PUBLIC LIBRARY CORE COLLECTION:

NONFICTION

FOURTEENTH EDITION

CORE COLLECTION SERIES

Formerly
STANDARD CATALOG SERIES

EVE-MARIE MILLER, GENERAL EDITOR

CHILDREN'S CORE COLLECTION

MIDDLE & JUNIOR HIGH CORE COLLECTION

SENIOR HIGH CORE COLLECTION

PUBLIC LIBRARY CORE COLLECTION: NONFICTION

PUBLIC LIBRARY CORE COLLECTION: FICTION

PUBLIC LIBRARY CORE COLLECTION: NONFICTION

A Selection Guide to Reference Books
and
Adult Nonfiction

FOURTEENTH EDITION

Former title:

Public Library Catalog

EDITED BY

EVE-MARIE MILLER,

LIZA OLDHAM

AND

CHRISTI SHOWMAN FARRAR

H. W. WILSON
A Division of EBSCO Publishing, Inc.
IPSWICH, MASSACHUSETTS

Printed in the United States of America

ISBN 978-0-8242-1151-6

Library of Congress Cataloging-in-Publication Data

Public library core collection. Nonfiction : a selection guide to reference books and adult nonfiction / edited by Eve-Marie Miller, Christi Showman Farrar and Liza Oldham. -- Fourteenth edition.
    pages cm. -- (Core collection series)
  Includes index.
  ISBN 978-0-8242-1151-6
  1. Public libraries--United States--Book lists. I. Miller, Eve-Marie. II. Farrar, Christi Showman. III. Oldham, Liza.
  Z1035.P934 2013
  025.2'187473--dc23   2012033119

CONTENTS

PREFACE

PUBLIC LIBRARY: NONFICTION CORE COLLECTION, formerly entitled Public Library Catalog, is a list of recommended reference and nonfiction books for adults, in classified order. The Core Collections are also available in electronic format on the web, updated weekly.

What's new in this Edition?

Each new edition of PUBLIC LIBRARY: NONFICTION CORE COLLECTION is a mixture of the old and the new. Older titles, some in updated versions, are included if they remain the best titles in their field. Newer titles reflect new topics of interest and new interpretations of traditional knowledge. This edition of the Core Collection features extensive revision in the areas of computers and technology, math, science, sociology, medicine, and law. Crafts, art, religion, and psychology have also received comprehensive evaluation. Reference materials in all subject fields have been updated.

History

The first of several installments of the "Standard Catalog" for the general library was published in 1918. It was called STANDARD CATALOG: SOCIOLOGY SECTION. Additional installments were issued over the next fourteen years, covering Biography; Fiction; Fine Arts; History and Travel; Science and Useful Arts; Literature and Philology; and Philosophy, Religion and General Works. Finally, a fully integrated first edition of the STANDARD CATALOG FOR PUBLIC LIBRARIES was assembled and published in 1934. The contents were displayed in classified order, according to the Dewey Decimal Classification. The name was changed to PUBLIC LIBRARY CATALOG with the publication of the fifth edition in 1969, and then to PUBLIC LIBRARY CORE COLLECTION: NONFICTION with the thirteenth edition in 2008.

Although a Fiction Section was issued in 1923, followed by supplements in 1928 and 1931, fiction was omitted from the first edition of the complete Catalog in 1934. A new expanded edition of the Fiction Section was published as FICTION CATALOG in 1942. In its preface that Catalog was referred to as "a companion volume to the Standard Catalog for Public Libraries." This complementary relationship has continued to the present. PUBLIC LIBRARY CORE COLLECTION: NONFICTION has always listed works of literary criticism and literary history and books about literary technique.

Scope and Purpose

This volume lists nonfiction books published in the United States, or published in other countries and distributed in the United States. It excludes non-print materials; periodicals; non-English items (with the exception of dictionaries), and works of an ephemeral nature. All books were in print at the time of listing. Original paperback editions are included. Entries for hardcover editions provide information about the availability of paperback reprints where possible. This volume comprises over 12,000 book titles with multiple subject access.

The Core Collection is intended to serve the needs of public and undergraduate libraries and stand as a basic or "opening day" collection. The newer titles help in identifying areas in a collection that can be updated or strengthened. Retention of useful material from the previous edition enables the librarian to make informed decisions about weeding a collection. With its classified arrangement, complete bibliographical data, and descriptive and critical annotations, the Core Collection provides useful information for the acquisitions librarian, the reference librarian, and the cataloger. Entries provide information about the availability of electronic versions of books listed.

Preparation

Books included in this edition were selected by experienced librarians representing public library systems and academic libraries across the United States who also act as a committee of advisors on library policy and trends. The names of participating librarians and their affiliations are listed in the Acknowledgments.

Organization

The Core Collection is organized into two parts: the Classified Collection; and an Author, Title, and Subject Index.

Part 1. Classified Collection. This is arranged according to the Dewey Decimal Classification. Within classes, arrangement is by main entry, with complete bibliographical and cataloging information given for each book. The classified arrangement, along with the descriptive and critical annotations, provides a useful guide to book selection. Entries include such information as price and ISBN to facilitate acquisitions.

Part 2. Author, Title, and Subject Index. This is a comprehensive key to the Classified List with entries for authors, titles, and subjects.

ACKNOWLEDGMENTS

H. W. Wilson and EBSCO Publishing express special gratitude to the following librarians who both advised the company in editorial matters and assisted in the selection of titles for this Core Collection:

Advisory Board

James E. Bobick
Author and Consultant
Pittsburgh, Pennsylvania

Gail de Vos
University of Alberta
Edmonton, Alberta, Canada

Mary Griffin
Omaha Public Library
Omaha, Nebraska

Steven Jablonski
Skokie Public Library
Skokie, Illinois

Brett W. Lear
Martin County Library
System
Stuart, Florida

John J. Meier
Penn State University
University Park,
Pennsylvania

Mary Rasner
Library Consultant
Melrose, Massachusetts

The following EBSCO Publishing staff members were integral to the successful transition of the Core Collections.

Melissa Alicea
Terry Berube
Rebecca Borichevsky
David Brickner
Kathy Brown
Nathaniel Brown
Lee Bryars
Mike Bucco
Joe Calderone
Nicole Casellini
Chris Corcoran
Gary Crespo
Linda Diering
Peter Devney
Leonard Dube
Sheila Dykstra
Scott Farrar
Dave Flynn
Ken Goodridge
Nicole Grande
Kimberly Hawlena
Syed Husain
Mohan Joyappa

Elshad Kasumov
Jaideep Majumdar
Laura Mansfield
Gina Mathews
Nate Meloon
Jameson Morely
Rob Opiela
Beverly Pajer
David Patterson
Jason Rozen
Jennifer Sawtelle
Mihir Shah
Emily Tragert
Ron Trevarrow
Margaret Whittaker
Chuck Williams
Emily Williams
Michael Woodring
Brittany Wylde
Abstracting & Indexing Department
Comprehensive Subject Indexing Department

DIRECTIONS FOR USE OF THE CORE COLLECTION

Part 1. Classified Collection

The Classified Collection is arranged by the Dewey Decimal Classification in numerical order from 000 to 999. Individual biographies are classed at 92 and follow the 920s (collective biography). An Outline of Classification, which serves as a table of contents for the Classified Collection, is reproduced below. It should be noted that many topics can be classified in more than one discipline. If a particular title is not found where it might be expected, the Index should be consulted to determine if it is classified elsewhere.

Within classes, works are arranged alphabetically under main entry, usually the author. Works of individual biography are arranged alphabetically under the biography's subject.

Each listing consists of a full bibliographical description. Prices, which are always subject to change, have been obtained from the publisher and are as current as possible. Entries include recommended subject headings derived from the *Sears List of Subject Headings*, a suggested classification number from the *Abridged Dewey Decimal Classification and Relative Index*, a brief description of the contents, and, whenever possible, an evaluation from a quoted source.

Part 2. Author, Title, and Subject Index

The Index is a single alphabetical list of all the books entered in the Core Collection. Each book is entered under author; title (if distinctive); and subject. The classification number, displayed in boldface type, is the key to the location of the main entry for the book in the Classified Collection.

Appropriate added entries are made for joint authors and editors. "See" references are made from forms of names or subjects that are not used as headings. "See also" references are made to related or more specific headings.

Standards Used

Anglo-American Cataloguing Rules, 2nd ed., 2002 revision, 2005 update. Chicago: American Library Association, 2005.

Dewey, Melvil. *Abridged Dewey Decimal Classification and Relative Index*. 15th ed. Edited by Joan S. Mitchell, et al. Dublin, Ohio: OCLC, 2012.

McCarthy, Susan and Joseph Miller, eds. *Sears List of Subject Headings*. 20th ed. New York: The H. W. Wilson Company, 2010.

Outline of Classification

Reproduced below is the Second Summary of the Dewey Decimal Classification. * As Part 1 of this Core Collection is arranged according to this classification, the outline will serve as a table of contents for it. Please note, however, that the inclusion of this outline is not to be considered a substitute for consulting the Dewey Decimal Classification itself.

* Reproduced from Edition 15 of the Abridged Dewey Decimal Classification and Relative Index, published in 2012, by permission of OCLC Online Computer Library Center, Inc., owner of copyright.

PUBLIC LIBRARY CORE COLLECTION: NONFICTION
FOURTEENTH EDITION
CLASSIFIED COLLECTION

000 COMPUTER SCIENCE, KNOWLEDGE & SYSTEMS

001 Knowledge

Major, David C.
100 one-night reads; a book lover's guide. {by} David C. Major and John S. Major. Ballantine Bks. 2001 312p pa $12.95   **001**
  1. Best books 2. Books and reading
  ISBN 0-345-43994-5
                                LC 2001-16135
The authors "offer recommendations in nonfiction, general fiction, fantasy, humor, mystery, history, public affairs, memoirs, science, and travel. Most are by English or U.S. authors and were published in the 20th century. Each three-page entry includes a description of the book, information about the author, and an evaluation of what makes the book distinctive. Suggestions for additional writings by the author are often included." Libr J
  Includes bibliographical references

001.1 Intellectual life

Levine, Lawrence W.
  The **opening** of the American mind; canons, culture, and history. Beacon Press 1996 xxiv, 212p hardcover o.p. pa $18   **001.1**
  1. Higher education 2. Multiculturalism
  ISBN 0-8070-3119-4 pa
                                LC 96-33866
"Levine's presentation is eloquent, eminently reasonable, and gratifyingly optimistic." Booklist
  Includes bibliographical references

001.4 Research; statistical methods

Feldman, Burton
  The **Nobel** Prize; a history of genius, controversy, and prestige. Arcade Pub. 2000 489p il $29.95; pa $15.95   **001.4**
  1. Nobel Prizes 2. Nobel Prizes -- History
  ISBN 1-55970-537-X; 1-55970-592-2 pa
                                LC 00-42002
The author provides a "history of the prizes awarded in the sciences, social sciences, and humankind's . . .

peace efforts. This is the first comprehensive critical history of the prizes to appear, and it's very good." Libr J
  Includes bibliographical references

Tufte, Edward R.
  The **visual** display of quantitative information; 2nd ed; Graphics Press 2001 197p il $40   **001.4**
  1. Statistics -- Graphic methods
  ISBN 0-9613921-4-2
                                LC 2001-271866
  This book focuses "on statistical graphics, charts, tables. Theory and practice in the design of data graphics, 250 illustrations of the best (and a few of the worst) statistical graphics, with . . . analysis of how to display data for precise, effective, quick analysis." Publisher's note

★ Awards, honors, & prizes; 28th ed; Gale Res. 2v
  v1 $385; v2 $420   **001.4**
  1. Awards
  ISBN 978-1-414419-00-8 v1; 1-414419-00-7 v1; 978-1-414419-01-5 v2; 1-414419-01-5 v2
  Volume one is an alphabetical directory of organizations in the United States and Canada sponsoring awards, honors and prizes in a wide range of endeavors from academic awards to prizes in sports. Volume two provides coverage of awards originating in other countries

Nobel Prize winners; an H.W. Wilson biographical dictionary. editor, Tyler Wasson; consultants, Gert H. Brieger {et al.} Wilson, H.W. 1987 xxxiv, 1165p il $145   **001.4**
  1. Biography -- Dictionaries 2. Biography, Collective 3. Nobel Prizes 4. Nobel prizes 5. Reference books
  ISBN 0-8242-0756-4
                                LC 87-16468
  This reference book "begins with an alphabetical listing of winners, a listing of prize categories (broken down chronologically by years), an article on Alfred Nobel, and another on the process by which the prizes are awarded. . . . Included are all winners (persons and institutions) from 1901-1986 in entries of 1200-1500 words." SLJ

001.9 Controversial knowledge

Bullard, Thomas E.
  The **myth** and mystery of UFOs. University Press of Kansas 2010 417p il $35   **001.9**
  1. Unidentified flying objects
  ISBN 978-0-7006-1729-6; 0-7006-1729-9
                                LC 2010-26289

"Bullard is well known in the UFO community because he leaves the door open that there may be some basis in reality behind UFO stories while also contending that the UFO field is fertile ground for rumor and legend. His bibliography is impressive, and the book is a full account of UFO sightings and the development of 'Ufology.' He concludes that there is enough evidence to suggest that UFOs deserve a place in academic inquiry, with more scientific research needed. . . . Those interested in the UFO phenomenon will find tons of interesting material to ponder and a different way of looking at it." Libr J

Includes bibliographical references

Shermer, Michael

Why people believe weird things; pseudoscience, superstition, and other confusions of our time. foreword by Stephen Jay Gould. rev and expanded; Freeman, W.H. 2002 xxvi, 349p il pa $16 **001.9**
1. Belief and doubt 2. Creative ability in science 3. Parapsychology 4. Pseudoscience 5. Science
ISBN 0-8050-7089-3

LC 2002-68784

The author "explores the very human reasons people find otherworldly phenomena, conspiracy theories, and cults so appealing. In . . . [the] chapter, 'Why Smart People Believe in Weird Things' he takes on science luminaries like physicist Frank Tippler and others, who hide their spiritual beliefs behind the trappings of science." Publisher's note

Includes bibliographical references

001.94 Mysteries

Ellis, Richard

★ **Imagining** Atlantis. Knopf 1998 322p il maps hardcover o.p. pa $13 **001.94**
1. Atlantis
ISBN 0-375-70582-1 pa

LC 97-48432

"Engaging, lucid, and full of lore, Ellis's book makes a convincing case that Atlantis was merely a morality tale of Plato's, and along the way provides insight into our enduring preoccupation with things vanished and lost." New Yorker

Includes bibliographical references

Wilson, Colin

The **Atlantis** blueprint; unlocking the ancient mysteries of a long-lost civilization. [by] Colin Wilson and Rand Flem-Ath. Delacorte Press 2001 xxv, 415p il maps hardcover o.p. pa $16 **001.94**
1. Atlantis 2. Civilization, Ancient
ISBN 0-385-33479-6; 0-440-50898-3 pa

LC 00-47449

The authors "propose a single, geo-historical theory that links the Egyptian, Chinese and South American pyramids and other sacred sites. According to this argument, these civilizations received templates from Atlantis that contained crucial geodesic, geological and geometric information. Furthermore, Atlantean mariners, based in Antarctica, sailed the globe over 100,000 years ago and established more than 60 sacred sites around the world." Publ Wkly

002 The book

Basbanes, Nicholas A.

★ **Patience** & fortitude; a roving chronicle of book people, book places, and book culture. HarperCollins Pubs. 2001 636p il hardcover o.p. pa $19.95 **002**
1. Book collecting 2. Books 3. Books and reading 4. Libraries
ISBN 0-06-019695-5; 0-06-051446-9 pa

LC 2001-16935

"Basbanes's fund of stories will delight readers who value books for more than just a good story, have a yen for second-hand books plucked from dusty shops or look to book catalogs for suspense and excitement." Publ Wkly

Includes bibliographical references

Buzbee, Lewis

The **yellow**-lighted bookshop; a memoir, a history. Graywolf Press 2006 216p $17 **002**
1. Authors 2. Booksellers and bookselling 3. Nonfiction writers 4. Novelists 5. Short story writers
ISBN 1-55597-450-3

LC 2005-938151

This "is a tribute to those who crave the cozy confines of a bookshop." Booklist

Darnton, Robert

The **case** for books; past, present, and future. PublicAffairs 2009 218p il $23.95 **002**
1. Books and reading -- History
ISBN 978-1-58648-826-0

"These essays bring balance and a refreshing perspective to the nervous predictions over the future of print." Libr J

Includes bibliographical references

Kelly, Stuart

The **book** of lost books; an incomplete history of all the great books you will never read. Random House 2006 344p $24.95 **002**
1. Books and reading 2. Lost books -- History 3. Lost literature
ISBN 1-4000-6297-7

LC 2005-51653

"Prodigiously informative, if occasionally dense, 'The Book of Lost Books' is less a book one reads than a vade mecum one consults. But every page is a garden of delights." N Y Times Book Rev

002.07 Education, research, related topics

Lansky, Aaron

Outwitting history; the amazing adventures of a man who rescued a million Yiddish books. Algonquin Books of Chapel Hill 2004 316p **002.07**
1. Book collecting 2. Book collectors 3. Distributors 4. Yiddish language
ISBN 1-56512-429-4

LC 2004-51587

"The book is a testimony to [Lansky's] love of Judaism and literature and his desire to make a difference in the world." Publ Wkly

Includes bibliographical references

003   Systems

Taleb, Nassim

The **black** swan; the impact of the highly improbable. [by] Nassim Nicholas Taleb. 2nd ed; Random House Trade Paperbacks 2010 xxxiii, 444p il pa $17   **003**
  1. Forecasting
  ISBN 978-0-8129-7381-5; 0-8129-7381-X
                                              LC 2010-292618
Examines the role of the unexpected, discussing why improbable events are not anticipated or understood properly, and how humans rationalize the black swan phenomenon to make it appear less random.

The author "is really a philosopher in a businessman's clothing and his irreverent writing style, with its frequent first-person asides and tangential musings that go on for pages, actually helps make heavy intellectual discussions more accessible." Risk Management

Includes bibliographical references

004   Computer science; computer programming, programs, data; special computer methods

Dyson, George

Turing's cathedral; the origins of the digital universe. George Dyson. Pantheon Books 2012 xxii, 401 p. (hardback) $29.95   **004**
  1. Computable functions   2. Computer science -- History 3. Computers -- History 4. Historical literature 5. Institute for Advanced Study (Princeton, N.J.) 6. Random access memory 7. Turing machines
  ISBN 9780375422775
                                              LC 2011030265
In this book, "science historian George Dyson shines light on the critical period when computers came into being. He begins with British mathematician Alan Turing's . . . 1936 description of a machine designed to resolve a problem in mathematical logic. . . . Dyson focuses on US efforts, when . . . a group of engineers, scientists and mathematicians gathered together by Hungarian-American polymath John von Neumann . . . bent their minds to the making of the IAS machine." (New Scientist)

Gerstner, Louis V.

Who says elephants can't dance? inside IBM's historic turnaround. HarperBusiness 2002 372p il $27.95   **004**
  1. Computer industry
  ISBN 0-06-052379-4
                                              LC 2002-27523
This is the "tale of the rise, fall and rise of IBM. . . . [The author] became IBM's CEO in 1993, when the gargantuan company was near collapse. The book's opening section

snappily reports Gerstner's decisions in his first 18 months on the job. . . . The following sections describe the marathon fight to make IBM once again 'a company that mattered.' . . . The book is a well-rendered self-portrait of a CEO who made spectacular change on the strength of personal leadership." Publ Wkly

Hally, Mike

Electronic brains; stories from the dawn of the computer age. Joseph Henry 2005 xxiii, 275p $27.95   **004**
  1. Computers -- History
  ISBN 0-309-09630-8
                                              LC 2005-16583
"Inspired by a popular BBC radio series of the same name, this book details the postwar computer development boom, concentrating on the personalities instead of the technology. . . . Major historical events serve as the backdrop to Hally's history; The Manhattan Project's atomic researches, presidential elections, wars and revolutions all figure into the computer's development. The book has its techie moments, but this is an informative and entertaining read." Publ Wkly

Henderson, Harry

Encyclopedia of computer science and technology; Rev ed; Facts On File 2009 580p il $87.50 **004**
  1. Computer science   2. Computer science -- Encyclopedias 3. Computers 4. Computers -- Encyclopedias 5. Information technology 6. Reference books
  ISBN 978-0-8160-6382-6; 0-8160-6382-6
                                              LC 2008-29156
"The A-to-Z entries run from several paragraphs to two pages in length and provide highly accessible, jargon-free explanations of hardware, software, programming language, notable figures, crucial inventions, and hotly debated civil-liberties issues in a field outpacing legislation. One of the most user-friendly and enlightening books for field outsiders, this handy volume promotes clear understanding of a complex subject." Libr J

Includes bibliographical references

Ifrah, Georges

The **universal** history of computing; from the abacus to the quantum computer. translated from the French, and with notes by E.F. Harding, assisted by Sophie Wood {et al.} Wiley 2000 410p il hardcover o.p. pa $16.95   **004**
  1. Computers -- History 2. Data processing -- History 3. Electronic data processing -- History
  ISBN 0-471-39671-0; 0-471-44147-3 pa
                                              LC 00-47771
The author covers "the history of computing from its earliest time to today's supercomputers. After extensive coverage of numbers and the calculating techniques of early history, he discusses in great detail modern calculating machines. . . . Ifrah's erudite book adds new and interesting findings to the topic." Libr J

Includes bibliographical references

Markoff, John

★ **What** the dormouse said--how the sixties counterculture shaped the personal computer industry. Viking Penguin 2005 xxiii, 310p il $25.95; pa $16 **004**

1. Computers -- History 2. Computers and civilization 3. Counter culture 4. Microcomputers -- History 5. Nineteen sixties
ISBN 0-670-03382-0; 0-14-303676-9 pa

LC 2004-61181

"This book is a rare treat and a must-read for everyone who has had the pleasure of using the mysterious friend called the PC." Choice

Includes bibliographical references

Vamosi, Robert

When gadgets betray us; the dark side of our infatuation with new technologies. Basic Books 2011 222p **004**

1. Computer crimes 2. Computer security 3. Computers -- Health aspects 4. Computers -- Social aspects 5. Electronic apparatus and appliances 6. Software failures
ISBN 978-0-465-01958-8

LC 2010-43829

"The book is about hardware hacking and new kinds of identity fraud." (Publisher's note) Index.

"Read this, and you'll never again ignore the default security settings on accounts or your devices again. Gadget geeks and lay readers would benefit from Vamosi's information." Libr J

Includes bibliographical references

Computer sciences; Roger R. Flynn, editor in chief. Macmillan 2002 4v set $325 **004**

1. Computer science
ISBN 0-02-865566-4

LC 2002-754

This set "includes 286 signed entries written by more than 125 contributors. . . . Many articles are enhanced by sidebars, glossary definitions, black-and-white illustrations, cross-references, and bibliographic or Internet resources. Additional features include time lines, a glossary, and an index to the set. Intended for general readers and high school students, this encyclopedia will appeal to anyone curious about this complex field or its impact on today's world." Choice

004.1 General works on specific types of computers

Johnson, George

A **shortcut** through time; the path to a quantum computer. Knopf 2003 204p il hardcover o.p. pa $13 **004.1**

1. Computers 2. Quantum theory
ISBN 0-375-41193-3; 0-375-72618-7 pa

LC 2002-73013

"Johnson has presented the fascinating science of quantum computing and its future development in a down-to-earth style." Libr J

Includes bibliographical references

004.67 Wide-area networks

Lessig, Lawrence

The **future** of ideas; the fate of the commons in a connected world. Random House 2001 352p hardcover o.p. pa $15 **004.67**

1. Copyright 2. Copyright and electronic data processing 3. Information society 4. Intellectual property 5. Internet 6. Internet -- Law and legislation
ISBN 0-375-72644-6 pa

LC 2001-31968

"Some of Lessig's sweeping proposals are sure to spark a lively debate, but his well-reasoned, clearly written argument is powerful." Publ Wkly

005 Computer programming, programs, data

Campbell-Kelly, Martin

★ **From** airline reservations to Sonic the Hedgehog; a history of the software industry. MIT Press 2003 372p il $42.50; pa $16.95 **005**

1. Computer software industry
ISBN 0-262-03303-8; 0-262-53262-X pa

LC 2002-75351

The author presents a "history of the software industry from the 1950s to 1995. Dividing the business into three sectors (software contracting, corporate software precuts, and mass-market software products), he examines the key products and players in each. . . . The result is a well-rounded look at the software industry from a business perspective." Libr J

Includes bibliographical references

005.8 Data security

Jennings, Charles

The **hundredth** window; protecting your privacy and security in the age of the Internet. {by} Charles Jennings and Lori Fena; foreword by Esther Dyson. Free Press 2000 xxv, 278p hardcover o.p. pa $19.95 **005.8**

1. Computer security 2. Internet -- Security measures
ISBN 0-684-83944-X; 978-0-7432-5498-4 pa; 0-7432-5498-8 pa

LC 00-22527

The authors "look at the typical day of a high-tech user, noting the myriad ways in which such an individual exposes information about personal income, health, buying preferences, and daily activities. They counsel online consumers on how to protect their privacy by encrypting e-mail, checking for security provisions on Web sites, and updating browsers." Booklist

006.3 Artificial intelligence

Baker, Stephen
Final Jeopardy; man vs. machine and the quest to know everything. Houghton Mifflin Harcourt 2011 268p $24 **006.3**
1. Artificial intelligence 2. Database management 3. Natural language processing (Computer science) 4. Watson (Computer)
ISBN 978-0-547-48316-0; 0-547-48316-3
LC 2010051653
"In February 2011, the world watched as a computer named Watson handily beat the two greatest Jeopardy champions of all time. The contest was reminiscent of when IBM's Deep Blue defeated chess grandmaster Garry Kasparov, but Jeopardy was a much more difficult game for a computer to master. Although Baker . . . reviews the match in his last chapter, his primary focus here is on the compelling story of Watson's creation and education. . . . This is a thought-provoking view of one of IBM's major contributions to the computing field." Libr J
Includes bibliographical references

006.7 Multimedia systems

Tortorella, Neil
Starting your career as a freelance web designer. Allworth Press 2011 251p il pa $19.95 **006.7**
1. Vocational guidance 2. Web sites -- Design
ISBN 978-1-58115-859-5
LC 2011019292
"This is not a book about how to design websites; it is about managing the financial, legal, and business realities of being a freelance web designer. . . . Part One deals with the fundamentals of being a freelancer, including analyzing one's abilities and talents, formulating a business plan, understanding taxes and insurance, and finding trusted business advisers. In Part Two, Tortorella discusses the necessary proficiencies of the portfolio, proposals, project management, and marketing. . . . Tortorella's contribution is the nuts-and-bolts handbook for success in the field of freelance web design and will find a ready audience with the fledgling right-brain designer or the college student considering web design as a career." Libr J
Includes bibliographical references

011 Bibliographies and catalogs

Ellington, Elisabeth
A year of reading; a month-by-month guide to classics and crowd-pleasers for you and your book group. by H. Elisabeth Ellington and Jane Freimiller. Sourcebooks 2002 314p pa $14.95 **011**
1. Best books 2. Books and reading
ISBN 1-57071-935-7
LC 2002-6926
"Five titles designated as crowd pleasers, classics, challenges, memoirs, or potluck options are provided for each month. . . . There are brief descriptions of each book,

thought-provoking discussion questions, information about the authors, video and Internet resources, and lists of related readings. Literary discussion groups will welcome this invaluable resource." Booklist

Pearl, Nancy
Book lust; recommended reading for every mood, moment, and reason. Sasquatch Books 2003 287p pa $16.95 **011**
1. Best books 2. Books and reading
ISBN 1-57061-381-8
LC 2003-45796
Pearl's "recommendations are arranged under an alphabetical, subjective, but certainly comprehensive system of categories, which range from 'Academic Mysteries' to 'World War II Nonfiction' and from 'First Novels' to 'Three-Hanky Readers.' Within each category, Pearl's commentaries are concise and sound. A book difficult to put down and easy to be guided by." Booklist

Saricks, Joyce G.
★ Read on--audiobooks; reading lists for every taste. Libraries Unlimited 2011 145p pa $30 **011**
1. Audiobooks -- Catalogs 2. Libraries -- Special collections -- Audiobooks
ISBN 978-1-59158-804-7 pa; 978-1-59158-807-8 ebook
LC 2010051372
"More than 300 selections, fiction and nonfiction, are grouped into five chapters according to their primary appeal: language (including voice), mood, story, characters, or setting. Within each category, titles are listed by shared themes, such as full-cast readings or armchair travel. . . . All libraries that circulate audiobooks should shelve this guide alongside." Booklist
Includes bibliographical references

Guide to reference books; edited by Robert Balay; associate editor, Vee Friesner Carrington; with special editorial assistance by Murray S. Martin. 11th ed; American Lib. Assn. 1996 xxvii, 2020p $275 **011**
1. Reference books 2. Reference books -- Bibliography
ISBN 0-8389-0669-9
LC 95-26322
Nearly 16,000 entries provide details on general reference works and on reference books in the humanities, social and behavioral sciences, history and area studies, and science, technology, and medicine. Electronic resources are included.

★ Magazines for libraries; for the general reader and school, junior college, college, university and public libraries; reviewing the best publications for all serials collections since 1969. edited by Cheryl LaGuardia; created by Bill Katz. 19th ed; ProQuest 2010 995p $520 **011**
1. Periodicals 2. Periodicals -- Bibliography 3. Periodicals -- United States 4. Reference books
ISBN 978-1-60030-135-3

"Annotated classified guide to recommended periodicals for the general reader and school, college, and public libraries. Provides comparative evaluations and grade and age-level recommendations for all periodicals included." N Y Public Libr Book of How & Where to Look It Up

★ Recommended reference books for small and medium-sized libraries and media centers, Vol. 30; Shannon Graff Hysell, associate editor. 2010 ed; Libraries Unlimited 2010 344p $75   **011**
1. Best books 2. Reference books 3. Reference books -- Bibliography 4. Reference books -- Reviews
ISBN 978-1-59884-592-1
Each annual volume includes reviews of about 550 titles chosen by the editor as the most valuable reference titles published during the previous year.

Reference sources for small and medium-sized libraries; Jack O'Gorman, editor. 7th ed; American Library Association 2008 329p pa $88   **011**
1. Reference books 2. Reference books -- Bibliography
ISBN 978-0-8389-0943-0; 0-8389-0943-4
                          LC 2007-40026
"Intended as a guide for college and large secondary school libraries as well as for public libraries. Items are grouped in subject categories and further subdivided by type of reference source or other suitable subdivision. Sections were prepared by individual compilers or teams of compilers. Good annotations; coverage of various subject fields is unusually even for a work of this kind; index of names and titles." Guide to Ref Books. 11th edition
Includes bibliographical references

011.6 General bibliographies and catalogs of works for young people and people with disabilities; for specific types of libraries

Rosow, La Vergne
★ **Accessing** the classics; great reads for adults, teens, and English language learners. Libraries Unlimited 2006 301p pa $40   **011.6**
1. Best books 2. Reading -- Remedial teaching 3. Remedial reading 4. Young adults' literature -- Book lists
ISBN 1-56308-891-6; 978-1-56308-891-9
                          LC 2005-30838
"The intended audience is wide-ranging and includes anyone who wishes to foster language and literacy skills. Essential reading." Booklist
Includes bibliographical references

Safford, Barbara Ripp
Guide to reference materials for school library media centers; 6th ed; Libraries Unlimited 2010 236p $60   **011.6**
1. Children's reference books 2. Instructional materials centers 3. Reference books -- Bibliography 4. School libraries -- Catalogs
ISBN 978-1-59158-277-9; 1-59158-277-6
                          LC 2009-51190

"This volume has been updated to include web-based reference offerings as well as listings of older sources, provided that their content is still valid. . . . This title profiles resources recommended for use by school librarians for collection management, readers' advisory, teaching, general reference materials, the social sciences and humanities, and science and technology. This volume is an excellent starting point for new school librarians, as well as for those who are building a library from scratch." SLJ
Includes bibliographical references

Silvey, Anita
100 best books for children. Houghton Mifflin 2004 184p $20   **011.6**
1. Best books 2. Children's literature 3. Children's literature -- Bibliography 4. Reference books
ISBN 0-618-27889-3
                          LC 2003-56899
The author's "long experience as a book reviewer and editor makes her list pretty much spot-on. . . . Each title gets a short essay that not only discusses the book and what it has meant to its audience but that also supplies wonderful behind-the-scenes information. . . . A helpful list, 'Beyond the 100 Best,' points parents in the right direction for more good reads." Booklist
Includes bibliographical references

015 Bibliographies and catalogs of works from specific places

Forthcoming books. Bowker   **015**
1. Bibliography 2. Reference books
This supplement to Books in print, and Subject guide to Books in print, provides a cumulative author-title-subject index to books that are to appear in the next five-month period. Information includes price, publisher, ISBN and LC control numbers and expected publication date

016 Bibliographies and catalogs of works on specific subjects

Adamson, Lynda G.
Notable women in American history; a guide to recommended biographies and autobiographies. Greenwood Press 1999 450p $52.95   **016**
1. American diaries -- Women authors 2. Autobiography -- Women authors 3. Reference books 4. Women -- Biography -- Dictionaries 5. Women -- United States 6. Women -- United States -- Biography 7. Women -- United States -- Correspondence
ISBN 0-313-29584-0
                          LC 98-55350
This volume "concentrates on women who made contributions to U.S. history from the colonial period through 1998. The 500 women covered were born in America or became naturalized citizens; had a full-length biography or autobiography published since 1970; and, in the case of

twentieth-century actors, authors, and poets, have been recognized by their peers." Booklist

Notable women in world history; a guide to recommended biographies and autobiographies. Greenwood Press 1998 401p $52.95   **016**

1. Autobiography -- Women authors 2. Autobiography -- Women authors -- Bibliography 3. Diaries -- Women authors 4. Diaries -- Women authors -- Bibliography 5. Reference books 6. Women -- Biography 7. Women -- Biography -- Bibliography 8. Women -- Biography -- Dictionaries 9. Women -- Correspondence 10. Women -- Correspondence -- Bibliography

ISBN 0-313-29818-1

LC 97-33136

"The entries are arranged alphabetically by last name with appropriate cross-references for alternative designations. Each contains the woman's name, key dates, occupation or avocation, and birthplace. A short biographical sketch about parents, education, general achievement, and recognition or awards follows. Women of all time periods are included. . . . Because it includes only those born outside the U.S., it complements sources on American women. Notable Women in World History is a useful addition to academic, public, and high-school libraries. It would be especially useful for women's studies collections." Booklist

Bleiler, Richard

★ **Reference** and research guide to mystery and detective fiction; [by] Richard J. Bleiler. 2nd ed; Libraries Unlimited 2003 828p $78   **016**

1. Detective and mystery stories 2. Detective and mystery stories -- Bibliography 3. Detective and mystery stories -- History and criticism 4. Detective and mystery stories -- Reference books -- Bibliography 5. Mystery fiction -- Bibliography 6. Reference books

ISBN 1-56308-924-6

LC 2003-58905

"Separate chapters cover sources as diverse as maps and atlases, writers' associations and awards, character indexes, calendars, and quotations in addition to guides, encyclopedias, and dictionaries." Choice

Includes bibliographical references

Bouricius, Ann

The **romance** readers' advisory; the librarian's guide to love in the stacks. American Lib. Assn. 2000 107p pa $56   **016**

1. Libraries -- Special collections -- Love stories 2. Love stories -- Appreciation 3. Love stories -- Bibliography 4. Love stories -- History and criticism 5. Love stories -- Stories, plots, etc 6. Love stories, American -- Bibliography -- Methodology 7. Love stories, English -- Bibliography -- Methodology 8. Reader guidance 9. Readers' advisory service 10. Reading interests 11. Reference books 12. Romance novels

ISBN 0-8389-0779-2

LC 99-57295

The author provides "information about the highly popular romance genre and its diverse subgenres; addresses key issues regarding the establishment of a romance collection; and, in a series of reading lists, recommends outstanding romances of all flavors for avid fans and new converts." Booklist

Burgess, Michael

Reference guide to science fiction, fantasy, and horror; [by] Michael Burgess, Lisa R. Bartle. 2nd ed; Libraries Unlimited 2002 605p $75   **016**

1. Fantasy fiction -- History and criticism 2. Fantasy fiction -- History and criticism -- Bibliography 3. Fantasy fiction -- Reference books -- Bibliography 4. Horror tales -- History and criticism 5. Horror tales -- History and criticism -- Bibliography 6. Horror tales -- Reference books -- Bibliography 7. Reference books 8. Science fiction -- Bibliography 9. Science fiction -- History and criticism 10. Science fiction -- History and criticism -- Bibliography 11. Science fiction -- Reference books -- Bibliography

ISBN 1-56308-548-8

LC 2002-151707

A guide to "amateur and professional reference materials in the related fields of science fiction, fantasy, and horror. . . . The book is divided into 32 sections . . . including 'Encyclopedias and Dictionaries,' 'Magazine and Anthology Indexes,' 'Subject Bibliographies,' 'Character Dictionaries and Author Cyclopedias,' and 'Film and Television Catalogs.' . . . Complete bibliographic citations are followed by literature and readable annotations that vary from a brief note to three or four lengthy paragraphs. The annotations consist of description and succinct analysis of the strengths and weaknesses of each item. . . . 'Major On-Line Resources,' is a particularly valuable examination of 20 Web sites." Booklist

Includes bibliographical references

Burt, Daniel S.

The **biography** book; a reader's guide to nonfiction, fictional, and film biographies of the 500 most fascinating individuals of all time. Oryx Press 2001 629p $83.95   **016**

1. Biography 2. Biography -- Bibliography 3. Reference books

ISBN 1-57356-256-4

LC 00-10116

This "book provides annotated bibliographies of works on international historical figures. Entries are arranged alphabetically by person and begin with a paragraph on the individual's life and significance. Each entry contains a birth and death date, and recommended autobiographical and biographical studies. Primary sources include letters, memoirs, diaries, interviews, etc. Biographical novels, fictional portraits, films, documentaries, and theatrical performances are also identified. . . . A wonderful resource for students, biography lovers, and librarians." SLJ

Includes bibliographical references

Frolund, Tina

★ **Genrefied** classics; a guide to reading interests in classical literature. Libraries Unlimited 2007 xxiv, 365p $45   **016**

1. Fiction -- Bibliography 2. Humanities -- Bibliography 3. Humanities literature -- Bibliography 4. Literature

5. Reference books
ISBN 1-59158-172-9; 978-1-59158-172-7

LC 2006-33740

"By identifying the genre characteristics of more than 400 classic fiction works, and organizing titles according to these features, this guide helps readers find the type of books they enjoy." Publisher's note

Includes bibliographical references

Herald, Diana Tixier

Fluent in fantasy; the next generation. [by] Diana Tixier Herald and Bonnie Kunzel. Libraries Unlimited 2008 312p $52   **016**
1. Fantasy fiction 2. Fantasy fiction -- Bibliography 3. Reference books
ISBN 978-1-59158-198-7; 1-59158-198-2

LC 2007-28840

"More than 2,000 titles are arranged by author in 14 thematic chapters, including 'Epic Fantasy,' 'Arthurian Legend,' and 'Time Travel Romance.'. . . An essential collection development and readers'-advisory tool." Booklist

Includes bibliographical references

★ **Strictly** science fiction; a guide to reading interests. [by] Diana Tixier Herald, Bonnie Kunzel. Libraries Unlimited 2002 xxii, 297p $55   **016**
1. Fiction in libraries -- United States 2. Libraries -- United States -- Special collections -- Science fiction 3. Readers' advisory services -- United States 4. Reading interests -- United States 5. Reference books 6. Science fiction 7. Science fiction -- Bibliography 8. Science fiction -- History and criticism
ISBN 1-56308-893-2

LC 2002-3186

"Good indexing, by author, title, subject, and character name, along with chapters devoted to books written for children and young adults and genre-blended books (such as science fiction/romance or science fiction/mystery), sets this reference apart." Libr J

Includes bibliographical references

Hollands, Neil

Read on . . . fantasy fiction; reading lists for every taste. Libraries Unlimited 2007 210p pa $30 **016**
1. Fantasy -- Bibliography 2. Fantasy fiction -- Bibliography 3. Fantasy fiction, American 4. Fantasy fiction, English 5. Reference books
ISBN 978-1-59158-330-1; 1-59158-330-6

LC 2007-7841

"Librarians who do readers advisory for teens or adults will wonder how they ever got along without this funny, opinionated, wide-angle guide." SLJ

Husband, Janet

Sequels; an annotated guide to novels in series. [by] Janet G. Husband & Jonathan F. Husband. 4th ed; American Library Association 2009 782p pa $95   **016**
1. Fiction 2. Fiction -- Bibliography 3. Reference books 4. Sequels (Literature)
ISBN 978-0-8389-0967-6

LC 2009-16426

"A selective, annotated list of the best, most enduring, and most popular novels in series. Short stories and children's books are excluded; classics, mysteries, and science fiction are included. Each work is listed in the best current edition, in the preferred order for reading. Arranged by author, with a title and subject index." Ref Sources for Small & Medium-sized Libr. 5th edition

Includes bibliographical references

Morris, Vanessa Irvin

The **readers'** advisory guide to street literature; Vanessa Irvin Morris; foreword by Teri Woods. American Library Association 2012 xxiii, 138 p.p ill. ALA readers' advisory series (alk. paper) $48.00   **016**
1. Fiction in libraries 2. Readers' advisory services -- United States 3. Street life -- Fiction -- Bibliography 4. Urban fiction, American -- Bibliography 5. Urban fiction, American -- History and criticism 6. Young adult fiction, American -- Bibliography
ISBN 0838911102; 9780838911105

LC 2011029685

In this book, author Vanessa Irvin "Morris presents a[n] . . . overview of the genre [of street literature]. From exploring the genre's roots . . . to articulating the appeal of the books, this . . . volume covers unique . . . material. For example, there is an entire chapter on teen-friendly street lit as well as material on collection development. Appendixes include a list of publishers and unannotated book lists." (Booklist)

Ottemiller, John H.

Ottemiller's index to plays in collections; an author and title index to plays appearing in collections published between 1900 and 1985. 7th ed; Scarecrow Press 1988 564p $80   **016**
1. Drama -- Bibliography -- Indexes 2. Drama -- Indexes 3. Reference books
ISBN 0-8108-2081-1

LC 87-34160

This index analyzes 1,350 collections and "covers plays by 2,555 authors. The arrangement is by playwright, with lists of plays and collections in which each is designated by symbols. A list of collections analyzed and key to symbols and a title index complete the volume." Nichols. Guide to Ref Books for Sch Media Cent. 4th edition

Pawuk, Michael G.

★ **Graphic** novels; a genre guide to comic books, manga, and more. foreword by Brian K. Vaughn. Libraries Unlimited 2007 xxxv, 633p il $65   **016**
1. Comic books, strips, etc. 2. Graphic novels 3. Graphic novels -- Bibliography 4. Reference books
ISBN 1-59158-132-X; 978-1-59158-132-1

LC 2006-34156

"This guide is intended to help you start, update, or maintain a graphic novel collection and advise readers about the genre. It covers more than 2,400 titles, including series titles, and organizes them according to genre, subgenre, and theme—from super-heroes and adventure to crime, humor, and nonfiction. Reading levels, awards/recognition, and core titles are identified; and tie-ins with gaming, film, anime, and television are noted." Publisher's note

Includes bibliographical references

Pearl, Nancy

★ **Now** read this III; a guide to mainstream fiction. [by] Nancy Pearl and Sarah Statz Cords. Libraries Unlimited 2010 xxiii, 405p $60   **016**
1. Best books 2. Fiction 3. Fiction -- Bibliography 4. Reference books
ISBN 978-1-59158-570-1

LC 2009-49898

An annotated list of over 500 books categorized by setting, story, characterization, or language. "This volume covers books published since 2002, with heavy emphasis on the last three years. Appendixes provide bridges to other genres, book award information, further resources, and advice for book groups, and everything is thoroughly indexed by author, title, and subject." Booklist

Includes bibliographical references

Ramsdell, Kristin, 1940-

Romance fiction; a guide to the genre. Libraries Unlimited 1999 435p $47.50   **016**
1. Love stories 2. Love stories -- Bibliography 3. Love stories -- History and criticism 4. Reference books
ISBN 1-56308-335-3

LC 99-10207

"Part 1 has several chapters that discuss the definition and appeal of romance and contain general information about advising readers and building collections. Part 2, 'The Literature,' has chapters devoted to 13 specific subgenres of romance, from contemporary to ethnic/multicultural. . . . Part 3, 'Research Aids,' surveys the secondary literature (histories and critical guides, dissertations, biographical sources, etc.), periodicals, organizations, awards, publishers, and other resources. . . . Libraries will want to hold on to their copies of Happily Ever After, which this new edition builds upon rather than supersedes." Booklist

Riechel, Rosemarie

Easy information sources for ESL, adult learners, & new readers. Neal-Schuman Publishers 2009 285p pa $65   **016**
1. English as a second language -- Bibliography 2. English language -- Study and teaching -- Foreign speakers 3. High interest-low vocabulary books 4. High interest-low vocabulary books -- Bibliography 5. Libraries -- Special collections 6. Public libraries -- Book lists 7. Public libraries -- Services to adults 8. Remedial reading
ISBN 978-1-55570-650-0; 1-55570-650-9

LC 2008-40028

"This work is aimed at educators and librarians working with adults whose English is poor. Advice on ways to use children's nonfiction for adults; reference interview strategies; book selection, placement, and utilization; collection development; and readers' advisory enables this work to not only suggest sources but also offer new ways of serving this growing and diverse population." Booklist

Includes bibliographical references

Thompson, Jason

★ **Manga**: the complete guide. Ballantine Books/ Del Rey Manga 2007 592p il pa $19.95   **016**
1. Graphic novels -- Bibliography 2. Manga -- Bibliography 3. Reference books
ISBN 978-0-345-48590-8

Former manga editor at Viz, Thompson reviews more than 900 manga titles that have been translated and published in the U.S. This book includes only original manga series published in Japan and then translated into English for U.S. publication. Titles include series that are no longer in print. The book also includes sidebar discussions on the many genres included in manga, including the age and genre divisions and such topics as otaku (hard-core fans), underground manga, and more. Separate sections cover yaoi and gay manga, and adult manga (often called hentai). It also includes an artist index. Each review includes a description of the series, how many volumes it has, an age rating, and content indicators.

Trott, Barry

Read on . . . crime fiction; reading lists for every taste. Libraries Unlimited 2008 146p pa $30 **016**
1. Crime -- Fiction 2. Detective and mystery stories 3. Mystery and detective fiction -- Bibliography 4. Mystery fiction -- Bibliography 5. Reference books
ISBN 978-1-59158-373-8

LC 2007-33858

The author organizes recommended crime fiction titles by "five 'appeal characteristics' commonly employed by RA professionals: story, character, setting, mood, and language. Under these broad categories, he offers an assortment of creatively titled reading lists ('Serf and Turf: Medieval Mysteries') that illustrate aspects of one of the appeal factors. Arrows designate one title per list selected as a good starting point for that category. . . . Both readers' advisors and crime-fiction fans will find all sorts of inventive ways to use this book, including, of course, compiling their own lists of titles or categories that should have been represented." Booklist

All music guide to classical music; the definitive guide to classical music. edited by Chris Woodstra, Gerald Brennan, Allen Schrott. Backbeat Books 2005 1607p $34.95   **016**
1. Music -- Discography
ISBN 0-87930-865-6

LC 2005-23988

"The 1500 A-to-Z entries include established composers, performers, and ensembles of every style and era. . . . The final 25 pages are devoted to one-page discussions of form in classical music, historical periods (ten divisions), and genres such as ballet, film music, and opera. . . . This is an excellent resource for both classical novices and aficionados. There is simply no other single volume on the market as inclusive." Libr J

American foreign relations since 1600; a guide to the literature. Robert L. Beisner, editor. 2nd ed; ABC-CLIO 2003 2v set $255   **016**
1. Reference books
ISBN 1-57607-080-8

LC 2003-8684

"The arrangement is essentially chronological, with the first of 32 chapters covering reference works and bibliographies and the second chapter, overviews and synthesis. Individual chapter editors . . . include journal articles, essays in collections, and dissertations. . . . Each chapter begins with a brief statement of the editor's selection criteria. Works in related specialties are listed for their influence on foreign relations, including Native American relations, gender and ethnic issues, and religious groups. . . . This is an excellent book; imaginative users will find ways to apply these listings to a wide variety of projects." Libr J

Includes bibliographical references

★ Fiction core collection; edited by John Greenfieldt. 16th ed.; H. W. Wilson Co. 2010 1307p $265   **016**
1. Best books 2. Fiction 3. Fiction -- Bibliography 4. Reference books
ISBN 978-0-8242-1103-5

LC 2009-27909

This volume "features classic and contemporary works of fiction recommended for a general adult audience, written in or translated into English. The best authors and their most widely read works in literary and popular fiction, old and new, are listed, including mysteries, science fiction, fantasy, Westerns, and romance. . . . More than 8,000 titles [are] listed, with entries providing complete bibliographic data, price, descriptive annotations, and evaluative quotations from a review when available." Publisher's note

Printed sources; a guide to published genealogical records. edited by Kory L. Meyerink. Ancestry 1998 840p $49.95   **016**
1. Genealogy -- Bibliography 2. Reference books
ISBN 0-916489-70-1

LC 98-10852

The book opens with an "introductory chapter that highlights categories of research, the evaluation of records, interlibrary loan, and even the Dewey Decimal system. Editor Meyerink then divides the book into four sections encompassing background information (how-to-books, atlases), finding aids, printed original records, and compiled records (family histories, periodicals)." Libr J

What do I read next? 2011; a reader's guide to current genre fiction. 2011 ed; Gale / Cengage Learning 2011 2v ea $230   **016**
1. Best books 2. Fiction 3. Fiction -- Bibliography 4. Popular literature 5. Reference books
ISBN 978-1-4144-6136-6 v1; 978-1-4144-8763-2 v2

A guide to locating new fiction titles in specific genres. Arranged by author within six genre sections, each entry provides publisher and publication date, series name, major characters, time period, geographic setting, review citations, and related books.

016.6   Bibliographies of technology (Applied sciences)

Covert, Jack
★ The **100** best business books of all time; what they say, why they matter, and how they can help you. [by] Jack Covert and Todd Sattersten. Portfolio 2009 335p il $25.95   **016.6**
1. Best books 2. Business 3. Business -- Bibliography 4. Management
ISBN 978-1-59184-240-8

LC 2008-36664

"Covert and Sattersten operate 800-CEO-READ, a specialty business-book retailer. Out of the countless business books they have read every year for a quarter century, they have culled 100 of the best and presented them in review format. . . . This list and the fine reviews are proof positive that business books can offer a rich treasure of stories and inspiration." Booklist

Includes bibliographical references

020   Library and information sciences

Gleick, James
The **information**. Pantheon Books 2011 526p il $29.95   **020**
1. Information science 2. Information society -- History
ISBN 978-0-375-42372-7; 0-375-42372-9

LC 2010-23221

"As he traces the evolution of intertwined ideas, [Gleick] provides vivid portraits of [Claude] Shannon and other pioneers of our Information Age, including Charles Babbage, whose unbuilt 19th-century 'Analytical Engine' anticipated modern computers, and Alan Turing, whose machines helped the Allies crack German codes during World War II." Wall Street J

Includes bibliographical references

Johnson, Marilyn
★ **This** book is overdue! how librarians and cybrarians can save us all. Harper 2010 272p $24.99   **020**
1. Knowledge management 2. Librarians 3. Libraries and society 4. Libraries and the Internet 5. Library science
ISBN 978-0-06-143160-9; 0-06-143160-5

LC 2010-07860

"In an information age full of Google-powered searches, free-by-Bittorrent media downloads and Wiki-powered knowledge databases, the librarian may seem like an antiquated concept. . . . [The author] is here to reverse that notion with a topical, witty study of the vital ways modern librarians uphold their traditional roles as educators, archivists, and curators of a community legacy. . . . Johnson's wry report is a must-read for anyone who's used a library in the past quarter century." Publ Wkly

Includes bibliographical references

Kroski, Ellusa

Web 2.0 for librarians and information professionals. Neal-Schuman Publishers 2008 209p il pa $75   **020**

1. Web 2.0 2. Web 2.0 -- Library applications

ISBN 978-1-55570-614-2; 1-55570-614-2

LC 2007-43249

"Whether you are just beginning the journey in the transformation of the Web or want to begin implementing this exciting tool in your library, this outstanding resource will take the mystery out of these concepts and be an excellent addition to your reference section." Libr Media Connect

Includes glossary and bibliographical references

Lankes, R. David

The **atlas** of new librarianship. MIT Press; Association of College & Research Libraries 2011 408p il $55   **020**

1. Librarianship 2. Libraries and community 3. Library science

ISBN 978-0-262-01509-7

LC 2010-22788

The author initiates a "conversation about librarianship and its future. He builds this conversation using an atlas, or topical mapping, to engage librarians in exploring their profession, their mission, and their future. . . . Grounding the atlas in the why of librarianship, Lankes argues that libraries serve not only as repositories providing access to information but as fertile ground for actively using collections, resources, and information to create knowledge and foster learning via ongoing conversations with our communities. He invites librarians to expand librarianship beyond the support of information seeking, access, and literacy and toward participation in and co-ownership of a community's knowledge-creation processes. . . . Essential for all librarians." Libr J

Includes bibliographical references.

The Bowker annual library and book trade almanac 2008; 53rd ed.; Information Today 2008 863p $199.95   **020**

1. Book industry 2. Libraries

ISBN 978-1-57387-321-5; 1-57387-321-7

"A compendium of statistical and directory information relating to most aspects of librarianship and the book trade. Professional reports from the field; international library news; library legislation; grants; survey articles of developments during the preceding year." Ref Sources for Small & Medium-sized Libr. 6th edition

★ Core technology competencies for librarians and library staff; a LITA guide. Susan M. Thompson, editor. Neal-Schuman Publishers 2009 248p il pa $65   **020**

1. Automation of library processes -- Teaching 2. In-service education 3. Information technology 4. Information technology -- Study and teaching 5. Librarians -- In-service training 6. Librarians -- Qualifications 7. Libraries -- Technological innovations 8. Library education 9. Library employees -- In-service

training 10. Technological innovations

ISBN 978-1-55570-660-9

LC 2008-46174

In this book, "a coterie of experts identify competencies for technology specialists and describe several competency implementation programs. Useful for everyone from the systems librarian to the 'lone information technology librarian.'" Am Libr

Includes bibliographical references

Library literature & information science index. Wilson, H.W.   **020**

1. Library science -- Bibliography 2. Reference books

This is a single-alphabet author and subject index to materials in library and information science published in the United States and abroad. Over 200 journals are indexed each year. Other materials indexed include selected state journals, conference proceedings, pamphlets, and library school theses. This index also includes monographs and book reviews

Library mashups; exploring new ways to deliver library data. edited by Nicole C. Engard. Information Today, Inc. 2009 334p il map pa $39.50 **020**

1. Internet resources 2. Web sites -- Design

ISBN 978-1-57387-372-7

LC 2009-25999

"Editor Engard assembles 21 articles from 25 international contributors to focus on mashups within the library environment. Readers with little knowledge of mashups will find chapters such as 'What Is a Mashup?' and 'Behind the Scenes: Some Technical Details on Mashups' especially helpful. Other portions of this book cover topics such as mashups in library Web sites, mashups of catalog data, and mashups and media (e.g., photos)." Booklist

Includes bibliographical references

021.2   Relationships with the community

Brookover, Sophie

Pop goes the library; using pop culture to connect with your whole community. [by] Sophie Brookover and Elizabeth Burns. Information Today, Inc. 2008 298p il pa $39.50   **021.2**

1. Libraries -- Special collections -- Popular culture 2. Libraries and community

ISBN 978-1-57387-336-9

LC 2008-19509

"This work defines how popular culture can contribute to any library. . . . The authors explore what popular culture is and, more importantly, what it is not. Also examined are what it means to create a popular-culture collection and how to use popular culture to generate staff and public support. . . . This book is required reading." Booklist

Includes bibliographical references

Hill, Chrystie

Inside, outside, and online; building your library community. foreword by Steven Cohen. American Library Association 2009 175p pa $48   **021.2**

1. Libraries -- Evaluation 2. Libraries and community

3. Library administration
ISBN 978-0-8389-0987-4; 0-8389-0987-6

LC 2008-52520

In this "how-to manual, author Hill makes a . . . case for community building as an essential form of service in public libraries, both for their survival and relevance and also for the needs of those Americans who find themselves 'bowling alone.' She outlines five steps in the process she recommends public libraries follow to build communities: assess, deliver, engage, iterate, and sustain." Booklist

Includes bibliographical references

Librarians as community partners; an outreach handbook. edited by Carol Smallwood. American Library Association 2010 204p pa $55 **021.2**
1. Cultural programs 2. Libraries -- Public relations 3. Libraries and community
ISBN 978-0-8389-1006-1

LC 2009-20359

"Thirty-seven public, school, and academic librarians here share 'how we did outreach good' and produce a joyful collection. . . . Beyond a bounty of ideas are practical suggestions and examples that can be used for the library to approach organizations, groups, and governmental entities for grant applications. While the creative is foremost, the financial and efficient are also addressed with the essential details of who did what, how it was funded, and the nature of follow-up. . . . Even the smallest library with a handful of staff could benefit from this book." Libr J

Includes bibliographical references

021.7 Promotion of libraries, archives, information centers

Thenell, Jan

The **library's** crisis communications planner; a PR guide for handling every emergency. American Library Association 2004 77p il pa $25 **021.7**
1. Archives -- Safety measures -- Handbooks, manuals, etc 2. Archives -- Security measures -- Handbooks, manuals, etc 3. Crisis management -- Handbooks, manuals, etc 4. Libraries -- Public relations 5. Libraries -- Safety measures -- Handbooks, manuals, etc 6. Libraries -- Security measures -- Handbooks, manuals, etc 7. Libraries and mass media
ISBN 0-8389-0870-5

LC 2004-10891

Offering "advice, firsthand experience, scenarios, and guidelines for communicating effectively before, during, and after a crisis or crisis-producing events, ... [the author's] guide is a ready-made workshop on how to establish and maintain relationships with the media, including how to write a press release, how to keep all staff informed and aware of what to do when an emergency occurs, and how to make sure library board members and other community stakeholders are notified and/or involved. Whether or not you have a public relations office or officer, this slim volume is a must for your professional shelf." Libr J

Includes bibliographical references

023 Personnel management (Human resource management)

Giesecke, Joan

★ **Fundamentals** of library supervision; [by] Joan Giesecke and Beth McNeil. 2nd ed.; American Library Association 2010 189p il pa $55 **023**
1. Libraries -- Administration 2. Personnel management
ISBN 978-0-8389-1016-0

LC 2009-28890

"The authors give advice on how to build relationships with bosses, peers, and reports; establish good communication skills; create a healthy work climate; motivate others; and build a team. . . . Each chapter includes a succinct bibliography, allowing the new manager to continue his or her education—especially useful for more complex topics like project management." Libr J

Includes bibliographical references

Stanley, Mary J.

Managing library employees; a how-to-do-it manual. Neal-Schuman Publishers 2008 247p il pa $59.95 **023**
1. Administration -- Handbooks, manuals, etc. 2. Libraries -- Handbooks, manuals, etc. 3. Library personnel management 4. Personnel -- Administration 5. Personnel management
ISBN 978-1-55570-628-9; 1-55570-628-2

LC 2007-51961

"Oriented to librarians who do not have a human resources department in the library, Managing Library Employees is for the nonexpert trying to come to terms with managing a library's largest expenditure and asset—its employees. The chapters are divided into subtopics posed as questions. . . . The chapters also provide information on writing an effective job description, designing a disciplinary procedure, and identifying potential issues that might lead to a lawsuit. . . . This useful guide for everyday situations should be on any library director or manager's professional reference shelf." Booklist

Includes bibliographical references

Tucker, Dennis C.

Crash course in library supervision; meeting the key players. [by] Dennis C. Tucker and Shelley Elizabeth Mosley. Libraries Unlimited 2008 139p il pa $30 **023**
1. Administration -- Handbooks, manuals, etc. 2. Libraries -- Administration
ISBN 978-1-59158-564-0; 1-59158-564-3

LC 2007-30131

This book "covers the basics for new public library administrators, with an emphasis on interpersonal relations. . . . The book should prove valuable to all new library administrators." Booklist

Includes bibliographical references

025 Operations of libraries, archives, information centers

Bolan, Kimberly

Technology made simple; an improvement guide for small and medium libraries. [by] Kimberly Bolan and Robert Cullin. American Library Association 2007 213p il $40 **025**
1. Information technology 2. Libraries -- Automation
ISBN 0-8389-0920-5; 978-0-8389-0920-1
LC 2006-13191

The authors present an "overview of basic public library technologies. . . . Using examples from a plethora of small- and medium-sized libraries to illustrate how such specific issues as self-check, hiring for attitude, tech policies, staff and public training, and formal planning can be approached as doable and nonthreatening to the non-specialist, this guide is an excellent demonstration of how order can make big issues approachable. . . . Libraries should purchase it for their staff collections but also make reading and implementing various suggestions part of their work plans." Voice Youth Advocates
Includes bibliographical references

Burke, John J., 1875-1936

Neal-Schuman library technology companion; a basic guide for library staff. [by] John J. Burke. 3rd ed.; Neal-Schuman Publishers 2009 279p il **025**
1. Information technology 2. Libraries -- Automation 3. Technological innovations
ISBN 978-1-55570-676-0
LC 2009-23646

"Separated into five parts, the work begins with a discussion of the basics, followed by descriptions of the tools, such as computers and networks. Next addressed are how to put technology to work and how to build and maintain the technology environment. The final chapter talks about future trends. . . . [This is] a valuable reference manual for practicing librarians and textbook for a library-school course. The work addresses all aspects of librarianship and technology—teaching, security, databases, social networking, and more." Booklist
Includes bibliographical references

Cohn, John M.

The **complete** library technology planner; a guidebook with sample technology plans and RFPs on CD-ROM. [by] John M. Cohn and Ann L. Kelsey; with a foreword by Keith Michael Fiels. Neal-Schuman Publishers 2010 xxiv, 163p il pa $99.95 **025**
1. Automation of library processes -- Handbooks, manuals, etc. 2. Information technology 3. Libraries -- Automation 4. Planning, Library
ISBN 978-1-55570-681-4; 1-55570-681-9
LC 2009-41008

"This book provides a comprehensive wealth of information for libraries in need of creating or updating a technology plan. Whether your goal is to introduce an integrated library system (ILS) or transfer from an existing system to a new one, Cohn and Kelsey make clear the strategic planning process involved and provide the tools needed to create a plan, including how to meet funding requirements, implement the plan, and evaluate its success. The accompanying CD-ROM contains 38 sample technology plans and requests for proposals (RFPs) that have been collected from 32 different libraries." Libr J
Includes bibliographical references

Kovacs, Diane K.

The **Kovacs** guide to electronic library collection development; essential core subject collections, selection criteria, and guidelines. 2nd ed; Neal-Schuman Publishers 2009 xxiii, 303p il pa $150 **025**
1. Collection development 2. Digital libraries 3. Digital libraries -- Collection development 4. Information systems -- Selection 5. Virtual library
ISBN 978-1-55570-664-7; 1-55570-664-9
LC 2009-27772

"Chapters cover general collection guidelines and licensing basics; especially useful are individual sections citing specific Web sites for e-collection sources in ready reference, business, medicine, biology, engineering, physical and earth sciences, and the social sciences and humanities. Kovacs . . . is a very diligent researcher, and her latest title again offers librarians much useful information. " Booklist
Includes bibliographical references

Pearl, Nancy

More book lust; recommended reading for every mood, moment, and reason. Sasquatch Books 2005 286p pa $16.95 **025**
1. Best books 2. Books and reading
ISBN 1-57061-435-0
LC 2004-66292

The author presents a list of "books she or someone else really enjoyed reading, presented in more than 100 lists covering a delightful range of topics, from the biographical or geographical (Winston Churchill, Africa) to favorite writers categorized as 'too good to miss'. . . . If you're clueless about what to read next, you'll find something to pique your interest here." Publ Wkly
Includes bibliographical references

More technology for the rest of us; a second primer on computing for the non-IT librarian. Nancy Courtney, editor. Libraries Unlimited 2010 172p il pa $50 **025**
1. Digital libraries. 2. Digital preservation. 3. Libraries -- Information technology. 4. Libraries -- Technological innovations. 5. Libraries and the Internet.
ISBN 978-1-59158-939-6 pa; 1-59158-939-8 pa; 978-1-59158-941-9 ebook; 1-59158-941-X ebook
LC 2009051166

"11 chapters provide readings on technology topics of interest to today's librarian. Each chapter, authored by a different practicing librarian, describes how the specific technology works and addresses its current and potential use in the library. . . . This book is a one-stop resource for gaining a basic overview of topics such as Web services, digital data preservation and curation, cloud computing, learning management systems, content management systems, metadata repurposing using XSLT, and more." Booklist

Includes bibliographical references

025.04   Information storage and retrieval systems

Dornfest, Rael

Google hacks; [by] Rael Dornfest, Paul Bausch, and Tara Calishain. 3rd ed.; O'Reilly 2006 xxxii, 510p il $24.99   **025.04**

1. Google (Web site) 2. Internet searching

ISBN 0-596-52706-3; 978-0-596-52706-8

LC 2006-285771

This guide to the search engine Google gives instructions on how to use such tools as Google Earth, Google Maps, Google Blog Search, Video Search, and Music Search, as well as different ways of using Google products, such as using Google to keep track of new blog posts and building customized Google maps.

Jaeger, Paul T.

★ **Public** libraries and internet service roles; measuring and maximizing Internet services. [by] Charles R. McClure and Paul T. Jaeger. American Library Association 2009 112p il map $65 **025.04**

1. Internet 2. Internet -- Public libraries 3. Librarianship -- Social aspects 4. Libraries and the Internet 5. Public libraries 6. Public libraries -- Aims and objectives 7. Public libraries -- Social aspects

ISBN 978-0-8389-3576-7; 0-8389-3576-1

LC 2008-26622

The authors "summarize the existing research on the meanings of social roles and expectations of public libraries and the results of studies detailing those roles and expectations in relation to the Internet. . . . Their book raises our awareness of some very critical issues and is required reading for anyone who cares about public libraries." Booklist

Includes bibliographical references

Norlin, Elaina

Usability testing for library websites; a hands-on guide. [by] Elaina Norlin, CM! Winters. American Lib. Assn. 2002 69p il pa $35   **025.04**

1. Library Web sites -- Testing 2. User interfaces (Computer systems) -- Testing 3. Web sites 4. Web sites -- Design 5. Web sites -- Evaluation 6. Web sites -- Reviews

ISBN 0-8389-3511-7

LC 2001-33817

"Four goals are explored in improving library sites: usefulness, effectiveness, learn-ability, and user satisfaction. . . . Steps for recruitment of a testing team, development of sample questions and tasks, and evaluation of results are included." SLJ

Includes bibliographical references

Pariser, Eli

The **filter** bubble; what the Internet is hiding from you. Penguin Press 2011 294p $25.95 **025.04**

1. Information organization 2. Information systems 3. Internet 4. Internet -- Censorship 5. Invisible Web 6. Semantic Web 7. World Wide Web

ISBN 978-1-59420-300-8; 1-59420-300-8

LC 2011010403

The author examines "the personalization of search-engine results. . . . He is most concerned with its political and social implications, and particularly with what he believes to be its high toll on serendipitous discovery." (N Y Times Book Rev) Index.

"The distinction between citizen and consumer forms the core of [this book] . . . . Are we consumers whose role in society is primarily to purchase and use products, or are we citizens who make informed decisions in an attempt to make life better for ourselves and the world? The Internet, as Eli Pariser convincingly argues in the book, is hurtling toward a consumer model, existing primarily to sell people stuff at the expense of everything else. Pariser is focused on the 'personalization' model, as well as the 'filter bubble' that gives the book its name. The biggest companies on the Internet, specifically Google and Facebook, are changing the Internet to match users' specific interests, habits, and purchasing preferences, often without us even knowing we're getting personalized content. Pariser isn't simply a disgruntled anticapitalist, though—he lays out the societal and cognitive reasons this particular form of personalization is threatening, using anecdotes, data, philosophy, and social as well as cognitive psychology." A V Club

Includes bibliographical references

Gale directory of databases. Gale Res. 2008 2v in 4 parts set $585   **025.04**

1. Information systems -- Directories 2. Reference books

ISBN 978-0-7876-9755-6; 0-7876-9755-9

"Descriptive entries include such details as producer name and contact information, summary of content, database language, geographic coverage, year first available, time span, updating, availability, rates, and more." Publisher's note

★ The **United States** government internet directory; edited by Peggy Garvin. Bernan Press 2010 627p pa $65   **025.04**

1. Government information -- Directories 2. Internet resources -- Directories 3. Reference books 4. Web sites -- Directories

ISBN 978-1-59888-421-0

This directory "contains more than 2,000 Web site records, organized into 20 subject-themed chapters; provides descriptions and URLs for each site; . . . includes information about the sponsoring agency; notes the useful or unique aspects of the site; lists some of the major government publications hosted on the site; evaluates the most important and frequently sought sites; provides a roster of congressional members with members' Web sites includes a one-page 'Quick Guide' to the major federal agencies and the leading online library, data source, and finding aid sites; [and] highlights the Freedom of Information Act Web pages to access U.S. federal executive agency records." Publisher's note

025.1 Administration

Gerding, Stephanie K.

Winning grants; a how-to-do-it manual for librarians with multimedia tutorials and grant development tools. [by] Pamela H. MacKellar and Stephanie K. Gerding. Neal-Schuman Publishers 2010 xxi, 242p il **025.1**
1. Fund raising 2. Grants-in-aid
ISBN 978-1-55570-700-2

LC 2010017965

"This great all-around resource should be a staple for those just entering the challenging world of grant seeking and for the well-rounded library collection." Libr J

Includes bibliographical references

Landau, Herbert B.

The **small** public library survival guide; thriving on less. American Library Association 2008 159p pa $42 **025.1**
1. Libraries and community 2. Library finance 3. Public libraries 4. Public libraries -- Administration
ISBN 978-0-8389-3575-0; 0-8389-3575-3

LC 2008-7425

This "volume covers many topics of interest to staff in small public libraries. Written in a conversational, accessible style, information is presented in short chapters with relevant examples and sample documents. . . . Covering topics from low-budget programming to building 'noncash support from the community,' this text has something for almost everyone involved in the operations of a small public library. . . . Easy and enjoyable to read." Voice Youth Advocates

Includes bibliographical references

Larson, Jeanette C.

★ The **public** library policy writer; a guidebook with model policies on CD-ROM. [by] Jeanette C. Larson and Herman L. Totten. Neal-Schuman Publishers 2008 xxi, 280p $75 **025.1**
1. Administration -- Handbooks, manuals, etc. 2. Libraries -- Administration 3. Library rules and regulations 4. Public libraries 5. Public libraries -- Administration
ISBN 978-1-55570-603-6; 1-55570-603-7

LC 2008-17622

"This guidebook is written mainly for small to medium-sized library directors who need to analyze current policies, revise or update those still in use, and develop new ones. The book is organized by administrative and service areas such as employment practices, staff and patron conduct, use of materials, collection development, and access to facilities. . . . This practical tool should be useful to administrators, staff, and library boards." Booklist

Includes bibliographical references

Laughlin, Sara

The **quality** library; a guide to staff-driven improvement, better efficiency, and happier customers. [by] Sara Laughlin and Ray W. Wilson. American Library Association 2008 144p il pa $55 **025.1**
1. Customer services 2. Libraries -- Administration

3. Libraries -- Management 4. Library administration 5. Management 6. Planning, Library 7. Total quality management
ISBN 978-0-8389-0952-2; 0-8389-0952-3

LC 2007-30710

"Building on an earlier publication, The Library's Continuous Improvement Fieldbook: 29 Ready-to-Use Tools . . . Laughlin and Wilson have created a manual for administrators and employees who want to improve their libraries by improving their processes. . . . This can be a useful guide for libraries whose governing bodies are looking for business-like solutions and for managers who want to heed input from those who do the job." Booklist

Includes bibliographical references

Our new public, a changing clientele; bewildering issues or new challenges for managing libraries? edited by James R. Kennedy, Lisa Vardaman, and Gerard B. McCabe. Libraries Unlimited 2008 305p $45 **025.1**
1. Academic libraries -- Administration 2. Libraries -- Administration 3. Libraries and students 4. Library administration
ISBN 978-1-59158-407-0

LC 2007-35907

"Several chapters in this . . . title discuss the milennials—children of the baby boomers—and digital natives and how they have already had an impact on library service. . . . Each chapter offers practical advice based on experiences, and each includes a list of references. Library managers and those aspiring to be managers will find help in providing services for a younger demographic." Booklist

Includes bibliographical references

025.17 Administration of collections of special materials

★ No shelf required; e-books in libraries. edited by Sue Polanka. American Library Association 2011 182p pa $65 **025.17**
1. Electronic books
ISBN 978-0-83891-054-2

LC 2010-14045

"Following a chapter on e-book history are chapters discussing e-books and students' learning; e-books in school, public, and academic libraries; and e-book acquisitions and management. . . . An essential guide to a topic of high importance." Booklist

Includes bibliographical references

025.2 Acquisitions and collection development

Alabaster, Carol

Developing an outstanding core collection; a guide for libraries. 2nd ed; American Library Association 2010 191p il pa $60 **025.2**
1. Best books 2. Libraries -- Collection development 3. Public libraries -- Collection development 4. Reference

books
ISBN 978-0-8389-1040-5

LC 2009-40342

The author suggests "that the general public needs materials beyond current best-sellers and ready-reference works; that those materials should be high-quality, enduring pieces; and that librarians are the best persons to decide what constitutes appropriate core collections for their communities. . . . [She also] addresses the technological changes that drastically affect reading habits and our ability to satisfy the needs of 'the people's university.' . . . [This book is] required reading for all those charged with the task of adult collection development." Booklist

Includes bibliographical references

Baker, Nicholson

Double fold; libraries and the assault on paper. Random House 2001 370p il hardcover o.p. pa $14   **025.2**

  1. Libraries -- Special collections 2. Libraries -- United States -- Special collections -- Newspapers 3. Library resources -- Conservation and restoration 4. Newspaper and periodical libraries -- United States 5. Newspapers -- Conservation and restoration 6. Paper 7. Paper -- Preservation -- United States

ISBN 0-375-72621-7 pa

LC 00-59171

Baker criticizes libraries for discarding books, magazines and newspapers and disputes the arguments for doing so "that libraries are running out of space, and that paper, because of its acid content, is rapidly turning to dust. . . . What the Library of Congress spends in a year on microfilming would, (according to Baker), buy a storage facility 'the size of a Home Depot, which would hold a century of newsprint.' . . . Librarians, he says, 'have lied to us shamelessly about the extent of paper's fragility, and they continue to lie about it.'" N Y Times Book Rev

Includes bibliographical references

Brenner, Robin E.

★ **Understanding** manga and anime. Libraries Unlimited 2007 335p il pa $40   **025.2**

  1. Anime 2. Libraries -- Collection development 3. Libraries -- Special collections -- Graphic novels 4. Manga -- Study and teaching

ISBN 978-1-59158-332-5; 1-59158-332-2

LC 2007-9773

The author "provides thorough explanations of manga and anime vocabulary, potential censorship issues because of cultural disparities, and typical Manga conventions. . . . No professional collection could possibly be complete without this all-inclusive and exceptional work." Voice Youth Advocates

Charles, John A.

The **mystery** readers' advisory; the librarian's clues to murder and mayhem. [by] John Charles, Joanna Morrison, [and] Candace Clark. American Library Association 2002 227p pa $45   **025.2**

  1. Detective and mystery stories 2. Detective and mystery stories -- Bibliography 3. Fiction in libraries -- United States 4. Libraries -- United States -- Special

collections -- Detective and mystery stories 5. Mystery and detective fiction 6. Mystery fiction -- Bibliography 7. Reader guidance 8. Readers' advisory service 9. Readers' advisory services -- United States 10. Reference books 11. Reference services (Libraries)

ISBN 0-8389-0811-X; 978-0-8389-0811-2

LC 01-45083

"Covering everything a librarian would need to know to successfully build and promote a mystery collection, the authors include chapters on weeding and marketing the collection, with a great section on how to do a readers' advisory interview. . . . The text is peppered with authors and titles to know and plenty of plot teasers to fill your reading list. There are thorough discussions of the different subgenres, from police procedural to romantic suspense and other genre blends. . . . The lists of mystery periodicals, reference sources, and Web sites are well-rounded and up-to-date." Voice Youth Advocates

Includes bibliographical references

Foerstel, Herbert N.

★ **Banned** in the U.S.A; a reference guide to book censorship in schools and public libraries. rev and expanded ed; Greenwood Press 2002 xxvii, 296p $54.95   **025.2**

  1. Book selection -- United States 2. Books -- Censorship 3. Censorship 4. Censorship -- United States 5. Libraries -- Censorship 6. Public libraries -- Book selection -- United States 7. Public libraries -- Censorship -- United States 8. Public schools -- Censorship -- United States 9. Textbooks -- Censorship -- United States

ISBN 0-313-31166-8

LC 2001-55620

"Librarians and teachers need this book, but patrons who want to better understand the threats to their First Amendment rights should be led to it as well." SLJ

Includes bibliographical references

Gallaway, Beth

★ **Game** on! gaming at the library. Neal-Schuman Publishers 2009 306p il pa $55   **025.2**

  1. Electronic games -- Collections 2. Libraries -- Special collections 3. Multimedia library services 4. Video games 5. Video games and children 6. Video games and teenagers

ISBN 978-1-55570-595-4; 1-55570-595-2

LC 2009-14110

"An essential guide for any librarian who plans on embracing the video-game phenomenon, or at the very least, understanding it. . . . [The chapters] are well organized and contain an abundance of practical information. The sections on selection, collection, and circulation of video games include relevant advice on policy, cataloging, marketing, storage, and displays. . . . The annotated list of video games for a core collection is wonderful for selection purposes." SLJ

Includes bibliographical references

Goldsmith, Francisca

The **readers'** advisory guide to graphic novels. American Library Association 2010 124p pa $45 **025.2**

1. Graphic novels 2. Graphic novels -- Bibliography 3. Libraries -- Special collections -- Graphic novels

ISBN 978-0-8389-1008-5; 0-8389-1008-4

LC 2009-25239

"After dispelling the two main myths that ghettoize graphic novels—they are just for adolescents and they are far less complex than texts without pictures—Goldsmith emphasizes that GNs are a format and not a genre. She suggests active and passive ways to offer readers' advisory (RA) from face-to-face encounters with patrons to book displays and book groups and offers guidance on helping established GN readers to find new titles they might enjoy. . . . All in all it is a valuable and quite readable resource that belongs in every library's professional collection." Voice Youth Advocates

Includes glossary and bibliographical references

Greiner, Tony

★ **Analyzing** library collection use with Excel. American Library Association 2007 167p il pa $40 **025.2**

1. Circulation analysis 2. Excel (Computer program) 3. Libraries -- Collection development 4. Library circulation 5. Use studies

ISBN 978-0-8389-0933-1; 0-8389-0933-7

LC 2006-101539

The authors "show how to use Excel® to translate circulation and collection data into meaningful reports for making collection management decisions." Publisher's note

Includes bibliographical references

Serchay, David S.

The **librarian's** guide to graphic novels for adults. Neal-Schuman Publishers 2010 320p il $65 **025.2**

1. Graphic novels -- Administration 2. Graphic novels -- Collections 3. Libraries -- Special collections -- Graphic novels

ISBN 978-1-55570-662-3

LC 2009-41011

"This book will inspire librarians—and others—with little knowledge of graphic novels (GNs) for adults to pick one up and see what all the buzz is about. Serchay puts forth a complete guide that will enable any librarian, whether a GN novice or seasoned fan, to establish a brand-new collection, fully understanding what GNs are, where to purchase them, how to catalog them, and how to review, promote, and maintain the new collection." Libr J

Includes bibliographical references

Slote, Stanley J.

★ **Weeding** library collections; library weeding methods. 4th ed; Libraries Unlimited 1997 xxi, 240p il $69 **025.2**

1. Collection development 2. Discarding of books, periodicals, etc. 3. Libraries -- Collection development

ISBN 1-56308-511-9

LC 96-54865

"The author demonstrates how weeding strengthens a collection and increases circulation. . . . Four weeding methods are presented: the book card method, the spine-marking method, the historical reconstruction method, and the computer-assisted method. Slote gives precise instructions for each method, enhanced with illustrations." Book Rep

Includes bibliographical references

White, Andrew C.

★ **E-metrics** for library and information professionals; how to use data for managing and evaluating electronic resource collections. Neal-Schuman Publishers 2006 249p il pa $75 **025.2**

1. Digital libraries 2. Internet -- Statistics

ISBN 1-55570-514-6

LC 2004-54678

"Designed to introduce readers to e-metrics ('the measurements of the use and activity of networked information'), this book is made up of 10 chapters that are divided among three major sections. Part 1 supplies a definition of e-metrics, explores their use in libraries, and discusses vendor-supplied electronic data reports. Part 2 explains why libraries need e-metrics, focusing on how they can be used for public relations, collection management, and library administration. Part 3 offers ways that libraries can build local e-metrics. Chapters cover the capturing and processing of statistics, infrastructure and technical requirements, and staffing needs. With its coherent structure, well-articulated language, and illustrative material (tables, figures, and examples), this book has much to recommend it." Booklist

Includes bibliographical references

Graphic novels beyond the basics; insights and issues for libraries. Martha Cornog and Timothy Perper, editors. Libraries Unlimited 2009 xxx, 281p il pa $45 **025.2**

1. Comic books, strips, etc. -- History and criticism 2. Graphic novels -- History and criticism 3. Libraries -- Special collections -- Graphic novels

ISBN 978-1-59158-478-0; 1-59158-478-7

LC 2009-16189

Editors Cornog and Perper have collected essays by experts Robin Brenner, Francisca Goldsmith, Trina Robbins, Michael R. Lavin, Gilles Poitras, Lorena O'English, Michael Niederhausen, Erin Byrne, and Cornog herself, all about graphic novels in libraries. Topics covered range from the appeal of superheroes to manga, the appeal of comics to women and girls, anime, independent comics, dealing with challenges to the material, and more. Appendices provide resource information on African American-interest graphic novels, Latino-interest graphic novels, LGBT-interest graphic novels, religious-themed graphic novels, a bibliography of books about graphic novels in libraries, and online resources.

"Whether you are serious about the genre, interested in the history, or looking for ammunition, this book should be on your shelf. The wealth of knowledge and research that went into these essays is impressive, and reading this book will put you on the road to becoming an expert." Libr Media Connect

Includes bibliographical references

★ Intellectual freedom manual; 8th ed; American Library Association 2010 xxii, 439 p.p   **025.2**
    1. Intellectual freedom -- United States -- Handbooks, manuals, etc. 2. Libraries -- Censorship -- United States -- Handbooks, manuals, etc.
    ISBN 0838935907; 9780838935903
                         LC 2010016157
"All libraries should have a copy of this book to use when writing or revising policies; indispensable." Libr J

025.3   Bibliographic analysis and control

Maxwell, Robert L.
    FRBR; a guide for the perplexed. American Library Association 2008 151p il pa $50   **025.3**
    1. FRBR (Conceptual model)
    ISBN 978-0-8389-0950-8; 0-8389-0950-7
                         LC 2007-27845
This book explains "Functional Requirements for Bibliographic Records (FRBR), an evolving conceptual model developed to assist users in navigating library catalogs to find the information they want and need. Maxwell . . . explains and illustrates the FRBR model, details why the document and model are important for the future of information organization, and explains what a catalog based on FRBR principles might look like. He also briefly illustrates the use of Functional Requirements for Authority Data (FRAD)." Booklist
    Includes bibliographic references

Mitchell, Anne M.
    ★ **Cataloging** and organizing digital resources; a how-to-do-it manual for librarians. Neal-Schuman Publishers 2005 219p il pa $75   **025.3**
    1. Cataloging 2. Cataloging -- Handbooks, manuals, etc. 3. Digital libraries 4. Information systems 5. Information systems -- Cataloging 6. Reference books
    ISBN 1-55570-521-9
                         LC 2005-903
This "volume addresses the ways a library can manage electronic collections. The goal is to provide an overview of management concerns and issues regarding bibliographic control in an online environment and to suggest tools that are available. The 10 chapters address such topics as development of digital libraries, organization of work flow, alternatives to cataloging, cataloging rules and records, online monographs and serials, integration of resources, and trends. Each chapter offers an introduction; guidelines, instructions, or strategies; and a summary and references. The writing is clear, with plentiful examples that include figures and titles." Booklist

Oliver, Chris
    ★ **Introducing** RDA; a guide to the basics. American Library Association 2010 117p il   **025.3**
    1. Cataloging 2. Cataloging -- Standards 3. Descriptive cataloging -- Standards
    ISBN 978-0-8389-3594-1
                         LC 2010021719
Practical advice for catalogers and library administrators on how to make the transition from the Anglo-American cataloging rules (AACR) to Resource description and access (RDA).
    This is "a useful guide that provides a clear explanation of what RDA is all about. . . . Highly recommended for novice and experienced catalogers." Libr J
    Includes bibliographical references

025.4   Subject analysis and control

Dewey, Melvil
    ★ **Dewey** decimal classification and relative index; devised by Melvil Dewey. ed 22; OCLC 2003 4v set $375   **025.4**
    1. Classification, Dewey decimal 2. Dewey Decimal Classification
    ISBN 0-910608-70-9
                         LC 2003-50872

Library of Congress/Cataloging Policy and Support Office
    Library of Congress subject headings; prepared by the Policy and Standards Division, Library Services. 31st ed; Library of Congress 2009 5v   **025.4**
    1. Subject headings
    This work contains the headings and cross-references established and applied by the Library of Congress.

McCarthy, Susan
    ★ **Sears** list of subject headings; Joseph Miller, editor; Susan McCarthy, associate editor. 20th ed; H.W. Wilson Co. 2010 liii, 847p $150   **025.4**
    1. Reference books 2. Subject headings
    ISBN 978-0-8242-1105-9; 0-8242-1105-7
                         LC 2010-5731
"The Sears List of Subject Headings delivers a core list of key headings, together with patterns and examples to guide the cataloger in creating additional headings as required. It features: agreement with the Dewey Decimal Classification system to ensure that subject headings conform with library standards; [a] thesaurus-like format; accompanying list of canceled and replacement headings; and legends within the list that identify earlier forms of headings; scope notes accompanying . . . headings where clarification of the specialized use of a term may be required." Publisher's note
    Includes bibliographical references

025.5   Services for users

Buker, Derek M.
    The **science**-fiction and fantasy readers' advisory; the librarian's guide to cyborgs, aliens, and sorcerers. American Lib. Assn. 2002 230p pa $50   **025.5**
    1. Fantasy fiction 2. Fantasy fiction -- Bibliography 3. Fiction in libraries -- United States 4. Libraries -- United States -- Special collections -- Fantasy fiction 5. Libraries -- United States -- Special collections -- Science fiction 6. Reader guidance 7. Readers' advisory service 8. Readers' advisory services -- United States 9. Reference books 10. Reference services (Libraries) 11.

Science fiction 12. Science fiction -- Bibliography
ISBN 0-8389-0831-4; 978-0-8389-0831-0

LC 2002-1494

A "well-organized, humorous guide to providing readers' advisory to customers wanting science fiction or fantasy recommendations. . . . The book is divided into two parts, one dealing with science fiction and one with fantasy, and further divides these genres into their many subgenres, providing short annotated lists of recommended titles as well as longer lists without annotations. . . . What this guide does best is demonstrate the wide scope of science fiction and fantasy literature; it gives many suggestions and recommendations across this broad range." SLJ

Includes bibliographical references

Evans, G. Edward

Introduction to library public services; [by] G. Edward Evans and Thomas L. Carter. 7th ed; Libraries Unlimited 2009 401p il $65; pa $50   **025.5**

1. Library circulation 2. Library services 3. Public services (Libraries) 4. Reference services (Libraries) 5. Reference services -- Handbooks, manuals, etc.
ISBN 978-1-59158-596-1; 978-1-59158-595-4 pa

LC 2008-37445

"Each chapter covers the role, purpose, and philosophy related to major functional areas of public service, including points to ponder, forms and flowcharts, review questions and suggested readings." Publisher's note

Ford, Charlotte

Crash course in reference. Libraries Unlimited 2008 143p il   **025.5**

1. Reference books 2. Reference services (Libraries) 3. Reference services -- Handbooks, manuals, etc.
ISBN 978-1-59158-463-6

LC 2007-52948

"A basic explanation of reference services for those with little formal LIS training working in small rural libraries or others who have been working in other areas and wish to brush up on their skills, this author provides an introduction to reference services including search strategies." Publisher's note

Includes bibliographical references

Hernon, Peter

Assessing service quality; satisfying the expectations of library customers. [by] Peter Hernon + Ellen Altman. 2nd ed; American Library Association 2010 206p il pa $65   **025.5**

1. Consumer satisfaction 2. Customer services -- Quality control 3. Evaluation research (Social action programs) 4. Information services -- Quality control 5. Libraries -- Public relations 6. Library services 7. Public services (Libraries) 8. Public services (Libraries) -- Evaluation 9. Social service -- Quality control
ISBN 978-0-8389-1021-4; 0-8389-1021-1

LC 2009-40332

The authors "concentrate on how to assess service quality and customer satisfaction. Here they suggest . . . ways to think about library services, clarify the distinction between service quality and customer satisfaction, present strategies for developing a customer service plan, identify procedures

to measure service quality and satisfaction, and . . . challenge conventional thinking about these powerful principles. . . . Kudos to these authors for providing an essential resource for librarians who understand that folks who walk into their libraries are not patrons but customers." Libr J

Includes bibliographical references

Jerrard, Jane

★ **Crisis** in employment; a librarian's guide to helping job seekers. foreword by Denise Davis. American Library Association 2009 66p il pa $40   **025.5**

1. Entrepreneurship 2. Job hunting 3. Libraries and community 4. Library-community relations 5. Reference services (Libraries) 6. Unemployment 7. Vocational guidance 8. Vocational guidance -- Information services 9. Vocational guidance in libraries
ISBN 978-0-8389-1013-9

LC 2009-16684

This "special report provides suggestions for providing low-cost assistance to job-seeking unemployed library users. With examples from various public libraries, the report offers advice for planning, how to get the most out of resources at hand, dealing with the need for additional computers, suggestions for community partnerships, and how to best assist users who need to become computer literate for a successful job search." Libr J

Includes bibliographical references

Katz, William A.

★ **Introduction** to reference work; 8th ed; McGraw-Hill 2001 2v v1 $82.81; v2 $85   **025.5**

1. Reference books 2. Reference books -- Bibliography 3. Reference services (Libraries)
ISBN 978-0-07-244107-9 v1; 0-07-244107-0 v1; 978-0-07-244143-7 v2; 0-07-244143-7 v2

Volume one opens with a general introduction to the reference process and online reference services. Types of services include: bibliographies; indexing and abstracting services; encyclopedias; ready-reference; biographies; government documents. Volume two covers community reference services; interviewing; online searching; and library and bibliographic instruction, as well as evaluation of reference services

Kern, M. Kathleen

★ **Virtual** reference best practices; tailoring services to your library. American Library Association 2009 148p il pa $50   **025.5**

1. Reference services (Libraries) 2. Reference services -- Automation
ISBN 978-0-8389-0975-1

LC 2008-15379

The author "offers advice and assistance for libraries considering VR. . . . Kern's guidebook includes useful forms and exercises for every aspect of the VR process from a market assessment of the library's community served to an evaluation of the service. . . . Even those [libraries] which already offer virtual reference will find assistance and suggestions to improve their services." Voice Youth Advocates

Includes bibliographical references

Moyer, Jessica E.

Research-based readers' advisory; with contributions by Amanda Blau and others. American Library Association 2008 278p pa $50   **025.5**
1. Reader guidance 2. Reference services (Libraries)
ISBN 978-0-8389-0959-1; 0-8389-0959-0

LC 2007-49421

"Following a survey of the current state of RA, 11 chapters cover topics such as 'Nonfiction Readers and Nonfiction Advisory,' 'Romance and Genre Readers,' and 'Tools for Readers' Advisory.' Each chapter begins with a 'Research View,' in which Moyer summarizes the latest literature. Following the 'Research View' is a 'Librarian's View,' in which an impressive array of contributors talk about practical applications." Booklist

Includes bibliographical references

★ The **readers'** advisory handbook; edited by Jessica E. Moyer and Kaite Mediatore Stover. American Library Association 2010 220p pa $55   **025.5**
1. Best books 2. Reference services (Libraries)
ISBN 978-0-8389-1042-9

LC 2009-45793

"This great generalist title offers guidelines not only on readers' advisory (RA) but on related matters of collection development and marketing books to different reading audiences. . . . [The authors] gather information and instruction from 15 contributing public and school librarians on self-education, managing and improving groups of selectors, making quick but thorough evaluations of different types of materials, writing reviews, and working with book groups as well as other kinds of programming." Libr J

Includes bibliographical references

Ross, Catherine Sheldrick

Conducting the reference interview; a how-to-do-it manual for librarians. [by] Catherine Sheldrick Ross, Kirsti Nilsen, and Marie L. Radford. 2nd ed; Neal-Schuman Publishers Inc. 2009 290p il pa $75   **025.5**
1. Electronic reference services (Libraries) 2. Reference interview 3. Reference services (Libraries) 4. Reference services -- Automation
ISBN 978-1-55570-655-5

LC 2009-17660

This book aims to teach librarians how "to understand the needs of public, academic and special library users across any virtual setting—email, text messaging, social networking websites—as well as in traditional and face-to-face models of communication." Publisher's note

Includes bibliographical references

Saricks, Joyce G.

The **readers'** advisory guide to genre fiction; 2nd ed; American Library Association 2009 352p pa $65   **025.5**
1. Best books 2. Fiction 3. Fiction -- Bibliography 4. Reference services (Libraries)
ISBN 978-0-8389-0989-8

LC 2008-51029

"Each section includes three or four specific genres . . . and features a definition and introduction to the genre, the characteristics of the genre's appeal, suggested authors and titles, and other practical information. Well-crafted back matter add to the ease of navigation. This very readable text employs a playful tone that reflects Saricks's love of her work and will inspire readers to use RA techniques in a variety of ways. [This is] a useful tool for both new library employees and established practitioners." Voice Youth Advocates

Includes bibliographical references

Spratford, Becky Siegel

The **horror** readers' advisory; the librarian's guide to vampires, killer tomatoes, and haunted houses. [by] Becky Siegel Spratford [and] Tammy Hennigh Clausen. American Library Association 2004 161p il pa $36   **025.5**
1. Fiction in libraries -- United States 2. Horror fiction -- History and criticism 3. Horror tales 4. Horror tales -- Bibliography 5. Libraries -- United States -- Special collections -- Horror tales 6. Readers' advisory services -- United States 7. Reference services (Libraries)
ISBN 0-8389-0871-3

LC 2003-25530

This is a "guide to horror fiction, explaining its appeal and advising on how librarians unfamiliar with the genre can broaden their own knowledge and build a viable collection. The text briefly outlines the characteristics of the main categories, or subgenres, including the usual monsters and occult creatures; extreme suspense of all types; hauntings and possession; and a section on classic works of horror, along with tips for interviewing readers of each subgenre. . . . [This] small, helpful book will be a boon to readers' advisors needing fresh meat for horror fans." Libr J

Includes bibliographical references

Willis, Mark R.

★ **Dealing** with difficult people in the library. American Lib. Assn. 1999 195p pa $28   **025.5**
1. Public libraries
ISBN 0-8389-0760-1

LC 99-20426

"Besides the angry patron, [Willis] considers situations including suspected child abuse, censorship, problems with Internet users, homeless persons in the library, and parents who treat the library as a convenient, free baby-sitting service. In separate sections he focuses on communicating and preventing problems from occurring, and he includes sample policy statements." Booklist

Includes bibliographical references

Virtual reference service; from competencies to assessment. edited by R. David Lankes . . . [et al.] Neal-Schuman Publishers 2008 206p il $75   **025.5**
1. Reference services (Libraries)
ISBN 978-1-55570-528-2

LC 2007-24104

"Featuring essays from the 2005 7th Annual Virtual Reference Desk Conference, this book focuses on the evolving aspects of virtual reference theory, research, and practice. .

. . The topics explored include the implementation and expansion of virtual reference programs, and the training and assessment that is necessary to ensure the success of these services. . . . This is a valuable resource for library practitioners involved with reference services." Am Ref Books Annu, 2008

Includes bibliographical references

025.7   Physical preparation for storage and use

Lavender, Kenneth

★ **Book** repair; a how-to-do-it manual. Kenneth Lavender. 2nd ed; Neal-Schuman Publishers Inc. 2011 xiv, 265 p.p il How-to-do-it manuals (alk. paper) $80   **025.7**
1. Bookbinding -- Repairing -- Handbooks, manuals, etc
2. Books -- Conservation and restoration -- Handbooks, manuals, etc
ISBN 1555707475; 1555707483; 9781555707477; 9781555707484

LC 2011022636

Author Kenneth Lavender provides a "step-by-step manual . . . on basic book repair techniques and sound preservation practices . . . [which] offers illustrated sections on cleaning, mending, hinge and spine repair, strengthening paperbacks, and more. . . . A full discussion of when and how to make repairs is provided, as is a discussion of alternative conservation practices that will enable each librarian to develop procedures appropriate to his or her library." (Publisher's note)

Covering both basic book repair techniques and . . . conservation practices, this . . . manual offers illustrated sections on cleaning, mending, hinge and spine repair, strengthening paperbacks, [etc.]. . . . Chapters cover: wet and water-damaged books; mold and mildew; repair of book linings and pamphlet bindings; using acid-free materials to repair damaged books; lining paper objects; affordable repair tools and supplies. . . . A full discussion of when and how to make repairs, and alternative conservation practices that enable each librarian to develop procedures appropriate to his or her library are also provided. Publisher's note

Includes bibliographical references and index.

Schechter, Abraham A.

Basic book repair methods; illustrated by the author. Libraries Unlimited 1999 102p il pa $37 **025.7**
1. Bookbinding -- Repairing 2. Books -- Conservation and restoration 3. Preservation of library materials -- Handbooks, manuals, etc.
ISBN 1-56308-700-6

LC 98-50950

Photographs accompany step-by-step instructions for common preservation techniques, from the cleaning of pages and their readhesion, to case reattachment and rebacking.

025.8   Maintenance and preservation of collections

Halsted, Deborah D.

★ **Disaster** planning; a how-to-do-it manual for librarians with planning templates on CD-ROM. Neal-Schuman Publishers 2005 xx, 247p il pa $85   **025.8**
1. Accidents -- Prevention 2. Disaster relief 3. Disasters -- Handbooks, manuals, etc. 4. Library resources -- Conservation and restoration
ISBN 1-55570-486-7

LC 2003-65152

"Step-by-step instructions discuss creating a working disaster team, establishing a communications strategy, identifying relief and recovery agencies, developing response plans, and examining issues of cutting-edge library security. . . . This valuable resource is an important addition to most professional collections." Booklist

Includes bibliographical references

026   Specific kinds of institutions

★ Directory of special libraries and information centers, [2008] a guide to more than 35,000 special libraries, research libraries, information centers, archives, and data centers maintained by government agencies . . . Matthew Miskelly, content project editor. 34th ed.; Thompson/Gale 2008 3v set $1260   **026**
1. Reference books 2. Special libraries -- Directories
ISBN 978-0-7876-9679-5; 0-7876-9679-X

"Volume 1, in three parts, provides . . . contact and descriptive information on more than 35,800 subject-specific resource collections maintained by various government agencies, businesses, publishers, educational and nonprofit organizations, and associations around the world. . . . Volume 2, Geographic and Personnel Indexes, provides access to profiled libraries by geographic region, as well as by the professional staff that are cited in each listing." Publisher's note

027   General libraries, archives, information centers

Ryback, Timothy W.

Hitler's private library; the books that shaped his life. Alfred A. Knopf 2008 xx, 278p il map $25.95   **027**
1. Heads of state 2. Nazi leaders
ISBN 978-1-4000-4204-3; 1-4000-4204-6

LC 2008-22010

"Thanks to [Ryback's] imaginative research—and his willingness to investigate a very creepy subject—we come closer to one of the most elusive men ever to shape world history." New Repub

Includes bibliographical references

★ American library directory 2008-2009; 61st ed; Information Today 2008 2v set $299.95 **027**
1. CD-ROMs 2. Libraries -- Directories 3. Reference books
ISBN 978-1-57387-320-8; 1-57387-320-9
"Includes U.S. and Canadian public, academic, and special libraries arranged by state or province, city, and institution. Gives personnel and statistical data, subject interests, and special collections." Ref Sources for Small & Medium-sized Libr. 6th edition

027.4 Public libraries

Matthews, Joseph R.
Scorecards for results; a guide for developing a library balanced scorecard. Libraries Unlimited 2008 112p pa $45 **027.4**
1. Libraries -- Administration 2. Library administration 3. Organizational effectiveness -- Evaluation 4. Performance -- Evaluation 5. Public libraries 6. Public libraries -- Evaluation 7. Strategic planning
ISBN 978-1-59158-698-2
LC 2008-3689
"A balanced scorecard (BSC) is 'a process and culture for choosing, using, and revising measures' to help libraries focus on the success of their mission. ... [The author] has developed a BSC workbook for public libraries. ... Individual chapters here detail the six steps in developing and using a balanced scorecard, with sample vision statements, strategic themes, and performance measures." Libr J
Includes bibliographical references

McCook, Kathleen de la Peña
★ **Introduction** to public librarianship. Neal-Schuman Publishers 2004 406p il **027.4**
1. Public librarianship 2. Public libraries 3. Public libraries -- United States
ISBN 1-55570-475-1
LC 2004-46012
"The book is a necessary addition to all professional collections, not to collect dust, but to become respectfully dog-eared and coffee-stained through repeated use." Florida Libraries
Includes bibliographical references

027.5 Government libraries

Conaway, James
America's library; the story of the Library of Congress, 1800-2000. foreword by James Billington; introduction by Edmund Morris. Yale Univ. Press 2000 226p il $48 **027.5**
1. National libraries -- Washington (D.C.) -- History -- 19th century 2. National libraries -- Washington (D.C.) -- History -- 20th century
ISBN 978-0-300-08308-8; 0-300-08308-4
LC 99-58751
This history of the Library of Congress is organized "around that tiny, hardy band of men and women who have used both political acumen and intellectual vision to build the library's collections and establish those services that make the LC library to both Congress and nation. Richly supplemented with photographs, this history reaches out to touch all who love libraries." Booklist
Includes bibliographical references

027.6 Libraries for special groups and organizations

Moller, Sharon Chickering
Library service to Spanish speaking patrons; a practical guide. Libraries Unlimited 2001 207p pa $30 **027.6**
1. Hispanic Americans -- Databases 2. Hispanic Americans -- Information services 3. Hispanic Americans -- Library resources 4. Hispanic Americans and libraries 5. Libraries -- Services to Hispanic Americans 6. Libraries -- Special collections -- Hispanic Americans 7. Libraries and Hispanic Americans 8. Public libraries 9. Public libraries -- Services to Hispanic Americans
ISBN 1-56308-719-7
LC 00-45090
"Intended to stimulate discussion among library service planners and to offer counsel to service providers, this book should become required reading in any jurisdiction with an underserved Latino population." Voice Youth Advocates
Includes bibliographical references

Roberts, Elizabeth Ann
Crash course in library services to people with disabilities; [by] Ann Roberts and Richard J. Smith. Libraries Unlimited 2010 158p pa $30 **027.6**
1. Libraries and the handicapped
ISBN 978-1-59158-767-5
LC 2009-23985
"Librarians who are striving to fill the information needs of people with different mental and physical challenges will find that this title answers many of their questions. ... Among the topics that are discussed are the implications of the Americans with Disabilities Act; marketing, programs, and services; assistive technologies; and the particular needs of older adults and people with mental and physical disabilities." Booklist
Includes bibliographical references

027.62 Libraries for specific age groups

Fiore, Carole D.
★ **Fiore's** summer library reading program handbook. Neal-Schuman Publishers 2005 xxiii, 312p pa $65 **027.62**
1. Books and reading 2. Children -- Reading -- Study and teaching -- Activities and projects 3. Children's libraries 4. Children's reading -- Projects 5. Young adults -- Reading -- Study and teaching -- Activities and

projects 6. Young adults' reading -- Projects
ISBN 1-55570-513-8

LC 2004-31104

"This research-laden handbook . . . serves as a 'comprehensive program-planning and implementation tool' for public libraries seeking to revamp, revise, or develop a summer library reading program. . . . This is an invaluable resource, both for its concrete guidance and its abstract exploration of the meaning of summer library programs." Bull Cent Child Books

Includes bibliographical references

Vaillancourt, Renee J.

Bare bones young adult services; tips for public library generalists. American Lib. Assn. 2000 142p il pa $33 **027.62**

1. Libraries -- Services to young adults 2. Libraries and students 3. Public libraries 4. Public libraries -- Services to teenagers -- United States 5. Young adults' libraries 6. Young adults' library services
ISBN 0-8389-3497-8

LC 99-35643

The author "provides guidelines for forming Teen Advisory Boards and focus groups, dealing with unruly adolescent patrons, providing homework support, as well as some basic programming ideas. She also discusses collection development and suggests resources that specialize in reviewing teen-level materials." SLJ

Includes bibliographical references

028   Reading and use of other information media

Basbanes, Nicholas A.

★ **Every** book its reader; the power of the printed word to stir the world. HarperCollins 2005 360p il $29.95; pa $15.95 **028**

1. Best books 2. Books and reading
ISBN 0-06-059323-7; 978-0-06-059323-0; 0-06-059324-5 pa; 978-0-06-059324-7 pa

LC 2005-46164

The author "focuses on peoples' reading habits and on the books they have read, both obscure and renowned, as well as on the importance of particular books in specific contexts. Basbanes begins by interviewing some of the best-read people alive, among them David McCullough, Harold Bloom, Helen Vendler, and Elaine Pagels; he also mentions a wide variety of contemporary and historical personages. The loosely related stories are often inspirational, making this an engrossing read." Libr J

Includes bibliographical references

Dirda, Michael

Book by book; notes on reading and life. Henry Holt 2006 170p $17 **028**

1. Best books 2. Books and reading 3. Reading -- Social aspects
ISBN 978-0-8050-7877-0; 0-8050-7877-0

LC 2005-55451

The author "writes a guide to reading and its life lessons ranging widely and pithily through the universal themes of learning, school, work, love, childhood and spiritual guidance. Dirda's message is simple: if reading is to be life enhancing, we need to focus our attention on books that are rewarding. . . . For those who enjoy books about reading, and for all those seeking to encourage others to read, Dirda's brief yet suggestive book will inspire." Publ Wkly

Hooper, Brad

The **short** story readers' advisory; a guide for librarians. American Lib. Assn. 2000 135p pa $32 **028**

1. Libraries -- United States -- Special collections -- Short stories 2. Reader guidance 3. Readers' advisory service 4. Readers' advisory services -- United States 5. Short stories 6. Short stories -- Bibliography 7. Short stories -- History and criticism 8. Short stories, English
ISBN 0-8389-0782-2

LC 99-85751

This work contains over 200 critical essays covering short story authors past and present. A step-by-step guide on how to interview readers in order to match their tastes with appropriate stories is included.

Maatta, Stephanie L.

A **few** good books; using contemporary readers' advisory strategies to connect readers with books. Neal-Schuman Publishers 2010 xix, 387p pa $69.95 **028**

1. Books and reading -- History 2. Reader guidance 3. Reference services (Libraries)
ISBN 978-1-55570-669-2; 1-55570-669-X

LC 2009-40999

"This comprehensive and up-to-date guide is a treasure trove of practical advice and resources that will help make the RA experience even more effective and enjoyable." Libr J

Includes bibliographical references

028.1   Reviews

Szymborska, Wislawa

Nonrequired reading; prose pieces. translated from the Polish by Clare Cavanagh. Harcourt 2002 233p $24 **028.1**

1. Books and reading
ISBN 0-15-100660-1

LC 2002-2440

"The skillful simplicity and lyric quality of these essays make them distinctive. With her poet's gift for compression, Szymborska captures large concepts and brilliantly reduces them to pithy, two-page essays." Libr J

Includes bibliographical references

028.5   Reading and use of other information media by young people

Allyn, Pam

What to read when; the books and stories to read with your child, and all the best times to read them. Avery 2009 318p pa $16.95   **028.5**
1. Children -- Books and reading
ISBN 978-1-58333-334-1

LC 2008-54501

The author "provides many ways to promote a love of reading to children and offers top-ten lists of reasons to read to kids that incorporate practical, easy-to-use tips to encourage literacy from a young age. . . . This is an indispensable guide to choosing age-appropriate books for children. Allyn provides a list of more than 300 titles on 50 themes including such issues as adoption, feelings about school, sharing, and coping with illness. This valuable resource for children's librarians, educators, and parents is highly recommended." Libr J

Helbig, Alethea

Dictionary of American children's fiction, 1995-1999; books of recognized merit. [by] Alethea K. Helbig and Agnes Regan Perkins. Greenwood Press 2002 614p $115   **028.5**
1. American fiction -- 20th century -- Bio-bibliography -- Dictionaries 2. American fiction -- 20th century -- Dictionaries 3. Best books 4. Best books -- United States 5. Children's libraries -- Book lists 6. Children's literature -- Dictionaries 7. Children's stories, American -- Bio-bibliography -- Dictionaries 8. Children's stories, American -- Dictionaries 9. Reference books
ISBN 0-313-30389-4

LC 2001-23871

"The extensive, detailed index is an excellent resource for locating fiction about a wide range of specific topics, characters, authors, and genres." Booklist
Includes bibliographical references

Dictionary of American young adult fiction, 1997-2001; books of recognized merit. {by} Alethea K. Helbig and Agnes Regan Perkins. Greenwood Press 2004 xxii, 558p $75   **028.5**
1. American fiction 2. American fiction -- 20th century -- Bio-bibliography -- Dictionaries 3. American fiction -- 20th century -- Dictionaries 4. Best books 5. Children's literature -- Book lists 6. Reference books 7. Young adult fiction 8. Young adult fiction, American -- Bio-bibliography -- Dictionaries 9. Young adult fiction, American -- Dictionaries 10. Young adult libraries -- Book lists 11. Young adult literature -- Bio-bibliography 12. Young adult literature -- Dictionaries 13. Young adults -- Books and reading 14. Youth -- Books and reading
ISBN 0-313-32430-1

LC 2003-56804

"The 290 books included {in this volume} have been recognized by one or more of the following: Alex Award, ALA Best Books for Young Adults, Booklist, NYPL, and the Michael L. Printz Award. Approximately 60 of the listed books are adult books considered appropriate for young adults by the award committees. The 741 entries, which include books, their authors, major characters, and settings, are listed alphabetically and range in length from a couple of paragraphs to a bit more than a page. Book entries describe plot, themes, and characters, as well as relevant literary awards, while author entries consist of a brief biography and bibliography. . . . {The information is collected} usefully for selectors of young adult fiction, reader's advisers, teachers, and libraries supporting young adult fiction teaching." Libr J
Includes bibliographical references

The Cambridge guide to children's books in English; [edited by] Victor Watson; advisory editors, Elizabeth L. Keyser, Juliet Partridge, Morag Styles. Cambridge Univ. Press 2001 814p il $75 **028.5**
1. Children -- Books and reading 2. Children's literature 3. Children's literature -- Encyclopedias 4. Children's literature, American 5. Children's literature, American -- History and criticism 6. Children's literature, Commonwealth (English) 7. Children's literature, Commonwealth (English) -- History and criticism 8. Children's literature, English 9. Children's literature, English -- History and criticism 10. Reference books
ISBN 0-521-55064-5

LC 00-65163

This reference provides an "overview of historic and contemporary children's books published in English. The entries include authors, illustrators, and significant works primarily from Britain, the US, Canada, Australia, New Zealand, India, and Africa. . . . Major themes, such as fairy tales, fantasy, folktales, legends, mythology, and young adult fiction, are covered as well as less-expected entries on topics such as bias, the bush, disability, ecology, and nudity in children's books. Nonbook media are also covered by entries on animated cartoons, comics, superheroes, and television for children." Choice
Includes bibliographical references

031   General encyclopedic works in specific languages and language families

Jacobs, A. J.

The **know**-it-all; one man's humble quest to become the smartest person in the world. Simon & Schuster 2004 386p $25   **031**
1. Authors 2. Humorists 3. Journalists 4. Memoirists
ISBN 0-7432-5060-5

LC 2004-48233

This "book stems from the author's herculean effort to read every volume of the majestic Encyclopaedia Britannica. . . . Jacobs turns his quest for intellectual enlightenment into alphabetically ordered, humorous ruminations on all persons and events of his life. . . . Plenty of good fun pours out of this prose." Booklist
Includes bibliographical references

Kett, Joseph F.

The **new** dictionary of cultural literacy; [by] E.D. Hirsch, Joseph F. Kett, James Trefil. Completely rev

and updated, 3rd ed; Houghton Mifflin 2002 647p
il maps $29.95   **031**
   1. Civilization -- Dictionaries 2. Encyclopedias and
dictionaries 3. English language -- Dictionaries 4.
Reference books
   ISBN 0-618-22647-8
LC 2002-27609

"The text is divided into sections by subject—e.g., fine
arts, world politics, life sciences—each with a brief introduction; access is also aided by a thorough index. The entries themselves are complete, concise, and clearly written as
well as extensively and effectively cross-referenced." Libr J

Lih, Andrew

   The **Wikipedia** revolution; how a bunch of no-
bodies created the world's greatest encyclopedia. Hyperion 2009 246p il map $24.99   **031**
   1. Electronic encyclopedias 2. User generated content
   ISBN 978-1-4013-0371-6; 1-4013-0371-4
LC 2008-51137

"Wikipedia is a revolutionary phenomenon, changing
fundamentally the landscape of networked collaboration,
e-learning, and, as librarians know all too well, mediated information provision. Depicted here is a Wikipedia insider's
narrative of the development of Wikipedia. . . . [Lih] characterizes this revolution as only partly technological. The real
revolution is social—an apt point when one considers the
philosophical underpinnings of this resource, the articles'
neutral point of view, while remaining a free resource anyone can use and distribute." Libr J
   Includes bibliographical references

★ The new encyclopaedia Britannica; 15th ed.; En-
   cyclopædia Britannica 2009 32v il map apply to
   publisher for price   **031**
   1. Encyclopedias and dictionaries 2. Reference books
   ISBN 978-1-59339-837-8
"In three sections: Propaedia, or outline of knowledge;
Macropaedia, with longer in-depth articles covering major
topics; and Micropaedia, with shorter A-to-Z ready reference entries. Britannica's reputation as the basic encyclo-
dia for all libraries and reference collections is based on the
writing and knowledge of thousands of expert contributors
and consultants. Updated between major editions by the Britannica Book of the Year." NY Public Libr Book of How &
Where to Look It Up
   Includes bibliographical references

★ The World Book encyclopedia. World Book, Inc.
   2010 22v il map set $1,044   **031**
   1. Encyclopedias and dictionaries 2. Reference books
   ISBN 978-0-7166-0110-4
LC 2009-29267

"A 22-volume, highly illustrated, A-Z general encyclopedia for all ages, featuring sections on how to use World
Book, other research aids, pronunciation key, a student
guide to better writing, speaking, and research skills, and
comprehensive index." Publisher's note
   Includes bibliographical references

031.02   Books of miscellaneous facts

Feldman, David

   When do fish sleep? and other imponderables
of everyday life; illustrated by Kassie Schwan.
Harper & Row 1989 260p il hardcover o.p. pa
$12.95   **031.02**
   1. Questions and answers
   ISBN 0-06-016161-2; 0-06-074093-0 pa
LC 89-45038

"Feldman offers answers to such 'imponderables' as
Why are rented bowling shoes so ugly? and Why do doctors tap on our backs during physical exams? Delightful and
informative browsing fare." Booklist

   Why do clocks run clockwise? and other impon-
derables; mysteries of everyday life. explained by
David Feldman; illustrated by Kas Schwan. Harper &
Row 1987 251p il hardcover o.p. pa $12.95 **031.02**
   1. Questions and answers
   ISBN 0-06-015781-X; 0-06-074092-2 pa
LC 87-45045

The author "answers such recurring questions as 'What
causes the ringing sound in your ears?' 'Why do nurses wear
white?' and 'Why doesn't a "two-by-four" measure two
inches by four inches?' Feldman answers them as authoritatively and truthfully as he can, relying on as trustworthy
sources as he can find and sometimes, when the query submits to no single answer, fielding several different probable
responses." Booklist

Kane, Joseph Nathan

   ★ **Famous** first facts; a record of first happenings, discoveries, and inventions in American history. [by] Joseph Nathan Kane, Steven Anzovin, &
Janet Podell. 6th ed.; Wilson, H.W. 2006 1307p il
$185   **031.02**
   1. Encyclopedias and dictionaries 2. Reference books
   ISBN 978-0-8242-1065-6; 0-8242-1065-4
LC 2006-3096

Over 7500 entries cover first occurences in American
history, organized into 16 chapters each divided into sections. Sections are alphabetically organized, and individual
entries are organized chronologically within each section.
Includes five indexes: subject index, index by years, index
by days, index to personal names, and geographical index
   "Besides serving as an essential ready-reference source,
the book is also fun to read out loud to colleagues—when
was bubble gum first manufactured in the U.S.? When was
the spray can introduced?" Booklist

Famous first facts, international edition; a record
   of first happenings, discoveries, and inventions
   in world history. {edited by} Steven Anzovin & Janet Podell. Wilson, H.W. 2000 837p
   $140   **031.02**
   1. Encyclopedias and dictionaries 2. Reference books
   ISBN 0-8242-0958-3
LC 99-86869

This work "contains more than 5000 firsts from hundreds of countries and ranging in time from 3.5 billion years

ago (the age of the oldest continental land discovered) to 2001 (the scheduled date of completion of the first building over 1500 feet tall). . . . {It} groups related entries under broad subject categories (arranged alphabetically) and sub-categories. Within each category or sub-category, entries are arranged chronologically." Publisher's note

★ The New York Public Library desk reference; 4th ed; Hyperion 2002 999p il maps $34.95 **031.02**
　　1. Encyclopedias and dictionaries 2. Reference books
　　ISBN 0-7868-6846-5

　　　　　　　　　　　　　LC 2002-27480
　　Divided into chapters, this reference features charts, tables, lists, and illustrations providing information in such categories as signs and symbols, mathematics and science basics, the arts, grammar and punctuation, etiquette, personal finance, first aid, and household tips.

The New York Times 2011 almanac; edited by John W. Wright with editors and reporters of the Times. Penguin Reference 2010 1004p map pa $12.95 **031.02**
　　1. Almanacs 2. Reference books 3. Statistics
　　ISBN 978-0-14-311894-7
　　This almanac contains a "chronology of the year; major news stories of the year; U.S. history; U.S. presidential bi-ographies; world history; world geography; economic and climate data; major awards in the arts, sciences, and sports; and a wide variety of U.S. demographic information. . . . It is well organized, the table layout is easy to read, and the type-face does not invite eye strain." Am Ref Books Annu, 1998

Time almanac 2011. Time Home Entertainment 2010 864p il map $34.95; pa $13.99 **031.02**
　　1. Almanacs 2. Reference books
　　ISBN 978-1-60320-164-3; 978-1-60320-165-0 pa
　　Contains statistical and factual material with a general topical arrangement and subject index. Illustrated with news photos and maps.

★ The world almanac and book of facts, 2011. World Almanac Books 2010 1008p il map $34.95 **031.02**
　　1. Almanacs 2. Reference books
　　ISBN 978-1-60057-133-6
　　"This is the most comprehensive and well-known of almanacs. . . . Contains a chronology of the year's events, consumer information, historical anniversaries, annual cli-matological data, and forecasts. Color section has flags and maps. Includes detailed index." N Y Public Libr Book of How & Where to Look It Up

032.02　Books of miscellaneous facts

★ Guinness world records. Guinness World Records il **032.02**
　　1. Curiosities and wonders 2. Reference books
　　"Ready reference for current record holders in all fields, some esoteric. Index provides access to information ar-ranged in broad subject categories. Must be replaced annu-ally." N Y Public Libr. Ref Books for Child Collect

050　General serial publications

Humanities index. Wilson, H.W. **050**
　　1. Humanities -- Periodicals -- Indexes 2. Reference books
　　A subject index to over 500 periodicals in a broad range of subject fields in the humanities. Author and subject en-tries are arranged in a single alphabet. Complete biblio-graphic information is given with each entry. Book reviews are indexed by author in a separate section.

051　General serial publications in specific languages and language families

Meyerowitz, Rick
　　Drunk stoned brilliant dead; the writers and art-ists who made the National Lampoon insanely great. Abrams 2010 319p il $40 **051**
　　1. American wit and humor 2. Satire
　　ISBN 978-0-8109-8848-4; 0-8109-8848-8
　　This is the "first Lampoon book that celebrates the wild, eye-intoxicating diversity of its illustrations, photography, cartoons, comic strips, graphics—parodies of everything from matchbooks to Marvel Comics to modern art. In toto this volume is a testament to the dazzling design expertise of its formative art directors, Michael Gross and David Kaestle. Rick Meyerowitz, a charter member of the Lampoon crew . . . , has in effect edited a magnificent 320-page issue of the magazine that reprints much of its finest work. And in brief, funny, and for once malice-free memoirs from its principals, the collection evokes the sparkling camaraderie that drove it. If you grew up with the Lampoon, this book is a trip down memory lane like no other; if not, it will demonstrate that the much-maligned 70s could produce humor that has never been surpassed." Vanity Fair

Readers' guide to periodical literature. Wilson, H.W. **051**
　　1. Periodicals -- Indexes
　　A cumulative author and subject index to over 300 pe-riodicals. Coverage includes computers, business, health, fashion, politics, education, science, sports, arts and litera-ture with criticism of individual dramatic works, videodiscs and videotapes, operas, ballets, musicals, movies, phono-graph records, dance, and television and radio programs. A free pamphlet: How to use the Reader's guide to periodical literature, is available for download in PDF format from publisher's website or upon request.
　　"This is a modern index of the best type." Sheehy. Guide to Ref Books. 10th edition

060　General organizations and museology

★ Directories in print. Gale Res. 2v **060**
　　1. Directories 2. Reference books
　　This work "describes approximately 15,500 active ros-ters, guides and other print and nonprint address lists pub-lished in the United States and worldwide. Hundreds of ad-ditional directories (defunct, suspended and directories that

cannot be located) are cited, with status notes, in the title/ keyword index." Publisher's note

★ The Europa world of learning; 59th ed; Routledge 2008 2v set $950 **060**
    1. Colleges and universities -- Directories 2. Reference books 3. Societies -- Directories
    ISBN 978-185743-471-2

"The standard international directory for the nations of the world, covering learned societies, research institutes, libraries, museums and art galleries, and universities and colleges. Includes for each institution address, officers, purpose, foundation date, publications, etc." Ref Sources for Small & Medium-sized Libr. 6th edition

060.4 Special topics of general organizations

Robert, Henry Martyn
  ★ **Robert's** Rules of order newly revised. Perseus Pub. 2000 various paging $37.50 **060.4**
    1. Parliamentary practice
    ISBN 0-7382-0384-X; 978-0-7382-0384-3
                   LC 2004-351757

"Long the standard compendium of parliamentary law, explaining methods of organizing and conducting the business of societies, conventions, and other assemblies. Includes convenient charts and tables." Ref Sources for Small & Medium-sized Libr. 6th edition

  ★ **Webster's** New World Robert's rules of order; simplified and applied. by Robert McConnell Productions. 2nd ed; Hungry Minds 2001 xx, 409p pa $10.99 **060.4**
    1. Parliamentary practice
    ISBN 0-7645-6399-8
                   LC 2001-92064

This explains the rules of parliamentary procedure, discussing the concepts behind each rule and including examples. This revised edition includes procedures for conducting meetings online, voting by mail and by e-mail, and adopting election procedures

Sturgis, Alice
The **standard** code of parliamentary procedure; original edition by Alice Sturgis. 4th ed; McGraw-Hill 2001 xxiv, 285p pa $14.95 **060.4**
    1. Parliamentary practice
    ISBN 0-07-136513-3
                   LC 2001-265929

This guide to the rules of parliamentary procedure includes explanations of their purpose and examples of their use. Also considers ways the Internet and other technologies have rewritten rules of meetings.

061 General organizations

★ Encyclopedia of associations; 46th ed; Gale Res. 2008 3v in 5 v1 $835; v2 $650; v3 $660 **061**
    1. Reference books 2. Societies -- Directories 3. Trade and professional associations
    ISBN 978-1-4144-2006-6 v1; 1-4144-2006-4 v1; 978-1-4144-2010-3 v2; 1-4144-2010-2 v2; 978-1-4144-2011-0 v3; 1-4144-2011-0 v3

This is a guide to more than 23,000 nonprofit American membership organizations of national scope

★ The Foundation directory; compiled by The Foundation Center. 2008 edition; Foundation Center 2008 2730p $215 **061**
    1. CD-ROMs 2. Endowments -- Directories 3. Reference books
    ISBN 978-1-59542-176-9

"Provides detailed information concerning independent, corporate, community, and private foundations with assets of at least $2 million or annual giving of at least $200,000. Geographical arrangement. Entries give date founded; names of officers, contact, and donors; foundation type; financial data; fields of interest; types of support; limitations; application information; and number of staff. Six indexes: Donors, officers, and trustees; Geographic; Types of support; Subject; Foundations new to edition; Foundations name index." Guide to Ref Books. 11th edition

★ National trade and professional associations of the United States; 43rd ed; Columbia Bks. 2008 1423p pa $299 **061**
    1. Trade and professional associations
    ISBN 1-88087-356-7; 978-1-88087-356-4

"Includes nearly 6500 organizations arranged by subject. Indexed by title, key word, geographical location, size of budget, and executive officers. Particularly valuable for its data on the annual budget as well as such general information as date of establishment, address, headquarters staff, size of membership, publications, and telephone number." Ref Sources for Small & Medium-sized Libr. 6th edition

069 Museology (Museum science)

★ Museums of the world; [editors: Nikolaus Himmler, Ruth Lochar, Hildegard Toma] 15th rev. and enl. ed; K.G. Saur 2008 2v il set $749 **069**
    1. Museums -- Directories 2. Reference books
    ISBN 978-3-598-20695-5; 3-598-20695-X

This set "covers more than 54,500 museums in 202 countries, listed hierarchically by country and place, and within places alphabetically by name. A separate chapter records some 500 museum associations in 132 countries." Publisher's note

★ The Official museum directory. National Register Pub. 2v set $297 **069**
    1. Museums -- Directories 2. Reference books
    ISBN 978-0-87217-756-7

This directory contains "listings on more than 8,100 museums operating in 87 different fields, ranging from science museums to zoos to historic homes to fine arts. It is one of the most trusted and accessible sources for museum professionals to identify vendors, access unique collections and exhibitions, and contact directors and curators. Volume 1 lists institutions by state, and contains a number of indexes: an alphabetic index to institutions, an index to personnel, an index to institutions by category, an index to institutions by collection, and new listings. Volume 2 is a guide to more than 2,100 vendors, their products, and their services, subdivided by category. . . . This product is one of the most useful and up-to-date reference works in the area of museums, especially in relation to current personnel and exhibitions." Recomm Ref Books for Small & Medium-sized Libr & Media Cent, 2003

070　Documentary media, educational media, news media; journalism; publishing

Angell, Roger

Let me finish. Harcourt 2006 302p $25　　**070**
1. Authors 2. Biography, Individual 3. Short story writers 4. Sportswriters
ISBN 0-15-101350-0; 978-0-15-101350-0
　　　　　　　　　　　　　　　　LC 2005-33067
"The assembled pieces add up to a fine memoir." Publ Wkly

Bragg, Rick

★ **All** over but the shoutin' Pantheon Bks. 1997 xxii, 329p hardcover o.p. pa $14　　**070**
1. Authors 2. Biography, Individual 3. Journalists 4. Memoirists
ISBN 0-679-44258-8; 0-679-77402-5 pa
　　　　　　　　　　　　　　　　LC 97-9918
"Honest, unsentimental, and so elegantly spare it nearly hurts to read, this memoir by Pulitzer Prize-winning journalist Bragg recounts a dirt-poor childhood in Alabama and the debt he owes his mother." Libr J

Brokaw, Tom

A **long** way from home; growing up in the American heartland. Random House 2002 272p $24.95; pa $12.95　　**070**
1. Journalists 2. National characteristics, American 3. Television journalists -- United States -- Biography 4. Television news anchors 5. Television news anchors -- United States -- Biography
ISBN 0-375-50763-9; 0-375-75935-2 pa
　　　　　　　　　　　　　　　　LC 2002-31865
"Peppered with photographs . . . this tribute to an idyllic childhood should please Brokaw's loyal fans." Publ Wkly

Cronkite, Walter

A **reporter's** life. Knopf 1997 384p il $26.95; pa $15　　**070**
1. Biography, Individual 2. Radio reporters 3. Television news anchors
ISBN 0-394-57879-1; 0-345-41103-X pa
　　　　　　　　　　　　　　　　LC 96-21053
Cronkite's "memoir is a short course on the flow of events in the second half of this century—events the world knows more about because of Walter Cronkite's work, and some of which might not have happened without it." N Y Times Book Rev

Gabler, Neal

Winchell; gossip, power, and the culture of celebrity. Knopf 1994 681p il hardcover o.p. pa $17　　**070**
1. Biography, Individual 2. Columnists 3. Political commentators 4. Radio personalities 5. Television personalities
ISBN 0-679-76439-9 pa
　　　　　　　　　　　　　　　　LC 93-44259
"At the peak of his career during the 1930s and 1940s, Walter Winchell was America's most powerful and feared journalist; when he died in 1972, he had been long forgotten. Gabler's biography brings back to life the man credited with inventing the gossip column and with creating today's celebrity culture." Libr J
Includes bibliographical references

Kovach, Bill

Blur; how to know what's true in the age of information overload. [by] Bill Kovach and Tom Rosenstiel. Bloomsbury 2010 227p $26　　**070**
1. Journalism -- Objectivity
ISBN 978-1-59691-565-7
　　　　　　　　　　　　　　　　LC 2010-19766
"Kovach and Rosenstiel combine journalism and civics in this valuable and insightful resource to help Americans adapt to an era that demands that readers become their own editors and news aggregators." Booklist
Includes bibliographical references

Levy, Edmond

Making a winning short; how to write, direct, edit, and produce a short film. Holt & Co. 1994 290p pa $17　　**070**
1. Motion pictures -- Production and direction 2. Short films
ISBN 0-8050-2680-0
　　　　　　　　　　　　　　　　LC 94-6621
"Using examples from his own career, Levy . . . explains all aspects of creating a short film, from the development of the idea to what food and drink to provide for actors and crew. After Levy's easy-to-follow lessons are finished, he offers a list of film festivals that accept short films, titles of short films that he believes to be some of the finest examples of the genre, and a reading list. . . . A worthy addition to all performing arts collections." Libr J

O'Faolain, Nuala

Are you somebody; the accidental memoir of a Dublin woman. Holt & Co. 1998 215p hardcover o.p. pa $13　　**070**
1. Authors 2. Columnists 3. Memoirists 4. Novelists 5. Women journalists -- Ireland -- Biography
ISBN 0-8050-5664-4 pa
　　　　　　　　　　　　　　　　LC 97-29725
This is a "moving and painfully honest memoir." Libr J

Ross, Lillian

Here but not here; a love story. Counterpoint 2001 240p il pa $15　　**070**
1. Authors, American 2. Journalists 3. Magazine editors

4. Periodical editors -- United States -- Biography 5. Women journalists -- United States -- Biography

ISBN 1-582-43110-8; 978-1-582-43110-9

LC 00-65948

"Ross writes directly and with great feeling about her years with Shawn. . . . It is a remarkable and very moving love story, composed like most great love stories of both passion and regret." Booklist

Schorr, Daniel

Staying tuned; a life in journalism. Pocket Bks. 2001 354p il hardcover o.p. pa $14 **070**

1. Journalists -- United States -- Biography 2. Political commentators 3. Television reporters

ISBN 0-671-02088-9 pa

LC 2001-21014

Schorr tells of his life as a reporter for CBS, CNN and National Public Radio.

"Schorr's memoir is as much an inside look at the famous world figures of the latter half of the twentieth century as it is the story of one man's life and career." Booklist

Thompson, Hunter S.

★ **Fear** and loathing in America; the brutal odyssey of an outlaw journalist, 1968-1976. foreword by David Halberstam; edited by Douglas Brinkley. Simon & Schuster 2000 xxv, 756p il $30; pa $15 **070**

1. Authors 2. Columnists 3. Journalists 4. Journalists -- United States -- Correspondence 5. Nonfiction writers 6. Novelists 7. Satirists

ISBN 0-684-87315-X; 0-684-87316-8 pa

LC 00-47012

"During the period covered in this collection, Thompson was a vital, deliriously erratic force in journalism, covering the turbulent 1968 Democratic National Convention in Chicago, the 1968 election of Richard M. Nixon, the 1972 campaign, Watergate, the falls of Nixon and Saigon." N Y Times Book Rev

★ Gale directory of publications and broadcast media; 143rd ed; Gale Res. 2008 5v maps set $1050 **070**

1. Newspapers -- Directories 2. Periodicals -- Directories 3. Reference books

ISBN 978-0-7876-9669-6; 0-7876-9669-2

Identifies specific print and broadcast sources of news and advertising for trade, business, labor, and professionals. Arrangement is geographic with a thumbnail description of each local market. Indexes are classified (by format and subject matter) and alphabetical (by name and keyword).

★ Reporting Iraq; an oral history of the war by the journalists who covered it. edited by Mike Hoyt, John Palattella, and the staff of the Columbia Journalism Review. Melville House 2007 191p il pa $21.95 **070**

1. Iraq War, 2003- -- Personal narratives 2. Reporters and reporting

ISBN 978-1-93363-334-3; 1-93363-334-4

"44 reporters casually and directly discuss all angles of the War in Iraq, including their own shock, fear and incomprehension, in this compilation of interviews conducted by

The Columbia Journalism Review. . . . This vital, breathtaking collection may be the closest contemporary reporting gets to cutting through the fog of war." Publ Wkly

070.1   Documentary media, educational media, news media

Henderson, Harry

Power of the news media. Facts on File 2004 316p il $45 **070.1**

1. Broadcast journalism 2. Press

ISBN 0-8160-4768-5

LC 2003-18900

The author's "format—breaking topics into quick-hit subsections—makes it an ideal source for students researching a particular aspect of news media. . . . Every American should have a working knowledge of the topic, and this book is a recommended resource." Voice Youth Advocates

Includes bibliographical references

Wenger, Debora Halpern

Advancing the story; broadcast journalism in a multimedia world. [by] Debora Halpern Wenger and Deborah Potter. 2nd ed.; CQ Press 2011 xxxi, 380p il pa $36.95 **070.1**

1. Broadcast journalism

ISBN 978-1-60871-714-9

LC 2010049469

"While stressing basics of good journalism with emphasis on attention to detail, [the] authors explain how technology has changed the approach to content preparation among those invested in the Internet and integrated technology." Journalism and Mass Communication Educator [review of 2008 edition]

Includes bibliographical references

070.4   Journalism

Friedlander, Edward Jay

Feature writing for newspapers and magazines; the pursuit of excellence. [by] Edward Jay Friedlander, John Lee. 6th ed.; Pearson/A&B 2008 334p pa $86.80 **070.4**

1. Journalism

ISBN 0-205-48466-2; 978-0-205-48466-9

LC 2007-20885

Through suggestions and examples this guide for the novice writer provides tips from Pulitzer Prize-winning journalists and other magazine and newspaper feature writers.

Fuller, Jack

What is happening to news; the information explosion and the crisis in journalism. The University of Chicago Press 2010 214p $25 **070.4**

1. Information society 2. Journalism 3. Journalism -- United States 4. Journalistic ethics

ISBN 978-0-226-26898-9; 0-226-26898-5; 978-0-226-26899-6 ebook

LC 2009039090

"This worthy addition to the journalism bookshelf will stand the test of time." Choice

Includes bibliographical references

Johnson, Marilyn

★ The **dead** beat; lost souls, lucky stiffs, and the perverse pleasures of obituaries. HarperCollins 2006 244p il $24.95   **070.4**

1. Obituaries

ISBN 0-06-075875-9

LC 2005-52817

"Johnson handles her offbeat topic with an appropriate level of humor, while still respecting the gravity of mortality." Publ Wkly

Includes bibliographical references

Tobin, James

Ernie Pyle's war; America's eyewitness to World War II. Free Press 1997 312p il pa $15   **070.4**

1. Biography, Individual 2. Journalists 3. World War, 1939-1945

ISBN 0-684-83642-4; 978-0-7432-8476-9 pa; 0-7432-8476-3 pa

LC 97-6165

"Living and working among the troops he so vividly chronicled, Pyle offered a unique insider's perspective of the harsh reality experienced by the common soldier during World War II. . . . A respectful and insightful biography of a giant among journalists." Booklist

Includes bibliographical references

Reporting America at war; an oral history. compiled by Michelle Ferrari with commentary by James Tobin. Hyperion 2003 241p il $23.95   **070.4**

1. Reporters and reporting 2. War

ISBN 1-401-30072-3

LC 2003-49966

"Beginning with Edward R. Morrow's live reports during the London blitz and ending with an epilogue on the second war in Iraq, this oral history contains transcripts of interviews with 11 top correspondents. Murrow is one of three deceased reporters included (the others are Martha Gellhorn and Homer Bigart), along with Walter Cronkite, Andy Rooney, Frank Gibney, Malcolm Browne, David Halberstam, Morley Safer, Ward Just, Gloria Emerson, Chris Hedges and Christiane Amanpour. . . . Tobin's introductions and transitional and informational interpolations within the transcripts hold this informative volume together." Publ Wkly

Includes bibliographical references

★ Reporting Vietnam. Library of Am. 1998 2v il maps v1-v2 ea $35; v2 pa $17.95   **070.4**

1. Journalism -- United States -- History -- 20th century 2. Reporters and reporting 3. Vietnam War, 1961-1975 4. Vietnamese Conflict, 1961-1975 -- Press coverage -- United States

ISBN 1-88301-158-2 v1; 1-88301-159-0 v2; 1-88301-190-6 v2 pa

LC 98-12267

"This book will help readers understand better what it was like to live through that tumultuous period of American history." Publ Wkly

Includes bibliographical references

070.449

Deford, Frank

Over time; my life as a sportswriter. Frank Deford. Atlantic Monthly Press 2012 354 p.   **070.449**

ISBN 0802120156; 9780802120151

This memoir by sports journalist Frank Deford describes his life-long career. It describes how Deford joined Sports Illustrated in 1962, . . . In 1990, he was Editor-in-Chief of The National Sports Daily, . . . But then . . . writing ten novels, winning an Emmy . . . and . . . read[ing] commentary on NPRs Morning Edition. . . . From the Mad Men-like days of SI in the 60s, and the bush years of the early NBA, to Deford's visit to apartheid South Africa with Arthur Ashe, and his friend's . . . death. . . . Interwoven through his personal history, Deford . . . traces the entire arc of American sportswriting from the lurid early days of the Police Gazette, through Grantland Rice and Red Smith and on up to ESPN. (Publishers note)

070.5   Publishing

Appelbaum, Judith

★ **How** to get happily published; 5th ed; HarperPerennial 1998 380p pa $15.95   **070.5**

1. Authors and publishers 2. Publishers and publishing

ISBN 0-06-273509-8

LC 97-41128

Covers the mechanics of writing and manuscript preparation, selling the book to a publisher, stages of publication and the self-publishing option, promotional ideas, and possible markets such as poetry and children's books.

Germano, William P.

Getting it published; a guide for scholars and anyone else serious about serious books. {by} William Germano. University of Chicago Press 2001 197p $35; pa $15   **070.5**

1. Authors and publishers 2. Authorship -- Marketing 3. Publishers and publishing

ISBN 0-226-28843-9; 0-226-28844-7 pa

LC 00-46715

The author "deconstructs and demystifies what publishers and editors actually do and what authors should look for in finding the right house for their subject and in putting the right words in their contract. He also does a lot of hand-holding through the review process and the production of the manuscript." Booklist

Includes bibliographical references (p. 193) and index

Graham, Katharine

Personal history. Knopf 1997 642p il $35; pa $15.95   **070.5**

1. Authors 2. Biography, Individual 3. Journalists 4.

Memoirists 5. Newspaper executives
ISBN 0-394-58585-2; 0-375-70104-4 pa

LC 96-49638

"Throughout this easy-to-read story, Graham writes about her personal life and the lives of others, ranging from presidents to household help, with sympathy and grace." Libr J

Herman, Jeff

Jeff Herman's guide to book publishers, editors, & literary agents 2008; who they are! what they want! how to win them over! 18th ed.; Three Dog Press; Distributed to the book trade by Watson-Guptill 2008 991p $29.95 **070.5**

1. Authors and publishers 2. Publishers and publishing
ISBN 978-0-9772682-2-1; 0-9772682-2-5

Herman provides "portraits of more than 100 agents plus tips on writing query letters and nonfiction book proposals, dealing with rejections, ghostwriting, and self-publishing. With an excellent glossary and sample author-agent and collaboration agreements." Libr J

Includes bibliographical references

Marcus, Leonard S.

Minders of make-believe; idealists, entrepreneurs, and the shaping of American children's literature. Houghton Mifflin Co. 2008 402p $28 **070.5**

1. Children -- Books and reading 2. Children -- Books and reading -- History 3. Children's literature -- History and criticism 4. Children's literature -- Publishing -- United States -- History -- 20th century 5. Publishers and publishing
ISBN 978-0-395-67407-9; 0-395-67407-7

LC 2008-00589

"Marcus' approach and tone are always, and irresistibly, well informed, sensible, and intelligent. . . . It is hard to imagine any issue that he has overlooked, and the resulting book is, in a word, indispensable." Booklist

Includes bibliographical references

Nasaw, David

The **chief**: the life of William Randolph Hearst. Houghton Mifflin 2000 687p il $35; pa $16 **070.5**

1. Newspaper editors 2. Newspaper executives 3. Newspaper publishing -- United States -- History -- 19th century 4. Newspaper publishing -- United States -- History -- 20th century 5. Publishers and publishing -- United States -- Biography
ISBN 0-395-82759-0; 0-618-15446-9 pa

LC 99-462122

"Few publishers have loomed as large in their lifetimes, or cast as long a shadow after death, as William Randolph Hearst. . . . Nasaw's judicious and comprehensive biography sensibly seeks to understand its subject, not to judge him." New Yorker

Includes bibliographical references

Pettegree, Andrew

The **book** in the Renaissance. Yale University Press 2010 421p il $40 **070.5**

1. Book industries and trade -- Europe -- History -- 16th century 2. Book industry 3. Books -- Europe -- History -- 1400-1600 4. Printing 5. Printing -- Europe -- History -- 16th century 6. Reformation -- Europe 7. Renaissance
ISBN 978-0-300-11009-8; 0-300-11009-X

LC 2009-26513

The author's "treatment is both thorough and engaging, ably situating the social, economic, and historical within the stories of individuals involved." Libr J

Includes bibliographical references

Poynter, Dan

★ The **self**-publishing manual; how to write, print and sell your own book. 16th ed; Para Pub. 2007 463p pa $19.95 **070.5**

1. Publishers and publishing
ISBN 978-1-568601-42-7; 1-568601-42-5

"Poynter gives the basics for producing a commercially successful manuscript, taking the reader step-by-step through printing a book, determining its value, promoting and advertising, fulfilling orders, and coping with being published. There are appendixes on printers, professional organizations, and fulfillment warehouses." Libr J

Rose, M. J.

How to publish and promote online; {by} M. J. Rose and Angela Adair-Hoy. St. Martin's Griffin 2001 266p pa $13.95 **070.5**

1. Authorship -- Computer network resources 2. Authorship -- Internet resources 3. Electronic publishing -- United States 4. Publishers and publishing 5. Self-publishing -- United States
ISBN 0-312-27191-3

LC 00-45833

The authors "provide encouragement and tips for aspiring authors hoping to publish their works electronically." Booklist

2009 guide to literary agents; 18th annual ed.; Writer's Digest 2008 362p il pa $27.99 **070.5**

1. Authors and publishers -- Directories 2. Reference books
ISBN 978-1-58297-548-1; 1-58297-548-5

"An invaluable tool for writers in search of an agent, this guide is indexed by agency, agent, format, subject, and geographic location. Submission procedures, fees, contracts and what to ask a prospective agent are covered." Libr J

★ American book trade directory 2008-2009; 54th ed; Information Today 2008 1850p $299.95 **070.5**

1. Book collecting 2. Book industry 3. Publishers and publishing -- Directories 4. Reference books
ISBN 978-1-57387-317-8; 1-57387-317-9

"Includes lists of booksellers, wholesalers, and publishers in the United States, with related information on the book trade in Canada, the United Kingdom, and Ireland. Bookstores are arranged under state and city with speciality of each noted. Separate lists include exporters, importers, and dealers in foreign books. Index of retailers and wholesalers in the United States and Canada." Ref Sources for Small & Medium-sized Libr. 6th edition

★ The Columbia guide to digital publishing; edited by William E. Kasdorf. Columbia Univ. Press 2003 lxi, 750p $65; pa $34.95   **070.5**
1. Electronic publishing
ISBN 0-231-12498-8; 0-231-12499-6 pa
                                        LC 2002-41462
This volume begins with an introductory chapter on "the role of digital publishing in various facets of the publishing industry. . . . Other chapters address topics such as: the technical infrastructure, mark-up, content management, digital rights management, e-books, archiving issues, legal issues, accessibility, and international issues." The Indexer
Includes bibliographical references

International literary market place 2009. Information Today 2008 1800p pa $259   **070.5**
1. Publishers and publishing -- Directories 2. Reference books
ISBN 978-1-57387-325-3; 1-57387-325-X
This directory of the international book publishing industry covers over 180 countries worldwide and profiles "more than 15,000 book-related concerns around the globe, including . . . 10,500 publishers and literary agents; 1,100 major booksellers and book clubs; 1,500 major libraries and library associations . . . and thousands of other book-related concerns—including trade organizations, distributors, dealers, literary associations, trade publications, book trade events, and other resources . . . organized in a country-by-country format." Publisher's note

Literary market place 2009. Bowker 2008 2v pa $309   **070.5**
1. Publishers and publishing -- Directories 2. Reference books
ISBN 978-1-57387-329-1; 1-57387-329-2
"Directory of U.S. and Canadian book publishers and related businesses such as book clubs, literary agents, translators, and manufacturers. Gives names of executives and addresses, telephone numbers, and fields of specialization for each publishing company." N Y Public Libr Book of How & Where to Look It Up

The Publish-it-yourself handbook; [literary tradition and how to] edited by Bill Henderson. 25th anniversary ed.; Pushcart Press 1998 346p il pa $18   **070.5**
1. Publishers and publishing
ISBN 1-888-88903-9
An anthology of articles about how to publish without the assistance of commercial or vanity publishers.

Publishers, distributors & wholesalers of the United States 2009. Bowker 2008 2v set $475   **070.5**
1. Publishers and publishing -- Directories 2. Reference books
ISBN 978-0-8352-4966-9
This directory provides information on "more than 150,000 U.S. publishers, wholesalers, distributors, software firms, audiocassette producers, museum and association imprints, and trade organizations that publish." Publisher's note

070.92   Biography regardless of area, region, place

Koppel, Ted
Off camera; private thoughts made public. Knopf 2000 320p hardcover o.p. pa $14   **070.92**
1. Television journalists -- United States -- Diaries 2. Television moderators 3. Television news anchors
ISBN 0-375-72708-6 pa
                                        LC 00-34919
The television journalist of Nightline presents a daily diary for 1999 chronicling "the controversial events from the century's last year, such as the Clinton impeachment trial and the Columbine High School shootings. . . . The subtitle of the book may lead some readers to expect a bit of muckraking, but they will be disappointed. . . . Yet one does not get the sense that Koppel is restraining himself or hiding anything, merely that this is a person who lives his life with integrity so that his private thoughts are full of the same." Libr J

Levy, Bernard Henri
★ **Who** killed Daniel Pearl? Melville House Pub 2003 454p $25.95; pa $16.95   **070.92**
1. Homicide 2. Journalists 3. Kidnapping
ISBN 0-9718659-4-9; 0-9749609-4-2 pa
                                        LC 2003-13576
Levy reports on "the murder of the Wall Street Journal correspondent Daniel Pearl. . . . [He] follows the trail of the kidnappers to the highest reaches of Osama bin Laden's Al Qaeda and Pakistan's Inter-Services Intelligence agency, and to the links he claims exist between them." N Y Times Book Rev

O'Faolain, Nuala
Almost there; the onward journey of a Dublin woman. Riverhead Bks. 2003 275p $24.95; pa $14   **070.92**
1. Authors 2. Columnists 3. Memoirists 4. Novelists
ISBN 1-57322-241-0; 1-57322-374-3 pa
                                        LC 2002-36722
This "is a thought-provoking work that differs markedly from the self-serving memoirs we frequently see." Libr J

Pearl, Mariane
★ A **mighty** heart; the brave life and death of my husband, Danny Pearl. [by] Mariane Pearl, with Sarah Crichton. Scribner 2003 278p $25; pa $13   **070.92**
1. Journalists
ISBN 0-7432-4442-7; 0-7432-6237-9 pa
                                        LC 2003-60143
"On January 23, 2002, Danny Pearl, the South Asia bureau chief of the Wall Street Journal stationed in Pakistan, left his Karachi home to go to some meetings. It was the last time his wife, fellow journalist Mariane, saw him alive. . . . This memoir, written by his widow, begins the morning of his abduction and takes us through the confirmation of his abduction, the efforts to free him, and his assassination. . . . Plenty of words have been written about the Pearl abduction, but these are by far the most personal and most poignant." Booklist

Politkovskaya, Anna, 1958-2006

Is journalism worth dying for? translated by Arch Tait. Melville House 2011 468 p. [8] p. of plates **070.92**

ISBN 978-1-935554-40-0 pa; 1-935554-40-9 pa
LC 2011922469

'This book is written by "Anna Politkovskaya [who] won international fame for her courageous reporting. . . . Beginning with a brief introduction by the author about her pariah status, the book contains essays that characterize . . . Politkovskaya more fully than she allowed in her other books. From deeply personal statements about the nature of journalism, to . . . reports from Chechnya, to . . . pieces of memoir, to, finally, the first translation of the series of investigative reports that Politkovskaya was working on at the time of her murder—pieces many believe led to her assassination." (Publisher's note)

Thompson, Hunter S.

The **kingdom** of fear; loathsome secrets of a star-crossed child in the final days of the American century. Simon & Schuster 2003 xx, 354p il hardcover o.p. pa $16 **070.92**

1. Authors 2. Columnists 3. Journalists 4. Journalists -- United States -- Biography 5. Nonfiction writers 6. Novelists 7. Satirists
ISBN 0-684-87323-0; 978-0-684-87324-4; 0-684-87324-9 pa
LC 2002-191228

In this book the American journalist writes about his life and career experiences

"Just as Thompson paved his own way in writing about politics, sports, news and culture throughout the 1960s and '70s, he now offers an autobiography that is typically unorthodox in style but still revealing previously unknown facts about its subject. Wavering between the uproarious and the lunatic, it's vintage Thompson through and through." Publ Wkly

071 Geographic treatment of journalism and newspapers

Baker, Nicholson

The **World** on Sunday; graphic art in Joseph Pulitzer's newspaper (1898-1911) [by] Nicholson Baker and Margaret Brentano. Bulfinch Press 2005 131p il $50 **071**

1. Members of Congress 2. Newspaper executives
ISBN 0-8212-6193-2
LC 2005-00224

This book collects 85 examples of graphic art from the Sunday edition of the New York World

This volume "offers a kaleidoscopic tour through an ebullient moment in American history when the country was emerging from the shadowy gaslight age and bursting into the glare of the modern. It is a big, lush, coffee-table-size book suffused with gaiety and the optimism of an age blissfully unaware of darknesses soon to come. . . . The World on Sunday is the result of a heroic piece of cultural preservation." N Y Rev Books

Burns, Eric

Infamous scribblers; the founding fathers and the rowdy beginnings of American journalism. Public Affairs 2006 467p hardcover o.p. pa $15.95 **071**

1. Constitutional history 2. Journalism 3. Newspapers -- United States 4. Sensationalism in journalism
ISBN 978-1-58648-334-0; 1-58648-334-X; 978-1-58648-428-6 pa; 1-58648-428-1 pa
LC 2005-53542

"From the sniping feuds among Boston's first papers to sex scandals involving Alexander Hamilton and Thomas Jefferson, the snappy patter gives clear indication of how much Burns . . . relishes telling his story." Publ Wkly
Includes bibliographical references

Campbell, W. Joseph

Getting it wrong; ten of the greatest misreported stories in American journalism. University of California Press 2010 269p il $60; pa $24.95 **071**

1. Journalism -- Objectivity 2. Journalistic ethics
ISBN 978-0-520-25566-1; 0-520-25566-6; 978-0-520-26209-6 pa; 0-520-26209-3 pa
LC 2009047705

This "provocative book provides a wealth of case studies in the complexity of journalism and history. It reinforces the truism that journalists, authors and book reviewers alike should all be more skeptical—and definitely more humble." Am Journalism Rev
Includes bibliographical references

Ellison, Sarah

War at the Wall Street journal; inside the struggle to control an American business empire. Houghton Mifflin Harcourt 2010 274p $27 **071**

1. Broadcasting executives 2. Electronic publishers 3. Magazine executives 4. Motion picture executives 5. Newspaper executives 6. Publishing executives
ISBN 978-0-547-15243-1; 0-547-15243-4
LC 2009-46266

"Sarah Ellison has written a definitive, indeed cinematic, account of the News Corporation's conquest and occupation of this venerable business publication, and of the subterranean battle of motives and moods in the Bancroft family psychodrama." N Y Times Book Rev
Includes bibliographical references

McChesney, Robert W.

The **death** and life of American journalism; the media revolution that will begin the world again. [by] Robert W. McChesney, John Nichols. Nation Books 2010 352p il $26.95 **071**

1. Journalism
ISBN 978-1-56858-605-2; 1-56858-605-1
LC 2010-282015

The author provides "a compelling blueprint for rejuvenating meaningful journalism in the US. This is really two books in one. First, it is an immensely readable history of—and insightful deconstruction of myths surrounding—freedom of the press and a cogent analysis of how press freedom was narrowly redefined in the 20th century to protect the business of newspapering from government interference. Second, it is a visionary manifesto for government subsidy of American journalism, a 'massive public intervention to produce a public good.'" Choice

Includes bibliographical references

McMillian, John

Smoking typewriters; the Sixties underground press and the rise of alternative media in America. [by] John McMillian. Oxford University Press 2011 277p il $27.95   **071**

    1. Alternative press 2. Journalism -- United States -- History -- 20th century 3. Nonfiction 4. Radicalism 5. Underground press publications

    ISBN 978-0-19-531992-7

                            LC 2010-26243

The book "argues that for young people seeking to engender new forms of culture and politics, alternative newspapers of the era held a singular power to embody principles of participatory democracy, radical journalism, and youth empowerment—and in the process reflected, reinforced, and peddled some of the period's most representative values. Thus 'Smoking Typewriters' offers a[n] . . . argument that the underground press was one of the New Left's most important counterinstitutions. The book combines institutional history, social and cultural analysis, and fresh retellings of both major and lesser-known episodes within the underground press to offer a kaleidoscopic narrative of colorful story lines and revolving, idiosyncratic characters." (Journal of American History)

This is a "readable, richly detailed study of the hundreds of anti-establishment 1960s newspapers—from the Los Angeles Free Press to Rag (Austin, Texas) and The Paper (East Lansing, Mich.)—that 'educated, politicized and built communities among disaffected youths in every region of the country.' . . . A welcome book on the '60s—a nostalgia trip for those who were there and a vivid work of history for anyone curious about the journalism that jolted a decade." Kirkus

Includes bibliographical references

Ostertag, Bob

People's movements, people's press; the journalism of social justice movements. Beacon Press 2006 232p il $23.95   **071**

    1. Alternative press 2. Social movements

    ISBN 0-8070-6164-6; 978-0-8070-6164-0

                            LC 2005-31735

"Readers interested in the intersection of the media and social movements will appreciate this insightful book." Booklist

Includes bibliographical references

Ritchie, Donald A.

Reporting from Washington; the history of the Washington press corps. Oxford University Press 2005 390p il $30   **071**

    1. Journalism -- Objectivity 2. Journalism -- Political aspects -- United States 3. Press -- Government policy 4. Press and politics -- United States -- History -- 20th century 5. Reporters and reporting 6. Reporters and reporting -- United States -- History -- 20th century

    ISBN 0-19-517861-0

                            LC 2004-18892

The author "focuses on the period from 1932, when the rising influence of radio and FDR's aggressive politicking broke the dominance of newspapers, until 2001, when the terrorist attacks on the U.S. refocused attention on the government and the press. . . . Ritchie presents a rich perspective on the people who write the first draft of history, investigating and then breaking the Teapot Dome and Watergate scandals, among others." Booklist

Includes bibliographical references

The New new journalism; conversations with America's best nonfiction writers on their craft. [edited and with an introduction by] Robert S. Boynton. Vintage Books 2005 xxxiv, 456p pa $13.95 **071**

    1. Journalism

    ISBN 1-400-03356-X

                            LC 2004-57161

The author "offers interviews with 19 writers who detail how and why they produce their work. . . . A fascinating book that makes the reader want to go out and get every book the writers have written as well as those mentioned as sources of inspiration." Booklist

Includes bibliographical references

Written into history; Pulitzer Prize reporting of the twentieth century from the New York times. edited and with an introduction by Anthony Lewis. Times Bks. 2001 xxv, 355p hardcover o.p. pa $17   **071**

    1. Journalism 2. Journalism -- United States 3. Pulitzer Prizes 4. Pulitzer prizes

    ISBN 0-8050-6849-X; 0-8050-7178-4 pa

                            LC 2001-35555

"For anyone interested in recent history or journalism at its best, this book will prove worthwhile." Publ Wkly

080   General collections

Adler, Mortimer J.

How to think about the great ideas; from the great books of Western civilization. {by} Mortimer J. Adler; edited by Max Weismann. Open Court 2000 xxiv, 530p pa $24.95   **080**

    ISBN 0-8126-9412-0

                            LC 99-45251

This volume contains the transcripts of 52 half-hour segments of Adler's 1953-1954 television program The great ideas

"The book showcases Adler's ideas about all the big categories—truth, beauty, freedom, love, sex, art, justice, rationality, humankind's nature, Darwinism, government." Publ Wkly

Andrews, Robert

Famous lines; a Columbia dictionary of familiar quotations. Columbia Univ. Press 1997 xxiii, 625p $38.95   **080**

    1. Quotations 2. Reference books

    ISBN 0-231-10218-6

                            LC 96-43879

This work "contains more than 6,000 witticisms, enduring observations, and incendiary statements from all kinds of people from antiquity to yesterday. Besides identifying the source, Andrews . . . provides details of the first publication, specific chapter and scene, and even the character speaking. Besides quotes from Shakespeare and Oscar Wilde, readers will find fascinating quotes from Monty Python, Gloria Steinem, and maybe your favorite author, for example, Agatha Christie. The more than 500 subject headings include homelessness, AIDS, sexual harassment, murder, and war." Booklist

Includes bibliographical references

Elder, Robert K.

Last words of the executed; with a foreword by Studs Terkel. The University of Chicago Press 2010 301p ebook $22.50; $22.50   **080**
  1. Capital punishment 2. Capital punishment -- United States -- History 3. Death -- Quotations 4. Last words
  ISBN 978-0-226-20269-3 ebook; 978-0-226-20268-6
                        LC 2009-38402
  "Whatever side in the argument [over the death penalty] one habitually takes, this book is recommended reading, so that in addition to learning how we put people to death, one can also put to the test the firmness of one's convictions." N Y Rev Books

Includes bibliographical references

Essay and general literature index. Wilson, H.W. **080**
  1. Essays -- Indexes 2. Literature -- Indexes 3. Reference books
This subject-author index provides access to essays and articles in collections and anthologies published in English. Some 300 volumes are indexed annually plus more than 20 selected annuals and serials
  "A boon to librarians. . . . A must for all academic and large public libraries." Am Ref Books Annu

081   General collections in specific languages and language families

McPhee, John A.

Irons in the fire; {by} John McPhee. Farrar, Straus & Giroux 1997 215p $22; pa $14   **081**
  ISBN 0-374-17726-0; 0-374-52545-5 pa
                        LC 96-32358
  "John McPhee's essays are proof that the kind of journalism that can effortlessly put a topic into perfect perspective will never go out of style." N Y Times Book Rev

Pauling, Linus C.

Linus Pauling in his own words; selections from his writings, speeches, and interviews. edited by Barbara Marinacci; introduction by Linus Pauling. Simon & Schuster 1995 320p hardcover o.p. pa $20   **081**
  1. Biography, Individual 2. Chemists 3. College teachers 4. Nobel laureates for chemistry 5. Nobel laureates for peace 6. Science 7. Writers on science
  ISBN 0-6848-1387-4 ps
                        LC 95-31123

This book "attempts to follow the life and career of Dr. Pauling through his own writings, interspersed with narrative by the editor. The book succeeds wonderfully. Linus Pauling is unique among modern scientists, both for winning two Nobel Prizes and for his political and social views. Through his writings, the breadth and depth of his work become clear to the reader." Sci Books Films

Includes bibliographical references

082   General collections in English

Quotations for all occasions; compiled by Catherine Frank. Columbia Univ. Press 2000 260p $55; pa $18.95   **082**
  1. Quotations 2. Quotations, English
  ISBN 0-231-11290-4; 0-231-11291-2 pa
                        LC 00-24048
This title "organizes its 1500-plus quotes into three sections that cover 150 different occasions. 'Every Year' contains quotes for such annual events as holidays, birthdays, days of the week, and seasons, while 'Occasionally' encompasses quotes for less frequent events, like going back to school, breaking up, quitting smoking, and school reunions. The final section is for 'Once in a Lifetime' experiences, such as turning 16, getting a first car, menopause, and retirement." Libr J

Includes bibliographical references

★ The Yale book of quotations; edited by Fred R. Shapiro; foreword by Joseph Epstein. Yale University Press 2006 1104p $50   **082**
  1. Quotations
  ISBN 978-0-300-10798-2; 0-300-10798-6
                        LC 2006-12317
The more than 12,000 "range over literature, history, popular culture, sports, computers, science, politics, law, and the social sciences, and although American quotations are emphasized, the book's scope is global. The authors represented are as diverse as William Shakespeare, John Lennon, Jack Dempsey, both Presidents Bush, J.K. Rowling, Rita Mae Brown, Confucius, Warren Buffet, and Deng Xiaoping. The entries are arranged by author, then chronologically and alphabetically by source title within the same year. A significant effort was made to trace the first published occurrence of a quotation, and whenever possible the wording is taken from the original source. . . . Electronic products such as the Times Digital Archive, JSTOR, Proquest Historical Newspapers and American Periodical Series, LexisNexis, Newspaperarchive.com, Questia, Eighteenth Century Collections Online, and Literature Online were all used." Libr J

098   Prohibited works, forgeries, hoaxes

Bosmajian, Haig A.

★ **Burning** books; [by] Haig Bosmajian. McFarland 2006 233p $39.95   **098**
  1. Book burning
  ISBN 0-7864-2208-4; 978-0-7864-2208-1
                        LC 2005-35201

"This work provides a detailed account of book burning worldwide over the past 2000 years. The book burners are identified, along with the works they deliberately set aflame." Publisher's note

Includes bibliographical references

Katsoulis, Melissa

Literary hoaxes; an eye-opening history of famous frauds. Skyhorse Pub. 2009 328p $22.95 **098**
1. Literary forgeries
ISBN 978-1-60239-794-1

LC 2009-30421

"The book is by no means comprehensive, nor does it intend to be, but it is an excellent and informative survey of a fascinating and often newsworthy subject." Booklist

100 PHILOSOPHY

100　Philosophy, parapsychology and occultism, psychology

Blackburn, Simon

★ **Think**: a compelling introduction to philosophy. Oxford Univ. Press 1999 312p $25 **100**
1. Philosophy
ISBN 0-19-210024-6

LC 00-265266

The author explores such areas as knowledge, mind, free will, identity, God, goodness and justice. "His method is to introduce what other philosophers—primarily Plato, Descartes, Locke, Berkeley, Leibniz, Hume, and Kant—have had to say about these themes. . . . Readers new to the subject could very well be captivated." Libr J

Includes bibliographical references

Ferry, Luc

A **brief** history of thought; Luc Ferry; translated by Theo Cuffe. HarperPerennial 2012 304p. **100**
ISBN 9780062074249

This book "offers a thematic introduction to continental philosophy constructed around the biggest questions: how can we lead a meaningful life knowing that we will die but without the consolation of religion? . . . The author's episodic treatment starts with the Stoic concept of man as a fragment of a harmonious cosmos, moves on to Descartes, Rousseau, and Kant and their establishment of philosophy based on reason and individual freedom, climaxes with Nietzsche's demolition of modernist certitudes--a stance he finds both thrilling and unsatisfying--and ponders the abiding need to embrace a world we must ultimately lose." (Publishers Weekly)

Rorty, Amelie Oksenberg

★ The **many** faces of philosophy; reflections from Plato to Arendt. edited by Amélie Oksenberg

Rorty. Oxford Univ. Press 2003 xxix, 512p $40; pa $24.95 **100**
1. Philosophy
ISBN 0-19-513402-8; 0-19-517655-3 pa

LC 2002-30342

This is a collection of "self-reflective musings by canonical Western philosophers, culled from letters, prefaces, memoirs, political tracts, and replies to critics. . . . No single-volume collection of philosophical autobiographies spans the entire history of philosophy as this one does." Choice

Includes bibliographical references

Russell, Bertrand

★ The **problems** of philosophy. Hackett Pub. Co 1990 167p $27.95; pa $8.95 **100**
1. Philosophy
ISBN 978-0-87220-099-9; 0-87220-099-X; 978-0-87220-098-2 pa; 0-87220-098-1 pa

LC 90-81389

The author discusses: appearance and reality, matter, idealism, theories of knowledge, universals, intuition, and truth.

"The work is concise, free from technical terms and perfectly clear to the general reader with no prior knowledge of the subject." Booklist

Includes bibliographical references

★ A Companion to world philosophies; edited by Eliot Deutsch and Ron Bontekoe; advisory editors, Tu Weiming {et al.} Blackwell 1997 587p hardcover o.p. pa $34.95 **100**
1. African philosophy 2. Asian philosophy 3. Oriental philosophy 4. Philosophy
ISBN 0-631-21327-9 pa

LC 96-36179

This volume "focuses on non-Western philosophies. . . . The editors have drawn together leading authors in the fields of Chinese, Indian, Buddhist, Islamic, Polynesian, and African philosophy to produce an excellent single-volume survey. . . . The essays are of a uniformly high quality and are accessible even to those with little background in non-Western philosophies." Libr J

103　Dictionaries, encyclopedias, concordances of philosophy

Blackburn, Simon

The **Oxford** dictionary of philosophy; 2nd ed.; Oxford University Press 2005 407p il $45 **103**
1. Philosophy -- Dictionaries 2. Reference books
ISBN 0-19-861014-9; 978-0-19-861014-4

LC 2006-271895

This dictionary "contains over 2,500 entries, including biographies of nearly 500 influential philosophers. The dictionary provides . . . coverage of not only Western philosophical traditions, but also themes from Chinese, Indian, Islamic, and Jewish philosophy." Publisher's note

Includes bibliographical references

★ The Cambridge dictionary of philosophy; edited by Robert Audi. 2nd ed; Cambridge Univ.

Press 1999 xxxv, 1001p il hardcover o.p. pa
$32.99   **103**
1. Philosophy -- Dictionaries 2. Reference books
ISBN 0-521-63136-X; 0-521-63722-8 pa
LC 99-12920
This work contains some 4,400 entries including 50 on
major contemporary philosophers. Wide coverage of Western philosophy as well as non-Western and non-European
philosophers is included. The rapidly growing fields of philosophy of mind and applied ethics are also covered

★ Encyclopedia of philosophy; Donald M. Borchert,
   editor in chief. 2nd ed; Macmillan Reference
   USA 2005 10v il set $995   **103**
   1. Philosophy 2. Philosophy -- Encyclopedias 3.
   Reference books
   ISBN 0-02-865780-2
LC 2005-18573
For a fuller review, see: Booklist, June 1 & 15, 2006
"Among the many topics covered are African, Islamic,
Jewish, Russian, Chinese, and Buddhist philosophies; bio-
ethics and biomedical ethics; art and aesthetics; epistemol-
ogy; metaphysics; peace and war; social and political phi-
losophy; the Holocaust; feminist thought; and much more.
Additionally, . . . [it] also features 1,000 biographical entries
on major figures in philosophical thought throughout his-
tory." Publisher's note
Includes bibliographical references

★ The Oxford companion to philosophy; edited by
   Ted Honderich. 2nd ed., new ed; Oxford University Press 2005 1056p il $60   **103**
   1. Philosophers 2. Philosophy 3. Philosophy --
   Encyclopedias 4. Reference books
   ISBN 0-19-926479-1
LC 2005-275452
"Including more than 2200 alphabetically arranged entries from nearly 300 contributors, . . . [this book] provides
an encyclopedic view of philosophy's past and present, its
ideas, disputes (the editor himself contributes an article on
unlikely philosophical propositions), and key figures, living
and dead. . . . This title makes an excellent companion for
standard multivolume subject encyclopedias." SLJ
Includes bibliographical references

109   History and collected biography

Durant, William James
   ★ The **story** of philosophy; the lives and opin-
   ions of the great philosophers. by Will Durant. [2nd
   ed]; Simon & Schuster 1933 412p hardcover o.p.
   pa $15   **109**
   1. Authors 2. Dramatists 3. Educators 4. Essayists
   5. Historians 6. Literary critics 7. Logicians 8.
   Mathematicians 9. Nobel laureates for literature 10.
   Nonfiction writers 11. Novelists 12. Philosophers 13.
   Philosophy -- History 14. Poets 15. Psychologists 16.
   Writers on religion 17. Writers on science
   ISBN 0-671-69500-2; 0-671-20159-X pa
A selective account of western thinkers from Socrates
and Kant to Schopenhauer and Dewey.

King, Peter J.
   ★ **One** hundred philosophers; the life and work
of the world's greatest thinkers. Barron's Educ. Ser.
2004 192p il pa $19.95   **109**
   1. Philosophers
   ISBN 0-7641-2791-8
LC 2003-110643
The author "has done a masterful job in presenting the
life and work of what he calls 'the world's greatest thinkers.' . . . The concise and clearly written description of the
thinker's life and ideas are just what a student or a layperson
needs to gather an overview of the thinker's life and intellectual contributions." Am Ref Books Annu, 2005
Includes bibliographical references

Russell, Bertrand
   A **history** of Western philosophy; and its connection with political and social circumstances from
the earliest times to the present day. Simon & Schuster 1945 xxiii, 895p hardcover o.p. pa $25   **109**
   1. Authors 2. Bishops 3. Catholic Church 4. Essayists
   5. Historians 6. Mathematicians 7. Memoirists
   8. Nobel laureates for literature 9. Novelists 10.
   Philosophers 11. Philosophy -- History 12. Political
   and social philosophers 13. Saints 14. Science --
   History 15. Statesmen 16. Stoics 17. Theologians 18.
   Writers on law 19. Writers on politics 20. Writers on
   religion 21. Writers on science
   ISBN 0-671-31400-9; 0-671-20158-1 pa
"My purpose is to exhibit philosophy as an integral part
of social and political life; not as the isolated speculations of
remarkable individuals." Preface

Solomon, Robert C.
   A **passion** for wisdom; a very brief history of
philosophy. {by} Robert C. Solomon, Kathleen M.
Higgins. Oxford Univ. Press 1997 137p hardcover
o.p. pa $12.95   **109**
   1. Philosophy -- History
   ISBN 0-19-511209-1 pa
LC 96-42034
The authors "provide a multicultural account of philosophical thought and developments across nearly 4000
years. The volume is necessarily simplified but not simplistic, and the thoughts themselves are given precedent over the
biographies of the thinkers." SLJ
Includes bibliographical references

World philosophers and their works; editor, John K.
Roth; managing editor, Christina J. Moose; project editor, Rowena Wildin. Salem Press 2000 3v
il set $331   **109**
   1. Philosophers
   ISBN 0-89356-878-3
LC 99-55143
The editor "presents substantial entries that for 226
philosophers give brief biographies, justify the inclusion of each thinker, list their most important works, analyze their lifework, and locate them within the context of
philosophy." Choice
Includes bibliographical references

111　Ontology

Barrow, John D.

The **book** of nothing; vacuums, voids, and the latest ideas about the origins of the universe. Pantheon Bks. 2001 361p il hardcover o.p. pa $15 **111**

1. Nothing (Philosophy) 2. Science -- History 3. Vacuum 4. Zero (The number)

ISBN 0-375-72609-8 pa

LC 00-58894

This volume traces the concept of nothing "from a Babylonian place holder, a Mayan decoration in the empty space where no number fell and an Indian dot signifying all the current aspects of zero, to one of the most essential elements in mathematics, physics and cosmology." Publ Wkly

The **infinite** book; a short guide to the boundless, timeless, and endless. Pantheon Books 2005 328p il $26 **111**

1. Infinite

ISBN 0-375-42227-7

LC 2004-60206

The author "approaches the subject [of infinity] from the viewpoints of mathematics, physics, and scientific cosmology and also delves into philosophers' and theologians' reflections concerning infinity. . . . Well suited to a general audience, this book requires no specialized knowledge of mathematics or science." Libr J

Includes bibliographical references

Eco, Umberto

History of beauty; translated by Alastair McEwen. Rizzoli Int. Pubs. 2004 438p il $40 **111**

1. Aesthetics 2. Aesthetics -- History 3. Art -- Philosophy 4. Arts -- Philosophy

ISBN 0-8478-2646-5

The editor "traces the protean subject of beauty in art, literature, philosophy, the mass media, and other humanities from ancient times to the present, setting forth various Western cultural aesthetic ideals ranging from ancient Greek to modern American. . . . This is not a quick, one-time coffee-table read but a nearly flawless presentation of the history of a fascinating and elusive idea that will delight and enlighten general readers as well as scholars." Libr J

Includes bibliographical references

Heidegger, Martin

★ **Being** and time; translated by John Macquarrie & Edward Robinson. Harper & Row 1962 589p hardcover o.p. pa $19.99 **111**

1. Ontology 2. Phenomenology

ISBN 0-06-063850-8; 0-06-157559-3 pa

"All of Heidegger's work revolves around the essential inquiry: what is the nature of being? In his most important book, . . . he distinguishes between two types of being: human existence (Dasein) and nonhuman presence (Vorhandensein)." Reader's Ency. 4th edition

Includes bibliographical references

Watson, Lyall

Dark nature; a natural history of evil. HarperCollins Pubs. 1996 318p hardcover o.p. pa $19 **111**

1. Biology -- Philosophy 2. Evolution 3. Good and evil 4. Human beings 5. Philosophy of nature

ISBN 0-06-092790-9 pa

LC 96-1663

The author "ranges through philosophy, psychology, anthropology, history, ecology and especially biology. . . . Watson believes that aggression is in our genes and examines such phenomena as war, rape and murder as manifestations of that aggression. But while he firmly believes that humans are made up of both good and evil and that natural selection is completely amoral, he is sanguine about humans as the world's first ethical animals with the capability of making moral decisions." Publ Wkly

Includes bibliographical references

★ Encyclopedia of aesthetics; editor in chief, Michael Kelly. Oxford Univ. Press 1998 4v set $495 **111**

1. Aesthetics -- Encyclopedias 2. Reference books

ISBN 0-19-511307-1

LC 98-18741

"Drawing from experts in the areas of philosophy, art, history, psychology, feminist theory, legal theory, and many more, the encyclopedia presents 600 signed essays alphabetically arranged. Most entries include a headnote clarifying the topic. Entries range from the philosophical essay on ugliness, to the more reality-based article on the impact of AIDS on the arts. Comprehensive coverage includes key figures, concepts, periods, theories, and movements in the history of aesthetics." Am Libr

On ugliness; edited by Umberto Eco; translated by Alastair McEwen. Rizzoli 2007 455p il $45 **111**

1. Aesthetics 2. Art -- Philosophy 3. Arts -- Philosophy 4. Ugliness 5. Ugliness in art

ISBN 978-0-8478-2986-6; 0-8478-2986-3

LC 2007-930249

In this "collection of images and written excerpts from ancient times to the present, all woven together with a provocative commentary and translated by Alastair McEwen, . . . [the editor] asks: Is repulsiveness, too, in the eye of the beholder? And what do we learn about that beholder when we delve into his aversions? Selecting stark visual images of gore, deformity, moral turpitude and malice, and quotations from sources ranging from Plato to radical feminists, Eco unfurls a taxonomy of ugliness. As gross-out contests go, it's both absorbing and highbrow." N Y Times Book Rev

Includes bibliographical references

113　Cosmology (Philosophy of nature)

Teilhard de Chardin, Pierre

★ The **phenomenon** of man; with an introduction by Julian Huxley. Harper & Row 1959 318p hardcover o.p. pa $14.95 **113**

1. Evolution 2. Human beings 3. Universe

ISBN 0-06-090495-X pa

The author integrates scientific findings with the tenets of Christian faith in this study of human evolution and destiny

Whitehead, Alfred North

★ **Process** and reality; an essay in cosmology. corrected ed; Free Press 1978 xxxi, 413p hardcover o.p. pa $18.95 **113**
 1. Science -- Philosophy 2. Universe
 ISBN 0-02-934570-7 pa

LC 77-90011

This book presents a condensed scheme of cosmological ideas developed by confrontation with various topics of experience. The aesthetic, moral and religious interests are thus brought into relation with those elements of knowledge which have their origin in natural science

Wilson, Edward O.

★ **In** search of nature. Island Press 1996 214p il $22; pa $15 **113**
 1. Biological diversity 2. Human beings 3. Human ecology 4. Philosophy of nature 5. Sociobiology
 ISBN 1-55963-215-1; 1-55963-216-X pa

LC 96-11226

"Concerned people of all ages should enjoy the reasoning provided by the dedicated scientific writing presented in this attractive book." Sci Books Films
 Includes bibliographical references

115   Time

Gorst, Martin

★ **Measuring** eternity; the search for the beginning of time. Broadway Bks. 2002 338p il $23.95; pa $13.95 **115**
 1. Time
 ISBN 0-7679-0827-9; 0-7679-0844-9 pa

LC 2001-37556

"For the most part Gorst avoids retrospective judgments on what now seem to be spectacular errors of calculation. Instead, he peppers his account with snippets and asides that bring the protagonists to life and make the story of time surprisingly easy to trace." New Sci
 Includes bibliographical references

121   Epistemology (Theory of knowledge)

Blackburn, Simon

★ **Truth**; a guide. Simon Blackburn. Oxford University Press 2005 xxi, 238p $25 **121**
 1. Truth
 ISBN 0-19-516824-0

LC 2004-19800

This book "traverses a broad terrain, exploring many points of the map of human knowledge and thinkers of all stripes." N Y Times Book Rev
 Includes bibliographical references

Hecht, Jennifer Michael

Doubt: a history; the great doubters and their legacy of innovation, from Socrates and Jesus to Thomas Jefferson and Emily Dickinson. HarperSanFrancisco 2003 xxi, 551p il $27.95; pa $16.95 **121**
 1. Belief and doubt
 ISBN 0-06-009772-8; 0-06-009795-7 pa

LC 2004-266061

The author's "brief but splendid study of the great Renaissance skeptic Montaigne is alone worth the price of the book. Hecht's warm prose, lucid insights, and impeccable research combine for a lively, thoughtful, and first-rate study of a neglected idea." Libr J

Locke, John

★ **An essay** concerning human understanding; edited by Roger Woolhouse. Penguin Books 1997 xxvii, 784p pa $17 **121**
 1. Theory of knowledge 2. Thought and thinking
 ISBN 0-14-043482-8

LC 98-175907

This essay, first published 1690, deals "with the nature and scope of human knowledge. Its basic premise is the empirical origin of ideas, which can be described as the raw material with which the mind works. Locke's essay contributed greatly to the growth of 18th-century empiricism." Reader's Ency. 4th edition
 Includes bibliographical references

Sartre, Jean Paul

★ **Truth** and existence; original text established and annotated by Arlette Elkaïm-Sartre; translated by Adrian van den Hoven; edited and with an introduction by Ronald Aronson. University of Chicago Press 1992 xlix, 94p hardcover o.p. pa $11 **121**
 1. Theory of knowledge
 ISBN 0-226-73523-0 pa

LC 92-5889

This book "presents Sartre's ontology of truth in terms of his characteristic key moral questions of freedom, action, and bad faith. Here is Sartre the existentialist at his most original and most provocative." Univ Press Books for Public and Second Sch Libr
 Includes bibliographical references

Wilson, Edward O.

★ **Consilience**; the unity of knowledge. Knopf 1998 332p $27.50; pa $15 **121**
 1. Philosophy 2. Science -- Philosophy 3. Theory of knowledge
 ISBN 0-679-45077-7; 0-679-76867-X pa

LC 97-2816

The author's "extraordinarily clear, evocative imagery and elegant sentences make us see how a consilient world of knowledge might look. . . . Wilson's book of faith in the dream of reason and objective knowledge is a tour de force." Publ Wkly
 Includes bibliographical references

128   Humankind

Abram, David

The **spell** of the sensuous; perception and language in a more-than-human world. Pantheon Bks. 1996 326p hardcover o.p. pa $14.95   **128**
  1. Language and languages   2. Mind and body   3. Perception   4. Philosophy of nature
  ISBN 0-679-77639-7 pa

                                LC 95-31466

This book grew out of Abram's "explorations of magic and sorcery in indigenous cultures and the relationship between magic and the natural world. Where he leads the reader after this is tough to summarize: Edmund Husserl, Maurice Merleau-Ponty, Balinese sorcerers, origins of the alphabet, Kant, Newton. Word by word this is readable and connected to a fascinating thesis: that our perceptions grew from the natural world around us, and we can 'return to our senses' and be reinvigorated, reformed, by the experience." Libr J
  Includes bibliographical references

Bloom, Howard

The **Lucifer** principle; a scientific expedition into the forces of history. Atlantic Monthly Press 1995 466p hardcover o.p. pa $16   **128**
  1. Culture   2. Evolution   3. Good and evil   4. History -- Philosophy   5. Human beings   6. Modern civilization
  ISBN 0-87113-664-3 pa

                                LC 94-11464

"A disturbing book, but its broad generalities wear down the sharp edges of its arguments, leaving something that becomes food for thought rather than reason to despair." Booklist
  Includes bibliographical references

Christian, Brian

The **most** human human; what talking with computers teaches us about what it means to be alive. Doubleday 2011 303p $27.95; ebook $13.99 **128**
  1. Artificial intelligence   2. Human beings   3. Philosophical anthropology   4. Turing test
  ISBN 978-0-385-53306-5; 978-0-385-53307-2 ebook

                              LC 2010-48572

"In a fast-paced, witty, and thoroughly winning style, Christian documents his experience in the 2009 Turing Test, a competition in which judges engage in five-minute instant-message conversations with unidentified partners, and must then decide whether each interlocutor was a human or a machine. . . . This fabulous book demonstrates that we are capable of experiencing and sharing far deeper thoughts than even the best computers—and that too often we fail to achieve the highest level of humanness." Publ Wkly

Devlin, Keith J.

Goodbye, Descartes; the end of logic and the search for a new cosmology of the mind. Wiley 1997 301p hardcover o.p. pa $14.95   **128**
  1. Artificial intelligence   2. Authors   3. College teachers   4. Dissenters   5. Essayists   6. Linguistics   7. Linguists   8. Logic   9. Mind and body   10. Nonfiction writers   11. Philosophy of mind   12. Social critics   13. Writers on

politics
  ISBN 0-471-14216-6; 0-471-25186-0 pa

                                LC 96-25493

"An excellent book that should be read by everyone who has ever wondered how we communicate with one another but find it so frustrating to interact with computers." Libr J
  Includes bibliographical references

Frayn, Michael

The **human** touch; our part in the creation of a universe. Metropolitan Books 2007 505p $32.50   **128**
  1. Cosmology   2. Philosophy   3. Science -- Philosophy   4. Subjectivity
  ISBN 978-0-8050-8148-0; 0-8050-8148-8

                                LC 2006-48204

"Beginning with a description of the continual 'traffic' between humans and the universe, Frayn shapes a cohesive introduction to philosophy that includes elements of science, determinism, physics, mathematics, psychology, linguistics, and epistemology." Libr J
  Includes bibliographical references

Irvine, William Braxton

On desire; why we want what we want. [by] William B. Irvine. Oxford University Press 2005 322p $24   **128**
  1. Desire
  ISBN 0-19-518862-4

                                LC 2005-05938

The author "explains how desire–really a multitude of desires, uninvited and unannounced–manifests itself, how it can be identified and parsed, and how it can be mastered in a way that offers the best chance at self-fulfillment. He uses modern psychology to delineate desire but then shows how the world's great religions–here mainly Christianity and Buddhism, but also Hinduism, Islam, and Judaism–address this phenomenon. He advocates no particular approach, admitting instead that different tacks probably work for different people. And he never lets the reader think that mastering desire will be easy. This is that rare book that should appeal to a wide range of readers without necessarily trying to do so." Booklist

Louv, Richard

The **nature** principle; human restoration and the end of nature-deficit disorder. Algonquin Books of Chapel Hill 2011 317p $24.95   **128**
  1. Environmental influence on humans   2. Nature   3. Nature -- Psychological aspects
  ISBN 9781565125810; 1565125819

                                LC 2011-3626

An "exploration of nature's significance in our lives and what role it will play in the future. . . . [Louv discusses] seven precepts of natural power, introducing such concepts as the 'purposeful place,' where natural history is as highly valued as human history. While the author comes across as a bit self-obsessed and the book is written to suburban and urban audiences, his writing style is clear and raises many valid points. . . . Louv heartily exhorts readers to become more engaged in the world around them, as citizen naturalists out to discover their own bioregions. Taking time to find and create an everyday Eden is not only beneficial to the individual, but to the community as a whole." Kirkus

Includes bibliographical references and index.

Terkel, Studs

Will the circle be unbroken? reflections on death, rebirth, and a hunger for faith. New Press (NY) 2001 xxiv, 407p $25.95 **128**
1. Death 2. Faith
ISBN 1-56584-692-3

"Terkel talks to 60 people about their encounters with death. His subjects range from emergency room doctors and paramedics to public figures such as author Kurt Vonnegut and guitarist Doc Watson. A stirring celebration of life and exploration of death." Booklist

Trachtenberg, Peter

The **book** of calamities; five questions about suffering and its meaning. Little, Brown 2008 450p $23.99 **128**
1. Suffering
ISBN 978-0-316-15879-4; 0-316-15879-8
LC 2008-13351

This book "succeeds because it asks the right questions, calls on the experience of articulate witnesses and—through skillful narrative and trenchant observation—beguiles the reader into facing heartbreaking reality." Publ Wkly

Includes bibliographical references

★ The Oxford companion to the mind; edited by Richard L. Gregory. 2nd ed; Oxford University Press 2005 1004p il $75 **128**
1. Neurophysiology 2. Philosophy 3. Psychology 4. Psychology -- Dictionaries 5. Reference books
ISBN 0-19-866224-6
LC 2004-275127

This book "contains over 1000 alphabetically arranged entries on all aspects of the mind, including topics in neurophysiology, communication, psychology, and philosophy, as well as people relevant to the field." Libr J

130　Parapsychology and occultism

Dolnick, Barrie

Luck; understanding luck and improving the odds. [by] Barrie Dolnick and Anthony H. Davidson. Harmony Books 2007 236p $19.95 **130**
1. Chance 2. Superstition
ISBN 978-0-307-34750-3; 0-307-34750-8
LC 2007-13235

This "mini reference examines the concept of luck throughout history as observed by a variety of religious sects and practiced in many cultures. The authors help readers develop a personal-luck profile and detail how to apply astrology, numerology, and even herbology toward increasing the odds in one's favor. A practical section on gambling advises readers how to play cards, dice, or the roulette wheel with caution." Libr J

Includes bibliographical references

Goodman, Linda

Linda Goodman's star signs; the secret codes of the universe: forgotten rainbows and forgotten melodies of ancient wisdom. St. Martin's Press 1987 xli, 477p il hardcover o.p. pa $17.95 **130**
1. Astrology 2. New Age movement 3. Occultism 4. Parapsychology
ISBN 0-312-19203-7 pa
LC 87-28375

"Goodman explains numerology, lexigrams (secret codes of words, names, and titles), the power of sound, and the power of color. . . . Along with explanations of karma and other modes of spiritual growth, she interweaves her own experiences with avatars and gurus, as well as common folk who are on their own spiritual path." Booklist

133.1　Apparitions

Aykroyd, Peter

A **history** of ghosts; the true story of seances, mediums, ghosts, and ghostbusters. by Peter H. Aykroyd; with Angela Narth; foreword by Dan Aykroyd. Rodale 2009 237p il $25.99 **133.1**
1. Ghosts 2. Spiritualism
ISBN 978-1-60529-875-7; 1-60529-875-1
LC 2009-18360

The author's "grandfather was a spiritualist: he believed the human personality survives after bodily death, and practiced regular communication with ghosts—much of which he documented in journals. Aykroyd broadens the discussion with historical figures like Sir Arthur Conan Doyle, creator of Sherlock Holmes, who joined the Society of Psychical Research three weeks after his father's death. . . . This is a smart consideration of the paranormal and a curious artifact of the Aykroyd legacy." Publ Wkly

Includes bibliographical references

Brown, Alan

Haunted Georgia; ghosts and strange phenomena of the Peach State. Stackpole Books 2008 138p il pa $10.95 **133.1**
1. Ghosts
ISBN 978-0-8117-3443-1; 0-8117-3443-9
LC 2007-25887

"This collection draws from the state's historic past, with stories of phantom pirates from the coast and restless Civil War spirits from Sherman's March and Andersonville Prison. Unusual creatures, such as the devilish Wog of Winder and the monstrous Hogzilla of River Oak Plantation, make appearances. There's also the fatal pillar in Augusta, the haunted orphanage in Savannah, the ghost of Mary MacRae searching for her lost love on St. Simon's Island, and dozens more." Publisher's note

Includes bibliographical references

Haunted Kentucky; ghosts and strange phenomena of the Bluegrass State. illustrated by Alan Brown. Stackpole Books 2009 120p il pa $10.95 **133.1**

1. Ghosts

ISBN 978-0-8117-3584-1; 0-8117-3584-2

LC 2009-3415

"This volume includes stories about the headless ghost of Old Fort Herrod, the vanishing hitchhiker of Meshack Road, the Great Meat Storm of 1876, and the sinister witch's grave at Pilot's Knob Cemetery. A host of strange creatures also wander the state, among them Goat Man, Lizard Man, and the Herrington Lake Monster." Publisher's note

Includes bibliographical references

Haunted South Carolina; ghosts and strange phenomena of the Palmetto State. illustrations by Marc Radle. Stackpole Books 2010 115p il pa $10.95 **133.1**

1. Ghosts

ISBN 978-0-8117-3635-0; 0-8117-3635-0

LC 2009-32601

"The stories of phantoms from the Indian conflicts, the American Revolution, and the Civil War still wandering the landscape of South Carolina are recounted here. Other strange phenomena include Messie the Lake Murray Monster, the trinocular Third Eye Man, the halfheaded Lost Cadet, the Ghost Hound of Goshen, and the bloodsucking Boo Hag." Publisher's note

Includes bibliographical references

Haunted Tennessee; ghosts and strange phenomena of the volunteer state. illustrations by Heather Adel Wiggins. Stackpole Books 2009 138p il pa $10.95 **133.1**

1. Ghosts

ISBN 978-0-8117-3540-7; 0-8117-3540-0

LC 2008-40678

"Readers will encounter the spirits of the Battle of Shiloh, the Fiddlin' Snake Man of Johnson County, Andrew Jackson at the Hermitage, Hank Williams at Ryman Auditorium, and Elvis Presley at Graceland. Strange creatures are also featured, including Bigfoot, the famed Wampus Cat, and the legendary Bell Witch." Publisher's note

Includes bibliographical references

Haunted Texas; ghosts and strange phenomena of the Lone Star State. illustrations by Heather Adel Wiggins. Stackpole Books 2008 122p il pa $10.95 **133.1**

1. Ghosts

ISBN 978-0-8117-3500-1; 0-8117-3500-1

LC 2007-48786

"This collection, drawn from the deserts of the west to the beaches of the Gulf Shore, includes eerie tales of the spirits that haunt the Alamo, Old Rip the horned toad, UFO sightings in north Texas, the never-ending ride of El Muerto, the ghost on board the USS Lexington, and the watchful specter of Miss Bettie at Galveston's Ashton Villa." Publisher's note

Includes bibliographical references

Farnsworth, Cheri

Haunted Connecticut; ghosts and strange phenomena of the Constitution State. by Cheri Revai. Stackpole Books 2006 119p il pa $10.95 **133.1**

1. Ghosts

ISBN 978-0-8117-3296-3; 0-8117-3296-7

LC 2006-9390

"Stories of supernatural occurrences in Connecticut, including the curse on Dudleytown, the spirit of Hanna Cranna who causes car crashes in Monroe, the phantom black dog of Meriden, buried-alive Midnight Mary, the lost village of Bara-Hack, and . . . more." Publisher's note

Includes bibliographical references

Haunted Hudson Valley; ghosts and strange phenomena of New York's Sleepy Hollow country. illustrations by Marc Radle. Stackpole Books 2010 121p il pa $10.95 **133.1**

1. Ghosts

ISBN 978-0-8117-3621-3; 0-8117-3621-0

LC 2009-40866

"'The whole neighborhood abounds with local tales, haunted spots, and twilight superstitions,' wrote Washington Irving in the 1820s. This part of New York, straddling the Hudson River from New York City to Albany, is still rife with stories of the paranormal, including a temperance reformer who haunts the Bull's Head Inn, a floating ball of fire at the College of Saint Rose, the ghost girl of the Bardavon Opera House in Poughkeepsie, the spirits of West Point, UFOs at Indian Point 3 nuclear power plant, and the phantoms of Smalley's Inn in Carmel." Publisher's note

Includes bibliographical references

Haunted Massachusetts; ghosts and strange phenomena of the Bay State. [by] Cheri Revai, illustrations by Heather Adel Wiggins. Stackpole Books 2005 119p il pa $10.95 **133.1**

1. Ghosts

ISBN 978-0-8117-3221-5; 0-8117-3221-5

LC 2004-25254

A "look at unexplained phenomena in Massachusetts, including the wandering spirit of lost child Lucy Keyes, the monkey-like Dover Demon, the ghost that leaves tips at Stone's Public Tavern, hauntings in Lizzie Borden's house, the Black Flash phantom in Provincetown, and . . . more." Publisher's note

Includes bibliographical references

Haunted New York; ghosts and strange phenomena of the Empire State. [by] Cheri Revai; illustrations by Heather Adel Wiggins. Stackpole Books 2005 117p il pa $10.95 **133.1**

1. Ghosts

ISBN 978-0-8117-3249-9; 0-8117-3249-5

LC 2005-9365

A "look at supernatural phenomena in New York, including the ghost of a British soldier at Fort Ontario, Champ the Lake Champlain monster, the haunted castle of Captain Beardslee, spirits in Manhattan's oldest house, the alien abduction at the Brooklyn Bridge, and many more." Publisher's note

Includes bibliographical references

Haunted New York City; ghosts and strange phenomena of the Big Apple. [by] Cheri Revai; illustrations by Heather Adel Wiggins. Stackpole Books 2008 120p il pa $10.95   **133.1**
  1. Ghosts
  ISBN 978-0-8117-3471-4; 0-8117-3471-4
               LC 2007-25890
"Stories of the paranormal from the five boroughs are compiled in this volume, including the phantom searching for lost gold in the Parrish House in the Bronx, the demonic flying Coney Island Monster in Brooklyn, the haunted St. Paul's Chapel in Manhattan, the raving ghost of Mount Olivet Cemetery in Queens, the restless spirits that peer from the windows of the Kreischer Mansion in Staten Island, and many others." Publisher's note

Includes bibliographical references

Godfrey, Linda S.
  Haunted Wisconsin; ghosts and strange phenomena of the badger state. Stackpole Books 2010 122p il pa $10.95   **133.1**
  1. Ghosts
  ISBN 978-0-8117-3636-7; 0-8117-3636-9
              LC 2010-914
"Readers will encounter Kenosha's Headless Nun, the Man Bat of Lacrosse, Rocky the Rock Lake Monster, and John Dillinger's phantom. They will explore Aztalan's ancient mounds, the ghostly bars and taverns of Madison and Milwaukee, and the creepy town of Caryville, one of the most haunted places in America." Publisher's note

Includes bibliographical references

Guiley, Rosemary Ellen
  ★ The **encyclopedia** of ghosts and spirits; foreword by Troy Taylor. 3rd ed; Facts on File 2007 564p il $75   **133.1**
  1. Ghosts 2. Ghosts -- Encyclopedias 3. Parapsychology 4. Reference books
  ISBN 978-0-8160-6737-4; 0-8160-6737-6
              LC 2006-103302
This work examines famous hauntings, historical personages and happenings, and various legends and myths about ghosts and spirits throughout the world. Recent events, new findings about old myths and updated information on major figures in the field are covered.

"Believers and skeptics alike seeking information on various phenomena will find this book useful." Booklist

Includes bibliographical references

Martinelli, Patricia A.
  Haunted Delaware; ghosts and strange phenomena of the First State. illustrations by Heather Adel Wiggins. Stackpole Books 2006 119p il pa $10.95   **133.1**
  1. Ghosts
  ISBN 978-0-8117-3297-0; 0-8117-3297-5
              LC 2005-29805

"Tales of unexplained phenomena in Delaware, including the evil murderess Patty Cannon, the judge who was buried twice, the vengeful phantom dog of Frederica, the wizard of Belltown who sold his soul to the Devil, the Girl of the Dunes waiting on her lost love, and . . . more. Includes information on ghost tours in the region." Publisher's note

Includes bibliographical references

Haunted New Jersey; ghosts and strange phenomena of the Garden State. [by] Patricia A. Martinelli and Charles A. Stansfield, Jr. Stackpole Books 2004 120p il pa $10.95   **133.1**
  1. Ghosts
  ISBN 978-0-8117-3156-0; 0-8117-3156-1
              LC 2003-23431
This is a "look at unexplained phenomena in New Jersey, featuring information on ghost tours in the state." Publisher's note

Includes bibliographical references

Nesbitt, Mark
  Haunted Pennsylvania; ghosts and strange phenomena of the Keystone State. [by] Mark Nesbitt and Patty A. Wilson; illustrations by Heather Adel Wiggins. Stackpole Books 2006 133p il pa $10.95   **133.1**
  1. Ghosts
  ISBN 978-0-8117-3298-7; 0-8117-3298-3
              LC 2006-10129
"A collection of . . . stories, including the Civil War ghosts of Gettysburg, spirits at John Brown's tannery, the fiddling ghost of Potter County, hauntings at the Eastern State Penitentiary, the mysterious indelible handprint, and many more." Publisher's note

Includes bibliographical references

Norman, Michael
  Haunted America; {by} Michael Norman and Beth Scott. TOR Bks. 1994 411p maps hardcover o.p. pa $7.99   **133.1**
  1. Ghosts
  ISBN 0-8125-5054-4 pa
              LC 94-28984
"This collection of chilling tales of the supernatural includes at least one story from each state and from the English-speaking Canadian provinces. The stories recount sightings of ghostly apparitions and mysterious happenings, and their history and evolution is documented." Libr J

Includes bibliographical references

Okonowicz, Ed
  Haunted Maryland; ghosts and strange phenomena of the Old Line State. illustrations by Heather Adel Wiggins. Stackpole Books 2007 137p il pa $10.95   **133.1**
  1. Ghosts
  ISBN 978-0-8117-3409-7; 0-8117-3409-9
              LC 2006-102022
"Tales of unexplained phenomena in Maryland, including the bleeding stone of White House Farm, the vengeful ghost of Bigg Lizz, the Chesapeake sea monster fondly

known as Chessie, America's most haunted lighthouse, the mysterious 'Toaster' who visits Edgar Allan Poe's grave, and . . . more." Publisher's note

Includes bibliographical references

Ramsland, Katherine M.

Ghost; investigating the other side. {by} Katherine Ramsland. St. Martin's Press 2001 322p il $25.95; pa $6.99 **133.1**

1. Ghosts 2. Ghosts -- United States

ISBN 0-312-26164-0; 0-312-98373-5 pa

LC 2001-41725

"Although prepared to dismiss many so-called paranormal occurrences in favor of natural explanations, {the author} nevertheless encounters, experiences, and investigates a variety of inexplicable visual, photographic, and verbal manifestations. Both skeptics and believers will be intrigued by this first-person exploration of ghostly visitations." Booklist

Includes bibliographical references

Stansfield, Charles A.

Haunted Arizona; ghosts and strange phenomena of the Grand Canyon State. [by] Charles A. Stansfield, Jr.; illustrations by Marc Radle. Stackpole Books 2010 138p il pa $10.95 **133.1**

1. Ghosts

ISBN 978-0-8117-3620-6; 0-8117-3620-2

LC 2009-33322

"Tales in this volume include the spirits of Tombstone, the ghost train of Curly Bill, the mysterious appearances of the Blue Lady, and the phantoms that crossed the Atlantic to haunt London Bridge." Publisher's note

Includes bibliographical references

Haunted Jersey shore; ghosts and strange phenomena of the Garden State coast. [by] Charles A. Stansfield, Jr.; illustrations by Heather Adel Wiggins. Stackpole Books 2006 115p il pa $10.95 **133.1**

1. Ghosts

ISBN 978-0-8117-3267-3; 0-8117-3267-3

LC 2005-19596

A "look into the haunted history of the New Jersey coastline, with tales of pirates and treasure, loves lost at sea, Civil War ghosts, and monsters and other strange beings that lurk in the countryside." Publisher's note

Includes bibliographical references

Haunted Maine; ghosts and strange phenomena of the Pine Tree State. [by] Charles A. Stansfield, Jr. Stackpole Books 2007 117p il pa $10.95 **133.1**

1. Ghosts

ISBN 978-0-8117-3373-1; 0-8117-3373-4

LC 2006-18546

A "look at spooky legends and stories of the paranormal, including the guardian spirit of Portland Head Light, the preacher and the cats from Hell, the ghost of Marie Antoinette, the ghost who toasts independence, and the logger who befriended the Devil." Publisher's note

Includes bibliographical references

Haunted Ohio; ghosts and strange phenomena of the Buckeye State. [by] Charles A. Stansfield Jr.; illustrations by Heather Adel Wiggins. Stackpole Books 2008 102p il pa $10.95 **133.1**

1. Ghosts

ISBN 978-0-8117-3472-1; 0-8117-3472-2

LC 2007-37709

"From across the plains to the metropolitan centers of Cleveland, Columbus, and Cincinnati come a variety of stories and legends, including the phantom in Dayton's Woodland Cemetery who perches atop his tombstone, the pitiful spirits of the Millfield miners, the fearsome ghost of boatman Mike Fink, and many more." Publisher's note

Includes bibliographical references

Haunted Southern California; ghosts and strange phenomena of the Golden State. Stackpole Books 2009 118p il pa $10.95 **133.1**

1. Ghosts

ISBN 978-0-8117-3539-1; 0-8117-3539-7

LC 2008-30857

"This region includes the Central Coast, the San Joaquin Valley, and metropolitan Los Angeles and San Diego, where readers will encounter the spirits of gold prospectors, cowboys, Spanish padres, and movie stars, as well as the phantom camels of Fort Tejon, the shape-shifting witch of Tulare, underwater UFOs, ghosts aboard the Queen Mary, and the tragic specter of Marilyn Monroe." Publisher's note

Includes bibliographical references

Haunted Vermont; ghosts and strange phenomena of the Green Mountain State. [by] Charles A. Stansfield, Jr.; illustrations by Heather Adel Wiggins. Stackpole Books 2007 115p il pa $10.95 **133.1**

1. Ghosts

ISBN 978-0-8117-3399-1; 0-8117-3399-8

LC 2006-34011

"A collection of . . . stories from the Green Mountain state, including the Barre Vampire, the Thetford Horror, the spirit of Robert Lincoln, the ghostly sentries of Bennington Monument, and many others." Publisher's note

Includes bibliographical references

Haunted northern California; ghosts and strange phenomena of the Golden State. [by] Charles A. Stansfield, Jr.; illustrations by Heather Adel Wiggins. Stackpole Books 2009 136p il pa $10.95 **133.1**

1. Ghosts

ISBN 978-0-8117-3586-5; 0-8117-3586-9

LC 2009-3157

"This region includes the North and Central coasts, the Santa Clara and Sacramento valleys, the East Bay, and the Northern Sierra, where readers will experience strange encounters at Alcatraz, in the abandoned town of Bodie, and aboard the aircraft carrier Hornet. Also included are stories of the legendary Bear Man, Native American ghost danc-

ers, and the spirits of novelist Jack London, the bandit Black Bart, and the ill-fated Donner party." Publisher's note
Includes bibliographical references

Taylor, L. B.

Haunted Virginia; ghosts and strange phenomena of the Old Dominion. [by] L.B. Taylor, Jr. Stackpole Books 2009 120p il pa $10.95   **133.1**
1. Ghosts
ISBN 978-0-8117-3541-4; 0-8117-3541-9
LC 2008-35174
"This volume includes stories on the female stranger of Gadsby's Tavern in Alexandria, the mysterious stone showers in Newport, the ghost hound of the Blue Ridge, Mad Lucy of Williamsburg, and the spirits of native sons Thomas Jefferson, Robert E. Lee, and Edgar Allan Poe." Publisher's note
Includes bibliographical references

Taylor, Troy

Haunted Illinois; ghosts and strange phenomena of the prairie state. illustrations by Heather Adel Wiggins. Stackpole Books 2008 140p il pa $10.95   **133.1**
1. Ghosts
ISBN 978-0-8117-3499-8; 0-8117-3499-4
LC 2007-40206
"This volume explores the supernatural side of the Prairie State, with stories on the horrors of an old slave house, the numerous spirits of Alton's McPike Mansion, the cemetery where the dead walk, the Spring Valley Vampire, the ghosts of the Bartonville Asylum, Chicago's famous Resurrection Mary, and the spirit world of Abraham Lincoln." Publisher's note
Includes bibliographical references

Thuma, Cynthia

Haunted Florida; ghosts and strange phenomena of the Sunshine State. [by] Cynthia Thuma and Catherine Lower; illustrations by Heather Adel Wiggins. Stackpole Books 2008 101p il pa $10.95   **133.1**
1. Ghosts
ISBN 978-0-8117-3498-1; 0-8117-3498-6
LC 2007-40121
"This compilation of supernatural tales shows Florida to be a place rife with eerie occurences and ghostly denizens. Stories include the spirit of Uncle Charlie at Fernandina Beach's Palace Saloon, the infamous Chupacabras of south Florida, a count's strange obsession with his dead wife, and the mysterious Skunk Ape of Collier County." Publisher's note
Includes bibliographical references

Wilson, Patty A.

Haunted North Carolina; ghosts and strange phenomena of the Tar Heel State. illustrations by Heather Adel Wiggins. Stackpole Books 2009 138p il pa $10.95   **133.1**
1. Ghosts
ISBN 978-0-8117-3585-8; 0-8117-3585-0
LC 2009-19333

"Readers will encounter the spirit of infant Virginia Dare in the form of a white deer, shipwreck survivors guided by ghosts to safety, a Halifax County reverend's encounter with the Devil, phantom marauders at Hannah's Creek Swamp, the spirit who directed his will from the grave, hauntings in the State Capitol, and mysterious figures at Devil's Stairs." Publisher's note
Includes bibliographical references

Haunted West Virginia; ghosts & strange phenomena of the mountain state. illustrations by Heather Adel Wiggins. Stackpole Books 2007 138p il pa $10.95   **133.1**
1. Ghosts
ISBN 978-0-8117-3400-4; 0-8117-3400-5
LC 2007-347
"Stories of supernatural occurences in West Virginia, including the restless spirits of Harpers Ferry, the legendary Mothman of Point Pleasant, the ghosts of Twistabout Ridge, the phantom hitchhikers on the West Virginia Turnpike, and . . . more." Publisher's note
Includes bibliographical references

133.4   Demonology and witchcraft

Adler, Margot

Drawing down the moon; witches, Druids, goddess-worshippers, and other pagans in America. [Rev and updated ed]; Penguin Books 2006 646p il pa $18   **133.4**
1. Paganism 2. Witchcraft
ISBN 0-14-303819-2; 978-0-14-303819-1
LC 2006-43786
A survey of goddess worship and witchcraft movements discussing their basic philosophies and practices
"Despite its clear anti-Judaic and anti-Christian bias, this book is recommended for general and college audiences interested in religion, the occult, and modern social phenomena." Choice {review of 1979 edition}
Includes bibliographical references

Carlson, Laurie M.

A **fever** in Salem; a new interpretation of the New England witch trials. Dee, I.R. 1999 197p hardcover o.p. pa $14.95   **133.4**
1. Epidemic encephalitis -- Massachusetts -- Salem -- History -- 17th century 2. Witchcraft 3. Witchcraft -- Massachusetts -- Salem -- History -- 17th century
ISBN 1-56663-253-6; 1-56663-309-5 pa
LC 99-27520
"Carlson's compelling narrative begs for assessment by medical experts. A valuable purchase for libraries seeking more than a basic summary of the witch trials." Libr J
Includes bibliographical references

Guiley, Rosemary Ellen

The **encyclopedia** of demons and demonology; foreword by John Zaffis. Facts On File 2009 302p il $82.50; pa $24.95   **133.4**
1. Demonology 2. Demonology -- Encyclopedias 3.

Reference books 4. Witchcraft
ISBN 978-0-8160-7314-6; 0-8160-7314-7; 978-0-8160-7315-3 pa; 0-8160-7315-5 pa

LC 2008-52488

"This encyclopedia delineates beliefs about demons and demonology. The text emerges from an exploration of the darker aspects of folklore, myths, culture, and religion, covering major issues, people, and events in a historical and phenomenological perspective. Its over 400 A-to-Z entries cover topics such as demons in different cultures and religious traditions, possession, exorcism, and demon types. . . . Clear, concise, and balanced, this will attract a range of non-scholarly audiences, especially those interested in the occult, paranormal, folklore, myths, and religion. A solid addition to public libraries." Libr J

Includes bibliographical references

The **encyclopedia** of witches, witchcraft, and Wicca; 3rd ed; Facts On File 2008 436p il $85; pa $24.95 **133.4**
1. Reference books 2. Witchcraft -- Encyclopedias 3. Witchcraft -- History 4. Witches
ISBN 978-0-8160-7103-6; 0-8160-7103-9; 978-0-8160-7104-3 pa; 0-8160-7104-7 pa

LC 2008-8917

"Spanning centuries and continents, the book defines 480 of witchcraft's and wizardry's major historical events, figures, tools, sites, symbols, and abstract terms. The highly engaging, alphabetically organized entries run several paragraphs in length and deftly clarify a term's etymology as well as its spiritual, historical, or spell-making significance." Libr J

Includes bibliographical references

Hutton, Ronald

The **triumph** of the moon; a history of modern pagan witchcraft. Oxford Univ. Press 1999 486p $55.50; pa $17.95 **133.4**
1. Neopaganism 2. Witchcraft
ISBN 0-19-820744-1; 0-19-285449-6 pa

LC 99-31586

This "history of paganism in 19th- and 20th-century Britain centers on Wicca, the system of witchcraft Gerald B. Gardner introduced to a startled public in the 1950s. . . . Hutton's exceptional work is by far the most scholarly, comprehensive and judicious analysis of the subject yet published." Publ Wkly

Includes bibliographical references

Karlsen, Carol F.

★ The **devil** in the shape of a woman; witchcraft in colonial New England. Norton 1987 360p hardcover o.p. pa $16.95 **133.4**
1. Witchcraft
ISBN 0-393-02478-4; 0-393-31759-5 pa

LC 87-16615

The author presents a "social history of witchcraft in Puritan New England (1620-1725). She unearths detailed evidence which demonstrates that prosecuted and accused witches generally were older, married women who had violated the religious and/or economic Puritan social hierarchy.

. . . A well-written, provocative addition to the . . . scholarship on New England witchcraft." Libr J

Includes bibliographical references

Robisheaux, Thomas

The **last** witch of Langenburg; murder in a German village. [by] Thomas Robisheaux. W. W. Norton & Co. 2009 427p il map **133.4**
1. Homicide 2. Murder -- Germany -- History 3. Witchcraft 4. Witchcraft -- Germany -- History
ISBN 0-393-06551-0; 9780393065510

LC 2008-43052

This "account of one of Europe's last witch panics draws on court documents, eyewitness testimonies, and an early autopsy report to chronicle the 1672 trial of Anna Schmeig and her family, who were accused of sorcery when a neighbor girl died after eating one of Anna's butter cakes." (Publisher's note) Bibliography. Index.

The author "gives us the story of one of the last witch hunts in Europe. In 1672, in a German village, a young woman who had just given birth to her second child died after eating a Shrovetide cake made by her neighbor. Stories of witches poisoning innocents were common in the Franconia region. The neighbor was arrested, and the entire family charged with witchcraft. You can't beat a witch hunt for drama. Every childhood nightmare is called to mind—the dark forest on the edge of town, the inaccessibility of God and, worse, our own friends and family. Forget memoir; this is nonfiction." Seattle Times

Includes bibliographical references

133.5 Astrology

Goodman, Linda

Linda Goodman's sun signs. Taplinger 1968 xxiii, 549p $29.95 **133.5**
1. Astrology 2. Zodiac
ISBN 0-8008-4900-0

The author tells how to identify and deal with people according to their astrological signs

"This book is part astrology, part psychology, and always entertaining." Libr J

Lewis, James R.

★ The **astrology** book; the encyclopedia of heavenly influences. 2nd ed; Visible Ink Press 2003 928p il pa $24.95 **133.5**
1. Astrology 2. Astrology -- Encyclopedias 3. Natal astrology 4. Reference books
ISBN 1-57859-144-9

"Although aimed at the believer, Lewis' work may be confidently consulted by the skeptic seeking basic information about astrology." Booklist

Miller, Susan

Planets and possibilities; explore the worlds beyond your sun sign. Warner Bks. 2001 418p il $30; pa $15.95 **133.5**
1. Astrology
ISBN 0-446-52434-4; 0-446-67806-6 pa

The author provides "character analysis of each sign. The cosmic gifts, relationship trends, financial tendencies, and career tendencies associated with each sign are all described in detail. The mythology of each sign is included as well, nicely rounding out the book." Libr J

Snodgrass, Mary Ellen

Signs of the zodiac; a reference guide to historical, mythological, and cultural associations. illustrated by Raymond Miller Barrett, Jr. Greenwood Press 1997 243p il $46.95   **133.5**
  1. Astrology 2. Zodiac
  ISBN 0-313-30276-6

LC 97-5598

"After brief descriptions of zodiacal variants from other parts of the world, plus chapters on the historical foundations of astrology and its pervasiveness in the arts and sciences, Snodgrass treats each sign to a full workover: major stars in each, mythological background and symbology, commonly accepted character traits of those born under its influence, and thumbnail biographies of select prominent people who exemplify those traits." SLJ

Includes bibliographical references

133.6   Palmistry

Reid, Lori

The **art** of hand reading. DK Pub. 1996 120p il hardcover o.p. pa $15   **133.6**
  1. Hand 2. Palmistry
  ISBN 0-7894-4837-8 pa

LC 96-15506

This volume uses color photographs of hands and handprints to analyze all the significant lines, mounts, and markings on hands. It shows how the different areas of the palm reveal the balance between instinctive desires and powers of intellect and reason

133.8   Psychic phenomena

Bader, Christopher D.

Paranormal America; ghost encounters, UFO sightings, Bigfoot hunts, and other curiosities in religion and culture. [by] Christopher D. Bader, F. Carson Mencken, and Joseph O. Baker. New York University Press 2010 264p il $70; pa $20   **133.8**
  1. Curiosities and wonders 2. Faith 3. Parapsychology 4. Subcultures
  ISBN 978-0-8147-9134-9; 978-0-8147-9135-6 pa; 978-0-8147-8642-0 ebook

LC 2010-16525

Authors "Christopher D. Bader, F. Carson Mencken, and Joseph O. Baker take their readers on a . . . journey into 'the world of people who devote themselves to the "quest"' for contact with angels, aliens, and other unusual beings. . . . To flesh out the findings of the 2005 Baylor Religion Survey, a national random sample of American religious beliefs (two of the authors were principle investigators), and to understand who is attracted to paranormal beliefs, Bader, Menck-

en, and Baker accompany bigfoot hunters into the woods and listen to stories about alien abductions and ghostly apparitions. . . . By drawing on both the Baylor survey and qualitative research, these three sociologists conclude that 'the paranormal is normal' and challenge the stereotype that those drawn to the paranormal come from the margins of society." (Journal of American History)

The authors "examine America's belief in paranormal phenomena inside and outside of mainstream religion—from UFOs and Bigfoot to speaking in tongues and guardian angels. They look at how belief affects lives, examining common stereotypes faced by believers and considering whether belief in a mainstream religion makes one likely to ascribe to more otherworldly occurrences. . . . While this academic work showcases an astounding amount of research, the quick pacing and engaging language keep it from being a dry report of BRS findings. It is accessible to any reader with an interest in the convergence of paranormal beliefs and religion." Libr J

Includes bibliographical references

Sheldrake, Rupert

Dogs that know when their owners are coming home; and other unexplained powers of animals. Crown 1999 352p il hardcover o.p. pa $14   **133.8**
  1. Extrasensory perception 2. Extrasensory perception in animals 3. Pets 4. Pets -- Psychic aspects
  ISBN 0-609-80533-9 pa

LC 99-25439

"The author reports the results of five years of extensive research as he followed up on anecdotal accounts from pet owners on the homing abilities of lost pets, animals that show premonitions of earthquakes or epileptic seizures, and the fact that animals anticipate the arrival home of their owners." Booklist

Includes bibliographical references

The **sense** of being stared at; and other aspects of the extended mind. Crown 2003 369p il hardcover o.p. pa $13.95   **133.8**
  1. Extrasensory perception 2. Extrasensory perception in animals
  ISBN 1-4000-5129-0 pa

LC 2002-9943

"A most unusual book—fascinating, scientifically sound, and fun to read—it posits that ESP and 'other aspects of the extended mind' are not paranormal but natural functions. Every library should make room on its shelves for this one." Libr J

Includes bibliographical references

133.9   Spiritualism

Blum, Deborah

Ghost hunters; William James and the search for scientific proof of life after death. Penguin Press 2006 370p $25.95; pa $15   **133.9**
  1. Parapsychology 2. Philosophers 3. Psychologists 4. Spiritualism 5. Spiritualism -- History 6. Writers on science
  ISBN 1-59420-090-4; 978-1-59420-090-8; 0-14-

303895-8 pa; 978-0-14-303895-5 pa

LC 2006-44948

In this book, the author examines the Victorian era conflict between science and religion "by reviewing the history of the British Society for Psychical Research and its U.S. counterpart, the American Society for Psychical Research, both of which aimed to find scientific proof of the existence of the supernatural. . . . Her clearly written presentation of the history, frauds, and personalities involved in this unique slice of Victorian life is recommended for all history of science collections." Libr J

Includes bibliographical references

Moody, Raymond A.

★ **Life** after life; the investigation of a phenomenon--survival of bodily death. [by] Raymond A. Moody, Jr.; with a new preface by Melvin Morse and a foreword by Elizabeth Kübler-Ross. HarperSanFrancisco 2001 xxviii, 175p pa $14   **133.9**

1. Death 2. Future life 3. Near-death experiences

ISBN 0-06-251739-2

LC 00-46156

The author "investigates more than one hundred case studies of people who experienced 'clinical death' and were subsequently revived." Publisher's note

Roach, Mary

★ **Spook**; science tackles the afterlife. Norton 2005 311p il $24.95   **133.9**

1. Death 2. Future life 3. Religion and science 4. Soul

ISBN 0-393-05962-6

LC 2005-14450

The author investigates a range of theories and beliefs about the soul's migration after death.

"Roach perfectly balances her skepticism and her boundless curiosity with a sincere desire to know. . . . She is an original who can enliven any subject with wit, keen reporting and a sly intelligence." Publ Wkly

Includes bibliographical references

141   Idealism and related systems and doctrines

Berlin, Isaiah

The **roots** of romanticism; edited by Henry Hardy. Princeton Univ. Press 1999 171p pa $19.95 **141**

1. Arts -- Philosophy 2. Romanticism

ISBN 0-691-00713-6; 978-0-691-08662-0 pa; 0-691-08662-0 pa

LC 98-41657

This is an edited transcript of the lectures "and the supporting bibliographic notes from which Berlin worked on his idea of romanticism. . . . Arguing that the concept flows from late 18th-century German thought and society, Berlin addresses romanticism's effect on the Enlightenment, the roles played by Hamann, Herder, and other early Romanticists in the codification of the movement, the more distilled approaches of Kant and Schiller, and romanticism's lingering effects on Western intellectual posture. . . . An excellent resource for both beginning researcher and seasoned scholar." Libr J

Includes bibliographical references

★ The essential transcendentalists; edited and introduced by Richard G. Geldard. J.P. Tarcher/Penguin 2005 265p pa $15.95   **141**

1. Transcendentalism

ISBN 1-58542-434-X

LC 2005-44016

This study "is divided into three main sections. . . . The first is 'Primary Texts,' with selections from the writings of Sampson Reed, James Marsh, Amos Alcott (father of Louisa May), and Ralph Waldo Emerson. The second, 'Individual Voices,' introduces selections from Frederic Hedge, Margaret Fuller, and Henry David Thoreau. The last is 'The Transcendental Heritage,' which features the works of Walt Whitman, Emily Dickinson, Wallace Stevens, Loren Eiseley, and Annie Dillard. This is a highly informed, elegantly written, fascinating story told through commentary, historical overview, and selections from classic works. It belongs in all libraries." Libr J

Includes bibliographical references

142   Critical philosophy

Barrett, William

★ **Irrational** man; a study in existential philosophy. Doubleday 1958 278p hardcover o.p. pa $12.95   **142**

1. Existentialism

ISBN 0-385-03138-6 pa

This discussion of existentialism traces its origins and analyzes the contributions of chief exponents of existentialist thought—Nietzsche, Kierkegaard, Heidegger and Sartre.

Sartre, Jean Paul

★ **Being** and nothingness; an essay on phenomenological ontology. translated and with an introduction by Hazel E. Barnes. Philosophical Lib. 1956 638p   **142**

1. Existentialism

This is "Sartre's major attempt to systematize his theoretical analysis of the human condition and human consciousness which underlies 'Existentialism.'" Reader's Ency. 4th edition

Existentialism and human emotions. Philosophical Library; Distributed to the book trade by Citadel Press 1957 96p pa $9.95   **142**

1. Existentialism

ISBN 0-8065-0902-3 pa

Existentialism from Dostoevsky to Sartre; rev and expanded; New Am. Lib. 1975 384p pa $15.95   **142**

1. Authors 2. Biographers 3. Dramatists 4. Essayists 5. Existentialism 6. Nobel laureates for literature 7. Nonfiction writers 8. Novelists 9. Philosophers 10. Poets 11. Short story writers 12. Theologians 13. Writers on religion

ISBN 0-452-00930-8

This book contains selections from the basic writings of Dostoevsky, Kierkegaard, Nietzsche, Rilke, Ortega y Gasset, Jaspers, Heidegger, Sartre and Camus.

146 Naturalism and related systems and doctrines

Dennett, Daniel Clement

Darwin's dangerous idea; evolution and the meanings of life. {by} Daniel C. Dennett. Simon & Schuster 1995 586p il hardcover o.p. pa $16 **146**
1. Authors 2. College teachers 3. Evolution 4. Geologists 5. Mathematicians 6. Natural selection 7. Paleontologists 8. Writers on science
ISBN 0-684-82471-X pa

LC 94-49158

"Current controversies associated with the origin of life, sociobiology, punctuated equilibrium, the evolution of culture and language, and evolutionary ethics are investigated rigorously within the context of Darwinian science and philosophy. Dennett challenges the ideas of several imminent scientists, including Roger Penrose and Stephen Jay Gould, who, Dennett asserts, tend to limit the power or implications of Darwin's dangerous ideas." Libr J

Includes bibliographical references

150 Psychology

Colman, Andrew M.

★ A **dictionary** of psychology; 2nd ed; Oxford University Press 2006 861p il $45; pa $17.95 **150**
1. Psychology 2. Psychology -- Dictionaries 3. Reference books
ISBN 978-0-19-280632-1; 0-19-280632-7; 978-0-19-861035-9 pa; 0-19-861035-1 pa

LC 2005-31810

"This work defines the most common as well as the most important issues facing psychology today.... [The book features] over 11,000 cross-referenced entries, covering everything from anxiety and cognitive impairment to hypolexia (another name for dyslexia) and postpartum depression.... For professionals and students of psychology, this is a good place to start their research." SLJ

Includes bibliographical references

Cordon, Luis A.

★ **Popular** psychology; an encyclopedia. Greenwood Press 2005 274p il $75 **150**
1. Psychology -- Encyclopedias 2. Psychology -- Popular works 3. Reference books
ISBN 0-313-32457-3

LC 2004-17426

This book "provides a concise guide for anyone seeking to understand the true scientific nature of psychology." Libr Media Connect

Includes bibliographical references

Glasser, William

Choice theory; a new psychology of personal freedom. HarperCollins Pubs. 1998 340p il $24; pa $13.95 **150**
1. Choice (Psychology) 2. Interpersonal relations 3. Psychology
ISBN 0-06-019109-0; 0-06-093014-4 pa

LC 97-36025

"Choice theory helps its users avoid confrontation and ask pertinent questions. It sees conscious or unconscious desire for external control as the main problem in the four major personal relationships: husband-wife, parent-child, teacher-student, and manager-worker.... Combining choice theory and reality therapy in his practice, Glasser has been able to shorten the durations of his treatment programs substantially. As he presents them here, his theories and approaches can be applied in education and business as well as for self-help." Booklist

Kübler-Ross, Elisabeth

The **wheel** of life; a memoir of living and dying. Scribner 1997 286p il hardcover o.p. pa $13 **150**
1. Biography, Individual 2. College teachers 3. Death -- Psychological aspects 4. Psychiatrists 5. Writers on medicine
ISBN 0-684-84631-4 pa

LC 97-6435

In this autobiography "Kübler-Ross describes her growing-up years in Switzerland as one of a set of triplet sisters, her fight to become a doctor, and later, the even stronger opposition she met when she began her research on death and dying. Despite the weightiness inherent in working with and writing about mortality, the book has a light, almost airy feel to it, which goes along with the author's central theme that death is merely a transformation." Booklist

The **Corsini** encyclopedia of psychology and behavioral science; co-editors, W. Edward Craighead, Charles B. Nemeroff. 3rd ed; Wiley 2001 4v il set $800 **150**
1. Psychology 2. Psychology -- Encyclopedias 3. Reference books
ISBN 0-471-23949-6

LC 99-58006

"Despite its poor indexing, this edition of Corsini is an essential, solid, and important reference work in psychology and behavioral science." Choice

Includes bibliographical references

★ The **Gale** encyclopedia of psychology; Bonnie R. Strickland, executive editor. 2nd ed; Gale Group 2001 701p il $191.50 **150**
1. Psychology -- Encyclopedias 2. Reference books
ISBN 0-7876-4786-1

LC 00-34736

Coverage includes noteworthy people, movements, theories, and important case studies and experiments. The articles, ranging from 25 to 1,500 words examine such diverse topics as abnormal psychology, bipolar disorder, Sigmund Freud and insomnia.

Salem health; psychology & mental health. editor, Nancy A. Piotrowski. Salem Press 2010 5v il set $495 **150**
1. Psychology -- Encyclopedias 2. Reference books
ISBN 978-1-58765-556-2
"The well-written, well-researched, concise text offers an easily accessible collection of information." Choice
Includes bibliographical references

150.19 Systems, schools, viewpoints

Bettelheim, Bruno
★ **Freud** and man's soul. Knopf 1983 111p hardcover o.p. pa $9 **150.19**
1. Psychoanalysis 2. Psychoanalysts 3. Writers on medicine
ISBN 0-394-71036-3 pa

LC 82-47809

The author argues that Freud was a great humanist and that mistranslation of his work has lead American psychoanalysis astray.

Buhle, Mari Jo
★ **Feminism** and its discontents; a century of struggle with psychoanalysis. Harvard Univ. Press 1998 432p $39.95; pa $21.50 **150.19**
1. Feminism 2. Psychoanalysis 3. Psychoanalysis and feminism 4. Women -- Psychology
ISBN 0-674-29868-3; 0-674-00403-5 pa

LC 97-32397

Buhle bases her "historical study on the premise that feminism and psychoanalytic theory, each in its own way concerned with understanding the 'self,' developed in continuous dialogue with each other. The author's captivating, energetic writing style reflects the often spirited, surprisingly tenacious relationship of these two theories." Booklist
Includes bibliographical references

Freud, Sigmund
★ The **Freud** reader; edited by Peter Gay. Norton 1989 832p hardcover o.p. pa $21.95 **150.19**
1. Psychoanalysis
ISBN 0-393-31403-0 pa

LC 89-2949

This "work includes some 50 of Freud's texts, organized chronologically with headnotes. The selections range from case studies and theoretical discussions about dreams, anxiety and anal eroticism to essays on lay analysis and religion as humankind's obsessional neurosis." Libr J
Includes bibliographical references

★ The **basic** writings of Sigmund Freud; translated and edited by A.A. Brill. Modern Lib. 1995 973p $24.95 **150.19**
1. Dreams 2. Psychoanalysis
ISBN 0-679-60166-X

LC 95-13411

Fromm, Erich
★ **On** being human; foreword by Rainer Funk. Continuum 1994 180p hardcover o.p. pa $29.95 **150.19**
1. Humanism 2. Psychoanalysis 3. Social psychology
ISBN 0-8264-0576-2; 0-8264-1005-7 pa

LC 93-9243

This volume includes the author's writings on humanism, social psychology, and psychoanalysis from the 1960s, based on Fromm's lectures, works written for specific occasions, and manuscripts intended as books.

Gay, Peter
★ A **Godless** Jew; Freud, atheism, and the making of psychoanalysis. Yale Univ. Press 1987 182p hardcover o.p. pa $17 **150.19**
1. Atheism 2. Psychoanalysis 3. Psychoanalysis and religion 4. Psychoanalysts 5. Writers on medicine
ISBN 0-300-04008-3; 0-300-04608-1 pa

LC 87-8267

The author "reviews the various claims for the Jewishness of psychoanalysis and finds them to be wholly without merit. Paradoxically, he argues that Freud's position as an outsider—an atheist and Jew—enabled him to pierce the taboo topics of sexuality and the unconscious which led to his momentous discoveries." Publ Wkly
Includes bibliographical references

Hayman, Ronald
A **life** of Jung. Norton 2001 xxi, 522p il hardcover o.p. pa $18.95 **150.19**
1. Jungian psycholgy -- History 2. Psychiatrists 3. Psychoanalysis -- History 4. Psychoanalysts -- Switzerland -- Biography 5. Psychologists 6. Writers on medicine
ISBN 0-393-32322-6 pa

LC 00-54802

"One of the many strengths of this candid and discerning biography is that Hayman enlists . . . provocative, alarming material to build a careful, nuanced portrait of his subject that neither excuses nor excoriates his actions and words." Publ Wkly
Includes bibliographical references

Jung, C. G.
★ **Man** and his symbols; {by} Carl G. Jung {et al.} Doubleday 1964 320p il $30; pa $7.99 **150.19**
1. Art -- Psychology 2. Dreams 3. Psychology 4. Self 5. Symbolism
ISBN 0-385-05221-9; 0-440-35183-9 pa
"The basic ideas of Jungian psychology are presented in popular language in six essays by Dr. Jung and {four} of his pupils; these are correlated to dreams and symbols and are shown in their archetypal relationships to ancient myths, present-day thought and art." Libr J
Includes bibliographical references

Memories, dreams, reflections; recorded and edited by Aniela Jaffé; translated from the German

by Richard and Clara Winston. rev ed; Vintage Bks.
1989 430p pa $14 **150.19**
1. Psychiatrists 2. Psychologists 3. Writers on
medicine
ISBN 0-679-72395-1

LC 88-37040
"This volume of recollections reveals the intellectual
and spiritual development of an eminent Swiss psychologist and psychiatrist while only touching upon the outward
events of his long and productive life. . . . An important,
firsthand document for readers who wish to understand this
seminal writer and thinker." Booklist
Includes bibliographical references

★ The **basic** writings of C. G. Jung; edited with
an introduction by Violet Staub de Laszlo. Modern
Lib. 1993 xxxiii, 691p $21.95 **150.19**
1. Psychoanalysis
ISBN 0-679-60071-X

LC 93-17801
This volume contains excerpts from Symbols of transformation, On the nature of the psyche, Relations between
the ego and the unconscious, Psychological types, Psychology of the transference, and Psychology and religion. It also
includes Archetypes of the collective unconscious, Psychological aspects of the mother archetype, On the nature of
dreams, On the psychogenesis of schizophrenia, Introduction to the religious and psychological problems of alchemy,
and Marriage as a psychological relationship.

The **essential** Jung; selected and introduced by
Anthony Storr. Princeton Univ. Press 1983 447p
hardcover o.p. pa $18.95 **150.19**
1. Psychoanalysis
ISBN 0-691-02935-0 pa

LC 82-61441
Storr's "selections from Jung's writings are lucid and accessible; linked by skillful explanatory passages, they provide both interested laypersons and students with a perspective on Jung." Libr J
Includes bibliographical references

The **portable** Jung; edited with an introduction
by Joseph Campbell; translated by R. F. C. Hull. Viking 1971 xli, 659p hardcover o.p. pa $17 **150.19**
1. Psychoanalysis
ISBN 0-14-015070-6 pa
A collection of writings spanning the career of
the pioneering psychoanalyst. Includes a chronology
and bibliography.

May, Rollo
★ The **discovery** of being; writings in existential psychology. Norton 1983 192p hardcover
o.p. **150.19**
1. Existentialism 2. Psychotherapy

LC 83-4282
The author "provides the reader with principles of his
existential psychotherapy; delineates his view of the cultur-
al-historical context that gave rise to both psychoanalysis

and existentialism; and sets forth what he considers to be the
contributions to therapy of an existential approach." Choice
Includes bibliographical references

Rogers, Carl R.
★ A **way** of being. Houghton Mifflin 1980
395p hardcover o.p. pa $15 **150.19**
1. Humanism 2. Psychology
ISBN 0-395-75530-1 pa

LC 80-20275
"This is a book rich in theoretical insights and experien-
tial sharing, and full of invigorating optimism." Libr J
Includes bibliographical references

Skinner, B. F.
★ **About** behaviorism. Knopf 1974 256p hardcover o.p. pa $12 **150.19**
1. Behaviorism
ISBN 0-394-71618-3 pa
The author defines, analyzes and defends the science of
behaviorism with chapters exploring the causes of behavior,
operant behavior, verbal behavior, thinking, causes and reasons, knowledge, emotion and self.

Thurschwell, Pamela
Sigmund Freud; 2nd ed.; Routledge 2009 162p
$95; pa $22.95 **150.19**
1. Psychoanalysis 2. Psychoanalysts 3. Writers on
medicine
ISBN 978-0-415-47368-2; 978-0-415-47369-9 pa
"The book contains chapters on early theories, interpretation, sexuality, case histories, maps of the mind, society
and religion, and psychoanalysis's aftermath, including feminist criticism and a remarkable summary of Jacques Lacan's
role." Booklist [review of 2000 edition]
Includes bibliographical references

150.9 History, geographic treatment, biography

Kagan, Jerome
An **argument** for mind. Yale University Press
2006 287p $27.50; pa $17 **150.9**
1. College teachers 2. Nonfiction writers 3.
Psychologists 4. Psychology -- History 5. Psychology
-- History -- 20th century
ISBN 978-0-300-11337-2; 0-300-11337-4; 978-0-300-
12603-7 pa; 0-300-12603-4 pa

LC 2005-33441
"Jerome Kagan writes elegantly, with humor . . . and with
profound intellectual depth and range." Sci Books Films
Includes bibliographical references

152.1 Sensory perception

Ackerman, Diane
A **natural** history of the senses. Random House
1990 331p hardcover o.p. pa $14.95 **152.1**
1. Senses and sensation
ISBN 0-394-57335-8; 978-0-679-73566-3 pa; 0-679-

73566-6 pa

LC 89-43416

"Ackerman celebrates the senses by examining their biological bases and the various and bizarre ways we have come to indulge them. Her catalog of the senses is itself a sensuous journey, with prose rich in imagery and rhythm. Ackerman's book is a provocative and entertaining treat whose details will bestir the reader's imagination." Libr J

Includes bibliographic references

Herz, Rachel S.

The **scent** of desire; discovering our enigmatic sense of smell. [by] Rachel Herz. William Morrow 2007 xxi, 266p $24.95; pa $13.95　　**152.1**

1. Smell

ISBN 978-0-06-082537-9; 0-06-082537-5; 978-0-06-082538-6 pa; 0-06-082538-3 pa

LC 2007-33563

"This is one of those all-too-rare books that is involving, well written, and solidly grounded in research." Libr J

Includes bibliographical references

152.14　Visual perception

Hoffman, Donald D.

Visual intelligence; how we create what we see. Norton 1998 294p il hardcover o.p. pa $17.95　　**152.14**

1. Human information processing 2. Neuropsychology 3. Perception 4. Vision 5. Visual perception

ISBN 0-393-31967-9 pa

LC 98-6181

This book offers "wit, insight and charm. . . . An outstanding example of creative popular science." Publ Wkly

Includes bibliographical references

152.4　Emotions

Ackerman, Diane

A **natural** history of love. Random House 1994 xxiii, 358p hardcover o.p. pa $14　　**152.4**

1. Love 2. Sexual behavior

ISBN 0-679-76183-7 pa

LC 94-171385

"Ackerman sets out on her exploration by reviewing the lessons provided across time by such lovers as Antony and Cleopatra, Orpheus and Eurydice, Dido and Aeneas, Abelard and Heloise and Romeo and Juliet. During this journey, she explores the neurophysiology of love. . . . With dazzling poetic charm and insight, she uses history, literature, science, psychology, and personal experience as tools to illuminate the vigor and vehemence of the thrilling, devastating, and comforting phenomenon of love." Libr J

Bloom, Paul

How pleasure works; the new science of why we like what we like. W. W. Norton 2010 280p il $26.95　　**152.4**

1. Pleasure

ISBN 978-0-393-06632-6; 0-393-06632-0

LC 2010-05803

Bloom "presents essentialism as a weighty determinant of our pleasures. . . . [He] probes the history of sentimental objects, the contact and context that give them meaning; how we hope that qualities of the things we eat will pervade us; the ways in which we are attracted to the process of making art and storytelling; and the strange case of giving and receiving pain. A heartening, well-developed argument." Kirkus

Includes bibliographical references

Clark, Taylor

Nerve; poise under pressure, serenity under stress, and the brave new science of fear and cool. Little, Brown and Company 2011 310p $25.99; ebook $12.99　　**152.4**

1. Anxiety 2. Fear

ISBN 978-0-316-04289-5; 978-0-316-12686-1 ebook

LC 2010-38835

"A compassionate psychological page-turner." Kirkus

Includes bibliographical references

Damasio, Antonio R.

Looking for Spinoza; joy, sorrow, and the feeling rain. {by} Antonio Damasio. Harcourt 2003 355p il $28; pa $15　　**152.4**

1. Authors 2. Emotions 3. Essayists 4. Philosophers 5. Writers on religion

ISBN 0-15-100557-5; 0-15-602871-9 pa

LC 2002-11347

This is a "discussion of the difference between emotions (of the body) and feelings (of the mind), various sites in the brain that trigger these states, and the . . . synthesis of the homeostatic process, memory, sensory input, imagination, and foresight that links the unconscious to consciousness and feelings to reasoning." Booklist

Includes bibliographical references

De Waal, Frans

The **age** of empathy; nature's lessons for a kinder society. with drawings by the author. Harmony Books 2009 291p il　　**152.4**

1. Animal behavior 2. Empathy

ISBN 0-307-40776-4; 978-0-307-40776-4

The author "examines what he calls the behavioral 'glue' of primate societies: empathy, sympathy, a sense of fair play, and trust. In tracing the origins and evolution of empathy, de Waal points out that our ability to take another's perspective is an automatic impulse with a long evolutionary history in the mammalian line. . . . This insightful work . . . will appeal to a wide variety of general readers interested in the links between human evolution and animal behavior."

The author "examines what he calls the behavioral 'glue' of primate societies: empathy, sympathy, a sense of fair play, and trust. In tracing the origins and evolution of empathy, de Waal points out that our ability to take another's perspective

is an automatic impulse with a long evolutionary history in the mammalian line. . . . This insightful work . . . will appeal to a wide variety of general readers interested in the links between human evolution and animal behavior." Libr J
Includes bibliographical references

Fromm, Erich
★ The **art** of loving; Centennial ed; Continuum 2000 130p $18.95   **152.4**
1. Love
ISBN 0-8264-1260-2
LC 00-21030
"An astonishingly simple presentation of an abstract subject." Booklist

Gardner, Daniel
The **science** of fear; why we fear the things we shouldn't-- and put ourselves in greater danger. Dutton 2008 339p $24.95   **152.4**
1. Fear
ISBN 978-0-525-95062-2; 0-525-95062-1
LC 2008-03024
Gardner "analyses everything from the media's predilection for irrational scare stories to the cynical use of fear by politicians pushing a particular agenda. . . . [He] never falls into the trap of becoming frustrated and embittered by the waste and needless worry that he is documenting. A personal anecdote about an unwise foray into a Nigerian slum in search of a stolen wallet disposes of the idea that the author is immune to the foibles he describes. What could easily have been a catalogue of misgovernance and stupidity instead becomes a cheery corrective to modern paranoia." Economist
Includes bibliographical references

Gilligan, Carol
★ The **birth** of pleasure. Knopf 2002 253p $24; pa $13   **152.4**
1. Interpersonal relations 2. Intimacy (Psychology) 3. Love 4. Man-woman relationships
ISBN 0-679-44037-2; 0-679-75943-3 pa
LC 2001-50329
Gilligan's "mastery of literary sources and her intelligent but nonacademic writing style make this an enjoyable, challenging work." Publ Wkly
Includes bibliographical references

Goleman, Daniel
★ **Emotional** intelligence; 10th anniversary ed.; Bantam Books 2006 xxiv, 358p il $29; pa $18   **152.4**
1. Education -- Curricula 2. Emotionally disturbed children 3. Emotions 4. Industrial relations 5. Intellect 6. Marriage 7. Medicine 8. Parenting 9. Temperament
ISBN 978-0-553-80491-1; 0-553-80491-X; 978-0-553-38371-3 pa; 0-553-38371-X pa
LC 2006-283929
The author explains "how to develop our emotional intelligence in ways that can improve our relationships, our parenting, our classrooms, and our workplaces. Goleman as-

sures us that our temperaments may be determined by neurochemistry, but they can be altered." Booklist
Includes bibliographical references

Jamison, Kay R.
Exuberance; the passion for life. by Kay Redfield Jamison. Knopf 2004 405p il $24.95   **152.4**
1. Happiness 2. Joy
ISBN 0-375-40144-X
LC 2004-46561
The author "examines the contagious nature of exuberance, which she defines as 'a psychological state characterized by high mood and high energy,' offering diverse examples that range from John Muir and FDR to Mary Poppins and Peter Pan. Having in mind the simply put idea that 'those who are exuberant act,' the author details the energetic efforts of scientists, naturalists, politicians and even her meteorologist father." Publ Wkly
Includes bibliographical references

Jeffers, Susan J.
Feel the fear--and do it anyway; [by] Susan Jeffers. Ballantine Books 2007 214p il pa $13.95 **152.4**
1. Fear
ISBN 978-0-345-48742-1
LC 2007-271292
"By mixing positive thinking with situational exercises that examine basic fear responses, psychologist Jeffers shows that fear is what you make of it and that in most cases it is unfounded." Libr J
Includes bibliographical references

Lerner, Harriet Goldhor
★ The **dance** of anger; a woman's guide to changing the patterns of intimate relationships. [by] Harriet Lerner. Perennial Currents 2005 239p il pa $13.95   **152.4**
1. Anger 2. Women -- Psychology
ISBN 0-06-074104-X
LC 2004-60074
The author examines the ways women express anger, as well as how women's anger is viewed by society and throughout history.

Levy, Alexander
The **orphaned** adult; understanding and coping with grief and change after the death of our parents. Perseus Bks. 1999 190p hardcover o.p. pa $15.95   **152.4**
1. Bereavement 2. Bereavement -- Psychological aspects 3. Death 4. Loss (Psychology) 5. Parents -- Death
ISBN 0-7382-0361-0 pa
LC 99-64773
"Incorporating his own personal experience with the accounts of others who have lost their parents, psychologist Levy examines this profound life-changing event with compassion and understanding." Libr J

Lewis, Thomas

★ A **general** theory of love; [by] Thomas Lewis, Fari Amini, Richard Lannon. Random House 2000 274p il hardcover o.p. pa $13   **152.4**
1. Love 2. Love -- Physiological aspects
ISBN 0-375-70922-3 pa
                LC 99-49930
The authors "aim to help physicians treat patients by showing how the many and varied aspects of love, including the lack and the warping of it, affect patients' problems and strengths and by discussing what must, therefore, be involved in treating patients." Booklist
Includes bibliographical references

Nettle, Daniel

Happiness; the science behind your smile. Oxford University Press 2005 216p il $21; pa $13.95   **152.4**
1. Happiness
ISBN 0-19-280558-4; 978-0-19-280558-4; 0-19-280559-2 pa; 978-0-19-280559-1 pa
                LC 2004-30585
"With absolute clarity and admirable brevity, Nettle explores the pursuit of happiness and, happily, makes good sense of it all." Publ Wkly
Includes bibliographical references

Orloff, Judith

Emotional freedom; liberate yourself from negative emotions and transform your life. Harmony Books 2009 401p $24.95   **152.4**
1. Emotions 2. Self-realization
ISBN 978-0-307-33818-1
                LC 2008-21482
"In Part 1, Orloff presents four components of emotion—biology, energy, spirituality, and psychology—and provides a 20-question assessment to highlight individuals' strengths and weaknesses. . . . Orloff divides Part 2 into seven chapters, each devoted to a difficult negative emotion. Throughout, Orloff details how one can use the four components of emotion to transform negative emotions into positive ones and become a more centered and emotionally healthy person. . . . This well-written book is full of good advice for anyone who wants to take more control of his or her emotional life." Libr J

Tavris, Carol

Anger; the misunderstood emotion. rev ed; Simon & Schuster 1989 383p pa $14   **152.4**
1. Anger
ISBN 0-671-67523-0
                LC 89-33129
The author contends that anger is a complex, socially learned response that is not necessarily cathartic.

153   Conscious mental processes and intelligence

Baars, Bernard J.

In the theater of consciousness; the workspace of the mind. Oxford Univ. Press 1997 193p il $35; pa $14.95   **153**
1. Consciousness 2. Intellect 3. Theory of knowledge
ISBN 0-19-510265-7; 0-19-514703-0 pa
                LC 96-10379
The author "does a masterful job of explicating the issues and distinctions related to consciousness providing representative charts, graphs, and figures to relate both theory and data. . . . A most accessible and up-to-date introduction to current ideas about consciousness, and a valuable work for general readers." Choice
Includes bibliographical references

Carter, Rita

★ **Exploring** consciousness. University of Calif. Press 2002 320p il $34.95   **153**
1. Consciousness
ISBN 0-520-23737-4
                LC 2002-25900
This work explores the nature, origins, and purpose of consciousness from philosophical, scientific, and experiential perspectives.
"A treasure trove of fact, argument and opinion, doing an excellent job of conveying both research and controversies. The general reader will find it filled with stimulating material." New Sci
Includes bibliographical references

Damasio, Antonio R.

The **feeling** of what happens; body and emotion in the making of consciousness. Harcourt Brace & Co. 1999 386p il $28; pa $15   **153**
1. Consciousness 2. Consciousness -- Physiological aspects 3. Emotions 4. Emotions -- Physiological aspects
ISBN 0-15-100369-6; 0-15-601075-5 pa
                LC 99-26357
The author contends "that consciousness arises from our ability to map relations between the self and others through our emotions. This bold attempt to mend the classical breach between emotion and reason is all the more compelling for its poetic expression." Publ Wkly
Includes bibliographical references

Eagleman, David

Incognito; the brains behind the mind. Pantheon 2011 290p il $26.95   **153**
1. Brain 2. Subconsciousness
ISBN 978-0-307-37733-3
                LC 2010053184
"Eagleman's main theme is that what one calls 'me,' the conscious mind, is only the tip of the iceberg, and that most of the interesting and important things the brain does are inaccessible to the brain's 'owner.' . . . What Eagleman does is explain the idea to the neophyte through discussion of dozens of fascinating, engaging examples. . . . Eagleman's prose is vivid and, more important, accessible." Choice
Includes bibliographical references

Edelman, Shimon

★ The **happiness** of pursuit; what neuroscience can teach us about the good life. Shimon Edelman. Basic Books 2012 x, 237 p.p **153**

1. Cognition 2. Ego 3. Emotions (Psychology) & cognition 4. Happiness 5. Mind-Body Relations, Metaphysical 6. Nonfiction 7. Self 8. Thinking 9. Thought and thinking
ISBN 0465022243; 9780465022243
LC 2011039326

This book by psychologist Shimon Edelman offers a fundamental understanding of pleasure and joy via the brain. Using the concept of the mind as a computing device, he unpacks how the human brain is highly active, involved in patterned networks, and constantly learning from experience. As our brains predict the future through pursuit of experience, we are rewarded both in real time and in the long run. Essentially, as Edelman discovers, it's the journey, rather than the destination, that matters. Edelman makes the case for these claims by constructing a conceptual toolbox that offers readers a glimpse of the computations underlying the mind's faculties: perception, motivation and emotions, action, memory, thinking, social cognition, learning and language. (Publishers note)

Hallinan, Joseph T.

Why we make mistakes; how we look without seeing, forget things in seconds, and are all pretty sure we are way above average. Broadway Books 2009 283p $24.95 **153**

1. Errors 2. Failure (Psychology)
ISBN 978-0-7679-2805-2; 0-7679-2805-9
LC 2008-30818

"Hallinan examines 13 pitfalls that make us vulnerable to mistakes: 'we look but don't always see,' 'we like things tidy' and 'we don't constrain ourselves' among them. Each chapter takes on a different drawback, packing in an impressive range of intriguing and practical real-world examples. . . He also looks at the serious consequences of multitasking and data overload on what is at best a two or three-track mind." Publ Wkly
Includes bibliographical references

Hofstadter, Douglas R.

I am a strange loop. Basic Books 2007 412p il 26.95 **153**

1. College teachers 2. Computer scientists 3. Consciousness 4. Intellect 5. Self 6. Self (Philosophy) 7. Soul 8. Writers on science
ISBN 978-0-465-03078-1; 0-465-03078-5

The author's model of self is neither "spiritual—he's not a religious man—nor is it locked into the cold neurological materialism of cellular mechanics. . . . [The book] scales some lofty conceptual heights, but it remains very personal, and it's deeply colored by the facts of Hofstadter's later life." Time
bibliography: p. 377-82

Kandel, Eric R.

★ **In** search of memory; the emergence of a new science of mind. W. W. Norton & Company 2006 510p il $29.95 **153**

1. College teachers 2. Memory 3. Nervous system 4. Neurosciences 5. Neuroscientists 6. Nobel laureates for physiology or medicine
ISBN 0-393-05863-8; 978-0-393-05863-5
LC 2005-28565

The author "recounts his own revolutionary research in establishing the molecular chemistry of short-term memory and the cellular dynamics of long-term memory, highlighting particularly the potential of his findings for the treatment of Alzheimer's and other mental disorders. But even as he outlines the biomechanics of memory, Kandel shares his personal reminiscences of the years during which he unraveled those mysteries. . . . An autobiography of exceptional substance." Booklist
Includes bibliographical references

Karpf, Anne

The **human** voice; how this extraordinary instrument reveals essential clues about who we are. Bloomsbury 2006 399p $24.95 **153**

1. Elocution 2. Voice
ISBN 1-58234-299-7; 978-1-58234-299-3
LC 2006-9698

This "book is packed with information . . . backed up by prolific references to relevant research." Times Lit Suppl
Includes bibliographical references

Pinker, Steven

★ **How** the mind works. Norton 1997 660p il hardcover o.p. pa $18.95 **153**

1. Brain 2. Emotions 3. Evolution 4. Intellect 5. Natural selection 6. Psychology 7. Reasoning
ISBN 978-0-393-33477-7 pa
LC 97-1855

Pinker "has a gift for making enormously complicated mechanisms—and human foibles—accessible." Publ Wkly
Includes bibliographical references

Sagan, Carl

The **dragons** of Eden; speculations on the evolution of human intelligence. Random House 1977 263p il hardcover o.p. pa $7.50 **153**

1. Brain 2. Genetics 3. Intellect
ISBN 0-345-34629-7 pa
LC 76-53472

In this study of human intellect "Sagan is principally preoccupied with the neocortex, with its left hemisphere, responsible for language and logic, a right hemisphere in charge of intuition and spatial dimension, and a corpus callosum that mediates and synthesizes the two." Atl Mon
Includes bibliographical references

Schulz, Kathryn

Being wrong; adventures in the margin of error. Ecco 2010 405p il $26.99; pa $20.99 **153**

1. Decision making 2. Error 3. Errors 4. Errors --

Psychological aspects 5. Expertise 6. Fallibility
ISBN 978-0-06-117604-3; 0-06-117604-4; 978-0-06-199793-8 pa; 0-06-199793-5 pa

The author discusses "how we make mistakes, how we behave when we find we have been wrong, and how our errors change us. . . . Schulz writes with such lucidity and wit that her philosophical enquiry becomes a page-turner." Publ Wkly

Includes bibliographical references

153.1　Memory and learning

Foer, Joshua

Moonwalking with Einstein; the art and science of remembering everything. Penguin Press 2011 307p $26.95　　　　　**153.1**
1. Memory 2. Memory disorders -- Treatment
ISBN 978-1-59420-229-2

LC 2010-30265

"Mr. Foer writes in these pages with fresh enthusiasm. His narrative is smart and funny and . . . it's informed by a humanism that enables its author to place the mysteries of the brain within a larger philosophical and cultural context." N Y Times (Late N Y Ed)

Includes bibliographical references

Goldman, Bob

Brain fitness; anti-aging strategies for achieving super mind power. {by} Robert M. Goldman with Ronald Klatz and Lisa Berger. Doubleday 1999 333p il hardcover o.p. pa $14.95　　　　**153.1**
1. Aging 2. Aging -- Prevention 3. Cognition -- Age factors 4. Memory 5. Memory -- Age factors 6. Sleep 7. Sleep -- Age factors 8. Stress (Physiology) 9. Stress management
ISBN 0-385-48869-6 pa

LC 98-18785

This is an "exploration of techniques—mental workouts, memory training, physical exercises, and nutrition and dietary supplements—that readers can use to maximize their concentration, memory, imagination, energy, intelligence, and creativity while decreasing fatigue and stress and preventing Alzheimer's disease and other brain diseases." Libr J

Includes bibliographical references

Schacter, Daniel L.

Searching for memory; the brain, the mind, and the past. Basic Bks. 1996 398p il hardcover o.p. pa $17.50　　　　　**153.1**
1. Brain 2. False memory syndrome 3. Memory
ISBN 0-465-07552-5 pa

LC 96-19521

"This is an excellent book on an important topic: it is exceptionally well written; its examples of defects in memory are fascinating, as are the theories based on them; and its arguments are illustrated with opposite pictures, reproduced

from works by many modern artists, and passages from novels." N Y Times Book Rev

Includes bibliographical references

The **seven** sins of memory; how the mind forgets and remembers. Houghton Mifflin 2001 272p il hardcover o.p.　　　　　**153.1**
1. Memory 2. Memory disorders 3. Recollection (Psychology)
ISBN 0-618-04019-6; 0-618-21919-6 pa

LC 00-53885

Schacter discusses "the 'different ways in which memory can get us into trouble.' . . . We forget things over time (transience). We often forget where we put our house keys because we were preoccupied with something else (absent-mindedness). We can't remember someone's name (blocking). We mistake an idealized version of our past for a real recollection (misattribution) or claim an 'implanted' memory as our own when it has been suggested by someone else (suggestibility). Our memories are often . . . influenced by our current beliefs (bias). In some cases, we obsessively remember traumatic or painful events that we'd much rather forget (persistence)." (N Y Times Book Rev) Index.

The author discusses "the curious processes of memory by classifying its malfunctions into seven categories: transience, absent-mindedness, blocking, misattribution, suggestibility, bias, and persistence. Schacter illustrates each of these 'sins' with examples of routine misfortunes common to all." Libr J

Includes bibliographical references

153.3　Imagination, imagery, creativity

Csikszentmihalyi, Mihaly

Creativity; flow and the psychology of discovery and invention. HarperCollins Pubs. 1996 456p hardcover o.p. pa $15　　　　　**153.3**
1. Creative ability 2. Creative thinking
ISBN 0-06-092820-4 pa

LC 96-4116

"Utilizing the interviews garnered from 91 respondents (ranging from philosopher Mortimer Adler to biologist Edward O. Wilson to politician Eugene McCarthy), the author . . . demonstrates the processes that these acknowledged creative thinkers and doers go through and the characteristics that make them stand out. . . . Csikszentmihalyi also deals with creativity and aging and ways to enhance one's own personal creativity." Libr J

Includes bibliographical references

Gardner, Howard

Creating minds; an anatomy of creativity seen through the lives of Freud, Einstein, Picasso, Stravinsky, Eliot, Graham, and Gandhi. Basic Bks. 1993 464p il hardcover o.p. pa $22.50　　　　**153.3**
1. Artists 2. Authors 3. Biography, Collective 4. Choreographers 5. Composers 6. Creative ability 7. Dance teachers 8. Dancers 9. Dramatists 10. Editors 11. Essayists 12. Journalists 13. Literary critics 14. Memoirists 15. Nobel laureates for literature 16. Nobel laureates for physics 17. Pacifists 18. Painters

19. Physicists 20. Poets 21. Political leaders 22. Psychoanalysts 23. Writers on medicine 24. Writers on politics
ISBN 0-465-01455-0; 0-465-01454-2 pa
LC 92-56172

In seven "case studies, Gardner focuses on highly creative figures who lived in the same era but who exemplify different human intelligences. He postulates that each of their major innovations involved an intersection of the maturity and confidence of a master with the sensibilities and impulsiveness of a child. This scholarly and insightful study is highly recommended." Libr J
Includes bibliographical references

Gawain, Shakti
★ **Creative** visualization; use the power of your imagination to create what you want in your life. 30th anniversary ed.; Nataraj Pub./New World Library 2008 175p $25; pa $12.95 **153.3**
1. Imagination 2. Self-realization
ISBN 978-1-577-31636-7; 1-577-31636-3; 978-1-577-31229-1 pa; 1-577-31229-5 pa
LC 2008-14400

"The author asserts that people can achieve an ideal existence simply through mental visualization." Libr J
Includes bibliographical references

May, Rollo
★ The **courage** to create. Norton 1975 143p hardcover o.p. pa $11.95 **153.3**
1. Consciousness 2. Courage 3. Creative ability
ISBN 0-393-31106-6 pa
The author argues that creativity is an act of encounter and draws on examples from literature, art, and psychoanalysis.

153.35

Bissell, Tom
Magic hours; essays on creators and creation. Tom Bissell. Believer Books 2012 301 p. **153.35**
ISBN 1936365766; 9781936365760

In this book of essays, award-winning essayist Tom Bissell explores the highs and lows of the creative process. He takes us from the set of The Big Bang Theory to the first novel of Ernest Hemingway to the final work of David Foster Wallace; from the films of Werner Herzog to the film of Tommy Wiseau to the editorial meeting in which Paula Fox's work was relaunched into the world. Originally published in magazines such as The Believer, The New Yorker, and Harper's, these essays represent ten years of Bissell's . . . writing on every aspect of creation--be it Iraq War documentaries or video-game character voices. . . . What are sitcoms for exactly? Can art be both bad and genius? Why do some books survive and others vanish? (Publishers note)

153.4 Thought, thinking, reasoning, intuition, value, judgment

Gladwell, Malcolm
Blink: the power of thinking without thinking. Little, Brown and Co 2005 277p il $25.95 **153.4**
1. Decision making 2. Intuition
ISBN 0-316-17232-4
LC 2004-13916

Gladwell "has a dazzling ability to find commonality in disparate fields of study. . . . Each case study is satisfying, and Gladwell imparts his own evident pleasure in delving into a wide range of fields and seeking an underlying truth." Publ Wkly
Includes bibliographical references

Herbert, Wray
On second thought; outsmarting your mind's hard-wired habits. Crown Publishers 2010 289p $25 **153.4**
1. Thought and thinking
ISBN 0-307-46163-7; 978-0-307-46163-6
LC 2010-03073

"The brain is like a dual processor, [Herbert] argues—one part is logical, deliberate, and cautious, while the other is much older and primitive. The latter is the heuristic brain—fast, impressionistic, and sometimes irrational. After years of evolution, the brain has become hardwired with mental shortcuts that help us quickly navigate our daily lives. However, they can also distort our thinking and lead to poor decision making. . . . Heuristics are neither good nor bad—the trick, Herbert says, is in recognizing when to question an instant response." Libr J

Kahneman, Daniel, 1934-
Thinking, fast and slow; Daniel Kahneman. Farrar, Straus and Giroux 2011 499p. ill. **153.4**
1. Decision making 2. Intuition 3. Reasoning 4. Thought and thinking
ISBN 0374275637; 9780374275631
LC 2011027143

In this book, the author "challenges the idea that people are generally rational and demonstrates that emotions such as fear and love explain many of the departures from rationality. He also makes the . . . point that luck plays a much larger role in our successes and failures than we are inclined to believe." (Science). "A large part of [the] book is devoted to stories illustrating the various illusions to which supposedly rational people succumb. Each story describes an experiment, examining the behavior of students or citizens who are confronted with choices under controlled conditions. The subjects make decisions that can be precisely measured and recorded. . . . The stories demonstrate how far our behavior differs from the behavior of the mythical 'rational actor' who obeys the rules of classical economics." (New York Review of Books)

Shermer, Michael
The **believing** brain; from ghosts and gods to politics and conspiracies--how we construct beliefs

and reinforce them as truths. Times Books 2011 385p il $28   **153.4**

1. Belief and doubt 2. Cognitive neuroscience 3. Knowledge, Theory of 4. Theory of knowledge
ISBN 9780805091250; 0805091254

LC 2010-30706

This book discusses the science of the human brain in relation to belief formation. "[T]he book is clearly less about the examples than about the theory Shermer uses to explain them all. . . . Shermer's theory looks like this: The human mind is inherently a 'belief engine'; we perceive endless bits of information, and we must posit beliefs as ways of organizing and making sense of them. . . . Having found a possible explanation, we then seek confirming evidence and deepenings of the patterns and agents we believe we have discerned. The result, Shermer claims, is that we live much of the time in 'belief-dependent realism,' which is to say that our beliefs are shaping what we see in the world, rather than the world shaping our beliefs. . . . Shermer also believes in a dividing line between benign or helpful beliefs and malignant ones (like religion)." (Commonweal)

"A timely, reasoned reflection on the nature of belief, offering a levelheaded corrective to the divisiveness of extreme partisanship." Kirkus

Includes bibliographical references and index.

Watts, Duncan J.
Everything is obvious; once you know the answer. Crown Business 2011 335p il $26   **153.4**

1. Common sense 2. Reasoning 3. Thought and thinking
ISBN 978-0-385-53168-9; 0-385-53168-0

LC 2010031550

This book argues that "common sense can be an unreliable guide to the social world." (N Y Times Book Rev) Bibliography. Index.

The author posits "that common sense is a shockingly unreliable guide to truth and yet we rely on it virtually to the exclusion of other methods of reasoning. Mr. Watts, a former sociology professor and physicist who is now a researcher for Yahoo, has written a fascinating book that ranges through psychology, economics, marketing and the science of social networks. He is especially interested in the mistakes we make when we reason about how people influence one another—such as our tendency to think of groups in terms of representative or important members rather than as whole entities. . . . The enterprise of prediction-making is another casualty of the limits of common sense. Mr. Watts suggests that the entire field of business strategy suffers from a delusion that the future can be forecast with enough numerical precision to enable accurate planning. One solution he endorses is a systematic process of imagining detailed alternative narratives of the future." Wall Street J

Includes bibliographical references

153.6   Communication

Pease, Allan
The **definitive** book of body language; [by] Allan & Barbara Pease. Bantam Books 2006 386p il $23   **153.6**

1. Body language 2. Nonverbal communication
ISBN 0-553-80472-3; 978-0-553-80472-0

LC 2006-42657

"The book is amply and wittily illustrated with celebrity photographs. . . . This is a fascinating book." N Y Times Book Rev

Includes bibliographical references

153.7   Perceptual processes

Chabris, Christopher
The **invisible** gorilla; and other ways our intuitions deceive us. [by] Christopher Chabris and Daniel Simons. Crown 2010 306p $27; pa $14 **153.7**

1. Memory 2. Perception 3. Thought and thinking
ISBN 978-0-307-45965-7; 0-307-45965-9; 978-0-307-45966-4 pa; 0-307-45966-7 pa

LC 2009-45325

The authors "won a 2004 Ig Nobel Prize for their widely reported 'gorilla experiment,' which showed that when people focus on one thing, it's easy to overlook other things—even a woman in a gorilla suit. . . . [In this book,] they explore this habit of 'inattentional blindness' and other common ways in which we distort our perception of reality. Their readable book offers surprising insights into just how clueless we are about how our minds work and how we experience the world." Kirkus

Includes bibliographical references

Ellard, Colin
★ **You** are here; why we can find our way to the moon but get lost in the mall. Doubleday 2009 328p il map $25   **153.7**

1. Animal orientation 2. Direction sense 3. Orientation (Physiology) 4. Orientation (Psychology) 5. Space perception
ISBN 978-0-385-52806-1; 0-385-52806-X

LC 2009-07822

Ellard argues that in the modern age the human sense of navigation and direction has diminished greatly.

"If you're looking for an eye-opening, if somewhat embarrassing, book to help understand why you keep getting lost when you know you shouldn't and what you can do about it well, here you are." Booklist

Includes bibliographical references

Greenspan, Stanley I.
The **first** idea; how symbols, language, and intelligence evolved from our early primate ancestors to modern humans. [by] Stanley I. Greenspan, Stuart G.

Shanker. 1st Da Capo Press ed; Da Capo Press 2004 504p $25 **153.7**
    1. Evolution 2. Theory of knowledge
    ISBN 0-7382-0680-6
                                  LC 2004-10658
"This book should appeal most to readers working in psychology and child development, but its revolutionary ideas no doubt will lead to lively and well-publicized debates." Publ Wkly
Includes bibliographical references

Klein, Stefan
    The **secret** pulse of time; making sense of life's scarcest commodity. translated by Shelley Frisch. Marlowe & Co. 2007 xxi, 343p il $25 **153.7**
    1. Perception 2. Time 3. Time management
    ISBN 978-1-6009-4017-0; 1-6009-4017-X
"Sure to give readers fresh perspective on their everyday lives, Klein's concepts are well illustrated in copious examples from literature and popular culture, and Frisch's fluid, flawless translation makes his text as captivating as it is enlightening." Publ Wkly
Includes bibliographical references

Zimbardo, Philip G.
    The **time** paradox; the new psychology of time that will change your life. [by] Philip Zimbardo and John Boyd. Free Press 2008 358p il $27 **153.7**
    1. Time perception
    ISBN 978-1-4165-4198-1; 1-4165-4198-5
                                  LC 2008-2149
This is an "investigation of how attitudes toward time affect every aspect of human life. The authors help readers determine their personal time zone before revealing how to 'reclaim yesterday, enjoy today, and master tomorrow.' Balance never seemed so attainable." Libr J
Includes bibliographical references

153.8   Will (Volition)

Akst, Daniel
    We have met the enemy; self-control in an age of excess. Penguin Press 2011 303p $26.95 **153.8**
    1. Consumption (Economics) 2. Quality of life -- Social aspects 3. Quality of life -- United States 4. Self-control 5. Self-control -- Social aspects 6. Supply and demand
    ISBN 978-1-59420-281-0
                                  LC 2010-28525
"Akst combines the disciplines of history, philosophy, psychology, economics, and literature in examining this phenomenon and inspires readers to view self-control in a positive light. Essential for all people concerned with their own overindulgences and with the future of society in general." Libr J
Includes bibliographical references

Cialdini, Robert B.
    ★ **Influence**: the psychology of persuasion; Rev. ed.; 1st Collins business essentials ed; Collins 2007 320p il pa $17.95 **153.8**
    1. Persuasion (Psychology)
    ISBN 0-06-124189-X; 978-0-06-124189-5
The author "explains the psychology of why people say 'yes'—and how to apply these understandings." Publisher's note
Includes bibliographical references

Dennett, Daniel Clement
    Freedom evolves; {by} Daniel C. Dennett. Viking 2003 347p il $24.95; pa $17 **153.8**
    1. Decision making 2. Free will and determinism
    ISBN 0-670-03186-0; 0-14-200384-0 pa
                                  LC 2002-28085
"Drawing on evolutionary biology, neuroscience, economic game theory, philosophy and Richard Dawkins's meme, the author argues that there is indeed such a thing as free will, but it 'is not a preexisting feature of our existence, like the law of gravity.' . . . This book comprises a kind of toolbox of intellectual exercises favoring cultural evolution, the idea that culture, morality and freedom are as much a result of evolution by natural selection as our physical and genetic attributes. Yet genetic determinism, he argues, does not imply inevitability, as his critics may claim, nor does it cancel out the soul. . . . Dennett clearly relishes pushing other scientists' buttons. Though natural selection itself is still a subject of controversy, the author . . . most certainly is in the vanguard of the philosophy of science." Publ Wkly
Includes bibliographical references

Dutton, Kevin
    Split-second persuasion; the ancient art and new science of changing minds. Houghton Mifflin Harcourt 2011 296p il $26 **153.8**
    1. Persuasion (Psychology)
    ISBN 978-0-15-101279-4
                                  LC 2010-5739
"This is a well-researched, wide-ranging treatise on the psychology of persuasion. The first section reviews research from an impressive variety of disciplines, from neuroscience to the biological and social sciences. The second section focuses on the author's main theme—split-second persuasion—a powerful 'superstrain' of persuasion that occurs quickly. Written for a less-experienced audience, the book is clear and nontechnical." Choice
Includes bibliographical references

Iyengar, Sheena
    The **art** of choosing. Twelve 2010 329p il $25.99 **153.8**
    1. Choice (Psychology) 2. Decision making
    ISBN 978-0-446-50410-2; 0-446-50410-6
                                  LC 2009-37664
"In 'The Art of Choosing,' a broad and fascinating survey of current research on the subject, Iyengar stitches together personal anecdotes, examples from popular culture, and scientific evidence to explain the complex calculus that goes into our everyday choices, from picking our favorite soda to choosing our medical insurance. She also writes

about the ways in which her blindness — Iyengar lost her sight as a teenager — has given her a unique perspective on the subject." Salon

Lehrer, Jonah

How we decide. Houghton Mifflin Harcourt 2009 302p $25   **153.8**
1. Decision making
ISBN 978-0-618-62011-1; 0-618-62011-7
LC 2008036769
"Lehrer is a delight to read, and this is a fascinating book . . . that will help everyone better understand themselves and their decision making." Publ Wkly
Includes bibliographical references

Levine, Robert

The **power** of persuasion; how we're bought and sold. Wiley 2003 278p hardcover o.p. pa $14.95   **153.8**
1. Interpersonal relations 2. Persuasion (Psychology)
ISBN 0-471-26634-5; 0-471-76317-9 pa
LC 2002-9952
The author "opens by demonstrating that all of us . . . can be persuaded under the right circumstances. He goes on to study financial manipulation and the use of the sense of obligation . . . and then proceeds to a nuts-and-bolts analysis of salesmanship by describing what he learned and did (and had done to him) as an automobile salesman. . . . Inevitably, he moves to cults, the Moonies and the ultimate persuasion horror story, Jonestown." Publ Wkly
Includes bibliographical references

Partnoy, Frank

Wait; the art and science of delay. Frank Partnoy. PublicAffairs 2012 xii, 290 p.p   **153.8**
1. Decision making 2. Procrastination
ISBN 1610390040; 9781610390040; 9781610390057
LC 2012010970
In this book, author Frank Partnoy weaves together findings from hundreds of scientific studies and interviews with wide-ranging experts to craft a picture of effective decision-making that runs counter to our . . . fast-paced world. Even as technology exerts new pressures to speed up our lives, it turns out that the choices we make--unconsciously and consciously, in time frames varying from milliseconds to years--benefit profoundly from delay. As this . . . book reveals, taking control of time and slowing down our responses yields better results in almost every arena of life--even when time seems to be of the essence. (Publishers note)

153.9   Intelligence and aptitudes

Beilock, Sian L.

Choke; what the secrets of the brain reveal about getting it right when you have to. Free Press 2010 294p il $26; ebook $12.99   **153.9**
1. Failure (Psychology) 2. Success
ISBN 978-1-4165-9617-2; 978-1-4391-0962-5 ebook
LC 2010-10595
"A star golfer misses a critical putt; a brilliant student fails to ace a test; a savvy salesperson blows a key presenta-

tion. Each of these people has suffered the same bump in mental processing: They have just choked under pressure. . . . By studying how the brain works when we are doing our best — and when we choke — Beilock has formulated practical ideas about how to overcome performance lapses at critical moments." Science Daily

Bloom, Harold

Genius; a mosaic of one hundred exemplary creative minds. Warner Bks. 2002 814p il $35.95; pa $19.95   **153.9**
1. Authors 2. Genius 3. Gifted persons 4. Literature -- History and criticism
ISBN 0-446-52717-3; 0-446-69129-1 pa
LC 2002-16808
"Although the book is a delight to read, its real value lies in the author's ability to provoke the reader into thinking about literature, genius, and related topics. No similar work discusses literary genius in this way or covers this many writers." Libr J
Includes bibliographical references

Calvin, William H.

How brains think; evolving intelligence, then and now. Basic Bks. 1996 184p il hardcover o.p. pa $14   **153.9**
1. Brain 2. Comparative psychology 3. Intellect 4. Thought and thinking
ISBN 0-465-07278-X pa
LC 96-21086
Calvin's book "offers an exquisite distillation of his key ideas. He's a member of that rare breed of scientists who can translate the arcana of their fields into lay language, and he's one of the best." N Y Times Book Rev
Includes bibliographical references

Gould, Stephen Jay

★ The **mismeasure** of man; rev & expanded ed; Norton 1996 444p il hardcover o.p. pa $15.95   **153.9**
1. Ability -- Testing 2. Intelligence tests
ISBN 0-393-31425-1 pa
LC 95-44442
The author examines the history of various scientific methods used to measure intelligence. He demonstrates how the research was used to perpetuate the myth of the intellectual superiority of the white male

Kurzweil, Ray, 1948-

★ The **singularity** is near; when humans transcend biology. [by] Ray Kurzweil. Viking 2005 652p il $29.95; pa $18   **153.9**
1. Evolution 2. Genetics 3. Nanotechnology 4. Robots
ISBN 0-670-03384-7; 0-14-303788-9 pa
LC 2004-61231
The book provides an "argument that a sudden acceleration in the growth of knowledge is about to make immortality technologically feasible. . . . A part of the argument concerns the transformation the human body will undergo as a result of the explosive increase of knowledge he believes is imminent.

Nanotechnology will enable the design of nanobots . . . that will 'have myriad roles within the human body, including reversing human aging (to the extent that this task will not already have been completed through biotechnology, such as genetic engineering).' . . . But this will still not be immortality, and perfecting the human body is a phase in a much larger transformation. . . . 'Ultimately, the entire universe will become saturated with our intelligence.'" (New York Review of Books)

"Anyone can grasp Mr. Kurzweil's main idea: that mankind's technological knowledge has been snowballing, with dizzying prospects for the future. The basics are clearly expressed. But for those more knowledgeable and inquisitive, the author argues his case in fascinating detail." N Y Times (Late N Y Ed)

Includes bibliographical references

Murdoch, Stephen

IQ; a smart history of a failed idea. J. Wiley and Sons 2007 269p $24.95   **153.9**

    1. Intelligence tests
    ISBN 978-0-471-69977-4; 0-471-69977-2

                     LC 2006-32488

The author "traces now ubiquitous but still controversial attempts to measure intelligence to its origins in the late 19th and early 20th centuries. . . . This is a thoughtful overview and a welcome reminder of the dangers of relying on such standardized tests." Publ Wkly

Includes bibliographical references

Stanovich, Keith E.

What intelligence tests miss; the psychology of rational thought. Yale University Press 2009 308p il $30   **153.9**

    1. Intelligence tests 2. Thought and thinking
    ISBN 978-0-300-12385-2; 0-300-12385-X

                     LC 2008-37325

Stanovich "argues that IQ tests measure cognitive efficiency but not the degree to which subjects make rational decisions. He explains that individuals with high IQs are as likely as others to go for quick, easy answers, adopt beliefs that preclude rational thinking, or be unaware of the rules of chance and probability—a concept Stanovich terms dysrationalia. . . . This is an important book for much the same reason that Daniel Goleman's bestselling Emotional Intelligence has proven so useful: it is based on sound evidence and allows for better prediction and education for success." Libr J

Includes bibliographical references

154.2   The subconscious

Kandel, Eric R.

The **age** of insight; the quest to understand the unconscious in art, mind, and brain : from Vienna 1900 to the present. Eric R. Kandel. Random House 2011 636 p.   **154.2**

    1. Perception 2. Subconsciousness 3. Subconsciousness in art
    ISBN 9781400068715; 9781588369307

                     LC 2011025274

In this book, [n]euroscientist and Nobel laureate [Eric R.] Kandel has crafted a . . . [work which examines] the interplay among art, psychology and brain science. The author, who fled Vienna as a child, has remained captivated by Austrian artists Gustav Klimt, Oskar Kokoschka and Egon Schiele, each of whom was profoundly influenced by Sigmund Freud and by the emerging scientific approach to medicine in their day. Kandel describes the psychological and biological insights reflected in their paintings, as well as the neuroscience behind how the beholder perceives the paintings. He concludes by calling for a new, interdisciplinary approach to understanding the mind, one that combines the humanities with the natural and social sciences. (Scientific American)

Tallis, Frank

Hidden minds; a history of the unconscious. Arcade Pub. 2002 194p $25.95   **154.2**

    1. Psychology 2. Subconsciousness 3. Subconsciousness -- History
    ISBN 1-55970-643-0

                     LC 2002-74566

"Highly readable and possessing a surprising degree of depth, this book manages to be both entertaining and informative." Libr J

Includes bibliographical references

Vedantam, Shankar

The **hidden** brain; how our unconscious minds elect presidents, control markets, wage wars, and save our lives. Spiegel & Grau 2009 270p $26; pa $16   **154.2**

    1. Discrimination -- Psychological aspects 2. Motivation (Psychology) 3. Perception 4. Selectivity (Psychology) 5. Subconsciousness
    ISBN 978-0-385-52521-3; 0-385-52521-4; 978-0-385-52522-0 pa; 0-385-52522-2 pa

                     LC 2009-19717

"A tour into dark realms of the psyche by a personable guide." Kirkus

Includes bibliographical references

154.6   Sleep phenomena

Freud, Sigmund

★ **Interpretation** of dreams; translated by Joyce Crick; edited with an introduction by Ritchie Robinson. Oxford University Press 2008 514p il pa $14.95   **154.6**

    1. Dreams 2. Psychoanalysis
    ISBN 978-0-19-953758-7; 0-19-953758-5

Groundbreaking analysis of dreams as manifestations of suppressed unconscious desires.

Lewis, James R.

★ The **dream** encyclopedia; [by] James R. Lewis and Evelyn Dorothy Oliver. 2nd ed.; Visible Ink Press 2009 xxi, 410p il pa $24.95   **154.6**
1. Dreams -- Encyclopedias 2. Reference books
ISBN 978-1-57859-216-6

LC 2009-5132

This "reference examines more than 250 dream-related topics, from art to history to science, including how factors such as self-healing, ESP, literature, religion, sex, cognition and memory, and medical conditions can all have an effect on dreams. Dream symbolism and interpretation is examined in historical, cultural, and psychological detail." Publisher's note

Includes bibliographical references

155   Differential and developmental psychology

Bailey, Rebecca Anne

Easy to love, difficult to discipline; the 7 basic skills for turning conflict into cooperation. {by} Becky A. Bailey. Morrow 2000 285p hardcover o.p. pa $12.95   **155**
1. Child rearing 2. Discipline of children 3. Parent and child 4. Parenting 5. Self-control
ISBN 0-06-000775-3 pa

LC 99-44313

"Bailey contends that the difficult but rewarding task of guiding children's behavior starts only when parents are able to discipline themselves and become models of self-control. . . . Bailey's underlying message is positive and hopeful, supported with humorous anecdotes and helpful solutions." Publ Wkly

Includes bibliographical references

155.2   Individual psychology

Cain, Susan

Quiet; Susan Cain. Crown Publishers 2012 x, 333 p.p   **155.2**
1. Extraversion 2. Interpersonal relations 3. Introversion 4. Introverts
ISBN 9780307352149; 9780307452207

LC 2010053204

It was the author's intent to discuss "the one-third to one-half of the population who are introverts. She defines the term broadly, including 'solitude-seeking' and 'contemplative,' but also 'sensitive,' 'humble,' and 'risk-averse.' Such individuals, she claims . . . are 'disproportionately represented among the ranks of the spectacularly creative.' Yet the American school and workplace make it difficult for those who draw strength from solitary musing by overemphasizing teamwork. . . . She notes [that] introverts can negotiate as well as, or better than, alpha males and females because they can take a firm stand 'without inflaming [their] counterpart's ego.' Cain provides tips to parents and teachers of children who are introverted or seem socially awkward and isolated. She suggests, for instance, exposing them gradu-

ally to new experiences that are otherwise overstimulating." (Publishers Weekly)

Csikszentmihalyi, Mihaly

★ **Flow**: the psychology of optimal experience. Harper Perennial 2008 303p pa $14.95   **155.2**
1. Applied psychology 2. Attention 3. Happiness
ISBN 978-0-06-133920-2; 0-06-133920-2

This book offers a discussion of "'flow,' a field of behavioral science examining connections between satisfaction and daily activities. [According to the author], a flow state ensues when one is engaged in self-controlled, goal-related, meaningful actions. . . . This thoroughly researched study is an intriguing look at the age-old problem of the pursuit of happiness and how, through conscious effort, we may more easily attain it." Libr J

Dimitrius, Jo-Ellan

Reading people; how to understand people and predict their behavior--anytime, anyplace. {by} Jo-Ellan Dimitrius and Mark Mazzarella. Random House 1998 281p hardcover o.p. pa $14.95 **155.2**
1. Body language 2. Nonverbal communication 3. Personality 4. Personality assessment -- Miscellanea 5. Physiognomy
ISBN 0-345-42587-1 pa

LC 98-4934

"Dimitrius shares the people-reading techniques she developed over 15 years as a jury consultant. In so doing, she provides a wealth of tips and strategies for ferreting out people's real viewpoints, motives and character traits." Publ Wkly

Ehrenreich, Barbara

★ **Bright**-sided; how the relentless promotion of positive thinking has undermined America. Metropolitan Books/Henry Holt and Co. 2009 235p $23   **155.2**
1. Happiness 2. Optimism 3. Self-confidence 4. Success 5. Success in business
ISBN 978-0-8050-8749-9; 0-8050-8749-4

LC 2009-23588

"The author's tough-minded and convincing broadside raises troubling questions about many aspects of contemporary American life. . . . Bright, incisive, provocative thinking." Kirkus

Includes bibliographical references

Hamer, Dean H.

Living with our genes; why they matter more than you think. {by} Dean Hamer and Peter Copeland. Doubleday 1998 355p hardcover o.p. pa $14.95   **155.2**
1. Behavior genetics 2. Personality 3. Personality -- Genetic aspects 4. Temperament 5. Temperament -- Physiological aspects
ISBN 0-385-48584-0 pa

LC 97-29818

"The authors devote chapters to the most compelling of human behaviors and conditions: sex, worry, anger, thrill-seeking, addiction, intelligence, eating and aging. They explore the biochemistry underlying the characteristics in question, and ask how much of that biochemistry is under genetic control. . . . This thought-provoking book's explanations of how our genes 'express' themselves is sure to capture the imaginations of readers." Publ Wkly

Includes bibliographical references

Harris, Judith Rich

No two alike; human nature and human individuality. W.W. Norton & Co. 2006 322p il $26.95 **155.2**
1. Individual differences 2. Individuality 3. Personality
ISBN 0-393-05948-0

LC 2005-25837

"Harris makes behavioral genetics and evolutionary psychology enjoyable and accessible to general readers as well as scholars." Libr J

Includes bibliographical references

Helgoe, Laurie A.

Introvert power; why your inner life is your hidden strength. [by] Laurie Helgoe. Sourcebooks 2008 xxiv, 256p il pa $15.95 **155.2**
1. Introversion and extroversion
ISBN 978-1-4022-1117-1; 1-4022-1117-1

LC 2008-4967

Shows readers how to use introversion not as a weakness but as a source of power.

"The author's voice is vivid and engaging, and she skillfully draws real-life examples of awkward scenarios introverts find themselves in when forced to play a role in society or the workplace. Readers will find much insight, as well as a comforting sense of being understood and validated." Publ Wkly

Includes bibliographical references

Keltner, Dacher

Born to be good; the science of a meaningful life. W. W. Norton & Co. 2009 336p il $25.95 **155.2**
1. Altruism 2. Cooperation 3. Helping behavior 4. Interpersonal relations
ISBN 978-0-393-06512-1

LC 2008-42492

"A landmark book in the science of emotion and its implications for ethics and human universals, this is essential for all libraries." Libr J

Includes bibliographical references

Lunden, Joan

Wake-up calls; making the most out of every day. McGraw-Hill 2000 230p il $19.95; pa $12 **155.2**
1. Change (Psychology) 2. Conduct of life 3. Self-actualization (Psychology) 4. Self-realization
ISBN 0-07-136126-X; 0-07-137970-3 pa

A collection of aphorisms and life principles the author feels may inspire readers faced with stress, change, and adversity.

Maslow, Abraham Harold

★ **Toward** a psychology of being; {by} Abraham H. Maslow. 3rd ed; Wiley 1998 244p $45 **155.2**
1. Motivation (Psychology) 2. Personality 3. Self-actualization (Psychology)
ISBN 0-471-29309-1

LC 98-3766

The author presents his theory of psychological health and motivation and explains his belief that human beings can be loving and creative, and capable of pursuing the highest values and aspirations

Myers, Isabel Briggs

★ **Gifts** differing; understanding personality type. [by] Isabel Briggs Myers with Peter B. Myers. Davies-Black Pub 1995 228p il pa $16.95 **155.2**
1. Personality
ISBN 0-89106-074-X

LC 95-4184

This is a guide to the 16 personality types distinguished in the Myers-Briggs Type Indicator.

Pinker, Steven

The **blank** slate; the denial of human nature in modern intellectual life. Viking 2002 509p $27.95; pa $16 **155.2**
1. Nature and nurture
ISBN 0-670-03151-8; 0-14-2003344 pa

LC 2002-22719

The author "attacks the notion that an infant's mind is a blank slate, arguing instead that human beings have an inherited universal structure shaped by the demands made upon the species for survival, albeit with plenty of room for cultural and individual variation." Publ Wkly

Includes bibliographical references

Seligman, Martin E. P.

★ **Learned** optimism; how to change your mind and your life. Vintage Books 2006 319p pa $14.95 **155.2**
1. Adjustment (Psychology) 2. Self-perception
ISBN 1-4000-7839-3; 978-1-4000-7839-4

LC 2006-277713

Seligman "has written a lively, very accessible book. . . . Presented for lay readers, this book can be highly recommended to professionals as well for its lucid and informative introduction to cognitive therapy and its approach to issues of mood and depression." Libr J

Includes bibliographical references

Shenk, David

The **genius** in all of us; why everything you've been told about genetics, talent, and IQ is wrong. Doubleday 2010 302p il $26.95 **155.2**
1. Ability 2. Genes 3. Heredity 4. Intellect 5. Intellect -- Genetic aspects
ISBN 978-0-385-52365-3; 0-385-52365-3

LC 2009-18376

Shenk "tells engaging stories, lucidly explains complex research and offers fresh insights into the nature of exceptional performance. . . . [This is a] deeply interesting and important book." N Y Times Book Rev

Includes bibliographical references

Triandis, Harry C.

Fooling ourselves; self-deception in politics, religion, and terrorism. Harry C. Triandis. Praeger Publishers 2009 xxvi, 246p Contributions in psychology (alk. paper) $49.95   **155.2**

1. Culture -- Psychological aspects 2. Psychology -- Cross-cultural studies 3. Psychology and religion 4. Self-deception 5. Social psychology
ISBN 9780313364389; 0313364389

LC 2008033679

In this book, author Harry C. Triandis shows how and why self-deception takes place, and its subtle and profound effects on our everyday lives. Self-deception occurs because we often see the world the way we would like it to be, rather than the way it is. Our brains so long for things the way we want them, we might not even be aware we are fooling ourselves. . . . Across cultures and around the world, self-deception is a phenomenon that has subtle and profound effects on everyday life, explains Triandis, . . . former president of the International Association of Cross-Cultural Psychology. In this work, he not only explains how and why self-deceptions occur in three areas -- politics, religion, and terrorism -- but also how to recognize and reduce the frequency of fooling ourselves. (Publisher's note)

Weber, Robert J.

The **created** self; reinventing body, persona, spirit. Norton 2000 350p il hardcover o.p. pa $14.95   **155.2**

1. Change (Psychology) 2. Psychology 3. Self 4. Self-presentation
ISBN 0-393-32121-5 pa

LC 99-37480

The author contends that "having a self enables the individual to pursue creative endeavors, which though often adaptive from an evolutionary standpoint, actually extend beyond what can be explained in terms of biological, reproductive aims. Using the model of the self developed by William James . . . Weber attempts to show that the self is a constantly developing, 'unitary system', consisting of bodily awareness, persona and spirit, over which the individual has control." Publ Wkly
Includes bibliographical references

Young-Eisendrath, Polly

The **self**-esteem trap; raising confident and compassionate kids in an age of self-importance. Little, Brown 2008 248p $25.99   **155.2**

1. Child psychology 2. Self-esteem
ISBN 978-0-316-01311-6; 0-316-01311-0

LC 2008-2224

The author argues that "those born between 1970 and 2000 (Gen Me-ers) . . . are a vastly discontented group who find their lives unsatisfying and feel entitled to success owing to an overestimation of what the world will bring. She views this as a cultural problem begun in the 1980s when the collapse of the traditional parental hierarchy coincided with a hyperfocus on self-esteem. . . . This is well written, accessible, soundly researched, and beautifully insightful." Libr J
Includes bibliographical references

155.3 Sex psychology; psychology of people by gender or sex, by sexual orientation

Eldredge, Niles

★ **Why** we do it; rethinking sex and the selfish gene. Norton 2004 269p il $24.95   **155.3**

1. Evolution 2. Genes 3. Human evolution 4. Sex (Biology) 5. Sociobiology
ISBN 0-393-05082-3

LC 2003-27564

"This book, while written for the lay reader, is appropriate for a scientific audience as well. It could be used as supplementary reading in college courses in animal behavior." Sci Books & Films

Lerner, Harriet Goldhor

The **dance** of deception; pretending and truth-telling in women's lives. HarperCollins Pubs. 1993 254p hardcover o.p.   **155.3**

1. Truthfulness and falsehood 2. Women -- Psychology

LC 92-53376

"Patriarchal culture teaches women to pretend and sometimes deceive, Lerner says, and in her study of the role this dissembling plays in women's lives, she shows how 'pretending reflects deep prohibitions, real and imagined, against a more direct and forthright assertion of self.' . . . She acknowledges that truth telling is not easy, yet her discussion of the many ways women lie and how lying affects them clearly shows the benefits of honesty and makes her prescription appealing." Booklist
Includes bibliographical references

Pincott, J.

Do gentlemen really prefer blondes? bodies, behavior and brains: the science behind sex, love, and attraction. [by] Jena Pincott. Delacorte Press 2008 351p il $20   **155.3**

1. Dating (Social customs) 2. Sexual behavior
ISBN 978-0-385-34215-5; 0-385-34215-2

LC 2008-23933

The author "argues that desire is strongly rooted in evolutionary biases and consults a variety of studies . . . to reveal the extent to which hormones dictate human behavior." Publ Wkly
Includes bibliographical references

Riggle, Ellen D. B.

A **positive** view of LGBTQ; Ellen D.B. Riggle and Sharon S. Rostosky. Rowman & Littlefield 2011 193p.   **155.3**

1. Gender identity 2. Positive psychology 3. Sexual minorities
ISBN 9781442212817; 9781442212831

LC 2011027007

The book explores "the strengths and benefits of Lesbian, Gay, Bisexual, Transgender, and Queer (LGTBQ) identities. . . . Focusing on how LGTBQ-identified individuals can cultivate a sense of well-being and a personal identity that allows them to flourish in all areas of life, the authors explore a variety of themes. Through personal stories from people with a variety of backgrounds and gender and sexual identities, readers will learn more about expressing gender and sexuality; creating strong and intimate relationships; exploring unique perspectives on empathy, compassion, and social justice; belonging to communities and acting as role models and mentors; and, enjoying the benefits of living an authentic life." (Publisher's note)

155.4 Psychology of specific ages

Barnet, Ann B.

The **youngest** minds; parenting and genes in the development of intellect and emotion. {by} Ann B. Barnet and Richard J. Barnet. Simon & Schuster 1998 352p il hardcover o.p. pa $22.95   **155.4**
1. Child development 2. Child psychology 3. Child rearing 4. Child rearing -- Social aspects 5. Children -- Intelligence levels 6. Emotions in children 7. Emotions in infants 8. Infants -- Intelligence levels 9. Language acquisition 10. Nature and nurture
ISBN 978-0-684-85440-3; 0-684-85440-6
           LC 98-13450
The authors debate "the relative importance of genetics vs. environment in shaping human personality. Explaining recent work in language acquisition and emotional development . . . they provide an accessible summary of our current state of knowledge of brain development and chemistry while placing significantly greater emphasis on the role played by environmental factors." Publ Wkly
Includes bibliographical references

Brazelton, T. Berry

★ **To** listen to a child; understanding the normal problems of growing up. photographs by B.A. King. Addison-Wesley 1984 184p il hardcover o.p.   **155.4**
1. Asthma 2. Child development 3. Child psychology 4. Children -- Health and hygiene 5. Emotionally disturbed children 6. Parent-child relationship 7. Sleep
           LC 84-6174
"Brazelton's sensible, authoritative, clear approach provides parents with the kinds of information they need to relax over the long pull, and to understand and cope with day-to-day difficulties." Publ Wkly

The **irreducible** needs of children; what every child must have to grow, learn, and flourish. {by} T. Berry Brazelton, Stanley I. Greenspan. Perseus Bks. 2000 xx, 228p hardcover o.p. pa $14   **155.4**
1. Child development 2. Child psychology 3. Child rearing
ISBN 0-7382-0516-8 pa
           LC 2001-2290
This is "a practical, well-organized volume, of value to parents, physicians, teachers, sociologists, and others who wish to improve children's lives locally and globally." Booklist
Includes bibliographical references

Bruer, John T.

★ The **myth** of the first three years; a new understanding of early brain development and lifelong learning. Free Press 1999 244p il hardcover o.p. pa $18.95   **155.4**
1. Child development 2. Educational psychology 3. Learning, Psychology of 4. Pediatric neuropsychology 5. Psychology of learning
ISBN 0-7432-4260-2 pa
           LC 99-34934
Bruer offers a critique of recent thinking about early childhood development and learning. Specifically, he identifies as myth the notion that "a child's experiences and environment during his first three years play a crucial role in determining the course of his later life." Commentary
Includes bibliographical references

Elkind, David

★ The **power** of play; how spontaneous, imaginative activities lead to happier, healthier children. Da Capo Lifelong 2007 240p $24   **155.4**
1. Play
ISBN 0-7382-1053-6; 978-0-7382-1053-7
           LC 2006-35592
"Prescribing the trinity of play, love, and work, . . . [the author] shows how the integration of these elements at various stages of development, from infancy to adolescence, leads to happier, well-adjusted individuals with a greater potential for academic success. Elkind will connect with parents when he reveals that 'Toys R Not Us' and argues that less is more; that children should use toys for inspiration, not distraction." Libr J
Includes bibliographical references

Gopnik, Alison

The **scientist** in the crib; minds, brains, and how children learn. [by] Alison Gopnik, Andrew N. Meltzoff, Patricia K. Kuhl. Morrow 1999 279p hardcover o.p. pa $14   **155.4**
1. Child development 2. Cognition 3. Cognition in children 4. Learning, Psychology of 5. Psychology of learning
ISBN 0-688-17788-3 pa
           LC 99-24247
The authors examine "how children learn to understand and use language, control their emotions and arouse the emotions of others, and establish relationships. . . . Prospective and actual parents stand to learn much that may be helpful to them and their children from this lively book." Booklist
Includes bibliographical references

Linn, Susan

The **case** for make believe; saving play in a commercialized world. New Press 2008 258p $24.95   **155.4**
1. Advertising and children 2. Imagination 3. Play
ISBN 978-1-56584-970-9; 1-56584-970-1
           LC 2007-42435
"Puppeteer and therapist Linn draws on years of work at Boston Children's Hospital to make a thoughtful case for creative play. She distinguishes between children who are familiar with concepts of imagination and make-believe versus those who know only how to play with manufactured toys linked to media campaigns or within the constructs of rule-driven environments. . . . None of this will be news to

most parents, but Linn seeks to discover what it means for children to no longer spend time pretending to be someone or somewhere else. Her research is comprehensive, her first-hand knowledge is impressive, and her examples are damning in their conclusions." Booklist

Includes bibliographical references

Louv, Richard

Last child in the woods; saving our children from nature-deficit disorder. Algonquin Books of Chapel Hill 2005 323p $24.95   **155.4**
    1. Child psychology 2. Environment and children 3. Environmental influence on humans 4. Nature -- Psychological aspects
    ISBN 1-56512-391-3

                                        LC 2004-66034
"Louv's book is a call to action, full of warnings—but also full of ideas for change." Publ Wkly

Includes bibliographical references

Piaget, Jean

★ The **moral** judgment of the child; {translated by Marjorie Gabain} Free Press 1948 418p hardcover o.p. pa $15   **155.4**
    1. Child psychology 2. Ethics 3. Human behavior
    ISBN 0-684-83330-1 pa

Piaget studies, not the moral behavior of children, but their ideas about right and wrong, the rules of a game, adult authority, and cooperation and justice

Segal, Nancy L.

Entwined lives; twins and what they tell us about human behavior. Plume 2000 396p il pa $16 **155.4**
    1. Nature and nurture 2. Twins 3. Twins -- Psychology
    ISBN 0-452-28057-5; 978-0-452-28057-1

                                        LC 99-59376
"This elegantly written study cogently distills and makes available to the general reader a wealth of research from the fields of behavioral genetics, evolutionary psychology and social science." Publ Wkly

Includes bibliographical references

★ **Indivisible** by two; lives of extraordinary twins. Harvard University Press 2005 280p il $24.95   **155.4**
    1. Biography, Collective 2. Twins 3. Twins -- Psychology
    ISBN 0-674-01933-4; 978-0-674-01933-1

                                        LC 2005-45979
The author "makes use of a particularly powerful research method for answering . . . vexing questions about why our own and other people's lives turn out the way they do. Segal studies twins—identical, that is, from a single fertilized egg, and fraternal, from two eggs fertilized by different sperm—as well as pseudotwins, children of the same age who are raised together. She does so with a passion that derives in part from the fact that she is a fraternal twin herself." N Y Rev Books

Seligman, Martin E. P.

The **optimistic** child; {by} Martin E.P. Seligman with Karen Reivich, Lisa Jaycox, and Jane Gillham.

Houghton Mifflin 1995 336p il hardcover o.p. pa $14.95   **155.4**
    1. Child psychology
    ISBN 0-395-69380-2; 978-0-618-91809-6 pa; 0-618-91809-4 pa

                                        LC 95-12619
The author "discounts prevalent theory that children who are encouraged by others to feel good about themselves will do well. Instead, he proposes that self-esteem comes from mastering challenges, overcoming frustration and experiencing individual achievement. In clear, concise prose peppered with anecdotes, dialogues, cartoons and exercises, Seligman offers a concrete plan of action based on techniques of self-evaluation and social interaction." Publ Wkly

Includes bibliographical references

White, Burton L.

★ The **new** first three years of life; 20th anniversary ed; Fireside Bks. 1995 384p il pa $14 **155.4**
    1. Child psychology 2. Infants -- Development
    ISBN 0-684-80419-0

                                        LC 95-18297
"White describes the seven developmental phases of the first three years of life. He provides parents with a comprehensive treasury of techniques for enhancing development and establishing discipline that are refreshingly straight-forward and based on real-world experience." Publ Wkly

155.44   Children by status and relationships

Wright, Lawrence

Twins; and what they tell us about who we are. Wiley 1997 202p $22.95; pa $14.95   **155.44**
    1. Nature and nurture 2. Twins
    ISBN 0-471-25220-4; 0-471-29644-9 pa

                                        LC 97-38827
"Wright does an admirable job of sorting through the differing research in a well-reasoned, clearheaded manner." Publ Wkly

Includes bibliographical references

155.45   Exceptional children; children by social and economic levels, by ethnic or national group

Winner, Ellen

Gifted children; myths and realities. Basic Bks. 1996 449p il hardcover o.p. pa $21   **155.45**
    1. Gifted children
    ISBN 0-465-01759-2 pa

                                        LC 95-49279
This study considers the following questions: "are gifted children gifted in all subject areas? Are artistically gifted children gifted or talented? Does giftedness depend on IQ? What role do environment and biology play in giftedness? Are gifted children psychological and social misfits? In her analyses, Winner cites and explains a broad range of recent research, including extensive notes and references with each chapter. She then offers her recommendations for dealing with gifted children in America's educational systems." Libr J

155.5 Psychology of young people twelve to twenty

American Academy of Child and Adolescent Psychiatry

Your adolescent; emotional, behavioral and cognitive development from early adolescence through the teen years. David B. Pruitt, editor-in-chief. HarperCollins Pubs. 1999 xxiii, 374p hardcover o.p. pa $18 **155.5**

1. Adolescent psychology 2. Parent-child relationship
ISBN 0-06-095676-3 pa

LC 98-34587

"In addition to discussing the milestones of normal development, common family, behavioral, physical, and emotional disorders are described and treatment options are discussed. . . . This is the most encyclopedic general treatment of the topic to be issued in years and will be a useful starting point for many parents." Libr J

155.6 Psychology of adults

Ackerman, Diane

Deep play; illustrations by Peter Sis. Random House 1999 235p il hardcover o.p. pa $13 **155.6**

1. Play -- Psychological aspects 2. Self-actualization (Psychology)
ISBN 0-679-77135-2 pa

LC 98-35067

The author contends that "deep play, 'ecstatic' play, transcends practical concerns and grants us passage to the sacred and the holy. Art is deep play, so is religion, the contemplation of nature, and playing sports; in short, pursuits that are all-consuming and inspire feelings of awe and a profound sense of connection with the universe. By turns anecdotal and philosophic, Ackerman vividly recounts her own 'deep play' experiences." Booklist

Includes bibliographical references

Engel, Beverly

The **nice** girl syndrome; stop being manipulated and abused--and start standing up for yourself. John Wiley & Sons 2008 245p $24.95 **155.6**

1. Conduct of life 2. Self-confidence 3. Self-esteem 4. Women -- Psychology
ISBN 978-0-470-17938-3; 0-470-17938-4

LC 2008-8382

The author argues "that while society superficially rewards nice girls, they suffer deeply in their intimate and work relationships by losing personal power and parading inauthentic selves. . . . Most useful for its thorough treatment for how 'nice girls' are socialized and for Engel's concise antidote (the four 'Power C's': confidence, competence, conviction and courage) this book will challenge, entertain and empower its readers." Publ Wkly

Includes bibliographical references

Friday, Nancy

My mother/my self; the daughter's search for identity. Delta Trade Paperbacks 1997 425p pa $17 **155.6**

1. Mother-daughter relationship 2. Mothers 3. Women -- Psychology
ISBN 0-385-32015-9; 978-0-385-32015-3

LC 98-115632

The author explores the psychological aspects of the mother-daughter relationship.

Lerner, Harriet Goldhor

The **dance** of intimacy; a woman's guide to courageous acts of change in key relationships. Harper & Row 1989 255p hardcover o.p. pa $14 **155.6**

1. Human relations 2. Interpersonal relations 3. Self 4. Women -- Psychology
ISBN 0-06-091646-X pa

LC 88-45519

The author explains "how to operate more effectively in key relationships—whether it be with a distant or unfaithful spouse, a depressed sister, a difficult mother, an alcoholic father, an uncommitted lover, a dying parent, or a family member that we have written off." Publisher's note

Includes bibliographical references

Levinson, Daniel J.

The **seasons** of a man's life; by Daniel J. Levinson {et al.} Knopf 1978 363p hardcover o.p. pa $15 **155.6**

1. Men -- Psychology 2. Middle age
ISBN 0-394-533901-0 pa

LC 77-20978

The Levinson theory divides a man's "life cycle into five overlapping eras. . . . Each era is marked by periods of stability during which life structures are built. These stable periods alternate with transition periods during which life structures change." Saturday Rev

Includes bibliographical references

The **seasons** of a woman's life; in collaboration with Judy D. Levinson. Knopf 1996 438p hardcover o.p. pa $23 **155.6**

1. Businesswomen 2. Homemakers 3. Middle age 4. Middle aged women 5. Women -- Psychology
ISBN 0-345-31174-4 pa

LC 95-20893

"This work asks whether there is a human life cycle and a process of adult growth similar to the process of child development, and how gender affects the lives of individual women and women in general. The Levinson team interviewed 15 homemakers, 15 women with corporate-financial careers, and 15 women with academic careers. Their stories are the core of Levinson's book." Booklist

Includes bibliographical references

155.67   People in late adulthood

Alford, Henry

How to live; a search for wisdom from old people (while they are still on this earth) Twelve 2009 262p $23.99   **155.67**

1. Aged -- Attitudes 2. Aging 3. Aging -- Psychological aspects 4. Authors 5. Elderly 6. Essayists 7. Humorists 8. Wisdom

ISBN 978-0-446-19603-1; 0-446-19603-7

LC 2008-15576

The author "embarks on a quest to find wisdom. Alford notes that Benjamin Franklin helped pen the Constitution at age 81 and Michelangelo completed the Pietà at 91. Who better to consult than septuagenarians, octogenarians, and nonagenarians? He interviews well-known figures—literary critic Harold Bloom, comedian Phyllis Diller, spiritual leader Ram Dass, and playwright Edward Albee—as well as lesser-known yet equally captivating people. . . . Alford is a master of turns of phrase, diction, dialog, and technique. Essential reading." Libr J

155.7   Evolutionary psychology

Clark, William R.

Are we hardwired? the role of genes in human behavior. by William R. Clark & Michael Grunstein. Oxford Univ. Press 2000 322p il hardcover o.p. pa $24.95   **155.7**

1. Behavior genetics 2. Nature and nurture

ISBN 0-19-513826-0; 978-0-19-517800-5 pa; 0-19-517800-9 pa

LC 99-54699

The authors offer an "overview of the current evidence supporting genetic causes for general behavioral tendencies, such as aggression, consumption, sexual preferences, and, most controversial, intelligence. Case studies of identical twins separated as infants provide some of the most compelling proofs." Libr J

Includes bibliographical references

Ridley, Matt

The **agile** gene; how nature turns on nurture. Perennial 2004 326p pa $13.99   **155.7**

1. Genetics 2. Nature and nurture

ISBN 978-0-06-000679-2; 0-06-000679-X

"In February 2001 it was announced that the human genome contains not 100,000 genes, as originally postulated, but only 30,000. This . . . revision led some scientists to conclude that there are simply not enough human genes to account for all the different ways people behave: we must be made by nurture, not nature. . . . [Ridley argues that] nurture depends on genes, too, and genes need nurture. Genes not only predetermine the broad structure of the brain, they also absorb formative experiences, react to social cues, and even run memory. They are consequences as well as causes of the will." Publisher's note

Includes bibliographical references

155.8   Ethnopsychology and national psychology

Levi-Strauss, Claude

★ The **savage** mind. University of Chicago Press 1966 290p il hardcover o.p. pa $18   **155.8**

1. Anthropology 2. Ethnopsychology

ISBN 0-226-47484-4 pa

"An anthropological study of the nature of thought, concepts and systems as they occur in various cultures." Chicago Public Libr

Includes bibliographical references

155.9   Environmental psychology

Attig, Thomas

The **heart** of grief; death and the search for lasting love. Oxford Univ. Press 2000 xx, 289p hardcover o.p. pa $15.95   **155.9**

1. Bereavement 2. Bereavement -- Psychological aspects 3. Bereavement -- Psychological aspects -- Case studies 4. Death 5. Death -- Psychological aspects 6. Grief 7. Grief -- Case studies 8. Loss (Psychology)

ISBN 0-19-511873-1; 0-19-515625-0 pa

LC 99-49842

"A reassuring and useful book for those grieving or counseling those who grieve." Libr J

Benson, Herbert

★ The **relaxation** response; by Herbert Benson, with Miriam Z. Klipper. Updated & expanded [ed.]; Quill 2001 liv, 179p il pa $13.99   **155.9**

1. Rest 2. Stress (Physiology) 3. Stress (Psychology)

ISBN 0-380-81595-8

LC 2003-269877

This guide to relieving stress is "recommended for patients suffering from heart conditions, hypertension, chronic pain, and other ailments. A classic." Libr J

Includes bibliographical references

Berns, Nancy

★ **Closure**; the rush to end grief and what it costs us. Temple University Press 2011 213p $75.50; pa $24.95; ebook $24.95   **155.9**

1. Bereavement 2. Loss (Psychology)

ISBN 978-1-43990-576-0; 1-43990-576-2; 978-1-43990-577-7 pa; 1-43990-577-0 pa; 978-1-43990-578-4 ebook; 1-43990-578-9 ebook

LC 2011002611

"'Closure' as a signifier for the end of grief has come into wide use, and Berns, who experienced a profound loss when she gave birth to a stillborn son, is here to reinforce what most of us intuitively know: feeling bad about losing a loved one never really ends. By commodifying the concept of closure in order to sell products and services, however, society has put pressure on us to conform to the prevailing 'feeling rules,' suggesting that disappointment, loss, and grief can and should come to an arbitrary end. . . . Berns wisely counsels us to find other language and perspectives for living with grief, and this lucid debunking of the current use of the word 'closure' is a breath of fresh air, recommended for both general readers and specialists." Libr J

Includes bibliographical references

Brehony, Kathleen A.

After the darkest hour; how suffering begins the journey to wisdom. {by} Kathleen Brehony. Holt & Co. 2000 274p il hardcover o.p. pa $14   **155.9**

    1. Adjustment (Psychology) 2. Life change events -- Psychological aspects 3. Self-actualization (Psychology) 4. Suffering

    ISBN 0-8050-6436-2 pa

                    LC 00-29577

  "Brehony provides stories and anecdotes throughout the book of people both known and unknown who have gotten through traumatic situations and have learned something from them. . . . Peppered throughout with inspirational quotations, this book teeters on the brink of self-help sentiment, but it succeeds where others might fail in its practicality." Booklist

Includes bibliographical references

Buchholz, Ester Schaler

The **call** of solitude; alonetime in a world of attachment. Simon & Schuster 1997 365p hardcover o.p. pa $22   **155.9**

    1. Solitude

    ISBN 0-684-87280-3 pa

                    LC 97-20698

  "Buchholz's wide-ranging discussion, slanted toward professionals but accessible to interested general readers, may overreach on occasion, but she is often convincing in her timely and provocative advocacy of 'alonetime.'" Publ Wkly

Includes bibliographical references

Dresser, Norine

Saying goodbye to someone you love; your journey through end-of-life and grief. [by] Norine Dresser, Fredda Wasserman. DemosHealth Pub. 2010 210p pa $16.95   **155.9**

    1. Bereavement 2. Death

    ISBN 978-1-932603-85-9

                  LC 2010-2096

  The authors "draw from their experience as hospice workers to illustrate how people have brought up the subject of death with the dying, made end-of-life decisions, and planned (or not held) a funeral service. Dresser and Wasserman not only offer comfort and companionship but provide practical suggestions for conversation starters, ideas for memorials, and a whole section on handling the grief of children. Essential for anyone experiencing end-of-life issues." Libr J

Includes bibliographical references

Edelman, Hope

Motherless daughters; the legacy of loss. 2nd ed; Da Capo Press 2006 pa $15.95   **155.9**

    1. Bereavement 2. Loss (Psychology) 3. Mother-daughter relationship

    ISBN 978-0-7382-1026-1

                  LC 2005-33840

"Writing of her own experiences of losing her mother when she was 17, and the grief of hundreds of women she interviewed who lost their mothers through death, abandonment or another form of separation . . . Edelman marshals a wealth of anecdotal evidence, supplemented with psychological research about bereavement, that indicates that one's longing for a mother never disappears." Publ Wkly

Includes bibliographical references

Motherless mothers; how mother loss shapes the parents we become. HarperCollins 2006 xxxiii, 410p hardcover o.p. pa $14.95   **155.9**

    1. Bereavement 2. Loss (Psychology) 3. Mother-daughter relationship 4. Parenting

    ISBN 0-06-053246-7 pa; 978-0-06-053246-8 pa

                  LC 2005-52812

  Edelman "presents emotionally charged concepts in clear, memorable terms (e.g., reaching the 'neon number' of a mother's age of death) to encourage frank, cathartic discussion." Publ Wkly

Includes bibliographical references

Emswiler, Mary Ann

Guiding your child through grief; {by} Mary Ann Emswiler and James P. Emswiler. Bantam Bks. 2000 286p il pa $13.95   **155.9**

    1. Bereavement 2. Bereavement in children 3. Child rearing 4. Death 5. Loss (Psychology)

    ISBN 0-553-38025-7

                  LC 00-23645

  "Thoroughly researched and bolstered with the wisdom of bereavement experts nationwide, this fine guide does those working through the loss of loved ones an enormous service. It should rank amongst the first line of defense and support for those facing a death in the family." Publ Wkly

Includes bibliographical references

Gilbert, Sandra M.

  ★ **Death's** door; modern dying and the ways we grieve. Norton 2006 580p il $29.95; pa $17.95   **155.9**

    1. Bereavement 2. Death 3. Death -- Social aspects 4. Grief 5. Mourning customs

    ISBN 0-393-05131-5; 978-0-393-05131-5; 0-393-32969-0 pa; 978-0-393-32969-8 pa

                  LC 2004-65430

  "Those who have experienced the death of a loved one will recognize themselves in this meticulously researched, comprehensively organized, and exceptionally caring examination of society's attitudes about mortality and mourning." Booklist

Includes bibliographical references

Gonzales, Laurence

Surviving survival; the art and science of resilience. Laurence Gonzales. W.W. Norton 2012 272 p. (hardcover) $26.95   **155.9**

    1. Disasters -- Psychological aspects 2. Resilience (Personality trait) 3. Resourcefulness

    ISBN 0393083187; 9780393083187

                  LC 2012015592

This book "looks deeply into the mental processes that enable us to cope with the trauma that often sets in during and after a challenge to our survival. . . . [Laurence] Gonzales narrates plenty of grim and gruesome tales, not all of them elective; his survivors are those who have suffered war and terrorism as well as falls off mountains and into choppy surf." The book includes "explanations of the science behind, for instance, how the amygdala works." (Kirkus)

Gosling, Sam

Snoop; what your stuff says about you. Basic Books 2008 263p il map $25 **155.9**
1. Materialism 2. Personal paraphernalia 3. Social perception 4. Social psychology
ISBN 978-0-465-02781-1; 0-465-02781-4
LC 2007-52071

"Unlike many current books on behaviour, Snoop does not contain a single brain scan or discussion of neural activity. Instead, it adopts a shamelessly social approach, focusing on how people behave in the real world rather than in a brain scanner, and presents explanations at the level of individual personalities and social interactions. It works, not least because it has the huge advantage of being exclusively concerned with the one topic that most people find endlessly fascinating: themselves." New Sci
Includes bibliographical references

Karr-Morse, Robin

Scared sick; Robin Karr-Morse with Meredith S. Wiley. Basic Books 2012 xvii, 301p **155.9**
1. Psychic trauma
ISBN 9780465013548; 9780465028122
LC 2011029405

This book presents an "investigation of the importance of attachment between baby and caretaker—usually the mother—in setting the path to physical and mental health. . . . [The authors] write that without that bond, there is danger that a baby will be stressed, triggering the hypothalamus-pituitary-adrenal axis and flooding the baby's developing nervous system with flight-or-fight hormones. The baby, unable to flee or fight, may succumb to trauma, defined as being frozen in fear. Such trauma is the root of being 'scared sick': suffering ills that may not appear until later in life. Among many others, these can include autism, Alzheimer's, addiction, ADHD, schizophrenia, PTSD, suicide, chronic pain, obesity, heart disease, diabetes and cancer." (Kirkus)

Kingma, Daphne Rose

The ten things to do when your life falls apart; an emotional and spiritual handbook. New World Library 2010 xxiv, 214p pa $14.95 **155.9**
1. Adjustment (Psychology) 2. Suffering
ISBN 978-1-57731-698-5
LC 2010-1049

The author "writes for readers whose lives are being wrenched apart by sudden job loss, the death of a loved one, financial ruin, or a dire medical diagnosis. When any of these things happens, either separately or simultaneously, Kingma offers a list of ten ways whereby readers can eventually learn that their difficulties have meaning and purpose. . . . For those lost in the turbulence of life, Kingma offers a genuine hand through." Libr J

Kosko, Bart

★ Noise. Viking 2006 252p il $24.95 **155.9**
1. Noise
ISBN 0-670-03495-9; 978-0-670-03495-6
LC 2006-44708

The author "discusses the science and subjectivity of noise, achieving a high 'wow' factor in a highly entertaining disclosure of surprising facts and concepts." Booklist
Includes bibliographical references

Kübler-Ross, Elisabeth

★ On children and death. Macmillan 1983 279p hardcover o.p. pa $12 **155.9**
1. Child psychology 2. Children 3. Death 4. Parent and child 5. Terminally ill children
ISBN 0-684-83939-3 pa
LC 83-11252

A look at how one copes with a child's death by disease, accident or murder.

★ On death and dying. Scribner Classics 1997 286p il $23; pa $13 **155.9**
1. Death 2. Terminal care
ISBN 0-684-84223-8; 0-684-83938-5 pa
LC 97-177294

A look at the psychological, sociological and theological issues faced by the terminally ill and their caregivers.

Lazare, Aaron

On apology. Oxford University Press 2004 306p $24; pa $13.95 **155.9**
1. Apologizing
ISBN 0-19-517343-0; 0-19-518911-6 pa
LC 2004-43470

"Everybody on earth could benefit from this small but essential book." Publ Wkly
Includes bibliographical references

Pastoureau, Michel

Black; the history of a color. translated from the French by Jody Gladding. Princeton University Press 2009 210p il $35 **155.9**
1. Black
ISBN 978-0-691-13930-2; 0-691-13930-X
LC 2008-25145

"This handsome, strikingly designed, richly illustrated book traces the history of the color black in Europe. . . . [The author] takes special care to define what the universe of color might have been for earlier societies, and carefully follows black's changing social status from archetypical color of darkness, death, and monastic virtue to preferred color of royalty and Romantic melancholy. . . . This book is well researched, skillfully written, and a pleasure to read." Choice
Includes bibliographical references

Prochnik, George

In pursuit of silence; listening for meaning in a world of noise. Doubleday 2010 342p $26 **155.9**
1. Noise 2. Noise -- Psychological aspects 3. Silence
ISBN 978-0-385-52888-7; 0-385-52888-4
LC 2009-41991

"Prochnik's quest for the many meanings of silence takes him on an adventure of profound listening. A Trappist monk says that silence offers a 'radical confrontation with ourselves'; anti-noise policymakers in Europe explain noise-mapping projects; and deaf students reveal unexpected ways of observing space and light. To understand silence, one must understand noise as well, and Prochnik, an advocate for quiet, takes himself to a car-audio competition where boom-car enthusiasts compete in decibel production. He investigates the unexpected paradoxes at the heart of our relationship with sound: we create noise in order to soundproof ourselves, and we create noise by clamoring for silence. There is a difference between mere noise control and genuine silence, and Prochnik makes an eloquent case for the latter, whether in the form of personal contemplation or communal spaces of tranquillity." New Yorker

Includes bibliographical references.

Ripley, Amanda

The **unthinkable**; who survives when disaster strikes and why. Crown Publishers 2008 xx, 266p il $24.95 **155.9**
1. Disaster relief 2. Disasters 3. Survival skills
ISBN 978-0-307-35289-7
LC 2007-40315

Ripley "offers an elementary discussion of disaster and survival, drawing on both survivors' personal accounts and scientific studies that reveal how the human brain functions under duress. She shows how individuals and groups react when such disasters as shipwrecks, fires, terrorist attacks, and tsunamis occur, detailing the traits survivors demonstrate that help them respond effectively. . . . Offering tips on how we can boost our odds, her self-help approach to survival will attract readers." Libr J

Includes bibliographical references

Sife, Wallace

The **loss** of a pet; 3rd ed; Howell Book House 2005 260p il pa $14.99 **155.9**
1. Bereavement 2. Death 3. Pets
ISBN 0-7645-7930-4
LC 2005-12603

The author "addresses the pet owner whose grief at a pet's death is largely misunderstood or even ridiculed by friends, associates and society in general. . . . Sife is to be commended for offering information that is not only compassionate but concise, wide-ranging and, above all, practical." Publ Wkly {review of 1993 edition}

Wickersham, Joan

The **suicide** index; putting my father's death in order. Harcourt 2008 316p $25; pa $14.95 **155.9**
1. Father-daughter relationship 2. Suicide
ISBN 978-0-1510-1490-3; 0-1510-1490-6; 978-0-1560-3380-0 pa; 0-1560-3380-1 pa
LC 2007-29299

"Wickersham's memoir unravels the twisted branches of family ties in the aftermath of her father's suicide as she attempts to answer the question, Why did he do it? . . . Wickersham's effort is worth the read. . . . This book is beautifully written and haunts the reader long after it's closed. Recommended." Libr J

Zimbardo, Philip G.

The **Lucifer** effect; understanding how good people turn evil. [by] Philip Zimbardo. Random House 2007 xx, 551p il $27.95 **155.9**
1. Good and evil 2. Good and evil -- Psychological aspects 3. Social psychology
ISBN 978-1-4000-6411-3; 1-4000-6411-2
LC 2006-50388

The author "masterminded the famous Stanford Prison Experiment, in which college students randomly assigned to be guards or inmates found themselves enacting sadistic abuse or abject submissiveness. In this penetrating investigation, he revisits . . . the SPE study and applies it to historical examples of injustice and atrocity, especially the Abu Ghraib outrages by the U.S. military. . . . Combining a dense but readable and often engrossing exposition of social psychology research with an impassioned moral seriousness, Zimbardo challenges readers to look beyond glib denunciations of evil-doers and ponder our collective responsibility for the world's ills." Publ Wkly

Includes bibliographical references

156   Comparative psychology

Fouts, Roger

Next of kin; what chimpanzees have taught me about who we are. {by} Roger Fouts with Stephen Tukel Mills; introduction by Jane Goodall. Morrow 1997 420p il hardcover o.p. pa $14 **156**
1. Animal communication 2. Chimpanzees 3. Washoe (Chimpanzee)
ISBN 0-380-72822-2 pa
LC 97-15144

This is an account of a study known as Project Washoe where a female chimpanzee was taught American Sign Language.

"What makes this book an exceptional popularization of scientific research is the authors' ability to charm with a fascinating story while also teaching why the story is so fascinating." Booklist

Includes bibliographical references

Miller, Peter

The **smart** swarm; how understanding flocks, schools, and colonies can make us better at communicating, decision making, and getting things done. Avery 2010 xx, 283p $26 **156**
1. Animal behavior 2. Decision making 3. Human behavior
ISBN 978-1-58333-390-7
LC 2009-48619

The author "examines hives, mounds, colonies, and swarms, whose complex systems of engagement and collective decision making have catalyzed innovations in engineering and can suggest solutions to such problems as climate change. . . . Miller informs, engages, entertains, and even surprises in this thought-provoking study of problem making and problem solving, and through the comparison of human and insect scenarios, shows how social cues and signals can either bring about social cooperation or destruction." Publ Wkly

Includes bibliographical references

Peterson, Dale

The **moral** lives of animals. Bloomsbury Press 2010 342p **156**

1. Animal behavior 2. Animal intelligence 3. Animal psychology 4. Ethics 5. Moral motivation
ISBN 978-1-59691-424-7

LC 2010024662

Peterson "examines the moral behavior observed in animals and argues that human beings are not the only species to live by the principles of cooperation, kindness, and empathy." (Publisher's note) Bibliography. Index.

The author "develops his thoughts on how morality evolved in mammals, including humans. He initially concentrates on where morality comes from, covering basic concepts, linguistic bias, definitions of morality, and a theory of morality's structure. Rules of morality follow with topics such as authority, violence, sex, possession, and communication. . . . Although written for a general audience, this book challenges readers to absorb new information in an area unfamiliar to most. It is definitely worth the effort and is highly recommended for high school-age readers and up." Libr J

Includes bibliographical references

Waal, Frans de

Our inner ape; a leading primatologist explains why we are who we are. photographs by the author. Riverhead Books 2005 274p il $24.95 **156**

1. Bonobo -- Behavior 2. Chimpanzees -- Behavior 3. Comparative psychology 4. Human behavior 5. Primates -- Behavior 6. Psychology, Comparative
ISBN 1-57322-312-3

LC 2005-42768

"Readers might be surprised at how much these apes and their stories resonate with their own lives, and may well be left with an urge to spend a few hours watching primates themselves at the local zoo." Publ Wkly

Includes bibliographical references

158 Applied psychology

Bloomfield, Harold H.

Making peace with your past; the six essential steps to enjoying a great future. {by} Harold H. Bloomfield with Philip Goldberg. HarperCollins Pubs. 2000 269p hardcover o.p. pa $13 **158**

1. Applied psychology 2. Autobiographical memory 3. Self-realization
ISBN 0-06-093314-3 pa

LC 99-89719

The author "addresses the syndrome Freud called 'repetition compulsion'—humans' tendency to re-create what they have not worked through. . . . With revealing exercises, Bloomfield shows readers how to rediscover 'the passion to live {their} highest destiny.'" Libr J

Includes bibliographical references

Burns, David D.

Feeling good; the new mood therapy. preface by Aaron T. Beck. Rev and updated; Avon Bks. 1999 xxxii, 706p il pa $15 **158**

1. Depression (Psychology) 2. Psychotherapy
ISBN 0-380-73176-2

LC 99-461798

"The author . . . writes simply, clearly, and without any jargon; better yet, he has a sense of compassion and a sense of humor, and is aware of his own limitations." Libr J {review of 1980 edition}

Includes bibliographical references

Canfield, Jack

The **success** principles; how to get from where you are to where you want to be. by Jack Canfield with Janet Switzer. HarperCollins Publishers 2005 xxxiii, 473p il $24.95 **158**

1. Success
ISBN 0-06-059488-8

LC 2004-54259

A self-improvement guide for business professionals, teachers, students, parents, or anyone interested in promoting themselves within today's success-oriented culture shares sixty-four principles on how to reach desired goals.

The author "has an easy style and talks directly to readers, responding to potential 'what ifs' and 'buts' with encouragement and sound advice. The book's layout is superb—small paragraphs are punctuated by italicized quotes, questions for self-study, and several appropriate cartoons." Libr J

Includes bibliographical references

Carnegie, Dale

★ **How** to win friends and influence people; editorial consultant, Dorothy Carnegie, editorial assistance, Arthur R. Pell. Pocket Books 1982 276p pa $6.99 **158**

1. Applied psychology 2. Success
ISBN 0-671-72365-0; 978-0-671-72365-1

LC 94-176452

An examination of the psychology of business and social success.

Covey, Stephen R.

★ The **7** habits of highly effective people; restoring the character ethic. [Rev. ed.]; Free Press 2004 372p il $26; pa $15.95 **158**

1. Conduct of life 2. Success
ISBN 0-7432-7245-5; 0-7432-6951-9 pa

LC 2004-57494

The author describes seven habits designed to help people solve personal and professional problems.

The **8th** habit; from effectiveness to greatness. Free Press 2004 408p il $26 **158**

1. Self-realization 2. Success
ISBN 0-684-84665-9

LC 2004-56371

"Though conceived for individuals, Covey's book will be of tremendous importance to organizations and businesses." Libr J

Includes bibliographical references

First things first; to live, to love, to learn, to leave a legacy. {by} Stephen R. Covey, A. Roger Merrill, Rebecca R. Merrill. Simon & Schuster 1994 360p il hardcover o.p. pa $14 **158**
1. Conduct of life 2. Life skills 3. Time management
ISBN 0-684-80203-1 pa
LC 94-2305

The authors "offer a 'principle-centered' approach to time management that emphasizes what 'represents our vision, values, principles, mission, conscience, direction—what we feel is important and how we lead our lives.' The authors argue that central to our lives are 'four needs and capacities—to live, to love, to learn, to leave a legacy.' The ideas here are not only clearly explained but are reinforced by scenarios from the authors' lives and self-directed activities for the reader." Libr J

Includes bibliographical references

Dyer, Wayne W.
★ The **power** of intention; learning to co-create your world your way. Hay House 2004 259p $24.95; pa $14.95 **158**
1. Intentionalism
ISBN 1-401-90215-4; 1-401-90216-2 pa
LC 2003-14622

The author argues that "there are seven faces, or energy fields, of intention: creativity, kindness, love, beauty, expansion, abundance and receptivity. Drawing on a variety of spiritual traditions and gurus, Dyer . . . describes how to surmount the barriers that may get in the way of connecting to this power, such as negative thinking, relying on the opinion of others or retaining a controlling ego." Publ Wkly

Foster, Rick
How we choose to be happy; the 9 choices of extremely happy people--their secrets, their stories. Rev; Berkley Publishing Group 2004 xxi, 228p pa $14.95 **158**
1. Happiness
ISBN 978-0-399-52990-0; 0-399-52990-X

The authors "interviewed happy people from all walks of life, from the United States to Eastern Europe. The resulting personal stories, writing exercises, and quotes together inform and instruct the reader in the nine principles discovered by the authors in their travels." Libr J

Gegax, Tom
Winning in the game of life; self-coaching secrets for success. RH Publishing 2003 318p pa $14 **158**
1. Self-realization 2. Success
ISBN 978-0-9740675-0-6; 0-9740675-0-4

"For Gegax, creating a winning life plan requires defining a mission and taking steps that balances career, friends, community, and family into an integrated whole." Booklist

Gilbert, Daniel
★ **Stumbling** on happiness; [by] Daniel Gilbert. Alfred A. Knopf 2006 277p il **158**
1. Happiness
ISBN 1-4000-4266-6; 1-4000-7742-7 pa; 978-1-4000-4266-1; 978-1-4000-7742-7 pa
LC 2005044459

This book argues that "events that we anticipate will give us joy make us less happy than we think; things that fill us with dread will make us less unhappy, for less long, than we anticipate." (N Y Times Book Rev) Index.

"The book is a sly, irresistible romp down, or through, memory lane—past, present, and future. It is not only wildly entertaining but also hilarious . . . and yet full of startling insight, imaginative conclusions, and even bits of wisdom." Booklist

Includes bibliographical references

Goleman, Daniel
★ **Social** intelligence; the new science of human relationships. Bantam Books 2006 403p il $28; pa $14 **158**
1. Emotions 2. Emotions -- Social aspects 3. Intellect 4. Intellect -- Social aspects 5. Interpersonal relations
ISBN 0-553-80352-2; 978-0-553-80352-5; 0-553-38449-X pa; 978-0-553-38449-9 pa
LC 2006-45971

The author "argues for a new social model of intelligence drawn from the emerging field of social neuroscience. . . . Goleman illuminates new theories about attachment, bonding, and the making and remaking of memory as he examines how our brains are wired for altruism, compassion, concern and rapport." Publ Wkly

Includes bibliographical references

Hay, Louise L.
★ **You** can heal your life. Hay House 1987 226p pa $14.95 **158**
1. Health self-care 2. Holistic medicine 3. Mind and body 4. Self-realization
ISBN 0-937611-01-8
LC 88-200391

The author's "key message in this . . . work is: 'If we are willing to do the mental work, almost anything can be healed.' Louise explains how limiting beliefs and ideas are often the cause of illness." Publisher's note

Includes bibliographical references

Hodgkinson, Tom
How to be idle. HarperCollins Publishers 2005 286p il $18.95 **158**
1. Conduct of life 2. Laziness
ISBN 0-06-077968-3
LC 2004-59932

The author "presents 24 essays defending life's idle pleasures, which are, he says, vilified by our modern society. He meditates on sleeping in, fishing, smoking and drinking, and even waxes poetic about the hangover. The whole book is soaked with nostalgia for the turn-of-the-century English gentleman's lifestyle; Hodgkinson defends his arguments by

quoting Jerome K. Jerome, G.K. Chesterton and, of course, that icon of British foppery, Oscar Wilde." Publ Wkly
Includes bibliographical references

Klauser, Henriette Anne

Write it down, make it happen; knowing what you want--and getting it! Scribner 2000 250p hardcover o.p. pa $12 **158**
1. Applied psychology 2. Goal (Psychology) 3. Planning
ISBN 0-684-85002-8 pa

LC 99-43551

The author "instructs her readers to write down their most extravagant wishes and, merely by the act of recording them, make them come true. . . . Her technique is intended to clarify goals, increase self-confidence, and dispel self-doubt, and she describes how it has dramatically improved her life and the lives of her friends and acquaintances." Libr J
Includes bibliographical references

May, Rollo

★ **Freedom** and destiny. Norton 1981 275p hardcover o.p. pa $14 **158**
1. Applied psychology 2. Fate and fatalism 3. Free will and determinism
ISBN 0-393-31842-7 pa

LC 81-4009

This book examines "the continuing tension in our lives between the possibilities freedom offers and the various limitations imposed upon us by our particular fate or destiny." America
Includes bibliographical references

McGraw, Phillip C.

Life strategies; doing what works, doing what matters. Hyperion 1999 282p il $21.95; pa $13.95 **158**
1. Change (Psychology) 2. Success 3. Success -- Psychological aspects
ISBN 0-7868-6548-2; 0-7868-8459-2 pa

LC 98-46748

"McGraw claims that people in dire situations have serious problems, including denial and choosing initial assumptions without testing them for accuracy. To create a life strategy that works, McGraw lays out his ten 'Life Laws' along with checklists and 18 assignments." Libr J

Michels, Barry

The **tools**; Phil Stutz and Barry Michels. Spiegel & Grau 2012 271 p. (alk. paper) $25.00 **158**
1. Change (Psychology) 2. Self-actualization (Psychology)
ISBN 067964444X; 9780679644446; 9780679644453
LC 2011044717

In this book, "psychiatrist [Phil] Stutz and psychotherapist [Barry] Michels promote a rapid and streamlined method of self-improvement. Michels . . . teaches readers to end procrastination and negativity by tapping into higher forces. . . . [T]he authors' techniques are designed to access intense intrapersonal areas. The 'Inner Authority' tool, for example, involves imagining the Jungian Shadow to reach greater self-expression." (Publishers Weekly)

Miller, Caroline Adams

★ **Creating** your best life; the ultimate life list guide. [by] Caroline Adams Miller and Dr. Michael B. Frisch. Sterling Pub. 2009 276p il $19.95; pa $14.95 **158**
1. Happiness 2. Success
ISBN 978-1-4027-6259-8; 1-4027-6259-3; 978-1-4027-7998-5 pa; 1-4027-7998-4 pa

LC 2010-275766

"Instead of making New Year's resolutions, it may be more beneficial to assemble a goal-setting list. So believe positive psychologist/life coach Miller and clinical psychologist Frisch . . . who have put together dozens of interactive exercises and assessments to guide readers in self-discovery and life-list creation. Whether or not readers follow through with every assignment, they will undoubtedly be inspired to think about goals and live more consciously and productively." Libr J
Includes bibliographical references

Myers, Betsy

Take the lead; motivate, inspire, and bring out the best in yourself and everyone around you. [by] Betsy Myers with John David Mann. Atria 2011 240p $25; ebook $11.99 **158**
1. Leadership 2. Motivation (Psychology)
ISBN 978-1-4391-6067-1; 978-1-4391-6395-5 ebook
LC 2011015072

Myers "look at characteristics and traits that enable individuals to motivate, inspire, and influence individuals and groups. [She] explores what constitutes successful modern leadership, focusing on qualities of emotional intelligence, which she maintains are as essential to leadership effectiveness as more tactical management abilities. The author organizes the book around seven leadership traits: authenticity, connection, respect, clarity, willingness to collaborate, an openness to continuous learning, and the courage to do the right thing. . . . Written in an intelligent but conversational and approachable tone, this inspirational primer is a perfect read for anyone seeking to understand, develop, or unleash his or her genuine leadership potential." Publ Wkly
Includes bibliographical references

Peck, M. Scott

Further along the road less traveled; the unending journey toward spiritual growth: the edited lectures. Simon & Schuster 1993 255p hardcover o.p. pa $14 **158**
1. Applied psychology 2. Human relations 3. Psychology of religion 4. Self-realization 5. Spiritual life
ISBN 0-684-84723-X pa

LC 93-31322

The author "discusses 'growing up'—becoming self-aware, working through cycles of blame and toward wholesale forgiveness—and then the self-examination we each must undergo in order to groom ourselves for the most important step of all: the search for God." Booklist

★ The **road** less traveled; a new psychology of love, traditional values, and spiritual growth.

25th anniversary ed; Simon & Schuster 2002 315p
$22.95 **158**
1. Applied psychology 2. Interpersonal relations 3.
Love 4. Maturation (Psychology) 5. Self-actualization
(Psychology) 6. Spirituality 7. Values
ISBN 0-7432-3825-7

LC 2002-75858

This book attempts to bring together "psychology and
religion. It is divided into four areas—discipline, love, religion and growth, and grace—and within each Peck tackles
the . . . struggle between stagnation and progress which goes
on in all of us throughout our lives." Libr J

The **road** less traveled and beyond; spiritual
growth in an age of anxiety. Simon & Schuster 1997
314p $23; pa $14 **158**
1. Applied psychology 2. Self-realization 3. Spiritual
life
ISBN 0-684-81314-9; 0-684-83561-4 pa

LC 96-43391

In this volume Peck "continues his journey through the
existential conflicts and baffling paradoxes on the meandering road of personal development. . . . Through copious detailed references from his previous books, he allows readers
unfamiliar with them to understand and enjoy the present
work, which completes his Road trilogy." Publ Wkly

Prager, Dennis

Happiness is a serious problem; a human nature
repair manual. ReganBooks 1998 179p hardcover
o.p. pa $13 **158**
1. Happiness
ISBN 0-06-098735-1 pa

LC 97-35404

The author "uses the pursuit of happiness as a central
motif but generally instructs in the modern art of self-improvement. The 31 short chapters . . . are cogent, complete,
and preach a nonreligious yet morally guided moderation
that should appeal across a wide range of patron groups."
Libr J

Richardson, Brenda Lane

What mama couldn't tell us about love; healing
the emotional legacy of slavery; celebrating our light.
{by} Brenda Lane Richardson and Brenda Wade.
HarperCollins Pubs. 1999 xxviii, 241p hardcover
o.p. pa $13.95 **158**
1. African American women 2. Afro-American women
-- Attitudes 3. Afro-American women -- Mental health
4. Afro-American women -- Psychology 5. Healing
-- United States 6. Intimacy (Psychology) -- United
States 7. Love 8. Man-woman relationships -- United
States 9. Oppression (Psychology) -- United States
10. Slavery -- United States -- History 11. Women --
Psychology
ISBN 0-06-09379-9 pa

LC 99-12127

The authors present a "self-help guide on relationships
and intimacy for African American women. What makes
this work unique is that it makes the direct connection
between slavery and emotional health. . . . The resource
sections on assistance for individual or group work, men-

tal health organizations, and sisterly support are valuable
additions." Booklist
Includes bibliographical references

Robbins, Tony

★ **Awaken** the giant within; how to take immediate control of your mental, emotional, physical
& financial destiny! [by] Anthony Robbins. Summit
Bks. 1991 539p il hardcover o.p. pa $16 **158**
1. Applied psychology 2. Success
ISBN 0-671-72734-6; 0-671-79154-0 pa

LC 91-27218

The author offers advice and techniques for achieving
personal success.
"Robbins' system is somewhat elaborate, but his advice
is based on common sense and on psychological and sociocultural reality." Booklist

★ **Unlimited** power; the new science of personal
achievement. [by] Anthony Robbins. 1st Fireside
ed.; Simon & Schuster 1997 425p il pa $15 **158**
1. Applied psychology 2. Success
ISBN 0-684-84577-6

LC 97-35403

The author offers advice and techniques for achieving
personal and professional success using neurolinguistic
programming (NLP).

Salzberg, Sharon

Real happiness; learn the power of meditation:
a 28-day program. Workman Publishing 2011 208p
pa $14.99 **158**
1. Meditation
ISBN 978-0-7611-5925-4

LC 2010-52087

The author "provides a 28-day program for incorporating meditation into one's life. Written for beginners, the
book explains breathing and sitting techniques, the science
behind the practice, and 12 guided meditations. Interspersed
throughout are FAQs from Salzberg's students regarding
their difficulties with the practice. The accompanying CD
includes nine meditations to guide readers through breathing, walking, emotional, and loving-kindness exercises. This
is one of the best guides for anyone interested in exploring
meditation or mindfulness." Libr J
Includes bibliographical references

Schwartz, David Joseph

★ The **magic** of thinking big; 1st Fireside ed.;
Simon & Schuster 1987 192p pa $14.95 **158**
1. Success
ISBN 0-671-64678-8

LC 87-8516

In this motivational book, the author presents a "program for getting the most out of your job, your marriage and
family life, and your community." Publisher's note

Siegel, Bernie S.

Prescriptions for living; inspirational lessons for a joyful, loving life. HarperCollins Pubs. 1998 xxiv, 210p hardcover o.p. pa $14　　　**158**
1. Self-realization 2. Self-realization -- Religious aspects 3. Spiritual life
ISBN 0-06-092936-7 pa

LC 98-39059

"Among the topics Siegel covers are how to find peace of mind; how to love, encourage, and forgive other people as well as yourself; and how to thrive in bad times and survive the good times. For those ready to be uplifted by the soothing repetition of time-tested homilies, Siegel delivers the goods." Booklist

Stone, Douglas

Difficult conversations; how to discuss what matters most. {by} Douglas Stone, Bruce Patton, Sheila Heen. Viking 1999 xxi, 250p il hardcover o.p. pa $14　　　**158**
1. Communication 2. Interpersonal relations
ISBN 0-14-028852-X pa

LC 98-33346

The authors "blend a daunting array of disciplines into highly readable and practical advice." Booklist

Tolle, Eckhart

A **new** earth; awakening to your life's purpose. Dutton/Penguin Group 2005 315p $24.95　　　**158**
1. Self-realization 2. Spiritual life
ISBN 978-0-525-94802-5; 0-525-94802-3

LC 2005-23358

"According to Tolle, . . . humans are on the verge of creating a new world by a personal transformation that shifts our attention away from our ever-expanding egos." Publ Wkly
Includes bibliographical references

The **power** of now; a guide to spiritual enlightenment. New World Library 1999 193p $22.95; pa $14　　　**158**
1. Self-realization 2. Spiritual life
ISBN 978-1-57731-152-2; 1-57731-152-3; 978-1-57731-480-6 pa; 1-57731-480-8 pa

LC 99-42366

"The author describes his transition from despair to self-realization soon after his 29th birthday. Tolle took another ten years to understand this transformation, during which time he evolved a philosophy that has parallels in Buddhism, relaxation techniques, and meditation theory. . . In The Power of Now he shows readers how to recognize themselves as the creators of their own pain, and how to have a pain-free existence by living fully in the present." Publisher's note

Ury, William

Getting past no; negotiating with difficult people. {by} William L. Ury. Bantam Bks. 1991 161p hardcover o.p. pa $14.95　　　**158**
1. Negotiation
ISBN 0-553-37131-2 pa

LC 91-10101

"Ury presents a five-step agenda to deal successfully with opponents, be they unruly teenagers, labor leaders, terrorists or international politicians. Strategies focus on self-discipline, or tactics for defusing the adversary's attacks, and suggestions for developing options designed to lead to a mutually satisfactory agreement." Publ Wkly
Includes bibliographical references

Viscott, David S.

Emotional resilience; simple truths for dealing with the unfinished business of your past. by David Viscott. Harmony Bks. 1996 358p il hardcover o.p. pa $15　　　**158**
1. Attitude (Psychology) 2. Human behavior
ISBN 0-517-88825-4 pa

LC 96-407

The author outlines his 10 step self help program. "His method, which includes truth telling, acceptance of self and others, letting go of the past and of false expectations, and taking responsibility for one's life, is for those trapped in emotionally confining situations, whether personal relationships, educational impasses, or financial situations." Booklist

158.1　　Personal improvement and analysis

Ban Breathnach, Sarah

A **man's** journey to simple abundance; [by] Sarah Ban Breathnach and friends; edited by Michael Segell. Scribner 2000 448p $22　　　**158.1**
1. Conduct of life 2. Men 3. Men -- Conduct of life
ISBN 0-7432-0061-6

LC 00-45012

"A collection of 50-plus pieces on men's experiences. . . . The book's sections cover family, emotional and moral concerns, men's roles and obligations, success and failure, amusements and obsessions, and the deepest values in life. . . . Contributors include respected novelists (Rick Bass, Jim Harrison, Reynolds Price), journalists (Roy Blount, Harold Evans), pop-culture figures (Sting, director Garry Marshall), and representatives of religious and spiritual movements." Booklist
Includes bibliographical references

Viorst, Judith

★ **Imperfect** control; our lifelong struggles with power and surrender. Simon & Schuster 1998 446p hardcover o.p. pa $14　　　**158.1**
1. Control (Psychology) 2. Psychology
ISBN 0-684-84814-7 pa

LC 97-37302

"Referring to the works of social scientists, psychologists, and philosophers as well as literary examples and personal experiences, Viorst shows how issues of power and surrender confront and affect us throughout our lives. . . . Her book is very readable, with traces of the author's special brand of humor woven throughout." Libr J
Includes bibliographical references

★ The power of habit; by Charles Duhigg. Random House 2012 xx, 371 p.p　　　**158.1**
1. Change (Psychology) 2. Habit 3. Habit -- Social

aspects
ISBN 9780679603856; 9781400069286

LC 2011029545

In this book, science writer Charles Duhigg explores the reasons why we find it so hard to change ingrained behaviour." . . . [H]abits usually start with a simple sensory cue . . . which sets up a craving in the brain's reward centres. This yearning overrides the regions involved in self-control. . . . From nail-biting to alcoholism, Duhigg offers . . . insights into the triggers that set people on a downward spiral, and proven ways to fight those urges. . . . Habitual behaviours can propagate through an organisation or society, he argues, offering convincing anecdotes that cover everything from the success of Starbucks to the civil rights movement. . . . [Duhigg examines the] way advertising hijacks your brain's reward centres to set off a new, irresistible habit." (New Scientist)

158.2 Interpersonal relations

Goodman, Ellen

I know just what you mean; the power of friendship in women's lives. {by} Ellen Goodman, Patricia O'Brien. Simon & Schuster 2000 300p il $25; pa $14 **158.2**
1. Female friendship 2. Friendship 3. Women -- Psychology
ISBN 0-684-84287-4; 0-7432-0171-X pa

LC 00-24859

"Heavy on insight and light on psychological jargon, this book is an intelligent, observant read." Publ Wkly

Hallowell, Edward M.

Connect. Pantheon Bks. 1999 xx, 328p hardcover o.p. pa $13.95 **158.2**
1. Achievement motivation 2. Interpersonal relations 3. Performance 4. Quality of life
ISBN 0-7434-0621-4 pa

LC 99-13082

The author "urges readers to 'make time for connectedness,' which he alternately defines as having person-to-person interaction or being involved with something greater than oneself." Libr J

Stengel, Richard

You're too kind; a brief history of flattery. Simon & Schuster 2000 315p $25; pa $14 **158.2**
1. Flattery 2. Flattery -- History
ISBN 0-684-85491-0; 0-684-85492-9 pa

"Charting the uses of flattery and the social contexts in which it is used from biblical times to the present, Stengel . . . illustrates that more than mere praise, flattery is praise with a motive, be it benign or grasping. . . . Enjoyable and informative." Libr J
Includes bibliographical references

160 Philosophical logic

Copi, Irving M.

★ **Introduction** to logic; [by] Irving M. Copi, Carl Cohen. 13th ed; Pearson/Prentice-Hall 2008 670p il $104 **160**
1. Logic
ISBN 978-0-13-614139-6; 0-13-614139-0

LC 2007-41752

This introduction to logic covers language, fallacies, definitions, categories, arguments, deduction, probability and other areas of logical inquiry such as thought and reasoning.

170 Ethics (Moral philosophy)

Aristotle

★ **Nicomachean** ethics; translation (with historical introduction) by Christopher Rowe; philosophical introduction and commentary by Sarah Broadie. Oxford University Press 2002 468p pa $29.95 **170**
1. Ethics
ISBN 978-0-19-875271-4; 0-19-875271-7

LC 2002-283430

According to Aristotle's ethical treatises, "happiness is the goal of life. Pleasure, fame, and wealth, however, will not bring one the highest happiness, which is achieved only through the contemplation of philosophic truth, because it exercises man's peculiar virtue, the rational principle." Reader's Ency. 3d edition
Includes bibliographical references

Carter, Stephen L.

Integrity. Basic Bks. 1996 277p hardcover o.p. pa $14 **170**
1. Conduct of life 2. Ethics 3. Integrity
ISBN 0-06-092807-7 pa

LC 95-44538

The author seeks to define "integrity in both personal and political terms. . . . Mr. Carter divides true integrity into three parts: discernment, steadfastness and forthrightness. Anyone who wants to act with integrity must first think hard about what is right and wrong. . . . Once the right course of action suggests itself, it should be acted upon, even if doing so is risky or unpleasant. . . . People of integrity, finally, are willing to defend what they do in public." N Y Times Book Rev
Includes bibliographical references

Coles, Robert

★ **Lives** of moral leadership. Random House 2000 247p hardcover o.p. pa $13.95 **170**
1. Conduct of life 2. Conduct of life -- Case studies 3. Ethics 4. Leadership 5. Leadership -- Moral and ethical aspects -- Case studies
ISBN 0-375-75835-6 pa

LC 00-27858

Drawing on interviews he conducted over the past four decades with public and private figures, Coles reflects on the meaning of moral leadership in the United States.

Comte-Sponville, Andre

A **small** treatise on the great virtues; the uses of philosophy in everyday life. translated by Catherine Temerson. Metropolitan Bks. 2001 352p $27.50; pa $16   **170**

1. Ethics 2. Virtues
ISBN 0-8050-4555-4; 0-8050-4556-2 pa
LC 2001-30299

"His subject demands a sober seriousness, but Comte-Sponville still manages to avoid taking himself too seriously: humility makes it into his litany of virtues, as does humor. A laudable renewal of the ancient quest for ethical wisdom." Booklist

Includes bibliographical references

Edelman, Marian Wright

The **measure** of our success; a letter to my children and yours. HarperPerennial 1993 97p pa $10   **170**

1. Child rearing 2. Ethics 3. Human behavior
ISBN 0-06-097546-6; 978-0-06-097546-3
LC 92-54846

The author presents her "beliefs on child rearing and moral values. . . . She includes a personal letter to her three sons, who were born into a family with a shared African American and Jewish heritage, and offers 25 lessons, or 'road maps,' for life." Libr J

Fleming, Thomas

The **morality** of everyday life; rediscovering an ancient alternative to the liberal tradition. University of Missouri Press 2004 270p $44.95   **170**

1. Ethics
ISBN 0-8262-1509-2
LC 2003-23962

"Writing much more accessibly and knowledgeably than most modern, professional philosophers, Fleming revivifies the body of thought with which civilization was created and without which it is disintegrating." Booklist

Includes bibliographical references

Gaines, Patrice

Moments of grace; meeting the challenge to change. Crown 1997 206p hardcover o.p. pa $15   **170**

1. Conduct of life 2. Conversion 3. Faith
ISBN 0-609-80171-6 pa
LC 96-25404

"Gaines manifests an intelligent and mellow wisdom. She treats her own insight into her travails as spiritual awakenings, or gifts from God. Without preaching or cheerleading, she points out the powerful, life-changing lessons available in her experiences and in those of others." Publ Wkly

Gottlieb, Daniel

Learning from the heart; lessons on living, loving, and listening. Sterling Pub. 2008 170p $17.95   **170**

1. Conduct of life
ISBN 978-1-4027-4999-5; 1-4027-4999-6
LC 2007-35100

"Having rebuilt his life after an accident that left him a quadriplegic in his thirties, . . . [the author] here shares his observations on what makes us human. . . . An uplifting book abounding with encouragement for daily living; recommended for public libraries." Libr J

Haidt, Jonathan

The **happiness** hypothesis; finding modern truth in ancient wisdom. Basic Books 2005 297p il $26; pa $15.95   **170**

1. Happiness
ISBN 978-0-465-02801-6; 0-465-02801-2; 978-0-465-02802-3 pa; 0-465-02802-0 pa
LC 2005-21163

"Using the wisdom culled from the world's greatest civilizations as a foundation, social psychologist Haidt comes to terms with 10 Great Ideas, viewing them through a contemporary filter to learn which of their lessons may still apply to modern lives. . . . Fascinating stuff, accessibly expressed." Booklist

Includes bibliographical references

Hauser, Marc D.

★ **Moral** minds; how nature designed our universal sense of right and wrong. Ecco 2006 489p il $27.95   **170**

1. Ethics
ISBN 978-0-06-078070-8; 0-06-078070-3
LC 2006-41324

"Hauser has picked a subject that philosophers have vented about since philosophy began, and knows it. He explores Kant and Hume and Rawls in some detail and uses their insights to characterize different aspects of the human mental apparatus that can become involved in moral judgments. But while he pays respects to these thinkers of the past, he does not kowtow to them." Humanist

Includes bibliographical references

Kalman, Maira

And the pursuit of happiness. Penguin Group 2010 471p il $29.95   **170**

1. Democracy 2. Happiness 3. National characteristics, American
ISBN 978-1-59420-267-4

"First published as an illustrated, 12-part blog in the New York Times, artist-author Kalman's . . . meditation on democracy is now available in a single volume. Despite its original episodic publication, the book coheres beautifully in terms of both artistic unity and the careful evolution of its overarching theme. Each chapter—beginning with the January inauguration of Barack Obama, an event that was the catalyst for the book—represents a month of Kalman's yearlong quest, which included visits to both coasts. Thus, the month of February is devoted to her loving celebration of Abraham Lincoln; March to 'the essence of democracy, the town meeting'; and so on to December, which concerns George Washington and, finally, a tender and loving evocation of happiness itself. Kalman's art and its wonderful interaction with her hand-lettered text is every bit as idiosyncratic as her approach to her subject, and the result is an achievement that evokes her widely praised picture books for children." Booklist

Kübler-Ross, Elisabeth

★ **Life** lessons; two experts on death and dying teach us about the mysteries of life and living. [by] Elisabeth Kübler-Ross and David Kessler. Scribner 2000 224p $24; pa $13   **170**
    1. Conduct of life 2. Death
    ISBN 0-684-87074-6; 0-684-87075-4 pa
                          LC 00-57387
"As in each of their previous individual works, the authors provide useful and accessible information." Libr J

McMahon, Darrin M.

★ **Happiness**; a history. Atlantic Monthly Press 2005 544p il $27.50   **170**
    1. Happiness
    ISBN 0-8711-3886-7
                         LC 2005-48009
Utilizing different types of sources including "art and architecture, music and theology, literature and myth . . . [the author] traces the transformation of the concept of happiness through more than 2000 years of Western thought. . . . Filled with ample and provoking commentary, this work keeps the reader engaged and makes valuable contributions to the concept of happiness with each successive chapter." Libr J
Includes bibliographical references

Reader's Digest Association

Everyday greatness; inspiration for a meaningful life. insights and commentary by Steven R. Covey; compiled by David K. Hatch. Rutledge Hill Press 2006 445p $24.99   **170**
    1. Conduct of life
    ISBN 978-1-4016-0241-3; 1-4016-0241-X
                        LC 2006-19786
"The stories, which the authors have gleaned from Reader's Digest, illustrate 21 principles such as integrity, gratitude, respect, and perseverance. Covey provides commentary, reflections, and further insights on how readers can apply each principle to their own lives in today's world. Truly inspiring." Libr J
Includes bibliographical references

Schoch, Richard W.

The **secrets** of happiness; three thousand years of searching for the good life. Scribner 2006 243p $23; pa $13.95   **170**
    1. Happiness
    ISBN 978-0-7432-9292-4; 0-7432-9292-8; 978-0-7432-9293-1 pa; 0-7432-9293-6 pa
                        LC 2006-44375
"The essence of happiness, Schoch believes, is not simply feeling good—a state some today consider an entitlement. Rather, it lies in one's quest to create a better world. First highlighting the Greek philosopher Epicurus, the Roman Stoic Seneca and medieval Islamic scholar Abu Hamid al-Ghazali, Schoch explains that although these three thinkers had very different experiences, they were united in their search for a more fulfilling life under sometimes adverse conditions. Schoch then explores the ideas found in eight sacred and secular traditions, including Buddhism, Hinduism, Christianity and Epicureanism. . . . Schoch writes in an informed, lively style and his nonjudgmental stance will appeal to many who seek not easy self-help but to wrestle with issues of meaning and values." Publ Wkly
Includes bibliographical references

Tutu, Desmond

Made for goodness; and why this makes all the difference. [by] Desmond M. Tutu and Mpho A. Tutu; edited by Douglas C. Abrams. HarperOne 2010 206p $25.99   **170**
    1. Christian life 2. Conduct of life 3. Good and evil 4. Religious life
    ISBN 978-0-06-170659-2
                        LC 2010-3774
"The book is founded on the broad notion that we are created with the freedom to choose good or evil but also incline fundamentally to the good. . . . A crucially important book from the Nobel Peace Prize winner; a witness to our tumultuous times." Libr J

Wolfe, Alan

Moral freedom; the impossible idea that defines the way we live now. Norton 2001 256p hardcover o.p. pa $14.95   **170**
    1. Ethics 2. Ethics -- United States -- Public opinion 3. Public opinion 4. Public opinion -- United States 5. Values
    ISBN 0-393-04843-8; 0-393-32302-1 pa
                        LC 00-51969
"Wolfe here discusses the results of a national public opinion poll he helped design on American beliefs about values, which he supplemented with detailed interviews of people from eight different U.S. communities. These ranged widely, from the Castro district of San Francisco to San Antonio." Libr J
Includes bibliographical references

Encyclopedia of applied ethics. Academic Press 1998 4v set $790   **170**
    1. Ethics -- Encyclopedias 2. Reference books
    ISBN 0-12-227065-7
                        LC 97-74395
"Arranged in an A-Z format, the set describes 282 topics in 5000- to 6000-word articles. Coverage includes most of the 'hot topics' of our day from abortion and adoption to zoos. Typical of the broad coverage, 'Aids in the Developing World' includes a glossary description of clinical research, a discussion of sex education, and comments on resource allocation." Libr J

★ **Encyclopedia of ethics;** edited by Lawrence C. Becker and Charlotte B. Becker. 2nd ed; Routledge 2001 3v set $370   **170**
    1. Ethics 2. Ethics -- Encyclopedias 3. Reference books
    ISBN 0-415-93672-1
                        LC 2001-19657
"The coverage of ethical theory as pursued among English-speaking philosophers remains the scope of this set. Entries are listed in word-by-word alphabetical order. A list of entries gives a convenient overview of headwords and see references. A subject index provides a guide to subjects discussed in the text of the entries, including persons; and a

citation index provides an author-by-author listing of writers, and some editors, cited in the bibliographies of all 581 entries." Booklist
Includes bibliographical references and index

★ Ethics; edited by John K. Roth. Rev. ed.; Salem Press 2005 3v set $331   **170**
1. Ethics 2. Ethics -- Encyclopedias 3. Reference books
ISBN 1-58765-170-X
LC 2004-21797
For a fuller review, see: Booklist, June 1 & 15, 2005
The aim of this set is "to provide accessible entry points for those grappling with ethical issues and concerns. The 1000-plus articles cover people, events, organizations, trends, and issues. . . . This well-organized, highly useful work will be popular with researchers and general readers." SLJ
Includes bibliographical references

Global values 101; a short course. edited by Kate Holbrook . . . [et al.] Beacon Press 2006 276p pa $14   **170**
1. Social values
ISBN 0-8070-0305-0
LC 2005-13091
"For Personal Choice and Global Transformation, the exceedingly popular and controversial Harvard undergraduate religion course that spawned this book, . . . [the editors] invited about a dozen people—'from janitors to billionaires, from professors to corporate CEOs to nuns'—to their class each semester to answer tough, well-informed questions posed by their students. Transcripts of 16 of those conversations comprise this timely, thought-provoking volume that opens with historian Howard Zinn and closes with independent journalist Amy Goodman." Libr J
Includes bibliographical references

This I believe; the personal philosophies of remarkable men and women. edited by Jay Allison and Dan Gediman, with John Gregory and Viki Merrick; photographs by Nubar Alexanian. H. Holt 2006 xxi, 281p il $23   **170**
1. Belief and doubt 2. Conduct of life
ISBN 978-0-8050-8087-2; 0-8050-8087-2
LC 2006-43522
This collection of essays from a popular radio series "draws transcripts from both the original series and its newer version, including some remarkable statements from the likes of dancer/choreographer Martha Graham, autistic academic Temple Grandin, writer and physicist Alan Lightman, novelist and social critic Thomas Mann, economic historian Arnold Toynbee, and feminist writer Rebecca West. Astonishing to hear and astonishing to read and reread, this work is a wonderful addition to any library." Libr J

This I believe II; more personal philosophies of remarkable men and women. edited by Jay Allison and Dan Gediman; with John Gregory and Viki Merrick; additional editing by Emily Botein . . . [et al.] Henry Holt 2008 268p $23   **170**
1. Belief and doubt 2. Biography, Collective 3.

Conduct of life
ISBN 978-0-8050-8768-0; 0-8050-8768-0
LC 2008-10110
"Many [of these essays] will leave you breathless. And those that don't astonish may simply humble you." Christ Sci Monit

171 Ethical systems

Moeller, Hans-Georg
The **moral** fool; a comparative case for amorality. Columbia University Press 2009 212p   **171**
1. Moral conditions 2. Social ethics 3. Social values
ISBN 9780231145084; 9780231145091
LC 2008050513
"This engaging and often difficult study is a well-conceived critique of ethical and moral thinking from an amoral perspective or standpoint. . . . Throughout this study Moeller considers controversial ethical and moral problems from his amoral perspective: civil rights, abortion, religious and just wars, capital punishment, ethnic cleansing, segregation, sexual orientation, political purges, and more. . . . The author's amoral slant on these subjects is difficult to contest; this is a landmark study that anyone who champions ethics and morality must confront. Very highly recommended." Libr J
Includes bibliographical references

Rand, Ayn
★ The **virtue** of selfishness; a new concept of egoism. with additional articles by Nathaniel Branden. Centennial ed; Signet/New American Library 2005 173p pa $7.99   **171**
1. Egoism 2. Objectivism (Philosophy)
ISBN 0-451-16393-1
The author "sets forth the moral principles of Objectivism, the philosophy that holds man's life—the life proper to a rational being—as the standard of moral values and regards altruism as incompatible with man's nature, with the creative requirements of his survival, and with a free society." Publisher's note

172 Applied ethics

Ignatieff, Michael
The **lesser** evil; political ethics in an age of terror. Princeton University Press 2004 212p $29.95; pa $16.95   **172**
1. International relations -- Moral and ethical aspects 2. Political ethics 3. Terrorism
ISBN 0-691-11751-9; 0-691-12393-4 pa
The author "presents an overview of how democracies have dealt with terrorist movements in the past and how they might best approach the terrorist threat today. . . . This should be required reading for all informed citizens as we face an uncertain future." Libr J
Includes bibliographical references

Sandel, Michael J.

Justice; what's the right thing to do? Farrar, Straus & Giroux 2009 308p $25; pa $15 **172**
1. Ethics 2. Justice 3. Values
ISBN 978-0-374-18065-2; 0-374-18065-2; 978-0-374-53250-5 pa; 0-374-53250-8 pa
LC 2009-25438
This book is based on a course the author teaches at Harvard University and a companion to series on public television. Sandel examines different philosophical approaches to justice and seeks to show how they relate to contemporary political debates on such issues as same-sex marriage, reparations for slavery, surrogate motherhood and immigration reform.

"The author has a talent for making the difficult—Kant's 'categorical imperative' or Rawls's 'difference principle'—readily comprehensible, and his relentless, though never oppressive, reason shines throughout the narrative. Sparkling commentary from the professor we all wish we had." Kirkus
Includes bibliographical references

174 Occupational ethics

Callahan, David

The **cheating** culture; why more Americans are doing wrong to get ahead. Harcourt 2004 353p $26; pa $14 **174**
1. Business ethics 2. Social ethics
ISBN 0-15-101018-8; 0-15-603005-5 pa
LC 2003-15529
"If all business school students could be required to read one book, this should be it." Choice
Includes bibliographical references

Conway, Erik M.

Merchants of doubt; how a handful of scientists obscured the truth on issues from tobacco smoke to global warming. [by] Naomi Oreskes and Erik M. Conway. Bloomsbury Press 2010 355p $27 **174**
1. Science -- Ethical aspects
ISBN 978-1-59691-610-4; 1-59691-610-9
LC 2009-43183
"A well-documented, pulls-no-punches account of how science works and how political motives can hijack the process by which scientific information is disseminated to the public." Kirkus
Includes bibliographical references

Fox, Michael W.

Beyond evolution; the genetically altered future of plants, animals, the earth--humans. Lyons Press 1999 256p $24.95 **174**
1. Agricultural biotechnology -- Moral and ethical aspects 2. Agricultural biotechnology -- Social aspects 3. Bioethics 4. Genetic engineering 5. Genetic engineering -- Moral and ethical aspects 6. Genetic engineering -- Social aspects
ISBN 1-55821-901-3
LC 99-12866

The author "argues that biotechnology—coupled with industrial, chemical-based agriculture—will only accelerate the adverse environmental and consumer-health consequences of factory farming." Publ Wkly
Includes bibliographical references and index

Gentile, Mary C.

Giving voice to values; how to speak your mind when you know what's right. Yale University Press 2010 xliv, 273p $26 **174**
1. Business ethics 2. Leadership 3. Values
ISBN 978-0-300-16118-2
LC 2010011905
Gentile "offers a powerful action-oriented manifesto for living with integrity, fighting for one's convictions, and building a more ethical workplace." Publ Wkly
Includes bibliographical references

Lutz, Tom

Doing nothing; a history of loafers, loungers, slackers and bums in America. Farrar, Straus and Giroux 2006 384p $25 **174**
1. Conduct of life 2. Flaneurs 3. Laziness 4. Leisure -- History
ISBN 0-8654-7650-0; 978-0-8654-76
LC 2005-27230
"With layabouts such as Theodore Dreiser, the Beats, and our epoch's own Anna Nicole Simpson on offer, cultural-history mavens won't be able to pass Lutz up." Booklist

Munson, Ronald

★ Raising the dead; organ transplants, ethics, and society. Oxford Univ. Press 2002 288p $55; pa $19.95 **174**
1. Medical ethics 2. Transplantation of organs, tissues, etc -- Moral and ethical aspects 3. Transplantation of organs, tissues, etc -- Social aspects 4. Transplantation of organs, tissues, etc.
ISBN 0-19-513299-8; 0-19-517801-7 pa
LC 2001-36119
"Lucid and compelling writing on a much-debated topic." Booklist
Includes bibliographical references

Preer, Jean L.

Library ethics; [by] Jean Preer. Libraries Unlimited 2008 255p il pa $45 **174**
1. Ethics 2. Librarians -- Ethics 3. Librarians -- Professional ethics 4. Library science -- Moral and ethical aspects
ISBN 978-1-59158-636-4
LC 2008-21122
"This title takes an inclusive look at why library ethics are needed in the 21st century. This highly practical, substantial, and carefully planned resource is designed to help information professionals figure out their professional values and where they stand when faced with ethical dilemmas. . . . New practitioners entering the field would be wise to use this book as their first professional bible. Those already in the library profession may find this title to be a good refresher." Libr Media Connect
Includes bibliographical references

United States/President's Council on Bioethics

★ **Human** cloning and human dignity; the report of the President's Council on bioethics. with a foreword by Leon R. Kass, chairman. PublicAffairs 2002 350p il pa $14   **174**
1. Bioethics 2. Cloning
ISBN 1-58648-176-2

This "report focuses on three major issues: cloning to produce children (reproductive uses), cloning for biomedical research (therapeutic uses), and various public policies that could be enacted. The council members were divided on their recommendations regarding human cloning, so both a majority and a minority opinion are presented here." Libr J
Includes bibliographical references

Wilmut, Ian

★ The **second** creation; Dolly and the age of biological control. [by] Ian Wilmut, Keith Campbell and Colin Tudge. Harvard University Press 2001 360p il pa $16.95   **174**
1. Cloning 2. Cloning -- Moral and ethical aspects
ISBN 978-0-674-00586-0

The scientists responsible for cloning the ewe Dolly "tell the full story of how they did it. . . . To demystify cloning (now called nuclear transfer by experts), the authors trace the history of cell biology and embryology, the linked sciences that made it possible, explaining in lucid terms the fundamental principles that brought Dolly and her successors to life." Booklist

Clones and clones; facts and fantasies about human cloning. edited by Martha C. Nussbaum and Cass R. Sunstein. Norton 1998 351p $26.95; pa $15.95   **174**
1. Bioethics 2. Cloning 3. Reproductive technology
ISBN 0-393-04648-6; 0-393-32001-4 pa
LC 97-51781

This is a collection of essays and short stories on cloning. The contributors include Richard Dawkins; Eric A. Posner and Richard A. Posner; Andrea Dworkin; William N. Estridge and Edward Stein; and Richard A. Epstein.
"The spectrum of authors and their varying perspectives in fact and fiction are assets to anyone who hopes to understand this broad issue and its vast cultural implications." Publ Wkly
Includes bibliographical references

★ Encyclopedia of bioethics; Stephen G. Post, editor in chief. 3rd ed; Macmillan Reference USA 2003 5v set $595   **174**
1. Bioethics 2. Bioethics -- Encyclopedias 3. Medical ethics -- Encyclopedias 4. Reference books
ISBN 0-02-865774-8
LC 2003-15694

"This new edition of a classic work, which addresses timely issues such as same-sex marriages and direct advertising of prescription drugs, belongs in all academic libraries and all but the smallest public libraries. It is an outstanding resource for students, professionals, and the interested public." Booklist
Includes bibliographical references

The Ethics of organ transplants; the current debate. edited by Arthur L. Caplan and Daniel H. Coelho. Prometheus Bks. 1998 350p il pa $20   **174**
1. Medical ethics 2. Transplantation of organs, tissues, etc -- Moral and ethical aspects 3. Transplantation of organs, tissues, etc.
ISBN 1-57392-224-2
LC 98-31722

The editors "have selected 35 articles that are representative of the ethical issues surrounding organ transplantation. . . . In many cases, the editors have selected companion articles that illustrate contrasting viewpoints on a particular issue." Libr J

174.2   Medical and health professions

Caplan, Arthur L.

Smart mice, not-so-smart people; an interesting and amusing guide to bioethics. Rowman & Littlefield 2006 210p $21.95; pa $14.95   **174.2**
1. Medical ethics
ISBN 978-0-7425-4171-9; 0-7425-4171-1; 978-0-7425-4172-6 pa; 0-7425-4172-X pa
LC 2006-14275

The author discusses "issues at the center of the new genetics, cloning in the laboratory and in the media, stem cell research, experiments on human subjects, blood donation and organ transplantation, and healthcare delivery." Publisher's note

Elliott, Carl

White coat, black hat; adventures on the dark side of medicine. Beacon Press 2010 224p $24.95 **174.2**
1. Conflict of interests -- United States 2. Drug industry 3. Drugs -- Effectiveness -- Evaluation 4. Medical ethics 5. Medical ethics -- United States 6. Medicine -- United States 7. Pharmaceutical industry -- United States
ISBN 978-0-8070-6142-8
LC 201006119

The author argues that "over the past twenty-five years, the practice of medicine has been subverted by the business of medicine, sacrificing old-style doctoring to fit the values of consumer capitalism. In this . . . narrative, physician and moral philosopher Carl Elliott traces the evolutionary path of this new direction in health care." (Publisher's note) Index.

Elliott "examines the part played by the pharmaceutical industry in constructing 'a medical system in which deception is often not just tolerated but rewarded.' While some abuses—including the use of subjects to test drugs without informed consent—are not new, these practices continue despite the existence of regulatory institutional-review boards set up by Congress, because these too have now become profit centers. Elliott writes that pharmaceutical companies hire PR specialists who not only supply educational materials to promote products, they also train medical professionals to be 'opinion leaders' and even write papers in their name." Kirkus
Includes bibliographical references

Scott, Christopher Thomas

Stem cell now; from the experiment that shook the world to the new politics of life. [by] Christopher Thomas Scott; foreword by Donald Kennedy. Pi Press 2006 243p il $24.95 **174.2**

1. Stem cell research

ISBN 0-13-173798-8; 978-0-13-173798-3

LC 2005-23266

"This book is illuminating reading for everyone who wants to understand a hot-button topic that will dominate the political, medical and religious arenas for years to come." Publ Wkly

Includes bibliographical references

Tucker, Todd

★ The **great** starvation experiment; the heroic men who starved so that millions could live. Free Press 2006 270p il $26 **174.2**

1. Centenarians 2. College teachers 3. Human experimentation in medicine 4. Human experimentation in medicine -- United States -- History -- 20th century 5. Physiologists 6. Physiology, Experimental 7. Starvation 8. World War, 1939-1945 -- Conscientious objectors

ISBN 0-7432-7030-4; 978-0-7432-7030-4

LC 2006-278255

"As WWII neared an end, 36 idealistic conscientious objectors, members of the Civilian Public Service, volunteered to be systematically starved. The project, headed by Dr. Ancel Keys, was designed to develop an understanding of the physiology and psychology of starvation and to provide strategies to manage the mass starvation that might follow the war's end in Europe. Tucker . . . provides a fascinating and moving history of the experiment, centering on the lives and experiences of the volunteers and the formidable obstacles they overcame." Publ Wkly

Includes bibliographical references and index

Washington, Harriet A.

★ **Medical** apartheid; the dark history of medical experimentation on Black Americans from colonial times to the present. Doubleday 2006 501p il hardcover o.p. pa $17 **174.2**

1. African Americans -- Health and hygiene 2. African Americans -- Medical care 3. Human experimentation in medicine

ISBN 0-385-50993-6; 978-0-385-50993-0; 0-7679-1547-X pa; 978-0-7679-1547-2 pa

LC 2005-51873

The author offers a "history of medical experimentation on and mistreatment of black Americans in this stunning work, which is both broad in scope and well documented." Booklist

Includes bibliographical references

176 Ethics of sex and reproduction

Green, Ronald Michael

Babies by design; the ethics of genetic choice. Yale University Press 2007 279p il hardcover o.p. pa $19 **176**

1. Genetic engineering 2. Genetic engineering -- Moral and ethical aspects 3. Human reproductive technology -- Moral and ethical aspects 4. Medical genetics 5. Medical genetics -- Moral and ethical aspects 6. Reproductive technology

ISBN 978-0-300-12546-7; 0-300-12546-1; 978-0-300-14308-9 pa; 0-300-14308-7 pa

LC 2007-19927

"By providing examples, contextualizing issues within the framework of stories in popular fiction, and presenting a balanced view of the topics, the author allows the reader to fully explore the issues embedded in the scientific transformation created by the genomic revolution." Sci Books Films

Includes bibliographical references

Mundy, Liza

Everything conceivable; how assisted reproduction is changing men, women, and the world. Alfred A. Knopf 2007 xx, 406p $26.95 **176**

1. Human reproductive technology -- Moral and ethical aspects 2. Human reproductive technology -- Social aspects 3. Reproductive technology

ISBN 978-1-4000-4428-3; 1-4000-4428-6

LC 2006-51432

The author "opens a mind-boggling Pandora's box to issues that surely give us pause. This book is destined to become a bible for those seeking to examine the many ways of making babies and the complex questions that result." Dallas Morning News

Includes bibliographical references

Stock, Gregory

Redesigning humans; our inevitable genetic future. Houghton Mifflin 2002 277p $24; pa $14 **176**

1. Genetic engineering 2. Genetic engineering -- Moral and ethical aspects 3. Genetics 4. Human genetics -- Moral and ethical aspects 5. Human reproductive technology -- Moral and ethical aspects 6. Reproductive technology

ISBN 0-618-06026-X; 0-618-34083-1 pa

LC 2001-51890

The author gives an "overview of the new biotechnology that will allow scientists to delay aging and to insert genes that enhance physical and cognitive performance, combat disease or improve looks into embryos. Stock thoughtfully weighs the ethical dilemmas such advances present, arguing that the real threat is not frivolous abuse of technology but the fact that we don't know the long-term effects of these genetic changes." Publ Wkly

Includes bibliographical references and index

Wilmut, Ian

★ **After** Dolly; the uses and misuses of human cloning. Norton 2006 335p il $24.95; pa $15.95 **176**

1. Cloning 2. Human cloning 3. Human reproductive

technology -- Moral and ethical aspects 4. Reproductive technology
ISBN 0-393-06066-7; 978-0-393-06066-9; 0-393-33026-5 pa; 978-0-393-33026-7 pa
LC 2006-2030
In this "account of the program that eventuated in Dolly, . . . [Wilmut] covers a variety of the social, medical, and scientific implications of cloning. . . . Wilmut, aided by science writer Highfield, well explains potentially confusing issues, in the end making a strong enough case to convince us that Dolly neither lived nor died in vain." Booklist
Includes bibliographical references

177   Ethics of social relations

Armstrong, Karen

Twelve steps to a compassionate life. Alfred A. Knopf 2010 222p $22.95; ebook $11.99   177
1. Compassion 2. Conduct of life 3. Ethics 4. Sympathy 5. Twelve-step programs
ISBN 978-0-307-59559-1; 978-0-307-59563-8 ebook
LC 2010-36870
"Armstrong weaves together the teachings of diverse religions in a graceful, approachable manner. A commendable effort well-executed." Kirkus
Includes bibliographical references

Campbell, Jeremy

The **liar's** tale; a history of falsehood. Norton 2001 363p $26.95; pa $15.95   177
1. Truthfulness and falsehood 2. Truthfulness and falsehood -- History
ISBN 0-393-02559-4; 0-393-32361-7 pa
LC 2001-30286
"This challenging romp through the underbelly of intellectual history . . . is fascinating and troublesome." NY Times Book Rev
Includes bibliographical references and index

Sullivan, Evelin E.

The **concise** book of lying; {by} Evelin Sullivan. Farrar, Straus & Giroux 2001 334p il $25; pa $15   177
1. Deception 2. Deception -- Social aspects 3. Truthfulness and falsehood 4. Truthfulness and falsehood -- Social aspects
ISBN 0-374-12868-5; 0-312-42047-1 pa
LC 2001-18760
The author discusses lying in history and literature. She examines what impels people to lie and what the results of lying might be.
"Anyone interested in the history and philosophy of human nature will appreciate this compelling and cleverly written volume." Libr J
Includes bibliographical references and index

179   Other ethical norms

Baur, Gene

Farm Sanctuary; changing hearts and minds about animals and food. Simon & Schuster 2008 286p il $25   179
1. Animal welfare 2. Livestock industry
ISBN 978-0-7432-9158-3; 0-7432-9158-1
LC 2008-297873
A founder of an organization dedicated to promoting the compassionate treatment of animals and combating factory farming addresses the ethics of breeding animals for food, exposing inhumane practices utilized by typical food-production companies.
"Baur's report is not for the faint of heart, but it is critical reading for anyone willing to ask about the origin of their food, and readers are rewarded with tales of animals who have been saved, and the surprising things that have been learned about farm animals from close observation of their habits. A life-altering read." Booklist
Includes bibliographical references

Beers, Diane L.

★ **For** the prevention of cruelty; the history and legacy of animal rights activism in the United States. Swallow Press/Ohio University Press 2006 312p il $34.95; $19.95   179
1. Animal rights movement 2. Animal rights movement -- History 3. Animal welfare -- United States
ISBN 0-8040-1086-2; 978-0-8040-1086-3; 0-8040-1087-0 pa; 978-0-8040-1087-0 pa
LC 2006-4294
This "study of the animal advocacy movement in the U.S. since the ASPCA's founding in 1866 fills a glaring historical gap with exceptional style, accuracy and insight." Publ Wkly
Includes bibliographical references

Blum, Deborah

The **monkey** wars. Oxford Univ. Press 1994 306p hardcover o.p. pa $19.95   179
1. Animal experimentation 2. Animal rights
ISBN 0-19-510109-X pa
LC 94-12439
"The 'wars' between scientific researchers and animal-rights activists have several aspects: fanaticism, propaganda, pragmatism, and idealism. Blum has written a beautifully balanced account of the major individuals and organizations involved. She points out the different shades of belief and approaches in the conflict and shows how these have developed over the years." Booklist
Includes bibliographical references

Coetzee, J. M.

The **lives** of animals; {by} J.M. Coetzee; {reflections by} Marjorie Garber {et al.}; edited and introduced by Amy Gutmann. Princeton Univ. Press 1999 127p $29.95; pa $13.95   179
1. Animal rights 2. Animal welfare
ISBN 0-691-00443-9; 0-691-07089-X pa
LC 98-39591

"This hybrid collection of fiction and essays is a provocative version of Socratic philosophy. It begins with a story about a Doris Lessing-like author who visits her conflicted son and his antagonistic wife while lecturing at the university where they teach. The mother's hobbyhorse, that Animals R Us, embarrasses the academic couple, and her suggestion that they are like Nazis because they eat meat infuriates them. Other distinguished academics carry on this dialogue in playful fiction and sober commentary, in which the most eloquent part may be the descriptions of communication with animals." New Yorker

Includes bibliographical references

Fox, Michael W.

Inhumane society; the American way of exploiting animals. introduction by Cleveland Amory. St. Martin's Press 1990 268p hardcover o.p. pa $18.95   179

1. Animal welfare
ISBN 0-312-30213-4 pa

LC 89-70299

This book "is very readable and takes a strong stance while presenting a creditably balanced treatment of the issues." Libr J

Includes bibliographical references

Greek, C. Ray

Sacred cows and golden geese; the human cost of experiments on animals. {by} C. Ray Greek and Jean Swingle Greek; foreword by Jane Goodall. Continuum 2000 256p $24.95; pa $18.95   179

1. Animal experimentation 2. Animal experimentation -- Moral and ethical aspects
ISBN 0-8264-1226-2; 0-8264-1402-8 pa

LC 99-57157

This "covers the history of animal experimentation, legislation that promulgates it, the real cost to humans, and alternatives. It is a well-written, if disturbing, book." Libr J

Includes bibliographical references (p. {227}-251) and index

Hall, Stephen S.

Wisdom; from philosophy to neuroscience. Alfred A. Knopf 2010 333p $27.95   179

1. Decision making 2. Neuropsychology
ISBN 978-0-307-26910-2; 0-307-26910-2

LC 2009-27438

"Those searching for easy tips on achieving wisdom will not find them here, but diligent readers will be rewarded. A steady stream of insights into the psychology and neurological mechanisms of wise decision-making and the researchers uncovering them." Kirkus

McCain, John S.

Why courage matters; the way to a braver life. [by] John McCain with Mark Salter. Random House 2004 209p il $16.95   179

1. Courage
ISBN 1-400-06030-3

LC 2003-58626

Senator McCain tells his favorite stories of courage. "In offering anecdotes of individuals whose actions embody the rarity of true courage, his well-drawn examples range from Navajo leaders to Colorado River explorers to Jewish freedom fighter Hannah Senesh and Burmese dissident and Nobel Peace Prize-recipient Aung San Suu Kyi. He reflects on the wellsprings of courage, defining it as conscious self-sacrifice 'for the sake of others or to uphold a virtue,' encompassing actions that may be spurred by honor, outrage, a sense of duty, one's conscience, or moral obligation." SLJ

Miller, William Ian

Faking it. Cambridge University Press 2003 290p $42; pa $18.99   179

1. Honesty 2. Identity (Psychology) 3. Impostors and imposture 4. Social role
ISBN 0-521-83018-4; 0-521-61370-1 pa

LC 2003-43750

"In this refreshing book, Miller . . . considers the human propensity for fraudulence and the correlative fear of being found out. He makes us laugh as he describes trying to wing it in his class on property law or eyeing an attractive woman a few pews up during prayer, and he entertains us with stories of adults who overestimate their sexual prowess and children who find out that saying 'please' doesn't buy them what they were told it would." Libr J

Includes bibliographical references

Rudacille, Deborah

★ The **scalpel** and the butterfly; the conflict between animal research and animal protection. University of California Press 2001 389p pa $21.95 179

1. Animal experimentation 2. Animal welfare
ISBN 978-0-520-23154-2; 0-520-23154-6

LC 2001-27339

The author gives a "history of the conflict between anti-vivisectionists and research scientists. She begins with French physician Claude Bernard. . . . Rudacille then documents the rise of the animal welfare movement in Britain and the United States and legislation designed to govern the use of animals in research. . . . The author also discusses the Nazi 'science' of eugenics and explores the ethical implications of such new scientific developments as xenotransplantation." Libr J

Includes bibliographical references

Shevelow, Kathryn

For the love of animals; the rise of the animal protection movement. Henry Holt and Co. 2008 352p il $27.50   179

1. Animal rights movement 2. Animal welfare -- England -- History
ISBN 978-0-8050-8090-2; 0-8050-8090-2

LC 2007-47353

The author "documents the history of animal cruelty and the slow, controversial and much maligned rise of the animal protection movement in 17th and 18th-century England. . . . This is a fascinating, often disturbing and frequently funny book, a must read for anyone concerned with the treatment of animals and a call to action for the next generation of animal rights activists." Publ Wkly

Includes bibliographical references

Tillich, Paul

★ The **courage** to be; with an introduction by Peter J. Gomes. 2nd ed; Yale Univ. Press 2000 197p pa $12.95   **179**

1. Anxiety 2. Courage 3. Existentialism 4. Ontology

ISBN 0-300-08471-4

LC 00-102364

The author offers advice on how to conquer the anxiety caused by the loss of meaning in one's life.

Wise, Steven M.

★ **Drawing** the line; science and the case for animal rights. Perseus Bks. 2002 322p $26; pa $18   **179**

1. Animal rights

ISBN 0-7382-0340-8; 0-7382-0810-8 pa

Wise "sets out to determine whether animals ranging from dolphins to his family dog . . . have mental abilities meriting {legal} protection. . . . The key to granting any of them rights, Wise argues, is whether they possess 'practical autonomy'—desires and the ability to act to satisfy them." Christ Sci Monit

Includes bibliographical references

Encyclopedia of animal rights and animal welfare; edited by Marc Bekoff; foreword by Jane Goodall. 2nd ed.; Greenwood Press 2010 2v il set $165   **179**

1. Animal rights -- Encyclopedias 2. Animal welfare -- Encyclopedias 3. Reference books

ISBN 978-0-313-35255-3; 0-313-35255-0

LC 2009-22275

"This encyclopedia shows why both animal rights and animal welfare matter around the world. . . . More than 200 entries are included that cover 50 or so topics ranging from activism, animal welfare, anthrozoology, companion animals, and law and animals to pain, stress, and suffering; sports; and animal and wildlife ethics." Libr J

Includes bibliographical references

179.7   Respect and disrespect for human life

Durkheim, Emile

★ **Suicide,** a study in sociology; translated by John A. Spaulding and George Simpson; edited with an introduction by George Simpson. Free Press 1951 405p maps hardcover o.p. pa $18.95   **179.7**

1. Suicide

ISBN 0-684-83632-7 pa

Durkheim's "Suicide is a major sociological classic, one that is still read today, not so much for its data, which are limited and out-of-date, but for the brilliance of his analysis of suicide rates and other data that had been initially obtained for administrative rather than scientific purposes." Reader's Adviser

Includes bibliographical references

Filene, Peter G.

In the arms of others; a cultural history of the right-to-die in America. Dee, I.R. 1998 282p il hardcover o.p. pa $15.95   **179.7**

1. Death 2. Euthanasia 3. Euthanasia -- History -- United States 4. Right to die 5. Sick

ISBN 1-56663-268-4 pa

LC 97-42583

"A fine general overview of the right-to-die question." Libr J

Includes bibliographical references

Humphry, Derek

★ **Final** exit; the practicalities of self-deliverance and assisted sucide for the dying. 3rd ed; Delta Trade Paperbacks 2002 xxviii, 220p pa $13.95   **179.7**

1. Assisted suicide 2. Euthanasia 3. Right to die 4. Suicide

ISBN 0-385-33653-5

LC 2002-19403

This offers information about how to commit suicide for the terminally ill and about the legality and ethics of assisted suicide and euthanasia.

Kiernan, Stephen P.

★ **Last** rights; rescuing the end of life from the medical system. St. Martin's Press 2006 301p $25.95   **179.7**

1. Death 2. Terminal care

ISBN 978-0-312-34224-1; 0-312-34224-1

LC 2006-47449

"Anyone who has stood helplessly by as physicians insisted that a battery of tests and interventions could prolong the life of a loved one, only to see those expensive efforts fail, is certain to be moved by Kiernan's presentation." Booklist

Includes bibliographical references

Marcus, Eric

Why suicide? answers to 200 of the most frequently asked questions about suicide, attempted suicide, and assisted suicide. HarperSanFrancisco 1996 240p pa $14   **179.7**

1. Suicide

ISBN 0-06-251166-1

LC 95-33431

The author's "questions range from 'Does everyone have thoughts of suicide?' to 'What are the arguments against legalizing doctor-assisted suicide?' His responses reflect not only a knowledgeable and well-informed consideration of suicidology but also empathetic treatment. The typical response aims to educate by giving factual information and/or practical advice as well as to console by providing personal stories from suicide survivors." Libr J

Includes bibliographical references

McKhann, Charles F.

A **time** to die; the place for physician assistance. Yale Univ. Press 1999 268p $42; pa $19   **179.7**

1. Assisted suicide 2. Euthanasia

ISBN 0-300-07631-2; 0-300-08698-9 pa

LC 98-22193

The author "believes that physician-assisted suicide is not only desirable but inevitable. Humanity is divided in two parts, he says: those who have seen a loved one die a miserable death and those who have not. . . . McKhann argues level-headedly about patients, doctors, and laws." Booklist

Includes bibliographical references

Peck, M. Scott

Denial of the soul; spiritual and medical perspectives on euthanasia and mortality. Harmony Bks. 1997 242p hardcover o.p. pa $19   **179.7**
1. Death 2. Euthanasia 3. Medical ethics 4. Right to die 5. Suicide
ISBN 0-609-80134-1 pa

       LC 97-157271

"Peck is a wonderful writer, engaging, intelligent, and full of stories from his long psychiatric practice; as usual, he takes on big issues with seriousness, sensitivity, and balance." Libr J

Wanzer, Sidney H.

★ **To** die well; your right to comfort, calm, and choice in the last days of life. Da Capo 2007 209p $24; pa $15   **179.7**
1. Euthanasia 2. Right to die 3. Terminal care -- Ethical aspects
ISBN 0-7382-1083-8; 978-0-7382-1083-4; 0-7382-1163-X pa; 978-0-7382-1163-3 pa

The authors present "what individuals can do to achieve a peaceful death for themselves and their loved ones. Using a combination of patient stories and their own expert discussions, the authors describe the legal rights of terminally ill patients to end their medical care. They also address the controversial issue of hastening the death of terminally ill patients. . . . More useful than the many other recent books on death and dying, this influential volume should be on the shelves of every public and university library." Libr J

Wiesenthal, Simon

★ The **sunflower**; on the possibilities and limits of forgiveness. [by] Simon Wiesenthal; with a symposium edited by Harry James Cargas and Bonny V. Fetterman. rev and expanded ed, 2nd pa. ed; Schocken Books 1998 289p pa $14   **179.7**
1. Forgiveness 2. Genocide 3. Holocaust, 1933-1945 -- Personal narratives 4. World War, 1939-1945 -- Concentration camps 5. World War, 1939-1945 -- Personal narratives, Jewish
ISBN 0-8052-1060-1

       LC 99-198049

"The responses to the author's question are as varied as their authors. The mystery of evil and atonement remain, and the reader is left challenged on these most basic issues of meaning in human life." Publ Wkly

Yount, Lisa

★ **Right** to die and euthanasia; rev ed; Facts on File 2007 312p il $45   **179.7**
1. Assisted suicide 2. Euthanasia 3. Right to die
ISBN 978-0-8160-6275-1

       LC 2006-33424

This reference source contains an overview of the subjects, a chronology of significant events (including the Terri Schiavo case), biographical information on important figures, a glossary of terms, and an annotated bibliography.

180   History, geographic treatment, biography

Gottlieb, Anthony

The **dream** of reason; a history of western philosophy from the Greeks to the Renaissance. Norton 2000 468p $27.95; pa $17.95   **180**
1. Philosophy -- History
ISBN 0-393-04951-5; 0-393-32365-X pa

       LC 00-49012

"This eloquent book offers a lively chronicle of the evolution of Western philosophy." Publ Wkly

Includes bibliographical references and index

★ Encyclopedia of classical philosophy; edited by Donald J. Zeyl; associate editors, Daniel T. Devereux and Phillip K. Mitsis. Greenwood Press 1997 614p $119.95   **180**
1. Ancient philosophy 2. Ancient philosophy -- Encyclopedias 3. Biography, Collective 4. Philosophers -- Biography 5. Reference books
ISBN 0-313-28775-9

       LC 96-2562

"This encyclopedia fills a void in philosophical reference works that has existed for too long, and it will likely become a standard in the field." Libr J

181   Eastern philosophy

Buber, Martin

★ **I** and thou; translated by Ronald Gregor Smith. Scribner 2000 126p $22; pa $11   **181**
1. God 2. Jewish philosophy 3. Ontology
ISBN 0-7432-0133-7; 0-7432-0133-7 pa

In this book, the author "conceived the individual as in permanent relationship with all forms of life, finding his fulfillment in the reciprocity of the relationship—the 'Thou' being God." Reader's Adviser

Confucius

★ The **Analects**; [by] Confucius; translated by Arthur Waley; with an introduction by Sarah Allan. Knopf 2000 xxxi, 257p $19   **181**
1. Chinese ethics 2. Chinese philosophy
ISBN 0-375-41204-2

       LC 00-53460

"One of the Chinese 'Four Books.' A brief, unsystematic collection of fragmentary writings attributed to Confucius and his school. . . . It is one of the most influential works in the history of Chinese thought." Reader's Ency

Includes bibliographical references

183   Sophistic, Socratic, related Greek philosophies

Stone, I. F.

★ The **trial** of Socrates. Anchor Bks. 1989 282p pa $14.95   **183**

1. Philosophers

ISBN 0-385-26032-6; 978-0-385-26032-9

The author attempts "to show that Athens was totally committed to free speech and did not normally place any check on it, and, therefore, that the trial of Socrates was a singular aberration which might be explicable, if finally not justifiable." Commentary

Includes bibliographical references

Waterfield, Robin

Why Socrates died; dispelling the myths. W. W. Norton & Co. 2009 253p il map $27.95   **183**

1. Hellenism 2. Philosophers 3. Philosophy, Ancient 4. Trials

ISBN 978-0-393-06527-5

LC 2009-4317

This "account of the trial and execution of the philosopher draws on Greek sources to separate truth from myth, . . . [arguing for] Socrates' character as a deeply moral thinker whose convictions strongly contrasted those of his former student, Alcibaides." (Publishers note)

The author "sets out to explain why Socrates died: he discusses his trial, but also offers an informed and well-written account of classical Athenian history." Times Higher Ed

Includes bibliographical references

184   Platonic philosophy

Hare, R. M.

Plato. Oxford Univ. Press 1982 82p hardcover o.p. pa $9.95   **184**

1. Authors 2. Essayists 3. Philosophers

ISBN 0-19-287585-X pa

LC 83-159441

The author examines the chief Platonic concepts in their political and intellectual contexts

185   Aristotelian philosophy

Adler, Mortimer J.

Aristotle for everybody; difficult thought made easy. Macmillan 1978 206p hardcover o.p. pa $13   **185**

1. Philosophers 2. Writers on science

ISBN 0-684-83823-0 pa

LC 78-853

Adler traces "in the simplest language and with occasional modern analogues, the logic and growth of Aristotle's basic doctrines." Publ Wkly

Includes bibliographical references

187   Epicurean philosophy

Lucretius Carus, Titus

On the nature of things: De rerum natura; [by] Lucretius; edited and translated by Anthony M. Esolen. Johns Hopkins Univ. Press 1995 296p pa $25   **187**

1. Ancient philosophy 2. Poetry -- By individual authors

ISBN 978-0-8018-5055-4; 0-8018-5055-X

LC 94-25165

"Writing in the waning days of the Roman Republic— as Rome's politics grew individualistic and treacherous, its high-life wanton, its piety introspective and morbid—Lucretius sets forth a rational and materialistic view of the world which offers a retreat into a quiet community of wisdom and friendship." Publisher's note

188   Stoic philosophy

Marcus Aurelius

★ **Meditations**; a new translation, with an introduction, by Gregory Hays. Modern Lib. 2002 lvii, 191p $19.95   **188**

1. Ethics 2. Philosophy, Ancient 3. Stoics

ISBN 0-679-64260-9

LC 2001-57947

"An emperor and Stoic philosopher records his thoughts as he struggles for composure and order in the face of national disaster." Good Read

189   Medieval western philosophy

Davies, Brian

The **thought** of Thomas Aquinas. Oxford Univ. Press 1992 391p hardcover o.p. pa $44.95   **189**

1. Doctrinal theology 2. Saints 3. Theologians

ISBN 0-19-826753-3 pa

LC 91-35671

"Davies aims to cover the whole programme of the Summa in 370 pages. This necessarily means that, though his writing is admirably clear and never cryptic, much of what he says is extremely concise, and some topics get less airing than others." Times Lit Suppl

Includes bibliographical references

Rubenstein, Richard E.

Aristotle's children; how Christians, Muslims, and Jews rediscovered ancient wisdom and illuminated the Dark Ages. Harcourt 2003 368p $27 **189**

1. Faith and reason -- Christianity -- History of doctrines 2. Medieval philosophy 3. Philosophers 4. Scholasticism 5. Writers on science

ISBN 0-15-100720-9

LC 2003-6582

"Although the book purports to trace Aristotle's influence on Christianity, Islam and Judaism, it devotes more attention to Christianity. Even so, Rubenstein's lively prose, his lucid insights and his crystal-clear historical analyses make this a first-rate study in the history of ideas." Publ Wkly

Includes bibliographical references and index

Thomas

★ **Selected** writings; edited and translated with an introduction and notes by Ralph McInerny. Penguin Bks. 1998 xxxviii, 841p pa $14.95   **189**
1. Catholic Church and philosophy -- Early works to 1800
ISBN 0-14-043632-4

Arranged chronologically, this collection of theological and philosophical writings brings together sermons, commentaries, responses to criticism and lengthy extracts from the Summa theologia.

The Renaissance philosophy of man; {by} Petrarca {and others}; selections in translation, edited by Ernst Cassirer, Paul Oskar Kristeller, John Herman Randall, Jr. University of Chicago Press 1948 405p hardcover o.p. pa $17.50   **189**
1. Authors 2. Medieval philosophy 3. Philosophers 4. Poets 5. Writers on science
ISBN 0-226-09604-1 pa

This book provides English translations from selected writings of six early Italian Renaissance philosophers from about the middle of the fourteenth century to the end of the sixteenth. Francesco Petrarca, Lorenzo Valla, Marsilio Ficino, Giovanni Pico della Mirandola, Pietro Pomponazzi, and Juan Luis Vives are represented. An introduction accompanies each of the translations

190   Modern western and other noneastern philosophy

Berlin, Isaiah

★ The **sense** of reality; studies in ideas and their history. edited by Henry Hardy; with an introduction by Patrick Gardiner. Farrar, Straus & Giroux 1997 xx, 278p hardcover o.p. pa $13   **190**
1. Authors 2. Communism 3. Dramatists 4. Essayists 5. History -- Philosophy 6. Modern philosophy 7. Nationalism 8. Nobel laureates for literature 9. Novelists 10. Philosophers 11. Poets 12. Russian literature -- History and criticism 13. Short story writers 14. Social activists 15. Socialism
ISBN 0-374-52569-2 pa

LC 96-39829

Berlin maintains that "the great goods of human life are diverse and conflicting. . . . Values like self-realization and social cohesion, economic progress and settled communities cannot always be made compatible. Sometimes we must choose between them. In the nine seminal essays collected in 'The Sense of Reality' ranging over such diverse subjects as the Romantic movement, Marxism, Kant's influence on nationalism and the thought of Rabindranath Tagore, Berlin argues with rare wisdom and passion that every such choice entails a loss." N Y Times Book Rev

Includes bibliographical references

Critchley, Simon

The **book** of dead philosophers. Vintage Books 2009 xxxviii, 265p il pa $15.95   **190**
1. Death 2. Philosophers 3. Philosophers -- Death 4. Philosophy
ISBN 978-0-307-39043-1

LC 2008-47719

"A primer on just about every notable philosophical figure in history, this book challenges readers to learn from the philosophers' conduct in life and the circumstances of their deaths. . . . It is a witty and generous gift that will leave readers perhaps a little less afraid of death and more appreciative of life." Publ Wkly

Includes bibliographical references (p. 286-98)

Gay, Peter

The **rise** of modern paganism. Norton 1995 xviii, 555, xvp pa $19.95   **190**
1. Enlightenment 2. Modern philosophy
ISBN 0-393-31302-6

Voume one of a two volume series examining the ideas, experiences and impact of leading Enlightenment figures in 18th century Europe and America.

The **science** of freedom. Norton 1996 xx, 705, xviiip pa $19.95   **190**
1. Enlightenment 2. Modern philosophy
ISBN 0-393-31366-2

Volume two of a two-volume series examining the ideas, experiences and impact of leading Enlightenment figures in 18th century Europe and America.

Himmelfarb, Gertrude

The **moral** imagination; from Edmund Burke to Lionel Trilling. Ivan R. Dee 2006 259p $26   **190**
1. Modern philosophy 2. Political science
ISBN 1-56663-624-8

LC 2005-19838

The author "specializes in Victorian Britain and profiles some of its leading writers and statesmen, along with philosophical forerunners and descendants, to probe the complexities of two centuries of conservative thought. . . . Himmelfarb's stylish blend of literary criticism and intellectual history yields a stimulating reappraisal of a multifaceted and influential worldview." Publ Wkly

Includes bibliographical references

The **roads** to modernity; the British, French, and American enlightenments. Knopf 2004 284p $25   **190**
1. Enlightenment
ISBN 1-400-04236-4

LC 2003-60576

"This is a book with important ideological implications that deserves to be read and debated across the political spectrum." Publ Wkly

Includes bibliographical references

Magee, Bryan

The **story** of philosophy. DK Pub. 1998 240p il
hardcover o.p. pa $20   **190**
  1. Philosophy 2. Philosophy -- History
  ISBN 0-7894-3511-X; 0-7894-7994-X pa
                                  LC 98-3780
"Writing with a clear and lively style, Magee provides an
excellent introduction to the topic." SLJ
  Includes bibliographical references

Miller, Jim

Examined lives; [by] James Miller. Farrar,
Straus and Giroux 2011 422p ill. $28   **190**
  1. Biography, Collective 2. Conduct of life
  3. Philosophers -- Biography 4. Philosophy --
  Psychological aspects
  ISBN 978-0-374-15085-3
                          LC 201014385
This book, a "New York Times" Notable Book for 2011,
looks at the lives of "12 philosophers: Socrates, Plato, Diogenes the Cynic, . . . Aristotle, Seneca, Augustine, Montaigne, Descartes, Rousseau, Kant, Emerson and Nietzsche.
In each case, he explores the life selectively, looking for
'crux' points and investigating how ideas of the philosophical life have changed. Few readers will be astounded to learn
that philosophers make as much of a mess of their lives as
anyone else. But [James] Miller . . . shows us philosophers
becoming ever more inclined to reflect on these failings, and
suggests that this makes their lives more rather than less
worth studying." (N Y Times)

Nadler, Steven M.

The **best** of all possible worlds; a story of philosophers, God, and evil. [by] Steven Nadler. Farrar,
Straus and Giroux 2008 300p $25   **190**
  1. Essayists 2. God 3. Good and evil 4. Mathematicians
  5. Modern philosophy 6. Philosophers 7. Theologians
  ISBN 978-0-374-22998-6; 0-374-22998-8
                        LC 2008-29143
This book "is written simply and clearly, without condescension, flashiness or oversimplification. But it's a demanding book nonetheless, and you need to pay attention. You'll
be amply rewarded if you do." Washington Post Book World
  Includes bibliographical references

Sedgwick, Peter

★ **Descartes** to Derrida; an introduction to European philosophy. Blackwell 2001 310p $76.95; pa
$33.95   **190**
  1. Modern philosophy 2. Philosophy, European 3.
  Philosophy, Modern
  ISBN 0-631-20142-4; 0-631-20143-2 pa
                          LC 00-57917
"This book should take a place as one of the key texts
in humanities programs throughout the English-speaking
world." Choice
  Includes bibliographical references

★ The Columbia history of Western philosophy; edited by Richard H. Popkin. Columbia Univ. Press
1999 xxvi, 836p $64.50   **190**
  1. Philosophy -- History
  ISBN 0-231-10128-7
                          LC 98-15219
"This survey's coverage of medieval Islamic, Jewish,
and Christian philosophy is particularly strong." Choice
  Includes bibliographical references

Great thinkers of the Western world; edited by Ian
P. McGreal. HarperCollins Pubs. 1992 572p
$47   **190**
  1. Philosophy 2. Science 3. Theology
  ISBN 0-06-270026-X
                          LC 91-38362
"This guide to 116 selected authors . . . spans the ancient Greeks to the first half of the twentieth century. . . .
The guide is arranged chronologically by the birthdate of
the writer. Each entry contains birth and death dates, a list of
the writer's major ideas, an essay of three to five pages, and
a short annotated list of secondary sources. . . . Its readable
essays . . . are accessible to the layperson." Booklist

★ The Oxford history of Western philosophy; edited by Anthony Kenny. Oxford Univ. Press 1994
407p il maps hardcover o.p. pa $15   **190**
  1. Philosophy -- History
  ISBN 0-19-824278-6; 0-19-289329-7 pa
                          LC 94-9858
"The illustrations have been wisely chosen to show the
constant play between art and idea. Some familiarity with
analytic philosophy would be useful to gain the most from
the text, but this is a significant addition to the literature."
Libr J
  Includes bibliographical references

191   Philosophy of United States and Canada

Dewey, John

★ The **philosophy** of John Dewey; edited with
an introduction and commentary by John J. McDermott. University of Chicago Press 1981 2v in 1 pa
$25   **191**
  1. Philosophers 2. Psychologists 3. Writers on science
  ISBN 0-226-14401-1
                          LC 80-39766
A digest of extracts from the American philosopher's
most important works.

Rand, Ayn

★ The **voice** of reason; essays in objectivist
thought; edited and with an introduction by Leonard
Peikoff; and with additional essays by Leonard Peikoff and Peter Schwartz. New Am. Lib. 1989 353p
hardcover o.p. pa $18   **191**
  1. American philosophy 2. Objectivism (Philosophy)
  ISBN 0-45-300634-5; 0-45-201046-2 pa
                          LC 88-18192

The late author opposed liberalism and championed "capitalism, self-interest, and objective reality against collectivism, altruism, and mysticism. . . . These lectures, newspaper columns, and magazine articles are entirely characteristic of her—surprisingly emotional and dogmatic for a professed rationalist. Additional essays by editor Peikoff and disciple Peter Schwartz are of a piece." Booklist

Includes bibliographical references

Romano, Carlin

America the philosophical; Carlin Romano. Knopf 2012 672 p. **191**
1. Critics -- United States 2. Intellectuals -- United States 3. Journalists -- United States 4. Philosophers -- United States 5. Philosophical literature 6. Philosophy -- United States
ISBN 0679434704; 9780679434702
LC 2011034753

This book offers a "diagnosis of the condition of philosophical thinking in America today. . . . [Carlin Romano] realizes that philosophy has traditionally been the ballpark for white men to play in, so he . . . add[s] to the team some prominent women, African Americans, Native Americans, gays and others. But he begins with the famous white men (William James, George Santayana, John Dewey et al.) and looks at key figures later on--John Rawls and Richard Rorty among them." (Kirkus)

192   Philosophy of British Isles

Edmonds, David

Wittgenstein's poker; the story of a ten-minute argument between two great philosophers. {by} David Edmonds and John Eidinow. Ecco Press 2001 340p il $24; pa $13.95 **192**
1. Logicians 2. Nonfiction writers 3. Philosophers
ISBN 0-06-621244-8; 0-06-093664-9 pa
LC 2002-276301

"On the Cambridge University campus in 1946, two of the twentieth-century's most notable philosophers, Ludwig Wittgenstein and Karl Popper, squared off in an intense 10-minute clash rumored to have culminated with Wittgenstein brandishing a red-hot poker. The authors explain what the fight was about and how it reflects the development of philosophy. Ivory-tower drama at its crackling best." Booklist

Includes bibliographical references (p. {317}-327) and index

193   Philosophy of Germany and Austria

Hegel, Georg Wilhelm Friedrich

★ The **philosophy** of Hegel; edited with an introduction by Carl J. Friedrich. Modern Lib. 1954 552p pa $10.75 **193**
ISBN 0-07-553655-2 pa
Contents: The philosophy of history; The history of philosophy; The science of logic; Philosophy of right and law, or natural law and political science outlines; Lectures on aesthetics; The phenomenology of the spirit (1807); Political essays; Bibliography

Kant, Immanuel

★ **Basic** writings of Kant; edited and with an introduction by Allen W. Wood. Modern Lib. 2001 xxv, 478p pa $15.95 **193**
1. Philosophy
ISBN 0-375-75733-3
LC 2001-18303

This volume presents the essential works of the philosopher including "selected excerpts from his most frequently taught essays and book-length publications, including 'Critique of Pure Reason, Critique of Judgment,' and 'Eternal Peace.'" Publisher's note

★ **Critique** of pure reason; translated by Marcus Weigelt. Rev ed; Penguin 2003 lxxvi, 708p pa $20 **193**
1. Reason 2. Theory of knowledge
ISBN 978-0-14-044747-7; 0-14-044747-4

In this philosophical work Kant "attempted to define the possibility and limits of our knowledge. He denied that we can ever know how the world 'really' is. However, he tried to show that science nevertheless has a sort of universal validity, insofar as it consists of sense experience, which comes from the world, coupled with the mind, which orders this sense experience according to the 'categories of the understanding' and the intuitions of space and time." Reader's Ency. 4th edition

Krell, David Farrell

Basic writings; from Being and time (1927) to The task of thinking (1964) edited, with general introduction and introductions to each selection by David Farrell Krell. rev and expanded ed; HarperSanFrancisco 1993 452p pa $17.95 **193**
ISBN 0-06-063763-3
LC 91-58187

Nietzsche, Friedrich Wilhelm

★ **Basic** writings of Nietzsche; introduction by Peter Gay; translated and edited, with commentaries, by Walter Kaufmann. Modern Lib. 2000 xxiv, 862p pa $14.95 **193**
ISBN 0-679-78339-3
LC 00-64578

"Gathers the complete texts of five of Nietzsche's most important works, from his first book to his last: The Birth of Tragedy, Beyond Good and Evil; On the Genealogy of Morals; The Case of Wagner; and Ecce Homo. . . . Included also are seventy-five aphorisms, selections from Nietzsche's correspondence, and variants from drafts for Ecce Homo." Publisher's note

★ **Thus** spoke Zarathustra; a book for everyone and nobody. [by] Friedrich Nietzsche; translated with an introduction and notes by Graham Parkes. Oxford University Press 2005 xliii, 335p pa $14.95 **193**
ISBN 0-19-280583-5
LC 2005-19431

A philosophical narrative in which Nietzsche "transforms the ancient Persian philosopher Zarathustra . . . into a mouthpiece for his own views. Nietzsche develops his doctrine of the 'Ubermensch' in a prophetic, quasi-biblical style. Nietzsche's Zarathustra announces the death of God, and preaches a new 'faithfulness to the earth,' which includes a new respect for the body . . . and attentiveness to this world rather than the next. He also attacks pity and virtue as weapons of weakness." Reader's Ency. 4th edition

Includes bibliographical references

The **portable** Nietzsche; selected and translated, with an introduction, prefaces, and notes, by Walter Kaufmann. Viking 1954 687p hardcover o.p. pa $17   **193**

ISBN 0-14-015062-5 pa

Includes the complete texts of Thus spake Zarathustra, Twilight of the idols, The antichrist, and Nietzsche contra Wagner. Selections from other works, notes and letters complete the volume

The **will** to power; a new translation by Walter Kaufmann and R. J. Hollingdale; edited with commentary by Walter Kaufmann; with facsimiles of the original manuscript. Random House 1967 xxxii, 576p hardcover o.p. pa $16   **193**

ISBN 0-394-70437-1 pa

Safranski, Rudiger

Nietzsche; a philosophical biography. translated by Shelley Frisch. Norton 2001 409p $29.95; pa $18.95   **193**

1. Authors 2. Essayists 3. Philosophers

ISBN 0-393-05008-4; 0-393-32380-3 pa

LC 2001-52130

"With brilliant insights and impressive scholarship, Safranski . . . here makes a major contribution to understanding and appreciating the lasting significance of Friedrich Nietzsche." Libr J

Includes bibliographical references

Solomon, Robert C.

What Nietzsche really said; {by} Robert C. Solomon and Kathleen M. Higgins. Schocken Bks. 2000 263p hardcover o.p. pa $13   **193**

1. Authors 2. Essayists 3. Philosophers

ISBN 0-8052-1094-6 pa

LC 99-33796

The authors offer an "overview of Friedrich Nietzsche's life, thought, and influence. . . . Particularly helpful are their brief annotations of Nietzsche's 14 books and short analyses of the thinkers who influenced him." Libr J

Includes bibliographical references

194   Philosophy of France

Gray, Francine du Plessix

Simone Weil. Viking 2001 248p il $19.95 **194**

1. Essayists 2. Philosophers -- France -- Biography 3.

Political and social philosophers

ISBN 0-670-89998-4

LC 00-51367

"Part intellectual primer and part case study, this slim, sympathetic biography makes us question whether we value Weil's thinking despite the example of her punishing, courageous, profoundly exasperating life, or because of it." New Yorker

Includes bibliographical references

196   Philosophy of Spain and Portugal

Ortega y Gasset, Jose

★ **What** is philosophy? translated from the Spanish by Mildred Adams. Norton 1961 252p hardcover o.p. pa $10.95   **196**

1. Philosophy

ISBN 0-393-00126-1 pa

This volume by the influential Spanish philosopher, essayist and critic "consists of a series of lectures begun in 1929 at the University of Madrid. Interrupted when the University was closed as a result of political troubles, they were resumed in a Madrid theatre. Part of the lectures had been given earlier in Buenos Aires." N Y Times Book Rev

200   RELIGION

200   Religion

Armstrong, Karen

A **history** of God; the 4000 year quest of Judaism, Christianity, and Islam. Knopf 1993 xxiii, 460p maps hardcover o.p. pa $15.95   **200**

1. Christianity 2. God 3. Islam 4. Judaism

ISBN 0-345-38456-3 pa

LC 92-38318

This is a study of ideas and experiences of God in Judaism, Christianity and Islam from Abraham to the twentieth century

"Public librarians should be aware that conservative readers may be offended by this book, and even religious scholars may find Armstrong's rather one-sided 'death of God' optimism about humanity a bit passé. Otherwise, this is an excellent and informative book." Libr J

Bowker, John

World religions; contributing consultants: David Bowker [et al.] DK Pub. 1997 200p il maps $35; pa $16.95   **200**

1. Religion 2. Religions

ISBN 0-7894-1439-2; 0-7566-1772-3 pa

LC 96-38277

Each chapter begins with an "introduction and is followed by one-or-two page sections that explain the basic tenets of the faith, symbols, events, people, buildings, works of art, and the differences and similarities to other religions. Hinduism, Buddhism, Judaism, Christianity, and Islam are included as are Jainism, Sikhism, Chinese and Japanese religions, and Native religions." SLJ

Chittister, Joan
The **gift** of years; growing older gracefully. BlueBridge 2008 222p $19.95   **200**
1. Aged -- Conduct of life 2. Aged -- Psychology 3. Aging -- Psychological aspects 4. Aging -- Religious aspects 5. Aging -- Social aspects 6. Elderly
ISBN 978-1-933346-10-6; 1-933346-10-8
LC 2008-00332
"This collection of inspirational reflections, 'not meant to be read in one sitting, or even in order, but one topic at a time,' abounds in gentle insights and arresting aphorisms." Publ Wkly
Includes bibliographical references

Dawkins, Richard
★ The **God** delusion. Houghton Mifflin Co. 2006 406p $27; pa $15.95   **200**
1. Atheism 2. God 3. Irreligion 4. Religion
ISBN 978-0-618-68000-9; 0-618-68000-4; 978-0-618-91824-9 pa; 0-618-91824-8 pa
LC 2006-15506
"Both fans of Dawkins and his many opponents will want to read this book." Libr J
Includes bibliographical references

De Botton, Alain, 1969-
Religion for atheists; Alain de Botton. Pantheon Books 2012 320p. ill.   **200**
1. Atheism 2. Atheists 3. Criticism (Philosophy) 4. Philosophy 5. Philosophy & religion 6. Religion -- Philosophy 7. Religions 8. Religious life
ISBN 9780307379108
LC 2011021286
It was the author's intent to demonstrate "that the supernatural claims of religion are entirely false -- but that it still has some very important things to teach the secular world." The author "suggests that rather than mocking religion, agnostics and atheists should instead steal from it—because the world's religions are packed with good ideas on how we might live and arrange our societies. Blending deep respect with total impiety, [Alain] de Botton (a non-believer himself) proposes that we look to religion for insights into how to, among other concerns, build a sense of community, make our relationships last, overcome feelings of envy and inadequacy, inspire travel and reconnect with the natural world." (Publisher's note)

Dennett, Daniel Clement
Breaking the spell; religion as a natural phenomenon. [by] Daniel C. Dennett. Viking 2006 448p il $25.95   **200**
1. Religion
ISBN 0-670-03472-X
LC 2005-42415
"A book certain to spark heated controversy." Booklist
Includes bibliographical references

Dreyfus, Hubert L., 1929-
All things shining; reading the Western classics to find meaning in a secular age. [by] Hubert Dreyfus and Sean Dorrance Kelly. Free Press 2011 254p $26; ebook $12.99   **200**
1. Meaning (Philosophy) 2. Religion 3. Religions
ISBN 978-1-4165-9615-8; 1-4165-9615-1; 978-1-4391-0170-4 ebook; 1-4391-0170-1 ebook
LC 2010021750
This book contains "readings of authors including Homer, Dante, Descartes and Kant, as well as the novelists Herman Melville and David Foster Wallace." (N Y Times (Late N Y Ed)) Index.
"A provocative, illuminating and inspirational exhortation to 'Ask not why the gods have abandoned you, but why you have abandoned the gods.'" Kirkus
Includes bibliographical references

Hall, Timothy L.
★ **American** religious leaders. Facts on File 2003 430p il $65   **200**
1. Clergy -- United States -- Biography 2. Religious biography 3. Religious leaders -- United States -- Biography
ISBN 0-8160-4534-8
LC 2002-2454
"This is a perfect source for fast, basic information for anyone who wishes a two-minute reading synopsis on an American religious leader. It should be within arm's reach of any reference librarian working an information desk or a telephone." Am Ref Books Annu, 2003
Includes bibliographical references

Hexham, Irving
Understanding world religions. Zondervan 2011 512p il map $39.99; ebook $30.99   **200**
1. Religions
ISBN 978-0-310-25944-2; 0-310-25944-4; 978-0-310-31448-6 ebook; 0-310-31448-8 ebook
LC 2010013103
This "world religions text explores various religions under the broad categories of African Religions, the Yogic Traditions (including Buddhism), and the Abrahamic traditions." Publisher's note
Includes bibliographical references

Hitchens, Christopher
God is not great; how religion poisons everything. Twelve 2007 307p $24.99   **200**
1. Atheism 2. Religion
ISBN 978-0-44657-980-3; 0-44657-980-7
LC 2006-23039
In this work Hitchens catalogs "the major arguments against religion, which he deems a pernicious force. First, he writes, faith misrepresents the origin of the cosmos as well as that of humanity; second, it fosters servility, solipsism, and sexual repression; and, third, it is based on wishful thinking. Hitchens spares no targets in this manifesto, criticizing both Western and Eastern faiths." Libr J
Includes bibliographical references

Hutchison, William R.

Religious pluralism in America; the contentious history of a founding ideal. Yale University Press 2003 262p $32.50; pa $18 **200**
1. Religious pluralism
ISBN 0-300-09813-8; 0-300-10516-9 pa
LC 2002-151893

The author "illuminates the cultural transformations that enabled twentieth-century Americans to embrace belatedly the religious diversity that emerged in the nineteenth-century influx of Catholic and Jewish immigrants and in the rise of new American-born faiths such as Mormonism and Transcendentalism. . . . Though he acknowledges the concerns of critics worried about the moral balkanization of a society lacking shared religious premises, Hutchison hails America's new religious pluralism as a great achievement. A balanced and informative narrative." Booklist
Includes bibliographical references

King, Barbara J.

Evolving God; a provocative view on the origins of religion. Doubleday 2007 262p il $24.95 **200**
1. Religion 2. Social change
ISBN 978-0-385-51104-9; 0-385-51104-3
LC 2006-270101

The author "contends that religion, conceived as a system not of beliefs but of actions, not as theology but as worship, is a consequence of primate evolution. . . . In conclusion, she weighs the popular debate over evolution, noting high skepticism about human evolution and high belief in God, and questions the compulsion to choose either evolution or belief. Anyone who recognizes that compulsion, internal or external, may profit from reading this brilliant book." Booklist
Includes bibliographical references

Messadie, Gerald

A **history** of the devil; translated from the French by Marc Romano. Kodansha Int. 1996 377p hardcover o.p. pa $16 **200**
1. Demonology 2. Devil
ISBN 1-56836-198-X pa
LC 95-4949

"Messadie's highly engaging and provocative cultural history is essential for most libraries." Libr J
Includes bibliographical references

Prothero, Stephen R.

God is not one; the eight rival religions that run the world--and why their differences matter. [by] Stephen Prothero. HarperOne 2010 388p $26.99; ebook $9.99 **200**
1. Religions
ISBN 978-0-06-157127-5; 0-06-157127-X; 978-0-06-199120-2 ebook; 0-06-199120-1 ebook
LC 2009053372

Prothero argues that each of the major world religions have different worldviews and approaches to spiritual questions. The book contains chapters on Islam (the way of submission); Christianity (the way of salvation); Confucianism (the way of propriety); Hinduism (the way of devotion); Buddhism (the way of awakening); Yoruba religion (the way

of connection); Judaism (the way of exile and return); Daoism (the way of flourishing); Atheism (the way of reason).

"Provocative, thoughtful, fiercely intelligent and, for both believing and nonbelieving, formal and informal students of religion, a must-read." Booklist
Includes bibliographical references

Religious literacy; what every American needs to know--and doesn't. [by] Stephen Prothero. HarperSanFrancisco 2007 296p $24.95 **200**
1. Religions 2. Religions -- Dictionaries 3. Religious education -- United States
ISBN 978-0-06-084670-1; 0-06-084670-4
LC 2006-41310

"In this book, the author combines a lively history of the rise and fall of American religious literacy with a set of proposed remedies based on his hope that 'the Fall into religious ignorance is reversible.' He also includes a useful multicultural glossary of religious definitions and allusions, in which religious illiterates can find the prodigal son, the promised land, the Quakers and the Koran." Washington Post Book World
Includes bibliographical references

Turner, Alice K.

The **history** of hell. Harcourt Brace & Co. 1993 275p il hardcover o.p. pa $22 **200**
1. Hell
ISBN 0-15-600137-3 pa
LC 93-9909

"Belief in a hell or some sort of afterlife has been intrinsic to the religions of the world ever since the first stories were shared aloud and incised in clay tablets. Turner's richly illustrated history surveys the myriad forms hell has taken in the West from Sumer to Rome and beyond." Booklist

Weber, Eugen

Apocalypses; prophesies, cults, and millennial beliefs through the ages. [by] Eugen Weber. Harvard Univ. Press 1999 294p $27.50; pa $16.95 **200**
1. End of the world 2. End of the world -- History of doctrines 3. Millennialism -- History of doctrines 4. Millennium
ISBN 0-674-04080-5; 0-674-00395-0 pa
LC 99-18001

"Weber traces millennial beliefs as professed through the ages. From ancient and pre-Christian times to the present day, humankind has had an unshakable belief that the end is at hand. . . . Weber has an excellent grasp of his subject, an accessible style, and an understated sense of humor." Booklist
Includes bibliographical references

Williams, Juan

This far by faith; stories from the African-American religious experience. [by] Juan Williams and Quinton Dixie. Morrow 2003 326p il hardcover o.p. pa $15.95 **200**
1. African Americans -- History 2. African Americans -- Religion
ISBN 0-06-018863-4; 0-06-093424-7 pa
LC 2002-71884

"Brief topical articles and captioned illustrations supplement the main text, creating a balanced, readable, and nuanced introduction to the power of faith to sustain the African American community." Libr J

★ Encyclopedia of religion; Lindsay Jones, editor in chief. 2nd ed; Macmillan Reference USA 2005 15v il set $1295 **200**
1. Reference books 2. Religion 3. Religions -- Encyclopedias
ISBN 0-02-865733-0
LC 2004-17052
"Treats theoretical (e.g., doctrines, myths, theologies, ethics), practical (e.g., cults, sacraments, meditations), and sociological (e.g., religious groups, ecclesiastical forms) aspects of religion; includes extensive coverage of non-Western religions. Signed articles by some 1,400 contributors worldwide end with bibliographies. Many composite entries treat two or more related topics. . . . Has quickly become the standard work." Guide to Ref Books. 11th edition [review of 1993 edition]
Includes bibliographical references

★ Encyclopedia of religious rites, rituals, and festivals; Frank A. Salamone, editor. Routledge 2004 487p il $150 **200**
1. Reference books 2. Religions 3. Religions -- Encyclopedias 4. Rites and ceremonies 5. Rites and ceremonies -- Encyclopedias
ISBN 0-415-94180-6
LC 2003-20389
"The entries can be understood by readers unfamiliar with the topics covered, but the work is suitable for all levels of scholars." Choice
Includes bibliographical references

National Geographic concise history of world religions; an illustrated time line. edited by Tim Cooke. National Geographic 2011 352 p. col. ill. **200**
1. Ethics 2. Religion -- History -- Chronology 3. Religion and ethics 4. Religions 5. Religions -- History 6. World history
ISBN 1426206984; 1426206992; 9781426206986; 9781426206993
LC 2011276808
This book continues the "Concise History" series with [a] . . . take on major religions and lesser-known faiths of all times and nations. . . . [It] . . . offers a . . . global perspective on the history of faith in the Americas, Europe, Asia and Oceania, and Africa and the Middle East. . . . [I]llustrations illuminate the faithful, their houses of worship, and the articles and artifacts of faith. . . . 50 feature essays explore in detail the origins, development and influence of faith; 325 images document all aspects of the religious experience, from architecture and icons to exemplary individuals and acts of devotion; and quotes throughout chapters are drawn from prayers and sermons that embody the religious attitudes of each era. (Publisher's Note)

Religions of the world; a comprehensive encyclopedia of beliefs and practices. J. Gordon Melton,

Martin Baumann, editors; Todd M. Johnson, world religious statistics; Donald Wiebe, introduction. 2nd ed.; ABC-CLIO 2010 6v il map set $595 **200**
1. Reference books 2. Religions -- Encyclopedias
ISBN 978-1-59884-203-6; 978-1-59884-204-3 ebook
LC 2010-29403
"With its currency and particular emphasis, this work warrants the attention of virtually every academic and public library." Booklist
Includes bibliographical references

The encyclopedia of cults, sects, and new religions; {edited by} James R. Lewis. 2nd ed; Prometheus Bks. 2002 951p il $180 **200**
1. Cults 2. Cults -- United States -- Encyclopedias 3. Reference books 4. Sects -- Encyclopedias 5. Sects -- United States -- Encyclopedias
ISBN 1-57392-888-7
LC 2002-19180
This reference contains "information on approximately 1,000 religious groups, ranging from small churches with less than a hundred members (Chishti Order of America) to organizations such as the Assemblies of God that number in the millions. Most entries are relatively short. The more controversial religions, as well as religious groups that have had a high profile lately, receive more lengthy treatments. Also included are entries on broader religious movements such as the New Age and the Charismatic Movement. . . . Each article outlines the history of the group, its founders and leaders, its main teachings, and an approximate number of followers or congregations. The explanations are clearly written, interesting and understandable, without too much scholarly jargon." Booklist
Includes bibliographical references

200.1 Systems, scientific principles, psychology of religion

Barrett, Justin L.
Born believers; the science of children's religious belief. Justin L. Barrett. Free Press 2012 x, 302 p.p **200.1**
1. Child development 2. Child psychology 3. Children -- Religious life 4. Faith -- Psychology 5. God 6. Psychological literature 7. Psychology, Religious
ISBN 1439196540; 9781439196540
LC 2011039581
In this book, the author looks at cross-cultural studies of children conducted by experts in the 'cognitive science of religion.' The studies indicate that, from an early age, humans know the difference between inanimate objects and agents--people or forces that can move or make things move. As they develop, children are prone to see agents as powerful forces unlike humans. By four or five, kids see a purpose, not only in objects, but also in creatures, rocks, rivers and mountains. . . . In the second part of the book, the author indicts atheism by arguing that if one accepts natural selection then one cannot reject the natural religion of childhood--it must have survival value. (Kirkus)

200.9 History, geographic treatment, biography

Almond, Gabriel Abraham

★ **Strong** religion; the rise of fundamentalisms around the world. {by} Gabriel A. Almond, R. Scott Appleby, and Emmanuel Sivan. University of Chicago Press 2003 281p il $49; pa $19   **200.9**
  1. Fundamentalism 2. Religious fundamentalism
  ISBN 0-226-01497-5; 0-226-01498-3 pa
                                    LC 2002-13665
This "may be the single most cogent sociohistorical analysis of the modern religious phenomenon called fundamentalism. . . . This foundational work is essential for academic and major public libraries." Libr J
  Includes bibliographical references

Armstrong, Karen

★ The **battle** for God; fundamentalism in Judaism, Christianity, and Islam. Knopf 2000 442p $29.95; pa $15.95   **200.9**
  1. Christian fundamentalism 2. Church history -- Modern period, 1500- 3. Fundamentalism -- History 4. Islam -- History 5. Islamic fundamentalism 6. Islamic fundamentalism -- History 7. Judaism 8. Judaism -- History 9. Orthodox Judaism -- Israel -- History 10. Religious fundamentalism
  ISBN 0-679-43597-2; 0-345-39169-1 pa
                                    LC 99-34022
This is a "study of fundamentalism among Jews (in Israel), Christians (American Protestants), and Muslims (Sunni Egyptians and Shiite Iranians). Armstrong argues that all strains of fundamentalism, despite their differences, are fearful defenses against modernity. . . . The author is sympathetic to the human need for spiritual meaning, but she points out that the intellectual flaws of fundamentalist beliefs are customarily accompanied by paranoia, anger, and aggression—which, in turn, frequently betray the message of the faith." New Yorker
  Includes bibliographical references

★ The **great** transformation; the beginning of our religious traditions. Knopf 2006 469p il map $30   **200.9**
  1. Religion -- History
  ISBN 0-375-41317-0
                                    LC 2005-47536
"This could very possibly be one of the greatest intellectual histories ever written." Libr J
  Includes bibliographical references

Balmer, Randall Herbert

Religion in twentieth century America; {by} Randall Balmer. Oxford Univ. Press 2001 142p il $28   **200.9**
  ISBN 0-19-511295-4
                                    LC 00-60674
"This title is accessible and reliable, brief and lively, and makes a fine addition to most libraries." SLJ
  Includes bibliographical references

Butler, Jon

Religion in American life; a short history. [by] Jon Butler, Grant Wacker, and Randall Balmer. Updated ed.; Oxford University Press 2008 496p il pa $19.95   **200.9**
  ISBN 978-0-19-533329-9; 0-19-533329-2
                                    LC 2007-24915
This volume begins by describing the state of religious affairs in the old and new worlds. The survey continues with a look at the religious landscape of 19th-century America and concludes with an examination of current religious beliefs and practices.

Kugel, James L.

In the valley of the shadow; on the foundations of religious belief (and their connection to a certain, fleeting state of mind) Free Press 2011 237p   **200.9**
  1. Cancer -- Religious aspects 2. College teachers 3. Hebraists
  ISBN 978-1-4391-3009-4; 978-1-4391-3010-0 pa; 978-1-4391-5055-9 ebook
                                    LC 2010-28086
The author invites readers to witness the exploration on religion that he undertook after being diagnosed with an aggressive, and likely fatal, form of cancer.
  "Written with eloquence suitable to a scholar of Biblical poetry, Kugel's memoir-cum-meditation will appeal to thoughtful Jewish and non-Jewish readers alike." Libr J
  Includes bibliographical references

Leon, Luis D.

Religion and American cultures; an encyclopedia of traditions, diversity, and popular expressions. Gary Laderman and Luis León, editors; foreword by Amanda Porterfield. ABC-CLIO 2003 3v set $285   **200.9**
  1. Reference books
  ISBN 1-57607-238-X
                                    LC 2003-8644
"This resource explores the various ways Americans approach religion. Its first volume features chapters on ethnic groups and sectarian beliefs, the second comprises essay entries on distinct practices, and the third collects primary documents. Cotton Mather, Shirley MacLaine, and Elijah Muhammad are represented, along with such pivotal documents as The Maryland Toleration Act and the American Indian Religious Freedom Act." Libr J
  Includes bibliographical references

Melton, J. Gordon

★ **Melton's** encyclopedia of American religions; [by] J. Gordon Melton; James Beverley, associate editor; Constance Jones, assistant editor; Pamela S. Nadell, assistant editor; foreword by Rodney Stark. 8th ed.; Gale, Cengage Learning 2009 xxvi, 1386p il map $380   **200.9**
  1. Reference books 2. Sects -- Encyclopedias
  ISBN 978-0-7876-9696-2
                                    LC 2008-37465
This encyclopedia features "coverage on more than 2,300 North American religious groups in the U.S. and

Canada—from Adventists to Zen Buddhists. Information on these groups is presented in two . . . sections. These sections contain essays and directory listings that describe the historical development of religious families and give . . . information about each group within those families, including, when available, rubrics for membership figures, educational facilities and periodicals." Publisher's note

Includes bibliographical references

Moore, R. Laurence

Selling God; American religion in the marketplace of culture. Oxford Univ. Press 1994 317p hardcover o.p. pa $19.95 **200.9**
1. Christianity and economics
ISBN 0-19-509838-2 pa

LC 93-19624

The author "is balanced and nonpedantic, treating religion as a cultural element of history." N Y Times Book Rev

Includes bibliographical references

Naipaul, V. S.

The **masque** of Africa; glimpses of African belief. Alfred A. Knopf 2010 241p $26.95; ebook $26.95 **200.9**
ISBN 978-0-307-27073-3; 0-307-27073-4; 978-0-307-59449-5 ebook; 0-307-59449-1 ebook

LC 2010-01256

This is a "book for outsiders, for those who may never visit Africa or may know it only superficially. But it is also a book in which Africans themselves may find something to learn. Naipaul is a difficult, imperfect narrator who does not care to be liked, but he is an honest one and doesn't dissemble. Somehow, by the end of it all, and despite his best efforts, I have grown to like him." Observer (London)

Queen, Edward L.

Encyclopedia of American religious history; [by] Edward L. Queen II, Stephen R. Prothero, and Gardiner H. Shattuck, Jr.; foreword by Martin E. Marty, editorial adviser; book producer, Marie A. Cantlon. 3rd ed.; Facts On File 2009 3v il set $250 **200.9**
1. Reference books
ISBN 978-0-8160-6660-5

LC 2007-52350

This reference source presents over 800 articles examining different religions, religious leaders, events, and other topics that helped shape the history of religion in America. The coverage extends from Puritan America to the moral majority.

Wolfe, Alan

The **transformation** of American religion; how we actually live our faith. Free Press 2003 309p $26 **200.9**
ISBN 0-7432-2839-1

LC 2003-44870

"This provocative book is a must-read for a wide variety of readers." Choice

Includes bibliographical references

Believer, beware; first person dispatches from the margins of faith. selected by Jeff Sharlet, Peter Manseau, and the editors of Killing the Buddha. Beacon Press 2009 263p pa $16 **200.9**
1. Faith
ISBN 978-0-8070-7739-9; 0-8070-7739-9

LC 2008-47403

"The editors are among the smart, candid, and insightful authors whose personal narratives form the book's 35 brief chapters. The selections represent a wide range of experiences from cheating on bar mitzvah prep to discovering hunger as spiritual food in a Ramadan fast, from sabotaging Bible camp to stumbling upon barbershop theology. Contributions reflect the scope of religious diversity, including orthodox Judaism, Roman Catholicism, Islam, Zen Buddhism and even a meditation on agnosticism. Some are funny, others heartbreaking, and some are simply revelatory." Publ Wkly

Includes bibliographical references

★ The Cambridge illustrated history of religions; edited by John Bowker. Cambridge Univ. Press 2002 336p il $40 **200.9**
1. Religions
ISBN 0-521-81037-X

LC 2001-37866

"The major religions get thoroughgoing treatment, with short introductions also given to the Zoroastrianism; the religions of Greece, Rome, Egypt, and Mesopotamia; aboriginal religions; and new religious movements. . . . Christianity receives a separate chapter as well as substantial treatment in chapters on Chinese, Korean, and Japanese religions. . . . This volume presents a large amount of information in an engaging way, offering much scholarly insight for the lay reader." Libr J

Includes bibliographical references

★ Eastern religions; origins, beliefs, practices, holy texts, sacred places. general editor, Michael D. Coogan; [contributors] Vasudha Narayanan . . . [et al.] Oxford University Press 2005 552p il $35; pa $19.95 **200.9**
1. Buddhism 2. Confucianism 3. Hinduism 4. Shinto 5. Taoism
ISBN 0-19-522190-7; 978-0-19-522190-9; 0-19-522191-5 pa; 978-0-19-522191-6 pa

LC 2004-30376

This is an introduction "to major South Asian and East Asian religious traditions. Four expert authors introduce Hinduism, Buddhism, Taoism, Confucianism, and Shinto. To aid comparison, each article has parallel sections on origins and historical development, aspects of the divine, sacred texts, sacred persons, ethical principles, sacred space, sacred time, death and the afterlife, and society and religion. The clear, crisp prose avoids academic jargon without losing the complexity and richness of the traditions being examined." Libr J

Includes bibliographical references

★ Encyclopedia of fundamentalism; Brenda E. Brasher, editor. Routledge 2001 558p il $125   **200.9**

1. Fundamentalism 2. Religious fundamentalism

ISBN 0-415-92244-5

LC 2001-19951

This reference covers "fundamentalism, from definition, history, and beliefs to movements and churches, significant individuals, and expressions in various world religions. Creationism, fascism, rock music, and the Taliban are a sample of the topics covered. The contributors provide clear, readable explanations. . . . This beautifully laid-out work is the one to have." Libr J

Includes bibliographical references

201   Specific aspects of religion

Barr, Stephen M.

★ **Modern** physics and ancient faith. University of Notre Dame Press 2003 312p il hardcover o.p. pa $18   **201**

1. Physics 2. Physics -- Religious aspects -- Christianity 3. Religion and science

ISBN 0-268-03471-0; 978-0-268-02198-6 pa; 0-268-02198-8 pa

LC 2002-151565

The author "argues that the great discoveries of modern physics are more compatible with the central teachings of Christianity and Judaism about God, the cosmos, and the human soul than with the atheistic viewpoint of scientific materialism." Publ Wkly

Includes bibliographical references

Campbell, David E.

American grace; how religion divides and unites us. [by] Robert D. Putnam [and] David E. Campbell, with the assistance of Shaylyn Romney Garrett. Simon & Schuster 2010 673p il map $30   **201**

1. Religion -- Social aspects 2. Religion and sociology -- United States

ISBN 978-1-4165-6671-7; 1-4165-6671-6

LC 2010-27838

The book examines "the place of religion in contemporary American society. Relying on a 2006–2007 survey of their own, but also employing an array of other survey data and monographic studies, Robert D. Putnam and David E. Campbell give a[n] . . . account of . . . the religious demography of the United States and offer . . . views on how religion has shaped contemporary American social and political values and identities. They provide . . . analysis while eschewing social science jargon and technicality. . . . The author's "account of how we got to where we are . . . [focuses on] the 1960s and its discontents." (Journal of American History)

"An essential resource for anyone trying to understand twenty-first-century America." Booklist

Includes bibliographical references

Campbell, Joseph

★ **Creative** mythology. Arkana 1991 730p pa $18   **201**

1. Mythology in literature

ISBN 978-0-14-019440-1; 0-14-019440-1

"This volume explores the whole inner story of modern culture since the Dark Ages, treating modern man's unique position as the creator of his own mythology." Publisher's note

Includes bibliographical references

★ **Occidental** mythology. Arkana 1991 564p pa $18   **201**

1. Mythology

ISBN 978-0-14-019441-8; 0-14-019441-X

"A systematic . . . comparison of the themes that underlie the art, worship, and literature of the Western world." Publisher's note

Includes bibliographical references

★ **Oriental** mythology. Arkana 1991 561p pa $18   **201**

1. Oriental mythology

ISBN 978-0-14-019442-5; 0-14-019442-8

"An exploration of Eastern mythology as it developed into the distinctive religions of Egypt, India, China, and Japan." Publisher's note

Includes bibliographical references

★ **Primitive** mythology. Arkana 1991 504p pa $18   **201**

1. Mythology

ISBN 978-0-14-019443-2; 0-14-019443-6

The author "discusses the primitive roots of mythology, examining them in light of . . . discoveries in archaeology, anthropology, and psychology." Publisher's note

Includes bibliographical references

★ The **power** of myth; [by] Joseph Campbell, with Bill Moyers; Betty Sue Flowers, editor. Doubleday 1988 231p il hardcover o.p. pa $29.95   **201**

1. Mythology 2. Religious art 3. Spiritual life

ISBN 0-385-24773-7; 0-385-24774-5

LC 88-4218

This companion to a public television series records conversations between Campbell and Bill Moyers. Campbell reflects on themes and symbols from world religions and mythologies and explores their relevance for his own spiritual journey.

"Campbell is the hero on his own voyage of discovery. This well-bound book on lovely paper with helpful illustrations from art is highly recommended for all libraries." Choice

Coles, Robert

The **secular** mind. Princeton Univ. Press 1999 189p $45; pa $15.95   **201**

1. Religion and science 2. Secularism 3. Secularism -- United States

ISBN 0-691-05805-9; 0-691-08862-4 pa

LC 98-39388

"This is a potent and powerful work readers will think about and return to again and again." Publ Wkly

Consolmagno, Guy

God's mechanics; how scientists and engineers make sense of religion. Jossey-Bass 2007 245p $24.95 **201**
1. Religion and science
ISBN 978-0-7879-9466-2; 0-7879-9466-9
LC 2007-19067
"Combining personal memoir with conversations within the techie world, Consolmagno describes questions about the universe and the meaning of life that attract techies into religious belief and practice, concluding that 'techies are not looking for proof. They're looking for confidence.'" Publ Wkly

Davis, Kenneth C.

Don't know much about mythology; everything you need to know about the greatest stories in human history but never learned. HarperCollins Publishers 2005 545p $26.95; pa $14.95 **201**
1. Mythology
ISBN 0-06-019460-X; 978-0-06-019460-4; 0-06-093257-0 pa; 978-0-06-093257-2 pa
LC 2005-43341
The author "examines the myths created by societies ranging from Egypt, Greece and Rome to Africa, India and the Americas, proceeding . . . by way of question and answer as he surveys each mythmaking culture. . . . His survey provides a superb starting point for entering the world of mythology." Publ Wkly
Includes bibliographical references

Deloria, Vine

Evolution, creationism, and other modern myths; a critical inquiry. [by] Vine Deloria, Jr. Fulcrum 2002 274p $24.95; pa $18.95 **201**
1. Creationism 2. Evolution 3. Evolution (Biology) -- Religious aspects 4. Natural history -- Religious aspects 5. Religion and science
ISBN 1-55591-159-5; 1-55591-458-6 pa
LC 2002-8171
The author "argues that both sides in the evolution-versus-creationism debate are wrong. . . . This intellectual duel finds only mistaken orthodoxies in the field, for creationism has no scientific basis, but evolution is far from proven. . . . Certain to be controversial, likely to outrage the faithful of both camps, and a stunning good read." Booklist
Includes bibliographical references

Frank, Adam

The **constant** fire; beyond the science vs. religion debate. University of California Press 2009 288p $24.95 **201**
1. Religion and science 2. Religion and science -- History
ISBN 978-0-520-25412-1; 0-520-25412-0
LC 2008-25402

"An elegant reimagining of the relationship between science and spirituality. . . . Challenges the assumption that science and religion are implacable foes." Chron Higher Educ
Includes bibliographical references (p. 269-281) and index

Frazer, James George

The **golden** bough; a study in magic and religion. a new abridgment from the second and third editions; edited with an introduction by Robert Fraser. Oxford University Press 1998 xlix, 858p pa $17.95 **201**
1. Mythology 2. Religions 3. Superstition
ISBN 978-0-19-283541-3; 0-19-283541-6
LC 2001-522510
A "study of the beliefs and institutions of mankind, and the progress through magic and religion to scientific thought. . . . First published in 1890, The Golden Bough was eventually issued in a twelve-volume edition (1906-15) which was abridged in 1922 by the author and his wife. That abridgement has never been reconsidered for a modern audience. In it some of the more controversial passages were dropped, including Frazer's daring speculations on the Crucifixion of Christ. For the first time this one-volume edition restores Frazer's bolder theories." Publisher's note
Includes bibliographical references

Glucklich, Ariel

Dying for heaven; holy pleasure and suicide bombers--why the best qualities of religion are also its most dangerous. HarperCollins 2009 345p $25.99 **201**
1. Suicide bombers 2. Terrorism -- Religious aspects
ISBN 978-0-06-143081-7
LC 2009-5174
"Extremely well written, and at times quite funny . . . this book is an absolute necessity for a public seeking to understand religious nuance and zealotry; it deserves careful attention and a broad readership." Libr J
Includes bibliographical references

Haidt, Jonathan

The **righteous** mind; why good people are divided by politics and religion. Jonathan Haidt. Pantheon Books 2012 419 p. $28.95 **201**
1. Ethics 2. Political psychology 3. Psychological literature 4. Psychology, Religious 5. Social psychology
ISBN 9780307377906
LC 2011032036
The core of the book [by Jonathan Haidt] is an attempt at a Darwinian explanation of morality, contending that moral behavior emerges from a natural process of competition among human groups. . . . A part of "The Righteous Mind" is a . . . critique of . . . [a] primitive type of rationalism. . . . Much of his book is an attempt to apply the findings of evolutionary psychology to the political gridlock that . . . exists in the United States. (New Republic)

Jordan, Michael

Dictionary of gods and goddesses; 2nd ed; Facts on File 2004 402p il $45   **201**

1. Goddesses 2. Gods 3. Gods and goddesses -- Dictionaries 4. Reference books

ISBN 0-8160-5923-3

LC 2004-13028

The author's "alphabetical list includes gods and goddesses from a variety of religions. Each entry provides a brief description with cross-references where appropriate; some supply translations of the names. Longer entries include origin, dates of observance, synonyms, geographic location of the cult center, art references by type (e.g., stone carvings), and literary sources. . . . This [is] a usable, well-written resource for short descriptions of cross-cultural deities." Choice

Includes bibliographical references

Karabell, Zachary

Peace be upon you; the story of Muslim, Christian, and Jewish coexistence. Random House 2007 343p map $26.95   **201**

1. Christianity and other religions 2. Interfaith relations 3. Islam -- Relations 4. Judaism -- Relations 5. Religions -- Relations

ISBN 978-1-4000-4368-2; 1-4000-4368-9

LC 2006-31501

"This outstanding book . . . combines in a single volume centuries of interaction among the three great monotheistic religions." Choice

Includes bibliographical references (p. 317-326)

Kimball, Charles

When religion becomes lethal; the explosive mix of politics and religion in Judaism, Christianity, and Islam. Jossey-Bass 2011 254p $27.95; ebook $14.99   **201**

1. Christianity and politics 2. Islam -- Relations 3. Islam and politics 4. Judaism and politics 5. Religion and politics 6. Religious fundamentalism

ISBN 978-0-470-58190-2; 0-470-58190-5; 978-1-1180-3056-1 ebook

LC 2010052515

The author "begins with a careful overview of how, in sacred text and history, religion and politics interact in Judaism, Christianity, and Islam. He then examines the constructive and destructive ways adherents of the faiths have interpreted and acted on their traditions in the public square, focusing specifically on Israel, the U.S., Iraq, and Iran." Sojourners

Includes bibliographical references (p. 229-232)

Leeming, David Adams

★ The **Oxford** companion to world mythology. Oxford University Press 2006 xxxvii, 469p $65 **201**

1. Mythology 2. Mythology -- Dictionaries 3. Reference books

ISBN 0-19-515669-2

LC 2005-14216

"This volume presents approximately 2,000 concise entries in dictionary format. Leeming, . . . in an attempt to be 'inclusive and reasonably comprehensive,' ranges far outside the Western tradition to cover figures and folklore from Africa, Asia, and the Americas, as well as from the sacred narratives of religions. . . . Approximately 100 black-and-white illustrations, along with a few color plates, provide examples of artistic renderings of various myths. . . . This work should find a place in any general reference collection." Choice

Includes bibliographical references

A **dictionary** of Asian mythology; [by] David Leeming. Oxford Univ. Press 2001 232p $39.95; pa $29   **201**

1. Asian mythology -- Dictionaries 2. Mythology, Asian 3. Reference books

ISBN 0-19-512052-3; 0-19-512053-1 pa

LC 00-62389

"This concise dictionary references the mythologies of India, China, Tibet, Central and Southeast Asia, and Japan. The authoritative text is clearly written, thorough in coverage, and stylistically distinguished." Libr J

Includes bibliographical references

Mercatante, Anthony S.

The **Facts** on File encyclopedia of world mythology and legend; [by] Anthony S. Mercatante & James R. Dow. 3rd ed; Facts On File 2008 2v il set $150   **201**

1. Folklore 2. Mythology 3. Mythology -- Encyclopedias 4. Reference books

ISBN 978-0-8160-7311-5

LC 2007-51965

"Jammed with information and filled with both impressive scholarship and entertaining tidbits . . . it is highly recommended for all libraries." Libr J

Includes bibliographical references

Niebuhr, Gustav

Beyond tolerance; searching for interfaith understanding in America. Viking 2008 xxxviii, 218p $25.95   **201**

1. Interfaith relations 2. Religions -- Relations 3. Religious tolerance 4. Violence -- Religious aspects

ISBN 978-0-670-01956-4; 0-670-01956-9

LC 2007-40479

"Niebuhr brings his reporter's eye for detail to this work, which he populates with people and organizations who strive to find religious meaning in our diverse lives. This is no dry, academic exposition. Written for a general audience, it is also valuable for scholars wishing to see an America many might have thought was calcifying into an insular continent, worshipping hard gods or God." Libr J

Includes bibliographical references (p. 208-212)

Robinson, Marilynne, 1943-

Absence of mind; the dispelling of inwardness from the modern myth of the self. Yale University Press 2010 158p   **201**

1. Modern philosophy 2. Philosophy, Modern 3. Religion and science 4. Thought and thinking

ISBN 0-300-14518-7; 978-0-300-14518-2

LC 2009044020

"From Freud to Steven Pinker, much of what passes for scientific writing in the modern period, [Robinson] argues, is scientific in name only. Real science is forever searching after truth. Parascience, by contrast, is dogmatic, forever pretending it is in the 'clutch of certitudes.'" (Bookforum) Index.

"The title refers to what Robinson argues is missing from modern thought: the mind, the individual subjective experience of perception and reflection. Science, she says, has leapt from biology, theory and real science to 'parascientific' statements of faith.... Parascience, Robinson says, grew out of 19th century positivism. She discusses Auguste Comte as an early progenitor of parascience, moves to Freud, whose ideas have been largely discredited but whose influence remains prevalent, and then to contemporary parascience writers like Richard Dawkins, Daniel Dennett and E. O. Wilson. All of them, she says, use the language of science to claim legitimacy for their inconsistent, nonscientific statements of faith about what it means to be human.... Beneath the complex philosophical argument, Robinson makes a profound defence of the Imago Dei and of love. This book resounds with wisdom, passion and prophetic anger." Christian Week

Includes bibliographical references

Stark, Rodney

For the glory of God; how monotheism led to reformations, science, witch-hunts, and the end of slavery. Princeton Univ. Press 2003 488p il $45; pa $18.95 **201**

1. Church history 2. Monotheism 3. Reformation 4. Religion and science 5. Slavery 6. Witchcraft
ISBN 0-691-11436-6; 0-691-11950-3 pa
LC 2002-31746

A "provocative volume—lucid and tightly reasoned." Booklist

Includes bibliographical references and index

One true God; historical consequences of monotheism. Princeton Univ. Press 2001 319p il $47.50; pa $19.95 **201**

1. God 2. Monotheism
ISBN 0-691-08923-X; 0-691-11500-1 pa
LC 2001-21128

Stark seeks "a theoretical understanding of monotheism that will be . . . 'sociologically useful.' . . . Stark's theory has monotheism—the belief that there is just one God, just one giver of supernatural blessings and curses—as its object. He wants to explain monotheism's origins and development, to show its main effects upon the behavior and attitudes of social groups, and to account for the fact that monotheists are sometimes aggressively intolerant of those who do not share their beliefs and at other times civilly forebearing." Commonweal

Includes bibliographical references and index

★ Encyclopedia of science and religion; J. Wentzel Vrede van Huyssteen, editor in chief. Macmillan Ref. 2003 2v set $280 **201**

1. Reference books 2. Religion and science 3. Religion and science -- Encyclopedias
ISBN 0-02-865704-7
LC 2002-152471

"Thousands of books have been written about the relationship between science and religion, but few can be characterized as reference resources. This two-volume set helps fill that niche with more than 400 scholarly articles written by experts from around the world." Libr J

Includes bibliographical references

The History of science and religion in the western tradition; an encyclopedia. Gary B. Ferngren, general editor; Edward J. Larson, Darrel W. Amundsen, co-editors; Anne-Marie E. Nakhla, assistant editor. Garland 2000 xxi, 586p $195 **201**

1. Religion and science 2. Religion and science -- History
ISBN 0-8153-1656-9
LC 00-25153

This is a collection of articles "grouped under ten headings covering everything from the relationship of science and religion to the approaches taken by specific religious traditions, from alchemy to chemistry to materialism to spiritualism. Ferngren . . . and his coeditors take the stand that the historical relationship between science and religion follows a complex model rather than the popularly understood model of unalterable conflict. The result is a work, well worth reading through or browsing, that is filled with respect for the roles and methodologies of both religion and science." Libr J

Includes bibliographical references and index

203   Public worship and other practices

Davidson, Linda Kay

Pilgrimage: from the Ganges to Graceland: an encyclopedia; [by] Linda Kay Davidson and David M. Gitlitz. ABC-CLIO 2002 2v il maps set $185 **203**

1. Pilgrims and pilgrimages
ISBN 1-57607-004-2
LC 2002-10119

"This splendid encyclopedia is a delight to read and pleasing to view." Booklist

Includes bibliographical references and index

Manseau, Peter

Rag and bone; a journey among the world's holy dead. Henry Holt and Co. 2009 243p il $25 **203**

1. Relics
ISBN 978-0-8050-8652-2; 0-8050-8652-8
LC 2008-39465

"Manseau embarks on a global odyssey in search of the 'dismembered toes, splinters of shinbone, stolen bits of hair, burned remnants of an anonymous rib cage, and other odds and ends' belonging to saints and other sacred figures. The result is an entertaining, sometimes affecting inquiry into man's yearning for spiritual transcendence through the worship of holy relics, real or otherwise — from the Shroud of Turin . . . to more obscure bits of clothing and body parts. The book could have been ghoulish, but Manseau's irreverent approach and enthusiasm keep the tone surprisingly light." N Y Times Book Rev

★ How to be a perfect stranger; the essential religious etiquette handbook. edited by Stuart M. Matlins & Arthur J. Magida. 5th ed.; SkyLight Paths Pub. 2011 402p pa $19.99 **203**
1. Etiquette 2. Rites and ceremonies
ISBN 978-1-59473-294-2

LC 2010-31668

This guide "provides brief overviews of many religions: services, life-cycle events, home celebrations. It explains rituals so that those unfamiliar with them will know what to expect, how to dress, whether to bring a gift, and so on. It also has a glossary, explains various religious calendars, and lists religious festivals." Booklist

204 Religious experience, life, practice

Colegate, Isabel
A **pelican** in the wilderness; hermits and solitaries. Counterpoint 2002 284p il hardcover o.p. pa $15.95 **204**
1. Hermits 2. Solitude
ISBN 1-58243-121-3; 1-58243-238-4 pa

LC 2001-47242

This "is a study of the soul that wants to be alone and knows how to do it; frequently met (so to say) in religion, the urge is also found in celebrities (J.D. Salinger, Howard Hughes)." N Y Times Book Rev

Coles, Robert
★ The **spiritual** life of children. Houghton Mifflin 1990 358p il hardcover o.p. pa $14 **204**
1. Children -- Religious life
ISBN 0-395-59923-7 pa

LC 90-40097

"One of the delights of his presentation is the combination of the children's searching comments and the struggle the author makes to hear beyond his own conceptions." J Youth Serv Libr
Includes bibliographical references

Lundberg, C. David
Unifying truths of the world's religions; practical principles for living and loving in peace. Heavenlight Press 2010 426p pa $18.95 **204**
1. Religions 2. Truth -- Religious aspects
ISBN 978-0-979-63082-8

This book presents a list of 33 inspirational principles that appear in the sacred texts of different eastern and western religions.

209 Sects and reform movements

★ **Belief** beyond boundaries; Wicca, Celtic spirituality and the new age. edited by Joanne Pearson. Ashgate 2002 339p il maps $94.95; pa $29.95 **209**
1. Cults
ISBN 0-7546-0744-5; 0-7546-0820-4 pa

LC 2001-53654

"Though somewhat academic in tone, this is a solid overview of several New Age spiritual movements." Libr J
Includes bibliographical references

210 Philosophy and theory of religion

Huxley, Aldous
★ The **perennial** philosophy. Harper & Row 1945 312p hardcover o.p. pa $14 **210**
1. Philosophy and religion 2. Religion -- Philosophy
ISBN 0-06-057058-X pa

An anthology of and commentary on Chinese, Latin, Greek, Catholic and Protestant mysticism

James, William
★ The **varieties** of religious experience; a study in human nature. introduction by Reinhold Niebuhr. Simon & Schuster 2004 398p pa $15 **210**
1. Conversion 2. Mysticism 3. New Thought 4. Psychology 5. Religion -- Philosophy 6. Religious life 7. Spiritual healing
ISBN 978-0-7432-5787-9; 0-7432-5787-1

LC 2004-42870

"Based on material James had collected on the psychology and philosophy of religion for lectures at the University of Edinburgh in 1901 and 1902. The varieties of religious experience contains numerous descriptions of religious states of consciousness, which James presented from a pragmatic point of view." HarperCollins Reader's Ency of Am Lit. 2nd edition
Includes bibliographical references

211 Concepts of God

Armstrong, Karen
The **case** for God. Knopf 2009 406p $27.95 **211**
1. Apologetics 2. Christian life 3. God 4. God -- History of doctrines 5. Religious life
ISBN 978-0-307-26918-8

LC 2009-14044

"'Magisterial' is the adjective of choice to describe Armstrong's work; her usual confident sweep across times and cultures rises above the 'answer-the-atheists' tired angle to make a passionate footnoted argument for the human need for a God." Publ Wkly
Includes bibliographical references

Jacoby, Susan
Freethinkers: a history of American secularism. Metropolitan Books 2004 417p il $27.50; pa $16 **211**
1. Secularism
ISBN 0-8050-7442-2; 0-8050-7776-6 pa

LC 2003-59294

"Enlightening, invigorating, and responsibly yet passionately argued, Jacoby's unparalleled history of American secularism offers a much needed perspective on today's most urgent social issues." Booklist
Includes bibliographical references

Russell, Sharman Apt

Standing in the light; my life as a pantheist. Basic Books 2008 306p map $25; pa $16.95   **211**

1. Atheism 2. Authors 3. Children's authors 4. College teachers 5. Nonfiction writers 6. Novelists 7. Pantheism

ISBN 978-0-465-00517-8; 0-465-00517-9; 978-0-465-01380-7 pa; 0-465-01380-5 pa

LC 2008-03958

"This quietly arresting book . . . offers a braided narrative, weaving Russell's own spiritual autobiography with a thoughtfully selected intellectual history of pantheism and accounts of forays into the natural world, as she endeavors to work with other civic-minded folk to preserve the native habitat of their homes in New Mexico's Gila River Valley. Gradually, generously, and in fits and starts—rather like her own quest—Russell's encounter with an indifferent cosmos grows slyly compelling." Bookforum

Includes bibliographical references

212 Existence of God, ways of knowing God, attributes of God

Overman, Dean L.

A **case** for the existence of God. Rowman & Littlefield 2008 xxxii, 229p $24.95   **212**

1. God 2. God -- Proof, Cosmological 3. Religion and science

ISBN 978-0-7425-6312-4; 0-7425-6312-X

LC 2008-21731

"Drawing on modern cosmology and information theory, Overman exposes fallacies that have infested skeptics' thinking since Hume and Kant. Clearer reasoning establishes an astonishing harmony between quantum physics and religious orthodoxy, so providing a credible defense for free will and moral judgment. Still, readers looking for certainty will not find it here: Overman acknowledges that the believer must make a leap of faith. . . . The intensely personal character of spiritual conversion emerges in the lives of the nine remarkable believers—including St. Augustine and Pascal, Dostoyevsky and Weil—whose testimonies resonate with passionate conviction. A book for readers willing to wrestle with the largest questions." Booklist

Includes bibliographical references

215 Science and religion

Ecklund, Elaine Howard

Science vs. religion; what scientists really think. Oxford University Press 2010 228p $27.95   **215**

1. Religion and science 2. Scientists -- Attitudes 3. Universities and colleges -- United States -- Faculty

ISBN 978-0-19-539298-2; 0-19-539298-1

LC 2009-34731

Ecklund's "outstanding research, articulately presented, and judicious recommendations make this a valuable work for all who care about the subject of science and religion." Libr J

Includes bibliographical references

Hagerty, Barbara Bradley

Fingerprints of God; the search for the science of spirituality. Riverhead Books 2009 323p $26.95   **215**

1. Religion and science

ISBN 978-1-59448-877-1

LC 2009-3921

The author attempts to answer "questions about the science of spiritual experience. Along the way she tells the story of her own intriguing spiritual evolution. . . . Throughout the book, one is struck by the humility Hagerty brings to her subject—something lacking in many contemporary debates over the meaning of faith and the existence of God—and her skepticism about the science offered up as proof of spiritual experience. . . . Hagerty's engaging book poses a provocative challenge to anyone who has ever wondered where faith comes from, and what it can do for—and to—us." Washington Post Book World

Includes bibliographical references

220 Bible

Jacobs, A. J.

The **year** of living biblically; one man's humble quest to follow the Bible as literally as possible. A.J. Jacobs. Simon & Schuster 2007 388p ill. (pbk.) $16; (hbk.) $25   **220**

1. Authors 2. Biography, Individual 3. Humorists 4. Journalists 5. Memoirists

ISBN 9780743291484; 9780743291477; 0743291476

LC 200709573

It was the author's intent to "follow the more than 800 rules found in the Hebrew Bible and to chronicle the experience. Jacobs spends 388 days investigating how a 21st-century New Yorker can live the lifestyle outlined in the Old Testament. Repeatedly, he tries to follow literal meanings only to find that he has misinterpreted the ritual, moral, agricultural, and sacrificial laws. For example, he throws pebbles at a man in Central Park, intending to replicate a stoning, but after consulting with his team of religious advisers discovers that in biblical times, stoning actually meant pushing the victim off a cliff. . . . He concludes that people today practice 'cafeteria religion,' picking and choosing which rules to follow." (Library Journal)

"Throughout his journey, Jacobs comes across as a generous and thoughtful (and, yes, slightly neurotic) participant observer, lacing his story with absurdly funny cultural commentary as well as nuanced insights into the impossible task of biblical literalism." Publ Wkly

Includes bibliographical references (p. [343]-348) and index.

Pelikan, Jaroslav Jan

★ **Whose** Bible is it? a history of the Scriptures through the ages. [by] Jaroslav Pelikan. Viking 2004 274p il $24.95   **220**

ISBN 0-670-03385-5

LC 2004-58049

The author "offers a masterly overview of [the] complex development of the Bible over the ages. . . . This engaging, concise, and highly readable work demonstrates that the most influential book in Western civilization has always held different meanings for different peoples." Christ Sci Monit

Includes bibliographical references

★   The Oxford illustrated history of the Bible; edited by John Rogerson. Oxford Univ. Press 2001 395p il $40   **220**
ISBN 0-19-860118-2

                            LC 2001-272513

This volume offers an "overview of the origins of the Bible we know (consisting of the Old and New Testaments and the Apocrypha), the transmission and translation of the texts, and the historical and contemporary interpretation and influence of the Bible. Enhancing this overview are numerous color and black-and-white illustrations." Libr J

Includes bibliographical references

220.3   Encyclopedias and topical dictionaries

Abingdon Press

The **New** Interpreter's dictionary of the Bible; [edited by Katharine Doob Sakenfeld et al.] Abingdon Press 2009 5v il map set $400   **220.3**
1. Reference books
ISBN 978-0-687-33346-2

"A scholarly encyclopedic dictionary designed for the preacher, scholar, student, teacher, and general reader, referring to both the King James Version and the Revised Standard Version, to the Apocrypha, the Pseudepigrapha, the Dead Sea Scrolls, and other ancient manuscripts. . . . Important for modern biblical study." Guide to Ref Books. 11th edition

Includes bibliographical references

Oxford University Press

The **Oxford** companion to the Bible; edited by Bruce M. Metzger, Michael D. Coogan. Oxford Univ. Press 1993 xxi, 874p il map $70   **220.3**
1. Bible (as subject) -- Dictionaries 2. Reference books
ISBN 0-19-504645-5

                            LC 93-19315

"The many contributors read as a veritable who's who among biblical scholars. Although this companion is not meant to be an exhaustive reference, it is a highly reliable guide." Booklist

Society of Biblical Literature

The **HarperCollins** Bible dictionary; general editor, Paul J. Achtemeier; associate editors, Roger S. Boraas {et al.} with the Society of Biblical Literature. HarperSanFrancisco 1996 xxiv, 1256p il $47.95   **220.3**
1. Reference books
ISBN 0-06-060037-3

                            LC 96-25424

This volume features a "two-column format, with 16 single-column articles interspersed throughout (including 'Art in the Biblical Period,' 'Jesus Christ,' and 'The temple'), and it is well illustrated. Many of the longer articles include a brief bibliography. . . . Though not a flawless work (e.g.,

the article 'Manasseh' treats only the 14th king of Judah but neither the patriarch nor the tribe of Israel that also bear the name), it is outstanding in terms of scholarship and writing." Libr J

Eerdmans dictionary of the Bible; David Noel Freedman, editor-in-chief; Allen C. Myers, associate editor; Astrid B. Beck, managing editor. Eerdmans 2000 xxxiii, 1425p il maps $45   **220.3**
1. Bible (as subject) -- Dictionaries 2. Reference books
ISBN 0-8028-2400-5

                            LC 00-56124

"Up-to-date, comprehensive, and well written, the EDB is highly recommended." Libr J

Includes bibliographical references

The Oxford encyclopedia of the books of the Bible; Michael D. Coogan, editor in chief. Oxford University Press 2011 2 v. ill., maps   **220.3**
ISBN 9780195377378; 0195377370

                            LC 2011013649

This reference book provides "overviews of scholarship on some of the most important topics of study in the field of biblical studies. The 'Encyclopedia' contains almost 120 . . . entries, ranging in length from 500 to 10,000 words, on each of the canonical books of the Bible, major apocryphal books of the New and Old Testaments, important noncanonical texts, and thematic essays on topics such as canonicity, textual criticism, and translation. 'Books of the Bible' has . . . cross-references to other . . . points of interest within the Encyclopedia, and . . . lists of abbreviations and an index. . . . Illustrations of various types supplement the text. . . . Bibliographies for all entries [are also included]." (Publisher's note)

Zondervan illustrated Bible dictionary; [edited by] J.D. Douglas and Merrill C. Tenney; revised by Moises Silva. Zondervan 2011 1571 p. col. ill., maps $29.99   **220.3**
ISBN 9780310229834

                            LC 2010034210

This reference book provides a visual . . . journey for anyone interested in learning more about the world of the Bible. Through the articles, sidebars, charts, maps, and full-color images included in this volume, the text of the Old and New Testaments [is enhanced]. . . . As a condensation of the Zondervan Pictorial Encyclopedia of the Bible, the information contained within this reference work is . . . biblically sound. The material is based completely on the NIV [New International Version] and cross-referenced to the King James Version, and it contains over 7,200 entries, 500 full-color photographs, charts, and illustrations, 75 full-color maps, and a Scripture index. (Publishers note)

220.4   Texts, versions, translations

Daniell, David
The **Bible** in English. Yale University Press 2003 xx, 899p $40   **220.4**
  1. Bible -- History 2. Bible -- Versions
ISBN 0-300-09930-4
                LC 2002-153177
  "This book is a vibrant history of the more than 350 English translations of the Bible and what they meant to their translators, readers, and times. The fascinating story ranges from the translations of William Tyndale (who was martyred in 1536 for his work), to Coverdale's translation, the Geneva Bibles, the King James Bible, and the many American translations in the twentieth century." Univ Press Books for Public and Second Sch Libr, 2004
  Includes bibliographical references

220.5   Modern versions and translations

Bible
  ★ The **Bible**: Authorized King James Version; with an introduction and notes by Robert Carroll and Stephen Prickett. Oxford University Press 2008 lxxiv, 1039, 248, 445p il map pa $18.95   **220.5**
ISBN 978-0-19-953594-1
                LC 2008-273825
  The authorized or King James Version originally published 1611.

  The **HarperCollins** study Bible; New Revised Standard Version, including the Apocraphal/Deuterocanonical books with concordance. general editor, revised edition, Harold W. Attridge; general editor, original edition, Wayne A. Meeks; associate editors, Jouette M. Bassler [et al.] with the Society of Biblical Literature. Fully rev and updated; HarperSanFrancisco 2006 lxvi, 2204p il map $44.95   **220.5**
  ISBN 978-0-06-078685-4; 0-06-078685-X
                LC 2007-277226
  "This edition of the Bible—newly annotated by the Society of Biblical Studies—is definitely for a wide audience. It is interdenominational, incorporates the latest in biblical scholarship, and is sensitive to unnecessary gender specificity." Booklist

  ★ The **New** American Bible; translated from the original languages with critical use of all the ancient sources including the revised Psalms and the revised New Testament. authorized by the Board of Trustees of the Confraternity of Christian Doctrine and approved by the Administrative Committee Board of the National Conference of Catholic Bishops and the United States Catholic Conference. Oxford University Press 2006 xxiii, 1514p $39.99   **220.5**
  ISBN 978-0-19-528904-6; 0-19-528904-8

"Roman Catholic version based on modern English translations; replaces the Douay edition." N Y Public Libr Book of How & Where to Look It Up

  The **Oxford** study Bible; Revised English Bible with the Apocrypha. edited by M. Jack Suggs, Katharine Doob Sakenfeld, James R. Mueller. Oxford University Press 1992 xxviii, 199, 1597p map hardcover o.p. pa $34.99   **220.5**
  ISBN 0-19-529001-1; 0-19-529000-3 pa
                LC 92-137886
  An annotated version of the Revised English Bible. "This volume combines a cultural guide to the biblical world and an annotated Bible. Its notes feature the reflections of Protestant, Roman Catholic, and Jewish scholars." Publisher's note

  ★ The **new** Jerusalem Bible; [general editor: Henry Wansbrough] Doubleday 1985 2108p map $45; pa $29.95   **220.5**
  ISBN 0-385-14264-1; 978-0-385-14264-9; 0-385-24833-4 pa; 978-0-385-24833-4 pa
                LC 85-16070
  "Derives from the French version edited at the Dominican Ecole Biblique de Jerusalem and known as 'La Bible de Jerusalem.' The introductions and notes are 'a direct translation from the French, though revised and brought up to date in some places' but translation of the Biblical text goes back to the original languages." Guide to Ref Books. 11th edition

Bloom, Harold, 1930-
  The **shadow** of a great rock; a literary appreciation of the King James Bible. Yale University Press 2011 311p $28   **220.5**
  1. Bible -- Concordances, English -- New King James 2. God in literature 3. Literary critiques 4. Religion & literature
ISBN 978-0-300-16683-5; 0-300-16683-4
                LC 2011003148
  This book is Harold Bloom's . . . tribute to the strength of [the King James Bible]. . . . Like Shakespeare, Bloom writes, the Bible "represents the fullness of life and can give you more life." . . . Bloom's literary appreciation turns out to be a wrestling with religious questions as well. . . . For Bloom, the Tanakh is above all a story of great personalities, the most memorable of them being Jacob, Joseph, and David. . . . But the transcendent personality . . . is that of God himself. Bloom describes God as "an outrageous fellow," and cautions that "we cannot know his nature because it is not nature." He is the strangest, most transgressive character ever created, and therefore more disturbing than anything in Shakespeare or Dostoyevsky. (Yale Review)
  "Bloom approaches the King James Bible seeking not religious truth but literary beauty. And he marvels at how much he finds, particularly given the undistinguished committee who—under royal commission—completed this landmark translation of scripture 400 years ago. As a linguistically sophisticated scholar, Bloom moves adroitly between the KJB and the earlier translations of Tyndale and Coverdale, expressing astonishment at how often the KJB translators, despite their missteps, improve on the work of their talented predecessors." Booklist

Bragg, Melvyn

The **book** of books; the radical impact of the King James Bible, 1611-2011. Counterpoint 2011 370p il $28 **220.5**

ISBN 978-1-58243-781-1; 1-58243-781-5

LC 2011-12432

"Bragg pays eloquent homage to the literary grandeur of the scriptures that shaped his own outlook. But this heartfelt and far-reaching tribute makes its special mark in tracing the links between the KJB and revolutions in science, politics and society, from the savants of the Royal Society to Abolitionists and Martin Luther King." Independent (UK)

Includes bibliographical references

Brake, Donald L.

A **visual** history of the English Bible; the tumultuous tale of the world's bestselling book. Baker Books 2008 349p il $29.99 **220.5**

ISBN 978-0-8010-1316-4

LC 2008-5492

"Refreshingly readable and lavishly illustrated, this volume is essential to anyone wanting to understand the Bible and its hazardous progress through the ages." Publ Wkly

Includes bibliographical references

Cruden, Alexander

★ **Cruden's** Complete concordance; with index to proper names and their meanings. edited by A.D. Adams, C.H. Irwin, S.A. Waters. Zondervan Pub. House 1968 803p $24.99; pa $8.99 **220.5**

ISBN 0-310-22920-0; 0-310-48971-7 pa

"The special value of this title is that Cruden provides an index to the Apocrypha. Note that some reprints of the work omit the Apocrypha in the concordance." Ref Sources for Small & Medium-sized Libr. 5th edition

Ferrell, Lori Anne

The **Bible** and the people. Yale University Press 2008 273p il map $32.50 **220.5**

ISBN 978-0-300-11424-9

LC 2008-26769

"The Christian Bible is not only a physical object but also a delivery system for spiritual and secular ideas, according to cultural historian Ferrell. . . . Examining the English Bible collection at the Huntington Library, Ferrell discusses these Bibles' historical, political, and social impact on Christian belief and practice in Great Britain and America from the Middle Ages to the present. . . . Written for a general audience, this is an engaging and accessible overview of the history of the English Bible." Libr J

Includes bibliographical references

Strong, James

The **strongest** Strong's exhaustive concordance of the Bible; 21st century ed, fully rev and corrected by John R. Kohlenberger III and James A. Swanson; Zondervan 2001 1742p maps $34.99 **220.5**

1. Greek language, Biblical -- Dictionaries -- English 2. Hebrew language -- Dictionaries -- English

ISBN 0-310-23343-7

LC 2001-26577

"Kohlenberger has teamed with James A. Swanson to produce a volume that cross-indexes a . . . database with exhaustive Hebrew and Greek dictionaries and adds Nave's Topical Bible Reference System (essentially a Bible dictionary with subjects, persons, places, and biblical books in alphabetic order). . . . Charts plot the chronology of events in the Old and New Testament, miracles and parables of Jesus, and messianic prophecies. There is a harmony (parallels) of gospel stories, lists of biblical kings, weights and measures, Old Testament feasts, sacred days, sacrifices, and the major social concerns of the Mosaic Covenant. There is also a chart of the Hebrew Calendar. The work is based on the King James Version of the Bible and is generally conservative." Am Ref Books Annu, 2003

220.6   Interpretation and criticism (Exegesis)

Beal, Timothy

The **rise** and fall of the Bible; the unexpected history of an accidental book. [by] Timothy Beal. Houghton Mifflin Harcourt 2011 244p il $25 **220.6**

ISBN 978-0-15-101358-6

LC 2010-5734

"The author's attempt to reclaim a sense of the Bible as a rich source of history and spiritual depth is refreshing given today's mass-marketing of scripture. The narrative is well-written and engaging." Kirkus

Includes bibliographical references

Bowker, John

The **complete** Bible handbook; an illustrated companion. DK Pub. 1998 544p il maps $39.95; pa $25 **220.6**

ISBN 0-7894-3568-3; 0-7894-8154-5 pa

LC 98-4478

In this volume "every book of the Bible (including Jewish Apocrypha) has its own entry, and there are supplementary entries on specific stories, theological concerns, history (Routes of the Exodus), or background (Gods and Goddesses of the Ancient Near East). In his introduction, Bowker presents a well-balanced summary of the Bible as a piece of literature and as scripture in our time and in history. . . . One of the book's strengths is its abundance of pictures." Voice Youth Advocates

Includes bibliographical references

Manser, Martin H.

Critical companion to the Bible; a literary reference. [by] Martin H. Manser; associate editors, David Barratt, Pieter J. Lalleman, Julius Steinberg. Facts On File, Inc. 2009 488p il $75 **220.6**

1. Bible as literature

ISBN 978-0-8160-7065-7

LC 2008-29257

"This reference provides an excellent introduction to not only the literary but also the theological studies of the Bible through the ages." Booklist

Includes bibliographical references

Wray, T. J.

What the Bible really tells us; the essential guide to biblical literacy. Rowman & Littlefield Publishers 2011 249p $24.95; ebook $23.99 **220.6**

ISBN 978-0-7425-6253-0; 978-1-4422-1293-0 ebook
LC 2011011778

"Wray devotes a couple of introductory chapters to the biblical world and the tools and methods scholars use in their exegetical work. But her intention is to get people reading the Bible, not to offer an academic, verse-by-verse commentary. Subsequent chapters, therefore, explore what the Bible says about such issues as wealth, heaven, hell, sex, and the environment, dispelling many commonly held assumptions and pointing out where disagreements in interpretation lie along the way. Wray succeeds in sharing the wisdom of the Bible by making it accessible, interesting, and fun." Booklist

Includes bibliographical references

220.7 Commentaries

Reader's Digest Association, Inc.

Reader's digest complete guide to the Bible; an illustrated book-by-book companion to the Scriptures. Reader's Digest Assn. 1998 448p il maps $29.95 **220.7**

ISBN 0-7621-0073-7
LC 98-6836

This volume describes events, people, and themes of the Bible, and includes approximately 400 color illustrations and 25 maps and charts.

Society of Biblical Literature

★ The **HarperCollins** Bible commentary; general editor, James L. Mays; associate editors, Joseph Blenkinsopp {et al.}; with the Society of Biblical Literature. rev ed; HarperSanFrancisco 2000 xxvi, 1203p il $49.50 **220.7**

ISBN 0-06-065548-8
LC 00-20818

This work is "outstanding in terms of scholarship and writing." Libr J

Includes bibliographical references

★ Oxford Bible commentary; edited by John Barton and John Muddiman. Oxford Univ. Press 2001 xxv, 1386p maps $79.95 **220.7**

ISBN 0-19-875500-7
LC 2001-21139

"An international, interfaith group of scholars is responsible for this rich, far-reaching commentary, which is most profitably studied alongside a copy of the New Revised Standard Version upon which it is based." Choice

Includes bibliographical references

220.8 Nonreligious subjects treated in Bible

Knust, Jennifer Wright

★ **Unprotected** texts; the Bible's surprising contradictions about sex and desire. HarperOne 2010 343p $25.99; ebook $20.99 **220.8**

1. Sexual behavior
ISBN 978-0-06-172558-6; 978-0-06-201082-7 ebook

"Knust's impressive and highly readable analysis of Old and New Testament Bible stories explores mores of ancient cultures, which supported prostitution and polygamy along with slavery and patriarchy. In doing so, she makes a convincing case for religious leaders and others to take greater care and responsibility in extracting wisdom needed for healing contemporary society. . . . For those wanting to understand the Bible as a chronicle of human conduct for achieving the goals of survival, peace, and fulfillment, this is a treasure." Booklist

Includes bibliographical references

Murphy, Cullen

The **Word** according to Eve; women and the Bible in ancient times and our own. Houghton Mifflin 1998 302p $24; pa $14 **220.8**

1. Bible and feminism 2. Feminism 3. Women in the Bible
ISBN 0-395-70113-9; 0-618-00192-1 pa
LC 98-18015

This is an examination of feminist Biblical scholarship. Murphy "divides his study into Old Testament scholarship and New Testament and early church history." N Y Times Book Rev

Includes bibliographical references

220.9 Geography, history, chronology, persons of Bible lands in Bible times

Currie, Robin

The **letter** and the scroll; what archaeology tells us about the Bible. [by] Robin Currie and Stephen Hyslop. National Geographic 2009 335p il map $40 **220.9**

1. Bible (as subject) -- Antiquities
ISBN 978-1-4262-0514-9
LC 2009-8572

"This gorgeous book . . . covering the people and events of the Bible, placed into their archaeological context, will delight and inform those who are interested in the Bible from a religious, cultural, or historical perspective. . . . [The book] investigates a variety of topics—such as cities, languages, luxury goods, wars, taxes, writings, and ancient art— through artifacts and archaeological evidence to provide an extensive background for the reader." Libr J

Includes bibliographical references

Freund, Richard A.

Digging through the Bible; understanding biblical people, places, and controversies through archae-

ology. Rowman & Littlefield 2008 381p il map
$44.95   **220.9**

ISBN 978-0-7425-4644-8; 0-7425-4644-6

LC 2008-18594

"It is often the work of biblical literalists to find harmonies and agreements in the scriptural record. Others seek, and celebrate, the differing views of the biblical writers. Freund . . . has put together a masterful and eminently readable study of these differences, not to resolve them, but rather to explore the rich traditions that produced these writings. In an invaluable introductory chapter, he leads the reader through the world of biblical archeology, examining the methods of textual criticism and historical research. He then explores the biblical and archeological foundations for our understandings of such notables as Abraham, David, Jesus, Mary and many others." Publ Wkly

Includes bibliographical references

Kee, Howard Clark

The **Cambridge** companion to the Bible; Bruce Chilton, general editor; Howard Clark Kee . . . [et al.] 2nd ed; Cambridge University Press 2008 724p il $100; pa $34.99   **220.9**

ISBN 978-0-521-86997-3; 978-0-521-69140-6 pa

LC 2008-270190

"This is an excellent, single-volume resource for serious students of the Bible. . . . The text is generally accessible; extensive maps and illustrations add to its popular appeal." Booklist [review of 1997 edition]

Includes bibliographical references

Tischler, Nancy M.

Men and women of the Bible; a readers guide. Greenwood Press 2002 267p il $59.95   **220.9**

ISBN 0-313-31714-3

LC 2002-75347

This resource provides "information on 100 biblical characters and their cultural significance in Western civilization. . . . Entries are arranged alphabetically from Aaron to Zephaniah, concisely written, and adhere to a uniform pattern. Subjects are listed by name with the addition of etymological information. A synopsis of the relevant biblical story follows, utilizing the King James version of the Bible. . . . The author also includes information on each person as a character in later works, including Western literature, legend, and painting." Booklist

Includes bibliographical references

Oxford Bible atlas; edited by Adrian Curtis. 4th ed.; Oxford University Press 2007 229p il map $35   **220.9**

1. Reference books

ISBN 0-19-100158-9; 978-0-19-100158-1

This atlas includes "81 full-color illustrations as well as 27 maps—e.g., of Jerusalem and the Holy Land, the Middle East and the eastern Mediterranean lands—all with terrain modeling. The text is divided into four main sections: 'The Setting,' 'The Hebrew Bible,' 'The New Testament,' and 'Archaeology in Bible Lands.' . . . [This is] a handsome background resource for Bible study." Libr J

Includes bibliographical references

The Oxford history of the biblical world; edited by Michael D. Coogan. Oxford Univ. Press 1998 643p il maps $60; pa $19.95   **220.9**

1. Ancient civilization

ISBN 0-19-508707-0; 0-19-513937-2 pa

LC 98-16042

"Organized chronologically, the essays explore the many cultures of ancient Canaan, Israel, Judea, and Palestine from 10,000 B.C.E. to the rise of Islam in the seventh century C.E. Illustrations, maps, charts, chronologies, and bibliographies enhance the uniformly well-written essays. But the strengths of the work are its currency and breadth of coverage and perspective." Libr J

Includes bibliographical references

221   Old Testament (Tanakh)

Bible/O.T.

★ **Tanakh**; a new translation of the Holy Scriptures according to the traditional Hebrew text. Jewish Publ. Soc. 1985 xxvi, 1624p $35; pa $22   **221**

ISBN 0-8276-0252-9; 0-8276-0366-5 pa

LC 85-10006

This volume represents a "collaboration between rabbis from the Orthodox, Conservative, and Reform branches of Judaism, and scholars in Semitic languages and biblical studies. The translators relied on the Hebrew tenth-century Masoretic text that is Judaism's standard. The Torah, Prophets, and Writings are here in a single volume." Publisher's note

Friedman, Matti

The **Aleppo** Codex; a true story of obsession, faith, and the pursuit of an ancient Bible. Matti Friedman. Algonquin Books of Chapel Hill 2012 298 p.   **221**

ISBN 1616200405; 9781616200404

LC 2012002327

This book by Matti Friedman unveils the journey of a sacred text--the tenth-century annotated bible known as the Aleppo Codex--from its hiding place in a Syrian synagogue to the newly founded state of Israel. Based on . . . independent research . . . the book proposes a new theory of what happened when the codex left Aleppo, Syria, in the late 1940s and eventually surfaced in Jerusalem, mysteriously incomplete. . . . Along the way, he raises critical questions about who owns historical treasures and the role of myth and legend in the creation of a nation." (Publishers note)

Kugel, James L.

How to read the Bible; a guide to scripture, then and now. Free Press 2007 819p il map $35   **221**

ISBN 978-0-7432-3586-0; 0-7432-3586-X

LC 2007-23466

"Kugel has written a wonderful book, one that lays bare the worlds both of modern biblical scholarship and of ancient biblical interpretation with wit and erudition." Commentary

Includes bibliographical references

Telushkin, Joseph

Biblical literacy; the most important people, events, and ideas of the Hebrew Bible. Morrow 1997 xxviii, 628p $29.95 **221**

1. Jewish ethics

ISBN 0-688-14297-4

LC 97-6645

"Biblical truths that many a reader may have glossed over before stand out, thanks to this superb book, and, more important, misunderstandings are cleared up and previously mistranslated words correctly rendered." Booklist

Includes bibliographical references

The Jewish Bible. The Jewish Publication Society 2008 291p il map pa $22 **221**

ISBN 978-0-8276-0851-1; 0-8276-0851-9

LC 2008-10794

"One in a series of concise reference books on different aspects of Judaism, this includes a history of the Jewish scriptures, translations through the centuries, how to read the Bible, summaries of each book, and an extensive glossary." Univ Press Books for Public and Second Sch Libr, 2009

Includes bibliographical references

222   Historical books of Old Testament

Armstrong, Karen

In the beginning; a new interpretation of Genesis. Knopf 1996 195p hardcover o.p. pa $14 **222**

ISBN 0-345-40604-4 pa

LC 96-26170

Armstrong "interprets selected accounts of Genesis using an archetypal approach to literature so as to offer insights into the problematic nature of human religion, especially the problems of separation between humans and God. . . . The text of Genesis (NRSV) makes up a third of the book's volume." Libr J

Includes bibliographical references

Bible/O.T./Genesis

The **book** of Genesis; illustrated by R. Crumb. W.W. Norton 2009 un il map $24.95 **222**

1. Comic books, strips, etc. 2. Graphic novels

ISBN 978-0-393-06102-4; 0-393-06102-7

LC 2009-14303

An illustrated adaptation of the entire book of Genesis, providing the biblical accounts of the Creation, Adam and Eve, Cain and Abel, Noah and the ark, the Tower of Babel, and other people and events.

"This is the Bible that distressed 19th-century English philanthropist and man of letters Thomas Bowdler: not stories for sweet-faced kiddies, but sex and blood. . . . We could not expect less from the patriarch of underground comix— themselves notorious for sex and violence and deals gone sour. Indeed, Crumb's muscular, detailed black-and-white seems ideally suited to Old Testament scuffles and seaminess." Libr J

Bible/O.T./Pentateuch

★ The **Torah**: the five books of Moses; a new translation of the Holy Scriptures according to the

Masoretic text; first section. Jewish Publication Society 1963 393p $20; pa $15 **222**

ISBN 0-8276-0015-1; 0-8276-0680-X pa

This "translation of Genesis, Exodus, Leviticus, Numbers, and Deuteronomy was prepared . . . to present a version of the Bible that takes into account modern insights and knowledge of ancient times. . . . Of chief value to persons of the Jewish religion but of interest to Bible scholars of any religion." Booklist

The **book** of J; translated from the Hebrew by David Rosenberg; interpreted by Harold Bloom. Vintage Books 1991 340p pa $12 **222**

ISBN 0-679-73624-7; 978-0-679-73624-0

This volume "contains three works: David Rosenberg's translation of those parts of the Pentateuch that have been attributed to the J Writer (most of Genesis and Exodus, parts of Numbers and Deuteronomy), Bloom's introduction, and, following the translation, his [commentary]." Voice Lit Suppl

The **contemporary** Torah; a gender-sensitive adaptation of the JPS translation. revising editor, David E.S. Stein; consulting editors, Adele Berlin, Ellen Frankel, and Carol L. Meyers. Jewish Publication Society 2006 xlii, 412p $28 **222**

ISBN 0-8276-0796-2; 978-0-8276-0796-5

LC 2006-40608

A modern adaptation of the Jewish Publication Society's translation of the Torah. "In places where the ancient audience probably would not have construed gender as pertinent to the text's plain sense, the editors changed words into gender-neutral terms; where gender was probably understood to be at stake, they left the text as originally translated, or even introduced gendered language where none existed before. They made these changes regardless of whether words referred to God, angels, or human beings." Publisher's note

The **five** books of Moses; Genesis, Exodus, Leviticus, Numbers, Deuteronomy. a new translation with introductions, notes, and commentary by Everett Fox. Schocken Bks. 1995 xxxi, 1024p hardcover o.p. pa $27.50 **222**

ISBN 0-8052-1119-5 pa

LC 95-10143

This translation "captures the beautiful, majestic, and dynamic character of biblical Hebrew. . . . An essential purchase for all libraries." Libr J

Dershowitz, Alan M.

The **Genesis** of justice; ten stories of biblical injustice that led to the Ten Commandments and modern law. Warner Bks. 2000 273p $28; pa $14.95 **222**

1. Justice 2. Justice -- Biblical teaching

ISBN 0-446-52479-4; 0-446-67677-2 pa

LC 99-50220

"For believers of all faiths, as well as nonbelievers, this is an outstanding work." Libr J

Includes bibliographical references

Feiler, Bruce S.

Abraham; a journey to the heart of three faiths. [by] Bruce Feiler. Morrow 2002 224p $23.95; pa $12.95 **222**

    1. Biblical characters 2. Large print books 3. Prophets

    ISBN 0-380-97776-1; 0-06-052509-6 pa

        LC 2002-70309

    "Feiler explores how Christian, Judaic, and Islamic understandings of Abraham, a patriarch to all three faiths, express interfaith disagreements. On the way to a passionate, prayerful argument for interfaith peace, Feiler mixes theological meditation, adventurous travelogue, and sly wit." Booklist

Hazony, David

The Ten commandments; how our most ancient moral text can renew modern life. Scribner 2010 288p $26; ebook $12.99 **222**

    ISBN 978-1-4165-6235-1; 978-1-4165-62511 ebook

        LC 2009-43129

    The author "uses the biblical text as a point of departure for 10 wide-ranging essays, examining each commandment as a contribution to constructing the good society. . . . Hazony has succeeded in extending the Ten Commandments to an impressive vision of how to attain the good society." Publ Wkly

    Includes bibliographical references

Kass, Leon

The beginning of wisdom; reading Genesis. {by} Leon R. Kass. Free Press 2003 576p $35 **222**

    ISBN 0-7432-4299-8

        LC 2002-45593

    The author "sees Genesis as a text that offers wisdom about the nature of man and how we ought to live, while it also calls for interpretation, reflection, and judgment. . . . Kass presents many enlightening insights, the result of his attempts to understand the text on its own terms and relating it to contemporary concerns, especially tradition and parenthood. While not everyone will agree with his interpretations, which tend to the conservative, Kass offers much to be pondered by thoughtful readers, both academics and, especially, educated laypeople." Libr J

    Includes bibliographical references

Klinghoffer, David

The discovery of God; Abraham and the birth of monotheism. Doubleday 2003 348p map $26; pa $14.95 **222**

    1. Biblical characters 2. Jews -- History -- To 70 A.D. 3. Judaism -- History -- To 70 A.D. 4. Monotheism 5. Monotheism -- History 6. Prophets

    ISBN 0-385-49973-6; 0-385-49974-4 pa

        LC 2002-31566

    This book "makes no attempt to prove the historical accuracy of the stories from Genesis, but rather advances an impassioned argument for their relevance." Natl Rev

    Includes bibliographical references

McKenzie, Steven L.

King David; a biography. Oxford Univ. Press 2000 232p il maps $41.50 **222**

    1. Kings

    ISBN 0-19-513273-4

        LC 99-44315

    McKenzie "views David as a ruthless, brutal usurper who would be well at home among many modern-day rulers. . . . Much of this portrait is inevitably speculation, and it is likely to outrage David's defenders. Still, given the limitations of written sources, McKenzie effectively coats his assertions with a veneer of credibility." Booklist

    Includes bibliographical references

Moyers, Bill

Genesis: a living conversation. Doubleday 1996 361p il hardcover o.p. pa $22.95 **222**

    ISBN 0-385-49043-7 pa

        LC 96-15318

    Companion volume to the PBS series led by Bill Moyers in which writers and religious thinkers discussed episodes from the first book of the Bible. Among the participants are Burton Visotzky, a rabbi who initiated the conversations which gave rise to the series, "Elaine Pagels, Karen Armstrong, . . . John Barth, and Oscar Hijuelos. The book is divided by biblical tale (Adam and Eve, Cain and Abel, the blinding of Isaac) with five or six of the participants discussing the moral, literary, and personal meanings of the stories." Booklist

225 New Testament

Brown, Raymond Edward

An introduction to the New Testament; by Raymond E. Brown. Yale University Press 1997 xxxviii, 878p map $55 **225**

    ISBN 978-0-300-14016-3; 0-300-14016-9

    Brown's book "culminates his life's work and synthesizes the best of his generation's historical-critical scholarship clearly and cogently for beginners and advanced students alike." N Y Times Book Rev

Wilson, A. N.

Paul: the mind of the Apostle. Norton 1997 273p hardcover o.p. pa $16.95 **225**

    1. Apostles 2. Saints 3. Writers on religion

    ISBN 0-393-31760-9 pa

        LC 96-47834

    "Wilson's insights fascinate and provoke. Even as rich and incisive a portrait as this one cannot provide a complete understanding of Paul or the turbulent time in which he lived, but readers will come away seeing the enigmatic apostle as an imaginative transformer who shaped a worldwide religious movement." Booklist

    Includes bibliographical references

225.9   Geography, history, chronology, persons of New Testament lands in New Testament times

Murphy-O'Connor, J.
Paul; a critical life. {by} Jerome Murphy-O'Connor. Clarendon Press 1996 416p maps hardcover o.p. pa $21   **225.9**
   1. Apostles 2. Biography, Individual 3. Saints 4. Writers on religion
   ISBN 01-9-285342-2 pa
                                              LC 95-49173
"This is likely to become the standard work on Paul's life for the next generation and is warmly recommended as such." Choice
Includes bibliographical references

Ruden, Sarah
Paul among the people; the Apostle reinterpreted and reimagined in his own time. Pantheon Books 2010 214p $25; ebook $25   **225.9**
   1. Apostles 2. Christian life -- History -- Early church, ca. 30-600 3. Saints 4. Theology, Doctrinal in literature 5. Writers on religion
   ISBN 978-0-375-42501-1; 978-0-307-37902-3 ebook
                                              LC 2009-20969
"In 'reimagining' Paul with the aid of her intimate knowledge of classical literature, Ruden hasn't only helped us to better understand him and his message in the context of his time (as indispensable as that service is). She has also brought Paul to us, to our time. . . . In an uncanny way, her book is animated by the apostle's style: his urgency, his argumentative agility, his bluntness, his exasperation, his vision of great felicity." Natl Rev
Includes bibliographical references

226   Gospels and Acts

Bonhoeffer, Dietrich
★ The **cost** of discipleship; containing material not previously translated. rev and unabridged ed; Macmillan 1959 hardcover o.p. pa $12   **226**
   ISBN 0-684-81500-1 pa
The first part of the book "is an exposition of the conception of discipleship that is to be found in the Synoptic Gospels, together with an interpretation of the Sermon on the Mount. The second part consists of Bonhoeffer's attempt to show how the terminology used by the evangelists has been translated into the language of the Church of the Apostle Paul." Magill. Masterpieces of Christ Lit in Summary Form

Chilton, Bruce
Mary Magdalene; a biography. Doubleday 2005 220p map $23.95   **226**
   1. Biography, Individual 2. Saints 3. Women in Christianity -- History -- Early church, ca. 30-600
   ISBN 0-385-51317-8
                                              LC 2005-45446
Through an "examination of available texts (canonical gospels, the most important noncanonical gospels, and other early Christian writings) and sober speculation, Chil-

ton traces [Mary Magdalene's] . . . relationship to Jesus and claims that it was she who taught Jesus the power of vision, anointing, and touch and the disciples that Jesus had overcome death; without her, according to Chilton, resurrection might never have become a central Christian teaching. He also traces her later legend, the ambivalence of Gnosticism toward her, her medieval cult and denigration, and 20th-century reassessments." Libr J

Kloppenborg, John S.
Q, the earliest Gospel; an introduction to the original stories and sayings of Jesus. Westminster John Knox Press 2008 170p il pa $19.95   **226**
   1. Q hypothesis (Synoptics criticism)
   ISBN 978-0-664-23222-1; 0-664-23222-1
                                              LC 2008-8394
The author is an "authority on the Q Gospel, a 'sayings gospel' that is thought to be a source (from the German Quelle for source) for the Gospels of Matthew and Luke. No copy of Q has been found, but scholars have recreated it through analysis of the three synoptic Gospels, looking for common elements and focusing on the sayings of Jesus. This book is a succinct introduction to Q, addressing questions about its composition and importance. . . . A complete reconstruction of Q is included as well as notes and a bibliography." Libr J

Wroe, Ann
Pontius Pilate. Modern Library 2000 412p $26; pa $14.95   **226**
   1. Colonial administrators 2. Government officials
   ISBN 0-375-50305-6; 0-375-75397-4 pa
                                              LC 99-43000
"As long as readers don't take this as accurate history but enjoy it as a well-written, imaginative, and creative portrait of Pilate and his times, the book serves a useful purpose." Libr J
Includes bibliographical references

226.3   Mark

Bible/N.T./Gospels
The **three** Gospels; {by} Reynolds Price. Scribner 1996 288p $23; pa $13   **226.3**
   ISBN 0-684-80336-4; 0-684-83281-X pa
                                              LC 95-39948
"Although there is so much to appreciate in these commentaries and in the translated texts, the best part of the book . . . is left to last: Price's own joyously written account of Jesus' life." Booklist

227   Epistles

Borg, Marcus J.
The **first** Paul; reclaiming the radical visionary behind the Church's conservative icon. [by] Marcus

J. Borg, John Dominic Crossan. HarperOne 2009
230p $24.99; pa $13.99   **227**
1. Apostles 2. Saints 3. Writers on religion
ISBN 978-0-06-143072-5; 0-06-143072-2; 978-0-06-
143073-2 pa; 0-06-143073-0 pa
LC 2009-004881
"The great epistolary apostle is revealed as neither anti-
Semitic, anti-sex, nor misogynist, but a preacher of social
and political equality." Booklist
Includes bibliographical references

228   Revelation (Apocalypse)

Pagels, Elaine H., 1943-
    Revelations; visions, prophecy, and politics in the
book of Revelation. Elaine Pagels. Viking 2012 246
p.   **228**
1. Church history 2. Eschatology 3. Judaism -- History
4. Nonfiction 5. Religion & politics -- History
ISBN 9780670023349
LC 2011037551
This book presents an interpretation of the Book of Revelation from the Christian Bible, touching on its narrative,
themes, and historical background. "[Elaine] Pagels . . .
shows that Revelation, far from being meant as a hallucinatory prophecy, is actually a coded account of events that
were happening at the time John was writing. The author
determines that based on historical conflicts between Jewish
and Gentile followers of Jesus Christ, the Revelation is essentially an anti-Christian polemic. (New Yorker)

229   Apocrypha, pseudepigrapha,
intertestamental works

Bible/O.T./Apocrypha
    ★ The **Apocrypha**; new revised standard ver-
sion. Cambridge University Press 1993 262p pa
$14.99   **229**
ISBN 978-0-521-50776-9; 0-521-50776-6
"These books form part of the sacred literature of the
Alexandrian Jews. . . . Some of them form an historical link
between the Old and New Testament, others have a linguistic value in connexion with the Hellenistic phraseology of
the latter. The narratives of Apocrypha are partly historical
records, and partly allegorical." Oxford Univ. Press

Pagels, Elaine H.
    ★ **Beyond** belief; the secret Gospel of Thomas.
{by} Elaine Pagels. Random House 2003 241p
$26.95   **229**
1. Christianity
ISBN 0-375-50156-8
LC 2002-36840
"Even those who possess only a nodding acquaintance
with Gnostic writings will find themselves stimulated by
the author's arguments and perhaps transformed by her
conclusions. A fresh and exciting work of theology and
spirituality." Booklist
Includes bibliographical references

230   Christianity

Holifield, E. Brooks
    ★ **Theology** in America; Christian thought from
the age of the Puritans to the Civil War. Yale University Press 2003 617p hardcover o.p. pa $23   **230**
1. Doctrinal theology
ISBN 0-300-09574-0; 978-0-300-10765-4 pa; 0-300-
10765-X pa
LC 2003-42289
"In this majestic achievement, Holifield . . . provides a
first-rate, richly evocative and unrivaled history of theology
in America. . . . This masterfully narrated, splendid book will
become the definitive study of the development of American
theology." Publ Wkly
Includes bibliographical references

Kung, Hans
    Great Christian thinkers. Continuum 1994 235p
hardcover o.p. pa $19.95   **230**
1. Apostles 2. Bishops 3. Church history 4.
Philosophers 5. Religious leaders 6. Saints 7. Social
reformers 8. Theologians 9. Theology 10. Writers
on religion
ISBN 0-8264-0848-6 pa
LC 94-883
The author "attempts a new approach to the introduc-
tion-to-theology genre by critically tracing the developing
thought of key, usually 'paradigm-shifting,' theologians
(Paul, Origen, Augustine, Aquinas, Luther, Schleiermacher,
and Karl Barth) in relation to their social, intellectual, and
religious environment. He explores the significance of their
life and work for the Christian world in an interesting, quite
understandable manner." Libr J
Includes bibliographical references

Lewis, C. S.
    ★ **Mere** Christianity; a revised and amplified
edition, with a new introduction, of the three books,
Broadcast talks, Christian behaviour, and Beyond
personality. HarperSanFrancisco 2001 xx, 227p
$19.95; pa $10   **230**
1. Christian philosophy
ISBN 0-06-065288-8; 0-06-065292-6 pa
LC 00-49862
This omnibus edition includes most of C. S. Lewis' writings on Christian theology and moral philosophy

Teilhard de Chardin, Pierre
    ★ The **divine** milieu; an essay on the interior
life. Harper & Row 1960 144p hardcover o.p. pa
$14   **230**
1. Christian philosophy
ISBN 978-0-06-093725-6 pa; 0-06-093725-4 pa
In this book Father de Chardin describes his
spiritual philosophy.

Oxford companion to Christian thought; edited by
    Adrian Hastings {et al.}   Oxford Univ. Press
2000 xxviii, 777p $75   **230**
1. Reference books 2. Theology 3. Theology --

Dictionaries
ISBN 0-19-860024-0

LC 2001-267818

This volume focuses "on the movement of ideas among Christians. The articles (more than 500) by 268 scholars (mostly British) range in length from half a column . . . to seven pages. . . . They broadly cover the themes . . . persons . . . places . . . and historical periods . . . that characterize Christian thought." Choice

Includes bibliographical references

231 Christian doctrinal theology

Cairns, Scott

The **end** of suffering; finding purpose in pain. Paraclete Press 2009 126p pa $15.99   **231**
    1. Suffering   2. Suffering -- Religious aspects -- Christianity
    ISBN 978-1-55725-563-1; 1-55725-563-6

LC 2009-18728

The author "offers a profoundly touching and deeply considered treatment of the notion of suffering, especially grief, in a Christian's life. For Cairns, suffering is not about the presence of evil; instead, it provides occasions where God can be known more intimately. . . . Eloquent in its simplicity, Cairns's brief book is a superb treatment of the thorny issues of suffering and grief." Libr J

Includes bibliographical references

Price, Reynolds

Letter to a man in the fire; does God exist and does He care? Scribner 1999 108p $20; pa $11 **231**
    1. God 2. Suffering
    ISBN 0-684-85626-3; 0-684-85627-1 pa

LC 98-54197

This book "consists of Price's response to a 1997 letter he received from a medical student stricken with cancer. Price telephoned and then followed up with this long, eloquent letter on the nature of suffering and the justice and righteousness of God." Publ Wkly

231.7 Relation to the world

Humes, Edward

Monkey girl; evolution, education, religion, and the battle for America's soul. HarperCollins Publishers 2007 380p $25.95   **231.7**
    1. Creationism 2. Evolution
    ISBN 978-0-06-088548-9; 0-06-088548-3

LC 2006-50263

Humes "may be the most successful so far in making a complicated issue accessible and in putting human faces on both sides of the evolution divide. Clearly based on exhaustive reporting that takes the reader from the hard benches of a Harrisburg, Pa., federal district courtroom to the kitchen tables of Dover families whose children were taunted as 'monkey girls,' Humes' fast-moving, richly detailed book reads like a suspense novel." Chicago Tribune

Lewis, C. S.

Miracles; a preliminary study. HarperSanFrancisco 2001 294p pa $13.95   **231.7**
    1. Miracles
    ISBN 0-06-065301-9; 978-0-06-065301-9

LC 00-49863

"Mr. Lewis casts his net fairly wide and, under the guise of a book on miracles, offers a rational justification both of theism and of doctrinal Christianity." Times Lit Suppl

Miller, Kenneth R.

Finding Darwin's God; a scientist's search for common ground between God and evolution. Cliff St. Bks. 1999 338p il hardcover o.p.   **231.7**
    1. Evolution 2. Evolution (Biology) 3. Evolution (Biology) -- Religious aspects -- Christianity 4. Religion and science
    ISBN 0-06-017593-1; 0-06-123350-1 pa

LC 99016754

This work seeks to establish that "evolution is scientifically true. Miller, a practicing Roman Catholic, attempts to demonstrate that it is also compatible with a belief in God." (Christ Sci Monit) Index.

The author "explains the difference between evolution as validated scientific fact and as an evolving theory. He illustrates his contentions with examples from astronomy, geology, physics and molecular biology, confronting the illogic of creationists with persuasive reasons based on the known physical properties of the universe. . . . Then standing firmly on Darwinian ground, he turns to take on, with equal vigor, his outspoken colleagues in science who espouse a materialistic, agnostic or atheistic vision of reality." Publ Wkly

Includes bibliographical references

Scott, Robert A.

Miracle cures; saints, pilgrimage, and the healing powers of belief. University of California Press 2010 xxix, 235p il map $24.95; ebook $20 **231.7**
    1. Health -- Psychological aspects 2. Middle Ages -- History 3. Miracles -- Christianity 4. Placebo (Medicine) 5. Psychophysiology 6. Spiritual healing
    ISBN 978-0-520-26275-1; 978-0-520-94620-0 ebook

LC 2009-37269

The author "illuminates the Christian practice of pilgrimages to healing shrines from medieval to contemporary times. He also explores the contemporary phenomenon of 'virtual pilgrimage' on the Internet as a foil to the practice of physical pilgrimage. The author carefully weaves detailed textual and historiographic work with the latest social scientific findings on pain, and environmental and behavioral factors that promote health and shape the experience of illness. . . . Readers at all levels should enjoy this engaging but sophisticated book." Choice

Includes bibliographical references

Wintz, Jack

Will I see my dog in heaven? God's saving love for the whole family of creation. Paraclete Press 2009 153p pa $14.99   **231.7**
    1. Animals -- Religious aspects 2. Future life
    ISBN 978-1-55725-568-6

LC 2009-259

The author, a Franciscan friar, argues that "God's promise of a new creation at the end of time extends to the animal companions we have known and loved in this life. . . . Strongly recommended." Libr J

Includes bibliographical references

Woodward, Kenneth L.

The **book** of miracles; the meaning of the miracle stories in Christianity, Judaism, Buddhism, Hinduism, Islam. Simon & Schuster 2000 429p hardcover o.p. pa $16   **231.7**
1. Miracles
ISBN 0-7432-0029-2 pa

LC 99-88083

"A great resource for studies in comparative religions and interfaith dialog." Libr J

Includes bibliographical references

232   Jesus Christ and his family

Gordon, Mary

Reading Jesus; a writer's encounter with the Gospels. Pantheon Books 2009 205p $24.95   **232**
ISBN 978-0-375-42457-1

LC 2009-04975

Gordon "examines her faith by closely reading, in a kind of literary lectio divina (sacred reading), the four Christian gospels that recount the life of Christ. The accounts by evangelists Matthew, Mark, Luke and John of the life of Jesus have a common subject and amazingly different treatments. Gordon tackles the power and puzzle of the Christian gospels with measure and imagination, providing welcome relief for those left cold by scholarly or fundamentalist parsing." Publ Wkly

Vermes, Geza

The **changing** faces of Jesus. Viking 2001 324p map hardcover o.p. pa $15.86   **232**
ISBN 0-14-026524-4 pa

LC 00-43897

"Vermes's vast knowledge of first century Judaism ensures that this work will become one of the most important works in historical Jesus studies, and his readable style makes it useful for both public and academic library patrons." Libr J

Includes bibliographical references

232.9   Family and life of Jesus

Benedict XVI, Pope, 1927-

Jesus of Nazareth. part two; Holy week, from the entrance into Jerusalem to the Resurrection. by Joseph Ratzinger, Pope Benedict XVI. Ignatius Press 2011 362p $24.95   **232.9**
1. Biography, Individual 2. Holy Week
ISBN 978-1-58617-500-9; 1-58617-500-9

This is "the second volume in [the author's] 'Jesus of Nazareth' series. . . . [This book] is a worthy contribution to the field not only because it was written by a pope, but also because it combines solid scholarship with deep spirituality. As such it joins the Jesus of history to the Christ of faith in an accessible narrative. This volume explores the drama of Holy Week. . . . The focus is on the meaning of the events, with a strong reiteration of recent church teaching against imputing guilt for Jesus' death to the Jews of that time or now." Publ Wkly

Chilton, Bruce

Rabbi Jesus; an intimate biography. Doubleday 2000 xxii, 330p il maps hardcover o.p. pa $14.95   **232.9**
1. Christianity
ISBN 0-385-49793-8 pa

LC 00-31548

The author presents a "wonderfully fresh presentation of the implications of Jesus's being a Jewish male living in the context of first-century Judaism." Libr J

Includes bibliographical references

Fredriksen, Paula

Jesus of Nazareth, King of the Jews; a Jewish life and the emergence of Christianity. Knopf 1999 327p hardcover o.p. pa $14   **232.9**
ISBN 0-679-76746-0 pa

LC 99-31054

"To Fredriksen, Jesus was an observant Jew immersed in a context bounded by Galilee and Jerusalem. He was crucified as an imperial Roman deterrent to unruly inhabitants of a region prone to rebellion, and the emergence of Christianity is a work of creative theological reinterpretation as much as of historical memory." Booklist

Includes bibliographical references

Girzone, Joseph F.

A **portrait** of Jesus. Doubleday 1998 179p il hardcover o.p. pa $11.95   **232.9**
1. Christian life 2. Christian life -- Catholic authors
ISBN 0-385-48477-1 pa

LC 98-15618

"This is popular liberal Catholic theology, more filled with forgiveness and fellowship than shaming and hierarchy. Many a non-Catholic and even non-Christian may embrace it, too." Booklist

Meier, John P.

A **marginal** Jew; rethinking the historical Jesus. Doubleday 1991 3v maps v1 $45; v2 $42.50; v3 $45   **232.9**
ISBN 0-385-26425-9 v1; 0-385-46992-6 v2; 0-385-46993-4 v3

LC 91-10538

The first three volumes in a projected series of four devoted to an examination of the historical Jesus and his Jewish environment

The author "summarizes the first two volumes of A Marginal Jew and forecasts the next while meticulously documenting his understanding of the relations between the historical Jesus, his historical companions, and his historical competitors—Pharisees, Sadducees, Essenes, and others. . . . The only thing common about Meier's project is fascination with the character of Jesus. Those who share that will find this dense, academic work worth their effort." Booklist {review of volume 3}

Includes bibliographical references

Pelikan, Jaroslav Jan

★ The **illustrated** Jesus through the centuries. Yale Univ. Press 1997 254p il $25   **232.9**

ISBN 0-300-07268-6

LC 97-7360

In this revision of Jesus through the centuries (1985) the author "has abridged the text and turns to illustrations to convey his interpretations. . . . Very beautiful and very appealing for the general reader, this edition by no means replaces the scholarship and documentation of the first; those notations and references are missing in the illustrated edition. However, the illustrations enhance this interesting and insightful text." Libr J

Wilson, A. N.

Jesus. Norton 1992 269p $22.95   **232.9**

ISBN 0-393-03087-3

LC 92-37046

The author attempts to understand Jesus as a historical figure and ethical teacher within the context of first-century Judaism.

232.91   Mary, mother of Jesus

Pelikan, Jaroslav Jan

★ **Mary** through the centuries; her place in the history of culture. Yale Univ. Press 1996 267p il $40; pa $14.95   **232.91**

1. Doctrinal theology 2. Saints

ISBN 0-300-06951-0; 0-300-07661-4 pa

LC 96-24726

"Although volumes have been written about the Virgin Mary from a wide variety of perspectives, it is rare to find a scholarly work that is easily accessible to the general, educated reader." Choice

Includes bibliographical references

233   Humankind

Jacobs, Alan

Original sin; a cultural history. HarperOne 2008 286p $24.95; pa $14.99   **233**

1. Sin 2. Sin, Original -- History of doctrines 3. Sin, Original, in literature

ISBN 978-0-06-078340-2; 0-06-078340-0; 978-0-06-087257-1 pa; 0-06-087257-8 pa

LC 2008-06582

This is "a playful, wide-ranging, erudite meditation on the nagging question of whether human beings enter the world predisposed to evil and sinfulness. . . . Original Sin has a great deal to offer both the general reader and those already well versed in this most controversial of theological arenas." America

Includes bibliographical references

235   Spiritual beings

Pagels, Elaine H.

★ The **origin** of Satan; {by} Elaine Pagels. Random House 1995 214p hardcover o.p. pa $12   **235**

1. Church history -- 30-600, Early church 2. Devil

ISBN 0-679-73118-0 pa

LC 95-7983

Pagels "shows herself to be a masterful guide through the risk-laden complexities of biblical studies." Publ Wkly

Includes bibliographical references

Woodward, Kenneth L.

Making saints; how the Catholic Church determines who becomes a saint, who doesn't, and why. Simon & Schuster 1990 461p il hardcover o.p. pa $21.50   **235**

1. Catholic Church 2. Christian saints 3. Saints

ISBN 0-684-81530-3 pa

LC 90-10117

A study of the politics and procedures of the modern process of canonization in the Roman Catholic church.

This is "the most comprehensive, critical and up-to-date look at saint making so far written." N Y Times Book Rev

Includes bibliographical references

Wray, T. J.

The **birth** of Satan; tracing the devil's biblical roots. [by] T.J. Wray, Gregory Mobley. Palgrave Macmillan 2005 211p $24.95   **235**

1. Devil

ISBN 1-4039-6933-7

LC 2005-43046

The authors find Satan's "origins in a biblical character and in early Jewish and Christian writings outside of the scriptures. They try to understand why we as a species strive to feel fearful, why being frightened—vicariously, at least—is so appealing. . . . A thoughtful, informative examination." Booklist

Includes bibliographical references

236   Eschatology

Brown, Samuel Morris

In heaven as it is on earth; Samuel Morris Brown. Oxford University Press 2012 xii, 392 p illustrations   **236**

ISBN 9780199793570

LC 2011002848

'This book examines Mormonism "through the lens of founder Joseph Smith's profound preoccupation with the specter of death. Revisiting historical documents and scripture from this . . . perspective, Brown offers . . . insight into the origin and meaning of some of Mormonism's earliest beliefs and practices. The world of early Mormonism was besieged by death--infant mortality, violence, and disease were rampant. A prolonged battle with typhoid fever, punctuated by painful surgeries including a threatened leg amputation, and the sudden loss of his beloved brother Alvin cast a long shadow over Smith's own life. Smith embraced and was deeply influenced by the culture of 'holy dying'--with its emphasis on deathbed salvation, melodramatic bereavement, and belief in the Providential nature of untimely death--that sought to cope with the widespread mortality of the period." (Publisher's note)

Eire, Carlos M. N.
A **very** brief history of eternity; [by] Carlos Eire. Princeton University Press 2010 268p il $24.95; ebook $24.95   **236**
1. Civilization, Western 2. Eternity 3. Eternity -- History of doctrines 4. Western civilization
ISBN 978-0-691-13357-7; 978-1-4008-3187-6 ebook
    LC 2009-22951
The author's "skill at engaging readers conceals the rigorous, thoughtful research and methodology that went into this volume. . . . This thought-provoking book is sure to be a classic." Choice
Includes bibliographical references

Miller, Lisa
Heaven; our 2000-year-old fascination with the afterlife. Harper 2010 331p $25.99   **236**
1. Future life 2. Heaven
ISBN 978-0-06-055475-0; 0-06-055475-4
    LC 2009-26063
In this "sweeping historical and literary geography of heaven . . . [Miller] talks to priests, a Dominican monk, Muslim clerics, rabbis, and professors (and even visits a psychic, who channels a balding Ed Asner look-alike — no one she knows, though she racks her brain). She doesn't ignore pop culture, either, touching on everything from The Lovely Bones to the hugely popular Left Behind series. . . . But once she has finished reporting and researching, Miller's book loses its hard journalistic edge and becomes something else: a memoir. Her own qualms about faith have danced around the edges of the story, but finally they come front and center. What Miller ultimately concludes may surprise you. It certainly surprised her." Entertainment Wkly

Spong, John Shelby
Eternal life; a new vision: beyond religion, beyond theism, beyond heaven and hell. Harper One 2009 xx, 268p $24.99   **236**
1. Death 2. Eternity 3. Future life
ISBN 978-0-06-076206-3
    LC 2008-51443
This book "offers new insights into religion's big questions about life and death, making an invaluable contribution to both religious scholarship and faithful exploration." Publ Wkly
Includes bibliographical references

Wright, N. T.
Surprised by hope; rethinking heaven, the resurrection, and the mission of the church. HarperOne 2008 332p $24.95   **236**
1. Eschatology 2. Future life 3. Future life -- Christianity 4. Hope 5. Hope -- Religious aspects -- Christianity
ISBN 978-0-06-155182-6; 0-06-155182-1

"Readers will need a Bible handy to appreciate this work fully, as Wright prefers to cite rather than print Scripture. His prose, deep but not murky, is lightened by glints of humor. For any library serving patrons who are willing to think a bit about religion." Libr J
Includes bibliographical references

239   Apologetics and polemics

De civitate Dei./English
Concerning the city of God against the pagans; [by] St. Augustine; translated by Henry Bettenson; with a new introduction by G.R. Evans. Penguin Books 2003 lxxi, 1097p pa $16   **239**
1. Apologetics
ISBN 978-0-14-044894-8; 0-14-044894-2
    LC 2004-269353
"Written as an eloquent defence of the faith at a time when the Roman Empire was on the brink of collapse, it examines the ancient pagan religions of Rome, the arguments of the Greek philosophers and the revelations of the Bible. Pointing the way forward to a citizenship that transcends worldly politics and will last for eternity, City of God represents a dramatic turning point in the unfolding of Christian doctrine. The new introduction by Gill Evans examines the text in the light of contemporary Greek and Roman thought and political change." Publisher's note
Includes bibliographical references

Keller, Timothy J.
The **reason** for God; belief in an age of skepticism. Dutton 2008 293p $24.95   **239**
1. Apologetics 2. Faith 3. Skepticism
ISBN 978-0-525-95049-3; 0-525-95049-4
    LC 2007-43745
"Using literature, philosophy, and pop culture, the author gives . . . reasons for a strong belief in God. . . . [The author] presents a religious view without being overly critical of the secular side presented in other books. . . . This book presents a valid, well-written, and well-researched argument." Libr J

241   Christian ethics

Anderson, Gary A.
Sin; a history. Yale University Press 2009 253p $30; pa $20   **241**
1. Sin 2. Sin -- Biblical teaching 3. Sin -- Christianity
ISBN 978-0-300-14989-0; 0-300-14989-1; 978-0-300-16809-9 pa; 0-300-16809-8 pa
    LC 2009012342
This book "is a significant contribution both to scriptural interpretation and to theology proper, and an object lesson in how to do both well. . . . The richness and precision of Anderson's engagement with the texts he treats cannot be adequately conveyed in a short review, which is why you should read his book." Commonweal
Includes bibliographical references

Chapman, Gary D.

Love as a way of life; seven keys to transforming every aspect of your life. [by] Gary Chapman. Doubleday 2008 239p $19.95; pa $13.95 **241**
1. Interpersonal relations -- Religious aspects 2. Love -- Religious aspects
ISBN 978-0-385-51858-1; 0-385-51858-7; 978-1-4000-7259-0 pa; 1-4000-7259-X pa
LC 2007-50546

"All self-help books run the risk of cliché, but Chapman manages to make tried-and-true material feel fresh through carefully chosen examples from his pastoral counseling practice and his own life. . . . Although Christian faith provides the scaffolding for his program and a concluding chapter makes the need for God's help explicit, Chapman's judicious counsel can be implemented by people of many religious traditions." Publ Wkly
Includes bibliographical references

Pagels, Elaine H.

★ **Adam,** Eve, and the serpent. Random House 1988 xxviii, 189p hardcover o.p. pa $12 **241**
1. Christianity 2. Church history -- 30-600, Early church 3. Sexual behavior
ISBN 0-679-72232-7 pa
LC 87-43227

"Pagels writes with a rare combination of formidable knowledge and easy fluency. The old controversies she discusses become, in her hands, matters of immediate interest." Economist
Includes bibliographical references

Price, Reynolds

A **serious** way of wondering; the ethics of Jesus imagined. Scribner 2003 146p hardcover o.p. pa $14.95 **241**
1. Christian ethics
ISBN 0-7432-3008-6; 0-7432-3009-4 pa
LC 2003-41506

"In three . . . apocryphal gospel stories, Price's Jesus engages in conversations about homosexuality, suicide and the plight of women in male-dominated societies. . . . Elegant and passionate, Price's provocative parables provide no simple answers to the saccharine question 'What would Jesus do?' Rather, they compel us to imagine creatively our engagements with Jesus' teachings and the impact of those teachings on our lives." Publ Wkly
Includes bibliographical references

242   Devotional literature

Augustine

★ **Confessions**; translated with an introduction and notes by Henry Chadwick. Oxford University Press 1998 xxviii, 311p pa $7.95 **242**
ISBN 978-0-19-283372-3; 0-19-283372-3

"These confessions were written at the end of the fourth century by the most distinguished of the Latin fathers as a revelation of his spiritual experience. They have been a source of religious inspiration through the centuries." Pratt Alcove
Includes bibliographical references

Kempis, Thomas à

The **imitation** of Christ; {by} Thomas à Kempis. Vintage Books 1998 xliii, 242p pa $12.95 **242**
ISBN 978-0-375-70018-7; 0-375-70018-8

This devotional classic originally written in Latin in the 15th century "traces in four books the gradual progress of the soul to Christian perfection, its detachment from the world, and its union with God." Oxford Companion to Engl Lit. Concise edition

King, Martin Luther, Jr., 1929-1968

Thou, dear God; Martin Luther King, Jr. ; foreword by Julius R. Scruggs ; edited and introduced by Lewis V. Baldwin. Beacon Press 2012 245 p. **242**
1. Prayers
ISBN 9780807086032
LC 2011031431

This book "is the first and only collection of sixty-eight prayers by Martin Luther King, Jr. Arranged thematically in six parts--with prayers for spiritual guidance, special occasions, times of adversity, times of trial, uncertain times, and social justice--Baptist minister and King scholar Lewis Baldwin introduces the book and each section with short essays. Included are both personal and public prayers King recited as a seminarian, graduate student, preacher, pastor, and, finally, civil rights leader, along with a special section that reveals the biblical sources that most inspired King. Collectively they illustrate how King turned to private prayer for his own spiritual fulfillment and to public prayer as a way to move, inspire, and reaffirm a quest for peace and social justice." (Publisher's note)

Rennebohm, Craig

Souls in the hands of a tender God; stories of the search for home and healing on the streets. [by] Craig Rennebohm with David Paul. Beacon Press 2008 208p $23.95; pa $18 **242**
1. Mental health -- Religious aspects 2. Mental illness 3. Spiritual healing
ISBN 978-0-8070-0042-7; 0-8070-0042-6; 978-0-8070-0043-4 pa; 0-8070-0043-4 pa
LC 2007-31506

"For decades Rennebohm, a Protestant pastor, has walked the streets of Seattle, making contact with mentally ill homeless people and slowly drawing them into 'circles of care' so they can find safe housing, receive medical and psychological help and rejoin the human community. In this collaboration with Paul, Rennebohm interweaves themes of the Spirit working in desperate lives, the unshakable dignity of human souls and the necessity of companionship for healing as he vividly portrays the lost people he encounters. . . . As well as a guide to how others can help be healing presences to the mentally ill, this hopeful book is a meditation on faith in a broken world." Publ Wkly
Includes bibliographical references

★ The little flowers of St. Francis of Assisi; written by Ugolino di Monte Santa Maria; edited by and adapted from a translation by W. Heywood; with a new preface by Madeleine L'Engle. Vintage Books 1998 xxxviii, 120p pa $13   **242**

1. Saints 2. Writers on religion

ISBN 978-0-375-70020-0; 0-375-70020-X

LC 97-48815

These "simple anecdotes exemplify St. Francis' love of nature, man and of God." Bookman's Manual

Includes bibliographical references

248   Christian experience, practice, life

Brizendine, Judy

Stunned by grief; remapping your life when loss changes everything. BennettKnepp Publishing 2011 274p il pa $18.95   **248**

1. Adjustment (Psychology) 2. Bereavement 3. Loss (Psychology) 4. Spiritual healing

ISBN 978-0-9831688-1-2

"A former market analyst and interior designer, . . . [the author] found her world turned upside down when her husband died. She uses her own experience combined with the advice of psychologists, grief counselors, the Bible, and fellow mourners to provide a sort of roadmap for the unwelcome journey of grief. In bite-size pieces, she covers the progression of grief, the intrinsic anger and guilt felt in the process, and the possibility of dealing with and planning a new future. . . . This book will comfort and support anyone new to grief and will serve as a companion in times of loneliness. Realistic, practical, and highly recommended." Libr J

Includes bibliographical references

Lewis, C. S.

Letters to Malcolm: chiefly on prayer. 1964 124p hardcover o.p. pa $13   **248**

1. Christian life 2. Prayer

ISBN 978-0-15-602766-3

The author's "reflections on prayer are here set down in the form of thoughtful and engaging letters to his friend Malcolm." Cincinnati Public Libr

★ The **Screwtape** letters; with, Screwtape proposes a toast. HarperSanFrancisco 2001 209p $22.95; pa $11.95   **248**

1. Christian life 2. Satire

ISBN 0-06-065289-6; 0-06-065293-4 pa

LC 00-49860

"A popular work on Christian moral and theological problems. . . . It is in the form of a series of letters in which a devil, Screwtape, advises his nephew, Wormwood, on how to deal with his human 'patients.'" Reader's Ency. 4th edition

Lucado, Max

Fearless; imagine your life without fear. Thomas Nelson 2009 221p $24.99   **248**

1. Fear -- Religious aspects

ISBN 978-0-8499-2139-1

LC 2009-707

The author offers a faith-based primer on how to live without fear.

"Skillful as a surgeon, . . . [Lucado] discerns and identifies the cancer of fear that touches every human being, and with like precision speaks healing words that cut right to the heart. While there exists no fast fix or simple cure for the fear-bound individual, Lucado's tempered counsel and faith-driven remedies will offer day-by-day spiritual medicine of the most potent kind." Publ Wkly

Includes bibliographical references

Peale, Norman Vincent

★ The **power** of positive living. Fawcett Columbine 1996 224p pa $13.95   **248**

1. Applied psychology 2. Pastoral psychology 3. Success

ISBN 0-449-91166-7; 978-0-449-91166-2

LC 96096721

In this volume "Peale strings together dozens of personal success stories ('success' is always materialistic) that make readers feel good. Believing (in yourself, others, values, God) is all-important, and the stories of wealthy business executives who made it on their own grab center stage." Libr J

Zondervan dictionary of Christian spirituality; Glen G. Scorgie, general editor; consulting editors: Simon Chan, Gordon T. Smith, James D. Smith III. Zondervan 2011 852p $39.99   **248**

1. Christianity -- Dictionaries 2. Reference books

ISBN 978-0-310-29066-7

LC 2010037314

"The first section presents six to seven-page entries on topics such as spiritual theology, human personhood, education and spiritual formation, and liturgical spirituality. Also included are articles describing the history of Christian spirituality from 100 C.E. to the present. Each article is followed by a bibliography and a further-reading list. The second section is a dictionary with entries on a broad variety of subjects: biblical figures, popes, mystics, saints, philosophers, spiritual leaders, and educators, as well as concepts and areas of concern including poverty, humanism, suffering, vows, the Kingdom of God, and peace." Libr J

Includes bibliographical references

248.2   Religious experience

Armstrong, Karen

Visions of God; four medieval mystics and their writings. Bantam Bks. 1994 228p pa $19   **248.2**

1. Authors 2. Christian literature -- Collections 3. Hermits 4. Mysticism 5. Mystics 6. Writers on religion

ISBN 0-553-35199-0

LC 94-20217

"The collection is eminently readable and should serve to make these important sources more accessible to a general audience. The selections are arranged chronologically, but Armstrong's reflections also place them in a 'developmental sequence.'" Booklist

Includes bibliographical references

Downing, David C.

Into the region of awe; mysticism in C. S. Lewis. InterVarsity Press 2005 207p $17 **248.2**

1. Authors 2. Children's authors 3. Essayists 4. Literary critics 5. Mysticism 6. Novelists 7. Satirists 8. Theologians

ISBN 0-8308-3284-X; 978-0-8308-3284-2

LC 2004-29844

This is a "book on the writer/thinker's complex attitudes toward mysticism and mystical experience. Downing is keenly responsible in his approach to Lewis's biography and background and candid about Lewis's reservations about mysticism in his own theology; the author's affection for his subject ably informs this sensitive reading of Lewis's life and writings." Libr J

Includes bibliographical references

248.4 Christian life and practice

Carter, Jimmy

Living faith. Times Bks. 1996 256p hardcover o.p. pa $13 **248.4**

1. Biography, Individual 2. Christian life 3. Governors 4. Large print books 5. Nobel laureates for peace 6. Presidents 7. Presidents -- United States

ISBN 0-8129-3034-7 pa

LC 96-20993

In this "spiritual autobiography, the former president . . . traces the growth and development of his faith through his career in the Navy and various political offices, and through his work with Habitat for Humanity (which builds housing for poor Americans) and the Carter Center (an international peacemaking organization). Carter also discusses the impact that Soren Kierkegaard and Reinhold Niebuhr have had on his life." Publ Wkly

Sources of strength; meditations on scripture for a living faith. Times Bks. 1997 252p hardcover o.p. pa $14.99 **248.4**

1. Christian life 2. Meditations

ISBN 0-8129-3236-6 pa

LC 97-27501

This "is a collection of 52 brief Bible lessons—one for each week of the year—written by former president Jimmy Carter. All were used in adult Sunday school classes he taught himself. Carter's lessons are open-minded and socially progressive while remaining unapologetically conservative and Christian theologically. . . . The lessons are grouped in nine categories, such as 'What We Believe' and 'Christians in the World,' but each lesson stands well on its own." Libr J

Chittister, Joan

Following the path; the search for a life of passion, purpose, and joy. Image 2012 188 p. $18.00 **248.4**

ISBN 030795398X; 9780307953988

This book considers the questions "What am I supposed to do with my life?" and "How do I know when I've found my purpose?" [which] can seem endless and overwhelming. . . . [Author] Sister Joan [Chittister] brings the insights of her years of teaching and contemplation to bear on this issue. She examin[es] . . . spiritual calling and gifts, change and discernment. (Publisher's note) This book "is meant to give someone in the process of making a life decision at any age—in early adulthood, at the point of middle-age change and later, when we find ourselves at the crossroads without a name—some ideas against which to pit their own minds, their own circumstances." (Author's note)

Girzone, Joseph F.

Never alone; a personal way to God. Doubleday 1994 115p il hardcover o.p. pa $10.95 **248.4**

1. Christian life 2. Spiritual life

ISBN 0-3854-7683-3 pa

LC 93-38725

Girzone's "empathy for the loneliness and insecurity of being human guides readers toward a more satisfying religious experience than that provided by organized religions, which he continues to criticize for not sufficiently following the living message of Jesus' life." Booklist

Heim, Tami

@stickyjesus; how to live out your faith online. Toni Birdsong, Tami Heim. Abingdon Press 2012 224 p. **248.4**

1. Christian life -- Meditations

ISBN 1426741898; 9781426741890

LC 2011044377

This book instructs Christian readers in incorporating technology, computers, and the Internet into their faith. The book is a fusion of discipleship, faith sharing, marketing, and a Get Started 101 on Twitter, Facebook and blogging. "@stickyJesus@ . . . challenges Christ followers to regain [their] God-given dominion on earth, which includes the Internet. With knowledge, skills, and Holy Spirit guidance, [the authors] encourage believers to dig in and learn how to navigate this online world. . . . The book also includes personal testimonies. . . . These are real people and ministries (about a dozen) making a difference because they walk, talk and connect differently online." (Publisher's Note)

Martin, James

The Jesuit guide to almost everything; a spirituality for real life. HarperOne 2010 420p il $26.99; ebook $11.99 **248.4**

1. Catholic Church 2. Christian life 3. Priests 4. Religious leaders 5. Saints 6. Spiritual life 7. Spiritual life -- Catholic Church 8. Writers on religion

ISBN 978-0-06-143268-2; 978-0-06-198140-1 ebook

LC 2009030505

"In this digestible account of all things Jesuit, James Martin, S.J., encapsulates the uniquely Ignatian concept of spirituality. Translating the essence of the Jesuit philosophy into layman's terms, he uses both traditional stories and personal anecdotes to vividly illustrate the Jesuit approach to God, friendship, social justice, decision-making, prayer, simplicity, obedience, and self-actualization. Martin's engaging, intimate tone will appeal to anyone interested in understanding the history, the efficacy, and the universality of the Jesuit mission and way of life." Booklist

Includes bibliographical references

Riess, Jana

Flunking sainthood; a year of breaking the Sabbath, forgetting to pray, and still loving my neighbor. Paraclete Press 2011 179p pa $16.99   **248.4**
1. Christian life 2. Failure (Psychology) 3. Spiritual life 4. Success
ISBN 978-1-55725-660-7

LC 2011022595

The author "intended to devote an entire year ('a year-long experiment') to mastering 12 different spiritual challenges, including praying at fixed times during the day, exhibiting gratitude, observing the Sabbath, practicing hospitality according to the rules set by St. Benedict, abstaining from eating meat, and amply demonstrating her generosity. But nothing turned out as planned. . . . Although her spiritual quest falls far short, she can still proffer spiritual lessons. Anyone who has failed to live up to expectations, which means most everyone, will love this book." Booklist
Includes bibliographical references

248.8   Guides to Christian life for specific groups of people

Hendey, Lisa M.

A **book** of saints for Catholic moms; 52 companions for your heart, mind, body, and soul. Lisa M. Hendey. Ave Maria Press 2011 xiv, 334 p.p ill.   **248.8**
1. Christian saints -- Prayers and devotions 2. Mothers -- Prayers and devotions
ISBN 1594712735; 9781594712739

LC 2011025284

In this book, Lisa M. Hende familiarizes readers with saints — one for each week of the year — who are relevant to nearly every aspect of a Catholic mother's life, divided into categories of heart, mind, body and soul. She offers related Scripture verses for the week as well as practical suggestions and activities. . . . [The book covers] topics such as "overflowing mounds of dirty laundryo or serious issues such as mental illness and single parenthood. . . . Hendey . . . details the saints' trials and triumphs that . . . people struggle with the same intrinsic issues today. Although many of the individual saints are patrons to various groups or issues . . . Hendey . . . relat[es] each saint's legacy to common dilemmas faced by mothers." (Our Sunday Visitor)

252   Texts of sermons

King, Martin Luther

★ **Strength** to love; foreword by Coretta Scott King. Fortress 2010 168p il pa $20   **252**
1. Sermons
ISBN 978-0-8006-9740-2

A collection of sermons addressing social injustice and racism.

★ American sermons; the pilgrims to Martin Luther King, Jr. Library of Am. 1999 939p $40   **252**
1. Sermons
ISBN 1-88301-165-5

LC 98-34295

"To peruse this work is to become reacquainted with the literary eloquence of our distant and recent past and to observe what has happened to rhetoric itself over the centuries." N Y Times Book Rev
Includes bibliographical references

253   Pastoral office and work (Pastoral theology)

McKibben, Bill

Eaarth; making a life on a tough new planet. Times Books 2010 253p $24   **253**
1. Climate -- Environmental aspects 2. Climatic changes 3. Environmental degradation 4. Global warming 5. Greenhouse effect 6. Greenhouse effect, Atmospheric 7. Human influence on nature
ISBN 978-0-8050-9056-7; 0-8050-9056-8

LC 2009-30040

The author "demonstrates how global warming has already occurred and is irreversible. He describes a new 'Eaarth,' where the cumulative effects of the release of carbon dioxide in the atmosphere have already changed the planet. . . . McKibben envisions a future in which humanity transitions from unfettered growth and a dependence on external markets for sustenance and fossil-fuel-driven energy, to smaller, self-contained communities, growing food locally and generating sustainable distributed electricity. An absolute must-read." Kirkus
Includes bibliographical references

255   Religious congregations and orders

Norris, Kathleen

The **cloister** walk. Riverhead Bks. 1996 384p hardcover o.p. pa $12.95   **255**
1. Catholic Church -- Liturgy 2. Monasticism and religious orders 3. Spiritual life
ISBN 1-57322-584-3 pa

LC 96-863

The author relates her experiences as a lay oblate at St. John's Abbey, a Benedictine monastery in Collegeville, Minnesota. The narrative is arranged chronologically according to the rhythm of the Catholic liturgical calendar
"Kathleen Norris knows about faith. She also knows a lot about doubt. . . . As a married Protestant woman, Norris appears to be an improbable candidate to live in a community of celibate men. Yet as she 'walks' with the Benedictine monks, spending days in continual reading, prayer, and singing, she gains new perspectives on their life and her own." Christ Sci Monit

261.2 Christianity and other systems of belief

Carroll, James

Constantine's sword; the church and the Jews: a history. Houghton Mifflin 2001 756p $28; pa $16   **261.2**

1. Catholic Church -- Relations -- Judaism   2. Christianity and antisemitism -- History 3. Christianity and other religions 4. Judaism 5. Judaism -- Relations -- Catholic Church
ISBN 0-395-77927-8; 0-6142-1908-0 pa
                                    LC 00-61329

"This magisterial work will satisfy Jewish and Christian readers alike, challenging both to a renewed conversation with one another." Publ Wkly
Includes bibliographical references and index

Kertzer, David I.

The **Popes** against the Jews; the Vatican's role in the rise of modern anti-semitism. Knopf 2001 355p $27.95; pa $15   **261.2**

1. Antisemitism 2. Catholic Church -- Relations -- Judaism 3. Holocaust, Jewish 4. Judaism -- Relations -- Catholic Church
ISBN 0-375-40623-9; 0-375-70605-4 pa
                                    LC 2001-33728

"This is a devastating indictment, and fair-minded critics will find flaws in Kertzer's methodology and sweeping conclusions. Nevertheless, he has opened a window that should be opened." Booklist
Includes bibliographical references

261.5 Christianity and secular disciplines

Barbour, Ian G.

When science meets religion; enemies, strangers, or partners? HarperSanFrancisco 2000 205p pa $16.95   **261.5**

1. Religion and science
ISBN 0-06-060381-X
                                    LC 99-55579

The author "guides readers through a four-fold typology of the science/religion relationship—Conflict, Independence, Dialogue and Integration. . . . Barbour's own sympathies are markedly on the side of dialogue and integration, but he makes an unusually sucessful effort to represent other perspectives in a fair light." Publ Wkly
Includes bibliographical references

Grant, Edward

★ Science and religion, 400 B.C. to A.D. 1550; from Aristotle to Copernicus. Greenwood Press 2004 xxvi, 307p il $67.95   **261.5**

1. Religion and science 2. Religion and science -- History
ISBN 0-313-32858-7
                                    LC 2004-17429

Noble, David F.

The **religion** of technology; the divinity of man and the spirit of invention. Knopf 1997 273p hardcover o.p. pa $14.95   **261.5**

1. God 2. Religion and science 3. Technology -- Social aspects 4. Technology and civilization
ISBN 0-14-027916-4 pa
                                    LC 96-48019

"This is a dense, fascinating study of technology and Christianity." Libr J
Includes bibliographical references

Olson, Richard

★ Science and religion, 1450-1900; from Copernicus to Darwin. [by] Richard G. Olson. Greenwood Press 2004 292p il $65   **261.5**

1. Religion and science 2. Religion and science -- History
ISBN 0-313-32694-0
                                    LC 2004-47501

The issues discussed "should be especially helpful to those who are interested in the historical background to current science-religion issues being debated in the United States." Sci Books Films
Includes bibliographical references

261.7 Christianity and political affairs

Dionne, E. J.

Souled out; reclaiming faith and politics after the religious right. Princeton University Press 2008 251p pa $17.95; $24.95   **261.7**

1. Christian conservatism 2. Christian fundamentalism 3. Christianity and politics 4. Christianity and politics -- United States 5. Religious right -- United States 6. Right and left (Political science)
ISBN 0-691-14329-3 pa; 978-0-691-13458-1; 0-691-13458-8; 978-0-691-14329-3 pa
                                    LC 2007-45172

This "is an astute and important review of the intersection of faith and public policy." America
Includes bibliographical references

Zagorin, Perez

How the idea of religious toleration came to the West. Princeton University Press 2003 371p il hardcover o.p. pa $24.95   **261.7**

1. Religious tolerance 2. Religious tolerance -- Christianity -- History
ISBN 0-691-09270-2; 978-0-691-12142-0; 0-691-12142-7 pa
                                    LC 2002-42565

"A deeply scholarly but ultimately engaging argument for the origins of religious toleration in Western culture since the Enlightenment." Libr J
Includes bibliographical references

261.8 Christianity and socioeconomic problems

Martin, William C.

With God on our side; the rise of the religious right in America. {by} William Martin. Broadway Bks. 1996 418p il $27.50; pa $15 **261.8**
1. Christian fundamentalism 2. Christianity and politics 3. Conservatism 4. Evangelists 5. Inspirational writers 6. Religion and politics 7. Religious fundamentalism
ISBN 0-553-06745-1; 0-553-06749-4 pa

LC 96-2919

"Unlike some companion volumes to television documentaries, Martin's well-written, superbly organized work stands on its own. . . . {It} is required reading for anyone seeking to understand the rise of the Religious Right. . . . Nothing has been published that can match Martin's book in sweep and substance." Christ Century

Includes bibliographical references

262 Ecclesiology

Chaves, Mark

Ordaining women; culture and conflict in religious organizations. Harvard Univ. Press 1997 237p hardcover o.p. pa $18.50 **262**
1. Christian sociology 2. Ordination of women 3. Religion and sociology 4. Women in Christianity
ISBN 0-674-64146-9 pa

LC 97-12518

The author provides a "study of the 19th- and 20th-century ordination policies and practices of many Christian groups in the United States, including the Roman Catholic Church." Libr J

Includes bibliographical references

Meyers, Robin R.

Saving Jesus from the church; how to stop worshiping Christ and start following Jesus. HarperOne 2009 243p $24.99 **262**
1. Christian life 2. Christianity
ISBN 978-0-06-156821-3; 0-06-156821-X

LC 2008-51766

"In a progressive rather than negatively critical mode, in strong contrast to much of Far Right Protestantism, . . . [the author] suggests with typical elegance that a recovery of true Christianity emphasizes compassion over condemnation, blessing over sin, and equity over individual prosperity. Highly recommended." Libr J

Includes bibliographical references

Reese, Thomas J.

Inside the Vatican; the politics and organization of the Catholic Church. Harvard Univ. Press 1996 317p il $30; pa $16.95 **262**
1. Catholic Church 2. Councils and synods 3. Papacy 4. Popes
ISBN 0-674-93260-9; 0-679-93261-7 pa

LC 96-26641

The author examines "the internal workings of the Vatican both as city-state and the headquarters of the Roman Catholic Church. . . . With its wealth of information, historical background, and analysis, Reese's work should be an important addition for a variety of libraries." Libr J

Includes bibliographical references

Wills, Garry, 1934-

Papal sin; structures of deceit. Doubleday 2000 326p **262**
1. Catholic Church 2. Papacy
ISBN 0-385-49410-6; 0-385-49411-4 pa

LC 99-54851

In Part I—"'Historical Dishonesties'—{Wills claims that the Catholic} hierarchy has persistently lied . . . about what the church did and did not do during the Holocaust. Part 2—'Doctrinal Dishonesties'—argues that recent popes . . . have cared more about retaining their grip on authority than about the needs of those whom they claim to serve. In the last two parts of the book—'The Honesty Issue' and 'The Splendor of Truth'—Wills writes about his heroes: Lord Acton, Cardinal Newman and St. Augustine. He offers them as exemplars to whom the church might turn." (N Y Times Book Rev) Index.

The author "argues that the Church is not merely the clergy but the whole body of believers. His examination of papal policies on such topics as the Holocaust, clerical celibacy, and the role of women finds that the Church has often distorted history and Scripture in the attempt to bolster its authority. There's an undertone of grief to this rationally argued book, which ends with a wistful vision of the Church as it might be." New Yorker

Includes bibliographical references

262.001 Philosophy and theory

Meyers, Robin

The underground church; reclaiming the subversive way of Jesus. Robin Meyers. 1st ed. Jossey-Bass 2012 xiv, 266 p.p (cloth) $24.95 **262.001**
1. Christianity 2. Church history
ISBN 1118061594; 9781118061596

LC 2011039903

In this book, "[Robin] Meyers . . . offers a number of subversive ideas . . . reminding readers that Jesus came to feed the hungry, wage nonviolence, and generally afflict the comfortable in his day. . . . Hospitality is a cardinal Christian virtue. So is nonviolence, but it's so hard that most fail at a practice that demands discipline and sacrifice. Meyers calls for other practices . . . including low or no-interest moneylending and tithing." (Publishers Weekly)

264 Public worship

Episcopal Church/Book of common prayer

★ The Book of common prayer and administration of the sacraments and other rites and ceremonies of the church; together with the Psalter or Psalms of David according to the use of the Episcopal Church.

Church Hymnal Corp, Seabury Press 1979 1001p
pew ed., black $19   **264**
  ISBN 0-89869-081-1

                                             LC 81-204603
The official liturgy of the Episcopal Church.

Lucatero, Heliodoro

  ★ The **living** Mass; changes to the Roman missal and how we worship. Liguori 2011 64p il pa
$4.99   **264**
  1. Catholic Church -- Liturgy
  ISBN 978-0-7648-2007-6
This book seeks to answer questions about the changes
made to the Roman Missal "as well as to give some insight
into the history of the development of the Roman Missal
from early Church times, through the Middle Ages, through
the different Church councils, and up to the present day. A
comparison of each change features old and new text side-
by-side with the changes highlighted in bold type." Publisher's note
  Includes bibliographical references

270 History, geographic treatment, biography of Christianity; Church history; Christian denominations and sects

Chidester, David

  Christianity; a global history. HarperSanFrancisco 2000 627p il hardcover o.p. pa $21.95 **270**
  1. Christianity 2. Church history
  ISBN 0-06-251708-2; 0-06-251770-8 pa
                                            LC 00-37006
"Highly recommended for religion and history collections looking for a work that anchors modern sensibilities to
ancient ideas." Libr J
  Includes bibliographical references

Cox, Harvey Gallagher

  The **future** of faith; [by] Harvey Cox. HarperOne 2009 245p $24.99 **270**
  1. Christianity 2. Christianity -- 20th century 3. Christianity -- Forecasting 4. Church history 5. Holy
Spirit
  ISBN 978-0-06-175552-1; 0-06-175552-4
                                        LC 2008-54429
Presents an interpretation of why Christian beliefs and
dogma are giving way to new grassroots movements rooted
in social justice and spiritual experience.
  This "spirited portrait of our religious landscape challenges us to think in new ways about faith." Publ Wkly
  Includes bibliographical references

Craughwell, Thomas J.

  Saints behaving badly; the cutthroats, crooks,
trollops, con men, and devil-worshippers who became saints. Doubleday 2006 190p $15.95 **270**
  1. Christian saints
  ISBN 0-385-51720-3; 978-0-385-51720-1
                                        LC 2006-299594

The author presents a "review of 32 less-than-perfect
saints, among them St. Olga, St. Mary of Egypt, and Thomas
a Becket. Relying on a wide range of sources—including his
own expertise—he writes concise and informative profiles
of these holy people that chronicle their respective rises to
sainthood and end with what inspired them to abandon their
wicked ways." Libr J
  Includes bibliographical references

Jenkins, Philip

  Jesus wars; how four patriarchs, three queens,
and two emperors decided what Christians would believe for the next 1,500 years. HarperOne 2010 328p
map $26.99   **270**
  1. Christian civilization 2. Church history -- 30-600,
Early church 3. Church history -- Primitive and early
church, ca. 30-600 4. Councils and synods 5. Doctrinal
theology 6. Theology, Doctrinal -- History -- Early
church, ca. 30-600
  ISBN 978-0-06-176894-1
The author focuses "not only on the theological definitions of the nature of Christ, promulgated by various
Christian political and ecclesiastical leaders from the fourth
through the seventh centuries, but also on the political
machinations, violent persecutions, and scheming that made
'wars' of these debates. . . . In showing general readers how
he finds fresh ideas and the resurrections of past teachings
invigorating to religious studies, Jenkins provides an accessible book, and one with mild suspense and intrigue." Libr J
  Includes bibliographical references and index

  ★ The **lost** history of Christianity; the thousand-
year golden age of the church in the Middle East, Africa, and Asia--and how it died. HarperOne 2008
315p map $26.95   **270**
  1. Christian civilization 2. Church history -- 30-600,
Early church 3. Church history -- Primitive and early
church, ca. 30-600 4. Civilization, Arab 5. Civilization,
Christian
  ISBN 978-0-06-147280-0; 0-06-147280-8
A lost history revealing that, for centuries, Christianity's
center was actually in the Middle East, Asia, and Africa,
with significant communities extending as far as China.
  "This is an important counterweight to previous histories
that have focused almost exclusively on Christianity in the
West." Publ Wkly
  Includes bibliographical references

  The **new** faces of Christianity; believing the
Bible in the global south. Oxford University Press
2006 252p $26   **270**
  1. Christianity 2. Christianity -- Africa 3. Christianity
-- Asia 4. Christianity -- Forecasting 5. Forecasting
  ISBN 978-0-19-530065-9; 0-19-530065-3
                                        LC 2006-15490
Jenkins explores the growth of Christianity in Africa,
Asia and Latin America.
  "Those interested in religious trends across the globe,
the Muslim-Christian friction, and world politics will benefit
from this resource." Libr J
  Includes bibliographical references

MacCulloch, Diarmaid

★ **Christianity**; the first three thousand years. Viking 2010 1161p il map $45   **270**

1. Church history

ISBN 978-0-670-02126-0; 0-670-02126-1

LC 2009-40184

"It is difficult to imagine a more comprehensive and surprisingly accessible volume on the subject than MacCulloch's. . . . Want a refresher on the rise of the papacy? It is here. On Charlemagne and Carolingians? That is here, too. On the Fourth Crusade and its aftermath? Look no farther." N Y Times Book Rev

Includes bibliographical references

Martin, James

My life with the saints. Loyola Press 2006 411p $22.95   **270**

1. Biography, Individual 2. Christian saints 3. Priests 4. Spiritual life

ISBN 0-8294-2001-0

LC 2005-28466

The author "relates how he discovered various 'saints' and how each has affected his life. . . . Despite a theme built on a particular facet of Catholic belief, Martin's animated style and wide-ranging experiences make this a book readers of diverse backgrounds will enjoy." Publ Wkly

Includes bibliographical references

Tickle, Phyllis

The **great** emergence; how Christianity is changing and why. Baker Books 2008 172p il $17.99 **270**

1. Christianity

ISBN 978-0-8010-1313-3; 0-8010-1313-5

LC 2008-21706

"This is a must-read for anyone seeking to understand the face and future of Christianity." Publ Wkly

Includes bibliographical references

270.09 Areas, regions, places in general; biography

McBrien, Richard P.

Lives of the saints; from Mary and Francis of Assisi to John XXIII and Mother Teresa. HarperSanFrancisco 2001 xxiii, 646p il hardcover o.p. pa $19.95   **270.09**

1. Christian saints 2. Christian saints -- Biography

ISBN 0-06-123283-1 pa

LC 00-53933

"This work goes beyond the Roman Catholic Church's list of saints to include those of the Orthodox, Anglican, and Lutheran churches. Concise and well-researched biographical sketches are arranged by feast days, with access provided by indexes for saints, personal names, and subjects. Complementing the biographies are thoughtful essays on the history of saints, their place in religious history, and canonization; a series of seven tables on feast days, patron saints, iconography, and papal canonization." Libr J

Includes bibliographical references

270.1 Historical periods

Riley, Gregory J.

The **river** of God; a new history of Christian origins. HarperSanFrancisco 2001 252p hardcover o.p. pa $14.95   **270.1**

1. Christianity -- Origin 2. Church history -- 30-600, Early church

ISBN 0-06-066979-9; 0-06-066980-2 pa

LC 2001-16888

"This volume will become one of the most important books on the subject." Libr J

Includes bibliographical references

Encyclopedia of early Christianity; edited by Everett Ferguson. 2nd ed; Garland 1997 2v il maps set $245; pa set $55   **270.1**

1. Christianity -- Encyclopedias 2. Church history -- 30-600, Early church -- Dictionaries 3. Reference books

ISBN 0-8153-1663-1; 0-8153-3319-6 pa

LC 96-36865

"Covers persons, places, doctrines, practices, art, liturgy, heresies, and schisms from the time of Jesus to approximately 600 CE. Articles by . . . specialists include bibliographies and cross-references. Extensive subject index. Intended for general readers, students, and professionals in fields outside religion who want information concerning early Christianity." Guide to Ref Books. 11th edition {entry for 1990 edition}

270.2 Period of ecumenical councils, 325-787

Wills, Garry

Saint Augustine. Viking 1999 xx, 152p $19.95   **270.2**

1. Bishops 2. Christian saints -- Algeria -- Hippo (Extinct city) -- Biography 3. Philosophers 4. Saints 5. Theologians 6. Writers on religion

ISBN 0-670-88610-6

LC 98-50317

Wills begins "by addressing centuries of misconceptions. Though his admiration for the saint is occasionally tainted by defensiveness, his account of Augustine's search for a faith and a philosophy engages our sympathy. He also conveys the turbulence of the era, when the Roman Empire was beleaguered by barbarians and the Catholic Church by heretics, and shows how Augustine's responses to the troubles of his time have shaped Christianity down to our own." New Yorker

Includes bibliographical references

270.6   Period of Reformation and Counter-Reformation, 1517-1648

MacCulloch, Diarmaid
The **Reformation**; a house divided. Viking 2004 xxiv, 792p il map $34.95; pa $18   **270.6**
1. Reformation
ISBN 0-670-03296-4; 0-14-303538-X pa
LC 2003-61607
The author "has produced the definitive survey for this generation. . . . This well-written book is a joy to read, with new facts and interpretations on nearly every page." Libr J
Includes bibliographical references

271   Religious congregations and orders in church history

Butcher, Carmen Acevedo
Man of blessing; a life of St. Benedict. Paraclete Press 2006 180p map $21.95   **271**
1. Monks 2. Saints 3. Writers on religion
ISBN 1-55725-485-0; 978-1-55725-485-6
LC 2005-35827
This is the "story of the life of St. Benedict of Nursia, who founded Western monasticism in the sixth century and later became the patron saint of Europe. . . . The book's readability will make it easy for patrons to escape into late Roman culture and find peace in a monastic simplicity." Libr J
Includes bibliographical references

Johnson, Mary
An **unquenchable** thirst; Mary Johnson. Spiegel & Grau 2011 xv, 526p.p   **271**
1. Memoirists 2. Missionaries 3. Nuns 4. Orators 5. Teachers
ISBN 9780385527477; 9781588369864 (ebook); 9780385527484
LC 2010038858
This book presents a "memoir of one woman's experience in Mother Teresa's order, the Missionaries of Charity. . . . As she progressed in the order and became Sister Donata, the issues she faced became darker: a sexually predatory subordinate, theological disputes, an increasingly rigid system of rules and regulations and a love affair with a priest. Throughout the book, the author describes her interactions with Mother Teresa, but she does not try to pass off their relationship as especially close. . . . As it became increasingly clear to [Mary] Johnson that the Missionaries of Charity's vision and management were diverging from her own beliefs and values, she struggled with her place in the order and eventually made the decision to leave after two decades of service." (Kirkus)

Merton, Thomas
Intimate Merton; his life from his journals. edited by Patrick Hart and Jonathan Montaldo. HarperSanFrancisco 1999 374p il hardcover o.p. pa $16   **271**
1. Authors 2. Monks 3. Nonfiction writers 4. Poets

5. Writers on religion
ISBN 0-06-251629-9 pa
LC 99-33239
"This is a one-volume condensation of Merton's journals, which have been published over the last few years; its seven chapters correspond to the seven volumes of Merton's complete journals. . . . {The editors} have maintained all of Merton's central themes—including controversial ones, like the relationship with the nurse identified as 'M.' and Merton's doubts about his vocation." Libr J

Spink, Kathryn
Mother Teresa; a complete authorized biography. HarperSanFrancisco 1997 306p il hardcover o.p. pa $15.95   **271**
1. Biography, Individual 2. Missionaries 3. Missions -- India 4. Nobel laureates for peace 5. Nuns
ISBN 0-06-251553-5 pa
LC 97-41349
"Spink's biography benefits from her own 18-year involvement with the work of the Missionaries of Charity Order as well as from the intimate relationship she developed over the years with Mother Teresa. . . . A final chapter in the book provides glimpses of Mother Teresa's affection for Princess Diana, a brief description of Mother Teresa's funeral and a short account of the election of Sister Nirmal as her successor." Publ Wkly

272   Persecutions in general church history

Kamen, Henry
The **Spanish** Inquisition; a historical revision. Yale Univ. Press 1998 369p il $45; pa $14.80 **272**
1. Antisemitism 2. Inquisition 3. Jews -- Spain
ISBN 0-300-07522-7; 0-300-07880-3 pa
LC 97-32451
In this revision of his 1965 study, the author "restates his original argument. . . . He reaffirms his contention that an all-powerful, torture-mad Inquisition is largely a 19th-century myth. In its place he portrays a poor, understaffed institution whose scattered tribunals had only a limited reach and whose methods were more humane than those of most secular courts. . . . As for the Inquisition's much-vaunted role as Big Brother and its responsibility for intellectual decline, Kamen rejects this hypothesis out of hand. . . . {He} also dismisses the notion that the Inquisition enjoyed widespread popular support." N Y Times Book Rev
Includes bibliographical references

Perez, Joseph
★ The **Spanish** Inquisition; a history. trans. by Janet Lloyd. Yale University Press 2005 248p $26; pa $17   **272**
1. Inquisition
ISBN 0-300-10790-0; 0-300-11982-8 pa
LC 2004-114614
The author "tells the history of the Spanish Inquisition from its medieval beginnings to its nineteenth-century ending. . . . He explores the inner workings of its councils, and shows how its officers, inquisitors, and leaders lived and

worked." Univ Press Books for Public and Second Sch Libr, 2006

Includes bibliographical references

277   Christianity in North America

Bawer, Bruce

Stealing Jesus; how fundamentalism betrays Christianity. Crown 1997 340p hardcover o.p. pa $14   **277**

1. Christian fundamentalism 2. Christianity
ISBN 0-609-80222-4 pa

LC 97-20111

The author "contends that fundamentalist Christianity, what he calls the 'Church of Law,' has been preaching a message of wrath and judgment to modern American culture that Bawer believes is incompatible with Jesus' message of love. . . . [His] graceful prose and lucid insights make this a must-read book for anyone concerned with the relationship of Christianity to contemporary American culture." Publ Wkly

Boyle, Gregory J.

Tattoos on the heart; the power of boundless compassion. [by] Gregory Boyle. Free Press 2010 217p $25; pa $14; ebook $11.99   **277**

1. Christian life 2. Church work 3. Church work with juvenile delinquents -- California -- East Los Angeles 4. Priests 5. Youth workers
ISBN 978-1-4391-5302-4; 1-4391-5302-7; 978-1-4391-5315-4 pa; 1-4391-5315-9 pa; 978-1-4391-7177-6 ebook; 1-4391-7177-7 ebook

LC 2009-32970

"Jesuit priest Boyle recounts his two decades of working with 'homies' in Los Angeles County, which contains 1,100 gangs with nearly 86,000 members. Boyle's Homeboy Industries is the largest gang intervention program in the country, offering job training, tattoo removal, and employment to members of enemy gangs." Publ Wkly

Dochuk, Darren

From Bible belt to sunbelt; plain-folk religion, grassroots politics, and the rise of evangelical conservatism. W.W. Norton 2011 520p il   **277**

1. Christianity and politics -- Evangelicalism 2. Conservatism 3. Conservatism -- Religious aspects -- Christianity -- History -- 20th century 4. Evangelicalism 5. Evangelicalism -- Southern California
ISBN 0-393-06682-7; 978-0-393-06682-1

LC 2010032740

"A five-decade history of the evangelical movement in southern California [argues that] . . . the influx of migrants from the Bible Belt during the Great Depression ultimately led to the rise of the New Right and modern conservatism in the late twentieth century." (Publisher's note) Bibliography. Index.

"Well-written and documented, a supremely helpful guide in sorting out how we arrived at that odd state of affairs." Kirkus

Includes bibliographical references and index

Luhrmann, T. M.

When God talks back; understanding the American evangelical relationship with God. by T.M. Luhrmann. Alfred A. Knopf 2012 464 p.   **277**

1. Christianity -- United States 2. Evangelicalism -- Psychology -- Case studies 3. Psychology, Religious -- United States -- Case studies 4. Sociology literature
ISBN 9780307264794

LC 2011040116

The book provides an "analysis of evangelical communities in America. [Author T. M.] Luhrmann . . . entered the Vineyard Christian Fellowship openly . . . and she was both welcome and eventually somewhat transformed. . . . She begins by describing the current evangelical movement--how widespread it is, how God has become an intimate friend rather than a harsh judge and how evangelicals largely avoid theodicy. She sketches the history of the Vineyard and attributes to the 1960s counterculture some of the spiritual energy that animates the evangelical movement. As the title suggests, the author devotes much of her discussion to the conversation between believers and their God, a conversation facilitated by specific techniques of prayer." (Kirkus)

Marty, Martin E.

Pilgrims in their own land; 500 years of religion in America. Penguin Books 1985 500p il pa $18   **277**

ISBN 0-14-008268-9; 978-0-14-008268-5

LC 85-3596

This book examines "the force of religion in the United States since colonial times. Marty considers not only the religious beliefs and rituals brought to America by the various European settlers, but also those of native Americans. The clashes between Protestant, Catholic, Judaic, and other religious groups are perceived in light of their influence upon the development of this nation up to the present." Booklist

Includes bibliographical references

★ **Yearbook** of American & Canadian churches, 2008; edited by Eileen W. Lindner. Seventy-sixth issue; Abingdon Press 2008 440p pa $55   **277**

1. Christian sects -- North America 2. Reference books 3. Religious institutions -- Directories 4. Religious newspapers and periodicals
ISBN 978-0-687-65149-8; 0-687-65149-2

"Directory, statistical, and historical information on many religious and ecumenical organizations and service agencies, accredited seminaries, colleges and universities, and depositories of church history materials. Also a list of religious periodicals." Ref Sources for Small & Medium-sized Libr. 6th edition

Includes bibliographical references

280   Denominations and sects of Christian church

Atwood, Craig D.

★ **Handbook** of denominations in the United States; [by] Craig D. Atwood, Frank S. Mead, Samuel S. Hill. 13th ed.; Abingdon Press 2010 416p il $24 **280**

1. Sects
ISBN 978-1-4267-0048-4; 1-4267-0048-2

LC 2010-07092

"History and present structure of Christian religious bodies in the United States. Reports on doctrines of different churches. Includes bibliography and index." NY Public Libr Book of How & Where to Look It Up

Includes bibliographical references

★ The encyclopedia of Protestantism; Hans Hillerbrand, editor. Routledge 2004 4v set $695 **280**

1. Protestantism 2. Protestantism -- Encyclopedias 3. Reference books
ISBN 0-415-92472-3

LC 2003-11582

"Nearly 500 contributors provide descriptions and explanations of matters of theology, culture, eminent lives, material artifacts, and comparative religions; the A-to-Z entries range from 'Apocalypticism' to 'Latin America,' 'Pilgrim's Progress,' and 'Women Clergy.' . . . [This work] is an excellent resource to engage in the exploration of humanities, policy issues, and concerns beyond the specifically religious while also providing deep analyses of theological matters." Libr J

Includes bibliographical references

282 Roman Catholic Church

Buckley, William F.
★ **Nearer,** my God; an autobiography of faith. Harcourt Brace & Co. 1998 xx, 313p il pa $14 **282**

1. Authors 2. Columnists 3. Journalists -- United States -- Biography 4. Magazine editors 5. Novelists
ISBN 0-15-600618-9

LC 98-16194

"As we might expect, Nearer My God is rich in anecdote, witty, and animated by what Buckley refers to as his 'polemical inclinations.'. . . But what gives it unity as a book, and not just a loose collection of pieces bound in cloth, is the warmth and the depth of Buckley's faith, at once complex and many-sided." Christ Today

Buttiglione, Rocco
Karol Wojtyla; the thought of the man who became Pope John Paul II. translated by Paolo Guietti and Francesca Murphy. Eerdmans 1997 384p $35 **282**

1. Catholic Church 2. Christian sociology 3. Popes
ISBN 0-8028-3848-0

LC 97-23188

The author traces the Pope's "intellectual development, offering a critique of his literary works and a detailed analysis of how he was influenced by Thomism and phenomenology, which he sought to reconcile while emphasizing individual freedom of conscience. . . . Recommended for general collections for its broad sweep complementary to other biographies on the pope." Libr J

Carroll, James
Toward a new Catholic Church; the promise of reform. Houghton Mifflin 2002 130p pa $8.95 **282**

1. Catholic Church
ISBN 0-618-31337-0

LC 2002-27262

The author "has a reform agenda . . . consisting of five proposals: expand the faithful's biblical literacy in sophistication and depth; purge the church's political pretensions and behavior; reformulate Christology to emphasize Jesus as revelator rather than savior; run the church democratically; and repent of anti-Semitism, sexism, homophobia, and other ills by admitting the church has sinned. . . . An important statement." Booklist

Includes bibliographical references

Collins, Paul
The **modern** Inquisition; seven prominent Catholics and their struggles with the Vatican. Overlook Press 2002 260p $29.95 **282**

1. Catholic Church 2. Catholics -- History 3. Catholics -- History -- 20th century 4. Dissenters, Religious -- History 5. Dissenters, Religious -- History -- 20th century
ISBN 1-58567-270-X

LC 2002-25223

This work is an "assessment of the Roman Catholic Church's treatment of its theologians who reflect contrary views from those of the Congregation for the Doctrine of the Faith (CDF). . . . In eight passionately written essays, {Collins} considers the lives, work, and trials of several priests and sisters whose ideas were reviewed by the CDF. . . . Among them Hans Kung, Lavinia Byrne, Charles Curran, Jeannine Gramick and Robert Nugent, Tissa Balusaria, and the author himself." Libr J

Includes bibliographical references

Duffy, Eamon
Saints & sinners; a history of the popes. 3rd ed.; Yale Nota Bene/Yale University Press 2006 474p il pa $22 **282**

1. Catholic Church -- History 2. Papacy
ISBN 978-0-300-11597-0

This illustrated volume is a companion piece to a six-part television series of the same name. The book offers an overview of the 2,000-year history of the papacy.

Gillis, Chester
Roman Catholicism in America. Columbia Univ. Press 1999 365p il $60; pa $20.50 **282**

1. Catholic Church -- United States
ISBN 0-231-10870-2; 0-231-10871-0 pa

LC 99-17945

This is "an excellent survey." Libr J
Includes bibliographical references

Guiley, Rosemary Ellen
The **encyclopedia** of saints. Facts on File 2001 419p il $82.50; pa $24.95 **282**

1. Christian saints -- Dictionaries 2. Reference books
ISBN 0-8160-4133-4; 0-8160-4134-2 pa

LC 00-69176

This volume offers "accounts of the lives and experiences of more than 400 principal saints, from early martyrs such as Lucy of Syracuse to recently canonized saints such as Katherine Drexel. Entries provide a biographical overview, a record of the saint's religious journeys and mystical experiences, a discussion of personal philosophies and important theological influences, as well as his or her patronage, feast days and popular role within the Church." Publisher's note

John Paul

★ **Crossing** the threshold of hope; edited by Vittorio Messori. Knopf 1994 244p hardcover o.p. pa $15 **282**

1. Apologetics 2. Catholic Church 3. Christian life 4. Faith

ISBN 0-679-76561-1 pa

LC 94-78675

In this book the Pope responds to written questions by an Italian Catholic journalist originally planned for a television interview which never took place. The questions addressed include: what is the papacy?; when and how should one pray?; is there proof of God's existence?; is Jesus the Son of God?; why is there so much evil in the world?; why does God tolerate suffering?; is only Rome right?; and what are human rights?

"This is a book to be read for insights, perspectives, connections, formulations that spark meditation and enrich our understanding." Commonweal

Kung, Hans

The **Catholic** Church; a short history. translated by John Bowden. Modern Lib. 2001 xxv, 221p $19.95; pa $9.95 **282**

1. Catholic Church

ISBN 0-679-64092-4; 0-8129-6762-3 pa

LC 00-67568

"About as good a brief presentation of the 'liberal' view of church history as anyone could reasonably expect." Booklist

Maxwell-Stuart, P. G.

Chronicle of the popes; the reign-by-reign record of the papacy from St. Peter to the present. Thames & Hudson 1997 240p il maps $34.95 **282**

1. Catholic Church -- History 2. Papacy 3. Popes

ISBN 0-500-01798-0

LC 97-60230

This survey examines the lives and deeds of the 264 popes from St. Peter to John Paul II.

This history of the papacy "provides a good selection of illustrations with a lightweight text." N Y Times Book Rev

Includes bibliographical references

Medwick, Cathleen

Teresa of Avila; the progress of a soul. Knopf 1999 282p hardcover o.p. pa $12.95 **282**

1. Authors 2. Christian saints 3. Christian saints -- Spain -- Avila -- Biography 4. Memoirists 5. Mystics 6. Nuns 7. Saints 8. Writers on religion

ISBN 0-385-50129-3 pa

LC 99-18921

In this biography of the sixteenth-century Spanish nun, "Medwick traces Teresa's early years, her entrance into the genteel life of the Convent of the Incarnation in Avila, her second conversion as a person of prayer, and her subsequent trials as a founder of reformed monasteries of women under the austere rule of Mount Carmel." Commonweal

Includes bibliographical references

Steinfels, Peter

A **people** adrift; the crisis of the Roman Catholic Church in America. Simon & Schuster 2003 xxi, 392p hardcover o.p. pa $15 **282**

1. Catholic Church -- United States

ISBN 0-684-83663-7; 0-7432-6144-5 pa

LC 2003-54208

"Steinfels sounds a call for a reasoned common ground that respects the richness of tradition and also reflects the reality of the practices and needs of more than 60 million American Catholics, rather than the agendas of any number of the small but vocal groups within Catholicism. This book will be hailed by many, and with good reason." Publ Wkly

Includes bibliographical references

Wills, Garry

Why I am a Catholic. Houghton Mifflin 2002 390p $26; pa $14 **282**

1. Catholic Church 2. Papacy

ISBN 0-618-13429-8; 0-618-38048-5 pa

LC 2002-283644

The author "begins with a very personal, though brief, look at his life as a Catholic, which includes time spent as a Jesuit novice, then proceeds with a detailed defense of his views on the church and its papacy. He concludes with an explanation of the Apostles' Creed, which he regards as the true foundation of his faith." Publ Wkly

Includes bibliographical references

★ **Catholic** Almanac, 2008; Matthew Bunson, D.Min., general editor. Our Sunday Visitor 2008 640p pa $28.95 **282**

1. Almanacs 2. Catholic Church -- Directories 3. Catholic church -- Periodicals 4. Reference books

ISBN 978-1-59276-334-4; 1-59276-334-0

"Includes much miscellaneous information, e.g., annual survey of news, ecclesiastical calendar, glossary of terms in Catholic use, the Catholic church in various countries of the world, statistics, directory of information, etc." Guide to Ref Books. 11th edition

The **HarperCollins** encyclopedia of Catholicism; general editor, Richard P. McBrien; associate editors, Harold W. Attridge {et al.} HarperSanFrancisco 1995 xxxviii, 1349p il maps $47.50 **282**

1. Catholic Church -- Dictionaries 2. Catholic Church -- Encyclopedias 3. Reference books

ISBN 0-06-065338-8

LC 94-39972

"This encyclopedic dictionary contains 4700 entries by 277 experts. . . . Broad-ranging topics in Catholic theology, history, culture, art, canon law, literature, etc., are replete with cross references, photos, maps, tables, diagrams, and charts." Libr J

★ New Catholic encyclopedia; prepared by an editorial staff at the Catholic University of America. 2nd ed; Gale Group 2003 15v il maps set $1,981 **282**
1. Catholic Church 2. Catholic Church -- Encyclopedias 3. Catholic church -- History 4. Church history -- Middle Ages, 600-1500 5. Church history -- Modern period, 1500- 6. Reference books 7. Religion -- History
ISBN 978-0-7876-4004-0; 0-7876-4004-2
LC 2002-924

This encyclopedia "covers the history of the eastern churches, the churches of the Protestant Reformation, and other ecclesial communities as well as the Christian roots based in ancient Israel and Judaism. No comprehensive resource on Catholicism can be complete without touching on other world religions as well, including Islam, Buddhism, and Hinduism. This resource provides entries not only on the doctrine, organization, and history of the church, but also on the people, institutions, and social changes that have affected the church over the years. Arranged alphabetically, the entries run in length from half a page to several pages in length. All entries provide the name of the contributor and a bibliography. Cross-references to related articles are located throughout the work. Adding to the usefulness of the set are more than 3,000 black-and-white photographs, maps, and charts that complement the scholarly articles." Am Ref Books Annu, 2003

★ The Official Catholic directory 2008. National Register Pub. 2008 2109p $335 **282**
1. Catholic Church -- Directories 2. Reference books
ISBN 978-0-87217-550-1; 0-87217-550-1

"Contains a large amount of useful and detailed directory, institutional, and statistical information about the organization, clergy, churches, missions, schools, religious orders, etc., of the Catholic church in the U.S. and its possessions. Coverage varies." Guide to Ref Books. 11th edition

283 Anglican churches

Winner, Lauren F.
Still; Lauren F. Winner. HarperOne 2012 256p. **283**
ISBN 978-0-06-176811-8; 9780061768118
LC 2011017200

In this book, "the author explores her emotional landscape as she struggles to move beyond the depression that plagues her following her mother's death and her own divorce. [She e]xamin[es] feelings of grief, failure, and doubt that she never expected to encounter after her conversion from Judaism to Christianity. . . . Narrative accounts of visiting her mother's grave; 'the failed cool-professor moment;' infiltrating a synagogue, in costume, to participate in Purim; and a church visit that results in her holding hands with 'one of the people from whom Jesus would have cast a demon' all provide a . . . window into a seeker trying to find equilibrium in a stage of faith and life that is neither beginning nor end, but, she fears, 'an extended sojourn into the spiritual equivalent of middle school.'" (Publishers Weekly)

287 Methodist churches; churches related to Methodism

Tomkins, Stephen
★ **John** Wesley; a biography. Eerdmans 2003 208p pa $20 **287**
1. Evangelists 2. Methodist Church 3. Methodist Church -- England -- Clergy -- Biography 4. Theologians 5. Writers on religion
ISBN 0-8028-2499-4
LC 2003-54328

In this biography of the founder of the Methodist religion "Tomkins presents a keenly engaging portrait of a great man full of contradictoriness. Wesley insisted he was loyal to the Church of England yet consented to his followers setting up establishments and engaging in practices that flouted Anglican authority. . . . He altered the face of Christianity in the West by inspiring modern evangelicalism and Pentecostalism. A fascinating figure, fascinatingly limned." Booklist
Includes bibliographical references

289 Other denominations and sects

Stein, Stephen J.
The **Shaker** experience in America; a history of the United Society of Believers. Yale Univ. Press 1992 xx, 554p il $65; pa $21 **289**
1. Shakers
ISBN 0-300-05139-5; 0-300-05933-7 pa
LC 91-30836

A historical look at the evolution of Shakerism focusing on the movement's cultural values, religion and artifacts

289.3 Latter-Day Saints (Mormons)

Abanes, Richard
★ **One** nation under gods; a history of the Mormon Church. Four Walls Eight Windows 2002 xxv, 651p il $32; pa $22 **289.3**
1. Church of Jesus Christ of Latter-day Saints 2. Mormon Church -- Controversial literature
ISBN 1-56858-219-6; 1-56858-283-8 pa
LC 2001-40430

"This well-researched and readable history will be of interest to anyone seeking an objective Mormon history." Libr J
Includes bibliographical references

Book of Mormon
★ The **Book** of Mormon; another testament of Jesus Christ. [translated by Joseph Smith, Jr.] Doubleday 2004 586p $24.95 **289.3**
1. Church of Jesus Christ of Latter-day Saints 2. Mormons
ISBN 0-385-51316-X
LC 2004-51982

"Based on golden plates which Joseph Smith claimed were revealed to him, and which he unearthed from Cumorah Hill, New York, this book is roughly similar in structure to the Bible. . . . Emphasized are the doctrines of pre-existence, perfection, the afterlife, and Christ's second coming." Haydn. Thesaurus of Book Dig

Bushman, Richard L.

Joseph Smith and the beginnings of Mormonism. University of Ill. Press 1984 262p maps hardcover o.p. pa $16.95   **289.3**

    1. Church of Jesus Christ of Latter-day Saints 2. Mormon leaders

    ISBN 0-252-06012-1 pa

                                 LC 84-2451

The author surveys the historical background of the Mormon church with particular emphasis on the spiritual growth of its founder, Joseph Smith.

"Resulting from many years of careful research and reflections, this book will stand for decades as a major contribution in the field." Choice

Includes bibliographical references

Mormonism; a very short introduction. [by] Richard Lyman Bushman. Oxford University Press 2008 130p il pa $11.95   **289.3**

    1. Church of Jesus Christ of Latter-Day Saints 2. Church of Jesus Christ of Latter-day Saints 3. Mormon Church 4. Mormon leaders

    ISBN 978-0-19-531030-6

                            LC 2007-44444

This is an "outstanding, reliable overview of Mormon history and beliefs." Libr J

Includes bibliographical references (p. 121-123)

Givens, Terryl

By the hand of Mormon; the American scripture that launched a new world religion. [by] Terryl L. Givens. Oxford Univ. Press 2002 230p il maps hardcover o.p. pa $16.95   **289.3**

    ISBN 0-19-513818-X; 0-19-516888-7 pa

                            LC 2001-53118

The author "investigates the history and theology of the Book of Mormon, which he calls 'perhaps the most religiously influential, hotly contested, and, in the secular press at least, intellectually under-investigated book in America.' Givens persuasively demonstrates how the Book of Mormon was trumpeted by early Latter-day Saints more for the fact of its existence . . . than for its content per se." Publ Wkly

Includes bibliographical references

Gutjahr, Paul C.

The **Book** of Mormon; a biography. Paul C. Gutjahr. Princeton University Press 2012 xix, 255 p.p Lives of great religious books   **289.3**

    ISBN 9780691144801

                            LC 2011044063

This book presents a history of the Book of Mormon. To explain this book—now published in 150 million copies in 110 languages—[Paul C.] Gutjahr recounts the life of Joseph Smith, whose status as the prophet of the Church of Jesus Christ of Latter-Day Saints rests upon his claim that he translated the Book of Mormon from ancient gold plates delivered to him by an angel. . . . [This] . . . book chronicles the travails of an immigrant band of ancient Israelites who jour-

ney to the Americas, where they welcome the Risen Christ after his resurrection in Jerusalem but who then descend into apostasy and internecine war. Undeterred by skeptics allegations of fraud, a small army of missionaries have made the book a powerful proselytizing tool, attracting millions . . . to their faith. (Booklist)

Hardy, Grant

★ **Understanding** the Book of Mormon; a reader's guide. Oxford University Press 2010 336p $29.95   **289.3**

    ISBN 978-0-19-973170-1

                            LC 2009-26675

In this analysis of the Book of Mormon's narrative structure, the author describes the work's "characters, events, and ideas, as he explores the story and its messages. He identifies the book's literary techniques, such as characterization, embedded documents, allusions, and parallel narratives." Publisher's note

Includes bibliographical references

Krakauer, Jon

Under the banner of heaven; a story of violent faith. Doubleday 2003 xxxii, 665p map $26; pa $14.95   **289.3**

    1. Church of Jesus Christ of Latter-day Saints

    ISBN 0-385-50951-0; 1-4000-3280-6 pa

                            LC 2003-43824

"In 1984, Brenda Lafferty and her baby daughter Erica were found murdered in their Utah home, victims of a 'removal revelation' that her Mormon brother-in-law had supposedly received from God. Krakauer . . . aims to explain why and how this crime happened by recounting the history of Mormonism from its conception by Joseph Smith in the 19th century and tracing the origins of its extremist sects through to the present day." Libr J

Includes bibliographical references

Ostling, Richard N.

Mormon America; the power and the promise. [by] Richard N. Ostling and Joan K. Ostling. Rev. ed.; HarperOne 2007 xxvi, 469p il map pa $17.95   **289.3**

    1. Church of Jesus Christ of Latter-day Saints

    ISBN 978-0-06-143295-8

                          LC 2008-275419

"This thorough, thoughtful treatment of LDS beliefs and practices, written by non-Mormons, is a boon to members and interested lay readers alike." Libr J

Includes bibliographical references

Remini, Robert Vincent

Joseph Smith. Viking 2002 190p $19.95 **289.3**

    1. Mormon leaders 2. Mormons 3. Mormons -- United States -- Biography

    ISBN 0-670-03083-X

                            LC 2001-56762

"A masterful evenhanded précis that will engross history and religion readers alike." Booklist

Includes bibliographical references

289.5   Church of Christ, Scientist (Christian Science)

Eddy, Mary Baker

★ **Science** and health, with key to the Scriptures; Trustees under the will of Mary Baker G. Eddy. Christian Science Pub. Soc. 2000 pa $9.95   **289.5**
1. Christian Science
ISBN 978-0-87952-259-9; 0-87952-259-3
This work is the foundation of the Christian Science religion, setting forth Mrs. Baker's interpretations of the Holy Scriptures and the method of healing. It has not been revised since her death in 1910.

Fraser, Caroline

God's perfect child; living and dying in the Christian Science Church. Metropolitan Bks. 1999 561p il hardcover o.p. pa $16   **289.5**
1. Christian Science   2. Christian Science -- Controversial literature   3. Christian Science -- History   4. Christian Science leaders   5. Writers on religion
ISBN 0-8050-4431-0 pa
LC 99-17535
This "history traces the roots of the Christian Science church to nineteenth-century Calvinism, Emersonian self-reliance, and the remarkable life of its grandiose, anxiety-ridden founder, Mary Baker Eddy. . . . A work of compelling skepticism and scholarship." New Yorker
Includes bibliographical references

Gill, Gillian

Mary Baker Eddy. Perseus Bks. 1998 xxxv, 713p il hardcover o.p. pa $24   **289.5**
1. Christian Science   2. Christian Science -- History   3. Christian Science leaders   4. Christian Scientists -- United States -- Biography   5. Writers on religion
ISBN 0-7382-0227-4 pa
LC 98-86397
This "biography of Christian Science's founder offers detailed depictions of her early years of obscurity, her multiple marriages, the controversies she endured, and the inspiration that sustained her." Libr J
Includes bibliographical references

Schoepflin, Rennie B.

Christian Science on trial; religious healing in America. Johns Hopkins Univ. Press 2002 301p il $39.95   **289.5**
1. Christian Science   2. Christian Science -- History   3. Medical care -- Law and legislation -- United States   4. Medicine -- Religious aspects -- Christian Science
ISBN 0-8018-7057-7
LC 2001-8512
"A historical examination of Christian Science's evolution during the late 19th and early 20th centuries and the faith's struggle for existence and respectability in the midst of organized American medicine's efforts to curtail its influence." Libr J
Includes bibliographical references and index

289.6   Society of Friends (Quakers)

Hamm, Thomas D.

★ The **Quakers** in America. Columbia Univ. Press 2003 293p il $48.50; pa $27   **289.6**
1. Quakers -- United States   2. Society of Friends
ISBN 0-231-12362-0; 0-231-12363-9 pa
LC 2002-41422
The author provides an "introduction to Quaker origins abroad, their influences on American politics and culture, as well as their beliefs and traditions as they are played out on American soil. Though this is a serious history with a glossary, chronology, and 40 pages of notes, cartoons and anecdotes leaven the text. For both public and academic libraries." Libr J
Includes bibliographical references

289.7   Mennonite churches

Hostetler, John A.

Amish society; 4th ed; Johns Hopkins Univ. Press 1993 435p il maps hardcover o.p. pa $20   **289.7**
1. Amish
ISBN 0-8018-4441-X; 0-8018-4442-8
LC 92-19304
This book discusses the sectarian origins of the Amish, immigration history, family and community life, population trends, farming practices, technological innovations, education, medicine and the effects of government regulation.

Kraybill, Donald B.

Concise encyclopedia of Amish, Brethren, Hutterites, and Mennonites; Donald B. Kraybill. Johns Hopkins University Press 2010 302p ill., maps   **289.7**
ISBN 9780801896576; 0801896576
LC 2009046015
In this book author "[Donald B.] Kraybill [provides an] . . . overview of the beliefs and cultural practices of Amish, Brethren, Hutterites, and Mennonites in North America. Found throughout Canada, Central America, Mexico, and the United States, these religious communities include more than 200 different groups with 800,000 members in 17 countries. Through 340 short entries, Kraybill offers readers information on a wide range of topics related to religious views and social practices. With . . . consideration of how these diverse communities are related, this compact reference provides a . . . synopsis of these groups in the twenty-first century." (Publisher's note)

★ **On** the backroad to heaven; Old Order Hutterites, Mennonites, Amish, and Brethren. {by} Donald B. Kraybill, Carl F. Bowman. Johns Hopkins Univ. Press 2001 330p il maps $57; pa $16.95   **289.7**
1. Amish   2. Hutterian Brethren   3. Mennonites   4. Old Order Mennonites
ISBN 0-8018-6565-4; 0-8018-7089-5 pa
LC 00-10406
"This look at the history, similarities and differences between four groups of Old Order faithful in North Ameri-

ca—Hutterites, Mennonites, Amish and Brethren—is fascinating. . . . A book that, in one volume, tackles history, sociology and future trends—and does it well." Christ Century

Includes bibliographical references

The **riddle** of Amish culture; rev ed; Johns Hopkins Univ. Press 2001 397p il maps $65; pa $16.95 **289.7**

1. Amish 2. Amish -- Canada 3. Amish -- Pennsylvania -- Lancaster County 4. Amish -- United States

ISBN 0-8018-6771-1; 0-8018-6772-X pa

LC 00-13054

The author examines the history and culture of the Amish, discussing such topics as the social structure of Amish society, rites of redemption and purification, recreation and social gatherings, work, technology, public relations, and social change

Mackall, Joe

Plain secrets; an outsider among the Amish. Beacon Press 2007 xxxiv, 208p $24.95; pa $13 **289.7**

1. Amish 2. Amish -- Ohio -- Ashland County 3. Authors 4. Biography, Individual 5. College teachers 6. Essayists 7. Journalists 8. Memoirists

ISBN 0-80701-064-2; 978-0-80701-064-8; 0-80701-065-0 pa; 978-0-80701-065-5 pa

LC 2007-924329

"This is a loving portrait, warts and all, of an often-misunderstood people." Booklist

Includes bibliographical references

289.9 Denominations and sects not provided for elsewhere

Holden, Andrew

★ **Jehovah's** Witnesses; portrait of a contemporary religious movement. Routledge 2002 206p $80; pa $23.95 **289.9**

1. Jehovah's Witnesses

ISBN 0-415-26609-2; 0-415-26610-6 pa

LC 2001-45726

"This ethnographic study, academic in tone and British in orientation, offers several chapters of general information about the faith and analyzes its relationship to the wider society." Libr J

Includes bibliographical references

292 Classical religion (Greek and Roman religion)

Graves, Robert

★ The **Greek** myths; Combined ed; Penguin Books 1992 782p pa $19.95 **292**

1. Classical mythology

ISBN 0-14-017199-1

A collection of the author's interpretations of Greek myths based on anthropological and archaeological findings.

★ The Oxford dictionary of classical myth and religion; edited by Simon Price and Emily Kearns. Oxford University Press 2003 599p maps $39.95; pa $17.95 **292**

1. Classical mythology -- Dictionaries 2. Mythology, Classical 3. Reference books

ISBN 0-19-280288-7; 0-19-280289-5 pa

LC 2004-298013

"Instead of separating mythology and Judeo-Christian religion into separate references, this work covers all religious life in the ancient Greco-Roman world. The result is a generally accessible and academically current compendium of information on gods and holy beings, religious practices, festivals, sacred sites, myths, authors, and texts of the period. The reader will find not only Athena and Zeus but also Jesus Christ and St. Augustine, Mani and Zoroaster." Libr J

294 Religions of Indic origin

Dalrymple, William

Nine lives; in search of the sacred in modern India. A.A. Knopf 2010 275p il map $26.95 **294**

1. Religious biography -- India

ISBN 978-0-307-27282-9; 0-307-27282-6

LC 2010-06362

"Throughout the book, Dalrymple showcases his knowledge of the breadth of India and his fearless willingness to penetrate its sometimes unsavory nooks and crannies, rendering this a truly heartfelt work for readers craving a deeper connection to India and its rich spiritual heritage. A remarkable feat of journalism." Kirkus

Includes bibliographical references

Iyengar, B. K. S.

Light on life; the yoga journey to wholeness, inner peace, and ultimate freedom. [by] B.K.S. Iyengar, with John J. Evans and Douglas Abrams. Rodale 2005 xxii, 282p il $24.95; pa $15.95 **294**

1. Yoga

ISBN 1-59486-248-6; 978-1-59486-248-9; 1-59486-524-8 pa

LC 2005-15700

The author "expounds the philosophy of yoga—its metaphysics, of which yoga poses, or asanas, represent the physical component. . . . Not the book with which to begin the yoga journey, it is highly recommended for those advanced on the path and interested in learning from a master of flexibility and wisdom." Publ Wkly

294.3 Buddhism

Armstrong, Karen

Buddha. Viking 2001 xxix, 205p map hardcover o.p. pa $13 **294.3**

1. Authors, Italian -- To 1500 -- Biography 2. Buddhist leaders 3. Philosophers

ISBN 0-670-89193-2; 0-14-303436-7 pa

LC 00-43808

"Armstrong interprets the mythologized story of the Buddha's abandonment of his life of comfort and privilege; commitment to practicing advanced forms of yoga and nearly fatal asceticism; enlightenment beneath a bodhi tree; and 45 years of wandering and teaching until his death in 483. And as she does so, she lucidly explains his revelations and influence." Booklist

Includes bibliographical references

Bernstein, Richard

Ultimate journey; retracing the path of an ancient Buddhist monk who crossed Asia in search of enlightenment. Knopf 2001 352p il maps hardcover o.p. pa $14   **294.3**
1. Buddhism 2. Buddhist monks 3. Priests, Buddhist -- China -- Biography
ISBN 0-679-78157-9 pa

LC 2001-267521

"In 629, a Buddhist monk named Hsuan Tsang set out from China, crossing Asia in search of Buddhist truth. Bernstein . . . decided to retrace the monk's journey over the silk road to Pakistan and India and back to China. In this entertaining and well-written account, more travel literature than religious study, he juxtaposes his account of Hsuan Tsang's experiences with descriptions of his own trials." Libr J

Includes bibliographical references

Bstan-'dzin-rgya-mtsho, Dalai Lama XIV, 1935-

★ **How** to be compassionate; a handbook for creating inner peace and a happier world. [by] His Holiness the Dalai Lama; translated from oral teachings and edited by Jeffrey Hopkins. Atria Books 2011 xi, 147 p.p $14   **294.3**
1. Buddhism 2. Compassion 3. Religious life
ISBN 1451623917; 9781451623901; 9781451623925

LC 2011281813

In this book, the Tibetan Buddhist spiritual leader the Dalai Lama demonstrates that "the surest path to true happiness lies in being intimately concerned with the welfare of others," or "in compassion." (Publisher's note) The author "works . . . from the Buddhist places (awareness, nonattachment) to speak to general readers about habits that make for unhappiness (anger, for one) and the attitudes that increase contentment." (Library Journal)

Light on politics and even lighter on the more abstruse points of Tibetan Buddhism, this is a fine and accessible book for the everyday reader. Libr J

Includes bibliographical references (p. [145]-147)

Crane, George

Bones of the master; a Buddhist monk's search for the lost heart of China. Bantam Bks. 2000 293p il maps hardcover o.p. pa $14.95   **294.3**
1. Buddhism 2. Buddhist monks 3. Priest, Buddhist -- China -- Biography
ISBN 0-553-37908-9 pa

LC 99-37868

This is an account of the friendship between Crane and Tsung Tsai, a Buddhist monk, and their journey to Mongolia to bury the bones of the monk's teacher

"Crane chronicles their perilous and miraculous adventures, the beauty of Mongolia's wilderness of wind and sand,

and Tsung Tsai's transcendent determination with uncommon clarity, wit, vitality, and love." Booklist

Dalai Lama

Violence and compassion; {by} the Dalai Lama and Jean-Claude Carrière. Doubleday 1996 248p hardcover o.p. pa $11.50   **294.3**
1. Buddhism
ISBN 0-385-50144-7 pa

LC 95-30694

"This is a rich and invigorating volume, full of ponderable wisdom." Booklist

Johnson, Tim

Tragedy in crimson; how the Dalai Lama conquered the world but lost the battle with China. Nation Books 2011 333p map pa $26.99   **294.3**
1. Buddhism and politics -- China -- Tibet 2. Buddhist leaders 3. Journalists 4. Nobel laureates for peace 5. Political leaders
ISBN 978-1-56858-601-4

LC 2010-37497

"A current, objective, basic primer on the Free Tibet movement and the Dalai Lama was sorely needed, and . . . [the author] has provided exactly that." Natl Rev

Includes bibliographical references

Keown, Damien

★ A **dictionary** of Buddhism; contributors, Stephen Hodge, Charles Jones, Paoli Tinti. Oxford Univ. Press 2003 357p il maps hardcover o.p. pa $15.95   **294.3**
1. Buddhism
ISBN 0-19-860560-9; 978-0-19-280062-6 pa; 0-19-280062-0 pa

LC 2003-276701

"The entries are short . . . but such accessibility is the very reason why this should be on the bookshelf of every student of Buddhism." Publ Wkly

Kerouac, Jack

Some of the dharma. Viking 1997 419p hardcover o.p. pa $20   **294.3**
1. Buddhism
ISBN 0-14-028707-8 pa

LC 97-12870

"Begun in December 1951 as a notebook for his Buddhist studies, this work records Kerouac's reactions to a variety of Buddhist texts. Over the course of five years, it grew to include poems, prayers, dialogs, meditations, and notes on his reading, as well as commentary on family, friends, and meaningful concerns in his life. . . . Long anticipated by Kerouac scholars, this major work belongs in all literature collections." Libr J

Olson, Carl

Historical dictionary of Buddhism. Scarecrow Press 2009 xxix, 327p il map $105; ebook $105   **294.3**
1. Buddhism -- Dictionaries 2. Buddhism -- History 3.

Reference books

ISBN 978-0-8108-5771-1; 0-8108-5771-5; 978-0-8108-6317-0 ebook; 0-8108-6317-0 ebook

LC 2009-7383

This dictionary covers "Buddhist concepts, significant figures, movements, schools, places, activities, and periods. . . . [It also features] a chronology, an introductory essay, a bibliography, and over 700 cross-referenced dictionary entries." Publisher's note

Includes bibliographical references

Sogyal

The **Tibetan** book of living and dying; edited by Patrick Gaffney and Andrew Harvey. rev and updated ed; HarperSanFrancisco 2002 441p il $28.95; pa $17.95   **294.3**

1. Buddhism 2. Buddhism -- China -- Tibet -- Doctrines 3. Death 4. Death -- Religious aspects -- Buddhism 5. Intermediate state -- Buddhism 6. Religious life -- Buddhism

ISBN 0-06-250793-1; 0-06-250834-2 pa

LC 2002-523084

The author "is well qualified to pass on his tradition. He does this beautifully, in limpid prose free of the scholastic list making that deadens many Tibetan Buddhist primers." N Y Times Book Rev {review of 1992 edition}

Includes bibliographical references (p. 415-418) and index

Sutin, Lawrence

★ **All** is change; the two-thousand year journey of Buddhism to the West. Little, Brown 2006 403p il $25.99   **294.3**

1. Buddhism

ISBN 978-0-316-74156-9; 0-316-74156-6

LC 2006-40824

"Greeks and Buddhists in India found common metaphysical ground 2,000 years ago, and Sutin also documents parallels between Buddist and Gnostic teachings in this vital study of a remarkable spiritual migration." Booklist

Includes bibliographical references

Suzuki, Daisetz Teitaro

★ **Manual** of Zen Buddhism. Grove Press 1960 192p il pa $13   **294.3**

1. Buddhist art 2. Zen Buddhism

ISBN 0-8021-3065-8

In this volume, D. T. Suzuki has brought together some of Zen Buddhism's original sources. Included are the sutras or sermons of the Buddha: the gathas or hymns; the philosophical puzzles known as koan; and the dharanis or invocations to expel evil spirits. In addition to the written selections there are reproductions of Buddhist drawings and paintings, including religious statues found in Zen temples

Thondup, Tulku

Enlightened journey; Buddhist practice as daily life. edited by Harold Talbott. Shambhala Publs. 1995 268p pa $16.95   **294.3**

1. Buddhism 2. Rdzogs-chen (Rñin-ma-pa) 3. Spiritual life -- Rñin-ma-pa (Sect)

ISBN 1-57062-021-0

LC 94-36154

This is an "exposition on one of the more important sects of Tibetan Buddhism. As such, it comprises 15 talks and articles by Thondup, {a} leader and teacher of the Nyingma school of Tibetan Buddhism. His purpose here is to show how daily life can become the basis of Buddhist spiritual training, and each talk is an introduction to various aspects of Buddhism, covering such topics as meditation as a means to arouse compassion and the importance of suffering to reach enlightenment." Libr J

Includes bibliographical references

Thurman, Robert A. F.

Why the Dalai Lama matters; his act of truth as the solution for China, Tibet, and the world. [by] Robert Thurman. Beyond Words Pub. 2008 xxiv, 231p il map $23   **294.3**

1. Buddhism 2. Buddhist leaders 3. Nobel laureates for peace 4. Political leaders

ISBN 978-1-58270-220-9; 1-58270-220-9

LC 2008-8529

The author presents an "introduction to Buddhism and the Tibetan concept of the Dalai Lama before focusing on the current 'living embodiment of the Buddha'—a man born as Tenzin Gyatso—the 14th Dalai Lama. Thurman sympathetically renders his lifelong friend as a 'simple Buddhist monk,' a teacher, philosopher, scientist and the political representative of the Tibetan people. . . . The book concludes with a five-step plan to broker peace between Tibet and China—an agenda simultaneously pragmatic and idealistic, demonstrating truly the talent and power of faith." Publ Wkly

Includes bibliographical references

Watts, Alan

The **way** of Zen. Vintage Books 1999 236p il pa $13.95   **294.3**

1. Zen Buddhism

ISBN 0-375-70510-4

This is an historical and cultural survey of Zen, tracing its origins in Indian and Chinese thought. The author describes the Zen way of living and its techniques for overcoming the mind's conflict between symbolic thought and actual experience.

294.5   Hinduism

Goldberg, Philip

American Veda; from Emerson and the Beatles to yoga and meditation: how Indian spirituality changed the West. Doubleday Religion 2010 398p il $26; ebook $26   **294.5**

1. Hinduism 2. Vedanta 3. Yoga

ISBN 978-0-385-52134-5; 978-0-307-71961-4 ebook

LC 2010-11040

"From meditating movie stars, scandalous gurus, and psychedelic drugs to genuine spiritual breakthroughs and devotion to helping others, Goldberg's history of 'American Veda' takes measure of a powerful, if underappreciated, force." Booklist

Includes bibliographical references

Mahabharata/Bhagavadgita

★ **Bhagavad** Gita; a new translation. [translated by] Stephen Mitchell. Harmony Bks. 2000 223p hardcover o.p. pa $13.95   **294.5**
ISBN 0-609-60550-X; 0-609-81034-0 pa
LC 00-28286

"An eighteen-part discussion between the god Krishna, an avatar of Vishnu appearing as a charioteer, and Arjuna, a warrior about to enter battle, on the nature and meaning of life. Sometimes called the New Testament of Hinduism, it is an interpolation in the great Hindu epic the Mahabharata." Reader's Ency. 4th edition

Sivananda Yoga Vedanta Center (London, England)

Yoga mind & body. DK Pub. 2008 168p il pa $15   **294.5**
1. Yoga
ISBN 978-0-7566-3674-6
LC 2008-489063

"This guide stresses the five points of exercise, breathing, meditation, diet, and relaxation for improved health and happiness. In addition to basic yoga poses, Yoga Mind & Body provides meditation tools, stress relief exercises, and recipes for healthful nutrition." Publisher's note

294.6   Sikhism

Singh, Patwant

The **Sikhs**. Knopf 2000 276p il hardcover o.p. pa $14   **294.6**
1. Sikhs 2. Sikhs -- History
ISBN 0-375-40728-6; 0-385-50206-0 pa
LC 99-31807

The author "traces Sikh history from its origins in the 15th century through Indira Gandhi's 1984 storming of the Golden Temple. . . . Sikhs, he argues, have for centuries been an embattled people because their culture and religion defy the predominant religions in the region, as well as the Indian caste system with its ruling elite." Publ Wkly

Includes bibliographical references

296   Judaism

Freedman, Samuel G.

Jew vs. Jew; the struggle for the soul of American Jewry. Simon & Schuster 2000 397p $26; pa $14   **296**
1. Jews -- United States 2. Jews -- United States -- Identity 3. Jews -- United States -- Social conditions -- 20th century 4. Judaism 5. Judaism -- 20th century 6. Judaism -- United States
ISBN 0-684-85944-0; 0-684-85945-9 pa
LC 00-33907

The author "describes the paradoxical situation faced by today's American Jews, living in a country where religious freedom has yielded unreconcilable devisiveness. . . . This is a helpful guide for anyone seeking an understanding of intra-Jewish conflicts in contemporary America." Libr J

Includes bibliographical references

Kushner, Harold S.

To life! a celebration of Jewish being and thinking. Warner Books 1994 304p pa $14.99   **296**
1. Judaism
ISBN 0-446-67002-2; 978-0-446-67002-9
LC 94-25828

The author discusses the meaning of Jewish customs and ceremonies and the purpose of prayer. Antisemitism, Jewish-Christian relations, and the importance of Israel to contemporary Jews are also examined.

"This is a very easy book to read, to discuss, even to argue about, and Kushner's celebration is everything his many readers could have hoped it would be." Booklist

Robinson, George

Essential Judaism; a complete guide to beliefs, customs and rituals. Pocket Bks. 2000 xxi, 644p hardcover o.p. pa $20   **296**
1. Judaism
ISBN 0-671-03480-4; 0-671-03481-2 pa
LC 99-55288

This book "attempts to provide the essentials of Judaism for novices, outsiders and those who, like Robinson, rediscovered their heritage as adults. It's an excellent introductory resource, vast but accessibly organized." Publ Wkly

Includes bibliographical references

Sarna, Jonathan D.

★ **American** Judaism; a history. Yale University Press 2004 xx, 490p il $35   **296**
1. Jews -- United States 2. Jews -- United States -- History 3. Judaism 4. Judaism -- United States -- History
ISBN 0-300-10197-X
LC 2003-14464

"This comprehensive and insightful study of the American Jewish experience is much more than just a record of events. It is an account of how people shaped events: establishing and maintaining communities, responding to challenges, and working for change. It is compelling reading for Jews and non-Jews alike." Booklist

Includes bibliographical references

Wouk, Herman

This is my God: the Jewish way of life. Little, Brown 1987 345p hardcover o.p. pa $16.95   **296**
1. Judaism
ISBN 0-316-95514-0 pa
LC 87-3245

The author, an orthodox Jew, writes a personal declaration of faith. He explains holy days, fasts, and presents the historical background of Judaism.

American Jewish year book 2007. American Jewish
    Com. $49.95   **296**
    1. Jews -- Periodicals 2. Jews -- United States
    ISBN 978-0-87495-142-4; 0-87495-142-9
"An almanac of Jewish life and culture including population statistics, directories of Jewish organizations and periodicals, a religious calendar, necrology, coverage of international Jewish politics and communities, and periodicals."
Ref Sources for Small & Medium-sized Libr. 6th edition

★ The Cambridge history of Judaism; v1 edited by
    W.D. Davies [and] Louis Finkelstein. Cambridge
    Univ. Press 1984 461p v1 il maps $194   **296**
    1. Judaism 2. Judaism -- History
    ISBN 0-521-21880-2
                                          LC 77-85704
"The first of . . . four volumes on the history of the Jews
from the destruction of the Temple in 586 BC to the closure of the Mishnah in AD 250, the work deals not solely
with Judaism . . . but with the entire material history of
the Jews in the Land of Israel as well as in Babylonia and
Egypt." Choice
    Includes bibliographical references

Encyclopaedia Judaica; Fred Skolnik, editor-in-
    chief; Michael Berenbaum, executive editor. 2nd
    ed; Macmillan Reference USA in association
    with the Keter Pub. House 2007 22v il map **296**
    1. Jews 2. Judaism 3. Judaism -- Encyclopedias 4.
    Reference books
    ISBN 0-02-865928-7; 978-0-02-865928-2
                                          LC 2006020426
This "is a welcome addition to reference collections. By
documenting the modern Jewish experience while retaining
links with its rich past, it provides users with information
about all aspects of Jewish religion and culture." Booklist
    Includes bibliographical references

★ The New encyclopedia of Judaism; editor-in-
    chief, Geoffrey Wigoder; coeditors, Fred Skolnik
    & Shmuel Himelstein. New York Univ. Press
    2002 856p il $79.95   **296**
    1. Judaism -- Dictionaries 2. Reference books
    ISBN 0-8147-9388-6
                                          LC 2002-16614
    This reference "seeks to present a balanced picture,
offering current thinking among scholars in Reform, Conservative, and Orthodox movements and a roster of contributors hailing from Israel, England, and the United States.
While the scholarship is solid, the material is readily accessible to a popular audience, and the work is magnificently
illustrated." Libr J
    Includes bibliographical references

★ The Oxford dictionary of the Jewish religion;
    editors in chief, R.J. Zwi Werblowsky, Geoffrey
    Wigoder. Oxford University Press 1997 764p
    $125   **296**
    1. Judaism -- Dictionaries 2. Reference books
    ISBN 0-19-508605-8
                                          LC 96-45517

"The 2400 entries in this dictionary include unsigned but
revised articles from the editors' Encyclopedia of the Jewish
Religion (1966), as well as . . . new signed articles covering
[topics] . . . and biographies related to the Jewish religion
and interfaith relations." Libr J

Reader's guide to Judaism; editor, Michael Terry.
    Fitzroy Dearborn Pubs. 2000 718p $135   **296**
    1. Jewish religious literature 2. Judaism 3. Judaism
    -- Encyclopedias 4. Reference books
    ISBN 1-57958-139-0
                                          LC 2001-274119
    This "work covers over 400 topics, including interfaith
relations, historical periods, philosophical and mystical
movements, important figures, and more. Preceding each essay is a bibliography of five to ten English-language titles. .
. . Written by librarians and scholars . . . these 1000 to 2000-
word essays include a descriptive and often analytical overview of each book. . . . This is an excellent tool for building
Judaica collections in public and academic libraries." Libr J
    Includes bibliographical references

296.09   History, geographic treatment, biography

Cole, Peter
    ★ **Sacred** trash; [by] Adina Hoffman & Pe-
    ter Cole. Nextbook : Schocken 2011 283p. ill.,
    ports.   **296.09**
    1. Cairo Genizah 2. Judaism -- History -- Sources
    ISBN 978-0-8052-4258-4; 0-8052-4258-9
                                          LC 201016751
    This is an account of the discovery, about 120 years ago,
of a cache of documents in the storeroom of a synagogue in
Cairo. The cache, referred to as a geniza, includes "letters,
wills, bills of lading, prayers, marriage contracts and writs
of divorce, Bibles, money orders, court depositions, business inventories, leases, magic charms and receipts." (N Y
Times Book Rev)

★ The Cambridge history of Judaism; v3 edited by
    William Horbury, John Sturdy and W.D. Davies.
    Cambridge Univ. Press 1999 1254p v3 il maps
    $190   **296.09**
    1. Judaism -- History
    ISBN 0-521-24377-7
    This third volume of a four-volume history "contains
thirty-two essays on aspects of Judaism in the early Roman
period, primarily the period between Pompey and Vespasian
but often ranging into the rabbinic period." J Relig
    Includes bibliographical references

296.1   Sources

Abegg, Martin G.
    The **Dead** Sea scrolls; a new translation. [by]
    Michael O. Wise, Martin G. Abegg Jr., and Edward

M. Cook. Rev ed; HarperSanFrancisco 2005 662p
pa $24.95 **296.1**
ISBN 0-06-076662-X

LC 2005-46285

"An engaging necessity for updating Dead Sea Scrolls collections." Booklist

Includes bibliographical references

Golb, Norman

Who wrote the Dead Sea scrolls? the search for the secret of Qumran. Scribner 1995 446p il maps hardcover o.p. pa $22 **296.1**
1. Judaism -- History
ISBN 0-684-80692-4 pa

LC 94-23295

"This is an archival book that should be considered for any collection dealing with the Dead Sea Scrolls. It is well written and can be read by the interested person as well as by the professional scholar." Choice

Includes bibliographical references

Schiffman, Lawrence H.

Reclaiming the Dead Sea scrolls; the history of Judaism, the background of Christianity, the lost library of Qumran. with a foreword by Chaim Potok. Jewish Publ. Soc. 1994 xxvii, 529p il maps **296.1**
1. Judaism -- History

LC 94-26489

Schiffman provides a "description and evaluation of the scrolls, the archeology of Qumran (the site near the Dead Sea from which the scrolls originated), the history and nature of the Jewish community that lived at Qumran and the setting of the scrolls in Jewish history and thought from the second century B.C. through the first century A.D." N Y Times Book Rev

Includes bibliographical references

Shanks, Hershel

The **mystery** and meaning of the Dead Sea scrolls. Random House 1998 xxi, 246p il maps hardcover o.p. pa $14 **296.1**
ISBN 0-679-78089-0 pa

LC 97-29391

"Shanks looks at the key questions surrounding the Dead Sea Scrolls (who wrote them, what they say, and what they mean vis-à-vis Judaism and Christianity) and gives readers the most up-to-date information along with his own best guesses about what it all means, easily incorporating many divergent theories." Booklist

Includes bibliographical references

The Encyclopedia of the Dead Sea scrolls; {edited by} Lawrence H. Schiffman and James C. VanderKam. Oxford Univ. Press 2000 2v set $295 **296.1**
ISBN 0-19-508450-0

LC 99-55300

"In addition to individual texts, coverage extends to the archeological sites themselves; important historical figures (Moses) and groups (Essenes, Pharisees) as they are represented in the scrolls; scholars important to Dead Sea scroll

research . . . and methods employed both to date and to preserve these ancient documents." Booklist

296.3 Theology, ethics, views of social issues

Kushner, Harold S.

★ **When** bad things happen to good people; with a new preface by the author. 20th anniversary ed; Schocken Bks. 2001 202p $21 **296.3**
1. Providence and government of God 2. Suffering
ISBN 0-8052-4193-0

LC 2001-531062

"A bright and happy infant, Rabbi Kushner's first-born son gradually succumbed to progeria, 'rapid aging': he never grew beyond three feet tall, looked like a hairless, wizened old man, and died in his teens. This book is his father's attempt to make sense out of his son's fate, his own pain, and the pain of others enduring undeserved misfortunes." Libr J

Telushkin, Joseph

Jewish wisdom; ethical, spiritual, and historical lessons from the great works and thinkers. {by} Rabbi Joseph Telushkin. Morrow 1994 xxiv, 663p $26 **296.3**
1. Jewish ethics 2. Jews -- Quotations 3. Judaism
ISBN 0-688-12958-7

LC 94-9186

"Organized by subject, this is a collection of teachings and quotations from the Talmud, the Bible, rabbinical commentaries, and ancient and modern religious and secular writings. Writers include Elie Wiesel, Isaac Bashevis Singer, Hebrew poet Hayim Bialik, Cynthia Ozick, Emile Zola, Albert Einstein, Bruno Bettelheim, Gertrude Stein, Irving Howe, and Maimonides. . . . Jews—and even non-Jews— will find the book a treasure." Booklist

Includes bibliographical references

296.4 Traditions, rites, public services

Eisenberg, Ronald L.

★ The **JPS** guide to Jewish traditions; [by] Ron Eisenberg. The Jewish Publication Society 2004 xxiii, 806p $40 **296.4**
1. Judaism -- Encyclopedias 2. Reference books
ISBN 0-8276-0760-1

LC 2004-6399

This "work covers the major elements of Jewish life, including life-cycle events (birth, bar and bat mitzvah, marriage, divorce, parenting, and death), the Sabbath and holidays, the synagogue, prayer, and the Bible and Jewish literature. . . . The author has done a masterful job in distilling the major beliefs and practices of a 3,000-year-old religion into lively and informative prose and in creating an accessible, essential reference work." Booklist

Includes bibliographical references

Goldman, Ari L.

Being Jewish; the spiritual and cultural practice of Judaism today. Simon & Schuster 2000 286p $25   **296.4**

1. Fasts and feasts -- Judaism 2. Jewish holidays 3. Jewish way of life 4. Judaism -- Customs and practices 5. Life cycle, Human -- Religious aspects -- Judaism

ISBN 0-684-82389-6

LC 00-44047

"An excellent resource." Booklist

Includes bibliographical references

Shulevitz, Judith

The **Sabbath** world; glimpses of a different order of time. Random House 2010 246p $26 **296.4**

1. Rest -- Religious aspects 2. Rest -- Religious aspects -- Christianity 3. Rest -- Religious aspects -- Judaism 4. Sabbath 5. Time -- Religious aspects 6. Time -- Religious aspects -- Christianity 7. Time -- Religious aspects -- Judaism

ISBN 978-1-4000-6200-3; 1-4000-6200-4

LC 2009-26417

"In personal terms, and without sanctimony, [the author] explores the history of the Sabbath, its philosophical foundations, its consolations, its purposes, and, in doing so, writes a swift, penetrating book intent on shattering the habits of mindless workaholism and the inability to recognize the blessings of rest, reflection, spirit, and family." New Yorker

Wieseltier, Leon

Kaddish. Knopf 1998 588p $27.50; pa $16   **296.4**

1. Funeral rites and ceremonies 2. Grief 3. Jewish mourning customs 4. Judaism -- Customs and practices

ISBN 0-375-40389-2; 0-375-70362-4 pa

LC 98-15881

"When his father died in 1996 . . . Wieseltier began to observe the Jewish rituals of the traditional year of mourning. His own mourning led him to an in-depth study of the history and meaning of Kaddish in Judaism. Wieseltier provides a work of history, philosophy and spiritual memoir that demonstrates how the practice of religion meets the needs of a troubled soul." Publ Wkly

296.7 Religious experience, life, practice

Diamant, Anita

Pitching my tent; on marriage, motherhood, friendship, and other leaps of faith. Scribner 2003 223p hardcover o.p. pa $15   **296.7**

1. Jewish women 2. Jewish women -- United States -- Anecdotes 3. Jews -- United States -- Anecdotes 4. Judaism -- United States

ISBN 0-7432-4616-0; 0-7432-4617-9 pa

LC 2003-45440

"This collection of short essays, culled primarily from the Boston Globe Sunday Magazine and then reworked, . . . [are] organized around such themes as love and marriage, child rearing, friendship and living a religious life. . . . The book's strength lies in its woman-to-woman conversational tone, especially in the opening section about married life and

its dark side. . . . These morsels will make a tasty snack for Diamant's admirers." Publ Wkly

Isaacs, Ronald H.

★ **Kosher** living; it's more than just the food. [by] Ron Isaacs. Jossey-Bass 2005 xlvii, 286p $22.95   **296.7**

1. Judaism -- Customs and practices

ISBN 0-7879-7642-3

LC 2004-26727

"The book not only covers the expected Jewish topics— circumcision, marriage, prayer, Shabbat, synagogue behavior and more—but also . . . [items] such as employer-employee relations, shopping and even war. . . . This resource offers timeless wisdom through a contemporary lens." Publ Wkly

Includes bibliographical references

Kushner, Harold S.

How good do we have to be? a new understanding of guilt and forgiveness. Little, Brown 1996 181p hardcover o.p. pa $11.95   **296.7**

1. Forgiveness 2. Good and evil 3. Guilt

ISBN 0-316-51933-2 pa

LC 95-25350

"This is one psychological self-help book that deserves the popularity it is likely to achieve." Booklist

Who needs God; [by] Harold Kushner. Fireside 2002 212p pa $14   **296.7**

1. God -- Judaism

ISBN 0-7432-3477-4

The author "believes that 'human life has meaning . . . but only in religious terms.' According to this crucial realization, it is religion that connects us to God and community." Libr J

Levy, Naomi

To begin again; a journey toward comfort, strength, and faith in difficult times. Knopf 1998 267p hardcover o.p. pa $12.95   **296.7**

1. Bereavement 2. Bereavement -- Religious aspects -- Judaism 3. Consolation (Judaism) 4. Jewish way of life 5. Judaism -- Customs and practices

ISBN 0-345-41383-0 pa

LC 98-16024

"A wise and practical guide for readers of any religious persuasion." Libr J

Reuben, Steven Carr

★ **Becoming** Jewish; the challenges, rewards, and paths to conversion. [by] Steven Carr Reuben and Jennifer S. Hanin; [foreword by Bab Saget] Rowman & Littlefield Publishers 2011 256p $22.95; ebook $22.95   **296.7**

1. Conversion 2. Converts to Judaism

ISBN 978-1-4422-0848-3; 978-1-4422-0849-0 ebook

LC 2011014083

"The authors explain such details as finding the right denomination, choosing a rabbi, selecting a Hebrew name, and the need to learn Hebrew. They also discuss Jewish culture and beliefs, holidays, and traditions. Chapters on telling family and friends about the decision to convert, raising Jewish children, kabbalah, anti-Semitism, and Israel help those converting understand important issues. . . . Written in a casual, friendly style with good humor and warmth, this accessible guide will help anyone considering conversion to Judaism." Booklist

297   Islam, Babism, Bahai Faith

Armstrong, Karen

★ **Islam**; a short history. Modern Lib. 2000 xxxiv, 222p maps $19.95; pa $11.95   **297**
1. Islam 2. Islam -- History
ISBN 0-679-64040-1; 0-8129-6618-X pa
LC 00-25285
This history of the Islamic faith focuses on the religion's attitude toward politics.
The author "does an admirable job of presenting Islamic history from an objective, unbiased point of view." Libr J
Includes bibliographical references

Muhammad; a prophet for our time. Atlas Books/HarperCollins Publishers 2006 249p map $21.95; pa $14.95   **297**
1. Biography, Individual 2. Islam 3. Islamic leaders 4. Prophets 5. Writers on religion
ISBN 0-06-059897-2; 978-0-06-059897-6; 0-06-115577-2 pa; 978-0-06-115577-2 pa
LC 2006-45864
This is a biography of the founder of Islam.
"Readers of these pages cannot escape the genius of Muhammad and his aim for peace and compassion among nations and among Muslims themselves. . . . Recommended for all libraries." Libr J
Includes bibliographical references

Aslan, Reza

★ **No** god but God; the origins, evolution, and future of Islam. Random House 2005 xxiv, 310p $25.95; pa $14.95   **297**
1. Islam
ISBN 1-4000-6213-6; 0-8129-7189-2 pa
LC 2004-54053
"Beginning with an exploration of the religious climate in the years before the Prophet's Revelation, Aslan traces the story of Islam from the Prophet's life and the so-called golden age of the first four caliphs all the way through European colonization and subsequent independence. . . . This is an excellent overview that doubles as an impassioned call to reform." Booklist
Includes bibliographical references

Barrett, Paul M.

American Islam; the struggle for the soul of a religion. Farrar, Straus & Giroux 2006 304p $25 **297**
1. Biography, Collective 2. Islam 3. Muslims -- United States
ISBN 978-0-374-10423-8; 0-374-10423-9
LC 2006-11404

"In the post-9/11 world Muslims have frequently been stereotyped as monolithically murderous. . . . The heated debates among Muslims themselves about violence committed under the banner of Islam are often drowned out in the fray. Paul M. Barrett's timely and engaging new book brings some of those voices in the United States to life." N Y Times (Late N Y Ed)
Includes bibliographical references

Bawer, Bruce

Surrender; appeasing Islam, sacrificing freedom. Doubleday 2009 321p $24.95   **297**
1. Civil rights -- Public opinion 2. Freedom of speech 3. Islam -- Public opinion 4. Islam -- Relations 5. Public opinion -- Europe
ISBN 978-0-385-52398-1; 0-385-52398-X
LC 2008-35743
"Bawer files a hefty brief of case reports on Muslim campaigns against free speech, primarily in western Europe but also in Canada and the U.S. Official infatuation with political correctness (PC), the determination that no one ever be offended, and multiculturalism, the dogma that all cultural perspectives are equally and universally valid, undergird what Bawer believes amounts to a surrender of Western liberal traditions. What may seal the fate of free speech, he argues, are the apparent inabilities of Western ruling elites to be offended by Muslims rioting, threatening by fatwa, and murdering non-Muslims . . . and to assert the priority of Western liberal values in the West. . . . Sublimely literate and rational, Bawer is no crank, however angry he gets." Booklist
Includes bibliographical references

Ben Jelloun, Tahar

Islam explained. New Press (NY) 2002 120p hardcover o.p. pa $13.95   **297**
1. Islam 2. Islam -- Apologetic works 3. Islam -- Appreciation 4. Islam -- Essence, genius, nature
ISBN 1-56584-781-4; 1-56584-897-7 pa
LC 2002-30500
"Cast in the form of an extended conversation between Ben Jelloun and his young daughter. . . . Father and child discuss the history of Islam, what it means to be a Muslim today, the challenges facing the Islamic world, and terrorism. . . . Its openness and emotional honesty, particularly when discussing the tragedy of 9/11, make it a valuable addition to a growing public discourse. As an introduction to the religion, it is spotty, but as a liberal Muslim voice of reconciliation, heartbreak, and compassion, it is priceless." Booklist

Campo, Juan Eduardo

Encyclopedia of Islam; [by] Juan E. Campo. Facts On File 2008 750p il map $85   **297**
1. Islam 2. Islam -- Encyclopedias 3. Reference books
ISBN 978-0-8160-5454-1; 0-8160-5454-1
LC 2008-5621
"In about 600 A-to-Z entries, this encyclopedic guide explores the terms, concepts, personalities, historical events, and institutions that helped shape the history of this religion and the way it is practiced today." Publisher's note
Includes bibliographical references

Ernst, Carl W.

Following Muhammad; rethinking Islam in the contemporary world. University of North Carolina Press 2003 244p il $24.95; pa $16.95   **297**
1. East and West 2. Islam
ISBN 0-8078-2837-8; 0-8078-5577-4 pa
LC 2003-11162
The author "informs readers of the roles played by colonialism, Christian missionary efforts, and Western conceptions of just what 'religion' is, all in relation to American conceptions of Islam." Libr J
Includes bibliographical references

Esposito, John L.

Islam; the straight path. Rev. 3rd ed., updated with new epilogue; Oxford University Press 2005 304p map pa $39.95   **297**
1. Islam
ISBN 0-19-518266-9
LC 2004-61688
This "survey text introduces the faith, belief, and practice of Islam from its earliest origins up to its contemporary resurgence." Publisher's note
Includes bibliographical references

What everyone needs to know about Islam. Oxford Univ. Press 2002 204p $18.95   **297**
1. Islam 2. Islam -- Essence, genius, nature
ISBN 0-19-515713-3
LC 2002-8387
In question-and-answer format the author presents information on a variety of aspects of Islam. The "format allows readers to skip ahead to areas that interest them, including hot-button issues such as 'Why are Muslims so violent?' or 'Why do Muslim women wear veils and long garments?' In his answers, which are anywhere from a paragraph to several pages long, Esposito elegantly educates the reader through what the Qur'an says, how Muslims are influenced by their local cultures, and how the unique politics of Islamic countries affects Muslims' views." Publ Wkly
Includes bibliographical references

Fuller, Graham E.

A **world** without Islam. Little, Brown and Co. 2010 328p $25.99   **297**
1. East and West 2. Islam -- History 3. Islam -- Relations 4. Islamic civilization
ISBN 978-0-316-04119-5; 978-0-316-07201-4 ebook
LC 2009-54078
"A cogent argument demonstrating that a knowledgeable awareness of the rich dynamics that drive societies will better help diffuse tensions." Kirkus
Includes bibliographical references

Gardell, Mattias

In the name of Elijah Muhammad; Louis Farrakhan and the Nation of Islam. Duke Univ. Press 1996 482p $59.95; pa $23.95   **297**
1. Black Muslim leaders 2. Black Muslims 3. Civil rights activists
ISBN 0-8223-1852-0; 0-8223-1845-8 pa
LC 96-22666

"Some will appreciate the author's brief critical airing of claims of pre-Columbian Africans in America and accounts of Muslims and the slave trade, but he is at his best when focusing on the leaders and on the changing theology of the Nation of Islam (NOI) and similar African American groups in the 20th-century US. The book is balanced and well researched." Choice
Includes bibliographical references

Gordon, Matthew

Understanding Islam; origins, beliefs, practices, holy texts, sacred places. [by] Matthew S. Gordon. Sterling Pub. Co. 2010 112p pa $9.95   **297**
1. Islam
ISBN 978-1-90748-616-6
LC 2010-2376
This "exploration of Islam's history, beliefs, and practices . . . [addresses] issues such as political Islam, Islam and Israel, and Islamic fundamentalism." Publisher's note
Includes bibliographical references

Grieve, Paul

★ A **brief** guide to Islam; history, faith and politics: the complete introduction. Carroll & Graf 2006 433p il map pa $13.95   **297**
1. Islam
ISBN 0-7867-1804-8; 978-0-7867-1804-7
LC 2006-282191
"If you read only one book about Islam this year, this should be it." Publ Wkly

Griswold, Eliza

The **tenth** parallel; dispatches from the fault line between Christianity and Islam. Farrar, Straus and Giroux 2010 317p il map $27; ebook $12.99 **297**
1. Christianity and other religions 2. Christianity and other religions -- Islam 3. Islam -- Relations -- Christianity
ISBN 978-0-374-27318-7; 0-374-27318-9; 978-1-4299-7966-5 ebook; 1-4299-7966-6 ebook
LC 2010-1480
This "is a beautifully written book, full of arresting stories woven around a provocative issue—whether fundamentalism leads to violence—which Griswold investigates through individual lives rather than caricatures or abstractions." N Y Times Book Rev
Includes bibliographical references

Hazleton, Lesley

After the prophet; the epic story of the Shia-Sunni split in Islam. Doubleday 2009 239p map $26.95   **297**
1. Caliphs 2. Imams 3. Islam -- History 4. Islamic leaders 5. Prophets 6. Shi'ah 7. Spouses of prominent persons 8. Sunnis 9. Writers on religion
ISBN 978-0-385-52393-6
LC 2009-6498
"In June 632, the founder of Islam died without having clearly designated a successor. It seemed obvious to some that Muhammad's first cousin, Ali, who occupied the place of a son in the prophet's circle, would assume leadership. But Aisha, Muhammad's favorite, youngest, and most force-

ful wife, favored her father, and others backed Muhammad's greatest warrior. Ali would succeed, but not until 25 years later. Thus began the turmoil that eventuated in the bisection of Muslims into Sunni and Shia and that Hazleton describes in a new masterpiece of a kind of history seldom seen these days, in which the telling of a complicated, eventful story takes precedence over constant quotation of documents and squabbling with other historians." Booklist

Includes bibliographical references

Islam in der Gegenwart./English.

★ **Islam** in the world today; a handbook of politics, religion, culture, and society. edited by Werner Ende and Udo Steinbach. Cornell University Press 2010 1114p il $85   **297**
   1. Islam -- History 2. Islamic civilization
   ISBN 978-0-8014-4571-2
                             LC 2009-39910
This is "one of the most authoritative works on Islam in the modern world. . . . The volume is divided into three parts; the first is a historical overview of the Islamic world from its beginnings in the seventh century to the present, including a description of the different sects and movements of Islam and their influence in the world today. The second, and most extensive, section discusses the political role of Islam in the modern world, Islamic economics, social systems, and law. . . . The final section describes Islamic culture and civilization, including art, literature, and architecture, and their intersection with the West." Libr J

Includes bibliographical references

Johnson, Ian

A **mosque** in Munich; Nazis, the CIA, and the Muslim brotherhood in the West. Houghton Mifflin Harcourt 2010 318p $27   **297**
   1. Cold War 2. Cold war 3. Islam and politics 4. Islamic fundamentalism 5. Islamic fundamentalism -- Germany 6. Mosques 7. Mosques -- Germany
   ISBN 978-0-15-101418-7; 0-15-101418-3
                             LC 2009-35285
"Mr. Johnson brings to life a previously overlooked episode in the Muslim Brotherhood's story and thus in the story of Islamism as a whole: How a radical European beachhead came to be established in Munich. It should be said that the story takes some confusing turns; even alert readers may find themselves flipping to the list of characters at the back of the book, or to the index, to help them follow the narrative. But many of the details are astonishing and the larger implications for our own time disturbing." Wall Street J

Includes bibliographical references

Karsh, Efraim

Islamic imperialism; a history. Yale University Press 2006 276p map $30   **297**
   1. Imperialism 2. Islam -- History 3. Islam and politics 4. Jihad
   ISBN 0-300-10603-3
                             LC 2005-34836
The author "surveys for a general audience the region's Islamic political past. Parallel to his narrative, Karsh frequently contrasts the universalistic proclamations of Islam with cycles of imperial consolidation and fragmentation.

After recounting the Prophet Muhammad's religio-political establishment of Islam, and the discord about his legacy that continues today, Karsh narrates the battles over Muhammad's caliphate that eventuated in the Umayyad and Abbasid Empires. Karsh's commentary often looks forward to contemporary ideologues of Islam who ransack history to justify grievances. . . . An informative foundation for further exploration of Islamic history." Libr J

Kepel, Gilles

Jihad; the trail of political Islam. translated by Anthony F. Roberts. Harvard Univ. Press 2002 454p $33.95; pa $15.95   **297**
   1. Islam -- 20th century 2. Islam and politics 3. Jihad
   ISBN 0-674-00877-4; 0-674-01090-6 pa
                             LC 2002-17181
"Kepel argues that the terrorism seen today throughout the world results from the failure of Islamic fundamentalism and not its success. . . . Fascinating despite its copious detail." Booklist

Lewis, Bernard

★ The **crisis** of Islam; holy war and unholy terror. Modern Library 2003 xxxii, 184p map hardcover o.p. pa $13.95   **297**
   1. Islam and politics 2. Islamic fundamentalism 3. Jihad 4. Terrorism 5. Terrorism -- Religious aspects 6. Terrorism -- Religious aspects -- Islam 7. War -- Religious aspects -- Islam
   ISBN 0-679-64281-1; 0-8129-6785-2 pa
                             LC 2002-45219
"Written in an easily accessible style, this analysis provides a digestible overview for Westerners still asking why." Booklist

Includes bibliographical references

Naipaul, V. S.

Beyond belief; Islamic excursions among the converted peoples. Random House 1998 408p hardcover o.p. pa $15   **297**
   1. Islam 2. Islamic countries -- Description
   ISBN 0-375-70648-8 pa
                             LC 97-37350
"Retracing a voyage he made in 1979, the novelist and essayist journeys through Indonesia, Iran, Pakistan and Malaya, using Islam as a window on the animism, nationalism, capitalism and other isms he encounters there." N Y Times Book Rev

Nasr, Seyyed Hossein

Islam: religion, history, and civilization. HarperSanFrancisco 2002 xx, 198p pa $12.95   **297**
   1. Islam 2. Islamic civilization
   ISBN 0-06-050714-4
                             LC 2002-32810
This introduction to the world of Islam explores the following topics: What is Islam?; The doctrines and beliefs of Islam; Islamic practices and institutions; The history of Islam; Schools of Islamic thought; Islam in the contemporary world; Islam and other religions; The spiritual and religious significance of Islam.

"Provides compelling analysis of contemporary Islam and its conflicts without overwhelming the reader with information." Booklist

Includes bibliographical references

Nasr, Vali

★ The **Shia** revival; how conflicts within Islam will shape the future. Norton 2006 287p map $25.95   **297**

1. Islam and politics   2. Islam and politics -- Middle East   3. Shi'ah   4. Shiah   5. Shi'ah   6. Sunnites

ISBN 0-393-06211-2; 978-0-393-06211-3

LC 2006-12361

"So enlightening and perspective altering that no one concerned about the Middle East should miss reading it." Booklist

Includes bibliographical references

The Many faces of Islam; perspectives on a resurgent civilization. Nissim Rejwan {editor} University Press of Fla. 2000 282p $55   **297**

1. Islam   2. Islam -- 20th century   3. Islam -- Appreciation   4. Islam -- Essence, genius, nature   5. Islam and world politics

ISBN 0-8130-1807-2

LC 00-32587

The editor offers "perspectives on modern Islamic culture and religious practice. Seeking to dispel the perception that Islamic fundmentalism and extremism represent Islam in its entirety, Rejwan surveys the issues and provides numerous excerpts from modern writers and scholars, Muslim and non-Muslim, summarizing the many problems and dilemmas facing contemporary Muslims." Univ. Press Books for Public and Second Sch Libr, 2001

★ The Oxford dictionary of Islam; John L. Esposito, editor in chief. Oxford Univ. Press 2003 359p hardcover o.p. pa $18.95   **297**

1. Islam -- Dictionaries   2. Reference books

ISBN 0-19-512558-4; 0-19-512559-2 pa

LC 2002-30261

"This is an excellent resource for ready-reference collections in any library." Libr J

Includes bibliographical references

The Oxford history of Islam; {edited by} John Esposito. Oxford Univ. Press 1999 749p il map $49.95   **297**

1. Islam   2. Islam -- History

ISBN 0-19-510799-3

LC 99-13219

"Contributors treat, among other things, Muslim history, law, and society; art and architecture; and regional differences. Chapters on the 'Globalization of Islam' and 'Contemporary Islam' are particularly relevant to current events. . . . An ideal one-volume source." Libr J

Includes bibliographical references

297.092   Biography

Smith, Jane Idleman

Islam in America; {by} Jane I. Smith. Columbia Univ. Press 1999 251p il $60; pa $20.50   **297.092**

1. Islam   2. Islam -- United States

ISBN 0-231-10966-0; 0-231-10967-9 pa

LC 98-31943

The author discusses "the basic tenets of the Muslim faith, surveys the history of Islam in this country, and profiles the lifestyles, religious practices, and worldviews of American Muslims. Sections of the book cover the role of women in American Islam, raising and educating children, the use of products acceptable to Muslims, appropriate dress and behavior, concerns about prejudice and unfair treatment, and other issues related to life in {America}." Univ Press Books for Public and Second Sch Libr, 2001

Includes bibliographical references

297.1   Islam

Koran

★ The **meaning** of the glorious Koran; an explanatory translation by Marmaduke Pickthall; with an introduction by William Montgomery Watt. A.A. Knopf 1992 xxiv, 693p il $22   **297.1**

ISBN 0-679-41736-2; 978-0-679-41736-1

LC 92-52928

"The sacred scripture of Islam, regarded by Muslims as the Word of God, and except in sura I.—which is a prayer to God—and some few passages in which Muhammad or the angels speak in the first person, the speaker throughout is God." Ency Britannica

Wagner, Walter H.

Opening the Qur'an; introducing Islam's holy book. University of Notre Dame Press 2008 547p $45   **297.1**

ISBN 978-0-268-04415-2; 0-268-04415-5

LC 2008-27221

This "work makes an important contribution to the contemporary Muslim-Christian conversation." Catholic Hist Rev

Includes bibliographical references

The Qur'an: an encyclopedia; edited by Oliver Leaman. Taylor & Francis Group 2006 xxvii, 771p $280; pa $45   **297.1**

1. Reference books

ISBN 0-415-32639-7; 978-0-415-32639-1; 0-415-77529-9 pa; 978-0-415-32639-1 pa

"The objective of this encyclopedia is to fill a gap between general introductions and more technical works and provide the non-specialist with a resource covering all aspects of the text and its reception." Booklist

Includes bibliographical references

297.4 Sufism (Islamic mysticism)

Ernst, Carl W.

The **Shambhala** guide to Sufism. Shambhala Publs. 1997 xxi, 264p il pa $18.95   **297.4**
1. Sufism
ISBN 1-57062-180-2

LC 97-10189

This guide to Sufism "covers its beginnings, its basic philosophies, and its place in Islam." Libr J
Includes bibliographical references

297.8 Islamic sects and reform movements

Evanzz, Karl

The **messenger**: the rise and fall of Elijah Muhammad. Pantheon Bks. 1999 667p hardcover o.p. pa $18   **297.8**
1. Afro-Americans -- Biography 2. Black Muslim leaders 3. Black Muslims -- Biography 4. Civil rights activists
ISBN 0-679-77406-8 pa

LC 99-11826

A "critical biography of one of America's leading black nationalists of the 20th century. One of the founders of the Nation of Islam (NOI), Muhammad helped convert thousands of African Americans to the religion popularly known as the Black Muslims. Evanzz concludes that Muhammad was essentially a con man who used his considerable powers of persuasion to get rich and seduce women. Especially fascinating is Evanzz's extensive use of FBI files to make his case." Libr J
Includes bibliographical references

Levinsohn, Florence Hamlish

Looking for Farrakhan. Dee, I.R. 1997 305p $25   **297.8**
1. Biography, Individual 2. Black Muslim leaders 3. Black Muslims
ISBN 1-56663-157-2

LC 97-11335

Levinsohn's "biography, which reflects on the black experience and how it changed young Eugene Walcott into Louis Farrakhan, leader of the Nation of Islam, attempts to make sense of this prominent figure in American politics." Libr J

299 Religions not provided for elsewhere

Pagels, Elaine H.

★ The **Gnostic** Gospels; by Elaine Pagels. Random House 1979 xxxvi, 182p hardcover o.p. pa $12   **299**
1. Gnosticism
ISBN 0-679-72453-2 pa

LC 79-4764

An examination of the origins of early Christianity based on Gnostic texts rediscovered in the 20th century.

Pagels "writes for the layman, which is refreshing, and she does so lucidly, which is a challenge, especially when 'gnosticism' was regarded by its own adherents to be for the initiated only." Christ Sci Monit
Includes bibliographical references

Reitman, Janet

★ **Inside** Scientology. Houghton Mifflin Harcourt 2011 xx, 444p $28   **299**
1. Scientology
ISBN 978-0-618-88302-8; 0-618-88302-9

LC 2010-49837

An expose "culled from hundreds of interviews with active Scientologists and defectors alike. Reitman brings an almost clinical detachment to the religion's story, from its birth in the sci-fi imagination of founder L. Ron Hubbard to its current Hollywood heyday. Her revelations—including abuse allegations against church leader David Miscavige and details about the organization's aggressive courtship of Tom Cruise—come with impressive backup." Entertainment Wkly
Includes bibliographical references

Wilkinson, Richard H.

★ The **complete** gods and goddesses of ancient Egypt. Thames & Hudson 2003 256p il $39.95 **299**
1. Egyptian mythology 2. Goddesses, Egyptian 3. Gods and goddesses 4. Gods, Egyptian
ISBN 0-500-05120-8

LC 2002-110321

"Wilkinson's gorgeously illustrated book adds new dimension to popular literature on ancient Egypt. . . . And once readers open the book to look at the pictures, they well may stay to read the well-organized, comprehensive, clearly written text." Booklist
Includes bibliographical references

★ The Gnostic Bible; edited by Willis Barnstone and Marvin Meyer. Rev. ed.; Shambhala 2009 881p pa $29.95   **299**
1. Gnosticism
ISBN 978-1-59030-631-4; 1-59030-631-7

LC 2008-36431

"The book provides Gnostic texts from their Jewish origins, into early Christianities, on into the medieval world. Though it concentrates on the early Jewish-Christian matrix of early Gnosticism, the collection . . . manifests the breadth and depth of Gnostic variations in neo-Platonist, Manichean, Mandean, Islam, and Cathar movements." Choice
Includes bibliographical references

299.5 Religions of East and Southeast Asian origin

I ching

★ The **classic** of changes; a new translation of the I Ching as interpreted by Wang Bi. translated by Richard John Lynn. Columbia Univ. Press 1994 602p $27.95; pa $17.95   **299.5**
1. Divination
ISBN 0-231-08294-0; 0-231-08295-9 pa

LC 93-43999

"Most available editions of the I Ching are based on the James Legge translation, a work produced over 140 years ago and characterized by romanticized and idiomatic Victorian English. Although not more accurate or revealing than the Legge, this new translation is welcome because of its crisp usage of modern-day English." Libr J

Lao-tzu

★ **Tao** te ching; the new translation from Tao te ching: the definitive edition. translation by Jonathan Star. Jeremy P. Tarcher/Penguin 2008 103p pa $10   **299.5**

ISBN 978-1-58542-618-8

LC 2007-44948

"Chinese Taoist text attributed to Lao Tzu, supposedly an elder contemporary of Confucius (551?-479 BC). . . . A brief work in eighty-one-paragraphs in both verse and prose, it probably dates from the 4th or 3rd century BC, although some believe it may be as early as the 6th century BC. Because of its concise, poetic language, its meaning is subject to many interpretations. It is generally agreed that it is both a mystical book about union with the absolute, and a political handbook on how to rule and survive in chaotic times." Reader's Ency. 4th edition

Yang Lihui

★ **Handbook** of Chinese mythology; [by] Lihui Yang and Deming An, with Jessica Anderson Turner. ABC-CLIO 2005 293p il $75   **299.5**

1. Asian mythology

ISBN 1-57607-806-X

LC 2005-13851

"This volume provides useful information to the reader. The authors' credibility and in-depth scholarship offer a rare opportunity to experience Chinese mythology through Chinese eyes." Booklist

Includes bibliographical references

299.6 Religions originating among Black Africans and people of Black African descent

Chevannes, Barry

Rastafari: roots and ideology. Syracuse Univ. Press 1994 298p hardcover o.p. pa $19.95 **299.6**

1. Ras Tafari movement 2. Rastafari movement

ISBN 0-8156-0296-0 pa

LC 94-18608

"Vital for students of African American religions and Caribbean religions, but also of interest to anthropologists, sociologists, and historians." Choice

Includes bibliographical references

★ The **Encyclopedia** of African and African-American religions; Stephen D. Glazier, editor. Routledge 2000 xx, 452p il maps $150   **299.6**

1. African Americans -- Religion 2. African Americans -- Religion -- Encyclopedias 3. Blacks -- America -- Religion 4. Blacks -- Religion 5. Reference books

ISBN 0-415-92245-3

LC 00-59136

"This encyclopedia is a good starting point for understanding the complex interrelationships among African, African American, and European religious beliefs, practices, and traditions in a global context." Libr J

299.7 Religions of North American native origin

Castaneda, Carlos

The **teachings** of Don Juan; a Yaqui way of knowledge. University of Calif. Press 1968 196p $32.50; pa $16.95   **299.7**

1. Hallucinogenic drugs and religious experience 2. Mystics 3. Yaqui Indians -- Religion

ISBN 0-520-21755-1; 0-520-21757-8 pa

"This book is the record of a young anthropologist's experiences as the apprentice of a [Yaqui] Indian sorcerer. Over a period of four years, Mr. Castaneda paid intermittant visits to Don Juan, first in Arizona, then in Sonora, Mexico." N Y Times Book Rev

Nabokov, Peter

Where the lightning strikes; the lives of American Indian sacred places. Viking 2005 350p hardcover o.p. pa $17   **299.7**

1. Geographical perception 2. Indians of North America -- Religion 3. Indians of North America -- Social life and customs 4. Native Americans -- Religion 5. Sacred space 6. Sacred space -- United States

ISBN 0-670-03432-0; 0-14-303881-8 pa

LC 2005-42227

The author presents "16 'biographies of place,' each of a habitat illustrating the bond between North American Indian cultures and their environment perpetuated by myths, legends, and rituals. . . . The author's careful documentation of unbroken reverence for these sacred places powerfully illuminates Native American attachment to the earth itself." Booklist

Includes bibliographical references

Popol vuh

★ **Popol** vuh; the Mayan book of the dawn of life. translated by Dennis Tedlock; with commentary based on the ancient knowledge of the modern Quiché Maya. rev ed; Simon & Schuster 1996 388p il maps pa $15   **299.7**

1. Mayas -- Religion 2. Native Americans -- Religion

ISBN 0-684-81845-0

LC 95-46822

A modern translation of the 16th century Mayan holy book.

"Tedlock's translation splendidly combines scholarship, imagination, and literary sensitivity. His photographs (derived from field work in Guatemala) vividly illustrate the text, and the notes (based on his collaboration with a contemporary Quiché shaman) fascinate and inform." Libr J

Includes bibliographical references

300 SOCIAL SCIENCES, SOCIOLOGY & ANTHROPOLOGY

300 Social sciences

Isserman, Maurice

The **other** American: the life of Michael Harrington. PublicAffairs 2000 449p $28.50; pa $14   **300**

1. Authors 2. College teachers 3. Inspirational writers 4. Nonfiction writers 5. Political scientists 6. Political scientists -- United States -- Biography 7. Social critics 8. Social scientists -- United States -- Biography 9. Socialists -- United States -- Biography 10. Writers on politics

ISBN 1-89162-030-4; 1-58648-036-7 pa

LC 99-56654

This biography of the leftist social critic and author of the influential The other America (1962) is "also a veritable Zagat's guide through the left sectarian factions of the last three-quarters of the 20th century." N Y Times Book Rev

Includes bibliographical references

Oxford University Press

★ **Dictionary** of the social sciences; edited by Craig Calhoun. Oxford Univ. Press 2002 563p $75   **300**

1. Reference books 2. Social sciences 3. Social sciences -- Dictionaries

ISBN 0-19-512371-9

LC 00-68151

This dictionary provides "definitions of key terms, offering entries that also discuss the intellectual issues behind the terms' usage. The entries cover all the social sciences except for law, education, and public administration. . . . Some 275 biographies are included." Libr J

Includes bibliographical references

Rosenblatt, Roger

★ **Kayak** morning; Roger Rosenblatt. Ecco 2012 160p.   **300**

ISBN 9780062084033

In this memoir, the author questions "why [he] cannot come to terms with his grief [over the death of his 38-year-old daughter] two and a half years later. As [Roger] Rosenblatt, a writer and professor of English and writing at Stony Brook University, takes up kayaking near his home in Quogue on Long Island, he begins to contemplate his connection to nature and his place in it by observing the sea. The kayak becomes a metaphorical conveyance as he floats from one topic to the next . . . everything from life versus death to personal memories and classical literature. . . . The piece . . . combines short vignettes, poetic verses, snippets of conversations and meaningful quotations." (Publishers Weekly)

Social sciences index. Wilson, H.W.   **300**

1. Reference books 2. Social sciences -- Periodicals -- Indexes

"Author-subject index to over 400 periodicals in the social sciences. Specific subject headings and many cross-references aid research. Book reviews indexed by author in a separate section." Ref Sources for Small & Medium-sized Libr. 6th edition

301 Sociology and anthropology

Best, Joel

Stat-spotting; a field guide to identifying dubious data. University of California Press 2008 132p il $19.95   **301**

1. Statistics

ISBN 978-0-520-25746-7; 0-520-25746-4

LC 2008-17175

This "is an easily digestible guide to understanding how simple miscalculations, botched translations and inappropriate graphics misled the American public. This concise book helps readers understand how politicians and the media twist statistics to match the goals of their agenda. Author Joel Best describes how things like bloating figures by misplacing a decimal point or using enlarged graphics to visually distract readers from analyzing the data objectively. If you want a better understanding of the reality behind those charts and graphs you see in books, on television and in the media then you need to read this book." Univ Press Books for Public and Second Sch Libr, 2009

Includes bibliographical references

Encyclopedia of sociology; Edgar F. Borgatta, editor-in-chief, Rhonda Montgomery, managing editor. 2nd ed; Macmillan Ref. USA 2000 5v set $575   **301**

1. Reference books 2. Sociology 3. Sociology -- Encyclopedias

ISBN 0-02-864853-6

LC 00-28402

This set includes about 400 articles covering all fields and subfields of sociology: social psychology, social demography, social anthropology, social history, social geography, social ecology, certain branches of political science, political economy, and sociolinguistics. More recent studies include affirmative action, alernative lifestyles, genocide, information society, sexually transmitted diseases and terrorism

Required reading; sociology's most influential books. edited by Dan Clawson. University of Mass. Press 1998 221p hardcover o.p. pa $17.95 **301**

1. Best books 2. Reference books 3. Sociology -- Bibliography

ISBN 1-55849-153-8 pa

LC 98-11944

This volume "identifies and discusses 17 of the 'most influential' books in sociology written during the last 25 years. . . . The power of this book lies in reconsiderations by eminent sociologists of important titles in light of a quarter of a century's worth of political, social, and economic change." Libr J

Includes bibliographical references

World of sociology; Joseph M. Palmisano, editor. Gale Group 2001 2v il set $160 **301**

1. Reference books 2. Sociology -- Encyclopedias

ISBN 0-7876-4965-1

LC 00-48399

This is a "subject-specific guide to concepts, theories, discoveries, pioneers, issues and ethical questions associated with sociology. It includes approximately 1,000-1,500 alphabetically arranged topical essays, definitions and biographies." Publisher's note

Includes bibliographical references

302 Specific topics in sociology and anthropology

Friedman, Jenny Lynn

The **busy** family's guide to volunteering; do good, have fun, make a difference as a family! Robins Lane Press 2003 206p pa $14.95 **302**

1. Family 2. Family -- Time management 3. Family -- United States 4. Voluntarism -- United States 5. Volunteer work

ISBN 1-589-04012-0

LC 2003-12054

"Each chapter includes book resources for parents and children as well as contact information to many agencies, both public and private and in multiple fields, such as social service, environment, and politics. . . . Written for parents, The Busy Family's Guide would also be appropriate for adolescents who wish to involve themselves and their families in meaningful work. Highly recommended for public libraries." LibrJ

Includes bibliographical references

Gladwell, Malcolm

Outliers; the story of success. Little, Brown and Co. 2008 309p $27.99 **302**

1. Success 2. Successful people

ISBN 978-0-316-01792-3; 0-316-01792-2

LC 2008-32824

Gladwell's "subject is success — an 'outlier' is a superachiever, like Bill Gates or the four Beatles, and Gladwell wants to know what sets these titans apart. It's not mere talent, he insists, offering up instead one thrilling, exquisitely unfurled counterargument after another. . . . There are both brilliant yarns and life lessons here: Outliers is riveting science, self-help, and entertainment, all in one book." Entertainment Wkly

Includes bibliographical references

The **tipping** point; how little things can make a big difference. Malcolm Gladwell. Little, Brown 2000 viii, 279 p $27.99 **302**

1. Causation 2. Contagion (Social psychology) 3. Context effects (Psychology) 4. Social psychology

ISBN 0316316962; 9780316316965

LC 99047576

It was the author's intent to demonstrate "that ideas, products, messages and behaviors 'spread just like viruses do.' . . . [Malcolm Gladwell] follows the growth of word-of-mouth epidemics" triggered with the help of three pivotal types. These are Connectors, sociable personalities who bring people together; Mavens, who like to pass along knowledge; and Salesmen, adept at persuading the unenlightened. (Paul Revere, for example, was a Maven and a Connector). . . . [The book] offers a smorgasbord of . . . snippets summarizing research on topics such as conversational patterns, infants' crib talk, judging other people's character, cheating habits in schoolchildren, memory sharing among families or couples, and the dehumanizing effects of prisons. (Publishers Weekly)

302.2 Communication

Biedermann, Hans

★ **Dictionary** of symbolism; cultural icons and the meanings behind them. translated by James Hulbert. Meridan Book 1994 465p il pa $25 **302.2**

1. Reference books 2. Signs and symbols

ISBN 0-452-01118-3

LC 93-30616

This dictionary "incorporates symbols that originated in Asia, Africa, Europe and the 'New World.' There are almost 600 entries from mythology, fairy tale, psychology, religion, and sociology, plus historical and legendary figures. With 2000 black-and-white illustrations, the book is highly attractive. The symbols are accompanied by thorough interpretations based on various sources." SLJ

Includes bibliographical references

Tannen, Deborah

You just don't understand; women and men in conversation. Quill 2001 342p pa $13.95 **302.2**

1. Conversation 2. Sex differences (Psychology)

ISBN 978-0-06-095962-3; 0-06-095962-2

"Aside from the vivid examples and lively prose, what makes this book particularly engaging is that the author makes linguistics . . . interesting and usable." N Y Times Book Rev

Includes bibliographical references

302.23 Media (Means of communication)

Alterman, Eric

What liberal media? the truth about bias and the news. Basic Books 2003 322p $25; pa $15 **302.23**

1. Journalism -- Objectivity 2. Journalistic ethics 3. Right and left (Political science)

ISBN 0-465-00176-9; 0-465-00177-7 pa

LC 2002-152568

"Whether readers agree with Alterman or not, his writing on the business of opinion making is eye-opening. This book will be required reading for anyone in politics or journalism, or anyone curious about their complicated nexus." Publ Wkly

Includes bibliographical references

Charnock, Elizabeth

E-habits; what you must do to optimize your professional digital presence. McGraw-Hill 2010 250p il $22.95; ebook $22.95 **302.23**

1. Internet -- Social aspects 2. Social networking
ISBN 978-0-07-162995-9; 0-07-162995-5; 978-0-07-174055-5 ebook; 0-07-174055-4 ebook

LC 2010001201

The author aims to show readers how to present themselves "in the best possible light with every electronic action—whether on the Internet or within [their] own organization[s]. Elizabeth Charnock . . . reveals what everyday activities—looking for a job, applying for a loan, searching for romance, e-mailing coworkers—tell others about us." Publisher's note

Durham, M. Gigi

The **Lolita** effect; the media sexualization of young girls and what we can do about it. [by] M. Gigi Durham, Ph.D. Overlook Press 2008 320p $24.95; pa $14.95 **302.23**

1. Body image 2. Girls -- Sexual behavior 3. Girls -- United States 4. Mass media 5. Parenting 6. Teenage girls in popular culture -- United States -- History
ISBN 978-1-5902-00636; 1-5902-0063-2; 978-1-5902-0215-9 pa; 1-5902-0215-5 pa

In this "exploration of the media's exploitation of girls, Durham exposes the links between destructive teenage self-images and the popular, highly sexed, and negative representations of girls in magazines, television programs, and movies. . . . [Her] provocative and erudite study of the demeaning way society views girls serves to both alarm and educate; consider it required reading for parents and their daughters." Booklist

Includes bibliographical references

Gladstone, Brooke

The **influencing** machine; Brooke Gladstone on the media. illustrated by Josh Neufeld; with additional penciling by Randy Jones and Susann Ferris-Jones. W. W. Norton 2011 xxii, 170p ill. (chiefly col.) (hbk.) $23.95; (hbk.) $16.95 **302.23**

1. Broadcast journalism -- Comic books, strips, etc. 2. Broadcast journalism -- Graphic novels 3. Graphic novels 4. Journalism -- Comic books, strips, etc. 5. Journalism -- Graphic novels
ISBN 0393077799; 9780393077797

LC 2011009820

This work of graphic nonfiction explores the history of media's influence. . . . [F]rom the "Acta Diurna" posted in ancient Rome to the outcries over President Adams's Alien and Sedition Acts and McCarthy's Red Scare, [Brooke] Gladstone traces not only the birth of the press, but also its various muzzles. The press will not always stay silent, as she illustrates with Daniel Ellsberg and the Pentagon Papers. . . . Yet government opacity still abounds, and Gladstone pointedly wonders if secrecy really makes us safer. . . . Gladstone points to seven key biases that cognizant media consumers should worry about: commercial, bad news, status quo, access, visual, narrative, and fairness. These dovetail . . . into a . . . discussion of war journalism. (Publishers Weekly)

"Gladstone's is an indispensible guide to our ever-evolving media landscape that's brought vividly to life." Publ Wkly

Includes bibliographical references (p. 163-170).

Gonzalez, Juan, 1969-

News for all the people; Juan Gonzalez and Joseph Torres. Verso 2011 432p $29.95 **302.23**

1. African American journalists 2. Hispanic American journalists 3. Historical literature 4. Journalists 5. Mass media 6. Press -- United States
ISBN 978-1-84467-687-3

This book provide[s] a history of the development of "the American system of news," with emphasis on the government's role . . . and . . . construct[s] an account of the struggle across the "fundamental fault-line" of race and ethnicity that shaped both mainstream and dissident media. . . . The stories of Hispanic, Native-American, African-American, and Asian-American journalists risking lives and well-being to raise their voices, constitute the true heart of this book. Some of the pioneers' names are reasonably familiar, . . . [b]ut there are dozens of others rescued from obscurity, ranging from Joaquín de Lisa and Joseph Antonio Boniquet, founders in 1809 of El Mensajero of New Orleans, to Ruben Salazar of Los Angeles, assassinated while covering a riot in 1970. (Columbia Journalism Review)

Jones, Gerard

Killing monsters; why children need fantasy, super heroes, and make-believe violence. foreword by Lynn Ponton. Basic Bks. 2002 261p $25; pa $15 **302.23**

1. Children 2. Fantasy 3. Fantasy in children 4. Fantasy in mass media 5. Heroes in mass media 6. Mass media 7. Mass media and children 8. Monsters in mass media 9. Popular culture -- Psychological aspects 10. Violence 11. Violence in mass media
ISBN 0-465-03695-3; 0-465-03696-1 pa

LC 2001-52667

"Although not an academic, the author has done his homework. He presents his case convincingly, and the concluding notes provide support." SLJ

Includes bibliographical references

McLuhan, Marshall

★ The **global** village; transformations in world life and media in the 21st century. [by] Marshall McLuhan and Bruce R. Powers. Oxford Univ. Press 1989 220p il hardcover o.p. pa $14.95 **302.23**

1. Mass media 2. Technology -- Social aspects 3. Technology and civilization
ISBN 0-19-507910-8 pa

LC 88-22718

This book "was written, according to Powers, between 1974 and 1980 . . . and 'put together' between 1976 and 1984. McLuhan's thesis has always been that electronic technologies have been altering and reconstituting people in ways they don't understand and causing them to lose their private identities. This book probes the same theme from different angles, but with the same McLuhanesque all-over-the-place reasoning." Libr J

Includes bibliographical references

Palfrey, John

Born digital; understanding the first generation of digital natives. [by] John Palfrey and Urs Gasser. Basic Books 2008 375p $25.95 **302.23**

1. Information society 2. Information society -- Social aspects 3. Information technology 4. Internet -- Social aspects 5. Internet and children 6. Internet and teenagers 7. Technological innovations -- Social aspects

ISBN 9780465005154

LC 2008-21538

The authors "document the myriad ways downloading, text-messaging, Massively Multiplayer Online Games-playing, YouTube-watching youth are transforming society. Energetic, expert, and forward-looking, the authors serve as envoys between the generations, addressing issues that worry parents and educators, from privacy and safety concerns to the quality of digital information, the psychological and physical effects of information overload and excessive on-line time, and legal and ethical issues, all the while stressing the need for digital literacy and critical thinking." Booklist

Includes bibliographical references

Postman, Neil

Amusing ourselves to death; public discourse in the age of show business. Viking 1985 184p hardcover o.p. pa $14 **302.23**

1. Mass media 2. Television broadcasting

ISBN 0-14-009438-5 pa

LC 85-5335

The author argues that the constant exposure to television has contributed to a decline in America's intellectual life.

"A sustained, withering and thought-provoking attack on television and what it is doing to us." Publ Wkly

Includes bibliographical references

History of the mass media in the United States; an encyclopedia. edited by Margaret A. Blanchard; commissioning editor Carol J. Burwash. Fitzroy Dearborn Pubs. 1998 xxxii, 752p il $150 **302.23**

1. Mass media 2. Mass media -- United States -- History

ISBN 1-57958-012-2

LC 98-233183

This volume examines the ways in which mass media affects and is affected by United States society. From the 1690s to 1990, the alphabetically arranged entries cover subjects ranging from newspaper history to media coverage of wars, court cases, legislation and interest groups.

"Beautifully designed, with a nice clear typeface, this work is also enhanced by superb illustrations and well-chosen photographs. . . . This volume is outstanding." Booklist

302.3   Social interaction within groups

King, Larry

How to talk to anyone, anytime, anywhere; the secrets of good communication. [by] Larry King with Bill Gilbert. Crown 1994 220p hardcover o.p. pa $12.95 **302.3**

1. Communication 2. Conversation

ISBN 0-517-88453-4 pa

LC 94-31458

King "shows you how to break the ice with strangers, what to say at a wedding or a funeral, and how to sell yourself to a prospective employer—or interview a prospective employee. He gives his secrets for how to survive if you have to appear on radio or television, and how to recover from making a blooper." Publisher's note

Locke, John L.

The **de**-voicing of society; why we don't talk to each other anymore. Simon & Schuster 1998 256p hardcover o.p. pa $18.95 **302.3**

1. Communication 2. Conversation 3. Conversation analysis -- Social aspects

ISBN 0-684-85574-7 pa

LC 98-14921

"Locke offers a pointed diagnosis of the isolated society created by disembodied interaction. Ever more atomized and shackled to video screens, modern people watch and type, rather than talk. The loss, argues Locke, can be discerned in the purposes of talk, specifically gossip, in creating relationships and social networks. . . . An insightful lamentation about a palpable social pandemic." Booklist

Includes bibliographical references

Sciolino, Elaine

La seduction; how the French play the game of life. Times Books/Henry Holt 2011 338p il **302.3**

1. Seduction 2. Sex customs -- France -- History

ISBN 0-8050-9115-7; 9780805091151

LC 2010049572

According to the author, "seduction plays a crucial role in how the French relate to one another—not just in romantic relationships but also in how they conduct business, enjoy food and drink, define style, engage in intellectual debate, elect politicians, and project power around the world. While sexual repartee and conquest remain at the heart of seduction, for the French seduction has become a philosophy of life, even an ideology, that can confuse outsiders. In [this book, Sciolino looks at] . . . how seduction works in all areas, analyzing its limits as well as its power." (Publisher's note)

The author "deals with the subtle and cultural ways seduction shapes all aspects of French life. She takes a broad approach and writes less about the sexual associations of the word and more about the pleasure game the French play in order to 'attract or influence, to win over, even if just for fun.' Ms. Sciolino's pedigree as a commentator on things French is first class. She was a student in France in 1969 and returned to live and work there as a correspondent for Newsweek, then later as the Bureau Chief of The New York Times in Paris, and now as a correspondent for the paper. She finds French life permeated with the seduction factor, and in a journalistic fashion looks at it in an array of fields, including politics, foreign affairs, literature, history, film, advertising, beauty, scent, fashion, entertaining, food and wine, and sex, and makes her mostly French victims unveil some rules and secrets." Daily Beast

Includes bibliographical references

302.4 Social interaction between groups

Maalouf, Amin

In the name of identity; violence and the need to belong. translated from the French by Barbara Bray. Arcade Pub. 2001 164p $22.95 **302.4**
1. Group identity 2. Identity (Psychology) 3. Violence
ISBN 1-55970-593-0

LC 2001-24929

"This is an important addition to contemporary literature on diversity, nationalism, race and international politics." Publ Wkly

302.5 Relation of individual to society

Olds, Jacqueline

The **lonely** American; drifting apart in the twenty-first century. [by] Jacqueline Olds and Richard S. Schwartz. Beacon Press 2008 228p $24.95 **302.5**
1. Loneliness 2. Loneliness -- United States 3. Social isolation -- United States
ISBN 978-0-8070-0034-2; 0-8070-0034-5

LC 2008-19339

The authors "paint a tragic picture of a nation of individual units—families, couples and, increasingly, single people—that have all but ceased to function as a society. While the authors focus largely on the psychological impact of all this isolation, they also explain its physical toll on Americans and their world. Not only is social isolation an indicator for substance abuse, violent crime and early death, it is also linked to greater consumption of consumer goods. . . . In keeping with their profession as psychoanalysts, Olds and Schwartz maintain a kind and caring tone throughout The Lonely American, neither scolding nor scoffing at the nation of individuals Americans have become." PopMatters

Includes bibliographical references and index.

303 Social processes

Macpherson, Heidi Slettedahl

Britain and the Americas; culture, politics, and history: a multidisciplinary encyclopedia. edited by Wil Kaufman and Heidi Slettedahl Macpherson. ABC-CLIO 2005 3v il set $270 **303**
1. Reference books
ISBN 1-85109-431-8

LC 2004-24655

"Included in the scope of this interdisciplinary work are historical events (Boston Tea Party, Falklands War, Yalta Conference); places (Brazil, Jamestown, Ontario); and economic, social, political, and cultural forces (Fur trade; Nuclear weapons; Reggae; Slave trade, Atlantic; Treaties, Britain-U.S.). . . . There are more than 400 signed entries in alphabetical order, and each includes see also's and references. The entries average about two pages, with the longest, Cold War and Explorers, British in the Americas, at seven pages each. There is one combined subject and person index in volume 3. While the references are helpful and well researched, the work could benefit from one comprehen-

sive bibliography. Well written and engaging enough to be used for research or to be read on its own for enjoyment's sake." Booklist

303.3 Coordination and control

Corning, Peter

The **fair** society; [by] Peter Corning. University of Chicago Press 2011 237p $27.50 **303.3**
1. Basic needs 2. Fairness 3. Nonfiction 4. Social contract 5. Social ethics 6. Social justice 7. Social policy
ISBN 978-0-226-11627-3; 0-226-11627-1

LC 2010021771

It was the author's intent to demonstrate "that human nature has evolved in such a way as to create a natural revulsion to [unfair situations] . . . He recounts various evolutionary arguments for the notion that our hunter-gatherer ancestors possessed a deep sense of fairness and developed 'a pattern of egalitarian sharing' in which dominance behaviors were actively resisted by coalitions of other group members." . . .Corning endeavors to show that the capitalist system as currently practiced in the United States and elsewhere is manifestly unfair. . . . he proposes a new type of society founded on a biosocial contract, which he describes as a truly voluntary bargain among various (empowered) stakeholders over how the benefits and obligations in a society are to be apportioned among the members' that is grounded in our growing understanding of human nature and the basic purpose of a human society.'" (American Scientist)

"Corning argues that both capitalism and socialism fail the fairness test—both in theory and in practice—and he calls for a new social contract based on three complementary fairness principles: equality in relation to our basic needs, equity (or merit) in relation to our personal efforts and accomplishments, and reciprocity—an obligation for everyone to contribute a fair share in return for the benefits they receive from society. Corning also proposes a set of transformative economic and political reforms that would move us toward the ideal of what he terms a Fair Society, including full employment and a 'basic needs guarantee' for all of our people, a shift in our economic system toward stakeholder (versus shareholder) capitalism, a strong effort to promote cooperative, not-for-profit community development and, not least, a lifelong community service ethic that would include a year or two of national service for all who are able to do so." Politics and Life Sciences

Includes bibliographical references

Huxley, Aldous

★ **Brave** new world revisited. Harper & Row 1958 147p hardcover o.p. pa $11.95 **303.3**
1. Brainwashing 2. Culture 3. Propaganda 4. Totalitarianism
ISBN 0-06-089852-6 pa

In response to his 1932 novel Brave new world "Huxley reconsiders his prophecies and fears that some of these may be coming true much sooner than he thought." Oxford Companion to Engl Lit. 5th edition

Rosenberg, Tina

Join the club; how peer pressure can transform the world. W.W. Norton & Company 2011 xxiv, 402p $25.95   **303.3**

1. Peer pressure 2. Social change 3. Social groups
ISBN 978-0-393-06858-0

LC 2010-52146

"A solid, sweeping examination of peer pressure as a force for social change." Kirkus
Includes bibliographical references

Sowell, Thomas

The **quest** for cosmic justice. Free Press 1999 214p $25; pa $14   **303.3**

1. Equality 2. Justice 3. Social justice
ISBN 0-684-86462-2; 0-684-86463-0 pa

LC 99-31470

The author "presents his case in clear, convincing, and accessible language." Libr J
Includes bibliographical references

Surowiecki, James

The **wisdom** of crowds; why the many are smarter than the few and how collective wisdom shapes business, economies, societies and nations. Doubleday 2004 xxi, 296p $24.95; pa $14   **303.3**

1. Consensus (Social sciences) 2. Crowds 3. Intellect 4. Social psychology
ISBN 0-385-50386-5; 0-385-72170-6 pa

LC 2003-70095

The author "analyzes the concept of collective wisdom and applies it to various areas of the social sciences, including economics and politics. . . . This work is an intriguing study of collective intelligence and how it works in contemporary society." Libr J
Includes bibliographical references

Wills, Garry

Certain trumpets; the call of leaders. Simon & Schuster 1994 336p il hardcover o.p. pa $16 **303.3**

1. Leadership 2. Abolitionists 3. Authors 4. Baseball executives 5. Choreographers 6. Christian Science leaders 7. Civil rights activists 8. Clergy 9. Columnists 10. Computer software executives 11. Dance teachers 12. Dancers 13. Diplomats 14. Dramatists 15. Emperors 16. Generals 17. Governors 18. Handicapped 19. Heads of state 20. Humanitarians 21. Journalists 22. Kings 23. Leadership 24. Mayors 25. Members of Congress 26. Newspaper editors 27. Nobel laureates for peace 28. Nonfiction writers 29. Philanthropists 30. Philatelists 31. Philosophers 32. Political and social philosophers 33. Political leaders 34. Popes 35. Power (Social sciences) 36. Presidential candidates 37. Presidents 38. Social activists 39. Social reformers 40. Spouses of presidents 41. Statesmen 42. United Nations officials 43. Writers on politics 44. Writers on religion
ISBN 0-671-65702-X; 978-0-684-80138-4 pa; 0-684-80138-8 pa

LC 94-6526

The author "has chosen 16 figures who exemplify a distinctive leadership type—for example, military (Napoleon),

charismatic (King David), saintly (Catholic worker activist Dorothy Day). Each leader is contrasted with an 'anti-type' who, in Wills's judgment, failed to capitalize on strengths similar to those of his or her successful counterpart. . . . Wills pairs Martha Graham with Madonna, Socrates with Ludwig Wittgenstein, Eleanor Roosevelt with Nancy Reagan in a wise, witty, entertaining look at the psychology of leaders and their followers." Publ Wkly
Includes bibliographical references

Young-Bruehl, Elisabeth

The **anatomy** of prejudices. Harvard Univ. Press 1996 632p hardcover o.p. pa $18.95   **303.3**

1. Prejudices
ISBN 0-674-03191-1 pa

LC 95-43754

"Clearly written and accessible to general as well as scholarly readers, this is a major work in personality and culture that asserts the plurality rather than the unity of prejudice." Libr J
Includes bibliographical references

303.4   Social change

Baker, Stephen

The **numerati**. Houghton Mifflin Co. 2008 244p $26   **303.4**

1. Data processing 2. Human behavior -- Mathematical models 3. Mathematical models 4. Mathematical statistics -- Data processing 5. Privacy -- Social aspects 6. Social interaction -- Mathematical models
ISBN 978-0-618-78460-8; 0-618-78460-8

LC 2008-17830

The author "spotlights a new breed of entrepreneurial mathematicians (the numerati) engaged in harnessing the avalanche of private data individuals provide when they use a credit card, donate to a cause, surf the Internet—or even make a phone call. . . . An intriguing but disquieting look at a not too distant future when our thoughts will remain private, but computers will disclose our tastes, opinions, habits and quirks to curious parties, not all of whom have our best interests at heart." Publ Wkly
Includes bibliographical references

Carr, Nicholas

The **big** switch; rewiring the world, from Edison to Google. W. W. Norton & Company 2008 278p $25.95; pa $16.95   **303.4**

1. Computers and civilization 2. Information technology 3. Internet 4. Technological innovations
ISBN 978-0-393-06228-1; 0-393-06228-7; 978-0-393-33394-7 pa; 0-393-33394-9 pa

LC 2007-38084

The author "examines the future of the Internet, which he says may one day completely replace the desktop PC as all computing services are delivered over the Net as a utility, the Internet morphing into one giant 'World Wide Computer.'" Booklist
Includes bibliographical references

Diamond, Jared M.

★ **Guns,** germs, and steel; the fates of human societies. [by] Jared Diamond. Norton 2005 518p il map $24.95   **303.4**

1. Environmental influence on humans 2. Ethnology 3. Food supply 4. Social change 5. Technology and civilization

ISBN 0-393-06131-0; 978-0-393-06131-4

LC 2005-284261

"This book poses a simple but profound question about the distribution of wealth and power in the modern world: 'Why weren't Native Americans, Africans, and Aboriginal Australians the ones who decimated, subjugated, or exterminated Europeans and Asians?'. . . To explore the discrepancies in technological and cultural development he looks not at peoples but at places, and at the natural resources available to different indigenous populations since 11,000 B.C. The scope and the explanatory power of this book are astounding." New Yorker [review of 1997 edition]

Includes bibliographical references

Ferris, Timothy

The **science** of liberty; democracy, reason and the laws of nature. Harper 2010 368p $26.99 **303.4**

1. Democracy 2. Liberty -- History 3. Science -- History 4. Science -- Political aspects 5. Science and civilization

ISBN 978-0-06-078150-7; 0-06-078150-5

LC 2009-27505

The author "argues that science and the rise of 'science societies' are the fundamental drivers of liberty and democracy. . . . Ferris traces the dual scientific and democratic revolutions from their Renaissance, Enlightenment, and early modern origins to the titanic twentieth-century battles between the liberal democracies and their fascist and communist rivals. Ferris also explores the scientific orientation of the United States' founders, such as Thomas Jefferson and Benjamin Franklin, and its relevance to their constitutional thinking and their noble 'experiment' of a new nation. The Science of Liberty is sweeping and provocative, even if many may still doubt that science can extinguish prejudices, parochialisms, and illiberal impulses." Foreign Affairs

Includes bibliographical references

Gershon, Ilana

The **breakup** 2.0; disconnecting over new media. Cornell University Press 2010 214p il $22.95 **303.4**

1. Dating (Social customs) 2. Digital media 3. Rejection (Psychology) 4. Technological innovations

ISBN 978-0-8014-4859-1; 0-8014-4859-X

LC 2010001008

"Gershon interviewed over 70 people (many of them college students) to examine how they used chatting, email, texting, and social networking websites in conjunction with their relationships and found that opinions and social rules governing the intersection of romance and technology are still highly variable. Why would some people rather break up through email, while others prefer instant messaging? What kind of problems arise when a couple has different ideas about how to digitally negotiate the end of their relationship? . . . Though written with an academic focus, this is an intriguing read for anyone interested in how social con

ventions for new media develop and the ways that technology is changing romantic relationships." Libr J

Includes bibliographical references

Heath, Chip

Switch; how to change things when change is hard. [by] Chip Heath and Dan Heath. Broadway Books 2010 305p $26; pa $15.95; ebook $11.99   **303.4**

1. Change (Psychology)

ISBN 978-0-385-52875-7; 978-0-307-74235-3 pa; 978-0-307-59016-9 ebook

LC 2009-27814

This book "offers many insights about human behavior and psychology that marketing professionals, communications experts, and public-policy makers might all appreciate." Futurist

Includes bibliographical references

Hessler, Peter

Country driving; a journey through China from farm to factory. Harper 2010 438p map $27.99   **303.4**

1. Highway transportation 2. Journalists 3. Transportation, Automotive -- China

ISBN 978-0-06-180409-0; 0-06-180409-6

LC 2009-27502

"Full of exotic detail, solid reporting, and ironic observation, Country Driving offers a personal snapshot of the world's second superpower hurtling through the 21st century." Boston Globe

Includes bibliographical references

Hoffman, Abbie

The **best** of Abbie Hoffman; foreword by Norman Mailer; edited by Dan Simon with the author. Four Walls Eight Windows 1989 421p il hardcover o.p. pa $18.95   **303.4**

1. Popular culture -- United States 2. Radicalism 3. Radicalism -- United States

ISBN 0-941423-27-1; 0-941423-42-5 pa

LC 89-23585

This volume contains selections from Revolution for the hell of it, Woodstock Nation, Steal this book, and New writings.

Ladd, Brian

Autophobia; love and hate in the automotive age. University of Chicago Press 2008 227p il $22.50   **303.4**

1. Automobiles 2. Automobiles -- Social aspects 3. Environmental degradation 4. Transportation, Automotive -- United States

ISBN 978-0-226-46741-2; 0-226-46741-4

LC 2008-14520

Ladd "documents a century of expanding U.S. reliance on vehicles powered by oil, most of which has to be imported. He frames his analysis in familiar concepts: the automotive industry as employer, urban migration from cities by families relying on automobiles for transportation, traffic/ congestion/roadways, and damage to the environment from burning fossil fuels. . . . [The author shows] how the car is completely woven into the fabric of our cultural and economic history. As such, he writes, we have accepted the dark side of the automobile—pollution, congestion, high energy costs, and accidental loss of life—in exchange for personal mobility." Libr J

Includes bibliographical references

Lanier, Jaron

★ **You** are not a gadget; a manifesto. Alfred A. Knopf 2010 209p $24.95   **303.4**
1. Digital media -- Social aspects 2. Information technology 3. Information technology -- Social aspects 4. Technological innovations 5. Technological innovations -- Social aspects 6. Technology and civilization 7. Web sites -- Design
ISBN 0-307-26964-7; 978-0-307-26964-5
                     LC 2009-20298

The author, an artist and computer scientist, offers an examination of the way the World Wide Web "is transforming our lives. . . . [He maintains that] the web's first designers made crucial choices (such as making one's presence anonymous) that have had enormous—and often unintended— consequences. What's more, these designs quickly became 'locked in,' a permanent part of the web's very structure. Lanier discusses the technical and cultural problems that [he believes] can grow out of poorly considered digital design and warns that our financial markets and sites like Wikipedia, Facebook, and Twitter are elevating the 'wisdom' of mobs and computer algorithms over the intelligence and judgment of individuals. . . . [Lanier argues that] a new humanistic technology is necessary." (Publisher's note)

"In the nineteen-eighties, Lanier belonged to what he calls a 'merry band' of Internet pioneers who believed that the digital revolution would mean a groundswell of creativity. But, he argues in this manifesto, around the turn of this century the dream was hijacked by 'digital Maoists,' who value the crowd above the individual. Their influence, he writes, has led to an online culture of mashups, 'pervasive anonymity' (which encourages bullying and moblike behavior), open access (so that individual ownership is devalued or lost), and social-networking sites that reduce 'the deep meaning of personhood.' He fears that these characteristics are perilously close to 'lock-in': becoming permanent features of the Web. Lanier's detractors have accused him of Ludditism, but his argument will make intuitive sense to anyone concerned with questions of propriety, responsibility, and authenticity." New Yorker

Linden, Eugene

The **ragged** edge of the world; encounters at the frontier where modernity, wildlands, and indigenous peoples meet. Viking 2011 260p $26.95   **303.4**
1. Ethnology
ISBN 978-0-670-02251-9
                     LC 2010043578

"Traveling to the rain forests of Borneo and to the Amazon, the Antarctic, and Africa, Linden provides firsthand accounts of cargo cults in New Guinea, practices of Pygmy tribes in Africa, and conservation efforts in Cuba—some of which show positive responses to deforestation and loss of habitat for wildlife, while others reveal the downward spiral to extinction for rain forests and many animal species. He

highlights cultural extinction as much as environmental devastation to habitats. . . . Linden provides an original look at globalization and its impact on various cultures and species throughout the world. Anyone interested in global environmental issues will find this book informative." Libr J

Otto, Shawn

Fool me twice; fighting the assault on science in America. [by] Shawn Lawrence Otto. Rodale 2011 376p $25.99   **303.4**
1. Learning and scholarship 2. Science -- Study and teaching 3. Science -- United States
ISBN 978-1-60529-217-5; 1-60529-217-6
                     LC 2011033902

The author "explores the devaluation of science in America. His exhaustively researched text explains the three-pronged attack on science: how right-wing Christian fervor discredits evolution; how post-modernism and cultural sensitivity makes people believe that objective truth doesn't exist; and how corporations discredit scientists in order to further economic agendas. . . . The accessible book will inform scientists about what has happened to their field, provide an overview for laypeople, and allow educators to equip themselves to address these issues for the next generation and reverse this troubling trend." Publ Wkly

Includes bibliographical references

Pagel, Mark

Wired for culture; origins of the human social mind. Mark Pagel. W. W. Norton & Company 2012 416 p.   **303.4**
1. Culture 2. Dawkins, Richard, 1941- 3. Evolution (Biology) 4. Evolution (Biology) & the social sciences 5. Evolutionary genetics 6. Human evolution 7. Language & languages 8. Memes 9. Scientific literature 10. Social evolution
ISBN 0393065871; 9780393065879
                     LC 2011044465

This book frames cultural development in the language of Richard Dawkins's selfish gene theory, in which genes are replicators that build individual bodies as vehicles for their own survival. Dawkins . . . coined the term "meme" as the cultural analogue of a gene. [Mark] Pagel . . . [argues that m]emes . . . have built vehicles around themselves made up of groups of people. We live inside "cultural survival vehicles" that allow us to collectively survive. . . . Pagel argues that there are thousands of such vehicles, each adapted to different environments, exemplified by humanity's . . . languages. . . . [He] explores the implications of the emerging consensus across . . . religion, the arts and economics, . . . consciousness, deception, conflict and the very idea of truth. (New Scientist)

Penenberg, Adam L.

Viral loop; from Facebook to Twitter, how today's smartest businesses grow themselves. Hyperion 2009 274p il $25.99   **303.4**
1. Electronic commerce 2. Marketing 3. Social networking
ISBN 978-1-4013-2349-3; 1-4013-2349-9

From Google to Facebook, the author delves into how a "viral loop," a situation where using a product means needing to share it with others, can make an online business a success.

"Solidly researched and briskly-written, Penenberg at once captures a great business and tech story, as well as a defining moment in our online culture." Publ Wkly

Includes bibliographical references

Reeves, Byron

Total engagement; using games and virtual worlds to change the way people work and businesses compete. [by] Byron Reeves [and] J. Leighton Read. Harvard Business Press 2009 274p $29.95 **303.4**

1. Games 2. Group relations training 3. Play 4. Work

ISBN 978-1-4221-4657-6; 1-4221-4657-X

LC 2009-35808

The authors "discuss how game design can be a great interface for office work. They describe how using avatars (virtual personal characters) and online games can increase employee engagement and productivity and facilitate team building, collaboration, and leadership skills. They anticipate online games changing how people will work, and they view virtual-world work interfaces as inevitable and definitive." Choice

Includes bibliographical references

Shirky, Clay

Cognitive surplus; creativity and generosity in a connected age. Penguin Press 2010 242p $25.95 **303.4**

1. Information society 2. Mass media -- Social aspects 3. Social media 4. Social networking

ISBN 978-1-59420-253-7; 1-59420-253-2

LC 2009-53882

Shirky "argues that new technology is making it possible for people to collaborate in ways that have the potential to change society. By 'cognitive surplus,' the author refers to the free time of the world's educated citizenry, which amounts to more than one trillion hours per year. . . . [He] discusses the many factors that have given rise to social media and suggests the conditions that will best allow voluntary groups to take advantage of the world's aggregate free time to benefit society. . . . [Shirky] may be overly optimistic about the possible benefits of social media, but he makes clear their growing global importance. An informed look at the social impact of the Internet." Kirkus

Includes bibliographical references

Solnit, Rebecca

A **paradise** built in hell; the extraordinary communities that arise in disasters. Viking 2009 353p $27.95 **303.4**

1. Disasters 2. Disasters -- Psychological aspects 3. Disasters -- Social aspects

ISBN 978-0-670-02107-9; 0-670-02107-5

LC 2009-04101

"An engaging book, full of fascinating detail, 'Paradise' especially deserves a close reading by political leaders at every level, as well as the news media who cover disasters." Christ Sci Monit

Includes bibliographical references

Tapscott, Don, 1947-

Macrowikinomics; rebooting business and the world. [by] Don Tapscott and Anthony D. Williams. Portfolio/Penguin 2010 424p $27.95 **303.4**

1. Information technology 2. Online social networks 3. Technological innovations

ISBN 978-1-59184-356-6

LC 2010023338

The authors "present a new framework for understanding social and economic innovations applicable to the spectrum of industries under which people utilize emerging Web applications to foster a more economically, socially, and ecologically sustainable world. . . . [This book] addresses an important issue and is good preparation for an epoch of staggering technological leaps." Choice

Includes bibliographical references

Toffler, Alvin

★ **Future** shock. Bantam Books 1990 561p pa $7.99 **303.4**

1. Adaptation (Biology) 2. Children 3. Democracy 4. Education 5. Family 6. Interpersonal relations 7. Modern civilization -- 1950- 8. Social change 9. Technology and civilization

ISBN 978-0-553-27737-1; 0-553-27737-5

According to the author, "future shock is 'the dizzying disorientation brought on by the premature arrival of the future.' . . . Toffler outlines some interesting strategies for survival, writing in a clear popular style." Publ Wkly

Includes bibliographical references

Turkle, Sherry

Alone together. Basic Books 2011 360p $28.95 **303.4**

1. Attention 2. Communication & technology -- Evaluation 3. Communication & technology -- Social aspects 4. Human-computer interaction 5. Information technology 6. Information technology -- Social aspects 7. Interpersonal relations 8. Online social networks -- Psychological aspects 9. Online social networks -- Social aspects 10. Social criticism

ISBN 978-0-465-01021-9; 0-465-01021-0

LC 2010-30614

This book is the third in a trilogy, part of a project [author Sherry Turkle] . . . has been working on since she joined MIT in 1976 and noticed that the people there were using the language of psychology to talk about their machines. . . . Turkle picks out the contradictions of the networked life that everyone has now come to take for granted, but adolescents especially: the desire for attention and the desire to hide, constantly online but dreading the exposure of a phone call. . . . Turkle argues that people risk impairing the quality of their thought and communication by so often resorting to media designed only for short, simplified messages. (London Review of Books)

"Turkle argues that people are increasingly functioning without face-to-face contact. For all the talk of convenience and connection derived from texting, e-mailing, and social networking, Turkle reaffirms that what humans still instinctively need is each other, and she encounters dissatisfaction and alienation among users. . . . Turkle's prescient book makes a strong case that what was meant to be a way to

facilitate communications has pushed people closer to their machines and further away from each other." Publ Wkly
Includes bibliographical references

Wasik, Bill

And then there's this; how stories live and die in viral culture. Viking Press 2009 202p il $25.95   **303.4**

1. Blogs 2. Information society 3. Internet -- Social aspects 4. Weblogs
ISBN 978-0-670-02084-3; 0-670-02084-2
LC 2009-04100

In the spring of 2003 the author "sent out an anonymous e-mail to several dozen folks regarding their potential participation in an impromptu mass gathering. Wasik's 'flash mobs,' as the events would be called, became rousing successes. Satellite groups started staging their own irreverent be-ins. Mainstream media soon reported on this oddball phenomena at length. . . . What interested Wasik wasn't whether he could coordinate absurdist goofs but the way these pranks were reported through a short-attention news filter. Thus began a series of controlled explorations on how far he could push the viral nature of information dissemination." Time Out N Y
Includes bibliographical references and index.

Werth, Barry

Banquet at Delmonico's; how evolution conquered Gilded Age America. Random House 2009 xxxi, 362p $27   **303.4**

1. Evolution 2. Philosophers 3. Social Darwinism
ISBN 978-1-4000-6778-7; 1-4000-6778-2
LC 2008-16567

"Werth effortlessly brings each eccentric character to life through colorful details and well-chosen anecdotes, while taking us on a whirlwind tour of Gilded Age politics and society. Banquet at Delmonico's crackles with energy and wit." N Y Times Book Rev
Includes bibliographical references

★ The **Radical** reader; a documentary history of the American radical tradition. edited by Timothy Patrick McCarthy and John McMillian; foreword by Eric Foner. New Press 2003 688p $65; lib bdg $21.95   **303.4**

1. Radicalism 2. Radicalism -- United States -- History -- Sources
ISBN 1-56584-827-6; 1-56584-682-6 lib bdg
LC 2002-41051

"By bringing many hard-to-find documents under one cover, this anthology will excite readers in discussing why radicals from all walks of life have made progressive ideals meaningful to Americans. Recommended for college, high school, and public libraries." Libr J
Includes bibliographical references

303.48   Causes of change

Anderson, Terry H.

The **movement** and the sixties. Oxford Univ. Press 1995 500p il hardcover o.p. pa $19.95 **303.48**

1. Demonstrations 2. Radicalism 3. Radicalism -- United States
ISBN 0-19-510457-9 pa
LC 94-16344

Anderson's "sweeping study is a valuable, refreshingly unbiased reassessment of the '60s legacy." Publ Wkly
Includes bibliographical references

Diamandis, Peter H.

Abundance; the future is better than you think. Peter H. Diamandis and Steven Kotler. Free Press 2012 386 p. $26.99   **303.48**

1. Future, The 2. Scientific literature 3. Technological forecasting 4. Technological innovations -- Forecasting 5. Technology -- Social aspects
ISBN 9781451614213; 1451614217
LC 2011039926

This book discusses technological innovations, looking at how they could help in finding solutions for world problems, from poverty and disease to climate change and pollution. . . . Peter Diamandis, founder of the X Prize Foundation, and journalist Steven Kotler argue that innovation can provide 9 billion people with a world of plenty. . . . [Lowell Wood envisions a] toilet that would burn faeces to evaporate urine, thus preventing water pollution while generating surplus energy that could power cellphones and lights. . . . Abundance extols the potential of 3D printers to make almost any kind of product at home. (New Scientist)

Moreno, Jonathan D.

The **body** politic; Jonathan D. Moreno. Bellevue Literary Press 2011 207p.   **303.48**

ISBN 9781934137383 pa; 1934137383 pa
LC 2011026354

In this book, a "Kirkus Reviews" Best Book of the Year, the author uses the term "'biopolitics,' popularized by [philosopher] Michel Foucault . . . to describe historical and current debates over issues ranging from abortion and health care to stem cells and genetically modified organisms. . . . [He] unpacks . . . distrust of technology, on both the political right and left. . . . Both extremes place 'human dignity' as central to their trepidation toward technology, but they have starkly contrasting ideas of what such a concept embodies. The far-left greens fear the effects of technology on social justice, while the neoconservatives are more concerned with technology as a source of alienation from what makes us truly human. . . . Ultimately, Moreno shows that the disarming features of modern biology reflect those of all science as a human endeavor." (washingtonindependentreveiwof-books.com)

Morozov, Evgeny

The **net** delusion; Evgeny Morozov. Public Affairs 2011 xvii, 409 p.p   **303.48**

1. Freedom of information 2. Internet -- Political

aspects 3. Internet -- Social aspects
ISBN 978-1-58648-874-1; 1-58648-874-0

LC 2010039066

This book challenges "[t]he idea that the internet was fomenting revolution and promoting democracy in Iran . . . [and the] belief that communications technology, and the internet in particular, is inherently pro-democratic. In this gleefully iconoclastic book, Evgeny Morozov takes a stand against this cyber-utopian view, arguing that the internet can be just as effective at sustaining authoritarian regimes. By assuming that the internet is always pro-democratic, he says, Western policymakers are operating with a 'voluntary intellectual handicap' that makes it harder rather than easier to promote democracy. . . . He starts with the events in Iran, which illustrate his argument in microcosm. . . . Mr Morozov catalogues many similar examples of the internet being used with similarly pacifying consequences today, as authoritarian regimes make an implicit deal with their populations: help yourselves to pirated films, silly video clips and online pornography, but stay away from politics." (Economist)

Postman, Neil

Technopoly; the surrender of culture to technology. Knopf 1992 222p hardcover o.p. pa $12 **303.48**
1. Technology -- Social aspects 2. Technology and civilization
ISBN 0-679-74540-8 pa

LC 91-53121

Postman's "style is comfortable, his exposition incisive, and his reasoning hard to ignore." Christ Sci Monit
Includes bibliographical references

Silver, Brian L.

The **ascent** of science. Oxford Univ. Press 1998 534p il hardcover o.p. pa $53 **303.48**
1. Discoveries in science 2. Science -- History 3. Science -- Philosophy 4. Thought and thinking
ISBN 0-19-513427-3

LC 97-15430

The author discusses a "variety of topics, from Pythagorean musings and lodestones to quantum mechanical puzzles and DNA structures. Yes, chaos theory and cosmology are included too. All this is sandwiched between interesting references to historical matters, philosophical positions, some controversies, and to Shakespeare, Shelley, and Shaw also. A book commendable for its breadth, depth, and vision." Choice
Includes bibliographical references

Tenner, Edward

Our own devices; the past and future of body technology. Alfred A. Knopf 2003 336p hardcover o.p. pa $14.95 **303.48**
1. Body, Human (Philosophy) 2. Body, Human -- Social aspects 3. Human beings -- Effect of technological innovations on 4. Technological innovations 5. Technological innovations -- Social aspects 6. Technology 7. Technology -- Social aspects 8. Technology and civilization
ISBN 0-375-40722-7; 0-375-70707-7 pa

LC 2002-40694

"For a work that covers such a broad topic, this book is a page-turner, largely due to its clear prose and the author's approach to the material. While not lavishly illustrated, there seems to be a picture every time one is needed to illustrate the technology being discussed." SLJ
Includes bibliographical references

Encyclopedia of mathematics and society; Sarah J. Greenwald , Jill E. Thomley, [editors] Salem Press 2012 3 v. (xxxi, 1191 p.)p **303.48**
1. Mathematics -- Social aspects
ISBN 1587658445; 1587658453; 1587658461; 158765847X; 9781587658440; 9781587658457; 9781587658464; 9781587658471

LC 2011021856

This encyclopedia of mathematics focus[es] on how the basic concepts of figures relate to everyday life. As the editors phrase it, the purpose of these compact volumes is to weave multilayered connections between society, history, people, applications, and mathematics. . . . [T]opics covered include Cooking, Earthquakes, Mathematics and Religion, and Skydiving. While some purely mathematical principles are discussed, they are always placed in relation to the larger context of human affairs, such as in the essay Algebra in Society. Pieces open with boldface headword(s), a classification of the subject matter, and a one-line summary of the material to follow. A short bibliography and cross-references follow. (Libr J)

303.483

Johnson, Clay

The **information** diet; Clay A. Johnson. 1st ed. OReilly Media 2012 ix, 150p.p **303.483**
ISBN 9781449304683; 1449304680

LC 2011410787

This book examines how humans have "become gluttons for texts, instant messages, emails, RSS feeds, downloads, videos, status updates, and tweets. We're all battling a storm of distractions, buffeted with notifications and tempted by tasty tidbits of information. And just as too much junk food can lead to obesity, too much junk information can lead to cluelessness. 'The Information Diet' shows you how to thrive in this information glut--what to look for, what to avoid, and how to be selective. In the process, author Clay Johnson explains the role information has played throughout history, and why following his prescribed diet is essential for everyone who strives to be smart, productive, and sane." (Publisher's note)

303.49 Social forecasts

Kaku, Michio

Physics of the future; how science will shape human destiny and our daily lives by the year 2100. Doubleday 2011 389p il $28.95; ebook $12.99 **303.49**
1. Forecasting 2. Science 3. Science -- History -- 21st

century 4. Science -- Social aspects
ISBN 978-0-385-53080-4; 978-0-385-53081-1 ebook

LC 2010-26569

"The book's lively, user-friendly style should appeal equally to fans of science fiction and popular science." Booklist

Includes bibliographical references

Rees, Martin J.

Our final hour; a scientist's warning: how terror, error, and environmental disaster threaten humankind's future in this century on earth and beyond. [by] Martin Rees. Basic Books 2003 228p $25; pa $15 **303.49**

1. Disasters -- Forecasts 2. End of the world 3. Twenty-first century -- Forecasts

ISBN 0-465-06862-6; 0-465-06863-4 pa

LC 2003-301

This is an "assessment of the risks associated with myriad scientific advances, from nuclear weapons to genetic engineering. . . . Rees' most arresting futuristic scenarios involve biotechnologies that will change the very essence of human nature, and he also offers some chilling observations regarding bioterror and bioerror, certain that one or the other will kill a million people by 2020. Chilling predictions of doom are interrupted by compelling insights into various scientific discoveries." Booklist

Includes bibliographical references

Toffler, Alvin

Powershift; knowledge, wealth, and violence at the edge of the 21st century. Bantam Bks. 1990 xxii, 585p hardcover o.p. pa $7.99 **303.49**

1. Forecasting 2. Modern civilization -- 1950- 3. Power (Social sciences) 4. Social change 5. Twenty-first century

ISBN 0-553-29215-3 pa

LC 90-1068

The author "argues that the control of knowledge has become the principal means to create wealth and power. Aided by the widespread use of computers and other communications technologies, this 'powershift,' Toffler predicts, will dramatically alter the world's political balance." Libr J

Includes bibliographical references

Zakaria, Fareed

The post-American world. W.W. Norton & Company 2008 292p $25.95 **303.49**

1. Economic forecasting 2. Globalization 3. Globalization -- United States 4. International economic relations 5. International relations -- Forecasting 6. World politics -- Forecasting

ISBN 978-0-393-06235-9; 0-393-06235-X

LC 2008-01306

"This is a relentlessly intelligent book that eschews simpleminded projections from crisis to collapse." N Y Times Book Rev

Includes bibliographical references

303.6 Conflict and conflict resolution

Bergen, Peter L.

Holy war, Inc. inside the secret world of Osama bin Laden. Free Press 2001 242p hardcover o.p. pa $14 **303.6**

1. Jihad 2. Terrorism 3. Terrorism -- Government policy -- United States 4. Terrorism -- Religious aspects -- Islam

ISBN 0-7432-0502-2; 0-7432-3495-2 pa

LC 2001-54732

"Although it may be impossible to fully understand bin Laden, Bergen does an admirable job of portraying him as a person, not just the face of terrorism. Readers will come away from this book understanding why bin Laden has been successful and how difficult it will be to dismantle his organization of terror." Booklist

Includes bibliographical references

Camus, Albert

The rebel; an essay on man in revolt. with a foreword by Sir Herbert Read; a revised and complete translation of L'homme révolté by Anthony Bower. Vintage Bks. 1991 306p pa $12 **303.6**

1. Authors 2. Essayists 3. Memoirists 4. Nihilism 5. Novelists 6. Philosophers 7. Political and social philosophers 8. Revolutionaries 9. Revolutions 10. Short story writers 11. Writers on politics

ISBN 0-679-73384-1

LC 91-50022

The author describes how the theories of philosophers have been used with disastrous effect by political leaders from the French Revolution through the nihilist revolutions of Russia and the governments of Lenin, Hitler and Stalin. The conclusion calls for a return to a political philosophy having as its aim the happiness and development of living human beings.

Carr, Caleb

The lessons of terror; a history of warfare against civilians: why it has always failed and why it will fail again. Random House 2002 272p hardcover o.p. pa $12.95 **303.6**

1. Terrorism 2. Terrorism -- History

ISBN 0-375-76074-1 pa

LC 2002-280604

The author argues "that terrorism must be viewed in terms of 'military history, rather than political science or sociology,' and that the refusal to label terrorists as soldiers, rather than criminals, is a mistake. . . . This often fascinating, accessible tome skillfully contends that the terrorizing of civilians has a long and controversial history but, as an inferior method, is prone to failure." Publ Wkly

Includes bibliographical references

Dershowitz, Alan M.

Why terrorism works; understanding the threat, responding to the challenge. Yale Univ. Press 2002 271p $24.95; pa $16 **303.6**

1. Terrorism 2. Terrorism -- Prevention
ISBN 0-300-09766-2; 0-300-10153-8 pa
LC 2002-6387

The author "argues forcefully that the attacks of September 11 were largely of our own doing—the international community, Dershowitz says, repeatedly rewards terrorists with appeasement and legitimization, refusing to take the necessary steps to curtail attacks. . . . These penetrating arguments force readers to consider how we got to September 11, how far we are willing to pursue terrorists and how much freedom we are willing to give up for our security." Publ Wkly

Includes bibliographical references

Herbst, Philip

Talking terrorism; a dictionary of the loaded language of political violence. Greenwood Press 2003 220p $49.95 **303.6**

1. Political violence -- Dictionaries 2. Prejudices -- United States -- Dictionaries 3. Reference books 4. Terrorism -- Dictionaries
ISBN 0-313-32486-7
LC 2003-44071

"This work is original, refreshing, and insightful. It attempts to discern the why of terrorism and political violence from the perspective of language." Choice

Includes bibliographical references

Sontag, Susan

Regarding the pain of others. Farrar, Straus & Giroux 2003 131p hardcover o.p. pa $12 **303.6**

1. Atrocities 2. Documentary photography 3. Photojournalism 4. Photojournalism -- Social aspects 5. Violence 6. War and society 7. War in art -- Social aspects 8. War photography 9. War photography -- Social aspects
ISBN 978-0-312-42219-6
LC 2002-192527

"All libraries, regardless of type, size, or demographics, should own this book." Libr J

Confronting fear; a documentary history of terrorism. edited by Isaac Cronin. Thunder's Mouth Press 2002 561p pa $18.95 **303.6**

1. Terrorism 2. Terrorism -- History 3. Terrorism -- History -- Sources
ISBN 1-56025-399-1
LC 2002-18005

"Cronin provides a rare overview for the public to understand this important and disturbing subject." Choice

Violence in America; an encyclopedia. Ronald Gottesman, editor; Richard Maxwell Brown, consulting editor {et al.} Scribner 1999 3v set $400 **303.6**

1. Reference books 2. Violence -- Encyclopedias 3. Violence -- United States
ISBN 0-684-80487-5
LC 99-52027

This reference "on the social, historical, biological, and cultural aspects of violence in the United States offers 600 entries on topics ranging from violence, homicide, and race and ethnicity to women, child abuse, labor and unions, sociobiology, 'ultimate fighting,' television, gun violence, and various events and persons." Libr J

Includes bibliographical references

304 Factors affecting social behavior

Sagan, Carl

Shadows of forgotten ancestors; a search for who we are. {by} Carl Sagan, Ann Druyan. Random House 1992 505p hardcover o.p. pa $15.95 **304**

1. Evolution 2. Life -- Origin
ISBN 0-345-38472-5 pa
LC 92-50155

"Despite a preference for the overly dramatic phrase at the expense of scientific clarity, the argument is coherent throughout." Libr J

Includes bibliographical references

304.2 Human ecology

Brand, Stewart

★ Whole earth discipline; an ecopragmatist manifesto. Viking 2009 325p $25.95 **304.2**

1. Biotechnology -- Environmental aspects 2. Climate -- Environmental aspects 3. Climatic changes -- Environmental aspects 4. Human ecology 5. Urban ecology
ISBN 9780670021215
LC 2009-13386

Brand "provides readers with the most necessary survival tool in this era of increasing climate change: well-researched, accurate information and a guide with which to use it. . . . Breathtaking in scope and implication—a must-read." Kirkus

Cerveny, Randall S.

Weather's greatest mysteries solved! [by] Randy Cerveny. Prometheus Books 2009 328p il map $26.98 **304.2**

1. Climate 2. Climatology
ISBN 978-1-59102-720-1; 1-59102-720-9
LC 2009-04493

The author discusses "the investigative process, theories, and the techniques of weather and climate research. Presenting the issues as unsolved mysteries, he engages readers and explains how science is conducted. Each short chapter contains a fictional vignette personalizing a weather or climate-related mystery." Choice

Includes bibliographical references

Diamond, Jared M.

★ **Collapse**: how societies choose to fail or succeed. Viking 2005 575p il $29.95; pa $17 **304.2**

1. Environmental policy 2. Social change
ISBN 0-670-03337-5; 0-14-303655-6 pa

LC 2004-57152

The author "examines storied examples of human economic and social collapse, and even extinction, including Easter Island, classical Mayan civilization and the Greenland Norse. He explores patterns of population growth, overfarming, overgrazing and overhunting, often abetted by drought, cold, rigid social mores and warfare, that lead inexorably to vicious circles of deforestation, erosion and starvation prompted by the disappearance of plant and animal food sources. . . . Readers will find his book an enthralling, and disturbing, reminder of the indissoluble links that bind humans to nature." Publ Wkly

Includes bibliographical references

Faris, Stephan

Forecast; the consequences of climate change, from the Amazon to the Arctic, from Darfur to Napa Valley. Henry Holt 2009 242p $25 **304.2**

1. Climate -- Environmental aspects 2. Climatic changes 3. Global environmental change -- Social aspects 4. Greenhouse effect
ISBN 978-0-8050-8779-6; 0-8050-8779-6

LC 2008-28558

This book "is a skillful amalgam of reporting and analysis. Faris's stories, from polar bear hunts around Hudson Bay to the melting glaciers of the Himalayas, are always about human as well as ecological affairs—and are far more compelling than any number of computer model simulations of climate change." Orion

Includes bibliographical references

Gessner, David

My green manifesto; down the Charles River in pursuit of a new environmentalism. David Gessner. 1st ed.; Milkweed Editions 2011 225 p. $15 **304.2**

1. Environmental protection 2. Environmental protection -- Massachusetts -- Charles River 3. Environmentalism 4. Environmentalism -- Massachusetts -- Charles River
ISBN 9781571313249 pa

LC 2011012994

In this book, the author canoes down Boston's Charles River with Dan Driscoll, an upbeat, pot-smoking, environmental planner, who has spent nearly 20 years fighting to revitalize the once famously polluted river. . . . [David] Gessner sets out to find a new environmentalism, something that is a part of [his] everyday life, not running roughshod over it. For Gessner, environmentalism begins with a connection to a particular place. . . . And while his friend's fight to bring a bit of the natural world back to the banks of the Charles may not account for much in the long run, Gessner believes that committing to a lifelong environmental fight is an act of personal fulfillment. (Publishers Wkly)

Gilding, Paul

The **great** disruption; why the climate crisis will bring on the end of shopping and the birth of a new world. Bloomsbury Press 2011 292p $25 **304.2**

1. Economic development 2. Human ecology 3. Social change
ISBN 978-1-60819-223-6

LC 2010-35843

"Gilding's confidence in our ability to transform disaster into a 'happiness economy' may astonish readers, but the book provides a refreshing, provocative alternative to the recent spate of gloom-and-doom climate-change studies." Publ Wkly

Includes bibliographical references

Gore, Al

Earth in the balance; ecology and the human spirit. [by] Al Gore. Houghton Mifflin 2000 xxiv, 407p il maps $26 **304.2**

1. Environmental policy 2. Environmental protection 3. Human ecology
ISBN 0-618-05664-5

LC 00-38311

"The author exhibits little of the clichéd myopia of his profession and is aware of the political obstacles posed by such an integrated approach. He identifies the root of our current problems as spiritual. If civilization is to persist, he maintains, it must make the rescue of the environment its organizing principle." N Y Times Book Rev

Includes bibliographical references

Hertsgaard, Mark

Hot; living through the next fifty years on earth. Houghton Mifflin Harcourt 2011 339p $25 **304.2**

1. Climate -- Environmental aspects 2. Climatic changes 3. Global environmental change 4. Global warming 5. Greenhouse effect 6. Human beings -- Effect of climate on
ISBN 978-0-618-82612-4; 0-618-82612-2

LC 2010-12416

"The author notes that we have entered the 'second era of global warming.' Even if greenhouse-gas emissions ceased today, the consequences would continue for hundreds of years. Consequently, the author persuasively argues that we need to begin adapting to those changes, which does not mean that mitigating global warming is no longer important; in fact, it grows more urgent every day. . . . Starkly clear and of utmost importance. " Kirkus

Includes bibliographical references

Jensen, Derrick

What we leave behind; [by] Derrick Jensen and Aric McBay. Seven Stories Press 2009 453p pa $24.95 **304.2**

1. Pollution 2. Refuse and refuse disposal
ISBN 978-1-58322-867-8

LC 2008-47287

Jensen and McBay argue that "the global industrial system . . . produces massive amounts of unsustainable and toxic wastes. . . . The authors focus on some of these harmful products, discuss reasons why our culture produces so much waste, and explain why individual action is insufficient to solve our enormous problems. . . . This compelling book has a refreshing style, at once very personal and very passionate. It is also thorough, with historical, scientific, statistical, and anecdotal evidence filtered through a lot of anger and some quirky humor." Libr J

Includes bibliographical references

Owen, David

Green metropolis; why living smaller, living closer, and driving less are the keys to sustainability. Riverhead Books 2009 357p $25.95   **304.2**
1. Green technology 2. Human ecology 3. Sustainable architecture 4. Urban ecology 5. Urban ecology -- Social aspects
ISBN 978-1-59448-882-5; 1-59448-882-7
LC 2009-17116

This is "a compelling analysis of the world's environmental predicament that upends orthodox opinion and points the way to practical solutions." Publ Wkly

Includes bibliographical references

Smith, Laurence C.

The **world** in 2050; four forces shaping civilization's northern future. Dutton 2010 322p il map $26.95   **304.2**
1. Climate -- Environmental aspects 2. Forecasting
ISBN 978-0-525-95181-0
LC 2010-29553

"Smith demonstrates the breadth of geography and emerges as a champion of the discipline. His engaging style and understandable prose will appeal to a wide range of readers interested in social and environmental sciences." Libr J

Includes bibliographical references

Wohlforth, Charles

The **fate** of nature; rediscovering our ability to rescue the earth. Thomas Dunne Books/St. Martin's Press 2010 434p map $27.99   **304.2**
1. Conservation of natural resources 2. Conservation of natural resources -- Alaska 3. Environmental protection 4. Human ecology 5. Human ecology -- Alaska 6. Natural history -- Alaska
ISBN 978-0-312-37737-3; 0-312-37737-1
LC 2009-45779

The author "considers the consequences of Captain John Cook's hasty visit to the gulf in 1778, the Russian conquest of coastal Alaska, . . . the crash of the herring fisheries, and the cruel fates of the region's indigenous peoples. But Wohlforth believes that our 'consuming nature' is balanced by the impulse to understand and cherish the living world, which is borne out in his compelling profiles of whale biologist Eva Saulitis; Geerat Vermeij, a blind evolutionary scientist who discovered an arms race among crustaceans; and various environmental heroes. . . . By analyzing competition and evolution, culture and economics, habits of living and of mind, science and suffering, Wohlforth brings a truly ecological perspective to the global debate over how to protect the biosphere." Booklist

Includes bibliographical references

304.5   Genetic factors

Taylor, Shelley E.

The **tending** instinct; how nurturing is essential for who we are and how we live. Times Bks. 2002 290p $25; pa $16   **304.5**
1. Nurturing behavior 2. Sex differences 3. Sex differences (Psychology) 4. Sociobiology 5. Stress (Psychology)
ISBN 0-8050-6837-6; 0-8050-7289-6 pa
LC 2002-19879

The author "launched a series of innovative experiments that led her to believe that humans are biologically wired to nurture. She thus devised no less than a whole new psychology of women, presented in this accessible and well-grounded work." Libr J

Includes bibliographical references

304.6   Population

★ The American people; Census 2000. [edited by] Reynolds Farley and John Haaga. Russell Sage 2005 456p il map $35   **304.6**
ISBN 0-8715-4273-0
LC 2005-50433

This book "is more than just a compilation of tables and charts of raw census data. It is an interpretative guide to understanding the demographic breakdown of American society. Chapters include: 'Gender Inequalities', 'Cohorts and Socioeconomic Progress' and 'The Lives and Times of the Baby Boomers.' Editors Farley and Haaga show trends in American culture that will not be found anywhere else." Univ Press Books for Public and Second Sch Libr, 2006

Includes bibliographical references

★ Encyclopedia of genocide and crimes against humanity; Dinah L. Shelton, editor in chief. Macmillan Reference 2004 3v il map set $415 **304.6**
1. Atrocities 2. Genocide -- Encyclopedias 3. Reference books
ISBN 0-02-865847-7
LC 2004-6587

"The editorial team has cast its net wide to create an outstanding comprehensive sourcebook that will be the standard resource for many years." Booklist

Includes bibliographical references

Encyclopedia of the U.S. Census; Margo J. Anderson, editor. CQ Press 2000 xxiv, 424p il $140   **304.6**
ISBN 1-56802-428-2
LC 00-30522

The alphabetically arranged articles "explain the history, methodology, and results of U.S. censuses since 1790. . . . Maps, tables, and charts show how the composition of the population has changed, where the center of population has moved over time, and how the address lists and census tracts are developed." Booklist

Includes bibliographical references and index

304.8 Movement of people

Brownstone, David M.

★ **Facts** about American immigration; [by] David M. Brownstone and Irene M. Franck. Wilson, H.W. 2001 xxx, 818p il $105 **304.8**

1. Immigrants -- United States
ISBN 0-8242-0959-1

LC 00-53422

"Coverage begins with the earliest Americans and continues to today's immigrants. An overview places the process of immigration in a wide historical context covering efforts to restrict immigration, a portrait of the immigrant journey over the centuries, and a chronology. The main section of the book covers emigration from Europe, Africa, Asia, the Americas, and Oceania." Publisher's note

Includes bibliographical references

Sowell, Thomas

Migrations and cultures; a world view. Basic Bks. 1996 516p hardcover o.p. pa $23 **304.8**

1. Culture 2. Ethnic groups 3. Ethnic relations 4. Immigration and emigration 5. Race
ISBN 0-465-04589-8 pa

LC 95-44316

In this book the author seeks "to determine how migrations have transformed nations and continents over the course of human history. . . . He believes the habits and beliefs that migrants bring to a new homeland, what he calls their cultural capital, are far more important in determining their fate than the homeland's economy, culture or politics. . . . This is a lively and provocative book that is important reading for anyone who thinks we have too many immigrants or too few, who favors affirmative action and multicultural programs or opposes them." N Y Times Book Rev

Includes bibliographical references

Urrea, Luis Alberto

★ The **devil's** highway; a true story. Luis Alberto Urrea. Little, Brown 2004 xii, 239p (pbk.) $13.99 **304.8**

1. Human smuggling -- Mexican-American Border Region 2. Illegal aliens -- Crimes against -- Mexican-American Border Region 3. Illegal aliens -- Mexican-American Border Region -- Crimes against
ISBN 9780316746717; 9780316010801

LC 2003058930

This book tracks the paths of 26 Mexican men who in 2001 scrambled across the border into an area of the Arizona desert known as the Devil's highway. Only 12 made it safely across. . . . Their enemies were many: the U.S. Border Patrol ('La Migra'); gung-ho gringo vigilantes bent on taking the law into their own hands; the Mexican Federales; rattlesnakes; severe hypothermia and the remorseless sun. . . . But while many point to the group's smugglers . . . as the prime villains of the tragedy, [Luis Alberto] Urrea unloads on . . . "the politics of stupidity that rules both sides of the border." Mexican and U.S. border policy is backward, Urrea finds, and it does little to stem the flow of immigrants. Since the policy results in Mexicans making the crossing in increasingly forbidding areas, it contributes to the conditions that kill those who attempt it. (Publishers Weekly)

305 Groups of people

Baldwin, Neil

★ **Henry** Ford and the Jews; the mass production of hate. PublicAffairs 2001 416p il $27.50; pa $16 **305**

1. Antisemitism 2. Antisemitism -- United States 3. Automobile executives 4. Automobile industry 5. Automobile industry and trade -- United States -- History 6. Industrialists -- United States 7. Jews -- United States 8. Philanthropists
ISBN 1-891620-52-5; 1-58648-163-0 pa

LC 2001-41679

"The strength of this biography lies in context: by emphasizing Ford's background, influences and the world around the auto manufacturer, Baldwin . . . brings a fresh approach to what has long been known about one of America's most famous anti-Semites." Publ Wkly

Includes bibliographical references

Gates, Henry Louis

★ The **African**-American century; how Black Americans have shaped our country. {by} Henry Louis Gates, Jr. and Cornel West. Free Press 2000 414p il hardcover o.p. pa $16 **305**

1. African Americans 2. African Americans -- Biography 3. African Americans -- Intellectual life 4. African Americans -- Intellectual life -- 20th century
ISBN 0-684-86414-2; 0-684-86415-0 pa

LC 00-63596

"Gates and West have listed and written biographies of their choices of the 100 most important and influential [African Americans] of the . . . twentieth century. In their opinion the subjects that they have selected have made significant impacts and contributions to American society. . . . The entries are arranged by decade and by the person's period of prominence in society, 1900-1909 through 1990-1999. Profiles include Madame C.J. Walker, Langston Hughes, Carter G. Woodson, Paul Robeson, Thurgood Marshall, and Colin Powell." MultiCult Rev

Includes bibliographical references

Hrabowski, Freeman A.

Overcoming the odds; raising academically successful African American young women. {by} Freeman A. Hrabowski III {et al.} Oxford Univ. Press 2002 272p $25 **305**

1. African American women 2. African Americans -- Education
ISBN 0-19-512642-4

LC 2001-32152

This volume "focuses on young black women overcoming the stereotypical image: high-school dropout, unwed mother, welfare recipient. Based on interviews with students and parents, the book answers the question, What does it take to succeed academically?" Booklist

Includes bibliographical references

Pickett, Kate

The **spirit** level; [by] Richard Wilkinson and Kate Pickett. Bloomsbury Press 2010 330p il $28 **305**

1. Equality 2. Nonfiction 3. Quality of life 4. Social classes 5. Social mobility 6. Social policy

ISBN 9781608190362; 1608190366

LC 2009-30428

It was the author's intent to rank the quality of life in twenty-three countries, mainly European, but with Singapore, Israel, and the United States also on the list. To evaluate the well-being of each society, Richard Wilkinson and Kate Pickett use indices ranging from obesity and incarceration rates to teenage births and the feelings people have about their fellow countrymen. They then relate these variables to how income is distributed in each society. . . . Linking social indicators to economic disparities, the authors conclude that 'reducing inequality is the best way of improving the quality of the social environment.'" (New York Review of Books)

The authors "make an eloquent case that the income gap between a nation's richest and poorest is the most powerful indicator of a functioning and healthy society. . . . Felicitous prose and fascinating findings make this essential reading." Publ Wkly

Includes bibliographical references (p. 27-1297) and index.

Reef, Catherine

Working in America. Facts On File 2007 xxviii, 484p il map $80 **305**

1. Labor -- United States 2. Labor -- United States -- History

ISBN 978-0-8160-6239-3; 0-8160-6239-0

LC 2006-31191

"Each chapter begins with a . . . narrative that chronicles the experience of workers in the United States—from factory workers, cowboys, seamstresses, and newsboys to truck drivers, migrant farm workers, computer programmers, and genetic engineers. Chronologies of important events follow, along with eyewitness testimonies on the experience of working in a wide range of professions and trades—from Thomas Jefferson, Malcolm X, Samuel Gompers, Charlotte Perkins Gilman, Jesse Jackson, Cesar Chavez, and Jane Addams, as well as a wide range of American workers." Publisher's note

Includes bibliographical references

Rubin, Richard

Confederacy of silence; a true tale of the new old South. Atria Bks. 2002 438p $26; pa $14 **305**

1. Journalists -- United States -- Biography

ISBN 0-671-03666-1; 0-671-03667-X pa

LC 2002-510321

"Rubin's memoir exposes the racial polarity of the Delta in clear, effective prose." Publ Wkly

★ After the storm; black intellectuals explore the meaning of Hurricane Katrina. edited by David Dante Troutt. New Press 2006 xxvii, 164p il $22.95 **305**

1. African Americans -- Social conditions 2. Hurricane

Katrina, 2005

ISBN 978-1-59558-116-7; 1-59558-116-2

LC 2006-8883

The contributors "assess why Katrina was handled as it was (and still is), how inevitable future crises should be handled differently, and how redevelopment of New Orleans should occur. Angry, learned, focused, readable, essential." Libr J

Includes bibliographical references

My sister, guard your veil; my brother guard, your eyes; uncensored Iranian voices. Lila Azam Zanganeh, editor. Beacon Press 2006 132p il pa $12 **305**

1. Women -- Iran

ISBN 0-8070-0463-4; 978-0-8070-0463-0

LC 2005-27496

This "volume features frank interviews with an array of reputable Iranians—intellectuals, artists, and writers, some of whom live in exile. Their compelling personal experiences, views, and opinions answer some persistent questions about the lives of ordinary people in Iran and challenge established myths and stereotypes. . . . This volume opens a window on the irrepressible talents, aspirations, and energy of Iranians both at home and abroad, despite their adverse conditions" MultiCult Rev

305.23   Young people

Bronson, Po

Nurtureshock; new thinking about children. [by] Po Bronson & Ashley Merryman. Twelve 2009 336p **305.23**

1. Child development 2. Child psychology 3. Child rearing 4. Parenting

ISBN 9780446504126

LC 2009006290

This book describes "what recent research has to say about child-rearing." (N Y Times Book Rev) Index.

The authors "clearly and concisely dispel myths about childhood development, drawing on a body of convincing research. An eye-opener in the best sense." Libr J

Includes bibliographical references

Canada, Geoffrey

Fist, stick, knife, gun; a personal history of violence in America. Beacon Press 1995 179p pa $13 **305.23**

1. Children 2. Children -- United States 3. Violence

ISBN 0-8070-0422-7; 978-0-8070-0423-4 pa; 0-8070-0423-5 pa

LC 94-41357

"A more powerful depiction of the tragic life of urban children and a more compelling plea to end 'America's war against itself' cannot be imagined." Publ Wkly

Reaching up for manhood; transforming the lives of boys in America. Beacon Press 1998 160p hardcover o.p. pa $12.50 **305.23**

1. African American boys -- Psychology 2. African

American boys -- Social conditions 3. African American children 4. Boys -- Psychology 5. Boys -- United States -- Psychology 6. Boys -- United States -- Social conditions 7. Masculinity -- United States 8. Youth -- United States
ISBN 0-8070-2316-7 pa

LC 97-19919

The author "grew up on tough South Bronx streets, where he witnessed friends dying by the handful. Recounting his childhood at midlife, he powerfully depicts what children face in today's world, especially the crippling problems of African American boys." Libr J

Coles, Robert

★ **Children** of crisis; selections from the Pulitzer Prize-winning five-volume Children of crisis series; with a new introduction by the author. Little, Brown 2003 714p il $35; pa $22.45   **305.23**
1. Children -- United States 2. Children of the rich -- United States 3. Children with social disabilities -- United States 4. Poor children -- United States 5. Socially handicapped children
ISBN 0-316-15547-0; 0-316-15102-5 pa

LC 2003-47522

These are selections of Coles' social study of "African American children caught in the throes of the South's racial integration; the young children of impoverished sharecroppers, migrant workers, and mountaineers in Appalachia; children whose families were transformed by the migration from South to North, from rural to urban communities; Latino, Native American, and Eskimo children in the poorest communities of the American West; the children of America's wealthiest families, wrestling with the burden of their own privilege." Publisher's note

Konner, Melvin

The **evolution** of childhood. Belknap Press of Harvard University Press 2010 943p $39.95 **305.23**
1. Child development 2. Children 3. Children -- Anthropometry 4. Emotions in children 5. Evolution 6. Human evolution 7. Nonfiction
ISBN 978-0-674-04566-8; 0-674-04566-1

LC 2009050775

It was the author's intent 'to describe 'the foundations of psychosocial growth' in an evolutionary context. A goal of the book is to provide the basis for understanding the modification of that biological heritage in interaction with the environment. . . . [Melvin] Konner's focus is on how 'the laws and facts of biology underlie normally developing social behavior' . . . [The book] is divided into five broad sections: evolution (focused on the phylogenetic origins of childhood), maturation (the genetic, physiological, and anatomical bases of psychosocial growth), socialization (the evolving social context of ontogeny), enculturation (the transmission and evolution of culture), and a conclusion. Between each of the first four major parts of the book, there is a transition essay.' (Current Anthropology)

This book "explores the biological evolution of human behavior and specifically the behavior of children. Melvin Konner . . . weaves a compelling web of theories and studies across a remarkable array of disciplines, from experimental genetics to ethnology. He ranges back to the earliest, egg-laying mammals, discusses topics as seemingly modern as

cross-gender identity conflicts, and draws on scientific work examining all manner of species with which humans share distinct characteristics. . . . To read this book is to be in the company of a helpful and hopeful teacher who is eager to share what he's found." Atl Mon

Includes bibliographical references

Kozol, Jonathan

Ordinary resurrections; children in the years of hope. Harper Perennial 2001 388p pa $14 **305.23**
1. Children
ISBN 978-0-06-095645-5; 0-06-095645-3

"Kozol tells of his continued visits with the children who attend the afterschool program at St. Ann's Episcopal Church in the racially segregated, impoverished South Bronx." SLJ

Includes bibliographical references

Mintz, Steven

★ **Huck's** raft; a history of American childhood. Belknap Press of Harvard University Press 2004 445p il $29.95   **305.23**
1. Child rearing -- United States 2. Children -- United States 3. Children -- United States -- History
ISBN 0-674-01508-8

LC 2004-42220

The author "revisits the treatment of children from the Puritan era up to the edge of the millennium, . . . showing that we have alternately vilified our offspring . . . and glorified them. . . . In addition, the roles children have assumed in the workforce have fluctuated with the needs of the era—economic expansion led to harsh child labor, while its aftermath, prosperity, led to an interest in child welfare. . . . Mintz's thorough yet accessibly written study delves into the external forces that have shaped the lives of our young while also probing the internal developments in their collective consciousness." Libr J

Includes bibliographical references

Orenstein, Peggy

Cinderella ate my daughter; dispatches from the frontlines of the new girlie-girl culture. HarperCollins 2011 244p $25.99   **305.23**
1. Femininity 2. Girls -- Psychology 3. Mother-daughter relationship 4. Mothers and daughters
ISBN 0061711527; 9780061711527

LC 2010-28724

Orenstein examines aspects and manifestations of sexualized girlhood such as child beauty pageants and Disney Princess dolls. Bibliography. Index.

The author "finds today's pink and princess-obsessed girl culture grating when it threatens to lure her own young daughter, Daisy. In her quest to determine whether princess mania is merely a passing phase or a more sinister marketing plot with long-term negative impact, Orenstein travels to Disneyland, American Girl Place, the American International Toy Fair; visits a children's beauty pageant; attends a Miley Cyrus concert; tools around the Internet; and interviews parents, historians, psychologists, marketers, and others. . . . With insight and biting humor, the author explores her own conflicting feelings as a mother as she protects her offspring and probes the roots and tendrils of the girlie-girl movement." Publ Wkly

Includes bibliographical references

Orme, Nicholas

Medieval children. Yale Univ. Press 2001 387p il $39.95; pa $19.95   **305.23**

1. Children -- England -- History 2. Children -- History 3. Middle Ages 4. Social history -- Medieval, 500-1500

ISBN 0-300-08541-9; 0-300-09754-9 pa

LC 2001-26172

This is an "examination of the daily lives of medieval children from diverse classes and backgrounds. . . . Orme's exacting research gives the book weight, and his affectionate, eloquent prose carries its immediate manner from history to sociology to philosophy and back again." Booklist

Includes bibliographical references and index

Shachtman, Tom

★ **Rumspringa**; to be or not to be Amish. North Point Press 2006 286p hardcover o.p. pa $16 **305.23**

1. Amish 2. Amish -- Customs and practices 3. Teenagers -- Religious life 4. Teenagers -- Religious life -- United States 5. Teenagers -- United States -- Social life and customs

ISBN 0-86547-687-X; 978-0-86547-687-5; 0-86547-742-6 pa; 978-0-86547-742-1 pa

LC 2006-4329

"Shachtman is like a maestro, masterfully conducting an orchestra of history, anthropology, psychology, sociology, and journalism together in a harmonious and evocative symphony of all things Amish." Christ Sci Monit

Includes bibliographical references

Simmons, Rachel

★ **Odd** girl out; the hidden culture of aggression in girls. Harcourt 2002 296p $25; pa $14 **305.23**

1. Aggressiveness (Psychology) 2. Aggressiveness in children 3. Girls 4. Girls -- Psychology

ISBN 0-15-100604-0; 0-15-602734-8 pa

LC 2001-6864

The author "does an excellent job of articulating to adults exactly the pain and subtle warfare that many teen girls experience." Booklist

Includes bibliographical references

305.231   Child development

Brazelton, T. Berry

Touchpoints three to six; your child's emotional and behavioral development. [by] T. Berry Brazelton, Joshua D. Sparrow. Perseus Bks. 2001 xxiii, 502p il hardcover o.p. pa $18   **305.231**

1. Child development 2. Child psychology 3. Child rearing 4. Preschool children

ISBN 0-7382-0199-5; 0-7382-0678-4 pa

LC 2001-92010

"Destined to become required reading for parents and early childhood educators, this is a valuable addition to any public library." Libr J

Includes bibliographical references

305.235   Young people twelve to twenty

Flanagan, Caitlin

Girl land; Caitlin Flanagan. Little, Brown and Co. 2012 209 p.   **305.235**

1. Adolescence 2. Teenage girls -- Psychology 3. Teenage girls -- United States

ISBN 9780316065986

LC 2011024934

The book discusses "[t]he transition from girl to woman [which according to the author] is an experience that has changed radically over the generations: everything from how a girl learns about her period to how she expects to be treated by boys and men. Girls today observe these passages very differently, and yet the landmarks themselves have remained remarkably constant—proof, [Caitlin] Flanagan believes, of their significance. In a world where protections of girls' privacy and personal freedom seem to disappear every day, the ultimate challenge modern parents face is finding a way to defend both." (Publisher's note)

Hine, Thomas

The **rise** and fall of the American teenager. Bard 1999 322p $24; pa $14   **305.235**

1. Adolescence 2. Adolescence -- United States 3. Teenagers 4. Teenagers -- United States

ISBN 0-380-97358-8; 0-380-72853-2 pa

LC 99-24381

In this social history Hine "writes about ways the culture has affected what teenage has meant for youth and how youth have been perceived, as in World War II when teenagers readily took on roles supporting the war effort. Interesting, enjoyable, and multifaceted, Hine's work defies pigeonholing by covering anthropology, psychology, communications, and sociology." Libr J

Includes bibliographical references

305.24   Adults

Sheehy, Gail

★ **New** passages; mapping your life across time. Random House 1995 xxv, 498p hardcover o.p. pa $15.95   **305.24**

1. Adulthood 2. Aging 3. Middle age 4. Socialization

ISBN 0-345-40445-9 pa

LC 94-43996

This work is "grounded in the economic and psychological realities that make adult life so complex today. The major themes of this book are accurate and important." N Y Times Book Rev

Includes bibliographical references

Taylor, D. J.

Bright young people; the lost generation of London's jazz age. Farrar, Straus and Giroux 2009 361p il $27   **305.24**

1. Bohemianism

ISBN 978-0-374-11683-5; 0-374-11683-0

LC 2008-31366

The author "chronicles the doings of London's gilded youth in the Roaring Twenties. Even if you think you know a lot (or enough) about them; even if you've read the acerbic novels of the early Evelyn Waugh or plowed your way through Anthony Powell's A Dance to the Music of Time, there's bound to be material here you haven't seen or heard of." Washington Post Book World

Includes bibliographical references

305.244   People in middle adulthood

Sheehy, Gail

Understanding men's passages; discovering the new map of men's lives. Random House 1998 xxvi, 292p hardcover o.p. pa $14   **305.244**

1. Impotence 2. Masculinity -- United States 3. Maturation (Psychology) 4. Men -- Psychology 5. Middle age 6. Middle aged men -- United States 7. Sexual behavior

ISBN 0-345-40690-7 pa

LC 98-9942

"Sheehy's advice, bolstered with demographic research, group interviews, medical commentary and personal testimony, is tough and wise." N Y Times Book Rev

Includes bibliographical references

305.26   People in late adulthood

Carter, Jimmy

The **virtues** of aging. Ballantine Pub. Group 1998 140p hardcover o.p. pa $11.95   **305.26**

1. Aging 2. Large print books

ISBN 0-345-42826-9; 0-345-42592-8 pa

LC 98-25298

"At age 56, Jimmy Carter 'involuntarily retired' when he was defeated for a second term as president by Ronald Reagan in 1980. . . . Carter sketches how he and Rosalynn created new careers and new lives for themselves—as authors, educators, and senior family members and as a couple growing old together. He adds statistics about the aging population, makes suggestions for healthy living, and defines successful aging." Libr J

Friedan, Betty

The **fountain** of age. Simon & Schuster 1993 671p hardcover o.p. pa $26.95   **305.26**

1. Old age 2. Women -- United States

ISBN 0-671-89853-1 pa

LC 93-4090

"Betty Friedan's metaphorical fountain of age spouts research, observation, conjecture, evangelical fervor, revolutionary rhetoric, and denial. The result is a pool of optimism in which the mother of the woman's movement examines the unlifted face of age and finds it lovable." New Repub

Includes bibliographical references

Jacoby, Susan

Never say die; the myth and marketing of the new old age. Pantheon Books 2011 332p $27.95 **305.26**

1. Aged -- United States 2. Aging 3. Elderly 4. Old age

ISBN 978-0-307-37794-4; 0-307-37794-6

LC 2010-17123

In this book, author "Susan Jacoby turns an . . . eye on the marketers of longevity—pharmaceutical companies, lifestyle gurus, and scientific businessmen who suggest that there will soon be a 'cure' for the 'disease' of aging. She separates wishful hype from realistic hope in a[n] . . . appraisal of subjects that include the explosion of Alzheimer's cases, the impact of possible cuts in Social Security on the economic future of aging boomers, and the fact that women make up most of the 'oldest old.' Finally, Jacoby raises the fundamental question of whether living longer is a desirable thing unless it means living better, and she considers the profound moral and ethical concerns raised by increasing longevity." (Publisher's note)

The author "offers an important reality check for Americans enamored of the images of healthy, active seniors featured in advertisements." Booklist

Includes bibliographical references

Lawrence-Lightfoot, Sara

The **third** chapter; passion, risk, and adventure in the 25 years after 50. Farrar, Straus and Giroux 2009 260p $25   **305.26**

1. Aging 2. Elderly -- United States 3. Old age

ISBN 978-0-374-27549-5; 0-374-27549-1

LC 2008-29147

"New opportunities for creativity and self-fulfillment await men and women between the ages of 50 and 75. . . . [The author] coins the term 'Third Chapter' to describe the rich possibilities as illustrated in her extended interviews with 40 well-educated, affluent Americans. Founding her thesis on classic formulations of life-stage development, particularly that of Erik Erikson, the author offers a wide range of models for people who feel burned out, restless or dissatisfied with their lives, describing how each of her subjects became 'a different person.' . . . Readers feeling that something is missing from their lives, that there is something more they can contribute, will find this book a helpful guide." Publ Wkly

Includes bibliographical references

Pillemer, Karl A.

30 lessons for living; tried and true advice from the wisest Americans. [by] Karl Pillemer. Hudson Street Press 2011 271p $25.95   **305.26**

1. Aging 2. Conduct of life 3. Elderly -- United States 4. Happiness 5. Old age

ISBN 978-1-59463-084-2

LC 2011017113

"Who better to teach lessons on living . . . than the thousands of Americans over the age of 65 who have successfully navigated the territories of marriage, career, money, and aging? By conducting innumerable interviews, Pillemer found that their advice upends contemporary wisdom: they suggest marrying a person like oneself, choosing a career for intrinsic rewards, and spending more time with one's children. The author skillfully weaves a prevailing theme (e.g., parenting, aging fearlessly) with self-disclosing statements from interviewees to create a compelling, inspirational book. One of the best of its kind. " Libr J

Includes bibliographical references

Vaillant, George E.

Aging well; surprising guideposts to a happier life from the landmark Harvard study of adult development. Little, Brown 2002 373p $24.95; pa $14.95   **305.26**
1. Aging 2. Aging -- Psychological aspects -- United States -- Longitudinal studies 3. Aging -- Social aspects -- United States -- Longitudinal studies
ISBN 0-316-98936-3; 0-316-09007-7 pa
LC 2001-30651
The author "offers much valuable information about aging, and his judgment calls (his term) are perceptive, understanding, and often tinged with delightful humor." Booklist
Includes bibliographical references

★ Encyclopedia of aging; David J. Ekerdt, editor in chief. Macmillan Ref. USA 2002 4v set $450   **305.26**
1. Aged 2. Aged -- Encyclopedias 3. Aging 4. Aging -- Encyclopedias 5. Elderly -- Encyclopedias 6. Gerontology 7. Gerontology -- Encyclopedias 8. Reference books
ISBN 0-02-865472-2
LC 2002-2596
This includes "400-plus concise and readable entries that offer excellent introductions to important concepts." Libr J
Includes bibliographical references

305.31   Men

Bly, Robert

★ Iron John; a book about men. DaCapo Press 2004 268p pa $15   **305.31**
1. Men -- Psychology
ISBN 0-306-81376-9
LC 2004-56137
"Drawing vitally upon such diverse sources as ancient mythology, classic literature (including his own poetry), anthropology, psychology, and even the responses of the real-life men who have participated in his seminars ('gatherings'), Bly staunchly redefines male identity, emphasizing the importance of what he calls 'warrior energy' and all its positive implications." Booklist
Includes bibliographical references.

Bordo, Susan

The male body; a new look at men in public and in private. Farrar, Straus & Giroux 1999 358p il hardcover o.p. pa $16   **305.31**
1. Body, Human -- Social aspects 2. Gay men 3. Masculinity 4. Masculinity in popular culture 5. Men 6. Men in popular culture 7. Personal appearance 8. Sexual harassment
ISBN 0-374-52732-6 pa
LC 99-25386
"Bordo sets out to map the ambivalent attitudes that exist in the American cultural imagination toward male bodies and, in particular, toward the penis and its 'symbolic double,' the phallus. . . . Part memoir, part elegy, this feminist

guided tour of the male body concludes with real hope for improved relations between the sexes." Publ Wkly
Includes bibliographical references

Men and masculinities; a social, cultural, and historican encyclopedia. edited by Michael Kimmel and Amy Aronson. ABC-CLIO 2004 2v set $255   **305.31**
1. Men 2. Sex role
ISBN 1-57607-774-8
LC 2003-20729
This reference covers "individuals, creative works and characters, theories, and events that over centuries have shaped the notion of American masculinity and its implications for men and women." Booklist

305.38   Specific groups of men

Cose, Ellis

The envy of the world; on being a Black man in America. Washington Sq. Press 2002 163p $22; pa $13   **305.38**
1. African American men -- Attitudes 2. African American men -- Psychology 3. African American men -- Social conditions 4. African Americans 5. Self-defeating behavior -- United States 6. Social values -- United States
ISBN 0-7434-2715-7; 0-7434-2817-x pa
LC 2001-52073
The author's "stated objective of opening a discussion on how racism affects individuals makes this book interesting reading for a broad range of readers." Booklist

McCall, Nathan

Makes me wanna holler; a young black man in America. Random House 1994 404p hardcover o.p. pa $14.95   **305.38**
1. African Americans -- Biography 2. Biography, Individual 3. Essayists 4. Journalists 5. Memoirists
ISBN 0-679-74070-8 pa
LC 93-30654
The author relates the "story of his rise from poverty to success as a journalist at the Washington Post. He uses graphic language, blunt descriptions, honest expression, introspection, and careful observation to describe his early years in Portsmouth, Virginia, as a young black male, the recipient of a 12-year prison sentence for armed robbery, whose life was dangerously out of control. Insensitivity, alienation, racial hatred, drugs (especially crack), guns, rape, robbery, the black American as an endangered species—McCall covers it all in a depressing yet spellbinding documentary." Libr J

305.4   Women

Adovasio, J. M.

The invisible sex; uncovering the true roles of women in prehistory. by J .M. Adovasio, Olga

Soffer & Jake Page. Collins 2007 320p il map
$26.95   **305.4**
1. Feminist archaeology 2. Prehistoric peoples 3. Sex
role 4. Sex role -- History 5. Sexual division of labor
-- History 6. Women, Prehistoric
ISBN 978-0-06-117091-1; 0-06-117091-7
                                         LC 2006-50582
In this study of prehistoric culture, the authors argue
"that women invented all kinds of critical materials, including the clothing necessary for life in colder climates, the
ropes used to make rafts that enabled long-distance travel
by water, and nets used for communal hunting. Even more
important, women played a central role in the development
of language and social life—in short, in our becoming human." Publisher's note
Includes bibliographical references (p. 283-290)

Beauvoir, Simone de
★ The **second** sex; translated and edited by
H. M. Parshley; with an introduction by Margaret
Crosland. Knopf 1993 lv, 786p $23; pa $17 **305.4**
1. Women
ISBN 0-679-42016-9; 0-679-72451-6 pa
                                         LC 92-54303
This "thorough analysis of women's secondary status in
society, became a classic of feminist literature." Reader's
Ency. 3d edition

Berg, Barbara J.
Sexism in America; alive, well, and ruining our future. Lawrence Hill Books 2009 412p
$24.95   **305.4**
1. Sex role 2. Sexism 3. Women -- United States
ISBN 978-1-55652-776-0
                                         LC 2009-11473
"This book is Berg's extremely persuasive dismissal of
the claim that the United States is a 'post-feminist, post-ra-
cial' society. Using testimonies from her survey of hundreds
of American women, as well as extensively documented
research, . . . [the author] gives a rapid-fire account of the
advancement of women's rights and the continuing backlash
on feminist progress from the 1950s to the present. Berg's
feminist critique of seemingly gender-neutral events are a
revelation. . . . Equally insightful is Berg's analysis of the
setbacks facing the third wave of feminists in the United
States." Libr J
Includes bibliographical references

Collins, Gail
America's women; four hundred years of dolls,
drudges, helpmates, and heroines. Morrow 2003
556p il $27.95; pa $15.95   **305.4**
1. Women -- United States -- History
ISBN 0-06-018510-4; 0-06-122722-6 pa
                                         LC 2003-51011
This is a history of American women from colonial times
to the present

"Collins elegantly and eruditely celebrates the hard-won
victories, overwhelming obstacles, and selfless contributions
of a captivating array of influential women." Booklist
Includes bibliographical references

When everything changed; the amazing journey
of American women from 1960 to the present. Little,
Brown and Co. 2009 471p il $27.99   **305.4**
1. Feminism -- United States -- History -- 20th century
2. Women -- United States -- Biography 3. Women
-- United States -- History 4. Women -- United States
-- Social conditions 5. Women -- United States -- Social
life and customs
ISBN 978-0-316-05954-1; 0-316-05954-4
                                         LC 2008-54933
"Collins can be deadly serious and great fun to read at
the same time. A revelatory book for readers of both sexes,
and sure to become required reading for any American wom-
en's-studies course." Kirkus
Includes bibliographical references

Coontz, Stephanie
A **strange** stirring; The Feminine Mystique and
American women at the dawn of the 1960s. Basic
Books 2010 222p $25.95   **305.4**
1. Authors 2. Feminism 3. Feminism -- United States
-- History -- 20th century 4. Feminists 5. Nonfiction
writers 6. Organization officials 7. Women -- Social
conditions 8. Women -- United States -- Social
conditions -- 20th century
ISBN 978-0-465-00200-9; 0-465-00200-5
                                         LC 2010-22163
The book "documents the circumstances of middle-class
American women in the early 1960s and the impact of Betty
Friedan's The Feminine Mystique (1963). Stephanie Coontz
makes it clear that although Friedan, and many observers
since, have exaggerated the book's role in launching the second wave of the feminist movement, thousands of women
were profoundly affected by it. . . . [Stephanie] Coontz begins with a stark look at the circumstances facing women in
the early 1960s, including legal discrimination and widely
held cultural beliefs about women's nature and proper role.
. . . The book ends with a chapter on the circumstances of
women today. Despite the gains of the feminist movement,
gender expectations still limit women's possibilities." (Journal of American History)
The author "analyzes the impact of Betty Friedan's
groundbreaking 1963 book, The Feminine Mystique, on
the generation of white, middle-class women electrified by
Friedan's argument that beneath the surface contentment,
most housewives harbored a deep well of insecurity, self-
doubt, and unhappiness. . . . This perceptive, engrossing,
albeit specialized book provides welcome context and background to a still controversial bestseller that changed how
women viewed themselves." Publ Wkly
Includes bibliographical references

Fleet, Carole Brody
Widows wear stilettos; a practical and emotional
guide for the young widow. by Carole Brody Fleet

with Syd Harriet. New Horizon Press 2009 223p pa
$14.95 **305.4**
1. Widows
ISBN 978-0-88282-339-3; 0-88282-339-6

A guide for women who have "experienced the loss of
a partner at a young age. Fleet's presentation is frank and
interspersed with bits of honest humor. The text is easy to
read, with charts and tips sprinkled throughout. Fleet, with
psychotherapist Harriet, provides information on how to
organize details such as funeral arrangements, wills, social
security, and insurance at a time when organization is the last
thing a new widow may want to face. She discusses emotional, physical, and spiritual health and finishes by focusing
on living the rest of your life. This is a book about hope, and
women will want to read it and share it with others, regardless of marital status or age." Libr J

Fox-Genovese, Elizabeth

Within the plantation household; black and
white women of the Old South. University of N.C.
Press 1988 544p il $49.95; pa $19.95 **305.4**
1. Plantation life 2. Slavery -- Southern States 3.
Slavery -- United States 4. Women -- Southern States
ISBN 0-8078-1808-9; 0-8078-4232-X pa
LC 88-40139

"An illuminating and solid book of social history, with
appeal to those who take a serious interest in historical
research." Booklist
Includes bibliographical references

Freedman, Estelle B.

No turning back; the history of feminism and the
future of women. Ballantine Bks. 2002 446p hardcover o.p. pa $15.95 **305.4**
1. Feminism 2. Feminism -- History 3. Women --
Social conditions
ISBN 0-345-45053-1 pa
LC 2002-280895

This "work goes beyond previous studies in being interdisciplinary, international, and a pleasure to read." Libr J
Includes bibliographical references

Friedan, Betty

★ The **feminine** mystique; with a new introduction. Norton 1997 xlviii, 452p hardcover o.p. pa
$15.95 **305.4**
1. Feminism 2. Women -- United States
ISBN 0-393-32257-2 pa
LC 97-8877

An "analysis of the dilemma facing the educated American woman; the post-war emphasis on the feminine image of
the role as wife and mother has caused the American woman
to lose her identity, says the author." Cincinnati Public Libr
Includes bibliographical references

Goodwin, Jan

Price of honor; Muslim women lift the veil of silence on the Islamic world. rev ed; Plume Bks. 2003
351p il pa $16 **305.4**
1. Muslim women
ISBN 0-452-28377-9
LC 2002-28257

The author "examines the movement that is aggressively
spreading a fundamentalist version of Islam throughout
much of the world. Her interviews with Muslim women in
ten countries both fascinate and disturb, for their candor reveals the movement's profound and often devastating effects
on them. . . . A necessary purchase." Libr J [review of 1994
edition]

Greer, Germaine

The **madwoman's** underclothes; essays and occasional writings. Atlantic Monthly Press 1987 xxvii, 305p hardcover o.p. pa $12.95 **305.4**
1. Authors 2. Essayists 3. Feminism 4. Feminists
5. Literary critics 6. Women -- Social conditions 7.
Writers on politics
ISBN 0-87113-308-3 pa
LC 87-11475

A collection of the British feminist's nonfiction writings
spanning her career from the 1960s to the 1980s.

Roberts, Cokie

We are our mothers' daughters. Morrow 1998
197p $19.95; pa $11 **305.4**
1. Feminism 2. Sex discrimination 3. Women --
United States -- History
ISBN 0-688-15198-1; 0-688-16967-8 pa
LC 98-14816

"Roberts uses the vantage point of mother, daughter and
exasperated observer as she discusses the evolution of wom-
en's roles over the past few generations. . . . Although there's
no sophisticated analysis or new material here, Roberts is at
her best when describing the ambivalences and ambitions of
a woman's life." N Y Times Book Rev

Rodriguez, Deborah

Kabul Beauty School; an American woman goes
behind the veil. Random House 2007 275p $24.95;
pa $14.95 **305.4**
1. Beauty shops 2. Hairstylists 3. Relief workers 4.
School administrators 5. Women -- Afghanistan 6.
Women -- Afghanistan -- Social conditions
ISBN 978-1-4000-6559-2; 1-4000-6559-3; 978-0-
8129-7673-1 pa; 0-8129-7673-8 pa
LC 2006-50384

"Rodriguez's experiences will delight readers as she recounts such tales as two friends acting as 'parents' and negotiating a dowry for her marriage to an Afghan man or her students puzzling over a donation of a carton of thongs. Most
of all, they will share her admiration for Afghan women's
survival and triumph in chaotic times." SLJ

Ulrich, Laurel

Well-behaved women seldom make history; [by] Laurel Thatcher Ulrich. Alfred A. Knopf 2007 xxxiv, 284p il $24 **305.4**

1. Authors 2. Biographers 3. Essayists 4. Feminism 5. Novelists 6. Poets 7. Short story writers 8. Suffragists 9. Women -- History 10. Women in literature

ISBN 978-1-4000-4159-6; 1-4000-4159-6

LC 2006-100581

This book "is by no means jargon-ridden or academic in tone. Ulrich's style is plain and direct, agreeable but without frills, and she moves efficiently right along. The book is a pleasure to read." Washington Post Book World

Includes bibliographical references

Wolf, Naomi

★ The **beauty** myth; how images of beauty are used against women. Perennial 2002 348p pa $14.95 **305.4**

1. Feminine beauty (Aesthetics) 2. Femininity 3. Personal appearance 4. Sex role 5. Women

ISBN 0-06-051218-0

LC 2002-72516

The author "presents a provocative and persuasive account of the pervasiveness of the beauty ideal in all facets of Western culture." Libr J

Includes bibliographical references

Xinran

Message from an unknown Chinese mother; stories of loss and love. translated from Chinese by Nicky Harman. Scribner 2011 xxvii, 239p $25; ebook $11.99 **305.4**

1. Children -- China 2. Mothers

ISBN 978-1-4516-1089-5; 978-1-4516-1095-6 ebook

The author "collects the heartbreaking stories of Chinese women forced to give up their baby girls because of the one-child-only policy or feudal traditions that prefer boys, in an oral history written for those abandoned daughters. . . . This is a brutally honest book written for those relinquished children, so that they will know how much their birth mothers loved them and how—in the words of one mother who gave up her daughter—'they paid for that love with an endless stream of bitter tears.'" Publ Wkly

Zeitz, Joshua

Flapper; a madcap story of sex, style, celebrity, and the women who made America modern. Crown Publishers 2006 338p il $24.95 **305.4**

1. Popular culture -- United States 2. Women -- United States

ISBN 1-4000-8053-3; 978-1-4000-8053-3

LC 2005-24297

"An essential exploration of the women Zeitz deems 'the first thoroughly modern American[s].'" Booklist

Includes bibliographical references

Bitchfest; ten years of cultural criticism from the pages of Bitch magazine. edited by Lisa Jervis and Andi Zeisler. Farrar, Straus & Giroux 2006 372p pa $16 **305.4**

1. Criticism 2. Culture 3. Feminism 4. Feminist criticism 5. Popular culture 6. Popular culture -- United States

ISBN 978-0-374-11343-8 pa; 0-374-11343-2 pa

LC 2005-36156

"This work represents an alternating mix of the most hilarious, alarming, and unexpected essays from Bitch magazine's first ten years. . . . Readers new to this feminist quarterly will find the articles, almost without exception, original, intelligent, and well written. This compilation has staying power." Libr J

Includes bibliographical references

★ The Columbia documentary history of American women since 1941; edited by Harriet Sigerman. Columbia University Press 2003 690p $94; pa $34.50 **305.4**

1. Feminism 2. Feminism -- United States -- History -- Sources 3. Women -- United States -- History -- 20th century -- Sources 4. Women -- United States -- History -- Sources 5. Women's rights 6. Women's rights -- United States -- History -- Sources

ISBN 0-231-11698-5; 0-231-11699-3 pa

LC 2002-41395

This collection of public and private primary sources includes such topics as employment opportunities, "the ideas and changes brought about by the women's movement, the challenges to and defense of reproductive rights, the backlash against feminism in the name of family values, and new visions for women's lives in the twenty-first century." Publisher's note

Includes bibliographical references

Encyclopedia of women in the American West; Gordon Morris Bakken and Brenda Farrington, editors. Sage 2003 xxiii, 381p il $125 **305.4**

1. Women -- West (U.S.)

ISBN 0-7619-2356-X

LC 2003-6729

"There is a clear need for this encyclopedia. . . . Recommended for academic and public libraries and all libraries with a special interest in the western region and women's studies." Libr J

Includes bibliographical references and index

★ The Greenwood encyclopedia of women's issues worldwide; Lynn Walter, editor-in-chief. Greenwood Press 2003 6v il maps set $550 **305.4**

1. Reference books 2. Women -- Social conditions -- Encyclopedias

ISBN 0-313-32787-4

LC 2004-695024

"Readers looking for information on women's everyday lives around the world will welcome this country-by-country survey." Booklist

Includes bibliographical references

No small courage; a history of women in the United States. edited by Nancy Cott. Oxford Univ.

Press 2000 646p il maps hardcover o.p. pa
$21.95 **305.4**
1. Women -- United States -- History
ISBN 0-19-513946-1; 978-0-19-517323-9 pa; 0-19-517323-6 pa

LC 00-21130

"By examining the flow of American history as it has affected women {the authors} illuminate aspects of the past that have often been neglected." Booklist
Includes bibliographical references

The Oxford encyclopedia of women in world history;
Bonnie G. Smith, editor in chief. Oxford University Press 2008 4v il set $595 **305.4**
1. Reference books 2. Women -- History -- Encyclopedias
ISBN 978-0-19-514890-9; 0-19-514890-8

LC 2007-34939

"These four volumes combine scholarship from the . . . fields of world history and women's history to produce a thoughtful, thorough, and accessible survey of women in world history to which some 900 researchers from 50-plus countries have contributed. . . . Smith does an admirable job of summarizing and synthesizing a vast academic literature in clear, jargon-free language that will engage scholars and general readers alike." Libr J
Includes bibliographical references

Women in the Middle Ages; an encyclopedia. edited by Katharina M. Wilson and Nadia Margolis.
Greenwood Press 2004 2v il set $199.95 **305.4**
1. Middle Ages -- Encyclopedias 2. Reference books 3. Women -- History -- Encyclopedias
ISBN 0-313-33016-6

LC 2004-53042

"In addition to entries on renowned women, there is a . . . number of articles covering topics such as footbinding, clothing, medicine, law, literary motifs, and geography-specific information. Terminology is defined in context, making the work readily accessible to high school students and lay readers." Libr J
Includes bibliographical references

★ Women's letters; America from the Revolutionary War to the present. edited by Lisa Grunwald & Stephen J. Adler. Dial Press 2005 824p il hardcover o.p. pa $18 **305.4**
1. American letters -- Women authors 2. Biography, Collective 3. Women -- Biography 4. Women -- United States -- Correspondence 5. Women -- United States -- History -- Sources
ISBN 0-385-33553-9; 0-385-33556-3 pa

LC 2005-41446

"This is a delightful collection of belles letters in the most literal sense of the term." Publ Wkly
Includes bibliographical references

The essential feminist reader; edited and with an introduction by Estelle B. Freedman. Modern Library 2007 472p pa $17.95 **305.4**
1. Feminism
ISBN 0-8129-7460-3; 978-0-8129-7460-7

This collection of writings by feminist authors "features primary source material from around the globe, including short works of fiction and drama, political manifestos, and the work of less well-known writers." Publisher's note
Includes bibliographical references

305.409 History, geographic treatment, biography

Bumiller, Elisabeth
May you be the mother of a hundred sons; a journey among the women of India. Random House 1990 306p il hardcover o.p. pa $13.95 **305.409**
1. Women -- India
ISBN 0-449-90614-0 pa

LC 89-27120

"In addition to the usual discussion of arranged marriages, movie stars, and Indira Gandhi, India's late prime minister, Bumiller portrays a wide cross section of Indian society. Her discussion of bride burning, family planning, village health programs, the outlook of village women, and female infanticide will generate much comment and discussion. Essential for libraries with women's studies and Third World collections." Libr J
Includes bibliographical references

305.42 Social role and status of women

Brownmiller, Susan
In our time; memoir of a revolution. Dial Press (NY) 1999 360p hardcover o.p. pa $15.95 **305.42**
1. Feminism 2. Feminism -- United States -- History -- 20th century 3. Feminists -- United States 4. Women's movement 5. Women's rights -- United States -- History -- 20th century
ISBN 0-385-31831-6 pa

LC 99-39344

This book focuses on the women's movement between 1967 and 1977.
"A riveting blend of eyewitness accounts and keen analysis, this is history at its most vital and a stirring testament to our ability to come together to combat social injustice, no matter how deeply entrenched it has become." Booklist

Friedan, Betty
Life so far. Simon & Schuster 2000 399p il hardcover o.p. pa $17 **305.42**
1. Authors 2. Feminism 3. Feminism -- United States -- History 4. Feminists 5. Feminists -- United States -- Biography 6. Nonfiction writers 7. Organization officials
ISBN 0-684-80789-0; 978-0-7432-9986-2 pa; 0-7432-9986-8 pa

LC 00-23920

In this memoir, "Friedan reminisces over a life of social activism that has included helping to found the National Organization for Women, the National Abortion and Reproductive Rights Action League, and the National Women's Political Caucus, as well as writing the pivotal The Feminine Mystique." Libr J

Sommers, Christina Hoff

Who stole feminism? how women have betrayed women. Simon & Schuster 1994 320p il hardcover o.p. pa $14 **305.42**

1. Feminism

ISBN 0-684-80156-6 pa

LC 94-4734

The author's "critique of what she calls 'gender feminism' exposes numerous examples of distorted data and totalitarian methodology in the work of such feminist leaders as Susan Faludi, Catherine MacKinnon, and a cabal of likeminded academics. Controversial, to be sure, but objectively presented and impossible to dismiss." Booklist

Includes bibliographical references

Steinem, Gloria

★ **Moving** beyond words. Simon & Schuster 1994 319p hardcover o.p. pa $19.95 **305.42**

1. Authors 2. Feminism 3. Feminists 4. Journalists 5. Magazine editors 6. Memoirists

ISBN 0-671-51052-5 pa

LC 94-4839

"Ms. Steinem's enduring contribution to the women's movement has been her ability to popularize feminist issues to a wide and often wary audience." N Y Times Book Rev

Includes bibliographical references

Outrageous acts and everyday rebellions; 2nd ed; Holt & Co. 1995 xxii, 406p pa $17 **305.42**

1. Authors 2. Feminism 3. Feminists 4. Journalists 5. Magazine editors 6. Memoirists

ISBN 0-8050-4202-4

LC 95-31711

In addition to material addressing specific feminist issues, this collection includes personal accounts of political leaders and noted women.

Zucchino, David

Myth of the welfare queen; a Pulitzer Prize-winning journalist's portrait of women on the line. Scribner 1997 366p hardcover o.p. pa $21.95 **305.42**

1. African American women 2. Poor -- United States 3. Public welfare 4. Women -- United States

ISBN 0-684-85006-5 pa

LC 97-9104

This book, "a harrowing description of daily subsistence living with very little chance of change, is a powerful exposé of the welfare myth." Libr J

305.48 Specific groups of women

Boyer, Ruth McDonald

Apache mothers and daughters; four generations of a family. University of Okla. Press 1992 xx, 393p il maps hardcover o.p. pa $19.95 **305.48**

1. Apache Indians 2. Apache Indians -- Social life and customs 3. Women -- Biography

ISBN 0-8061-2922-0 pa

LC 92-54149

"The voice throughout the narrative is an Apache one, emphasizing the continuation of Chiricahua culture. . . . It's a treat for anyone interested in cultural change and persistence." Libr J

Includes bibliographical references

Brooks, Geraldine

Nine parts of desire; the hidden world of Islamic women. Anchor Bks. (NY) 1995 255p hardcover o.p. pa $14 **305.48**

1. Muslim women 2. Women -- Islamic countries 3. Women in Islam

ISBN 0-385-47577-2 pa

LC 94-17496

"The author's revelations about these women's lives behind the veil are frank, enraging, and captivating." New Yorker

Includes bibliographical references

Mah, Adeline Yen

Falling leaves; a true story of an unwanted Chinese daughter. Wiley 1998 278p il $22.95 **305.48**

1. Physicians 2. Women physicians -- California -- Biography

ISBN 0-471-24742-1

LC 97-40144

"Although the focus of this memoir is the author's struggle to be loved by a family that treated her cruelly, it is more notable for its portrait of the domestic affairs of an immensely wealthy, Westernized Chinese family in Shanghai as the city evolved under the harsh strictures of Mao and Deng. . . . In recounting this painful tale, Yen Mah's unadorned prose is powerful, her insights keen and her portrait of her family devastating." Publ Wkly

Scroggins, Deborah

Wanted women; faith, lies, and the war on terror : the lives of Ayaan Hirsi Ali and Aafia Siddiqui. by Deborah Scroggins. Harper 2011 p. cm. **305.48**

1. Muslim women -- Political activity 2. Muslim women -- Social conditions 3. Religion -- Islam -- History

ISBN 9780060898977

LC 2011022153

This book explores the topics of "militant Islam, Muslim women's rights, and the war on terror--brought into focus through two lives on opposite sides: activist Ayaan Hirsi Ali and religious extremist Aafia Siddiqui. . . . Ayaan Hirsi Ali, a Somali-born former member of the Dutch Parliament and the author of the international bestseller 'Infidel,' was raised as a Muslim fundamentalist in Kenya. A feminist, political analyst, writer, and fierce critic of her former religion, she champions the West in what she insists must be a war against Islam. . . . Aafia Siddiqui, a native of Pakistan, moved to the United States to pursue a doctorate in neuroscience. A decade later, she returned to Pakistan, where her involvement with al-Qaeda, including her marriage to one of the 9/11 plotters, led the CIA to regard her as one of the most dangerous terrorists in the world." (Publisher's note)

305.5   People by social and economic levels

Boo, Katherine

★ **Behind** the beautiful forevers; Katherine Boo. Random House 2011 xxii, 256 p.p   **305.5**
1. India 2. India -- Economic conditions -- 1947- 3. Nonfiction 4. Slums -- India 5. Urban poor -- India -- Mumbai
ISBN 1400067553; 9780679645504; 9781400067558
LC 2011019555

This book examines the stark lives of the inhabitants of Annawadi, a slum across from Mumbai's Sahar Airport, to reveal the . . . inequality and urban poverty still endemic in India's democracy. Using recorded and videotaped conversations, interviews, documents, and the assistance of interlocutors, [Katherine] Boo profiles the lives of some of the slum dwellers from November 2007 to March 2011. . . . [Boo] claims she witnessed most of the events described in the book. (Library Journal)

Brooks, David

The **social** animal; the hidden sources of love, character, and achievement. Random House 2011 424p $27; ebook $13.99   **305.5**
1. Character 2. Elite (Social sciences) 3. Social status
ISBN 978-1-4000-6760-2; 1-4000-6760-X; 978-0-679-60393-1 ebook; 0-679-60393-X ebook
LC 2010045785

"Brooks offers fictional characters Harold and Erica to illustrate how humans communicate, are educated, and succeed—or don't. Synthesizing research on human unconsciousness, Brooks meshes sociology, psychology, and economics to show how character is formed and how we strive for happiness and success. . . . [The author] offers a new look at the assumptions we make about life and a close, deep examination of the failure of social and economic policies that do not take into account the complexities of human behavior, treating us as if we were totally rational and guided by our thoughts rather than some combination of intellect and emotion." Booklist
Includes bibliographical references

Ehrenreich, Barbara

★ **Nickel** and dimed; on (not) getting by in boom-time America. Metropolitan Bks. 2001 221p hardcover o.p. pa $15   **305.5**
1. Labor -- United States 2. Minimum wage 3. Minimum wage -- United States 4. Poverty 5. Poverty -- United States 6. Unskilled labor -- United States
ISBN 0-8050-6388-9; 0-8050-8838-5 pa
LC 00-52514

"No real answers to the problem but a compelling sketch of its reality and pervasiveness." Libr J

Epstein, Joseph

Snobbery: the American version. Houghton Mifflin 2002 274p $25; pa $14   **305.5**
1. Snobs and snobbishness 2. Snobs and snobbishness -- United States 3. Social status -- United States
ISBN 0-395-94417-1; 0-618-34073-4 pa
LC 2001-51623

"Every bracing page is a mirror in which readers can't help but recognize themselves, and each offers a quotable quip . . . and much to think about." Booklist
Includes bibliographical references and index

Freeman, Joshua Benjamin

Working-class New York; life and labor since World War II. [by] Joshua B. Freeman. New Press (NY) 2000 409p il $35; pa $19.95   **305.5**
1. Labor unions 2. Labor unions -- New York (State) -- New York -- History -- 20th century 3. Working class 4. Working class -- New York (State) -- New York -- History -- 20th century
ISBN 1-56584-575-7; 1-56584-712-1 pa
LC 99-87940

"Freeman charts the postwar rise and eventual fall of Manhattan working-class life and culture. . . . Strong narrative drive, attention to detail and historical insight make this a superb addition to studies of postwar culture, urbanology and labor history." Publ Wkly
Includes bibliographical references

Hayes, Christopher

Twilight of the elites; America after meritocracy. Christopher Hayes. Crown Publishers 2012 292 p.   **305.5**
1. Business and politics -- United States 2. Corporate power -- United States 3. Elite (Social sciences) -- United States 4. Power (Social sciences) 5. Twilight of the Elites: America After Meritocracy (Book)
ISBN 9780307720450; 9780307720474
LC 2012002435

This book looks at the meritocracy and income inequality in the U.S. Combining "political analysis," "social commentary," and "historical understanding," this book "describes how the society we have come to inhabit – utterly forgiving at the top and relentlessly punitive at the bottom – produces leaders who are out of touch with the people they have been trusted to govern." (Amazon.com)

Jadhav, Narendra

★ **Untouchables**; my family's triumphant journey out of the caste system in modern India. Scribner 2005 307p $26   **305.5**
1. Caste
ISBN 0-7432-7079-7
LC 2005-44166

"This moving story of perseverance from a sector of India rarely represented to American readers will be a standard text on Indian and Dalit themes for years to come." Libr J

LeBlanc, Adrian Nicole

Random family; love, drugs, trouble, and coming of age in the Bronx. Scribner 2003 408p $25 **305.5**
1. Family -- New York (State) -- New York -- Case studies 2. Inner cities -- New York (State) -- Case studies 3. Poor -- New York (N.Y.) 4. Urban poor -- New York (State) -- New York -- Case studies 5. Youth -- Drug use -- New York (State) -- New York 6. Youth -- New York (N.Y.) 7. Youth -- New York (State) -- New

York -- Biography
ISBN 0-684-86387-1

LC 2002-26673

"A painstaking feat of reporting and empathy that resulted from 10 years of hanging out with a hard-pressed, loosely defined family in the Bronx." N Y Times Book Rev

Maharidge, Dale

Someplace like America; tales from the new Great Depression. photographs by Michael S. Williamson; with a foreword by Bruce Springsteen. University of California Press 2011 244p il $29.95   **305.5**
1. Poverty 2. Unemployed 3. Working class
ISBN 978-0-520-26247-8; 0-520-26247-6

LC 2010-53750

"Maharidge and Williamson continue their heartfelt chronicle of the travails facing America's poor and homeless in this follow-up to the 1995 Journey to Nowhere. Presenting new stories from today's 'Great Depression' and updating their accounts of those impoverished during the recession of the '80s and the supposed boom years of the '90s, this book evokes the Depression-era collaboration of Walker Evans and James Agee. . . . At the core of the narrative are the individuals who've found themselves dispossessed, hopping freight trains to look for work, waiting in food bank lines, huddling in shanties hand-built from scraps and billboard tarps, and mourning the closings of the steel mills where they once worked. Williamson's gritty photographs—of blind storefronts, abandoned lots choked with weeds, faces lined with dirt and worry, stalwart families, and squatters hunched over meager campfires—are an equally eloquent testimonial." Publ Wkly
Includes bibliographical references.

Painter, Nell Irvin

★ **Sojourner** Truth; a life, a symbol. Norton 1996 370p il hardcover o.p. pa $15.95   **305.5**
1. Abolitionists 2. African American women -- Biography 3. Biography, Individual 4. Feminism 5. Memoirists
ISBN 0-393-02739-2; 0-393-31708-0 pa

LC 95-47595

"Painter persuasively offers us the real woman behind the myth." Publ Wkly
Includes bibliographical references

Phillips, Kevin P.

★ **Wealth** and democracy; a political history of the American rich. {by} Kevin Phillips. Broadway Bks. 2002 xxii, 473p $29.95; pa $16.95   **305.5**
1. Political corruption 2. Political corruption -- United States 3. Representative government and representation 4. Representative government and representation -- United States 5. Wealth 6. Wealth -- United States
ISBN 0-7679-0533-4; 0-7679-0534-2 pa

LC 2001-52656

"Phillips's astute analysis of the effects of wealth and capital upon democracy is both eye-opening and disturbing." Publ Wkly
Includes bibliographical references

Rothkopf, David J.

Superclass; the global power elite and the world they are making. [by] David Rothkopf. Farrar, Straus and Giroux 2008 400p   **305.5**
1. Elite (Social sciences) 2. Power (Social sciences)
ISBN 978-0-374-27210-4

LC 2007-36569

"Neither hand-wringing nor worshipful, this book delivers an unsettling account of what the immense and growing power of this superclass bodes for the future." Publ Wkly
Includes bibliographical references (p. 235-355)

Veblen, Thorstein

★ The **theory** of the leisure class; edited with an introduction and notes by Martha Banta. Oxford University Press 2007 pa $15.95   **305.5**
1. Social classes
ISBN 978-0-19-280684-0; 0-19-280684-X

LC 2007-8544

In this economic treatise, "Veblen held that the feudal subdivision of classes had continued into modern times, the lords employing themselves uselessly . . . while the lower classes labored at industrial pursuits to support the whole of society. The leisure class, Veblen said, justifies itself solely by practicing 'conspicuous leisure and conspicuous consumption'; he defined waste as any activity not contributing to material productivity." Benet Reader's Ency. 4th edition

Wyman, Mark

Hoboes; bindlestiffs, fruit tramps, and the harvesting of the West. Hill and Wang 2010 336p il map $28   **305.5**
1. Migrant labor 2. Tramps
ISBN 978-0-8090-3021-7

LC 2009-20834

"A vigorous, well-written multicultural history of the West as it really was." Kirkus
Includes bibliographical references

Zubok, Vladislav

Zhivago's children; the last Russian intelligentsia. [by] Vladislav Zubok. Belknap Press of Harvard University Press 2009 453p il $35   **305.5**
1. Authors 2. Communist leaders 3. Heads of state 4. Intellectuals -- Soviet Union 5. Intellectuals -- Soviet Union -- History 6. Nobel laureates for literature 7. Novelists 8. Poets 9. Political leaders 10. Short story writers 11. Socialism -- Soviet Union 12. Translators
ISBN 978-0-674-03344-3; 0-674-03344-2

LC 2008-53107

This "is a thorough, scholarly examination of a vital era in Russian history whose themes of human rights, freedom and dissent will resonate among experts and lay readers alike." Washington Post
Includes bibliographical references

305.8   Ethnic and national groups

American Jewish Historical Society

American Jewish history; edited by Jeffrey S. Gurock. Routledge 1998 8v in 13 set $1,705 **305.8**
1. Jews -- History 2. Jews -- United States 3. Jews -- United States -- History
ISBN 0-415-91933-9

"This set is a compilation of 211 articles . . . chosen to relate the history of American Jews to that of other Americans or to that of Jews all over the world. . . . The wide range of issues discussed in the set includes anti-Semitism among the suffragettes, Jewish-black relations, the role of synagogue sisterhoods, and the political and cultural impact of Zionism. American Jewish History is a unique source." Booklist

Asante, Molefi K.

The **African**-American atlas; black history and culture--an illustrated reference. [by] Molefi K. Asante and Mark T. Mattson. Macmillan 1998 251p il maps $135 **305.8**
1. African Americans -- History 2. Afro-Americans 3. Afro-Americans -- History
ISBN 0-02-864984-2
LC 98-25556

"The authors introduce African-American history by interweaving information about the people and events that influenced our nation's development with maps, charts, reproductions, and photographs." SLJ
Includes bibliographical references

Avakian, Monique

★ **Atlas** of Asian-American history. Facts on File 2002 214p il maps $85 **305.8**
1. Asian Americans -- History
ISBN 0-8160-3699-3
LC 00-49509

This "overview of the political, social, and cultural history of Asian Americans opens with a discussion of the Asian heritage and ends with comments on Asian America today. Personal anecdotes throughout range from the Chinese miners in 19th-century California to modern day health-care workers from India. Sixty full-color maps, 100 historical photos, and 34 line drawings and graphs lead the reader through discussions of the people of China, Japan, Korea, India, the Philippines, and Southeast Asia." Libr J
Includes bibliographical references

Bayoumi, Moustafa

How does it feel to be a problem? being young and Arab in America. Penguin Press 2008 290p $24.95; pa $15 **305.8**
1. Arab American youth 2. Arab Americans -- Ethnic identity 3. Arab Americans -- Social conditions 4. Race awareness -- United States 5. Young men -- Psychology 6. Young men -- United States
ISBN 978-1-59420-176-9; 978-0-14-311541-0 pa
LC 2007-49272

The author "wondered how younger generations of Arab Americans were faring in a post-9/11 U.S. against the backdrop of fear and suspicion. By focusing on the lives of seven young people living in Brooklyn, Bayoumi offers a reveal-ing portrait of life for people who are often scrutinized but seldom heard from." Booklist
Includes bibliographical references

Beckerman, Gal

When they come for us we'll be gone; the epic struggle to save Soviet Jewry. Houghton Mifflin Harcourt 2010 598p il $30 **305.8**
1. Jews -- Persecutions 2. Jews -- Persecutions -- Soviet Union 3. Jews -- Russia 4. Jews -- Soviet Union -- History 5. Jews -- Soviet Union -- Politics and government
ISBN 978-0-618-57309-7; 0-618-57309-7
LC 2010-05735

"Beckerman tells a complex tale set in the United States, Israel and the Soviet Union. Some of the most potent historical forces of the century shaped the departure of 1.3 million Jews from the Soviet Union: the Holocaust, assimilation, the human rights movements, the birth of Israel and the Cold War. . . . The author is gifted at weaving this very human and very political tale together. He lays out how this struggle intersected with other movements, including the drive for democracy in the Soviet Union and the fight for civil rights in the United States. All the while, he keeps the reader mindful of Cold War politics. Beckerman also teases out the Jewish role in the rise of U.S. neoconservatism, tracking such figures as Richard Perle and Paul Wolfowitz as they learn the political trade." Cleveland Plain Dealer
Includes bibliographical references

Berlin, Ira

The **making** of African America; the four great migrations. Viking 2010 304p $27.95 **305.8**
1. African Americans -- History 2. African Americans -- Migrations -- History 3. Internal migration 4. Migration, Internal -- United States -- History 5. Slave trade 6. Slave trade -- United States
ISBN 978-0-670-02137-6; 0-670-02137-7
LC 2009-28366

"This . . . book proposes a new framework for African American history. Breaking with what he calls the 'master narrative' that frames the subject as an ongoing struggle for freedom and equality, Ira Berlin argues that the experience of relocation and the formation of new communities in new contexts have been pivotal in the making and remaking of African American society. . . . Based on secondary sources, this . . . book briskly narrates four hundred years of history, highlighting the 'four great migrations.' . . . 'The Making of African America' aims to show how migrations reorganized culture and social life. Each of his four major relocations yields a new African America." (Journal of American History)

"Berlin's neat synthesis offers the sharp insights and provocative commentary of one of the foremost historians of black America. Essential for library collections, general readers, and scholars of African American history." Libr J
Includes bibliographical references

Bishop, Bill

The **big** sort; why the clustering of like-minded America is tearing us apart. with Robert G. Cushing. Houghton Mifflin 2008 370p il map $25   **305.8**

1. Group identity -- Political aspects 2. Minorities 3. Minorities -- United States 4. Political culture -- United States 5. Regionalism -- Political aspects 6. Regionalism -- United States 7. Segregation -- United States 8. Social conflict -- United States

ISBN 978-0-618-68935-4; 0-618-68935-4

LC 2007-43907

"Bishop's argument is meticulously researched—surveys and polls proliferate—and his reach is broad. . . . [The] portrait of our 'post materialistic' society will . . . generate chatter [and] the idea is catchy." Publ Wkly

Includes bibliographical references

Biss, Eula

Notes from no man's land; American essays. Graywolf Press 2009 230p   **305.8**

1. Authors 2. Essayists 3. Group identity -- United States 4. Poets

ISBN 1-55597-518-6; 978-1-55597-518-0

LC 20080935599

"This essay collection won the 2008 Graywolf Press Nonfiction Prize." (Libr J)

"These essays are about many things, but the theme of race runs through them all. They are not 'about' race, however, not in the way essays are usually 'about' something. Instead of presenting her opening gambits and using the body of the essay to support her initial points, Biss finds her jumping-off point and examines her observations and experiences. Although her juxtapositions are occasionally forced, it is impossible to remain unmoved by Biss's work." Libr J

Blackmon, Douglas A.

Slavery by another name; the re-enslavement of Black people in America from the Civil War to World War II. Doubleday 2008 466p il $29.95; pa $16.95   **305.8**

1. African American prisoners 2. African Americans -- Civil rights 3. African Americans -- Civil rights -- History -- 19th century 4. African Americans -- Civil rights -- History -- 20th century 5. African Americans -- Crimes against -- History 6. African Americans -- Employment -- History 7. Convict labor -- United States -- History 8. Slavery -- United States -- History 9. Slavery -- United States -- History

ISBN 978-0-385-50625-0; 0-385-50625-2; 978-0-385-72270-4 pa; 0-385-72270-2 pa

LC 2007-34500

The author "gives a groundbreaking and disturbing account of a sordid chapter in American history—the lease (essentially the sale) of convicts to commercial interests between the end of the 19th century and well into the 20th. . . . [The] book reveals in devastating detail the legal and commercial forces that created this neoslavery along with deeply moving and totally appalling personal testimonies of survivors." Publ Wkly

Includes bibliographical references (p. 444-459)

Chang, Iris

★ The **Chinese** in America; a narrative history. Viking 2003 496p il hardcover o.p. pa $16 **305.8**

1. Chinese Americans -- History

ISBN 0-670-03123-2; 0-14-200417-0 pa

LC 2002-44858

The author recounts "the immigration of Chinese people to the U.S. from the early nineteenth century to the end of the twentieth. . . . Chang threads personal stories of individuals she came across in her research into her book, making it a much more human account. . . . This is history at its most dramatic and relevant." Booklist

Includes bibliographical references

Chesler, Phyllis

The **new** anti-Semitism; the current crisis and what we must do about it. Jossey-Bass 2003 307p $24.95; pa $15.95   **305.8**

1. Antisemitism 2. Arab-Israeli conflict 3. Israel-Arab conflicts 4. Public opinion -- Arab countries 5. September 11 terrorist attacks, 2001 6. Zionism -- Public opinion

ISBN 0-7879-6851-X; 0-7879-7803-5 pa

LC 2003-6448

The author "addresses what she sees as a re-emergence of virulent anti-Jewish hatred cloaked in 'political correctness,' closely linked to anti-American attitudes, sustained by many liberal feminists, intellectuals and Jewish leftists, acted upon by Islamic terrorists and jihadists, and fueled by a 'demonization of Jews' in the media. One of the main thrusts of Chesler's argument is that in our contemporary world anti-Zionism is nearly inseparable from anti-Semitism, and that while there are valid criticisms to be made of Israeli policies—for instance, she sees the West Bank settlements as an impediment to peace—many of these critiques are, she contends, rooted in a profound and socially accepted anti-Semitism." Publ Wkly

Includes bibliographical references

Cleaver, Eldridge

Soul on ice. Delta Trade Paperbacks 1999 242p pa $15   **305.8**

1. African Americans

ISBN 978-0-385-33379-5; 0-385-33379-X

In a collection of essays and open letters written from California's Folsom State Prison, the author writes about the forces which shaped his life.

There are sections "on the Watts riots, on Cleaver's religious conversion, on the black man's stake in the Vietnam War, on fellow-writers and white women." Saturday Rev

Cose, Ellis

Color-blind; seeing beyond race in a race-obsessed world. HarperCollins Pubs. 1997 260p hardcover o.p. pa $13   **305.8**

1. Affirmative action programs 2. Race discrimination

ISBN 0-06-092887-5 pa

LC 96-34433

Issues discussed include racial classification and discrimination, race and genetics, achieving educational parity, affirmative action in colleges and the workplace, and the concept of a color-blind society. The author concludes by proposing twelve steps toward a race-neutral nation.

"Bolstered by research data and his own personal experience, Cose convincingly illuminates why race still remains a determining factor of success in America." Libr J

Includes bibliographical references

Curtis, Edward E.

Muslims in America; a short history. Oxford University Press 2009 144p il pa $12.95   **305.8**
1. Ethnic relations 2. Islam -- History 3. Islam -- United States -- History 4. Muslims 5. Muslims -- United States 6. Muslims -- United States -- History
ISBN 978-0-19-536756-0
LC 2008-47566

The author "has authored a fine and succinct history that spans centuries. . . . Although geared toward non-Muslims, American Muslims would also learn a great deal from reading about their own history. . . . [Readers] will undoubtedly be intrigued by Curtis's compelling little read." Publ Wkly

Includes bibliographical references

Dash, Leon

Rosa Lee; a mother and her family in urban America. Plume 1997 279p il pa $15   **305.8**
1. African Americans -- Social conditions
ISBN 0-452-27896-1; 978-0-452-27896-7
LC 97-11543

"What makes Rosa Lee, Leon Dash's report on a particular Washington ghetto family, so convincing and so valuable is [Dash's] intimacy with his subjects, an intimacy that very few writers about the underclass have ever achieved." N Y Rev Books

Diner, Hasia R.

A **time** for gathering; the second migration, 1820-1880. Johns Hopkins Univ. Press 1992 313p il hardcover o.p. pa $20.95   **305.8**
1. Jews -- History 2. Jews -- United States 3. Jews -- United States -- History 4. Judaism
ISBN 0-8018-4344-8; 0-8018-5121-1 pa
LC 91-45368

This second volume in a five-volume history of American Jewry focuses on the German-speaking Jewish immigrants who came to the United States in the nineteenth century.

Du Bois, W. E. B.

★ The **souls** of Black folk; edited with an introduction and notes by Brent Hayes Edwards. Oxford University Press 2007 xxxvi, 223p il pa $12.95   **305.8**
1. African Americans
ISBN 978-0-19-280678-9; 0-19-280678-5
LC 2006-35193

"A collection of fifteen essays and sketches by W.E.B. Du Bois. In it he describes the lives of African American farmers, sketches the role of music in their churches, details the history of the Freedman's Bureau, discusses the career of Booker T. Washington, and advocates a commitment to higher education for the most talented African American youth." Benet's Reader's Ency of Am Lit

Includes bibliographical references

Everett, Daniel Leonard

Don't sleep, there are snakes; life and language in the Amazonian jungle. [by] Daniel L. Everett. Pantheon Books 2008 283p il $26.95   **305.8**
1. College teachers 2. Indians of South America -- Amazon River region 3. Linguists 4. Pirahã Indians
ISBN 978-0-375-42502-8; 0-375-42502-0
LC 2008-16306

The author "has crafted a fascinating account of his 30 years of linguistics work among the Pirahã (pronounced pee-da-HAN) Indians, a tribal group living along the Maici and Marmelos Rivers in a remote area of western Brazil. . . . With a clear, detail-rich writing style, Everett provides evocative ethnographic descriptions of Pirahã life and culture as well as perceptive linguistic analysis." Libr J

Includes bibliographical references

Faber, Eli

A **time** for planting; the first migration, 1654-1820. Johns Hopkins Univ. Press 1992 188p il hardcover o.p. pa $14.95   **305.8**
1. Jews -- History 2. Jews -- United States 3. Jews -- United States -- History 4. Sephardim -- History
ISBN 0-8018-4343-X; 0-8018-5120-3 pa
LC 91-45341

This is the initial volume in a five-volume series tracing the history of Jews in the United States from the seventeenth century to the period following World War II. It focuses on the Sephardic Jews who settled in New Amsterdam, Newport, Rhode Island, Philadelphia, Charleston and other colonial towns.

Feingold, Henry L.

A **time** for searching; entering the mainstream, 1920-1945. Johns Hopkins Univ. Press 1992 338p il hardcover o.p. pa $21.95   **305.8**
1. Jews -- History 2. Jews -- United States 3. Jews -- United States -- History 4. Judaism
ISBN 0-8018-4346-4; 0-8018-5123-8 pa
LC 91-45367

This fourth volume in The Jewish People in America series addresses the period from the end of World War I to World War II. The author discusses "the emergence of anti-Semitism, second-generation Jewish acculturation and secularization, political behavior, and Zionism, . . . aiming to explain the disarray of the American Jewish community during the Holocaust." Libr J

Includes bibliographical references

Flavell, Julie

When London was capital of America. Yale University Press 2010 305p il map $32.50   **305.8**
1. Americans -- England 2. Americans -- England -- London 3. Americans -- England -- London -- History
ISBN 978-0-300-13739-2; 0-300-13739-7
LC 2009-53163

"Beautifully reimagining a city that was a distant but integral part of American life, Flavell's book is essential reading for anyone interested in the colonial period." N Y Times Book Rev

Includes bibliographical references

Franklin, John Hope

★ **From** slavery to freedom; a history of African Americans. [by] John Hope Franklin, Evelyn Higginbotham. 9th ed.; McGraw-Hill 2010 xxv, 710p il map $100.63   **305.8**
    1. African Americans -- History 2. Slavery -- United States
    ISBN 978-0-07-296378-6; 0-07-296378-6
                   LC 2009-42935
A survey of African-Americans' history from slavery to the present.

Gates, Henry Louis

In search of our roots; how 19 extraordinary African Americans reclaimed their past. Crown Publishers 2008 438p il map $27.50   **305.8**
    1. African Americans 2. Genealogy
    ISBN 978-0-307-38240-5
                   LC 2008-11860
"Bright, inquisitive take on the multifarious murky stories and relationships that make up the history of a dispossessed people." Kirkus
    Includes bibliographical references

Life upon these shores; looking at African American history, 1513-2008. Knopf 2011 487p il $50   **305.8**
    1. African Americans -- History
    ISBN 978-0-307-59342-9
                  LC 2011014277
"With nearly 900 illustrations (formal portraits, news photos, historic lithographs, broadsides, flyers, posters, newspaper clippings, advertisements) complemented by a succinct but informing text, Harvard professor Gates (Black in Latin America) provides a visual sojourn through African-American history, a generally upbeat march from Juan Garrido, accompanying Cortés in 1519, to Barack Obama taking the presidential oath in 2008. Gathered in this chronologically arranged compendium, with its focus on the accomplishments and moments of achievement in the African-American community, is a wealth of materials about the historical, political, social, literary, and scientific events influencing American social and political culture." Publ Wkly
    Includes bibliographical references

Gibbon, Piers

Tribe; endangered peoples around the world. [by] Piers Gibbon with Jane Houston. Firefly Books 2010 192p il $45   **305.8**
    1. Acculturation 2. Ethnology
    ISBN 978-1-55407-742-7; 1-55407-742-7
                 LC 2011-380573
Presents the cultures, beliefs, and societal patterns of over two hundred indigenous peoples and describes their degrees of integration with other societies and the integrity of their indigenous identities. Contains some images of nudity.
    This is "a wonderful compendium of diversity and a useful platform for thought, providing an opportunity to pose questions to ourselves. . . . It reminds us that there is so much that we still don't know, so much more to the world than we see in our homes and high streets; that the world is won-

drous and precious and has an innate value that must be both defended and empowered if it is to survive." Geographical
    Includes bibliographical references

Goodman, Jordan

The **devil** and Mr. Casement; one man's battle for human rights in South America's heart of darkness. Farrar, Straus and Giroux 2010 322p il map $30   **305.8**
    1. Atrocities 2. Diplomats 3. Human rights 4. Human rights -- Peru 5. Imperialism -- Social aspects 6. Indians of South America -- Social conditions 7. Native Americans -- South America 8. Revolutionaries 9. Rubber industry workers 10. Spies
    ISBN 978-0-374-13840-0; 0-374-13840-0
                  LC 2009-29528
"An incisive rendering of an important episode in the ongoing battle for the rights of individuals." Kirkus
    Includes bibliographical references

Griffin, John Howard

★ **Black** like me; the definitive Griffin estate edition, corrected from original manuscripts. foreword by Studs Terkel; with historic photographs by Don Rutledge; and an afterword by Robert Bonazzi. 2nd Wings Press ed., with index; Wings Press 2006 243p il $29.95   **305.8**
    1. African Americans -- Southern States 2. Prejudices
    ISBN 978-0-930324-73-5
The author, "who is white, a Catholic, and a Texan, conceived and carried out the unusual notion of blackening his skin with a newly developed pigment drug and traveling through the Deep South as a Negro. This book, part of which appeared in the Negro magazine Sepia, is a journal account of that experience." New Yorker
    Includes bibliographical references

Gross, Ariela J.

What blood won't tell; a history of race on trial in America. [by] Ariela J. Gross. Harvard University Press 2008 368p $29.95   **305.8**
    1. Minorities 2. Minorities -- Legal status, laws, etc. -- United States 3. Race discrimination 4. Race discrimination -- Law and legislation -- United States 5. Race discrimination -- Laws and regulations
    ISBN 978-0-674-03130-2; 0-674-03130-X
                  LC 2008011271
This book examines "the legal fight of nonwhite citizens not to be counted as black under the . . . 'one drop' rule of racial categorization—a stigma that could lock them out of all sorts of social benefits, from business contracts to rights of inheritance and land ownership." Bookforum
    Includes bibliographical references

Gross, Jan Tomasz

Fear: anti-Semitism in Poland after Auschwitz; an essay in historical interpretation. [by] Jan T. Gross. Random House 2005 303p il $25.95 **305.8**
    1. Antisemitism 2. Holocaust, 1933-1945 3. Jews --

Persecutions 4. Jews -- Poland
ISBN 0-375-50924-0; 978-0-375-50924-7
LC 2005-52913
"This is a masterful work that sheds necessary light on a tragic and often-ignored aspect of postwar history." Booklist
Includes bibliographical references

Hahn, Steven

A **nation** under our feet; Black political struggles in the rural South, from slavery to the great migration. Steven Hahn. Belknap Press of Harvard University Press 2003 610p il $35; pa $18.95 **305.8**
1. African Americans -- Political activity 2. African Americans -- Social conditions -- To 1964 3. African Americans -- Southern States -- Politics and government -- 19th century 4. African Americans -- Southern States -- Politics and government -- 20th century
ISBN 0-674-01169-4; 0-674-01765-X pa
LC 2003-45326
This book "is one of the most important works in American social history to appear in recent years." Nation
Includes bibliographical references

Heap, Chad C.

Slumming; sexual and racial encounters in American nightlife, 1885-1940. [by] Chad Heap. University of Chicago Press 2009 420p il map $35 **305.8**
1. Sexual behavior
ISBN 978-0-226-32243-8; 0-226-32243-2
LC 2007-10881
"From its appearance as a 'fashionable dissipation' centered on the immigrant and working-class districts of 1880s New York through its spread to Chicago and into the 1930s nightspots frequented by lesbians and gay men, Slumming charts the development of this popular pastime, demonstrating how its moralizing origins were soon outstripped by the artistic, racial, and sexual adventuring that typified Jazz-Age America. Vividly recreating the allure of storied neighborhoods such as Greenwich Village and Bronzeville, with their bohemian tearooms, rent parties, and 'black and tan' cabarets, Heap plumbs the complicated mix of curiosity and desire that drew respectable white urbanites to venture into previously off-limits locales." Bookmarks
Includes bibliographical references

Hendrickson, Paul

Sons of Mississippi; a story of race and its legacy. Knopf 2003 343p il map $26; pa $15 **305.8**
1. African Americans -- Mississippi 2. Police brutality
ISBN 0-375-40461-9; 0-375-70425-6 pa
LC 2002-29857
"The number of telling quotes, interviews with friends and family, primary and secondary sources, allusions to art and history, and gut reactions Hendrickson offers are what really make the book. . . . He repeatedly comes up with electric interview material, and deftly places these men within the defining events of their times, when 'a 100-year-old way of life was cracking beneath them.'" Publ Wkly
Includes bibliographical references

Hill, Anita, 1956-

Reimagining equality; stories of gender, race, and finding home. Beacon Press 2011 xxiv, 195p $25.95 **305.8**
1. African American women 2. African Americans -- Housing 3. African Americans -- Social conditions 4. Houses -- Buying and selling
ISBN 978-0-8070-1437-0
LC 2011020232
The author "addresses the prime mortgage debacle, specifically how 'owning a home, and thus acquiring this piece of the American Dream has become increasingly difficult for people of color and single women,' and presents an indictment of subprime and predatory lending." Publ Wkly
Includes bibliographical references

Lasch-Quinn, Elisabeth

Race experts; how racial etiquette, sensitivity training, and New Age therapy hijacked the civil rights revolution. Norton 2001 267p $25.95 **305.8**
1. African Americans 2. African Americans -- Civil rights -- History -- 20th century 3. Civil rights movements -- United States -- History -- 20th century 4. Cross-cultural counseling -- United States 5. Diversity in the workplace -- United States 6. Etiquette -- United States -- Psychological aspects 7. Group relations training 8. Interpersonal relations -- United States 9. Multicultural education -- United States 10. Multiculturalism 11. Multiculturalism -- United States
ISBN 0-393-04873-X
LC 2001-30913
The author "probes the intersection of the civil rights struggle and modern social psychology, in particular the human potential movement. She highlights the 'overthrow of the social code of segregation' and the adoption of an etiquette of black assertiveness and white submissiveness that has produced a 'harangueflagellation' ritual that does not advance the goal of racial equality. . . . This is sure to be a controversial book among readers interested in race issues." Booklist
Includes bibliographical references

Lukas, J. Anthony

Common ground; a turbulent decade in the lives of three American families. Knopf 1985 659p il maps hardcover o.p. pa $18 **305.8**
1. Busing (School integration) 2. School integration
ISBN 0-394-74616-3 pa
LC 85-127
"By focusing on three families—one of them welfare black, one upper-middle-class white and one working-class Irish—a veteran journalist recreates the school-busing struggles of Boston in the 1970s, and delineates . . . the moral complexities of caste and class in America." Newsday

Malek, Alia

A **country** called Amreeka; Arab roots, American stories. Free Press 2009 305p il $25 **305.8**
1. Arab Americans -- Social conditions 2. Immigrants -- United States
ISBN 978-1-4165-8972-3
LC 2008-55091

"In this superb snapshot of the Americans of Arab-speaking descent, individuals with roots in Jordan, Yemen, the Palestinian territories and Lebanon share their stories and demonstrate the extent to which, even as they play football, work assembly lines and hold public office, they remain shut out of the national narrative. With a remarkable ability to capture her subjects' voices, . . . [the author] sketches illuminating responses to her question: 'What does American history look and feel like in the eyes and skin of Arab Americans?'" Publ Wkly

Includes bibliographical references

McWhorter, John H.

Losing the race; self-sabotage in Black America. [with a new afterword by the author] Perennial 2001 299p pa $13.95   **305.8**
1. African Americans -- Education 2. African Americans -- Psychology 3. African Americans -- Social conditions 4. African Americans -- Social conditions -- 1975- 5. Self-defeating behavior 6. Success -- Psychological aspects
ISBN 978-0-06-093593-1; 0-06-093593-6
LC 2001-24092

McWhorter discusses what he sees as "a cult of anti-intellectualism 'that has infected black America. . . . He concluded [black students] were held back by three defeatist thought patterns': the Cult of Victimology, which leads blacks to blame their problems on racism; the Cult of Separatism, which makes blacks think that whatever whites do, they should do the opposite; and the Cult of Anti-Intellectualism, which holds that scholastic excellence is a white thing." Time

Includes bibliographical references

Minutaglio, Bill

In search of the blues; a journey to the soul of Black Texas. foreword by Linda Jones. University of Texas Press 2010 167p il $50; pa $24.95   **305.8**
1. African Americans -- Texas 2. Blues music
ISBN 978-0-292-72247-7; 0-292-72247-8; 978-0-292-72289-7 pa; 0-292-72289-3 pa
LC 2009-44161

This volume includes "profiles of football coach Ray Rhodes and rumors of a lynched ancestor in Mexia, and of Fahim Minkah, a former Black Panther once considered the most dangerous black militant in the Dallas area — who now devotes his life to ridding neighborhoods of drug dealers. . . . There are portraits of neighborhoods, streets and clubs and, of course, blues musicians such as T-Bone Walker, Lightnin' Hopkins and Buckwheat Zydeco, all painted with Minutaglio's closely-observed, deeply reported and beautifully written prose. . . . [This is] not only a celebration of the blues, black culture and black Texans but a celebration of extraordinary journalism and writing." San Antonio Express-News

Monterrey, Manuel

Americanos; Latino life in the United States. [by] Edward James Olmos, Lea Ybarra, Manuel Monterrey; preface by Edward James Olmos; introduction

by Carlos Fuentes. Little, Brown 1999 176p il $39; pa $25   **305.8**
1. Hispanic Americans 2. Hispanic Americans -- Social conditions 3. Hispanic Americans -- Social conditions -- Pictorial works 4. Hispanic Americans -- Social life and customs 5. Hispanic Americans -- Social life and customs -- Pictorial works
ISBN 0-316-64914-7; 0-316-64909-0 pa
LC 98-51930

This work includes essays, poetry, and commentary in English and Spanish by such authors as Carlos Fuentes and Maya Angelou and over 200 photographs of Latin Americans from many parts of the United States.

"This is a beautiful, vibrant . . . book; it may also be one of the more socially important books to appear in some time." Booklist

Murray, Charles

Coming apart; Charles Murray. Crown Forum 2012 407 p.   **305.8**
1. Nonfiction 2. Social classes -- United States 3. Social mobility -- United States 4. Whites -- United States -- Economic conditions 5. Whites -- United States -- Social conditions
ISBN 0307453421; 9780307453426; 9780307453440
LC 2011501987

This book argues that a new upper class and a new lower class have diverged so far in core behaviors and values that they barely recognize their underlying American kinship." It argues that [t]he top and bottom of white America increasingly live in different cultures, . . . with the powerful upper class living in enclaves surrounded by their own kind, ignorant about life in mainstream America, and the lower class suffering from erosions of family and community life." (Publisher's note)

"Though it provides much to argue with, the book is a timely investigation into a worsening class divide no one can afford to ignore." (Publishers Weekly)

Includes bibliographical references and index

Nagel, Joane

American Indian ethnic renewal; Red power and the resurgence of identity and culture. Oxford Univ. Press 1996 298p il hardcover o.p. pa $21.95 **305.8**
1. Indians of North America -- Political activity 2. Indians of North America -- Politics and government 3. Indians of North America -- Social conditions 4. Native Americans
ISBN 0-19-512063-9 pa
LC 94-23948

The author "argues that American Indian political activism, especially the Red Power movement of the 1970s, was directly responsible for both a cultural renaissance among Indian peoples and major changes in federal Indian policy." Libr J

Includes bibliographical references

Overmyer-Velázquez, Mark

Latino America; a state-by-state encyclopedia. edited by Mark Overmyer-Velázquez; foreword by

Stephen Pitti. Greenwood Press 2008 2v il map set
$175 **305.8**
1. Hispanic Americans -- Encyclopedias 2. Hispanic
Americans -- History 3. Hispanic Americans -- Social
conditions 4. Reference books
ISBN 978-0-313-34116-8; 0-313-34116-8
LC 2008-26044
This work "charts the historical and contemporary con-
tributions of Latinos throughout the United States. The en-
cyclopedia approaches its material from a geographical per-
spective, with a chapter devoted to each of the fifty states. . .
. This is an informative resource that fills a needed gap." Ref
& User Services Quarterly
Includes bibliographical references

Packard, Jerrold M.
American nightmare; the history of Jim Crow. St.
Martin's Press 2002 291p $24.95; pa $14.95 **305.8**
1. African Americans -- History -- 1863-1877 2.
African Americans -- History -- 1877-1964 3. African
Americans -- Segregation 4. African Americans --
Segregation -- Southern States -- History
ISBN 0-312-26122-5; 0-312-30241-X pa
LC 2001-41960
"This is a clear, concise, historical narrative of a draco-
nian reality." Publ Wkly
Includes bibliographical references (p. {275}-280)
and index

Page, Joseph A.
The **Brazilians**. Addison-Wesley 1995 540p il
map hardcover o.p. pa $22.50 **305.8**
1. Brazilian national characteristics 2. Religion
ISBN 0-201-44191-8 pa
LC 94-45812
The author "probes deep into the layers of Spanish, Portuguese, Dutch, African and Indian heritage that make Brazil
so alluring and paradoxical. . . . In this magnetizing study,
Page also explores the meld of Catholicism and Pentecostalism, of native Indian healers and modern medicine, of
African rhythms and Western music. He discusses the environmental and investment scenes as well as the addiction to
soccer and to the telenovelas of the powerful Globus media
empire." Publ Wkly
Includes bibliographical references

Painter, Nell Irvin
The **history** of White people. W.W. Norton 2010
496p il map $27.95 **305.8**
1. Whites 2. Whites -- Race identity 3. Whites --
United States -- History
ISBN 978-0-393-04934-3; 0-393-04934-5
LC 2009-34515
The author "examines the history of 'whiteness' as a racial category and rhetorical weapon: who is considered to be
'white,' who is not, what such distinctions mean, and how
notions of whiteness have morphed over time in response
to shifting demographics, aesthetic tastes, and political
exigencies. . . . Painter's narrative succeeds as an engaging and sophisticated intellectual history, as well as an elo-

quent reminder of the fluidity (and perhaps futility) of racial
categories." Booklist
Includes bibliographical references

Reed, Ishmael
Another day at the front; dispatches from the
race war. Basic Bks. 2002 xliv, 189p $24; pa
$14.95 **305.8**
1. African Americans -- Civil rights 2. Hispanic
Americans -- Social conditions 3. Muslims -- United
States 4. Racism 5. Racism -- United States
ISBN 0-465-06891-X; 0-465-06892-8 pa
LC 2002-10563
The author "gathers a series of original and revamped essays from recent years on a variety of topics, from the Confederate flag to NPR, with the underlying theme that African
Americans have been living in a police state for the past 300
years. These brief essays, written in Reed's lively hit-and-
run style, are certainly provocative, particularly as he jabs at
many well-known critics both black and white." Libr J

Roberts, Dorothy
Fatal invention; how science, politics, and big
business re-create race in the twenty-first century.
New Press 2011 388p $29.95 **305.8**
1. Genomics 2. Human population genetics 3. Physical
anthropology 4. Race
ISBN 9781595584953; 1595584951
LC 2011012830
The author "examines the development and contemporary consequences of 'race as a political system,' bringing
science, law, commerce, and race ideologies, virtual thickets
of controversy, under one canopy. . . . Roberts is consistently
lucid. Her book is alarming but not alarmist, controversial
but evidential, impassioned but rational." Publ Wkly
Includes bibliographical references and index.

Robinson, Eugene
Disintegration; the splintering of Black America.
Doubleday 2010 254p $24.95 **305.8**
1. African Americans -- Economic conditions 2. African
Americans -- Race identity 3. African Americans --
Social conditions
ISBN 978-0-385-52654-8; 0-385-52654-7
LC 2010-20405
"This book will have great appeal to African Americans
and others concerned about issues of race and equality."
Libr J
Includes bibliographical references

Sabar, Ariel
My father's paradise; a son's search for his Jew-
ish past in Kurdish Iraq. Algonquin Books of Chapel
Hill 2008 332p il map $25.95 **305.8**
1. College teachers 2. Jews -- Iraq 3. Jews, Kurdish 4.
Journalists 5. Linguists 6. Memoirists 7. Sephardim
ISBN 978-1-56512-490-5; 1-56512-490-1
LC 2008-24811
Sabar writes about his father's early life as a Sephardic
Jew in Iraq and his father's authorship of a dictionary of
Neo-Aramaic.

This "is an engaging account of a wonderful, enlightening journey, a voyage with the power to move readers deeply even as it stretches across differences of culture, family, and memory." Christ Sci Monit

Includes bibliographical references

Shapiro, Edward S.

A time for healing; American Jewry since World War II. Johns Hopkins Univ. Press 1992 313p il hardcover o.p. pa $14.95 **305.8**

1. Jews -- United States 2. Jews -- United States -- History 3. Judaism

ISBN 0-8018-4347-2; 0-8018-5124-6 pa

LC 91-38385

This volume is the fifth and last in The Jewish People in America, a series sponsored by the American Jewish Historical Society. "This history of American Jewry after 1945 has two broad themes. One is the rapid social and economic mobility of American Jews. . . . The other major theme is the adaptation of Jews to unprecedented conditions of affluence and freedom." Preface

Includes bibliographical references

Sharfstein, Daniel J.

The invisible line; three American families and the secret journey from black to white. Penguin Press 2011 396p il $27.95 **305.8**

1. Miscegenation -- United States -- History 2. Race -- Social aspects -- United States 3. Race awareness 4. Race awareness -- United States 5. Racially mixed people 6. Racially mixed people -- United States

ISBN 978-1-59420-282-7; 1-59420-282-6

LC 2010-29647

"This popular history makes vivid use of primary documents to reconstruct the sagas of three families who crossed the color line from black to white. They negotiated this transition by means of legal challenges and such racial categories as 'Melungeons' and 'Black Dutch,' or simply by staying quiet when neighbors made assumptions based on cues of class and complexion. . . . This is an important reconsideration of the porousness of racial categories . . . and also a powerful evocation of the peril and insecurity that blacks faced both before and after the Civil War." New Yorker

Includes bibliographical references

Sokol, Jason

★ There goes my everything; white Southerners in the age of civil rights, 1945-1975. Knopf 2006 433p il $27.95 **305.8**

1. African Americans -- Civil rights 2. African Americans -- Civil rights -- Southern States -- History -- 20th century 3. Civil rights movements -- Southern States -- History -- 20th century 4. Whites -- Southern States -- Attitudes -- History -- 20th century

ISBN 0-307-26356-8; 978-0-307-26356-8

LC 2005-44488

"This chronicle of the destruction of the white Southern hierarchy belongs in all libraries, public and academic." Libr J

Includes bibliographical references

Sorin, Gerald

A time for building; the third migration, 1880-1920. Johns Hopkins Univ. Press 1992 306p il hardcover o.p. pa $14.95 **305.8**

1. Jews -- History 2. Jews -- United States 3. Jews -- United States -- History

ISBN 0-8018-4345-6; 0-8018-5122-X pa

LC 91-40700

This volume, the third in The Jewish People in America, a series sponsored by the American Jewish Historical Society, focuses on Eastern European Jewish immigration to the United States between 1880 and 1920.

Takaki, Ronald T.

Strangers from a different shore; a history of Asian Americans. [by] Ronald Takaki. Updated and rev ed, 1st Back Bay ed; Little, Brown 1998 591p il pa $16.95 **305.8**

1. Asian Americans -- History 2. Asian Americans -- Social conditions

ISBN 0-316-83130-1

LC 98-218270

This work discusses the Chinese transcontinental railroad workers, the plantation workers in the Hawaii canefields, the Japanese Americans in the U.S. internment camps during World War II, the Hmong refugees in Wisconsin and the stereotypical image of Asian American youth as model students.

Tatum, Beverly Daniel

Why are all the Black kids sitting together in the cafeteria? and other conversations about race. Basic Bks. 2003 294p pa $15.95 **305.8**

1. African Americans -- Race identity

ISBN 0-465-08361-7

"Tatum explains the development of racial identity. To illustrate her point she uses anecdotes about her sons, excerpts from research interviews and essays written by her students." Libr J

Thorpe, Helen

Just like us; the true story of four Mexican girls coming of age in America. Scribner 2009 387p $27.99 **305.8**

1. Hispanic American women 2. Illegal aliens 3. Mexican Americans

ISBN 978-1-4165-3893-6

LC 2009-22722

"Thorpe does a masterful job of exploring issues of class, race, and culture in the American amalgam through the lives of four young Mexican women." Booklist

Walker, Clarence Earl

Mongrel nation; the America begotten by Thomas Jefferson and Sally Hemings. [by] Clarence E. Walker. University of Virginia Press 2008 128p $22.95 **305.8**

1. African Americans -- Race identity 2. Architects 3. Essayists 4. Miscegenation -- United States -- History 5. Mistresses 6. Presidents 7. Racially mixed people 8. Racially mixed people -- United States 9. Slaves 10.

Vice-presidents 11. Whites -- Race identity -- United States
ISBN 978-0-8139-2777-0; 0-8139-2777-3; 978-0-8139-2778-7 pa; 0-8139-2778-1 pa

LC 2008-24042

The author "uses the contradictions between Jefferson's writings on race and his 38-year relationship with his slave Sally Hemings as a prism through which to view the complexities of American race relations. . . Walker maintains that unless the nation can fully recognize the Jefferson-Hemings relationship, it can never have a true sense of its identity." Booklist

Includes bibliographical references

West, Cornel

Race matters; with a new preface by the author. Beacon Press 2001 108p $20   **305.8**
1. Black Muslim leaders 2. Civil rights activists 3. Government officials 4. Supreme Court justices
ISBN 0-8070-0972-5; 978-0-8070-0972-7

LC 2001-025310

In this collection of essays the author "addresses a number of issues of concern to black Americans: the Los Angeles riots after the Rodney King verdict; Malcolm X; Clarence Thomas and Anita Hill, and black street life. . . . West's essays have the feel of a fine sermon, with thought-provoking ideas and new ways of looking at the same old problems." Libr J

Wilson, Jennifer

Running away to home; our family's journey to Croatia in search of who we are, where we came from, and what really matters. St. Martin's Press 2011 320p il $25.99; ebook $12.99   **305.8**
ISBN 978-0-312-59895-2; 978-1-4299-8908-4 ebook

LC 2011024841

"Travel writer Wilson, her architect husband, and their two small children spent a family sabbatical in Mrkopalj, Croatia, an unlikely destination for most folks but the birthplace of Wilson's great-grandparents. Wilson and family arrived in the village speaking little Croatian but soon became part of the community. She relates how they explored the area, tracked down distant relatives, and became immersed in the traditions of daily life. . . . This thoughtful, amusing tale reads like a novel and will have wide appeal." Libr J

Wohlforth, Charles

The **whale** and the supercomputer; on the northern front of climate change. 1st ed; North Point Press 2004 322p $25; pa $14   **305.8**
1. Climate 2. Climatic changes 3. Inuit
ISBN 0-86547-659-4; 0-86547-714-0 pa

LC 2003-19448

"While the book's main focus is on climate change in the Arctic, . . . [the author includes] discussions of the worldview of the Inupiat in contrast to that of Western scientists, the conflict between rural and urban culture, the philosophy of science, and the machinations surrounding funding for science. Wohlforth writes beautifully, managing to wax philosophical while providing detailed notes for those skeptical of the points he makes." Sci Books Films

Includes bibliographical references

Womack, Ytasha

Post Black; how a new generation is redefining African American identity. [by] Ytasha L. Womack; foreword by Derek T. Dingle. Lawrence Hill Books 2010 206p il pa $16.95   **305.8**
1. African Americans -- Race identity 2. African Americans -- Social conditions
ISBN 978-1-55652-805-7; 1-55652-805-1

LC 2009-29619

This is "an engaging and ambitious discussion of African American identity in the 21st century." Publ Wkly

Includes bibliographical references

Woodward, C. Vann

The **strange** career of Jim Crow; 3rd rev ed; Oxford Univ. Press 1974 233p hardcover o.p. pa $17.95   **305.8**
1. African Americans -- Segregation
ISBN 0-19-514690-5 pa

An account of segregation in the South which analyzes events from 1877 to the Nixon administration.

Zeskind, Leonard

Blood and politics; the history of the white nationalist movement from the margins to the mainstream. Farrar, Straus and Giroux 2009 xxiv, 645p $37.50   **305.8**
1. Nationalism -- United States 2. Racism 3. White supremacy movements
ISBN 978-0-374-10903-5; 0-374-10903-6

LC 2008-46131

"Zeskind's rigorously researched and eloquent book is a definitive history of white nationalism and contains alarming warnings for a resurgence in racist politics." Publ Wkly

Includes bibliographical references

★ The African American almanac; Christopher A. Brooks, editor; foreword by Benjamin Jealous. 11th ed; Gale Cengage Learning 2011 1601p il map $297   **305.8**
1. African Americans 2. Reference books
ISBN 978-1-4144-4547-2

"Reference covering the cultural and political history of Black Americans. Includes generous amount of statistical information and biographies of Black Americans, both historical and contemporary." N Y Public Libr. Book of How & Where to Look It Up

★ Antisemitism; a historical encyclopedia of prejudice and persecution. Richard S. Levy, editor. ABC-CLIO 2005 2v il   **305.8**
1. Antisemitism -- Encyclopedias 2. Reference books
ISBN 1-85109-439-3

LC 2005-9480

This is "a balanced, well-written, exceedingly useful, and often compelling tool. . . . Levy's encyclopedia is crucial for any library serving a thinking public." Choice

Includes bibliographical references

Black firsts: 4,000 ground-breaking and pioneering historical events; [edited by] Jessie Carney

Smith. 2nd ed rev and expanded; Visible Ink Press 2003 787p il $58; pa $24.95   **305.8**
1. African Americans -- History 2. African Americans -- History -- Miscellanea 3. Blacks -- History -- Miscellanea 4. World records -- United States -- Miscellanea
ISBN 1-57859-153-8; 1-57859-142-2 pa
LC 2002-154346
"The chapters survey broad fields such as 'Arts and Entertainment,' 'Government: Local,' and 'Science and Medicine' and are broken down into more specific subject headings. 'Arts and Entertainment,' for example, encompasses 'Architecture,' 'Dance,' 'Music,' and 'Television,' among others. Under each of these headings, firsts are arranged chronologically. Each is described in an entry ranging from a line or two to half a page, and sources are always cited. . . . Many of the sidebars highlight achievements by women. . . . Black firsts remains an important part of the reference collection." Booklist
Includes bibliographical references

Encyclopedia of African American history, 1619-1895; from the colonial period to the age of Frederick Douglass. editor in chief, Paul Finkelman. Oxford University Press 2006 3v il set $395   **305.8**
1. African Americans -- History -- Encyclopedias 2. Reference books
ISBN 0-19-516777-5; 978-0-19-516777-1
LC 2005-33701
This encyclopedia, the first of two sets focusing on African-American history, documents "blacks' experiences from the first slave ships to Frederick Douglass's death. The set offers depth, reaching most important persons, events, and developments through 1895 but is written for easy access with multiple cross references, chronologies, topical outlines, and a comprehensive index." Libr J
Includes bibliographical references

Encyclopedia of African American history, 1896 to the present; from the age of segregation to the twenty-first century. editor in chief, Paul Finkelman. Oxford University Press 2009 5v il set $595   **305.8**
1. African Americans -- History -- Encyclopedias 2. Reference books
ISBN 978-0-19-516779-5
LC 2008-34263
This resource "excels at gathering discussions of similar or related topics by academics under one heading." Libr J
Includes bibliographical references

★ Encyclopedia of African-American culture and history; the Black experience in the Americas. Colin A. Palmer, editor in chief. 2nd ed.; Macmillan Reference USA 2006 6v il map set $695   **305.8**
1. African Americans -- Encyclopedias 2. Reference books
ISBN 0-02-865816-7
LC 2005-13029

"Readers can find comparative analyses of social movements, languages, religions and family structures in the context of an interdisciplinary framework." Publisher's note
Includes bibliographical references

Encyclopedia of Muslim-American history; edited by Edward E. Curtis, IV. Facts on File 2010 628p 2v il set $195   **305.8**
1. Muslims -- United States 2. Muslims -- United States -- Encyclopedias 3. Reference books
ISBN 978-0-8160-7575-1; 978-1-4381-3040-8 ebook
LC 2009-24875
The editor "has assembled a fascinating and timely resource detailing the history and contributions of Muslim Americans in the United States. More than 300 articles, written by scholars, historians, and experts in Islam and American history, outline the long legacy and impact that Muslim Americans have had since their earliest arrival on slave ships in the 18th century. . . . A necessary and timely resource to remind us of the vital contributions that Muslim Americans have made to our culture and society since its founding." Libr J
Includes bibliographical references

Encyclopedia of modern ethnic conflicts; edited by Joseph R. Rudolph, Jr. Greenwood Press 2003 xxvi, 375p il map $74.95   **305.8**
1. Culture conflict 2. Culture conflict -- Encyclopedias 3. Culture conflict -- Encyclopedias 4. Ethnic relations 5. Ethnic relations -- Encyclopedias 6. Ethnic relations -- Political aspects 7. Ethnic relations -- Political aspects -- Encyclopedias 8. Reference books 9. World politics -- 1989- 10. World politics -- 1995-2005 -- Encyclopedias
ISBN 0-313-31381-4
LC 2002-70025
These "essays explore the history and issues that were the root causes of 38 major ethnic conflicts, the attempts to 'manage' them, and the impact they have had on the politics of the region in question. . . . Organized alphabetically by country or geographic area, the entries include a time line of significant events in the region, followed by a general discussion of the area. . . . Students will find this volume to be a useful tool in understanding the history and causes behind some of the major events in today's world." SLJ
Includes bibliographical references

Family affair; what it means to be African American today. [edited by] Gil L. Robertson IV. Bolden 2009 407p pa $16   **305.8**
1. African Americans -- Race identity
ISBN 978-1932841-35-0; 1-932841-35-0
LC 2008-45716
"This thoughtful collection of short essays, addressing a wide range of issues and emotions facing African Americans, should become a well-thumbed nightstand fixture." Publ Wkly

★ Freedom on my mind; the Columbia documentary history of the African American experience. Manning Marable, general editor; Nishani Frazier

and John McMillian, assistant editors. Columbia University Press 2003 734p $80   **305.8**
1. African Americans -- History -- Sources
ISBN 0-231-10890-7

LC 2003-51605

This "anthology features the works of noteworthy figures of African American history and culture . . . and provides a tapestry of personal correspondence, excerpts from slave narratives and autobiographies, leaflets, speeches, oral histories and interviews, political manifestos, song lyrics, and important statements of black institutions and organizations. . . . A necessary text of readings for both introductory and advanced African American studies courses." Choice

Includes bibliographical references

★ The Greenwood encyclopedia of African American civil rights; from emancipation to the twenty-first century. Charles D. Lowery and John F. Marszalek, editors; Thomas Adams Upchurch, associate editor; foreword by David J. Garrow. Greenwood Press 2003 2v il set $175   **305.8**
1. African Americans -- Civil rights -- Encyclopedias 2. Reference books
ISBN 0-313-32171-X

LC 2003-40837

"Entries are alphabetically arranged and cross-referenced, and each is followed by a selected bibliography. Many of the entries focus on seminal political issues of the 1950s and 1960s—Black Power, March on Washington, Voter Education Project—but also cover important developments both before and after this time. Other entries are biographical, ranging from politicians to writers, artists, actors, musicians, and athletes. Important literary documents are covered, including not only novels, plays, and political treatises but also journals." Booklist

Letters from Black America; edited by Pamela Newkirk. Farrar, Straus, and Giroux 2009 372p il $30   **305.8**
1. African Americans -- Social conditions 2. American letters -- African American authors
ISBN 978-0-374-10109-1; 0-374-10109-4

LC 2008-41265

"This anthology features the writings of individuals who range from highly celebrated to barely literate and presents stories that are of vital historical importance and touchingly personal. Newkirk divides the letters by topic—covering family, courtship and romance, politics and social justice, education and scholarship, war, art and culture, and the African diaspora—and offers concise introductions to each. . . . While this unique collection of letters represents a frank depiction of the black experience, the great achievement is that these writings often go far beyond race and class to simply tell the story of the human experience in America." Libr J

Includes bibliographical references

Those who forget the past; the question of anti-Semitism. edited and with an introduction by Ron Rosenbaum; afterword by Cynthia Ozick. Ran-

dom House Trade Paperbacks 2004 lxix, 649p pa $16.95   **305.8**
1. Antisemitism
ISBN 0-8129-7203-1

LC 2003-65542

"This is an important and vital contribution to efforts to comprehend what is new and what is the same in this ancient virus of ignorance and hatred." Booklist

Includes bibliographical references

305.868   Spanish Americans

Meier, Matt S.
  Notable Latino Americans; a biographical dictionary. {by} Matt S. Meier with Conchita Franco Serri and Richard A. Garcia. Greenwood Press 1997 431p il $73.95   **305.868**
1. Biography, Collective 2. Hispanic Americans -- Biography -- Dictionaries 3. Hispanic Americans -- Dictionaries 4. Reference books
ISBN 0-313-29105-5

LC 96-27392

This dictionary "offers 127 biographies of men and women of Latino descent who were born in or immigrated to the United States and have made a noteworthy impact. The majority of those profiled are writers, sports figures, actors, or political activists, though some lesser-known personalities in the sciences, education, and the arts are also included. The entries average three pages and generally include a picture and a short bibliography of additional sources." Libr J

Morales, Ed
  Living in Spanglish; the search for a new Latino identity in America. St. Martin's Press 2002 310p $25.95; pa $14.95   **305.868**
1. Hispanic Americans 2. Hispanic Americans -- Ethnic identity 3. Hispanic Americans -- Social conditions 4. Pluralism (Social sciences) -- United States 5. Racially mixed people 6. Racially mixed people -- United States -- Social conditions
ISBN 0-312-26232-9; 0-312-31000-5 pa

LC 2001-48867

"To the author, Spanglish isn't just . . . {an} increasingly common linguistic mélange. . . . It is the breakdown of the either/or of a black/white worldview through the inevitable mingling of race and culture. . . . The author meditates on his own coming to terms with Latino identity as well as positing the larger point that 'We have spent the last several centuries preparing for our role as the first wholly postmodern culture.'. . . His ideas are provocative and engaging." Booklist

305.891   Other Indo-European peoples

Walsh, Mikey
  Gypsy boy; my life in the secret world of the Romany Gypsies. Mikey Walsh. Thomas Dunne Books/ St. Martin's Press 2012 278 p.   **305.891**
1. Romanies -- England -- Biography 2. Romanies -- England -- Social life and customs 3. Young gay men

-- England -- Biography
ISBN 9780312622084; 9781250011978

LC 2011038168

This memoir, a number-one best-seller in the UK following its 2009 release, was written under a pseudonym to protect . . . [author Mikey] Walsh [who] has ongoing concerns for his safety after leaving the highly secretive Romany Gypsy community 15 years ago. . . . He claims his ultraviolent father once put a contract out on his life. He was born into a roving caravan of outsiders, brutally abused as a child (both physically by his father and sexually by an uncle), and never received any formal education growing up. He is also gay. (Booklist)

305.892   Semites

Smith, Helmut Walser
   The **butcher's** tale; murder and anti-Semitism in a German town. Norton 2002 270p il maps $25.95; pa $14.95   **305.892**
   1. Antisemitism 2. Antisemitism -- Germany -- Könitz 3. Blood accusation -- Germany -- Könitz 4. Homicide 5. Trials (Murder) -- Germany -- Könitz
   ISBN 0-393-05098-X; 0-393-32505-9 pa

LC 2002-22883

The author "does a masterful job exploring the history of the blood libel . . . as well as of community and how people band together to bring about great good or in the case of Konitz genuine evil. . . . Although classed by the publisher as history/Judaica, this powerful volume will also appeal to true-crime readers and anyone interested in the dynamics that can turn a peaceful community into a place of hatred and violence." Publ Wkly
   Includes bibliographical references (p.) and index

Wasserstein, Bernard
   On the eve; the Jews of Europe before the Second World War. Bernard Wasserstein. Simon & Schuster 2012 xxi, 552 p.p   **305.892**
   1. Antisemitism -- Europe -- History -- 20th century 2. Jews -- Europe -- History -- 20th century 3. Jews -- Europe -- Social conditions -- 20th century 4. Jews -- Persecutions -- Europe -- History -- 20th century 5. Nineteen thirties 6. Nineteen twenties 7. World War, 1939-1945 -- Causes
   ISBN 1416594272; 9781416594277; 9781416594284; 9781439101698

LC 2011020529

This book by Bernard Wasserstein "presents a new . . . interpretation of the collapse of European Jewish civilization even before the Nazi onslaught. In the 1930s, as Europe spiraled toward the Second World War, the continent's Jews faced an existential crisis. The harsh realities of the age . . . devastated Jewish communities and shattered the lives of individuals. The Jewish crisis was as much the result of internal decay as of external attack. . . . [Wasserstein] focuses not on the anti-Semites but on the Jews . . . refut[ing] the common misconception that they were unaware of the gathering forces of their enemies. . . . It explores their hopes, anxieties, and ambitions, their family ties, social relations, and intellectual creativity. (Publishers note)

305.896   Africans and people of African descent

Du Bois, W. E. B.
   ★ The **Oxford** W. E. B. Du Bois reader; edited by Eric J. Sundquist. Oxford Univ. Press 1996 680p pa $34.95   **305.896**
   1. African Americans
   ISBN 0-19-509178-7

LC 95-21307

This reader covers Du Bois's "writing career, from the 1890s through the early 1960s. The volume selects key essays and longer works that portray the range of Du Bois's thought on such subjects as African American culture, the politics and sociology of American race relations, art and music, black leadership, gender and women's rights, Pan-Africanism and anti-colonialism, and Communism in the U.S. and abroad." Publisher's note
   Includes bibliographical references

Gates, Henry Louis
   The **future** of the race; by Henry Louis Gates, Jr. and Cornel West. Knopf 1996 196p hardcover o.p. pa $12.95   **305.896**
   1. African Americans -- Intellectual life 2. African Americans -- Social conditions 3. Authors 4. Civil rights activists 5. Editors 6. Essayists 7. Historians 8. Nonfiction writers 9. Novelists 10. Sociologists
   ISBN 0-679-44405-X; 0-679-76378-3 pa

LC 96-14450

"Gates and West explore the challenge of W.E.B. Du Bois's famous essay 'The Talented Tenth' and consider the future of African American society in light of it. . . . The authors examine the responsibility of the successful and talented black middle and upper classes to uplift the impoverished. . . . The text includes DuBois's 'The Talented Tenth' and, reprinted for the first time, his 1948 critique of it." Libr J
   Includes bibliographical references

Kennedy, Randall
   Nigger; the strange career of a troublesome word. Pantheon Bks. 2002 226p hardcover o.p. pa $12   **305.896**
   1. African American musicians 2. African Americans 3. African Americans -- Music -- History and criticism 4. African Americans -- Race identity 5. African Americans -- Social conditions 6. Popular music -- United States -- History and criticism 7. Racism
   ISBN 0-375-42172-6; 0-375-71371-9 pa

LC 2001-36442

Kennedy examines the history of the use of the racial epithet in American society by both African Americans and whites and its implications for race relations.
   "An insightful and highly provocative book that raises vital questions about the relationship between language, politics, social norms and how society and culture confront racism." Publ Wkly
   Includes bibliographical references

Loury, Glenn C.
The **anatomy** of racial inequality. Harvard Univ. Press 2001 226p il $22.95   **305.896**
1. African Americans -- Civil rights 2. African Americans -- Economic conditions 3. African Americans -- Social conditions 4. African Americans -- Social conditions -- 1975- 5. Race discrimination -- Political aspects -- United States 6. Race discrimination -- United States
ISBN 0-674-00625-9
LC 2001-39192
"Loury argues that the image white Americans have of black Americans as less than full citizens influences policy far more than who African-Americans actually are. Although much of Loury's argument is theoretical . . . he grapples eloquently and vigorously with such concrete examples as affirmative action, arguments about racial IQ differences and racial profiling." Publ Wkly
Includes bibliographical references

The New York Public Library African American desk reference. Wiley 1999 606p il $40   **305.896**
1. African Americans 2. African Americans -- Encyclopedias 3. African Americans -- History 4. Afro-Americans 5. Reference books
ISBN 0-471-23924-0
This reference is "arranged into 19 chapters covering topics such as slavery, education, health, law, science and technology, the arts, and sports. Chapters include numerous tables, lists, photographs, and sidebars and end with sources for additional information. Quotations are sprinkled throughout." Booklist
Includes bibliographical references

★ Remembering Jim Crow; African Americans tell about life in the segregated South. edited by William H. Chafe [et al.] New Press (NY) 2001 xxxv, 346p il $55; pa $16.95   **305.896**
1. African Americans -- Civil rights -- Southern States -- History 2. African Americans -- Segregation 3. African Americans -- Segregation -- Southern States -- History 4. African Americans -- Southern States
ISBN 1-56584-697-4; 1-56584-778-4 pa
LC 2001-31224
This work offers "views into the thoughts, activities, and anxieties of black Americans. . . . Included are two one-hour CDs of the radio documentary produced by American Radio Works, a transcript of the audio program, 50 rare segregation-era photographs, biographical information, and suggestions for further reading. This [is a] superb primary source." Libr J
Includes bibliographical references

305.9 People by occupation and miscellaneous social statuses; people with disabilities and illnesses, gifted people

Allport, Alan
Demobbed; coming home after the Second World War. Yale University Press 2009 265p il $38 **305.9**
1. Veterans 2. War and society -- Great Britain 3.

World War, 1939-1945 -- Great Britain 4. World War, 1939-1945 -- Veterans
ISBN 9780300140439; 0-300-14043-6
LC 2009-26511
"Looking at the experiences of returning British servicemen after World War II, Alan Allport acknowledges time and again that there are almost no comprehensive, statistically non-dubious studies to draw upon in trying to figure out how many soldiers returned shell-shocked, or how many marriages broke up as a direct result of reunited ex-newlyweds discovering a lack of compatibility. Instead, he acknowledges the stumbling blocks and gets on with it, drawing on a wide range of contemporary publications, anecdotes, and letters to extrapolate a dazzling, largely anecdotal portrait of a society in transition." A V Club
Includes bibliographical references

Martinez, Ruben
★ The **new** Americans; photographs by Joseph Rodríguez. New Press 2004 251p il $25   **305.9**
ISBN 1-565-84792-X
LC 2003-70621
"Masterfully evoking such diverse settings as a Palestinian wedding in Chicago, a raucous ball game in Guatemala City and a torpid migrant trailer camp in California, Martínez's writing is clear-eyed and incisive—and sometimes heartbreaking and hilarious." Publ Wkly
Includes bibliographical references

Nugent, Benjamin
American nerd; the story of my people. Scribner 2008 224p $20   **305.9**
1. Creative ability 2. Creative ability -- History -- 20th century 3. Gifted children 4. Gifted persons 5. Popular culture -- United States 6. Stereotypes (Social psychology)
ISBN 978-0-7432-8801-9; 0-7432-8801-7
A study of the nerd in American popular culture and throughout history discussed in such contexts as the rise of online gaming, the science fiction club, ethnicity, Asperger's syndrome, autism, and high school and college debating.
"In a lighthearted, often laugh-out-loud manner, Nugent challenges us to reexamine our long-held belief of what it means to be a nerd and to reposition the nerd as, if not an American hero, at least an American antihero. Great fun and remarkably insightful between the laughs." Booklist

Pipher, Mary Bray
The **middle** of everywhere; the world's refugees come to our town. {by} Mary Pipher. Harcourt 2002 xxv, 390p $25; pa $14   **305.9**
1. Refugees 2. Refugees -- United States -- Social conditions
ISBN 0-15-100600-8; 0-15-602737-2 pa
LC 2001-5863
The author "writes in rich, empathetic language and with a keen, observant eye for detail and nuance." Publ Wkly
Includes bibliographical references

Shannon, Lisa
A **thousand** sisters; my journey into the worst place on earth to be a woman. [by] Lisa J. Shannon;

foreword by Zainab Salbi. Seal Press 2010 335p il $24.95   **305.9**
1. Women -- Congo (Republic)
ISBN 978-1-58005-296-2

LC 2009-25391

"Shannon presents images of the uncensored horror stories that, to many Congolese, have become regrettably routine: Congo's vile colonial history and the Rwandan genocide spillover that has caused the murders of more than five million Congolese people; children forced to kill and rape in their own communities; daily child deaths from easily curable illnesses; grisly murders of men and children in front of their wives and mothers; families burned alive inside their homes; women who must choose between rape and watching their children starve. . . . Juxtaposing brutality with beauty, Shannon's direct prose is a stirring reminder that these horrors are real and ongoing. An alarming and inspiring message that will hopefully spur much-needed action." Kirkus
Includes bibliographical references

Stephenson, Michael
The **last** full measure; how soldiers die in battle. Michael Stephenson. Crown Publishers 2012 xvi, 464 p.p $28.00; $28.00   **305.9**
1. Battle casualties -- History 2. Historical literature 3. Military art & science -- History 4. Military history 5. Military personnel 6. Weapons -- History
ISBN 0307395847; 0307952770; 9780307395849; 9780307952776

LC 2011005874

In this book, "[Michael] Stephenson . . . provides . . . descriptions of the ways in which soldiers have died in battle throughout history. Arranged chronologically, the book begins with analyses of ancient weapons and armor, and the deaths and destruction they caused, and then proceeds through history to discuss modern warfare. The physical and psychological effects of weapons are constant themes." (Library Journal)

306   Culture and institutions

Ault, James M.
Spirit and flesh; life in a fundamentalist Baptist church. Knopf 2004 435p $27.95   **306**
1. Baptists 2. Christian fundamentalism 3. Fundamentalist churches
ISBN 0-375-40242-X

LC 2003-65650

This "is a mix of ethnography and spiritual autobiography that deserves a hearing from fundamentalism's cultured despisers." N Y Times Book Rev

Bork, Robert H.
Slouching towards Gomorrah; modern liberalism and American decline. ReganBooks 1996 382p il hardcover o.p. pa $14.95   **306**
1. Liberalism 2. Social values
ISBN 0-06-039163-4; 0-06-057311-2 pa

LC 96-31277

"Forthright and magisterial, this is a fine summary of 'social conservativism.'" Booklist
Includes bibliographical references

Burd-Sharps, Sarah
★ The **measure** of America; American human development report, 2008-2009. written, compiled, and edited by Sarah Burd-Sharps, Kristen Lewis, and Eduardo Borges Martins; with forewords by Amartya Sen and William H. Draper III. Social Science Research Council 2008 245p il map $75; pa $24.95   **306**
1. Quality of life -- United States -- Statistics 2. Reference books
ISBN 978-0-231-15494-9; 0-231-15494-1; 978-0-231-15495-6 pa; 0-231-15495-X pa

LC 2008-20177

"Based on 2005 US government information, this . . . report focuses on three major concepts: longevity (life expectancy), knowledge (school enrollment and educational attainment), and standard of living (median income). Furthermore, the index is divided according to state, congressional district, gender, race, and ethnicity. This very timely report articulates clearly the state of the country, using a multifaceted perspective; it is written in a straightforward, engaging manner. Colorful graphics, charts, tables, and maps illustrate potentially complex concepts." Choice
Includes bibliographical references

Carter, Jimmy
Our endangered values; America's moral crisis. Simon & Schuster 2005 212p $25   **306**
1. Christianity and politics 2. Christianity and politics -- United States 3. Church and state 4. Church and state -- United States 5. Social values 6. Social values -- United States 7. United States -- Politics and government -- 2001-
ISBN 0-7432-8457-7

LC 2005-54051

"This book is an eloquent personal testament that deserves a wide readership, regardless of political affiliation." Libr J

Chang, Jeff
Can't stop, won't stop; a history of the hip-hop generation. introduction by D.J. Kool Herc. St. Martin's Press 2005 546p il hardcover o.p. pa $16 **306**
1. Hip-hop 2. Rap (Music) -- History and criticism 3. Rap music
ISBN 0-312-30143-X; 0-312-42579-1 pa

LC 2004-56656

"A fascinating, far-reaching must for pop-music and pop-culture collections." Booklist
Includes bibliographical references, discography, and filmography.

Charnas, Dan

The **big** payback; the history of the business of hip-hop. New American Library 2010 660p il $24.95 **306**

1. Hip-hop 2. Music industry 3. Rap music
ISBN 978-0-451-22929-8; 0-451-22929-0

LC 2010-16062

On this four-decade-long journey from the studios where the first rap records were made to the boardrooms where the big deals were inked, "The Big Payback" tallies the list of who lost and who won along the 40-year road to hip-hop's dominance.

This "history of the rap industry is a classic of music-business dirt-digging as well as a kind of pulp epic. . . . Tomorrow's Diddys should sleep with this book under their pillow." Rolling Stone

De Grazia, Victoria

Irresistible empire; America's advance through twentieth-century Europe. Belknap Press of Harvard University Press 2005 586p il $29.95 **306**

1. Consumers 2. Consumers -- Europe 3. Consumption (Economics) 4. Consumption (Economics) -- Europe -- History -- 20th century 5. Hegemony
ISBN 0-674-01672-6

LC 2004-59943

The author "contends that U.S. companies—and consumerism—have been making inroads in Europe for the past hundred years. She argues that an early, and major, U.S. innovation treated foreign territories as extensions of domestic markets. . . . De Grazia writes clearly, giving an uncommon perspective on the ways and means by which the U.S. and Europe drew close after WWII." Publ Wkly

Includes bibliographical references

Dionne, E. J.

Stand up, fight back; Republican toughs, Democratic wimps, and the politics of revenge. Simon & Schuster 2004 243p $24 **306**

1. Political culture -- United States 2. Political parties -- United States 3. United States -- Politics and government -- 2001-
ISBN 0-7432-5858-4

LC 2004-45155

The author "proffers perhaps the most cogent analysis to date of why Democrats have lost the battle to the right, and how they might regain control of the debate." Publ Wkly

Includes bibliographical references

Gennari, John

Blowin' hot and cool; jazz and its critics. University of Chicago Press 2006 480p $35 **306**

1. Jazz -- History and criticism 2. Jazz music -- History and criticism 3. Music -- Social aspects -- United States
ISBN 0-226-28922-2

LC 2005-30539

"Gennari's book does for jazz critics what most of them were unable to do for themselves, but with a postmodern twist: The scholar demystifies and historicizes the journalists. The first sustained scholarly book exclusively about jazz criticism—and, not least, about the passions that have driven and surrounded it—Blowin' Hot and Cool is thorough, ab-

sorbing and original, an obsessive study of professional obsessives that will circumvent the need for any other." Nation

Includes bibliographical references

Gioia, Ted

The **birth** (and death) of the cool. Speck Press 2009 256p $25 **306**

1. Jazz musicians 2. Lifestyles 3. Popular culture -- United States
ISBN 978-1-933108-31-5

LC 2009-18827

"Describing 'cool' as a set of 'beliefs, values, and behavior patterns' rooted in the personal and musical styles of Bix Beiderbecke, Lester Young and Miles Davis (with a healthy dose of Bugs Bunny), Gioia argues that while their ironic detachment once held sway, earnestness has made its way back on top. His narrative history of cool hits intriguing touchstones, such as Lee Strasberg and Frank Sinatra, while a time line appendix provides even more cultural referents— for the new sincerity as well, culminating with the arrival of Susan Boyle and Twitter." Publ Wkly

Includes bibliographical references

Johnson, Steven

★ **Everything** bad is good for you; how today's pop culture is actually making us smarter. Riverhead Books 2005 238p il $23.95; pa $14 **306**

1. Intellect 2. Popular culture 3. Popular culture -- United States 4. Reality television programs 5. Video games
ISBN 1-57322-307-7; 1-59448-194-6 pa

LC 2005-42769

This "is a brisk, witty read, well versed in the history of literature and bolstered with research." Time

Includes bibliographical references

Lasch, Christopher

The **revolt** of the elites; and the betrayal of democracy. Norton 1995 276p $22; pa $14.95 **306**

1. Democracy 2. Elite (Social sciences) 3. Elite (Social sciences) -- United States
ISBN 0-393-03699-5; 0-393-31371-9 pa

LC 94-37270

Lasch "argues that democracy today is threatened not by the masses, as José Ortega y Gasset (The Revolt of the Masses) had said, but by the elites. These elites—mobile and increasingly global in outlook—refuse to accept limits or ties to nation and place. Lasch contends that, as they isolate themselves in their networks and enclaves, they abandon the middle class, divide the nation, and betray the idea of a democracy for all America's citizens." Publisher's note

Includes bibliographical references

Marshall Cavendish Corporation

Encyclopedia of social issues; editor, John K. Roth. Marshall Cavendish 1997 6v il maps set $459.95 **306**

1. Canada -- Social conditions -- Encyclopedias 2. Reference books
ISBN 0-7614-0568-2

LC 96-38361

"This encyclopedia on current U.S. and Canadian social issues covers topics in government and politics, social policy, information, economics, human rights, health, law, environment, religion, etc." Libr J

Marzollo, Jean

Fathers & babies; how babies grow and what they need from you from birth to 18 months. illustrated by Irene Trivas. HarperPerennial 1993 235p il pa $13.95 **306**

1. Father and child 2. Father-child relationship 3. Infants -- Care
ISBN 0-06-096908-3

LC 92-53386

Marzollo covers "infant development from the physical and social to the intellectual, psychological and creative. . . . Her book provides step-by-step instructions on fixing bottles, bathing and feeding, changing a diaper, toilet training, helping a child develop langauge skills, and disciplining the older baby." Libr J

Mead, Margaret

★ **Coming** of age in Samoa; a psychological study of primitive youth for Western civilisation. foreword by Franz Boas. Morrow 1928 297p il hardcover o.p. pa $14 **306**

1. Adolescence 2. Samoan Islands -- Social life and customs 3. Sex differences (Psychology)
ISBN 0-688-05033-6 pa
An anthropological study of adolescent Samoan girls

Misiroglu, Gina Renee

American countercultures; an encyclopedia of nonconformists, alternative lifestyles, and radical ideas in U.S. history. Gina Misiroglu, editor. M.E. Sharpe 2009 3v il set $299 **306**

1. Counter culture -- Encyclopedias 2. Counterculture -- United States 3. Popular culture -- United States 4. Popular culture -- United States -- Encyclopedias 5. Radicals -- United States 6. Reference books
ISBN 978-0-7656-8060-0; 0-7656-8060-2

LC 2008-26227

"Offers readers a unique reference that pulls together disparate elements of our historic nonconformity. By doing so it helps provide clarity and definition to just how deeply countercultures are woven into the American fabric. In addition, it is one of those references that, while being useful and fact filled, is also fascinating to read and fun to browse." Against the Grain
Includes filmography and bibliographical references

Morgan, Peter W.

The **appearance** of impropriety; how ethics wars have undermined American government, business, and society. [by] Peter W. Morgan, Glenn H. Reynolds. Free Press 1997 272p hardcover o.p. pa $16.95 **306**

1. Business ethics 2. Political ethics
ISBN 0-7432-4266-1 pa

LC 97-19251

"Examples the authors give, concerning plagiarism and election-posturing 'anti-crime' legislation, are so deliciously preposterous that the reader is well primed for the concluding recommendations for reform." Booklist
Includes bibliographical references

Talbot, David

Season of the witch; enchantment, terror, and deliverance in the City of Love. David Talbot. Free Press 2012 xvii, 452 p.p **306**

1. City and town life -- California -- San Francisco -- History -- 20th century 2. Counterculture -- California -- San Francisco -- History -- 20th century 3. Culture conflict -- California -- San Francisco -- History -- 20th century 4. Political culture -- California -- San Francisco -- History -- 20th century 5. Social change -- California -- San Francisco -- History -- 20th century 6. Social problems -- California -- San Francisco -- History -- 20th century
ISBN 1439108218; 9781439108215

LC 2011032082

In this book, author David Talbot "recounts the . . . story of San Francisco in the turbulent years between 1967 and 1982. . . . The cool gray city of love was the epicenter of the 1960s cultural revolution. But by the early 1970s, San Francisco's ecstatic experiment came crashing down from its starry heights. The city was rocked by savage murder sprees, mysterious terror campaigns, political assassinations, street riots, and finally a terrifying sexual epidemic. . . . David Talbot takes us deep into the riveting story of his city's ascent, decline, and heroic recovery. He draws intimate portraits of San Francisco's legendary demons and saviors. . . . He reveals how the city emerged from the trials of this period with a new brand of San Francisco values. (Publishers note)

Underhill, Paco

The **call** of the mall; a walking tour through the crossroads of our shopping culture. Simon & Schuster 2004 227p hardcover o.p. pa $14 **306**

1. Consumers 2. Consumers -- Attitudes 3. Consumption (Economics) 4. Consumption (Economics) -- United States 5. Shopping centers and malls 6. Shopping malls
ISBN 0-7432-3591-6; 0-7432-3592-4 pa

LC 2003-64960

The author takes readers on a "tour of a typical Saturday at a large, regional mall. He examines the routes there, the shopping center itself, the stores, food, entertainment, ambience, and the customers. He shows why the mall is the way it is and how it could be improved. He provides insight into how the stores are arranged, how they display merchandise, and the different ways that men and women respond to this environment." SLJ

Victorian house

Inside the Victorian home; a portrait of domestic life in Victorian England. W.W. Norton 2004 xxviii, 499p il $34.95 **306**

1. Family -- England -- History -- 19th century
ISBN 0-393-05209-5

LC 2003-27693

"Room by room, Flanders walks us through the typical home of upper-middle-class Britain, explaining its use, its décor, the habits of occupants, and more. The result is a genteel yet absorbing and thoroughly researched book. . . . Fearsomely entertaining and yet a wonderful addition to academic literature, this book is sure to become a classic." Libr J

Includes bibliographical references

Wann, David

The **new** normal; an agenda for responsible living. St. Martin's Griffin 2011 274p il pa $14.99 **306**
1. Conduct of life 2. Lifestyles 3. Quality of life 4. Social values
ISBN 978-0-312-57543-4

LC 2010-37913

"Wann pulls from the disciplines of biology, anthropology, history, and psychology to make his case that the current paradigm of bigger and more is not working. He proposes the 'Era of Emerging Restoration,' in which healthy families, communities, and ecosystems are the best measures of wealth. . . . This is one of the best approaches to promoting a sustainable world." Libr J

Includes bibliographical references

Worldmark encyclopedia of cultures and daily life; editors, Timothy L. Gall and Janeen Hobby. 2nd ed.; Gale 2009 5v il map set $551 **306**
1. Ethnology -- Encyclopedias 2. Manners and customs -- Encyclopedias 3. Reference books
ISBN 978-1-4144-4882-4

LC 2009-4744

This encyclopedia "covers more than 500 cultures from around the world. . . . The five volumes covering four geographical areas—Africa, Americas, Asia and Oceania, and Europe—are arranged alphabetically by country with information about the various cultures and communities that exist within their borders. . . . Each article begins with a block containing key country facts: location, population, language, religion, related articles, and pronunciation assistance. . . . A well-organized, easy-to-use research tool." SLJ

Includes bibliographical references

306.2   Cultural institutions

Freeman, Joanne B.

Affairs of honor; national politics in the new republic. Yale Univ. Press 2001 xxiv, 376p $29.95; pa $16.95 **306.2**
1. Elite (Social sciences) -- United States -- Political activity -- History -- 18th century 2. Honor -- Political aspects -- United States -- History -- 18th century 3. Political culture -- United States -- History -- 18th century 4. Politics and culture -- United States -- History -- 18th century
ISBN 0-300-08877-9; 0-300-09755-7 pa

LC 2001-915

"Freeman's prose is lively, and she balances entertaining narrative with sharp analysis." Publ Wkly

Includes bibliographical references (p. 347-364) and index

Goldwag, Arthur

The **new** hate; a history of fear and loathing on the populist right. Arthur Goldwag. Pantheon Books 2012 368 p. $27.95 **306.2**
1. Conspiracy theories -- Political aspects -- United States 2. Hate groups -- Political aspects -- United States 3. Politics and culture -- United States 4. Right-wing extremists -- United States
ISBN 0307379698; 9780307379696

LC 2011028589

The author [Arthur] Goldwag . . . delivers a . . . history of organized hate groups and their role in U.S. politics. Less about prejudice than America's relentless quest for scapegoats, he traces the American conspiratorial tradition from colonial times--where the Puritans feared Jesuit conspiracies as much as Indian ambushes--to the present, covering the movements and vitriolic commentary against the Masons, Catholics, Jews, Communists, and Muslims. . . . Goldwag combines his research with contemporary analysis to explain what conspiracy theories all have in common and to show how the new hate is the same as the old, though it's now hiding in plain sight. (Publishers Wkly)

Maddow, Rachel

Drift; the unmooring of American military power. Rachel Maddow. Crown 2012 275 p. **306.2**
1. Militarism -- United States 2. National security -- United States 3. Political culture -- United States 4. Social criticism
ISBN 9780307460981; 9780307461001

LC 2012000998

The author "examines how the country has lost control of its national-security policy. The author holds Dick Cheney . . . responsible, . . . associating . . . [him] with the presidential prerogative of war-making powers. . . . American forces are now accompanied by . . . private contractors who perform functions that used to be reserved to the military, without either accountability or military control. . . . She grounds her argument in the Founding Fathers' debates about going to war." (Kirkus)

Stern, Kenneth S.

A **force** upon the plain; the American militia movement and the politics of hate. [by] Kenneth S. Stern; with a new foreword by the author. University of Oklahoma Press 1997 303p pa $16.95 **306.2**
1. Militia movements 2. Radicalism 3. Resistance to government
ISBN 0-8061-2926-3; 978-0-8061-2926-6

LC 96-41861

Stern "links militias to preexisting racist groups such as the Ku Klux Klan, Aryan Nations, and Posse Comitatus. . . . This book provides an excellent introduction to the latest incarnation of racist and paranoid politics." Libr J

306.3 Economic institutions

Fukuyama, Francis

Trust; the social virtues and the creation of prosperity. Free Press 1995 458p hardcover o.p. pa $16 **306.3**

1. Economic conditions 2. Economics 3. Economics -- Ethical aspects 4. International economic relations 5. Virtue

ISBN 0-684-82525-2 pa

LC 95-19320

The author "compares how selected modern economies organize themselves, and he argues that these same societies depend on 'civil society' and the creation and maintenance of 'social capital' for their vitality and economic success. By social capital he means the set of intermediate institutions, such as businesses, unions, and voluntary organizations (churches, charities, clubs) that facilitate trust beyond the more traditional family oriented structures to socialize people into their culture and transmit both knowledge and values. . . . Fukuyama proposes that natural cultural laws are important determinants of a nation's wealth. This stimulating, well-documented volume will be widely read and discussed." Choice

Includes bibliographical references

Nathans, Sydney

To free a family; Sydney Nathans. Harvard University Press 2012 330 p. [20] p of plates, ill, maps **306.3**

1. African American women -- Massachusetts -- Cambridge -- Biography 2. Family reunions -- Massachusetts -- Cambridge -- History -- 19th century 3. Fugitive slaves -- Northeastern States -- Biography 4. Women slaves -- North Carolina -- Orange County -- Biography

ISBN 9780674062122

LC 2011023122

This book "tells the . . . story of Mary Walker, who in August 1848 fled her owner for refuge in the North and spent the next seventeen years trying to recover her family. . . . This story is anchored in two . . . collections of letters and diaries, that of her former North Carolina slaveholders and that of the northern family--Susan and Peter Lesley--who protected and employed her. Sydney Nathan's . . . narrative reveals Mary Walker's . . . persistence as well as the sustained collaboration of black and white abolitionists who assisted her. Mary Walker and the Lesleys ventured half a dozen attempts at liberation, from ransom to ruse to rescue, until the end of the Civil War reunited Mary Walker with her son and daughter." (Publisher's note)

Postma, Johannes

The Atlantic slave trade. Greenwood Press 2003 xxii, 177p map $45 **306.3**

1. Slave trade 2. Slave trade -- Africa -- History 3. Slave trade -- America -- History 4. Slave trade -- Europe -- History

ISBN 0-313-31862-X

LC 2002-35338

The author "covers the entire Atlantic slave trade era, from the 1400s to the final abolition of chattel slavery in the New World in 1888. The focus is on Africa and the entire New World. While he describes the many horrors of the Middle Passage, he also examines how the slave trade contributed to the development of the modern international economy. The last chapters discuss the efforts to abolish the slave trade and its legacy." SLJ

Includes bibliographical references

Reich, Robert B.

The future of success. Knopf 2001 289p $26; pa $14 **306.3**

1. Information society 2. Information society -- United States 3. Quality of life 4. Quality of work life -- United States 5. Work 6. Work and family -- United States.

ISBN 0-375-41112-7; 0-375-72512-1 pa

LC 00-40552

The author provides an "analysis of the new economy and how it is affecting lives. . . . He argues that the current economic opportunities afforded by new communication, transportation, and information technologies have produced a workforce that is unable to perform individual, family, and community roles effectively in a job market that is frenzied, economically divergent, and socially stratified." Libr J

Includes bibliographical references

Segal, Ronald

★ Islam's Black slaves; the other Black diaspora. Farrar, Straus & Giroux 2001 273p maps hardcover o.p. pa $14 **306.3**

1. African diaspora 2. Slave trade 3. Slavery 4. Slavery -- Islamic countries -- History 5. Slavery and Islam -- History

ISBN 0-374-22774-8; 0-374-52797-0 pa

LC 00-62256

"The strength of this account is the meticulous documentation of what is fact and what is surmise. The dramatic narrative is sure to spark discussion and further research." Booklist

306.4 Specific aspects of culture

Blanning, T. C. W.

The triumph of music; the rise of composers, musicians and their art. [by] Tim Blanning. Belknap Press of Harvard University Press 2008 416p il $29.95 **306.4**

1. Music -- Social aspects 2. Musicians 3. Musicians -- Social conditions

ISBN 978-0-674-03104-3; 0-674-03104-0

LC 2008-26753

"This is not intended to be a history of music; it is a brilliantly written history of the steady growth of the power of music and its performers." Libr J

Includes bibliographical references (p. 343-352)

Chidester, Brian

Pop surf culture; music, design, film, and fashion from the Bohemian surf boom. [by] Brian Chidester and Domenic Priore; forewords by Kathy Zukerman

(aka Gidget) and Billy Al Bengston (aka Moondoggie) Santa Monica Press 2008 271p il $39.95 **306.4**
1. Popular culture -- United States 2. Surfing
ISBN 978-1-59580-035-0; 1-59580-035-2
LC 2008-01803
"Throughout, the authors have the good sense to realize that the power of the surfing story is as much in the showing—the rich visual panorama—as in the telling. No walls of narrative here; every page is crowded with images of the corresponding period. . . . More than a catalog of beach-blanket movies or a survey of surf music, it connects the historical dots between the surf culture we experienced domestically, the economic culture that made it marketable, and the foreign cultures that made it possible in the first place." PopMatters
Includes bibliographical references

Ekirch, A. Roger
★ **At** day's close; night in times past. Norton 2005 447p il $25.95 **306.4**
1. Night 2. Night -- Social aspects 3. Social history
ISBN 0-393-05089-0
LC 2005-2784
"This history finds Ekirch reminding us of how preindustrial Westerners lived during the nocturnal hours, when most were plunged into almost total darkness. . . . A rich weave of citation and archival evidence, Ekirch's narrative is rooted in the material realities of the past, evoking a bygone world of extreme physicality and preindustrial survival stratagems." Publ Wkly
Includes bibliographical references

Elliott, Carl
Better than well; American medicine meets the American dream. foreword by Peter D. Kramer. Norton 2003 xxi, 357p $26.95; pa $14.95 **306.4**
1. American national characteristics 2. Medical innovations -- Social asepcts -- United States 3. National characteristics, American 4. Self-perception 5. Social medicine 6. Social medicine -- United States
ISBN 0-393-05201-X; 0-393-32565-2 pa
LC 2002-15947
This is an "engaging and provocative book. . . . As Elliott considers Americans' yearning for self-improvement and fulfillment, he takes readers on a refreshingly quirky journey, its twists and turns dotted with cultural and literary references." Christ Sci Monit
Includes bibliographical references

Fadiman, Anne
★ The **spirit** catches you and you fall down; a Hmong child, her American doctors, and the collision of two cultures. Anne Fadiman. Farrar, Straus & Giroux 1997 xi, 339p $25; (pbk.) $15 **306.4**
1. Culture conflict 2. Epilepsy 3. Epilepsy in children 4. Hmong (Asian people) 5. Hmong (Asian people) -- Medicine 6. Hmong American children -- Medical care -- California 7. Hmong Americans -- Medicine 8. Intercultural communication 9. Medical care 10. Social medicine -- United States 11. Transcultural

medical care -- California -- Case studies
ISBN 0374267812; 9780374533403
LC 97005175
This book presents an anthropological exploration of the Hmong population in Merced County, California. Following the case of Lia (a Hmong child with a progressive and unpredictable form of epilepsy), Fadiman maps out the controversies raised by the collision between Western medicine and holistic healing traditions of Hmong immigrants. Unable to enter the Laotian forest to find herbs for Lia that will "fix her spirit," her family becomes resigned to the Merced County emergency system, which has little understanding of Hmong animist traditions. [Anne] Fadiman reveals the rigidity and weaknesses of these two ethnographically separated cultures. (Library Journal)

Gross, Michael
Starstruck: when a fan gets close to fame; [by] Michael Joseph Gross. Bloomsbury 2005 239p $23.95; pa $14.95 **306.4**
1. Celebrities 2. Fans 3. Popular culture
ISBN 1-58234-316-0; 1-59691-094-1 pa
LC 2004-30339
The author "interviews fans, collectors, celebrities and publicists in an effort to paint a broad portrait of changing celebrity culture. . . . Gross's writing is honest and humane, and his book is an entertaining look at modern celebrity culture." Publ Wkly

Leonard, Annie
The **story** of stuff; how our obsession with stuff is trashing the planet, our communities, and our health--and a vision for change. [by] Annie Leonard with Ariane Conrad. Free Press 2010 xxxiv, 317p il $26 **306.4**
1. Consumption (Economics) 2. Material culture
ISBN 978-1-4391-2566-3
LC 2009-42207
"Leonard explains that our consumer goods undergo extraction, production, distribution, consumption, and disposal processes that are trashing the planet, diminishing our resources, exploiting workers, and contributing to high levels of disease and death. She advocates an international cooperative effort to develop domestic and international policies and laws that will reverse our planet's ecological decline and leave a sustainable world for future generations. . . . An important work for consumers of all ages." Libr J

Levine, Mark
Heavy metal Islam; rock, resistance, and the struggle for the soul of Islam. Three Rivers Press 2008 296p il pa $13.95 **306.4**
1. Heavy metal (Music) 2. Music -- Islamic countries 3. Popular music -- Social aspects -- Egypt 4. Popular music -- Social aspects -- Islamic countries 5. Popular music -- Social aspects -- Middle East 6. Popular music -- Social aspects -- Morocco
ISBN 978-0-307-35339-9; 0-307-35339-7
LC 2008-02801
This is "a deeply felt, informed volume that's both hopeful and emotionally honest. . . . Anyone—regardless of musical preference—who wants an eye-level glimpse into the

Middle East should pick up Heavy Metal Islam. Headbanging optional." Paste
Includes bibliographical references

McGonigal, Jane

Reality is broken; why games make us better and how they can change the world. Penguin Press 2011 388p il	**306.4**

    1. Computer games -- Social aspects
    ISBN 1594202850; 9781594202858

                    LC 2010029619

McGonigal argues "that videogames are increasingly fulfilling genuine human needs. . . . [She also argues that] we can use the lessons of game design to fix what is wrong with the real world." (Publisher's note) Index.

"If the world of gaming seems alien to you, this book will crack it wide open. For experienced gamers, it will likely inspire you to play or even invent better, more meaningful games. Despite her expertise, McGonigal's book is never overly technical, and as with a good computer game, anyone, regardless of gaming experience, is likely to get sucked in." New Sci
Includes bibliographical references

Pollan, Michael

The **botany** of desire; Michael Pollan. Random House 2001 xxv, 271 p.p $24.95; pa $13.95 **306.4**

    1. Apples 2. Economic botany 3. Human-plant relationships 4. Marijuana 5. Potatoes 6. Tulips
    ISBN 0-375-50129-0; 0-375-76039-3 pa;
    9780375760396; 9780375501296

                    LC 00066479

In this book, author "Michael Pollan . . . demonstrates how people and domesticated plants have formed a similarly reciprocal relationship. He . . . links four fundamental human desires--sweetness, beauty, intoxication, and control--with the plants that satisfy them: the apple, the tulip, marijuana, and the potato. In telling the stories of four familiar species, Pollan illustrates how the plants have evolved to satisfy humankind's most basic yearnings. And just as we've benefited from these plants, we have also done well by them. So who is really domesticating whom?" (Publisher's note)

"Pollan intertwines history, anecdote, and revelation as he investigates the connection between four plants that have thrived under human care—apples, tulips, marijuana, and potatoes—and the four human desires they satisfy in return: sweetness, beauty, intoxication, and control. . . . Pollan's dynamic, intelligent, and intrepid parsing of the wondrous dialogue between plants and humans is positively paradigm-altering." Booklist
Includes bibliographical references and index.

Rose, Frank

The **art** of immersion; how the digital generation is remaking Hollywood, Madison Avenue, and the way we tell stories. W.W. Norton & Co. 2011 354p $26.95	**306.4**

    1. Internet -- Social aspects 2. Internet entertainment
    3. Internet marketing
    ISBN 978-0-393-07601-1

                    LC 2010-38676

The author "theorizes that we are encountering a profound shift in the way we play, consume, and communicate. He explains that our experiences with television, movies, games, and advertisements are becoming increasingly more immersive and consumer-driven. . . . This engrossing study of how new media is reshaping the entertainment, advertising, and communication industries is an essential read for professionals in the fields of digital communications, marketing, and advertising, as well as for fans of gaming and pop culture." Libr J
Includes bibliographical references

Trumble, Angus

The **finger**; a handbook. Farrar, Straus and Giroux 2010 300p il $28	**306.4**

    1. Fingers 2. Hand in art
    ISBN 978-0-374-15498-1; 0-374-15498-8

                    LC 2009-42220

On the whole, The Finger is a deft, enjoyable and often provocative investigation into some overlooked and interrelated aspects of human experience. Washington Post
Includes bibliographical references

Science, technology, and society; an encyclopedia. Sal Restivo, editor in chief. Oxford University Press 2005 xxiv, 701p $165	**306.4**

    1. Reference books 2. Science -- Encyclopedias 3. Science -- Social aspects 4. Technological innovations -- Social aspects 5. Technology -- Encyclopedias 6. Technology -- Social aspects
    ISBN 0-19-514193-8; 978-0-19-514193-1

                    LC 2004-31121

"This is an excellent source for readers needing an overview of societal issues raised by science, technology, and medicine." Choice
Includes bibliographical references

306.44   Language

Lepore, Jill

A is for American; letters and other characters in the newly United States. Knopf 2002 241p il $25; pa $13	**306.44**

    1. Americanisms 2. Americanisms -- History 3. Architects 4. Artisans 5. Artists 6. English language -- 18th century 7. English language -- 19th century 8. English language -- Social aspects 9. English language -- Social aspects -- United States 10. English language -- United States -- History 11. Essayists 12. Indian leaders 13. Inventors 14. Lexicographers 15. Metalworkers 16. National characteristics, American -- History 17. Painters 18. Slaves 19. Sociolinguistics 20. Teachers of the deaf 21. Telecommunications executives 22. Writers on law
    ISBN 0-375-40449-X; 0-375-70408-6 pa

                    LC 2001-38057

"Each man's story delivers a wealth of irony along with valuable history. . . . Some familiar accounts, some not well known, but all told with a fresh eye to their national significance." Booklist
Includes bibliographical references

306.7   Sexual relations

Bader, Michael J.

Arousal, the secret logic of sexual fantasies. Thomas Dunne Bks./St. Martin's Press 2002 293p $23.95; pa $14.95   **306.7**

1. Sexual behavior

ISBN 0-312-26933-1; 0-312-30242-8 pa

LC 2001-51290

"Bader covers how arousal works, how fantasies assist in arousal, the role of fantasies in therapy, and the social meaning of fantasies. Throughout, he gives numerous case studies, examples, and sensible and compassionate conjectures about particular fantasies and the fantasizing process. Bader is a clear, graceful writer, and he makes his points with rare facility in a way useful to both lay people and therapeutic professionals." Libr J

Includes bibliographical references

Barash, David P.

The **myth** of monogamy; fidelity and infidelity in animals and people. [by] David P. Barash, Judith Eve Lipton. Freeman, W.H. 2001 227p $24.95; pa $15   **306.7**

1. Adultery 2. Marriage 3. Sex customs 4. Sexual behavior 5. Sexual behavior in animals

ISBN 0-7167-4004-4; 0-8050-7136-9 pa

This is "guaranteed to entertain and may even pique thoughtful readers' interests." Sci Books Films

Includes bibliographical references

Bergner, Daniel

The **other** side of desire; four journeys into the far realms of lust and longing. Ecco 2009 208p $24.95   **306.7**

1. Compulsive behavior 2. Psychosexual disorders 3. Sexual behavior

ISBN 978-0-06-088556-4; 0-06-088556-4

The author "approaches deviance with a reporter's notepad. He selects four areas: foot fetishism, sadomasochism, pedophilia, and an obsession for amputees. In each case, he finds and follows a devotee. In the process, Bergner does what science cannot: He illuminates peculiar longings. His method is at first descriptive and finally poetic. The message of the book is in the interplay among personal narratives that prove alternately bizarre and mundane." Slate

Bernstein, Richard

The **East,** the West, and sex; a history of erotic encounters. Knopf 2009 325p il $27.95   **306.7**

1. Asian national characteristics 2. East and West 3. Erotica 4. Orientalism 5. Sex -- Cross-cultural studies 6. Sex -- History 7. Sex in popular culture

ISBN 978-0-375-41409-1

LC 2008-55079

"This probing, absorbing and eclectic study critically challenges morally and politically correct interpretations of the Western sexual exploitation of the East." Publ Wkly

Includes bibliographical references

Hooks, Bell

Salvation; Black people and love. Morrow 2001 xxiv, 225p hardcover o.p. pa $12.95   **306.7**

1. African Americans -- Psychology 2. African Americans -- Social conditions 3. African Americans -- Social life and customs 4. Friendship -- United States 5. Interpersonal relations 6. Love 7. Love -- United States 8. Man-woman relationships -- United States

ISBN 0-06-095949-5 pa

LC 00-61648

The author contends "that there is a crisis of 'lovelessness' in the black community. . . . [In this exploration of love] she addresses its meaning in black experience today and offers a plan of action for 'black survival and self-determination.'" Libr J

Kipnis, Laura

How to become a scandal; adventures in bad behavior. Metropolitan Books 2010 209p il $24 **306.7**

1. Celebrities 2. Conduct of life 3. Deviant behavior 4. Scandals

ISBN 978-0-8050-8979-0; 0-8050-8979-9

LC 2010-05036

The author "picks through the mortifying carnage of other people's lives, exploring why we both relish and condemn bad behavior. Divided in two parts, 'Downfalls' and 'Uproars,' this slight and easy-to-digest book covers four major popular-culture scandals of the last two decades. These include those of love-crazed, diaper-wearing astronaut Lisa Nowak; the dishonorable judge Sol Wachtler; whistle-blower Linda Tripp; and the 'overimaginative,' so-called memoirist James Frey. . . . Light and fun." Kirkus

Includes bibliographical references

Levine, Judith

Harmful to minors; the perils of protecting children from sex. foreword by Joycelyn Elders. University of Minn. Press 2002 xxxv, 299p $25.95   **306.7**

1. Child sexual abuse 2. Sex education 3. Sex instruction -- United States 4. Sexual behavior

ISBN 0-8166-4006-8

LC 2001-6553

"Levine argues that sex is not necessarily bad for minors, and that puritanical attitudes often backfire. . . . She notes the disturbing trend toward pathologizing young children's eroticized play and criticizes mainstream America for letting the Christian right steer sex education toward an emphasis on abstinence. Compounding that, she says, the right wing has expunged abortion discussions. . . . It's a good start to confronting some vital questions." Publ Wkly

Includes bibliographical references

McConnachie, James

The **book** of love; the story of the Kamasutra. Metropolitan Books 2008 267p il $27.50; pa $17   **306.7**

1. Sexual behavior

ISBN 978-0-8050-8818-2; 0-8050-8818-0; 978-0-8050-9019-2 pa; 0-8050-9019-3 pa

LC 2007-47172

"In an impressively researched, charming volume, McConnachie traces the Kamasutra's history from its creation by the third-century sage Vatsyayana as a guide to the good life for urbane dandies. . . . Since not a single posture is described, consider it G-rated." Booklist

Includes bibliographical references

Reinisch, June

★ The **Kinsey** Institute new report on sex; what you must know to be sexually literate. [by] June M. Reinisch with Ruth Beasley; edited and compiled by Debra Kent. St. Martin's Press 1990 xx, 540p il hardcover o.p. pa $18.95   **306.7**

    1. Sexual behavior

    ISBN 0-312-06386-5 pa

                  LC 90-41444

This volume offers information about sexual matters, divided into general areas, including "body image and self esteem, problems with sexual functioning, sex and aging, contraception, [and] sexually transmitted diseases." Libr J

Shlain, Leonard

Sex, time, and power; how women's sexuality shaped human evolution. Viking 2003 xx, 420p il $25.95; pa $16   **306.7**

    1. Evolution 2. Evolution (Biology) 3. Human evolution 4. Mate selection 5. Sex (Biology) 6. Sexual attraction 7. Social evolution 8. Women -- Sexual behavior

    ISBN 0-670-03233-6; 0-14-200467-7 pa

                  LC 2002-41186

The author "takes an evolutionary approach to solving the conundrums of misogyny and patriarchy, guiding his . . . readers through . . . speculations about the purpose of such seemingly impractical, even dangerous traits as bipedalism, menstruation, the perils of childbirth, and the helplessness of infants. . . . Lucid and compelling, Shlain asks startling and crucial questions about human nature and presents truly imaginative and mind-stretching answers." Booklist

Includes bibliographical references

Wolf, Naomi

Promiscuities; the secret struggle for woman-hood. Random House 1997 xxx, 286p hardcover o.p. pa $15   **306.7**

    1. Girls -- Sexual behavior 2. Women -- Sexual behavior

    ISBN 0-449-90764-3 pa

                  LC 96-46724

"Wolf offers some astute and eminently realizable suggestions for a new approach to sexual education, even healing." Booklist

Includes bibliographical references

★ The Continuum complete international encyclopedia of sexuality; edited by Robert T. Francoeur and Raymond J. Noonan; associate editors, Africa: Beldina Opiyo-Omolo . . . [et al.] ; foreword by Robert T. Francoeur; preface by Timothy Perper; introduction by Ira L. Reiss. Continuum 2004 1419p map $225   **306.7**

    1. Sex -- Encyclopedias 2. Sex customs -- Encyclopedias

    3. Sexual behavior

    ISBN 0-8264-1488-5

                  LC 2003-6391

"Covered here are the sexual attitudes and behavior of more than 60 countries . . . including most large and influential nations like the United States, China, Russia, South Africa, India, Japan, and Mexico. . . . This unique compilation of specialized knowledge is recommended for research collections in the social sciences, where it could be useful for reference as well as a secondary source for cross-cultural research." Libr J

Includes bibliographical references

Longing to tell; Black women talk about sexuality and intimacy. {compiled by} Tricia Rose. Farrar, Straus & Giroux 2003 415p $25; pa $15 **306.7**

    1. African American women 2. Women -- Sexual behavior

    ISBN 0-374-19061-5; 0-312-42372-1 pa

                  LC 2002-32541

"By letting the women speak for themselves and following the histories with a passionate afterword, Rose provides a collection that is as compelling as it is sorely needed." Publ Wkly

Includes bibliographical references

Sugar in my bowl; real women write about real sex. edited by Erica Jong. Ecco 2011 238p il $21.99; ebook $9.99   **306.7**

    1. Sex 2. Sexual behavior 3. Women -- Sexual behavior

    ISBN 9780061875762; 0061875767; 9780062092205 ebook; 0062092200 ebook

                  LC 2011012689

A "frank collection of personal essays, short fiction and cartoons celebrating female desire. The approaches to the still-taboo topic of feminine sexuality—at least, for women writers seeking approbation from the literary establishment—are, as Jong notes, 'as varied as sexuality itself' and as exuberantly diverse as the contributors themselves. They range from such emerging talents as Elisa Albert and J.A.K. Andres to such luminaries as Rebecca Walker, Eve Ensler, Susan Cheever, Anne Roiphe and Fay Weldon, and represent a multiethnic, multigenerational swath of some of the finest women writers in the United States. Most of the pieces deal with the perennial themes of sexual coming-of-age, social and religious sexual hang-ups and lusty obsessions for male bodies (as well as female ones). Some deal with lesser-discussed—but no less important—subjects like procreative sex and eroticism in old age. Still others fearlessly explore fetishism, childhood masturbation, kink, [and] sexual addiction." Kirkus

Yes means yes! visions of female sexual power & a world without rape. [by] Jaclyn Friedman & Jessica Valenti [editors]; foreword by Margaret Cho. Seal Press 2008 361p pa $16.95   **306.7**

    1. Rape 2. Sex role 3. Sexism 4. Women -- Sexual behavior

    ISBN 978-1-58005-257-3; 1-58005-257-6

                  LC 2008-20989

The editors "present an extraordinary, eye-opening essay collection that focuses on the importance of sexual identity and ownership in the struggle against rape in the U.S., as well as a number of related issues, including sexual pleasure, self-esteem and the mixed societal messages that turn 'nice guys' bad." Publ Wkly

Includes bibliographical references

306.76 Sexual orientation, transgenderism, intersexuality

Bronski, Michael

★ A **queer** history of the United States. Beacon Press 2011 xx, 287p $27.95   **306.76**

1. Homosexuality -- United States -- History

ISBN 978-0-8070-4439-1

LC 2010-50225

"This enthralling history spans 500 years of evolving perspectives on sexuality in America—from the European setters' violent responses to the more fluid gender roles of Native Americans to how the birth control pill, which separated sex from reproduction, contributed to the cause of LGBT liberation. . . . A savvy political, legal, literary (and even fashion) history, Bronski's narrative is as intellectually rigorous as it is entertaining." Publ Wkly

Faderman, Lillian

Gay L.A. a history of sexual outlaws, power politics, and lipstick lesbians. [by] Lillian Faderman and Stuart Timmons. Basic Books 2006 431p il $27.50   **306.76**

1. Gay liberation movement 2. Gay liberation movement -- California -- Los Angeles 3. Gays -- California -- Los Angeles 4. Homosexuality 5. Homosexuality -- California -- Los Angeles

ISBN 978-0-465-02288-5; 0-465-02288-X

LC 2006-23470

This history of lesbian and gay life in Los Angeles "stretches from the humane tolerance of pre-contact indigenous peoples, through the 20th-century crisis years of homophobia and AIDS and ultimately into the victories and setbacks in this century. . . . Full of fascinating anecdotes (including much on Hollywood), wise and fair analysis, and significant and inspiring examples of courageous resistance recaptured from the unwritten histories of the past, Gay L.A. deserves a prominent place in every library." Libr J

Includes bibliographical references

Fellows, Will

Gay bar; the fabulous, true story of a daring woman and her boys in the 1950s. [by] Will Fellows and Helen P. Branson; introduction by Blanche M. Baker. University of Wisconsin Press 2010 xx, 166p il $26.95; ebook $14.95   **306.76**

1. Gay men 2. Restaurants

ISBN 978-0-299-24850-5; 978-0-299-24853-6 ebook

LC 2010011528

This is "the firsthand, contemporary account by a straight woman, Branson, who owned a gay bar in 1950s Los Angeles. . . . The book shows Branson to be a compassionate and astute observer of gay mores, now providing a rare primary source of gay life in an era from which such information is

hard to obtain. Researchers will find material on the relationships between gay men and women, what gay parties were like, and the distinct house rules that Branson set up for patronage of her bar, among other topics. . . . General readers of memoir or LGBT lit, as well as historians, will find Gay Bar to be a charming, informative read." Libr J

Includes bibliographical references

Gambone, Philip

Travels in a gay nation; portraits of LGBTQ Americans. University of Wisconsin Press 2010 294p pa $26.95; ebook $16.95   **306.76**

1. Bisexuals 2. Gay men 3. Lesbians 4. Transgendered people

ISBN 978-0-299-23684-7 pa; 978-0-299-23683-0 ebook

LC 2009041591

"The 44 profiles here are of artists, writers, activists, politicians, and intellectuals. Gambone's interviewees are diverse in many ways (age, gender, race, background), but they are all people of noted accomplishment, the best-known probably being Dorothy Allison, Tammy Baldwin, Kate Clinton, Barney Frank, and George Takei, but at least half the names should be familiar to most LGBT readers. Gambone is a smart interviewer with a laid-back, engaging style, and he knows how to bring out the most interesting qualities of his subjects." Libr J

Marcus, Eric

Is it a choice? answers to the most frequently asked questions about gay and lesbian people. 3rd ed; HarperSanFrancisco 2005 258p pa $14.95 **306.76**

1. Gay men 2. Homosexuality 3. Lesbians

ISBN 978-0-06-083280-3; 0-06-083280-0

LC 2005-52527

"Straightforward answers for both straight and lesbian/ gay readers to fundamental questions about definitions and origins of homosexuality and bisexuality, lesbian and gay life, and lesbians and gay men in American culture. Highly useful." Libr J [review of 1993 edition]

Includes bibliographical references

Mondimore, Francis Mark

A **natural** history of homosexuality. Johns Hopkins Univ. Press 1996 282p il hardcover o.p. pa $18.95   **306.76**

1. Homosexuality 2. Sex (Biology)

ISBN 0-8018-5440-7 pa

LC 96-16191

"The information in the book is basic, accurate, wideranging, up-to-date, and compassionate." Choice

Includes bibliographical references

Robb, Graham

★ **Strangers**: homosexual love in the nineteenth century. W.W. Norton 2004 341p il $26.95; pa $15.95   **306.76**

1. Homosexuality

ISBN 0-393-02038-X; 0-393-32649-7 pa

LC 2003-66239

The author "has produced a brilliant work of social archaeology. . . . In excavating the long-buried lives of our gay great-great-granduncles and lesbian great-great-grandaunts, Robb has done more than make a major historical contribution. He has, as it were, provided their distant nieces and nephews, gay and straight, with a family tree that we have never had before." N Y Times Book Rev

Encyclopedia of lesbian and gay histories and cultures. Garland 2000 2v il set $450 **306.76**
1. Homosexuality -- Encyclopedias 2. Lesbianism -- Encyclopedias 3. Reference books
ISBN 978-0-8153-3354-8; 0-8153-3354-4

"The volumes consist of short, signed entries arranged alphabetically. This set, which should become the standard in its field, will be a useful addition to all public and academic libraries." Am Libr

★ Encyclopedia of lesbian, gay, bisexual, and transgender history in America; Marc Stein, editor in chief. Thomson Learning 2003 3v set $380 **306.76**
1. Bisexuals -- United States -- History -- Encyclopedias 2. Gays -- United States -- History -- Encyclopedias 3. Homosexuality 4. Homosexuality -- United States -- History -- Encyclopedias 5. Lesbianism 6. Reference books 7. Transsexuals -- United States -- History -- Encyclopedias
ISBN 0-684-31261-1

LC 2003-17434

"Stein puts together an impressive set. . . . This information is available elsewhere, but this resource gathers it in one easy-to-use source." Voice Youth Advocates
Includes bibliographical references

Persistence; all ways butch and femme. [edited by] Ivan E. Coyote and Zena Sharman. Arsenal Pulp Press 2011 312 p. **306.76**
1. Biography, Collective 2. Lesbians -- Identity 3. Lesbians' writings, Canadian
ISBN 9781551523972 pa

LC 2010671168

In this book, honored as a Stonewall Honor Book by the American Library Association and Lambda Literary Award finalist, [c]ontributors such as Jewelle Gomez (The Gilda Stories), Thea Hillman (Intersex), S. Bear Bergman (Butch is a Noun), Chandra Mayor (All the Pretty Girls), Amber Dawn (Sub Rosa), Anna Camilleri (Brazen Femme), Debra Anderson (Code White), Anne Fleming (Anomaly), Michael V. Smith (Cumberland), and Zoe Whittall (Bottle Rocket Hearts) explore the parameters, history, and power of a multitude of butch and femme realities. . . . [The book] look[s] at what the words butch and femme can mean in today's ever-shifting gender landscape, with one eye on the past and the other on what is to come. (Publishers note)

St. James Press gay & lesbian almanac; editor, Neil Schlager; with foreword by R. Ellen Greenblatt. St. James Press 1998 680p il $147 **306.76**
1. Gay men 2. Gay men -- United States -- Biography 3. Gay men -- United States -- History 4. Homosexuality, Male -- United States -- History 5. Lesbianism -- United States -- History 6. Lesbians 7. Lesbians -- United States -- Biography 8. Lesbians -- United States --

History
ISBN 1-55862-358-2

LC 98-6156

This volume's "sections include a chronology, an annotated list of organizations, significant historical documents important to the gay and lesbian movement, and in-depth discussions of gay and lesbian involvement in such fields as politics, film, music, science, sports, travel, leisure, and visual and performing arts. Each section includes biographical profiles of prominent people in each field and extensive bibliographies of books, articles, and Web sites." Am Libr
Includes bibliographical references and index

306.8   Marriage and family

Brower, Sam
Prophet's prey; my seven-year investigation into Warren Jeffs and the Fundamentalist Church of Latter-Day Saints. [preface by Jon Krakauer] Bloomsbury USA 2011 323p il $27 **306.8**
1. Christian fundamentalism 2. Church of Jesus Christ of Latter-day Saints 3. Mormon leaders 4. Polygamy
ISBN 978-1-60819-275-5; 1-60819-275-X

"Private investigator Brower gives readers a firsthand look at the investigation that brought down prophet Warren Jeffs and the cultlike Fundamentalist Church of Jesus Christ of Latter Day Saints. . . . This compelling story of one man's crusade against a pedophile prophet will appeal to readers of current events and religious history as well as to crime fans." Libr J

Celani, David P.
Leaving home; the art of separating from your difficult family. Columbia University Press 2005 156p $24.95 **306.8**
1. Adult child abuse victims
ISBN 0-231-13476-2

LC 2004-51980

The author "explains how children in abusive or neglectful homes develop both wounded and hopeful selves and why they compulsively pick the worst possible mate or make self-destructive decisions. Full of compassion and encouragement, this book will prepare readers to leave home and to live a life free of interpersonal failures." Libr J
Includes bibliographical references

Garner, Abigail
★ **Families** like mine; children of gay parents tell it like it is. HarperCollins 2004 256p hardcover o.p. pa $13.95 **306.8**
1. Children of gay parents 2. Gay parents 3. Homosexuality 4. Parent-child relationship 5. Parenting
ISBN 0-06-052757-9; 0-06-052758-7 pa

LC 2003-56975

This book "should quickly become a mainstay resource for many family service agencies and public libraries serving LGBT patrons." Booklist
Includes bibliographical references

Howey, Noelle

Dress codes of three girlhoods--my mother's, my father's, and mine. Picador 2002 332p $24; pa $14   **306.8**
    1. Parent-child relationship 2. Transsexualism
ISBN 0-312-26921-8; 0-312-42220-2 pa
            LC 2001-59060
"Howey manages to entertain, console, and enlighten readers. The book is impossible to ignore, and impossible to put down." SLJ

Moats, David R.

Civil wars; a battle for gay marriage. [by] David Moats. Harcourt 2004 288p $25; pa $14   **306.8**
    1. Gay couples -- Legal status, laws, etc -- United States 2. Gay couples -- Legal status, laws, etc -- Vermont 3. Same-sex marriage 4. Same-sex marriage -- Law and legislation -- United States 5. Same-sex marriage -- Law and legislation -- Vermont 6. Same-sex marriage -- United States 7. Same-sex marriage -- Vermont
ISBN 0-15-101017-X; 0-15-603003-9 pa
            LC 2003-19811
"Moats offers an insightful account of the fierce battle that led to the legalization of civil unions in Vermont in 2001." Booklist

Phillips, Kathy J.

The **moon** in the water; reflections on an aging parent. Vanderbilt University Press 2008 139p il $19.95   **306.8**
    1. Aging parents 2. Caregivers 3. Parent-child relationship
ISBN 978-0-8265-1586-5; 0-8265-1586-X
            LC 2007-26255
"By turns witty, compassionate, wise, and intensely personal, Phillips's book is perfect for our 'sandwich generation,' facing the care of elderly parents and trying to continue spiritual journeys even in the face of the end." Libr J
Includes bibliographical references

Pickhardt, Carl E.

The **everything** parent's guide to children and divorce; reassuring advice to help your family adjust. Adams Media 2006 287p pa $14.95   **306.8**
    1. Children of divorced parents
ISBN 1-59337-418-6; 978-1-59337-418-1
            LC 2005-26454
The author "exlains divorce's effects on kids and cogently analyzes many topics, presenting particularly excellent support for divorcing parents." Libr J

Ray, Barbara E.

Not quite adults; why 20-somethings are choosing a slower path to adulthood, and why it's good for everyone. [by] Rick Settersten and Barbara E. Ray. 1st ed. Delacorte Press 2010 xxiii, 239 p.p (paperback) $15.00   **306.8**
    1. Adulthood 2. Youth -- United States
ISBN 0553807404; 9780440339793; 9780553807400
            LC 2010027109

This authors of this book "document the many ways that touch points of adulthood . . . are happening years later for people currently in their twenties and thirties than for their parents and grandparents" as well as "the vast disparity of resources and opportunities . . . between 'swimmers,' as the authors term college-educated youth with strong family support and wide social networks, and 'treaders,' a larger group of young people suffering chronic, generational resource deficits." (Library Journal)

Drawing on eight years of data and more than 500 interviews with young people between 18 and 34, Richard Settersten and Barbara Ray dismantle the common belief that this generation has been coddled into laziness. Rather, these young adults have come of age at a particularly merciless moment. . . . "Not Quite Adults" offers a valuable portrait of the diverging destinies of young people today. Economist
Includes bibliographical references

Scott, Laura S.

Two is enough; a couple's guide to living childless by choice. Seal Press 2009 254p pa $16.95   **306.8**
    1. Childlessness
ISBN 978-1-58005-263-4
            LC 2009-4841
The author discusses "people choosing to forgo having children. She bases her observations on an extensive survey, exploring the decision-making process that relates not only to the ramifications of this decision but also to living a childless life in a pronatal world. Scott discusses this emotionally wrought topic in a measured, neutral tone that will appeal to those making these decisions and their extended families." Libr J
Includes bibliographical references

Smith, Janna Malamud

A **potent** spell; mother love and the power of fear. Houghton Mifflin 2003 289p $25; pa $14   **306.8**
    1. Child care 2. Mother and child 3. Motherhood -- Psychological aspects 4. Mothers 5. Mothers -- Psychology
ISBN 0-618-06349-8; 0-618-44673-7 pa
            LC 2002-27632
"Smith concludes by asserting that what the child needs most is a mother who is free, who believes she is living her own life, and who has adequate food, sleep, wages, education, safety, opportunity, institutional support, health care, child care, and emotional support. To say that the best mother is a free woman is simplistic yet radical when considered in historical context." Choice
Includes bibliographical references

Vickery, Amanda

Behind closed doors; at home in Georgian England. Yale University Press 2009 382p il $45 **306.8**
    1. Households -- England -- History 2. Material culture -- Great Britain -- History 3. Sex role -- England -- History -- 18th century 4. Social control -- England -- History 5. Social status -- England
ISBN 978-0-300-15453-5; 0-300-15453-4
            LC 2009-18592
"Vickery's greatest achievement is to upend the notion that the home was divided into separate spheres in which men were responsible for brick and stone while women

ruled over domestic life. Instead, Vickery brilliantly shows that these boundaries were fluid and mutable. . . . [This work] demonstrates that rigorous academic work can also be nosy, gossipy and utterly engaging." N Y Times Book Rev

Includes bibliographical references

Warner, Judith

★ **Perfect** madness; motherhood in the age of anxiety. Riverhead Books 2005 327p $23.95; pa $15   **306.8**

1. Dual-career families 2. Motherhood 3. Mothers 4. Mothers -- United States -- Social conditions

ISBN 1-573-22304-2; 1-594-48170-9 pa

LC 2004-56615

"Writing from the perspective of her first few years of motherhood spent in France and her subsequent return to the U.S., Warner ponders the cultural factors driving the madness of pursuing perfect motherhood and the toll it is taking on American women." Booklist

Includes bibliographical references

Because I said so; 33 mothers write about children, sex, men, aging, faith, race, and themselves. from the editors of Mothers who think [Camille Peri & Kate Moses]. HarperCollins 2005 xxi, 372p $24.95; pa $13.95   **306.8**

1. Mothers

ISBN 0-06-059878-6; 0-06-059879-4 pa

LC 2004-62007

"Women will appreciate the humor and candor, and men will gain insight into the stunning challenges of motherhood." Booklist

Includes bibliographical references

Maybe baby; 28 writers tell the truth about skepticism, infertility, baby lust, childlessness, ambivalence, and how they made the biggest decisions of their lives. edited by Lori Leibovich; foreword by Anne Lamott. HarperCollins 2006 266p $24.95; pa $13.95   **306.8**

1. Childlessness 2. Parenting 3. Pregnancy

ISBN 0-06-073781-6; 978-0-06-073781-8; 0-06-073782-4 pa; 978-0-06-073782-5 pa

LC 2005-52686

"This work, an outgrowth of a Salon.com series that ran in 2003, considers one of modern life's great issues: parenthood. Divided into three sections ('No,' 'Maybe,' and 'Yes'), the 28 essays personalize the choices found in broader society today. . . . These superbly written essays are recommended for all libraries, especially gender studies and sociology collections." Libr J

306.81   Marriage and marital status

Klinenberg, Eric

Going solo; the extraordinary rise and surprising appeal of living alone. Eric Klinenberg. Penguin Press 2012 273 p.   **306.81**

1. Living alone -- United States 2. Single people -- United States 3. Single people -- United States --

Psychology

ISBN 9781594203220

LC 2011031522

This book explores why more than 50 percent of American adults are single--and why they usually prefer to live that way. . . . The author examines both ends of the age spectrum in an attempt to understand the social implication of this trend. He finds that among relatively affluent young adults in the 25-to-34 age bracket, living solo is seen as a rite of passage into adulthood--a period allowing more sexual freedom, a chance to explore relationships without commitment and a major focus on career building. A similar increase in solitary living is becoming the norm among the elderly. . . . [Eric] Klinenberg suggests that public support is needed to provide affordable, urban assisted-living facilities in which the elderly can maintain their independence for as long as possible. (Kirkus)

Roiphe, Anne Richardson

Married; a fine predicament. {by} Anne Roiphe. Basic Bks. 2002 285p $25; pa $14.95   **306.81**

1. Marriage

ISBN 0-465-07066-3; 0-465-07067-1 pa

LC 2002-3506

The author writes "about how marriage and women's lives have changed since the 1950s, and about constants in human nature and the beleaguered but not yet improved upon institution of marriage. . . . Roiphe's rumination is a bit indulgent and soft with hearsay, yet it is timely, clever, candid, generous, and free of sentiment or trivialization." Booklist

Waite, Linda J.

The **case** for marriage; [by] Linda J. Waite and Maggie Gallagher. Doubleday 2000 260p hardcover o.p. pa $14.95   **306.81**

1. Man-woman relationships -- United States 2. Marriage 3. Marrie couples -- United States -- Psychology 4. Married people 5. Single people 6. Single people -- United States -- Psychology

ISBN 0-7679-0632-2 pa

LC 00-22672

The authors defend marriage and enumerate what they consider the benefits of the institution.

"Waite and Gallagher overstate contemporary attacks on marriage, but they make a valid point that the revered institution has suffered stings lately." Booklist

Includes bibliographical references

306.85   Family

Gore, Al

Joined at the heart; the transformation of the American family. [by] Al and Tipper Gore. Holt & Co. 2002 417p il $26; pa $16   **306.85**

1. Family 2. Family -- United States

ISBN 0-8050-6893-7; 0-8050-7450-3 pa

LC 2002-27252

The authors "examine subjects as diverse as the increased divorce rate, the parent-teen gap, dual-income households and the health problems associated with sleep deprivation. They divide the book into themes, including love, communication, work, play and community, and show how these factors influence one another, taking a holistic approach to the underlying problems affecting today's families." Publ Wkly

Includes bibliographical references

Hite, Shere

The **Hite** report on the family; growing up under patriarchy. Grove Press 1995 xxiv, 424p hardcover o.p. pa $14   **306.85**
1. Family 2. Parent and child 3. Parent-child relationship 4. Sexual behavior
ISBN 0-8021-3451-3 pa

          LC 94-42157

This study "based on some 3000 questionnaires completed by children and adults in 16 countries (50% from the U.S.), focuses on the child's developing psychosexual identity and the impact of this process on adulthood. . . . Her respondents' testimonies, organized around specific themes, touch on all manner of taboo subjects." Publ Wkly

Includes bibliographical references

Hochschild, Arlie Russell

The **outsourced** self; intimate life in market times. Arlie Russell Hochschild. Metropolitan Books 2012 300 p. ill.   **306.85**
1. Capitalism 2. Contracting out 3. Families -- Economic aspects -- United States -- History 4. Free enterprise 5. International trade 6. Interpersonal relations and culture -- United States -- History 7. Social criticism 8. Turner (Me.)
ISBN 080508889X; 9780805088892

          LC 2011044135

In this book, sociologist [Arlie Russell] Hochschild . . . compares Turner, Maine—the self-sufficient farming village where she spent summers as a child—with the global marketplace, where . . . outsourc[ing is common]. . . . [Some of] Hochschild's . . . chapters center on surrogate motherhood: at India's Akanksha Clinic, . . . surrogates are instructed to think of their wombs as . . .something exterior to themselves, and are forbidden to breast feed the babies they're paid to carry for strangers. Hochschild makes the . . . observation that many pressing for a greater expansion of the free market, gutting of regulations, and cuts in social services are the same people who call for stronger family values, perhaps unaware of the way the market distorts them. (Publishers Weekly)

Westheimer, Ruth

The **value** of family; a blueprint for the 21st century. [by] Ruth Wertheimer and Ben Yagoda. Warner Bks. 1996 211p hardcover o.p. pa $12.99 **306.85**
1. Family 2. Family -- United States 3. Social values
ISBN 0-446-67336-6 pa

          LC 96-15154

"A humane, levelheaded, eye-opening look at changing family dynamics." Publ Wkly

Includes bibliographical references

Winik, Marion

The **lunch**-box chronicles; notes from the parenting underground. Pantheon Bks. 1998 229p hardcover o.p. pa $15   **306.85**
1. Parenting 2. Single parent family 3. Single parents 4. Single-parent families
ISBN 0-375-70170-2 pa

          LC 97-26753

"Winik brings together in winning fashion her decidedly nonmainstream attitude, laugh-out-loud humor, and refreshing candor." Booklist

306.87   Intrafamily relationships

Tannen, Deborah

I only say this because I love you; how the way we talk can make or break family relationships throughout our lives. Random House 2001 xxvii, 336p hardcover o.p. pa $15.95   **306.87**
1. Communication 2. Communication in the family 3. Family
ISBN 0-345-40752-0 pa

          LC 00-68851

"With lively prose and genuine concern for people, Tannen brings linguistic concepts—metamessage, re-framing, indirect request—to bear on dozens of situations to help lay readers strengthen family ties." Libr J

Includes bibliographical references

306.872   Spousal relationship

Yalom, Marilyn

A **history** of the wife. HarperCollins Pubs. 2001 441p il hardcover o.p. pa $14.95   **306.872**
1. Housewives -- History 2. Marriage 3. Marriage -- History 4. Married women -- History 5. Women -- History
ISBN 0-06-093156-6 pa

          LC 00-58153

Yalom "has apparently written the first truly comprehensive history of the Western female spousal experience; indeed, there are precious few long views of either marriage or the family to which this book can be compared." Libr J

306.874   Parent-child relationship

Crews, Kambri

Burn down the ground; a memoir. Kambri Crews. Villard 2012 xiv, 334 p.p   **306.874**
1. Abusive men 2. Children of deaf parents -- Biography 3. Dysfunctional families 4. Memoirs
ISBN 0345516028; 9780345516022

          LC 2011040828

The author provides an account of her dysfunctional childhood and the father who both charmed and victimized her family. As the hearing child of two deaf adults, Crews grew up between worlds. . . . But not long after they moved from their tin-shed shelter into a mobile home, Crews began to see evidence of domestic abuse that took the form of mysterious bruises on her mother's face and inexplicably cruel behavior in her brother. Her home life continued to show signs of ugly undercurrents, yet only silence prevailed, and the author threw herself into school and a full-time job. . . . At age 31, she received the shattering news that her father had stabbed his girlfriend. (Kirkus)

Cusk, Rachel
A **life's** work; on becoming a mother. Picador 2002 213p $22; pa $13   **306.874**
1. Motherhood 2. Mothers 3. Parenting
ISBN 0-312-26987-0; 0-312-31130-3 pa
            LC 2001-54894
"This is not a happy guide; instead, it is a penetrating, sometimes joyful and amusing, sometimes frightening and disturbing look at pregnancy and motherhood." Booklist

Gross, Gretchen
But dad! a survival guide for single fathers of tween and teen daughters. Gretchen Gross and Patricia Livingston. Rowman & Littlefield Publishers 2012 192 p.   **306.874**
1. Fathers and daughters 2. Parenting 3. Single fathers 4. Teenage girls
ISBN 9781442212671; 9781442212688
            LC 2011044670
This book offers a guide to being a single father to a tween or teenage daughter. . . . Whether rendered a one-man show by divorce, death, or deployment, single fathers face a slew of unique challenges when parenting adolescent girls. They must navigate issues like menstruation, female social development (including the great, dreaded D-word: Dating), the establishment of positive male role models, and more subtle issues, like negotiating new forms of father-daughter physical contact. In addition to these dad-and-daughter topics, the book also contains . . . information on general parenting areas, such as fiscal responsibility and setting boundaries. (Publishers Weekly)

Holroyd, Michael
A **book** of secrets; Michael Holroyd. Farrar, Straus and Giroux 2011 xiv, 258p.p ill.   **306.874**
1. Biography, Collective 2. Fairfax, Eve 3. Gifted women 4. Illegitimate children 5. Keppel, Alice 6. Trefusis, Violet 7. Women -- Biography
ISBN 0-374-11558-3; 978-0-374-11558-6 0-374-11558-3
            LC 2011003839
In this book, a "Publisher's Weekly" Best Nonfiction title for 2011, author "[Michael] Holroyd brings a company of unknown women into the light. From Alice Keppel, the mistress of both the second Lord Grimthorpe and the Prince of Wales; to Eve Fairfax, a muse of Auguste Rodin; to the novelist Violet Trefusis, the lover of Vita Sackville-West--these women are always on the periphery of the respectable world. Also on the margins is the . . . biographer, who on occasion turns an . . . eye upon himself as part of his investigations in the maze of biography." (Publisher's note)

Pipher, Mary Bray
Another country; navigating the emotional terrain of our elders. [by] Mary Pipher. Riverhead Bks. 1999 xx, 328p hardcover o.p. pa $13.95   **306.874**
1. Adult children of aging parents -- United States -- Family relationships 2. Aging parents 3. Aging parents -- Care -- United States 4. Aging parents -- United States -- Family relationships 5. Aging parents -- United States -- Psychology 6. Loss (Psychology) in old age -- United States 7. Parent-child relationship
ISBN 1-57322-784-6 pa
            LC 98-31877
The author is interested in studying "the aging process in order to promote meaningful connections between the generations and more cultural support for pursuing them. . . . Pipher describes strategies for dealing with illness, physical decline, the death of a husband or wife and the emotional problems that arise for both the elderly and their families. . . . One of the strengths of this excellent study is that Pipher includes examples of troubled as well as rewarding marital and parent/child relationships." Publ Wkly

Taffel, Ron
The **second** family; how adolescent power is challenging the American family. [by] Ron Taffel with Melinda Blau. St. Martin's Press 2001 204p $23.95; pa $12.95   **306.874**
1. Parent and teenager 2. Parenting 3. Popular culture 4. Teenagers 5. Teenagers -- Social networks
ISBN 0-312-26137-3; 0-312-28493-4 pa
            LC 00-45993
This book is "required reading for anyone interacting with adolescents today." Voice Youth Advocates

306.89   Separation and divorce

Green, Janice
Divorce after 50; your guide to the unique legal & financial challenges. Nolo 2010 370p pa $29.99   **306.89**
1. Divorce -- Law and legislation
ISBN 978-1-4133-1081-8; 1-4133-1081-8
            LC 2009-21435
The author "explores the special legal, monetary, and emotional burdens of a marital split that occurs after age 50. She covers how to select and work with an attorney, the choice of legal mechanisms for terminating a marriage, and how to work out a fair division of marital property. . . . This book fills a gap on the self-help divorce shelf. Essential for public libraries." Libr J

Moffett, Kay
Not your mother's divorce; a practical, girlfriend-to-girlfriend guide to surviving the end of an early marriage. [by] Kay Moffett and Sarah Touborg. Broadway Bks. 2003 259p pa $12.95   **306.89**
1. Divorce 2. Divorce -- Psychological aspects 3. Young women -- Conduct of life 4. Young women --

Life skills guides 5. Young women -- Psychology
ISBN 0-7679-1350-7

LC 2003-58531

The authors "help young divorcées tackle both legal and emotional problems. . . . Overwhelming issues like mutual photographs, wedding rings, and family, as well as legal counsel, mediators, and even Internet divorce, are discussed with authority and sensitivity. The authors realize that each person is different and comes out of her relationship with a different set of circumstances, so they also provide many personal stories—including their own." Libr J

Wallerstein, Judith S.

Second chances; men, women, and children a decade after divorce. [by] Judith S. Wallerstein and Sandra Blakeslee. Houghton Mifflin 2004 329p il pa $14   **306.89**
1. Children of divorced parents 2. Divorce
ISBN 0-618-44689-3; 978-0-618-44689-6

LC 2004-273131

In 1971 the author "began a study of 131 children and adolescents from 60 families and their divorcing parents, in Marin County, California. . . . The researchers reinterviewed all family members 18 months later, again 5 years after divorce, and again 10 years after divorce. . . . 'Second Chances' is Ms. Wallerstein's account of the course and consequences of divorce for these parents and children." N Y Times Book Rev

Includes bibliographical references

306.9   Institutions pertaining to death

Schechter, Harold

The **whole** death catalog; a lively guide to the bitter end. Ballantine Books 2009 304p il pa $18   **306.9**
1. Death
ISBN 978-0-345-49964-6

LC 2009-13779

The author "offers readers a scholarly yet wildly hilarious romp through the cultural history of death and dying. It is not only rollicking entertainment but also provides a wealth of practical and historical information about death." Libr J

Includes bibliographical references

Encyclopedia of death and dying; edited by Glennys Howarth and Oliver Leaman. Routledge 2001 xxii, 534p il $140   **306.9**
1. Death 2. Death -- Encyclopedias 3. Reference books 4. Thanatology
ISBN 0-415-18825-3

LC 2001-19234

"This work will enrich all academic and public library collections." Libr J

Includes bibliographical references and index

Handbook of death & dying; Clifton D. Bryant, editor in chief. Sage Publications 2003 2v il set $350   **306.9**
1. Death
ISBN 0-7619-2514-7

LC 2003-14864

This is "a collection of 103 comprehensive essays clustered in 10 general areas. . . . In the first volume the section 'Death in the Cultural Context' treats issues in confronting death, with essays on fear of death, death in popular culture, spiritualism, and more. The 12 essays that make up 'Death in the Social Context' consider topics such as trends in mortality, accidental death, and terrorism. Suicide, capital punishment, euthanasia, and the hospice movement are among other topics in the first volume. The second volume deals with the response to death. . . . The substantive essays are generally between 9 to 15 pages, with extensive bibliographies." Booklist

307   Communities

Wilkerson, Isabel

★ The **warmth** of other suns; the epic story of America's great migration. Random House 2010 622p $30; ebook $30   **307**
1. African Americans -- History 2. African Americans -- Migrations -- History -- 20th century 3. Internal migration 4. Migration, Internal -- United States -- History -- 20th century 5. Rural-urban migration -- United States -- History -- 20th century
ISBN 978-0-679-44432-9; 0-679-44432-7; 978-0-679-60407-5 ebook; 0-679-60407-3 ebook

LC 2009-49753

An "account of the Great Migration, the 55-year stretch (1915–70) during which 6 million black Americans fled the Jim Crow South. Wilkerson, a Pulitzer Prize-winning journalist, uses the journeys of three of them — a Mississippi sharecropper, a Louisiana doctor, and a Florida laborer — to etch an indelible and compulsively readable portrait of race, class, and politics in 20th-century America. History is rarely distilled so finely." Entertainment Wkly

Includes bibliographical references

Encyclopedia of the great Black migration; edited by Steven A. Reich. Greenwood Press 2006 3v il set $325   **307**
1. African Americans -- History -- Encyclopedias 2. African Americans -- Migrations 3. Internal migration -- Encyclopedias 4. Migration, Internal 5. Reference books 6. Rural-urban migration
ISBN 0-313-32982-6; 978-0-313-32982-1

LC 2005-33783

"This encyclopedia deals with its topic in social, economic, cultural, and political contexts, covering the migrations since the time of the Exodusters of 1879 moving into Kansas and the Middle West to the return migrations sparked by deindustrialization at the end of the twentieth century." Booklist

Includes bibliographical references

307.24   Movement from rural to urban communities

Saunders, Doug

Arrival city; Doug Saunders. Pantheon Books 2010 356p. ill.   **307.24**

ISBN 9780375425493

LC 2010029651

In this book, the author examines global urbanization. He concentrates on the slums and satellite communities that act as portals from villages to cities and, in turn, revitalize village economies. . . . Citing the statistical relationship between urbanization and falling poverty rates, as well as historical precedents like Paris, . . . Saunders insists urban migration means improvement overall, and that the arrival city serves as a springboard for the integration of new populations. While the picture of urbanization veers from gloomier forecasts by analysts like Mike Davis (Planet of Slums), it does so by eschewing direct questioning of the global economic system driving much of this migration." (Publishers Weekly)

307.7   Specific kinds of communities

Carr, Patrick J.

Hollowing out the middle; the rural brain drain and what it means for America. [by] Patrick J. Carr and Maria J. Kefalas. Beacon Press 2009 239p map $26.95; pa $16   **307.7**

1. Brain drain -- United States -- History -- 20th century 2. Cities and towns -- Middle Western States 3. Cities and towns -- United States 4. Youth -- United States 5. Youth -- United States -- Social conditions

ISBN 978-0-8070-4238-0; 978-0-8070-0614-6 pa

LC 2009-10392

"Whatever the future may hold, the authors alert readers to this major change with clarity and compassion." Publ Wkly

Includes bibliographical references

Grandin, Greg

Fordlandia; the rise and fall of Henry Ford's forgotten jungle city. Metropolitan Books 2009 416p il map   **307.7**

1. Automobile executives 2. Philanthropists 3. Planned communities -- Brazil 4. Plantations

ISBN 0-8050-8236-0; 978-0-8050-8236-4

LC 2008049642

This is an account of Henry Ford's attempt to recreate small-town America in the . . . Amazon. In 1927, Ford . . . bought a tract of land twice the size of Delaware in the Brazilian Amazon. . . . Ford's early success in imposing time clocks and square dances on the jungle soon collapsed, as indigenous workers . . . turned the place into a . . . tropical boomtown. (Publisher's note) Index.

Grandin's account is an epic tale of a clash between cultures, values, man, and nature. Booklist

Includes bibliographical references

Green, Hardy

The **company** town; the industrial Edens and Satanic mills that shaped the American economy. Basic Books 2010 248p il $26.95   **307.7**

1. Cities and towns 2. Company towns -- United States -- History 3. Industrial relations 4. Industrial relations -- United States -- History 5. Industries -- United States 6. Industries -- United States -- History

ISBN 978-0-465-01826-0

LC 2010-13434

"The book provides a valuable perspective on a well-worn history, detailing the heinous, lofty, and occasionally absurd ways companies have tried to shape their workers' lives beyond factory walls." Publ Wkly

Includes bibliographical references

Mumford, Lewis

The **city** in history; its origins, its transformation, and its prospects. Harcourt Brace & World 1961 657p il hardcover o.p. pa $29   **307.7**

1. Cities and towns -- History 2. City and town life 3. Civilization -- History

ISBN 0-15-618035-9 pa

More than a history of the forms and functions of the city throughout the ages, this is a portrait of the development of man as a religious, a political, an economic, a cultural, and a sexual being.

The **culture** of cities. Greenwood Press 1981 586p il lib bdg $57.95   **307.7**

1. Cities and towns 2. City planning 3. Regional planning

ISBN 0-313-22746-2

LC 80-23130

Traces the growth of cities from medieval times to the twentieth century.

Wilson, David Sloan

The **neighborhood** project; using evolution to improve my city, one block at a time. Little, Brown and Company 2011 432p $25.99; ebook $12.99   **307.7**

1. Cities and towns -- Civic improvement 2. Cities and towns -- Growth

ISBN 978-0-316-03767-9; 978-0-316-17525-8 ebook

LC 2011002752

"Although the book meanders—Wilson gives a vivid, in-depth description of several scientific studies, and offers a biography for each scientist he cites—the tangents are mostly pleasurable and provide more evidence for how lives, like ideas, intersect in fascinating ways." Publ Wkly

Includes bibliographical references

307.76   Urban communities

Duany, Andres

Suburban nation; the rise of sprawl and the decline of the American Dream. {by} Andres Duany,

Elizabeth Plater-Zyberk, and Jeff Speck. North Point Press 2000 289p il $35; pa $18 **307.76**
1. Cities and towns 2. City planning 3. Community development, Urban -- United States 4. Suburbs -- United States 5. Urban policy -- United States 6. Urban renewal 7. Urban renewal -- United States 8. Urbanization 9. Urbanization -- United States
ISBN 0-86547-557-1; 0-86547-606-3 pa

LC 99-52186

The authors, town planners associated with the New Urbanism movement, argue that American suburbs have failed on ecological, economic, aesthetic, and social levels. Drawing on their experiences with a variety of community development projects, they advocate a return to more traditional planning principles.

Smith, P. D.
★ City; a guidebook for the urban age. P.D. Smith. Bloomsbury 2012 383 p. **307.76**
1. Cities and towns -- History 2. City life -- History 3. Sociology, Urban -- History
ISBN 1608196763; 9781608196760

LC 2011051430

This book is an illustrated guide to 7,000 years of urban life for an age when more than half of the world's population lives in cities. From the earliest Sumerian city of Eridu to the wired eco-cities of the future, [P.D.] Smith embarks on a multicentury tour highlighting urban history, customs, infrastructure, architecture, language, markets, crime, parks, cemeteries, transportation, food, and leisure activities across cultures. He . . . provid[es] panoramic yet focused views of a particular subject, such as . . . the development of language from cuneiform script to 16th-century street speech and its effect on cockney, to the new London dialect of the 21st century, Jafaican. (Publishers Weekly)

310 Collections of general statistics

United Nations/Statistical Office
★ Statistical yearbook 2006; 51st ed; U.N. Publs. 2008 836p $150 **310**
1. Reference books 2. Statistics
ISBN 978-9-2106-1228-9; 9-2106-1228-0

An annual giving statistics under the following headings: Population; Manpower; Production summary; Agriculture; Forestry; Fishing; Mining, quarrying; Manufacturing; Construction; Electricity, gas consumption; Transport; Communications; Internal trade; External trade; Balance of payments; International economic aid; Wages and prices; National income; Public finance; Housing statistics; Education, culture.

★ The Europa world year book 2008; 49th ed; Europa 2008 2v $1,295 **310**
1. Political science 2. Reference books 3. Statistics
ISBN 978-1-85743-451-4; 1-85743-451-X

"The best annual directory of the nations of the world. For each country it includes demographic and economic statistics, and facts about constitution and government, political parties, press, trade and industry, publishers, etc. Also incorporates a substantive section with listings and infor-

mation about international organizations." Ref Sources for Small & Medium-sized Libr. 6th edition

★ The statesman's yearbook 2011; the politics, cultures and economies of the world. edited by Barry Turner. 147th ed; Palgrave Macmillan 2010 xxxi, 1573p il map $285 **310**
1. Political science 2. Reference books 3. Statistics
ISBN 978-0-230-20603-8

"Descriptive and statistical information about international organizations and countries of the world--brief history, area, political status, economy, etc." N Y Public Libr. Ref Books for Child Collect. 2d edition

Includes bibliographical references

317 General statistics of North America

United States/Bureau of the Census
County and city data book, 2007; a statistical abstract supplement. [by the] Economics and Statistics Administration, U.S. Census Bureau. Claitor's Publishing Division 2007 various paging map $75; pa $58 **317**
1. Cities and towns -- United States 2. Reference books
ISBN 978-1-59804-424-9; 1-59804-424-9; 978-1-59804-423-2 pa; 1-59804-423-0 pa

"Presents the latest available census figures for each county, and for the larger cities in the United States. Also has summary figures for states, geographical regions, urbanized areas, standard metropolitan areas, and unincorporated places." Guide to Ref Books. 11th edition

★ Statistical abstract of the United States, 2011; [by the] U.S. Dept. of Commerce, Economics and Statistics Administration, U.S. Census Bureau. 130th ed; U.S. Census Bureau 2010 1010p il map $43; pa $39 **317**
1. Reference books
ISBN 978-0-16-086682-1; 978-0-16-086681-4 pa

"Compendium of statistics on the social, political and economic organization of the U.S. presented in tables. Lists other sources of such information." N Y Public Libr. Ref Books for Child Collect. 2d edition

★ Canadian almanac & directory 2011; 164th ed; Grey House Publishing Canada 2010 various paging il map $350 **317**
1. Almanacs 2. Reference books
ISBN 978-1-59237-589-9

"Contains reliable legal, commercial, governmental, statistical, astronomical, departmental, ecclesiastical, financial, educational, and general information." Guide to Ref Books. 11th edition

★ Historical statistics of the United States; earliest times to the present. [by] Susan B. Carter . . . [et

al.]. Millennial ed; Cambridge University Press
2006 5v il set $990   **317**
1. Reference books
ISBN 0-521-81791-9; 978-0-521-81791-2
LC 2005-27089
"Each of the 39 chapters begins with an essay on the
'quantitative history' of the topic and comments on the reliability of the data and possible limits to interpretation. Included are approximately 1900 tables and 170 maps, graphs,
and time lines; the text is fully cross-referenced and indexed.
. . . A bargain for all libraries supporting research." Libr J
Includes bibliographical references

320 Political science (Politics and government)

Aristotle
★ **Politics**. Oxford University Press 1998 480p
pa $12.95   **320**
1. Political science
ISBN 978-0-19-283393-8
"Discussion of public affairs by the most eminent of the
Greek philosophers in terms applicable to many of the prob-
lems of modern political science." Pratt Alcove

Brookhiser, Richard
What would the Founders do? our questions,
their answers. Basic Books 2006 261p $26   **320**
1. Politicians -- United States 2. Presidents -- United
States 3. Statesmen -- United States 4. United States
-- Politics and government -- 2001-
ISBN 0-465-00819-4; 978-0-465-00819-3
The author "uses the Founders' written and oral statements to imagine their thoughts concerning contemporary
issues ranging from stem cells and terrorism to censorship
and gay marriage. The short answers he gives for each question can be serious or witty and are often infused with interesting historical facts." Libr J
Includes bibliographical references

Carroll Publishing Company
★ **Government** phone book USA; a comprehensive guide to federal, state, county, and local government offices in the United States. editorial data
provided by Carroll Publishing Co. 16th ed; Omnigraphics 2008 2538p map lib bdg $317   **320**
1. Reference books 2. State governments -- Directories
ISBN 978-0-7808-0696-2; 0-7808-0696-4
"Despite ever-increasing access to directory information
on the Internet, comprehensive direct contact information
for government offices at all levels is still often time-consuming to collate, making this set a useful addition to reference collections." Am Ref Books Annu, 2006

Fukuyama, Francis
The **origins** of political order; from prehuman
times to the French Revolution. Farrar, Straus and
Giroux 2011 585p $35   **320**
1. Comparative government 2. Democracy 3.
Democracy -- History 4. State, The 5. State, The --

History
ISBN 978-0-374-22734-0; 0-374-22734-9
LC 2010-38534

Kaplan, Robert D.
Warrior politics; why leadership demands a pa-
gan ethos. Random House 2002 xxii, 198p $22.95;
pa $12   **320**
1. International relations 2. International relations
-- Political aspects 3. International relations --
Psychological aspects 4. Leadership 5. Political ethics
ISBN 0-375-50563-6; 0-375-72627-6 pa
LC 2001-31862
"This is a provocative, smart and polemical work that
will stimulate lively discussion." Publ Wkly
Includes bibliographical references

Nathan, John
Japan unbound; a volatile nation's quest for
pride and purpose. Houghton Mifflin 2004 271p
$25   **320**
ISBN 0-618-13894-3
LC 2003-60559
The author "explores the dynamics of cultural continuity and change in Japan driven in part by economic stagnation. . . . The author also confronts the reader with the
links between a loss of personal pride and purpose as a result
of economic uncertainty, and the search for a new basis of
pride and purpose in the form of heightened nationalism. .
. . This book is a must for general and specialized library
collections." Choice
Includes bibliographical references

Paine, Thomas
★ **Rights** of man; and, Common sense. Knopf
1994 lii, 306p $19   **320**
1. Political science
ISBN 0-679-43314-7
LC 94-5989
This volume combines Rights of man with Common
sense which was "published anonymously at Philadelphia
(Jan. 10, 1776). . . . Over 100,000 copies were sold by the
end of March, and it is generally considered the most impor-
tant literary influence on the movement for independence."
Oxford Companion to Am Lit. 5th edition
Includes bibliographical references

Purdy, Jedediah
A **tolerable** anarchy; rebels, reactionaries, and
the making of American freedom. Alfred A. Knopf
2009 294p $23.95   **320**
1. American national characteristics 2. Freedom 3.
Liberty -- Philosophy 4. National characteristics,
American
ISBN 978-1-4000-4447-4; 1-4000-4447-2
LC 2008-49552
"Purdy's thesis is a work in progress by an inventive
mind in evolution, a didactic and synoptic tour of American
thoughts on freedom." N Y Times Book Rev
Includes bibliographical references

Smith, Hedrick
The **power** game; how Washington works. Random House 1988 xxii, 793p pa $16.95   **320**
1. Power (Social sciences)
ISBN 0-345-41048-3 pa

LC 87-42669
Smith "has an insider's awareness of the alliances, machinations and turf-battles that make the capital work; he knows what he is talking about." Economist
Includes bibliographical references

★ Washington information directory, 2009-2010. CQ Press 2009 994p il $140   **320**
1. Reference books
ISBN 978-1-60426-531-6
"This substantial and user-friendly guide . . . [is] a vital resource for navigating Washington's intricate bureaucratic web." Libr J

320.092   Biography

Judt, Tony
Thinking the twentieth century; Tony Judt, with Timothy Snyder. Penguin 2012 414 p.   **320.092**
1. Arab-Israeli conflict -- Peace 2. College teachers 3. Criticism 4. Economics 5. Hayek, Friedrich A. von (Friedrich August), 1899-1992 6. Historians 7. History -- Philosophy 8. Jews -- Crimes against 9. Jews -- Intellectual life 10. Nonfiction writers 11. Political philosophy 12. Political science 13. United States -- Politics & government -- 1989-
ISBN 9781594203237

LC 2011031473
The book is a history of twentieth-century thought. It begins with . . . [author Tony Judt's] reflections on Jewish idealism and Jewish suffering in Europe and ends with a devastating account of the failure of American politics in the post-cold war world. It is also an intellectual autobiography. . . . [Topics include] the argument . . . for a one-state solution in Israel . . . [and] the interwar Austrian historical setting of Friedrich Hayek's ideas about economics and state planning. . . . [In the book, written while Judt was suffering from Lou Gehrig's Disease,] the idea of justice swung . . . to the fore. (N Y Review of Books)

320.1   The state

Cicero, Marcus Tullius
The **republic;** and, The laws; [by] Cicero; translated by Niall Rudd; with an introduction and notes by Jonathan Powell and Niall Rudd. Oxford University Press 1998 xliii, 242p pa $12.95   **320.1**
1. Political science 2. State, The
ISBN 978-0-19-283236-8; 0-19-283236-0

LC 97-23394
"Cicero's The Republic is an impassioned plea for responsible government written just before the civil war that ended the Roman Republic in a dialogue following Plato. Drawing on Greek political theory, the work embodies the mature reflections of a Roman ex-consul on the nature of political organization, on justice in society, and on the qualities needed in a statesman. Its sequel, The Laws, expounds the influential doctrine of Natural Law, which applies to all mankind, and sets out an ideal code for a reformed Roman Republic, already half in the realm of utopia." Publisher's note
Includes bibliographical references

Hobbes, Thomas
★ **Leviathan;** edited with an introduction and notes by J.C.A. Gaskin. Oxford University Press 2008 lv, 508p pa $9.95   **320.1**
1. Political science 2. State, The
ISBN 978-0-19-953728-0
"A treatise on the origin and ends of government. . . . This work, a defense of secular monarchy, written while the Puritan Commonwealth ruled England, contains Hobbes's famous theory of the sovereign state." Benet's Reader's Ency. 4th edition

Machiavelli, Niccolo
★ The **prince**. Knopf 1992 xxxi, 190p $16   **320.1**
1. Political ethics 2. Political science
ISBN 0-679-41044-9

LC 91-53225
"A handbook of advice on the acquisition, use, and maintenance of political power, dedicated to Lorenzo de Medici." Haydn. Thesaurus of Book Dig

Rousseau, Jean-Jacques
★ The **social** contract; translated by Maurice Cranston. Penguin Books 2006 167p pa $10 **320.1**
1. Political science
ISBN 978-0-14-303749-1; 0-14-303749-8

LC 2006-43772
"A treatise on the origins and organization of government and the rights of citizens. Rousseau's thesis states that, since no man has any natural authority over another, the social contract, freely entered into, creates natural reciprocal obligations between citizens." Benet's Reader's Ency. 4th edition
Includes bibliographical references

Runciman, David
Political hypocrisy; the mask of power, from Hobbes to Orwell and beyond. Princeton University Press 2008 272p il $29.95   **320.1**
1. Authors 2. Essayists 3. Hypocrisy 4. Political and social philosophers 5. Political ethics 6. Political science -- Philosophy 7. Politics 8. Power (Social sciences)
ISBN 978-0-691-12931-0; 0-691-12931-2

LC 2007-46793
"A very intelligent, subtle, and learned guide to the classics and to the preeminent historical examples of hypocrisy from Mandeville and Hobbes, to Jefferson and the Victorians." Times Lit Suppl
Includes bibliographical references (p. 245-258)

320.4   Structure and functions of government

Han, Lori Cox

Handbook to American democracy; Lori Cox Han and Tomislav Han. Facts On File 2011 224 p.   **320.4**
ISBN 0816078548; 9780816078547
LC 2011005185

The authors address the foundations of American democracy and the three branches of American government. The books introduce offices, history, and issues in eight chapters each (e.g., The Founding Fathers and the American Revolution, How Congress Is Organized, and Vice Presidents, Presidential Advisers, and America's First Ladies). The material is complemented by black-and-white photos and sidebars on legal cases, laws and legislation, statistics, maps, biographies of major figures such as Henry VIII, and other primary materials, and chapters close with a summary. . . . [The volumes] each include an individual glossary, index, selected bibliography, and table of contents. (Libr J)

Starks, Glenn L.

How your government really works; a topical encyclopedia of the federal government. [by] Glenn L. Starks and F. Erik Brooks. Greenwood Press 2008 334p il $75   **320.4**
1. Federal government -- United States 2. Reference books
ISBN 978-0-313-34761-0
LC 2008-24134

The authors' aim is to "bridge the gap between the government's ideal, balanced structure, laid out in the Constitution, and its actual institutionalized form today. . . . Coverage of the government's inner workings includes such subjects as executive-branch appointments, domestic and foreign policy development and execution, the federal budget, the legislative process, the Congressional committee system, the drawing of Congressional districts, the levels of the federal judiciary, aides in all three branches, and the various government offices and oversight agencies." Publisher's note
Includes bibliographical references

320.5   Political ideologies

Allitt, Patrick

★ The **conservatives**; ideas and personalities throughout American history. Yale University Press 2009 325p $35   **320.5**
1. Conservatism 2. Conservatism -- United States -- History 3. Government 4. Politics
ISBN 978-0-300-11894-0; 0-300-11894-5
LC 2008-42559

"From present-day questions of taxation and big government, Allitt traces conservative principles to the earliest days of the republic. . . . Cutting across the stereotypes of present-day conservatism, this nuanced, thoughtful history should educate the unaffiliated and help the disillusioned recover." Publ Wkly
Includes bibliographical references

Atkins, Stephen E.

★ **Encyclopedia** of modern worldwide extremists and extremist groups. Greenwood Press 2004 xxviii, 404p il $75   **320.5**
1. Cults 2. Radicalism 3. Radicals 4. Religious fanaticism 5. Religious fundamentalism 6. Right and left (Political science)
ISBN 0-313-32485-9
LC 2003-64256

"Focusing on post-1945, with 85 percent of the information coming from the period since 1980, the 285 entries encompass people and organizations on every continent, many not widely known. . . . The arrangement is alphabetical, with see and see also references leading the reader futher. The information is accurate, clearly written, and relatively current. . . . It is also objective and balanced." Booklist
Includes bibliographical references

Brown, Archie

★ The **rise** and fall of communism. Ecco 2009 720p il map $35.99   **320.5**
1. Communism 2. Communism -- History
ISBN 0-06-113879-7; 978-0-06-113879-9

Brown has crafted a readable and judicious account of Communist history, from its theoretical beginnings in 19th-century Europe to its practical collapse at the end of the 1980s, that is both controversial and commonsensical. . . . Given the immense sweep of time, ideology and geography he strives to cover in 600-odd pages--as Brown observes, almost every one of his chapters could be a book on its own--The Rise and Fall of Communism is a work of considerable delicacy and nuance. Salon
Includes bibliographical references

Ezekiel, Raphael S.

The **racist** mind; portraits of American Neo-Nazis and Klansmen. Viking 1995 xxxv, 330p hardcover o.p. pa $20   **320.5**
1. Racism 2. White supremacy movements
ISBN 0-14-023449-7 pa
LC 94-45177

"White supremacy groups are examined in this brutally honest portrait of hate and fear, based on personal interviews and interactions. A disturbingly provocative look at the frightening ignorance existing in the 1990s." Booklist
Includes bibliographical references

Halstead, Ted

The **radical** center; the future of American politics. [by] Ted Halstead and Michael Lind. Doubleday 2001 264p $24.95; pa $13   **320.5**
ISBN 0-385-50045-9; 0-385-72029-7 pa
LC 2001-28285

"Sure to have its detractors across the political spectrum, this book adds many fresh insights to our currently stale political discourse." Libr J
Includes bibliographical references

Micklethwait, John

The **right** nation; conservative power in America. [by] John Micklethwait and Adrian Wooldridge.

Penguin Press 2004 450p il maps $25.95; pa $16 **320.5**

1. Conservatism 2. Conservatism -- United States -- History -- 20th century 3. Right and left (Political science) 4. Right and left (Political science) -- History -- 20th century

ISBN 1-594-20020-3; 0-14-303539-8 pa

LC 2003-70749

The authors' "analysis shows that American conservatives differ from their European counterparts. While both are nationalistic and suspicious of state power, preferring liberty over equality, American conservatives are more liberal in regard to hierarchy, pessimism, and elitism. . . . Political junkies on both sides of the political spectrum will enjoy and gain from the analysis." Libr J

Includes bibliographical references

Pipes, Daniel

★ **Militant** Islam reaches America. Norton 2002 309p hardcover o.p. pa $15.95 **320.5**

1. Islam and politics 2. Islam and politics -- United States 3. Islamic fundamentalism 4. Islamic fundamentalism -- United States 5. Muslims -- United States 6. Muslims -- United States -- Political activity

ISBN 0-393-05204-4; 0-393-32531-8 pa

LC 2002-6482

"Pipes argues that Islam is not an inherent threat to Western civilization, but that militant Islam . . . is the greatest threat since the cold war. He goes on to explore the threats posed to America by an influx of Muslim immigrants, extol the benefits of racial profiling, and argue that the only viable form of Islamic belief is 'secularist' Islam, which embraces Western values and eschews traditional Islamic ones. . . . It's controversial and often interesting stuff." Booklist

Includes bibliographical references

Potter, Will

Green is the new red. City Lights Books 2011 301 p. **320.5**

ISBN 9780872865389

LC 2010053209

It was the author's intent to demonstrate that "the U.S. government is using post-9/11 anti-terrorism resources to target environmentalists and animal rights activists. . . . Tracing funds from animal-exploiting corporations to Congress and the passing of the big business-friendly Animal Enterprise Terrorism Act, Potter reports on an increased usage of the terrorism enhancement in court cases. . . . [Will] Potter warns of the crumbling of the "legal wall separating 'terrorist' from 'dissident' or 'undesirable' and concludes his account with a call to action and a decry of the injustice that results in the 'terrorist' label being put on those who threaten American corporate interests." (Publishers weekly)

★ The neocon reader; edited, with and [sic] introduction by Irwin Stelzer. Grove Press 2005 328p pa $15 **320.5**

1. Conservatism 2. Conservatism -- United States

ISBN 0-8021-4193-5

LC 2004-54063

This is a "collection of essays that reflect the breadth and depth of neo-conservative thought. Among the contributors are academics James Q. Wilson, Robert Kagan, and both Kristol (the father of neo-conservatism) and his son, William Kristol . . . journalists David Brooks, Charles Krauthammer, and George Will, and former and current political figures such as Jeane Kirkpatrick and Condoleeza Rice. The essays are informative and challenging and, taken as a whole, present a reasonably complete portrait of the neo-conservative approach." Libr J

Includes bibliographical references

320.53 Collectivism and fascism

Atkins, Stephen E.

★ **Encyclopedia** of modern American extremists and extremist groups. Greenwood Press 2002 xxiv, 375p $74.95 **320.53**

1. Cults 2. Cults -- United States 3. Radicalism 4. Radicalism -- United States 5. Right and left (Political science)

ISBN 0-313-31502-7

LC 2001-57729

"This is an excellent reference tool." Recomm Ref Books for Small & Medium-sized Libr & Media Cent, 2003

Includes bibliographical references

320.54 Nationalism, regionalism, internationalism

Hazony, Yoram

The **Jewish** state; the struggle for Israel's soul. Basic Bks. 2000 433p hardcover o.p. pa $18 **320.54**

1. Jews -- Israel -- Identity 2. Post-Zionism 3. Zionism 4. Zionism -- History -- 20th century

ISBN 0-465-02902-7 pa

LC 00-21814

"An extremely well-thought-out treatise, The Jewish State screams out for attention and is strongly recommended for anyone interested in contemporary Israeli politics." Libr J

Peres, Shimon

The **imaginary** voyage; with Theodor Herzl in Israel. in collaboration with Patrick Girard. Arcade Pub. 1999 256p $23.95 **320.54**

1. Writers on politics 2. Writers on religion 3. Zionism 4. Zionist leaders

ISBN 1-55970-468-3

LC 99-24365

Peres "takes the reader on an imaginary journey around present-day Israel with Theodor Herzl (1860-1904), the father of modern Zionism. The imaginary Herzl proves a good foil to whom Peres explains concisely how Israel has evolved." Publ Wkly

320.6   Policy making

Collins, Gail

As Texas goes; how the Lone Star State hijacked the American agenda. Gail Collins. Liveright Pub. Corporation 2012 267 p.   **320.6**

ISBN 0871404079; 9780871404077

LC 2012007794

This book is a study of Texas's government and its discontents. New York Times columnist [Gail] Collins . . . argues . . . [that Texas] is a disastrous model of public policy that inspired the Republican Party's national platform: a rickety economic boom based on insecure, poverty-level jobs and massive state incentives to corporations; financial deregulation that led to banking meltdowns; a raft of ill-advised education nostrums, from the prototype of the No Child Left Behind Act to abstinence-only sex-ed programs and textbook guidelines that frown on evolution; skimpy public services, high rates of poverty and inequality, and low rates of health coverage and graduation. Collins's book is really an indictment of . . . the rural conservative populism that favors small government, low taxes, and lax regulation. . . . (Publishers Weekly)

321.8   Democratic government

Feldman, Noah

After Jihad; America and the struggle for Islamic democracy. Farrar, Straus and Giroux 2003 260p $24; pa $14   **321.8**

1. Democracy -- Religious aspects -- Islam 2. Islam and politics 3. Islam and world politics 4. Religion and politics -- Islamic countries

ISBN 0-374-17769-4; 0-374-52933-7 pa

LC 2002-192524

Feldman "wonders if democracy 'can be made to flourish in the lands where Islam prevails?' The answer, according to the author, is a resounding yes. Furthermore, he argues . . . that the West in general and the U.S. in particular must encourage democratic growth even at the expense of existing relations with autocratic Islamic regimes viewed as our traditional allies. . . . Certain to spur debate, this thought-provoking discourse couldn't be published at a more appropriate time." Booklist

Includes bibliographical references

321.9   Authoritarian government

Arendt, Hannah

★ Origins of totalitarianism; new ed with added prefaces; Harcourt Brace Jovanovich 1973 xliii, 527p pa $19   **321.9**

1. Antisemitism 2. Imperialism 3. Totalitarianism

ISBN 0-15-670153-7

In this book, the author documents her "belief that Nazism and Communism had their roots in the anti-Semitism and imperialism of the 19th century." Benet's Reader's Ency. 4th edition

Includes bibliographical references

Paxton, Robert O.

★ The anatomy of fascism; [by] Robert Paxton. Knopf 2004 321p $26; pa $15   **321.9**

1. Fascism

ISBN 1-4000-4094-9; 1-4000-3391-8 pa

LC 2004-100489

"While there are countless studies on fascism, readers will be hard pressed to find anything more in-depth from a scholar with Paxton's credentials." Libr J

Includes bibliographical references

322   Relation of the state to organized groups and their members

Buruma, Ian

Taming the gods; religion and democracy on three continents. Princeton University Press 2010 142p $19.95   **322**

1. Church and state 2. Democracy 3. Democracy -- Religious aspects 4. Religion and state

ISBN 978-0-691-13489-5; 0-691-13489-8

LC 2009-31550

The author "tackles the vexing issue of the religious challenge to liberal democracy. . . . Buruma is that rare bird equally at home not only in Europe and America, but also in East and West. He devotes a chapter to Europe and America, one to China and Japan, and a third to Europe again, but this time focused on its confrontation with Islam. Throughout all, Buruma sounds a recurrent note: the toxicity of blending religion and politics, whether when religion usurps the mantle of politics or politics usurps that of religion." Globe and Mail

Includes bibliographical references

Djupe, Paul A.

Encyclopedia of American religion and politics; [by] Paul A. Djupe and Laura R. Olson. Facts on File 2003 512p il $85   **322**

1. Reference books 2. Religion and politics 3. Religion and politics -- United States 4. Religion and politics -- United States -- Encyclopedias

ISBN 0-8160-4582-8

LC 2002-33921

"The encyclopedia is timely and accessible. . . . Recommended for most reference collections in public libraries." Libr J

Includes bibliographical references

Preston, Andrew

Sword of the spirit, shield of faith; religion in American war and diplomacy. by Andrew Preston. Alfred A. Knopf 2012 815 p.   **322**

1. Historical literature 2. Religion and international relations -- United States -- History 3. United States -- History, Military -- Religious aspects

ISBN 9781400043231

LC 2011035138

It was the author's intention to provide an "examination of the consistent application of the founding religious principles to American foreign policy, from the colonists' sense of a Protestant exceptionalism to President Obama's 'Good Niebuhr Policy.' . . . [Author Andrew] Preston explores this fascinating paradox of a nation founded on freedom of religion yet exhibiting, in its relations with the wider world, a profound belief in a Judeo-Christian sense of 'exceptional virtue.' . . . Its founding Reformation Protestant society eventually developed tenets of pluralism, libertarianism, a deep suspicion of despotism and hostility to arbitrary power, a faith-based progressivism, nationalism and even isolationism, all of which Preston explores systematically." (Kirkus)

Tobin, Jacqueline
★ **From** Midnight to Dawn; the last tracks of the underground railroad. [by] Jacqueline Tobin with Hettie Jones. Doubleday 2006 272p il hardcover o.p. pa $14 **322**
    1. Abolitionists 2. Slavery -- United States 3. Underground railroad
    ISBN 978-0-385-51431-6; 0-385-51431-X; 978-1-4000-7936-0 pa; 1-4000-7936-5 pa
                        LC 2006-46304
"There's an enlightening portrait of Josiah Henson (the model for Stowe's Uncle Tom) as a political activist, a fascinating look at the pioneering journalist and early feminist Mary Ann Shadd and an intriguing section on the deep 'Canadian connection to Harpers Ferry,' as John Brown meets with the fugitives in Chatham. Accessible and fluidly written, the book will appeal to general readers." Publ Wkly
Includes bibliographical references

Winters, Michael Sean
God's right hand; Michael Sean Winters. HarperOne 2012 384p. **322**
    1. Biography & Autobiography -- Political 2. Baptists -- United States -- Clergy -- Biography 3. Christianity and politics -- United States 4. Church and state -- United States 5. Fundamentalism 6. Religious right -- United States
    ISBN 9780061970672
                        LC 2011031293
The book offers a "biography of the . . . conservative pastor who reshaped the landscape of American politics—Jerry Falwell. At a time when the Tea Party movement is dominating much of America's social and political discourse, the story of Falwell's Moral Majority will resonate strongly. Indeed, Falwell's language may sound familiar to anyone who has heard recent speeches by figures like Sarah Palin, Rick Perry, or Michelle Bachmann. . . . He was a man of strong views—and he knew that those views were shared by millions of Americans who were disengaged with public life. Falwell led them into the public square, articulated a coherent rationale for their involvement with politics, and made them the largest and most organized constituency in the contemporary Republican Party." (Publisher's note)

322.4 Political action groups

Chalmers, David Mark
Hooded Americanism: the history of the Ku Klux Klan; 3rd ed; Duke Univ. Press 1987 477p il hardcover o.p. pa $24.95 **322.4**
    ISBN 0-8223-0772-3 pa
                        LC 86-29133
This book recounts the history of the Klan. It describes the sociological and psychological forces behind the Klan, and sets forth its dogmas.
"The book is written in a breezy, journalistic style. . . . Especially instructive and sobering is Chalmers' account of the role of the Klan in politics." J Am Hist
Includes bibliographical references

Esposito, John L.
Unholy war; terror in the name of Islam. Oxford Univ. Press 2002 196p hardcover o.p. pa $15.95 **322.4**
    1. Anti-Americanism 2. Islam and politics 3. Islam and world politics 4. Jihad 5. Terrorism 6. Terrorism -- Religious aspects 7. Terrorism -- Religious aspects -- Islam
    ISBN 0-19-515435-5; 0-19-516886-0 pa
                        LC 2001-58009
The author "explains the teachings of Islam—the Quran, the example of the Prophet, Islamic law—about jihad or holy war, the use of violence, and terrorism. He chronicles the rise of extremist groups and examines their frightening worldview and tactics." Publisher's note
Includes bibliographical references

Gandhi, Mahatma
★ **Gandhi** on non-violence; selected texts from Mohandas K. Gandhi's Non-violence in peace and war. edited with an introduction by Thomas Merton; preface by Mark Kurlansky. New Directions 2007 101p pa $13.95 **322.4**
    1. Nonviolence 2. Passive resistance
    ISBN 978-0-8112-1686-9
                        LC 2007-32262
In an introductory essay Merton "considers Gandhi's ideas, not in relation to their Indian context, but in terms of their applicability to all men's lives. Brief quotations from Gandhi's writings make up most of the book." Asia: a Guide to Paperbacks
Includes bibliographical references

Gerges, Fawaz A.
★ **Journey** of the Jihadist; inside Muslim militancy. Harcourt 2006 312p $25; pa $15 **322.4**
    1. Islamic fundamentalism 2. Jihad 3. Terrorism 4. Terrorism -- Religious aspects 5. Terrorism -- Religious aspects -- Islam
    ISBN 0-15-101213-X; 978-0-15-101213-8; 0-15-603170-1 pa; 978-0-15-603170-7 pa
                        LC 2005-37759
In this "account of the development of militant Islamist praxis and ideology in the contemporary Middle East, Gerges . . . explains what the jihadists are about and what they intend to accomplish. . . . The author's ability to explain

complex issues in a jargon-free and easy-flowing narrative makes this book one of the best, most useful, and most timely volumes for nonspecialist readers." Libr J

Includes bibliographical references

Hamilton, Neil A.

Rebels and renegades; a chronology of social and political dissent in the United States. Routledge 2002 361p il $100   **322.4**

1. Protest movements -- United States -- History 2. Radicalism 3. Radicalism -- United States -- History 4. Radicals -- United States -- History 5. Right and left (Political science) 6. Social reformers -- United States -- History

ISBN 0-415-93639-X

LC 2002-8916

The author "examines the historical role that radicals and reactionaries have played in shaping American society and culture. Arranged in nine chapters, the book features a chronological format that begins in 1620 with the Pilgrims and ends with the September 11, 2001 terrorist attacks. Each chapter opens with an overview of the time period, and individual entries consist of one- or two-page descriptions of radicals, their activities, and their impact." Libr J

Includes bibliographical references

Ronson, Jon

Them: adventures with extremists. Simon & Schuster 2002 330p $24; pa $13   **322.4**

1. Conspiracies 2. Radicalism

ISBN 0-7432-2707-7; 0-7432-3321-2 pa

LC 2001-47411

This book "is at times funny, other times unsettling, but always astonishing. So difficult to accept are Ronson's narratives that any conclusions must be left up to the reader." Booklist

323   Civil and political rights

Arsenault, Raymond

★ **Freedom** riders; 1961 and the struggle for racial justice. Oxford University Press 2006 690p il map $32.50   **323**

1. African Americans -- Civil rights 2. African Americans -- Civil rights -- Southern States -- History -- 20th century 3. African Americans -- Segregation 4. African Americans -- Segregation -- Southern States 5. Civil rights -- Constitutional history 6. Civil rights activists -- Southern States -- History 7. Civil rights movements -- Southern States 8. Civil rights workers -- Southern states -- History 9. Civil rights workers -- United States -- History -- 20th century 10. Segregation in transportation 11. Segregation in transportation -- Southern States -- History

ISBN 0-19-513674-8; 978-0-19-513674-6

LC 2005-18108

This is a history of the "six months [in 1961] in which black and white volunteers descended on the South to challenge segregated travel." N Y Times (Late N Y Ed)

Includes bibliographical references

Berry, Mary Frances

My face is black is true; Callie House and the struggle for ex-slave reparations. Knopf 2006 314p il $26.95; pa $14.95   **323**

1. African American women -- Biography 2. African Americans -- Reparations 3. Biography, Individual 4. Laundry workers 5. Needleworkers 6. Social activists

ISBN 1-4000-4003-5 Knopf; 0-307-27705-4 pa, Vintage; 978-0-307-27705-3 pa, Vintage

LC 2004-51330

The author "unearths the intriguing story of Callie House (1861–1928), a Tennessee washerwoman and seamstress become activist, and the organization she led, the National Ex-Slave Mutual Relief, Bounty and Pension Association. . . . Students and scholars of African-American history, as well as those engaged in the current reparations debates, will be deeply informed by the rise and fall of the Ex-Slave Association." Publ Wkly

Includes bibliographical references

Brinkley, Douglas

Rosa Parks. Viking 2000 246p hardcover o.p. pa $13   **323**

1. African American women -- Biography 2. African American women civil rights workers -- Alabama -- Montgomery -- Biography 3. African Americans -- Civil rights 4. African Americans -- Civil rights -- Alabama -- Montgomery -- History -- 20th century 5. Civil rights activists 6. Civil rights workers -- Alabama -- Montgomery -- Biography 7. Montgomery (Ala.) -- Biography 8. Segregation in transportation -- Alabama -- Montgomery -- History -- 20th century

ISBN 0-670-89160-6; 0-14-303600-9 pa

LC 00-35916

"Rosa Parks' story takes readers from rural Alabama to the Montgomery Industrial School for Girls, marriage to barber Raymond Parks, quiet activism in the '30s and '40s, a first experience of integration at the Highlander Folk School, arrest in 1955 and the bus boycott, a move to Detroit, and more than 20 years on the staff of Rep. John Conyers (D-Mich.)." Booklist

Includes bibliographical references

Cleaver, Eldridge

Target zero; a life in writing. edited by Kathleen Cleaver; foreword by Henry Louis Gates, Jr.; afterword by Cecil Brown. Palgrave Macmillan 2005 xxvi, 336p $27.95; pa $16.95   **323**

1. Civil rights activists 2. Dissenters 3. Memoirists

ISBN 978-1-4039-6237-9; 1-4039-6237-5; 978-1-4039-7657-4 pa; 1-4039-7657-0 pa

LC 2005-51252

"The book's four parts chart Cleaver's life through his essays, short stories, letters, interviews, and poems, many previously unpublished. . . . This well-crafted reader . . . is a rich experience." Choice

Includes bibliographical references

Dershowitz, Alan M.

★ **Rights** from wrongs; a secular theory of the origins of rights. Basic Books 2004 261p $24 **323**

1. Civil rights 2. Human rights

ISBN 0-465-01713-4

LC 2004-20006

The author "asserts that human rights derive from the world's experience with 'wrongs,' i.e., injustice. Only after seeing genocide, for example, did the notion develop that this was a violation of human rights. Dershowitz . . . has a rare ability to develop complex ideas in readable prose. . . . Whether conservative or liberal, absolutist or relativist, readers will find areas of disagreement, but most will concur that a talented and creative legal mind is at work." Publ Wkly

Includes bibliographical references

Devine, Carol

Human rights; the essential reference. {by} Carol Devine, Carol Rae Hansen, Ralph Wilde {et al.}; edited by Hilary Poole. Oryx Press 1999 311p il $73.95 **323**

1. Human rights

ISBN 1-57356-205-X

LC 99-24395

"This volume is divided into four sections; the first 'traces the evolution of our modern concept of human rights' beginning with the ancient Greeks and continuing through World War II to the adoption of the Universal Declaration of Human Rights by the United Nations General Assembly in 1948. Part two is a thorough examination of this historical document, article by article. Part three provides a detailed overview of the contemporary human-rights movement. . . . The final section consists of short essays on 33 of the most pressing human-rights issues today." SLJ

Includes bibliographical references

Dyson, Michael Eric

I may not get there with you: the true Martin Luther King, Jr. Free Press 2000 404p $25; pa $15 **323**

1. African American civil rights workers -- Biography 2. African Americans -- Biography 3. African Americans -- Civil rights 4. African Americans -- Civil rights -- History -- 20th century 5. Baptists -- United States -- Clergy -- Biography 6. Civil rights activists 7. Civil rights movements -- United States -- History -- 20th century 8. Clergy 9. Nobel laureates for peace 10. Nonfiction writers

ISBN 0-684-86776-1; 0-684-83037-X pa

LC 99-40478

Dyson "believes that the ministry fostered King's rhetorical gifts but also encouraged his authoritarian personality. We learn much about his flaws, and about conflict, dissent, and generational differences within the black community, as Dyson insists that King, properly understood, remains a controversial figure." New Yorker

Includes bibliographical references

Hartman, Saidiya V.

★ **Lose** your mother; a journey along the Atlantic slave route. [by] Saidiya Hartman. Farrar, Straus and Giroux 2007 270p il $25; pa $14 **323**

1. College teachers 2. Historic sites -- Ghana 3. Literary critics 4. Philologists 5. Slave trade 6. Slave trade -- Ghana

ISBN 978-0-374-27082-7; 0-374-27082-1; 978-0-374-53115-7 pa; 0-374-53115-3 pa

LC 2006-29407

This "is a groundbreaking book for its ability to combine autobiography, history, and politics in an unprecedented style. . . . Hartman's book is not just to be read by historians of slavery or the Atlantic World, but by all of those who desire to write of the past." Rev Am Hist

Includes bibliographical references

King, Martin Luther

The **autobiography** of Martin Luther King, Jr; edited by Clayborne Carson. Warner Bks. 1998 400p il $25; pa $15.95 **323**

1. African Americans -- Biography 2. African Americans -- Civil rights 3. African Americans -- Civil rights -- History -- 20th century 4. Baptists -- United States -- Clergy -- Biography 5. Civil rights activists 6. Civil rights workers -- United States -- Biography 7. Clergy 8. Nobel laureates for peace 9. Nonfiction writers

ISBN 0-446-52412-3; 0-446-67650-0 pa

LC 98-35704

"Carson, director of Martin Luther King Jr. Papers Project, brings together selections from King's writings, speeches, and recordings to create this fascinating 'autobiography' of the famed civil rights leader and Nobel Peace Prize winner. The writings trace King's struggles with religion, philosophy, and the racial politics of the U.S." Booklist

Includes bibliographical references

Kotz, Nick

★ **Judgment** days; Lyndon Baines Johnson, Martin Luther King, Jr., and the laws that changed America. Houghton Mifflin 2005 522p $26 **323**

1. Civil rights activists 2. Clergy 3. Members of Congress 4. Nobel laureates for peace 5. Nonfiction writers 6. Presidents 7. Senators 8. Vice-presidents

ISBN 0-618-08825-3

LC 2004-59852

This is a "narrative of how President Johnson and King temporarily overcame their mutual suspicion to battle successfully for the Civil Rights Acts of 1964 and 1968 and the 1965 Voting Rights Act. . . . This book is an informed political investigation of these two civil rights warriors and the cause for which they fought and, in King's case, died." Libr J

Lourie, Richard

Sakharov; a biography. University Press of New England 2002 465p il $35 **323**

1. Dissenters 2. Dissenters -- Soviet Union 3. Human rights workers -- Soviet Union 4. Nobel laureates for peace 5. Physicists 6. Physicists -- Soviet Union 7. Political and social philosophers 8. Political prisoners

-- Soviet Union

ISBN 1-58465-207-1

LC 2001-5246

"Utilizing newly accessible KGB files as well as Sakharov's personal correspondence, Lourie provides a revealing portrait of an extraordinary man to whom the world owes a great debt." Booklist

Includes bibliographical references

Maddex, Robert L.

International encyclopedia of human rights; freedoms, abuses, and remedies. CQ Press 2000 xxxii, 404p il $156.25   **323**

1. Civil rights 2. Civil rights -- Encyclopedias 3. Human rights 4. Human rights -- Encyclopedias 5. Reference books

ISBN 1-56802-490-8

LC 00-42941

"Beginning its coverage with the 1948 Universal Declaration of Human Rights, the volume includes definitions of more than 150 important concepts . . . entries on decisions of national and international bodies; descriptions of well over 100 documents . . . information about agencies and organizations involved in human rights; and biographies of some key individuals." Booklist

Includes bibliographical references

Nader, Ralph

The **good** fight; declare your independence & close the democracy gap. ReganBooks 2004 294p $25.95   **323**

1. Political participation -- United States 2. Social movements 3. Social movements -- United States 4. United States -- Politics and government -- 2001-

ISBN 0-06-075604-7

LC 2005-295013

Activist and presidential candidate Ralph Nader discusses how political engagement benefits society.

"Nader's voice is full of anger and frustration. He rages as much as reasons. This will no doubt please those who already follow him." NY Times Book Rev.

Includes bibliographical references

Schulz, William F.

In our own best interest; how defending human rights benefits us all. foreword by Mary Robinson. Beacon Press 2001 235p $25; pa $15   **323**

1. Human rights

ISBN 0-8070-0226-7; 0-8070-0227-5 pa

LC 2001-392

According to the author, "defending human rights pays off not only in terms of justice, but also in ways that can include greater economic growth, a more protected environment, better public health, and a generally less violent world." America

Includes bibliographical references

Shipler, David K.

The **rights** of the people; how our search for safety invades our liberties. Alfred A. Knopf 2011 366p $27.95; ebook $13.99   **323**

1. Civil rights 2. Civil rights -- United States 3. Law

enforcement 4. Rule of law -- United States

ISBN 978-1-4000-4362-0; 978-0-307-59550-8 ebook

LC 2010-34255

The book "offers provocative real-life accounts of how privacy has been sacrificed in the modern era. The outlines of some of the stories he tells are familiar, such as the arrest of Brandon Mayfield, a Muslim lawyer in Portland, Oregon, whose fingerprint the FBI erroneously 'matched' to fingerprints from the Madrid train bombing in 2004. . . . [David K.] Shipler's goal is not to reformulate legal doctrine but to show us, through the experience of Americans subject to intrusive police tactics, where existing doctrine has left us; we live in a world where a federal judge can resignedly say, as Shipler quotes US District Judge Paul Friedman, 'I don't think that there's much left of the Fourth Amendment in criminal law.' As Shipler . . . illustrates, the dual wars on drugs and terror have brought us to this point. Time and again, constitutional law has bent to the imperatives of the state in conflict." (New York Review of Books)

"Identifying five periods in American history when the Bill of Rights has been under particular assault, Shipler . . . argues that we are in the middle of a sixth, a post-9/11 era in which our liberties are once again endangered. . . . A timely call for vigilance, for insisting on the protections the Framers provided against an always overreaching government." Kirkus

Includes bibliographical references

Sugrue, Thomas J.

Sweet land of liberty; the forgotten struggle for civil rights in the North. Random House 2008 xxviii, 688p il $35   **323**

1. African American civil rights workers 2. African Americans -- Civil rights 3. African Americans -- Civil rights -- History -- 20th century 4. Civil rights movements -- Northeastern States 5. Civil rights movements -- United States -- History -- 20th century 6. Civil rights workers -- United States -- History -- 20th century

ISBN 978-0-679-64303-6; 0-679-64303-6

LC 2008-2081

The author "shows that black exclusion, poverty, and racial violence permeated America on both sides of the Mason-Dixon Line. . . . This splendid read brims with insights broadening and deepening understanding of the black-white mold of modern America. Highly recommended and essential for collections on U.S. history, social movements, race relations, or civil rights." Libr J

Includes bibliographical references

323.1   Civil and political rights of nondominant groups

Boyd, Herb

★ **We** shall overcome; a living history of the civil rights struggle told in words, pictures and the voices of the participants. Sourcebooks 2004 272p il $45   **323.1**

1. African Americans -- Civil rights

ISBN 1-402-20213-X

LC 2004-12509

"Through text, images, and actual recordings (found on 2 CDs), Boyd . . . presents some of the major events in the Civil Rights Movement, including the murder of Emmett Till, the march on Washington, and the life and death of Martin Luther King Jr." Libr J

Includes bibliographical references

Branch, Taylor

★ **Pillar** of fire; America in the King years, 1963-65. Simon & Schuster 1998 746p il hardcover o.p.   **323.1**

1. African Americans -- Civil rights 2. Afro-Americans -- Civil rights -- History -- 20th century 3. Civil rights activists 4. Clergy 5. Nobel laureates for peace 6. Nonfiction writers

ISBN 0-684-84809-0 pa

LC 97-46076

"Branch began telling the story of the civil rights movement in his . . . Parting the Waters: America in the King Years, 1954-63. Here he picks up where he left off, narrating the history of the years 1963-65, when the movement won . . . the Civil Rights Act of 1964 and the Voting Rights Act of 1965." (Commonweal) Bibliography. Index.

"Branch's research is impeccable and his knowledge of his material solid. . . . The book is significant for marshaling so much information, particularly the profiles of all the many individuals involved in the race issues of that time." Booklist

Includes bibliographical references

Egerton, John

Speak now against the day; the generation before the civil rights movement in the South. University of North Carolina Press 1995 704p il pa $27.50 **323.1**

1. African Americans -- Civil rights

ISBN 0-8078-4557-4; 978-0-8078-4557-8

This "book is a stunning achievement: a sprawling, engrossing, deeply moving account." N Y Times Book Rev

Includes bibliographical references

Euchner, Charles C.

Nobody turn me around; a people's history of the 1963 march on Washington. Beacon Press 2010 226p $26.95   **323.1**

1. African Americans -- Civil rights 2. Civil rights demonstrations

ISBN 978-0-8070-0059-5

LC 2009-46943

Draws on the oral histories of more than one hundred participants to provide a behind-the-scenes look at the historic 1963 March on Washington that culminated in Martin Luther King Jr.'s "I Have a Dream" speech.

"A sweeping, comprehensive look at a pivotal march in American history." Booklist

Includes bibliographical references

Fairclough, Adam

Better day coming; Blacks and equality, 1890-2000. Viking 2001 384p il $26.95; pa $16 **323.1**

1. African Americans -- Civil rights 2. African Americans -- Civil rights -- History -- 20th century 3. African Americans -- Civil rights -- Southern States -- History -- 20th century 4. Civil rights movements --

Southern States -- History -- 20th century 5. Civil rights movements -- United States -- History -- 20th century

ISBN 0-670-87592-9; 0-14-200129-5 pa

LC 00-51342

"Although it adds little to what experts in the field already know, this well-written work is a fine general introduction to the topic." Libr J

Includes bibliographical references (p. {337}-369) and index

Goff, Keli

Party crashing; how the hip-hop generation declared political independence. Basic Books 2008 294p pa $16.95   **323.1**

1. African Americans -- Political activity

ISBN 978-0-465-00332-7; 0-465-00332-X

LC 2007-45697

"Goff argues that members of the post-Civil Rights—the hip-hop—generation, without personal memories of the Civil Rights Movement, have different political motivations from their parents and think more independently about politics than previous generations of African Americans. . . . Interviews with prominent leaders in politics and popular culture, such as Colin Powell and Russell Simmons, lend credibility to the work." Libr J

Includes bibliographical references

Greenhaw, Wayne

Fighting the devil in Dixie; how civil rights activists took on the Ku Klux Klan in Alabama. Lawrence Hill Books 2011 316p il $26.95 **323.1**

1. African Americans -- Civil rights

ISBN 978-1-56976-345-2

LC 2010-30114

"The author skillfully weaves a rich historical tapestry from his deeply engaged, firsthand observations. Impressively captures stark, stunning history in the making." Kirkus

Includes bibliographical references

Guinier, Lani

The **miner's** canary; enlisting race, resisting power, transforming democracy. {by} Lani Guinier and Gerald Torres. Harvard Univ. Press 2002 392p $28.95; pa $16.95   **323.1**

1. Coalition (Social sciences) 2. Minorities 3. Minorities -- United States -- Political activity 4. Political participation -- United States

ISBN 0-674-00469-8; 0-674-01084-1 pa

LC 2001-39629

The authors "grapple intelligently and with passionate wit with such explosive topics as racial profiling and the elusiveness of racial identification and identity . . . making this one of the most provocative and challenging books on race produced in years." Publ Wkly

Includes bibliographical references

Halberstam, David

★ The **children**. Fawcett Books 1999 783p il pa $18.95   **323.1**

1. African Americans -- Civil rights 2. Civil rights activists 3. Clergy 4. College teachers 5. Educators 6. Local government officials 7. Mayors 8. Members

of Congress 9. Physicians 10. Psychiatrists 11. School administrators 12. Social activists 13. Songwriters
ISBN 978-0-449-00439-5; 0-449-00439-2

This is a "recreation of the early days of the civil rights movement. . . . The author focuses on a small group of young African Americans who attended the Reverend James Lawson's workshop for nonviolent demonstrators in Nashville in 1959, then went on to play active roles in the movement. . . . A masterful achievement in reporting, research and understanding." Publ Wkly

Includes bibliographical references

Joseph, Peniel E.

Dark days, bright nights; from Black power to Barack Obama. BasicCivitas Books 2010 277p $26   **323.1**

1. African American leadership 2. African Americans -- Civil rights 3. African Americans -- History -- 1964- 4. African Americans -- Politics and government 5. Black Muslim leaders 6. Black power 7. Black power -- United States 8. Civil rights activists 9. Democracy -- United States 10. Lawyers 11. Nobel laureates for peace 12. Presidents 13. Senators 14. State legislators
ISBN 978-0-465-01366-1; 0-465-01366-X

LC 2009-37946

This is a "discussion of black power's successes and its contributions to the civil rights movement. . . . Joseph examines two paths to black social justice—'black power' and the pulpit-driven civil rights movement—which popular history has traditionally pitted in opposition. . . . [This] book is a vivid and welcome recasting of the history—and the myriad interpretations—of the movement." Booklist

Includes bibliographical references

★ **Waiting** 'til the midnight hour; a narrative history of Black power in America. Henry Holt and Co. 2006 399p il hardcover o.p. pa $17   **323.1**

1. African Americans -- Civil rights 2. African Americans -- Civil rights -- History -- 20th century 3. African Americans -- Politics and government 4. Black power 5. Black power -- United States -- History -- 20th century 6. Civil rights activists 7. Civil rights movements 8. Revolutionaries
ISBN 978-0-8050-7539-7; 0-8050-7539-9; 978-0-8050-8335-4 pa; 0-8050-8335-9 pa

LC 2005-46765

"Rather than simply detailing the history of radical organizations, Joseph . . . also profiles several famous leaders and uses their stories to spearhead a discussion of the intellectual and practical history of Black Power as a political movement. . . . Enthusiastically recommended for public and academic libraries." Libr J

Includes bibliographical references

Katznelson, Ira

★ **When** affirmative action was white; an untold history of racial inequality in twentieth-century America. W.W. Norton 2005 238p $25.95   **323.1**

1. Affirmative action programs 2. African Americans -- Civil rights -- History -- 20th century 3. African Americans -- Economic conditions 4. Race discrimination 5. Race discrimination -- United States

-- History -- 20th century
ISBN 0-393-05213-3

LC 2004-24359

"Katznelson offers a penetrating . . . analysis, supported by vivid examples and statistics." N Y Times Book Rev

Includes bibliographical references

King, Martin Luther

Where do we go from here; chaos or community? [by] Martin Luther King, Jr.; [foreword by Coretta Scott King; introduction by Vincent Harding] Beacon Press 2010 xxiv, 223p $24.95; pa $14   **323.1**

1. African Americans -- Civil rights 2. Racism
ISBN 978-0-8070-0076-2; 978-0-8070-0067-0 pa

LC 2009035950

The author reaffirms his belief in the power of nonviolence to achieve full citizenship for black people in America and defines his attitude toward the Black Power movement and the white backlash.

Why we can't wait; [by] Martin Luther King, Jr. Harper & Row 1964 178p il hardcover o.p. pa $6.95   **323.1**

1. African Americans -- Civil rights
ISBN 0-06-012395-8; 0-451-52753-4 pa

The author first reviews the background of the 1963 civil rights demands. He then describes the strategy of the Birmingham campaign and outlines future action.

★ A **testament** of hope; the essential writings of Martin Luther King, Jr. edited by James Melvin Washington. Harper & Row 1986 xxvi, 676p hardcover o.p. pa $23.95   **323.1**

1. African Americans -- Civil rights 2. Nonviolence
ISBN 0-06-250931-4; 0-06-064691-8 pa

LC 85-45370

"King's most important writings are gathered together in one source. The arrangement is topical: philosophy, sermons and public addresses, essays, interviews and excerpts of his books. The material within each of these categories is arranged chronologically. Included are Dr. King's writings on nonviolence, integration and politics." SLJ

Includes bibliographical references

Lewis, Andrew B.

The **shadows** of youth; the remarkable journey of the civil rights generation. Hill and Wang 2009 356p $28   **323.1**

1. African American civil rights workers -- Biography 2. African American college students -- Political activity -- History -- 20th century 3. African Americans -- Biography 4. African Americans -- Civil rights 5. African Americans -- Civil rights -- History -- 20th century 6. Civil rights movements -- United States -- History 7. Civil rights movements -- United States -- History -- 20th century 8. Political activists
ISBN 978-0-8090-8598-9; 0-8090-8598-4

LC 2009-9980

The author "offers an engaging look at some of the major figures in the budding civil rights movement: John Lewis, son of a poor tenant cotton farmer; Marion Barry, ambitious son of poor southern parents; Diane Nash, from a middle-class Chicago family; Stokely Carmichael, who learned black culture from his Caribbean roots and politics from a leftist friend; and Julian Bond, born of black privilege. Lewis chronicles the coming together of these young people, and others, in the formation of the Student Nonviolent Coordinating Committee." Booklist

Includes bibliographical references (p. 329-335)

Litwack, Leon F.

How free is free? The long death of Jim Crow. Harvard University Press 2009 187p $18.95 **323.1**
1. African Americans -- Civil rights 2. African Americans -- Segregation 3. African Americans -- Southern States 4. Blacks 5. Civil rights movements -- Southern states 6. Liberty 7. Segregation
ISBN 978-0-674-03152-4

LC 2008-36468
"An interesting analysis of the dynamics of race and class and how they continue to affect progress." Booklist
Includes bibliographical references

McGuire, Danielle L.

At the dark end of the street; Black women, rape, and resistance: a new history of the civil rights movement, from Rosa Parks to the rise of Black Power. Alfred A. Knopf 2010 324p il $27.95; e-book $27.95 **323.1**
1. African American women 2. African American women -- Civil rights -- History -- 20th century 3. African American women -- Violence against 4. African Americans -- Civil rights 5. Civil rights movements -- Southern States -- History -- 20th century 6. Rape 7. Rape -- Political aspects -- Southern States
ISBN 978-0-307-26906-5; 978-0-307-59447-1 e-book

LC 2010-12072
"McGuire restores to memory the courageous black women who dared seek legal remedy, when black women and their families faced particular hazards for doing so. McGuire brings the reader through a dark time via a painful but somehow gratifying passage in this compelling, carefully documented work." Publ Wkly
Includes bibliographical references and index

Prucha, Francis Paul

The **great** father; the United States government and the American Indians. University of Neb. Press 1984 2v il hardcover o.p. pa $60 **323.1**
1. Indians of North America -- Government relations 2. Native Americans -- Government relations
ISBN 0-8032-8734-8 pa

LC 83-16837
"Beginning with the American Revolution and continuing to 1980, Prucha . . . brilliantly chronicles the history of relations between the federal government and Native Americans, in a work that belongs in all public and academic libraries." Libr J
Includes bibliographical references

Spagna, Ana Maria

Test ride on the Sunnyland bus; a daughter's civil rights journey. University of Nebraska Press 2010 270p il pa $19.95 **323.1**
1. African Americans -- Civil rights 2. Boycotts 3. Civil rights activists
ISBN 978-0-8032-1712-6

LC 2009034320
This book "chronicles the story of an American family against the backdrop of one of the civil rights movement's lesser-known stories. In January 1957, Joseph Spagna and five other young men waited to board a city bus called the Sunnyland in Tallahassee, Florida. Their plan was simple but dangerous: ride the bus together—three blacks and three whites—get arrested, and take their case to the U.S. Supreme Court. Fifty years later Ana Maria Spagna sets off on a journey to understand what happened and why." Publisher's note

Sullivan, Patricia

Lift every voice; the NAACP and the making of the Civil Rights Movement. New Press 2009 514p il $26.95 **323.1**
1. African Americans -- Civil rights 2. African Americans -- Civil rights -- History -- 20th century 3. Civil rights -- United States -- History -- 20th century
ISBN 978-1-59558-446-5

LC 2009-9473
The author "delivers a solidly researched examination of the organization's growth and influence, leaving us with a vital account of 100 years of foundational civil rights activism." Publ Wkly
Includes bibliographical references

Wallace, Anthony F. C.

The **long** bitter trail; Andrew Jackson and the Indians. consulting editor, Eric Foner. Hill & Wang 1993 143p maps hardcover o.p. pa $11 **323.1**
1. Generals 2. Indians of North America -- Government relations 3. Indians of North America -- History 4. Native Americans -- Government relations 5. Presidents
ISBN 0-8090-1552-8 pa

LC 92-32609
A "retelling of the story of the Trail of Tears. This refers to the forced removal in the 1830s of thousands of Indians, particularly the Cherokee and the Choctaw, from the American east to west of the Mississippi River. The author expands his focus to examine the relocation of numerous Indian groups. Central to the story is Andrew Jackson, who assumed the presidency confronted with a government divided over the question of Indian removal and who soon became one of its major proponents." Publ Wkly

Watson, Bruce

Freedom summer; the savage season that made Mississippi burn and made America a democracy. Viking 2010 369p il $27.95 **323.1**
1. African Americans -- Civil rights 2. African Americans -- Suffrage
ISBN 978-0-670-02170-3

LC 2009-47211
This book "combines a political overview of the Mississippi civil rights struggle in the summer of 1964 with more

than 50 personal accounts from those who were there, both the famous (including Sidney Poitier, Pete Seeger, John Lewis, Stokely Carmichael) and the lesser known, including the more than 200 volunteer students from the North who lived and worked with local residents and taught in the Freedom Schools in converted shacks and church basements. . . . The personal interviews, some from people telling their stories for the first time, make gripping drama, as they recount the standoffs, the struggle for voter registration, the reign of terror that encompassed church burnings and murders." Booklist

Includes bibliographical references

Williams, Juan

Eyes on the prize: America's civil rights years, 1954-1965; [by] Juan Williams with the Eyes on the prize production team; introduction by Julian Bond. Viking 1987 300p il hardcover o.p. pa $20   **323.1**
1. African Americans -- Civil rights
ISBN 0-670-81412-1; 0-14-009653-1 pa

LC 86-40271

"Highly recommended both as a socio-historical document and as a heartfelt, poignant remembrance of a movement and its activists." Booklist

Includes bibliographical references

The Eyes on the prize civil rights reader; documents, speeches, and firsthand accounts from the black freedom struggle, 1954-1990. general editors, Clayborne Carson {et al.} Penguin Bks. 1991 764p pa $18   **323.1**
1. African Americans -- Civil rights
ISBN 0-14-015403-5

LC 91-9507

"An anthology of primary material important in the historiography of this country's civil rights movement. . . . Not simply for reference use, this compilation makes provocative cover-to-cover reading and is extremely worthy of consideration by every library." Booklist

Includes bibliographical references

★ Reporting civil rights. Library of Am. 2003 2v ea $40   **323.1**
1. African Americans -- Civil rights 2. African Americans -- Civil rights -- History -- 20th century -- Sources 3. African Americans -- Civil rights -- Press coverage 4. Civil rights movements -- Press coverage -- United States 5. Civil rights movements -- United States -- History -- 20th century -- Sources 6. Journalism
ISBN 1-931082-28-6 v1; 1-931082-29-4 v2

LC 2002-27459

"An important anthology for readers interested in the history of the civil rights movement." Booklist

Voices in our blood; America's best on the civil rights movement. edited by Jon Meacham. Random House 2001 561p hardcover o.p. pa $16.95   **323.1**
1. African Americans -- Civil rights 2. African-Americans -- Civil rights -- History -- 20th century -- Sources 3. Civil rights movements -- United States --

History -- 20th century -- Sources
ISBN 0-375-75881-X pa

LC 00-41474

A "collection of acclaimed 'voices' narrating the environment, origin, and progress of the Civil Rights movement, as told by reporters, artists, novelists, historians, and authors such as Maya Angelou, Eudora Welty, James Baldwin, Richard Wright, Willie Morris, Robert Penn Warren, Alice Walker, Murray Kempton, E. B. White, William Faulkner, Ralph Ellison, and Rebecca West." Libr J

323.4   Specific civil rights; limitation and suspension of civil rights

Conroy, John

Unspeakable acts, ordinary people; the dynamics of torture. University of California Press 2001 304p pa $19.95   **323.4**
1. Persecution 2. Police brutality 3. Torture
ISBN 0-520-23039-6

LC 2001-33218

The author "interviews torturers, torture victims, and government officials from such diverse locations as Israel, Northern Ireland, and a Chicago police interrogation room, focusing on how torture is performed and why." Booklist

Includes bibliographical references

McCoy, Alfred W.

★ A **question** of torture; CIA interrogation from the Cold War to the War on Terror. Metropolitan Books 2006 290p il $25; pa $15   **323.4**
1. Intelligence service -- United States 2. Torture
ISBN 978-0-8050-8041-4; 0-8050-8041-4; 978-0-8050-8248-7 pa; 0-8050-8248-4 pa

LC 2005-51124

The author "shows how, since 1950, the CIA and various nations have augmented traditional physical torture with psychological abuse techniques of 'sensory disorientation' and 'self-inflicted pain,' which he documents with some gruesome first-person accounts by victims and with stories of doctors who conducted horrific experiments." Libr J

Includes bibliographical references

Pipes, Richard

Property and freedom. Knopf 1999 328p hardcover o.p. pa $15   **323.4**
1. Affirmative action programs 2. Freedom 3. Liberty -- History 4. Property 5. Property -- History 6. Right of property -- History
ISBN 0-375-70447-7 pa

LC 98-41728

This is a "survey of the Western philosophical stance toward property, primarily concerning its origins, justification of possession, and wisdom of redistribution. . . . After rendering compact constitutional histories of England and Russia, Pipes usefully provides concrete, rather than theoretical, illustrations of the liberty-property nexus in action. An incisive essay." Booklist

Includes bibliographical references

Razac, Olivier

Barbed wire; a political history. translated from the French by Jonathan Kneight. New Press 2002 132p $22.95; pa $13.95 **323.4**
1. Barbed wire 2. Barbed wire -- Political aspects 3. Concentration camps -- History 4. Wire fencing -- West (U.S.) -- History 5. Wire obstacles -- History
ISBN 1-56584-735-0; 1-56584-812-8 pa
LC 2002-19536
"First introduced in 1874 as an inexpensive means of fencing off U.S. prairie land, barbed wire quickly became not only a way to manage livestock but a means to contain Native Americans on reservations. . . . Arguing that barbed wire is 'the political management of space,' Razac traces how it radicalized trench warfare during WWI . . . and, electrified, literally defined the space of Nazi concentration camps. . . . The simplicity and clarity of Razac's prose reinforces the enormous power and originality of his ideas, making this a vital work of cultural criticism." Publ Wkly
Includes bibliographical references

323.44 Freedom of action (Liberty)

Etzioni, Amitai

The **limits** of privacy. Basic Bks. 1999 280p hardcover o.p. pa $21 **323.44**
1. Common good 2. Privacy, Right of -- United States 3. Public interest 4. Public interest -- United States 5. Right of privacy
ISBN 0-465-04090-X pa
LC 98-47082
The author addresses the right to privacy and the common good. Topics discussed include HIV testing of infants, sex offender laws, deciphering encrypted messages, I.D. cards, and medical records
"Etzioni advocates rethinking privacy and placing it in the context of the common good. This book provides a valuable and informative analysis of a timely and interesting topic." Booklist
Includes bibliographical references

Fischer, David Hackett

Liberty and freedom. Oxford University Press 2004 851p il $50 **323.44**
1. American national characteristics 2. Freedom 3. Liberty -- History 4. National characteristics, American
ISBN 0-19-516253-6
LC 2004-5197
This "beautifully illustrated book shifts subtly from a rich graphic survey, incorporating painting, flags and sculpture, to a broader chronicle of the many ways Americans have articulated their most cherished ideals." Publ Wkly
Includes bibliographical references

Foner, Eric

The **story** of American freedom. Norton 1998 422p il hardcover o.p. pa $16.95 **323.44**
1. African Americans -- Civil rights 2. Civil rights -- United States -- History 3. Cold war 4. Conservatism 5. Democracy -- United States -- History 6. Freedom 7. Human rights -- United States -- History 8. Labor

movement 9. Liberty -- History 10. Slavery -- United States 11. Women -- Social conditions
ISBN 0-393-31962-8 pa
LC 98-3290
"The book's strongest claim to distinction lies . . . in its succinct, information-packed, wonderfully readable account of the twists and turns in 20th-century American history." N Y Times Book Rev
Includes bibliographical references

Stone, Geoffrey R.

★ **Perilous** times; free speech in wartime from the Sedition Act of 1798 to the war on terrorism. Norton 2004 xx, 730p il $35 **323.44**
1. Freedom of speech
ISBN 0-393-05880-8
LC 2004-17871
The author "delivers rich material in an engaging, character-based narrative. Stone offers deep insight into rhetorical history and the men and women who made it—resisters like Clement Vallandingham, Emma Goldman, Fred Korematsu and Daniel Ellsberg; presidents faced with wartime dilemmas; and the prosecutors, defenders and Supreme Court justices who shaped our understanding of the First Amendment today." Publ Wkly
Includes bibliographical references

323.6 Citizenship and related topics

Ellis, Richard

To the flag; the unlikely history of the Pledge of Allegiance. [by] Richard J. Ellis. University Press of Kansas 2005 297p il hardcover o.p. pa $15.95 **323.6**
1. Patriotism -- United States -- History
ISBN 0-7006-1372-2; 0-7006-1521-0 pa
LC 2004-23110
The author provides an "account not only of the pledge's 19th century beginnings, but also of its recent use as a political tool. A must read for political junkies of any age!" Univ Press Books for Public and Second Sch Libr, 2006

LearningExpress (Organization)

★ **Pass** the U.S. citizenship exam; 3rd ed.; LearningExpress 2008 151p il map pa $12.95 **323.6**
1. Citizenship
ISBN 978-1-57685-619-2
LC 2007-48381
This book covering the civics test and the N-400 "includes bilingual lessons, quizzes, translated civics terms/definitions, sample questions/forms, embassy data, and more." Libr J

United States/Dept. of Homeland Security/U.S. Citizenship and Immigration Services

★ The **citizen's** almanac; fundamental documents, symbols, and anthems of the United States.

U.S. Citizenship and Immigration Services, [Office of Citizenship] 2007 102p il pa $7.50   **323.6**
1. Citizenship
ISBN 0-16-078027-6; 978-0-16-078027-1

LC 2008-354023

"Featuring historical speeches, songs, landmark Supreme Court decisions, and more; all public libraries should point patrons here." Libr J

324   The political process

Larson, Edward J.

A **magnificent** catastrophe; the tumultuous election of 1800, America's first presidential campaign. Free Press 2007 335p il $27   **324**
1. Architects 2. Essayists 3. Political culture -- United States -- History -- 18th century 4. Political culture -- United States -- History -- 19th century 5. Presidents 6. Presidents -- United States -- Election -- 1800 7. Secretaries of the treasury 8. Statesmen 9. Vice-presidents
ISBN 978-0-7432-9316-7; 0-7432-9316-9

LC 2007-16017

The author "recreates the dramatic presidential race of 1800, which, Larson says, stamped American democracy with its distinctive partisan character as Republicans and Federalists battled for the presidency. . . . [This is] an invaluable study of a crucial chapter in the lives of the founding fathers—and of the nation." Publ Wkly
Includes bibliographical references

Schoen, Douglas E.

The **power** of the vote; electing presidents, overthrowing dictators, and promoting democracy around the world. William Morrow 2007 396p pa $25.95   **324**
1. Democracy 2. Political campaigns 3. Political consultants 4. Presidents -- United States -- Election
ISBN 978-0-06-123188-9; 0-06-123188-6

LC 2006-52877

The author presents an account of his work as a political strategist.

Traister, Rebecca

Big girls don't cry; the election that changed everything for American women. Free Press 2010 336p $26   **324**
1. Feminism 2. Feminism -- Political aspects 3. Governors 4. Hospital administrators 5. Lawyers 6. Mayors 7. Presidential candidates 8. Presidents -- United States -- Election -- 2008 9. Secretaries of state 10. Senators 11. Spouses of presidents 12. Women -- Political activity 13. Women in politics -- United States
ISBN 978-1-4391-5028-3; 1-4391-5028-1

LC 2010-09631

This is "a passionate, visionary and very personal account of the cultural ferment that accompanied the election of '08." N Y Times Book Rev
Includes bibliographical references

★   Historical atlas of U.S. presidential elections 1788-2004; [by] J. Clark Archer . . . [et al.] CQ Press 2006 164p map $150   **324**
1. Elections -- United States -- Maps 2. Elections -- United States -- Statistics 3. Presidents -- United States -- Election -- Maps 4. Presidents -- United States -- Election -- Statistics 5. Reference books
ISBN 1-56802-955-1; 978-1-56802-955-9

LC 2006-42406

"Offering detailed geographic and historical visual evidence of every presidential election held in the US, this book is a required source of reference." Choice
Includes bibliographical references

★   Political handbook of the world 2011; edited by Thomas C. Muller, William R. Overstreet, Judith F. Isacoff, Tom Lansford. CQ Press 2011 1832p $325   **324**
1. Political parties 2. Political science -- Handbooks, manuals, etc. 3. Reference books
ISBN 978-1-60871-734-7

"Provides data for each country on chief officials, government and politics, political parties, and news media. Sections devoted to intergovernmental organizations and to issues concerned with particular regions; e.g., Middle East, Latin America. Index to geographical, organizational, and personal names." Ref Sources for Small & Medium-sized Libr. 6th edition

324.2   Political parties

McGerr, Michael E.

A **fierce** discontent; the rise and fall of the Progressive movement in America, 1870-1920. [by] Michael McGerr. Oxford University Press 2005 395p pa $19.95   **324.2**
1. Progressivism (United States politics)
ISBN 978-0-19-518365-8; 0-19-518365-7

LC 2004-30592

The author "examines the social, cultural and political currents of a movement that, through its early successes and ultimate failure, has defined today's 'disappointing' political climate. . . . In three parts, McGerr illuminates the origins of Progressive thought, the movement's meteoric ascent in American life and its descent into 'the Red scare, race riots, strikes and inflation,' positing that the Progressive vision of remaking America in its own middle-class image eventually sparked a backlash that persists to this day. . . . Simply put, this is history at its best." Publ Wkly
Includes bibliographical references

McGregor, Richard

The **Party**; the secret world of China's communist rulers. Harper 2010 302p il map   **324.2**
1. Communism -- China 2. Economic policy -- China
ISBN 9780061708770; 9780061998089

McGregor "examines China's Communist Party, with a focus on the large role it has played in the nation's competition with the United States." (Publisher's note) Index.

"An astute, well-crafted work that should be enormously useful in understanding China's role in the world." Kirkus

Includes bibliographical references

324.273 Parties founded or in existence after 1945

Gould, Lewis L.

★ **Grand** Old Party; a history of the Republicans. Random House 2003 597p il $35 **324.273**

ISBN 0-375-50741-8

LC 2003-46604

This is an "account of the Grand Old Party that spans its earliest days under Abraham Lincoln to its conservative bent today. Much of the book documents the shifts of its platform. . . . Gould also discusses the leadership qualities, farsighted policies, conservative federal spending, and willingness to provide social programs at the cost of future generations of four Republican presidents—Lincoln, Theodore Roosevelt, Eisenhower, and Reagan." Libr J

Includes bibliographical references

324.5 Nominating candidates

Congressional Quarterly, Inc.

National party conventions, 1831-2008. CQ Press 2010 375p il pa $65 **324.5**

1. Political conventions 2. Political parties

ISBN 978-1-60426-540-8

LC 2009040264

This volume offers information about Republican and Democratic Party national conventions including sites, delegates, chief officers and keynote speakers, party organization and rules, credential fights, platform fights, ballots, and candidates.

324.6 Election systems and procedures; suffrage

Benenson, Bob

Elections A to Z; 3rd ed.; CQ Press 2008 xxxvi, 704p il $85 **324.6**

1. Elections -- United States -- Encyclopedias 2. Reference books

ISBN 978-0-87289-366-5

LC 2007-41388

"Topics include individuals, current and defunct political parties, and significant events in election history. Landmark court cases on this topic are also discussed. . . . Public libraries and media centers will find this a convenient and useful addition to their collections." Am Ref Books Annu, 2008

Includes bibliographical references

Congressional Quarterly, Inc.

Guide to U.S. elections; 6th ed.; CQ Press 2010 2v il map set $420 **324.6**

1. Elections -- United States -- Statistics 2. Reference books

ISBN 978-1-60426-536-1

LC 2009-33938

This is a compilation of data drawn from different sources on gubernatorial, congressional, and presidential elections.

"The clearly written, analytical essays . . . focus on key issues such as reapportionment and redistricting, campaign finance, political party development, party conventions, politics and war, the electoral process, and the ethnic and gender composition of Congress. . . . It is an important resource for students and researchers needing historical or contemporary election data and analysis." Choice

Includes bibliographical references

★ **Presidential** elections 1789-2008. CQ Press 2010 295p il map pa $65 **324.6**

1. Presidents -- United States -- Election

ISBN 978-1-60426-541-5

LC 2009-40267

This book offers information about the electoral college, electoral votes and popular votes in each presidential election, voter turnout, primary returns, and Democratic and Republican Party conventions.

Dudden, Faye E.

Fighting chance; the struggle over woman suffrage and Black suffrage in Reconstruction America. Oxford University Press 2011 287p il $34.95 **324.6**

1. African Americans -- Suffrage 2. Reconstruction (1865-1876) 3. Women -- Suffrage

ISBN 978-0-19-977263-6; 0-19-977263-0

LC 2010053188

"Likely to be a classic study, it is recommended for all readers in American studies and Reconstruction history." Libr J

Includes bibliographical references

Henderson, Harry

Campaign and election reform. Facts on File 2004 316p $45 **324.6**

1. Campaign funds -- Law and legislation -- United States 2. Campaign funds -- United States 3. Election law -- United States 4. Elections -- United States

ISBN 0-8160-5136-4

LC 2003-6485

"Beginning with the Declaration of Independence and ending with the 2002 Bipartisan Campaign Reform Act, coverage includes the Electoral College and the complicated world of campaign-finance reform as well as the technology used to record individual voter records. Legislation and court cases that have determined the current electoral process in our country are reviewed and explanations of the legal battles waged during the 2000 presidential election between George Bush and Al Gore are included. . . . A solid one-stop resource." SLJ

Includes bibliographical references

League of Women Voters (U.S.)

Choosing the president 2008; a citizen's guide to the electoral process. [by] League of Women Voters;

edited by Bob Guldin. Lyons Press 2008 178p il pa
$14.95   **324.6**
    1. Elections -- United States   2. Presidents -- United
States -- Election
    ISBN 978-1-59921-214-2; 1-59921-214-5
                       LC 2007-51852
    "An essential text for understanding the process, laws,
and issues that impact a U.S. presidential election. . . . Covers political parties, media, money, campaigning, primaries,
conventions, and election day processes." Libr J
    Includes videography and bibliographical references

Rubin, Aviel D.
    Brave new ballot; the battle to safeguard democ-
racy in the age of electronic voting. Morgan Road
Books 2006 280p $24.95   **324.6**
    1. Voting machines
    ISBN 0-7679-2210-7; 978-0-7679-2210-4
                       LC 2006-41917
    The author "found himself at center stage of the de-
bate surrounding the safety and security of electronic voting when he and his grad students exposed serious failings
in the code in electronic voting machines manufactured by
Diebold. . . . Rubin thoroughly analyzes the vulnerabilities
of electronic voting and offers an absorbing account of how
his involvement in the e-voting controversy affected his life
and career, in what he describes as a scenario from a bad
Hollywood script. In this highly accessible book, Rubin offers readers a look at the weaknesses of electronic voting
systems and the need for paper records." Booklist
    Includes bibliographical references

Walters, Ronald W.
    Freedom is not enough; black voters, black can-
didates, and American presidential politics. Rowman
& Littlefield 2005 239p $27.95; pa $24.95   **324.6**
    1. African Americans -- Suffrage   2. Presidents --
United States -- Election
    ISBN 0-7425-3837-0; 978-0-74253-837-5; 978-0-
7425-4806-0 pa; 0-7425-4806-6 pa
                       LC 2005-8343
    The book "examines the impact of the black vote on
presidential elections . . . [and] offers useful background
information on black voting habits and how the black vote
is both obtained and obstructed, with an emphasis on voter
turnout rather than the issues blacks should base their votes
upon." Libr J
    Includes bibliographical references

324.7   Conduct of election campaigns

Greenberg, Stanley B.
    Dispatches from the war room; in the trench-
es with five extraordinary leaders. Thomas Dunne
Books/St. Martin's Press 2009 501p il $29.95 **324.7**
    1. Biography, Individual   2. Cabinet members   3.
College teachers   4. Diplomats   5. Generals   6.
Governors   7. Human rights activists   8. Leadership
9. Members of Parliament   10. Military officials   11.
Nobel laureates for peace   12. Political consultants   13.
Political leaders   14. Political leadership   15. Political

prisoners   16. Political scientists   17. Presidents   18.
Prime ministers   19. World politics   20. World politics
-- 1989-
    ISBN 978-0-312-35152-6; 0-312-35152-6
                       LC 2008-29884
    "While there is plenty of talk about focus groups and
polling numbers, Greenberg doesn't get bogged down in
jargon, and the strength of the book lies in his insider perspective on the leaders who helped shape this century."
Publ Wkly
    Includes bibliographical references

Harding, James
    Alpha dogs; the Americans who turned political
spin into a global business. Farrar, Straus, and Giroux
2008 252p $25; pa $15   **324.7**
    1. Globalization   2. Political campaigns -- United States
-- History   3. Political consultants   4. Politics   5. Public
relations   6. Public relations and politics
    ISBN 978-0-374-10367-5; 0-374-10367-4; 978-0-374-
53175-1 pa; 0-374-53175-7 pa
                       LC 2007-47953
    "Harding draws on over 200 interviews to reconstruct
the behind-the-scenes history of the Sawyer Miller Group's
meteoric rise to power and influence, offering an intimate
look at the firm's involvement in global politics. . . . This
fascinating book vividly renders political history with clear
insight and rich detail." Publ Wkly
    Includes bibliographical references

324.9   History and geographic treatment of elections

Dershowitz, Alan M.
    Supreme injustice; how the high court hijacked
election 2000. Oxford Univ. Press 2001 275p il
hardcover o.p. pa $14.95   **324.9**
    1. Baseball executives   2. Children of presidents   3.
Conservationists   4. Contested elections -- Florida   5.
Contested elections -- United States   6. Elections   7.
Energy industry executives   8. Governors   9. Members
of Congress   10. Nobel laureates for peace   11.
Presidential candidates   12. Presidents   13. Presidents
-- United States -- Election -- 2000   14. Senators   15.
Vice-presidents
    ISBN 0-19-514827-4; 0-19-515807-5 pa
                       LC 2001-32193
    "This well-reasoned and controversial book asks central
questions about American democracy and the role of citizens
and courts in our society." Libr J
    Includes bibliographical references

Karabell, Zachary
    The **last** campaign; how Harry Truman won the
1948 election. Knopf 2000 308p hardcover o.p. pa
$14   **324.9**
    1. District attorneys   2. Governors   3. Presidential
candidates   4. Presidents   5. Presidents -- United States
-- Election -- 1948   6. Senators   7. Vice-presidents
    ISBN 0-375-70077-3 pa
                       LC 99-28567

This is an account of the presidential campaign which pitted Truman against Dewey.

"The author is strongest discussing the impact of the press, polls, and radio and describing the importance of the convention, which was then 'a mix of high politics, low politics and entertainment.'" Libr J

Includes bibliographical references

Morris, Roy

Fraud of the century; Rutherford B. Hayes, Samuel Tilden, and the stolen election of 1876. {by} Roy Morris, Jr. Simon & Schuster 2003 311p il hardcover o.p. pa $14 **324.9**

1. Contested elections -- United States -- History -- 19th century 2. Elections -- Corrupt practices -- United States -- History -- 19th century 3. Generals 4. Governors 5. Lawyers 6. Political corruption 7. Political corruption -- United States -- History -- 19th century 8. Political leaders 9. Presidential candidates 10. Presidents 11. Presidents -- United States -- Election 12. Presidents -- United States -- Election -- 1876

ISBN 0-7432-2386-1; 978-0-7432-5552-3; 0-7432-5552-6 pa

LC 2002-36507

"Morris has an eye for detail and a lively writing style that make this highly detailed, first-rate work of history read more like a whodunnit than a historical examination." Libr J

Includes bibliographical references

325 International migration and colonization

Cannato, Vincent J.

American passage; the history of Ellis Island. [by] Vincent J. Cannato. Harper 2009 487p il $27.99 **325**

1. Immigrants -- United States 2. Immigrants -- United States -- History

ISBN 978-0-06-074273-7; 0-06-074273-9

LC 2008-52245

"The author reaches back to the island's beginnings in the early 19th century, when, then named Gibbet Island, it served as a venue for hanging convicted pirates. Cannato then chronicles the many different people—immigrants, immigration officials, politicians and others—who made Ellis Island what it was in the early 20th century. . . . Ambitious in scope and rooted in solid storytelling." Kirkus

Includes bibliographical references

Daniels, Roger

Coming to America; a history of immigration and ethnicity in American life. 2nd ed; Perennial 2002 515p il map pa $17.95 **325**

1. Ethnology -- United States -- History 2. Minorities 3. Minorities -- United States -- History

ISBN 0-06-050577-X

LC 2002-72436

"After discussing the topic of immigration in general and sociological theories of why people migrate between countries, Daniel discusses each racial or national group that

came to the United States during the various eras of the nation's history." SLJ {review of 1990 edition}

Includes bibliographical references

Handlin, Oscar

The **uprooted**; 2nd ed; Little, Brown 1973 333p hardcover o.p. pa $18.99 **325**

1. Acculturation

ISBN 0-316-34313-7 pa

This account of the American immigrant experience and the acculturation process describes employment, religion, ghetto life, benevolent societies, boss politics, family life, and social alienation.

Yans-McLaughlin, Virginia

Ellis Island and the peopling of America; the official guide. [by] Virginia Yans-McLaughlin and Marjorie Lightman, with the Statue of Liberty-Ellis Island Foundation. New Press (NY) 1997 209p il maps pa $19.95 **325**

ISBN 1-56584-364-9

LC 96-54713

Photographs, time lines, charts and historical documents from the Ellis Island Museum accompany a text that places immigration policy in its historical context.

326 Slavery and emancipation

Berlin, Ira

Generations of captivity; a history of African-American slaves. Belknap Press 2003 374p maps $29.95; pa $16.95 **326**

1. Slavery -- United States 2. Slavery -- United States -- History 3. Slaves -- United States -- History

ISBN 0-674-01061-2; 0-674-01624-6 pa

LC 2002-28142

"Berlin has given us a moving, insightful account of slavery in the United States. Readers will not soon forget the story he has told, nor should they." N Y Times Book Rev

Includes bibliographical references and index

Blight, David W.

A **slave** no more; two men who escaped to freedom: including their own narratives of emancipation. Harcourt 2007 307p il map **326**

1. African Americans -- Biography 2. Biography, Individual 3. Diarists 4. Freedmen 5. Slavery -- United States 6. Slaves

ISBN 978-0-15-101232-9; 0-15-101232-6

LC 2007-14467

"Required reading for scholars or even casual students, this signal [sic] contribution is essential for any collection on slavery, emancipation, or African American or U.S. history and literature." Libr J

Includes bibliographical references

DeWolf, Thomas Norman

Inheriting the trade; a Northern family confronts its legacy as the largest slave-trading dynasty in U.S. history. Beacon Press 2008 262p $24.95; pa $16   326

1. Biography, Individual 2. County government officials 3. Local government officials 4. Slave trade 5. Slave trade -- Cuba -- History 6. Slave trade -- New England -- History 7. Slave trade -- West Africa -- History 8. Slave traders 9. Slavery -- United States
ISBN 978-0-8070-7281-3; 0-8070-7281-8; 978-0-8070-7282-0 pa; 0-8070-7282-6 pa

LC 2007-19708
"A companion book to the PBS documentary POV: Traces of the Trade, this is the memoir of the DeWolfe family's learning and acknowledgement of their legacy in the African slave trade of American history. The family retraces the slave trade journey from the North, through Africa and the Caribbean, to the South. This story chronicles their journey, how they dealt with the shame of the family's past, and how slavery in the United States has contributed to racism in the world today." Univ Press Books for Public and Second Sch Libr, 2009
Includes bibliographical references

Douglass, Frederick
★ **Frederick** Douglass: selected speeches and writings; edited by Philip S. Foner; abridged and adapted by Yuval Taylor. Hill Bks. 1999 789p hardcover o.p. pa $32.95   326

1. African Americans -- Civil rights -- History -- 19th century 2. Antislavery movements -- United States -- History -- 19th century 3. Slaves -- United States -- Social conditions -- 19th century 4. Speeches, addresses, etc., American
ISBN 1-55652-352-1 pa

LC 99-23180
Based on Foner's five-volume The life and writings of Frederick Douglass (1950-1975), this volume "covers Douglass' speeches and writings over a 54-year period. The breadth and depth of his focus and concerns reflected in more than 2,000 speeches, editorials, articles, and letters provide a wellspring of knowledge about the man and his intellect." Booklist
Includes bibliographical references

Gallay, Alan
The **Indian** slave trade; the rise of the English empire in the American South, 1670-1717. Yale Univ. Press 2002 444p maps $35; pa $18   326

1. Indian slaves -- Southern States -- History -- 17th century 2. Indians of North America -- Southern States -- Social conditions 3. Indians, Treatment of 4. Indians, Treatment of -- Southern States -- History -- 17th century 5. Native Americans -- Southern States 6. Slave trade 7. Slave trade -- Great Britain -- History -- 17th century 8. Slave trade -- Southern States 9. Slave trade -- Southern States -- History -- 17th century
ISBN 0-300-08754-3; 0-300-10193-7 pa

LC 2001-5270
"Powerfully argued and densely detailed. . . . Gallay's stunning and engrossing work, aimed especially at advanced students and scholars, seems to spur a renewed debate on the origins and meaning of racial slavery." Choice
Includes bibliographical references and index

Hochschild, Adam
★ **Bury** the chains; prophets, slaves, and rebels in the first human rights crusade. Houghton Mifflin 2005 468p il $26.95   326

1. Antislavery movements -- Great Britain -- History -- 18th century 2. Antislavery movements -- Great Britain -- History -- 19th century 3. Slavery
ISBN 0-618-10469-0

LC 2004-54091
The author "brings drama and incredible research to this thrilling look at the little-celebrated abolition movement in Britain and its reverberations throughout modern democracies." Booklist
Includes bibliographical references

Horton, James Oliver
★ **Slavery** and the making of America; [by] James Oliver Horton [and] Lois E. Horton. Oxford University Press 2004 254p il maps $35; pa $18.95   326

1. African Americans -- History 2. African Americans -- History -- To 1863 3. Slavery -- History 4. Slavery -- United States
ISBN 0-19-517903-X; 0-19-530451-9 pa

LC 2004-13617
"The oft-told tale is made fresh through up-to-date slavery scholarship, the extensive use of slave narratives and archival photos and, especially, a focus on individual experience." Publ Wkly

Johnson, Charles Richard
Africans in America: America's journey through slavery; {by} Charles Johnson, Patricia Smith, WGBH series Research Team. Harcourt Brace & Co. 1998 494p il $30; pa $15   326

1. African Americans -- History 2. Slavery -- United States
ISBN 0-15-100339-4; 0-15-600854-8 pa

LC 98-20829
"This is an impressively researched book . . . that includes photographs, drawings, and posters." Booklist
Includes bibliographical references

Johnson, Walter
Soul by soul; life inside the antebellum slave market. Harvard Univ. Press 1999 283p il $28.50; pa $15.95   326

1. Slave records -- Louisiana -- New Orleans 2. Slave trade 3. Slavery -- Louisiana -- New Orleans -- History -- 19th century 4. Slavery -- United States
ISBN 0-674-82148-3; 0-674-00539-2 pa

LC 99-46696
This is an examination of the antebellum slave market. "Using slave narratives, court records, planters' letters, and more, Johnson enters the slave pens and showrooms of the New Orleans slave market to observe how slavery turned men and women into merchandise and how slaves resisted such efforts to steal their humanity." Libr J
Includes bibliographical references and index

Jordan, Don

White cargo; the forgotten history of Britain's white slaves in America. [by] Don Jordan and Michael Walsh. New York University Press 2008 320p il map hardcover o.p. pa $20   **326**
1. Contract labor 2. Indentured servants -- United States -- History 3. Slavery -- History 4. Slavery -- United States -- History -- 17th century 5. Slavery -- United States -- History -- 18th century 6. Whites -- United States -- History
ISBN 978-0-8147-4272-3; 0-8147-4296-3; 978-0-8147-4296-9 pa; 0-8147-4296-3 pa
LC 2007-37976
This "is a colorful series of portraits of villains and victims, exploiters and exploited, rendered with bemused outrage." Choice
Includes bibliographical references

Schneider, Dorothy

Slavery in America; [by] Dorothy Schneider and Carl J. Schneider. Rev ed; Facts on File 2007 554p il map $80; pa $21.95   **326**
1. Slavery -- Law and legislation 2. Slavery -- United States 3. Slaves -- Biography
ISBN 0-8160-6241-2; 978-0-8160-6241-6; 0-8160-6839-9 pa; 978-0-8160-6839-5 pa
LC 2006-24798
This book recounts the history of slavery, "as well as the Reconstruction period that followed, by examining, chapter by chapter, many of its aspects: the slave catchers and their coffles in Africa, the crowded slave ships, slave auctions, life and labor on plantations, escape attempts and insurrections, and the Civil War and eventual emancipation." Publisher's note
Includes bibliographical references

White, Shane

★ The sounds of slavery; discovering African American history through songs, sermons, and speech. [by] Shane White and Graham White. Beacon Press 2005 xxii, 241p hardcover o.p. pa $17   **326**
1. African Americans -- History 2. African Americans -- Songs and music 3. Oral communication -- History 4. Plantation life 5. Plantation life -- Southern States 6. Slavery -- History 7. Slavery -- Social aspects 8. Slavery -- United States
ISBN 0-8070-5026-1; 0-8070-5027-X pa
LC 2004-21447
"Drawing on WPA interviews with former slaves, slave narratives, and other historical documents from the 1700s through the 1850s, the authors provide the context for the field calls, work songs, sermons, and other sounds and utterances of slaves on American plantations. The authors also focus on recollections of the wails of slaves being whipped, the barking of hounds hunting down runaways, and the keening of women losing their children to the slave block. The combination of the CD and the book brings vibrancy and texture to a complex history that has been long neglected." Booklist
Includes discography and bibliographical references

Wills, Garry

'Negro president' Jefferson and the slave power. Houghton Mifflin 2003 274p il $25; pa $14   **326**
1. Architects 2. Essayists 3. Presidents 4. Slavery -- United States 5. Vice-presidents
ISBN 0-618-34398-9; 0-618-48537-6 pa
LC 2003-56710
"Wills makes a valuable contribution to our understanding of Jefferson and the new American nation." Choice
Includes bibliographical references

Winch, Julie

A gentleman of color: the life of James Forten. Oxford Univ. Press 2002 501p il hardcover o.p. pa $18.95   **326**
1. Abolitionists 2. African American abolitionists 3. African American businesspeople -- History 4. African American businesspeople -- Pennsylvania -- Philadelphia 5. African American soldiers 6. African American soldiers -- History 7. African Americans 8. African Americans -- Biography 9. African Americans -- Pennsylvania -- History 10. Free African Americans -- History 11. Free African Americans -- Pennsylvania -- Philadelphia 12. Philanthropists 13. Sailmakers 14. Sailmakers -- Pennsylvania -- Philadelphia
ISBN 0-19-508691-0; 0-19-516340-0 pa
LC 2001-36215
The author "has done a masterful job of researching and piecing together Forten's life. . . . But the strength of the book—aside from rediscovering Forten—is the careful and often surprising research into the complexity of African-American life in the 18th and early 19th centuries." Publ Wkly
Includes bibliographical references

Encyclopedia of slave resistance and rebellion; edited by Junius P. Rodriguez. Greenwood Press 2006 2v il set $199.95   **326**
1. African Americans -- History 2. Reference books 3. Slavery -- History 4. Slavery -- United States 5. Slavery -- United States -- Encyclopedias
ISBN 0-313-33271-1; 978-0-313-33271-5
LC 2006-31210
This encyclopedia "focuses solely on the history of resistance in slave societies, most notably in the Americas. The 20-page introduction provides a solid examination of the history of resistance to slavery and begins to examine some of the cultural issues that both maintained slavery and downplayed resistance. . . . The text will serve as a good accompaniment to reference materials on slavery, so that readers understand that with slavery went resistance." Booklist
Includes bibliographical references

Remembering slavery; African Americans talk about their personal experiences of slavery and emancipation. edited by Ira Berlin, Marc Favreau, and Steven F. Miller. New Press (NY) 1998 355p hardcover o.p. pa $16.95   **326**
1. African Americans -- History -- Sources 2. Slavery -- United States
ISBN 1-56584-587-0 pa

This "book-and-tapes collection of slave narratives, drawn from slave narratives and audio recordings of former slaves collected by the Federal Writers' Project (FWP) during the 1930s and 1940s (some of which have been remastered and included in two 60-minute cassettes with the book), brings slavery to life as few recent books have done." Libr J

Includes bibliographical references

327 International relations

Bobbitt, Philip

The **shield** of Achilles; war, peace, and the course of history. Knopf 2002 xxxii, 919p $40; pa $19.95 **327**

1. International relations 2. National state 3. Peace 4. State, The 5. War
ISBN 0-375-41292-1; 0-385-72138-2 pa

LC 2001-38085

"This work will be a valuable and intriguing look at where we have been and where we might be going." Booklist
Includes bibliographical references

Brands, H. W.

What America owes the world; the struggle for the soul of foreign policy. Cambridge Univ. Press 1998 335p $65; pa $23 **327**

ISBN 0-521-63031-2; 0-521-63968-9 pa

LC 97-38837

"With the end of the Cold War, a long time debate has been resumed between two schools of thought, the exemplarists and the vindicators. The former . . . contends that the US owes the world the example of a humane democratic and prosperous society. The vindicators go beyond example and, through active measures, coercion, and force, support what is right in the world. The literature offers examples of the two schools analyzed in Brands's intellectual history. . . . This is a valuable contribution to the intellectual history of American foreign policy." Choice
Includes bibliographical references and index

Burk, Kathleen

Old world, new world; Great Britain and America from the beginning. Atlantic Monthly Press 2008 830p il map $35 **327**

ISBN 978-0-87113-971-9

This is "the most reliable, lucidly narrated and generous history of the mutual entanglement of Britain and America we are likely to have for some time." Times Lit Suppl
Includes bibliographical references

Cohen, Stephen F.

Failed crusade; America and the tragedy of post-Communist Russia. Norton 2000 304p hardcover o.p. pa $14.95 **327**

ISBN 0-393-32226-2 pa

LC 00-35501

"In part 1, Cohen describes the arrogant missionary crusade to impose U.S. political and economic institutions on the former Soviet Union. . . . Part 2 gathers 10 Cohen cri-

tiques of this American crusade published between 1992 and 1998. . . . In part 3, Cohen urges that the goal of U.S. policy should be to reduce the risk of nuclear disaster by stabilizing this giant nuclear power." Booklist
Includes bibliographical references

Dreyfuss, Robert

Devil's game; how the United States helped unleash fundamentalist Islam. 1st ed.; Metropolitan Books 2005 388p $27.50 **327**

1. Islamic fundamentalism
ISBN 0-8050-7652-2

LC 2005-43881

This "is a stunning summary of missed opportunities and signals ignored." Libr J
Includes bibliographical references

Feingold, Russ

While America sleeps; Russ Feingold. Crown Publishers 2011 viii, 304 p col. ill., maps **327**

1. Political culture -- United States -- History -- 21st century 2. Progressivism (United States politics) -- History -- 21st century 3. September 11 Terrorist Attacks, 2001 -- Influence 4. Terrorism -- Government policy -- United States -- History -- 21st century
ISBN 9780307952523; 9780307952547

LC 2011051735

In this book, former U.S. Senator Russ "Feingold revisits the U.S. reaction in the wake of the [September 2001 terrorist] attacks, which set off an 'unfortunate trend' in soured international relations that is only presently being arrested under President Obama. While Feingold graciously allows former President Bush accolades for his initial words of resolve and restraint after 9/11, he grew increasingly alarmed by the hysterical fear gripping Washington, and cast the lone vote against the Patriot Act. . . . In the post-9/11 Risk game, as he calls it, Feingold urged the government not to lose sight of other important strategic spots like Yemen, Indonesia and Somalia. . . . [H]e first urged the troop withdrawal from Iraq in 2005. . . . He has been a vocal proponent for 'restoring the rule of law' to the presidency and of Obama's health-care legislation." (Kirkus)

Gaddis, John Lewis, 1941-

George F. Kennan; An American Life. John Lewis Gaddis. Penguin Press 2011 xi, 784p.p 16 p. of plates **327**

1. Ambassadors -- United States -- Biography 2. Authors 3. Biographies 4. Biography, Individual 5. Centenarians 6. Cold War -- Diplomatic history 7. Containment (Political science) 8. Diplomats 9. Diplomats -- United States -- Biography 10. Historians 11. Kennan, George F. (George Frost), 1904-2005 12. Marshall Plan 13. Nonfiction writers 14. World Politics -- 1945-1989
ISBN 1594203121; 9781594203121

LC 2011021786

The book presents a biography of U.S. statesman George F. Kennan, which the author composed using "Kennan's . . . diary . . . the 300-plus boxes of other papers by Kennan now open for research at Princeton . . . interviews with the former diplomat and his associates . . . [and] family papers still in the possession of Kennan's daughter." The author "sides largely with Kennan's critics, such as former secretary of state Dean Acheson, in the heated debate over Kennan's advocacy in 1957-1958 for US 'disengagement' from the cold war in Europe." Other topics include Kennan's "response to the Vietnam War . . . [his] struggle[s] to control his emotions" and his marriage. (New York Review of Books)

Gates, Robert M.

From the shadows; the ultimate insider's story of five presidents and how they won the Cold War. Simon & Schuster 1996 604p il hardcover o.p. pa $16 **327**

1. Cold War 2. Cold war
ISBN 0-684-83497-9 pa

LC 95-51704

This is an "often entertaining, frequently self-serving but always thoughtful account of the United States' long effort to contain the Soviet Union." N Y Times Book Rev

Includes bibliographical references

Gelb, Leslie H.

Power rules; how common sense can rescue American foreign policy. Harper 2009 334p **327**

1. International relations 2. National security -- United States 3. Power (Social sciences) 4. Power (Social sciences) -- United States
ISBN 0-06-171454-2; 978-0-06-171454-2

LC 2008-51977

According to Leslie Gelb, "Washington risks losing the essential lifeblood of its national security—its power—unless American leaders relearn the lessons of how to use that power. . . . [The author argues that] America's future power must be based on the principle of mutual indispensability: Washington is the indispensable leader because it alone can galvanize coalitions to solve major international problems (and all nations know this), while other key nations are indispensable partners in getting the job done. The reality is this: succeed together or fail apart." (Publisher's note) Index.

This book "is filled with gritty, shrewd, specific advice on foreign policy ends and means. . . . Gelb's ruminations are welcome and stimulating." N Y Times Book Rev

Includes bibliographical references

Gerges, Fawaz

Obama and the Middle East; the end of America's moment? Fawaz Gerges. Palgrave Macmillan 2011 292 p. **327**

1. Political science -- General 2. Political science -- International Relations -- Diplomacy 3. Political science -- International Relations -- General
ISBN 0230113818; 9780230113817

LC 2011019900

This book by Fawaz A. Gerges provides an assessment of Obama's current foreign policy . . . The 2011 Arab Spring upended the status quo in the Middle East and poses new challenges for the United States. . . . Gerges . . . reaches back to the post-World War II era to explain the issues that have challenged the Obama administration and examines the president's responses, from his negotiations with Israel and Palestine to his drawdown from Afghanistan and withdrawal from Iraq. Evaluating the president's engagement with the Arab Spring, his decision to order the death of Osama bin Laden, his intervention in Libya, his relations with Iran, and other key policy matters. . . . Gerges' conclusion is [that] the United States is near the end of its moment in the Middle East. The cynically realist policy it has employed since World War II--continued by the Obama administration--is at the root of current bitterness and mistrust. (Publishers note)

Gutman, Roy

How we missed the story; Osama bin Laden, the Taliban, and the hijacking of Afghanistan. United States Institute of Peace 2008 321p map $26 **327**

1. September 11 terrorist attacks, 2001 2. Terrorism 3. Terrorism -- Government policy -- United States 4. Terrorists
ISBN 978-1-60127-024-5; 1-60127-024-0

LC 2007-32944

This "is a powerfully well-researched work that will have lasting value. It is unique in providing as detailed an analysis of the politics and personalities in Afghanistan (and Pakistan) as it does for those in Washington, DC and merging the two into a single stream. Specialists on either of these two foreign cultures will find much to learn from his interviews and new documentation. More general readers will be attracted by [Gutman's] clear exposition of a very complex situation, one that is populated by larger than life personalities." Middle East J

Includes bibliographical references

Halberstam, David

War in a time of peace; Bush, Clinton, and the generals. Scribner 2001 543p $28; pa $16 **327**

1. Diplomats 2. Governors 3. Intervention (International law) 4. Members of Congress 5. Parents of presidents 6. Presidents 7. United Nations officials 8. Vice-presidents 9. Vietnamese Conflict, 1961-1975 -- Influence
ISBN 0-7432-0212-0; 0-7432-2323-3 pa

LC 2001-38416

"This is vintage Halberstam, combining sharp portraits of the political players . . . with nuanced reportage of the events they shape and are shaped by." Publ Wkly

Includes bibliographical references

Hart, Gary

The **fourth** power; a grand strategy for the United States in the 21st Century. Oxford University Press 2004 187p $22 **327**

1. International security 2. Military policy -- United States 3. National security 4. National security -- United States 5. United States -- Foreign relations -- 2001- 6. World politics -- 1989- 7. World politics -- 1991-
ISBN 0-19-517683-9

LC 2004-1444

The author "fears that containment of communism has been supplanted by a blatant strategy of empire as the basis of American foreign policy. . . . As an alternative, Hart promotes a foreign policy designed to advance the 'fourth power'—that is, the power of core American values, including representative government and individual liberty. . . . Hart states his case with eloquence and generally sound reasoning, and his assertions deserve to be seriously considered." Booklist

Hastedt, Glenn P.

★ **Encyclopedia** of American foreign policy; by Glenn Hastedt. Facts on File　2003　562p　il map $85　　　　**327**

1. Reference books

ISBN 0-8160-4642-5

LC 2003-49186

In this reference, Hastedt "addresses the four major foreign policy themes: selection of a grand strategy, the role of the public voice, the policymaking process, and the influence of the past. The more than 475 entries, all by Hastedt, are arranged alphabetically and include people, agencies, documents, and events rather than broader issues and ideological constructs of US foreign policy. Entries are quite readable and rarely run longer than a page; most are also cross-referenced and have bibliographies." Choice

Includes bibliographical references

Herring, George C., 1936-

From colony to superpower; U.S. foreign relations since 1776. Oxford University Press　2008　1035p　il map　$35　　　　**327**

ISBN 978-0-19-507822-0; 0-19-507822-5

LC 2008-07996

The author "recaptures a quarter-millennium of American foreign policy with fluidity and felicity." N Y Times Book Rev

Includes bibliographical references (p. 965-995)

Hirsh, Michael

At war with ourselves; why America is squandering its chance to build a better world. Oxford University Press　2003　288p　hardcover o.p.　pa $15.95 **327**

1. American national characteristics 2. Globalization 3. Globalization -- Political aspects

ISBN 0-19-515269-7; 0-19-517602-2　pa

LC 2002-193013

"Hirsh outlines a sensible basis for détente between the warring hegemonists and internationalists, an America that leads without bullying." N Y Times Book Rev

Includes bibliographical references

Jacques, Martin

When China rules the world; the end of the western world and the birth of a new global order. Penguin Press　2009　xxv, 550p　il map　$29.95　　　**327**

1. Forecasting 2. Globalization

ISBN 978-1-59420-185-1; 1-59420-185-4

LC 2009-27298

This "comprehensive and richly detailed analysis will be an indispensable resource for anyone who wants to understand contemporary China." New Statesman

Includes bibliographical references

Kagan, Robert

★ **Dangerous** nation. Knopf　2006　527p $30　　　　**327**

ISBN 0-375-41105-4

LC 2006-45264

This "is a first-rate work of history, based on prodigious reading and enlivened by a powerful prose style." Economist

Includes bibliographical references

Kaplan, Robert D.

Monsoon; the Indian Ocean and the future of American power. Random House　2010　366p　map $28　　　　**327**

1. National security -- Indian Ocean region 2. National security -- United States

ISBN 978-1-4000-6746-6; 1-4000-6746-4

LC 2009-49752

"The book's political and economic focus and forecasts are smart and brim with aperçus on the intersection of power, politics, and resource consumption (especially water), and give full weight to the impact of colonialism. An ambitious and prescient study equally at ease analyzing the work of the Indian poet Rabindranath Tagore, the finer points of the Indian state of Gujarat's flirtation with fascism, and the economic impact of the Asian tsunami on Indonesia." Publ Wkly

Includes bibliographical references

Kinzer, Stephen

All the Shah's men; an American coup and the roots of Middle East terror. John Wiley & Sons　2003　258p　il map　hardcover o.p.　pa $14.95　　　**327**

1. Prime ministers

ISBN 0-471-26517-9; 0-471-67878-3　pa

LC 2003-9968

"This comprehensive . . . account of the nationalization of the Anglo-Iranian Oil Company under the leadership of Mohammad Mossadegh in 1951 . . . is a valuable and informative work." Choice

Includes bibliographical references

Kissinger, Henry

Does America need a foreign policy? towards a diplomacy for the 21st century. Simon & Schuster　2001　318p　maps　$30; pa $15　　　**327**

1. Large print books 2. United States -- Foreign relations -- Forecasting

ISBN 0-684-85567-4; 0-684-85568-2　pa

LC 2001-20564

Kissinger "surveys Europe, Latin America, Asia, Africa and the Middle East, giving the historical context, raising the issues in each region, and then searching out some ideas on what a wise American policy would do about them." Christ Sci Monit

Includes bibliographical references

LaFeber, Walter

The **clash**; a history of U.S.-Japan relations. Norton 1997 xxii, 508p il maps hardcover o.p. pa $16.95 **327**

ISBN 0-393-31837-0 pa

LC 96-48565

LaFeber presents an overview of U.S.-Japan relations from the 1850s to the present. He argues that "amid all the changes in the American-Japanese relationship, two fundamental continuities persist: . . . different conceptions of capitalism and divergent approaches to China." Booklist

Includes bibliographical references

Mann, Jim

About face; a history of America's curious relationship with China, from Nixon to Clinton. Knopf 1999 433p il $30; pa $16 **327**

1. Actors 2. College teachers 3. Diplomats 4. Governors 5. International relations specialists 6. Members of Congress 7. Nobel laureates for peace 8. Nonfiction writers 9. Parents of presidents 10. Presidential advisers 11. Presidents 12. Secretaries of state 13. Senators 14. United Nations officials 15. Vice-presidents 16. Writers on politics

ISBN 0-679-45053-X; 0-679-76861-0 pa

LC 98-6285

"Mann's descriptions of the behind-the-scenes jockeying among U.S. policy makers—the micropolitics behind the geopolitics—are so entertaining that his book will appeal to readers beyond foreign policy junkies." Publ Wkly

Includes bibliographical references

Moynihan, Daniel Patrick

On the law of nations. Harvard Univ. Press 1990 211p $37; pa $10.95 **327**

1. International law

ISBN 0-674-63575-2; 0-674-63576-0 pa

LC 90-33227

"In the seven essays in this volume, Moynihan traces U.S. attitudes toward international law from the American Revolution to the current administration, and he makes a powerful argument for a return to the conventions of international behavior set out by Woodrow Wilson and the United Nations." Libr J

Nolan, Cathal J.

The **Greenwood** encyclopedia of international relations. Greenwood Press 2002 4v maps set $475 **327**

1. International relations -- Encyclopedias 2. Reference books

ISBN 0-313-30743-1

LC 2002-19495

This alphabetically arranged set covers the history of international relations in over 6,000 entries.

This "work dwells primarily on the deeds of the great powers since the 1648 Peace of Westphalia. . . . Lively, objective writing characterizes the first-rate historical essays. . . . This work belongs in all academic and large public libraries." Libr J

Includes bibliographical references

Pillar, Paul R.

Terrorism and U.S. foreign policy. Brookings Institution Press 2001 272p $26.95 **327**

1. Terrorism 2. Terrorism -- Prevention

ISBN 0-8157-0004-0

LC 00-13070

"Pillar is most useful when he shows that the disunity within the Muslim world indicates that any successful struggle against terrorism must include all kinds of deal-making in order to play off groups and states against one another." N Y Times Book Rev

Includes bibliographical references and index

Purdy, Jedediah

Being America; liberty, commerce, and violence in an American world. Knopf 2003 337p $24; pa $14 **327**

1. International relations

ISBN 0-375-41307-3; 0-375-72755-8 pa

LC 2002-116390

The author's theme is "globalization in its social, economic and, above all, intellectual aspects, his goal is an answer to the oft-repeated question 'Why do they hate us?' In 2001 Purdy went to see for himself, traveling through the Middle East and Asia, talking to students, business executives, ethnic nationalists, religious fanatics. This is his report on the bad news." N Y Times Book Rev

Includes bibliographical references

Schoultz, Lars

That infernal little Cuban republic; the United States and the Cuban Revolution. University of North Carolina Press 2009 745p map **327**

ISBN 0-8078-3260-X; 978-0-8078-3260-8

LC 2008036714

This is a "history of US-Cuba relations since World War II." (Nation) Index.

"This is a gripping, expertly told story of one of the most complicated foreign policy relationships in the western hemisphere." Publ Wkly

Includes bibliographical references

Talbott, Strobe

The **Russia** hand; a memoir of presidential diplomacy. Random House 2002 478p il $29.95; pa $15.95 **327**

1. Diplomats 2. Diplomats -- United States -- Biography 3. Government officials 4. Governors 5. Journalists 6. Nonfiction writers 7. Political consultants -- United States -- Biography 8. Presidents

ISBN 0-375-50714-0; 0-8129-6846-8 pa

LC 2001-48843

Talbott writes of his experiences as "President Bill Clinton's top adviser and operative for relations with the former Soviet Union. . . . 'The Russia Hand' recounts the major and minor crises over issues like the expansion of NATO, the removal of missiles from Ukraine, Western military action against the Bosnian Serbs, the . . . confrontation over Kosovo, the question of antimissile defense." N Y Times (Late N Y Ed)

Includes bibliographical references

Tuchman, Barbara Wertheim

★ **Stilwell** and the American experience in China, 1911-45; [by] Barbara W. Tuchman. Grove Press 2001 621p map pa $20   **327**
1. Generals 2. Presidents 3. Sino-Japanese Conflict, 1937-1945 4. World War, 1939-1945 -- China
ISBN 0-8021-3852-7; 978-0-8021-3852-1

LC 2001-40154

Using the career of General "Vinegar Joe" Stilwell as a vehicle, this is a history of America's relations with China from the end of the Manchu Empire to the rise of Mao Tse-tung.

Unger, Craig

House of Bush, house of Saud; the secret relationship between the world's two most powerful dynasties. Scribner 2004 356p il $26; pa $15   **327**
1. Political leaders 2. September 11 terrorist attacks, 2001
ISBN 0-7432-5337-X; 0-7432-5339-6 pa

LC 2004-274217

The author "pieces together the highly unusual and close personal and financial relationships between the Bush family and the ruling family of Saudi Arabia—and questions the implications for Bush's preparedness, or possible lack thereof, for September 11. . . . Unger also questions whether Bush grew so complacent about the Saudis that his administration ignored then White House terrorism czar Richard Clarke's repeated warnings and recommendations about the Saudis and al-Qaeda." Publ Wkly

Includes bibliographical references

Wise, David

Tiger trap; America's secret spy war with China. Houghton Mifflin Harcourt 2011 292p il $28   **327**
1. Chinese espionage 2. Intelligence service 3. Intelligence service -- China
ISBN 978-0-547-55310-8; 0-547-553102

LC 2010-42025

"For decades during the Cold War, the most captivating spy-vs.-spy battle was the one waged between Moscow and Washington. With the rise of China, a new player has entered the game. These days, it seems, not a month goes by without an intelligence case involving alleged Chinese spies stealing American industrial secrets, or reports that China tried to pay an American to join the CIA, or Chinese hackers (perhaps from the government) breaking into the Gmail accounts of U.S. officials and human rights activists. Move over U.S.S.R., China is America's espionage enemy No. 1. . . . Wise is a master of page-turning nonfiction, and from that perspective 'Tiger Trap' doesn't disappoint. His book paints a sobering, sometimes pathetic picture of American law enforcement and counterintelligence forces that appear woefully incapable of coping with the challenge from China. Some of the cases Wise details seem right out of the Keystone Kops." Washington Post

Includes bibliographical references

327.092   Biography

Notable U.S. ambassadors since 1775; a biographical dictionary. edited by Cathal J. Nolan. Greenwood Press 1997 430p $109.95   **327.092**
1. Ambassadors -- United States 2. Biography, Collective 3. Diplomats -- Biography -- Dictionaries 4. Diplomats -- Dictionaries 5. Reference books 6. United States -- Foreign relations -- Dictionaries
ISBN 0-313-29195-0

LC 96-50291

This work contains historical-biographical profiles of 58 architects of U.S. foreign policy.

"Following a preface that describes the editor's selection criteria, each entry begins with full birth and death dates and locations, education, family background, and career progression. The larger issues during diplomatic assignments are described fully, as well as the difficulties in achieving success." Booklist

327.1   Foreign policy and specific topics in international relations

Abrams, Irwin

The **Nobel** Peace Prize and the laureates; an illustrated biographical history, 1901-2001. Centennial ed; Science Hist. Publs. 2001 350p il pa $35 **327.1**
1. Biography -- Dictionaries 2. Nobel Prizes 3. Nobel Prizes -- History 4. Pacifists -- Biography 5. Peace -- Awards -- History 6. Reference books
ISBN 0-88135-388-4

LC 2001-49554

This reference work "provides a biography with bibliographic references (and a photograph) of each individual winner of the Nobel Peace Prize from its inception in 1901 through the 2001 award. . . . The introductory material and all the biographical entries are concise, well-written, meet high academic standards, and are enjoyable as well." Choice

Includes bibliographical references

Emmott, Bill

Rivals; how the power struggle between China, India and Japan will shape our next decade. Harcourt 2008 342p il map $26; pa $15.95   **327.1**
1. Balance of power 2. International relations
ISBN 978-0-15-101503-0; 0-15-101503-1; 978-0-15-603362-6 pa; 0-15-603362-3 pa

LC 2007-52804

"Former Economist editor Emmott discusses foreign relations among China, India, and Japan, as seen through the lens of economics. . . . Examining each country in turn, Emmott reviews reforms that have spurred the torrid economic pace or, in Japan's case, overcome depression in the 1990s. The strains created by phenomenal growth, both internationally in competition for raw materials and domestically in politics, bear on the author's main concern: the possibility of war between these nations. . . . Factoring in the influence of the U.S. and ultimately proposing nine policies to help ensure peace, Emmott displays an informative grip and strategic fluency benefiting those tracking trends in Asian economics and politics." Booklist

Includes bibliographical references

Rhodes, Richard

The **twilight** of the bombs; recent challenges, new dangers, and the prospects for a world without nuclear weapons. Alfred A. Knopf 2010 366p il $27.95 **327.1**

1. Arms control 2. Arms race 3. Nuclear disarmament 4. Nuclear nonproliferation 5. Nuclear weapons
ISBN 978-0-307-26754-2; 0-307-26754-7

LC 2010-03901

"Rhodes documents events from the end of the Cold War to 2003 that, he believes, point toward the feasibility of eradicating nuclear weapons. He chronicles the underpublicized drama of the era: the efforts to contain the spread of nuclear weapons after the Soviet Union's collapse, the nuclear disarmament of South Africa, the fallout from India's and Pakistan's nuclear tests, and the negotiations with North Korea over its nuclear ambitions. In Rhodes's telling, big personalities clash and cooperate, jokes and epiphanies punctuate the debate, and offbeat details energize the narrative." Washington Post

Includes bibliographical references

Schlesinger, Arthur M. (Arthur Meier), 1917-2007

★ **War** and the American presidency; [by] Arthur M. Schlesinger, Jr. W. W. Norton 2004 160p **327.1**

1. Baseball executives 2. Children of presidents 3. Democracy -- United States 4. Energy industry executives 5. Governors 6. Iraq War, 2003 7. Iraq War, 2003- 8. Presidents 9. War and emergency powers -- United States
ISBN 0393060020; 0393327698

LC 200409872

This book "explores the war in Iraq, the presidency, and the future of democracy." (Publisher's note) Index.

"This intelligent collection of essays, sketching historical congruities (most conspicuously between the Bush administration and Nixon's original 'imperial presidency') as well as incongruities, includes a compelling discussion of the challenges inherent to history's lens." Booklist

327.12 Espionage and subversion

Andrew, Christopher M.

Defend the realm; the authorized history of MI5. [by] Christopher Andrew. Alfred A. Knopf xxii, 1032p il $40 **327.12**

1. Intelligence service -- Great Britain
ISBN 978-0-307-26363-6; 0-307-26363-0

LC 2009-25463

"This unique publication is definitive and fascinating. Definitive because, after decades of ill-informed or partial accounts this book fully defines and describes its subject; no future writer can ignore it. Fascinating because of the fluent clarity of Andrew's narrative, his eye for colourful individual detail and the sheer interest of his subjects. . . . This book

is essential reading for anyone with even the slightest interest in intelligence in the modern period." Spectator

Includes bibliographical references

Bamford, James

The **shadow** factory; the ultra-secret NSA from 9/11 to the eavesdropping on America. Doubleday 2008 395p $27.95 **327.12**

1. Electronic surveillance 2. Electronic surveillance -- United States 3. Intelligence service 4. Intelligence service -- United States
ISBN 978-0-385-52132-1; 0-385-52132-4

LC 2008-26448

The book is "full of technical details and insider politics for those who follow such things, but Bamford's overarching theme is the grand scale of the threat to privacy." San Francisco Chron

Includes bibliographical references

Dorril, Stephen

MI6; inside the covert world of Her Majesty's secret intelligence service. Free Press 2000 907p $40; pa $22 **327.12**

1. Intelligence service -- Great Britain 2. Intelligence service -- Great Britain -- History -- 20th century
ISBN 0-7432-0379-8; 0-7432-1778-0 pa

LC 00-29385

This study of the British secret intelligence service "focuses on the years since World War II, when MI6 was dedicated to winning the cold war. . . . The book is invaluable for readers who want to separate spy fact from spy fiction." Booklist

Garton Ash, Timothy

The **file**; a personal history. Random House 1997 262p hardcover o.p. pa $14 **327.12**

1. Authors 2. Essayists 3. Historians 4. Intelligence service -- Germany (East) 5. Nonfiction writers 6. Secret service -- Germany (East)
ISBN 0-679-77785-7 pa

"The author went to Berlin to study in 1978 and soon came under the scrutiny of the Stasi, the notorious East German secret police. In 1993, Garton Ash had the opportunity to examine the secret file kept on him. Comparing the file reports with his private diary of the time, he finds distortions, fabrications, and surprising omissions in the file. . . . This work makes an important contribution to the literature of the new Europe." Libr J

Grose, Peter

Operation Rollback; America's secret war behind the Iron Curtain. Houghton Mifflin 2000 256p il map $25; pa $15 **327.12**

1. Authors 2. Centenarians 3. Cold War 4. Cold war 5. Communist countries -- Foreign relations -- United States 6. Diplomats 7. Historians 8. Nonfiction writers
ISBN 0-395-51606-4; 0-618-15458-2 pa

LC 99-89830

"Thorough, thought-provoking and entertaining, this is a work that casts considerable light on a topic that has long lingered in the shadows." Publ Wkly

Includes bibliographical references

Gup, Ted

Book of honor; covert lives and classified deaths at the CIA. Doubleday 2000 390p il hardcover o.p. pa $15   **327.12**

    1. Spies 2. Spies -- United States -- Biography

    ISBN 0-385-49541-2 pa

                              LC 99-89017

This exposé "reveals the names—and personal stories—of some three dozen CIA agents who died in the line of duty and whose identities have been kept secret—sometimes for decades. . . . Gup's sleuthing is a remarkable coup, full of high-level intrigue, cover-ups and drama." Publ Wkly

Hamrick, S. J.

Deceiving the deceivers; Kim Philby, Donald Maclean & Guy Burgess. Yale University Press 2004 297p $29.95   **327.12**

    1. Biography, Individual 2. Diplomats 3. Espionage 4. Espionage, Soviet -- Great Britain 5. Memoirists 6. Spies

    ISBN 0-300-10416-2; 978-0-300-10416-5

                           LC 2004-53695

In this "analysis of one of the most famous Cold War espionage cases, Hamrick . . . asserts that British Intelligence had identified Donald Maclean as a Soviet agent earlier than the accepted date of spring 1951. . . . {Hamilton's} subversive recasting of the Philby-Maclean-Burgess case will fascinate and challenge all those interested in Cold War history." Publ Wkly

Includes bibliographical references

Haynes, John Earl

Spies; the rise and fall of the KGB in America. [by] John Earl Haynes, Harvey Klehr, and Alexander Vassiliev; with translations by Philip Redko and Steven Shabad. Yale University Press 2009 liii, 650p il $35; pa $24   **327.12**

    1. Cold war 2. Espionage -- Soviet Union 3. Espionage, Soviet -- United States -- History 4. Russian espionage 5. Spies 6. Spies -- Soviet Union -- History 7. Spies -- United States -- History

    ISBN 978-0-300-12390-6; 0-300-12390-6; 978-0-300-16438-1 pa; 0-300-16438-6 pa

                           LC 2008-45628

This history of Soviet espionage in the United States "offers a remarkable portrait of the KGB's efforts—drawn largely from the KGB's own files. This achievement is possible only because Alexander Vassiliev, a former KGB agent, was allowed extensive access to the raw espionage files for two years in the mid-1990s. . . . Spies is chockablock with poignant individual tales." Newsweek

Includes bibliographical references

Venona; decoding Soviet espionage in America. [by] John Earl Haynes and Harvey Klehr. Yale Univ. Press 1999 487p $35; pa $14.95   **327.12**

    1. Communism -- United States 2. Communism -- United States -- History -- Sources 3. Cryptography -- United States -- History -- Sources 4. Diplomats 5. Espionage, Soviet -- United States -- History -- Sources 6. Lawyers 7. Russian espionage 8. Spies -- Soviet

Union -- History -- Sources 9. Spies -- United States -- History -- Sources

    ISBN 0-300-07771-8; 0-300-08462-5 pa

                           LC 98-51464

"The Venona Project, a U.S. secret revealed only in 1995, decrypted Soviet intelligence's wartime cable traffic. . . . The authors systematically recount Venona's references to approximately 350 Soviet spies in U.S. government and industry—some of them highly placed, most notoriously Alger Hiss. . . . Venona may open a fundamental revision of U.S. history." Booklist

Herrington, Stuart A.

Traitors among us; inside the spy catcher's world. Harcourt 2000 409p il pa $14   **327.12**

    1. Intelligence service -- United States 2. Intelligence service -- United States -- History -- 20th century 3. Russian espionage 4. Soldiers 5. Spies 6. Spies -- Communist countries -- History -- 20th century

    ISBN 0-15-601117-4

                           LC 00-38893

"Herrington, former head of the U.S. Army Counterintelligence Unit . . . offers a fascinating view of life as a spy catcher in West Berlin during the height of the Cold War. His description of the search for and capture of Clyde Conrad and James Hall . . . (who for 13 years handed over America's secret war plans to the Soviets) surpasses any spy fiction." Libr J

Laird, Thomas

Into Tibet; the CIA's first atomic spy and his secret expedition to Lhasa. Grove Press 2002 364p il $26; pa $15   **327.12**

    1. American espionage 2. Espionage, American -- China -- Tibet

    ISBN 0-8021-1714-7; 0-8021-3999-X pa

                           LC 2001-58459

The author "traces the story of two CIA agents, Douglas Mackiernan and Frank Bessac, sent on an intelligence expedition to Tibet in 1949-1950. . . . Focusing on the heart-stopping details of the expedition itself, Laird gives the now familiar story of callous CIA manipulation an absorbing twist." Publ Wkly

Includes bibliographical references

Prados, John

Presidents' secret wars; CIA and Pentagon covert operations from World War II through the Persian Gulf. rev & expanded ed; Dee, I.R. 1996 572p pa $18.95   **327.12**

    1. Intelligence service -- United States

    ISBN 1-56663-108-4

                           LC 95-49737

The author argues that presidents have too much freedom of action in covert operations, and discusses such operations with regard to the Cold War, Asia, Cuba, Vietnam, Angola, Afghanistan, Nicaragua, and the Persian Gulf

Richelson, Jeffrey

The **wizards** of Langley; inside the CIA's Directorate of Science and Technology. {by} Jeffrey T.

Richelson. Westview Press 2001 386p il hardcover
o.p. pa $17   **327.12**
    1. Intelligence service -- United States
    ISBN 0-8133-4059-4 pa
    The author "provides a richly detailed account of the
agency's work." Libr J

Smith, W. Thomas
    ★ **Encyclopedia** of the Central Intelligence
Agency; [by] W. Thomas Smith Jr. Facts on File
2003 282p il $60; pa $19.95   **327.12**
    1. Reference books
    ISBN 0-8160-4666-2; 0-8160-4667-0 pa
    This encyclopedia includes "more than 500 historical,
biographical, and general entries about the intelligence-
gathering, covert-action agency established in 1947. . . .
Current through March 2003, the encyclopedia also covers
predecessor organizations such as the World War II-era Office of Strategic Services (OSS). . . . The work covers terrorism extensively." Booklist
    Includes bibliographical references

Stafford, David
    Spies beneath Berlin. Overlook Press 2003 211p
il $24.95; pa $15.95   **327.12**
    1. Cold war 2. Espionage 3. Operation Stopwatch\
Gold, Berlin, Germany, 1955-1956
    ISBN 1-58567-361-7; 1-58567-549-0 pa
                  LC 2002-34628
    This is the "story of the secret tunnel beneath the Rus-
sian sector of Berlin that existed for more than a year in the
mid-1950s and enabled the British and Americans to tap into
all area Russian telephone conversations. But this amazing intelligence achievement was complicated by another
development: the KGB knew about the tunnel through the
traitorous activities of its undercover agent, George Blake,
but could not reveal that they knew for fear that they might
compromise the invaluable Blake. . . . What a great story!
And Stafford tells it exceedingly well in sprightly prose.
This book belongs in all collections that cover Cold War espionage." Libr J
    Includes bibliographical references and index

Taubman, Philip
    Secret empire; Eisenhower, the CIA, and the hid-
den story of America's space espionage. Simon &
Schuster 2003 xx, 441p il $27; pa $15   **327.12**
    1. Aerial reconnaissance 2. Aerial reconnaissance,
American -- History -- 20th century 3. Cold war 4.
Space surveillance -- United States -- History -- 20th
century
    ISBN 0-684-85699-9; 0-684-85700-6 pa
                  LC 2002-42937
    "This book functions marvelously as a history of sci-
ence, detailing the research, engineering and policy decisions behind the U2 and Corona, but it's also an excellent
social history of the Cold War in the 1950s and early '60s.
It's a page-turner as well." Publ Wkly
    Includes bibliographical references

Theoharis, Athan G.
    Chasing spies; how the FBI failed in counterin-
telligence but promoted the politics of McCarthyism
in the Cold War years. {by} Athan Theoharis. Dee,
I.R. 2002 307p $27.50   **327.12**
    1. Intelligence service -- United States
    ISBN 1-56663-420-2
                  LC 2001-47399
    The author "argues that Hoover's FBI was much more
interested in promoting an anti-Communist agenda, which
would enhance the credibility of the agency and its political
influence, than in countering Soviet espionage. . . . Theoharis's book is an outstanding contribution to the growing
historical literature on the Cold War and a potent warning to
anyone who thinks we have heard the last word on the Cold
War." Libr J
    Includes bibliographical references

Trulock, Notra
    Code name Kindred Spirit; inside the Chinese
nuclear espionage scandal. Encounter Bks. 2002
xxi, 385p il $26.95   **327.12**
    1. Computer scientists 2. Espionage, Chinese -- New
Mexico -- Los Alamos -- History -- 20th century 3.
Espionage, Chinese -- New Mexico -- Los Alamos
-- History -- 21st century 4. Intelligence officers 5.
Intelligence officers -- United States 6. Intercontinental
ballistic missiles -- United States 7. Nuclear weapons
-- United States 8. Spies
    ISBN 1-89355-451-1
                  LC 2002-67856
    Trulock was the head of the Department of Energy's "in-
telligence office during the investigation into whether Los
Alamos scientist Wen Ho Lee had given nuclear warhead
secrets to China. . . . This detailed account reveals that the
spy hunt didn't focus solely on Lee, or even on Los Alamos.
. . . While he denies knowledge as to whether Lee 'did it,'
the author drops hints that Lee and his wife may have been
double agents. . . . He provides a unique look into the American intelligence community and an unsettling perspective on
the lax attitude toward national security." Publ Wkly
    Includes bibliographical references

Vise, David A.
    The **bureau** and the mole; the unmasking of
Robert Philip Hanssen, the most dangerous double
agent in FBI history. Atlantic Monthly Press 2002
272p il $25; pa $14   **327.12**
    1. Espionage 2. FBI agents 3. Intelligence agents --
United States -- Biography 4. Spies 5. Spies -- Russia
(Federation) -- Biography
    ISBN 0-87113-834-4; 0-8021-3951-5 pa
                  LC 2001-53872
    "In February 2001, FBI special agent Bob Hanssen was
arrested as a double agent for Russian intelligence in what
turned out to be the biggest sellout of U.S. national security
secrets in the long history of the bureau. . . . {The author}
details how Hanssen did it and how he got caught." Booklist
    Includes bibliographical references

Weinstein, Allen

The **haunted** wood; Soviet espionage in America--the Stalin era. {by} Allen Weinstein, Alexander Vassiliev. Random House 1999 xxviii, 402p il hardcover o.p. pa $23   **327.12**

1. Russian espionage 2. Spies
ISBN 0-375-75536-5 pa

LC 98-11801

"This is a relentlessly powerful book and an eye-opener for all readers." Libr J

Includes bibliographical references

Wise, David

Cassidy's run; the secret spy war over nerve gas. Random House 2000 228p il hardcover o.p. pa $15   **327.12**

1. Disinformation -- United States 2. Espionage, American -- Soviet Union -- History 3. Intelligence service -- United States 4. Russian espionage 5. Spies
ISBN 0-8129-9263-6 pa

LC 99-15802

The "reconstruction of a hitherto unknown counterespionage case. Joseph Cassidy's double life began in August 1959. . . . For 20 years Cassidy, a master sergeant, worked for the United States during the day and pretended to work for the Soviet Union at night. . . . The F.B.I. decided to use this double agent to undermine the Soviet chemical weapons industry." N Y Times Book Rev

Spy: the inside story of how the FBI's Robert Hanssen betrayed America. Random House 2002 309p $24.95; pa $13.95   **327.12**

1. Espionage 2. FBI agents 3. Spies
ISBN 0-375-50745-0; 0-375-75894-1 pa

LC 2002-31867

"A relentless reporter and true expert on the world of spying, Wise recounts Hanssen's story and the hunt to catch him in precise, if sometimes overwhelming detail." N Y Times Book Rev

327.2   Diplomacy

Kissinger, Henry

Diplomacy. Simon & Schuster 1994 912p il maps hardcover o.p. pa $22   **327.2**

1. Actors 2. Cabinet members 3. Cold war 4. College presidents 5. Communist leaders 6. Diplomacy 7. Emperors 8. Generals 9. Governors 10. Handicapped 11. Heads of state 12. Historians 13. Members of Congress 14. Members of Parliament 15. Memoirists 16. Nazi leaders 17. Nobel laureates for literature 18. Nobel laureates for peace 19. Nonfiction writers 20. Philatelists 21. Political leaders 22. Presidents 23. Prime ministers 24. Princes 25. Senators 26. Statesmen 27. Vice-presidents 28. Vietnam War, 1961-1975 29. World War, 1914-1918 30. World War, 1939-1945 -- Children 31. World politics
ISBN 0-671-51099-1 pa

LC 93-44001

"This is an important contribution to the theoretical literature on foreign affairs and will also serve quite ably as a one-volume synthesis of modern diplomatic history. All libraries should have this impressive book." Libr J

Includes bibliographical references

328   The legislative process

Barone, Michael

★ The **almanac** of American politics 2010; the senators, the representatives and the governors: their records and election results, their states and districts. [by] Michael Barone, Richard E. Cohen. National Journal Group 2009 1726p il map $97.95; pa $79.95   **328**

1. Almanacs 2. Reference books
ISBN 978-0-89234-119-1; 978-0-89234-120-7 pa

"Provides essential data for the assessment of each representative and senator in Congress. Specifics include political background on the state or congressional district, biographies, voting records, group ratings (by such groups as Americans for Democratic Action and Americans for Constitutional Action), and recent election results. Provides information on the governor of each state. Arranged by state. Congressional district maps." Ref Sources for Small & Medium-sized Libr. 6th edition

Congressional Quarterly, Inc.

★ **CQ's** politics in America, 2010; the 111th Congress. by Congressional Quarterly staff; Chuck McCutcheon and Christina L. Lyons, editors. Congressional Quarterly, Inc. 2009 xxvi, 1214p il $125; pa $89   **328**

1. Elections -- United States 2. Reference books
ISBN 978-1-60426-602-3; 978-1-60426-603-0 pa

Provides an analysis of every lawmaker in the 111th Congress, including biographical data, contact information, election results, and committee assignments.

"An outstanding, highly detailed guide to contemporary politics." Libr J

★ **Congress** A to Z; 5th ed.; CQ Press 2008 xxxiv, 704p il map $85   **328**

1. Reference books
ISBN 978-0-87289-558-4

LC 2008-11284

This work provides information on the structure and work of Congress in some 340 alphabetical entries.

Congress and the Nation; a review of government and politics in the postwar years. Congressional Quarterly 1965   **328**

1. Legislation

"Overview and detailed coverage of presidential, legislative, and political events in every major subject area." N Y Public Libr Book of How & Where to Look It Up

★ **Guide** to Congress; 6th ed.; CQ Press 2008 2v il map set $350 **328**
ISBN 978-0-8728-9295-8
LC 2007-33245
"To really understand Congress, there is nothing better than these large volumes." Booklist
Includes bibliographical references

Hamilton, Lee H.

How Congress works and why you should care. Indiana University Press 2004 156p $29.95; pa $14.95 **328**
ISBN 0-253-34425-5; 0-253-21695-8 pa
LC 2003-17926
This "primer details the history of Congress, its importance and some of the critical actions it has taken. . . . Hamilton also describes the 'complicated and untidy' process by which Congress really works and why we 'need more people who know how to practice the art of politics.' . . . Parents should send this primer off with their kids to college." Publ Wkly
Includes bibliographical references

Kaiser, Robert Greeley

So damn much money; the triumph of lobbying and the corrosion of American government. [by] Robert G. Kaiser. Knopf 2009 398p il $27.95 **328**
1. Lobbying 2. Lobbying -- United States 3. Lobbyists 4. Political corruption 5. Political corruption -- United States
ISBN 978-0-307-26654-5; 0-307-26654-0
LC 2008-33862
"Lobbying, Kaiser writes, is a business of 'huge numbers and vague standards,' forever reorienting itself in an effort to skate just inside the limits of legality. Kaiser follows the career of Gerald S. J. Cassidy, a kid from a poor family who became a lawyer for migrant workers, an aide to George McGovern, and, latterly, a lobbyist for universities, cranberries, defense contractors, and Taiwan. Cassidy pioneered the use of earmarks, fought to save the Seawolf submarine, and took congressmen to N.C.A.A. Final Four games. . . . Kaiser's account dwells less on blatant corruption than on what is perfectly, depressingly legal." New Yorker
Includes bibliographical references

Remini, Robert Vincent

★ **Daniel** Webster; the man and his time. {by} Robert V. Remini. Norton 1997 796p il $26; pa $14 **328**
1. Biography, Individual 2. Lawyers 3. Secretaries of state 4. Statesmen
ISBN 0-393-04552-8; 0-375-72715-9 pa
LC 97-24371
This work explores the life and times of the influential politician and statesman of antebellum America.
"Remini tends to exaggerate Webster's personal peccadilloes, but it cannot be said that he underestimates his subject's importance to American political culture. For

Remini, Webster's muscular nationalism, embroidered with Lincoln's democratic eloquence, provided the foundation for a strong and enduring union." Choice
Includes bibliographical references

Robert C. Byrd Center for Legislative Studies

Congress investigates; a critical and documentary history. edited by Roger A. Bruns, David L. Hostetter, Raymond W. Smock; Robert C. Byrd Center for Legislative Studies. Rev. ed; Facts on File 2011 2v il set $195 **328**
1. Governmental investigations -- United States 2. Reference books
ISBN 978-0-8160-7679-6; 978-1-4381-3545-8 ebook
LC 2010020268
The editors "have gathered here information on congressional investigations from the Colonial period to the 21st century. The entries, written by U.S. historians and archivists, each offer an overview, chronology, documents, excerpts from congressional committee reports and testimony, and a bibliography; many also include black-and-white illustrations, photographs, or political cartoons. They cover well-known events such as the Teapot Dome scandal, the burning of Washington in 1814, the Hurricane Katrina inquiry of 2005–06, and several lesser-known happenings—General St. Clair's defeat of 1792–93 and the Pujo Committee on the 'Money Trust,' for example. . . . This well-researched and richly detailed resource provides an excellent overview of major congressional investigations and will be a quality addition to a high school, public, or undergraduate academic library." Libr J
Includes bibliographical references

Stathis, Stephen W.

Landmark debates in Congress; from the Declaration of independence to the war in Iraq. CQ Press 2009 514p il map $145 **328**
1. American speeches 2. Parliamentary practice 3. Reference books
ISBN 978-0-87289-976-6; 0-87289-976-4
LC 2008-41380
"Presenting excerpts of speeches delivered in the House of Representatives and the Senate, this volume seeks to give readers 'a window into how Congress, seemingly constituting a cross-section of society, has wrestled with some of the most thorny questions facing American democracy.' Such monumental issues as war, slavery, impeachment of the President, amendments to the Constitution, and other bones of contention illuminate the legislative process. . . . A depiction of real people struggling to solve real problems, this book helps to humanize 'the marble men'—and women—of our national legislative body." Libr J
Includes bibliographical references

Treese, Joel D.

Biographical directory of the American Congress, 1774-1996; the Continental Congress, September 5, 1774, to October 21, 1788, and the Congress of the United States, from the First through the 104th

Congress, March 4, 1789, to January 3, 1997. CQ Staff Directories 1997 2108p il $295 **328**
   1. Biography, Collective 2. Reference books
   ISBN 0-87289-124-0
   This directory provides brief biographies of members of Congress from the Continental Congress through the 104th Congress. Each entry includes date and place of birth, education and employment, some entries also give additional biographical references
   This is "an indispensable reference tool for students and scholars of U.S. history and politics. . . . It is the most comprehensive biographical source on congressional members." Am Ref Books Annu, 1998

Official Congressional directory, 2009-2010; 111th Congress convened January 6, 2009. Joint Committee on Printing, United States Congress. U.S. Government Printing Office 2009 xxiv, 1207p map $55; pa $45 **328**
   1. Reference books
   ISBN 978-0-16-083728-9; 978-0-16-083727-2 pa
   "Covers biographical information, committee assignments of members of Congress, and officers of Congress." N Y Public Libr Book of How & Where to Look It Up

328.2   Initiative and referendum

Broder, David S.
   Democracy derailed; initiative campaigns and the power of money. Harcourt 2000 260p map hardcover o.p. pa $14 **328.2**
   1. Democracy 2. Democracy -- United States 3. Referendum 4. Referendum -- United States
   ISBN 0-15-601410-6 pa
                LC 99-54190
   "The initiative process, available in half the states and hundreds of cities, allows for the placement on election ballots of legislative proposals that emanate directly from sources outside the legislative branch of government. . . . {The author explores how} lawyers, campaign consultants, signature-gathering firms, and other players sell their services to affluent interest groups or wealthy individuals who mask private policy and business agendas under the guise of political reform." Libr J
   Includes bibliographical references

330   Economics

Adler, Moshe
   Economics for the rest of us; debunking the science that makes life dismal. New Press 2009 217p il $24.95; ebook $24.95 **330**
   1. Economics 2. Income 3. Salaries, wages, etc.
   ISBN 978-1-59558-101-3; 978-1-59558-527-1 ebook
                LC 2009-24968
   "Only occasionally relying on graphs or tables, Adler provides an accessible summary of quite complex debates in economic theory." Choice
   Includes bibliographical references

Dubner, Stephen J., 1963-
   ★ **Freakonomics**; a rogue economist explores the hidden side of everything. [by] Steven D. Levitt and Stephen J. Dubner. William Morrow 2005 242p hardcover o.p. pa $15.99 **330**
   1. Economics 2. Economics -- Psychological aspects 3. Economics -- Sociological aspects
   ISBN 0-06-073132-X; 0-06-073133-8 pa
               LC 2004-65478
   The authors "evaluate intriguing questions such as 'What do Schoolteachers and Sumo Wrestlers Have in Common?' 'How is the Ku Klux Klan Like a Group of Real Estate Agents?' 'Where Have All the Criminals Gone?' and 'What Makes a Perfect Parent?' . . . This excellent, readable book will enlighten many library patrons." Booklist
   Includes bibliographical references

Ferguson, Niall
   ★ The **ascent** of money; a financial history of the world. Penguin Press 2008 441p $29.95 **330**
   1. College teachers 2. Economic history 3. Economics -- History 4. Historians 5. International finance 6. International finance -- History 7. Money 8. Money -- History
   ISBN 978-1-59420-192-9; 1-59420-192-7
   The author "presents the history of money within these contexts: the rise of money and the history of credit, and the histories of the bond market, the stock market, insurance, the real-estate market, and international finance. There is an ease to his prose that leaves this complicated subject interesting to and approachable by any general reader." Booklist
   Includes bibliographical references

Levitt, Steven D.
   Superfreakonomics; global cooling, patriotic prostitutes, and why suicide bombers should buy life insurance. [by] Steven D. Levitt & Stephen J. Dubner. William Morrow 2009 270p $29.99; pa $15.99; ebook $9.99 **330**
   1. Economics 2. Economics -- Psychological aspects 3. Economics -- Sociological aspects
   ISBN 978-0-06-088957-9; 0-06-088957-8; 978-0-06-088958-6 pa; 0-06-088958-6 pa; 978-0-06-195993-6 ebook; 0-06-195993-6 ebook
               LC 2009035852
   The authors "assert that the unifying principle in the various topics they address is people responding to incentives in ways that are not necessarily predictable or manifest. Major themes are explored using a wide range of examples, e.g., life and death issues, terrorism, altruism, medical care, crime, and the environment. . . . Levitt and Dubner succeed in applying economic analysis to timely topics with stimulation, wit, and humor. Best of all, their book will appeal to a broad segment of the population." Choice
   Includes bibliographical references

Oxford University Press
   The **Oxford** encyclopedia of economic history; Joel Mokyr, editor in chief. Oxford University Press 2003 5v set $695 **330**
   1. Economic history -- Encyclopedias 2. Reference

books
ISBN 0-19-510507-9

LC 2003-8992

This encyclopedia includes "over 900 contributions from 800 scholars to explore key concepts of economics, firms and individuals, institutions, countries, and cities. Although scholarly in tone, this volume is an excellent starting point for those wishing to trace ideas and industries across chronological boundaries." Libr J

Includes bibliographical references and index

Sowell, Thomas

Basic economics; a common sense guide to the economy. 4th ed.; Basic Books 2011 689p $39.95 **330**
1. Economics
ISBN 978-0-465-02252-6

Thomas Sowell explains the principles of economics in plain jargon for the general public, answering questions like: Why are homeless people sleeping on the sidewalks of New York in the winter, when the abandoned apartment buildings have four times as many dwelling units as there are homeless people in the city? Why did Russians have to import food to feed people in Moscow, when Russia itself had vast amounts of some of the richest farmland in Europe?

"Sowell's volume does a fantastic job in cultivating the reader's 'economic imagination.'" Choice

Taylor, Timothy

The **instant** economist; Timothy Taylor. Plume 2012 x, 260p.p ill. pa $16 **330**
1. Economics
ISBN 978-0-452-29752-4

LC 2011033416

This book provides an introduction to "[e]conomics [which] isn't just about numbers: It's about politics, psychology, history, and so much more. We are all economists-when we work, save for the future, invest, pay taxes, and buy our groceries. Yet many of us feel lost when the subject arises. . . . Timothy Taylor tackles all the key questions and hot topics of both microeconomics and macroeconomics, including: Why do budget deficits matter? What exactly does the Federal Reserve do? Does globalization take jobs away from American workers? Why is health insurance so costly?" (Publisher's note)

Wheelan, Charles J.

★ **Naked** economics; {by} Charles Wheelan; foreword by Burton G. Malkiel. Norton 2002 xxii, 260p $25.95; pa $15.95 **330**
1. Economics
ISBN 0-393-04982-5; 0-393-32486-9 pa

LC 2002-23580

This is an introduction to economics. Index.

The author explains the essentials of economics, defining "terms like GDP and inflation, explaining how they work and what the short- and long-term impact might be. . . . This is a thoughtful, well-written introduction to economics, with the author projecting a genuine excitement for his material." Libr J

Includes bibliographical references

330.1   Systems, schools, theories

Appleby, Joyce

The **relentless** revolution; a history of capitalism. [by] Joyce Appleby. W.W. Norton 2010 494p $29.95 **330.1**
1. Capitalism 2. Capitalism -- History 3. Economic conditions 4. Economic history
ISBN 978-0-393-06894-8; 0-393-06894-3

LC 2009-35676

"Whether masterfully discussing the significance of agricultural progress that made capitalism possible, or touching lightly on the impact of Amazon and e-mail, Appleby offers consistently illuminating commentary. A useful introduction to a vast, complex topic." Kirkus

Includes bibliographical references

Heilbroner, Robert L.

★ The **worldly** philosophers; the lives, times, and ideas of the great economic thinkers. Rev. 7th ed.; Simon & Schuster 1999 365p pa $16 **330.1**
1. Authors 2. Capitalism 3. Depressions 4. Economics 5. Economists 6. Imperialism 7. Journalists 8. Nonfiction writers 9. Patrons of the arts 10. Political and social philosophers 11. Social critics 12. Utopias 13. Writers on politics
ISBN 0-684-86214-X

LC 99-14050

The author traces the story of economics and the great economists from Adam Smith, Malthus, Ricardo, the Utopians, Marx, Veblen and Keynes to those working with the problems of our contemporary world.

Keynes, John Maynard

★ The **general** theory of employment, interest and money. Harcourt Brace & Co. 1936 403p hardcover o.p. pa $15 **330.1**
1. Economics 2. Interest (Economics) 3. Money
ISBN 0-15-634711-3 pa

This work "revolutionized economic theory by showing how unemployment could occur 'involuntarily.' For 30 years after the Second World War governments of western nations pursued 'Keynesian' full-employment policies." Oxford Companion to Engl Lit. 5th edition

Marx, Karl

★ **Capital**: an abridged edition; edited with an introduction and notes by David McLellan. Oxford University Press 2008 xxxii, 499p pa $16.95 **330.1**
1. Capital 2. Economics
ISBN 978-0-19-953570-5

LC 2008-274361

This abridged edition of Marx's three-volume "denunciation of mid-Victorian capitalist society . . . offers virtually all of Volume 1, which Marx himself published in 1867; excerpts from a . . . translation of 'The Result of the Immediate Process Production'; and a selection of key chapters from Volume 3, which Engels published in 1895." Publisher's note

Patel, Raj

The **value** of nothing; how to reshape market society and redefine democracy. Picador 2010 250p pa $14   **330.1**

1. Democracy 2. Economic policy 3. Free enterprise

ISBN 978-0-312-42924-9

LC 2009-41546

The author "lays bare the social, political, and environmental damage caused by free markets and the commoditization of every facet of any market society. . . . Patel debunks the myth that markets are the perfect form of social organization, effectively arguing that the tyranny they exert can and must be replaced by strategies benefiting all humanity and ensuring our very survival. This work is written calmly and sensibly enough that it could change some readers' minds, although it will leave free-market apologists spluttering. Highly recommended." Libr J

Includes bibliographical references

Sandel, Michael J.

What money can't buy; the moral limits of markets. Michael J. Sandel. Farrar Straus & Giroux 2012 244 p.   **330.1**

1. Business ethics 2. Capitalism 3. Economics -- Philosophy

ISBN 0374203032; 9780374203030

LC 2011052182

In this book author Michael J. Sandel takes on . . . the . . . ethical questions . . . Is there something wrong with a world in which everything is for sale? If so, how can we prevent market values from reaching into spheres of life where they dont belong? What are the moral limits of markets? In recent decades, market values have crowded out nonmarket norms in almost every aspect of life—medicine, education, government, law, art, sports, even family life and personal relations. Without quite realizing it, Sandel argues, we have drifted from having a market economy to being a market society. . . . What is the proper role of markets in a democratic societ— and how can we protect the moral and civic goods that markets don't honor and that money can't buy? (Publishers note)

Smith, Adam

★ The **wealth** of nations; introduction by Robert Reich; edited, with notes, marginal summary, and enlarged index by Edwin Cannan. Modern Library 2000 xxvi, 1154p pa $15.95   **330.1**

1. Economics

ISBN 0-679-78336-9; 978-0-679-78336-7

LC 00-64573

This treatise "is the first comprehensive treatment of the whole subject of political economy, and is remarkable for its breadth of view. . . . In it, the author presents an attack on the mercantile system, and an advocacy of freedom of commerce and industry." Oxford Companion to Engl Lit. 6th edition

Includes bibliographical references

330.12   Systems

McMillan, John

Reinventing the bazaar; a natural history of markets. Norton 2002 278p $25.95; pa $15.95 **330.12**

1. Capitalism 2. Capitalism -- History 3. Economic history 4. Evolutionary economics

ISBN 0-393-05021-1; 0-393-32371-4 pa

LC 2002-521

The author "examines how markets in ancient times evolved and shows how countries experimented with markets, some successfully and some not. . . . He takes a refreshingly commonsense approach to his subject, doesn't talk down to his readers, and refrains from excessive economic jargon." Libr J

Includes bibliographical references

Soto, Hernando de

The **mystery** of capital; why captitalism triumphs in the West and fails everywhere else. Basic Bks. 2000 276p il $27.50; pa $17   **330.12**

1. Capitalism

ISBN 0-465-01614-6; 0-465-01615-4 pa

LC 00-34301

The author contends that "the poor do not really 'own' the property they work, because they are not registered as owning it, and because of this, they cannot turn it into capital. . . . The market is restricted and the growth of wealth retarded. His solution is simple: give the poor title to the property they own de facto, and their countries will become capital rich." N Y Times Book Rev

330.9   Economic situation and conditions

Bartiromo, Maria

The **weekend** that changed Wall Street; an eyewitness account. [by] Maria Bartiromo, with Catherine Whitney. Portfolio Penguin 2010 232p $26.95   **330.9**

1. Bank failures 2. Global Financial Crisis, 2008-2009

ISBN 978-1-59184-351-1

LC 2010026892

"Bartiromo lays out the facts of the Lehman Brothers downfall using both her own account and those of the most powerful people on Wall Street. . . . The most fascinating aspects of . . . [this book] were not so much the details of the collapse . . . but the book's early focus on the lavish lives of those involved in the Wall Street game; Bartiromo details the parties they threw, the apartments they owned that resembled art galleries and the confidence they exuded, which came across not only in their business conversations, but also in the casual talks between the author and her trusting subjects." Risk Management

Includes bibliographical references

De Graaf, John

What's the economy for, anyway? why it's time to stop chasing growth and start pursuing happiness. [by] John de Graaf and David K. Batker; foreword by

James Gustave Speth. Bloomsbury Press 2011 292p
il $25 **330.9**

    1. Economic development 2. Happiness

    ISBN 978-1-60819-510-7; 1-60819-510-4

                     LC 2011017438

De Graaf and Batker "examine new ways to think about
economic processes, specifically as they relate to human
happiness and well-being. The authors show that the indicators of performance developed during World War II—the
'Gross National Product'—have become both obscurantist
and counterproductive. They argue that human purposes
and needs ought to provide the basis for much more broadly
based measures of performance, which would consider what
is the greatest good and benefit for the greatest number of
people over the longest period of time. . . . An entertaining
presentation of important ideas and information about how
lives could be improved." Kirkus

    Includes bibliographical references

Epping, Randy Charles

The **21st** century economy; a beginner's guide:
with 101 easy-to-learn tools for surviving and thriving in the new global marketplace. Vintage Books
2009 316p pa $14.95 **330.9**

    1. Economic conditions 2. Globalization 3.
International finance 4. International trade

    ISBN 978-0-307-38790-5

                     LC 2008-41554

This is an "explanation of the workings of our modern
economy and hundreds of terms, such as subprime debt,
CDO, IMF, money supply, and discount rate. . . . [The au-
thor] is able to explain the global economy in language that
most readers will find both understandable and interesting."
Libr J

Huffington, Arianna

Third World America; how our politicians are
abandoning the middle class and betraying the American dream. Crown Publishers 2010 276p $23.99;
ebook $9.99 **330.9**

    1. Economic policy -- United States 2. Social policy
-- United States

    ISBN 978-0-307-71982-9; 978-0-307-71997-3 ebook

                     LC 2010-26871

The author "argues that overspending on war at the
expense of domestic issues and the alarming decline of
the middle class are troubling signals that the U.S. is losing its economic, political, and social stability—a stability
that has always been maintained by the middle class. . . .
An engaging analysis of troubling economic and political
trends." Booklist

Lanchester, John

    ★ **I.O.U.** why everyone owes everyone and
no one can pay. Simon & Schuster 2010 260p
$25 **330.9**

    1. Economic conditions 2. Economic history 3.
Financial crises 4. Global Financial Crisis, 2008-2009
5. International finance

    ISBN 978-1-4391-6984-1; 1-4391-6984-5

                     LC 2009-36465

    This book is "equal parts history, economic primer, and
social commentary—that manages to be, by turns, acidic,
frightening, and sharply funny." Entertainment Wkly

    Includes bibliographical references

Lewis, Michael

The **big** short; inside the doomsday machine.
W.W. Norton 2010 266p **330.9**

    1. Financial crises 2. Financial crises -- United States
3. Global Financial Crisis, 2008-2009

    ISBN 0-393-07223-1; 0-393-33882-7 pa; 978-0-393-
07223-5; 978-0-393-33882-9 pa

                     LC 201004804

This is a study of the financial crisis that began in 2008.
Michael Lewis, the author of Liar's Poker (1989) contends
that "the roots of the meltdown of 2008 can be found in the
1980s, . . . when complex financial products like mortgage
derivatives were developed." (N Y Times (Late N Y Ed))

"'The Big Short' manages to give us the truest picture
yet of what went wrong on Wall Street—and why. At times,
it reads like a morality play, at other times like a modern-day
farce. But as with any good play, its value lies in the way it
reveals character and motive and explores the cultural context in which the plot unfolds." Washington Post

Liveris, Andrew

Make it in America; the case for re-inventing the
economy. Wiley 2011 xxi, 208p il $24.95; ebook
$16.99 **330.9**

    1. Economic forecasting 2. Industrial policy -- United
States 3. Manufactures

    ISBN 978-0-470-93022-9; 0-470-93022-5;
9781118019405 ebook

                     LC 2010045654

The author "calls for a national strategy to revive manufacturing. We need manufacturing jobs, he says, if we are
to keep a growing population busy and start paying off our
debts to the rest of the world." Wall Street J

    Includes bibliographical references

Madrick, Jeffrey G.

Age of greed; the triumph of finance and the decline of America, 1970 to the present. [by] Jeff Madrick. Alfred A. Knopf 2011 464p il $30; ebook
$14.99 **330.9**

    1. Capitalists and financiers 2. Financial crises 3.
Financial crises -- United States -- History 4. Wealth 5.
Wealth -- Moral and ethical aspects

    ISBN 978-1-4000-4171-8; 978-0-307-59671-0 ebook

                     LC 2011003399

This book "is a fascinating and deeply disturbing tale of
hypocrisy, corruption, and insatiable greed. But more than
that, it's a much-needed reminder of just how we got into the
mess we're in—a reminder that is greatly needed when we
are still being told that greed is good." New York Rev Books

    Includes bibliographical references

McLean, Bethany

All the devils are here; the hidden history of the
financial crisis. [by] Bethany McLean and Joe Noc-
era. Portfolio/Penguin 2010 380p il $32.95 **330.9**

    1. Financial crises -- United States 2. Global Financial

Crisis, 2008-2009 3. International finance 4. Mortgage-backed securities 5. Mortgages

ISBN 978-1-59184-363-4; 1-59184-363-4

LC 2010-32893

This is an "account of the late financial meltdown, when, in the words of one analyst, 'we went from a collective belief in soundness to a collective belief in insolvency.' . . . Hard-hitting reporting and fluent writing bring the utter devastation of the Great Recession to life." Kirkus

Includes bibliographical references

Paulson, Henry M.

★ **On** the brink; inside the race to stop the collapse of the global financial system. Business Plus 2010 478p il $28.99   **330.9**

1. Economic policy -- United States 2. Financial crises -- United States 3. Global Financial Crisis, 2008-2009 4. Investment bankers 5. Secretaries of the treasury

ISBN 978-0-446-56193-8; 0-446-56193-2

LC 2009-939043

"This is the ultimate insider's account of the crisis, and, owing to its evenhanded tone and penetrating insights into government actions, it will also remain an important contribution to the historical record of the crisis, essential reading for everyone interested in knowing what happened." Libr J

Perino, Michael A.

The **hellhound** of Wall Street; how Ferdinand Pecora's investigation of the Great Crash forever changed American finance. [by] Michael Perino. Penguin Press 2010 341p il $27.95   **330.9**

1. Financial crises 2. Judges 3. Lawyers 4. Regulatory agency officials 5. Stock exchanges 6. Stock market crash, 1929

ISBN 978-1-59420-272-8

LC 2010-19157

The author "recounts the 1933 investigation into Wall Street abuses by the Senate Committee on Banking and Currency, focusing on the 10-day interrogation by chief counsel Ferdinand Pecora of executives of National City Bank (precursor to Citigroup). . . . Perino's book is a trenchant, entertaining study of the New Deal's heroic beginnings, one with obvious relevance to latter-day efforts to rein in Wall Street's excesses." Publ Wkly

Includes bibliographical references

Rajan, Raghuram G.

Fault lines; how hidden fractures still threaten the world economy. Princeton University Press 2010 260p   **330.9**

1. Economic history -- 21st century 2. Global Financial Crisis, 2008-2009 3. Income distribution -- United States -- History

ISBN 9780691146836; 9780691152639; 9781400834211

LC 2010-6031

Some have blamed the global financial crisis of 2008-2009 on "bankers who took irrational risks and left the rest of us to foot the bill. . . . Rajan argues that serious flaws in the economy are also to blame, and warns that a potentially more devastating crisis awaits us if they aren't fixed. Rajan [aims to] show how the individual choices that collectively brought about the economic meltdown—made by bankers, government officials, and ordinary homeowners—were rational responses to a flawed global financial order in which the incentives to take on risk are . . . out of step with the dangers those risks pose. He traces [what he views as] the deepening fault lines in a world overly dependent on the indebted American consumer to power global economic growth and stave off global downturns. He [argues that] . . . America's growing inequality and thin social safety net create tremendous political pressure to encourage easy credit and keep job creation robust, no matter what the consequences to the economy's long-term health; and . . . [that] the U.S. financial sector, with its skewed incentives, is the critical but unstable link between an overstimulated America and an underconsuming world. . . . . He outlines the hard choices [he believes] we need to make to ensure a more stable world economy and restore lasting prosperity." (Publisher's note) Bibliography. Index.

The author "explains the financial market panic of 2008 and argues that the weaknesses or fault lines in the world economy that led to financial collapse and recession persist. . . . Economists who can challenge their peers while remaining accessible to the general reader are rare, but Rajan belongs to this elite group. No short summary can do justice to this well-written, insightful, and nuanced study." Choice

Includes bibliographical references

Reich, Robert B.

Aftershock; the next economy and America's future. Alfred A. Knopf 2010 174p il $25; ebook $11.99   **330.9**

ISBN 978-0-307-59281-1; 0-307-59281-2; 978-0-307-59452-5 ebook

LC 2010-04134

Reich "argues that America will not have a sustained economic recovery until the middle class has more buying power. In this call for reform, the author writes that the increasing concentration of wealth among a small percentage of Americans was the main culprit in the destabilization of the U.S. economy in 2008. . . . Lucid and cogent." Kirkus

Includes bibliographical references

Sachs, Jeffrey D.

The **price** of civilization; reawakening American virtue and prosperity. Random House 2011 324p il $27; ebook $12.99   **330.9**

1. Economic policy -- United States 2. Environmental responsibility -- United States 3. Social responsibility of business -- United States

ISBN 9781400068418; 140006841X; 9780679605027 ebook; 0679605029 ebook

LC 2011014631

The author "explores the economic, political, social, and psychological roots of the U.S.'s 30-year journey 'from decades of consensus and high achievement to an era of deep division and growing crisis.' He indicts America's elites for abandoning social responsibility, politicians for giving up on solving problems, the media for distraction and hyper-commercialization, and citizens for surrendering to that distraction. He urges mindfulness, clear goals for political reform, and significant tax changes, and he suggests that the millennial generation will lead the way to a restoration of the nation's highest aspirations." Booklist

Includes bibliographical references (p. [277]-307) and index.

Sorkin, Andrew Ross

★ **Too** big to fail; the inside story of how Wall Street and Washington fought to save the financial system from crisis--and themselves. Viking 2009 xx, 600p il $32.95; pa $18　　**330.9**
1. Financial crises 2. Financial crises -- United States 3. Global Financial Crisis, 2008-2009
ISBN 978-0-670-02125-3; 0-670-02125-3; 978-0-14-311824-4 pa; 0-14-311824-2 pa

LC 2009-36494

This is an account of the recent financial crisis.

"Sorkin boasts of the hours spent interviewing, emailing, inspecting telephone call logs, billing time sheets and even expense reports [for this book], and his reward is the fullest and most convincing account of the Lehman debacle. Conversations are reconstructed, and an air of authenticity created by the accumulation of thousands of small facts." Times Lit Suppl

Includes bibliographical references

330.973　Economic conditions--United States

Ferguson, Charles

Predator nation; corporate criminals, political corruption, and the hijacking of America. Charles Ferguson. Crown Business 2012 vii, 369 p.p ill. $27.00　　**330.973**
1. Banks and banking -- United States 2. Equality -- United States 3. Financial crises -- United States 4. Global Financial Crisis, 2008-2009
ISBN 030795255X; 9780307952554

LC 2011052366

In this book, "author Charles H. Ferguson . . . explains how a predator elite took over the country, step by step, and he exposes the networks of academic, financial, and political influence, in all recent administrations, that prepared the predators' path to conquest." Topics include the decline of the manufacturing industry, fraud in the finance industry, and income inequality in the U.S. (Publisher s note)

331　Economics of labor, finance, land, energy

Crawford, Matthew B.

Shop class as soulcraft; an inquiry into the value of work. Penguin Press 2009 246p il $25.95　**331**
1. Manual work 2. Mechanics (Persons) 3. Philosophers 4. Work
ISBN 978-1-59420-223-0

LC 2009-1789

The author "extols the value of making and fixing things in this masterful paean to what he calls 'manual competence,' the ability to work with one's hands. . . . With wit and humor, the author deftly mixes the details of his own experience as a tradesman and then proprietor of a motor-

cycle repair shop with more philosophical considerations." Publ Wkly

Includes bibliographical references

De Botton, Alain

The **pleasures** and sorrows of work. Pantheon Books 2009 326p il $26　　**331**
1. Labor 2. Work 3. Work -- Social aspects
ISBN 978-0-375-42444-1

LC 2008-46060

"De Botton's sprightly mix of reportage and rumination expands beyond the workplace to investigate the broader meaning of life." Publ Wkly

Lichtenstein, Nelson

State of the Union: a century of American labor. Princeton Univ. Press 2002 336p il hardcover o.p. pa $18.95　　**331**
1. Labor -- United States 2. Labor unions
ISBN 0-691-11654-7 pa

LC 2001-36863

The author "analyzes the history of the labor movement from the 1930's to the present in the context of U.S. economics, politics, and democracy and from this he formulates ideas about where labor may find opportunities in this new century." Libr J

Includes bibliographical references

Murolo, Priscilla

From the folks who brought you the weekend; a short, illustrated history of labor in the United States. {by} Priscilla Murolo and A.B. Chitty; illustrations by Joe Sacco. New Press (NY) 2001 xx, 364p hardcover o.p. pa $17.95　　**331**
1. Labor -- History 2. Labor -- United States 3. Labor -- United States -- History 4. Labor movement 5. Labor movement -- History 6. Labor movement -- United States -- History 7. Working class 8. Working class -- History 9. Working class -- United States -- History
ISBN 1-56584-776-8 pa

LC 2001-30978

"Brandishing little-known facts, the authors reshape common views of social history." Publ Wkly

Includes bibliographical references

Murray, R. Emmett

★ The **lexicon** of labor; more than 500 key terms, biographical sketches, and historical insights concerning labor in America. Rev. and updated ed.; New Press 2010 235p pa $16.95　　**331**
1. Labor -- United States -- Dictionaries 2. Reference books
ISBN 978-1-59558-226-3

LC 2010-8276

This is an "encyclopedia of 500 entries for terms, concepts, people, legislation, places, and events in U.S. labor history." Booklist

Includes bibliographical references

The Adams resume almanac. Adams Media Corp. 1996 768p pa $19.95 **331**

1. Applications for positions 2. Résumés (Employment)

ISBN 1-55850-618-7

LC 96-15500

This "guide reviews résumé layouts and various formats and strategies, along with 600 samples and 25 cover letters. With the disk, the job seeker can actually generate a résumé." Libr J

Resumes and cover letters that have worked; {edited by Anne McKinney} PREP Pub. 1996 270p pa $25 **331**

1. Applications for positions 2. Résumés (Employment)

ISBN 1-88528-804-2

LC 95-19458

"The superior, readable samples, customized to professionals, college graduates, and career changers, distinguish this work from others." Libr J

331.1   Labor force and market

Damp, Dennis V.

★ The **book** of U.S. government jobs; where they are, what's available, and how to complete a Federal resume. 11th ed.; Bookhaven Press 2011 308p il pa $27.95 **331.1**

1. Civil service -- United States

ISBN 978-0-943641-29-4

LC 2011903343

This is "an essential guide to securing well-paying federal positions. [Its] . . . 11 chapters offer highly detailed instruction on where to locate and how to apply for federal jobs. Featuring tips for interview and exam performance, the accessible text presents instructive narratives and helpful sidebar hints. . . . Other chapters clarify the qualifications necessary for securing positions with the police, the postal service, and the homeland security administration." Libr J

Includes bibliographical references

Taylor, Nick

★ **American**-made; the enduring legacy of the WPA: when FDR put the nation to work. Bantam Books 2008 630p il $27 **331.1**

1. Governors 2. Handicapped 3. Job creation -- United States -- History -- 20th century 4. New Deal, 1933-1939 5. Philatelists 6. Presidents

ISBN 978-0-553-80235-1; 0-553-80235-6

LC 2007-34563

"Lavishly illustrated, the book also has a list of New Deal organizations, a partial list of construction projects, a New Deal chronology, and endnotes. It will be a boon to all 20th-century history collections." Libr J

Includes bibliographical references

Woodward, Bob

Maestro: Greenspan's Fed and the American boom. Simon & Schuster 2000 270p il $25; pa $14 **331.1**

1. Bankers 2. Economists 3. Government officials 4. Monetary policy -- United States 5. Monetary policy -- United States -- History -- 20th century 6. Presidential advisers 7. Regulatory agency officials

ISBN 0-7432-0412-3; 0-7432-0562-6 pa

LC 00-52627

The author discusses the influence exerted over the American economy by Alan Greenspan, chairman of the Federal Reserve Board.

"In a surprisingly short book, Woodward lucidly explains the axes of intellectual and political disagreement over monetary policy, productivity growth, irrational exuberance and more, shedding new light on major conflicts of the Greenspan era and demystifying this most political of ostensibly technical institutions." N Y Times Book Rev

Includes bibliographical references

331.13   Discrimination in employment, labor shortages, unemployment

Snyder, Don J.

The **cliff** walk; a memoir of a lost job and a life found. Little, Brown 1997 265p $23.95; pa $12.95 **331.13**

1. Authors 2. Biography, Individual 3. Carpenters 4. College teachers

ISBN 0-316-80308-1; 0-316-80348-0 pa

LC 96-51163

"When the author is fired by Colgate University, he never doubts that his brilliance and charm will soon gain him entrance to a new ivory tower. Instead, he is forced to move his family of five to Maine in the off season. With his pride and his checking account steadily eroding, he concocts wild schemes—stealing golf balls from a nearby course with his son, and secretly contemplating selling his unborn child. Finally, Snyder gives his last seventeen hundred dollars to a dying woman so she can take her children to Disney World. This dire act propels him into a real job—building a house— and toward a vision of self that depends more on strength than on prestige." New Yorker

331.2   Conditions of employment

Lowenstein, Roger

While America aged; how pension debts ruined General Motors, stopped the NYC subways, bankrupted San Diego, and loom as the next financial crisis. Penguin Press 2008 274p $25.95 **331.2**

1. Defined benefit pension plans 2. Pensions 3. Pensions -- United States 4. Retirement income 5. Retirement income -- United States

ISBN 978-1-594-20167-7; 1-59420-167-6

LC 2007-42508

"A chilling anatomy of one bad decision followed by another—and another." Kirkus

Includes bibliographical references

Schultz, Ellen

Retirement heist; how companies plunder and profit from the nest eggs of American workers. [by]

Ellen E. Schultz. Portfolio/Penguin 2011 245p
$26.95 **331.2**
 1. Corporations 2. Life insurance 3. Pensions
 ISBN 978-1-59184-333-7; 1-59184-333-2
LC 2011015064
"Readers are no stranger to the grumblings of their corporate overlords: Pensions are untenable; health-care costs too high; retiree benefits hurt competitiveness. But according to . . . Schultz, employee pensions actually make money for corporations, and the funds diverted from them help feather the beds of multimillionaire executives. She exposes all this and more in a rapid-fire narrative. Individual stories of retired men and women (some with more than 40 years of service) robbed of their nest eggs put a human face on the proceedings. . . . Essential reading for anyone who works for a living." Kirkus
Includes bibliographical references

Shulman, Beth
 The **betrayal** of work; how low-wage jobs fail 30 million Americans and their families. New Press (NY) 2003 255p $25.95 **331.2**
 1. Labor -- United States 2. Minimum wage 3. Work
 ISBN 1-56584-733-4
LC 2003-43413
The author "analyzes one of the downsides of the 'new economy': the large number of American jobs that pay poverty-level wages, have few or no benefits, and create childcare nightmares." Libr J
Includes bibliographical references

Terkel, Studs
 Working; people talk about what they do all day and how they feel about what they do. The New Press 1997 589p pa $16.95 **331.2**
 1. Labor -- United States 2. Work
 ISBN 978-1-56584-342-4; 1-56584-342-8
Based on interviews, this study describes the working lives and feelings of people engaged in occupations ranging from interstate truck driver to stockbroker to bookbinder to corporation president.
 This "is not a dry, academic treatise but a sensitive portrayal of the experience of working, with all its pain, tension, frustrations, and occasional satisfactions." Best Sellers

331.3 Labor force by personal attributes

Levine, Marvin J.
 Children for hire; the perils of child labor in the United States. Praeger Pubs. 2003 233p $49.95 **331.3**
 1. Agricultural laborers -- United States 2. Child labor 3. Child labor -- United States 4. Children -- Health and hygiene -- United States 5. Industrial safety -- United States 6. Teenagers -- Employment 7. Working class -- Education -- United States 8. Youth -- Employment 9. Youth -- Employment -- United States 10. Youth -- Health and hygiene -- United States
 ISBN 1-56720-433-3
LC 2002-29767

The author defines the problem of child labor and "analyzes the working conditions of people under 18, the legal context for their employment and exploitation, and the impact of such labor upon the education and development of America's young people. An important work about a hidden social problem." Libr J
Includes bibliographical references and index

331.4 Women workers

Chang, Leslie T.
 Factory girls; from village to city in a changing China. Spiegel & Grau 2008 420p map $26; pa $16 **331.4**
 1. Manufacturing industries 2. Manufacturing industries -- Employees -- China 3. Migrant labor 4. Women -- China 5. Women migrant labor -- China 6. Young women -- Employment -- China
 ISBN 978-0-385-52017-1; 0-385-52017-4; 978-0-385-52018-8 pa; 0-385-52018-2 pa
LC 2008-12880
This "is an exceptionally vivid and compassionate depiction of the day-to-day dramas, and the fears and aspirations, of the real people who are powering China's economic boom." N Y Times Book Rev
Includes bibliographical references

Featherstone, Liza
 Selling women short; the landmark battle for workers' rights at Wal-Mart. Basic Bks. 2004 282p $25 **331.4**
 1. Sex discrimination 2. Sex discrimination against women -- United States 3. Sex discrimination in employment -- Law and legislation -- United States 4. Sex discrimination in employment -- United States
 ISBN 0-465-02315-0
LC 2004-10298
Using an "investigation of the class action suit Dukes v. Wal-Mart Stores, Inc. and . . . interviews with female workers, Featherstone indicts Wal-Mart for low wages, discriminatory policies and sexist practices. . . . This is a clearly written and compelling book." Publ Wkly
Includes bibliographical references

Kessler-Harris, Alice
 ★ **Out** to work; a history of wage-earning women in the United States. 20th anniversary ed; Oxford Univ. Press 2003 414p il pa $19.95 **331.4**
 1. Women -- Employment -- History 2. Women -- Employment -- United States -- History 3. Working class women -- United States -- History
 ISBN 0-19-515709-5
LC 2003-267644
"This work remains a landmark in the field of analyzing the history of women's work in the United States from Colonial times to the Reagan era." Libr J
Includes bibliographical references

331.6   Workers by ethnic and national origin

Bacon, David

Illegal people; how globalization creates migration and criminalizes immigrants. Beacon Press 2008 261p $25.95; pa $18   **331.6**

1. Alien labor 2. Alien labor -- United States 3. Globalization 4. Globalization -- Economic aspects 5. Globalization -- Social aspects 6. Illegal aliens 7. Illegal aliens -- United States 8. Labor movement 9. Labor movement -- United States 10. Labor policy 11. Labor policy -- United States 12. Migrant labor
ISBN 978-0-8070-4226-7; 978-0-8070-4230-4 pa
LC 2008-15394

The author "follows the lives of undocumented workers at the Westin Suite Hotel in California and a Smithfield meatpacking plant in North Carolina, who travel back and forth from Mexico to the U.S. He examines the economic and social forces in both countries that lure workers to a market where they can earn higher wages but are vulnerable to exploitation. . . . A fascinating look at trade and immigration policies and the people directly affected by them." Booklist
Includes bibliographical references

Breslin, Jimmy

The **short** sweet dream of Eduardo Gutierrez. Crown 2002 213p hardcover o.p. pa $12   **331.6**

1. Alien labor, Mexican -- New York -- New York -- Biography 2. Construction workers 3. Illegal aliens -- New York -- New York -- Biography
ISBN 1-400-04682-3 pa
LC 2001-47283

"A true-life account of an illegal Mexican immigrant who died on a New York construction site, and of the dreary lives and modest ambitions common to Mexicans in this country." N Y Times Book Rev

331.7   Labor by industry and occupation

Farr, J. Michael

★ **100** fastest-growing careers; your complete guidebook to major jobs with the most growth and openings. [by] Michael Farr. 11th ed.; JIST Works 2010 402p il pa $17.95   **331.7**

1. Occupations 2. Vocational guidance
ISBN 978-1-5935-7783-4

This volume "provides information about pay, outlook, education, and skills needed to obtain some of the most promising jobs in the world of work." Publisher's note
Includes bibliographical references

Ferguson Publishing

The **top** 100; the fastest growing careers for the 21st century. 5th ed.; Ferguson 2011 388p $75; pa $19.95   **331.7**

1. Occupations 2. Vocational guidance
ISBN 978-0-8160-8367-1; 0-8160-8367-3; 978-0-8160-8359-6 pa; 0-8160-8359-2 pa; 978-1-4381-3767-4 ebook; 1-4381-3767-2 ebook
LC 2011004455

This book provides information "on jobs projected to experience the fastest growth, the greatest opportunity, and the best earnings through 2018, according to statistics from the U.S. Department of Labor. . . . Each job article describes the job duties; required education, training, and skills; expected earnings; and . . . more." Publisher's note

Fisher, James Terence

On the Irish waterfront; the crusader, the movie, and the soul of the port of New York. [by] James T. Fisher. Cornell University Press 2009 370p il map $29.95   **331.7**

1. Authors 2. Catholic Church -- Missions 3. Church work with the working class 4. Dramatists 5. Irish Americans 6. Irish Americans -- Employment 7. Novelists 8. Priests 9. Screenwriters 10. Short story writers 11. Social reformers 12. Stevedores
ISBN 978-0-8014-4804-1; 0-8014-4804-2
LC 2009-13058

The author presents a "history of the New York-New Jersey waterfront depicted in Elia Kazan's Oscar-winning 1954 film, On the Waterfront. Fischer's impeccable research delves into the real-life stories behind the characters, particularly Pete Corridan, the crusading Catholic priest who tried to reform the longshoremen's union and the recently deceased Bud Schulberg, who adapted Malcolm Johnson's 1949 Pulitzer Prize-winning 'Crime on the Waterfront' newspaper series for the screen. . . . This engaging narrative is essential reading for both labor historians and cinema buffs, plus anyone studying the waterfront, working-class and immigrant history, anticommunism, blacklisting, and the House Un-American Activities Committee." Libr J
Includes bibliographical references

J.G. Ferguson Publishing Company

★ **Encyclopedia** of careers and vocational guidance; 15th ed.; Ferguson 2010 5v il set $249.95   **331.7**

1. Occupations -- Encyclopedias 2. Reference books 3. Vocational guidance -- Encyclopedias
ISBN 978-0-8160-8313-8; 0-8160-8313-4
LC 2010-17724

"These five volumes contain more than 700 . . . [articles] on careers in nearly 100 industries. Each three to five-page entry provides a concise and engaging profile of fields like accounting, animal care, computers, the environment, publishing, sales, and the visual arts. Included in each job entry are an overview, a history, a description, requirements, employers, advancement, earnings, work environment, outlook, and more." Libr J [review of 2008 edition]
Includes bibliographical references

United States/Bureau of Labor Statistics

★ **Occupational** outlook handbook 2010-2011. U.S. Dept. of Labor Bureau of Labor Statistics 2010 877p il $39   **331.7**

1. Occupations 2. Reference books 3. Vocational guidance
ISBN 978-0-16-084318-1

"Gives information on employment trends and outlook in more than 800 occupations. Indicates nature of work, qualifications, earnings and working conditions, how to enter, where to go for more information, etc." Guide to Ref Books. 11th edition

331.702 Choice of vocation

McKenna, Amy

Nontraditional careers for women and men; more than 30 great jobs for women and men with apprenticeships through PhDs. by Andrew Morkes and Amy McKenna. College & Career Press 2012 280 p. $19.95 **331.702**

1. Men -- Employment -- United States -- Juvenile literature 2. Vocational guidance -- United States -- Juvenile literature 3. Women -- Employment -- United States -- Juvenile literature

ISBN 0974525197; 9780974525198

LC 2011046915

This book is chock-full of career articles encompassing a wide variety of fields. Each career article includes salary information, skills needed, minimum education level, employment outlook, information about the career, certification and licensing information, tips for getting a job in this career, and industry resources. (Voice of Youth Advocates)

331.8 Labor unions, labor-management bargaining and disputes

Dray, Philip

There is power in a union; the epic story of labor in America. Doubleday 2010 772p il $35; ebook $35 **331.8**

1. Industrialization 2. Industrialization -- United States -- History 3. Labor movement 4. Labor movement -- United States -- History 5. Labor unions -- United States 6. Labor unions -- United States -- History

ISBN 978-0-385-52629-6; 0-385-52629-6; 978-0-385-53360-7 ebook

LC 201002357

This is a "narrative history of American labor. . . . From the textile mills of Lowell, Massachusetts . . . to the triumph of unions in the twentieth century and their waning influence today, the contest between labor and capital for their share of American bounty has shaped our national experience. Philip Dray's ambition is to show us the vital accomplishments of organized labor in that time and illuminate its central role in our social, political, economic, and cultural evolution." (Publisher's note) Bibliography. Index.

The author "follows organized labor from the struggles of early 19th-century female textile workers to the present-day retreat of organized labor following the failed 1981 air traffic controllers' strike. . . . Packed with vivid characters and dramatic scenes, Dray's fine recap of a neglected but vital tradition has much to say about labor's current straits." Publ Wkly

Includes bibliographical references

Dubofsky, Melvyn

★ **Labor** in America; a history. [by] Melvyn Dubofsky, Foster Rhea Dulles. 7th ed; Harlan Davidson 2005 472p il pa $34.95 **331.8**

1. Labor -- United States 2. Labor unions 3. Working class

ISBN 978-0-88295-998-6; 0-88295-998-0

LC 2003-13265

A study of the social and political impact of the American labor movement since colonial times.

Shaw, Randy

Beyond the fields; Cesar Chavez, the UFW, and the struggle for justice in the 21st century. University of California Press 2008 347p il **331.8**

1. Agricultural laborers 2. Labor leaders 3. Social action 4. Social action -- United States -- History -- 20th century 5. Social justice -- United States

ISBN 0520251075; 0520268040; 9780520251076; 9780520268043

LC 2008-31252

This book explores the impact of César Chávez and the United Farm Workers "on 21st-century social justice movements. Beyond the Fields [aims to show] . . . how Chávez and the UFW's imprint can be found in the modern reshaping of the American labor movement, the building of Latino political power, the transformation of Los Angeles and California politics, the fight for environmental justice, and the . . . movement for immigrant rights. [According to the author], many of the ideas, tactics, and strategies that Chávez and the UFW initiated or revived—including the boycott, the fast, clergy-labor partnerships and door-to-door voter outreach—are now so commonplace that their roots in the farmworkers' movement [are] forgotten. . . . UFW volunteers and staff were dedicated to furthering economic justice, and many devoted their post-UFW lives to working for social change." (Publisher's note) Index.

"Shaw's book is the product of extensive research, and it's invaluable for anyone interested in the evolution of unionization over the past forty years." Washington Monthly

Includes bibliographical references and index

Stepan-Norris, Judith

Left out; Reds and America's industrial unions. [by] Judith Stepan-Norris, Maurice Zeitlin. Cambridge Univ. Press 2002 375p $75; pa $27 **331.8**

1. Labor -- United States 2. Labor unions -- United States 3. Labor unions -- United States -- Political activity 4. Labor unions and communism -- United States -- History

ISBN 0-521-79212-6; 0-521-79840-X pa

LC 2001-37655

"In 1947, ten 'Communist-dominated unions' were expelled from the CIO. The mythology that developed is that these unions sacrificed the interests of the American worker to the foreign policy dictates of the Stalin-era Soviet Union. The authors, both sociologists, use statistical analysis of contracts to argue that these unions actually had the most democracy, the most pro-labor contracts, and the best track record in fighting for gender and racial equality in the labor movement." Libr J

Includes bibliographical references

Zieger, Robert H.

American workers, American unions; the twentieth century. {by} Robert H. Zieger & Gilbert J. Gall. 3rd ed; Johns Hopkins Univ. Press 2002 292p pa $17.95   **331.8**

1. Labor -- United States 2. Labor unions 3. Labor unions -- United States -- History -- 20th century
ISBN 0-8018-7078-X

           LC 2002-3250

"This standard work of American labor history from the Gilded Age onward has been updated to almost the present, with the last paragraph discussing September 11. Zieger's strength lies in his striving for a balanced survey." Libr J
Includes bibliographical references

★ Historical encyclopedia of American labor; edited by Robert Weir and James P. Hanlan. Greenwood Press 2003 2v set $175   **331.8**
1. Industrial relations -- United States -- History 2. Industrial relations -- United States -- History -- Encyclopedias 3. Labor -- United States -- Encyclopedias 4. Labor -- United States -- History 5. Labor -- United States -- History -- Encyclopedias 6. Labor laws and legislation -- United States -- History -- Encyclopedias 7. Labor movement -- Encyclopedias 8. Labor movement -- United States -- History 9. Labor movement -- United States -- History -- Encyclopedias 10. Reference books
ISBN 0-313-31840-9

           LC 2003-52847

This "encyclopedia includes approximately 400 entries designed for the general researcher, students, and lay readers interested in learning more about such topics as unions, union leaders, union history, important laws and court cases, and labor terminology. An appendix contains excerpts from over 50 primary documents." Libr J
Includes bibliographical references

★ St. James encyclopedia of labor history worldwide; major events in labor history and their impact. with introductions by Willie Thompson and Daniel Nelson; Neil Schlager, editor; produced by Schlager Groups. St. James Press 2003 2v set $260   **331.8**
1. Labor movement -- Encyclopedias 2. Reference books
ISBN 1-558-62542-9

           LC 2003-294

"This reference promises to fill an important niche for larger public and academic libraries." Libr J

331.88   Labor unions (Trade unions)

Gorn, Elliott J.

Mother Jones; the most dangerous woman in America. Hill & Wang 2001 408p il hardcover o.p. pa $14   **331.88**
1. Centenarians 2. Labor leaders 3. Women in the labor movement -- United States -- Biography 4. Women labor leaders -- United States -- Biography 5. Women

labor union members -- United States -- Biography 6. Working class women -- United States -- Biography
ISBN 0-8090-7094-4 pa

           LC 00-44997

This is a biography of union organizer and labor leader Mary Harris Jones, known more popularly as Mother Jones.

Gorn "has successfully separated fact from myth . . . situating Jones's story within a wider cultural frame." Publ Wkly
Includes bibliographical references

332   Financial economics

Gasparino, Charles

The **sellout**; how three decades of Wall Street greed and government mismanagement destroyed the global financial system. Harper Business 2009 553p $27.99   **332**
1. Financial crises -- United States -- History 2. Global Financial Crisis, 2008-2009 3. Wall Street 4. Wall Street (New York, N.Y.)
ISBN 978-0-06-169716-6; 0-06-169716-8

           LC 2009-28097

"Of all the books documenting the financial crisis . . . The Sellout tells it better than most. Filled with very little of the boring, complex financial jargon that comprises many books of the genre, this tome makes for a surprisingly entertaining and easy read." Risk Management
Includes bibliographical references

Mayer, Robert

Quick cash; the story of the loan shark. Northern Illinois University Press 2010 293p $35   **332**
1. Loans 2. Usury
ISBN 978-0-8758-0430-9; 0-8758-0430-6

           LC 2010014718

This book "traces high-interest lending from the late 19th century through the latest financial crisis. While the book focuses on Chicago, it does reference lending practices throughout the South and New York City. Chapters delve into the social issues of the early 20th century that created a market for these high-interest loans, the various government policies that tried to regulate the lenders, and the legal and economic changes that gave rise to the current methods of payday lending since the 1980s. . . . [The author] has created an original and multidisciplinary look at subprime lending in the United States that is accessible to a wide variety of readers, including students and professionals." Libr J
Includes bibliographical references

332.024   Personal finance

Armstrong, Frank

The **retirement** challenge--will you sink or swim? a complete, do-it-yourself toolkit to navigate

your financial future. FT Press 2009 266p il pa
$21.99   332.024
1. Personal finance 2. Retirement
ISBN 0-13-236132-9; 978-0-13-236132-3
LC 2008-29134
"With a companion web site (www.sink-swim.com), this
planning guide takes readers through the steps: determining
retirement age, setting up retirement funds, forecasting financial needs, and much, much more." Libr J

Bradford, Stacey L.
The **Wall** Street Journal: financial guidebook for
new parents. Three Rivers Press 2009 196p il pa
$14.95   332.024
1. Parents 2. Personal finance
ISBN 978-0-307-40707-8; 0-307-40707-1
LC 2008-50657
The author "presents a relevant and witty overview of
the awesome task facing new parents—affording their kids.
She covers all the major issues, including child tax credits,
the Family and Medical Leave Act of 1993, flexible spending accounts, and 529 plans; even wills, trusts, and disability
insurance are considered." Libr J

D'Agnese, Joseph
The **money** book for freelancers, part-time, and
the self-employed; the only personal finance system for people with not-so-regular jobs. [by] Joseph
D'Agnese & Denise Kiernan. Three Rivers Press
2010 306p il pa $15   332.024
1. Personal finance 2. Self-employed
ISBN 978-0-307-45366-2; 0-307-45366-9
LC 2009-31596
"The authors describe how one can maximize financial
security without compromising success by addressing debts,
taxes, emergency funds, and retirement savings using their
'Freelance Finance System.' They preach commonsense
ideas such as accountability and restraint but also describe
plenty of clever ways to make one's money go further. . .
. Developed from the personal experiences of the authors,
this book is fun and relevant. . . . Recommended for anyone
who is self-employed now or is facing a new work-life situation." Libr J

Glink, Ilyce R.
50 simple things you can do to improve your personal finances; how to spend less, save more, and
make the most of what you have. Three Rivers Press
(NY) 2001 222p pa $14   332.024
1. Finance, Personal 2. Personal finance
ISBN 0-8129-2742-7
LC 00-66675
The author gives advice on such topics as personal
budgets and savings, credit and debt, investments, insurance, taxes, marriage, partnerships and children, and
retirement planning.

Hirshman, Susan L.
Does this make my assets look fat? a woman's
guide to finding financial empowerment and success.

St. Martin's Press 2010 302p il $24.99; ebook
$11.99   332.024
1. Investments 2. Personal finance 3. Women -- United
States
ISBN 978-0-312-38553-8; 0-312-38553-6; 978-1-
4299-5006-0 ebook; 1-4299-5006-4 ebook
LC 2010-21668
"Comparing getting one's financial house in order to dieting, Hirshman . . . presents chapters on assessing personal
finance fitness and gives comprehensive definitions and explanations of, as well as practical suggestions on, various
investment strategies." Libr J

Jason, Julie
★ The **AARP** Retirement Survival Guide; how
to make smart financial decisions in good times and
bad. Sterling Pub. Co. 2009 340p pa $14.95 **332.024**
1. Pensions 2. Personal finance 3. Retirement income
ISBN 978-1-4027-4341-2
LC 2008-20577
This guide to retirement "includes a solid grounding
in the basics (such as the infamous What's your number?
discussion), careful outlines of how to approach retirement
income products as well as the stock market, and approaches
to taxes and to potential advisors." Booklist
Includes bibliographical references

Kessel, Brent
It's not about the money; unlock your money type
to achieve spiritual and financial abundance. Harper-
One 2008 xxi, 299p il $24.95; pa $14.99 **332.024**
1. Applied psychology 2. Money 3. Personal finance
4. Self-perception
ISBN 978-0-06-123406-4; 978-0-06-123405-7 pa
LC 2007-18380
The author "offers 'holistic financial advice' in this Bud-
dhist-influenced . . . [book] promising both a better financial
strategy and greater fulfillment and happiness. . . . Readers
interested in an Eastern-influenced approach will find useful
advice on how to think about money, as well as insight into
what makes us tick." Publ Wkly
Includes bibliographical references

McNaughton, Deborah
The **essential** credit repair handbook; [a quick
and handy guide for anyone who wants to get and
stay out of debt] Career Press 2011 224p pa
$14.99   332.024
1. Consumer credit 2. Debt 3. Personal finance
ISBN 978-1-60163-160-2 pa; 1-60163-160-X pa;
978-1-60163-666-9 ebook; 1-60163-666-0 ebook
LC 2011010730
This book discusses "how to: dispute late payments,
charge-offs, and collection accounts; rebuild your life after
a bankruptcy, foreclosure, or short sale; re-establish your
credit in spite of a bad credit report; set new financial goals;
[and] understand the latest credit card laws and regulations.
. . . [This is a] guide for people who are getting over bankruptcy, foreclosure, short sale, or any financial hardship affecting their credit and are looking to rebuild or re-establish
their credit." Publisher's note
Includes bibliographical references

Miller, Mark

The **hard** times guide to retirement security; practical strategies for money, work, and living. Wiley 2010 223p il pa $16.95; ebook $11.99 **332.024**

1. Retirement income

ISBN 978-1-57660-362-8 pa; 978-0-470-90834-1 ebook

LC 2010-14478

This guide to retirement after the financial crisis touches upon "issues such as insuring against the risk of outliving your assets, recalibrating damaged retirement portfolios, managing the risk of health-care expenses in retirement, and career strategies for workers who are 50 years old and up." Publisher's note

Orman, Suze

The **money** class; learn to create your new American dream. Spiegel & Grau 2011 281p $26; ebook $13.99   **332.024**

1. Personal finance 2. Wealth

ISBN 978-1-4000-6973-6; 978-0-679-60470-9 ebook

LC 2011-1394

"Organized into nine 'classes,' with each class/chapter further divided into related lessons, . . . [this book is] upbeat and no-nonsense, offering lessons on family matters, home-ownership, saving for college, emergencies, retirement, and more. Orman firmly guides readers when dealing with parenting issues or underwater mortgages. . . . After finishing Orman's book, and completing her exercises, readers will have a very clear sense of how they can achieve what she has rechristened the 'New American Dream.'" Publ Wkly

Pond, Jonathan D.

Grow your money! 101 easy tips to plan, save, and invest. Collins 2008 xlv, 352p $26.95 **332.024**

1. Investments 2. Public finance 3. Retirement income

ISBN 978-0-06-112140-1; 0-06-112140-1

LC 2007-24071

The author offers "investment and financial definitions, debt-management strategies, retirement and home-ownership considerations, tax tips, and more, enabling lay readers to understand these seemingly daunting and complex issues." Libr J

Quinn, Jane Bryant

Making the most of your money now; the classic bestseller. Completely rev. for the new economy; Simon & Schuster hardcover ed.; Simon & Schuster 2010 1242p $35   **332.024**

1. Investments 2. Personal finance

ISBN 978-0-7432-6996-4; 0-7432-6996-9

LC 2009-32610

This guide includes information about investing, buying a home, life and health insurance, retirement planning, checklists for life changes, finding a financial advisor, and financing college.

"This is an excellent primer, especially for those new to managing their money." Libr J

Romans, Christine

How to speak money; the language and knowledge you need now. Ali Velshi and Christine Romans. John Wiley & Sons 2012 xviii, 190 p.p   **332.024**

1. Business & economics -- Personal Finance -- General 2. Finance, Personal 3. Money

ISBN 9781118114957

LC 2011033518

In this book about personal finance, [a]uthors and CNN financial experts Ali Velshi and Christine Romans speak the global language of money. . . . Speaking money affects every area of your life. It's more than simply your savings or the investments you may have. It involves the way you think about money, the way you teach your children about it, and the way you were taught about it yourself. It's about the way you spend it, save it, invest it, use it, need it and want it. The book will . . . [cover] the male and female spending and investing disparity, . . . emerging international economies, . . . [the] hurdle of student debt, . . . [and explain] how to plan appropriately for retirement. (Publishers note)

Schwab-Pomerantz, Carrie

It pays to talk; how to have the essential conversations with your family about money and investing. [by] Carrie Schwab-Pomerantz and Charles R. Schwab. Crown Business 2003 386p il hardcover o.p. pa $14   **332.024**

1. Communication in the family 2. Finance, Personal 3. Investments 4. Personal finance

ISBN 0-609-61028-7; 1-4000-4960-1 pa

LC 2002-5994

The authors "share their insights on money, investing and the conversations that need to accompany these. Their focus is on the importance of conducting different lifestage conversations (e.g., how to financially approach being single, getting married, raising children, helping parents), and this . . . primer provides one-stop shopping for the many phases of financial understanding and planning. . . . This educational volume provides a useful framework that a family can refer to when approaching those often difficult but necessary conversations about finances." Publ Wkly

Includes bibliographical references

Solin, Daniel R.

The **smartest** retirement book you'll ever read. Penguin Group 2009 255p $21.95   **332.024**

1. Investments 2. Personal finance 3. Retirement income

ISBN 978-0-399-53520-8

LC 2009014075

The author "offers short chapters on a variety of retirement subjects, each concluding with a pithy summarization. . . [It is] clearly written and easy to understand, tackling such topics as stocks, bonds, annuities, pensions, and cash withdrawal strategies." Libr J

Includes bibliographical references

Tobias, Andrew P.

★ The **only** investment guide you'll ever need; [by] Andrew Tobias. Completely updated and rev.; Houghton Mifflin Harcourt 2011 306p il pa $14.95 **332.024**

1. Investments 2. Personal finance
ISBN 978-0-547-44725-4

LC 2010-41533

This book offers advice on such topics as personal investments, tax strategies, life insurance, stock market trading, college funds, real estate, and inheritance.

Walsh, Peter

Lighten up; love what you have, have what you need, be happier with less. Free Press 2011 288p $26; pa $15; ebook $12.99 **332.024**

1. Conduct of life 2. Happiness 3. Personal finance
ISBN 978-1-4391-5514-1; 978-1-4391-5515-8 pa; 978-1-4391-6008-4 ebook

LC 2010030244

The author "coaches readers in dealing with psychological clutter tied to money and finances so they can live thrifty lives that are also liberating, pleasurable, and rewarding. . . . At the crux of this book are three audits designed to instigate life changes: a financial audit combined with assessments of the physical junk filling our homes and the emotional junk causing tension in our lives. Throughout, Walsh challenges readers to face not just the physical clutter overwhelming their homes but also the psychological underpinnings to their habits and attitudes, to confront family members, and to establish tough boundaries within the limits of their family's means. . . . Motivated readers will find plenty of helpful tips to jump-start their self-transformations." Publ Wkly

Weltman, Barbara

★ **J.K.** Lasser's guide for tough times; tax and financial solutions to see you through. John Wiley 2009 224p pa $18.95 **332.024**

1. Income tax 2. Investments 3. Personal finance 4. Taxation
ISBN 978-0-470-40232-0; 0-470-40232-6

LC 2008-32269

"Besides tax and financial advice for coping with a down economy, Weltman examines steps being taken by the federal government (mortgage relief, stimulus packages) to ease the recession." Libr J

Yeager, Jeff

The **cheapskate** next door; the surprising secrets of Americans living happily below their means. Broadway Books 2010 231p pa $12.99; ebook $12.99 **332.024**

1. Finance, Personal 2. Personal finance 3. Thriftiness
ISBN 978-0-7679-3132-8 pa; 978-0-307-59247-7 ebook

LC 2009-42287

"The amazing fact about this book is that in addition to his instructions making perfect sense, like no other book of its kind, this one can be read simply for the humor of the author's prose." Booklist

The **ultimate** cheapskate's road map to true riches; a practical (and fun) guide to enjoying life

more by spending less. Broadway Books 2008 241p pa $12.95 **332.024**

1. Personal finance
ISBN 978-0-7679-2695-9; 0-7679-2695-1

LC 2007-34883

"From 'cheapskate shops' to inexpensive hobbies (e.g., bird watching), this lighthearted but practical 'road map' shows how to save up your money." Libr J

332.1 Banks

Ahamed, Liaquat

Lords of finance; the bankers who broke the world. Penguin Press 2009 564p il $32.95 **332.1**

1. Bankers 2. Biography, Collective 3. Cabinet members 4. Capitalists and financiers 5. Financiers 6. International finance -- History -- 20th century 7. Nazi leaders
ISBN 978-1-59420-182-0

LC 2008-44512

"A grand, sweeping narrative of immense scope and power." N Y Times Book Rev

Includes bibliographical references

Farrell, Greg

Crash of the titans; greed, hubris, the fall of Merrill Lynch, and the near-collapse of Bank of America. Crown Business 2010 471p $27; pa $17; ebook $12.99 **332.1**

1. Bank failures 2. Corporate mergers and acquisitions
ISBN 978-0-307-71786-3; 978-0-307-71787-0 pa; 978-0-307-71788-7 ebook

LC 2010485623

This is an account of the decline of Merrill Lynch & Co. and Bank of America Corp. The author claims that "at the moment they should have been minding their balance sheets, . . . many of the financial industry's masters of the universe were preoccupied with their bonuses, expense accounts, and office renovations." Businessweek

Includes bibliographical references

Johnson, Simon

13 bankers; the Wall Street takeover and the next financial meltdown. [by] Simon Johnson and James Kwak. Pantheon Books 2010 304p il $26.95; pa $15.95; ebook $11.99 **332.1**

1. Bank failures 2. Banks and banking -- United States 3. Finance -- United States 4. Financial crises 5. Financial crises -- United States
ISBN 978-0-307-37905-4; 0-307-37905-1; 978-0-307-47660-9 pa; 0-307-47660-X pa; 978-0-307-37922-1 ebook

LC 2010-00168

Johnson and Kwak examine not only how Wall Street's ideology, wealth, and political power among policy makers in Washington led to the financial debacle of 2008, but also what the lessons learned portend for the future.

"The book is a thoughtful, stimulating read on a topic of much ongoing debate and concern." Choice

Includes bibliographical references

Meltzer, Allan H.

★ A **history** of the Federal Reserve; v1 with a foreword by Alan Greenspan. University of Chicago Press 2002 800p v1 $75; pa $25   **332.1**

1. Federal Reserve banks
ISBN 0-226-51999-6; 0-226-52000-5 pa

LC 2002-72007

The author "provides a definitive history of the U.S. Federal Reserve from its founding in 1913 to its establishment as a separate, independent entity in 1951. Using meeting minutes, correspondence, and internal Federal Reserve documents, he traces the reasons behind Federal Reserve policy decisions, highlights the impact that individuals and events had on the Fed, and examines the Fed's influence on international affairs. . . . This well-written and thoroughgoing account is recommended for academic, business, and public libraries." Libr J

Includes bibliographical references

Overtveldt, Johan van

Bernanke's test; Ben Bernanke, Alan Greenspan, and the drama of the central banker. Agate 2009 287p il $26   **332.1**

1. Bankers 2. Banks and banking -- United States 3. Economic policy -- United States 4. Economists 5. Government officials 6. Monetary policy -- United States 7. Presidential advisers 8. Regulatory agency officials
ISBN 978-1-932841-37-4; 1-932841-37-7

LC 2008-45741

"Anyone who wants to understand the role of the Fed in the current crisis will find this an accessible primer." Publ Wkly

Includes bibliographical references

Parks, Tim

Medici money; banking, metaphysics, and art in fifteenth-century Florence. W. W. Norton & Co. 2005 273p il map $22.95   **332.1**

1. Art patronage -- Italy -- Florence -- History 2. Art, Renaissance -- Italy -- Florence 3. Bankers 4. Banks and banking 5. Banks and banking -- Italy -- Florence 6. Political leaders
ISBN 0-393-05827-1

LC 2004-30516

"The general reader will learn from this book a great deal about the era, and those who bestrode it, without getting bogged down in excessive scholarly detail." Natl Rev

Includes bibliographical references

Rockefeller, David

Memoirs. Random House 2002 517p $35; pa $17.95   **332.1**

1. Bankers 2. Bankers -- United States 3. Banks and banking -- United States -- History 4. Philanthropists
ISBN 0-679-40588-7; 0-8129-6973-1 pa

LC 2002-24800

"Rockefeller's style is restrained and self-deprecating; the account of his attempts to modernize and globalize Chase makes for excellent business history, and his sketch of his complicated relationship with his brother is especially convincing." New Yorker

Wessel, David

★ **In** Fed we trust; Ben Bernanke's war on the great panic. Crown Business 2009 323p $26.99   **332.1**

1. Banks and banking 2. Economists 3. Financial crises -- United States 4. Global Financial Crisis, 2008-2009 5. Government officials 6. Monetary policy -- United States 7. Regulatory agency officials
ISBN 978-0-307-45968-8; 0-307-45968-3

LC 2009-289789

This book reviews events of 2008 as the U. S. government attempted to stave off financial panic.

The author "has written a gripping blow-by-blow account of how the top brass at the Federal Reserve and Treasury flailed against financial collapse. . . . [The story] is a thrilling one, deftly told by a veteran journalist with access to those involved. Mr Wessel has an eye for enlivening detail, . . . and he has a knack for making finance accessible to the layman without boring the specialist." Economist

Includes bibliographical references

332.3   Credit and loan institutions

Grind, Kirsten

The **lost** bank; the story of Washington Mutual --the biggest bank failure in American history. Kirsten Grind. Simon & Schuster 2012 389 p.   **332.3**

1. Bank failures -- United States -- History 2. Banks and banking -- Washington (State) -- Seattle -- History 3. Dimon, Jamie, 1956- 4. Global Financial Crisis, 2008-2009 5. Greenspan, Alan, 1926- 6. Historical literature 7. Killinger, Kerry 8. Savings and loan association failures -- United States -- History 9. Savings and loan associations -- Washington (State) -- Seattle -- History 10. Subprime mortgage default 11. Subprime mortgages 12. Washington Mutual Inc.
ISBN 1451617925; 9781451617924; 9781451617931; 9781451617948

LC 2011048587

In this book, reporter [Kirsten] Grind chronicles the rise of Washington Mutual from a sleepy Seattle-based thrift to America's biggest savings and loan bank, its reckless plunge into the can't-lose subprime mortgage market, and its 2008 failure. . . . [The book includes] personalities like Kerry Killinger, WaMu's . . . CEO, and Jamie Dimon, the . . . JPMorgan leader who swallowed WaMu, . . . [as well as the] WaMu salespeople. . . . Grind pens a . . . guide to the delusions and frauds powering the debacle, from Fed chief Alan Greenspan's . . . economic forecasts down to the falsified documents that put people with no income, assets, or perhaps even pulses into mortgages they could never repay. (Publishers Weekly)

332.4   Money

Rickards, James

Currency wars; the making of the next global crisis. Portfolio/Penguin 2011 288p $26.95 **332.4**

1. Financial crises 2. Foreign exchange 3. Monetary

policy
ISBN 978-1-59184-449-5

LC 2011026906

The author "tells us we are in a new currency war that could destroy faith in the U.S. dollar; he examines that war through the lens of economic policy, national security, and historical precedent. As a national security issue, he tells a fascinating story of his involvement with the Pentagon and other agencies in designing and participating in a war game using currencies and capital markets, instead of ships and planes, to gain early warning of attacks on the U.S. dollar. . . . He presents a compelling case for his views and offers thought-provoking information for library patrons. This is a must-read book." Booklist

Includes bibliographical references

332.6 Investment

Bernstein, William

The **four** pillars of investing; lessons for building a winning portfolio. [by] William J. Bernstein. McGraw Hill 2010 331p il $30 **332.6**

1. Investments

ISBN 978-0-07-174705-9

The author discusses "the four pillars—the theory of investing, the history of investing, the psychology of investing, and the business of investing. . . . Using humor, Bernstein advises readers to employ sound tenets of investing to manage risk while building a foundation of assests for the long term." Libr J

Includes bibliographical references

The **investor's** manifesto; preparing for prosperity, Armageddon, and everything in between. [by] William J. Bernstein. Wiley 2010 xxii, 201p il $24.95; ebook $24.95 **332.6**

1. Investments 2. Securities 3. Stocks

ISBN 978-0-470-50514-4; 978-0-470-55807-2 ebook

LC 2009-20116

"Touching on lessons from the dot.com and 2008 market sell-offs, . . . [the author] discusses market and investor psychology, asset allocation, the unpredictability of returns, how to keep costs low, and, ultimately, how to avoid dying poor." Libr J

Includes bibliographical references

Boeckh, J. Anthony

The **great** reflation; how investors can profit from the new world of money. John Wiley & Sons 2010 xxii, 314p il $34.95 **332.6**

1. Business cycles 2. Financial crises 3. Investments 4. Personal finance

ISBN 978-0-470-53877-7

LC 2009-54227

"After laying out the post-2008 state of the U.S. economy and the inflation/deflation dangers as the Federal Reserve attempts to stimulate activity in the shadow of massive debt deleveraging, economist Boeckh then presents various investing scenarios." Libr J

Includes bibliographical references

Buffett, Mary

Warren Buffett and the art of stock arbitrage; proven strategies for arbitrage and other special investment situations. [by] Mary Buffett & David Clark. Scribner 2010 153p $25; ebook $11.99 **332.6**

1. Financiers 2. Investments

ISBN 978-1-4391-9882-7; 978-1-4516-0645-4 ebook

LC 2011280299

Analyzes Buffett's techniques for arbitrage and special situations investing and offers step-by-step instructions on how to take advantage of such events as spin-offs, liquidations, recapitalizations, and tender offers.

"The writing is concise and straightforward, the examples are current and clear, and there are simple formulas on how to determine risk in both arbitrage and valuing liquidations." Libr J

Includes glossary

Cohan, William D.

Money and power; how Goldman Sachs came to rule the world. Doubleday 2011 658p $30.50; ebook $14.99 **332.6**

1. Banks and banking 2. Investments 3. Securities

ISBN 978-0-385-52384-4; 978-0-385-53497-0 ebook

This is a history of the New York-based banking and investment firm from its founding in 1869 to the present.

"The book offers the best analysis yet of Goldman's increasingly tangled web of conflicts. . . . The writing is crisp and the research meticulous, drawing on reams of documents made publicly available by congressional committees and the Financial Crisis Inquiry Commission." Economist

Includes bibliographical references

Cortese, Amy

Locavesting; the revolution in local investing and how to profit from it. John Wiley 2011 252p $22.95; ebook $10.99 **332.6**

1. Community development 2. Investments 3. Small business

ISBN 978-0-470-91138-9; 978-1-1180-8578-3 ebook

LC 2011005647

"With the recent crash of the financial markets, many investors are looking for new places to put their money. At the same time, many small businesses are finding it ever more difficult to get credit. Cortese . . . covers this current confluence, providing examples of how investing in local small businesses can be beneficial to all parties. . . . Various types of funding methods are discussed, including cooperatives, credit unions, local stock exchanges, community development funds, public venture capital, and raising money through social networking. . . . Timely and easy to read, this is a nice introduction to something many of us have never considered. A good choice for public libraries and fruitful reading for small businesses and investors." Libr J

Includes bibliographical references

Cramer, James J.

Confessions of a street addict. Simon & Schuster 2002 339p $26; pa $14 **332.6**

1. Hedging (Finance) 2. Journalism, Commercial 3. Securities industry 4. Stockbrokers 5. Stocks 6. Wall

Street 7. Wall Street (New York, N.Y.)
ISBN 0-7432-2487-6; 0-7432-2488-4 pa

LC 2002-22902

The author "recounts his turbulent dual career as hedge fund manager and media pundit. . . . This is a lively, informative portrait of the highest levels of finance and media in the last decade." Publ Wkly

Downes, John

★ **Finance** and investment handbook; [by] John Downes, Jordan Elliot Goodman. 8th ed.; Barron's Educational Series 2010 1152p il $39.99   **332.6**
1. Investments 2. Personal finance
ISBN 978-0-7641-6269-5; 0-7641-6269-1

LC 2010-31548

This "volume presents a financial dictionary with definitions of more than 5,000 terms, an analysis of . . . investment opportunities, guidelines for non-experts on what to look for when reading corporate reports and financial news sources, . . . [a] directory of hundreds of publicly traded corporations in the United States and Canada, and a directory listing the names and addresses of brokerage houses, mutual funds families, banks, . . . information on federal and state regulators, and other major financial institutions." Publisher's note
Includes bibliographical references

Fox, Justin

★ The **myth** of the rational market; a history of risk, reward, and delusion on Wall Street. Harper Business 2009 382p $27.99; pa $16.99   **332.6**
1. Economics 2. Economics -- History 3. Economics -- Psychological aspects 4. Rational expectations (Economic theory) 5. Wall Street (New York, N.Y.)
ISBN 978-0-06-059899-0; 0-06-059899-9; 978-0-06-059903-4 pa; 0-06-059903-0 pa

LC 2008-52718

"A must-read for anyone interested in the markets, our economy or government, this dense but spellbinding work brings modern finance and economics to life." Publ Wkly
Includes bibliographical references

Hagstrom, Robert G.

The **Warren** Buffett way; 2nd ed; John Wiley 2005 xxiii, 245p il $24.95; pa $14.95   **332.6**
1. Financiers 2. Investments
ISBN 0-471-64811-6; 0-471-74367-4 pa

LC 2004-13841

This edition "encompasses Buffett's numerous investments and accomplishments over the past ten years, as well as the timeless and highly successful investment strategies and techniques he has always used to come out a market winner." Publisher's note
Includes bibliographical references

Hudson, Michael

The **monster**; how a gang of predatory lenders and Wall Street bankers fleeced America--and spawned a global crisis. [by] Michael W. Hudson. Times Books 2010 365p $26; ebook $12.99 **332.6**
1. Banks and banking -- Corrupt practices 2. Global

Financial Crisis, 2008-2009 3. Mortgages
ISBN 978-0-8050-9046-8; 978-1-4299-4004-7 ebook

LC 2010-3223

The author "exposes the source of the so-called toxic subprime mortgages that led to the 2008 financial crisis. He picks his way through a warren of mortgage brokers and lending companies that sat just outside banking regulations in the years following the savings and loan crisis. The book concentrates on the practices of mortgage lenders FAMCO and Ameriquest Mortgage, at one point the largest U.S. subprime lender. . . . This is essential reading for anyone concerned with the mortgage crisis." Libr J
Includes bibliographical references

Kelly, Kate

Street fighters; the last 72 hours of Bear Stearns, the toughest firm on Wall Street. Portfolio 2009 247p hardcover o.p. pa $16   **332.6**
1. Bank failures 2. Financial crises -- United States 3. Investment banking 4. Investments 5. Wall Street (New York, N.Y.)
ISBN 978-1-5918-4273-6; 1-5918-4273-5; 978-1-5918-4318-4 pa; 1-5918-4318-9 pa

LC 2009-07694

This is an account of the collapse of the Bear Stearns investment bank in March 2008.

"Enlivened by graphic descriptions of executive disarray and cameo profiles of scrambling financiers as they come to appreciate the magnitude of the disaster they unleashed . . . this riveting account puts the ensuing worldwide financial crises in stark perspective." Publ Wkly
Includes bibliographical references

Lowenstein, Roger

The **end** of Wall Street. Penguin Press 2010 xxv, 339p $27.95   **332.6**
1. Financial crises -- United States 2. Global Financial Crisis, 2008-2009 3. Wall Street (New York, N.Y.) 4. Wall Street -- History
ISBN 978-1-59420-239-1; 1-59420-239-7

LC 2009-50864

Lowenstein "examines the past three years of economic collapse, chronicling actions and inactions from dozens of villains and a few heroes. . . . [He] identifies more than 100 key players, almost all of them middle-aged white males from Wall Street, private mortgage companies, law firms, federal government agencies and the U.S. Congress. The narrative consistently demonstrates how almost all of those who could have halted the coming recession by employing common sense instead decided that the housing market would never collapse." Kirkus
Includes bibliographical references

Lutnick, Howard

On top of the world; Cantor Fitzgerald and 9/11: a story of loss and renewal. {by} Howard Lutnick and Tom Barbash. HarperCollins Pubs. 2002 282p il $25.95; pa $14.95   **332.6**
1. September 11 terrorist attacks, 2001
ISBN 0-06-051029-3; 0-06-051030-7 pa

LC 2002-27550

The bond-trading firm Cantor Fitzgerald lost 658 employees on September 11, 2001. "'On Top of the World' sets out to tell the story of Cantor Fitzgerald's tragedy, and its survival, largely from its chairman's point of view; the book is interspersed with . . . passages in {Howard} Lutnick's own voice." N Y Times Book Rev

Mahar, Maggie

★ **Bull!**: a history of the boom, 1982-1999; what drove the breakneck market--and what every investor needs to know about financial cycles. HarperBusiness 2003 xxii, 486p il $27.95; pa $16.95 **332.6**
1. Business cycles 2. Wall Street (New York, N.Y.)
ISBN 0-06-056413-X; 0-06-056414-8 pa
LC 2003-51131
This is a "history of the 1982-99 bull market in U.S. stocks. {The author} explains that this bull market got its initial impetus from both the undervaluation of equities during the 1970s and the end of the Cold War. . . . Mahar concludes by summarizing how investors who haven't seen a bear market for 17 years might plan their investing strategies. Mahar takes complicated topics and explains them clearly for the average reader. Her exceptional book is most highly recommended to even the smallest public or academic library." Libr J
Includes bibliographical references

Malkiel, Burton Gordon

★ A **random** walk down Wall Street; the time-tested strategy for successful investing. [by] Burton G. Malkiel. Rev. ed.; W.W. Norton & Co. 2011 445p il $29.95 **332.6**
1. Investments 2. Stocks
ISBN 978-0-393-08143-5
LC 2010-41866
The author argues "that it is extremely rare for an individual investor to consistently beat the stock-market averages. Investors are better off buying and holding an index fund than attempting to buy and sell individual securities or actively managed mutual funds. . . . This readable investment guide for individuals offers information on the full range of new investment products available, the results of current research by academics and other marketplace professionals, and a section on investment strategies for retired investors or those anticipating retirement. This excellent book offers important information for individual investors and is a valuable resource for library patrons." Booklist

McGee, Suzanne

Chasing Goldman Sachs; how the masters of the universe melted Wall Street down--and why they'll take us to the brink again. Crown Publishers 2010 398p $27; ebook $13.99 **332.6**
1. Banks and banking 2. Finance -- United States -- History 3. Financial crises -- United States 4. Global Financial Crisis, 2008-2009 5. Investment banking -- United States
ISBN 978-0-307-46011-0; 0-307-46011-8; 978-0-307-46012-7 ebook
LC 2009-53440

This "is an exceptionally lucid, well-written account of how and why the financial system broke down." Washington Post
Includes bibliographical references

Siegel, Jeremy J.

★ **Stocks** for the long run; the definitive guide to financial market returns and long-term investment strategies. 4th ed.; McGraw-Hill 2008 380p il $34.95 **332.6**
1. Stocks
ISBN 978-0-07-149470-0; 0-07-149470-7
LC 2007-42478
This guide to investments "provides extensive coverage including efficient markets, market anomalies, historical returns, securities valuation, behavioral finance, and derivatives. . . . This book should be in the library of every serious investor." Choice
Includes bibliographical references

Tett, Gillian

Fool's gold; how the bold dream of a small tribe at J.P. Morgan was corrupted by Wall Street greed and unleashed a catastrophe. Free Press 2009 293p $26; pa $16 **332.6**
1. Credit derivatives 2. Financial crises -- United States 3. Housing -- United States -- Finance 4. Investments 5. Wall Street (New York, N.Y.)
ISBN 978-1-4165-9857-2; 1-4165-9857-X; 978-1-4391-0013-4 pa; 1-4391-0013-6 pa
LC 2009-5127
Traces the relationship between a team of JP Morgan banking gurus and the current financial crisis, documenting their invention of a bold variety of allegedly risk-free investments that sparked a frenzy in the banking world and may have directly contributed to the market crash.
Tett "deploys a remarkable sense of pacing, generating real suspense over rapidly inflating debt on bank balance sheets; by the time Lehman Brothers fails, the book has become a bonafide page-turner. . . . Tett's explosive, illuminating narrative is the one to read for anyone confused by the present financial mess." Publ Wkly
Includes bibliographical references

332.7 Credit

Acharya, Viral V.

Guaranteed to fail; Fannie Mae, Freddie Mac, and the debacle of mortgage finance. [by] Viral V. Acharya [et al.] Princeton University Press 2011 232p il $24.95; ebook $24.95 **332.7**
1. Business failures 2. Financial crises 3. Housing 4. Mortgages
ISBN 978-0-691-15078-9; 978-1-4008-3809-7 ebook
LC 2011000247
"The authors of Guaranteed to Fail are specialists in applied financial and housing economics. They believe in the necessity of choosing among three options: should Fannie Mae and Freddie Mac exist? Should there be a private-public partnership of mortgage guarantees? Should government

end housing subsidies? . . . The authors argue that overextension in housing came from the private sector, Congress, and government-sponsored enterprises." Choice

Includes bibliographical references

Andrews, Edmund L.

Busted; life inside the great mortgage meltdown. W. W. Norton 2009 220p $25.95   **332.7**

1. Adjustable rate mortgages 2. Houses -- Buying and selling 3. Housing -- Prices 4. Housing -- United States -- Finance 5. Journalists 6. Mortgages 7. Real estate

ISBN 978-0-393-06794-1; 0-393-96794-7

LC 2009-09074

This is an "examination of the housing crisis, a story that turned personal when New York Times economics reporter Andrews got caught up in the housing bubble after falling in love with a woman and a house." Publ Wkly

Atwood, Margaret

Payback; debt and the shadow side of wealth. House of Anansi Press 2008 230p   **332.7**

1. Debt 2. Debt -- Moral and ethical aspects 3. Debt -- Social aspects 4. Debt in literature 5. Wealth

ISBN 978-0-88784-800-1

This volume collects novelist Margaret Atwood's Massey Lectures, originally broadcast on the CBC. She investigates the "subject of debt, exploring debt as an ancient and central motif in religion, literature, and the structure of human societies." (Publisher's note) Bibliography. Index.

"Delivered with . . . [Atwood's] trademark wit and imagination, this is a meditation that challenges conventional thinking on one of the most morally pressing issues we face." Booklist

Includes bibliographical references

Leonard, Robin

★ **Credit** repair; by Robin Leonard and Attorney John Lamb. 9th ed.; Nolo 2009 268p il pa $24.99   **332.7**

1. Consumer credit

ISBN 978-1-4133-1019-1; 1-4133-1019-2

LC 2009-4833

This book offers advice on assessing your debt situation, avoiding overspending, handling existing debts, cleaning your credit file, how credit reports are used, and building and maintaining good credit.

Morgenson, Gretchen

Reckless endangerment; how outsized ambition, greed, and corruption led to economic armageddon. [by] Gretchen Morgenson, Joshua Rosner. Times Books 2011 331p il $30; ebook $12.99   **332.7**

1. Financial crises 2. Financial crises -- United States -- 21st century 3. Global Financial Crisis, 2008-2009 4. Mortgages 5. Subprime mortgage loans

ISBN 978-0-8050-9120-5; 978-1-4299-6577-4 ebook

LC 2010047594

"A sobering account of some sordid recent history that's so clear and detailed that pros and novices will find its account rich and informative, and deeply depressing." Publ Wkly

Scurlock, James D.

Maxed out; hard times, easy credit, and the era of predatory lenders. Scribner 2007 248p il $24 **332.7**

1. Consumer credit 2. Credit -- United States 3. Credit cards -- United States 4. Debtor and creditor

ISBN 978-1-4165-3251-4; 1-4165-3251-X

LC 2006-51246

Scurlock presents a critique of the credit industry in the United States.

This is an "astute indictment of the credit industry. . . . Not all financial experts share Scurlock's pessimism about an indebted society. But he builds a persuasive case that deserves serious attention." Christ Sci Monit

Includes bibliographical references

333   Economics of land and energy

Clover, Charles

The **end** of the line; how overfishing is changing the world and what we eat. New Press 2006 386p $26.95   **333**

1. Commercial fishing

ISBN 978-1-59558-109-9; 1-59558-109-X

LC 2006-12058

"Clover's hard-hitting approach will probably anger some, but his argument that we will soon run out of fish unless we take drastic measures . . . is persuasive." Publ Wkly

Includes bibliographical references

333.3   Private ownership of land

Haden, Jeff

★ The **complete** dictionary of real estate terms explained simply; what smart investors need to know. Atlantic Pub. Group 2006 286p pa $21.95   **333.3**

1. Real estate -- Dictionaries 2. Reference books

ISBN 978-0-910627-01-6; 0-910627-01-0

LC 2006-29746

"A licensed real estate broker defines over 2400 terms for potential home buyers and sellers." Libr J

Includes bibliographical references

Irwin, Robert

Tips & traps for negotiating real estate; 3rd ed.; McGraw-Hill 2010 246p pa $17; ebook $17 **333.3**

1. Houses -- Buying and selling 2. Negotiation 3. Real estate business 4. Real estate investment

ISBN 978-0-07-175040-0 pa; 978-0-07-175088-2 ebook

LC 2010029971

This guide to negotiating real estate transactions covers "getting a better price in a down market; negotiating a quick sale; dealing with reluctant lenders; keeping the upper hand when buying a foreclosed property; [and] talking a seller into financing your purchase." Publisher's note

333.7 Natural resources and energy

Duncan, Dayton

The **national** parks; America's best idea: an illustrated history. with a preface by Ken Burns; picture research by Susanna Steisel and Aileen Silverstone. Alfred A. Knopf 2009 403p il map $50 **333.7**
1. National parks and reserves -- United States 2. Nature conservation
ISBN 978-0-307-26896-9

LC 2009-20880
The author delves "into the history of the park idea, from the first sighting by white men in 1851 of the valley that would become Yosemite and the creation of the world's first national park at Yellowstone in 1872, through the most recent additions to a system that now encompasses nearly four hundred sites and 84 million acres." Publisher's note
Includes bibliographical references

Goleman, Daniel

Ecological intelligence; how knowing the hidden impacts of what we buy can change everything. Doubleday 2009 276p $26 **333.7**
1. Consumers 2. Environmental protection 3. Industries
ISBN 0-385-52782-9; 978-0-385-52782-8

LC 2008-41811
"Brimming with intriguing, useful, and galvanizing information, this is an exceptionally sharp, innovative, and realistic approach to raising the demand for environmentally safe merchandise." Booklist

Miller, Char

Gifford Pinchot and the making of modern environmentalism. Island Press (Washington, D.C.) 2001 458p il $28 **333.7**
1. Conservation of natural resources -- United States -- History 2. Conservationists 3. Conservationists -- United States 4. Foresters 5. Governors 6. Politicians -- United States
ISBN 1-55963-822-2

LC 2001-5665
"Charismatic, progressive, and controversial, Gifford Pinchot (1865-1946) established and directed the Forest Service under Theodore Roosevelt, lobbied hard for responsible logging practices, expressed prescient warnings about pollution, and called for sustainable energy. Miller's animated biography portrays Pinchot in all his fervor, and environmentalism in all its complexity." Booklist
Includes bibliographical references (p.)

Speth, James Gustave

The **bridge** at the end of the world; capitalism, the environment, and crossing from crisis to sustainability. Yale University Press 2008 295p il $28 **333.7**
1. Capitalism 2. Environmental policy
ISBN 978-0-300-13611-1; 0-300-13611-0

LC 2007-43584
This book "is a superb synthesis of the great economic questions of our time: how to reconcile markets with environmental sustainability; efficiency with equality; and trade and global openness with socially defensible standards of living." Am Prospect
Includes bibliographical references

Wilkins, Thurman

John Muir; apostle of nature. University of Okla. Press 1995 xxvii, 302p il maps hardcover o.p. pa $21.95 **333.7**
1. Authors 2. Biography, Individual 3. Naturalists 4. Writers on nature
ISBN 0-8061-2797-X pa

LC 95-11426
"Wilkins follows Muir from his Scottish boyhood, clouded by a harsh, fundamentalist father, to an adolescence of arduous farmwork in Wisconsin to a lifelong career of exploration and study of wildernesses, particularly those of the western U.S., and vividly relates some of Muir's more perilous adventures on cliffside and snowfield. . . . An affectionate, uncluttered tale of an American folk hero." Booklist
Includes bibliographical references

Encyclopedia of global resources; editor, Craig W. Allin. Salem Press 2010 4v il map set $395 **333.7**
1. Natural resources -- Encyclopedias 2. Reference books
ISBN 978-1-58765-644-6; 1-58765-644-2

LC 2010-1984
"This four-volume set provides a wide variety of perspectives about Earth's natural resources and explains the interrelationships among resource exploitation, environmentalism, geology, and biology. Allin . . . presents 576 articles on resources such as oil and tar sands, nations from Argentina to Zimbabwe, government laws and conventions, and historical events. . . . [This encyclopedia] offers real value and sheds important light on where we derive our mineral and biological resources, how they are processed, what they are used for, and how they fit into the global economy." Libr J
Includes bibliographical references

333.72 Conservation and protection

Beavan, Colin

No impact man; the adventures of a guilty liberal who attempts to save the planet, and the discoveries he makes about himself and our way of life in the process. Farrar, Straus, and Giroux 2009 274p $25; pa $15 **333.72**
1. Bloggers 2. Conservationists 3. Environmental protection 4. Environmental protection -- Citizen participation 5. Global warming -- Environmental aspects 6. Journalists 7. Nature -- Effect of human beings on -- New York (N.Y.)
ISBN 978-0-374-22288-8; 0-374-22288-6; 978-0-312-42983-6 pa; 0-312-42983-5 pa

LC 2009-10188
"An inspiring, persuasive argument that individuals are not helpless in the battle against environmental degradation and global warming." Kirkus
Includes bibliographical references

Brinkley, Douglas

The **quiet** world; saving Alaska's wilderness kingdom, 1879-1960. Harper 2011 576p il map $29.99; ebook $23.99   **333.72**

1. Environmental protection 2. Natural history -- Alaska 3. Nature conservation

ISBN 978-0-06-200596-0; 978-0-06-203533-2 ebook

This book "brims over with information and insight, passion and insistence and some carelessness. In fact, it's a bit like Alaska itself: large, formidable, raw and ultimately unforgettable." Washington Post

Includes bibliographical references

Kostigen, Thomas M.

The **green** book; the everyday guide to saving the planet one simple step at a time. Elizabeth Rogers and Thomas M. Kostigen; with a foreword by Cameron Diaz and William McDonough. Three Rivers Press 2007 xix, 201p $13.95   **333.72**

1. Environmental protection -- Citizen participation 2. Environmentalism

ISBN 9780307381354; 0307381358

LC 2007013222

It was the authors' intent to "address the fact that Americans endanger the balance of the ecosystem by the amount of waste we produce, the amount of water we use, and the amount of energy we consume." In order to influence readers' behavior, they present observations and suggestions for living green from celebrities including Robert Redford, Ellen DeGeneres, Jennifer Aniston, Faith Hill, and Dale Earnhardt Jr. (Booklist) Topics include ATM receipts . . . [t]urn[ing] off the tap while you brush your teeth . . . [and] voice-mail service for your home phone. (Publisher's notes)

McDaniel, Carl N.

Wisdom for a livable planet; the visionary work of Terri Swearingen, Dave Foreman, Wes Jackson, Helena Norberg-Hodge, Werner Fornos, Herman Daly, Stephen Schneider, and David Orr. Trinity University Press 2005 277p hardcover o.p. pa $17.95   **333.72**

1. Environmental sciences

ISBN 1-595-34008-4; 1-595-34009-2 pa

LC 2004-19081

The author personalizes "critical environmental issues via profiles of eight 'visionaries' agitating for a more livable planet. . . . His subjects are prominent in the areas of hazardous waste incineration, biodiversity, sustainable agriculture, appropriate technology, population control, rational economic planning, climate concerns and environmental education. . . . The stories of these eight ecological warriors are profoundly appealing in that they show the diverse ways that people can commit to a common cause." Publ Wkly

Includes bibliographical references

McKibben, Bill

★ The **Bill** McKibben reader; pieces from an active life. Henry Holt 2008 442p pa $18 **333.72**

1. Environmental protection 2. Environmental protection -- Citizen participation

ISBN 978-0-8050-7627-1 pa; 0-8050-7627-1 pa

LC 2007-39609

This is a "collection of essays gleaned from books and periodicals published between 1982 and 2007. Most of the 44 essays come from a diverse array of magazines, including The New Yorker, Mother Jones, Outside, Gourmet, and Christian Century. . . . Essays are loosely divided into categories that include consumerism, activism, the changing planet, the meaning of community, and the sufficiency of nature. . . . Readers new to McKibben will be entertained, informed, and perhaps even inspired to make the positive changes that McKibben desires for the world." Libr J

Nelson, Gaylord

Beyond Earth Day; fulfilling the promise. [by] Gaylord Nelson with Susan Campbell and Paul Wozniak; with a foreword by Robert Kennedy, Jr. University of Wisconsin Press 2002 xx, 201p il map $26.95   **333.72**

1. Earth Day 2. Environmental movement 3. Environmentalism

ISBN 0-299-18040-9

LC 2002-2806

"The Earth Day founder presents exceptionally lucid explanations of a host of current ecoissues." Booklist

Includes bibliographical references

★ **American** earth; environmental writing since Thoreau. edited by Bill McKibben; foreword by Al Gore. Literary Classics of the United States 2008 1047p il $40   **333.72**

1. Ecocriticism 2. Ecology in literature 3. Environmental literature 4. Environmental movement 5. Environmental protection 6. Environmentalism 7. Literature -- Collections 8. Nature conservation

ISBN 978-1-59853-020-9; 1-59853-020-8

LC 2007-940683

This book "can be read as a survey of the literature of American environmentalism, but above all, it should be enjoyed for the sheer beauty of the writing." Publ Wkly

Includes bibliographical references

Green volunteers; the world guide to voluntary work in nature conservation. editor, Fabio Ausenda. 7th ed; Green Volunteers; distributed by Universe Pub 2009 255p pa $16.95   **333.72**

1. Nature conservation -- Directories 2. Reference books 3. Volunteer work -- Directories

ISBN 978-88-89060-14-8; 88-89060-14-X

LC 2008-943207

This book "lists over 200 projects worldwide for those who want to experience active conservation work as a volunteer. Projects are in a variety of habitats and countries, lasting from one week to one year or more. Projects involve volunteer work in wildlife rehabilitation centers, national parks, and protected areas, and general conservation work with a variety of animal species." Publisher's note

333.73 Land

Biggers, Jeff

Reckoning at Eagle Creek; the secret legacy of coal in the heartland. Nation Books 2010 300p il $26.95   **333.73**

1. Coal mines and mining 2. Coal mines and mining -- Illinois -- Eagle Creek Region 3. Mountain life -- Illinois

ISBN 978-1-56858-421-8; 1-56858-421-0

LC 2009-32686

Biggers "takes a look at coal and its role in the history of southern Illinois as well as its human and environmental costs. Biggers also tells a personal story as he chronicles the saga of his family's strip-mined homestead in an area that one day would be a part of the Shawnee National Forest. . . . A lot of history is presented here in a personal style by a cultural historian with a keen eye. A valuable read for followers of environmental history." Libr J

Includes bibliographical references

333.79 Energy

McGraw, Seamus

The **end** of country. Random House 2011 245p $26; ebook $13.99   **333.79**

1. Energy policy 2. Energy resources

ISBN 978-1-4000-6853-1; 978-0-679-60431-0 ebook

LC 2010035972

"In 2006, in a hardscrabble part of Pennsylvania that had long lost its allure as a farming and industrial area, geologists began investigating the Marcellus Shale. It turned out to be the richest deposit of natural gas ever discovered anywhere. When his widowed mother was approached about permitting natural-gas exploration on their farm, journalist McGraw had to weigh their need for money against the future prospects of the farmland. Chronicling the impact of the find on his mother and her neighbors, McGraw's research led to this impressively detailed, highly engaging look at issues of energy policy, economics, and sociology that arose when a bucolic town was suddenly faced with the 'traveling circus' of energy exploration. . . . A completely engaging look at how energy policy affected a quiet, rural town." Booklist

Yergin, Daniel

The **quest**; energy, security and the remaking of the modern world. Penguin Press 2011 804p il map $37.95   **333.79**

1. Climatic changes 2. Energy policy 3. Energy resources 4. Environmental literature 5. Globalization 6. Historical literature 7. Money -- Political aspects 8. Power resources -- Political aspects

ISBN 978-1-59420-283-4; 1-59420-283-4

LC 2011013100

"This book combines four books. The first . . . provides global history of oil, natural gas, and nuclear power from 1991 to 2011. . . . The second part of 'The Quest' traces a path from the discovery of climate change as an esoteric interest of a few scientists in the nineteenth century to the introduction of new climate change policies . . . intended to make a profound transformation of the energy foundations that support the world economy.n . . . 'The Quest's third part looks at nuclear and renewable alternatives to fossil fuels. . . . When Yergin looks to the future in his fourth book, he asks how the economic benefits from an average megawatt of power can be increased while at the same time reducing its negative effects on the environment and health." (New York Review of Books)

This book "is a masterly piece of work and, as a comprehensive guide to the world's great energy needs and dilemmas, it will be hard to beat." Economist

Includes bibliographical references

333.8 Subsurface resources

Goodstein, David L.

Out of gas; the end of the age of oil. {by} David Goodstein. Norton 2004 140p il $21.95; pa $13.95   **333.8**

1. Petroleum 2. Petroleum industry and trade 3. Petroleum reserves

ISBN 0-393-05857-3; 0-393-32647-0 pa

LC 2003-10376

"Goodstein's predictions are based on a sophisticated understanding of physics and thermodynamics, and on a simple observation about natural resources." N Y Times Book Rev

Includes bibliographical references and index

333.91 Water and lands adjoining bodies of water

Dean, Cornelia

Against the tide; the battle for America's beaches. Columbia Univ. Press 1999 279p il $60; pa $18.95   **333.91**

1. Beach erosion -- United States 2. Beaches 3. Coast changes -- United States 4. Coastal zone management -- United States 5. Coasts 6. Seashore ecology

ISBN 0-231-08418-8; 0-231-08419-6 pa

LC 98-50755

Dean discusses the ecology of American beaches and contends that they are threatened by coastal development and erosion

"This thoroughly researched and thoughtful book is destined to become a classic of environmental science writing." Libr J

Includes bibliographical references

Fishman, Charles

The **big** thirst; Charles Fishman. Free Press 2011 388p. ebook $12.99; $26.99   **333.91**

1. Water resources development 2. Water supply

ISBN 978-1-4391-2493-2 ebook; 978-1-4391-0207-7

LC 2010033989

This book presents an "assessment of the current politics, economics, and culture of water." It was the author's intent to demonstrate "that the water we have now is all the water we will ever have and that our 'golden age' of 'abundant, safe, and cheap' water may soon end, thanks to deteriorating infrastructure, . . . rising urban populations, and climate change. Both 'water complacency' and 'water poverty' are rampant. . . . Among his many case studies are Las Vegas water extravaganzas and India's lack of 24/7 water even in its booming cities, which keeps millions of girls out of school to collect and carry each day's water supply. . . . Fishman praises tap water, observes that water consciousness is 'infectious,' and declares that most water problems are, in fact, solvable." (Booklist)

This is a "lively and invaluable assessment of the current politics, economics, and culture of water. Lyrical in his descriptions of the beauty and wonder of water, Fishman is rigorous when explaining that the water we have now is all the water we will ever have and that our 'golden age' of 'abundant, safe, and cheap' water may soon end, thanks to deteriorating infrastructure (7 billion gallons leak out of our water systems every day), rising urban populations, and climate change." Booklist

Includes bibliographical references and index.

Harden, Blaine

A **river** lost; the life and death of the Columbia. Norton 1996 271p maps $25; pa $14.95   **333.91**
1. Economic development 2. Pollution 3. Water resources development
ISBN 0-393-03936-6; 0-393-31690-4 pa
LC 95-38618

In this look at the development of Columbia River region, the author "examines the changes—sociological, environmental, economic and aesthetic—that the taming of this great river wrought. His wonderful account touches on the destruction of Native American cultures dependent on the river and its salmon, and on the near extinction of the salmon themselves. Also fairly portrayed are the people and industries currently dependent on both the managed river and massive government subsidies." Publ Wkly

Includes bibliographical references

Rothfeder, Jeffrey

Every drop for sale; our desperate battle over water in a world about to run out. Tarcher/Putnam 2001 205p hardcover o.p. pa $14.95   **333.91**
1. Water supply 2. Water-supply -- Economic aspects
ISBN 1-58542-114-6; 978-1-58542-367-5 pa;
1-58542-367-X pa
LC 2001-27903

"Like the drip of water on stone, Rothfeder's steady exposition of horrors will wear down any reader's doubts that water is the next flashpoint of global politics, human rights and health issues." Publ Wkly

Includes bibliographical references

Ward, Diane Raines

Water wars; drought, flood, folly, and the politics of thirst. Riverhead Bks. 2002 280p $24.95; pa $14   **333.91**
1. Hydraulic engineering 2. Water -- Political aspects 3. Water rights 4. Water supply 5. Water-supply -- International cooperation 6. Water-supply -- Management
ISBN 1-57322-229-1; 1-57322-995-4 pa
LC 2002-21301

"Ward writes with the sensibilities and concerns of an environmentalist. But unexpectedly, delightfully, she's an environmentalist who loves the scale, ingenuity and power of engineering." N Y Times Book Rev

Includes bibliographical references

333.95   Biological resources

Barrow, Mark V.

Nature's ghosts; confronting extinction from the age of Jefferson to the age of ecology. [by] Mark V. Barrow, Jr. University of Chicago Press 2009 497p il $35   **333.95**
1. Biologists 2. Endangered species 3. Endangered species -- Law and legislation 4. Extinct animals 5. Extinction (Biology) 6. Wildlife conservation 7. Wildlife conservation -- United States -- History
ISBN 978-0-226-03814-8; 0-226-03814-9
LC 2008-49085

The author "retraces the history of the earliest European and North American naturalists, from those who refused to believe that species comprising a perfect, stable world could go extinct, to the acceptance of extinction at the hands of humans and the legal mechanisms created to halt it. . . . Professionals in ecology, conservation biology, and wildlife management and readers interested in natural history will find this book hard to put down." Choice

Includes bibliographical references

Chadwick, Douglas H.

The **company** we keep; America's endangered species. {by} Douglas H. Chadwick and Joel Sartore. National Geographic Soc. 1996 157p il hardcover o.p. pa $16   **333.95**
1. Endangered species 2. Environmental policy -- United States 3. Wildlife conservation
ISBN 0-7922-7132-7 pa
LC 96-18874

"The book is not built solely around the photographs. But the pictures are collectively a good storyteller. They're well-edited, and accompanied by maps and charts that help explain how man is threatening many species." Christ Sci Monit

Includes bibliographical references

Cousteau, Jacques Yves

The **human,** the orchid, and the octopus; exploring and conserving our natural world. [by] Jacques Cousteau and Susan Schiefelbein. Bloomsbury 2007 305p hardcover o.p. pa $16   **333.95**
1. Authors 2. Divers 3. Human influence on nature 4. Nature -- Effect of human beings on 5. Nature conservation 6. Naval officers 7. Nonfiction writers 8. Oceanographers 9. Oceanography
ISBN 978-1-59691-417-9; 1-59691-417-3; 978-1-59691-418-6 pa; 1-59691-418-1 pa
LC 2007-18824

"Cousteau's reverence for life's miracles . . . shines through in this eloquent testimony on the importance of pursuing higher ideals, particularly the preservation of the oceans and the natural world for future generations." Publ Wkly

Includes bibliographical references

Ellis, Richard

Tuna; a love story. Alfred A. Knopf 2008 334p il $27.95; pa $16 **333.95**

1. Artists 2. Authors 3. Bluefin tuna 4. Children's authors 5. Commercial fishing 6. Endangered species 7. Illustrators 8. Tuna 9. Tuna fisheries 10. Tuna fishing -- Environmental aspects

ISBN 978-0-307-26715-3; 0-307-26715-6; 978-0-307-38710-3 pa; 0-307-38710-0 pa

LC 2007-52253

"Ellis loves this fish. His rapt description of the physiology that makes tunas one of the fastest things in the ocean . . . lends emotional urgency to his account of the collapsing tuna fishery." Orion

Includes bibliographical references

Fraser, Caroline

Rewilding the world; dispatches from the conservation revolution. Metropolitan Books 2009 400p map $28.50 **333.95**

1. Biodiversity conservation 2. Ecology 3. Endangered species 4. Restoration ecology 5. Wildlife conservation

ISBN 978-0-8050-7826-8; 0-8050-7826-6

LC 2009-32989

"Heavily researched with endnotes for those looking for more information, this truly is an essential read for conservationists, biologists, and anyone interested in the natural world." Libr J

Includes bibliographical references

Goodall, Jane

★ The **ten** trusts; what we must do to care for the animals we love. {by} Jane Goodall and Marc Bekoff. HarperSanFrancisco 2002 xx, 200p hardcover o.p. pa $14.95 **333.95**

1. Animal rights 2. Animal welfare 3. Human influence on nature 4. Wildlife conservation

ISBN 0-06-251757-0; 0-06-055611-0 pa

LC 2002-68717

"An accessible, compelling, and important exposé." Booklist

Includes bibliographical references

Greenberg, Paul

Four fish; the future of the last wild food. Penguin Press 2010 284p $25.95 **333.95**

1. Bass (Fish) 2. Codfish 3. Commercial fishing 4. Fish culture 5. Salmon 6. Tuna

ISBN 978-1-59420-256-8

LC 2010-1276

"The narrative is grounded in common sense and anchored by first-rate, on-scene reporting from the Yukon and Mekong Rivers, Lake Bardawil in the Sinai Peninsula and the waters off the coasts of Long Island, Greece, Hawaii and the Shetland Islands. Hugely informative, sincere and infectiously curious and enthusiastic." Kirkus

Includes bibliographical references

Hoekstra, Jonathan M.

The **atlas** of global conservation; changes, challenges and opportunities to make a difference. [by] Jonathan Hoekstra ... [et al.]; edited by Jennifer L. Molnar. University of California Press 2010 234p il map $49.95 **333.95**

1. Atlases 2. Conservation of natural resources 3. Environmental protection 4. Globalization 5. Reference books

ISBN 978-0-520-26256-0

LC 2009-23617

"Focusing primarily on biomes and ecosystems, this valuable atlas promotes a deeper understanding of the challenges involved in preserving and maintaining these habitats and resources. Basically an analysis of the current state of the globe, the book highlights conservation challenges through chapters on habitats, species distributions, deforestation, global warming, coastal development, and pollution. . . . The book is unique and well done." Voice Youth Advocates

Includes bibliographical references

Kurlansky, Mark

Cod; a biography of the fish that changed the world. Penguin Bks. 1998 294p il pa $14 **333.95**

1. Codfish 2. Commercial fishing 3. Cooking -- Fish

ISBN 0-14-027501-0

LC 97-12165

Kurlansky discusses the history of commercial cod fishing and the plight of the Atlantic fish and fisheries today as the cod faces extinction.

This book offers "maximum readability, plenty of handsome illustrations, and a 40-page appendix of superlatively annotated recipes." Booklist

Includes bibliographical references

Lebbin, Daniel J.

The **American** Bird Conservancy guide to bird conservation; [by] Daniel J. Lebbin, Michael J. Parr, and George H. Fenwick; with a foreword by Jonathan Franzen. University of Chicago Press 2010 446p il map $45; ebook $27 **333.95**

1. Birds -- United States 2. Wildlife conservation

ISBN 978-0-226-64727-2; 0-226-64727-7; 978-0-226-6472-6 ebook

LC 2010007646

The authors survey "the comprehensive status of bird conservation in the Americas, primarily focusing on North America. . . . 'WatchList Birds' provides accounts for 212 US birds—priority species for conservation—with a color plate, map, and text sections on distribution, threats, conservation, and action. 'Habitats' gives an overview of 12 major North American habitats (tundra, wetlands, grasslands, etc.) and includes several prime site descriptions within each, accompanied by the same features as the 'WatchList' accounts. The third major section, 'Threats,' includes sections such as 'Habitat Loss,' 'Pollution and Toxics,' and 'Climate Change,' and describes problems, solutions, and actions. . . . A beautiful production visually, the book is inviting as well as an unprecedented, rewarding conservation reference source." Choice

Includes glossary and bibliographical references

McNamee, Thomas

The **return** of the wolf to Yellowstone. Holt & Co. 1997 354p il maps hardcover o.p. pa $15   **333.95**
1. Endangered species 2. Wolves
ISBN 0-8050-5792-7 pa
LC 96-39702

"An advocate for the reintroduction of the gray wolf to Yellowstone National Park, McNamee kept careful watch over the legal wrangling that accompanied this controversial endeavor, the challenges of its execution, and the complex questions it has raised, then recorded the entire story in this vivid day-by-day chronicle." Booklist

Includes bibliographical references

Owens, Delia

The **eye** of the elephant; an epic adventure in the African wilderness. [by] Delia and Mark Owens. Houghton Mifflin 1992 305p il hardcover o.p. pa $16   **333.95**
1. Elephants 2. Endangered species 3. North Luangwa National Park (Zambia) 4. Wildlife conservation
ISBN 0-395-42381-3; 0-395-68090-5 pa
LC 92-17691

This is an account of the authors' efforts to save elephants in the Luangwa Valley of Zambia from poachers by involving and educating the local people.

This "is a provocative, disturbing, and eminently readable work." Nat Hist

Includes bibliographic references

Wilson, Edward O.

The **diversity** of life. Harvard Univ. Press 1992 424p il maps $31.50   **333.95**
1. Biological diversity 2. Ecology 3. Nature conservation
ISBN 0-674-21298-3
LC 92-9018

"Identifying five natural events that have disrupted evolution and global diversity (climatic changes, meteorite strikes), Wilson maintains that the present sixth great extinction is being caused by human neglect and ignorance. This important book is highly recommended." Libr J

Includes bibliographical references

★ The **future** of life. Knopf 2002 xxiv, 229p il $22; pa $13   **333.95**
1. Endangered species 2. Environmental degradation 3. Nature conservation
ISBN 0-679-45078-5; 0-679-76811-4 pa
LC 2001-38316

Wilson "proposes that there is yet time to avoid a grand planetary environmental crash provided we get serious, acknowledge a duty of stewardship and recognize an emotional affiliation . . . with other kinds of life." NY Times Book Rev

Life on earth; an encyclopedia of biodiversity, ecology, and evolution. edited by Niles Eldredge. ABC-CLIO 2002 2v set $185   **333.95**
1. Biological diversity 2. Biological diversity --

Encyclopedias 3. Ecology 4. Reference books
ISBN 1-57607-286-X
LC 2002-15852

"Four introductory essays outline the definition, importance, and preservation of biodiversity. Many of the 194 articles are about specific phyla or species . . . or important concepts. . . . Others address issues that will appeal to students and general readers. . . . Articles are clearly written, usually define specialized terms, and include bibliographies of books and popular and scholarly periodical articles." Booklist

Includes bibliographical references

★ **Sustaining** life; how human health depends on biodiversity. edited by Eric Chivian and Aaron Bernstein; Center for Health and the Global Environment Harvard Medical School; foreword by Edward O. Wilson; prologue by Kofi Annan. Oxford University Press 2008 542p il map $34.95   **333.95**
1. Biological diversity 2. Environmental health
ISBN 978-0-19-517509-7; 0-19-517509-3
LC 2007-20609

"A collaborative survey of biodiversity issues written and/or reviewed for accuracy by more than 100 scientists, this volume is motivated by its UN sponsors' sense of the world populace's indifference to the consequences of environmental degradation. Conceiving that implicating human health with the health of other species may enlist its concern, the authors collectively warn that present extinction rates are abnormally high. Seven categories of endangered species stand in as portents of the dire effects to ecosystems when extinction occurs. . . . Abundantly illustrated, this is a valuable, urgent resource suited to any general-interest library." Booklist

Includes bibliographical references (p. 445-514)

335 Socialism and related systems

Butterworth, Alex

The **world** that never was; a true story of dreamers, schemers, anarchists and secret agents. Pantheon Books 2010 482p il $30; ebook $30   **335**
1. Anarchism -- History 2. Anarchism and anarchists
ISBN 978-0-375-42511-0; 978-0-307-37903-0 ebook
LC 2009-48115

"A narrative taut with intrigue and freighted with contemporary significance." Booklist

Includes bibliographical references

Rudahl, Sharon

A **dangerous** woman; the graphic biography of Emma Goldman. The New Press 2007 115p il $17.95   **335**
1. Anarchism and anarchists -- Graphic novels 2. Anarchists 3. Biographical graphic novels 4. Essayists 5. Family planning advocates 6. Graphic novels 7. Memoirists 8. Writers on politics
ISBN 978-1-59558-064-1
LC 2007-15415

Emma Goldman was a revolutionary activist, speaker, writer, and feminist and anarchist. An immigrant to the U.S., she spoke out against inhumane working conditions, taught contraception, and opposed conscription for World War I. She founded the Free Speech League (a precursor to the ACLU), and the magazine Mother Earth. When she was deported to Russia just after the Bolshevik Revolution, she became disillusioned with the authoritarianism she found there, and she ended up supporting the fight against fascism in the Spanish Civil War. Rudahl based her graphic novel on Goldman's autobiography. The book includes nudity, sexual situations, and some violence.

335.4 Marxian systems

Marx, Karl

★ The **Communist** manifesto; [by] Karl Marx and Friedrich Engels; with an introduction and notes by Gareth Stedman Jones. Penguin Books 2002 287p pa $7 **335.4**
1. Communism
ISBN 0-14-044757-1
This document "analyzes history in terms of class conflict, predicts the imminent overthrow of the ruling bourgeoisie by the oppressed proletariat, and envisions a resulting classless society in which personal property would be abolished. The 'Manifesto' calls upon the proletariat of the world to unite and strengthen itself for this final revolution." Benet's Reader's Ency 4th edition
Includes bibliographical references

Pipes, Richard

★ **Communism**: a history. Modern Lib. 2001 175p hardcover o.p. pa $10.95 **335.4**
1. Communism
ISBN 0-679-64050-9; 0-8129-6864-6 pa
LC 2001-275458
"As a brief, polemical diatribe . . . this short account of communism should provoke and instruct." Libr J
Includes bibliographical references

Priestland, David

The **red** flag; a history of communism. Grove Press 2009 xxvii, 675p il $30 **335.4**
1. Communism
ISBN 978-0-8021-1924-7
"Starting with the origins of communist ideology in the French Revolution, . . . [this book] presents an interesting analysis of Marx's thinking as being shaped as much by Romanticism as by the Enlightenment. Priestland also examines communist governments and movements in Africa, Asia, Europe and Latin America as well as the Soviet Union, and discusses the Nazi-Soviet pact as well as Stalin's ban on anti-fascist activity in Europe, concluding with a level-headed account of the communist collapse." New Statesman
Includes bibliographical references

Wheen, Francis

Karl Marx; a life. Norton 2000 431p il $27.95; pa $14.95 **335.4**
1. Communism 2. Communists -- Biography 3.

Political and social philosophers 4. Writers on politics
ISBN 0-393-04923-X; 0-393-32157-6 pa
LC 99-87466
"Following Marx from his childhood in Trier, Germany, through his exile in London, Wheen . . . takes readers from hovel to grand house, from the International Working Man's Association to Capital, from obscurity to notoriety and back again." Publ Wkly
Includes bibliographical references

336.2 Taxes

★ **J.K.** Lasser's your income tax 2009; prepared by the J.K. Lasser Tax Institute. Wiley 2008 xxviii, 816p il pa $18.95 **336.2**
1. Income tax
ISBN 978-0-470-28002-7; 0-470-28002-6
This "guide offers line-by-line instructions on filling out tax forms and what to do to prepare throughout the year." Libr J

337 International economics

Friedman, Thomas L.

The **Lexus** and the olive tree; Updated and expanded ed; Farrar, Straus, Giroux 2000 xxi, 469p $30 **337**
1. Business and politics 2. Capitalism -- Social aspects 3. Free trade 4. Intercultural communication 5. International economic relations 6. Technological innovations -- Economic aspects 7. Technological innovations -- Social aspects
ISBN 978-0-374-18552-7; 0-374-18552-2
LC 00-29411
Friedman "explains, with anecdotes as well as analyses, what the instant electronic global economy is and what it may take to live there." N Y Times Book Rev

Stiglitz, Joseph E.

Globalization and its discontents. Norton 2002 xxii, 282p $24.95; pa $15.95 **337**
1. Foreign trade regulation 2. Globalization 3. Globalization -- Economic aspects -- Developing countries 4. International economic integration 5. International economic relations 6. International finance
ISBN 0-393-05124-2; 0-393-32439-7 pa
LC 2002-23148
"This smart, provocative study contributes significantly to the ongoing globalization debate." Publ Wkly
Includes bibliographical references

Zizek, Slavoj

First as tragedy, then as farce. Verso 2009 157p pa $12.95 **337**
1. Capitalism 2. Communism 3. Globalization
ISBN 978-1-84467-428-2
"An earnest and timely challenge, Zizek's critique of capitalism and repositioning of communist thought is both

insightful and well-reasoned, and guaranteed to rile readers across the political and theoretical spectrum." Publ Wkly
Includes bibliographical references

338   Production

Clark, Taylor

Starbucked;   a double tall tale of caffeine, commerce, and culture. Little, Brown 2007 297p $25.99   **338**
1. Coffee -- Social aspects 2. Coffee industry 3. Coffee industry -- History 4. Coffeehouses
ISBN 978-0-316-01348-2; 0-316-01348-X
LC 2007-13074

This "is a breezily written business yarn with plenty of big-picture punch." Christ Sci Monit
Includes bibliographical references

Cook, John

Our noise; the story of Merge Records, the indie label that got big and stayed small. [by] John Cook with Mac McCaughan and Laura Ballance. Algonquin Books of Chapel Hill 2009 289p il pa $18.95   **338**
1. Rock music -- History and criticism
ISBN 978-1-56512-624-4; 1-56512-624-6
LC 2009-12495

This is "an oral history of Merge Records, featuring interviews from its founders (McCaughan and Ballance), its numerous signees (featuring members of Lambchop, Spoon, the Arcade Fire, and more), and various admirers and business partners (like Dischord Records founder/Fugazi frontman Ian MacKaye). Author John Cook alternates his chapters between recounting the history of the Merge label and then profiling one particular band. . . . For still being in the game after putting out two decades worth of classic albums . . . , it's obvious that Merge—with its success and its struggles—is still wanting nothing more than to make some peers of its own. In our rushed digital age of today, there's something profoundly sweet about such a simple sentiment." PopMatters

Schwantes, Carlos A.

The West the railroads made; [by] Carlos A. Schwantes, James P. Ronda. University of Washington Press in association with Washington State Historical Society and the John 2008 xx, 229p il map $39.95   **338**
1. Railroads -- United States
ISBN 978-0-295-98769-9
LC 2007-29363

"Sprinkled throughout with marvelous reproductions of photos, maps, artwork and railroad memorabilia, this book highlights a fascinating era in our history. . . . A stunning work using well chosen archival resources to tell the story." Univ Press Books for Public and Second Sch Libr, 2009
Includes bibliographical references

★ Encyclopedia of American business; general editor, W. Davis Folsom; associate editor, Stacia N.

VanDyne. Rev. ed.; Facts On File 2011 2v set $150   **338**
1. Business -- Encyclopedias 2. Reference books
ISBN 978-0-8160-8112-7
LC 2010-28372

"Five general areas of business are covered: accounting, banking, finance, marketing, and management. This encyclopedia focuses on the terms, concepts, and associations that one is most likely to encounter in business." Publisher's note
Includes bibliographical references

338.1   Specific kinds of industries

Astyk, Sharon

A nation of farmers; defeating the food crisis on American soil. [by] Sharon Astyk & Aaron Newton. New Society Publishers 2009 392p il pa $19.95   **338.1**
1. Food relief 2. Food supply
ISBN 978-0-86571-623-0
LC 2009-483077

The authors "argue that it is both possible and necessary to stop the harm caused by industrial agriculture. They show how the food crisis is tied to the energy crisis, global warming, and resource depletion and conclude that worldwide food shortages are imminent. . . . This outstanding and well-written compendium of insights and recommendations, of fervent idealism and practical solutions, is highly recommended." Libr J
Includes bibliographical references

Berry, Wendell

Citizenship papers. Shoemaker & Hoard 2003 189p $24; pa $15   **338.1**
1. Agriculture -- Environmental aspects 2. Agriculture -- Government policy 3. Agriculture and state -- United States 4. Economic policy -- United States 5. Environmental economics
ISBN 1-593-76000-0; 1-593-76037-X pa
LC 2003-13811

"Berry's recent essays may restate what he has said before—that agribusiness and the new globalism are inimical to human thriving—but they say it better, and through different immediate subjects, saliently including sound sheep raising and 9/11, than ever before." Booklist

Hamilton, Lisa M.

Deeply rooted; unconventional farmers in the age of agribusiness. Counterpoint 2009 313p $25 **338.1**
1. Farmers
ISBN 978-1-5937-6180-6; 1-5937-6180-5
LC 2008-50526

Hamilton "profiles farmers and ranchers who believe that 'agriculture is not an industry' but, rather, 'a fundamental act that determines whether we as a society will live or die.'. . . Hamilton's in-depth portraits of independent farmers offer invaluable perspectives on American agriculture, past and present, while offering hope for a life-sustaining future." Booklist
Includes bibliographical references

Hesterman, Oran B.

Fair food; growing a healthy, sustainable food system for all. PublicAffairs 2011 302p il $24.99; ebook $9.99 **338.1**

1. Food industry 2. Food supply 3. Sustainable agriculture

ISBN 978-1-61039-006-4; 978-1-61039-007-1 ebook

LC 2010-53129

Hesterman "writes that our food system is broken and will not be able to continue supporting the world population for much longer. The author's deft explanation of our current cultivation and consumption of food should have families moving away from their supermarket aisles and into farmers' markets and community-supported agriculture programs. Hesterman urges much-needed change on the federal level, as well. . . . Guides and resources are included to help the average consumer source food locally, and the author also includes a breakdown of federal legislation and how it should be amended. A thorough, inspiring guide on how to restructure the food system for a long and healthy future, for consumers and legislators alike." Kirkus

Includes bibliographical references

Hewitt, Ben

The **town** that food saved; how one community found vitality in local food. Rodale 2009 234p $24.99 **338.1**

1. Entrepreneurship 2. Food industry 3. Food supply 4. Sustainable agriculture

ISBN 978-1-60529-686-9; 1-60529-686-4

LC 2009-34294

"Adroitly balancing professional neutrality with personal commitment, Hewitt engagingly examines this paradigm shift in the way a community feeds its citizens." Booklist

The essential agrarian reader; the future of culture, community, and the land. edited by Norman Wirzba. University Press of Kentucky 2003 276p il $27 **338.1**

1. Agriculture -- Economic aspects 2. Agriculture -- Environmental aspects 3. Agriculture -- Moral and ethical aspects 4. Agriculture -- Social aspects 5. Human ecology

ISBN 0-8131-2285-6

LC 2003-8808

"In this collection of . . . essays, farmers, philosophers, scientists, and environmentalists look at the ways in which industrial agriculture, unchecked consumerism, and the squandering of natural resources have caused great harm. . . . The contributors . . . are leaders in their fields, and have lucid, expressive writing styles. Highly recommended." Libr J

Includes bibliographical references

338.2 Extraction of minerals

Burrough, Bryan

The **big** rich; the rise and fall of the greatest Texas oil fortunes. Penguin Press 2009 466p il $29.95; pa $16 **338.2**

1. Biography, Collective 2. Energy industry executives

3. Financiers 4. Football executives 5. Petroleum industry 6. Petroleum industry and trade -- Texas -- History -- 20th century 7. Philanthropists

ISBN 978-1-59420-199-8; 1-59420-199-4; 978-0-14-311682-0 pa; 0-14-311682-7 pa

LC 2008-27043

"Full of schadenfreude and speculation—and solid, timely history too." Kirkus

Includes bibliographical references

House, Silas

Something's rising; Appalachians fighting mountaintop removal. [by] Silas House and Jason Howard; foreword by Lee Smith. University Press of Kentucky 2009 xiv, 306 p.p $27.95 **338.2**

1. Celebrities -- Appalachian Region, Southern -- Interviews 2. Coal mines and mining 3. Environmentalism -- Appalachian Region, Southern 4. Landscape protection 5. Landscape protection -- Appalachian Region, Southern -- Citizen participation 6. Mountaintop mining 7. Mountaintop removal mining -- Environmental aspects -- Appalachian Region, Southern

ISBN 978-0-8131-2546-6; 0813125464; 9780813125466

LC 2008049846

The authors focus on "the long-growing mining crisis in Central Appalachia. Twelve Appalachians—among them a college student, former union organizers, community activists and the octogenarian 'mother of folk,' Jean Ritchey—provide firsthand accounts of a disappearing way of life, a vital ecology in rapid decline, an industry that refuses to take responsibility for the devastation it causes (blowing the tops off mountains is only the latest, most destructive technique), and a nation too hooked on cheap energy to help. . . . This important collection illuminates the ongoing betrayal of the American mining town." Publ Wkly

Includes bibliographical references (p. [287]-290) and index

LeCain, Timothy J.

Mass destruction; the men and giant mines that wired America and scarred the planet. Rutgers University Press 2009 273p il map $26.95 **338.2**

1. Copper industry and trade -- History 2. Copper mines and mining 3. Copper mines and mining -- Environmental aspects 4. Copper mines and mining -- Western States 5. Mining engineering 6. Mining engineers

ISBN 978-0-8135-4529-5; 0-8135-4529-3

LC 2008-35434

The author writes "about the history, the engineering challenges, the successes of production and resulting consumption, and the environmental consequences of open-pit copper mining, mainly in the first half of the 20th century. . . . This book provokes serious second thoughts about the future of the exploitation of nature's bounty, and it should appeal to a wide audience." Choice

Includes bibliographical references and index

Maass, Peter

Crude world; the violent twilight of oil. Alfred A. Knopf 2009 276p il $27 **338.2**

1. Petroleum industry 2. Petroleum industry and trade

ISBN 978-1-4000-4169-5

LC 2009-12303

"An absorbing, relentlessly discouraging account of the disastrous effect of oil wealth on nearly everyone." Kirkus

Includes bibliographical references (p. 233-62)

Margonelli, Lisa

Oil on the brain; adventures from the pump to the pipeline. Doubleday 2007 324p hardcover o.p. pa $14.95 **338.2**

1. Petroleum industry 2. Petroleum industry and trade -- Environmental aspects 3. Petroleum industry and trade -- Social aspects 4. Petroleum industry and trade -- United States

ISBN 0-385-51145-0; 978-0-385-51145-2; 0-7679-1697-2 pa; 978-0-7679-1697-4 pa

LC 2006-20789

Margonelli examines how oil travels from petroleum fields to neighborhood gas stations.

The author "adds something fresh to the discussion by eschewing the popular (but dreary) doomsday angle in favor of an 'adventures in . . .' approach. . . . By giving voice to the people who are the links in the global oil chain, Margonelli invites us to leapfrog all the rhetoric, dry statistics, and dire pronouncements about oil in order to truly understand it." Fast Company

Includes bibliographical references

Yergin, Daniel

★ The prize; the epic quest for oil, money & power. Free Press 2008 908p il map $22 **338.2**

1. Petroleum industry 2. World politics

ISBN 978-1-4391-1012-6; 1-4391-1012-3

LC 2009-291302

This is a "history of the oil industry, from the first oil well ever drilled (near Titusville, Pennsylvania, in 1859) to the Iraqi invasion of Kuwait. It recalls advances in technology, innovations in salesmanship, and wars and truces among corporations and nations." New Yorker

Includes bibliographical references

338.4   Secondary industries and services

Almond, Steve

★ Candyfreak: a journey through the chocolate underbelly of America. Algonquin Books of Chapel Hill 2004 266p $21.95 **338.4**

1. Authors 2. Candy 3. Chocolate 4. Humorists 5. Journalists 6. Short story writers

ISBN 1-56512-421-9

LC 2003-70801

The author tells how candy "shaped his childhood and continues to define his life in ways large and small. . . . Once hundreds of American confectioners delivered regional favorites to consumers, but now the big three of candy—Hershey, Mars, and Nestlé—control the market. To find out what happened to those candies of yesteryear, Almond talks to candy collectors and historians and visits a few of the remaining independent candy companies. . . . Flavored with the author's amusingly tart sense of humor, Candyfreak is an intriguing chronicle of the passions that candy inspires and the pleasures it offers." Libr J

Includes bibliographical references

Avorn, Jerry

★ Powerful medicines; the benefits, risks, and costs of prescription drugs. Knopf 2004 448p $27.50 **338.4**

1. Drug industry 2. Drugs 3. Drugs -- Prescribing 4. Pharmaceutical industry -- United States 5. Prescription pricing

ISBN 0-375-41483-5

LC 2003-66119

The author explains "the current American prescription-drug debacle, placing it within the larger context of overall medical cost concerns. He . . . discusses what often goes awry when overworked physicians can't keep abreast of voluminous research, when patients are underinformed about generic drug availability, and when profits provide the sole motivation for pharmaceutical research. . . . A comprehensive, interesting read." Booklist

Includes bibliographical references

Burhans, Dirk E.

Crunch! a history of the great American potato chip. [by] Dirk Burhans. University of Wisconsin Press 2008 203p il $26.95 **338.4**

1. Potato chips

ISBN 978-0-299-22770-8

LC 2008-11962

"A wonderfully readable history that spans popular culture, local history, agriculture, economics, business and biography. Pass the chips please!" Univ Press Books for Public and Second Sch Libr, 2009

Includes bibliographical references

Callahan, Daniel

Taming the beloved beast; how medical technology costs are destroying our health care system. Princeton University Press 2009 267p $29.95 **338.4**

1. Medical care -- Cost control 2. Medical care -- Costs 3. Medical care, Cost of -- United States 4. Medical technology 5. Medical technology -- Economic aspects

ISBN 978-0-691-14236-4; 0-691-14236-X

LC 2009-1503

According to Callahan, . . . Americans want universal health care but are divided over how to obtain it. While bringing insightful ethical, social, political, and economic perspectives to this timely, well-documented discourse of the ballooning costs of American health care and Medicare, Callahan concentrates on the growing costs of medical technology, which, along with uncontrolled governmental health-care spending, threaten to drag this country into financial crisis. Libr J

Includes bibliographical references and index

Lewis, Michael

The **new** new thing; a Silicon Valley story. Norton 1999 268p $25.95   **338.4**

1. Businessmen -- United States -- Biography 2. Computer software executives 3. Computer software industry 4. Computer software industry -- United States -- History

ISBN 0-393-04813-6

LC 99-43412

This "is a splendid, entirely satisfying book, intelligent and fun and revealing and troubling in the correct proportions, resolutely skeptical but not at all cynical, brimming with fabulous scenes as well as sharp analysis." NY Times Book Rev

Mitford, Jessica

★ The **American** way of death revisited. Knopf 1998 296p hardcover o.p. pa $14   **338.4**

1. Cremation 2. Funeral rites and ceremonies 3. Funeral rites and ceremonies -- Economic aspects -- United States 4. Undertakers and undertaking 5. Undertakers and undertaking -- United States

ISBN 0-679-77186-7 pa

LC 97-49349

"Very interesting, informative, and easy to read, this book is written with wit, solid information, and refreshing bluntness." Libr J

Petersen, Melody

Our daily meds; how the pharmaceutical companies transformed themselves into slick marketing machines and hooked the nation on prescription drugs. Farrar, Straus and Giroux 2008 432p $26   **338.4**

1. Drug industry 2. Drugs -- Prescribing 3. Pharmaceutical industry -- Corrupt practices 4. Pharmaceutical industry -- United States 5. Pharmaceutical services -- Marketing

ISBN 978-0-374-22827-9; 0-374-22827-2

LC 2008-2097

The author shows how corporate salesmanship has triumphed over science inside the biggest pharmaceutical companies and, in turn, how this promotion driven industry has taken over the practice of medicine and is changing American life.

"Petersen takes readers beyond glossy advertising and celebrity endorsements to glimpse the alarming dark side of the American pharmaceutical industry." Libr J

Includes bibliographical references (p. 409-412)

Rudacille, Deborah

Roots of steel; the boom and bust of an American mill town. Pantheon Books 2010 290p $27   **338.4**

1. Steel industry

ISBN 9780375423680; 978-0-375-42368-0

LC 2009020962

"Rudacille has delivered a book that would do Studs Terkel proud, partaking of his oral-historical approach to the past at turns, imbued with his pro-labor spirit throughout. Required reading for activists and for those wondering where things went wrong for America's working people." Kirkus

Includes bibliographical references

Suisman, David

Selling sounds; the commercial revolution in American music. Harvard University Press 2009 356p il $29.95   **338.4**

1. Music -- United States 2. Music -- United States -- History and criticism 3. Music industry 4. Music trade -- United States

ISBN 978-0-674-03337-5; 0-674-03337-X

LC 2008-55620

"A fascinating, well-written, richly detailed story of how music became a commodity in America. . . . [Suisman's] scholarship is amazingly wide-ranging." Washington Times

Includes bibliographical references

Vlasic, Bill

Once upon a car; the fall and resurrection of America's big three auto makers--GM, Ford, and Chrysler. William Morrow 2011 394p   **338.4**

1. Automobile industry

ISBN 978-0-06-184562-8; 978-0-06-204222-4 ebook

LC 2011020572

The author "examines the perfect storm of overseas competition, economic downturn, rising gas prices, union pressures, legacy costs, and lumbering bureaucracy that brought the U.S. auto industry to its knees. He takes us into the boardrooms and inside the heads of such people as Rick Wagoner, former GM CEO, who was ousted by Steve Rattner; Obama's 'car czar,' Bill Ford Jr., great-grandson of Henry Ford and chairman of Ford Motor Company; and billionaire financier Kirk Kerkorian, who at different times held 10-percent stakes in both GM and Ford. This is an engrossing look at big business in crisis, forever changed but never willing to give up." Booklist

Includes bibliographical references

Washington, Harriet A.

Deadly monopolies; the shocking corporate takeover of life itself, and the consequences for your health and our medical future. Doubleday 2011 433p il $28.95; ebook $14.99   **338.4**

1. Drug industry 2. Drugs -- Marketing 3. Medical ethics

ISBN 978-0-385-52892-4; 978-0-385-53405-5 ebook

LC 2011013033

"Extensively documented with minimal scientific jargon, this book is recommended for any reader interested in the future of our health system." Libr J

Includes bibliographical references

338.5 General production economics

Galbraith, John Kenneth

★ The **great** crash, 1929; with a new introduction by the author; foreword by James K. Galbraith. Houghton Mifflin Co. 2009 206p pa $14.95 **338.5**

1. Great Depression, 1929-1939

ISBN 978-0-547-24816-5

Beginning with the bull market of Coolidge and Hoover and continuing through the stock market crash, the author analyzes its causes and speculates about the chances of another crash.

Reinhart, Carmen M., 1955-

This time is different; eight centuries of financial folly. [by] Carmen M. Reinhart, Kenneth S. Rogoff. Princeton University Press 2009 xlv, 463p il $35   **338.5**
1. Business cycles 2. Financial crises 3. Fiscal policy 4. International finance
ISBN 978-0-691-14216-6; 0-691-14216-5
LC 2009-22616

The authors "have compiled an impressive database, which covers eight centuries of government debt defaults from around the world. They have also collected statistics on inflation rates from every country where information is available and on banking crises and international capital flows over the past couple of centuries. This lengthy historical study gives what they call a 'panoramic view' of the unending cycle of boom and bust, showing how claims that 'this time is different' are invariably proven wrong. . . . [This] is an important addition to the literature of financial history." Wall Street J
Includes bibliographical references (p. 400-433)

Panic; the story of modern financial insanity. [edited by] Michael Lewis. W. W. Norton & Company 2009 391p il $27.95; pa $18.95   **338.5**
1. Finance -- Psychological aspects 2. Financial crises 3. Investments -- Psychological aspects
ISBN 978-0-393-06514-5; 978-0-393-33798-3 pa
LC 2008-39523

The editor "has compiled an anthology of articles related to five major financial crises in recent decades: the 1987 stock market crash, the Russian default, the Asian currency crisis, the Internet bubble and . . . the subprime mortgage collapse (the final article included is from January 2008). For each crisis, Lewis offers articles from journals, books, transcripts, and newspapers, all written immediately before, during, or after the event. . . . Timely and highly readable, this work includes in one accessible source two decades' worth of some of the best writing on the various crises and panics." Libr J

The value of a dollar; prices and incomes in the United States, 1860-2009. [edited] by Scott Derks. 4th ed; Grey House Pub. 2009 690p il $155   **338.5**
1. Cost and standard of living 2. Prices 3. Reference books 4. Salaries, wages, etc.
ISBN 978-1-59237-403-8

"Both great-grandparents and serious students in historical research will benefit from this book. It will be an especially valuable study to students of American history, economics, and even mathematics." Libr J
Includes bibliographical references

The value of a dollar: colonial era to the Civil War, 1600-1865; [edited by] Scott Derks and Tony Smith. Grey House Pub. 2005 436p il $155   **338.5**
1. Cost and standard of living 2. Prices 3. Reference

books 4. Salaries, wages, etc.
ISBN 1-59237-094-2; 978-1-59237-094-8
LC 2006-275331

"This source is an engaging statistical summary that looks at the history of the American people through the eyes of everyday workers and consumers. The 265 years it covers are presented in six chronological chapters: '1600-1749: The Development of the Colonies,' '1750-1774: The Run up to the War of American Independence,' and so on, ending with the close of the Civil War in 1865. . . . [This book] will find a happy audience among students, researchers, and general browsers. It offers a fascinating and detailed look at early American history from the viewpoint of everyday people trying to make ends meet." Booklist
Includes bibliographical references

338.7   Business enterprises

Abrams, John

Companies we keep; employee ownership and the business of community and place. foreword by William Greider. 2nd ed.; Chelsea Green Pub. Co. 2008 333p il pa $17.95   **338.7**
1. Business ethics 2. Employee ownership 3. Management
ISBN 978-1-60358-000-7
LC 2008-25075

The author posits a "business model based on community, goodwill, craftsmanship, and not-so-big growth, outlining the steps he took to help his own firm become a 'more democratic, more responsible, more permanent kind of company.'" Libr J
Includes bibliographical references

Angwin, Julia

Stealing MySpace; the battle to control the most popular website in America. Random House 2009 371p il $27   **338.7**
1. Electronic commerce 2. Internet industry 3. MySpace (Web site) 4. Online social networks
ISBN 978-1-4000-6694-0; 1-4000-6694-8
LC 2008-23504

"This engrossing look at how MySpace became a media powerhouse will find a solid audience of business history, technology and entrepreneurship readers." Publ Wkly
Includes bibliographical references

Arden, Lynie

★ The **work**-at-home sourcebook; 10th ed.; Live Oak Pubns 2009 400p il pa $19.95   **338.7**
1. Home-based business
ISBN 978-0-911781-20-5

"Each entry in this helpful listing of firms that hire freelancers and franchises that can be home-based includes contact information and advice on how to get one's foot in the door. The book also features directories of marketplaces for handicrafts and online certification programs." Libr J

Auletta, Ken
Googled; the end of the world as we know it. Penguin Press 2009 384p $27.95 **338.7**
1. Computer scientists 2. Information technology executives 3. Internet executives 4. Internet industry 5. Internet searching 6. Social responsibility of business 7. Web search engines
ISBN 978-1-594-20235-3
LC 2009-24770
The author's "thorough reporting and declarative writing provide a crisp, informative read. . . . Auletta displays the skill of a responsible journalist in both researching and crafting this snapshot of today's technological landscape. " Christ Sci Monit
Includes bibliographical references

Brenner, Joel Glenn
The **emperors** of chocolate; inside the secret world of Hershey and Mars. Random House 1999 366p il hardcover o.p. pa $14.95 **338.7**
1. Candy industry -- United States -- History 2. Chocolate 3. Chocolate candy -- United States -- Marketing -- History 4. Chocolate industry -- United States -- History 5. Competition -- United States -- Case studies 6. Food industry executives
ISBN 0-7679-0457-5 pa
LC 98-21610
"Brenner examines the candy industry, focusing on the rivalry between Hershey and Mars. Milton Hershey was and Forrest Mars is highly secretive and eccentric, and they both amassed huge fortunes. A wonderful inside look at successful businessmen." Booklist
Includes bibliographical references

Brinkley, Douglas
★ **Wheels** for the world; Henry Ford, his company, and a century of progress, 1903-2003. Viking 2003 xxii, 858p il $34.95; pa $18 **338.7**
1. Automobile executives 2. Automobile industry 3. Automobile industry and trade -- United States -- History -- 20th century 4. Philanthropists
ISBN 0-670-03181-X; 0-14-200439-1 pa
LC 2003-33066
"Car lovers will appreciate this amazing account of the birth of the automobile industry, including funny anecdotes about the trusty Model T, the evolution of the V-8 engine, the artistic design of the Thunderbird, sophistication of the Lincoln Continental, and popularity of the Mustang." Booklist
Includes bibliographical references

Bruck, Connie
When Hollywood had a king; the reign of Lew Wasserman, who leveraged talent into power and influence. Random House 2003 512p il hardcover o.p. pa $16.95 **338.7**
1. Chief executive officers -- United States -- Biography 2. Motion picture executives 3. Motion picture industry 4. Talent agents
ISBN 0-375-50168-1; 978-0-8129-7217-7 pa; 0-8129-7217-1 pa
LC 2003-41418

"Those who are interested in comprehensive details about the inner workings of the entertainment industry—its history, business, customs, people, and gossip—will find this a fascinating read and a solid resource." Libr J
Includes bibliographical references

Burrows, Peter
Backfire: Carly Fiorina's high-stakes battle for the soul of Hewlett-Packard. Wiley 2003 296p il $27.95 **338.7**
1. Computer industry 2. Computer industry -- United States 3. Computer industry executives 4. Consolidation and merger of corporations -- United States -- Case studies 5. Corporations -- Investor relations -- United States -- Case studies 6. Electronic industries -- United States 7. Telecommunications executives
ISBN 0-471-26765-1
LC 2002-156443
This is an account "of the bitter boardroom fight that erupted after Hewlett-Packard announced plans to merge with Compaq in the late summer of 2001 . . . [with a focus on] the charismatic Carleton S. Fiorina, who became one of the highest-ranking women in American business in 1999 when she was tapped as the first outside chief executive of the Hewlett-Packard company. . . . [This] is a riveting, colorful, fast-paced account of the Compaq battle." N Y Times Book Rev
Includes bibliographical references

Casnocha, Ben
My start-up life; what a (very) young CEO learned on his journey through Silicon Valley. Ben Casnocha ; foreword by Marc Benioff. Jossey-Bass 2007 xiv, 189 p.p (cloth) $24.95 **338.7**
1. Computer software industry -- United States 2. Entrepreneurship -- United States 3. Internet software industry -- United States 4. New business enterprises -- United States -- Management
ISBN 0787996130; 9780787996130
LC 2007007866
This book is written by "Ben Casnocha [who] discovered he was entrepreneur at age 12 and hasn't slowed down since. In this . . . instructive book, Ben dissects the entrepreneurship 'gene,' explaining that everyone has inherited it if they have an idea to make the world a better place. In Casnocha's case, he found a better way for city governments to communicate with constituents on the Web. Six years later, Comcate has dozens of municipal clients, a growing staff, and a record of excellence. This book is the story of his start-up, but also a conversation with his mentors, clients and fellow entrepreneurs about how to make a business idea work and how to have the time of your life trying." (Publisher's note)

Cohen, Rich
The **fish** that ate the whale; the life and times of America's banana king. Rich Cohen. Farrar, Straus and Giroux 2012 xiii, 270 p.p **338.7**
1. Banana trade -- Louisiana -- New Orleans -- History 2. Biographies 3. Jewish businesspeople -- Louisiana -- New Orleans -- Biography
ISBN 0374299277; 9780374299279
LC 2011041207

This biography describes the life of the 20th-century American fruit businessman Samuel Zemurray. [H]e worked as . . . a banana hauler, a dockside hustler, and a plantation owner. He battled and conquered the United Fruit Company, becoming a symbol of the best and worst of the United States. . . . Starting with nothing but a cart of freckled bananas, he built a sprawling empire . . . connected to the birth of modern American diplomacy, public relations, business, and war. (Publisher's note)

Coll, Steve
★ **Private** empire; ExxonMobil and American power. Steve Coll. Penguin Press 2012 685 p. $36.00   338.7
1. Big business -- United States 2. Corporate history 3. Corporate power -- United States 4. Petroleum industry and trade -- Political aspects -- United States
ISBN 1594203350; 9781594203350
LC 2011044722
In this book "two-time Pulitzer winner [Steve] Coll . . . demonstrates how the merger of Exxon and Mobil has allowed the company to wield more power and wealth than even the American government, in the manner of John D. Rockefeller. . . . The Exxon-Mobil merger in 1999 created a global behemoth and also provoked small wars at drilling spots where the poor and disenfranchised deeply resented the foreign workers on native soil and disrupted the extraction by violence and insurgency." (Kirkus)

Kealing, Bob
Tupperware, unsealed; Brownie Wise, Earl Tupper, and the home party pioneers. University Press of Florida 2008 250p il $28   338.7
1. Containers 2. Household products industry executives 3. Sales personnel
ISBN 0-8130-3227-X; 978-0-8130-3227-6
LC 2007-47539
The author "explores the origins of the Tupperware industry as seen through the insightful genius of Brownie Wise, the impetus behind the home party craze that catapulted Tupperware revenues into the millions. . . . This work proves to be a valuable contribution to the growing body of literature that focuses on the individual contributions of women to US business and industry." Choice
Includes bibliographical references

Kirkpatrick, David
The **Facebook** effect; the inside story of the company that is connecting the world. Simon & Schuster 2010 372p il $26   338.7
1. Internet -- Social aspects 2. Internet executives 3. Internet industry 4. Online social networks 5. Social networking
ISBN 978-1-4391-0211-4; 1-4391-0211-2
LC 2009-51983
The author was encouraged by Mark Zuckerberg, the founder and chief executive of Facebook.com, to write this book and was granted extensive access to him and his associates. Their cooperation has resulted in a mostly sympathetic—at times, gushingly laudatory—account of the company, though Mr. Kirkpatrick does not shy away from dissecting its missteps and successive disputes over pri-

vacy. He gives the reader a detailed understanding of how the company grew from a 2004 Harvard dorm-room project into the world's second-most-visited site after Google. (N Y Times (Late NY Ed))
Includes bibliographical references

Krass, Peter
Carnegie. Wiley 2002 612p il $35; pa $19.95   338.7
1. Charities -- History 2. Industrialists -- United States 3. Metal industry executives 4. Philanthropists 5. Philanthropists -- United States 6. Steel industry and trade -- History 7. Steel industry and trade -- United States -- History
ISBN 0-471-38630-8; 0-471-46883-5 pa
LC 2002-10162
"From bobbin boy in a cotton mill to one of American history's most famous characters, Carnegie's life was one of contradictions. In his lifetime, Carnegie gave away a staggering $350 million, setting a standard for social conscience. Krass used original sources such as letters, diaries, and other writings by primary and peripheral characters in Carnegie's life to penetrate the public persona and show the man who crusaded for universal literacy and world peace." Booklist
Includes bibliographical references

Kurlansky, Mark, 1948-
Birdseye; the adventures of a curious man. Mark Kurlansky. Doubleday 2012 251 p.   338.7
1. Businessmen -- United States -- Biography 2. Frozen foods industry -- United States -- History 3. Inventors -- United States -- Biography
ISBN 0385527055; 9780385527057; 9780385535885
LC 2011044891
This book explains that [t]here was far more to American inventor Clarence Birdseye (1886-1956) than met the eye; he was slight and cheerful but restlessly curious. He was drawn into a life of travel to remote parts of the continent in search of adventure and new experiences. He invented tools and processes, notably that which enabled quick freezing of foodstuffs and revolutionized culinary habits. Birdseye launched not just the frozen-vegetable company that bears his now-famous name but an entire industry. [Mark] Kurlansky, whose past works include the popular histories Salt and Cod, paints a complete picture of Birdseye's unusual career and accomplishments. (Libr J)

Levy, Steven
In the plex; how Google thinks, works, and shapes our lives. Simon & Schuster 2011 424p $26; ebook $12.99   338.7
1. Google (Web site)
ISBN 978-1-4165-9658-5; 1-4165-9658-5; 978-1-4165-9671-4 ebook; 1-4165-9671-2 ebook
LC 2010049964
The author presents a behind-the-scenes story of the Internet search engine company Google.
This is "the most comprehensive, intelligent and readable analysis of Google to date. Levy is particularly good on how those behind Google think and work. . . . [This work]

teems with original insight into Google's most controversial affairs." New Sci

Includes bibliographical references

Lutz, Bob, 1932-

Car guys vs. bean counters; the battle for the soul of American business. [by] Bob Lutz. Portfolio/Penguin 2011 241p il $26.95 **338.7**

1. Automobile executives 2. Automobile industry 3. Automobile industry and trade -- United States -- Finance 4. Corporate turnarounds

ISBN 978-1-59184-400-6; 1-59184-400-2

LC 2011010720

The author "describes how he was pulled out of retirement to turn around a bankrupt General Motors in 2008, recounting how he transitioned the company away from office politics and penny pinching." Publisher's note

Magner, Mike

Poisoned legacy; the human cost of BP's rise to power. Mike Magner. St. Martin's Press 2011 432 p. $18 **338.7**

1. Petroleum industry and trade -- Moral and ethical aspects 2. Petroleum refineries -- Accidents -- United States 3. Petroleum workers -- Health and hygiene -- United States

ISBN 9780312554941

LC 2010054461

In this book, an exposé of the British oil giant, BP, gives a comprehensive rundown of the [2010] Gulf oil well explosion and leak, and of the rushed scheduling, substandard engineering, skipped tests, and faulty equipment that precipitated that disaster. That's just the capstone of [Mike Magners] detailed account of BP's misadventures in North America, which include a 2005 explosion at the company's Texas refinery that killed 15 people, a 200,000-gallon leak from a corroded Alaskan oil pipeline, a steady drip of workplace accidents, fatalities, and pollution violations and a drumbeat of callow apologies, lawsuits, fines, and criminal probes. (Publishers Wkly)

Mazzeo, Tilar J.

The **secret** of Chanel No. 5; the intimate history of the world's most famous perfume. Harper 2010 281p il $25.99 **338.7**

1. Chanel No. 5 perfume 2. Cosmetics industry executives 3. Fashion designers 4. Perfumers 5. Perfumes

ISBN 978-0-06-179101-7; 0-06-179101-6

LC 2010-15284

This "'unauthorized biography of a scent' unearths the roots of the creation and fame of Coco Chanel's famous perfume. . . . Mazzeo's lush prose covers relevant aspects of Coco Chanel's life, from the stark beauty of the orphanage where she was raised to the glamour and luxury of her adulthood, to the scents that wove through her life and shaped the development of her signature perfume. However, the book never bogs down in the details—despite the extensive research showcased in the bibliography—and a smooth pacing keeps it moving along at a fast clip." Libr J

Includes bibliographical references

Micklethwait, John

The **company**; a short history of a revolutionary idea. [by] John Micklethwait and Adrian Wooldridge. Modern Library 2003 xxiii, 227p hardcover o.p. pa $14.95 **338.7**

1. Business -- History 2. Business enterprises 3. Business enterprises -- History 4. Commerce -- History 5. Corporations 6. Corporations -- History 7. Economic history 8. Entrepreneurship -- History 9. Incorporation -- History

ISBN 0-679-64249-8; 0-8129-7287-2 pa

LC 2002-26429

In this history of the joint-stock company, Micklethwait and Wooldridge "trace its progress from Assyrian partnership agreements through the 16th- and 17th-century European 'charter companies' that opened trade with distant parts of the world, to today's multinationals. The authors' breadth of knowledge is impressive. They infuse their engaging prose with a wide range of cultural, historical and literary references, with quotes from poets to presidents. . . . Moreover, the authors argue that for all the change companies have engendered over time, their force has been for an aggregate good." Publ Wkly

Includes bibliographical references

Orbanes, Philip

The **game** makers; the story of Parker Brothers from Tiddledy Winks to Trivial Pursuit. {by} Philip E. Orbanes. Harvard Business School Press 2003 272p il $29.95 **338.7**

ISBN 1-591-39269-1

LC 2003-10768

This is a study of the Parker Brothers, who developed such games as Monopoly, Clue and Risk. The author contends that the games "reflect the American world view of the 20th century. Life is a ruthless struggle in which there are many losers, but it takes place within a framework of unbendable and fairminded rules." Economist

Includes bibliographical references

Saxon, A. H.

P. T. Barnum: the legend and the man. Columbia Univ. Press 1989 437p il hardcover o.p. pa $22.50 **338.7**

1. Circus executives

ISBN 0-231-05687-7 pa

LC 89-982

"Working primarily from Barnum's letters, business papers, family members' and associates' diaries, and legal documents, Saxon has pieced together a picture of the legendary circus owner. Saxon's detailed coverage of Barnum's life . . . is rich with anecdotes yet scholarly enough to please any researcher. Saxon succeeds admirably in capturing the essence of Barnum." Booklist

Includes bibliographical references

Spector, Robert

Amazon.com; get big fast. HarperBusiness 2000 xxii, 263p hardcover o.p. pa $16 **338.7**

1. Booksellers and bookselling 2. Electronic commerce -- United States -- History 3. Internet 4. Internet

bookstores -- United States -- History
ISBN 0-06-662042-2 pa

LC 99-87599

"Spector looks at a Seattle company that has turned retailing and customer service upside down. Online bookseller Amazon.com almost instantly became a part of America's popular culture, but Amazon.com has yet to turn a profit." Booklist

Includes bibliographical references

Stross, Randall E.

Planet Google; how one company's all-encompassing vision is transforming our lives. [by] Randall Stross. Free Press 2008 275p $26   **338.7**
1. Google (Web site) 2. Information organization 3. Internet industry 4. Internet searching 5. Web search engines
ISBN 1-41654-691-X; 978-1-41654-691-7

LC 2008-18788

This is "an outstanding business history of Google from its humble beginnings through the dot-com era to current times." Libr J

Includes bibliographical references (p. 201-257)

Vaidhyanathan, Siva

The **Googlization** of everything; (and why we should worry) University of California Press 2011 265p $26.95; ebook $22   **338.7**
1. Google (Web site) 2. Internet -- Social aspects 3. Internet industry
ISBN 978-0-520-25882-2; 978-0-520-94869-3 ebook

LC 2010-27772

The author "shows how Google's methods of capturing, storing and filtering information are often elitist and increasingly invasive. . . . Citing some of the company's most controversial headlines, from the toddler who was captured naked in his grandmother's garden with Google Street View to the settlement between Google and the Author's Guild over copyrights, the author unmasks the monster behind the friendly interface with the suspense of a horror novel. An urgent reminder to look more closely at dangers that lurk in plain sight. " Kirkus

Includes bibliographical references

Vise, David A.

★ The **Google** story; [by] David A. Vise and Mark Malseed. Updated ed.; Delacorte Press 2008 330p il hardcover o.p. pa $15   **338.7**
1. Computer scientists 2. Information technology executives 3. Internet executives
ISBN 978-0-385-34272-8; 978-0-385-34273-5 pa

LC 2009-285529

The authors present a business history of the Internet search engine company, focusing particular attention on the story of founders Larry Page and Sergey Brin.

★ Standard and Poor's register of corporations, directors, and executives. Standard & Poor's Corp. 3v   **338.7**
1. Corporations -- Directories 2. Executives -- Directories 3. Reference books

This "reference provides essential information on virtually all of the nation's corporations and their key people. Updated with supplements in April, July, and October. Volume 1: Profiles of more than 55,000 corporations in alphabetical order. Volume 2: Brief biographies of directors and executives. Volume 3: Indexes according to geography, industry, and other parameters." N Y Public Libr Book of How & Where to Look It Up

338.8   Combinations

Bown, Stephen R.

Merchant kings; when companies ruled the world, 1600-1900. [by] Stephen Bown. Thomas Dunne Books 2010 314p il map $26.99   **338.8**
1. Merchants 2. Multinational corporations
ISBN 978-0-312-61611-3

LC 2010-34783

The author "has produced a magnificent description of the six great companies, and their leaders, that dominated the 'Heroic Age of Commerce.' Bown demonstrates how the corporations served as stalking horses for kings and parliaments while enriching shareholders and the powerful managers themselves. . . . Bown presents a fascinating look at the men who exploited resources and native peoples while laying the foundations of empires." Publ Wkly

Includes bibliographical references

MacIntosh, Julie

Dethroning the king; the hostile takeover of Anheuser-Busch, an American icon. Wiley 2010 408p il $27.95   **338.8**
1. Beverage industry executives 2. Corporate mergers and acquisitions
ISBN 978-0-470-59270-0

LC 2010-32279

"In a narrative that reads as fast as any fiction thriller, . . . MacIntosh details the 2008 takeover of the iconic Anheuser-Busch brewing company by Belgian corporation InBev, focusing particularly on the company's importance to the St. Louis region; its management, or lack thereof, by the Busch family (particularly the August Busches III and IV); and the broader unsettled economic climate of 2008." Libr J

Includes bibliographical references

339.2   Distribution of income and wealth

Bernstein, William

The **birth** of plenty; how the prosperity of the modern world was created. [by] William J. Bernstein. McGraw-Hill 2004 420p il $29.95   **339.2**
1. Economic conditions 2. Economic history 3. Quality of life 4. Wealth
ISBN 0-07-142192-0

LC 2003-26155

The author "examines the four factors that fell into place to create a formula for human progress: property rights, scientific rationalism, capital markets, and transportation and communication. From the rise of common law to the invention of the steam engine, from the creation of currencies to shipbuilding, this is an in-depth history of the rise of prosperity." Booklist

Includes bibliographical references

Milanovic, Branko

The **haves** and the have-nots; a short and idiosyncratic history of global inequality. Basic Books 2010 258p il map $27.95   **339.2**

1. Income distribution 2. Poverty 3. Poverty -- History 4. Wealth 5. Wealth -- History

ISBN 978-0-465-01974-8; 0-465-01974-9

LC 2010-29295

"Students, practitioners, and anyone interested in economics and the issue of inequality would enjoy this." Libr J

Includes bibliographical references

Noah, Timothy

The **great** divergence; America's growing inequality crisis and what we can do about it. Timothy Noah. Bloomsbury 2012 264 p.   **339.2**

1. Economic history 2. Equality -- United States 3. Historical literature 4. Income distribution -- United States 5. Poverty -- United States 6. Wealth -- United States

ISBN 9781608196333

LC 2011048447

This book examines the political dimensions of the outrageous disparity in incomes that has developed since 1979. This inequality, writes the author, is worse than it has been in any other period of American history, and it is completely out of line with America's trading partners and allies. . . . [Timothy] Noah discusses the rise and fall of the trade-union movement and demonstrates that turning points in that movement were also turning points in the growth of income inequality. While after the end of World War II it was normal for the president to sit down with labor and business officials to discuss the economy, it no longer is. . . . Noah also calls out financial deregulation as a major offender. (Kirkus)

Ridley, Matt

The **rational** optimist; how prosperity evolves. Fourth Estate, Harper 2010 438p il $26.99   **339.2**

1. Connectionism 2. Cost and standard of living 3. Optimism 4. Practical reason 5. Progress -- History 6. Reason 7. Wealth

ISBN 978-0-06-145205-5

LC 2010-4907

The author posits that as long as civilization engages in exchange and specialization, we will be able to reinvent ourselves and responsibly use earthly resources ad infinitum. . . . Ridley puts current perceptions about violence, wealth, and the environment into historical perspective, reaching back thousands of years to advocate global free trade, smaller government, and the use of fossil fuels. He confidently takes on the experts, from modern sociologists who fret over the current level of violence in the world to environmentalists who disdain genetically modified crops. An ambitious and sunny paean to human ingenuity, this is an argument for why ambitious optimism is morally mandatory. Publ Wkly

Includes bibliographical references

339.4   Factors affecting income and wealth

Banerjee, Abhijit

Poor economics; a radical rethinking of the way to fight global poverty. [by] Abhijit V. Banerjee and Esther Duflo. PublicAffairs 2011 303p $26.99 **339.4**

1. Economic assistance -- Developing countries 2. Foreign aid 3. Poverty 4. Poverty -- Prevention

ISBN 978-1-58648-798-0; 1-58648-798-1

LC 2010-50938

This book "draws on a variety of evidence, not limiting itself to the results of randomised trials, as if they are the only route to truth. And the authors' interest is not confined to 'what works', but also to how and why it works. Indeed, Ms Duflo and Mr Banerjee, perhaps more than some of their disciples, are able theorists as well as thoroughgoing empiricists." Economist

Includes bibliographical references

Cohen, Lizabeth

A **consumer's** republic; the politics of mass consumption in postwar America. Knopf 2003 567p il $35; pa $16.95   **339.4**

1. Consumer behavior -- United States 2. Consumers 3. Consumption (Economics) 4. Consumption (Economics) -- United States

ISBN 0-375-40750-2; 0-375-70737-9 pa

LC 2002-141599

"Without question, this is a difficult, demanding, and dense book—but it is also a greatly significant contribution to business literature. . . . Cohen submits a copiously researched, brilliantly conceived, and ultimately quite instructive study of American economics since the Depression." Booklist

Includes bibliographical references

Gerth, Karl

As China goes, so goes the world; how Chinese consumers are transforming everything. Hill and Wang 2010 258p il $26; ebook $12.99   **339.4**

1. Consumers 2. Consumption (Economics)

ISBN 978-0-8090-3429-1; 978-1-4299-6246-9 ebook

LC 2010-12647

"Nuanced, balanced and accessible—essential reading for anyone trying to make sense of China today." Kirkus

Includes bibliographical references

Miller, Geoffrey F.

Spent; sex, evolution, and consumer behavior. [by] Geoffrey Miller. Viking 2009 374p $26.95   **339.4**

1. Consumer behavior 2. Consumers 3. Consumption (Economics)

ISBN 978-0-670-02062-1; 0-670-02062-1

LC 2008-51554

"Since evolutionary psychology seeks to examine how natural selection acts on psychological and mental traits, Miller applies this knowledge to help us understand what actually motivates us to buy. He pokes fun at popular culture and at the things we buy and flaunt to inflate our self-esteem and try to make ourselves more attractive. Personality research can inform the study of consumer behavior, and

Miller shows us how having a better understanding of our own personalities will help us avoid the pitfalls of runaway consumerism." Libr J

Includes bibliographical references

Novogratz, Jacqueline

The **blue** sweater; bridging the gap between rich and poor in an interconnected world. Jacqueline Novogratz. Rodale Distrib. to the trade by Macmillan 2009 x, 262 p.p $15.99   **339.4**
1. Charities 2. Economic assistance 3. Microfinance 4. Poverty
ISBN 1594869154 (hardcover); 9781594869150 (hardcover)

LC 2008043621

This book, [p]art coming-of-age story, part blueprint for effecting real change, . . . explores what it means to create meaningful solutions to global poverty and release human potential in an interconnected world. For [author] Jacqueline Novogratz it all started back home in Alexandria, Virginia, with the blue sweater . . . she outgrew . . . and gave . . . to Goodwill. Eleven years later in Africa, she spotted a young boy wearing that very sweater, with her name still on the tag inside. . . . Novogratz relates her experiences over two decades, first in Africa and later in India and Pakistan. She began as a banker and philanthropist, and now works as a venture capitalist, trying to effect real change in countries where the average citizen lives on less than $4 a day. (Publishers note)

Rivlin, Gary

Broke, USA; from pawnshops to Poverty, Inc.: how the working poor became big business. Harper 2010 358p $26.99   **339.4**
1. Poor -- United States
ISBN 978-0-06-173321-5

LC 2010-2874

"A timely, important, and deeply disturbing look at the cycle of debt of the nation's most vulnerable." Publ Wkly

Includes bibliographical references

Waldfogel, Joel

Scroogenomics; why you shouldn't buy presents for the holidays. Princeton University Press 2009 173p $9.95   **339.4**
1. Consumption (Economics) 2. Gifts
ISBN 9780691142647

LC 2009-6177

The author "assesses holiday gift giving through the lens of economic tenets such as opportunity costs and deadweight loss. The result is a short but engaging manifesto on the inefficiency of the tradition, concluding with several solutions to increase satisfaction for both givers and receivers." Libr J

Includes bibliographical references

340   Law

Feinman, Jay M.

★ **Law** 101; 3rd ed.; Oxford University Press 2010 363p $27.95   **340**
1. Law -- United States
ISBN 978-0-19-539513-6

LC 2010-487303

This book "covers the main subjects taught in the first year of law school. Readers are introduced to every aspect of the legal system, from constitutional law and the litigation process to tort law, contract law, property law, and criminal law." Publisher's note

Nolo (Firm)

★ **Nolo's** encyclopedia of everyday law; answers to your most frequently asked legal questions. by Shae Irving & Nolo editors. 8th ed.; Nolo 2011 494p pa $34.99   **340**
1. Law -- United States
ISBN 978-1-4133-1321-5 pa; 1-4133-1321-3 pa; 978-1-4133-1347-5 ebook; 1-4133-1347-7 ebook

LC 2010-31328

This offers answers to frequently asked legal questions about such topics as credit and debt, workplace rights, wills, divorce, bankruptcy, social security, tenant's rights, child custody and visitation, patents and trademarks, travel, partnerships, healthcare directives and powers of attorney.

Tucker, Virginia

Finding the answers to legal questions; a how-to-do-it manual. [by] Virginia Tucker and Marc Lampson. Neal-Schuman Publishers 2011 274p pa $75   **340**
1. Law -- Research
ISBN 978-1-55570-718-7

LC 2010-36421

"Comprehensive and easily understood by the non-lawyer, this book would be a useful addition to the reference collections of public libraries." Catholic Library World

Includes bibliographical references

★ Black's law dictionary; Bryan A. Garner, editor in chief. 9th ed.; West 2009 xxxi, 1920p $80 **340**
1. Law -- Dictionaries 2. Reference books
ISBN 978-0-314-19949-2

LC 2009-459279

This law dictionary contains more than 45,000 terms, including archaic terms and references to statutes and cases.

Legal systems of the world; a political, social, and cultural encyclopedia. edited by Herbert M. Kritzer. ABC-CLIO 2002 4v il maps set $385   **340**
1. Administration of justice 2. Comparative law 3. Law -- Encyclopedias 4. Reference books
ISBN 1-57607-231-2

LC 2002-2659

"Written by an international team of more than 350 legal scholars, the more than 400 signed entries cover legal systems of countries from around the world, Australia, and the provinces of Canada; transnational systems (International Court of Justice); general systems (Islamlic law, indigenous, and folk legal systems); and key concepts. Each country profile includes a map with an inset of its location on the globe, general information about the country, its history, diagrams of its court structure, the evolution of its legal framework, its current structure, staffing or how judges are appointed, any specialized judicial bodies (i.e. military court), and the impact that the legal system has had on the country. Articles conclude with references and a bibliography. Academic and public libraries will find this source invaluable for comparative studies in legal and judicial systems."—"The Best of the Best Reference Sources." Am Libr

Includes bibliographical references

340.5   Legal systems

Miller, William Ian

Eye for an eye. Cambridge University Press 2005 266p $28; pa $19.99 **340.5**

1. Justice 2. Primitive law 3. Punishment

ISBN 978-0-521-85680-5; 0-521-85680-9; 978-0-521-70467-0 pa; 0-521-70467-7 pa

LC 2005-8077

"Analyzing the law of the talion—an eye for an eye, tooth for a tooth—literally, William Ian Miller presents . . . [a] meditation on the concept of 'pay back.'" Publisher's note

Includes bibliographical references

341.23   United Nations

Fasulo, Linda M.

★ An **insider's** guide to the UN; [by] Linda Fasulo. 2nd ed; Yale University Press 2009 262p il pa $17 **341.23**

ISBN 978-0-300-14197-9; 0-300-14197-1

LC 2008-52231

This "guide to the United Nations surveys the world body's programs and activities, and covers key issues including human rights, climate change, counterterrorism, nuclear proliferation, peacekeeping, and UN reform. It also offers guidelines for setting up a Model UN." Publisher's note

Includes bibliographical references

Moore, John Allphin

★ **Encyclopedia** of the United Nations; [by] John Allphin Moore, Jr., Jerry Pubantz. 2nd ed.; Facts On File 2008 2v il set $125 **341.23**

1. International relations -- Encyclopedias 2. Reference books

ISBN 978-0-8160-6913-2

LC 2007-29559

This set features entries on "the United Nations's institutions, procedures, policies, specialized agencies, historic personalities, initiatives, and involvement in world affairs. . . . The appendixes contain important UN documents, such as the Charter of the United Nations, the Universal Declaration of Human Rights, the Statute of the International Court of

Justice, and the recent Security Council Resolution." Publisher's note

Includes bibliographical references

Osmanczyk, Edmund Jan

Encyclopedia of the United Nations and international agreements; [by] Jan Edmund Osmancyzk; edited and revised by Anthony Mango. 3rd ed; Routledge 2002 4v set $550 **341.23**

1. International relations -- Encyclopedias 2. Reference books

ISBN 0-415-93920-8

LC 2002-10761

"An alphabetically arranged treasure trove of information on the United Nations, its specialized agencies, and many intergovernmental and non-governmental organizations. This especially valuable resource for smaller collections includes the full or partial texts of some 3,000 international agreements, conventions, and treaties as well as definitions of political, economic, military, geographical, and diplomatic terms. Analytical and agreements-conventions-treaties indexes." Ref Sources for Small & Medium-sized Libr. 6th edition [entry for 1990 edition]

Includes bibliographical references and index

341.5   Disputes and conflicts between states

Bass, Gary J.

Freedom's battle; the origins of humanitarian intervention. Alfred A. Knopf 2008 509p $35 **341.5**

1. Humanitarian intervention

ISBN 978-0-307-26648-4; 0-307-26648-6

LC 2007-52252

This "history of nineteenth-century campaigns to stop atrocities in Greece, Syria, and Bulgaria is a corrective to the idea that humanitarian interventions are a product of the 'dreamy interlude' between 1989 and 9/11. The compelling narrative, rich with accounts of parliamentary debate and battlefield confrontation, presents a world of familiar political and military concerns, from the pressure of nonstop media coverage to the importance of a clear exit strategy. Bass's thesis that humanitarianism long preceded the crises of Bosnia and Rwanda is persuasive." New Yorker

Includes bibliographical references

342   Branches of law; laws, regulations, cases; law of specific jurisdictions, areas, socioeconomic regions

Amar, Akhil Reed

★ **America's** constitution; a biography. Random House 2005 657p il $29.95; pa $16.95 **342**

1. Constitutional history -- United States

ISBN 1-400-06262-4; 0-8129-7272-4 pa

LC 2004-61464

"Only rarely do you find a book that embodies scholarship at its most solid and invigorating; this is such a book." Publ Wkly

Includes bibliographical references

Beeman, Richard

★ **Plain,** honest men; the making of the American Constitution. [by] Richard Beeman. Random House 2009 514p il $30   **342**

1. Constitutional history -- United States
ISBN 978-1-4000-6570-7; 1-4000-6570-4

LC 2008-28841

"Masterfully told American history for the scholar and general reader alike." Kirkus

Includes bibliographical references

Berkin, Carol

A **brilliant** solution; inventing the American Constitution. Harcourt 2002 310p $26; pa $14 **342**

1. Constitutional history -- United States 2. Statesmen -- United States -- History -- 18th century
ISBN 0-15-100948-1; 0-15-602872-7 pa

LC 2002-5648

This history of the 1787 Constitutional Convention "emphasizes the importance of the delegates' anxieties, showing how they insinuated themselves into some of the compromises, such as the equality of the states in the Senate. Shrewd at integrating biographical detail on the delegates into their debates, Berkin fares well in comparison with previous historians on the topic." Booklist

Bezanson, Randall P.

How free can the press be? University of Illinois Press 2003 258p $34.95   **342**

1. Freedom of speech
ISBN 0-252-02866-X

LC 2003-2148

The author "ponders the contradictions of a free press in this study of nine historical court cases involving free speech. He critically explores the thorny issues surrounding freedom of the press and the press's use of First Amendment protections. Drawing on selected Supreme Court and lower court cases to illustrate his argument, Bezanson articulates important legal questions pertaining to First Amendment rights." Libr J

Includes bibliographical references

Bray, Ilona M.

How to get a green card; by Ilona Bray and Loida Nicolas Lewis; updated by Ruby Lieberman. 9th ed; Nolo 2010 334p il pa $39.99   **342**

1. Aliens -- United States
ISBN 978-1-4133-1103-7

This guide covers different ways to get a green card, alternatives to a green card, fiancé and fiancée visas, visa lotteries, applying for refugee status and political asylum, and immigration applications.

★ **U.S.** immigration made easy; [by] Ilona Bray. 15th ed.; Nolo 2011 596p il pa $44.99   **342**

ISBN 978-1-4133-1207-2

This guide "discusses immigration paperwork, green cards, and other types of temporary visas and when to involve a lawyer." Libr J

Breyer, Stephen G.

Active liberty; interpreting our democratic Constitution. [by] Stephen Breyer. Knopf 2005 161p $21   **342**

1. Constitutional law -- United States 2. Judicial process -- United States 3. Law -- United States -- Interpretation and construction 4. Liberty
ISBN 0-307-26313-4

LC 2005-44242

The Supreme Court Justice presents his view on the Constitution of the United States.

"This will be essential reading at a possibly watershed moment for the Supreme Court." Publ Wkly

Includes bibliographical references

Carpenter, Dale

Flagrant conduct; the story of Lawrence v. Texas : how a bedroom arrest decriminalized gay Americans. Dale Carpenter. W. W. Norton & Company 2012 345 p.   **342**

1. Gays -- Legal status, laws, etc. -- United States 2. Homosexuality -- Law and legislation -- Texas -- Criminal provisions 3. Lawrence v. Texas (Supreme Court case) 4. Trials (Sodomy) -- Texas
ISBN 9780393062083

LC 2011047245

This book looks at the 2003 landmark Lawrence v. Texas Supreme Court case [which] established the right of homosexuals to engage in private sexual conduct. After setting the sociopolitical and legal scene, [Dale] Carpenter . . . describes the 1998 arrest of John Lawrence and Tyron Garner and the ensuing events as gay rights groups in Houston grasped the potential of the case as a national test. Chapters introduce participants, describe the so-called crime, compare differing accounts of the arrest, follow court events, and explain the stakes. Carpenter . . . discuss[es] legal strategies and Supreme Court arguments, and the elite lawyers and strategists of the defense team . . . in stark contrast to the ill-prepared Harris County district attorney. (Libr J)

Ford, Richard T.

Rights gone wrong; Richard Thompson Ford. Farrar, Straus and Giroux 2011 272p.   **342**

ISBN 9780374250355

LC 2011010705

It was the author's intent to demonstrate "that both the progressive left and the colorblind right are guilty of the same error: defining discrimination too abstractly and condemning it too categorically, with similarly perverse results. According to Ford," the urge to condemn discrimination in all its forms . . . has led people on the left and the right to reject reasonable, prudent and innocent distinctions." It has also led activists, judges and government officials to concentrate on eliminating even trivial forms of discrimination at the expense of more effective means to social justice, like expanding economic opportunities for the poor. (N Y Times)

Hennessey, Jonathan

The **United** States Constitution; a graphic adaptation. written by Jonathan Hennessey; art by Aaron

McConnell. Hill and Wang 2008 149p il $35; pa
$16.95 **342**
    1. Constitutional history -- United States -- Graphic
novels 2. Graphic novels
    ISBN 978-0-8090-9487-5; 0-8090-9487-8; 978-0-
8090-9470-7 pa; 0-8090-9470-3 pa
                  LC 2008-17927
    The author and illustrator go "through the entire U. S.
Constitution, article by article, amendment by amendment,
explaining their meaning and implications—in comics format. Avoiding the didactic, the book succeeds in being both
consistently entertaining and illuminating." Publ Wkly
    Includes bibliographical references

Maddex, Robert L.

    The **U.S.** Constitution A to Z; 2nd ed.; CQ Press
2008 xxix, 736p il map $85 **342**
    1. Constitutional history -- United States --
Encyclopedias 2. Constitutional law -- United States
-- Encyclopedias 3. Reference books
    ISBN 978-0-87289-764-9
                  LC 2008-21902
    "Maddex offers over 200 articles about issues (abortion,
gun control), legal concepts (due process, privacy), landmark cases (Roe v. Wade, Brown v. Board of Education)
and people (John Adams, Thurgood Marshall) related to the
Constitution. . . . The unique feature of this work is its collection of source materials. . . . It is an excellent, concise
reference." Choice [review of 2002 edition]
    Includes bibliographical references

Madison, James

    ★ The **Constitutional** Convention; a narrative
history from the notes of James Madison. [edited by]
Edward J. Larson and Michael P. Winship. Modern
Library 2005 229p pa $13.95 **342**
    1. Constitutional history -- United States
    ISBN 0-8129-7517-0
                  LC 2005-41649
    "This book tells the convention's turbulent story in
Madison's own words, drawn from the notes he took at the
scene and giving us a daily blow-by-blow. . . . [The editors]
steer readers through the fierce debates with helpful explanations and editorial asides, as well as a cogent epilogue,
making this primary source far more than a tidy civics lesson." Publ Wkly
    Includes bibliographical references

Maier, Pauline

    Ratification; the people debate the Constitution,
1787-1788. Simon & Schuster 2010 589p il map
$30 **342**
    1. Constitutional history -- United States
    ISBN 978-0-684-86854-7; 0-684-86854-7
                  LC 2010-27709
    "Maier's monumental study, filled with penetrating con-
clusions, stands presently as the authoritative account of the
ratification of the Constitution." Libr J
    Includes bibliographical references

Meyerson, Michael

    Liberty's blueprint; how Madison and Hamilton
wrote the Federalist Papers, defined the constitution,
and made democracy safe for the world. [by] Michael
I. Myerson. Basic Books 2008 309p $26.95 **342**
    1. Constitutional history -- United States 2.
Constitutional law -- United States 3. Members of
Congress 4. Presidents 5. Secretaries of state 6.
Secretaries of the treasury 7. Statesmen
    ISBN 978-0-465-00264-1; 0-465-00264-1
                  LC 2007-35376
    "This fine book is the fullest and most insightful account
we have of the collaboration between Alexander Hamilton
and James Madison." J Am Hist
    Includes bibliographical references

Noonan, John Thomas

    Narrowing the nation's power: the Supreme
Court sides with the states; {by} John T. Noonan,
Jr. University of Calif. Press 2002 203p $34.95; pa
$14.95 **342**
    1. Government liability -- United States -- States 2.
State governments 3. State governments -- United
States -- Privileges and immunities
    ISBN 0-520-23574-6; 0-520-24068-5 pa
                  LC 2002-19473
    "In this highly recommended work, the author convinc-
ingly sounds the alarm." Libr J
    Includes bibliographical references

Nussbaum, Martha Craven

    Liberty of conscience; in defense of America's
tradition of religious equality. [by] Martha Nussbaum. Basic Books 2008 406p $28.95 **342**
    1. Freedom of religion 2. Freedom of religion -- United
States 3. Liberty of conscience
    ISBN 978-0-465-05164-9; 0-465-05164-2
                  LC 2007-38176
    "Nussbaum writes engagingly and with generosity; her
critiques, particularly those of opinions written by Justices
Scalia and Thomas, are pointed but respectful, and she demonstrates warm regard for Supreme Court plaintiffs who
have braved persecution as they have followed the dictates
of conscience." Publ Wkly

Rabban, David M.

    Free speech in its forgotten years. Cambridge
Univ. Press 1997 404p il $60; pa $22 **342**
    1. Constitutional history 2. Constitutional law -- United
States 3. Freedom of speech
    ISBN 0-521-62013-9; 0-521-65537-4 pa
                  LC 97-15281
    The author "focuses on free speech issues between the
Civil War and World War I. Through an impressive marshaling of controversies, cases, and litigants, he persuasively argues that libertarian radicalism and the Free Speech League
. . . deserve much of the credit for pushing valuable First
Amendment issues to the forefront of American social, political, and legal circles. . . . This enlightening work fills a
void in First Amendment civil liberties studies." Libr J
    Includes bibliographical references and index

Rehnquist, William H.

All the laws but one; civil liberties in wartime. Knopf 1998 254p il $27.50; pa $14   **342**

1. Civil rights 2. Civil rights -- United States -- History -- 19th century 3. Constitutional history 4. Japanese Americans -- Evacuation and relocation, 1942-1945 5. National security -- United States 6. War 7. World War, 1914-1918 8. World War, 1939-1945

ISBN 0-679-44661-3; 0-679-76732-0 pa

LC 98-12641

This is "Supreme Court Chief Justice Rehnquist's narrative of the conflict between civil liberties and military necessity. . . . Fully two-thirds of the book covers Civil War issues. . . . One chapter discusses World War I espionage and draft resistance cases; three, the World War II internment of Japanese Americans and the imposition of martial law in Hawaii. . . . Far from a complete survey of wartime civil liberties—reviewing only cases that reached the Supreme Court before 1950—this is nonetheless both enlightening and entertaining." Booklist

Includes bibliographical references

Schultz, David A.

Encyclopedia of the United States Constitution; [by] David Schultz. Facts On File 2009 2v il set $150   **342**

1. Constitutional law -- United States 2. Constitutional law -- United States -- Encyclopedias 3. Reference books

ISBN 978-0-8160-6763-3; 0-8160-6763-5

LC 2008-23349

"This reference source can help high-school students, the general public, and other interested parties comprehend the fundamental concepts, evolutionary character, and historic people and events that have shaped the [Constitution.] . . . The alphabetically arranged entries cover terms, events, people, landmark cases, and issues that help explain the Constitution's history. The appendix provides the Declaration of Independence, the Articles of Confederation, the Constitution, and the Bill of Rights as well as 'Other Amendments to the Constitution,' a 'U.S. Constitution Time Line,' and instructions on locating court cases." Booklist

Includes bibliographical references

Simon, James F.

What kind of nation; Thomas Jefferson, John Marshall, and the epic struggle to create a United States. Simon & Schuster 2002 348p $27.50; pa $14   **342**

1. Architects 2. Biographers 3. Constitutional history 4. Constitutional history -- United States 5. Essayists 6. Executive power 7. Executive power -- History 8. Political questions and judicial power -- United States -- History 9. Presidents 10. Secretaries of state 11. Separation of powers 12. Supreme Court justices 13. Vice-presidents 14. Writers on law

ISBN 0-684-84870-8; 0-684-84871-6 pa

LC 2001-55027

"Simon's enlivening account proves that writing about constitutional law needn't be the dry preserve of academics." Booklist

Includes bibliographical references

Strebeigh, Fred

Equal; women reshape American law. W.W. Norton 2009 582p $35   **342**

1. Sex discrimination against women -- Law and legislation -- United States 2. Trials 3. Trials -- United States 4. Women -- Law and legislation 5. Women's rights 6. Women's rights -- United States

ISBN 978-0-393-06555-8; 0-393-06555-3

LC 2008-44463

"This book generates a genuine appreciation for the legal entrepreneurs who fought long and hard to make possible the careers of many a professional woman." Wilson Quarterly

Includes bibliographical references

United States/Constitution

★ The **Constitution** of the United States of America; analysis and interpretation: analysis of cases decided by the Supreme Court of the United States to June 28, 2002. prepared by the Congressional Research Service, Library of Congress; Johnny H. Killian, George A. Costello, Kenneth R. Thomas, co-editors; David M. Ackerman, Henry Cohen, Robert Meltz, contributors. U.S. Govt. Ptg. Office 2004 xxii, 2608p $215   **342**

1. Constitutional law -- United States

ISBN 978-0-16-072379-7; 0-16-072379-5

LC 2005-414932

"Sometimes known by its short title, the Constitution Annotated provides commentary on every article, section, and clause of the basic instrument, as well as the amendments, with citations to selected United States Supreme Court decisions construing these provisions." Introd to U.S. Govt Info Sources. 5th edition

Includes bibliographical references

Vile, John R.

The **Constitutional** Convention of 1787; a comprehensive encyclopedia of America's founding. ABC-CLIO 2005 2v il set $185   **342**

1. Constitutional history -- United States -- Encyclopedias 2. Constitutional law -- United States -- Encyclopedias 3. Reference books

ISBN 1-85109-669-8

LC 2005-24214

This "resource covers the people, events, committees, ideology, and documents related to the drafting of the Constitution." SLJ

Includes bibliographical references

Encyclopedia of constitutional amendments, proposed amendments, and amending issues, 1789-2010; 3rd ed.; ABC-CLIO 2010 2v set $165   **342**

1. Constitutional history -- United States -- Encyclopedias 2. Constitutional law -- United States -- Encyclopedias 3. Reference books

ISBN 978-1-59884-316-3; 1-59884-316-8; 978-1-59884-317-0 ebook; 1-59884-317-6 ebook

LC 2010-2113

The author "discusses the Constitution, its 27 ratified amendments, and the approximately 11,700 amendments proposed within the titular time frame to present 'a unique window into American history and politics.' The alphabetical format and detailed index make information access a breeze, and the six appendixes provide a reprint of the Constitution along with charts of the number of proposals by decade, key events, and names of individuals submitting the proposals." Libr J

Includes bibliographical references

Waldman, Steven

Founding faith; providence, politics, and the birth of religious freedom in America. Random House 2008 277p $26 **342**

1. Founding Fathers of the United States -- Religious life 2. Freedom of religion 3. Freedom of religion -- United States

ISBN 978-1-4000-6437-3; 1-4000-6437-6

LC 2007-21710

This "is an excellent book about an important subject: the inescapable—but manageable—intersection of religious belief and public life. With a grasp of history and an understanding of the exigencies of the moment, Waldman finds a middle ground between those who think of the Founders as apostles in powdered wigs and those who assert, equally inaccurately, that the Founders believed religion had no place in politics." Newsweek

Includes bibliographical references

Weiner, Mark Stuart

Black trials; citizenship from the beginnings of slavery to the end of caste. [by] Mark S. Weiner. Alfred A. Knopf 2004 421p $26.95; pa $16.95 **342**

1. African Americans -- Civil rights 2. African Americans -- Legal status, laws, etc -- History 3. Trials

ISBN 0-375-40981-5; 0-375-70884-7 pa

LC 2004-40860

The author "examines how court proceedings involving black people—and whites trying to assist them—have served as windows onto race relations and the power of whites over blacks in the U.S. from its earliest days. . . . This book is the best of its kind—a serious, deeply felt reflection on the weight of history on contemporary affairs." Publ Wkly

Includes bibliographical references

Wexler, Jay

Holy hullabaloos; a road trip to the battlegrounds of the church/state wars. Beacon Press 2009 251p pa $20 **342**

1. Church and state 2. Church and state -- United States 3. Freedom of religion 4. Religious minorities

ISBN 978-0-8070-0044-1; 0-8070-0044-2

LC 2008-47405

"This is a rare treat, a combination of thoughtful analysis and quirky humor that illuminates an issue that rarely elicits a laugh—and that is central to the American body politic." Publ Wkly

Includes bibliographical references

Wise, Steven M.

Though the heavens may fall; the landmark trial that led to the end of human slavery. Da Capo Press 2005 282p il $25; pa $17.95 **342**

1. Slavery 2. Slavery -- Law and legislation 3. Slavery -- Legal history -- Great Britain 4. Slaves 5. Trials

ISBN 0-7382-0695-4; 0-306-81450-1 pa

LC 2004-25346

The author "has an eye for evocative detail and an interest in the trappings and procedures of an 18th-century courtroom that do as much to engage the reader as the drama of the trials themselves." N Y Times Book Rev

Includes bibliographical references

★ The Debate on the Constitution; Federalist and Antifederalist speeches, articles, and letters during the struggle over ratification. Library of Am. 1993 2v ea $35 **342**

1. Constitutional history -- United States

ISBN 0-940450-42-9; 0-940450-64-X

LC 92-25449

In addition to the documents themselves, these volumes contain "brief biographical notes on the various speakers and writers, a chronology of key events in American independence and the establishment of the new governmental system, notes on contemporary state constitutions, and notes explicating the text of the reprinted documents." Christ Sci Monit

Encyclopedia of the American Constitution; edited by Leonard W. Levy and Kenneth L. Karst. 2nd ed; Macmillan Ref. USA 2000 6v set $595 **342**

1. Constitutional law 2. Constitutional law -- United States 3. Constitutional law -- United States -- Encyclopedias 4. Reference books

ISBN 0-02-864880-3

LC 00-29203

This "reference contains approximately 3000 contributions from academics, lawyers, and judges concerning key constitutional law cases and legislative developments relating to constitutional issues (e.g., abortion, welfare rights, and affirmative action)." Libr J

Includes bibliographical referencess

★ Encyclopedia of the First Amendment; edited by John R. Vile, David L. Hudson Jr., David Schultz. CQ Press 2009 2v il set $275 **342**

1. Reference books

ISBN 978-0-87289-311-5; 0-87289-311-1

LC 2008-36077

This "is an excellent resource for anyone who wants to learn more about broadcast regulation, the establishment of religion clause, students' rights, or a myriad of other topics involving the First Amendment and its political, cultural, and legal significance." Booklist

Includes bibliographical references

★ The Federalist; edited, with introduction and notes, by Jacob E. Cooke. Wesleyan Univ. Press 1982 xxx, 672p pa $27.95 **342**

ISBN 0-8195-6077-4

LC 82-2815

"From 27 Oct. 1787 to 2 April 1788, 77 essays were published in the semi-weekly 'Independent Journal' of New York, entitled 'The Federalist,' and signed first 'A Citizen of New York' then 'Publius.' Eight more were added when they were collected in book form {in 1789}. . . . They were so acute and massively learned in their exposition of the true intent of the Constitution, that even the courts have accepted them as authoritative comments in doubtful cases; and they are held by all the civilized world as among the noblest storehouses of political philosophy in existence. A classic textbook of political science." Ency Americana

The Oxford guide to United States Supreme Court decisions; edited by Kermit L. Hall, James W. Ely, Jr. 2nd ed.; Oxford University Press 2009 499p $35 **342**
1. Constitutional law 2. Constitutional law -- United States 3. Reference books
ISBN 978-0-19-537939-6
LC 2008-23763
The editors "assemble the scholarship of 161 field specialists, who summarize the Supreme Court's 440 most significant cases. Scholar-signed, multiparagraph entries are alphabetized by case name, include argued and decided dates, and detail vote divisions. The book closes with a glossary, an appendix containing the complete Constitution, a chronology of justices since 1789, and a list of presidential appointments. An outstanding single-volume reference." Libr J
Includes bibliographical references

The annotated U.S. Constitution and Declaration of Independence; edited by Jack N. Rakove. Belknap Press 2009 354p il $24.95 **342**
1. Constitutional history -- United States 2. Constitutional law -- United States
ISBN 978-0-674-03606-2; 0-674-03606-9
LC 2009-22907
The author "presents both the Declaration and the Constitution with carefully laid out annotation that's accessible to general readers as well as high school and college students. His extended introduction provides a readable and instructive analysis of how the writing of the Constitution progressed, especially on matters concerning representation, executive power, and creation of the amendments. His annotations often rely upon contemporary usage and meaning from the time of the Declaration of Independence and Constitution . . . and he compares such usage to other documents of the time." Libr J
Includes bibliographical references

343   Military, defense, public property, public finance, tax, commerce (trade), industrial law

Benedict, Jeff
Little pink house; a true story of defiance and courage. Grand Central Publishing 2009 397p il $26.99 **343**
1. Eminent domain 2. Eminent domain -- United States -- Cases 3. Nurses
ISBN 978-0-446-50862-9; 0-446-50862-4
LC 2008-17650

"Benedict has pieced together a fascinating narrative, using e-mail messages, planning documents, interviews and personal diaries to produce a sordid account of ruthless local politicians working hand-in-medical-glove with big business to drive hardworking Americans from their homes." N Y Times Book Rev

Fishman, Stephen
Working for yourself; law & taxes for independent contractors, freelancers & consultants. 8th ed.; Nolo 2011 360p pa $39.99 **343**
1. Self-employed
ISBN 978-1-4133-1331-4 pa; 978-1-4133-1357-4 ebook
LC 2010-38423
"There's a good chance having a side business will mean being an independent contractor, a freelancer, or a consultant. This thorough and well-organized volume will guide individuals through the legal and tax issues that come with the territory. From deciding on legal structures to drafting contracts to collecting payment from deadbeat clients, this is excellent information." Libr J
Includes bibliographical references

344   Labor, social service, education, cultural law

Hull, N. E. H.
★ **Roe** v. Wade; the abortion rights controversy in American history. [by] N.E.H. Hull and Peter Charles Hoffer. 2nd ed., rev. & expanded.; University Press of Kansas 2010 370p $39.95; pa $19.95 **344**
1. Abortion -- Law and legislation 2. District attorneys 3. Pro-choice activists
ISBN 978-0-7006-1753-1; 0-7006-1753-1; 978-0-7006-1754-8 pa; 0-7006-1754-X pa
LC 2010-21294
This book "highlights the abortion issue's historical background; highlights Roe v. Wade's core issues, essential personalities, and key precedents; tracks the case's path through the courts; clarifies the jurisprudence behind the court's ruling in Roe; and gauges its impact on American society and subsequent challenges to it in Webster v. Reproductive Services (1989) and Casey v. Planned Parenthood (1992). . . . [It includes] chapters covering abortion politics and legal battles in the post-9/11 era." Publisher's note
Includes bibliographical references

James, Vaughn E.
The **Alzheimer's** advisor; a caregiver's guide to dealing with the tough legal and practical issues. AMACOM - American Management Association 2009 300p pa $19.95 **344**
1. Alzheimer's disease 2. Caregivers 3. Medicine -- Law and legislation
ISBN 978-0-8144-0924-4; 0-8144-0924-5
LC 2008-20258

The author "deals with the often overlooked but difficult legal and financial responsibilities associated with caring for elders with memory loss and/or dementia." Libr J

Includes bibliographical references

Joel, Lewin G.

Every employee's guide to the law; what you need to know about your rights in the workplace--and what to do if they are violated. {by} Lewin G. Joel III. 3rd ed, rev and updated; Pantheon Bks. 2001 431p pa $16 **344**
1. Employee rights -- United States -- Popular works 2. Employees -- Civil rights 3. Employer and employee 4. Labor -- Law and legislation 5. Labor laws and legislation -- United States -- Popular works
ISBN 0-375-71445-6
LC 2001-21501

The author offers legal advice on such subjects as employee interviews, wages, hours, health and safety, sexual harassment, privacy, discrimination, and benefits.

Lombardo, Paul A.

Three generations, no imbeciles; eugenics, the Supreme Court, and Buck v. Bell. Johns Hopkins University Press 2008 365p il **344**
1. Constitutional history 2. Constitutional law -- United States 3. Eugenics 4. Eugenics -- United States -- History -- 20th century 5. Forced sterilization 6. Insanity -- Jurisprudence -- United States 7. Mentally handicapped 8. Sterilization (Birth control) 9. Sterilization, Eugenic
ISBN 0-8018-9010-1; 978-0-8018-9010-9
LC 2008-6546

This book examines the case of Buck v. Bell, covering the events of the trial and the 1927 Supreme Court decision that upheld Virginia's 1924 Eugenical Sterilization Act, which called for compulsory sterilization of the "feeble-minded." Index.

The author "traces a seminal 1927 Supreme Court case arising from the attempt by authorities in Virginia to force the sterilization of a woman believed to be mentally and socially 'insufficient.'" Libr J

Includes bibliographical references

Matthews, Joseph L.

★ **Social** security, Medicare & government pensions; get the most out of your retirement & medical benefits. with Dorothy Matthews Berman. 16th ed.; Nolo 2011 482p pa $29.99 **344**
1. Medicare 2. Pensions 3. Social security
ISBN 978-1-4133-1327-7 pa; 1-4133-1327-2 pa; 978-1-4133-1353-6 ebook; 1-4133-1353-1 ebook
LC 2010-38404

This guide discusses such topics as how to claim social security benefits, social security disability, civil service and veterans benefits, and Medicare procedures.

Nather, David

★ The **new** health care system; everything you need to know. Thomas Dunne Books 2010 230p pa $12.99 **344**
1. Health insurance 2. Medicaid 3. Medical care -- Government policy 4. Medicare
ISBN 978-0-312-64934-0

In this "primer on health-care reform, . . . Nather explains how insurance works, what the big changes are, and when everything will happen. It's a conversational guide that tells readers how to sign up for Medicare, and what to do if they're uninsured, or if they work for a small business versus a large company. . . . Nather's book, which includes a useful glossary, provides an excellent snapshot of how the post-reform health-care system should work as it stands now." Booklist

Nourse, Victoria F.

In reckless hands; Skinner v. Oklahoma and the near-triumph of American eugenics. W.W. Norton & Company 2008 240p il map $24.95 **344**
1. Constitutional law -- United States 2. Eugenics 3. Eugenics -- United States -- History -- 20th century 4. Prisoners 5. Sterilization (Birth control) 6. Sterilization, Eugenic 7. Thieves
ISBN 978-0-393-06529-9; 0-393-06529-4
LC 2008-13140

The author "provides a legal history of the Supreme Court case that served to increase the recognition of individual rights, although it fell short of ending the practice and debate of eugenics in the US. . . . This book deserves attention from those interested in the history and politics of the legal system." Choice

Includes bibliographical references

Sack, Steven Mitchell

The **employee** rights handbook; effective legal strategies to protect your job from interview to pink slip. 3rd ed., rev. & enlarged ed.; Legal Strategies Publications 2010 620p $39.95 **344**
1. Employee rights 2. Labor -- Law and legislation
ISBN 978-0-9636306-7-4
LC 2010-926886

The author "advises readers on topics from avoiding prehiring abuses and protecting on-the-job rights through postemployment litigation and finding and hiring a lawyer. . . . Readers looking for an all-in-one employee legal primer or layperson's quick reference should find this a useful tool." Libr J

Steingold, Fred

The **employer's** legal handbook; by Fred S. Steingold; edited by Alayna Schroeder. 9th ed.; Nolo 2009 374p pa $49.99 **344**
1. Labor -- Law and legislation
ISBN 978-1-4133-1023-8; 1-4133-1023-0
LC 2009-11075

This guide for employers discusses "how to comply with the most recent workplace laws and regulations, run a safe and fair workplace and avoid lawsuits." Publisher's note

Includes bibliographical references

345 Criminal law

Bogira, Steve

Courtroom 302; a year behind the scenes in an American criminal courthouse. Knopf 2005 404p hardcover o.p. pa $16 **345**

1. Administration of criminal justice 2. Courts 3. Criminal courts -- Illinois -- Chicago 4. Criminal justice, Administration of -- Illinois -- Chicago 5. Criminals -- Illinois -- Chicago

ISBN 0-679-43252-3; 0-679-75206-4 pa

LC 2004-57636

Bogira provides "a balanced view of the realities of the day-to-day, assembly-line grind that marks so much of the process from arrest to final disposition. . . . The brilliance of Bogira's insights will lead many to hope that he will follow this debut with proposals to cure the many ills he has diagnosed." Publ Wkly

Includes bibliographical references

Boyle, Kevin

Arc of justice; a saga of race, rights, and murder in the Jazz Age. Holt & Co. 2004 415p il $26; pa $15 **345**

1. African Americans -- Civil rights 2. African Americans -- Civil rights -- History -- 20th century 3. African Americans -- Michigan -- Detroit 4. Lawyers 5. Memoirists 6. Physicians 7. State legislators 8. Trials (Homicide) 9. Trials (Murder) 10. Writers on law

ISBN 0-8050-7145-8; 0-8050-7933-5 pa

LC 2004-47352

Boyle "has brilliantly rescued from obscurity a fascinating chapter in American history that had profound implications for the rise of the Civil Rights movement." Publ Wkly

Includes bibliographical references

Dunne, Dominick

Justice; crimes, trials, and punishments. Crown 2001 337p hardcover o.p. pa $14 **345**

1. Trials 2. Trials (Murder) -- United States

ISBN 0-609-80963-6 pa

LC 2001-28214

"Fascinating stuff, though less than complimentary about the American system of justice." Booklist

Feige, David

Indefensible; one lawyer's journey into the inferno of American justice. Little, Brown and Co. 2006 276p $24.95 **345**

1. Administration of criminal justice 2. Lawyers 3. Writers on law

ISBN 978-0-316-15623-3; 0-316-15623-X

LC 2006-1283

The author "takes us through a typically harrowing day as a public defender, dealing with arbitrary judges and clients who are often victims of the judicial system. . . . Feige skillfully shares his wisdom and his humanity and sheds light on a justice system that too often works irrationally." Publ Wkly

Geis, Gilbert

★ Crimes of the century; from Leopold & Loeb to O.J. Simpson. {by} Gilbert Geis and Leigh B. Bienen. Northeastern Univ. Press 1998 227p $40; pa $18.95 **345**

1. Carpenters 2. Children of prominent persons 3. Crime -- United States 4. Diplomats 5. Football players 6. Kidnap victims 7. Kidnappers 8. Lawyers 9. Murder victims 10. Murderers 11. Scottsboro case 12. Sportscasters 13. Trials 14. Trials -- United States

ISBN 1-55553-360-4; 1-55553-427-9 pa

LC 98-23180

The authors discuss "five of the most famous crimes and trials of the 20th century. The cases of Leopold and Loeb, the Scottsboro boys, the Lindbergh kidnapping, Alger Hiss, and O.J. Simpson. . . . Though each case is covered from crime through punishment (or acquittal) in fewer than 50 pages, the depth of historical detail and legal analysis is remarkable. The authors are particularly adept at placing these crimes within both their immediate historical settings and the larger societal issues." Libr J

Includes bibliographical references

Geoghegan, Thomas

In America's court; how a civil lawyer who likes to settle stumbled into a criminal trial. New Press (NY) 2002 206p $23.95; pa $15.95 **345**

1. Administration of criminal justice 2. Attorneys 3. Criminal courts -- United States -- Anecdotes 4. Criminal justice, Administration of -- United States -- Anecdotes 5. Criminal law 6. Lawyers 7. Lawyers -- United States -- Anecdotes 8. Practice of law -- United States -- Anecdotes

ISBN 1-56584-732-6; 1-56584-817-9 pa

LC 2002-20065

The author "describes participating in a criminal trial after arranging to assist in the defense of a young man accused of committing a felony murder. As the trial proceeds, he talks about his work as a civil lawyer, what it means to be a lawyer, and the issues lawyers face." Libr J

Hoffer, Peter Charles

The Salem witchcraft trials; a legal history. University Press of Kan. 1997 165p hardcover o.p. pa $12.95 **345**

1. Legal history -- Massachusetts 2. Trials 3. Witchcraft

ISBN 0-7006-0858-3; 0-7006-0859-1 pa

LC 97-19986

"Hoffer discusses the legal nature of the charges of witchcraft, the evidential and procedural characteristics of the trials of the accused, and the roles and attitudes of the ministers and magistrates who controlled the proceedings. . . . Hoffer offers little that is new in terms of interpretation, but he presents it well and in a manner easily grasped by the general reader." Choice

Includes bibliographical references

Kadri, Sadakat

The **trial**; a history, from Socrates to O. J. Simpson. Random House 2005 459p il $29.95   **345**
1. Trials 2. Trials -- History
ISBN 0-375-50550-4
LC 2005-42925

This "history of the trial from ancient times to the present provides . . . [a] history of the various forms and purposes of trials throughout Western civilization. . . . The result is a magnificent book suitable for all sorts of people, from inquisitive high school students to blue-chip lawyers." Choice
Includes bibliographical references

Lewis, Anthony

★ **Gideon's** trumpet. Random House 1964 262p hardcover o.p. pa $12.95   **345**
1. Law -- United States
ISBN 0-679-72312-9 pa

An account of the case of a Florida man convicted of burglary which brought about a historic decision of the Supreme Court decreeing that in all states a defendant is entitled to counsel.

Lipstadt, Deborah E.

The **Eichmann** trial. Nextbook/Schocken 2011 237p $24.95   **345**
1. Holocaust, 1933-1945 2. Holocaust, Jewish (1939-1945) 3. Nazi leaders 4. War crime trials 5. War criminals
ISBN 978-0-8052-4260-7; 0-8052-4260-0
LC 2010-28620

"Lipstadt has done a great service by untethering the trial from [Hannah] Arendt's polarizing presence, recovering the event as a gripping legal drama, as well as a hinge moment in Israel's history and in the world's delayed awakening to the magnitude of the Holocaust." N Y Times Book Rev
Includes bibliographical references

Mack, Raneta Lawson

A **layperson's** guide to criminal law. Greenwood Press 1999 201p $69.95   **345**
1. Criminal law 2. Criminal law -- United States -- Popular works
ISBN 0-313-30556-0
LC 98-53382

This explanation of the basics of criminal law includes numerous hypothetical situations that place some of the more difficult concepts in an "everyday" context. An overview of the criminal trial process, from the arrest to the final verdict is also provided

Malcolm, Janet

Iphigenia in Forest Hills; anatomy of a murder trial. Yale University Press 2011 155p $25   **345**
1. Dentists 2. Internists 3. Murder victims 4. Murderers 5. Trials (Homicide) 6. Trials (Murder) -- Queens (New York, N.Y.)
ISBN 978-0-300-16746-7; 0-300-16746-6
LC 2010-35851

"Malcolm's book chronicles the fate of Mazoltuv Borukhova, a 35-year-old doctor and a member of the Bukharan Jewish sect who stands accused of hiring an assassin to kill her ex-husband, Daniel Malakov. On the morning of Oct. 28, 2007, Malakov was shot to death in a park in Queens, N.Y., in front of his and Borukhova's 4-year-old daughter. . . . Malcolm shows us what happens when the abstract ideals of the law are applied, as they always are, by human beings. We meet one judge who, acting out of incompetence or malice, makes an inexplicable and terrible child-custody decision. Another proves less interested in serving justice than in wrapping up proceedings in time for his Caribbean vacation. A lawyer who, on the stand, appears to be 'intelligent and well-spoken' turns out to be both negligent and delusional. . . . All told, it's such a damning portrait of American jurisprudence that Malcolm scarcely need editorialize. As lawyers would say, res ipsa loquitur: the thing speaks for itself." Boston Globe

Newton, Michael A.

Enemy of the state; the trial and execution of Saddam Hussein. [by] Michael A. Newton & Michael P. Scharf. St. Martin's Press 2008 305p il $26.95   **345**
1. Presidents 2. Trials
ISBN 978-0-312-38556-9; 0-312-38556-0
LC 2008-21087

The authors "provided judicial assistance to the trial of Saddam Hussein and other Ba'athists, including training of judicial personnel, writing rules for the Iraqi Tribunal, and observing the nine-month trial proceedings. Here, they write of their experiences and provide perspective on the trial, which began in October 2005, including gavel-to-gavel coverage of the proceedings. . . . Their insiders' account is directed toward general adult audiences and will effectively aid them in understanding this crucial phase as Iraq struggles toward its future." Libr J
Includes bibliographical references

Rabinowitz, Dorothy

★ **No** crueler tyrannies; accusation, false witness, and other terrors of our times. Simon & Schuster 2003 239p $25; pa $13   **345**
1. Child sexual abuse 2. Child sexual abuse -- Investigation -- United States 3. Child witnesses -- United States 4. False testimony -- United States 5. Interviewing in child abuse -- United States 6. Trials (Child sexual abuse) -- United States 7. Trials (Child sexual abuse) -- United States
ISBN 0-7432-2834-0; 0-7432-2840-5 pa
LC 2002-44670

This book "reexamines high-profile cases of the 1980s and 1990s involving mass sexual abuse. Demonstrating that overzealous prosecutors and indifferent courts led to the prosecution of many innocents, Rabinowitz provides . . . analyses of the major cases, especially those that involved child-care workers. . . . This gripping, well-written book about social injustice and public hysteria is recommended for social science and law collections." Libr J

Spence, Gerry

The **smoking** gun; day by day through a shocking murder trial with Gerry Spence: a true story. Scribner 2003 435p hardcover o.p. pa $7.99   **345**
1. Trials (Homicide) 2. Trials (Murder) -- Oregon --

Newport
ISBN 0-7432-4696-9; 978-0-7434-7052-0; 0-7434-7052-4

LC 2003-42722

"This disquieting book shows that the facts don't speak for themselves, innocence is rarely presumed and justice is far from a first priority in America's courtrooms. Spence is a gifted storyteller and his rhetorical skills are mesmerizing. The blizzards of argument and counterargument that would be tedious reading in less talented hands are neatly incorporated into this thrilling account of injustice barely averted." Publ Wkly

Temkin, Moshik, 1971-
The **Sacco**-Vanzetti Affair; America on trial. Yale University Press 2009 316p il $35   345
  1. Sacco-Vanzetti Trial, Dedham, Mass., 1921 2. Sacco-Vanzetti case 3. Sacco-Vanzetti trial, Dedham (Mass.), 1921 4. Trials (Homicide) 5. Trials (Murder) -- Massachusetts -- Dedham
  ISBN 978-0-300-12484-2; 0-300-12484-8

LC 2008-45606

This "study of the trial and appeals of these two condemned murderers and of the life and times of the country, which feared foreign contamination, surpasses all prior analyses of this subject in terms of scope, erudition, and objectivity. . . . This book discusses many fascinating elements of controversy, not least the long-term views held by Sacco and Vanzetti's defenders and accusers and how their participation in the search for justice was perceived by their peers." Libr J
  Includes bibliographical references

Turow, Scott
  ★ **Ultimate** punishment; a lawyer's reflections on dealing with the death penalty. Farrar, Straus and Giroux 2003 164p $18   345
  1. Capital punishment
  ISBN 0-374-12873-1

LC 2003-7873

"In 2000 Governor George Ryan of Illinois declared a moratorium on executions. . . . Ryan established a commission to study the state's capital punishment system and propose reforms. In 2002 the commission issued its report. . . . Among the people Ryan appointed to the commission was Scott Turow, a . . . novelist and practicing attorney, with experience in death penalty cases. He was, at the time of his appointment, a self-described 'agnostic' on capital punishment. Ultimate Punishment is Turow's account of his struggle to resolve for himself the question, Should we retain the death penalty?" Christ Century
  Includes bibliographical references

Walsh, John Evangelist
  Moonlight; Abraham Lincoln and the Almanac trial. St. Martin's Press 2000 166p il $22.95   345
  1. Lawyers 2. Members of Congress 3. Presidents 4. State legislators 5. Trials 6. Trials (Murder) -- Illinois -- Beardstown
  ISBN 0-312-22922-4

LC 99-59606

This is "the story of how Abraham Lincoln secured the acquittal of murder suspect William 'Duff' Armstrong, the son of an old New Salem friend, by making use of an almanac to discredit a witness's description of the position of the moon on the night in question." Libr J
  Includes bibliographical references

Watson, Bruce
  ★ **Sacco** and Vanzetti; the men, the murders and the judgment of mankind. Viking 2007 433p il $25.95; pa $16   345
  1. Anarchism -- History 2. Anarchists 3. Sacco-Vanzetti Trial, Dedham, Mass., 1921 4. Sacco-Vanzetti case 5. Trials (Homicide)
  ISBN 978-0-670-06353-6; 0-670-06353-3; 978-0-14-3114284 pa; 0-14-311428-X pa

LC 2006-103092

The author "has written a well-researched page-turner. Highly recommended." Libr J
  Includes bibliographical references

346   Private law

American Bar Association
  ★ The **American** Bar Association legal guide for small business; everything you need to know about small business, from start-up to employment to financing and selling. 2nd ed.; Random House Reference 2010 472p pa $16.99   346
  1. Small business
  ISBN 978-0-375-72303-2; 0-375-72303-X

LC 2009-49394

Topics covered "include legal forms of operating businesses, buying an existing business or a franchise, hiring and firing employees, managing temps and independent contractors, dealing with contracts and scams, taxes of all types, and, finally, closing, selling, or bequeathing the business." Libr J [review of 2000 edition]

Butler, Rebecca P.
  ★ **Copyright** for teachers & librarians in the 21st century. Neal-Schuman Publishers 2011 274p il pa $70   346
  1. Copyright 2. Fair use (Copyright)
  ISBN 978-1-55570-738-5

LC 2011012600

"Library educator Rebecca Butler explains fair use, public domain, documentation and licenses, permissions, violations and penalties, policies and ethics codes, citations, creation and ownership, how to register copyrights, and gives tips for staying out of trouble." Publisher's note
  Includes bibliographical references

Elias, Stephen
  Chapter 13 bankruptcy; keep your property & repay debts over time. [by] Stephen Elias &

Robin Leonard. 10th ed.; Nolo 2010 486p il pa $39.99 **346**

1. Bankruptcy

ISBN 978-1-4133-1069-6; 1-4133-1069-9

LC 2009-21416

Answers questions about bankruptcy that range from how to face the reality of being in debt and possible alternatives to filing procedures and strategies for rebuilding credit after the process is complete.

★ The **foreclosure** survival guide; keep your house or walk away with money in your pocket. 2nd ed.; Nolo 2009 304p pa $24.99 **346**

1. Foreclosure

ISBN 978-1-4133-1059-7; 1-4133-1059-1

LC 2009-11885

"Elias explains how foreclosure works, what options there may be for keeping a home when in default, and what to do when that is not possible. He includes instruction on negotiating a workout with a lender as well as chapters on how to use bankruptcy to avoid foreclosure. . . . Straightforward and timely." Libr J

Fishman, Stephen

The **public** domain; how to find & use copyright-free writings, music, art & more. 5th ed.; Nolo 2010 462p il map pa $39.99 **346**

1. Copyright

ISBN 978-1-4133-1205-8; 1-4133-1205-5

LC 2009-39940

This book offers "information about finding copyright-free writings, music, art, photography, software, maps, databases, videos, and more." Publisher's note

Leonard, Robin

★ **Solve** your money troubles; debt, credit & bankruptcy. by Robin Leonard & Margaret Reiter. 12th ed.; Nolo 2009 520p pa $24.99 **346**

1. Credit 2. Debtor and creditor

ISBN 978-1-4133-1022-1; 1-4133-1022-2

LC 2009-10728

This guide offers advice on how to manage debts, including how to create a budget, negotiate with creditors, and rebuild your credit.

Lessig, Lawrence

Remix; making art and commerce thrive in the hybrid economy. Penguin Press 2008 xxii, 327p $25.95 **346**

1. Copyright 2. Copyright and electronic data processing 3. Cultural industries

ISBN 978-1-59420-172-1

LC 2008-32392

As Lessig "sees it, if intellectual-property law is left as it is an entire generation will be criminalized. He argues that the ways in which young people break copyright laws help them to become the sort of people we want them to be— creative and collaborative. Kids today are simply not going to give up downloading music and using copyrighted material in YouTube videos: they belong to a culture for which 'remix' is 'the essential art.' Lessig's proposals for revising

copyright are compelling, because they rethink intellectual-property rights without abandoning them." New Yorker

Includes bibliographical references

Pakroo, Peri

★ The **small** business start-up kit; by Peri H. Pakroo; edited by Marcia Stewart. 6th ed.; Nolo 2010 352p pa $29.99 **346**

1. Business enterprises 2. Commercial law 3. Small business

ISBN 978-1-4133-1099-3; 1-4133-1099-0

LC 2009-37822

"In addition to covering essential legal basics, . . . [the author] advises on picking a business name and the best location, drafting and using contracts, managing business finances using technology, choosing the right business structure, and reaching customers using social media. . . . The CD-ROM includes contact information for state agencies that deal with businesses and taxes." Libr J

Pascoe, Peggy

What comes naturally; miscegenation law and the making of race in America. Oxford University Press 2009 404p il map **346**

1. Interracial marriage 2. Interracial marriage -- United States -- History 3. Miscegenation -- Law & legislation 4. Miscegenation -- United States -- History 5. Racially mixed people 6. Racially mixed people -- Legal status, laws, etc. -- United States 7. Sociology literature

ISBN 0-19-509463-8; 978-0-19-509463-3

LC 2008-18035

"Peggy Pascoe's book, 'What Comes Naturally,' has won five major book awards--two from the American Historical Association, two from the Organization of American Historians, and one from the Law and Society Association; it was also a finalist for another from the American Studies Association. . . . It . . . [examines] laws banning interracial marriage in the United States, . . . informed by sociological, anthropological, and feminist theories of race-making, the state, law, and the intersections of race, class, and gender." (Contemporary Sociology)

This compelling history of the United States miscegenation law demonstrates its centrality to maintaining white supremacy in the century following the Civil War. Pascoe, broadening her focus beyond black-white relations, considers Western states' prohibition of marriage between whites and American Indians, Chinese, Japanese, and Filipinos, as well as blacks. She weaves a fascinating story out of significant court cases.T New Yorker

Includes bibliographical references and index

Pressman, David

Patent it yourself; your step-by-step guide to filing at the U.S. Patent Office. 14th ed.; Nolo 2009 596p il pa $49.99 **346**

1. Inventions 2. Patents

ISBN 978-1-4133-1058-0; 1-4133-1058-3

LC 2009-11888

This guide for the amateur inventor covers patent searching, filing and infringement.

Stim, Richard

Contracts; the essential business desk reference. Nolo 2011 477p pa $39.99; ebook $39.99   **346**

1. Contracts 2. Reference books

ISBN 978-1-4133-1281-2 pa; 1-4133-1281-0 pa; 978-1-4133-1289-8 ebook; 1-4133-1289-6 ebook

LC 2010-21161

The author "helps laypeople navigate the sometimes murky waters of contractual agreements. Stim dedicates sections to writing different types of contracts, a dictionary of terms found in contracts and similar legal documents, and how to enforce these agreements once they're made. The bulk of the book is an alphabetized list of terms related to legal words and concepts. There is also a well-thought-out section on statutes of limitations on contract claims by state as well as contract sample documents scattered throughout." Libr J

★ **Patent,** copyright & trademark; 11th ed.; Nolo 2010 636p il pa $44.99   **346**

1. Copyright 2. Patents 3. Trademarks

ISBN 978-1-4133-1200-3; 1-4133-1200-4

LC 2009-48208

The author explains concepts, issues, and terms concerning intellectual property, discusses trade secrets, copyright, patent, and trademark law, and provides sample forms.

Encyclopedia of crime and punishment; edited by David Levinson. Sage Publs. 2002 4v set $600   **346**

1. Administration of criminal justice 2. Crime -- Encyclopedias 3. Criminal justice, Administration of -- Encyclopedias 4. Criminology -- Encyclopedias 5. Reference books

ISBN 0-7619-2258-X

LC 2002-1220

"The 439 signed entries cover 13 major themes: crimes and related behaviors, law and justice, policing, forensics, corrections, victimology, punishment, social and cultural context, international aspects, concepts and theories, research methods and information, organizations and institutions, and special populations. . . . {This is} easy to understand and useful for beginning research in the field of criminal justice." Booklist

Includes bibliographical references

346.01   Persons and domestic relations

American Civil Liberties Union

★ The **rights** of women; the authoritative ACLU guide to women's rights. [by] Lenora M. Lapidus, Emily J. Martin, and Namita Luthra. 4th ed.; New York University 2009 412p $75; pa $19   **346.01**

1. Women -- Law and legislation 2. Women's rights

ISBN 978-0-8147-5230-2; 0-8147-5230-6; 978-0-8147-5229-6 pa; 0-8147-5229-2 pa

LC 2008-47033

Topics covered include "employment, education, housing, and public accommodations. This handbook also examines the specific issues of trafficking, violence against women, welfare reform, and reproductive freedom." Publisher's note

Includes bibliographical references

Clifford, Denis

A **legal** guide for lesbian and gay couples; by Denis Clifford, Frederick Hertz, and Emily Doskow. 15th ed; Nolo 2010 333p pa $34.99   **346.01**

1. Gay couples -- Legal status, laws, etc.

ISBN 978-1-4133-1091-7; 1-4133-1091-5

LC 2009-37846

This handbook addresses "legal issues with which gay and lesbian couples are certain to contend . . . [including] advice for GLBT parents and prospective parents. Moreover, it addresses other legal considerations such as finanical arrangements. Indispensable for gay and lesbian readers, as well as for attorneys who may lack familiarity in this area." Libr J

Includes bibliographical references

Doskow, Emily

★ **Nolo's** essential guide to divorce; 3rd ed.; Nolo 2010 496p il pa $24.99   **346.01**

1. Divorce -- Law and legislation

ISBN 978-1-4133-1255-3; 1-4133-1255-1

LC 2010-8698

The author "covers the before, during, and after of divorce, counseling readers on the types of divorces, how to make decisions about living arrangements and the division of property, and how custody decisions are made. She advocates minimizing conflict but includes sections on domestic violence and kidnapping if the worst happens. Appendixes contain state-to-state grounds for divorce and financial inventory forms." Libr J

Sember, Brette McWhorter

★ **Seniors'** rights; your legal guide to living life to the fullest. Sphinx Pub 2004 243p pa $19.95   **346.01**

1. Elderly -- Law and legislation 2. Older people -- Civil rights -- United States -- Popular works 3. Older people -- Legal status, laws, etc -- United States -- Popular works 4. Retirees -- Civil rights -- United States -- Popular works 5. Retirees -- Legal status, laws, etc -- United States -- Popular works

ISBN 1-572-48386-5

LC 2004-10704

"The author endeavors to help seniors understand their rights involving medical care, bank accounts, retirement accounts, housing, and discrimination. . . . The first step to protecting your rights, as she indicates, is understanding them, and this book will help seniors achieve that goal." Booklist

Sherman, Charles Edward

Make any divorce better! specific steps to make things smoother, faster, less painful, and save you a lot of money. [by] Ed Sherman; [foreword by Warren Farrell] Nolo Press Occidental 2008 177p il $24.95   **346.01**

1. Divorce -- Law and legislation

ISBN 978-0-944508-64-0; 0-944508-64-2

LC 2007-930632

The author "offers an insider's guide to making divorce go smoothly, quickly, painlessly, and inexpensively, revealing how the law works against divorcing couples and showing how to beat the system. . . . His no-nonsense guide to the legalities and practicalities of divorce is highly recommended for all public libraries." Libr J

Woodhouse, Violet

★ **Divorce** & money; how to make the best financial decisions during divorce. with Dale Fetherling. 10th ed.; Nolo 2011 511p pa $34.99 **346.01**
    1. Divorce -- Law and legislation
    ISBN 978-1-4133-1314-7 pa; 1-4133-1314-0 pa; 978-1-4133-1337-6 ebook; 1-4133-1337-X ebook
                         LC 2010-31198
A guide to financial problems that arise as a result of divorce proceedings.

Women's legal guide; editor, Barbara R. Hauser with Julie A. Tigges. Fulcrum 1996 526p hardcover o.p. pa $22.95 **346.01**
    1. Women 2. Women -- Law and legislation
    ISBN 1-55591-303-2 pa
                         LC 95-46893
"This is a collection of essays written by women attorneys for women who need legal information. Family- and health- related issues such as divorce, family violence, and reproductive rights are covered, as are business topics of particular concern to women. . . . Estate planning, sexual discrimination, dealing with disabilities, and the rights of lesbian women are considered as well. The writing is consistently clear, objective, and practical." Libr J
    Includes bibliographical references

346.04 Property

Crews, Kenneth D.

★ **Copyright** law for librarians and educators; creative strategies and practical solutions. with contributions from Dwayne K. Buttler . . . [et al.] 2nd ed; American Library Association 2012 xii, 192 p.p ill. (alk. paper) $57 **346.04**
    1. Copyright -- United States 2. Fair use (Copyright) -- United States 3. Legal literature 4. Librarians -- United States -- Handbooks, manuals, etc 5. Press law 6. Teachers -- United States -- Handbooks, manuals, etc
    ISBN 0838910920; 9780838910924
                        LC 2011027604
Author Kenneth D. Crews' book "allows readers to get up to speed on current interpretations of the Digital Millennium Copyright Act from a librarian-educator viewpoint." It also "draws on cutting-edge case law in 18 discrete areas of copyright, including specialized and controversial music and sound recording issues. [This guide offers] information professionals . . . the tools they need to take control of their rights and responsibilities as copyright owners and users." (Publisher's note)
    The author addresses 18 areas of copyright in 5 parts. He begins with the scope of protectable works as well as works without copyright protection. Next, he discusses the rights of ownership, including duration and exceptions. He then explains fair use and its related guidelines. Part 4 focuses on the TEACH Act, Section 108, and responsibilities and liabilities. Lastly, Crews examines special issues such as the Digital Millennium Copyright Act.a Booklist
    Includes bibliographical references and index.

Elias, Stephen

★ **Trademark**; legal care for your business & product name. by Stephen Elias & Richard Stim. 9th ed.; Nolo 2010 448p il pa $39.99 **346.04**
    1. Trademarks
    ISBN 978-1-4133-1256-0; 1-4133-1256-X
                        LC 2010-9267
The authors explain "how to: choose a distinctive name or logo that others can't copy; search for other marks that might conflict with your own; register your mark with the U.S. Patent and Trademark Office; protect your marks from unauthorized use by others; resolve trademark disputes outside the courtroom; [and] create an Internet presence with an eye on trademark law." Publisher's note

Fishman, Stephen

★ **Copyright** handbook; what every writer needs to know. 10th ed.; Nolo 2008 527p il pa $39.99 **346.04**
    1. Copyright
    ISBN 978-1-4133-0893-8; 1-4133-0893-7
                        LC 2008-7882
"Designed as a practical handbook for writers and publishers. Includes a list of legal aid groups and sample forms." Guide to Ref Books. 11th edition
    Includes bibliographical references

Hyde, Lewis

Common as air; revolution, art, and ownership. Farrar, Straus and Giroux 2010 306p $26 **346.04**
    1. Arts 2. Copyright 3. Culture 4. Information commons 5. Intellectual property 6. Patents
    ISBN 978-0-374-22313-7; 0-374-22313-0
                       LC 2010-02388
This is "an eloquent and erudite plea for protecting our cultural patrimony from appropriation by commercial interests." N Y Times Book Rev
    Includes bibliographical references

Portman, Janet

★ **Every** tenant's legal guide; by Janet Portman and Marcia Stewart. 6th ed.; Nolo 2009 445p il pa $34.99 **346.04**
    1. Landlord and tenant
    ISBN 978-1-4133-1015-3; 1-4133-1015-X
                        LC 2009-4832
This guide explains how to find and inspect a home, negotiate clauses in a lease or rental agreement, understand rules on rent increases and late rent, get repairs and maintenance, protect privacy rights, fight discrimination, deal with environmental hazards, security deposits, evictions and legal procedures.

Stewart, Marcia

★ **Every** landlord's legal guide; by Marcia Stewart and Ralph Warner & Janet Portman. 10th ed.; Nolo 2010 462p pa $44.99   **346.04**

1. Landlord and tenant
ISBN 978-1-4133-1197-6; 1-4133-1197-0

LC 2009-39934

This guide covers how to "screen and choosing tenants; prepare leases and rental agreements; collect and returning deposits; avoid discrimination charges; keep up with repairs and maintenance; hire the right property manager; minimize your liability; [and] deal with problem tenants." Publisher's note

Strauss, Steven D.

Landlord and tenant. Norton 1998 155p $25; pa $14   **346.04**

1. Landlord and tenant 2. Landlord and tenant -- United States -- Popular works
ISBN 0-393-04585-4; 0-393-31730-7 pa

LC 97-33617

This book covers the legal rights and responsibilities of tenants and landlords including such topics as what to look for in an apartment or lease, how to evict tenants or avoid eviction, and how to break a lease

Wherry, Timothy Lee

★ **Intellectual** property; everything the digital-age librarian needs to know. American Library Association 2008 141p il $50   **346.04**

1. Copyright 2. Patents 3. Trademarks
ISBN 978-0-8389-0948-5; 0-8389-0948-5

LC 2007-13893

The author "explains the difference between patents, copyrights, and trademarks and when one would want to obtain any one or a combination of the three. He goes on to instruct readers on how technology has simplified the process of both searching and acquiring these three types of intellectual property protection. . . . This informative and necessary volume is a must have for any professional reference collection." Voice Youth Advocates

346.05   Inheritance, succession, fiduciary trusts, trustees

Clifford, Denis

★ **Make** your own living trust; 10th ed.; Nolo 2011 338p pa $39.99   **346.05**

1. Estate planning 2. Inheritance and succession
ISBN 978-1-4133-1316-1 pa; 1-4133-1316-7 pa; 978-1-4133-1344-4 ebook; 1-4133-1344-2 ebook

LC 2010-38422

"Explains what trusts are, how they work, and who should use them. The CD provides a basic living trust, and AB living trust, plus other key forms." Publisher's note

★ **Plan** your estate; 10th ed; Nolo 2010 539p pa $44.99   **346.05**

1. Estate planning
ISBN 978-1-4133-1201-0

This guide covers basic estate planning, probate avoidance, living wills, federal estate and gift taxes, trusts, durable powers of attorney, and more.

Shotwell, Barbara

Pass it on; a practical approach to the fears and facts of planning your estate. [by] Barbara Shotwell and Nancy R. Greenway. Hyperion 2000 286p il $22.95; pa $14.95   **346.05**

1. Estate planning 2. Estate planning -- Caricatures and cartoons 3. Estate planning -- Humor 4. Estate planning -- United States -- Popular works
ISBN 0-7868-6580-6; 0-7868-8494-0 pa

LC 99-49481

The authors explain "the essential estate-planning documents, various kinds of trusts, retirement plans, business considerations, and the probate process. . . . The text is replete with cartoons, quotes, illustrative song titles, and anecdotes that add levity and accessibility without oversimplifying the treatment of the subject." Libr J

Strauss, Steven D.

Wills and trusts. Norton 1998 176p $25; pa $14   **346.05**

1. Estate planning 2. Trusts and trustees 3. Trusts and trustees -- United States -- Popular works 4. Wills 5. Wills -- United States -- Popular works
ISBN 0-393-04583-8; 0-393-31728-5 pa

LC 97-33619

"Strauss specializes in transforming the arcane and obtuse into everyman's lingo and comprehension." Booklist

346.07   Commercial law

Elias, Stephen

★ **How** to file for Chapter 7 bankruptcy; by Stephen Elias, Albin Renauer, & Robin Leonard. 16th ed.; Nolo 2009 555p il pa $39.99   **346.07**

1. Bankruptcy
ISBN 978-1-4133-1060-3; 1-4133-1060-5

LC 2009-21419

This guide offers advice on such topics as personal debt, property liability, asset protection, rebuilding credit, and filling out and filing forms.

347   Procedure and courts

Breyer, Stephen G.

Making our democracy work; a judge's view. [by] Stephen Breyer. Alfred A. Knopf 2010 270p il $26.95   **347**

1. Judicial review -- United States 2. Judicial review -- United States -- History 3. Political questions and judicial power -- United States 4. Separation of powers -- United States
ISBN 978-0-307-26991-1; 0-307-26991-4

LC 2010-16839

"A sitting Justice explains how the Supreme Court won the public trust and what it must do to keep it. Employing a succession of cases from Marbury v. Madison to Bush v. Gore, Breyer . . . offers a short, highly accessible course on the evolution of judicial review, the doctrine permitting the Court to invalidate laws conflicting with the Constitution. . . . Speaking out without talking down, Breyer renders a signal service to his fellow citizens." Kirkus

Includes bibliographical references

Faigman, David L.

Laboratory of justice; the Supreme Court's 200-year struggle to integrate science and the law. Times Books, Henry Holt 2004 417p $27.50; pa $17 **347**
1. Constitutional law -- United States 2. Science -- Governmental policy
ISBN 0-8050-7274-8; 0-8050-7845-2 pa
LC 2003-57049

"This insightful and accessible study throws light on how new ways of understanding the world produce new readings of our Constitution." Publ Wkly

Includes bibliographical references

Finkelman, Paul

★ **Landmark** decisions of the United States Supreme Court; [by] Paul Finkelman, Melvin I. Urofsky. 2nd ed.; CQ Press 2008 791p il $250 **347**
1. Constitutional law -- United States
ISBN 978-0-87289-409-9
LC 2007-42588

This "provides the historical context and constitutional perspective of more than 1,000 of the most important Supreme Court cases." Publisher's note

Includes bibliographical references

Friedman, Barry

The **will** of the people; how public opinion has influenced the Supreme Court and shaped the meaning of the Constitution. Farrar, Straus and Giroux 2009 614p **347**
1. Judicial process -- United States -- Public opinion 2. Public opinion 3. Public opinion -- United States
ISBN 0374220344; 0374532370 pa; 9780374220341; 9780374532376 pa
LC 2008054247

This is an account of the relationship between popular opinion and the Supreme Court from the Declaration of Independence to the end of the Rehnquist court in 2005. (Publisher's note) Index.

This book is a thought-provoking and authoritative history of the Supreme Court's relationship to popular opinion. . . . Friedman's contribution to [the] discussion is the breadth and detail of his historical canvas, and it's a significant one." N Y Times Book Rev

Includes bibliographical references

Hall, Timothy L.

Supreme Court justices; a biographical dictionary. Facts on File 2001 566p $65 **347**
1. Judges -- Dictionaries 2. Judges -- United States 3. Judges -- United States -- Biography -- Dictionaries 4. Reference books
ISBN 0-8160-4194-6
LC 00-65415

This work offers "sketches of the lives of members of the Court through the Clinton presidency. . . . Includes a wide array of appendixes that would be valuable at a reference desk. . . . Of greatest interest is the excellent bibliography, grouped by general works, then by justice in alphabetical order. . . . This book would be useful in any public or academic library." Choice

Includes bibliographical references

Leiter, Richard A.

Landmark Supreme Court cases; the most influential decisions of the Supreme Court of the United States. [by] Gary Hartman, Roy M. Mersky, [and] Cindy Tate Slavinski. Facts on File 2004 594p $70; pa $21.95 **347**
1. Law -- United States
ISBN 0-8160-2452-9; 0-8160-6923-9 pa
LC 2003-57776

This is "an excellent source for beginning researchers. . . . The discussion of the case's significance and its implications will be useful for students." SLJ

Includes bibliographical references

Marshall, Thurgood

Thurgood Marshall; his speeches, writings, arguments, opinions, and reminiscences. edited by Mark Tushnet; foreword by Randall Kennedy. Hill Bks. 2001 xxvi, 548p $40; pa $24.95 **347**
1. African Americans -- Biography 2. African Americans -- Civil rights 3. Civil rights 4. Civil rights activists 5. Judges -- United States -- Biography 6. Lawyers 7. Race discrimination 8. Solicitors general 9. Supreme Court justices
ISBN 1-55652-385-8; 1-55652-386-6 pa
LC 2001-16793

"In a career ranging from his trial and appellate work for the NAACP to his tenure as an associate justice of the Court, Marshall wrought revolutionary changes in U.S. law and politics, and this collection of his legal briefs, writings, speeches, and judicial opinions, plus a never-before-published oral interview, gives us a superior analysis of the advocate, the democrat, the dissenter, and the unflagging fighter for equality." Libr J

Includes bibliographical references

O'Brien, David M.

Storm center; the Supreme Court in American politics. 8th ed; W.W. Norton 2008 xx, 458p il pa $29.85 **347**
ISBN 978-0-393-93218-8; 0-393-93218-4
LC 2008-7373

The author discusses "the day-to-day workings of the Court justices and their law clerks, how cases are accepted for hearing, what negotiations and compromises go on, how case opinions get written—and what happens to American society when two conservative presidents, Reagan and Bush, appoint the majority of justices." Publisher's note

Includes bibliographical references

Shesol, Jeff

★ **Supreme** power; Franklin Roosevelt vs. the Supreme Court. W. W. Norton & Co. 2010 644p il $27.95   **347**

1. Governors 2. Handicapped 3. Philatelists 4. Political questions and judicial power -- United States -- History 5. Presidents
ISBN 978-0-393-06474-2; 0-393-06474-3

LC 2009-46365

The book examines the interaction between U.S. President Franklin Delano Roosevelt and the Supreme Court. "FDR took up the idea of expanding the number of justices on the Court. This was the famous 'court-packing plan.' The story of the plan and the . . . political battle over it . . . [is] told . . . by Jeff Shesol in his . . . [book] 'Supreme Power.' Shesol looks at the battle through the eyes of all the major players--FDR and his advisers, the congressional leadership that was handed the unappealing job of putting the plan into effect, the congressional opposition, the many politicians and interest groups that organized over the plan, and the justices themselves." (New York Review of Books)

This "is an impressive and engaging book—an excellent work of narrative history. It is deeply researched and beautifully written. Even readers who already know the outcome will find it hard not to feel the suspense that surrounded the battle, so successfully does Shesol recreate the atmosphere of this great controversy." N Y Times Book Rev

Includes bibliographical references

Smith, Jean Edward

John Marshall; definer of a nation. Holt & Co. 1996 736p il hardcover o.p. pa $22   **347**

1. Biographers 2. Biography, Individual 3. Secretaries of state 4. Supreme Court justices 5. Writers on law
ISBN 0-8050-5510-X pa

LC 96-15072

"Mr. Smith's splendid biography deserves a large readership mostly because it has recovered Marshall the man." N Y Times Book Rev

Includes bibliographical references

Toobin, Jeffrey R.

★ The **nine**; inside the secret world of the Supreme Court. [by] Jeffrey Toobin. Doubleday 2007 369p il $27.95   **347**

1. Judicial review -- United States 2. Law -- Political aspects 3. Political questions and judicial power -- United States
ISBN 978-0-385-51640-2

LC 2007-20287

"Beautifully written, this is an essential purchase for all libraries interested in the contemporary Supreme Court." Libr J

Includes bibliographical references

Warner, Ralph E.

★ **Everybody's** guide to small claims court; by Ralph Warner. 13th ed.; Nolo 2010 480p pa $29.99   **347**

1. Small claims court
ISBN 978-1-4133-1102-0; 1-4133-1102-4

LC 2009-41947

Presents resources and step-by-step instructions for defending one's case in small claims court, and discusses specific kinds of cases, such as motor vehicle repair and purchase, vehicle accident, and landlord-tenant cases.

Williams, Juan

Thurgood Marshall; American revolutionary. Times Bks. 1998 459p il hardcover o.p. pa $16 **347**

1. African Americans -- Biography 2. African Americans -- Civil rights 3. Civil rights activists 4. Judges -- United States -- Biography 5. Lawyers 6. Solicitors general 7. Supreme Court justices
ISBN 0-8129-3299-4 pa

LC 98-9735

"Williams presents Marshall as a revolutionary 'of grand vision,' but this well-rounded portrait of the man also addresses his vanities and warts, from his ascension to his deflation and subsequent redemption. This is a must read for all Americans concerned with the struggle for civil and individual rights." Booklist

Includes bibliographical references

★ Great American trials; Edward W. Knappman, editor; Stephen G. Christianson and Lisa Paddock, consulting legal editors. 2nd ed; Gale Group 2002 2v il set $170   **347**

1. Trials
ISBN 0-7876-4901-5

Featuring approximately 360 trials from the 1800s to the present, entries "cover the principals involved, the crime charged, the verdict and sentence, and the significance and impact of each trial." Publisher's note

Includes bibliographical references

★ The Oxford companion to the Supreme Court of the United States; editor in chief, Kermit L. Hall; editors, James W. Ely, Jr., Joel B. Grossman. 2nd ed.; Oxford University Press 2005 xxv, 1239p il $65   **347**

1. Reference books
ISBN 0-19-517661-8

LC 2004-29463

This encyclopedia includes over 1200 articles "on all aspects of the court's history, justices, operations, and cases. Over 300 experts contributed the entries, which vary in length; some have bibliographic references. The organization . . . [includes] alphabetical entries, portraits of the justices, cross-references, and indexes by both case name and topic." Choice

348   Laws, regulations, cases

Stathis, Stephen W.

Landmark legislation, 1774-2002; major U.S. acts and treaties. {by} Stephen Stathis. CQ Press 2003 22, 429p $130   **348**

1. Legislation 2. Legislation -- United States
ISBN 1-56802-781-8

LC 2003-3531

"This well-organized volume will allow users to quickly find a description of important legislation and determine where they can locate the full text. . . . This will be a useful source for academic and public libraries." Booklist

Includes bibliographical references

★ Major acts of Congress; Brian K. Landsberg, editor in chief. Macmillan Reference USA 2004 3v il set $290 **348**
1. Law -- United States -- Encyclopedias 2. Reference books
ISBN 0-02-865749-7

LC 2003-18747

This "will be a top-tier reference work for students and laypersons researching federal legislation." Booklist

Includes bibliographical references

★ U.S. laws, acts, and treaties; edited by Timothy L. Hall. Salem Press 2003 3v set $188 **348**
1. Law -- United States
ISBN 1-58765-098-3

LC 2002-156063

This "is a collection of 433 major U.S. acts of Congress and U.S. treaties covering the time period from 1776 through 2002, beginning with the Declaration of Independence and ending with the Homeland Security Act. . . . The essays, chronologically arranged and varying in length from 500 to 2,000 words, cover the historical origins and main provisions of each law or treaty. . . . This set presents a good coverage of landmark laws and treaties in a concise, easy-to-read, and easy-to-use work. It is geared toward high-school and undergraduate students but would also make a useful and functional reference tool for public libraries." Booklist

Includes bibliographical references

349 Law of specific jurisdictions, areas, socioeconomic regions, regional intergovernmental organizations

Clark, David Scott

The **Oxford** companion to American law; editor in chief, Kermit L. Hall; editors, David S. Clark {et al.} Oxford Univ. Press 2002 xxvi, 912p $75 **349**
1. Law -- History 2. Law -- United States 3. Law -- United States -- Encyclopedias
ISBN 0-19-508878-6

LC 2002-284010

The alphabetically arranged "entries consider how law, legal institutions, and court decisions are related to social demands and legal responses. . . . The volume also includes standard legal terms and key legal concepts, such as verdicts and venues, as well as biographical statements about leading individuals in the legal profession. . . . With a substantial breadth of information and analysis, this volume is accessible to every reader. All libraries will find it an invaluable reference source." Libr J

Includes bibliographical references

Friedman, Lawrence Meir

American law in the 20th century; {by} Lawrence M. Friedman. Yale Univ. Press 2002 722p $38 **349**
1. Law -- United States 2. Law -- United States -- History -- 20th century
ISBN 0-300-09137-0

LC 2001-3332

The author "examines the American legal system as an integral part of the larger society, both reflecting and causing changes therein. By adopting such a focus, the author makes his book accessible to readers who are not legal scholars." Booklist

Includes bibliographical references

★ Gale encyclopedia of American law; 3rd ed.; Gale/Cengage Learning 2011 14v il map set $1604 **349**
1. Law -- United States -- Encyclopedias 2. Reference books
ISBN 978-1-4144-3684-5; 1-4144-3684-X; 978-1-4144-4302-7 ebook; 1-4144-4302-1 ebook

LC 2010-45527

Explains legal terms and concepts in everyday language, covering a wide variety of persons, entities, and events that have shaped the U.S. legal system and influenced public perceptions of it.

★ Gale encyclopedia of everyday law; Jeffrey Wilson, editor. 2nd ed.; Thomson Gale 2006 2v set $325 **349**
1. Law -- United States
ISBN 1-4144-0353-4

LC 2006-10071

This encyclopedia includes "descriptions of each issue's historical background, covering important statutes and cases; profiles of various U.S. laws and regulations; details of how laws and regulations vary from state to state, and; . . . bibliographies, including print and Web resources and lists of relevant organizations." Publisher's note

Includes bibliographical references

★ National survey of state laws; Richard A. Leiter, editor. 6th ed; Thomson Gale 2008 808p $140 **349**
1. Law -- United States
ISBN 978-0-7876-9874-4; 0-7876-9874-1

Summarizes state laws on 50 subjects, divided into general legal categories: business and consumer, criminal, education, employment, family, general civil, real estate, and tax.

351 Public administration

Kettl, Donald F.

The **next** government of the United States; why our institutions fail us and how to fix them. W. W. Norton & Co. 2009 288p il $25.95 **351**

1. Administrative agencies

ISBN 978-0-393-05112-4; 0-393-05112-9

LC 2008-38584

"Kettl's cogent and unbiased analysis of the failure of government institutions posits that current challenges, whether in health care or disaster response, have outgrown the capacity of monolithic government agencies, even while the size of government continues to swell. . . . He presents a balanced and unpartisan analysis of the Hurricane Katrina debacle, examining human error and generations of poor decision making as well as the intricacies of federalism and the organizational complexity of government institutions." Publ Wkly

Includes bibliographical references

Phillips, Kevin P.

Arrogant capital; Washington, Wall Street, and the frustration of American politics. {by} Kevin Phillips. Little, Brown 1994 231p hardcover o.p. pa $18.99 **351**

1. Political corruption

ISBN 0-316-70602-7 pa

LC 94-10035

Phillips "makes a convincing case that voters see Washington as the enemy because they can't crack the interlock between interest-group power and the political system." N Y Times Book Rev

Includes bibliographical references

351.076 Review and exercise

Civil service arithmetic and vocabulary; [by] Joe Krasowski . . . [et al.] 15th ed.; Arco/Thomson Learning 2005 347p pa $14.95 **351.076**

1. Civil service -- Examinations

ISBN 0-7689-1697-6; 978-0-7689-1697-3

Contains basic instructions for working every type of math problem found on the exams. The vocabulary section includes a review of vocabulary words, verbal analogies, and sentence completion problems.

352.13 Administration of subordinate jurisdictions

★ Counties USA; a directory of United States counties. Darren L. Smith, managing editor. Omnigraphics 2006 840p il map $149 **352.13**

1. County government 2. Reference books

ISBN 978-0-7808-0821-8

This is "an excellent choice, offering multiple uses as a country directory, demographic source, and gazetteer." Choice [review of 2003 edition]

★ The book of the states; [compiled by] the Council of State Governments. 2010 ed; Council of State Governments 2010 627p il map $125 **352.13**

1. State governments

ISBN 978-0-87292-7667

"In addition to general articles on various aspects of state government, this source provides many statistical and directory data, the principal state officials, and such information as the nickname, motto, flower, bird, song, and tree of each state." Ref Sources for Small & Medium-sized Libr. 6th edition

352.23 Chief executives

Raphael, Ray

Mr. president; how and why the founders created a chief executive. by Ray Raphael. Alfred A. Knopf 2012 324 p. **352.23**

1. Historical literature 2. Presidents -- United States 3. Presidents -- United States -- History -- 18th century 4. United States. Constitutional Convention (1787)

ISBN 9780307595270

LC 2011033471

The author presents a biography of the Constitutional Convention and the herculean task faced by the representatives. The author paints a picture of heroes--Edmund Randolph, George Mason, James Wilson and James Madison, among others--noting that the founders developed a government presupposing that George Washington would be the first chief executive. . . . In order to show how their views evolved as they toiled, Raphael explores the founders' writings in chronological order. . . . They struggled with questions of popular or legislative election, term of office and re-eligibility before they ever began to worry about the powers the executive would wield. (Kirkus)

Fellow citizens; the Penguin book of U.S. presidential inaugural addresses. edited with an introduction and commentaries by Robert V. Remini and Terry Golway. Penguin Books 2008 476p $16 **352.23**

1. American speeches 2. Presidents -- United States -- Inaugural addresses

ISBN 978-0-14-311453-6; 0-14-311453-0

LC 2008-19970

"Two distinguished historians round up every presidential inaugural address and preface it with commentary on the rhetoric and historical context of the discourse. . . . Reflecting the major events of American history, as well as a rhetorical evolution from prolixity to brevity, this . . . is a great resource." Booklist

Includes bibliographical references

★ Guide to the presidency; Michael Nelson, editor. 4th ed; CQ Press 2008 2v il map set $355 **352.23**

1. Presidents -- United States

ISBN 978-0-8728-9364-1; 0-8728-9364-2

LC 2007-25322

"The history of the presidency; the powers of the office . . . ; the president as a public figure; relations with other branches of government; life in the White House; and many other topics are covered in 37 chapters authored by academic scholars." Booklist

Includes bibliographical references

My fellow citizens; the inaugural addresses of the presidents of the United States, 1789-2009. with an introduction by Arthur M. Schlesinger, Jr. and commentary by Fred L. Israel. Facts On File 2010 428p $45 **352.23**
1. Presidents -- United States -- Inaugural addresses
ISBN 978-0-8160-8253-7; 0-8160-8253-7
LC 2009-32184
"Features the original text of all 56 inaugural speeches, each with an explanatory essay." Publisher's note

State of the union; presidential rhetoric from Woodrow Wilson to George W. Bush. CQ Press 2007 1185p il $140 **352.23**
1. American speeches 2. Presidents -- United States -- Inaugural addresses 3. Presidents -- United States -- Messages
ISBN 978-0-87289-433-4; 0-87289-433-9
LC 2006-35973
"This volume includes over 100 full-text addresses delivered by Presidents from 1913 to 2006 and comes complete with prefatory notes for context." Libr J

Includes bibliographical references

★ The presidency A to Z; Gerhard Peters, editor; John T. Woolley, editor; Michael Nelson, advisory editor. 4th ed.; CQ Press 2008 675p il map $85 **352.23**
1. Presidents -- United States -- Encyclopedias 2. Reference books
ISBN 978-0-87289-367-2; 0-87289-367-7
LC 2007-31322
"Volume 1 traces the history of the office from the creation of the United States Constitution to present-day duties and responsibilities. . . . Volume 2 examines the interaction between the President and the other branches of government. It also includes biographies of Presidents, Vice Presidents, and First Ladies and concludes with tables listing the popular and electoral votes in presidential elections, party nominees for President, and cabinet members. . . . Students of history, political science, and public policy will find it useful when looking for background information about the office of the President." Libr J

Includes bibliographical references

352.3   Executive management

Moynihan, Daniel Patrick
Secrecy; the American experience. {by} Daniel Patrick Moynihan; introduction by Richard Gid Powers. Yale Univ. Press 1998 262p il $38; pa $16 **352.3**
1. Executive power 2. Executive privilege (Government

information) -- United States -- History -- 20th century 3. National security -- United States 4. Official secrets -- United States -- History -- 20th century 5. Security classification (Government documents) -- United States -- History -- 20th century
ISBN 0-300-07756-4; 0-300-08079-4 pa
LC 98-8144
"Using his background as chairman of the bipartisan Commission on Protecting and Reducing Government Secrecy, Moynihan provides a fascinating account of the development of secrecy as a mode of regulation for the U.S. government since World War I: how it was born, how world events shaped it, how it has adversely affected momentous political decisions—dropping the bomb on Hiroshima, the Bay of Pigs fiasco, the Iran-contra affair—and how it has eluded efforts to curtail or end it." America

Includes bibliographical references

353   Specific fields of public administration

Gentry, Curt
J. Edgar Hoover; the man and the secrets. Norton 1991 846p il hardcover o.p. pa $17.95 **353**
1. Biography, Individual 2. FBI officials
ISBN 0-393-32128-2 pa
LC 90-30576
The author "has based his account of Hoover on more than 300 interviews and on access to previously classified FBI documents. . . . Gentry paints a portrait of Hoover as the 'indispensable man,' with many provocative revelations about his political dealings." Libr J

Includes bibliographical references

★ The United States government manual 2009/2010; Office of the Federal Register, National Archives and Records Administration. For sale by the Supt. of Docs., U.S. G.P.O. 2009 674p pa $35 **353**
1. Reference books
ISBN 978-1-59804-516-1
"Official handbook of the Federal government describing the purposes and programs of most Government agencies and listing the top personnel." N Y Public Libr. Ref Books for Child Collect. 2d edition

353.9   Public administration of safety, sanitation, waste control

Hilts, Philip J.
★ Protecting America's health; the FDA, business, and one hundred years of regulation. University of North Carolina Press 2004 394p pa $19.95 **353.9**
1. Drug industry 2. Food -- Law and legislation 3. Food adulteration and inspection
ISBN 978-0-8078-5582-9; 0-8078-5582-0
"This fascinating look at the inside story reveals how disastrous unfettered capitalism would be without reasonable regulation." Booklist

Includes bibliographical references

355 Military science

Arnold, James R.

Jungle of snakes; a century of counterinsurgency warfare from the Philippines to Iraq. Bloomsbury Press 2009 291p map $28 **355**

1. Counterinsurgency 2. Military history

ISBN 978-1-59691-503-9; 1-59691-503-X

LC 2008-54018

The author "studies past insurgency responses to help clarify the U.S. efforts in Iraq. The author investigates four counterinsurgencies that either proved successful in putting down rebellion—the United States in the Philippines following war with Spain in 1898; the British response to the Malayan Emergency in 1948—or disastrous—the French invasion of Algeria in 1830; the U.S. quagmire in Vietnam—and offers lessons to be drawn from them. . . . A reasonably argued work that delivers needed insight and historical precedent to the current war debate." Kirkus

Includes bibliographical references

Axelrod, Alan

★ The **encyclopedia** of the American armed forces. Facts on File 2005 2v il set $175 **355**

1. Reference books

ISBN 0-8160-4700-6

LC 2004-20549

"The four sections each document a major branch of the United States military: Army, Navy, Marine Corps, and Air Force. Each branch has an initial list of entries, a list of branch-specific abbreviations and acronyms, and a short bibliography." Choice

Includes bibliographical references

Bacevich, Andrew J.

Washington rules; America's path to permanent war. [by] Andrew J. Bacevich. Metropolitan Books 2010 286p $25 **355**

1. Military policy -- United States

ISBN 978-0-8050-9141-0; 0-8050-9141-6

LC 2010-06302

This book "is a tough-minded, bracing and intelligent polemic against some 60 years of American militarism." N Y Times Book Rev

Includes bibliographical references

Belfiore, Michael

★ The **department** of mad scientists; how DARPA is remaking our world, from the Internet to artificial limbs. Smithsonian Books/Harper 2009 xxiii, 295p $26.99; ebook $12.99 **355**

1. Science -- Governmental policy 2. Science and state -- United States

ISBN 978-0-06-157793-2; 0-06-157793-6; 978-0-06-195937-0 ebook; 0-06-195937-5 ebook

LC 2009-18015

"Founded by Eisenhower in response to Sputnik and the Soviet space program, DARPA [Defense Advanced Research Projects Agency] mixes military officers with sneaker-wearing scientists, seeking paradigm-shifting ideas in varied fields—from energy, robotics, and rockets to peopleless operating rooms, driverless cars, and planes that can fly halfway around the world in just hours. DARPA gave birth to the Internet, GPS, and mind-controlled robotic arms. . . . Michael Belfiore was given unprecedented access to write this first-ever popular account of DARPA." Bookmarks

Includes bibliographical references

Boot, Max

★ **War** made new; technology, warfare, and the course of history, 1500 to today. Gotham Books 2006 624p il map $24.95 **355**

1. Military art and science 2. Military art and science -- Technological innovations 3. Military history 4. Military history, Modern

ISBN 978-1-592-40222-9; 1-592-40222-4

LC 2006-15518

"Throughout, Boot provides a vivid and engaging mix of historical narrative and analysis, showing the bloody real-world results of abstract decisionmaking about the nature and degree of a country's military preparedness. His twelve case studies, stretching from the defeat of the Spanish Armada to the current situation in Iraq, point to a variety of disparate lessons but some themes that are surprisingly constant over time and space." Commentary

Buckley, Gail Lumet

★ **American** patriots; the story of Blacks in the military from the Revolution to Desert Storm. [by] Gail Buckley. Random House 2001 xxiv, 534p il hardcover o.p. pa $15.95 **355**

1. African American soldiers 2. African American soldiers -- Biography 3. African American soldiers -- History

ISBN 0-375-50279-3; 0-375-76009-1 pa

LC 00-51825

This is an account "of blacks in the U.S. military, both at home and abroad, from the 1770s to the 1990s. . . . This readable, spirited story deserves a place in every U.S. history collection, as well as in the black or military collections." Libr J

Includes bibliographical references

Carroll, James

House of war; the Pentagon and the disastrous rise of American power. Houghton Mifflin Co. 2006 657p il $30 **355**

1. Arms race -- United States 2. Militarism -- United States -- History -- 20th century 3. Military policy -- United States 4. Pentagon

ISBN 0-618-18780-4; 978-0-618-18780-5

LC 2005-24014

"Chronicling the ascent of America's military establishment from 1943 to the aftermath of 9/11, Carroll uses the Pentagon as a metaphor for a U.S. political culture that values military power over human rights and seeks to project U.S. influence and values abroad by force, if necessary, whether invited by other countries or not. . . . Certain to be a widely read and discussed book, this is worthy of space on the shelves of all libraries." Libr J

Includes bibliographical references

Clausewitz, Carl von

★ **On** war; {by} Carl von Clausewitz; edited and translated by Michael Howard and Peter Paret; introductory essays by Peter Paret, Michael Howard and Bernard Brodie; with commentary by Bernard Brodie. Princeton Univ. Press 1976 717p $95; pa $26.95 **355**

    1. Military art and science 2. War

    ISBN 0-691-05657-9; 0-691-01854-5 pa

"Drawing on the experiences of Frederick the Great and Napoleon, Clausewitz tried to analyze the workings of military genius by isolating the factors that decide success in war. His conclusions have remained generally applicable, and since his work contains a minimum of technical discussion, it has retained a wide appeal." Ency Britannica

Cohen, Eliot A.

Conquered into liberty. Free Press 2011 405p il map $30; ebook $14.99 **355**

    1. Guerrilla warfare 2. Nonfiction

    ISBN 978-0-7432-4990-4; 978-1-4516-2733-6 ebook

    LC 2011023717

It was the author's intent to demonstrate "that there is more to the American military heritage than the U.S.' conventional war-fighting and its European antecedents. We should expand the concept of 'American' to include pre-revolutionary times, and so include nearly 200 years of frontier fighting . . . . In . . . [an] examination of 18th-century warfare along the northeastern seaboard . . . Cohen sees two less-appreciated sources for the way Americans currently fight. First was the birth of a unique strain of raiding, ambushing, subversion, living off the land, ad hoc alliance-building with indigenous peoples, long-range reconnaissance, and patrolling behind enemy lines. Second, writes Cohen, was the very fact that these non-traditional tactics were rooted in the distinctiveness of colonial society. . . . Cohen believes that this legacy endures." (National Review)

This is "an engaging account of the wars fought on the 'Great Warpath.' These were the trails, especially around Lakes George and Champlain, which marked a kind of western border for early settlers. The author recounts the eight major battles in those successive campaigns. He includes two naval battles: Plattsburgh, during the War of 1812, and Valcour Island in 1776, both of which he presents as decisive but underrated contributions to securing the young republic from foreign threat. . . . A delightful-to-read piece of American history." Kirkus

    Includes bibliographical references

Daalder, Ivo H.

In the shadow of the Oval Office; profiles of the national security advisers and the presidents they served: from JFK to George W. Bush. [by] Ivo H. Daalder and I.M. Destler. Simon & Schuster 2009 386p $27 **355**

    1. National security -- United States 2. Presidents -- United States -- Staff

    ISBN 978-1-416-55319-9; 1-416-55319-3

    LC 2008-40699

"A revealing, unsettling look at how our presidents receive advice on foreign policy." Kirkus

    Includes bibliographical references

De Pauw, Linda Grant

Battle cries and lullabies; women in war from prehistory to the present. University of Okla. Press 1998 395p il hardcover o.p. pa $21.95 **355**

    1. Military history 2. Women -- History 3. Women and war 4. Women soldiers

    ISBN 0-8061-3288-4 pa

    LC 98-21219

"Though the book never directly states its larger claims, the wealth of evidence it provides renders the controversy over women in combat almost quaint—their presence on and near the battlefield is ancient, inescapable and irreversible." Publ Wkly

    Includes bibliographical references

Dower, John W.

Cultures of war; Pearl Harbor, Hiroshima, 9-11, Iraq. New Press 2010 596p il $29.95 **355**

    1. Iraq War, 2003- 2. Military policy -- United States 3. September 11 terrorist attacks, 2001 4. War and civilization 5. War and society -- United States 6. World War, 1939-1945

    ISBN 978-0-393-06150-5; 0-393-06150-7

    LC 2010-20395

The author "draws astute ironies between Pearl Harbor and 9/11 in terms of the overweening arrogance of military superpowers. The author moves back and forth between these two definitive eras in history, providing a brilliant examination of the willful self-delusion and selective reasoning involved in the highest levels of decision making—from Japan's spectacularly ill-advised bombing of Pearl Harbor to the Bush Administration's bundling of 'weapons of mass destruction' and Osama bin Laden as justification for invasion of Iraq. . . . An unrelenting, incisive, masterly comparative study." Kirkus

    Includes bibliographical references and index.

Fredriksen, John C.

American military leaders; from colonial times to the present. ABC-CLIO 1999 2v il set $175 **355**

    1. Indians of North America -- Biography 2. Indians of North America -- Biography -- Juvenile literature 3. Soldiers -- United States

    ISBN 1-57607-001-8

    LC 99-27929

"Prominent men and women of the military are the scope of this reference work. Coverage includes the most famous of leaders such as Grant, Patton, and Schwarzkopf; but what makes the source so outstanding is its inclusion of forgotten leaders such as Native American Stand Watie, aviator Jackie Cochran, and army educator Alden Partridge. Biographies range from two to three pages, concluding with a bibliography. Photographs and illustrations are included, and both a subject index and a list of leaders organized by their military titles can be found at the end of volume two." Am Libr

    Includes bibliographical references

Gaddis, John Lewis

Surprise, security, and the American experience. Harvard University Press 2004 150p $18.95 **355**

    1. National security -- United States 2. Preemptive

attack (Military science) 3. Strategy
ISBN 0-674-01174-0

LC 2003-56935

"This compact, provocative history of an idea-in-action has the potential to alter the U.S.'s collective self-image." Publ Wkly

Includes bibliographical references

Gordin, Michael D.

Red cloud at dawn; Truman, Stalin, and the end of the atomic monopoly. Farrar, Straus and Giroux 2009 402p il map $27 **355**

1. Arms race 2. Arms race -- History -- 20th century 3. Communist leaders 4. Heads of state 5. Nuclear weapons 6. Nuclear weapons -- History 7. Political leaders 8. Presidents 9. Senators 10. Vice-presidents 11. World politics -- 1945-1955

ISBN 978-0-374-25682-1; 0-374-25682-9

LC 2009-01424

The author "brings considerable scholarship to the subject of how the Soviets succeeded in building an atomic bomb. He weaves an impressively wide range of sources, including new material from ex-Soviet and western archives, into a brilliant narrative about the intelligence war." Hist Today

Includes bibliographical references

Hanson, Victor Davis

The **father** of us all; war and history, ancient and modern. Bloomsbury 2010 259p $25 **355**

1. Military history 2. War

ISBN 978-1-60819-165-9; 1-60819-165-6

LC 2009-41714

"This anthology brings together 13 of Hanson's essays and reviews, revised and re-edited. They have appeared over the past decade in periodicals from the American Spectator to the New York Times. Hanson's introductory generalization that war is a human enterprise that seems inseparable from the human condition structures such subjects as an eloquent answer to the question 'Why Study War?', a defense of the historicity of the film 300, about the Persian Wars, in a masterpiece of envelope pushing, and a comprehensive and dazzling analysis of why America fights as she does. . . . The pieces are well written, sometimes elegantly so, and closely reasoned." Publ Wkly

Includes bibliographical references

The **soul** of battle; from ancient times to the present day, how three great liberators vanquished tyranny. Anchor Books 2001 480p pa $16.95 **355**

1. Army officers 2. Generals 3. Memoirists 4. Military history 5. Secretaries of war

ISBN 0-385-72059-9; 978-0-385-72059-5

LC 00-63979

"Hanson narrates the success of three military campaigns--Epaminondas defeat of the Spartans in the fourth century B.C., Sherman's march through Georgia and the Carolinas during the Civil War, and Patton's race into Germany at the head of the Third Army in 1944-45. . . . In Hanson's view, the individual traits of spontaneity and creativity

that are nourished in a free society are assets, not hindrances, in warfare." Booklist

Includes bibliographical references

Hastings, Max

Warriors; portraits from the battlefield. Knopf 2006 xxiii, 354p il maps $27.50 **355**

1. Biography, Collective 2. Military history 3. Soldiers 4. Soldiers -- Biography 5. War

ISBN 1-4000-4441-3; 978-1-4000-4441-2

LC 2005-44302

The author "selects memoirs and biographies about 15 combatants (one of them a woman) and distills accounts of their lives and trenchant observations about their personalities. . . . Filled with poignant psychological insight, Hastings' remarkable sketches will provoke greater-than-average demand from the military affairs readership." Booklist

Includes bibliographical references

Hirshson, Stanley P.

General Patton: a soldier's life. HarperCollins Pubs. 2002 xxii, 826p il maps $34.95; pa $18.95 **355**

1. Army officers 2. Generals

ISBN 0-06-000982-9; 0-06-000983-7 pa

LC 2002-68881

The author attempts "to round out the unknown familial aspects of Patton's life and {provide a} . . . context for understanding the enigmatic commander. . . . Those interested in Patton will find Hirshson's book valuable reading." Libr J

Includes bibliographical references

Karpin, Michael I.

The **bomb** in the basement; how Israel went nuclear and what that means for the world. [by] Michael Karpin. Simon & Schuster 2006 404p il map $26; pa $15 **355**

1. Nuclear weapons

ISBN 0-7432-6594-7; 978-0-7432-6594-2; 0-7432-6595-5 pa; 978-0-7432-6595-9 pa

LC 2005-51689

"For all those interested in understanding how Israel's idealistic origins dovetail with its hawkish position in the game of nuclear deterrence and fraught relationship with other countries in the Middle East, this well-researched study is a must-read." Publ Wkly

Includes bibliographical references

Kennett, Lee B.

Sherman; a soldier's life. [by] Lee Kennett. HarperCollins Pubs. 2001 426p il maps hardcover o.p. pa $14.95 **355**

1. Generals 2. Generals -- United States -- Biography 3. Memoirists 4. Secretaries of war

ISBN 0-06-093074-8 pa

LC 2001-16687

This is a "well-balanced analytical biography." Publ Wkly

Includes bibliographical references

Kindsvatter, Peter S.

American soldiers; ground combat in the World Wars, Korea, and Vietnam. foreword by Russell F. Weigley. University Press of Kan. 2003 432p il $34.95 **355**

1. Combat 2. Soldiers 3. Soldiers -- United States
ISBN 0-7006-1229-7

LC 2002-12957

"Mining twentieth-century foot soldiers' memoirs and novels, Kindsvatter integrates this literature of personal experience into a generalized assessment of what combat was like and how men reacted to it. . . . Kindsvatter's illuminating work is about coping with . . . fear at the foxhole level, and it . . . powerfully conveys the psychology and military sociology of combat in the draft-era armies." Booklist
Includes bibliographical references

Langewiesche, William

The **atomic** bazaar; the rise of the nuclear poor. Farrar, Straus and Giroux 2007 179p map $22 **355**

1. Arms control 2. Nuclear nonproliferation 3. Nuclear weapons 4. World politics -- 21st century
ISBN 978-0-374-10678-2; 0-374-10678-9

LC 2006-102539

"Langewiesche's bracing expose of nuclear criminality blasts away the ubiquitous misinformation usually attendant on this alarming subject." Booklist

Lipsky, David

Absolutely American; four years at West Point. Houghton Mifflin 2003 317p il $25 **355**

ISBN 0-618-09542-X

LC 2002-191339

"The book must have been extremely hard to organize. And yet it reads with a novelistic flow. . . . It turns out that how teenagers get turned into leaders is not a simple story, but it is wonderfully told in this book." N Y Times Book Rev

Phillips, Charles

★ **Encyclopedia** of wars; [by] Charles Phillips and Alan Axelrod. Facts on File 2005 3v map set $300 **355**

1. Military history 2. Military history -- Encyclopedias 3. Reference books
ISBN 0-8160-2851-6

LC 2003-28010

Phillips and Axelrod "have produced a very readable and . . . well-researched book that both scholars and history buffs will enjoy." Booklist
Includes bibliographical references

Rhodes, Richard

Arsenals of folly; the making of the nuclear arms race. Alfred A. Knopf 2007 386p il $28.95 **355**

1. Arms race 2. Cold War 3. Nuclear weapons
ISBN 978-0-375-41413-8; 0-375-41413-4

LC 2007-17613

"This historical record, drawing upon many firsthand accounts and interviews, details pivotal events in world his-

tory and should be necessary reading for anyone interested in 20th-century history." Libr J
Includes bibliographical references

Rose, Gideon

How wars end; why we always fight the last battle: a history of American intervention from World War I to Afghanistan. Simon & Schuster 2010 413p $27 **355**

1. Disengagement (Military science) 2. Military planning -- United States 3. Military policy -- United States 4. War 5. War -- Termination
ISBN 978-1-4165-9053-8; 1-4165-9053-6

LC 2010-34817

"Surveying the settlements of America's wars since WWI, Rose analyzes reasons for the manner and substance of their conclusions. . . . Public spirited and accessible, Rose's presentation should impress anyone hoping for better management of war and peace by Washington." Booklist
Includes bibliographical references

Rosenbaum, Ron

How the end begins; the road to a nuclear World War III. Simon & Schuster 2011 304p $28; ebook $14.99 **355**

1. Nuclear warfare 2. Nuclear weapons 3. World War III
ISBN 978-1-4165-9421-5; 978-1-4391-9007-4 ebook

LC 2010-22474

This book "raises fundamental questions more acutely than dozens of other recent books on the nuclear problem. There is much to learn from it." N Y Times Book Rev
Includes bibliographical references

Ruggero, Ed

Duty first; West Point and the making of American leaders. HarperCollins Pubs. 2001 342p il $27.50; pa $14.95 **355**

1. Leadership 2. Military education -- United States
ISBN 0-06-019317-4; 0-06-093133-7 pa

LC 00-59775

In this report about the contemporary West Point experience, the author "tries to explain precisely what makes the United States Military Academy, better known as West Point, a breeding ground for future leaders." Publ Wkly

Singer, P. W.

Wired for war; the robotics revolution and conflict in the twenty-first century. Penguin Press 2009 499p il $29.95 **355**

1. Military art and science 2. Military weapons 3. Robotics -- Military applications 4. Robots
ISBN 978-1-59420-198-1; 1-59420-198-6

This is "a vivid picture of the current controversies and dazzling possibilities of war in the digital age." Kirkus
Includes bibliographical references

Sunzi bing fa

★ The **illustrated** art of war; [by] Sun Tzu; the definitive English translation by Samuel B.

Griffith. Oxford University Press 2005 272p il map
$29.95　　**355**
1. Military art and science
ISBN 0-19-518999-X; 978-0-19-518999-5
LC 2005-10651
An illustrated version of The art of war, a military treatise written in China during the 6th century BC discussing
different military tactics and strategies.

Sutherland, Jonathan
★ **African** Americans at war; an encyclopedia.
[by] Jonathan D. Sutherland. ABC-CLIO 2004 2v
set $185　　**355**
1. African American soldiers 2. African Americans --
Biography -- Encyclopedias 3. Reference books
ISBN 1-57607-746-2
LC 2003-21501
"There are more than 250 [alphabetically arranged]
entries conveying biographical, thematic, and conceptual
information. Well-known leaders (Colin Powell), groups
(Buffalo Soldiers), specific units [and battles] . . . have their
own entries. . . . This is a superb resource for any . . . library
looking to enrich its history, military or African American
studies collections." Booklist

★ Amazons to fighter pilots; a biographical diction-
ary of military women. Reina Pennington, edi-
tor; foreword by Gerhard Weinberg. Greenwood
Press 2003 2v il set $175　　**355**
1. Reference books 2. Women soldiers -- Biography
-- Dictionaries
ISBN 0-313-29197-7
LC 2002-44777
"This peerless work, situated at the nexus of military his-
tory and women's studies, is an essential companion to more
male-biased biographical resources." Choice
Includes bibliographical references

★ Barron's how to prepare for the ASVAB; Armed
Services Vocational Aptitude Battery. compiled
by the Editorial Department of Barron's Educational Series, Inc; edited by Terry L. Duran.
8th ed.; Barron's Educ. Ser. 2006 484p il pa
$18.99　　**355**
ISBN 0-7641-3281-4; 978-0-7641-3281-0
This study guide includes practice examinations and a
review of pertinent subject areas.

The Book of war; edited by John Keegan. Viking
1999 492p hardcover o.p. pa $17　　**355**
1. Military history
ISBN 0-14-029655-7 pa
LC 99-42660
This is an "anthology of eyewitness and participant writ-
ing covering 25 centuries, from Thucydides' history of the
Peloponnesian War to a small-unit engagement between
British and Iraqi infantry in the Persian Gulf war." N Y
Times Book Rev
Includes bibliographical references

★ Dictionary of military terms; a guide to the language of warfare and military institutions. compiled by Trevor N. Dupuy {et al.} 2nd ed; Wilson, H.W. 2003 271p il $85　　**355**
1. Military art and science -- Dictionaries 2. Military
history -- Dictionaries 3. Naval art and science
-- Dictionaries 4. Naval history -- Dictionaries 5.
Reference books
ISBN 0-8242-1025-5
LC 2002-32960
"This is a very readable book for the general reader and
will make a great addition to public, academic, and some
high-school libraries as well as being useful for military
professionals." Booklist

Dictionary of wars; George Childs Kohn, editor.
3rd ed.; Facts on File 2006 692p il $85; pa
$22.95　　**355**
1. Military history -- Dictionaries 2. Reference books
ISBN 0-8160-6577-2; 978-0-8160-6577-6; 0-8160-
6578-0 pa; 978-0-8160-6578-3 pa
LC 2005-58936
"Entries include the dates of events and a brief summary
of their causes, effects, and consequences. The straightforward writing style emphasizes basic facts rather than arguments justifying or opposing each conflict. This, along with
the occasional cross-references and helpful and complete
general and geographic indexes, makes the encyclopedia accessible to most students." SLJ

★ Encyclopedia of American military history; Spencer C. Tucker, general editor; associate editors
David Coffey, John C. Fredriksen, Justin D. Murphy. Facts on File 2003 3v il maps set $225 **355**
1. Reference books
ISBN 0-8160-4355-8
LC 2002-29658
"More than 1,200 entries cover military leaders, wars,
campaigns, battles, events, famous soldiers, military branches, key technological developments, overviews of weapons
systems, and more. It covers the period from the colonial
wars to the present, and gives special attention to the minorities and women who have contributed significantly to
American military success." Publisher's note
Includes bibliographical references

★ Facts about the American wars; edited by John
S. Bowman. Wilson, H.W. 1998 750p il maps
$110　　**355**
ISBN 0-8242-0929-X
LC 97-40298
"An introduction explains the text's layout and approach
to each war. The reader samples every conflict from the
Franco-Spanish War of the mid-1500s to the Persian Gulf
War of 1991. Most wars covered have maps; illustrations; or
photographs; each has a separate bibliography. The details
provided for each war are most impressive." Book Rep
Includes bibliographical references

Magill's guide to military history; editor, John Powell; managing editor, Christina J. Moose; project

editor, Rowena Wildin. Salem Press 2001 5v il set $473 **355**
1. Generals -- Biography -- Dictionaries 2. Military history 3. Military history -- Dictionaries 4. Reference books
ISBN 0-89356-014-6
LC 00-66072
This "is a worldwide, illustrated, alphabetical survey of war, weapons, battles, civilizations, people and their place in military history, ancient times to the 21st century. Its 1,518 entries and over 300 thorough essays with keywords in bold-face are all indexed by category in volume 5." Choice
Includes bibliographical references

★ Voices of war; stories of service from the home front and the front lines. edited by Tom Wiener. National Geographic Society 2004 336p il $30; pa $6.95 **355**
1. Veterans 2. Veterans -- United States -- Biography
ISBN 0-7922-7838-0; 0-7922-4204-1 pa
LC 2004-49986
This book showcases "the oral histories collected by the Veteran's History Project, the Library of Congress's nation-wide effort to collect and preserve the stories not only of war veterans, but also of those who served in support of the frontline troops. . . . The personal accounts cover the major conflicts of the 20th century, from World War I to the Persian Gulf War, and include letters, diaries, and journals. The chapters are nicely arranged to show the commonalities of military experience, e.g., basic training, daily life, combat, the home front, and returning home." Libr J

★ War: from ancient Egypt to Iraq; editorial consultant, Saul David. DK 2009 512p il $50 **355**
1. Military history -- Encyclopedias 2. Reference books 3. War -- Encyclopedias
ISBN 978-0-7566-5572-3
LC 2010-278612
"From the Punic wars to the Crusades to the wars of the league of Cognac and modern conflicts like those in the former Yugoslavia, War is an outstanding catalog of conflict. Each of the seven chapters . . . opens with a time line and is peppered with sidebars of military superlatives such as youngest commanders, famous female warriors, and even landmark war movies. . . . An essential reference title for all libraries." Libr J

The encyclopedia of Middle East wars; the United States in the Persian Gulf, Afghanistan, and Iraq conflicts. Spencer C. Tucker, editor; Priscilla Mary Roberts, editor, documents volume; foreword by Anthony C. Zinni. ABC-CLIO 2010 1887p 5v il map set $495 **355**
1. Afghan War, 2001- -- Encyclopedias 2. Iraq War, 2003- -- Encyclopedias 3. Middle East -- Military history -- Encyclopedias 4. Persian Gulf War, 1991 -- Encyclopedias 5. Reference books
ISBN 978-1-85109-947-4; 978-1-85109-948-1 ebook
LC 2010-33812
"An essential resource for anyone seeking detailed information and in-depth reading on U.S. actions and involve-

ment in the Middle East region during the last 15 years." Libr J
Includes bibliographical references

355.009 History, geographic treatment, biography

Brands, H. W.
★ The **man** who saved the union; Ulysses Grant in war and peace. H. W. Brands. Doubleday 2012 736 p. $35.00 **355.009**
1. Biographies 2. Generals -- United States -- Biography 3. Presidents -- United States -- Biography 4. United States -- Politics & government -- 1865-1877
ISBN 0385532415; 9780385532419
LC 2011043795
This book offers a biography of U.S. President Ulysses S. Grant. Here, "Pulitzer [prize] finalist [H. W.] Brands . . . treats Grants entire life, showing its full arc. He breaks with earlier interpretations . . . , concluding that Grant did the best he could in trying circumstances, particularly in the area of civil and minority rights." (Library Journal)

Keegan, John
★ **Fields** of battle; the wars for North America. Knopf 1996 348p il maps hardcover o.p. pa $15 **355.009**
1. Battles
ISBN 0-679-42413-X; 0-679-74664-1 pa
LC 96-154385
The author "demonstrates how North America's geography has influenced its history: how its mountain chains and river systems have determined where people fought, and fought repeatedly. For example, the defenses that Cornwallis built at Yorktown to deter American forces were improved and reused by the Confederates almost a century later. Keegan's tour of the continent skips the Mexican War, and his book is atypically discursive. For Americans, the charm is the familiarity of its sites—Brooklyn, Pittsburgh, Laramie, and other home towns." New Yorker

★ New York at war; Steven H. Jaffe. Basic Books 2012 p. cm. **355.009**
1. War
ISBN 9780465029709; 9780465036424
LC 2012000454
In this book historian Steven H. Jaffe offers a . . . history of New York City from a local, military perspective. Beginning with an Indian attack on one of Henry HudsonBs crewmen (who in 1609 became the first recorded fatality of an act of war in the regionss history), Jaffe describes, in turn, each of the city's encounters with war over the past four centuries. . . . [including] how New York became hugely powerful . . . during the Civil War . . . during the build-up to World War I . . . during World War II, and in the atomic era.s The book's scope discusses the impact of military and ethnic conflicts in the city "stretching from the colonial era to 9/11 and beyond." (Publisher's note)

The Oxford companion to American military history; editor in chief, John Whiteclay Chambers II; edi-

tors, Fred Anderson [et al.] Oxford Univ. Press 1999 xxxiv, 916p il maps $75 **355.009**
1. Reference books 2. United States -- Military history -- Dictionaries
ISBN 0-19-507198-0

LC 99-21181

This reference work covers "battles and soldiers, ships and weapons, services and doctrines—as well as the social and cultural impact of the U.S. military at home and around the world. . . . There are entries on relevant acts of Congress and on diplomatic policies such as the Monroe Doctrine and the Marshall Plan; on peace and antiwar movements; on war in film, literature, music, and photography; and on war viewed through the disciplinary lenses of anthropology, economics, gender studies, and psychology." Publisher's note
Includes bibliographical references

Reader's guide to military history; edited by Charles Messenger. Fitzroy Dearborn Pubs. 2001 xxxvi, 948p $135 **355.009**
1. Military history 2. Military history -- Sources
ISBN 1-57958-241-9

LC 2002-275907

Topics covered "include land, sea, and air services; conflicts; types of warfare; military theory; prominent military leaders; and national armed services. . . . {This} is a unique, well-designed reference tool." Booklist
Includes bibliographical references

355.02 War and warfare

Hedges, Chris
War is a force that gives us meaning. PublicAffairs 2002 211p $23 **355.02**
1. War 2. War (Philosophy)
ISBN 1-58648-049-9

LC 2002-68136

"This should be required reading in this post-9/11 world." Libr J
Includes bibliographical references

355.3 Organization and personnel of military forces

Geraghty, Tony
Soldiers of fortune; a history of the mercenary in modern warfare. Pegasus Books 2009 392p il $27.95 **355.3**
1. Mercenary soldiers
ISBN 978-1-60598-048-5; 1-60598-048-X
"Covering the 1960s to the present, with revealing interviews, Geraghty looks at the virtues and failings of the world's second-oldest profession. . . . This serious study should find its way to most readers of military history." Libr J
Includes bibliographical references

Paglen, Trevor
Blank spots on the map; the dark geography of the Pentagon's secret world. Dutton/Penguin Group 2009 324p il map **355.3**
1. Intelligence service -- United States 2. Military bases
ISBN 9780525951018

LC 2008042862

The author "explores the clandestine activities of the U.S. military and the CIA, giving readers a thorough and provocative tour of places that officially do not exist. Paglen has a brisk reporting style and is an engaging storyteller. His journey into what he calls the 'black world' of classified locations—from research facilities to secret prisons—this time takes him across the country and around the world." Libr J
Includes bibliographical references

355.4 Military operations

Kilcullen, David
The **accidental** guerrilla; fighting small wars in the midst of a big one. Oxford University Press 2009 xxviii, 346p il map $27.95 **355.4**
1. Counterinsurgency 2. Guerrilla warfare 3. Military history, Modern -- 20th century 4. Military history, Modern -- 21st century 5. War on Terrorism, 2001- 6. War on terrorism
ISBN 978-0-19-536834-5

LC 2008-54870

This "excellent book has an anthropologist's sense of social dynamics and a reporter's eye for telling detail. . . . [The author's] account of how the Americans use soft and hard power to pacify parts of eastern Afghanistan . . . should be compulsory reading in military academies on both sides of the Atlantic." Economist
Includes bibliographical references

355.6 Military administration

Vogel, Steve
The **Pentagon**; a history: the untold story of the wartime race to build the Pentagon--and to restore it sixty years later. Random House 2007 xxv, 626p il map $32.95 **355.6**
1. Public buildings -- United States
ISBN 978-1-4000-6303-1; 1-4000-6303-5

LC 2006-50873

Vogel's "work recounts the construction of one of the world's most iconic buildings—the Pentagon. But more compelling by far, he relates the human stories underlying this huge construction effort. . . . All this would of itself be enough to warrant a book but Vogel plunges on to an appropriate second story: the terrorist assault of 9/11 and the Pentagon's subsequent resurrection. This section of the book, due perhaps to the proximity of the event, is all the more compelling." New York Post
Includes bibliographical references

355.8 Military equipment and supplies (Matériel)

Baggott, J. E.
The **first** war of physics; the secret history of the atom bomb, 1939-1949. [by] Jim Baggott. Pegasus Books 2010 576p il $35 **355.8**
1. Atomic bomb 2. Atomic bomb -- History
ISBN 978-1-60598-084-3; 1-60598-084-6
"Baggott contributes a novel perspective to the story, looking at the Anglo-American, German, and Soviet atomic programs, and as such provides a broad thematic history." Libr J
Includes bibliographical references

Light, Michael
100 suns, 1945-1962. Knopf 2003 208p il $49.95 **355.8**
1. Documentary photography 2. Nuclear weapons -- Pictorial works 3. Nuclear weapons -- Testing
ISBN 1-4000-4113-9
LC 2003-106275
"The 'suns' Light presents to readers in this . . . photography collection are manmade: aboveground atomic detonations captured on film both in the Nevada desert and at sea, terrifyingly beautiful images that remind readers of the apocalyptic might of nuclear weapons." Booklist
Includes bibliographical references

Preston, Diana
Before the fallout; from Marie Curie to Hiroshima. Walker 2005 438p il $27 **355.8**
1. Atomic bomb 2. Atomic bomb -- History 3. Science -- Moral and ethical aspects
ISBN 0-8027-1445-5
LC 2004-61953
"Avidly researched and gracefully constructed, Preston's revelatory history is rich in telling moments, powerful personalities, intense confrontations, and indelible images of the devastation delivered by nuclear weapons, our Damoclean sword." Booklist
Includes bibliographical references

356 Specific kinds of military forces and warfare

Carney, John T.
No room for error; the covert operations of America's special tactics units from Iran to Afghanistan. {by} John T. Carney Jr. and Benjamin F. Schemmer. Ballantine Books 2003 334p il map $25.95 **356**
1. Air force officers 2. Authors 3. Military art and science 4. Special forces (Military science) -- United States 5. Writers on the military
ISBN 0-345-45333-6
LC 2002-28158
The author's "dramatic tales place special operations history in perspective, particularly as the war in Afghanistan has been led by special forces units." Publ Wkly
Includes bibliographical references

Clancy, Tom
Special forces; a guided tour of U.S. Army Special Forces. written with John Gresham. Berkley Bks. 2001 366p il pa $16 **356**
1. Special forces (Military science) -- United States -- History
ISBN 0-425-17268-6
LC 00-65121
"The book covers recruitment and training of personnel . . . equipment, which includes an exotic mixture of high, low, and no tech components; and the variety of missions special forces execute." Booklist
Includes bibliographical references

Haney, Eric L.
★ **Inside** Delta Force; the story of America's elite counterterrorist unit. Delacorte Press 2002 324p il hardcover o.p. pa $14 **356**
1. Terrorism -- Prevention
ISBN 0-385-33603-9; 0-385-33936-4 pa
LC 2001-58408
The author relates his "experiences during the formation and early operations of 1st Special Forces Operational Detachment-Delta. . . . He served three times in Beirut guarding the American ambassador, participated in the invasion of Grenada, served in several Central American countries and narrowly escaped death during the abortive rescue attempt of the American hostages in Iran. . . . Readers of other special forces memoirs will find this one distinctive for Haney's attention to interservice rivalries . . . that he believes compromised several missions, as well as for Haney's nuanced, often disgusted descriptions of the human cost of war." Publ Wkly

357 Mounted forces and warfare

Cotterell, Arthur
Chariot; from chariot to tank, the astounding rise and fall of the world's first war machine. Overlook Press 2005 344p il map $29.95 **357**
1. Military art and science
ISBN 1-58567-667-5
LC 2004-65980
"This work is a welcome addition to a collection specializing in military history or ancient history but will appeal to general readers as well because the writing is accessible despite the plethora of detail." Libr J
Includes bibliographical references

358 Air and other specialized forces and warfare; engineering and related services

Engelberg, Stephen
Germs; America's secret war against biological weapons. Judith Miller, Stephen Engelberg, William Broad. Simon & Schuster 2001 382p $27; pa $14 **358**
1. Biological warfare 2. Biological warfare -- Research -- United States 3. Biological warfare -- Safety measures

-- United States
ISBN 0-684-87158-0; 0-684-87159-9 pa
LC 2001-42690
Three reporters survey the history of biological weapons and recount incidents of their use by terrorist groups. They explain why advances in biology and the spread of germ weapons poses grave risks as countries such as Iran, Iraq and North Korea continually engage in research

Guillemin, Jeanne
★ **Biological** weapons; from the invention of state-sponsored programs to contemporary bioterrorism. Columbia University Press 2005 258p $75; pa $22.95 **358**
1. Biological warfare 2. Biological weapons 3. Bioterrorism
ISBN 0-231-12942-4; 0-231-12943-2 pa
LC 2004-51911
This is a "history of biological weaponry, beginning with the British, American and Japanese programs that predate WWII. . . . Admirably free of finger-pointing, shrillness and Luddite tendencies, the book ranks high as a historical introduction to the subject and a handbook on contemporary remedies." Publ Wkly
Includes bibliographical references

Lockwood, Jeffrey A.
Six-legged soldiers; using insects as weapons of war. Oxford University Press 2009 xx, 377p il $27.95 **358**
1. Biological warfare 2. Insects -- War use 3. Insects as carriers of disease 4. Insects as carriers of plant disease
ISBN 978-0-19-533305-3; 0-19-533305-5
LC 2008-6935
"Both science and military history buffs will learn much from Lockwood." Publ Wkly
Includes bibliographical references (p. 315-322)

Tucker, Jonathan B.
★ **War** of nerves; chemical warfare from World War I to al-Qaeda. Pantheon Books 2006 479p il $30; pa $17.95 **358**
1. Chemical warfare 2. Chemical warfare -- History 3. Chemical weapons
ISBN 0-375-42229-3; 978-0-375-42229-4; 1-4000-3233-4 pa; 978-1-4000-3233-4 pa
LC 2005-50053
This "book makes a sobering case for a less poisonous world." N Y Times Book Rev
Includes bibliographical references

Weapons of mass destruction; an encyclopedia of worldwide policy, technology, and history. Eric A. Croddy and James J. Wirtz, editors. ABC-CLIO 2004 2v il set $185 **358**
1. Biological warfare 2. Chemical warfare 3. Nuclear weapons
ISBN 1-85109-490-3
LC 2004-24651
"No other reference source covers such a wide array of topics related to WMD. It will dispel many myths

but will also draw attention to the lethal consequences of WMD." Booklist
Includes bibliographical references

358.4   Air forces and warfare

Boyne, Walter J.
★ **Beyond** the wild blue; a history of the United States Air Force, 1947-1997. St. Martin's Press 1997 442p il $29.95; pa $19.95 **358.4**
1. Military aeronautics
ISBN 0-312-15474-7; 0-312-18705-X pa
LC 96-53507
In this "history of the evolution of the air force, from its beginning as a separate arm of the military in 1947 through its many roles and changes since then, Boyne asserts that the air force's effort and sacrifice won us the Cold War. . . . While his slant may be seen as controversial, this is a large, thorough, and valuable history." Libr J
Includes bibliographical references

Jacobsen, Annie
Area 51; an uncensored history of America's top secret military base. Little, Brown 2011 523p il map $27.99 **358.4**
ISBN 978-0-316-13294-7; 0-316-13294-2
"Seventy-five miles north of Las Vegas sits a land parcel in the middle of the desert. Called Area 51, the parcel is just outside of the abandoned Nevada Test and Training Range, where more than 100 atmospheric bomb tests were conducted in the 1950s. Officially, the U.S. government has never acknowledged the existence of Area 51. Unofficially, it has become a place associated with conspiracy theories, alien landings and tiny spaceships. Journalist Annie Jacobsen . . . [reveals] that the site has remained classified for many years — not because of aliens or spaceships, but because the government once used the site for top-secret nuclear testing and weapons development. . . Jacobsen details how several agencies — including the Atomic Energy Commission, the Department of Defense and the CIA — once used the site to conduct controversial and secretive research on aircraft and pilot-related projects." NPR
Includes bibliographical references

359   Sea forces and warfare

Bruce, Anthony
An **encyclopedia** of naval history; [by] Anthony Bruce and William Cogar. Fitzroy Dearborn 1998 440p il $100 **359**
1. Naval history -- Encyclopedias 2. Reference books
ISBN 1-579-58109-9
An "encyclopedia of world naval history from the 15th century to the present. Its 1,000 articles cover all manner of detail from sea battles and great commanders to warship evolution, naval technology and tactics, organizations, and naval-oriented details of specific campaigns. Although international in scope, the work clearly emphasizes the US and Britain." Choice

Crowley, Roger

Empires of the sea; the siege of Malta, the battle of Lepanto, and the contest for the center of the world. Random House 2008 336p il map $30; pa $16 **359**

1. Christianity and other religions 2. Christianity and other religions -- Islam 3. Islam -- Relations -- Christianity 4. Lepanto, Battle of, 1571 5. Naval battles

ISBN 978-1-4000-6624-7; 1-4000-6624-7; 978-0-8129-7764-6 pa; 0-8129-7764-5 pa

LC 2007-33794

This book "is well-crafted narrative history in the best sense of the word, lucid, colorful, and beautifully written. . . . Crowley draws on a wealth of sources reflecting a multiplicity of viewpoints and the results are convincing." Journal of Military History

Includes bibliographical references

Grant, R. G.

Battle at sea; 3,000 years of naval warfare. written by R.G. Grant. DK Pub. 2008 360p il map $40 **359**

1. Naval art and science 2. Naval history

ISBN 978-0-7566-3973-0

LC 2008-10019

"This oversized book . . . is perhaps the most comprehensive one-volume history of war at sea, covering engagements large and small, from 1200 B.C.E. to the present day. . . . Highly recommended." Libr J

Toll, Ian W.

★ **Six** frigates; the epic history of the founding of the U.S. Navy. Norton 2006 560p il map $27.95 **359**

ISBN 978-0-393-05847-5; 0-393-05847-6

LC 2006-20769

This is "a must-read for fans of naval history and the early American Republic." Publ Wkly

Includes bibliographical references

★ **Naval** warfare; an international encyclopedia. edited by Spencer C. Tucker; associate editors, John Fredriksen {et al.}; introduction by James C. Bradford. ABC-CLIO 2002 3v il maps set $295 **359**

1. Naval art and science -- Encyclopedias 2. Naval biography -- Encyclopedias 3. Naval history -- Encyclopedias 4. Reference books

ISBN 1-57607-219-3

LC 2002-4401

This set "explores the history of combat at sea, from ancient Greek galleys to the sophisticated ships of the U.S. Sixth Fleet. More than 1500 signed entries . . . describe the three key eras: Age of Galley Warfare, Age of Sail, and Age of Steam or Modern Era. . . . Each new development is examined in painstaking detail." Libr J

Includes bibliographical references

359.9   Specialized combat forces; engineering and related services

Couch, Dick

The **warrior** elite; the forging of Seal Class 228. photographs by Cliff Hollenbeck. Crown 2001 319p il hardcover o.p. pa $14.95 **359.9**

1. United States -- Navy -- Commando troops -- Training of

ISBN 1-4000-4695-5 pa

LC 2001-28368

This is an account of the Basic Underwater Demolition course, (BUD) training for the U.S. Navy Sea Air Land Team (SEALs)

This book "is unique. Couch, a Vietnam-era SEAL and retired naval reserve captain was given the most complete access possible. . . . On view is much serious thought by serious thinkers on the making of warriors at the dawn of the twenty-first century." Booklist

Parrish, Thomas

★ The **submarine**; a history. Viking 2004 576p il $29.95; pa $16 **359.9**

1. Submarines 2. Submarines (Ships) -- History

ISBN 0-670-03313-8; 0-14-303519-3 pa

LC 2003-70515

"This brilliant, dramatic account of submarines and the men who sailed in them is a required acquisition for every military history collection." Choice

Includes bibliographical references

361   Social problems and services

Heintzelman, Greta

Critical companion to Tennessee Williams; [by] Greta Heintzelman, Alycia Smith Howard. Facts on File 2005 436p il $65; pa $19.95 **361**

1. Authors 2. Dramatists 3. Novelists 4. Short story writers

ISBN 0-8160-4888-6; 0-8160-6429-6 pa

LC 2004-7362

The authors "offer an excellent resource for those studying Williams's life and extensive body of work." Choice

Includes bibliographical references

★ **Social** issues in America; an encyclopedia. James Ciment, editor. M.E. Sharpe 2006 8v il set $499 **361**

1. Reference books

ISBN 0-7656-8061-0; 978-0-7656-8061-7

LC 2005-18778

"Anyone who wants to know more about the problems the world faces and, in particular, any student who has an assignment to learn about a particular social issue will find this set useful." Booklist

Includes bibliographical references

361.2   Social action

Rieff, David

A **bed** for the night; humanitarianism in crisis. Simon & Schuster 2002 367p $26; pa $15   **361.2**
1. Humanitarianism 2. International agencies 3. International relief 4. War relief
ISBN 0-684-80977-X; 0-7432-5211-X pa
     LC 2002-29432
Readers "will come away from this passionate, eloquent argument with a distinctly clearer understanding of the complex moral issues facing humanitarian aid in a world filled with brutality and suffering." Publ Wkly
Includes bibliographical references

361.6   Governmental action

Hancock, LynNell

Hands to work; the stories of three families racing the welfare clock. Morrow 2002 308p $25.95; pa $13.95   **361.6**
1. Poor -- New York (N.Y.) 2. Poor women -- New York (State) -- New York -- Case studies 3. Public welfare 4. Public welfare -- New York (State) -- New York -- Case studies 5. Welfare recipients -- Employment -- New York (State) -- New York -- Case studies 6. Welfare recipients -- New York (State) -- New York -- Case studies
ISBN 0-688-17388-8; 0-06-051216-X pa
     LC 2001-31730
This "study depicts welfare in America today through the stories of three women from the South Bronx—Alina, Brenda, and Christine—who were affected by the 1996 Personal Responsibility Act . . . which limits lifetime federal financial assistance to five years for families and two years for singles. . . . Attention-holding and articulate, this important book on how America treats residents who are 'down and out' is highly recommended." Libr J
Includes bibliographical references

Katz, Michael B.

The **price** of citizenship; redefining America's welfare state. Metropolitan Bks. 2001 469p hardcover o.p. pa $17   **361.6**
1. Public welfare 2. Social policy -- United States
ISBN 0-8050-6929-1 pa
     LC 00-46906
Katz "has written a defining history of post-Nixon transformations of America's welfare state, including its nonprofit and private sectors (private pensions, health insurance, etc.)." Publ Wkly

361.7   Private action

World volunteers; the world guide to humanitarian and development volunteering. [editors, Fabio Ausenda, Erin McCloskey] 4th ed., fully rev. and updated; Green Volunteers; distributed by Universe Pub 2008 255p pa $16.95   **361.7**
1. Reference books 2. Volunteer work -- Directories
ISBN 978-88-89060-13-1; 8-88-906013-1
"For people of all ages, this book lists many humanitarian aid projects ranging in length from a week to months. It gives all the information needed to contact specific organizations as well as necessary qualifications, allowable age ranges, and more. Free updates via the Internet come with the purchase." Libr J

361.9   History, geographic treatment, biography

Elshtain, Jean Bethke

Jane Addams and the dream of American democracy; a life. Basic Bks. 2001 xxii, 329p il hardcover o.p. pa $20   **361.9**
1. Authors 2. Essayists 3. Nobel laureates for peace 4. Pacifists 5. Philanthropists 6. Social welfare leaders 7. Women social reformers -- United States -- Biography 8. Women social workers -- United States -- Biography
ISBN 0-465-01913-7 pa
     LC 2001-43493
In this biography of the founder of the settlement-house movement, "Elshtain gives a moving account of a stunningly creative woman occupied cognitively, emotionally and spiritually with the ways an elite in a cosmopolitan society riven by inequality might offer succor to others." N Y Times Book Rev
Includes bibliographical references

362   Specific social problems and services

Booth, Martin

Opium; a history. St. Martin's Press 1998 381p hardcover o.p. pa $14.95   **362**
1. Opium
ISBN 0-312-20667-4 pa
     LC 98-14951
"An excellent historical treatment of the development, use, and misuse of the drug, as well as of society's efforts to control it." Libr J
Includes bibliographical references

Critser, Greg

Fat land; how Americans became the fattest people in the world. Houghton Mifflin 2003 232p il $24; pa $13   **362**
1. Obesity
ISBN 0-618-16472-3; 0-618-38060-4 pa
     LC 2002-32282
The author "succeeds in letting laypersons grasp agricultural policy, astute marketing ploys, lipid chemistry, human physioloy, and the follies of institutional feeding schemes and weight-loss quackery." Choice

Manguso, Sarah

The **two** kinds of decay. Farrar, Straus and Giroux 2008 184p $22; pa $14   **362**

1. Authors 2. Editors 3. Guillain-Barré syndrome 4. Poets 5. Polyradiculoneuritis

ISBN 978-0-374-28012-3; 0-374-28012-6; 978-0-312-42844-0 pa; 0-312-42844-8 pa

LC 2008-1766

"What makes this lightning-quick book extraordinary is not just Manguso's deadpan delivery of often unthinkable details, nor her poet's struggle with the damaging metaphors of disease, but the compassion she acquires as she comes to understand her pain in relation to the pain of others." Publ Wkly

★ America's top doctors. Castle Connolly Medical $79.95; pa $29.95   **362**

1. Physicians -- Directories 2. Reference books

ISBN 1-883769-38-8; 1-883769-36-1 pa

LC 2003-100260

This guide identifies and provides information about more than 4,000 top specialists for care and treatment of more than 2,000 diseases and medical conditions, provides information about accessing and using clinical trials, and explains services provided at the National Institutes of Health and how to get the most from your specialist's appointment

362.1   People with illnesses and disabilities

Blumenthal, David

The **heart** of power; health and politics in the Oval Office. [by] David Blumenthal and James A. Morone. University of California Press 2009 484p il $26.95   **362.1**

1. Medical care -- Government policy 2. Medical policy -- United States -- History 3. Presidents -- United States -- Health

ISBN 978-0-520-26030-6; 0-520-26030-9

LC 2008-54361

"More than an excellent primer on American health policy, the book offers a thorough, incisive look at the presidency as an institution and the men who have occupied the office." Publ Wkly

Includes bibliographical references

Chase, Marilyn

★ The **Barbary** plague; the Black Death in Victorian San Francisco. Random House 2003 276p map $25.95; pa $13.95   **362.1**

1. Plague 2. Plague -- California -- San Francisco -- History -- 20th century

ISBN 0-375-50496-6; 0-375-75708-2 pa

LC 2002-68102

This is "a pleasure to read, full of people, dramatic situations, individual foibles and collective hard work. I closed the book wishing it had been longer." N Y Times Book Rev

Coste, Joanne Koenig

Learning to speak Alzheimer's; a groundbreaking approach for everyone dealing with the disease.

Houghton Mifflin 2003 240p il hardcover o.p. pa $14   **362.1**

1. Alzheimer's disease 2. Alzheimer's disease -- Patients -- Care -- Popular works 3. Alzheimer's disease -- Patients -- Rehabilitation -- Popular works 4. Caregivers 5. Caregivers -- Popular works

ISBN 0-618-22125-5; 0-618-48517-1 pa

LC 2003-51141

"Key elements of Coste's approach include simplifying the environment for the patient, capitalizing on his or her remaining skills, and making an effort to understand what life must be like for the memory impaired. Because such Alzheimer's behaviors as agitation and physical aggression are often rooted in frustration, she also offers caregivers techniques to help patients compensate for cognitive and sensory losses. . . . Directions for simple activities, recipes for nutritious 'finger foods,' and tips for hiring home caregivers are included. . . . A fine addition to Alzheimer's and caregiving collections." Libr J

Includes bibliographical references

Crosby, Molly Caldwell

Asleep; the forgotten epidemic that remains one of medicine's greatest mysteries. Berkley Books 2010 291p il $24.95   **362.1**

1. Encephalitis 2. Epidemic encephalitis -- History 3. Epidemics

ISBN 978-0-425-22570-7; 0-425-22570-4

LC 2009-34928

"Crosby is a fine storyteller, peppering her case studies with facts about the history of neurology and details about 1910s New York. She also provides fully realized portraits of not only her case studies' patients, but also the brilliant doctors who treated them. . . . A capable, readable account of a medical mystery." Kirkus

Includes bibliographical references

Douglas, Kirk

My stroke of luck. Morrow 2002 196p il hardcover o.p. pa $12.95   **362.1**

1. Actors

ISBN 0-06-001404-0 pa

LC 2002-727755

"Entertaining and uplifting, Douglas's story is a lesson in survival, one that will entice readers whether or not they have had similar illnesses. . . . This book is a natural for the 65-plus crowd." Publ Wkly

Epstein, Helen

The **invisible** cure; Africa, the West, and the fight against AIDS. Farrar, Straus and Giroux 2007 326p il $26   **362.1**

1. AIDS (Disease) 2. AIDS (Disease) -- Africa 3. AIDS (Disease) -- Social aspects -- Africa

ISBN 978-0-374-28152-6; 0-374-28152-1

LC 2006-35679

In this book, the author "avoids both the patronizing and the 'culturally sensitive' demeanors that infect much of the debate on AIDS in Africa. Ms. Epstein, whose essays in the New York Review of Books over the past decade have provided some of the most illuminating reporting on AIDS in Africa, here offers one of the most personal, thorough, and conclusive studies of this human plague that has utterly devastated a continent. 'The Invisible Cure' is largely a comparison between AIDS in Uganda, which has instituted a variety of successful policies thwarting the disease, and South Africa, which has one of the highest HIV incidence rates in the world." N Y Sun

Fisher, Mary

Sleep with the angels; a mother challenges AIDS. Moyer Bell 1994 220p il $24.95; pa $12.95 **362.1**
1. AIDS (Disease) 2. AIDS (Disease) -- Social aspects
ISBN 1-55921-105-9; 1-55921-103-2 pa

LC 93-27216

"Fisher learned she was HIV+ in July 1991 and began telling her story in public in 1992. . . . Presented in chronological order from May 4, 1992 through June 28, 1993, the transcripts of these 24 speeches . . . include her famous address to the 1992 Republican National Convention in Houston. . . . Utilizing her position as a privileged heterosexual non-drug using white woman, she forces her audiences to confront the reality of the epidemic." Libr J

Garrett, Laurie

Betrayal of trust; the collapse of global public health. Hyperion 2000 754p il $30; pa $16.95 **362.1**
1. Epidemiology -- Popular works 2. Medical care 3. Medical policy 4. Public health 5. World health
ISBN 0-7868-6522-9; 0-7868-8440-1 pa

LC 00-33425

This book examines contemporary "health systems in the former Soviet Union, India, central Africa, and the United States." N Y Times Book Rev

Greenspan, Stanley I.

The **child** with special needs; encouraging intellectual and emotional growth. [by] Stanley I. Greenspan, Serena Wieder, with Robin Simons. Addison-Wesley 1998 496p $32 **362.1**
1. Child psychology 2. Child psychology -- United States 3. Developmental psychology -- United States 4. Developmentally disabled children -- Mental health -- United States 5. Developmentally disabled children -- United States -- Life skills guides 6. Developmentally disabled children -- United States -- Psychology 7. Handicapped children 8. Parents of children with disabilities -- United States
ISBN 0-201-40726-4

LC 97-32101

This offers advice to parents on helping children with such disabilities as cerebral palsy, autism, retardation, ADD, and language problems.

This "is an important work for libraries." Libr J
Includes bibliographical references

Gruber, Jonathan

Health care reform; what it is, why it's necessary, how it works. Jonathan Gruber, with HP Newquist ; illustrated by Nathan Schreiber. Hill and Wang 2011 151 p. **362.1**
1. Health care reform -- United States 2. Medical care -- United States 3. Medical policy -- United States
ISBN 0809053977; 0809094622; 9780809053971;

9780809094622

LC 2011020495

This book is [a] cartoon-driven examination of what's wrong with the American way of health care--and why the legislative reform of 2010 was necessary. (Kirkus) It delivers information . . . through an earnest but informal lecture by a cartoon version of an expert--in this case [Jonathan] Gruber, an MIT economics professor who helped craft Massachusetts's successful health care reform plan as well as the Affordable Care Act, which has been the subject of so much confusion and deliberate misinformation. He begins the presentation by confronting a small group of people with the enormous medical bills they could receive after medical treatment, then moves from the individual to the national level to show that our present system is unfair and unsustainable. (Publishers Wkly)

Havemann, Joel

A **life** shaken; my encounter with Parkinson's disease. foreword by Stephen G. Reich. Johns Hopkins Univ. Press 2002 181p il $26; pa $14.95 **362.1**
1. Parkinson's disease -- Patients -- United States -- Biography 2. Parkinson's disease -- Personal narratives
ISBN 0-8018-6928-5; 0-8018-7888-8 pa

LC 2001-4650

The author "chronicles the physical and emotional effects . . . {Parkinson's} disease has had on his life since his diagnosis in 1990. While he briefly discusses PD's history, possible causes, medical and surgical treatments, and research progress, it is the account of his personal struggle that is the heart of this book." Libr J
Includes bibliographical references and index

Hurley, Dan

Diabetes rising; how a rare disease became a modern pandemic, and what to do about it. foreword by Zachary T. Bloomgarden. Kaplan Pub. 2010 xxiii, 312p $26.95 **362.1**
1. Diabetes
ISBN 978-1-60714-458-8

LC 2009-29382

The author, "diagnosed at age 18 with type 1 diabetes, recounts the 3500-year history of the disease, its possible causes, and the latest promising treatments and cures with a professional writer's skills and a patient's passion. . . . [This is] a compelling layperson's overview of diabetes research, enlivened by multiple interviews with scientists in the field. Diabetics and those who love them will find this a fascinating and hope-filled read." Libr J
Includes bibliographical references

Kaufman, Francine R.

★ **Diabesity**; the obesity-diabetes epidemic that threatens America--and what we must do to stop it. [by] Francine Ratner Kaufman. Bantam Books 2005 326p $27; pa $15 **362.1**
1. Diabetes 2. Obesity
ISBN 0-553-80384-0; 0-553-38379-5 pa

LC 2004-54189

The author "explains how obesity triggers diabetes, the devastating long-term effects on the human body, and what means of prevention and treatment are available. She also relates the history of diabetes as it has evolved with changes in culture and lifestyle and explains what can be done through education and healthcare systems to improve individuals' health. Kaufman's sympathetic, nonjudgmental accounts of her patients highlight the many factors contributing to the problem, and her compassion and dedication shine through." Libr J

Kaufman, Sharon R.

★ --And a time to die; how American hospitals shape the end of life. Scribner 2005 400p $28 **362.1**
1. Death 2. Death -- Social aspects -- United States 3. Hospital care -- Psychological aspects 4. Terminal care 5. Terminal care -- Ethical aspects
ISBN 0-7432-6476-2

LC 2004-52530
The author "reveals the dilemmas of hospital death in America today: the shift to patients' control of decision making despite the doctors' greater knowledge; the ethics and practical effects of resuscitation versus pain relief; the complexities of assessing 'quality of life' while guessing at the desires of an unconscious patient. . . . This deeply probing study lays bare the cultural and institutional assumptions and rhetoric that frame our search for 'a good death.'" Publ Wkly
Includes bibliographical references

Kessler, Lauren

Dancing with Rose; finding life in the land of Alzheimer's. Viking 2007 260p $24.95 **362.1**
1. Alzheimer's disease 2. Caregivers
ISBN 0-670-03859-8; 978-0-670-03859-6

LC 2006-35699
"Invaluable intelligence, especially for anyone considering a residential facility for a loved one." Booklist

Monette, Paul

Borrowed time; an AIDS memoir. Harcourt Brace Jovanovich 1988 342p $22; pa $13 **362.1**
1. AIDS (Disease) 2. AIDS (Disease) -- Personal narratives 3. Authors 4. Memoirists 5. Novelists 6. Poets
ISBN 0-15-113598-3; 0-15-600581-6 pa

LC 88-7215
"The memoir transcends the particulars of the AIDS epidemic to stand as an eloquent testimonial to the power of love and the devastation of loss." Publ Wkly

Orbach, Susie

Bodies. Picador 2009 216p pa $14 **362.1**
1. Body dysmorphic disorder 2. Body image 3. Body, Human, in popular culture
ISBN 978-0-312-42720-7; 0-312-42720-4

LC 2008-50352
The author "delves into the touchy subject of commercial exploitation of 'the body' and explores how modern culture is eroding individual appreciation of the unaltered human form. She uses specific case studies from her own practice to show the long-term effects that can result from body dissatisfaction. . . . Orbach's timely analysis is a key addition to the growing discussion of what is becoming a national trend, the favoring of delusion over reality, a troubling

tendency that is threatening to steadily encompass all facets of American life." Booklist
Includes bibliographical references

Price, Reynolds

A whole new life. Atheneum Pubs. 1994 213p $23; pa $13 **362.1**
1. Authors 2. Cancer -- Personal narratives 3. College teachers 4. Essayists 5. Novelists 6. Short story writers
ISBN 0-684-87255-2; 0-7432-3854-0 pa

LC 93-35967
Price gives an "account of his 'mid-life collision with cancer and paralysis.' In 1984, he was found to have a malignant tumor of the spinal cord, and three surgeries and radiation therapy arrested the growth but left him unable to walk. Although he has not written an essay on illness per se, he embraces elements of an essay as he pauses to ponder nature's systemic breakdowns, the importance of friendships in times of stress, or how to handle pain psychologically. His book is primarily a chronological narrative of events in the treatment of his disease and his rehabilitation." Booklist

Reid, T. R.

The healing of America; a global quest for better, cheaper, and fairer health care. Penguin Press 2009 277p il $25.95 **362.1**
1. Health care reform -- United States 2. Insurance, Health 3. Medical care -- Europe 4. Medical care -- Government policy 5. Medical policy -- United States
ISBN 9781594202346

LC 2009-9555
"Reid's concise—and surprisingly humorous—study is recommended to anyone following the ongoing debate over health-care reform." Libr J
Includes bibliographical references

Relman, Arnold

A second opinion; rescuing America's health-care: a plan for universal coverage serving patients over profit. [by] Arnold S. Relman. PublicAffairs 2007 205p $24 **362.1**
1. Health care reform 2. Medical care -- Government policy
ISBN 978-1-58648-481-1; 1-58648-481-8

LC 2006-103332
This book is the author's "call to reform America's profit-driven health-care system, which fails to cover a large segment of the population. His solution is a single-payer network that provides universal coverage and uses salaried community-based physicians. This thought-provoking book is recommended for all who are interested in health care." Libr J
Includes bibliographical references

Rovner, Julie

★ Health care policy and politics A to Z; 3rd ed.; CQ Press 2008 314p il $93.75 **362.1**
1. Medical care -- Government policy -- Encyclopedias 2. Public health -- Encyclopedias 3. Reference books
ISBN 978-0-87289-776-2; 0-87289-776-1

LC 2008-31429

This reference explores changes made in the nation's health system by the private sector, Congress, federal and state courts, and state legislatures. Entries cover such topics as prescription drug benefits, key programs and agencies, committees and organizations, statistics, and the history and background shaping major health policies.

Schultz, Nancy Lusignan

Mrs. Mattingly's miracle; the prince, the widow, and the cure that shocked Washington City. Yale University Press 2011 274p il   **362.1**
  1. Biography, Individual 2. Breast -- Cancer -- Patients 3. Breast cancer 4. Cancer patients 5. Catholic Church 6. Catholic Church -- United States 7. Historical literature 8. Mattingly family 9. Miracles 10. Priests 11. Spiritual healing
  ISBN 0-300-11846-5; 978-0-300-11846-9
                                            LC 2010-39308
This book focuses on Ann Carbery Mattingly, who [i]n March of 1824, . . . in Washington, DC, . . . had suffered from breast cancer for seven years, [and] lay near death. . . . Prince Alexander Leopold Hohenlohe-Waldenburg-Schillingfüst, a thirty-year-old German cleric, was contacted. . . . As he said mass in Europe, . . . she was miraculously healed. . . . This is the story that Nancy Lusignan Schultz, . . . fleshes out. . . . [Moreover,] she . . . argues that the controversy the miracle created illuminates a key turning point in the life of American Catholicism. . . . The Mattingly miracle coincided with a demographic transformation of the Catholic community in which an Anglo-American community became a church of immigrants and much more European in focus. (Journal of Religion)

"In the predawn hours of a March day in 1824 . . . Ann Carbery Mattingly, the widowed sister of DC's mayor and somewhat of a local celebrity, rose from bed in the family's Foggy Bottom mansion (now the site of DAR Constitution Hall) suddenly healed of the advanced breast cancer that had kept her holed up for seven years. The bells of nearby Georgetown College announced the news. Believers exulted. Others lifted fists and cried foul. Doctors could offer no medical explanation, but Mattingly knew who had cured her: a German faith healer whom she had petitioned to say Mass for her that morning. Nancy Lusignan Schultz's recounting of this story and of the anti-fanatical sentiment it exacerbated on the East Coast feels flimsy and scattershot in places but succeeds at infusing Washington's ragtag days with an aura of supernatural intrigue and makes for a fine field guide to local Catholic lore." Washingtonian

Includes bibliographical references and index

Shah, Sonia

  ★ The **body** hunters; testing new drugs on the world's poorest patients. New Press 2006 242p $24.95   **362.1**
  1. Drug industry 2. Medical ethics
  ISBN 1-56584-912-4; 978-1-56584-912-9
                                            LC 2005-58394
The author "uncovers a series of recent unethical drug trials conducted on impoverished and sick people in the developing world. . . . Meticulously researched and packed with documentary evidence, Shah's tautly argued study will

provoke much needed public debate about this disturbing facet of globalization." Publ Wkly
  Includes bibliographical references

Shilts, Randy

  ★ And the band played on; politics, people, and the AIDS epidemic. 20th anniversary ed.; St Martin's Griffin 2007 630p pa $17.95   **362.1**
  1. AIDS (Disease)
  ISBN 978-0-312-37463-1
The author traces the history of the AIDS epidemic in the United States.
  "Shilts successfully weaves comprehensive investigative reporting and commercial page-turner pacing, political intrigue and personal tragedy into a landmark work." Publ Wkly
  Includes bibliographical references

Silver, Daniel B.

  Refuge in hell; how Berlin's Jewish hospital outlasted the Nazis. Houghton Mifflin 2003 xxii, 311p $24   **362.1**
  1. Holocaust, 1933-1945 2. Jews -- Germany
  ISBN 0-618-25144-8
                                            LC 2003-47896
  "This enlightening work is essential for public and academic libraries." Libr J
  Includes bibliographical references and index

Smith, Tom

  A **balanced** life; 9 strategies for coping with the mental health problems of a loved one. Hazelden 2008 147p pa $14.95   **362.1**
  1. Mentally ill
  ISBN 978-1-59285-662-6
                                            LC 2008-18794
  "Through extensive research and his own experience with his daughter's mental illness and subsequent suicide, . . . [the author] suggests nine strategies for coping, including helping loved ones find and continue to take their medication, urging them to maintain a supportive relationship with a therapist, and recognizing the warning signs. . . . Smith provides empathetic information that has the potential to buoy people up." Libr J
  Includes bibliographical references

Sommer, Alfred

  Getting what we deserve; health and medical care in America. Johns Hopkins University Press 2009 133p il map $21.95   **362.1**
  1. Medical care -- Government policy 2. Public health -- United States 3. Social medicine
  ISBN 978-0-8018-9387-2; 0-8018-9387-9
                                            LC 2009-6039
  "Opposing what we've been led to believe about the health-care situation in the United States, . . . [the author] posits that there's less complexity than meets the eye and that solutions are possible. . . . First illustrating how much improvement there was in life expectancy in the 20th century even before the advent of antibiotics and advanced technology, he proceeds to emphasize the importance of environment—e.g., hygiene, pollution, smoking—in creat-

ing public health problems and the relatively simple steps to improvement. . . . Sommer keeps it short and clear, with plenty of understandable graphs and charts. His common-sense points will interest consumers trying to understand the ongoing debate as well as policymakers." Libr J

Includes bibliographical references

Sotile, Wayne M.

Thriving with heart disease; a unique program for you and your family: live happier, healthier, longer. {by} Wayne M. Sotile with Robin Cantor-Cooke. Free Press 2003 303p $25; pa $13 **362.1**
1. Heart -- Diseases -- Psychological aspects -- Popular works 2. Heart diseases
ISBN 0-7432-4364-1; 0-7432-4365-X pa

LC 2002-45587

This book presents "advice on diet, exercise, mental health, sexual function, and spirituality. . . . Besides addressing the emotional consequences of recovering from a heart attack or heart failure, the text also discusses the ramifications of adjusting to implanted devices. . . . Sotile's guide will appeal to patients and family members . . . and is highly recommended for all academic, consumer health, and public libraries." Libr J

Includes bibliographical references

Starr, Paul

★ **Remedy** and reaction; the peculiar American struggle over health care reform. Yale University Press 2011 324p $28.50 **362.1**
1. Health insurance 2. Medical care -- Government policy
ISBN 978-0-300-17109-9

LC 2011019577

The author "recounts the long and largely unsuccessful fight to provide all Americans with health care. . . . Starr shows how the window of opportunity for health-care reform has opened several times in the last 100 years and how each time it has been slammed shut by powerful interests including the American Medical Association, big insurance companies, and the conservative politicians they support. . . . This is a must-read in order to understand why health-care reform has been and continues to be so difficult to achieve in America." Libr J

Includes bibliographical references

Steinberg, Jonny

Sizwe's test; a young man's journey through Africa's AIDS epidemic. Simon & Schuster 2008 349p il $26 **362.1**
1. AIDS (Disease) 2. AIDS (Disease) -- South Africa
ISBN 978-1-4165-5269-7; 1-4165-5269-3

LC 2007-29672

The author "becomes intertwined with his subject, but balances critical distance and compassion with gleanings from his own psychological barriers to HIV testing that further deepen the concern and understanding he accords to Sizwe's story." Publ Wkly

Includes bibliographical references

Torrey, E. Fuller (Edwin Fuller), 1937-

The **insanity** offense; how America's failure to treat the seriously mentally ill endangers its citizens. W.W. Norton 2008 265p il **362.1**
1. Mentally ill -- Institutional care
ISBN 0-393-06658-4; 978-0-393-06658-6

LC 2008-2697

"Released en masse from institutions beginning in the 1960s, the most severely ill are most likely to become homeless, incarcerated, victimized, and/or violent. Torrey details how civil liberties suits have prevented such people from being involuntarily institutionalized, leaving them a danger both to themselves and to others. . . . Chilling and well documented, this text has many no-nonsense solutions to protect the mentally ill themselves as well as society as a whole." Publ Wkly

Includes bibliographical references

Warner, Mark L.

The **complete** guide to Alzheimer's-proofing your home; rev ed; Purdue Univ. Press 2000 477p il $54.95 **362.1**
1. Alzheimer's disease 2. Home accidents
ISBN 1-55753-202-8

LC 99-462016

"A generous directory of relevant products and manufacturers and a helpful glossary further distinguish this superlative resource for home caregivers." Booklist {review of 1998 edition}

Includes bibliographical references

★ **AIDS** sourcebook; basic consumer health information about human immunodeficiency virus (HIV) and acquired immunodeficiency syndrome (AIDS), featuring updated statistics and facts about risks, prevention, screening, dia. edited by Ivy L. Alexander. 4th ed; Omnigraphics 2008 707p il $87 **362.1**
1. AIDS (Disease)
ISBN 978-0-7808-0997-0; 0-7808-0997-1

LC 2007-34967

★ **Consumers'** guide to hospitals; by the editors of Consumers' checkbook magazine. Center for the Study of Services 2002 359p il pa $19.95 **362.1**
1. Hospitals -- United States
ISBN 978-1-88812-412-5; 1-88812-412-1

LC 2002-104079

This guide presents statistics about U.S. hospitals with comparisons on death rates, estimated rates of complications, ratings of physicians, and outcome ratings for particular conditions and diseases. It includes advice on choosing a hospital and cutting costs and lists resources

Encyclopedia of AIDS; a social, political, cultural, and scientific record of the HIV epidemic. edited by Raymond A. Smith; forewords by James W.

Curran, Peter Piot; photo editor, Jane Rosett. Fitzroy Dearborn Pubs. 1998 xli, 601p il $135 **362.1**
1. AIDS (Disease) -- Encyclopedias 2. Reference books
ISBN 1-57958-007-6

LC 98-200474

This reference covers "aspects of the global HIV/AIDS crisis, primarily for the period 1991-96. The contents are organized into eight broad domains covering basic science and epidemiology; transmission and prevention; pathology and treatment; impacted populations; government and activism; policy and law; culture and society; and the global epidemic." Choice

Encyclopedia of public health; edited by Lester Breslow. Macmillan Ref. USA 2001 4v set $475　　　　　　　　　　　　　　　　　　　**362.1**
1. Public health 2. Public health -- Encyclopedias 3. Reference books
ISBN 0-02-865354-8

LC 2001-31501

"Information on more than 900 programs, services, organizations, health behaviors, and the prevalence, epidemiology, and costs of communicable diseases. Although the work focuses on the United States, there are also references to worldwide problems." Libr J

362.109　History, geographic treatment, biography

Brawley, Otis Webb
How we do harm; Otis Webb Brawley with Paul Goldberg. St. Martin's Press 2012 256p. **362.109**
1. Health care reform -- United States 2. Medical care -- United States 3. Medical policy -- United States
ISBN 9780312672973

LC 2011035843

In this book, Dr. Otis Webb Brawley, M.D., explores "how medicine is really practiced in America. Brawley tells of doctors who select treatment based on payment they will receive, rather than on demonstrated scientific results; hospitals and pharmaceutical companies that seek out patients to treat even if they are not actually ill (but as long as their insurance will pay); a public primed to swallow the latest pill, no matter the cost; and rising healthcare costs for unnecessary—and often unproven—treatments that we all pay for. Brawley calls for rational healthcare, healthcare drawn from results-based, scientifically justifiable treatments, and not just the peddling of hot new drugs." (Publisher's note)

362.196　Specific conditions

Baroni, Bill
Fat kid got fit; Bill Baroni with Damon DiMarco ; with a foreword by Howard Eisenson. Lyons Press 2012 x, 245p.p **362.196**
1. Biography & autobiography -- Personal Memoirs 2. Health & fitness -- General 3. Health & fitness -- Weight Loss 4. Overweight persons -- New Jersey -- Biography

5. Weight loss
ISBN 9780762770472

LC 2011028047

This book tells the story of "Bill Baroni [who] was just twenty years old, [when] he was convinced he was dying. He thought he was having a heart attack because it felt like he had an elephant sitting on his chest. It turned out to be only indigestion, but more than that, it was the wake up call he needed to save his life. Bill weighed 320 pounds and was hooked on junk food. He set about to change his life forever. . . . He lost his weight using common sense. It took dedication, and even some gumption. But it worked! He lost 120 pounds and, more importantly, he has kept it off! He has maintained a healthy 185 pounds for fifteen years. At 65, he is trim, handsome, and healthy." (Publisher's note)

"[Baroni] traces his own path and, with humor and style, passes the information he learned along to readers. This can work for anyone." (Libr J)

Includes bibliographical references (p. 241-245).

Cody, Joshua
[Sic] W.W. Norton 2011 266 p. **362.196**
ISBN 9780393081060

LC 2011026035

In this book "Joshua Cody, a . . . young composer, was about to receive his PhD when he was diagnosed with an aggressive cancer. Facing a bone-marrow transplant and full radiation, he charts his struggle: the fury, the tendency to self-destruction, and the ruthless grasping for life and sensation; the encounter with a strange woman on Canal Street that leads to sex at his apartment; the detailed morphine fantasy complete with a bride called Valentina while, in reality, hospital staff are pinning him to his bed." (Publisher's note)

Forrest, Emma
Your voice in my head; a memoir. Other Press 2011 215 p. **362.196**
1. Authors 2. Biography, Individual 3. Journalists 4. Novelists 5. Screenwriters
ISBN 1590514467; 9781590514467; 978-1-59051-446-7; 1-59051-446-7

LC 201030930

This book presents a memoir by writer Emma Forrest which details a period in her life in which, despite "the support of her parents . . . as well as a precocious career in journalism and a first novel . . . already on the way, she became a bulimic and an obsessive cutter, and soon began walking 'hand in hand with the thought of suicide.' She also had a knack for acquiring terrible boyfriends whose bad behavior inspired her to hurt herself more, and who sometimes aided and abetted the abuse." Particular focus is given to "the therapist who ultimately changed her life, a man she refers to as Dr. R. . . . [and his] unexpected death." Also included are "letters from Dr. R.'s other patients . . . [and] a sermon by her rabbi." (N Y Times)

Zimmer, Carl
A **planet** of viruses; Carl Zimmer. University of Chicago Press 2011 x, 109p.p col. ill. **362.196**
1. Bacteriophages 2. Scientific literature 3. Virus diseases 4. Viruses
ISBN 9780226983356 pa; 0226983358 pa;

9780226983363; 9780226983332

LC 2010036742

"This . . . book explores the hidden world of viruses. . . . Here Carl Zimmer, popular science writer and author of Discover magazine's award-winning blog The Loom, presents the latest research on how viruses hold sway over our lives and our biosphere, how viruses helped give rise to the first life-forms, how viruses are producing new diseases, how we can harness viruses for our own ends, and how viruses will continue to control our fate for years to come. In this . . . tour of the frontiers of biology, . . . we learn that some treatments for the common cold do more harm than good; that the world's oceans are home to an astonishing number of viruses; and that the evolution of HIV is now in overdrive, spawning more mutated strains than we care to imagine." (Publisher's note)

362.28 Suicide

Ackerman, Diane

A **slender** thread. Random House 1997 305p hardcover o.p. pa $14   **362.28**
1. Crisis centers 2. Hotlines (Telephone counseling) 3. Social work 4. Suicide
ISBN 0-679-77133-6 pa

LC 96-8721

This is an account of the author's work as a volunteer counselor at a suicide-prevention and crisis center in a New York college town

"In a narrative that is lush with her signature gift for metaphor and delight in the senses and taut with the drama of her often frightening negotiations with people in the throes of every imaginable form of crisis, Ackerman illuminates the bewildering workings of the resilient human psyche." Booklist

Evans, Glen

★ The **encyclopedia** of suicide; {by} Glen Evans, Norman L. Farberow; foreword by Alan L. Berman. 2nd ed; Facts on File 2003 xxxiii, 329p $65   **362.28**
1. Reference books 2. Suicide -- Dictionaries
ISBN 0-8160-4525-9

LC 2002-27166

Arranged in A-Z format, over 500 entries cover such aspects as causes, history and psychology of suicide. Also covered are philosophical and religious issues as well as sociological viewpoints and research and treatment concerns.

362.29 Substance abuse

Black, Claudia

Straight talk from Claudia Black; what recovering parents should tell their kids about drugs and alcohol. Hazelden 2003 131p il pa $12.95 **362.29**
1. Alcoholics -- Family relationships 2. Alcoholism 3. Children of alcoholics 4. Children of drug addicts 5. Drug abuse 6. Parents -- Alcohol use 7. Parents

-- Drug use
ISBN 1-59285-041-3

LC 2003-50831

The author discusses "brain chemistry, generational vulnerability, and phenomena such as multiple addictions, tolerance levels, relapse, and blackouts. The emphasis then moves to . . . advice about self-forgiveness, making amends for past behavior, and new ways of relating to loved ones. . . . This candid and hope-filled book merits strong consideration by large public libraries and specialized collections given the prevalence of some form of addictive behavior in families." Libr J

Includes bibliographical references

Cermak, Timmen L.

Marijuana: what's a parent to believe? Hazelden 2003 253p il pa $12.95   **362.29**
1. Drug abuse -- Prevention 2. Marijuana 3. Parenting 4. Teenagers -- Drug use 5. Youth -- Drug use
ISBN 1-59285-039-1

LC 2003-50917

The author "describes the world of difference between experimenting with marijuana at age 12 and age 20. Rejecting the 'just say no' approach, as well as the legalization model, he urges schools to adopt programs that will teach kids social and emotional competence, not just drug education." Libr J

Includes bibliographical references

Courtwright, David T.

Forces of habit; drugs and the making of the modern world. Harvard Univ. Press 2001 277p $24.95; pa $16.95   **362.29**
1. Drug abuse 2. Psychotropic drugs 3. Psychotropic drugs -- History 4. Substance abuse -- Economic aspects 5. Substance abuse -- History 6. Substance abuse -- Prevention 7. Substance abuse -- Social aspects
ISBN 0-674-00458-2; 0-674-01003-5 pa

LC 00-61466

"Reasoned and informative, Courtwright's book is a cogent source of dispassionate information on drugs and their role in society." Booklist

Includes bibliographical references

Feiling, Tom

Cocaine nation; how the white trade took over the world. Pegasus Books 2010 350p $27.95 **362.29**
1. Cocaine 2. Cocaine abuse 3. Cocaine industry 4. Drug traffic
ISBN 978-1-60598-101-7; 1-60598-101-X

"Studying the cultivation, distribution, and use of cocaine, . . . [the author] probes the drug's meteoric rise in sales and traces traffic from Colombian coca fields to Miami, Kingston, Tijuana, London, and New York. He follows consumers, traders, producers, police officers, doctors, and custom officials. . . . Packed with facts and figures, this is a well-researched survey of the subject." Publ Wkly

Includes bibliographical references

Ford, Betty

Healing and hope; six women from the Betty Ford Center share their powerful journeys of addiction and recovery. Putnam 2003 275p $24.95; pa $14 **362.29**

1. Alcoholism 2. Drug abuse 3. Drug addicts -- Rehabilitation 4. Substance abuse -- Patients -- Rehabilitation -- Case studies

ISBN 0-399-15138-9; 0-425-19830-8 pa

LC 2003-47041

The author presents and comments on the recovery stories of six women who have gone through the Betty Ford Center program, including those of a housewife, a schoolteacher, and a former gang member

"With its six powerful personal stories and Ford's warm, authoritative overview, this is a solid popular introduction to the experience of recovery from addiction." Booklist

Henderson, Elizabeth Connell

Understanding addiction. University Press of Miss. 2000 209p il hardcover o.p. pa $12 **362.29**

1. Compulsive behavior 2. Drug abuse

ISBN 1-57806-240-3 pa

LC 00-42856

The author writes "on how addictions develop, how the addicted brain works, and what the different effects of the major addictive drugs are, and on genetic, psychological, and behavioral factors involved in addiction." Booklist

Includes bibliographical references

Pampel, Fred C.

★ **Drugs** and sports. Facts on File 2007 284p $45 **362.29**

1. Athletes -- Drug use 2. Doping in sports

ISBN 0-8160-6575-6; 978-0-8160-6575-2

LC 2006-20536

This is an overview of the history of drug use among athletes "from the performance-enhancement methods of the ancient Greeks to the recent accusations of drug use among high-profile professional athletes." Publisher's note

Includes bibliographical references

Reding, Nick

Methland; the death and life of an American small town. Bloomsbury 2009 255p $25 **362.29**

1. Methamphetamine 2. Methamphetamine abuse

ISBN 978-1-59691-650-0; 1-59691-650-8

LC 2008-45398

The author traces "rise of meth use across the Midwest, focusing on Oelwein, an Iowa railroad town (pop. 6,772) that by 2005 had been 'destroyed' by the drug. . . . An important report on an extremely dangerous drug and the consequences of addiction." Kirkus

Includes bibliographical references

Streatfeild, Dominic

Cocaine; an unauthorized biography. Thomas Dunne Bks./St. Martin's Press 2002 510p il $27.95; pa $15 **362.29**

1. Cocaine 2. Cocaine -- History 3. Drug abuse 4. Drug traffic

ISBN 0-312-28624-4; 0-312-42226-1 pa

"Thorough, engrossing, balanced, and entertaining, it is important social history in palatable form." Booklist

Includes bibliographical references

★ Drug abuse sourcebook; basic consumer health information about the abuse of cocaine, club drugs, hallucinogens, heroin, inhalants, marijuana, and other illicit substances, prescription medications, and over-the-counter medi. edited by Joyce Brennfleck Shannon. 3rd ed; Omnigraphics 2010 645p il $95 **362.29**

1. Drug abuse 2. Reference books

ISBN 978-0-7808-1079-2

LC 2010-748

"Provides basic consumer health information about the abuse of illegal drugs and misuse of prescription and over-the-counter medications, with facts about addiction, treatment, and recovery. Includes index, glossary of related terms and directory of resources." Publisher's note

Includes bibliographical references

Drugs and controlled substances; information for students. Stacey Blachford, Kristine Krapp, editors. Gale Group 2003 xxvi, 495p il $115 **362.29**

1. Drug abuse 2. Drug abuse -- Juvenile literature 3. Drugs

ISBN 0-7876-6264-X

LC 2002-10925

Provides detailed information about the composition, history, effects, uses and abuses of common drugs, including illegal drugs and addictive substances, as well as commonly abused classes of prescription drugs.

"In addition to the well-written essays, sidebars discussing legal issues, misconceptions, history, and news stories add depth to each topic. . . . Currency, scope, and authority are the hallmarks of this highly recommended reference work." Booklist

Includes bibliographical references

362.292   Alcohol

Dorris, Michael

★ The **broken** cord; with a foreword by Louise Erdrich. Harper & Row 1989 300p il hardcover o.p. pa $14 **362.292**

1. Alcoholism 2. Father-son relationship 3. Native Americans

ISBN 0-06-016071-3; 0-06-091682-6 pa

LC 88-45893

"The alarming statistics and consequences of fetal alcohol syndrome are skillfully interwoven with the human story of one of its victims in 'The Broken Cord.' Mr. Dorris's prose is clear and affecting." N Y Times Book Rev

Includes bibliographical references

★ **Alcohol** and temperance in modern history; an international encyclopedia. Jack S. Blocker, Jr., David M. Fahey, and Ian R. Tyrrell, editors. ABC-CLIO 2003 2v il set $185 **362.292**

1. Alcohol 2. Alcohol -- Encyclopedias 3. Alcoholic beverage industry -- Encyclopedias 4. Alcoholism -- Encyclopedias 5. Drinking of alcoholic beverages -- Encyclopedias 6. Temperance 7. Temperance --

Encyclopedias
ISBN 1-576-07833-7

LC 2003-8679

"The editors present the history of beverage alcohol as commercial product, cultural icon, behavioral solvent, medical/social research, and political issue. Their book admirably fits many purposes, covering many eras and having an international focus. The comprehensive entries (with three levels of coverage: international, regional, and country-specific) trace the history of the subject, 18th century to the present. . . . A storehouse of scholarship." Choice

Includes bibliographical references

362.4 People with physical disabilities

Iezzoni, Lisa

When walking fails; mobility problems of adults with chronic conditions. University of California Press 2003 355p il $60; pa $19.95 **362.4**
1. Chronic diseases 2. Movement disorders
ISBN 0-520-23742-0; 0-520-23819-2 pa

LC 2002-152225

"Iezzoni grounds her readable and compelling discussion with case histories and interviews of people who struggle with policy and environmental barriers in addition to their own physical impairments. . . . This is a valuable work for academic and public libraries." Libr J

Includes bibliographical references

Sacks, Oliver W.

Seeing voices; a journey into the world of the deaf. [by] Oliver Sacks. Vintage Books 2000 222p il pa $13.95 **362.4**
1. Deaf 2. Sign language
ISBN 0-375-70407-8

LC 00-42340

"With his philosopher's penchant for profound discovery and his neurologist's knowledge of biology and the brain, Sacks offers provocative connections and acute observations about the nature of language and culture." Booklist

Includes bibliographical references

★ The **Encyclopedia** of blindness and vision impairment; [by] Jill Sardegna [et al.] 2nd ed; Facts on File 2002 333p $65 **362.4**
1. Blind -- Dictionaries 2. Blind, Apparatus for the -- Dictionaries 3. Blindness -- Dictionaries 4. People with visual disabilities -- Dictionaries 5. Reference books 6. Vision Disorders 7. Vision disorders -- Dictionaries
ISBN 0-8160-4280-2

LC 2001-55653

"This volume incorporates a history of blindness and vision impairment with an A-to-Z presentation of health issues, types of surgery, medications, medical terminology, social issues, myths and misconceptions, economic issues, and current research trends." Publisher's note

Includes bibliographical references

★ **Encyclopedia** of disability; general editor, Gary L. Albrecht. Sage Publications 2006 5v il set $850 **362.4**
1. Disability studies 2. Handicapped -- Encyclopedias 3. Physically handicapped 4. Reference books 5. Sociology of disability
ISBN 0-7619-2565-1

LC 2005-18301

"Almost 200 of the entries are biographical, treating individuals from Homer and Socrates to Helen Keller and Franklin Roosevelt. Others treat history . . . types of disability . . . [and] attitudes and conditions affecting daily life. . . . [This encyclopedia draws] in readers from a wide range of studies and interests . . . helping them to see disability in an entirely new way." Booklist

Includes bibliographical references

362.5 Poor people

Kozol, Jonathan

Rachel and her children; homeless families in America. Three Rivers Press 2006 303p pa $13.95 **362.5**
1. Homeless persons
ISBN 0-307-34589-0

LC 2007-281899

"While the individual stories that Kozol tells so affectingly point out the vivid realities of urban poverty, the book also supplies statistics that detail the more abstract--and inhuman--attitudes that contemporary society assumes when attempting to deal with its victims." Booklist

Includes bibliographical references

Reef, Catherine

Poverty in America. Facts on File 2006 xxix, 386p il map $80 **362.5**
1. Poor -- United States 2. Poverty -- United States 3. Poverty -- United States -- History 4. Public welfare 5. Social work
ISBN 978-0-8160-6062-7; 0-8160-6062-2

LC 2006-6896

This book "examines the lives and experiences of the poor throughout the United States from colonial times to the present, covering trends, events, facts, figures, and anything else related to this topic." Publisher's note

Includes bibliographical references

Vollmann, William T.

★ **Poor** people. Ecco 2007 314p il $29.95; pa $16.95 **362.5**
1. Authors 2. Novelists 3. Poor 4. Poverty 5. Short story writers
ISBN 0-06-087882-7; 978-0-06-087882-5; 0-06-087884-3 pa; 978-0-06-087884-9 pa

LC 2006-48547

The author "brings to bear his keen powers of observation on the world around him and, not incidentally, on himself; he is unabashed about allowing his emotional reactions to inform his thoughts about what it means to be poor. This remarkable book is sui generis and should be in all collections." Libr J

★ Encyclopedia of homelessness; David Levinson, editor. Sage Publications 2004 2v il $295 **362.5**

1. Homelessness -- Encyclopedias 2. Reference books

ISBN 0-7619-2751-4

LC 2004-9279

"Entries cover homelessness in 8 major U.S. cities and 30 cities and nations around the world, as well as causes of homelessness; historical aspects; housing, policy, health and lifestyle issues; and service systems." Booklist

Includes bibliographical references

362.6   People in late adulthood

Carnot, Edward J.

Is your parent in good hands? protecting your aging parent from financial abuse and neglect. Capital Books 2004 261p pa $18.95   **362.6**

1. Adult children -- Legal status, laws, etc -- United States 2. Aged -- Crimes against -- United States -- Prevention 3. Aging parents 4. Aging parents -- Care -- United States 5. Aging parents -- Legal status, laws, etc -- United States 6. Caregivers 7. Caregivers -- Law and legislation -- United States 8. Elder abuse 9. Elderly -- Care

ISBN 1-931868-37-9

LC 2003-12140

The author "offers advice for adult children who may live far from their elderly parents about the importance of planning, how to find reliable caregivers, how to use the legal system when abuse occurs, and how to keep track of a parent's condition from a distance. This cautionary tale belongs in all aging collections." Libr J

Includes bibliographical references and index

Delehanty, Hugh

★ **Caring** for your parents; the complete AARP guide. [by] Hugh Delehanty & Elinor Ginzler; foreword by Mary Pipher. Rev. and expanded ed.; Sterling Pub. 2008 xvii, 238p il pa $12.95   **362.6**

1. Aging parents 2. Elderly -- Care

ISBN 1-4027-5857-X; 978-1-4027-5857-7

LC 2008-277441

The authors "provide information on everything from the first difficult conversations with parents about their changing situation to coping with terminal illness and death. The book has a wealth of data on long-distance caregiving, financial matters, community-based and professional case management, Medicare, and age-related physical changes." Libr J

Includes bibliographical references

Hogan, Paul Ross

Stages of senior care; your step-by-step guide to making the best decisions. by Paul Hogan and Lori Hogan. McGraw-Hill 2009 292p il pa $18.95 **362.6**

1. Aging parents 2. Elderly -- Care

ISBN 978-0-07-162109-0

LC 2009-20572

This is "a helpful guide for families choosing among home care-giving and other assisted-living options for aging or ailing parents." Publ Wkly

Includes bibliographical references

362.7   Young people

Adamec, Christine A.

★ The **encyclopedia** of adoption; [by] Christine Adamec, Laurie C. Miller, M.D. 3rd ed; Facts on File 2007 xxxvi, 394p $75   **362.7**

1. Adoption 2. Adoption -- Encyclopedias 3. Reference books

ISBN 0-8160-6329-X; 978-0-8160-6329-1

LC 2005-55514

"Beginning with a brief history of adoption as a concept and touching on key issues in past history and recent times, this book looks at the development of adoption and adoption law in the U.S. . . . It includes entries that discuss not just adoption but also the related institutions of foster care, group homes, and orphanages." Booklist [review of 2000 edition]

Includes bibliographical references

Caughman, Susan

You can adopt; an Adoptive Families guide. [by] Susan Caughman and Isolde Motley; with the editors and readers of Adoptive Families magazine. Ballantine Books 2009 296p il pa $16   **362.7**

1. Adoption

ISBN 978-0-345-50401-2; 0-345-50401-1

LC 2009-20252

"This thorough and honest resource stands out among other books on the topic in both its comprehensiveness and the authors' candor in discussing potentially controversial adoption-related issues. Domestic or international adoption? An infant or an older child? A sibling group? What about adopting transracially? These questions and many more are addressed here via a straightforward text interspersed with firsthand, sometimes wrenching accounts by adoptive parents, birth parents, and adoptees themselves." Booklist

Includes bibliographical references

Gammage, Jeff

China ghosts; my daughter's journey to America, my passage to fatherhood. William Morrow 2007 255p il $25.95   **362.7**

1. Adoption 2. Adoptive parents 3. Journalists

ISBN 978-0-06-124029-4; 0-06-124029-X

LC 2007-61204

"A father's account of going to China with his wife to adopt their first and second daughters. . . . Gammage, a staff writer for the Philadelphia Inquirer, had been happily married without children for many years, although he knew his wife really wanted children. By the time they discovered they couldn't have biological children, the best option was adopting from China. While there were tensions over their first daughter's medical problems (an infected scalp injury), both adoptions went reasonably smoothly. Back home, Gammage wrestled with his mixed feelings about the birth parents and his burden of good fortune, that guilty knowledge that his own happiness came from someone else's misfortune. Realizing that his own relationship to China was being shaped by the process of raising two Chinese girls, he ends this upbeat memoir by wondering about the impact of this new wave of immigrants on the future of Sino-American relations." Publ Wkly

Gilman, Lois
★ The **adoption** resource book; 4th ed; HarperPerennial 1998 576p pa $16.95   **362.7**
1. Adoption
ISBN 0-06-273361-3
                                    LC 98-21174
This offers information about adoption strategies including international adoptions, private and agency adoptions, and financing and lists more than 1,000 agencies and support groups

Kozol, Jonathan
Amazing grace; the lives of children and the conscience of a nation. HarperPerennial 1996 284p pa $14.95   **362.7**
1. Inner cities 2. Poor -- New York (N.Y.) 3. Socially handicapped children
ISBN 0-06-097697-7; 978-0-06-097697-2
Kozol's "powerfully understated report takes us inside rat-infested homes that are freezing in winter, overcrowded schools, dysfunctional clinics, soup kitchens. . . . While his narrative offers no specific solutions, it forcefully drives home his conviction: a civilized nation cannot allow this situation to continue." Publ Wkly
Includes bibliographical references

Leach, Penelope
★ **Child** care today; getting it right for everyone. Alfred A. Knopf 2009 350p $25.95   **362.7**
1. Child care
ISBN 978-1-4000-4256-2
                                    LC 2008-38373
The author "evaluates the state of child care in the Western world in the context of caring for children (as opposed to rearing children). . . . There's no doubt Child Care Today will become the bible on the subject. Stock up." Booklist
Includes bibliographical references

Thompson, Robert Smith
Empires on the Pacific; World War II and the struggle for the mastery of Asia. Basic Bks. 2001 434p $30; pa $18.95   **362.7**
1. Child welfare -- United States 2. World War, 1939-1945 -- Asia
ISBN 0-465-08575-X; 0-465-08576-8 pa
                                    LC 2001-36561
In this study, Thompson asserts that "the U.S. had strong political and economic interests in East Asia and saw Japan as a danger to those interests. . . . The author makes his points by telling only one side of the story, but his alternate view of our 'last good war' is bound to attract attention and may generate controversy." Booklist
Includes bibliographical references

Tough, Paul
Whatever it takes; Geoffrey Canada's quest to change Harlem and America. Houghton Mifflin Co. 2008 296p il map   **362.7**
1. African American children -- Education 2. Education -- United States 3. Organization officials 4. Poor -- Social conditions 5. Poverty 6. Poverty -- Prevention 7. Social welfare leaders
ISBN 0-618-56989-8; 978-0-618-56989-2
                                    LC 2008-13303
This is an account of Geoffrey Canada's creation of "the Harlem Children's Zone, a ninety-seven-block . . . [area] in central Harlem where he is testing new . . . ideas about poverty in America." (Publisher's note) Index.
"Tough profiles educational visionary Geoffrey Canada, whose Harlem Children's Zone—currently serving more than 7,000 children and encompassing 97 city blocks—represents an audacious effort to end poverty within underserved communities. . . . This book gives readers a solid look at the problems facing poor communities and their reformers, as well as good cause to be optimistic about the future." Publ Wkly
Includes bibliographical references

Tucker, Neely
Love in the driest season; a family memoir. Crown Publishers 2004 242p il hardcover o.p. pa $14   **362.7**
1. Adoption 2. Biography, Individual 3. Children's rights advocates 4. Intercountry adoption 5. Journalists 6. Librarians
ISBN 0-609-60976-9; 1-4000-8160-2 pa
                                    LC 2002-154095
"This story about the adoption of a tiny, critically ill Zimbabwean orphan appeals to the head as much as the heart." Christ Sci Monit

Child abuse sourcebook; edited by Joyce Brennfleck Shannon. 2nd ed.; Omnigraphics 2009 631p il $93   **362.7**
1. Child abuse 2. Reference books
ISBN 978-0-7808-1037-2
                                    LC 2009-27489
The editor "differentiates between abuse and neglect, defines the warning signs of various abuses, details intercession and prevention techniques, and offers positive parenting strategies and additional intervention resources. This difficult subject, with its many complicated facets, is explained with candor and sensitivity." Libr J
Includes bibliographical references

362.73 Institutional and related services

Bernstein, Nina
The **lost** children of Wilder; the epic struggle to change foster care. Pantheon Bks. 2001 482p hardcover o.p. pa $15   **362.73**
1. Child welfare 2. Child welfare -- New York (State) -- New York 3. Foster children -- Legal status, laws, etc -- New York (State) -- New York 4. Foster children

-- New York (State) -- New York 5. Foster home care
ISBN 0-679-75834-8 pa

LC 00-57456

"Bernstein explores the genesis and aftermath of the landmark 1973 legal case filed by young ACLU attorney Marcia Lowry against the New York State foster-care system. Known as Wilder for its 14-year-old African-American plaintiff, Shirley 'Pinky' Wilder, the suit claimed Jewish and Catholic child welfare services had a lock on foster care funding and placements. . . . This viscerally powerful history of institutionalized child abuse and the criminalization of poverty, of civil rights and social change, is compelling and essential reading." Publ Wkly

Includes bibliographical references

362.76   Abused and neglected young people

Bartholet, Elizabeth

Nobody's children; abuse and neglect, foster drift, and the adoption alternative. Beacon Press 1999 304p hardcover o.p. pa $17.50   **362.76**
1. Adoption 2. Adoption -- United States 3. Child abuse 4. Child abuse -- United States 5. Child welfare 6. Child welfare -- Government policy -- United States 7. Children -- Institutional care 8. Children -- Institutional care -- United States 9. Foster home care 10. Foster home care -- United States 11. Kinship care -- United States
ISBN 0-8070-2319-1 pa

LC 99-22976

This is a critique "of American child welfare policy. Examining legislation from all parts of the United States, Bartholet questions why 'family preservation ideology still reigns supreme when children rather than adult women are involved.' . . . Clear and consistent." Libr J

Includes bibliographical references

362.82   Families

Dalpiaz, Christina M.

Breaking free, starting over; parenting in the aftermath of family violence. Praeger 2004 232p $39.95   **362.82**
1. Children of abused wives 2. Domestic violence 3. Family violence 4. Parenting 5. Victims of family violence
ISBN 0-275-98167-3

LC 2003-62436

This guide provides "techniques for reparenting children who've been exposed to domestic violence. Lacking a safe haven, many of these children exhibit significant behavior, communication, and self-management problems." Libr J

Includes bibliographical references and index

Denham, Wes

Arrested; what to do when your loved one's in jail. Chicago Review Press 2010 263p il pa $16.95   **362.82**
1. Prisoners
ISBN 978-1-55652-834-7; 1-55652-834-5

LC 2009-42270

This book is an "extended checklist for those coping with the incarceration of a family member or significant friend, from the time the phone rings with news of the arrest onward. Denham shares the jargon, procedures, tricks, and traps in his coverage of jail visits, bail, public defenders, jail medical care, and legal and jail costs, and he outlines a decision-making process that considers the well-being of the entire family. . . .Hard-hitting, blunt, and practical, this book is packed with inside knowledge of the jail experience. It's a necessary purchase for criminal justice collections in public libraries." Libr J

Includes bibliographical references

Dutton, Donald G.

The **batterer**; a psychological profile. {by} Donald G. Dutton with Susan K. Golant. Basic Bks. 1995 209p hardcover o.p. pa $15   **362.82**
1. Domestic violence 2. Football players 3. Men -- Psychology 4. Sportscasters 5. Wife abuse
ISBN 0-465-03388-1 pa

LC 95-9556

The authors draw on the O. J. Simpson trial "to help elucidate their points regarding wife batterers. . . . Dutton and Golant provide an excellent introduction to the psychology of wife abusers, examining the different types of abusers: psychopathic, overcontrolled, and cyclical. They then narrow the focus to the cyclical abuser (the Dr. Jekyll/Mr. Hyde type exemplified by Simpson) and examine the different factors that go into making such an abuser." Libr J

Includes bibliographical references

Fessler, Ann

★ The **girls** who went away; the hidden history of women who surrendered children for adoption in the decades before Roe v. Wade. Penguin Press 2006 354p hardcover o.p. pa $16   **362.82**
1. Adoption 2. Adoption -- United States 3. Birthmothers
ISBN 1-59420-094-7; 0-14-303897-4 pa

LC 2005-58179

"These knowing oral histories are an emotional boon for birth mothers and adoptees struggling to make sense of troubled pasts." Publ Wkly

Includes bibliographical references

Forward, Susan

Toxic parents: overcoming their hurtful legacy and reclaiming your life; {by} Susan Forward with Craig Buck. Bantam Bks. 1989 326p hardcover o.p. pa $16   **362.82**
1. Child abuse
ISBN 978-0-553-38140-5; 0-553-38140-7

LC 89-6812

The authors identify types of hurtful parents, including alcoholics, verbal and physical abusers, and those who emotionally neglect their children. They also offer advice to adult child abuse victims on how to overcome the harm done

Weiss, Elaine

★ **Family** & friends' guide to domestic violence; how to listen, talk, and take action, when someone you care about is being abused. Volcano Press 2003 143p pa $17.95 **362.82**

    1. Domestic violence
    ISBN 1-88424-422-X

                         LC 2003-4642

This is a "guide for family and friends, with practical tips for communicating with a likely victim of abuse, including how to broach the subject." Libr J

Includes bibliographical references

Surviving domestic violence; voices of women who broke free. Volcano Press 2004 214p pa $17.95 **362.82**

    1. Abused wives -- United States -- Case studies 2. Abused wives -- United States -- Psychology 3. Conjugal violence -- United States 4. Domestic violence 5. Wife abuse -- United States
    ISBN 1-88424-427-0

                       LC 2003-27829

The author tells the "stories of 12 survivors, ranging in age and socioeconomic circumstances. She concludes each case study with a reflective commentary that emphasizes the strength and courage of these women." Libr J

Includes bibliographical references

Domestic violence sourcebook; edited by Joyce Brennfleck Shannon. 3rd ed.; Omnigraphics 2009 665p il $84 **362.82**

    1. Domestic violence 2. Reference books
    ISBN 978-0-7808-1038-9; 0-7808-1038-4

                       LC 2009-4386

"Provides basic consumer health information about the physical, mental, and social effects of violence against intimate partners, children, teens, parents, and the elderly, along with prevention and intervention strategies." Publisher's note

Includes bibliographical references

Encyclopedia of domestic violence; [edited by] Nicky Ali Jackson. Routledge 2007 789p $190 **362.82**

    1. Domestic violence -- Encyclopedias 2. Reference books
    ISBN 0-415-96968-9; 978-0-415-96968-0

                      LC 2006-103335

"The 138 A-Z entries fall into seven categories, including Child Abuse and Elder Abuse, Domestic Violence and the Law, and several others. . . . Each article is several pages long, with cross-references to other articles in the volume and with substantial bibliographies." Booklist

Includes bibliographical references

362.83   Women

Kristof, Nicholas D.

★ **Half** the sky; turning oppression to opportunity for women worldwide. [by] Nicholas D. Kristof and Sheryl WuDunn. Alfred A. Knopf 2009 xxii, 294p il $27.95; ebook $15.95; pa $15.95 **362.83**

    1. Women -- Crimes against -- Developing countries 2. Women -- Developing countries 3. Women -- Developing countries -- Social conditions 4. Women's rights 5. Women's rights -- Developing countries
    ISBN 9780307267146; 9780307273154; 9780307387097

                       LC 2009-12270

Kristof and WuDunn address what they consider to be "our era's most pervasive human rights violation: the oppression of women in the developing world. They show that a little help can transform the lives of women and girls abroad and that the key to economic progress lies in unleashing women's potential." (Publisher's note) Index.

This book "is a call to arms, a call for help, a call for contributions, but also a call for volunteers. It asks us to open our eyes to this enormous humanitarian issue. It does so with exquisitely crafted prose and sensationally interesting material." Washington Post Book World

Includes bibliographical references

362.88   Victims of war

Crompton, Vicki

Saving beauty from the beast; how to protect your daughter from an unhealthy relationship. by Vicki Crompton and Ellen Zelda Kessner. Little, Brown 2003 259p il $22.95; pa $13.95 **362.88**

    1. Abused women 2. Parenting
    ISBN 0-316-09058-1; 0-316-73552-3 pa

                       LC 2002-19153

This book "illuminates the problems of dangerous relationships by describing their characteristics, mapping out warning signs of abuse and offering sound advice for parents seeking to empower their daughters. The authors interviewed psychologists, counselors and girls who have had violent boyfriends; the girls' stories, as well as first-person accounts from parents and abusive boyfriends, are woven throughout the text. . . . This book serves as both fervent friend and practical coach to parents whose daughters may be facing abuse." Publ Wkly

Includes bibliographical references

Feinberg, Kenneth R.

What is life worth? the unprecedented effort to compensate the victims of 9/11. Public Affairs 2005 xxv, 213p $24 **362.88**

    1. Government officials 2. Lawyers 3. September 11 terrorist attacks, 2001
    ISBN 1-58648-323-4

                       LC 2005-47699

"Feinberg's willingness to put himself into the book makes what could have been an alternately dry and self-serving case study crackle with care, frustration, intellectual energy and good writing." Publ Wkly

362.883   Rape

Sebold, Alice

Lucky. Back Bay Books 2002 246p pa $11.95   **362.883**
1. Rape
ISBN 0-316-09619-9

When the author "was a college freshman at Syracuse University, she was attacked and raped on the last night of school. . . . Sebold launches her memoir headlong into the rape itself, laying out its visceral physical as well as mental violence, and from there spins a narrative of her life before and after the incident, weaving memories of parental alcoholism together with her post-rape addiction to heroin. In the midst of each wrenching episode, from the initial attack to the ensuing courtroom drama, Sebold's wit is as powerful as her searing candor." Publ Wkly

★ **Encyclopedia of rape**; edited by Merril D. Smith. Greenwood Press 2004 xxvii, 301p $75 **362.883**
1. Rape -- Encyclopedias 2. Reference books
ISBN 0-313-32687-8

LC 2004-44213

"The alphabetically arranged entries cover the physiological, political, and psychological aspects of rape, and supply biographical sketches of notorious rapists and their victims from ancient times to the present. The language used is at times graphic, and by its nature the volume is intended for adult readers, but entries are written with an unflinching regard for facts, avoiding sensationalism. . . . Users at all levels will find this volume a useful resource for scholarly information on recent high-profile rape cases, and it will also serve as an entry point for further research on rape and its subtopics." Choice
Includes bibliographical references

363   Other social problems and services

Charles, Daniel

Lords of the harvest; biotech, big money, and the future of food. Perseus Bks. 2001 348p il hardcover o.p. pa $17.50   **363**
1. Agricultural industry 2. Biotechnology 3. Farm produce 4. Food -- Biotechnology 5. Genetic engineering 6. Genetic engineering industry
ISBN 0-7382-0773-X pa

The author "covers the history of genetic engineering in plant crops from the early 1980s to the present. . . . What makes this book particularly interesting are the author's tales of the key individuals and groups involved in the biotechnology controversy. . . . This carefully researched and balanced account is intended to help the reader understand the how and the why of genetic engineering rather than make an argument for or against it." Libr J
Includes bibliographical references

Halpern, Jake

Braving home; dispatches from the Underwater Town, the Lava-Side Inn, and other extreme locales. Houghton Mifflin 2003 240p il $23; pa $13   **363**
1. Authors 2. Home 3. Journalists
ISBN 0-618-15548-1; 0-618-44662-1 pa

LC 2002-191262

"The book is like a stay-at-home adventure, with all the excitement but none of the hardship. . . . This is the perfect book for armchair travelers interested in virtual visits to 'extreme locations.'" Booklist
Includes bibliographical references

363.1   Public safety programs

Cummins, Ronnie

★ **Genetically** engineered food; a self-defense guide for consumers. [by] Ronnie Cummins and Ben Lilliston; foreword by Frances Moore Lappé. [2nd, rev ed]; Marlowe & Co 2004 237p pa $14.95 **363.1**
1. Farm produce 2. Food -- Biotechnology
ISBN 1-569-24469-3

LC 2004-45565

The authors "discuss genetically engineered or modified food focusing on the scientific, political, economic, and health issues. . . . [They] include information on what consumers can do, from smart shopping to grassroots lobbying, to reduce the threat of genetically engineered food." Booklist [review of 2000 edition]
Includes bibliographical references

Eban, Katherine

Dangerous doses; how counterfeiters are contaminating America's drug supply. Harcourt 2005 462p il $25   **363.1**
1. Consumer education 2. Counterfeits and counterfeiting 3. Drugs
ISBN 0-15-101050-1

LC 2004-25581

The author "documents the flaws in the U.S. drug-distribution system that too often result in Americans getting diluted and contaminated drugs. . . . She details in particular the dramatic workings of Operation Stone Cold in Florida, a task force informally called the Horsemen of the Apocalypse, assigned to investigate trafficking in counterfeit drugs. This riveting page-turner provides a fascinating behind-the-scenes look at drug sales and distribution." Booklist

Nestle, Marion

Pet food politics; the Chihuahua in the coal mine. University of California Press 2008 219p il $18.95   **363.1**
1. Food contamination 2. Food industry and trade -- Safety measures 3. Pets -- Feeding and feeds 4. Pets -- Food 5. Product recall
ISBN 978-0-520-25781-8; 0-520-25781-2

LC 2008-3995

This book "provides a vivid and detailed account of the [contaminated pet food] affair and its aftermath. The book . . . deserves a wider readership." Economist

Includes bibliographical references

Pringle, Peter

★ **Food,** inc; Mendel to Monsanto--the promises and perils of the biotech harvest. Simon & Schuster 2003 239p hardcover o.p. pa $13   **363.1**
1. Agricultural biotechnology 2. Farm produce 3. Food -- Biotechnology 4. Genetically modified foods
ISBN 0-7432-2611-9; 0-7432-6763-X pa
LC 2003-42823

"This is a book to satisfy curiosity and engender concern, and any of its chapters would provide an excellent subject for discussion groups." SLJ

Puleo, Stephen

Dark tide; the great Boston molasses flood of 1919. Beacon Press 2003 263p il $23   **363.1**
1. Industrial accidents
ISBN 0-8070-5020-2
LC 2003-10433

"On January 15, 1919, a fifty-foot tall steel tank filled with 2.3 million gallons of molasses collapsed on Boston's waterfront, disgorging its contents as a fifteen-foot high wave of molasses that briefly traveled at thirty-five miles per hour. The Great Boston Molasses Flood claimed the lives of twenty-one people and scores of animals, injured 150, and caused widespread destruction. Tracing the era from the tank's construction in 1915 through the multiyear lawsuit that followed the tragedy, Dark Tide uses the drama of the flood to examine the sweeping changes brought about by World War I, Prohibition, the Anarchist movement, the Red Scare, Immigration, and the role of big business in society." Univ Press Books 2004

Includes bibliographical references

Wilson, Bee

Swindled; the dark history of food fraud, from poisoned candy to counterfeit coffee. Princeton University Press 2008 384p il map $26.95   **363.1**
1. Consumer protection -- History 2. Food -- Safety measures 3. Food contamination 4. Food industry 5. Food industry and trade -- History 6. Product counterfeiting 7. Public health -- History
ISBN 978-0-691-13820-6
LC 2008-9688

"In this day and age of tainted milk, pet food and genetically altered food, Bee Wilson has given us an immensely readable history from the 1820's to the 21st century. Timely and purposeful, this book should bring many people to the whole foods world." Univ Press Books for Public and Second Sch Libr, 2009

Includes bibliographical references (351-361)

Genetically modified foods; debating biotechnology. edited by Michael Ruse, David Castle. Prometheus Bks. 2002 355p il $20   **363.1**
1. Agricultural biotechnology 2. Farm produce 3.

Food -- Biotechnology 4. Genetically modified foods
ISBN 1-57392-996-4
LC 2002-70510

In this collection of essays the first section focuses on "the history and the science of genetically modified foods. The next section focuses on the morality of modifying organisms for human use. . . . Succeeding sections include articles discussing religious attitudes toward genetically modified food, legal issues involving patenting and environmental damage, risk assessment, and possible environmental threats and benefits." Publisher's note

Includes bibliographical references and index

363.17   Hazardous materials

Iversen, Kristen

★ **Full** body burden; growing up in the nuclear shadow of Rocky Flats. Kristen Iversen. Crown Publishers 2012 400 p. ill. $25.00   **363.17**
1. Nuclear weapons plants -- Health aspects -- Colorado 2. Plutonium -- Health aspects -- Colorado 3. Radioactive pollution -- Colorado -- Jefferson County 4. Radioactive waste sites -- Cleanup -- Colorado
ISBN 030795563X; 9780307955630
LC 2011045902

This book is about [t]he Rocky Flats nuclear weapons plant near Denver [that] began production in 1953; within four years, the plutonium factory had its first major accident, the first of many. In fact, by the end of its forty-year run, the plant would gain notoriety as [the most contaminated site in America.] Kristen [Iversen], the author . . . , grew up in the radioactive shadow of this secret facility and she witnessed at close quarters the disastrous effects of its activities. Here, she combines . . . personal experiences and . . . investigative reporting to expose [the U.S.] government's betrayal of its responsibility to its citizens.s (Barnes & Noble)

363.19   Product hazards

Nestle, Marion

★ **Safe** food; bacteria, biotechnology, and bioterrorism. University of Calif. Press 2003 350p il $27.50   **363.19**
1. Bioterrorism 2. Food -- Biotechnology 3. Food -- Safety measures 4. Food adulteration and inspection 5. Terrorism
ISBN 0-520-23292-5
LC 2002-27172

The author "argues that ensuring safe food involves more than washing hands or cooking food to higher temperatures. It involves politics. When it comes to food safety, billions of dollars are at stake, and industry, government, and consumers collide over issues of values, economics, and political power—and not always in the public interest." Publisher's note

Includes bibliographical references

363.2   Police services

Bell, Suzanne

★ **Encyclopedia** of forensic science; foreword by Barry A.J. Fisher; preface by Robert C. Shaler. rev ed; Facts on File 2008 402p il $85   **363.2**

1. Forensic sciences   2. Forensic sciences -- Encyclopedias 3. Reference books

ISBN 978-0-8160-6799-2; 0-8160-6799-6

LC 2008-5862

"In addition to explaining the science of forensics, Bell . . . reviews various disciplines related to forensic science, among them entomology, odontology, and psychology. Other entries cover professional organizations, government agencies, famous names in the field of forensics, evidence, and legal issues. . . . With its clear language and brief entries [this] volume will provide readers with a nuts-and-bolts understanding of the real world of forensic science." Booklist [review of 2003 edition]

Includes bibliographical references

Brenner, John C.

★ **Forensic** science; an illustrated dictionary. CRC Press 2003 286p $79.95   **363.2**

1. Criminal investigation   2. Forensic sciences   3. Forensic sciences -- Dictionaries   4. Reference books

ISBN 0-8493-1457-7

LC 2003-55804

"In this dictionary of over 2,000 forensic words and terms . . . the terms are drawn from criminal and forensic disciplines and include court and legal terms. Definitions, ranging from a few sentences to a paragraph, are complete but neither so technical nor scientific that novices will have trouble understanding the definition. When a definition incorporates a large number of subdefinitions, all are included under the umbrella term for ease in finding. . . . A quick reference for forensic scientists and a good source of information for armchair enthusiasts." Choice

Includes bibliographical references

Englert, Rod

Blood secrets; a forensic expert reveals how blood spatter tells the crime scene's story. [by] Rod Englert, with Kathy Passero; foreword by Ann Rule. Thomas Dunne Books 2010 286p il $25.99; ebook $12.99   **363.2**

1. Blood   2. Criminal investigation   3. Evidence, Criminal   4. Forensic hematology   5. Forensic sciences

ISBN 978-0-312-56400-1; 0-312-56400-7; 978-1-4299-2921-9 ebook; 1-4299-2921-9 ebook

LC 2009-40294

"Englert deftly balances real-life examples and detailed scientific analysis, giving readers a richer understanding of this developing avenue of forensic science." Publ Wkly

Includes bibliographical references

Geary, Rick

J. Edgar Hoover; a graphic biography. Hill and Wang 2008 102p il $16.95   **363.2**

1. Biographical graphic novels   2. FBI officials   3.

Graphic novels

ISBN 978-0-8090-9503-2; 0-8090-9503-3

LC 2007-25193

Rick Geary has written a biography of J. Edgar Hoover, who served in the federal government for 55 years and under eight presidents, most notably as director of the Federal Bureau of Investigation. He was appointed to that position on May 10, 1924. Geary covers Hoover's sometimes controversial career, including his refusal to involve the FBI directly into investigations of crimes against civil rights workers and the 1963 bombing in Birmingham, Alabama, and the bureau's investigation of Martin Luther King, Jr. He tastefully discusses Hoover's undercover sexual life.

"As solid, thrilling and informative a guide to the life of the America's most powerful authoritarian as one could ask for." Kirkus

Kessler, Ronald

The **FBI**; inside the world's most powerful law enforcement agency. Pocket Bks. 1993 492p il hardcover o.p. pa $6.99   **363.2**

ISBN 0-671-78658-X pa

LC 93-5207

"Kessler details how the bureau solved prominent cases such as Watergate and the World Trade Center bombing; covered up many detrimental internal cases; and introduced and employed ultra-modern forensic technologies for criminal investigations." Libr J

Includes bibliographical references

Neme, Laurel A.

Animal investigators; how the world's first wildlife forensics lab is solving crimes and saving endangered species. foreword by Richard Leakey. Scribner 2009 230p il $25   **363.2**

1. Endangered species   2. Endangered species -- United States   3. Forensic sciences   4. Poaching   5. Wild animal trade   6. Wildlife conservation   7. Wildlife crimes

ISBN 978-1-4165-5056-3; 1-4165-5056-9

LC 2008-56004

"Illegal wildlife trafficking is worth an estimated $20 billion a year. That makes it the third most lucrative criminal activity, coming in just behind drug and human trafficking and, incredibly, ahead of arms smuggling. . . . Animal Investigators documents this black market in unflinching and often depressing detail. But the book is more than just a journey into the criminal underworld, a litany of dismal statistics or a roll-call of cowardly, greedy intermediaries. Instead, Laurel A. Neme centres her book on a more inspiring place: the US Fish and Wildlife Service Forensics Lab in Ashland, Oregon, the world's only laboratory dedicated to solving crimes against wildlife." New Sci

Includes bibliographical references

Theoharis, Athan G.

★ The **FBI** & American democracy; a brief critical history. University Press of Kansas 2004 195p il $24.95   **363.2**

1. Abuse of administrative power -- United States -- History   2. Criminal investigation -- United States -- History   3. Intelligence service -- United States --

History 4. Internal security -- United States -- History
ISBN 0-7006-1345-5

LC 2004-6077

"This clear, thoughtful presentation is strongly recommended for both public libraries and academic institutions."
Libr J

Includes bibliographical references

Wagner, E. J.

The **science** of Sherlock Holmes; from Baskerville Hall to the Valley of Fear, the real forensics behind the great detective's greatest cases. Wiley 2006
244p il $24.95; pa $16.95 **363.2**
1. Criminal investigation 2. Forensic sciences 3. Forensic sciences -- History 4. Holmes, Sherlock (Fictitious character)
ISBN 0-471-64879-5; 978-0-471-64879-6; 0-470-12823-2 pa; 978-0-470-12823-7 pa

LC 2005-22236

The author discusses forensic science in Arthur Conan Doyle's stories of the 'consulting detective' Sherlock Holmes. She compares Holmes's investigative techniques to those used in actual cases such as the killing of Lizzie Borden's parents in 1892, the 1902 murder of Joseph Browne Elwell, and the disappearance of Dr. George Parkman in 1849.

This book "will intrigue readers with incredible stories and amazing tales from the early days of forensic science." Christ Sci Monit

Includes bibliographical references

★ Encyclopedia of law enforcement. Sage Publications 2005 3v set $310 **363.2**
1. Law enforcement -- Encyclopedias 2. Reference books
ISBN 0-7619-2649-6

LC 2004-21803

Sullivan "has edited an outstanding set on law enforcement issues." Choice

Includes bibliographical references

The FBI: a comprehensive reference guide; edited by Athan G. Theoharis with Tony G. Poveda, Susan Rosenfeld, Richard Gid Powers. Oryx Press 1999 409p $89.95 **363.2**
ISBN 0-89774-991-X

LC 98-26642

This work provides a "chronological history of and guide to the FBI that includes information about the facilities, the organizational structure, and biographies of key individuals. This reference source will not only please FBI enthusiasts, but it also serves as an excellent resource for those interested in U.S. history, criminal justice, and American culture. Also included is an extensive chronology of key events, a subject index, and an authoritative bibliography." Am Libr

From the secret files of J. Edgar Hoover; edited with commentary by Athan Theoharis. Dee, I.R. 1991
370p $24.95; pa $19.90 **363.2**
1. Anticommunist movements 2. FBI officials 3. Internal security -- United States 4. Subversive activities
ISBN 0-929587-67-7; 1-56663-017-7 pa

LC 91-3478

After a history of the Federal Bureau of Investigation, the first section of the book "presents selected files examining the alleged and real sexual indiscretions of JFK, Robert Kennedy, Eleanor Roosevelt, and Martin Luther King Jr. . . . Subsequent chapters examine the FBI's 'investigative' techniques, its relationship with Presidents and the McCarthy committee, and the uses of public relations and the role of the director." Libr J

363.25 Detection of crime (Criminal investigation)

Conklin, Barbara Gardner

Encyclopedia of forensic science; a compendium of detective fact and fiction. [by] Barbara Gardner Conklin, Robert Gardner, and Dennis Shortelle. Oryx Press 2002 329p il $64.95 **363.25**
1. Criminal investigation 2. Criminal investigation -- Encyclopedias 3. Forensic sciences -- Encyclopedias 4. Reference books
ISBN 1-57356-170-3

LC 2001-36638

This "illustrates the various ways that evidence can be extracted from a crime scene (e.g., ballistics, toxicology). . . . Though events in Great Britain and France are covered, the book's 85 entries focus on 19th-and 20th-century America. . . . Both famous and infamous people are listed, but what makes this book different and interesting is the inclusion of novelists (e.g., Patricia Cornwell, Jeffery Deaver, and Sir Arthur Conan Doyle) and their characters, who use forensics to solve crimes. . . . This is a solid resource." Libr J

Includes bibliographical references

Lee, Henry C.

Blood evidence; how DNA is revolutionizing the way we solve crimes. [by] Henry C. Lee, Frank Tirnady. Perseus Bks. 2003 xxx, 418p $26 **363.25**
1. DNA fingerprinting 2. Forensic sciences
ISBN 0-7382-0602-4

LC 2002-105970

"This volume is an excellent introduction to the science and use of DNA analysis." Publ Wkly

Includes bibliographical references

Weiner, Tim

Enemies; the history of the FBI at war. Tim Weiner. 1st ed. Random House 2011 537 p. (alk. paper) $30 **363.25**
1. Espionage -- United States -- History -- 20th century 2. Historical literature 3. United States -- Politics & government -- 20th century
ISBN 9780679643890; 9781400067480

LC 2011005353

This book, delivers an . . . often frightening history of what has been, in effect, America's secret police. The history of the FBI is easily divided into two periods: the J. Edgar Hoover period and after. In 1924, before he was 30, Hoover took over a tiny, tawdry Bureau and built it into a fearsome empire he ruled as a personal fiefdom until his death in 1972. . . . Weiner focuses on the FBI's activities investigating and attempting to prevent subversion and terrorism and writes little about the Bureau's pursuit of gangsters and white-collar criminals, which has taken up far fewer resources than the public supposes. A major theme is the difference between investigations intended to support criminal prosecutions and those intended to disrupt potential subversive activity. (Kirkus)

363.28   Services of special kinds of security and law enforcement agencies

Mackay, James A.

   Allan Pinkerton; the first private eye. {by} James Mackay. Wiley 1997 256p il $35   **363.28**

    1. Biography, Individual 2. Private investigators
    ISBN 0-471-19415-8

                       LC 97-21271

   "Though Pinkerton started the first U.S. detective agency after successfully uncovering a counterfeit ring, little was known about him. The author does an excellent job of tracing Pinkerton's early life and his arrival in the United States from Scotland. Then he examines better-known aspects of Pinkerton's career—his part in Lincoln's train ride through Baltimore, investigation of the Confederate spy Rose Greenhow, and association with Gen. George McClellan, his mentor and hero." Libr J

   Includes bibliographical references

363.3   Other aspects of public safety

Maclean, John N.

   Fire and ashes; on the front lines of American wildfire. Holt & Co. 2003 238p il map $25; pa $14   **363.3**

    1. Wildfires
    ISBN 0-8050-7212-8; 0-8050-7591-7 pa

                      LC 2002-38704

   "This work tells of two infernos: a 1999 conflagration in Nevada and a 1953 case of arboreal arson in California that took 15 lives when the fire exhibited unexpected behavior. . . . Careful in analysis, Maclean turns visceral when imparting the sudden terror of life-ending flames, or, as for a survivor of the 1949 Mann Gulch disaster whom he visits, a life-searing whirlwind. A solid choice that will be in demand, particularly during the West's summer fire season." Booklist

363.31   Censorship

Green, Jonathon

   ★ The **encyclopedia** of censorship; [by] Jonathon Green, Nicholas J. Karolides. rev ed; Facts on File 2005 xxii, 698p $85   **363.31**

    1. Censorship -- Encyclopedias 2. Reference books
    ISBN 0-8160-4464-3

                    LC 2004-53211

   "The crowded roster of those who have been affected by censorship, as well as the books, films, and other works attacked, are found in these . . . pages. Controversies that have arisen over the years are given historical context; highly valuable national wrap-ups treat the culture, law, and predominant trends of diverse lands." Libr J

   Includes bibliographical references

363.32   Social conflict

Allison, Graham T.

   Nuclear terrorism; the ultimate preventable catastrophe. [by] Graham Allison. Times Books\Henry Holt 2004 263p il $24   **363.32**

    1. Nuclear terrorism -- United States -- Prevention 2. Nuclear warfare 3. Terrorism
    ISBN 0-8050-7651-4

                    LC 2004-47427

   "Allison's comprehensive but accessible treatment of this vital subject is a major contribution to public understanding." N Y Times Book Rev

   Includes bibliographical references

Anderson, Sean

   Historical dictionary of terrorism; [by] Sean K. Anderson, with Stephen Sloan. 3rd ed; Scarecrow Press 2009 lxxvi, 800p $115   **363.32**

    1. Reference books 2. Terrorism 3. Terrorism -- Dictionaries
    ISBN 978-0-8108-5764-3; 0-8108-5764-2

                    LC 2009-3226

   "The dictionary encompasses individuals, groups, events, doctrines, and concepts such as Power law, which is the mathematical relation between the numbers and intensity of events. . . . This is an accurate, objective, and clearly written resource that will be useful in public and academic libraries." Booklist

   Includes bibliographical references (p. 713-798)

Aust, Stefan

   Baader-Meinhof; the inside story of the R.A.F. translated from the German by Anthea Bell. Rev ed; Oxford University Press 2009 xxi, 457p il $29.95   **363.32**

    1. Terrorism
    ISBN 978-0-19-537275-5; 0-19-537275-1

                    LC 2008-49401

   "The quintessential radical leftist terrorist group, founded in 1970 and eventually known as the Red Army Faction, Baader-Meinhof was responsible for 34 deaths in Germany over a 30-year period. . . . Exhaustively detailing the group's exploits from 1970 until the prison suicides of the leaders in 1977, Aust offers fascinating insights into both the spectacular and the mundane aspects of life in a terrorist cadre." Libr J

Baker, Stewart A.

   Skating on stilts; why we aren't stopping tomorrow's terrorism. Hoover Institution Press 2010 370p $19.95   **363.32**

    1. Right of privacy 2. Terrorism
    ISBN 978-0-8179-1154-6

                    LC 2010-20763

Baker "makes a persuasive case against the privacy absolutists." Los Angeles Times

Includes bibliographical references

Bobbitt, Philip

Terror and consent; the wars for the twenty-first century. Alfred A. Knopf 2008 672p il $35 **363.32**

1. Terrorism 2. Terrorism -- Government policy -- United States 3. United States -- Foreign relations -- 2001-

ISBN 1-4000-4243-7; 978-1-4000-4243-2

LC 2007-34194

The author examines "the relationship between the emergent constitutional order and the emergence of modern 'market state terrorism,' which, mirroring the market state and availing itself of the same technological advances, may be lethal enough to pose an existential threat to the very possibility of government by consent of the governed." Booklist

Includes bibliographical references

Burns, Vincent

★ **Terrorism**; a documentary and reference guide. [by] Vincent Burns and Kate Dempsey Peterson; foreword by James K. Kallstrom. Greenwood Press 2005 xxxvii, 293p il $75 **363.32**

1. Terrorism

ISBN 0-313-33213-4

LC 2005-3390

This is a "volume of 70 documents, some never before in print, pertaining to terrorism and the US. Readings include speeches, policy statements, letters, reports, and laws. . . . An easy-to-use resource that is full of pertinent information, this volume should be read all the way from the introduction . . . to the resources section." Choice

Includes bibliographical references

Combs, Cindy C.

★ **Encyclopedia** of terrorism; [by] Cindy C. Combs and Martin Slann. Rev ed; Facts on File 2007 478p il map $95 **363.32**

1. Reference books 2. Terrorism 3. Terrorism -- Encyclopedias

ISBN 0-8160-6277-3; 978-0-8160-6277-5

LC 2006-15853

This encyclopedia provides articles on "the events, people, organizations, and places that have played a major role in international terrorism. Each entry is placed within its . . . historical context to help readers understand the wide-ranging motivations behind terrorist actions." Publisher's note

Includes bibliographical references

Dershowitz, Alan M.

★ **Preemption**; a knife that cuts both ways. W.W. Norton 2006 348p il $24.95 **363.32**

1. Civil rights 2. Military art and science 3. Preemption 4. Preemptive attack (Military science) 5. Violence -- Prevention

ISBN 0-393-06012-8

LC 2005-27728

The author "examines preemptive war, preventative detention, and restrictions on dangerous speech, and claims that in the absence of general legal principles (or even a healthy debate) about preemptive action, society's current trend away from deterrence and toward prevention (as accelerated by the 'war on terrorism') threatens longstanding notions of individual liberty and state sovereignty. . . . This book is an academic and accessible framing of an important debate." Booklist

Includes bibliographical references

Dickey, Christopher

Securing the city; inside America's best counterterror force--the NYPD. Simon & Schuster 2009 321p $26 **363.32**

1. Civil rights 2. Intelligence service agents 3. Law enforcement -- Public opinion 4. Local government officials 5. Police -- New York (N.Y.) 6. Police officials 7. Terrorism 8. Terrorism -- Prevention

ISBN 978-1-4165-5240-6; 1-4165-5240-5

LC 2008-43085

"Vivid and thought-provoking. . . . The general reader can enjoy a book that has the pace and drama of a thriller, and for the specialist, . . . there is much to ponder." Economist

Includes bibliographical references

Elshtain, Jean Bethke

Just war against terror; the burden of American power in a violent world. Basic Books 2003 240p $23; pa $14 **363.32**

1. Islamic fundamentalism 2. Just war doctrine 3. September 11 Terrorist Attacks, 2001 4. Terrorism 5. Terrorism -- United States 6. War on terrorism 7. World politics -- 21st century

ISBN 0-465-01910-2; 0-465-01911-0 pa

LC 2002-154549

"While this volume is not a radical departure from the abundance of post-September 11 books, it presents well the moral case for U.S. military engagement in the world and gives credence to those who advocate the use of force as a response to terrorism." Publ Wkly

Includes bibliographical references

Harris, Shane

The **watchers**; the rise of America's surveillance state. Penguin Press 2010 418p il $27.95; pa $17 **363.32**

1. Intelligence service -- United States 2. National security -- United States 3. Terrorism 4. Terrorism -- United States -- Prevention

ISBN 978-1-59420-245-2; 978-0-14-311890-9 pa

LC 2009-37205

The author examines the development of domestic surveillance programs in the United States intended to prevent terrorist attacks.

"A sharply written, wise analysis of the complex mashup of electronic sleuthing, law, policy and culture." Kirkus

Includes bibliographical references

Herridge, Catherine

The **next** wave; on the hunt for al Qaeda's American recruits. Crown Forum 2011 258p il $25 **363.32**

1. Islamic fundamentalism 2. Muslims -- United States

3. Terrorism -- Religious aspects 4. Terrorists
ISBN 978-0-307-88525-8; 0-307-88525-9

LC 2010-53585

A "report on a new generation of terrorists and the American-born Islamic cleric Anwar al-Awlaki, who has inspired many of them to commit violent acts. Now believed to be in Yemen, al-Awlaki was targeted for killing by the U.S. government in 2010. He is linked to three of the 9/11 hijackers, the massacre at Foot Hood, the attempted Christmas Day 2009 bombing and the cargo printer plot in October 2010. Drawing on documents and interviews, the author shows how the charismatic al-Awlaki has become a leading al-Qaeda propagandist, using the Internet to recruit alienated American youths, many newly arrived in America, to join the terrorist cause. . . . A sobering view of why the 9/11 nightmare continues a decade later. " Kirkus

Includes bibliographical references

Kronenwetter, Michael

★ **Terrorism**: a guide to events and documents. Greenwood Press 2004 298p il $55   **363.32**
1. Terrorism
ISBN 0-313-32578-2

LC 2004-6619

"Kronenwetter's book is seminal to an understanding of terrorism. Honest, insightful, and easily understood, his book articulates the core ideals of terrorism and expertly presents its philosophical motivations within a historical context." Choice

Includes bibliographical references

Merriman, John M.

The **dynamite** club; how a bombing in fin-de-siecle Paris ignited the age of modern terror. Houghton Mifflin Co. 2009 259p il map $26   **363.32**
1. Anarchism -- France -- History 2. Anarchism and anarchists 3. Anarchists 4. Bombings 5. Terrorism 6. Terrorism -- History
ISBN 978-0-618-55598-7; 0-618-55598-6

LC 2008-49470

"Because he neither makes excuses for anyone nor takes simplistic ideological swipes, Merriman is a solid guide through these dark back lanes of European history." Houston Chron

Includes bibliographical references

Pedahzur, Ami

The **Israeli** secret services and the struggle against terrorism. Columbia University Press 2009 215p il $27.50   **363.32**
1. Counterterrorism -- Israel 2. Intelligence service -- Israel 3. Secret service -- Israel 4. Terrorism
ISBN 978-0-231-14042-3; 0-231-14042-8

LC 2008-25949

"Dividing the potential responses to terrorism into four categories (defensive, reconciliatory, criminal justice and war), the author tracks the development of an Israeli war model and demonstrates that rather than sending terrorists running, the approach leads to an escalating cycle of terrorism, citing many examples in which Israels elimination of threats has created the impetus for more violence. . . . While Pedahzur's style leans toward the dryly academic, his

insights are so well reasoned and relevant that the pages almost turn themselves." Publ Wkly

Includes bibliographical references

★ **Homeland security**; edited by Norris Smith and Lynn M. Messina. H.W. Wilson Co 2004 197p il $50   **363.32**
1. Emergency management 2. National security -- United States 3. Terrorism 4. Terrorism -- Prevention
ISBN 0-8242-1033-6

LC 2003-70366

"This book looks at the Office of Homeland Security, evaluating its effectiveness and its impact on civil liberties, law enforcement, and Americans' peace of mind." Publisher's note

Includes bibliographical references

The **Sage** encyclopedia of terrorism; editor, Gus Martin. 2nd ed; SAGE Publications 2011 xxv, 689p il $125   **363.32**
1. Reference books 2. Terrorism -- Encyclopedias
ISBN 978-1-4129-8016-6

LC 2011009896

This encyclopedia explores the impact of terrorism on economics, public health, religion and pop culture, and also includes details of ethical issues and debates relating to terrorism.

363.325   Terrorism

Graff, Garrett M.

The **threat** matrix; Garrett M. Graff. 1st ed. Little, Brown and Company 2011 666 p. ill. **363.325**
1. Intelligence service -- United States 2. Terrorism -- United States -- Prevention 3. War on Terrorism, 2001-2009
ISBN 9780316068611

LC 2010053237

In this book, author Garrett M. "Graff shows how . . . [Former FBI Director Louis Freeh's] leadership slowed intelligence operations preceding 9/11 and in what ways the agency still suffers from his tenure. Graff . . . track[s] the ways that the FBI adapted as terrorism changed. He takes seriously even ridiculous threats, such as an absurd letter penned by a Filipino teenager and the realization that the FBI lacked a file on the Japanese cult that released sarin gas in Tokyo even though they were listed in the Manhattan phone book. Some episodes . . . [include a] discussion of the events behind a July 2001 memo's theory that terrorists were in the U.S. training at civil aviation facilities. Graff's focus, though it covers a time span from J. Edgar Hoover's death to the present day, rests particularly on the massive intelligence failures in the 10 years preceding 9/11, and after." (Publishers Weekly)

McDermott, Terry

The **hunt** for KSM; inside the pursuit and takedown of the real 9/11 mastermind, Khalid Sheikh Mohammed. Terry McDermott and Josh Meyer. Little, Brown and Co. 2012 350 p.   **363.325**
1. September 11 Terrorist Attacks, 2001 2. Terrorism

-- United States -- Prevention 3. Terrorists -- Islamic countries

ISBN 9780316186599

LC 2011041533

This book follows [t]he cat-and-mouse game between American investigators and Khalid Sheikh Mohammed, architect of the 9/11 attacks and other terrorist spectaculars. . . . Journalists [Terry] McDermott . . . and [Josh] Meyer (the L.A. Timess chief terrorism reporter) present a police procedural starring an FBI agent, Frank Pellegrino, Port Authority detective Matt Besheer, and the inter-agency anti-terrorism experts who tracked KSM and his confederates for a decade before his 2003 capture. . . . The author's . . . profile of Khalid Sheikh Mohammed depicts a resourceful, charismatic man . . . and paints a . . . portrait of the workaday terrorist life of fund-raising, recruitment, bomb-rigging, and general plotting, all carried out while dodging a global manhunt. (Publishers Weekly)

Theoharis, Athan G.

Abuse of power; Athan G. Theoharis. Temple University Press 2011 xvi, 212p (hbk: alk. paper) $29.95   **363.325**
1. Cold War 2. Electronic surveillance 3. Intelligence service 4. September 11 Terrorist Attacks, 2001 5. Wiretapping

ISBN 9781439906644; 9781439906651; 9781439906668

LC 2010042416

In this book, "[Athan G.] Theoharis continues his investigation of U.S. government surveillance and historicizes the 9/11 response. Criticizing the U.S. government's secret activities and policies during periods of 'unprecedented crisis,' he recounts how presidents and FBI officials exploited concerns about foreign-based internal security threats. Drawing on information sequestered until recently in FBI records, Theoharis shows how these secret activities in the World War II and Cold War eras expanded FBI surveillance powers and, in the process, eroded civil liberties without substantially advancing legitimate security interests. . . . [T]his . . . book speaks to the costs and consequences of still-secret post-9/11 surveillance programs and counterintelligence failures [and] . . . makes the case that the abusive surveillance policies of the Cold War years were repeated in the government's responses to the September 11 attacks." (Publisher's note)

Willman, David

The **mirage** man; David Willman. Bantam Books 2011 xiii, 448p ill.   **363.325**

ISBN 9780553807752; 9780345530219

LC 2011006232

This book "offers . . . [an] account of the . . . FBI investigation into the 'anthrax attacks' as the [George W.] Bush administration strove to use the public panic to strengthen their case to go to war, while the culprit was, in all likelihood, a military microbiologist named Bruce Ivins. . . . [It] traces Ivins's unhappy life, how he endured childhood abuse and privation to become a successful scientist only to find his life unraveling as a result of his . . . obsessions and fixations with women. . . . [David] Willman pivots to focus on the flawed investigation . . . and how . . . Ivins benefited both financially and professionally from the public paranoia about anthrax as

his research into an anthrax vaccine became a national priority." (Publishers Weekly)

363.33   Control of firearms

Henderson, Harry

★ **Gun** control; rev ed; Facts on File 2005 316p il $45   **363.33**
1. Gun control

ISBN 0-8160-5660-9

LC 2004-50651

This examination of the history and issues of gun control "includes an annotated bibliography, chronology, glossary, biographical listing, a chapter on how to research the topic, laws and court cases, and a list of applicable organizations and agencies." Publisher's note

Sugarmann, Josh

Every handgun is aimed at you; the case for banning handguns. New Press (NY) 2001 238p il $24.95; pa $14.95   **363.33**
1. Gun control 2. Gun control -- United States 3. Pistols -- United States

ISBN 1-56584-629-X; 1-56584-705-9 pa

LC 00-60547

"The book begins with a brief historical survey that argues . . . that handguns did not become widespread in the U.S. until the Civil War, when the introduction of the Colt pistol and westward expansion fueled gun sales and deaths. But most of the book's focus is on present-day issues such as crime and self-defense." Publ Wkly

Utter, Glenn H.

Encyclopedia of gun control and gun rights. Oryx Press 2000 xxiii, 376p il $77.95   **363.33**
1. Firearms -- Law and legislation -- United States 2. Gun control 3. Gun control -- United States 4. Weapons

ISBN 1-57356-172-X

LC 99-43449

A "listing of the court cases, personalities, laws, and groups involved in the regulation of guns. The book begins with an essay on the issues in the gun-control battle and a short guide to the court cases and groups involved, placing them in the opposing camps. The entries, which are balanced and well written, include photographs and charts." Libr J

Includes bibliographical references (p. 361-364) and index

Guns in American society; an encyclopedia of history, politics, culture, and the law. edited by Gregg Lee Carter. ABC-CLIO 2002 2v set $185 **363.33**
1. Firearms ownership -- United States 2. Gun control 3. Gun control -- United States 4. Violence -- United States

ISBN 1-576-07268-1

LC 2002-14682

"The entries range widely, including many individuals past and present, both in and out of government. A variety of federal and state court cases are covered, as are the ordinances promoted by gun control advocates or opponents, and good background is provided on many issues. . . . [This encyclopedia] should serve as the standard reference on many aspects of guns, gun ownership, and gun control in the United States." Libr J

363.34   Disasters

De Villiers, Marq

The **end**; natural disasters, manmade catastrophes, and the future of human survival. Thomas Dunne Books/St. Martin's Press 2008 362p il $26.95   **363.34**
1. Disaster relief 2. Human ecology 3. Natural disasters
ISBN 978-0-312-36569-1; 0-312-36569-1
LC 2008-39096
The author presents an analysis of humanity's role in catastrophic natural disasters to consider whether or not such threats are increasing and how they can be managed.
"This book effectively summarizes the latest scientific thought on disasters, and de Villiers's entrancing prose will hook even the most reluctant reader." Libr J
Includes bibliographical references

Downey, Tom

The **last** men out; life on the edge at Rescue 2 firehouse. H. Holt 2004 300p il $25; pa $15 **363.34**
1. Fire fighters 2. World Trade Center terrorist attack, 2001
ISBN 0-8050-7169-5; 0-8050-7844-4 pa
LC 2003-67770
"Downey's descriptions burn into the pages with searing intensity. Writing with verve and energy in a gritty style, he explores all extremes of the firemen's world, from triumphant moments of heroism to bitter tragedies." Publ Wkly

Halberstam, David

Firehouse. Hyperion 2002 201p $22.95; pa $14   **363.34**
1. Fire fighters 2. World Trade Center terrorist attack, 2001
ISBN 1-4013-0005-7; 0-7868-8851-2 pa
"A journalist's homage to firefighters, their values, their culture and their courage during the martyrdom imposed on the New York Fire Department by the catastrophe of the attack on the World Trade Center." N Y Times Bk Rev

Hemingway, Lorian

A **world** turned over; a killer tornado and the lives it changed forever. Simon & Schuster 2002 244p $23; pa $12   **363.34**
1. Tornadoes 2. Tornadoes -- Mississippi -- Jackson 3. Tornadoes -- Mississippi -- Jackson -- Psychological aspects
ISBN 0-684-85634-4; 0-7432-4767-1 pa
LC 2002-73346
"On March 3, 1966, a devastating tornado struck the Candlestick Shopping Center in South Jackson, Miss., flattening buildings and killing 14 people. Because her family had just moved away from their home across the road from the shopping center, Hemingway . . . missed the disaster. All her life she has been obsessed with it, however, and in 2000

she went back to learn about it from childhood friends who were there. . . . Hemingway skillfully draws the reader into the nightmare." Publ Wkly

Pilkey, Orrin H., 1934-

The **rising** sea; [by] Orrin H. Pilkey and Rob Young. Island Press/Shearwater Books 2009 203p il map $25.95   **363.34**
1. Coast changes 2. Coasts 3. Greenhouse effect 4. Ocean 5. Sea level
ISBN 978-1-59726-191-3; 1-59726-191-2
LC 2009-06152
"This book's title represents the most obvious effect of global warming: the incursion of ocean water onto land due to thermal expansion and, more ominously, the melting of mountain glaciers and polar ice sheets. This phenomenon is often dismissed as inconsequential (or even denied), but as the authors convincingly demonstrate with stories of distress at vulnerable locations (e.g., the Maldives), it is already ravaging coastlines directly and indirectly, helped by human intrusion. . . . This book offers a wealth of opportunities for further reading. Its greatest strength is the cogent, well-organized, layman-friendly narrative that makes up each chapter." Sci Books Films
Includes bibliographical references

Smith, Dennis

Report from ground zero; the story of the rescue efforts at the World Trade Center. Viking 2002 366p il maps $24.95; pa $14   **363.34**
1. Fire fighters 2. September 11 terrorist attacks, 2001 3. World Trade Center (New York, N.Y.) 4. World Trade Center terrorist attack, 2001
ISBN 0-670-03116-X; 0-452-28395-7 pa
LC 2002-19840
Based on his personal observations and interviews with other rescue workers, the author describes the efforts of the New York City Fire Department to rescue survivors of the September 11 attack on the World Trade Center.

Tougias, Mike

Ten hours until dawn; the true story of heroism and tragedy aboard the Can Do. [by] Michael Tougias. St. Martins Press 2005 322p il map $24.95 **363.34**
1. Blizzards 2. Rescue work 3. Shipwrecks
ISBN 0-312-33435-4
The author "delivers a well-researched, vividly written tale of brave men overwhelmed by the awesome forces of nature." Publ Wkly

Welky, David

The **thousand**-year flood; the Ohio-Mississippi disaster of 1937. University of Chicago Press 2011 355p il $27.50   **363.34**
1. Disaster relief 2. Floods -- Mississippi River 3. Floods -- Ohio River valley 4. New Deal, 1933-1939
ISBN 978-0-226-88716-6; 0-226-88716-2; 978-0-226-88718-0 ebook
LC 2011014875

"Vividly written and carefully documented, . . . [this book] masterfully brings a turning point in American history back to life." Wilson Quarterly

Includes bibliographical references

Zebrowski, Ernest

★ **Category** 5; the story of Camille, lessons unlearned from America's most violent hurricane. [by] Ernest Zebrowski & Judith A. Howard. University of Michigan Press 2005 276p il map $27.95 **363.34**

1. Hurricanes

ISBN 0-472-11525-1

LC 2005-28583

"Partly a narrative and partly a pondering of how people and authorities prepare for predictable risk, the work focuses on the areas devastated by the maelstrom: Plaquemines Parish, Louisiana; Mississippi's Gulf Coast; and faraway Nelson County, Virginia. . . . The authors sound a pessimistic note about society's short-term memory in their sobering, able history of Camille." Booklist

Includes bibliographical references

Zeilinga de Boer, Jelle

★ **Earthquakes** in human history; the far-reaching effects of seismic disruptions. [by] Jelle Zeilinga de Boer and Donald Theodore Sanders. Princeton University Press 2005 278p il maps $24.95 **363.34**

1. Earthquakes 2. Earthquakes -- History

ISBN 0-691-05070-8

LC 2004-40122

The authors provide "facts and insights on geologic processes and the effects of . . . natural disasters on the course of human history. Narratives on especially impactful earthquakes include events in the Holy Land, Ancient Greece, England, Portugal, Missouri, San Francisco, Japan, Peru and Chile, and Nicaragua. The influence of the earthquakes on religion, politics, economy, wars, and literature is portrayed in fascinating prose, embellished with carefully selected photos, drawings, and maps." Choice

Includes bibliographical references

363.37 Fire hazards

Golway, Terry

So others might live; a history of New York's bravest; the FDNY from 1700 to the present. Basic Bks. 2002 368p $27.50; pa $17 **363.37**

1. Fire extinction -- New York (State) -- New York -- History 2. Fire fighters -- New York (State) -- New York 3. Fire fighting

ISBN 0-465-02740-7; 0-465-02741-5 pa

The author describes the New York City Fire Department's "emergence from amateur bucket brigades into the beginnings of a specialized force and up to the present, never letting a memorable figure or vivid moment escape his narrative." Libr J

Includes bibliographical references (p. 357-360) and index

363.4 Controversies related to public morals and customs

Behr, Edward

Prohibition; thirteen years that changed America. Arcade Pub. 1996 262p il hardcover o.p. pa $13.95 **363.4**

1. Prohibition

ISBN 1-55970-394-6 pa

LC 96-24063

"This is an excellent and honest book that does not flinch at unpalatable facts." N Y Times Book Rev

Includes bibliographical references

Lerner, Michael A.

Dry Manhattan; Prohibition in New York City. Harvard University Press 2007 351p $28.95 **363.4**

1. Prohibition 2. Prohibition -- New York (N.Y.)

ISBN 978-0-674-02432-8; 0-674-02432-X

LC 2006-50885

This book is "in all important respects exemplary, a singularly useful and revealing contribution to our understanding of a time from which the nation probably never will recover." Washington Post Book World

Includes bibliographical references

Okrent, Daniel

★ **Last** call; the rise and fall of Prohibition, 1920-1933. Scribner 2010 468p $30 **363.4**

1. Drinking of alcoholic beverages 2. Drinking of alcoholic beverages -- United States -- History -- 20th century 3. Prohibition 4. Prohibition -- United States -- History -- 20th century

ISBN 978-0-7432-7702-0; 0-7432-7702-3

LC 2009-51127

"Okrent's style is bracing and wry, his research is vast and impressive and his insight is penetrating. Intoxicating." Kirkus

Includes bibliographical references

Watman, Max

Chasing the white dog; an amateur outlaw's adventures in moonshine. Simon & Schuster 2010 292p $25 **363.4**

1. Brewing 2. Distillation 3. Distilling, Illicit 4. Liquors 5. Sportswriters

ISBN 978-1-4165-7178-0; 1-4165-7178-7

LC 2009-24657

"No matter where the chase takes him, from policing a lobster pot full of boiling molasses to getting schnockered at a conference for hobby distillers, Watman is a hands-on, no-holds-barred participant. He gamely learns to race cars to absorb the moonshine/NASCAR culture, and sits through the trial of a group of large-scale bootleggers in a multistate investigation. He profiles local color like Daytona 500 winner Junior Johnson, onetime moonshiner, famous for inventing the 'bootleg turn' to outrun the feds; and 'whitecollar' distillers like George Stranahan in Colorado." PopMatters

363.45   Drug traffic

Chouvy, Pierre-Arnaud

   Opium; uncovering the politics of the poppy. Harvard University Press 2010 256p il map $27.95 **363.45**

   1. Drug traffic 2. Opium

   ISBN 0-674-05134-3; 978-0-674-05134-8

                  LC 2009-44012

   "Chouvy outlines the history of opium trafficking, beginning in ancient times when it was likely traded on the Silk Road. After eras in which Turkey, China and Southeast Asia played dominant roles in the market, recent data indicate that 93 percent of the world's poppy supply is grown in Afghanistan. While packed with meticulous details, the book is a bit hard to follow due to unfamiliar names, political factions and geographic locations. Chouvy achieves more clarity in his analysis of why the opium trade continues to thrive, explaining the strong correlation between war and drug economies. . . . He also explains how the United States has sometimes hampered its own efforts to suppress the drug trade, claiming the CIA has cooperated with international drug lords to gain influence and intelligence." Seattle Times

   Includes bibliographical references

Gibler, John

   To die in Mexico; dispatches from inside the drug war. City Lights Books 2011 218p pa $15.95 **363.45**

   1. Crime -- Mexico 2. Drug traffic

   ISBN 978-0-87286-517-4; 0-87286-517-7

                  LC 2011-02970

   The author "recounts an endless litany of violence that has exploded during the tenures of Carlos Salinas, Ernesto Zedillo, Vicente Fox and, especially, Felipe Calderon. The various drug cartels—the Gulf cartel, the Zetas, the Sinaloa Cartel, among others—have only grown stronger over the years. . . . Hence, drugs are big business, especially for the banks, who launder the spectacular profits. The corruption of organized crime has infiltrated every segment of Mexican society, as Gibler demonstrates here, visiting prisons and civic groups, who express an utter sense of hopelessness and despair. However, the author has found fighting spirits, such as young murdered men's mothers who show up bravely and demand a police reckoning; and the journalists mourning their murdered fellow colleagues at El Diario de Juarez. Gibler argues passionately to undercut this 'case study in failure.' . . . With legality, both U.S. and Mexican society could address real issues of substance abuse through education and public-health initiatives." Kirkus

   Includes bibliographical references

Schou, Nicholas

   Orange sunshine; the Brotherhood of Eternal Love and its quest to spread peace, love, and acid to the world. Thomas Dunne Books 2010 306p il $24.99 **363.45**

   1. Dissenters 2. Drug traffic 3. Narcotics dealers

   ISBN 978-0-312-55183-4; 0-312-55183-5

                  LC 2009-40284

   "Blue Cheer. Window Pane. Orange Sunshine. Maui Wowie. These were the brand names of the psychedelic counterculture of the 1960s and '70s, a culture led by the Brotherhood of Eternal Love. Chances are, if a brand of acid, pot or hashish was known to stoners, it first made its way into the underground market via the Brotherhood. Originally a marijuana-dealing motorcycle gang of toughs, the Brotherhood had a mass religious experience with LSD in 1965-they believed they'd found a lysergic shortcut to God. They resolved, under the charismatic leadership of John 'the Farmer' Griggs, whom Timothy Leary called 'the holiest man ever to live in this country,' to become apostles of acid with a mission to turn on the entire world. . . . A fascinating read for any audience and essential history for anyone interested in the roots of psychedelia." Kirkus

   Includes bibliographical references

363.46   Abortion

Palmer, Louis J.

   ★ **Encyclopedia** of abortion in the United States; [by] Louis J. Palmer, Jr. and Xueyan Z. Palmer. 2nd ed.; McFarland & Co. 2009 624p il $150 **363.46**

   1. Abortion -- Encyclopedias 2. Reference books

   ISBN 978-0-7864-3838-9; 0-7864-3838-X

                  LC 2008-31047

   "Ranging in length from a single paragraph to several pages, the A-to-Z entries define noteworthy events, significant figures, state and federal legislation, prochoice and prolife organizations, case specifics, abortion methods, and contraceptive devices. . . . This balanced, unblinking, and comprehensive subject reference makes complex legal details accessible to the lay reader." Libr J

   Includes bibliographical references

Press, Eyal

   ★ **Absolute** convictions; my father, a city, and the conflict that divided America. Henry Holt and Co. 2006 292p il map hardcover o.p. pa $15 **363.46**

   1. Abortion 2. Abortion providers 3. Gynecologists 4. Pro-life movement

   ISBN 0-8050-7731-6; 978-0-312-42657-6 pa; 0-312-42657-7 pa

                  LC 2005-34064

   The author "manages the extraordinary feat of bringing light to a political issue that for far too long has generated nothing but blistering heat." N Y Times Book Rev

   Includes bibliographical references

Reagan, Leslie J.

   When abortion was a crime; women, medicine, and law in the United States, 1867-1973. University of Calif. Press 1997 387p il hardcover o.p. pa $19.95 **363.46**

   1. Abortion 2. Women -- United States

   ISBN 0-520-21657-1 pa

                  LC 96-22568

   This is a history of abortion in the United States from its criminalization between 1860 and 1880 to Roe v. Wade in 1973

   "Important and original, vigorously written even down to the footnotes, {this book} manages with apparent ease to combine serious scholarship . . . and broad appeal." Atl Mon

   Includes bibliographical references

Rose, Melody

★ **Abortion**; a documentary and reference guide. Greenwood Press 2008 258p il $85   **363.46**
1. Abortion 2. Abortion -- United States -- History
ISBN 978-0-313-34032-1; 0-313-34032-3
LC 2007-37489
This "reference work explores the evolution of America's abortion debate in a . . . selection of over 40 primary documents by doctors, feminists, religious leaders, politicians, extremists, and judges from the 19th century to the present day." Publisher's note
Includes bibliographical references

Solinger, Rickie

Beggars and choosers; how the politics of choice shapes adoption, abortion, and welfare in the United States. Hill & Wang 2001 290p hardcover o.p. pa $14   **363.46**
1. Abortion 2. Abortion -- Social aspects -- United States 3. Pro-choice movement 4. Pro-choice movement -- United States 5. Women -- United States -- Social conditions -- 20th century 6. Women's rights 7. Women's rights -- United States
ISBN 0-8090-2860-3 pa
LC 2001-16652
"The juxtaposition of choice and class when considering women's reproductive rights makes for insightful reading." Libr J
Includes bibliographical references

Tribe, Laurence H.

Abortion: the clash of absolutes; new ed; Norton 1992 318p pa $12.95   **363.46**
1. Abortion
ISBN 0-393-30956-8
LC 93-111762
The author examines both pro-life and pro-choice arguments and analyzes major court and legislative decisions

Weddington, Sarah Ragle

A **question** of choice. Putnam 1992 306p il hardcover o.p. pa $15   **363.46**
1. Abortion 2. Feminists 3. Lawyers 4. Nonfiction writers 5. Presidential aides 6. Pro-choice activists 7. State legislators
ISBN 0-14-017798-1 pa
LC 92-14311
"Starting with her years at the University of Texas Law School at Austin, Weddington, the attorney who won Roe v. Wade, traces the history of her involvement with this . . . Supreme Court case and its aftermath." Libr J
Includes bibliographical references

Abortion wars; a half century of struggle, 1950-2000. edited by Rickie Solinger. University of Calif. Press 1998 413p hardcover o.p. pa $21.95   **363.46**
1. Abortion
ISBN 0-520-20952-4 pa
LC 97-12261

"A collection of 18 essays written by abortion providers, journalists, reproductive-rights activists, legal strategists, and philosophers. In the introduction the editor makes it clear that the book is 'unabashedly a pro-rights book.' . . . The time line alone is so valuable that it's practically worth the price of the book." SLJ

363.5   Housing

Loewen, James W.

★ **Sundown** towns; a hidden dimension of American racism. New Press 2005 562p il $29.95 **363.5**
1. African Americans -- Segregation 2. Cities and towns -- United States 3. Discrimination in housing 4. Discrimination in housing -- United States 5. Racism -- United States
ISBN 1-56584-887-X
LC 2005-43855
"This book is sure to become a landmark in several fields and a sure bet among Loewen's many fans." Publ Wkly
Includes bibliographical references

Satter, Beryl

Family properties; race, real estate, and the exploitation of Black urban America. Metropolitan Books 2009 495p il $30   **363.5**
1. African Americans -- Chicago (Ill.) 2. African Americans -- Housing -- Illinois -- Chicago 3. African Americans -- Relations with Jews 4. Discrimination in housing 5. Discrimination in housing -- Illinois -- Chicago 6. Housing policy -- Illinois -- Chicago 7. Lawyers 8. Social activists
ISBN 978-0-8050-7676-9; 0-8050-7676-X
LC 2008-33005
The author "leaps from the particulars of one man's story to become a panoramic retelling of the Chicago real-estate wars during a period when, after the postwar migration of Southern blacks, that city was the most segregated in the North." N Y Times (Late N Y Ed)
Includes bibliographical references

363.6   Public utilities and related services

Amery, Colin

★ **Vanishing** histories; 100 endangered sites from the World Monuments Watch. by Colin Amery, with Brian Curran; foreword by John Berendt; preface by Bonnie Burnham and Marilyn Perry. Abrams 2001 207p il maps $60   **363.6**
1. Cultural property -- Protection 2. Historic preservation 3. Historic sites 4. Historic sites -- Conservation and restoration 5. Monuments 6. Monuments -- Conservation and restoration
ISBN 0-8109-1435-2
LC 2001-22622
"The World Monuments Fund, which has been monitoring the state of precious architectural and artistic sites since 1965, established the World Monuments Watch in 1995 to heighten awareness of endangered cultural sites in the hope

of garnering the support necessary for their preservation. Architectural expert Amery and conservator Curran present the histories of 100 such monuments in a volume as notable for the beauty of its photographs as for the urgency of its message." Booklist

Farabee, Charles R.

National park ranger; an American icon. {by} Charles R. "Butch" Farabee Jr. Roberts Rinehart Publishers 2003 180p il pa $18.95 **363.6**

1. National parks and reserves -- United States 2. Park rangers -- United States -- History

ISBN 1-570-98392-5

LC 2003-1022

"In this study of the vocation of park ranger since Maryland's park caretakers in 1696 to the present day, former ranger Farabee not only explores a ranger's role but also touches on the establishment of the National Park Service, the introduction of women rangers, and early resource management. Readers will enjoy the abundance of archival photographs, ranger profiles, and numerous other features." Libr J

Includes bibliographical references

Powell, James Lawrence

Dead pool; Lake Powell, global warming, and the future of water in the west. University of California Press 2009 283p il map $27.50 **363.6**

1. Environmental policy -- Western States 2. Global warming -- Environmental aspects 3. Greenhouse effect 4. Water supply 5. Water-supply -- Western States

ISBN 978-0-520-25477-0; 0-520-25477-5

LC 2008-15854

"This is a well-written book about the management of the Colorado River and by simile, waters in the western US in general. In the first two-thirds of the work, Powell . . . covers the development of the Colorado River Storage Project by the Bureau of Reclamation. . . . The last third of the book discusses the implications of global warming for the Colorado River and, in particular, the miscalculations of the Bureau of Reclamation regarding the amount of water available in the system under the predicted higher temperatures." Choice

Includes bibliographical references

Simpson, John W.

Dam! water, power, politics, and preservation in Hetch Hetchy and Yosemite National Park. [by] John Warfield Simpson. Pantheon Books 2005 356p il maps $28.50 **363.6**

1. Environmentalism -- United States 2. Water resources development 3. Water supply 4. Water-supply -- California -- San Francisco

ISBN 0-375-42231-5

LC 2004-65016

The author "argues for the restoration of Yosemite's Hetch Hetchy Valley. . . . Simpson's research is exemplary, and he deftly explores this case study of the nexus of politics, business and the environment. And he's lyrical when recounting his trips to Yosemite and describing the transformative beauty of the wilderness area." Publ Wkly

363.7 Environmental problems

Achenbach, Joel

A hole at the bottom of the sea; the race to kill the BP oil gusher. Simon & Schuster 2011 276p $25.99; ebook $12.99 **363.7**

1. BP Deepwater Horizon Explosion and Oil Spill, 2010 2. Drilling platforms 3. Offshore oil well drilling 4. Oil spills

ISBN 978-1-4516-2534-9; 978-1-4516-2538-7 ebook

LC 2011-8104

The author "appears equally well-informed and comfortable discussing encounters between managers, engineers and roustabouts, and the effect of White House politics in Washington on oil-spill containment operations in the Gulf of Mexico. . . . In Achenbach's masterful hands, the story takes on fresh drama and meaning." Washington Post Book World

Includes bibliographical references and index.

Berners-Lee, Mike

How bad are bananas? the carbon footprint of everything. Greystone Books 2011 232p il pa $16.95 **363.7**

1. Carbon 2. Greenhouse effect

ISBN 978-1-55365-831-3 pa; 978-1-55365-832-0 ebook

Discusses the carbon footprint—the carbon emissions used to manufacture and transport—of everyday items, including paper bags and imported produce, and provides information to help build carbon considerations into everyday purchases.

"A book like this risks being preachy or overly serious, but Berners-Lee approaches his topics with humor and curiosity. He rarely advocates radical change. Rather, he gives readers information." Christ Sci Monit

Includes bibliographical references

Blatt, Harvey

America's environmental report card; are we making the grade? MIT Press 2004 277p il maps $27.95; pa $13.95 **363.7**

1. Environmental policy -- United States 2. Pollution -- United States

ISBN 0-262-02572-8; 0-262-52467-8 pa

LC 2004-40261

The author "breaks down environmental issues into their components, describing different aspects of the problem, offering solutions and suggesting a prognosis. . . . Frank but hopeful, serious but readable, this is an excellent environmental science primer." Publ Wkly

Includes bibliographical references

Blauvelt, Robert P.

Encyclopedia of pollution; [by] Alexander E. Gates and Robert P. Blauvelt. Facts on File 2011 2v il map set $170 **363.7**

1. Pollution 2. Pollution -- Encyclopedias 3. Reference books

ISBN 978-0-8160-7002-2

LC 2009048190

Bloom, Jonathan

American wasteland; how America throws away nearly half of its food (and what we can do about it) Da Capo Press 2010 360p il $26   **363.7**
1. Food industry 2. Food supply 3. Salvage 4. Waste (Economics)
ISBN 978-0-7382-1364-4
LC 2010-15075
"An eye-opening account of what used to be considered a sin—the willful waste of perfectly edible food. . . . An urgent, necessary book." Kirkus
Includes bibliographical references

Braasch, Gary

Earth under fire; how global warming is changing the world. Updated ed; University of California Press 2009 xxx, 267p il pa $24.95   **363.7**
1. Climate -- Environmental aspects 2. Greenhouse effect
ISBN 978-0-520-26025-2
"What sets Earth Under Fire apart from other books on the same topic are the inspiring photographs. These images are an effective tool that helps the reader understand what the implications of climate change are—for people, for other organisms, and for entire ecosystems." Sci Books Films
Includes bibliographical references

Carson, Rachel, 1907-1964

★ **Silent** spring; introduction by Linda Lear; afterword by Edward O. Wilson. 40th anniversary ed; Houghton Mifflin 2002 378p il   **363.7**
1. Pesticides -- Environmental aspects 2. Pesticides and wildlife
ISBN 0-618-24906-0 pa; 0-618-25305-X
In The silent spring, Carson "contended that the indiscriminate use of weed killers and insecticides constituted a hazard to wildlife and to human beings. Her provocative work inspired many subsequent environmental studies." Reader's Ency. 4th edition

Flannery, Tim F.

★ The **weather** makers; how man is changing the climate and what it means for life on Earth. [by] Tim Flannery. Atlantic Monthly Press 2006 357p il maps hardcover o.p. pa $15   **363.7**
1. Climate 2. Climatic changes 3. Global warming 4. Greenhouse effect
ISBN 0-8711-3935-9; 0-8021-4292-3 pa
LC 2005-52350
"This work is distinctive in its marriage of science to an act-now attitude and should energize environmentally minded readers." Booklist
Includes bibliographical references (p. 289-297)

Freudenburg, William R.

Blowout in the Gulf; the BP oil spill disaster and the future of energy in America. [by] William R. Freudenburg and Robert Gramling. MIT Press 2010 254p il $18.95   **363.7**
1. Drilling platforms 2. Offshore oil well drilling 3.

Oil spills
ISBN 978-0-262-01583-7
LC 2010-937510
The authors "set the deadly BP blowout within a technologically precise history of oil in America, from the first primitively constructed well on land to the development of offshore rigs, explaining that the Deepwater Horizon was actually a technical marvel—if only its operation hadn't been compromised. . . . Science, commerce, and the politics of oil are all newly illuminated here, accompanied by invaluable explanations of the risks of offshore drilling and a pragmatic look at the energy conundrums we now face." Booklist
Includes bibliographical references

Friedman, Thomas L.

★ **Hot,** flat, and crowded; why we need a green revolution--and how it can renew America. Farrar, Straus & Giroux 2008 438p il $27.95   **363.7**
1. Climate -- Environmental aspects 2. Climatic changes -- Government policy 3. Energy resources 4. Environmental movement 5. Environmental policy -- United States 6. Green movement 7. Renewable energy sources -- United States
ISBN 978-0-374-16685-4; 0-374-16685-4
LC 2008-930589
"Friedman's big, passionate, and solidly specific ecological primer, social manifesto, and realistic plan for a green revolution aimed at restoring America's greatness and securing a sustainable future should serve as a playbook for innovators and civic leaders." Booklist

George, Rose

★ The **big** necessity; the unmentionable world of human waste and why it matters. Metropolitan Books 2008 288p il $26   **363.7**
1. Feces 2. Hygiene 3. Sanitation 4. Sanitation -- History 5. Sewage 6. Sewage disposal
ISBN 978-0-8050-8271-5; 0-8050-8271-9
LC 2008-29999
The author "breaks the embarrassed silence over the economic, political, social and environmental problems of human waste disposal. . . . From the depths of the world's oldest surviving urban sewers in to Japan's robo-toilet revolution, George leads an intrepid, erudite and entertaining journey through the public consequences of this most private behavior." Publ Wkly
Includes bibliographical references

Gonzalez, Juan

Fallout; the environmental consequences of the World Trade Center collapse. New Press (NY) 2002 150p $20   **363.7**
1. Environmental health 2. Pollution 3. World Trade Center terrorist attack, 2001
ISBN 1-56584-754-7
LC 2002-72404
González discusses the pollution caused when the World Trade Center collapsed after the terrorist attacks on September 11, 2001. He believes that substances such as asbestos, lead, mercury, dioxins, furans, and diesel fuel were released into the surrounding environment

"This book is a tragic indictment of the breakdown of public trust when it was needed most." Libr J

Gore, Al

★ **Our** choice; a plan to solve the climate crisis. Rodale 2009 414p il map pa $26.99   **363.7**
1. Environmental policy 2. Environmental protection 3. Greenhouse effect 4. Human ecology
ISBN 978-1-59486-734-7; 1-59486-734-8

LC 2009-38291

The former vice president addresses key environmental issues while profiling and evaluating possible solutions.

This "is an inviting and momentous compendium of environmental discovery . . . that addresses one of the greatest threats our species has encountered with intelligence, knowledge, wisdom, and faith in human empowerment. This is a book that should be displayed and talked about everywhere." Booklist

★ An **inconvenient** truth; the planetary emergency of global warming and what we can do about it. Rodale 2006 325p il map pa $23.95   **363.7**
1. Ecology 2. Environmental policy -- United States 3. Environmental protection 4. Global warming 5. Greenhouse effect 6. Human ecology
ISBN 978-1-59486-567-1; 1-59486-567-1

LC 2006-926537

"Gore has put together a coherent account of a complex topic that Americans desperately need to understand. . . . By telling the story of climate change with striking clarity . . . Al Gore may have done for global warming what [Rachel Carson's] Silent Spring [1962] did for pesticides." N Y Rev Books

Grossman, Elizabeth

★ **High** tech trash; digital devices, hidden toxins, and human health. Island Press/Shearwater Books 2006 334p hardcover o.p. pa $21.95 **363.7**
1. Electronic apparatus and appliances 2. Electronic apparatus and appliances -- Environmental aspects 3. Refuse and refuse disposal 4. Waste electronic apparatus and appliances
ISBN 1-55963-554-1; 978-1-55963-554-7; 1-59726-190-4 pa; 978-1-59726-190-6 pa

LC 2006-4549

The author "traces the toxic substances (lead, mercury, phosphorus, brominated flame retardants, and others) used in digital devices, along with their health hazards. Each of the book's nine chapters has notes and references; there is also an appendix on how to recycle computers. . . . [Grossman] has made a valiant effort to consolidate the information that general, nontechnical readers interested in the subject . . . would find very useful." Sci Books Films
Includes bibliographical references

Hansen, James E.

Storms of my grandchildren; the truth about the coming climate catastrophe and our last chance to save humanity. [by] James Hansen; illustrations by Makiko Sato. Bloomsbury USA 2009 304p il $25   **363.7**
1. Climate -- Environmental aspects 2. Environmental

influence on humans 3. Greenhouse effect
ISBN 978-1-60819-200-7

LC 2009-44553

"Rich in invaluable insights into the geopolitics as well as the geophysics of climate change, Hansen's guaranteed-to-be-controversial manifesto is the most comprehensible, realistic, and courageous call to prevent climate change yet. It belongs in every library." Booklist
Includes bibliographical references

Hosansky, David

The **environment** A-Z. CQ Press 2000 320p il maps $58   **363.7**
1. Environmental policy -- Encyclopedias 2. Environmental sciences -- Encyclopedias 3. Reference books
ISBN 1-568-02583-1

LC 00-62163

"Covering mostly the last 30 years, with some treatment of earlier events when essential to provide perspective, the alphabetic entries include general issues and topics, federal agencies and laws, and individual persons . . . who have influenced environmental decisions. A few international bodies are included, and of course issues like global warming are of broader than national scope, but in these cases the emphasis is primarily on how U.S. policies relate to the agencies and issues. Most entries are one or two pages in length, and are clearly and concisely written." Am Ref Books Annu, 2002
Includes bibliographical references and index

Humes, Edward

Eco barons; the dreamers, schemers and millionaires who are saving our planet. Ecco 2009 367p $25.99   **363.7**
1. Conservationists 2. Environmentalists
ISBN 978-0-06-135029-0; 0-06-135029-X

"The millionaires of the subtitle are Doug Tompkins, who put Esprit clothing profits to work protecting Argentina's Patagonia; Roxanne Quimby, who used Burt's Bees cosmetics earnings to purchase vast wild lands in Maine; and Ted Turner, whose CNN fortune allowed him to become America's single largest landowner, with 15 immense ranches managed for native species. Others featured in the book get the job done through sheer tenacity. . . . Although too fast-paced for much nuance, this book is full of captivating facts and well-told tales of environmentalism's human side." Libr J

Hunter, Robert

Thermageddon: countdown to 2030. Arcade Pub. 2003 276p $24.95   **363.7**
1. Greenhouse effect
ISBN 1-55970-667-8

LC 2002-38349

This book "is a solid achievement by one of Canada's most important environmentalists." Quill & Quire
Includes bibliographical references

Jacobs, Chip

Smogtown; the lung-burning history of pollution in Los Angeles. [by] Chip Jacobs & William J. Kelly. Overlook Press 2008 384p il $26.95   **363.7**
1. Air pollution
ISBN 978-1-58567-860-0
"This friendly, accessible history should appeal to any American environmentalist." Publ Wkly
Includes bibliographical references

Jones, Van

The **green**-collar economy; how one solution can fix our two biggest problems. with Ariane Conrad. HarperOne 2008 237p $25.95; pa $14.99   **363.7**
1. Environmental policy -- United States   2. Environmental protection 3. Social policy -- United States
ISBN 978-0-06-165075-8; 0-06-165075-7; 978-0-06-165076-5 pa; 0-06-165076-5 pa
The author "argues that developing a sustainable energy industry in America would lessen our dependency on non-renewable and foreign energy sources, as well as provide local and well-paid employment. With a resource list to help individuals become involved." Libr J
Includes bibliographical references

Keizer, Garret

The **unwanted** sound of everything we want; a book about noise. PublicAffairs 2010 385p $27.95   **363.7**
1. Noise 2. Noise -- Psychological aspects 3. Sound 4. Sound -- Psychological aspects
ISBN 1586485520; 9781586485528

LC 2010-05391
This book examines the "political, social, and environmental costs of [noise]." (Publisher's note) Bibliography. Index.
This "book explores the unforeseen (and sometimes unwanted) side effects of our inventive natures. We usually use the word noise as a pejorative, a term denoting unwanted sound: somebody's loud music, a blaring car alarm, the din from a nearby airport. But, as Keizer points out, noise is often—perhaps even usually—a product of human achievement, invention, or ambition. In broad terms, you can't have civilization without noise. . . . An enlightening look at an issue most of us ignore." Booklist
Includes bibliographical references

Kirby, David

Animal factory; the looming threat of industrial pig, dairy, and poultry farms to humans and the environment. St. Martin's Press 2010 492p $26.99 **363.7**
1. Agriculture -- Environmental aspects 2. Livestock industry
ISBN 978-0-312-38058-8; 0-312-38058-5
"Thanks to Kirby's extraordinary journalism, we have the most relatable, irrefutable, and unforgettable testimony yet to the hazards of industrial animal farming." Booklist

Kolbert, Elizabeth

★ **Field** notes from a catastrophe; man, nature, and climate change. Bloomsbury Pub. 2006 210p il map hardcover o.p. pa $14.95   **363.7**
1. Climate 2. Global environmental change 3. Global warming 4. Greenhouse effect
ISBN 1-59691-125-5; 978-1-59691-125-3; 1-59691-130-1 pa; 978-1-59691-130-7 pa

LC 2005-30972
"On the burgeoning shelf of cautionary but occasionally alarmist books warning about the consequences of dramatic climate change, Kolbert's calmly persuasive reporting stands out for its sobering clarity." Publ Wkly
Includes bibliographical references

Lynas, Mark

High tide; the truth about our climate crisis. Picador 2004 xxxiii, 345p il map pa $14   **363.7**
1. Greenhouse effect
ISBN 0-312-30365-3

LC 2004-44661
"In a series of . . . travel narratives, Lynas shows the human side of global warming, taking readers to Britain, North and South America, China, and the South Pacific. He introduces them to folks whose houses and roads are falling crazily through melting permafrost, who are going hungry because fishing lakes have disappeared, and who are becoming refugees because their grasslands have turned to desert. . . . The author clearly explains why these are not isolated incidents, but interrelated parts of a worldwide set of phenomena that soon will affect us all." SLJ
Includes bibliographical references

McKay, Kim

True green @ work; 100 ways you can make the environment your business. [by] Kim McKay and Jenny Bonnin, with Tim Wallace. National Geographic Society 2008 141p il pa $19.95   **363.7**
1. Business enterprises   2. Conservation of natural resources 3. Consumption (Economics) 4. Environmental protection 5. Management
ISBN 978-1-4262-0263-6; 1-4262-0263-6

LC 2008-301223
The authors "outline practical steps to help executives and office workers take the right ecosteps. The superb design features striking topography and gorgeous photos." Libr J
Includes bibliographical references

Mongillo, John F.

Encyclopedia of environmental science; by John Mongillo and Linda Zierdt-Warshaw. Oryx Press 2000 450p il $99.95   **363.7**
1. Environmental sciences 2. Environmental sciences -- Encyclopedias 3. Reference books
ISBN 1-57356-147-9

LC 00-32657
This encyclopedia covers "the major topics of agriculture, atmosphere, biomes, ecology, endangered plant and wildlife species, energy, law and regulations, water, and wetlands. . . . The 1000 entries are arranged alphabetically and

range from several paragraphs to two pages in a clear and straightforward style with plenty of cross references." Libr J
Includes bibliographical references

Mooney, Chris
    Storm world; hurricanes, politics, and the battle over global warming. Harcourt 2007 392p il map $26   **363.7**
    1. Climatology 2. Global warming 3. Global warming -- Political aspects 4. Greenhouse effect 5. Hurricanes 6. Hurricanes -- Social aspects
    ISBN 978-0-15-101287-9; 0-15-101287-3
                LC 2007-09742
    "This is certainly one of the most thought-provoking and accessible accounts of climate change to appear since Katrina." Booklist
    Includes bibliographical references

Moore, Charles
    Plastic ocean; how a sea captain's chance discovery launched a determined quest to save the oceans. [by] Capt. Charles Moore with Cassandra Phillips. Avery 2011 358p il map $26   **363.7**
    1. Marine pollution 2. Plastics
    ISBN 978-1-58333-424-9; 1-58333-424-6
                LC 2011034559
    "The author is an impassioned, fiercely inquisitive writer, detailing the many unorthodox ways he's managed to get these issues into the news and in peer-reviewed science journals. . . . Fast-paced and electrifying, Moore's story is 'gonzo science' at its best." Kirkus
    Includes bibliographical references

Pooley, Eric
    The **climate** war; true believers, power brokers, and the fight to save the earth. Hyperion 2010 481p $27.99   **363.7**
    1. Climate -- Environmental aspects 2. Climatic changes -- Government policy 3. Climatic changes -- Political aspects 4. Conservationists 5. Environmental policy 6. Environmentalists -- Political activity 7. Lawyers 8. Members of Congress 9. Nobel laureates for peace 10. Presidential candidates 11. Senators 12. Vice-presidents
    ISBN 978-1-4013-2326-4
                LC 2010-12422
    This "is a fascinating, well-researched, behind-the-scenes account of the political twists and turns and efforts of corporate bosses and climate activists. Pooley . . . puts a human face on the topic and writes a gripping account— whether one reads it cover to cover or consults individual chapters in any order." Choice
    Includes bibliographical references

Rogers, Heather
    Gone tomorrow; the hidden life of garbage. New Press 2005 288p il $23.95   **363.7**
    1. Refuse and refuse disposal
    ISBN 1-56584-879-9
                LC 2005-41562
    The author "analyzes the contents of America's garbage and its disposal while also revealing the corporate strategies

behind the disposable-goods explosion and assessing the ecological toll of our consumer habits." Booklist
    Includes bibliographical references

Royte, Elizabeth
    ★ **Garbage** land; on the secret trail of trash. Little, Brown 2005 311p hardcover o.p. pa $14.99   **363.7**
    1. Refuse and refuse disposal
    ISBN 0-316-73826-3; 0-316-15461-X pa
                LC 2004-24732
    "There's little waste in Royte's winning words. . . . Seldom has garbage been handled with such care." Christ Sci Monit
    Includes bibliographical references

Seidl, Amy
    Early spring; an ecologist and her children wake to a warming world. Beacon Press 2008 172p $24.95   **363.7**
    1. Climate -- Environmental aspects 2. Climatic changes -- Environmental aspects 3. Ecologists 4. Foundation officials 5. Global warming 6. Greenhouse effect 7. Human influence on nature 8. Nature -- Effect of human beings on 9. Social activists
    ISBN 978-0-8070-8584-4; 0-8070-8584-7
                LC 2008-08101
    "Seidl blends a well-researched environmental study with observations of small-town Vermont life, even as she reaches beyond New England by keeping her discussion of global warming artfully broadminded. . . . At once deeply personal and solidly scientific, Seidl's chronicle manages to be concerned without being cloying." Booklist
    Includes bibliographical references

Speth, James Gustave
    Red sky at morning; America and the crisis of the global environment. Yale University Press 2004 299p $24; pa $16   **363.7**
    1. Ecology 2. Environmental policy -- United States 3. Environmental protection 4. Globalization
    ISBN 0-300-10232-1; 0-300-10776-5 pa
                LC 2003-20223
    Speth "presents an authoritative, trenchant analysis of the worsening global environmental crisis." Choice
    Includes bibliographical references

Stager, Curt
    Deep future; Curt Stager. Thomas Dunne Books 2011 284p ill.   **363.7**
    ISBN 9780312614621; 9780312614638
                LC 2010040381
    This book, a 'Kirkus Reviews' Best Nonfiction of 2011 title, presents an "exploration of the impact of climate change over geological time. [Curt] Stager takes the long view of global climate change . . . [and] examines both moderate and extreme scenarios. . . . A key point is that humanity has the ability to moderate the release of carbon, shaping the long-range impact on climate. While we are already past the point where significant global warming can be prevented, the author points out that cutting carbon now preserves some for a future era when its release could help prevent another

ice age -- a global disaster every bit as threatening to the human race as warming." (Kirkus)

Walker, Gabrielle

The **hot** topic; what we can do about global warming. [by] Gabrielle Walker and Sir David King. Harcourt 2008 276p il map pa $14   **363.7**
   1. Climatic changes 2. Global warming -- Economic aspects 3. Global warming -- Environmental aspects 4. Greenhouse effect
   ISBN 978-0-15-603318-3

                     LC 2007-45080

"This is the best overview of global warming that this reviewer has read. . . . What is most valuable about this book is that the text clearly explains to lay readers a very complex and highly controversial topic." Libr J
Includes bibliographical references

Watts, Jonathan

When a billion Chinese jump; how China will save mankind--or destroy it. Scribner 2010 435p map pa $17; ebook $9.99   **363.7**
   1. Environmental policy -- China
   ISBN 978-1-4165-8076-8 pa; 1-4165-8076-X pa; 978-1-4391-4193-9 ebook; 1-4391-4193-2 ebook

                     LC 2010-29901

"Watts' comprehensive, revealing study is eye-opening, not only for the way it illuminates how China's population growth and rapid modernization affect the environment, but also for its exposure of the way Western waste contributes to the problem." Booklist
Includes bibliographical references

Winston, Mark L.

Nature wars; people vs. pests. Harvard Univ. Press 1997 210p $27.50; pa $15.95   **363.7**
   1. Human influence on nature 2. Pest control 3. Pesticides -- Environmental aspects
   ISBN 0-674-60541-1; 0-674-60542-X pa

                     LC 97-17302

"Winston provides case studies demonstrating alternative methods of pest control, explaining how political, social, economic, and biologic interactions behind pest-management decisions have contributed to our failure to replace toxic chemicals as our first method of choice. . . . Winston has written a convincing and necessary book." Libr J
Includes bibliographical references

Wyman, Bruce C.

★ The **Facts** on File dictionary of environmental science; [by] Bruce Wyman, L. Harold Stevenson. 3rd ed.; Facts on File 2007 498p il $49.50 **363.7**
   1. Environmental sciences -- Dictionaries 2. Reference books
   ISBN 0-8160-6437-7; 978-0-8160-6437-3

                     LC 2006-45697

This dictionary contains over 5,000 cross-referenced entries reflecting the diversity of subjects that are relevant to the environmental field.

Encyclopedia of environmental issues; editor, Craig W. Allin. Rev. ed.; Salem Press 2011 4v il map set $495   **363.7**
   1. Environmental sciences -- Encyclopedias 2. Pollution -- Encyclopedias 3. Reference books
   ISBN 978-1-58765-735-1; 978-1-58765-740-5 ebook

                     LC 2011004176

"This set would be useful to general readers and students alike and would be a worthwhile resource for high-school, public, and undergraduate libraries." Booklist
Includes bibliographical references

Encyclopedia of global change; environmental change and human society. Andrew S. Goudie, editor in chief; David J. Cuff, associate editor. Oxford Univ. Press 2002 2v il maps set $350   **363.7**
   1. Environmental sciences -- Encyclopedias 2. Global environmental change 3. Global environmental change -- Social aspects 4. Human influence on nature -- Encyclopedias 5. Nature -- Effect of human beings on 6. Reference books
   ISBN 0-19-510825-6

                     LC 00-58918

"This encyclopedia of environmental science and its impact on human society reflects the global changes that have taken place during the past century. The selection of the various topics cuts across many disciplines in the social, political, and natural sciences. The physical, biological, and chemical changes in the atmosphere, in the water, and on land are related to health, industry, economics, and human welfare. Some of the topics discuss climate models, including cyclones and winter storms. . . . The importance of the world-wide effort to manage whole ecosystems and its impact on human society are also explained. . . . Topics that are discussed briefly include dams, deforestation, earth motions, El Niño, extinction of species, fires, fishing, the Gaia hypothesis, the greenhouse effect, and biological diversity." Sci Books Films
Includes bibliographical references

★ **Famous** first facts about the environment; edited by Ronald J. Formica; contributors, Victoria S. Chase {et al.} Wilson, H.W. 2002 573p $150   **363.7**
   1. Environmental sciences 2. Environmental sciences -- Miscellanea
   ISBN 0-8242-0974-5

                     LC 2001-17704

This "volume lists 4000 entries of international environmental 'firsts'. . . . Entries are first listed under a major subject category, such as air pollution, climate and weather, hazardous waste, population growth, and storms, which are then broken down into various subdivisions. . . . This unique work should be purchased by any size library that needs an account of environmental 'firsts.'" Libr J
Includes bibliographical references

363.738   Pollutants

Johansen, Bruce E.

The **dirty** dozen: toxic chemicals and the earth's future. Praeger 2003 297p $49.95   **363.738**

1. Environmental health 2. Industrial waste 3. Organochlorine compounds -- Environmental aspects 4. Organochlorine compounds -- Health aspects 5. Persistent pollutants -- Environmental aspects 6. Persistent pollutants -- Health aspects 7. Pollution
ISBN 0-275-97702-1

LC 2002-29872

This study examines the history, industrial uses, and harmful effects of "the 12 most commonly used persistent organic pollutants (POPs). Also called organochlorines, they are pervasive in air, water, food, animals, pesticides, solvents, and numerous household products. They are responsible for cancer, respiratory ailments, birth defects, other illnesses, and death in humans and animals." Libr J

Includes bibliographical references

Lapierre, Dominique

Five past midnight in Bhopal; {by} Dominique Lapierre, Javier Moro; translated from the French by Kathryn Spink. Warner Bks. 2002 403p il map $25.95   **363.738**

1. Bhopal Union Carbide Plant Disaster, Bhopal, India, 1984 2. Pesticides industry -- Accidents
ISBN 0-446-53088-3

LC 2002-100974

The authors relate "the story of Bhopal, India, where in 1984 16,000 to 30,000 people were killed and half a million maimed as the result of a deadly gas leak of methyl isocyanate from a Union Carbide pesticide manufacturing plant." America

Lerner, Steve

Sacrifice zones; the front lines of toxic chemical exposure in the United States. Steve Lerner; foreword by Phil Brown. MIT Press 2010 xiv, 346p (hardcover : alk. paper) 29.95   **363.738**

1. Chemical spills -- Health aspects -- United States -- Case studies 2. Environmental toxicology -- United States -- Case studies 3. Hazardous substances -- Health aspects -- United States -- Case studies 4. Hazardous waste sites -- United States -- Case studies 5. Pollution -- United States -- Case studies
ISBN 0262014408; 9780262014403

LC 2009051289

In this book, author "Steve Lerner tells the stories of twelve communities, from Brooklyn to Pensacola, that rose up to fight the industries and military bases causing disproportionately high levels of chemical pollution. He calls these low-income neighborhoods 'sacrifice zones'—repurposing a Cold War term coined by U.S. government officials to designate areas contaminated with radioactive pollutants during the manufacture of nuclear weapons. And he argues that residents of a new generation of sacrifice zones, tainted with chemical pollutants, need additional regulatory protections." (Publisher's note)

363.739   Pollution of specific environments

Woodard, Colin

Ocean's end; travels through endangered seas. Basic Bks. 2000 300p hardcover o.p. pa $15   **363.739**

1. Marine pollution 2. Marine resources 3. Marine resources conservation
ISBN 0-465-01571-9 pa

LC 99-51771

The author contends "that pollution, harmful fishing practices, ignorance and global warming are destroying the world's oceans. . . . He uncovers a colorful cast of scientists, officials, activists, divers and religious missionaries who attest to the human and economic costs of ecological decline." Publ Wkly

Includes bibliographical references

363.8   Food supply

Soussan, Michael

Backstabbing for beginners; my crash course in international diplomacy. Nation Books 2008 332p il $25.95   **363.8**

ISBN 978-1-56858-397-6; 1-56858-397-4

LC 2008-31698

"Soussan brings provocative wit, a keen eye for detail and a knack for revealing anecdotes to this important account of the rampant greed, hypocrisy and cynicism festering behind the United Nations' humanitarian credo." Publ Wkly

Includes bibliographical references

Stuart, Tristram

Waste; uncovering the global food scandal. W.W. Norton & Co. 2009 xxii, 451p il $27.95   **363.8**

1. Food industry 2. Recycling 3. Waste minimization
ISBN 978-0-393-06836-8

The author "shows how we could have much more food overnight simply by not tossing away so much of it. This simple concept ingeniously unites many food scandals that often do not get the attention they deserve: the mould that destroys a third or more of Third World harvests; . . . [and] the millions of tonnes of edible food wasted by modern food processing and 'sell-by' dates. . . . Usefully, Stuart offers examples of what we could be doing better, from processing technologies to offal sausages." New Sci

Includes bibliographical references

363.9   Population problems

Black, Edwin

★ **War** against the weak; eugenics and America's campaign to create a master race. Four Walls Eight Windows 2003 xxviii, 550p il $27; pa $18 **363.9**

1. Eugenics 2. Eugenics -- History 3. Human reproduction -- Government policy 4. Sterilization (Birth control)
ISBN 1-568-58258-7; 1-568-58321-4 pa

LC 2003-48857

The author reveals that the American eugenics movement "was extensive, systematic, well funded, and supported by major political and intellectual leaders; perhaps most startling, it directly inspired the rise of Nazism in Hitler's Germany. . . . This chilling and well-researched book is highly recommended." Libr J

Includes bibliographical references

Bruinius, Harry

★ **Better** for all the world; the secret history of forced sterilization and America's quest for racial purity. Knopf 2006 401p il hardcover o.p. pa $16.95; ebook $16.95   **363.9**

1. Eugenics 2. Eugenics -- United States -- History 3. Racism -- United States -- History 4. Sterilization (Birth control)

ISBN 0-375-41371-5; 0-375-71305-0 pa; 978-0-307-42496-9 ebook

LC 2005-44150

"Bruinius' account of one of America's dirty little secrets is . . . a real page-turner." Booklist

Includes bibliographical references

May, Elaine Tyler

America and the pill; a history of promise, peril, and liberation. Basic Books 2010 214p $25.95 **363.9**

1. Birth control 2. Birth control -- United States -- History 3. Oral contraceptives 4. Oral contraceptives -- Social aspects 5. Women -- Social conditions 6. Women -- United States -- Social conditions -- 20th century

ISBN 978-0-465-01152-0

LC 2009-46957

The author describes "the now extravagant-seeming hopes and fears the pill first elicited, how the pill became a symbol of the 1960s sexual revolution without demonstrably affecting it, how feminists used the pill to push for an analogue for men as part of their gender-egalitarian agenda, and how reaction to the pill's ill effects on many women contributed to the late-twentieth-century dissipation of respect for professional and institutional authority. . . . Understanding that the book is fundamentally, nonargumentatively pro-pill, one couldn't ask for a better short history of its subject." Booklist

Includes bibliographical references and index

Tone, Andrea

Devices and desires; a history of contraceptives in America. Hill & Wang 2001 366p hardcover o.p. pa $15   **363.9**

1. Birth control 2. Birth control -- United States -- History 3. Contraceptives -- United States -- History

ISBN 0-8090-3817-X; 0-8090-3816-1 pa

LC 00-50547

"Part 1 examines the 'contraceptive entrepreneurs' who practiced what was for many years an illegal trade, regulated by no one. In part 2, 'From Smut to Science,' Tone considers the development of relatively reliable contraceptive techniques, . . . part 3, 'The Medicalization of Contraceptives,' covers birth control pills, Norplant, and intrauterine devices." Booklist

★ **Family** planning sourcebook; edited by Amy Marcaccio Keyzer. Omnigraphics 2000 520p $78   **363.9**

1. Birth control 2. Birth control -- United States 3. Contraception -- United States

ISBN 0-7808-0379-5

LC 00-53029

"Basic consumer health information about planning for pregnancy and contraception, including traditional methods, barrier methods, hormonal methods, permanent methods, future methods, emergency contraception, and birth control choices for women at each stage of life." Publisher's note

364   Criminology

Nash, Jay Robert

The **great** pictorial history of world crime. History 2004 2v il set $249   **364**

1. Crime -- Encyclopedias 2. Reference books

ISBN 1-928831-20-6

LC 2004-100992

"Each of these topical sections opens with a general overview and then explores individual crimes in chronological order. As befits the title, there are thousands of black-and-white photographs and illustrations and although their quality varies they are, by and large, helpful and interesting. . . . [This is] the most comprehensive true crime book available." SLJ

Newton, Michael

★ The **encyclopedia** of serial killers; 2nd ed.; Facts On File 2006 515p il $85; pa $19.95   **364**

1. Criminals -- Encyclopedias 2. Homicide -- Encyclopedias 3. Reference books

ISBN 0-8160-6195-5; 0-8160-6196-3 pa

LC 2005-3800

The author "covers hundreds of serial murder cases from early history to the present, among them Jack the Ripper, the Green River Killer, Robert Lee Yates, and Aileen Wuornos. A good starting point for those needing basic information." Libr J

Includes bibliographical references

Rosen, Fred

★ The **historical** atlas of American crime. Facts on File 2005 xx, 296p il map $75; pa $24.95 **364**

1. Crime -- United States

ISBN 0-8160-4841-X; 0-8160-4842-8 pa

LC 2004-11346

The author "brings a fresh point of view to American crime by placing it within the larger context of American history; at the same time he observes multiple disciplines (e.g., history, economics, literature) through the lens of crime." Choice

Includes bibliographical references

Simpson, Colton

Inside the Crips; life inside L.A.'s most notorious gang. [by] Colton Simpson with Ann Pearlman.

St. Martin's Press 2005 xxiii, 323p $24.95; pa
$14.95 **364**

1. Gang members

ISBN 0-312-32929-6; 0-312-30930-X pa

LC 2005-42704

The author "provides an insider's perspective on day-to-
day life in the Crips, the gang's history (including quite a bit
about its rival, the Bloods), and the plight of growing up in
the 'hood while wanting a better life. . . . This unvarnished
portrayal of gang life is enlightening and even inspiring
about a subject badly in need of illumination." Booklist

Zuckoff, Mitchell

Ponzi's scheme; the true story of a financial legend. Random House 2005 390p il $25.95; pa
$14.95 **364**

1. Swindlers

ISBN 1-400-06039-7; 0-8129-6836-0 pa

LC 2004-46770

The author "chronicles Ponzi's mercurial rise and fall as
he conjured up one get-rich-quick scheme after another. . . .
Zuckoff provides not only a definitive portrait of Ponzi's life
but also insights into immigrant life and the social world of
early 20th-century Boston." Publ Wkly

Includes bibliographical references

★ Encyclopedia of crime & justice; Joshua Dressler,
editor in chief. 2nd ed; Macmillan Ref. USA
2001 4v set $475 **364**

1. Administration of criminal justice 2. Crime --
Encyclopedias 3. Criminals -- Encyclopedias 4.
Reference books

ISBN 0-02-865319-X

"The signed essays are written by respected scholars in
the fields of law, sociology, and criminal justice and range in
length from 800 to 12,000 words. . . . This set will be in high
demand by 'issues' researchers as well as by researchers in
the fields of law and criminal justice." Booklist

★ Encyclopedia of criminology; Richard A. Wright,
J. Mitchell Miller, editors. Fitzroy Dearborn
2005 3v set $495 **364**

1. Crime -- Encyclopedias 2. Reference books

ISBN 1-579-58387-3

LC 2004-4861

"More than 500 essays contributed by more that 300 international scholars fall into 12 major substantive areas in
the discipline, including criminal behavior (124 essays), the
justice system (121), criminal law (61), theories of criminal
behavior (49), and prominent figures in the field (44). . . .
This reference source is destined to become a standard in
the field." Choice

Includes bibliographical references

Famous American crimes and trials; edited by
Frankie Y. Bailey and Steven Chermak. Praeger
2004 5v il set $375 **364**

1. Administration of criminal justice

ISBN 0-275-98333-1

LC 2004-50548

This set "examines 70 cases, beginning in 1607 with the
trial of accused heretic Quaker Mary Dyer and ending with

the 2001 execution of convicted Oklahoma City bomber
Timothy McVeigh. . . . This work has definite multidisciplinary appeal." Choice

Includes bibliographical references

364.1 Criminal offenses

Atwood, Roger

★ **Stealing** history; tomb raiders, smugglers, and
the looting of the ancient world. St. Martin's Press
2004 337p il map hardcover o.p. pa $15.95 **364.1**

1. Antiquities -- Collection and preservation 2.
Archaeological thefts 3. Archaeological thefts -- Peru
-- Sipan 4. Archaeological thefts -- Peru -- Sipán 5. Art
thefts 6. Cultural property -- Protection

ISBN 0-312-32406-5; 0-312-32407-3 pa

LC 2004-50862

The author's "ability to bring a story dramatically to life
and his keen interest in stemming the illegal antiquities trade
makes this an important book for anyone interested in archeology, preservation or the potentially tangled provenance of
works they love." Publ Wkly

Includes bibliographical references

Bergreen, Laurence

Capone; the man and the era. Simon & Schuster
1994 701p il hardcover o.p. pa $19 **364.1**

1. Biography, Individual 2. Bootleggers 3. Mobsters

ISBN 0-684-82447-7 pa

LC 94-5941

"Mr. Bergreen has written a book objective and rigorous
enough to meet scholarly standards, yet colorful enough to
engross the general reader." N Y Times Book Rev

Includes bibliographical references

Bonanno, Bill

Bound by honor; a mafioso's story. St. Martin's
Press 1999 282p il $24.95; pa $6.99 **364.1**

1. Mafia 2. Mafia -- New York (State) -- New York
-- Biography 3. Mobsters 4. Organized crime -- New
York (State) -- New York 5. Television producers

ISBN 0-312-20388-8; 0-312-97147-8 pa

LC 99-14049

"Bonanno not only details Mob infighting and the struggles among rival East Coast Mob families; he also offers
specifics concerning Mob influence on Presidents Kennedy,
Johnson, and Nixon as well as on other important political
figures, such as J. Edgar Hoover . . . and Morris Udall. Even
the Mob's involvement in JFK's assassination is spelled
out. . . . Straightforward rather than chatty, the book paints
a revealing picture of Mob family politics and government
intervention." Booklist

Breslin, Jimmy

The **good** rat; a true story. Ecco 2008 270p
$24.95 **364.1**

1. Mafia 2. Mafia -- New York (N.Y.) -- History -- 20th
century 3. Organized crime 4. Organized crime -- New
York (N.Y.) -- History

ISBN 978-0-06-085666-3; 0-06-085666-1

"Breslin is a delighted tour guide through the underworld. . . . Nobody does it better." Booklist

Bugliosi, Vincent

★ **Helter** skelter; the true story of the Manson murders. {by} Vincent Bugliosi with Curt Gentry. 25th anniversary ed; Norton 1994 528p il $25; pa $13.95   **364.1**
1. Homicide 2. Murderers 3. Prisoners
ISBN 0-393-08700-X; 0-393-32223-8 pa
LC 94-20957
"This book by the prosecutor at the Tate-LaBianca murder trial tells the inside story of the Manson Family murders, the investigations, and the trial." Libr J

Burns, Sarah

The **Central** Park Five. Alfred A. Knopf 2011 240p il map $25.95   **364.1**
1. Administration of criminal justice 2. Crime -- New York (N.Y.) 3. Criminal justice, Administration of -- New York (N.Y.) 4. False accusation 5. Investment bankers 6. Nonfiction 7. Rape 8. Rape victims 9. Victims of crimes
ISBN 978-0-307-26614-9; 0-307-26614-1
LC 2010039661
This book recounts the public frenzy surrounding the April 19, 1989, attack on Trisha Meili in Central Park. The 28-year-old investment banker was out for a run when she was . . . raped, beaten and left for dead. The assault, pinned on a group of black and Hispanic boys aged 13 to 16 who'd been misbehaving in the park that night, incited media diatribes about civic decay. . . . [C]ourt cases found five of the boys guilty in 1990. Then, in 2002, convicted rapist and murderer Matias Reyes confessed to the attack and the five convictions were overturned. [Sarah] Burns's deconstruction of how justice was hijacked is part police procedural, part courtroom drama, part cultural critique . . . Burns . . . reveals how twinning the case trumped investigating the evidence." Particular focus is given to media and public resistance to Reyes's confession: so entrenched was the wilding narrative that many refused to give it up. (Maclean's)
"An important cultural document, and unquestionably worth reading. . . . Burns's gripping tale may serve as an allegory for some of the most pressing criminal justice issues of our time." N Y Times Book Rev
Includes bibliographical references

Butterfield, Fox

All God's children; the Bosket family and the American tradition of violence. Avon Bks. 1996 389p il map pa $15   **364.1**
1. Violence
ISBN 0-380-72862-1
Willie Bosket is an inmate "in New York's Woodbourne Correction Center. . . . Butterfield, with Willie's encouragement, set out to trace Bosket's family tree. . . . Butterfield focuses on Edgefield Country in Central South Carolina, where Bosket's family served as slaves." Newsweek
Includes bibliographical references

Capote, Truman

★ **In** cold blood; a true account of a multiple murder and its consequences. Random House 2002 343p $22; pa $13   **364.1**
1. Homicide 2. Murder -- Kansas -- Case studies 3. Murderers
ISBN 0-375-50790-6; 0-679-74558-0 pa
LC 2002-282920
"Truman Capote called his account of the 1959 murder of a Kansas farm family a nonfiction novel. Using information he collected through interviews with townspeople and the killers, Capote created a vivid portrait of the criminals and graphically described the crime, the criminals' escape to Mexico, capture, trial, appeals, and hanging." HarperCollins Reader's Ency of Am Lit. 2nd edition

Carney, Scott

The **red** market; on the trail of the world's organ brokers, bone thieves, blood farmers, and child traffickers. William Morrow 2011 254p il $25.99 **364.1**
1. Organ trafficking 2. Procurement of organs, tissues, etc.
ISBN 978-0-06-193646-3; 0-06-193646-4
LC 2010-47807
"The 'red market' of Scott Carney's lucid and alarming book refers to the various medical activities through which the human body can generate a profit: surrogate motherhood, organ transplantation, drug testing, baby selling and blood farming, to mention just a few items on Mr. Carney's disturbing list. The buyers of red-market goods are usually well-to-do Westerners, while the sellers tend to come from developing countries. A surprisingly large number of the sellers are women, and many appear to be forced into the business. Middlemen, beyond taking large profits, encourage the trade by assuring buyers that the transaction is conducted ethically. . . . [This] is not an abstract philosophical meditation or an ethnographic treatise, though it has elements of both. It is a work of investigative journalism, written by an experienced health reporter who lived in India for more than 10 years. Mr. Carney knows how to tell a story and digs deeply." Wall Street J
Includes bibliographical references

Carrere, Emmanuel

The **adversary**; a true story of monstrous deception. translated by Linda Coverdale. Picador USA 2002 191p pa $13   **364.1**
1. Homicide
ISBN 0-312-42060-9; 978-0-312-42060-4
LC 2001-50066
"In telling Romand's story, [the author] also writes of the process of creating this book. By injecting himself into the narrative, Carrere has managed to make this appalling story both fascinating and highly readable." Libr J

Dash, Mike

The **first** family; terror, extortion, revenge, murder, and the birth of the American mafia. Random House 2009 375p il map $27   **364.1**
1. Biography, Individual 2. Mafia 3. Mafia -- History 4. Mafia -- United States -- History 5. Mobsters 6. Organized crime 7. Organized crime -- United States

-- History
ISBN 978-1-4000-6722-0

LC 2009-5681

"Essential for students of organized crime in America. Murder and mayhem buffs will enjoy it too." Kirkus

Includes bibliographical references (p. 350-357)

De Vito, Carlo

★ The **encyclopedia** of international organized crime. Facts on File 2005 386p il $75; pa $24.95   **364.1**

1. Organized crime -- Encyclopedias 2. Reference books
ISBN 0-8160-4848-7; 0-8160-4849-5 pa

LC 2003-24724

"This alphabetically arranged volume covers organized crime units in a variety of countries including, but not limited to, the US, Mexico, China, England, and Australia. Not only does this reference tool span a wide geographical area, it also covers a lengthy time period, from the mid-19th century to the present. . . . Presented in an interesting, straightforward manner, this easy-to-read book is also enjoyable." Choice

Includes bibliographical references

Dolnick, Edward

The **rescue** artist; a true story of art, thieves, and the hunt for a missing masterpiece. HarperCollins Publishers 2005 270p il $25.95; pa $14.95 **364.1**

1. Art thefts 2. Artists 3. Painters
ISBN 0-06-053117-7; 978-0-06-053117-1; 0-06-053118-5 pa; 978-0-06053118-8 pa

LC 2004-62060

This is an "account of the 1994 theft of one of the world's most famous paintings, The Scream. . . . This is a tightly woven, fast-paced story." SLJ

Includes bibliographical references

Douglas, John E.

The **cases** that haunt us; from Jack the Ripper to JonBenet Ramsey, the FBI's legendary mindhunter sheds light on the mysteries that won't go away. [by] John Douglas, Mark Olshaker. Pocket Books 2001 487p il pa $7.99   **364.1**

1. Criminal psychology 2. Homicide
ISBN 978-0-671-01706-4; 0-671-01706-3

The authors discuss "eight controversial cases that include the Lindbergh baby kidnapping, the Boston Strangler, the Zodiac Killer, and the JonBenet Ramsey killing." Libr J

Dray, Philip

At the hands of persons unknown; the lynching of Black America. Random House 2002 528p il hardcover o.p. pa $14.95   **364.1**

1. African Americans -- Crimes against -- Southern States 2. African Americans -- Southern States 3. Lynching 4. Lynching -- Southern States -- History
ISBN 0-375-75445-8 pa

LC 2001-40366

"Dray balances moral indignation with a sound understanding of history and politics. The result is vital, hard-hitting cultural history." Publ Wkly

Includes bibliographical references

Drew, Elizabeth

The **corruption** of American politics; what went wrong and why. Overlook Press 2000 286p pa $15.95   **364.1**

1. Campaign funds -- United States 2. Political corruption 3. Political corruption -- United States
ISBN 1-585-67049-9; 978-1-585-67049-9

LC 00-22068

The author argues "that the prevalence of soft money has lowered the quality of leadership in Washington. The most successful politicians are no longer the best executives or the best legislators, she says, but rather the best fund-raisers. . . . One of the most skillfully written, as well as insightful, looks inside the Beltway to appear in a very long time." Publ Wkly

Fisher, Kenneth L.

How to smell a rat; the five signs of financial fraud. [by] Ken Fisher with Lara Hoffmans. Wiley 2009 209p $24.95   **364.1**

1. Fraud 2. Investments 3. Swindlers and swindling
ISBN 978-0-470-52653-8

LC 2009-21631

"With five straightforward rules that would have saved any investor from Bernie Madoff, . . . [Fisher] gives readers a secure plan for fraudproof investing, worthwhile for novices and sophisticated financiers alike. . . . Much more than what to avoid, Fisher's concise guide should be highly illuminating and confidence-building for anyone with a bank account." Publ Wkly

Includes bibliographical references

Geary, Rick

The **Lindbergh** child; America's hero and the crime of the century. written and illustrated by Rick Geary. NBM/ComicsLit 2008 un il map pa $15.95   **364.1**

1. Air force officers 2. Air pilots 3. Generals 4. Graphic novels 5. Homicide -- Graphic novels 6. Kidnapping -- Graphic novels 7. Memoirists 8. Mystery graphic novels
ISBN 978-1-56163-529-0

Charles Lindbergh was an American hero following his solo crossing of the Atlantic in an airplane. He married into a wealthy family, he and his wife had a baby, they were building their dream home. Then, one night, the baby was abducted from the house. Geary's account retraces all the highly publicized events, ransom notes (false and otherwise), as well as the string of colorful characters who all claimed they could help but instead snookered the Lindberghs. While Bruno Hauptmann was arrested, tried, convicted, and executed, there remain many questions about what really happened. Geary brings them up for readers to consider.

"A good example of the origins of modern forensics, crime-scene investigation, and celebrity hysteria, this work is an excellent choice for most collections." SLJ

Glenny, Misha

McMafia; a journey through the global criminal underworld. Alfred A. Knopf 2008 375p il map $27.95 **364.1**

1. Globalization -- Social aspects 2. Organized crime 3. Transnational crime
ISBN 978-1-4000-4411-5; 1-4000-4411-1

LC 2007-30522

"Readers yearning for a deeper understanding of the real-life, international counterparts to The Sopranos need look no further than Glenny's engrossing study." Publ Wkly
Includes bibliographical references

Goldhagen, Daniel Jonah

Worse than war; genocide, eliminationism, and the ongoing assault on humanity. [by] Daniel Jonah Goldhagen. PublicAffairs 2009 658p il **364.1**

1. Genocide 2. Genocide -- Psychological aspects 3. Mass murder 4. Prejudices 5. Racism 6. Racism -- Psychological aspects
ISBN 1-58648-769-8; 978-1-58648-769-0

LC 2009-28035

This is an investigation into the phenomenon of genocide and mass killing—explaining why genocides begin, are sustained, and end; why societies support them and why they happen so frequently; and how the international community should and can successfully stop them.

The author "convincingly disparages bureaucratic 'banality of evil' explanations of genocide and spotlights the ideologies of leaders who exploit ordinary citizens' hate-filled beliefs to instigate mass murder. It's not easy reading, but Goldhagen's vehemence and the sheer weight of horrors that he recounts move one's conscience." Publ Wkly
Includes bibliographical references

Gourevitch, Philip

A cold case. Picador USA 2002 183p il pa $12 **364.1**

1. Homicide 2. Murder investigation -- New York (State) -- New York -- Case studies 3. Murderers
ISBN 0-312-42002-1; 978-0-312-42002-4

LC 2002-66767

"In 1970, Frankie Koehler shot and killed two men after a barroom brawl in Hell's Kitchen and then disappeared; twenty-seven years later, Andy Rosenzweig, the chief investigator for the Manhattan D.A., set out to solve one last case before he retired. Gourevitch reconstructs not only the crime but an era of cops and criminals that's fast passing into myth." New Yorker

Guinn, Jeff

Go down together; the true, untold story of Bonnie and Clyde. Simon & Schuster 2009 467p il $27 **364.1**

1. Biography, Individual 2. Criminals 3. Murderers 4. Outlaws
ISBN 978-1-4165-5706-7; 1-4165-5706-7

LC 2008-53342

"As Guinn relates, Bonnie and Clyde didn't commit many of the acts—particularly the murders—they were accused of. Their crime spree only lasted from spring 1932 to May 1934. But in the worst of the Depression, Americans ate up accounts of the Barrow exploits as a form of entertainment. The gang fed the newspapers terrific stuff, including the staged photo of Bonnie holding a gun and smoking a cigar. For folks living hardscrabble lives, the fact that the gang robbed the same bankers who were foreclosing on their farms made the exploits of Bonnie and Clyde even sweeter. Guinn succeeds marvelously in recreating the spirit of the times, the desperation of unemployment and financial ruin." PopMatters
Includes bibliographical references

Hiss, Tony

The view from Alger's window; a son's memoir. Knopf 1999 241p il hardcover o.p. pa $13 **364.1**

1. Children of prominent persons 2. Diplomats 3. Fathers and sons -- United States -- Biography 4. Journalists 5. Lawyers 6. Nonfiction writers 7. Prisoners -- United States -- Biography 8. Trials (Perjury) -- New York (State) -- New York
ISBN 0-375-70128-1 pa

LC 98-50911

"A poignant, wonderfully written and deeply troubling memoir." N Y Times Book Rev

Hooper, Chloe

Tall man; the death of Doomadgee. Scribner 2009 258p $24 **364.1**

1. Aboriginal Australians 2. Australian aborigines -- Crimes against 3. Australian aborigines -- Criminal justice system 4. Police -- Australia 5. Prisoners -- Australia 6. Prisoners -- Death
ISBN 978-1-4165-6159-0; 1-4165-6159-5

LC 2008-38308

"In 2004, in a remote Aboriginal community in northern Australia, Cameron Doomadgee, a drunk young indigenous man, was arrested and, a few hours later, died in his prison cell. A witness claimed that the six-foot-seven-inch arresting officer beat Doomadgee to death. The officer claimed that Doomadgee fell accidentally and that the extent of his injuries (which included broken ribs and a ruptured liver) wasn't apparent. Through the story of the manslaughter trial, Hooper lays bare Australia's institutional racism and the grim conditions of Aboriginal life there. A novelist, she finds a muscular music even when confronting sordid truths." New Yorker

Ifill, Sherrilyn A.

On the courthouse lawn; confronting the legacy of lynching in the twenty-first century. Beacon Press 2007 xx, 204p il $25.95; pa $16 **364.1**

1. Lynching 2. Lynching -- United States -- History 3. Reconciliation
ISBN 978-0-8070-0987-1; 0-8070-0987-3; 978-0-8070-0988-8 pa; 0-8070-0988-1 pa

LC 2006-16618

The author explores the continued effects of lynching. Ifill contends that "the lynchings implicated average white citizens, some of whom actively participated in the violence while many others witnessed the lynchings but did nothing to stop them. Ifill observes that this history of complicity has become embedded in the social and cultural fabric of local communities, who either supported, condoned, or ignored the violence. She . . . [presents] ideas to help communities heal. . . . Ifill argues that reconciliation and reparation efforts must also be locally based in order to bring both black and white Americans together in an efficacious dialogue." (Publisher's note) Index.

"An intriguing, immodest proposal that itself warrants discussion—and action." Kirkus

Includes bibliographical references

James, Bill

Popular crime; reflections on the celebration of violence. Scribner 2011 482p il $30   **364.1**
  1. Crime 2. Crime -- United States -- History 3. Homicide
  ISBN 978-1-4165-5273-4; 1-4165-5273-1
                                                 LC 2010-36180

This is a "very entertaining book, and it will instigate arguments even as it scores many important points. . . . James's layman status is a big part of this book's bracing charm. And his real point is more universal. He loves crime books and wants you to love them, too, and not just because they're a good way to pass the time in a motel room or airport. He wants you to take them seriously, as he does, and consider the ways they reflect and reshape the culture, what they say about our justice system and our very concept of justice." Washington Post Book World

Javers, Eamon

Broker, trader, lawyer, spy; inside the secret world of corporate espionage. Harper 2010 306p $26.99; ebook $11.99   **364.1**
  1. Business intelligence 2. Espionage
  ISBN 978-0-06-169720-3; 978-0-06-196938-6 ebook
                                                 LC 2009031010

"Javers traces spying activity, which began in Washington, D.C., in 1790, when the city became the capital, through the Civil War, when Allan Pinkerton was chasing Confederate spies, to Allen Dulles and the CIA developing drugs to enhance interrogations and in 2002 capturing traitor Robert Hanssen. The author also offers a fascinating explanation of the role of spies in today's world economy with hundreds of firms globally in the corporate espionage business using as operatives alumni from the FBI, CIA, Secret Service, British M15 and Russian KGB, and military intelligence officers. . . . This is a must-read, excellent book." Booklist

Includes bibliographical references

Jentz, Terri

★ **Strange** piece of paradise. Farrar, Straus & Giroux 2006 542p il $27   **364.1**
  1. Criminal investigation 2. Offenses against the person 3. Screenwriters 4. Violent crimes
  ISBN 0-374-13498-7; 978-0-374-13498-3
                                                 LC 2005-27240

"This book opens 15 years after a horrifyingly brutal assault in which Jentz and a Yale classmate, asleep at an Oregonian campground, were first run over and then attacked by a hatchet-wielding stranger. Jentz first returned to Oregon in 1992 to reclaim the self she lost at 19 and conduct her own investigation into the crime, for which no one was ever prosecuted. Her story is simultaneously riveting and disturbing—not an embellished memoir but a straightforward, chronological account based on notes, crime reports, newspaper accounts, hospital records, lab reports, and the author's own memory of events." Libr J

Jones, Ann

Women who kill. Beacon Press 1996 448p pa $16   **364.1**
  1. Criminals 2. Homicide
  ISBN 0-8070-6775-X
                                                 LC 95-46961

The author examines murders committed by women throughout American history, discussing such cases as Lizzie Borden, Alice Crimmins, and Jean Harris. The cases discussed shed light on women's status in American society

Keefe, Patrick Radden

The **snakehead;** an epic tale of the Chinatown underworld and the American dream. Doubleday 2009 414p map   **364.1**
  1. Businesspeople 2. Human trafficking -- United States 3. Illegal aliens 4. Illegal aliens -- United States 5. Smugglers 6. Smuggling
  ISBN 0-307-27927-8 pa; 0-385-52130-8; 978-0-307-27927-9 pa; 978-0-385-52130-7
                                                 LC 2008-50049

This book tells the story of human smuggling and trafficking among Fujianese immigrants to the United States. It focuses on Cheng Chui Ping, a Chinese immigrant who came to New York in the early 1980s. Her path to the American "dream began with an underground bank . . . run out of a noodle shop. . . . She became known as Sister Ping and built a global people-smuggling conglomerate that stretched from China's Fujian province to Africa, Europe, and South America, relying on one of Chinatown's . . . gangs to protect her power and profits. Sister Ping's empire came to light in 1993, when [the Golden Venture], a ship loaded with 300 near-starving immigrants ran aground off Queens. It took . . . nearly ten years to untangle the criminal network and home in on its mastermind." (Publisher's note) Index.

"This is one of the freshest accounts of modern-day migration I've read, one filled with moral ambiguity, one that doesn't pretend to have the answers, one that . . . feels like essential reading." Washington Post Book World

Includes bibliographical references

Kelly, Robert J.

Encyclopedia of organized crime in the United States; from Capone's Chicago to the new urban underworld. Greenwood Press 2000 xxx, 358p $64.95   **364.1**
  1. Organized crime 2. Organized crime -- United States -- Encyclopedias
  ISBN 0-313-30653-2
                                                 LC 99-33801

This reference source "describes and analyzes issues, criminal personalities, and trends throughout the 20th century. Kelly also examines the conditions that produced criminal activities and organizations. More than 250 entries provide in-depth information on major underworld figures, from Al Capone to Lucky Luciano to John Gotti, as well as key criminal events, from rub outs to FBI stings." Libr J

Includes bibliographical references

Lebsock, Suzanne

A **murder** in Virginia; Southern justice on trial. Norton 2003 442p il $26.95; pa $15.95 **364.1**
1. Trials (Homicide)
ISBN 0-393-04201-4; 0-393-32606-3 pa
LC 2002-15946

"On a warm afternoon in June 1895, a 56-year-old white woman was brutally murdered in Lunenburg County, VA. Despite the absence of any truly incriminating eyewitness testimony or physical evidence, four blacks—three women and one man—were arrested and tried for the murder. Lebsock . . . recreates the subsequent trials, introducing the defendants, their prosecutors, and the witnesses and placing the proceedings within the context of the black and white communities and deteriorating conditions for African Americans in the post-Reconstruction South. Here historical narrative is every bit as intriguing as fictional mystery but more edifying for the information it gives its readers concerning race relations and criminal justice in the latter part of the 19th century." Libr J

Includes bibliographical references

Lehr, Dick

The **fence**; a police cover-up along Boston's racial divide. Harper 2009 383p il map $25.99; pa $14.99 **364.1**
1. Police brutality 2. Police corruption
ISBN 978-0-06-078098-2; 0-06-078098-3; 978-0-06-078099-9 pa; 0-06-078099-1 pa

The author "details one of the most controversial cases in the annals of the Boston Police Department, involving a brutal assault on a black plainclothes officer by his fellow cops and the resulting 1998 civil rights trial against the police force. Not only does Lehr paint the racial and political turbulence of Boston at the time, but he explores the cultural backgrounds of the black officer, Michael Cox; his attacker and fellow officer, Kenny Conley; and Robert 'Smut' Brown, a drug dealer involved in the killing that started it all. . . . Jolting, nightmarish and potent, this true cop yarn bests any bogus reality show or overblown tabloid tale with its hardboiled spin." Publ Wkly

Includes bibliographical references

Levitt, Len

NYPD confidential; power and corruption in the country's greatest police force. Thomas Dunne Books 2009 304p $25.99 **364.1**
1. Police -- New York (N.Y.) 2. Police corruption
ISBN 978-0-312-38032-8; 0-312-38032-1
LC 2009-7602

"Using the administrations of recent New York City police commissioners Raymond W. Kelly (twice), William J. Bratton, Howard Safir, and Bernard Kerick as a frame, Levitt . . . pries into the inner workings of the NYPD. Levitt spins a fascinating tale of politics, rivalries, infighting, counterterrorism, and corruption inside the police department of America's largest city." Libr J

Includes bibliographical references

Longman, Jere

Among the heroes; United Flight 93 and the passengers and crew who fought back. HarperCollins Pubs. 2002 288p il $24.95; pa $13.95 **364.1**
1. Aircraft accident victims -- United States 2. Heroes -- United States 3. Hijacking of aircraft -- United States 4. Hijacking of airplanes 5. September 11 terrorist attacks, 2001 6. United Airlines Flight 93 Hijacking Incident, 2001 7. Victims of terrorism -- United States
ISBN 0-06-009908-9; 0-06-009909-7 pa
LC 2002-68530

This is an account of the United Airlines flight which was hijacked on September 11, 2001 and crashed in Pennsylvania before reaching its intended target.

This book "gives us an incredibly detailed and personal tale of that horrific episode." Booklist

Includes bibliographical references

Mallon, Thomas

★ **Mrs.** Paine's garage and the murder of John F. Kennedy. Pantheon Bks. 2002 211p $22; pa $13 **364.1**
1. Homemakers 2. Members of Congress 3. Murderers 4. Presidents 5. Senators 6. Spouses of prominent persons
ISBN 0-375-42117-3; 0-15-602755-0 pa
LC 2001-36157

"A journalistic inquiry into Ruth Paine, the woman who welcomed Marina Oswald—and sometimes her husband, Lee—into her suburban Dallas home in 1963; it offers a new theory about the antecedents of the assassination." N Y Times Book Rev

Matthews, Joe

Bringing Adam home; the abduction that changed America. [by] Les Standiford with Detective Sergeant Joe Matthews. Ecco 2011 291p il map **364.1**
1. Children 2. Homicide 3. Kidnap victims 4. Kidnapping 5. Murder victims
ISBN 0-06-198390-X; 978-0-06-198390-0
LC 2010-43572

"This is the ultimate cold case—tragic, high-profile, and, finally, successfully solved. Six-year-old Adam Walsh was abducted from a crowded Sears store in Hollywood, Florida, in 1981. Later, he was murdered and decapitated. Identifying Adam's killer took 25 years. His parents turned into tireless advocates for missing and abused children; Adam's father, John Walsh, moved from a sales job to being the executive producer and host of America's Most Wanted. This forceful account . . . gives readers the ultimate insider's account of the grueling search for Adam's killer and for the evidence to convict him. While many true-crime books claim to shine a light on society by examining one particular case, this account actually does." Booklist

McGinniss, Joe

★ **Fatal** vision. New American Library 1989 684p il pa $7.99 **364.1**
1. Homicide 2. Murderers 3. Surgeons
ISBN 978-0-451-16566-4; 0-451-16566-7

"This is a wisely observant, well-written, and understated book." Harpers

Includes bibliographical references

Murakami, Haruki

Underground; translated from the Japanese by Alfred Birnbaum and Philip Gabriel. Vintage Bks. 2001 366p map pa $14   **364.1**

1. Terrorism 2. Terrorism -- Japan

ISBN 0-375-72580-6

LC 00-69310

"On March 20, 1995, followers of the religious cult Aum Shinrikyo unleashed lethal sarin gas into cars of the Tokyo subway system. Many died, many more were injured. This is {Murakami's} . . . account of this episode." Publ Wkly

Olsen, Jack

I: the creation of a serial killer. St. Martin's Press 2002 365p il $24.95; pa $6.99   **364.1**

1. Homicide 2. Murderers 3. Serial murderers -- West (U.S.)

ISBN 0-312-24198-4; 0-312-98384-0 pa

LC 2001-58892

"A truly horrifying account of a serial killer, told with shocking candor." Booklist

Pepper, William F.

An **act** of state; the execution of Martin Luther King. Norton 2003 334p il map $25   **364.1**

1. Civil rights activists 2. Clergy 3. Conspiracies 4. Conspiracies -- United States 5. Nobel laureates for peace 6. Nonfiction writers 7. Political corruption -- United States

ISBN 1-85984-695-5

This book continues the author's examination of the life and death of Martin Luther King Jr.

"Forget everything you think you know, Pepper insists. James Earl Ray did not pull the trigger. . . . Pepper gradually introduces the vast cast of characters in a dizzying murder conspiracy that winds from a Memphis bar through the shadows of organized crime to the far reaches of national government. He carefully maps each player's place and role in the tangled web and doggedly tries to stick to a straightforward narrative. . . . Pepper attempts nothing less than a rewrite of history, and a spurring of further investigation." Publ Wkly

Includes bibliographical references

Queen, William

Under and alone; the true story of the undercover agent who infiltrated America's most violent outlaw motorcycle gang. Random House 2005 270p il $24.95   **364.1**

1. Gangs 2. Motorcycle gangs 3. Police

ISBN 1-400-06084-2

LC 2004-51176

"The strength and white-hot intensity of the writing make this read like a movie, and Hollywood is certain to take note." Publ Wkly

Raab, Selwyn

★ **Five** families; the rise, decline, and resurgence of America's most powerful Mafia empires. Thomas Dunne Books 2005 765p il $29.95   **364.1**

1. Mafia 2. Mafia -- New York (N.Y.) -- History -- 20th century 3. Organized crime 4. Organized crime -- New York (State)

ISBN 0-312-30094-8

LC 2005-48416

"With vivid characterizations of a cavalcade of thugs, Raab's account is the most lively and informative Mafia history in years." Booklist

Includes bibliographical references

Reppetto, Thomas A.

American Mafia; a history of its rise to power. {by} Thomas Reppetto. H. Holt 2003 318p il $26; pa $15   **364.1**

1. Mafia

ISBN 0-8050-7210-1; 0-8050-7798-7 pa

LC 2003-56736

"Though this book doesn't answer every question about the Mafia in America, it does present a thought-provoking depiction of the Mob devoid of the sensationalism prevalent in many other portrayals." Publ Wkly

Includes bibliographical references

Rule, Ann

Dead by sunset; perfect husband, perfect killer? Simon & Schuster 1995 429p il hardcover o.p. pa $7.99   **364.1**

1. Homicide 2. Trials 3. Trials (Homicide)

ISBN 0-671-00113-2 pa

LC 95-38326

"Rule's writing is crisp and well paced, full of details that give the reader clear insight into circumstances and surroundings, as well as motive." Libr J

--and never let her go; Thomas Capano, the deadly seducer. Pocket Star Books 2000 680p il pa $7.99   **364.1**

1. District attorneys 2. Homicide 3. Lawyers 4. Missing persons 5. Murder victims 6. Murderers 7. Secretaries 8. State government employees 9. Trials (Homicide)

ISBN 0-671-86871-3; 978-0-671-86871-0

"In June 1996, Anne Marie Fahey, a 30-year-old secretary to the governor of Delaware, disappeared and was reported missing by her family. In the weeks that followed, a charming, successful, and well-connected attorney, Tom Capano, was charged with her murder. Rule . . . tells the riveting story of the three-year secret affair between Fahey and Capano and a cruel obsession that led to murder." Booklist

Saviano, Roberto

Gomorrah; translated from the Italian by Virginia Jewiss. Farrar, Straus & Giroux 2007 301p map $25   **364.1**

1. Camorra -- History 2. Organized crime 3. Organized

crime -- Italy -- Naples (Province)
ISBN 978-0-374-16527-7; 0-374-16527-0

LC 2007-31004

This "is an eyepopping, hair-raising, stomach-turning book. The mob has never looked so bad—or read so well." Christ Sci Monit

Selby, Scott Andrew

Flawless; inside the largest diamond heist in history. by Scott Andrew Selby and Greg Campbell. Sterling Pub. Co. 2010 319p il map $24.95 **364.1**
1. Diamonds 2. Theft
ISBN 978-1-4027-6651-0

LC 2009-40766

The authors "provide an engrossing nonfiction thriller with a truly improbable story at its center, but they also provide a colorful look at the shadowy world of the diamond trade—how they're graded, sold, secured and stolen." Kirkus
Includes bibliographical references

Shteir, Rachel

The **steal**; a cultural history of shoplifting. Penguin Press 2011 256p $25.95 **364.1**
1. Shoplifting 2. Shoplifting -- History
ISBN 9781594202971; 1594202974

LC 2010047842

"As with any specialized crime enterprise, the technology and vocabulary of the trade make for particularly giddy reading. Luckily for readers, Shteir has keen inside-dopester instincts and 'The Steal' is best when she follows them." Boston Globe
Includes bibliographical references.

Sifakis, Carl

★ The **mafia** encyclopedia; 3rd ed; Facts on File 2005 510p il $65; pa $21.95 **364.1**
1. Mafia -- Dictionaries 2. Reference books
ISBN 0-8160-5694-3; 0-8160-5695-1 pa

LC 2004-58487

"Sifakis provides detailed, informed, and colorful information." Libr J

Smith, Jennie Erin

Stolen world; a tale of reptiles, smugglers and skulduggery. Crown 2011 322p il $25; ebook $25 **364.1**
1. Animal dealers 2. Rare animals 3. Rare reptiles 4. Reptiles 5. Smuggling 6. Wild animal trade 7. Wild animal trade -- Corrupt practices 8. Wildlife smuggling
ISBN 978-0-307-38147-7; 0-307-38147-1; 978-0-307-72026-9 ebook; 0-307-72026-8 ebook

LC 2010-9548

"Smith's affection for these unsavory people gives the book an intriguing moral ambiguity (which might make some environmentalists cringe), but the subculture's brazen shenanigans make for a convoluted, fascinating tale." Publ Wkly

Stewart, James B.

Blind eye; how the medical establishment let a doctor get away with murder. Simon & Schuster 1999 334p il hardcover o.p. pa $14 **364.1**
1. Homicide 2. Murderers 3. Physicians 4. Physicians -- United States -- Biography 5. Serial murderers -- United States -- Biography 6. Serial murders -- United States -- Case studies 7. Serial murders -- Zimbabwe -- Case studies
ISBN 0-684-86563-7 pa

LC 99-37044

This is "not only a fascinating look at a psychopath masquerading as a healer but also a disturbing exposé of the system that fails to protect the public." Libr J

Storia della mafia./English

History of the mafia; translated by Antony Shugaar. Columbia University Press 2009 328p $32.95 **364.1**
1. Mafia
ISBN 978-0-231-13134-6; 0-231-13134-8

LC 2009-11765

"For anyone who has grown weary of the fond treatment of the Mafia in American popular culture this book is a tonic. Lupo's myth-busting history explores why the Mafia survived despite Fascist repression, the 'maxitrial' in Palermo in the nineteen-eighties, and frequent predictions that it would disappear as Italy modernized. While Lupo's focus is on Sicily, he also sketches the development of the Mafia's stateside branches, occasioning the fascinating reminder that the crime network's first American port of call was not New York or New Jersey but New Orleans." New Yorker
Includes bibliographical references

Utley, Robert Marshall

Billy the Kid; a short and violent life. {by} Robert M. Utley. University of Neb. Press 1989 302p il hardcover o.p. pa $16 **364.1**
1. Biography, Individual 2. Outlaws
ISBN 0-8012-9558-8 pa

LC 89-30022

Examines the career of the young outlaw whose life and death were an expression of the violence prevalent on the American frontier

"Robert M. Utley does what countless books, movies, television shows, musical compositions, and paintings have failed to do: he successfully strips off the veneer of legendry to expose the reality of Billy the Kid." Univ Press Books for Public Libr
Includes bibliographical references

Walsh, John

Public enemies; the host of America's most wanted targets the nation's most notorious criminals. {by} John Walsh with Philip Lerman. Pocket Bks. 2001 310p il $24.95; pa $7.99 **364.1**
1. Crime 2. Crime -- United States -- Case studies 3. Criminal investigation -- United States -- Case studies 4. Criminals 5. Criminals -- United States -- Case studies 6. Violent crimes -- United States -- Case studies
ISBN 0-671-01995-3; 0-671-01996-1 pa

LC 2001-34027

"From the media-popular 'Railroad Killer' to a remorse-less member of the Symbionese Liberation Army with 25 years on the lam, to '70s iconoclast Ira Einhorn, who murdered his girlfriend and hid her body for 18 months in a steamer trunk, this title captures the television show's highlights." Publ Wkly

Ward, Nathan

Dark harbor; the war for the New York waterfront. Farrar, Straus and Giroux 2010 250p map $26   **364.1**
1. Homicide 2. Journalists 3. Labor unions 4. Labor unions -- Corrupt practices -- New York (N.Y.) 5. Organized crime 6. Organized crime -- New York (N.Y.) -- History -- 20th century 7. Stevedores 8. Stevedores -- Labor unions -- New York (N.Y.)
ISBN 978-0-374-28622-4; 0-374-28622-1
LC 2009-45680
"The author deftly marshals vast amounts of research to tell his story, including original interviews with players from the era, and he richly evokes the atmosphere of mid-century New York. A lucid, illuminating history of the epicenter of organized crime in America." Kirkus
Includes bibliographical references

Weisman, Steve

★ **50** ways to protect your identity and your credit; everything you need to know about identity theft, credit cards, credit repair, and credit reports. Prentice Hall 2005 xxii, 232p il pa $19.95   **364.1**
1. Consumer credit 2. Credit cards 3. Credit reports 4. Identity theft
ISBN 0-13-146759-X
LC 2004-112968
"This book takes a comprehensive look at the phenomenon of identity theft, explaining what it is, how it happens, how to protect yourself from it, and what to do if it does happen to you. . . . Full of good information presented in usable form, Weisman's book is recommended for public libraries." Libr J

Welch, Craig

Shell games; rogues, smugglers, and the hunt for nature's bounty. William Morrow 2010 274p il map $25.99   **364.1**
1. Poaching 2. Smuggling
ISBN 978-0-06-153713-4; 0-06-153713-6
LC 2009-38980
"Welch covers the wildlife crime beat in Puget Sound, where shellfish poachers wreak havoc on the region's once bountiful, now imperiled marine ecosystem. Writing with the sizzle of a mystery novelist, Welch portrays a complex, driven, and irresistible cast of real-life characters, from fish cops Ed Volz and Kevin Harrington to Doug Tobin, a larger-than-life Native American fisherman. . . . Welch's utterly compelling true tale of black-market trade in endangered ocean wildlife is astounding and infuriating." Booklist
Includes bibliographical references

Wittman, Robert

Priceless; how I went undercover to rescue the world's stolen treasures. [by] Robert K. Wittman

with John Shiffman. Crown Publishers 2010 324p il $25; ebook $25   **364.1**
1. Art thefts 2. Criminal investigation
ISBN 978-0-307-46147-6; 978-0-307-46149-0 ebook
LC 2009-49083
This "book has the excitement of an espionage novel. It's suspenseful, thought provoking, and funny." ARTnews

★ The best American crime reporting, 2010; guest editor, Stephen J. Dubner; series editors, Otto Penzler and Thomas H. Cook. Ecco/HarperCollins Pub. 2010 359p pa $14.99   **364.1**
1. Crime 2. Criminals
ISBN 978-0-06-149086-6
A collection of some of the most noted works of crime journalism from the past year.
"From sitting face-to-face with a cartel hitman to an unsolved kidnapping, the stories collected here are some of the best depictions of the worst of humanity." Publ Wkly

364.15   Offenses against the person

Brown, Elaine

The **condemnation** of Little B. Beacon Press 2002 391p hardcover o.p. pa $19   **364.15**
1. African American juvenile delinquents -- Georgia -- Atlanta -- Public opinion 2. Discrimination in criminal justice administration -- Georgia -- Atlanta 3. Homicide 4. Murder -- Georgia -- Atlanta 5. Murder in mass media
ISBN 0-8070-0975-X pa
LC 2001-37943
"Packed with detail, strong arguments and flashes of brilliance, Brown's book is extraordinarily powerful." Publ Wkly
Includes bibliographical references

Hirsch, James S.

Hurricane: the miraculous journey of Rubin Carter. Houghton Mifflin 2000 358p il $25; pa $14   **364.15**
1. Boxers (Persons) 2. Capital punishment -- United States -- Case studies 3. Crime -- United States -- Case studies 4. Human rights activists 5. Judicial error -- United States -- Case studies 6. Prisoners 7. Victims of crimes
ISBN 0-395-97985-4; 0-618-08728-1 pa
LC 99-52703
"Scrupulously researched and expertly crafted, Hirsch's updated account of Carter's life is both a rich portrait of a complex man and a clear-eyed telling of a remarkable life." Publ Wkly

Kersten, Jason

Journal of the dead; a story of friendship and murder in the New Mexico desert. HarperCollins 2003 236p il map $24.95; pa $12.95   **364.15**
1. Hikers 2. Homicide 3. Murder victims 4. Murderers
ISBN 0-06-018470-1; 0-06095-922-3 pa
LC 2003-40714

The author "tells the story of Coughlin and Kodikian with quiet authority, lending unexpected dignity to the whole affair. The result is a ruminative, wholly absorbing book." N Y Times Book Rev

King, Joyce
Hate crime: the story of a dragging in Jasper, Texas. Pantheon Bks. 2002 225p $24   **364.15**
1. African American men -- Crimes against -- Texas -- Jasper 2. African Americans -- Southern States 3. Hate crimes 4. Hate crimes -- Texas -- Jasper 5. Homicide 6. Murder -- Texas -- Jasper 7. Murder victims 8. Racism -- Texas -- Jasper
ISBN 0-375-42132-7

LC 2001-58074

The author "provides both objective reporting and sensitive insight into the players on both sides of America's racial divide." Booklist

Larson, Erik
★ The **devil** in the white city; murder, magic, and madness at the fair that changed America. Erik Larson. Crown 2003 xi, 447p ill., maps $25.95 **364.15**
1. Devil in the White City, The (Book) 2. Homicide 3. Larson, Erik 4. Murderers
ISBN 0609608444; 9780609608449

LC 20020154046

"This nonfiction tale of Chicago World't Fair of 1893 focuses primarily on two men: Daniel H. Burnham, the architect who was the driving force behind the fair, and Henry H. Holmes, a sadistic serial killer working under the cover of the busy fair. . . Burnham and his partner, John Root, the leading architects in Chicago, were tapped for the job, and they in turn called on Frederick Law Olmstead, Louis Sullivan, and Richard M. Hunt to help them build the world's greatest fair. . . . Unbeknownst to any of them, Holmes, a charismatic, handsome doctor, had arrived in the city and built a complex with apartments, a drugstore, and a vault, which he used to trap his victims until they suffocated." (Booklist)

This is an account of how "H.H. Holmes (born Herman Webster Mudgett) dispatched somewhere between 27 and 200 people, mostly single young women, in the churning new metropolis of Chicago; many of the murders occurred during (and exploited) the city's finest moment, the World's Fair of 1893. Larson's breathtaking new history is a novelistic yet wholly factual account of the fair and the mass murderer who lurked within it." Publ Wkly

Includes bibliographical references (p. [423]-429) and index.

Salamon, Julie
Facing the wind; a true story of tragedy and reconciliation. Random House 2001 302p hardcover o.p. pa $13.95   **364.15**
1. Brooklyn (New York, N.Y.) -- Social conditions 2. Family violence -- New York (State) -- New York 3. Homicide 4. Murder -- New York (State) -- New York 5. Uxoricide -- New York (State) -- New York
ISBN 0-375-75940-9 pa

LC 00-42532

"In 1978, Bob Rowe, an out-of-work Brooklyn lawyer, killed his two sons, his daughter and wife by bashing their heads in with a baseball bat. He was found not guilty by reason of insanity, and after several years in a mental institution was released. He later remarried and had another daughter. Although journalist Salamon . . . did not interview Rowe before his death in 1997, this expertly crafted account is informed by diligent research and interviews with his second wife, Colleen, as well as with a women's support group to which Rowe's first wife, Mary, had belonged." Publ Wkly

Schiller, Lawrence
Perfect murder, perfect town. HarperCollins Pubs. 1999 621p hardcover o.p. pa $7.99 **364.15**
1. Beauty contest winners 2. Children 3. Children -- Crimes against -- Colorado -- Boulder -- Case studies 4. Computer industry executives 5. Homemakers 6. Homicide 7. Murder -- Investigation -- Colorado -- Boulder -- Case studies 8. Murder victims 9. Parents of murdered children
ISBN 0-06-109696-2 pa

LC 99-207248

Schiller argues that the "Boulder Police Department bungled the investigation, in large part out of ego and inexperience." N Y Times Book Rev

Stiles, T. J.
★ **Jesse** James; last rebel of the Civil War. Knopf 2002 510p il maps $27.50; pa $16 **364.15**
1. Outlaws 2. Outlaws -- West (U.S.) -- Biography 3. Thieves
ISBN 0-375-40583-6; 0-375-70558-9 pa

LC 2002-25493

"This is a well-written and often surprising reinterpretation of the life of a legendary and enigmatic figure." Booklist
Includes bibliographical references

Thornhill, Randy
A **natural** history of rape; biological bases of sexual coercion. [by] Randy Thornhill and Craig T. Palmer. MIT Press 2000 251p $35; pa $16.95   **364.15**
1. Human evolution 2. Men -- Sexual behavior 3. Rape
ISBN 0-262-20125-9; 0-262-70083-2 pa

LC 99-31685

The authors aim "to show that human rape is a 'natural, biological phenomenon that is a product of the human evolutionary heritage.' . . . Rape, they argue, was favored by natural selection to give sexually dispossessed males the chance to have children, or males with mates the chance to have extra children. . . . They further claim that attempts to root out rape will not succeed until one accepts its evolutionary origin and uses this . . . knowledge as a basis for social policy." New Repub
Includes bibliographical references

Worrall, Simon
The **poet** and the murderer; a true story of literary crime and the art of forgery. Dutton 2002 270p il $23.95; pa $14 **364.15**
1. Forgers 2. Forgery 3. Forgery -- Utah -- Salt Lake City 4. Forgery of manuscripts -- Utah -- Salt Lake City

5. Homicide 6. Murderers
ISBN 0-525-94596-2; 0-452-28402-3 pa
LC 2001-53878

"In 1997, Sotheby's unveiled what experts believed was a newly discovered poem, 'That God Cannot Be Understood,' by Emily Dickinson. A few weeks later, the . . . discovery was revealed a forgery by a man who had already convincingly forged documents by more than 100 literary and historical figures, including Daniel Boone and Betsy Ross. This book examines the psychology of . . . forger and murderer (he killed two people who threatened his unmasking) Mark Hofmann." Booklist

★ The Ultimate Jack the Ripper companion; an illustrated encyclopedia. {compiled by} Stewart P. Evans & Keith Skinner. Carroll & Graf Pubs. 2000 692p il $35; pa $16   **364.15**
1. Homicide 2. Murderers 3. Serial murders -- England -- London -- History -- 19th century
ISBN 0-7867-0768-2; 0-7867-0926-X pa
LC 00-711560

This is a collection of primary and secondary source material pertaining to the Whitechapel murders.

"This volume is undoubtedly the single largest resource on this case ever published." Libr J

Includes bibliographical references

364.152   Homicide

Blum, Howard
American lightning; terror, mystery, moviemaking, and the crime of the century. Crown Publishers 2008 339p il $24.95   **364.152**
1. Bombings 2. Detectives 3. Lawyers 4. Memoirists 5. Motion picture directors 6. State legislators 7. Terrorism 8. Writers on law
ISBN 978-0-307-34694-0
LC 2008-2974

"Blum's prose is tight, his speculations unfailingly sound and his research extensive—all adding up to an absorbing and masterful true crime narrative." Publ Wkly

Includes bibliographical references

Bowden, Charles
Murder city; Ciudad Juarez and the global economy's new killing fields. photographs by Julian Cardona. Nation Books 2010 320p il $27.50 **364.152**
1. Drug traffic 2. Drug traffic -- Mexico 3. Homicide 4. Homicide -- Mexico
ISBN 978-1-56858-449-2; 1-56858-449-0
LC 2010-01716

"Bowden uses his tremendous talents to tell a haunting, darkly poetic story of a city's horrifying descent into madness and anarchy. A potent book that readers won't soon forget, and a warning of what can come of an insatiable market that knows no borders." Kirkus

Braude, Joseph
The **honored** dead; Joseph Braude. 1st ed. Spiegel & Grau 2011 xvi, 318p.p   **364.152**
ISBN 9780385527033; 0385527039; 9780679604327

ebook
LC 2010046496

This book recounts the author's experiences as a journalist with 'embed-style access' to a police precinct in Casablanca, [Morocco]. . . . The Judiciary Police, an FBI-like agency, were . . . proud of their low crime rate compared to the United States, although bedeviled by a pesky sect of Islamist militants. . . . The particular murder that fascinated the author during this period involved a 41-year-old homeless Berber man, Ibrahim Dey, who was beaten to death in a warehouse where he had been sleeping for five years—ostensibly for theft. Dey was well liked and considered a majdub, or someone who brings fortune to others, and his best friend, Muhammad Bari, whom Braude befriended, swore to vindicate the suspicious murder." (Kirkus)

Brown, Ethan
Shake the devil off; a true story of the murder that rocked New Orleans. Henry Holt and Co. 2009 286p il $25   **364.152**
1. Bartenders 2. Homicide 3. Murder -- Louisiana -- New Orleans 4. Murder victims 5. Murderers 6. Soldiers
ISBN 978-0-8050-8893-9; 0-8050-8893-8
LC 2009-06698

Drawing the parallel between Katrina's aftermath and Bowen's unraveling psyche, Brown creates a riveting portrait of a gruesome crime while detailing the heart of a city in distress. A grim murder-suicide story delivered with skill and verve. Kirkus

Includes bibliographical references

Bryan, Patricia L.
Midnight assassin; a murder in America's heartland. [by] Patricia L. Bryan & Thomas Wolf. Algonquin Books of Chapel Hill 2005 278p $23.95 **364.152**
1. Farmers 2. Homemakers 3. Trials (Homicide)
ISBN 1-565-12306-9
LC 2004-59782

Bryan and Wolf offer "not only an interesting trial drama but also a look into social attitudes of rural America at the beginning of the 20th century, especially toward women." Libr J

Includes bibliographical references

Burke, Timothy M.
The **Paradiso** files; Boston's unknown serial killer. Steerforth Press 2008 346p il $24.95 **364.152**
1. Homicide 2. Murderers 3. Sex offenders
ISBN 978-1-58642-140-3; 1-58642-137-9
LC 2007-42576

"Burke tells a compelling story, with chilling accounts of Paradiso's crimes gleaned from victims' accounts and evidence that never made it to court. . . . The story transcends Boston with an insider's view of the criminal justice system." Boston Globe

Buruma, Ian
★ **Murder** in Amsterdam; the death of Theo van Gogh and the limits of tolerance. Penguin Press 2006 278p $24.95   **364.152**
1. College teachers 2. Ethnic relations 3. Motion

picture directors 4. Political leaders 5. Sociologists 6. Television producers 7. Toleration

ISBN 1-59420-108-0; 978-1-59420-108-0

LC 2006-43606

This is a "shrewd, subtly argued inquiry into the tensions and resentments underlying two of the most shocking events in the recent history of the Netherlands." N Y Times (Late N Y Ed)

Includes bibliographical references

Buss, David M.

The **murderer** next door; why the mind is designed to kill. Penguin Press 2005 278p $24.95 **364.152**

1. Homicide

ISBN 1-59420-043-2

LC 2005-43105

The author argues "that murder is the product of evolutionary forces and that the homicidal act, in evolutionary terms, conveys advantages to the killer. . . . Well argued and unsettling." Booklist

Includes bibliographical references

Collins, Paul

The **murder** of the century; Paul Collins. Crown 2011 viii, 325p ill. **364.152**

ISBN 9780307592200; 0307592200

LC 2011009390

This book discusses "a sensational 1897 murder case that fascinated the public as it played out across the front pages of the New York Citys leading newspapers: Joseph Pulitzer's 'New York World' and William Randolph Hearst's 'New York Journal.' After a group of children discovered the ghastly severed trunk of William Guldensuppe, a Turkish bath-house attendant, the rival news organs spared no expense to ferret out the culprits, eventually tracking the purchase of an oilcloth used to wrap the torso to Mrs. Augusta Nack, a German immigrant midwife and rumored back-room abortionist. Guldensuppe had been Nack's lover before being replaced by Martin Thorn, a hotheaded barber. Things failed to progress smoothly." (Kirkus)

Cullen, Dave

Columbine. Twelve 2009 417p $26.99 **364.152**

1. Columbine High School Massacre, Littleton, Colo., 1999 2. School shootings 3. School shootings -- Colorado

ISBN 978-0-446-54693-5; 0-446-54693-3

LC 2008-31441

This is an account of the shootings at Columbine High School in 1999.

This book "is an excellent work of media criticism, showing how legends become truths through continual citation; a sensitive guide to the patterns of public grief . . . and, at the end of the day, a fine example of old-fashioned journalism." N Y Times Book Rev

Includes bibliographical references

Diebel, Linda

Betrayed; the assassination of Digna Ochoa. Carroll & Graf 2006 513p il $27 **364.152**

1. Homicide 2. Homicide -- Mexico 3. Human rights

activists 4. Lawyers 5. Murder victims

ISBN 0-7867-1753-X; 978-0-7867-1753-8

LC 2006-275515

"Digna Ochoa, a Mexican human rights lawyer, died of a gunshot wound to the back of her head on October 19, 2001. The investigation into her death was reopened in 2005 after initially being ruled a suicide. Diebel . . . writes that there is no doubt that Ochoa was murdered for defending those tortured and harassed by the Mexican army." Libr J

Includes bibliographical references

Hakkakiyan, Ru'ya

Assassins of the Turquoise Palace. Grove Press 2011 322p **364.152**

1. Assassination 2. Political crimes and offenses 3. Trials (Homicide)

ISBN 0-8021-1911-5; 978-0-8021-1911-7

Heidenry, John

Zero at the bone; the playboy, the prostitute, and the murder of Bobby Greenlease. St. Martin's Press 2009 230p il $25.99; pa $14.99 **364.152**

1. Children 2. Homicide 3. Kidnap victims 4. Kidnappers 5. Kidnapping 6. Kidnapping -- Missouri -- Saint Louis 7. Murder -- Missouri -- Saint Louis 8. Murder victims 9. Murderers

ISBN 978-0-312-37679-6; 0-312-37679-0; 978-0-312-64196-2 pa; 0-312-64196-6 pa

LC 2009-7677

An account of the 1953 kidnapping and murder of 6-year-old Bobby Greenlease by Carl Austin Hall and Bonnie Brown Heady.

This is "a tough, gripping chiller of a book, written straightforwardly yet cloaked with the trappings of pulp fiction." N Y Times (Late N Y Ed)

Includes bibliographical references

Higham, Scott

Finding Chandra; a true Washington murder mystery. [by] Scott Higham and Sari Horowitz. Scribner 2010 287p il map $26 **364.152**

1. County government officials 2. Government employees 3. Homicide 4. Interns 5. Mayors 6. Members of Congress 7. Missing persons 8. Murder -- Washington (D.C.) 9. Murder victims 10. Prisoners 11. State legislators

ISBN 978-1-4391-3867-0; 1-4391-3867-2

LC 2009-50721

"A well-reported, well-written chronicle of a botched criminal investigation and its disturbing aftermath." Kirkus

Junger, Sebastian

★ A **death** in Belmont. Norton 2006 266p il $23.95 **364.152**

1. Authors 2. Homemakers 3. Homicide 4. Journalists 5. Maintenance workers 6. Murder victims 7. Murderers 8. Nonfiction writers

ISBN 0-393-05980-4

"In [Albert] DeSalvo's dark world, Junger's clear, beautifully reasonable writing is the literary equivalent of night-vision goggles." Time

Includes bibliographical references

Kraybill, Donald B.

Amish grace; how forgiveness transcended tragedy. [by] Donald B. Kraybill, Steven M. Nolt, [and] David L. Weaver-Zercher. Jossey-Bass 2007 237p $24.95 **364.152**

1. Amish 2. Amish -- Doctrines 3. Amish School Shooting, Nickel Mines, Pa., 2006 4. Forgiveness 5. Forgiveness -- Religious aspects -- Christianity

ISBN 978-0-7879-9761-8; 0-7879-9761-7

This book explains "Amish reaction to the horrific Nickel Mines shootings. . . . This anguished and devastating account of a national tragedy and a hopeful, life-affirming lesson in how to live is itself a marvel of grace." Booklist

Includes bibliographical references

Larson, Erik

★ **Thunderstruck**. Crown Publishers 2006 463p il map $25.95 **364.152**

1. Biography, Individual 2. Electrical engineers 3. Homeopathic physicians 4. Homicide 5. Inventors 6. Murderers 7. Nobel laureates for physics 8. Radio 9. Telegraph, Wireless -- History

ISBN 1-4000-8066-5; 978-1-4000-8066-3

LC 2006-11908

This book "alternates the story of Marconi's quest for the first wireless transatlantic communication amid scientific jealousies and controversies with the tale of [Dr. Hawley Harvey Crippen,] a mild-mannered murderer caught as a result of the invention. . . . A thrilling read." SLJ

Includes bibliographical references

Leake, John

Entering Hades; the double life of a serial killer. Farrar, Straus & Giroux 2007 350p il $25 **364.152**

1. Authors 2. Biography, Individual 3. Criminals 4. Dramatists 5. Homicide 6. Journalists 7. Murderers 8. Novelists 9. Serial murderers

ISBN 978-0-374-14845-4; 0-374-14845-7

LC 2007-08644

The author "has written the definitive book—dispassionate, superbly detailed—on Jack Unterweger." N Y Times Book Rev

Includes bibliographical references

May, Gary

The **informant**; the FBI, the Ku Klux Klan, and the murder of Viola Liuzzo. Yale University Press 2005 431p il $35 **364.152**

1. Civil rights activists 2. Civil rights workers 3. Homicide 4. Homicide -- Alabama 5. Informers 6. Murder victims

ISBN 0-300-10635-1

LC 2005-2067

"This is popular history at its best and shines a long overdue light on a dark chapter in the FBI's past." Publ Wkly

Includes bibliographical references

Maynard, Joyce

★ **Internal** combustion; the true story of a marriage and a murder in the Motor City. Jossey-Bass 2006 490p il $24.95 **364.152**

1. Elementary school teachers 2. Homicide 3. Murderers

ISBN 978-0-7879-8226-3; 0-7879-8226-1

LC 2006-17098

"Though she was unable to get Nancy or most of her immediate family to talk to her, Maynard seems to have formed a surprisingly complete picture of their lives." Libr J

Includes bibliographical references

Parry, Richard Lloyd

People who eat darkness; the true story of a young woman who vanished from the streets of Tokyo and the evil that swallowed her up. Richard Lloyd Parry. Farrar, Straus and Giroux 2012 454 p. **364.152**

1. Murder -- Investigation -- Japan -- Tokyo 2. Nonfiction 3. Young women -- Crimes against -- Japan -- Tokyo

ISBN 9780224079174 Jonathan Cape; 0224079174 Jonathan Cape; 0374230595 Farrar, Straus and Giroux; 9780374230593 Farrar, Straus and Giroux

LC 2011047019

This true crime book by Richard Lloyd Parry tells the story of how Lucie Blackman—tall, blond, twenty-one years old—stepped out into the vastness of Tokyo in the summer of 2000, and disappeared forever. The following winter, her dismembered remains were found buried in a seaside cave. . . . [The author], an award-winning foreign correspondent, covered Lucie's disappearance and followed the massive search for her, the long investigation, and the even longer trial. Over ten years, he earned the trust of her family and friends, won unique access to the Japanese detectives and Japan's convoluted legal system, and delved deep into the mind of the man accused of the crime, Joji Obara, described by the judge as unprecedented and extremely evil. (Publishers note)

Rivard, Robert

Trail of feathers: searching for Philip True; a reporter's murder in Mexico and his editor's search for justice. Public Affairs 2005 417p il $27.50 **364.152**

1. Criminal justice, Administration of -- Mexico 2. Homicide 3. Huichol Indians 4. Journalists 5. Murder victims 6. Reporters and reporting

ISBN 1-58648-222-X

LC 2005-45822

"This is a fascinating look at an intriguing man and an alien culture." Libr J

Includes bibliographical references

Rule, Ann

Too late to say goodbye; a true story of murder and betrayal. Free Press 2007 456p il $26 **364.152**

1. Homemakers 2. Homicide 3. Murder victims

ISBN 978-0-7432-3852-6; 0-7432-3852-4

LC 2007-9168

"Rule's meticulous 2½ years of research provides a cinematically satisfying look into how police in two jurisdictions worked together to prove Corbin was a serial murderer of women who tried to leave him." USA Today

Sides, Hampton

★ **Hellhound** on his trail; the stalking of Martin Luther King, Jr., and the international hunt for his assassin. Doubleday 2010 459p il $28.95 **364.152**
1. Assassination 2. Biography, Individual 3. Civil rights activists 4. Clergy 5. Murderers 6. Nobel laureates for peace 7. Nonfiction writers
ISBN 978-0-385-52392-9; 0-385-52392-0
LC 2009-43659
"Sides begins with Ray's escape from a maximum security prison in Missouri the prior April. In short, crisp chapters, Sides then cuts back and forth between Ray's movements during the ensuing year and King's increasing challenges during the same period, as a fraying civil rights movement struggled to transform hard-won legal equality into economic justice. Along the way, we're treated to vignettes featuring J. Edgar Hoover's vicious anti-King smear tactics; George Wallace's race-driven politics of hate during the 1968 presidential campaign; and an embittered Lyndon Johnson's estrangement from King over the ongoing war in Vietnam. None of this is new, but Sides ensures that it's still compulsively readable." Milwaukee Journal Sentinel
Includes bibliographical references

Starr, Douglas

The **killer** of little shepherds; a true crime story and the birth of forensic science. A.A. Knopf 2010 300p il $26.95 **364.152**
1. Criminologists 2. Forensic sciences 3. Forensic sciences -- History 4. Homicide 5. Law enforcement officials 6. Murderers 7. Physicians 8. Serial murders -- France 9. Trials (Homicide) 10. Trials (Murder) -- France
ISBN 978-0-307-26619-4; 0-307-26619-2
LC 2010-14930
This book is "like an episode of CSI: 19th-Century France. As he prowled the countryside, Joseph Vacher preyed on young shepherds, ultimately slaughtering four times as many people as Jack the Ripper. How the bumbling French authorities finally pieced together the evidence — while learning to study bodies and crime scenes for clues and to compare details about the killings — represents, Starr says, nothing less than the birth of forensic science. In gripping, almost novelistic chapters, he alternates between Vacher and Alexandre Lacassagne, the criminologist who helped crack the case." Entertainment Wkly
Includes bibliographical references

Stashower, Daniel

The **beautiful** cigar girl; Mary Rogers, Edgar Allan Poe, and the invention of murder. Dutton 2006 326p il $25.95 **364.152**
1. Authors 2. Essayists 3. Homicide 4. Murder victims 5. Poets 6. Short story writers
ISBN 0-525-94981-X; 978-0-525-94981-7
LC 2006-19335
The author "tells the story of New York City cigar store clerk Mary Rogers, whose violent death in 1841 brought on a frenzy of sensational newspaper stories and prompted

the interest of Edgar Allan Poe. . . . [He] details how the mystery surrounding Rogers's murder became the inspiration for Poe's story 'The Mystery of Marie Rogêt.' . . . Well researched and accessible, here is a gripping story that is hard to put down." Libr J
Includes bibliographical references

Summerscale, Kate

The **suspicions** of Mr. Whicher; a shocking murder and the undoing of a great Victorian detective. Walker & Company 2008 360p il map $24.95 **364.152**
1. Biography, Individual 2. Centenarians 3. Children 4. Detectives 5. Homicide 6. Murder -- England 7. Murder victims 8. Murderers 9. Nurses
ISBN 978-0-8027-1535-7; 0-8027-1535-4
LC 2008-00247
This is the story of Inspector Jonathan Whicher of Scotland Yard, who investigated the 1860 murder of three-year-old Francis Saville Kent in the village of Road, Wiltshire.
The author's "clean writing makes . . . [this book] so dynamic that she can't be accused of 'freezing' the past—instead, she has done a masterly job of reviving it, with all its curiosities and contradictions. But, most strikingly, she has created an enthralling mystery by overlaying the fictional tools of misdirection and suspense onto a nonfiction narrative." Am Scholar
Includes bibliographical references

Swanson, James L.

★ **Manhunt**; the 12-day chase for Lincoln's killer. William Morrow 2006 448p il $26.95 **364.152**
1. Actors 2. Lawyers 3. Members of Congress 4. Murderers 5. Presidents 6. State legislators
ISBN 0-06-051849-9
LC 2005-44911
While this book "belongs in the history section . . . it's as gripping a page-turner as anything you'll find on the mystery shelf." Entertainment Weekly
Includes bibliographical references

364.16 Offenses against property

Wambaugh, Joseph

Fire lover; a true story. Morrow 2002 338p $25.95; pa $7.99 **364.16**
1. Arson 2. Arson -- California -- Case studies 3. Arsonists 4. Firefighters 5. Pyromania -- California -- Case studies
ISBN 0-06-009527-X; 0-06-009528-8 pa
LC 2002-20139
"Wambaugh's painstaking research which included interviews with law-enforcement officers, survivors, and victims' families, is astonishing." Booklist

364.3   Offenders

Paradis, Cheryl

The **measure** of madness; inside the disturbed and disturbing criminal mind. Citadel Press 2010 272p pa $16.95   **364.3**

1. Criminal psychology 2. Forensic sciences

ISBN 978-0-8065-3105-2

LC 2010-924994

The author "has spent more than two decades evaluating mentally ill and violent individuals and giving expert testimony in court. Here she details criminal cases in which the prosecution or defense asked her to establish whether defendants were competent to stand trial, or to vet such psychiatric defenses as insanity and extreme emotional disturbance. The cases, all tried in New York City, are fascinating, unsettling and often horrifying. . . . The author also discusses the psycho-legal issues of cases involving juveniles and abused wives. . . . A welcome inside account." Kirkus

Includes bibliographical references

Rhodes, Richard

Why they kill; the discoveries of a maverick criminologist. Knopf 1999 371p $26.95; pa $14   **364.3**

1. College teachers 2. Criminal behavior -- Research -- Methodology 3. Criminal psychology 4. Criminal psychology -- Case studies 5. Criminals 6. Violence 7. Violent crimes -- Case studies

ISBN 0-375-40249-7; 0-375-70248-2 pa

LC 99-18920

The author discusses the history of violence and the work of social scientist Lonnie H. Athens. "Athens interviewed prisoners in maximum security prisons in Iowa, California and elsewhere, predominantly men. . . . His hope was to bypass inmates' typical narratives and get to what they actually thought and felt when they assaulted or raped or killed." N Y Times Book Rev

Includes bibliographical references and index

364.4   Prevention of crime and delinquency

Stuntz, William J.

The **collapse** of American criminal justice. Belknap Press of Harvard University Press 2011 413p il $35   **364.4**

1. Administration of criminal justice 2. African Americans -- Civil rights 3. Crime prevention 4. Crime prevention -- United States 5. Criminal justice, Administration of -- United States

ISBN 978-0-674-05175-1; 0-674-05175-0

LC 2011006905

This is "a fascinating, passionate, compassionate, often brilliant book. Flawless? No. But it's a work that deserves to have a significant influence on American criminal-justice thinkers from across the political spectrum." Natl Rev

Includes bibliographical references

364.66   Capital punishment

Christianson, Scott

The **last** gasp; the rise and fall of the American gas chamber. University of California Press 2010 325p il $27.50   **364.66**

1. Capital punishment -- United States 2. Executions & executioners 3. Gas chambers -- History

ISBN 978-0-520-25562-3

LC 2009-52476

The book "provides an . . . account of the origins and relatively short career of the gas chamber, both as a mode of execution in the United States and as a means of Nazi-run genocide in Europe during World War II. . . . Christianson interweaves the American execution chronology with Adolf Hitler's deployment of Zyklon-B. . . . Christianson argues that the American chemical industry and American policy makers sympathetic to its interests . . . deserve an as-yet unrecognized share of responsibility for the Nazi genocide for their promotion of the market for cyanide, their cozy relationship with Nazi leaders during the buildup to the war, and their insufficient support of European Jews during the war." (Journal of American History)

The author "charts the 75-year history of gas chamber execution as well as its intersection with eugenics, the Holocaust, and America's ongoing capital punishment debate. . . . Though the gas chamber hasn't been used in America since 1999, Christianson makes a chilling argument for its—and the death penalty's—abolition." Publ Wkly

Includes bibliographical references

Heard, Alex

The **eyes** of Willie McGee; a tragedy of race, sex, and secrets in the Jim Crow South. Harper 2010 404p il $26.99   **364.66**

1. Alleged criminals 2. Capital punishment 3. Discrimination in capital punishment 4. Discrimination in criminal justice administration 5. Trials 6. Veterans

ISBN 978-0-06-128415-1; 0-06-128415-7

LC 2009-51769

"McGee was mourned in poems, novels and memoirs. But while he clearly did not get a fair trial, was he innocent? Was Willette Hawkins really the guilty party? 'The Eyes of Willie McGee' leaves us wondering, and wondering how many other ghosts remain in Jim Crow's closet." Los Angeles Times

Henderson, Harry

★ **Capital** punishment; 3rd ed; Facts on File 2006 316p il $45   **364.66**

1. Capital punishment

ISBN 0-8160-5708-7

LC 2005-13671

A look at both sides of this controversial issue from social, political, ethical, and religious perspectives. Includes a glossary, bibliographies, and Internet sources.

Prejean, Helen

★ The **death** of innocents; an eyewitness account of wrongful executions. Random House 2005 310p $25.95   **364.66**

1. Capital punishment 2. Capital punishment -- Moral

and ethical aspects 3. Machinists 4. Murderers 5. Prisoners 6. Wrongful death
ISBN 0-679-44056-9

LC 2004-54154

The author "reexamines the cases of two men she fervently believes were executed for crimes they did not commit. . . . In addition to providing a searing indictment of capital punishment, Prejean also exposes the fundamental inadequacies of the American court system. Expect demand for this extremely thought-provoking book." Booklist

Includes bibliographical references

Solotaroff, Ivan

The **last** face you'll ever see; the private life of the American death penalty. HarperCollins Pubs. 2001 232p hardcover o.p. pa $12.95   **364.66**
1. Capital punishment 2. Capital punishment -- United States 3. Death row -- United States 4. Executions and executioners -- United States
ISBN 0-06-093103-5 pa

LC 2001-16604

"Entertainingly written, well researched and documented, this is important reading for death-penalty activists, pro and con, and other concerned citizens." Booklist

Includes bibliographical references

365   Penal and related institutions

Abbott, Jack Henry

In the belly of the beast; letters from prison. with an introduction by Norman Mailer. Random House 1981 166p hardcover o.p. pa $12   **365**
1. Prisoners 2. Prisons -- United States
ISBN 0-679-73237-3 pa

LC 80-6038

Abbott's "letters belong with the best prison literature, not because of their accounts of atrocity, but for their disturbing picture of daily life behind bars." Time

Applebaum, Anne

★ **Gulag**; a history. Doubleday 2003 677p il maps $35   **365**
1. Concentration camps 2. Concentration camps -- Soviet Union -- History 3. Convict labor 4. Forced labor -- Soviet Union -- History 5. Prisons -- Soviet Union -- History
ISBN 0-7679-0056-1

LC 2002-41344

This "describes how, largely under Stalin's watch, a regulated, centralized system of prison labor—unprecedented in scope—gradually arose out of the chaos of the Russian Revolution. . . . Applebaum details camp life, including strategies for survival; the experiences of women and children in the camps; sexual relationships and marriages between prisoners; and rebellions, strikes and escapes. . . . Applebaum's lucid prose and painstaking consideration of the competing theories about aspects of camp life and policy are always compelling." Publ Wkly

Includes bibliographical references

Ferro, Jeffrey

★ **Prisons**; Rev. ed; Facts On File, Inc. 2011 312p $45   **365**
1. Prisons 2. Prisons -- United States
ISBN 978-0-8160-8236-0; 978-1-4381-3398-0 ebook

LC 2010-49855

This book "examines the state of U.S. prisons and related issues. It focuses on the development of prisons in the United States and how the competing goals of punishment and rehabilitation have shaped the evolution of criminal correction. An overview presents statistics on U.S. prisons and explores the issues behind those statistics, including racial disparity among prisoners and the causes of recidivism. The financial costs of running prisons and the mixed record of private prisons are examined, and laws and legislation relating to issues of incarceration are reviewed." Publisher's note

Includes bibliographical references

Figes, Orlando

Just send me word; a true story of love and survival in the Gulag. Orlando Figes. Metropolitan Books/Henry Holt and Company 2012 333 p.   **365**
1. Biographies 2. Fiancées -- Soviet Union 3. Fiancées -- Soviet Union -- Correspondence 4. Imprisonment -- Soviet Union 5. Labor camps -- Russia (Federation) -- Pechora (Komi) 6. Love-letters 7. Political prisoners -- Russia (Federation) -- Pechora (Komi) 8. Political prisoners -- Russia (Federation) -- Pechora (Komi) -- Correspondence
ISBN 0805095225; 9780805095227

LC 2011048355

In this book, [d]rawing on more than 1,200 letters between Lev and Svetlana Sveta Mishchenko, and interviews with the couple, veteran historian Figes . . . tells their remarkable tale of love and devotion during the worst years of the USSR. Having fallen in love as physics students at Moscow University, they were separated for 13 years: first while Lev seized in WWII, and then after he was sentenced to a Siberian labor camp for the crime of serving as a translator for a German officer while a POW. Lev's letters illustrate the extreme hardships of the Stalinist camps. . . . Her letters express her extraordinary devotion and determination to visit Lev, which she managed to do four times, despite the long trek, subterfuges, necessary bribes, and dangers involved in the illegal journeys. (Publishers Weekly)

Goewey, David

Crash out; the true tale of a Hell's kitchen kid & the bloodiest escape in Sing Sing history. Crown 2005 304p il $24.95   **365**
1. Escapes
ISBN 1-4000-5469-9

LC 2005-7531

The author details the "biggest prison break (crash out) in Sing Sing history, on Easter Sunday 1941. The story tracks back to a Hell's Kitchen gang that ran a series of headline-grabbing robberies; the crew, who would lead the crash out, were imprisoned after a 1939 heist from Consolidated Edison. Goewey's research is impressive: he interviewed the surviving guard on duty during the prison break, gained access to a scrapbook of news clips housed in the Ossining Historical Society, and combed the WPA Guide to New York

City and case files from New York's Department of Records and Information Services. His writing produces a grim but fascinating snapshot of Depression-era crime." Booklist

Hubner, John

Last chance in Texas; the redemption of criminal youth. Random House 2005 xxv, 277p $25.95 **365**
1. Juvenile delinquency
ISBN 0-375-50809-0

LC 2005-42892

"Readers of this eye-opening account will find themselves reflecting on their own attitudes about juvenile justice as it's administered today." Booklist

Khlevniuk, Oleg V.

The **history** of the Gulag; from collectivization to the great terror. foreword by Robert Conquest; translated by Vadim A. Staklo. Yale University Press 2004 418p il $45 **365**
1. Concentration camps 2. Concentration camps -- Soviet Union -- History 3. Convict labor 4. Forced labor -- Soviet Union 5. Political prisoners -- Soviet Union
ISBN 0-300-09284-9

LC 2004-10969

This "is a fascinatingly detailed depiction of that horrific symbol of the 20th century, the Soviet prison camp system." Publ Wkly

Includes bibliographical references

Kizny, Tomasz

Gulag; life and death inside the Soviet concentration camps. Firefly Books 2004 495p il maps $69.95 **365**
1. Concentration camps 2. Convict labor 3. Documentary photography -- Soviet Union 4. Political prisoners -- Soviet Union
ISBN 1-55297-964-4

LC 2005-357207

This book "contains 550 black-and-white photographs of life in the Soviet Gulag. . . . The photos gathered here range from official archival snapshots, showing both inmates and their captors, to scenes of enormous construction projects and snowbound ruins. Kizny has added his own photographs of the abandoned camps or work projects and included a brief history of the camps and personal accounts of survivors. These rare and historically significant photographs can only hint at the appalling horrors committed within the camps, and the importance of the book cannot be overstated." Booklist

Oshinsky, David M.

★ **Worse** than slavery; Parchman Farm and the ordeal of Jim Crow justice. Free Press 1996 306p il hardcover o.p. pa $14 **365**
1. Administration of criminal justice 2. Prisons -- United States 3. Race discrimination
ISBN 0-684-83095-7 pa

LC 95-52880

"Oshinsky's beautifully constructed narrative brings to vivid life one of the most shameful chapters in American history." New Yorker

Includes bibliographical references

Rees, Sian

The **floating** brothel; the extraordinary true story of an eighteenth-century ship and its cargo of female convicts. Hyperion 2002 236p il maps $23.95 **365**
1. Convict ships -- Great Britain -- History -- 18th century 2. Female offenders -- Great Britain -- History -- 18th century 3. Penal colonies 4. Penal colonies -- Australia -- New South Wales -- History -- 18th century 5. Penal colonies -- Great Britain -- History -- 18th century 6. Prisoners 7. Prisoners, Transportation of -- Great Britain -- History -- 18th century 8. Women criminals 9. Women prisoners -- Great Britain -- History -- 18th century
ISBN 0-7868-6787-6

LC 2001-46338

"Rees uses every scrap of information she can muster to produce a lively, vibrant sense of these women as they must have lived their lives." Publ Wkly

Includes bibliographical references

Solzhenitsyn, Aleksandr

★ The **Gulag** Archipelago, 1918-1956 v1; an experiment in literary investigation. [by] Aleksandr I. Solzhenitsyn; translated from the Russian by Thomas P. Whitney; foreword by Anne Applebaum. Harper Perennial Modern Classics 2007 xx, 660p pa $21.95 **365**
1. Political prisoners
ISBN 978-0-06-125371-3; 0-06-125371-5

The first volume of the author's three-volume "'literary investigation' of the network of Soviet prison camps as they existed between 1918 and 1956. . . . A mixture of autobiography, history, and analysis, the relentlessly grim picture of life inside the camps forms the basis for an attack not only on Stalinism and Leninism but also on the whole process of substituting Western rational and secular ideas for Russia's traditional mysticism." Benét's Reader's Ency. 4th edition

★ The **Gulag** Archipelago, 1918-1956 v2; an experiment in literary investigation. [by] Aleksandr I. Solzhenitsyn; translated from the Russian by Thomas P. Whitney; foreword by Anne Applebaum. Harper Perennial Modern Classics 2007 712p il map pa $21.95 **365**
1. Political prisoners
ISBN 978-0-06-125372-0; 0-06-125372-3

This second volume of a two-volume series describes "the story of Solzhenitsyn's entrance into the Soviet prison camps, where he would remain for nearly a decade." Publisher's note

★ The **Gulag** Archipelago, 1918-1956 v3; an experiment in literary investigation. [by] Aleksandr I. Solzhenitsyn; translated from the Russian by Harry Willetts; foreword by Anne Applebaum. Harper

Perennial Modern Classics 2007 558p il map pa
$21.95   **365**
  1. Political prisoners
  ISBN 978-0-06-125373-7; 0-06-125373-1
  The final volume of a three-volume series, this book contains the author's "account of resistance within the Soviet
labor camps and his own release after eight years." Publisher's note

Wynn, Jennifer
  Inside Rikers; stories from the world's largest
penal colony. St. Martin's Press 2001 223p $24.95;
pa $13.95   **365**
  1. Prisoners 2. Prisoners -- New York (State) -- New
York
  ISBN 0-312-26179-9; 0-312-29158-2 pa
                                              LC 2001-19261
  "Wynn's study is ultimately a call for much-needed prison reform, with emphasis on rehabilitation rather than mere
incarceration, and she makes her case well." Booklist
  Includes bibliographical references

Encyclopedia of American prisons; editors, Marilyn D. McShane, Frank P. Williams III. Garland
  1996 xxv, 532p il $160   **365**
  1. Administration of criminal justice -- Dictionaries
  2. Crime -- United States -- Dictionaries 3. Prisons --
  Dictionaries 4. Prisons -- United States -- Encyclopedias
  5. Reference books
  ISBN 0-8153-1350-0
                                              LC 95-41593
  This encyclopedia "traces the history and development
of the major prisons in the United States and provides an
overview of prison issues such as convicts with AIDS, prisoners' rights, and juveniles behind bars." Libr J

★ Encyclopedia of prisons & correctional facilities;
  Mary Bosworth, editor. Sage Publications 2005
  2v il set $310   **365**
  1. Prisons -- United States -- Encyclopedias 2.
  Reference books
  ISBN 0-7619-2731-X
                                              LC 2004-21802
  The entries in this encyclopedia "revolve around 12
themes, among them theories of punishment, prison architecture, prison populations, juvenile justice, prison reform,
treatment programs, and race, gender, and class. . . . Those
interested in understanding the US's complex system of
incarceration will find this encyclopedia a vital reference
tool." Choice
  Includes bibliographical references

366   Secret associations and societies

Ridley, Jasper Godwin
  ★ The **Freemasons**; a history of the world's
most powerful secret society. [by] Jasper Ridley. Arcade Pub. 2001 357p $25.95; pa $14.95   **366**
  ISBN 1-55970-601-5; 1-55970-654-6 pa
                                              LC 2001-45745

  The author "traces the origins of freemasonry back to
the craft guilds in medieval Europe, and then he chronicles
their growth and evolution through the modern era. . . . This
work of popular history sheds light on a frequently obscure
subject." Booklist
  Includes bibliographical references

368   Insurance

Boyd, Roddy
  Fatal risk; a cautionary tale of AIG's corporate
suicide. Wiley 2011 349p   **368**
  1. Financial crises 2. Insurance 3. Insurance executives
  ISBN 978-0-470-88980-0
                                              LC 2011-01512
  "A vivid portrait of the giant insurer at the center of the
2008 financial crisis." Wall Street J

368.32   Life insurance

Beard, Patricia
  After the ball; Gilded Age secrets, boardroom
betrayals, and the party that ignited the great Wall
Street scandal of 1905. HarperCollins 2003 402p il
$25.95; pa $14.95   **368.32**
  1. Businessmen -- New York (N.Y.) -- History -- 20th
century 2. Financiers 3. Philanthropists 4. Scandals
-- United States 5. Wall Street (New York, N.Y.)
  ISBN 0-06-019939-3; 0-06-095892-8 pa
                                              LC 2003-44987
  The author "details the great Equitable Life Assurance
scandal of 1905 that captured the national spotlight and
shook Wall Street. The death in 1899 of Equitable's president and founder, Henry Hyde, created a power vacuum
in one of the era's richest and most powerful companies.
Hyde's chosen successor, his son James Hazen Hyde,
quickly became embroiled in a struggle for control of the
company with the 'old guard.' James's extravagant lifestyle
and expensive tastes came to be used against him. . . . The
saga is complete with betrayal, romance, accounting fraud,
sneaky backroom deals, and connections to some of the most
powerful men of the era, including President Theodore Roosevelt. Well written and documented, this fast-paced book
reads like a novel." Libr J
  Includes bibliographical references

368.4   Government-sponsored insurance

Altman, Nancy J.
  ★ The **battle** for Social Security; from
FDR's vision to Bush's gamble. Wiley 2005 362p
$24.95   **368.4**
  1. Social security
  ISBN 978-0-471-77172-2; 0-471-77172-4
                                              LC 2005-20700
  The author "traces the history of Social Security from
its introduction in 1935, and provides a thoughtful, well-re-

searched case against the . . . [Bush] administration's efforts to reduce Social Security protection." Booklist

Includes bibliographical references

Frank, Joshua

The **people's** pension; the struggle to defend social security since Reagan. Eric Laursen, Joshua Frank; [edited by] 674-A 23rd Street. AK Press 2012 818 p. ill. (alk. paper) $13.99   **368.4**

ISBN 9781849351010

LC 2012933068

This book looks at the issue of Social Security in terms of the U.S. 2012 presidential election. In "the aftermath of the debt reduction deal between Barack Obama and congressional Republicans, the 2012 election promises to be a kind of referendum on the size and role of government—including economic support programs like Social Security. . . . Eric Laursen suggests that the only solution for Social Security is taking it out of the government's hands altogether." (Barnes and Noble)

United States/Social Security Administration

★ **Social** Security handbook; overview of Social Security programs. Bernan Press 2010 697p pa $60   **368.4**

1. Social security

ISBN 978-1-59888-425-8

"Detailed explanation without commentary of the federal retirement, survivors, disability, black lung benefits, supplementary security income, and health insurance programs, who is entitled to benefits, and how such benefits may be obtained." Ref Sources for Small & Medium-sized Libr. 6th edition

370   Education

Education index. Wilson, H.W.   **370**

1. Education -- Periodicals -- Indexes 2. Reference books

A cumulative index to more than 500 English-language periodicals, yearbooks, and monographs. The main body consists of subject and author entries arranged in one alphabet. In addition there is an author listing of citations to book reviews

"A cornerstone for information and research in the field of education." Am Ref Books Annu, 1982

★ Encyclopedia of education; James W. Guthrie, editor in chief. 2nd ed; Macmillan Ref. USA 2003 8v il set $850   **370**

1. Education -- Encyclopedias 2. Education -- Encyclopedias and dictionaries 3. Reference books

ISBN 0-02-865594-X

LC 2002-8205

This set includes over 850 signed articles covering educational policy and curriculum issues, learning assessment, standards, history and culture, legislation, and profiles of schools, people, and organizations.

"The writing is well edited and accessible." Booklist

Includes bibliographical references

★ The Greenwood dictionary of education; edited by John W. Collins III and Nancy Patricia O'Brien; foreword by Catherine Snow. Greenwood Press 2003 431p $59.95   **370**

1. Education 2. Education -- Dictionaries 3. Reference books

ISBN 0-89774-860-3

LC 2003-51766

"The editors asked . . . experts in various fields of education (e.g., early childhood education, curriculum, adult education, and language acquisition) to write definitions for the volume's 2600 terms, which are used in education research, practice, and theory. . . . It also contains . . . information on how to use the volume, an alphabetical arrangement of entries, cross references, a bibliography of sources, lists of contributing editors and contributors arranged by field, and a list of contributors arranged by initials (so that users can identify entry authors). . . . No library, whether public or academic, should be without this reference source." Libr J

Uncle Tom or new Negro; African Americans reflect on Booker T. Washington and Up from slavery one hundred years later. edited by Rebecca Carroll. Broadway Books/Harlem Moon 2006 320p pa $15.95   **370**

1. African American educators 2. African Americans -- Biography 3. Authors 4. Civil rights activists 5. Educators 6. Memoirists 7. Nonfiction writers 8. Slaves

ISBN 0-7679-1955-6; 978-0-7679-1955-5

LC 2005-50161

"This collection of 20 commentaries by contemporary writers offers new perspectives on Booker T. Washington's autobiography and his place in the struggle for racial equality. Among the commentators are Debra Dickerson, Julianne Malveaux, Bill Ethanson, Ronald Walkers, Earl Ofari Hutchinson, and John McWhorter. The book also includes the complete text of Up from Slavery." Booklist

Includes bibliographical references

370.1   Philosophy and theory, education for specific objectives, educational psychology

Dewey, John

Democracy and education; an introduction to the philosophy of education. Free Press 1997 378p pa $17.95   **370.1**

1. Education -- Philosophy

ISBN 0-684-83631-9; 978-0-684-83631-7

"The author's aim here is to detect and state the ideas implied in a democratic society and to apply those ideas to the problems of education." Boston Transcr

370.15   Educational psychology

Levine, Melvin D.

A **mind** at a time; {by} Mel Levine. Simon & Schuster 2002 352p $26; pa $14   **370.15**

1. Child development 2. Cognition in children 3.

Educational psychology 4. Individual differences in children 5. Learning 6. Learning disabilities
ISBN 0-7432-0222-8; 0-7432-0223-6 pa

LC 2001-57670

The author discusses "eight areas of learning (the memory system, the language system, the spatial ordering system, the motor system, etc.). He provides chapters describing how each type of learning works and advises parents and teachers on how to help kids struggling in these areas. . . . This is a must-read for parents and educators who want to understand and improve the school lives of children." Publ Wkly

Includes bibliographical references

370.2   Miscellany

★ Private independent schools, 2010; 63rd ed; Bunting and Lyon 2010 xxix, 300, 21p il $115 **370.2**
1. Private schools -- Directories 2. Reference books
ISBN 978-0-913094-63-1

"Describes some 1,000 American and 100 foreign boarding and day schools, from kindergarten through high school, plus one-year post-high school programs. Roughly a quarter of the entries are descriptive; the remainder give the school's size, age range, application procedures, administrative control, cost, and special programs, plus a brief statement of its philosophy. A classification grid, arranged by state, identifies institutions with specific characteristics, such as military programs, church affiliation, and restriction to one sex. Separate section on summer programs emphasizing academics, recreation, or travel." Guide to Ref Books. 11th edition

370.9   History, geographic treatment, biography

Hirsch, E. D.

The **schools** we need and why we don't have them; {by} E.D. Hirsch, Jr. Doubleday 1996 317p hardcover o.p. pa $14.95   **370.9**
1. Education -- Aims and objectives 2. Education -- Philosophy 3. Education -- Social aspects 4. Education -- Theories and principles 5. Education -- United States 6. Educational sociology 7. School reform
ISBN 0-385-49524-2 pa

LC 96-2192

This "book presents a sophisticated, scholarly and often compelling argument and it deserves serious consideration, whatever one's political predilections." N Y Times Book Rev

Includes bibliographical references

Postman, Neil

The **end** of education; redefining the value of school. Knopf 1995 209p hardcover o.p. pa $13.95   **370.9**
1. Education -- Aims and objectives 2. Education -- United States 3. Multiculturalism 4. School reform 5. Technology and civilization
ISBN 0-679-75031-2 pa

LC 94-46605

"Beautifully written, breathtakingly high-minded, this is Postman's best book on American education." Booklist

Includes bibliographical references

371.01   Specific kinds of schools

Gross, Martin L.

The **conspiracy** of ignorance; the failure of American public schools. HarperCollins Pubs. 2000 291p hardcover o.p. pa $14   **371.01**
1. Education -- United States 2. Public schools -- United States 3. Public schools -- United States -- Evaluation 4. School failure -- United States
ISBN 0-06-019458-8; 0-06-093260-0 pa

LC 99-34783

Gross examines the current state of public schools in the United States and argues for the need for reform

371.04   Alternative schools

Rupp, Rebecca

★ The **complete** home learning sourcebook; the essential resource guide for homeschoolers, parents, and educators covering every subject from arithmetic to zoology. Three Rivers Press (NY) 1998 865p pa $29.95   **371.04**
1. Activity programs in education 2. Children's literature 3. Home schooling 4. Home schooling -- United States -- Handbooks, manuals, etc
ISBN 0-609-80109-0

LC 98-38440

Arranged by subject, this resource reviews: books, videos, magazines, catalogs, timelines, kits, hands-on activities, board games, CD-ROMs, and educational web sites. Icons denote format and intended age group of each resource

371.1   Schools and their activities

Barzun, Jacques

Begin here; the forgotten conditions of teaching and learning. editor, Morris Philipson. University of Chicago Press 1991 222p $24.95; pa $21   **371.1**
1. Education -- United States 2. Psychology of learning 3. Teaching
ISBN 0-226-03846-7; 0-226-03847-5 pa

LC 90-25877

"Some of the topics Barzun addresses include the inadequate ways in which reading is taught; the demeaning methods of teacher training; the counterfeit 'social studies' programs which are the offshoot of combined geography and history curriculums; the benefits of reading the classics; and how television affects learning." Libr J

Includes bibliographical references

Kozol, Jonathan

Letters to a young teacher. Crown Publishers 2007 288p hardcover o.p. pa $14   **371.1**
1. Authors 2. Education, Primary 3. Educators 4. Nonfiction writers 5. Social critics 6. Social reformers 7. Teachers -- United States 8. Teaching
ISBN 978-0-307-39371-5; 0-307-39371-2; 978-0-307-39372-2 pa; 0-307-39372-0 pa

LC 2007-2689

"The book will delight and encourage first-year (or for that matter, 40th-year) teachers who need Kozol's reminders of the ways that their beautiful profession can bring joy and beauty, mystery and mischievous delight into the hearts of little people in their years of greatest curiosity." Publ Wkly

Includes bibliographical references

Parini, Jay

The **art** of teaching. Oxford University Press 2005 160p $17.95   **371.1**
1. Authors 2. Biographers 3. College teachers 4. Essayists 5. Literary critics 6. Novelists 7. Poets 8. Teachers 9. Teaching 10. Vocational guidance
ISBN 0-19-516969-7

LC 2004-5443

The author offers "musings about teaching's demands and what it takes to not lose one's other, creative self while meeting those demands in this memoir-cum-advice book for novice instructors. . . . This warm guide should inform, entertain, and inspire young teachers as they seek to 'waken a student to his or her potential.'" Publ Wkly

371.2   School administration; administration of student academic activities

Kohn, Alfie

The **schools** our children deserve; moving beyond traditional classrooms and tougher standards. Houghton Mifflin 1999 344p $24; pa $14   **371.2**
1. Education -- Aims and objectives 2. Education -- Aims and objectives -- United States 3. Education -- United States 4. Educational change -- United States 5. School improvement programs -- United States
ISBN 0-395-94039-7; 0-618-08345-6 pa

LC 99-31122

The author challenges the "back-to-basics" approach to education and test-driven "tougher standards," advocating instead the teaching of creative and critical thinking skills

"Parents as well as educators should read this remarkable book." Libr J

Includes bibliographical references (p.) and index

371.3   Methods of instruction and study

Britton, Lesley

Montessori play & learn; a parents' guide to purposeful play from two to six. with an introduction by Joy Starrey Turner. Crown 1992 144p il pa $19.95   **371.3**
1. Montessori method of education 2. Parenting
ISBN 0-517-59182-0

LC 92-5446

This describes educational activities for two to six year olds according to the Montessori method which parents can introduce at home

Montessori, Maria

★ The **Montessori** method; introduction by J. McV. Hunt. Schocken Bks. 1964 xxxix, 376p il hardcover o.p. pa $14   **371.3**
1. Montessori method of education
ISBN 0-8052-0922-0 pa

This is an introduction to the author's teaching methods. The Montessori system emphasizes the development of individuality in the child and the careful training of the senses. Education is controlled by interpersonal relations between the children rather than between teacher and child

AV market place 2008. Information Today 1700p il pa $199.95   **371.3**
1. Audiovisual materials -- Directories 2. Reference books
ISBN 978-1-57387-316-1; 1-57387-316-0

371.82   Specific groups of students; schools for specific groups of students

Mortenson, Greg

Stones into schools; promoting peace with books, not bombs, in Afghanistan and Pakistan. Viking 2009 420p il map $26.95   **371.82**
1. Education -- Afghanistan 2. Education -- Pakistan 3. Humanitarian assistance -- Developing countries 4. Humanitarian assistance, American 5. Humanitarian intervention 6. Humanitarians 7. Mountaineers 8. Peace-building 9. Schools -- Afghanistan 10. Schools -- Pakistan
ISBN 978-0-670-02115-4

LC 2009-30812

In this follow-up to Three cups of tea (2009), the author "continues the story of how the Central Asia Institute (CAI) built schools in northern Afghanistan. Descriptions of the harsh geography and more than one near-death experience impress readers as new faces join Mortenson's loyal 'Dirty Dozen' as they carefully plot a course of school-building through the Badakshan province and Wakhan corridor. . . . To blandly call this book inspiring would be dismissive of all the hard work that has gone into the mission in Afghanistan as well as the efforts to fund it. Mortenson writes of nothing less than saving the future, and his adventure is light years beyond most attempts." Booklist

★ **Three** cups of tea; one man's mission to fight terrorism and build nations--one school at a time. [by] Greg Mortenson and David Oliver Relin. Viking 2006 338p il map $25.95; pa $16   **371.82**
1. Education -- Afghanistan 2. Education -- Pakistan 3. Humanitarian assistance 4. Humanitarian intervention 5. Humanitarians 6. Mountaineers 7. Schools -- Afghanistan 8. Schools -- Pakistan
ISBN 0-670-03482-7; 978-0-670-03482-6; 0-14-303825-7 pa; 978-0-14-303825-2 pa

LC 2005-43466

"Laced with drama, danger, romance, and good deeds, Mortenson's story serves as a reminder of the power of a good idea and the strength inherent in one person's passion-

ate determination to persevere against enormous obstacles."
Christ Sci Monit

Perez, William
   We are Americans; undocumented students
pursuing the American dream. foreword by Daniel Solorzano. Stylus 2009 xxxiv, 161p $70; pa
$22.50   **371.82**
   1. Discrimination in education 2. Illegal aliens
   ISBN 978-1-57922-375-5; 978-1-57922-376-2 pa
                                            LC 2009-26206
   The author "plumbs the stories of students living with
the constant threat of deportation for an answer to the question, 'What does it mean to be an American?' Raised in
this country by parents who gained access illegally, the 16
high school, college and postgraduate students profiled here
(standing in for 65,000 nationwide) have each embraced
our language, culture and collective dream, but are denied
pathways to success. . . . No matter what one's position is
on legalizing immigrants, this collection of inspiring, heartbreaking stories puts a number of unforgettable faces to the
issue, making it impossible to defend any one side in easy
terms or generalities." Publ Wkly
   Includes bibliographical references

371.9   Special education

Chura, David
   I don't wish nobody to have a life like mine; tales
of kids in adult lockup. Beacon Press 2010 xxiii,
216p $24.95; pa $14   **371.9**
   1. Juvenile delinquency 2. Juvenile transfer 3.
   Prisoners -- Education 4. Prisons and prisoners
   ISBN 978-0-8070-0064-9; 978-0-8070-0123-3 pa
                                            LC 2009027664
   Shares the experiences of teenagers incarcerated in an
adult prison in New York, as well as those of the men and
women hired to teach and watch over them.
   "Chura offers a compelling personal look at the failings
of the juvenile justice system." Booklist

Hayden, Torey L.
   Beautiful child; [by] Torey Hayden. HarperCollins Pubs. 2002 326p hardcover o.p. pa $7.99 **371.9**
   1. Special education 2. Special education teachers --
   United States
   ISBN 0-380-81339-4; 0-06-050887-6 pa
                                            LC 2001-39928
   This is "the story of a scruffy seven-year-old, Venus,
who is so unresponsive that Hayden searches for signs of
deafness, brain damage or mental retardation. . . . Hayden
sets Venus's bittersweet and complex story against the backdrop of other students. . . . In this first-person narrative,
Hayden also shares her own thoughts, worries and strained
relationship with a mismatched classroom aide, creating a
rich tapestry of the dynamics of a group of special needs
youngsters and the adults who try to help them." Publ Wkly

Kozol, Jonathan
   Savage inequalities; children in America's schools. HarperPerennial 1992 261p pa
$14.95   **371.9**
   1. Public schools 2. Segregation in education 3.
   Socially handicapped children
   ISBN 0-06-097499-0; 978-0-06-097499-2
   "Jonathan Kozol has written an impassioned book, laced
with anger and indignation, about how our public education
system scorns so many of our children. 'Savage Inequalities'
is also an important book, and warrants widespread attention" N Y Times Book Rev
   Includes bibliographical references

Salzman, Mark
   True notebooks. Alfred A. Knopf 2003 330p
hardcover o.p. pa $13.95   **371.9**
   1. Asian studies specialists 2. Authors 3. Creative
   writing 4. Juvenile delinquency 5. Memoirists 6.
   Novelists
   ISBN 0-375-41308-1; 0-375-72761-2 pa
                                            LC 2002-43435
   "While teaching writing to 17-year-olds detained in
Los Angeles Central Juvenile Hall, Salzman found himself surprised by the boys' talent. The teens' heartwarming,
funny voices are included in his irresistible, provocative
memoir." Booklist

Siegel, Bryna
   Helping children with autism learn; treatment
approaches for parents and professionals. Oxford
Univ. Press 2003 498p $30; pa $18.95   **371.9**
   1. Autism 2. Autistic children -- Education 3.
   Communicative disorders in children -- Treatment 4.
   Learning disabilities -- Treatment 5. Special education
   ISBN 0-19-513811-2; 0-19-532506-0 pa
                                            LC 2002-151673
   "Carefully tailoring her book to multiple audiences, with
free use of commentary and introductory notes, Siegel . .
. excels at showing what parents and educators need to do
to reach autistic children. She includes a valuable section
on having successful individualized educational programs
(IEPs), the standard for children with special needs." Libr J
   Includes bibliographical references

Siegel, Lawrence M.
   The **complete** IEP guide; how to advocate for
your special ed child. 7th ed.; Nolo 2011 380p pa
$34.99   **371.9**
   1. Handicapped children 2. Individualized instruction
   3. Special education
   ISBN 978-1-4133-1313-0 pa; 1-4133-1313-2 pa;
   978-1-4133-1336-9 ebook; 1-4133-1336-1 ebook
                                            LC 2010-38386
   This legal guide offer strategies and advice for parents
of children who need an individualized education program.
Includes information on special education laws and eligibil-
ity rules, how to draw up a blueprint of a child's educational
needs, and what to look for in a special education program.

Turkington, Carol

★ The **encyclopedia** of learning disabilities; [by] Carol Turkington, Joseph R. Harris, American Bookworks. 2nd ed; Facts on File 2006 304p $75; pa $19.95   **371.9**

1. Learning disabilities -- Encyclopedias 2. Reference books

ISBN 0-8160-6399-0; 978-0-8160-6399-4; 0-8160-6400-8 pa; 978-0-8160-6400-7 pa

LC 2005-53045

This book "offers a wealth of information useful to teachers, health-care providers, and parents as they seek to communicate and learn about particular developmental and learning problems." Booklist

Includes bibliographical references

★ The directory for exceptional children; a comprehensive listing of special-needs schools, programs and facilities, 2007-08. 16th ed.; Sargent Pubs. 2007 1151p $75   **371.9**

1. Exceptional children -- Education -- Directories 2. Reference books

ISBN 978-0-87558-160-6; 0-87558-160-9

"Contains 14 sections on facilities for specific handicaps (residential facilities for mentally retarded persons, speech and hearing clinics, etc.); within each section, entries are arranged geographically. Each entry includes names of directors, medical directors, and admissions officers, as well as information on which handicaps are targeted; grades served; academic orientation and curriculum; therapy offerings; enrollment; staff; fees and financial aid; summer programs; and organizational structure; plus descriptive text. List of associations, foundations, and societies for specific disabilities; directory of state agency personnel." Guide to Ref Books. 11th edition

372   Specific levels of education

Dewey, John

★ The **school** and society, and The child and the curriculum; introduction by Philip W. Jackson. University of Chicago Press 1990 xli, 209p hardcover o.p. pa $11   **372**

1. Elementary education

ISBN 0-226-14396-1 pa

LC 90-43528

Both of these works stress the functional relationship between classroom learning activities and real life experiences and analyze the social and psychological nature of the learning process. They present and defend the underlying tenets of Dewey's philosophy of education.

372.4   Reading

Fertig, Beth

Why cant U teach me 2 read? three students and a mayor put our schools to the test. Farrar, Straus and Giroux 2009 354p $27   **372.4**

1. Handicapped students 2. Reading -- Remedial

teaching 3. Reading disability

ISBN 978-0-374-29905-7; 0-374-29905-6

LC 2009-11520

This is "an overall excellent, thoroughly grounding survey of the state of literacy and education." Publ Wkly

Includes bibliographical references

Flesch, Rudolf Franz

★ **Why** Johnny can't read--and what you can do about it. Harper & Row 1955 222p hardcover o.p. pa $13   **372.4**

1. Phonetics -- Study and teaching 2. Reading

ISBN 0-06-091340-1 pa

The author advocates the alphabetic-phonetic system of teaching children to read. He includes step-by-step directions and phonetic drills for use by parents.

372.6   Language arts (Communication skills)

Maguire, James

★ **American** bee; the National Spelling Bee and the culture of word nerds: the lives of five top spellers as they compete for glory and fame. Rodale 2006 371p $24.95   **372.6**

1. English language -- Spelling 2. Spelling bees

ISBN 978-1-59486-214-4; 1-59486-214-1

LC 2005-37443

"From the nail-biting denouement of the 2004 Bee, Maguire . . . moves on to brief sketches of some past winners and then takes an informative and wryly humorous look at the English language itself and the evolution of the American spelling bee from Puritan pastime to major media event." Libr J

Includes bibliographical references

Seeger, Pete

Pete Seeger's storytelling book; by Pete Seeger and Paul Du Bois Jacobs. Harcourt 2000 264p $24; pa $14   **372.6**

1. Storytelling 2. Tales

ISBN 0-15-100370-X; 0-15-601311-8 pa

LC 00-29599

"The tales themselves, tape-recorded by Seeger and rewritten by Jacobs . . . are grouped roughly by origin. They range from family stories to versions of Bible tales to stories inspired by songs, history, legends, and Seeger's own imagination. In an introduction to each chapter, Seeger explains the source of the tales and offers suggestions for scouting similar ones. Each story, ready to read aloud or tell, concludes with possible variations, themes, morals, and, sometimes, music." Booklist

374   Adult education

John, Lauren Z.

★ **Running** book discussion groups; a how-to-do-it manual. [by] Lauren Zina John. Neal-Schuman Publishers 2006 250p pa $55   **374**

1. Book discussion groups -- Handbooks, manuals, etc.

2. Books and reading 3. Discussion groups
ISBN 1-55570-542-1; 978-1-55570-542-8

LC 2006-704

This is a "step-by-step guide to the tasks and responsibilities librarians are likely to encounter as book-group leaders conducting booktalks both on-site and online. . . . This is essential reading for anyone who may be considering taking on the role of a book-discussion-group leader and a refresher for the more experienced among us." Booklist

Includes bibliographical references

378 Higher education (Tertiary education)

College Entrance Examination Board

★ **Book** of majors 2011; [by] the College Board. 5th ed; Henry Holt 2010 1328p pa $26.99   **378**
1. Colleges and universities -- Curricula 2. Colleges and universities -- United States -- Directories 3. Reference books
ISBN 978-0-8744-7904-1

Provides information on over nine hundred college majors, including related fields, prior high school subjects, possible courses of study, and career options and trends for graduates.

★ **College** handbook 2011; [by] the College Board. Henry Holt 2010 2214p pa $29.99   **378**
1. Colleges and universities -- United States -- Directories 2. Reference books
ISBN 978-0-8744-7903-4

This work offers "detailed information for college-bound students on such subjects as freshman admissions requirements and procedures, enrollment, majors, expenses, financial aid, and many other areas of interest." N Y Public Libr. Book of How & Where to Look It Up

Dreifus, Claudia

Higher education? how colleges are wasting our money and failing our kids--and what we can do about it. [by] Andrew Hacker and Claudia Dreifus. Times Books 2010 271p il $26   **378**
1. College costs 2. College teachers -- United States 3. Colleges and universities -- Faculty 4. Education, Higher -- United States -- Finance 5. Higher education
ISBN 978-0-8050-8734-5; 0-8050-8734-6

LC 2010-07219

Hacker and Dreifus "draw up a powerful, if rambling, indictment of academic careerism. The authors are not shy about making biting judgments along the way. . . . [They conclude] with capsule summaries of, as they put it, 'Schools We Like'—that is, schools that offer superior undergraduate educations at relatively low cost." Wall Street J

Includes bibliographical references

Kravets, Marybeth

★ The **K** & W guide to colleges for students with learning disabilities or attention deficit hyperactivity disorder; [by] Marybeth Kravets and Imy F. Wax. 10th ed.; Random House 2010 831p pa $29.99 **378**
1. Colleges and universities -- United States --

Directories 2. Learning disabilities 3. Reference books
ISBN 978-0-375-42961-3

This guide "includes profiles of over 300 schools, advice from specialists in the field of learning disabilities, and strategies to help students find the best match for their needs." Publisher's note

Logue, Robert

★ **Fiske** guide to colleges, 2012; [by] Edward B. Fiske with Robert Logue and the Fiske guide to colleges staff. 28th ed.; Sourcebooks 2011 xxxv, 812p pa $23.99   **378**
1. College choice 2. Colleges and universities -- United States -- Directories 3. Reference books
ISBN 978-1-4022-0962-8

This guide to over 310 of the best colleges and universities nationwide includes information on admissions, costs, financial aid, housing, social life, and academic strengths and weaknesses.

Martinez Aleman, Ana M.

★ **Women** in higher education; an encyclopedia. Ana M. Martinez Alemán and Kristen A. Renn, editors. ABC-CLIO 2002 xxiv, 637p il $85   **378**
1. Higher education 2. Women -- Education 3. Women -- Education (Higher) 4. Women -- Education (Higher) -- United States 5. Women in education 6. Women in education -- United States
ISBN 1-57607-614-8

LC 2002-11570

This resource "on women and higher education presents multipage essays organized in nine sections covering historical and cultural contexts, gender theory, feminism, curriculum, policy, and women as students, faculty, administrators, and employees. . . . Destined to become a classic." Choice

Includes bibliographical references

Williams, Juan

★ **I'll** find a way or make one; a tribute to historically Black colleges and universities. by Juan Williams and Dwayne Ashley. Amistad/HarperCollins 2004 xxiv, 453p il $35   **378**
1. African American universities and colleges 2. African Americans -- Education
ISBN 0-06-009453-2

LC 2004-46450

The authors "explore America's 107 historically black colleges and universities, in existence for 172 years, showing how the schools were created and how black and white abolitionists united to educate newly freed slaves." Libr J

Includes bibliographical references

★ **American** universities and colleges; 19th ed; Praeger 2010 2v set $194.95   **378**
1. Colleges and universities -- United States -- Directories 2. Reference books
ISBN 978-0-313-36607-9; 978-0-313-36608-6 ebook

LC 2010-6880

This reference work "provides basic information on more than 1800 accredited 'degree-granting baccalaureate-or-above institutions' in the United States. Entries are alphabetically arranged by state and include a wide variety of contact, descriptive, and statistical information on institutional history, freshman class data, admissions deadlines, number of degrees conferred, library collections, institutional structure, ethnic makeup of the student body, and library collections. . . . A very well-organized work containing concise and helpful information, this two-volume set serves as a good ready-reference source." Libr J

Includes bibliographical references

★ Barron's profiles of American colleges, 2011; compiled and edited by the College Division of Barron's Educational Series. 29th ed.; Barron's Educational Series, Inc. 2010 1652p map pa $28.99   378
1. Colleges and universities -- United States -- Directories 2. Reference books
ISBN 978-0-7641-9768-0

This college guide contains "information on enrollments, tuition and fees, academic programs, campus environment, available financial aid, and [more.] . . . Every accredited four-year college in the United States is profiled, and readers are directed to a . . . Web site featuring a FREE ACCESS college search engine that presents exclusive online information to help students match their academic plans and aptitudes with the admission requirements and academic programs of each school." Publisher's note

★ Peterson's four-year colleges 2012; 42nd ed.; Peterson's 2011 1987p il pa $32.95   378
1. Colleges and universities -- United States -- Directories 2. Reference books
ISBN 978-0-7689-3279-9

This reference compiles profiles of over 2,500 accredited institutions in the United States with four year undergraduate degree programs.

★ Peterson's two-year colleges 2012; 42nd ed; Peterson's Publishing 2011 498p il pa $29.95 378
1. Colleges and universities -- United States -- Directories 2. Reference books
ISBN 978-0-7689-3278-2

This reference compiles profiles of over 1,500 accredited institutions in the United States with two year associate degree programs.

★ The college blue book; 37th ed; Gale/Cengage Learning 2010 6v map set $519   378
1. Colleges and universities -- United States -- Directories 2. Reference books
ISBN 978-0-02-866143-8

This is a "guide to thousands of 2 and 4-year schools in the U.S. and Canada, their programs, degrees, and financial aid sources." Publisher's note

378.1 Organization and activities in higher education

Albom, Mitch, 1958-

Tuesdays with Morrie; an old man, a young man, and life's greatest lesson. Mitch Albom. Doubleday 1997 192 p. pa $13.99; $20.00   **378.1**
1. Amyotrophic lateral sclerosis 2. Amyotrophic lateral sclerosis -- Patients -- United States -- Biography 3. College teachers 4. Death -- Psychological aspects 5. Death -- Psychological aspects -- Case studies 6. Sociologists 7. Teacher-student relationships -- United States -- Case studies 8. Teachers and students -- Colleges and universities
ISBN 076790592X pa; 0385484518

LC 96052535

This book discusses the author's relationship with his former teacher and mentor, "sociologist Morrie Schwartz. Here [Mitch] Albom recounts how . . . as the old man was dying, he renewed his warm relationship with his revered mentor. This is the . . . record of the teacher's battle with muscle-wasting amyotrophic lateral sclerosis, or Lou Gehrig's disease. The dying man, largely because of his life-affirming attitude toward his death-dealing illness, became a sort of thanatopic guru, and was the subject of three Ted Koppel interviews on Nightline. That was how the author first learned of Morrie's condition. Albom . . . calls his weekly visits to his teacher his last class, and the present book a term paper. The subject: The Meaning of Life . . . Albom does not present a full transcript of the regular Tuesday talks. Rather, he expands a little on the professor's aphorisms." (Kirkus)

"As a student at Brandeis University in the late 1970s, Albom was especially drawn to his sociology professor, Morris Schwartz. On graduation he vowed to keep in touch with him, which he failed to do until 1994, when he saw a segment about Schwartz on the TV program Nightline, and learned that he had just been diagnosed with Lou Gehrig's disease. By then a sports columnist for the Detroit Free Press . . . Albom was idled by the newspaper strike in the Motor City and so had the opportunity to visit Schwartz in Boston every week until the older man died. Their dialogue is the subject of this moving book." Publ Wkly

Ehrenhaft, George

★ **Barron's** ACT; [by] George Ehrenhaft ... [et al.] 16th ed.; Barrons 2010 688p il pa $18.99 **378.1**
1. ACT assessment 2. Colleges and universities -- Entrance requirements
ISBN 978-0-7641-4482-0

A guide to achieving higher scores on the ACT which includes subject reviews and practice exams with answers.

Green, Sharon

★ **Barron's** SAT; [by] Sharon Weiner Green, Ira K. Wolf. 25th ed.; Barron's Educational Series 2010 920p il pa $18.99   **378.1**
1. Colleges and universities -- Entrance requirements 2. Scholastic Assessment Test
ISBN 978-0-7641-4436-3

"This manual explains all of the important tactics and strategies for taking the SAT and provides a . . . review of all test topics. It also presents a diagnostic test and five full-length SAT practice tests with all questions answered and explained." Publisher's note

Includes bibliographical references

Pekar, Harvey

Students for a Democratic Society; a graphic history. written by Harvey Pekar; art by Gary Dumm; edited by Paul Buhle. Hill & Wang 2008 214p il $22; pa $16 **378.1**
    1. College students -- Political activity -- Graphic novels
    2. Graphic novels
    ISBN 978-0-8090-9539-1; 978-0-8090-8939-0 pa
                     LC 2007-40641

Students for a Democratic Society formed as an organization in 1960, but had its roots as a New Left group in the League for Industrial Democracy, founded in 1905 with members such as Jack London and Upton Sinclair. The members in 1960 included Al Haber and Tom Hayden, and one of their most famous documents is the Port Huron Statement of 1962. By the late 1960s, with opposition to the Vietnam War in full swing, a radical subgroup called the Weathermen became more violent. Graphic novelist Pekar is joined by members of the SDS in telling the story of the organization, which dissolved soon after its 1969 convention. The book includes some harsh language and violence.

"The book acts like a sophisticated handbook on an often misunderstood organization. It's good comics and excellent history." Publ Wkly

Rosenfeld, Seth

Subversives; the FBI's war on student radicals, and Reagan's rise to power. Seth Rosenfeld. Farrar, Straus and Giroux 2012 752 p. ill., map (alk. paper) $40.00 **378.1**
    1. College students -- Political activity -- California -- Berkeley -- History 2. Student movements -- California -- Berkeley -- History 3. Subversive activities -- California -- Berkeley -- History
    ISBN 0374257000; 9780374257002
                     LC 2011041204

This book "traces the FBI's secret involvement with three iconic figures at Berkeley during the 1960s: the ambitious neophyte politician Ronald Reagan, the fierce but fragile radical Mario Savio, and the liberal university president Clark Kerr. Through these converging narratives, the award-winning investigative reporter Seth Rosenfeld tells . . . of FBI surveillance, illegal break-ins, infiltration, planted news stories, poison-pen letters, and secret detention lists." (Publisher's note)

Shachtman, Tom

Airlift to America; how Barack Obama, Sr., John F. Kennedy, Tom Mboya, and 800 East African students changed their world and ours. St. Martin's Press 2009 273p il $24.99 **378.1**
    1. College students
    ISBN 978-0-312-57075-0
                     LC 2009-13186

"In the late 1950s, before Kenya's independence from Britain, Kenyan leader Tom Mboya and American philanthropist William Scheinman joined to develop a cadre of educated young people to staff the government and schools. Between 1959 and 1963, nearly 800 African students were flown to the U.S. to be educated and to return to become the 'founding brothers and sisters' of their East African nations. Among them were Wangari Maathai, who went on to become an environmentalist and 2004 Nobel Peace Prize winner, and Barack Obama Sr., father of the future president of the U.S. Shachtman provides historical perspective of cold war politics in African nations, countervailing loyalties to European colonial powers, and the appeal of U.S. ideals of independence." Booklist

Includes bibliographical references

Steinberg, Jacques

The **gatekeepers**; inside the admissions process of a premier college. Viking 2002 xxiii, 292p hardcover o.p. pa $15 **378.1**
    1. College applications 2. Universities and colleges -- United States -- Admission -- Case studies
    ISBN 0-670-03135-6; 0-14-200308-5 pa
                     LC 2002-16884

"This insightful and readable book should be purchased by all academic and large public libraries." Libr J

Includes bibliographical references

Toor, Rachel

Admissions confidential; an insiders account of the elite college selection process. St. Martin's Press 2001 256p $23.95; pa $12.95 **378.1**
    1. College applications 2. Universities and colleges -- United States -- Admission
    ISBN 0-312-28405-5; 0-312-30235-5 pa
                     LC 2001-34892

"Toor tells all—and it's not necessarily a pretty picture. It's a funny, often irreverent overview of her work. . . . The students don't leap off the page, but Toor certainly does." Booklist

Fiske guide to getting into the right college; [by] Edward B. Fiske & Bruce G. Hammond. 4th ed.; Sourcebooks 2010 352p pa $16.99 **378.1**
    1. College choice 2. Colleges and universities -- Entrance requirements 3. Colleges and universities -- Finance
    ISBN 978-1-4022-4309-7

This guide includes advice and information on constructing applications, writing essays, interviews, the application process, using the Internet when applying for college, and finanical aid.

378.3   Student aid and related topics

College Entrance Examination Board

    ★ **Getting** financial aid 2011; [by the] College Board. 5th ed; College Board 2010 986p il pa $21.99 **378.3**
    1. College costs 2. Student loan funds
    ISBN 978-0-8744-7905-8

This guide covers over 3000 two- and four-year institutions. Provides information on what each college really costs, describes aid packages and includes tips on application procedures.

Collinge, Alan

The **student** loan scam; the most oppressive debt in U.S. history, and how we can fight back. Beacon Press 2008 167p $22.95   **378.3**
1. Student loan funds 2. Student loans
ISBN 978-0-8070-4229-8; 0-8070-4229-3
LC 2008-12230
"Comprehensive and stirring, this extraordinary book is whistle-blowing at its finest." Publ Wkly
Includes bibliographical references

Schlachter, Gail A.

★ **Financial** aid for the disabled and their families, 2010-2012; [by] Gail Ann Schlachter, R. David Weber. Reference Service Press 2010 480p $40   **378.3**
1. Physically handicapped 2. Scholarships
ISBN 978-1-58841-204-1
"Provides information on a wide range of funding needs in such areas as education, career development, research, and travel. Includes multiple indexes; cross-referenced." N Y Public Libr Book of How & Where to Look It Up

★ Peterson's how to get money for college; financing your future beyond federal aid. 28th ed.; Peterson's 2010 863p pa $33.95   **378.3**
1. College costs 2. Scholarships 3. Student loan funds
ISBN 978-0-7689-2886-0
A resource for anyone looking to supplement his or her federal financial-aid package with funds from colleges and universities, this directory features information on need-based and non-need gifts, loans, and more.

379   Public policy issues in education

Greenawalt, Kent

★ **Does** God belong in public schools? Princeton University Press 2005 261p $29.95   **379**
1. Church and state 2. Education and state -- United States 3. Establishment clause 4. Religion in the public schools 5. Religion in the public schools -- Law and legislation -- United States 6. Religion in the public schools -- United States 7. School prayer
ISBN 0691121117
LC 2004-45779
The author "considers issues ranging from the teaching of evolution to parents' rights that their children not be exposed to offensive curriculum. He grounds his analyses in a review of the history and purposes of schooling. . . . His legal and philosophical lines of scholarship come together to produce a nonpartisan consideration of the crucial issues facing US courts and the country." Choice
Includes bibliographical references

Kozol, Jonathan

★ The **shame** of the nation; the restoration of apartheid schooling in America. Crown Publishers 2005 404p $25; pa $14.95   **379**
1. De facto school segregation 2. Segregation in education
ISBN 1-4000-5244-0; 1-4000-5245-9 pa
LC 2005-8626
"Readers interested in public education will appreciate— and be challenged by—this compelling book." Booklist
Includes bibliographical references

Ravitch, Diane

★ The **death** and life of the great American school system; how testing and choice are undermining education. Basic Books 2010 283p $26.95 **379**
1. Educational accountability -- United States 2. Educational tests and measurements 3. Educational tests and measurements -- United States 4. Public schools -- United States 5. School choice
ISBN 978-0-465-01491-0; 0-465-01491-7
LC 2009-50406
The author "provides an important and highly readable examination of the educational system, how it fails to prepare students for life after graduation, and how we can put it back on track. . . . Anyone interested in education should definitely read this accessible, riveting book." Libr J
Includes bibliographical references

379.1   Specific elements of support and control of public education

DelFattore, Joan

What Johnny shouldn't read; textbook censorship in America. Yale Univ. Press 1992 209p $40; pa $16.95   **379.1**
1. Censorship 2. Censorship -- Case studies 3. Textbooks -- Evaluation
ISBN 0-300-05709-1; 0-300-06050-5 pa
LC 92-3585
The author "thoughtfully presents six specific cases and their immediate and long-term effects in order to open the eyes and, hopefully, to raise the voices of those who treasure intellectual freedom." Booklist
Includes bibliographical references

381   Commerce (Trade)

Bond, Robert E.

★ **Bond's** franchise guide; Robert E. Bond, publisher; Michelle Yang, Jennifer Young, editor[s] 2008 ed., 19th ed; Source Book Publications 2008 447p il pa $34.95   **381**
1. Franchises (Retail trade)
ISBN 978-1887137591; 1887137599
This guide to over 1000 franchise opportunities in 45 categories gives background, capital requirements, support and training information as well as specifics on expansion in the U.S and Canada.

Cassidy, John

Dot.con; the greatest story ever sold. HarperCollins Pubs. 2002 372p hardcover o.p. pa $13.95 **381**
1. Electronic commerce 2. Electronic commerce -- United States -- Finance 3. Electronic trading of securities -- United States 4. Internet 5. Internet industry -- United States -- Finance 6. Stocks 7. Stocks -- United States
ISBN 0-06-000881-4 pa
LC 2001-51449
"A history of the dot-com bubble by a financial writer for The New Yorker, with insightful observations about the Federal Reserve and severe views on its chairman, Alan Greenspan." N Y Times Book Rev

How markets fail; the logic of economic calamities. Farrar, Straus and Giroux 2009 390p il **381**
1. Banks and banking 2. Financial crises 3. Monetary policy 4. Stock exchanges
ISBN 0374173206; 9780374173203
LC 2009029529
"Cassidy describes the rising influence of what he calls utopian economics—thinking that is blind to how real people act and that denies the many ways an unregulated free market can produce disastrous unintended consequences." (Publisher's note) Index.
"The author focuses primarily on the rise and fall of free market ideology and the mostly unrealistic ideal of a self-correcting marketplace. An excellent comprehensive history of the economic thought that led to this kind of utopian economics provides a refresher course in Adam Smith, Friedrich August von Hayek, Kenneth Arrow and Hyman Minsky." Publ Wkly
Includes bibliographical references

Dolin, Eric Jay

Fur, fortune, and empire; the epic history of the fur trade in America. W.W. Norton & Co. 2010 442p il map $29.95 **381**
1. Frontier and pioneer life -- North America 2. Fur trade 3. Fur trade -- North America -- History 4. Fur trade -- Western States -- History
ISBN 978-0-393-06710-1
LC 2010016212
This is an "overview of the American fur trade from Colonial times until the beginnings of the conservation movement of the late 19th century. . . . From the Iroquoian 'Beaver Wars' of the mid-1600s to the brutal Russian domination of Alaskan native hunters, Dolin successfully shows how America's natural history is a vital part of our collective national history." Libr J
Includes bibliographical references

Eltis, David

Atlas of the transatlantic slave trade; [by] David Eltis and David Richardson; foreword by David Brion Davis; afterword by David W. Blight. Yale University Press 2010 xxvi, 307p il map $50 **381**
1. Atlases 2. Reference books 3. Slave trade -- Maps
ISBN 978-0-300-12460-6
"For nearly 20 years, the Trans-Atlantic Slave Trade Database project has been diligently tabulating all the slave ship crossings of the Atlantic Ocean, from 1500 to 1900. . . . With 189 informative and handsome maps, Eltis and Richardson relay and interpret the information contained in this rich database, mixing in beautiful historical illustrations and key passages from relevant texts. An accessible narrative, meanwhile, expands on the information in the maps. . . . This marvelous book will change how people think of the slave trade." Foreign Affairs

Grippo, Robert M.

Macy's; the store, the star, the story. Square One Publishers 2009 186p il $29.95; pa $24.95 **381**
1. Department stores 2. Merchants
ISBN 978-0-7570-0212-0; 0-7570-0212-9; 978-0-7570-0309-7 pa; 0-7570-0309-5 pa
LC 2008-41870
An illustrated history of the department store launched "in 1858 under the ownership of former Nantucket seaman Rowland H. Macy. . . . The author provides great historical context through the bottom-of-the-page illustrated footers chronicling events, celebrities, and politics of that era." Booklist

Hopp, Steven L.

★ Animal, vegetable, miracle; a year of food life. [by] Barbara Kingsolver, with Steven L. Hopp and Camille Kingsolver; original drawings by Richard A. Houser. HarperCollins Publishers 2007 370p il $26.95; pa $15.99 **381**
1. Agriculture and energy 2. Eating customs 3. Farm life
ISBN 978-0-06-085255-9; 0-06-085255-0; 978-0-06-085256-6 pa; 0-06-085256-9 pa
LC 2006-53516
"This is a serious book about important problems. Its concerns are real and urgent. It is clear, thoughtful, often amusing, passionate and appealing. It may give you a serious case of supermarket guilt, thinking of the energy footprint left by each out-of-season tomato, but you'll also find unexpected knowledge and gain the ability to make informed choices about what—and how—you're willing to eat." Washington Post Book World
Includes bibliographical references

Marcus, James

Amazonia. New Press 2004 261p $24.95 **381**
1. Electronic commerce 2. Electronic commerce -- United States -- History 3. Internet bookstores -- United States -- History
ISBN 1-565-84870-5
LC 2003-66505
"While the quotidian world of everyday work might have seemed uninteresting, Marcus makes it fun to peek inside company workings to see how Amazon.com invented itself. And the literati name-dropping from interviews, parties, and the like lends a tone of friendly gossip to this tale." Libr J

Mitchell, Stacy

Big-box swindle; the true cost of mega-retailers and the fight for America's independent businesses. Beacon Press 2006 318p $24.95; pa $15   **381**
1. Chain stores 2. Retail trade 3. Small business
ISBN 978-0-8070-3500-9; 0-8070-3500-9; 978-0-8070-3501-6 pa; 0-8070-3501-7 pa
LC 2006-13818
Mitchell's "call to action reveals the hidden costs of those 'low prices' promoted by the big-box bullies and gives hope to local entrepreneurs and concerned citizens alike." Booklist
Includes bibliographical references

Spector, Robert

The **mom** & pop store; how the unsung heroes of the American economy are surviving and thriving. Walker Pub. Co. 2009 293p $26   **381**
1. Business enterprises 2. Small business
ISBN 978-0-8027-1605-7
LC 2009-19198
"Lively lessons about business ethics and practices that Fortune 500 companies, the author suggests, would be wise to follow." Kirkus
Includes bibliographical references

Stanton, Maureen

Killer stuff and tons of money; seeking history and hidden gems in flea-market America. Penguin Press 2011 326p $26.95   **381**
1. Antiques 2. Flea markets
ISBN 978-1-59420-293-3; 1-59420-293-1
LC 2010-53099
Before Stanton "reconnected with her pseudonymous old college friend, 'Curt Avery,' who had become a professional antiques dealer, she was 'the self-anointed Queen of the Flea-Market Dollar Table.' Like many Americans, she was on the lookout for an appealing bargain and just as happy with an inexpensive reproduction as the real thing. When she and Avery met again in 2000, she agreed to fly across the country to attend an auction where some old bottles that he coveted were on offer. He asked her to be his proxy bidder while he hid at the back and signaled his bids. This was her introduction to a fascinating subculture, which she calls 'the flea realm.' Over the years, she attended many fairs and flea markets with Avery as what she calls a 'participant observer,' getting up before dawn to help him set up displays, grabbing food on the run and camping out next to his truck at night. . . . A treasure-trove of a book, especially for would-be antiquers." Kirkus
Includes bibliographical references

Whitaker, Jan

Service and style; how the American department store fashioned the middle class. St. Martin's Press 2006 342p il $35   **381**
1. Department stores 2. Middle class
ISBN 978-0-312-32635-7; 0-312-32635-1
LC 2006-40542
"At their peak, department stores were the nation's largest booksellers and many major chains also sold groceries. But it was clothes that made the stores a prime destination for women of all social classes, and Whitaker discusses at significant length the subtle movements through which major chains from one end of the country to the other cultivated their reputations for being up-to-date with the latest Paris fashions, then tapped into additional markets for young adult and children's wear. More than 100 photographs and illustrations are integrated into the text, aptly demonstrating the lengths to which stores went in order to present themselves as elegant yet modern and convenient." Publ Wkly
Includes bibliographical references

★ **Consumer sourcebook**; 21st ed; Gale Res. 2008 1762p $423   **381**
1. Consumer protection
ISBN 978-0-7876-9625-2; 0-7876-9625-0
This directory describes "programs and services available to the American consumer at little or no cost. Lists federal, state, county, and local governmental agencies, nongovernmental consumer organizations and associations, and consumer affairs and customer services departments of corporations. Describes consumer publications and multimedia products and provides consumer tips and recommendations." Ref Sources for Small & Medium-sized Libr. 6th edition

Wal-Mart; the face of twenty-first-century capitalism. edited by Nelson Lichtenstein. New Press 2006 349p il $60; pa $21.95   **381**
1. Discount houses (Retail trade) 2. Discount stores 3. Labor unions -- United States 4. Wages -- United States
ISBN 1-59558-035-2; 1-59558-021-2 pa
LC 2005-49147
This collection of essays discusses the retailer Wal-Mart. "With numerous charts and graphs that keep the data flowing, this assemblage thoroughly dissects the Wal-Mart global high-tech phenomenon through overarching historical, cultural, and economic perspectives." Booklist
Includes bibliographical references

382   International commerce (Foreign trade)

Rose, Sarah

For all the tea in China; how England stole the world's favorite drink and changed history. Viking 2010 261p $25.95   **382**
1. Horticulturists 2. Tea
ISBN 978-0-670-02152-9; 0-670-02152-0
LC 2009-41482
An account of mid-19th-century botanist Robert Fortune's mission to travel to China's remote Wu Yi Shan hills to steal closely guarded secrets of tea horticulture and manufacturing describes his encounters with pirates, threatening weather, and unethical people.
"With her probing inquiry and engaging prose, Sarah Rose paints a fresh and vivid account of life in rural 19th-century China and Fortune's fateful journey into it." Washington Post
Includes bibliographical references

Snyder, Rachel Louise

Fugitive denim; a moving story of people and pants in the borderless world of global trade. W.W. Norton & Company 2008 352p $26.95; pa $16.95 **382**

1. Clothing industry 2. Clothing trade 3. Denim 4. International trade 5. Jeans (Clothing)
ISBN 978-0-393-06180-2; 0-393-06180-9; 978-0-393-33542-2 pa; 0-393-33542-9 pa
LC 2007-24335

"Snyder's investigation is an essential read for those curious about fashion or the globe-spanning business that produces their clothes." Publ Wkly

Includes bibliographical references

383 Communications and transportation

Bobrow, Jerry

Barron's comprehensive postal exam, 473/473-C; contributing author and consultant, Michele Spence. Barron's Educational Series 2006 327p il pa $16.99 **383**

1. Postal service -- Examinations
ISBN 0-7641-3412-4; 978-0-7641-3412-8
LC 2006-40108

"Six full-length model exams plus a diagnostic test are presented to prepare applicants for a variety of jobs in the U.S. Postal Service. . . . The author also provides special drills designed to improve test-taking skills in memory, speed, and following oral directions." Publisher's note

Damp, Dennis V.

★ **Post** office jobs; explore and find jobs, prepare for the 473 postal exam, and locate all job opportunities. 5th ed., completely rev.; Bookhaven Press 2009 256p il pa $24.95 **383**

1. Postal service -- Examinations 2. Postal service -- Vocational guidance
ISBN 978-0-943641-27-0; 0-943641-27-6

This is a guide to Postal Service careers including professional and administrative positions, mail carrier, maintenance, postal inspectors, and clerical positions. It includes information on preparing for postal exams, applications, resumes, and interviews.

★ National five digit zip code and post office directory. U.S. Postal Service 2v maps pa $45 **383**
1. Zip code
ISBN 978-1-59804-282-5; 1-59804-282-3

"Besides ZIP codes and post offices, this directory includes information on the organization of the Postal Service, addressing, parcel weights and sizes, delivery statistics, and other matters." Recomm Ref Books in Paperback. 2d edition

384 Communications

Knopper, Steve

Appetite for self-destruction; the spectacular crash of the record industry in the digital age. Free Press 2009 301p $26 **384**

1. Compact disc industry 2. Music industry 3. Music trade 4. Sound recording industry -- History
ISBN 978-1-4165-5215-4; 1-4165-5215-4
LC 2008-38739

Knopper "provides a wide-angled, morally complicated view of the current state of the music business. He doesn't let those rippers and burners among us—that is, those who download digital songs without paying for them, and you know who you are—entirely off the hook. But he suggests that with even a little foresight, record companies could have adapted to the Internet's brutish and quizzical new realities and thrived." N Y Times Book Rev

Includes bibliographical references

Slide, Anthony

The **new** historical dictionary of the American film industry. Scarecrow Press 1998 266p hardcover o.p. pa $19.95 **384**

1. Motion picture industry 2. Motion picture industry -- United States -- Dictionaries 3. Motion pictures -- Dictionaries 4. Reference books
ISBN 1-57886-015-6 pa
LC 97-35737

This reference "covers studios, companies, clubs and associations, and related concepts. Lots here that is not found elsewhere." Booklist

Includes bibliographical references

Wu, Tim

The **master** switch; the rise and fall of information empires. Alfred A. Knopf 2010 366p il $27.95 **384**

1. Information technology 2. Information technology -- History 3. Mass media -- History 4. Telecommunication 5. Telecommunication -- History
ISBN 978-0-307-26993-5; 0-307-26993-0
LC 2010-04137

"Policy quibbles aside, there's a sharp insight and a surprising fact on nearly every page of Wu's masterful survey. Above all, Wu shows that each new communications technology spawns the same old quest for power." Boston Globe

Includes bibliographical references

384.1 Telegraphy

Gordon, John Steele

A **thread** across the ocean; the heroic story of the transatlantic cable. Walker & Co. 2002 240p il $26 **384.1**

1. Cables, Submarine -- Atlantic -- History 2. Financiers 3. Submarine cables 4. Telegraph 5. Telegraph -- Great Britain -- History 6. Telegraph -- United States

-- History
ISBN 0-8027-1364-5

LC 2002-66385

The author "has written a lively, engaging account of the extraordinary efforts that brought about this remarkable scientific, technological, and business feat." Libr J

Includes bibliographical references

★ National e-mail and fax directory; Louise Gagne, project editor. 24th ed.; Gale Cengage Learning 2010 3v set $255   **384.1**
1. Electronic mail systems -- Directories 2. Fax transmission -- Directories 3. Reference books
ISBN 978-1-4144-4157-3

This directory provides "access to nearly 130,000 fax numbers and more than 85,000 e-mail addresses for U.S. companies, organizations and government agencies." Publisher's note

384.3   Computer communication

Blum, Andrew

Tubes; a journey to the center of the Internet. Andrew Blum. Ecco 2012 294 p.   **384.3**
1. Information highway 2. Information technology 3. Internet -- History 4. Internet -- Social aspects 5. Telecommunication systems
ISBN 0061994936; 9780061994937

LC 2012009519

In this book, "journalist Andrew Blum goes inside the Internet's physical infrastructure . . . revealing an utterly fresh look at the online world we think we know. It is a . . . tactile realm of unmarked compounds . . . where glass fibers pulse with light and creaky telegraph buildings . . . become communication hubs once again. From the room in Los Angeles where the Internet first flickered to life. . . . [to] a ten-thousand-mile undersea cable just two thumbs wide [that] connects Europe and Africa, to the wilds of the Pacific Northwest, where Google, Microsoft, and Facebook have built monumental data centersBlum chronicles the . . . Internet's development, explains how it all works, and takes . . . [an] in-depth look inside its hidden monuments." (Publishers note)

384.5   Wireless communication

Murray, James B.

Wireless nation; the frenzied launch of the cellular revolution in America. Perseus Bks. 2001 338p hardcover o.p. pa $17.95   **384.5**
1. Cellular telephones
ISBN 0-7382-0391-2 pa

An account of the development and growth of the communications industry with speculations about its future.

384.54   Radiobroadcasting

Fisher, Marc

★ **Something** in the air; radio, rock, and the revolution that shaped a generation. Random House 2007 374p il $27.95   **384.54**
1. Radio broadcasting 2. Radio broadcasting -- United States -- History
ISBN 978-0-375-50907-0; 0-375-50907-0

LC 2006-47353

"There's not a bit of dead air in this well-written and researched history of radio and its pivotal role in the emergence of American youth culture." Publ Wkly

Includes bibliographical references

Heil, Alan L.

Voice of America; a history. Columbia University Press 2003 538p $75; pa $26.50   **384.54**
1. International broadcasting -- United States 2. Radio broadcasting
ISBN 0-231-12674-3; 0-231-12675-1 pa

LC 2002-41019

This is a "history of America's largest publicly funded overseas broadcasting network. . . . From the crises in eastern Europe to the student uprising in Tiananmen Square, Mr Heil provides countless examples of people clinging to their shortwave radios to listen to VOA and other international broadcasters, in spite of intense jamming, to know what was really going on in their own countries. . . . Readers fascinated by the technical intricacies of radio and the arcana of Washington's broadcasting policies will no doubt be riveted." Economist

Includes bibliographical references

Johns, Adrian

Death of a pirate; British radio and the making of the information age. W. W. Norton & Company 2010 305p il $26.95   **384.54**
1. Pirate radio broadcasting 2. Politicians 3. Social activists
ISBN 978-0-393-06860-3; 0-393-06860-9

LC 2010-24525

Johns "portrays the British radio pirates not in the warm glow of sentimental memory that the period usually enjoys but in the historian's cold bright light. 'Death of a Pirate' is, in its way, a treasure." Wall Street J

Includes bibliographical references

★ **Broadcasting** & cable yearbook 2009. Reed Business Information 2008 2v set $275   **384.54**
1. Cable television 2. Radio broadcasting
ISBN 978-1-60030-121-6

"The most comprehensive directory to the Fifth Estate, covering the history and continuing growth of every field in the industry. There are nine major sections: 'The Fifth Estate,' 'Radio,' 'Television,' 'Cable,' 'Satellites,' 'Programming,' 'Advertising and Marketing,' 'Technology,' and 'Professional Services.' Includes extensive equipment listings and a buyer's guide. The standard directory of AM and FM radio stations in the United States, Canada, Mexico, and the Caribbean and of U.S. and Canadian television stations." Ref Sources for Small & Medium-sized Libr. 6th edition

★ The Museum of Broadcast Communications encyclopedia of radio; editor, Christopher H. Sterling;
consulting editor, Michael Keith. Fitzroy Dearborn 2004 xl, 1650p 3v il set $375 **384.54**
1. Radio -- Encyclopedias 2. Radio broadcasting --
Encyclopedias 3. Radio programs -- Encyclopedias 4.
Reference books
ISBN 1-579-58249-4
LC 2003-15683
"A premise of this unique encyclopedia is that radio
broadcasting is so pervasive that its importance can be easily overlooked. More than 600 articles provide ample illustration of the role this medium plays throughout the world.
From radio's invention to radio on the Internet, the cross-
referenced and thoroughly indexed articles analyze over
100 years of topics, programs, issues, people, and places,
and provide leads to further reading. Some 250 photographs
'give visual context to an often unseen world.' Scholars, old-
time-radio admirers, and curious readers will appreciate the
unparalleled comprehensiveness of this source."—"The Top
20 Reference Titles of the Year." Am Libr, May 2004

385 Railroad transportation

Ambrose, Stephen E.
Nothing like it in the world; the men who built
the transcontinental railroad, 1863-1869. Simon &
Schuster 2000 471p $28; pa $16 **385**
1. Railroad construction workers -- United States --
History -- 19th century 2. Railroads -- United States
3. Railroads -- United States -- History -- 19th century
ISBN 0-684-84609-8; 0-7432-0317-8 pa
LC 00-41005
This is an account of the construction of the trans-
continental railroad by the Central Pacific and Union
Pacific companies.
"Ambrose's scholarship seems impeccable. . . . He
writes a brisk, colloquial, straightforward prose that not only
is easy to read but also bears the reader on shoulders of won-
der and excitement." N Y Times Book Rev
Includes bibliographical references

Bain, David Haward
Empire express; building the first transcontinen-
tal railroad. Viking 1999 797p il maps hardcover
o.p. pa $30 **385**
1. Railroads -- United States 2. Railroads -- United
States -- History
ISBN 0-670-80889-X; 0-14-008499-1 pa
LC 99-33375
"Bain knits together excellent storytelling and exhaus-
tive research in a rich contextual tale of vision, ambition,
and, ultimately, political and personal corruption." Libr J
Includes bibliographical references

Hayes, Derek
Historical atlas of the North American railroad.
University of California Press 2010 224p il map
$39.95 **385**
1. Historical atlases 2. Railroads -- Canada -- Maps

3. Railroads -- North America -- History 4. Railroads
-- North America -- Maps 5. Railroads -- United States
-- Maps 6. Reference books
ISBN 978-0-520-26616-2
LC 2009-943592
"With 400-plus color maps ranging from 1821 to President Obama's report 'A Vision for High Speed Rail,' this
historical atlas reveals the richly variegated visual culture
of railroad mapping in the US and Canada. Always utilitarian, railroad maps are differentiated into four types: those
required to survey the land for construction and attracting investments, timetable maps for passengers, maps in
advertising, and engineering maps. . . . The wealth of visual information, comprehensive coverage, and optimistic
stance for the future of railroads on the North American
continent make this an important purchase for all reference
collections." Choice
Includes bibliographical references

McCommons, James
Waiting on a train; the embattled future of passenger rail service. foreword by James Howard Kun-
stler. Chelsea Green Pub. Company 2009 285p map
pa $17.95 **385**
1. Railroads -- United States 2. Transportation
ISBN 978-1-60358-064-9; 1-60358-064-6
LC 2009-30142
"McCommons spent almost all of 2008 riding Amtrak
trains back and forth across the country, telling folks he met
along the way that he was doing research for a book on the
future of passenger rail. . . . [The resulting work] is part
travel log, chronicling both the horrors and the pleasures of
riding Amtrak, and part solid political and business reporting
on the rail industry that hardly any other journalist is doing."
Washington Monthly

White, Richard
Railroaded; the transcontinentals and the making
of modern America. Norton 2011 xxxix, 660p il
map $35 **385**
1. American national characteristics 2. Land settlement
-- United States 3. National characteristics, American
4. Railroads -- United States 5. Railroads -- United
States -- History -- 19th century
ISBN 978-0-393-06126-0; 0-393-06126-4
LC 2010-54054
"Excellent big-picture, popularly written history of the
Howard Zinn mold, backed by a mountain of research and
statistics." Kirkus
Includes bibliographical references

Wolmar, Christian
Blood, iron, & gold; how the railroads trans-
formed the world. PublicAffairs 2009 376p il map
$28.95 **385**
1. Railroads -- History
ISBN 978-1-58648-834-5
LC 2009-38340
This is "a fascinating study not just of a transportation
system, but of the Promethean spirit of the modern age."
Publ Wkly
Includes bibliographical references

386   Inland waterway and ferry transportation

Bernstein, Peter L.

Wedding of the waters; the Erie Canal and the making of a great nation. W.W. Norton 2005 448p il map $24.95; pa $15.95   **386**
1. Transportation -- United States -- History
ISBN 0-393-05233-8; 0-393-32795-7 pa

LC 2004-22792

The author discusses the building of the Erie Canal and how, in his opinion, it changed the course of American history.

This "is an important window into a vital and too often neglected period in the American past." Foreign Affairs

Includes bibliographical references

Karabell, Zachary

★ **Parting** the desert; the creation of the Suez Canal. Knopf 2003 310p il map $27.50   **386**
1. Diplomats
ISBN 0-375-40883-5

LC 2002-34209

Karabell "has written a thorough and entertaining work. . . . The author is quite comfortable discussing any issue, period, or personality in the canal's history, and many of the references in his 150-title bibliography are from primary sources. This is simply an excellent book." Libr J

387.7   Air transportation

Blatner, David

The **flying** book; everything you've ever wondered about flying on airplanes. Walker & Co. 2003 248p il $22   **387.7**
1. Aeronautics -- History -- Popular works   2. Aeronautics, Commercial -- Popular works 3. Airplanes 4. Airplanes -- Popular works   5.   Commercial aeronautics
ISBN 0-8027-1378-5

"Engaging, upbeat, and fact-filled, The Flying Book features an open, airy design with lots of charts and sidebars." SLJ

Includes bibliographical references

Fallows, James

China airborne; James Fallows. Pantheon Books 2012 xiii, 268 p.p   **387.7**
1. Aeronautics -- China 2. Aeronautics, Commercial -- China 3. Aerospace industries -- China
ISBN 0375422110; 9780375422119

LC 2011046805

This book analyzes the problems and promises of China's economic development through an examination of the efforts to create a world-class aerospace industry. With its unprecedented manufacturing prowess, China has become a world economic power. But how real and sustainable is the development? The test, writes the author, is how well China succeeds in its current effort to build an aerospace industry . . . However, this is no easy task. . . . developing internationally recognized standards of safety and inspection, ensuring adequate air space above China for a busy airline industry,

developing and manufacturing airplanes, and their millions of components, that can compete with established manufacturers such as Boeing and Airbus. (Kirkus Reviews)

Mondor, Colleen Catherine

The **map** of my dead pilots; Colleen Mondor. Lyons Press 2012 256p   **387.7**
ISBN 9780762773619

LC 2011033005

This book explores the author's experiences "as operations manager for a commercial airline servicing Alaskas remote villages and hamlets. . . . [Colleen] Mondor has had a bird's-eye view of the rigors of flying cargo that often as not included carcasses as well as crates, sleds as well as the dogs that hauled them, and passengers who had no other means of traversing a state whose isolation was both allure and aggravation. The men who flew these missions are—and, all too sadly, were—a lethal combination of danger junkies and hotshots, dreamers and schemers, dedicated professionals and determined daredevils who reveled in the challenges that Alaskaas climate and terrain threw their way." (Booklist)

Walsh, Kenneth T.

Air Force One; a history of the presidents and their planes. Hyperion 2003 261p il $24.95 **387.7**
1. Presidents -- United States
ISBN 1-401-30004-9

LC 2002-38751

Walsh "presents a narrative account of life on Air Force One that is part history and part journalistic profile. Beginning with Franklin D. Roosevelt, the first President to fly while in office, through George W. Bush, Walsh highlights the decisions made and crises that happened aboard this 'flying White House.' The author's hypothesis is that the plane's close quarters and relaxed atmosphere allow each President to bring his own distinct personality to the activities and decisions." Libr J

Includes bibliographical references

388   Transportation

McPhee, John A.

Uncommon carriers; [by] John McPhee. Farrar, Straus & Giroux 2006 248p $24   **388**
1. Freight 2. Freight and freightage 3. Transport workers 4. Transportation
ISBN 0-374-28039-8; 978-0-374-28039-0

LC 2006-7953

"McPhee's eye for idiosyncratic detail keeps the stories . . . lively and frequently moves them in interesting directions." Publ Wkly

388.1   Roads

Conover, Ted

The **routes** of man; how roads are changing the world, and the way we live today. Alfred A. Knopf 2010 333p il map $26.95   **388.1**
1. Authors 2. Journalists 3. Nonfiction writers 4.

Roads 5. Roads -- Social aspects 6. Travel -- Social aspects 7. Voyages and travels
ISBN 978-1-4000-4244-9; 1-4000-4244-5

LC 2009-24007

"A readable, fact-filled, well-written exploration of how roads work, for good and ill, and what their future likely holds." Kirkus
Includes bibliographical references

388.3 Vehicular transportation

Sperling, Daniel
Two billion cars; driving toward sustainability. [by] Daniel Sperling [and] Deborah Gordon. Oxford University Press 2009 304p il $24.95 **388.3**
1. Alternative fuel vehicles 2. Automobile industry 3. Automobiles -- Environmental aspects 4. Automobiles -- Fuel consumption 5. Motor vehicles -- Fuel consumption
ISBN 978-0-19-537664-7; 0-19-537664-1

LC 2008-21647

"With statistical data, charts, graphs, and erudite analysis, Sperling and Gordon present the most thorough study of the automobile industry general readers could hope to find." Booklist
Includes bibliographical references and index

390 Customs, etiquette, folklore

★ The Greenwood encyclopedia of daily life; a tour through history from ancient times to the present. Joyce E. Salisbury, general editor. Greenwood Press 2004 6v il map set $599.95 **390**
1. Civilization -- Encyclopedias 2. Manners and customs -- Encyclopedias 3. Manners and customs -- History 4. Reference books
ISBN 0-313-32541-3

LC 2003-54724

This "work provides an overview of the material, domestic, recreational, religious, political, intellectual, and economic aspects of daily life in a selection of cultures from six broad historical periods. . . . Each of the six volumes gives a survey of the historical period in each culture covered, which is representative rather than exhaustive, then covers aspects of daily life from broad topics to narrower." Libr J
Includes bibliographical references

391 Customs

Ashenburg, Kathy
The **dirt** on clean; an unsanitized history. [by] Katherine Ashenburg. North Point Press 2007 358p il $24; pa $15 **391**
1. Bathing customs -- History 2. Hygiene 3. Hygiene -- History 4. Personal grooming
ISBN 978-0-86547-690-5; 0-86547-690-X; 978-0-

374-53137-9 pa; 0-374-53137-4 pa

LC 2007-32334

"Brimming with lively anecdotes, this well-researched, smartly paced and endearing history of Western cleanliness holds a welcome mirror up to our intimate selves, revealing deep-seated desires and fears spanning 2000-plus years." Publ Wkly
Includes bibliographical references

Calasibetta, Charlotte Mankey
★ The **Fairchild** dictionary of fashion; {by} Charlotte Mankey Calasibetta, Phyllis Tortora; illustrated by Bina Abling. 3rd ed; Fairchild Publs. 2003 522p il $75 **391**
1. Fashion design -- Dictionaries 2. Reference books
ISBN 1-5636-7235-9

LC 2002-103884

This work provides definitions of fashion terms, line drawings, and biographical sketches of designers.

Crowe, Lauren Goldstein
The **towering** world of Jimmy Choo; a glamorous story of power, profits and the pursuit of the perfect shoe. [by] Lauren Goldstein Crowe and Sagra Maceira de Rosen. Bloomsbury USA 2009 228p il $26; pa $15 **391**
1. Clothing industry executives 2. Fashion design 3. Shoes
ISBN 978-1-59691-391-2; 1-59691-391-6; 978-1-60819-040-9 pa; 1-60819-040-4 pa

LC 2008-44378

"A fascinating, well-written chronology that draws a chillingly accurate behind-the-scenes portrait of a contemporary fashion brand." Booklist
Includes bibliographical references

De Marly, Diana
★ **Dress** in North America. v1 Holmes & Meier 1990 221p v1 il $59.95 **391**
1. Costume -- History
ISBN 0-8419-1199-1

LC 90-4905

"Volume 1 of this projected three-volume series is a historical narrative of the development of clothing styles and industries in Colonial America. Beautifully reproduced art works, mostly portrait paintings, are accompanied by excellent fashion commentary." Libr J
Includes bibliographical references

DeJean, Joan E.
The **essence** of style; how the French invented high fashion, fine food, chic cafes, style, sophistication, and glamour. Free Press 2005 303p il $25; pa $15 **391**
1. Cookery, French -- History 2. Fashion -- France -- History 3. Fashion -- History 4. Kings
ISBN 0-7432-6413-4; 0-7432-6414-2 pa

LC 2005-40019

"An unusual and delightfully educational perspective on snob appeal." Booklist
Includes bibliographical references

Kelly, Clinton

Dress your best; the complete guide to finding the style that's right for your body. [by] Clinton Kelly and Stacy London. Three Rivers Press 2005 255p il pa $18.95 **391**

1. Clothing and dress 2. Fashion
ISBN 0-307-23671-4

LC 2005-13681

This fashion guide describes specific male and female body types, and the kinds of outfits that match well with them. "Each type's section opens with a photo of an average-looking model sporting a basic swimsuit, along with comments from the model and the authors. . . . Ladies and gentlemen, start your shopping engines—and don't leave home without this book!" Publ Wkly

Nunn, Joan

Fashion in costume, 1200-2000; 2nd ed; New Amsterdam Bks. 2000 280p pa $18.95 **391**

1. Costume -- History
ISBN 1-56663-279-X

LC 99-47516

This history of American and European costume covers men's, women's, and children's dress, accessories and jewelry, fabrics, and color. Discusses how historical, social, economic, and artistic events influence fashion

Paterek, Josephine

★ **Encyclopedia** of American Indian costume. Norton 1996 516p il pa $24.95 **391**

1. Native American costume -- Encyclopedias 2. Reference books
ISBN 0-393-31382-4

Paterek describes "the clothing used for everyday, war, rites, and ceremonies for men, women, and children in hundreds of tribes in diverse climates stretching over centuries. Well-organized text and 400 drawings and authentic photos plus the cultural essays prefacing the 10 regional groupings and each tribe put the costumes in historical, social, and geographic context. Appendixes cover terminology and the materials used in clothing. The excellent bibliographies in this classic work both document and encourage further reading." Am Libr

Includes bibliographical references

★ Encyclopedia of clothing and fashion; Valerie Steele, editor in chief. Scribner 2005 3v set $395 **391**

1. Costume -- Encyclopedias 2. Fashion -- Encyclopedias 3. Reference books
ISBN 0-684-31394-4

LC 2004-10098

Alphabetically arranged entries range "from a half page for some particular items, clothing types, fibers , and techniques . . . to multiple pages for Cross dressing; Dandyism; Hats, men's and Hats, women's; Kimono; Street style and Twentieth century fashion, among others. Articles on designers or people who influenced fashion . . . are a significant part of the content, as are articles with a historical slant. . . . Many of the articles are entertaining as well as enlightening. . . . Encyclopedia of Clothing and Fashion is an excit-

ing and unique resource that excels in depth and range of coverage." Booklist

391.6 Personal appearance

Etcoff, Nancy L.

Survival of the prettiest; the science of beauty. {by} Nancy Etcoff. Doubleday 1999 325p il hardcover o.p. pa $14 **391.6**

1. Beauty, Personal -- Social aspects 2. Natural selection 3. Personal appearance 4. Sexual attraction 5. Sexual behavior
ISBN 0-385-47942-5 pa

LC 98-41332

"Topics as wide-ranging as penis- or breast-enlargement surgery and the basics of haute couture are treated with wit and insight. Etcoff's arguments are certain to initiate a great deal of discussion." Publ Wkly

Includes bibliographical references

Peiss, Kathy Lee

Hope in a jar; the making of America's beauty culture. {by} Kathy Peiss. Metropolitan Bks. 1998 334p il hardcover o.p. pa $15.95 **391.6**

1. Beauty culture -- United States -- History 2. Cosmetics 3. Cosmetics -- United States -- History 4. Personal appearance
ISBN 0-8050-5551-7 pa

LC 97-42706

This is a "social history of the origin and development of the U.S. cosmetics industry. . . . An engrossing, highly readable book that should be welcomed by scholars and general readers alike." Libr J

Includes bibliographical references

392 Customs of life cycle and domestic life

Gollaher, David

Circumcision; a history of the world's most controversial surgery. [by] David L. Gollaher. Basic Bks. 2000 253p hardcover o.p. pa $18 **392**

1. Circumcision 2. Circumcision -- History
ISBN 0-465-02653-2 pa

LC 99-40015

This history of circumcision discusses Jewish, Muslim, and tribal rituals, medical procedures and complications, reasons for the procedure, and its social significance in various cultures and eras.

Jellison, Katherine

It's our day; America's love affair with the white wedding, 1945-2005. University Press of Kansas 2008 297p il $29.95 **392**

1. Marriage customs and rites
ISBN 978-0-7006-1559-9

LC 2007-35444

The author "takes an in-depth look at the history and popularity of the American 'white wedding' and in doing so provides a unique exploration of late 20th- and early 21st-century American culture. She starts right after World War II and progresses through celebrity, royal, and movie weddings to the 'reality weddings' of today and how the ritual of a white wedding has been adapted in many same-sex marriages. . . . An enlightening and fascinating read, her book is sure to be of interest in most libraries." Libr J

Includes bibliographical references

Mead, Rebecca

One perfect day; the selling of the American wedding. Penguin Press 2007 245p $25.95; pa $15 **392**

1. Weddings 2. Weddings -- Social aspects
ISBN 978-1-59420-088-5; 978-0-14-311384-3 pa
LC 2006-52461

"Part investigative journalism, part social commentary, Mead's wry, insightful work offers an illuminating glimpse at the ugly underbelly of our Bridezilla culture." Publ Wkly

Monger, George

★ **Marriage** customs of the world; from henna to honeymoons. [by] George P. Monger. ABC-CLIO 2004 327p il $85 **392**

1. Marriage customs and rites
ISBN 1-576-07987-2
LC 2004-17586

This is "an encyclopedia of marriage rites, traditions, and beliefs from around the world, ranging from ancient practices to contemporary ceremonies." Publisher's note

Includes bibliographical references

393 Death customs

Jokinen, Tom

Curtains; adventures of an undertaker-in-training. Da Capo Press 2010 279p pa $15.95 **393**

1. Funeral rites and ceremonies 2. Undertakers and undertaking
ISBN 978-0-306-81891-2; 0-306-81891-4
LC 2010-920629

"The narrative pinballs between the many roles Jokinen takes on within the industry—hearse driver, embalming assistant, theatrically solemn host who gestures at coat racks and restrooms. All the while, Jokinen dutifully remains the voice of the curious reader, channeling skepticism, the weirds and awe into laugh-out-loud observations grounded in just enough research to provide context without weighing down the plot." PopMatters

Kammen, Michael G.

Digging up the dead; a history of notable American reburials. [by] Michael Kammen. University of Chicago Press 2010 260p il $25 **393**

1. Burial 2. Burial -- United States 3. Exhumation 4. Funeral rites and ceremonies 5. Funeral rites and ceremonies -- United States
ISBN 978-0-226-42329-6; 0-226-42329-8
LC 2009-23515

"Kammen has a good sense of the details that make historical stories memorable. His occasional flashes of humor

add a winsome, professionally geeky element to the telling." Dallas Morning News

Includes bibliographical references

Laderman, Gary

Rest in peace; a cultural history of death and the funeral home in twentieth-century America. Oxford Univ. Press 2003 245p il hardcover o.p. pa $21.95 **393**

1. Funeral supplies industry 2. Undertakers and undertaking 3. Undertakers and undertaking -- United States
ISBN 0-19-513608-X; 978-0-19-518355-9 pa; 0-19-518355-X pa
LC 2002-6682

This book explores "the world of death specialists, the development of their profession in post-Civil War America, and the profession's role in American culture. . . . The topics covered . . . include embalming, the repatriation of wartime remains, the rise of corporate facilities, the AIDS epidemic, and cultural representations such as The Night of the Living Dead and Six Feet Under. . . . Laderman's respect, even affection, for the profession is clearly evident, but he maintains objectivity throughout. Especially impressive is his treatment of {Jessica} Mitford, whose accusations he challenges politely but thoroughly." Libr J

Includes bibliographical references

Pringle, Heather Anne

The mummy congress; science, obsession, and the everlasting dead. {by} Heather Pringle. Hyperion 2001 368p il hardcover o.p. pa $13.95 **393**

1. Body, Human -- Social aspects 2. Forensic anthropology 3. Human remains (Archaeology) 4. Mummies 5. Physical anthropology
ISBN 0-7868-6551-2; 0-7868-8463-0 pa
LC 00-54487

"Besides outstanding members of the scientific association that gathers as the Mummy Congress, Pringle limns the many varieties of mummies, from the world's oldest, preserved by the high-altitude climate of the Andes, to modern Communist dictators, self-mummifying Buddhists, and the subjects of extreme cosmetic surgery. More astounding than all the fright flicks about shambling, gauze-wrapped menaces wound together." Booklist

Includes bibliographical references

394 General customs

Visser, Margaret

The gift of thanks; the roots and rituals of gratitude. Houghton Mifflin Harcourt 2009 458p $27 **394**

1. Gratitude
ISBN 978-0-15-101331-9
LC 2009-14018

"A book to be thankful for—sympathetic to human foible, deeply learned and a pleasure to read." Kirkus

Includes bibliographical references

394.1   Eating, drinking; using drugs

Burns, Eric

★ The **spirits** of America; a social history of alcohol. Temple University Press 2004 352p $29   **394.1**

1. Alcoholic beverages 2. Drinking of alcoholic beverages 3. Drinking of alcoholic beverages -- United States -- History 4. Social history

ISBN 1-592-13214-6

LC 2003-50790

Burns "presents an enjoyable and informative examination of the role of alcoholic beverages in American society." Libr J

Includes bibliographical references

Collingham, E. M.

★ **Curry**; a tale of cooks and conquerors. Oxford University Press 2006 315p il maps $28 **394.1**

1. Eating customs 2. Food habits -- India -- History

ISBN 978-0-19-517241-6; 0-19-517241-8

LC 2005-16641

The author "with incredibly engrossing detail, unravels the tantalizing mystery of 'curry' in its innumerable forms, which have ravished the taste buds in far-flung kitchens and dining rooms." MultiCult Rev

Includes bibliographical references

Cowen, Tyler

An **economist** gets lunch; new rules for everyday foodies. Tyler Cowen. Dutton 2012 x, 293 p.p   **394.1**

1. Food -- Moral & ethical aspects 2. Food habits -- Economic aspects 3. Food industry and trade 4. Food preferences -- Economic aspects 5. Locavores 6. Social criticism

ISBN 0525952667; 9780525952664

LC 2011035174

In this book, economist Tyler Cowen steers his audience through the contemporary world of eating and drinking. Like many staunch foodies, he respects the local. He much prefers the tamales from a roadside vendor in Nicaragua to those offered in a tourist restaurant. Not only does the roadside vendor produce a tastier product; the food is also less processed and less depleting of energy spent on transportation. Cowen finds that, despite what logic may suggest, the most expensive food is not necessarily the best. And he reveals that the same principle holds true in urban America as well as in the Third World. He expands this insight with a survey of barbecue restaurants in the U.S. (Booklist)

Fernandez-Armesto, Felipe

Near a thousand tables; a history of food. Free Press 2002 258p $25; pa $14   **394.1**

1. Food -- History

ISBN 0-7432-2644-5; 0-7432-2740-9 pa

LC 2002-23318

This is a "well-written, thought-provoking overview of food history." Libr J

Includes bibliographical references and index

Gately, Iain

Tobacco; the story of how tobacco seduced the world. Grove Press 2002 403p il $25; pa $15 **394.1**

1. Tobacco 2. Tobacco -- History 3. Tobacco -- Social aspects -- History

ISBN 0-8021-1705-8; 0-8021-3960-4 pa

LC 2001-54493

"An entertaining story of humanity's Faustian bargain with tobacco." Booklist

Includes bibliographical references

Grimes, William

Appetite city; a culinary history of New York. North Point Press 2009 368p il $30   **394.1**

1. Cookery -- New York (N.Y.) 2. Cooking -- New York (N.Y.) 3. Eating customs 4. Food -- Social aspects 5. Food habits -- New York (N.Y.) 6. Restaurants

ISBN 978-0-86547-692-9; 0-86547-692-6

LC 2008-54288

This "lively, profusely illustrated history veers in one fascinating direction after another, from the proliferation of oyster houses in the 1800s to the original recipe for chop suey. . . . [Grimes] gets personal in the final chapter, describing the scene of the late 1990s and early 2000s from his frontline perspective as the restaurant critic for the New York Times. . . . All the material is so fascinating that you'll wish every chapter was at least twice as long, but it's hard to imagine a more entertaining introduction to the subject." Publ Wkly

Includes bibliographical references

Holland, Barbara

The **joy** of drinking. Bloomsbury 2007 150p il $15   **394.1**

1. Drinking of alcoholic beverages

ISBN 978-1-59691-337-0; 1-59691-337-1

LC 2006-39322

"Mixing fact, fable, anecdote, and personal opinion with irresistible panache, cultural historian Barbara Holland's The Joy of Drinking distills thousands of years of humankind's lusty relationship with alcohol . . . into a slim, sparkling history." Elle

Mayle, Peter

French lessons; adventures with knife, fork, and corkscrew. Knopf 2001 227p il $24; pa $12.95   **394.1**

1. Eating customs

ISBN 0-375-40590-9; 0-375-70561-9 pa

Mayle "relives some of his most precious moments reveling in the cuisine of his adopted homeland. . . . {He tells} savory, sensual, positively transporting stories about his encounters with Gallic gustatory delights and about his growing appreciation of the central place food occupies in French life." Booklist

McWilliams, James E.

Just food; where locavores get it wrong and how we can truly eat responsibly. Little, Brown and Company 2009 258p $25.99   **394.1**
1. Eating customs 2. Food industry 3. Natural foods
ISBN 978-0-316-03374-9

LC 2009-15514

The author "argues for moderation and compromise in today's raging food fights. Until recently, the author was a locavore—one who eats locally produced food. Though he still believes that it is a dietary commitment with many virtues, he argues that it's also a feeble, ineffective way to feed the world's hungry billions. . . . McWilliams presents some appealing alternatives to the views of both the agrarian romantics on the left and the agribusiness capitalists on the right. . . . Rich in research, provocative in conception and nettlesome to both the right and the left." Kirkus
Includes bibliographical references

Pollan, Michael

★ The **omnivore's** dilemma; a natural history of four meals. Penguin Press 2006 450p $26.95; pa $16   **394.1**
1. Agriculture -- United States 2. Eating customs 3. Food consumption -- United States 4. Food supply -- United States
ISBN 1-59420-082-3; 0-14-303858-3 pa

LC 2005-56557

The author "defines the Omnivore's Dilemma as the confusing maze of choices facing Americans trying to eat healthfully in a society that he calls 'notably unhealthy.' He seeks answers to this dilemma by taking readers through the industrial, organic, and hunter-gatherer stages of the food chain. . . . This folksy narrative provides a wealth of information about agriculture, the natural world, and human desires." Libr J
Includes bibliographical references

Schlosser, Eric

★ **Fast** food nation; the dark side of the all-American meal. Houghton Mifflin 2001 356p il $25   **394.1**
1. Convenience foods 2. Cookery, American 3. Food industry 4. Large print books 5. Restaurants
ISBN 0-395-97789-4

LC 00-53886

"Schlosser documents the effects of fast food on America's economy, its youth culture, and allied industries. . . . Starting with a young woman who makes minimum wage working at a Colorado fast-food restaurant, Schlosser relates the oft-told story of Ray Kroc's founding of McDonald's. The author also tells about the development of the franchise method of business ownership and the health and nutrition implications of fast-food consumption." Booklist
Includes bibliographical references

Spencer, Colin

British food; an extraordinary thousand years of history. Columbia Univ. Press 2003 400p il $35   **394.1**
1. Cookery -- Great Britain -- History 2. Food -- History

3. Food habits -- Great Briatain -- History
ISBN 0-231-13110-0

LC 2003-48492

"Spencer traces the country's lamentable decline in cuisine through the Reformation, Puritanism, and the Industrial Revolution, noting that Britons gradually lost a knowledge of wild foodstuffs and the time in their day to gather and cook more than the most convenient foods. . . . Readers may . . . find the glossary and appendixes of British edible flora and traditional dishes to be particularly valuable." Libr J
Includes bibliographical references

Standage, Tom

An **edible** history of humanity. Walker & Company 2009 269p il map $26   **394.1**
1. Agriculture 2. Eating customs 3. Food
ISBN 978-0-8027-1588-3; 0-8027-1588-5

LC 2009-5610

"This meaty little volume [is] cogent, informative and insightful." Kirkus
Includes bibliographical references

A **history** of the world in 6 glasses. Walker & Co. 2005 311p il $25   **394.1**
1. Beverages 2. Beverages -- History 3. Coffee -- History 4. Drinking of alcoholic beverages -- History 5. Tea -- History 6. World history
ISBN 0-8027-1447-1

LC 2004-61209

Standage "has the ability to connect the smallest detail to the big picture and a knack for summarizing vast concepts in a few sentences." Publ Wkly
Includes bibliographical references

Stern, Jane

Two for the road; our love affair with American food. [by] Jane and Michael Stern. Houghton Mifflin 2006 292p $24   **394.1**
1. Cookbook writers 2. Cookery -- United States 3. Cookery, American 4. Cooking 5. Food critics
ISBN 0-618-32963-3; 978-0-618-32963-2

LC 2005-31611

This is "a book to be savored while sitting in the Formica and vinyl booth of your favorite diner eating meatloaf and real mashed potatoes." Libr J

United States/Works Progress Administration

The **food** of a younger land; a portrait of American food: before the national highway system, before chain restaurants, and before frozen food, when the nation's food was seasonal, regional, and traditional: from the lost WPA fil. edited and illustrated by Mark Kurlansky. Riverhead Books 2009 397p il $27.95   **394.1**
1. Cookery -- United States -- History -- 20th century 2. Cooking 3. Eating customs 4. Food habits -- United States -- History
ISBN 978-1-59448-865-8

LC 2009-8100

"In the late 1930s the WPA farmed out a writing project with the ambition of other New Deal programs: an encyclopedia of American food and food traditions from coast-to-coast similar to the federal travel guides. After Pearl Harbor, the war effort halted the project for good; the book was never published, and the files were archived in the Library of Congress. . . . [The editor] brought the unassembled materials to light and created this version of the guide that never was. . . . This extraordinary collection—at once history, anthropology, cookbook, almanac and family album—provides a vivid and revitalizing sense of the rural and regional characteristics and distinctions that we've lost and can find again here." Publ Wkly

Includes bibliographical references

★ Tobacco in history and culture; an encyclopedia. Jordan Goodman, editor in chief. Thomson Gale 2005 2v il set $275   **394.1**
1. Reference books 2. Smoking -- History 3. Tobacco -- Encyclopedias 4. Tobacco -- History
ISBN 0-684-31405-3
           LC 2004-7109

"This makes an excellent starting point for readers looking for quick entrance to the vast body of knowledge of the history and diversity of tobacco uses, tobacco health, addiction, social control issues, advertising, production, and distribution, among other topics." Choice

Includes bibliographical references

394.26   Holidays

Baker, James W.
Thanksgiving; the biography of an American holiday. foreword by Peter J. Gomes. University of New Hampshire Press 2009 273p il pa $26.95   **394.26**
1. Thanksgiving Day
ISBN 978-1-58465-801-6
           LC 2009-12348

The author shows "how Thanksgiving is seen through each generation's reality, having morphed from a holiday for pilgrim hats and turkeys to a cause for Native American protests to a holy day to several ancient holidays combined and a full-scale orgy of food and football. . . . [This is] an enjoyable, fascinating read both for students and for anyone looking for a good story." Libr J

Includes bibliographical references

Christianson, Stephen G.
★ The **international** book of days; edited by Lynn M. Messina; contributors, Jennifer Peloso, Norris Smith, Laura Ware. H.W. Wilson 2004 xxxi, 889p il map $140   **394.26**
1. Festivals 2. Holidays
ISBN 0-8242-0975-3
           LC 2004-42285

This "book presents an international tour of holidays and major historical events. Organized by day of the year, the book covers some 1500 key events in world history." Libr J

Forbes, Bruce David
Christmas; a candid history. University of California Press 2007 179p il $19.95; pa $12.95 **394.26**
1. Christmas 2. Christmas -- History
ISBN 978-0-520-25104-5; 978-0-520-25802-0 pa
           LC 2007-00366

The author "presents a brief social history of Christmas from pre-Christian winter celebrations to the commercialization of the holiday in American popular culture. The growth of the holiday to include Christmas cards, music and movies are included in this easy to read overview." Univ Press Books for Public and Second Sch Libr, 2008

Includes bibliographical references

Gulevich, Tanya
★ **Encyclopedia** of Christmas and New Year's celebrations; illustrated by Mary Ann Stavros-Lanning. Omnigraphics 2003 xx, 977p il $68   **394.26**
1. Christmas 2. Christmas -- Encyclopedias 3. New Year 4. New Year -- Encyclopedias
ISBN 0-7808-0625-5
           LC 2003-40580

The author "covers a variety of secular and sacred aspects of Christmas and New Year's celebrations. . . . This encyclopedic work is useful for those schools where folklore is covered, or for those interested in origins of the holidays." Libr Media Connect

Includes bibliographical references

Hillstrom, Laurie
The **Thanksgiving** book; [by] Laurie C. Hillstrom. Omnigraphics 2008 328p il $65   **394.26**
1. Thanksgiving Day
ISBN 978-0-7808-0403-6
           LC 2007-25708

"This book is definitely a wonderful tribute to the holiday of Thanksgiving." Am Ref Books Annu, 2008

Includes bibliographical references

Rajtar, Steve
★ **United** States holidays and observances; by date, jurisdiction, and subject, fully indexed. McFarland & Co. 2003 165p $45   **394.26**
1. Festivals 2. Holidays 3. Holidays -- United States 4. Special days -- United States
ISBN 0-7864-1446-4
           LC 2002-154293

This "concentrates on observances and holidays established by statute in the U.S. and American Samoa, District of Columbia, Guam, the Northern Mariana Islands, Puerto Rico, and the U.S. Virgin Islands. In addition, UN-designated holidays are included. . . . The text is arranged by month, and chapters for each month are divided into 'Observances with Variable Dates' and 'Observances with Fixed Dates.' Each entry identifies the observance as federal or specific to a state and offers a description that ranges in length from three or four lines to a quarter page. . . . [This] would be a good addition to ready-reference desks in public libraries and information centers in schools." Booklist

Stuever, Hank

Tinsel; a search for America's Christmas present. Houghton Mifflin Harcourt 2009 231p $24 **394.26**
1. Christmas
ISBN 978-0-547-13465-9; 0-547-13465-7

LC 2009-13746

"In 2006, Stuever set out to characterize the experience of Christmas—its aesthetics, economics, and metaphysics—in an average Texas town. The resulting dissection of the holiday is cultural anthropology at its most exuberant. According to Stuever, fakery, not excess, is the signature of the modern American Christmas." New Yorker

Includes bibliographical references

★ **Chase's calendar of events 2011**; the ultimate go-to guide for special days, weeks and months. McGraw-Hill 2011 752p il pa $75 **394.26**
1. Almanacs 2. Calendars 3. Holidays 4. Reference books
ISBN 978-0-07-174026-5

"Day-by-day listing of national and state holidays, religious observances, special events, festivals and fairs, and historical anniversaries and birthdays. Covers U.S. events primarily, but some international occasions and anniversaries are included." N Y Public Libr Book of How & Where to Look It Up

Encyclopedia of holidays and celebrations; a country-by-country guide. Matthew Dennis, editor. Facts on File 2006 3v il map set $275 **394.26**
1. Festivals 2. Holidays
ISBN 0-8160-6235-8; 978-0-8160-6235-5

LC 2005-27700

This is "a three-volume guide that explores holidays and festivals in 206 countries. Volumes I and II are organized alphabetically by country, and volume III contains overviews of major internationally observed holidays and religions. . . . This welcome addition to multicultural studies is attractively laid out, easy to use, great for browsing as well as fact finding, and is highly recommended for high school, public, and college libraries." Ref & User Services Quarterly

Includes bibliographical references

★ **Holiday symbols and customs**; 4th ed.; Omnigraphics 2009 1321p $94 **394.26**
1. Festivals 2. Holidays
ISBN 978-0-7808-0990-1

LC 2008-28403

"Describes the origins of 323 holidays around the world. Explains where, when, and how each event is celebrated, with detailed information on the symbols and customs associated with the holiday. Includes contact information and web sites for related organizations." Publisher's note

Includes bibliographical references

★ **Holidays, festivals, and celebrations of the world dictionary**; detailing more than 3,000 observances from all 50 states and more than 100 nations: a compendious reference guide to popular, ethnic, religious, national, and ancient holidays. . . edited

by Cherie D. Abbey. 4th ed.; Omnigraphics 2010 1323p $144 **394.26**
1. Festivals -- Dictionaries 2. Holidays -- Dictionaries 3. Reference books
ISBN 978-0-7808-0994-9

LC 2009-41138

"A comprehensive dictionary that describes more than 3,000 holidays and festivals celebrated around the world. Features both secular and religious events from many different cultures, countries, and ethnic groups. Includes contact information for events; multiple appendices with background information on world holidays; extensive bibliography; multiple indexes." Publisher's note

395   Etiquette (Manners)

Allert, Tilman

The **Hitler** salute; on the meaning of a gesture. translated by Jefferson Chase. Metropolitan Books/Henry Holt and Company 2008 115p il $20; pa $13 **395**
1. Manners and customs 2. National socialism 3. National socialism -- Social aspects -- Germany 4. Political customs and rites -- Germany 5. Salutations -- Germany
ISBN 978-0-8050-8178-7; 0-8050-8178-X; 978-0-312-42830-3 pa; 0-312-42830-8 pa

In this "study of the Third Reich's preferred greeting, . . . [the author] asserts that the Hitler salute played a key role in the Nazis' ability to disengage the moral scruples of the German populace. . . . Straightforward in its analysis yet profound in its conclusions, this uncommon selection sheds elusive light on the question of how Nazi ideology managed to penetrate even the most ordinary social interactions." Booklist

Includes bibliographical references

Baldrige, Letitia

★ **Letitia** Baldrige's new manners for new times; a complete guide to etiquette. illustrations by Denise Cavalieri Fike. Scribner 2003 xxvi, 709p il $35 **395**
1. Etiquette
ISBN 0-7432-1062-X

LC 2003-65666

"Combining correctness, consideration, and common sense in equal measure, Baldrige advises readers on proper ways to approach intricate situations. She addresses same-sex unions, pregnant brides, blended and extended families, and sexual harassment with aplomb." Libr J

Blyth, Catherine

The **art** of conversation; a guided tour of a neglected pleasure. Gotham Books 2009 289p $22.50 **395**
1. Conversation
ISBN 978-1-592-40419-3; 1-592-40419-7

LC 2008-24276

"Adopting a chatty, conversational manner to write about conversation, Blyth mixes personal anecdotes into a salmagundi of selected quotes from anthropology, history, literature, philosophy and pop culture to analyze and give advice on the dynamics of good conversation, not to mention the perfect riposte for every situation. She examines everything from small talk to pillow talk, from riotous raconteurs to crashing bores, from flattery to false smiles. . . . Witty, eloquent and insightful, Blyth's book is a delightful encouragement to rediscover conversation as the best communication technology." Publ Wkly

Dresser, Norine
   Multicultural manners; essential rules of etiquette for the 21st century. Rev ed; John Wiley & Sons 2005 285p map pa $16.95   **395**
   1. Etiquette 2. Manners and customs
   ISBN 978-0-471-68428-2; 0-471-68428-7
                              LC 2004-27079
   "From body language and table manners to classroom behavior and gift giving, this guide to etiquette provides fascinating information about relations in our multicultural society." Booklist
   Includes bibliographical references

Forni, Pier Massimo
   The **civility** solution; what to do when people are rude. [by] P.M. Forni. St. Martin's Press 2008 xxi, 166p $19.95   **395**
   1. Courtesy 2. Etiquette
   ISBN 978-0-312-36849-4; 0-312-36849-6
                              LC 2008-9448
   "In Part 1 . . . [the author] describes some of the causes of rudeness (e.g., anger, fear, inflated self-worth) and the negative consequences of rude behavior in daily life. . . . In Part 2, Forni provides over 70 examples of situations in which rudeness arises and solutions for dealing with them. Readers who have been criticized in public or annoyed by a loud cell phone conversation get realistic help." Libr J
   Includes bibliographical references

Martin, Judith
   ★ **Miss** Manners' guide to excruciatingly correct behavior; illustrated by Gloria Kamen. freshly updated; Norton 2005 858p il $35   **395**
   1. Etiquette
   ISBN 0-393-05874-3
                              LC 2005-00264
   "Miss Manners is always as entertaining as she is civilized." Booklist

Morrison, Terri
   ★ **Kiss,** bow, or shake hands; the bestselling guide to doing business in more than 60 countries. [by] Terri Morrison and Wayne A. Conaway. 2nd ed.; Adams Media 2006 593p il pa $24.95   **395**
   1. Business communication 2. Business etiquette 3. Negotiation
   ISBN 1-59337-368-6
                              LC 2006-13587
   "The definitive reference for doing business around the world." Libr J

Oliver, Vicky
   301 smart answers to tough business etiquette questions. Skyhorse Pub. 2010 370p pa $12.95 **395**
   1. Business etiquette
   ISBN 978-1-61608-141-6; 1-61608-141-4
                              LC 2010021474
   This guide to business etiquette covers "making a good first impression (and how to fix a bad one!); how to behave in elevators, airplanes, and supply closets; surviving cabs, commutes, and coffee shops; why time is not necessarily money everywhere on the planet; pre-approved conversational topics from A to Z; dining rules and regulations for the twenty-first century; what to do when you are suddenly unemployed; [and] electronic communication." Publisher's note
   Includes bibliographical references

Outcalt, Todd
   Your beautiful wedding on any budget. Sourcebooks 2009 227p pa $12.99   **395**
   1. Weddings
   ISBN 978-1-4022-1788-3
                              LC 2008-46864
   "A terrific resource for couples trying to start their marriage on a financially sound footing. The Methodist pastor offers suggestions for building a wedding fund and creative cost-cutting measures based on his debt-free wedding seminars and blog." Libr J

Post, Peggy
   ★ **Emily** Post's Etiquette; 17th ed.; HarperCollins Publishers 2004 876p $39.95   **395**
   1. Etiquette
   ISBN 0-06-620957-9
                              LC 2004-40508
   "The classic reference for which fork to use has been expanded to include such modern situations as dating, living together, second marriages, and co-ed business traveling." N Y Public Libr Book of How & Where to Look It Up

   ★ **Emily** Post's wedding etiquette; 5th ed.; HarperCollins 2006 xxiv, 405p il $27.95   **395**
   1. Etiquette 2. Marriage customs and rites 3. Weddings
   ISBN 978-0-06-074503-5; 0-06-074503-7
                              LC 2005-40387
   This guide to wedding planning covers such topics as multicultural and interfaith marriages, second marriages, engagements, prewedding events, postwedding duties, financial matters, working with consultants, and responsibilities of participants, and includes flow charts and ckecklists.

Truss, Lynne
   Talk to the hand; the utter bloody rudeness of the world today, or six good reasons to stay home and bolt the door. Gotham Books 2005 206p $20 **395**
   1. Civilization 2. Conduct of life 3. Etiquette
   ISBN 1-59240-171-6
   The author "examines the death of civil language, the transfer of customer service from those who serve the customers to the customers themselves, the refusal to live by any rules but one's own, the pervasiveness of profanity, the dismissal of criticism, and the universal lack of responsibil-

ity. Each examination is not merely an opportunity to rant but a thoughtful and well-researched effort to understand the behavior." Libr J

Includes bibliographical references

Vivaldo, Denise

Do it for le$$! weddings; how to create your dream wedding without breaking the bank. Sellers Pub., Inc. 2008 272p il pa $19.95 **395**

1. Weddings

ISBN 978-1-4162-0519-7

LC 2008-923779

The author "focuses on receptions—venues, logistics, and menus (including numerous recipes). Detailed information and instructive illustrations make this a solid choice for those catering their own affairs." Libr J

Includes bibliographical references

Warner, Diane

How to have a big wedding on a small budget; cut your wedding costs in half. 4th ed; Betterway Bks. 2003 185p il pa $12.99 **395**

1. Weddings

ISBN 1-55870-646-1

LC 2002-26191

The author provides consumer tips on such subjects as invitations, dresses, food, flowers, and pictures

Weiss, Mindy

★ The **wedding** book; the big book for your big day. by Mindy Weiss with Lisbeth Levine. Workman Pub. Company, Inc. 2007 485p il $35; pa $19.95 **395**

1. Weddings

ISBN 978-0-7611-5094-7; 978-0-7611-3960-7 pa

LC 2008-15510

This book offers wedding planning advice on topics such as announcing the wedding, setting up a budget, planning the ceremony, wedding parties, and designing the dress and tuxedo.

This "comprehensive, well-organized guide offers good details on contracts and setting priorities." Libr J

★ **Bride's** book of etiquette; by the editors of Bride's magazine. Rev. ed.; Perigee 2003 333p il pa $19.95 **395**

1. Etiquette 2. Marriage customs and rites 3. Weddings

ISBN 0-399-52866-0

LC 2002-35534

A guide to planning a wedding ceremony and reception, from announcements to honeymoon plans.

398 Folklore

Bane, Theresa

Encyclopedia of vampire mythology. McFarland & Company, Inc., Publishers 2010 199p $75 **398**

1. Reference books 2. Vampires -- Encyclopedias

ISBN 978-0-7864-4452-6

LC 2010-15576

The "introduction presents a survey of the vampire myth's historical roots and continued evolution. Subsequent entries, organized alphabetically by vampire name, include phonetic pronunciations and define the many tangible and intangible vampiric forms that hail from every continent around the globe. . . . A thorough resource for dark mythologists and vampire enthusiasts." Libr J

Includes bibliographical references

Bernstein, Peter L.

The **power** of gold; the history of an obsession. Wiley 2000 432p $27.95; pa $16.95 **398**

1. Gold

ISBN 0-471-25210-7; 0-471-00378-6 pa

LC 00-36647

The author "recounts the magical, religious, and artistic qualities of gold and moves through the invention of coins, the transformation of gold into money, and the history of the gold standard." Libr J

Includes bibliographical references

Guiley, Rosemary Ellen

The **encyclopedia** of vampires & werewolves; foreword by Jeanne Keyes Youngson. 2nd ed; Facts On File 2011 430p il $85; pa $24.95 **398**

1. Monsters -- Encyclopedias 2. Reference books 3. Vampires 4. Vampires -- Encyclopedias 5. Werewolves 6. Werewolves -- Encyclopedias

ISBN 978-0-8160-8179-0; 0-8160-8179-4; 978-0-8160-8180-6 pa; 0-8160-8180-8 pa; 978-1-4381-3632-5 ebook; 1-4381-3632-3 ebook

LC 2010034839

"Entries describe supposed true historical accounts, how vampires and werewolves come into existence, beliefs about vampires and werewolves, and real-life creatures and cases that may have inspired their legends. . . . Fictional vampires from a range of media are discussed, along with the people who helped create them." Publisher's note

Includes bibliographical references

Hurston, Zora Neale

★ **Folklore,** memoirs, and other writings. Library of Am. 1995 1001p il $35 **398**

1. African Americans -- Folklore 2. Authors 3. Biography, Individual 4. Dramatists 5. Folklorists 6. Memoirists 7. Novelists 8. Short story writers

ISBN 0-940450-84-4

LC 94-21384

"This is the first time the unexpurgated version of Hurston's 1942 autobiography, Dust Tracks on the Road, is being published; sections deemed too provocative (dealing with politics, race, and sex) have been restored. Mules and Men (1935) is a collection of African American folklore she gleaned on travels in the South, while Tell My Horse (1938) tenders her personal findings on African-based religion in Jamaica and Haiti. Additionally, 22 magazine and book articles with anthropological themes . . . that have never been gathered into book form are corralled here." Booklist

Melton, J. Gordon

★ The **vampire** book; the encyclopedia of the undead. Completely revamped, fully rev. and ex-

panded, 3rd ed.; Visible Ink Press 2010 909p il pa
$29.95   **398**
  1. Reference books 2. Vampires -- Encyclopedias
ISBN 978-1-57859-281-4

                                       LC 2010-24263
"This vampire lore tome covers legends from around the
world, both classical and current, presenting an overview of
the historical, literary, mythological, biographical, and popular aspects of vampires. . . . This book is an excellent and
comprehensive addition to any collection serving readers
interested in learning more about the vampire in time, place,
and society. Aficionados of vampires in popular culture will
enjoy it." Libr J
  Includes bibliographical references

Prahlad, Anand
  ★ The **Greenwood** encyclopedia of African
American folklore; edited by Anand Prahlad. Green-
wood Press 2005 xl, 1557p 3v il set $299.95 **398**
  1. African Americans -- Folklore 2. African Americans
-- Folklore -- Encyclopedias 3. African Americans --
Social life and customs 4. African Americans -- Social
life and customs -- Encyclopedias 5. Folklore -- United
States 6. Reference books
ISBN 0-313-33035-2

                                       LC 2005-19214
For a fuller review, see: Booklist, Feb. 1, 2006
"The three volume set gives special attention to music,
art, folktales, spiritual beliefs, foodways, proverbs, and other
topics central to African American folklore, and discusses
the Caribbean and African roots of traditional African American culture." Libr Media Connect
  Includes bibliographical references

  ★ Encyclopedia of American folklife; Simon J.
  Bronner, editor. M.E. Sharpe 2006 4v il set
  $399   **398**
  1. Folklore 2. Folklore -- United States -- Encyclopedias
  3. Reference books
ISBN 0-7656-8052-1; 978-0-7656-8052-5

                                       LC 2005-32119
This encyclopedia "provides a survey of the cultural patterns and experiences of diverse communities throughout
the United States and the territories of Guam, Samoa, and
Puerto Rico as well as other countries and ethnic groups that
have influenced American social practices. . . . The encyclopedia covers crafts, foods, architecture, remedies, customs,
holidays, narratives, speech, and stereotypes, with an emphasis on contemporary practices." Libr J
  Includes bibliographical references

World folklore for storytellers; tales of wonder, wisdom, fools, and heroes. Josepha Sherman, editor.
  Sharpe Reference 2010 368p il $95   **398**
  1. Folklore 2. Storytelling
ISBN 978-0-7656-8174-4

                                       LC 2009-10525
This is "a wonderfully wide-ranging collection of nearly
200 ethnically diverse folktales. Particularly vital is that the
stories are organized thematically rather than geographically, allowing for broader symbolic and anthropological comparisons. Each narrative runs several pages, includes a brief

explanatory introduction, and consistently concludes with
at least two bibliographic references. Pockets of multipage
color plates offer images from native folktale anthologies
and other relevant artistic renderings." Libr J
  Includes bibliographical references

398.2   Folk literature

Ackroyd, Peter
  The **death** of King Arthur; Thomas Malory's Le
morte d'Arthur. Sir Thomas Malory; a retelling by
Peter Ackroyd. Viking 2011 316p $26.95   **398.2**
  1. Authors 2. Britons -- Fiction. 3. Great Britain --
Kings and rulers -- Fiction. 4. Kings 5. Knights and
knighthood -- Great Britain -- Fiction.
ISBN 978-0-670-02307-3; 0-670-02307-8

                                       LC 2011-21800
"Ackroyd takes the daunting Middle English verse and
retells the ancient legends in modern English prose. He also
omits most of Malory's medieval tales as perhaps too creaky
for modern minds, or maybe simply to make his retelling a
niftier little book. All the essential stories are here, among
them: Arthur lifting the great sword Excalibur from the stone
to become king; the adulterous quarter-century-long love affair of Queen Guinevere and Arthur's most powerful and
trusted knight, Lancelot du Lake; the love of Tristram and
Isolte; Sir Galahad and the search for the Holy Grail; the
awesome power of the wizard Merlin, the exquisite evil of
Morgan le Fay, Arthur's half-sister, and finally the doom of
Camelot and the death of Arthur at the hand of Sir Mordred,
his own son born from an incestuous union of Arthur and
Morgan le Fay. . . . Ackroyd tells these stories in such simple, vivid language that they seem as new as they must have
when first heard around the peat fires of cold and gloomy
England perhaps 1,000 years ago. And they're still a lot of
fun." Dallas Morning News

Armstrong, Karen
  ★ A **short** history of myth. Canongate 2005
159p hardcover o.p. pa $14   **398.2**
  1. Mythology 2. Mythology -- History
ISBN 1-84195-716-X; 1-84195-800-X pa
This is an "overview of the ever-evolving partnership
between myth and man from Paleolithic times to the present. Succinct and cleanly written, it is hugely readable and,
in its journey across the epochs of human experience, often
moving. . . . Armstrong's exposition is streamlined and uncluttered without being simplistic." N Y Times Book Rev
  Includes bibliographical references

Asma, Stephen T.
  On monsters; an unnatural history of our worst
fears. Oxford University Press 2009 351p il
$27.95   **398.2**
  1. Monsters
ISBN 978-0-19-533616-0

                                       LC 2009-7219
The author "is insightful and entertaining in his discussion of monsters of the deep, supernatural doppelgangers,
zombies, and vampires, and intense in his discussion of
Freud and the science of monstrous feelings. . . . Asma's far-

reaching book of monsterology is original, captivating, and profoundly elucidating." Booklist

Includes bibliographical references

Brunvand, Jan Harold

The **vanishing** hitchhiker; American urban legends and their meaning. Norton 1981 208p hardcover o.p. pa $13.95　　　　**398.2**
1. Folklore -- United States 2. Legends -- United States
ISBN 0-393-95169-3 pa
LC 81-4744

A collection of modern urban folktales with an ironic or supernatural twist. The author reports on how such tales are disseminated and discusses their inherent messages for contemporary society

Bulfinch, Thomas

★ **Bulfinch's** mythology; foreword by Alberto Manguel. Modern Library pbk. ed.; Modern Library 2004 862p pa $17.95　　　　**398.2**
1. Chivalry 2. Emperors 3. Folklore -- Europe 4. Mythology
ISBN 0-375-75147-5
LC 2005-271850

"The classic work on mythology, Bulfinch's gives brief summations of Greek, Roman, Norse, Arthurian, and other miscellaneous myths and includes notes on the 'Iliad,' the 'Odyssey,' and the 'Aeneid.'" N Y Public Libr Book of How & Where to Look It Up

Includes bibliographical references

Gawain and the Grene Knight (Middle English poem)

Sir Gawain and the Green Knight; a new verse translation. [translated by] Simon Armitage. W. W. Norton & Company 2007 198p $25.95; pa $14.95　　　　**398.2**
1. Arthurian romances 2. Poetry -- By individual authors
ISBN 978-0-393-06048-5; 0-393-06048-9; 978-0-393-33415-9 pa; 0-393-33415-5 pa
LC 2007-28520

Armitage "clearly feels a special kinship with the Gawain poet. He captures his dialect and his landscape and takes great pains to render the tale's alliterative texture and drive.... His vernacular translation isn't literal—sometimes he alliterates different letters, sometimes he foreshortens the number of alliterations in a line, sometimes he changes lines altogether and so forth—but his imitation is rich and various and recreates the gnarled verbal texture of the Middle English original, which is presented in a parallel text." N Y Times Book Rev

Lavers, Chris

The **natural** history of unicorns. William Morrow 2009 258p il $26.99　　　　**398.2**
1. Natural history -- Early works to 1900 2. Unicorns
ISBN 978-0-06-087414-8; 0-06-087414-7

This "is an erudite, scholarly book which uses the unicorn to illuminate millennia of social and geographical change. Unicorns appear in many guises in many cultures. . . . Lavers's achievement is to show how each of these is a

chimera based on startlingly accurate reports of real animals, carried over trade routes. . . . Lavers's book offers revelations not only about mythical creatures, but about the extent and effects of globalisation in ancient times. It's eminently readable, too." New Sci

Includes bibliographical references p. 245-248)

Lynch, Patricia Ann

★ **Native** American mythology A to Z. Facts on File 2004 130p il map $40　　　　**398.2**
1. Indian mythology 2. Native Americans -- Folklore
ISBN 0-8160-4891-6
LC 2004-47115

This book presents "coverage of the deities, legendary heroes and heroines, important animals, objects, and places that make up the mythic lore of the many peoples of North America from northern Mexico into the Arctic Circle." Publisher's note

Includes bibliographical references

Malory, Thomas

★ **Le** morte D'arthur, or, The hoole book of Kyng Arthur and of his noble knyghtes of the Rounde Table; authoritative text, sources and backgrounds, criticism. [by] Sir Thomas Malory; edited by Stephen H.A. Shepherd. Norton 2004 lii, 954p pa $16.95　　　　**398.2**
1. Kings
ISBN 0-393-97464-2
LC 2002-26534

"The work is a skillful selection and blending of materials taken from the mass of Arthurian legends. The central story consists of two main elements: the reign of King Arthur ending in catastrophe and the dissolution of the Round Table; and the quest of the Holy Grail." Oxford Companion to Engl Lit

Includes bibliographical references

Orenstein, Catherine

★ **Little** Red Riding Hood uncloaked; sex, morality, and the evolution of a fairy tale. Basic Bks. 2002 289p il hardcover o.p. pa $14.95　　　　**398.2**
1. Fairy tales -- History and criticism
ISBN 0-465-04126-4 pa; 0-465-04125-6
LC 2002-4240

"Once upon a time, Red Riding Hood was a good little girl. When she foolishly strayed from the path in the forest and spoke to strangers, she fell prey to the wicked wolf, but fortunately, the heroic woodcutter rescued her just in time. . . . With wit and insight, Orenstein makes us look again at the old childhood story, how it has changed and what that says about us. From Perrault and the Brothers Grimm to Bruno Bettelheim and Andrea Dworkin, the lively informal narrative surveys the stories and the scholarship in terms of folklore, psychology, feminism, and pornography." Booklist

Includes bibliographical references

Favorite folktales from around the world; edited by Jane Yolen. Pantheon Bks. 1986 498p hardcover o.p. pa $18   **398.2**
1. Fairy tales 2. Folklore
ISBN 0-394-75188-4 pa

LC 86-42644

"Selections include tales from the American Indians, the brothers Grimm, Italo Calvino's Italian folk-tales, as well as stories from Iceland, Afghanistan, Scotland, and many other countries. Yolen provides each section with a relevant introduction, often including historical and literary factors, thus alerting readers as to what to look for." SLJ

The Greenwood encyclopedia of folktales and fairy tales; edited by Donald Haase. Greenwood Press 2008 3v il set $299.95   **398.2**
1. Fairy tales 2. Fairy tales -- Encyclopedias 3. Folklore 4. Folklore -- Encyclopedias 5. Reference books 6. Tales
ISBN 978-0-313-33441-2

LC 2007-31698

"Meticulously documented and firmly grounded in scholarly research, most articles feature straightforward language and sufficient background material to be accessible to lay readers and novice researchers." Booklist
Includes bibliographical references

398.209

Wroe, Ann
    Orpheus; the song of life. Ann Wroe. Overlook 2012 262 p. Hardcover $26.95   **398.209**
1. Orpheus (Greek mythology) 2. Orpheus (Greek mythology) in literature
ISBN 0224091360 Jonathan Cape; 1590207785 Overlook; 9780224091367 Jonathan Cape; 9781590207789 Overlook

LC 2011508687

In this book, author "Ann Wroe goes in search of the mythical figure of Orpheus. . . . She traces the man, and the power he represents, through . . . his birth in Thrace, his studies in Egypt, his voyage with the Argonauts to fetch the Golden Fleece, his love for Eurydice and journey to Hades, and his terrible death." Publisher's Note

398.8   Rhymes and rhyming games

★ The Oxford dictionary of nursery rhymes; edited by Iona and Peter Opie. 2nd ed; Oxford Univ. Press 1997 xxix, 559p il $55   **398.8**
1. Nursery rhymes -- Dictionaries 2. Reference books
ISBN 0-19-860088-7

LC 98-140995

"The novice as well as the professional will find it an enjoyable read, as well as a learning experience." Am Ref Books Annu, 1999

398.9   Proverbs

Manser, Martin H.
    ★ The **Facts** on File dictionary of proverbs; associate editors, Rosalind Fergusson, David Pickering. 2nd ed.; Facts On File 2006 499p $55; pa $19.95   **398.9**
1. Proverbs
ISBN 0-8160-6673-6; 978-0-8160-6673-5; 0-8160-6674-4 pa; 978-0-8160-6674-2 pa

LC 2006-24535

This dictionary "includes more than 1,700 English-language proverbs . . . that are widely recognized today. Arranged alphabetically, entries provide the meaning of each proverb, the date it was first recorded, variant forms of the proverb, other proverbs that are similar and opposite to it in meaning, and examples of the proverb's use." Publisher's note
Includes bibliographical references

400   LANGUAGE

400   Language

Crystal, David
    ★ The **Cambridge** encyclopedia of language; 3rd ed; Cambridge University Press 2010 516p il map $99; pa $45   **400**
1. Language and languages 2. Language and languages -- Encyclopedias 3. Linguistics 4. Reference books
ISBN 978-0-521-51698-3; 978-0-521-73650-3 pa

LC 2010-502889

"A valuable and concise . . . handbook for linguistic beginners, linguistic researchers looking for a quick overview and, most of all, the general reader interested in language." Linguist List
Includes bibliographical references

Kenneally, Christine
    The **first** word; the search for the origins of language. Viking 2007 357p $26.95   **400**
1. Evolution 2. Language and languages
ISBN 978-0-670-03490-1; 0-670-03490-8

LC 2007-3182

The author "explains difficult ideas concisely and clearly, and she maintains a firm grip on the steering wheel, moving the overall argument along in a straight line. Above all, she is scrupulously fair-minded." N Y Times (Late N Y Ed)
Includes bibliographical references

Pinker, Steven
    The **language** instinct; how the mind creates language. Harper Perennial 2007 526p il pa $15.95   **400**
1. Language and languages
ISBN 978-0-06-133646-1; 0-06-133646-7

The author "argues that an 'innate grammatical machinery of the brain' exists, which allows children to 'reinvent' language on their own. Basing his ideas on Noam Chomsky's Universal Grammar theory, Pinker describes language as a 'discrete combinatorial system' that might easily have evolved via natural selection. Pinker steps on a few toes . . . but his work, while controversial, is well argued, challenging, often humorous, and always fascinating." Libr J

Includes bibliographical references

401 Philosophy and theory

Crystal, David

★ **How** language works; how babies babble, words change meaning, and languages live or die. Overlook Press 2006 500p $32.50   **401**
  1. Language and languages 2. Linguistics
  ISBN 1-58567-848-1

Crystal "offers an impeccably organized guide to language and communication that brings clarity to a scholarly subject, and is sure to become a standard reference." Publ Wkly

Includes bibliographical references

Pinker, Steven

Words and rules; the ingredients of language. Perennial 2000 349p il pa $15   **401**
  1. Grammar 2. Language and languages
  ISBN 978-0-06-095840-4; 0-06-095840-5

This book "with its crisp prose and neat analogies, makes required reading for anyone interested in cognition and language." Publ Wkly

Includes bibliographical references

The **stuff** of thought; language as a window into human nature. Viking 2007 499p il $29.95   **401**
  1. Language and languages 2. Language and languages -- Philosophy 3. Thought and thinking
  ISBN 978-0-670-06327-7; 0-670-06327-4
       LC 2007-26601

The author's "vivid prose and down-to-earth attitude will once again attract an enthusiastic audience outside academia." Publ Wkly

Includes bibliographical references

Yang, Charles

★ The **infinite** gift; how children learn and unlearn the languages of the world. Scribner 2006 275p il $25   **401**
  1. Language and languages
  ISBN 978-0-7432-3756-7; 0-7432-3756-0

The author explains the "process by which children acquire language. He discusses everything from the sounds they hear in the womb to how they distinguish between different languages at three months to their mastery of their language by age five. Throughout this learning process, posits Yang, a child has tested the grammar and sounds that exist in many other languages (and would presumably have no trouble acquiring them) but ultimately settles on the relevant one, and soon after, can no longer distinguish between or articulate nonrelevant sounds. . . . Anyone with the slightest interest in the English language should read his book." Libr J

410 Linguistics

Crystal, David

★ **Language** and the internet; 2nd ed.; Cambridge University Press 2006 304p $29.99   **410**
  1. Internet 2. Language and languages
  ISBN 978-0-521-86859-4; 0-521-86859-9
       LC 2006-12916

"Covering a range of Internet genres, including e-mail, chat, and the Web, this is . . . [an] account of how the Internet is radically changing the way we use language." Publisher's note

Includes bibliographical references

★ A **dictionary** of language; 2nd ed; University of Chicago Press 2001 390p il pa $17.50   **410**
  1. Language and languages -- Dictionaries 2. Linguistics -- Dictionaries 3. Reference books
  ISBN 0-226-12203-4
       LC 00-69076

This dictionary "offers explanations of the most frequently used linguistic terms, particularly those that can occur in texts read by beginners and by interested laypersons. . . . There are also entries concerned with graphology, shorthand writing, and similar peripheral, but interesting, topics. The impression that this dictionary has been written mainly for the general public is enhanced by the humorous jocose caricatures interspersed throughout the text, but the information is still solid. The author has succeeded in creating a handy dictionary that will serve students and laypeople equally well, for both browsing and study." Am Ref Book Annu, 2002

Deutscher, Guy

Through the language glass; why the world looks different in other languages. Metropolitan Books / Henry Holt and Co. 2010 304p il $28; ebook $14.99   **410**
  1. Language and languages 2. Linguistics
  ISBN 978-0-8050-8195-4; 978-1-4299-7011-2 ebook
       LC 2010-1042

Deutscher "combines erudition, wry humor, and serious interpretation in this elegant and charmingly accessible study of the relation among language, culture, and thought and of how we have engaged in and reflected upon language over the years." Libr J

Includes bibliographical references

418 Standard usage (Prescriptive linguistics)

Deheane, Stanislas

Reading in the brain; the science and evolution of a cultural invention. Viking 2009 388p il $27.95   **418**
  1. Reading 2. Reading -- Physiological aspects 3. Reading, Psychology of
  ISBN 978-0-670-02110-9; 0-670-02110-5
       LC 2009-09389

"Dense with ideas and experiments, but richly rewarding for readers willing to put in the effort." Kirkus

Includes bibliographical references

Grossman, Edith

Why translation matters. Yale University Press 2010 135p   **418**

1. Literature -- Translations   2. Translating and interpreting

ISBN 0-300-12656-5; 978-0-300-12656-3

LC 2009-26510

Grossman "argues for the cultural importance of translation and a more encompassing and nuanced appreciation of the translator's role." (Publisher's note) Index.

"In the end, Grossman warmly (after all) and gratefully rehearses the twofold answer to the question of her title: translation matters because it is an expression and an extension of our humanity, the secret metaphor of all literary communication; and because the creation of any literary translation is (or at least must be) an original writing, not a pathetic shadow or tracing of the inaccessible 'original' but the creation, indeed, of a second — and as we have seen, a third and a ninth — but always a new work, in another language." N Y Times Book Rev

Includes bibliographical references

419   Sign languages

Chambers, Diane P.

Communicating in sign; creative ways to learn American Sign Language (ASL) written by Diane P. Chambers, with Lee Ann Chearney; edited by D. Keith Robertson; illustrations by Paul M. Setzer; with an introduction by Bernard Bragg. Fireside 1998 165p il pa $12   **419**

1. American Sign Language   2. Sign language

ISBN 0-684-83520-7

LC 97-51145

"By combining vocabulary, grammar, syntax, expression, and movement with commentary on etiquette and other cultural issues, Chambers . . . has created a general resource intended for the lay public." Libr J

Includes bibliographical references

Costello, Elaine

Random House Webster's American Sign Language dictionary: unabridged. Random House Reference 2008 xxxii, 1200p $55   **419**

1. Reference books   2. Sign language -- Dictionaries

ISBN 978-0-375-42616-2; 0-375-42616-7

This dictionary includes "over 5,600 signs for the novice and experienced user alike. It includes complete descriptions of each sign, plus full-torso illustrations. There is also a subject index for easy reference as well as alternate signs for the same meaning." Publisher's note

Gallaudet University

★ The **Gallaudet** dictionary of American Sign Language; Clayton Valli, editor in chief; illustrated by Peggy Swartzel Lott, Daniel Renner, and Rob

Hills. Gallaudet University Press 2005 xli, 558p il $49.95   **419**

1. Reference books   2. Sign language -- Dictionaries

ISBN 1-56368-282-6; 978-1-56368-282-7

LC 2005-51129

"This is a very valuable language resource for parents, students, and teachers learning ASL as a first language and as a second language." Choice

Includes bibliographical references

Grayson, Gabriel

Talking with your hands, listening with your eyes; a complete photographic guide to American Sign Language. Square One Pubs. 2002 373p il pa $26.95   **419**

1. American Sign Language   2. Deaf -- Means of communication -- United States   3. Deaf -- United States -- Social conditions   4. Sign language

ISBN 0-7570-0007-X

LC 2002-1125

"An outstanding, user-friendly resource for those interested in learning ASL." SLJ

Sternberg, Martin L. A.

American Sign Language; a comprehensive dictionary. illustrated by Herbert Rogoff. Unabridged; HarperCollins Pubs. 1998 xxi, 983p il $60; pa $24   **419**

1. Reference books   2. Sign language   3. Sign language -- Dictionaries

ISBN 0-06-271608-5; 0-06-273634-5 pa

LC 98-26649

Arranged alphabetically, this dictionary features 7,000 sign entries, with cross-references and more than 12,000 illustrations.

Tennant, Richard A.

The **American** Sign Language handshape dictionary; {by} Richard A. Tennant, Marianne Gluszak Brown; illustrated by Valerie Nelson-Metlay. Gallaudet Univ. Press 1998 407p il $39.95   **419**

1. American Sign Language -- Dictionaries   2. Sign language

ISBN 1-56368-043-2

LC 97-48389

This work organizes "signs by handshape rather than alphabetically by English word order. In so doing, it acts best as a recognition tool for the ASL learner, leading the user quickly to specific signs without having first to refer to an English-equivalent word." Libr J

420   Specific languages

Bragg, Melvyn

The **adventure** of English; the biography of a language. Arcade Pub. 2004 322p il pa $27.95   **420**

1. English language -- History

ISBN 1-55970-710-0

LC 2003-19583

The author offers a "biography of the English language, highlighting key individuals, places, and literature that advanced it, as well as the political and social trends that influenced it. . . . Bragg discusses its evolution in the English colonies, devoting four chapters to the United States and one each to India, the West Indies, and Australia. . . . Well researched yet more accessible to a wide audience than scholarly treatments by linguists or historians." Libr J

Bryson, Bill
Made in America; an informal history of the English language in the United States. Avon Books 1996 417p pa $14.95 **420**
  1. Americanisms 2. English language -- History
  ISBN 978-0-380-71381-3; 0-380-71381-0
"For Bryson's wonderfully sane and reasoned discussion of the issues surrounding 'politically correct' language alone, this book is a worthwhile read." Libr J
Includes bibliographical references

Crystal, David
★ The **Cambridge** encyclopedia of the English language; 2nd ed; Cambridge Univ. Press 2003 499p il hardcover o.p. pa $35 **420**
  1. English language
  ISBN 0-521-82348-X; 0-521-53033-4 pa
    LC 2003-272259
This "volume is divided into six broad topics that cover the English language's history, vocabulary, grammar, writing and speech systems, usage, and acquisition. Within these major topics, the book is divided into logical subtopics and finally into the basic unit of the text—the two-page spread. . . . The clear and spirited text is stunning, enhanced with over 500 illustrations, making this a particularly rich reference work and a browser's dream." Libr J {review of 1995 edition}

★ **English** as a global language; 2nd ed; Cambridge Univ. Press 2003 212p il maps $45; pa $15 **420**
  1. Communication, International 2. English language -- Foreign countries 3. English language -- Social aspects 4. English language -- Social aspects -- English-speaking countries 5. English language -- Social aspects -- Foreign countries 6. Language, Universal
  ISBN 0-521-82347-1; 0-521-53032-6 pa
    LC 2003-282119
"This is a fascinating and useful book. . . . a fine introduction for a wide variety of potential users." Choice
Includes bibliographical references

Hitchings, Henry
The **language** wars; a history of proper English. Farrar, Straus and Giroux 2011 408p $28 **420**
  1. English language -- History 2. English language -- Usage
  ISBN 978-0-374-18329-5; 0-374-18329-5
    LC 2011-10701
"As the author points out, there is probably not a person alive who does not have some bee in his bonnet about the way other people speak and write. Maybe it is the errant apostrophe, the splitting of the poor old infinitive, or the use

of 'like' as a comma. Or perhaps it is the exclamation mark, once known as the 'shriek mark'. Mr Hitchings's book is a corrective to some of these linguistic prejudices. It is bracing to learn, for example, that the prohibition on splitting the infinitive is fairly recent. Pre-Victorians did not object. Chaucer was a splitter, and even Shakespeare had a go. Same story with the apostrophe: in the 18th-century authors were sprinkling apostrophes over everything. . . . Mr Hitchings reviews such matters with cool erudition. He is resolutely relaxed about usage, understanding that correctitude and intelligibility are not the same." Economist
Includes bibliographical references

McCrum, Robert
★ The **story** of English; [by] Robert McCrum, Willam Cran [and] Robert MacNeil. 3rd rev ed; Penguin Bks. 2003 xxi, 468p pa $16 **420**
  1. English language -- History
  ISBN 0-14-200231-3
    LC 2002-29818
A "companion to the PBS television series of the same name. . . . The text covers the history of our language from its roots in Latin through its transplanting to other shores and its infusions from other cultures and languages. . . . Good for browsing, this book is a must for word and history buffs." SLJ [review of 1986 edition]
Includes bibliographical references

Metcalf, Allan A.
Predicting new words; the secrets of their success. {by} Allan Metcalf. Houghton Mifflin 2002 206p il $22 **420**
  1. English language -- New words 2. English language -- Terms and phrases 3. Lexicology 4. New words
  ISBN 0-618-13006-3
    LC 2002-68593
This book traces the origins of an "array of words and phrases: Marlboro Man, Frankenfood, blurb, skycap, quark, scofflaw. It also introduces us to a fascinating array of would-be words, coinages that never quite caught on. . . . The book is jam-packed with treats for word lovers." Booklist

421 Writing system, phonology, phonetics of standard English

Stahl, Dean
★ **Abbreviations** dictionary; {by} Dean Stahl, Karen Kerchelich; originated by Ralph De Sola. 10th ed; CRC Press 2001 1529p $79.95 **421**
  1. Abbreviations -- Dictionaries 2. Abbreviations, English 3. Acronyms 4. Reference books 5. Signs and symbols
  ISBN 0-8493-9003-6
    LC 00-58549
"The classic status of this title endures: abbreviations are again joined by a dazzling array of acronyms, contractions, initials, nicknames, short forms, signs, and symbols. Its 15,000 new terms swell the dictionary to nearly 300,000 entries. Domestic and international terms are harvested from diverse fields, criminology to music. Computing, technology, and government draw special attention due to active

abbreviating. Entries are alphabetically and numerically ordered." Choice

★ Acronyms, initialisms, & abbreviations dictionary; 40th ed; Gale Res. 2008 4v set $1,190 **421**
1. Acronyms -- Dictionaries 2. Reference books
ISBN 978-1-4144-1902-2; 1-4144-1902-3
A guide to acronyms, initialisms, abbreviations, contractions, alphabetic symbols, and similar condensed apellations.

422   Etymology of standard English

Crystal, David
The **story** of English in 100 words; David Crystal. St. Martin's Press 2012 260 p. **422**
1. English language -- Etymology 2. English language -- Foreign elements 3. English language -- Foreign words and phrases
ISBN 9781250003461; 9781466805088
LC 2012003038
This book presents information about how English grows, changes, adopts and plays. . . . The author . . . teach[es] 100 lessons about English by picking out 100 words from our history, telling us their origin story and showing us how they've changed and spawned. Roughly chronological-beginning in the fifth century, ending in the 21st-[David] Crystal's text begins with what may be the first written word in our language, raihan, the word for roe-deer, and ends with something awfully recent, twittersphere. In between are not just the stories of individual words but the stories of how words become words. Why do we sometimes spell yogurt with an -h? Has there always been a difference between disinterested and uninterested? Why do only poets use certain words like swain? (Kirkus)

Guinagh, Kevin
Dictionary of foreign phrases and abbreviations; translated and compiled by Kevin Guinagh. 3rd ed; Wilson, H.W. 1983 261p $70 **422**
1. English language -- Foreign words and phrases 2. English language -- Foreign words and phrases -- Dictionaries 3. Quotations 4. Reference books
ISBN 0-8242-0675-4
LC 82-8486
This dictionary "contains more than 5,000 foreign phrases, proverbs, and abbreviations frequently used in written and spoken English. Provides translations and pronunciations, and for some entries brief explanatory notes; includes a list of phrases by languages." Ref Sources for Small & Medium-sized Libr. 6th edition

Hendrickson, Robert
★ The **Facts** on File encyclopedia of word and phrase origins; 4th ed., [Updated and expanded ed.]; Facts On File 2008 948p $95; pa $27.95 **422**
1. English language -- Etymology -- Dictionaries 2. English language -- Terms and phrases 3. Reference books
ISBN 978-0-8160-6966-8; 978-0-8160-6967-5 pa
LC 2007-48223

"Because the entries have both scholarly value and the capacity to entertain, the book is ideal for both linguists and lay readers." Libr J

Hitchings, Henry
The **secret** life of words; how English became English. Farrar, Straus and Giroux 2008 440p $27 **422**
1. English language -- Etymology 2. English language -- Lexicography -- History
ISBN 978-0-374-25410-0; 0-374-25410-9
LC 2008-26055
"Hitchings here provides a colorful, thematic history of the English language. Treating borrowings and coinages as psychological windows to history, the author takes the reader on a tour of the lexicon from Anglo-Saxon to the present day and shows how new words answer linguistic needs. . . . Hitchings treats the reader to some 3,000 word histories. . . . With 90-plus pages of notes, sources, and useful indexes, this is a fine choice for libraries and a 'smorgasbord' for language aficionados." Choice
Includes bibliographical references

Korach, Myron
Common phrases and where they come from; [by] Myron Korach in collaboration with John B. Mordock. Lyons Press 2001 200p hardcover o.p. pa $9.95 **422**
1. English language -- Etymology 2. English language -- Terms and phrases
ISBN 1-58574-682-7 pa
LC 00-69016
Korach and Mordock "show how much our culture relies on idiomatic speech to enliven discourse, a point further demonstrated by the more than 150 well-known phrases whose interesting histories they have provided. The arrangement of phrases is loosely thematic, with one to several paragraphs devoted to each." Libr J

Manser, Martin H.
The **Facts** on File dictionary of allusions; David H. Pickering, associate editor. Facts on File 2008 532p $75; pa $18.95 **422**
1. Allusions 2. Literature -- Dictionaries 3. Reference books
ISBN 978-0-8160-7105-0; 0-8160-7105-5; 978-0-8160-7907-0 pa; 0-8160-7907-2 pa
LC 2007-51375
"In approximately 4,000 entries, this . . . resource explores well-known events, places, people, and phenomena whose names have acquired linguistic significance, conveying a particular message beyond a mere reference to the objects referred to. Entries are drawn from a . . . range of sources, including Shakespeare and the Bible; Greek, Roman, and Norse mythology; texts from literature through the ages; historical events; popular culture; and film and television. Individual entries contain pronunciation guides, definitions, examples, information on derived forms, and more." Publisher's note
Includes bibliographical references

★ The **Facts** on File dictionary of foreign words and phrases; [by] Martin H. Manser; associate editors: Alice Grandison and David H. Pickering. 2nd ed., [New ed.]; Facts on File 2008 469p $55; pa $19.95 **422**

1. English language -- Foreign words and phrases -- Dictionaries 2. Reference books
ISBN 978-0-8160-7035-0; 978-0-8160-7036-7 pa

LC 2007-29711

This dictionary includes more than 4,500 entries for terms that have entered the English lexicon from foreign languages in the fields of language and literature, religion, law, politics, economics, music, entertainment and cuisine. Examples or quotations are provided to illustrate usage.

"This is a captivating title to browse." SLJ

Includes bibliographical references

Morris, William

Morris dictionary of word and phrase origins; [by] William and Mary Morris; foreword by Isaac Asimov. 2nd ed; Harper & Row 1988 669p $38 **422**

1. English language -- Etymology 2. English language -- Etymology -- Dictionaries 3. English language -- Terms and phrases
ISBN 0-06-015862-X

LC 87-45651

"Traces the origins of several thousand words and phrases commonly used in the English language, including slang terms and clichés not usually found in more formal works. Entries are listed alphabetically by the first word in the phrase, with an index at the end." Ref Sources for Small & Medium-sized Libr. 6th edition

Quinion, Michael

★ **Ballyhoo,** buckeroo, and spuds; ingenious tales of words and their origins. Smithsonian Books 2004 288p $19.95 **422**

1. English language -- Etymology 2. English language -- Terms and phrases
ISBN 1-588-34219-0

LC 2004-52235

A look at common English "words and phrases most readers will probably have wondered about. We're all familiar with the phrase 'happy as a clam.' but why a clam? We know what a 10-gallon hat is, but how did it get its name? And what the heck is a ballyhoo, anyway? The book is simply organized—alphabetically, of course—and endlessly illuminating. Quinion's research and documentation are impeccable, and when he needs to make a leap of imagination, he does so gracefully. For word lovers, this book is indispensable." Booklist

Includes bibliographical references

Rosten, Leo

The **new** joys of Yiddish; revisions and commentary by Lawrence Bush; illustrations by R. O. Blechman. Rev ed; Crown 2001 xxxii, 458p il $35; pa $18 **422**

1. English language -- Foreign words and phrases 2.

Yiddish language
ISBN 0-609-60785-5; 0-609-80692-0 pa

LC 2001-28366

This "work explores the nuances and complexities of language, clarifying the interrelationship between Yiddish and English (Yinglish, according to Rosten). The lengthy alphabetical listing not only presents multiple spellings, pronunciation guides, definitions, and cross references but also illustrates usage with background information, anecdotes, and jokes, as well as breezy erudition in the form of tidbits of cultural history, Talmudic and biblical references, tips on pronunciation, and thoughtful commentary. . . . The revision incorporates additional material on modern Yiddish literature and culture and updates on changes in American Jewish life and faith. Also included as an appendix is an English-Yiddish dictionary." Libr J

Includes bibliographical references

Steinmetz, Sol

★ The **Barnhart** dictionary of etymology; Robert K. Barnhart, editor; Sol Steinmetz, managing editor. Wilson, H.W. 1988 xxvii, 1284p $115 **422**

1. English language -- Etymology 2. English language -- Etymology -- Dictionaries 3. Reference books
ISBN 0-8242-0745-9

LC 87-27994

This dictionary "focuses on words used in contemporary American English and words of American origin and incorporates current American scholarship. Entries give spelling variations, pronunciation for difficult words, part of speech, definition, and information on word origins. Written for a wide audience, this is a very attractive, readable work suited for most library users." Ref Sources for Small & Medium-sized Libr. 6th edition

Adonis to Zorro; Oxford dictionary of reference and allusion. edited by Andrew Delahunty and Sheila Dignen. 3rd ed.; Oxford University Press 2010 406p $34.95 **422**

1. Allusions 2. Reference books
ISBN 978-0-19-956745-4; 0-19-956745-X

LC 2010-549367

"This guide to allusions and common references is a moderately priced volume well worth adding to a public, school, community college, or college shelf. Neat and user-friendly, the 1,900 entries, their provenance, definitions, models, and starred cross-references identify a range of familiar terms, from 'Terminator' to 'hobbit,' and from 'My Lai' to the 'sword of Damocles' and 'thirty pieces of silver.' The text makes clever use of fonts, dingbats, and point count to identify authors, sources, and dates." Choice

★ From bonbon to cha-cha; Oxford dictionary of foreign words and phrases. edited by Andrew Delahunty. 2nd ed; Oxford University Press 2008 411p $24.95; pa $18.99 **422**

1. English language -- Foreign words and phrases 2. English language -- Foreign words and phrases -- Dictionaries 3. Reference books
ISBN 978-0-19-954369-4; 0-19-954369-0; 978-0-19-954368-7 pa; 0-19-954368-2 pa

LC 2008-482026

This reference "offers coverage of more than 6,000 foreign words and phrases that are in regular use in English today." Publisher's note

More word histories and mysteries; from aardvark to zombie. from the editors of the American Heritage dictionaries. Houghton Mifflin 2006 288p il pa $12.95   **422**

1. English language -- Etymology 2. Reference books
ISBN 978-0-618-71681-4; 0-618-71681-5
LC 2006020835

This "emphasizes the huge number of source languages from which English draws its vast vocabulary—from Sanskrit to French and beyond. The introductory pages give the reader a brief overview of the methods and aims of etymology and a potted history of the origins of English. . . . The editors then present an alphabetical listing of words and their etymology. Each of the 300-plus entries is about half a page to a page long and briefly outlines the origins of the word, its use, and the evolution of its meaning. . . . The book's informative yet informal writing style would appeal to the amateur enthusiast, and accessibility is further enhanced by a useful glossary of linguistic terms." Libr J

Word histories and mysteries; from abracadabra to Zeus. from the editors of the American Heritage dictionaries. Houghton Mifflin Co. 2004 xvi, 348p il pa $12.95   **422**

1. English language -- Etymology 2. Reference books
ISBN 978-0-618-45450-1; 0-618-45450-0
LC 2004014798

"The 400 alphabetically arranged entries here illustrate the diversity from which the English language draws its vocabulary, particularly from the prehistoric base that linguists call Proto-Indo-European. As a result, the editors aim to demonstrate links between the ancient base and modern English. . . . An overall quality resource." Libr J

423   Dictionaries of standard English

Adelson-Goldstein, Jayme
The **Oxford** picture dictionary; [by] Jayme Adelson-Goldstein and Norma Shapiro. 2nd ed.; Oxford University Press 2008 285p il pa $16.95 **423**

1. English language -- Dictionaries 2. Picture dictionaries 3. Reference books
ISBN 978-0-19-436976-3; 0-19-436976-5
LC 2007-41017

This picture dictionary features "4,000 words and phrases illustrated with . . . artwork." Publisher's note

Ammer, Christine
The **American** Heritage dictionary of idioms. Houghton Mifflin 1997 729p $32; pa $14.95 **423**

1. Americanisms 2. Americanisms -- Dictionaries 3. English language -- Idioms 4. English language -- Idioms -- Dictionaries 5. English language -- Terms and phrases 6. Reference books
ISBN 0-395-72774-X; 0-618-24953-2 pa
LC 97-12390

"In addition to idioms, the dictionary includes common figures of speech, formula phrases such as 'take care,' emphatic redundancies whose word order cannot be reversed such as 'cease and desist,' common proverbs, colloquialisms, and slang phrases. Each expression is defined briefly and then illustrated by a short, simple sentence showing how it is used in context." SLJ
Includes bibliographical references

Corbeil, Jean-Claude
★ **Merriam**-Webster's visual dictionary; [by] Jean-Claude Corbeil, Ariane Archambault; [illustrators, Jean-Yves Ahern . . . [et al.] Merriam-Webster 2006 952p il map $39.95   **423**

1. English language -- Dictionaries 2. Picture dictionaries 3. Reference books
ISBN 978-0-8777-9051-8; 0-8777-9051-5

"Logically organized into 17 broad categories (e.g., astronomy, humans, animals, clothing, and society), with numerous subcategories to make finding the needed terms easy, this is the only visual dictionary that includes definitions with the terms. And its price is very reasonable for such a substantial book. Essential." Libr J

Davidson, Mark
★ **Right**, wrong, and risky; a dictionary of today's American English usage. Norton 2006 570p $29.95   **423**

1. Americanisms 2. English language -- Dictionaries 3. English language -- Usage 4. Reference books
ISBN 0-393-06119-1
LC 2005-17628

The author "offers a dictionary that 'views the real world of today's American English, identifying usage questions that are debatable, citing conflicting answers, and offering risk-free solutions for each conflict.' . . . Browsers will enjoy the colorful, interesting backstories on the origins of terms such as ground zero, on the sudden warming to the phrase girl talk, and on the widely misunderstood use of the word Neanderthal." Booklist
Includes bibliographical references

Espy, Willard R.
Words to rhyme with; a rhyming dictionary. 3rd ed.; Facts On File 2006 683p $75; pa $19.95 **423**

1. English language -- Rhyme
ISBN 0-8160-6303-6; 978-0-8160-6303-1; 0-8160-6304-4 pa; 978-0-8160-6304-8 pa
LC 2005-51122

"Including a primer of prosody, a list of more than 80,000 words that rhyme, a glossary defining 9,000 of the more eccentric rhyming words, and a variety of exemplary verses, one of which does not rhyme at all." Title page

Garner, Bryan A.
★ **Garner's** modern American usage; 3rd ed; Oxford University Press 2009 lx, 942p $45   **423**

1. Americanisms -- Dictionaries 2. English language 3. English language -- Usage 4. English language -- Usage -- Dictionaries 5. Reference books
ISBN 978-0-19-538275-4
LC 2009-9539

"One would be tempted to say that this is clearly one of the best works on the topic, but doing so would be using one of Garner's weasel words (intensives such as clearly that 'actually have the effect of weakening a statement'). Suffice it to say that it is highly recommended for most libraries." Booklist

Includes bibliographical references (p. 925-938)

Houghton Mifflin Co.
★ The **American** Heritage guide to contemporary usage and style. Houghton Mifflin 2005 512p $19.95 **423**
1. English language -- Usage 2. English language -- Usage -- Dictionaries
ISBN 978-0-618-60499-9; 0-618-60499-5

LC 2005-16513

"Drawing on the authoritative knowledge of its lexicographers and the considered collective judgment of a panel of noted writers, the book offers guidance on the simple (the pronunciations of bouquet); the perplexingly redundant (free gift); the often imprecisely used (impeach); the no longer distinct (healthful/healthy); the needless but persistent (irregardless); the easily confused (stationary/stationery); the unfortunately conflated (lay/lie); and many more pitfalls. Articles embodying the precision and lucidity of dictionary definitions explain the history of a word's or expression's usage issue, how and why the issue exists, and the preferred usage." Booklist

Little, Brown & Co. Inc.
★ **Bartlett's** Roget's thesaurus. Little, Brown 1996 xxxii, 1415p $21.95; pa $16.95 **423**
1. Americanisms 2. English language -- Synonyms and antonyms 3. Reference books
ISBN 0-316-10138-9; 0-316-73587-6 pa

LC 96-18343

This thesaurus "reflects the current state of American English, including terminology from the worlds of composers and television, with such sub-categories as 'Living Things,' 'The Arts,' 'Feelings.' But what really makes the book a joy to use is the tremendously useful lists—everything from phobias to styles and periods of furniture." Am Libr

Lutz, William
The **Cambridge** thesaurus of American English; {by} William D. Lutz. Cambridge Univ. Press 1994 515p $25 **423**
1. Americanisms 2. Americanisms -- Dictionaries 3. English language -- Synonyms and antonyms
ISBN 0-521-41427-X

LC 93-31878

This thesaurus lists "over 200,000 synonyms and antonyms. . . . Lutz concentrates on idioms, verb phrases, and slang. Phrases are listed under the 'main' word in the phrase. 'Play it by ear,' for example, is found under the noun ear instead of the verb play. . . . The Cambridge is a welcome addition to the list of modern thesauruses and highly recommended for users who need a concise work that provides quick and easy access." Libr J

Merriam-Webster Inc.
★ **Merriam**-Webster's collegiate dictionary; Eleventh ed; Merriam-Webster 2003 1623p il $23.95 **423**
1. English language -- Dictionaries 2. Reference books
ISBN 0-87779-808-7

LC 2003-3674

This edition includes over 165,000 entries, 10,000 new words and meanings, 38,000 etymologies, a handbook of style, an essay on the English language, a special section on signs and symbols, and a free one-year subscription to the Collegiate Web site.

★ **Merriam**-Webster's collegiate thesaurus; 2nd ed.; Merriam-Webster 2010 16a, 1162p $21.95 **423**
1. English language -- Synonyms and antonyms 2. Reference books
ISBN 978-0-8777-9269-7; 0-8777-9269-0

LC 2009-42161

"Employs a conventional dictionary arrangement, and gives synonyms, related terms, idiomatic equivalents, antonyms, and contrasted words as applicable. Cross-references in small capitals." Guide to Ref Books. 11th edition

★ **Webster's** third new international dictionary of the English language, unabridged; editor in chief, Philip Babcock Gove and the Merriam-Webster editorial staff. Merriam-Webster 2002 144a, 2662p il $129 **423**
1. English language -- Dictionaries 2. Reference books
ISBN 0-87779-201-1

LC 2003-272164

"Clear, accurate definitions are given in historical order. Outstanding for its numerous illustrative quotations, impeccable authority, and etymologies, Webster's third is regarded as the most reliable, comprehensive general unabridged dictionary." Ref Sources for Small & Medium-sized Libr. 6th edition

Mugglestone, Lynda
Lost for words; the hidden history of the Oxford English Dictionary. Yale University Press 2005 xxi, 273p il $30 **423**
ISBN 0-300-10699-8

LC 2004-29344

"Serious word lovers will appreciate . . . [this book's] fascinating revelations." Booklist

Includes bibliographical references

Princeton Language Institute
★ **Roget's** 21st century thesaurus in dictionary form; the essential reference for home, school, or office. edited by the Princeton Language Institute; Barbara Ann Kipfer, head lexicographer. 3rd ed; Bantam Dell 2005 962p $15; pa $5.99 **423**
1. English language -- Synonyms and antonyms 2. Reference books
ISBN 0-385-33895-3; 0-440-24269-X pa

This thesaurus, cross referencing each word with the same concept, provides 500,000 synonyms and antonyms in a dictionary format and includes recently coined and common slang terms and commonly used foreign terms.

Upton, Clive

★ **Oxford** rhyming dictionary; {by} Clive Upton, Eben Upton. Oxford University Press 2004 659p $37.95 **423**
1. English language -- Rhyme
ISBN 0-19-280115-5

LC 2004-53133

In this dictionary "an index of words leads to numbered sections of phonic groupings of end, double, and triple syllable rhymes, with proximate groupings of near rhymes. But the index (95,000 words) . . . provides many word variations." Choice

Winchester, Simon

The **professor** and the madman; a tale of murder, insanity, and the making of the Oxford English dictionary. HarperCollins Pubs. 1998 242p il $22; pa $13 **423**
1. Editors 2. English language -- Lexicography -- History -- 19th century 3. Lexicographers 4. Mentally ill 5. Murderers 6. Surgeons 7. United States -- History -- Civil War, 1861-1865 -- Veterans -- Biography
ISBN 0-06-017596-6; 0-06-099486-X pa

LC 98-10204

The author relates the "story of the Oxford English Dictionary's first editor and the expatriate American murderer who contributed more than 10,000 quotations as examples. Best of all, among the entertaining tangents one learns a great deal about the making of that grandest of all reference works." Libr J

Includes bibliographical references

★ The American Heritage dictionary of the English language; 5th ed.; Houghton Mifflin Harcourt 2011 xxvii, 2084p il map **423**
1. Definitions 2. Encyclopedias & dictionaries 3. English language 4. English language -- Dictionaries 5. English language -- Usage 6. English language -- Usage -- Dictionaries 7. Reference books
ISBN 9780547041018

LC 2011004777

This book, the fifth edition of The American Heritage Dictionary of the English Language (AHD) includes 10,000 new words, with color photos in the margin to illustrate the definitions. Countries all have a small map with their location and major cities. . . . [U]sage notes . . . . have been updated . . . AHD also includes example sentences, and many of these have been lengthened with the addition of quotations from writers . . . Synonyms for words have been added . . . The purchase of this print edition contains a passkey for a free app version, and there is a free online version at www.ahdictionary.com. (Booklist)

★ Concise Oxford American thesaurus. Oxford University Press 2006 996p $19.95 **423**
1. English language -- Synonyms and antonyms 2. Reference books
ISBN 0-19-530485-3; 978-0-19-530485-5

LC 2005-35868

This "thesaurus contains over 15,000 entries with more than 350,000 synonyms and is . . . arranged with the typical synonyms listed first. . . . This simple arrangement makes this thesaurus particularly user-friendly." Libr J

★ Dictionary of confusable words; {edited by} Adrian Room. Fitzroy Dearborn Pubs. 2000 251p $35 **423**
1. English language -- Synonyms and antonyms 2. English language -- Usage
ISBN 1-57958-271-0

A "guide to potentially confusing words. . . . The brief entries give definitions of each of the terms. Each word is then used in at least one sample sentence, clarifying the differences between like terms. The definitions and examples are in simple language and are easy to understand." Libr J

Historical thesaurus of the Oxford English dictionary; with additional material from A Thesaurus of Old English. [edited by] Christian Kay [et al.] Oxford University Press 2009 3952p 2v set $395 **423**
1. English language -- Synonyms and antonyms 2. Reference books
ISBN 978-0-19-920899-9

LC 2009-935029

"The knowledge compiled in this 40-year project is stunning, and promises to revolutionize the study of the language by making wholly new kinds of questions possible." Choice

Includes bibliographical references

★ New Oxford American dictionary; 3rd ed.; Oxford University Press 2010 xxvi, 2018p il map $60 **423**
1. Americanisms -- Dictionaries 2. English language -- Dictionaries 3. Reference books
ISBN 978-0-19-539288-3

LC 2010-20033

"This dictionary arranges definitions by most current usage and provides additional guidance in usage notes. Although U.S. English is the focus here, regionalisms from other English-speaking areas are also included. More than 1000 illustrations (e.g., photos, drawings, diagrams) clarify definitions. . . . A labor of love and an unparalleled gift to writers and readers worldwide, the New Oxford American Dictionary should be on the reference shelves of every library." Libr J

★ Oxford American writer's thesaurus; compiled by Christine A. Lindberg. 2nd ed.; Oxford University Press 2008 xxvi, 1052p $40 **423**
1. English language -- Synonyms and antonyms 2. Reference books
ISBN 978-0-19-534284-0; 0-19-534284-4

LC 2008-31259

"This expansive reference . . . is a functional treasure." Libr J

★ The Oxford English dictionary; 2nd ed; Oxford Univ. Press 1989 20v apply to publisher for price **423**
1. CD-ROMs 2. English language -- Dictionaries 3.

Reference books
ISBN 0-19-861186-2

LC 88-5330

"This is an etymological or word-source dictionary. In addition to definitions, this work gives the history of 290,500 words, both current and archaic, in the English language. Slang entries are very limited. Word histories include early forms, variant forms and roots, and first or exemplary usages in English from ancient to modern times. Short explanatory notes are provided for more common words." N Y Public Libr Book of How & Where to Look It Up

The Oxford dictionary of American English. Oxford University Press 2005 828p il map $27.50; pa $19.95   **423**
1. Americanisms -- Dictionaries 2. English language -- Dictionaries 3. Reference books
ISBN 978-0-19-431714-6; 0-19-431714-5; 978-0-19-439949-4 pa; 0-19-439949-4 pa

LC 2005-174

This dictionary provides "explanations, illustrations, and related information not given in ordinary dictionaries. All entries use carefully worded definitions and provide contextual examples of usage, grammar, and idioms." Publisher's note

Includes bibliographical references

★ Oxford dictionary of English idioms; 3rd ed., Oxford pbk ed.; Oxford University Press 2010 408p pa $16.95   **423**
1. English language -- Idioms 2. Reference books
ISBN 978-0-19-954378-6

LC 2010-935315

This book "contains entries for over 6,000 idioms. . . . These include a range of idioms such as 'the elephant in the corner,' 'go figure,' 'step up to the plate,' 'a walk in the park,' and 'win ugly.'" Publisher's note

★ Random House Webster's college dictionary; [Rev and updated ed]; Random House Reference 2005 xxvi, 1597p il map $26.95   **423**
1. English language -- Dictionaries 2. Reference books
ISBN 0-375-42600-0

LC 2005-280097

"Each entry in the dictionary presents spelling, along with alternatives, syllabication, pronunciation used in conversational speech (with alternatives), and part of speech. Entries also include meanings and definitions, with the most common usage listed first; historical, technical, or other usages of the term; date of first usage, including place of origin; and other related words that use the same root or stem. . . . The dictionary includes over 207,000 definitions, many of them so new they are not yet found in competing products. . . . For libraries seeking a wide variety of dictionaries, this work will prove especially useful for its inclusion of recent terms and idioms." Am Ref Books Annu, 2001 [entry for 2001 edition]

★ Random House Webster's unabridged dictionary; 2nd ed.; Random House 2005 xxvi, 2230p il map $59.95   **423**
1. English language -- Dictionaries 2. Reference books
ISBN 0-375-42599-3

This dictionary contains over 315,000 entries. A newwords section and an essay on the growth of English are included. 2,400 spot maps and illustrations complement the text

★ Roget's international thesaurus; 6th ed; HarperResource 2001 xxv, 1248p $20.95; pa $16.95 **423**
1. English language -- Synonyms and antonyms 2. Reference books
ISBN 0-06-273693-0; 0-06-093544-8 pa

LC 2002-276277

This edition includes 330,000 words and phrases organized into 1,075 categories and a pinpoint reference system that directs the user from a comprehensive index to the numbered category of the right word. Cross-references throughout lead to other categories. Also included are supplemental word lists that supply the names of things which have no synonyms (measurements, wines, state mottoes) as well as quotations that amplify the meanings of selected words.

★ Shorter Oxford English dictionary on historical principles; [editor-in-chief, Lesley Brown] 6th ed.; Oxford University Press 2007 2v il map set $175   **423**
1. English language -- Dictionaries 2. Reference books
ISBN 978-0-19-923324-3; 0-19-923324-1

LC 2007-37226

This dictionary "has more than half a million definitions drawn from the Oxford English Corpus database of more than 1.5 billion words. . . . It includes 'all words in current English from 1700 to the present day, plus the vocabulary of Shakespeare, the Authorized Version of the Bible and other major works from before 1700.'" Booklist
Includes bibliographical references

425   Grammar of standard English

Huddleston, Rodney D.

★ The **Cambridge** grammar of the English language; {by} Rodney Huddleston, Geoffrey K. Pullum in collaboration with Laurie Bauer {et al.} Cambridge Univ. Press 2002 1842p il $160   **425**
1. English language -- Grammar
ISBN 0-521-43146-8

LC 2001-25630

This "comprehensive and detailed look at the principles of the English language . . . {is} an authoritative addition to the fields of both English grammar and linguistics." Libr J
Includes bibliographical references

427   Historical and geographic variations, modern nongeographic variations of English

Ayto, John

The **Oxford** dictionary of slang. Oxford University Press 2003 pa $16.95   **427**

ISBN 0-19-860763-6

LC 427

"The 10,000 slang terms defined here originated mainly in the United States, Britain, Australia, or New Zealand and include both old and new coinages. The dictionary's arrangement is topical in thesaurus fashion." Libr J

Crystal, David

By hook or by crook; a journey in search of English. Overlook Press 2008 314p il map $27.95 **427**

1. English language -- Dialects

ISBN 978-1-59020-061-2; 1-59020-061-6

Combines personal reflections, historical allusions, and traveler's observations about the author's encounters with language and its users throughout the English-speaking world.

"In a conversational style that includes plenty of quirky facts, Crystal captures the exploratory, seductive, teasing, quirky, tantalizing nature of language study, and in doing so illuminates the fascinating world of words in which we live." Publ Wkly

Includes bibliographical references

The **stories** of English. Overlook Press 2004 584p il map $35   **427**

1. English language -- History

ISBN 1-585-67601-2

LC 2004-54727

The author "traces the diverse and unpredictable influences that have shaped English into an unruly family of dialects, creoles, and patois. . . . Crystal acknowledges the emergence during the fourteenth and fifteenth centuries of a prestigious standard version of English. Yet he shows in instance after instance that the tempests of linguistic change have often overwhelmed the custodians of the King's English, compelling them to accommodate forces they could not control. And though he never loses his focus on language, Crystal allows some of its more colorful users—including Chaucer, Shakespeare, Samuel Johnson, and Thomas Jefferson—to bring their personalities and voices into the chronicle." Booklist

Includes bibliographical references

Dickson, Paul

★ **Slang!** the topical dictionary of Americanisms. Walker & Co. 2006 418p $24.95   **427**

1. Americanisms -- Dictionaries 2. English language -- Slang -- Dictionaries 3. Reference books

ISBN 0-8027-1531-1; 978-0-8027-1531-9

"Informative, reliable, entertaining, and modern, this topical slang dictionary complements the more staid slang lexicons and more scholarly general dictionaries." Booklist

Includes bibliographical references

Do you speak American ?(Television program)

Do you speak American? [by] Robert MacNeil and William Cran. 1st Harvest ed.; Harcourt 2005 228p map pa $13   **427**

1. Americanisms 2. English language -- Dialects

ISBN 978-0-15-603288-9; 0-15-603288-0

LC 2005-23093

"Whether talking to crab fishermen in Maryland or country-and-western singers in Tennessee, the authors discover that regional dialects are thriving despite the uniformity of our national tastes in clothing, fast-food chains, and movies. . . . The authors show how mobility, immigration, and racial and ethnic mixing are rapidly and profoundly changing the language. . . . This is colorful, witty, and insightful commentary on American speech patterns." Booklist

Includes bibliographical references

Holder, R. W.

★ **How** not to say what you mean; a dictionary of euphemisms. 4th ed.; Oxford University Press 2007 410p pa $18.95   **427**

1. Euphemism -- Dictionaries 2. Reference books

ISBN 978-0-19-920839-5; 0-19-920839-5

LC 2007-37558

"Here are almost five thousand euphemistic expressions listed in alphabetical order, ranging from well-known favorites such as 'push up the daisies,' 'fly-by-night,' 'red light district,' 'take to the cleaners,' 'get lucky,' and 'five-fingered discount,' to less amusing expressions from the bureaucratic and military world such as 'restructuring,' 'collateral damage,' and 'extrajudicial killing.' For each word or expression, Holder includes examples from . . . authors, along with . . . explanations of the words' origins and meaning." Publisher's note

Includes bibliographical references

McMahon, Sean

★ **Brewer's** dictionary of Irish phrase & fable; [by] Sean McMahon and Jo O'Donoghue. Brewer's 2009 867p $34.95   **427**

1. Allusions 2. Folklore -- Ireland 3. Irish literature -- Dictionaries 4. Reference books

ISBN 978-0-550-10565-3

"Entries explore the island's history, literature, language, folklore and mythology . . . [with a] mix of people, places, historical events, facts and phrases. . . . 6,000 entries focus on the phrase and fable of Ireland, from ancient myth to modern politics." Publisher's note

Metcalf, Allan A.

How we talk; American regional English today. {by} Allan Metcalf. Houghton Mifflin 2000 206p il hardcover o.p. pa $14   **427**

1. Americanisms 2. English language -- Dialects -- United States 3. English language -- Dictionaries 4. English language -- Spoken English -- United States 5. English language -- United States -- Pronunciation 6. English language -- Variation -- United States 7. Reference books

ISBN 0-618-04362-4 pa

LC 00-59777

The author "discusses the origins of American regional dialects and explains why different parts of the country use different words to mean the same thing (carry versus tote, for example) or why the same words are pronounced differently in the South as opposed to the North. For fiction writers hoping to create authentic-sounding dialogue, this book could function as an indispensable guide." Booklist

Spears, Richard A.

★ **McGraw**-Hill's dictionary of American slang and colloquial expressions; 4th ed.; McGraw-Hill 2006 xxix, 546p pa $19.95   **427**
1. Americanisms   2. English language -- Slang -- Dictionaries   3. Reference books
ISBN 0-07-146107-8; 978-0-07-146107-8

LC 2005-52220

This book offers "definitions of more than 12,000 slang and informal expressions from various sources, ranging from golden oldies such as . . . golden oldie, to recent coinages like shizzle (gangsta), jonx (Wall Street), and ping (the Internet). Each entry is followed by examples illustrating how an expression is used in everyday conversation and, where necessary, International Phonetic Alphabet pronunciations are given, as well as cautionary notes for crude, inflammatory, or taboo expressions." Publisher's note

Includes bibliographical references

Dictionary of American slang; Barbara Ann Kipfer, editor; Robert L. Chapman, founding editor. 4th ed., fully rev. and updated; Collins 2007 592p $45   **427**
1. Americanisms   2. English language -- Slang -- Dictionaries   3. Reference books
ISBN 978-0-06-117646-3; 0-06-117646-X

This dictionary of American slang terms "features pronunciation guides, word origins, examples of appropriate usage as well as a . . . highlighting system that lets you know which terms should be used with caution, and never in polite company." Publisher's note

★ The new Partridge dictionary of slang and unconventional English; Tom Dalzell (senior editor) and Terry Victor (editor) Routledge 2006 2v set $220   **427**
1. English language -- Slang -- Dictionaries   2. Reference books
ISBN 0-415-21258-8; 978-0-415-21258-8

"Entries list the term, identify its part of speech, explain its meaning, identify the country of origin, and cite sources or provide quotations showing how the term is used. . . . This dictionary informs, but it also entertains." Booklist

Includes bibliographical references

428   Standard English usage (Prescriptive linguistics)

Chalker, Sylvia

★ The **Oxford** dictionary of English grammar; {by} Sylvia Chalker, Edmund Weiner. Oxford Univ. Press 1994 448p il hardcover o.p. pa $15.95   **428**
1. English language -- Dictionaries   2. English language -- Grammar   3. English language -- Grammar -- Dictionaries   4. Reference books
ISBN 0-19-280087-6 pa

LC 94-19818

"Offering 1,000 grammatical terms and their meanings, this title is a comprehensive reference tool and an updated guide to grammatical and linguistic terms, including entries related to phonetics and semantics. Its emphasis is on the terminology of current mainstream grammar, including Chomskyan generative grammar." Choice

Dunn, Patricia A.

Grammar rants.   Heinemann/Boynton/Cook Publishers 2011 xvi, 134 p   **428**
ISBN 0867096055; 9780867096057

LC 2011005689

This book presents an analysis of debates and complaints concerning the moral and social implications of grammar. "Each chapter includes actual rants along with . . . editorial commentary, instructional activities and classroom lessons" intended to facilitate student discussion on the social aspects of grammar and the assumptions people make when they encounter incorrect usage. According to the publisher, these "lessons will promote savvy writing by empowering students and teachers to see for themselves how best to raise the quality of their written and spoken language without resorting to ranting." (Publisher's note)

Florey, Kitty Burns

Sister Bernadette's barking dog; the quirky history and lost art of diagramming sentences. Melville House 2006 154p $19.95   **428**
1. English language -- Grammar
ISBN 978-1-933633-10-7; 1-933633-10-7

LC 2006-24703

The author "writes with verve about the nuns who taught her to render the English language as a mess of slanted lines, explains how diagrams work, and traces the bizarre history of the men who invented this odd pedagogical tool. And unlike so many of today's microhistorians, who seek to demonstrate how zippers, azaleas, or hopscotch explain the world, Florey is refreshingly content to recount her tale without any suggestion that the diagramming of sentences somehow illuminates the American character. It's a great read." Slate

Fowler, H. W.

★ **Fowler's** modern English usage; first edition by H.W. Fowler. Rev. 3rd ed.; Oxford University Press 2004 xxi, 873p $35   **428**
1. English language -- Etymology   2. English language -- Idioms   3. English language -- Usage   4. Reference books
ISBN 0-19-861021-1; 978-0-19-861021-2

LC 2005-271630

This alphabetically arranged guide gives "advice on grammar, syntax, style, and choice of words." Publisher's note

O'Conner, Patricia T.

★ **Woe** is I; the grammarphobe's guide to better English in plain English. Riverhead Bks. 2003 240p $19.95; pa $14   **428**
1. English language -- Grammar 2. English language -- Usage
ISBN 1-57322-252-6; 1-59448-006-0 pa
LC 2003-41416

This guide to good English offers advice on punctuation, usage, style and grammar as well as e-mail.

"The author doesn't take herself or the subject matter too seriously, offering a delightful romp through the intricacies of our language. . . . She knows her subject, can convey her message with wit and ease, and does it all in a compact, easy-to-read format. In short, this is an entertaining and useful grammar reference." Libr J

Includes bibliographical references

Peters, Pam

★ The **Cambridge** guide to English usage. Cambridge University Press 2004 608p il $35 **428**
1. English language -- Australia -- Usage 2. English language -- Canada -- Usage 3. English language -- United States -- Usage 4. English language -- Usage 5. Reference books
ISBN 0-521-62181-X
LC 2004-301888

"Considering the abundance of peculiarities and challenges in English usage, Cambridge will strengthen even a library well stocked with other guides. It is a serious book for those serious about language." Booklist

Strumpf, Michael

The **grammar** bible; everything you always wanted to know about grammar but didn't know whom to ask. [by] Michael Strumpf and Auriel Douglas. Holt 2004 489p pa $18   **428**
1. English language -- Grammar
ISBN 0-8050-7560-7
LC 2003-57129

The authors move "from the parts of speech to the parts of the sentence and then to spelling, vocabulary, and punctuation, even encompassing thorny issues (e.g., sexist language, split infinitives) and complex grammatical terms (e.g., objective complements, gerund phrases). The authors also include a useful list of collocations and intersperse informative and often amusing 'Hot Line' queries throughout. . . This book is thorough, combining practical information not easily found in trade books, and is lively without trying to be too witty, cute, or humorous." Libr J

Includes bibliographical references

Wilson, Kenneth G.

The **Columbia** guide to standard American English. Columbia Univ. Press 1993 482p hardcover o.p. pa $26   **428**
1. Americanisms 2. Americanisms -- Dictionaries 3. English language -- Dictionaries 4. English language

-- Usage 5. English language -- Usage -- Dictionaries 6. Reference books
ISBN 0-231-06988-X; 978-0-231-06989-2 pa; 0-231-06989-8 pa
LC 92-37887

"The 6,500 entries in this book provide a unique approach to spoken and written English. Wilson diagrams five levels of speech, from intimate to oratorical, and three levels of writing, from informal to formal. His descriptive discussion of usage is intended to assist in making choices. . . . Cross references are numerous, and a helpful guide to pronunciation is included." Am Libr

433   Dictionaries of standard German

★ Random House Webster's German-English, English-German dictionary; Rev. ed; Random House Reference 2006 547p $12.95   **433**
1. German language -- Dictionaries 2. Reference books
ISBN 0-375-72194-0; 978-0-375-72194-6

In addition to more than 60,000 entries this dictionary also includes notes on pronunciation, lists of abbreviations, tables of irregular verbs and lists of geographical names.

440   French and related Romance languages

Nadeau, Jean-Benoit

★ The **story** of French; [by] Jean-Benoît Nadeau [and] Julie Barlow. St. Martin's Press 2006 483p map $25.95   **440**
1. French language 2. French language -- History
ISBN 9780312341831; 0312341830
LC 2006-49348

This book explores the origins and evolution of the French language.

This is "a well-told, highly accessible history of the French language that leads to a spirited discussion of the prospects for French in an increasingly English-dominated world." N Y Times (Late N Y Ed)

Includes bibliographical references

443   Dictionaries of standard French

Correard, Marie-Helene

★ The **Oxford**-Hachette French dictionary; French-English, English-French. edited by Marie-Hélène Corréard, Valerie Grundy. 4th ed.; Oxford University Press/Hachette Livre 2007 xxxviii, 1945p $55   **443**
1. French language -- Dictionaries 2. Reference books
ISBN 978-0-19-861422-7; 0-19-861422-5
LC 2007-14213

This work provides coverage of French and English vocabulary in general as well as scientific and technical areas with over 350,000 words and phrases and over 530,000 translations. Supplementary material includes information on French society and culture, including famous places, people and much practical information for those planning to reside in France.

463   Dictionaries of standard Spanish

Houghton Mifflin Co.

The **Concise** American Heritage Spanish dictionary; 2nd ed; Houghton Mifflin 2001 xxiv, 616p $14   **463**
1. English language -- Dictionaries -- Spanish 2. Reference books 3. Spanish language -- Dictionaries 4. Spanish language -- Dictionaries -- English
ISBN 0-618-11769-5

LC 00-66461

"This bilingual dictionary includes more than 70,000 words and phrases. The emphasis on American English and Latin American Spanish as well as the informative guides and tables will assist students of either language." Booklist

470   Latin and related Italic languages

Ostler, Nicholas

Ad infinitum; a biography of Latin. Walker & Company 2007 382p il map $27.95   **470**
1. Latin language 2. Latin language, Postclassical -- History 3. Latin language, Preclassical to ca. 100 B.C
ISBN 978-0-8027-1515-9; 0-8027-1515-X

"In four parts, Ostler covers the origins and development of Latin in the Roman world, Latin's "taking over the church," its medieval continuation and fracturing into vernaculars, and a nuanced rebirth in the Renaissance and its legacy in the contemporary world. Incredibly well documented, with examples from antiquity to the modern era." Libr J

473   Dictionaries of classical Latin

Stone, Jon R.

★ **Latin** for the illiterati; a modern phrase book for an ancient language. 2nd ed.; Routledge 2009 xxii, 338p pa $24.95   **473**
1. Latin language -- Dictionaries 2. Reference books
ISBN 978-0-415-77767-4; 0-415-77767-4

"Organized alphabetically within the categories of verba (common words and expressions), dicta (common phrases and familiar sayings), and abbreviations, this . . . [is a] compendium of more than 7,000 Latin words, expressions, phrases, and sayings taken from the world of art, music, law, philosophy, theology, medicine and the theatre, as well as . . . [remarks and] advice from ancient writers such as Virgil, Ovid, Cicero, and more." Publisher's note
Includes bibliographical references

★ **More** Latin for the illiterati; exorcizing the ghosts of a dead language. Routledge 1999 201p $75; pa $17.95   **473**
1. Latin language -- Church Latin 2. Latin language -- Dictionaries 3. Latin language -- Dictionaries -- English

4. Latin language -- Medical Latin 5. Latin language -- Terms and phrases 6. Law -- Dictionaries 7. Reference books
ISBN 0-415-92210-0; 0-415-92211-9 pa

LC 98-43820

This dictionary focuses on "three areas: medicine, law, and religion. Translations are brief and literal. The dictionary concludes with some of the same information given in Latin for the Illiterati as well as newer miscellaneous information, including Latin selections (with English translations) from the Roman Catholic liturgy." Libr J
Includes bibliographical references

★ Oxford Latin dictionary; edited by P. G. W. Glare. Oxford Univ. Press 1982 xxiii, 2126p   **473**
1. Latin language -- Dictionaries 2. Latin language -- Dictionaries -- English 3. Reference books
ISBN 0198642245

LC 8208162

This dictionary looks at the meaning and development of more than 40,000 classical Latin words and phrases.
"Authorized in 1931 and begun two years later, {this dictionary} appeared in eight fascicles published between 1968 and 1982. These have been combined in a single volume." Wilson Libr Bull

492.4   Hebrew

Zilkha, Avraham

★ **Modern** English-Hebrew dictionary. Yale Univ. Press 2002 457p $55; pa $30   **492.4**
1. English language -- Dictionaries -- Hebrew 2. Hebrew language -- Dictionaries 3. Reference books
ISBN 0-300-09004-8; 0-300-09005-6 pa

LC 2001-26830

This dictionary includes 30,000 entries, with listings for translating words with multiple meanings, newly coined and slang words, common idioms, vocalization of Hebrew words, acronyms, and gender identification and plural forms of irregular nouns.

495.1   Chinese

Cheng & Tsui English-Chinese lexicon of business terms with pinyin; compiled by Andrew C. Chang = [Jianqiao Ying Han shang yong ci hui pin ying ci dian / Zhang Jiezhou bian] Cheng & Tsui Co. 2001 442p $36.95   **495.1**
1. Business -- Dictionaries 2. Chinese language -- Dictionaries 3. Reference books
ISBN 978-0-88727-394-0; 0-88727-394-7

LC 2001-94244

"A book to hand to your patrons who need to know the Chinese expressions for terms such as Chief Executive Officer, market penetration, and stockholder. More than 9,000 English-language words and phrases are listed with their Chinese simplified characters, with pinyin transliteration equivalents." Booklist

495.7 Korean

Berlitz Korean compact dictionary. Berlitz Publishing 2006 672p pa $12.95   **495.7**
1. Korean language -- Dictionaries 2. Reference books
ISBN 978-981-246-949-6; 981-246-949-4
This book has "45,000 entries that aim to capture the core words of the language. This dictionary features bold, blue headwords [for navigation]." Publisher's note

499 Non-Austronesian languages of Oceania, Austronesian languages, miscellaneous languages

Okrent, Arika
In the land of invented languages; Esperanto rock stars, Klingon poets, Loglan lovers, and the mad dreamers who tried to build a perfect language. Spiegel & Grau 2009 342p il $26   **499**
1. Artificial languages 2. Esperanto 3. Klingon (Artificial language) 4. Languages, Artificial 5. Loglan (Artificial language)
ISBN 978-0-385-52788-0; 0-385-52788-8
LC 2008-38732
The author "explores some of the themes and shortcomings of 900 years worth of artificial languages. . . . [Her] prose is a model of clarity and grace; through it, she conveys fascinating insights into why natural language, with its corruptions, ambiguities and arbitrary conventions, trips so fluently off our tongues." Publ Wkly
Includes bibliographical references

Pukui, Mary Kawena
Hawaiian dictionary; Hawaiian-English, English-Hawaiian. [by] Mary Kawena Pukui, Samuel H. Elbert. rev & enl ed; University of Hawaii Press 1986 xxvi, 572p $32.95   **499**
1. Hawaiian language -- Dictionaries 2. Reference books
ISBN 0-8248-0703-0
LC 85-24583
"The Hawaiian-English part now comprises 29,000 entries. It is the most comprehensive and up-to-date dictionary for the language." Guide to Ref Books. 11th edition
Includes bibliographical references

500 SCIENCE

500 Natural sciences and mathematics

Aczel, Amir D.
The artist and the mathematician; the story of Nicolas Bourbaki, the genius mathematician who never existed. Thunder's Mouth Press 2006 239p il $23.95   **500**
1. Mathematicians 2. Mathematics -- History -- 20th century
ISBN 978-1-56025-931-2; 1-56025-931-0

"In 1934, a small group of mostly French mathematicians met to reinvent a new math based on a pedagogy of rigorous proofs, clarity, and logical thinking. The group invented a fictitious persona, 'Nicolas Bourbaki,' as a pseudonym under which to author their collective work. Presenting the fascinating story behind the publication of over 40 tomes . . . , Aczel describes the group's cultural context, eccentricities, informal rules, and practices of engagement and offers biographical sketches of such influential members as Andr Weil and Alexandre Grothendieck. Writing in an accessible, conversational style that excludes mathematical proofs, Aczel paints a clear picture of the Bourbaki movement and how it has influenced the way mathematics should be discussed and learned." Libr J

Angier, Natalie
The canon; a whirligig tour of the beautiful basics of science. Houghton Mifflin Company 2007 293p $27   **500**
1. Science
ISBN 978-0-618-24295-5; 0-618-24295-3
LC 2006-26871
If Angier "reaches for a joke too often instaed of relying on her admirably supple prose, she's still a matchless scientific decathlete, able to perform with equal adroitness whether examining the infinitesimal or the infinite." Fortune
Includes bibliographical references

Bais, Sander
In praise of science; curiosity, understanding, and progress. MIT Press 2010 192p il $24.95 **500**
1. Science
ISBN 978-0-262-01435-9; 0-262-01435-1
LC 2009-35675
"Over the course of four short chapters, Sander Bais illustrates in entertaining and often poetic ways not only how all of the sciences are connected to each other, but how they comprise a vital (if not the most vital) endeavor humans has ever undertaken. . . . Among others, the stories in In Praise of Science include the origin of Santa Claus, the history of quantum theory, the invention of the lightning rod, and religious attacks that distorted the theory of evolution and facts surrounding HIV and AIDS. The polemical nature of Bais' arguments might spark debate for some readers, but he never comes across as ranting. He employs many (at times lengthy) quotes from a variety of sources, and near the end of the book there's a tendency to let the quotes make the case for him. But for the vast majority of the book, Bais seems like the quirky professor everyone loves and/or wishes they had, one who inspires lifelong interests." PopMatters
Includes bibliographical references

Bronowski, Jacob
Science and human values; revised edition with a new dialogue, The abacus and the rose. Harper & Row 1965 119p il hardcover o.p. pa $12   **500**
1. Science
ISBN 0-06-097281-5 pa
Contains the following three essays, which were first given as lectures at the Massachusetts Institute of Technology in 1953: The creative mind; The habit of truth; The sense

of human dignity. The abacus and the rose was originally broadcast by the BBC Third Programme in 1962

The dialogue "discusses the theme that 'science is as integral a part of the culture of our age as the arts are.'" Sci Am

Brooks, M.

13 things that don't make sense; the most baffling scientific mysteries of our time. [by] Michael Brooks. Doubleday 2008 240p $23.95   **500**
    1. Science
    ISBN 978-0-385-52068-3; 0-385-52068-9
                   LC 2008-12443
This "book examines such mysteries as dark matter and dark energy, the prospect of life on Mars, sex and death, free will and the placebo effect, among other head-scratchers. . . . This elegantly written, meticulously researched and thought-provoking book provides window into how science actually works, and is sure to spur intense debate." New Sci
Includes bibliographical references

Bryson, Bill

★ A **short** history of nearly everything. Broadway Bks. 2003 544p $27.50; pa $15.95   **500**
    1. Science 2. Science -- Popular works
    ISBN 0-7679-0817-1; 0-7679-0818-X pa
                   LC 2003-46006
"Neither oversimplified nor overstuffed, this exceptionally skillful tour of the physical world covers the basic principles and still has room for profiles of some of the more engaging scientists." N Y Times Book Rev
Includes bibliographical references

Cole, K. C.

Mind over matter; conversations with the cosmos. Harcourt 2003 319p $25; pa $14   **500**
    1. Cosmology 2. Science
    ISBN 0-15-100816-7; 0-15-602956-1 pa
                   LC 2003-982
"These three-page tidbits may not tax your scientific thought processes, but they'll certainly make you think." Libr J

Dawkins, Richard

A **devil's** chaplain; reflections on hope, lies, science, and love. Houghton Mifflin 2003 263p il $24; pa $14   **500**
    1. Evolution 2. Religion and science 3. Science -- Philosophy
    ISBN 0-618-33540-4; 0-618-48539-2 pa
                   LC 2003-50859
This is "a collection of essays that span 25 years of writing on evolution, education and science versus nonsense. . . . Dawkins is creative, articulate and, above all, emotional." N Y Times Book Rev
Includes bibliographical references

Dyson, Freeman J.

The **scientist** as rebel; [by] Freeman Dyson. New York Review Books 2006 360p $27.95   **500**
    1. College teachers 2. Physicists 3. Science 4. Science -- History 5. Science -- Moral and ethical aspects 6.

Writers on science
    ISBN 978-1-59017-216-2; 1-59017-216-7
                   LC 2006-22081
This is a "collection of 33 previously published and frequently updated essays and reviews. Organized into sections on contemporary issues in science, war and peace, history of science and scientists, and personal and philosophical ruminations, these works demonstrate Dyson's far-ranging interests and skill in writing for educated and curious generalists, qualities that ensure this volume's wide appeal." Booklist
Includes bibliographical references

Eiseley, Loren C.

The **unexpected** universe. 1969 239p hardcover o.p. pa $14   **500**
    1. Natural history 2. Science
    ISBN 0-15-692850-7 pa
This volume contains personal interpretative meditations on mankind's relationship to nature.

Feynman, Richard Phillips

★ The **meaning** of it all; thoughts of a citizen scientist. Basic Books 2005 133p pa $13.95   **500**
    1. Religion 2. Science
    ISBN 0-465-02394-0
"Originally delivered as a three-part lecture series at the University of Washington in 1963, this collection touches on such far-ranging topics as the existence or nonexistence of God; the Constitution; and UFOs. . . . These memorable lectures confirm that Feynman's gift of insight extended from the subatomic world to the cosmic, and to the very human as well." Publ Wkly

The **pleasure** of finding things out; the best short works of Richard P. Feynman. by Richard P. Feynman; edited by Jeffrey Robbins; foreword by Freeman Dyson. Perseus Bks. 1999 270p hardcover o.p. pa $15.95   **500**
    1. Science
    ISBN 0-7382-0349-1 pa
                   LC 99-64775
These lectures and interviews are "expositions about [Feynman's] life, about technical topics in computing and physics, and about science's general place in society." Booklist

Flatow, Ira

Present at the future; from evolution to nanotechnology, candid and controversial conversations on science and nature. Collins 2007 354p il $24.95   **500**
    1. Science
    ISBN 978-0-06-073264-6; 0-06-073264-4
                   LC 2007-14583
This is "an entertaining and thought-provoking read that leaves you feeling more informed and as though you might have a little more to offer during your next dinner-party conversation." Sci Books Films

Gardner, Martin

★ **Did** Adam and Eve have navels? discourses on reflexology, numerology, urine therapy and other dubious subjects. Norton 2000 333p il hardcover o.p. pa $15.95   **500**

1. Science

ISBN 0-393-32238-6 pa

LC 00-34870

This is a collection of the author's pieces culled from the Skeptical Inquirer. Gardner "gives succinct and amusing critiques of a number of the fallacies that abound in alternative medicine (including the very peculiar urine-therapy treatment) and many other 'dubious subjects.'" Libr J

Includes bibliographical references

Goldacre, Ben

Bad science; quacks, hacks, and big pharma flacks. Faber and Faber 2010 288p il pa $15   **500**

1. Errors 2. Medical misconceptions

ISBN 978-0-86547-918-0

LC 2010-14401

The author "has written a very funny and biting book critiquing what he calls 'Bad Science.' Under this heading he includes homeopathy, cosmetics manufacturers whose claims about their products defy plausibility, proponents of miracle vitamins, and drug companies and physicians who design faulty studies and manipulate the results. . . . While it is a very entertaining book, it also provides important insight into the horrifying outcomes that can result when willful anti-intellectualism is allowed equal footing with scientific methodology." Boston Globe

Includes bibliographical references

Gould, Stephen Jay

The **flamingo's** smile; reflections in natural history. Norton 1985 476p il hardcover o.p. pa $15.95   **500**

1. Natural history

ISBN 0-393-30375-6 pa

LC 85-4916

In this collection "the theme is history, both natural and human. . . . The essays are marked by Gould's usual careful scholarship and erudition and clear and nontechnical language." Sci Books Films

Includes bibliographical references

Gribbin, John R.

★ **Almost** everyone's guide to science; the universe, life and everything. [by] John Gribbin with Mary Gribbin. Yale Univ. Press 1999 232p $30; pa $11.95   **500**

1. Science 2. Science -- Popular works

ISBN 0-300-08101-4; 0-300-08460-9 pa

LC 99-26755

In this "general guide to science for the layperson . . . Gribbin combines biographies and history, on the one hand, with the major theories in science, on the other. . . . The text is clear, is based on solid research, and clearly reflects a lifetime love for science." Sci Books Films

Includes bibliographical references

Henderson, Mark

100 most important science ideas; key concepts in genetics, physics and mathematics. [by] Mark Henderson, Joanne Baker, Tony Crilly. Firefly Books 2009 431p il $19.95   **500**

1. Genetics 2. Mathematics 3. Physics

ISBN 978-1-55407-527-0

This book aims to encourage the reader to explore "the 100 most important, groundbreaking ideas that have emerged from the scientific disciplines of genetics, physics, and mathematics. Divided into three sections, each written by one of the authors . . . this work presents complex scientific topics in a simple, understandable way. . . . Text boxes, entertaining quotations, frequent diagrams, and everyday examples hold the reader's attention and make this work engaging to anyone interested in the world of science." Libr J

Highfield, Roger

The **science** of Harry Potter; how magic really works. Viking 2002 xxii, 322p hardcover o.p. pa $15   **500**

1. Authors 2. Children's authors 3. Fantasy writers 4. Magic 5. Magic -- Popular works 6. Novelists 7. Potter, Harry (Fictitious character) 8. Science 9. Science -- Popular works 10. Young adult authors

ISBN 0-670-03153-4; 0-14-200355-7 pa

LC 2002-28878

"Fans of such science popularizers as Gould and Asimov will certainly get a kick out of Highfield's utterly fascinating take on the subject." Booklist

Includes bibliographical references

Kipfer, Barbara Ann

How it happens; the extraordinary processes of everyday things. Random House Reference 2005 322p il pa $16.95   **500**

1. Science

ISBN 0-375-72082-0

LC 2005-40453

This "trivia miscellany describes hundreds of processes, from popcorn popping to radio signal transmission to tango dancing." Publisher's note

Maddox, John Royden

What remains to be discovered; mapping the secrets of the universe, the origins of life, and the future of the human race. [by] John Maddox. Kessler Bks./ Free Press 1998 434p hardcover o.p. pa $22.95 **500**

1. Discoveries in science 2. Research -- Miscellanea 3. Science 4. Science -- History

ISBN 0-684-82292-X; 978-0-684-86300-9 pa; 0-684-86300-6 pa

LC 98-29137

The author reflects "on the nature of science, both its successes and its challenges. . . . By focusing on some of the 'big' fields of science—cosmology, quantum mechanics, cell biology, genetics, evolution and neuroscience, for example—he has crafted a primer worthy of study. But this is not an introduction for the uninitiated." Publ Wkly

Includes bibliographical references

Marshall, I. N.

Who's afraid of Schrodinger's cat? all the new science ideas you need to keep up with the new thinking. [by] Ian Marshall & Danah Zohar, with contributions by F. David Peat. Morrow 1997 xxx, 402p map hardcover o.p. pa $15   **500**
1. Science
ISBN 0-688-16107-3 pa

LC 96-20769

This "is an alphabetically organized, heavily cross-listed compendium of brief descriptions of new areas of science, such as 'Artificial Intelligence,' 'The Edge of Chaos,' 'Mesons' and 'Transpersonal Psychology.' While the 201 entries are weighted toward new areas of physics, the book does justice to every area of natural and social science." Sci Books Films

Oakes, Elizabeth H.

★ **International** encyclopedia of women scientists. Facts on File 2002 448p il $82.50   **500**
1. Reference books 2. Women scientists -- Dictionaries
ISBN 0-8160-4381-7

LC 2001-23100

This volume "covers more than 500 scientists. Dating back to 400 BCE, it treats current, historical, and minority women scientists. The entries . . . include biographical information that provides detailed descriptions of education, research, and notable accomplishments. Oakes also supplies an impressive, expansive set of indexes: general alphabetical, field of specialization, country of birth, country of major scientific activity, and year of birth." Choice
Includes bibliographical references

Park, Robert L.

Voodoo science; the road from foolishness to fraud. Oxford Univ. Press 2000 230p hardcover o.p. pa $17.95   **500**
1. Fraud 2. Fraud in science -- United States 3. Science 4. Science -- Social aspects -- United States
ISBN 0-19-513515-6; 978-0-19-514710-0 pa; 0-19-514710-3 pa

LC 99-40911

The author "aims to expose various beliefs and schemes put forth in the popular press and other places as scientifically real and factual. . . . {He} turns a critical eye on cold fusion, magnet therapy, homeopathy, perpetual motion, and other recent examples of fringe science. . . . Park's book should be required reading for all science writers, journalists, and politicians." Libr J

Pohl, Frederik

Chasing science; science as a spectator sport. TOR Bks. 2000 251p $23.95; pa $14.95   **500**
1. Science 2. Science -- Popular works
ISBN 0-312-86711-5; 0-7653-0829-0 pa

LC 00-57768

In order to witness science in action, Pohl traveled to a variety of sites, museums, laboratories, and observatories around the world. This is an account of his experiences and impressions.

Randall, Lisa

Knocking on heaven's door; how physics and scientific thinking illuminate the universe and the modern world. Ecco 2011 xxi, 442p il $29.99; ebook $14.99   **500**
1. Physics 2. Science
ISBN 978-0-06-172372-8; 978-0-06-209689-0 ebook

LC 2011010521

"To explain how science works, Randall analyzes the way two researchers at Bell Labs turned the annoying static coming through their radio telescope into a cosmic breakthrough. For in this piquant episode—and others that Randall examines—science advances by testing theoretical ingenuity against technologically acquired data. . . . Randall offers an insider's perspective into this cutting-edge science. Yet she illuminates that science with lucid language, laced with references to popular culture, political controversy, and even comic-strip art. The general reader's indispensable passport to the frontiers of science." Booklist
Includes bibliographical references

Ray, C. Claiborne

The **New** York Times second book of science questions and answers; 225 new, intriguing, and just plain bizarre inquiries into everyday scientific mysteries. drawings by Victoria Roberts; edited by Henry Fountain. Anchor Bks. (NY) 2003 228p il pa $13   **500**
1. Science
ISBN 0-385-72258-3

LC 2002-26192

"This eclectic volume of 228 questions with 200-word answers entices readers' interest in science. . . . There is no index and not much structure in this volume, but its charm and interest make up for its informality." Sci Books Films
Includes bibliographical references

Sagan, Carl

Billions and billions; thoughts on life and death at the brink of the millennium. Random House 1997 241p hardcover o.p. pa $14.95   **500**
1. Science
ISBN 0-345-37918-7 pa

LC 96-52730

This collection of essays covers such topics as: "the invention of chess, life on Mars, global warming, abortion, international affairs, the nature of government, and the meaning of morality. Writing with clarity and an understanding of human nature, Sagan offers hope for humanity's future." Libr J
Includes bibliographical references

★ **Broca's** brain; reflections on the romance of science. Random House 1979 347p hardcover o.p. pa $7.99   **500**
1. Astronomy 2. God 3. Machinery 4. Nobel laureates for physics 5. Philosophy 6. Physicians 7. Physicists 8. Psychologists 9. Religion 10. Science 11. Writers on science
ISBN 0-345-33689-5 pa

LC 78-21810

The author "is a lucid, logical writer with a gift for explaining science to the layman and infecting the reader with his own boundless enthusiasm and curiosity." Natl Rev

Includes bibliographical references

Wiggins, Arthur W.

The **five** biggest ideas in science; [by] Charles M. Wynn [and] Arthur W. Wiggins; with cartoon commentary by Sidney Harris. Wiley 1997 200p il maps pa $15.95   **500**

1. Science

ISBN 0-471-13812-6

LC 96-27469

Presents five basic scientific hypotheses: the atomic model, the periodic law, the big bang theory, plate tectonics, and evolution.

"Each 'Big Idea' is thoroughly described. . . . In explaining the thinking that led to each 'Big Idea,' the authors clearly outline the scientific method and demystify the process." Libr J

Includes bibliographical references

★ The **five** biggest unsolved problems in science; [by] Arthur W. Wiggins [and] Charles M. Wynn; with cartoon commentary by Sidney Harris. J. Wiley & Sons 2003 234p il pa $14.95   **500**

1. Science 2. Science -- Miscellanea

ISBN 0-471-26808-9

LC 2003-284262

"The problems discussed in this volume are the dueling concepts of mass and masslessness (physics), the passage from chemicals to living matter (chemistry), the complete structure of the proteome (biology), long-range weather forecasting (geology), and the expansion of the universe (astronomy)." Sci Books Films

Includes bibliographical references

History of modern science and mathematics; Brian S. Baigrie, editor. Scribner 2002 4v il set $605   **500**

1. Mathematics -- History 2. Science -- History

ISBN 0-684-80636-3

LC 2002-4042

This "set attempts to synthesize the history of scientific developments in anthropology, astronomy, biology, chemistry, mathematics, physics, psychology, and the earth sciences. . . . This work ranges from the 17th century to the present without trying to include the most recent developments." Libr J

Includes bibliographical references

★ Oxford dictionary of scientific quotations; edited by W.F. Bynum and Roy Porter; assistant editors, Sharon Messenger, Caroline Overy. Oxford University Press 2005 712p $60; pa $18.95   **500**

1. Quotations 2. Science

ISBN 0-19-858409-1; 0-19-861443-8 pa

LC 2005-277260

"This hefty volume is a great reference but it is also a great read—open it up to any page and expand the mind with a sampling of scientific ideas and philosophy." Choice

Scientific American's ask the experts; answers to the most puzzling and mindblowing science questions. by the editors of Scientific American. HarperCollins Pubs. 2003 267p il pa $14.95   **500**

1. Science

ISBN 0-06-052336-0

LC 2004-555579

This "is a book that answers questions big, little, and in between. . . . The book uses the familiar question-and-answer format, with a table of contents allowing the reader to flip to a specific question. The questions are answered by a variety of experts. . . . This is one of those books you put on your reference shelf, and pull out whenever the subject turns to matters of scientific interest. Great for trivia buffs, too." Booklist

★ The best American science and nature writing 2010; edited and with an introducion by Freeman Dyson; Tim Folger, series editor. Houghton Mifflin Harcourt 2010 xxv, 385p pa $14.95   **500**

1. Nature 2. Science

ISBN 978-0-547-32784-6

A collection of 26 essays on science and nature topics from the past year.

"Each of the authors—many familiar to readers of publications such as the New Yorker (from which Elizabeth Kolbert merits two entries) and the New York Review of Books—writes clearly, on occasion elegantly, and often with a contagious passion." Publ Wkly

The handy science answer book; compiled by the Carnegie Library of Pittsburgh; [edited by] Naomi E. Balaban and James E. Bobick. 4th ed.; Visible Ink Press 2011 679p il pa $21.95   **500**

1. Science 2. Technology

ISBN 978-1-57859-321-7

LC 2011-429

"The text is divided into various subject areas including physics and chemistry, space, earth, climate and weather, minerals and other materials, energy, technology, and environment, gathering answers to reference questions. . . . A comprehensive index . . . makes the material accessible and easy to find. Pages are full of fascinating tidbits, complemented by illustrations, photos, charts, graphs, and maps." Voice Youth Advocates

Includes bibliographical references

500.2   Physical sciences

Ball, Philip

Nature's patterns; a tapestry in three parts. Oxford University Press 2009 308p il $29.95   **500.2**

1. Chaos (Science) 2. Chaotic behavior in systems 3. Evolution (Biology) 4. Exterior forms 5. Pattern formation (Biology) 6. Patterns (Mathematics) 7. Shape

ISBN 978-0-19-923796-8; 0-19-923796-4

LC 2009-280579

"From the curl of a ram's horn to patterns of spider webs and the development of an embryo, Mr Ball examines the possible causes of the shapes and forms we observe. His book contains a lot of fascinating detail about the different physical, chemical and evolutionary processes at work." Economist

Includes bibliographical references

Notable women in the physical sciences; a biographical dictionary. edited by Benjamin F. Shearer and Barbara S. Shearer. Greenwood Press 1997 479p il $55 **500.2**
1. Biography, Collective 2. Physical sciences 3. Reference books 4. Women scientists -- Biography -- Dictionaries 5. Women scientists -- Dictionaries
ISBN 0-313-29303-1

LC 96-9024

"Featuring biographical essays on 96 world and U.S. women scientists, this volume includes women who made a significant contribution to the physical sciences from antiquity to the present, though the emphasis is on 20th-century women. . . . Disciplines include astronomy, astrophysics, biochemistry, chemistry, and physics. The essays average five pages in length and describe obstacles encountered and achievements experienced by each scientist. Each entry provides a chronology, a descriptive essay, and a bibliography." Choice

500.5 Space sciences

Launius, Roger D.
Smithsonian atlas of space exploration; [by] Roger D. Launius & Andrew K. Johnston. Collins 2009 230p il map $34.99 **500.5**
ISBN 978-0-06-156526-7

LC 2009-649

This book "relates the story of space exploration in text, photographs, illustrations, and maps from the earliest times to the present. Written at a level geared to the general reader, this topically arranged work is divided into seven parts. . . . Each part contains a number of two or four-page subsections covering topics ranging from the earliest observatories of the ancient world to the possibilities for space flight in the future. . . . Distinguished by outstanding color illustrations and photographs, the very reasonably priced atlas should appeal to a broad audience." Booklist

Includes bibliographical references

Zimmerman, Robert
The **chronological** encyclopedia of discoveries in space. Oryx Press 2000 410p il maps $95 **500.5**
1. Astronautics
ISBN 1-57356-196-7

"Over 1,000 entries record the date of launch, name of the spacecraft(s), summary of the mission, names of the crew members, experiments, problems, and discoveries in a clear and concise fashion. Seemingly every single space mission is included, encompassing spaceflight with and without human crews, military and civilian ventures, public and commercial ventures, planetary probes, and communications satellites. . . . An excellent, cross-referencing system within the text, as well as extensive subject indices by satellite, mission, and nation or consortia, helps the reader

follow particular interests in detail. . . . There is no comparable source to this volume for its comprehensiveness and conciseness." Sci Books Films

Includes bibliographical references

Space sciences; Pat Dasch, editor in chief. Macmillan Ref. USA 2002 4v il set $395 **500.5**
1. Reference books 2. Space sciences
ISBN 0-02-865546-X

LC 2002-1707

"A comprehensive and usable survey of space exploration, this marvelous encyclopedia works equally well as a multivolume set and as four standalone volumes. . . . The photographs are excellent." Libr J

Includes bibliographical references

501 Philosophy and theory

Costa, Rebecca D.
The **watchman's** rattle; thinking our way out of extinction. with a foreword by E.O. Wilson. Vanguard Press 2010 347p $26.95 **501**
1. Civilization 2. Complexity (Philosophy) 3. Problem solving
ISBN 978-1-59315-605-3; 1-59315-605-7

LC 2010-927900

Explains why the human brain has such difficulty dealing with complex global problems and provides a method for surmounting these limitations in order to end the blights of worldwide recession, global warming, fast-spreading viruses, famine, and poverty.

This book "will give concerned readers new hope in human capability." Libr J

Includes bibliographical references

Dawkins, Richard
Unweaving the rainbow; science, delusion, and the appetite for wonder. Houghton Mifflin 1998 336p $26; pa $14 **501**
1. Science -- Philosophy
ISBN 0-395-88382-2; 0-618-05673-4 pa

LC 98-40879

Dawkins is a "witty popularizer, whether he is offering a crash course in DNA fingerprinting, explaining the origins of 'mad cow disease' in weird proteins that spread like self-replicating viruses or discussing male birdsong as an auditory aphrodisiac for female birds." Publ Wkly

Includes bibliographical references

Dawkins, Richard, 1941-
The **magic** of reality; how we know what's really true. illustrated by Dave McKean. 1st Free Press hardcover ed; Free Press 2011 271p il map **501**
1. Nature 2. Reality 3. Science -- Philosophy
ISBN 1439192812; 1451628927 ebook;
9781439192818; 9781451628920 ebook

LC 2011025607

"In this outstanding 'graphic science book,' evolutionary biologist Dawkins . . . teams up with illustrator Dave McKean . . . to examine questions in everyday science, such as: why seasons occur; what things are made of; and whether there's life on other planets. They explain the answers from mythological and cultural points of view before diving into the chemistry, biology, and physics—all in language that advanced middle school, or most high school, students can absorb." Publ Wkly

Deutsch, David

The **beginning** of infinity; explanations that transform the world. Viking Adult 2011 487p il $30 **501**

1. Infinite 2. Memetics 3. Science -- Philosophy
ISBN 978-0-670-02275-5; 0-670-02275-6

LC 2011004120

The book discusses the interaction between humans and the universe they inhabit, challenging concepts such as "the Earth is a maternally inclined spacefaring vessel . . . [and] the utter insignificance of human beings in the cosmic scheme of things. . . . Our cosmic importance derives from our capacity to acquire knowledge, and use it to transform our lives and surroundings. . . . In the short term, this means that we should seek to understand and control the Earth's entire ecosystem. . . . In the medium term we should colonize the Moon, followed by the other planets in our solar system. In the longer term we should aim for the stars -- and even beyond: Deutsch argues in some detail that extremely empty intergalactic space is easily capable of sustaining a high population of technologically advanced space-dwellers." (TLS)

"Anyone who loves to grapple with profound ideas should love reading this very ambitious and challenging look at the history and (possibly unlimited) future of human understanding." Sci Books Films

Includes bibliographical references

Mitchell, Melanie

Complexity; a guided tour. Oxford University Press 2009 349p il map $29.95 **501**

1. Complexity (Philosophy) 2. Science -- Philosophy
ISBN 978-0-19-512441-5; 0-19-512441-3

LC 2008023794

The sciences of complexity "seek to explain how large-scale complex, organized, and adaptive behavior can emerge from simple interactions among myriad individuals. . . . Based on her work at the Santa Fe Institute and drawing on its interdisciplinary strategies, Mitchell [attempts to] bring clarity to the workings of complexity across a . . . range of biological, technological, and social phenomena, seeking out the general principles or laws that apply to all of them. She explores as well the relationship between complexity and evolution, artificial intelligence, computation, genetics, information processing, and [other fields]." (Publisher's note) Bibliography. Index.

The author offers a "snapshot of the growing field of complex-systems science. . . . Mitchell explores the historical roots of this area in the work of visionaries such as Henri Poincaré and Edward Lorenz in dynamical-systems theory, and of John von Neumann, Alan Turing and others in computation. . . . The book hits its stride in its latter half, with an insightful survey of recent developments in complex-network theory and scaling in biology." Nature

Includes bibliographical references (p. 326-336)

Olson, Randy

★ **Don't** be such a scientist; talking substance in an age of style. Island Press 2009 206p il pa $19.95 **501**

1. College teachers 2. Communication 3. Communication in science 4. Marine biologists 5. Motion picture directors 6. Science 7. Science -- Study and teaching 8. Science in motion pictures
ISBN 978-1-59726-563-8; 1-59726-563-2

LC 2009-7081

The author argues "that 'scientists need artists.' He delves into the principle of 'arouse and fulfill,' suggesting that while scientists are great with the fulfillment part, the power of art can help arouse the interest of the broader audience." Publisher's note

Includes bibliographical references

Poe, Mya

Learning to communicate in science and engineering; case studies from MIT. [by] Mya Poe, Neal Lerner, and Jennifer Craig; foreword by James Paradis. MIT Press 2010 256p il $35 **501**

1. Communication 2. Engineering -- Study and teaching 3. Science -- Study and teaching 4. Writing
ISBN 978-0-262-16247-0

LC 2009-24788

"Case studies and pedagogical strategies to help science and engineering students improve their writing and speaking skills while developing professional identities." Barnes and Noble

Includes bibliographical references

Stannard, Russell

The **end** of discovery. Oxford University Press 2010 228p il $24.95 **501**

1. Physics 2. Science -- Philosophy 3. Theory of knowledge
ISBN 978-0-19-958524-3; 0-19-958524-5

LC 2010-930293

The author "believes that science will eventually come to an end, and that we are living in a 'transient age of human development' in which scientific discoveries can be made. But science won't end because we know everything; it will end because we know everything we can know. . . . [This is] a book worth reading. Lucid and provocative, it is a very polite corrective to both the superstitions of the layman . . . and the triumphalism of the experts." New Statesman

This will change everything; ideas that will shape the future. edited by John Brockman; [introduction by Daniel C. Dennett] HarperCollins 2010 xxiii, 390p pa $14.99 **501**

1. Forecasting 2. Science
ISBN 978-0-06-189967-6

"With contributions from Ian McEwan, Steven Pinker, Lee Smolin, Craig Venter, Richard Dawkins and 130 others of their ilk, the book is like an intellectual lucky dip." New Sci

502   Miscellany

Ochoa, George

The **Wilson** chronology of science and technology; [by] George Ochoa and Melinda Corey. Wilson, H.W. 1997 440p $105   **502**
1. Reference books 2. Science -- History 3. Technology -- History
ISBN 0-8242-0933-8

LC 97-22060

This chronology begins in 2,500,000 B.C. and continues into 1997. "Within each year, entries are arranged alphabetically according to one of 13 categories: archaeology; astronomy, space science, and space exploration; biology, biochemistry, agriculture, and ecology; chemistry; earth sciences (geology, oceanography, meteorology) and earth exploration; mathematics; medicine; miscellaneous; paleontology; physics; psychology, neuroscience, and artificial intelligence; social sciences (anthropology, sociology, economics, political science) and linguistics; and technology and engineering." Publisher's note
Includes bibliographical references

502.8   Auxiliary techniques and procedures; apparatus, equipment, materials

Instruments of science; an historical encyclopedia. editors, Robert Bud, Deborah Jean Warner; associate editor, Stephen Johnston; managing editor, Betsy Bahr Peterson; picture editor, Simon Chaplin. Garland 1998 xxv, 709p il $175   **502.8**
1. Reference books 2. Scientific apparatus and instruments -- Encyclopedias 3. Scientific apparatus and instruments -- History -- Encyclopedias
ISBN 0-8153-1561-9

LC 97-15296

This "encyclopedia presents 325 historically significant scientific instruments from antiquity to the present. Instruments used for testing and monitoring in addition to those used for research are studied, including laboratory organisms such as E coli. Each of the signed entries explains how the instrument works and how it is used, as well as tracing its invention, development, and distribution. . . . Beautiful illustrations accompany many of the entries." Am Libr
Includes bibliographical references

503   Dictionaries, encyclopedias, concordances

McGraw-Hill Publishing Company

McGraw-Hill concise encyclopedia of science & technology; 6th ed.; McGraw-Hill 2009 2v il map set $295   **503**
1. Reference books 2. Science -- Encyclopedias 3. Technology -- Encyclopedias
ISBN 978-0-07-161366-8

LC 2008-50987

This encyclopedia features over 7100 articles on branches of technology and science ranging from acoustics to zoology.

Trefil, James S.

The **nature** of science; an A-Z guide to the laws and principles governing our universe. {by} James Trefil. Houghton Mifflin 2003 xxx, 433p il $35 **503**
1. Reference books 2. Science -- Encyclopedias
ISBN 0-618-31938-7

LC 2002-27364

The author presents a "collection of the 200 most important scientific laws and principles governing our universe, from DNA, mimicry, and molecular clocks to the conservation of energy, quantum mechanics, Godel's incompleteness theorems, and the big bang. . . . Trefil has included a wonderful must-read introduction, biographies, pictures, diagrams, time lines, and anecdotes to provide human stories behind nature's laws. The comprehensive index, small glossary, and cross-disciplinary time-line provide good search help and historical relationships." Choice

Academic Press dictionary of science and technology; edited by Christopher Morris. Academic Press 1992 xxxii, 2432p il $99.95   **503**
1. Reference books 2. Science -- Dictionaries 3. Technology -- Dictionaries
ISBN 0-12-200400-0

LC 90-29032

"With over 133,000 entries, this title provides current, concise definitions of the specialized vocabulary used in 124 designated fields from acoustical engineering to zoology. . . . This authoritative, attractive dictionary will be useful to anyone seeking to understand the language of science and technology." Am Libr

★ The **American** Heritage science dictionary; [rev. ed]; Houghton Mifflin Harcourt 2008 695p il $21.95   **503**
1. Reference books 2. Science -- Dictionaries
ISBN 978-0-618-88274-8; 0-618-88274-X

LC 2008-276195

This science dictionary has 8,500 entries in all areas of science and includes biographical entries, cross-references, photographs, drawings, tables, and charts.

The **Encyclopedia** of science and technology; James S. Trefil, general editor; contributing editors, Harold Morowitz, Paul Ceruzzi. Routledge 2001 554p il maps $50   **503**
1. Reference books 2. Science 3. Science -- Encyclopedias 4. Technology 5. Technology -- Encyclopedias
ISBN 0-415-93724-8

LC 2001-19983

This reference includes "1000 entries, arranged alphabetically and color-coded to indicate whether the topic is related to life science, physical science, or technology. Accessible to the general reader, the articles range widely. . . . The excellent cross references direct the reader to related articles that cover either more fundamental or more advanced information. . . . A true pleasure to browse and read; highly recommended." Libr J
Includes bibliographical references and index

Encyclopedia of science, technology, and ethics; edited by Carl Mitcham. Macmillan Reference USA 2005 4v il map set $450   **503**
1. Reference books 2. Science -- Ethical aspects 3. Science -- Ethical aspects -- Encyclopedias 4. Technology -- Encyclopedias
ISBN 0-02-865831-0
LC 2005-6968
This "multivolume work on ethics provides a superb introduction to the issues presented." Booklist
Includes bibliographical references

Gale encyclopedia of science; K. Lee Lerner & Brenda Wilmoth Lerner, editors. 4th ed.; Thomson Gale 2008 6v il set $685   **503**
1. Reference books 2. Science -- Encyclopedias
ISBN 978-1-4144-2877-2; 1-4144-2877-4
LC 2006-37485
"From algae to zooplankton, assembly lines to Y2K, and from Agent Orange to weapons of mass destruction, this encyclopedia covers every aspect of the scientific world. . . . It is designed to 'instruct, challenge, and excite' a wide range of users and is a good starting point to answer any scientific question." Libr Media Connect
Includes bibliographical references

McGraw-Hill dictionary of scientific and technical terms; 6th ed; McGraw-Hill 2003 2380p il $150   **503**
1. Reference books 2. Science 3. Science -- Dictionaries 4. Technology 5. Technology -- Dictionaries
ISBN 0-07-042313-X
LC 2002-26436
"This continues to be the most comprehensive science and technology dictionary for the student, researcher, and layperson." Booklist

Van Nostrand's concise encyclopedia of science; Christopher G. De Pree, Alan Axelrod, editors; with a foreword by Glenn D. Considine. Wiley 2003 821p il $40   **503**
1. Engineering 2. Engineering -- Encyclopedias 3. Reference books 4. Science 5. Science -- Encyclopedias
ISBN 0-471-36331-6
LC 2002-34327
"This encyclopedia is a great resource for quick and short answers to many scientific questions. There are no references, so it is not a good conduit to further information, but if you need a book that will provide concise answers quickly, this is it." Sci Books Films
Includes bibliographical references

★ Van Nostrand's scientific encyclopedia; 10th ed.; Wiley 2008 3v il map set $450   **503**
1. Reference books 2. Science -- Encyclopedias
ISBN 978-0-471-74338-5
LC 2007-46658
This encyclopedia contains articles contains over 10,000 entries on topics such as biology, chemistry, earth science, mathematics and engineering, anatomy and physiology, physics, botany, and space science.

The new encyclopedia of science; 2nd ed; Oxford University Press 2003 9v il set $299   **503**
1. Reference books 2. Science 3. Science -- Encyclopedias 4. Science -- Encyclopedias, Juvenile
ISBN 0-19-521918-X
LC 2003-41937
This set "consists of nine volumes, eight of them devoted to a particular field of modern science: 'Matter and Energy,' 'Animals and Plants,' 'Chemistry in Action,' 'Stars and Atoms,' 'Earth and Other Planets,' 'Ecology and Environment,' 'Computing,' and 'Evolution and Genetics.' The set is intended for both general readers with quick questions and students interested in specific scientific topics. . . . The text is written for the less well informed reader and should be accessible to most. The layout is bright and appealing." Booklist

505 Serial publications

★ General science index. Wilson, H.W.   **505**
1. Reference books 2. Science -- Periodicals -- Indexes
"Cumulative subject index to English-language science journals covering 150 essential periodicals. Its accessible subject headings, extremely broad coverage, and identification of articles on current topics in widely owned periodicals are helpful for high school and college students and public library patrons alike." Ref Sources for Small and Medium-sized Libr. 6th edition

506 Organizations and management

Seeing further; the story of science, discovery, and the genius of the Royal Society. edited & introduced by Bill Bryson; contributing editor, Jon Turney. William Morrow 2010 506p il $35; ebook $21.99   **506**
1. Discoveries in science 2. Science 3. Science -- History
ISBN 978-0-06-199976-5; 978-0-06-203622-3 ebook
Bryson "presents a remarkable collection of essays celebrating the 350th anniversary of the founding of the Royal Society of London and its many contributions to science. Society members have included such illustrious names as Darwin, Newton, Leibniz, and Francis Bacon, to name a few. The volume's 23 contributors are both uniformly excellent and remarkable for their diversity." Publ Wkly
Includes bibliographical references (p. 486-489)

507.8 Use of apparatus and equipment in study and teaching

Johnson, George
The **ten** most beautiful experiments. Alfred A. Knopf 2008 192p il $22.95   **507.8**
1. Science -- Experiments 2. Science -- History
ISBN 978-1-4000-4101-5; 1-4000-4101-5
LC 2007-27839
"Writing up Luigi Galvani's study of frog's legs, James Joule's of heat, Albert Michelson's of light's speed, and Rob-

ert Millikan's of the electron's charge, Johnson exerts classic appeal to science readers: presenting the lone genius making a great discovery. Good to go in any library." Booklist

Includes bibliographical references

Sheldrake, Rupert

Seven experiments that could change the world; a do-it-yourself guide to revolutionary science. {2nd ed}; Park St. Press 2002 303p pa $16.95   **507.8**
1. Science -- Experiments 2. Science -- Experiments -- Popular works
ISBN 0-89281-989-8

                          LC 2002-728157

"Sheldrake questions many tenets of the mechanistic-materialistic orthodoxy governing most science today and proposes certain practical experiments to raise further doubts about it. He presents experiments by which we can determine how some pets know when their owners are coming home, how homing pigeons find their way, how insect colonies operate, how people know that they are being stared at from behind and how phantom limbs sometimes seem to amputees to be still attached. . . . Finally, he offers details of experiments by which even those who are not trained scientists can measure some of these possibly paranormal phenomena. A well-reasoned, accessible and provocative book." Publ Wkly

Includes bibliographical references (p. 284-296) and index

Experiment central; understanding scientific principles through projects. John T. Tanacredi & John Loret, general editors. U.X.L 2000 6v il set $347   **507.8**
1. Science -- Experiments
ISBN 1-4144-0522-7

                          LC 99-54142

Demonstrates scientific concepts by means of experiments, including step-by-step instructions, lists of materials, troubleshooter's guide, and interpretation and explanation of the results.

508   Natural history

Ackerman, Diane

Cultivating delight; a natural history of my garden. HarperCollins Pubs. 2001 261p hardcover o.p. pa $13.95   **508**
1. Gardens 2. Large print books 3. Natural history
ISBN 0-06-050536-2 pa

                        LC 2001-16607

Although Ackerman's "book is presented as a gardening journal, with sections on the four seasons, her musings know no bounds and verge on stream-of-consciousness. One typical chapter ranges over topics that include landscape architecture, lawns, fences, autumn colors, childhood memories, the difference between labyrinths and mazes, the history and definition of gardens, and compost, all peppered with quotations from a dozen authors." Libr J

Asma, Stephen T.

Stuffed animals & pickled heads; the culture and evolution of natural history museums. Oxford Univ. Press 2001 302p il hardcover o.p. pa $16.95 **508**
1. Museums 2. Natural history
ISBN 0-19-513050-2; 0-19-516336-2 pa

                        LC 00-40674

The author discusses the development of natural history museums, beginning with the "'cabinets of curiosities', put together in the 17th century. . . . The cabinets changed when Darwin's theory of evolution became widely accepted in the late 19th century, with less emphasis on the exceptional, more on showing how each species fitted into the supposed scheme of things." Economist

Includes bibliographical references

Carroll, Sean B.

Remarkable creatures; epic adventures in the search for the origins of species. Houghton Mifflin Harcourt 2009 331p il map $26; pa $14.95 **508**
1. Evolution 2. Evolution (Biology) -- History 3. Naturalists 4. Naturalists -- History
ISBN 978-0-15-101485-9; 0-15-101485-X; 978-0-547-24778-6 pa; 0-547-24778-8 pa

                        LC 2008-25438

"A stirring introduction to the wonder of evolutionary biology." Kirkus

Includes bibliographical references

Darwin, Charles

★ The **voyage** of the Beagle; journal of researches into the natural history and geology of the countries visited during the voyage of H.M.S. Beagle round the world. introduction by Steve Jones. Modern Lib. 2001 468p il pa $12.95   **508**
1. Natural history
ISBN 0-375-75680-9

                        LC 00-46294

This journal records the author's five year voyage around the world as a naturalist aboard H.M.S. Beagle. The trip was influential in the formulation of Darwin's theories of evolution. During the journey he collected data on wildlife, geological formations, weather, and local customs.

De Villiers, Marq

Sahara: a natural history; {by} Marq de Villiers and Sheila Hirtle. Walker & Co. 2002 326p il maps $28; pa $13   **508**
1. Natural history -- Africa 2. Natural history -- Sahara
ISBN 0-8027-1372-6; 0-8027-7678-7 pa

                        LC 2002-71391

"Insightful and intelligent, this fascinating book will appeal to anyone with a curiosity about the world's largest desert and the people who inhabit it." Booklist

Includes bibliographical references

Dunne, Pete

Bayshore summer; finding Eden in a most unlikely place. photographs by Linda Dunne. Houghton Mifflin Harcourt 2010 262p il $24   **508**
1. Authors 2. Bird watchers 3. Natural history -- New

Jersey 4. Outdoor life
ISBN 978-0-547-19563-6; 0-547-19563-X

LC 2009-27928

"This delightful book, written in the first person, introduces readers to the places that Pete Dunne loves in South Jersey along Delaware Bay. Each chapter relates a particular excursion of his and manages to include an ample amount of natural history, along with regional human history, environmental controversies, and appreciation of the local culture. . . . The book is written with an easygoing style and humor, presenting scientific information in an accessible form, along with local history and culture, with a dose of environmentalism and regret for the loss of the old ways of life for the local population thrown in." Sci Books Films
Includes bibliographical references

Flannery, Tim F.

The **eternal** frontier; an ecological history of North America and its peoples. {by} Tim Flannery. Atlantic Monthly Press 2001 404p il maps $27.50; pa $16 **508**
1. Ecology -- North America 2. Natural history -- North America
ISBN 0-87113-789-5; 0-8021-3888-8 pa

LC 2001-18841

"This book weaves ecological, cultural, and social history together in a marvelous way." Sci Books Films

Fothergill, Alastair

Planet Earth; as you've never seen it before. [by] Alastair Fothergill [et al.]; foreword by David Attenborough. University of California Press 2007 309p il map $39.95 **508**
1. Habitat (Ecology)
ISBN 978-0-520-25054-3; 0-520-25054-0

LC 2006-50073

In this collection of over 400 photographs of natural landscapes and wildlife, the author "takes readers on a kaleidoscopic tour of the flora, fauna and natural history of the Earth's poles, forests, plains, deserts, mountains and oceans." Publ Wkly

Gould, Stephen Jay

★ **Bully** for brontosaurus; reflections in natural history. Norton 1991 540p il hardcover o.p. pa $15.95 **508**
1. Evolution 2. Natural history
ISBN 0-393-30857-X pa

LC 91-6916

A collection of essays from the author's monthly columns in Natural History magazine
"These pithy essays focus on evolution and the workings of science. Gould's fans . . . will find these works fascinating, literate, and often challenging—vintage Gould." Libr J

Leonardo's mountain of clams and the Diet of Worms; essays on natural history. Harmony Bks. 1998 422p il hardcover o.p. pa $15 **508**
1. Evolution 2. Evolution (Biology) 3. Natural history
ISBN 0-609-80475-8 pa

LC 98-11500

"Gould's incomparable style, by turns colloquial, humorous, ironic and insightful, allows readers to revel in his unabashed and contagious enthusiasm." N Y Times Book Rev
Includes bibliographical references

The **lying** stones of Marrakesh; penultimate reflections to natural history. Harmony Bks. 2000 372p il hardcover o.p. pa $15 **508**
1. Evolution 2. Natural history
ISBN 0-609-80755-2 pa

LC 99-36148

In this collection of essays Gould "chronicles the history of paleontology through a biographical lens, then trains his scientific acumen and keen humor on such subjects as Mozart's Requiem and the tragic 1911 Triangle Shirt Factory fire." Booklist

★ The **richness** of life; the essential Stephen Jay Gould. edited by Paul McGarr and Steven Rose; with an introduction by Steven Rose and a foreword by Oliver Sacks. Norton 2007 654p il $35 **508**
1. Evolution 2. Natural history
ISBN 978-0-393-06498-8; 0-393-06498-0

LC 2006-29208

"For collections that have room for only one volume of his writing, this is the essential one." SLJ
Includes bibliographical references

Keynes, R. D.

Fossils, finches, and Fuegians; Darwin's adventures and discoveries on the Beagle. by Richard Keynes. Oxford Univ. Press 2003 428p il maps $35 **508**
1. Natural history 2. Naturalists 3. Travel writers 4. Writers on science
ISBN 0-19-516649-3

LC 2002-154176

"Keynes shows readers how his great-grandfather's belief in the immutability of species slowly began to change during his travels. Handsomely illustrated with sketches and paintings made by Darwin and others associated with the Beagle, this is an excellent introduction to the events that led 20 years later to On the Origin of Species." Publ Wkly
Includes bibliographical references

Kress, W. John

The **weeping** goldsmith; discoveries in the secret land of Myanmar. foreword by Wade Davis. Abbeville Press 2009 272p il map $45 **508**
1. Natural history -- Myanmar
ISBN 978-0-7892-1032-6

LC 2008-55031

"A visually stunning and involving chronicle of . . . Kress' daunting and revelatory explorations and discoveries in Myanmar, a land of beauty and tyranny, imperiled biodiversity and resilience." Booklist
Includes bibliographical references

Leopold, Aldo

A **Sand** County almanac; and sketches here and there. illustrated by Charles W. Schwartz; introduc-

tion by Robert Finch. Oxford Univ. Press 1987 xxviii, 228p il hardcover o.p. pa $9.95   **508**
   1. Natural history -- United States 2. Nature
conservation
   ISBN 0-19-505305-2; 0-19-505928-X pa
                        LC 87-22015
The essays in the first section of the book record natural
changes observed by the author on his Wisconsin farm during the course of a year. In the other two sections are personal experiences ranging over a wide expanse of country
and forty years in time.
   This "collection of poetic vignettes about run-down
farmland and wilderness trips, seasoned with erudite historical reflections . . . has added a significant ethical concept to
the prophecies of Thoreau, John Muir and other voices in the
wilderness." N Y Times Book Rev

Lincoln, Roger J.
   ★ The **Cambridge** illustrated dictionary of natural history; {by} R. J. Lincoln and G. A. Boxshall;
illustrations by Roberta Smith. Cambridge Univ.
Press 1987 413p il hardcover o.p. pa $29   **508**
   1. Natural history -- Dictionaries 2. Reference books
   ISBN 0-521-39941-6 pa
                        LC 87-8018
This "is principally a dictionary of taxonomic groups
down to the level of family, with common names cross-referenced to Latin ones, and frequent illustrations. Technical
terms are few, and paleontology is given less attention than
current classes of plants, animals, and microorganisms." Recomm Ref Books in Paperback. 2d edition

Matthiessen, Peter
   End of the earth; voyaging to Antarctica. Na-
tional Geographic Soc. 2003 242p il maps $26 **508**
   1. Animals -- Antarctica 2. Animals -- Antarctica --
Antarctic Peninsula 3. Emperor penguin -- Antarctica
-- Antarctic Peninsula
   ISBN 0-7922-5059-1
                        LC 2003-51254
This account of the author's voyage describes the wildlife he encountered in the region
   "Vivid and empathic accounts of the high drama and
petty rivalries of Antarctic exploration alternate with Matthiessen's own adventures as he shares his indelible impressions of this cold, white wonderland in the hope that they
will inspire readers to appreciate the beauty and bounty of
the earth's 'shimmering web of biodiversity' enough to defend and preserve it." Booklist
   Includes bibliographical references

Muir, John
   Nature writings; the story of my boyhood and
youth, my first summer in the Sierra, the mountains of
California, Stickeen, selected essays. Library of Am.
1997 888p il $35   **508**
   1. Authors 2. Natural history -- United States 3.
Naturalists 4. Writers on nature
   ISBN 1-88301-124-8
                        LC 96-9664
Muir "is at his best . . . when he is looking intently at
something, walking around it, sniffing the air, looking again.

As a writer he is a kind of visionary sensualist, a seer who
reveals what lies in plain sight." Commentary

Nicholls, Steve
   Paradise found; nature in America at the time of
discovery. University of Chicago Press 2009 524p
$30   **508**
   1. Human influence on nature 2. Natural history --
North America 3. Nature -- Effect of human beings on
-- North America
   ISBN 978-0-226-58340-2; 0-226-58340-6
                       LC 2008-36076
   The author "turns to the writings of forgotten early naturalists to gain understanding both of the natural abundance
of the New World when the first Europeans arrived and of
how so much of this living bounty was destroyed so quickly.
. . . Not only does Nicholls present arresting material, he also
offers fresh interpretations and connections in this grandly
spanning and affecting look to the past for guidance in facing a future of further diminishment." Booklist
   Includes bibliographical references and index

Quammen, David
   The **boilerplate** rhino; nature in the eye of the
beholder. Scribner 2000 287p hardcover o.p. pa
$13   **508**
   1. Natural history 2. Nature
   ISBN 0-7432-0032-2 pa
                        LC 99-56894
   In this "collection of David Quammen's columns for
Outside magazine, the focus is on man's interaction with
nature. Sometimes Quammen interacts with the nature he's
writing about; at other times he just thinks about it, reads
up and summarizes what he's read." N Y Times Book Rev
   Includes bibliographical references

Safina, Carl
   The **view** from Lazy Point; a natural year in an
unnatural world. with drawings by Trudy Nicholson;
maps by Jon Luoma. Henry Holt and Co. 2011 401p
il map $32; ebook $16.99   **508**
   1. Coastal ecology 2. Conservationists 3. Environmental
degradation 4. Human ecology 5. Human ecology --
Philosophy 6. Marine biologists 7. Marine ecology
   ISBN 978-0-8050-9040-6; 0-8050-9040-1; 978-1-
4299-5035-0 ebook; 1-4299-5035-8 ebook
                        LC 2009-40108
   A conservationist explores various global regions to
investigate examples of environmental degradation and renewal while identifying a link between environmental dangers and human rights issues.
   "A superb work of environmental reportage and
reflection." Kirkus
   Includes bibliographical references

Shetterly, Susan Hand
   Settled in the wild; notes from the edge of
town. Algonquin Books of Chapel Hill 2010 240p
$21.95   **508**
   1. Natural history -- Maine 2. Wildlife
   ISBN 1565126181; 9781565126183
                        LC 2009-30802

Shetterly "notes the interplay of humanity and wilderness through fishing, forestry, conservation, preservation, hunting, trapping, development and wildlife rehabilitation, but also in quiet, personal appreciation. Shetterly is a less verbose Thoreau, allowing nature's wisdom to seep through her simple yet thorough observations." Kirkus

Wallace, Joseph
A **gathering** of wonders; behind the scenes at the American Museum of Natural History. St. Martin's Press 2000 288p il $24.95; pa $14.95   **508**
1. Natural history
ISBN 0-312-25221-8; 0-312-28039-4 pa
LC 00-25481
This describes the American Museum of Natural History "through its most famous, colorful or important scientists and administrators, from the 1880s to the 1970s." Publ Wkly

Webster, Raymond B.
★ **African** American firsts in science and technology; foreword by Wesley L. Harris. Gale Group 1999 462p $80   **508**
1. African American inventors 2. Afro-American inventors -- Biography -- Juvenile literature 3. Afro-American scientists -- Biography -- Juvenile literature 4. Afro-Americans 5. Inventors 6. Scientists
ISBN 0-7876-3876-5
LC 99-27346
Presents capsule accounts of notable first achievements by African Americans, arranged in the categories "Agriculture and Everyday Life," "Dentistry and Nursing," "Life Science," "Math and Engineering," "Medicine," "Physical Science," and "Transportation."

Natural history; the ultimate visual guide to everything on Earth. [senior project editor, Kathryn Hennessy] DK 2010 648p il map $50   **508**
1. Natural history 2. Reference books
ISBN 978-0-7566-6752-8; 0-7566-6752-6
LC 2010-283659
"This is an international encyclopedia of life-forms—e.g., fossils, fungi, plants, animals, mammals—that includes vital facts and two to three sentences about each as well as more than 5000 color illustrations in all. Each grouping is introduced by an essay that puts it in biological and evolutionary perspective." Libr J

Nature writing; the tradition in English. edited by Robert Finch and John Elder. Norton 2002 1152p $39.95   **508**
1. Natural history 2. Natural history literature
ISBN 0-393-04966-3
LC 2001-55825
This anthology of nature writings from 1789 to 1987 includes such authors as Henry David Thoreau, John Muir, Annie Dillard, and Barry Lopez.

508.2   Seasons

Ackerman, Diane
Dawn light; dancing with cranes and other ways to start the day. W.W. Norton 2009 240p il $24.95   **508.2**
1. Authors 2. Environmental influence on humans 3. Essayists 4. Human beings -- Effect of environment on 5. Meditations 6. Memoirists 7. Nature 8. Nonfiction writers 9. Poets 10. Seasons 11. Writers on nature
ISBN 978-0-393-06173-4
LC 2009-23459
"This collection of essays is arranged seasonally from spring to winter and ranges geographically between Palm Beach, FL, and Ithaca, NY. Essays cover everything from the behavior of doves in Florida at dawn and Monet's use of light in his art to a discussion of festivals that take place at dawn and teaching young whooping cranes to migrate. . . . These pieces are accessible and lyrically written, and they flow well, one after another, making reading the book a true pleasure." Libr J

509   History, geographic treatment, biography

Adler, Robert E.
★ **Science** firsts: from the creation of science to the science of creation; [by] Robert Adler. Wiley 2002 232p il $24.95   **509**
1. Discoveries in science 2. Science -- History 3. Scientists
ISBN 0-471-40174-9
LC 2002-727233
The author tells the engaging and inspiring stories of thirty-five landmark scientific discoveries from the first accurate prediction of an eclipse in 585 B.C. to the cloning of Dolly the sheep.

Al-Khalili, Jim
The **house** of wisdom; how Arabic science saved ancient knowledge and gave us the Renaissance. Penguin Press 2011 xxix, 302p il map $29.95 **509**
1. Medieval civilization 2. Science -- Arab countries 3. Science -- Philosophy
ISBN 978-1-59420-279-7; 1-59420-279-6
LC 2010-53136
"There is a commonly held view that during the Middle Ages, Arabic scientists focused mainly on translating into Arabic the scientific knowledge of ancient civilizations while contributing little to scientific advancement. Physicist al-Khalili . . . challenges this theory by documenting the remarkable contributions of Arabic astronomers, mathematicians, physicians, physicists, chemists, and philosophers, who were scholars at a scientific academy in Baghdad known as the House of Wisdom. . . . Al-Khalili brings to life a vibrant intellectual period of Islamic history when there was not only tolerance for other religions and cultures but a synergy between science and Islam. Anyone interested in the early history of science or the development of the scientific method before Galileo will find this an engaging study." Libr J
Includes bibliographical references

Crease, Robert P.

The **great** equations; breakthroughs in science from Pythagoras to Heisenberg. W.W. Norton & Co. 2009 315p il $25.95 **509**

1. Equations 2. Science -- History 3. Science -- Philosophy

ISBN 978-0-393-06204-5; 0-393-06204-X

LC 2008-42494

The author "explores 10 rather beautiful equations. He begins with the beguiling simplicity of the equation that bears Pythagoras' name . . . and moves on to Newton's second law of motion and law of universal gravitation, the second law of thermodynamics, Maxwell's celebrated equations, discoveries by Einstein and Schrödinger and, finally, Heisenberg's famous uncertainty principle. . . . Any reader who aspires to be scientifically literate will find this a good starting place." Publ Wkly

Includes bibliographical references

The **prism** and the pendulum; the ten most beautiful experiments in science. Random House 2003 xxii, 244p il hardcover o.p. pa $14.95 **509**

1. Science -- Experiments 2. Science -- History

ISBN 1-400-06131-8; 0-8129-7062-4 pa

LC 2003-54765

Each scientific experiment discussed here "is followed by an 'interlude,' or commentary, on how the experiment qualifies as most beautiful and how art and science both give meaning to the term 'beauty.'" Sci Books Films

Dolnick, Edward

The **clockwork** universe; Isaac Newton, the Royal Society, and the birth of the modern world. HarperCollins 2011 378p il $27.99; ebook $23.99 **509**

1. Mathematicians 2. Physicists 3. Science 4. Scientists -- Great Britain -- History 5. Writers on science

ISBN 978-0-06-171951-6; 978-0-06-204226-2 ebook

LC 2010-24321

"Colorful, entertainingly written and nicely paced—a fine introductory text on Newton and the scientific revolution." Kirkus

Includes bibliographical references

Fara, Patricia

★ **Science**; a four thousand year history. Oxford University Press 2009 408p il map pa $18.95; $34.95 **509**

1. Science -- History 2. Science and civilization

ISBN 019922689X; 0199580278 pa; 9780199226894; 9780199580279 pa; 978-0-19-922689-4; 978-0-19-958027-9 pa; 0-19-958027-8 pa; 0-19-922689-X

LC 2008-50975

This "book explores how science has become so powerful by describing the financial interests and imperial ambitions behind its success. . . . [Fara challenges] notions of European superiority by emphasising the importance of scientific projects based around the world. . . . [This] volume challenges scientific supremacy itself, arguing that science is successful not because it is always indubitably right, but because people have said that it is right. Science dominates modern life, but perhaps the globe will be better off by limit-

ing science's powers and undoing some of its effects." (Publisher's note) Index.

"This survey of 4,000 years of scientific discovery from Babylon to the present confirms that historians of science often have quite different perspectives from those of the actual practitioners. . . . Readers learn about the contributions of famous scientists as though they were almost puppets responding to religious, social, and practical influences in both their choices of research topics and their methods of investigation—in contrast to their possessing an inherent desire to better understand the behavior of nature. In this highly readable book that tells a magnificent story, Fara . . . weaves together the bits and pieces in a unique way." Choice

Includes bibliographical references

Flowers, Charles

★ **Instability** rules; the ten most amazing ideas of modern science. Wiley 2002 228p $24.95 **509**

1. Astronomers 2. Biochemists 3. College teachers 4. Geneticists 5. Geophysicists 6. Mathematicians 7. Meteorologists 8. Molecular biologists 9. Nobel laureates for physics 10. Nobel laureates for physiology or medicine 11. Physicists 12. Psychoanalysts 13. Science -- History 14. Science -- Popular works 15. Writers on medicine

ISBN 0-471-38042-3

LC 2001-6729

Green, Bill

Boltzmann's tomb; travels in search of science. Bellevue Literary Press 2011 208p il **509**

1. College deans 2. College teachers 3. Discoveries in science 4. Religious scholars 5. Scientists 6. Voyages and travels

ISBN 1-934137-35-9; 978-1-934137-35-2

This book discusses Green's visits to "the workplaces and graves of . . . famous scientists whose lives and research were affected in some way by unpredicted events." (Sci Books Films) Index.

"This book is very readable and should be especially appealing to young people contemplating a life in science." Sci Books Films

Gribbin, John R.

The **fellowship**; Gilbert, Bacon, Harvey, Wren, Newton, and the story of a scientific revolution. [by] John Gribbin. Overlook Press 2007 335p il $29.95 **509**

1. Scientists

ISBN 1-58567-831-7; 978-1-58567-831-0

LC 2008-530551

"Gribbin is an ideal and entertaining narrator for this lively story of intellectual discovery and brotherhood." Publ Wkly

Includes bibliographical references

The **scientists**; a history of science told through the lives of its greatest inventors. [by] John Gribbin.

Random House 2003 xxii, 646p il hardcover o.p.
pa $16.95 **509**
1. Science -- History 2. Scientists
ISBN 1-4000-6013-3; 0-8129-6788-7 pa
LC 2003-46607
"Replete with scientific clarity, Gribbin's work is the
epitome of what a general-interest history of science should
be." Booklist
Includes bibliographical references

Hofstadter, Dan
The **Earth** moves; Galileo and the Roman Inqui-
sition. W.W. Norton 2009 240p il **509**
1. Astronomers 2. Astronomy 3. Astronomy --
Religious aspects -- Christianity 4. Catholic Church --
Doctrines -- History -- 17th century 5. Catholic Church
-- Italy -- History 6. Inquisition 7. Inquisition -- Italy 8.
Popes 9. Science, Renaissance 10. Writers on science
ISBN 0-393-06650-9; 978-0-393-06650-0
LC 2009-4325
This book examines the Inquisition in relation to Gali-
leo's arrest, trial, conviction, and the legal processes in-
volved. Bibliography. Index.
This book "allows a clear understanding of one of the
major events in the history of science." Sci Books Films
Includes bibliographical references

Holmes, Richard
★ The **age** of wonder; how the romantic generation discovered the beauty and terror of science. Pantheon Books 2009 xxi, 552p il $40; pa $17.95 **509**
1. Science -- Great Britain -- History
ISBN 978-0-375-42222-5; 978-1-4000-3187-0 pa
LC 2008-49587
"In this big two-hearted river of a book, the twin energies of scientific curiosity and poetic invention pulsate on
every page." N Y Times Book Rev
Includes bibliographical references

Horvitz, Leslie Alan
Eureka!: scientific breakthroughs that changed
the world. Wiley 2002 246p il $24.95 **509**
1. Biochemists 2. Broadcasting engineers 3. Chemists
4. Clergy 5. College teachers 6. Discoveries in science
7. Geophysicists 8. Inventors 9. Mathematicians
10. Mathematics teachers 11. Meteorologists
12. Microbiologists 13. Molecular biologists 14.
Naturalists 15. Nobel laureates for physics 16. Nobel
laureates for physiology or medicine 17. Physicists 18.
Science -- History 19. Travel writers 20. Writers on
medicine 21. Writers on science
ISBN 0-471-40276-1
LC 2001-46890
This examines twelve scientific discoveries and their
discoverers, including Joseph Priestley and oxygen, Friedrich Kekulé and the structure of carbon compounds, Dmitri
Mendeleev and the periodic table, Isaac Newton and grav-
ity, Einstein and the theory of relativity, Philo Farnsworth
and television, Alexander Fleming and penicillin, Charles
Townes and the laser, Alfred Wegener and continental drift,
Darwin and the origin of species, Watson and Crick and the
double helix, and Benoit Mandelbrot and fractal geometry.

Jardine, Lisa
Ingenious pursuits; building the scientific revolution. Talese 1999 444p il hardcover o.p. pa
$16 **509**
1. Science -- History 2. Science, Renaissance
ISBN 0-385-72001-7 pa
LC 99-41985
In this history of science in the 17th and early 18th centuries the author "chronicles improvements in the tools of
observation (telescopes, microscopes) and measurement
(clocks) that were used by a pungent cast of characters who
collaborated and squabbled with one another as they sorted
out comets and discovered microbes." New Yorker
Includes bibliographical references

Lightman, Alan P.
★ The **discoveries**; great breakthroughs in 20th
century science. [by] Alan Lightman. Pantheon
Books 2005 553p il $32.50; pa $16.95 **509**
1. Discoveries in science -- History -- 20th century 2.
Science -- Historiography 3. Science -- History 4.
Science -- History -- Sources
ISBN 0-375-42168-8; 0-375-71345-X pa
LC 2005-40854
This book "chronicles 25 landmark findings in astron-
omy, physics, chemistry, and biology in the 20th century.
Beginning with Max Planck's quantum theory and ending
with Paul Berg's recombinant DNA, these breakthroughs are
academically and playfully explored via the nature of the un-
known, the circumstances and influences of discovery, and,
most originally, the actual words of the scientists." Libr J
Includes bibliographical references

Piel, Gerard
The **age** of science; what scientists learned in
the 20th century. with illustrations by Peter Bradford.
Basic Bks. 2001 xx, 460p il maps $40 **509**
1. Science -- History 2. Science -- History -- 20th
century
ISBN 0-465-05755-1
LC 2001-43178
This "survey explores quantum mechanics, subatomic
particles, astrophysics, genetics, cell biology, planetary
geology, and evolution. . . . While it generally succeeds in
making science intelligible to the lay reader, this book is still
challenging if rewarding." Libr J
Includes bibliographical references

Reynolds, Moira Davison
American women scientists; 23 inspiring biographies, 1900-2000. McFarland & Co. 1999 149p il
hardcover o.p. pa $24.95 **509**
1. Women scientists 2. Women scientists -- United
States 3. Women scientists -- United States -- History
-- 20th century
ISBN 0-7864-0649-6; 0-7864-2161-4 pa
LC 99-14603
"Four-to-six page profiles of 23 of the century's premier women scientists, representing a wide variety of disciplines. The entries are arranged chronologically beginning
with Cornelia Clapp (1849-1934) and ending with Mary

Good (1931-). . . . Each entry includes a black-and-white portrait." SLJ

Includes bibliographical references

Snyder, Laura J.

The **philosophical** breakfast club; four remarkable friends who transformed science and changed the world. Broadway Books 2011 439p il map $27; ebook $27   **509**

1. Astronomers 2. Clergy 3. Economists 4. Mathematicians 5. Philosophers 6. Photographers 7. Science -- Philosophy 8. Scientists 9. Scientists -- Great Britain -- History 10. Writers on science

ISBN 978-0-7679-3048-2; 978-0-7679-3048-2 ebook

LC 2010-25790

This book "gives a unique view of the background and times in which these men lived, and a peek at the implications that their work and philosophy had on today's modern science." Sci Books Films

Includes bibliographical references

Teresi, Dick

Lost discoveries; the ancient roots of modern science, from the Babylonians to the Maya. Simon & Schuster 2002 453p il $27; pa $15   **509**

1. Ancient civilization 2. Science -- History 3. Science, Ancient

ISBN 0-684-83718-8; 0-7432-4379-X pa

LC 2002-75457

"Teresi offers a great deal of fascinating material largely ignored by many histories of science." Publ Wkly

Includes bibliographical references

Walker, Mark

Nazi science; myth, truth, and the German atomic bomb. Perseus 2001 325p il pa $22.50   **509**

1. Atomic bomb 2. National socialism 3. Science -- Germany

ISBN 0-7382-0585-0; 978-0-7382-0585-4

"Although scholarly, this will be accessible to general readers." Libr J

Includes bibliographical references

Whitfield, Peter

Landmarks in western science; from prehistory to the atomic age. Routledge 1999 256p il $65 **509**

1. Science -- History

ISBN 0-415-92533-9

LC 99-24976

This survey "highlights significant discoveries and turning points in mathematics, astronomy, physics, medicine, geology, and many other fields." Publisher's note

Includes bibliographical references

The Chronology of science; from Stonehenge to the human genome project. consulting editor, Lisa Rosner. ABC-CLIO 2002 566p $85   **509**

1. Science -- History 2. Scientists

ISBN 1-57607-954-6

LC 2001-7692

The chronologies are "divided into subject areas, including astronomy, biology, chemistry, ecology, mathematics,

and physics; 16 feature essays on critical scientific discoveries . . . [are included as well as] biographies of key scientists." Publisher's note

Includes bibliographical references

Encyclopedia of the scientific revolution; from Copernicus to Newton. editor Wilbur Applebaum. Garland 2000 xxxv, 758p il $160   **509**

1. Reference books 2. Science -- Europe -- History -- 16th century 3. Science -- Europe -- History -- 17th century 4. Science -- History -- Encyclopedias

ISBN 0-8153-1503-1

LC 00-25149

A "collection of articles on the progress of scientific discovery in the 16th and 17th centuries. . . . The 437 entries vary in length from just half a page to five pages, and each has a short bibliography directing the reader to recent articles and monographs as well as primary sources." Libr J

Includes bibliographical references

The History of science in the United States; an encyclopedia. edited by Marc Rothenberg. Garland 2000 xx, 615p $160   **509**

1. Reference books 2. Science -- History -- Encyclopedias 3. Science -- United States -- History

ISBN 0-8153-0762-4

LC 99-43757

"This book will become a standard reference and belongs in every high school, college, and public library." Sci Books Films

Includes bibliographical references

Notable black American scientists; Kristine M. Krapp, editor. Gale Res. 1999 xxvi, 349p il $125   **509**

1. African American scientists -- United States -- Biography -- Dictionaries 2. African Americans -- Biography -- Dictionaries 3. Reference books 4. Scientists -- Dictionaries

ISBN 0-7876-2789-5

LC 98-36338

The "contributors to this compilation of 254 bibliographic profiles emphasize the achievements of black scientists and physicians, men and women, from Colonial times to the present, in the territory that is now the US. . . . Each entry begins with basic information about each subject— name, year of birth and death (if deceased), and specialty. A biographical essay follows." Choice

Includes bibliographical references

★ The Oxford companion to the history of modern science; editor in chief, J.L. Heilbron; editors, James Bartholomew {et al.} Oxford Univ. Press 2003 xxviii, 941p il $110   **509**

1. Science -- History

ISBN 0-19-511229-6

LC 2002-153783

This reference on the history of science from the Renaissance through the 20th century includes some 600 articles covering "a broad spectrum of topics in all scientific disciplines (e.g., biotechnology, geology) as well as disciplines that influenced science, such as religion and politics. Also included are the biographies of 100 leading figures (e.g., Isaac Newton, Marie Curie) and coverage of scientific instruments (e.g., microscopes, Geiger counters). Organized alphabetically, the well-written articles include plenty of cross references. Over 100 black-and-white illustrations appear within their appropriate articles, but the eight pages of color illustrations in the middle of the volume are not associated with any article." Libr J

Includes bibliographical references

Reader's guide to the history of science; edited by Arne Hessenbruch. Fitzroy Dearborn Pubs. 2000 xxix, 934p $135 **509**
1. Reference books 2. Science 3. Science -- History -- Encyclopedias
ISBN 1-884964-29-X

LC 2001-270888

"This volume contains about 600 entries on various aspects of the history of science, including individuals (e.g., Galileo), disciplines (e.g., astronomy), and broad topics (e.g., religion)." Libr J

Includes bibliographical references

Science and its times; understanding the social significance of scientific discovery. Neil Schlager, editor; Josh Lauer, associate editor. Gale Group 2000 8v set $625 **509**
1. Science -- History
ISBN 0-7876-3932-X

LC 00-37542

This set addresses "a wide variety of scientific developments with explanations of underlying factors and their effects on politics, economics, culture and daily life. [It includes] more than 20 topical essays, 25 full biographies and 85 sketches of notable people in each volume." Publisher's note

510   Mathematics

Adam, John A.
★ A **mathematical** nature walk. Princeton University Press 2009 248p il $27.95 **510**
1. Mathematical analysis 2. Mathematics 3. Mathematics in nature
ISBN 978-0-691-12895-5; 0-691-12895-2

LC 2008-44828

"The general reader will find here a remarkably lucid explanation of how mathematicians create a formulaic model that mimics the key features of some natural phenomenon. . . . Ordinary math becomes adventure." Booklist

Includes bibliographical references

Barrow, John D.
100 essential things you didn't know you didn't know; math explains your world. W.W. Norton & Co. 2009 284p il $25.95; pa $15.95 **510**
1. Mathematics
ISBN 978-0-393-07007-1; 978-0-393-33867-6 pa

LC 2008-55910

"For those who find something mysterious and intriguing in solving an equation, this collection is a fascinating

look into the mind of a professional mathematician and the way in which math can be not simply a row of numbers but a way of looking at the world." SLJ

Includes bibliographical references

Blastland, Michael
★ The **numbers** game; the commonsense guide to understanding numbers in the news, in politics, and in life. [by] Michael Blastland and Andrew Dilnot. Gotham Books 2009 210p il $22 **510**
1. Mathematics 2. Number concept 3. Statistics
ISBN 978-1-59240-423-0; 1-59240-423-5

LC 2008-30130

The authors "embark on a monumental task of interpreting numerical data and showing how its misinterpretation often leads to misinformation. . . . The authors take a close look at statistics that are accepted at face value—many stemming from scientific or medical discoveries." Publ Wkly

Includes bibliographical references

Boyer, Carl B.
A **history** of mathematics; [by] Carl B. Boyer and Uta Merzbach. 3rd ed.; Wiley 2010 xx, 668p il pa $39.95 **510**
1. Mathematics -- History
ISBN 978-0-470-52548-7

LC 2010-3424

"This good general history of mathematics is understandable to the student as well as authoritative for the mathematician." Malinowsky. Best Sci & Technol Ref Books for Young People

Includes bibliographical references

Chemical Rubber Company
★ **CRC** standard mathematical tables and formulae; [editor-in-chief,] Daniel Zwillinger. 31st ed.; CRC Press 2003 910p il $59.95 **510**
1. Mathematics -- Tables
ISBN 1-58488-291-3

"This standard mathematical handbook contains both textual and tabular material. The contents include constants and conversion factors; algebra; combinatorial analysis; geometry; trigonometry; logarithmic, exponential, and hyperbolic functions; analytical geometry; calculus; differential equations; special functions; numerical methods; probability and statistics; and financial tables." Malinowsky. Best Sci & Technol Ref Books for Young People

Includes bibliographical references

Cusick, Thomas W.
Mathematics made simple; 6th ed; Broadway Books 2003 281p il pa $12.95 **510**
1. Mathematics
ISBN 978-0-7679-1538-0; 0-7679-1538-0

LC 2003-41923

"This book serves as a review of arithmetic, and an introduction to algebra, geometry, and trigonometry. Combinations and permutations are covered . . . in the Probability chapter. The exercises and answers in this book provide readers with opportunities to test their mastery of each step in these common branches of mathematics." Introduction

Darling, David J.

The **universal** book of mathematics; from Abracadabra to Zeno's paradoxes. [by] David Darling. Wiley 2004 383p il $40 **510**

1. Mathematics -- Encyclopedias 2. Reference books

ISBN 0-471-27047-4

LC 2003-24670

"The book's entries include numerous mathematical terms, brief biographies of mathematicians from ancient times to the present, and famous mathematical problems (both solved and unsolved), as well as problems and puzzles of a more recreational nature. It is a spirit of whimsy, the fanciful, and the outrageous that makes this book much more than a dry encyclopedia of mathematical terms, however. Darling's writing style and choice of entries make this an easy book to pick up and page through." Choice

Includes bibliographical references

Devlin, Keith J.

The **math** gene; how mathematical thinking evolved and why numbers are like gossip. {by} Keith Devlin. Basic Bks. 2000 328p il hardcover o.p. pa $17 **510**

1. Mathematics 2. Number concept

ISBN 0-465-01619-7 pa

LC 2001-520984

"Is the human brain hardwired for mathematical thinking? Just as we have an instinct for language acquisition, Devlin argues that we also possess an innate ability for logical and algorithmic reasoning. This book is an eye-opener for all math phobics." Libr J

Includes bibliographical references

Dewdney, A. K.

200 [percent] of nothing; an eye-opening tour through the twists and turns of math abuse and innumeracy. Wiley 1993 182p il hardcover o.p. pa $15.95 **510**

1. Mathematics

ISBN 0-471-57776-6; 0-471-14574-2 pa

LC 92-42173

The author discusses the media abuse of numbers "as well as 'percentage pumping,' 'irrational ratios,' 'compound blindness,' 'filtering,' and 'dimensional dementia.'" Libr J

Includes bibliographical references

A **mathematical** mystery tour; discovering the truth and beauty of the cosmos. Wiley 1999 218p il $22.95; pa $15.95 **510**

1. Mathematics 2. Mathematics -- History

ISBN 0-471-23847-3; 0-471-40734-8 pa

LC 98-36470

Dewdney "addresses two closely related, long-pondered questions. Why is mathematics so uncannily effective in describing the physical universe? Is 'new' mathematics invented, or is it a preexisting something that is discovered?. . . He explores these fundamental questions via discussions of the mathematical work of Pythagoras, the medieval Arab mathematicians, modern theoretical physicists, and modern mathematicians." Libr J

Dunham, William

The **mathematical** universe; an alphabetical journey through the great proofs, problems, and personalities. Wiley 1994 314p il hardcover o.p. pa $19.95 **510**

1. Mathematicians 2. Mathematics 3. Mathematics -- History

ISBN 0-471-17661-3 pa

LC 93-46702

In this history of mathematics, "Dunham sheds light not only on the personalities—eccentric, vain, brilliant—of major mathematicians, but also on contemporary social issues, such as multiculturalism and gender equity. Readers who want to understand the cultural significance of mathematics would do well to begin with this book." Booklist

Includes bibliographical references

Glazer, Evan

★ **Real**-life math; everyday use of mathematical concepts. [by] Evan M. Glazer and John W. McConnell. Greenwood Press 2002 165p il $49.95 **510**

1. Mathematics

ISBN 0-313-31998-7

LC 2001-58635

The authors "have written this book as a reply to students' complaints that they'll never use the mathematical concepts they're being taught. They look at dozens of mathematical concepts and . . . show how these math ideas relate to the world in which students live. . . . The book is thorough and accurate." Libr Media Connect

Includes bibliographical references

Huber, Michael R.

Mythematics; solving the twelve labors of Hercules. Princeton University Press 2009 183p il $24.95 **510**

1. Hercules (Legendary character) 2. Problem solving

ISBN 978-0-691-13575-5

LC 2009-8535

The author takes the ancient Greeks' "early interest in puzzles and the descriptions of Hercules' various labors and reinterpreted each of those labors in terms of several 'tasks,' after which he gives a 'solution' to the mathematical problem(s) implicit in each of the tasks. . . . Given that we tend to think of early Greek mathematics in terms of geometry or, possibly, number theory, the breadth of mathematics required for the various tasks may be surprising." Sci Books Films

Includes bibliographical references

Kanigel, Robert

The **man** who knew infinity; a life of the genius Ramanujan. Washington Sq. Press 1992 438p map il pa $15 **510**

1. Mathematicians

ISBN 0-671-75061-5; 978-0-671-75061-9

LC 91-37763

"Kanigel deserves high praise for a work of arduous research and rare insight." Booklist

Includes bibliographical references

Livio, Mario

Is God a mathematician? Simon & Schuster 2009 308p il $26 **510**

1. Logic, Symbolic and mathematical 2. Mathematicians -- Psychology 3. Mathematics -- Philosophy 4. Symbolic logic

ISBN 978-0-7432-9405-8; 0-7432-9405-X

LC 2008-45850

Livio "provides apt quotations and helpful explanations within an enjoyable narrative. This is a good popularization of some decidedly nontrivial questions." Libr J

Includes bibliographical references

Mahajan, Sanjoy

Street-fighting mathematics; the art of educated guessing and opportunistic problem solving. MIT Press 2010 134p il pa $25 **510**

1. Approximate computation 2. Problem solving

ISBN 978-0-262-51429-3; 0-262-51429-X

LC 2009-28867

The author argues that the key to solving complex arithmetic questions "lies in having informal tools on hand that let us attack the problem. Though the result may not be perfectly precise, he believes, intuitive mathematical reasoning is often sufficient for our needs. . . . [The book] is not organized around traditional math topics, such as differential equations, but ways of thinking: reasoning by analogy, visualizing geometric problems, and more. Readers can then answer all manner of questions: Guessing the number of babies in the United States, calculating the bond angles in methane, or determining the drag that air exerts on a 747." Dr. Dobb's

Includes bibliographical references

Pasles, Paul C.

Benjamin Franklin's numbers; an unsung mathematical odyssey. Princeton University Press 2008 254p il $26.95 **510**

1. Authors 2. Diplomats 3. Inventors 4. Mathematics 5. Members of Congress 6. Scientists 7. Statesmen 8. Writers on science

ISBN 978-0-691-12956-3; 0-691-12956-8

LC 2006-102508

The author "documents the famous scientist-statesman's lively interest in numerical enigmas, most particularly those known as Magic Squares. . . . An unexpected but welcome perspective on the genial genius of Philadelphia." Booklist

Includes bibliographical references

Paulos, John Allen

Beyond numeracy; ruminations of a numbers man. Knopf 1991 285p il hardcover o.p. pa $14 **510**

1. Mathematics 2. Mathematics -- Dictionaries

ISBN 0-679-73807-X pa

LC 90-44999

"This well-written and easy-to-follow book gently guides readers through many interesting mathematical topics." SLJ

Includes bibliographical references

A **mathematician** reads the newspaper. Anchor Books 1996 212p il pa $13.95 **510**

1. Mathematics

ISBN 0-385-48254-X

LC 95-46049

The author uses newspaper features "as vehicles for explaining mathematical concepts and how they figure in the business of being a well-informed citizen. For instance, he uses stories on the economy to illustrate prediction, regression analysis, statistics, and game theory and how those tools are used to both illuminate and obfuscate underlying truth." Booklist

Includes bibliographical references

Pickover, Clifford A.

The **math** book; from Pythagoras to the 57th dimension, 250 milestones in the history of mathematics. Sterling Pub. 2009 527p $29.95 **510**

1. Mathematics -- History

ISBN 978-1-4027-5796-9

LC 2008-43214

"Pickover's love of mathematics shines through the text and images, and it is likely that the reader will catch at least some of his enthusiasm." Choice

Includes bibliographical references

Rudman, Peter Strom

The **Babylonian** theorem; the mathematical journey to Pythagoras and Euclid. [by] Peter S. Rudman. Prometheus Books 2010 248p il $26 **510**

1. Mathematicians 2. Mathematics -- History 3. Mathematics, Ancient 4. Mathematics, Babylonian 5. Mathematics, Egyptian 6. Philosophers 7. Writers on science

ISBN 978-1-59102-773-7; 1-59102-773-X

LC 2009-39196

"Topics covered include Pythagorean triplets, . . . similar triangles, square-root calculations, and calculations of the volume of a pyramid. . . . This is a well-researched volume on what forms of mathematics existed when similar ideas developed again and again in different cultures. The book's numerous mathematical equations would delight any math student." Sci Books Films

Includes bibliographical references

Seife, Charles

★ **Proofiness**; the dark arts of mathematical deception. Viking 2010 295p il map $25.95 **510**

1. Mathematics 2. Mathematics -- Social aspects 3. Pseudoscience

ISBN 978-0-670-02216-8

LC 2010-12127

The author "examines the many ways that people fudge with numbers, sometimes just to sell more moisturizer but also to ruin our economy, rig our elections, convict the innocent and undercount the needy. . . . [This book] reveals the truly corrosive effects on a society awash in numerical mendacity. This is more than a math book; it's an eye-opening civics lesson." N Y Times Book Rev

Includes bibliographical references

Stewart, Ian

The **magical** maze; seeing the world through mathematical eyes. Wiley 1998 268p il $24.95; pa $16.95 **510**

1. Mathematical recreations 2. Mathematics
ISBN 0-471-19297-X; 0-471-35065-6 pa

LC 98-13185

Stewart presents various mathematical puzzles and problems through the metaphorical structure of a maze.

Chapters "contain good discussions of such topics as modular arithmetic, Marilyn vos Savant's Monty-Hall problem, depth-first and other search strategies, static and dynamic symmetry, Turing machines, optimization, fractals, and chaos. This is an excellent mix of topics and the material is very much up-to-date." Choice

Szpiro, George G.

Numbers rule; the vexing mathematics of democracy from Plato to the present. Princeton University Press 2010 226p **510**

1. Democracy -- History 2. Mathematics 3. Voting
ISBN 978-0-691-13994-4

LC 2009-28615

Szpiro "traces the quest of philosophers, statesmen and mathematicians throughout history to create a more perfect democracy and adapt to the ever-changing demands of each new generation by analyzing the mathematical anomalies in voting results." (Publisher's note) Index,

The author "presents a refreshingly different presentation of the mathematics of voting and apportionment. Topics are organized chronologically, and historical contexts are presented in an engaging way. Unlike mathematics textbooks, the book reads like a collection of stories describing the origin of many mathematical ideas. The mathematical content is not trivial, and it is well written, very clear, and should be accessible to readers with an understanding of arithmetic and a willingness to play with numbers." Choice

Includes bibliographical references

Poincare's prize; the hundred-year quest to solve one of math's greatest puzzles. Dutton 2007 309p $24.95 **510**

1. Mathematicians 2. Mathematics
ISBN 978-0-525-95024-0; 0-525-95024-9

LC 2007-12792

The author "recounts the story of how a geometrical puzzle worthy of the most voracious sphinx finally yielded to an eccentric Russian genius who has since refused the honors and million-dollar prize proffered by an astonished world. The mathematical puzzle, readers learn, originated with the French polymath Henri Poincaré, whose revolutionary topology generated a tantalizing conjecture about how multidimensional bodies might all be transformed into spheres. . . . Never has mathematics provided more fascinating human drama!" Booklist

Includes bibliographical references

Tanton, James S.

★ **Encyclopedia** of mathematics; [by] James Tanton. Facts on File 2005 568p il $75 **510**

1. Mathematics -- Encyclopedias 2. Reference books
ISBN 0-8160-5124-0

LC 2004-16785

This encyclopedia "offers more than 800 entries from abacus and compound interest to Bertrand Russell and vector along with essays on the history and evolution of equations and algebra, calculus, functions, geometry, probability and statistics, and trigonometry." SLJ

Includes bibliographical references

Tobias, Sheila

Overcoming math anxiety; rev and expanded; Norton 1993 260p il $23; pa $14.95 **510**

1. Mathematics
ISBN 0-393-03577-8; 0-393-31307-7 pa

LC 93-3648

The author explains common misconceptions about mathematical concepts, analyzes what makes math seem difficult, discusses alleged sex differences in brain function in relation to math, and describes math programs aimed at women

★ A **Dictionary** of quotations in mathematics; compiled and edited by Robert A. Nowlan. McFarland & Co. 2002 314p pa $45 **510**

1. Mathematics -- Quotations 2. Mathematics -- Quotations, maxims, etc 3. Quotations
ISBN 0-7864-1284-4

LC 2002-5268

"For anyone writing a term paper, professional paper, or giving a presentation, whether in mathematics, science, or a related discipline, this reference will be a useful resource. For the rest of us, this book is a delightful read all by itself." Am Ref Books Annu, 2003

Includes bibliographical references

God created the integers; the mathematical breakthroughs that changed history. edited and with commentary by Stephen Hawking. Running Pr. 2005 1160p il $29.95; pa $21.95 **510**

1. Biography, Collective 2. Mathematicians 3. Mathematicians -- Biography 4. Mathematics 5. Mathematics -- History
ISBN 0-7624-1922-9; 978-0-7624-1922-7; 0-7624-3004-4 pa; 978-0-7624-3004-8 pa

LC 2005-924493

This "is a wonderful resource providing insight into both the mathematics and the personalities involved." Sci Books Films

Includes bibliographical references

Sherlock Holmes in Babylon; and other tales of mathematical history. edited by Marlow Anderson, Victor Katz, Robin Wilson. Mathematical Association of America 2004 387p il maps $51.95 **510**

1. Mathematics -- History

ISBN 0-88385-546-1

LC 2003-113541

This "is a compilation of journal articles written by various mathematical historians and published by the Mathematical Association of America over the past 100 years. The stories deal with many important and fundamental topics from ancient up through 18th-century mathematics. The papers are all self-contained, so the reader with some degree of mathematical maturity can jump around in the book." Sci Books Films

Includes bibliographical references

511   General principles of mathematics

Berlinski, David

The **advent** of the algorithm; the idea that rules the world. Harcourt 2000 345p $28; pa $14 **511**

1. Algorithms

ISBN 0-15-100338-6; 0-15-601391-6 pa

LC 98-43755

Berlinski "chronicles the discovery of algorithms, the codes that control computers, vividly profiling the key thinkers involved. He also identifies the hidden sources of the algorithm's power as a calculating tool, and exposes its defects as a scientific metaphor for explaining the human intellect." Booklist

Includes bibliographical references

Kaplan, Robert

The **nothing** that is; a natural history of zero. illustrations by Ellen Kaplan. Oxford Univ. Press 2000 225p $40; pa $11.95 **511**

1. Zero (The number)

ISBN 0-19-512842-7; 0-19-514237-3 pa

LC 99-29000

"Kaplan presents cultural, philosophical, historical, and mathematical developments that either encouraged or discouraged the recognition of the role of zero in counting and computation." Sci Books Films

Michael, T. S.

How to guard an art gallery and other discrete mathematical adventures. Johns Hopkins University Press 2009 257p il $60; pa $25 **511**

1. Algorithms 2. Computer science 3. Mathematical analysis

ISBN 978-0-8018-9298-1; 0-8018-9298-8; 978-0-8018-9299-8 pa; 0-8018-9299-6 pa

LC 2009-00435

"The time-honored story problem, central to mathematics and an expression of its fascination or frustration (depending on the student's success), is the protagonist of this delightful work on discrete mathematics. Written for . . . [readers with a knowledge of] algebra and geometry, the text contains 7 chapters, each one devoted to a different story problem and its variations. Pick's formula, art gallery problems, quadratic residues of primes and squares, and stamps and coins and Sylvester's formula are some of the problems

presented, with each chapter consisting of a group of problems of increasing difficulty." Sci Tech Book News

Includes bibliographical references

Seife, Charles

Zero; the biography of a dangerous idea. Viking 2000 248p il hardcover o.p. pa $15 **511**

1. Zero (The number)

ISBN 0-670-88457-X; 0-14-029647-6 pa

LC 99-36693

"The zero emerges as a daunting intellectual riddle in this . . . chronicle of a once controversial concept as Seife deftly traces the gradual acceptance of the zero and its role as catalyst for the evolution of everything from business to physics to moral thought." Booklist

Includes bibliographical references

511.3   Mathematical logic (Symbolic logic)

Stillwell, John

Roads to infinity; the mathematics of truth and proof. A K Peters 2010 203p il $39 **511.3**

1. Infinite 2. Logic, Symbolic and mathematical 3. Set theory 4. Symbolic logic

ISBN 978-1-56881-466-7; 1-56881-466-6

LC 2010-14077

"This book offers an introduction to modern ideas about infinity and their implications for mathematics. It unifies ideas from set theory and mathematical logic, and traces their effects on mainstream mathematical topics of today, such as number theory and combinatorics." Publisher's note

Includes bibliographical references

512   Algebra

Livio, Mario

The **equation** that couldn't be solved; how mathematical genius discovered the language of symmetry. Simon & Schuster 2005 353p il $26.95 **512**

1. Galois theory 2. Group theory 3. Mathematicians 4. Symmetry

ISBN 0-7432-5820-7

LC 2005-44123

"Even the mathematically fainthearted can learn a great deal about symmetry from this book." Sci Books Films

Includes bibliographical references

Singh, Simon

Fermat's enigma; the epic quest to solve the world's greatest mathematical problem. foreword by John Lynch. Anchor Books 1998 315p il pa $13.95 **512**

1. College teachers 2. Mathematicians 3. Number theory

ISBN 0-385-49362-2

"This vivid account is fascinating reading for anyone interested in mathematics, its history, and the passionate quest for solutions to unsolved riddles." SLJ

Includes bibliographical references

512.7 Number theory

Clawson, Calvin C.

Mathematical mysteries; the beauty and magic of numbers. Perseus Bks. 1999 313p il pa $18.95 **512.7**

1. Number theory

ISBN 0-7382-0259-2; 978-0-7382-0259-4

LC 99-66854

"A writer in love with his subject, Clawson offers the perfect antidote to the phobias and misconceptions surrounding mathematics." Booklist

Includes bibliographical references

Conway, John Horton

The **book** of numbers; [by] John Horton Conway, Richard K. Guy. Copernicus 1996 310p il $35 **512.7**

1. Number theory

ISBN 0-387-97993-X

LC 95-32588

"The authors take such joy in the order and patterns of numbers that you can't help being fascinated by what is actually a fairly difficult subject." Libr J

Includes bibliographical references

Derbyshire, John

Prime obsession; Bernhard Riemann and the greatest unsolved problem in mathematics. Plume 2004 422p il pa $16 **512.7**

1. Mathematicians 2. Number theory

ISBN 978-0-452-28525-5; 0-452-28525-9

The author "first takes readers through . . . mathematical fundamentals in order to give them a good understanding of Riemann's discovery and its consequences. Interspersed with the hardcore math, other chapters profile Riemann the man and trace the history of mathematics in relation to his still-unproven hypothesis. Derbyshire shows how after 150 years, the world's greatest minds still haven't found a solution." Libr J

Reid, Constance

From zero to infinity; what makes numbers interesting. 5th ed, 50th anniversary ed; A K Peters 2006 188p il pa $19.95 **512.7**

1. Number theory

ISBN 978-1-568812-73-1; 1-568812-73-6

LC 2005-27860

"This book covers selected topics in number theory. Partly expository, it nonetheless challenges the reader's mind in clever and nonthreatening ways." Sci Books Films

Sabbagh, Karl

★ The **Riemann** hypothesis; the greatest unsolved problem in mathematics. Farrar, Straus & Giroux 2002 340p il $25; pa $14 **512.7**

1. Mathematicians 2. Number theory

ISBN 0-374-25007-3; 0-374-52935-3 pa

LC 2003-101178

"Sabbagh introduces contemporary mathematicians who are working on the problem, one of whom claims, to pro-

fessional skepticism, to be on the verge of vindicating the hypothesis. Another is working away in search of a single counterexample that would refute it. Such pursuits, which often consume mathematicians' entire lives, may seem incomprehensible or even pointless to the innumerate—but that's a prejudice brilliantly dispelled through Sabbagh's interviews, which are interwoven with his not overly numerical tour of the hypothesis. The drive and competitiveness of mathematicians clearly emerge from Sabbagh's narrative." Booklist

513 Arithmetic

Bellos, Alex

Here's looking at Euclid; a surprising excursion through the astonishing world of math. Free Press hardcover ed.; Free Press 2010 319p il $25; ebook $11.99 **513**

1. Number concept

ISBN 978-1-4165-8825-2; 978-1-4165-9634-9 ebook

LC 2009-36815

The author "offers a lively romp through many different fields of mathematics as he incorporates ancient discoveries and modern developments alike. Topics include geometry, number theory, the development of sudoku, numerous aspects of pi and its calculation, statistics, probability and its application to gambling, and many other historical tidbits." Libr J

Includes bibliographical references

Kogelman, Stanley

The **only** math book you'll ever need; [by] Stanley Kogelman and Barbara R. Heller. rev ed.; HarperPerennial 1995 xx, 268p il pa $15 **513**

1. Mathematics

ISBN 978-0-06-272507-3; 0-06-272507-6

Step-by-step operations are reviewed in problems encountered on a daily basis such as comparing credit cards, evaluating investments, estimating interest rates, and converting area measurements.

515 Analysis

Ouellette, Jennifer

The **calculus** diaries; how math can help you lose weight, win in Vegas, and survive a zombie apocalypse. [illustrations by Jason Torchinsky] Penguin Books 2010 318p il pa $15 **515**

1. Calculus 2. Mathematics

ISBN 978-0-14-311737-7; 0-14-311737-8

LC 2010-25843

The author "shows how she learned to apply calculus to everything from gas mileage to dieting, from the rides at Disneyland to shooting craps in Vegas." Publisher's note

Includes bibliographical references

516　Geometry

Gorini, Catherine A.

The **Facts** on File geometry handbook; Rev ed; Facts on File 2009 342p il $40　　**516**
1. Geometry
ISBN 978-0-8160-7389-4

LC 2009-5775

This includes a glossary of over 3,000 entries with labeled diagrams, biographies of over 300 scientists and mathematicians from ancient times to the present, a chronology of geometry history, charts, tables, recommended reading and websites.

Mlodinow, Leonard

Euclid's window; the story of geometry from parallel lines to hyperspace. Free Press 2001 306p il hardcover o.p. pa $15　　**516**
1. Astronomers 2. Authors 3. College teachers 4. Geometry 5. Geometry -- History 6. Mathematicians 7. Nobel laureates for physics 8. Philosophers 9. Physicists 10. Writers on science
ISBN 0-684-86524-6 pa

LC 00-54351

"This engaging history does an excellent job of explaining the importance of the study of geometry without making the reader learn any geometry." Libr J
Includes bibliographical references

O'Rourke, Joseph

How to fold it; the mathematics of linkages, origami, and polyhedra. Cambridge University Press 2011 177p il $80; pa $27.99　　**516**
1. Mathematics 2. Origami
ISBN 978-0-521-76735-4; 0-521-76735-0; 978-0-521-14547-3 pa; 0-521-14547-3 pa

LC 2011001236

The author explains "folding problems starting from high school algebra and geometry and introducing more advanced concepts in tangible contexts as they arise. He shows how variations on these basic problems lead directly to the frontiers of current mathematical research and offers ten . . . unsolved problems for the enterprising reader." Publisher's note

516.2　Euclidean geometry

Kaplan, Ellen

Hidden harmonies; the lives and times of the Pythagorean theorem. [by] Robert Kaplan and Ellen Kaplan. Bloomsbury Press 2011 290p il $25 **516.2**
1. Mathematics -- History 2. Pythagorean theorem
ISBN 978-1-59691-522-0; 1-59691-522-6

LC 2010-19959

The authors discuss "the famous theorem that relates the sides of a right triangle. Going through many of the apparently hundreds of proofs of it, the Kaplans sinuously weave personalities into the history of proving Pythagoras correct. . . . Showing the theorem's endless versatility, the Kaplans

and their logic- and symbol-permeated text will engage those who delight in doing the math." Booklist
Includes bibliographical references

Livio, Mario

The **golden** ratio; the story of phi, the world's most astonishing number. Broadway Bks. 2002 294p hardcover o.p. pa $14.95　　**516.2**
1. Geometry 2. Golden section
ISBN 0-7679-0815-5; 0-7679-0816-3 pa

LC 2002-23084

The author examines the history and myths of phi, the "golden ratio" of 1.6180339887 that has been related to phenomena as diverse as the arrangements of petals on roses and the breeding patterns of rabbits.

"Overall, an enjoyable work, amply supported by index, extensive references, and ten appendixes presenting mathematical elaborations of text material." Choice
Includes bibliographical references

Maor, Eli

The **Pythagorean** theorem; a 4,000-year history. Princeton University Press 2007 259p il map $24.95　　**516.2**
1. Mathematics -- History 2. Pythagorean theorem
ISBN 978-0-691-12526-8; 0-691-12526-0

LC 2006-50969

"This [is an] interesting and well-written book. . . . I recommend the book highly to students, teachers, and the intelligent general reader interested in a very old, beautiful, and useful result." Sci Books Films
Includes bibliographical references

516.22　Plane geometry

Blatner, David

The **joy** of pi. Walker & Co. 1997 129p il hardcover o.p. pa $12　　**516.22**
1. Pi
ISBN 0-8027-1332-7; 0-8027-7562-4 pa

LC 97-23705

The author discusses the history of the number π, as well as the process of "calculating the ratio of a circle's circumference to its diameter, which has advanced from measuring lengths of string and the 'brute force' of measuring polygons to feeding supercomputers sophisticated algorithms. Sidebars . . . abound, containing a factoid, joke, or doggerel inspired by π." Booklist
Includes bibliographical references

519.2　Probabilities

Aczel, Amir D.

Chance: a guide to gambling, love, the stock market & just about everything else. Thunder's Mouth Press 2004 161p il $23　　**519.2**
1. Chance 2. Probabilities
ISBN 1-56858-316-8

LC 2004-304723

The author "explains the elements of probability theory for lay readers. . . . [He] points out that some of the results of probabilistic calculations can seem contrary to common sense and can even surprise experienced mathematicians and scientists such as himself; nevertheless, the results are mathematically sound and must be accepted. . . . It is not often that one can recommend a mathematics book as good-quality 'light' reading, but this work fits the bill." Libr J

Includes bibliographical references

Devlin, Keith J.

The **unfinished** game; Pascal, Fermat, and the seventeenth-century letter that made the world modern. [by] Keith Devlin. Basic Books 2008 191p il $24.95 **519.2**

1. Game theory 2. Mathematicians 3. Probabilities 4. Theologians 5. Writers on religion

ISBN 978-0-465-00910-7; 0-465-00910-7

LC 2008-12222

"This informative book is a lively, quick read for anyone who wonders about the science of predicting what's next and how deeply it affects our lives." Publ Wkly

Includes bibliographical references

Mlodinow, Leonard

The **Drunkard's** walk; how randomness rules our lives. Pantheon Books 2008 252p il $24.95 **519.2**

1. Chance 2. Probabilities 3. Random variables

ISBN 978-0-375-42404-5; 0-375-42404-0

LC 2007-42507

"Mlodinow will help readers sort out Mark Twain's 'damn lies' from meaningful statistics and the choices we face every day." Publ Wkly

Includes bibliographical references

Rosenthal, Jeffrey

Struck by lightning; the curious world of probabilities. [by] Jeffrey S. Rosenthal. HarperCollins Canada 2005 263p il pa $19.95 **519.2**

1. Chance 2. Probabilities

ISBN 0-309-09734-7; 978-0-309-09734-5

LC 2005-37021

Rosenthal discusses ways in which probability theory affects such areas of everyday life as crime, travel, gambling, politics, and disease.

"The lighthearted presentation ensures that readers will not feel burdened by all the knowledge they are gaining and the concluding summary—disguised as a final exam—is sure to deliver an A to everyone, which is what Rosenthal deserves for this clever book." Publ Wkly

Santos, Aaron

How many licks? or, How to estimate damn near anything. Running Press 2009 175p il pa $14.95 **519.2**

1. Probabilities

ISBN 978-0-7624-3560-9; 0-7624-3560-7

"No matter how you feel about math, Santos' puzzle-solving prowess shows you just how much you can do when you put on your thinking cap." Am Profile

519.3   Game theory

Highfield, Roger

★ **Supercooperators**; altruism, evolution, and why we need each other to succeed. [by] Martin A. Nowak, with Roger Highfield. Free Press 2011 330p $27 **519.3**

1. Cooperative societies 2. Evolution 3. Evolution (Biology) -- Mathematical models 4. Game theory

ISBN 978-1-4391-0018-9; 1-4391-0018-7

LC 2010-35517

"Nowak aims to tackle the mysteries of nature with paper, pencil and computer. By looking at phenomena as diverse as H.I.V. infection and English irregular verbs, he has formally defined five distinct mechanisms that have helped give rise to cooperative behavior, from the first molecules that joined to self-replicate, to the first cells that formed multicellular organisms, all the way to human societies, which exhibit a degree of cooperation unmatched in all creation. In Nowak's view, figuring out how cooperation comes about and breaks down, as well as actively pursuing the 'snuggle for existence,' is the key to our survival as a species." N Y Times Book Rev

Includes bibliographical references

519.5   Statistical mathematics

Cohen, I. Bernard

The **triumph** of numbers; how counting shaped modern life. W. W. Norton 2005 209p il $24.95; pa $14.95 **519.5**

1. Mathematical statistics -- History 2. Science -- History 3. Statistics 4. Statistics -- History

ISBN 0-393-05769-0; 978-0-393-05769-0; 0-393-32870-8 pa; 978-0-393-32870-7 pa

LC 2004-27322

"This book presents a persuasive narrative on how numbers have maintained a prominent role not only in science and government throughout time, but in the daily operations of life." Sci Books Films

Includes bibliographical references

Everitt, Brian

★ The **Cambridge** dictionary of statistics; [by] B.S. Everitt, A. Skrondal. 4th ed.; Cambridge University Press 2010 468p il $59 **519.5**

1. Reference books 2. Statistics -- Dictionaries

ISBN 978-0-521-76699-9

LC 2010-502891

"This field-specific dictionary explains nearly 4000 terms, concepts, and models relevant to fields employing theoretical, applied, scientific, and survey-related probability methods." Libr J

520   Astronomy and allied sciences

Bakich, Michael E.

★ The **Cambridge** encyclopedia of amateur astronomy. Cambridge Univ. Press 2003 342p il $69   **520**

1. Astronomy -- Encyclopedias 2. Reference books
ISBN 0-521-81298-4

LC 2002-31551

"Any amateur astronomer, or anyone with an interest in seeing what nonprofessionals can do if they are dedicated, would enjoy this book." Sci Books Films

Includes bibliographical references

Bartusiak, Marcia

The **day** we found the universe. Pantheon Books 2009 337p il $27.95   **520**

1. Astronomers 2. Astronomy -- History 3. Astronomy -- History -- 20th century
ISBN 978-0-375-42429-8; 0-375-42429-6

LC 2008-34377

"This is a superb book that interweaves the fascinating story of a major scientific quest with a cast of characters, situations, painstaking observations, and imaginative thinking that reminds us all of the human side of scientific endeavors and the ways in which the universe itself continuously surprises us." Sci Books Films

Includes bibliographical references

Couper, Heather

The **history** of astronomy; [by] Heather Couper & Nigel Henbest; foreword by Arthur C. Clarke. Firefly Books 2007 285p il $59.95; pa $29.95 **520**

1. Astronomy -- History
ISBN 978-1-55407-325-2; 1-55407-325-1; 978-1-55407-537-9 pa; 1-55407-537-8 pa

LC 2008-272095

This "history is pieced together through astronomer interviews and visits to historically important astronomy sites around the world. . . . This is a copiously illustrated, straightforwardly written volume that will appeal to readers with and without an astronomy background. In addition to covering astronomy through the ages, the authors do an admirable job explaining current astronomical discoveries and personalities." Choice

Darling, David J.

★ The **universal** book of astronomy from the Andromeda Galaxy to the zone of avoidance; [by] David Darling. Wiley 2003 570p il $40   **520**

1. Astronomy -- Dictionaries 2. Reference books
ISBN 0-471-26569-1

LC 2003-13941

"Designed for nonspecialists, Darling's volume fills a niche in astronomy ready reference. . . . The volume is . . . highly readable and provides bonuses in 22 star charts outlining all 88 constellations in both north and south celestial hemispheres, instructional aids throughout the text, and charts that accompany entries for many stars, galaxies, and clusters and show size, position, etc." Choice

Includes bibliographical references

Davidson, Keay

Carl Sagan; a life. Wiley 1999 xx, 540p hardcover o.p. pa $24.95   **520**

1. Astronomers 2. Astronomers -- United States 3. Astrophysicists 4. Authors 5. Essayists 6. Novelists 7. Science fiction writers 8. Writers on science
ISBN 0-471-39536-6 pa

LC 99-36206

The author profiles the life and scientific career of the influential American astronomer.

"Sagan is presented in such a way that readers can decide whether to view him admirably or with a dose of skepticism." Booklist

Includes bibliographical references

Ferris, Timothy

Seeing in the dark; how backyard stargazers are probing deep space and guarding earth from interplanetary peril. Simon & Schuster 2002 379p il hardcover o.p. pa $14   **520**

1. Astronomers 2. Astronomy
ISBN 0-684-86579-3; 0-684-86580-7 pa

LC 2002-20693

"This book should turn many novices on to astronomy and captivate those already fascinated by the heavens." Publ Wkly

Finkbeiner, Ann K.

A **grand** and bold thing; the extraordinary new map of the universe ushering in a new era of discovery. [by] Ann Finkbeiner. Free Press 2010 223p $27; ebook $12.99   **520**

1. Astronomical instruments 2. Astrophysicists 3. College teachers
ISBN 978-1-416-55216-1; 978-1-4391-9647-2 ebook

LC 2010-8533

"Finkbeiner reveals the story behind today's most exciting astronomical research program: the Sloan Digital Sky Survey, a massive technological undertaking whose results have allowed everyone, from astronomers to high school students, to create and work with 'the most complete map of the universe ever.' The SDSS began with astronomer Jim Gunn. . . . This delightful book reveals just how much SDSS has changed how astronomers work, and how they—and we—see the universe." Publ Wkly

Includes bibliographical references

Garfinkle, David

Three steps to the universe; from the sun to black holes to the mystery of dark matter. [by] David Garfinkle & Richard Garfinkle. The University of Chicago Press 2008 265p il $25   **520**

1. Black holes (Astronomy) 2. Dark matter (Astronomy)
ISBN 978-0-226-28346-3; 0-226-28346-1

LC 2008-8659

The authors "explore some of the knottiest problems facing modern cosmologists in this tough but informative primer to modern cosmology. . . . Arguing that 'it is necessary to jump the barrier of user-friendliness and discover the fascinating world beyond that layer of comfort,' the Garfinkles aren't afraid to get technical, but this smart, rewarding read is helped by a welcome voice, a feel for narrative and a useful glossary." Publ Wkly

Includes bibliographical references

Kanipe, Jeff

The **cosmic** connection; how astronomical events impact life on Earth. Prometheus Books 2009 296p il $27.95 **520**

1. Astronomy
ISBN 978-1-59102-667-9; 1-59102-667-9

LC 2008-31877

"This extremely well written book would be an engaging read for any person with even the slightest interest in astronomy." Sci Books Films

Includes bibliographical references

Miller, Arthur I.

Empire of the stars; obsession, friendship, and betrayal in the quest for black holes. Houghton Mifflin 2005 364p il $26 **520**

1. Astronomers 2. Astrophysicists 3. Black holes (Astronomy) 4. Mathematicians 5. Nobel laureates for physics 6. Writers on science
ISBN 0-618-34151-X

LC 2004-60909

This history of the discovery of black holes focuses on the bitter rivalry between Indian astrophysicist Subrahmanyan Chandrasekhar and Cambridge astrophysicist Sir Arthur Eddington.

"Astronomy buffs and readers fascinated by the history of science will find this a compelling read." Publ Wkly

Includes bibliographical references

Plait, Philip C.

Death from the skies! these are the ways the world will end . . . [by] Philip Plait. Viking 2008 326p il $25.95 **520**

1. End of the world
ISBN 978-0-670-01997-7; 0-670-01997-6

LC 2008-22943

"The book is extremely informative: Plait explains not only what can destroy the planet but also how it would happen. It's a crash course in astronomy as well as a cautionary tale about the (possibly brief) future of our world." Booklist

Raymo, Chet

An **intimate** look at the night sky. Walker & Co. 2001 242p il $25; pa $16 **520**

1. Astronomy
ISBN 0-8027-1369-6; 0-8027-7670-1 pa

"A delightful, inspiring introduction to astronomy." Booklist

Includes bibliographical references

Ridpath, Ian

★ **Stars** and planets; the most complete guide to the stars, planets, galaxies, and the solar system. illustrated by Wil Tirion. Fully rev. and expanded

ed.; Princeton University Press 2007 400p il pa $19.95 **520**

1. Astronomy 2. Planets 3. Stars
ISBN 978-0-691-13556-4; 0-691-13556-8

This book features "charts covering all 88 constellations in the Northern and Southern hemispheres; data and notes on all bright stars and other objects of interest; . . . Moon maps and descriptions of the main lunar features; [and] tips on choosing and using binoculars and telescopes." Publisher's note

Sagan, Carl

Conversations with Carl Sagan; edited by Tom Head. University Press of Mississippi 2006 xxv, 167p $50; pa $20 **520**

1. Astronomers 2. Astrophysicists 3. Authors 4. Essayists 5. Novelists 6. Science fiction writers 7. Writers on science
ISBN 1-57806-735-9; 1-57806-736-7 pa

LC 2005-48747

The editor "has selected 16 engaging conversations from such popular venues as Rolling Stone, Psychology Today, The Charlie Rose Show, and NPR, and it's a boon to connect with Sagan's knowledge, wisdom, and generosity . . . after his early death at 62." Booklist

Includes bibliographical references

Pale blue dot; a vision of the human future in space. Ballantine Books 1997 360p pa $14.95 **520**

ISBN 978-0-345-37659-6; 0-345-37659-5

"In a tour of our solar system, galaxy and beyond . . . Sagan meshes a history of astronomical discovery, a cogent brief for space exploration and an overview of life. . . . His exploration of our place in the universe is illustrated with photographs, relief maps and paintings, including high-resolution images made by Voyager 1 and 2, as well as photos taken by the Galileo spacecraft, the Hubble Space Telescope and satellites orbiting Earth." Publ Wkly

Includes bibliographical references

Schaaf, Fred

The **50** best sights in astronomy and how to see them; observing eclipses, bright comets, meteor showers, and other celestial wonders. John Wiley 2007 280p il pa $19.95 **520**

1. Astronomy 2. Astronomy -- Amateurs' manuals 3. Astronomy -- Observers' manuals
ISBN 978-0-471-69657-5; 0-471-69657-9

LC 2006-36221

The author "begins with some basic information and terminology (altazimuth system, for example, or right ascension) and then plunges right in with the most easily accessible astronomical sight, the starry sky above our heads. For each sight, he not only explains what it is and the best conditions under which to observe it, he also tells us about its historical, mythological, or scientific importance and explores how these far-off wonders can have a very real effect on our humble home world. This could so easily have been a dry-as-dust tome, but Schaaf's enthusiasm overflows every page." Booklist

Includes bibliographical references

Scientific American (Periodical)

The **Amateur** astronomer; edited by Shawn Carlson. Wiley 2001 271p il pa $16.95 **520**

1. Astronomy

ISBN 0-471-38282-5

LC 00-47773

A collection of articles on the subject of astronomy published in Scientific American magazine from the 1950s to the 1990s.

"Carlson provides fascinating assessments of both how much and how little was known 50 years ago, and he charts the evolution of theories and the rise and resolution of controversies, thus offering invaluable insights into the history of scientific thought and methodology. Technically precise yet always clear, these popular science columns remain vital and exciting." Booklist

Includes bibliographical references

Sobel, Dava

A **more** perfect heaven; how Copernicus revolutionized the cosmos. Walker Pub. 2011 273p il map $25 **520**

1. Astronomers 2. Astronomy

ISBN 978-0-8027-1793-1

LC 2011024772

"Dava Sobel excels in telling the story of Nicholas Copernicus and his almost-shelved masterpiece, On the Revolutions. Along the way, she brings the social and political milieu of the times into sharp relief providing context for the sheer audacity of his insights into planetary motion and his reticence in pursuing their dissemination." Sci Books Films

Includes bibliographical references

History of astronomy; an encyclopedia. edited by John Lankford. Garland 1997 594p il $155 **520**

1. Astronomy -- History 2. Astronomy -- History -- Encyclopedias 3. Reference books

ISBN 0-8153-0322-X

LC 96-28558

"Focusing on developments since the Scientific Revolution, the signed articles . . . fall into five broad categories: an historical overview of astronomy, astronomy in national contexts (e.g., Chinese astronomy), the history of observatories, the social history of astronomy (e.g., Women in Astronomy), and biographies. . . . Recommendations for further reading are well chosen and current. An excellent and much-needed work." Libr J

Patrick Moore's data book of astronomy; edited by Patrick Moore and Robin Rees. Cambridge University Press 2011 576p il map $55 **520**

1. Astronomy 2. Reference books

ISBN 978-0-521-89935-2

LC 2010031372

"Readers with no prior interest in amateur astronomy will find a lot to captivate here. It also contains clearly written, up-to-date sections explaining what all these various celestial objects are, and how we've come to know them. . . . This work offers so much more than a handbook for backyard telescopes; it is an atlas for the Universe around us that will surprise every time you dip in." Times Higher Ed

★ Universe; general editor, Martin Rees. DK 2008 512p il pa $27.95 **520**

1. Cosmology

ISBN 978-0-7566-3670-8; 0-7566-3670-1

LC 2008-299650

This is "a visually stunning reference that makes browsing irresistible. Every page of this oversized volume is full color, with an eye-pleasing balance of text and graphics." Libr J

521 Astronomy

Goodstein, David L.

Feynman's lost lecture; the motion of planets around the sun. {by} David L. Goodstein and Judith R. Goodstein. Norton 1996 191p il $35; pa $19.95 **521**

1. Astrophysics 2. Authors 3. Nobel laureates for physics 4. Physicists 5. Planets 6. Universe 7. Writers on science

ISBN 0-393-03918-8; 0-393-31995-4 pa

LC 95-38719

This "book consists of four chapters. The first and largest is a brief history of the establishment of the Copernican cosmology, which Feynman gave as a lecture to the freshman class at Caltech. Feynman then revisits the work of Isaac Newton and the watershed proof of the Scientific Revolution that separated the ancient world from the modern. There is also a chapter with some wonderful reminiscences of Feynman." Libr J

Includes bibliographical references

Rubin, Alan E.

Disturbing the solar system; impacts, close encounters, and coming attractions. Princeton Univ. Press 2002 361p il $29.95 **521**

1. Catastrophes (Geology) 2. Gravitation 3. Gravity 4. Life on other planets

ISBN 0-691-07474-7

LC 2001-55197

"After relating a brief history of the solar system, Alan Rubin describes how astronomers determined our location in the Milky Way. He provides . . . accounts of the energetic interactions among planetary bodies, the generation of the Earth's magnetic field, the effects of other solar-system objects on our climate, the moon's genesis, the heating of asteroids, and the origin of the mysterious tektites. . . . He chronicles the history of the search for life on Mars and describes cutting-edge lines of astrobiological inquiry." Publisher's note

Includes bibliographical references and index

522 Techniques, procedures, apparatus, equipment, materials

Dickinson, Terence

★ The **backyard** astronomer's guide; [by] Terence Dickinson & Alan Dyer. 3rd ed; Firefly Books 2008 368p il $49.95 **522**
1. Astronomy
ISBN 978-1-55407-344-3; 1-55407-344-8

The authors provide guidance "on the right types of telescopes and other equipment; photographing the stars through a telescope; and star charts, software and other references. They cover daytime and twilight observing, planetary and deep-sky observing, and . . . more." Publisher's note
Includes bibliographical references

Katz, Jonathan I.

The **biggest** bangs; the mystery of gamma-ray bursts, the most violent explosions in the universe. Oxford Univ. Press 2002 218p il $28 **522**
1. Gamma ray bursts
ISBN 0-19-514570-4
LC 2001-36545

"Discovered in the 1960s, gamma-ray bursts were not as easily measured or explained as quasars and pulsars. Besides recounting the journey to our current understanding of these bursts—which are thought to be explosions from neutron stars either hitting each other or being dragged into a black hole—physicist Katz also elucidates the scientific thinking process." Booklist
Includes bibliographical references

Kerrod, Robin

★ **Hubble**; the mirror on the universe. [by] Robin Kerrod & Carole Stott. 3rd ed. updated, rev. and expanded.; Firefly Books 2011 224p il pa $29.95 **522**
1. Hubble Space Telescope
ISBN 978-1-55407-972-8; 1-55407-972-1
LC 2011292195

"Kerrod provides an excellent overview of Hubble's accomplishments (along with a history of the evolution of the telescope), thoughtfully organizing the spellbinding images from space, and clearly and avidly explaining exactly which phenomena they depict." Booklist

Schilling, Govert

Flash! the hunt for the biggest explosions in the universe. translated by Naomi Greenberg-Slovin. Cambridge Univ. Press 2002 291p il $28 **522**
1. Black holes (Astronomy) 2. Gamma ray bursts
ISBN 0-521-80053-6
LC 2002-283188

"Everday examples are frequently used to illustrate the more difficult concepts. Those who want more details will appreciate the glossary and references to the scientific literature. Almost without realizing it, readers will also get a good introduction to elementary astronomy as a bonus. A must-read for anyone interested in GRBs!" Choice
Includes bibliographical references and index

523 Specific celestial bodies and phenomena

Chartrand, Mark R.

The **Audubon** Society field guide to the night sky; astronomical charts by Wil Tirion. Knopf 1991 714p il map $19.95 **523**
1. Astronomy 2. Stars
ISBN 0-679-40852-5
LC 91-52708

This guide "begins with monthly star charts and constellation star charts . . . then gives photographs of the constellations; and finally, provides detailed information on each constellation including stars, galaxies, and nebulae. . . . Other information includes hints on observing ther sky; dates of solar and lunar eclipses, meteor showers, and comets, and the Messier catalog. . . . Students interested in astronomy will find lots of observing tips and information." Voice Youth Advocates
Includes bibliographical references

Gribbin, John R.

Stardust; supernovae and life: the cosmic connection. {by} John Gribbin with Mary Gribbin. Yale Univ. Press 2000 238p $35; pa $13.95 **523**
1. Cosmochemistry 2. Life (Biology) 3. Supernovae 4. Supernovas 5. Universe
ISBN 0-300-08419-6; 0-300-09097-8 pa
LC 00-35944

"A fine summary of the origin of our elemental constitution." Booklist
Includes bibliographical references

★ Firefly **atlas** of the universe; foreword by Arnold Wolfendale. 3rd ed.; Firefly Books 2005 288p il $49.95 **523**
1. Astronomy
ISBN 1-55407-071-6
LC 2006-275758

This work begins with a "general historical overview, followed by individual sections on the solar system, the sun, the stars, the structure of the universe and our galaxy's place in it, and over 20 useful star maps, all incorporating the newest scientific data." Libr J [review of 2003 edition]

523.1 The universe, galaxies, quasars

Aczel, Amir D.

God's equation; Einstein, relativity, and the expanding universe. Delta Trade Paperbacks 2000 236p il pa $12 **523.1**
1. Cosmology 2. Nobel laureates for physics 3. Physicists 4. Relativity (Physics)
ISBN 978-0-385-33485-3; 0-385-33485-0

"Though Aczel's analysis of Einstein's work requires familiarity with advanced mathematics, that analysis makes up only a minor portion of his book, and most readers will appreciate the author's inclusion of the great physicist's letters to astronomer Erwin Freundlich." Publ Wkly
Includes bibliographical references

Bojowald, Martin

Once before time; a whole story of the universe. Alfred A. Knopf 2010 309p il $27.95; ebook $27.95 **523.1**

1. Beginning 2. Cosmology 3. Physicists 4. Quantum gravity 5. Space and time
ISBN 978-0-307-27285-0; 978-0-307-59425-9 ebook
LC 2010-15937

"Cutting-edge physics made accessible for readers who pay close attention." Kirkus

Includes bibliographical references

Cox, Brian

Wonders of the universe; [by] Brian Cox and Andrew Cohen. Harper Design 2011 256p il $29.99; ebook $14.99 **523.1**

1. Cosmology
ISBN 978-0-06-211054-1; 978-0-06-211561-4 ebook

The author "uses the evidence found in the natural world on Earth to . . . explain the truth of the cosmos. . . . [He shows] how the vast and unfathomable phenomena of deep space can be explained, and even experienced, by re-examining the familiar here on Earth." Publisher's note

Croswell, Ken

The **alchemy** of the heavens; searching for meaning in the Milky Way. illustrations by Philippe Van. Anchor Bks. (NY) 1995 340p il hardcover o.p. pa $14.95 **523.1**

1. Galaxies 2. Universe
ISBN 0-385-47214-5 pa
LC 94-30452

A "well-written, crystal-clear presentation. . . . This work will snare all general reading interests." Booklist

Includes bibliographical references

Dauber, Philip M.

The **three** big bangs; comet crashes, exploding stars, and the creation of the universe. [by] Philip M. Dauber, Richard A. Muller. Perseus Books 1997 207p il pa $15 **523.1**

1. Catastrophes (Geology) 2. Cosmology 3. Supernovas
ISBN 978-0-201-15495-5; 0-201-15495-1

The authors discuss the origins of the universe and of life on Earth.

"Dauber and Muller have not only chosen three 'hot topics' in . . . astronomy but also have masterfully woven the underlying scientific strands together. They paint a colorful picture of the theories and techniques of modern astronomy." Choice

Includes bibliographical references

Davies, P. C. W.

The **last** three minutes; conjectures about the ultimate fate of the universe. {by} Paul Davies. Basic Bks. 1994 162p il hardcover o.p. pa $14 **523.1**

1. Cosmology 2. End of the world 3. Universe
ISBN 0-465-03851-4 pa
LC 94-6345

"The reader will discover that science can sometimes be more creative than art, more stimulating than philosophy, more revelatory than any religion, and more frightening than any fiction thriller." Choice

Includes bibliographical references

Ferguson, Kitty

Measuring the universe; our historic quest to chart the horizons of space and time. Walker & Co. 1999 342p il $27; pa $16.95 **523.1**

1. Cosmological distances 2. Cosmology 3. Measurement 4. Mensuration
ISBN 0-8027-1351-3; 0-8027-7592-6 pa
LC 99-19476

"Starting with Eratosthenes and his calculation of the earth's circumference using the shadows cast in a well, and moving through Stephen Hawking's work on black holes, Ferguson tells the tale of our search for our place in the universe. This book is nicely illustrated with photos, tables, and diagrams." Libr J

Includes bibliographical references and index

Ferris, Timothy

The **whole** shebang; a state-of-the-universe(s) report. Simon & Schuster 1997 393p hardcover o.p. pa $16 **523.1**

1. Cosmology 2. Universe
ISBN 0-684-81020-4; 0-684-83861-3 pa
LC 96-49768

The author "reviews the current state of scientific cosmology, including the now-considerable overlap between astronomical findings and the theories of elementary particle physicists. . . . Ferris adheres to the orthodox Big Bang theory, giving little attention to its critics, but he is candid about the many uncertainties in modern cosmology. He writes clearly, often with considerable eloquence." Libr J

Includes bibliographical references

Frank, Adam

About time; cosmology and culture at the twilight of the Big Bang. Free Press 2011 xxi, 406p il $26 **523.1**

1. Big bang theory 2. Cosmology 3. Life -- Origin 4. Space and time
ISBN 978-1-4391-6959-9; 1-4391-6959-4; 978-1-4391-6961-2 ebook
LC 2011011345

"Frank offers a unique and fascinating look at complex concepts with an accessible style that is both matter-of-fact and thoroughly entertaining." Publ Wkly

Includes bibliographical references

Gates, Evalyn

Einstein's telescope; the hunt for dark matter and dark energy in the universe. W.W. Norton 2009 305p il $25.95; pa $16.95 **523.1**

1. Astrophysics 2. Dark energy (Astronomy) 3. Dark matter (Astronomy) 4. Gravitational lenses
ISBN 978-0-393-06238-0; 978-0-393-33801-0 pa
LC 2008-44455

"Gates writes with a freshness and clarity that make complex ideas such as relativity, lensing, black holes, and the cosmic web understandable." Libr J

Includes bibliographical references

Gleiser, Marcelo

The **prophet** and the astronomer; a scientific journey to the end of time. Norton 2002 256p il $26.95; pa $15.95 **523.1**

1. Cosmology 2. End of the universe 3. End of the world 4. Religion and science
ISBN 0-393-04987-6; 0-393-32431-1 pa

LC 2002-538

"Gleiser ponders the dark parallels between the apocalyptic visions of ancient seers and the cosmic predictions of modern scientists. . . . Gleiser's musings . . . occasionally will baffle the nonspecialist, but most readers will consider a few moments of perplexity a small price to pay for the opportunity to probe humanity's oldest nightmares and newest aspirations." Booklist

Includes bibliographical references

Greene, Brian R.

★ The **fabric** of the cosmos; space, time, and the texture of reality. Knopf 2004 569p il $28.95; pa $15.95 **523.1**

1. Cosmology
ISBN 0-375-41288-3; 0-375-72720-5 pa

LC 2003-58918

"Frogs in bowls, falling eggs, loaves of bread, pennies on balloons, ping pong balls in molasses, and babushka dolls are just some of the analogies used to explain complex concepts cleverly. After reading this book, you will never look at a starry night sky the same way again." Libr J

Includes bibliographical references

Gribbin, John R.

The **birth** of time; how astronomers measured the age of the universe. [by] John Gribbin. Yale Univ. Press 2000 237p $40; pa $11.95 **523.1**

1. Cosmology
ISBN 0-300-08346-7; 0-300-08914-7 pa

LC 99-52835

The author "recounts the history of the problem and describes the people who have worked on it. Since the age of the universe is inextricably linked to its size, he devotes most of his work to dealing with methods that have been used, are being used, and are proposed as future means to determine cosmic distances." Libr J

Includes bibliographical references

The **origins** of the future; ten questions for the next ten years. [by] John Gribbin. Yale University Press 2006 292p $27.50 **523.1**

1. Cosmology 2. Evolution 3. Life -- Origin
ISBN 978-0-300-11998-5; 0-300-11998-4

LC 2006-11062

"In each of this book's 10 chapters, . . . [the author] describes different eras in the evolution of our universe. Each chapter opens with a question setting forth that chapter's theme. . . . Gribbin lays out the history of the universe and takes care to show its intricate workings for us to admire." Sci Books Films

Includes bibliographical references

Hawking, Stephen W.

Black holes and baby universes and other essays; [by] Stephen Hawking. Bantam Bks. 1993 182p hardcover o.p. pa $18 **523.1**

1. Cosmology 2. Science -- Philosophy
ISBN 0-553-37411-7 pa

LC 93-8269

A collection of essays and speeches ranging from autobiographical sketches to theoretical discussions of black holes, relativity and quantum mechanics.

The author "sprinkles his explanations with a wry sense of humor and a keen awareness that the sciences today delve not only into the far reaches of the cosmos, but into the inner philosophical world as well." N Y Times Book Rev

★ A **briefer** history of time; [by] Stephen Hawking and Leonard Mlodinow. Bantam Dell 2005 162p il $25 **523.1**

1. Cosmology
ISBN 0-553-80436-7

LC 2005-42949

The authors describe concepts about space and time, black holes, the origin and nature of the universe, the uncertainty principle, and the unification of physics. It also discusses string theory, dark matter, and dark energy.

"Hawking and Mlodinow provide one of the most lucid discussions of this complex topic ever written for a general audience. Readers will come away with an excellent understanding of the apparent contradictions and conundrums at the forefront of contemporary physics." Publ Wkly

Includes bibliographical references

Hooper, Dan

Dark cosmos; in search of our universe's missing mass and energy. HarperCollins Publishers 2006 240p il pa $14.95; $24.95 **523.1**

1. Astrophysics 2. Cosmology 3. Dark energy (Astronomy) 4. Dark matter (Astronomy)
ISBN 978-0-06-113033-5 pa; 0-06-113033-8 pa; 978-0-06-113032-8; 0-06-113032-X

LC 2006-44333

This book discusses "dark matter" and "dark energy," invisible substances which scientists speculate may make up over 95% of the universe.

"Hooper's clear presentation in very simple, jargon-free prose should appeal especially to young people just starting to get excited about the mysteries that still await them in science." Publ Wkly

Impey, Chris

How it began; a time-traveler's guide to the universe. Chris Impey. W.W. Norton 2012 434 p. **523.1**

1. Cosmology -- Popular works 2. Space and time -- Popular works
ISBN 9780393080025

LC 2011052855

This book about the universe follow[s] atoms through generation after generation of stellar cores from the Big Bang onward. [Author Chris] Impey's time travelers are astronomers doing cosmic archeology in which the farther out in the universe one goes, the farther back in time one can see. Impey begins close to home, and closest in time, with the formation of our solar system. . . . Moving outward in the universe (and back in time toward the Big Bang), Impey discusses how to measure stellar distances and detect planets orbiting other stars. Stretching farther back, Impey explores galactic evolution, relativity, the large-scale structure of the universe, and the Big Bang. Fictional vignettes narrated by a space/time traveler . . . bookend each chapter to personalize the material. (Publishers Wkly)

How it ends; from you to the universe. W.W. Norton 2010 352p il $26.95   **523.1**
   1. Death 2. End of the universe 3. End of the world 4. Universe
   ISBN 978-0-393-06985-3; 0-393-06985-0
                      LC 2009-47265
"Although dealing with a gruesome subject, Impey's book is a lighthearted romp through all the ways that life and everything else in the universe may end. Along the way, the author not only educates the reader in biology and astronomy, but also provides some tantalizing glimpses into possible future scenarios that avoid such gruesome endings." Sci Books Films
   Includes bibliographical references

Jastrow, Robert

★ **God** and the astronomers; 2nd ed; Norton 1992 149p il hardcover o.p. pa $12.95   **523.1**
   1. Astronomy 2. Cosmology 3. Religion and science
   ISBN 0-393-85006-4 pa
                      LC 92-32186
The author considers the theological implications of the big bang theory of creation, and summarizes the evidence for the theory including the relativity theory, the life story of stars, and the discovery of the retreat of the galaxies. Includes chapters by a Catholic astronomer and a Jewish theologian with their viewpoints on the origin and destiny of the universe

Kaku, Michio

Parallel worlds; a journey through creation, higher dimensions, and the future of the cosmos. Doubleday 2005 428p il hardcover o.p. pa $15.95 **523.1**
   1. Big bang theory 2. Cosmology 3. String theory
   ISBN 0-385-50986-3; 1-4000-3372-1 pa
                      LC 2004-56039
"This is a riveting popular treatment of the string revolution in physics written by a pioneering theorist in the field. Kaku expounds comprehensibly on why astrophysicists love strings and branes and the way they resolve various vexatious cosmological paradoxes." Booklist

Kanipe, Jeff

Chasing Hubble's shadows; the search for galaxies at the edge of time. Hill and Wang 2006 205p il $24; pa $15   **523.1**
   1. Galaxies 2. Hubble Space Telescope
   ISBN 0-8090-3406-9; 0-8090-3407-7 pa
                      LC 2005-9652
The author's "breathless writing conveys his own excitement over the revelations that new advances in astronomy

can tell us about our planet and our place in the universe." Publ Wkly

Lightman, Alan P.

Ancient light; our changing view of the universe. {by} Alan Lightman. Harvard Univ. Press 1991 170p il hardcover o.p. pa $14.95   **523.1**
   1. Astronomers 2. Cosmology 3. Universe
   ISBN 0-674-03363-9 pa
                      LC 91-12459
The author discusses the development of modern cosmology, the big bang model, and recent challenges to that model
"Lightman's book is a short and simple introduction to modern cosmology, with a strong emphasis upon observation and its interaction with theory. . . . Its merits are that it is accurate and does not go further than current observations warrant." Nat Hist
   Includes bibliographical references

O'Dell, C. Robert

The **Orion** Nebula; where stars are born. Belknap Press of Harvard University Press 2003 170p il $27.95   **523.1**
   1. Orion Nebula
   ISBN 0-674-01183-X
                      LC 2003-50332
"An excellent book for collections of any library serving general readers." Choice

Panek, Richard

★ The **4** percent universe; dark matter, dark energy, and the race to discover the rest of reality. Houghton Mifflin Harcourt 2011 297p $26   **523.1**
   1. Astrophysics 2. Cosmology 3. Dark energy (Astronomy) 4. Dark matter (Astronomy) 5. Physics
   ISBN 978-0-618-98244-8; 0-618-98244-2
                      LC 2010-25838
The author offers an insider's view of the quest for what could be the ultimate revelation: the true substance of the unseen dark matter and energy that makes up some 96% of our universe.
"This is a story about not just science, but also scientists, with enough dueling personalities, epic failures, inspirational triumphs, and out-and-out rivalries to carry a Hollywood blockbuster—should Hollywood ever turn its attention to the world of cosmology." Ad Astra
   Includes bibliographical references

Potter, Christopher

You are here; a portable history of the universe. HarperCollins 2009 294p $26.99   **523.1**
   1. Cosmology 2. Science -- History 3. Science -- Philosophy
   ISBN 978-0-06-113786-0; 0-06-113786-3
   An exploration of the universe and our relationship to it.
"A well-executed, consistently readable layperson's exposition of the state of scientific knowledge. . . . One of the best short surveys of science and its history in recent years." Kirkus
   Includes bibliographical references (p. 275-279)

Primack, Joel R.

The **view** from the center of the universe; discovering our extraordinary place in the cosmos. [by] Joel R. Primack and Nancy Ellen Abrams. Riverhead Books 2006 386p il $26.95   **523.1**
    1. Cosmology 2. Cosmology -- History 3. Physics -- Philosophy
    ISBN 1-5944-8914-9; 978-1-5944-8914-3
           LC 2005-55262
"This very important and fascinating book powerfully describes the scope and depth of human connections to our universe." Sci Books Films
    Includes bibliographical references

Rees, Martin J.

Just six numbers; the deep forces that shape the universe. {by} Martin Rees. Basic Bks. 2000 173p il hardcover o.p. pa $14.95   **523.1**
    1. Big bang theory 2. Cosmology
    ISBN 0-465-03673-2 pa
           LC 00-268248
"A brief, readable, and profoundly instructive account of where cosmological knowledge stands at this moment." New Yorker
    Includes bibliographical references

Our cosmic habitat; [by] Martin Rees. Princeton Univ. Press 2001 205p il $35; pa $14.95   **523.1**
    1. Cosmic physics 2. Cosmology
    ISBN 0-691-08926-4; 0-691-11477-3 pa
           LC 2001-27835
"In the crowded field of popular writing about the universe, Rees is genuinely in the forefront—an accomplished scientist with the superior writing skills that enable him to connect with nonspecialists." Booklist
    Includes bibliographical references

Seife, Charles

Alpha and omega; the search for the beginning and end of the universe. Viking 2003 294p il hardcover o.p. pa $15   **523.1**
    1. Astronomy 2. Cosmology
    ISBN 0-670-03179-8; 978-0-14-200446-3; 0-14-200446-4 pa
           LC 2002-44853
"Seife provides lucid explanations of very complicated topics for the science buff or well-rounded general reader." Publ Wkly
    Includes bibliographical references

Singh, Simon

Big bang: the origins of the universe. Fourth Estate 2005 532p il $27.95   **523.1**
    1. Big bang theory 2. Cosmology
    ISBN 0-00716-220-0
    The author "presents a brief history of the origins of the universe. . . . He begins with a historical overview of how scientific thought changed from mythology to cosmology, then moves to the debate between the steady state model of an eternal universe and the Big Bang theory, which saw the universe as beginning at a unique moment that was followed by rapid extension. . . . This readable book provides an accessible overview of this complex scientific theory." Libr J

Smoot, George

Wrinkles in time; witness to the birth of the universe. [by] George Smoot and Keay Davidson; with a new preface. Harper Perennial 2007 331p il pa $14.95   **523.1**
    1. Cosmology
    ISBN 978-0-06-134444-2; 0-06-134444-3
           LC 2008-530705
"Smoot and Davidson present a historical review of cosmology that takes the reader from the work of Galileo to the recent . . . work on 'COBE' (the Cosmic Background Explorer satellite). An excellent nontechnical study of research into what makes the universe the way it is, the book provides a detailed discussion of the search for and the eventual discovery of what are called the 'wrinkles in time' from the viewpoint of the authors' own experiences in the field." Choice [review of 1993 edition]
    Includes bibliographical references

Steinhardt, P. J.

Endless universe; beyond the Big Bang. [by] Paul J. Steinhardt and Neil Turok. Doubleday 2007 284p il $24.95   **523.1**
    1. Cosmology
    ISBN 0-385-50964-2; 978-0-385-50964-0
           LC 2006-25256
"This volume is not light reading, but the authors lighten the load with stories of how they met and collaborated on an M-theory (a string theory derivative) based cyclical model of the universe. . . . The illustrations, which play a key role in the book, introduce the reader to difficult material through simplified analogies." Sci Books Films
    Includes bibliographical references

Tyson, Neil De Grasse

Origin : fourteen billion years of cosmic evolution; {by} Neil deGrasse Tyson, Donald Goldsmith. W.W. Norton 2004 345p il $27.95   **523.1**
    1. Cosmology 2. Evolution 3. Life -- Origin
    ISBN 0-393-05992-8
           LC 2004-12201
"Amateur astronomers—in fact, any reader who enjoys popular science—will find fascinating information presented in clear but never patronizing language." Libr J
    Includes bibliographical references

Universe down to Earth. Columbia Univ. Press 1994 277p il $60; pa $19   **523.1**
    1. Cosmology 2. Universe
    ISBN 0-231-07560-X; 0-231-07561-8 pa
           LC 93-32259
"This book is a genuine joy to read. . . . It is at once witty and profound in its treatment of some of the most 'far-out' concepts of the universe." Sci Books Films
    Includes bibliographical references

Vilenkin, Alexander

Many worlds in one; the search for other universes. [by] Alex Vilenkin. Hill and Wang 2006 235p il $24   **523.1**

1. Cosmology

ISBN 978-0-8090-9523-0; 0-8090-9523-8

LC 2005-27057

The author discusses the "creation of the universe, its likely demise and the growing belief among cosmologists that there are an infinite number of universes. Vilenkin does an impressive job of presenting the background information necessary for lay readers to understand the ideas behind the big bang and related phenomena. . . . Drawing on the work of Stephen Hawking and recent advances in string theory, Vilenkin gives us a great deal to ponder." Publ Wkly

Includes bibliographical references

Weintraub, David A.

How old is the universe? Princeton University Press 2011 370p il $29.95   **523.1**

1. Cosmology 2. Solar system 3. Universe

ISBN 978-0-691-14731-4

LC 2010-9117

"This is no-nonsense science writing that will be enjoyed for years: David Weintraub is an expert guide, laying out the evidence in just the right amount of detail." New Sci

523.2   Planetary systems

Baker, David

The **50** most extreme places in our solar system; [by] David Baker and Todd Ratcliff. Belknap Press 2010 290p il $27.95   **523.2**

1. Extreme environments 2. Solar system

ISBN 978-0-674-04998-7; 0-674-04998-5

LC 2010-06126

The authors "discuss phenomena like the potential for diamond rain on Uranus and Neptune and the hardiness of extremophile life forms. As planetary scientists, they write clearly about the most extreme physical aspects of solar system bodies such as planets, moons, and comets, but deftly mix in more familiar comparisons from planet Earth as well." Choice

Includes bibliographical references

Boss, Alan P.

The **crowded** universe; the search for living planets. [by] Alan Boss. Basic Books 2009 227p il $26   **523.2**

1. Astrophysicists 2. Exobiology 3. Extrasolar planets 4. Life on other planets

ISBN 978-0-465-00936-7; 0-465-00936-0

LC 2008-37149

The author "argues that based on what we already know about planetary systems, in the coming years we will find abundant Earths, including many that are indisputably alive." Publisher's note

Daniels, Patricia

The **new** solar system; ice worlds, moons, and planets redefined. foreword by Robert Burnham. National Geographic Society 2009 223p il map $35   **523.2**

ISBN 978-1-4262-0462-3; 1-4262-046-20

LC 2009-10117

This is "a sumptuously illustrated book describing the history, composition, and exploration of the solar system. Aimed at a general audience, the text is highly readable and contains numerous side notes providing fascinating anecdotes and facts about the planets, the sun, and astronomers." Choice

Includes bibliographical references

Jayawardhana, Ray

Strange new worlds; the search for alien planets and life beyond our solar system. Princeton University Press 2011 255p il $24.95   **523.2**

1. Astronomy -- History 2. Extrasolar planets 3. Life on other planets 4. Solar system

ISBN 978-0-691-14254-8; 0-691-14254-8

LC 2010940350

An astronomer discusses the search for extrasolar planets and extraterrestrial life. Bibliography. Index.

"Everything you need to know about alien planet discovery is insightfully described in this engaging book, which will appeal to astronomers, general science buffs, and armchair UFOlogists." Libr J

Includes glossary and bibliographical references

Lang, Kenneth R.

The **Cambridge** guide to the solar system; Kenneth R. Lang. Cambridge University Press 2003 452p il $60   **523.2**

ISBN 0-521-81306-9

LC 2002-31562

"The photographs are stunning, the numerous charts and graphs are exemplary, and the narrative is bulging with all the important information about the solar system that is available to date. The author has done a wonderful job of making many of the complicated scientific concepts accessible to the layperson." Booklist

Includes bibliographical references

Lorenz, Ralph

Titan unveiled; Saturn's mysterious moon explored. [by] Ralph Lorenz and Jacqueline Mitton. Princeton University Press 2008 243p il map $29.95; pa $19.95   **523.2**

ISBN 978-0-691-12587-9; 0-691-12587-2; 978-0-691-14633-1 pa; 0-619-14633-0 pa

LC 2007-938922

This book "provides the general reader with a lively narrative that combines a reliable, nontechnical account of the Cassini-Huygens mission with personal and often intimate insights into these efforts to explore a fascinating planetary analogue to the Earth." Am Sci

Includes bibliographical references

Sobel, Dava

The **planets**. Viking 2005 270p il $24.95; pa $13
523.2

1. Planets 2. Solar system
ISBN 0-670-03446-0; 0-14-200116-3 pa

"For newcomers to planetary astronomy, 'The Planets' offers a nimble summary of the latest findings on each planet's features and geology. For those who avidly followed the journeys of the Mariners, Voyagers and Vikings through interplanetary space, it lets us fall in love with the heavens all over again." N Y Times Book Rev

Includes bibliographical references

523.3 Specific parts of solar system

Mackenzie, Dana

The **big** splat; or, How our moon came to be. Wiley 2003 232p il $24.95
523.3

ISBN 0-471-15057-6

LC 2003-535402

"Mackenzie's account of humanity's long relationship with Earth's only natural satellite, from a probable lunar calendar found in the Lascaux caves to the new 'giant impact' theory of the moon's origin, is magnetically readable, preternaturally clear, and amazingly concise." Booklist

Includes bibliographical references

523.4 Planets, asteroids, trans-Neptunian objects of solar system

Beebe, Reta F.

Jupiter; the giant planet. {by} Reta Beebe. 2nd ed; Smithsonian Institution Press 1997 261p il hardcover o.p. pa $17.95
523.4

ISBN 1-56098-685-9 pa

LC 96-38604

The author describes the history of discoveries about Jupiter, its atmosphere and interior composition. Includes findings from the 1994 collision of Comet Shoemaker-Levy/9 and observations of the Galileo probe.

Boyle, Alan

The **case** for Pluto; how a little planet made a big difference. Wiley 2010 258p il $22.95; ebook $14.99
523.4

1. Solar system
ISBN 978-0-470-50544-1; 0-470-50544-3; 978-0-470-54188-3 ebook

LC 2009-15961

This volume examines the history of the discovery of planets. Boyle "chronicles the decision by the International Astronomical Union in 2006 to redefine the definition of a planet. . . . [Boyle argues] that Pluto has unjustly been cast out of the 'Planet Family' and recast as a 'dwarf planet.'" Sci Books Films

Includes bibliographical references

Grinspoon, David Harry

Venus revealed; a new look below the clouds of our mysterious twin planet. Addison-Wesley 1997 355p il hardcover o.p. pa $20
523.4

ISBN 0-201-32839-9 pa

LC 96-38448

The author "makes science fun, not forbidding." Booklist

Jones, Barrie William

Pluto; sentinel of the outer solar system. [by] Barrie W. Jones. Cambridge University Press 2010 231p il $35.99
523.4

1. Kuiper Belt 2. Solar system -- Origin
ISBN 978-0-521-19436-5; 0-521-19436-9

LC 2010-15480

This is "a detailed, matter-of-fact, and thoroughly accessible look at Pluto's origins, its history, and what it can tell us about our solar system—especially its outer reaches. . . . The author writes in a clear, matter-of-fact style, including sidebars on related subjects from Kepler's laws of planetary motion to calculating a planet's surface temperature using nothing more complex than high school algebra." Publ Wkly

Includes glossary and bibliographical references

Kessler, Andrew

Martian summer; robot arms, cowboy spacemen, and my 90 days with the Phoenix Mars Mission. Pegasus 2011 340p il $27.95
523.4

1. Phoenix Mars Mission (U.S.) 2. Space flight to Mars
ISBN 978-1-60598-176-5; 1-60598-176-1

The author chronicles the three months he spent in Mission Control for NASA's Phoenix Mars Mission, a project that lead to the discovery of liquid water on Mars, as well as a giant frozen ocean trapped beneath the planet's north pole.

"The author provides some fascinating glimpses of the real work of a space mission: planning activities for the lander, dealing with peremptory orders from NASA and JPL, interpreting the sometimes ambiguous data and occasionally letting one's hair down for a party." Kirkus

Tyson, Neil De Grasse

The **Pluto** files; the rise and fall of America's favorite planet. W.W. Norton 2009 194p il $23.95; pa $15.95
523.4

1. Astrophysicists 2. Classification of sciences 3. Museum administrators
ISBN 978-0-393-06520-6; 0-393-06520-0; 978-0-393-33732-7 pa; 0-393-33732-4 pa

LC 2008-40436

An exploration of the controversy surrounding Pluto and its planet status from an astrophysicist at the heart of the controversy.

The author "uses an engaging mix of facts, photographs, cartoons, illustrations, songs, e-mails, and humor to explain what's up (and down) with Pluto." Christ Sci Monit

Includes bibliographical references

Weintraub, David A.

Is Pluto a planet? a historical journey through the solar system. Princeton University Press 2007 254p il $27.95   **523.4**

    1. Planets 2. Solar system

    ISBN 0-691-12348-9; 978-0-691-12348-6

                  LC 2006-929630

    Weintraub "provides a very interesting and thought-provoking history concerning the whole idea of planets, and I recommend the book highly to anyone interested in the solar system." Sci Books Films

    Includes bibliographical references

523.43   Mars

Morton, Oliver

    Mapping Mars; science, imagination, and the birth of a world. Picador 2002 357p il maps $30; pa $16   **523.43**

    ISBN 0-312-24551-3; 0-312-42261-X pa

    The author "traces scientists' efforts to map and understand the surface of Mars. . . . Morton writes eloquently and displays a breadth of knowledge not often found in science writing." Publ Wkly

    Includes bibliographical references (p. 333-345) and index

Sheehan, William

    Mars; the lure of the red planet. {by} William Sheehan & Stephen James O'Meara. Prometheus Bks. 2001 406p il $28   **523.43**

    ISBN 1-57392-900-X

                  LC 00-67358

    The authors look "at the personalities of the great astronomers who gazed at Mars and, in particular, the aspects of or mysteries about Mars that captivated them. . . . An informative overview of sky watchers' enduring fascination with Mars." Booklist

    Includes bibliographical references

523.44   Asteroids (Planetoids)

Peebles, Curtis

    Asteroids; a history. Smithsonian Institution Press 2000 280p il $29.95; pa $17.95   **523.44**

    1. Asteroids

    ISBN 1-56098-389-2; 1-56098-982-3 pa

                  LC 00-20733

    Surveys the equipment, techniques, and controversies of 200 years of asteroid research. Prominent theorists are profiled. Impact threats and the mystery of the dinosaurs' extinction are discussed.

    "For a book aimed at general audiences, Peeble's excellent review of asteroids is unusually well documented. . . . {His} book clearly has a place on the bookshelves of specialists, students, and advanced amateurs." Choice

    Includes bibliographical references

523.48   Neptune

Brown, Mike

    How I killed Pluto and why it had it coming; Mike Brown. Spiegel & Grau 2010 xiii, 267p 1 ill. (pbk.) $15.00; (alk. paper) o.p.; (alk. paper) o.p.; (ebook) $12.99   **523.48**

    1. Astronomers 2. College teachers 3. Discoveries in science 4. Discoveries in science -- Anecdotes 5. Planets 6. Solar system

    ISBN 9780385531108; 0385531087; 9780385531085; 9780385531092

                  LC 2010015074

    This book relates the story of astronomist Mike Brown's research that led to the demotion of Pluto as a planet. "The solar system most of us grew up with included nine planets, with Mercury closest to the sun and Pluto at the outer edge. Then, in 2005, astronomer Mike Brown made the discovery of a lifetime: a tenth planet, Eris, slightly bigger than Pluto. But instead of adding one more planet to our solar system, Brown's find ignited a firestorm of controversy that culminated in the demotion of Pluto from real planet to the newly coined category of 'dwarf' planet. Suddenly Brown was receiving hate mail from schoolchildren and being bombarded by TV reporters—all because of the discovery he had spent years searching for and a lifetime dreaming about." (Publisher's note)

    "Deftly pulling readers along on his journey of discovery and destruction, Brown sets the record straight and strongly defends his science with a conversational, rational, and calm voice that may change the public's opinion of scientists as poor communicators." Publ Wkly

523.5   Meteors, solar wind, zodiacal light

Bevan, A. W. R.

    Meteorites: a journey through space and time; [by] Alex Bevan and John de Laeter. Smithsonian Institution Press 2002 215p il maps $35.95   **523.5**

    1. Meteorites

    ISBN 1-58834-021-X

                  LC 2001-49551

    "Informative and visually appealing, this title meets any library's need for a basic source on meteorites." Booklist

    Includes bibliographical references

Cokinos, Christopher

    The **fallen** sky; an intimate history of shooting stars. Jeremy P. Tarcher/Penguin 2009 518p $27.95   **523.5**

    1. Bird watchers 2. College teachers 3. Meteorites 4. Meteorites -- History

    ISBN 978-1-58542-720-8; 1-58542-720-9

                  LC 2009-17493

    "In 1894, fifteen years before his storied expedition to the North Pole, Robert Peary crossed a treacherous expanse of ice in Greenland in search of another prize: a massive meteorite laden with rare metals from outer space. In this hefty, industrious book, Cokinos retraces Peary's steps, and those of other meteor 'obsessives,' in an idiosyncratic hunt of his own." New Yorker

Includes bibliographical references

523.6   Comets

Sagan, Carl

Comet; [by] Carl Sagan and Ann Druyan. Random House 1985 398p il hardcover o.p. pa $23   **523.6**

1. Comets

ISBN 0-345-41222-2

LC 85-8308

"The authors explore the myth and science of comets in a lavishly illustrated, slightly oversize volume that is both fascinating and authoritative." Booklist

Includes bibliographical references

523.7   Sun

Berman, Bob

The **sun's** heartbeat; and other stories from the life of the star that powers our planet. Little, Brown and Co. 2011 290p il $25.99; ebook $12.99 **523.7**

ISBN 978-0-316-09101-5; 0-316-09101-4; 978-0-316-17539-5 ebook

LC 2010044207

Provides facts about the star at the center of our solar system and describes the life of the sun, from its birth and life as a self-sustaining ultra-H-Bomb fusion explosion, to its spectacular and anticipated future death.

"An engaging consciousness-raiser that entertains as it informs about our neighborhood nuclear furnace." Booklist

Includes bibliographical references

Clark, Stuart

The **sun** kings; the unexpected tragedy of Richard Carrington and the tale of how modern astronomy began. Princeton Univ. Press 2007 211p il $24.95   **523.7**

1. Astronomers 2. Astronomy -- History 3. Astronomy -- History -- 19th century 4. Photographers 5. Writers on science

ISBN 978-0-691-12660-9; 0-691-12660-7

LC 2006-940123

"Clark's parade of historical characters dramatize the narrative nicely, and Clark conveys the significance of their scientific observations with plenty of context and thorough references, making this a fascinating work for both casual stargazers and serious astronomy buffs." Publ Wkly

Includes bibliographical references

Cohen, Richard

Chasing the sun; the epic story of the star that gives us life. Random House 2010 xxxi, 574p il $35; ebook $17.99   **523.7**

1. Astronomy -- History 2. Science and civilization

ISBN 978-1-4000-6875-3; 1-4000-6875-4; 978-1-

58836-934-5 ebook

LC 2010-05885

"A remarkably comprehensive and engrossing synthesis of the sun's influence on science, art, religion, literature, mythology and politics. . . . Ever enthusiastic, Cohen provides illuminating personal anecdotes, but he includes just the right amount of detail, never allowing the material to sprawl untethered." Kirkus

Includes bibliographical references

Golub, Leon

★ **Nearest** star; the surprising science of our sun. {by} Leon Golub & Jay M. Pasachoff. Harvard Univ. Press 2001 267p il $29.95; pa $16.95 **523.7**

ISBN 0-674-00467-1; 0-674-01006-X pa

LC 00-63213

This is "a brilliant, richly illustrated survey." Booklist

Includes bibliographical references

523.8   Stars

Bakich, Michael E.

★ The **Cambridge** guide to the constellations. Cambridge Univ. Press 1995 320p il maps hardcover o.p. pa $29   **523.8**

1. Constellations

ISBN 0-521-44921-9 pa

LC 94-4678

"This book is the ultimate constellation reference book that brings together a variety of information about constellations, including: the size, visibility and relative brightness of all eighty-eight constellations; former location of extinct constellations; the number of visible stars in each constellation, and more." Univ Press Books for Public and Second Sch Libr

Includes bibliographical references

Ferguson, Kitty

Prisons of light; black holes. Cambridge Univ. Press 1996 214p il hardcover o.p. pa $17   **523.8**

1. Black holes (Astronomy)

ISBN 0-521-49518-0; 0-521-62571-8 pa

LC 96-11729

The author discusses the origin, properties, and behavior of black holes and reviews the scientific evidence for their existence.

"The typical reader will find this book an easily understood overview of an interesting subject. . . . A clear and accurate introduction to black holes for the general science reader." Sci Books Films

Includes bibliographical references

Hirshfeld, Alan

Parallax; the race to measure the cosmos. {by} Alan W. Hirshfeld. Freeman, W.H. 2001 314p il $23.95; pa $16   **523.8**

1. Cosmological distances 2. Parallax -- Stars 3. Stars

ISBN 0-7167-3711-6; 0-8050-7133-4 pa

LC 00-68147

This book chronicles the efforts to secure the first distance to a star through detection of stellar parallax. Scientists involved in the challenge included Tycho Brahe, Robert Hooke, James Bradley and William Herschel

This "is a lively gallery of colorful and, of course, calculating characters. . . . A delightful history of a crucial advance in knowledge." Booklist

Includes bibliographical refeerences and index

Kaler, James B.

Extreme stars; at the edge of creation. Cambridge Univ. Press 2001 236p il maps $40   **523.8**

1. Stars

ISBN 0-521-40262-X

LC 00-58522

"Each chapter covers extreme stars of a different kind, including the faintest, the coolest, the brightest, the largest, the smallest, the youngest, the oldest, and the strangest. . . . {Kaler} piques the curiosity of the novice, while encouraging knowledgeable readers to think about stars from a different perspective. There is a wealth of information, much of it not available elsewhere at this semipopular level." Choice

Kerrod, Robin

The **star** guide; learn how to read the night sky star by star. 2nd ed; Wiley 2005 160p il $29.95   **523.8**

1. Reference books 2. Stars -- Atlases

ISBN 0-471-70617-5

LC 2004-22953

The presentation for this instructional guide to stargazing "is structured around monthly star maps (for midlatitude observers) in two-page spreads, with a follow-up feature on that month's outstanding constellation. . . . Photos featuring Hubble Space Telescope spectaculars, supplemented by tips for viewing the sun, moon, and planets, round out this attractive book on basic astronomy." Booklist

Scagell, Robin

Stargazing with binoculars; [by] Robin Scagell, David Frydman. 2nd ed., updated and rev.; Firefly Books 2011 208p il pa $19.95   **523.8**

1. Astronomy 2. Binoculars 3. Stars

ISBN 978-1-55407-821-9; 1-55407-821-0

LC 2011-288021

This is a "guide to using binoculars to view the night sky for newcomers to astronomy. The book includes reviews of the wide range of binoculars on the market and provides advice on features to consider before making a purchase. The authors guide the beginner through the first steps of using binoculars to observe the night sky, describe what will be visible and show how to find specific objects." Publisher's note

Tirion, Wil

★ The **Cambridge** star atlas; 3rd ed; Cambridge Univ. Press 2001 90p il maps $25   **523.8**

1. Reference books 2. Stars 3. Stars -- Atlases

ISBN 0-521-80084-6

LC 20010622030

"Recommended for anyone who plans to observe with the naked eye, binoculars, or small telescope... The printing is excellent, and the pages easily lie flat." Choice

Includes bibliographical references

Tyson, Neil De Grasse

Death by black hole; and other cosmic quandaries. Norton 2007 384p $24.95; pa $15.95   **523.8**

1. Black holes (Astronomy) 2. Cosmology 3. Exobiology 4. Religion and science 5. Solar system 6. Space biology

ISBN 978-0-393-06224-3; 0-393-06224-4; 978-0-393-33016-8 pa; 0-393-33016-8 pa

LC 2006-22058

"A wonderfully informed viewpoint on the slowly expanding boundaries of human knowledge." Boston Globe

Includes bibliographical references

523.9   Satellites and rings; eclipses, transits, occultations

Sheehan, William

The **transits** of Venus; by William Sheehan, John Westfall. Prometheus Books 2004 407p il $28   **523.9**

ISBN 1-59102-175-8

LC 2003-22420

"This volume is a tour de force not only of the history of observing Venus, but of much of astronomy itself." Sci Books Films

Includes bibliographical references

Wulf, Andrea

Chasing Venus; the race to measure the heavens. Andrea Wulf. Alfred A. Knopf 2012 xxvi, 304 p.p (hardback) $26.95   **523.9**

1. Astronomy -- History -- 18th century 2. Geodetic astronomy -- History -- 18th century 3. Historical literature 4. Scientists -- History

ISBN 0307700178; 0307958612; 9780307700179; 9780307958617

LC 2011049136

This book "is concerned with Venus's 1761 and 1769 transits, when the international science community dispatched a remarkable set of expeditions to remote parts of the world to observe and measure the planet's passages across the sun. Their primary objective was to use newly acquired observational data to improve knowledge of the distance between Earth and the Sun and the solar system's dimensions. Many of the traveling scientists underwent great travails, and several died." (Library Journal)

525   Earth (Astronomical geography)

Our changing planet; the view from space. edited by Michael D. King . . . [et al.] Cambridge University Press 2007 390p il map $47   **525**

1. Environmental sciences 2. Human influence on nature 3. Remote sensing

ISBN 978-0-521-82870-3; 0-521-82870-8

LC 2008-295497

Examines what orbital imagery tells us about the atmosphere, land, ocean, and polar ice caps of our planet and the ways that it changes naturally, and in response to human activity.

"This is a very fine compilation of System Earth through the eyes and experience of remote sensing experts—beautifully made and a pleasure to read." Environmental Geology

526 Mathematical geography

Alder, Ken

The **measure** of all things; the seven-year odyssey and hidden error that transformed the world. Free Press 2002 422p $27; pa $15 **526**

1. Arc measures -- History 2. Astronomers 3. Geography 4. Meter (Unit) -- History 5. Metric system
ISBN 0-7432-1675-X; 0-7432-1676-8 pa

LC 2002-70267

"In 1792, two astronomers set out from Paris in opposite directions to measure the meridian and thereby define the length of the meter. Alder's marvelous account of their quest is a dramatic tale of revolution, science, and human error." Libr J

Includes bibliographical references

Danson, Edwin

Weighing the world; the quest to measure the Earth. Oxford University Press 2005 289p il $29.95 **526**

1. Science -- History 2. Surveying
ISBN 978-0-19-518169-2; 0-19-518169-7

LC 2004-66284

The author "enlivens data about geodetic surveying, transforming them into greatly interesting dramas of science." Booklist

Includes bibliographical references

Ferreiro, Larrie D.

Measure of the Earth; the enlightenment expedition that reshaped our world. Basic Books 2011 353p il map $28 **526**

1. Geodesy 2. Geodesy -- Europe -- History 3. Scientific expeditions 4. Scientific expeditions -- Europe -- History -- 18th century
ISBN 978-0-465-01723-2; 0-465-01723-1; 978-0-465-02345-5 ebook; 0-465-02345-2 ebook

LC 2011007173

This book "reads like a script from an Indiana Jones adventure film. . . . [It is] very well written and will interest any reader as it gives insight into the 18th Century and introduces some fascinating and unforgettable characters." Sci Books Films

Includes bibliographical references

Nicastro, Nicholas

Circumference; Eratosthenes and the ancient quest to measure the globe. St. Martin's Press 2008 223p il map $23.95 **526**

1. Arc measures 2. Astronomers 3. Earth sciences -- Measurement 4. Geographers 5. Mathematics, Greek 6. Measurement 7. Weights and measures 8. Weights

and measures, Ancient 9. Writers on science
ISBN 978-0-312-37247-7; 0-312-37247-7

LC 2008-25773

"Nicastro delivers the deeply human story of a multitalented genius whose tenure as the head of Alexandria's famed library occasioned remarkable achievements in literature, history, linguistics, and philosophy despite the political turmoil that periodically rocked the Ptolemaic world." Booklist

Includes bibliographical references

Raymo, Chet

Walking zero; discovering cosmic space and time along the Prime Meridian. Walker & Co. 2006 194p il maps $22.95 **526**

1. Authors 2. College teachers 3. Longitude 4. Longitude -- Prime meridian 5. Novelists 6. Physicists 7. Writers on science
ISBN 0-8027-1494-3; 978-0-8027-1494-7

LC 2006-282372

This is the author's "expression of his personal exploration of space, time, and scientific history, inspired partly by his walking the footpaths of southeast England in close proximity to the 0 degrees longitude line. . . . . This work is a thought-provoking, highly enlightening discussion of some of the most fascinating concepts in physics, astronomy, and geology, among other subjects." Sci Books Films

Includes bibliographical references

Sobel, Dava

★ **Longitude**; the true story of a lone genius who solved the greatest scientific problem of his time. with a new foreword by Neil Armstrong. Hardcover anniversary ed., [10th anniversary ed., 2005 anniversary ed.]; Walker & Co. 2005 184p il $19 **526**

1. Clock and watch makers 2. Longitude 3. Mechanical engineers
ISBN 0-8027-1462-5; 978-0-8027-1462-6

"In 1714, Britain's Parliament offered the modern equivalent of $12 to anybody who could develop a means of determining longitude at sea. While the likes of Isaac Newton and Edmund Halley sought to calculate longitude by celestial measurement, John Harrison, an uneducated clockmaker, solved the problem with his invention of the chronometer. Science writer Sobel tells this story in a way that enables readers 'to see the globe anew.'" Libr J

Includes bibliographical references

Winchester, Simon

The **map** that changed the world; William Smith and the birth of modern geology. illustrations by Soun Vannithone. HarperCollins Pubs. 2001 329p il map $26; pa $13.95 **526**

1. Civil engineers 2. Geologists 3. Geologists -- Great Britain -- Biography 4. Geology, Stratigraphic -- History 5. Stratigraphic geology 6. Writers on science
ISBN 0-06-019361-1; 0-06-093180-9 pa

LC 2001-16603

"In the early years of the nineteenth century, William Smith created the first geological map of Great Britain, a time-consuming, solitary project that helped establish geology as one of the 'fundamental fields of study.' . . . Winchester tells Smith's story, including the dramatic ups and downs of his personal life. . . . This is just the kind of creative non-fiction that elevates a seemingly arcane topic into popular fare." Booklist

★ 100 maps; the science, art and politics of cartography throughout history. edited by John O. E. Clark; introduction by Jeremy Black. Sterling 2006 256p il map $24.95   **526**

1. Maps

ISBN 1-4027-2885-9

"This atlas contains 100 attractively presented maps, each with a story appended explaining its qualities: scientific, imaginative, propagandistic, etc. . . . The maps range across history from an ancient clay tablet map drawn more than 4,000 years ago in a country now known as Iraq to maps of the tsunami of 2004. . . . This well-wrought production will appeal to both advanced readers and neophytes." Choice

Includes bibliographical references

528   Ephemerides

United States Naval Observatory

★ **Astronomical** almanac for the year 2011; and its companion The astronomical almanac online: data for astronomy, space sciences, geodesy, surveying, navigation and other applications. U.S. Govt. Ptg. Office 2010 various pagings $40   **528**

1. Nautical almanacs 2. Reference books

ISBN 9780-70-774103-1

"With basic information contributed by the ephemeris offices of a number of countries, this collection of tables is the authoritative source for annual astronomical data from the movement of heavenly bodies to the calculation of calendars." Ref Sources for Small & Medium-sized Libr. 6th edition

529   Chronology

Aveni, Anthony F.

Empires of time; calendars, clocks, and cultures. [by] Anthony Aveni. rev ed; University Press of Colo. 2002 332p il pa $22.95   **529**

1. Archaeoastronomy 2. Time

ISBN 0-87081-672-1

LC 2002-7120

The author "traces the modern calendar's roots back to Greek pastoral poetry and prehistoric African bone markings, then compares Western, Chinese, Maya, Inca and tribal time systems. He also fathoms our division of time into days, weeks, months, seasons and years for clues to our psychology and worldview." Publ Wkly

Includes bibliographical references

Barnett, Jo Ellen

Time's pendulum; from sundials to atomic clocks, the fascinating history of timekeeping and

how our discoveries changed the world. Harcourt Brace 1999 334p il map pa $15   **529**

1. Time

ISBN 0-15-600649-9

LC 98-49612

The author "shows how our notion of time is relative on a very human level. Time has undergone a long process of standardization over the centuries, she explains. . . . Barnett's book is a triumph of interdisciplinary scholarship that could appeal to a wide variety of readers." Publ Wkly

Includes bibliographical references

Falk, Dan

★ **In** search of time; the science of a curious dimension. Thomas Dunne Books, St. Martin's Press 2008 329p il $25.95; pa $15.99   **529**

1. Science and civilization 2. Time

ISBN 978-0-312-37478-5; 0-312-37478-X; 978-0-312-60351-9 pa; 0-312-60351-7 pa

LC 2008-24875

"The book's scope is audaciously broad. Relying on reportage and humour to offset writing that is occasionally prolix, Falk deftly weaves together elements of religion, anthropology, philosophy, and physics into an engaging narrative." Quill Quire

Includes bibliographical references

Galison, Peter Louis

★ **Einstein's** clocks and Poincare's maps; empires of time. by Peter Galison. Norton 2003 389p il $23.95   **529**

1. Mathematicians 2. Nobel laureates for physics 3. Physicists 4. Relativity (Physics) 5. Time

ISBN 0-393-02001-0

LC 2002-155114

"Galison shows how Einstein's work was influenced by French cartographer Henri Poincaré and by the physicist's own experience working in a Bern patent office, where the numerous patent requests for devices designed to coordinate distant clocks may have prompted further inquiry into the problem of simultaneity, which lies at the heart of relativity. Few books have ever made Einstein's theories more accessible—or more engrossing—for general readers." Booklist

Includes bibliographical references

Gleick, James

Faster; the acceleration of just about everything. Pantheon Bks. 1999 324p il hardcover o.p. pa $14   **529**

1. Time

ISBN 0-679-77548-X pa

LC 99-21640

The author's "shrewd dissection of the 'psychology of hurriedness' leads to many provocative observations." Booklist

Richards, E. G.

Mapping time; the calendar and its history. Oxford Univ. Press 1999 xxi, 438p il hardcover o.p. pa $43.50 **529**

1. Calendars 2. Time

ISBN 0-19-286205-7 pa

LC 98-24957

"An overview of astronomy, time, clocks, writing, arithmetic, and other theoretical issues lays the groundwork for a description of calendar systems from prehistory to the present. Illustrations, charts, and diagrams, including algorithms for the conversion of calendar systems, are also provided." Libr J

Includes bibliographical references

Sims, Michael

Apollo's fire; a day on Earth in nature and imagination. Viking 2007 xxiv, 296p $24.95 **529**

1. Astronomy 2. Days 3. Time

ISBN 978-0-670-06328-4; 0-670-06328-2

LC 2007-6024

The author "takes a single day and guides readers through the history of what we know, and what we've imagined, about sunrises, clouds and other natural phenomena. . . . His delightful tour of day and night skies will inspire many readers to look up with a marveling new perspective." Publ Wkly

Includes bibliographical references

530   Physics

Ananthaswamy, Anil

The **edge** of physics; a journey to Earth's extremes to unlock the secrets of the universe. Houghton Mifflin Harcourt 2010 322p il $25 **530**

1. Cosmology 2. Physics 3. Physics -- Experiments 4. Voyages and travels

ISBN 978-0-618-88468-1; 0-618-88468-8

LC 2009-20225

"A meticulous, accessible update of the latest ideas and instruments that contribute to the clarification of an increasingly puzzling universe." Kirkus

Includes bibliographical references

Balibar, Sebastien

The **atom** and the apple; twelve tales from contemporary physics. translated by Nathanael Stein. Princeton University Press 2008 190p il $24.95 **530**

1. Physics

ISBN 978-0-691-13108-5

LC 2008-18027

This "is a delightful ramble through many areas of science as well as through the experiences, opinions, passions and frustrations of a leading research physicist. . . . It is a very refreshing read that will do much to bring an understanding of scientific culture to the reader." Times Higher Ed

Includes bibliographical references

Bernstein, Jeremy

Oppenheimer; portrait of an enigma. Dee, I.R. 2004 223p il $25 **530**

1. College teachers 2. Government officials 3. Physicists 4. Physicists -- United States -- Biography

ISBN 1-566-63569-1

LC 2003-66652

The author "recounts Oppenheimer's eclectic life as it evolved in the US through his education and service at several prestigious institutions. . . . The book is not a review of Oppenheimer's contributions to physics or the development of the atomic bomb; rather, it provides insight into the human side of a brilliant individual, all things considered. Of course, his leadership of the Manhattan Project, and his persecution by Congress for alleged communist sympathies, defined Oppenheimer's career. Bernstein provides personalized insights into both." Choice

Includes bibliographical references

Brennan, Richard P.

Heisenberg probably slept here; the lives, times, and ideas of the great physicists of the 20th century. Wiley 1997 274p il $22.95; pa $14.95 **530**

1. Authors 2. Biography, Collective 3. College teachers 4. Mathematicians 5. Nobel laureates for chemistry 6. Nobel laureates for physics 7. Physicists 8. Physicists -- Biography 9. Physics -- History 10. Writers on science

ISBN 0-471-15709-0; 0-471-29585-X pa

LC 96-42935

"Brennan provides an accessible view of some tough areas of science by knowing what to leave out, and the way he links the continuing quest of physics through the century is admirable." New Sci

Includes bibliographical references

Buchanan, Mark

Nexus: small worlds and the groundbreaking science of networks. Norton 2002 235p $25.95; pa $14.95 **530**

1. Patterns (Mathematics) 2. System analysis

ISBN 0-393-04153-0; 0-393-32442-7 pa

LC 2002-518

The author "introduces readers to the dynamics of networks and shows how these networks affect behaviors in both the natural and the social world. . . . {Buchanan} finds the same patterns taking shape in food chains, in the neuronal networks of insects, in the architecture of the Internet and in the cultural backgrounds of elite CEOs. . . . Buchanan's ability as an affable, easygoing storyteller makes up for myriad digressions, and the narrative is, at times, spellbinding." Publ Wkly

Includes bibliographical references

Close, F. E.

Nothing; a very short introduction. [by] Frank Close. Oxford University Press 2009 157p pa $11.95 **530**

1. Cosmology 2. Nothing (Philosophy) 3. Physics -- Philosophy 4. Physics -- Philosophy -- History

ISBN 978-0-19-922586-6; 0-19-922586-9

LC 2009-281157

This history of "nothing" covers the "history of the vacuum: how the efforts to make a better vacuum led to the discovery of the electron; the ideas of Newton, Mach, and Einstein on the nature of space and time; the mysterious aether and how Einstein did away with it; and the . . . [idea] that the vacuum is filled with the Higgs field." Publisher's note
Includes bibliographical references

Cole, K. C.

   First you build a cloud; and other reflections on physics as a way of life. Harcourt Brace & Co. 1999 231p il pa $14   **530**
   1. Physics
   ISBN 0-15-600646-4

              LC 98-47050

   "Cole offers reflections on the place of physics in modern life. . . . Especially compelling are the essays on the aesthetic force behind scientific endeavors—the beauties of theory. For readers without scientific background, Cole gracefully introduces relativity, quantum theory, optics, astrophysics, and other significant disciplines, never getting bogged down in unnecessary explanation." Booklist
   Includes bibliographical references

Conant, Jennet

   Tuxedo Park; a Wall Street tycoon and the secret palace of science that changed the course of World War II. Simon & Schuster 2002 330p il $26; pa $14   **530**
   1. Atomic bomb   2. Atomic bomb -- United States -- History -- 20th century   3. Foundation officials   4. Investment bankers   5. Physicists   6. Physicists -- United States -- Biography   7. Research -- New York (State) -- Tuxedo Park -- History -- 20th century   8. World War, 1939-1945 -- Science -- United States
   ISBN 0-684-87287-0; 0-684-87288-9 pa

              LC 2002-21001

   "Conant displays a real feel for the personal lives and sensibilities of the era's leading scientists and industrialists in a fascinating, never-before-told bit of American history." Booklist
   Includes bibliographical references

Darling, David J.

   Gravity's arc; the story of gravity, from Aristotle to Einstein and beyond. [by] David Darling. J. Wiley 2006 278p $24.95   **530**
   1. Biography, Collective   2. General relativity (Physics) -- History   3. Gravitation   4. Gravity   5. Physicists -- Biography
   ISBN 0-471-71989-7; 978-0-471-71989-2

              LC 2005-30772

   This is a "historical review of the human understanding of gravity from the ancient Greeks to the 21st century. Included are examinations of Greek philosophers and their debates, medieval and Arabic developments, Galileo, Tycho, Kepler, Newton, Eotvos, [and] Einstein. . . . The writing style is clear and reader friendly. . . . Read this book to learn about gravity and experience a model scientific exposition for the scientist and general reader alike." Sci Books Films
   Includes bibliographical references

Deutsch, David

   The **fabric** of reality; the science of parallel universes--and its implications. Allen Lane/The Penguin Press 1997 390p il hardcover o.p. pa $16   **530**
   1. Cosmology   2. Life   3. Physics -- Philosophy   4. Reality   5. Universe
   ISBN 0-14-027541-X

              LC 97-6171

   "A thoroughly mesmerizing scientific/philosophical view of reality." Libr J
   Includes bibliographical references

Einstein, Albert

   Ideas and opinions; with an introduction by Alan Lightman; based on Mein weltbild, edited by Carl Seelig, and other sources; new translations and revisions by Sonja Bargmann. Modern Lib. 1994 418p $16.95; pa $13   **530**
   ISBN 0-679-60105-8; 0-517-88440-2 pa

              LC 94-2115

   This is a collection of the scientist's general writings on such subjects as freedom, education, religion, politics and government, the Jewish people, and Germany

   ★ The **evolution** of physics; the growth of ideas from early concepts to relativity and quanta. by Albert Einstein and Leopold Infeld. Simon & Schuster 1938 320p il hardcover o.p. pa $13   **530**
   1. Physics -- History   2. Quantum theory   3. Relativity (Physics)
   ISBN 0-671-20156-5 pa
   An "exposition for the layman of the growth of ideas in physical science." Publ Wkly

   The **ultimate** quotable Einstein; collected and edited by Alice Calaprice; with a foreword by Freeman Dyson. Princeton University Press 2011 xxviii, 578p il $24.95; ebook $24.95   **530**
   1. Quotations
   ISBN 978-0-691-13817-6; 0-691-13817-6; 978-1-4008-3596-6 ebook

              LC 2010002855

   This collection of Einstein's quotes includes "sections titled 'On and to Children' and 'On Race and Prejudice,' and a brief selection of Einstein's wry verses. The comments are few on the matters of physics and mathematics, concentrating more on personal, social, political, philosophical, and educational subjects." Choice
   Includes bibliographical references

Feynman, Richard Phillips

   ★ **Six** easy pieces; essentials of physics explained by its most brilliant teacher. [by] Richard P. Feynman; originally prepared for publication by Robert B. Leighton and Matthew Sands; introduction by Paul Davies. Basic Books 2005 xxix, 144p il pa $13.95   **530**
   1. Atoms   2. Energy conservation   3. Gravitation   4. Physics   5. Quantum theory
   ISBN 978-0-465-02392-9

This book reprints six chapters from Feynman's Lectures on Physics. "In these six chapters, Feynman introduces the general reader to the following: atoms, basic physics, the relationship of physics to other topics, energy, gravitation, and quantum force." Publisher's note

Folsing, Albrecht

Albert Einstein; a biography. translated from the German by Ewald Osers. Viking 1997 882p il hardcover o.p. pa $20 **530**
1. Biography, Individual 2. Nobel laureates for physics 3. Physicists
ISBN 0-14-023719-4 pa
LC 96-26341
This biography traces "Einstein's life from early childhood through his final years at Princeton's Institute for Advanced Study. It gives equal detail to his technical accomplishments and personal life, including his role as an international spokesman for Zionism and pacifism. It also includes a more honest picture of his relationships with women." Libr J
Includes bibliographical references

Gleick, James

Isaac Newton. Pantheon Bks. 2003 272p il hardcover o.p. pa $13 **530**
1. Biography, Individual 2. Mathematicians 3. Physicists 4. Scientists 5. Writers on science
ISBN 0-375-42233-1; 1-4000-3295-4 pa
LC 2002-192696
This "is now the biography of choice for the interested layman. Gleick copes with the complex tapestry of Newton's interests by teasing them apart into individual chapters, assembled into a smooth chronological flow. . . . Newton the man emerges from the shadows." N Y Times Book Rev
Includes bibliographical references

Goldberg, Dave

A **user's** guide to the universe; surviving the perils of black holes, time paradoxes, and quantum uncertainty. [by] Dave Goldberg and Jeff Blomquist. Wiley 2010 296p il $24.95 **530**
1. Physics
ISBN 978-0-470-49651-0; 0-470-49651-7
Surveys the major discoveries of modern physics, from relativity to the Large Hadron Collider. The authors discuss subjects such as special relativity, quantum mechanics, randomness, time travel, and the expanding universe. Illustrated with cartoons
"With a large measure of humor and a minimum of math (one equation), physics professor Goldberg and engineer Blomquist delve into the fascinating physics topics that rarely make it into introductory classes. . . . This nearly-painless guide is . . . involved and scientific, aimed at science hobbyists rather than science-phobes." Publ Wkly
Includes bibliographical references

Hirshfeld, Alan

The **electric** life of Michael Faraday. Walker & Co. 2006 258p il $24 **530**
1. Biography, Individual 2. Chemists 3. Physicists 4.

Writers on science
ISBN 0-8027-1470-6
LC 2005-25533
In this biography of the English scientist, the author "explains Faraday's status as one of the most inspirational and significant figures of science. . . . A vibrant portrayal that emphasizes Faraday's qualities of wonder, acuity, and diligence, which propelled him to greatness." Booklist
Includes bibliographical references

Johnson, George

Strange beauty: Murray Gell-Mann and the revolution in twentieth-century physics. Knopf 1999 434p il hardcover o.p. pa $15 **530**
1. College teachers 2. Nobel laureates for physics 3. Nuclear physics 4. Physicists 5. Writers on science
ISBN 0-679-75688-4 pa
LC 99-19952
This is a biography of the American physicist who was awarded the Nobel prize in 1969 for his work on the interaction of elementary particles and their classification
"While it is necessarily dense in parts, this book is free of mathematics and is accessible to the advanced lay reader." Libr J
Includes bibliographical references

Kaku, Michio

Physics of the impossible; a scientific exploration into the world of phasers, force fields, teleportation, and time travel. Doubleday 2008 xxi, 329p $26.95 **530**
1. Physics
ISBN 978-0-385-52069-0; 0-385-52069-7
LC 2007-30290
"There is a surprising amount of heavyweight, cutting-edge science woven into the fabric of the book. String theory, dark energy, metamaterials and quantum theory are just a few topics—Physics of the Impossible is, in fact, an easy-to-read physics primer in disguise." New Sci
Includes bibliographical references

Kragh, Helge

Quantum generations; a history of physics in the twentieth century. Princeton Univ. Press 1999 494p $65; pa $22.95 **530**
1. Physics -- History 2. Physics -- History -- 20th century
ISBN 0-691-01206-7; 0-691-09552-3 pa
LC 99-17903
The author "details the explosive course physics has taken from the introduction of X rays in the mid-1890's to superstring theory in the present day. . . . {He} explains not only how the groundbreaking ideas of physics progressed but also how they are actively applied." Publisher's note
Includes bibliographical references

Krauss, Lawrence Maxwell

★ **Fear** of physics; a guide for the perplexed. [by] Lawrence M. Krauss. Rev ed; Basic Books 2007 257p il pa $29.95 **530**

1. Physicists 2. Physics

ISBN 978-0-465-00218-4; 0-465-00218-8

LC 2007-04700

This overview describes what physics is and the work of physicists.

"The writing style genuinely keeps the reader interested. . . . This book is a great resource if you want insight into what physics really is and what physicists do." Sci Books Films

Includes bibliographical references

Leiter, Darryl J.

A to Z of physicists; {by} Darryl J. Leiter, with Sharon L. Leiter. Facts on File 2003 388p il $45 **530**

1. Biography -- Dictionaries 2. Biography, Collective 3. Physicists 4. Physicists -- Biography

ISBN 0-8160-4798-7

LC 2002-14709

"The essays are well written, but the book's greatest strength is the space it devotes to currently active physicists." Choice

Includes bibliographical references

Ohanian, Hans C.

Einstein's mistakes; the human failings of genius. W.W. Norton & Company 2008 394p il $24.95 **530**

1. Errors, Scientific 2. Nobel laureates for physics 3. Physicists 4. Physics 5. Physics -- History 6. Physics -- Philosophy 7. Science -- History

ISBN 978-0-393-06293-9; 0-393-06293-7

LC 2008-13155

This "clearly written, fascinating, and exciting book is a gem." Sci Books Films

Includes bibliographical references

Rosen, Joe

★ **Encyclopedia** of physics. Facts on File 2004 386p il $75 **530**

1. Physics -- Encyclopedias 2. Reference books

ISBN 0-8160-4974-2

LC 2003-14963

The entries "cover physical concepts, prominent physicists (modern and historical), and physics laboratories, societies, and organizations. The alphabetically arranged entries are supplemented with 11 topical essays that aim to shed some light on physics in a philosophical or practical way. These essays cover such topics as beauty, the nature of the relationship between physics and philosophy, and the desire among some physicists to find the unifying laws governing all physical concepts. . . . The entries are well written, accurate, and include equations where appropriate." Booklist

Includes bibliographical references

Suplee, Curt

Physics in the 20th century; edited by Judith R. Franz and John S. Rigden. Abrams 1999 223p il $49.50; pa $19.95 **530**

1. Physics 2. Physics -- History -- 20th century

ISBN 0-8109-4364-6; 0-8109-9084-9 pa

LC 98-41306

In this overview of physics Suplee "leads us through the structure and function of atoms, the astonishing intimacy of light and matter, the often amusing improbabilities of quantum mechanics, the architecture of exotic materials, the elusive lives of subatomic particles that are the stuff of all creation, and chaos and order in nature—until we arrive at a vision of the entire universe. He does it without equations or misleading analogies, and often with humor." N Y Times Book Rev

Westfall, Richard S.

The **life** of Isaac Newton. Cambridge Univ. Press 1993 328p il hardcover o.p. pa $16 **530**

1. Biography, Individual 2. Mathematicians 3. Physicists 4. Scientists 5. Writers on science

ISBN 0-521-47737-9 pa

LC 92-33777

In this book the author has "reduced his longer 1980 biography of Newton (Never at Rest) to a size that is more suitable for general audiences. The result is a work whose faults lie only in the paucity of source materials that all Newton biographers face. . . . Westfall's book comes as close to presenting the man as the impersonal evidence allows without undue extrapolation." Sci Books Films

Includes bibliographical references

White, Michael

Stephen Hawking; a life in science. {by} Michael White and John Gribbin. New updated ed; Joseph Henry Press 2002 348p pa $17.95 **530**

1. Astrophysics 2. Biography, Individual 3. College teachers 4. Handicapped 5. Physicists 6. Writers on science

ISBN 0-309-08410-5

LC 2002-11961

This book "sets out to show how natural talent combined with immense willpower have enabled Hawking to live a surprisingly active and interesting life and at the same time be a distinguished astrophysicist. It tries hard to express abstract concepts in ordinary language and tells enough about Hawking's relations with the world for readers to grasp that living close to such determination is not always easy. . . . Highly recommended." Choice

Includes bibliographical references

The Cambridge companion to Newton; edited by I. Bernard Cohen and George E. Smith. Cambridge Univ. Press 2002 500p il $65; pa $23 **530**

1. Mathematicians 2. Physicists 3. Physics -- Europe -- History -- 17th century 4. Physics -- Europe -- History -- 18th century 5. Science -- Europe -- History -- 17th century 6. Science -- Europe -- History -- 18th century 7. Writers on science

ISBN 0-521-65177-8; 0-521-65696-6 pa

LC 2001-37836

This is "the best available brief overview of Newton's contributions to mechanics, cosmology, optics, mathematics, alchemy, and theology. The contributors have produced 16 well-written and admirably focused chapters. Some will be challenging for nonspecialist readers, but even those that discuss mechanics in detail are so well organized and clearly written that they amply repay close attention." Choice

Includes bibliographical references

530.01   Philosophy and theory

Cole, K. C.

The **hole** in the universe; how scientists peered over the edge of emptiness and found everything. Harcourt 2001 274p il hardcover o.p. pa $14 **530.01**
1. Infinite 2. Physics 3. Quantum theory 4. Space sciences
ISBN 0-15-601317-7 pa

LC 00-44947

Cole discusses the history of nothing, "combining the history of zero (a mathematical nothing) with that of the vacuum (a physical nothing). . . . Until Einstein showed that light needed no tangible medium through which to travel, theorists filled the vacuum with 'ether'—the 'enfant terrible' of substances, as Einstein put it. It was subsequently banished." Atl Mon

Includes bibliographical references

530.092

Kaiser, David

How the hippies saved physics; science, counterculture, and the quantum revival. David Kaiser. 1st ed. W.W. Norton 2011 xxvi, 372 p.p ill. (hardcover) $26.95 **530.092**
1. Counter culture 2. Counterculture -- United States 3. Quantum theory
ISBN 0393076369; 9780393076363

LC 2010053415

This book by David Kaiser looks at "a coterie of physicists who, during the 1970s, embraced New Age fads and sometimes went on to make dramatic discoveries. . . . They explored complex, hitherto ignored areas such as Bell's theorem and quantum entanglement while annoying the establishment by exploring their links to the paranormal. The end result was a transformation in cutting-edge physics and major discoveries in quantum information science, now a thriving industry." (Kirkus Reviews)

In 1975 several Berkeley graduate students organized an informal "Fundamental Fysiks Group." They attracted like-minded hip doctorates, so discussions mixed quantum theory with the latest counterculture delights from LSD to Eastern mysticism to ESP. They received generous media attention, including a Time cover story. . . . With financial support from unexpected sources such as the CIA (worried about possible Soviet PSI weapons) and various young millionaires including Werner Erhard, they explored complex, hitherto ignored areas such as Bell's theorem and quantum entanglement while annoying the establishment by exploring their links to the paranormal. The end result was a trans-

formation in cutting-edge physics and major discoveries in quantum information science, now a thriving industry. Readers will enjoy this entertaining chronicle of colorful young scientists whose sweeping curiosity turned up no hard evidence for psychic phenomena but led to new ways of looking into the equally bizarre quantum world. Kirkus

Includes bibliographical references

530.1   Theories and mathematical physics

Baggott, Jim

The **quantum** story; [by] Jim Baggott. Oxford University Press 2011 469p il $29.95 **530.1**
1. Physics -- History 2. Physics literature 3. Quantum theory 4. Quantum theory -- History
ISBN 978-0-19-956684-6; 0-19-956684-4

This book explores the history of the development by physicists of the theoretical particle called the Higgs boson as a possible explanation of many unanswered questions about the universe. It was the author's intention to "place the Higgs within a broader context of physical theory. . . . The particle is the cornerstone of the 'standard model,' a 40-year-old mathematical blueprint for the way elementary particles behave. Mr [Jim] Baggott captures its development in 40 key moments." (Economist)

"Quantum theory—challenging, disconcerting and heavy on math—is not going to be pinned down and dissected for lay readers without a lot of kicking and screaming. Baggott succeeds, however, imbuing the narrative with important context, his own communicable enthusiasm and the instances of dense theoretical exposition mediated by historical and biographical storytelling. His survey runs roughly chronologically, starting with Max Planck's contention that energy is composed of a definite number of equal finite packages, through Einstein, Bohr, Heisenberg, Dirac, Feynman, Hawking et al. the author then looks at the Standard Model and the more amorphous superstring theory." Kirkus

Includes bibliographical references

Bodanis, David

E; a biography of the world's most famous equation. Walker & Company 2005 337p il $25 **530.1**
1. Force and energy 2. Nobel laureates for physics 3. Physicists 4. Relativity (Physics) 5. Space and time
ISBN 0-8027-1463-3

The author relates the story of "Einstein's formulation of the equation in 1905 and its association ever after with relativity and nuclear energy. Parallel with the science, Bodanis populates his tale with dramatic lives." Booklist [review of 2000 edition]

Bolles, Edmund Blair

Einstein defiant; genius versus genius in the quantum revolution. Joseph Henry Press 2004 348p il $27.95 **530.1**
1. Nobel laureates for physics 2. Physicists 3. Quantum theory 4. Quantum theory -- History 5. Relativity (Physics)
ISBN 0-309-08998-0

LC 2003-23735

"This carefully researched book achieves a nice balance between science and history. The author provides enough scientific information to illuminate the unfolding drama for nonscientists and constructs a marvelously choreographed tale of how just about every physicist of note in the last century contributed to the debate." Sci Books Films

Includes bibliographical references

Carroll, Sean M.

★ From eternity to here; the quest for the ultimate theory of time. [by] Sean Carroll. Dutton 2009 438p il $25   **530.1**

1. Space and time
ISBN 978-0-525-95133-9; 0-525-95133-4
LC 2009-23828

"Understanding time requires an acquaintance with entropy, relativity, cosmology, thermodynamics and statistical mechanics, which Carroll enthusiastically delivers at great length. Not for the scientifically disinclined, but determined readers will come away with a rewarding grasp of a complex subject." Kirkus

Includes bibliographical references

Close, F. E.

The **infinity** puzzle; quantum field theory and the hunt for an orderly universe. [by] Frank Close. Basic Books 2011 435p il $28.99   **530.1**

1. Infinite 2. Quantum theory
ISBN 978-0-465-02144-4; 978-0-465-02803-0 ebook
LC 2011022966

Close "offers a compelling history and sociology of modern particle theory. We discover the motivations and achievements of a rich cast of brilliant individuals, and get enough of the science to grasp what they were trying to do. Where Close really shines is in exposing the fraught process of recognition in science, focusing on key players such as Pakistani theoretical physicist Abdus Salam and the man after whom the famous boson is named, British physicist Peter Higgs." Nature

Includes bibliographical references

Davies, P. C. W.

About time; Einstein's unfinished revolution. {by} Paul Davies. Simon & Schuster 1995 316p il hardcover o.p. pa $14   **530.1**

1. Astrophysics 2. Nobel laureates for physics 3. Physicists 4. Relativity (Physics) 5. Space and time
ISBN 0-684-81822-1 pa
LC 94-40281

This "is intelligent, fascinating, and eminently readable." Sci Books Films

Includes bibliographical references

Einstein, Albert

The **meaning** of relativity; 5th ed; Princeton University Press 2005 xxiv, 166p il pa $16.95 **530.1**

1. Relativity (Physics)
ISBN 0-691-12027-7
LC 2004-111082

"Though few can understand it, most readers in physics and librarians in charge of science collections know this book as one of the landmarks of modern knowledge. . . .

The book is not intended for general reading. Instead it is addressed to . . . those whose training enables them to understand the mathematical expressions of relativity." N Y Public Libr. New Tech Books

★ A **stubbornly** persistent illusion; the essential scientific works of Albert Einstein. [edited, with commentary, by Stephen Hawking] Running Press 2007 468p il $29.95   **530.1**

1. Nobel laureates for physics 2. Philosophy 3. Physicists 4. Physics -- Philosophy 5. Relativity (Physics)
ISBN 978-0-7624-3003-1; 0-7624-3003-6
LC 2007-935658

The editor presents with introductions writings by Albert Einstein on relativity, the history of physics and philosophy.

"Hawking adds a brief but effective introduction to each section, making this gem of a collection really shine." Publ Wkly

Includes bibliographical references

Ford, Kenneth William

101 quantum questions; what you need to know about the world you can't see. [by] Kenneth W. Ford. Harvard University Press 2011 291p il $24.95 **530.1**

1. Quantum theory
ISBN 978-0-674-05099-0
LC 2010-34791

"Ford explains the essential concepts of quantum reality, our small-fast world, full of uncertainty and probability, where all matter can exist in more than one state simultaneously. Ford brings interesting and entertaining anecdotal and historical material into his answers, organizing and shaping his book around 15 subjects. By using humor and straight talk to answer questions that often bedevil the nonscientist who attempts to grasp this knotty subject, Ford has created an entertaining read and an excellent companion piece to more detailed popular treatments of modern physics." Publ Wkly

Includes bibliographical references

Fritzsch, Harald

An **equation** that changed the world; Newton, Einstein, and the theory of relativity. translated by Karin Heusch. University of Chicago Press 1994 279p il $32.50; pa $16   **530.1**

1. Mathematicians 2. Nobel laureates for physics 3. Physicists 4. Relativity (Physics) 5. Writers on science
ISBN 0-226-26557-9; 0-226-26558-7 pa
LC 94-3876

"Many readers will applaud Fritzsch for this lively but profoundly insightful book." Booklist

Includes bibliographical references

Gell-Mann, Murray

The **quark** and the jaguar; adventures in the simple and the complex. Holt & Co. 1995 392p il pa $17   **530.1**

1. Particles (Nuclear physics) 2. Science -- Philosophy
ISBN 0-8050-7253-5

"While the topics are technical in nature, Gell-Mann's presentation is clear and will be readily understood by scholars and informed lay readers." Libr J

Gilder, Louisa

The **age** of entanglement; when quantum physics was reborn. Alfred A. Knopf 2008 443p il $27.50   **530.1**
1. Quantum theory
ISBN 978-1-4000-4417-7; 1-4000-4417-0

LC 2008-11796

This is "the story of quantum mechanics and its lively cast of supporters. . . . Gilder's history is rife with curious characters and dramatizes how difficult it was for even these brilliant scientists to grasp the paradigm-changing concepts of quantum science." Publ Wkly

Includes bibliographical references

Greene, B. (Brian), 1963-

★ The **hidden** reality; parallel universes and the deep laws of the cosmos. [by] Brian Greene. Alfred A. Knopf 2011 370p il $29.95   **530.1**
1. Cosmology   2.   General relativity (Physics)   3. Physics -- Philosophy 4. Quantum theory 5. Relativity (Physics)
ISBN 0-307-26563-3; 978-0-307-26563-0

LC 2010-42710

The Hidden Reality aims to show how major developments in different branches of fundamental theoretical physics—relativistic, quantum, cosmological, unified, computational—have all led us to consider one or another variety of parallel universe. Index.

The author "explores the possibility that there is not one big uncharted universe, but many. Those universes take the form of Swiss cheese, suds in a bubble bath, passageways right out of 'Star Trek,' and realms right next to us. The danger of writing a mind-blower like 'The Hidden Reality' is that, if the author isn't careful, it can become mind-numbing to read. A caution here upfront: There are points where Greene walks perilously close to that precipice. Black holes, parallel universes, the idea that we and our world may have doppelgängers in different dimensions are heady concepts. For some, such conjecture is religious heresy; for others, it aims to answer the ultimate questions as to how and why we are here, with science, not faith, forming a necessary and—so far—inadequate, bridge to explore the mystery. What Greene . . . does exceedingly well is to lay out the prevailing theories, advanced by the brightest human minds, as to how the whole of everything may be ordered." Christ Sci Monit

Includes bibliographical references

Gribbin, John R.

In search of Schrodinger's cat; quantum physics and reality. Bantam Bks. 1984 302p il pa $15.95   **530.1**
1. Quantum theory 2. Reality
ISBN 0-553-34253-3

LC 84-2975

This history of quantum mechanics discusses the work of Huygens, Einstein, Schrödinger, Bohr, Planck and Everett.

This book "contains many vignettes from the history of science and many insights into the researchers and the work

that has led to our current understanding of the quantum theory. Excellent analogies and graphic illustrations are used to present difficult ideas." Sci Books Films

Includes bibliographical references

Schrodinger's kittens and the search for reality; solving the quantum mysteries. {by} John Gribbin. Little, Brown 1995 261p il hardcover o.p. pa $14.95   **530.1**
1. Light 2. Nobel laureates for physics 3. Physicists 4. Quantum theory 5. Reality
ISBN 0-316-32819-7 pa

LC 95-75652

In this sequel to In search of Schrödinger's cat, Gribbin attempts to "explain recent experimental and theoretical findings about the . . . nature of the submicroscopic world of the atom. The 'Copenhagen interpretation' of quantum mechanics offered by Niels Bohr and his colleagues has prevailed for almost 70 years, but there {are} . . . competing interpretations. Gribbin reviews this . . . {field and} indicates his personal preference for one of the new theoretical models." Libr J

Includes bibliographical references

Guillen, Michael

Five equations that changed the world; the power and poetry of mathematics. Hyperion 1995 277p hardcover o.p. pa $14.95   **530.1**
1. Chemists 2. College teachers 3. Mathematicians 4. Mathematics 5. Mathematics -- History 6. Nobel laureates for physics 7. Physicists 8. Physics 9. Physics -- History 10. Writers on science
ISBN 0-7868-6103-7; 0-7868-8187-9 pa

LC 95-15199

"A seamless blend of dramatic biography and mathematical documentary that links the personal with the scientific." Publ Wkly

Hawking, S. W. (Stephen W.), 1942-

★ The **grand** design; [by] Stephen Hawking and Leonard Mlodinow. Bantam Books 2010 198p il $28; ebook $28   **530.1**
1. Cosmology 2. Life -- Origin 3. Quantum theory 4. Science -- Philosophy 5. String theory 6. Universe
ISBN 978-0-553-80537-6; 0-553-80537-1; 978-0-553-90707-0 ebook; 0-553-90707-7 ebook

"The three central questions of philosophy and science: Why is there something rather than nothing? Why do we exist? Why this particular set of laws and not some other? . . . Along with Caltech physicist Mlodinow . . . Hawking deftly mixes cutting-edge physics to answer those key questions. . . . This is an amazingly concise, clear, and intriguing overview of where we stand when it comes to divining the secrets of the universe." Publ Wkly

Includes bibliographical references

Hawking, Stephen W.

The **nature** of space and time; [by] Stephen Hawking and Roger Penrose. [New ed.]; Princeton

University Press 2010 145p il pa $14.95; ebook
$14.95   **530.1**
1. Astrophysics 2. Quantum theory 3. Space and time
ISBN 978-0-691-14570-9 pa; 978-1-4008-3474-7
ebook

This volume "takes the form of a debate between Hawking and Penrose at Cambridge in 1994. At the center of the
discussion is a pair of powerful theories: the quantum theory of fields and the general theory of relativity. The issue
is how—if at all—one can merge the two into a quantum
theory of gravity. . . . A substantial background in theoretical
physics is needed for full comprehension." Libr J
Includes bibliographical references

★ The **universe** in a nutshell; [by] Stephen
Hawking. Bantam Bks. 2001 216p il $35   **530.1**
1. Quantum theory
ISBN 0-553-80202-X
                                    LC 2001-35757
Hawking "explains the basic laws of physics that govern
the universe, beginning with a brief history of the concept
of relativity, and then he is off and running to explore time,
space, the future, and the possibility of time travel, among
other fundamental rules of the universe's road. Admirers of
Hawking's previous book will continue to appreciate his
ability not only to air fresh, provocative ideas but also to
say what he means clearly and without watering down his
material or condescending to his audience—he even injects
humor into his narrative. The profuse, beautifully rendered
illustrations contribute greatly to the reader's understanding
of his points." Booklist

Kakalios, James
The **amazing** story of quantum mechanics; a
math-free exploration of the science that made our
world. Gotham Books 2010 318p il $26   **530.1**
1. Quantum theory
ISBN 978-1-59240-479-7; 1-59240-479-0
                                    LC 2010-29568
"Though the book does not quite live up to the subtitle's
promise of a 'math-free' text, readers need no more than
basic algebra to accompany comic-book heroes into well-
illustrated explanations of quantum packets of light energy,
of the wave functions of particles, and even of the angular
spin inherent in both energy and matter. These basic principles illuminate the solid-state physics of semiconductors,
the atomic magnetism of MRIs, and the nanotechnology of
high-capacity storage batteries. And all of this conceptual
heavy lifting comes with entertaining episodes from DC
Comics and H. G. Wells' fiction. Physics has never been
more fun!" Booklist
Includes bibliographical references

Kaku, Michio
Hyperspace; a scientific odyssey through parallel
universes, time warps, and the tenth dimension. illustrations by Robert O'Keefe. Oxford Univ. Press
1994 359p il $35   **530.1**
1. Relativity (Physics) 2. Space and time
ISBN 0-19-508514-0
                                    LC 93-7910

This is an "overview of the major scientists, discoveries, and ideas involved in an ongoing quest for synthesizing
quantum mechanics and relativity physics into a superstring
theory of our entire universe." Libr J
Includes bibliographical references

Kumar, Manjit
★ **Quantum**; Einstein, Bohr and the great debate
about the nature of reality. W.W. Norton 2010 448p
il $27.95   **530.1**
1. Quantum theory 2. Quantum theory -- History
ISBN 978-0-393-07829-9; 0-393-07829-9
                                    LC 2009-51249
"A staggering account of the scientific revolution that
still challenges our notions of reality. . . . Kumar evokes the
passion and excitement of the period and writes with sparkling clarity and wit. Expertly delineates complex scientific
issues in nontechnical language, using telling detail to weave
together personal, political and scientific elements." Kirkus
Includes bibliographical references

Lloyd, Seth
★ **Programming** the universe; a quantum computer scientist takes on the cosmos. Knopf 2006
221p il $25.95   **530.1**
1. Microcomputers 2. Microcomputers -- Programming
3. Quantum computers 4. Quantum theory
ISBN 1-4000-4092-2; 978-1-4000-4092-6
                                    LC 2005-50408
"Exploring big questions in accessible, comprehensive
fashion, Lloyd's work is of vital importance to the general-
science audience." Booklist
Includes bibliographical references

Nadis, Steve
The **shape** of inner space; string theory and
the geometry of the universe's hidden dimensions.
Shing-tung Yau and Steve Nadis; illustrations by
Xianfeng (David) Gu and Xiaotian (Tim) Yin. Basic
Books 2010 xix, 377 p.p $30   **530.1**
1. Fourth dimension 2. Geometry 3. Hyperspace 4.
String models 5. String theory
ISBN 978-0-465-02023-2; 0-465-02023-2;
9780465020232; 0465020232
                                    LC 2010009956
"It is a testimony to [Yau's] careful prose (and no doubt
to the skills of co-author Steve Nadis) that this book so compellingly captures the essence of what pushes string theorists
forward in the face of formidable obstacles. It gives us a
rare glimpse into a world as alien as the moons of Jupiter,
and just as fascinating. . . . Yau and Nadis have produced
a strangely mesmerizing account of geometry's role in the
universe." New Scientist
Includes bibliographical references (p. 331-343)
and index

Parker, Barry R.
Albert Einstein's vision; remarkable discoveries
that shaped modern science. [by] Barry Parker. Prometheus Books 2004 286p il $28   **530.1**
1. Nobel laureates for physics 2. Physicists 3. Quantum

theory 4. Relativity (Physics)
ISBN 1-59102-186-3

LC 2004-3990

"The book takes the ideas generated by Einstein, before his death in 1955, and follows the work of other scientists as they continued to build modern physics and cosmology." Sci Books Films

Includes bibliographical references

Rigden, John S.

★ **Einstein** 1905; the standard of greatness. Harvard University Press 2005 173p il $21.95; pa $14.95 **530.1**

1. Nobel laureates for physics 2. Physicists 3. Quantum theory

ISBN 0-674-01544-4; 0-674-02104-5 pa

LC 2004-54049

"The book is a delight to read, with a lot of interesting, useful information." Choice

Includes bibliographical references

Smolin, Lee

The **trouble** with physics; the rise of string theory, the fall of a science, and what comes next. Houghton Mifflin Co. 2006 392p il $26 **530.1**

1. Physics -- Methodology 2. Science -- Methodology 3. String models 4. String theory

ISBN 978-0-618-55105-7; 0-618-55105-0

LC 2006-07235

"This is a well-written, critical profile of the theoretical physics community, free of equations, from the perspective of a member." Libr J

Includes bibliographical references

Susskind, Leonard

The **black** hole war; my battle with Stephen Hawking to make the world safe for quantum mechanics. Little, Brown 2008 470p il $27.99; pa $15.99 **530.1**

1. Black holes (Astronomy) 2. College teachers 3. General relativity (Physics) 4. Handicapped 5. Physicists 6. Quantum theory 7. Relativity (Physics) 8. Space and time 9. Writers on science

ISBN 978-0-316-01640-7; 0-316-01640-3; 978-0-316-01641-4 pa; 0-316-01641-1 pa

LC 2007-48355

The author "delves into the related and disturbingly dangerous subject of black holes. Here, he describes disagreements that he and his Dutch friend, Gerard d'Hooft, had with the famous British mathematician/physicist Stephen Hawking on his predictions regarding the interaction of objects with black holes. This book provides an anecdotal, highly readable discussion of the background to black holes and the consequences of their existence." Choice

Includes glossary

Thorne, Kip S.

Black holes and time warps; Einstein's outrageous legacy. Norton 1994 619p il hardcover o.p. pa $18.95 **530.1**

1. Astrophysics 2. Black holes (Astronomy) 3. Physics

4. Physics -- Philosophy 5. Relativity (Physics)
ISBN 0-393-31276-3 pa

LC 93-2014

This book is "about black holes, white holes, wormholes, parallel universes, time travel, 10-dimensional space-time, the origin and fate of the universe and a lot of other subjects dear to science fiction fans." N Y Times Book Rev

Includes bibliographical references

Toomey, David M.

The **new** time travelers; a journey to the frontiers of physics. [by] David Toomey. W. W. Norton 2007 391p il $28 **530.1**

1. Space and time

ISBN 978-0-393-06013-3; 0-393-06013-6

LC 2007-11307

This book on the physics of time travel "illustrates dimension-bending concepts with space-time diagrams, M. C. Escher drawings, and the plot of H.G. Wells' Time Machine. Toomey gets a grip on bending the fourth dimension by historically chronicling physicists who have theorized about time travel . . . . If you dream of getting outside your personal light cone, Toomey shows how it might be imagined." Booklist

Includes bibliographical references

Wertheim, Margaret

Physics on the fringe; Smoke rings, circlons, and alternative theories of everything. Margaret Wertheim. Walker & Company 2011 336 p. il **530.1**

1. Biographies 2. Physics 3. Science 4. Theory of everything (Physics) 5. Vortex motion

ISBN 0802715133; 9780802715135

This book describes work done by amateur . . . [scientists], people rejected by the academic establishment and rejecting orthodox academic beliefs. . . . Margaret Wertheim's book discusses her encounters with the natural philosophers. . . . Her leading character is Jim Carter, and her main theme is the story of his life and work. . . . Carter's . . . belief in a theory of the universe [is] based on endless hierarchies of circlons. Circlons are mechanical objects of circular shape. The history of the universe is a story of successive generations of circlons arising by processes of reproduction and fission. He verified the behavior of circlons by doing experiments with smoke rings at his home. (New York Review of Books)

The author offers a look into the hearts and minds of the "outsider" physicists: solitary figures who, usually with little or no formal training, strive to explain our world. Wertheim builds the book around the affable Jim Carter, explorer, self-taught physicist, trailer park owner, and proponent of circlon synchronicity, with atoms shaped like tiny circles of coiled spring. . . . This sympathetic portrayal of one outsider's work offers an entry point into a fascinating corner of pseudoscience. Publ Wkly

Includes bibliographical references

Wolfson, Richard

  Simply Einstein; relativity demystified. Norton 2003 261p il $24.95   **530.1**

    1. Relativity (Physics)

    ISBN 0-393-05154-4

                     LC 2002-2984

  "Wolfson's economical and vivid tutorial should open doors for lay readers encountering Einstein's principles for the first time. His popular style, with a minimum of math, should make this a must-have book for Einstein buffs as well." Publ Wkly

  Includes bibliographical references

530.11   Relativity theory

Barbour, Julian B.

  The **end** of time; the next revolution in physics. [by] Julian Barbour. Oxford Univ. Press 2000 371p il hardcover o.p. pa $17.95   **530.11**

    1. Quantum theory 2. Relativity (Physics) 3. Space and time

    ISBN 0-19-511729-8; 0-19-514592-5 pa

                     LC 99-44319

  This "book is about time and its history—how it is treated in various physical theories. . . . Barbour asks what time really is. His answer, in light of all we know of the physics involved: nothing; time does not exist." NY Times Book Rev

  Includes bibliographical references

Gott, J. Richard

  Time travel in Einstein's universe; the physical possibilities of travel through time. {by} J. Richard Gott, III. Houghton Mifflin 2001 291p il hardcover o.p. pa $14   **530.11**

    1. Fourth dimension 2. Space and time 3. Time travel

    ISBN 0-395-95563-7; 0-618-25735-7 pa

                     LC 00-54243

  "Gott tackles the complexities of attempting to turn the fantasy of time travel into a theoretical possibility in a lively and lucid discussion." Booklist

  Includes bibliographical references

Magueijo, Joao

  Faster than the speed of light; the story of a scientific speculation. Perseus Bks. 2003 279p il $26   **530.11**

    1. Light 2. Light -- Speed 3. Physics 4. Physics -- Research

    ISBN 0-7382-0525-7

                    LC 2002-112394

  In this study theoretical physicist Magueijo presents the idea that light traveled faster in the early universe than it does today. He also documents the reactions other scientists are having to this theory, which contradicts Einstein's theory of relativity.

  "Breaking the old speed limit posted by . . . Albert Einstein in his 20s, this book deploys a racy and provocative text to convey its popularized content of a new cosmology. Jocular, ironic, witty, self-centered, even indignant, Magueijo is all too ready to castigate his adversaries." Sci Am

530.12   Quantum mechanics (Quantum theory)

Parker, Barry R.

  Quantum legacy; the discovery that changed our universe. {by} Barry Parker. Prometheus Bks. 2002 282p il $29   **530.12**

    1. Quantum theory

    ISBN 1-57392-993-X

                   LC 2002-67966

  The author describes the theory of quantum mechanics, its practical applications, and the work of such scientists as Max Planck, Albert Einstein, Niels Bohr, Werner Heisenberg, Erwin Schrodinger, and Richard Feynman

530.4   States of matter

Frankel, Felice

  On the surface of things; images of the extraordinary in science. [by] Felice Frankel and George M. Whitesides. Harvard University Press 2007 160p il pa $26.50   **530.4**

    1. Optical images 2. Surfaces (Physics)

    ISBN 978-0-674-02688-9

  Text and photographs explore the way light interacts with various surfaces.

  "Materials science bears an unfortunate reputation for dullness, dealing as it does with the stuff of everyday life. A ramble through the pages of this poetic volume, however, exposes the field's underlying luster." Sci Am [review of 1997 ed.]

  Includes bibliographical references

530.8   Measurement

Barrow, John D.

  The **constants** of nature; from Alpha to Omega --the numbers that encode the deepest secrets of the universe. Pantheon Books 2002 352p il $26; pa $15   **530.8**

    1. Measurement 2. Physical constants -- Popular works

    ISBN 0-375-42221-8; 1-4000-3225-3 pa

                   LC 2002-75975

  "Barrow traces scientists' evolving understanding of natural constants, like the speed of light, in this erudite and enthralling work of popular science." Publ Wkly

  Includes bibliographical references

Robinson, Andrew

  The **story** of measurement. Thames & Hudson 2007 224p il map $34.95   **530.8**

    1. Measurement 2. Mensuration -- History

    ISBN 978-0-500-51367-5; 0-500-51367-8

                   LC 2007-921450

  "Robinson has the knack to explain any number of complex concepts lucidly and with simplicity, without being condescending. . . . He has produced a highly readable book." Times Lit Suppl

  Includes bibliographical references

535 Light and related radiation

Park, David

The **fire** within the eye; a historical essay on the nature and meaning of light. Princeton Univ. Press 1997 377p il hardcover o.p. pa $19.95   **535**
1. Light 2. Optics
ISBN 0-691-05051-1 pa
    LC 96-45573
A history of the concept and science of light from classical times to the present. Cultural, philosophical, intellectual and theological perspectives are explored and works by Aristotle, Grosseteste, Plotinus and Bohr are among those discussed

"Whether it is Fermat and Huygens on optics or Faraday and Maxwell on electromagnetism, the writing is lively and informed. . . . The very readable style and helpful glossary, along with an excellent bibliography and references, make this work suitable for . . . general readers." Choice

Pendergrast, Mark

Mirror mirror; a history of the human love affair with reflection. Basic Books 2003 404p il $27.50; pa $17   **535**
1. Mirrors 2. Mirrors -- History 3. Reflecting telescopes 4. Reflection (Optics)
ISBN 0-465-05470-6; 0-465-05471-4 pa
    LC 2003-2544
"Those with a historical and scientific bent may profitably read this book for insight into the manufacture of mirrors—along with descendents the telescope and microscope—down through the ages. . . . Whether for pleasure or profit, this well-written, entertaining book, packed with historical information, should be read!" Choice
Includes bibliographical references

536 Heat

Segre, Gino

A **matter** of degrees; what temperature reveals about the past and future of our species, planet, and universe. Viking 2002 300p il $24.95; pa $15 **536**
1. Temperature 2. Temperature measurements -- Popular works
ISBN 0-670-03101-1; 0-14-200278-X pa
    LC 2001-46942
The author "first gives background on the inventors of the thermometer, which prepares the way for the major discoveries in the 1800s about the nature of heat. . . . Segre recounts heat's role in the earth's formation, climate history, and thermophilic life on the ocean bottom, and . . . the temperature of stellar interiors." Booklist
Includes bibliographical references and index

Shachtman, Tom

Absolute zero and the conquest of cold. Houghton Mifflin 1999 261p hardcover o.p. pa $14 **536**
1. Low temperature research 2. Low temperatures --

Research 3. Thermodynamics
ISBN 0-395-93888-0; 0-618-08239-5 pa
    LC 99-33305
The author "analyzes the social impact of the chill factor, explains the science of cold and tells the curious tales behind inventions like the thermometer, the fridge and the thermos flask." N Y Times Book Rev
Includes bibliographical references

Von Baeyer, Hans Christian

Maxwell's demon; why warmth disperses and time passes. Random House 1998 xxi, 207p hardcover o.p. pa $15   **536**
1. Maxwell's demon 2. Thermodynamics 3. Time
ISBN 0-375-75372-9 pa
    LC 97-41543
The author "traces the development of the laws of thermodynamics in a narrative spanning a period from 13th-century perpetual motion machines to contemporary thinking about laser technology, information theory, and algorithmic randomness. . . . The star of the story is James Clerk Maxwell's molecule-manipulating demon, who conceivably could challenge the Second Law of Thermodynamics." Choice
Includes bibliographical references

537 Electricity and electronics

Bodanis, David

Electric universe; the shocking true story of electricity. Crown Publishers 2004 308p hardcover o.p. pa $31   **537**
1. Electricity 2. Force and energy
ISBN 1-4000-4550-9; 0-307-33598-4 pa
    LC 2004-11275
"As a storyteller, author David Bodanis is wonderful. . . . This book is directed at a general audience, but it should be required reading for all scientific professionals." Sci Books Films
Includes bibliographical references

538 Magnetism

Livingston, James D.

Driving force; the natural magic of magnets. Harvard Univ. Press 1996 311p il maps hardcover o.p. pa $16.95   **538**
1. Magnetism 2. Magnets
ISBN 0-674-21645-8 pa
    LC 95-39595
"A stimulating variety of science, history, and technology delivered enthusiastically." Booklist
Includes bibliographical references

539.7 Atomic and nuclear physics

Aczel, Amir D.

Present at the creation; the story of CERN and the Large Hadron Collider. [by] Amir Aczel. Harmony Books 2010 271p il $25.99; ebook $12.99 **539.7**

1. Large Hadron Collider (France and Switzerland)

ISBN 978-0-307-59167-8; 978-0-307-59168-5 ebook

LC 2010-14835

Aczel "has produced an excellent review of past, current, and possible future theories of particle physics and how they relate to the field of cosmology. He uses the Large Hadron Collider (LHC), the most energetic particle accelerator ever built, as a focal point for a discussion of these theories." Choice

Includes bibliographical references

Feynman, Richard Phillips

QED; the strange theory of light and matter. [by] Richard Feynman. Princeton Univ. Press 1985 158p $55; pa $15.95 **539.7**

1. Electrons 2. Light 3. Quantum theory

ISBN 0-691-08388-6; 0-691-02417-0 pa

LC 85-42685

The author attempts to describe the interaction between light and electrons.

"Feynman describes with accuracy, insight, self-deprecating humor, and clarity the centerpiece of modern elementary particle theory—quantum electrodynamics. . . . 'QED' will challenge the mind." Christ Sci Monit

Greene, Brian R.

★ The **elegant** universe; superstrings, hidden dimensions, and the quest for the ultimate theory. [by] Brian Greene. Vintage Books 2000 448p il pa $15.95 **539.7**

1. Cosmology 2. String theory

ISBN 0-375-70811-1; 978-0-375-70811-4

LC 99-42018

The author "makes the terribly complex theory of strings accessible to all. He possesses a remarkable gift for using the everyday to illustrate what may be going on in dimensions beyond our feeble human perception." Publ Wkly

Includes bibliographical references

Gribbin, John R.

Q is for quantum; an encyclopedia of particle physics. [by] John Gribbin; edited by Mary Gribbin; illustrations by Jonathan Gribbin; timelines by Benjamin Gribbin. Free Press 1998 545p il $35; pa $20 **539.7**

1. Particles (Nuclear physics) -- Dictionaries 2. Particles (Nuclear physics) -- Popular works 3. Reference books

ISBN 0-684-85578-X; 0-684-86315-4 pa

LC 98-9918

"There are entries for people (Feynman, Richard Phillips; Huygens, Christiaan; Oppenheimer, Robert), places (Brookhaven National Laboratory, Fermilab), and historical highlights (Manhattan Project). . . . Following the entries is a bibliography that lists the books referred to in the text, together with others; the more technical titles are indicated with an asterisk. The volume concludes with time lines of birth dates of famous scientists, key dates in physical sciences, and key dates in history." Booklist

Includes bibliographical references

The **search** for superstrings, symmetry, and the theory of everything; {by} John Gribbin. Little, Brown 1999 212p $23; pa $14.95 **539.7**

1. Nuclear physics 2. Particles (Nuclear physics)

ISBN 0-316-32975-4; 0-316-32614-3 pa

LC 98-34711

"Diligent readers without any specialized knowledge of physics or mathematics will come away with a flavor of the latest ideas theorists are grappling with." Publ Wkly

Includes bibliographical references

Kane, Gordon

The **particle** garden; our universe as understood by particle physicists. Addison-Wesley 1995 224p il hardcover o.p. pa $15 **539.7**

1. Nuclear physics 2. Particles (Nuclear physics)

ISBN 0-201-40826-0 pa

LC 94-25804

"This is an accurate, well-written, up-to-date account of particle physics by an expert in the field." Sci Books Films

Lederman, Leon M.

The **God** particle; if the universe is the answer, what is the question? [by] Leon Lederman with Dick Teresi. Houghton Mifflin 1993 434p hardcover o.p. pa $15.95 **539.7**

1. Particles (Nuclear physics) 2. Science -- Philosophy 3. Universe

ISBN 0-395-55849-2; 978-0-618-71168-0 pa; 0-618-71168-6 pa

LC 92-43583

The author "pokes fun at the theorists and dazzles us with descriptions of the seemingly impossible experiments he and his fellow genius tinkerers executed to prove the existence of those massless, charmed, and strange entities, quarks and leptons." Booklist

Includes bibliographical references

Lincoln, Don

★ The **quantum** frontier; the Large Hadron Collider. foreword by Leon Lederman. Johns Hopkins University Press 2009 172p il map $25 **539.7**

1. Colliders (Nuclear physics) 2. Large Hadron Collider (France and Switzerland) 3. Particles (Nuclear physics) 4. Quantum theory

ISBN 978-0-8018-9144-1; 0-8018-9144-2

LC 2008-22647

"This book provides a most enjoyable and interesting introduction to the LHC." Sci Books Films

Includes bibliographical references

Malley, Marjorie Caroline

Radioactivity; a history of a mysterious science. [by] Marjorie C. Malley. Oxford University Press 2011 xxi, 267p il map $21.95 **539.7**
1. Radioactivity
ISBN 978-0-19-976641-3

LC 2010038979

"Malley presents a timely tale about the discovery of radioactivity, the development of our knowledge of the physical universe, and the way radioactivity has changed our world. . . . [She] manages to make the periodic table and the giants involved in its creation interesting. . . . Malley does a wonderful job of demonstrating how scientific discovery functions, as opposed to the usual approach in which facts and figures are given as tidbits along a chronology." Libr J
Includes bibliographical references

Sample, Ian

Massive. Basic Books 2010 260p $25.95 **539.7**
1. Higgs bosons 2. Higgs, Peter 3. Large Hadron Collider (France and Switzerland) 4. Particles (Nuclear physics) 5. Physics -- Research -- History 6. Physics literature
ISBN 978-0-465-01947-2

LC 2010023132

This book looks at the history of physics, focusing on the creation of the theoretical Higgs Boson particle and subsequent attempts to validate its existence experimentally. The story of the Higgs Boson is traced by Guardian" science journalist Ian Sample from its inception as a theory by Peter Higgs in 1964 to the construction of particle accelerators attempting to prove the hypothesis. Mr [Ian] Sample also tracked down many of those involved, including Mr [Peter] Higgs." (Economist)

This book "offers a larger window into the minds that dreamed of the Higgs and the culture that shaped their search . . . and is accessible for the curious science layperson." Sci News
Includes bibliographical references

Seife, Charles

Sun in a bottle; the strange history of fusion and the science of wishful thinking. Viking 2008 294p il map $25.95 **539.7**
1. Nuclear fusion
ISBN 978-0-670-02033-1; 0-670-02033-8

LC 2008-13135

"Ever since the first hydrogen bomb tests in the 1950s, scientists have hoped to reproduce the sun's magic in a controlled fashion, unlocking an unlimited source of energy. But the dream has been elusive. With great explanatory skill, Seife . . . explains how fusion works and why it is so hard to get power out of it. Seife reviews the parade of hubristic and sometimes comic or outright dishonest claims that fusion scientists have made over the decades." Sci News
Includes bibliographical references

Stewart, Ian

Why beauty is truth; a history of symmetry. Basic Books 2007 290p il $26.95 **539.7**
1. Mathematics -- History 2. Symmetry 3. Symmetry

(Physics)
ISBN 978-0-465-08236-0; 0-465-08236-X

LC 2006-38274

"Beginning with the early struggles of the Babylonians to solve quadratics, Stewart guides his readers through the often-tangled history of symmetry, illuminating for non-specialists how a concept easily recognized in geometry acquired new meanings in algebra. . . . An exciting foray for any armchair physicist!" Booklist
Includes bibliographical references

540   Chemistry and allied sciences

Cobb, Cathy

Creations of fire; chemistry's lively history from alchemy to the atomic age. [by] Cathy Cobb and Harold Goldwhite. Perseus Pub. 2001 475p il pa $20.95 **540**
1. Chemistry -- History
ISBN 0-7382-0594-X; 978-0-7382-0594-6

LC 2001-99001

This history "begins with chemistry in the Stone Age and ends with current areas of interest such as superheavy elements and the polymerase chain reaction. Along the way, the coverage includes alchemy, cold fusion, and . . . topics like the contributions of Lise Meitner and Marie Lavoisier. . . . This book's light and often humorous style makes it especially appealing to the general reader." Libr J
Includes bibliographical references

The **joy** of chemistry; the amazing science of familiar things. [by] Cathy Cobb & Monty L. Fetterolf. Prometheus Books 2005 393p il hardcover o.p. pa $19 **540**
1. Chemistry
ISBN 1-591-02231-2; 1-591-02771-3 pa

LC 2004-20144

The authors cover "the material of a general chemistry course along with organic, inorganic and analytical chemistry and biochemistry; there's even a chapter on forensic chemistry. . . . They explain everything from flatulence (the chemical composition of intestinal gas) to pizza cheese (why mozzarella rather than, say, parmesan?)." Publ Wkly
Includes bibliographical references

Coffey, Patrick

Cathedrals of science; the personalities and rivalries that made modern chemistry. Oxford University Press 2008 379p il $29.95 **540**
1. Chemical weapons 2. Chemistry -- History 3. Chemistry -- History -- 20th century 4. Chemists 5. College teachers 6. Discoveries in science 7. Nobel laureates for chemistry 8. Science -- Ethical aspects 9. Science -- Moral and ethical aspects
ISBN 978-0-19-532134-0; 0-19-532134-0

LC 2007-48304

The author writes about the careers of such chemists as Gilbert Lewis, Irving Langmuir, Fritz Haber, Glenn Seaborg, Harold Urey, Linus Pauling, and Dorothy Wrinch.

This is "is an engaging, well-written, balanced account of 13 chemists who built modern chemistry." Choice
Includes bibliographical references

Greenberg, Arthur

From alchemy to chemistry in picture and story. Wiley-Interscience 2007 xxiii, 637p il $69.95 **540**
1. Chemistry -- History
ISBN 978-0-471-75154-0; 0-471-75154-5
LC 2006-33564

According to the author, this "is a combination of his two previous books, A Chemical History Tour and The Art of Chemistry, with some additions and revisions. . . . One could open the book at almost any page to learn something about the remarkable history of the chemical sciences." Sci Books Films
Includes bibliographical references

The **art** of chemistry; myths, medicines, and materials. Wiley 2003 357p $59.95 **540**
1. Alchemy 2. Chemistry -- History 3. Medicine -- History
ISBN 0-471-07180-3
LC 2002-9950

"A very interesting mix of information. Although it is not something that a reader would sit down and read through in one sitting, each of the eight sections was interesting by itself." Sci Books Films
Includes bibliographical references

Le Couteur, Penny

Napoleon's buttons; how 17 molecules changed history. [by] Penny Le Couteur, Jay Burreson. Jeremy P. Tarcher/Penguin Books 2003 375p il hardcover o.p. pa $14.95 **540**
1. Chemistry
ISBN 1-58542-220-7; 1-58542-331-9 pa
LC 2002-032247

"Napoleon's Buttons is a fascinating attempt at recognizing the role of chemistry in the wider world. With its many structural diagrams, the book can resemble a course in organic chemistry, but the chemist-authors are good guides. . . . The best chapter is the one on dyes." Quill & Quire
Includes bibliographical references

Quinn, Susan

Marie Curie; a life. Addison-Wesley 1996 509p il pa $21 **540**
1. Chemists 2. Nobel laureates for physics 3. Physicists 4. Women scientists
ISBN 0-201-88794-0; 978-0-201-88794-5
LC 96-167

This a biography of the Polish-born scientist who was twice the recipient of the Nobel Prize for her work with radium.

"A well-written, evenhanded story of dedication, disappointment, tragedy, and extraordinary achievement." Booklist
Includes bibliographical references

Rittner, Don

★ **Encyclopedia** of chemistry; [by] Don Rittner and Ronald A. Bailey. Facts on File 2005 342p il $75 **540**
1. Chemistry -- Encyclopedias 2. Reference books
ISBN 0-8160-4894-0
LC 2004-11242

This encyclopedia "offers more than 2000 articles on topics from ABO blood groups to zwitterionic compound." SLJ
Includes bibliographical references

CRC handbook of chemistry and physics; a ready-reference book of chemical and physical data. editor-in-chief, W.M. Haynes; associate editor, David R. Lide. CRC 2010 various pagings il $149.95 **540**
1. Chemistry -- Tables 2. Physics -- Tables 3. Reference books
ISBN 978-1-4398-2077-3

A "reference book containing much-used information on mathematics, chemistry, and physics, including tables, physical constants of chemical elements and compounds, definitions, formulae, etc." AAAS Sci Book List for Young Adults
Includes bibliographical references

★ Lange's handbook of chemistry; 16th ed.; McGraw-Hill 2005 various paging il $150 **540**
1. Chemistry -- Tables
ISBN 0-07-143220-5; 978-0-07-143220-7

"A standard reference source for both students and professional chemists. Sections for: organic compounds; general information, conversion tables, and mathematics; inorganic chemistry; properties of atoms, radicals, and bonds; physical properties; thermodynamic properties; spectroscopy; electrolytes, electromotive force, and chemical equilibrium; physiochemical relationships; polymers, rubbers, fats, oils, and waxes; and practical laboratory information." Guide to Ref Books. 11th edition

A dictionary of chemistry; edited by John Daintith. 6th ed.; Oxford University Press 2008 584p il pa $17.95 **540**
1. Chemistry -- Dictionaries 2. Reference books
ISBN 978-0-19-920463-2; 0-19-920463-2
LC 2008-274475

This book covers "biochemistry, chemoinformatics, forensic chemistry, metallurgy, and geology. The dictionary includes chronologies, biographies, illustrations, tables, chemical structures, feature articles, and eight appendixes." Choice

541 Chemistry

Atkins, Peter

Reactions; the private life of atoms. by Peter Atkins. Oxford University Press 2011 191 p. $24.95 **541**
1. Chemical reactions
ISBN 978-0-19-969512-6; 0-19-969512-1;

9780199695126; 0199695121

LC 2011275047

The author "provides detailed descriptions of the reactions that occur in everyday life, using language that, while elevated, will be accessible for the armchair scientist. Each chapter focuses on a particular type of reaction, including: precipitation, neutralization, combustion, reduction, oxidation separately and in combination, catalysis, and more." Publ Wkly

Atkins, Peter William

The **periodic** kingdom; a journey into the land of the chemical elements. Basic Bks. 1995 161p il hardcover o.p. pa $14   **541**

1. Chemical elements 2. Periodic law

ISBN 0-465-07266-6 pa

LC 95-7362

"Depicting the periodic table of elements as a map, Atkins explores the territories that it represents, from metallic 'deserts' to the hydrogen 'island.' Basic chemistry has never been presented in a more creative and readily comprehensible manner." Libr J

Includes bibliographical references

546   Inorganic chemistry

Aldersey-Williams, Hugh

Periodic tales; a cultural history of the elements, from arsenic to zinc. Ecco 2011 428p il $29.99 **546**

1. Chemical elements 2. Periodic law

ISBN 978-0-06-182472-2; 0-06-182472-0

"Because Aldersey-Williams's ultimate subject is human civilization rather than simply the elements, he gives himself room to expound on just about everything, treating the components of the table as though they were 'sorted by an anthropologist.' So his book is organized (loosely) into five sections: power (elements hoarded as riches or used to exert control); fire (elements that can best be understood by what happens when they are burned); craft (elements used to create and the cultural meaning we ascribe to them); beauty (elements used to 'colour our world'); and earth (elements that have marked the place where they were discovered in a notable way). It's an ambitious project. . . . [The book] is swollen with names, places, and long-forgotten (or simply unknown to most of us) figures, with zigzagging detours into almost every subject imaginable. It is almost more of a question of what the book does not touch upon than what it does." Boston Globe

Includes bibliographical references

Bernstein, Jeremy

Plutonium; a history of the world's most dangerous element. National Academies Press 2007 194p il map $27.95   **546**

1. Plutonium

ISBN 978-0-309-10296-4; 0-309-10296-0

LC 2006-38466

"Bernstein's book should play a useful role by helping to demystify plutonium and by encouraging interested members of the public and Congress to start constructing a more

rational policy to deal with the dangers posed by this man-made element." Am Sci

Includes bibliographical references

Gray, Theodore

★ The **elements**; a visual exploration of every known atom in the universe. photographs by Theodore Gray and Nick Mann. Black Dog & Leventhal Publishers 2009 240p il $29.95   **546**

1. Chemical elements 2. Chemical elements -- Pictorial works 3. Periodic law

ISBN 1-57912-814-9; 978-1-57912-814-2

LC 2009-34931

This is a collection of "photographic representations of the 118 elements in the periodic table. . . . [The book also contains] facts, figures, and stories of the elements as well as data on the properties of each, including atomic weight, density, melting and boiling point, valence, electronegativity, and the year and location in which it was discovered." (Publisher's note) Index.

This is a collection of "photographic representations of the 118 elements in the periodic table. . . . Organized in order of appearance on the periodic table, each element is represented by a spread that includes a . . . full-page, full-color photograph that most closely represents it in its purest form. . . . [Also included are] facts, figures, and stories of the elements as well as data on the properties of each, including atomic weight, density, melting and boiling point, valence, electronegativity, and the year and location in which it was discovered." Publisher's note

Includes bibliographical references

Kean, Sam

★ The **disappearing** spoon; and other true tales of madness, love, and the history of the world from the periodic table of the elements. Little, Brown and Co. 2010 391p $24.99   **546**

1. Chemical elements

ISBN 978-0-316-05164-4; 0-316-05164-0

LC 2009-40754

"Kean's traipse among the elements leads him through a warren of subjects, as he examines how these basic building blocks have factored prominently in astronomy, biology, literature, history, politics, and even cryptozoology. With the anecdotal flourishes of Oliver Sacks and the populist accessibility of Malcolm Gladwell, but without the latter's occasional facileness, he makes even the most abstract concepts graspable for armchair scientists. His keen sense of humor is a particular pleasure." Entertainment Wkly

Includes bibliographical references

Rigden, John S.

Hydrogen; the essential element. Harvard Univ. Press 2002 280p il $28; pa $15.95   **546**

1. Hydrogen 2. Science -- History

ISBN 0-674-00738-7; 0-674-01252-6 pa

LC 2001-51708

The author chronicles "how one enduring conundrum—that of explaining the element hydrogen—has challenged two centuries of brilliant scientists. . . . In the process, he clarifies for general readers the nature of the scientific enterprise, in which elegant theories must meet the test of empirical verification." Booklist

Includes bibliographical references

Zoellner, Tom

Uranium; war, energy, and the rock that shaped the world. Viking 2009 337p $26.95; pa $16 **546**

1. Uranium

ISBN 978-0-670-02064-5; 0-670-02064-8; 978-0-14-311672-1 pa; 0-14-311672-X pa

LC 2008-29023

This is an overview of the radioactive mineral.

"Zoellner vividly conveys both the potential benefits and the harm that uranium holds for human civilization. . . . Policymakers and citizens alike need to read 'Uranium.'" Washington Post Book World

Includes bibliographical references

548   Crystallography

Holden, Alan

Crystals and crystal growing; {by} Alan Holden and Phylis Morrison; introduction by Philip Morrison. MIT Press 1982 318p il pa $19.95   **548**

1. Crystals

ISBN 0-262-58050-0

LC 81-23639

"An excellent introduction to crystallography (and, incidentally, to much basic physics) written in plain language." Libr J

549   Mineralogy

Chesterman, Charles W.

★ The **Audubon** Society field guide to North American rocks and minerals; scientific consultant, Kurt E. Lowe. Knopf 1979 850p il $19.95   **549**

1. Minerals 2. Rocks

ISBN 0-394-50269-8

LC 78-54893

"Pocket guide providing color photos and descriptions of some 232 mineral species and forty types of rocks. Includes guide to mineral environments, glossary, bibliography, and indexes by name and locality." Ref Sources for Small & Medium-sized Libr. 5th edition

Johnsen, Ole

Minerals of the world. Princeton Univ. Press 2002 439p il pa $24.95   **549**

1. Crystals 2. Minerals

ISBN 0-691-09537-X

LC 2001-97695

The author "provides descriptive information for the identification of more than 500 minerals. . . . This book follows the standard mineralogy textbook approach in which the mineral sections are arranged according to mineral composition and structure. . . . The book's suitability as a field guide is completed by the addition of hundreds of excellent color photographs and drawings. . . . The content material is solid, and superb illustrations on high-quality paper make for an attractive volume." Choice

Klein, Cornelis

Manual of mineral science; [by] Cornelis Klein, Barbara Dutrow. 23rd ed; Wiley 2007 xxi, 675p il $150.95   **549**

1. Minerals

ISBN 978-0-471-72157-4; 0-471-72157-3

LC 2007-273750

This is a standard introductory reference book for the use of students and collectors. It covers physical, chemical, determinative, and descriptive mineralogy, discusses mineral occurrence, association, and use, and includes both a subject and mineral index

Pellant, Chris

Rocks and minerals; Helen Pellant, editorial consultant; photography by Harry Taylor. 2nd American ed; Dorling Kindersley 2002 256p il pa $20   **549**

1. Minerals 2. Rocks

ISBN 0-7894-9106-0; 978-0-7894-9106-0

This field guide to identification of rocks and minerals includes techniques for collection and classification, and facts about physical and chemical composition and formation.

Pough, Frederick H.

★ A **field** guide to rocks and minerals; photographs by Jeff Scovil. 5th ed; Houghton Mifflin 1996 396p il hardcover o.p. pa $20   **549**

1. Minerals 2. Rocks

ISBN 0-395-72778-2; 0-395-91096-X pa

LC 94-49005

This illustrated guide utilizes traditional identification methods and includes discussions of crystallography, mineralogy and home laboratory techniques.

550   Earth sciences

Facts on File, Inc.

★ The **Facts** on File dictionary of earth science; Rev. ed.; Facts on File 2006 388p il map $55 **550**

1. Earth sciences -- Dictionaries 2. Reference books

ISBN 0-8160-6000-2

LC 2006-42340

In this reference work more than 3700 "cross-referenced entries . . . cover all aspects of Earth science: geomorphology, stratigraphy, mineralogy, petrology, climatology, oceanography, paleontology, hydrology, geophysics, cartography, surveying, and soil science. Key concepts in physics, chemistry, biology, and mathematics are also defined." Publisher's note

Includes bibliographical references

Hazen, Robert M.

★ The **story** of Earth; the first 4.5 billion years, from stardust to living planet. Robert M. Hazen. Viking 2012 306 p.   **550**

1. Earth -- Origin 2. Earth sciences 3. Evolution

(Biology) 4. Scientific literature
ISBN 0670023558; 9780670023554

LC 2011043713

This book by Robert M. Hazen argues that Earth's living and nonliving spheres have co-evolved over the past four billion years. . . . The author updates evidence collected by mineralogists over the last two centuries. Describing the discoveries of organisms in places long considered inhospitable [to life] -- in superheated volcanic vents, acidic pools, Arctic ice and stratospheric dust, he argues for the dating of the origin of life more than a billion years earlier than estimates based on Nobel Prize winner Harold Urey's groundbreaking experiments. These appeared to support the view that life originated 2.5 billion years ago in an oceanic environment with the creation of organic molecules. (Kirkus)

Kusky, Timothy M.

Encyclopedia of earth science; [by] Timothy Kusky. Facts on File 2005 510p il map $75 **550**
1. Earth sciences -- Encyclopedias 2. Reference books
ISBN 0-8160-4973-4

LC 2004-4389

"Kusky's encyclopedia will appeal to a broad audience, from high school students to researchers." Choice
Includes bibliographical references

Morton, R. L.

Music of the earth; volcanoes, earthquakes, and other geological wonders. [by] Ron L. Morton. Perseus Pub. 2002 312p il pa $26 **550**
1. Earth sciences
ISBN 978-0-7382-0870-1; 0-7382-0870-1

"An entertaining and readable account of the earth that is full of humor and anecdotes." Sci Books Films
Includes bibliographical references

Smithsonian Institution

★ **Earth**; editor-in-chief, James F. Luhr. Compact ed.; DK Pub. 2007 520p il map pa $24.95 **550**
ISBN 978-0-7566-3332-5; 0-7566-3332-X

LC 2007282646

Presents an overview of the Earth, discussing its internal structure, the major features of its lands, mountains, and oceans, its climate, weather, and place in the universe.

Williams, David B.

Stories in stone; travels through urban geology. Walker 2009 260p il **550**
1. Urban geology
ISBN 978-0-8027-1622-4

LC 2009-5609

The author "describes the mineralogy and history of some of the world's most common building materials. . . . Each chapter showcases a different stone. By describing how the stones formed and how they are used, this book reveals that natural and cultural history may lie no farther than the building next door." Sci News
Includes bibliographical references

551 Geology, hydrology, meteorology

Flannery, Tim

Here on Earth; a natural history of the planet. [by] Tim Flannery. Atlantic Monthly Press 2011 316p il **551**
1. Earth sciences 2. Earth sciences -- History 3. Evolution 4. Evolution -- History
ISBN 080211976X; 9780802119766

The author expands on the proposition that humans inherently exhaust their resources, triggering all manner of ecological and societal trauma. To evaluate the idea, he ranges over the entirety of human existence, remarking within each subtopic he raises—for example, the Aborigines' relation to Australian ecosystems—the ramifications of human use of available natural resources. Booklist
Includes bibliographical references

Lamb, Simon

Devil in the mountain; a search for the origin of the Andes. Princeton University Press 2004 335p il $29.95 **551**
1. Geology -- Andes
ISBN 0-691-11596-6

LC 2003-64124

The author gives "a clear, solid lecture on geological theory and practice with a few personal snapshots of the unseen hazards of fieldwork and occasional local color. . . . Those interested in geology will find it informative and its conclusion satisfying." Publ Wkly
Includes bibliographical references

Lambert, David

The **field** guide to geology; [by] David Lambert and the Diagram Group. New ed.; Checkmark Books 2006 304p il map $39.95; pa $16.95 **551**
1. Geology
ISBN 0-8160-6509-8; 978-0-8160-6509-7; 0-8160-6510-1 pa; 978-0-8160-6510-3 pa

LC 2006-48533

This is an "overview of the processes that forged the planet and the technologies that have revolutionized the way that scientists investigate Earth's systems." Publisher's note
Includes bibliographical references

Newton, David E.

Encyclopedia of air. Greenwood Press 2003 252p il $79.95 **551**
1. Aeronautics 2. Air 3. Atmosphere 4. Atmosphere -- Encyclopedias 5. Meteorology 6. Meteorology -- Encyclopedias 7. Reference books
ISBN 1-57356-564-4

LC 2003-44076

"Entries discuss the science of air (biology, chemistry, meteorology, physics), its technology (air bag, airbrush, air conditioner), and even its social, mythological, and cultural aspects. Newton also includes biographical entries and descriptions of related organizations and associations." Choice
Includes bibliographical references

Interdisciplinary encyclopedia of marine sciences; edited by James W. Nybakken, William W.

Broenkow, Tracy L. Vallier. Grolier 2002 3v set
$349   **551**
1. Marine sciences -- Encyclopedias 2. Oceanography
3. Reference books
ISBN 0-7172-5946-3

LC 2002-192707

"More than 800 alphabetical enries vary in length from
250 to 2500 words and discuss topics ranging from 'Abyssal
Gigantism' to 'Zooxanthellae'. The . . . articles cover the
subdiscipline of oceanography (biological, chemical, geological, and physical) in addition to economics, marine life,
and ecology of the oceans. Technologies used to explore this
environment and biographies of important individuals are
also included. Each accessible, signed entry concludes with
a list of related articles and suggestions for further reading
that will be useful for students." SLJ

Includes bibliographical references and index

551.09   History, geographic treatment, biography of geology

Oldroyd, D. R.

Thinking about the earth; a history of ideas in
geology. Harvard Univ. Press 1996 xxx, 410p il
maps $55.50   **551.09**
1. Geology 2. Geology -- History
ISBN 0-674-88382-9

LC 95-48234

"The sections on mountain-building, seismology, and,
especially, the Gaia hypothesis . . . are new to the history of
geology. Because of this book, these subjects will now be
added to the standard lists of topics that are required reading
for the 'complete' geologist." Choice

Includes bibliographical references

551.2   Volcanoes, earthquakes, thermal waters and gases

Calderazzo, John

Rising fire: volcanoes and our inner lives. Lyons
Press 2004 268p $22.95   **551.2**
1. Volcanoes
ISBN 1-59228-389-6

"Calderazzo climbs volcanoes, presents dramatic accounts of major eruptions, portrays people who live within
a volcano's reach, and muses on the impact volcanoes have
had on humankind's sense of the sacred." Booklist

Carson, Rob

Mount St. Helens: the eruption and recovery of
a volcano; with selected photographs by Geff Hinds,
Cheryl Haselhorst and Gary Braasch. Sasquatch Bks.
1990 160p il hardcover o.p. pa $19.95   **551.2**
1. Volcanoes -- United States
ISBN 1-57061-248-X pa

LC 90-31009

The author "describes the eruption of Mount St. Helens
in 1980, and goes on to report what has happened in the devastated area since then. . . . Mr. Carson has a lively story to

tell and does it well. The photographs . . . provide beauty as
well as information." Atl Mon

Feldman, Jay

★ **When** the Mississippi ran backwards; empire,
intrigue, murder, and the new Madrid earthquakes.
Free Press 2005 307p il maps $27   **551.2**
1. Earthquakes -- Missouri -- New Madrid region 2.
Earthquakes -- United States
ISBN 0-7432-4278-5

LC 2004-57537

"Through four historical figures, Feldman recreates the
frontier world of 1811-12, when the New Madrid earthquakes devastated the lower Ohio and mid-Mississippi valleys. . . . Synthesizing lives and times, Feldman composes
a fluent, coherent narrative that culminates in the War of
1812." Booklist

Includes bibliographical references

Gates, Alexander E.

★ **Encyclopedia** of earthquakes and volcanoes;
[by] Alexander E. Gates, PH.D and David Ritchie.
3rd ed.; Facts on File 2007 346p il map $75 **551.2**
1. Earthquakes 2. Earthquakes -- Encyclopedias
3. Reference books 4. Volcanoes 5. Volcanoes --
Encyclopedias
ISBN 0-8160-6302-8

LC 2005-46619

"The book's entries cover information on key environmental issues, economic dilemmas, ethical concerns, advances in research and technology, organizations, and individuals who have left their mark on the fields of volcanology
and seismology." Publisher's note

Includes bibliographical references

Oppenheimer, Clive

Eruptions that shook the world. Cambridge University Press 2011 392p il map $30   **551.2**
1. Volcanoes
ISBN 978-0-521-64112-8

LC 2011004246

The author "pieces together our volcanic past by connecting major historic and prehistoric eruptions to the course
of human civilization. . . . A fascinating work that will engage not just volcano experts but also those with an interest
in history, climatology, archaeology, and geochronology."
Libr J

Includes bibliographical references

Scarth, Alwyn

Vesuvius: a biography.   Princeton University
Press 2009 342p il map $29.95   **551.2**
1. Volcanism -- Italy 2. Volcanoes
ISBN 978-0-691-14390-3; 0-691-14390-0

LC 2009-925151

"Vesuvius has been central to Western civilization's
unfolding understanding of volcanoes. While the detailed
descriptions of historic eruptions here are valuable, if rep-
etitious, the real strength of the book lies in the quotations
from primary sources. These range from Pliny the Younger's
description of the C.E. 79 eruption that destroyed Pompeii
and Herculaneum, to medieval and Counter-Reformation

reactions invoking the supernatural (after a brief naturalistic approach in the Renaissance), to the beginnings of a modern scientific understanding of volcanoes in the late 18th century with the work of Sir William Hamilton, the British envoy in Naples. The chronology concludes with current concerns about the safety of the increasing population around Vesuvius." Libr J

Includes bibliographical references

Winchester, Simon

Krakatoa: the day the world exploded, August 27, 1883. HarperCollins Pubs. 2003 416p il maps $25.95; pa $13.95   **551.2**
1. Large print books 2. Volcanoes
ISBN 0-06-621285-5; 0-06-083859-0 pa

"As a rich blend of science and history, this book is highly recommended for most public and academic libraries." Libr J

551.21   Volcanoes

Thompson, Dick

Volcano cowboys; the rocky evolution of a dangerous science. St. Martin's Press 2000 326p il map $26.95; pa $14.95   **551.21**
1. Volcanoes 2. Volcanological research -- History -- 20th century
ISBN 0-312-20881-2; 0-312-28668-6 pa
                                                           LC 00-26158
This describes the work of U.S. Geological Survey scientists in predicting volcanic eruptions, focusing on the eruptions of Mount St. Helens in 1980 and Mount Pinatubo in 1991

"An informative book about science's communication with the lay public." Booklist

Includes bibliographical references

551.3   Surface and exogenous processes and their agents

Fredston, Jill A.

Snowstruck; in the grip of avalanches. [by] Jill Fredston. Harcourt 2005 342p il $24; pa $14 **551.3**
1. Avalanches 2. Biography, Individual 3. Mountaineers 4. Safety educators 5. Snow and ice climbing 6. Survival skills
ISBN 978-0-15-101249-7; 0-15-101249-0; 978-0-15-603254-4 pa; 0-15-603254-6 pa
                                                           LC 2005-20454
"As avalanche experts, . . . [the author and her husband] are often called upon to forecast, trigger, and teach about avalanches as well as rescue survivors—or, sadly, more often to recover remains. Fredston's decades of experience distilled into this instructive and personal narrative will leave readers with a newfound appreciation for the force, the fury, and the cold sorrow of avalanches." Libr J

Gosnell, Mariana

Ice; the nature, the history, and the uses of an astonishing substance. Knopf 2005 560p il $30 **551.3**
1. Ice
ISBN 0-679-42608-6
                                                           LC 2005-45126
The author "opens with a description of the sound and sight of a small lake freezing, expanding from there to discuss the seasonal advance and retreat of ice, as on the Great Lakes or Lake Baikal. Taking the next natural step, the persistence of ice through the summer, brings Gosnell to the 1800s origin of glaciology in Louis Agassiz's study of Mont Blanc's Mer de Glace, and subsequently into the contemporary specialty of ice cores in ice-age research. En route through the science, which Gosnell condenses from the technical literature, the author imparts eclectic information through excerpts from poems, adventure and disaster stories, and discussions of ice sports and diversions." Booklist

Pollack, H. N.

A **world** without ice; [by] Henry Pollack. Avery 2009 287p il map $26; pa $16 **551.3**
1. Glaciers 2. Greenhouse effect 3. Ice
ISBN 978-1-58333-357-0; 978-1-58333-407-2 pa
                                                           LC 2009-30326
"Seldom has a scientist written so well and so clearly for the lay reader. Pollack's explanations of how researchers can tell that the climate is warming faster than normal are free of the usual scientific jargon and understandable. All readers concerned about global warming and students writing papers on the topic will want this excellent and important volume." Libr J

Includes bibliographical references

Stewart, Ian

★ **In** pursuit of the unknown; 17 equations that changed the world. Ian Stewart. Basic Books 2012 x, 342 p.p **551.3**
1. Equations -- History 2. Mathematics -- History 3. Physics -- History
ISBN 9780465029747; 0465029736; 9780465029730
                                                           LC 2011944850
In this book, [t]he author shows how mathematics has played a crucial role in the ascent of humanity, but were merely steps in the technological advances that followed. He begins with Pythagoras' Theorem [which] . . . laid the basis for navigation and astronomy. He ends with the Black-Scholes Equation, the mathematical formula that created the possibility for computerized derivatives trading and arguably the recent economic meltdown, and urges the need for more regulation of financial markets. [Ian] Stewart provides . . . explanations of how the equations work . . . [and] uses them to elaborate his thesis that mathematics . . . does not in itself change the world. (Kirkus)

551.46   Oceanography and submarine geology

Ballard, Robert D.

The **eternal** darkness; a personal history of deepsea exploration. {by} Robert D. Ballard with Will

Hively. Princeton Univ. Press 2000 388p il maps $55; pa $18.95   551.46

1. Underwater exploration 2. Underwater exploration -- History

ISBN 0-691-02740-4; 0-691-09554-X pa

LC 99-43072

Ballard "blends his personal experiences exploring hydrothermal vents and shipwrecks with stories of earlier deep-sea pioneers, focusing especially on the technology. . . . Ballard's volume is easy to read and will be an excellent addition to collections at all levels on oceanography, history of science, and exploration." Libr J

Includes bibliographical references and index

Broad, William

The **universe** below; discovering the secrets of the deep sea. {by} William J. Broad; illustrations by Dimitry Schidlovsky. Simon & Schuster 1997 432p il maps hardcover o.p. pa $15   551.46

1. Oceanography 2. Underwater exploration

ISBN 0-684-83852-4 pa

LC 96-50337

"Intensively researched and crisply told, this is an illuminating, stimulating portrait of one of Earth's last frontiers." Publ Wkly

Includes bibliographical references

Carson, Rachel

The **sea** around us. Oxford Univ. Press 2003 274p il maps $45   551.46

1. Ocean 2. Oceanography

ISBN 0-19-514701-4

LC 2002-29299

Beginning with a description of how the earth acquired its oceans, the book covers such topics as how life began in the primeval sea, the hidden lands, the life discovered in the abyss by highly delicate sounding apparatus, currents and tides, the formation of volcanic islands, and mineral resources

Casey, Susan

The **wave**; in pursuit of the rogues, freaks and giants of the ocean. Doubleday 2010 326p il map $27.95   551.46

1. Ocean waves 2. Oceanography 3. Surfing

ISBN 978-0-7679-2884-7; 0-7679-2884-9

LC 2010-10193

Casey "estimates that freak waves might have a hand in sinking about two dozen large ships every year. She embarked on a five-year odyssey to meet the people who know these monsters best—from salvagers working a graveyard of ships off the South African coast to a convention of wave scientists, from researchers and mariners who have battled these beasts to surfers who roam the world in search of the ultimate thrill. Reading the 'The Wave' is almost like riding one, paddling in the expositional surf of vivid imagery and colorful description, thrown at you in ever-escalating surges." Cleveland Plain Dealer

Includes bibliographical references

Day, Trevor

Oceans; illustrations by Richard Garratt. rev ed; Facts on File 2008 318p il map $70   551.46

1. Marine biology 2. Ocean 3. Oceanography

ISBN 0-8160-5932-2; 978-0-8160-5932-4

LC 2006-100769

This volume describes the oceans of the world with regard to their geography, geology, history, chemistry, biology, ecology, exploration, relationship to the atmosphere, economic resources, and management.

Earle, Sylvia A.

The **world** is blue; how our fate and the ocean's are one. National Geographic 2009 303p il map $26   551.46

1. Biological diversity 2. Human influence on nature 3. Marine biology 4. Marine ecology 5. Marine pollution 6. Nature -- Effect of human beings on 7. Oceanography

ISBN 978-1-4262-0541-5; 1-4262-0541-4

LC 2009-23972

The author "illustrates, in ways both humorous and discomforting, how our cavalier attitude toward the ocean and its inhabitants is causing our slow but certain destruction. Even more importantly, Earle offers solutions and discusses ongoing actions that have been taken to reverse this frightening cycle of obliteration. Even those who do not consider themselves environmentalists will find themselves easily caught up in Earle's heroic fight to save our 'blue world.'" Choice

Includes bibliographical references (p. 286-303)

Ebbesmeyer, Curtis

Flotsametrics and the floating world; how one man's obsession with runaway sneakers and rubber ducks revolutionized ocean science. [by] Curtis Ebbesmeyer and Eric Scigliano. Smithsonian Books 2009 286p il $26.99   551.46

1. Marine debris 2. Ocean currents 3. Oceanographers

ISBN 978-0-06-155841-2; 0-06-155841-9

LC 2008-38805

Ebbesmeyer's "primary interest is ocean currents, especially gyres—great circular, interlocking currents that sweep the Earth's waters with clockwork regularity—and the flotsam they carry around the planet. Everything from athletic shoes and bathtub toys to messages in bottles and corpses have provided data to help Ebbesmeyer trace currents. He recounts how flotsam guided colonization and exploration, from Norse explorers to Christopher Columbus (the first to master the North Atlantic Subtropical Gyre). Today, Ebbesmeyer says, the human propensity for creating garbage has also made flotsam an environmental concern." Publ Wkly

Includes bibliographical references

Ellis, Richard

★ **Encyclopedia** of the sea; written and illustrated by Richard Ellis. Knopf 2000 380p il $35 551.46

1. Marine ecology -- Encyclopedias 2. Ocean -- Encyclopedias 3. Oceanography -- Encyclopedias 4. Reference books

ISBN 0-375-40374-4

LC 99-42401

"The alphabetically arranged text consists of short paragraphs on topics in marine biology, oceanography, fisheries, geography, and maritime and naval history. . . . Eight pages of Ellis's color paintings . . . and hundreds of his own illustrations enhance the text. . . . The handy format makes the book useful as a ready-reference source for public and college libraries." Libr J

Kunzig, Robert

The **restless** sea; exploring the world beneath the waves. Norton 1999 336p il maps $24.95 **551.46**
1. Ocean
ISBN 0-393-04562-5

LC 98-38704

The author "chronicles the history of oceans from the Big Bang to the present. Although some of the material Kunzig sets down as fact is still hotly debated, his writing is clear and easy to understand. His descriptions of the ocean are visual, almost poetic." Libr J

McCutcheon, Scott

The **Facts** on File marine science handbook; {by} Scott McCutcheon and Bobbi McCutcheon. Facts on File 2003 266p il maps $35; pa $17.95 **551.46**
1. Marine sciences
ISBN 0-8160-4812-6; 0-8160-4883-5 pa

LC 2003-275

"The information given in the entries is for the most part general in nature and not too full of scientific jargon, which makes it easy to understand . . . The charts and tables area is quite interesting and useful with its miscellaneous information about ocean currents, size of the oceans, fish catches, and so on." Am Ref Books Annu, 2004
Includes bibliographical references

Prager, Ellen J.

Chasing science at sea; racing hurricanes, stalking sharks, and living undersea with ocean experts. [by] Ellen Prager. University of Chicago Press 2008 162p il $22.50; pa $13 **551.46**
1. Ocean 2. Oceanography
ISBN 978-0-226-67870-2; 0-226-67870-9; 978-0-226-67874-0 pa; 0-226-67874-1 pa

LC 2007-49486

This book "assembles anecdotes from colleagues such as marine biologists, geologists and engineers. Their tales range from divers chasing parrotfish poo with plastic bags to oceanographers seeing an actual step in the surface of the sea at the edge of the Gulf Stream. In bringing these briny tales together, Prager explores some of their common themes to convey why many of us study the ocean—and why it matters." Times Higher Ed
Includes bibliographical references

Roberts, Callum

The **ocean** of life; the fate of man and the sea. Callum Roberts. Viking 2012 405 p. **551.46**
1. Marine ecosystem health 2. Nonfiction 3. Ocean -- History 4. Ocean and civilization 5. Ocean mining -- Environmental aspects
ISBN 067002354X; 9780670023547

LC 2012000252

In this book, Callum Roberts warns that the oceans have changed more in [the] last thirty years than in all of human history before. . . . [He] documents the loss of large sea animals, such as whales, sharks and turtles, the destruction of coral reefs and the broader ocean environment . . . and . . . anticipates further devastation from the onset of deep-sea mining in the near future. While environmentalists are keenly aware of the danger man poses to animal species, Roberts suggests that the oceans have always played a significant role in human survival. He writes that the view of our ancestors as a plucky species of big-game hunters has a certain mythological ring to it. However, our early survival may have depended mainly on water creatures for sustenance. (Kirkus Reviews)

Stow, Dorrik A. V.

★ **Oceans**: an illustrated reference; [by] Dorrik Stow. University of Chicago Press 2006 256p il map $55 **551.46**
1. Marine biology 2. Ocean 3. Oceanography
ISBN 0-226-77664-6

LC 2004-55333

This "reference work presents a thorough overview of the physical, geological, chemical, and biological properties of the world's oceans. . . . [The author's] up-to-date and well-organized volume would make a valuable introduction to a huge field of knowledge." Libr J
Includes bibliographical references

Ulanski, Stan L.

The **Gulf** Stream; tiny plankton, giant bluefin, and the amazing story of the powerful river in the Atlantic. [by] Stan Ulanski. University of North Carolina Press 2008 212p il map $28; pa $22 **551.46**
1. Gulf Stream
ISBN 978-0-8078-3217-2; 0-8078-3217-0; 978-0-8078-8709-7 pa; 0-8078-8709-9 pa

LC 2008-4746

This "book provides the layperson a synopsis of the physical origin, general biology, and rich exploration history of the Gulf Stream. Ulanski . . . offers a concise, engaging blend of science and history for anyone interested in learning about the general flow dynamics, the intricate food webs, and the human use and exploitation of this vital western-boundary current of the North Atlantic Ocean." Choice
Includes bibliographical references

Winchester, Simon

Atlantic; great sea battles, heroic discoveries, titanic storms, and a vast ocean of a million stories. Harper 2010 495p il map $27.99 **551.46**
1. Ocean and civilization
ISBN 978-0-06-170258-7; 0-06-170258-7

LC 2010-15229

"Writing the history of the Atlantic Ocean — from tectonic labor pains to its lead role in modern European and American history — might be one of the more difficult tasks Simon Winchester has set for himself. . . . Luckily, the author comes armed with a knowledge almost as vast and deep as his subject, as well as a clever yet functional organizational scheme that divides his oceanic biography Atlantic into the seven ages of a man's life as proposed by Shakespeare. A formidable writer and storyteller, Winchester still gets distracted by the occasional unworthy anecdote or superfluous specificity, but for all the densely packed information in this work, the one thing it never becomes, quite appropriately, is dry." Entertainment Wkly

551.48 Hydrology

Montgomery, David R.

★ The **rocks** don't lie; a geologist investigates Noah's flood. David R. Montgomery. W.W. Norton 2012 320 p. (hardcover) $26.95   **551.48**
1. Paleohydrology 2. Paleolimnology
ISBN 0393082393; 9780393082395
LC 2012015146

In this book, geologist David R. Montgomery "offers a . . . critique of creationist worldviews (including Noah's flood) . . . , reflecting on both ancient and modern debates . . . . He admits that geologists have often stifled dissent and stubbornly rejected the idea that massive floods could have ever occurred, discounting such ideas as myths though there have, in fact, been many throughout human history." (Library Journal)

Pielou, E. C.

Fresh water. University of Chicago Press 1998 275p il maps $24; pa $14   **551.48**
1. Hydrology 2. Water
ISBN 0-226-66815-0; 0-226-66816-9 pa
LC 97-51562

This "is a wonderful natural history of one of life's necessities, a refreshing break from grand theory and special pleading of many a science book. . . . Sometimes Pielou gets political. . . . But the mind-boggling details always hold the attention best." New Scientist
Includes bibliographical references (p. {247}-267) and index

551.5 Meteorology

Buckley, Bruce

★ **Weather**: a visual guide; [by] Bruce Buckley, Edward J. Hopkins [and] Richard Whitaker. Firefly Books 2004 303p il maps $29.95; pa $27.95 **551.5**
1. Meteorology 2. Weather
ISBN 1-55297-957-1; 978-1-55297-957-0; 1-55407-430-4 pa; 978-1-55407-430-3 pa
LC 2004-303909

This is "a comprehensive academic resource with information and glorious color photographs on virtually every aspect of weather." SLJ

Rittner, Don

A to Z of scientists in weather and climate. Facts on File 2003 256p il $45   **551.5**
1. Climatologists -- Biography -- Dictionaries 2. Meteorologists -- Biography -- Dictionaries 3. Meteorology 4. Scientists
ISBN 0-8160-4797-9
LC 2002-152435

This reference "includes 115 biographical sketches of individuals throughout history, around the world, and working in a variety of disciplines, who have contributed to an understanding of climate and weather. Entries, informative and clearly written . . . consist of a text of 750 to 2,000 words that includes the subject's early history, educational background, positions held, prizes and awards, and major contributions to weather and climate studies." Choice
Includes bibliographical references and index

Walker, Gabrielle

An **ocean** of air; why the wind blows and other mysteries of the atmosphere. Harcourt 2007 272p il map $25   **551.5**
1. Atmosphere
ISBN 978-0-15-101124-7; 0-15-101124-9
LC 2006-32359

The author "brings a new perspective to centuries-old stories of wonder and discovery and sheds light on the personalities of the 19th and 20th centuries who have also contributed to the world's body of knowledge. Witty and full of fascinating information, this is a captivating book." Libr J
Includes bibliographical references

Williams, Jack

★ The **AMS** weather book; the ultimate guide to America's weather. University of Chicago Press 2009 316p il map $35   **551.5**
1. Climate 2. Meteorology 3. Weather
ISBN 978-0-226-89898-8; 0-226-89898-9
LC 2008-35916

This book "provides a clearly written, profusely illustrated narrative guide to weather that affects the US. . . . Topics in this 12-chapter volume range from how rainbows are formed and what makes the wind blow, to climate change and how weather satellites work. In addition, Williams highlights profiles of meteorologists and other scientists influential in weather prediction and research, including many women and minorities. This work, with its attractive, easy-to-understand graphics, offers a useful, engaging basic introduction to a wide variety of weather-related topics." Choice
Includes glossary

Encyclopedia of atmospheric sciences;   editor-in-chief, James R. Holton; editors, Judith A. Curry, John A. Pyle. Academic Press 2003 6v il set $1,400   **551.5**
1. Atmosphere 2. Atmosphere -- Encyclopedias 3. Meteorology 4. Reference books
ISBN 0-12-227090-8
LC 2002-114120

This reference set "includes the work of 400 scientists worldwide. The 330 authoritative and concise articles review such complex subjects as weather prediction, climate change and variability, and atmospheric chemistry. Beautifully illustrated with maps, charts, photos and illustrations." Libr J
Includes bibliographical references

551.51 Composition, regions, dynamics of atmosphere

Bowen, Mark

Thin ice; unlocking the secrets of climate in the world's highest mountains. Henry Holt 2005 463p il $30; pa $17 **551.51**
1. Climate -- Research 2. Climatic changes 3. Climatology -- Research 4. Geologists 5. Upper atmosphere
ISBN 0-8050-6443-5; 0-8050-8135-6 pa
LC 2005-40426
"This book will appeal to mountaineering and climatology buffs, but should be read by everyone concerned about the future of our planet." Publ Wkly

De Villiers, Marq

Windswept; the story of wind and weather. Walker & Co. 2006 344p il $25 **551.51**
1. Weather 2. Winds
ISBN 0-8027-1469-2
LC 2005-23115
The author "explains the science clearly, and he describes the workings of wind, weather and the natural world with enormous gusto. He is a greedy observer, with plenty of wind and storms to watch from his seaside home in Eagle Head, Nova Scotia. Simply as a catalog of statistics, [the book] is a grabber." N Y Times (Late N Y Ed)

551.55 Atmospheric disturbances and formations

Davies, Pete

Inside the hurricane; face to face with nature's deadliest storms. Holt & Co. 2000 264p hardcover o.p. pa $14 **551.55**
1. Hurricanes
ISBN 0-8050-6611-X pa
LC 00-29562
The author "surveys the 1999 Atlantic hurricane season, focusing on the experiences of a small group of hurricane researchers and forecasters. . . . Vivid and engrossing; recommended for both public and academic libraries." Libr J
Includes bibliographical references

Emanuel, Kerry A.

★ **Divine** wind; the history and science of hurricanes. [by] Kerry Emanuel. Oxford Univ. Press 2005 285p il $45 **551.55**
1. Hurricanes
ISBN 0-19-514941-6
LC 2004-13078
This is a study of hurricanes.
"A gripping popular treatment of peril, that will have great resonance in light of recent disasters." Booklist
Includes bibliographical references

Longshore, David

Encyclopedia of hurricanes, typhoons, and cyclones; New ed; Facts on File 2008 468p il map $75 **551.55**
1. Cyclones 2. Cyclones -- Encyclopedias 3. Hurricanes 4. Hurricanes -- Encyclopedias 5. Reference books 6. Storms 7. Typhoons 8. Typhoons -- Encyclopedias
ISBN 978-0-8160-6295-9; 0-8160-6295-1
LC 2007-32336
This encyclopedia describes named hurricanes, typhoons and cyclones, explains meteorological terms and instruments, and includes biographical data, a chronology, and a list of hurricane safety procedures.
"This is an excellent basic reference work that belongs in all school, public, and academic libraries." Sci Books Films
Includes bibliographical references

551.57 Hydrometeorology

Hamblyn, Richard

The **invention** of clouds; how an amateur meteorologist forged the language of the skies. Picador 2002 292p il pa $15 **551.57**
1. Chemists 2. Clouds 3. Meteorologists 4. Meteorology
ISBN 0-312-42001-3; 978-0-312-42001-7
LC 2002-25152
"A remarkable, remarkably pleasing story." Booklist
Includes bibliographical references

Mergen, Bernard

Snow in America. Smithsonian Institution Press 1997 xxi, 321p il $24.95; pa $16.95 **551.57**
1. Snow
ISBN 1-56098-780-4; 1-56098-381-7 pa
LC 97-12247
This study traces the development of snow technology, explains the importance of snow surveys for climate regulation, and looks at the ski industry, water usage, winter fashions and street cleaning. The author also explores snow in popular culture and its role in the emotional development of the American character.

551.6 Climatology and weather

Allaby, Michael

★ The **Facts** on File weather and climate handbook. Facts on File 2002 290p il $35; pa $17.95 **551.6**
1. Climate 2. Climatology 3. Weather
ISBN 0-8160-4517-8; 0-8160-4961-0 pa
LC 2001-50114
"This work is a comprehensive, handy reference tool for weather and climate. The glossary is especially comprehensive . . . {and} is recommended for all reference collections." Am Ref Books Annu, 2003
Includes bibliographical references

Collier, Michael

Floods, droughts, and climate change; [by] Michael Collier and Robert H. Webb. University of Arizona Press 2002 153p il map pa $17.95   **551.6**
1. Climate 2. Climatic changes -- Environmental aspects 3. Climatology
ISBN 0-8165-2250-2
LC 2002-5314

"Packed with illustrations and balanced between general and specific information, Collier and Webb's work superbly outlines and makes accessible a subject that is complex even for experts in the field." Booklist
Includes bibliographical references

Cox, John D.

Climate crash; abrupt climate change and what it means for our future. Joseph Henry Press 2005 215p il maps hardcover o.p. pa $15.95   **551.6**
1. Climate -- Environmental aspects 2. Climatic changes -- Environmental aspects 3. Paleoclimatology
ISBN 0-309-09312-0; 0-309-10199-9 pa
LC 2005-2387

"The author stresses the speed with which climate has changed in the past 100,000 years and the potential for climate to change radically over a span of decades or even less. . . . I recommend Climate Crash highly as an introduction to one of the most exciting developing sciences of the present time." Sci Books Films
Includes bibliographical references

DeBuys, William Eno

A **great** aridness; climate change and the future of the American southwest. [by] William deBuys. Oxford University Press 2011 369p il map   **551.6**
1. Climate -- Environmental aspects 2. Droughts 3. Water supply
ISBN 978-0-19-977892-8
LC 2011033298

The author discusses "the untenable water situation in the Southwest. . . . While he focuses on the environmental science of heat and aridity, he also acknowledges the uncertain nature of climate variability itself. . . . With wide-eyed wonder and the clearest of prose, deBuys explains why we should care about these places, the people he portrays, and the conundrums over land and water he illuminates." Booklist
Includes bibliographical references

Dow, Kirstin

The **atlas** of climate change; mapping the world's greatest challenge. [by] Kirstin Dow and Thomas E. Downing. Rev. and updated.; University of California Press 2007 112p il map pa $21.95   **551.6**
1. Atlases 2. Climate -- Environmental aspects -- Maps 3. Reference books
ISBN 978-0-520-25558-6
LC 2010-483727

"This atlas examines the causes of climate change and considers its possible impact on subsistence, water resources, ecosystems, biodiversity, health, coastal megacities, and cultural treasures. It reviews historical contributions to greenhouse gas levels, progress in meeting international

commitments, and local efforts to meet the challenge of climate change." Publisher's note
Includes bibliographical references

Dumanoski, Dianne

★ The **end** of the long summer; why we must remake our civilization to survive on a volatile Earth. Crown Publishers 2009 311p $25   **551.6**
1. Climate -- Environmental aspects
ISBN 978-0-307-39607-5; 0-307-39607-X
LC 2009-281272

An environmental journalist discusses the possible ecological consequences beyond global warming resulting from modern human activity and describes the possibility of massive instability and climate swings, including a possible return to ice ages of the past.

"A passionate, precise account of climate change and a persuasive strategy for dealing with 'Nature's return to center stage as a critical player in human history.'" Kirkus
Includes bibliographical references

Fagan, Brian M.

The **long** summer: how climate changed civilization. Basic Books 2003 284p il hardcover o.p. pa $16   **551.6**
1. Civilization -- History 2. Climate
ISBN 0-465-02281-2; 0-465-02282-0 pa
LC 2003-13917

"This book is highly recommended for general audiences considering the implications and the challenges posed by human-induced global climate change." Sci Books Films
Includes bibliographical references

Fleming, James Rodger

Fixing the sky; the checkered history of weather and climate control. [by] James Rodger Fleming. Columbia University Press 2010 325p il $27.95 **551.6**
1. Climatic changes 2. Global warming 3. Human influence on nature 4. Weather control
ISBN 978-0-231-14412-4
LC 2010-15482

This book "should be read by all who want a better understanding of global climate change and the debate over geoengineering our environment." Sci Books Films
Includes bibliographical references

Goodell, Jeff

How to cool the planet; geoengineering and the audacious quest to fix Earth's climate. Houghton Mifflin Harcourt 2010 262p $26   **551.6**
1. Climate -- Environmental aspects 2. Climate change mitigation 3. Climatic changes -- Environmental aspects 4. Engineering geology 5. Environmental engineering 6. Greenhouse effect
ISBN 978-0-618-99061-0; 0-618-99061-5
LC 2009-46565

"There is no trace of climate alarmism or political advocacy here. Goodell takes a detailed look at the range of hard choices humanity faces and explores how complicated moral and ethical considerations will dictate our response.

Goodell is also a skilled writer. He splices complicated ideas into pithy turns of phrase." Business Week

Includes bibliographical references

Linden, Eugene

The **winds** of change; climate, weather, and the destruction of civilizations. Simon & Schuster 2006 302p il map $26 **551.6**

1. Climate 2. Climatic changes 3. Social change 4. Weather 5. Weather -- Social aspects

ISBN 0-684-86352-9; 978-0-684-86352-8

LC 2005-54434

"Relatively restrained in tone, and consequently more persuasive by its sobriety, Linden's presentation of scientists' theories on historical climate change will provoke readers concerned about the implications of global warming for modern civilization." Booklist

Ludlum, David M.

The **Audubon** Society field guide to North American weather. Knopf 1991 656p il maps $19.95 **551.6**

1. Weather forecasting

ISBN 0-679-40851-7

LC 91-52707

"The opening essays provide in-depth information on topics such as clouds, snowstorms, floods, etc. About half of the book is comprised of labelled, high-quality photographs. The third section gives description, environment, season, range, and significance of each type of weather. Clear diagrams, simple definitions, and a readable text make this an excellent selection." SLJ

Lynas, Mark

★ **Six** degrees; our future on a hotter planet. National Geographic 2008 335p $26 **551.6**

1. Climate -- Environmental aspects 2. Environmental influence on humans 3. Greenhouse effect

ISBN 978-1-4262-0213-1

LC 2007-30864

"In 2001, the Intergovernmental Panel on Climate Change released a landmark report projecting average global surface temperatures to rise between 1.4 degrees and 5.8 degrees Celsius (roughly 2 to 10 degrees Fahrenheit) by the end of this century. Based on this forecast, author Mark Lynas outlines what to expect from a warming world, degree by degree." Publisher's note

Includes bibliographical references

Lyons, Walter A.

The **handy** weather answer book. Visible Ink Press 1997 397p il pa $19.95 **551.6**

1. Weather

ISBN 0-7876-1034-8

LC 96-30555

This book provides "answers to more than 1,000 frequently asked questions about the weather. It also provides information on such . . . topics as hurricanes, droughts, flash floods, volcanoes . . . the greenhouse effect, Aurora Borealis and St. Elmo's fire." Publisher's note

Includes bibliographical references

Pearce, Fred

With speed and violence; why scientists fear tipping points in climate change. Beacon Press 2007 xxvi, 278p $24.95; pa $15 **551.6**

1. Climate -- Environmental aspects 2. Climatic changes 3. Greenhouse effect

ISBN 978-0-8070-8576-9; 0-8070-8576-6; 978-0-8070-8577-6 pa; 0-8070-8577-4 pa

LC 2006-19901

"Important reading for policymakers, climate-change skeptics and anyone planning a future beyond the next decade." Kirkus

Includes bibliographical references

Philander, S. George

Our affair with El Nino; how we transformed an enchanting Peruvian current into a global climate hazard. Princeton University Press 2004 275p il maps hardcover o.p. pa $17.95 **551.6**

1. Climate 2. Climatic changes 3. El Nino Current 4. El Niño Current

ISBN 0-691-11335-1; 0-691-12622-4 pa

LC 2003-44235

"This is an exceptional book, enjoyable to read and educational at several levels. El Niño is the springboard for a book that thoroughly explains the phenomenon and even goes far beyond it." Sci Books Films

Includes bibliographical references

Weart, Spencer R.

★ The **discovery** of global warming. Harvard University Press 2003 228p il $24.95; pa $14.95 **551.6**

1. Greenhouse effect

ISBN 0-674-01157-0; 0-674-01637-8 pa

LC 2003-40703

The author "reports the history of global warming theory, including the internal conflicts plaguing the research community and the role government has had in promoting climate studies. . . . Without resorting to fear-mongering, Weart gives an informed history and offers his readers solutions to consider." Publ Wkly

Includes bibliographical references

The encyclopedia of weather and climate change; a complete visual guide. University of California Press 2010 512p il map $39.95 **551.6**

1. Climate -- Environmental aspects -- Encyclopedias 2. Meteorology -- Encyclopedias 3. Reference books

ISBN 978-0-520-26101-3

LC 2009-943908

"Major sections fall under the following headings: Engine, Action, Extremes, Watching, Climate, and Change. Chapters within the sections begin with a broad overview of a particular topic, then move on to greater detail. The regional climate guide, focusing on 43 specific locations around the world, is particularly noteworthy. . . . The profuse illustrations carry the information; this title could be just the thing for visual learners." Libr J

Includes glossary

551.63   Weather forecasting and forecasts, reporting and reports

Cullen, Heidi

The **weather** of the future; heat waves, extreme storms, and other scenes from a climate-changed planet. HarperCollins 2010 329p il map $25.99; pa $15.99   **551.63**
    1. Climate -- Environmental aspects 2. Climatic changes -- Forecasting 3. Forecasting 4. Global environmental change 5. Weather forecasting
    ISBN 978-0-06-172688-0; 0-06-172688-5; 978-0-06-172694-1 pa; 0-06-172694-X pa

"A lively and troubling but not entirely doomsday scenario of our warmer future, which will hopefully persuade readers to pay greater attention." Kirkus
    Includes bibliographical references

Monmonier, Mark S.

Air apparent; how meteorologists learned to map, predict, and dramatize weather. {by} Mark Monmonier. University of Chicago Press 1999 309p il $27.50; pa $17   **551.63**
    1. Meteorology 2. Weather forecasting 3. Weather forecasting -- Technique
    ISBN 0-226-53422-7; 0-226-53423-5 pa
                                                            LC 98-25797

The author presents a "history of more than 200 years of weather maps, an account that embraces technological advances from the telegraph and mercury barometer to the satellite and Doppler radar." Booklist
    Includes index

551.69   Geographic treatment of climate

Tape, Ken D.

The **changing** arctic landscape; Ken D. Tape. University of Alaska Press 2010 viii, 56p ill. (some col.), col. maps (cloth : alk. paper) $35.00   **551.69**
    1. Climatic changes -- Environmental aspects -- Alaska -- Pictorial works
    ISBN 9781602230804; 1602230803
                                                            LC 2009035478

It was the author's intent to demonstrate "how the work of several generations of earth scientists can be integrated into a picture of arctic Alaska landscapes that are responding to both natural and human influences. Decades-old photos from pioneering studies of the geology, vegetation, glaciers, and landforms of Brooks Range and North Slope were used to select specific environments for change detection. . . . The author concludes that the changes are consisted with a warming climate, but the argument for warming is not as solid as the argument for the changes themselves." (Environment)

551.7   Historical geology

Alvarez, Walter

T. rex and the Crater of Doom. Princeton Univ. Press 1997 185p il $35   **551.7**
    1. Catastrophes (Geology) 2. Dinosaurs 3. Geology -- History 4. Mass extinction of species
    ISBN 0-691-01630-5
                                                            LC 96-49208

This book "gets the facts across in a lighthearted, almost playful manner. But it's also solid science, a clear and efficient exposition." N Y Times Book Rev
    Includes bibliographical references

Bjornerud, Marcia

Reading the rocks; the autobiography of the earth. Basic Books 2005 237p $26   **551.7**
    1. Geology
    ISBN 0-8133-4249-X
                                                            LC 2004-22738

"This wonderful book should be examined by anyone with a curiosity about the natural history of our planet and how one science in particular has done such an impressive job of deciphering key mysteries of its origin and evolution." Sci Books Films
    Includes bibliographical references

Fortey, Richard A.

★ **Earth**; an intimate history. by Richard Fortey. Knopf 2004 429p il hardcover o.p. pa $19 **551.7**
    1. Stratigraphic geology
    ISBN 0-375-40626-3; 0-375-70620-8 pa
                                                            LC 2004-46470

The author "relates his walks in places that visually reveal the deep earth (Vesuvius, Hawaii, the Grand Canyon) as well as sites, which, if not so spectacular, contain puzzling elements that provoked great interpretive controversies. . . . The Alps, the Scottish Highlands, Newfoundland, the Deccan Traps of India—these are among Fortey's destinations as he explains the theory of plate tectonics, showing how the theory came to be, as well as the continents and oceans whose skein of connections it explains. This is a marvelously inviting presentation." Booklist
    Includes bibliographical references

Hancock, Graham

Underworld: the mysterious origins of civilization; photographs by Santha Faiia. Crown 2002 769p il maps $27.50; pa $16.95   **551.7**
    1. Ancient civilization 2. Prehistoric peoples 3. Stratigraphic geology
    ISBN 1-4000-4612-2; 1-4000-4951-2 pa

The author presents theories on how "civilization rose about 17,000 years ago (rather than about 6,000) and vanished beneath a rising sea level, leaving its traces in flood myths in Sumerian and Vedic texts, in early maps of the Age of Discovery, and more plausibly, in submerged ruins. Hancock throws up a fantastic amount of data on these points in this work, ranging from his personal textual interpretations to his dives at coastal sites in Malta, India, Japan, and the Bahamas." Booklist
    Includes bibliographical references

Macdougall, J. D.

Frozen earth; the once and future story of ice ages. [by] Doug Macdougall. University of California Press 2004 256p il $24.95; pa $15.95 **551.7**

1. Glacial epoch 2. Global environmental change 3. Ice Age 4. Paleoclimatology

ISBN 0-520-23922-9; 0-520-24824-4 pa

LC 2004-8502

The author "presents the scientific history behind ice ages, emphasizing the roles of four great scientists in the field: Louis Agassiz, James Croll, Milutin Milankovitch, and Harlan Bretz. . . . Macdougall's account promotes a welcome reasoning attitude toward ice-age research and its relevance to global warming." Booklist

Includes bibliographical references

Nature's clocks; how scientists measure the age of almost everything. University of California Press 2008 271p il $40; pa $17.95 **551.7**

1. Geochronometry 2. Geological time 3. Radiocarbon dating 4. Radioisotopes in geology

ISBN 978-0-520-24975-2; 978-0-520-26161-7 pa

LC 2007-46955

"Rich in historical titbits, this book is a delightful study of how scientists figured out analytical techniques that revealed the history of the Earth." New Sci

Includes bibliographical references

A **short** history of planet earth; mountains, mammals, fire, and ice. Wiley 1996 266p il maps hardcover o.p. pa $16.95 **551.7**

1. Life -- Origin 2. Stratigraphic geology

ISBN 0-471-19703-3 pa

LC 95-46399

In "this survey of four-and-a-half billion years of Earth's past . . . MacDougall traces the rise of continents and the origins of life in each era. He discusses tectonic plates, the major extinctions and their probable causes, climate and the Ice Ages, and he speculates on the future of our planet. To compress Earth's history into a single, lucidly written volume is a major achievement." Publ Wkly

Includes bibliographical references

Richet, Pascal

A **natural** history of time; translated by John Venerella. University of Chicago Press 2007 471p il $29 **551.7**

1. Geological time

ISBN 978-0-226-71287-1; 0-226-71287-7

LC 2006-33992

"How old is the Earth? Mr. Richet sets out to explore humanity's attempts to answer this most perplexing of questions, which acted as a spur and a baffle to human ingenuity for 2,500 years. . . . The book is translated from the French— capably, considering how much scientific terminology it contains, but not gracefully—and . . . can be rough going. Still, 'A Natural History of Time' more that repays the effort it requires. Not only does it shed light on key advances in the history of science, from the ancient Greeks to the X-ray, it reminds us of the real heroism and nobility of the scientific enterprise." N Y Sun

Seeley, Thomas D.

Honeybee democracy. Princeton University Press 2010 273p $29.95 **551.7**

1. Bees 2. Democracy 3. Honeybee -- Behavior

ISBN 978-0-691-14721-5

LC 2010-10265

Seeley's "enthusiasm and admiration for honeybees is infectious. His accumulated research seems truly masterly, doing for bees what E. O. Wilson did for ants." N Y Times Book Rev

Includes bibliographical references

552 Petrology

Coenraads, Robert Raymond

Rocks and fossils; a visual guide. [by] Robert R. Coenraads. Firefly Books 2005 304p il $29.95 **552**

1. Fossils 2. Minerals 3. Rocks

ISBN 1-55407-068-6

In this "introduction to geology and paleontology . . . [the author presents] facts of how fossils are formed, how rocks are formed, and how plate tectonics work. . . . A science work perfectly suited for general use." Booklist

553.6 Other economic materials

Kurlansky, Mark

★ **Salt**: a world history. Penguin Books 2003 484p il map pa $16 **553.6**

1. Salt

ISBN 0-14-200161-9

LC 2004-270006

"Throughout his engaging, well-researched history, Kurlansky sprinkles witty asides and amusing anecdotes. A piquant blend of the historic, political, commercial, scientific and culinary, the book is sure to entertain as well as educate." Publ Wkly

Includes bibliographical references

Welland, Michael

Sand; the never-ending story. University of California Press 2009 343p il map $24.95 **553.6**

1. Geology 2. Sand

ISBN 978-0-520-25437-4

LC 2008-9084

The author "discusses the science, geology, and cultural significance of sand as a critical ingredient in so many aspects of our lives. Learn about arenophiles, sand forensics, extraterrestrial sand, Udden-Wentworth scale, Bagnold formula, and how sand shapes our environment. . . . Anyone who has walked on a beach, run up a sand dune, or built a sand castle will be fascinated by this excellent book." Libr J

Includes bibliographical references

553.7   Water

Kandel, Robert S.

★ **Water** from heaven; the story of water from the big bang to the rise of civilization, and beyond. [by] Robert Kandel. Columbia Univ. Press 2003 311p il maps $29.95; pa $24   **553.7**
1. Hydrologic cycle 2. Water 3. Water-supply
ISBN 0-231-12244-6; 0-231-12245-4 pa
              LC 2002-31229
"While dense with facts and figures, Kandel's aquatic history is riveting, an exhaustive and complex examination of our most precious chemical compound." Publ Wkly
Includes bibliographical references

Newton, David E.

Encyclopedia of water. Greenwood Press 2002 401p il $75   **553.7**
1. Reference books 2. Water -- Encyclopedias
ISBN 1-57356-304-8
              LC 2002-70031
"The 236 entries in this book comprise an A-Z overview of water's manifold roles in human society and the natural world throughout history." Publisher's note
Includes bibliographical references

Solomon, Steven

Water; the epic struggle for wealth, power, and civilization. Harper 2010 596p il map $27.99 **553.7**
1. Water 2. Water and civilization 3. Water-supply -- Government policy 4. World history
ISBN 978-0-06-054830-8; 0-06-054830-4
              LC 2009-27500
"Solomon's unprecedented inquiry into the history, science, and politics of water use provides fascinating and ample testimony to the need to place a higher value on water and its preservation." Booklist
Includes bibliographical references

Water: science and issues; E. Julius Dasch, editor in chief. Macmillan Ref. USA 2003 4v il maps set $395   **553.7**
1. Reference books 2. Water -- Encyclopedias
ISBN 0-02-865611-3
"This reference contains more than 300 topical entries . . . about a wide array of topics surrounding the nature, sources, use, desecration, and protection of this most valuable resource. . . . At the beginning of each volume are several tables: metric conversions; symbols, abbreviations, and acronyms; and geologic eras, periods and epochs. Entries range in length from 500 to 2,500 words and include short bibliographies of print and electronic sources. Pages have wide margins, which contain picture captions, definitions of key terms, and boxes of important facts and explanations. . . . The scientific and social aspects of water are well introduced in this set, which is recommended for high-school, public, and undergraduate libraries." Booklist
Includes bibliographical references

553.8   Gems

Hart, Matthew

Diamond: a journey to the heart of an obsession. Walker & Co. 2001 276p il maps $26   **553.8**
1. Diamonds
ISBN 0-8027-1368-8
              LC 2001-26348
Hart's "account of the glittering business of mining and marketing diamonds is also a story of avarice, theft, aesthetics, monopoly, and war. A thoroughly entrancing book." Booklist
Includes bibliographical references

Oldershaw, Cally

★ **Firefly** guide to gems. Firefly Bks. 2004 224p il map $14.95   **553.8**
1. Gems 2. Precious stones
ISBN 1-55297-814-1
This book "opens with extensive introductory material including history, various properties, and lore. Then, each gem is presented with text and charts of specific chemical properties. While most gems are discussed on a single page, some that are well known have longer articles." SLJ

Zoellner, Tom

The **heartless** stone; a journey through the world of diamonds, deceit, and desire. St. Martins Press 2006 293p map hardcover o.p. pa $16   **553.8**
1. Diamonds
ISBN 0-312-33969-0; 978-0-312-33969-2; 0-312-33970-4 pa; 978-0-312-33970-8 pa
              LC 2005-33037
The author "probes how 'blood diamonds' are used to fund vicious civil wars in Africa; how De Beers, seeing new markets to exploit, linked diamonds to the ancient yuino ceremony in Japan and played on caste obsession in India; and how India is pushing Belgium and Israel out of the gem trade. . . . This is a superior piece of reportage." Publ Wkly
Includes bibliographical references

557   Earth sciences of North America

McPhee, John A.

Annals of the former world; [by] John McPhee. Farrar, Straus & Giroux 1998 695p maps $35; pa $20   **557**
1. Geology -- United States
ISBN 0-374-10520-0; 0-374-51873-4 pa
              LC 97-39660
"As in any McPhee work, there are gemlike sentences, richly rhythmic paragraphs, nicely burnished synecdoches, metaphors as pungent as wasabi and, behind those felicities, vast amounts of painstaking research." N Y Times Book Rev

559.9   Earth sciences of extraterrestrial worlds

Sykes, Bryan

DNA USA; a genetic portrait of America. Bryan Sykes. Liveright Pub. Corp. 2012 369 p.   **559.9**
1. Human genetics -- Popular works 2. Human population genetics -- United States -- Popular works
ISBN 0871404125; 9780871404121

LC 2011053182

In this book, America's gorgeous mosaic emerges from its DNA in this . . . treatise on genetics and genealogy. Oxford geneticist [Bryan] Sykes . . . traveled across the United States collecting DNA samples, recording family histories. . . . The resulting chromosomal portraits, painted by analyzing markers that correlate with African, European, or Asian-Native American populations, reveal DNA tell-tales of unsuspected centuries-old migrations and mixings: Mexican-American Catholics descended from Spanish Jews; white Southerners with substantial African-American ancestry; possible journeys from Europe to North America 10,000 years ago, Sykes gives . . . explanations of new genetic techniques and their startling success at tracing familial ties across continents and millennia. (Publishers Weekly)

560   Paleontology

Fortey, Richard A.

★ **Fossils**; the key to the past. [by] Richard Fortey. 3rd ed; Smithsonian Institution Press 2002 232p il maps $55; pa $27.50   **560**
1. Fossils
ISBN 1-58834-023-6; 1-58834-048-1 pa

LC 2001-49439

In this volume, fossils "from earliest Precambrian forms onward are discussed, emphasizing evolutionary trends and extinctions, and relationships with habitat environments and geologic processes, such as volcanism and meteorite impacts, are evaluated. . . . Aspects of preservation, discovery, collection, and identification are discussed." Choice {review of 1991 edition}

Includes bibliographical references

Trilobite! eyewitness to evolution. by Richard Fortey. Knopf 2000 284p il $26; pa $14   **560**
1. Evolution 2. Fossils 3. Trilobites
ISBN 0-375-40625-5; 0-375-70621-6 pa

LC 00-34908

The author's "unabashed trilobite-centric view of the evolution of life on Earth is full of personal anecdotes and asides, but it's also full of excellent science." Libr J

Includes bibliographical references

Poinar, George O.

The **quest** for life in amber; {by} George and Roberta Poinar. Addison-Wesley 1994 219p il hardcover o.p. pa $18   **560**
1. Amber 2. Fossils
ISBN 0-201-48928-7

LC 94-3043

This is an account of the authors' search for and work with amber, a fossilized resin. The Poinars also include details of their scientific analyses of the insects trapped within this host material

This is "one of those books that educates the general reader about a scientific topic without requiring very much scientific background. Although educational, it is also highly entertaining and should be read for pleasure as much as for knowledge." Choice

Includes bibliographical references

Rea, Tom

Bone wars; the excavation and celebrity of Andrew Carnegie's dinosaur. University of Pittsburgh Press 2001 276p il $25   **560**
1. Dinosaurs 2. Diplodocus 3. Fossils 4. Metal industry executives 5. Paleontology -- United States -- History -- 20th century 6. Philanthropists
ISBN 0-8229-4173-2

LC 2001-3336

This describes the history of the excavation of the dinosaur fossil Diplodocus carnegii in 1899 which was financed by Andrew Carnegie.

"Rea pieces together countless bits of information to construct an overall picture of this period of scientific discovery." Booklist

Includes bibliographical references and index

Thompson, Ida

★ The **Audubon** Society field guide to North American fossils; with photographs by Townsend P. Dickinson; visual key by Carol Nehring. Knopf 1982 846p il maps flexible bdg $19.95   **560**
1. Fossils
ISBN 0-394-52412-8

LC 81-84772

"This softbound field guide to fossils is divided into a section of color photographs followed by a section of detailed descriptions. It covers 420 fossils of marine and freshwater invertebrates, insects, plants, and vertebrates that are likely to be found by the amateur." Malinowsky. Best Sci & Technol Ref Books for Young People

Wallace, David Rains

The **bonehunters'** revenge; dinosaurs, greed, and the greatest scientific feud of the gilded age. Houghton Mifflin 1999 366p il $25; pa $14   **560**
1. Fossils 2. Fossils -- Collection and preservation -- West (U.S.) -- History -- 19th century 3. Paleontologists 4. Paleontologists -- United States -- Biography 5. Zoologists
ISBN 0-395-85089-4; 0-618-08240-9 pa

LC 99-31904

This is an account of the rivalry between 19th century paleontologists Edward Drinker Cope and Othniel Charles Marsh.

"This curious century-old feud comes alive with momentum and understanding in Wallace's skillful hands." Booklist

Includes bibliographical references

Encyclopedia of paleontology; editor, Ronald Singer. Fitzroy Dearborn Pubs. 1999 2v il set $295 **560**
1. Fossils -- Encyclopedias 2. Paleontology 3.

Reference books
ISBN 1-88496-496-6

LC 00-271769

This work has "328 articles that cover all areas of pale-ontology, including 79 biographies for individuals such as Jean Agassiz, Charles Darwin, and Louis Leakey. The articles are extremely well written, with line drawings, photographs, charts, and other illustrative matter, plus a list of works cited and a further reading list." Booklist

Includes bibliographical references

Travels with the fossil hunters; edited by Peter Whybrow. Cambridge Univ. Press 2000 211p il $40   **560**

1. Fossils 2. Fossils -- Collection and preservation 3. Scientific expeditions 4. Scientists

ISBN 0-521-66301-6

LC 99-30134

A collection of essays by paleontologists from London's Natural History Museum describing their work in such places as China, India, the Sahara, Latvia, and Antarctica

"The essayists give enough details of their quests to explain their presence in these places and keep science buffs entertained. . . . Heightening the impact of the stories is an abundance of beautiful, colorful photos of the places, the people, and the fossils." SLJ

567.9   Reptiles

Fiffer, Steve

Tyrannosaurus Sue; the extraordinary saga of the largest, most fought over T. rex ever found. foreword by Robert T. Bakker. Freeman, W.H. 2000 248p hardcover o.p. pa $14.95   **567.9**

1. Dinosaurs 2. Paleontologists

ISBN 0-7167-9462-4 pa

LC 00-21596

In 1990 "South Dakota fossil-hunters Sue Hendrickson and Peter Larson dug up an exceptional T. rex—only the 12th tyrannosaur ever found, and the biggest and best-preserved to date. . . . The ensuing legal, political and scientific imbroglio set Native Americans against the federal government, the government against itself, the feds against established scientists and the world's great research universities against independent operators like Larson. Fiffer's thorough account should prove irresistible to readers with even a marginal interest in the legendary lizards." Publ Wkly

Gillette, David D.

Seismosaurus; the earth shaker. with illustrations by Mark Hallett. Columbia Univ. Press 1994 205p il maps $60; pa $21.95   **567.9**

1. Dinosaurs

ISBN 0-231-07874-9; 0-231-07875-7 pa

LC 93-40318

"Seismosaurus (Sam, for short) is a new dinosaur discovered by hikers in New Mexico and excavated by the author. . . . Gillette's step-by-step story of the discovery of the first bones of the Seismosaurus details how it was named, unearthed, funded, and shared with the scientific community. He discusses how Sam fits in among the better-known

Jurassic specimens as well as the potential uses for some exciting new field sensing techniques." Booklist

Includes bibliographical references

Horner, John R.

How to build a dinosaur; extinction doesn't have to be forever. [by] Jack Horner and James Gorman. Dutton 2009 246p il $25.95   **567.9**

1. Dinosaurs 2. Evolution 3. Evolutionary paleobiology

ISBN 978-0-525-95104-9; 0-525-95104-0

LC 2008-48042

"Dinosaurs could walk the earth again within five years, says paleontologist Jack Horner. It won't happen the way it did in Jurassic Park, the novel and movie inspired in part by Horner's work. No active DNA from history's big lizards is likely ever to be found, he says. But birds carry dinosaur DNA. As embryos, they sprout the beginnings of teeth, claws, and a lizard tail before certain genes cancel and redirect that growth. Horner's dream these days is to bring out a chicken's inner dinosaur by turning off those controlling secondary genes. . . . The great value of How to Build a Dinosaur is that it illuminates how the work of paleontologists has changed in the past few decades." Week

Includes bibliographical references

Larson, Peter L.

Rex appeal; the amazing story of Sue, the dinosaur that changed science, the law, and my life. {by} Peter Larson, Kristin Donnan. Invisible Cities Press 2002 404p il $26.95   **567.9**

1. Dinosaurs 2. Fossils 3. Paleontologists 4. Tyrannosaurus rex -- South Dakota

ISBN 1-931229-07-4

LC 2002-24207

Larson's "team discovered the largest and most complete Tyrannosaurus rex skeleton that the world had seen. Almost immediately, however, the team . . . became embroiled in a dispute with the U.S. government about who owns the fossil, during which the skeleton was seized by the National Guard. . . . The book recounts the heated legal battles but focuses primarily on Larson's adventures in South Dakota, where his group eventually found six more T. rex fossils." Publ Wkly

Includes bibliographical references

Nothdurft, William E.

The lost dinosaurs of Egypt; {by} William Nothdurft with Josh Smith {et al.} Random House 2002 242p il maps $24.95; pa $13.95   **567.9**

1. Dinosaurs 2. Dinosaurs -- Egypt -- Bahariya Oasis 3. Fossils 4. Paleontological excavations -- Egypt -- Bahariya Oasis 5. Paleontology -- Cretaceous

ISBN 0-375-50795-7; 0-375-75979-4 pa

LC 2002-75172

"Between 1910 and 1914, Ernst Stromer . . . unearthed a wealth of dinosaur fossils in Egypt's Bahariya Oasis. Thirty years later, Stromer's discoveries were destroyed in a WWII Allied bombing raid, and the oasis lay neglected for decades until Josh Smith, a Penn State doctoral candidate in paleontology, decided to retrace Stromer's footsteps in 1999. . . . {This} account highlights Stromer's discoveries . . . and chronicles recent findings by Smith and his colleagues. . .

. An engaging mix of history and desert drama, this . . . is first-rate popular science." Publ Wkly

Paul, Gregory S.
The **Princeton** field guide to dinosaurs. Princeton University Press 2010 320p il map $35 **567.9**
1. Dinosaurs
ISBN 978-0-691-13720-9; 0-691-13720-X
LC 2010-14916
"Though not a field guide to stuff in your backpack, this exciting addition to dinosaur reference is essential for high school through university libraries and is highly recommended for all students of dinosaurs." Libr J
Includes bibliographical references

Sampson, Scott D.
Dinosaur odyssey; fossil threads in the web of life. University of California Press 2009 332p il map $29.95 **567.9**
1. Dinosaurs 2. Fossils 3. Paleontology
ISBN 978-0-520-24163-3; 0-520-24163-0
LC 2009-6150
"This book draws scientifically accurate pictures in a style that is accessible to researchers and general readers alike." Libr J
Includes bibliographical references

★ Dinosaurs; edited by John J. Meier. H.W. Wilson Co. 2011 221p il pa $55 **567.9**
1. Dinosaurs
ISBN 978-0-8242-1107-3
LC 2011007540
A collection of articles discussing dinosaurs "from their origins and evolution to their much-debated extinction. . . . Coverage includes . . . background information distilled from the fossil record as well as more speculative and theoretical material." Publisher's note
Includes bibliographical references

Encyclopedia of dinosaurs; edited by Philip J. Currie, Kevin Padian. Academic Press 1997 xxx, 869p il $110.95 **567.9**
1. Dinosaurs -- Encyclopedias 2. Reference books
ISBN 0-12-226810-5
LC 97-23430
"Organized alphabetically by subject, the signed articles cover kinds of dinosaurs, biology, geology, research, and museums where dinosaurs are on display, including a worldwide list of museums and sites." Libr J

★ The Scientific American book of dinosaurs; Gregory S. Paul, editor. St. Martin's Press 2000 424p il maps $32.95; pa $19.95 **567.9**
1. Dinosaurs
ISBN 0-312-26226-4; 0-312-31008-0 pa
LC 2001-269051
This book features information on "how dinosaurs evolved, how they looked, where they lived, how they behaved, and why they died . . . {as well as} stories about the first discoveries of dinosaur fossils, the beginnings of dinosaur paleontology, how the field has changed with modern

technology, the most sensational finds, and the latest theories." Publisher's note
Includes bibliographical references

568   Fossil birds

Shipman, Pat
Taking wing; Archaeopteryx and the evolution of bird flight. Simon & Schuster 1998 336p il hardcover o.p. pa $22.95 **568**
1. Archaeopteryx 2. Birds -- Flight
ISBN 0-684-84965-8 pa
LC 97-27527
"Shipman brings to her excellent book the authority of a paleontologist and the talent of an accomplished writer on science for popular audiences." N Y Times Book Rev
Includes bibliographical references

569   Fossil mammals

Lister, Adrian
★ **Mammoths**; giants of the ice age. [by] Adrian Lister and Paul Bahn; foreword by Jean M. Auel. Rev ed; University of California Press 2007 192p il $29.95 **569**
1. Extinct animals 2. Mammoths
ISBN 978-0-520-25319-3; 0-520-25319-1
LC 2007-26369
This book integrates "research to piece together the story of mammoths, mastodons, and their relatives, icons of the Ice Age." Publisher's note
Includes glossary and bibliographical references

569.9   Humans and related genera

Johanson, Donald C.
Lucy's legacy; the quest for human origins. [by] Donald Johanson and Kate Wong. Harmony Books 2009 309p il map $25 **569.9**
1. Human origins
ISBN 978-0-307-39639-6; 0-307-39639-8
LC 2008-39907
"In 1974 paleontologist Donald C. Johanson found a female skeleton 3.2 million years old that exhibited both ape and human characteristics. Johanson and Kate Wong . . . recount the stunning discovery of Lucy, and then they venture far beyond that to bring readers up-to-date on what has been unearthed since and the implications of these new finds for what it means to be human. . . . Conversational, knowledgeable, flowing logically from one topic to the next, the book is packed with information of the kind that will be especially intriguing to general readers." Sci Am
Includes bibliographical references

Sarmiento, Esteban
★ The **last** human; a guide to twenty-two species of extinct humans. created by G.J. Sawyer and Viktor Deak; text by Esteban Sarmiento, G.J. Sawyer,

Richard Milner; with contributions by Donald C. Johanson, Meave Leakey, and Ian Tattersall. Yale University Press 2006 256p il map $45 **569.9**

1. Evolution 2. Fossil hominids 3. Human beings 4. Human evolution

ISBN 978-0-300-10047-1; 0-300-10047-7

"This is fascinating stuff, not least because it drives home just how much of our knowledge about the past is based on inference." New Sci

Includes bibliographical references

570 Biology

Carson, Rachel

Lost woods; the discovered writing of Rachel Carson. edited and with an introduction by Linda Lear. Beacon Press 1998 267p hardcover o.p. pa $16 **570**

1. Bird watching 2. Marine ecology 3. Nature 4. Wildlife conservation

ISBN 0-8070-8547-2 pa

LC 98-20058

This is a collection of previously unpublished essays, speeches, field notes, letters, and other writings by the pioneering environmentalist.

These excerpts provide readers "with samples of some of the most lyrical, clear scientific writing available in the fields of biology, ecology, and wildlife and wilderness conservation." SLJ

Includes bibliographical references

Gould, Stephen Jay

An urchin in the storm; essays about books and ideas. Norton 1987 255p il hardcover o.p. pa $11.95 **570**

1. Biology 2. Biology -- Book reviews 3. Books -- Reviews

ISBN 0-393-30537-6 pa

LC 87-21718

This collection of Gould's book reviews is arranged in broad subject areas: evolutionary theory, biological determinism, time and geology.

Lear, Linda J.

Rachel Carson; witness for nature. [by] Linda Lear. Holt & Co. 1997 634p il hardcover o.p. pa $20 **570**

1. Authors 2. Biography, Individual 3. College teachers 4. Conservationists 5. Environmental movement 6. Marine biologists 7. Writers on nature 8. Writers on science

ISBN 0-8050-3428-5 pa

LC 97-8324

This "is the most exhaustive account so far of Carson's private, professional and public lives." N Y Times Book Rev

Includes bibliographical references

Mayr, Ernst

★ This is biology; the science of the living world. Harvard Univ. Press 1997 327p il hardcover o.p. pa $17.95 **570**

1. Biology

ISBN 0-674-88469-8 pa

LC 96-42192

This is an overview of the major concepts and issues surrounding biology from Aristotle to the present. Topics discussed include genetics, cytology, evolution, development, and biodiversity

"This is an extremely well-thought-out and eminently scholarly work. . . . Mayr is definitely a grand old man of biology, and this book demonstrates his grasp of the development of the field." Sci Books Films

Includes bibliographical references

Serafini, Anthony

The epic history of biology. 1993 395p il hardcover o.p. pa $25 **570**

1. Biology 2. Biology -- History

ISBN 0-7382-0577-X pa

LC 93-27895

This volume traces the origins and evolution of the discipline "of biology from prehistoric times through the modern revolution in molecular biology." Sci Books Films

Includes bibliographical references

570.1 Philosophy and theory

Capra, Fritjof

The web of life; a new scientific understanding of living systems. Anchor Bks. (NY) 1996 347p il hardcover o.p. pa $14.95 **570.1**

1. Life (Biology) 2. System theory

ISBN 0-385-47676-0 pa

LC 96-12576

This is "a rewarding synthesis that will challenge serious readers." Publ Wkly

Includes bibliographical references

Keller, Evelyn Fox

Making sense of life; explaining biological development with models, metaphors, and machines. Harvard Univ. Press 2002 388p il $29.95 **570.1**

1. Biology -- Philosophy 2. Developmental biology 3. Life (Biology)

ISBN 0-674-00746-8

LC 2001-51559

The author "analyzes the history of developmental biology. She explains the type of information scientists have accepted, why changes in acceptance may occur and, on a broader scale, what it means to understand the natural world. . . . While Keller's prose is graceful and informed, her thesis is complex and unlikely to be fully appreciated by those without significant grounding in philosophy and biology." Publ Wkly

Includes bibliographical references

Lovelock, James

★ The **ages** of Gaia; a biography of our living earth. Norton 1988 xx, 252p il hardcover o.p. pa $13.95 **570.1**
1. Biology -- Philosophy 2. Biosphere 3. Gaia hypothesis 4. Life (Biology)
ISBN 0-393-31239-9 pa

LC 87-36567

"Gaia is the Greek goddess of the earth. For James Lovelock she is the embodiment of a hypothesis: the earth is not merely the abode of life but is a single living organism. He proposes that all living species are components of that organism, as cells are components of the human body." N Y Times Book Rev

Includes bibliographical references

Margulis, Lynn

What is life? foreword by Niles Eldredge. University of California Press 2000 288p il pa $24.95 **570.1**
1. Biological diversity 2. Biology -- Philosophy 3. Life (Biology) 4. Life -- Origin
ISBN 0-520-22021-8

LC 00-25833

"Continuing Margulis's contention that organelles within cells, such as mitochondria, were originally free-living organisms that fused with others to form complex cells and bodies, the authors extend this concept to the Earth as a superorganism. Although following traditional evolutionary pathways, the authors argue that life has played a role in its own evolution." Choice

Includes bibliographical references

Thomas, Lewis

The **lives** of a cell; notes of a biology watcher. Viking 1974 153p hardcover o.p. pa $13 **570.1**
1. Biology -- Philosophy
ISBN 0-14-004743-3 pa

In this collection of twenty-nine short essays "the author does not confine his scientist's eye to a microscope. He takes a much wider view of the world, looking at insect behavior and the possibility of intelligent life in outer space or bird songs and the evolution of language. He also offers a modest proposal for saving ourselves from nuclear self-destruction." Time

Includes bibliographical references

Yoon, Carol Kaesuk

Naming nature; the clash between instinct and science. W.W. Norton 2009 344p il $27.95 **570.1**
1. Biology -- Classification 2. Biology -- Nomenclature 3. Names
ISBN 978-0-393-06197-0; 0-393-06197-3

LC 2009-14332

This is "a wondrous history of taxonomy—the science of ordering and naming living things—and how it has disconnected us from the natural world. . . . Yoon is an outstanding science writer who takes a seemingly dull topic and rivets unsuspecting readers to the page. Superb." Kirkus

Includes bibliographical references

Bulletproof feathers; how science uses nature's secrets to design cutting-edge technology. edited by Robert Allen. University of Chicago Press 2010 192p il $35 **570.1**
1. Biomimetics 2. Bionics 3. Robotics 4. Robots
ISBN 978-0-226-01470-8

LC 2009037097

This book "is a fascinating introduction to the field of biomimetics, or bionics. Biomimetics refers to efforts to understand the design and complexity of natural, biological systems and the application of this knowledge to achieve useful new technologies. . . . This book, beautifully illustrated with many real-world examples and explanatory diagrams, will be a joy to read for any fan of science and technology." Choice

Includes bibliographical references

571 Internal biological processes and structures

Roach, Mary

★ **Packing** for Mars; the curious science of life in the void. W.W. Norton 2010 334p il **571**
1. Space biology
ISBN 0-393-06847-1; 978-0-393-06847-4

LC 2010-17113

This book examines space travel and life without gravity. (Publisher's note)

The author "explores the organic aspects of the space program, such as the dangerous bane of space motion sickness and the challenges of space hygiene. . . . She devotes one chapter to space food and another to zero-gravity elimination, which is a serious matter, even with a term like 'fecal popcorning.' An impish and adventurous writer with a gleefully inquisitive mind and a standup comic's timing, Roach celebrates human ingenuity (the odder the better), and calls for us to marshal our resources, unchain our imaginations, and start packing for Mars." Booklist

Includes bibliographical references

571.1 Animals

Widmaier, Eric P.

Why geese don't get obese (and we do) how evolution's strategies for survival affect our everyday lives. Freeman, W.H. 1998 213p il hardcover o.p. pa $14.95 **571.1**
1. Animals -- Adaptation 2. Comparative physiology 3. Evolution (Biology) 4. Physiology, Comparative -- Popular works
ISBN 0-7167-3649-7 pa

LC 98-2698

This book examines "the evolution of normal human and animal physiology, why we work the way we do, and a few conditions where adaptations from our ancestors are not so useful in modern life, for example, diabetes, stress, and the obesity mentioned in the title. What really makes this book stand out are the lucid explanations of how scientific method

. . . is used to learn about human and animal physiology."
Libr J

Includes bibliographical references

571.4   Biophysics

Vogel, Steven

Cats' paws and catapults; mechanical worlds of nature and people. illustrated by Kathryn K. Davis with the author. Norton 1998 382p il $27.50; pa $15.95   **571.4**

1. Biomechanics 2. Human engineering 3. Mechanics
ISBN 0-393-04641-9; 0-393-31990-3 pa

LC 97-44807

"Composed of curiosity and counter-intuition, this amply illustrated work should attract anyone interested in biology." Booklist

Includes bibliographical references

571.6   Cell biology

Harold, Franklin M.

The **way** of the cell; molecules, organisms, and the order of life. Oxford Univ. Press 2001 305p il hardcover o.p. pa $17.95   **571.6**

1. Biochemistry 2. Cells 3. Cytology 4. Life (Biology)
ISBN 0-19-513512-1; 0-19-516338-9 pa

LC 00-56670

"Harold tackles the largest of questions (What is life?) within the smallest of settings (the cell) in order to consider where and why a strictly genetic approach to life leads us astray." Booklist

Includes bibliographical references

Loewenstein, Werner R.

The **touchstone** of life; molecular information, cell communication, and the foundations of life. Oxford Univ. Press 1999 366p il $45; pa $17.95 **571.6**

1. Cell interaction 2. Cells 3. Cellular signal transduction 4. Evolution 5. Information theory in biology
ISBN 0-19-511828-6; 0-19-514057-5 pa

LC 97-43408

"Loewenstein writes engagingly, and he provides the background material a nonspecialist needs to follow the intricate story." N Y Times Book Rev

Includes bibliographical references

Rensberger, Boyce

Life itself; exploring the realm of the living cell. illustrations by Nigel Orme. Oxford Univ. Press 1996 290p il hardcover o.p. pa $16.95   **571.6**

1. Cells 2. Molecular biology
ISBN 0-19-512500-2 pa

LC 96-33679

This is "an elegant, authoritative, yet felicitously written book that will appeal to anyone who is interested in how cells work." New Sci

Includes bibliographical references

571.7   Biological control and secretions

Foster, Russell G.

Rhythms of life; the biological clocks that control the daily lives of every living thing. Yale University Press 2004 276p il $30; pa $18   **571.7**

1. Biological rhythms
ISBN 0-300-10574-6; 978-0-300-10574-2; 0-300-10969-5 pa; 978-0-300-10969-6 pa

LC 2004-105609

The authors "survey the biological clocks that dictate circadian rhythms, the daily cycles that affect creatures from cockroaches to humans. . . . Biology buffs will marvel at the fascinating material." Publ Wkly

Includes bibliographical references

571.8   Reproduction, development, growth

Carroll, Sean B.

Endless forms most beautiful; the new science of evo devo and the making of the animal kingdom. with illustrations by Jamie W. Carroll, Josh P. Klaiss, Leanne M. Olds. W.W. Norton & Co. 2005 350p il $25.95   **571.8**

1. Evolution
ISBN 0-393-06016-0

LC 2004-29388

The author's "highly detailed and well-illustrated technical discussions are enriched by his appreciation for the philosophical, aesthetic, and ethical implications of the biological wonders he decodes, adding up to a vital and enjoyable introduction to a field with profound implications." Booklist

Includes bibliographical references

Haycock, David Boyd

Mortal coil; a short history of living longer. Yale University Press 2008 308p il   **571.8**

1. Aging 2. Death 3. Immortality (Philosophy) 4. Longevity 5. Medicine -- Philosophy
ISBN 0-300-11778-7; 9780300117783

LC 2007-35341

This book "explores the medical, scientific, and philosophical theories behind the quest for the prolongation of human life. [According to Haycock], it was a conundrum that intrigued Sir Francis Bacon and underpinned the scientific revolution; ideas of ultimate perfectibility, indefinite progress, and worldly rather than heavenly immortality fed directly into the spirit of the Enlightenment and even further into the nineteenth and twentieth centuries. In today's world of genetic research, cryonics, and nanotechnology, we still seek the same elusive philosopher's stone." (Publisher's note) Index.

This book is "fully successful in managing to drum up excitement for the future of human development while steering clear of propaganda." PopMatters

Includes bibliographical references

572 Biochemistry

Morton, Oliver
★ **Eating** the sun; how plants power the planet. HarperCollins 2008 457p il $28.95 **572**
1. Discoveries in science 2. Photosynthesis
ISBN 978-0-00-716364-9; 0-00-716364-9
LC 2008-23433
This book "is a work of flowing prose that makes vivid why our leafy nub of cosmic dust, swirling around an average star, is an extraordinarily beautiful and rare place to reside in the universe." Christ Sci Monit
Includes bibliographical references

The Facts on File dictionary of biochemistry; edited by John Daintith. Facts on File 2002 247p il $49.50; pa $19.95 **572**
1. Biochemistry -- Dictionaries 2. Reference books
ISBN 0-8160-4914-9; 0-8160-4915-7 pa
LC 2002-35203
"General areas included in the Dictionary of Biochemistry are basic organic and physical chemistry, classes of compounds, cytology and histology, nutrition and metabolism, and natural-product chemistry. Examples of specific entries are Beta-pleated sheet; cyano-bacteria; Enzyme; G protein; Guanine; Isomerase; McClintock, Barbara; Pollution; Sex determination; Sugar; Vector; and Zeolite. Appendixes provide a chronology of major events in the development of biochemistry and molecular biology, a table of the genetic code, amino acid structures, the periodic table, chemical elements, the Greek alphabet, and suggested Web pages." Booklist
Includes bibliographical references

572.8 Biochemical genetics

Bodmer, W. F.
★ The **book** of man; the Human Genome Project and the quest to discover our genetic heritage. [by] Walter Bodmer, Robin McKie. Oxford University Press 1997 259p il map pa $42 **572.8**
1. Gene mapping
ISBN 0-19-511487-6; 978-0-19-511487-4
LC 96-37423
This "is highly readable, clear and accurate." New Sci

Carroll, Sean B.
★ The **making** of the fittest; DNA and the ultimate forensic record of evolution. with illustrations by Jamie W. Carroll and Leanne M. Olds. W.W. Norton & Co. 2006 301p il map $25.95 **572.8**
1. DNA 2. Evolution 3. Evolution (Biology)
ISBN 978-0-393-06163-5; 0-393-06163-9
LC 2006-17197
The author presents "discoveries gathered from DNA evidence that confirm Charles Darwin's theory of evolution 'beyond any reasonable doubt.' . . . Readers will gain insight into the evolutionary process and expand their knowledge of how the 'fittest' species were made, from fish that live in

subfreezing water to birds that communicate via ultraviolet colors." Libr J
Includes bibliographical references

Cook-Deegan, Robert M.
The **gene** wars; science, politics, and the human genome. Norton 1994 416p il $25; pa $14.95 **572.8**
1. Gene mapping
ISBN 0-393-03572-7; 0-393-31399-9 pa
LC 93-10762
This "account of the Human Genome Project is as much about the politics, economics, and personalities as it is about the science of this . . . project to map the 100,000 chromosome sequences of the human genome." Libr J
Includes bibliographical references

Danchin, Antoine
The **Delphic** boat; what genomes tell us. translated by Alison Quayle. Harvard Univ. Press 2002 368p $35 **572.8**
1. Genomes
ISBN 0-674-00930-4
LC 2002-27273
"Danchin conducts intelligent amateurs surprisingly far into the {book's} central issues. This timely book offers hope that the rhetoric and hype of the antagonists fighting over the genome agenda will not drown out rational dialogue." Booklist
Includes bibliographical references

Francis, Richard C.
Epigenetics; the ultimate mystery of inheritance. W.W. Norton 2011 234p il $25.95 **572.8**
1. Adaptation (Biology) 2. Genetics
ISBN 978-0-393-07005-7; 0-393-07005-0
LC 2011-00696
The author "sets out to dethrone the notion that genes are the 'directors' of the 'plays' that are our lives, orchestrating our development and determining our risk for disease and sundry physical and behavioral traits. Yes, genes are important, writes the author, but they are subject to regulation by forces that can turn them on or off, sometimes for a lifetime, sometimes across generations. These forces can come via the cell housing of the genes, other parts of the body or the environment, in each instance initiating the actions of chemicals that bind (or unbind) one or more parts of a gene, preventing (or activating) its transcription. This is an 'epigenetic' process—epigenetics is the science that studies the ways in which DNA can undergo long-term regulatory changes that do not involve mutations of the genes themselves. To illustrate, Francis provides a dizzying array of examples." Kirkus
Includes bibliographical references

Lewontin, Richard C.
The **triple** helix; gene, organism, and environment. [by] Richard Lewontin. Harvard Univ. Press 2000 136p il $25; pa $15 **572.8**
1. Developmental biology -- Philosophy 2. Ecology 3. Ecology -- Philosophy 4. Evolution 5. Evolution (Biology) 6. Genetic code 7. Molecular biology 8.

Molecular biology -- Philosophy
ISBN 0-674-00159-1; 0-674-00677-1 pa
LC 99-53879

In this book the author "demonstrates how all organisms, including humans, are the product of intricate interactions between their genes and the environment in which they live. . . . Although the issues Lewontin addresses are huge, he writes about them in a manner fully accessible to the non-specialist." Publ Wkly

Includes bibliographical references

Morange, Michel

A **history** of molecular biology; translated by Matthew Cobb. Harvard Univ. Press 1998 336p $39.95; pa $22.50   **572.8**

1. Molecular biology 2. Molecular biology -- History
ISBN 0-674-39855-6; 0-674-00169-9 pa
LC 97-47158

"Molecular biology is responsible for the recent high-profile developments in cloning, genetic engineering, DNA fingerprinting, etc. Morange . . . covers the birth of the field at the beginning of this century, the discovery of DNA and the deciphering of the genetic code, and the practical applications resulting from the revelations of the last 50 years." Libr J

Includes bibliographical references

Rabinow, Paul

Making PCR; a story of biotechnology. University of Chicago Press 1996 190p il $22.50; pa $14   **572.8**

1. Chemical reactions 2. Polymers
ISBN 0-226-70146-8; 0-226-70147-6 pa
LC 95-49103

"An intriguing read that raises many questions about our understanding of the twisting process of discovery itself." New Sci

Includes bibliographical references

Segrè, Gino

Ordinary geniuses; Max Delbruck, George Gamow, and the origins of genomics and big bang cosmology. Gino Segrè. Viking 2011 xxi, 330 p.p $27.95   **572.8**

1. Molecular biologists -- United States -- Biography 2. Physicists -- United States -- Biography
ISBN 9780670022762; 0670022764
LC 2011009309

The author "explores the extraordinary lives and scientific accomplishments of two far-from-ordinary men, Max Delbrück and George Gamow. . . . An exuberant dual biography that integrates developments in quantum physics, cosmology and genetics since the 1920s with the lives of these two scientists." Kirkus

Includes bibliographical references (p. 309-318) and index

Sulston, John

The **common** thread; a story of science, politics, ethics, and the human genome. [by] John Sulston,

Georgina Ferry. Joseph Henry Press 2002 310p il $24.95   **572.8**
ISBN 0-309-08409-1
LC 2002-14007

The author gives an "account of the excitement, hard work, vision, and daring needed to move from worm biology to recommending sequencing of the human genome, while senior and influential colleagues argued vigorously against it. He speaks forcefully of the necessity of keeping the sequence public and freely available. . . . {This title is} recommended for almost any library, particularly those with readers willing to go beyond sound bites and media hype." Libr J

Includes bibliographical references

Watson, James D., 1928-

★ The **double** helix; a personal account of the discovery of the structure of DNA. Scribner 1998 226p il   **572.8**

1. Biochemistry -- Research 2. DNA 3. DNA -- Research -- History 4. Genetic code -- Research -- History 5. Molecular biologists -- Biography 6. Molecular biology -- Research -- History
ISBN 0684852799; 074321630X
LC 980136787

This book is a "personal, day-by-day account of how Watson, [Francis] Crick and their collaborators in the years between 1951 and 1963 hit upon the famous 'double helix' model of the 'DNA' [deoxyribonucleic acid] molecule, the fundamental genetical material." America

573.6   Reproductive system

Friedman, David M.

A **mind** of its own; a cultural history of the penis. Penguin Books 2003 358p il pa $16   **573.6**

1. Penis
ISBN 978-0-14-200259-9; 0-14-200259-3

This is a social and medical history of the male organ. Topics discussed include religious teachings about sex, efforts to overcome male impotence throughout history, attitudes toward masturbation, and racial stereotypes relating to phallus size.

"This valuable analysis of the origins of male sexuality and how the conception of maleness has shaped understanding of female sexuality isn't just educational . . . it's entertaining." Booklist

Includes bibliographical references

573.8   Nervous and sensory systems

Hughes, Howard C.

Sensory exotica; a world beyond human experience. MIT Press 1999 345p $40; pa $18.95 **573.8**

1. Comparative physiology 2. Echolocation (Physiology) 3. Electroreceptors 4. Magnetoreception 5. Physiology, Comparative 6. Senses and sensation
ISBN 0-262-08279-9; 0-262-58204-X pa
LC 98-51875

This is a compendium of stories and information regarding the vast array of sensory systems that are utilized by different species, ranging from insects to aquatic mammals to humans. . . . Hughes does an excellent job of presenting the facts and the science behind the vast array of sensory systems." Sci Books Films

Includes bibliographical references

Iacoboni, Marco

Mirroring people; the new science of how we connect with others. Farrar, Straus and Giroux 2008 308p il $25   **573.8**
    1. Nervous system 2. Neurons
    ISBN 978-0-374-21017-5; 0-374-21017-9
             LC 2007-47322

The author introduces "readers to the world of mirror neurons and what they imply about human empathy, which, the author says, underlies morality. . . . Iacoboni's expansive style and clear descriptions make for a solid introduction to cutting-edge neurobiology." Publ Wkly

Includes bibliographical references

575   Specific parts of and physiological systems in plants

Browne, Janet

Charles Darwin; v1 a biography. Princeton Univ. Press 1996 605p v1 il pa $25.95   **575**
    1. Naturalists 2. Travel writers 3. Writers on science
    ISBN 0-691-02606-8
             LC 95-53319

This first volume of a two-part biography of Darwin focuses on his early years, leading up to his marriage and his moving out of London to the countryside of Kent.

The author "captures the spirit of a quietly revolutionary scientist whose ingrained Victorian prejudices were at odds with his radical ideas." Publ Wkly

Includes bibliographical references

Dawkins, Richard

River out of Eden; a Darwinian view of life. illustrations by Lalla Ward. Basic Bks. 1995 172p il hardcover o.p. pa $14   **575**
    1. Evolution 2. Genetics
    ISBN 0-465-06990-8 pa
             LC 94-37146

The author "explores the evolution of humans from a single ancestor; evolutions of specific organs (e.g., eyes) and coadaptation of species (e.g., wasps and orchids); nature's physical and behavioral mechanisms to maximize survival of DNA; and, finally, the ultimate results when our DNA reaches out in space. His arguments and examples are clear, compelling, and often amusing." Libr J

Includes bibliographical references

576   General and external biological phenomena

Dawkins, Richard

★ The **selfish** gene; 30th anniversary ed; Oxford University Press 2006 xxiii, 360p il pa $15.95 **576**
    1. Evolution 2. Genetics
    ISBN 978-0-19-929115-1; 0-19-929115-2 pa
             LC 2007-271478

The author examines evolution and contends that genes that benefit individual members of a species will be passed on to future generations, rather than those which may benefit the entire group

576.5   Genetics

Beckwith, Jonathan R.

Making genes, making waves; a social activist in science. Harvard Univ. Press 2002 242p il $27.95   **576.5**
    1. College teachers 2. Ethicists 3. Geneticists -- United States -- Biography 4. Genetics 5. Microbiologists 6. Political activists -- United States -- Biography 7. Science -- Social aspects
    ISBN 0-674-00928-2
             LC 2002-22747

"The text traces Beckwith's development as both a scientist and an activist, essentially in a chronological narrative form, with a few chapters providing expanded coverage of specific examples of the interaction between scientific research and societal effects. Those working in scientific fields or students who plan to pursue such a career would enjoy this book." Sci Books Films

Includes bibliographical references

Endersby, Jim

A **guinea** pig's history of biology. Harvard University Press 2007 499p il $27.95; pa $18.95 **576.5**
    1. Biology -- History 2. Genetics 3. Genetics -- History 4. Heredity
    ISBN 978-0-674-02713-8; 0-674-02713-2; 978-0-674-03227-9 pa; 0-674-03227-6 pa
             LC 2007-20824

"This book would be of interest to anyone fascinated or intrigued by genetics or biological research, as well as any professional or lay student of history and science." Sci Books Films

Includes bibliographical references

Henig, Robin Marantz

The **monk** in the garden: how Gregor Mendel and his pea plants solved the mystery of inheritance. Houghton Mifflin 2000 292p il $24; pa $14 **576.5**
    1. Geneticists 2. Geneticists -- Austria -- Biography
    ISBN 0-395-97765-7; 0-618-12741-0 pa
             LC 00-24341

The author explores "Mendel's personality and experiments. The latter lasted but a few years in the 1850s and 1860s, ending when Mendel became the abbot of his monastery in what is now Brno in the Czech Republic. Henig crisply conveys how the laws of inheritance that Mendel derived from his statistical analysis remained unnoticed until several botanists who discovered them independently in 1900 also learned that Mendel found them first. This biography itself rediscovers a scientist often mentioned but insufficiently known." Booklist

Keller, Evelyn Fox

The **century** of the gene. Harvard Univ. Press 2000 186p il $25; pa $15.95 **576.5**

1. Genetics 2. Genetics -- History -- 20th century
ISBN 0-674-00372-1; 0-674-99825-1 pa

LC 00-38319

"In this tight, clearly written survey, Keller does a wonderful job of explaining and demonstrating how our knowledge of genetics has accumulated to the extent that we can fathom what we don't understand." Publ Wkly

Includes bibliographical references

Tudge, Colin

The **impact** of the gene; from Mendel's peas to designer babies. Hill & Wang 2001 375p $27; pa $15 **576.5**

1. Geneticists 2. Genetics 3. Genetics -- Popular works
ISBN 0-374-17523-3; 0-8090-5743-3 pa

LC 00-67306

This is a "narrative on the development of genetics from Gregor Mendel's 19th-century pea experiments to the present. . . . Tudge manages to weave the contributions of hundreds of scientists into a story that is coherent, logical, and readable. He also tackles the social implications of genetics . . . and offers thoughtful and persuasive discussions of difficult topics such as evolutionary psychology." Libr J

Includes bibliographical references

Genetics; Richard Robinson [editor in chief] Macmillan Ref. USA 2003 4v set $395 **576.5**

1. Genetic Diseases, Inborn -- English 2. Genetic Techniques -- English 3. Genetics -- Encyclopedias 4. Genetics -- English 5. Molecular Biology -- English 6. Reference books
ISBN 0-02-865606-7

LC 2002-3560

This set contains "approximately 250 signed entries from Accelerated aging: Progeria to Zebrafish. Articles range from a few paragraphs to a few pages in length and focus on a variety of topics, including inheritance, genes and chromosomes, genetic diseases, biotechnology, history, careers, and the ethical, legal, and social issues associated with genetically modified foods and cloning. The entries appear in alphabetical order and include cross-references to related entries. Most have a list of suggested readings and Internet resources. . . . The clear and well-written articles are informative and should meet the needs of most students." Booklist

Includes bibliographical references

★ **Genetics & inherited conditions**; editor, Jeffrey A. Knight. Salem Press 2010 3v il set $395 **576.5**

1. Genetics -- Encyclopedias 2. Medical genetics -- Encyclopedias 3. Reference books
ISBN 978-1-587-65650-7; 1-587-65650-7

LC 2010-5289

"The subjects covered include all aspects of genetics, such as diseases, biology, genetic engineering, social issues,

and more. . . . Articles covering diseases and syndromes include such information as definition, risk factors, etiology and genetics, symptoms, screening and diagnosis, treatment and therapy, and prevention and outcomes. For other types of articles, essays are preceded by a brief summary of the significance of the topic and definitions of key terms." Booklist

Includes bibliographical references

576.8 Evolution

Ayala, Francisco J.

Darwin's gift to science and religion. Joseph Henry Press 2007 237p il map $24.95 **576.8**

1. Creationism 2. Evolution 3. Evolution (Biology) 4. Intelligent design (Teleology) 5. Natural selection 6. Naturalists 7. Travel writers 8. Writers on science
ISBN 978-0-309-10231-5; 0-309-10231-6

LC 2007-05821

"This elegant book provides the single best introduction to Darwin and the development of evolutionary biology now available." Publ Wkly

Includes bibliographical references

Browne, Janet

★ **Darwin's** Origin of species; a biography. Atlantic Monthly Press 2007 174p hardcover o.p. pa $14 **576.8**

1. Naturalists 2. Travel writers 3. Writers on science
ISBN 0-87113-953-7; 978-0-87113-953-5; 0-8021-4346-6 pa; 978-0-8021-4346-4 pa

LC 2007-275116

"This excellent introduction is highly recommended for all readers who want to better understand the heated debates that this book still causes today." Publ Wkly

Includes bibliographical references

Coyne, Jerry A.

★ **Why** evolution is true. Viking 2009 xx, 282p il map $27.95 **576.8**

1. Evolution
ISBN 978-0-670-02053-9

LC 2008-33973

Presents the threads of modern work in genetics, paleontology, geology, molecular biology, and anatomy that demonstrate the stamp of the evolutionary processes first proposed by Darwin.

"Readers looking to understand the case for evolution and searching for a response to many of the most common creationist claims should find everything they need in this powerful book, which is clearer and more comprehensive than the many others on the subject." Publ Wkly

Includes bibliographical references

Darwin, Charles

The **Beagle** letters; edited by Frederick Burkhardt; with an introduction by Janet Browne. Cambridge University Press 2008 xxx, 470p il map $32 **576.8**

1. Evolution
ISBN 978-0-521-89838-6; 0-521-89838-2

LC 2009-417801

"The complete correspondence both to and from Charles Darwin during his five years circumnavigating the globe on the HMS Beagle, beginning in 1831, documents his growth as a naturalist and offers a picture of life in the England he left behind. . . . It is fascinating to watch Darwin attempt to come to grips with the huge amount of data he collected and make sense of the patterns he observed. We get an intimate look at an adventurous young Darwin, so unlike his more familiar, sedentary older self who would write On the Origin of Species." Publ Wkly

Includes bibliographical references

★ The **Darwin** reader; edited by Mark Ridley. 2nd ed; Norton 1996 315p il pa $21.30 **576.8**
1. Evolution 2. Natural selection
ISBN 0-393-96967-3

LC 95-50297

This collection presents excerpts from Darwin's most important works including Origin of the species, The descent of man and Coral reef. Illustrations are taken from the original editions.

On the origin of species; David Quammen, general editor. Illustrated ed.; Sterling Pub. 2008 544p il $35 **576.8**
1. Evolution 2. Heredity 3. Human origins 4. Natural selection
ISBN 978-1-4027-5639-9

LC 2008-6902

"As a milestone not only in the history of science but also in cultural history, On the Origin of Species belongs in every library, high school and above. . . . [Quammen] offers a gloriously illustrated and richly annotated volume, which testifies to the book's enduring legacy. Throughout the text, relevant sidebars from other of Darwin's writings, including his Autobiography, field notes from the HMS Beagle, and his myriad letters, are presented for their insight. Illustrations include historical images, such as sketches, woodcuts, and portraits of people and places, but also included are contemporary photographs of the flora and fauna that Darwin described." Libr J

Includes bibliographical references

★ The **origin** of species by means of natural selection, or, The preservation of favored races in the struggle for life. Modern Library 1993 689p $21.95 **576.8**
1. Evolution 2. Heredity 3. Human origins 4. Natural selection
ISBN 0-679-60070-1

LC 93-3598

The classic exposition of the "theory of evolution by natural selection. Darwin argues that every species develops or evolves from a previous one and that all life is a continuing pattern. His objects of study were the variations from generation to generation in domestic plants and animals. . . . While subsequent investigation has superseded some of Darwin's arguments, Origin of Species remains one of the most influential books ever published." Reader's Ency. 4th edition

Davies, P. C. W.

The **eerie** silence; renewing our search for alien intelligence. [by] Paul Davies. Houghton Mifflin Harcourt 2010 241p il $27 **576.8**
1. Extraterrestrial beings 2. Life on other planets 3. Unidentified flying objects
ISBN 978-0-547-13324-9; 0-547-13324-3

LC 2010-3088

"After 50 years of scanning the skies for signs of extraterrestrial intelligence, astronomers have only silence to report — an eerie silence, Davies argues. Part history of the search, part road map for its future and (large) part mind-stretching exercise, the book provides Davies' perspective on profound questions that have implications far beyond alien hunting." Sci News

Includes bibliographical references

The **fifth** miracle; the search for the origin and meaning of life. {by} Paul Davies. Simon & Schuster 1999 304p il hardcover o.p. pa $14 **576.8**
1. Life 2. Life -- Origin
ISBN 0-684-86309-X pa

LC 98-33421

"Life on earth—God's fifth miracle according to Genesis—may have begun with rock-eating microbes far below the surface of Mars. So suggests Davies in this provocative investigation into the origins of life. . . . In his remarkably lucid style, Davies lays out the evidence for a universe inherently friendly to life. A ground-breaking book." Booklist

Includes bibliographical references

Dawkins, Richard

★ The **ancestor's** tale; a pilgrimage to the dawn of evolution. with additional research by Yan Wong. Houghton Mifflin 2004 673p il $28; pa $16.95 **576.8**
1. Evolution 2. Evolution (Biology) -- History 3. Evolution (Biology) -- Philosophy
ISBN 0-618-00583-8; 0-618-61916-X pa

LC 2004-59864

The author "sets out on a pilgrimage tracing the history of the human species back to the very origins of life, marking along the way 39 rendezvous points where the human genealogical path crosses that of other terrestrial species. . . . Lively and daring, a book certain to draw even casual readers deep into the adventure—and controversy—of science." Booklist

Includes bibliographical references

The **greatest** show on Earth; the evidence for evolution. Free Press 2009 470p il map $30 **576.8**
1. Evolution 2. Evolution (Biology)
ISBN 978-1-4165-9478-9; 1-4165-9478-7

LC 2009-25330

"A pleasure in the face of so much scientific ignorance—biology rendered accessible and relevant to the utmost degree." Kirkus

Includes bibliographical references

Eiseley, Loren C.

★ The **immense** journey; [by] Loren Eisley. Random House 1957 210p hardcover o.p. pa $10   **576.8**

    1. Evolution 2. Human origins

    ISBN 0-394-70157-7 pa

    Dr Eiseley's "style is beautiful, compelling in impact and poetic in its imagery. His subject is one of the epics of natural science—the 'immense journey' of life as known on this planet." Christ Sci Monit

Fortey, Richard A.

★ **Life**; a natural history of the first four billion years of life on earth. [by] Richard Fortey. Knopf 1998 346p il $32.59; pa $15   **576.8**

    1. Evolution 2. Evolution (Biology) 3. Life -- Origin

    ISBN 0-375-40119-9; 0-375-70261-X pa

                   LC 97-49466

    This work is "written for readers with no science. It will help them understand the specialized and often technical books on evolution that make headlines but leave most people wondering why." N Y Times Book Rev

    Includes bibliographical references

Goodwin, Brian C.

How the leopard changed its spots; the evolution of complextiy. Princeton Univ. Press 2001 252p il pa $25.95   **576.8**

    1. Biology 2. Evolution 3. Evolution (Biology) 4. Genetics 5. Morphology 6. Self-organizing systems 7. System theory

    ISBN 0-691-08809-8; 978-0-691-08809-9

                   LC 00-51652

    "Although light on data, this is a serious presentation for the informed lay reader of the philosophical direction some avant-garde biological thought is taking." Libr J

    Includes bibliographical references

Gould, Stephen Jay

★ **Hen's** teeth and horse's toes. Norton 1983 413p il hardcover o.p. pa $15.95   **576.8**

    1. Evolution

    ISBN 0-393-31103-1 pa

                   LC 82-22259

    The theme of this collection is "biological evolution. {The author} has grouped the 30 essays into seven categories: Sensible Oddities, Personalities, Adaptation and Development, Teilhard and Piltdown, Science and Politics, Extinction and a Zebra Trilogy." America

    Includes bibliographical references

The **panda's** thumb; more reflections in natural history. Stephen Jay Gould. Norton 1980 343p il hardcover o.p. pa $15.95   **576.8**

    1. Evolution 2. Natural selection

    ISBN 0-393-30819-7 pa

                   LC 80-15952

    In these essays "a variety of creatures, including humans, dinosaurs, pandas, turtles, and microscopic organisms, are considered in light of their reflection of Darwin's theory. One intriguing theme which runs throughout the selections

is how imperfectly designed anatomy or haphazardly applied anatomical evolution best supports Darwinism." Booklist

    Includes bibliographical references

The **structure** of evolutionary theory. Belknap Press 2002 xxii, 1433p il $39.95   **576.8**

    1. Evolution 2. Evolution (Biology) 3. Punctuated equilibrium (Evolution)

    ISBN 0-674-00613-5

                   LC 2001-43556

    This is a "history and analysis of classical and twentieth-century evolutionary theory." Booklist

    Includes bibliographical references and index

Hooper, Judith

Of moths and men; an evolutionary tale: the untold story of science and the peppered moth. Norton 2002 xx, 377p il $26.95; pa $15.95   **576.8**

    1. College teachers 2. Entomologists 3. Evolution 4. Evolution (Biology) 5. Fraud 6. Fraud in science 7. Geneticists 8. Moths 9. Natural selection 10. Naturalists 11. Peppered moth

    ISBN 0-393-05121-8; 0-393-32525-3 pa

                   LC 2002-26315

    "A fascinating look at the people behind scientific theories." Booklist

    Includes bibliographical references

Jones, Steve

Darwin's ghost; the origin of species updated. Random House 2000 xxix, 377p il hardcover o.p. pa $15.95   **576.8**

    1. Evolution 2. Natural selection

    ISBN 0-345-42277-5 pa

                   LC 99-53246

    Jones "has updated Charles Darwin's On the origin of species (1859) so that the fact of organic evolution is both understandable and relevant to today's general reader. . . . Very informative and cogently argued, this book is an important addition to the natural history literature." Libr J

    Includes bibliographical references

Kaufman, Marc

First contact; scientific breakthroughs in the hunt for life beyond Earth. Simon & Schuster 2011 213p il $26; ebook $12.99   **576.8**

    1. Life on other planets

    ISBN 978-1-4391-0900-7; 978-1-4391-3030-8 ebook

                   LC 2010-44630

    Kaufman "takes us from beneath the surface of our planet, where scientists hunt for and study 'extremophile' microbes that alter our views of what is necessary for life to exist, to observatories and labs searching deep space for extraterrestrial signals or exoplanets, planets outside the solar system. Not only does the book suggest the breadth of the effort, it reveals how each aspect reveals ideas and science never before suspected. . . . [The author] does what excellent science reporters do—he translates at times difficult concepts into language those of us who barely passed 'Bonehead Chemistry' can understand." Seattle Post-Intelligencer

    Includes bibliographical references

Keller, Michael

Charles Darwin's On the Origin of Species; a graphic adaptation. [by] Michael Keller; art by Nicolle Rager Fuller. Rodale 2009 192p il $19.99; pa $14.99 **576.8**

1. Evolution (Biology) 2. Evolution -- Graphic novels 3. Graphic novels 4. Heredity -- Graphic novels 5. Human origins -- Graphic novels 6. Natural selection 7. Natural selection -- Graphic novels 8. Naturalists 9. Travel writers 10. Writers on science

ISBN 978-1-60529-697-5; 1-60529-697-X; 978-1-60529-948-8 pa; 1-60529-948-0 pa

LC 2009-11387

"The graphic novel follows Origin's original chapters, combining snippets of Darwin's text with quotes from letters, illustrative examples from his time and from the present, and occasional invented dialog. Fuller's images of people seem clumsy, but her full-color plants, animals, charts, maps, and scientific accoutrements are attractive and effective.... [This] version well conveys both the science and the wonder of Origin." Libr J

Koerner, David

Here be dragons; the scientific quest for extraterrestrial life. [by] David Koerner, Simon LeVay. Oxford Univ. Press 2000 264p il hardcover o.p. pa $24.95 **576.8**

1. Life -- Origin 2. Life on other planets

ISBN 0-19-514600-X pa

LC 99-38170

In this book the authors explore "the origin of life and its occurrence outside Earth. . . . They offer a broad overview of up-to-date research and thought on topics ranging from the chemistry of life's origins to the search for extra-solar planets, the process of evolution, and the nature of life and the cosmos." Booklist

Includes bibliographical references

Larson, Edward J.

Evolution: the remarkable history of a scientific theory. Modern Library 2004 337p il $21.95; pa $14.95 **576.8**

1. Evolution 2. Evolution (Biology) -- Philosophy

ISBN 0-679-64288-9; 0-8129-6849-2 pa

LC 2003-64888

This is an "overview of evolutionary thought from ancient speculations to the emergence of a neo-Darwinian synthesis. It focuses on those essential facts, events, and ideas that have contributed to the successes of scientific evolutionism. . . . Larson is to be commended for stressing the value of both scientific inquiry and the evolutionary framework. This outstanding book is highly recommended for all academic and public libraries." Libr J

Includes bibliographical references

Margulis, Lynn

Symbiotic planet; a new look at evolution. Basic Bks. 1998 147p il hardcover o.p. pa $14 **576.8**

1. Evolution 2. Evolution (Biology) 3. Gaia hypothesis 4. Symbiogenesis 5. Symbiosis

ISBN 0-465-07272-0 pa

LC 98-38921

"From the origin of life to the classification and phylogeny of living organisms, from a discussion of Gaia—the belief that Earth operates like a living being—to a discussion of the underlying reasons for sex, iconoclastic biologist Margulis . . . takes on many of the big questions in biology. . . . In a book that is part autobiography and part biological primer, Margulis . . . advances the idea that a large part of organic evolution can be explained by symbiosis." Publ Wkly

Includes bibliographical references

Mayr, Ernst

What evolution is. Basic Bks. 2001 318p il maps hardcover o.p. pa $16 **576.8**

1. Evolution 2. Evolution (Biology)

ISBN 0-465-04426-3 pa

LC 2001-36562

"A wise and illuminating examination, by an illustrious evolutionary biologist, that sorts out the complexities of evolution." N Y Times Book Rev

Includes bibliographical references

McCalman, Iain

Darwin's armada; four voyages and the battle for the theory of evolution. W.W. Norton & Co. 2009 422p il map **576.8**

1. Biologists 2. Botanists 3. Essayists 4. Evolution 5. Naturalists 6. Travel writers 7. Writers on science

ISBN 0-393-06814-5; 978-0-393-06814-6

LC 2009-16055

"This geographically expansive account of the rise of evolutionary theory traces the lives and travels of four titans of nineteenth-century biology: Darwin, the botanist Joseph Hooker, the physiologist Thomas Huxley, and Alfred Russel Wallace, a fearless globetrotter whose dangerous and often unpleasant journeys in the Amazon and the Malay Archipelago were the source of biological epiphanies and tens of thousands of specimens. Though these stories have been told before, McCalman's central conceit—that the four naturalists, who all travelled at length in the Southern Hemisphere, share a 'special bond of the salt'—supplies a fresh, antipodean perspective."

"This geographically expansive account of the rise of evolutionary theory traces the lives and travels of four titans of nineteenth-century biology: Darwin, the botanist Joseph Hooker, the physiologist Thomas Huxley, and Alfred Russel Wallace, a fearless globetrotter whose dangerous and often unpleasant journeys in the Amazon and the Malay Archipelago were the source of biological epiphanies and tens of thousands of specimens. Though these stories have been told before, McCalman's central conceit—that the four naturalists, who all travelled at length in the Southern Hemisphere, share a 'special bond of the salt'—supplies a fresh, antipodean perspective." New Yorker

Includes bibliographical references

Novacek, Michael J.

Terra; our 100-million-year-old ecosystem--and the threats that now put it at risk. [by] Michael Novacek. Farrar, Straus and Giroux 2007 xxiv, 451p il map $27 **576.8**

1. Ecology 2. Environmental degradation 3. Evolution

4. Human influence on nature
ISBN 978-0-374-27325-5; 0-374-27325-1

LC 2007-9126

The author takes a "look at what humans have done over time and in more recent years. Combining paleontology, evolutionary biology, and environmental science, he shows how these three perspectives can bring us to a better understanding of the 'mass extinction event' that threatens this planet if changes aren't implemented now." Libr J

Includes bibliographical references

Palumbi, Stephen R.

The **evolution** explosion; how humans cause rapid evolutionary change. Norton 2001 277p il $24.95; pa $14.95   **576.8**
1. Antibiotics 2. Breeding 3. Drug resistance in microorganisms 4. Evolution 5. Evolution (Biology) 6. Human influence on nature 7. Nature -- Effect of human beings on 8. Pesticide resistance 9. Pesticides
ISBN 0-393-02011-8; 0-393-32338-2 pa

LC 00-67004

This describes human causes of rapid evolutionary change, focusing on bacteria which have evolved strains resistant to antibiotics and insects resistant to pesticides.

"Palumbi's writing is lively and lucid, and his analogies are felicitous." Booklist

Includes bibliographical references

Pennock, Robert T.

Tower of Babel; the evidence against the new creationism. MIT Press 1999 429p hardcover o.p. pa $21.95   **576.8**
1. Creationism 2. Evolution 3. Evolution (Biology) 4. Evolution (Biology) -- Religious aspects -- Christianity 5. Historical linguistics 6. Religion and science 7. Science -- Philosophy
ISBN 0-262-16180-X; 0-262-66165-9 pa

LC 98-27286

By "disentangling the scientific issues from the religious and philosophic ones, Pennock has made a valuable contribution to a too-often-overheated debate." Booklist

Includes bibliographical references

Powell, James Lawrence

Night comes to the Cretaceous; dinosaur extinction and the transformation of modern geology. [by] James L. Powell. Freeman, W.H. 1998 250p il map $22.95   **576.8**
1. Catastrophes (Geology) 2. Dinosaurs 3. Extinction (Biology) 4. Mass extinction of species
ISBN 0-7167-3117-7

LC 98-13192

The author "summarizes arguments for and against the controversial 'impact theory' of the extinction of the dinosaurs first proposed by Nobel physicist Luis Alvarez and his geologist son Walter and others in 1980. . . . Powell's book is written for a broad audience. It is slow reading in places, but explanations added in parentheses clarify technical materials." Sci Books Films

Includes bibliographical references

Rose, Michael R.

Darwin's spectre; evolutionary biology in the modern world. Princeton Univ. Press 1998 233p hardcover o.p. pa $20.95   **576.8**
1. Evolution 2. Evolution (Biology) -- Social aspects 3. Natural selection 4. Natural selection -- Social aspects
ISBN 0-691-05008-2 pa

LC 98-11494

Rose "outlines the elements of evolutionary theory and then examines its contemporary applications in agriculture, where it is manifested in genetically engineered crops and animals, and in the new and developed field of 'Darwinian medicine,' which is transforming our understanding of pathogens and how to treat certain diseases." Libr J

Includes bibliographical references

Sasselov, Dimitar

The **life** of super-Earths; Dimitar Sasselov. Basic Books 2012 xvi, 202 p.p ill.   **576.8**
1. Exobiology 2. Extrasolar planets 3. Life -- Origin 4. Life on other planets 5. Science -- Astrophysics & Space Science. 6. Science -- Life Sciences -- Biological Diversity 7. Synthetic biology
ISBN 9780465021932; 9780465023400

LC 2011036888

This book discusses the research supporting the claim for extra-terrestrial life beyond Earth. Author Dimitar "Sasselov (Astronomy/Harvard Univ.) reviews the hard evidence in favor . . . before proceeding to explain discoveries and simulations that suggest we are not alone. No telescope has directly observed an extra-solar planet, but the author delivers a[n] . . . explanation of how instruments and, since 2009, a satellite are detecting subtle changes in a stars light or movement that reveal not only the presence of planets (600 so far) but their size, orbits and a hint of their composition. Sasselov maintains that the minority of 'super-earths' possess conditions favorable to life: proper temperature, protective atmosphere, volcanism and tectonic movements." (Kirkus)

Schopf, J. William

Cradle of life; the discovery of earth's earliest fossils. Princeton Univ. Press 1999 367p il $55; pa $20.95   **576.8**
1. Evolutionary paleobiology 2. Fossils 3. Life -- Origin 4. Micropaleontology 5. Paleontology -- Precambrian
ISBN 0-691-00230-4; 0-691-08864-0 pa

LC 98-42443

"Schopf's chapter on the evolution of biochemical pathways is a fascinating and wonderfully clear exposition of a difficult topic." Libr J

Includes bibliographical references

Small, Meredith F.

What's love got to do with it? the evolution of human mating. Anchor Bks. (NY) 1995 xx, 249p hardcover o.p. pa $14.95   **576.8**
1. Evolution 2. Sex (Biology) 3. Sexual behavior 4. Sociobiology
ISBN 0-385-47702-3 pa

LC 95-1359

"Extensively documented and indexed, Small's text is . . . highly readable." Libr J

Includes bibliographical references

Stott, Rebecca

★ **Darwin's** ghosts; the secret history of evolution. Rebecca Stott. Spiegel & Grau 2012 xviii, 396 p.p   **576.8**

1. Evolution (Biology) -- History 2. Naturalists -- Biography 3. Scientists -- Biography
ISBN 1400069378; 9781400069378

LC 2011041951

This book draws for readers stories of the people who came before [Charles] Darwin and who presented ideas that were precursors to the theory of evolution. While Darwin described as he saw it the process now known as evolution, he was standing on the shoulders of giants. Though for the most part he did not realize it, his theory had itself evolved from other ideas. Many of the thinkers and ideas presented in this book--each chapter covers a new individual--Darwin was not aware of until after the publication of On the Origin of Species. After receiving a critical letter, he compiled a list of his scientific predecessors to be included in the foreword of later editions. [Rebecca] Scott discusses many of them, including Aristotle, Al-Jahiz, Leonardo da Vinci, and Denis Diderot. (Libr J)

Switek, Brian

Written in stone; evolution, the fossil record and our place in nature. Bellevue Literary Press 2010 320p il pa $17.95   **576.8**

1. Evolution 2. Fossil hominids 3. Fossils 4. Human evolution
ISBN 978-1-934137-29-1 pa; 1-934137-29-4 pa

The author "presents a popular account of fossil discoveries, historical debates related to evolution, and how the unearthing of these missing links is filling in the gaps in evolutionary history. . . . Armchair scientists and general readers interested in evolution will enjoy this informative book." Libr J

Ward, Peter Douglas

Life as we do not know it; the NASA search for (and synthesis of) alien life. Peter D. Ward. Viking 2005 xxvii, 292p ill. hardcover o.p. (pbk.) $15.00; o.p.   **576.8**

1. Life -- Origin 2. Life on other planets
ISBN 9780143038498; 0670034584

LC 2005056299

This book "sets a research agenda aimed at unraveling science's most profound questions: What is life, and how does it exist? To that query, he adds this philosophical discussion: What is humanity's role in life's unfolding on Earth and in the rest of the Solar System? . . . [Author Peter] Ward begins with a generally agreed-upon set of criteria — life metabolizes, has complexity and organization, reproduces, develops, evolves, and is autonomous — but then proposes the controversial hypothesis that this definition should include viruses. . . . Ward leaves no solar-system world unvisited. He quickly dismisses Mercury but spends a number of pages discussing the possibility of life floating high in the sulfuric-acid-laced clouds of Venus. . . . Mars gets the most attention outside of Earth." (National Space Society)

The author "believes researchers might be taking the wrong approach by looking only for earthly DNA-based life forms. Truly alien life, he argues, might have completely different origins. . . . The science is neatly laid out, and readers willing to follow his daring, scientifically based speculations will find their imaginations spurred." Publ Wkly

Includes bibliographical references (p. [257]-278) and index

Rare earth; why complex life is uncommon in the universe. {by} Peter Ward, Don Brownlee. Copernicus 1999 xxviii, 333p il $27.50; pa $16.95 **576.8**

1. Exobiology 2. Life on other planets
ISBN 0-387-98701-0; 0-387-95289-6 pa

LC 99-20532

"Arguing that complex life is a rare event in the universe, this compelling book magnifies the significance—and tragedy—of species extinction." Libr J

Includes bibliographical references and index

Wilson, David Sloan

★ **Evolution** for everyone; how Darwin's theory can change the way we think about our lives. Delacorte Press 2007 390p $24   **576.8**

1. Evolution 2. Evolution (Biology) 3. Naturalists 4. Travel writers 5. Writers on science
ISBN 978-0-385-34021-2; 0-385-34021-4

LC 2006-23685

"Rather than catalog its successes, denounce its detractors or in any way present evolutionary theory as the province of expert tacticians like himself, Wilson invites readers inside and shows them how Darwinism is done, and at lesson's end urges us to go ahead, feel free to try it at home. The result is a sprightly, absorbing and charmingly earnest book that manages a minor miracle, the near-complete emulsifying of science and the 'real world,' ingredients too often kept stubbornly, senselessly apart." N Y Times Book Rev

Includes bibliographical references

Young, Christian C.

★ **Evolution** and creationism; a documentary and reference guide. [by] Christian C. Young and Mark A. Largent. Greenwood Press 2007 298p il $85   **576.8**

1. Creationism 2. Evolution 3. Evolution (Biology) 4. Religion and science -- History
ISBN 978-0-313-33953-0; 0-313-33953-8

LC 2007-10682

"This reference work provides over 40 of the most important documents to help readers understand the [evolution versus creationism] debate in the eyes of the people of the time. Each document is from a major participant in the debates from the predecessors of Darwin to the judges of influential court cases of the present day." Publisher's note

Includes bibliographical references

★ **Evolution;** the first four billion years. edited by Michael Ruse [and] Joseph Travis; with a foreword by Edward O. Wilson. Belknap Press

of Harvard University Press 2009 979p il map
$39.95   **576.8**
1. Evolution 2. Evolution (Biology)
ISBN 9780674031753

LC 2008-30270

"If ever there were an education in a book, there's one in
this massive volume." Booklist

Includes bibliographical references

577 Ecology

Buchmann, Stephen

The **forgotten** pollinators; {by} Stephen L. Buchmann and Gary Paul Nabhan; with a foreword by
Edward O. Wilson; illustrations by Paul Mirocha.
Island Press (Covelo) 1996 xx, 292p il $30; pa
$18   **577**
1. Biological diversity 2. Ecology 3. Environmental
protection 4. Fertilization of plants
ISBN 1-55963-352-2; 1-55963-353-0 pa

LC 96-802

The authors explore the "link between plants and their
pollinators. It is a disturbing story of disappearing insects
and diminishing plant reproduction, owing to overuse of
pesticide and fragmented habitat. The authors combine anecdotes from the field with discussions of ecology, entomology, botany, crop science and the economics of pollination."
Publ Wkly

Includes bibliographical references

Burdick, Alan

★ **Out** of Eden; an odyssey of ecological invasion. Farrar, Straus & Giroux 2005 324p il $25; pa
$14   **577**
1. Biological invasions 2. Biotic communities 3.
Ecology
ISBN 0-374-21973-7; 0-374-53043-2 pa

LC 2005-922517

"A sober report, Burdick's work still sounds an
alarm for readers concerned with the way humans alter
nature." Booklist

Roston, Eric

The **carbon** age; how life's core element has
become civilization's greatest threat. Distributed to
the trade by Macmillan 2008 309p il $25.99 **577**
1. Atmosphere 2. Carbon
ISBN 978-0-8027-1557-9; 0-8027-1557-5

LC 2008-2754

"The first half traces carbon's history from the beginning
of the universe, the Big Bang, and the nucleosynthesis (the
formation of the elements) through the life cycle of stars,
and then covers the development of life and dynamics of the
'natural' carbon cycle of Earth. The second section spans the
last 150 years and delves into the impact of humans on the
climate in creating what Roston calls the 'industrial carbon
cycle.' Without using a great deal of scientific jargon, Roston
leads us patiently and clearly through this complex issue."
Libr J

Includes bibliographical references

Slobodkin, Lawrence B.

A **citizen's** guide to ecology. Oxford University
Press 2003 245p hardcover o.p. pa $14.95   **577**
1. Ecology 2. Human influence on nature 3. Nature
-- Effect of human beings on
ISBN 0-19-516286-2; 0-19-516287-0 pa

LC 2002-72826

"Slobodkin's sober examination of [the issues] . . . offers
the empowerment that arises from genuine knowledge about
problems." Booklist

Includes bibliographical references

Smil, Vaclav

The **earth's** biosphere; evolution, dynamics, and
change. MIT Press 2002 346p il maps $32.95; pa
$19.95   **577**
1. Biosphere
ISBN 0-262-19472-4; 0-262-69298-8 pa

LC 2001-58705

"A presentation marked by balance and clarity. . . . A
superior, comprehensive survey." Booklist

Includes bibliographical references

Stolzenberg, William

Where the wild things were; life, death, and
ecological wreckage in a land of vanishing predators.
Bloomsbury 2008 291p $24.99   **577**
1. Ecology 2. Endangered ecosystems 3. Endangered
species 4. Nature conservation 5. Predatory animals 6.
Predatory animals -- Ecology
ISBN 978-1-59691-299-1; 1-59691-299-5

LC 2008-2392

A look at how the disappearance of the world's great
predators has upset the delicate balance of the environment,
and what their disappearance portends for the future.

This "is one of those rare books that provide not just an
enriching story, but a new, clarifying lens through which to
understand the world around us." Christ Sci Monit

Includes bibliographical references

577.2 Specific factors affecting ecology

Montaigne, Fen

Fraser's penguins; a journey to the future in
Antarctica. Henry Holt and Co. 2010 288p il map
$26   **577.2**
1. Adélie penguin 2. Climate -- Environmental aspects
3. Climatic changes -- Antarctic regions 4. Ecologists
5. Endangered species 6. Global environmental change
7. Human influence on nature 8. Nature -- Effect of
human beings on -- Antarctic regions 9. Penguins
ISBN 978-0-8050-7942-5; 0-8050-7942-4

LC 2010-07151

The author "spent five months tracking penguins
through the breeding season on the northwestern Antarctica
peninsula with the scientist Bill Fraser, and his book is a
bittersweet account of the stark beauty of the continent and
the climate change that threatens its delicate ecosystem. . .
. Montaigne poetically portrays the daunting Antarctic landscape and gives readers an intimate perspective on its rug-

ged, audacious, and charming penguin and human inhabitants." Publ Wkly

Includes bibliographical references

577.3 Ecology of specific environments

Haskell, David George

The **forest** unseen; a year's watch in nature. David George Haskell. Viking 2012 268 p **577.3**

1. Natural history -- Tennessee 2. Nature observation -- Tennessee 3. Old growth forest ecology -- Tennessee 4. Old growth forests -- Tennessee 5. Philosophy of nature 6. Seasons -- Tennessee

ISBN 9780670023370

LC 2011037552

In this book, "biologist David Haskell uses a one-square-meter patch of old-growth Tennessee forest as a window onto the entire natural world. Visiting it almost daily for one year to trace nature's path through the seasons, he brings the forest and its inhabitants to . . . life. Each of this book's short chapters begins with a simple observation: a salamander scuttling across the leaf litter; the first blossom of spring wildflowers. From these, Haskell spins a . . . web of biology and ecology, explaining the science that binds together the tiniest microbes and the largest mammals and describing the ecosystems that have cycled for thousands--sometimes millions--of years." (Publisher's note)

Preston, Richard

The **wild** trees; a story of passion and daring. Random House 2007 294p il map $25.95; pa $16 **577.3**

1. Botanists 2. Coast redwood 3. College teachers 4. Redwood 5. Tree climbing

ISBN 978-1-4000-6489-2; 1-4000-6489-9; 978-0-8129-7559-8 pa; 0-8129-7559-6 pa

LC 2006-48646

The author tells the story of Steve Sillett, Marie Antoine and other naturalists and researchers who climb and explore giant redwoods in northern California.

"There is something so elementally boyish in searching out the biggest and tallest, poring over maps and measurements, dubbing these trees with names lifted from J.R.R. Tolkien's Middle Earth. . . . Preston knows how to fold the science into the seams of his narrative, and his dry humor crops up, pleasurably, at the edges of his observations." Cleveland Plain Dealer

577.34 Rain forest ecology

Lowman, Margaret

Life in the treetops; adventures of a woman in field biology. [by] Margaret D. Lowman. Yale Univ. Press 1999 219p il maps hardcover o.p. pa $13.95 **577.34**

1. Botanists 2. Ecologists -- Australia 3. Forest canopy ecology 4. Rain forest ecology 5. Women ecologists -- Australia 6. Women scientists

ISBN 0-300-07818-8; 978-0-300-07818-3; 0-300-

08464-1 pa; 978-0-300-08464-1 pa

LC 98-48691

Lowman "gives a funny, unassuming and deeply idiosyncratic chronicle of her trials and triumphs as a field biologist of tree canopies and other ecosystems in Australia, New England, Belize, Panama and elsewhere." N Y Times Book Rev

Includes bibliographical references

Royte, Elizabeth

The **Tapir's** morning bath; mysteries of the tropical rain forest and the scientists who are trying to solve them. Houghton Mifflin 2001 328p maps $25; pa $14 **577.34**

1. Panama -- Description 2. Rain forest ecology 3. Rain forest ecology -- Panama -- Barro Colorado Island 4. Rain forests -- Research -- Panama -- Barro Colorado Island

ISBN 0-395-97997-8; 0-618-25758-6 pa

LC 2001-24989

Royte discusses time spent with scientists studying the ecology of Barro Colorado, an island in the Panama Canal.

This is "a superb introduction to tropical ecology and theoretical biology, as well as original and thoroughly engaging travel writing." Publ Wkly

Includes bibliographical references

577.4 Grassland ecology

Manning, Richard

Grassland; the history, biology, politics, and promise of the American prairie. Viking 1995 306p hardcover o.p. pa $15 **577.4**

1. Environmental protection 2. Grassland ecology 3. Grasslands -- United States 4. Human influence on nature

ISBN 0-14-023388-1 pa

LC 95-10073

"Our culture's disrespect for grasslands has produced an environmental catastrophe, charges the author. By allowing overgrazing on public lands, our government is wiping out an ecosystem as vital as the Brazilian rain forests. In this sweeping exploration of the prairie, Manning . . . makes an eloquent plea to restore it." Publ Wkly

Includes bibliographical references

577.6 Aquatic ecology

Douglas, Marjory Stoneman

The **Everglades**; river of grass. illustrated by Robert Fink; [update by Michael Grunwald] 60th anniversary ed; Pineapple Press 2007 447p $19.95 **577.6**

ISBN 978-1-56164-394-3

LC 2007-28384

A natural history of South Florida focusing on the unique ecosystem of the Everglades. Discusses environmental changes, scientific research, and political responses to conservation efforts.

577.7   Marine ecology

Carson, Rachel

The **edge** of the sea; with illustrations by Bob Hines. Houghton Mifflin 1955 276p il hardcover o.p. pa $14   **577.7**

1. Marine biology 2. Seashore
ISBN 0-395-92496-0 pa

"The seashores of the world may be divided into three basic types: the rugged shores of rock, the sand beaches, and the coral reefs and all their associated features. Each has its typical community of plants and animals. The Atlantic coast of the United States [provides] clear examples of each of these types. I have chosen it as the setting for my pictures of shore life." Preface

Ellis, Richard

★ The **empty** ocean; plundering the world's marine life. written and illustrated by Richard Ellis. Island Press 2003 367p il hardcover o.p. pa $25   **577.7**

1. Endangered species 2. Fishing 3. Marine ecology
ISBN 1-55963-974-1; 1-55963-637-8 pa

"Rather than writing the 'Silent Spring' of the oceans, [Ellis] has produced a book that is likely to provide the inspiration and source materials for such a badly needed work ... It is also a splendid example of history illuminating ecology, with well-chosen facts that enable us to picture a largely invisible catastrophe." N Y Times Book Rev

Includes bibliographical references

578   Natural history of organisms and related subjects

Weidensaul, Scott

★ **Return** to wild America; a yearlong journey in search of the continent's natural soul. North Point Press 2005 xx, 394p il map $26; pa $15   **578**

1. Artists 2. Illustrators 3. Natural history -- North America 4. Ornithologists 5. Writers on nature
ISBN 0-8654-7688-8; 0-8654-7731-0 pa

LC 2005-47720

Fifty years after the publishing of Roger Tory Peterson's and James Fisher's Wild America, the author retraces Peterson and Fisher's steps "from Newfoundland's craggy coastline, down the East Coast, into Mexico and up the West Coast to Alaska.... This engrossing state-of-nature memoir, making a vibrant case for preserving America's wild past for future Americans, promises to become a classic in its own right." Publ Wkly

Includes bibliographical references

578.4   Adaptation

Barrington, Rupert

Life; extraordinary animals, extreme behaviour. [by] Martha Holmes and Mike Gunton; [with] Rupert Barrington ... [et al.] University of California Press 2010 311p il map   **578.4**

1. Adaptation (Biology) 2. Animal behavior
ISBN 0-520-26537-8; 978-0-520-26537-0

LC 2009-31158

"In 2009, to commemorate the 200th anniversary of Charles Darwin's birth, the BBC premiered the ten-episode television documentary Life to great acclaim. . . . Written by the documentary's producers, this impressive companion volume showcases species of fish, amphibians, reptiles, insects, birds, mammals, and plants that have developed unique or unusual strategies for solving 'the eternal problems of life': finding food, escaping predators, attracting mates, and raising young. . . . Even the most casual reader will be awed by the beauty, complexity, and ingenuity of nature as celebrated here." Libr J

Forbes, Peter

Dazzled and deceived; mimicry and camouflage. Yale University Press 2009 283p il map $27.50   **578.4**

1. Camouflage (Biology) 2. Mimicry (Biology)
ISBN 978-0-300-12539-9; 0-300-12539-9

LC 2009-23577

"Forbes has produced a colorful look at camouflage in nature and battle, with a focus on the two world wars. . . . [The book] straddles the worlds of evolutionary biology, art, and military strategy with a world-class cast of characters, among them Charles Darwin, Pablo Picasso, Vladimir Nabokov, Theodore Roosevelt, and Winston Churchill. A pivotal character is Abbott Handerson Thayer, the eccentric New England painter who studied the animals near his summer home in Dublin, N.H., and is one of the few artists to have a scientific law (Thayer's Law of Concealing Coloration) named after him." Boston Globe

Includes bibliographical references

578.6   Miscellaneous nontaxonomic kinds of organisms

Bright, Chris

Life out of bounds; bioinvasion in a borderless world. Norton 1998 287p il pa $13.95   **578.6**

1. Alien plants -- Control 2. Animal introduction 3. Biological diversity conservation 4. Biological invasions 5. Ecology 6. Nonindigenous pests -- Control 7. Plant introduction
ISBN 0-393-31814-1

LC 99-163011

"Bright discusses the increasingly urgent issue of invasive exotic plants and animals and their ecological impact worldwide on native species. An excellent introduction to the field, loaded with historical examples and heavily referenced." Libr J

Includes bibliographical references

Hamilton, Garry

Super species; the creatures that will dominate the planet. Firefly Books 2010 271p il $35 **578.6**

1. Biological invasions 2. Nonindigenous pests
ISBN 978-1-55407-630-7; 1-55407-630-7

LC 2011286604

"Well researched and written, with an abundance of excellent photos, this work provides an outstanding, balanced look at this group of species." Choice

Includes bibliographical references

578.68 Rare and endangered species

Ackerman, Diane

The **rarest** of the rare; vanishing animals, timeless worlds. Random House 1995 xxi, 184p hardcover o.p. pa $12 **578.68**

1. Endangered species 2. Rare animals
ISBN 0-679-77623-0 pa

LC 95-8499

"Every species that is endangered or becomes extinct deserves so poetic a chronicler as Ackerman." Libr J

578.7 Organisms characteristic of specific kinds of environments

Burt, William

Marshes; the disappearing Edens. Yale University Press 2007 179p il $35 **578.7**

1. Marshes 2. Wetland ecology -- North America 3. Wetlands -- North America
ISBN 978-0-300-12229-9; 0-300-12229-2

LC 2006-26961

This book combines photographs of marsh life with information about wetland habitat in North America.

"This well-structured, readable book will be valuable for students, teachers, researchers, and sundry readers interested in a unique kind of wetland. Reading this book is an excellent way to understand marshes as wild places." Choice

Includes bibliographical references

Carson, Rachel

Under the sea wind; introduction by Linda Lear; illustrations by Howard Frech. Penguin Books 2007 xx, 184p il pa $15 **578.7**

1. Marine biology
ISBN 978-0-14-310496-4

LC 2006-50707

A series of narratives describe the birds and sea creatures that inhabit the Eastern coasts of North America.

Cramer, Deborah

Smithsonian ocean; our water, our world. Smithsonian Books 2008 295p il map $39.95 **578.7**

1. Marine biology 2. Marine ecology 3. Ocean
ISBN 978-0-06-134383-4; 0-06-134383-8

LC 2008-15633

"With its hundreds of beautiful photographs, the volume is visually enchanting. It is also a vividly, accurately, and clearly written survey of the state of our understanding . . . of the history and current condition of the ocean." Sci Books Films

Includes bibliographical references

Crist, Darlene Trew

World ocean census; a global survey of marine life. [by] Darlene Trew Crist, Gail Scowcroft, James M. Harding, Jr. Firefly Books 2009 256p il map $40 **578.7**

1. Marine animals 2. Marine biology 3. Science -- Methodology
ISBN 978-1-55407-434-1; 1-55407-434-7

The authors "have produced a highly readable text with stunning photos that should fully engage the public imagination." Publ Wkly

Includes bibliographical references

DeStefano, Stephen

Coyote at the kitchen door; living with wildlife in suburbia. Harvard University Press 2010 196p il $24.95 **578.7**

1. Biologists 2. College teachers 3. Coyote 4. Coyotes 5. Suburban life 6. Urban animals 7. Urbanization 8. Urbanization -- Environmental aspects 9. Wildlife conservation
ISBN 978-0-674-03556-0; 0-674-03556-9

The author "examines the expanding field of 'urban ecology' in this pithy volume. Urban ecologists study changes in human-animal interactions caused by factors like sprawl, traffic, and noise pollution, in an attempt to understand why some species (the mountain lion, say) are badly disrupted by human developments, while others, such as the coyote, appear to be thriving—turning up in more and more Eastern back yards. DeStefano cites some alarming facts . . . but, having experienced the benefits of a suburban childhood, he refuses to reduce his thinking to a view in which wilderness preservation is the only solution." New Yorker

Includes bibliographical references

Koslow, J. Anthony

★ The **silent** deep; the discovery, ecology, and conservation of the deep sea. [by] Tony Koslow. University of Chicago Press 2007 270p il map $35 **578.7**

1. Conservation of natural resources 2. Deep-sea ecology 3. Marine ecology 4. Marine resources 5. Marine resources conservation
ISBN 978-0-226-45125-1; 0-226-45125-9

LC 2006-22282

"This important book should be read by everyone who cares about Earth's future." Choice

Includes bibliographical references

Wolfe, David W.

Tales from the underground; a natural history of subterranean life. Perseus Bks. 2001 221p il hardcover o.p. pa $18 **578.7**

1. Soil biology 2. Soil ecology 3. Soil microbiology 4. Underground ecology
ISBN 0-7382-0679-2 pa

The author discusses the ecology of life in the soil and the earth's rocky crust, including Darwin's experiments with earthworms, Lewis and Clark's first encounter with prairie dogs, the use of genetic tools, and the possible role of primitive underground microbes in evolution.

Wolfe "explains in a straightforward, readable style that there is probably as much biodiversity and even as much biomass below ground as above." New Sci

Includes bibliographical references

578.73   Specific kinds of nonaquatic environments

Jukofsky, Diane

Encyclopedia of rainforests; by Diane Jukofsky for the Rainforest Alliance. Oryx Press 2001 xxxi, 328p il $84.95   **578.73**

1. Rain forests -- Encyclopedias 2. Reference books

ISBN 1-57356-259-9

LC 2001-32154

"The text as a whole, which . . . includes sections on peoples, noted naturalists, and conservation efforts, . . . provides a fine introduction to the world of the rainforest and would be appreciated by any high school/undergraduate library." Libr J

Includes bibliographical references

579   Natural history of microorganisms, fungi, algae

Ben-Barak, Idan

The invisible kingdom; from the tips of our fingers to the tops of our trash, inside the curious world of microbes. Basic Books 2009 204p $24   **579**

1. Microbiology

ISBN 978-0-465-01887-1; 0-465-01887-4

LC 2009-19655

The author "gives an enthusiastic tour of single-celled life. . . . He touches on myriad microbes in a range of environments, from the abyss of the sea to the inside of humans, explaining how they defend themselves, eat, move, and reproduce." Booklist

Includes bibliographical references

Dunn, Rob

The wild life of our bodies; predators, parasites, and partners that shape our evolution. Harper 2011 290p $26.99   **579**

1. Evolution 2. Human ecology 3. Microorganisms 4. Parasites

ISBN 978-0-06-180648-3; 0-06-180648-X

LC 2010-43564

The author "shares the view of modern human life as a paradise lost, but the loss he laments is not merely of a vague sense of being one with nature. What we have sacrificed, he argues, is a physical connection with the species that shaped our bodies from our physique to the immune system. As humans became urban and industrial, we also separated ourselves from other species. Pets aside, we have laboured to rid our houses and cities of creatures — not just visible predators and pests but also the microbes on our countertops and hands. Some of these steps were sensible acts of self-preservation, but others were driven by an ideology of humans as separate from nature. Dunn . . . catalogues the dangers of that ideology." New Scientist

Includes bibliographical references

Sankaran, Neeraja

★ Microbes and people: an A-Z of microorganisms in our lives. Oryx Press 2000 297p il $62.95   **579**

1. Microbiology -- Dictionaries 2. Microbiology -- Encyclopedias 3. Reference books

ISBN 1-57356-217-3

LC 00-10117

"Because it provides very readable coverage of topics so much in the news lately, this dictionary will be much used in high school, undergraduate, and public libraries." Booklist

Includes bibliographical references

579.2   Viruses and subviral organisms

Crawford, Dorothy H.

The invisible enemy; a natural history of viruses. Oxford Univ. Press 2000 275p il hardcover o.p. pa $14.95   **579.2**

1. Medical virology 2. Viruses 3. Viruses -- Ecology

ISBN 0-19-850332-6; 0-19-856481-3 pa

LC 00-36756

"Crawford offers new knowledge and insights for any reader, regardless of the depth of their science education." New Sci

Includes bibliographical references

579.3   Prokaryotes (Bacteria)

Karlen, Arno

Biography of a germ. Pantheon Bks. 2000 178p hardcover o.p. pa $12   **579.3**

1. Borrelia burgdorferi 2. Lyme disease 3. Microorganisms

ISBN 0-385-72066-1 pa

LC 99-57304

"Karlen has created a vigorous, compact account of Bb's life and times." Publ Wkly

Zimmer, Carl

Microcosm; E. coli and the new science of life. Pantheon Books 2008 243p il $25.95   **579.3**

1. Bacteria 2. Escherichia coli 3. Genetics -- History 4. Microbiology 5. Molecular biology -- History

ISBN 978-0-375-42430-4; 0-375-42430-X

LC 2007-37155

The author "renders an absorbing picture of what E. coli says about the history and future of life." Booklist

Includes bibliographical references

579.5 Fungi

Hudler, George W.

Magical mushrooms, mischievous molds. Princeton Univ. Press 1998 248p il hardcover o.p. pa $18.95 **579.5**
1. Fungi
ISBN 0-691-07016-4 pa

LC 98-10163

The author shows how fungi "have dramatically influenced the course of human history. With chapters on yeasts used to make bread and to brew alcoholic beverages, on the medicinal uses of fungi from penicillin to possible treatments for AIDS, on edible mushrooms like the common button mushroom and the more exotic truffle, and on hallucinogenic mushrooms, Hudler takes readers on an enthralling and informative tour of this much maligned kingdom." Publ Wkly

Includes bibliographical references

579.6 Mushrooms

McKnight, Kent H.

A **field** guide to mushrooms, North America; [by] Kent H. McKnight and Vera B. McKnight; illustrations by Vera B. McKnight. Houghton Mifflin 1987 429p il hardcover o.p. pa $21 **579.6**
1. Mushrooms
ISBN 0-395-91090-0 pa

LC 86-27799

"More than 500 species [of mushrooms] are described and depicted. . . . Edibility of each species is noted and signified by marginal pictograms both in the text and on the color-plates. . . . Appended: a genial chapter of recipes by Anne Dow, glossary, selected references, and index." Booklist

Smith, Alexander Hanchett

The **mushroom** hunter's field guide; {by} Alexander H. Smith and Nancy Smith Weber. all color & enlarged; University of Mich. Press 1980 316p il $24.95 **579.6**
1. Mushrooms
ISBN 0-472-85610-3

LC 80-10514

This is a "field guide for both novices and experts alike. The introductory chapter explains basic terminology and what to look for when identifying fungi. More than 280 mushrooms are described, including identifying marks, edibility, habitat, native range, and type of spore. A color photograph . . . of each mushroom is most valuable for accurate information." Booklist

Includes bibliographical references

580 Natural history of plants and animals

★ Magill's encyclopedia of science; plant life. editor, Bryan D. Ness. Salem Press 2002 4v il map set $457 **580**
1. Botany -- Encyclopedias 2. Reference books
ISBN 1-58765-084-3

LC 2002-13319

This encyclopedia provides "information for any study related to plants, archaea, bacteria, algae, or fungi, from molecular-level processes to planet-wide economic or environmental issues. The 379 signed articles, about half of which are published with revisions and updated bibliographies from several of the publisher's earlier reference books, are arranged into a single alphabet." SLJ

Includes bibliographical references

581.6 Miscellaneous nontaxonomic kinds of plants

Angier, Bradford

Field guide to edible wild plants; revisions by David K. Foster; illustrations by Arthur J. Anderson; additional illustrations by Jacqueline Mahannah, Michelle L. Meneghini, and Kristen E. Workman. 2nd ed.; Stackpole Books 2008 282p il pa $21.95 **581.6**
1. Edible plants
ISBN 978-0-81173-447-9; 0-81173-447-1

LC 2007-40125

"Plants are arranged alphabetically by one of their common names. Each entry includes genus, family affiliation, other common names, a lengthy plant description (including many interesting facts about the plant), notes on distribution, and a statement concerning edibility and preparation of the plant parts." Libr J

Davis, Wade

One river; explorations and discoveries in the Amazon rain forest. Simon & Schuster 1996 537p il hardcover o.p. pa $16 **581.6**
1. Botanists 2. College teachers 3. Ethnobiologists 4. Ethnobotany 5. Hallucinogens 6. Medical botany 7. Writers on nature 8. Writers on science
ISBN 0-684-83496-0 pa

LC 96-21516

Davis "writes magnificently, with verve when describing his many adventurous field trips, accurately and efficiently when telling science or history, and with vivid fantasy when portraying hallucinogenic trances." N Y Times Book Rev

Includes bibliographical references

Gibbons, Euell

Stalking the wild asparagus; with illustrations by Margaret F. Schroeder; including a remembrance of the author by John McPhee. 25th anniversary ed; Hood, A.C. 1987 303p il hardcover o.p. pa $17.50 **581.6**
1. Cooking 2. Edible plants
ISBN 0-911469-036 pa

LC 87-16933

In this series of brief anecdotal essays the naturalist discourses on the identification and preparation of roots, flowers and plants, old Indian legends, and wilderness survival.

Sumner, Judith

The **natural** history of medicinal plants; foreword by Mark Plotkin. Timber Press 2000 235p il hardcover o.p. pa $24.95   **581.6**

1. Botany, Medical 2. Medical botany 3. Medicinal plants

ISBN 0-88192-483-0; 978-0-88192-957-7 pa; 0-88192-957-3 pa

LC 99-76555

Sumner presents an "accessible introduction to the world of medicinal plants. . . . Some of her most interesting revelations are about the relationships that animals have with plants." Booklist

Includes bibliographical references

Turner, Nancy J.

★ The **North** American guide to common poisonous plants and mushrooms; [by] Nancy J. Turner and Patrick von Aderkas. Timber Press 2009 375p il $29.95   **581.6**

1. Mushrooms 2. Mushrooms, Poisonous 3. Poisonous plants

ISBN 0-88192-929-8; 978-0-88192-929-4

LC 2008-35095

"The book is split into four main categories: mushrooms, wild plants, ornamental and crop plants, and houseplants. Each plant entry includes a . . . photograph to aid the task of identification, a description of the plant, notes on where they commonly occur, and a description of their toxic properties." Publisher's note

Includes bibliographical references

Van Wyk, Ben-Erik

★ **Food** plants of the world; an illustrated guide. Timber Press 2005 480p il $39.95   **581.6**

1. Edible plants

ISBN 0-88192-743-0; 978-0-88192-743-6

LC 2005-44048

For a fuller review, see: Booklist, Feb. 15, 2005

This is an "illustrated guide to more than 350 commercially important plants that are sources of cereals, nuts, fruits, vegetables, drinks, herbs, and spices." Choice

Includes bibliographical references

582.1   Herbaceous and woody plants, plants noted for their flowers

Symonds, George W. D.

The **shrub** identification book; the visual method for the practical identification of shrubs, including woody vines and ground covers. photos by A. W. Merwin. William Morrow & Company 1963 379p il pa $22   **582.1**

1. Shrubs

ISBN 978-0-688-05040-5; 0-688-05040-9

"Part I gives pictorial keys for thorns, leaves, flowers, fruit, twigs and bark of broad-leaved upright shrubs. Part II contains 200 master pages arranged under four categories, with data on habitat, blooming period, etc., accompanying the photographs." Wilson Libr Bull

Includes bibliographical references

582.13   Plants noted for their flowers

Heywood, V. H.

Flowering plant families of the world; [by] V.H. Heywood . . . [et al.] Updated & rev.; Firefly Books 2007 424p il map $59.95   **582.13**

1. Flowers

ISBN 978-1-55407-206-4; 1-55407-206-9

LC 2007-272849

"At the core of the book are . . . entries on 504 flowering plant families. Each entry describes distribution, anatomy, habitat, classification and commercial uses." Publisher's note

Includes bibliographical references

Spellenberg, Richard

National Audubon Society field guide to North American wildflowers, western region; 2nd ed rev; Knopf 2001 862p il map $19.95   **582.13**

1. Wild flowers

ISBN 0-375-40233-0

LC 2001-269242

"More than 940 . . . full-color images show the wildflowers of western North America close-up and in their natural habitats. . . . Images are grouped by flower color and shape and keyed to . . . descriptions that reflect current taxonomy." Publisher's note

Thieret, John W.

National Audubon Society field guide to North American wildflowers: eastern region; revising author, John W. Thieret; original authors, William A. Niering and Nancy C. Olmstead. Knopf 2001 879p il map $19.95   **582.13**

1. Wild flowers

ISBN 0-375-40232-2

LC 2001-269241

"Covers the area east of the Rockies and east of the Big Bend area of Texas to the Atlantic. Color photographs together with family and species descriptions make this a most useful field guide." Sci News {review of 1979 edition}

Wells, Diana

100 flowers and how they got their names; illustrated by Ippy Patterson. Algonquin Bks. 1997 257p il $17.95   **582.13**

1. Flowers 2. Popular plant names

ISBN 1-56512-138-4

LC 96-22296

The author "describes the mythology and history behind 100 favorite garden plants, emphasizing the exploits of botanists and plant explorers who brought them out of their native habitats." Libr J

Includes bibliographical references

582.16 Trees

Hugo, Nancy Ross

★ **Seeing** trees; Nancy Ross Hugo ; photography by Robert J. Llewellyn. 1st ed; Timber Press 2011 242p. col. ill. **582.16**

ISBN 9781604692198

LC 2010052455

This book, "[f]ocusing on widely grown trees, . . . describes the rewards of careful and regular tree viewing, outlines strategies for improving your observations, and describes some of the most visually interesting tree structures, including leaves, flowers, buds, leaf scars, twigs, and bark. . . . [P]rofiles of ten familiar species -- including such beloved trees as white oak, southern magnolia, white pine, and tulip poplar -- show you how to recognize and understand many of their most compelling (but usually overlooked) physical features." (Publisher's note)

Johnson, Hugh

The **world** of trees; consultant editor, John Grimshaw; preface by Thomas Pakenham. University of California Press 2010 400p il map $34.95 **582.16**

1. Trees

ISBN 978-0-520-24756-7

"The first section of the book provides general information on how trees grow, the life cycle of trees, their classification, and morphological characteristics. Next comes a compendium of more than 600 taxa of trees, divided into conifers and broadleaves. Beautiful color photographs, including portraits and landscape scenes, grace every page. The last section includes a guide to choosing trees for the landscape and a chart comparing the ornamental traits of trees throughout the seasons." Am Gardener

Little, Elbert Luther

★ The **Audubon** Society field guide to North American trees; [by] Elbert L. Little; photographs by Sonja Bullaty and Angelo Lomeo [et. al.]; visual key by Susan Rayfield and Olivia Buehl. Knopf 1980 2v il v1 $19.95; v2 $19.95 **582.16**

1. Trees -- North America

ISBN 0-394-50760-6 v1; 0-394-50761-4 v2

LC 79-3474

These "guides are unusual in that they contain many color photographs of parts of a living tree. The identification keys are easy to use, being based on an arrangement by leaf shapes, flowers, fruit, and fall leaves, and giving drawings of winter silhouettes. The eastern guide covers 364 species, the western guide describes 314 species; they divide the country at central Texas and the Rockies." Libr J

Nadkarni, Nalini

Between earth and sky; our intimate connections to trees. [by] Nalini M. Nadkarni. University of California Press 2008 322p il $45; pa $17.95 **582.16**

1. Trees

ISBN 978-0-520-24856-4; 978-0-520-26165-5 pa

LC 2008-2162

"This book presents a multifaceted, multidisciplined approach to the appreciation of trees that combines science, art, literature, poetry, and spirituality, including a discussion of the practical use of trees throughout history. . . . Beginning with a very enlightening chapter defining just what a tree is and describing the attributes of trees, the book thoroughly explores the human affinities to trees, explaining that trees fulfill human needs at every level of our existence. The chapters cover physical needs, security, health, recreation, time and history, symbols and language, and finally spirituality and mindfulness." Choice

Includes bibliographical references

Pakenham, Thomas

Remarkable trees of the world; text and photographs by Thomas Pakenham. Norton 2002 191p il $49.95; pa $27.95 **582.16**

1. Trees 2. Trees -- Pictorial works

ISBN 0-393-04911-6; 0-393-32529-6 pa

LC 2002-21934

The author presents descriptions and photographs of sixty exceptional trees from around the world.

"This beautiful and unique book is sure to be appreciated by nature lovers. And though it is a highly personal work and not a scientific text, it demonstrates keen and accurate observation; it could also serve as an excellent supplement to studies in science, history, and geography." SLJ

Includes bibliographical references

Sibley, David

The **Sibley** guide to trees; written and illustrated by David Allen Sibley. Alfred A. Knopf 2009 xxxviii, 426p il map $39.95 **582.16**

1. Trees -- North America

ISBN 978-0-375-41519-7

LC 2009-927625

This "is an outstanding book that should be available in all public libraries, schools, colleges, universities, and homes. The text is comprehensive and the illustrations are pertinent, accurate, and clear." Sci Books Films

Wells, Diana

Lives of the trees; an uncommon history. illustrated by Heather Lovett. Algonquin Books of Chapel Hill 2010 369p il $19.95 **582.16**

1. Trees

ISBN 978-1-56512-491-2; 1-56512-491-X

LC 2009-31669

"Wells explores people's relationship with about 100 trees and the stories behind their names." NPR

Includes bibliographical references

583   Dicotyledons

Anderson, Edward F.
★ The **cactus** family; with a foreword by Wilhelm Barthlott; and a chapter on cactus cultivation by Roger Brown. Timber Press 2001 776p il maps $99.95   **583**
1. Cactus 2. Cactus -- Pictorial works
ISBN 0-88192-498-9; 978-0-88192-498-5
LC 00-60700
This reference work on cactaceae covers 125 genera and 1810 species.
"While more than 1,000 photographs overall illustrate the extraordinary diversity and beautiful flowers of cacti, the main section—an alphabetically arranged reference—will arguably rank as the definitive work readers will use to examine and identify cactus genera, species, and subspecies." Booklist
Includes bibliographical references

Pappalardo, Joe
Sunflowers; the secret history; the unauthorized biography of the world's most beloved weed. Overlook Press 2008 256p il $22.95   **583**
1. Sunflowers
ISBN 978-1-58567-991-1; 1-58567-991-7
A "look at a flower so ubiquitous that its critical role in cultural development since the dawn of time often goes overlooked. A glib, upbeat writer and fiercely determined researcher, Pappalardo intrepidly investigates everything from the sunflower's genetic history and recent bioengineering discoveries to its influence on global economies from the U.S. to Uganda." Booklist

590   Animals

Botting, Douglas
Gerald Durrell; the authorized biography. Carroll & Graf Pubs. 1999 xx, 644p il $29.95; pa $16.95   **590**
1. Authors 2. Children's authors 3. Conservationists 4. Naturalists 5. Novelists 6. Wildlife conservationists -- Great Britain -- Biography 7. Writers on science 8. Zoologists -- Great Britain -- Biography
ISBN 0-7867-0655-4; 0-7867-0796-8 pa
LC 00-268642
A biography of the naturalist, writer, and founder of the Jersey Zoo.
"Given full access to Durrell's personal and professional papers, Botting clearly admires his subject yet presents an evenhanded account." Libr J
Includes bibliographical references

Lavers, Chris
Why elephants have big ears; understanding patterns of life on Earth. St. Martin's Press 2001 269p il $24.95; pa $13.95   **590**
1. Animal ecology 2. Animals 3. Animals -- Adaptation

4. Evolution 5. Evolution (Biology)
ISBN 0-312-26902-1; 0-312-30333-5 pa
LC 00-45997
"Lavers analyzes why animals look the way they do, why they live where they live, and why their physiology is either warm or cold-blooded. . . . He then examines the evolution of animal life and the corollary evolution of warmbloodedness." Booklist
Includes bibliographical references

590.73   Collections and exhibits of living mammals

Anthony, Lawrence
Babylon's ark; the incredible wartime rescue of the Baghdad Zoo. [by] Lawrence Anthony with Graham Spence. Thomas Dunne Books 2007 248p il hardcover o.p. pa $14.95   **590.73**
1. Iraq War, 2003- 2. Wildlife conservation 3. Zoos
ISBN 978-0-312-35832-7; 0-312-35832-6; 978-0-312-38215-5 pa; 0-312-38215-4 pa
LC 2006-50573
"This remarkable story recounts the recent wartime rescue of the once-world-renowned Baghdad Zoo through the experiences of a South African conservationist and heroic Iraqi zookeepers." Booklist

Baratay, Eric
★ **Zoo**: a history of zoological gardens in the West; [by] Eric Baratay, Elisabeth Hardouin-Fugier. Reaktion Bks. 2002 400p il $40   **590.73**
1. Zoos 2. Zoos -- History
ISBN 1-86189-111-3
In this history of zoos the authors "take a social history focus, examining how people view wild animals and how that has changed over time. . . . One can read the text or spend hours simply enjoying the images. Libraries that have other titles on zoos will still want to purchase this." Libr J
Includes bibliographical references

French, Thomas
Zoo story; life in the garden of captives. Hyperion 2010 288p $24.99   **590.73**
1. Zoos
ISBN 978-1-4013-2346-2
The author "chronicles the rise of Lowry Park from one of the worst zoos in the country to one of the best. . . . This behind-the-scenes look will both entertain and enlighten animal lovers. It is a story that needs to be told, and French does it superbly." Libr J
Includes bibliographical references

Hanson, Elizabeth
Animal attractions; nature on display in American zoos. Princeton Univ. Press 2002 243p il $29.95   **590.73**
1. Zoos 2. Zoos -- United States
ISBN 0-691-05992-6
LC 2001-55198

"If ever a book lived up to its title and subtitle, this one, an interesting and readable history of zoos and influences on their development in the US, certainly does." Choice

Includes bibliographical references (p.   )

Robinson, Phillip T.

★ **Life** at the zoo: behind the scenes with the animal doctors. Columbia University Press 2004 293p il $27.95; pa $17.95   **590.73**

1. Zoos

ISBN 0-231-13248-4; 0-231-13249-2 pa

LC 2004-43893

"It would be difficult to cover even one aspect, such as animal health, that might affect the overall management of a zoo, but Dr. Philip Robinson manages to provide an excellent coverage of just about everything that might be involved in the operation of a zoo." Sci Books Films

Includes bibliographical references

590.75   Museum activities and services

Milgrom, Melissa

Still life; adventures in taxidermy. Houghton Mifflin Harcourt 2010 285p $25   **590.75**

1. Taxidermists 2. Taxidermy

ISBN 978-0-618-40547-3

LC 2009-13511

"An animated initiation to the realm of taxidermy—its cultural significance, its hybrid status between art, craft and science, and the obsessive, idiosyncratic personalities who practice it. . . . Brimming with respect and immersive vitality." Kirkus

591.3   Genetics, evolution, age characteristics

Avise, John C.

Genetics in the wild; illustration by Trudy Nicholson. Smithsonian Institution Press 2002 248p il $27.95   **591.3**

1. Animal behavior 2. Animal genetics 3. Behavior genetics 4. Evolution 5. Evolutionary genetics 6. Genetics

ISBN 1-58834-069-4

LC 2002-17576

The author "demonstrates how scientists directly examine DNA to address long-standing questions about wild animals, plants, and microbes." Publisher's note

Includes bibliographical references

591.5   Behavior

American Museum of Natural History

Animal life; Charlotte Uhlenbroek, [editor in chief] DK Pub. 2008 512p il map $50   **591.5**

1. Animal behavior 2. Animals -- Pictorial works

ISBN 978-0-7566-3986-0; 0-7566-3986-7

LC 2008-300010

This book "provides an excellent overview of the animal world written at a level accessible to students and the general public. Introductory sections cover basics of animal life such as evolution, animal history, classification, and anatomy. Animal behavior receives the most extensive treatment, encompassing living space, hunting and feeding, defense mechanisms, sex and reproduction, birth and development, society, communication, and intelligence." Booklist

Balcombe, Jonathan

Pleasurable kingdom; animals and the nature of feeling good. Macmillan 2006 274p il $24.95; pa $14.95   **591.5**

1. Animal behavior 2. Pleasure

ISBN 1-4039-8601-0; 978-1-4039-8601-6; 1-4039-8602-9 pa; 978-1-4039-8602-3 pa

LC 2006-41734

This is an "examination of positive feelings in animals. . . . [The author] first defines what is meant by pleasure and why it is worthy of study, then looks at several potentially pleasure-causing activities: play, eating, sex, touching, and love. Full of examples both anecdotal and from refereed journals . . . this book not only makes a case for animal pleasure but calls for more research on the science of pleasure in animals, allowing humans to view them in a new way." Booklist

Includes bibliographical references

Second nature; the inner lives of animals. foreword by J.M. Coetzee. Palgrave Macmillan 2010 242p il $27.00; $27.00   **591.5**

1. Animal behavior 2. Animal intelligence 3. Animal psychology 4. Social behavior in animals

ISBN 0230613624; 9780230613621

LC 2009-30770

The author of Pleasurable Kingdom (2006) argues that animals are "sentient beings capable of feelings and pain and emotions." (Publisher's note) Index.

The author draws on the latest research, observational studies and personal anecdotes to reveal the full gamut of animal experience—from emotions, to problem solving, to moral judgment. Balcombe challenges the widely held idea that nature is red in tooth and claw, highlighting animal traits we have disregarded until now: their nuanced understanding of social dynamics, their consideration for others, and their strong tendency to avoid violent conflict. Publisher's note

Includes bibliographical references

The **exultant** ark; a pictorial tour of animal pleasure. University of California Press 2011 214p il $34.95   **591.5**

1. Animal behavior 2. Animals -- Pictorial works 3. Emotions in animals 4. Pleasure

ISBN 978-0-520-26024-5; 0-520-26024-4

LC 2010-43747

"As animal behaviourist Jonathan Balcombe sees it, too often the animal kingdom is portrayed solely as a realm of dire and perpetual struggle for survival. He argues that observations of playfulness or expressions of pleasure by non-human creatures of all stripes, feathers and fins are depicted as nothing more than evolutionary adaptation. The Exultant Ark, his pictorial exploration of pleasure among creatures from primate to porpoise, challenges this idea. It intersperses glorious images of animals preening, grooming and gallivanting with snippets of studies suggesting such behaviours belie an overly utilitarian interpretation." New Sci

Includes bibliographical references

Bekoff, Marc

Minding animals; awareness, emotions, and heart. {by} Marc Bekoff; with a foreword by Jane Goodall. Oxford Univ. Press 2002 xxiv, 230p il $27.50; pa $15.95   **591.5**

1. Animal behavior
ISBN 0-19-515077-5; 0-19-516337-0 pa

LC 2001-51341

"Chapters cover such broad topics as the richness of behavioral diversity, animal emotions, play and cooperation, and human intrusion into animals' lives. . . . The conversational writing style makes for a highly accessible book." Booklist

Includes bibliographical references

Wild justice; the moral lives of animals. [by] Marc Bekoff and Jessica Pierce. University of Chicago Press 2009 188p il $26; pa $17   **591.5**

1. Animal behavior 2. Animal intelligence 3. Animal psychology 4. Motivation in animals 5. Social behavior in animals
ISBN 978-0-226-04161-2; 0-226-04161-1; 978-0-226-04163-6 pa; 0-226-04163-8 pa

LC 2008-40173

The authors "discuss recent scientific studies documenting that great apes, monkeys, wolves, coyotes, hyenas, dolphins, whales, elephants, rats, and mice are capable of a wide range of moral behavior. They strongly urge the scientific and philosophical communities to recognize that these animals can act as moral agents within the context of their own social groups. This provocative and well-argued view of animal morality may surprise some readers as it challenges outdated assumptions about animals." Libr J

Includes bibliographical references

Berger, Joel

The **better** to eat you with; fear in the animal world. University of Chicago Press 2008 305p il map $29   **591.5**

1. Animal behavior 2. Animal ecology 3. Biologists 4. Biology -- Research 5. College teachers 6. Conservation biology 7. Fear 8. Fear in animals 9. Predation (Biology)
ISBN 978-0-226-04363-0; 0-226-04363-0

LC 2008-00418

This is "an engaging book about how an understanding of predator-prey dynamics can inform conservation biology." Times Higher Ed

Includes bibliographical references (p. 287-292)

Boysen, Sarah Till

The **smartest** animals on the planet; with a contribution from Deborah Custance. Firefly Books 2009 192p il map $35   **591.5**

1. Animal behavior 2. Animal intelligence
ISBN 978-1-5540-7456-3; 1-5540-7456-8

"Succinctly written and sumptuously illustrated with photographs and diagrams, this appealing book is sure to fascinate the general reader and inspire the science student considering a career in animal behavior or cognition." Libr J

Grandin, Temple

★ **Animals** in translation; using the mysteries of autism to decode animal behavior. [by] Temple Grandin and Catherine Johnson. Scribner 2010 356p $28; ebook $18.99   **591.5**

1. Animal behavior 2. Autism
ISBN 978-1-4391-8710-4; 978-1-4391-3084-1 ebook

"This fascinating book will teach readers to see as animals see, to be a little more visual and a little less verbal, and, as a unique analysis of animal behavior, it belongs in all libraries." Booklist

Includes bibliographical references

Griffin, Donald Redfield

Animal minds; beyond cognition to consciousness. {by} Donald R. Griffin. {Rev and expanded}; University of Chicago Press 2001 355p $27.50 **591.5**

1. Animal behavior 2. Animal psychology 3. Cognition in animals
ISBN 0-226-30865-0

LC 00-10006

"Griffin's book will enlighten, delight and even ruffle some feathers." Publ Wkly

Includes bibliographical references (p.) and index

Linden, Eugene

The **octopus** and the orangutan; more true tales of animal intrigue, intelligence, and ingenuity. Dutton 2002 242p $23.95; pa $14   **591.5**

1. Animal behavior 2. Animal intelligence
ISBN 0-525-94661-6; 0-452-28411-2 pa

LC 2002-67434

"Linden's chatty writing style, along with the science behind the stories that he occasionally slips in, makes for entertaining and enlightening reading." Booklist

Includes bibliographical references

Masson, J. Moussaieff

★ **When** elephants weep; the emotional lives of animals. {by} Jeffrey Moussaieff Masson and Susan McCarthy. Delacorte Press 1995 xxiii, 291p il hardcover o.p. pa $15.95   **591.5**

1. Animal behavior 2. Animal intelligence 3. Animal welfare 4. Comparative psychology
ISBN 0-385-31428-0 pa

LC 94-23819

The authors gather "the evidence to date for the existence of emotions and, hence, something approaching human consciousness in animals. . . . Masson and McCarthy do a commendable job of synthesizing the material they tackle . . . making it efficiently readable." Booklist

Includes bibliographical references

The **pig** who sang to the moon; the emotional world of farm animals. {by} Jeffrey Moussaieff Masson. Ballantine Books 2003 277p il $25.95; pa $13.95 **591.5**

1. Animal intelligence 2. Domestic animals 3. Domestic animals -- Behavior 4. Emotions in animals
ISBN 0-345-45281-X; 0-345-45282-8 pa

LC 2003-61773

"Masson is passionate in his beliefs, and a strong thread of animal rights runs through his entire narrative. Readers not convinced by his philosophy will learn quite a bit about the animals we mostly take for granted." Booklist

Includes bibliographical references

McCarthy, Susan

★ **Becoming** a tiger; how baby animals learn to live in the wild. HarperCollins 2004 418p hardcover o.p. pa $13.95 **591.5**

1. Animal behavior 2. Animal intelligence 3. Animals -- Infancy 4. Learning in animals
ISBN 0-06-620924-2; 0-06-093484-0 pa

LC 2003-67553

"McCarthy writes clearly and her penchant for humor . . . makes the book an easy read, both for students of learning and those who can't get enough of television's Animal Planet." Publ Wkly

Includes bibliographical references

Smoller, Jordan

The **other** side of normal; how biology is providing the clues to unlock the secrets of normal and abnormal behavior. Jordan Smoller. HarperCollins 2012 390 p. **591.5**

1. American Psychiatric Association 2. Behavior genetics 3. Biological psychiatry 4. Mental illness -- Diagnosis 5. Norm (Philosophy) 6. Psychology -- General 7. Psychobiology 8. Scientific literature
ISBN 0061492191; 9780061492198; 9780061492204

LC 2011040827

In this book, "[t]he author uses the 2010 announcement by the American Psychiatric Association of provisional plans to revise the Diagnostic and Statistical Manual of Mental Disorders as an opportunity to revisit the hot-button issue of what constitutes mental disease. In his opinion, one of the shortcomings of the DSM is its creation of 'categories from constellations of symptoms' without understanding how they connect to the 'functional organization of the mind and brain.'" (Kirkus)

Weiner, Jonathan

Time, love, memory; a great biologist and his quest for the origins of behavior. Knopf 1999 300p il $27.50; pa $14 **591.5**

1. Behavior genetics 2. Biophysicists 3. College teachers 4. Neuroscientists
ISBN 0-679-44435-1; 0-679-76390-2 pa

LC 98-43128

An exploration of the work of "one of the unsung pioneers of molecular biology: brash, eccentric physicist-turned-biologist Seymour Benzer. By studying tiny genetic mutations in the fruit fly, Benzer seeks to shed light on the question of whether genes determine behavior. Weiner . . . presents an elegant scientific detective story." Publ Wkly

Includes bibliographical references

Wynne, Clive D. L.

Do animals think? Princeton University Press 2004 268p il $26.95 **591.5**

1. Animal intelligence 2. Consciousness in animals
ISBN 0-691-11311-4

LC 2003-60019

The author "shows how bats, bees, pigeons, and dolphins perceive their worlds quite differently from the way humans do. . . . Readers will delight in this insightful, well-referenced book." Choice

Includes bibliographical references

★ Encyclopedia of animal behavior; edited by Marc Bekoff; foreword by Jane Goodall. Greenwood Press 2004 3v il set $349.95 **591.5**

1. Animal behavior
ISBN 0-313-32745-9

LC 2004-56073

This encyclopedia describes "what makes animals tick using techniques that range from molecular approaches to analysis of species. The 300 entries, some stretching to 7000 words, discuss topics as diverse as concept learning in pigeons and stress in dolphins." Libr J

Includes bibliographical references

591.56 Behavior relating to life cycle

Bagemihl, Bruce

Biological exuberance; animal homosexuality and natural diversity. illustrated by John Megahan. St. Martin's Press 1999 751p il map $40; pa $21.95 **591.56**

1. Animal behavior 2. Homosexuality
ISBN 0-312-19239-8; 0-312-25377-X pa

LC 98-28528

The author "challenges the belief that homosexuality is an aberration in nature by revealing the documented homosexual or transgendered behavior of 450 animal species. Contesting the idea that scarcity and functionality are the primary agents of biological change, biologist Bagemihl persuasively argues that abundance and extravagance are just as crucial to the mosaic of life." Publ Wkly

Includes bibliographical references

Wilcove, David S.

No way home; the decline of the world's great animal migrations. with illustrations by Louise Zemaitis. Island Press/Shearwater Books 2008 253p il map $24.95 **591.56**

1. Animal migration 2. Animals -- Migration 3. Endangered ecosystems 4. Environmental degradation
ISBN 978-1-55963-985-9; 1-55963-985-7

LC 2007-26205

"Absorbing and thought provoking, [this work] deserves to be widely read and used to promote conservation action." Science

Includes bibliographical references

Zuk, M.

Sexual selections; what we can and can't learn about sex from animals. {by} Marlene Zuk. University of Calif. Press 2002 239p il $40; pa $16.95   **591.56**

1. Sexual behavior in animals

ISBN 0-520-21974-0; 0-520-24075-8 pa

LC 2001-5771

"Fascinating and persuasive. Zuk is not an idealogue, just an unusually clear-eyed scholar." N Y Times Book Rev

Includes bibliographical references (p.)

591.59   Communication

Friend, Tim

Animal talk; breaking the codes of animal language. Free Press 2004 274p il $25; pa $15 **591.59**

1. Animal communication

ISBN 0-7432-0157-4; 0-7432-0158-2 pa

LC 2003-63107

"The author describes the methods of, and reasons behind, animal communication and demonstrates that human and animal communication are not so widely disparate as once believed. Friend also gives background details on the basics of communication theory, genetics, evolution, and the progression of scientific thought regarding animal communication. . . . His humorous and engaging prose style makes this a captivating read." Libr J

Includes bibliographical references

591.6   Miscellaneous nontaxonomic kinds of animals

Grice, Gordon

Deadly kingdom; the book of dangerous animals. Dial Press 2010 xxv, 324p il $27; ebook $27 **591.6**

1. Dangerous animals

ISBN 978-0-385-33562-1; 978-0-385-33562-1 ebook

LC 2009-33933

Describes the author's lifelong obsession with dangerous animals that prompted his amateur studies with virtually all dangerous creatures, from sharks and bears to alligators and spiders.

"This darkly fascinating book might add a few words to your vocabulary: anthropophagy (the eating of humans), or the verb to flense (to strip off skin). . . . Grice was clearly the sort of kid who left the house at dawn with a packed lunch and a bag full of bug jars. He peppers Deadly Kingdom with his own stories, and defends animals as only behaving as they are meant to." Maclean's

Includes bibliographical references

Quammen, David

★ **Monster** of God; the man-eating predator in the jungles of history and the mind. Norton 2003 513p maps $26.95; pa $15.95   **591.6**

1. Dangerous animals 2. Endangered species 3. Predatory animals

ISBN 0-393-05140-4; 0-393-32609-8 pa

LC 2003-7812

"Rich with personal stories that clarify humanity's true place in the universe, this book will leave the reader eager for more. . . . This has all the makings of a science book of the year. Highly recommended." Libr J

Includes bibliographical references

Todd, Kim

Tinkering with Eden; a natural history of exotics in America. illustrations by Claire Emery. Norton 2001 302p il hardcover o.p. pa $15.95   **591.6**

1. Animal introduction 2. Introduced animals -- United States

ISBN 0-393-32324-2 pa

LC 00-58740

"Exotics include such now prosaic, nonnative bird species as starlings, pigeons, and house sparrows. Todd's intriguing history of their introduction in the U.S., some deliberate . . . others accidental, develops into an essential look at the unexpected and, all too often, unwelcome impact exotics have on the ecosystem in which they thrive." Booklist

Includes bibliographical references

591.68   Rare and endangered animals

Weidensaul, Scott

The ghost with trembling wings; science, wishful thinking, and the search for lost species. North Point Press 2002 341p il maps $26; pa $15 **591.68**

1. Extinct animals 2. Rare animals 3. Rare plants

ISBN 0-374-24664-5; 0-86547-668-3 pa

LC 2001-54605

"Weidensaul is a graceful writer who works an amazing amount of scientific theory into his narrative." Booklist

Includes bibliographical references

591.7   Animal ecology, animals characteristic of specific environments

Heinrich, Bernd

Life everlasting; the animal way of death. Bernd Heinrich. Houghton Mifflin Harcourt 2012 xiv, 236 p.p   **591.7**

1. Animal behavior 2. Animal communication 3. Animal ecology 4. Animal life cycles 5. Animals -- Psychological aspects 6. Biodegradation 7. Nature -- Animals -- General 8. Nonfiction 9. Science -- Life Sciences -- Zoology -- Entomology

ISBN 0547752660; 9780547752662

LC 2012010583

This book explores the taboos and relevance of scavengers, the life-giving links that keep nature's systems humming along smoothly. After a friend asked if he could be buried on the author's woodland property in Maine, he re-examined his curiosity with the natural world . . . [Bernd] Heinrich presents five major sections outlining how bodies and plants are recycled and broken down: small to large . .

. north to south . . . plant undertakers . . . watery deaths . . . and changes (metamorphosis and death rituals). Above all, temperature affects how and what breaks down carrion as the flies and insects of summer are replaced by various birds in the winter. The author also tracks how trees decompose, a process that often begins before they die. (Kirkus Reviews)

Summer world; a season of bounty. Ecco 2009 253p il $26.95 **591.7**
1. Animal behavior 2. Animals 3. College teachers 4. Entomologists 5. Summer 6. Zoologists
ISBN 978-0-06-074217-1; 0-06-074217-8

A discussion of animal survival in the hot season explores the ways in which animals make the most of the summer's short span by efficiently compacting most of their procreative and survival activities.

"Heinrich presents natural science at its engaging best." Kirkus

Includes bibliographical references

Naskrecki, Piotr

The **smaller** majority; the hidden world of the animals that dominate the tropics. Belknap Press of Harvard University Press 2005 278p il $35 **591.7**
1. Animals -- Pictorial works 2. Animals -- Tropics 3. Invertebrates 4. Invertebrates -- Tropics
ISBN 0-674-01915-6; 978-0-674-01915-7
LC 2005-46060

"Naskrecki's exuberant, expert knowledge of this microscopic world has been distilled down to the most arresting details. Crisp, enjoyable prose, clearly explains complex biological processes." Publ Wkly

Includes bibliographical references

Zimmer, Carl

★ **Parasite** rex; inside the bizarre world of nature's most dangerous creatures. Free Press 2000 xxii, 298p il hardcover o.p. pa $14 **591.7**
1. Parasites
ISBN 0-7432-0011-X pa
LC 00-37593

This is a chronicle of the effects of parasites on plants and animals.

"The importance of Zimmer's book lies not only in its accessible presentation of the new science of evolutionary parasitology but in its thoughtful treatment of the global strategies and policies that scientists, health workers and governments will have to consider in order to manage parasites in the future." N Y Times Book Rev

Includes bibliographical references

591.9 Animals by specific continents, countries, localities

Bambaradeniya, Channa N. B.

The **illustrated** atlas of wildlife; [by] Channa Bambaradeniya [et al.] University of California Press 2009 288p il map $39.95 **591.9**
1. Atlases 2. Biogeography 3. Reference books 4.

Zoogeography
ISBN 978-0-520-25785-6; 0-520-25785-5
LC 2008-40625

"This gorgeous book, featuring detailed, customized maps and more than 800 photographs . . . and original artworks, presents a spectacular visual survey of wild animals across the globe and describes in detail their habitats, physical characteristics, diet, and behavior. . . . [It also includes] conservation and preservation data, information about human impact upon the world's complex ecosystems, and chronicles of the evolution and adaptation of animals over the ages." Education Digest

Includes glossary and bibliographical references

592 Specific taxonomic groups of animals

Attenborough, David

Life in the undergrowth. Princeton University Press 2006 288p il $29.95 **592**
1. Invertebrates
ISBN 0-691-12703-4
LC 2005-934727

"This wonderful exploration of invertebrates exceeds the requirements for a great nature book through the strength of its photographs and the quality of its prose." Publ Wkly

Hubbell, Sue

Waiting for Aphrodite; journeys into the time before bones. with illustrations by Liddy Hubbell. Houghton Mifflin 1999 242p il $24; pa $13 **592**
1. Invertebrates
ISBN 0-395-83703-0; 0-618-05684-X pa
LC 98-49811

"These essays on natural history discuss everything from the orange-humped crickets that are unique to Missouri and the iridescent butterflies of Costa Rica to the furry sea mice that live in the coastal waters near the writer's new house, in Maine. Hubbell is both a delighted home scientist and a glinting memoirist, and her observations are interspersed with accounts of her fresh life in the East." New Yorker

Includes bibliographical references and index

Stewart, Amy

The **earth** moved; on the remarkable achievements of earthworms. Algonquin Bks. 2004 223p $23.95; pa $12.95 **592**
1. Earthworms 2. Worms
ISBN 1-56512-337-9; 1-56512-468-5 pa
LC 2003-52379

The author explores "the impact worms have on humans and on our planet. . . . {She} educates on the vital roles these creatures play in growing crops, how they can neutralize the effects of nuclear waste on soil, and their ability to regenerate new body parts. . . . A book that's as enlightening as it is entertaining." SLJ

Includes bibliographical references

594   Mollusks and molluscoids

Ellis, Richard

The **search** for the giant squid. Penguin Bks. 1999 322p il pa $14.95   **594**

1. Squids

ISBN 0-14-028676-4; 978-0-14-028676-2

LC 98-10436

"Some of the appeal of this book is visual, as it presents 30 b&w photographs and 35 line drawings, many historical, several of the drawings by Ellis himself." Publ Wkly

Includes bibliographical references

Harasewych, M. G.

The **book** of shells; a life-size guide to identifying and classifying six hundred seashells. [by] M.G. Harasewych & Fabio Moretzsohn. University of Chicago Press 2010 655p il map $55   **594**

1. Mollusks 2. Reference books 3. Shells

ISBN 978-0-226-31577-5; 0-226-31577-0

LC 2009-34321

This book "provides an excellent introduction to the major classes of sea-living mollusks worldwide. Students and the lay enthusiast will find the 600 entries accessible and engaging. . . . A table lists the family, shell-size range, distribution, abundance, depth, habitat, feeding habit, and the presence or absence of an operculum. A color range map, genus and species and common name, a paragraph-long description of the species, a listing of related species, a color life-size illustration, and, for small shells, a larger, more detailed image complete the information." Booklist

Includes bibliographical references

595   Arthropods

Fortey, Richard

Horseshoe crabs and velvet worms; the story of the animals and plants that time has left behind. by Richard Fortey. Alfred A. Knopf 2012 320 p.   **595**

1. Arthropoda -- Conservation 2. Invertebrates -- Conservation 3. Limulus polyphemus -- Conservation 4. Plant conservation 5. Worms

ISBN 9780307263612

LC 2011039941

Written by paleontologist Richard Fortey, this book [is] about living creatures, about the old-timers, the survivors, the organisms and ecologies that, he writes, have survived many mass extinction events and are messengers from deep geological time. In this book the author travels the planet, looking at life forms that, as Darwin wrote, may almost be called living fossils. These include not just horseshoe crabs and velvet worms, which live in dead trees, but algae mats, lungfish, musk oxen, various herbs, sponges, jellyfish, clams and cockroaches. The life forms nothing can seem to kill. (N Y Times)

595.4   Chelicerates

Beccaloni, Jan

Arachnids. University of California Press 2009 320p il $39.95   **595.4**

1. Arachnida 2. Mites 3. Spiders 4. Ticks

ISBN 978-0-520-26140-2; 0-520-26140-2

LC 2009-18657

"This book is overflowing with scientific data and crystal-clear images of strange insects that are certain to make your skin crawl. Free of myths and misconceptions, this book delivers the real facts on the diverse arachnid family which includes a wide variety of scorpions, ticks, mites, and over 38,000 species of spiders. They vary from bizarre to beautiful and a few are even deadly but all are interesting and sure to spark your imagination." Shutterbug

Includes bibliographical references

595.7   Insects

Alcock, John

In a desert garden; love and death among the insects. with illustrations by Turid Forsyth. Norton 1997 186p il $27.50   **595.7**

1. Desert animals 2. Desert ecology 3. Insects 4. Natural history -- Arizona

ISBN 0-393-04118-2

LC 97-589

The focus of this "work is the author's own front yard in Tempe, Arizona, and its insect inhabitants. . . . Readers will gain insights into how science is practiced as the author's lively, often humorous observations of assorted beetles, bugs, wasps, bees, caterpillars, and butterflies are related to broad concepts of animal behavior, ecology, and survival." Libr J

Includes bibliographical references

Brock, James P.

★ **Kaufman** field guide to butterflies of North America; [by] Jim P. Brock and Kenn Kaufman; with the collaboration of Rick and Nora Bowers and Lynn Hassler. Houghton Mifflin 2006 391p il map pa $19.95   **595.7**

1. Butterflies

ISBN 0-618-76826-2; 978-0-618-76826-4

LC 2006-287515

"Each species is listed by common name and scientific name and receives a several-sentence description, including flight time and larval food plants. All except very local or accidental species also are shown on range maps. The illustrations are opposite the written description, with most species pictured in multiple images. . . . The illustrations are created by digital enhancement of photographs. . . . An essential purchase for all libraries." Booklist [review of 2003 edition]

Capinera, John L.

Field guide to grasshoppers, crickets, and katydids of the United States; [by] John L. Capinera, Ralph D. Scott, and Thomas J. Walker. Cornell University Press 2004 249p il maps hardcover o.p. pa $29.95 **595.7**

1. Crickets 2. Grasshoppers 3. Katydids
ISBN 0-8014-4260-5; 0-8014-8948-2 pa

LC 2004-10727

"The highlight is certainly the 50 pages of Scott's color illustrations. . . . For those who want to know what's plaguing them when locusts descend, this is the book." Publ Wkly
Includes bibliographical references

Carde, Ring T.

Encyclopedia of insects; editors, Vincent H. Resh, Ring T. Cardé. 2nd ed; Elsevier/Academic Press 2009 xxxiii, 1132p il map $120 **595.7**

1. Insects -- Encyclopedias 2. Reference books
ISBN 978-0-12-374144-8

This book covers "all aspects of insect anatomy, physiology, evolution, behavior, reproduction, ecology, and disease, as well as issues of exploitation, conservation, and management." Publisher's note
Includes bibliographical references

Eisner, Thomas

For love of insects. Belknap Press of Harvard University Press 2003 448p il $35; pa $19.95 **595.7**

1. Insects
ISBN 0-674-01181-3; 0-674-01827-3 pa

LC 2003-44399

"Ranging from a caterpillar who feeds on flowers while disguising as one by affixing petals to his back, to a beetle who can resist a pull 200 times his own weight, the book is full of little known information about how insects feed, fight, and reproduce." Univ Press Books for Public and Second Sch Libr, 2006
Includes bibliographical references

★ **Secret** weapons; defenses of insects, spiders, scorpions, and other many-legged creatures. [by] Thomas Eisner, Maria Eisner, Melody V.S. Siegler. Belknap Press of Harvard University Press 2005 372p il $29.95; pa $18.95 **595.7**

1. Animal defenses 2. Arachnida 3. Insects 4. Spiders
ISBN 0-674-01882-6; 0-674-02403-6 pa

LC 2005-41042

"This very readable and well-illustrated book will appeal to all those interested in disciplines like biology, entomology, and ecology." Choice
Includes bibliographical references

Ellis, Hattie

Sweetness & light; the mysterious history of the honeybee. Harmony Books 2004 243p il hardcover o.p. pa $13.95 **595.7**

1. Bee culture 2. Beekeeping 3. Bees 4. Honeybee
ISBN 1-4000-5405-2; 1-4000-5406-0 pa

LC 2004-4116

"What a delightful volume on the honeybee this is: Not only is the reader treated to a wealth of information on the biology, ecology, and economic importance of that insect, but

the interrelationship of the honeybee and humanity throughout history is very nicely presented." Sci Books Films
Includes bibliographical references

Evans, Arthur V.

An **inordinate** fondness for beetles; [by] Arthur V. Evans, Charles L. Bellamy; photography by Lisa Charles Watson; illustrations by Patricia Wynne. University of California Press 2000 208p il pa $31.95 **595.7**

1. Beetles 2. Beetles -- Pictorial works
ISBN 0-520-22323-3; 978-0-520-22323-3

LC 99-46118

"The incredible full-color photographs bring readers up close without a magnifying lens at hand, and the seemingly infinite variations within the species due to size, structure, and color are easily seen. . . . While the text is scientific, it is very readable." SLJ
Includes bibliographical references

Himmelman, John

Cricket radio; tuning in the night-singing insects. Belknap Press of Harvard University Press 2011 254p il $22.95 **595.7**

1. Crickets 2. Katydids
ISBN 978-0-674-04690-0

LC 2010-35203

The author explores "what moves crickets and katydids to sing, how they produce their distinctive sounds, how they hear the songs of others, and how they vary cadence, volume, and pitch to attract potential mates, warn off competitors, and evade predators." Publisher's note
Includes bibliographical references

Hölldobler, Bert

The **leafcutter** ants; civilization by instinct. [by] Bert Hölldobler and Edward O. Wilson. Norton 2010 160p il pa $19.95 **595.7**

1. Ants
ISBN 978-0-393-33868-3

LC 2010-16202

The authors "introduce the general reader to earth's most evolved animal society. With the colony's queen as its reproductive organ; the various ages and types of workers as the brain, heart, and other organs; and the communication among the ants similar to the communication of nerves and ganglia, a leafcutter ant colony can be truly considered as a superorganism." Booklist
Includes bibliographical references

The **superorganism**; the beauty, elegance, and strangeness of insect societies. [by] Bert Hölldobler and Edward O. Wilson; line drawings by Margaret C. Nelson. W.W. Norton & Company 2009 xxi, 522p il $55 **595.7**

1. Insect societies 2. Insects
ISBN 978-0-393-06704-0; 0-393-06704-1

LC 2008-38547

"This study covers mathematical analysis as well as field data, but in a straightforward manner that guides readers from one remarkable fact or concept to the next, inspiring wonder at the origin of our own societies." Publ Wkly

Includes bibliographical references

Keller, Laurent

The **lives** of ants; by Laurent Keller and Élisabeth Gordon; translated by James Grieve. Oxford University Press 2009 252p il $27.95; pa $15.95   **595.7**

1. Ants

ISBN 978-0-19-954186-7; 0-19-954186-8; 978-0-19-954187-4 pa; 0-19-954187-6 pa

LC 2008-943416

The authors "provide a lucid . . . overview of any evolution, ecology, biology, behavior, and genetics that easily communicates complex research in these areas to a wide audience." Sci Books Films

Includes bibliographical references

Laufer, Peter

The **dangerous** world of butterflies; the startling subculture of criminals, collectors, and conservationists. Lyons Press 2009 271p $24.95   **595.7**

1. Butterflies

ISBN 978-1-59921-555-6; 1-59921-555-1

LC 2009-03115

"Laufer wants you to do more than just love them; he wants you to have some notion of the extraordinary circumstances which butterflies live through every day, whether it is as part of a hotly contested captive breeding program, or a participant in a thousand-mile, five year Monarch migration, or death at the hands of the sinister traders in endangered insect species. . . . So consider yourself warned: The Dangerous World of Butterflies might change the way you notice the world. For a book such as this, that's the highest praise of all." PopMatters

Includes bibliographical references

Milne, Lorus Johnson

The **Audubon** Society field guide to North American insects and spiders; [by] Lorus and Margery Milne; visual key by Susan Rayfield. Knopf 1980 989p il $19.95   **595.7**

1. Insects 2. Spiders

ISBN 0-394-50763-0

LC 80-7620

The authors "have based their field guide on 702 excellent color photographs (75 of which are of spiders and other arachnids). In addition to some general information, the text (two thirds of the book) is made up of brief comments on each kind of arthropod pictured." Choice

Includes glossary

Moffett, Mark W.

Adventures among ants; a global safari with a cast of trillions. University of California Press 2010 280p il $29.95   **595.7**

1. Ants 2. Ants -- Behavior 3. Ants -- Ecology

ISBN 978-0-520-26199-0; 0-520-26199-2

LC 2009-40610

"This superb book by a first-class writer with an unsurpassed feel for ants begins at the ground level as we come face to face with the creatures, move into their minds, and

begin to understand what makes them tick. Moffett organizes his text around six ant lifestyles, each represented by an insect that dominates its habitat: Indian Marauder ants, African army ants, African Weaver ants, Amazon slavemaking ants, Neotropical leaf cutter ants, and the Argentine ant, a global invader. . . . This marvelous volume illustrated with the author's closeup photographs will delight biologists, naturalists, and general readers with a natural history bent." Libr J

Includes bibliographical references

Pyle, Robert Michael

★ The **Audubon** Society field guide to North American butterflies; visual key by Carol Nehring and Jane Opper. Knopf 1981 916p il $19.95 **595.7**

1. Butterflies

ISBN 0-394-51914-0

LC 80-84240

This guide "introduces more than 600 species of North American butterfly, including those native to the Hawaiian Islands. A section of brilliant color plates (more than 1,000 of them) featuring butterflies in their natural habitats, follows a general introduction and notes on text organization and use." Booklist

Mariposa road; the first butterfly big year. Houghton Mifflin Harcourt 2010 558p il map $27   **595.7**

1. Authors 2. Butterflies 3. Butterflies -- North America 4. Ecologists 5. Insects -- Migration 6. Writers on nature

ISBN 978-0-618-94539-9

LC 2010-5763

"This is engaging writing—always compelling, always approachable; it should inspire all of us to set out on our own long quests on the road." Sci Books Films

Raffles, Hugh

Insectopedia. Pantheon Books 2010 465p il $29.95   **595.7**

1. Human-animal relationships 2. Insects

ISBN 978-0-375-42386-4; 0-375-42386-9

LC 2009-24302

"In addition to the fine writing, Raffles includes many intriguing drawings and illustrations, as well as a fascinating Notes section. Because of his manner of organization, there is little reason to read the book in order; you can simply open it anywhere and discover a new way to reflect on not only insects but people." Seattle Times

Includes bibliographical references

Schappert, Phil

The **last** Monarch butterfly; conserving the Monarch butterfly in a brave new world. Firefly Books 2004 113p il pa $19.95   **595.7**

1. Monarch butterflies 2. Monarch butterfly 3. Wildlife conservation

ISBN 1-55297-969-5

LC 2005-357220

Overview of both eastern and western monarch butterflies, including their life cycle and migratory patterns. The impact of natural disasters and increasing residential and industrial development on monarch butterfly populations is also discussed.

"The narrative is enhanced by beautiful photographs and backed up by some 180 references to the scientific literature. . . . Let's hear it for the monarch, an amazing insect; if the reader has any doubts about that, this book will put them to rest." Sci Books Films

Stokes, Donald W.

The **butterfly** book; an easy guide to butterfly gardening, identification, and behavior. {by} Donald and Lillian Stokes and Ernest Williams. Little, Brown 1991 95p il maps pa $12.95 **595.7**
1. Butterflies
ISBN 0-316-81780-5

LC 91-15323

This book discusses plants which will attract butterflies, explains butterfly life cycles and behavior, and provides information for identification of over 140 species

Waldbauer, Gilbert

Insects through the seasons. Harvard Univ. Press 1996 289p il $27.50; pa $14.95 **595.7**
1. Cecropia moth 2. Insects 3. Moths 4. Seasons
ISBN 0-674-45488-X; 0-674-45489-8 pa

LC 95-35171

"The scientific information is excellent and the writing is fascinating." Sci Books Films
Includes bibliographical references

Millions of monarchs, bunches of beetles; how bugs find strength in numbers. Harvard Univ. Press 2000 264p il $27.50; pa $16.95 **595.7**
1. Insects 2. Insects -- Behavior 3. Social behavior in animals
ISBN 0-674-00090-0; 0-674-00686-0 pa

LC 99-42453

The author "examines many of the reasons that insects form groups. . . . Insects come together for a host of reasons, Waldbauer explains: to find mates, to avoid predators, to enhance their food-gathering abilities, to manipulate their environment and to subdue prey. In each case, Waldbauer provides evocative descriptions of particular species' behaviors while discussing the underlying evolutionary reasons for that behavior." Publ Wkly
Includes bibliographical references

★ **What** good are bugs? insects in the web of life. Harvard University Press 2003 384p il hardcover o.p. pa $17.50 **595.7**
1. Insects 2. Insects -- Ecology
ISBN 0-674-01027-2; 0-674-01632-7 pa

LC 2002-27335

This "is an excellent work about the beneficial insects, that vast majority of insect species of which we are generally unaware. . . . The author is an excellent writer and provides many interesting examples." Choice
Includes bibliographical references

Zuk, Marlene

Sex on six legs; lessons on life, love, and language from the insect world. [by] Marlene Zuk. Houghton Mifflin Harcourt 2011 262p $25 **595.7**
1. Insects 2. Sexual behavior in animals
ISBN 978-0-15-101373-9

LC 2010025829

"In Zuk's breezy style, disquisitions on the mating habits of damselflies or the genetics of fruit flies are made surprisingly palatable—and they yield unexpected insights into human interactions. Zuk approaches her subject with such humor and enthusiasm for the intricacies of insect life, even bug-phobes will relish her account." Publ Wkly
Includes bibliographical references

The **monarch** butterfly; biology & conservation. edited by Karen S. Oberhauser & Michelle J. Solensky. Cornell University Press 2004 248p il maps $39.95 **595.7**
1. Monarch butterflies 2. Monarch butterfly 3. Wildlife conservation
ISBN 0-8014-4188-9

LC 2004-884

"Covered is every facet of monarch breeding, migration, and overwintering, as well as population modeling and management. . . . The text is clearly written, and the mathematical formulas included in certain chapters are not essential to understanding the main ideas. The most up-to-date and comprehensive publication on monarch butterfly biology, this will be an important reference tool." Libr J
Includes bibliographical references

595.77   Flies (Diptera) and fleas

Spielman, A.

Mosquito; a natural history of man's most persistent and deadly foe. {by} Andrew Spielman and Michael D'Antonio. Hyperion 2001 247p il maps hardcover o.p. pa $12 **595.77**
1. Mosquitoes 2. Mosquitoes as carriers of disease
ISBN 0-7868-8667-6 pa

LC 2001-16815

The authors tell us about the mosquito's "life cycle, its natural enemies and predators, and, of course, its monumental impact on human history. . . . This is truly an unexpected delight, an informative, entertaining, and sometimes skin-crawly book that should appeal to anyone with a taste for popular science." Booklist

595.79   Hymenoptera

Holldobler, Bert

Journey to the ants; a story of scientific exploration. {by} Bert Hölldobler and Edward O. Wilson. Belknap Press 1994 228p il $27.50; pa $16.95 **595.79**
1. Ants
ISBN 0-674-48525-4; 0-674-48526-2 pa

LC 94-13386

"A skillful blend of natural lore, autobiography, and history." Libr J

The **ants**; [by] Bert Hölldobler and Edward O. Wilson. Belknap Press 1990 732p il $95 **595.79**
1. Ants
ISBN 0-674-04075-9
LC 89-30653
"Science is rarely good literature. 'The Ants' is an exalting exception." N Y Times Book Rev
Includes bibliographical references

597 Cold-blooded vertebrates

Behnke, Robert J.
★ **Trout** and salmon of North America; illustrated by Joseph R. Tomelleri; foreword by Thomas McGuane; introduction by Donald S. Proebstel; edited by George Scott. Free Press 2002 359p il maps $40 **597**
1. Salmon 2. Salmon -- North America 3. Trout 4. Trout -- North America
ISBN 0-7432-2220-2
LC 2002-69256
"Along with full and clearly written scientific explanations, statistics and analysis, the author provides anecdotal and historical details that make this not just a field guide, but a fascinating read for those interested in the natural world." Publ Wkly
Includes bibliographical references

Compagno, Leonard J. V.
Sharks of the world; [by] Leonard Compagno, Marc Dando, Sarah Fowler. Princeton University Press 2005 368p il map hardcover o.p. pa $29.95 **597**
1. Sharks
ISBN 0-691-12071-4; 0-691-12072-2 pa
LC 2004-111901
The authors cover "over 450 species, including many as-yet-unnamed species and some that are only known from a single specimen. Each is illustrated with both a line drawing and a beautifully rendered color painting; in most cases a ventral view of the head and illustrations of the teeth are included. . . . Packed with information, this is an invaluable guide for anyone interested in this fascinating group." Choice
Includes bibliographical references

Eilperin, Juliet
Demon fish; travels through the hidden world of sharks. Pantheon Books 2011 xxi, 295p il $26.95 **597**
1. Sharks
ISBN 978-0-375-42512-7
LC 2010-30264
Eilperin "describes her travels throughout Asia, South Africa, and the United States in search of shark information and folklore. . . . The author provides a well-written overview of current and past attitudes toward sharks and

discusses shark species, physiology, genetics, reproduction, evolution, navigation, and attacks on swimmers." Libr J
Includes bibliographical references

Ellis, Richard
Great white shark; [by] Richard Ellis and John E. McCosker; with photographs by Al Giddings and others, and paintings by Richard Ellis. HarperCollins 1991 270p il map hardcover o.p. pa $37.95 **597**
1. Sharks
ISBN 0-8047-2529-2 pa
LC 89-46528
The authors discuss the great white shark's "unique biology (it's warm blooded), size, distribution, and evolution. They also describe the sport of shark fishing and the efforts . . . [to save] the white from threats of extinction. Handsomely illustrated with Ellis's paintings and many simply awesome photographs, . . . the text has enough scientific fact for armchair icthyologists but not enough to confuse the casual reader." Libr J
Includes bibliographical references

Gilbert, Carter Rowell
★ **National** Audubon Society field guide to fishes, North America; [by] Carter R. Gilbert, James D. Williams. rev ed, 2nd ed, fully rev; Alfred A. Knopf 2002 607p il maps pa $19.95 **597**
1. Fishes -- North America
ISBN 0-375-41224-7
LC 2002-20773
This guide covers over 600 freshwater and saltwater species in detail, with notes on 771 more species.

McPhee, John A.
The **founding** fish; {by} John McPhee. Farrar, Straus & Giroux 2002 358p $25; pa $14 **597**
1. American shad 2. Shad 3. Shad fishing -- North America -- History
ISBN 0-374-10444-1; 0-374-52883-7 pa
LC 2002-25012
"McPhee is in great form here, as informative as always but also funny, unusually self-revealing, and quite passionate." Booklist

Page, Lawrence M.
★ **Peterson** field guide to freshwater fishes of North America north of Mexico; [by] Lawrence M. Page, Brooks M. Burr; illustrations by Eugene C. Beckham III . . . [et al.]; maps by Griffin E. Sheehy. 2nd ed.; Houghton Mifflin Harcourt 2011 663p il map pa $21 **597**
1. Fishes -- North America
ISBN 978-0-547-24206-4; 0-547-24206-9
LC 2010-49219
This guide to identifying different species of freshwater fish in North America includes "maps and information showing where to locate each species of fish—whether that species can be found in miles-long stretches of river or small pools that cover only dozens of square feet." Publisher's note
Includes glossary and bibliographical references

Pepperell, Julian G.

Fishes of the open ocean; a natural history & illustrated guide. illustrated by Guy Harvey. University of Chicago Press 2010 266p il map $35 **597**
1. Fishes 2. Marine ecology 3. Marine fishes
ISBN 978-0-226-65539-0; 0-226-65539-3

LC 2009032290

This book "details the biology and brief ecology of various open-ocean fishes. The first half of the book details the importance of pelagic fish in the oceans, the food web of oceanic life, and the relationship between form (fish shape) and function, along with a historical perspective of interactions between fish and humans. The second half of the book illustrates the distribution range, migratory patterns and behavior, reproductive patterns, and trophic information of various fishes. . . . the book is not exhaustive in detail, it provides a very useful overall description of various fishes and their life in the oceans." Choice

Includes bibliographical references

Prosek, James

Eels; an exploration, from New Zealand to the Sargasso, of the world's most amazing and mysterious fish. Harper 2010 287p il map **597**
1. Eels 2. Maori (New Zealand people) 3. Religion and sociology
ISBN 0-06-05661-6; 978-0-06-056611-1

LC 2010-06803

This is an account of the "life history and cultural associations of the freshwater eel." (Publisher's note)

This is "much more than a fish book. It is an impassioned defense of nature itself, rescued from the tired rhetoric of 1970s-style environmentalism by good, honest shoe-leather reporting. And yet it contains the untainted germ of Age-of-Aquarius eco-consciousness by centering on an essential question: Does a tidy scientific analysis of a creature really tell us all we need to know, or are there numinous qualities to every life-form that require a different kind of meditation?" N Y Times Book Rev

Includes bibliographical references

Rigney, Matt

In pursuit of giants; one man's global search for the last of the great fish. Matt Rigney. Viking 2012 336 p. ill., map $26.95 **597**
1. Endangered species -- Research 2. Fish populations -- Research 3. Fisheries -- History 4. Fishing -- History 5. Marine fishes -- Conservation 6. Marine fishes -- Ecology 7. Rare fishes -- Conservation 8. Wildlife conservation
ISBN 0670023353; 9780670023356

LC 2012003442

Author Matt Rigney, a member of the International Game Fish Association, debuts with this personal investigation into the decline of big-game fish like marlin, swordfish and bluefin tuna. His travels took him to the Mediterranean, Japan, Cabo San Lucas, Mexico, Georges Bank off Nova Scotia, the Great Barrier Reef, and New Zealand. Occasionally fishing along the way, the author sought those whose love for the ocean and its creatures mirrored his own. Everywhere he traveled he discovered a similar story: Corporations entered an area, manipulated or ignored government regulations, and, using long lines and huge nets, laid waste to massive populations of sea creatures. (Kirkus)

Schultz, Ken

Ken Schultz's field guide to saltwater fish. Wiley 2004 274p il pa $17.95 **597**
1. Fishes
ISBN 0-471-44995-4

LC 2003-15773

"Arranged alphabetically by species, each entry covers the identification, size/age, distribution, habitat, life history/behavior, and feeding habits of each fish." Publisher's note

Schweid, Richard

Consider the eel. University of North Carolina Press 2002 181p il map $24.95 **597**
1. Anguillidae 2. Eel fisheries 3. Eels
ISBN 0-8078-2693-6

LC 2001-48067

The author "tries to fill in the gaps in the eel's astonishing natural history and tie that to sketches of fishery traditions, folklore, literary excerpts and reportage. . . . Anyone with a curiosity about the sea will find Schweid's taste of the eel strangely appealing." Publ Wkly

Includes bibliographical references

Smith, C. Lavett

National Audubon Society field guide to tropical marine fishes of the Caribbean, the Gulf of Mexico, Florida, the Bahamas, and Bermuda. Knopf 1997 720p il maps $19.95 **597**
1. Tropical fish
ISBN 0-679-44601-X

LC 97-7690

This illustrated guide to tropical fishes describes nearly 1,200 species and includes color photographs, classification and identification information.

Steel, Rodney

Sharks of the world. Facts on File 2003 192p il $35 **597**
1. Sharks
ISBN 0-8160-5212-3

LC 2002-35228

This volume covers shark classification, anatomy, evolution, behavior, and reproduction.

Thomson, Keith Stewart

Living fossil; the story of the coelacanth. Norton 1991 252p il maps hardcover o.p. pa $9.95 **597**
1. Coelacanth
ISBN 0-393-30868-5 pa

LC 90-43053

"Brisk and engrossing, this is a winning mix of science and adventure." Booklist

597.3   Selachii, Holocephali, fleshy-finned fishes

Weinberg, Samantha

A **fish** caught in time; the search for the coelacanth. HarperCollins Pubs. 2000 xx, 220p il map hardcover o.p. pa $13   **597.3**

1. Coelacanth

ISBN 0-06-093285-6 pa

LC 99-44800

"In 1938, a fish believed to be extinct for 70 million years was caught off the South African coast, triggering the 'greatest scientific find of the century.' The search for the coelacanth . . . is a fascinating story, and Weinberg . . . tells it well." Libr J

Includes bibliographical references

597.8   Amphibians

Beltz, Ellin

Frogs: inside their remarkable world.   Firefly Books 2005 175p il $34.95   **597.8**

1. Frogs 2. Toads

ISBN 1-55297-869-9

LC 2006-365517

"Beltz presents an entertaining and comprehensive introduction to the order Anura (frogs and toads)." Booklist

Includes bibliographical references

Souder, William E.

A **plague** of frogs; unraveling an environmental mystery. [by] William Souder. University of Minnesota Press 2002 309p pa $18.95   **597.8**

1. Frogs

ISBN 0-8166-4178-1

The author examines "the disturbing increase in deformed frogs found in Minnesota in 1995. . . . So far, the biologists have not reached a consensus, but Souder's deep-drilling reportage of their work informs readers how these sentinels of science track 'indicator' species such as frogs." Booklist

Includes bibliographical references

597.9   Reptiles

Attenborough, David

Life in cold blood. Princeton University Press 2008 288p il $29.95   **597.9**

1. Amphibians 2. Reptiles

ISBN 978-0-691-13718-6; 0-691-13718-8

LC 2007-938089

"The writing is crisp and lively, the examples are up to date, and the photography is beautiful. . . . This is a very interesting book, which provides many examples of organisms some of us often overlook." Am Biology Teacher

Conant, Roger

★ A **field** guide to reptiles & amphibians; eastern and central North America. [by] Roger Conant and Joseph T. Collins; illustrated by Isabelle Hunt

Conant and Tom R. Johnson. 3rd ed, expanded; Houghton Mifflin 1998 616p il map $21   **597.9**

1. Amphibians 2. Amphibians -- Canada -- Identification 3. Amphibians -- United States -- Identification 4. Reptiles 5. Reptiles -- Canada -- Identification 6. Reptiles -- United States -- Identification

ISBN 0-395-90452-8

LC 98-13622

This guide describes 595 species and subspecies, featuring color photos, black and white drawings, and color distribution maps of reptiles and amphibians of the region. Also includes information on transporting live reptiles and amphibians.

Stebbins, Robert C.

A **field** guide to Western reptiles and amphibians; text and illustrations by Robert C. Stebbins. 3rd ed newly rev; Houghton Mifflin 2003 533p il map pa $22   **597.9**

1. Amphibians 2. Amphibians -- North America -- Identification 3. Amphibians -- West (U.S.) -- Identification 4. Reptiles 5. Reptiles -- North America -- Identification 6. Reptiles -- West (U.S.) -- Identification

ISBN 0-395-98272-3

LC 2002-27561

This "covers all the species of reptiles and amphibians found in western North America. More than 650 full-color paintings and photographs show key details for making accurate identifications. . . . Color range maps give species' distributions. . . . [Includes] information on conservation efforts and survival status." Publisher's note

Includes bibliographical references

Tyning, Thomas F.

A **guide** to amphibians and reptiles; edited by Donald W. Stokes and Lillian Q. Stokes; illustrations by Andrew Finch Magee; range maps by Thomas F. Tyning and Timothy J. Flanagan. Little, Brown 1990 400p il hardcover o.p. pa $14.95   **597.9**

1. Amphibians 2. Reptiles

ISBN 0-316-81713-9 pa

LC 89-28444

This guide covers common frogs, salamanders, alligators, snakes, turtles, and lizards.

597.92   Turtles

Ferri, Vincenzo

Tortoises and turtles. Firefly Bks. 2002 255p il pa $24.95   **597.92**

1. Turtles

ISBN 978-1-55209-631-4; 1-55209-631-9

"Turtle enthusiasts and students writing papers will find this guide and the additional resources it cites invaluable." Voice Youth Advocates

Includes glossary and bibliographical references

Safina, Carl

Voyage of the turtle; in pursuit of the Earth's last dinosaur. Holt 2006 383p il map $27.50; pa $17   **597.92**
1. Turtles
ISBN 978-0-8050-7891-6; 0-8050-7891-6; 978-0-8050-8318-7 pa; 0-8050-8318-9 pa

                             LC 2005-55023
"This is a well-written natural history/conservation narrative. General readers will enjoy the book and hopefully will become excited to learn more about critical environmental issues." Sci Books Films
Includes bibliographical references

Spotila, James R.

Sea turtles; a complete guide to their biology, behavior, and conservation. Johns Hopkins University Press 2004 227p il $24.95   **597.92**
1. Sea turtles
ISBN 0-8018-8007-6

                             LC 2004-8935
"The author is eloquent in his appeal for the conservation of sea turtles. The best single book on the subject." Booklist
Includes bibliographical references

597.96   Snakes

Badger, David

Snakes; text by David Badger; photography by John Netherton. Voyageur Press 1999 144p $35   **597.96**
1. Snakes 2. Snakes -- Pictorial works
ISBN 0-89658-408-9

                             LC 98-52379
"The first chapter is a general overview of humans and snakes. . . . The second chapter presents a primer on snake biology and behavior, and the very long third chapter is an overview of various families and species of snakes (mostly native to North America). The photographs are breathtaking in their composition, clarity, and sheer beauty." Booklist
Includes bibliographical references

Campbell, Jonathan

The **venomous** reptiles of the Western Hemisphere; by Jonathan A. Campbell and William W. Lamar, with contributions by Edmund D. Brodie III [et al.] Comstock Pub. Associates 2004 2v il maps set $149.95   **597.96**
1. Poisonous animals 2. Poisonous snakes 3. Reptiles
ISBN 0-8014-4141-2

                             LC 2003-7834
The authors "describe two species of lizards (the Gila monster and the beaded lizard) and 190 species of dangerously venomous snakes of North, Central and South America. Provided are . . . accounts of each species—from the smallest to the largest—complete with descriptions, habitats, and geographic distribution." Libr J
Includes bibliographical references

Ernst, Carl H.

Snakes in question; the Smithsonian answer book. [by] Carl H. Ernst and George R. Zug; illustrations by Molly Dwyer Griffin. Smithsonian Institution Press 1996 203p il hardcover o.p. pa $24.95   **597.96**
1. Snakes 2. Snakes -- Miscellanea
ISBN 1-56098-649-2 pa

                             LC 96-9367
"The questions and answer format is effective, and readers with no background and others more familiar with snake biology but seeking some biological information or specific data will find the text and tables useful. The careful answers are based on long-term observations as well as current research." Choice

Snakes of the United States and Canada; [by] Carl H. Ernst, Evelyn M. Ernst. Smithsonian Books 2003 668p il map $70   **597.96**
1. Snakes 2. Snakes -- Canada 3. Snakes -- United States
ISBN 1-58834-019-8

                             LC 2002-26924
"This current and comprehensive volume contains all the information currently available on the 131 species of snakes living in North America." Libr J
Includes bibliographical references

Greene, Harry W.

Snakes; the evolution of mystery in nature. with photographs by Michael and Patricia Fodgen. University of Calif. Press 1997 351p il $55; pa $29.95   **597.96**
1. Snakes
ISBN 0-520-20014-4; 0-520-22487-6 pa

                             LC 96-21928
The author examines the "biology and ecology of snakes. Throughout, facts on the form, function, habitat, and evolution of these reptiles are mixed with the author's experiences, and the over 200 natural-setting color photographs that complement the text are commendable in their own right." Libr J
Includes bibliographical references

Mattison, Christopher

★ **Snakes** of the world; [by] Chris Mattison. Facts on File 2003 190p il map $35   **597.96**
1. Snakes
ISBN 0-8160-5213-1

                             LC 2002-34737
Snake morphology, reproduction, diet, self-defense, ecology and behavior are discussed.
"Mattison provides an enjoyable introduction to snake biology and snake diversity for the interested general reader. . . . Many of the numerous color photographs are spectacular." Choice [review of 1986 edition]
Includes bibliographical references

The **new** encyclopedia of snakes. Princeton University Press 2007 272p il map $35   **597.96**
1. Reference books 2. Snakes -- Anatomy 3. Snakes

-- Behavior 4. Snakes -- Encyclopedias
ISBN 0-691-13295-X; 978-0-691-13295-2

LC 2007-922951

This encyclopedia "covers all aspects of snake biology and habitat. This is not a field guide aimed at snake identification. . . . But the work contains a wealth of information about our scaled friends, including patterns of distribution and matters relating to evolution and morphology, feeding, reproduction, and defensive strategies. . . . This captivating work will appeal to students and snake lovers everywhere." Libr J

Includes bibliographical references

Murphy, John C.

Tales of giant snakes; a historical natural history of anacondas and pythons. [by] John C. Murphy and Robert W. Henderson. Krieger 1997 221p il map $32.50   **597.96**
1. Anacondas 2. Pythons
ISBN 0-89464-995-7

LC 96-54033

Accounts of encounters between large snakes and humans include newspaper articles, adventure writings, and reports of explorers.

O'Shea, Mark

Venomous snakes of the world. Princeton University Press 2005 160p il map $29.95   **597.96**
1. Poisonous animals 2. Poisonous snakes 3. Snakes
ISBN 0-691-12436-1

LC 2005-920576

"Fascinating photographs and descriptions will make this title a favorite." Univ Press Books for Public and Second Sch Libr, 2006

Includes bibliographical references

Rubio, Manny

Rattlesnake; portrait of a predator. Smithsonian Institution Press 1998 xxvii, 239p il $49.95 **597.96**
1. Rattlesnakes
ISBN 1-56098-808-8

LC 98-22935

This book contains "more than 120 color photographs of various North American rattlesnakes. . . . The text discusses many aspects of rattlesnake evolution, anatomy and physiology, and ecology, including several chapters on interactions between snakes and people." Sci Books Films

Includes bibliographical references

598   Birds

Alderfer, Jonathan

★ **National** Geographic birding essentials; all the tools, techniques, and tips you need to begin and become a better birder. [by] Jonathan Alderfer and Jon L. Dunn. National Geographic 2007 224p il pa $15.95   **598**
1. Bird watching 2. Birds -- Identification
ISBN 978-1-4262-0135-6; 1-4262-0135-4

LC 2007-30960

This "book offers data on how to begin and how to improve your bird-watching skills. Chapters deal with the pleasures of birding, getting started, where and when birds are found, how common or rare they are at different seasons, parts of a bird, how to identify them, and variations in birds. . . . With a helpful glossary, this is an essential volume for all bird-watchers." Booklist

Includes bibliographical references

Attenborough, David

The **life** of birds. Princeton Univ. Press 1998 320p il $29.95   **598**
1. Birds 2. Birds -- Behavior
ISBN 0-691-01633-X

LC 98-30705

"Well illustrated with color photographs, Attenborough's latest goes a long way to converting all readers into bird lovers." Booklist

Includes bibliographical references

Beans, Bruce E.

Eagle's plume; the struggle to preserve the life and haunts of America's bald eagle. University of Nebraska Press 1997 318p il pa $17.95   **598**
1. Bald eagle 2. Birds -- Protection
ISBN 0-8032-6142-X; 978-0-8032-6142-6

LC 97-15433

This book "deals with the conservation of eagles and their habitat. [It] also contains details on the biology, behavior, and ecology of eagles." Sci Books Films

Includes bibliographical references

Bull, John L.

★ The **National** Audubon Society field guide to North American birds, Eastern region; [by] John Bull and John Farrand, Jr.; revised by John Farrand, Jr.; visual key by Amanda Wilson and Lori Hogan. rev ed; Knopf 1994 797p il maps pa $19.95   **598**
1. Birds -- North America
ISBN 0-679-42852-6

LC 94-7768

This pictorial guide to 508 eastern species arranges birds by color and shape to simplify identification. It also includes information on bird-watching and conservation status.

Burger, Joanna

Birds: a visual guide. Firefly Books 2006 304p il map $29.95   **598**
1. Birds 2. Birds -- Juvenile literature 3. Children's literature -- Works -- Grades two through six 4. Young adult literature -- Works
ISBN 978-1-55407-177-7; 1-55407-177-1

"Divided into six sections, the text considers all aspects of birds' lives. Basic anatomy, evolution, physiology, and intelligence are all touched on in the first section, while bird behavior . . . is covered in the second. A large section examines the taxonomy of birds . . . accompanied by a world map showing its distribution. Habitat, migration, and how birds fill their space are discussed in the fourth section, followed by a look at avian adaptations and lifestyles. The final section, on birds and humans, covers such disparate topics as birds in legend, bird-watching, captive birds, and habitat loss. Beautifully illustrated." Booklist

Clark, William S.
★ A **field** guide to hawks of North America; {by} William S. Clark and Brian K. Wheeler; illustrations by Brian K. Wheeler. 2nd ed; Houghton Mifflin 2001 316p il maps $30; pa $22   **598**
    1. Hawks
    ISBN 0-395-67068-3; 0-395-67067-5 pa
                           LC 2001-2477
"Accounts are presented for all 39 of North America's diurnal raptors, including eagles, falcons, and vultures. Each species account reviews details of plumages and molts, useful identification features, patterns of flight, and general behavior. . . . The guide also provides size data (weight, length, and wingspread) for all species, as well as the etymology of common and scientific names. Basically, the reference is essential for any student of raptors and useful for serious birders in general." Am Ref Books Annu, 2002
    Includes bibliographical references

Cocker, Mark
    Birders; tales of a tribe. Atlantic Monthly Press 2002 229p $24; pa $13   **598**
    1. Bird watchers 2. Bird watching
    ISBN 0-87113-844-1; 0-8021-3996-5 pa
                       LC 2001-56490
In a "memoir cum essay collection, the author brings the reader into the sometimes obsessive world of bird-watching. . . . Stories of the author and friends going to great lengths and distances to see rare birds, of birding in exotic locales, or of unmasking a fellow birder's claims to finding a rare species are both thought-provoking and amusing." Booklist
    Includes bibliographical references

Dunn, Erica H.
    Birds at your feeder; a guide to the feeding habits, behavior, distribution, and abundance. [by] Erica H. Dunn and Diane L. Tessaglia-Hymes; illustrations by Peter Burke; abundance maps by Jeffrey Price; sponsored by Cornell Laboratory of Ornithology [et al.] Norton 1999 418p il maps hardcover o.p. pa $15.95   **598**
    1. Birds -- Feeding and feeds -- North America 2. Birds -- North America
    ISBN 0-393-32231-9 pa
                      LC 98-35661
"For the 93 most widespread feeder species, the authors present several pages of excellent commentary plus two range maps and four bar graphs. For each bird, there is textual and graphic information on its abundance . . . food preferences, behavior, habits, a drawing of the bird, and more." Libr J
    Includes bibliographical references

Dunne, Pete
    Pete Dunne on bird watching; the how-to, where-to, and when-to of birding. Houghton Mifflin 2003 334p il pa $12   **598**
    1. Bird watching
    ISBN 0-395-90686-5
                      LC 2002-27558
This "book is a superlative introduction to bird watching." Libr J
    Includes bibliographical references

    Pete Dunne's essential field guide companion. Houghton Mifflin Co. 2006 710p $29.95   **598**
    1. Birds -- North America
    ISBN 978-0-618-23648-0; 0-618-23648-1
                      LC 2005-21110
This "title should appeal . . . to the serious birder striving to become more accomplished. No serious bird collection should be without it." Libr J

Floyd, Ted
    Smithsonian field guide to the birds of North America; [by] Ted Floyd; edited by Paul Hess and George Scott; designed by Charles Nix; maps by Paul Lehman; photographs by Brian E. Small . . . [et al.] HarperCollins Publishers 2008 512p il map pa $24.95   **598**
    1. Birds -- North America
    ISBN 978-0-06-112040-4; 0-06-112040-5
                      LC 2008-1395
"Ideal for beginners, but also has formidable resources for experienced birders. . . . Perfect for field use. Birders of any experience level will be happy with this volume on their bookshelf." Publ Wkly
    Includes bibliographical references

Gallagher, Tim
    The **grail** bird; hot on the trail of the Ivory-billed woodpecker. Houghton Mifflin 2005 272p il map $25; pa $14.95   **598**
    1. Ivory-billed woodpecker 2. Woodpeckers
    ISBN 0-618-45693-7; 0-618-70941-X pa
                      LC 2005-42792
"An engaging story of the triumph of conservation, this book is highly recommended for most collections." Libr J
    Includes bibliographical references

Hanson, Thor
    Feathers; the evolution of a natural miracle. Basic Books 2011 336p il   **598**
    1. Birds 2. Feathers
    ISBN 0-465-02013-5; 978-0-465-02013-3
                      LC 2011003272
Hanson "presents the natural history of feathers, applying the findings of paleontologists, ornithologists, biologists, engineers and art historians to answer questions about the origin of feathers, their evolution and their uses throughout the ages." (Publisher's note) Index.
    "Divided into sections that cover such categories as evolution, insulation, flight and adornment, 'Feathers' stretches from the ancient mists of the late Jurassic to the laboratories

of today's Smithsonian Museum, where 'snarge'—science slang for what's produced when a bird meets a plane—is analyzed for data. In between, you learn that a falcon thrown out of an airplane can dive at a speed of 242 miles per hour, that the word pen is itself derived from the Latin word for feather and that the most valuable cargo on the Titanic wasn't gold or jewels but more than 40 cases of plumes intended for women's hats, a fashion craze that nearly caused the extinction of several species and led to the formation of the Audubon Society, as well as America's first National Wildlife Refuge, Florida's Pelican Island. Mr. Hanson may be a scientist but he writes like a man who believes in the value of story. . . . [He] offers more than a fanciful, associative style. He is a very good explainer of serious biology." Wall Street J

Includes bibliographical references

Kaufman, Kenn

Kaufman field guide to birds of North America; with the collaboration of Rick and Nora Bowers and Lynn Hassler Kaufman. Houghton Mifflin 2005 392p il map pa $18.95   **598**

1. Birds -- North America
ISBN 0-618-57423-9; 978-0-618-57423-0

For this identification guide "Kaufman selected over 2000 digitally edited photographs, enhanced to improve contrast, color, and the like. The excellent result will appeal to beginning birders perhaps intimidated by illustrations. . . . Kaufman's text is simple and uncluttered, a plus for novices." Libr J

Kroodsma, Donald E.

The **singing** life of birds; the art and science of listening to birdsong. drawings by Nancy Haver. Houghton Mifflin 2005 482p il $28   **598**

1. Birdsongs
ISBN 0-618-40568-2

LC 2004-65130

"Kroodsma is a warm, encouraging guide to the world of birdsong, and his enthusiasm is contagious." Publ Wkly

Includes bibliographical references

Leahy, Christopher W.

The **birdwatcher's** companion to North American birdlife; illustrations by Gordon Morrison. Princeton University Press 2004 1039p il hardcover o.p. pa $19.95   **598**

1. Bird watching 2. Birds -- North America
ISBN 0-691-09297-4; 0-691-11388-2 pa

LC 2003-66383

"This alphabetical compendium of ornithology offers entries ranging from single-line definitions of avian terminology ('Erne') to 12-page essay-style articles ('Systemics') that concentrate primarily on the US and Canada. Entries include a substantial number of biographies and black-and-white drawings. . . . Comprehensive entries on conservation, evolution of birdlife, optical equipment, and human threats to birdlife provide welcome up-to-date information. . . . Leahy's style is by turns serious and scholarly or personal and whimsical, appropriate to a comprehensive reference

for both novice and expert birders. There is no recent comparable work." Choice

Includes bibliographical references

Lynch, Wayne

Penguins of the world; text and photographs by Wayne Lynch. 2nd ed.; Firefly Books 2007 175p il map $34.95; pa $24.95   **598**

1. Penguins
ISBN 978-1-55407-334-4; 1-55407-334-0; 978-1-55407-274-3 pa; 1-55407-274-3 pa

LC 2007-299218

This is a "look at Lynch's discoveries about these flightless seabirds in the field and in scientific journals, during day-to-day as well as birth-to-death observations, and from the smallest to the largest type. While Lynch presents detailed descriptions of everything from mating rituals to eating habits, the best parts of his book are the photographs. Lynch's gorgeous and gorgeously printed images . . . display such a refined visual sensibility that even without accompanying text, the images would still achieve Lynch's goal of presenting the scientific and aesthetic appeal of this unique family of birds." Publ Wkly

Includes bibliographical references

Montgomery, Sy

Birdology; lessons learned from a pack of hens, a peck of pigeons, cantankerous crows, fierce falcons, hip hop parrots, baby hummingbirds, and one murderously big cassowary. Free Press 2010 260p il $25   **598**

1. Authors 2. Birds 3. Journalists 4. Writers on nature
ISBN 978-1-4165-6984-8; 1-4165-6984-7

LC 2009-31303

"Montgomery assists a hummingbird rehabilitator in the delicate raising of two tiny orphans, and meets the 'most dangerous bird on earth,' the enormous, razor-clawed cassowary in Australia, one bird whose dinosaur ancestry is blazingly apparent. She also writes from unexpected perspectives about falcons, crows, pigeons, chickens, and parrots. . . . Inspired equally by all that we share with birds—similarities in intelligence, emotion, language, and music—and all that is mysterious (birds 'remain fundamentally wild'), Montgomery expresses profound appreciation for the living web of life in a book that both bird lovers and readers new to bird lore will find evocative, enlightening, and uplifting." Booklist

Includes bibliographical references

National Audubon Society

Bird; the definitive visual guide. Audubon; [senior editor, Peter Frances; contributors, BirdLife International, David Burnie] DK Pub. 2007 512p il map $50   **598**

1. Birds
ISBN 978-0-7566-3153-6; 0-7566-3153-X

LC 2007-282186

"From flyleaf to fore edge, the visuals are astounding. . . . An enclosed CD with bird calls and songs adds yet another dimension to a glorious work." Libr J

Nigge, Klaus

Whooping crane; images from the wild. introduction by Krista Schlyer. Texas A&M University Press 2010 217p il map $45 **598**
1. Cranes (Birds)
ISBN 978-1-60344-209-1; 1-60344-209-X
LC 2009048496

"On the flock's wintering grounds at Aransas National Wildlife Refuge in Texas, photographer Klaus Nigge has captured the daily activity of a single family over several weeks in two separate years, documenting their life in the salt marshes of the central Texas coast and, in one year, the happy arrival from the north of twin adolescents. . . . Then, with the backing of National Geographic magazine, he received unprecedented permission from the Canadian government to photograph the cranes' summer nesting sites in remote areas of Wood Buffalo National Park. . . . [This collection of his photos is divided into] three galleries, each containing portfolios of images of these magnificent birds in their natural habitat." Publisher's note

Includes bibliographical references

Peterson, Roger Tory

Peterson field guide to birds of Eastern and Central North America; [by] Roger Tory Peterson, with contributions from Michael DiGiorgio [et al.] 6th ed; Houghton Mifflin Harcourt 2010 445p il map $19.95 **598**
1. Birds -- Identification 2. Birds -- North America
ISBN 978-0-547-15246-2; 0-547-15246-9
LC 2009-37681

This guide to birds found east of the Rocky Mountains contains colored illustrations painted by the author, with a description of each species on the facing page. Views of young birds and seasonal variations in plumage are included.

★ **Peterson** field guide to birds of North America; with contributions from Michael DiGiorgio . . . [et al.] Houghton Mifflin Co. 2008 527p il map $26 **598**
1. Birds -- North America
ISBN 978-0-618-96614-1; 0-618-96614-5
LC 2007-39803

This guide to birds found in North America contains colored illustrations painted by the author, with a description of each species on the facing page. Views of young birds and seasonal variations in plumage are included. The book also includes a URL to video podcasts.

"This field guide is of high quality and should be in millions of birders' and other nature lovers' backpacks." Sci Books Films

Peterson field guide to birds of Western North America; with contributions from Michael DiGiorgio [et al.] 4th ed; Houghton Mifflin Harcourt 2010 493p il map pa $19.95 **598**
1. Birds -- North America 2. Birds -- Western Canada 3. Birds -- Western States
ISBN 978-0-547-15270-7; 0-547-15270-1
LC 2009-39158

This guide illustrates over 600 species of birds on 176 color plates. In addition, over 588 range maps are included.

Robbins, Chandler S.

Birds of North America; a guide to field identification. by Chandler S. Robbins, Bertel Bruun, and Herbert S. Zim; revised by Jonathan P. Latimer and Karen Stray Nolting and James Coe; illustrated by Arthur Singer. rev and updated; St. Martin's Press 2001 359p il maps $19.95; pa $15.95 **598**
1. Birds -- North America 2. Birds -- North America -- Identification
ISBN 1-58238-091-0; 1-58238-090-2 pa
LC 2001-271739

This resource includes over 800 species and 600 range maps; illustrations featuring male, female, and juvenile plumage; and sonograms picturing sound for song recognition. Feeding habits, migration routes, and characteristic flight patterns as well as American Ornithologists' classifications are also provided.

Roth, Sally

The **backyard** bird feeder's bible; the A-to-Z guide to feeders, seed mixes, projects, and treats. Rodale 2000 268p il $29.95; pa $18.95 **598**
1. Bird feeders 2. Birds 3. Birds -- Feeding and feeds
ISBN 0-87596-834-1; 0-87596-918-6 pa
LC 00-9063

This "truly is a comprehensive guide for bird enthusiasts." Booklist

Includes bibliographical references

Sibley, David

The **Sibley** field guide to birds of Eastern North America; written and illustrated by David Allen Sibley. Knopf 2003 431p il pa $19.95 **598**
1. Birds -- North America
ISBN 0-679-45120-X
LC 2002-114931

"All the qualities to be expected in a field guide are here. . . . Image reproduction is crisp, colors are distinct, shading shows well, and despite the very small size, range map colors are clear. . . . Sibley has accomplished the difficult task of condensing . . . [The Sibley guide to birds] to practical field size." Libr J

★ The **Sibley** field guide to birds of Western North America; written and illustrated by David Allen Sibley. Knopf 2003 473p il pa $19.95 **598**
1. Birds -- North America 2. Birds -- United States
ISBN 0-679-45121-8
LC 2002-114930

"All the qualities to be expected in a field guide are here. . . . Image reproduction is crisp, colors are distinct, shading shows well, and despite the very small size, range map colors are clear. . . . Sibley has accomplished the difficult task of condensing . . . [The Sibley guide to birds] to practical field size." Libr J

★ The **Sibley** guide to bird life & behavior; illustrated by David Allen Sibley; edited by Chris

Elphick, John B. Dunning, Jr., David Allen Sibley. Knopf 2001 588p il maps hardcover o.p. pa $39.95 **598**
　　1. Birds -- North America
　　ISBN 0-679-45123-4; 1-4000-4386-7 pa
　　　　　　　　　　　　　LC 2001-33903
　　This companion volume to The Sibley guide to birds provides "information about birds' lives and behavior. . . . Part 1 ('The World of Birds') discusses basic avian biology, including form, distribution, population, and conservation, in about 100 pages. Part 2 ('Bird Families of North America'), to which over 40 ornithologists contributed, uses a standard format to describe taxonomy, foraging, breeding, range, nests, eggs, longevity, conservation, and more." Libr J

　　The **Sibley** guide to birds; written and illustrated by David Sibley. Knopf 2000 544p il maps pa $35 **598**
　　1. Birds -- North America
　　ISBN 0-679-45122-6
　　　　　　　　　　　　　LC 00-41239
　　"The treatments of each of the 810 species have detailed paintings to show the natural variations in plumage (e.g., juveniles, male/female adults, seasonal and geographic changes). In all, there are more than 6,600 full-color illustrations. . . . The text for each species has a short summary of identification key points, description of vocalizations, and an up-to-date range map." Choice

　　Sibley's birding basics; written and illustrated by David Allen Sibley. Knopf 2002 154p il pa $15.95 **598**
　　1. Bird watching 2. Birds 3. Birds -- Identification
　　ISBN 0-375-70966-5
　　　　　　　　　　　　　LC 2002-20768
　　Sibley "explores general aspects of birding such as getting started, misidentification, voice, understanding feathers, age variation, ethics and conservation, taxonomy, and finding birds. If being a field naturalist is a craft, then this book is essential in helping to develop and understand the required skills." Libr J

Stokes, Donald W.
　　The **bird** feeder book; an easy guide to attracting, identifying, and understanding your feeder birds. {by} Donald and Lillian Stokes; illustrations of feeders by Gordon Morrison; range maps by Leslie Cowperthwaite. Little, Brown 1987 90p il maps pa $12.95 **598**
　　1. Bird watching
　　ISBN 0-316-81733-3
　　　　　　　　　　　　　LC 87-3016
　　"This guide for beginners features 72 dramatic color photographs of the most common backyard birds. The text offers chapters on attracting and identifying birds (which types of feeders to use, etc.), dealing with squirrels and other yard pests, and planting shrubbery layouts that offer food and nest sites. A nicely illustrated, logically organized handbook." Booklist
　　Includes bibliographical references

Tudge, Colin
　　The **bird**; a natural history of who birds are, where they came from, and how they live. Crown Publishers 2009 462p il $30 **598**
　　1. Birds
　　ISBN 978-0-307-34204-1
　　"The author writes with clarity and cheerful wit about the physics and mechanics of flight, evolution and the archaeological record [of birds] . . . [Tudge] covers the avian landscape like a tarp, from amusing anecdotes about bird behavior, to a critique of behavioralism, to the abuse of Darwin's theories, to the complex structure of avian taxonomy. . . Entertaining, charming and knowledgeable." Kirkus
　　Includes bibliographical references

Udvardy, Miklos D. F.
　　★ **National** Audubon Society field guide to North American birds, Western region; revised by John Farrand, Jr.; visual key by Amanda Wilson and Lori Hogan. rev ed; Knopf 1994 822p il maps pa $19.95 **598**
　　1. Birds -- North America
　　ISBN 0-679-42851-8
　　　　　　　　　　　　　LC 94-7415
　　This pictorial guide to 544 western species arranges birds by color and shape to simplify identification. It also includes information on bird-watching and conservation status.

Unwin, Mike
　　The **atlas** of birds; diversity, behavior, and conservation. Princeton University Press 2011 144p il map pa $22.95 **598**
　　1. Atlases 2. Birds 3. Reference books
　　ISBN 978-0-691-14949-3
　　　　　　　　　　　　　LC 2011920367
　　This "is neither a textbook nor an encyclopedia but rather a compendium of interesting factoids and bird trivia, with each two-page layout addressing one aspect of bird biology. This is a book for general readers who enjoy studying birds." Choice
　　Includes bibliographical references

Weidensaul, Scott
　　Living on the wind; across the hemisphere with migratory birds. North Point Press 1999 420p il hardcover o.p. pa $15 **598**
　　1. Birds -- Migration
　　ISBN 0-86547-591-1 pa
　　　　　　　　　　　　　LC 99-11693
　　"The book will be of interest to biologists and amateur naturalists; birders will particularly appreciate the discussion of key 'fallout' areas." Libr J
　　Includes bibliographical references

　　Of a feather; a brief history of American birding. Harcourt, Inc. 2007 358p il $25; pa $15 **598**
　　1. Bird watching 2. Bird watching -- United States
　　ISBN 978-0-15-101247-3; 0-15-101247-4; 978-0-15-603355-8 pa; 0-15-603355-0 pa
　　　　　　　　　　　　　LC 2007-07364

The author's "vivid descriptions of his own experiences should send many a reader out of doors to look for the small, contained miracle that is a bird." Publ Wkly

Includes bibliographical references

Williamson, Sheri L.

A **field** guide to hummingbirds of North America; {by} Sheri L. Williamson. Houghton Mifflin 2001 263p il maps $30; pa $22　　　　　**598**

1. Hummingbirds

ISBN 0-618-02495-6; 0-618-02496-4 pa

LC 2001-24473

"The habits, habitats, migratory patterns, physical traits, diet, mating practices, where to find them in short, all the information that a good wildlife guide offers are the stuff of Williamson's book. Clear, engaging prose and 180 full color photographs make this a natural for birdwatchers everywhere." Publ Wkly

Zickefoose, Julie

The **bluebird** effect; uncommon bonds with common birds. Julie Zickefoose. Houghton Mifflin Harcourt Co. 2012 355 p.　　　　　**598**

1. Bird watching -- United States -- Anecdotes 2. Birds -- Behavior -- United States -- Anecdotes 3. Birds -- United States -- Pictorial works 4. Birds -- Wounds and injuries -- Treatment -- Anecdotes 5. Human-animal relationships -- Anecdotes 6. Naturalists -- United States -- Anecdotes 7. Wildlife rehabilitation -- United States -- Anecdotes 8. Wildlife rehabilitators -- United States -- Anecdotes

ISBN 9780547003092

LC 2011036692

This book explores a naturalist's life with backyard birds. For most of my life, I've tried to fix broken birds, writes painter and songbird rehabilitator [Julie] Zickefoose . . . in this account of her rescues of cardinals, robins and more than 20 other bird species. . . . The birds are a disparate lot: the starlings with their imitations of car alarms and barking dogs; the potentially home-wrecking chickadees; the lean and sinewy ospreys; the barn sparrows that haunt the eaves of large home-improvement stores. . . . She keeps a pair of binoculars in each room of her house and travels to beaches, salt marshes and the Central Flyway to observe the behaviors of these wild birds. (Kirkus)

Arctic wings; birds of the Arctic National Wildlife Refuge. edited by Stephen Brown; foreword by Jimmy Carter; introduction by David Allen Sibley. Mountaineers Books 2006 192p il map $39.95; pa $27.95　　　　　**598**

1. Birds 2. Birds -- Alaska

ISBN 0-89886-975-7; 978-0-89886-975-0; 0-89886-976-5 pa; 978-0-8988-6976-7 pa

LC 2006-865

"The unique aspect of this book is the vivid photographs of bird behavior and the birds in their habitats, showing the importance of the habitats to the birds' continued existence. A great addition is a CD with 60 bird calls recorded on the refuge." Sci Books Films

Includes bibliographical references

★ The Princeton encyclopedia of birds; edited by Christopher Perrins. Princeton University Press 2009 656p il map pa $35　　　　　**598**

1. Birds 2. Birds -- Encyclopedias 3. Reference books

ISBN 978-0-691-14070-4; 0-691-14070-7

The editor "combines the work of 150 contributors and more than 1000 great color photographs, maps, and other illustrations to produce a stunning book that informs both amateurs and experts. Coverage includes form and function, distribution, diet, breeding biology, and conservation and environment." Libr J

Includes bibliographical references

★ The atlas of bird migration; tracing the great journeys of the world's birds. general editor Jonathan Elphick; foreword by Thomas E. Lovejoy. Firefly Books 2007 176p il map hardcover o.p. pa $24.95　　　　　**598**

1. Birds -- Behavior 2. Birds -- Migration

ISBN 978-1-55407-248-4; 1-55407-248-4; 978-1-55407-971-1 pa; 1-55407-971-3 pa

"The first section is a primer on bird migration and habitat usage patterns, consisting of short, illustrated essays on topics like the evolution of migration, the mechanics of flight, birds' navigational methods and how human development affects migration patterns. Succeeding sections examine different families of migrating birds according to geographical distribution, and each has carefully designed maps that show birds' seasonal ranges and migratory routes. The use of color to describe, clarify, distinguish and compare migration patterns is exceptional, and clear explanations of complicated topics (e.g., how birds fly) make it an excellent text for middle and high school students as well as adults." Publ Wkly

598.4　Miscellaneous orders of water birds

Safina, Carl

Eye of the albatross; visions of hope and survival. Holt & Co. 2002 377p il maps hardcover o.p. pa $16　　　　　**598.4**

1. Albatrosses

ISBN 0-8050-6229-7 pa

LC 2001-51644

The author "recounts his travels to remote portions of the northwest Hawaiian Islands to witness albatross breeding season, during which parent birds fly across entire oceans— as much as 25,000 miles—to hunt sufficient food to nourish their single chicks. . . . Safina's encyclopedic knowledge and spirited prose provide a stunningly intimate portrait of an environment." Publ Wkly

Includes bibliographical references

598.8   Perching birds (Passeriformes)

Heinrich, Bernd

  Mind of the raven; investigations and adventures with wolf-birds. Cliff St. Bks. 1999 380p il $25; pa $13   **598.8**
   1. Ravens 2. Ravens -- Anecdotes
   ISBN 0-06-017447-1; 0-06-093063-2 pa
                        LC 99-18129
  Heinrich "describes his field experiments in the feeding habits, play, intelligence, social structure, territoriality, and hunting methods of ravens as well as an array of topics from their skill as mimics to their suspected emotional natures. He brings alive the romance of field research, where the discipline of science is often harder to achieve than in the lab but is at least as rewarding. A splendid book." Libr J
  Includes bibliographical references

Young, Jon

  What the robin knows; how birds reveal the secrets of the natural world. Jon Young; with science and audio editing by Dan Gardoqui. Houghton Mifflin Harcourt 2012 xxviii, 241 p.p   **598.8**
   1. Bird watching 2. Birdsongs 3. Natural history -- New Jersey 4. Nature observation 5. Philosophy of nature 6. Songbirds -- Behavior
   ISBN 0547451253; 9780547451251
                        LC 2012002403
  In this book naturalist Jon Young teaches three basic premises: the robin, junco, and other songbirds know everything important about their environment, be it backyard or forest; by tuning in to their vocalizations and behavior, we can acquire much of this wisdom for our own pleasure and benefit; and the birds' companion calls and warning alarms are just as important as their songs. Birds are the sentries—and our key to understanding the world beyond our front door. Unwitting humans create a zone of disturbance that scatters the wildlife. Respectful humans who heed the birds acquire an awareness that radically changes the dynamic. We are welcome in their habitat. (Publishers note)

598.9   Falconiformes, Caprimulgiformes, owls

Gessner, David

  Return of the osprey; a season of flight and wonder. Algonquin Bks. 2001 286p map $23.95 **598.9**
   1. Osprey -- Massachusetts -- Cape Cod 2. Ospreys
   ISBN 1-56512-254-2
                        LC 00-68230
  "Over 90 percent of the osprey population in New England was wiped out between 1950 and 1975, and then DDT was banned. Gessner writes of the return of nesting ospreys to Cape Cod. . . . This beautifully written story of a season with birds of prey makes for engrossing reading as we learn about osprey life from a master essayist." Booklist
  Includes bibliographical references

599   Mammals

Elbroch, Mark

  Mammal tracks & sign; a guide to North American species. Stackpole Bks. 2003 779p il maps $44.95   **599**
   1. Animal tracks 2. Mammals
   ISBN 0-8117-2626-6
                        LC 2002-10549
  The author "brings an ideal combination of practical experience and careful research to this work. . . . A definitive treatment, Elbroch's book will set the standard for years to come and is essential to anyone interested in tracking this continent's mammals." Libr J
  Includes bibliographical references

  ★ The **Peterson** field guide to animal tracks; [by] Mark Elbroch and Olaus J. Murie. 3rd ed.; Houghton Mifflin Company 2005 hardcover o.p. pa $19.95   **599**
   1. Animal tracks
   ISBN 978-0-618-51742-8; 978-0-618-51743-5 pa
                        LC 2005-13108
  "Murie's handbook is recognized as the classic work on the subject. . . . The illustrated guide describes the tracks, droppings, and marks left on bones and leaves by an army of wild animals-bats, bears, rabbits, reptiles, moles, weasels, and others. A fascinating collection of miscellaneous information about the habits of these creatures is part of the descriptive text." Wynar. Ref Books in Paperback. 2d edition

Mares, Michael A.

  A **desert** calling; life in a forbidding landscape. Harvard Univ. Press 2002 318p il maps $29.95 **599**
   1. Desert animals 2. Mammals
   ISBN 0-674-00747-6
                        LC 2001-51786
  The author describes his studies of "small mammals in the deserts of North America, South America, Egypt, and Iran. . . . The wonder of field research and of the discoveries that result shines through his matter-of-fact tone." Booklist
  Includes bibliographical references (p.)

Mowat, Farley

  Woman in the mists: the story of Dian Fossey and the mountain gorillas of Africa. Warner Bks. 1987 380p il hardcover o.p. pa $19.95   **599**
   1. Authors 2. Gorillas 3. Murder victims 4. Primatologists 5. Writers on science
   ISBN 0-446-38720-7 pa
                        LC 87-40166
  The author has "organized Fossey's journals into a biography that quotes her writings so heavily as to be autobiographical. Much of the text parallels material in Fossey's Gorillas in the Mist but provides additional insights into her personal life, difficulties in maintaining funding, and the continuation of her work up to her death in 1985. This gripping, action-packed story is essential reading for all who understand the sacrifice of self for the preservation of other species." Libr J

Nowak, Ronald M.

Walker's mammals of the world; 6th ed; Johns Hopkins Univ. Press 1999 2v il set $135   **599**
1. Mammals   2. Mammals -- Classification   3. Reference books
ISBN 0-8018-5789-9

LC 98-23686

"A goal of the work . . . [is] to provide a quality photograph of a living representative of every genus of mammal. . . . Each genus entry contains information on the number of species known, key literature references, physical description, comparison of characteristics of representative species, description of habitat, general behavior, breeding and care of young, and information on the species' endangered status." Am Ref Books Annu, 2000

Includes bibliographical references

Owens, Mark

Secrets of the savanna; twenty-three years in the African wilderness unraveling the mysteries of elephants and people. [by] Mark and Delia Owens. Houghton Mifflin 2006 230p il map $26; pa $14.95   **599**
1. African elephant -- Conservation   2. Biologists   3. Conservationists   4. Elephants   5. Wildlife conservation
ISBN 978-0-395-89310-4; 0-395-89310-0; 978-0-618-87250-3 pa; 0-618-87250-7 pa

LC 2005-23842

"This book, full of adventure and a few hair-raising moments, deserves a wide readership." Libr J

Includes bibliographical references

Whitaker, John O.

★ National Audubon Society field guide to North American mammals; rev ed; Knopf 1996 937p il maps pa $19.95   **599**
1. Mammals
ISBN 0-679-44631-1

LC 95-81456

This field guide describes 390 species of mammals of North America and includes keys for identification, range maps, information on tracks and anatomy, and 375 color photos.

★ The Princeton encyclopedia of mammals; edited by David W. Macdonald. Princeton University Press 2009 936p il map pa $45   **599**
1. Mammals   2. Mammals -- Encyclopedias   3. Reference books
ISBN 978-0-691-14069-8; 0-691-14069-3

This encyclopedia features a "general introduction to mammals followed by . . . accounts of species and groups that . . . describe form, distribution, behavior, status, conservation, and more." Publisher's note

Includes bibliographical references

599.2   Marsupials and monotremes

Flannery, Tim F.

Chasing kangaroos; a continent, a scientist, and a search for the world's most extraordinary creature. Grove Press 2007 258p il map hardcover o.p. pa $14   **599.2**
1. Human ecology -- Australia   2. Kangaroos   3. Mammalogists   4. Natural history -- Australia   5. Writers on science
ISBN 978-0-8021-1852-3; 0-8021-1852-6; 978-0-8021-4371-6 pa; 0-8021-4371-7 pa

LC 2006-52628

"In a time where pride in one's country is a rarity, Flannery has written a love letter to his. . . . Just as much as Chasing Kangaroos is about the evolution of a creature, it's also Flannery's acknowledgement of Australia's inherent uniqueness, a uniqueness he begs is not casually lost in the growing conformity of the global landscape." Paste

599.5   Cetaceans and sea cows

Bortolotti, Dan

Wild blue; a natural history of the world's largest animal. Thomas Dunne Books 2008 315p il map $24.95   **599.5**
1. Blue whale   2. Whales
ISBN 978-0-312-38387-9; 0-312-38387-8

LC 2008-24933

The author "provides the most comprehensive title yet on blue whales for the general reader. Encapsulating everything from statistical analysis of geographic populations to the reports of whalers from centuries past, Wild Blue is an effective twenty-first-century fusion of marine biology and international politics." Booklist

Includes bibliographical references

Folkens, Pieter A.

National Audubon Society guide to marine mammals of the world; illustrated by Pieter A. Folkens; written by Randall R. Reeves [et al.] Knopf 2002 527p il maps $26.95   **599.5**
1. Marine mammals   2. Marine mammals -- Identification
ISBN 0-375-41141-0

LC 2001-38103

"Just about everything one could hope for in a guide can be found in this info-packed yet extremely user-friendly tome. . . . A liberal dose of superb, high-quality action color photographs shows the creatures in their natural surroundings." SLJ

Includes bibliographical references

Herzing, Denise L.

Dolphin diaries; my 25 years with spotted dolphins in the Bahamas. St. Martin's Press 2011 xxi, 314p $26.99; ebook $12.99   **599.5**
1. Dolphins
ISBN 978-0-312-60896-5; 978-1-4299-8744-8 ebook

LC 2011005995

"Tales of diving with wild dolphins, recalcitrant equipment, living on boats, and hurricanes really bring both the excitement and the drudgery of field research to life." Booklist

Includes bibliographical references

Hoare, Philip

The **whale**; in search of the giants of the sea. Ecco 2010 453p il map $27.99   **599.5**

1. Whales 2. Whaling

ISBN 978-0-06-197621-6; 0-06-197621-0

A "chronicle of the tragic interaction between humans and whales. Using Herman Melville's life and 'Moby-Dick' as touchstones, Hoare traces the whaling industry from its origins in 18th century New England to the present." Los Angeles Times

Includes bibliographical references

Kelsey, Elin

Watching giants; the secret lives of whales. with photographs by Doc White; additional photographs by François Gohier. University of California Press 2009 201p il $24.95   **599.5**

1. Whales 2. Whales -- Mexico -- Gulf of California

ISBN 978-0-520-24976-9; 0-520-24976-3

LC 2008-7782

"An appealing, agitating foray into the world of whales that ignites both protective instincts and a hungry curiosity to know more." Kirkus

Includes bibliographical references

Rothenberg, David

Thousand mile song; whale music in a sea of sound. Basic Books 2008 287p il $27.50   **599.5**

1. Whale sounds 2. Whales 3. Whales -- Behavior

ISBN 978-0-465-07128-9; 0-465-07128-7

LC 2007-48161

"Biologists know that whale songs, which may carry for hundreds of miles, change over time and are passed on from one generation to the next, but they don't fully understand what these complex sounds are for. . . . [The author] proposes that music played by humans can help us find answers. He tested this theory by playing his clarinet into an underwater speaker and recording the whales' responses on an underwater hydrophone. His intriguing book includes sonograms and a CD demonstrating that the orcas, belugas and humpbacks he played for seemed to interact with his music. . . . His paean to the beautiful music these great mammals make should lend further support to attempts to save the whales at a time when they are increasingly threatened." Publ Wkly

Includes bibliographical references

599.53   Dolphins and porpoises

Montgomery, Sy

Journey of the pink dolphins; an Amazon quest. Simon & Schuster 2000 317p il maps hardcover o.p. pa $16   **599.53**

1. Dolphins 2. Inia geoffrensis -- Amazon River Region

ISBN 0-7432-0026-8 pa

LC 99-45840

The author "recounts her Amazonian adventures in search of the botos, the famously elusive freshwater pink dolphins, a quest that yields not only invaluable scientific observations but profound insights into the significance of myth." Booklist

Includes bibliographical references

599.64   Bovids

Rinella, Steven

American buffalo; in search of a lost icon. Spiegel & Grau 2008 277p il map $24.95   **599.64**

1. American bison 2. American bison hunting -- History 3. Bison 4. Hunters 5. Journalists 6. National characteristics, American

ISBN 978-0-385-52168-0; 0-385-52168-5

LC 2008-13624

"In 2005, [Rinella] won an Alaska state lottery permit making him one of 24 hunters allowed to kill one wild buffalo each to thin out the Copper River herd in the Wrangell-Saint Elias National Park. The book's core is Rinella's entertaining and often harrowing account of that hunting trip into Alaska's frozen south-central wilderness, where he bagged his first buffalo. But entwined throughout that story line is an engaging back story — a stampede of facts and factoids, legends and lore, hard-core science and staggering history of North America's largest land animal. Everything you ever wanted to know about the buffalo — or didn't — going back to Pleistocene days." USA Today

Includes bibliographical references

599.67   Elephants

Ammann, Karl

Elephant reflections; photographs by Karl Ammann; text by Dale Peterson. University of California Press 2009 272p il $39.95   **599.67**

1. Elephants

ISBN 978-0-520-25377-3; 0-520-25377-9

LC 2008-42391

"Ammann's photographs capture an astonishing range of elephant behavior, but Peterson's text—with its scope, synthesis of history and observation, précis of the ivory trade and conservation—is what distinguishes this book. He spins the history of elephant research into mini-mysteries of how scientists struggled to understand elephants' secretive behaviors. . . . The photographs and text complement each other beautifully in their respective odes to the 'improbable' physicality of the elephant's body." Publ Wkly

Includes bibliographical references

Anthony, Lawrence

The **elephant** whisperer; my life with the herd in the African wild. [by] Lawrence Anthony with Graham Spence. Thomas Dunne Books/St. Martin's Press 2009 368p il $24.99   **599.67**

1. Elephants 2. Wildlife refuges

ISBN 978-0-312-56578-7

LC 2009-23815

This is the author's "robust portrait of Thula Thula, the game land he owns, in cooperation with a number of Zulu tribes, in Zululand—5,000 acres of raw landscape that is thought to have been part of the exclusive hunting grounds of the Zulu king. No longer, since Anthony now runs it as a conservationist lodge, but it continues to produce colorful tales of wild discovery. Most prominent are the many fascinating stories that surround his adoption of the elephants, an unruly bunch he endeavors to make at home on the reserve. With a combination of intuition and experience, the author intelligently discusses many aspects of elephant behavior." Kirkus

599.7   Carnivores

Nicholls, Henry

The **way** of the panda; the curious history of China's political animal. Pegasus Books 2011 319p il map $25   **599.7**
  1. Giant panda 2. Wildlife conservation
  ISBN 978-1-60598-188-8; 1-60598-188-5

"When the Chinese government brings Giant Pandas to the negotiating table, the stakes change. Whole populations and their leaders clamor for access to these animals, as if they were toddlers reaching for toys. Washington, London and Moscow have all succumbed to this awesome (a chorus of 'Awwwwwww!' accompanies every panda appearance) force. That is only one reason that Henry Nicholls refers to the Giant Panda as a political animal in his charmingly written 'The Way of the Panda.' At times everything concerning the creatures seems to have a political angle: not only their value as state gifts (with heavy strings attached) but also their precise scientific classification; their mating habits and offspring; and the efforts to ensure their preservation. The author compares the history of the panda in the modern world to that of China itself, complete with a 'great leap forward' in the 1960s, when the captive breeding of pandas first became possible." Wall Street J
  Includes bibliographical references

599.74   Land carnivores

Kitchener, Andrew

The **natural** history of the wild cats. Comstock 1991 xxi, 280p il maps hardcover o.p. pa $23.95   **599.74**
  1. Cats 2. Wild cats
  ISBN 0-8014-8498-7 pa

LC 90-45833
The author provides a "synthesis of what we know about cats, his account always strengthened by the comparative point of view. There are eight vivid chapters packed with graphs, maps and feline parameters. He includes a cat Who's Who in fine color photographs; it shows us most of the small cat species, plus three big cats that, unlike lions and tigers and leopards, are not in the public eye." Sci Am
  Includes bibliographical references

Thomas, Elizabeth Marshall

The **tribe** of tiger; cats and their culture. illustrated by Jared Taylor Williams. Simon & Schuster 1994 240p il hardcover o.p. pa $13.95   **599.74**
  1. Cats 2. Cats -- Anecdotes 3. Cats -- Behavior 4. Lions 5. Tigers
  ISBN 0-7434-2689-4 pa

LC 94-20195
The author offers a "look into the lives of various members of the cat family—small and large, domestic and wild, Old World and New. She begins with the evolution and spread of different feline species, explaining the physiology and behavior of cats, including house cats, as meat eaters, that is, in the light of their hunting instincts. She then examines the changes over a period of more than 30 years in the culture . . . of different lion communities in several parts of Africa. In conclusion, she discusses the need for tiger conservation." Booklist
  Includes bibliographical references

599.75   Cat family

Adamson, Joy

★ **Born** free; a lioness of two worlds. Pantheon Bks. 1987 220p il hardcover o.p. pa $14.95 **599.75**
  1. Lions
  ISBN 0-375-71438-3 pa

LC 86-42972
This is the "story of a lioness who bridged the gulf between two worlds, that of the jungle and of man. The author and her husband, a Kenya game warden, reared a cub to kill and fend for herself when she was returned to the jungle. At the same time they were able to preserve the bond of confidence and affection established with her as a pet." Cincinnati Public Libr

Vaillant, John

The **tiger**; a true story of vengeance and survival. Alfred A. Knopf 2010 329p il map $26.95; pa $15   **599.75**
  1. Human-animal relationships 2. Tiger hunting 3. Tigers 4. Tigers -- Behavior
  ISBN 978-0-307-26893-8; 0-307-26893-4; 978-0-307-38904-6 pa; 0-307-38904-9 pa; 978-0-307-59379-5 ebook; 0-307-59379-7 ebook

LC 2010-04068
"What makes 'The Tiger' a grand addition to the animal-pursuit subgenre is the sensitive way in which Vaillant . . . evokes his cat. Few writers have taken such pains to understand their monsters, and few depict them in such arresting prose." N Y Times Book Rev
  Includes bibliographical references

599.756   Tiger

Matthiessen, Peter

Tigers in the snow; introduction and photographs by Maurice Hornocker. Farrar, Straus & Giroux 1999 169p il hardcover o.p. pa $15   **599.756**
1. Endangered species 2. Endangered species -- Russia (Federation) -- Russian Far East 3. Tigers 4. Tigers -- Russia (Federation) -- Russian Far East
ISBN 0-86547-596-2 pa
LC 99-44866

"Mixing information about the lives of all the races of wild tigers with firsthand tales of his visits to Russia, the author brings an immediacy to his narrative that stirs the reader to awe of these great cats. . . . [An] evocative look at one of our rarest animals." Booklist
Includes bibliographical references

599.77   Dog family

Busch, Robert

The **wolf** almanac; a celebration of wolves and their world. by Robert H. Busch. New & rev ed; Lyons Press 2007 274p il map pa $19.95   **599.77**
1. Wolves
ISBN 978-1-59921-069-8; 1-59921-069-X

This offers information about "the evolution and history of wolves; their biology and physiology; their behavior and sociology; and their influence in ancient cultures and mythology. . . . The author also discusses the conservation politics of all wolf species." Publisher's note
Includes bibliographical references

Lopez, Barry Holstun

★ **Of** wolves and men; with photographs by John Bauguess; including a new afterword by the author and expanded bibliography. 1st Scribner Classics ed.; Scribner Classics 2004 323p il $45 **599.77**
1. Wolves
ISBN 0-7432-4936-4
LC 2004-45429

The author "infuses his natural history of the long relationship between wolves and humankind with both myth and science, then revisits the controversial subject of wolf reintroduction." Booklist
Includes bibliographical references

McAllister, Ian

The **last** wild wolves; ghosts of the rain forest. with contributions by Chris Darimont; introduction by Paul C. Paquet. University of California Press 2007 191p il map $39.95   **599.77**
1. Photography of animals 2. Rain forest animals 3. Wolves 4. Wolves -- Behavior
ISBN 978-0-520-25473-2; 0-520-25473-2
LC 2007-10887

"The text is particularly well written and engaging. . . . However, it is the dozens of unique photos sprinkled liberally throughout the book that provide the greatest appeal." Sci Books Films

Mowat, Farley

Never cry wolf. Back Bay Books 2001 246p pa $12.99   **599.77**
1. Wolves
ISBN 978-0-316-88179-1; 0-316-88179-1

"A biologist for the Canadian government describes his experiences in the Arctic watching and tracking the activities of a wolf family." Publ Wkly

Smith, Douglas W.

★ **Decade** of the wolf; returning the wild to Yellowstone. [by] Douglas W. Smith & Gary Ferguson. Lyons Press 2005 212p il maps $23.95; pa $16.95   **599.77**
1. Endangered species 2. Wolves 3. Wolves -- Reintroduction 4. Wolves -- Yellowstone National Park
ISBN 1-59228-700-X; 1-59228-886-3 pa
LC 2005-40767

"Well illustrated with black-and-white and color photographs, this intimate history of the return of the top predator to Yellowstone will find an eager audience." Booklist
Includes bibliographical references

599.78   Bears

Croke, Vicki

★ The **lady** and the panda; the true adventures of the first American explorer to bring back China's most exotic animal. [by] Vicki Constantine Croke. Random House 2005 372p il $25.95; pa $14.95   **599.78**
1. Explorers 2. Giant panda
ISBN 0-375-50783-3; 0-375-75970-0 pa
LC 2004-51356

"This well-written, exhaustively researched and documented book should be on every library's shelves." Libr J
Includes bibliographical references

Ellis, Richard

On thin ice; the changing world of the polar bear. Alfred A. Knopf 2009 400p il $28.95   **599.78**
1. Global environmental change 2. Global warming 3. Greenhouse effect 4. Polar bear
ISBN 978-0-307-27059-7; 0-307-27059-9
LC 2009-20017

This profile of the habitat and life cycle of the polar bear covers the species' venerated position in Inuit culture, its reproductive habits, and the environmental factors that are compromising its ability to survive.

"The real strength of the book is its focus on the polar bear as the poster child of global warming, of how tied the bears are to the arctic ice and what will happen if the ice melts, and of the national and international wrangling over the politics of climate change and the listing of the bear as an endangered species. The polar bear could not ask for a better champion than Ellis in this highly recommended work." Booklist
Includes bibliographical references

599.784   Grizzly bear (Brown bear)

Busch, Robert

The **grizzly** almanac; [by] Robert H. Busch. Lyons Press 2000 229p il maps hardcover o.p. pa $19.95   **599.784**
1. Grizzly bear
ISBN 1-58574-143-4; 1-59228-320-9 pa

LC 00-58587

The author "traces the evolution of the 'big bear' from its earliest days, describes its habitat and behavior, and recounts grizzly folklore and tales of grizzly attacks. Maintaining that the grizzly's reputation as a vicious killer is undeserved, he makes recommendations for a more peaceful coexistence with humans." Libr J

Includes bibliographical references

599.8   Primates

Bearzi, Maddalena

Beautiful minds; the parallel lives of great apes and dolphins. [by] Maddalena Bearzi & Craig B. Stanford. Harvard University Press 2008 351p $24.95; pa $14.95   **599.8**
1. Animal societies 2. Apes 3. Apes -- Behavior 4. Comparative psychology 5. Dolphins 6. Dolphins -- Behavior 7. Psychology, Comparative
ISBN 978-0-674-02781-7; 0-674-02781-7; 978-0-674-04627-6 pa; 0-674-04627-7 pa

LC 2007-46199

"Endowed through evolution with large brains, the great apes (chimpanzees, bonobos gorillas and orangutans) and the cetaceans (dolphins and whales) are second only to humans in intelligence. In this delightful and intriguing book, . . . [the authors] discuss the similarities between these groups." Publ Wkly

Includes bibliographical references

Goodall, Jane

★ **In** the shadow of man; photographs by Hugo van Lawick; [with a new preface; foreword by Richard Wrangham] Mariner Books 2009 xxx, 302p il map pa $15.95   **599.8**
1. Chimpanzees
ISBN 978-0-547-33416-5

LC 2009044848

The author describes the chimpanzee group she studied during ten years of field observation in the Gombe Stream Chimpanzee Reserve in Tanzania.

Through a window; my thirty years with the chimpanzees of Gombe. [with a new preface and a new afterword] Houghton Mifflin Harcourt 2010 xx, 337p il map pa $15.95   **599.8**
1. Chimpanzees
ISBN 978-0-547-33695-4; 0-547-33695-0

LC 2009045230

This continuation of In the shadow of man "tells two stories: first of how the chimps of Gombe in Tanzania have grown, changed and died, and second, how Goodall and her

dedicated group of Tanzanian observers have survived the rigours of the past thirty years. It is beautifully written, and evokes both sympathy and understanding of these animals." Times Lit Suppl

Includes bibliographical references

Morris, Desmond

Planet ape; [by] Desmond Morris with Steve Parker. Firefly Books 2009 288p il $49.95   **599.8**
1. Apes
ISBN 978-1-55407-566-9

Detail of the great apes, including: where they live, how they live and the challenges they face. Illustrations compare apes with human beings, including their anatomy, social life, physical and mental development, diet and communication.

"Published in a large format (approximately 10 by 11 inches) with hundreds of full-color glossy photographs and illustrations, this beautiful volume is a cross between a coffee-table book and a thorough compendium of ape behavior, anatomy, taxonomy, and lore. . . . The book reads well, is packed full of exciting information, and is just plain fun to browse for hours." Sci Books Films

Redmond, Ian

The **primate** family tree; the amazing diversity of our closest relatives. foreword by Jane Goodall. Firefly Books 2008 176p il map $35   **599.8**
1. Primates
ISBN 978-1-55407-378-8; 1-55407-378-2

The Primate Family Tree "is beautifully designed, and the contents are well organized and will be interesting to all. . . . This is a very attractive, interesting, and informative publication." Sci Books Films

Includes bibliographical references

Sapolsky, Robert M.

A **primate's** memoir. Scribner 2001 304p $25; pa $14   **599.8**
1. Baboons 2. Baboons -- Behavior -- Africa, East -- Anecdotes
ISBN 0-7432-0247-3; 0-7432-0241-4 pa

LC 00-63522

This is an account of the author's experiences observing baboons in Kenya.

"One closes Sapolsky's book a lot more knowledgeable about plenty of baboon-related matters. But mostly one has already begun to miss the company of this sometimes cranky but always impassioned, learned and winningly irreverent man." N Y Times Book Rev

Among African apes; stories and photos from the field. edited by Martha M. Robbins and Christophe Boesch. University of California Press 2011 182p il map pa $29.95; ebook $29.95   **599.8**
1. Apes
ISBN 978-0-520-26710-7 pa; 978-0-520-94883-9 ebook

LC 2010033131

This book on apes contains some violent content. "The authors want to raise awareness about the plight of African apes. To do so, they draw upon research careers that go back at least 30 years. Included in the text are day-to-day accounts of what it takes to organize and find a research site in Africa, what it's like to track a gorilla, what it's like to experience a chimp or bonobo community, and what happens to these communities as a result of their encounters with various human communities. . . . Rarely does a book so perfectly illustrate the scientific process. The interaction between researcher and subject comes alive in these pages." Sci Books Films

Includes bibliographical references

★ World atlas of great apes and their conservation; edited by Julian Caldecott and Lera Miles; foreword by Kofi A. Annan. University of California Press, in association with UNEP-WCMC 2005 456p il map $45   **599.8**
1. Apes 2. Atlases 3. Biogeography 4. Reference books 5. Wildlife conservation
ISBN 0-520-24633-0; 978-0-520-24633-1
LC 2006-272653

"Each great ape specie is given a separate chapter that contains information on behavior and ecology, communication and tool use, threats and conservation, and exceptionally detailed distribution maps. What sets this book apart is the section that details each country in which apes are found and exactly what conservation efforts are underway." Univ Press Books for Public and Second Sch Libr, 2006

Includes bibliographical references

599.88   Great apes and gibbons

Fossey, Dian
★ **Gorillas** in the mist. Houghton Mifflin 1983 326p il hardcover o.p. pa $14   **599.88**
1. Gorillas
ISBN 0-618-08360-X pa
LC 82-23332

This book "recounts some of the events of the thirteen years that I have spent with the mountain gorillas in their natural habitat and includes data from the fifteen years of continuing field study." Preface

Includes bibliographical references

Waal, Frans de
Bonobo; the forgotten ape. photographs, Frans Lanting. University of Calif. Press 1997 210p il maps $50; pa $29.95   **599.88**
1. Apes 2. Chimpanzees -- Behavior 3. Kanzi (Bonobo chimpanzee)
ISBN 0-520-20535-9; 0-520-21651-2 pa
LC 96-41095

The subject of this monograph is the bonobo, a species of ape. "In six chapters, de Waal describes the history of the discovery of bonobos as a separate species; he compares them with common chimps; he describes their natural habitat and their . . . use of sex as social currency, particularly in moderating aggression; he examines bonobo social structure in relation to that of common chimps and humans; and he finishes with an exploration of bonobos' highly developed sense of empathy." New Sci

Includes bibliographical references

599.885   Chimpanzees

Halloran, Andrew R.
The **song** of the ape; Andrew R. Halloran. 1st ed. St. Martin's Press 2012 x, 276p.p   **599.885**
1. Animal communication 2. Animal sounds 3. Chimpanzees -- Behavior 4. Chimpanzees -- Behavior -- Case studies 5. Chimpanzees -- Psychology 6. Primatologists -- Biography 7. Zoo keepers -- Biography
ISBN 9780312563110; 9781429933278
LC 2011041344

The premise for this book began when, "working as a zookeeper at a drive-through animal park in south Florida, [author and primatologist Andrew R.] Halloran witnessed the escape of a group of chimpanzees who capitalized on an unsecured boat to flee from their island habitat and an upstart group of rival chimps. To react so quickly and uniformly, the group, Halloran surmises, must have been communicating in a complex manner that allowed them to plan and orchestrate such an escape. To examine this idea further, Halloran . . . embarks on a . . . study of five of the chimps involved, delving into their histories, their calls, and the meaning of their calls. The result is an . . . account of communication development among these intelligent animals . . . showing how they communicate with each other on their own terms and how numerous factors cause dialects to emerge." (Publishers Weekly)

599.9   Humans

Fabian, Ann
The **skull** collectors; Ann Fabian. The University of Chicago Press 2010 xi, 270 p.p ill.   **599.9**
1. Anthropometry -- United States 2. Craniology -- History 3. Nonfiction 4. Race relations 5. Science & civilization -- History
ISBN 978-0-226-23348-2; 0-226-23348-0
LC 2009047712

This book tells the "story of [naturalist Samuel] Morton, his contemporaries, and their search for a scientific foundation for racial difference. From cranial measurements and museum shelves to heads on stakes, bloody battlefields, and the 'rascally pleasure' of grave robbing, [author Ann] Fabian paints a . . . picture of scientific inquiry in service of an agenda of racial superiority, and of a society coming to grips with both the deadly implications of manifest destiny and the mass slaughter of the Civil War. . . . Fabian also . . . traces the continuing implications of this history, from lingering traces of scientific racism to debates over the return of the remains of Native Americans that are held by museums to this day." (Publisher's note)

Olson, Steve
Mapping human history; discovering the past through our genes. Houghton Mifflin 2002 292p il $25; pa $14   **599.9**
1. Human beings 2. Human beings -- Migrations 3. Human genetics -- Variation 4. Human population genetics 5. Physical anthropology 6. Physical

anthropology and history

ISBN 0-618-09157-2; 0-618-35210-4 pa

LC 2001-51880

The author "traces the history of human civilization in five regions of the world—Africa, the Middle East, Asia, Australia, and Europe and the Americas, plus a final chapter on Hawaii—to explain how physical differences originated and to provide evidence of our essential sameness." Publ Wkly

Includes bibliographical references and index

599.93   Genetics, sex and age characteristics, evolution

Diamond, Jared M.

The **third** chimpanzee; the evolution and future of the human animal. {by} Jared Diamond. Harper-Collins Pubs. 1992 407p il maps hardcover o.p. pa $14.95   **599.93**

1. Anthropology 2. Evolution 3. Human influence on nature 4. Human origins 5. Social change

ISBN 0-06-018307-1; 978-0-06-084550-6 pa; 0-06-084550-3 pa

LC 91-50455

The author "argues that the human being is just a third species of chimpanzee but nevertheless a unique animal essentially due to its capacity for innovation, which caused a great leap forward in hominoid evolution. After stressing the significance of spoken language, along with art and technology, Diamond focuses on the self-destructive propensities of our species." Libr J

Includes bibliographical references

Dunbar, R. I. M.

Grooming, gossip, and the evolution of language; {by} Robin Dunbar. Harvard Univ. Press 1996 230p $25; pa $17.95   **599.93**

1. Evolution 2. Gossip 3. Human behavior 4. Human origins 5. Language and languages

ISBN 0-674-36334-5; 0-674-36336-1 pa

LC 96-15934

"Concisely and clearly written for lay readers, Dunbar exhibits a gift for argument and explanation." Publ Wkly

Includes bibliographical references

Gee, Henry

Jacob's ladder; the history of the human genome. Norton 2004 272p $25.95   **599.93**

1. Genetics 2. Genomes 3. Human genetics 4. Human genome

ISBN 0-393-05083-1

LC 2004-49504

This "is an abbreviated history of biology from Aristotle through the sequencing of the human genome. The narrative includes a general description of the major discoveries in cell, developmental, evolutionary, and genetic biology. . . . This book provides a good summary of the discoveries that are the basis of modern-day biology." Sci Books Films

Includes bibliographical references

Johanson, Donald C.

★ **From** Lucy to language; [by] Donald Johanson & Blake Edgar; principal photography, David L. Brill. Rev., updated, and expanded; Simon and Schuster 2006 288p il map $65   **599.93**

1. Fossil hominids 2. Human evolution 3. Human origins 4. Paleontology 5. Physical anthropology

ISBN 0-7432-8064-4; 978-0-7432-8064-8

LC 2007-270098

This is a "photographic showcase of the essential physical evidence of human origins. . . . Permitting a face-to-face encounter with human ancestors, this work furnishes essential information, [and] an incomparable visual experience." Booklist

Includes bibliographical references

Lucy: the beginnings of humankind; [by] Donald C. Johanson and Maitland A. Edey. Simon & Schuster 1981 409p il hardcover o.p. pa $16   **599.93**

1. Fossil mammals 2. Human origins

ISBN 0-671-72499-1 pa

LC 80-21759

In November 1974 at a place called Hadar in Ethiopia Donald Johanson "discovered the partial skeleton of an extremely primitive female, erect-walking primate or hominid. . . . The skeleton received the name 'Lucy.' Much later, Lucy received the scientific name, Australopithecus afarensis, and it was determined she was some 3.5 million years old. . . . This book is Johanson's own story of the events leading up to and subsequent to Lucy's discovery." Best Sellers

Includes bibliographical references

Jolly, Alison

Lucy's legacy; sex and intelligence in human evolution. Harvard Univ. Press 1999 518p il hardcover o.p. pa $18.95   **599.93**

1. Evolution 2. Human evolution 3. Intellect 4. Intelligence 5. Social evolution 6. Women -- Evolution

ISBN 0-674-00069-2; 0-674-00540-6 pa

LC 99-32252

"Lucy is the name given to the fossil skeleton of an Australopithecine, a human ancestor, discovered in Ethiopia. The name may be a misnomer, since there's no way yet of telling whether Lucy was female. No matter. Primatologist Jolly's interest is not so much in Lucy as in the crucial role that females in general have played in human evolution. . . . In clear and clever prose, Jolly shows us how we got so smart, what sex had to do with it, and how our brains have become the central force in evolution." Booklist

Includes bibliographical references

Jones, Steve

Y: the descent of men. Houghton Mifflin 2003 252p $25   **599.93**

1. Chromosomes 2. Evolution 3. Genetics 4. Human beings -- Origin 5. Human evolution 6. Human genetics 7. Human origins 8. Masculinity 9. Men -- Physiology 10. Y chromosome

ISBN 0-618-13930-3

LC 2002-27631

"Jones' sardonic wit enlivens the molecular foundations of maleness, explaining hormones, baldness, sperm count, and even lineages of bastardy in language that is both educational and entertaining. Great general-interest science material." Booklist

Includes bibliographical references

Klein, Richard G.

The **dawn** of human culture; {by} Richard G. Klein with Blake Edgar. Wiley 2002 288p il maps $27.95   **599.93**

1. Culture 2. Culture -- Origin 3. Human evolution 4. Human origins

ISBN 0-471-25252-2

LC 2002-277680

This book "traces the origin of modern humans from their five-million-year-old roots in East Africa up through the replacement of Neanderthals in Europe some 40,000 years ago. . . . The clarity and information conveyed by the illustrations are superb, adding substantially to the book's value as a reference guide. The index is excellent. The book will appeal to all readers interested in human evolution, regardless of how much paleoanthropological background they have, and will serve admirably for courses on human evolution at any level." Choice

Includes bibliographical references

Leakey, Richard E.

Origins reconsidered; in search of what makes us human. [by] Richard Leakey and Roger Lewin. Doubleday 1992 375p il hardcover o.p. pa $16.95   **599.93**

1. Anthropology 2. Evolution 3. Human origins 4. Prehistoric peoples

ISBN 0-385-46792-3 pa

LC 92-6661

"Leakey and Lewin discuss how conceptions of human anatomical and behavioral development have been radically altered within the last 12 years by new discoveries and research in other fields. They review the developments and assert Leakey's own hypotheses based on these discoveries. . . . This is an engrossing book written for the layperson, fully explaining anthropological terms and theories when necessary. It's a solid introduction to current theory concerning human development." SLJ

The **origin** of humankind; [by] Richard Leakey. Basic Bks. 1994 171p il maps hardcover o.p. pa $14.95   **599.93**

1. Evolution 2. Human origins 3. Prehistoric peoples

ISBN 0-465-05313-0 pa

LC 94-3617

This "is a worthwhile addition to many kinds of libraries—public, general, science, biological, and psychological." Sci Books Films

Includes bibliographical references

Marks, Jonathan

★ **What** it means to be 98[percent] chimpanzee; apes, people, and their genes. University of Calif. Press 2002 312p $27.50   **599.93**

1. Evolution 2. Genetics 3. Human beings 4. Human beings -- Animal nature 5. Human evolution 6. Human

genetics 7. Human molecular genetics

ISBN 0-520-22615-1

LC 2001-7085

"With plenty of entertaining sarcasm as well as scientific argument and moral indignation, Marks blasts the pretensions of grandiose geneticists pretty thoroughly out of the water. This may be the science book to read this year." Booklist

Includes bibliographical references

Ridley, Matt

Genome; the autobiography of a species in 23 chapters. HarperCollins Pubs. 2000 344p hardcover o.p. pa $14.95   **599.93**

1. Genetics 2. Genomes 3. Human genetics -- Popular works 4. Human genome -- Popular works

ISBN 0-06-019497-9; 978-0-06-089408-5 pa; 0-06-089408-3 pa

LC 99-40933

Ridley presents a "summation of our ever increasing understanding of the roles that genes play in disease, behavior, sexual differences, and even intelligence. More important, though, he addresses not only the ethical quandaries faced by contemporary scientists but the reductionist danger in equating inheritability with inevitability." New Yorker

Includes bibliographical references

Rothman, Barbara Katz

Genetic maps and human imaginations; the limits of science in understanding who we are. Norton 1998 272p $24.95   **599.93**

1. Genetics 2. Genomes 3. Human beings 4. Human beings -- Philosophy 5. Human genetics -- Philosophy 6. Human genome -- Research -- Moral and ethical aspects

ISBN 0-393-04703-2

LC 98-18800

A discussion of "the bioethics and consequences of mapping the human genome. . . . Rothman has concentrated on how 'genetic thinking' affects the way we see race, illness and cancer, and reproduction. Scientists may not like a couple of phrases Rothman has coined . . . but most other readers will probably find that the terms make sense as they read." Libr J

Includes bibliographical references

Schwartz, Jeffrey H.

What the bones tell us. University of Arizona Press 1998 292p pa $18.95   **599.93**

1. Physical anthropology

ISBN 0-8165-1855-6

LC 97-34147

This volume discusses "the nature and limits of osteology and paleontology and the scientific knowledge the two sciences provide. Part one describes the kinds of fossils and artifacts archaeologists find. [Part two addresses] . . . the places of Darwin, Huxley, and Raymond Dart in human evolutionary theory." Booklist

Includes bibliographical references

Stringer, Christopher B.

African exodus; the origins of modern humanity. {by} Christopher Stringer and Robin McKie. Holt & Co. 1997 xx, 282p il map hardcover o.p. pa $17 **599.93**
1. Evolution 2. Human origins
ISBN 0-8050-5814-1 pa

LC 96-37718
"This intellectually potent yet eminently accessible volume . . . stands tall. It provides broad insight into a complex field." Publ Wkly
Includes bibliographical references

Swisher, Carl C.

Java Man; how two geologists changed our understanding of human evolution. [by] Carl C. Swisher III, Garniss H. Curtis, Roger Lewin. University of Chicago Press 2001 256p il pa $16 **599.93**
1. Fossil hominids 2. Human origins
ISBN 978-0-226-78734-3; 0-226-78734-6

LC 2001-37337
The authors "offer a lively writeup of the technicalities of geochronology, bio-sketches of the discoverers of the erectus fossils, travelogues of their travel in Java, and their side of a spat with paleoanthropology celebrity Don Johansen. An engrossing contribution to the general-interest literature about human origins." Booklist
Includes bibliographical references

Sykes, Bryan

Adam's curse; a future without men. Norton 2004 318p il $25.95; pa $15.95 **599.93**
1. Chromosomes 2. Genetics 3. Human evolution -- Popular works 4. Sex (Biology) 5. Sex (Biology) -- Popular works 6. Sociobiology 7. Y Chromosome 8. Y chromosome -- Popular works
ISBN 0-393-05896-4; 0-393-32680-2 pa

LC 2004-3628
"This book incorporates many genres—scientific protocol, biography, harlequin romance, and historical fiction—all expertly executed by Sykes." Sci Books Films

The seven daughters of Eve. Norton 2001 306p il map hardcover o.p. pa $15.95 **599.93**
1. Evolution 2. Genetics 3. Human origins
ISBN 0-393-32314-5 pa
The author "contends that most Europeans can trace their roots back to seven women—seven daughters of Eve. One of them lived about 10,000 years ago, around the time farmers first cultivated European soil; the six others go back much farther, to Europe's early hunter-gatherers." N Y Times Book Rev

Tattersall, Ian

Extinct humans; by Ian Tattersall and Jeffrey H. Schwartz. Westview Press 2000 256p il hardcover o.p. pa $35 **599.93**
1. Evolution 2. Fossil hominids 3. Human evolution 4. Human origins
ISBN 0-8133-3918-9 pa

LC 00-22088

The authors explain "why the idea of the one-track, lineal descent of human beings is obsolete and the notion of a 'bushy' evolutionary history, like that of other genera, fits the fossil evidence better." Booklist
Includes bibliographical references

Masters of the planet; Ian Tattersall. Palgrave Macmillan 2012 272p. **599.93**
ISBN 9780230108752

LC 2011034415
'This book examines the evolution of humans. "When homo sapiens made their entrance 100,000 years ago they were confronted by a wide range of other early humans -- homo erectus, who walked better and used fire; homo habilis who used tools; and of course the Neanderthals, who were brawny and strong. . . . [Author Ian Tattersall] explores how the physical traits and cognitive ability of homo sapiens distanced them from the rest of nature. Even more importantly, 'Masters of the Planet' looks at how our early ancestors acquired these superior abilities; it shows that their strange and unprecedented mental facility is not, as most of us were taught, simply a basic competence that was refined over unimaginable eons by natural selection. Instead, it is an emergent capacity that was acquired quite recently and changed the world definitively." (Publisher's note)

The fossil trail; how we know what we think we know about human evolution. 2nd ed.; Oxford University Press 2009 xxiii, 327p il map pa $24.95 **599.93**
1. Evolution 2. Fossils 3. Human origins
ISBN 978-0-19-536766-9

LC 2008-13654
"The task of organising such complex material into a narrative account would have defeated most writers, but Tattersall has mastered it with remarkable skill." New Sci [review of 1995 edition]
Includes bibliographical references

The monkey in the mirror; essays on science and what makes us human. Harcourt 2002 203p hardcover o.p. pa $13 **599.93**
1. Evolution 2. Human evolution 3. Human origins 4. Science
ISBN 0-15-602706-2 pa

LC 2001-24122
"A perceptive and persuasive introduction to human origins." Booklist

Taylor, Timothy

The artificial ape; how technology changed the course of human evolution. Palgrave Macmillan 2010 256p il $27 **599.93**
1. Evolution 2. Human evolution 3. Human origins
ISBN 9780230617636

LC 2010-7924
The author "proposes that it was our early adoption of tools, objects, and, now, technology that changed us [from apes], demonstrating how: baby slings made out of animal fur freed up our arms up to use tools; clothes kept us warm, reducing our need for body hair; [and] shelter protected us from the elements and led our bodies to become slighter

and physically weaker. . . . Taylor shows how humans made choices that assumed greater control over their own evolution." Publisher's note

Includes bibliographical references

Tudge, Colin

The **time** before history; 5 million years of human impact. Scribner 1996 366p il maps hardcover o.p. pa $17.95　　　　　　　　　　**599.93**

1. Agriculture 2. Continental drift 3. Evolution 4. Human origins 5. Mammals 6. Naturalists 7. Travel writers 8. Writers on science

ISBN 0-684-83052-3 pa

LC 95-42026

"With majestic sweep and subtle wit, . . . Tudge brings an astonishing perspective to the story of humanity." Publ Wkly

Includes bibliographical references

Wade, Nicholas

Before the dawn; recovering the lost history of our ancestors. Penguin Press 2006 312p il map $24.95　　　　　　　　　　　　　　　　**599.93**

1. Evolution 2. Human evolution 3. Social change 4. Social evolution

ISBN 1-59420-079-3; 978-1-59420-079-3

LC 2005-55293

"This is highly recommended for readers interested in how DNA analysis is rewriting the history of mankind." Publ Wkly

Includes bibliographical references

Walker, Alan

The **wisdom** of the bones; in search of human origins. [by] Alan Walker and Pat Shipman. Knopf 1996 338p il maps hardcover o.p. pa $14　**599.93**

1. Evolution 2. Fossil hominids 3. Human origins

ISBN 0-679-74783-4 pa

LC 95-37525

"In 1984 Walker, along with colleague Richard Leakey and their 'hominidgang' of experienced Kenyan excavators, discovered a near-intact fossil of Homo erectus. The find was a veritable trove of theory-busting information, which the authors take up after recounting the scientists who preceded Walker in investigating the species. . . . A fluidly presented portrait of the people and process of paleoanthropology." Booklist

Includes bibliographical references

Wilson, Edward O., 1929-

★ The **social** conquest of earth; Edward O. Wilson. W. W. Norton & Co 2012 viii, 330 p.p　**599.93**

1. Evolution (Biology) -- Philosophy 2. Group selection (Evolution) 3. Human evolution -- Philosophy 4. Natural history literature 5. Social evolution -- Philosophy

ISBN 0871404133; 9780871404138

LC 2011052680

This book by Edward O. Wilson provides an explanation of why humans rule the Earth. After a respectful nod to the old favorites (big brains, tools, language, fire), the author maintains that these merely provide the background to our overpowering eusociality; we are the world's most intensely

social creatures, living in complex societies of mutually dependent individuals. . . . Wilson adds that another eusocial organism, the ant, dominated terrestrial life for 50 million years before humans appeared; it remains a close second. The author provides a . . . comparison of how this powerful . . . strategy vaulted two wildly different species to the top of the heap. . . . Group selection--as opposed to kin selection, i.e., the selfish gene à la Richard Dawkins--is the author's big idea. (Kirkus)

The Cambridge encyclopedia of human evolution; edited by Steve Jones, Robert Martin and David Pilbeam; executive editor, Sarah Bunney; foreword by Richard Dawkins. Cambridge Univ. Press 1993 506p il maps $120; pa $42 **599.93**

1. Evolution 2. Evolution -- Encyclopedias 3. Human origins 4. Reference books

ISBN 0-521-32370-3; 0-521-46786-1 pa

LC 92-18037

"This encyclopedia of the human species places modern man in evolutionary perspective, showing the descent of humankind from Mitochondrial Eve and its relationship to other living primates. Genetics, fossils, biology, brain function, disease, the biology, evolution, and ecology of humans and other modern primates are the major themes arranged topically in this encyclopedia. Excellent black-and-white photos, drawings, tables, and maps complement a work with over 70 contributors." Am Libr

★ The Double-edged helix; social implications of genetics in a diverse society. edited by Joseph S. Alper [et al.] Johns Hopkins Univ. Press 2002 293p hardcover o.p. pa $26.95　　　**599.93**

1. Bioethics 2. Genetic engineering 3. Genetics 4. Medical genetics

ISBN 0-8018-6964-1; 0-8018-7926-4 pa

LC 2001-6618

"Bringing the concerns of different communities together in a single volume makes it possible to appreciate the mosaic of human issues fully and forces us to anticipate the challenges that may arise—and that will require our attention—as the genetic revolution proceeds. . . . A much needed antidote to the current genetic hoopla." JAMA

Includes bibliographical references

The Genomic revolution; unveiling the unity of life. Michael Yudell and Robert DeSalle, editors. Joseph Henry Press 2002 272p $27.95　**599.93**

1. Genomes 2. Genomics -- Popular works 3. Human genome -- Popular works

ISBN 0-309-07436-3

LC 2002-4016

"The essays are well written and accessible to almost anyone interested in the areas represented. . . . All in all, a unique snapshot of a pivotal period in science and a valuable addition to most libraries. Summing up: Highly recommended." Choice

Includes bibliographical references

600 TECHNOLOGY

600 Technology (Applied sciences)

Arthur, W. Brian

★ The **nature** of technology; what it is and how it evolves. Free Press 2009 246p $27 **600**

1. Technology -- Economic aspects 2. Technology -- Philosophy 3. Technology -- Social aspects

ISBN 978-1-4165-4405-0; 1-4165-4405-4

LC 2009-7015

"What is technology in its nature, in its deepest essence? Where does it come from? How does it evolve? . . . [The author] tries to answer these and other questions. . . . Arthur's arguments will likely alter the reader's way of thinking about technology and its relationship to humanity." Publ Wkly

Includes bibliographical references

Burke, James

The **knowledge** web; from electronic agents to Stonehenge and back--and other journeys through knowledge. Simon & Schuster 1999 285p il $25; pa $14 **600**

1. Technology -- History

ISBN 0-684-85934-3; 0-684-85935-1 pa

LC 99-24539

Burke's "style matches his subject as he skips from one topic to another, moving at the speed of hypertext. . . . This manic, associative tour of the cultural underpinnings of technological advancement is fast, sexy and packed with information." Publ Wkly

Includes bibliographical references

Edgerton, David

The **shock** of the old; technology and global history since 1900. Oxford University Press 2007 270p il $26 **600**

1. Technology -- History 2. Technology -- Social aspects -- History -- 20th century

ISBN 978-0-19-532283-5; 0-19-532283-5

LC 2006-26435

This book "is a necessary reminder of just how important things are in our lives, and how important we are in the life of things." New Yorker

Includes bibliographical references (240-247)

Langone, John

★ The **new** how things work; everyday technology explained. art by Pete Samek, Andy Christie, and Bryan Christie. National Geographic Society 2004 272p il $35 **600**

1. Inventions 2. Inventions -- Popular works 3. Technology 4. Technology -- Popular works

ISBN 0-7922-6956-X

LC 2004-50438

"With eleven chapters, including 'At Home,' 'Building and Buildings,' 'Transportation,' 'At Play,' and 'Tools of Medicine,' the book covers . . . familiar items such as refrigerators and washing machines, planes and trains, elevators and escalators, as well as the not-so-familiar, such as laser surgery and DNA manipulation. . . . {Coverage of recent innovations range} from DVDs and MP3s to plasma screen TVs and wireless Internet technology." Publisher's note

Macaulay, David

The **new** way things work; [by] David Macaulay with Neil Ardley. Houghton Mifflin 1998 400p il $35 **600**

1. Inventions 2. Machinery 3. Technology

ISBN 0-395-93847-3

LC 98-14224

Arranged in five sections this volume provides information on "the workings of hundreds of machines and devices—holograms, helicopters, airplanes, mobile phones, compact disks, hard disks, bits and bytes, cash machines. . . . Explanations [are also given] of the scientific principles behind each machine—how gears make work easier, why jumbo jets are able to fly, how computers actually compute." Publisher's note

Woodford, Chris

Cool stuff and how it works; written by Chris Woodford [et al.] Dorling Kindersley Pub. 2005 256p il hardcover o.p. pa $19.99 **600**

1. Inventions 2. Inventions -- Juvenile literature 3. Young adult literature -- Works

ISBN 0-7566-1465-1; 0-7566-5834-9 pa

LC 2005-13587

This book "uses advanced imaging technology such as X rays, scanning electron micrographs, and infrared thermograms, along with traditional graphics, to reveal the workings of . . . [high-tech gadgets and appliances] from the Internet and computers to advanced textiles, space-age materials, and medical marvels. . . . This will rate high on the 'cool' factor, whether at home, school, or library." Booklist

609 History, geographic treatment, biography

Brown, David E.

Inventing modern America; from the microwave to the mouse. text by David E. Brown; foreword by Lester C. Thurow; introductions by James Burke. MIT Press 2001 209p il hardcover o.p. pa $19.95 **609**

1. Inventions 2. Inventions -- United States -- History -- 20th century 3. Inventors 4. Inventors -- United States

ISBN 0-262-02508-6; 0-262-52349-3 pa

LC 2001-44768

"Brown simplifies technical data and uses an enthusiastic, almost proselytizing tone. . . . Full color photographs, diagrams and intriguing tidbits . . . make this a good book for most to browse." Publ Wkly

Includes bibliographical references

Burke, James

Circles: 50 round trips through history, technology, science, culture. Simon & Schuster 2000 286p $24; pa $13 **609**

1. Science -- History 2. Technology -- History

ISBN 0-7432-0008-X; 0-7432-4976-3 pa

LC 00-57335

"Readers will be fascinated by Burke's route through the labyrinthine corridors of history. This book is ideal for dipping into, a few essays at a time." Publ Wkly

Includes bibliographical references

Denny, Mark

Ingenium; five machines that changed the world. Johns Hopkins University Press 2007 176p il $27 **609**

1. Force and energy 2. Inventions -- History 3. Machinery 4. Technology -- History

ISBN 978-0-8018-8586-0; 0-8018-8586-8

LC 2006-26085

The author "has authored a well-written, illustrated, and informative book that is readable to all but the mentally lazy." Choice

Includes bibliographical references

Macdonald, Anne L.

Feminine ingenuity; women and invention in America. {by} Anne Macdonald. Ballantine Bks. 1992 xxiv, 514p il hardcover o.p. pa $25 **609**

1. Inventions 2. Women inventors

ISBN 0-345-38314-1 pa

LC 91-55502

This is a "study of American women's contribution to science, engineering, and technology as represented in the issuance of U.S. patents. From the first patent issued to a woman in 1809, Macdonald traces the uphill struggle women have faced in their efforts to obtain equal rights—in the area of patent awards as well as in the broader educational, economic, and social arenas." Libr J

Includes bibliographical references

Petroski, Henry

The **evolution** of useful things. Knopf 1992 288p il hardcover o.p. pa $13.95 **609**

1. Inventions 2. Patents

ISBN 0-679-74039-2 pa

LC 91-39524

The author "provides an intricate look, in lay reader's terms, at the technology and basic rationale behind a number of items we often take for granted. The list is comprehensive: kitchen utensils, zippers, tools, paper clips, fast-food packaging, and more. The text is far from a recital of mere facts. Petroski's anecdotes and stories about individual designers and inventors are told with warm regard. He also provides illuminating thoughts on the theoretical, historical, and cultural frameworks that influenced these creations." Libr J

Includes bibliographical references

Popular mechanics magazine.

The **wonderful** future that never was; flying cars, mail delivery by parachute, and other predictions from the past. Gregory Benford and the editors of Popular mechanics. Hearst Communications 2010 207p il $24.95 **609**

1. Forecasting 2. Inventions -- History 3. Technological innovations

ISBN 978-1-58816-822-1

LC 2010-3998

"Profusely illustrated (there's something on nearly every page), the book is endlessly fascinating, a collage of snapshots of the present the way people saw it when it was still the distant future." Booklist

Tobin, James

Great projects; the epic story of the building of America: from the taming of the Mississippi to the invention of the Internet. Free Press 2001 322p il maps hardcover o.p. pa $31.95 **609**

1. Engineering -- History 2. Engineering -- Social aspects

ISBN 0-7432-1064-6; 1-4516-1301-6 pa

LC 2001-33016

"The clearly written, nontechnical narratives are lively and comprehensive." Libr J

Includes bibliographical references

Van Dulken, Stephen

Inventing the 19th century; 100 inventions that shaped the Victorian Age from aspirin to the Zeppelin. New York Univ. Press 2001 218p il $30 **609**

1. Inventions

ISBN 0-8147-8810-6

LC 2001-30831

This briefly describes the inventions of the 19th century with text and diagrams from the patent applications.

Inventing the 20th century; 100 inventions that shaped the world: from the airplane to the zipper. {by} Stephen Van Dulken; with an introduction by Andrew Phillips. New York Univ. Press 2000 246p il hardcover o.p. pa $17.95 **609**

1. Inventions

ISBN 0-8147-8808-4; 0-8147-8812-2 pa

LC 00-41141

This briefly describes inventions of the 20th century, arranged by decade, with text and diagrams from the patent applications.

"A fascinating compendium for trivia seekers." Publ Wkly

Includes bibliographical references

609.2 Biography

Vare, Ethlie Ann

Patently female; from AZT to TV dinners: stories of women inventors and their breakthrough ideas.

[by] Ethlie Ann Vare, Greg Ptacek. Wiley 2002 220p
il $27.95   **609.2**
1. Women inventors 2. Women inventors -- United
States
ISBN 0-471-02334-5

LC 2001-26950

The authors "detail how women's ideas like the cotton gin, automatic sewing machine and even the Brooklyn
Bridge have often been attributed to men and how history
books and museums like the Smithsonian and the National
Inventors Hall of Fame have ignored women's achievements." Publ Wkly

Includes bibliographical references

610   Medicine and health

Adler, Robert E.

Medical firsts; from Hippocrates to the human
genome. Wiley 2004 232p il $24.95   **610**
1. Medicine -- History
ISBN 0-471-40175-7

LC 2003-14212

"Adler ably combines good storytelling, clear and cogent scientific explanations [and] a respect for science over
superstition." Publ Wkly

Includes bibliographical references

Ball, Philip

The **devil's** doctor; Paracelsus and the world of
Renaissance magic and science. Farrar, Straus and
Giroux 2006 430p il map $27   **610**
1. Alchemists 2. Alchemy -- History 3. Biography,
Individual 4. Physicians 5. Science -- History -- 16th
century 6. Science and magic 7. Writers on science
ISBN 0-374-22979-1

LC 2005-19848

This biography "illuminates the life of alchemist, physician, theologian, and astrologer Paracelsus (1493-1541),
placing him . . . in the context of the Reformation. . . . Ball
captures and explains all of Paracelsus's idiosyncrasies and
contradictions in writing that is clear and enjoyable." Libr J

Includes bibliographical references

Bortolotti, Dan

Hope in hell; inside the world of Doctors Without Borders. Firefly Bks. 2004 303p il $29.95; pa
$19.95   **610**
1. Disaster relief 2. War relief
ISBN 1-55297-865-6; 1-55407-142-9 pa

LC 2005-357206

"Much of what Bortolotti reports is noticeably absent from the daily headlines, so this eye-opening account
is all the more chilling, and MSF's efforts achingly more
compelling." Booklist

Includes bibliographical references

Cassedy, James H.

Medicine in America: a short history. Johns
Hopkins Univ. Press 1991 187p hardcover o.p. pa
$18.95   **610**
1. Medicine -- United States -- History
ISBN 0-8018-4208-5 pa

LC 91-7058

This history of American medicine traces medical and
health-related matters from colonial times to the present

This book "is scholarly, well written, very useful, and
fills a void." Choice

Includes bibliographical references

Finger, Stanley

Doctor Franklin's medicine. University of Pennsylvania Press 2006 379p il $39.95   **610**
1. Authors 2. Biography, Individual 3. Diplomats 4.
Inventors 5. Medicine -- History 6. Medicine -- United
States -- History 7. Members of Congress 8. Scientists
9. Statesmen 10. Writers on science
ISBN 978-0-8122-3913-3; 0-8122-3913-X

LC 2005-45659

The author presents the "story of Benjamin Franklin's
contributions to modern medicine and hygiene. The book is
an important tribute to America's quintessential Enlightenment scholar and statesman." Choice

Includes bibliographical references

Friedman, Meyer

Medicine's 10 greatest discoveries; [by] Meyer
Friedman, Gerald W. Friedland. Yale Univ. Press
1998 363p il hardcover o.p. pa $14.95   **610**
1. Anesthesiologists 2. Anesthetics 3. Bacteriology
4. Biochemists 5. Biologists 6. Biophysicists 7.
Blood -- Circulation 8. Chemists 9. Cholesterol 10.
College teachers 11. DNA 12. Discoveries in science
13. Geologists 14. Human anatomy 15. Medical
innovations -- History 16. Medical scientists 17.
Medical scientists -- History 18. Medicine -- History
19. Microbiologists 20. Microscopists 21. Molecular
biologists 22. Nobel laureates for physics 23. Nobel
laureates for physiology or medicine 24. Pathologists
25. Penicillin 26. Physicians 27. Physicists 28.
Physiologists 29. Scientists 30. Surgeons 31.
Vaccination 32. Writers on medicine 33. Writers on
science 34. X-rays
ISBN 0-300-07598-7; 0-300-08278-9 pa

LC 98-19921

This describes such medical discoveries as the circula-
tion of blood by William Harvey, the X-ray by Roentgen,
Penicillin by Alexander Fleming, and DNA by Watson,
Crick and Maurice Hugh Frederick Wilkins.

Gale Group

★ The **Gale** encyclopedia of medicine; 4th ed;
Gale 2011 6v il set $875   **610**
1. Medicine -- Encyclopedias 2. Reference books
ISBN 978-1-4144-8646-8

LC 2010-53605

This "medical guide features information on more than
1,700 medical topics. . . . Disease/disorder articles typically
cover definition; description; causes and symptoms; diagno-

sis; treatments; prevention; and more. Test/treatment articles typically cover definition; purposes; precautions; preparation; risks; normal and abnormal results." Publisher's note

Includes bibliographical references

Groopman, Jerome E.

How doctors think; [by] Jerome Groopman. Houghton Mifflin Co. 2007 307p il $26   **610**

1. Diagnosis 2. Medical logic 3. Medicine 4. Medicine -- Decision making 5. Physicians 6. Physicians -- Psychology

ISBN 978-0-618-61003-7; 0-618-61003-0

LC 2006-35718

This book is comprised of a series of "essays that explore the rational and irrational factors that influence medical decision-making. By turns inspired and dismaying, it explains how even the best doctor can draw the wrong conclusion, and why that same doctor might also come up with a brilliant diagnosis that has eluded his peers. Uncertainty hovers over the practice of medicine, which Dr. Groopman, a clear writer and a humane thinker, presents as an art as well as a science, despite the spectacular advances in medical technology." N Y Times (Late N Y Ed)

Includes bibliographical references

Second opinions; stories of intuition and choice in a changing world of medicine. {by} Jerome Groopman. Viking 2000 243p hardcover o.p. pa $14   **610**

1. Diagnosis 2. Medicine 3. Medicine -- Case studies 4. Medicine -- Decision making 5. Medicine, Popular -- Miscellanea

ISBN 0-14-029862-2 pa

LC 99-36692

"Through vivid accounts of the dilemmas he has faced—not only as a doctor but as a patient, a parent, a grandson and a friend—the author illuminates the art, and the perils, of interpreting other people's symptoms." Newsweek

Your medical mind; how to decide what is right for you. [by] Jerome Groopman and Pamela Hartzband. Penguin Press 2011 308p $27.95   **610**

1. Decision making 2. Medicine 3. Physician-patient relationship

ISBN 978-1-59420-311-4

LC 2011019808

The authors "present readers with a fascinating look into medical decision making. Through detailed portraits of socially and ethnically diverse real-life individuals who must make medical choices, the authors show how patients' family history, culture, profession, and attitudes toward medicine and technology can shape their decisions about treatment. . . . This engaging, insightful, and illuminating book should be read by general audiences as well as medical and health-care professionals, who are often baffled by the choices their patients make." Libr J

Includes bibliographical references

Lown, Bernard

The **lost** art of healing. Ballantine Bks. 1999 xx, 344p pa $14.95   **610**

1. Holistic medicine 2. Physician-patient relationship

3. Sick

ISBN 0-345-42597-9

LC 98-96703

The author's "stimulating inquiry is sound medicine for doctors and patients alike." Publ Wkly

Includes bibliographical references

Meyers, Morton A.

Happy accidents; serendipity in modern medical breakthroughs. [by] Morton Meyers. Arcade Pub. 2007 390p il $29.95; pa $16.99   **610**

1. Medicine -- Research

ISBN 978-1-55970-819-7; 978-1-55970-845-6 pa

LC 2006-100551

The author "details dozens of medicines currently saving millions of lives that are the results of serendipity, which he defines as 'chance plus judgment'—medicines discovered while researchers were looking in quite another, often the opposite, direction. . . . Meyers' accounts of such happy accidents as the discoveries of the lifesaving anticoagulant Coumadin, the manic-depression therapeutic lithium, and others is a significant brief on creativity's critical role in medical research." Booklist

Includes bibliographical references

Orbinski, James

An **imperfect** offering; humanitarian action in the twenty-first century. Walker & Co. 2008 431p il $27   **610**

1. Biography, Individual 2. College teachers 3. Humanitarians 4. Medical assistance 5. Medical association officials 6. Physicians 7. War relief

ISBN 978-0-8027-1709-2; 0-8027-1709-8

"Orbinski was president of Doctors Without Borders when it received the Nobel Peace Prize in 1999, and this book echoes and expands on his acceptance speech. He argues that humanitarian action must be free of political influence, must not become a tool of war and must not be silent in the face of human-rights violations. . . . An important, consciousness-raising work." Kirkus

Includes bibliographical references

Pollack, Robert

The **missing** moment; how the unconscious shapes modern science. Houghton Mifflin 1999 240p $25   **610**

1. Medicine -- Philosophy 2. Medicine and psychology 3. Psychology

ISBN 0-395-70985-7

LC 99-26241

"The collective myth of science and of biomedicine, in Pollack's diagnosis, involves misplaced beliefs in the omnipotence of rational thought, absolute control over nature and triumph over death. With eloquence and wit, he contends that biomedicine's heroic goals of beating infectious microbes into total submission, of eradicating cancer and of dramatically extended life expectancy should give way to emphasis on disease prevention and methods to slow the aging process." Publ Wkly

Includes bibliographical references

Porter, Roy

The **greatest** benefit to mankind; a medical history of humanity. Norton 1998 831p il $35; pa $18.95 **610**

1. Medicine -- History 2. Social medicine -- History
ISBN 0-393-04634-6; 0-393-31980-6 pa

LC 98-10219

Porter's "study traces Western medical thought and practices from their origins in classical Greece to today's biomedical developments. Although scholarly, the text is elegantly written, accessible to the general reader, and filled with fascinating details." Libr J

Includes bibliographical references

Schweitzer, Albert

Out of my life and thought; an autobiography. translated by Antje Bultmann Lemke; foreword by Jimmy Carter; preface by Rhena Schweitzer Miller and Antje Bultmann Lemke. Johns Hopkins Univ. Press 1998 272p il $18.95 **610**

1. Hospital administrators 2. Missionaries 3. Missionaries, Medical -- Gabon -- Lambaréné (Moyen-Ogooué) -- Biography 4. Musicians -- Europe -- Biography 5. Musicologists 6. Nobel laureates for peace 7. Nonfiction writers 8. Physicians 9. Theologians 10. Theologians -- Europe -- Biography 11. Writers on religion
ISBN 0-8018-6097-0

LC 98-28166

This is "the autobiography of the world-famous missionary doctor, organist, philosopher, theologian, and Nobel Peace Prize winner." Booklist

Includes bibliographical references

Sloane, Sheila B.

Medical abbreviations & eponyms; 2nd ed; Saunders 1997 905p pa $41 **610**

1. Medicine -- Dictionaries 2. Reference books
ISBN 0-7216-7088-1

LC 96-28595

This dictionary provides a list of medical abbreviations, acronyms, symbols, and eponyms. Also included are definitions for common diseases, syndromes, and operations. An appendix which lists over 400 anticancer drug combinations is provided

Snyderman, Nancy

★ **Medical** myths that can kill you; and the 101 truths that will save, extend, and improve your life. [by] Nancy L. Snyderman. Crown Publishers 2008 273p $24.95; pa $14.95 **610**

1. Medical misconceptions
ISBN 978-0-307-40613-2; 978-0-307-40614-9 pa

LC 2007-46699

The author "examines some common medical myths—e.g., that only old people get heart attacks and strokes, that 'natural' means safe—explaining why they have become so prevalent, why they are wrong, and what sensible approaches people can take to avoid inadvertently damaging their health because of false beliefs. . . . Every page is filled

with useful facts in this fascinating and well-researched and written book accessible to all readers." Libr J

Includes bibliographical references

Teresi, Dick

★ The **undead**; organ harvesting, the ice-water test, beating heart cadavers: how medicine is blurring the line between life and death. Dick Teresi. Pantheon Books 2012 256 p. **610**

1. Attitude to Death 2. Brain death 3. Death 4. Death -- Autobiography 5. Persistent Vegetative State 6. Scientific literature 7. Tissue and Organ Harvesting
ISBN 9780375423710

LC 2011032025

"In this . . . look at how doctors determine the moment of death, skeptical science writer . . . [Dick] Teresi . . . relishes ripping into the 1968 Harvard team that formulated new criteria for determining death: 'loss of personhood,' or brain death. Doctors, Teresi says, can now 'declare a person dead in less time than it takes to get a decent eye exam' by testing reflexes: 'a flashlight in the eyes, ice water in the ears, and then an attempt to gasp for air' when the respirator is disconnected. Teresi interviews scientists who question the finality of brain death when the heart is still beating, and even the concept that personhood is located solely in the brain. . . . Teresi charges that the brain-death revolution is driven by the $20 billion-a-year organ transplant business." (Publishers Weekly)

The **Cambridge** illustrated history of medicine; edited by Roy Porter. Cambridge Univ. Press 1996 400p il maps hardcover o.p. pa $35 **610**

1. Medicine -- History
ISBN 0-521-44211-7; 0-521-00252-4 pa

LC 95-38000

This is a history of medicine from antiquity to the present. In ten "chapters, Roy Porter and his collaborators examine the changing form of medicine and . . . {the} technical successes that it has achieved." Sci Am

Includes bibliographical references

Current medical diagnosis and treatment 2008; [edited by] Stephen J. McPhee, Maxine A. Papadakis; senior editor, Lawrence M. Tirerney. 47th ed; McGraw-Hill Medical 2008 1672p il pa $69.95 **610**

1. Medicine -- Handbooks, manuals, etc.
ISBN 978-0-07-149430-4; 0-07-149430-8

"Provides concise information on the diagnosis and treatment of diseases and disorders for medical practitioners. Uses common medical terminology, but is generally understandable to the layperson." N Y Public Libr Book of How & Where to Look It Up

★ **Dorland's** illustrated medical dictionary; 32nd ed; Elsevier/Saunders 2011 xxvii, 2147p il $51.95 **610**

1. Medicine -- Dictionaries 2. Reference books
ISBN 978-1-4160-6257-8

LC 2011-9789

This standard reference includes terms used in medicine, surgery, dentistry, pharmacy, chemistry, nursing, veterinary science, biology, and medical biology. Pronunciation, derivation, and definitions are given.

"This is considered one of the most comprehensive medical dictionaries in print." N Y Public Libr Book of How & Where to Look It Up

Includes bibliographical references

Magill's medical guide; medical editors, Brandon P. Brown ... [et al.] 6th ed.; Salem Press 2011 6v il set $495   **610**
1. Medicine -- Encyclopedias 2. Reference books
ISBN 978-1-58765-677-4

LC 2010-31862

Covers diseases, disorders, treatments, procedures, specialties, anatomy, biology, and issues in an A-Z format, with sidebars addressing recent developments in medicine and concise information boxes for all diseases and disorders.

★ The Merck manual of diagnosis and therapy; Robert S. Porter, editor-in-chief; Justin L. Kaplan, senior assistant editor. 19th ed.; Merck Sharp & Dohme Corp. 2011 xxxii, 3754p il $79.95 **610**
1. Medicine -- Handbooks, manuals, etc. 2. Reference books
ISBN 978-0-911910-19-3
"A one-volume reference that attempts to cover all but the most obscure diseases. Sections are organized by type of disease or medical specialty." N Y Public Libr Book of How & Where to Look It Up

Mosby's medical dictionary; 8th ed.; Mosby/Elsevier 2009 various paging il pa $40.95   **610**
1. Medicine -- Dictionaries 2. Reference books
ISBN 978-0-323-05290-0

LC 2008-18950

"Many definitions are discursive. Emphasizes allied health professions, with . . . categories of entries in physical therapy, occupational therapy, and respiratory care." Guide to Ref Books. 11th edition

★ Taber's cyclopedic medical dictionary; Donald Venes, editor. 20th ed.; F.A. Davis Co. 2005 xxxv, 2788p il $39.95   **610**
1. Medicine -- Dictionaries 2. Reference books
ISBN 0-8036-1207-9
This work gives "definitions of medical terms and words. Pronunciation is given for all but very common terms and the etymology of most words is included. Appendixes include such information as emergency treatment, dietetic charts, Latin and Greek nomenclature, and normal reference laboratory values." Guide to Ref Books. 11th edition

Includes bibliographical references

Western medicine: an illustrated history; edited by Irvine Loudon. Oxford Univ. Press 1997 347p il $65; pa $27.50   **610**
1. Medicine -- History
ISBN 0-19-820509-0; 0-19-924813-3 pa

LC 97-218848

This history "extends from ancient Greece to the present. . . . The book consists of chapters by 20 historians from England, Germany, and the United States. An introductory chapter describes the long historical relationship between medicine and the visual arts. Seven subsequent chapters offer a chronological history of medicine, including a discussion of the influence of Islamic medicine on medieval and Renaissance physicians. The 11 final chapters deal with medicine in its social context, such as histories of childbirth, nursing, and mental illness." Libr J

Includes bibliographical references

610.28 Auxiliary techniques and procedures; apparatus, equipment, materials

Friedman, David M.
The **immortalists**; Charles Lindbergh, Dr. Alexis Carrel, and their daring quest to live forever. HarperCollins Ecco 2007 337p il $26.95   **610.28**
1. Air force officers 2. Air pilots 3. Biologists 4. Generals 5. Immortality 6. Life spans (Biology) 7. Longevity 8. Memoirists 9. Nobel laureates for physiology or medicine 10. Physicians 11. Preservation of organs, tissues, etc. 12. Surgeons 13. Writers on medicine
ISBN 978-0-06-052815-7; 0-06-052815-X

LC 2007-299304

The author "makes complex science accessible and serves as an absorbing cautionary tale on how two heroic reputations were marred by fascism and anti-Semitism." Publ Wkly

Gawande, Atul
★ The **checklist** manifesto; how to get things right. Metropolitan Books 2010 209p $24.50 **610.28**
1. Lists 2. Medical care -- Quality control
ISBN 978-0-8050-9174-8

LC 2009-46888

"Few medical writers working today can transmit the gore-drenched terror of an operation that suddenly goes wrong—a terror that has a special resonance when it is Dr. Gawande himself who makes the initial horrifying mistake. And few can make it as clear as he can what exactly is at stake in the effort to minimize calamities." N Y Times (Late N Y Ed)

Includes bibliographical references

Hanson, William
The **edge** of medicine; the technology that will change our lives. Palgrave Macmillan 2008 248p $24.95; pa $17   **610.28**
1. Medical innovations 2. Medical technology 3. Technological innovations
ISBN 978-0-230-60575-6; 0-230-60575-3; 978-0-230-61753-7 pa; 0-230-61753-0 pa

LC 2008-23688

The author "describes the latest medical technologies and procedures and how they are helping us achieve a healthier tomorrow. . . . This is a fascinating book, engaging the reader's attention from the first page." Sci Books Films

Topol, Eric

The **creative** destruction of medicine; Eric Topol. Basic Books 2012 xi, 303p.p **610.28**
1. Biomedical Technology 2. Delivery of Health Care -- trends 3. Diffusion of Innovation 4. Health Communication 5. Internet 6. Medical Informatics Applications 7. Nonfiction
ISBN 9780465025503; 9780465029341
LC 2011041162

This book offers information about what author and "chief academic officer at Scripps Health . . . Dr. Topol has studied [regarding] how academic healthcare organizations like Scripps can collaborate with for-profit companies to accelerate technological progress in medicine. . . . The author says that no single innovation will have a more profound effect than the conversion of biological data. . . . [The book] describe[es] dozens of medical technologies that show . . . promise. The book also provides . . . anecdotes about Dr. Topol's own sampling of these products, as both a doctor and stand-in patient. . . . Dr. Topol focuses much of his attention on the development of 'theranostics,' or the integrated use of treatments and diagnostics (especially genomic and protein information) to better guide therapy." (WSJ)

610.6 Organizations, management; medical personnel and relationships

Barken, Frederick M.

Out of practice; fighting for primary care medicine in America. ILR Press 2011 264p il $26.95 **610.6**
ISBN 978-0-8014-4976-5; 9780801449765
LC 2010041490

"Those seeking a readable, understandable, and personal primer on debates about primary care and American health care will be both educated and moved by this outstanding book." Libr J
Includes bibliographical references.

610.69 Medical personnel and relationships

American Medical Association

Directory of physicians in the United States; 41st ed; American Medical Association 2009 4v set $750 **610.69**
1. Physicians -- Directories 2. Reference books
ISBN 978-1-60359-009-9

This directory lists names, addresses, and zip codes; includes information on medical school of graduation; year first licensed in state; primary and secondary practice specialties; type of practice; American Board of Medical Specialties Certification; and Physician's Recognition Award status.

Newman, David H.

Hippocrates' shadow; secrets from the house of medicine. Scribner 2008 236p il $26 **610.69**
1. Physician-patient relationship
ISBN 1-4165-5153-0; 978-1-4165-5153-9
LC 2008-12485

"Newman shares information about the practice of medicine not generally known or discussed but which could have a significant impact on health care costs, access, and outcomes. With this book he makes a valuable contribution to the dialogue on reform of the US health care system." Choice
Includes bibliographical references

Pikula, Donna L.

★ **After** the diagnosis; how to look out for yourself or a loved one. Books 2 Help You 2006 xx, 275p pa $16.95 **610.69**
1. Medical care 2. Patients
ISBN 0-9768970-0-8; 978-0-9768970-0-2
LC 2006-274957

The author "is clear, thorough, and practical, providing step-by-step forms and checklists that can be used by patients in their own proactive healthcare journey." Libr J
Includes bibliographical references

Wischnitzer, Saul

★ **Barron's** guide to medical & dental schools; [by] Saul Wischnitzer with Edith Wischnitzer. 11th ed; Barron's Educ. Ser. 2006 695p il maps pa $18.99 **610.69**
1. Medicine -- Vocational guidance
ISBN 978-0-7641-3372-5; 0-7641-3372-1
LC 2005-57070

This guide profiles "AMA-accredited American and Canadian schools, ADA-accredited dental schools, as well as osteopathic schools, accredited by the American Osteopathic Association. Advice is also given on applying to schools, with specific recommended courses and procedures for maximizing chances of acceptance." Publisher's note

The official ABMS directory of board certified medical specialists, 2010; 42nd ed; Elsevier Saunders 2010 3v set $749 **610.69**
1. Physicians -- Directories 2. Reference books
ISBN 978-1-4377-0777-9

"For each physician, lists name, certification(s), type of practice, birth date and place, education, career history, teaching positions, military record, professional memberships, office address and phone number. Includes an outline of certification requirements for each specialty." Guide to Ref Books. 11th edition

611   Human anatomy, cytology, histology

Bainbridge, David

Beyond the zonules of Zinn; a fantastic journey through your brain. Harvard University Press 2008 338p il $25.95   **611**
   1. Brain 2. Nervous system 3. Neuroanatomy
   ISBN 978-0-674-02610-0; 0-674-02610-1
                                  LC 2007-21595
   "In this 'geographical tour' of the nervous system, readers will find an entertaining and enlightening history of neuroscience and a look at the anatomy of the brain. . . . The book's relaxed pace, interesting tangents and broad coverage make this book eminently suitable for anyone curious about the brain." Publ Wkly
   Includes bibliographical references

Balaban, Naomi E.

   The **handy** anatomy answer book; [by] Naomi E. Balaban and James E. Bobick. Visible Ink Press 2008 362p il pa $21.95   **611**
   1. Human anatomy 2. Physiology
   ISBN 978-1-57859-190-9
   "This book can provide an excellent way to read and self-test for health and human biology classes. Adults wanting to know more about the subjects covered will also find a wealth of useful and accessible information." Voice Youth Advocates

McElheny, Victor K.

   Drawing the map of life; inside the Human Genome Project. Victor K. McElheny. Basic Books 2010 xiii, 361 p.p   **611**
   1. Genomics
   ISBN 046504333X (alk. paper); 40018025006; 9780465043330 (alk. paper)
                                    LC 2010003339
   Drawing the Map of Life is the "story of the Human Genome Project from its origins, through the race to order the 3 billion subunits of DNA, to the surprises emerging as scientists seek to exploit the molecule of heredity." (Publisher's note) Index.
   McElheny's "description of the politics that led to the human genome project becoming the first megascale biology research program . . . is clear and illuminating. Similarly, McElheny does an impressive job at explaining the current and future benefits likely to arise from the genetics data flooding into scientists' laboratories." Publ Wkly
   Includes bibliographical references and index

Netter, Frank H.

   ★ **Atlas** of human anatomy; 4th ed.; Saunders/Elsevier 2006 548, 47p il $76.95   **611**
   1. Human anatomy
   ISBN 1-4160-3699-7; 978-1-4160-3385-1
                                    LC 2006-47497
   This human anatomy atlas features over 540 illustrations of the human body and its systems and organs.

Richardson, Ruth

   The **making** of Mr. Gray's Anatomy; bodies, books, fortune, fame. Oxford University Press 2008 322p il $29.95   **611**
   1. Anatomy 2. Biologists 3. Hospital administrators 4. Human anatomy 5. Medical illustrators 6. Medical publishing -- History 7. Medicine -- Great Britain -- History -- 19th century 8. Surgeons 9. Writers on science
   ISBN 978-0-19-955299-3; 0-19-955299-1
   The author "uses Gray's Anatomy as a springboard to present an interesting slice of scientific history." Publ Wkly

Roach, Mary

   ★ **Stiff**; the curious lives of human cadavers. Norton 2003 303p il $23.95; pa $13.95   **611**
   1. Dead 2. Dissection 3. Human experimentation in medicine 4. Large print books
   ISBN 0-393-05093-9; 0-393-32482-6 pa
                                    LC 2002-152908
   "For those who are interested in the fields of medicine or forensics and are aware of some of the procedures, this book makes excellent reading." SLJ
   Includes bibliographical references

Shubin, Neil

   Your inner fish; a journey into the 3.5-billion-year history of the human body. Pantheon Books 2008 229p il map $24   **611**
   1. Evolution 2. Human anatomy 3. Human evolution
   ISBN 978-0-375-42447-2; 0-375-42447-4
                                      LC 2007-24699
   This is a "look at how the human body evolved into its present state. . . . Shubin excels at explaining the science, making each discovery an adventure, whether it's a Pennsylvania roadcut or a stony outcrop beset by polar bears and howling Arctic winds." Publ Wkly
   Includes bibliographical references

   ★ **Gray's** anatomy; the anatomical basis of clinical practice. 40th ed.; Churchill Livingstone 2008 xxiv, 1551p il $209   **611**
   1. Human anatomy 2. Reference books
   ISBN 978-0-443-06684-9
   A comprehensive standard reference work with illustrations, descriptions and definitions.
   "Holds its place as a major and authoritative text on systematic anatomy. Recommended." Annals of Internal Medicine
   Includes bibliographical references

612   Human physiology

Brenkus, John

   The **perfection** point. HarperCollins 2010 242p $26.99; ebook $9.99   **612**
   1. Sports records
   ISBN 978-0-06-184545-1; 978-0-06-200884-8 ebook
   This is an "exploration of the limits of human athletic ability. . . . The book is full of startling facts: the current U.S.

record for holding one's breath, for example, is a breathtaking 7 minutes and 21 seconds. But here's the book's most arresting element: using a variety of disciplines, including physics and physiology, Brenkus extrapolates into the future, showing us when we will reach our absolute limit of performance. . . . Sure to spark debate in sporting and scientific circles, the book is engagingly written, well argued, and—even when the conclusions seem almost science fictiony—entirely plausible." Booklist

Holmes, Hannah
The **well**-dressed ape; a natural history of myself. Random House 2008 351p $25   **612**
1. Authors 2. Comparative physiology 3. Human beings 4. Journalists 5. Physical anthropology 6. Physiology, Comparative
ISBN 978-1-4000-6541-7
LC 2008-16582
Explores how the human animal—the eponymous well-dressed ape—fits into the natural world, even as we humans change that world in both constructive and destructive ways.
"A pellucid spin through the contours of the human brain and the folds of the human body." Kirkus
Includes bibliographical references

Mai, Larry L.
The **Cambridge** Dictionary of human biology and evolution; [by] Larry L. Mai, Marcus Young Owl, M. Patricia Kersting. Cambridge University Press 2005 648p il pa $60   **612**
1. Biology -- Dictionaries 2. Evolution -- Dictionaries 3. Reference books
ISBN 0-521-66486-1; 978-0-521-66486-8
LC 2004-43553
"This is one of those dictionaries that will keep even casual browsers intrigued." Choice

McCredie, Scott
Balance: in search of the lost sense. Little, Brown and Company 2007 296p il $24.99   **612**
1. Balance 2. Equilibrium (Physiology)
ISBN 978-0-316-01135-8; 0-316-01135-5
LC 2006-38089
"After the shock of seeing his fit father fall for no apparent reason, . . . McCredie became curious about the physiology of equilibrium. His extensive and creative research has led him to conclude that balance is the overlooked sixth sense and crucial to our survival. . . . McCredie offers practical advice for maintaining one's equilibrium and acuity and rekindles deep appreciation for life's incredible exactitude and grace." Booklist
Includes bibliographical references (p. 283-287)

McMillan, Beverly
Human body; a visual guide. Firefly Books 2006 304p il $29.95   **612**
1. Body, Human -- Juvenile literature 2. Human anatomy 3. Human anatomy -- Juvenile literature 4. Human physiology -- Juvenile literature 5. Physiology 6. Young adult literature -- Works
ISBN 978-1-55407-188-3; 1-55407-188-7

This book provides "scientific information on the human body, using microphotography, advanced medical imaging and annotated illustrations. The book reveals all the intricacy and beauty of the human body and shows the structure and functions of all the systems that make up a human being." Publisher's note
Includes bibliographical references

Wilson, Frank R.
The **hand**; how its use shapes the brain, language, and human culture. Pantheon Bks. 1998 397p il $30; pa $16   **612**
1. Hand 2. Hand -- Physiology
ISBN 0-679-41249-2; 0-679-74047-3 pa
LC 97-46427
The author "explores anatomy, anthropology, and evolution to show how the hand shapes human language and thought. He argues convincingly that a less rigid, more individualized approach to education will yield a student with a unified body and mind. His most inspiring evidence is blessedly anecdotal: interviews with people whose vocations involve the skilled use of their hands." New Yorker
Includes bibliographical references

The **Human** body; an illustrated guide to its structure, function, and disorders. editor-in-chief, Charles Clayman. Dorling Kindersley 1995 240p il $30   **612**
1. Human anatomy 2. Physiology 3. Popular medicine
ISBN 1-56458-992-7
LC 94-37165
"This absolutely stunning book succeeds immeasurably as a guide to the human body." Sci Books Films

612.1 Specific functions, systems, organs

Amidon, Stephen
The **sublime** engine; a biography of the human heart. [by] Stephen Amidon and Thomas Amidon. Rodale 2011 242p $24.99   **612.1**
1. Heart
ISBN 978-1-60529-584-8
LC 2010-30227
This book "presents a multifaceted picture of the heart's influences on mythology, science, and popular culture through the ages. In six lyrically written chapters, they trace humanity's perennial fascination with the heart through the eyes of history's greatest artists and medical explorers, beginning with the Greeks and fancifully ending with a peek into the future of cardiological innovation." Booklist
Includes bibliographical references

Randall, Otelio Sye
★ The **encyclopedia** of the heart and heart disease; [by] Otelio S. Randall, Nathan Segerson, Deborah S. Romaine. 2nd ed; Facts On File 2010 392p il $75   **612.1**
1. Heart 2. Heart -- Diseases 3. Heart -- Encyclopedias

4. Heart diseases -- Encyclopedias 5. Reference books
ISBN 978-0-8160-7751-9; 0-8160-7751-7

LC 2009-53594

This book "examines the function of the heart and the
cardiovascular system and the major diseases and disorders
that impact their health. . . . [It] discusses how to recognize
the signs and symptoms of heart disease and how heart disease is diagnosed and treated. The causes and factors that
contribute to heart disease are explained as well as preventive measures and steps to live a heart-healthy lifestyle."
Publisher's note
Includes bibliographical references

612.4   Hematopoietic, lymphatic, glandular, urinary systems

Arikha, Noga
Passions and tempers; a history of the humours.
Ecco 2007 xxi, 376p il $27.95   **612.4**
1. Body fluids 2. Medicine -- History
ISBN 978-0-06-073116-8; 0-06-073116-8
This is "an erudite book, drawing on historical and scientific sources in several languages, but a gracefully written
one. There are many superb illustrations [and] informative
notes. . . . One of the best things about Ms. Arikha's study, in
addition to its wealth of intriguing detail, is that it is thoughtful." N Y Sun

612.6   Reproduction, development, maturation

Angier, Natalie
Woman; an intimate geography. Houghton Mif-
flin 1999 398p $25   **612.6**
1. Physiology 2. Sex differences 3. Sex role 4.
Women -- Physiology 5. Women -- Psychology
ISBN 0-395-69130-3

LC 98-47634

"Angier proves a knowledgeable, witty guide on
our illustrative journey through hordes of cultures and
species." Ms
Includes bibliographical references

Benecke, Mark
The **dream** of eternal life; biomedicine, aging,
and immortality. translated by Rachel Rubenstein.
Columbia Univ. Press 2002 196p il $29.95   **612.6**
1. Death 2. Immortality 3. Life 4. Life sciences --
Philosophy 5. Longevity
ISBN 0-231-11672-1

LC 2001-47366

An "informative and engaging examination of aging and
the meaning of death." Booklist
Includes bibliographical references and index

Blum, Deborah
Sex on the brain; the biological differences between men and women. Viking 1997 xxii, 329p
hardcover o.p. pa $13.95   **612.6**
1. Sex (Biology) 2. Sex differences (Psychology)
ISBN 0-14-026348-9 pa

LC 96-52034

Blum "has a skilled journalist's ability to take abstract
and confusing genetic, hormonal, endocrinological and neuroscientific findings and make them intelligible." Publ Wkly
Includes bibliographical references

Chopra, Deepak
Ageless body, timeless mind; the quantum alternative to growing old. Harmony Bks. 1993 342p
hardcover o.p. pa $14   **612.6**
1. Aging 2. Holistic medicine 3. Longevity 4. Mind
and body
ISBN 0-517-88212-4 pa

LC 93-16766

Chopra argues that "the mind-body connection is a major player in all facets of health. . . . {He advises} readers to
realize that the body is a product of awareness, that beliefs,
thoughts, and emotions cause chemical reactions in cells,
and that if you change your perception, you can change the
experience of your body and the world." Booklist

Doubilet, Peter M.
Your developing baby, conception to birth;
[by] Peter M. Doubilet, Carol B. Benson, [and]
Roanne Weisman. McGraw-Hill 2008 194p il pa
$18.95   **612.6**
1. Embryology 2. Pregnancy
ISBN 978-0-07-148871-6; 0-07-148871-5

LC 2007-35278

"Using 250 diagnostic ultrasound images, . . . [the au-
thors] present a marvelous book charting the growth of
babies in the womb. Readers are taken through the entire
reproductive process, from ovulation through the third trimester. . . . This virtual tour of a life in the making will attract future parents in droves." Libr J

Eliot, Lise
Pink brain, blue brain; how small differences
grow into trouplesome gaps--and what we can do
about it. Houghton Mifflin Harcourt 2009 420p il
$25   **612.6**
1. Brain -- Sex differences 2. Child development 3.
Sex differences (Psychology)
ISBN 978-0-618-39311-4

LC 2009-14746

"This is an important book and highly recommended for
parents, teachers, and anyone who works with children."
Libr J
Includes bibliographical references

Hall, Stephen S.
★ **Size** matters; how height affects the health,
happiness, and success of boys--and the men they become. Houghton Mifflin Co. 2006 388p $26 **612.6**
1. Body image in men 2. Growth 3. Men --

Psychology 4. Personal appearance 5. Stature, Short --
Psychological aspects 6. Stature, Short -- Social aspects
ISBN 978-0-618-47040-2; 0-618-47040-9

LC 2006-07304

The author's "interpretations of complicated science are
readily accessible, and his journalistic style will suit both
popular and academic readers." Publ Wkly
Includes bibliographical references

Kirkwood, Tom

Time of our lives; the science of human aging. Oxford Univ. Press 1999 277p $49.95; pa
$32.50   **612.6**
1. Aging
ISBN 0-19-512824-9; 0-19-513926-7 pa

LC 98-46932

Kirkwood "conveys scientific matters lucidly and
thought provokingly, posing good questions to show what
is definitely known, disposing of myths, and pointing out
where more information needs to be ascertained." Booklist
Includes bibliographical references

Lachs, Mark

Treat me, not my age; a doctor's guide to getting
the best care as you or a loved one gets older. Viking
2010 386p il $27.95   **612.6**
1. Aging 2. Elderly -- Health and hygiene
ISBN 978-0-670-02210-6

LC 2010-17487

The author "discusses for seniors and their caregivers the
aging process, ageism in society, choosing and communicating with a physician, financial issues, medications, complementary and alternative medicine, and end-of-life planning.
Writing in a witty, conversational style, Lachs provides a
great deal of useful information." Libr J
Includes bibliographical references

Medina, John

The **clock** of ages; why we age--how we
age--winding back the clock. {by} John J. Medina.
Cambridge Univ. Press 1996 332p il hardcover o.p.
pa $25   **612.6**
1. Aging
ISBN 0-521-59456-1 pa

LC 95-40712

"This is the best biology book written for the lay public
to appear in many years." Libr J
Includes bibliographical references

Moalem, Sharon

How sex works; why we look, smell, taste,
feel, and act the way we do. Harper 2009 274p
$26.99   **612.6**
1. Sex (Biology) 2. Sexual behavior
ISBN 978-0-06-147965-6; 0-06-147965-9

The author "outlines the many theories for sexual attraction, monogamy, and even sexual orientation. . . . Moalem
writes about intercourse and sexuality in a candid, inviting
way for a change, bridging the gap between the scientist and
the layperson, reinvigorating the learning process (and the
bedroom) once again." PopMatters
Includes bibliographical references

Nilsson, Lennart

A **child** is born; [photography], Lennart Nilsson;
text, Lars Hamberger; translated from the Swedish by
Linda Schenck. 4th ed, completely rev and updated;
Delacorte Press 2003 239p il $35; pa $21   **612.6**
1. Childbirth 2. Embryology 3. Pregnancy
ISBN 0-385-33754-X; 0-385-33755-8 pa

LC 2003-43854

An illustrated look at male and female reproductive
anatomy and physiology, the processes of ovulation and fertilization, fetal development, and labor and delivery.

Roach, Mary

Bonk; the curious coupling of science and sex.
Norton 2008 319p il $24.95   **612.6**
1. Sex (Biology)
ISBN 978-0-393-06464-3; 0-393-06464-6

LC 2007-51990

"Tucked between the jokes and anecdotes, you will find
lessons on impotence, orgasm, unusual and unusually brave
scientists, and the sexual behaviour of other species, including a hilarious description of porcupine sex." New Sci
Includes bibliographical references (p. 307-319)

Rowe, John W.

Successful aging; {by} John W. Rowe and Robert L. Kahn. Pantheon Bks. 1998 265p hardcover
o.p. pa $13.95   **612.6**
1. Aging 2. Longevity
ISBN 0-440-50863-0 pa

LC 97-36900

The authors "report on a 10-year, MacArthur Founda-
tion-funded inquiry into 'successful aging'—that is, remaining healthy, vigorous, mentally acute, and independent
well into the ninth and tenth decades of life. . . . Separate
chapters illustrate, with the experience of the study's elderly
subjects, that good diet and exercise, maintaining and enhancing mental functions, positive social connections, and
productive work are essential to living well while living
longer." Booklist
Includes bibliographical references

Stein, Elissa

★ **Flow**; the cultural story of menstruation. [by]
Elissa Stein and Susan Kim. St. Martin's Griffin
2009 270p $27.99   **612.6**
1. Menstruation
ISBN 978-0-312-37996-4

LC 2009-17046

"There is probably no better book for moms who want
their daughters to respect themselves in every aspect, and
for female preteens and teens who would never say a word
about their moms reading a book about menses but surely
would like several sneak peeks into its pages." Booklist
Includes bibliographical references

Stipp, David

The **youth** pill; scientists at the brink of an anti-aging revolution. Current 2010 308p $26.95 **612.6**

1. Drug industry 2. Longevity

ISBN 978-1-61723-000-4; 1-61723-000-6

LC 2010-7114

The author possesses "a singular style, crafting complex explanations of scientific discoveries (and failures) into eminently enjoyable reading. Whether or not the notion of living energetically to the age of 150 appeals, Stipp makes the research compelling." Booklist

Includes bibliographical references

Weil, Andrew

Healthy aging; a lifelong guide to your physical and spiritual well-being. Alfred A. Knopf 2005 293p $27.95 **612.6**

1. Aging

ISBN 0-375-40755-3

LC 2005-45183

The author "explores common Western beliefs and attitudes about aging and urges readers to develop healthier perspectives. The 60-year-old author assesses the growing and lucrative field of anti-aging medicine, takes the position that aging is not reversible, and offers many ways for readers to prevent conditions and illnesses that limit mortality and ensure well-being into the later years. . . . The real value is Weil's courageous stand, one likely to meet resistance in a culture devoted to external indicators of eternal youth." Publ Wkly

Includes bibliographical references

Weiner, Jonathan

Long for this world; the strange science of immortality. Ecco/HarperCollins Publishers 2010 310p $27.99 **612.6**

1. Immortalism 2. Immortality 3. Immortality (Philosophy) 4. Longevity

ISBN 978-0-06-076536-1; 0-06-076536-4

This is "a brilliant and improbably funny look inside the mind-bending science of immortality. . . . [The author's] ability to write simply and swiftly about complex evolutionary processes makes him an ideal guide through the burgeoning field of gerontology." Village Voice

Includes bibliographical references

612.7   Musculoskeletal system, integument

Dickey, Colin

Cranioklepty; grave robbing and the search for genius. Unbridled Books 2009 308p il $25.95 **612.7**

1. Grave robbing 2. Phrenology 3. Skull

ISBN 978-1-932961-86-7

LC 2009-18527

The author relates the story of "the plucky grave robbers who stole the craniums of famed composers Haydn and Beethoven, Swedish mystic Emanuel Swedenborg, artist Francisco Goya, the English doctor and philosopher Sir Thomas Browne and others to sell, study or put on public display. The skull obsession was triggered by the infamous Gall system, created in the late 18th century by Franz Joseph Gall, who theorized that the bumps and dents of the skull could provide a measure of intelligence. . . . Blending science with historical drama, Dickey's book illuminates the mystery and controversy of a bizarre tradition throughout the ages." Publ Wkly

Includes bibliographical references

612.8   Nervous system

Aamodt, Sandra

Welcome to your brain; why you lose your car keys but never forget how to drive and other puzzles of everyday life. [by] Sandra Aamodt and Sam Wang. Bloomsbury USA 2008 220p il $24.95 **612.8**

1. Brain 2. Neurophysiology

ISBN 978-1-59691-283-0; 1-59691-283-9

LC 2007-26739

This is a "'user's guide' to our brains. . . . The text is divided into six main parts, covering the brain's basic structure and function, the senses, the brain's development, emotions, rational processes, and altered states. . . . Rather than didactically lecturing, the authors very effectively engage the reader in a comfortable, interesting, and informative dialog." Sci Books Films

Buonomano, Dean

Brain bugs; how the brain's flaws shape our lives. W. W. Norton & Co. 2011 310p $25.95 **612.8**

1. Brain 2. Memory

ISBN 978-0-393-07602-8

LC 2011014934

The author explains "that as the human brain has evolved over the past 100,000 years, it has added layer upon layer of networked neural connections to cope with a rapidly changing world. But, he writes, the brain's most detrimental malfunctions are often traceable to its most ancient structures—those that compose the limbic system. . . . Drawing on real-world examples and current research in neuroscience, Buonomano guides the reader through the unexpected ways in which our lives are influenced by the messiness of our busiest, most intricate, and often most error-prone organ." The Scientist

Includes bibliographical references

Carr, Nicholas G., 1959-

The **shallows**; what the Internet is doing to our brains. W.W. Norton 2010 276p $26.95 **612.8**

1. Internet 2. Internet -- Psychological aspects 3. Neurophysiology 4. Neuropsychology

ISBN 978-0-393-07222-8; 0-393-07222-3

LC 2010-07639

"Drawing from neuroscience, history and social-science research, Carr reviews evidence that learning how to solve a problem, how to play a piece of music or how to speak a language physically changes the brain. It's a mistake, he argues, to think of the brain as a hard drive that stores information; it's far more than that and changes dynamically as it processes information, altering itself as it confronts challenges — for better or worse. Reading a book, he notes, is vastly different from reading hyperlinked Internet text. Reading a book is solitary, requiring deep thought, analysis of the text and sustaining a narrative thread for the duration. By contrast, Internet reading invites shallow skimming for relevant passages, incessant clicking to hyperlinked articles and reliance on Google's search algorithms to determine relevance. . . . Carr argues that the result is an emerging nation of shallow and impatient readers." Seattle Times

Includes bibliographical references

Carter, Rita

The **human** brain book; [by] Rita Carter; Susan Aldridge, Martyn Page, Steve Parker; consultants, Chris Frith, Uta Frith, and Melanie Shulman. DK 2009 256p il $40   **612.8**
1. Brain 2. Reference books
ISBN 978-0-7566-5441-2
"This outstanding reference is filled with interesting, detailed information about every possible aspect of the human brain. Three-dimension images and other unique computer-generated visuals complement the massive volume, which also includes more than 50 brain-related diseases and disorders." National Science Teachers Association

Includes glossary

Chorost, Michael

World wide mind; the coming integration of humanity, machines and the Internet. Free Press 2011 242p il $26; ebook $12.99   **612.8**
1. Brain 2. Brain mapping 3. Communication 4. Computational neuroscience 5. Internet 6. Interpersonal communication 7. Telepathy 8. Thought and thinking
ISBN 978-1-4391-1914-3; 1-4391-1914-7; 978-1-4391-4120-5 ebook; 1-4391-4120-7 ebook
LC 2010-11875
This "is a thought-provoking story about how technology will connect with the brain ever more intimately, merging humanity and the internet, providing technologically shared experiences and emotions. It forces the reader to think again—not just about neuro-technology but also about communication, about how important eye-to-eye and body-to-body contact is." New Sci

Includes bibliographical references

Damasio, Antonio R.

The **Scientific** American book of the brain; from the editors of Scientific American; introduction by Antonio Damasio. Lyons Press 1999 340p il hardcover o.p. pa $19.95   **612.8**
1. Brain 2. Brain -- Diseases 3. Cognitive neuroscience 4. Neuropsychiatry 5. Neuropsychology
ISBN 1-58574-285-6 pa
LC 99-39387
The articles in this anthology "include overviews of research and clinical medicine and focused discussions of such specific diseases as Parkinson's, Alzheimer's, and depression. They not only present recent accomplishments and research but also show, most intriguingly, how brain scientists think about a problem and develop its solution." Booklist

Dement, William C.

The **promise** of sleep; a pioneer in sleep medicine explores the vital connection between health, happiness, and a good night's sleep. by William C. Dement with Christopher Vaughan. Delacorte Press 1999 524p il hardcover o.p. pa $15.95   **612.8**
1. Sleep 2. Sleep -- Popular works 3. Sleep disorders -- Popular works
ISBN 0-440-50901-7 pa
LC 98-23527
This work "offers scientific data on sleep, advice on sleep hygiene and a scenario for a restorative 'sleep camp'. Dement's outstanding book also includes helpful appendixes listing sleep-disorder clinics and Web sites." Libr J

Doidge, Norman

The **brain** that changes itself; stories of personal triumph from the frontiers of brain science. Viking 2007 427p $24.95   **612.8**
1. Brain 2. Neuroplasticity
ISBN 978-0-670-03830-5; 0-670-03830-X
LC 2006-49224
"A woman who perpetually feels like she's falling, a man addicted to hard-core pornography, an amputee with excruciating pain in his phantom elbow: all cured thanks to neuroplasticity, the brain's ability to rewire itself. Doidge provides a history of the research in this growing field, highlighting scientists at the edge of groundbreaking discoveries and telling fascinating stories of people who have benefited. An engaging read for anyone interested in the science behind how our surprisingly moldable brains are changed by our experiences." Psychology Today

Dowling, John E.

Creating mind; how the brain works. Norton 1998 212p il hardcover o.p. pa $17.50   **612.8**
1. Brain 2. Neurosciences
ISBN 0-393-97446-4 pa
LC 98-9365
"In this guide to the 'nuts and bolts' of the human brain, neurobiologist Dowling explains how basic brain functions work and are interconnected. He then explores in clear, concise prose the brain's major functions: vision, language, memory, emotion, perception, and consciousness. A good jumping off point for learning about neuroscience and its fascinating discoveries." Libr J

Includes bibliographical references

Eliot, Lise

What's going on in there? how the brain and mind develop in the first five years of life. Bantam Bks. 1999 533p hardcover o.p. pa $18   **612.8**
1. Brain 2. Developmental neurophysiology -- Popular works 3. Developmental psychobiology -- Popular works 4. Developmental psychology
ISBN 0-553-37825-2 pa
LC 99-35423
"This book is both theoretical and practical, combining scientific reportage with 'how-to' advice for new parents. . . . With clear, mostly simple language, {Eliot} guides readers through a fascinating array of new research—on infant balance, the development of language and memory, and the relationship between the birthing process and the brain." Libr J

Gazzaniga, Michael S.

Human; the science behind what makes us unique. Ecco 2008 447p $27.50   **612.8**

1. Brain 2. Cognitive neuroscience 3. Consciousness 4. Human beings 5. Neuropsychology

ISBN 978-0-06-089288-3; 0-06-089288-9

LC 2008-297703

"A savvy, witty guide to neuroscience today." Kirkus

Includes bibliographical references

Glynn, Ian

An **anatomy** of thought; the origin and machinery of mind. Oxford Univ. Press 2000 456p hardcover o.p. pa $17.95   **612.8**

1. Brain 2. Cognition 3. Consciousness 4. Intellect 5. Neuropsychology 6. Philosophy of mind

ISBN 0-19-513696-9; 0-19-515803-2 pa

LC 99-41218

Glynn offers a "summary of what we know about the brain—both its evolution and its mechanisms. Among the topics he covers are natural selection, molecular evolution, nerves and the nervous system, sensory perception, and the specific structures responsible for our intellect." Libr J

Includes bibliographical references

Greenfield, Susan

The **private** life of the brain; emotions, consciousness, and the secret of the self. Wiley 2000 258p $27.95; pa $16.95   **612.8**

1. Brain

ISBN 0-471-18343-1; 0-471-39975-2 pa

LC 99-46191

"Greenfield presents a subtle model in everyday language, introducing her readers skillfully to her precedents and rivals in neurobiology and cognitive science." Publ Wkly

Johnson, Steven

Mind wide open; your brain and the neuroscience of everyday life. Scribner 2004 274p il $25; pa $15   **612.8**

1. Brain 2. Neuropsychology 3. Neurosciences 4. Self-perception

ISBN 0-7432-4165-7; 0-7432-4166-5 pa

LC 2003-63308

"Johnson fills this book with important, big-picture ideas, including enough description of the details to give the reader a sense of the science without becoming overwhelmed. His knowledgeable and thoughtful approach makes neuroscience accessible to all." Choice

Includes bibliographical references

Lavie, P.

The **enchanted** world of sleep; {by} Peretz Lavie; translated by Anthony Berris. Yale Univ. Press 1996 270p il hardcover o.p. pa $14.35   **612.8**

1. Sleep

ISBN 0-300-06602-3; 0-300-07436-0 pa

LC 95-41304

The author "describes our historical fascination with sleep and reviews notable research in the field. Among the topics he covers are the physiological changes that occur during a normal period of sleep, sleep disorders, the purpose of dreams, and the 'evolution' of the sleep cycle from birth to old age." Libr J

Includes bibliographical references

LeDoux, Joseph E.

Synaptic self; how our brains become who we are. {by} Joseph LeDoux. Viking 2002 406p il $29.95; pa $16   **612.8**

1. Personality 2. Self

ISBN 0-670-03028-7; 0-14-200178-3 pa

LC 2001-45356

The author puts forth the theory that "it's the neural pathways—the synaptic relationships—in our brains that make us who we are. . . . Writing for a general audience, he succeeds in making his subject accessible to the dedicated nonspecialist. He offers absorbing descriptions of some of the most fascinating case studies in his field, provides insight into the shortcomings of psychopharmacology and suggests new directions for research on the biology of mental illness." Publ Wkly

Linden, David J.

The **accidental** mind. Belknap Press of Harvard University Press 2007 276p il $25.95   **612.8**

1. Brain 2. Brain -- Evolution 3. Neuropsychology

ISBN 978-0-674-02478-6; 0-674-02478-8

LC 2006-47905

This is an "important counterpoint to breathless paeans to brain design." Choice

Includes bibliographical references

The **compass** of pleasure; how our brains make fatty foods, orgasm, exercise, marijuana, generosity, vodka, learning, and gambling feel so good. Viking 2011 230p il $26.95   **612.8**

1. Neuropsychology 2. Pleasure

ISBN 978-0-670-02258-8

LC 2010-35380

The author "addresses provocative questions about the relationship between pleasure and addiction while exploring many of the broader implications of the nexus of the two. . . . Linden's conversational style, his abundant use of anecdotes, and his successful coupling of wit with insight makes the book a joy to read. Even the footnotes are sprinkled with hidden gems." Publ Wkly

Includes bibliographical references

McDermott, Terry

101 theory drive; a neuroscientist's quest for memory. Pantheon Books 2010 271p il $25.95 **612.8**

1. Biologists 2. Brain 3. College teachers 4. Medicine -- Research 5. Memory 6. Memory -- Research 7. Neurologists 8. Neurosciences

ISBN 978-0-375-42538-7; 0-375-42538-1

LC 2009-34251

The author "profiles UC-Irvine psychobiologist Gary Lynch and his decades-long effort to understand the biochemical processes and structural changes in neurons that underlie memory. . . . In McDermott's portrayal, Lynch comes off as a hippie-ish, hard-drinking, foul-mouthed visionary at odds with the neuroscientific establishment, who both inspires and exploits the students and post-docs under his sway. . . . This is an engrossing story of science and the brilliant, flawed people who make it." Publ Wkly

Includes bibliographical references

Palca, Joe

Annoying; the science of what bugs us. [by] Joe Palca and Flora Lichtman. Wiley 2011 272p $25.95

612.8

1. Aversion 2. Aversive stimuli 3. Discontent 4. Human physiology 5. Neuropsychology 6. Physiology

ISBN 978-0-470-63869-9

LC 2010-54046

Palca and Lichtman "skitter all over the map in pursuit of their subject, and at first their progress seems peculiarly random, like one of those robotic vacuums. But in the end they do indeed cover every part of the terrain: from physics and psychology to aesthetics, genetics and even treatment for the miserably, terminally annoyed." N Y Times (Late N Y Ed)

Includes bibliographical references

Pert, Candace

Molecules of emotion; why you feel the way you feel. {by} Candace B. Pert; with a foreword by Deepak Chopra. Scribner 1997 368p $25; pa $14 **612.8**

1. Emotions 2. Medicine -- Research 3. Mind and body 4. Psychosomatic medicine

ISBN 0-684-83187-2; 0-684-84634-9 pa

LC 97-17463

The author "has been at the forefront of key discoveries in the fields of neuroscience and AIDS therapy, and was intimately involved in the discovery of the brain's opiate receptors in 1972. Her memoir describes some of her breakthroughs while providing very real insight into the processes and politics at the core of modern science. . . . This is an important look at what really goes on inside the human body— and inside the scientific elite." Publ Wkly

Includes bibliographical references

Pollak, Charles

★ The **encyclopedia** of sleep and sleep disorders; [by] Charles P. Pollak, Michael J. Thorpy, Jan Yager. 3rd ed., updated and rev; Facts on File 2009 lv, 309p $75

612.8

1. Reference books 2. Sleep 3. Sleep -- Encyclopedias 4. Sleep disorders

ISBN 978-0-8160-6833-3; 0-8160-6833-X

LC 2007-30682

"Notable for the subject expertise of its authors, . . . [this encyclopedia] provides authoritative content on a topic of interest to many." Booklist

Includes bibliographical references

Randall, David K.

Dreamland; adventures in the strange science of sleep. David K. Randall. W.W. Norton 2012 304 p. $25.95; (hardcover) $25.95

612.8

1. Dreams 2. Sleep

ISBN 039308020X; 9780393080209

LC 2012014932

This book offers an examination of the science behind the little-known world of sleep. . . . [David K.] Randall ex-

plores the research that is investigating those dark hours that make up nearly a third of our lives. Taking readers from military battlefields to children's bedrooms, [the book] shows that sleep isn't as simple as it seems. Why did the results of one sleep study change the bookmaker's odds for certain Monday Night Football games? Do women sleep differently than men? And if you happen to kill someone while you are sleepwalking, does that count as murder? (Publisher's note)

Ratey, John J.

A **user's** guide to the brain; perception, attention, and the four theaters of the brain. Pantheon Bks. 2001 404p il hardcover o.p. pa $14.95 **612.8**

1. Brain 2. Brain -- Popular works 3. Neurochemistry -- Popular works 4. Neuropsychology -- Popular works

ISBN 0-375-70107-9 pa

LC 98-27796

"Far more than a map of the brain's exotic jungles, this study can serve as a life-enriching guide for keeping the richest mental fields in cultivation." Booklist

Includes bibliographical references

Restak, Richard M.

Mozart's brain and the fighter pilot; unleashing your brain's potential. by Richard Restak. Harmony Bks. 2001 220p il hardcover o.p. pa $12 **612.8**

1. Brain 2. Brain -- Popular works 3. Cognition -- Popular works 4. Mental health 5. Mental health -- Popular works

ISBN 0-609-81005-7 pa

LC 2001-24779

The author "offers 28 ways to improve mental fitness, including exercises to enhance memory, concentration, creativity, and analytical ability. . . . Restak's upbeat and enlightening guide will certainly be a popular addition to public libraries." Libr J

Scientific American (Periodical)

Best of the brain from Scientific American; edited by Floyd E. Bloom. Dana Press 2007 270p il $25

612.8

1. Brain 2. Nervous system

ISBN 978-1-93259-422-5; 1-93259-422-1

LC 2007-15128

"This collection of essays drawn from Scientific American and Scientific American Mind offers an excellent, readable overview of . . . brain research since 1999." Libr J

Includes bibliographical references

Tammet, Daniel

Embracing the wide sky; a tour across the horizons of the mind. Free Press 2009 292p il $25 **612.8**

1. Brain 2. Intellect 3. Memory 4. Savants (Savant syndrome)

ISBN 978-1-4165-6969-5; 1-4165-6969-3

LC 2008-30551

"In chapters on intelligence, memory, language, the perception of numbers as instinctual, and ways in which the brain works, Tammet relates savant capabilities to normal functions, theorizes from sound research about what enables savant capabilities, cashiers the notion of computers ever becoming genuinely intelligent, and offers tips on how to calculate and learn languages better." Booklist

Includes bibliographical references

Turkington, Carol

The **encyclopedia** of the brain and brain disorders; [by] Carol Turkington and Joseph R. Harris. 3rd ed; Facts On File 2009 434p $75   **612.8**

1. Brain 2. Brain -- Diseases 3. Brain -- Encyclopedias 4. Neurology 5. Reference books
ISBN 978-0-8160-6395-6; 0-8160-6395-8

LC 2007-33543

With a large focus on memory this edition discusses the functions and elements of the brain, how it works, how it breaks down, and various diseases and disorders that affect it.

Victoroff, Jeffrey Ivan

Saving your brain; the revolutionary plan to boost brain power, improve memory, and protect yourself against aging and Alzheimer's. [by] Jeff Victoroff. Bantam Bks. 2002 450p il hardcover o.p. pa $14.95   **612.8**

1. Aging 2. Alzheimer's disease 3. Alzheimer's disease -- Prevention 4. Brain 5. Brain -- Aging 6. Memory 7. Memory disorders -- Prevention
ISBN 0-553-10944-8; 0-553-37980-1 pa

LC 2001-56732

"Contradicting popular scientific opinion, the author argues memory loss may be a natural part of the aging process. Using his own clinical experiences and reviews of 14,000 research studies, {he} explores the many ways the human brain can be damaged and offers tips for improving brain function and preventing memory loss, from avoiding exposure to chemicals to not watching television." Libr J

Includes bibliographical references

Watson, Lyall

Jacobson's organ and the remarkable nature of smell. Norton 2000 255p il hardcover o.p. pa $19.95   **612.8**

1. Jacobson's organ 2. Nose 3. Smell
ISBN 0-393-04908-6; 978-0-393-33291-9 pa; 0-393-33291-8 pa

LC 99-56864

"Drawing on both biology and cultural history, Watson employs intriguing and instructive examples as he describes how humans, animals, and plants secrete and decode odors; and explains how smell is essential to sexuality, and underlies emotions and many other forms of subconscious knowledge." Booklist

Includes bibliographical references

Wolf, Maryanne

Proust and the squid; the story and science of the reading brain. HarperCollins 2007 308p il   **612.8**

1. Brain 2. Brain -- Evolution 3. Reading 4. Reading -- History 5. Reading comprehension
ISBN 0060186399; 9780060186395

Wolf evaluates the ways in which reading and writing have transformed the human brain. Index.

This book "is an eye-opening winner, and deserves a wide readership." Publ Wkly

Includes bibliographical references

Zimmer, Carl

Soul made flesh; the discovery of the brain--and how it changed the world. Free Press 2004 367p il $26   **612.8**

1. Brain 2. Medicine -- History -- 17th century
ISBN 0-7432-3038-8

LC 2003-63144

Zimmer tells "the story of the 'discovery' of the human brain by physician Thomas Willis. Exploring the effects of this breakthrough on 17th-century Oxford, the author traces and investigates the subsequent discoveries and theories in neurology and medicine that flowed from Willis and others (e.g., Harvey, Hobbes, Descartes, Boyle, and Locke) in Oxford and on the continent. . . . Zimmer's elegant writing combines these multiple perspectives to produce a fascinating tour-de-force of a man, a time, and a place that readers will greatly enjoy." Libr J

Includes bibliographical references and index

613   Personal health and safety

Ammer, Christine

The **encyclopedia** of women's health; foreword by JoAnn E. Manson and Elizabeth F. Brigham. 6th ed.; Facts On File 2009 480p il $75; pa $19.95 **613**

1. Reference books 2. Women -- Diseases -- Encyclopedias 3. Women -- Health and hygiene -- Encyclopedias
ISBN 978-0-8160-7407-5; 0-8160-7407-0; 978-0-8160-7408-2 pa; 0-8160-7408-9 pa

LC 2008-13641

"A welcome addition to all public libraries or any library with a consumer health-collection, this compact volume is useful to anyone interested in women's health." Booklist

Includes bibliographical references

Atkins, Robert C.

Dr. Atkins' age-defying diet revolution. St. Martin's Press 2000 335p hardcover o.p. pa $7.99 **613**

1. Aging 2. Aging -- Nutritional aspects 3. Health 4. Longevity -- Nutritional aspects 5. Nutrition
ISBN 0-312-97701-8 pa

LC 99-55690

The author "argues here that the use of supplements and a change in diet can eliminate many health problems, including cardiovascular disease, diabetes and stroke." Publ Wkly

Boston Women's Health Book Collective

★ **Our** bodies, ourselves; [by the] Boston Women's Health Book Collective. 40th anniversary ed.; Touchstone 2011 928p il pa $26; ebook $12.99   **613**

1. Women -- Health and hygiene 2. Women -- Psychology
ISBN 978-1-4391-9066-1 pa; 1-4391-9066-6 pa;

978-1-4391-9665-6 ebook; 1-4391-9665-6 ebook

LC 2011022749

This encyclopedia of women's health covers such topics as body image, food, alcohol and drugs, holistic healing, psychotherapy, occupational health, violence, relationships and sexuality, sexual health and controlling fertility, childbearing, aging and politics of women and health.

This is "the bible for women's health; an outstanding resource that belongs in all health collections." Libr J

Carlson, Karen J.

★ The **new** Harvard guide to women's health; {by} Karen J. Carlson, Stephanie A. Eisenstat, Terra Ziporyn. Belknap Press of Harvard University Press 2004 688p il $55; pa $24.95   **613**
1. Women -- Diseases 2. Women -- Health and hygiene
ISBN 0-674-01282-8; 0-674-01343-3 pa

LC 2003-63680

"The guide is an outstanding source for public and professional libraries." Booklist

Columbia University/Health Service

The **Go** ask Alice book of answers; a guide to good physical, sexual, and emotional health. [by] Columbia University's Health Education Program. Holt & Co. 1998 345p pa $15.95   **613**
1. Adolescence 2. College students -- Health and hygiene 3. College students -- Mental health 4. College students -- Sexual behavior 5. Sex education 6. Youth -- Health and hygiene
ISBN 0-8050-5570-3

LC 98-3318

"The title within the title refers to a Web site maintained by Columbia University Health Services. Set up to answer questions about relationships, sex, physical and mental health, nutrition, and related matters, the site eventually was opened to the general public as a quick-reference forum. The book's seven chapters round up queries the site has received and responses to them from Columbia-associated health educators." Booklist

Includes bibliographical references

Davis, Robert J.

The **healthy** skeptic; cutting through the hype about your health. University of California Press 2008 243p il $21.95   **613**
1. Consumer education 2. Health -- Information services 3. Quacks and quackery
ISBN 978-0-520-24918-9; 0-520-24918-6

LC 2007-37341

The author "shares his experience of researching current health trends. From exploring ancient health 'wisdom' to uncovering the real agendas of modern-day health promoters, Davis guides the reader in analyzing and thinking critically about health-related information. Readers are treated to ten chapters tackling topics like the effectiveness of sunscreens and the failure of diets. . . . This reviewer highly recommends Davis's book for all libraries wishing to promote healthy skepticism." Libr J

Includes bibliographical references

Delgado, Jane L.

The **Latina** guide to health; consejos and caring answers. foreword by Antonia Novello. Newmarket Press 2010 239p pa $15.95   **613**
1. Hispanic American women -- Health and hygiene
ISBN 978-1-55704-854-7; 1-55704-854-1

LC 2009-36591

This book "contains useful information about psychosocial and environmental issues, access to health care, common diseases and conditions, and medical decision-making. An excellent addition to all consumer health collections and home libraries." Libr J

Includes bibliographical references

Gay, Kathlyn

Encyclopedia of women's health issues. Oryx Press 2001 300p $74.95   **613**
1. Women -- Diseases 2. Women -- Health and hygiene
ISBN 1-57356-303-X

LC 2001-37342

This encyclopedia covers "the issues and history surrounding diseases and medical procedures faced by women; health concerns of different ethnic groups of women; information on organizations and programs that deal with women's health; profiles on the people who have pioneered women's health services and information; and legal decisions related to women's health." Publisher's note

Includes bibliographical references

Hall, Stephen S.

Merchants of immortality; chasing the dream of human life extension. Houghton Mifflin 2003 439p $25; pa $14   **613**
1. Longevity -- Popular works 2. Medicine -- Research
ISBN 0-618-09524-1; 0-618-49221-6 pa

LC 2002-192155

"A lucid, thorough report on the developments in biology—cloning, stem cells, 'longevity genes'—that may not bring about immortality but appear to carry hope of making life a little longer and a great deal nicer toward the end." N Y Times Book Rev

Includes bibliographical references

Kandel, Joseph

The **encyclopedia** of senior health and well being; {by} Joseph Kandel, Christine Adamec. Facts on File 2003 xxvi, 324p il $71.50   **613**
1. Aged -- Health and hygiene -- Encyclopedias 2. Elderly -- Diseases 3. Elderly -- Health and hygiene 4. Geriatrics -- Encyclopedias
ISBN 0-8160-4691-3

LC 2002-10485

This reference covers "health issues, diseases, global and ethnic factors concerning aging, common illnesses, and social issues that affect the daily lives of mature adults." Publisher's note

Includes bibliographical references

Kearns, David A.

Where hell freezes over. Thomas Dunne Books 2005 286p il map $24.95   **613**

1. Survival after airplane accidents, shipwrecks, etc.
ISBN 0-312-34205-5

LC 2005-45526

This is an "account of the crash of the Martin PBM seaplane George 1 in Antarctica in December 1946. . . . With intimate access to surviving sources, plus a depth of personal commitment, the author makes a compelling addition to survival literature." Publ Wkly

Includes bibliographical references

Love, Susan M.

Live a little! breaking the rules won't break your health. [by] Susan M. Love, Alice D. Domar with Leigh Ann Hirschman and a little help from the experts of BeWell; foreword by Nancy L. Snyderman. Crown 2009 234p il $25; pa $15   **613**

1. Women -- Health and hygiene
ISBN 978-0-307-40942-3; 978-0-307-40943-0 pa

LC 2009-499879

The authors "debunk some prevalent health myths that the general public has swallowed for years. On subjects ranging from sleep to stress, they offer quizzes as guides to determine where one places on a healthy lifestyle continuum. The extra value in this value-added tome arises from the reasoned and reasonable methods proposed for maintaining a healthy life that a person might also actually enjoy." Booklist

Includes bibliographical references

May, Jeffrey C.

Jeff May's healthy home tips; a workbook for detecting, diagnosing, & eliminating pesky pests, stinky stenches, musty mold, and other aggravating home problems. [by] Jeffrey C. May & Connie L. May. Johns Hopkins University Press 2008 187p il pa $16.95   **613**

1. Air pollution 2. Environmental health 3. Houses -- Maintenance and repair
ISBN 978-0-8018-8845-8; 0-8018-8845-X

LC 2007-40653

"This workbook aims to help you figure out what's making you sick around the home, offering checklists and space for personal notation. . . . Covering mold, pets, and other toxicity problems, the advice and tips are excellent. This information should be in every public library." Libr J

Includes bibliographical references

Null, Gary

For women only! your guide to health empowerment. {by} Gary Null and Barbara Seaman. Seven Stories Press 1999 xxiv, 1571p il $49.95; pa $29.95   **613**

1. Alternative medicine 2. Women -- Health and hygiene
ISBN 1-58322-015-1; 1-58322-278-2 pa

LC 99-39822

"The first 600 pages of this . . . {book} offer alternative practitioner Null's thoughts on the causes, symptoms,

prevention, and treatment of conditions and illnesses, from addiction and arthritis to violence and varicose veins. The remainder is Seaman's history of the women's health movement, featuring selections from . . . feminist writers." Booklist

Includes bibliographical references

Peck, Brian

The **baby** boomer body book; the complete health reference for our generation. Sourcebooks 2001 447p il pa $21.94   **613**

1. Aging 2. Health 3. Middle age 4. Middle aged persons -- Health and hygiene 5. Middle aged persons -- Health and hygiene -- Case studies
ISBN 1-57071-715-X

LC 00-66169

The author "draws on case histories from his practice to discuss age-related physical changes, memory problems, depression, dietary supplements, medical tests, and weight loss. Separate sections on men's and women's health issues cover sexual dysfunction and osteoporosis in men—an often unrecognized condition. Peck also addresses recreational drug use and midlife self-image. His breezy, approachable style will appeal to midlifers (especially men not attracted by conventional resources)." Libr J

Includes bibliographical references and index

Pollan, Michael

In defense of food; an eater's manifesto. Penguin Press 2008 244p $21.95; pa $16   **613**

1. Eating customs 2. Nutrition
ISBN 978-1-59420-145-5; 1-59420-145-5; 978-0-14-311496-3 pa; 0-14-311496-4 pa

LC 2007037552

"Pollan will succeed in making you think twice about what you are piling up in your grocery cart or on your plate." Christ Sci Monit

Includes bibliographical references

Weil, Andrew

Eight weeks to optimum health; a proven program for taking full advantage of your body's natural healing power. Knopf 1997 276p $25; pa $13.95   **613**

1. Alternative medicine 2. Health self-care 3. Nutrition
ISBN 0-679-44715-6; 0-449-00026-5 pa

LC 96-51918

The book's "strength lies in its design, which uses small easy steps to achieve big changes. . . . As a physician, Weil is careful to substantiate every claim, and he debunks some of today's more extreme alternative health theories." Libr J

Includes bibliographical references

Fitness over fifty; an exercise guide from the National Institute on Aging. with a foreword by John Glenn. Special illustrated ed; Healthy Living Bks. 2003 134p il pa $15.95   **613**

1. Aging 2. Exercise 3. Physical fitness
ISBN 1-57826-136-8

"A panel of experts in exercise for older adults explain the benefits of physical activity and present basic fitness routines (with illustrated step-by-step instructions) to improve endurance, strength, balance, and flexibility. There are also useful tips for finding a fitness professional, incorporating exercise into daily routines, computing target heart rates, and creating exercise plans and progress charts. Excellent for beginners." Libr J

Healthy women, healthy lives; a guide to preventing disease from the landmark Nurses' Health Study. senior editors, Susan E. Hankinson {et al.} Simon & Schuster 2001 xxviii, 546p il $26; pa $16
613
1. Women -- Diseases 2. Women -- Diseases -- Prevention 3. Women -- Health and hygiene
ISBN 0-684-85519-4; 0-7432-1774-8 pa
LC 2001-34154

"In 'Lowering the Risk of Disease', the risks of coronary heart disease, breast cancer, lung cancer, stroke, diabetes, colon cancer, osteoporosis, endometrial cancer, ovarian cancer, and skin cancer are discussed. Another chapter covers asthma, arthritis, age-related eye disease, and Alzheimer's disease. . . . The final chapters look at changing behaviors and making decisions that can affect women's health." Libr J
Includes bibliographical references

★ The Johns Hopkins medical guide to health after 50; the latest recommendations from the Hopkins specialists. medical editor, Simeon Margolis; prepared by the editors of The John Hopkins medical letter health after 50. Rebus 2002 704p il $39.95
613
1. Aged -- Health and hygiene 2. Elderly -- Diseases 3. Elderly -- Health and hygiene 4. Middle aged persons -- Diseases -- Prevention 5. Middle aged persons -- Health and hygiene
ISBN 0-929661-73-7
LC 2002-69670

This handbook "explains which measures you can take to increase longevity and protect yourself from the avoidable ailments of aging—and how to deal effectively with those ailments you can't avoid." Publisher's note

★ Mayo Clinic family health book; Scott Litin, editor-in-chief. 4th ed., completely rev. and updated; Time Inc. Home Entertainment 2009 1423p il $49.95
613
1. Medicine 2. Reference books
ISBN 978-1-60320-077-6; 1-60320-077-0
LC 2010-287052

This book covers over 1,000 illnesses and includes information on immunizations, breast health, genetics, sleep disorders, complementary and alternative medicine, pain management, and end-of-life issues.

Men's health concerns sourcebook; edited by Sandra J. Judd. 3rd ed.; Omnigraphics, Inc. 2009 663p il $84
613
1. Men -- Health and hygiene 2. Reference books
ISBN 978-0-7808-1033-4
LC 2009-24973

"The book offers a one-stop resource for obtaining an outline of many male health issues." Libr J
Includes bibliographical references

613.2 Dietetics

Agatston, Arthur
The **South** Beach diet; the delicious, doctor-designed, foolproof plan for fast and healthy weight loss. Rodale 2003 310p $24.95
613.2
1. Glycemic index 2. Low-carbohydrate diet 3. Reducing diets 4. Weight loss
ISBN 1-57954-646-3
LC 2002-154529

"The South Beach diet begins with a somewhat restrictive two-week program, generally producing a weight loss of from eight to 13 pounds. . . . Complete meal plans along with simple recipes comprise roughly half the book. Of course, there's no perfect diet that works for everyone but the enthusiasm of the conversational tone and the inviting manner make the book more appealing than many other diet tomes." Publ Wkly

Atkins, Robert C.
Dr. Atkins' new diet revolution. Avon Bks. 2002 540p il pa $7.99
613.2
1. Low-carbohydrate diet 2. Weight loss
ISBN 0-06-001203-X
LC 2002-278407

In this "holistic approach to health and well-being . . . Atkins promotes a diet of protein and fat in four stages: induction, ongoing weight loss, premaintenance, and maintenance. Case histories document his achievements. . . . Useful appendixes include menus, recipes, and a carbohydrate gram counter." Libr J
Includes bibliographical references

Bijlefeld, Marjolijn
★ **Encyclopedia** of diet fads; [by] Marjolijn Bijlefeld and Sharon K. Zoumbaris. Greenwood Press 2003 242p il $65; pa $25
613.2
1. Reducing diets -- Encyclopedias 2. Weight loss 3. Weight loss -- Encyclopedias
ISBN 0-313-32223-6; 0-313-36146-0 pa
LC 2002-192821

This volume "covers vitamins, calcium, cholesterol, dietary guidelines, and medical disorders (diabetes, anorexia). It includes just about every fad diet, diet creators (Beverly Hills, Atkins, Weight-Watchers), and specialized diets (macrobiotic, vegetarian, high protein). . . . Entries are well-written and give factual analysis along with criticism of diet claims." Choice
Includes bibliographical references

Burke, Louise
The **complete** guide to food for sports performance; a guide to peak nutrition for your sport. [by] Louise Burke, Greg Cox. 3rd ed., Updated and

expanded; Allen & Unwin 2010 xxii, 522p il pa
$24.95   **613.2**

1. Athletes -- Nutrition 2. Physical fitness
ISBN 978-1-7411-4390-4; 1-7411-4390-X

LC 2010-537626

"This book presents nutrition as an integrated part of
an athlete's total performance-enhancing package. General
nutrition and exercise physiology information are converted
into a plan for day-to-day practice for training and competition preparation. It outlines important differences in nutritional needs for different sports, including the timing of food
and liquid intake, and the best foods to achieve maximum
energy output." Publisher's note

Cox, Peter

You don't need meat. Thomas Dunne Bks. 2002
xxii, 378p il $24.95; pa $14.95   **613.2**

1. Meat -- Health aspects 2. Vegetarian cookery 3.
Vegetarian cooking 4. Vegetarianism
ISBN 0-312-27761-X; 0-312-30338-6 pa

LC 2001-54814

"Cox's defense of vegetarianism rests largely on health
and nutritional issues, but he uses plenty of anthropomor-
phic imagery to discourage eating animals. He cites low
rates of heart disease among Seventh-Day Adventists as empirical evidence for the better health of those who refuse to
eat meat. . . . A few recipes illustrate general principles of
vegetarian cooking." Booklist
Includes bibliographical references

Duyff, Roberta Larson

★ **American** Dietetic Association complete food
and nutrition guide; 2nd ed; Wiley 2002 658p il
$45; pa $24.95   **613.2**

1. Nutrition
ISBN 0-471-22924-5; 0-471-44144-9 pa
"Duyff gives sound advice." Libr J {review of 1996 edi-
tion}

Friedman, Howard S.

The **longevity** project; surprising discoveries for
health and long life from the eight-decade study. [by]
Howard S. Friedman and Leslie R. Martin. Hudson
Street Press 2010 248p $25.95   **613.2**

1. Longevity
ISBN 978-1-594630-75-0; 1-594630-75-5

LC 2010-22833

"Analyzing the data from the Terman study and following up on the 1500 participants, . . . [the authors] investigate
why some people live until old age while others die or become ill prematurely. Unlike most studies, this work looks
at key psychological factors, habits, and patterns that affect
health and longevity over time. Some of the authors' conclusions about achieving longevity are surprising. Factors
such as the study participants' sociability, conscientious-
ness, happiness, and religious involvement were analyzed to
show which patterns lead over time to an increased life span.
The authors have provided a well-written and easy-to-follow
analysis of this interesting study." Libr J
Includes bibliographical references

Guiliano, Mireille

French women don't get fat; secrets for enjoying
food, having fun, and being thin. Mireille Guiliano.
Knopf 2004 272p $24.95; pa $14   **613.2**

1. Beverage industry executives 2. Diet 3. Eating
habits 4. Food habits -- France 5. Reducing diets 6.
Women -- France
ISBN 1-400-04212-7; 0-375-71051-5 pa

LC 2004-48424

Guiliano's "book, with its amusing asides about her life
and work, occasional lapses into French and inspiring recipes . . . is a stirring reminder of the importance of joie de
vivre." Publ Wkly

Jones, Heather K.

Good Housekeeping drop 5 lbs; the small
changes, big results diet. edited [and foreword] by
Rosemary Ellis. Hearst Books 2010 270p il pa
$19.95   **613.2**

1. Metabolism 2. Weight loss
ISBN 978-1-58816-786-6

LC 2010-18434

The author "highlights five eating misbehaviors, including skipping meals and mindless munching. Throughout,
there are specific tips to help eliminate bad habits. . . . An
effective, attractive, and informative ready reference diet
manual. Readers will love the achievable results, and it is
refreshing to have a book that does not expect great sacrifice
and total lifestyle change." Libr J

Kolata, Gina

Rethinking thin; the new science of weight
loss--and the myths and realities of dieting. Farrar,
Straus, and Giroux 2007 257p $24   **613.2**

1. Health behavior 2. Reducing diets 3. Weight loss 4.
Weight loss -- Psychological aspects
ISBN 978-0-374-10398-9; 0-374-10398-4

LC 2006-33816

The author "traces the history of dieting fads back to the
19th century; discusses our changing ideas about the ideal
body (thinner and thinner); and, most importantly, explains
how genetic and biochemical understanding has (at least
among researchers) replaced the view of obesity as a lack of
self-control. . . . This book will change your thinking about
weight, whether you struggle with it or not." Publ Wkly
Includes bibliographical references

Kraus, Barbara

Barbara Kraus' calories and carbohydrates; 16th
ed; Signet Bks. 2005 490p pa $6.99   **613.2**

1. Food -- Composition
ISBN 978-0-451-21384-6; 0-451-21384-X
This lists the calorie and carbohydrate count of more
than 8,500 brand-name and natural foods, according to portion size, with cross references

Mindell, Earl

Dr. Earl Mindell's unsafe at any meal; how to
avoid hidden toxins in your food. {by} Earl Mindell

with Hester Mundis. rev and updated; Contemporary Bks. 2002 274p pa $14.95   **613.2**
1. Food -- Composition 2. Food additives 3. Natural foods 4. Nutrition
ISBN 0-658-02115-X

LC 2001-58223

The author discusses the food industry's chemical cover-ups and looks at "labelese," pros and cons of new products, genetically modified foods and natural foods fortified with vitamins, minerals, and antioxidants.

Murray, Michael T.

Encyclopedia of nutritional supplements; the essential guide for improving your health naturally. Prima Pub. 1996 564p pa $22.95   **613.2**
1. Dietary supplements 2. Dietary supplements -- Encyclopedias 3. Minerals 4. Minerals in human nutrition 5. Nutrition -- Encyclopedias 6. Nutrition -- Requirements 7. Reference books 8. Vitamins 9. Vitamins in human nutrition
ISBN 0-7615-0410-9

LC 96-3804

"Written to help users make sense of the voluminous information available on nutritional supplements, this book includes detailed profiles of all the major ones—vitamins, minerals, essential fatty acids, accessory nutrients, and glandular extracts—and tells how they can help one live longer, feel better, and fight the effects of aging. A concluding section counsels which nutritional supplements to take for a host of conditions, including high cholesterol, depression, and fatigue." Am Ref Books Annu, 1997
Includes bibliographical references

Nelson, Miriam E.

Strong women eat well; nutritional strategies for a healthy body and mind. {by} Miriam E. Nelson with Judy Knipe. Putnam 2001 268p il $24.95; pa $13.95   **613.2**
1. Nutrition 2. Women -- Health and hygiene 3. Women -- Nutrition
ISBN 0-399-14740-3; 0-399-52782-6 pa

LC 00-69677

"The main body of the work discusses each level of the Food Guide Pyramid—grains; fruits and vegetables; milk and meat products; and fats, oils, and sugars—as well as the importance of water. . . . A large number of recipes . . . provide ways to increase the use and intake of some foods that most of us may be hesitant to try." Libr J
Includes bibliographical references and index

Nesheim, Malden

Why calories count; from science to politics. Marion Nestle and Malden Nesheim. University of California Press 2012 288 p. California studies in food and culture (hardback : alk. paper) $29.95 **613.2**
1. Diet 2. Energy Intake -- physiology 3. Food Industry 4. Marketing 5. Obesity -- prevention & control 6. Politics
ISBN 9780520262881

LC 2011044785

This book is [n]either a diet nor a weight-loss book, . . . [but a] work [that] assists readers in evaluating diet claims,

formulating strategies to lose, gain, or maintain weight, and learning how to make healthy food choices. [Marion] Nestle . . . and [Malden] Nesheim . . . focus on the history of the calorie and its relationship to body weight, the science behind metabolism, how to estimate calories in a given portion, and . . . the role of big business in creating calorie-laden food and why it's less politically controversial to recommend exercising than cutting back on calories. (Libr J)

Nestle, Marion

★ **What** to eat. North Point Press 2006 611p $30   **613.2**
1. Diet 2. Health 3. Nutrition
ISBN 0-8654-7704-3; 978-0-8654-7704-9

LC 2006-07886

The author's "intelligent and reassuring approach will likely make readers venture more confidently through the jungle of today's super-sized stores." Publ Wkly
Includes bibliographical references

Nichter, Mimi

Fat talk; what girls and their parents say about dieting. Harvard Univ. Press 2000 263p $25; pa $16.95   **613.2**
1. Body image in adolescence 2. Girls -- Health and hygiene 3. Obesity 4. Obesity in adolescence 5. Reducing diets 6. Teenage girls -- Nutrition 7. Weight loss
ISBN 0-674-00229-6; 0-674-00681-X pa

LC 99-59521

The author "spent three years studying and interviewing teenage girls about their attitudes toward appearance, eating habits, and dieting. . . . Over two hundred girls were followed over a three-year period so that changing attitudes could be measured. The reader gains a better understanding of teenage girls through the readable narrative that describes the results of the study." Voice Youth Advocates
Includes bibliographical references

Reader's Digest Association, Inc.

Foods that harm, foods that heal; an A-Z guide to safe and healthy eating. chief consultants, Joe Schwarcz and Fran Berkoff. Reader's Digest Association 2004 416p il pa $15.95   **613.2**
1. Nutrition
ISBN 0-7621-0505-4; 978-0-7621-0605-9 pa; 0-7621-0605-0 pa

LC 2003-27879

"Alphabetical listings in this . . . resource span general categories of illnesses, food groups, additives, and normal life passages, such as aging. Other entries refer to specific medical conditions or individual dietary elements. . . . Each medical entry recommends helpful foods, followed by those that should be avoided." Booklist

Ronzio, Robert A.

★ The **encyclopedia** of nutrition and good health; {by} Robert Ronzio. 2nd ed; Facts on File 2003 726p $71.50   **613.2**
1. Nutrition -- Encyclopedias 2. Reference books
ISBN 0-8160-4966-1

LC 2002-35221

"The alphabetical entries cover a broad range of topics. Foods, their ingredients, and nutritional values are described. Specific diets (Atkins, Mediterranean) are discussed objectively, with the basic premise of the diet explained along with its pros and cons. Entries on foods and the components implicated in diseases and disorders explain how and why the problem occurs and offer dietary recommendations. Some articles reflect new health concerns. For example, the Transfatty acids entry gives a clear explanation of the health risks and offers alternative food options. There is useful information on the food pyramid and food labels. Medical terms, tests, and current research are also covered." Booklist

Includes bibliographical references

Sears, William

The **family** nutrition book; everything you need to know about feeding your children from birth through adolescence. Little, Brown 1999 416p il hardcover o.p. pa $19   **613.2**

1. Children -- Nutrition   2. Children -- Nutrition -- Popular works   3. Infants -- Nutrition   4. Infants -- Nutrition -- Popular works

ISBN 0-316-77715-3 pa

LC 98-51879

"The book progresses from an overview of nutrients (water and fiber among them) to an extensive evaluation of food groups, including discussions of vegetarianism, organic foods and decoding packaging labels. Additional sections address weight control and the specific roles various foods play in disease prevention, stamina building, etc. Reference tables and an updated food pyramid will prove indispensable to the reader." Publ Wkly

Includes bibliographical references

Shintani, Terry

The **good** carbohydrate revolution. Pocket Bks. 2002 432p il $23; pa $14   **613.2**

1. Diet   2. High-carbohydrate diet   3. Reducing diets

ISBN 0-7434-0598-6; 0-7434-0599-4 pa

LC 2001-55416

The author introduces a "way to control weight and blood sugar levels by eating more of the right kinds of carbohydrates. . . . Designed to maximize your health and keep you lean for life, Dr. Shintani's . . . program centers on 'good' carbohydrates such as whole-grain pasta, pita bread, corn, sweet potatoes, and brown rice, as well as an array of vitamin-rich fruits and vegetables." Publisher's note

Includes bibliographical references

Singh Khalsa, Dharma

Food as medicine; how to use diet, vitamins, juices, and herbs for a healthier, happier, and longer life. Atria Books 2003 358p $26; pa $14   **613.2**

1. Health   2. Longevity -- Nutritional aspects   3. Nutrition

ISBN 0-7434-4226-1; 0-7434-4228-8 pa

LC 2003-266194

This guide to nutritional therapy is based "on the seven principles of yoga nutritional therapy: body detoxification; the use of organic products; elimination of genetically engineered foods; eating only clean protein . . . fresh juices and supplements; cooking consciously and eating mindfully;

and a complete transition to a yoga nutrition therapy diet." Publ Wkly

Includes bibliographical references

Spencer, Colin

Vegetarianism; a history. Four Walls Eight Windows 2002 384p $28   **613.2**

1. Vegetarianism   2. Vegetarianism -- History

ISBN 1-56858-238-2

LC 2002-69298

The author "chronicles meat abstinence throughout history, describing its ancient origins and the myriad struggles of this growing movement." Publisher's note

Includes bibliographical references (p. 367-371) and index

Steward, H. Leighton

The **new** sugar busters! cut sugar to trim fat. {by} H. Leighton Steward . . . {et al.} {rev and updated}; 2003 367p il $24.95   **613.2**

1. Carbohydrates   2. Insulin   3. Sugar-free diet   4. Weight loss

ISBN 0-345-45537-1

LC 2003-272004

In this guide to reducing sugar in your diet "the authors consider childhood obesity and diabetes, discuss artificial sweeteners and alcohol, offer recipes from restaurants around the country and answer FAQs from Sugar Busters everywhere. For those with the willpower to cut out the convenience foods, this will be a helpful guide to eating better." Publ Wkly

Includes bibliographical references

Weil, Andrew

Eating well for optimum health; the essential guide to food, diet, and nutrition. Knopf 2000 307p $25   **613.2**

1. Food   2. Health   3. Nutrition

ISBN 0-375-40754-5

LC 99-52730

"Weil illuminates the often confusing and conflicting ideas circulating about good nutrition, addressing specific health issues and offering nutritional guidance to help heal and prevent major illnesses. Of particular value is his examination of recent fads, such as low-carbohydrate, vegan and 'Asian' diets, with an eye toward debunking the myths about them while highlighting their valuable aspects." Publ Wkly

Includes bibliographical references

Wenner, Paul F.

Garden cuisine; heal yourself and the planet through low-fat meatless eating. {by} Paul Wenner. Simon & Schuster 1997 367p il hardcover o.p. pa $21.95   **613.2**

1. Low fat diet   2. Low-fat diet   3. Vegetarian cooking

ISBN 0-684-83882-6 pa

LC 96-53990

The author "begins by outlining the ethical, health, and environmental benefits of reducing the amount of meat in our diets. He then proposes what is called the Garden Plan for a healthier lifestyle, including three weeks worth of menu plans, a shopping list, and an eight-page list of educational and organizational resources. Wenner's recommendations are easy to follow and commonsensical. . . . The recipes are, for the most part, light and easy to prepare." Libr J

Includes bibliographical references

Willett, Walter

Eat, drink and be healthy; the Harvard Medical School guide to healthy eating. {by} Walter C. Willett with P. J. Skerrett; contributions by Edward L. Giovannucci; recipes by Maureen Callahan. Simon & Schuster 2001 299p il $25; pa $13   **613.2**
1. Nutrition
ISBN 0-684-86337-5; 0-7432-2322-5 pa

LC 2001-20565

The author contends that the USDA Food Pyramid, which recommends 6 to 11 servings of carbohydrate-rich foods per day, is wrong and dangerous, and he offers an alternate nutritional plan emphasizing fruits, vegetables, fish, chicken, legumes, and whole grains

Diet and nutrition sourcebook; edited by Joyce Brennfleck Shannon. 3rd ed.; Omnigraphics 2006 633p il $87   **613.2**
1. Diet 2. Nutrition
ISBN 0-7808-0800-2; 978-0-7808-0800-3

LC 2005-31842

The Encyclopedia of vitamins, minerals, and supplements; [compiled by] Tova Navarra; foreword by Wendy Shankin-Cohen. 2nd ed; Facts on File 2004 xxiii, 353p $65   **613.2**
1. Dietary supplements -- Encyclopedias 2. Nutrition 3. Reference books 4. Vitamins
ISBN 0-8160-4998-X

LC 2003-61662

Over 900 entries in A-Z format focus on how to use vitamins, minerals, and food supplements "safely, their effects on nutrition, their uses as treatment for assorted health concerns, and common misconceptions about them. Articles on individual vitamins and minerals are detailed." Booklist

Includes bibliographical references

The Mayo Clinic diet; [by the weight loss experts at Mayo Clinic] Good Books 2010 254p il $25.99   **613.2**
1. Exercise 2. Health self-care 3. Nutrition 4. Weight loss
ISBN 978-1-5614-8676-2

"Part one, 'Lose It,' includes a two-week intro program designed to result in six to 10 pounds of weight loss, provided readers take up five new habits, including eating breakfast and upping their intake of whole grains, while quitting five old habits, like eating in front of the TV. Part two, 'Live It,' modifies those techniques to sustain one to two pounds of weight loss a week. Part three helps readers with immediate and long-term challenges like behavior modification and stress, as well as meal planning and eating out. Efficiently organized with convenient reference points, this is a worthy guide for any determined dieter." Publ Wkly

Nutrition and well-being A to Z; Delores C.S. James, editor in chief. Macmillan Reference USA 2004 2v il set $175   **613.2**
1. Health -- Encyclopedias 2. Nutrition -- Encyclopedias 3. Reference books
ISBN 0-02-865707-1

LC 2004-6088

This is "a no-nonsense, comprehensive encyclopedia that will be of use to students researching health and food-science topics." SLJ

Includes bibliographical references

Vegetarian Times vegetarian beginner's guide; by the editors of Vegetarian Times. Macmillan 1996 181p il pa $13.95   **613.2**
1. Vegetarianism
ISBN 0-02-860386-9

LC 96-4120

The authors "describe the various types of vegetarianism. Stressing the health value of the vegetarian lifestyle, especially in the treatment of various diseases, they point out the possible dangers of dairy foods, discuss whether to use vitamin supplements, and encourage the use of low-fat ingredients. Tips on the basic vegetarian pantry, along with two-weeks' worth of easy recipes and menus, are given for the beginner." Libr J

★ Vegetarian sourcebook; basic consumer health information about vegetarian diets, lifestyle, and philosophy . . . edited by Chad T. Kimball. Omnigraphics 2002 360p il $78   **613.2**
1. Vegetarianism
ISBN 0-7808-0439-2

LC 2002-70236

"This work answers questions that people might have about the healthfulness of a vegetarian diet as well as how to incorporate it into one's everyday life. . . . The articles in this volume are easy to read and come from authoritative sources." Am Ref Books Annu, 2003

Includes bibliographical references

The Yale guide to children's nutrition; William V. Tamborlane, editor-in-chief; Janet Z. Weiswasser, managing editor; editors, Teresa Fung, Nancy A. Held, Tara Prather Liskov; foreword by Jane E. Brody; recipes compiled with cooperation from the James Beard Foundation. Yale Univ. Press 1997 415p il hardcover o.p. pa $19.95   **613.2**
1. Children -- Nutrition
ISBN 0-300-06965-0; 0-300-07169-8 pa

LC 96-44774

"Comprehensive in its coverage, well organized, and easily understood, this book is highly recommended for any consumer health collection." Libr J

Includes bibliographical references

613.6 Personal safety and special topics of health

Bocij, Paul

Cyberstalking; harassment in the Internet age and how to protect your family. Praeger Publishers 2004 268p $39.95   **613.6**
1. Computer crimes
ISBN 0-275-98118-5; 978-0-275-98118-1
LC 2003-68988
"This is an extremely alarming book that focuses on the dark side of the Internet and makes it clear that we are all potential victims of cyberstalkers. . . . It's certain to be popular in libraries." Booklist
Includes bibliographical references

Drago, Dorothy A.

★ From crib to kindergarten; the essential child safety guide. Johns Hopkins University Press 2007 195p il $45; pa $15   **613.6**
1. Accidents -- Prevention 2. Parenting
ISBN 978-0-8018-8569-3; 0-8018-8569-8; 978-0-8018-8570-9 pa; 0-8018-8570-1 pa
LC 2006-20809
"In an effort to help readers 'recognize and reduce hazards so . . . children can be as safe from injury as possible,' Drago offers hundreds of tips on how to provide a safe environment for daily activities, concentrating on small children in the home setting. . . . This book is packed with indispensable advice and is an essential resource and reference guide for parents and caregivers." Libr J
Includes bibliographical references

Frist, Bill

When every moment counts; what you need to know about bioterrorism from the Senate's only doctor. {by} Bill Frist. Rowman & Littlefield 2002 181p il pa $14.95   **613.6**
1. Anthrax 2. Biological warfare 3. Bioterrorism -- Popular works 4. Chemical warfare 5. Ebola virus 6. Plague 7. Smallpox 8. Terrorism
ISBN 0-7425-2245-8
LC 2001-8752

Gervasi, Lori Hartman

Fight like a girl--and win; defense decisions for women. St. Martin's Griffin 2007 285p pa $14.99   **613.6**
1. Safety education 2. Self-defense for women
ISBN 978-0-312-35772-6; 0-312-35772-9
LC 2007-17216
"Although the author has a black belt in karate, she maintains that 90 percent of self-defense is awareness and common sense. She helps readers set up absolute rules and boundaries, sharpen their observation skills, and trust in their intuition. Physical fitness is stressed, and resources are provided for further training." Libr J
Includes bibliographical references

Perkins, John

Attack proof; the ultimate guide to personal protection. [by] John Perkins, Al Ridenhour, Matt Kovsky. 2nd ed.; Human Kinetics 2009 276p il pa $19.95   **613.6**
1. Crime prevention 2. Self-defense
ISBN 978-0-7360-7876-4; 0-7360-7876-2
LC 2009-1456
This self-defense book presents a "personal protection system, called guided chaos, for anticipating and fending off even the most brutal assaults. . . . [It includes] protection strategies for larger assailants, car and airline hijackings, workplace violence, multiple attackers, fighting on the ground and in stairwells, and attacks and defenses using guns, knives, sticks, and canes." Publisher's note
Includes bibliographical references

Sherwood, Ben

The survivors club; the secrets and science that could save your life. Grand Central Pub. 2009 383p il $25.99; pa $14.99   **613.6**
1. Accidents 2. Survival skills
ISBN 978-0-446-58024-3; 0-446-58024-4; 978-0-446-69885-6 pa; 0-446-69885-7 pa
LC 2008-16203
"Is the book science? Self-help? It's a weird amalgam of the two, but somehow it works. . . . The true-life stories are satisfying in a popcorny kind of way, but it's the science that fascinates." Entertainment Wkly

Stilwell, Alexander

★ The encyclopedia of survival techniques. Lyons Press 2007 192p il map pa $19.95   **613.6**
1. Survival skills 2. Wilderness survival
ISBN 978-1-59921-314-9
This guide covers preparation, basic skills, equipment, various terrains, natural disasters, and first aid.

Wiseman, John

SAS survival handbook; for any climate, in any situation. [by] John "Lofty" Wiseman. Rev. ed.; Collins 2009 576p il pa $19.99   **613.6**
1. Survival after airplane accidents, shipwrecks, etc. 2. Survival skills 3. Wilderness survival
ISBN 978-0-06-173319-2; 0-06-173319-9
LC 2009-502549
This book "is the Special Air Service's complete course in being prepared for any type of emergency. John Wiseman presents real strategies for surviving in any type of situation, from accidents and escape procedures, including chemical and nuclear to successfully adapting to various climates (polar, tropical, desert), to identifying edible plants and creating fire." Publisher's note

Survival wisdom & know-how; everything you need to know to subsist in the wilderness. from the editors of Stackpole Books; compiled by Amy Rost.

Black Dog & Leventhal Publishers 2007 480p il pa $19.95 **613.6**
1. Survival skills 2. Wilderness survival
ISBN 978-1-57912-753-4

LC 2007-25379

This oversized guide covers "every aspect of outdoor adventure and survival . . . Topics include Building Outdoor Shelter, Tracking Animals, Winter Camping, Tying Knots, Orienteering, Reading the Weather, Identifying Edible Plants and Berries, Surviving in the Desert, Bird Watching, Fishing and Ice Fishing, Hunting and Trapping, Canoeing, Kayaking, and White Water Rafting, First Aid, Wild Animals, Cookery, and . . . more." Publisher's note

Includes bibliographical references

613.7   Physical fitness

American College of Sports Medicine

★ **Complete** guide to fitness & health; Barbara Bushman, editor. Human Kinetics 2011 396p il pa $21.95 **613.7**
1. Exercise 2. Health 3. Physical fitness
ISBN 978-0-7360-9337-8; 0-7360-9337-0

LC 2011-6563

"Contributions from a range of academics (many affiliated with the ACSM) distill the current thinking on nutrition and exercise for all ages and for adults with chronic conditions such as arthritis and diabetes. They discuss how to determine your current levels of fitness, create a graduated fitness plan and coordinate it with proper eating habits, and measure your progress and maintain your optimum level. Chapters include recommendations for those with special health and medical conditions, such as diabetes, high cholesterol, high blood pressure, and arthritis. . . . Anyone who is serious about getting in shape will want this guide." Libr J

Includes bibliographical references

Bailey, Covert

Smart exercise; burning fat, getting fit. Houghton Mifflin 1994 292p hardcover o.p. pa $12 **613.7**
1. Exercise 2. Physical fitness
ISBN 0-395-66114-5 pa

LC 94-1667

This fitness guide discusses metabolism, dieting, muscle tone, aerobics, exercise machines, swimming, walking and the benefits and drawbacks of various sports.

Blair, Steven N.

Active living every day; {by} Steven N. Blair {et al.} Human Kinetics 2001 194p il pa $22.95 **613.7**
1. Exercise 2. Health 3. Physical fitness
ISBN 0-7360-3701-2

LC 00-47238

The authors "present a week-by-week, self-paced plan for couch potatoes to incorporate physical activity gradually into their daily lives. . . . There is also sensible advice on proper nutrition and additional interactive exercises on the net." Libr J

Includes bibliographical references and index

Bonifonte, Philip

T'ai chi for seniors; how to gain flexibility, strength, and inner peace. New Page Bks. 2004 213p il pa $16.99 **613.7**
1. Tai chi 2. Tai chi for the aged
ISBN 1-564-14697-9

LC 2003-60207

The author describes the ancient Chinese exercise that focuses "on easy, gentle movements that increase aerobic capacity, decrease blood pressure and stress, and improve balance and joint function. Along with a short history of various tai chi styles philosophies, the text features breathing techniques, warm-up exercises, movement forms, and meditation exercises with modifications for those with limited mobility." Libr J

Broad, William J.

The **science** of yoga; William J. Broad. Simon & Schuster 2012 xxxi, 298p ill. **613.7**
1. Health & Fitness -- General 2. Health & Fitness -- Yoga 3. Hatha yoga 4. Science -- Life Sciences -- General
ISBN 9781451641424; 9781451641431; 9781451641448

LC 2011020408

This book, "[f]ive years in the making, . . . draws on more than a century of . . . research to present the first impartial evaluation of a practice thousands of years old. It celebrates what's real and shows what's illusory, describes what's uplifting and beneficial and what's flaky and dangerous--and why. Broad illuminates how yoga can lift moods and inspire creativity. He exposes moves that can cripple and kill. . . . [The book] presents a . . . body of evidence that raises questions about whether humans have latent capabilities for entering states of suspended animation and unremitting sexual bliss. 'The Science of Yoga' takes us on a . . . tour of unknown yoga that goes from old archives in Calcutta to the world capitals of medical research, from storied ashrams to spotless laboratories, from sweaty yoga studios with master teachers to the cozy offices of yoga healers." (Publisher's note)

Callahan, Lisa

The **fitness** factor; every woman's key to a lifetime of health and wellbeing. Lyons Press 2002 xxi, 314p il $24.95 **613.7**
1. Exercise 2. Exercise for women 3. Physical fitness 4. Physical fitness for women 5. Women -- Health and hygiene
ISBN 1-58574-501-4

LC 2001-50729

In this guide the author stresses the importance of exercise in "preventing heart disease; beating osteoporosis; lowering cholesterol; decreasing cancer risk; losing weight; increasing energy; reducing stress; having better sex and much more." Publisher's note

Includes bibliographical references

Decker, Joe

The **world's** fittest you; four weeks to total fitness. {by} Joe Decker with Eric Neuhaus. Dutton 2004 286p il $24.95; pa $13.95   **613.7**

1. Exercise 2. Physical fitness

ISBN 0-525-94759-0; 0-451-21401-3 pa

LC 2004-299995

This is "a scientifically sound fitness guide that reads as if the author had taken exercise principles from a college exercise physiology textbook and condensed and repacked them into a program geared to the working adult." Libr J

Duke, Kacy

The **show** it love workout; celebrate the body you have, get the body you want. [by] Kacy Duke with Selene Yeager. McGraw-Hill 2008 254p il $24.95   **613.7**

1. Exercise 2. Health 3. Physical fitness

ISBN 978-0-07-149446-5; 0-07-149446-4

LC 2007-20141

The author "addresses not only the physical aspects of fitness but also the spiritual and emotional components needed to maintain it. . . . Each of the three parts ('I Am,' 'I Can,' and 'I Do') features motivational text, 'woman warrior' exercises, healthy recipes, milestones, and a workout log. . . . Her book creates the effect of having a personal trainer, and the general public will love it." Libr J

Fahey, Thomas D.

Basic weight training for men and women; 6th ed.; McGraw-Hill 2007 248p il pa $30.63   **613.7**

1. Weight lifting

ISBN 0-07-304688-4; 978-0-07-304688-4

LC 2005-53132

This is a "guide to developing a personalized weight-training program with both free weights and machines. Weight training concepts and specific exercises are grouped by body region, and many photographs, illustrations, diagrams, and figures demonstrate proper technique and form." Publisher's note

Includes bibliographical references

Hesson, James L.

★ **Weight** training for life; 9th ed.; Wadsworth/Cengage Learning 2010 178p il $59.95   **613.7**

1. Weight lifting

ISBN 978-0-495-55909-2; 0-495-55909-1

LC 2010291364

"The text contains hundreds of full-color photos demonstrating exercises and proper techniques. It also contains forms for writing goals, planning a personal weight-training program, and recording circumference, strength, and muscle endurance measurements." Publisher's note

Includes bibliographical references

Hines, Emmett W.

Fitness swimming; [by] Emmett Hines. 2nd ed.; Human Kinetics 2008 224p il pa $18.95   **613.7**

1. Physical fitness 2. Swimming

ISBN 978-0-7360-7457-5; 0-7360-7457-0

LC 2008-13353

The author "has created 60 . . . workouts and 16 sample programs, each arranged into suggested training zones to correspond to your fitness level and performance goals. . . . The text covers stretching, warm-up and cool-down methods, heart rate zone targets, expanded instruction for stroke efficacy, progressive drills, conditioning tips, and fitness assessments." Publisher's note

Includes bibliographical references

Isacowitz, Rael

Pilates. Human Kinetics 2006 343p il pa $19.95   **613.7**

1. Pilates method

ISBN 0-7360-5623-8; 978-0-7360-5623-6

LC 2006-7911

This guide to Pilates exercises includes information on mat work, breathing, and equipment.

Kolata, Gina

Ultimate fitness; the quest for truth about exercise and health. Farrar, Straus & Giroux 2003 292p il $24; pa $14   **613.7**

1. Exercise 2. Physical fitness

ISBN 0-374-20477-2; 0-312-42322-5 pa

LC 2002-192523

The author " investigates 30 years of the American physical fitness craze, looking at issues like athlete's heart, maximum heart rates, fat-burning zones, training, runner's high, weightlifting, walking, food, water, {and} the fitness business. . . . Fascinating historical information about fitness, understandable facts and figures, and a conversational writing style make this an enormously readable book." Libr J

Includes bibliographical references

Pagano, Joan

★ **Strength** training for women; tone up, burn calories, stay strong. Dorling Kindersley 2005 160p il pa $15   **613.7**

1. Physical fitness 2. Weight lifting 3. Women -- Health and hygiene

ISBN 0-7566-0595-4; 978-0-7566-0595-7

LC 2005-295208

The author "begins with a three-part fitness test and questionnaire to assess whether the reader should consult a doctor before beginning her program. For true beginners, she provides an anatomy chart that depicts the major muscle groups and the exercises that are best suited to them. She dispels fitness myths like 'lifting weights will bulk you up' and 'you can spot reduce,' and talks about the risk factors, exercise guidelines and restrictions of osteoporosis. . . . This book may be one of the best substitutes for pricey gym memberships and personal trainers." Publ Wkly

Reichmann, Rosie

Ageless yoga; yoga exercises for improving your life at any age! Astrolog 2001 192p il pa $18.95   **613.7**

1. Yoga

ISBN 9-6549-4124-4

The author discusses how her "program of gentle stretching and breathing techniques can be used to create specific workouts to relieve tension, increase flexibility, and reduce age-related functional losses in various parts of the body. Her readable text is illustrated with photos of the author demonstrating the poses, with modifications for those who must use a chair or mattress." Libr J

Reynolds, Gretchen

The **first** 20 minutes; surprising science reveals how we can exercise better, train smarter, live longer. Gretchen Reynolds. Hudson Street Press 2012 xvii, 266 p.p **613.7**

1. Exercise -- Physiological aspects 2. Exercise -- Popular Works 3. Exercise -- physiology -- Popular Works 4. Nonfiction 5. Physical Fitness -- Popular Works 6. Physical education and training -- Physiological aspects 7. Physical fitness 8. Reducing diets

ISBN 1594630933; 9781594630934

LC 2012000321

This book by Gretchen Reynolds offers findings about the mental and physical benefits of exercise, personal stories from scientists and laypeople alike, as well as researched-based prescriptions for readers, . . . show[ing] what kind of exerciseand how muchis necessary to stay healthy, get fit, and attain a smaller jeans size. Inspired by Reynolds's . . . Phys Ed column for The New York Times, this book explains how exercise affects the body in distinct ways and provides the tools readers need to achieve their fitness goals, whether that's a faster 5K or staying trim. (Publishers note)

Sivananda Yoga Vedanta Center (London, England)

★ **Yoga**; your home practice companion. DK 2010 256p il $25 **613.7**

1. Physical fitness 2. Yoga

ISBN 978-0-7566-5729-1; 0-7566-5729-6

LC 2010-291655

This is "one of the best yoga guides for all levels of experience. . . . The yogic principles of proper exercise, breathing, diet, and meditation are covered. . . . Color photo spreads of models depict easy-to-follow classic poses as well as corrective poses for physical ailments. Accompanying anatomical drawings demonstrate how yoga affects and benefits the musculoskeletal and nervous systems. . . . Readers are given all of the necessary information to start and maintain a home yoga practice. Best of all, the information is comprehensive without being overwhelming." Libr J

Taubes, Gary

Why we get fat and what to do about it. Alfred A. Knopf 2011 257p $24.95 **613.7**

1. Low-carbohydrate diet 2. Obesity 3. Obesity -- Etiology 4. Weight loss

ISBN 978-0-307-27270-6; 0-307-27270-2

LC 2010-34248

The author "assures readers that overweight and obesity are not character flaws but a disorder of fat accumulation; most of the book deals with this issue in detail. This brave, paradigm-shifting man uses logic and the primary literature to unhinge the nutritional mantra of the last 80 years that an imbalance of 'calories in versus calories out' leads to weight change." Choice

Includes bibliographical references

Fitness and exercise sourcebook; edited by Amy L. Sutton. 3rd ed; Omnigraphics 2007 663p il $87 **613.7**

1. Exercise 2. Physical fitness

ISBN 978-0-7808-0946-8; 0-7808-0946-7

LC 2006-36852

613.9   Birth control, reproductive technology, sex hygiene, sexual techniques

Block, Joel D.

Sex over 50; {by} Joel D. Block with Susan Crain Bakos. Parker Pub. 1999 302p $34; pa $15 **613.9**

1. Sexual behavior

ISBN 0-13-080968-3; 0-7352-0058-0 pa

LC 98-42503

"Highlighting the 'potent sexual benefits' that come with midlife, this light-hearted but informative guide by a psychotherapist and journalist presents exercises to reenergize a routine sex life, suggests how to create moods and fantasies, describes alternative forms of lovemaking (bondage, etc.), and covers the more mundane aspects of midlife sexuality (health issues, impotence, hormonal changes)." Libr J

Comfort, Alex

★ The **joy** of sex; foreword by Claire Rayner. Crown 2002 240p il $29.95; pa $10 **613.9**

1. Sex customs 2. Sex instruction 3. Sexual behavior

ISBN 1-400-04614-9; 0-7434-7774-X pa

LC 2002-67455

Describes with illustrations a variety of sexual behaviors, addresses causes and risks of sexually transmitted diseases, and emphasizes the importance of love.

Winikoff, Beverly

The **whole** truth about contraception; a guide to safe and effective choices. by Beverly Winikoff, and Suzanne Wymelenberg. Joseph Henry Press 1997 274p il pa $18.95 **613.9**

1. Birth control

ISBN 0-309-05494-X

LC 97-26488

This guide contains "information about all forms of contraception and their safety, effectiveness, and side effects. The authors discuss male and female reproductive anatomy and physiology as well as barrier, hormonal, intrauterine, surgical, and natural methods. . . . Including information about cost, the prevention of sexually transmitted diseases, choosing practitioners, and the proper use of the various methods makes this an extremely useful source." Libr J

Includes bibliographical references

614   Forensic medicine; incidence of injuries, wounds, disease; public preventive medicine

Bass, William M.

Death's acre; inside the legendary forensic lab the Body Farm where the dead do tell tales. [by] Bill

Bass and Jon Jefferson; foreword by Patricia Cornwell. Putnam 2003 304p il $24.95; pa $15   **614**

   1. Body, Human -- Identification 2. Crime laboratories -- Tennessee 3. Forensic anthropology 4. Forensic anthropology -- Tennessee 5. Forensic anthropology -- United States 6. Human skeleton -- Identification

   ISBN 0-399-15134-6; 0-425-19832-4 pa

                       LC 2003-46908

"The author explains the process of decomposition and how bones give clues to identify: approximate age, sex, height, and race, all of which are needed to bring the forensic scientist one step closer to putting a name to a corpse. He describes some of the cases he has been involved with and laughs at himself when he shares stories of mistakes and assumptions. Young adults will gain insight into the forensic process and appreciate Bass's dedication to the truth and his work." SLJ

Blum, Deborah

   The **poisoner's** handbook; murder and the birth of forensic medicine in Jazz Age New York. Penguin Press 2010 319p $25.95; pa $16   **614**

   1. Crime -- New York (N.Y.) -- History -- 20th century 2. Forensic sciences 3. Forensic sciences -- History 4. Forensic toxicology 5. Poisoning 6. Poisons and poisoning 7. Toxicology

   ISBN 978-1-59420-243-8; 1-59420-243-5; 978-0-14-311882-4 pa; 0-14-311882-X pa

                       LC 2009-26461

Chronicles the story of New York City's first forensic scientists to describe Jazz Age poisoning cases, including a family's inexplicable balding, Barnum and Bailey's Blue Man, and the crumbling bones of factory workers.

"Blum effectively balances the fast-moving detective story with a clear view of the scientific advances that her protagonists brought to the field. Caviar for true-crime fans and science buffs alike." Kirkus

   Includes bibliographical references

Maples, William R.

   Dead men do tell tales; [by] William R. Maples and Michael Browning. Doubleday 1994 292p il hardcover o.p. pa $15.95   **614**

   1. Anthropologists 2. College teachers 3. Forensic anthropology

   ISBN 0-385-47968-9 pa

                       LC 94-12290

Maples, a forensic anthropologist, "describes the remains (or, when burnt, cremains) presented to him, describes what he looks for, and guides us through his thinking and the search for additional clues and information. His most difficult, fascinating, and perplexing case dealt with a 1985 apparent double murder and burning, while among historic bodies, Maples dealt with those of Francisco Pizarro, Zachary Taylor, Czar Nicholas II, and Joseph Merrick, 'the Elephant Man.'" Booklist

Wecht, Cyril H.

   ★ **Tales** from the morgue; forensic answers to nine famous cases including the Scott Peterson & Chandra Levy cases. [by] Cyril Wecht and Mark Cur-

riden with Angela Powell. Prometheus Books 2005 314p il $26   **614**

   1. Criminal investigation 2. Forensic sciences

   ISBN 1-59102-353-X

                       LC 2005-17805

Pathologist Wecht "sorts out the evidence, or lack thereof, in the scandalous circumstances of Scott Peterson and Chandra Levy, explains why he thinks the JFK assassination was a conspiracy and agrees with the original Marilyn Monroe autopsy that found no signs of foul play. . . . What makes Wecht's arguments so persuasive is that he lets scientific facts—or at least his expert interpretation of them—do the talking." Publ Wkly

   Includes bibliographical references

Zugibe, Frederick T.

   Dissecting death; secrets of a medical examiner. [by] Frederick Zugibe and David L. Carroll. Broadway Books 2005 240p il $24.95; pa $14   **614**

   1. Criminal investigation 2. Forensic sciences 3. Medical jurisprudence

   ISBN 0-7679-1879-7; 0-7679-1880-0 pa

                       LC 2004-62889

The authors' "straightforward style makes for clear and fascinating reading, and the cases chosen are intriguing." Booklist

614.4   Incidence of and public measures to prevent disease

Alcabes, Philip

   Dread; how fear and fantasy have fueled epidemics from the Black Death to avian flu. PublicAffairs 2009 313p $26.95   **614.4**

   1. Anxiety 2. Communicable diseases 3. Epidemics 4. Epidemics -- History 5. Epidemics -- Social aspects 6. Fear 7. Fear -- Psychological aspects 8. Health behavior 9. Nosophobia

   ISBN 978-1-58648-618-1; 1-58648-618-7

                       LC 2009-00248

"Showing how even epidemics hinge on societal attitudes and expectations, Alcabes presents an engrossing, revealing account of the relationship between progress and plague." Publ Wkly

   Includes bibliographical references

Allen, Arthur

   Vaccine; the controversial story of medicine's greatest lifesaver. Norton 2007 523p il $27.95 **614.4**

   1. Communicable diseases -- Prevention 2. Vaccination 3. Vaccination -- History

   ISBN 0-393-05911-1; 978-0-393-05911-3

                       LC 2006-19480

The author "records the miracles, controversies, and tragedies that have accompanied the development of vaccines since Edward Jenner first combated smallpox in the 18th century. . . . This compelling narrative of the vaccine's undoubted triumphs and troubling challenges is highly recommended to serious readers interested in medicine and public health." Libr J

   Includes bibliographical references

Drexler, Madeline

Secret agents; the menace of emerging infections. Joseph Henry Press 2002 316p il $24.95   **614.4**

1. Communicable diseases 2. Communicable diseases -- United States 3. Epidemiology

ISBN 0-309-07638-2

LC 2001-7832

This discusses such topics as food-borne pathogens, antibiotic resistance, animals and insect-borne pathogens, pandemic influenza, infectious causes of chronic disease, and bioterrorism, including the threats of anthrax and smallpox

This is a "fascinating thought-provoking book. . . . A substantial contribution to public information about infectious diseases." Booklist

Includes bibliographical references

Garrett, Laurie

The **coming** plague; newly emerging diseases in a world out of balance. Penguin 1995 750p maps pa $20   **614.4**

1. AIDS (Disease) 2. Communicable diseases 3. Ebola virus 4. Epidemics 5. Viruses

ISBN 0-14-025091-3; 978-0-14-025091-6

"The author demonstrates that the emerging global village means not only superior communication and trade among nations but also the deadly swap of microbes. Analyzing the spread of both familiar diseases like cholera and new viruses like Ebola, this is 'a meticulously researched, genuinely disturbing' account." N Y Times Book Rev

Includes bibliographical references

Karlen, Arno

Man and microbes; disease and plagues in history and modern times. Simon & Schuster 1996 266p pa $14   **614.4**

ISBN 0-684-82270-9

LC 96-1705

Karlen presents a "report on the current global crisis of new and resurgent diseases. Covering cholera, leprosy, cancer, AIDS, viral encephalitis, lethal Ebola fever, streptococcal 'flesh-eating' infections and a host of other killers, he shows how the present wave of diseases arose with drastic environmental change, wars, acceleration of travel, the breakdown of public health measures, and microbial adaptation." Publ Wkly

Includes bibliographical references

Kirby, David

Evidence of harm; mercury in vaccines and the autism epidemic: a medical controversy. David Kirby. St. Martin's Press 2005 460p $26.95; pa $14.95   **614.4**

1. Autism 2. Autism in children -- Etiology 3. Organomercury compounds 4. Vaccination 5. Vaccination of children -- Complications

ISBN 0-312-32644-0; 0-312-32645-9 pa

LC 2004-51492

This book "addresses the front-page question: has a mercury-containing preservative called thimerosal, commonly used in children's vaccines, caused a national epidemic of juvenile autism? . . . This is the book for medical professionals and concerned parents to read. It's accessible in its

handling of medical topics and compelling in its recounting of the parents' fight to advance their agenda in the face of both political and scientific roadblocks." Publ Wkly

Includes bibliographical references

McKenna, Maryn

★ **Beating** back the devil; on the front lines with the disease detectives of the Epidemic Intelligence Service. Free Press 2004 303p hardcover o.p. pa $21.95   **614.4**

1. Epidemiology

ISBN 0-7432-5132-6; 1-4391-2310-1 pa

LC 2004-53214

"This book should serve as an effective antidote for anyone suffering from the misconception that epidemiologists must lead boring lives." Sci Books Films

Includes bibliographical references

Morris, Robert D.

The **blue** death; disease, disaster and the water we drink. HarperCollins Publishers 2007 310p il $24.95   **614.4**

1. Communicable diseases 2. Water purification 3. Water supply

ISBN 978-0-06-073089-5; 0-06-073089-7

LC 2006-49674

"A clear and convincing argument; recommended for public libraries." Libr J

Includes bibliographical references

Offit, Paul A.

★ **Deadly** choices; how the anti-vaccine movement threatens us all. Basic Books 2010 270p il $27.50   **614.4**

1. Vaccination 2. Vaccination of children 3. Vaccination of children -- Complications

ISBN 978-0-465-02149-9; 0-465-02149-2

LC 2010-22446

This "is a thorough dismantling of antivaccine notions and a sober warning about the resurgence of deadly childhood infections stemming from declining vaccination rates. Worried parents, especially, will find this a lucid, compelling riposte to antivaccine fear-mongering." Publ Wkly

Includes bibliographical references

Oldstone, Michael B. A.

Viruses, plagues, and history. Oxford Univ. Press 1998 211p il maps hardcover o.p. pa $15.95 **614.4**

1. AIDS (Disease) 2. Communicable diseases 3. Ebola virus 4. Epidemics 5. Influenza 6. Measles 7. Plague 8. Poliomyelitis 9. Smallpox 10. Viruses 11. Yellow fever

ISBN 0-19-511723-9; 0-19-513422-2 pa

LC 97-9545

The author "starts with accounts of smallpox, yellow fever, measles, and polio, providing lively, well-documented stories about those diseases and their investigators. He well understands historical contexts and developments, and he has interviewed scientists involved in pertinent clinical and research work when that was possible. . . . He moves on to Ebola and other terrifying fevers, mad cow disease, and influenza, thoughtfully exploring the problems mutation poses for prevention and treatment." Booklist

Includes bibliographical references

Peters, C. J.

Virus hunter; thirty years of battling hot viruses around the world. {by} C.J. Peters, with Mark Olshaker. Anchor Bks. (NY) 1997 323p il hardcover o.p. pa $14.95　　　　**614.4**

1. Army officers　2. Communicable diseases -- Prevention　3. Epidemiologists　4. Epidemiology　5. Medicine -- Research　6. Viruses

ISBN 0-385-48558-1 pa

LC 97-977

This book is "smoothly written and provides an interesting overview of its author's career and education in the workings of medical bureaucracies." Libr J

Ryan, Frank

Virus-X; tracking the new killer plagues: out of the present and into the future. Little, Brown 1997 430p il maps hardcover o.p. pa $15　　**614.4**

1. Communicable diseases　2. Epidemics　3. Epidemiology　4. Viruses

ISBN 0-316-76306-3 pa

LC 96-30495

"Of the many recent books about emerging diseases, this is one of the most interesting and disquieting, not only because of its gripping accounts of recent disease outbreaks such as hantavirus and AIDS but because of what it says about the nature of viruses." Libr J

Includes bibliographical references

Sears, Robert

The **vaccine** book; making the right decision for your child. [by] Robert W. Sears. Little, Brown 2007 278p pa $13.99　　　　**614.4**

1. Vaccination

ISBN 978-0-316-01750-3; 0-316-01750-7

LC 2007-22994

"The first 12 chapters discuss each vaccination in the childhood series, providing explanation of the relative disease, how the vaccine is made and points to assess a child's at-risk level when considering if the vaccine is necessary. . . . Additional chapters illuminate more controversial aspects of the debate, such as how vaccine safety is researched and what the findings are, side effects and how to minimize them, common myths and questions. . . . Sears' tone puts readers at ease as he clearly explains medical terms and elucidates debates." Publ Wkly

Includes bibliographical references

Walters, Mark Jerome

Six modern plagues and how we are causing them. Island Press 2003 206p $22; pa $14　**614.4**

1. Communicable diseases　2. Environmental health　3. Environmental health -- Popular works　4. Epidemiology　5. Epidemiology -- Popular works　6. Human ecology　7. Human ecology -- Popular works

ISBN 1-55963-992-X; 978-1-55963-992-7; 1-55963-714-5 pa; 978-1-55963-714-5 pa

LC 2003-15137

"A quick read and a great introduction to the topic." Libr J

Includes bibliographical references

Wills, Christopher

Yellow fever, black goddess; the coevolution of people and plagues. Addison-Wesley 1996 324p il hardcover o.p. pa $16.50　　　　**614.4**

1. Communicable diseases　2. Epidemics

ISBN 0-201-32818-6 pa

LC 96-23934

The author manages "to provide a good read while weaving seamlessly between historical accounts, scientific detective stories, and personal (or family) anecdotes." New Sci

Includes bibliographical references

Encyclopedia of pestilence, pandemics, and plagues; edited by Joseph P. Byrne; foreword by Anthony S. Fauci. Greenwood Press 2008 2v il map set $199.95　　　　**614.4**

1. Communicable diseases　2. Communicable diseases -- Encyclopedias　3. Diseases -- History　4. Epidemics　5. Epidemics -- Encyclopedias　6. Reference books

ISBN 978-0-313-34101-4

LC 2008-19487

"A useful resource, especially for those trying to learn about the cultural issues like news reporting on epidemic disease or societal reactions to leprosy, this well-written work would be a good starting point for research." Libr J

Includes bibliographical references

★ Encyclopedia of plague and pestilence; from ancient times to the present. George Childs Kohn, editor. 3rd ed; Facts On File 2008 529p il map $85　　　　**614.4**

1. Communicable diseases　2. Epidemics　3. Epidemics -- Encyclopedias　4. Reference books　5. Social history　6. Social medicine

ISBN 978-0-8160-6935-4; 0-8160-6935-2

LC 2006-41296

This encyclopedia provides "descriptions of more than 700 epidemics, listed alphabetically by location of the outbreak. Each . . . entry includes when and where a particular epidemic began, how and why it happened, whom it affected, how it spread and ran its course, and its outcome and significance." Publisher's note

Includes bibliographical references

614.5　Incidence of and public measures to prevent specific diseases and kinds of diseases

Barry, John M.

The **great** influenza; the epic story of the deadliest plague in history. Viking 2004 546p il $29.95; pa $16　　　　**614.5**

1. Epidemics -- History　2. Influenza　3. Influenza -- History

ISBN 0-670-89473-7; 0-14-303649-1 pa

LC 2003-57646

In this account of the 1918 influenza pandemic, the author "explores how the deadly confluence of biology (a swiftly mutating flu virus that can pass between animals and humans) and politics (President Wilson's all-out war effort in WWI) created conditions in which the virus thrived, killing more than 50 million worldwide and perhaps as many as 100 million in just a year." Publ Wkly

Includes bibliographical references

Cantor, Norman F.

In the wake of the plague; the Black death and the world it made. 1st Perennial ed.; Perennial/HarperCollins 2002 245p il map pa $13.95   **614.5**
  1. Plague
  ISBN 0-06-001434-2

LC 2001-51819

"By animating history and demonstrating our times' connections to even as remote an event as the Black Death, Cantor's erudite excursion proves most engrossing." Booklist

Includes bibliographical references

Carrell, Jennifer Lee

★ The **speckled** monster; a historical tale of battling smallpox. Dutton 2003 474p il $24.95; pa $16   **614.5**
  1. Authors 2. Essayists 3. Physicians 4. Poets 5. Smallpox 6. Smallpox -- History -- Popular works
  ISBN 0-525-94736-1; 0-452-28507-0 pa

LC 2003-137

The author focuses "on two early pioneers in the practice of smallpox inoculation: Lady Mary Wortley Montagu of London . . . and Dr. Zabdiel Boylston of Boston. Basing much of her reconstructed dialog on Montagu's letters from Turkey, where she observed the local practice of inoculation, and Boylston's medical case studies of African practices, Carrell makes these historical figures come alive." Libr J

Includes bibliographical references

Crosby, Molly Caldwell

The **American** plague; the untold story of yellow fever, the epidemic that shaped our history. Berkley Books 2006 308p il $24.95   **614.5**
  1. Yellow fever 2. Yellow fever -- History
  ISBN 0-425-21202-5; 978-0-425-21202-8

LC 2006050497

This is an "account of the 1878 yellow fever epidemic." (N Y Times Book Rev) Index.

The author "offers a forceful narrative of a disease's ravages and the quest to find its cause and cure." Publ Wkly

Includes bibliographical references

Dow, Unity

Saturday is for funerals; [by] Unity Dow & Max Essex. Harvard University Press 2010 218p $19.95   **614.5**
  1. AIDS (Disease) 2. AIDS (Disease) -- Botswana 3. AIDS (Disease) -- Treatment
  ISBN 978-0-674-05077-8

LC 2009-52264

"In 2000, the World Health Organization predicted that 85 percent of 15-year-olds in Botswana would eventually die of AIDS. Life expectancies were projected to be short-

ened by 44 years. But in 2006, Botswana began receiving antiretroviral drugs, and its health prospects turned around dramatically. Dow brings a legal and human-rights perspective and Essex brings a medical-research perspective to chronicling the extent of the devastation of HIV/AIDS and the lessons learned from treating the disease and beating back the dire predictions. . . . Together, they present a compelling look at the toll of AIDS in Africa and some hopeful developments." Booklist

Includes bibliographical references and index

Fenn, Elizabeth A.

Pox Americana; the great smallpox epidemic of 1775-82. Hill & Wang 2001 370p $25; pa $15   **614.5**
  1. Epidemics -- United States -- History -- 18th century 2. Smallpox 3. Smallpox -- United States -- History -- 18th century
  ISBN 0-8090-7820-1; 0-8090-7821-X pa

LC 2001-16886

The author describes the effects of smallpox during the American Revolution, including the disease's toll on Native Americans, the greater vulnerability of Americans as compared to the British, and the conditions which transmitted the disease.

"Noteworthy as scholarship, Fenn's insightful, readable narrative is a welcome addition to literature about the revolutionary period." Booklist

Includes bibliographical references

Foege, William F.

House on fire; the fight to eradicate smallpox. University of California Press/Milbank Memorial Fund 2011 218p il map $29.95   **614.5**
  1. Smallpox
  ISBN 978-0-520-26836-4

LC 2010-41703

"Foege's emphasis on the personal does enliven the myriad statistics he presents. But he seems a reluctant memoirist, uncomfortable with the spotlight, and as a consequence, the story gets bogged down, at times, by Foege's need to mention (and compliment) every colleague with whom he ever collaborated. Still, though Foege is anything but self-congratulatory, it is impossible to read 'House on Fire' without admiring him and feeling grateful for the gift he gave to mankind." Boston Globe

Includes bibliographical references

Greenfeld, Karl Taro

China syndrome; the true story of the 21st century's first great epidemic. HarperCollins 2006 442p map hardcover o.p. pa $14.99   **614.5**
  1. SARS (Disease)
  ISBN 0-06-058722-9; 978-0-06-058722-2; 0-06-058723-7 pa; 978-0-06-058723-9 pa

LC 2005-52684

"The story unfolds like a whodunnit, with a large cast of rogues, victims and heroes. . . . This book is a parable for our times." New Statesman

Includes bibliographical references

Halperin, Daniel

Tinderbox; How the West Sparked the AIDS Epidemic and How the World Can Finally Overcome It. Craig Timberg and Daniel Halperin. Penguin Press HC 2012 421 p. ill. (hardback) $29.95 **614.5**

1. Acquired Immunodeficiency Syndrome -- epidemiology -- Africa 2. Acquired Immunodeficiency Syndrome -- etiology -- Africa 3. Colonialism -- Africa 4. HIV Infections -- epidemiology -- Africa 5. HIV Infections -- etiology -- Africa 6. Western World -- Africa

ISBN 159420327X; 9781594203275

LC 2011040206

It was the authors' intent to "trace the history, growth and spread of HIV and present what will in the minds of many be a controversial approach to addressing the disease. . . . The key factor in the spread of the disease was the expansion of European colonialism in Africa. . . . [Craig] Timberg and [Daniel] Halperin examine how to confront it." (Kirkus Reviews)

Johnson, Steven

The **ghost** map; the story of London's most terrifying epidemic--and how it changed science, cities, and the modern world. Riverhead 2006 299p il map $26.95 **614.5**

1. Cholera 2. Physicians 3. Writers on medicine
ISBN 1-59448-925-4; 978-1-59448-925-9

LC 2006-23114

"From Snow's discovery of patient zero to Johnson's compelling argument for and celebration of cities, this makes for an illuminating and satisfying read." Publ Wkly

Includes bibliographical references

Kelly, John

The **great** mortality; an intimate history of the Black Death, the most devastating plague of all time. HarperCollins Publishers 2005 364p hardcover o.p. pa $14.95 **614.5**

1. Black death 2. Plague
ISBN 0-06-000692-7; 0-06-000693-5 pa

LC 2004-54213

"Western Europe is the primary focus of Kelly's compact history, which is 'intimate' in that it highlights many particular persons' passages through the crucible years, 1348-49. . . . Kelly proceeds chronologically, beginning with the plague's prehistory in north central Asia and its spread through China before empire-building Mongols brought it west. . . . This sweeping, viscerally exciting book contributes to a literature of perpetual fascination: the chronicles of pestilence." Booklist

Includes bibliographical references

Kolata, Gina

★ **Flu**; the story of the great influenza pandemic of 1918 and the search for the virus that caused it. Simon & Schuster 2001 330p il pa $15 **614.5**

1. Epidemiology 2. Influenza 3. Influenza -- History -- 20th century
ISBN 0-7432-0398-4; 978-0-7432-0398-2

LC 00-64861

"Clearly explaining both the science and the social toll of the pandemic, Kolata writes an admirable history and soberly spells out how the U.S. government is prepared—or unprepared—for a similar public health threat today." Publ Wkly

Includes bibliographical references

Marriott, Edward

Plague: a story of science, rivalry, and the scourge that won't go away. Metropolitan Bks. 2003 302p il hardcover o.p. $25 **614.5**

1. Plague
ISBN 0-8050-6680-2

LC 2002-26325

"The scientists' competition is the stuff of movies, gripping even though Marriott reveals the ending early." Booklist

Includes bibliographical references

Nolen, Stephanie

28: stories of AIDS in Africa. Walker 2007 375p map $25.95 **614.5**

1. AIDS (Disease) -- Personal narratives
ISBN 0-8027-1598-2; 978-0-8027-1598-2

Twenty-eight anecdotal stories that chronicle men, women, and children involved in every aspect of the African AIDS crisis.

This "is both an informative and a powerful read, which will help Western readers connect personally with a crisis that too often seems remote." Libr J

Includes bibliographical references

Oshinsky, David M.

★ **Polio**; an American story. Oxford University Press 2005 342p il $30; pa $16.95 **614.5**

1. Poliomyelitis -- History 2. Poliomyelitis vaccine
ISBN 0-19-515294-8; 0-19-530714-3 pa

LC 2004-25249

This book "is a rich and illuminating analysis that convincingly grounds the ways and means of modern American research in the response to polio." N Y Times Book Rev

Includes bibliographical references

Pisani, Elizabeth

The **wisdom** of whores; bureaucrats, brothels, and the business of AIDS. W. W. Norton & Co. 2008 372p $25.95 **614.5**

1. AIDS (Disease) -- Prevention 2. Sexual behavior
ISBN 978-0-393-06662-3; 0-393-06662-2

LC 2007-51396

The author discusses various aspects of international AIDS prevention.

This is "an eye-opening look at who gets AIDS how, when and where. . . . Delivers a strong, well-told and believable message." Kirkus

Includes bibliographical references

Preston, Richard

The **hot** zone. Random House 1994 300p hardcover o.p. pa $14 **614.5**

1. Animal experimentation 2. Ebola virus
ISBN 0-385-49522-6 pa

LC 94-13415

"Ebola, a lethal virus that slumbers in an unknown host somewhere in the rain forest, sneaked into the United States in 1989 in a shipment of primates that ended up in a monkey house in Reston, Virginia. This virus jumps between species easily, and takes only weeks to kill its victim, with gory hemorrhaging from various orifices. Preston tells the suspenseful tale of its detection, and gives vivid life to the members of the SWAT team that, for eighteen bio-hazardous days, combatted the strain now known as Ebola Reston." New Yorker

Rhodes, Richard

Deadly feasts; tracking the secrets of a terrifying new plague. Simon & Schuster 1997 259p il hardcover o.p. pa $13   **614.5**
 1. Prion diseases
 ISBN 0-684-84425-7 pa

LC 97-320

"Rhodes offers the first popular documentation of a disaster with profound implications." Booklist

Shah, Sonia

The **fever**; how malaria has ruled humankind for 500,000 years. Sarah Crichton Books/Farrar, Straus, and Giroux 2010 307p $26 **614.5**
 1. Malaria 2. Malaria -- History
 ISBN 978-0-374-23001-2; 0-374-23001-3

LC 2010-2374

"This fascinating, mordant pop-sci account tells us why malaria is one of the world's greatest scourges, killing a million people every year and debilitating another 300 million, and why we have remained complacent about it. . . . [This] is an absorbing account of human ingenuity and progress, and of their heartbreaking limitations." Publ Wkly
 Includes bibliographical references

Spurlock, Morgan

Don't eat this book; fast food and the supersizing of America. G. P. Putnam's Sons 2005 308p hardcover o.p. pa $14   **614.5**
 1. Convenience foods 2. Fast food restaurants -- United States 3. Food industry 4. Restaurants
 ISBN 0-399-15260-1; 0-425-21023-5 pa

LC 2005-43196

The author "describes America's obesity epidemic, its relation to the fast food industry, the industry's cozy relations to U.S. government agencies and how the problem is spreading worldwide. . . . His book is a powerful tool in his rip-roaring campaign to turn around America's love-hate relationship with fast food." Publ Wkly
 Includes bibliographical references

Tayman, John

 ★ The **Colony**; John Tayman. Scribner 2006 421p il maps $27.50 **614.5**
 1. Leprosy 2. Leprosy -- Hawaii -- Molokai
 ISBN 0-7432-3300-X

LC 2005-47767

This is a "history of the leper colony at the Hawaiian island Molokai. . . . Tayman's crisp, flowing writing and inclusion of personal stories and details make this an ut-

terly engrossing look at a heartbreaking chapter in Hawaiian history." Booklist

615   Pharmacology and therapeutics

AARP

The **AARP** guide to pills; essential information on more than 1,200 prescription and nonprescription medicines, including generics. editor in chief, Maryanne Hochadel. Sterling Pub. 2005 xxxvii, 981p il $24.95   **615**
 1. Drugs 2. Materia medica
 ISBN 1-4027-1740-7

LC 2005-54444

The content found in this drug reference handbook is based on the "Clinical Pharmacology database [http://www.clinicalpharmacology.com], produced by Gold Standard. . . . Each entry is accompanied by one or two photographs showing such things as the pill size, shape, color, markings, or packaging for common brands. Information is . . . laid out in the form of eight questions covering what each drug is for; what to tell health-care providers before taking the drug; how to take the drug; what to do if a dose is missed; how the drug interacts with other prescription, nonprescription, and illicit drugs as well as foods, beverages, and dietary supplements; what to watch for when taking the drug; what side effects are possible; and how the drug should be stored. . . . This volume is highly recommended and should be available in every public library branch in all communities across the country." Booklist

Chevallier, Andrew

Encyclopedia of herbal medicine; 2nd ed; DK Pub. 2000 336p il $40   **615**
 1. Materia medica 2. Medical botany
 ISBN 0-7894-6783-6

LC 2001-268250

This provides information about the current uses, cultivation, habitat, and folklore of over 550 herbs.
 This "volume remains a top choice for a library reference on the medicinal use of herbs for the public." Libr J

Consumer Reports Books (Firm)

 ★ **Consumer** drug reference 2008. Consumer Repts. Bks. 2008 1752p il $44.95   **615**
 1. Drugs
 ISBN 978-1-933524-11-5; 1-933524-11-1
 Including more than 12,000 medicines, "this work presents drug information to the patient in clear and easy-to-read language. The drugs are listed by their generic names. The drug monographs make up the greatest portion of the source. Information provided for each drug includes brand names, general description, risks to be considered before taking the medicine (e.g., allergies, pregnancy, breastfeeding), proper use, precautions to be taken while using the medicine, and side effects." Am Ref Books Annu, 1993

Dasgupta, Amitava

The **science** of drinking; how alcohol affects your body and mind. Rowman & Littlefield Publishers 2011 265p il $34.95; ebook $34.95 **615**

1. Alcohol -- Physiological effect 2. Drinking of alcoholic beverages

ISBN 978-1-4422-0409-6; 978-1-4422-0411-9 ebook

LC 2010-51613

The author "outlines what constitutes healthy drinking and its attendant health benefits, offers advice on how to drink responsibly, and provides insight into just how alcohol works on the brain and the body." Publisher's note

Includes bibliographical references

Foster, Steven

National Geographic desk reference to nature's medicine; [by] Steven Foster and Rebecca L. Johnson. National Geographic Society 2006 416p il map $40 **615**

1. Materia medica 2. Medical botany 3. Reference books

ISBN 978-0-7922-3666-5; 0-7922-3666-1

The authors "offer an engaging, authoritative, and succinct work on traditional and current medicinal uses for a variety of plants, guidelines for cultivation and preparation, recent research, and cautions. Using a two-page format for each plant, the volume is arranged alphabetically. Sidebars feature colored botanical drawings, color photographs, habitat maps, and interesting information that enlivens the understanding of human experience with the plants." Choice

Includes bibliographical references

Gorman, Jack M.

★ The **essential** guide to psychiatric drugs; Rev. and updated 4th ed; St. Martin's Press 2007 xxiv, 424p pa $19.95 **615**

1. Psychotropic drugs

ISBN 978-0-312-36879-1; 0-312-36879-8

LC 2007-32207

This guide covers psychotropic prescription medications, including information such as side effects and withdrawal symptoms.

"Since most psychiatric drugs are prescribed by nonpsychiatric physicians, this work will be useful for them and for nurse practitioners as well as for patients and families. Essential for all general libraries." Libr J

Includes bibliographical references

Graedon, Joe

The **people's** pharmacy guide to home and herbal remedies; [by] Joe Graedon and Teresa Graedon. St. Martin's Press 1999 428p hardcover o.p. pa $7.99 **615**

1. Dietary supplements 2. Herbs -- Therapeutic use 3. Vitamin therapy 4. Vitamins

ISBN 0-312-20779-4; 0-312-98139-2 pa

LC 99-26613

"The first section combines tested scientific research and accumulated folk wisdom to provide the health consumer with treatment suggestions for common ailments. Also included are possible causes and symptoms for selected condi-

tions, as well as contact information for product manufacturers. The second section lists the 50 most commonly used herbs, including their ingredients and information on usage, dose, adverse effects, and drug interactions." Libr J

Hager, Thomas

The **demon** under the microscope; from battlefield hospitals to Nazi labs, one doctor's heroic search for the world's first miracle drug. Harmony Books 2006 340p $24.95 **615**

1. Microbiologists 2. Nobel laureates for physiology or medicine 3. Sulfonamides 4. Writers on science

ISBN 1-4000-8213-7; 978-1-4000-8213-1

LC 2006-4510

The author "narrates the story of the race [by doctors such as Gerhard Domagk] to find the 'magic bullet' to eliminate diseases such as pneumonia, childbed fever, and gonorrhea. . . . Hager connects early innovations in medicine to the fortuitous and intuitive leaps that allowed early 20th-century researchers to create sulfa, the first antibiotic. . . . One is left with a sense of gratitude for the relative safety of modern medical practices." Libr J

Includes bibliographical references

Kuhn, Cynthia

Buzzed; the straight facts about the most used and abused drugs from alcohol to ecstasy. {by} Cynthia Kuhn, Scott Swartzwelder, Wilkie Wilson; with Leigh Heather Wilson and Jeremy Foster. 2nd ed; Norton 2003 345p il pa $16.95 **615**

1. Drug abuse 2. Drugs 3. Drugs of abuse -- Popular works

ISBN 0-393-32493-1

LC 2003-11411

"The book adopts a straight, neutral tone that reflects its commitment to providing unbiased, scientific fact. . . . Best of all, the descriptions are jargon-free, making this book a great choice for anyone looking for clear, reliable information about any kind of drug." Publ Wkly

Includes bibliographical references

Lax, Eric

The **mold** in Dr. Florey's coat; the story of the penicillin miracle. Henry Holt and Co. 2004 307p il hardcover o.p. pa $15 **615**

1. Penicillin

ISBN 0-8050-6790-6; 0-8050-7778-2 pa

LC 2003-56685

"In this fluent, entertaining report on the history of the arguably most significant medical discovery of the twentieth century, Lax delves into the lives of the colorful scientists who played significant roles in developing the antibiotic." Booklist

Includes bibliographical references

Miller, Richard Lawrence

The **encyclopedia** of addictive drugs. Greenwood Press 2002 491p $75 **615**

1. Drugs -- Encyclopedias 2. Drugs of abuse 3. Reference books

ISBN 0-313-31807-7

LC 2002-75332

"The more than 130 substances included are both natural and pharmaceutical products, all associated with misuse and addiction. Listed by common name, the initial citation includes pronunciation, Chemical Abstracts Service Registry Number, formal and informal names, drug type, U.S. availability, and more. The accompanying article discusses uses, drawbacks, abuse factors, drug interactions, cancer risks, and effects on pregnancy, and concludes with a bibliography." SLJ

Seaman, Barbara

The **greatest** experiment ever performed on women; exploding the estrogen myth. Hyperion 2003 332p $24.95   **615**
1. Estrogen 2. Estrogen -- Therapeutic use 3. Menopause 4. Menopause -- Hormone therapy 5. Oral contraceptives
ISBN 0-7868-6853-8

LC 2004-271241

"Seaman passionately and convincingly argues that women have been unneccessarily put at risk by doctors treating menopause as a disease." Publ Wkly

Talbott, Shawn

A **guide** to understanding dietary supplements; magic bullets or modern snake oil? {by} Shawn M. Talbott. Haworth Press 2003 xxv, 713p il $119.95; pa $59.95   **615**
1. Dietary supplements 2. Drug industry
ISBN 0-7890-1455-6; 0-7890-1456-4 pa

LC 2002-68770

This overview of the dietary supplement industry and its products "examines more than 140 supplements arranged under broad categories such as weight loss and joint health." Booklist
Includes bibliographical references

Taylor, Leslie

The **healing** power of rainforest herbs; a guide to understanding and using herbal medicinals. Leslie Taylor. Square One Publishers 2005 519p il pa $23.95   **615**
1. Herbs -- Therapeutic use 2. Tropical plants
ISBN 0-7570-0144-0

LC 2004-22843

The author "introduces readers to the rain forest environment, methods of plant preparation, and herbal recipes for treating common ailments. She describes approximately 75 plants in detail, providing scientific and common names, dosage, preparation, chemical composition, traditional and modern usage, clinical research, and contraindications and interactions." Libr J
Includes bibliographical references

Tone, Andrea

★ The **age** of anxiety; a history of America's turbulent affair with tranquilizers. Basic Books 2008 xx, 298p il $26.95   **615**
1. Antipsychotic drugs 2. Anxiety -- Treatment 3. Pharmaceutical industry -- United States 4.

Tranquilizing drugs
ISBN 978-0-46508-658-0; 0-46508-658-6

LC 2008-32718

"Through personal interviews with leading figures of the era and an examination of personal and commercial archives, Dr. Tone provides a credible, well-written story." Sci Books Films
Includes bibliographical references

Tucker, Holly

Blood work; a tale of medicine and murder in the scientific revolution. W.W. Norton 2011 xxix, 304p il $25.95   **615**
1. Blood -- Transfusion 2. Homicide 3. Human experimentation in medicine 4. Physicians 5. Science -- History
ISBN 978-0-393-07055-2; 0-393-07055-7

LC 2010-46340

This is "more than a simple medical history; it's a true crime picaresque, with Denis as a roguish, ethically-challenged antihero beset on all sides by intrigue and villainy. It's also a provocative exploration of the often strained relationship between science and the morality of the society it seeks to enlighten." PopMatters
Includes bibliographical references

★ The **Merck index**; an encyclopedia of chemicals, drugs, and biologicals. Maryadele J. O'Neil, editor; Patricia E. Heckelman, senior associate editor; Cherie B. Koch, associate editor; Kristin J. Roman, assistant editor; Catherine M. Kenny, editorial assistant; Maryann R. D'Arecca, administrative assistant. 14th ed.; Merck 2006 various paging il $125   **615**
1. Drugs -- Dictionaries 2. Materia medica -- Dictionaries 3. Reference books
ISBN 0-911910-00-X; 978-0-911910-00-1

"Technical descriptions of the preparation, properties, uses, commercial names, and toxicity of drugs and medicines." N Y Public Libr Book of How & Where to Look It Up

Physician's desk reference 2008; 62nd ed; Medical Economics 2007 3482p $94.95   **615**
1. Materia medica
ISBN 978-1-56363-660-8; 1-56363-660-3

"Latest available information intended for physicians on over 2,000 products. Covers dosage, contraindications, precautions, side effects, and undesirable interactions. The information is furnished by the manufacturers of the various products. Product identification in color." N Y Public Libr Book of How & Where to Look It Up

★ **Physician's desk reference** for nonprescription drugs, dietary supplements, and herbs 2008; 29th ed; Thomson Healthcare 2008 400p il $59.95   **615**
1. Nonprescription drugs
ISBN 978-1-5636-3662-2; 1-5636-3662-X

"A companion to the Physician's Desk Reference. Provides essential information on nonprescription drugs. Indexed by manufacturer, product name, product category, and active ingredients." N Y Public Libr Book of How & Where to Look It Up

615.5 Therapeutics

Bausell, R. Barker

Snake oil science; the truth about complementary and alternative medicine. Oxford University Press 2007 324p il $24.95   **615.5**

1. Alternative medicine 2. Medicine -- Research 3. Placebo (Medicine)

ISBN 978-0-19-531368-0; 0-19-531368-2

LC 2007-10217

The author builds a "case against CAM, beginning with a look at the history of CAMs and placebos, then the 'poorly trained scientists' and flawed studies (among more than 300 analyzed for this book) that have historically supported CAM's efficacy. . . . Entertaining and informative, with plenty of diverting anecdotal examples, Bausell offers non-professionals and pros a thorough look at the science on CAM, along with a complementary lesson in the methods of good medical research." Publ Wkly

Includes bibliographical references

Bruce, Debra Fulghum

Miracle touch; a complete guide to hands-on therapies that have the amazing ability to heal. {by} Debra Fulghum Bruce; foreword by Dolores Krieger. Three Rivers Press 2003 xxi, 216p pa $12.95 **615.5**

1. Alternative medicine 2. Touch 3. Touch -- Therapeutic use

ISBN 0-609-80734-X

LC 2002-7443

The author covers "the various types of TT {Therapeutic Touch}, including acupuncture and acupressure, massage, reflexology, and Reiki. For each therapy, they include how it originated, how it works, what it can treat, how therapists are trained and/or certified, and research or case studies. . . . This practical, well-written guide is recommended for most alternative health and consumer health collections." Libr J

Includes bibliographical references

Maleskey, Gale

Nature's medicines; from asthma to weight gain, from colds to high cholesterol: the most powerful all-natural cures. by Gale Maleskey, and the editors of Prevention Health Books. Rodale Press 1999 688p $31.95   **615.5**

1. Alternative medicine 2. Naturopathy

ISBN 1-57954-028-7

LC 99-15694

The first three sections of this health guide cover "vitamins, minerals, herbs, and emerging supplements. The major portion of {the book} follows, with an . . . A-Z listing of 61 substances, from Acidophilus to Zinc. Sidebars provide botanical names and highlight special instructions and cautions. Following this section is an A-Z listing of more than 75 health concerns." Booklist

McTaggart, Lynne

The **field**: the quest for the secret force of the universe. HarperCollins Pubs. 2002 288p hardcover o.p. pa $12.95   **615.5**

1. Alternative medicine 2. Mind and body

ISBN 0-06-093117-5 pa

LC 2002-17348

The author "describes scientific discoveries that she believes point to a unifying concept of the universe, one that reconciles mind with matter, classic Newtonian science with quantum physics and, most importantly, science with religion." Publ Wkly

Includes bibliographical references

Murray, Michael T.

Encyclopedia of natural medicine; {by} Michael T. Murray, Joseph Pizzorno. rev 2nd ed; Prima Pub. 1998 946p il pa $24.95   **615.5**

1. Naturopathy -- Encyclopedias 2. Reference books

ISBN 0-7615-1157-1

LC 97-50569

This volume is divided into three parts. Part I explains the philosophy and principles of natural medicine; Part II covers body systems, and specific health problems are dealt with in Part III.

Navarra, Tova

The **encyclopedia** of complementary and alternative medicine; foreword by Adam Perelman. Facts on File 2004 xxiii, 276p $75; pa $18.95   **615.5**

1. Alternative medicine -- Encyclopedias 2. Reference books

ISBN 0-8160-4997-1; 0-8160-6226-9 pa

LC 2003-43415

"The topics in this book . . . range from yoga, chiropractic, and homeopathy to herbal remedies, imagery and visualization, massage, medication, and naturopathy. . . . Besides the entries, this important resource offers appendixes that list professional and lay organizations and herbs used in varieties of medical disciplines, and a time line of the various therapies." Choice

Includes bibliographical references

O'Meara, Alex

Chasing medical miracles; the promise and perils of clinical trials. Walker & Co. 2009 263p $25; pa $16   **615.5**

1. Clinical trials 2. Clinical trials -- Law and legislation 3. Clinical trials -- Moral and ethical aspects 4. Drugs -- Testing 5. Journalists 6. Medicine -- Research 7. Pharmaceutical industry

ISBN 978-0-8027-1696-5; 0-8027-1696-2; 978-0-8027-1990-4 pa; 0-8027-1990-2 pa

"Must reading for anyone considering participating in a clinical trial, whether to test treatment for an illness they have been diagnosed with or not." Booklist

Includes bibliographical references

Pelletier, Kenneth R.

The **best** alternative medicine; What works? What does not? introduction by Andrew Weil. Simon & Schuster 2000 448p hardcover o.p. pa $15 **615.5**

1. Alternative medicine
ISBN 0-684-84207-6; 978-0-7432-0027-1 pa; 0-7432-0027-6 pa

LC 99-26629

Pelletier "explains alternative and complementary medicine including commonly used treatment modalities and 75 medical conditions and correlating therapies. What sets Pelletier's work apart in this genre are cited studies and references. The selected bibliography alone is more than 50 pages long." Libr J

Includes bibliographical references

Schneider, Edward L.

What your doctor hasn't told you and the health store clerk doesn't know; the truth about alternative treatment and what works. [by] Edward L. Schneider, M.D., & Leigh Ann Hirschman. Avery 2006 267p pa $19.95 **615.5**

1. Alternative medicine
ISBN 1-58333-252-9; 978-1-58333-252-8

LC 2006-42811

"Evaluating the latest medical research on topics ranging from arthritis, depression, menopause and male libido to heart disease, brain function and cancer, . . . [the author] outlines his recommendations for a combination of conventional and alternative treatments. . . . Schneider's balanced view of integrative therapies and his great fund of practical and medical advice are both reassuring and invigorating." Publ Wkly

Speid, Lorna

Clinical trials; what patients and healthy volunteers need to know. Oxford University Press 2010 186p il pa $19.95 **615.5**

1. Drugs -- Testing
ISBN 978-0-19-973416-0

LC 2010-9154

"If informed consent is the gold standard for clinical-trial participants, this book raises the bar to become the platinum standard. A must-have for anyone—healthy or sick—who is considering volunteering." Booklist

Includes bibliographical references

★ The **Gale** encyclopedia of alternative medicine; edited by Laurie J. Fundukian, editor. 3rd ed.; Gale, Cengage Learning 2009 4v il set $540 **615.5**

1. Alternative medicine -- Encyclopedias 2. Reference books
ISBN 978-1-4144-4872-5

LC 2008-16097

This encyclopedia "identifies 150 types of alternative medicine being practiced today, including reflexology, acupressure, acupuncture, chelation therapy, kinesiology, yoga, chiropractic, Feldenkrais, polarity therapy, detoxification,

naturopathy, Chinese medicine, biofeedback, Ayurveda and osteopathy." Publisher's note

Includes bibliographical references

The **Illustrated** encyclopedia of body-mind disciplines; Nancy Allison, editor. Rosen Pub. Group 1999 xxxii, 448p il $105.95 **615.5**

1. Alternative medicine 2. Alternative medicine -- Encyclopedias 3. Mind and body therapies 4. Mind and body therapies -- Encyclopedias
ISBN 0-8239-2546-3

LC 98-24969

This "text is divided into 16 sections, each of which begins with an introductory essay discussing the disciplines included in that section. Each discipline is described by a certified practitioner in terms of history, basic principles, and potential benefits and risks. Short resources/reading lists follow each discipline description." Libr J

Includes bibliographical references and index

Mayo Clinic book of alternative medicine; 2nd ed.; Time Inc. Home Entertainment Books 2010 208p il $25.95 **615.5**

1. Alternative medicine
ISBN 978-1-60320-836-9

"This is a good introductory overview of such mind-body therapies as biofeedback, guided imagery, muscle relaxation therapy, relaxed breathing, Tai Chi, acupuncture, healing touch, and yoga. Includes action plans for treating 20 common conditions from arthritis to stress." Libr J

615.8   Specific therapies and kinds of therapies

Campbell, Don G.

The **Mozart** effect; tapping the power of music to heal the body, strengthen the mind, and unlock the creative spirit. {by} Don Campbell. Avon Bks. 1997 332p il hardcover o.p. pa $14 **615.8**

1. Music -- Psychological aspects 2. Music therapy
ISBN 0-06-093720-3 pa

LC 97-27570

The author "uses case histories to show how music can enhance memory, learning, and creativity. Properly chosen and presented, music can also alleviate and in some cases apparently cure medical problems, he says." Booklist

Includes bibliographical references

Hugo, Lynne

Where the trail grows faint; a year in the life of a therapy dog team. University of Nebraska Press 2005 142p $22 **615.8**

1. Dogs 2. Elderly -- Care 3. Pet therapy
ISBN 0-8032-2432-X

LC 2004-24174

The author "shares insights she gained through the nursing home visits she made with her therapy dog, Hannah, a chocolate Labrador Retriever obtained from a rescue organization. . . . Recommended not only for dog lovers interested in learning more about the training and accomplishments of a therapy dog but also for nurses, social workers, gerontologists, and anyone facing the prospect of long-term care for aging parents." Libr J

Mitchell, Deborah R.

The **Botox** miracle; {by} Deborah Mitchell; consulting medical editor, Roberta D. Sengelmann. Pocket Bks. 2002 212p il $11   **615.8**
    1. Botulinum toxin 2. Skin -- Care
    ISBN 0-7434-6463-X

                                      LC 2003-544572

The author "describes how wrinkles develop and how Botox works to reduce or eliminate them. Covered are how to find a doctor, what to expect during treatment, the frequency of treatments, side effects, and possible complications. Also describes other wrinkle remedies for Botox-resistant areas. Simply written, this is a good introduction to the subject." Libr J

Quest, Penelope

Reiki for life; the complete guide to reiki practice for levels 1, 2 & 3. Jeremy P. Tarcher/Penguin 2010 310p il pa $16.95   **615.8**
    1. Reiki (Healing system)
    ISBN 978-1-58542-790-1

                                        LC 2009-51213

This book covers "basic routines, details about the power and potential of each level, special techniques for enhancing Reiki practice, and . . . direction on the use of Reiki toward spiritual growth. Penelope Quest also compares the origins and development of Reiki in the West and the East, revealing methods specific to the original Japanese Reiki tradition." Publisher's note
    Includes bibliographical references

Wise, Anna

Awakening the mind; a guide to mastering the power of your brain waves. Tarcher/Putnam 2002 255p il pa $16.95   **615.8**
    1. Brain 2. Mental healing 3. Spiritual healing
    ISBN 1-58542-145-6

                                        LC 2001-53501

"This work aims to help readers improve their mental powers by optimizing brain-wave patterns. . . . {Wise discusses} the four types of brain-wave patterns, or EEGs, giving readers 'subjective landmarks' to help them gauge their own patterns without an EEG biofeedback machine." Libr J

615.9 Toxicology

Barker, Rodney

And the waters turned to blood; the ultimate biological threat. Simon & Schuster 1997 346p il hardcover o.p. pa $14   **615.9**
    1. Algae 2. Ecologists 3. Poisons and poisoning
    ISBN 0-684-83845-1 pa

                                        LC 97-86

"Barker follows the work of Dr. JoAnn Burkholder, a scientist from North Carolina State University, as she attempts to obtain academic respect and funding for her research on a new species of dinoflagellate that is responsible for a number of major fish kills. . . . He presents a detailed discussion of Burkholder's struggles with state officials as she becomes convinced that the organism is toxic, not only to fish but also to humans. Written in a clear, non-technical style." Libr J

Boyd, David R.

Dodging the toxic bullet; how to protect yourself from everyday environmental health hazards. foreword by David Suzuki. Publishers Group West 2010 214p pa $16.95   **615.9**
    1. Environmental health 2. Toxicology
    ISBN 978-1-55365-454-4

The author "identifies the chemicals, toxins, and infectious agents found in the air we breathe, the food and water we consume, and the gadgets, products, and machinery we use, and he outlines the steps we can take to limit exposure and protect our health. Comparing environmental safety standards in Canada, the United States, Australia, and Europe, he points to areas that need improvement. . . . Boyd's powerful, well-documented book will shake readers out of their complacency and empower them to take action against environmental hazards." Libr J
    Includes bibliographical references

Callahan, Joan R.

★ **Biological** hazards; an Oryx sourcebook. Oryx Press 2002 385p il $64.95   **615.9**
    1. Communicable diseases 2. Environmental health 3. Environmental toxicology 4. Environmentally induced diseases 5. Poisons and poisoning
    ISBN 1-57356-385-4

                                        LC 2001-55184

This sourcebook provides "introductory information on a wide range of biological hazards. . . . Chapters divide hazards into categories: human pathogens in water, food, and air; those transmitted by contact; plant and animal pathogens and pests; venoms, toxins, and allergens; and animals that are a threat for predatory or other behavior. Another chapter provides information on controversial topics such as immunization and biological warfare. . . . The chapters that deal with different kinds of hazards offer extensive references and recommended readings. Lists of additional resources, including statistics and documents, print resources, nonprint resources, and organizations, comprise the final chapters." Booklist
    Includes bibliographical references

Emsley, John

The **elements** of murder; [a history of poison] Oxford University Press 2005 421p il $30; pa $19.95   **615.9**
    1. Poisoning 2. Poisons -- History 3. Poisons and poisoning 4. Toxicology
    ISBN 0-19-280599-1; 0-19-280600-9 pa

                                        LC 2005-299328

Reading this book "is like watching a hundred episodes of 'CSI,' but without having to sit through the tedious personal relationships of the characters. . . . Emsley mines what he calls 'the darker side of the periodic table' with consummate skill." N Y Times Book Rev
    Includes bibliographical references

Fagin, Dan

Toxic deception; how the chemical industry manipulates science, bends the law, and endangers your health. [by] Dan Fagin, Marianne Lavelle, and the Center for Public Integrity. Common Courage Press 1999 xxv, 271p pa $17.95 **615.9**
1. Chemical industry 2. Chemicals
ISBN 1-56751-162-7

LC 99-13742
This work examines "the regulatory foundations of four suspect chemicals—atrazine, alachor, formaldehyde, and perchloroethylene—and the chemical industry's role in the design and calculation of risk assessments. . . . This well-researched expose is recommended." Libr J
Includes bibliographical references

Grossman, Elizabeth

Chasing molecules; poisonous products, human health, and the promise of green chemistry. Island Press/Shearwater Books 2009 249p $26.95 **615.9**
1. Commercial products 2. Consumer goods 3. Consumption (Economics) -- Environmental aspects 4. Environmental chemistry 5. Environmental chemistry -- Industrial applications 6. Environmental toxicology 7. Molecular theory 8. Toxicology
ISBN 978-1-59726-370-2; 1-59726-370-2

LC 2009-28279
The author "tracks the migration of synthetic, petroleum-based molecules emitted by pesticides, cosmetics, food containers, and vinyl. . . . She accompanies scientists to China, the Great Lakes, and the Arctic, where these persistent and pernicious chemicals (82,000 and counting) are found in alarming quantities. . . . Green chemistry aims to replace hazardous synthetic chemicals with chemicals that are 'benign by design.' Grossman's clarion exposé should give this lifesaving initiative a big boost." Booklist
Includes bibliographical references

Markowitz, Gerald E.

Deceit and denial; the deadly politics of industrial pollution. {by} Gerald Markowitz and David Rosner. University of Calif. Press 2002 xx, 408p il $45; pa $19.95 **615.9**
1. Environmental health 2. Environmental health -- Social aspects 3. Industrial waste 4. Pollution 5. Pollution -- Health aspects
ISBN 0-520-21749-7; 0-520-24063-4 pa

LC 2001-58515
"This is a historical acccount of corporate control of the lead, plastics, and petroleum industries and the campaign of denial regarding the toxic effects on workers, consumers, and the general public of chemicals used in the manufacture of paint, toys, furniture, plastics, and other products. . . . This is not another diatribe about industrial pollution. Instead, it is a well-researched work that analyzes the conflict between industry's need to provide products that make life easier for consumers and the public's demand for legislation and standards to protect them from toxic pollution caused by the manufacture of these products. Recommended for health, environment, and law collections." Libr J
Includes bibliographical references

Smith, Rick

Slow death by rubber duck; the secret danger of everyday things. [by] Rick Smith, Bruce Lourie; with Sarah Dopp. Counterpoint 2009 328p il $25 **615.9**
1. Environmental health 2. Pollution 3. Toxicology
ISBN 978-1-58243-567-1
"The authors manage to stay this side of apocalyptic without sounding flippant. Not only is the book scary, it's hard to put down." Quill Quire
Includes bibliographical references

Turkington, Carol

The **encyclopedia** of poisons and antidotes; [by] Carol Turkington and Deborah Mitchell; foreword by Shirley K. Osterhout. 3rd ed; Facts On File 2009 324p $75 **615.9**
1. Poisoning 2. Poisoning -- Treatment 3. Poisons 4. Poisons and poisoning -- Encyclopedias 5. Reference books
ISBN 978-0-8160-6401-4; 0-8160-6401-6

LC 2008-50407
More than 600 "entries detail poisonous substances ranging from common household items to exotic plants and animals. Entries describe the nature of the toxin, the symptoms it causes, and available antidotes and treatments. Special topics covered include children and poisons, first aid for poisoning victims, food poisoning, and pets and poisons." Publisher's note
Includes bibliographical references

616 Diseases

Bacci, Ingrid

Effortless pain relief; a guide to self-healing from chronic pain. Free Press 2005 255p $24 **616**
1. Chronic pain
ISBN 0-7432-6075-9

LC 2005-295415
This book presents an "explanation of how stress creates chronic pain, along with . . . self-help techniques for reducing and even eliminating pain." Publisher's note

Bakalar, Nick

★ **Where** the germs are; a scientific safari. {by} Nicholas Bakalar. Wiley 2003 262p il $24.95 **616**
1. Bacteria 2. Germ theory of disease 3. Medical microbiology 4. Microbiology
ISBN 0-471-15589-6

LC 2003-271569
The author's "excellent chapter on childhood diseases and vaccines should be required reading for parents, and teenagers should be plunked down in a chair with the chapter on sexually transmitted diseases. . . . His writing is witty, and he gives all the details of germs and illnesses without medical school jargon." Publ Wkly
Includes glossary and bibliographical references

Biddle, Wayne

A **field** guide to germs; 2nd Anchor Books ed; Anchor Bks. (NY) 2002 209p il pa $13.95 **616**

1. Germ theory of disease 2. Medical microbiology -- Popular works 3. Microbiology
ISBN 1-400-03051-X

LC 2002-511927

"Relaying essential information about the 100 most prevalent, powerful, or literarily famous microbiological malefactors in dictionary-encyclopedia style, Biddle injects social and political history into the exposition to provide fuller understanding of germs, their roles in society, their histories, and their current statuses. . . . Eminently entertaining, the book yet has the serious purpose of showing how concerns other than science and the relief of human suffering have affected the course of medical history." Booklist {review of 1995 edition}

Includes bibliographical references

Collins, Francis S.

The **language** of life; DNA and the revolution in personalized medicine. Harper 2010 332p il $26.99 **616**

1. Genetic screening 2. Medical genetics
ISBN 978-0-06-173317-8; 0-06-173317-2

LC 2009-25832

"This readable book . . . can help anyone understand more about how genetics and our DNA contribute to our health." Libr J

Includes bibliographical references

Dillard, James

The **chronic** pain solution; your personal path to pain relief. [by] James N. Dillard with Leigh Ann Hirschman. Bantam Bks. 2002 xxiii, 439p il $24.95; pa $13.95 **616**

1. Chronic pain 2. Chronic pain -- Alternative treatment 3. Pain
ISBN 0-553-80183-X; 0-553-38111-3 pa

LC 2002-23225

The author discusses how pain affects your body and mind. He outlines treatment methods, from state-of-the-art microsurgery and pharmaceuticals to acupuncture, yoga and feedback. He provides chapters on various forms of pain, from arthritis and back pain to migraines and fibromyalgia and includes a pain-control diet.

Fields, Stanley

Genetic twists of fate; [by] Stanley Fields and Mark Johnston. MIT Press 2010 222p il map $24.95 **616**

1. Human genetics 2. Medical genetics
ISBN 978-0-262-01470-0; 0-262-01470-X

LC 2010-06926

"The authors introduce concepts of genetic analysis and pharmacogenomics in a simple and methodological way. The wide variety of chapter topics focus on diseases such as diabetes, Alzheimer's disease, and autism. . . . [This book] will stimulate thinking not only in scientists, but also in anybody interested in the utilization of science for the benefit of society." Sci Books Films

Includes bibliographical references

Gawande, Atul

Better; a surgeon's notes on performance. Metropolitan 2007 273p $24 **616**

1. Authors 2. Medical ethics 3. Medicine 4. Medicine -- Practice 5. Physicians 6. Writers on medicine
ISBN 978-0-8050-8211-1; 0-8050-8211-5

LC 2006-46962

"Mostly, and repeatedly, the question Gawande pose at the heart of each of his essays is deceptively straightforward and can-do: How do we get it right, or barring that, just an ioat better? . . . Gawande is unassuming in every way, and yet his prose is infused with steadfast determination and hope." Boston Globe

Groopman, Jerome E.

The **anatomy** of hope; how people prevail in the face of illness. [by] Jerome Groopman. Random House 2004 248p hardcover o.p. pa $14.95 **616**

1. Hope 2. Patients 3. Physician-patient relationship
ISBN 0-375-50638-1; 0-375-75775-9 pa

LC 2003-46692

The author "discovered that hope could actually cause physiological change, blocking pain and improving respiratory, circulatory, and motor function. He shares personal experiences from his own life and his patients' case histories that illustrate the power and importance of hope. . . . An excellent narrative for public libraries." Libr J

Includes bibliographical references

Harrington, Anne

The **cure** within; a history of mind-body medicine. W.W. Norton 2008 336p il $25.95 **616**

1. Medicine, Psychosomatic 2. Medicine, Psychosomatic -- History 3. Mental healing 4. Mind and body 5. Mind and body -- History 6. Psychosomatic medicine
ISBN 978-0-393-06563-3; 0-393-06563-4

LC 2007-30906

This is a history of alternative and complementary medicine.

The author "has produced a book that desperately needed to be written." N Y Times Book Rev

Includes bibliographical references (p. 299-321)

Koestler, Angela J.

★ **Understanding** chronic pain; [by] Angela J. Koestler, Ann Myers. University Press of Miss. 2002 162p il $28; pa $12 **616**

1. Chronic Disease -- therapy 2. Chronic pain -- Popular works 3. Pain 4. Pain -- therapy
ISBN 1-57806-439-2; 1-57806-440-6 pa

LC 2002-1017

The authors "provide basic information about cultural history, definitions, theories, and causes of pain. They describe treatment specialists and the usual and varied approaches to pain relief and the responsibility of self-care. . . . This is a compact and readable self-help handbook for patients and their families." Choice

Moalem, Sharon

Survival of the sickest; a medical maverick discovers why we need disease. [by] Sharon Moalem, with Jonathan Prince. William Morrow 267p $25.95 **616**

1. Diseases 2. Evolution 3. Genetics 4. Natural selection

ISBN 978-0-06-088965-4; 0-06-088965-9

LC 2006-50128

The author "uses numerous examples to show how analyzing history might help explain why a certain genetic trait that seems useless—even harmful—to us now made perfect sense in our ancestors' environment. He also introduces such recent research topics as host manipulation, noncoding DNA, and epigenetics. The particularly coherent writing style makes complex ideas accessible to people without a science background. With the book's emphasis on evolution's goals of survival and reproduction, readers will gain insights into why evolution may have selected for certain traits and why having that insight may better our lives." Libr J

Moyers, Bill

Healing and the mind; {by} Bill Moyers; Betty Sue Flowers, editor; David Grubin, executive editor; Elizabeth Meryman-Brunner, art research. Doubleday 1993 369p il hardcover o.p. pa $21.95 **616**

1. Medicine 2. Mind and body 3. Psychophysiology

ISBN 0-385-47687-6 pa

LC 92-31074

In this "companion volume to a PBS TV series, Moyers explores the roles of thoughts and emotions in illness and health through interviews with 16 doctors and scientists." Publ Wkly

Newton, David E.

Stem cell research. Facts on File 2007 284p il $45 **616**

1. Stem cell research 2. Stem cells -- Research

ISBN 978-0-8160-6576-9; 0-8160-6576-4

LC 2005-32803

"Covering court cases, legislation, and relevant policies, this volume also includes a chronology; a glossary; a guide to further research; an annotated bibliography . . . ; appendixes; as well as an index." Publisher's note

Includes bibliographical references

Parks, Tim

Teach us to sit still; a skeptic's search for health and healing. Rodale Books 2011 322p il **616**

1. Chronic pain 2. Mind and body

ISBN 1609611586; 9781609611583

LC 2011-08512

"In a hallmark of conversion narratives, the original mania reproduces itself as a mirror image: in the old days, hyperbolically anxious; in the new, hyperbolically anxious to enumerate the old anxiety. To his credit, Parks doesn't pretend otherwise. Moreover, his personal account, never preachy, engages some serious matters about contemporary life, notably what it's like to be a patient, as nearly all of us, sooner or later, are or will be." N Y Times Book Rev

Rosenfeld, Arthur

★ The **truth** about chronic pain; patients and professionals on how to face it, understand it, over-

come it. Basic Bks. 2003 299p hardcover o.p. pa $14.95 **616**

1. Chronic Disease 2. Chronic pain 3. Chronic pain -- Patients -- Interviews 4. Pain

ISBN 0-465-07138-4; 978-0-465-07139-5 pa; 0-465-07139-2 pa

LC 2002-151003

The author "interviews patients, healthcare professionals, ethicists, policymakers, and clergy to learn about pain from many viewpoints. The excellent result is an inspirational and moving book that sheds light on the issue and pleads for compassion." Libr J

Stephenson, Frank H.

DNA; how the biotech revolution is changing the way we fight disease. foreword by Herbert Boyer. Prometheus Books 2007 333p il $26 **616**

1. Biotechnology 2. DNA 3. Genetic engineering 4. Medical genetics

ISBN 1-59102-482-X; 978-1-59102-482-8

LC 2006-28339

"From heart disease to AIDS and cancer, . . . [the author describes] how the tools of biotechnology are being used to combat our most common afflictions. Stephenson examines a . . . variety of health threats and illnesses: HIV infection, the many forms of cancer, asthma, diabetes, Alzheimer's, obesity, and even erectile dysfunction." Publisher's note

Includes bibliographical references

Van Tilburg, Christopher

Mountain rescue doctor; wilderness medicine in the extremes of nature. St. Martin's Press 2007 293p il hardcover o.p. pa $14.95 **616**

1. Mountaineering 2. Rescue work

ISBN 978-0-312-35887-7; 0-312-35887-3; 978-0-312-35888-4 pa; 0-312-35888-1 pa

LC 2007-28304

The author "is a member of the Hood River Crag Rats, the oldest search-and-rescue (S&R) team in the United States. Both adults and teens will relish his vivid recountings of efforts to rescue sports enthusiasts who got lost or injured in the mountains." Libr J

Wynbrandt, James

The **encyclopedia** of genetic disorders and birth defects; [by] James Wynbrandt and Mark D. Ludman. 3rd ed; Facts On File 2007 682p $75 **616**

1. Abnormalities, Human 2. Birth defects -- Encyclopedias 3. Genetic disorders 4. Reference books

ISBN 978-0-8160-6396-3

LC 2006-100640

This "is an excellent resource for public and consumer-health libraries with limited budgets. It is a good starting point for research, too." Booklist

Includes bibliographical references

Disease management sourcebook; edited by Joyce Brennfleck Shannon. Omnigraphics 2008 649p il map $84 **616**

1. Chronic diseases 2. Consumer education

ISBN 978-0-7808-1002-0

LC 2008-4554

"An essential guide to navigating the health care rapids."
Libr J

Includes bibliographical references

Human diseases and conditions; Miranda Herbert
Ferrara, project editor. 2nd ed.; Charles Scribner's Sons/Gale Cengage Learning 2010 4v il
set $340   **616**
1. Medicine -- Encyclopedias 2. Reference books
ISBN 978-0-684-31238-5; 0-684-31238-7
                                        LC 2009-6533
"The entries include a brief definition and the phonetic
spelling of the term and cover what the disease or condition
is and its prevalence, etiology, symptoms, and prevention
and treatment. Some entries begin with a brief story about
someone who has the disease, and each ends with a list of
relevant resources of articles, books, web sites, or health
organizations, as well as cross-references. The illustrations
are in color, as are term definitions in the margins. . . . The
entries are accessible to patrons from a high school reading
level and above, and the colorful display adds appeal." Libr J
    Includes glossary and bibliographical references

Twelve breaths a minute; end-of-life essays. edited
by Lee Gutkind; foreword by Karen Wolk Feinstein; introduction by Francine Prose. Southern Methodist University Press 2011 267p
$23.95   **616**
1. Caregivers 2. Death 3. Terminal care 4. Terminally
ill
ISBN 978-0-87074-571-3; 0-87074-571-9
                                        LC 2010-45874
"A collection of creative nonfiction essays about end-of-
life issues. How depressing, a friend said. I thought the same
thing until I read one and then another and then another. Sad,
yes. But depressing? No. 'Twelve Breaths a Minute,' a book
commissioned by the Jewish Healthcare Foundation as part
of its ongoing end-of-life initiative, is uplifting. The 23 essays, chosen from among more than 400 submissions, also
are beautifully written. The writers are the sons, daughters
and parents who have had to deal with the deaths of family,
as well as members of the medical profession who have had
to balance the oath to save lives with the desires of a patient
to die without extraordinary medical measures. Sometimes
they are both." Pittsburgh Post-Gazette

616.02   Special topics of diseases

American Medical Association
★ **American** Medical Association family medi-
cal guide; 4th ed., completely rev. and updated; John
Wiley & Sons 2004 1184p il $45   **616.02**
1. Health self-care 2. Medicine
ISBN 0-471-26911-5
                                        LC 2004-5764
"This is a well-organized volume, considering the
amount of information it covers." Publ Wkly

American Red Cross
The **American** Red Cross first aid and safety
handbook; [prepared by] American Red Cross and
Kathleen A. Handal; foreword by Elizabeth Dole.
Little, Brown 1992 321p il hardcover o.p. pa
$18.95   **616.02**
1. First aid
ISBN 0-316-73645-7; 0-316-73646-5 pa
                                        LC 91-24847
This first aid guidebook is based on course materials used by the Red Cross and covers how to handle such
emergencies as allergic reactions, bleeding, choking, and
heart attacks.

Brody, Jane E.
Jane Brody's guide to the great beyond; a practical primer to help you and your loved ones prepare
medically, legally, and emotionally for the end of life.
[by] Jane Brody. Random House 2009 xxiv, 287p il
$26   **616.02**
1. Death 2. Terminal care 3. Terminally ill
ISBN 978-1-4000-6654-4
                                        LC 2008-16583
"With bulleted lists itemizing what needs to be done and
how to do it, short portraits and anecdotes throughout, Brody
covers the importance of preparation; the necessity of an advance directive and why a living will is not enough; funeral
plans; living with a bad prognosis and dealing with uncertainty; caregiving; hospice; communicating with doctors; assisted dying; organ donation and autopsy; and legacies. An
instructive, inspiring and reassuring work full of compassion
and humor (along with several cartoons from various New
Yorker illustrators), this volume belongs on every family's
bookshelf." Publ Wkly

Gupta, Sanjay
Cheating death; the doctors and medical miracles that are saving lives against all odds. with research by Caleb Hellerman. Wellness Central 2009
282p $24.99   **616.02**
1. Brain resuscitation 2. Cardiac resuscitation 3.
Critical care medicine 4. Death, Apparent 5. Lifesaving
6. Medicine, Experimental 7. Near-death experiences
ISBN 978-0-446-50887-2; 0-446-50887-X
                                        LC 2009-18588
The author "examines several case studies where patients have literally cheated death by surviving horrendous
accidents and diseases against all reasonable odds: a young
woman who suffered a skiing accident and was considered
clinically dead for three hours before a doctor attempted to
revive her; a 63-year-old scholar who collapsed of heart failure in a gym in New York; a Michigan teenager diagnosed
with virulent brain cancer. . . . Gupta offers fascinating cases
that challenge assumptions about where the line is between
life and death, tackling controversial subjects such as stem-
cell research and vegetative comas, near-death experiences
and fetal surgery." Booklist

Norton, Trevor

Smoking ears and screaming teeth; a celebration of scientific eccentricity and self-experimentation. Pegasus Books 2011 404p il $24.95   **616.02**
1. Eccentrics and eccentricities 2. Human experimentation in medicine 3. Medicine -- Research
ISBN 978-1-60598-254-0

"Though some chapters (e.g., 'A Diet of Worms') shouldn't be read over breakfast, Norton conveys more than just a carnival of the grotesque; he also introduces forgotten and under-appreciated scientists whose curious curiosity saved lives." Kirkus

Includes bibliographical references

Preston, Richard

Panic in level 4; cannibals, killer viruses, and other journeys to the edge of science. Random House 2008 xli, 188p il $26; pa $15   **616.02**
1. Medicine 2. Science
ISBN 978-1-4000-6490-8; 1-4000-6490-2; 978-0-8129-7560-4 pa; 0-8129-7560-X pa

LC 2007-41770

A collection of the author's science essays, all first published in the New Yorker.

"Whether hanging out with genetics entrepreneur J. Craig Venter, the restorers of the Cloisters' famous unicorn tapestries, or the sufferers of Lesch-Nyhan syndrome, Preston personifies perceptiveness and empathy in journalism." Booklist

American College of Physicians complete home medical guide; editor-in-chief David R. Goldmann; associate editor David A. Horowitz. 2nd American ed; DK Pub. 2003 1104p il $50   **616.02**
1. Health self-care 2. Medicine
ISBN 0-7894-9673-9

This guide discusses genetics, health, and health care; lifestyle issues such as diet, exercise, and substance abuse, medical examinations, lab tests and imaging techniques; drug treatment, surgery, and therapies. Illustrated with diagrams, anatomical artworks, and over 2000 photographs. A select listing of online medical sites is also included.

The Merck manual home health handbook; Robert S. Porter, editor-in-chief; Justin L. Kaplan, senior assistant editor; Barbara P. Homeier, assistant editor; editorial board, Richard K. Albert ... [et al.] [3rd ed.]; Merck Research Laboratories 2009 xlii, 2306p il $39.95   **616.02**
1. Medicine -- Handbooks, manuals, etc.
ISBN 978-0-9119-1030-8

LC 2009-923536

"An editorial board of 207 medical experts contributes to this comprehensive overview of medical practice today, with a special focus on geriatric medicine (including a chapter devoted to enhancing the quality of end-of-life care for patient, caregiver, friends and family). . . . Charts and illustrations aid the book's accessibility, making it Merck's most authoritative and easy-to-read home medical guide yet." Publ Wkly

616.07   Pathology

Nuland, Sherwin B.

How we die; reflections on life's final chapter. Knopf 1994 278p hardcover o.p. pa $14   **616.07**
1. Death
ISBN 0-679-74244-1 pa

LC 93-24590

"Nuland is one of those rare physicians who know a great deal about a great deal, not only medicine but also its history and, beyond that, literature and the humanities." Commentary

Pagana, Kathleen Deska

★ **Mosby's** diagnostic and laboratory test reference; [by] Kathleen Deska Pagana, Timothy James Pagana. 9th ed.; Mosby 2009 xxiii, 1078p il pa $46.95   **616.07**
1. Diagnosis 2. Nursing 3. Reference books
ISBN 978-0-323-05345-7

This handbook features alphabetically organized laboratory and diagnostic tests. "Each test entry includes, where relevant, alternate or abbreviated test names; type of test; normal findings; possible critical values; test explanation and related physiology; contraindications; potential complications; interfering factors; procedure and patient care (before, during, and after); and abnormal findings." Publisher's note

Includes bibliographical references

Sanders, Lisa

Every patient tells a story; medical mysteries and the art of diagnosis. Broadway 2009 xxvii, 276p $25   **616.07**
1. Diagnosis
ISBN 978-0-7679-2246-3; 0-7679-2246-8

LC 2008-41478

The author "discusses how doctors deal with diagnostic dilemmas. . . . Sanders not only collects difficult cases, she reflects on what each means for both patient and struggling physician. . . . Readers who enjoy dramatic stories of doctors fighting disease will get their fill, and they will also encounter thoughtful essays on how doctors think and go about their work, and how they might do it better." Publ Wkly

Includes bibliographical references

Segen, J. C.

The **patient's** guide to medical tests; everything you need to know about the tests your doctor orders. [by] Joseph C. Segen and Josie Wade. 2nd ed; Facts on File 2002 418p $44   **616.07**
1. Diagnosis
ISBN 0-8160-4651-4

LC 2002-18824

This "guide presents information on more than 1,000 commonly prescribed tests and procedures. Each entry includes a description of the test, patient preparation required, a description of the procedure itself, the reference range, what abnormal values may signify, and the approximate cost of each test." Publisher's note

Zuk, M.

Riddled with life; friendly worms, ladybug sex, and the parasites that make us who we are. Harcourt 2007 328p il $25   **616.07**

1. Adaptation (Biology) 2. Diseases 3. Host-parasite relationships 4. Human ecology 5. Human evolution 6. Medical parasitology 7. Parasites 8. Pathology
ISBN 978-0-15-101225-1; 0-15-101225-3

LC 2006-28642

"Zuk has an amazing gift for turning experiments and facts into stories. . . . She is urging the public to take a new look at disease, though it's one that's well supported by the research. There are moments where she's speculating ahead of the science a bit, but those moments are clearly marked. Riddled with Life will change the way you look at public and private health." PopMatters

Includes bibliographical references

The Johns Hopkins consumer guide to medical tests; what you can expect, how you should prepare, what your results mean. Simeon Margolis, medical editor. Rebus 2001 400p il $39.95   **616.07**

1. Diagnosis
ISBN 0-929661-63-X

LC 2001-19980

This is a "guide to over 170 medical tests. . . . The entries, generally about two pages long, list the test's purpose and special concerns, what the results may mean, pretest preparations, risks and complications, and estimated cost." Libr J

616.1   Specific diseases

Berra, Kathy

Heart attack! advice for patients by patients. {by} Kathleen Berra {et al.} Yale Univ. Press 2002 232p $32.50; pa $14.95   **616.1**

1. Heart diseases
ISBN 0-300-08980-5; 0-300-09190-7 pa

LC 2001-33256

This "book on the current state of the diagnosis and treatment of heart attacks includes 11 personal accounts by patients and 5 chapters by health professionals. . . . Succinct yet detailed, this collection should prove valuable to both health professionals and the general public." Booklist

Includes bibliographical references

Bloom, Miriam

Understanding sickle cell disease. University Press of Miss. 1995 126p il map hardcover o.p. pa $11.95   **616.1**

1. Sickle cell anemia
ISBN 0-87805-745-5 pa

LC 94-44275

"Although it imparts much technical information, the book is very much for the lay reader." Booklist

Includes bibliographical references

DeBakey, Michael E.

The **New** living heart diet; {by} Michael E. DeBakey {et al.} {Completely rev and updated}; Simon & Schuster 1996 414p pa $16   **616.1**

1. Cooking 2. Heart diseases -- Diet therapy
ISBN 0-684-81188-X

LC 95-40787

This book includes "information about risk factors for coronary heart disease and . . . dietary recommendations for preventing it. The first half relates such health considerations as cholesterol, diabetes and blood pressure to diet; menus and 300-plus recipes with complete nutritional analyses constitute the second half." Publ Wkly

Delgado, Jane L.

The **buena** salud guide for a healthy heart. Newmarket Press 2011 126p pa $9.95   **616.1**

1. Heart diseases 2. Hispanic Americans -- Health and hygiene
ISBN 978-1-55704-943-8

LC 2010-41609

In this book on heart health for Hispanics, the author "offers a 'Ten-Point Program for Health,' which briefly explains key areas concerning general well-being, then breaks down facts concerning heart health, including brief descriptions of aneurysm, heart murmur, stroke, and specific diagnostic tests and procedures, including cardiac MRI, heart surgery, and stress testing. . . . The well-organized text does not overwhelm while delivering information. . . . Essential reading for Hispanics and a crucial addition to any consumer health collection." Libr J

Gould, K. Lance

Heal your heart; how you can prevent or reverse heart disease. Rutgers Univ. Press 1998 xxxi, 274p il hardcover o.p. pa $20   **616.1**

1. Coronary heart disease -- Diet therapy 2. Coronary heart disease -- Exercise 3. Coronary heart disease -- Popular works 4. Coronary heart disease -- Prevention 5. Heart diseases
ISBN 0-8135-2896-8 pa

LC 97-39172

"Although Gould's lucid style . . . makes things easy for the reader, the uncluttered, well-labeled illustrations help substantially, too." Booklist

Includes bibliographical references

McGowan, Mary P.

Heart fitness for life; the essential guide to preventing and reversing heart disease. by Mary P. McGowan, with Jo McGowan Chopra. Oxford Univ. Press 1997 322p il hardcover o.p. pa $16.95 **616.1**

1. Heart diseases -- Prevention
ISBN 0-19-512909-1 pa

LC 97-29834

The author "seeks to cover all the bases of a heart-healthy lifestyle, particularly for those recovering from heart disease, by discussing diet, exercise, stress relief, smoking, and medications. The information is current, and much is drawn from the work of other experts in the field." Libr J

Includes bibliographical references

Ornish, Dean

Love & survival; the scientific basis for the healing power of intimacy. HarperCollins Pubs. 1998 284p il hardcover o.p. pa $14 **616.1**
  1. Health 2. Heart diseases
  ISBN 0-06-093020-9 pa

                        LC 98-141279

"Ornish argues that affection is crucial to health with research findings as well as clinical-anecdotal evidence. The second of six . . . chapters presents studies demonstrating that those who give and receive love are healthier than those who don't; this is intriguing and persuasive testimony that many may find squares with common sense. Succeeding chapters present the anecdotal evidence." Booklist

616.2   Diseases of respiratory system

Ackerman, Jennifer

Ah-choo! the uncommon life of your common cold. Twelve 2010 245p $22.99 **616.2**
  1. Cold (Disease)
  ISBN 978-0-446-54115-2; 978-0-446-57401-3 ebook
                        LC 2010-4794

The author "parses the variety and durability of the cold, its wellknown miseries, paradoxes (a highly active immune system may actually make you sicker with a cold), and myriad mysteries (why do poorer people get more colds? what roles do stress and sleep play? is our clean obsession making us more susceptible to sickness?) with the thoroughness of a scientist, the doggedness of a journalist, and the verve of a thriller writer. . . . There's a nifty collection of comforting recipes as well, including a nonalcoholic hot toddy (and a delicious sounding boozy one, too), banana pudding, and yes, chicken soup." Publ Wkly
  Includes bibliographical references

Adams, Francis V.

The **asthma** sourcebook; 3rd ed.; McGraw-Hill 2007 254p il $16.95 **616.2**
  1. Asthma
  ISBN 978-0-07-147652-2; 0-07-147652-0
                        LC 2006-22980

Contains a wide variety of information about asthma, providing a description of the disease, and discussing medications, treatments, and self-management.

Brody, Jane E.

Jane Brody's allergy fighter. Norton 1997 127p il hardcover o.p. pa $10 **616.2**
  1. Allergy 2. Respiratory system -- Diseases
  ISBN 0-393-31635-1 pa

                        LC 96-34499

"Discussing the elements that cause allergies, the various OTC and prescription medications that may relieve symptoms, and special strategies for dealing with allergies in children, Brody also supplies a glossary and an information and product guide." Publ Wkly

Freedman, Michael R.

Living well with asthma; {by} Michael R. Freedman, Samuel J. Rosenberg, Cynthia L. Divino. Guilford Press 1998 213p pa $15.95 **616.2**
  1. Asthma
  ISBN 1-57230-051-5

                        LC 97-48747

The authors consider the "potentially serious psychological aspects of having a chronic disease. Aimed directly at the asthma sufferer, it includes case studies of commonly encountered problems and discusses family and broader issues that can constrain one's life." Libr J
  Includes bibliographical references

Silber, Sherman J.

★ **How** to get pregnant; Rev. ed.; Little, Brown and Co. 2005 xl, 470p il $27.95; pa $18.99 **616.2**
  1. Infertility 2. Reproductive technology
  ISBN 0-316-01136-3; 978-0-316-01136-5; 0-316-06650-8 pa; 978-0-316-06650-1 pa
                        LC 2005-2585

The author "begins with a review of the female anatomy and the physiology of conception before progressing to mechanisms for 'beating your biological clock'; following is coverage of male reproductive physiology and detailed discussions of procedures currently available to help overcome previously unmanageable fertility problems." Libr J
  Includes bibliographical references

Lung disorders sourcebook; edited by Dawn D. Matthews. Omnigraphics 2002 678p il $78 **616.2**
  1. Lungs -- Diseases
  ISBN 0-7808-0339-6
                        LC 2002-16976

"This title is a great addition for public and school libraries because it provides concise health information on the lungs. Readers can start with this reference source and get satisfactory answers before proceeding to other medical reference tools for more in-depth information." Am Ref Books Annu, 2003

616.3   Diseases of digestive system

Achord, James L.

Understanding hepatitis. University Press of Miss. 2002 132p il $28; pa $12 **616.3**
  1. Hepatitis -- Popular works 2. Liver -- Diseases
  ISBN 1-57806-435-X; 1-57806-436-8 pa
                        LC 2001-49243

"The book is divided into seven sections: the liver and hepatitis; symptoms and complications of acute and chronic viral hepatitis; hepatitis A; hepatitis B; hepatitis C; other viruses and nonviral causes of hepatitis; and current research. . . . The book's all-encompassing and easy-to-read format helps readers better understand the scope of the disease." Choice
  Includes bibliographical references and index

Cardello, Hank

Stuffed; an insider's look at who's (really) making America fat. [by] Hank Cardello with Doug Garr. Ecco

Press 2009 257p $25.99 **616.3**

1. Eating customs 2. Food industry 3. Obesity
ISBN 978-0-06-136386-3; 0-06-136386-3

The author argues that "the obesity epidemic . . . is connected to food businesses that control 'almost everything the average American eats.' . . . He examines such factors as marketing and product packaging, the recent controversies involving branded school snacks and beverages, the use of trans fat in restaurants, and the various food lobbies." Publ Wkly

Chow, Cheryl

★ The **encyclopedia** of hepatitis and other liver diseases; [by] James H. Chow, Cheryl Chow. Facts on File 2005 372p $75   **616.3**

1. Hepatitis 2. Liver -- Diseases 3. Liver -- Diseases -- Encyclopedias 4. Reference books
ISBN 0-8160-5710-9; 978-0-8160-5710-8

LC 2005-18489

"With more than 150 entries, coverage ranges from symptoms, treatments, and research to tests, social issues, and much more. Appendixes list . . . relevant organizations, transplantation and Internet resources, and support groups for those with liver-related issues." Publisher's note

Includes bibliographical references

Green, Peter H. R.

Celiac disease; a hidden epidemic. [by] Peter H.R. Green and Rory Jones. Rev. and updated ed., 1st William Morrow ed.; William Morrow 2010 333p il $24.99   **616.3**

1. Celiac disease 2. Gluten-free diet
ISBN 978-0-06-172816-7

The authors explain "the diagnosis, genetics, and possible complications [of celiac disease], with seven chapters devoted to the gluten-free diet." Libr J

Includes bibliographical references

Minocha, Anil

★ The **encyclopedia** of the digestive system and digestive disorders; [by] Anil Minocha, Christine Adamec. 2nd ed; Facts on File 2010 xxvii, 353p il $75   **616.3**

1. Digestive organs -- Diseases 2. Digestive organs -- Encyclopedias 3. Gastrointestinal system -- Diseases 4. Gastrointestinal system -- Encyclopedias 5. Reference books
ISBN 978-0-8160-7661-1; 0-8160-7661-8

LC 2010-28790

"Entries explain the organs of the digestive system and how they work, the digestive process, disorders and infectious diseases of the digestive system, and how to maintain good digestive health." Publisher's note

Includes bibliographical references

Palmer, Melissa

Dr. Melissa Palmer's guide to hepatitis & liver disease. Avery 2004 470p il pa $16.95   **616.3**

1. Liver -- Diseases
ISBN 1-58333-188-3

LC 2003-63905

The author "discusses all facets of liver disease, from symptoms and tests to treatment options and lifestyle changes." Publisher's note

Pool, Robert

Fat; fighting the obesity epidemic. Oxford Univ. Press 2000 292p $27.50 **616.3**

1. Obesity 2. Obesity -- Molecular aspects
ISBN 0-19-511853-7

LC 00-36731

"This fascinating investigative journey into the history of obesity will go a long way toward removing the stigma attached to being overweight and will increase our understanding of the complex issues that contribute to the obesity epidemic." Libr J

Zonderman, Jon

Understanding Crohn disease and ulcerative colitis; {by} Jon Zonderman and Ronald Vender. University Press of Miss. 2000 116p il $28; pa $12   **616.3**

1. Inflammatory bowel diseases
ISBN 1-57806-202-0; 1-57806-203-9 pa

LC 99-52483

"After describing how the digestive system functions, {the authors} show how it can go wrong. They deal with related medical conditions and how Crohn disease and ulcerative colitis can affect persons of different ages differently. Treatment can involve careful dieting . . . and medical and surgical procedures." Booklist

Includes bibliographical references and index

616.4   Diseases of endocrine, hematopoietic, lymphatic, glandular systems; diseases of male breast

American Diabetes Association

★ **American** Diabetes Association complete guide to diabetes; 5th ed.; American Diabetes Association 2011 499p il pa $22.95   **616.4**

1. Diabetes
ISBN 978-1-58040-330-6

LC 2010-41272

This book describes types of insulin and the best ways to use them, insulin pumps and injection-free insulin techniques in research, new oral diabetes medications and therapies, the use of carbohydrate counting techniques as a meal planning tool as well as information on diabetes in the workplace, school, and day care.

★ **What** to expect when you have diabetes; 180 tips for living well with diabetes. by the American Diabetes Association. Good Books 2008 220p pa $9.95   **616.4**

1. Diabetes
ISBN 978-1-56148-630-4; 1-56148-630-2

LC 2008-16364

"Using a Q & A format, . . . [this book] tackles all aspects of the chronic disease, from causes to treatment options." Libr J

Beaser, Richard S.

The **Joslin** guide to diabetes; a program for managing your treatment. [by] Richard S. Beaser and Amy P. Campbell. Simon & Schuster 2005 431p il pa $16.95 **616.4**

1. Diabetes

ISBN 0-7432-5784-7

LC 2005-51021

The authors offer "information on diabetes management: insulin pumps, current diet plans, weight management and exercise, foot care, and long-term complications. The authors target children and adult diabetics and offer specific advice for pregnant women." Libr J

Crowe, Lynn

The **diabetes** manifesto; take charge of your life. [by] Lynn Crowe, Julie Stachowiak. Demos Medical Publisher 2011 266p pa $18.95 **616.4**

1. Diabetes

ISBN 978-1-932603-94-1

LC 2010-38543

The authors "strive to provide information that enables diabetics to gain a healthy perspective in managing daily tasks and accepting the inevitable setbacks that occur in the course of the disease. . . . Their well-written, tangible, and achievable advice is outstanding. An essential title for diabetes patients, their families, and health-care workers." Libr J

Includes bibliographical references

Ditkoff, Beth Ann

★ The **thyroid** guide; [by] Beth Ann Ditkoff, and Paul LoGerfo. HarperPerennial 2000 xx, 171p il pa $13.95 **616.4**

1. Thyroid gland -- Diseases 2. Thyroid gland -- Diseases -- Popular works

ISBN 0-06-095260-1

LC 99-34742

A guide to the detection, diagnosis and treatment of thyroid diseases.

Eisenstat, Stephanie A.

Every woman's guide to diabetes; what you need to know to lower your risk and beat the odds. [by] Stephanie A. Eisenstat, Ellen Barlow; David M. Nathan (consulting editor) Harvard University Press 2006 305p il $24.95 **616.4**

1. Diabetes 2. Women -- Diseases 3. Women -- Health and hygiene

ISBN 978-0-674-02304-8; 0-674-02304-8

LC 2006-49463

The authors "begin by explaining the differences between Type 1 and Type 2 diabetes, the risk factors and diagnosis of the disease, and treatment options. They also discuss complications that occur if the disease is not well controlled. They then address issues particular to women, e.g., gestational diabetes, the influence of hormonal cycles on the disease, birth control, and pregnancy." Libr J

Includes bibliographical references

Hirsch, James S.

★ **Cheating** destiny; living with diabetes, America's biggest epidemic. Houghton Mifflin Co. 2006 307p il $25 **616.4**

1. Diabetes

ISBN 978-0-618-51461-8; 0-618-51461-9

LC 2006-11239

The author, a Type 1 diabetic, demonstrates "the impact—personal, economic, scientific—of a disease that many say is the fastest-spreading epidemic of the century. . . . Hirsch has an insider's candor speaking about life with diabetes, the sensitivity of the parent of a child with a chronic illness, and the skill of a good journalist reporting on the medical, social, economic, and scientific details of what was once called 'the wasting disease.'" Booklist

Includes bibliographical references

Kaplan-Mayer, Gabrielle

Insulin pump therapy demystified; an essential guide for everyone pumping insulin. foreword by Gary Scheiner. Marlowe & Co. 2003 192p il pa $15.95 **616.4**

1. Diabetes 2. Diabetes -- Treatment 3. Insulin pumps

ISBN 0-56924-508-8

LC 2002-113886

"The author, a diabetic who uses the pump, explains how it works, how to decide if it is the right therapy, and how to live with it. Drawing on interviews with 75 pump users and diabetes experts, she discusses blood sugar monitoring, carbohydrate counting, record keeping, financial issues, and support. With practical information about sleeping and having sex while wearing a pump, this outstanding manual covers material not found in most diabetes books." Libr J

Includes bibliographical references

Mayo Clinic (Rochester, Minn.)

Mayo Clinic: the essential diabetes book. Time Inc. Home Entertainment 2009 222p il $25.95 **616.4**

1. Diabetes

ISBN 978-1-60320-049-3; 1-60320-049-5

"Chapter one presents disease facts, spelling out the differences between type I (largely heredity) and type II (the fast-rising kind, related to lifestyle issues like obesity). Subsequent chapters explain blood glucose levels, how to monitor them and how to control them with medication and diet. . . . The next chapters deal with food, exercise, self-motivation, and specific medical issues like insulin pumps and prescription treatments. . . . [This is a] thorough, friendly, fully-illustrated overview." Publ Wkly

Petit, William

★ The **encyclopedia** of endocrine diseases and disorders; [by] William Petit Jr., Christine Adamec. Facts on File 2005 xxiv, 326p $75 **616.4**

1. Endocrine glands -- Diseases 2. Endocrine glands -- Encyclopedias 3. Reference books

ISBN 0-8160-5135-6

LC 2004-4916

For a fuller review, see: Booklist, Aug. 1, 2005

"An introduction covers the function of the glands throughout life and discusses the role of each. More than 250 A-to-Z entries, ranging in length from one paragraph to two pages, provide details about specific conditions (acromegaly, myxedema coma), hormones (estrogen, lutenizing hormone), glands (pancreas, adrenal gland), procedures (ultrasound, gastric surgery for weight loss), and organizations (American Thyroid Association, Canadian Diabetes Association)." Libr J

Includes bibliographical references

Walker, Rosemary A.

Diabetes: a practical guide to managing your health; [by] Rosemary Walker & Jill Rodgers; US medical editor, David S. Schade. DK 2005 224p il $25   **616.4**

1. Diabetes
ISBN 0-7566-0359-5

This guide to living with diabetes covers such issues as medication, diet, and exercise.

Warshaw, Hope S.

The **diabetes** food & nutrition bible; a complete guide to planning, shopping, cooking, and eating. with foreword by Graham Kerr. American Diabetes Association 2001 324p il pa $18.95   **616.4**

1. Diabetes -- Diet therapy
ISBN 1-58040-037-X

                    LC 2001-22343

This book features information on counting carbohydrates, planning meals, vitamins, minerals, and methods of meal preparation. It includes more than 100 recipes.

Diabetes sourcebook; edited by Karen Bellenir. 4th ed.; Omnigraphics 2008 655p il $93   **616.4**

1. Diabetes
ISBN 978-0-7808-1005-1; 0-7808-1005-8

                    LC 2008-18819

616.5   Diseases of integument

Cram, David L.

Coping with psoriasis; a patient's guide to treatment. Addicus Bks. 2000 132p pa $14.95   **616.5**

1. Psoriasis
ISBN 1-886039-47-X

                    LC 0000-8220

This book "covers how the disease starts, choosing the right doctor, treatment options, the importance of treating the emotional symptoms, the role of special diets, alternative therapies, and advances in treatment." Publisher's note

Includes bibliographical references

Greenwood-Robinson, Maggie

Hair savers for women; a complete guide to preventing and treating hair loss. Three Rivers Press (NY) 2000 261p pa $14   **616.5**

1. Baldness -- Treatment 2. Hair -- Diseases 3. Women -- Health and hygiene
ISBN 0-609-80445-6

                    LC 99-39185

The author discusses "solutions and advances in treating female hair loss, from medicine to natural remedies, and

introduces women to . . . safe, clinically proven baldness remedies. For women whose hair loss persists, the book discusses surgical alternatives such as hair transplants and scalp reductions, as well as the pros and cons of hair weaves and wigs." Publisher's note

Includes bibliographical references

Mayes, Maureen D.

The **scleroderma** book; a guide for patients and families. Rev ed; Oxford University Press 2005 211p il $28   **616.5**

1. Scleroderma (Disease)
ISBN 0-19-516940-9

                    LC 2004-10878

"Neither the cause nor the cure of the autoimmune connective tissue disease is known. Mayes describes the two main types of scleroderma; discusses who is likely to get the malady, which affects the whole body, as well as sexuality and pregnancy; and zeroes in on such organs as the kidneys, GI tract, lungs, heart, joints, tendons, muscles, and nerves." Booklist [review of 1999 edition]

Includes bibliographical referneces

Panagotacos, Peter J.

The **complete** book of hair loss answers; your comprehensive guide to the latest and best techniques. [by] Peter Panagotacos. 2nd ed.; Midpoint Trade 2006 240p il pa $15   **616.5**

1. Hair -- Diseases
ISBN 0-9720028-7-1; 978-0-9720028-7-5

This book provides "coverage of normal hair growth, causes of hair loss, bogus treatments, cosmetic treatments, drugs that cause hair loss and promote hair growth, surgical restoration, and questions and answers from concerned men and women experiencing hair loss. . . . This straightforward, plainspoken, all-inclusive book is highly recommended for all libraries where patrons are looking for complete, truthful answers to their hair-loss problems." Libr J

Includes bibliographical references

Turkington, Carol

★ The **encyclopedia** of skin and skin disorders; [by] Carol Turkington, Jeffrey S. Dover; medical illustrations, Birck Cox. 3rd ed; Facts on File 2007 459p $75; pa $17.95   **616.5**

1. Reference books 2. Skin -- Diseases 3. Skin -- Encyclopedias
ISBN 0-8160-6403-2; 978-0-8160-6403-8; 0-8160-6404-0 pa; 978-0-8160-6404-5 pa

                    LC 2005-57402

"More than 1,100 entries cover everything from the sun, skin, and acne to skin cancer, cosmetics, and skin lotions." Publisher's note

Includes bibliographical references

Skin disorders sourcebook; edited by Allan R. Cook. Omnigraphics 1997 647p il $78   **616.5**

1. Skin -- Diseases
ISBN 0-7808-0080-X

                    LC 97-6570

616.6   Diseases of urogenital system

Genadry, Rene

A **woman's** guide to urinary incontinence; [by] Rene Genadry and Jacek L. Mostwin. Johns Hopkins University Press 2008 184p il $39.95; pa $15.95   **616.6**

1. Urinary incontinence 2. Women -- Diseases
ISBN 978-0-8018-8732-1; 0-8018-8732-1; 978-0-8018-8733-8 pa; 0-8018-8733-X pa

LC 2007-14818

The authors "have written an excellent resource for women with urinary incontinence and their caretakers. Wide in scope and thorough in coverage, the book describes the stages and types of incontinence, kinds of exams and tests, current drugs and methods of treatment, anticipated outcomes, and possible complications." Libr J

Loe, Meika

The **rise** of Viagra; how the little blue pill changed sex in America. New York University Press 2004 289p il $27.95   **616.6**

1. Impotence 2. Sex (Biology) 3. Sex -- United States 4. Sildenafil 5. Sildenafil -- Social aspects -- United States
ISBN 0-8147-5200-4

LC 2004-5125

This book contains "discourse relating to Viagra and the medicalization of sexual dysfunctions, first men's and later women's. Drawing heavily on academic theories, Loe . . . tells a fascinating and sometimes disturbing tale of products discovered before science understood why they worked, diseases expanded to the worried well, and experts keeping cozy and often covert company with pharmaceutical companies." Libr J

Includes bibliographical references

Marrs, Richard P.

Dr. Richard Marrs' fertility book; America's leading fertility expert tells you everything you need to know about getting pregnant. [by] Richard Marrs, and Lisa Friedman Bloch and Kathy Kirtland Silverman. Dell 1998 510p il pa $19   **616.6**

1. Infertility
ISBN 978-0-440-50803-8; 0-440-50803-7

This guide to infertility discusses causes and treatments, outlines assisted reproductive technologies, considers immunological problems as well as emotional and financial issues.

"A necessary primer for any couple faced with infertility, this is essential for public libraries." Libr J

Includes bibliographical references

616.7   Diseases of musculoskeletal system

Arnot, Bob

Wear and tear; stop the pain and put back the spring in your body. Simon & Schuster 2003 xxvii, 259p il $25; pa $13   **616.7**

1. Arthritis 2. Physical fitness
ISBN 0-7432-2555-4; 0-7432-2556-2 pa

LC 2002-30871

"The information will be useful to those who currently have joint problems and to younger people who want to prevent future damage." Publ Wkly

Includes bibliographical references

Lahita, Robert G.

Lupus Q&A; everything you need to know. [by] Robert G. Lahita and Robert H. Phillips. Rev ed; Avery 2004 240p pa $14.95   **616.7**

1. Systemic lupus erythematosus
ISBN 1-58333-196-4; 978-1-58333-196-5

LC 2004-40974

This book "discusses the different types of the disease. Because lupus can be so confusing, Lahita and Phillips also discuss medical disorders similar to it. They subsequently turn to the immune system, which is the body system most likely to be involved in lupus, to tests and diagnosis, and to descriptions of symptoms and complications, usefully conveyed in question-and-answer format." Booklist

Lane, Nancy E.

The **osteoporosis** book. Oxford Univ. Press 1998 206p il hardcover o.p. pa $13.95   **616.7**

1. Osteoporosis 2. Osteoporosis -- Popular works
ISBN 0-19-514238-1 pa

LC 98-19650

This work is "organized in two parts, with early chapters devoted to educating the lay reader on the life cycle of bone and reasons for its loss. Risk factors and different types of fractures are identified, and diagnostic tests are explained. Later chapters discuss the many types of estrogen replacement therapy and medications other than hormones to prevent and treat osteoporosis." Libr J

Includes bibliographical references

Marek, Claudia

The **first** year--fibromyalgia; an essential guide for the newly diagnosed. {by} Claudia Craig Marek; foreword by R. Paul St. Amand. Marlowe & Co. 2002 xxii, 369p pa $15.95   **616.7**

1. Fibromyalgia
ISBN 1-56924-521-5

LC 2002-141445

The author "aims to help newly diagnosed patients learn about fibromyalgia and develop coping skills over a one-year time frame. Typical questions a new patient might have (e.g., how to prepare for travel, how to communicate with health professionals and employers) are addressed in a highly readable and understandable style and presented in manageable learning bites. . . . What is especially good about this guide is that the authors' tone is not alarmist but calm and evenhanded in articulating important precautions." Libr J

Includes bibliographical references

Nelson, Miriam E.

Strong women, strong bones; everything you need to know to prevent, treat, and beat osteoporosis. [by] Miriam E. Nelson with Sarah Wernick. Rev ed; Perigee 2006 320p il pa $14.95   **616.7**

1. Osteoporosis
ISBN 978-0-399-53249-8; 0-399-53249-8
LC 2007-274321

The authors explain "how bones grow; osteoporosis risk factors; how to adjust the diet to include calcium, vitamin D, and other bone-essential nutrients; the types of weight-bearing exercises that should be performed to promote maximum bone health; and the latest osteoporosis treatment options." Libr J

Includes bibliographical references

Patarca, Roberto

★ The **concise** encyclopedia of fibromyalgia and myofascial pain. Haworth Medical Press 2002 201p $49.95; pa $24.95   **616.7**

1. Fibromyalgia 2. Fibromyalgia -- Encyclopedias 3. Myofascial pain syndromes 4. Reference books
ISBN 0-7890-1527-7; 0-7890-1528-5 pa
LC 2001-51687

This source of information on fibromyalgia and myofascial pain is in dictionary form and includes entries on symptoms, medication, condition, and findings on related disorders. Also covered are "advances in rheumatology, cardiovascular medicine, endocrinology, epidemiology, immunology, infectious diseases, neurology, psychiatry, and psychology that form the basis for new lines of research and therapeutic intervention." Publisher's note

Includes bibliographical references

Sayler, Mary Harwell

The **encyclopedia** of the muscle and skeletal systems and disorders; foreword by Lori Siegel. Facts on File 2005 xx, 389p $75   **616.7**

1. Musculoskeletal system -- Encyclopedias 2. Reference books
ISBN 0-8160-5447-9
LC 2003-26606

The author "writes each entry with wit and skill—amazing among health science encyclopedias. It will be useful to health care consumers and students for years to come." Choice

Includes bibliographical references

Starlanyl, Devin

Fibromyalgia & chronic myofascial pain syndrome; a survival manual. {by} Devin Starlanyl, Mary Ellen Copeland; foreword by Christopher R. Brown. 2nd ed; New Harbinger Publs. 2001 398p il $19.95   **616.7**

1. Fibromyalgia
ISBN 1-57224-238-8
LC 2001-132299

In this overview of fibromyalgia syndrome (FMS) and myofascial pain syndrome (MPS) the authors "offer information on the latest medications, tips for bodywork, and suggestions for coping with family and work, getting sup-

port, and dealing with the healthcare system." Libr J {review of 1996 edition}

Includes bibliographical references

Wallace, Daniel J.

Fibromyalgia: an essential guide for patients and their families; {by} Daniel J. Wallace, Janice Brock Wallace. Oxford Univ. Press 2003 196p il pa $12.95   **616.7**

1. Fibromyalgia
ISBN 0-19-514931-9
LC 2002-17096

This guide to fibromyalgia, a form of chronic neuromuscular pain, provides an explanation of the syndrome and its symptoms and also outlines recent advances in treatment and new drugs available.

The encyclopedia of arthritis; [by] Guy Taylor, C. Michael Stein. 2nd ed; Facts On File 2010 420p $75   **616.7**

1. Arthritis 2. Arthritis -- Encyclopedias 3. Reference books
ISBN 978-0-8160-7767-0; 0-8160-7767-3; 978-1-4381-3305-8 ebook; 1-4381-3305-7 ebook
LC 2010-12573

"Organized alphabetically by disease or treatment name, the entries run several pages and contain subheadings, clarifying symptoms, treatment options, and risk factors. Extremely detailed, each entry includes specialized medical terms but remains highly accessible. A superb glossary, an appendix of relevant websites, and an eight-page bibliography make this an essential reference." Libr J

Includes bibliographical references

616.8   Diseases of nervous system and mental disorders

B., David

★ **Epileptic**. Pantheon Books 2005 361p il $25; pa $18.95 **616.8**

1. Autobiographical graphic novels 2. Epilepsy -- Comic books, strips, etc. 3. Epilepsy -- Graphic novels 4. Graphic novels
ISBN 0-375-42318-4; 0-375-71468-5 pa
LC 2004-53419

The author's "artwork is magnificent—gorgeously bold, impressionistic representations of the world not as it is but as he's taught himself to perceive it. . . . B.'s illustrations constantly underscore his writing's wrenching psychological depth; readers can literally see how the chaos of his childhood shaped his vision and mind." Publ Wkly

Bruno, Richard L.

The **polio** paradox; uncovering the hidden history of polio to understand and treat post-polio syndrome and chronic fatigue. Warner Bks. 2002 350p il $25.95; pa $15.95   **616.8**

1. Poliomyelitis 2. Postpoliomyelitis syndrome
ISBN 0-446-52907-9; 0-446-69069-4 pa

The author "discusses the history and care of polio patients, the identification of and research into PPS {post-polio syndrome}, and the approach to treating the symptoms. . . . {He} also addresses chronic fatigue (CF), multiple sclerosis, fibromyalgia, Gulf War syndrome, and spina bifida disorders that share symptoms, brain changes, and stress links similar to PPS." Libr J

Includes bibliographical references

Chase, Victor D.

Shattered nerves; how science is solving modern medicine's most perplexing problem. Johns Hopkins University Press 2007 289p $27.50   **616.8**
1. Nervous system
ISBN 978-0-8018-8514-3; 0-8018-8514-0
LC 2006-9626

"Chase achieves his formidable aim, enabling the reader to make connections between scientific endeavor and its application to the lives of the vivid individuals to whom he introduces us." Cerebrum

Includes bibliographical references

Cram, David L.

Answers to frequently asked questions in Parkinson's disease; a resource book for patients and families. [by] David L. Cram, M.D. Acorn Pub. 2002 170p pa $19.95   **616.8**
1. Parkinson's disease
ISBN 0-9710988-8-3
LC 2002-1074

Duvoisin, Roger C.

Parkinson's disease; a guide for patient and family. [by] Roger C. Duvoisin, Jacob Sage. 5th ed; Lippincott Williams & Wilkins 2001 195p il pa $32.95   **616.8**
1. Parkinson's disease 2. Parkinson's disease -- Popular works
ISBN 0-7817-2977-7
LC 2001-29689

"The complications of advancing disease are particularly well described. While the reading level is high, the determined reader can find a great deal of detailed information not found in other guides." Libr J

Freed, Curt

Healing the brain; [by] Curt Freed and Simon LeVay. Times Bks. 2002 269p $26   **616.8**
1. Cellular therapy 2. Parkinson's disease 3. Parkinson's disease -- Treatment -- Popular works 4. Stem cells 5. Transplantation of organs, tissues, etc.
ISBN 0-8050-7091-5
LC 2002-19671

"Parkinson's patients and others interested in the issue will find this an absorbing account." Libr J

Gillies, Andrea

★ **Keeper**; one house, three generations, and a journey into Alzheimer's. Broadway Books 2010 323p $25; ebook $25 **616.8**
1. Alzheimer's disease 2. Caregivers 3. Journalists 4. Memoirists
ISBN 978-0-307-71911-9; 978-0-307-71913-3 ebook
LC 2010-6659

In this "chronicle of her troubled two years taking care of her mother-inlaw in the throes of dementia, . . . Gillies reveals the 'dehumanizing' toll of the disease on the whole family. Gillies, her husband, and three children moved to a rambling Victorian house in the wilds of a Scottish peninsula and took in Chris's parents, Edinburgh residents who had been showing signs of needing increasing care: irascible Morris had 'bad legs,' while his strong-willed wife, Nancy, at 79, was spiraling deeper into Alzheimer's. As Nancy's memory deteriorated the entire family unit began to collapse under the strain of constant caretaking. . . . [This] memoir is an invaluable resource on the stages of Alzheimer's, history, drugs, brain function, care-giving options, even literary works." Publ Wkly

Includes bibliographical references

Greene, Gayle

Insomniac. University of California Press 2008 503p $29.95 **616.8**
1. Insomnia 2. Sleep 3. Sleep disorders
ISBN 978-0-520-24630-0; 0-520-24630-6
LC 2007-8838

"Greene offers an enjoyable and informative account that will provoke even readers who get their full eight hours a night." Publ Wkly

Includes bibliographical references

Halpern, Sue M.

★ **Can't** remember what I forgot; the good news from the front lines of memory research. Harmony Books 2008 256p $24; pa $14.95   **616.8**
1. Alzheimer's disease 2. Memory 3. Memory disorders
ISBN 978-0-307-40674-3; 0-307-40674-1; 978-0-307-40788-7 pa; 0-307-40788-8 pa
LC 2007-33895

This "timely book offers a vivid, often amusing introduction to a science that touches us all." Publ Wkly

Includes bibliographical references

Hauser, Robert A.

Parkinson's disease: questions and answers; 4th ed; Merit Pub. Int. 2003 204p $34.95   **616.8**
1. Parkinson's disease
ISBN 1-873413-68-8

"Although primarily aimed at general clinicians, this manual may be useful for patients wishing more in-depth knowledge than what the consumer guides offer. Hauser . . . covers test, clinical characteristics, staging and classifications, medical management, and issues frequently missed in the lay literature." Libr J {review of 2000 edition}

Horstman, Judith

The **Scientific** American day in the life of your brain. Jossey-Bass 2009 236p il $25.95   **616.8**
1. Brain 2. Human behavior 3. Mind and body
ISBN 978-0-470-37623-2
LC 2009-13923

The author "reviews a full day of brainwork by accounting for the mental processes of everyday activities, arranged by hour. . . . Information-packed and fully referenced, this Scientific American publication is perfect for anyone with

interest in mind/body interaction, mental health or aging."
Publ Wkly

Includes bibliographical references

Kuhn, Daniel

Alzheimer's early stages; first steps for families,
friends and caregivers. 2nd ed; Hunter House 2003
306p hardcover o.p. pa $15.95   **616.8**
1. Alzheimer's disease 2. Alzheimer's disease --
Popular works 3. Caregivers
ISBN 0-89793-398-2; 0-89793-397-4 pa
                                    LC 2002-151932
This book covers "the importance of getting a diagnosis,
risk factors (including the role of depression), early symptoms, treatment and prevention, and information on physical health, safety concerns, caring for the caregiver, and financial and end-of-life planning—all illustrated with brief,
first-person narratives. Of special interest are chapters on
relationships, including telling others about the diagnosis,
and the . . . section on current available treatments. . . . Intelligently written with numerous references to professional
and consumer literature, this book is an excellent choice for
Alzheimer's and consumer health collections." Libr J

Includes bibliographical references

Kushner, Howard I.

★ A **cursing** brain? the histories of Tourette syndrome. Harvard Univ. Press 1999 303p il $32.50;
pa $16.95   **616.8**
1. Tourette syndrome 2. Tourette syndrome -- History
ISBN 0-674-18022-4; 0-674-00386-1 pa
                                    LC 98-38733
"A compassionate and absorbing work of medical history." Libr J

Includes bibliographical references

Lang, Anthony E.

★ **Parkinson's** disease; a complete guide for
patients and families. [by] William J. Weiner, Lisa M.
Shulman, Anthony E. Lang. 2nd ed.; Johns Hopkins
University Press 2007 278p il $55; pa $17.95 **616.8**
1. Parkinson's disease
ISBN 0-8018-8545-0; 978-0-8018-8545-7; 0-8018-
8546-9 pa; 978-0-8018-8546-4 pa
                                    LC 2006-18814
This book contains "information for managing this complex condition, including details on the use of medications,
diet, exercise, complementary therapies, and surgery." Publisher's note

Lieberman, A.

100 questions & answers about Parkinson {sic}
disease; {by} Abraham Lieberman, with Marcia Mc-
Call. Jones & Bartlett 2003 238p il pa $16.95 **616.8**
1. Parkinson's disease.
ISBN 0-7637-0433-4
                                    LC 2002-152130
A patient-oriented guide to the symptoms, diagnosis, and
treatment of Parkinson's disease
"Lieberman is particularly good at telling patients what
they should expect from their physicians, how they can select a competent movement disorders specialist, how they

can make the most of living with PD, and what they should
know about the new advances in medical, alternative, and
surgical therapies. An optimistic resource that should be
much in demand." Libr J

Shaking-up Parkinson disease; fighting like
a tiger, thinking like a fox: a book for the puzzled,
the hopeful, the willing and the prepared. by Abraham Lieberman. Jones & Bartlett 2002 250p il pa
$18.95   **616.8**
1. Parkinson's disease
ISBN 0-7637-1866-1
                                    LC 2001-25721
This book "explains PD and its symptoms (with steps
to alleviate them) and extensively covers treatment options
such as drugs and surgery. A plus is the author's discussion
of anxiety and depression as a biological rather than a psychological symptom of the disease. . . . Although nonreligious readers may be put off by the biblical quotes, this is
still an outstanding text." Libr J

Marks, David R.

The **headache** prevention cookbook; eating right
to prevent migraines and other headaches. [by] David
R. Marks, with Laura Marks. Houghton Mifflin 2000
208p pa $16   **616.8**
1. Diet therapy 2. Headache 3. Headache -- Diet
therapy 4. Headache -- Prevention
ISBN 0-395-96716-3
                                    LC 00-33435
The authors explain how ordinary foods may serve as
triggers for headache pain. To help readers with undiagnosed food sensitivities they include more than 100 easy-
to-prepare recipes.

Max, D. T.

The **family** that couldn't sleep; a medical mystery. Random House 2006 xxxi, 299p hardcover
o.p. pa $15.95   **616.8**
1. Fatal familial insomnia 2. Insomnia 3. Prion
diseases 4. Prions 5. Sleep disorders
ISBN 1-4000-6245-4; 978-1-4000-6245-4; 978-0-
8129-7252-8 pa; 0-8129-7252-X pa
                                    LC 2006-43885
This book discusses fatal familial insomnia and the history of one family in the Veneto region of Italy that has suffered from this disease for more than two centuries.
This is a "gracefully written medical detective story." N
Y Times (Late N Y Ed)

Includes bibliographical references

Moore, Elaine A.

Encyclopedia of Alzheimer's disease; with directories of research, treatment, and care facilities.
[by] Elaine A. Moore; with Lisa Moore; illustrations
by Marvin G. Miller. McFarland & Co. 2003 401p
il $75   **616.8**
1. Alzheimer's disease 2. Alzheimer's disease --
Encyclopedias 3. Alzheimer's disease -- United States

4. Reference books
ISBN 0-7864-1438-3

LC 2002-12202

"The first section of this encyclopedia explains terms (e.g., scientific, health plans, organizations) relating directly or indirectly to the disease. . . . The next section has three directories (treatment centers listed by state and city, research facilities by state, and resources) followed by an index. . . . For a comprehensive reference on Alzheimer's, the Moores' resource would be an excellent choice." Choice

Includes bibliographical references

Mosley, Anthony D.

The **encyclopedia** of Parkinson's disease; [by] Anthony D. Mosley and Deborah S. Romaine with Ali Samii. 2nd ed; Facts on File 2009 368p $75 **616.8**
1. Parkinson's disease 2. Parkinson's disease -- Encyclopedias 3. Reference books
ISBN 978-0-8160-7674-1; 0-8160-7674-X

LC 2008-56091

This encyclopedia "presents more than 650 entries explaining the complex issues and topics related to Parkinson's, including etiology, surgeries, research, medical terms, and much more." Publisher's note

Includes bibliographical references

Ramachandran, V. S.

The **tell**-tale brain; a neuroscientist's quest for what makes us human. W. W. Norton 2011 xxvi, 357p il $26.95   **616.8**
1. Brain 2. Nervous system
ISBN 978-0-393-07782-7

LC 2010-44913

"Ramachandran produces an exhilarating and at times funny text that invites discussion and experimentation." Kirkus

Includes bibliographical references

Sacks, Oliver W.

Uncle Tungsten; memories of a chemical boyhood. [by] Oliver Sacks. Knopf 2001 337p il hardcover o.p. pa $14   **616.8**
1. Large print books 2. Neurologists 3. Neurologists -- England -- Biography 4. Physicians 5. Writers on medicine 6. Writers on science
ISBN 0-375-40448-1; 0-375-70404-3 pa

LC 2001-33738

"Sacks' first scientific love was chemistry, and he presents an avid history of the field within a memoir that pays tribute to his uncle, who welcomed Sacks into his lab, thus encouraging his passion for chemistry and learning." Booklist

An **anthropologist** on Mars; seven paradoxical tales. [by] Oliver Sacks. Knopf 1995 327p il hardcover o.p. pa $14   **616.8**
1. Nervous system -- Diseases
ISBN 0-679-75697-3 pa

LC 94-26733

In this "collection of previously published essays, the noted neurologist describes his meetings with seven people whose 'abnormalities' in brain function generate new perspectives on the workings of that organ, the nature of experience and concepts of personality and consciousness. .

. . Writing with eloquent particularity and compassionate respect, Sacks enlarges our view of the nature of human experience." Publ Wkly

Includes bibliographical references

★ The **man** who mistook his wife for a hat and other clinical tales; [by] Oliver Sacks. Simon & Schuster 1998 243p il pa $14   **616.8**
1. Nervous system -- Diseases
ISBN 0-684-85394-9

LC 98-4723

"Sacks introduces the reader to real people who suffer from a variety of neurological syndromes which includes symptoms such as amnesia, uncontrolled movements, and musical hallucinations. Sacks recounts their stories in a riveting, compassionate, and thoughtful manner." Libr J

Includes bibliographical references

Schwartz, Maxime

How the cows turned mad; translated by Edward Schneider. University of Calif. Press 2003 238p hardcover o.p. pa $15.95   **616.8**
1. Prion diseases 2. Prion diseases -- History
ISBN 0-520-23531-2; 0-520-24337-4 pa

LC 2002-75514

"Writing with immense concentration and clarity, French molecular biologist Schwartz makes the long hunt for the unexpected culprit gene utterly engrossing." Booklist

Includes bibliographical references

Shenk, David

The **forgetting**: Alzheimer's, portrait of an epidemic. Doubleday 2001 290p $24.95; pa $13.95   **616.8**
1. Alzheimer's disease
ISBN 0-385-49837-3; 0-385-49838-1 pa

LC 2001-28012

The author "traces the development of knowledge about Alzheimer's in the work of individuals and such groups as the National Institute of Aging; describes various tests that help in identifying possible sufferers; and discusses the early, middle, and end stages of the malady. . . . Lucid and well organized, this is one of the best books on this increasingly prevalent illness." Booklist

Includes bibliographical references

Spence, J. David

How to prevent your stroke. Vanderbilt University Press 2006 218p il $39.95; pa $19.95 **616.8**
1. Stroke
ISBN 0-8265-1536-0; 978-0-8265-1536-0; 0-8265-1537-7 pa; 978-0-8265-1537-7 pa

LC 2005-35450

Spence "offers a well-organized and engaging narrative with just the right amount of information to help readers make informed decisions regarding cardiovascular disease prevention." Libr J

Includes bibliographical references

Tanzi, Rudolph E.

Decoding darkness; the search for the genetic causes of Alzheimer's disease. {by} Rudolph E.

Tanzi & Ann B. Parson. Perseus Bks. 2000 281p il
hardcover o.p. pa $16 **616.8**

1. Alzheimer's disease

ISBN 0-7382-0526-5 pa

"This is a gripping book with a vast amount of fascinating information." Booklist

Turkington, Carol

★ The **encyclopedia** of Alzheimer's disease;
[by] Carol Turkington and Deborah Mitchell; foreword by James E. Galvin. 2nd ed.; Facts On File
2010 302p $75 **616.8**

1. Alzheimer's disease -- Encyclopedias 2. Reference
books

ISBN 978-0-8160-7766-3; 0-8160-7766-5; 978-1-4381-2858-0 ebook; 1-4381-2858-4 ebook

LC 2009-6661

"Those who have been diagnosed (or have had a family member diagnosed) with Alzheimer's disease or another type of dementia will find the information in this book . . . both useful and enlightening. More than 500 entries provide information and explanations of conditions, medicines, situations, and medical terms associated with not only Alzheimer's disease but with other dementia disorders as well." Booklist

Includes bibliographical references

The **encyclopedia** of multiple sclerosis; [by]
Carol Turkington and Kaye D. Hooper in collaboration with Rosalind C. Kalb and Nancy Holland. Facts
On File 2005 336p $75 **616.8**

1. Multiple sclerosis -- Encyclopedias 2. Reference
books

ISBN 0-8160-5623-4; 978-0-8160-5623-1

LC 2004-22858

"Entries range in length from a brief paragraph to several pages. They include events, such as the MS Walk, and celebrities, such as Joan Didion and Lena Horne, who are living with MS. Five appendixes list 'Organizations,' 'National MS Society-Affiliated Clinical Facilities,' 'Clinical Trials in Multiple Sclerosis,' 'State Chapters of the National Multiple Sclerosis Society,' and 'International Multiple Sclerosis Societies.' . . . This is a very good, reasonably priced source for public and consumer health collections." Booklist

Includes bibliographical references

Weiner, Jonathan

His brother's keeper; a story from the edge of
medicine. HarperCollins 2004 356p $26.95 **616.8**

1. Amyotrophic lateral sclerosis -- Patients 2.
Carpenters 3. Mechanical engineers 4. Nervous system
-- Diseases 5. Sick

ISBN 0-06-00100-7-X

LC 2004-302468

"When Stephen Heywood, a 29-year-old carpenter, was
diagnosed with amyotrophic lateral sclerosis (also known as
Lou Gehrig's disease), his older brother, Jamie, launched his
own research project to search for a cure. . . . The story's
power derives from attention to small, human details, like
Stephen's first symptoms of losing strength in his fingers. . .
. Weiner can't give readers a happy ending for Stephen, but

he can—and does—offer a powerful account of equal parts
ambition and hope." Publ Wkly

Whitehouse, Peter J.

The **myth** of Alzheimer's; what you aren't being
told about today's most dreaded diagnosis. [by] Peter J. Whitehouse, with Daniel George. St. Martin's
Press 2008 319p il $25.95; pa $15.95 **616.8**

1. Alzheimer's disease

ISBN 978-0-312-36816-6; 0-312-36816-X; 978-0-312-36817-3 pa; 0-312-36817-8 pa

LC 2007-22176

"Part 1 surveys the history of Alzheimer's, including
myths and the commercialization of Alzheimer's by drug
companies and celebrities. The science of Alzheimer's and
treatments past and present, including the merits and effectiveness of current drugs, are detailed in Part 2, as is the
world of genetics and molecular medicine. In Part 3, the
authors present a new model for living with brain aging,
practical information on preparing for a doctor's visit, and a
prescription for successful and healthy aging across the life
span based on nutrition, avoiding environmental exposures,
building a cognitive reserve, and community-based activity.
. . . An important contribution to the literature." Libr J

Includes bibliographical references

Wilson, Daniel J.

★ **Living** with polio; the epidemic and its survivors. Daniel J. Wilson. University of Chicago Press
2005 299p il $29 **616.8**

1. Poliomyelitis

ISBN 0-226-90103-3

LC 2004-24170

The author "has drawn on 150 personal narratives, published and unpublished, weaving quotes from those accounts
with historical information on polio treatment and rehabilitation. The result is a vivid portrait of a devastating disease
and its repercussions, as well as a glimpse into the physical,
social, and psychological challenges of being physically disabled in mid-20th century America." Libr J

Includes bibliographical references

Managing stroke; a guide to living well after stroke.
edited by Paul R. Rao, Mark N. Ozer, John E.
Toerge; foreword by Don A. Olson. ABI Professional Publs. 2000 299p il $27 **616.8**

1. Stroke

ISBN 1-886236-24-0

"With information on physical therapy, occupational
therapy, and daily living skills, this is primarily a guide to
rehabilitation for stroke patients or their families rather than
a quick reference book or a guide to prevention." Libr J

★ **Sleep disorders sourcebook**; edited by Amy
L. Sutton. 2nd ed; Omnigraphics 2005 567p
$87 **616.8**

1. Consumer education 2. Sleep

ISBN 0-7808-0743-X; 978-0-7808-0743-3

LC 2004-28389

When Parkinson's strikes early; voices, choices, resources, and treatment. {edited by} Blake-Krebs

& Linda Herman. Hunter House 2001 270p il pa $15.95   **616.8**

1. Parkinson's disease 2. Parkinson's disease -- Popular works

ISBN 0-89793-340-0

LC 2001-16619

This "guide incorporates e-mailings from the members of the Parkinson's Information Exchange Network (PIEN), with detailed advice on diagnosis, treatment, and self-help options. The vivid essays, poetry, and stories personalize the disease's impact; the resources section is outstanding." Libr J

Includes bibliographical references

616.85   Miscellaneous diseases of nervous system and mental disorders

Ainsworth, Patricia

Understanding mental retardation; [by] Patricia Ainsworth, Pamela Baker. University Press of Mississippi 2004 200p $30; pa $12   **616.85**

1. Mental retardation

ISBN 1-578-06646-8; 1-578-06647-6 pa

LC 2003-25098

"The value of this work hinges on its accessible presentation: parents and caregivers are given up-to-date information that should enable them to anticipate hurdles, to advocate, and to access necessary support services. Precious few books address the history and needs of people with mental retardation so thoroughly for parents and caregivers." Libr J

Includes bibliographical references

Attwood, Tony

The **complete** guide to Asperger's syndrome. Jessica Kingsley Publishers 2006 397p il $29.95   **616.85**

1. Asperger's syndrome

ISBN 978-1-84310-495-7; 1-84310-495-4

LC 2006-20065

The author covers "topics such as friendship, bullying, special interests, and theory of mind. Each chapter begins with a quote from Hans Asperger himself and includes first-hand experiences from individuals with Asperger's, including Temple Grandin, Liane Holliday Willey, and Stephen Shore. . . . His work skillfully brings together the current information on this fascinating condition." Libr J

Includes bibliographical references

Barkley, Russell A.

Taking charge of adult ADHD; with Christine M. Benton. Guilford Press 2010 294p $40; pa $16.95   **616.85**

1. Attention deficit disorder

ISBN 978-1-60623-710-6; 978-1-60623-338-2 pa

LC 2010-5716

"Thirty short chapters are organized into five sections that deal with evaluation of adult ADHD, underlying mechanisms of ADHD and self-acceptance of the diagnosis, understanding medication as a treatment option, utilizing behavioral strategies to address specific deficits, and managing in key areas such as work, relationships, and health. . . . This is a comprehensive and scientifically based yet comprehensible manual for understanding and managing adult ADHD." Libr J

Includes bibliographical references

Barthelme, Frederick

Double down; reflections on gambling and loss. {by} Frederick and Steven Barthelme. Houghton Mifflin 2000 198p hardcover o.p. pa $15   **616.85**

1. Authors 2. College teachers 3. Compulsive gamblers -- Mississippi -- Psychology 4. Compulsive gambling -- Mississippi 5. Novelists 6. Short story writers

ISBN 0-395-95429-0; 978-0-15-601070-2 pa; 0-15-601070-4 pa

LC 99-23957

"Beautifully evoking the gamblers' addiction, their mesmerizing account is best read as a novel Camus might have imagined, with the writer/protagonists as their own lost characters. A work of high art; enthusiastically recommended." Libr J

Bass, Ellen

★ The **courage** to heal; a guide for women survivors of child sexual abuse. by Ellen Bass and Laura Davis. 20th anniversary edition; 4th revised edition; Collins Living 2008 xxxiv, 606p pa $22.95 **616.85**

1. Adult child sexual abuse victims 2. Child sexual abuse 3. Women -- Psychology

ISBN 978-0-06-128433-5; 0-06-128433-5

LC 2008-11616

"This book offers help and encouragement to women who were sexually abused in childhood. Through moving first-person narratives, it illustrates how to come to terms with the past and work constructively towards the future. Along the way it describes the effects of sexual abuse, maps the stages survivors pass through, and offers practical guidance on dealing with self-defeating behaviors and building self-esteem. . . . Compassionate and supportive." Libr J

Includes bibliographical references

Claude-Pierre, Peggy

The **secret** language of eating disorders; the revolutionary new approach to understanding and curing anorexia and bulimia. Vintage Books 1999 288p il pa $14.95   **616.85**

1. Eating disorders

ISBN 978-0-375-75018-2; 0-375-75018-5

According to the author, "the primary cause of an eating disorder is rooted in confirmed negativity condition, or CNC. . . . She discusses how CNC manifests itself and the stages of recovery from it, with appropriate intervention strategies. . . . Her message and tone are supportive and should comfort those, including desperate parents, dealing with these complex, puzzling afflictions." Booklist

Includes bibliographical references

Coleman, Penny

★ **Flashback**; posttraumatic stress disorder, suicide, and the lessons of war. Beacon Press 2006 223p

$23.95 **616.85**
1. Post-traumatic stress disorder 2. Veterans
ISBN 0-8070-5040-7

LC 2005-30606

For this book, the author, the former wife of a Vietnam veteran who committed suicide, "interviewed women whose husbands survived battles but succumbed to the effects of war, researched instances of PTSD dating back to the Civil War, and compiled statistical information pertaining to American soldiers serving in the Middle East. . . . An essential part of any public library collection." Libr J

Includes bibliographical references

Dalton, Katharina
Depression after childbirth; how to recognize, treat, and prevent postnatal depression. {by} Katharina Dalton, with Wendy Holton. 4th ed; Oxford Univ. Press 2001 240p il pa $19.95 **616.85**
1. Postpartum depression 2. Puerperal psychoses
ISBN 0-19-263277-9

LC 00-53754

This guide for women and their partners for recognizing, treating and preventing postpartum depression discusses such topics as the role of hormones, symptoms such as exhaustion and irritability, and careers and motherhood.

DePaulo, J. Raymond
Understanding depression; what we know and what you can do about it. {by} J. Raymond DePaulo, Leslie Alan Horvitz. Wiley 2002 296p il $24.95; pa $14.95 **616.85**
1. Depression (Psychology) 2. Depression, Mental 3. Manic-depressive illness
ISBN 0-471-39552-8; 0-471-43030-7 pa

LC 2001-45449

This describes the nature, causes, effects, and treatment of depression and manic-depressive illness.

"The chapters on finding the right treatment and how doctors make diagnoses will be extremely useful for those suffering from the disease. . . . Readers will find this an invaluable resource." Publ Wkly

Includes bibliographical references

England, Diane
The **post** traumatic stress disorder relationship; how to support your partner and keep your relationship healthy. Adams Media 2009 271p pa $14.95 **616.85**
1. Post-traumatic stress disorder
ISBN 978-1-59869-997-5

The author "worked with military families at a NATO base. Drawing on those experiences, she compassionately helps couples cope with post-traumatic stress disorder (PTSD). Whether the PTSD patient suffered trauma during military warfare, physical or sexual abuse, or natural disasters, the partner is affected and needs to learn how to interact with the affected partner. Timely and well done; essential in communities with returning Iraq and Afghanistan vets." Libr J

Includes bibliographical references

Frost, Randy O.
Stuff. Houghton Mifflin Harcourt 2010 290p
$27 **616.85**
1. Collectors and collecting 2. Compulsive hoarding 3. Identity (Psychology) 4. Nonfiction 5. Obsessive-compulsive disorder
ISBN 978-0-15-101423-1; 0-15-101423-X

LC 2009-28273

"Writing with authority and compassion, the authors tell the stories of diverse men and women who acquire and accumulate possessions to the point where their apartments or homes are dangerously cluttered with mounds of newspapers, clothing and other objects. . . . An absorbing, gripping, important report." Kirkus

Includes bibliographical references

Glenmullen, Joseph
Prozac backlash; overcoming the dangers of prozac, zoloft, paxil, and other antidepressants with safe, effective alternatives. Simon & Schuster 2000 383p hardcover o.p. pa $14 **616.85**
1. Antidepressants 2. Antidepressants -- Side effects 3. Depression (Psychology) 4. Depression, Mental -- Alternative treatment 5. Fluoxetine -- Side effects
ISBN 0-7432-0062-4 pa

LC 99-59911

The author presents a "survey of recent studies on the negative effects of antidepressants and their less-publicized alternatives. His title refers not to the growing skepticism toward psychiatric medications but to the brain's compensatory reactions to the artificial elevation of serotonin, including potentially permanent tics, dependence, sexual dysfunction, memory problems, sudden suicidal feelings and violence." Publ Wkly

Includes bibliographical references

Greenberg, Gary
Manufacturing depression; the secret history of a modern disease. Simon and Schuster 2010 432p
$27 **616.85**
1. Antidepressants 2. Depression (Psychology) 3. Depression, Mental 4. Psychotherapy -- United States -- History
ISBN 9781416569794; 1-4165-6979-0

LC 2009-24310

The author "ponders depression and its treatment through the ages. . . . [He] focuses heavily on the human element lurking behind the symptoms of depression and their context and meaning. During this tour of depression, the author engages in extended, illuminating discussions of a host of therapeutic techniques, the confounding power of the placebo effect, the evolution of psychopharmacology and the ways in which expectations shape response. A humanistic, witty exploration of the human response to depression." Kirkus

Includes bibliographical references

Grinker, Roy Richard
Unstrange minds; remapping the world of autism. Basic Books 2006 340p hardcover o.p. **616.85**
1. Autism
ISBN 0465027636; 0465027644; 9780465027637;

9780465027644

LC 2006-23003

Part 1 of this work examines "the history of the classification of psychiatric disorders. . . . The second part of the book explores the cultural issues related to autism in . . . India, South Korea, and South Africa and how the place of the autistic child is changing in those countries." (Sci Books Films) Index.

"The first part of the book is an expanded essay on the history of the classification of psychiatric disorders and how these definitions continue to evolve. . . . The second part of the book explores the cultural issues related to autism in societies as diverse as those of India, South Korea, and South Africa and how the place of the autistic child is changing in those countries. Grinker's experiences as a father of an autistic child are woven throughout the volume. . . . The text is scholarly, but easily read, and is useful not only for providing an understanding of autism, but also for understanding the issues associated with changing diagnoses of psychiatric disorders." Sci Books Films

Includes bibliographical references

Hallowell, Edward M.

Delivered from distraction; getting the most out of life with attention deficit disorder. [by] Edward M. Hallowell, John J. Ratey. Ballantine Books 2004 xxxiii, 380p $25.95; pa $14.95   **616.85**

1. Attention deficit disorder

ISBN 0-345-44230-X; 0-345-44231-8 pa

LC 2004-52815

"Defining ADD as a collection of traits, some positive, some negative, the authors intend to encourage those who have this condition or are raising children with it and advise on how to maximize their abilities and minimize characteristics, such as procrastination, that may hinder them at school or work. . . . Overall, this is an excellent resource." Publ Wkly

Includes bibliographical references

Driven to distraction; recognizing and coping with attention deficit disorder from childhood through adulthood. [by] Edward M. Hallowell and John J. Ratey. Simon & Schuster 1995 319p il pa $14   **616.85**

1. Attention deficit disorder

ISBN 0-684-80128-0

LC 94-40712

This study of Attention Deficit Disorder in children as well as in adults covers biology, neurology, pharmacology, clinical findings and personal and professional experiences.

"This is an absorbing look at efforts to understand troubling and exasperating behaviors." Booklist

Includes bibliographical references

Worry; controlling it and using it wisely. Pantheon Bks. 1997 331p hardcover o.p. pa $16.95 **616.85**

1. Anxiety 2. Worry

ISBN 0-345-42458-1 pa

LC 97-8609

"The book offers useful advice and entertaining stories, and readers can find something here to help them worry less." Booklist

Includes bibliographical references

Hornbacher, Marya

Wasted: a memoir of anorexia and bulimia. HarperCollins Pubs. 1998 268p hardcover o.p. pa $13.95   **616.85**

1. Anorexia nervosa 2. Bulimia

ISBN 0-06-018739-5; 978-0-06-085879-7 pa; 0-06-085879-6 pa

LC 97-21375

This "is a gritty, unflinching look at eating disorders. . . . Hornbacher is at her best when she zeroes in on the specifics of eating disorders and their origins." N Y Times Book Rev

Includes bibliographical references

Kramer, Peter D.

★ **Against** depression. Viking 2005 353p $25.95   **616.85**

1. Art and mental illness 2. Depression (Psychology) 3. Depression, Mental 4. Depression, Mental, in literature

ISBN 0-670-03405-3

LC 2004-61228

The author "examines the cultural roots of notions about depression and underscores the gap between what we know scientifically and what we feel about the illness. Kramer traces depression from Hippocrates through the Renaissance and Romantic 'cult of melancholy' to advances in medicine, psychiatry and psychotherapy, and at last to the disease we now know it to be. . . . Resolute but not preachy, this book is an important addition to the growing public health campaign against depression." Publ Wkly

Includes bibliographical references

Listening to Prozac; a psychiatrist explores mood-altering drugs and the new meaning of the self. Viking 1993 409p hardcover o.p. pa $15 **616.85**

1. Personality disorders 2. Psychiatry 3. Psychotherapy 4. Psychotropic drugs

ISBN 0-14-026671-2 pa

LC 92-50733

"Kramer's thesis is that Prozac, in addition to its antidepressant effects, can also act upon aspects of the personality that were previously conceptualized as enduring individual traits (i.e., sensitivity to rejection, social inhibition, and reactivity to stressors). Medication with Prozac appears to have beneficial effects on self-esteem, the ability to experience pleasure, and mental acuity. Kramer is favorable to Prozac, although he documents its side effects, unknown long-term affects, and controversial publicity." Choice

Machoian, Lisa

The **disappearing** girl; learning the language of teenage depression. Dutton 2005 xxiv, 244p $24.95; pa $15   **616.85**

1. Depression (Psychology) 2. Teenagers

ISBN 0-525-94866-X; 0-452-28710-3 pa

LC 2004-25777

The author "sets out to determine why so many young women seem to emotionally withdraw and to explain how parents and others can help them." Publ Wkly

Includes bibliographical references

Matsakis, Aphrodite

Vietnam wives; facing the challenges of life with veterans suffering post-traumatic stress. 2nd ed; Sidran Press 1996 440p pa $24.95   **616.85**

1. Post-traumatic stress disorder 2. Veterans 3. Vietnam War, 1961-1975

ISBN 1-88696-800-4

LC 96-15876

The author describes post-traumatic stress disorder (PTSD) as it effects Vietnam War veterans and their wives, often resulting in psychic numbness, sexual impotence, alcohol and drug addiction, family violence and depression. The book outlines therapy and coping techniques and includes a resource guide

McBride, Karyl

Will I ever be good enough? healing the daughters of narcissistic mothers. Free Press 2008 243p il $24   **616.85**

1. Mother-daughter relationship 2. Narcissism 3. Self-acceptance

ISBN 978-1-4165-5132-4; 1-4165-5132-8

LC 2008-14676

In this book aimed at women whose mothers have narcissistic personality disorder, "McBride presents specific steps toward recovery that daughters of any age can use as they grieve for the love and support they didn't receive, set healthy boundaries with their mothers and access an 'internal mother' as a source of self-comforting. The author provides parenting tips as well as advice on maintaining healthy love relationships and friendships—all of which tend to be weak points of the daughters of narcissistic mothers." Publ Wkly

Includes bibliographical references

Mondimore, Francis Mark

Adolescent depression; a guide for parents. Johns Hopkins Univ. Press 2002 287p il $45; pa $17.95   **616.85**

1. Adolescent psychology 2. Depression (Psychology) 3. Depression in adolescence -- Popular works

ISBN 0-8018-7058-5; 0-8018-7065-9 pa

LC 2001-7992

"The author provides a solid reference tool for anyone who works with adolescents. It is highly recommended for education professionals as well as public libraries." Voice Youth Advocates

Includes bibliographical references

Osborn, Ian

Tormenting thoughts and secret rituals; the hidden epidemic of obsessive-compulsive disorder. Pantheon Bks. 1998 325p hardcover o.p. pa $14.95   **616.85**

1. Obsessive-compulsive disorder -- Popular works 2. Obsessive-compulsive neurosis

ISBN 0-440-50847-9 pa

LC 97-31226

"Osborn shows that OCD is caused by a chemical imbalance in the brain and that behavior therapy and drugs, preferably together, can take care of it for most patients; Osborn personalizes this part of the discussion with case histories of individuals. . . . He concludes with a long list of OCD support groups and other helpful information." Booklist

Includes bibliographical references

Penzel, Fred

Obsessive-compulsive disorders; a complete guide to getting well and staying well. Oxford Univ. Press 2000 428p il $35   **616.85**

1. Obsessive-compulsive neurosis

ISBN 0-19-514092-3

LC 00-32419

This study of OCD (obsessive-compulsive disorder) outlines behavior patterns, discusses new antidepressants and behavior therapy techniques, and includes a do-it-yourself guide for a self-administered program of behavior therapy.

"New antidepressants and behavioral therapy techniques have led to great improvements in the condition of sufferers of this biologically based illness. Psychologist Penzel has written a do-it-yourself guide that outlines in great detail procedures for a self-administered program of behavioral therapy. . . . This title is the most useful of the recent books on OCD and is highly recommended to all public libraries." Libr J

Ronson, Jon

The **psychopath** test; Jon Ronson. Riverhead Books 2011 275 p.   **616.85**

1. Psychopaths

ISBN 978-1-59448-801-6; 1-59448-801-0

LC 201103133

This book provides an "exploration of psychiatry's attempts to understand and treat psychopathy, [in which] British journalist Ronson . . . reveals that psychopaths are more common than we'd like to think. Visiting Broadmoor Psychiatric Hospital, where some of Britain's worst criminal offenders are sent, Ronson discovers the difficulties of diagnosing the complex disorder when he meets one inmate who says he feigned psychopathy to get a lighter sentence, and instead has spent 12 years in Broadmoor. The psychiatric community's criteria for diagnosing psychopathy . . . is a checklist developed by the Canadian prison psychologist Robert Hare. Using Hare's rubric, which includes 'glibness,' 'grandiose sense of self-worth,' and 'lack of remorse,' Ronson sets off to interview possible psychopaths, many of them in positions of power, from a former Haitian militia leader to a power-hungry CEO." (Publishers Weekly)

Root, Benjamin A.

★ **Understanding** panic and other anxiety disorders; [by] Benjamin A. Root, Jr. University Press of Miss. 2000 109p il hardcover o.p. pa $12 **616.85**

1. Anxiety 2. Panic disorders

ISBN 1-57806-245-4 pa

LC 00-21977

"Root explains physical and mental problems that can mimic panic disorders and that the differentiating diagnosis in emergency room or clinic is often a major hurdle. The unpredictable nature of attacks in panic disorders and their frequent accompaniment, agoraphobia . . . add to the anxiety involved. Root describes those likely to suffer from panic attacks, discusses drug and psychotherapy treatments, and includes a chapter on pertinent research projects." Booklist

Sacks, Oliver

The **mind's** eye. Alfred A. Knopf 2010 263p il $26.95   **616.85**
1. Cognition disorders 2. Communicative disorders 3. Face perception 4. Nervous system 5. Neurology 6. Perception 7. Vision disorders
ISBN 978-0-307-27208-9; 0-307-27208-7
LC 2010-12791
Sacks "offers case histories of six individuals adjusting to major changes in their vision. A renowned pianist has lost the ability to read music scores and must cope with the fear of an ever-shrinking life as her vision worsens. A prolific writer develops 'word blindness' and is unable to read even what he himself writes, forcing him to develop memory books in his mind, adaptations that he later incorporates into his fiction writing. Sacks recalls his own struggle to cope with a tumor in his eye that left him unable to perceive depth. He includes diary entries and drawings of his harrowing experience. . . . [A] riveting exploration of how we use our vision to perceive and understand the world and our place in it and how our brains teach us to 'see' those things we need to lead a complete, fulfilled life." Booklist
Includes bibliographical references

Schreiber, Flora Rheta

Sybil. Warner Books 1995 460p il pa $7.99 **616.85**
1. Multiple personality
ISBN 978-0-446-35940-5; 0-446-35940-8
This is the "true story of Sybil I. Dorsett, a battered child possessed by 16 different personalities. . . . The author skillfully evokes Sybil's patient work during 11 years of psychoanalysis and her eventual success in integrating these selves into a unified personality." Libr J

Slone, Laurie B.

★ **After** the war zone; a practical guide for returning troops and their families. [by] Laurie B. Slone and Matthew J. Friedman. Da Capo Lifelong 2008 279p pa $14.95   **616.85**
1. Mental health 2. Post-traumatic stress disorder 3. Veterans
ISBN 978-1-60094-054-5; 1-60094-054-4
LC 2008-5555
"Far more than a practical guide, this is an informative, insightful, and riveting text that should be required reading for everyone because no one is left untouched by war. Essential for all libraries." Libr J
Includes bibliographical references

Solden, Sari

Journeys through ADDulthood; discover a new sense of identity and meaning while living with attention deficit disorder. Walker & Co. 2002 300p il $24; pa $13   **616.85**
1. Attention deficit disorder
ISBN 0-8027-1376-9; 0-8027-7679-5 pa
LC 2003-268751

"The material is organized into three stages: understanding the brain and primary symptoms of ADD, discovering one's true identity and accepting one's uniqueness, and learning to share one's self with others. . . . This important work stands out among the growing number of books on ADD for its focus on adults and the author's emphasis on learning how to come to terms with and live comfortably with the disease. Highly recommended for all public libraries." Libr J
Includes bibliographical references

Solomon, Andrew

The **noonday** demon; an atlas of depression. Scribner 2001 569p $28; pa $16   **616.85**
1. Depression (Psychology) 2. Depression, Mental
ISBN 0-684-85466-X; 0-684-85467-8 pa
LC 2001-18884
"The author draws on his own life story and other sources for a deeply moving and provocative exploration of depression." Booklist
Includes bibliographical references

Styron, William

Darkness visible; a memoir of madness. Random House 1990 84p hardcover o.p. pa $11 **616.85**
1. Authors 2. Depression (Psychology) 3. Depression (Psychology) -- Personal narratives 4. Essayists 5. Novelists
ISBN 0-679-73639-5 pa
LC 90-53141
This is an account of the author's experience of suicidal depression and his recovery
"The book's virtues—considerable—are twofold. First, it is a pitiless and chastened record of a nearly fatal human trial far commoner than assumed—and then a literary discourse on the ways and means of our cultural discontents." Publ Wkly

Turkington, Carol

★ The **encyclopedia** of autism spectrum disorders; [by] Carol Turkington, Ruth Anan. Facts on File 2007 324p $75   **616.85**
1. Autism 2. Autism -- Encyclopedias 3. Reference books
ISBN 0-8160-6002-9; 978-0-8160-6002-3
LC 2005-27227
"More than 300 entries address the different types of autism, causes and treatments, institutions, associations, leading scientists, research, social impact, and much more." Publisher's note
Includes bibliographical references

Wansink, Brian

Mindless eating; why we eat more than we think. Bantam Books 2006 276p il hardcover o.p. pa $14   **616.85**
1. Compulsive eating 2. Eating habits 3. Food habits -- Psychological aspects
ISBN 978-0-553-80434-8; 0-553-80434-0; 978-0-553-38448-2 pa; 0-553-38448-1 pa
LC 2006-47532

The author "explores some of the psychological aspects of overeating to explain why we in fact consume more than we believe we do. . . . Wansink's dual approach emphasizing food knowledge and self-knowledge offers a sensible route to permanent weight loss." Booklist

Includes bibliographical references

616.86   Substance abuse (Drug abuse)

Beattie, Melody

Beyond codependency; and getting better all the time. Hazelden Foundation 1989 252p pa $15.95   **616.86**
1. Applied psychology 2. Drug abuse
ISBN 0-89486-583-8
The author discusses "the process of recovering from the self-defeating behaviors adopted as survival tactics by adult children of families rendered dysfunctional by parental alcoholism or similar traumas." Publ Wkly

Includes bibliographical references

★ **Codependent** no more; how to stop controlling others and start caring for yourself. 2nd ed.; Hazelden 1992 250p pa $15.95   **616.86**
1. Codependency 2. Drug abuse 3. Health self-care
ISBN 0-89486-402-5
                                            LC 2004-351623
This guide offers advice on how to overcome codependency, aimed at the spouses and other caretakers of people who abuse drugs or alcohol.

Codependents' guide to the twelve steps. Simon & Schuster 1998 273p pa $14   **616.86**
1. Drug abuse
ISBN 0-671-76227-3; 978-0-671-76227-8
                                            LC 2004-270580
"Beattie offers an interpretation of the 12 steps based on her own experience as a recovering addict, codependent, and practicing therapist. This includes an excellent annotated bibliography of recovery titles." Libr J

Chopra, Deepak

Overcoming addictions; the spiritual solution. Harmony Bks. 1997 136p il hardcover o.p. pa $12   **616.86**
1. Drug abuse 2. Mind and body
ISBN 0-609-80195-3 pa
The author "addresses the topic of dependencies on psychoactive and mood-altering substances and guides the reader to replace addictive behavior with deeper sources of joy and spiritual fulfillment." Publisher's note

Goldfarb, Toni L.

American Lung Association 7 steps to a smoke-free life; [by] Edwin B. Fisher, Jr. with Toni L. Goldfarb. Wiley 1998 226p pa $14.95   **616.86**
1. Cigarette habit 2. Smoking cessation programs 3. Tobacco habit
ISBN 0-471-24700-6
                                            LC 97-38826

"Based on the American Lung Association's smoking cessation program, this book coaches smokers through discovering their own personal motivations and obstacles to quitting, planning effective strategies to meet and conquer the temptation to pick up a cigarette, and tailoring a cessation program to individual lifestyles." Libr J

Peele, Stanton

7 tools to beat addiction. Three Rivers Press 2004 275p pa $14   **616.86**
1. Alcoholism 2. Drug abuse
ISBN 1-400-04873-7
                                            LC 2003-23765
"Well written and well researched, this is sure to be an essential text in the addiction field." Libr J

Includes bibliographical references

Weil, Andrew

From chocolate to morphine; everything you need to know about mind-altering drugs. [by] Andrew Weil and Winifred Rosen. Rev ed; Houghton Mifflin 2004 291p pa 14.95   **616.86**
1. Psychotropic drugs
ISBN 0-618-48379-9
                                            LC 2004-57677
"Because drug use (legal or illegal) is not condemned, this volume may be considered unorthodox by some. . . . Aimed at young people, their parents and teachers, this book offers an alternative way of looking at drug use." Libr J

Includes bibliographical references

West, James W.

The **Betty** Ford Center book of answers; help for those struggling with substance abuse and for the people who love them. foreword by Betty Ford. Pocket Bks. 1997 206p pa $16.95   **616.86**
1. Alcoholism 2. Drug abuse 3. Substance abuse
ISBN 0-671-00182-5
                                            LC 96-41485
"Chapters include straighforward information on how to identify an alcoholic, intervention, effects of substance abuse on the brain and other parts of the body, treatment, prevention, and relapse." Libr J

616.89   Mental disorders

Amen, Daniel

Change your brain, change your life; the breakthrough program for conquering anxiety, depression, obsessiveness, anger, and impulsiveness. Times Bks. 1998 337p il hardcover o.p. pa $15   **616.89**
1. Anger 2. Anxiety 3. Brain 4. Brain -- Pathophysiology 5. Depression (Psychology) 6. Mental illness 7. Mental illness -- Chemotherapy 8. Mental illness -- Physiological aspects 9. Neuropsychiatry -- Popular works
ISBN 0-8129-2998-5 pa
                                            LC 98-15043
Using brain imaging technology the author identifies which brain systems are associated with specific problems.

In addition to changes in diet the author advocates the use of fragrances, music, lighting, and cognitive exercises in combating certain negative behaviors.

Carter, Rosalynn

Helping someone with mental illness; a compassionate guide for families, friends, and caregivers. {by} Rosalynn Carter, with Susan K. Golant. Times Bks. 1998 348p hardcover o.p. pa $15   **616.89**

    1. Consumer education 2. Mental illness 3. Mental illness -- Popular works
    ISBN 0-8129-2898-9 pa

LC 97-39218

"The chapters of part 1 relate what spurred Carter's involvement with mental-health issues and profile families dealing with mental illness. . . . Part 2 sketches scientific and technological advances that are empowering treatment and homes in on understanding schizophrenia, depression, manic-depression, and anxiety disorders—the four basic kinds of mental illness. The third part discusses intervention, prevention, caregiving, and advocating in respect to mental illness." Booklist

    Includes bibliographical references

Duke, Patty

A **brilliant** madness; living with manic-depressive illness. {by} Patty Duke and Gloria Hochman. Bantam Bks. 1992 285p hardcover o.p. pa $7.99   **616.89**

    1. Manic-depressive illness
    ISBN 0-553-56072-7 pa

LC 92-5878

This work "alternates between the actress's first-person description of her experiences as a manic-depressive and Ms. Hochman's informative narrative about this sickness. . . . Ms. Duke is a comforting guide through the terror of mental illness, and Ms. Hochman lightens a weighty topic with interesting, animated writing." N Y Times Book Rev

    Includes bibliographical references

Engel, Jonathan

American therapy; the rise of psychotherapy in the United States. Gotham Books 2008 351p $27.50   **616.89**

    1. Psychotherapy 2. Psychotherapy -- United States -- History
    ISBN 978-1-59240-380-6; 1-59240-380-8

LC 2008-23517

Engel "does a thorough job of synopsizing the history of psychology in general, and studiously relates how psychoanalysis—a European-born oddity—took the United States by storm a century ago." Baltimore City Paper

    Includes bibliographical references

Freeman, Daniel

Paranoia; the twenty-first century fear. [by] Daniel Freeman and Jason Freeman. Oxford University Press 2008 189p il $19.95 **616.89**

    1. Delusions 2. Paranoia
    ISBN 978-0-19-923750-0; 0-19-923750-6

LC 2008-35850

The authors note that "that an unfounded or exaggerated distrust of others, once believed only to be a mark of severe mental illness, is actually commonly experienced by ordinary people and appears to be on the rise. Estimates suggest that 1 in 4 of us, or about a quarter of the population, is routinely plagued by paranoid thoughts, and Freeman blames the media's affinity for repeated, graphic, extreme reports of threats along with unprecedented levels of city dwelling." U. S. News & World Report

    Includes bibliographical references (p. 163-179)

Hewetson, Ann

The **stolen** child; aspects of autism and Asperger syndrome. foreword by Susan J. Moreno. Bergin & Garvey Pubs. 2002 240p $26.95   **616.89**

    1. Asperger's syndrome 2. Autism
    ISBN 0-89789-844-3

LC 2001-43015

"A strong introductory text. . . . Hewetson, the mother of a son with high-ability autism, carefully balances the different approaches and does not promote one treatment over another as the cure for all people with ASD." Libr J

    Includes bibliographical references

Hicks, James Whitney

★ **Fifty** signs of mental illness; a guide to understanding mental health. Yale University Press 2005 389p hardcover o.p. pa $17   **616.89**

    1. Abnormal psychology 2. Mental illness
    ISBN 0-300-10657-2; 0-300-11694-2 pa

LC 2004-21535

"A reservoir of useful knowledge, this belongs in almost every library serving real people." Libr J

Kahn, Ada P.

★ The **encyclopedia** of mental health; [by] Ada P. Kahn, Jan Fawcett. 3rd ed; Facts On File 2008 520p $75   **616.89**

    1. Mental health 2. Mental health -- Encyclopedias 3. Mental illness -- Encyclopedias 4. Psychiatry -- Encyclopedias 5. Reference books
    ISBN 978-0-8160-6454-0; 0-8160-6454-7

LC 2006-102540

This encyclopedia covers "all aspects of general mental health topics . . . [and includes] definitions of theories, syndromes, symptoms, treatments, and contemporary issues." Publisher's note

    Includes bibliographical references

Linde, Paul R.

Danger to self; on the front line with an ER psychiatrist. University of California Press 2010 253p $24.95   **616.89**

    1. College teachers 2. Crisis intervention (Mental health services) 3. Emergency medicine 4. Mental illness 5. Mental illness -- Diagnosis 6. Mental illness -- Treatment 7. Psychiatric emergencies 8. Psychiatrists
    ISBN 978-0-520-24984-4; 0-520-24984-4

LC 2009-06144

The author "relates the challenges, joys, and potential gut-wrenching errors of his work as an emergency room psychiatrist at a public hospital, who is encountering those on the margins of society in the midst of illness. Few of the many recent books on therapy, psychoactive medications, and American mental health services put human faces on their subjects as Linde does. He writes with grace, honesty, and humility about the psychiatrist's task of judging the mind and heart of another human being while remaining convinced that medicine can play a role in restoration and healing." Libr J

Includes bibliographical references

Morey, Bodie

The **family** intervention guide to mental illness; recognizing symptoms & getting treatment. [by] Bodie Morey, Kim T. Mueser. New Harbinger Publications 2007 227p pa $17.95   **616.89**

1. Mental illness
ISBN 978-1-57224-506-8; 1-5722-4506-9

LC 2007-13002

The authors "guide readers through a step-by-step process for helping a mentally afflicted loved one. Chapters begin with a 'fundamental step' ('Discuss the situation openly,' 'Get a correct diagnosis'), and end with a list of 'good steps' ('Familiarize yourself with the symptoms') and 'missteps' ('Thinking that it's none of your business') which give readers extra guidance. . . . Comprehensive, compassionate and rooted in solid research, this easy-to-read guidebook is suitable for any family in search of answers." Publ Wkly

Includes bibliographical references

Neugeboren, Jay

Transforming madness; new lives for people living with mental illness. University of California Press 2001 390p pa $16.95   **616.89**

1. Mental illness 2. Mentally ill
ISBN 0-520-22875-8

The author "provides a literate, lively guide, rich in history, biography, and economics as well as psychology and neurochemistry." Libr J

Includes bibliographical references

Noll, Richard

The **encyclopedia** of schizophrenia and other psychotic disorders; foreword by Leonard George. 3rd ed.; Facts on File 2007 xx, 409p $75   **616.89**

1. Reference books 2. Schizophrenia -- Encyclopedias
ISBN 0-8160-6405-9; 978-0-8160-6405-2

LC 2005-56749

"Biologically related schizophrenic disorders, genetics, antipsychotic drug treatments, and pathophysiology are a few of the topics explored in the more than 600 entries. . . . The language is clear, making this volume equally suitable for use by patients, scholars, and general readers. A solid addition for health collections." Booklist

Includes bibliographical references

Osborne, Lawrence

American normal; the hidden world of Asperger syndrome. Copernicus 2002 224p $27.50   **616.89**

1. Asperger's syndrome
ISBN 0-387-95307-8

LC 2002-73782

"Osborne uses his considerable journalistic talents to interview a number of well-known and not so well-known people diagnosed with an enigmatic disorder known as Asperger's Syndrome. . . . Recommended for readers at all levels." Choice

Includes bibliographical references

Park, Clara Claiborne

Exiting nirvana; a daughter's life with autism. foreword by Oliver Sacks. Little, Brown 2001 225p il $23.95; pa $14.95   **616.89**

1. Artists 2. Autism 3. Autism -- Patients -- United States 4. Folk artists 5. Painters 6. Parents of autistic children -- United States
ISBN 0-316-69117-8; 0-316-69124-0 pa

LC 00-33554

"A perceptive, detailed, and empathetic account not of autism but of the experience of autism. . . . A warm, level-headed, neither overly optimistic nor overly glorified book that proves very rewarding." Booklist

Includes bibliographical references

Phillips, Adam

Going sane; maps of happiness. Fourth Estate 2005 xxi, 199p $24.95   **616.89**

1. Mental health 2. Psychoanalysis
ISBN 0-00-715539-5

LC 2005-40063

The author's "interdisciplinary research, which relies on imaginative writings (e.g., Shakespeare) and traditional psychological theory, makes clear that a viable definition of sanity is surprisingly elusive. This concept is further developed through his exploration of how madness and 'badness' coexist in contemporary society; Freudian issues are raised in the context of sexual and money madness, and modern mental illnesses and disorders (autism, schizophrenia, and depression) are also examined. Phillips concludes with an original blueprint on how a 'sane' life might be constructed, including commentaries on sane parenting and dealing with conflict and personal desires. Though stronger on description and analysis than on prescriptive advice, this book is well argued and stunningly thought-provoking." Libr J

Porter, Roy

★ **Madness**; a brief history. Oxford Univ. Press 2002 241p il hardcover o.p. pa $12.95 **616.89**

1. Mental Disorders -- history 2. Mental illness 3. Mental illness -- History 4. Mentally ill -- Care -- History 5. Psychiatry 6. Psychiatry -- History
ISBN 0-19-280267-4 pa

LC 2001-52329

This is a study on the many ways madness has been perceived and misperceived from antiquity to modern times. The author "also discusses topical issues, including the relationship between lunacy and creativity, the drive to institutionalize, which peaked in the mid-20th century; the rise and demise of psychoanalysis; and the development of the antipsychiatry movement. This book combines the appeal of history as narrative with the intellectual stimulation derived from cogent analysis." Libr J

Includes bibliographical references

Rogers, Carl R.

On becoming a person; a therapist's view of psychotherapy. Houghton Mifflin 1961 420p hardcover o.p. pa $16 **616.89**

1. Psychotherapy

ISBN 0-395-75531-X pa

This collection begins with "two talks in which Dr. Rogers gives some biographical data and outlines his progress toward his concept of client-centered therapy; succeeding chapters express his views on helping others toward personal growth, the therapeutic process, his philosophy of the fully functioning person, the place of research in psychotherapy, its implications for living and the new discipline of behavioral sciences." Booklist

Includes bibliographical references

Scull, Andrew T.

Madhouse; a tragic tale of megalomania and modern medicine. [by] Andrew Scull. Yale University Press 2005 360p il $30 **616.89**

1. Hospital administrators 2. Psychiatrists 3. Psychiatry 4. Psychiatry -- United States -- History

ISBN 0-300-10729-3

LC 2004-28567

This book describes the once well-received psychiatric treatments of Dr. Henry Cotton, who, in the early 20th century, promoted the use of invasive surgery, including the removal of internal organs, as a treatment for mental illness.

"The shameful episodes described in these histories deserve our attention. The well-documented stories offer dramatic pictures of the cavalier attitudes adopted toward the mentally ill by professional psychiatry." Sci Books Films

Includes bibliographical references

Shorter, Edward

A history of psychiatry; from the era of the asylum to the age of Prozac. Wiley 1997 436p il hardcover o.p. pa $30 **616.89**

1. Psychiatry 2. Psychiatry -- History

ISBN 0-471-24531-3 pa

LC 96-15292

This "social history of 200 years of psychiatry in the U.S., Great Britain, France, and Germany is informative and at times lively. . . . Dealing ably with the major trends, Shorter does not fail to also illuminate such engaging and horrifying byways as the 'fever cure' and ice pick lobotomy." Booklist

Includes bibliographical references

Sichel, Deborah

Women's moods; what every woman must know about hormones, the brain, and emotional health. {by} Deborah Sichel and Jeanne Watson Driscoll. Morrow 1999 352p hardcover o.p. pa $14 **616.89**

1. Women -- Health and hygiene 2. Women -- Psychology

ISBN 0-380-72852-4 pa

LC 99-25412

"Drawing on their own personal experiences, the experiences of their patients, and their own research as well as that of others, the authors discuss why the unique brain chemistry of women and the sensitivity of the brain to female hormones make women more susceptible to mood disorders and anxiety problems. They outline the program they use with their patients, which includes some medications and a great deal of self-care." Libr J

Includes bibliographical references

Slater, Lauren

Prozac diary. Penguin Bks. 1999 203p pa $15 **616.89**

1. Fluoxetine 2. Mental illness 3. Psychologists 4. Psychotropic drugs

ISBN 0-14-026394-2; 978-0-14-026394-7

LC 97-35727

The author "was among the first patients to be given Prozac, and she has now been on it, almost without interruption, for ten years. She credits the drug with enabling her, after an incapacitating adolescence, not only to taste and see but to complete a doctorate; marry; and, as director of a clinic, be useful. But she also ponders what it means to one's sense of self to be more or less permanently under the influence of a personality (and libido) altering drug." New Yorker

Stone, Michael H.

Healing the mind; a history of psychiatry from antiquity to the present. Norton 1997 516p il $49 **616.89**

1. Psychiatry

ISBN 0-393-70222-7

LC 96-28209

The author "chronicles the persons, movements, and events that have contributed to modern psychiatry. Starting with accounts of aberrant behavior in religious texts, he traces the diagnosis and treatment of mental illness from ancient Greece to present times." Libr J

Includes bibliographical references

Whitaker, Robert

Anatomy of an epidemic; magic bullets, psychiatric drugs, and the astonishing rise of mental illness in America. Crown Publishers 2010 404p il $26 **616.89**

1. Drugs -- Prescribing 2. Mental illness 3. Mental illness -- Epidemiology 4. Mental illness -- United States 5. Psychiatry 6. Psychiatry -- United States -- History 7. Psychotropic drugs 8. Psychotropic drugs -- Effectiveness

ISBN 978-0-307-45241-2; 0-307-45241-7

LC 2009-49467

This is the "first book to investigate the long-term outcomes of patients treated with psychiatric drugs, and Whitaker finds that, overall, the drugs may be doing more harm than good. Adhering to studies published in prominent medical journals, he argues that, over time, patients with schizophrenia do better off medication than on it. Children who take stimulants for ADHD, he writes, are more likely to suffer from mania and bipolar disorder than those who go unmedicated. Intended to challenge the conventional wisdom about psychiatric drugs, 'Anatomy' is sure to provoke a hot-tempered response, especially from those inside the psychiatric community." Salon

Includes bibliographical references

★ **Mad** in America; bad science, bad medicine, and the enduring mistreatment of the mentally ill. Perseus Bks. 2002 334p $27; pa $17.50 **616.89**

    1. Mental illness   2. Psychiatric hospitals   3. Schizophrenia   4. Schizophrenia -- United States -- Treatment   5. Schizophrenia -- United States -- Treatment -- History

    ISBN 0-7382-0385-8; 0-7382-0799-3 pa

                  LC 2001-98251

The author "argues that mental asylums in the U.S. have been run largely as 'places of confinement—facilities that served to segregate the misfits from society—rather than as hospitals that provided medical care.' . . . Whitaker's . . . book will appeal to those interested in medical history, as well as anyone fascinated by Western culture's obsessive need to define and subdue the mentally ill." Publ Wkly

    Includes bibliographical references

Whybrow, Peter C.

    A **mood** apart; the thinker's guide to emotion and its disorders. Perennial Bks 1998 xx, 363p il map pa $15   **616.89**

    1. Personality 2. Personality disorders 3. Self

    ISBN 978-0-06-097740-5

"Seldom has the inner emotional landscape of melancholic depression, mania and manic-depressive illness been mapped with so much clarity, empathy and sensitivity." Publ Wkly

Yalom, Irvin D.

    The **gift** of therapy; an open letter to a new generation of therapists and their patients. HarperCollins Pubs. 2002 xxi, 263p $23.95; pa $12.95   **616.89**

    1. Psychotherapist and patient 2. Psychotherapy

    ISBN 0-06-621440-8; 0-06-093811-0 pa

                  LC 2001-39319

"Yalom offers what he calls a series of tips for therapists, emphasizing process rather than content. . . . His 85 brief advices, while certainly helpful to therapists and patients, may also help any thoughtful person seeking to improve relationships with others and self-understanding." Booklist

    Includes bibliographical references

★ The Complete guide to mental health for women; edited by Lauren Slater, Jessica Henderson Daniel, and Amy Banks. Beacon Press 2003 403p $45; pa $24.95   **616.89**

    1. Mental health 2. Women -- Health and hygiene

    ISBN 0-8070-2924-6; 0-8070-2925-4 pa

                  LC 2003-10436

"Drawing on the latest thinking in psychiatry and psychology, and written for women of diverse backgrounds, this . . . guide to women's mental health provides a comprehensive and readable overview to the psychological issues that concern women most." Univ Press Books 2004

    Includes bibliographical references

The Gale encyclopedia of mental health; [by] Laurie J. Fundukian and Jeffrey Wilson, editors. 2nd ed.; Thomson Gale 2008 2v il set $389   **616.89**

    1. Mental health -- Encyclopedias 2. Mental illness

-- Encyclopedias 3. Psychiatry -- Encyclopedias 4. Reference books

    ISBN 978-1-4144-2987-8

                  LC 2007-26137

This encyclopedia "offers accessible information on mental health for consumers and high school or undergraduate students. . . . The set contains over 400 entries and over 200 color photographs, tables, and illustrations. . . . The disorders covered are mostly recognized by the American Psychiatric Association, with entries for conditions and disorders usually including symptoms and demographics—a great asset for those needing statistics quickly." Libr J

    Includes bibliographical references

616.9   Other diseases

Ashby, Bonnie

    ★ The **encyclopedia** of infectious diseases; [by] Carol Turkington, Bonnie Lee Ashby. 3rd ed; Facts On File 2007 412p $75   **616.9**

    1. Communicable diseases 2. Communicable diseases -- Encyclopedias 3. Reference books

    ISBN 0-8160-6397-4; 978-0-8160-6397-0

                  LC 2006-13795

"The alphabetically arranged volume covers diseases, treatment options, and relevant organizations. . . . Information is provided for each disease and includes its cause, symptoms, treatment, and prevention. Major diseases that have had an impact on the world's population (tuberculosis, AIDS) are covered . . . and include a history. This feature makes the volume useful to researchers and students." Booklist [review of 2003 edition]

    Includes bibliographical references

Edlow, Jonathan A.

    Bull's-eye: unraveling the medical mystery of Lyme disease. Yale University Press 2003 285p il hardcover o.p. pa $17   **616.9**

    1. Lyme disease 2. Lyme disease -- History

    ISBN 0-300-09867-7; 0-300-10370-0 pa

                  LC 2002-154119

"This well-documented book is . . . as important for the light it sheds on the nature of scientific inquiry within the contemporary social and political context as it is for its information about Lyme disease." Booklist

    Includes bibliographical references

Glynn, Ian

    The **life** and death of smallpox; [by] Ian and Jenifer Glynn. Cambridge Univ. Press 2004 278p il $25   **616.9**

    1. Smallpox

    ISBN 0-521-84542-4; 978-0-521-84542-7

                  LC 2005-29712€

The authors "describe the history of the disease from the time of the ancient Egyptian pharaohs to the last natural case, which occurred in Somalia in 1977. . . . This book is thoroughly researched and eminently readable. Although several books have been written on the history of smallpox this is the definitive work on the subject." Choice

    Includes bibliographical references

Kahn, Ada P.

The **encyclopedia** of stress and stress-related diseases; foreword by Delbert H. Meyer. 2nd ed; Facts on File 2005 438p il $75   **616.9**
1. Reference books 2. Stress (Physiology) 3. Stress (Physiology) -- Encyclopedias 4. Stress (Psychology) 5. Stress (Psychology) -- Encyclopedias
ISBN 0-8160-5937-3; 978-0-8160-5937-9

LC 2005-43668

In addition to describing how to identify and manage stress this work explores causes and a variety of traditional and alternative methods of treatment.

This book "includes authoritative, up-to-date, and practical encyclopedic information on more than 800 entries . . . related to stress, mental health, and coping in a world in which as many as '80 percent of visits to physicians' offices may result from stress in patients' lives.'" Libr J

Includes bibliographical references

Koplow, David A.

Smallpox: the fight to eradicate a global scourge. University of Calif. Press 2003 265p $30; pa $14.95   **616.9**
1. Smallpox 2. Smallpox -- Cultures and culture media 3. Smallpox -- Epidemiology 4. Smallpox -- Prevention
ISBN 0-520-23732-3; 0-520-24220-3 pa

LC 2002-5539

The author "provides a brief overview of the disease's history, its basic biology, biodiversity concerns, and the role of the World Health Organization in the virus's eradication. He concludes his timely book with a lengthy consideration of the pros and cons of eliminating the smallpox stockpiles." Libr J

Includes bibliographical references

Marshall, Ruth

No time to lose; a life in pursuit of deadly viruses. Peter Piot with Ruth Marshall. W.W. Norton & Co. 2012 387 p.   **616.9**
1. Acquired Immunodeficiency Syndrome -- history -- Belgium 2. Acquired Immunodeficiency Syndrome -- history -- England 3. Hemorrhagic Fever, Ebola -- history -- Belgium 4. Hemorrhagic Fever, Ebola -- history -- England 5. History, 20th Century -- Belgium 6. History, 20th Century -- England 7. History, 21st Century -- Belgium 8. History, 21st Century -- England 9. International Cooperation -- Belgium -- Autobiography 10. International Cooperation -- England -- Autobiography 11. Virology -- Belgium -- Autobiography 12. Virology -- England -- Autobiography
ISBN 039306316X; 9780393063165

LC 2012011911

This autobiographical book by medical scientist Peter Piot describes the authors career, from identifying the Ebola virus to pioneering AIDS research and policy. . . . In the 1970s, as a young man, Piot was sent to Central Africa as part of a team tasked with identifying a grisly new virus. Crossing into the quarantine zone on the most dangerous missions, he studied local customs to determine how this disease—the Ebola virus—was spreading. Later, Piot found himself in the field again when another mysterious epidemic broke out: AIDS. He traveled throughout Africa, leading the first international AIDS initiatives there. Then, as founder and director of UNAIDS, he negotiated policies with leaders from Fidel Castro to Thabo Mbeki and helped turn the tide of the epidemic. (Publishers note)

McKenna, Maryn

Superbug; the fatal menace of MRSA. Free Press 2010 271p $26 **616.9**
1. Methicillin-Resistant Staphylococcus aureus
ISBN 978-1-4165-5727-2; 1-4165-5727-X

LC 2009-37793

"McKenna suggests that vaccines might be the answer, but it seems a distant hope — and too late for the patients whose heartbreaking stories she tells. A meticulously researched, frightening report on a deadly pathogen." Kirkus

Includes bibliographical references

Preston, Richard

The **demon** in the freezer; a true story. Random House 2002 240p hardcover o.p. pa $7.99   **616.9**
1. Biological warfare 2. Smallpox 3. Terrorism
ISBN 0-375-50856-2; 0-345-46663-2 pa

The author explains "the chemical properties of the smallpox virus; how a single infected person . . . can set off an epidemic; and what this horrendous disease can be like. . . . We learn how the disease was eliminated by an international vaccination campaign in the 1970's; why there are reasons to believe that the Soviet Union grew staggering quantities of the virus, allegedly in part to arm intercontinental missiles; and how the virus might now be used by others as a 'strategic weapon.'" N Y Times Book Rev

Vanderhoof-Forschner, Karen

Everything you need to know about Lyme disease and other tick-borne disorders; foreword by Willy Burgdorfer. 2nd ed; Wiley 2003 270p il pa $15.95   **616.9**
1. Lyme disease 2. Lyme disease -- Treatment 3. Lyme disease -- United States 4. Ticks
ISBN 0-471-40793-3

LC 2003-45066

The author "discusses the status of Lyme disease as a public health threat; the nature and characteristics of ticks; the history of Lyme disease; its symptoms, diagnosis, and treatment; and the search for vaccines. . . . The author's writing is conversational and clear even when discussing complex topics, and her appendixes are outstanding." Libr J

Includes bibliographical references

Weintraub, Pamela

Cure unknown; inside the Lyme epidemic. St. Martin's Press 2008 xxiv, 408p $27.95   **616.9**
1. Lyme disease
ISBN 978-0-312-37812-7; 0-312-37812-2

LC 2008-7816

The author "deftly weaves top-notch research and reporting on this malevolent infection . . . with the personal narrative of a family's encounters with ignorance and bias while fighting a tenacious, disabling illness. The result is a compelling read that is also important journalism." Discover

Includes bibliographic references

Wolfe, Nathan

The **viral** storm; the dawn of a new pandemic age. Times Books 2011 304p il map $26; ebook $12.99 **616.9**

1. Diseases 2. Evolution 3. Viruses

ISBN 978-0-8050-9194-6; 978-1-4299-7359-5 ebook

LC 2011011321

The author presents "an eloquent argument for why we need better ways to predict and thus prevent major disease outbreaks. . . . Wolfe makes clear that most bugs are harmless; some are even helpful. But his wide experience confronting killer diseases in Africa and Asia makes for important, graphic reading and underscores his passion for prevention." Kirkus

Environmental health sourcebook; basic consumer health information about the environment and its effects on human health . . . 3rd ed.; Omnigraphics 2010 667p $85 **616.9**

1. Environmental health 2. Environmentally induced diseases 3. Reference books 4. Toxicology

ISBN 978-0-7808-1078-5

LC 2009-44771

"Chapters begin with definitions of each danger, their physiological impact, and accepted treatments or permissible exposure amounts. Following this are Q&A segments, where relevant questions are posed in bold and clearly answered with supporting statistics. . . . Highly recommended for public libraries." Libr J

Includes bibliographical references

616.95   Sexually transmitted diseases, zoonoses

Hayden, Deborah

Pox: genius, madness, and the mysteries of syphilis. Basic Bks. 2003 xx, 379p il hardcover o.p. pa $19.95 **616.95**

1. Syphilis

ISBN 0-465-02881-0 pa

LC 2002-15847

"A fascinating account . . . any book that combines genius, madness, sex, and disease is bound to find an audience." Libr J

Includes bibliographical references

Marr, Lisa

★ **Sexually** transmitted diseases; a physician tells you what you need to know. 2nd ed.; Johns Hopkins Univ. Press 2007 371p il $45; pa $18.95 **616.95**

1. Sexually transmitted diseases

ISBN 978-0-8018-8658-4; 0-8018-8658-9; 978-0-8018-8659-1 pa; 0-8018-8659-7 pa

LC 2006-100443

The author "begins with basic anatomy, symptoms, and the components of a medical examination for men and women. She then offers important advice about communications with sex partners and safe sex. The second part of her book discusses specific diseases and their symptoms, diagnosis, and treatment." Libr J

Includes bibliographical references

616.97   Diseases of immune system

Baron-Faust, Rita

The **autoimmune** connection; essential information for women on diagnosis, treatment and getting on with your life. [by] Rita Baron-Faust, Jill M. Buyon. McGraw-Hill 2004 411p il pa $16.95 **616.97**

1. Immune system

ISBN 0-07-143315-5; 978-0-07-143315-0

This volume "covers some 20 diseases, including autoimmune hepatitis, myasthenia gravis, antiphospholipid antibody syndrome, vasculitis, and premature ovarian failure. It also addresses in a single chapter some disorders that often 'travel' with autoimmune diseases (e.g., chronic fatigue syndrome, fibromyalgia, and endometriosis), which can further downgrade a patient's quality of life. . . . The up-to-date information provided here will be welcome in most women's health collections." Libr J

Includes bibliographical references

Cassell, Dana K.

The **encyclopedia** of autoimmune diseases; {by} Dana Cassell, Noel Rose. Facts on File 2002 364p il $71.50 **616.97**

1. Autoimmune diseases -- Encyclopedias 2. Reference books

ISBN 0-8160-4340-X

LC 2002-2029

This encyclopedia "includes more than 300 cross-referenced entries on immunity and autoimmunity. It provides information on autoimmune diseases, their prevalence, levels of severity, demographics, suspected causes, clinical features, possible complications, and treatments." Am Ref Books Annu, 2004

Includes bibliographical references

Cichocki, Mark

Living with HIV; a patient's guide. McFarland & Co. 2009 249p pa $35 **616.97**

1. AIDS (Disease) 2. Health self-care

ISBN 978-0-7864-3921-8; 0-7864-3921-1

LC 2009-8041

"Newly diagnosed patients will find this an excellent book for learning more about HIV, and others will find it a great reference work." Libr J

Includes bibliographical references

Gallo, Robert C.

Virus hunting; AIDS, cancer, and the human retrovirus: a story of scientific discovery. Basic Bks. 1991 352p hardcover o.p. pa $17.50 **616.97**

1. AIDS (Disease) 2. Cancer 3. Medicine -- Research

ISBN 0-465-09815-0 pa

LC 90-55600

The author describes his biomedical research of the cancer-causing retrovirus, how it led to the discovery of the AIDS virus, and the political and ethical controversies surrounding AIDS research

Grmek, Mirko D.

★ **History** of AIDS; emergence and origin of a modern pandemic. translated by Russell C. Maulitz and Jacalyn Duffin. Princeton Univ. Press 1990 279p hardcover o.p. pa $30 **616.97**
    1. AIDS (Disease)
    ISBN 0-691-02477-4 pa

                            LC 90-32514

In this "medical and social history of the disease, Dr. Grmek . . . speculates about the prehistory of AIDS, before its seemingly sudden appearance from nowhere in 1981. He argues that while today's runaway epidemic is a new phenomenon, the viruses that cause AIDS have infected people for many decades, if not for centuries." NY Times Book Rev
    Includes bibliographical references

Haynes, Antony J.

The **food** intolerance bible; a nutritionist's plan to beat food cravings, fatigue, mood swings, celiac disease, headaches, IBS, and deal with food allergies. [by] Antony J. Haynes, Antoinette Savill. Conari Press 2008 332p il pa $19.95 **616.97**
    1. Diet therapy 2. Food allergy
    ISBN 978-1-57324-359-9

The authors "explain factors that contribute to food intolerance and sensitivity. An appendix covers many tests available for diagnosing food intolerances and allergies." Libr J
    Includes bibliographical references

Lipkowitz, Myron

Encyclopedia of allergies; [by] Myron A. Lipkowitz, Tova Navarra. 2nd ed; Facts on File 2001 340p $65; pa $19.95 **616.97**
    1. Allergy -- Encyclopedias 2. Reference books
    ISBN 0-8160-4404-X; 0-8160-4405-8 pa

                            LC 00-49490

This guide to the symptoms and treatments of a variety of allergies includes over 1,000 entries that provide information on medications, occupational and environmental allergies, inherited allergies, and antihistamines, etc.

Nakazawa, Donna Jackson

The **autoimmune** epidemic; bodies gone haywire in a world out of balance and the cutting edge science that promises hope. Simon & Schuster 2008 328p $25 **616.97**
    1. Autoimmune diseases
    ISBN 978-0-7432-7775-4; 0-7432-7775-9

                        LC 2007-48306

The author provides information on autoimmune diseases "drawing on personal experience, extensive research, and interviews with medical personnel to look at what autoimmune diseases are, why they happen, and what may trigger them. Special attention is paid to the overwhelming number of seemingly harmless triggers that surround all of us every day. . . . Nakazawa articulates highly complicated medical processes in extremely comprehensible language." Libr J
    Includes bibliographical references

Null, Gary

AIDS: a second opinion. Seven Stories Press 2001 750p $34.95 **616.97**
    1. AIDS (Disease) 2. AZT (Drug) 3. HIV (Viruses) 4. Therapeutics, Physiological
    ISBN 1-58322-062-3

                        LC 00-51013

The author "argues that the AIDS drama has exposed problematic issues having to do with the functioning of U.S. medical institutions. . . . The book dissects the claims of the AZT and drug-cocktail approach to treating AIDS and offers a trilogy of treatment strategies based on wide views of how to enhance the immune system and improve overall functioning." Publisher's note
    Includes bibliographical references

Pescatore, Fred

The **allergy** and asthma cure; a complete 8-step nutritional program. Wiley 2003 251p $24.95; pa $15.95 **616.97**
    1. Allergy 2. Allergy -- Alternative treatment 3. Asthma 4. Asthma -- Alternative treatment 5. Asthma -- Diet therapy 6. Diet therapy 7. Food allergy 8. Food allergy -- Diet therapy
    ISBN 0-471-21468-X; 0-470-27541-3 pa
                        LC 2002-14024

Rumpf, Teri P.

The **Sjogren's** syndrome survival guide; [by] Teri P. Rumpf, Katherine Morland Hammitt. New Harbinger Publs. 2003 234p pa $15.95 **616.97**
    1. Sjogren's syndrome 2. Sjogren's syndrome -- Treatment
    ISBN 1-57224-356-2

This discusses Sjogren's syndrome, the most prevalent autoimmune disorder in the U.S., and includes medical information, methods of treatment, and advice on how to cope with the disorder.

Stratton, Stephen E.

The **encyclopedia** of HIV and AIDS; [by] Sarah Barbara Watstein, Stephen E. Stratton; foreword by Evelyn J. Fisher. 2nd ed; Facts on File 2003 660p **616.97**
    1. AIDS (Disease) -- Dictionaries 2. Reference books
    ISBN 0816048088

                        LC 2002-35220

"The coverage is . . . broad and the language is pitched for the intended audience of nonspecialists . . . vastly expanded and brought up to date. . . . Recommended." Choice
    Includes bibliographical references

Walsh, William E.

★ **Food** allergies; the complete guide to understanding and relieving your food allergies. Wiley 2000 286p pa $16.95 **616.97**
    1. Allergy 2. Food allergy
    ISBN 0-471-38268-X

                        LC 00-24608

"While providing an overview of the physiology and types of food allergies, Walsh concentrates on what he terms

'MALS' (monosodium glutamate, acidic foods, low-calorie sweeteners, and refined sugar), the most common allergens identified in his patients. He lists MALS foods, provides a sample elimination diet, and includes information on common fast-food restaurant choices." Libr J

Includes bibliographical references

Wood, Robert A.

★ **Food** allergies for dummies; by Robert A. Wood with Joe Kraynak. Wiley 2007 xxii, 358p il pa $19.99   **616.97**
1. Food allergy
ISBN 978-0-470-09584-3

LC 2007-920012

This guide covers such topics as how to identify food that triggers allergic reactions, how to care for a child who has food allergies, the symptoms of an allergic reaction, and travelling and eating out with food allergies.

616.99 Tumors and miscellaneous communicable diseases

Adrouny, A. Richard

Understanding colon cancer. University Press of Miss. 2002 146p il hardcover o.p. pa $12 **616.99**
1. Cancer 2. Colon (Anatomy) 3. Colon (Anatomy) -- Cancer -- Popular works
ISBN 1-57806-473-2 pa

LC 2002-788

The author "describes the anatomy and physiology of the colon. A detailed chapter makes clear the stages of the disease and how they affect the prognosis. Adrouny describes various surgical procedures, their results, and possible complications. . . . The understandable, thorough book concludes with a resources list and a glossary." Booklist

Includes bibliographical references

American Cancer Society

American Cancer Society's Guide to complementary and alternative cancer methods. American Cancer Soc. 2000 438p pa $24.95   **616.99**
1. Alternative medicine 2. Cancer
ISBN 0-944235-29-8; 0-944235-24-7 pa

LC 00-40596

"The first part of the book defines complementary and alternative methods and commonly used terms; it also explains how to evaluate treatment and discusses types of research, safety, and usage guidelines. The second section covers a wide range of treatment methodologies, arranged into five categories: Mind, Body, and Spirit; Manual Healing and Physical Touch; Herb, Vitamin, and Mineral; Diet and Nutrition; and Pharmacological and Biological Treatment." Libr J

Includes bibliographical references

★ **American** Cancer Society's complete guide to prostate cancer; edited by David G. Bostwick ...

[et al.] American Cancer Society, Health Promotion 2005 xxii, 394p il pa $19.95   **616.99**
1. Cancer 2. Prostate 3. Prostate gland -- Cancer
ISBN 0-944235-54-9

LC 2004-1540?

This "is an accessible and comprehensive survey that describes PCa and explains who is at risk, backing up its discussions with statistics." Libr J

Includes bibliographical references

Arnot, Bob

The **breast** health cookbook; fast and simple recipes to reduce the risk of cancer. recipes and menu by Barbara Sutherland and Rita Mitchell. Little Brown 2001 262p hardcover o.p. pa $14.95 **616.99**
1. Breast cancer 2. Cancer -- Diet therapy
ISBN 0-316-05133-0; 0-316-09528-1 pa

LC 00-046942

"In this companion volume to . . . The Breast Cancer Prevention Diet, Arnot offers an array of recipes featuring the foods most likely to help people avoid breast cancer (and prostate cancer as well). With more than 150 recipes from nutritionists Rita Mitchell and Barbara Sutherland, the book is structured around ethnic categories of diet Asian New American, Mediterranean along with suggested meals Recipes are provided for main courses, sandwiches, soups desserts and more. The recipes frequently involve soy products, which Arnot believes are key for preventing cancer. Publ Wkly

Bristow, Robert E.

A **guide** to survivorship for women with ovarian cancer; [by] F.J. Montz, Robert E. Bristow with assistance from Paula J. Anastasia. Johns Hopkins University Press 2005 209p $39.95; pa $15.95 **616.99**
1. Ovaries -- Cancer
ISBN 0-8018-8090-4; 0-8018-8091-2 pa

LC 2004-1961

The authors offer "information on diagnosis and treatment, including chemotherapy, surgery, radiation therapy, pain management, and alternative/complementary options . . . This important book should be included in all consumer health collections, as well as purchased by women affected by the disease." Libr J

Davis, Devra

The **secret** history of the war on cancer [by] Devra Davis. Basic Books 2007 505p il $27.95   **616.99**
1. Cancer 2. Cancer -- Treatment 3. Environmental health 4. Public health
ISBN 978-0-465-01566-5; 0-465-01566-2

This book argues that the so-called war on cancer focuses "on cancer treatment rather than prevention." (N Y Times (Late N Y Ed))

The author "reveals the serious risks posed by the many environmental carcinogens we're exposed to and the huge effort to suppress this crucial information." Booklist

Includes bibliographical references

Goodwin, Scott C.

What your doctor may not tell you about fibroids; new techniques and therapies--including break-through alternatives to hysterectomy. {by} Scott C. Goodwin, Michael Broder, and David Drum; foreword by Carla Dionne. Warner Books 2003 xxiv, 320p pa $14.95   **616.99**

1. Uterine fibroids

ISBN 0-446-67853-8

This book "discusses how fibroids grow, the diagnostic tests used to distinguish them from other conditions, and major symptoms. The roles of diet, exercise, stress reduction, and alternative treatments such as homeopathy and acupuncture are also covered. The book's greatest strength lies in the final chapters, which explain uterine fibroid embolization, myomectomy, and new alternative treatments, both invasive and drug-based." Libr J

Includes bibliographical references

Gordon, James Samuel

Comprehensive cancer care; integrating alternative, complementary and conventional therapies; the complete guide. {by} James Gordon and Sharon Curtin. Perseus Bks. 2000 hardcover o.p. pa $18.50   **616.99**

1. Cancer

ISBN 0-7382-0486-2 pa

"Based on a series of medical conferences exploring new approaches to cancer, this guide discusses a wide variety of cancer-fighting modalities. Throughout . . . {the authors} encourage readers to consider unfamiliar ideas, form effective patient/doctor partnerships and adopt empowered, informed patient attitudes." Publ Wkly

Gubar, Susan

Memoir of a debulked woman; enduring ovarian cancer. Susan Gubar. W.W. Norton & Co. 2012 288 p.   **616.99**

1. Cancer -- Psychological aspects 2. Cancer -- Surgery -- Complications 3. Memoirs 4. Ovaries -- Cancer -- Diagnosis 5. Ovaries -- Cancer -- Patients 6. Ovaries -- Cancer -- Patients -- United States -- Biography 7. Ovaries -- Cancer -- Treatment

ISBN 9780393073256

LC 2011053073

This book presents an account of the author's ovarian cancer treatment and a staunch protest against the state of contemporary approaches to the disease. In telling her personal story, feminist scholar Gubar . . . remains the academic, looking for understanding not just in the medical literature but also in Frida Kahlo's art, Margaret Edson's drama Wit, Barbara Creaturo's memoir Courage and other women's writings . . . . A brief . . . chapter on ovaries and how they have been regarded throughout history precedes her personal account. For her, the treatment began with debulking . . . followed by rounds of debilitating chemotherapy. The surgery launched a cascade of intestinal disasters, including perforation, abscesses, loss of bowel control and an ileostomy. (Kirkus)

Harpham, Wendy Schlessel

Diagnosis, cancer; your guide to the first months of healthy survivorship. illustrations by Ann Bliss Pilcher. Expanded and updated ed; W.W. Norton 2003 xxiii, 262p il pa $14.95   **616.99**

1. Cancer

ISBN 0-393-32460-5; 978-0-393-32460-0

LC 2002-156597

The author discusses current developments in cancer diagnosis and treatments for the newly diagnosed patient, with advice on decision making and emotional and practical problems

Henschke, Claudia I.

Lung cancer; myths, facts, choices--and hope. {by} Claudia I. Henschke, and Peggy McCarthy, with Sarah Wernick. Norton 2002 389p il $27.95; pa $16.95   **616.99**

1. Adaptation, Psychological 2. Lung Neoplasms -- etiology 3. Lung Neoplasms -- therapy 4. Lung cancer 5. Lungs -- Cancer -- Popular works 6. Quality of Life 7. Risk Factors

ISBN 0-393-04154-9; 0-393-32498-2 pa

LC 2002-513

The authors present a "guide to the basics of how lung cancer develops, risk factors, diagnosis, treatment options, and living well with lung cancer. . . . Treatment modalities detailed here include surgery, chemotherapy, and radiation, with additional chapters on alternative therapies such as acupuncture for pain and getting access to the latest treatment through clinical trials." Libr J

Hirshaut, Yashar

★ **Breast** cancer; the complete guide. [by] Yashar Hirshaut and Peter I. Pressman. 5th ed.; Bantam Books 2008 420p il pa $17   **616.99**

1. Breast cancer

ISBN 978-0-553-38591-5

LC 2008-32566

This guide gives "information on everything from the first suspicion, through diagnosis and treatments, to follow-up care and recurrence. . . . From selecting the best doctor to describing procedures and treatments, the authors answer all possible questions in a calm, rational manner." Libr J

Includes bibliographical references

Lerner, Barron H.

The **breast** cancer wars; hope, fear, and the pursuit of a cure in twentieth century America. Oxford Univ. Press 2001 383p il hardcover o.p. pa $16.95   **616.99**

1. Breast -- Cancer -- United States -- History -- 20th century 2. Breast cancer

ISBN 0-19-514261-6; 0-19-516106-8 pa

LC 00-63691

This is an account of the development of breast cancer treatments in the United States from the nineteenth-century to the present.

"Lerner's book is essential for women's studies and history of medicine collections, but no public or academic library could go wrong in adding it to its collection." Libr J

Includes bibliographical references

Link, John

The **breast** cancer survival manual; a step-by-step guide for the woman with newly diagnosed breast cancer. 4th ed.; H. Holt 2007 237p il pa $16 **616.99**

1. Breast cancer

ISBN 978-0-8050-8234-0; 0-8050-8234-4

LC 2006-51596

This book offers advice on how to get a second opinion, how to work with doctors, exploring different treatment options, and considering genetic testing.

Mukherjee, Siddhartha

★ The **emperor** of all maladies. Scribner 2010 571p il $30; ebook $14.99 **616.99**

1. Cancer 2. Cancer -- History

ISBN 978-1-4391-0795-9; 1-4391-0795-5; 978-1-4391-8171-3 ebook; 1-4391-8171-3 ebook

LC 2010-24114

The author explores how cancer has been perceived throughout history.

"Mukherjee's formidable intelligence and compassion produce a stunning account of the effort to disrobe the 'emperor of maladies.'" Publ Wkly

Includes bibliographical references

Olson, James Stuart

Bathsheba's breast; women, cancer, and history. by James S. Olson. Johns Hopkins Univ. Press 2002 302p $24.95; pa $16.95 **616.99**

1. Breast -- Cancer -- History 2. Breast cancer

ISBN 0-8018-6936-6; 0-8018-8064-5 pa

LC 2001-6265

"Olson examines the evolution of cancer research, the politics and economics of the disease, the gender dynamics of female patients and male physicians, and the rise of patient activism. The book chronicles advances in breast-cancer diagnosis and treatment and the uncertainty that women must face while making difficult choices." Libr J

Includes bibliographical references

Patt, Richard B.

★ The **complete** guide to relieving cancer pain and suffering; {by} Richard B. Patt, Susan S. Lang. rev and expanded ed; Oxford University Press 2004 446p il $30 **616.99**

1. Cancer 2. Pain

ISBN 0-19-513501-6

LC 2003-17317

The authors cover "cancer pain management, from pain undermanagement and the quality-of-life benefits of properly managed pain to types and causes of cancer pain, pain assessment, and medications. Also addressed are high-tech interventions, such as implantable pumps and nerve blocks; nondrug approaches, including relaxation and biofeedback;

the special problems of pain in children, teens, and the elderly; psychological aspects; and comfort to the dying." Libr J

Includes bibliographical references

Schwartz, Anna

Cancer fitness; exercise programs for cancer patients and survivors. {by} Anna L. Schwartz. Simon & Schuster 2004 283p il pa $13 **616.99**

1. Cancer 2. Exercise

ISBN 0-7432-3801-X

LC 2004-4534

This guide "details the physical and mental benefit of exercise before, during, and after cancer. Following review of the science behind her book (including selecte references), . . . {the author} explains how and when to star exercising and presents examples of safe and effective aero bic and strength-building exercises designed for both me and women, young and old. . . . This unique guide is highl recommended for all public, consumer health, and nursin collections." Libr J

Scott, Walter J.

Lung cancer; a guide to diagnosis and treatment Addicus Bks. 2000 156p il pa $14.95 **616.99**

1. Lung cancer

ISBN 1-886039-43-7

LC 00-802

Scott "explains how the lungs work, the different type of lung cancer, diagnosis, treatment, and end-of-life care. A appendix contains a list of chemotherapy agents, a resourc list, and a glossary." Libr J

Servan-Schreiber, David

Anticancer; a new way of life. Viking 2008 258p $25.95 **616.99**

1. Alternative medicine 2. Brain -- Cancer -- Patient 3. Cancer 4. Cancer -- Adjuvant treatment 5. Cancer - Alternative treatment 6. Cancer -- Prevention 7. Colleg teachers 8. Integrative medicine 9. Neuroscientists 10 Psychiatrists

ISBN 978-0-670-02034-8

LC 2008-1572

"Servan-Schreiber's book is as uplifting as it is informa tive." Libr J

Includes bibliographical references (p. 273-293)

Silver, Julie K.

After cancer treatment; heal faster, better, stron ger. Johns Hopkins University Press 2006 269 $45; pa $16.95 **616.99**

1. Cancer

ISBN 0-8018-8437-3; 978-0-8018-8437-5; 0-8018-8438-1 pa; 978-0-8018-8438-2 pa

LC 2005-3397

This book is "a hands-on guide to survival issues: ex ercise, diet, fatigue, mental health, spirituality, and how t seek assistance from both Western and alternative medicin Helpful lists (e.g., symptoms of grief vs. symptoms of de pression, problems that cancer survivors may encounter wit exercise) and bibliographies at the end of each chapter wi

assist readers in exploring their own survivorship issues."
Libr J

Includes bibliographical references

Silver, Marc

Breast cancer husband; how to help your wife
(and yourself) through diagnosis, treatment, and beyond. foreword by Frederick P. Smith. Rodale 2004
319p pa $14.95   **616.99**

1. Breast -- Cancer -- Patients -- Family relationships 2.
Breast -- Cancer -- Popular works 3. Breast -- Cancer
-- Psychological aspects 4. Breast cancer 5. Caregivers
6. Husbands
ISBN 1-579-54833-4

LC 2004-7914

"Silver's prose is funny, tender, and filled with rock-
solid advice." Libr J

Smith, Claire Bidwell

The **rules** of inheritance; a memoir. Claire
Bidwell Smith. Hudson Street Press 2012 298
p.   **616.99**

1. Bereavement -- Psychological aspects 2. Children of
cancer patients -- United States -- Biography 3. Daughters
-- United States -- Biography 4. Psychotherapists --
United States -- Biography 5. Women psychotherapists
-- United States -- Biography
ISBN 1594630887; 9781594630880

LC 2011025136

This memoir by Claire Bidwell Smith describes a young
woman who loses her family but finds herself in the process.
. . . Smith is just fourteen years old when both of her charismatic parents are diagnosed with cancer. With an impatience
typical of youth, Claire throws herself at anything she thinks
might help her cope with the weight of this harsh reality:
boys, alcohol, traveling, and the anonymity of cities like
New York and Los Angeles. By the time she is twenty-five
years old they are both gone and Claire is very much alone
in the world. (Publishers note)

Torrey, E. Fuller

Surviving prostate cancer; what you need to
know to make informed decisions. illustrations by
Carlton Stoiber. Yale University Press 2006 280p il
$25; pa $17   **616.99**

1. Cancer 2. Prostate 3. Prostate gland -- Cancer
ISBN 0-300-11640-3; 0-300-12607-7 pa

In this guide, the author "describes his own medical and
personal experiences while offering detailed explanations of
diagnostic and staging procedures, treatment options, potential complications, recurrence, risk factors, possible causes,
and other essential topics backed with numerous references
to the professional literature." Libr J

Includes bibliographical references

Turkington, Carol

★ The **encyclopedia** of breast cancer; [by] Carol Turkington, Karen Krag. Facts on File 2004 308p
$75   **616.99**

1. Breast cancer -- Encyclopedias 2. Reference books
ISBN 0-8160-5028-7

LC 2003-49533

"Few libraries will want to be without this all-in-one volume for the layperson. . . . Information is current, with several 2004 studies cited in the text and hundreds of journal articles from 1993 to 2003 listed in the bibliography." Booklist

The **encyclopedia** of cancer; [by] Carol Turkington, William LiPera. Facts on File 2005 448p
$75   **616.99**

1. Cancer -- Encyclopedias 2. Reference books
ISBN 0-8160-5029-5

LC 2004-43444

"The encyclopedia covers subjects ranging from adeno-
carcinoma to melanoma to Wilms' tumor. It includes such
cancer-related subjects as laetrile and lasers. . . . It also includes current national and global statistics, gender differences, and promising research. . . . This jargon-free, comprehensive encyclopedia provides essential information to help
patients and their families better understand the disease and
deal with the various shocks associated with cancer." Choice

Includes bibliographical references

The **encyclopedia** of men's reproductive cancer;
[by] Carol Turkington, Charles R. Pound. Facts on
File 2004 304p $75   **616.99**

1. Cancer -- Encyclopedias 2. Men -- Health and
hygiene 3. Reference books 4. Reproductive system
ISBN 0-8160-5030-9

LC 2004-10241

"This book is well organized and provides reliable general information." Booklist

Includes bibliographical references

The **encyclopedia** of women's reproductive cancer; [by] Carol Turkington, Mitchell Edelson. Facts
on File 2005 306p $75   **616.99**

1. Cancer -- Encyclopedias 2. Reference books 3.
Reproductive system 4. Women -- Health and hygiene
ISBN 0-8160-5031-7

LC 2004-43253

"More than 400 . . . entries discuss ovarian cancer, fal-
lopian tube cancer, uterine cancer, and endometrial cancer,
among others, as well as statistics, prevention, symptoms,
causes, treatments, and much more." Publisher's note

Includes bibliographical references

Weiss, Marisa C.

Living well beyond breast cancer; a survivor's
guide for when treatment ends and the rest of your
life begins. [by] Marisa C. Weiss, Ellen Weiss. Fully updated 2nd ed.; Rivers Press 2010 511p pa
$20   **616.99**

1. Adjustment (Psychology) 2. Breast cancer
ISBN 978-0-307-46022-6

LC 2009-20648

"In 23 chapters within five major categories (e.g., 'Treatment Over, on with Your Life' and 'Additional Care Beyond Treatment'), the authors . . . [discuss] the post-breast cancer landscape with their take on bone health, sexual matters, and the ever-present fear of another diagnosis, among other topics. . . . This book's straightforward presentation will help readers gain control over these often scary concepts." Libr J

Wheelwright, Jeff

The **wandering** gene and the Indian princess; Jeff Wheelwright. W.W. Norton & Co. 2012 304p　　　　　　　　　　　　　**616.99**
1. Breast Neoplasms -- genetics 2. Ethnic Groups -- genetics 3. Genes, BRCA1 4. Genetic Predisposition to Disease 5. History of Medicine 6. Religion
ISBN 9780393081916

LC 2011030178

This book tells the story of a "vibrant young Hispano woman, Shonnie Medina, [who] inherits a breast-cancer mutation known as BRCA1.185delAG. It is a genetic variant characteristic of Jews. The Medinas knew they were descended from Native Americans and Spanish Catholics, but they did not know that they had Jewish ancestry as well. The mutation most likely sprang from Sephardic Jews hounded by the Spanish Inquisition. The discovery of the gene leads to a fascinating investigation of cultural history and modern genetics by Dr. Harry Ostrer and other experts on the DNA of Jewish populations. Set in the isolated San Luis Valley of Colorado, this . . . book tells of the Medina family's five-hundred-year passage from medieval Spain to the American Southwest and of their surprising conversion from Catholicism to the Jehovah's Witnesses in the 1980s." (Publisher's note)

Breast cancer; beyond convention: the world's foremost authorities on complementary and alternative medicine offer advice on healing. edited by Mary Tagliaferri, Isaac Cohen, and Debu Tripathy. Atria Bks. 2002 478p il hardcover o.p. pa $16　　　　　　　　　　　　　**616.99**
1. Alternative medicine 2. Breast -- Cancer -- Alternative treatment 3. Breast -- Cancer -- Popular works 4. Breast cancer
ISBN 0-7434-1011-4; 0-7434-1012-2 pa

LC 2002-16930

This collection of essays "is intended to serve as a guide to the alternative therapies most often used by women with breast cancer. The book includes . . . chapters on approaches such as Chinese Medicine, vitamin and mineral supplementation, meditation and prayer. . . . Women with breast cancer looking for alternative therapies might find this book to be a good start in their own research." Publ Wkly
Includes bibliographical references

★ Breast cancer sourcebook; basic consumer health information about breast health and breast cancer ... edited by Karen Bellenir. 3rd ed.; Omnigraphics 2009 633p il map $84　　　　**616.99**
1. Breast cancer 2. Reference books
ISBN 978-0-7808-1030-3; 0-7808-1030-9

LC 2008-48392

"Provides basic consumer health information on risk factors, prevention, diagnosis, and treatment of breast cancer, along with facts about coping after treatment. Includes index, glossary of related terms and directory of resources." Publisher's note
Includes bibliographical references

Cancer sourcebook; basic consumer health information about major forms and stages of cancer, featuring facts about head and neck cancers, lung cancers, gastrointestinal cancers, genitourinary cancers, lymphomas, blood. edited by Karen Bellenir. 6th ed.; Omnigraphics 2011 1121p il $95　　　　　　　　　　　　　**616.99**
1. Cancer 2. Reference books
ISBN 978-0-7808-1145-4

LC 2011003804

This book "has a place in consumer-health collections as a convenient and timesaving source of authoritative information." Booklist
Includes bibliographical references

★ Everyone's guide to cancer therapy; how cancer is diagnosed, treated, and managed day to day. {by} Malin Dollinger {et al.} 4th ed; Andrews McMeel Pub. 2003 xxxiv, 925p il $29.95　**616.99**
1. Cancer
ISBN 0-7407-1856-8

LC 2002-28289

This offers information on cancer diagnosis and treatment options and includes chapters on cryotherapy, radio frequency treatment, genetic risk assessment, and managed care.

617　Surgery, regional medicine, dentistry, ophthalmology, otology, audiology

Alpert, Michelle J.

Spinal cord injury and the family; a new guide. [by] Michelle J. Alpert, Saul Wisnia. Harvard University Press 2008 338p il $35; pa $16.95　**617**
1. Spinal cord 2. Spinal cord -- Wounds and injuries
ISBN 978-0-674-02714-5; 0-674-02714-0; 978-0-674-02715-2 pa; 0-674-02715-9 pa

LC 2007-50307

This is a "basic guide for SCI patients and their families, covering a multitude of important issues from basic spine anatomy, how injuries occur, and the impact of the injury's location to the first days after an injury, the emotional turmoil of the patient and family, and adjusting to work or school. . . . This excellent overview with an emphasis on the physical effects of SCI will be invaluable to a growing, currently underserved audience." Libr J
Includes bibliographical references (p. 315-325)

Hollingham, Richard

Blood and guts; a history of surgery. foreword by Michael Mosley. Thomas Dunne Books/St. Martin's Press 2009 319p $27.99   **617**
1. Surgery -- History
ISBN 978-0-312-57546-5
     LC 2009-31307
"Hollingham makes no attempt to provide a complete history of surgery, but he offers a quick, entertaining read filled with operating-room dramas that end in disaster or triumph and a wide variety of heroes and villains. One warning: This is not for the squeamish." Kirkus
Includes bibliographical references

Mailhot, Claire B.

Surgery: a patient's guide from diagnosis to recovery; {by} Claire Mailhot, Melinda Brubaker, Linda Garratt Slezak. University of Calif. Press 1999 253p il $20   **617**
1. Surgery
ISBN 0-943671-19-1
"Starting from the moment of diagnosis, the authors walk readers through general topics common to all in-patient treatment, including getting a second opinion; decoding insurance policies; understanding surgical procedures, anesthesia, and medications; preadmission testing (e.g., blood work, chest X-rays); discharge; and home care." Libr J
Includes bibliographical references

Mason, Michael Paul

Head cases; stories of brain injury and its aftermath. Farrar, Straus and Giroux 2008 310p $25 **617**
1. Brain -- Wounds and injuries 2. Brain -- Wounds and injuries -- Patients -- Rehabilitation 3. Health services accessibility -- United States 4. Long-term care facilities
ISBN 978-0-374-13452-5; 0-374-13452-9
     LC 2007-32335
"The strange effects of neurological damage will draw fans of Oliver Sacks, but Mason's poignant and caring accounts of his clients' lives are sure to touch the hearts of a wide range of readers." Publ Wkly
Includes bibliographical references

McLanahan, Sandra A.

Surgery and its alternatives; how to make the right choices for your health. by Sandra A. McLanahan, David J. McLanahan; preface by Bernie S. Siegel. Twin Streams 2002 814p $35; pa $22   **617**
1. Alternative medicine 2. Surgery
ISBN 0-7582-0201-6; 1-57566-739-8 pa
     LC 2001-92972
The authors discuss "the surgical perspective for conditions that include many types of cancer, coronary artery disease, varicose veins, gallstones and hernias . . . {describing} the surgical techniques available, various anesthetics and preoperative tests. {Also outlined are} alternative methods to surgery as well as ways to utilize complementary medical strategies that improve both body and mind when an operation is necessary." Publ Wkly
Includes bibliographical references

Palmer, Sara

★ **Spinal** cord injury; a guide for living. [by] Sara Palmer, Kay Harris Kriegsman, Jeffrey B. Palmer; with contributions by John W. McDonald and Cristina L. Sadowsky. 2nd ed.; Johns Hopkins University Press 2008 xx, 352p il $45; pa $19.95 **617**
1. Spinal cord
ISBN 978-0-8018-8777-2; 0-8018-8777-1; 978-0-8018-8778-9 pa; 0-8018-8778-X pa
     LC 200735741
"Combining first-person accounts with up-to-date medical information, the book addresses all aspects of spinal cord injury—recovery and coping, sex and family matters, transportation and housing, employment and leisure—and reviews the challenges encountered by people with spinal cord injury throughout their lives." Publisher's note
Includes bibliographical references

Sayler, Mary Harwell

The **encyclopedia** of the back and spine systems and disorders; [by] Mary Harwell Sayler with Arya Nick Shamie. Facts On File 2007 354p $75   **617**
1. Back -- Encyclopedias 2. Reference books 3. Spine -- Encyclopedias
ISBN 978-0-8160-6678-0
     LC 2006-35678
"More than 250 . . . entries provide information on all aspects of the back and spine, including anatomy, metabolic processes, neurological systems, injuries, diseases and disorders, treatments, medicines, nutrition, exercise and lifestyle issues, current research, and . . . more." Publisher's note
Includes bibliographical references

Tilney, Nicholas L.

Invasion of the body; revolutions in surgery. Harvard University Press 2011 358p il   **617**
1. Surgery -- History
ISBN 978-0-674-06228-3
     LC 2011013287
"Touching on everything from sanitation-free barber surgeons to robotics, he discusses the evolving science of surgery, the growth of the profession, the individuals responsible for incremental developments and breakthroughs, the technologies now available, and the directions in which the field might be headed. . . . A broad subject is nicely condensed into a very readable book that should prove fascinating to both lay readers and professionals." Libr J
Includes bibliographical references

Current surgical diagnosis & treatment; edited by Gerard M. Doherty, Lawrence W. Way. 12th ed; Lange Medical Books/McGraw-Hill 2006 1453p il pa $66.95   **617**
1. Surgery
ISBN 978-0-07-142315-1; 0-07-142315-X
     LC 2006-278501
This book "covers over 1,000 diseases and disorders managed by surgeons . . . {and} emphasizes quick recall of major diagnostic features and succinct descriptions of disease processes, followed by procedures for definitive di-

agnosis and treatment, epidemiology, pathophysiology, and pathology." Publisher's note

Includes bibliographical references

617.1 Injuries and wounds

Ehrlich, Gretel

A **match** to the heart. Penguin Books 1995 200p pa $15 **617.1**

1. Authors 2. Editors 3. Essayists 4. Lightning 5. Novelists 6. Poets 7. Short story writers 8. Writers on nature

ISBN 0-14-017937-2

LC 93-34981

"Hit by lightning on a stormy August afternoon in 1991, Ms. Ehrlich was left with damage to her nervous system that resulted in constant fainting spells. . . . This eclectic chronicle of recovery offers excursions into neurobiology, cardiology, the lore and science of lightning and the medical literature of lightning injury, as well as musings on the Tibetan Book of the Dead and the healing power of the ocean." N Y Times Book Rev

Kuhn, Cynthia

Pumped; straight facts for athletes about drugs, supplements, and training. by Cynthia Kuhn, Scott Swartzwelder, and Wilkie Wilson. Norton 2000 190p il pa $14.95 **617.1**

1. Athletes -- Drug use 2. Dietary supplements 3. Doping in sports

ISBN 0-393-32129-0

LC 00-30455

The authors offer "advice regarding drugs and supplements. Some of them work but are dangerous; some are dangerous and don't work; many are harmless and have little effect other than to fill the coffers of the sellers. . . . This is an excellent book that provides a realistic overview on the topic of drugs, dietary supplements, and athletics." Booklist

Includes bibliographical references and index

Oakes, Elizabeth H.

The **encyclopedia** of sports medicine; [by] Elizabeth Oakes; foreword by Connie Lebrun. Facts on File 2005 322p il $75 **617.1**

1. Reference books 2. Sports medicine -- Encyclopedias

ISBN 0-8160-5334-0

LC 2003-24720

"This is an excellent resource for weekend, varsity high school and college, and professional athletes, and for trainers." Choice

Includes bibliographical references

★ Burns sourcebook . . . edited by Allan R. Cook. Omnigraphics 1999 604p il $78 **617.1**

1. Burns and scalds

ISBN 0-7808-0204-7

LC 99-24510

617.6 Dentistry

Wynbrandt, James

The **excruciating** history of dentistry; toothsome tales & oral oddities from Babylon to braces. St. Martin's Press 1998 248p il hardcover o.p. pa $14.95 **617.6**

1. Dentistry -- History 2. Dentistry -- Humor 3. Teeth -- Care and hygiene -- History 4. Teeth -- Humor

ISBN 0-312-26319-8 pa

LC 98-9794

The author "discusses the development of dentistry as a profession, the use of different anesthetics, and the evolution of dentures and dental prosthetics, among other topics. Much of the book is devoted to anecdotes illustrating discontinued dental practices." Libr J

Includes bibliographical references

★ Dental care and oral health sourcebook; edited by Amy L. Sutton. 3rd ed.; Omnigraphics 2008 xx, 647p il $93 **617.6**

1. Dentistry 2. Mouth -- Diseases

ISBN 978-0-7808-1032-7

LC 2008-38411

617.7 Ophthalmology

Barry, Sue

Fixing my gaze; a scientist's journey into seeing in three dimensions. [by] Susan R. Barry. Basic Books 2009 249p il $26 **617.7**

1. Behavioral optometry 2. Biography, Individual 3. Biologists 4. College teachers 5. Depth perception 6. Strabismus 7. Vision disorders 8. Visual training

ISBN 978-0-465-00913-8; 0-465-00913-1

LC 2009-08900

"Filled with clear diagrams that illustrate the difference between how the stereoblind and normally sighted people see, Fixing My Gaze introduces readers to a rare but interesting disability. It is also a testament both to human physiology and spirit that permits someone to live with—and then change—a uniquely altered view of the world." BookPage

Includes bibliographical references

Cassel, Gary H.

The **eye** book; a complete guide to eye disorders and health. [by] Gary H. Cassel, Michael D. Billig, Harry G. Randall. Johns Hopkins Univ. Press 1998 367p il hardcover o.p. pa $19.95 **617.7**

1. Eye -- Diseases 2. Eye -- Diseases -- Popular works 3. Eye -- Popular works

ISBN 0-8018-5835-6; 0-8018-5847-X pa

LC 97-35348

This "guide covers routine eye care and the more common eye diseases, providing up-to-date facts on refractive surgery, treatment for optical neuritis, and possible nutritional therapies for cataracts and macular degeneration." Libr J

Includes bibliographical references

Kornmehl, Ernest W.

★ **LASIK**: a guide to laser vision correction; [by] Ernest W. Kornmehl, Robert K. Maloney, Jonathan M. Davidorf. 2nd ed.; Addicus Books 2006 121p il pa $14.95 **617.7**

1. Eye -- Surgery
ISBN 1-886039-79-8; 978-1-886039-79-7

LC 2005-35027

"The color illustrations are clear and instructive, and the risks and complications associated with the procedure are well delineated." Libr J

Sacks, Oliver W.

The **island** of the colorblind; and, Cycad island. {by} Oliver Sacks. Knopf 1997 298p il maps hardcover o.p. pa $13 **617.7**

1. Caroline Islands -- Description 2. Color blindness 3. Guam -- Description 4. Parkinson's disease
ISBN 0-375-70073-0 pa

LC 96-34252

"As a travel writer, Sacks ranks with Paul Theroux and Bruce Chatwin. As an investigator of the mind's mysteries, he is in a class by himself." Publ Wkly
Includes bibliographical references

617.8 Otology and audiology

Burkey, John M.

Overcoming hearing aid fears; the road to better hearing. Rutgers Univ. Press 2003 175p il $44.95; pa $17.95 **617.8**

1. Hearing aids 2. Hearing aids -- Popular works
ISBN 0-8135-3309-0; 0-8135-3310-4 pa

LC 2003-432

The author "explains how the ear works and addresses the most common misconceptions and fears that people have about using hearing aids. He demonstrates the devices' advantages for both the wearers and those with whom they interact. He also discusses the various types of hearing aids, their cost, and the process of diagnosing hearing loss and obtaining the proper hearing aid. A practical guide, with advice to which readers should listen." Libr J
Includes bibliographical references and index

Myers, David G.

A **quiet** world; living with hearing loss. Yale Univ. Press 2000 211p $23 **617.8**

1. Deafness 2. Hearing aids 3. Hearing disorders
ISBN 0-300-08439-0

LC 00-38153

The author "explores the problems faced by the hard of hearing at home and at work and provides information on the new technology and groundbreaking surgical procedures that are available." Publisher's note

617.9 Operative surgery and special fields of surgery

Cheney, Annie

★ **Body** brokers; inside America's underground trade in human remains. Broadway Books 2006 205p $23.95; pa $14 **617.9**

1. Procurement of organs, tissues, etc.
ISBN 0-7679-1733-2; 978-0-7679-1733-9; 0-7679-1734-0 pa; 978-0-7679-1734-6 pa

LC 2005-54278

This book "speeds along like a circular saw through a thigh joint. It's a zippy, entertaining read, and more formal, scholarly works on the topic are not." N Y Times Book Rev
Includes bibliographical references

Finn, Robert

Organ transplants; making the most of your gift of life. O'Reilly & Assocs. 2000 311p pa $19.95 **617.9**

1. Transplantation of organs, tissues, etc -- Interviews -- Popular works 2. Transplantation of organs, tissues, etc -- Popular works 3. Transplantation of organs, tissues, etc.
ISBN 1-56592-634-X

LC 00-29837

This guide is "sprinkled with comments from actual recipients, their families, and members of the transplant teams. . . . Appendixes include Internet discussion groups, mailing lists and other web sites, pharmaceutical and financial assistance programs, and contact information for scores of transplant-related organizations." Libr J
Includes bibliographical references

Gilman, Sander L.

Making the body beautiful; a cultural history of aesthetic surgery. Princeton Univ. Press 1999 396p il hardcover o.p. pa $20.95 **617.9**

1. Body image -- Social aspects -- History 2. Cosmetic Techniques -- history 3. Cultural Characteristics 4. Plastic surgery 5. Surgery, Plastic -- Social aspects -- History 6. Surgery, Plastic -- history
ISBN 0-691-07053-9 pa

LC 98-48423

Gilman's "book shows a dazzling European erudition. . . . He tells a strange, macabre, and often richly comic story of shifting desires." N Y Rev Books
Includes bibliographical references

Perry, Arthur W.

★ **Straight** talk about cosmetic surgery; with a foreword by Michael F. Roizen. Yale University Press 2007 360p il $45; pa $18 **617.9**

1. Consumer education 2. Plastic surgery
ISBN 978-0-300-11999-2; 978-0-300-12104-9 pa

LC 2007-1333

In this guide to cosmetic surgery, the author "examines the latest innovations, provides sound advice for those considering any cosmetic procedure, and offers an overview of the field. . . . The author also advises on choosing a practitioner, cautioning patients to opt only for a board-certified plastic surgeon, and then discusses the consultation. . . .

The rest of the book covers specific procedures (e.g., Botox injections, facial surgery, body contouring) and techniques that do not work (e.g., enderomologie, 'antiaging' medicine). There are also chapters about cosmetic dentistry, hair restoration, and tattoo removal." Libr J
Includes bibliographical references

Reconstructive and cosmetic surgery sourcebook

Cosmetic and reconstructive surgery sourcebook; edited by Karen Bellenir. 2nd ed.; Omnigraphics 2007 512p il $78   **617.9**
1. Consumer education 2. Plastic surgery
ISBN 978-0-7808-0951-2; 0-7808-0951-3
LC 2007-18893

Rinzler, Carol Ann

The **encyclopedia** of cosmetic and plastic surgery; foreword by Robert T. Grant and by Stanley Darrow. Facts On File 2009 264p $75   **617.9**
1. Plastic surgery -- Encyclopedias 2. Reference books 3. Surgery, Plastic
ISBN 978-0-8160-6285-0; 0-8160-6285-4
LC 2008-16098
"Written for lay readers, this book is an easy-to-use reference source with good cross-referencing and indexing." Choice
Includes glossary and bibliographical references

★ **Transplantation** sourcebook; edited by Joyce Brennfleck Shannon. Omnigraphics 2002 628p il $78   **617.9**
1. Teenagers -- Health and hygiene 2. Transplantation of organs, tissues, etc.
ISBN 0-7808-0322-1
LC 2002-16975

618   Gynecology, obstetrics, pediatrics, geriatrics

Buckley, Julie A.

Healing our autistic children; a medical plan for restoring your child's health. with Lynn Vannucci; foreword by Jenny McCarthy. Palgrave Macmillan 2010 238p il pa $18   **618**
1. Autism
ISBN 978-0-230-61639-4
LC 2009-20239
The author "explains different options and how they work for the parents of children with autism-spectrum disorders (ASD). The book is set up in six chapters, each representing a visit to the child's doctor as a way to walk readers through beginning treatment and managing ongoing treatments. . . . Essential for parents of newly diagnosed children as a way to learn about medical treatments or as a guide to start treatment." Libr J
Includes bibliographical references

618.1   Gynecology and obstetrics

Boston Women's Health Book Collective

★ **Our** bodies, ourselves: menopause; [by] the Boston Women's Health Book Collective; with a preface by Vivian Pinn. Simon & Schuster 2006 350p il pa $15   **618.1**
1. Menopause 2. Women -- Health and hygiene
ISBN 978-0-7432-7487-6; 0-7432-7487-3
LC 2006-44362
"The authors consider menopause within the totality of women's health and as a natural process, not a medical problem. They detail typical menopausal symptoms, mainstream and alternative treatments, and risk factors for such conditions as osteoporosis, heart disease, cancer and diabetes as women age. . . . As a general reference on menopause, this volume will be embraced by a wide female audience." Publ Wkly
Includes bibliographical references

Clark, Rebecca A.

Planning parenthood; strategies for success in fertility assistance, adoption, and surrogacy. Rebecca A. Clark . . . [et al.] Johns Hopkins University Press 2009 237p il $45; pa $18.95   **618.1**
1. Adoption 2. Infertility 3. Reproductive technology 4. Surrogate mothers
ISBN 978-0-8018-9111-3; 0-8018-9111-6; 978-0-8018-9112-0 pa; 0-8018-9112-4 pa
LC 2008-23838
"This panoramic view of the many routes to parenthood is both practical and encouraging." Publ Wkly
Includes bibliographical references

Greer, Germaine

The **change**; women, aging and the menopause. Ballantine 1993 422p pa $23 **618.1**
1. Aging 2. Menopause 3. Self-realization 4. Women -- Psychology
ISBN 0-449-90853-4; 978-0-449-90853-2
This is a discussion of menopause in Western society. Greer looks at medical, psychological and social aspects of the cessation of menstruation and the aging process. She views the climacteric as an important turning-point in a woman's life.
"In a wise, witty and inspiring book, Greer rebukes doctors, psychiatrists—and women themselves—who blame the aging female for her menopausal distress. . . . Greer dispels all manner of myths and misconceptions about menopause." Publ Wkly
Includes bibliographical references

Henig, Robin Marantz

Pandora's baby; how the first test tube babies sparked the reproductive revolution. Houghton Mifflin 2004 326p $25   **618.1**
1. Fertilization in vitro 2. Fertilization in vitro, Human 3. Reproductive technology
ISBN 0-618-22415-7
LC 2003-6137?

The author "presents the history of in vitro fertilization and the moral, ethical, and political controversies of reproductive technologies." Booklist

Includes bibliographical references

Love, Susan M.

★ **Dr.** Susan Love's breast book; [by] Susan M. Love, with Karen Lindsey. 5th ed., 1st Da Capo Press ed.; Da Capo Press 2010 736p il pa $22   **618.1**
1. Breast
ISBN 978-0-7382-1359-0

LC 2010-21598

This book covers breast development, plastic surgery, common problems, and breast cancer diagnosis, treatment, and screening.

Dr. Susan Love's menopause and hormone book; making informed choices. {by} Susan M. Love with Karen Lindsey. Rev. pbk. ed.; Three Rivers Press (NY) 2003 420p il pa $15.95   **618.1**
1. Hormones 2. Menopause 3. Women -- Health and hygiene
ISBN 0-609-80996-2

LC 2002-15811

Moore, Michele

★ The **only** menopause guide you'll need; 2nd ed; Johns Hopkins University Press 2004 164p hardcover o.p. pa $15.95   **618.1**
1. Menopause 2. Menopause -- Popular works
ISBN 0-8018-8012-2; 0-8018-8013-0 pa

LC 2004-43483

In this guide the author "includes specific recommendations for coping with symptoms ranging from night sweats to low libido, and outlines menopausal women's 'major health concerns,' namely, osteoporosis, cancer and heart disease. . . . Women looking for a comforting guide to menopause, with practical information as well as a sense of spirituality, will find it here." Publ Wkly

Includes bibliographical references

Seaman, Barbara

The **no**-nonsense guide to menopause. Simon & Schuster 2008 482p $26.95; pa $17   **618.1**
1. Menopause
ISBN 978-0-7432-7678-8; 0-7432-7678-7; 978-0-7432-7679-5 pa; 0-7432-7679-5 pa

LC 2007-42420

"Seaman touches on nearly every aspect of women's health (nutrition, exercise, sleep, stress relief, vitamins and herbs, aging, appearance, etc.) as she helps readers frame key questions, evaluate research studies, consider treatment options and move gracefully through menopause and the years leading up to and following it. This volume sheds an invaluable light on a long-cloudy subject." Publ Wkly

Includes bibliographical references

Sheehy, Gail

The **silent** passage: menopause; Rev and updated with four brand-new chapters; Pocket Bks. 1998 xxvi, 293p pa $7.50   **618.1**
1. Menopause
ISBN 0-671-56777-2

LC 98-65873

The author examines the medical, psychological, and social aspects of menopause and includes interviews with women in various stages of menopause and with experts. Discussions of herbal remedies, exercise and diet, menopause in the workplace, estrogen and brainpower, and new frontiers in treatment are included.

Wallach, Edward E.

Hysterectomy: exploring your options; [by] Edward E. Wallach & Esther Eisenberg. Johns Hopkins University Press 2004 204p il $45; pa $16.95 **618.1**
1. Consumer education 2. Hysterectomy
ISBN 0-8018-7622-2; 0-8018-7623-0 pa

LC 2003-6239

This is a "guide to provide the information women need to determine whether a hysterectomy is the best alternative in their specific medical situation. Part 1 reviews the anatomy and physiology of the uterus and related structures, Part 2 discusses the specific conditions that may indicate the need for a hysterectomy, Part 3 addresses the surgery itself, and Part 4 details post-hysterectomy issues. The authors stress two important points: hysterectomy is often performed unnecessarily, and the surgery is almost always done as an elective. This important decision-making tool for women should be included in most consumer health and public library collections." Libr J

West, Stanley

The **hysterectomy** hoax; the truth about why many hysterectomies are unnecessary and how to avoid them. by Stanley West with Paula Dranov. 3rd ed; Next Decade 2002 243p il pa $19.95   **618.1**
1. Consumer education 2. Hysterectomy 3. Hysterectomy -- Popular works 4. Surgery, Unnecessary
ISBN 0-9700908-1-1

LC 2001-55868

"West, an infertility specialist, makes a strong case against hysterectomy unless a woman has cancer. Providing clear, illustrated explanations of female anatomy and physiology, he also thoroughly discusses fibroids, endometriosis, uterine prolapse, ovarian cysts, and precancerous conditions. West offers effective treatments that enable women to preserve their ovaries and uterus as these organs are important for sexuality and hormone production, even after menopause." Libr J {review of 1994 edition}

Wingert, Pat

Is it hot in here? Or is it me? the complete guide to menopause. [by] Pat Wingert & Barbara Kantrowitz. Workman Pub. 2006 532p il $29.95; pa $17.95   **618.1**
1. Menopause
ISBN 0-7611-4370-X; 978-0-7611-4370-3; 0-7611-3808-0 pa; 978-0-7611-3808-2 pa

This is a "guide to major menopausal complaints: hot flashes, sleep disorders, sexual dysfunction, bleeding, and mood and memory changes. There is also information on midlife health issues like osteoporosis, heart disease, and cancer, as well as evidence-based discussions of available treatment options. Q&A sections, case studies, material on what to tell your daughter, memory tests, and 'Looking Good' beauty tips, combined with the writers' reader-friendly, authoritative tone, make this book an outstanding addition to menopause and midlife health collections." Libr J

618.2   Obstetrics

Alcaniz, Lourdes

Waiting for bebe; a pregnancy guide for Latinas. Ballantine Books 2003 xxiii, 390p il pa $14.95   **618.2**

1. Childbirth 2. Hispanic American women -- Health and hygiene 3. Pregnancy

ISBN 0-345-45211-9

The author "includes Spanish terminology and specifically addresses herbs, foods, beverages, customs, and social beliefs indigenous to Latino culture. Her comprehensive text spans from preconception to post-labor and includes sections for the father-to-be, checklists, questions to ask the doctor, a section describing insurance options, and a really well-written portion on gestational diabetes and other pregnancy-related conditions that affect Hispanic women in particular. Practical but not preachy, this is sure to be of enormous help to mothers-to-be, especially first-time mothers." Libr J

Includes bibliographical references

Boston Women's Health Book Collective

★ **Our** bodies, ourselves: pregnancy and birth; [by] the Boston Women's Health Book Collective. Simon & Schuster 2008 370p il pa $15   **618.2**

1. Childbirth 2. Pregnancy

ISBN 978-0-7432-7486-9; 0-7432-7486-5

LC 2007-49498

This book includes "information on making health-care decisions (e.g., choosing a provider and a birth setting), nutrition, labor and delivery, Cesarean birth, recovery, feeding an infant, and life as a new mother. It also addresses special situations such as prenatal testing and pregnancy loss. . . . This is an excellent book for public and consumer health library collections; highly recommended." Libr J

Includes bibliographical references

Bruce, Debra Fulghum

★ **Making** a baby; everything you need to know to get pregnant. {by} Debra Fulghum Bruce and Samuel Thatcher. Ballantine Bks. 2000 379p pa $14.95   **618.2**

1. Infertility 2. Infertility -- Popular works 3. Pregnancy

ISBN 0-345-43543-5

The authors offer a guide to "babyboosting medicines, IVF, sperm injection, and egg donation. They explain how the male and female reproductive systems work and detail the many common, and sometimes hidden, threats to fertil-

ity. They offer practical, low-tech-solutions, such as lifestyle changes, as well as the more advanced therapies." Libr J

Includes bibliographical references

Curtis, Glade B.

★ **Your** pregnancy week by week; [by] Glade B. Curtis, Judith Schuler. 6th ed., fully rev. and updated; Da Capo/Lifelong Books 2008 648p il $23; pa $15.95   **618.2**

1. Pregnancy 2. Prenatal care

ISBN 978-0-7382-1108-4; 978-0-7382-1109-1 pa

This pregnancy guide includes information on fetal development, medical procedures and tests, nutrition, and exercise during pregnancy, and advice for fathers.

Epstein, Randi Hutter

Get me out; a history of childbirth from the Garden of Eden to the sperm bank. W.W. Norton 2010 302p il $24.95   **618.2**

1. Childbirth

ISBN 978-0-393-06458-2

LC 2009-34751

The author "provides a sharp, sassy history of childbirth. The book is as much a study in sociology as historical snapshot of human birthing practices and gynecological advances, with particular emphasis on developments in the late 19th- and 20th-century United States. . . . The author's engaging sarcasm . . . lends this chronicle a welcome punch and vitality often absent from medical histories." Kirkus

Includes bibliographical references

Greene, Alan R.

Raising baby green; the earth-friendly guide to pregnancy, childbirth, and baby care. [by] Alan Greene; with Jeanette Pavini and Theresa Foy DiGeronimo; illustrations by Val Lawton. Jossey-Bass 2007 306p il pa $16.95   **618.2**

1. Environmental protection 2. Infants -- Care 3. Pregnancy

ISBN 978-0-7879-9622-2; 0-7879-9622-X

LC 2007-23342

This "informative guide for raising children in the most environmentally friendly way possible makes for some fascinating (and surprising) reading. . . . An excellent choice for those who don't know where to begin when it comes to environmental parenting." Booklist

Includes bibliographical references

Kitzinger, Sheila

The **complete** book of pregnancy and childbirth; black-and-white photography by Marcia May. rev ed; Knopf 2003 448p $35; pa $19.95   **618.2**

1. Childbirth 2. Childbirth -- Popular works 3. Infants -- Care 4. Pregnancy 5. Pregnancy -- Popular works

ISBN 1-400-04108-2; 0-375-71047-7 pa

LC 2002-43433

After an overview of basic embryology the author covers health, nutrition and emotional well-being during pregnancy. Hospital facilities, home birthing rooms, drugs and exercise are discussed.

Kropp, Tori

The **joy** of pregnancy; the complete, candid, and reassuring companion for parents-to-be. Harvard Common Press 2008 xx, 412p il $26.95; pa $14.95 **618.2**
    1. Pregnancy
    ISBN 978-1-55832-305-6; 1-55832-305-8; 978-1-55832-306-3 pa; 1-55832-306-6 pa
                    LC 2007-46213
"Each chapter explains what's happening to your body (increased hormone levels) and your baby (its size and development) each month. Kropp covers topics like weight gain, which medications are safe to take, bed rest and genetic testing. . . . Years of experience working with pregnant women gives Kropp a reassuring voice, and her book is sure to leave readers feeling more prepared—and less frightened—about the journey of pregnancy." Publ Wkly
    Includes bibliographical references

Murkoff, Heidi Eisenberg

What to expect before you're expecting; by Heidi Murkoff and Sharon Mazel; foreword by Charles J. Lockwood. Workman Pub. 2009 275p il $23.95; pa $12.95 **618.2**
    1. Childbirth 2. Pregnancy 3. Prenatal care
    ISBN 978-0-7611-5552-2; 978-0-7611-5276-7 pa
                    LC 2009-7466
The authors "present a preconception program that includes tips on what to eat (and not eat), how to maintain a healthy weight and advice about preconception medical care, such as having a physical and dental checkup. . . . Couples who are trying to conceive will find plenty of useful ideas to consider and implement in the months preceding their baby's debut." Publ Wkly

★ **What** to expect when you're expecting; by Heidi Murkoff and Sharon Mazel; foreword by Charles J. Lockwood. 4th ed.; Workman 2008 xxiii, 614p il pa $14.95 **618.2**
    1. Childbirth 2. Pregnancy
    ISBN 978-0-7611-4857-9; 0-7611-4857-4
"The book is arranged by month, from pregnancy test through labor and delivery. Each section offers answers to frequently asked questions, along with features such as 'What You May Be Feeling' . . . This book remains an indispensable guide for pregnant women and their partners." Publ Wkly [review of 2002 edition]

Port, David

The **caveman's** pregnancy companion; a survival guide for expectant fathers. [by] David Port and John Ralston; Brian M. Ralston, consultant; Gideon Kendall, illustrator. Sterling 2006 227p il pa $12.95 **618.2**
    1. Childbirth 2. Fathers 3. Pregnancy
    ISBN 1-4027-3526-X; 978-1-4027-3526-4
This "pregnancy guide is based on the conceit that most men are 'twenty-first-century Cro-Magnons' at those times when an expectant father 'stops, scratches his head, and mutters to his woman, "I don't get it."' What is immediately obvious about the book, however, is that it is actually a superb overview of the birthing experience. . . . [It also covers] prenatal massages, amniocentesis and a wonderful range of easy meals to prepare for a tired spouse." Publ Wkly
    Includes bibliographical references

Puryear, Lucy J.

Understanding your moods when you're expecting; emotions, mental health, and happiness--before, during, and after pregnancy. Houghton Mifflin Co. 2007 240p $24 **618.2**
    1. Child care 2. Childbirth 3. Pregnancy 4. Women -- Psychology
    ISBN 978-0-618-34107-8; 0-618-34107-2
                    LC 2006-35606
Puryear "reassures readers with her authoritative, sensitive, and calming tone as she discusses what to expect during and after pregnancy. Medical facts are effectively interspersed with real-life scenarios. Tips offer down-to-earth coping advice in bite-sized chunks." Libr J

Riley, Laura

You & your baby: pregnancy; the ultimate week-by-week pregnancy guide. Meredith Books 2006 455p il pa $14.95 **618.2**
    1. Pregnancy 2. Prenatal care
    ISBN 0-696-22221-3; 978-0-696-22221-4
This "guide begins with the first clues that one might be pregnant and progresses week by week until the baby reaches three months. Major sections cover first, second, and third trimesters; labor and delivery; feeding your baby; and postpartum and baby care. The trimester sections are further broken down into weeks, with each week addressing baby, body, self, diet and exercise, and common questions. . . . This easy-to-read guide is excellent for any library." Libr J

Sember, Brette McWhorter

The **everything** guide to pregnancy over 35; from conquering your fears to assessing health risks--all you need to have a happy, healthy nine months. technical review by Bruce D. Rodgers and Diane E. Rodgers. Adams Media 2007 289p pa $14.95 **618.2**
    1. Childbirth 2. Middle age 3. Pregnancy
    ISBN 978-1-59869-245-7; 1-59869-245-3
                    LC 2007-15890
This guide to pregnancy over the age of thirty-five includes information on fertility treatments, prenatal care options, nutrition and exercise, prenatal testing, preparing for labor and delivery, and financial issues.
This "upbeat book gives a clear and honest overview of issues facing pregnant women over 35." Libr J

Van der Ziel, Cornelia

Big, beautiful & pregnant; expert advice and comforting wisdom for the expecting plus-size woman. Marlowe & Co. 2006 273p il pa $15.95 **618.2**
    1. Obesity 2. Pregnancy 3. Prenatal care
    ISBN 1-56924-319-0; 978-1-56924-319-0
                    LC 2006-7832

"This belongs in every library's pregnancy collection."
Libr J

Includes bibliographical references

Vincent, Peggy

★ **Baby** catcher; chronicles of a modern midwife. Scribner 2002 336p $26; pa $13   **618.2**

1. Midwives 2. Midwives -- Anecdotes

ISBN 0-7432-1933-3; 0-7432-1934-1 pa

LC 2001-54988

This is an account of a midwife specializing in home births who "over the course of 40 years, brought some 2,000 babies into the world. . . . A solid writer, Vincent doesn't preach the virtues of unmedicated birthing; she just lays consistent stories of women doing it—Christian Science moms, Muslim moms, spiritualist moms, lesbian moms, teen moms and just plain ordinary moms." Publ Wkly

The mommy docs' ultimate guide to pregnancy and birth; [by] Yvonne Bohn, Allison Hill, Alane Park with Melissa Jo Peltier. Da Capo Lifelong 2011 526p il pa $15.95   **618.2**

1. Childbirth 2. Infants -- Care 3. Pregnancy

ISBN 978-0-7382-1460-3

"Chapters are arranged from preparing for pregnancy to first, second, and third trimesters; birth; and early days at home. Additional chapters handle complications of early pregnancy, high-risk pregnancies, and 'frequently asked questions . . . and frequently repeated myths.' They offer reassurance for a healthy pregnancy even for those with health conditions such as hypertension or diabetes. Throughout, the authors deliver practical tips and emotional support for coping with both complicated and uncomplicated pregnancies as well as the things that can go wrong, such as miscarriages or infertility. . . . A great resource for anyone seeking information on pregnancy, childbirth, and the first weeks after birth." Libr J

Includes bibliographical references

618.3   Diseases, disorders, management of pregnancy, childbirth, puerperium

Kohn, Ingrid

A **silent** sorrow; pregnancy loss: guidance and support for you and your family. [by] Ingrid Kohn and Perry-Lynn Moffitt, with Isabelle A. Wilkins. 2nd ed; Routledge 2000 xx, 299p pa $16.95 **618.3**

1. Bereavement 2. Bereavement -- Psychological aspects 3. Miscarriage 4. Miscarriage -- Psychological aspects 5. Perinatal death -- Psychological aspects

ISBN 0-415-92481-2

LC 99-25720

The authors provide "suggestions to validate parents' grief; cope with the unique concerns of early loss, crisis pregnancies, stillbirth, and newborn death; find medical, religious, and family support; and manage their lives afterwards. The writing is insightful and the tone respectful and supportive." Libr J [review of 1993 edition]

Includes bibliographical references

Lerner, Henry M.

★ **Miscarriage**: a doctor's guide to the facts; why it happens and how best to reduce your risks. with contributions by Alice Domar; introduction by Robert Barbieri. Perseus Bks. 2003 291p pa $16.95   **618.3**

1. Miscarriage

ISBN 0-7382-0634-2

LC 2002-114586

This book provides "explanations to questions concerning the etiology, diagnosis, prevention, and treatment of miscarriage. His medical and scientific discussion, while exceedingly thorough, is easy to understand. . . . Especially helpful are the concluding chapters, which focus on dealing with the emotional trauma of miscarriage." Libr J

Paul, Annie Murphy

Origins; how the nine months before birth shape the rest of our lives. Free Press 2010 306p $26; ebook $12.99 **618.3**

1. Fetus 2. Fetus -- Development 3. Pregnancy 4. Pregnancy -- Psychological aspects 5. Prenatal diagnosis

ISBN 978-0-7432-9662-5; 0-7432-9662-1; 978-1-4391-7184-4 ebook; 1-4391-7184-X ebook

LC 2010-15249

"Just what effect do the things that women inhale, consume and experience have on a fetus? In 'Origins,' Annie Murphy Paul sets out to discover the answer. Along the way she explodes myths, reviews scientific evidence and explores the new frontier of fetal-origins research, the study of how we are shaped in utero by a combination of genes and environment." Wall Street J

Includes bibliographical references

Young, Bruce

Miscarriage, medicine & miracles; everything you need to know about miscarriage. [by] Bruce K. Young and Amy Zavatto. Bantam Books 2008 334p il $25   **618.3**

1. Miscarriage

ISBN 978-0-553-80550-5

LC 2007-48179

Young "specializes in the care of women with high-risk pregnancies. Along with writer Zavatto, he supplies . . . information about pregnancy loss and treatment options without underestimating the difficulties involved." Libr J

618.4   Childbirth

Block, Jennifer

Pushed; the painful truth about childbirth and modern maternity care. Da Capo Press 2007 316p il $26; pa $16 **618.4**

1. Childbirth 2. Maternal health services -- United States 3. Medical ethics 4. Natural childbirth 5. Prenatal care

ISBN 978-0-7382-1073-5; 0-7382-1073-0; 978-0-7382-1166-4 pa; 0-7382-1166-4 pa

The author "examines childbirth in the United States today. A normal physiological process, she argues, has become a medical procedure, often depriving women of the right to choose how they give birth. . . . Readers get objective analysis of informed consent, reproductive rights, and the rights of the fetus vs. the rights of the mother in this thought-provoking text." Libr J

Includes bibliographical references

Gaskin, Ina May

Ina May's guide to childbirth. Bantam Books 2003 348p il pa $14.95   **618.4**
1. Natural childbirth
ISBN 0-553-38115-6

LC 2002-29901

Gaskin "explains that the female body is well designed for normal birth and provides techniques for dealing with the discomforts of labor. A whole chapter devoted to women's birthing experiences supports her stance. More than a childbirth guide, this comprehensive book provides insight into the sociological and historical aspects of the natural childbirth movement." Libr J

Includes bibliographical references

Leboyer, Frederick

Birth without violence; new translation by Yvonne Fitzgerald. rev ed; Healing Arts Press 2002 131p il pa $16.95   **618.4**
1. Natural childbirth
ISBN 0-89281-983-9

LC 2002-3503

"The work's stylistic qualities, in addition to the beautiful photographs, jar the reader into thinking about childbirth in a unique and revolutionary way." Choice {review of 1975 edition}

Moore, Michele

Cesarean section; understanding and celebrating your baby's birth. [by] Michele Moore, Caroline de Costa. Johns Hopkins University Press 2003 149p il $49.95; pa $14.95   **618.4**
1. Cesarean section 2. Cesarean section -- Popular works 3. Childbirth
ISBN 0-8018-7336-3; 0-8018-7337-1 pa

LC 2002-13625

The authors "explain why C-sections are sometimes the best method of delivery and discuss the anesthesia, surgical procedure, recovery, and care of the mother and child when they return home. They also cover postpartum depression, planning for future births, and the possibility of vaginal birth after Cesarean section (VBAC). They provide a list of questions for women to ask their doctors, nutritional information, an Apgar score chart, a glossary, and a bibliography." Libr J

Includes bibliographical references

Murphy, Magnus

★ **Pelvic** health and childbirth; what every woman needs to know. by Magnus Murphy, and Carol L. Wasson; foreword by Linda Brubaker. Prometheus Books 2003 312p il pa $21   **618.4**
1. Cesarean section -- Complications 2. Childbirth 3. Delivery, Obstetric 4. Genital Diseases, Female -- etiology 5. Natural childbirth -- Complications 6. Pelvic Floor -- surgery 7. Pelvic floor -- Diseases

8. Pelvic floor disorders 9. Urinary Incontinence -- etiology 10. Urogynecology
ISBN 1-59102-078-6

LC 2003-5896

The author "has written a unique book about a neglected subject. It explains the symptoms and treatment as well as the advances in labor and delivery and the politics of childbirth, including the option of elective Cesarean birth. An excellent presentation of childbirth options." Libr J

Includes bibliographical references

Sloan, Mark

Birth day; a pediatrician explores the science, the history, and the wonder of childbirth. Ballantine Books 2009 370p il $25   **618.4**
1. Childbirth
ISBN 978-0-345-50286-5; 0-345-50286-8

LC 2009-662

"Sloan, who practices in Northern California, is a graceful writer, and his narrative . . . flows easily between memoir, anecdotal reporting and hard science. . . . Anyone interested in the complex and, yes, miraculous way we all make it into this world will find lots to wonder over and ponder here." Washington Post

Includes bibliographical references and index

618.92   Pediatrics

Ashin, Deborah

Take charge of your child's eating disorder; a physician's step-by-step guide to defeating anorexia and bulimia. [by] Pamela Carlton and Deborah Ashin. Marlowe & Co. 2007 226p pa $15.95   **618.92**
1. Eating disorders
ISBN 978-1-56924-263-6; 1-56924-263-1

LC 2006-25836

Carlton "presents practical support for parents of children with anorexia and bulimia. Underscoring the importance of a multidisciplinary treatment team, she provides useful advice on finding appropriate programs and getting insurance companies to pay for treatment. Quotes from teens and family members offer a reality check." Libr J

Includes bibliographical references

Barber, Marianne S.

The **parent's** guide to food allergies; clear and complete advice from the experts on raising your food-allergic child. [by] Marianne S. Barber, with Maryanne Bartoszek Scott and Elinor Greenberg; foreword by Hugh A. Sampson. Henry Holt 2001 356p il pa $17   **618.92**
1. Food allergy 2. Parenting
ISBN 0-8050-6600-4; 978-0-8050-6600-5

LC 00-53920

"A pediatric allergist, a psychologist, and a mother of a food-allergic child pool their expertise to offer advice on handling the emotions, stress, and adjustment required when dealing with such a serious illness." Libr J

Barkley, Russell A.

Taking charge of ADHD; the complete, authoritative guide for parents. rev ed; Guilford Press 2000
321p $42; pa $19.95   **618.92**
   1. Attention deficit disorder 2. Attention-deficit hyperactivity disorder -- Popular works 3. Child rearing
   4. Child rearing -- Popular works
   ISBN 1-57230-600-9; 1-57230-560-6 pa
                         LC 00-34130
The author "reports on his own theory, recent research, and strategies for parents in the challenge of raising children with attention problems. His view is that attention-deficit hyperactivity disorder (ADHD) is a 'disorder of self-regulation' and that the problems of inattention, overactivity, and lack of inhibition become a developmental disability when extreme. ADHD is described as a neurologically based disorder with a probable genetic base." Sci Books Films
   Includes bibliographical references and index

Bashe, Patricia Romanowski

The **oasis** guide to Asperger syndrome; advice, support, insight, and inspiration. [by] Patricia Romanowski Bashe and Barbara L. Kirby; forewords by Simon Baron-Cohen and Tony Attwood. 1st rev. ed., completely rev. and updated; Crown Publishers 2005
497p $27.50   **618.92**
   1. Asperger's syndrome 2. Autism
   ISBN 1-4000-8152-1
                       LC 2005-274486
"Bashe and Kirby acknowledge that every AS child is different, but with the help of numerous anecdotes from parents of AS children, they manage to provide a wide-ranging, indispensable guide." Publ Wkly
   Includes bibliographical references

Bracken, Jeanne Munn

Children with cancer; a reference guide for parents. Rev. and updated ed.; Oxford University Press 2010 569p pa $27.95   **618.92**
   1. Cancer 2. Children -- Diseases
   ISBN 978-0-19-514739-1
                       LC 2009-52038
"Introductory chapters define cancer and discuss causes and genetics; coverage of specific cancers (e.g., leukemia, bone cancers, neuroblastoma) follows. Part 2 covers treatments, including information about standard procedures, plus experimental and alternative therapies. Part 3 concerns coping: the emotional aspects of cancer, siblings, financial and legal matters, school, and survivors as well as death and dying. . . . Highly recommended, this will be very helpful to parents/caregivers of children with cancer." Libr J
   Includes bibliographical references

Brown, Ian, 1954-

The **boy** in the moon; Ian Brown. St. Martin's Press 2011 293p.   **618.92**
   1. Journalists
   ISBN 0312671830; 9780312671839
                       LC 2011378371
This book, based on "a series of pieces [the author wrote] about his son Walker [for The Globe and Mail],]

presents an "account of raising, loving, and trying to connect with and gain insight into his severely disabled son. . . . Walker was born with cardiofaciocutaneous (CFC) syndrome, an extremely rare genetic disorder. . . . The author writes of the struggle to raise a self-destructive child who could not speak and suffered numerous physical deformities and medical problems. . . . He seeks out and profiles other families with CFC children, interviews a genetic researcher who found mutations in three genes related to the disorder, looks for clues to CFC through an MRI of Walker's brain and travels to France to visit L'Arche, a faith-based organization that operates communities for the developmentally disabled." (Kirkus)

Chicoine, Brian

The **guide** to good health for teens & adults with Down syndrome; [by] Brian Chicoine & Dennis McGuire. Woodbine House 2010 391p il pa $29.95   **618.92**
   1. Down syndrome
   ISBN 978-1-890627-89-8
                       LC 2010-18783
"This excellent book provides a wealth of information for DS caregivers. . . . The authors describe diagnosis, treatment, and prevention of common health conditions impacting DS people and cover mental and emotional issues that can affect physical health. Sexuality and birth control are discussed, as is abuse prevention. The book also includes information on residential options as well as coverage of end of life issues." Libr J
   Includes bibliographical references

Cohen, Scott W.

Eat, sleep, poop; a common sense guide to your baby's first year--essential information from an award-winning pediatrician and new dad. Scribner 2010 291p il pa $16   **618.92**
   1. Infants -- Care
   ISBN 978-1-4391-1706-4; 1-4391-1706-3
                       LC 2009-37966
"Cohen is great at identifying parental concerns, and he responds with reassuring answers, providing just enough information to assuage worries. Of the multitude of baby guides out there, this is, hands down, one of the best in years." Libr J
   Includes bibliographical references

Cohen, Susan

Normal at any cost; tall girls, short boys, and the medical industry's quest to manipulate height. [by] Susan Cohen and Christine Cosgrove. Jeremy P. Tarcher/Penguin 2009 405p il $26.95   **618.92**
   1. Growth disorders -- Hormone therapy 2. Hormone therapy 3. Pediatrics 4. Size 5. Stature
   ISBN 978-1-58542-683-6; 1-58542-683-0
                       LC 2008-40786
"Solid reporting on the reckless use of medical technology for socially dubious ends. " Kirkus
   Includes bibliographical references

DeGrandpre, Richard J.

Ritalin nation; rapid-fire culture and the transformation of human consciousness. Norton 1999 284p hardcover o.p. pa $13.95   **618.92**

1. Attention deficit disorder   2. Attention-deficit hyperactivity disorder -- Social aspects -- United States   3. Diagnostic errors 4. Methylphenidate hydrochloride   5. Ritalin

ISBN 0-393-32025-1 pa

LC 98-20687

The author questions "psychiatry's identification of ADHD as a biologically based brain disease. He argues that societal adjustments and a change in human consciousness are the real antidotes for this development disorder. Viewing hyperactivity in a multidisciplinary context, Ritalin Nation is richly referenced and offers a critical perspective suited to academic and specialized collections." Libr J

Includes bibliographical references

Diller, Lawrence H.

Running on Ritalin; a physician reflects on children, society, and performance in a pill. Bantam Bks. 1998 386p hardcover o.p. pa $12.95   **618.92**

1. Attention deficit disorder   2. Attention-deficit hyperactivity disorder -- Alternative treatment   3. Attention-deficit hyperactivity disorder -- Chemotherapy   4. Attention-deficit-disordered children -- Education   5. Attention-deficit-disordered children -- Rehabilitation   6. Children -- Health and hygiene 7. Methylphenidate hydrochloride 8. Ritalin

ISBN 0-553-37906-2 pa

LC 98-232695

The author discusses Attention deficit disorder (ADD), "the effects of Ritalin and behavior therapy, societal and parental expectations, ADD in adults, and treatment options." Libr J

Includes bibliographical references

Edwards, Laurie

Life disrupted; getting real about chronic illness in your twenties and thirties. Walker & Company 2008 272p pa $14.99   **618.92**

1. Chronic diseases

ISBN 978-0-8027-1649-1; 0-8027-1649-0

LC 2008-245

The author, who "manages bronchiectasis, thyroid disease, and celiac disease, among other conditions, ably describes the realities of people living longer with chronic (often rare) illnesses. . . . Using her own life story, Edwards shares practical advice about going to college, looking for a job, finding a partner, and deciding whether to have children, all the while juggling demanding health issues." Libr J

Includes bibliographical references

Ferber, Richard

Solve your child's sleep problems; Completely rev. and updated ed.; Fireside 2006 440p pa $15.95   **618.92**

1. Children -- Health and hygiene 2. Sleep

ISBN 0-7432-0163-9

LC 2006-41406

The author argues "that most sleep disruptions in one to six-year-olds are caused by improper sleep association (e.g., being rocked instead of lying still). Suggested corrections, often backed with specific case studies, are considerate of children; ditto for advice on prebedtime routines. . . . Interruptions in sleep (e.g., bedwetting, nightmares), establishing schedules, and children's natural sleep rhythms are all explored." Libr J

Foa, Edna B.

If your adolescent has an anxiety disorder; an essential resource for parents. [by] Edna B. Foa and Linda Wasmer Andrews. Oxford University Press 2006 227p il $30; pa $9.95   **618.92**

1. Anxiety

ISBN 0-19-518150-6; 978-0-19-518150-0; 0-19-518151-4 pa; 978-0-19-518151-7 pa

LC 2005-23770

"This text covers seven different conditions—social anxiety disorder, generalized anxiety disorder, obsessive-compulsive disorder, posttraumatic stress disorder, separation anxiety disorder, panic disorder, and specific phobias—emphasizing the first four. . . . Each disorder is accompanied by a definition, contributing factors, treatment information, and case studies." Libr J

Includes bibliographical references

Frith, Uta

Autism: explaining the enigma; 2nd ed; Blackwell 2003 249p il $59.95; pa $26.95   **618.92**

1. Autism 2. Autism in children

ISBN 0-631-22900-0; 0-631-22901-9 pa

LC 2002-12932

This "book is valuable for educated parents interested in learning about autism in a larger historical context. Frith writes a great deal on the problem that autistic people have with 'mind blindness,' the inability to look at and see other people." Libr J

Includes bibliographical references

Hayden, Torey L.

Twilight children; three voices no one heard until a therapist listened. [by] Torey Hayden. William Morrow 2005 331p $24.95   **618.92**

1. Child abuse 2. Psychotherapy

ISBN 0-06-056088-6

LC 2004-47376

"The author documents the particulars of her approach to treating a volatile, manipulative nine-year-old abuse victim; a mute but sociable and atypically charismatic four-year-old; and, in a change of pace, an 82-year-old stroke victim. The dysfunctional family dynamics impacting each patient are explored, as are impediments to the therapist's interfacing with relatives." SLJ

Hilden, Joanne M.

★ Shelter from the storm; caring for a child with a life-threatening condition. {by} Joanne M. Hilden and Daniel R. Tobin, with Karen Lindsey. Perseus 2003 224p pa $15.95   **618.92**

1. Critically ill children -- Care 2. Critically ill children

-- Mental health 3. Terminally ill children
ISBN 0-7382-0534-6

This guide "empowers parents to ask the right questions so that they can get necessary information and make the best decisions about their child's care. It also supports them through death and the grieving process if treatment fails. Using a combination of medical advice and quotes from parents who have been there, the authors have created a sensitive and useful resource." Libr J

Includes bibliographical references

Ives, Martine

Caring for a child with autism; a practical guide for parents. {by} Martine Ives and Nell Munro; illustrations by Fiona Bleach. Kingsley, J. 2002 304p il pa $18.95   **618.92**
1. Autism 2. Autism in children
ISBN 1-85302-996-3

LC 2001-38436

This "guide answers the questions commonly asked by parents and carers following a diagnosis of autism, and discusses the challenges that can arise in home life, education and socializing." Publisher's note

Includes bibliographical references and index

Jackson, Luke

Freaks, geeks and Asperger syndrome; a user guide to adolescence. foreword by Tony Attwood. Kingsley, J. 2002 217p il pa $17.95   **618.92**
1. Adolescent psychology 2. Asperger's syndrome 3. Asperger's syndrome -- Patients 4. Asperger's syndrome -- Patients -- Family relationships 5. Autism 6. Autistic youth
ISBN 1-8431-0098-3

LC 2002-70930

"In this terrific book that is sure to inspire other adolescents with the same condition, 13-year-old Jackson offers a teenager's perspective on what it's like to live with Asperger's. He also writes about his younger brother, who has a more severe condition on the ASD spectrum." Libr J

Includes bibliographical references

Janes-Hodder, Honna

★ **Childhood** cancer; a parent's guide to solid tumor cancers. [by] Honna Janes-Hodder, Nancy Keene. 2nd ed; O'Reilly & Assocs. 2002 xx, 537p il pa $29.95   **618.92**
1. Cancer 2. Children -- Diseases 3. Tumors in children
ISBN 0-59650-014-9

LC 2002-72284

This guide provides information on solid tumor childhood cancers, including neuroblastoma, Wilms tumor, liver tumors, soft tissue sarcomas, bone sarcomas and retinoblastoma. Medical terminology, diagnosis, treatment and hospitalization are discussed.

Johnson, Christopher M.

Your critically ill child; life and death choices parents must face. by Christopher Johnson. New Horizon Press 2007 212p pa $15.95   **618.92**
1. Children -- Medical care 2. Terminally ill children
ISBN 978-0-88282-284-6; 0-88282-284-5

LC 2006-923968

The author explains how pediatric intensive care units "operate and tells parents what to expect while their child is a patient. Case histories illustrate what may happen, while suggestions for self-care and lists of questions coach parents to play an active role. Johnson tackles issues such as ethics and medical expenses with sensitivity. A unique and much-needed resource for parents." Libr J

Lederman, Judith

The ups and downs of raising a bipolar child; a survival guide for parents. {by} Judith Lederman, Candida Fink. Fireside Books 2003 320p $14   **618.92**
1. Child rearing 2. Depression (Psychology) 3. Manic-depressive illness 4. Manic-depressive illness in children
ISBN 0-7432-2940-1

LC 2003-50696

"This guide's main strength lies in its suggestions for handling everyday issues between parent and child—how to minimize the misery of frequent blood tests, what to tell siblings, and coping with teens who get into legal trouble." Libr J

Includes bibliographical references

Linden, Dana Wechsler

Preemies; the essential guide for parents of premature babies. {by} Dana Wechsler Linden, Emma Trenti Paroli, and Mia Wechsler Doron. Pocket Bks. 2000 578p il pa $24.95 **618.92**
1. Birth weight, Low -- Complications 2. Infants (Premature) 3. Infants (Premature) -- Care 4. Pregnancy -- Complications 5. Premature infants
ISBN 0-671-03491-X

LC 00-28554

This guide "covers risk factors, the first day, the first week, surgery, taking the baby home and many other topics. Each section contains personal observations from parents of preemies, insightful comments from 'the doctor's perspective' and information on procedures, equipment, common problems and other issues." Publ Wkly

Martin, Katherine L.

Does my child have a speech problem? Chicago Review Press 1997 160p il pa $16.95   **618.92**
1. Children -- Health and hygiene 2. Speech disorders
ISBN 1-55652-315-7

LC 96-35302

The author addresses stuttering, fluency and articulation issues. Listening and auditory processing skills are discussed.

"Martin's writing style is clear and engaging, making this slim volume a quick, easy read." Libr J

Includes bibliographical references

Ozonoff, Sally

A **parent's** guide to Asperger syndrome and high-functioning autism; how to meet the challenges and help your child thrive. {by} Sally Ozonoff, Geraldine Dawson, James McPartland. Guilford Press 2002 278p il $38; pa $17.95 **618.92**
1. Asperger Syndrome 2. Asperger's syndrome -- Popular works 3. Autism 4. Autism -- Popular works 5. Autistic Disorder 6. Parenting
ISBN 1-57230-767-6; 1-57230-531-2 pa
LC 2002-5507
"This is an excellent resource for parents of children of the higher end of the autistic spectrum. All educators, the authors provide the basics on diagnosis, causes, and treatment. What makes their title essential is their positive emphasis on finding and channeling a child's strengths, as well as a sensitive discussion of home life, school, and the social world and life as an adult." Libr J
Includes bibliographical references

Papolos, Demitri F.

★ The **bipolar** child; the definitive and reassuring guide to childhood's most misunderstood disorder. [by] Demitri F. Papolos and Janice Papolos. 3rd ed.; Broadway Books 2006 xxii, 474p il hardcover o.p. pa $16.99 **618.92**
1. Child psychology 2. Depression (Psychology) 3. Manic-depressive illness
ISBN 0-7679-2297-2; 0-7679-2860-1 pa
LC 2005-55312
The authors "detail the diagnosis, explain how to find good treatment and medications, and advise parents about ways to advocate effectively for their children in school." Publisher's note
Includes bibliographical references

Richman, Shira

Raising a child with autism; a guide to applied behavior analysis for parents. Kingsley, J. 2000 173p pa $19.95 **618.92**
1. Autism 2. Autistic children 3. Autistic children -- Behavior modification 4. Parent-child relationship 5. Parents of autistic children
ISBN 1-85302-910-6
LC 00-47818
"Behavior therapy consultant Richman clearly outlines the applied behavior analysis (ABA) activities that parents can use with ASD children. Included is helpful guidance for toilet training, daily living, and increasing communication and sibling interaction. Since ABA consultants may be out of the financial or geographic reach of many parents, having a strong resource like this is invaluable." Libr J
Includes bibliographical references

Ryder, Christopher S.

Take your pediatrician with you; keeping your child healthy at home and on the road. Johns Hopkins University Press 2007 xxiii, 621p il pa $16 **618.92**
1. Children -- Travel 2. First aid 3. Health self-care
ISBN 978-0-8018-8601-0; 0-8018-8601-5
LC 2006-23120

This book "covers common pediatric illnesses and conditions, first aid, and travel-associated illnesses, clearly telling parents when to treat at home and when to seek medical attention. He also supplies a chapter on bringing a child adopted abroad back to the United States. This is an excellent choice and a bargain for both libraries and parents." Libr J

Sandler, Adrian

Living with spina bifida; a guide for families and professionals. illustrations by Peter Bedick. University of N.C. Press 1997 xxvii, 262p il hardcover o.p. pa $19.95 **618.92**
1. Spina bifida
ISBN 0-8078-4657-0 pa
LC 96-47697
This guide covers "issues of clinical management, habilitation, and early intervention from an interdisciplinary, holistic, and family-based perspective. In a series of chapters arranged according to the developmental stages of childhood—from birth through infancy, school age, adolescence, and young adulthood—Sandler discusses relevant medical, health, and psychosocial aspects of spina bifida. He addresses such concerns as education, daily living, and family relationships." Publisher's note

Selikowitz, Mark

★ **Down** syndrome; the facts. 3rd ed.; Oxford University Press 2008 211p il pa $19.95 **618.92**
1. Down syndrome
ISBN 978-0-19-923277-2
LC 2008-3360
Discusses possible causes of Down's syndrome, development of the child with the disease, medical problems and educational strategies, and includes advice for parents about future pregnancies.

Seroussi, Karyn

Unraveling the mystery of autism and pervasive developmental disorder; a mother's story of research and recovery. Broadway Books 2002 289p pa $14.95 **618.92**
1. Autism
ISBN 0-7679-0798-1
LC 2001-35575
This is an account of the author's experiences with her son, who was diagnosed with autism at 19 months. She discusses various therapies and the possible connections between autism and diet.

Shabecoff, Alice

Poisoned profits; the toxic assault on our children. [by] Philip Shabecoff and Alice Shabecoff. Random House 2008 353p **618.92**
1. Children -- Health and hygiene 2. Environmental health 3. Pollution
ISBN 1-4000-6430-9; 978-1-4000-6430-4
LC 2007-32250
"After reading this well-documented and accessible analysis, which exposes the American institutions' willingness to ignore science and public health in favor of protect-

ing corporations' rising profit rates, many will be roused to action." Environmental Health Perspectives

Includes bibliographical references

Sicherer, Scott H.

★ **Understanding** and managing your child's food allergies. Johns Hopkins University Press 2006 312p il $45; pa $18.95   **618.92**

1. Food allergy 2. Parenting

ISBN 0-8018-8491-8; 978-0-8018-8491-7; 0-8018-8492-6 pa; 978-0-8018-8492-4 pa

LC 2006-5261

This "book provides parents with practical advice for managing a child's environment at home, at school, or out in the world at large. In Part 2, 'Diagnosing a Food Allergy,' the practice of taking a detailed medical history is espoused and case studies serve to bring the issue home. An action plan for anaphylaxis, a life-threatening type of allergic reaction, as well as a chapter on food allergy resources are included." Libr J

Includes bibliographical references

Terr, Lenore

Magical moments of change; how psychotherapy turns kids around. W. W. Norton 2008 304p $27.95   **618.92**

1. Child psychiatry 2. Psychotherapy

ISBN 978-0-393-70530-0; 0-393-70530-7

LC 2007-16745

The author "has compiled 48 vignettes offered by 33 psychiatrists dealing with myriad cases, from mild development problems to juvenile delinquency to schizophrenia, recounting the almost magical moments of breakthrough." Booklist

Includes bibliographical references

Thompson, Charlotte E.

Raising a child with a neuromuscular disorder; a guide for parents, grandparents, friends, and professionals. Oxford Univ. Press 1999 275p $25 **618.92**

1. Children -- Diseases 2. Musculoskeletal system -- Abnormalities 3. Musculoskeletal system -- Diseases 4. Neuromuscular diseases in children

ISBN 0-19-512843-5

LC 99-30834

Thompson "suggests ways parents can be strong advocates for their children. . . . In addition to a chapter with descriptions and treatments of various neuromuscular disorders, there is a brief overview on genetics, a table summarizing the characteristics of various neuromuscular diseases, and a glossary of medical terms." Libr J

Includes bibliographical references and index

Wing, Lorna

The **autistic** spectrum; a parents' guide to understanding and helping your child. Ulysses Press 2001 240p pa $14.95   **618.92**

1. Autism 2. Autistic children -- Care and treatment

ISBN 1-56975-257-5

"While the depth of information here may be overwhelming to the parents of a newly diagnosed child . . . it is an excellent choice for those who require a text with more substance." Libr J

Includes bibliographical references

Autism and pervasive developmental disorders sourcebook; edited by Sandra J. Judd. Omnigraphics 2007 631p il $87   **618.92**

1. Autism

ISBN 978-0-7808-0953-6; 0-7808-0953-X

LC 2007-28714

Children with autism; a parent's guide. edited by Michael D. Powers; foreword by Temple Grandin. 2nd ed; Woodbine House 2000 xxvii, 427p il pa $17.95   **618.92**

1. Autism 2. Autism -- Popular works 3. Autistic children -- Popular works

ISBN 1-89062-704-6

LC 00-35165

Coverage includes "daily and family life, early intervention, educational programs, legal rights, advocacy, and a look at the years ahead with a chapter on adults with autism. . . . {Information is also provided} on current diagnostic criteria, Applied Behavior Analysis, the Individuals with Disabilities Education Act (IDEA), autism advocacy via the Internet, and much more." Publisher's note

Includes bibliographical references and index

Children with spina bifida; a parents' guide. edited by Marlene Lutkenhoff. 2nd ed; Woodbine House 2008 395p il pa $21.95   **618.92**

1. Spina bifida

ISBN 978-1-890627-77-5

LC 2007-39480

"The chapters deal with issues parents will face, from prenatal diagnosis to adulthood—legal issues, education, health concerns, treatments, therapies, and causes. The extensive Resource Guide at the back of the book is remarkable." Libr J [review of 1999 edition]

Includes bibliographical references

The Gale encyclopedia of children's health; infancy through adolescence. Kristine Krapp and Jeffrey Wilson, editors. Thomson Gale 2005 2178p 4v il set $550   **618.92**

1. Children -- Diseases -- Encyclopedias 2. Children -- Health and hygiene -- Encyclopedias 3. Reference books

ISBN 0-7876-9241-7

LC 2005-3478

The encyclopedia "covers the prenatal stages to age 18. It contains approximately 600 articles that range from 500 to 4000 words each and address medical conditions such as hernias, ringworm, and strep throat as well as topics like acting out, bullies, single-parent homes, and even allowances and money management. . . . This clearly written encyclopedia will be useful for students conducting research and for parents wanting to learn more about their children's conditions." Libr J

Includes bibliographical references

618.97 Geriatrics

Mace, Nancy L.

★ The **36**-hour day; a family guide to caring for people with Alzheimer disease, other dementias, and memory loss in later life. [by] Nancy L. Mace, Peter V. Rabins. 4th ed.; Johns Hopkins University Press 2006 xxii, 324p $45; pa $16.95 **618.97**
1. Alzheimer's disease
ISBN 978-0-8018-8510-5; 0-8018-8510-8; 978-0-8018-8509-9 pa; 0-8018-8509-4 pa
LC 2006-9627
A guide designed for families of Alzheimer's sufferers. Current research on the brain, behavior and personality is included.

The Gale encyclopedia of senior health; a guide for seniors and their caregivers. Jacqueline L. Longe, editor. Gale 2009 5v il set $683 **618.97**
1. Elderly -- Health and hygiene -- Encyclopedias 2. Reference books
ISBN 978-1-4144-0383-0; 978-1-4144-4855-8 ebook
LC 2008-17305
This encyclopedia, "with its ambitious yet clearly defined scope of coverage, value-added features, and accurate and accessible entries written by experts, provides an excellent first stop for information seekers, and even libraries that own any other print resources on the topic will want to give it a careful look. It should quickly take its place as an indispensable reference both for health consumers and for students across the broad range of disciplines that now make up the field of aging." Booklist
Includes bibliographical references

620 Engineering and allied operations

Berlow, Lawrence H.

The **reference** guide to famous engineering landmarks of the world; bridges, tunnels, dams, roads, and other structures. Oryx Press 1997 250p il $73.95 **620**
1. Engineering -- History
ISBN 0-89774-966-9
LC 97-36051
"The main section is an alphabetically arranged, double-column compendium of facts and histories of 600 structures. The format of each entry begins with the structure's location and date of construction. Size is often given, including metric, and the basic facts of the construction are provided. . . . A biography section provides background on 52 significant engineers or designers. A chronology section begins with the oldest surviving dam in the world (in Egypt) and continues to 2010, when a monster skyscraper, Millennium Tower, will be completed in Tokyo." Booklist

Frenay, Robert

Pulse; the coming age of systems and machines inspired by living things. Farrar, Straus and Giroux 2006 545p $30 **620**
1. Bioengineering 2. Bionics 3. Human-machine systems
ISBN 9780374113278; 0-374-11327-0
LC 2005-22285
"A smorgasbord de luxe, Frenay's reportage is sustaining fare for environmentalists." Booklist
Includes bibliographical references

Hall, J. Storrs

★ **Nanofuture**; what's next for nanotechnology. foreword by K. Eric Drexler. Prometheus Books 2005 333p il $29 **620**
1. Nanotechnology
ISBN 1-59102-287-8
LC 2005-1789
"This book fills a niche as a brief, inspirational introduction to nanotechnology for budding nanoscientists as well as the general public." Choice

Molotch, Harvey Luskin

Where stuff comes from; how toasters, toilets, cars, computers, and many other things come to be as they are. [by] Harvey Molotch. Routledge 2003 324p il $35; pa $29.95 **620**
1. Engineering
ISBN 0-415-94400-7; 0-415-95042-2 pa
LC 2003-1191
The author examines "the complicated, dynamic relationships between inventor, society, corporation, regulator, shopkeeper, community, family and customer. . . . Myriad links, he argues, ultimately produce and constantly change what we want, buy, keep and throw away; thus, neither consumers nor producers are to be blamed for our numerous possessions. . . . Molotch's description of systemic person-product complexes could work to end blame-the-consumer guilt-mongering in the popular discourse." Publ Wkly
Includes bibliographical references

Petroski, Henry

Invention by design; how engineers get from thought to thing. Harvard Univ. Press 1996 242p il map hardcover o.p. pa $14.95 **620**
1. Engineering 2. Engineering -- Social aspects 3. Inventions
ISBN 0-674-46368-4 pa
LC 96-19227
"Every case study includes well-chosen pictures and schematic drawings to clarify how inventors resolve technical difficulties, and the carefully research text explains how they make their new creations economically feasible and socially acceptable." Booklist
Includes bibliographical references

Remaking the world; adventures in engineering. Knopf 1997 239p il hardcover o.p. pa $13 **620**
1. Engineering
ISBN 0-375-70024-2 pa
LC 97-29328
A collection of the author's essays originally written for American Scientist. "Several pieces are about particular engineers . . . or engineering projects (the Channel Tunnel, the

Ferris Wheel); others are provocative (the flaws of engineering software, the creep of technology)." Libr J
Includes bibliographical references

Success through failure; the paradox of design. Princeton University Press 2006 235p il hardcover o.p. pa $21.95   **620**

1. Design 2. Engineering 3. Engineering design 4. System failures (Engineering)
ISBN 978-0-691-12225-0; 0-691-12225-3; 978-0-691-13642-4 pa; 0-691-13642-4 pa

LC 2005-34126

An "engaging and readable book. . . . Petroski uses countless interesting case histories to show how failure motivates technological advancement." IEEE Spectrum
Includes bibliographical references

The **essential** engineer; why science alone will not solve our global problems. Alfred A. Knopf 2010 274p il $26.95   **620**

1. Engineering 2. Technological innovations 3. Technology and civilization
ISBN 978-0-307-27245-4; 0-307-27245-1

LC 2009-21216

"Petroski presents a book-length argument for the place of engineering in humanity's future, especially when it comes to ensuring that future in the face of climate change, natural disasters, dwindling oil supplies and other global problems. . . . Scientists get the credit for everything from the moon landing to the construction of the Large Hadron Collider, he complains, when in reality those and myriad other projects large and small couldn't have been achieved without the creative, intelligent and rigorous input of engineers." Washington Post Book World
Includes bibliographical references

Sale, Kirkpatrick
The **fire** of his genius: Robert Fulton and the American dream. Free Press 2001 242p il $24; pa $13   **620**

1. Engineers 2. Inventors 3. Inventors -- United States -- Biography 4. Marine engineers -- United States -- Biography 5. Steamboats -- History
ISBN 0-684-86715-X; 0-7432-2321-7 pa

LC 2001-23064

Sale examines the life of the American inventor, "explaining how his North River steamboat opened up the North American continent to settlement and how it became the key factor that influenced the beginnings of the American industrial revolution. . . . This is an informative, moving story that personalizes the relatively obscure life of a self-taught tinkerer who had a genius for self-promotion and exploiting the discoveries of others." Libr J
Includes bibliographical references

Sargent, Ted
The **dance** of molecules; how nanotechnology is changing our lives. Thunder's Mouth Press 2006 234p il $25; pa $15.95   **620**

1. Nanotechnology
ISBN 1-56025-809-8; 978-1-56025-809-4; 1-56025-

895-0 pa; 978-1-56025-895-7 pa

LC 2006-275492

"This book is an enjoyable way to obtain a basic understanding of nanotechnology." Sci Books Films
Includes bibliographical references

620.1   Engineering mechanics and materials

Brady, George S.
  ★ **Materials** handbook; an encyclopedia for managers, technical professionals, purchasing and production managers, technicians and supervisors. 15th ed; McGraw-Hill 2002 1244p $99.95   **620.1**

1. Materials -- Encyclopedias 2. Reference books
ISBN 978-0-07-136076-0; 0-07-136076-X

"Covers more than 15,000 minerals, animal and plant substances, and commercial and engineering materials. Uses, production methods, and trade names are included for common items. Most entries are shorter than half a page. The special chapter on structure and properties of materials includes charts, tables, and a glossary of terms. Uses both SI and U.S. customary units. Subject index is very important because the main text has no cross-references." Guide to Ref Books. 11th edition

Freinkel, Susan
Plastic; a toxic love story. Houghton Mifflin Harcourt 2011 324p $27 **620.1**

1. Plastics
ISBN 978-0-547-15240-0

LC 2010-43019

"At first a godsend, [plastic] reduced dependence on shrinking natural resources, such as the shell of the hawksbill turtle (combs) or elephants' ivory (billiard balls and piano keys.) Ultimately it democratized materialism, making everything available to everybody, cheaply. Now, the partner we've found in plastic 'can rightly inspire both our deepest admiration and our strongest disgust.' To describe its history, wonders and dangers, journalist Freinkel reviews eight products: the comb, the chair, the Frisbee, the IV bag, the disposable lighter, the grocery bag, the soda bottle and the credit card. You will not look casually at any of them again." Cleveland Plain Dealer
Includes bibliographical references

621   Applied physics

Alley, Richard B.
Earth; the operators' manual. W.W. Norton 2011 479p il $27.95 **621**

1. Energy development 2. Greenhouse effect 3. Renewable energy resources
ISBN 978-0-393-08109-1

LC 2010-54016

The author "presents a primer on combatting global warming. The book begins with a history of how fuel—from trees, whale oil, and petroleum—has been instrumental to civilization and how we tend to exhaust our sources. He goes on to explain how scientists study climate change and why the evidence is convincing, and ends with a call to action and an overview of possible solutions. . . . This optimistic book ought to convince even the most obstinate climate-change denier." Publ Wkly

Includes bibliographical references

American Society of Mechanical Engineers/History and Heritage Committee

Landmarks in mechanical engineering; {by} ASME International History and Heritage. Purdue Univ. Press 1997 364p il $62.95; pa $24.95 **621**

1. Engineering -- History 2. Mechanical engineering
ISBN 1-55753-093-9; 1-55753-094-7 pa

LC 96-31573

This collection of essays on "American 'industrial archaeology' discusses still-existing artifacts ranging from the Saugus Ironworks (1640s) to the Saturn V rocket. . . . {Areas considered} include pumping, mechanical and electrical power, power tranmission, minerals extraction and refining, manufacturing, food processing, materials handling, environmental control, water transportation through space transportation, research, communications and processing, and biomedical engineering." Choice

Includes bibliographical references

Krupp, Frederic D.

Earth, the sequel; the race to reinvent energy and stop global warming. [by] Fred Krupp and Miriam Horn. W. W. Norton & Co. 2008 279p $24.95; pa $15.95 **621**

1. Energy conservation 2. Global warming 3. Greenhouse effect 4. Power resources -- Research
ISBN 978-0-393-06690-6; 0-393-06690-8; 978-0-393-33419-7 pa; 0-393-33419-8 pa

LC 2008-01317

"This volume is a 'must read' for anyone involved or interested in the future of energy generation and the consequences of global warming. It is a careful and readable review of the research and development occurring now in the areas of solar energy." Sci Books Films

Includes bibliographical references

Marks' standard handbook for mechanical engineers; [edited by] Eugene A. Avallone, Theodore Baumeister, Ali Sadegh. 11th ed; McGraw-Hill 2006 1800p il $199.95 **621**

1. Mechanical engineering -- Handbooks, manuals, etc.
ISBN 978-0-07-142867-5; 0-07-142867-4

This volume presents concisely the basic scientific and technical data of mechanical engineering, covering theory, basic mechanism, standard practice, often-needed mathematical formulae and technical data.

621.3 Electrical, magnetic, optical,

communications, computer engineering; electronics, lighting

Kaplan, Steven M.

Wiley electrical and electronics engineering dictionary. John Wiley & Sons 2004 885p pa $73.50 **621.3**

1. Electric engineering -- Dictionaries 2. Electrical engineering -- Dictionaries 3. Electronics -- Dictionaries 4. Reference books
ISBN 0-471-40224-9

LC 2003-66068

This "will be an asset to any university library that supports an electrical and electronics engineering curriculum, or to any professional engineering library. . . . A superb resource." Choice

Includes bibliographical references

McPartland, Brian J.

National Electrical Code 2008 handbook; by Brian J. McPartland, Joseph F. McPartland and Frederic P. Hartwell. 26th ed.; McGraw-Hill 2009 1561p il $75 **621.3**

1. Electrical engineering -- Handbooks, manuals, etc. 2. Reference books
ISBN 978-0-07-154652-2

This handbook presents analysis and commentary on the National Electrical Code, as it pertains to wiring of appliances, buildings, emergency systems, and other types of electrical construction.

Shulman, Seth

★ The **telephone** gambit; chasing Alexander Graham Bell's secret. W. W. Norton & Co. 2008 256p il $24.95 **621.3**

1. Biography, Individual 2. Inventors 3. Teachers of the deaf 4. Telecommunications executives 5. Telephone 6. Telephone -- History
ISBN 978-0-393-06206-9; 0-393-06206-6

LC 2007-30904

The author argues that Alexander Graham Bell is not the true inventor of the telephone.

This book "does a neat job of painting, in rapid brush strokes, a portrait of the thrilling era of innovation in which Bell lived and also of the interesting circumstances of his life. . . . [He] also manages to lace his work with just enough technology to tell his story without losing the interest of any low-tech readers." Christ Sci Monit

Includes bibliographical references

★ American electricians' handbook; [by] Terrell Croft, Wilford I. Summers, [and] Frederic P Hartwell. 15th ed; McGraw-Hill 2008 various paging il $89.95 **621.3**

1. Electrical engineering -- Handbooks, manuals, etc.
ISBN 978-0-07-149462-5

"A Standard handbook, written to be in accordance with the latest ed. of the National Electrical code." Guide to Ref Books. 11th edition

National Electrical Code handbook; 11th ed; National Fire Protection Assn. 2008 1440p $130 **621.3**

1. Electrical engineering -- Handbooks, manuals, etc.

ISBN 978-0-87765-793-4; 0-87765-793-9

This "is a nationally accepted guide to the safe installation of electrical conductors and equipment, and is, in fact, the basis for all electrical codes used in the United States." Ref Sources for Small & Medium-sized Libr. 5th edition

Standard handbook for electrical engineers; 15th ed.; McGraw-Hill 2007 various pagings il $195 **621.3**

1. Electrical engineering -- Handbooks, manuals, etc.

ISBN 978-0-07-144146-9; 0-07-144146-8

Contains data on all branches of electrical engineering including material in the field of nuclear physics, plastics and resins, transistors and television.

621.31   Generation, modification, storage, transmission of electric power

Black & Decker Corp.

The **complete** guide to wiring; 4th ed.; Creative Pub. International 2008 351p il pa $24.99 **621.31**

1. Electric wiring

ISBN 978-1-58923-413-0; 1-58923-413-8

LC 2008-16519

"This book contains projects not commonly seen in other guides, such as remote controlled lighting and childproofing. Money-saving projects like replacing cords and installing programmable thermostats will provide a great service to budget-conscious patrons." Libr J

Fletcher, Seth

Bottled lightning; superbatteries, electric cars, and the new lithium economy. Hill and Wang 2011 260p $26 **621.31**

1. Electric batteries 2. Electronics 3. Lithium

ISBN 978-0-8090-3053-8; 0-8090-3053-5

LC 2010-47695

"Provides an entertaining, surprisingly eventful history of human efforts to harness energy in the form of battery power . . . . A fine, readable work of popular science." Kirkus

Includes bibliographical references

Schlesinger, Henry R.

The **battery**; how portable power sparked a technological revolution. [by] Henry Schlesinger. Smithsonian Books 2010 308p il $25.99 **621.31**

1. Electric batteries 2. Storage batteries

ISBN 978-0-06-144293-3

LC 2009-34303

"From its witty subtitle ('sparked,' get it?), to its lively writing style, to its sheer abundance of fascinating and frequently surprising stories, this is a delightful book." Booklist

Includes bibliographical references

621.319   Transmission

Cauldwell, Rex

Safe home wiring projects. Taunton Press 1997 151p il pa $19.95 **621.319**

1. Electric wiring

ISBN 1-56158-164-X

LC 97-5789

The author "starts by explaining basic electrical principles and shows which tools to use. A section on inspecting your home's electrical system is particularly helpful, describing various hazards and pitfalls. Other sections cover repairing wiring switches and receptacles and installing light fixtures, ceiling and bathroom fans and home entertainment systems. . . . This is an excellent title for beginners." Libr J

621.32   Lighting

Brox, Jane

Brilliant; the evolution of artificial light. Houghton Mifflin Harcourt 2010 360p $25 **621.32**

1. Lighting

ISBN 978-0-547-05527-5; 0-547-05527-7

LC 2009-35441

The author "examines our relationship with light, our attempts to harness it to brighten places we cannot see, and its impact on American psychology and culture. . . . This well-written, well-researched, and thought-provoking book has much to offer. The general reader with an interest in the (social) history of technology will find it . . . a source of inspiration for considering technology's impact on our lives." Libr J

Includes bibliographical references

621.381   Electronics

Goodman, Robert L.

How electronic things work--and what to do when they don't; 2nd ed; TAB Electronics 2003 xx, 426p il $24.95 **621.381**

1. Electronic apparatus and appliances -- Maintenance and repair

ISBN 0-07-138745-5

LC 2003-265249

"Explains the practical side of electronics—troubleshooting problems, testing, repair, and servicing. Although the reader may not learn all the basics of electronics here, there is certainly a lot to be learned about resolving typical problems with common household items." Libr J

Schultz, Mitchel E.

★ **Grob's** basic electronics; 11th ed.; McGraw-Hill 2011 xxvi, 1206p il $155.31 **621.381**

1. Electricity 2. Electronics

ISBN 978-0-07-351085-9; 0-07-351085-8

LC 2010-8273

An introductory text on the fundamentals of electricity and electronics for technicians in radio, television, and industrial electronics.

★ Standard handbook of electronic engineering; Donald Christiansen, editor, Charles K. Alexander, editor, Ronald K. Jurgen, associate editor. 5th ed.; McGraw-Hill 2005 various pagings il $157.50 **621.381**
1. Electronics -- Handbooks, manuals, etc.
ISBN 978-0-07-138421-6; 0-07-138421-9
LC 2005-47880
Covers essential principles, data, and design information on the components, circuits, equipment, and systems of electronics engineering. Emphasizes practical use of basic principles. Includes computer-aided design and electronic data processing.

The illustrated dictionary of electronics; Stan Gibilisco, editor-in-chief. 8th ed; McGraw-Hill 2001 791, [11]p il pa $44.95 **621.381**
1. Electronics -- Dictionaries 2. Reference books
ISBN 0-07-137236-9
LC 2001-272029
This illustrated dictionary contains nearly 28,000 entries—definitions, abbreviations, and acronyms—including terms in the fields of robotics, artificial intelligence, and personal computing as they relate to electronics. Also included is terminology in: lasers; television; radio; IC technology; digital and analog electronics; audio and video; power supplies; fiber optic communications, etc.

621.382   Communications engineering

Tompkins, Dave
How to wreck a nice beach; the vocoder from World War II to hip-hop: the machine speaks. Melville House/Stop Smiling Books 2010 334p il $35 **621.382**
1. Electronic music 2. Electronic music -- History and criticism 3. Musicians 4. Vocoder
ISBN 978-1-933633-88-6; 1-933633-88-3
LC 2009-50617
This is "much more than a labor of love: It's an intergalactic vision quest fueled by several thousand gallons of high-octane spiritual-intellectual lust. . . . [Tompkin's] biggest and most perilous adventure in How to Wreck a Nice Beach is the plunge deep into the throbbing radioactive heart of his own prose—a hallucinatory stew of Rimbaud, Tom Wolfe, Lester Bangs, and Bootsy Collins." New York
Includes bibliographical references

Weems, David B.
Designing, building, and testing your own speaker system with projects; 4th ed; McGraw-Hill hardcover o.p. pa $19.95 **621.382**
1. Intercommunication systems
ISBN 0-07-069428-1; 978-0-07-069429-3 pa; 0-07-069429-X pa
LC 96-30967
This manual offers instructions on building low cost high quality loudspeaker systems using the latest audio technology.

621.383   Specific communications systems

Silverman, Kenneth
★ **Lightning** man; the accursed life of Samuel F.B. Morse. Knopf 2003 503p il $35 **621.383**
1. Artists 2. Biography, Individual 3. Cipher and telegraph codes 4. Inventors 5. Painters 6. Telegraph
ISBN 0-375-40128-8
LC 2002-43613
This is a "biography of Samuel F.B. Morse, the inventor of the Morse code and the disputed inventor of the electromagnetic telegraph. . . . Silverman shows how Morse's never-ending battle with negative self-image, a result of his strict Calvinist upbringing, was the common thread that tied together the disparate events of his life. And Silverman's well-paced, character-driven storytelling brings Morse's raw, emotional persona to life. Strongly recommend for public libraries and for academic library collections at all levels." Libr J

621.384   Radio and radar

Carr, Joseph J.
Old time radios! restoration and repair. TAB Bks. 1991 256p il hardcover o.p. pa $19.95 **621.384**
1. Radio -- Repairing
ISBN 0-8306-3342-1 pa
LC 90-44411
This guide includes the history, theory and practical operation of old-time radio sets and detailed instructions and schematics for repairing and rebuilding them

★ The ARRL handbook for radio communications 2011; 88th ed.; American Radio Relay League 2010 various pagings il $49.95 **621.384**
1. Radio -- Handbooks, manuals, etc.
ISBN 978-0-87259-095-3
"Chapters cover fundamentals and changing technology in the field and include many tables, circuit diagrams, photographs, and occasional references." Guide to Ref Books. 11th edition

621.388   Television

Abramson, Albert
★ The **history** of television, 1942 to 2000; foreword by Christopher H. Sterling. McFarland & Co. 2003 309p il hardcover o.p. pa $75 **621.388**
1. Television -- History
ISBN 0-7864-1220-8; 978-0-7864-3243-1 pa; 0-7864-3243-8 pa
LC 2002-326
"No reference work available in print right now matches the attention to detail that is obvious here. A significant work on how the machinery of television has evolved, this . . . should stand as the authority for years to come." Libr J
Includes bibliographical references

Capelo, Gregory R.

VCR troubleshooting & repair; {by} Gregory R. Capelo, Robert C. Brenner. 3rd ed; Newnes 1998 434p il $34.95 **621.388**
1. Home video systems -- Maintenance and repair
ISBN 0-7506-9940-X
LC 97-27610

This is a guide to caring for VCRs including preventative maintenance, diagnosing problems and making repairs.

Davidson, Homer L.

TV repair for beginners; rev and expanded ed; McGraw-Hill 1998 376p il $44.95; pa $29.95 **621.388**
1. Television -- Repairing
ISBN 0-07-015805-3; 0-07-015806-1 pa
LC 97-25446

This is a guide to the operation and repair of standard TV components as well as universal remote transmitters, stereo TV, digital controls, new color circuits and picture tube sizes, and digital satellite receivers.

621.39 Computer engineering

Isaacson, Walter

★ Steve Jobs. Simon & Schuster 2011 656p il por **621.39**
1. Biography, Individual 2. Businesspeople -- United States -- Biography 3. Computer engineers -- United States -- Biography 4. Entrepreneurship 5. Executives 6. Inventors -- United States -- Biography
ISBN 9781451648546; 1451648537; 9781451648539; 9781451648553; 1451648553 ebook
LC 2011045006

This book discusses the "basic outlines of [Steve] Jobs' career. . . . He was the co-creator of the personal computer. . . . [A]gainst the backdrop of [Jobs'] abrasive personality, [Walter] Isaacson's book offers an overriding message . . . he was a creative genius whose profound understanding of consumer appetites allowed him to create technology that no one else imagined or even thought feasible." (Commentary)

"This is an encyclopedic survey of all that Mr. Jobs accomplished, replete with the passion and excitement that it deserves." N Y Times Book Rev

Includes bibliographical references and index.

Mueller, Scott

★ Upgrading and repairing PCs; 18th ed; Que Pub. 2007 1556p il $59.99 **621.39**
1. Microcomputers -- Maintenance and repair 2. Microcomputers -- Upgrading
ISBN 978-0-7897-3697-0; 0-7897-3697-7
LC 2007-34956

This guide to maintaining, upgrading, and repairing personal computers explains physical disassembly and reassembly, primary system components, input/output hardware, mass storage systems, maintenance, troubleshooting and diagnostics. It includes a technical reference, a glossary, and lists vendors of replacement parts.

621.43 Internal-combustion engines

Weil, Elizabeth

They all laughed at Christopher Columbus; an incurable dreamer builds the first civilian spaceship. Bantam Bks. 2002 230p il hardcover o.p. pa $13.95 **621.43**
1. Aerospace industry executives 2. Rocketry 3. Space flight
ISBN 0-553-38236-5 pa
LC 2002-18665

"Gary Hudson, the subject of the book, was a space enthusiast of the 1950s. He believed that NASA engineers were wrong in their approach to space travel. He was convinced that private industry could build a vehicle to deliver humans into space more cheaply and more effectively than the government. . . . He sketched a rough drawing of his idea for a space vehicle he called the Roton. It looked like a 60-foot nose cone with a helicopter blade." Sci Books Films

621.8 Machine engineering

Gurstelle, William

Adventures from the technology underground; catapults, pulsejets, rail guns, flamethrowers, tesla coils, air cannons, and the garage warriors who love them. Clarkson Potter 2006 224p $25; pa $13.95 **621.8**
1. Machine design
ISBN 1-4000-5082-0; 0-307-35125-4 pa
LC 2005-20412

The author takes "readers into the hidden communities of people involved in developing hurling machines (catapults and trebuchets), pulse jet engines, flamethrowers, tesla coil-powered electric current theater, air cannons, robots, high-powered rockets, and magnetic linear accelerator guns. . . . Gurstelle balances scientific explanations of the technologies with profiles of the people who built them and descriptions of the events at which they were showcased." Libr J

Includes bibliographical references

621.9 Tools

Hack, Garrett

Classic hand tools; photographs by John S. Sheldon. Taunton Press 1999 218p il $34.95; pa $24.95 **621.9**
1. Tools 2. Tools -- Collectors and collecting
ISBN 1-56158-273-5; 1-56158-507-6 pa
LC 99-23719

In this look at old, muscle-powered tools Hack discusses "how to maintain them; and, for some of the obscurer ones, what exactly their purposes are. The resulting book is surprisingly comprehensive, covering just about everything from scrapers to saws and including a most interesting chapter on antique-tool collecting." Booklist

Includes bibliographical references and index

Nagyszalanczy, Sandor

★ **Power** tools; an electrifying celebration and grounded guide. written and photographed by Sandor Nagyszalanczy. Taunton Press 2001 266p il $40; pa $24.95 **621.9**

    1. Power tools

    ISBN 1-56158-427-4; 1-56158-576-9 pa

                     LC 2001-33097

    This work covers the history, design, accessories and recent developments of portable and stationary power tools

    "Tool collectors and those considering tool purchases will find this title invaluable." Libr J

622   Mining and related operations

Reece, Erik

Lost mountain; a year in the vanishing wilderness: radical strip mining, and the devastation of Appalachia. foreword by Wendell Berry; photographs by John J. Cox. Riverhead Books 2006 250p il $24.95; pa $14 **622**

    1. Coal mines and mining 2. Human influence on nature 3. Strip mining -- Appalachian Region 4. Strip mining -- Environmental aspects

    ISBN 1-59448-908-4; 1-59448-236-5 pa

                     LC 2005-52921

    The author explores the effects of strip mining on the landscape of Eastern Kentucky.

    Reece "has written an impassioned account of a business rife with industrial greed, devious corporate ownership and unenforced environmental laws. It's also a heartrending account of the rural residents whose lives are being ruined by strip-mining's relentless, almost unfettered, encroachment." Publ Wkly

    Includes bibliographical references

623.4   Ordnance

Chivers, C. J.

The **gun**; the AK-47 and the evolution of war. Simon & Schuster 2010 481p il $28 **623.4**

    1. AK-47 rifle 2. Firearms 3. Machine guns 4. Military history 5. Rifles 6. War -- History

    ISBN 978-0-7432-7076-2; 0-7432-7076-2

                     LC 2010-20459

    This "is gripping and original interpretive history, highly recommended." Libr J

    Includes bibliographical references

Conant, Jennet

★ **109** East Palace; Robert Oppenheimer and the secret city of Los Alamos. Simon & Schuster 2005 425p map hardcover o.p. pa $14 **623.4**

    1. Atomic bomb 2. Atomic bomb -- United States -- History 3. College teachers 4. Government employees 5. Government officials 6. Office workers 7. Physicists

    ISBN 0-7432-5007-9; 0-7432-5008-7 pa

                     LC 2005-42497

    "Anyone interested in the history of atomic weapons will find this book totally engrossing." Sci Books Films

    Includes bibliographical references

Degroot, Gerard J.

The **bomb**; a life. Gerard J. DeGroot. Harvard 2005 xiii, 397p ill. (hbk.) o.p.; (pbk.) $23.50 **623.4**

    1. Nuclear weapons 2. Nuclear weapons -- History

    ISBN 0674017242; 9780674022355

                     LC 2004-57657

    This book "tells the story of . . . [the atom bomb] that--at least since 8:16 a.m. on August 6, 1945--has haunted our dreams and threatened our existence. The Bomb has killed hundreds of thousands outright, condemned many more to lingering deaths, and made vast tracts of land unfit for life. For decades it dominated the psyches of millions, becoming a touchstone of popular culture, celebrated or decried in mass political movements, films, songs, and books. [Author Gerard] DeGroot traces the life of the Bomb from its birth in turn-of-the-century physics labs of Europe to a childhood in the New Mexico desert of the 1940s, from adolescence and early adulthood in Nagasaki and Bikini, Australia and Kazakhstan to maturity in test sites and missile silos around the globe." (Publisher's note)

    This history of the nuclear age "begins with the bomb's development during WW II and ends with the aftermath of 9/11. . . . Ideal for both scholars and general readers, this promises to be a standard work for years to come." Choice

    Includes bibliographical references (p. [370]-375) and index.

Hodge, Nathan

A **nuclear** family vacation; travels in the world of atomic weaponry. [by] Nathan Hodge and Sharon Weinberger. Bloomsbury 2008 324p $24.99 **623.4**

    1. Arms control 2. Nuclear engineering 3. Nuclear nonproliferation 4. Nuclear weapons

    ISBN 978-1-59691-378-3; 1-59691-378-9

                     LC 2008-2013

    This "is a book that is both entertaining and informative. Hodge and Weinberger are shrewd and observant nuclear tour guides who are knowledgeable about their subject without being didactic." Am Sci

    Includes bibliographical references

Rhodes, Richard

★ **Dark** sun; the making of the hydrogen bomb. Simon & Schuster 1995 731p il hardcover o.p. pa $18 **623.4**

    1. Air force officers 2. Arms race 3. Cold War 4. Cold war 5. College teachers 6. Generals 7. Government officials 8. Hydrogen bomb 9. Physicists 10. Spies 11. Writers on science

    ISBN 0-684-82414-0

                     LC 95-11070

    "This meticulously documented treatise presents a gripping story." Libr J

★ The **making** of the atomic bomb. Simon & Schuster 1986 886p il hardcover o.p. pa $20 **623.4**

1. Atomic bomb

ISBN 0-684-81378-5 pa

LC 86-15445

"The book provides portraits of the many players from Szilard and Einstein to Oppenheimer. . . . The book is heavily documented and includes a 13-page bibliography. This is a definitive work, well written, with a gripping story. It is not an easy book to read, but is well worth the effort." Libr J

Yenne, Bill

Tommy gun; how General Thompson's submachine gun wrote history. Thomas Dunne Books 2009 340p il $26.99 **623.4**

1. Firearms 2. Generals 3. Inventors 4. Military engineers 5. Thompson submachine gun

ISBN 978-0-312-38326-8

LC 2009-17591

In this history of the Thompson gun, the author "describes the struggle to create and sustain a market for the gun and the struggle to counteract its reputation as a 'gangster gun' from its use by noted criminals like Al Capone and John Dillinger. Yenne mixes this history with a fascinating look at how popular culture, particularly feature films, has shaped the gun's story." Libr J

Includes bibliographical references (p. 325-328)

Gun digest 2009; edited by Ken Ramage. 63rd ed; Krause Publications 2008 568p il pa $29.99 **623.4**

1. Firearms 2. Shooting

ISBN 978-0-89689-647-5; 0-89689-647-1

This reference work covers information relating to shotguns, rifles, cartridges, sights and scopes, availability of arms and accessories, technical articles on hunting, gun control, foreign arms, etc.

Shooter's bible; Keith Sutton, editor. 99th ed; Stoeger 2007 576p il pa $24.95 **623.4**

1. Firearms -- Catalogs 2. Reference books

ISBN 978-0-8831-7343-5; 0-8831-7343-3

Contains specifications and manufacturers' current prices for a variety of firearms and accessories. Also includes articles on related subjects, gun finder index, and caliber finder index.

★ Weapons & warfare; editor, John Powell. 2nd ed.; Salem Press 2010 3v il map set $395 **623.4**

1. Military art and science 2. Military weapons 3. Reference books

ISBN 978-1-58765-594-4

LC 2009-50491

"Volume 1, Ancient & Medieval, . . . covers warfare from prehistoric times to approximately 1500; Volume 2, Modern, covers 1500 to the present. The organization is chronological by geographic region, and both volumes open with essays discussing weapons and forces used in that era of history, how and why those tools of warfare have evolved or been discontinued, and the military achievement of the forces, weapons, uniforms and armor, military organiza-

tions, and doctrine strategy and tactics. In the third volume, Culture and Concepts, essays cover social aspects of war, technological achievements used in warfare, and morality of behavior during war. . . . This useful overview of warfare's evolution will be appreciated by students as well as general readers." Libr J

623.7 Communications, vehicles, sanitation, related topics

Macy, Edward

Apache: inside the cockpit of the world's most deadly fighting machine. Atlantic Monthly Press 2008 xxvi, 374p il map $25 **623.7**

1. Afghan War, 2001- 2. Military airplanes

ISBN 978-0-8021-1894-3; 0-8021-1894-1

"Macy, now retired from the British army, spent an active tour in Afghanistan's Helmand Province flying Apache helicopter combat sorties in support of the NATO ground mission there. He loved the work, which was demanding, violent, and incredibly expensive. An absorbing, exciting chronicle of a 21st-century soldier fighting on the high-tech side of asymmetric warfare." Libr J

623.74 Vehicles

Fredriksen, John C.

Warbirds; an illustrated guide to U.S. military aircraft, 1915-2000. ABC-CLIO 1999 363p il $75 **623.74**

1. Aircraft industry -- United States 2. Airplanes, Military -- United States 3. Military airplanes

ISBN 1-57607-131-6

LC 99-16624

This guide "covers all fighters, bombers, trainers, patrol craft, transports, and helicopters manufactured and deployed by military or naval units. . . . There are 325 entries, each with a black-and-white photograph of the aircraft and a listing of performance, power plant, armament, and service dates and a brief narrative detailing the development, deployment, and eventual retirement of the machines." Booklist

623.8 Nautical engineering and seamanship

Stewart, Matthew

Monturiol's dream; the extraordinary story of the submarine inventor who wanted to save the world. Pantheon Books 2004 338p il map $25 **623.8**

1. Inventors 2. Physicists 3. Submarines

ISBN 0-375-41439-8

LC 2003-62368

"Utopian revolutionary Monturiol had a vision of a submarine to free coral divers from hardship and then free the world from the tumult of the atmosphere. Stewart . . . comes admirably close to capturing the transcendent weirdness of Monturiol's quest." Publ Wkly

Includes bibliographical references

Jane's fighting ships 2008-2009; edited by Stephen Saunders. Jane's Information Group 2008 il $915 **623.8**
1. Navies 2. Warships
ISBN 978-0-7106-2845-9
"Arranged alphabetically by country, subdivided by class of ship. Gives numbers and names of ships in each class; builders; dates of laying down, launching, and completion; a photograph of a ship in the class; and specifications for the class." Guide to Ref Books. 11th edition

623.88 Seamanship

Pawson, Des
The **handbook** of knots; Expanded ed.; DK 2004 176p il pa $17 **623.88**
1. Knots and splices 2. Rope
ISBN 0-7566-0374-9; 978-0-7566-0374-8
LC 2004-274491
"This is a step-by-step guide to tying and using more than 100 knots. . . . There's a chapter on rope construction, rope materials, and properties of ropes and their main uses. It's very informative and put together concisely." BAYA Book Rev [review of 1998 edition]

623.89 Navigation

Cutler, Thomas J.
Dutton's nautical navigation; [by] Thomas J. Cutler; with the U.S. Naval Institute Navigation Board. 15th ed; Naval Inst. Press 2004 447p il map $55 **623.89**
1. Navigation
ISBN 1-557502-48-X
LC 2003-11183
This guide for the coastal and seagoing mariner focuses on piloting, celestial navigation, radio navigation and dead reckoning.

624.2 Bridges

Blockley, D. I.
Bridges; the science and art of the world's most inspiring structures. Oxford University Press 2010 312p il $29.95 **624.2**
1. Bridges
ISBN 978-0-19-954359-5
"In this fascinating exploration for lay readers, Blockley lucidly explains both the basic forces at work on every bridge—tension, compression, and shear—and the structural elements combating those forces: beams, arches, trusses, and suspension cables. . . . Bold, insightful statements help make this a remarkable work." Publ Wkly
Includes bibliographical references

Petroski, Henry
Engineers of dreams; great bridge builders and the spanning of America. Knopf 1995 479p il hardcover o.p. pa $16 **624.2**
1. Bridge engineers 2. Bridges 3. Bridges -- United States 4. Civil engineering 5. Civil engineers
ISBN 0-679-76021-0 pa
LC 94-48893
"An exhilarating saga of ingenuity and sheer determination." Publ Wkly
Includes bibliographical references

625.2 Railroad rolling stock

Jensen, Joel
Steam: an enduring legacy; the railroad photographs of Joel Jensen. introduction by Scott Lothes; essay by John Gruber; afterword by Jeff Brouws. W. W. Norton & Company 2011 160p il $50 **625.2**
1. Railroads -- Pictorial works 2. Steam engines
ISBN 978-0-393-08248-7; 0-393-08248-2
"Jensen has been photographing trains and rail stations west of the Mississippi River for some 25 years, and this long-overdue collection of his work features black-and-white shots that capture the bygone majesty and sense of history inspired by these steam-powered machines, preserved and operated in the latter-day era by dedicated rail-fans. Besides the 150 photos, there are essays by John Gruber and Scott Lothes—both of the Center for Railroad Photography and Art—examining the economics and cultural importance of trains in America." BookPage

McDonnell, Greg
Locomotives; the modern diesel & electric reference. Boston Mills Press 2008 240p il $49.95; pa $29.95 **625.2**
1. Locomotives
ISBN 978-1-55046-493-1; 978-1-55407-896-7 pa
LC 2009417490
This book "covers all mainline models built for North American railroads from the mid-1970s to today, from EMD Dash 2s and GE Dash 7s to the latest 70 Series and Evolution Series models, as well as Green Goats, Gensets and mainline passenger electric-powered locomotives." Publisher's note

625.7 Roads

Sobey, Ed
A **field** guide to roadside technology. Chicago Review Press 2006 204p il pa $14.95 **625.7**
1. Electronic apparatus and appliances 2. Roads 3. Traffic signs and signals
ISBN 1-55652-609-1
LC 2006002979
"For those travelers who have ever wondered what certain poles, signs, wires, markings, pipes, and other devices that line our streets, highways, and interstates are called and what functions they serve, this is the perfect book. More than 150 individual items, grouped in categories, are identified and concisely and understandably explained, often citing

their unique characteristics and interesting facts. A small black-and-white photo of each device is included. The text is sufficiently detailed without being overly technical." SLJ

Includes bibliographical references

627 Hydraulic engineering

Finch, Phillip

Diving into darkness; a true story of death and survival. St. Martin's Press 2008 310p il $25.95 **627**
1. Divers 2. Diving
ISBN 978-0-312-38394-7; 0-312-38394-0
LC 2008-24271

"In January 2005, extreme diver David Shaw entered Bushman's Hole, a watery crater in the Kalahari Desert. Easing himself through a narrow fissure, he aimed himself at the bottom of the crater, roughly 900 feet below him. Soon after, his diving partner, Don Shirley, followed Shaw down. In less than an hour, one of the men was dead, and the other faced a harrowing 10-hour decompression, during which he scrambled for every breath. This is a dramatic and emotional story. . . . A solid addition to the sport-diving genre." Booklist

Hiltzik, Michael A.

Colossus; Hoover Dam and the making of the American century. Free Press 2010 496p il map $30 **627**
1. Civil engineers 2. Hoover Dam (Ariz. and Nev.)
ISBN 978-1-4165-3216-3; 1-4165-3216-1
LC 2009-33833

In this account of the Hoover Dam story, Hiltzik "explains the technological and physical difficulties posed by the dam project, but he also fixes the endeavor in its time and captures the personalities of the people involved. . . . The author is at his best in a masterly portrayal of Frank Crowe, the central figure in the dam's construction. A born engineer who demanded much from his workmen, Crowe had to solve a myriad of problems on the fly as he confronted the unexpected difficulties of an unprecedented project in an unprecedented location. . . . One of the nice things about nonfiction such as 'Colossus' is that the stories don't need to be believable; they just need to be true." Wall Street J

Includes bibliographical references and index

Matson, Tim

Earth ponds A to Z; an illustrated encyclopedia. illustrated by Frank Fretz. Countryman Press 2003 225p il pa $18.95 **627**
1. Ponds 2. Water supply engineering
ISBN 0-88150-494-7
LC 2002-67672

"From Acid Rain to Zooplankton . . . Tim Matson defines and explains . . . {over} two hundred terms associated with pond building and maintenance. . . . The reader will find descriptions and definitions of . . . pond elements, including: structural features; construction materials; water conditions and treatments; aquacultural topics and crops; environmental concerns; government support and regulatory agencies {and} landscaping." Publisher's note

Includes bibliographical references

628.4 Waste technology, public toilets, street cleaning

Humes, Edward

Garbology; our dirty love affair with trash. Edward Humes. Avery 2012 277 p. **628.4**
1. Consumption (Economics) -- United States 2. Environmental engineering -- United States 3. Refuse and refuse disposal -- United States 4. Salvage (Waste, etc.) -- China 5. Social criticism 6. Waste management
ISBN 1583334343; 9781583334348
LC 2012001701

In this book, Edward Humes . . . [makes the case] that the United States—the world's largest generator of trash—will soon confront a new crisis of garbage. . . . Humes spotlights a turning point in the history of American garbage: the postwar rise of consumer culture, birthed by a new generation of advertisers who saw their mission in life as persuading Americans to throw away perfectly good things in order to buy bigger, better replacements. . . . Humes argues that an economy whose health depends on how much disposable stuff people buy is driving us toward a precipice. Making and trashing all those things will generate economic activity and jobs, to be sure, but the waste-driven model of mass consumption also eats up tremendous amounts of increasingly scarce resources. (Bookforum)

628.9 Other branches of sanitary and municipal engineering

National Fire Protection Association

Fire protection handbook; Arthur E. Cote, editor-in-chief; Casey C. Grant, John R. Hall, Jr., Robert E. Solomon, asoociate editors; Pamela A. Powell, managing editor. 20th ed; National Fire Protection Assn. 2008 2v il $233.75 **628.9**
1. Fire prevention
ISBN 978-0-87765-758-3; 0-87765-758-0
LC 2007-928644

"A handbook of approved practice in the fields of fire prevention and fire protection. Will be useful to owners and superintendents of buildings, and to architects and engineers interested in designing safe buildings and planning for their protection against fire." Carnegie Libr of Pittsburgh

629 Other branches of engineering

Bizony, Piers

The **man** who ran the moon; James E. Webb and the secret history of Project Apollo. Thunder's Mouth 2006 242p il $24.95 **629**
1. Apollo project 2. Biography, Individual 3. Cold War 4. Diplomats 5. Government officials 6. Lawyers 7. NASA officials
ISBN 1-56025-751-2; 9781560257512
LC 2006-298038

"Emerging from the bureaucratic thickets with an ultimately praiseworthy portrait of Webb, this should circulate with the space program set." Booklist

Includes bibliographical references

Mullane, R. Mike

Riding rockets; the outrageous tales of a space shuttle astronaut. [by] Mike Mullane. Scribner 2006 368p il hardcover o.p. pa $15   **629**

1. Air force officers 2. Astronauts 3. Biography, Individual

ISBN 978-0-7432-7682-5; 978-0-7432-7683-2 pa; 0-7432-7683-3 pa

LC 2005-56123

This is a memoir by the American astronaut.

"A strong addition to science and space collections of any size." Booklist

Space exploration; edited by Christopher Mari. Wilson, H.W. 1999 157p pa $50   **629**

1. Astronautics -- United States 2. Astronauts 3. Reference shelf 4. Senators 5. Space stations 6. Technology

ISBN 0-8242-0963-X

LC 99-25424

629.1   Aerospace engineering

Branson, Richard

Reach for the skies; ballooning, birdmen, and blasting into space. Current 2011 343p il $26.95   **629.1**

1. Aeronautics -- History

ISBN 978-1-61723-003-5

LC 2010-52340

"The Virgin Atlantic Airlines founder and billionaire adventurer celebrates the exploits of airborne daredevils—his own prominently among them—in this lively history of aviation pioneers. Branson ranges from the Montgolfier brothers' 1783 invention of the hot-air balloon to today's nascent space tourism industry . . . highlighting men and women who risked their money and lives to advance aerial technology or just put on a good show. It's a colorful assemblage of engineers, test pilots, barnstormers, and fighter aces. . . . Branson's enthusiasm for avant-garde flight and his firsthand understanding of its rigors make this a rousing—sometimes even elevating—read." Publ Wkly

Includes bibliographical references

Hickam, Homer H.

★ **Rocket** boys; a memoir. [by] Homer H. Hickam, Jr. Delacorte Press 1998 368p $25.95; pa $14   **629.1**

1. Aerospace engineers 2. Aerospace engineers -- United States -- Biography 3. Authors 4. Authors, American 5. Memoirists 6. Novelists 7. Writers on science

ISBN 0-385-33320-X; 0-385-33321-8 pa

LC 98-19304

"Even if Hickam stretched the strict truth to metamorphose his memories into Stand By Me-like material for Hol-

lywood . . . the embellishing only converts what is a good story into an absorbing, rapidly readable one that is unsentimental but artful about adolescence, high school, and family life." Booklist

629.13   Aeronautics

Alexander, David E.

Why don't jumbo jets flap their wings? flying animals, flying machines, and how they are different. Rutgers University Press 2009 278p il $26.95   **629.13**

1. Aeronautics 2. Airplanes 3. Animal flight 4. Birds -- Flight 5. Flying-machines

ISBN 978-0-8135-4479-3; 0-8135-4479-3

LC 2008-35425

Alexander discusses the mechanics and physics of how animals and aircraft fly.

"Anyone interested in the flight of birds or insects or the flight of various types of aircraft will find this volume fascinating. . . . [This book] is very well written and approaches complex topics in a manner that readers at any level of expertise will find understandable and interesting." Sci Books Films

Includes glossary and bibliographical references

Berg, A. Scott

★ **Lindbergh**. Putnam 1998 628p il $30; pa $16 **629.13**

1. Air force officers 2. Air pilots 3. Air pilots -- United States -- Biography 4. Generals 5. Memoirists

ISBN 0-399-14449-8; 0-425-17041-1 pa

LC 98-18548

"The first biographer to be granted unfettered access to Lindbergh's private papers, Berg provides enough fresh detail to trace the roots of Lindbergh's personality, its strengths as well as its maddening flaws, all the way back to his turbulent boyhood." N Y Times Book Rev

Includes bibliographical references (p. {569}-612) and index

Butler, Susan

East to the dawn; the life of Amelia Earhart. Da Capo Press 1999 489p il map pa $15.95   **629.13**

1. Air pilots 2. Memoirists 3. Missing persons 4. Women air pilots 5. Women air pilots -- United States -- Biography

ISBN 978-0-306-81837-0

In this biography of the pilot and women's rights advocate "Butler shows a mastery of aviation history, and considerable sophistication about the technology of flight and navigation . . . The mountain of new material it marshals guarantees 'East to the Dawn' a permanent place on the shelf of Amelia Earhart references." N Y Times Book Rev

Includes bibliographical references

Chaikin, Andrew

Air and space; the National Air and Space Museum's story of flight. Little, Brown 1997 317p il $50; pa $29.95   **629.13**

1. Aeronautics -- Pictorial works
ISBN 0-8212-2082-9; 0-8212-2670-3 pa

LC 96-31929

This illustrated work connects artifacts on display at the Smithsonian's aeronautics museum with a brief history of air and space flight.

"A few photos, as of the DC-3, show the vehicle in its exhibit hall, but most pictures depict planes or rockets in action, right up through the latest images of the space age—Mars as viewed from Pathfinder. An enthusiast's delight." Booklist

Demetz, Peter

The **air** show at Brescia, 1909. Farrar, Straus & Giroux 2002 254p $24   **629.13**

1. Aeronautics -- History 2. Aeronautics -- Italy -- Brescia -- Exhibitions -- History 3. Authors 4. Brescia (Italy) -- History 5. Novelists 6. Poets 7. Short story writers
ISBN 0-374-10259-7

LC 2002-23259

This is an "account of a flying competition that took place in northern Italy during the early days of aviation. Attending the event, among other notables, were Franz Kafka and Italian poet Gabriele d'Annunzio. Kafka, who traveled to Brescia with several friends, including novelist and editor Max Brod, published a journalistic article about the show. . . . Those interested in aviation history as well as a glimpse of the young Kafka will greatly enjoy this serendipitous account." Publ Wkly

Includes bibliographical references

Gorn, Michael H.

Expanding the envelope; flight research at NACA and NASA. University Press of Ky. 2001 472p il $35   **629.13**

1. Aeronautics 2. Aeronautics -- Research -- United States
ISBN 0-8131-2205-8

LC 00-12287

"A history of government-sponsored flight research, from the testing of kites and gliders in the 19th century through the Wright brothers, the creation of the National Advisory Committee on Aeronautics, and NASA in the 20th century." Choice

Includes bibliographical references and index

Grant, R. G.

Flight: 100 years of aviation. DK Pub. 2002 440p il hardcover o.p. pa $24.95   **629.13**

1. Aeronautics -- History
ISBN 0-7894-8910-4; 0-7566-1902-5 pa

LC 2002-73935

"The impressive illustrations include over 300 gorgeous, full-color profiles of the world's major military and civilian aircraft and space vehicles." Libr J

Gubert, Betty Kaplan

Distinguished African Americans in aviation and space science; {by} Betty Kaplan Gubert, Miriam Sawyer, and Caroline M. Fannin. Oryx Press 2002 319p il $64.95   **629.13**

1. African American air pilots -- Biography 2. African American astronauts -- Biography 3. African American pilots 4. Astronauts
ISBN 1-57356-246-7

LC 2001-34821

This profiles 80 men and 20 women in aviation and space science covering 80 years of the 20th century.

"Libraries should not hesitate to add this title to their collections." Booklist

Includes bibliographical references

Haynsworth, Leslie

Amelia Earhart's daughters; the wild and glorious story of American women aviators from World War II to the dawn of the space age. {by} Leslie Haynsworth and David Toomey. Morrow 1998 322p il hardcover o.p. pa $14   **629.13**

1. Air pilots 2. Cosmetics industry executives 3. Women air pilots 4. Women air pilots -- United States -- Biography 5. Women astronauts 6. Women astronauts -- United States -- Biography
ISBN 0-380-72984-9 pa

LC 98-8727

This "study of American women aviators concentrates almost exclusively on the WASPs of World War II and the would-be female astronauts of the early 1960s." Booklist

Includes bibliographical references

Lindbergh, Charles

The **spirit** of St. Louis; [by] Charles A. Lindbergh. Scribner 1998 562p il hardcover o.p. pa $20   **629.13**

1. Aeronautics -- Flights 2. Air force officers 3. Air pilots 4. Air pilots -- United States -- Biography 5. Generals 6. Memoirists 7. Spirit of St. Louis (Airplane) 8. Transatlantic flights
ISBN 0-684-85277-2; 0-7432-3705-6 pa

LC 98-33556

This is an account of the first solo transatlantic flight from New York to Paris, as well as a detailed description of the preparation for the flight which in turn mirrors aviation of the 1920's.

Lovell, Mary S.

The **sound** of wings: the life of Amelia Earhart. St. Martin's Press 1989 xxv, 420p il hardcover o.p. pa $17.99   **629.13**

1. Air pilots 2. Biography, Individual 3. Memoirists 4. Missing persons 5. Women air pilots
ISBN 978-0-312-58733-8 pa

LC 89-34935

This biography concentrates on Earhart's "personality and character and the relationships with family and friends as they contributed to her accomplishments. . . . The book also contains excerpts from Last Flight, Earhart's reworked logbook and notes on the fateful 1937 flight." Libr J

Includes bibliographical references

Mortimer, Gavin

Chasing Icarus; the seventeen days in 1910 that forever changed American aviation. Walker & Co 2009 305p il $26   **629.13**

1. Aeronautics -- History
ISBN 978-0-8027-1711-5

The author "argues that three aeronautic events in 1910 vouchsafed the primacy of U.S. aviation and the triumph of heavier-than-air flight. Interweaving the events—Walter Wellman's failed attempt to cross the Atlantic in his dirigible, America; the International Balloon Cup Race, which embarked from St. Louis; and the country's first international aircraft contest, held above the Belmont Park racetrack in New York—Mortimer effectively places the reader at the vital center of all three. . . . A singular contribution to early aviation history." Libr J

Includes bibliographical references

Rich, Doris L.

Amelia Earhart; a biography. Smithsonian Institution Press 1989 321p il hardcover o.p. pa $16.95   **629.13**

1. Air pilots 2. Memoirists 3. Missing persons 4. Women air pilots
ISBN 1-56098-725-1 pa

LC 89-32181

A "fast-paced, richly detailed biography." Publ Wkly

Includes bibliographical references

Tobin, James

★ **To** conquer the air; the Wright Brothers and the great race for flight. Free Press 2003 433p il hardcover o.p. pa $16   **629.13**

1. Aeronautics -- History 2. Aircraft industry executives 3. Biography, Individual 4. Inventors
ISBN 0-684-85688-3; 0-7432-5536-4 pa

LC 2002-44778

"This book represents the most forceful argument to date for the brothers' monumental legacy to the history of flight. . . . This lucidly written and exhaustively researched study is recommended for all aviation collections and all libraries." Libr J

Includes bibliographical references

Trzebinski, Errol

The **lives** of Beryl Markham; Out of Africa's hidden free spirit and Denys Finch Hatton's last great love. Norton 1993 396p il maps hardcover o.p. pa $12   **629.13**

1. Air pilots 2. Biography, Individual 3. Horse trainers 4. Memoirists
ISBN 0-393-31252-6 pa

LC 93-9919

The author offers "confirmation of the rumor that Beryl's third husband actually wrote her best-selling memoir, West with the Night." Booklist

Includes bibliographical references

Smithsonian atlas of world aviation; charting the history of flight from the first balloons to today's most advanced aircraft. [compiled by] Dana Bell. HarperCollins 2008 230p il map $39.95 **629.13**

1. Aeronautics -- History 2. Historical atlases 3. Reference books
ISBN 978-0-06-125144-3; 0-06-125144-5

LC 2007-47574

"Bell's writing . . . adds immeasurably to the value of this atlas: it is articulate, clear, informative, and, above all, accurate." SLJ

Includes bibliographical references

629.130   Biography of flight

Jackson, Joe

Atlantic fever; Lindbergh, his competitors, and the race to cross the Atlantic. Joe Jackson. Farrar, Straus and Giroux 2012 x, 525 p.p   **629.130**

1. Aeronautics -- Competitions -- History -- 20th century 2. Air pilots -- Biography 3. Transatlantic flights -- History -- 20th century
ISBN 0374106754; 9780374106751

LC 2011046068

In this book, Joe Jackson places Lindbergh's historic flight of May 20-21, 1927, in the dramatic framework of the Great Atlantic Air Race, which began eight years earlier when Franco-American hotelier Ramond Orteig sponsored a $25,000 prize to the first aviator to cross the Atlantic. . . . Jackson traces the futile attempts to win the Orteig Prize until the spring of 1927, when a bevy of pilots stepped forth to compete for the honor no matter the cost. Jackson's compelling portraits of these contenders . . . place Lindbergh's successful bid in perspective. The reader is reminded that Lindy was the last contestant to arrive in New York but the first to depart, owing to the simplicity of his effort compared with the technical, funding, and personnel complexities of his rivals' preparations. (Libr J)

629.132   Mechanics of flight; flying and related topics

Tennekes, H.

The **simple** science of flight; from insects to jumbo jets. [by] Henk Tennekes. Rev and expanded ed; MIT Press 2009 201p il pa $21.95   **629.132**

1. Aerodynamics 2. Flight
ISBN 978-0-262-51313-5; 0-262-51313-7

LC 2009-12431

The author "explains to lay readers the aerodynamic principles that underlie the flight of everything, including paper airplanes, kites, gliders, and human powered aircraft. He also explains such concepts as lift, drag, wing loading, and cruising speed; and the impact of fuel efficiency, headwind, tailwind, and other factors." Booknews

Includes bibliographical references

629.133   Aircraft types

Botting, Douglas

Dr. Eckener's dream machine; the great Zeppelin and the dawn of air travel. Holt & Co. 2001 331p il maps $27.50; pa $16   **629.133**
1. Aeronautics -- Flights 2. Aircraft industry executives 3. Airships
ISBN 0-8050-6458-3; 0-8050-6459-1 pa
LC 2001-24770

Botting discusses the history of the Zeppelin, a rigid airship designed by a Prussian army officer, Ferdinand Count von Zeppelin, and the career of Hugo Eckener, who promoted and flew the dirigible.

"A truly exciting book, filled with colorful characters and plenty of derring-do and laced with just the right amount of sadness and tragedy." Booklist
Includes bibliographical references

Chiles, James R.

The **god** machine; from boomerangs to black hawks, the story of the helicopter. Bantam Dell 2007 354p il hardcover o.p. pa $16   **629.133**
1. Helicopters
ISBN 978-0-553-80447-8; 978-0-553-38352-2 pa
LC 2007-28575

This "is an engaging blend of pop science and pop culture." Publ Wkly
Includes bibliographical references

Spenser, Jay P.

The **airplane**; how ideas gave us wings. [by] Jay Spenser. HarperCollins 2008 340p il $25.95 **629.133**
1. Aeronautics 2. Aeronautics -- History 3. Airplanes -- Design and construction 4. Inventors
ISBN 978-0-06-125919-7; 0-06-125919-5
LC 2008-23423

This "is a very well written book that is organized in a way to make it both readable and informative. The writing makes it obvious that the author knows his subject and is fascinated by it." Sci Books Films
Includes bibliographical references

Jane's all the world's aircraft 2008-2009. Jane's Information Group 2008 973p il $915   **629.133**
1. Aeronautics
ISBN 978-0-7106-2837-4; 0-7106-2837-4

"Offers illustrations, descriptions, and specifications of aircraft of various countries of the world including: airplanes, drones, sailplanes, airships, military missiles, research rockets, space vehicles, aero-engines. Arranged in sections by: Aircraft; Lighter than air; Aero engines, then alphabetically by country of manufacture." Guide to Ref Books. 11th edition

629.2   Motor land vehicles, cycles

Sobey, Ed

A **field** guide to automotive technology. Chicago Review Press 2008 207p il pa $14.95   **629.2**
1. Automobiles 2. Mechanics
ISBN 978-1-55652-812-5
LC 2008046620

The author "helps readers identify items on, inside, and under the car, as well as under the hood, and explains what they do and why. He also painlessly reviews a few principles of science and mechanics here and there. The 130 entries range from basic to complex, from bumper and windshield to differential and constant velocity joint boot. . . . Most of the material concerns passenger vehicles, but there are also sections on off-road vehicles, motorcycles, buses, and human-powered conveyances." SLJ

629.222   Gasoline-powered, oil-powered, man-powered vehicles

Adler, Dennis

The **art** of the sports car; the greatest designs of the 20th century. written and with photographs by Dennis Adler. HarperCollins Pubs. 2002 236p il $44.95   **629.222**
1. Sports cars 2. Sports cars -- History
ISBN 0-06-018885-5
LC 2001-51810

In this illustrated history of the sports car the author provides an "account of the evolution of small cars with big engines, recounting the travails of famous auto designers, the engineering and styling innovations they pioneered and the races and road rallies at which cars proved (and advertised) themselves. His narrative dwells mostly on European makes such as Jaguar, Porsche and Ferrari, but also discusses the American Corvette and muscle cars like the Ford Thunderbird and the Dodge Challenger. . . . Hard-core aficionados will derive much gratification from the detailed descriptions of mechanical design and performance. . . . But just about anyone will be entranced at the pictures of classic cars meticulously restored, polished to a sheen and photographed on opulent country estates." Publ Wkly

Vuic, Jason

The **Yugo**; the rise and fall of the worst car in history. Hill & Wang 2010 262p il $26 **629.222**
1. Foreign automobiles
ISBN 978-0-8090-9891-0; 0-8090-9891-1
LC 2009-25612

A "meticulous and wide-ranging social history of a troubled car." Minneapolis Star Tribune
Includes bibliographical references

The Beaulieu encyclopedia of the automobile; editor in chief, Nick Georgano; foreword by Lord Montagu of Beaulieu. Fitzroy Dearborn Pubs. 2000 2v il set $325   **629.222**
1. Automobiles 2. Automobiles -- Encyclopedias 3.

Reference books
ISBN 1-57958-293-1

LC 2001-316285

"The most comprehensive automobile encyclopedia available today." Am Libr

629.223 Light trucks

Perry, Michael
Truck: a love story. HarperCollins Publishers 2006 281p $24.95 **629.223**
1. Trucks
ISBN 978-0-06-057117-7; 0-06-057117-9

LC 2006-43394

Perry "propels the story forward as if he were writing a novel, helped by a cast of characters who range from the lightly offbeat to the totally bizarre." Booklist

629.227 Cycles

Herlihy, David
★ **Bicycle**: the history; [by] David V. Herlihy. Yale University Press 2004 470p il $40 **629.227**
1. Bicycles
ISBN 0-300-10418-9

LC 2004-12992

Herlihy "takes us from the mathematician Jacques Ozanam's 1696 challenge to develop a 'human-powered carriage' to the creation of the draisine and the velocipede and eventually to the development of the bicycle. . . . The author demonstrates how the development and success of the bicycle were contingent on engineering, marketing, patents, the culture of various regions, and changing views of recreation and health; therefore, this book will also appeal to anyone interested in the history of those fields." Libr J
Includes bibliographical references

Sloane, Eugene A.
Sloane's complete book of bicycling; 25th anniversary ed; Simon & Schuster 1995 429p il pa $21.95 **629.227**
1. Bicycles 2. Cycling
ISBN 0-671-87075-0

LC 94-46788

Covers choosing a bicycle, repair and tools, preventive maintenance, safety tips for commuters, new technologies, bike touring, all-terrain and mountain bikes, and facts on health.

629.28 Tests, driving, maintenance, repair

Christensen, Lisa
Clueless about cars; an easy guide to car maintenance and repair. [by] Lisa Christensen, with Dan Laxter. Rev. and updated ed.; Firefly Books 2007 174p il pa $16.95 **629.28**
1. Automobiles -- Maintenance and repair
ISBN 978-1-55407-333-7; 1-55407-333-2

This book describes "each major system of the automobile, what can go wrong and how to prevent breakdowns. Step-by-step do-it-yourself instructions are provided for the most important engine maintenance routines and basic automotive repairs." Publisher's note

Downs, Todd
★ The **bicycling** guide to complete bicycle maintenance & repair; for road & mountain bikes. Expanded and rev. 6th ed.; Rodale 2010 395p il pa $23.99 **629.28**
1. Bicycles -- Maintenance and repair
ISBN 978-1-60529-487-2; 1-60529-487-X

LC 2010-26471

This illustrated guide includes step-by-step instructions for major and minor repairs and maintenance for many types of bicycles.

Kachur, Bridget
Every woman's quick & easy car care; a worry-free guide to car troubles, trials & travels. Storey Bks. 2002 262p il pa $14.95 **629.28**
1. Automobiles -- Maintenance and repair 2. Automobiles -- Maintenance and repair -- Popular works 3. Automobiles -- Popular works
ISBN 1-58017-451-5

LC 2002-1117

This "guide presents a complete lesson in Auto Mechanics 101, from identifying the different parts of the engine to improving gas mileage to checking the air pressure in tires. . . . {It features} illustrated tutorials on changing a tire, jump-starting a car, installing a car seat, replacing belts and hoses, changing the oil, detailing, winterizing, performing seasonal maintenance, and much more." Publisher's note

Ramsey, Dan
Teach yourself visually car care & maintenance; by Dan Ramsey and Judy Ramsey. Visual / Wiley 2009 210p il pa $24.95 **629.28**
1. Automobiles -- Maintenance and repair
ISBN 978-0-470-37727-7

LC 2009-920042

This book covers "how to change oil and other fluids; rotate tires; replace fuel pumps, air filters, and batteries; and . . . more." Publisher's note
Includes glossary

Vanderbilt, Tom
Traffic; why we drive the way we do (and what it says about us) Alfred A. Knopf 2008 402p $24.95 **629.28**
1. Automobile drivers 2. Automobile drivers -- Psychology 3. Automobile driving 4. City traffic 5. Traffic congestion
ISBN 978-0-307-26478-7

LC 2008-11507

"This may be the most insightful and comprehensive study ever done of driving behavior and how it reveals truths about the types of people we are." Booklist
Includes bibliographical references

Wilson, Hugo

Motorcycle owner's manual. DK Pub. 1997
112p il pa $10   **629.28**
    1. Motorcycles -- Maintenance and repair
    ISBN 0-7894-1615-8
                        LC 96-35925

This guide to motorcycle maintenance starts with simple
procedures and routines then goes on to basic servicing and
complex jobs.
    "Handy, attractive, and easy to follow." Booklist

Zinn, Lennard

Zinn & the art of road bike maintenance; illustrated by Todd Telander. 3rd ed.; Velo Press 2009
424p il pa $24.95   **629.28**
    1. Bicycles -- Maintenance and repair
    ISBN 978-1-934030-42-4
                        LC 2009-15195

This book covers the different components of a road
bike, lists the tools bike owners need to tackle simple and
advanced projects, and demonstrates with 295 illustrations
how to work on each part.

629.4   Astronautics

Angelo, Joseph A.

   ★ **Encyclopedia** of space exploration; {by} Joseph A. Angelo, Jr. Facts on File 2000 305p il $55;
pa $21.95   **629.4**
    1. Outer space -- Exploration -- Encyclopedias 2.
    Reference books
    ISBN 0-8160-3942-9; 0-8160-4902-5 pa
                        LC 99-59659

In an A to Z format, this reference "presents the most
recent lunar missions, the exploration of Mars, the latest
images and discoveries via the Hubble Space Telescope, a
special focus on Mission to planet Earth and the use of space
to monitor and protect the biosphere, an update on the International Space Station, a focus on asteroid detection and
negation systems, and the role of robotics and virtual reality
in exploring the solar system." Publisher's note
    Includes bibliographical references

   The **Facts** on File dictionary of space technology; [by] Joseph A. Angelo, Jr. rev ed; Facts on File
2004 474p $49.95; pa $19.95   **629.4**
    1. Astronautics -- Dictionaries 2. Reference books
    ISBN 0-8160-5222-0; 0-8160-5223-9 pa
                        LC 2003-49148

This dictionary contains approximately 1,500 cross-referenced entries that present the basic concepts and phrases
in the science of space, spaceflight, and space technology.
Among the topics covered are: abort modes; ballistic missile defense; launch vehicles; Milstar; ocean remote sensing;
robotics and space stations.

Brzezinski, Matthew

Red moon rising; Sputnik and the hidden rivalries that ignited the Space Age. Times Books 2007
322p il $26   **629.4**
    1. Artificial satellites 2. Artificial satellites, Russian 3.
    Astronautics -- Soviet Union 4. Astronautics -- United
    States 5. Cold War 6. Cold war 7. Space race
    ISBN 978-0-8050-8147-3; 0-8050-8147-X
                        LC 2007-08227

"Matthew Brzezinski's history of 1957 is not a potted
retelling of the space race highlights we have perhaps encountered once too often in television documentaries and
Sunday supplements, but a vivid and anecdotal account of
the nerve-wracking delays, tormented decisions and agonizing uncertainties that unquestionably lent a human, and even
heroic, aspect to his subject." Times Lit Suppl
    Includes bibliographical references

Burrows, William E.

This new ocean; the story of the first space age.
Random House 1998 723p il hardcover o.p. pa
$18.95   **629.4**
    1. Astronautics 2. Outer space -- Exploration
    ISBN 0-375-75485-7 pa
                        LC 98-3252

"'This New Ocean' is most distinguished by the successful integration of three different story lines: manned space
flight, the militarization of space and space science." N Y
Times Book Rev
    Includes bibliographical references

   The **survival** imperative; using space to protect
Earth. Forge Books 2006 317p $24.95   **629.4**
    1. Asteroids 2. Astronautics
    ISBN 978-0-765-31114-6; 0-765-31114-3
                        LC 2005-33803

"Presenting a case for establishing a new direction and
vision for our space program, longtime science technology
reporter Burrows . . . proposes that NASA undertake a program to detect and protect Earth from asteroids and comets,
provide advance notice of hurricanes and other natural disasters, pinpoint environmental pollution, furnish replacement
power sources, and even detect and deter nuclear attacks.
One of the best things about the book is the historical background Burrows includes—on the space program, nuclear
proliferation, and environmental concerns—as he builds
his argument for creating an overall defense strategy using
space." Libr J

Cadbury, Deborah

Space race; the epic battle between America and
the Soviet Union for dominion of space. HarperCollins 2006 370p il hardcover o.p. pa $15.95 **629.4**
    1. Astronautics -- Soviet Union 2. Astronautics --
    United States 3. Cold war
    ISBN 0-06-084553-8; 0-06-117628-1 pa
                        LC 2005-52693

"From the opening account of Washington and Moscow's race to grab the models, machines, drawings, and
personnel from Hitler's V-2 missile program at the end of
World War II to Sputnik and then to Neil Armstrong's moon-
walk, this is an utterly engrossing book—largely because of

the two characters around whom the story unfolds, and because Cadbury has the material to tell it from the inside." Foreign Affairs

Includes bibliographical references

Hardesty, Von

Epic rivalry; the inside story of the Soviet and American space race. [by] Von Hardesty and Gene Eisman; foreword by Sergei Khrushchev. National Geographic Society 2007 275p il map $28; pa $16.95 **629.4**

1. Astronautics -- Soviet Union 2. Astronautics -- United States 3. Astronautics -- United States -- History 4. Cold war 5. Space race
ISBN 978-1-4262-0119-6; 978-1-4262-0321-3 pa
LC 2007-17393

"This is a true saga, full of daring, danger, death, ego conflicts, and triumphs. . . . All readers should love this fabulous and profusely illustrated combined story." Sci Books Films

Includes bibliographical references

National Geographic Society (U.S.)

★ **National** Geographic encyclopedia of space; [compiled by] Linda K. Glover; with Andrew Chaikin . . . [et al.]; foreword by Buzz Aldrin. National Geographic Society 2004 400p il map $40 **629.4**

1. Astronautics 2. Astronomy -- Encyclopedias 3. Reference books
ISBN 0-7922-7319-2
LC 2004-55229

The essays in this encyclopedia "discuss deep space, our solar system and space travel. There are also sections on using space to study Earth and on the military and intelligence uses of space. The essays in general are readable and show the implications of astronomy for life on Earth, such as the impact of solar flares on the weather. . . . This volume will suit astronomy enthusiasts better than total novices. Everyone, however, can enjoy the gorgeous photos." Publ Wkly

Walsh, Patrick J.

Echoes among the stars; a short history of the U.S. space program. Sharpe, M.E. 2000 204p $35.95; pa $29.95 **629.4**

1. Astronautics -- United States 2. Astronautics -- United States -- History
ISBN 0-7656-0537-6; 0-7656-0538-4 pa
LC 99-38899

Walsh "recounts the early successes of the Mercury and Gemini missions that paved the way for the Apollo moon landings as well as the Skylab and Apollo-Soyuz mission that marked the end of the first era of U.S. manned space flight." Libr J

Includes bibliographical references

Williamson, Mark

The **Cambridge** dictionary of space technology. Cambridge Univ. Press 2001 464p il maps $50 **629.4**

1. Aerospace engineering 2. Astronautics 3. Astronautics -- Dictionaries 4. Astronomy 5.

Astronomy -- Dictionaries 6. Reference books
ISBN 0-521-66077-7
LC 00-59884

"This dictionary is a comprehensive reference on the words and phrases related to many aspects of the evolving field of space technology. The work contains material ranging from basic concepts to advanced applications and includes over 2,000 entries. The extraordinary breadth of coverage ensures that there are entries on all major space technology subject areas. While the emphasis on each entry is on defining the meaning of the word or phrase, entries have been written with the intention of enhancing the understanding of the subject for a variety of users, ranging from the practicing specialist to the layperson to the student." Sci Books & Films

629.43 Unmanned space flight

Zimmerman, Robert

The **universe** in a mirror; the saga of the Hubble Telescope and the visionaries who built it. Princeton University Press 2008 287p il $29.95 **629.43**

1. Hubble Space Telescope
ISBN 978-0-691-13297-6; 0-691-13297-6
LC 2007-943159

"Must reading for armchair astrophysicists." Booklist
Includes bibliographical references

629.45 Manned space flight

Barbree, Jay

Live from Cape Canaveral; covering the space race, from Sputnik to today. Smithsonian Books/Collins 2007 321p il $26.95 **629.45**

1. Astronautics -- United States
ISBN 978-0-06-123392-0; 0-06-123392-7
LC 2007-15247

"Barbree writes with infectious enthusiasm about the glory days of space exploration, and his book will be an enjoyable introduction for a new generation and a fond remembrance for boomers." Publ Wkly

Chaikin, Andrew

A **man** on the moon; the voyages of the Apollo astronauts. Viking 1994 670p il hardcover o.p. pa $18 **629.45**

1. Apollo project 2. Space flight to the moon
ISBN 0-670-81446-6; 978-0-14-311235-8 pa; 0-14-311235-X pa
LC 93-48680

In this chronicle of NASA's Apollo program "diary-like reports mix with first- and third-person accounts as Chaikin . . . delivers a chronological view of the missions and those who planned and flew them. Focusing closely on the Apollo astronauts, including Buzz Aldrin, Pete Conrad and Neil Armstrong, Chaikin gives his topic a sense of immediacy." Publ Wkly

Includes bibliographical references

French, Francis
In the shadow of the moon; a challenging journey to Tranquility, 1965-1969. [by] Francis French and Colin Burgess; with a foreword by Walter Cunningham. University of Nebraska Press 2007 425p il $29.95   **629.45**
    1. Apollo project 2. Astronautics -- Soviet Union 3. Astronautics -- United States 4. Astronautics -- United States -- History 5. Project Apollo 6. Space flight to the moon 7. Space race
    ISBN 978-0-8032-1128-5; 0-8032-1128-7
                 LC 2006-103047
    "This book will have an important place in the recorded history of space exploration." Sci Books Films
    Includes bibliographical references

Kevles, Bettyann
  ★ Almost heaven; the story of women in space. [by] Bettyann Holtzmann Kevles. MIT Press 2006 280p il pa $16.95   **629.45**
    1. Women astronauts
    ISBN 978-0-262-61213-5; 0-262-61213-5
                 LC 2006-41945
    This is a "history of the U.S. space program, with special emphasis on, and stories about, the women who have had the courage to venture into space. Each one is special, the book reveals; yet they all share a spirit of adventure and a willingness to put up with hardship in order to fulfill their dream." Sci Books Films
    Includes bibliographical references

Kranz, Eugene F.
  Failure is not an option; mission control from Mercury to Apollo 13 and beyond. {by} Gene Kranz. Simon & Schuster 2000 415p il $26   **629.45**
    1. Astronautics -- United States 2. Ground support systems (Astronautics) -- History 3. Manned space flight -- Systems engineering -- United States -- History 4. Space flight
    ISBN 0-7432-0079-9
                 LC 00-27720
    "A welcome contribution to the history of space flight. More than any previous book, it gives the view of that history as lived by the brotherhood of Mission Control. The writing, like Kranz himself, is brisk, unadorned and informative, but warmed from time to time by characteristic expressions of irony and humor." N Y Times Book Rev

Launius, Roger D.
  Frontiers of space exploration; 2nd ed; Greenwood Press 2004 245p il $45   **629.45**
    1. Astronautics -- International cooperation
    ISBN 0-313-32524-3
                 LC 2003-60402
    "The text includes a chronology, a general historical overview of space flight, 3 lengthy essays on space exploration, and 21 biographical essays. In addition, 26 primary documents trace U.S. space flight history, and there is an up-to-date listing of all U.S. space flights up to and including the Columbia disaster of January 2003. A fine annotated bibliography rounds out the volume." Booklist

Nelson, Craig
  ★ Rocket men; the triumph and tragedy of the first Americans on the moon. Viking 2009 404p il $27.95   **629.45**
    1. Apollo project 2. Astronautics -- United States 3. Astronautics -- United States -- History 4. Project Apollo 5. Space flight to the moon
    ISBN 978-0-670-02103-1
                 LC 2008-51175
    "A thorough recounting—as full in human terms as in scientific and technical detail—of NASA's first manned Moon landing. . . . The definitive account of a watershed in American history." Kirkus
    Includes bibliographical references

Pyle, Rod
  Destination moon; the Apollo missions in the astronauts' own words. HarperCollins Publishers 2005 192p il $24.95; pa $14.95   **629.45**
    1. Apollo project 2. Astronautics -- United States 3. Space flight to the moon 4. Space flight to the moon -- History
    ISBN 0-06-087349-3; 0-06-087350-7 pa
                 LC 2005-51350
    This "survey of the Apollo moon program includes a brief summary of each flight and attempted flight of the great effort, from the fatal fire on Pad 34 in 1967 to the landing of a scientist on the moon in Apollo 17 in 1972. . . . Space collections of all sizes should welcome Pyle's book, and smaller ones will find it invaluable." Booklist

Schefter, James L.
  The race; the uncensored story of how America beat Russia to the moon. by James Schefter. Doubleday 1999 303p il hardcover o.p. pa $14 **629.45**
    1. Apollo project 2. Astronautics 3. Space flight to the moon
    ISBN 0-385-49254-5 pa
                 LC 98-54430
    Schefter chronicles the early days of space flight competition describing "the subtle infighting among the astronauts, the complex nature of lesser-known people like manned-flight champion Bob Gilruth, and the American leaders struggling with military, scientific and public relations concerns." Publ Wkly

Wolfe, Tom
  ★ The right stuff. Picador 2008 352p pa $16   **629.45**
    1. Astronautics -- United States 2. Astronauts
    ISBN 0-312-42756-5; 978-0-312-42756-6
    This volume chronicles "the handful of adrenaline-junkie military test pilots who became the Mercury astronauts. Their story is juxtaposed against that of Chuck Yeager, the ace of aces pilot who broke the sound barrier but couldn't apply to the space program because he lacked a college degree. . . . A terrific read from beginning to end." Libr J

Zimmerman, Robert

Genesis: the story of Apollo 8; the first manned flight to another world. Dell 1999 350p il pa $7.99
629.45

1. Apollo project 2. Space flight to the moon
ISBN 978-0-440-23556-9; 0-440-23556-1

The author tells the story of "Apollo 8 from the time it blasted into space on December 21, 1968, until it splashed down in the Pacific nearly a week later. He focuses on three brave men—Frank Borman, Jim Lovell, and Bill Anders—who volunteered to ride an inadequately tested space vehicle equipped with a primitive computer on a journey of some quarter-million miles to orbit the Moon and return. He also focuses on the astronauts' wives." Choice

Includes bibliographical references

629.46   Engineering of unmanned spacecraft

Dickson, Paul

Sputnik: the shock of the century. Walker & Co. 2001 310p il $28
629.46

1. Artificial satellites 2. Artificial satellites, Russian -- Political aspects 3. Astronautics 4. Astronautics and state -- United States -- Public opinion 5. Sputnik satellites -- History
ISBN 0-8027-1365-3

LC 2001-26156

"Paul Dickson skillfully puts the story of Sputnik and its aftermath into . . . perspective in his informative and readable book." Christ Sci Monit

Includes bibliographical references

629.47   Astronautical engineering

Dyson, George

Project Orion; the true story of the atomic spaceship. Holt & Co. 2002 345p il $26; pa $16 **629.47**

1. Astronautics 2. Nuclear rockets
ISBN 0-8050-5985-7; 0-8050-7284-5 pa

LC 2001-46500

The author "charts the history of the failed Project Orion, which called for a massive rocket to be built atop a nuclear-powered piston. . . . Dyson's explanations of the nuclear science behind the system are lucid. A great strength of Dyson's project is the interviews he conducted with surviving Orion team members." Publ Wkly

Includes bibliographical references

Stine, G. Harry

Handbook of model rocketry; [by] G. Harry Stine and Bill Stine. 7th ed; Wiley 2004 363p il pa $22.95
629.47

1. Rockets (Aeronautics) -- Models
ISBN 978-0-471-47242-1; 0-471-47242-5

LC 2004-2230

"Stine, an authority on model rocketry, describes all aspects of the subject from basics to international com-

petition." Ref Sources for Small & Medium-sized Libr. 4th edition

Includes bibliographical references

629.8   Automatic control engineering

Bascomb, Neal

The **new** cool; a visionary teacher, his FIRST robotics team, and the ultimate battle of smarts. Crown Publishers 2010 337p il $25; ebook $12.99 **629.8**

1. Robots
ISBN 978-0-307-58889-0; 978-0-307-58891-3 ebook

LC 2010-21646

The author "charts the marathon play-by-play teamwork of a group of fourth-year Southern California students from Dos Pueblos High School Engineering Academy as they competed in a robot-building contest. Since 2002, physics teacher and mentor Amir Abo-Shaeer has administered an experimental science curriculum culminating in a team entry in 'FIRST' (For Inspiration and Recognition of Science and Technology), a worldwide robotics competition created by Dean Kamen. . . . Aside from a mind-numbing plethora of physics terminology, Bascomb skillfully translates the exhilarating challenge to the page via intricately descriptive, expertly paced sketches of the group and their combined handiwork. A nail-biting thrill ride for techies and armchair engineers." Kirkus

Includes bibliographical references

Brooks, Rodney Allen

Flesh and machines; how robots will change us. Pantheon Bks. 2002 260p il hardcover o.p. pa $14
629.8

1. Artificial intelligence 2. Human-machine systems 3. Robotics 4. Robots
ISBN 0-375-42079-7; 0-375-72527-X pa

LC 2001-36636

A "stimulating book written by one of the major players in the field . . . about the state of robotics and its short-term future. It also offers surprisingly deep glimpses into what it is to be human. Brooks appears to have gained a boundless appreciation for human beings by attempting to copy them." N Y Times Book Rev

Cook, David

Robot building for beginners. APress 2002 568p il pa $29.95
629.8

1. Robots -- Design and construction
ISBN 1-893115-44-5

This book contains instructions on how to build a robot. "General sources for tools and parts are provided in a consolidated list, and specific parts are recommended throughout the book. . . . {The book also features information on} basic safety precautions and essential numbering and measuring systems." Publisher's note

Gutkind, Lee

★ **Almost** human; making robots think. Norton 2007 284p il $25.95
629.8

1. Artificial intelligence 2. Autonomous robots 3.

Robots

ISBN 978-0-393-05867-3; 0-393-05867-0

LC 2006-101046

"Drawing on years of observational curiosity at Carnegie Mellon's Robotics Institute, both in the lab and in the field, Gutkind explores the people and ideas behind machines developed to do the impossible: operate autonomously. This so-called bleeding-edge robotics is illuminated through stories of success and failure, tension between engineers developing bodies and the coders programming their artificial intelligence, motivational cross-pollination between seasoned veterans and young grad students, and performance tests chock-full of moments of elation and depression. Readers are given a strong sense of the drama inherent in the discipline, whether advancing incrementally or by leaps and bounds." Libr J

Includes bibliographical references

Long, John

Darwin's devices; what evolving robots can teach us about the history of life and the future of technology. John Long. Basic Books 2012 273 p. **629.8**

1. Evolution (Biology) -- Simulation methods 2. Evolutionary robotics 3. Robots 4. Science -- General 5. Scientific literature 6. Technological forecasting

ISBN 0465021417; 9780465021413; 9780465029280

LC 2011051804

The author traces his path from a doctoral student studying the evolution of fish vertebrae to his present position as director of Vassar's Interdisciplinary Robotics Laboratory. . . . [John] Long explains how a blunder in an early version of his doctoral thesis led to his later work with robots. . . . Long's first self-propelled robot had a fairly simple design--an embedded minicomputer, one light sensor and a backbone built to mimic varying structural aspects of a marlin vertebrae. . . . More complex robots allowed him to model predator/prey relationships and target acquisition more realistically, and he was able to consider broader issues such as the relationship between goal-directed behavior and animal intelligence. (Kirkus)

McComb, Gordon

Robot builder's sourcebook. McGraw-Hill 2002 711p il pa $24.95 **629.8**

1. Robotics 2. Robots

ISBN 0-07-140685-9

LC 2002-31999

A "listing (with address, phone numbers, web sites) of over 2500 suppliers and manufacturers of robot components, materials, tools, and much more. There are even sources for tracking down older and hard-to-find parts. Also listed are books, journals, magazines, professional societies, and Internet resources, including education sites, competition information, and web sites where hobbyists can find examples of program code. Dozens of sidebars and articles on various robotics topics break up the directory feel. The author also indicates recommended sources based on his own experiences and identifies 'premium' sources that are dedicated to robot hobbyists." Libr J

Menzel, Peter

Robo sapiens: evolution of a new species; [by] Peter Menzel and Faith D'Aluisio. MIT Press 2000 239p il $29.95; pa $19.95 **629.8**

1. Artificial intelligence 2. Intelligent control systems 3. Robotics 4. Robots

ISBN 0-262-13382-2; 0-262-63245-4 pa

LC 00-33946

This book is a collection of "interviews, essays, illustrations, and numerous photographs of all aspects of current research and actual production locations using robots, some of which approach the 'intelligent' level. The coverage includes more than 100 different researchers and developers with their robots. . . . The interviews are interesting, and the range of applications areas is fascinating; from medicine to housecleaning, from game playing to dancing robots, there is something for everyone in this collection." Libr J

Includes bibliographical references

Rosheim, Mark E.

Robot evolution; the development of anthrobotics. Wiley 1994 423p il $140 **629.8**

1. Robots

ISBN 0-471-02622-0

LC 94-13687

This "book is highly recommended because of its content, organization, completeness, quality of illustrations, and value." Sci Books Films

Wood, Gaby

Edison's Eve; a magical history of the quest for mechanical life. Knopf 2002 xxviii, 304p il $24; pa $14 **629.8**

1. Artificial intelligence 2. Robots 3. Robots -- Design and construction -- History

ISBN 0-679-45112-9; 1-4000-3158-3 pa

LC 2002-25467

This is "a lively, elegant and surprising book, packed with curious details and enticing anecdotes." N Y Times Book Rev

630 Agriculture and related technologies

Berry, Wendell

Bringing it to the table; on farming and food. introduction by Michael Pollan. Counterpoint 2009 234p pa $14.95 **630**

1. Agriculture -- United States 2. Family farms 3. Sustainable agriculture

ISBN 978-1-58243-543-5

LC 2009-24437

"The essays [included] address such concerns as: How does organic measure up against locally grown? What are the differences between small and large farms, and how does that affect what you put on your dinner table? What can you do to support sustainable agriculture?" Publisher's note

Includes bibliographical references

Carpenter, Novella

Farm city; the education of an urban farmer. Penguin Press 2009 276p $25.95   **630**

1. Farmers 2. Journalists 3. Urban agriculture

ISBN 978-1-59420-221-6; 1-59420-221-4

LC 2008-54666

This is "easily the funniest, weirdest, most perversely provocative gardening book I've ever read. . . . Though always entertaining, . . . [Carpenter] occasionally lapses into the grating lingo of the blogger, but toward the end, as she contemplates the place of her garden in the greater scheme of life, she shows what she's capable of and the writing soars." N Y Times Book Rev

Despommier, Dickson D.

The **vertical** farm; feeding ourselves and the world in the 21st century. [by] Dickson Despommier. Thomas Dunne Books 2010 305p il map $25.99; ebook $12.99   **630**

1. Agriculture -- Environmental aspects 2. Land use 3. Urban agriculture

ISBN 978-0-312-61139-2; 978-1-4299-4604-9 ebook

LC 2010-29257

"A provocative introduction to a pragmatic approach to growing safe, nutritious, local food." Booklist

Includes bibliographical references

Hurt, R. Douglas

Problems of plenty; the American farmer in the twentieth century. Dee, I.R. 2002 192p $24.95; pa $13.95   **630**

1. Agriculture -- Economic aspects 2. Agriculture -- Government policy 3. Agriculture -- United States

ISBN 1-56663-463-6; 1-56663-462-8 pa

LC 2002-67431

The author argues "that farmers face the same fundamental issues they did a century ago: overproduction, low commodity prices coupled with high production costs, and ineffective government intervention that often encourages rather than discourages overproduction. . . . He focuses chiefly on macroeconomic threads into which he incorporates the influence of farm organizations, technological developments (especially the gasoline tractor and later biotechnology), and federal farm programs. . . . Hurt has produced a very solid, readable history which should be useful for collections in general agriculture, agricultural economics and history, or rural sociology." Choice

Includes bibliographical references and index

Macceca, Stephanie

George Washington Carver; agriculture pioneer. by Stephanie Macceca. Compass Point Books 2010 40 p. ill. (chiefly col.) Mission: science (library binding) $27.99   **630**

1. African American agriculturists -- Biography -- Juvenile literature 2. Agriculturists -- United States -- Biography -- Juvenile literature

ISBN 9780756543051

LC 2009034855

This book offers a biography of George Washington Carver who was "[b]orn into slavery, . . . earned a university graduate degree, and eventually became a world famous expert on plants. By experimenting with peanuts and other plants, he learned how to make many useful products from them. Carver taught students and farmers how to grow plants without damaging the soil." (Publisher's note) This book is a textbook that is intended to be used in the middle school classroom. It includes a glossary, vocabulary, and a timeline.

Fatal harvest; the tragedy of industrial agriculture. edited by Andrew Kimbrell. Island Press (Washington, D.C.) 2002 384p il $75; pa $45   **630**

1. Agricultural ecology 2. Agricultural ecology -- United States 3. Agriculture -- Environmental aspects 4. Agriculture -- Environmental aspects -- United States 5. Organic farming 6. Organic farming -- United States

ISBN 1-55963-940-7; 1-55963-941-5 pa

LC 2001-5800

The contributors to this "volume trace the shift from agrarian to industrial agriculture, assess how and why the latter is now wreaking environmental havoc, and analyze alternative practices." Booklist

Includes bibliographical references (p.   )

631.4   Soil science

Montgomery, David R.

Dirt; the erosion of civilizations. University of California Press 2007 285p il map $24.95; pa $16.95 **631.4**

1. Agricultural industries 2. Paleoecology 3. Soil and civilization 4. Soil degradation 5. Soil erosion

ISBN 978-0-520-24870-0; 0-520-24870-8; 978-0-520-25806-8 pa; 0-520-25806-1 pa

LC 2006-26602

"This is an excellent, clearly written addition to the field. The author explains the mechanisms that form the world's soils in terms that nonscientists can understand." Choice

Includes bibliographical references

Stoll, Steven

Larding the lean Earth; soil and society in nineteenth-century America. Hill & Wang 2002 287p il maps hardcover o.p. pa $15   **631.4**

1. Agriculture -- Environmental aspects 2. Agriculture -- Environmental aspects -- United States -- History -- 19th century 3. Land settlement -- United States 4. Land settlement -- United States -- History -- 19th century 5. Soil conservation 6. Soil conservation -- United States -- History -- 19th century 7. Soil fertility -- United States -- History -- 19th century

ISBN 0-8090-6431-6; 0-8090-6430-8 pa

LC 2002-23279

"Stoll blends biology and history in this . . . study of soil, which performs more ecological functions than most people realize and which is being lost at an alarming rate." Booklist

Includes bibliographical references

631.5   Cultivation and harvesting

Cummings, Claire Hope

★ **Uncertain** peril; Genetic engineering and the future of seeds. Beacon Press 2008 232p $24.95 **631.5**

1. Agriculture 2. Biotechnology 3. Consumer protection 4. Seeds

ISBN 978-0-8070-8580-6

LC 2007-26298

This "authoritative portrait of another way in which our planet is at peril provides stark food for thought." Publ Wkly

Includes bibliographical references

631.8   Fertilizers, soil conditioners, growth regulators

Pleasant, Barbara

★ The **complete** compost gardening guide; banner batches, grow heaps, comforter compost, and other amazing techniques for saving time and money, and producing the most flavorful, nutritious vegetables ever. [by] Barbara Pleasant & Deborah L. Martin. Storey Pub. 2008 319p il map $29.95; pa $19.95 **631.8**

1. Compost 2. Gardening

ISBN 978-1-58017-703-0; 978-1-58017-702-3 pa

LC 2007-49729

The authors "provide both a reference guide and an introduction to composting. The first section . . . includes a number of interesting facts, definitions, and even recipes (e.g., for Miracle Leaf Mold). The second section, on compost gardening techniques, examines easy methods of composting with piles, bins, and cans as well as more elaborate approaches involving pits and trenches. It also discusses the use of earthworms in composting. Finally, the third section treats in detail the kinds of plants that will do well in a composter's garden. . . . Essential reading for any gardener interested in composting, this should find its way into many public libraries with active gardening communities and academic and special libraries with an interest in horticulture and gardening." Libr J

632   Plant injuries, diseases, pests

Lockwood, Jeffrey A.

★ **Locust**; the devastating rise and mysterious disappearance of the insect that shaped the American frontier. Jeffrey A. Lockwood. 1st ed; Basic Books 2004 xxiii, 294p il $25; pa $14.95 **632**

1. Locusts 2. Rocky Mountain locust

ISBN 0-7382-0894-9; 0-465-04167-1 pa

LC 2003-25538

The author "tells the fascinating story of how the Rocky Mountain locust invasions shaped American life in the 1870s. . . . This book is great for natural-history lovers, American history lovers, mystery lovers, and all who love a well-told real-life tale." Sci Books Films

Mabey, Richard

Weeds; in defense of nature's most unloved plants. HarperCollins 2011 324p il $25.99; ebook $12.99 **632**

1. Weeds

ISBN 978-0-06-206545-2; 978-0-06-206547-6 ebook

LC 2011010483

"This lively, erudite work invites readers to take a new look at the lowly and unloved weed. Mabey explains how weeds have cunningly evolved to survive natural disasters, human devastation, climate change, and almost every attempt to eradicate them. He weaves together a complex, fascinating tale of history and botany that travels from the first farm fields of Mesopotamia to the bomb craters of the London Blitz and the lowly industrial outfields of our modern cities." Publ Wkly

Includes bibliographical references

Stewart, Amy

Wicked bugs; the louse that conquered Napoleon's army & other diabolical insects. etchings and drawings by Briony Morrow-Cribbs. Algonquin Books of Chapel Hill 2011 271p il $18.95 **632**

1. Insect pests 2. Mites 3. Spiders 4. Ticks

ISBN 978-1-56512-960-3

LC 2011-3629

"Ranging from verdant South American jungles to Manhattan's cold concrete canyons, Stewart amusingly but analytically profiles the baddest bugs around in quick but attention-grabbing snapshots of little creatures that pack a lot of punch. Bed bugs and bookworms, rat fleas and filth flies all come under Stewart's curious gaze as she exposes their evil habits and lethal charms. No alarmist setting out to stoke preexisting phobias, Stewart shares her natural fascination with the insect world to help readers recognize both the threats and the wonders that could be lurking in corner crevices or come wafting in on the next gentle breeze." Booklist

Includes bibliographical references

Waldbauer, Gilbert

Insights from insects; what bad bugs can teach us. Prometheus Books 2005 311p il $18 **632**

1. Insect pests 2. Insects

ISBN 1-59102-277-0

LC 2004-26928

The author "profiles a rogue's gallery of unhealthful, unprofitable and unsavory creatures from the mosquito and house fly to an array of agricultural scourges. From their ingenious strategies for wreaking havoc and evading retribution from predators, toxic plant chemicals, insecticides and eradication programs, he gleans lessons about the Darwinian struggle for survival and the complex, easily upset balance of ecosystems. Waldbauer's lucid, engaging style, informed by accessible discussions of his and other scientists' research, maintains a lab-coated tone of interested objectivity." Publ Wkly

Includes bibliographical references

634.9 Forestry

Brown, Daniel

Under a flaming sky; the great Hinckley fire-storm of 1894. [by] Daniel James Brown. Lyons Press 2006 256p il map $22.95   **634.9**
  1. Forest fires
  ISBN 1-59228-863-4; 978-1-59228-863-2

"On September 1, 1894, a firestorm consumed timber-boomtown Hinckley, Minnesota, and three nearby hamlets. Brown, grandson of an 11-year-old survivor, makes riveting, affecting, white-knuckle reading of that horrifying, internationally reported day's lethal passage." Booklist

Includes bibliographical references

Connors, Philip

Fire season; field notes from a wilderness lookout. Ecco 2011 246 p. (trade) $24.99   **634.9**
  1. Authors 2. Essayists 3. Fire lookout stations 4. Fire lookouts 5. Forest fires 6. Newspaper editors 7. Solitude 8. Writers on nature
  ISBN 0061859362; 9780061859366

The content of this book is based on author "Philip Connors[' time] . . . spent . . . in a seven-by-seven foot fire-lookout tower, ten thousand feet above the ground in one of the remotest territories of New Mexico. One of the least developed parts of the country, the first region designated as an official wilderness area in the world, the section he tends is also one of the most fire-prone, suffering more than thirty thousand lightning strikes each year. . . . Connors time up on the peak is filled with drama—there are fires large and small; spectacular midnight lightning storms and silent mornings awakening above the clouds; surprise encounters with long-distance hikers, smokejumpers, bobcats, black bears, and an abandoned, dying fawn." (Blackstone Audio)

For almost a decade, former Wall Street Journal reporter Connors has spent half a year keeping vigil over 20,000 square miles of desert, forest, and mountain chains from atop a tower 10,000 feet above sea level. One of a handful of seasoned, seasonal fire-watchers in New Mexico's Gila National Forest, Connors introduces us to his wilderness in this ruminative, lyrical, occasionally suspenseful account. Publ Wkly

Maclean, John N.

The Thirtymile fire; a chronicle of bravery and betrayal. Henry Holt 2007 241p il map $25 **634.9**
  1. Fire fighters 2. Wildfires
  ISBN 978-0-8050-7578-6; 0-8050-7578-X
                    LC 2006-45846

Maclean "interviewed families, survivors, investigators and fire experts, and the result is an evenhanded, lucid recreation of catastrophe and its aftermath. The author gives a human face to national headlines, capturing the dignity and sense of mission of the lost firefighters." Publ Wkly

Taylor, Murry A.

Jumping fire; a smokejumper's memoir of fighting wildfire. Harcourt 2000 445p il hardcover o.p. pa $14   **634.9**
  1. Fire fighters 2. Fire fighting 3. Forest fires 4. Smokejumpers
  ISBN 0-15-601397-5 pa
                    LC 99-87608

"The oldest smoke jumper in the 60-year history of Alaskan firefighting, Taylor gives a detailed and exciting account of his adventures parachuting into the wilderness to combat wildfires during the summer of 1991." Publ Wkly

635 Garden crops (Horticulture)

Adam, Judith

Landscape planning; practical techniques for the home gardener. 2nd ed., rev. and expanded; Firefly 2008 247p il $39.95; pa $29.95   **635**
  1. Landscape gardening
  ISBN 978-1-55407-381-8; 1-55407-381-2; 978-1-55407-258-3 pa; 1-55407-258-1 pa

"Adam's language is both practical and reflective of a love of gardening. A sound resource for any size collection." Libr J [review of 2002 edition]

American Horticultural Society

★ The American Horticultural Society gardening manual. Dorling Kindersley 2000 420p il map $40   **635**
  1. Gardening
  ISBN 0-7894-5952-3
                    LC 00-22644

"The book is divided into four parts, the first of which covers garden planning, illustrating various garden styles, hardscape choices, and advice on designing the space. . . Part 2, which is arranged by plant type . . . covers the care and maintenance of the plants. . . . Part 3 offers thumbnail descriptions, including hardiness zones and the mature size of reliable, recommended plants arranged by the season they are at their best. The final part summarizes the routine but essential tasks the gardener should do each month." Libr J

★ New encyclopedia of gardening techniques; American Horticultural Society editors, David J. Ellis . . . [et al.]; additional contributors, Simon Akeroyd . . . [et al.] Mitchell Beazley 2009 480p il map $45   **635**
  1. Gardening -- Encyclopedias 2. Reference books
  ISBN 978-1-84533-484-0

"Expert gardeners and garden writers have been assembled to execute this tour de force, which every serious gardener will want to repeatedly consult. Abundantly illustrated with thousands of illustrations and photographs, each clearly and sensibly written section of this volume offers helpful advice, step-by-step techniques, tips for identifying and correcting common problems, suggested plants for various situations, and lots of ideas." Booklist

Barrett, Judy

What can I do with my herbs? how to grow, use, and enjoy these versatile plants. art by Victor Z. Martin. Texas A&M University Press 2009 134p il pa $19.95 **635**

1. Herb gardening 2. Herbs
ISBN 978-1-60344-092-9; 1-60344-092-5

LC 2008-31016

A "look at forty common herbs and the creative and useful things people do with them. Each herb description includes the plant's history and a list of popular uses. . . . [Barrett conveys] information about how to successfully grow herbs (start a ginger plant with a root from the grocery store), how to enjoy herbs in the garden (watch the swallowtail butterflies and caterpillars that love fennel), and how to use them in the kitchen (substitute the yellow flowers of calendula for saffron). Along the way, she even shares some of her favorite recipes." Publisher's note

Bartholomew, Mel

All new square foot gardening; grow more in less space! Rev. ed; Cool Springs Press 2006 271p il pa $19.99 **635**

1. Vegetable gardening
ISBN 978-1-59186-202-4; 1-59186-202-7

LC 2005025355

"Retired civil engineer Bartholomew introduces his high-yield, small-space gardening method. He includes ingredients to what he calls the perfect growing medium and information on the garden size needed on a per person basis. A systematic layout with clear instructions and photographs makes this highly useful to beginners thinking about raised-bed gardens." Libr J

Beckett, Kenneth A.

Gardening basics; a complete guide to designing, planting, and maintaining gardens. {by Ken Beckett et al.; consulting editor, John E. Elsley} Sterling 1999 276p hardcover o.p. pa $19.95 **635**

1. Gardening
ISBN 0-8069-2429-2 pa

LC 99-20247

This is "a comprehensive introduction to gardening, with basic information on designing and creating family gardens, patio gardens, large gardens, and low-maintenance gardens. From fences to hedges to soil types to fundamental plants for most gardens, the contributors bring great expertise and detail." Booklist

Borchardt, Rudolf

The **passionate** gardener; English translation by Henry Martin. McPherson & Company 2006 340p $30 **635**

1. Authors 2. Essayists 3. Gardening 4. Gardens 5. Poets
ISBN 978-0-92970-173-8; 0-92970-173-9

LC 2006-04312

"A poet and philosopher who was 'both famous and obscure' during his lifetime (1877-1945), Borchardt was also a gardening enthusiast. He was intimately involved with the contemporary German literary scene, but 19th-century ideas and ideals continued to dominate his outlook when he wrote this series of essays from self-imposed exile in Italy in 1938. . . . Borchardt begins with a discourse on 'The Flower and the Human Being,' exploring the ancient origins of that rela-

tionship through mythology, legend and language. He goes on to philosophize about the different natures of wild and cultivated plants and about the relationship between plants and their native landscapes. Martin's translation captures the Germanic density and impassioned, freewheeling inquiry behind this difficult but rewarding addition to the garden reader's bookshelf." Publ Wkly

Chalker-Scott, Linda

The **informed** gardener. University of Washington Press 2008 221p il pa $18.95 **635**

1. Landscape gardening
ISBN 978-0-295-98790-3

LC 2007-47682

"This enjoyable book should find its way into the hands of almost every gardener—and may increase ILL for specifically cited scholarly papers." Libr J

Includes bibliographical references

Coleman, Eliot

Winter harvest handbook; year-round vegetable production using deep-organic techniques and unheated greenhouses. Chelsea Green Pub. Co. 2009 247p il map pa $29.95 **635**

1. Greenhouses 2. Organic farming 3. Vegetable gardening
ISBN 978-1-60358-081-6

LC 2008-53184

"Coleman's opus is as much a call to action for town planners to embrace local farms as it is a bible for small farmers. This book is for people who know what they're doing." N Y Times Book Rev

Includes bibliographical references

Damrosch, Barbara

The **garden** primer; illustrations by Linda Heppes Funk, Ray Maher, and Carol Bolt. 2nd ed.; Workman Pub. 2008 820p il map $28.95; pa $18.95 **635**

1. Gardening
ISBN 978-0-7611-4856-2; 978-0-7611-2275-3 pa

LC 2007-51425

This is a "book for the new gardener that clearly explains the basics of garden planning, plant care, and equipment. Detailed chapters on the different categories of plants—annuals, perennials, vegetables, fruits, lawns, shrubs, roses, vines, trees, wildflowers, and even house plants—give general advice on how to use and care for these varieties. A valuable book for public libraries." Libr J

Includes bibliographical references

Deardorff, David C.

What's wrong with my plant (and how do I fix it?) a visual guide to easy diagnosis and organic remedies. [by] David Deardorff and Kathryn Wadsworth. Timber Press 2009 451p il pa $24.95 **635**

1. Natural pesticides 2. Ornamental plants 3. Plant diseases
ISBN 978-0-88192-961-4; 0-88192-961-1

LC 2009-19447

"The book allows readers to select a suitable starting point that describes a plant's symptom—for example, wilting leaves or holes in the stems—and answer simple questions that eventually lead to a solution to the problem. . . . The book is divided into three parts. The first features clear keys that help identify the cause. . . . Once the problem is identified, the reader just goes to the suggested page in the second section, which contains a hierarchy of remedies. The third section, also referenced by individual page numbers in the previous two, contains excellent pictures of symptoms to help confirm the diagnosis of the problem and offer remedies. . . . [This book] is an important reference that will help gardeners successfully diagnose their own plant problems and make educated decisions about how to solve them." Am Gardener

Includes bibliographical references

Denckla, Tanya

The **organic** gardener's home reference; a plant-by-plant guide to growing fresh, healthy food. Storey Communications 1994 273p il hardcover o.p. pa $21.95   **635**

1. Organic gardening
ISBN 0-88266-839-0 pa

LC 93-22835

This work "covers vegetables, herbs, fruits and nuts, and pest and disease control. The book has a good introduction on garden stewardship, followed by chapters on vegetables, fruits and nuts, herbs, macro- and microdestructive agents with organic remedies, and allies and companions. For those who want to know about an edible plant, the book describes growth conditions, harvesting, storage requirements, growing tips, and selected varieties." Recomm Ref Books for Small & Medium-sized Libr & Media Cent, 1996

Includes bibliographical references

DiSabato-Aust, Tracy

The **well**-designed mixed garden; building beds and borders with trees, shrubs, perennials, annuals, and bulbs. Timber Press 2003 460p il map $39.95   **635**

1. Gardens -- Design 2. Landscape gardening
ISBN 0-88192-559-4

LC 2002-23191

The author focuses on "the mixed border, which incorporates permanent woody plants as well as perennials, annuals, and other plants that die back to the ground every year. . . . Particularly impressive are the author's designs for using the mixed-garden approach in small properties, such as townhouse gardens and around foundations. . . . The motivated gardener will find a wealth of information and ideas in this book." Libr J

Includes bibliographical references

Eck, Joe

Our life in gardens; [by] Joe Eck and Wayne Winterrowd. Farrar, Straus and Giroux 2009 322p il $30   **635**

1. Gardeners 2. Gardening
ISBN 978-0-374-16031-9; 0-374-16031-7

LC 2008-45349

"In nearly 50 erudite and entertaining essays stretching alphabetically from Agapanthus to Xanthorrhoea quadrangulate, Eck and Winterrowd share the history of their Ver-

mont garden, writing about the plants they have lived with, nurtured and nourished." Publ Wkly

Hatch, Peter J.

A **rich** spot of earth; Thomas Jefferson's revolutionary garden at Monticello. Peter J. Hatch ; foreword by Alice Waters. Yale University Press 2012 263 p. (clothbound : alk. paper) $35.00   **635**

1. Gardening -- History 2. Historic gardens 3. Nonfiction 4. Vegetable gardening -- Virginia
ISBN 9780300171143

LC 2011038043

This book presents an account of U.S. President Thomas Jefferson's garden at his estate, Monticello. "Beginning with an extensive examination of Jefferson's structural plans and implementation strategies for Monticello's complex system of vegetable gardens, [Peter J.] Hatch then chronicles his own lengthy effort at the helm of a vast restoration project that owes much of its success to the meticulous records Jefferson left behind. Along with providing plant profiles of the myriad vegetables cultivated there over the centuries, he also offers . . . insights into the arduous physical tasks involved in eighteenth-century gardening as well as Jefferson's prudent establishment of seed-saving techniques that continue to affect the marketplace." (Booklist)

Heffernan, Maureen

Burpee complete gardener; a comprehensive, up-to-date, fully illustrated reference for gardeners at all levels. [by] Maureen Heffernan [et al.]; edited by Barbara W. Ellis. Macmillan 1995 422p il $29.95   **635**

1. Gardening
ISBN 0-02-860378-8

LC 95-13141

This volume presents "information on 420 annuals, biennials, perennials, bulbs, roses, vegetables, herbs, ground covers, and vines. There's a description of each plant, along with growing instructions and its uses. Other chapters cover designing, starting, planting, and caring for a garden; tools and equipment; and pests and diseases." Booklist

Includes bibliographical references

Hill, Fionna

Microgreens; how to grow nature's own superfood. Firefly Books 2010 107p il pa $17.95 **635**

1. Salad greens
ISBN 978-1-55407-769-4

"Hill explains how to plant, raise, and harvest crops of delicious and highly nutritious microgreens. The book is informative and accessible, delivering in a buoyant voice all you need to know about the ultimate in local eating—making a meal of houseplants. It is nicely illustrated as well, with tantalizing photographs of microgreens at every stage, from seed to planting to plate. And there are more than a dozen recipes included here along with the chapters on plant care, individual crops of microgreens from amaranth to mustard to rocket, and involving children in the operation." Libr J

Includes bibliographical references

Hutchinson, Carolyn

Time-saving gardener; tips and essential tasks, season by season. Firefly Books 2008 144p il pa $19.95 **635**

1. Gardening

ISBN 978-1-55407-372-6; 1-55407-372-3

"For gardeners too busy to plan, this eminently practical book takes care of the distracting work of planning, organizing and prioritizing." Publ Wkly

Land, Leslie

The **New** York times 1000 gardening questions & answers; based on the column Gardeners Q & A. with additional material by Leslie Land; botanical illustrations by Bobbi Angell; how-to illustrations by Elayne Sears. Workman 2003 852p il $34.95; pa $19.95 **635**

1. Gardening

ISBN 0-7611-2886-7; 0-7611-1997-3 pa

LC 2002-34206

"The text uses a Q&A format to address a gamut of gardening topics. The result is a substantial reference work useful to novice and experienced gardeners alike, with the Q&As organized into five sections: 'Flowering Plants,' 'Landscaping,' 'Edible Plants,' 'Container Gardening,' and 'Maintenance.' The subtopics within each section are many and diverse, including historically appropriate plantings, houseplants, over-wintering, and organic vegetable growing, as well as standard topics such as deer damage, roses, pruning, soil types and amendment, and recommended plant lists for specific situations." Libr J

Markham, Brett L.

Mini farming; self sufficiency on a 1/4 acre. rev. and expanded; Skyhorse Pub. 2010 227p il pa $16.95 **635**

1. Agriculture 2. Farms 3. Self-reliance

ISBN 978-1-60239-984-6

LC 2009041561

"An excellent guide for gardeners wanting to eliminate most of their grocery bills. Markham's approach combines his own experience with the best practices from several raised-bed methods. Advice includes how to select vegetables that are calorie-dense and budget friendly, how to raise poultry, how to build both a plucker and a thresher, and how to preserve food." Libr J

Includes bibliographical references

Pleasant, Barbara

Starter vegetable gardens. Storey Pub. 2010 179p il pa $19.95 **635**

1. Vegetable gardening

ISBN 978-1-60342-529-2

LC 2009-49114

"From simple bag gardens to bountiful food cornucopias, each garden plan is ... laid out with precise lists of materials and plants based on detailed landscape plans suitable for small city gardens as well as larger suburban backyards. Along with year-by-year overviews that allow gardeners to anticipate growth and adapt to changes, Pleasant provides essential cultivation and maintenance techniques." Booklist

Reader's Digest Association

Beginner's guide to gardening; creating a beautiful yard from the ground up. Reader's Digest 2005 256p il $32.95 **635**

1. Landscape gardening

ISBN 0-7621-0498-8

LC 2004-45350

"Color photographs and line drawings illustrate step-by-step methods that help take the mystery out of plant propagation methods like sowing seeds and dividing perennials, so that beginners can acquire necessary skills. ... [Beginners] will find adequate information on how to mulch and prune, plant a container, maintain a lawn, or equip a greenhouse." Booklist

Reader, John

Potato; a history of the propitious esculent. Yale University Press 2009 336p $28 **635**

1. Potatoes

ISBN 978-0-300-14109-2

LC 2008-937284

This "meandering history looks at the potato as a plant of paradox. ... Reader traces the evolution of the potato from poisonous Andean weed to global staple, offering adept disquisitions on whatever captures his attention: the mysterious origins of agriculture, the economic history of Peru, the domestic arrangements of the Irish. ... This is a story of invisible systems and unintended consequences, concerned with how the New World transformed the Old." New Yorker

Includes bibliographical references

Smith, Charles W. G.

The **beginner's** guide to edible herbs; 26 herbs everyone should grow & enjoy. introduction by Edward C. Smith; photography by Saxon Holt. Storey Pub. 2010 145p il pa $12.95 **635**

1. Cooking -- Herbs 2. Herb gardening 3. Herbs

ISBN 978-1-60342-528-5

LC 2010-845

"While Smith's beginner's guide may be a gem of simplicity, it's also chock-full of supplemental information including sumptuous recipes and inventive tips for household applications. Each herb's profile covers the many ways it can be harvested and used, and Smith includes helpful at-a-glance charts summarizing pertinent cultural information such as soil and light requirements, mature height, and planting distances. Perfect for novice gardeners, Smith's compact guide can also be appreciated by experienced hands who want to get back to the basics." Booklist

Smith, Edward C.

★ The **vegetable** gardener's bible; discover Ed's high-yield W-O-R-D system for all North American gardening regions. 2nd ed., [Fully updated 10th anniversary ed.]; Storey Pub. 2009 351p il map $34.95; pa $24.95 **635**

1. Organic gardening 2. Vegetable gardening

ISBN 978-1-60342-476-9; 978-1-60342-475-2 pa

LC 2009-23862

The author "explains everything novice and experienced gardeners need to know to grow vegetables and herbs using his system of wide, deep, raised beds. He gives detailed instructions on siting, preparing, and planning a vegetable garden, then goes on to cover choosing plant varieties, starting seed, and growing plants. Smith discusses compost creation, companion planting, crop rotation, succession planting, and ecologically friendly methods of dealing with plant diseases and pests." Libr J

Includes bibliographical references

The **vegetable** gardener's container bible. Storey Pub. 2011 263p il map $29.95; pa $19.95 **635**
1. Container gardening 2. Vegetable gardening
ISBN 978-1-60342-976-4; 978-1-60342-975-7 pa
LC 2010-51167

The author discusses "how to choose the right plants, select containers and tools, care for plants throughout the growing season, control pests without chemicals, and . . . more." Publisher's note

Smith, Jeremy N.

Growing a garden city; how farmers, first graders, counselors, troubled teens, foodies, a homeless shelter chef, single mothers, and more are transforming themselves and their neighborhoods through the intersection of local. [by] Jeremy N. Smith; foreword by Bill McKibben; photographs by Chad Harder and Sepp Jannotta. Skyhorse Pub. 2010 225p il $24.95 **635**
1. Community gardens
ISBN 978-1-61608-108-9
LC 2010-12369

"Bright, vibrant, and buoyantly accessible, this effervescent celebration of the local food movement thrums with regional, national, and international implications." Booklist

Speichert, C. Greg

Encyclopedia of water garden plants; [by] Greg Speichert & Sue Speichert; foreword by Ann Lovejoy. Timber Press 2004 386p il $49.95 **635**
1. Aquatic plants 2. Freshwater plants 3. Landscape gardening 4. Water gardens
ISBN 0-88192-625-6
LC 2003-16619

"The authors devote separate chapters to hardy waterlilies, tropicals, lotus, marginal plants, irises, waterlily-like plants (such as water snowflakes), floaters, and submerged plants. . . . This is the most comprehensive guide to all types of water plants and would make an excellent addition to gardening collections." Libr J

Springer, Lauren

Passionate gardening; good advice for challenging climates. essays and photography by Lauren Springer & Rob Proctor. Fulcrum 2000 336p il $34.95 **635**
1. Gardening
ISBN 1-55591-348-2
LC 99-49511

The "authors dispense practical advice to gardeners facing difficult growing conditions, such as poor soil, dry shade, etc. . . . {They also} discuss what plants to select—whether

working with bulbs or ornamental grasses—and how to use them in conjunction with other plants." Libr J

Includes bibliographical references

Tucker, Arthur O.

The **encyclopedia** of herbs; a comprehensive reference to herbs of flavor and fragrance. [by] Arthur O. Tucker and Thomas DeBaggio; edited by Francesco DeBaggio. [2nd ed.]; Timber Press 2009 604p il $39.95 **635**
1. Herbs -- Encyclopedias 2. Reference books
ISBN 978-0-88192-994-2
LC 2009-16700

The authors "describe more than 500 herbs that are most common in home gardens, catalogs, restaurants, and markets used for flavor or fragrance, from the acorus (sweet flag) used in the Oil of Holy Ointment to Zingiber mioga (mioga ginger) used for soups and stir fry." Libr J

Includes bibliographical references

Warren, Susan

Backyard giants; the passionate, heartbreaking, and glorious quest to grow the biggest pumpkin ever. Bloomsbury USA 2007 245p il $24.95 **635**
1. Pumpkin
ISBN 978-1-59691-278-6; 1-59691-278-2

The author's "hilarious yet enlightening exposé reveals why and how these passionate, peculiar, and painstaking pumpkin growers are willing to put it all on the line for one big—one very big—payoff." Booklist

Includes bibliographical references

Wulf, Andrea

The **brother** gardeners; botany, empire, and the birth of an obsession. Alfred A. Knopf 2008 354p il map $35 **635**
1. Gardening 2. Horticulture
ISBN 978-0-307-27023-8; 0-307-27023-8
LC 2008-55080

"A garden will never look quite the same after you've read this book. . . . Wulf's book will be of interest to anyone with a garden, even if it's on a windowsill." Libr J

Includes bibliographical references

Wyman, Donald

Wyman's gardening encyclopedia; new expanded 2nd ed; Macmillan 1986 xxvi, 1221p il $65 **635**
1. Gardening -- Encyclopedias 2. Ornamental plants -- Encyclopedias 3. Reference books
ISBN 0-02-632070-3
LC 86-12509

Contains information on major horticultural practices, including use of pesticides and herbicides, and on ornamental and agricultural plant species. Includes scientific names according to Hortus third, with cross-references for common names.

Zachos, Ellen
  Down & dirty; 43 fun & funky first-time projects
& activities to get you gardening. Storey Pub. 2007
248p il map $30; pa $19.95   **635**
    1. Gardening
    ISBN 978-1-58017-642-2; 978-1-58017-641-5 pa
                                 LC 2006-23059
  This book "describes more than 40 'fun and funky' projects and activities designed for novice gardeners, including
children. . . . The book also includes . . . activities such as
some garden photography basics, and instructions for building a containerized water garden and using cold frames."
Am Gardener
    Includes bibliographical references

Encyclopedia of gardens; history and design. edi-
    tor, by Candice A. Shoemaker. Fitzroy Dearborn
    Pubs. 2001 3v set $385   **635**
    1. Gardens -- Encyclopedias 2. Reference books
    ISBN 1-57958-173-0
  "Produced under the auspices of the Chicago Botanic
Garden . . . this comprehensive resource provides information on garden history and design. The contributors . . .
describe and provide analysis of garden-related individuals,
places, and topics. The entries are alphabetically arranged
and vary in length from a page to more than 10 pages for
the entry United States. Depending on whether the entry
deals with an individual, a place, or a topic, it includes
an essay, a biography, a list of works, a chronology, and a
bibliography." Booklist

Great garden formulas; the ultimate book of mix-it-
    yourself concoctions for your garden. Joan Ben-
    jamin and Deborah L. Martin, editors; contrib-
    uting writers, Erin Hynes {et al.} Rodale Press
    1998 342p il map hardcover o.p. pa $17.95 **635**
    1. Organic gardening 2. Organic gardening -- Formulae
    ISBN 0-87596-848-1 pa
                                     LC 98-8915
  Organic recipes and techniques for gardeners to "improve their soil, fertilize their plants, reduce weeds and
pests, and even concoct a soothing hand cream to use when
the work is done. Grouped thematically by chapter, these
formulas employ either natural ingredients or simple chemicals such as Epsom salts, and most are easy to make and
use." Libr J
    Includes bibliographical references

Homegrown harvest; a season-by-season guide to a
    sustainable kitchen garden. Rita Pelczar, editor in
    chief. Rev. American ed.; American Horticultural
    Society 2011 304p il $32.50   **635**
    1. Vegetable gardening
    ISBN 978-1-84533-560-1
  "The American Horticultural Society shows temperate-
climate gardeners how to make their ways through the gardening year. The book is arranged by season, from early
spring to late winter, with how-to advice on growing vegetables and fruits, subdivided into tasks for the different
vegetable families and fruit trees, bushes, and vines in each
subseason, individualized for mild-winter, medium-temper-
ature, and cold-winter regions. . . . The book's sumptuous

tone, instructive photographs, and detailed directions should
give beginning gardeners the enthusiasm and confidence to
get started and organizationally challenged old-timers a sigh
of relief that they won't have to figure out what to do next."
Publ Wkly

Learn to garden; [contributors, Guy Barter ... [et al.]]
    1st American ed.; DK Pub. 2008 352p il pa
    $22.95   **635**
    1. Gardening
    ISBN 978-0-7566-3443-8; 0-7566-3443-1
                                   LC 2008-297619
  This book covers how to "plant perennials, annuals and
bulbs; prune trees and shrubs; make a new lawn or a gravel
garden; select and grow roses, grasses, and ferns; grow vegetables and herbs in containers; [and] keep pests and diseases under control." Publisher's note

★ Rodale's ultimate encyclopedia of organic gar-
    dening; the indispensible green resource for ev-
    ery gardener. edited by Fern Marshall Bradley,
    Barbara W. Ellis, and Ellen Phillips. Newly rev.
    and updated; Rodale 2009 707p il map pa
    $24.99   **635**
    1. Organic gardening -- Encyclopedias 2. Reference
    books
    ISBN 978-1-59486-917-4; 1-59486-917-0
                                   LC 2008-35329
  This volume presents alphabetically arranged entries
about topics relating to organic gardening.
  "The book marches through its business, Acer to Zucchini. The chart of common organic fertilizers is nifty, especially for those of us who can ferret out that blood meal
we've lost in the pantry. Scarification, permaculture, crop
rotation and cover crops are clarified. Diagrams are used judiciously." N Y Times Book Rev
    Includes bibliographical references

635.9   Flowers and ornamental plants

American Horticultural Society
  ★ **American** Horticultural Society encyclopedia
of plants and flowers; editors in chief, Christopher
Brickell & Trevor Cole. Rev and updated ed; DK
Pub. 2002 720p il $60   **635.9**
    1. Ornamental plants 2. Plants, Ornamental --
    Encyclopedias 3. Plants, Ornamental -- Pictorial works
    ISBN 0-7894-8993-7
                                   LC 2002-73553
  This "volume features design information, an illustrated
catalog of plants arranged by color as well as kind, and a
plant dictionary. With over 8000 trees, shrubs, water plants,
cacti, succulents, and more profiled here, there is something
for nearly every kind of garden." Libr J

  Pruning & training; Christopher Brickell, editor
in chief. DK Pub. 1996 336p il $35   **635.9**
    1. Plants -- Training 2. Pruning
    ISBN 1-56458-331-7
                                   LC 96-10836

"The authors begin by explaining how plants grow and offer general information on the principles of pruning and training and on tools and equipment. They follow this with chapters on ornamental trees, fruit trees, ornamental shrubs, soft fruits . . . climbing plants, and roses. In each category are instructions on basic techniques, initial training, and renovation. Also included is a dictionary of ornamental trees and shrubs. This comprehensive and practical guide lists more than 800 plants and contains more than 1,500 color photographs and illustrations." Booklist

Armitage, Allan M.

Armitage's native plants for North American gardens. Timber Press 2006 451p il $49.95 **635.9**
1. Gardening 2. Native plants for cultivation -- North America 3. Ornamental plants
ISBN 0-88192-760-0; 978-0-88192-760-3
LC 2005-22495
This book provides "information on more than 630 native species and cultivars of perennials, biennials, and annuals that are readily available to mainstream gardeners. . . . With more than 400 color photos, this is an essential reference book for nursery people and horticulturalists, home gardeners, and all libraries." Libr J
Includes bibliographical references

Armitage's vines and climbers. Timber Press 2010 212p il $29.95 **635.9**
1. Climbing plants 2. Ornamental plants
ISBN 978-1-60469-039-2
LC 2009-32437
This book is "written with authority, in simple language, with humor. Anyone trying to build a gardening library should think about adding this one." Philadelphia Inquirer
Includes bibliographical references

Bryant, Geoff

Annuals and perennials; a gardener's encyclopedia. [by] Geoff Bryant and Tony Rodd. Firefly Books 2011 304p il pa $19.95 **635.9**
1. Annuals (Plants) -- Encyclopedias 2. Perennials -- Encyclopedias 3. Reference books
ISBN 978-1-55407-837-0; 1-55407-837-7
LC 2011499056
This guide provides a selection table with characteristics, growth habits, and needs of each plant, as well as information on subspecies, hybrids, and cultivars.
"This well-designed and practical book deserves a green thumbs-up for public libraries and most gardeners." Libr J

Cave, Yvonne

★ **Succulents** for the contemporary garden. Timber Press 2003 176p il $29.95 **635.9**
1. Succulent plants
ISBN 0-88192-573-X
LC 2003-271441
"After defining succulents or xerophytes, Cave presents short discussions of succulent's cultivation, pests and diseases, and propagation. The real core of this work is the A-Z of genera, which lists 60 genera and hundreds of their species. Each entry contains a detailed description, with shape, size, color, and country of origin for each plant, often with a

beautiful close-up photograph and cultivation and propagation information. . . . This first-rate reference belongs in . . . libraries everywhere." Am Ref Books Annu, 2003

Courtier, Jane

Indoor plants; the essential guide to choosing and caring for houseplants. {by} Jane Courtier & Graham Clarke; consultant, Anne Halpin. Reader's Digest Assn. 1997 240p il $30 **635.9**
1. House plants 2. Indoor gardening
ISBN 0-89577-921-8
LC 96-42046
This discussion of houseplants includes information on care, feeding, temperature control, propagation, and pests and diseases. Display ideas are also provided.

Cullina, William

Understanding perennials; a new look at an old favorite. Houghton Mifflin Harcourt 2009 247p il $40 **635.9**
1. Perennials
ISBN 978-0-618-88346-2; 0-618-88346-0
LC 2008-36760
This book provides "a chance to learn what soil is composed of, why it's acid or alkaline and why you should care. Cullina will straighten out your understanding of roots, bulbs, rhizomes, stolons, corms and tubers; he clarifies osmosis, photosynthesis, secretory structures, nitrogen fixes and plant hormones. . . . [He] is an engaging, clear and congenial writer." N Y Times Book Rev
Includes bibliographical references

Darke, Rick

The **American** woodland garden; capturing the spirit of the deciduous forest. text and photography by Rick Darke. Timber Press 2002 377p il $49.95 **635.9**
1. Forest plants 2. Gardening 3. Woodland garden plants -- United States 4. Woodland gardening -- United States
ISBN 0-88192-545-4
LC 2002-20474
This "is both a pictorial and narrative account of a wooded locale in Pennsylvania that the author spent years studying, as well as a design and planting guide. . . . He explains the different elements of a woodland garden and thoroughly describes the plants (features, zones, and growth ranges) that will perform well. The author's photographs illustrate both the overall effect and the beauty of individual plants." Libr J
Includes bibliographical references

Dash, Mike

Tulipomania; the story of the world's most coveted flower and the extraordinary passions it aroused. Crown 2000 273p hardcover o.p. pa $13.95 **635.9**
1. Tulip mania, 17th century 2. Tulips
ISBN 0-609-80765-X pa
LC 99-39186
"The centerpiece of this story is a stunning two months, December 1636 and January 1637, when fortunes were made and lost in the Netherlands—in tulip bulb futures trading. Stripped to its basics, this would be a dry case study in

an economics textbook. But Dash adds depth to the tale by including relevant bits of botany, sociology and history, as well as glimpses of the personalities involved in the creation of the tulip market." Publ Wkly

Includes bibliographic references

DiSabato-Aust, Tracy

The **well**-tended perennial garden; planting & pruning techniques. Expanded ed; Timber Press 2006 383p il map $34.95   **635.9**

1. Perennials

ISBN 978-0-88192-803-7; 0-88192-803-8

LC 2006-10388

In addition to details on pruning and maintenance this work contains an A-Z encyclopedia of perennials.

Dirr, Michael

Dirr's hardy trees and shrubs; an illustrated encyclopedia. by Michael A. Dirr. Timber Press 1997 493p il $69.95   **635.9**

1. Landscape gardening 2. Shrubs 3. Shrubs -- Dictionaries 4. Trees 5. Trees -- Dictionaries

ISBN 0-88192-404-0

LC 96-54032

"Depicting both character and traits (fruit, flower, bark, or autumn color), the volume covers over 500 species and some additional varieties and cultivars. Each entry enumerates scientific name, common name, detailed plant description, environmental conditions, place in the landscape, i.e., woodlawn tree or lawn tree, and hardiness zones." Libr J

Dirr's trees and shrubs for warm climates; an illustrated encyclopedia. by Michael A. Dirr. Timber Press 2002 446p il map $69.95   **635.9**

1. Landscape gardening 2. Landscape plants -- Sunbelt States 3. Ornamental plants 4. Ornamental shrubs -- Sunbelt States 5. Ornamental trees -- Sunbelt States 6. Shrubs 7. Trees

ISBN 0-88192-525-X

LC 2001-35810

"This volume, in conjunction with Dirr's Hardy Trees and Shrubs, completes [the author's] coverage of the woody ornamentals cultivated in North America. In a witty and informative style, Dirr presents botanic, cultural, and landscaping details on over 400 species. Entries are accompanied by magnificent color photos." Libr J

Duffield, Mary Rose

Plants for dry climates; how to select, grow, and enjoy. {by} Mary Rose Duffield and Warren D. Jones. rev ed; Perseus Pub. 2001 216p il pa $27.50   **635.9**

1. Arid regions plants 2. Arid regions plants -- Pictorial works 3. Desert gardening 4. Desert gardening -- Mexico 5. Desert gardening -- Southwest, New 6. Desert plants 7. Gardening

ISBN 1-55561-251-2

LC 2001-280011

The authors "explore strategies for gardening in dry or arid climates. . . . They cover climate conditions and pre-design concerns such as possible planting restrictions by neighborhood covenants, the use of professional landscap-

ing services, costs, and maintenance. A detailed plant guide identifies more than 300 species best suited to arid gardens, explaining conditions in which they thrive or are compromised." Libr J

Includes bibliographical references

Ellis, Barbara W.

Covering ground; unexpected ideas for landscaping with colorful, low-maintenance ground covers. Storey Pub. 2007 224p il map $29.95; pa $19.95   **635.9**

1. Climbing plants 2. Grasses 3. Ornamental plants

ISBN 1-58017-664-X; 978-1-58017-664-4; 1-58017-665-8 pa; 978-1-58017-664-4 pa

LC 2007-335

"Divided into three main sections, the book addresses why one should consider using ground covers, types of plants for different areas, and planting, growing, and propagating. . . . Suitable for all gardening collections, this easy and fun read is essential for the home gardener looking for low-maintenance or problem-area ground covers." Libr J

★ **Taylor's** guide to annuals; how to select and grow more than 400 annuals, biennials, and tender perennials. Houghton Mifflin 1999 441p il pa $23   **635.9**

1. Annuals (Plants) 2. Flower gardening

ISBN 0-395-94352-3

LC 99-33188

This guide features information on over five hundred popular plants and cultivars for landscaping and gardening.

Taylor's guide to perennials; more than 600 flowering and foliage plants, including ferns and ornamental grasses. Houghton Mifflin 2001 490p il map pa $23   **635.9**

1. Flower gardening 2. Perennials

ISBN 0-395-98363-0

LC 00-33436

Text and numerous illustrations cover popular perennials, their cultivars, ornamental grasses, and ferns.

Fell, Derek

★ **Encyclopedia** of hardy plants; annuals, bulbs, herbs, perennials, shrubs, trees, vegetables, fruits & nuts. Derek Fell. Firefly Books 2007 224p il map $29.95   **635.9**

1. Plants -- Encyclopedias 2. Reference books

ISBN 978-1-55407-240-8; 1-55407-240-9

LC 2007-296324

This reference features descriptions of more than 700 hardy plants, each with color photos and hardiness zone ranges. Also contains indexes of both common plant names and botanical names.

Fisher, Kathleen

★ **Taylor's** guide to shrubs; how to select and grow more than 500 ornamental and useful shrubs

for privacy, ground covers, and specimen plantings. Houghton Mifflin 2001 441p il map pa $23 **635.9**
1. Ornamental shrubs 2. Shrubs
ISBN 0-618-00437-8

LC 00-36941

This guide covers information on popular shrubs and their cultivars and includes growing instructions.

Freeman, Mark

Gardening in your greenhouse; illustrations by Heather Bellanca. Stackpole Bks. 1998 200p il pa $19.95 **635.9**
1. Gardening 2. Greenhouse gardening 3. Greenhouses
ISBN 0-8117-2776-9

LC 98-4842

This work "begins with chapters on types of greenhouses, equipment, soil, air, water, heat, light, pests, and diseases. The rest of the book covers growing seedlings for transplanting into the outdoor garden and raising vegetables and herbs in the greenhouse. Freeman lists vegetable, flower, and herb species suitable for growing to maturity in a greenhouse." Libr J

Garden perennials

★ **Armitage's** garden perennials; 2nd ed., fully rev. and updated; Timber Press 2011 347p il $49.95 **635.9**
1. Perennials -- Encyclopedias 2. Reference books
ISBN 978-1-60469-038-5

LC 2011293867

This is an "illustrated compilation of 136 genera of garden-worthy perennials. Alphabetical entries feature illuminating descriptions of plant habits and forms, along with essential cultural advice. Armitage recommends countless varieties that can be depended on to perform well or are particularly lovely specimens. Appropriate U.S.D.A. zones and regions where the plants will thrive are noted, too. With its accessible writing style, abundant color photographs, and final section listing plants suggested for specific conditions or purposes, Armitage's latest work should be considered an essential addition to gardening collections." Booklist

Gift, Nancy

A **weed** by any other name; the virtues of a messy lawn, or learning to love the plants we don't plant. Beacon Press 2009 192p il $23.95 **635.9**
1. Weeds
ISBN 978-0-8070-8552-3; 0-8070-8552-9

LC 2008-41103

"Balancing her expertise and personal encounters, Gift details the practical choices she makes in allowing weeds to inhabit her lawn. The results of her philosophy: a nontoxic yard for pets and children, considerable savings in time and money, and a renewed habitat for butterflies, amphibians and birds that are becoming increasingly rare in many urban and suburban neighborhoods. Covering one calendar year in her life, the book details Gift's experiences with some common varieties of weeds, from the wild garlic of early spring to the chickweed greening flower beds in winter. . . . Gift argues that tolerance for unexpected plant species can do more to

help restore wildlife than an expensive array of birdhouses and feeders." National Wildlife
Includes bibliographical references

Greenlee, John

The **American** meadow garden; creating a natural alternative to the traditional lawn. photography by Saxon Holt. Timber Press 2009 278p il $34.95 **635.9**
1. Grasses 2. Landscape gardening
ISBN 978-0-88192-871-6; 0-88192-871-2

LC 2009-19438

"Meadow gardening is an exciting, fresh approach to horticulture. By taking advantage of native plant life and soil conditions, gardeners can create an ecologically friendly yard that requires less water and mowing. Greenlee . . . focuses on the conditions of regional types of American grasslands, emphasizing throughout that gardeners must first understand local ecology (using professional help where necessary) to be successful. With Holt's photographs, this is a large and colorful showcase of Greenlee's extensive knowledge and great passion for gardening." Libr J
Includes bibliographical references

Hansen, Eric

Orchid fever; a horticultural tale of love, lust, and lunacy. Pantheon Bks. 2000 288p hardcover o.p. pa $13 **635.9**
1. Nursery growers 2. Orchid industry 3. Orchids 4. Plant collectors
ISBN 0-679-77183-2 pa

LC 99-44582

"Most of Hansen's sketches are fundamentally vehicles for illustrating his serious and provocative argument against CITES (the Convention on International Trade in Endangered Species of Wild Fauna and Flora). According to the author, CITES thwarts orchid conservation and perversely legitimizes plant smuggling by botanical institutions." Libr J

Heffernan, Cecelia

★ **Flowers** A to Z; buying, growing, cutting, arranging. photography T.K. Hill. Abrams 2001 160p $49.50; pa $17.95 **635.9**
1. Flower arrangement 2. Flower gardening 3. Flowers 4. flowers
ISBN 0-8109-3348-9; 0-8109-2122-7 pa

LC 00-64282

"Recommendations for the best tools and containers are followed by in-depth profiles of 55 of the most popular garden and hothouse flowers, in which Heffernan shares such trade secrets as the flower's vase life and its cost at different seasons. . . .Straightforward directions are supported by close-up photographs." Booklist

Henry Doubleday Research Association

Rodale's illustrated encyclopedia of organic gardening; Henry Doubleday Research Association;

editor-in-chief, Pauline Pears. DK Pub. 2002 416p
il hardcover o.p. pa $25 **635.9**
1. Organic gardening
ISBN 0-7894-8908-2; 0-7566-0932-1 pa
LC 2002-73477
This "encyclopedia offers guidance on growing flowers,
herbs, and fruits and vegetables the organic, chemical-free
way." Booklist
Includes bibliographical references

Hewitt, Terry
The **complete** book of cacti & succulents. Dorling Kindersley 1993 176p il hardcover o.p. pa
$20 **635.9**
1. Cactus 2. Succulent plants
ISBN 1-56458-337-6; 0-7894-1657-3 pa
LC 93-22107
An illustrated look at the history and cultivation of
more than 300 plants. Ideas for containers and display
are included.

Hill, Lewis
Bulbs; four seasons of beautiful blooms. {by} Lewis &
Nancy Hill. Storey Communications 1994 218p il hardcover o.p. pa $19.95 **635.9**
1. Bulbs
ISBN 0-88266-877-3 pa
LC 94-14240
The authors "examine bulbs that will bloom in each of
four seasons, as well as give guidance on such subjects as
forcing bulbs successfully, pests and disease, and natural-
izing bulbs. They go into the 'big four' (crocuses, hyacinths,
narcissus and tulips) in wonderful detail and pique our interest in lesser-known bulbs." Publ Wkly
Includes bibliographical references

Hillier, Malcolm
Container gardening through the year; photography by Matthew Ward. Dorling Kindersley 1995
160p il hardcover o.p. pa $13.95 **635.9**
1. Container gardening
ISBN 0-7894-3296-X pa
LC 94-26717
"Hillier advises on how to match surprising plant
combinations with an array of containers. Various themes
(shape and proportion, texture, and harmonizing or contrasting colors) are represented in lovely color plates that
provide a pleasing supplement to Hillier's reassuring
guidance." Booklist

Hodgson, Larry
Perennials for every purpose; choose the plants
you need for your conditions, your garden, and your
taste. Rodale 2000 502p il $29.95; pa $19.95 **635.9**
1. Perennials
ISBN 0-87596-823-6; 0-87596-893-7 pa
LC 99-6968
"Preliminary chapters cover the basics such as getting
started, creating a design, and keeping plants healthy. The
highlight, however, is the 14 chapters that profile perennials
that can be used in unique situations (e.g., dry, wet, sunny,
shade, easy-care). Each plant profile includes a photograph,
a sidebar listing plant characteristics, and informative paragraphs detailing good companion plants, problems and solutions, and the top performers and recommended varieties for
each plant." Libr J
Includes bibliographical references

Joyce, David
Topiary and the art of training plants; illustrated
by Laura Stoddart. Firefly Bks. 2000 160p il $40;
pa $24.95 **635.9**
1. Landscape gardening 2. Ornamental plants
ISBN 1-55209-420-0; 1-55209-442-7 pa
The author "explains the technical steps necessary to
achieve an array of plant forms that will function in the garden as living sculptures. . . . Joyce's handbook offers an instructive tour that will surely fire up the imagination of keen
gardeners. A directory of recommended plants and suppliers
is included." Booklist

Kelaidis, Gwen Moore
Hardy succulents; tough plants for every climate. photography by Saxon Holt. Storey Pub. 2008
159p il map $29.95; pa $19.95 **635.9**
1. Succulent plants
ISBN 978-1-58017-701-6; 978-1-58017-700-9 pa
LC 2007-39890
The author "offers practical tips on siting, planting,
soil requirements, and care of succulents for every hardiness zone in a clear and confident voice. Advice on pairing succulents with perennials, using them as focal points
in the garden, and protecting them from the cold of winter
is dispensed in lively prose. . . . This delightful book will
be practical and inspiring for both novice and experienced
gardeners." Libr J

King, Michael
Gardening with grasses; {by} Michael King and
Piet Oudolf; foreword by Beth Chatto. Timber Press
1998 152p il $34.95 **635.9**
1. Grasses 2. Landscape gardening 3. Ornamental
grasses
ISBN 0-88192-411-3
LC 97-24467
The authors discuss the application of grasses "in contemporary settings from lawns to urban landscaping projects. . . . Plant lists for particular situations augment the text,
and the many color photographs illustrate the roles grasses
can play in a natural garden design." Libr J
Includes bibliographical references

Martin, Tovah
The **new** terrarium; creating beautiful displays
for plants and nature. [by] Tovah Martin and Kindra
Clineff. Clarkson Potter/Publishers 2009 176p il
$25 **635.9**
1. Terrariums
ISBN 978-0-307-40731-3; 0-307-40731-4
LC 2008-27713
"With beguiling photographs by Kindra Clineff, this at-
tractive volume contains everything you need to know about
growing plants under glass." N Y Times Book Rev

McGowan, Alice

Bulbs in the basement, geraniums on the window-sill; how to grow and overwinter 165 tender plants. [by] Alice McGowan, Brian McGowan. Storey Pub. 2008 208p il pa $17.95 **635.9**

1. Greenhouses 2. Ornamental plants 3. Perennials
ISBN 978-1-60342-042-6; 1-60342-042-8

LC 2008-22440

"After offering readers a brief history of gardening with 165 plants, the McGowans give advice on choosing a container, on container combinations, and on the best type of soil to use. They stress the importance of the correct temperature and give instructions on setting up a site. There's a color photograph of each plant, along with information on its shape, color, and foliage, what the genus comprises, and design ideas. There also are instructions on how to use the guide, as well as suggested reading." Booklist

Includes bibliographical references

Michener, David

Taylor's guide to ground covers; more than 400 flowering and foliage ground covers for every garden situation. {by} David Michener and Nan Sinton. completely rev and updated; Houghton Mifflin 2001 375p il maps pa $23 **635.9**

1. Climbing plants 2. Grasses 3. Ground cover plants 4. Ornamental plants
ISBN 0-618-03010-7

LC 2001-39566

"In this guide luscious photographs of 400 ground covers are paired with information about gardening zones and sun tolerance. . . . The splendor of the photography aside, the no-nonsense approaches are recommended." Am Ref Books Annu, 2003

O'Sullivan, Penelope

The **homeowner's** complete tree & shrub handbook; the essential guide to choosing, planting and maintaining perfect landscape plants. photography by Karen Bussolini. Storey Pub. 2007 408p il map $39.95; pa $29.95 **635.9**

1. Ornamental plants 2. Shrubs 3. Trees
ISBN 978-1-58017-571-5; 978-1-58017-570-8 pa

LC 2007-10718

This guide to planting trees and shrubs discusses planning the landscape and buying, planting and caring for trees and shrubs. Includes descriptions of 348 trees and shrubs.

"The real jewel of this volume is the extensive AZ directory of nearly 350 trees and shrubs, many offering more than one season of interest. There is even a handy pronounciation guide for every plant name." Libr J

Includes webliography and bibliographical references

Ondra, Nancy J.

Taylor's guide to roses; how to select, grow, and enjoy more than 380 roses. Houghton Mifflin 2001 474p il maps pa $23 **635.9**

1. Rose culture 2. Roses
ISBN 0-618-06888-0

LC 00-68248

Text and numerous full color illustrations describe classes of roses including floribundas, grandifloras, miniatures, and climbers. Suggestions are provided for carefree border and ground cover roses. Entries are given for each plant, noting its uses and limitations.

Pavord, Anna

Bulb. Mitchell Beazley 2009 544p il map $39.99 **635.9**

1. Bulbs
ISBN 978-1-84533-532-8

This book features "advice on the purchase and care of bulbs. The approximately 600 entries include detailed descriptions of the blooms, some comparisons with related cultivars, plant size, hardiness, native areas, and bloom season. . . . The entries are accompanied by photographs of individual blossoms. These are interspersed with lush two-page-spread images of gardens, masses of blooms, and single spectacular blooms. Pavord's writing style is delightfully conversational while providing important technical information for the gardener." Booklist

Includes bibliographical references

Pleasant, Barbara

★ The **complete** houseplant survival manual; essential know-how for keeping (not killing) more than 160 indoor plants. photography by Rosemary Kautzky. Storey Pub. 2005 365p il pa $24.95 **635.9**

1. House plants
ISBN 1-58017-569-4

LC 2005-14205

"Following an enlightening introduction that discusses the history, uses, and benefits that houseplants bestow, the manual is divided into three main sections. The first two are plant directories offering in-depth plant profiles of first flowering, then foliage, houseplants. The third is an extensive compilation of houseplant-care topics, from acclimatization to watering. With vivid color photographs, precise illustrations, appendixes listing helpful resources, definitions, and a cross-reference chart of botanical and common names, this is a must-have manual for anyone who shares home or office space with potted plants." Booklist

Scott, Aurelia C.

Otherwise normal people; inside the thorny world of competitive rose gardening. Algonquin Books of Chapel Hill 2007 235p $22.95 **635.9**

1. Flower shows 2. Roses
ISBN 978-1-56512-464-6; 1-56512-464-2

LC 2006-27489

"Among the stories of the rose maniacs she encounters, Scott interweaves intruiging pieces of rose history and other fascinating bits of trivia." American Gardener

Includes bibliographical references

Swindells, Philip

The **water** garden encyclopedia. Firefly Bks. 2003 256p il $45; pa $29.95 **635.9**

1. Hydroponics
ISBN 1-55297-715-3; 1-55297-717-X pa

LC 2003-271624

This book "offers a host of ideas for creating and maintaining many types of water gardens, from small containers with fountains to re-creations of natural landscape settings. . . . Instructions for making each type of garden are given through a combination of text and photographs that . . . illustrate each step in the process, from choosing and marking out the site to finishing the project with suitable aquatic plants. Accompanying each design idea are lists of water-loving plants suitable for that type of garden—including water lilies, reeds and rushes, bog plants, and floating and submerged aquatics—and there are chapters on how to buy, plant, fertilize, divide, propagate and care for these plants." Publ Wkly

The American Horticultural Society A-Z encyclopedia of garden plants; Christopher Brickell, H. Marc Cathey, editors-in-chief. Rev. US ed.; DK Pub. 2004 1099p il map $80   **635.9**
1. Ornamental plants -- Encyclopedias 2. Reference books
ISBN 0-7566-0616-0

                         LC 2004-559196
"Equal parts gem and tool, this book is like a diamond. Clear, concise, and thoroughly useful, it fits the needs of all gardeners." Am Ref Books Annu, 2005

Flora: a gardener's encyclopedia; over 20,000 plants. chief consultant, Sean Hogan. Timber Press 2003 2v il map set $99.95   **635.9**
1. Flowers 2. Ornamental plants -- Encyclopedias 3. Reference books
ISBN 0-88192-538-1

                         LC 2003-59663
"Although gardening books abound, none matches this work's range of detail." Libr J

The Hillier gardener's guide to trees & shrubs; editor, John Kelly; consultant editor, John Hillier. Reader's Digest Assn. 1997 640p il maps $50 **635.9**
1. Ornamental plants 2. Shrubs 3. Trees
ISBN 0-89577-973-0

                         LC 97-4282
"Alphabetically arranged plant directory covering more than 4000 plants with over 400 genres represented. . . . {It discusses} basic biology, theory and practice, selection and purchase, care and maintenance, pest and diseases, plant propagation, plant names, and plant selection." Libr J

★ Taylor's encyclopedia of garden plants; edited by Frances Tenenbaum. Houghton Mifflin 2003 464p il map $45   **635.9**
1. Ornamental plants -- Encyclopedias 2. Reference books
ISBN 0-618-22644-3

                         LC 2002-27630
"This beautifully illustrated encyclopedia offers North American gardeners a definitive resource for all their questions, from flowers to trees to shrubs." Publ Wkly

Taylor's master guide to gardening; editor-in-chief: Frances Tenenbaum; editors: Rita Buchanan, Roger Holmes; designer: Deborah Fillion; illus-

trator: Steve Buchanan; copy editor: Nancy J. Stabile. Houghton Mifflin 1994 612p il $60 **635.9**
1. Gardening 2. Landscape gardening
ISBN 0-618-15907-X

                         LC 93-48865
The first part of this book consists of a discussion of "30 topics (annuals, perennials, trees, design, color, containers, shade, water, etc.) . . . Next, a 200-page 'Gallery' of recommended plants is arranged alphabetically by Latin name, with photographs and climate zone numbers. The third section, a 300-page encyclopedia, list 3000 unillustrated species and cultivars with a short paragraph about each." Libr J
Includes bibliographical references

★ The plant finder; the right plants for every garden. senior consultants, Tony Rodd and Geoff Bryant. Firefly Books 2007 992p il map $49.95 **635.9**
1. Gardening 2. Landscape gardening 3. Ornamental plants
ISBN 978-1-55407-265-1; 1-55407-265-4

                         LC 2007-298960
This book "gives basic descriptions and growing conditions for more than 5,000 plants, with a focus on the temperate zones. . . . Beginning gardeners as well as plant fanatics may find this comprehensive volume an indispensable midwinter reference for yearly garden planning, as well as a useful outdoor planting companion come spring." Publ Wkly

636   Animal husbandry

Belozerskaya, Marina
   ★ The **Medici** giraffe; and other tales of exotic animals and power. Little, Brown and Co. 2006 414p il $24.99   **636**
1. Diplomatic gifts 2. Exotic animals 3. Human-animal relationships 4. Wild animal collecting 5. Wild animals as pets
ISBN 0-316-52565-0; 978-0-316-52565-7

                         LC 2006-09659
"This is a sumptuous read—smart, funny and utterly compelling." Publ Wkly
Includes bibliographical references

Grandin, Temple
   Animals make us human; creating the best life for animals. [by] Temple Grandin and Catherine Johnson. Houghton Mifflin Harcourt 2009 342p $26   **636**
1. Animal behavior 2. Emotions in animals
ISBN 978-0-15-101489-7; 0-15-101489-2

                         LC 2008-34892
"Packed with fascinating insights, unexpected observations and a wealth of how-to tips, Grandin's peppy work ably challenges assumptions about what makes animals happy." Publ Wkly

Halligan, Karen
   Doc Halligan's What every pet owner should know; prescriptions for happy, healthy cats and dogs.

illustrations by Liz Wells. HarperCollins Publishers 2007 324p il $24.95; pa $15.95 **636**

1. Cats 2. Dogs 3. Pets -- Health and hygiene

ISBN 978-0-06-089859-5; 0-06-089859-3; 978-0-06-089860-1 pa; 0-06-089860-7 pa

LC 2007-60869

"Emphasizing canine (and feline) wellness, . . . [the author] gives clear advice about preventing illness and injuries through sensible nutrition, regular grooming, dental care, and partnering with your veterinarian." Libr J

Katz, Jon

Dog days; dispatches from Bedlam Farm. Villard Books 2007 273p il $23.95 **636**

1. Authors 2. Domestic animals 3. Farm life 4. Farm life -- New York (State) 5. Journalists 6. Nonfiction writers 7. Novelists 8. Television producers

ISBN 978-1-4000-6404-5; 1-4000-6404-X

LC 2006-52804

This is a "collection of stories from upstate New York's Bedlam Farm. . . . Bedlam Farm, a cross between a working and a hobby farm, is the home of the animals that are . . . [the author's] inspiration. . . . A must-read for all animal lovers." Booklist

Wells, Jeff

All my patients have tales; favorite stories from a vet's practice. St. Martin's Press 2009 226p il $24.95; pa $13.99 **636**

1. Veterinary medicine

ISBN 978-0-312-53739-5; 0-312-53739-5; 978-0-312-60639-8 pa; 0-312-60639-7 pa

LC 2008-35868

"Newly minted veterinarian Wells is on one of his first calls—a cow trying to deliver a dead calf—when after two hours of unceasing labor, he decides to try another approach, and one of the on-looking farmers says, 'That's what you should have done to begin with!' So begins the education of a young vet, the on-the-job training that no amount of schooling can provide. . . . A move to Colorado didn't immediately improve his finances but did improve his buffalo-wrangling skills and his ability to remove porcupine quills from overzealous dogs and donkeys. Another winning veterinary memoir deserving of space next to the immortal James Herriot and his heirs." Booklist

636.08   Specific topics in animal husbandry

Gorant, Jim

The **lost** dogs; Michael Vick's pit bulls and their tale of rescue and redemption. Gotham Books 2010 287p il $26 **636.08**

1. Animal welfare 2. Dogs 3. Football players

ISBN 978-1-592-40550-3

LC 2010-19125

"Read about the injuries, the exhumation of dogs shot or hung, the bloodied ring, and the eyewitness account of Vick taking a little red dog . . . and swinging her around by the legs, smashing her to death—and see if you can stop shaking. . . . Riveting, heartbreaking, and finally hopeful, this is exemplary reporting; essential for anyone who cares

about animal welfare—or what it means to be responsibly human." Libr J

Includes bibliographical references

Niman, Nicolette Hahn

Righteous porkchop; finding a life beyond factory farms. Collins 2009 321p $23.99 **636.08**

1. Agriculture -- Environmental aspects 2. Animal welfare 3. Meat industry

ISBN 978-0-06-146649-6; 0-06-146649-2

LC 2008-27852

"Hoping to establish an active reform movement, Niman exposes herself to the horrors of cruel, indifferent treatment of animals at factory farms. There are fairly graphic and distressing descriptions of the practices, but . . . the crucial issue Niman is determined to deal with is the widespread pollution caused by these practices." Libr J

Includes bibliographical references

636.088   Animals for specific purposes

Sutherland, Amy

Kicked, bitten, and scratched; life and lessons at the world's premier school for exotic animal trainers. Viking 2006 320p hardcover o.p. pa $15 **636.088**

1. Animal trainers 2. Animals -- Training 3. Exotic animals

ISBN 0-670-03768-0; 978-0-670-03768-1; 0-14-311194-9 pa; 978-0-14-311194-8 pa

LC 2005-57474

"Readers will acquire new and enhanced respect for a little-studied profession." Booklist

636.089   Veterinary medicine

Goldstein, Martin

The **nature** of animal healing; the path to your pet's health, happiness, and longevity. Knopf 1999 357p hardcover o.p. pa $16 **636.089**

1. Holistic veterinary medicine 2. Pets 3. Pets -- Diseases -- Alternative treatment 4. Veterinary medicine

ISBN 0-345-43919-8 pa

LC 98-38193

"Goldstein outlines an approach to healing that revolves around strengthening the immune system through diet and such holistic healing techniques as acupuncture and homeopathy, so that an animal can heal itself. . . . This is a life-affirming book that should interest any pet owner." Publ Wkly

Pinney, Chris C.

★ The **complete** home veterinary guide. Mc-Graw-Hill 2004 736p il $29.95 **636.089**

1. Pets -- Diseases 2. Pets -- Health 3. Veterinary medicine

ISBN 0-07-141272-7

LC 2003-52668

This guide covers "preventive health care, diet, grooming, training, diseases, traveling with pets, selection, first aid, anatomy, {and} holistic pet care." Publisher's note

Schoen, Allen M.

Kindred spirits; how the remarkable bond between humans and animals can change the way we live. Broadway Bks. 2001 280p hardcover o.p. pa $14   **636.089**
1. Alternative veterinary medicine 2. Human-animal relationships 3. Pets 4. Pets -- Social aspects -- Anecdotes 5. Pets -- Therapeutic use -- Anecdotes 6. Veterinary acupuncture 7. Veterinary medicine
ISBN 0-7679-0431-1 pa

LC 00-57891

This book "covers the benefits of the human-animal bond; seven ways to foster a spiritual bond with your animal; wellness approaches, such as diet therapy and preventing and treating cancer the natural way; finding veterinary support; and how to let go when there is nothing further that can be done." Libr J

Includes bibliographical references

Black's veterinary dictionary; [edited by] Edward Boden. Rowman & Littlefield 1998 il $156   **636.089**
1. Reference books 2. Veterinary medicine -- Dictionaries
ISBN 978-0-389-21017-7; 0-389-21017-X

"Gives comprehensive coverage of terms in veterinary medicine and animal husbandry, as well as the anatomy and physiology of domesticated animals. Includes 'information on accidents, worldwide disease eradication campaigns, health promotion, the housing of animals, and pest control.'—Pref. Includes references and cross-references." Guide to Ref Books. 11th edition

The Merck veterinary manual; editor, Susan E. Aiello. 9th ed.; Merck 2005 xxxix, 2712p $45   **636.089**
1. Veterinary medicine -- Handbooks, manuals, etc.
ISBN 0-911910-50-6

"Technical manual for use by veterinarians in the diagnosis and treatment of animal diseases. Authoritative, up-to-date information presented in a brief, convenient format; includes recommended prescriptions." Ref Sources for Small & Medium-sized Libr. 6th edition

★ The Merck/Merial manual for pet health; Cynthia M. Kahn, editor. Home ed.; Merck & Co. 2007 xxvii, 1345p il $29.95; pa $22.95   **636.089**
1. Pets -- Health and hygiene 2. Veterinary medicine -- Handbooks, manuals, etc.
ISBN 978-0-911910-22-3; 0-911910-22-0; 978-0-911910-99-5 pa; 0-911910-99-9 pa

LC 2007-933381

"An in-depth, thoroughly indexed reference featuring high-quality information." Libr J

Petspeak; you're closer than you think to a great relationship with your dog or cat! by the editors of Pets, part of the family books. Rodale 2000 485p il $29.95; pa $16.95   **636.089**
1. Cats 2. Cats -- Behavior 3. Dogs 4. Dogs -- Behavior 5. Human-animal communication 6. Human-

animal relationships
ISBN 1-57954-077-5; 1-57954-337-5 pa

LC 00-9290

This volume "attempts to explain pet behavior to improve pet-owner relationships. Addressing the habits of both cats and dogs, this book helps make sense out of pet peculiarities and offers practical solutions and advice." Booklist

636.1   Horses

Edwards, Elwyn Hartley

The **encyclopedia** of the horse; photography by Bob Langrish, Kit Houghton. [Rev. and updated]; DK 2008 464p il $40   **636.1**
1. Horses -- Encyclopedias 2. Reference books
ISBN 978-0-7566-2894-9

The author "traces the evolution of the horse, covering every major breed of horse and pony as well as the contribution the horse has made to civilization. The Visual Breed Guide portrays more than 150 of the world's major breeds of horse and pony. . . . The origin, history, and uses of each breed are explained." Publisher's note

Faurie, Bernadette

The **horse** riding & care handbook. Lyons Press 2000 160p il hardcover o.p. pa $19.95   **636.1**
1. Horsemanship 2. Horses
ISBN 1-58574-058-6; 1-58574-517-0 pa

"Each section contains pictures or diagrams to clarify the explanations, from horse evolution and history with humans to markings, colors, and breeds. Topics such as tack, how to mount, a first riding lesson, and techniques of western riding are all simply described with wonderful graphics." Libr J

Richards, Susan

Chosen by a horse; a memoir. Soho Press 2006 248p $20   **636.1**
1. College teachers 2. Horses 3. Memoirists 4. Psychotherapists
ISBN 1-56947-419-2

LC 2005-52337

"Richards adopts an emaciated mare and her foal, overriding the small voice telling her that she already has three horses to care for and a herniated disk. Her experience with her new charges proves profoundly instructive in terms of how love can foster growth of the human spirit and help in overcoming pain and loss. The abused mare, Lay Me Down, proves to be one of those rare creatures that remain gentle despite years of mistreatment, responding profoundly to the kind treatment that is part of everyday life for Richards' animals. Fascinated by the affection this animal accords a stranger, Richards notes the mare's courage and slowly begins to emulate it in her own life, opening up to a love affair and its aftermath." Booklist

★ Storey's horse-lover's encyclopedia; an English and Western A-to-Z guide. edited by Deborah Burns. Storey Bks. 2001 471p il $37.50; pa $24.95   **636.1**
1. Horse breeds -- Encyclopedias 2. Horsemanship --

Encyclopedias 3. Horses 4. Horses -- Encyclopedias
ISBN 1-58017-336-5; 1-58017-317-9 pa

LC 00-46329

"The alphabetically arranged entries vary in length from a few sentences to a few pages, with the most thorough coverage going to extensive topics like breeding, foot care, and feeding. Most entries consist of one or two paragraphs and provide a good definition of the term at hand." Libr J

636.4   Swine

Montgomery, Sy

The **good** good pig; the extraordinary life of Christopher Hogwood. Ballantine Books 2006 228p il $21.95; pa $13.95   **636.4**
   1. Human-animal relationships 2. Pet owners 3. Pets 4. Pigs 5. Swine
   ISBN 0-345-48137-2; 978-0-345-48137-5; 0-345-49609-4 pa; 978-0-345-49609-6 pa

LC 2005-57094

This is a "description of the 14-year life of a 750-pound pet pig who was named after the conductor [Christopher Hogwood]. Anyone who has ever loved a pet can enjoy reading about the relationship between Montgomery and her Christopher." Sci Books Films

Rath, Sara

The **complete** pig. Voyageur Press 2000 144p $29.95   **636.4**
   1. Pigs 2. Swine 3. Swine breeds 4. Wild boar
   ISBN 0-89658-435-6

LC 99-45618

This book is "liberally illustrated with color photographs, lithographs, advertisements, and vintage photographs. A good bibliography rounds out a book that is not only fun but informative." Booklist
   Includes bibliographical references

636.6   Birds other than poultry

Lantermann, Werner

The **new** parrot handbook; everything about purchase, acclimation, care, diet, disease, and behavior of parrots, with a special chapter on raising parrots. 50 color photographs by outstanding animal photographers, 30 drawings by Fritz W. Köhler, and 35 maps indicating distribution; translated from the German by Rita and Robert Kimber; American advisory editor, Matthew M. Vriends. Barron's Educ. Ser. 1986 144p il maps pa $11.95   **636.6**
   1. Parrots
   ISBN 0-8120-3729-4

LC 86-17289

This book "is divided into two parts, the first about selecting, housing, and caring for a bird; the other devoted to breeding and behavior and including a large section of descriptions of individual species." Booklist
   Includes bibliographical references

636.7   Dogs

American Kennel Club

  ★ The **complete** dog book; American Kennel Club. 20th ed.; Ballantine Books 2006 xxi, 858p il $35   **636.7**
   1. Dogs
   ISBN 0-345-47626-3; 978-0-345-47626-5

LC 2005-48263

"The official guide to 124 AKC registered breeds and their history, appearance, selection, training, care and feeding, and first aid. Some color plates." N Y Public Libr. Ref Books for Child Collect. 2d edition

Arden, Andrea

  ★ **Dog**-friendly dog training; illustrations by Tracy Dockray. 2nd ed.; Wiley Pub. 2007 232p il $18.99   **636.7**
   1. Dogs -- Training
   ISBN 978-0-470-11514-5; 0-470-11514-9

LC 2007-7079

"This straightforward, color-illustrated book by a charter member of the APDT [Association of Pet Dog Trainers] focuses on a dog-friendly, positive approach [to training]. The essential title for libraries with tight budgets." Libr J

Budiansky, Stephen

The **truth** about dogs; an inquiry into the ancestry, social conventions, mental habits, and moral fiber of Canis familiaris. Viking 2000 263p il hardcover o.p. pa $13   **636.7**
   1. Dogs 2. Dogs -- Behavior 3. Dogs -- Psychology
   ISBN 0-14-100228-X pa

LC 00-34966

The author "uses scientific and genetic research to explain why dogs do what they do and are the way they are. In a conversational and entertaining way, the author shows how dog behavior is much more complex and interesting than we have previously thought, and how that behavior is firmly grounded in the breed's successful evolution." Booklist
   Includes bibliographical references

Burch, Mary R.

Citizen canine; ten essential skills every well-mannered dog should know. Kennel Club Books 2010 256p il pa $14.95   **636.7**
   1. Dogs -- Training
   ISBN 978-1-593786-44-1

LC 2009-28847

"Often a component of therapy dog assessment, the Canine Good Citizen (CGC) test has become a popular way to document a dog's manners. . . . [The author] outlines the ten test items and demonstrates how to teach your dog these skills. . . . This well-indexed guide is essential reading for dog owners, whether the goal is obedience training, therapy dog work, or simply polite pets." Libr J

Charleson, Susannah

Scent of the missing; love and partnership with a search-and-rescue dog. Houghton Mifflin Harcourt 2010 288p il $26   **636.7**

1. Rescue dogs

ISBN 978-0-547-15244-8; 0-547-15244-2

LC 2009-33783

"Humans have long used dogs, with their remarkable scenting abilities, to find lost, injured, or dead people. However, recent tragedies and disasters—9/11, Hurricane Katrina—have brought search-and-rescue recovery to the forefront. Charleson introduces us to this world as she trains her dog Puzzle to work with Dallas's elite Metro Area Rescue K9 unit. Interspersed with stories of such routine activities as housebreaking and walking on a leash are the hold-your-breath moments when the author describes actual rescue/recovery missions such as the shuttle Columbia explosion." Libr J

Coile, D. Caroline

Encyclopedia of dog breeds. Barron's Educational Series 2005 352p il $29.95   **636.7**

1. Dogs -- Encyclopedias 2. Reference books

ISBN 0-7641-5700-0

LC 2004-52977

"More than 150 breed descriptions are grouped along American Kennel Club divisions: the sporting group, the hound group, the working group, and so on. . . . Breed descriptions are organized into subsections entitled 'History,' 'Temperament,' 'Upkeep,' 'Health,' and 'Form and Function.'" Booklist

Coppinger, Raymond

Dogs; a new understanding of canine origin, behavior, and evolution. [by] Raymond Coppinger and Lorna Coppinger. University of Chicago Press 2002 352p il pa $18 **636.7**

1. Dogs

ISBN 0-226-11563-1

LC 2002-20404

"This important book belongs in all libraries." Booklist

Includes bibliographical references

Coren, Stanley

Why we love the dogs we do; how to find the dog that matches your personality. Free Press 1998 308p il hardcover o.p. pa $13   **636.7**

1. Dogs

ISBN 0-684-85502-X pa

LC 97-50333

"Coren offers insight into dog-and-owner personality conflicts and shows prospective owners how to choose the dog that is right for them. His book shows why some breeds of dogs turn out to be disasters for certain people, provides personality tests for readers to determine their own distinctive personality types, and includes amusing 'famous pet' anecdotes. Humanitarian, witty, and full of common sense, this is a perfect primer for novice dog owners." Booklist

Includes bibliographical references

De Vito, Dominique

★ World atlas of dog breeds; [by] Dominique De Vito with Heather Russell-Revesz and Stephanie Fornino. 6th ed.; T.F.H. Publications 2009 959p il $99.95   **636.7**

1. Dogs 2. Reference books

ISBN 978-0-7938-0656-0

LC 2008-55261

"Covering more than 420 breeds, the guide is easy to use, alphabetically arranged with ratings for a number of important breed characteristics such as compatibility with children, with other pets, grooming, and energy level. Beautiful photographs portray each breed, accompanied by origin and history, recognized by the seven foremost breed clubs and registries." Publ Wkly

Includes bibliographical references

Dibra, Bashkim

Dogspeak; how to learn it, speak it, and use it to have a happy, healthy, well-behaved dog. {by} Bash Dibra; with Mary Ann Crenshaw; illustrations by José Dennis. Simon & Schuster 1999 270p il hardcover o.p. pa $13 **636.7**

1. Dogs 2. Dogs -- Behavior 3. Dogs -- Training 4. Human-animal communication

ISBN 0-684-86548-3 pa

LC 99-30194

"Discusses the social, or pack, nature of dogs and explains eight factors important to pack dynamics: the dominance hierarchy aggression, territorial behavior, food guarding, flight behavior, chase behavior, socialization, and vocalization. Throughout, Dibra provides examples of how these factors come into play when training the family dog." Libr J

Dodman, Nicholas H.

Dogs behaving badly; an A to Z guide to understanding and curing behavioral problems in dogs. Bantam Bks. 1999 284p hardcover o.p. pa $13.95   **636.7**

1. Dogs

ISBN 0-553-37968-2 pa

LC 98-46042

The author covers "behavioral traits and problems from A (aggression) to Z (zoonosis) . . . he describes canine foibles such as chewing, barking, and eating everything they can find, he shows how these little problems can mutate into major behavioral abnormalities. Many of the definitions are illustrated with tales from the author's practice treating behavioral problems, making the book extremely user-friendly." Booklist

Eldredge, Debra

Dog owner's home veterinary handbook; [by] Debra M. Eldredge . . . [et al.] 4th ed; Wiley Pub. 2007 xxviii, 628p il $34.99   **636.7**

1. Dogs -- Diseases

ISBN 978-0-4700-6785-7; 0-4700-6785-3

LC 2007-16275

"The authors discuss all of the major organ systems with descriptions of normal functions and infectious and parasitic diseases. Writing in easy-to-understand terms, they identify emergency situations and explain first-aid care. . . . It contains information on Lyme disease and other recently recognized problems." Libr J [review of 1992 edition]

Fogle, Bruce

ASPCA complete dog care manual; foreword by Roger Caras. Dorling Kindersley 1993 192p il pa $14.95   **636.7**
    1. Dogs
    ISBN 1-56458-168-3; 978-0-7566-1743-X pa; 0-7566-1743-1 pa

                       LC 92-53474
This book "presents the history, grooming, training, and showing of canines while emphasizing basic nursing, first aid, and breeding. The author gives commonsense tips, answers myriad questions, promotes owners' responsibility for pets, and discourages buying puppies from pet shops and the cruel practice of docking tails. The . . . text is supplemented by detailed diagrams and clear instructions." SLJ

Dog owner's manual. DK Pub. 2003 288p il pa $25   **636.7**
    1. Dogs
    ISBN 0-7894-9321-7

                    LC 2002-41146
"Fogle's succinct writing style packs a tremendous amount of information into each sentence. Heavily illustrated with beautiful photographs." Booklist

★ **Dog**: the definitive guide for dog owners. Firefly Books 2010 384p il $39.95; pa $29.95 **636.7**
    1. Dogs
    ISBN 978-1-55407-779-3; 978-1-55407-700-7 pa
This is a "one-volume compendium on everything canine. He begins with an explanation of the dog's evolution, genetics, and classification. Then he delves into the human-dog relationship, giving . . . information and advice about selecting and training a new puppy, surviving its adolescence, enjoying its adulthood, coping with its declining years, and, finally, coming to grips with its demise. . . . [This is] an easy-to-read, attractive, indispensable guide for the novice and veteran dog owner alike." Libr J
    Includes bibliographical references

New dog; choosing wisely and ensuring a happily ever after. with Patricia Holden White. Firefly Books 2008 192p il $29.95; pa $19.95   **636.7**
    1. Dogs -- Training
    ISBN 978-1-55407-356-6; 1-55407-356-1; 978-1-55407-357-3 pa; 1-55407-357-X pa

                  LC 2008-299624
"In advising how to choose and welcome a new dog, . . . [the author's] attractive and sensible guide addresses training, behavior issues, and health care." Libr J

The **new** encyclopedia of the dog; photography by Tracy Morgan. 2nd American ed; Dorling Kindersley 2000 416p il $40   **636.7**
    1. Dog breeds -- Encyclopedias 2. Dogs -- Encyclopedias 3. Reference books
    ISBN 0-7894-6130-7

                LC 00-22642

This describes over 420 breeds and varieties of dogs, including their histories, temperments, and physical features.

Franklin, Jon

★ The **wolf** in the parlor; the eternal connection between humans and dogs. Henry Holt 2009 283p $25   **636.7**
    1. Dogs
    ISBN 978-0-8050-9077-2; 0-8050-9077-0

                LC 2009-2227
Building on evolutionary science, archaeology, behavioral science, and the firsthand experience of watching his own dog evolve from puppy to family member, Franklin posits that man and dog are more than just inseparable; they are part and parcel of the same creature.
"Among a plethora of books on breeding, disciplining, loving and lamenting the loss of man's best friend, this thoughtful discourse is a best of breed." Publ Wkly

Geeson, Eileen

Ultimate dog grooming; additional material by Barbara Vetter & Lia Whitmore. Firefly Books 2004 288p il $29.95; pa $27.95   **636.7**
    1. Dogs
    ISBN 1-55297-873-7; 1-55407-328-6 pa
The author "offers a three-part introduction to grooming for both owners and professionals. In Part 1, she briefly addresses what an owner needs to know about grooming as well as how to choose the right groomer. Part 2 is geared toward those who want to become professional groomers. . . . The bulk of the book offers well-done profiles of 170 dog breeds—arranged by coat type—that include worthwhile tips and hints. Supplementing the text are more than 500 color illustrations, ranging from detailed drawings to photographs." Libr J

Healy, Thomas

I have heard you calling in the night. Harcourt 2006 204p $22   **636.7**
    1. Alcoholism 2. Authors 3. Dogs 4. Nonfiction writers 5. Novelists
    ISBN 978-0-15-10125-6; 0-15-101259-8

                LC 2006-6363
"Novelist Healy was a raging, brawling drunk until, on a whim, he adopted a Doberman pinscher puppy he named Martin. He nursed Martin through illness and wounds; Martin in turn stood guard over him while he lay passed out in fields. Their bond, and the slight but persistent duty of caring for Martin enabled Healy to very fitfully begin to recover from his alcoholism and propensity to violence and gently nudged him toward an understanding of himself and God. Healy embeds the story in a memoir of his life in the slums of Glasgow, his relationship with his parents, his conflicted attitude toward the church and his many loves. . . . In Healy's heartfelt prose, this eccentric friendship becomes the core of a moving meditation on the mysterious nature of redemption." Publ Wkly

Herriot, James

James Herriot's dog stories. St. Martin's Press
1986 xxxiii, 426p il $23.95; pa $7.99   **636.7**
1. Authors 2. Dogs 3. Memoirists 4. Veterinarians
ISBN 0-312-43968-7; 0-312-92558-1 pa

LC 86-6637

Herriot "has gathered 50 recollections of canines, some
of them sentimental, a few tragic and at least one—the story
of a terrier male who abruptly becomes attractive to other
males—as odd as anything in the Decameron. Herriot recalls
that in his student days domestic animals were customarily
listed in descending order of importance: horse, ox, sheep,
pig, dog. In the latest work, he has brought his favorites to
the front and given them a new leash on life." Time

Katz, Jon

★ **Katz** on dogs; a commonsense guide to training and living with dogs. Villard 2005 xxviii, 240p
il $24.95   **636.7**
1. Dogs -- Training
ISBN 1-4000-6403-1

LC 2005-46209

Katz's "commonsense approach and skill as a storyteller
make this an appealing, informative book." Libr J
Includes bibliographical references

The **new** work of dogs; tending to life, love, and
family. Villard Bks. 2003 xxiii, 225p $19.95; pa
$13.95   **636.7**
1. Dogs 2. Dogs -- Behavior -- New Jersey -- Montclair
-- Anecdotes 3. Dogs -- New Jersey -- Montclair --
Anecdotes 4. Human-animal relationships -- New
Jersey -- Montclair -- Anecdotes
ISBN 0-375-50814-7; 0-375-76055-5 pa

LC 2002-44915

The author "explores the bond between dogs and their
owners. Focusing on 12 people-dog relationships in Montclair, N.J., and drawing on current research into attachment
theory, interviews with animal workers and psychiatrists, as
well as conversations with dog owners, Katz offers nuanced
portraits of what happens when humans depend on dogs to
satisfy their emotional needs. . . . In this well-written and
thoughtful account, Katz makes a convincing case that dog
owners must be more self-aware and responsible when they
use their pets as human substitutes." Publ Wkly

Kerasote, Ted

Merle's door; lessons from a freethinking dog.
Harcourt, Inc. 2007 398p $25   **636.7**
1. Dogs
ISBN 978-0-15-101270-1

LC 2006-38041

"In telling Merle's story, Kerasote also explores the science behind canine behavior and evolution, weaving in research on the human-canine bond and musing on the way
dogs see the world. Merle is a true character, yet Merle is
also Everydog. An absolute treasure of a book." Booklist
Includes bibliographical references

Kihn, Martin

Bad dog; a love story. Pantheon Books 2011
213p   **636.7**
1. Dogs
ISBN 978-0-307-37915-3; 978-0-307-37987-0 ebook

LC 2010035355

"Meet Hola, a gorgeous purebred Bernese mountain dog
so badly managed by her human that walks were 'a haphazard dance of death' and greetings 'full-body slam[s] . . . just
this side of actionable.' Now meet the human: Kihn, a Yale
grad with an M.B.A., a deep neurotic streak, and a serious
drinking problem. When his wife leaves, Kihn realizes he
must get his life under control, and that includes Hola. Soon
man and dog are enrolled in various training programs so
that Hola can earn her Canine Good Citizen certificate from
the American Kennel Club. . . . This sharply written, darkly
funny memoir-cum-dog story-cum-recovery tale is a quick,
absorbing read that will serve a wide audience well." Libr J

Kotler, Steven

A **small** furry prayer; dog rescue and the meaning of life. Bloomsbury 2010 307p il $24   **636.7**
1. Dogs
ISBN 978-1-608-19002-7; 1-608-19002-1

LC 2010-12019

The author "became involved with dog rescue when he
became involved with novelist Joy Nicholson, a committed rescuer; in a matter of weeks, they were compelled to
move their dogs . . . from California to Chimayo, NM, a
rough neighborhood but the only place they could afford
that offered enough room. As he recounts their life in Chimayo (the pack at times approaches 50, all entertainingly
delineated), Kotler seamlessly blends a history of Chimayo,
a well-articulated understanding of how humans and dogs
coevolved, and background on animal welfare efforts in this
country with his witty, sharp-edged, and rewarding reflections on life." Libr J
Includes bibliographical references

Lane, Marion

The **Humane** Society of the United States complete guide to dog care; {by} Marion S. Lane and the
staff of the Humane Society of the United States. Little, Brown 1998 390p il $24.95; pa $16.95 **636.7**
1. Dogs
ISBN 0-316-51305-9; 0-316-59547-0 pa

LC 97-44392

"Emphasizing the importance of companionship between dogs and owners, this guide offers activities and
ideas for including your dog in your lifestyle as much as
possible." Booklist

Lufkin, Elise

To the rescue; found dogs with a mission. photographs by Diana Walker; foreword by Bonnie Hunt.
Skyhorse Pub. 2009 150p il $19.95   **636.7**
1. Animals and the handicapped 2. Dogs
ISBN 978-1-60239-772-9

LC 2009-12164

"This feel-good book should please animal and dog-lovers, especially those who live with a working dog." Publ Wkly

Includes bibliographical references

McConnell, Patricia

For the love of a dog; understanding emotion in you and your best friend. Ballantine Books 2006 332p il hardcover o.p. pa $15.95   **636.7**
1. Dog owners 2. Dogs 3. Dogs -- Behavior 4. Dogs -- Psychology 5. Human-animal relationships
ISBN 0-345-47714-6; 978-0-345-47714-9; 0-345-47715-4 pa; 978-0-345-47715-6 pa
                                        LC 2006-45200
"This is not a book on how to train dogs, but McConnell's examination of cases from her veterinary practice, backed up by her scientific study of animal behavior, will help readers better understand their closest companions." Booklist

McGinnis, Terri

The **well** dog book; the classic, comprehensive handbook of dog care. illustrated by Pat Stewart. rev ed; Random House 1991 287p il pa $19   **636.7**
1. Dogs 2. Dogs -- Diseases
ISBN 0-679-77001-1 pa
                                        LC 91-52680
This illustrated manual introduces canine anatomy and offers training, grooming and nutrition guidelines. Diagnostic and preventive information is included

Monks of New Skete

How to be your dog's best friend; the classic training manual for dog owners. {by} the Monks of New Skete. completely rev and updated, 2nd ed; Little, Brown 2002 336p il $25.95   **636.7**
1. Dogs -- Training
ISBN 0-316-61000-3
                                        LC 2002-102894
This guide to dog training focuses on important aspects of the canine-human relationship, including discipline and choosing a breed that fits the owner's personality and lifestyle.

This book's "unique value lies in the monks' insights and thoughts about the human-canine bond. . . . Without devolving into New Age psychobabble, the monks make philosophical and spiritual observations that no dog lover could resist." Publ Wkly

Includes bibliographical references

Orlean, Susan

★ **Rin** Tin Tin. Simon & Schuster 2011 324p il $26.99; ebook $12.99   **636.7**
1. Dogs in motion pictures 2. Duncan, Lee 3. Nonfiction 4. Rin-Tin-Tin (Dog) 5. Working dogs
ISBN 978-1-4391-9013-5; 978-1-4391-9015-9 ebook
                                        LC 2011024476
This book discusses the story of Lee Duncan (1893-1960), a young American soldier and dog-lover who found the German shepherd puppy that became Rin Tin Tin (Rinty) in France, got the dog home and spent the rest of his life training and promoting Rinty, breeding other German shepherds. . . . [The author] also provides the biography of Dun-

can, as well as Bert Leonard, writer and producer, and she includes interviews with Duncan's daughter, the current keeper of the latest Rinty and scores of others. The author tells the story of silent films (where Rinty began his career), the transition to talkies and to color, the rise of television, the popularity of dog ownership in America (especially of German shepherds and collies--because of Lassie) and the evolving tastes of American youth.s (Kirkus)

"A terrific dog's tale that will make readers sit up and beg for more." Kirkus

Includes bibliographical references

Palika, Liz

K.I.S.S. guide to raising a puppy; foreword by Alan Gomberg. DK Pub. 2002 288p il pa $20 **636.7**
1. Dogs
ISBN 0-7894-8947-3
                                        LC 2001-58418
This guide provides instructions on feeding, grooming, exercising, trips to the vet, and other important aspects of caring for a puppy.

Pelar, Colleen

Living with kids and dogs--without losing your mind; a parent's guide to controlling the chaos. C & R 2005 164p il pa $16.95   **636.7**
1. Child rearing 2. Dogs -- Training 3. Parenting
ISBN 1-933562-66-8
"A certified dog trainer stresses building positive relationships between dogs and children and avoiding interactions that can lead to dog bites. Excellent advice." Libr J

Prevention Magazine Health Books

The **Doctor's** book of home remedies for dogs and cats; over 1,000 solutions to your pet's problems--from top vets, trainers, breeders, and other animal experts. by the editors of Prevention Magazine Health Books; edited by Matthew Hoffman. Rodale Press 1996 403p il hardcover o.p. pa $16.95 **636.7**
1. Cats 2. Dogs
ISBN 0-87596-010-4 pa
                                        LC 95-46481
This volume "provides hints for everyday pet healthcare. Each section includes descriptions and suggestions for coping with or curing ailments ranging from arthritis to shedding. Almost 100 different symptoms and problems are covered." Libr J

Rutherford, Clarice

How to raise a puppy you can live with; [by] Clarice Rutherford, David H. Neil. 4th ed., rev. & updated; Alpine Blue Ribbon Books 2005 153p il pa $11.95   **636.7**
1. Dogs -- Training
ISBN 1-57779-076-6
                                        LC 2005-41038
This book features "practical advice on puppy selection, development, training, and problem-solving." Libr J

Includes bibliographical references

Schaffer, Michael

One nation under dog; adventures in the new world of prozac-popping puppies, dog-park politics, and organic pet food. Henry Holt 2009 304p $24 **636.7**

1. Dogs 2. Pets

ISBN 978-0-8050-8711-6; 0-8050-8711-7

LC 2008-37397

"Schaffer examines the sometimes over-the-top attention Americans lavish on their canines in the form of designer clothing, dog parties, cutting-edge medical treatments, mental stimulation toys, professional pet sitters, luxurious pet hotels, pet cemeteries with grief counselors, and superpremium dog food made with ingredients fit for human consumption. But this is no scathing exposé—Schaffer is a willing participant, an inside observer, forcibly immersed in the ethos by his adoption of a rescued St. Bernard who suffered from separation anxiety. Nevertheless, he offers a serious investigation of the human-animal bond and the forces that have driven 'pet parents' to what some might consider extremes." Libr J

Taylor, David

Old dog, new tricks; understanding and retraining older and rescued dogs. Firefly Books 2006 176p il pa $19.95 **636.7**

1. Dogs -- Training

ISBN 1-55407-197-6; 978-1-55407-197-5

LC 2006-286105

"Chapters cover basic commands, dealing with aggressive and destructive behaviors, housebreaking problems, fears and phobias, excitable and unruly dogs, and feeding problems. With full-color photos throughout, this book should be readable and understandable to even the first-time dog owner." Libr J

Thomas, Elizabeth Marshall

The **social** lives of dogs; the grace of canine company. illustrated by Jared Taylor Williams. Simon & Schuster 2000 253p hardcover o.p. pa $13.95 **636.7**

1. Dog owners -- New Hampshire -- Anecdotes 2. Dogs 3. Dogs -- Behavior -- New Hampshire -- Anecdotes 4. Dogs -- Social aspects -- New Hampshire -- Anecdotes 5. Large print books

ISBN 0-7434-2236-8 pa

LC 99-87357

Thomas discusses how dogs interact with various members of the household, including other dogs and pets of other species.

The author "draws upon her extensive knowledge of the behavior and treatment of feral dogs in East Africa to explain the domestication of the dog. Appendixes containing advice on controlling dogs' behavior and on keeping parrots as pets conclude this entertaining and informative book." Libr J

Woestendiek, John

Dog, Inc. the uncanny inside story of cloning man's best friend. Avery 2010 310p il $26 **636.7**

1. Cloning 2. Dogs 3. Human-animal relationships

ISBN 978-1-58333-391-4; 1-58333-391-6

LC 2010-23697

"A valuable contribution illuminating the hubris and futility of trying to replicate dead pets (or people) that will appeal to dog lovers and those interested in cloning and science." Libr J

Dogs: the ultimate care guide; good health, loving care, maximum longevity. edited by Matthew Hoffman; medical advisor, Lowell Ackerman. Rodale Press 1998 450p il hardcover o.p. pa $19.95 **636.7**

1. Dogs

ISBN 1-57954-244-1 pa

LC 97-46600

Subjects covered range "from bringing up puppy, basic training, and emergency first aid, to easing common complaints." Booklist

The original dog bible; the definitive source for all things dog. edited by Kristin Mehus-Roe. 2nd ed.; Bowtie Press 2009 831p il pa $29.95 **636.7**

1. Dogs

ISBN 978-1-933958-82-8

LC 2008-44402

This book "opens with an astute and wonderfully illustrated survey of dogs' considerable role in history and popular culture, using both period and artifact photographs. Because it is more a guide to responsible dog ownership than a breed standards guide, the book is subsequently divided into eight segments and 34 chapters, which offer indispensable guidance on pet-relevant emergencies, travel, exercise, training, health regimens, and end-of-life concerns. An informative, extremely enjoyable read, regardless of pet ownership." Libr J

Includes bibliographical references

636.8 Cats

Cooper, Gwen

Homer's odyssey; a fearless feline tale, or how I learned about love and life with a blind wonder cat. Delacorte Press 2009 287p il $20 **636.8**

1. Cats

ISBN 978-0-385-34385-5; 0-385-34385-X

LC 2009-17602

A pet rescue volunteer and literacy outreach coordinator describes her relationship with a three-pound blind cat whose daredevil character and affectionate personality saw the author through six moves, a burglary, and the healing of her broken heart.

"This tender and affecting book reveals Homer's lessons about love and acceptance—and how he transformed Cooper into the woman she had always wanted to be." Publ Wkly

Edney, A. T. B.

ASPCA complete cat care manual; [by] Andrew Edney; foreword by Roger Caras. Dorling Kindersley 1992 192p il hardcover o.p. pa $14.95 **636.8**

1. Cats

ISBN 1-56458-064-4; 0-7566-1742-1 pa

LC 92-52783

"Cat care is made easy through step-by-step photographs that illustrate grooming, handling, detecting illness, first aid, and other concerns. Difficult-to-explain procedures, such as how to administer medication or transport an injured cat, are clearly understandable." Libr J

Includes bibliographical references

Herriot, James

James Herriot's cat stories; with illustrations by Lesley Holmes. St. Martin's Press 1994 161p $17.95 **636.8**

    1. Cats 2. Cats -- Anecdotes

    ISBN 0-312-11342-0

                    LC 94-20131

A "collection of favorite cat tales from Herriot's veterinary practice. Retired after over 50 years in practice, Herriot continues to entertain young and old alike with his storytelling ability. His current collection includes 'Alfred, the Sweet-Shop Cat,' 'Boris and Mrs. Bond's Cat Establishment,' 'Moses Found Among the Rushes,' and others." Libr J

McGinnis, Terri

The **well** cat book; the classic comprehensive handbook of cat care. illustrated by Pat Stewart. 2nd ed; Random House 1993 325p il hardcover o.p. pa $19 **636.8**

    1. Cats 2. Cats -- Diseases

    ISBN 0-679-77000-3 pa

                    LC 92-56834

The author provides "professional advice on nutrition, diagnosing illnesses, treating injuries, and preventing health problems. . . . {She also includes} information on new illnesses such as feline infectious peritonitis and feline immunodeficiency virus, and she clearly explains their symptoms. Among her work's other useful features is the chapter on emergency first aid. . . . Highly recommended for all pet care collections." Libr J

Morris, Desmond

Cat watching. Crown 1987 136p hardcover o.p. pa $8.95 **636.8**

    1. Cats

    ISBN 0-517-88053-9 pa

                    LC 86-23938

In question-and-answer format, the author examines mating, hunting behavior and physical characteristics of cats

Myron, Vicki

Dewey; a small-town library cat who touched the world. Grand Central Publisher 2008 277p il $19.99 **636.8**

    1. Cats

    ISBN 978-0-446-40741-0; 0-446-40741-0

                    LC 2008-4498

The story of Dewey Readmore Books, the beloved library cat of Spencer, Iowa.

"Myron's beguiling, poignant, and tender tale of survival, loyalty, and love is an unforgettable study in the mysterious and wondrous ways animals, and libraries, enrich humanity." Booklist

Richards, James R.

ASPCA complete guide to cats. Chronicle Bks. 1999 368p il pa $24.95 **636.8**

    1. Cats 2. Cats -- Diseases 3. Cats -- Health

    ISBN 0-8118-1929-9

                    LC 99-12354

This guide offers advice on feeding, grooming, veterinary care, litterbox training, and the special needs of kittens, old cats, and cats from shelters. The text is accompanied by over 450 illustrations and photos.

636.9 Other mammals

Westoll, Andrew

The **chimps** of Fauna Sanctuary; a true story of resilience and recovery. Houghton Mifflin Harcourt 2011 268p il $25 **636.9**

    1. Animal experimentation -- Moral and ethical aspects 2. Animal rescue 3. Chimpanzees 4. Chimpanzees -- Behavior 5. Wildlife refuges

    ISBN 978-0-547-32780-8; 0-547-32780-3

                    LC 2010049783

"This is both an inspiring and a disturbing book. It is inspiring because of the devotion of caregivers to welfare of the chimps; it is disturbing because of the callous treatment to which chimps in research are subjected." Sci Books Films

Includes bibliographical references

637 Processing dairy and related products

English, Ashley

Home dairy with Ashley English; all you need to know to make cheese, yogurt, butter & more. Lark Crafts 2011 135p il $19.95 **637**

    1. Dairy products

    ISBN 978-1-60059-627-8

                    LC 2010020669

"English is no slouch at demystifying the intricacies of home dairy; from the simplicities of churning out your own delectable butter to pressing your very first gouda, the author covers it all in clean, unpretentious, step-by-step instruction. Excellent for those looking to take a slight step off the grid." Kirkus

Includes bibliographical references

638 Insect culture

Hubbell, Sue

★ A **book** of bees; and how to keep them. drawings by Sam Potthoff. Houghton Mifflin 1998 193p il pa $13 **638**

    1. Bees

    ISBN 0-395-88324-5

                    LC 98-10191

"Following the seasons of the beekeeper's year the author imparts practical hints along with literary, mythological, entomological, and anecdotal commentary." Booklist

Jacobsen, Rowan

Fruitless fall; the collapse of the honey bee and the coming agricultural crisis. Bloomsbury USA 2008 279p il $25   **638**

1. Bee culture 2. Bees 3. Honeybee

ISBN 978-1-59691-537-4; 1-59691-537-4

LC 2008-26126

The author "celebrates the marvels of the honeybee, reveals the many ways we've endangered this essential pollinator, and calls for action to prevent a 'fruitless fall'." Booklist

Includes bibliographical references

Nordhaus, Hannah

The **beekeeper's** lament; how one man and half a billion honey bees help feed America. Harper Perennial 2011 269p il pa $14.99   **638**

1. Beekeepers 2. Beekeeping 3. Bees

ISBN 978-0-06-187325-6; 0-06-187325-X

"Nordhaus centers her account on John Miller, a migratory beekeeper who hauls truckloads of bees from crop to crop to help farmers who don't have natural pollinators. Honey bees are crucial to American agriculture, pollinating crops of 90 different fruits and vegetables. We would lose our almond crops almost entirely without bees, for example. Nordhaus meticulously details this process, demonstrating how modern apiculture affects everyone from keeper to bee to farmer to consumer. . . . [She] provides an almost overwhelming amount of information in a relatively short amount of space, but it's a fascinating read from cover to cover, and Miller makes a genuinely likable American hero." Stamford Advocate

639   Hunting, fishing, conservation, related technologies

Greenlaw, Linda

The **lobster** chronicles; life on a very small island. Hyperion 2002 238p $22.95; pa $13.95 **639**

1. Lobster fisheries

ISBN 0-7868-6677-2; 0-7868-8591-2 pa

In this companion to The hungry ocean, the author gives "up swordfishing to return to her parents' home on Isle Au Haut off the coast of Maine and fish for lobster. . . . She intersperses her narrative with plenty of eccentrics who live on her tiny island. . . . Self-speculation and uncertainties . . . nicely balance her delightfully cocky essays of island life." Publ Wkly

639.2   Commercial fishing, whaling, sealing

Dolin, Eric Jay

Leviathan; the history of whaling in America. W.W. Norton & Company 2007 479p il $27.95 **639.2**

1. Whaling -- History 2. Whaling -- United States -- History

ISBN 978-0-393-06057-7; 0-393-06057-8

LC 2007-06113

The author "chronicles the long history of whaling in North America, from the voyages of Capt. John Smith, who, like many after him, 'found this Whale-fishing a costly conclusion,' to the last voyage of the Wanderer, a whaler that set sail from the once-teeming port of New Bedford, Mass., in 1924 and promptly wrecked in the shallows before a crowd of curious onlookers. . . . Anyone whose knowledge of whaling begins and ends with 'MobyDick' will get a solid education from Mr. Dolin, who fills in the historical record and sets the stage for the glory years when men like Melville set out from Nantucket, New Bedford, Sag Harbor and dozens of other ports on voyages lasting as long as four years." N Y Times (Late N Y Ed)

Includes bibliographical references

Fagan, Brian M.

Fish on Friday; feasting, fasting, and the discovery of the New World. [by] Brian Fagan. Basic Books 2006 338p il maps hardcover o.p. pa $16.95   **639.2**

1. Commercial fishing 2. Fish as food 3. Fisheries -- North America -- History

ISBN 0-465-02284-7; 0-465-02285-5 pa

LC 2005-21322

The author "traces the rise of the European fishing industry. He posits the root of popular demand for fish in the early church's cycle of fasts and feasts. . . . Fagan intersperses his account with delightfully rendered, updated versions of ancient and modern fish-based recipes from Roman, British, and Jamaican traditions." Booklist

Greenlaw, Linda

The **hungry** ocean; a swordboat captain's journey. Hyperion 1999 265p map $22.95; pa $14   **639.2**

1. Fishing

ISBN 0-7868-6451-6; 0-7868-8541-6 pa

LC 98-51985

The author "details a 30-day swordfishing trip from Gloucester to the Grand Banks. Greenlaw describes her boat, equipment, and various electronic gear, including the 'temperature bird' that is lowered to measure the temperature at the fishing depth, as well as her technique for finding just the right area to fish. . . . An exciting and detailed look inside the commercial fishing industry." Libr J

Kurlansky, Mark

★ The **last** fish tale; the fate of the Atlantic and survival in Gloucester, America's oldest fishing port and most original town. Riverhead Books 2009 xxix, 269p il map pa $16   **639.2**

1. Commercial fishing

ISBN 978-1-59448-374-5

The author "provides a delightful, intimate history and contemporary portrait of the quintessential northeastern coastal fishing town: Gloucester, Mass., on Cape Anne. Illustrated with his own beautifully executed drawings, Kurlansky's book vividly depicts the contemporary tension between the traditional fishing trade and modern commerce, which in Gloucester means beach-going tourists." Publ Wkly

Includes bibliographical references

639.3   Culture of cold-blooded vertebrates

Alderton, David

Firefly encyclopedia of the vivarium. Firefly Books 2007 224p il $39.95   **639.3**

1. Amphibians 2. Insects 3. Invertebrates 4. Reptiles 5. Terrariums

ISBN 978-1-55407-300-9; 1-55407-300-6

"With its vibrant photographs and easy reading level, this text is suggested for school and public libraries that are in need of a basic guide." Booklist

Includes bibliographical references

Halverson, Anders

An **entirely** synthetic fish; how rainbow trout beguiled America and overran the world. Anders Halverson. Yale University Press 2010 xxi, 257 p.p   **639.3**

1. Fisheries -- United States 2. Introduced fishes -- United States 3. Rainbow trout 4. Rainbow trout industry -- United States -- History

ISBN 0300140878; 9780300140873

LC 2009036200

Halverson provides an "account of the rainbow trout and why it has become the most commonly stocked and controversial freshwater fish in the United States. Discovered in the remote waters of northern California, rainbow trout have been artificially propagated and distributed for more than 130 years by government officials eager to present Americans with an opportunity to get back to nature by going fishing. . . . Dubbed 'an entirely synthetic fish' by fisheries managers, the rainbow trout has been introduced into every state and province in the United States and Canada and to every continent except Antarctica, often with devastating effects on the native fauna, [according to the author]." (Publisher's note) Bibliography. Index.

This is not one of those whiny, hand-wringing catalogs of environmental gloom and doom. With prose as engaging as it is thoughtful, Halverson has crafted an absorbing cautionary tale of ecological trial and error, documenting our tardy but increasing understanding of biological interdependence and its immeasurable value. Washington Post

Includes bibliographical references (p. 211-244) and index

639.34   Fish culture in aquariums

Alderton, David

Encyclopedia of aquarium & pond fish. Dorling Kindersley 2005 400p il hardcover o.p. pa $24.95   **639.34**

1. Fishes 2. Fishes -- Encyclopedias 3. Reference books

ISBN 0-7566-0941-0; 0-7566-3678-7 pa

The author "has created the definitive work on the subject, with photos to match." Libr J

Jennings, Greg

The **new** encyclopedia of the saltwater aquarium. Firefly Books 2007 304p il $49.95   **639.34**

1. Fishes -- Encyclopedias 2. Marine aquariums 3. Reference books

ISBN 978-1-55407-182-1; 1-55407-182-8

LC 2007-296089

"Over 150 species of reef fish, invertebrates and algae are described: their distribution in the wild, size, behavior, diet, aquarium requirements and compatibility. A large, full color photograph appears for each featured species, with personal recommendations on the fish considered best for the beginner." Publisher's note

Includes bibliographical references

Maitre-Allain, Thierry

★ **Aquariums**; the complete guide to freshwater and saltwater aquariums. [by] Thierry Maitre-Allain and Christian Piednoir; [English translation by Matthew Clarke] Firefly Books 2006 281p il $39.95 **639.34**

1. Aquariums 2. Marine aquariums

ISBN 1-55407-085-6

The authors "walk the novice through all aspects of setting up and maintaining an underwater habitat. . . . Beautiful photos clearly illustrate this good all-in-one handbook that will fill the needs of beginning aquarists." Booklist

Includes bibliographical references

Mills, Dick

Aquarium fish. DK 2004 72p il pa $5 **639.34**

1. Aquariums 2. Fishes

ISBN 0-7566-0611-X; 978-0-7566-0611-4

LC 2004-303366

This book offers advice on choosing fish for aquariums, aquarium equipment, decoration, feeding, and health care, and describes various species of tropical, coldwater, freshwater, and marine fishes.

"Accurate, clear, and concise writing is enhanced with wonderful color photographs on each page." Voice Youth Advocates [review of 1996 edition]

Sandford, Gina

Aquarium owner's manual. DK Publishing 2003 256p il pa $25   **639.34**

1. Aquariums

ISBN 0-7894-9677-1

Full color pictures accompany information on creating, stocking, and maintaining a home aquarium. Types of fish, water, and aquarium environments are discussed.

639.9   Conservation of biological resources

Apfelbaum, Steven I.

Nature's second chance; restoring the ecology of Stone Prairie Farm. Beacon Press 2009 242p $25.95   **639.9**

1. Ecologists 2. Prairie ecology 3. Sustainable living

ISBN 978-0-8070-8582-0

LC 2008-13071

"Ecologist Apfelbaum wanted to put into practice what he learned about restoring damaged ecosystems on land of his own. He purchased a 150-year-old farmhouse and eventually, thanks to the success of his visionary consulting business, Applied Ecological Services, acquired 80 acres of southern Wisconsin farmland. By dint of ardent research and relentless hard work, Apfelbaum and his partner, Susan Marie Lehnhardt, transformed land long depleted by corn crops, pesticides, and invasive species into a thriving prairie resplendent with wildflowers and resurgent birds, butterflies, and wildlife. . . . [The] book is as rich in farming adventure, environmental ideas, and profound insights as a restored prairie is rich in life and beauty." Booklist

DeNapoli, Dyan

The **great** penguin rescue; 40,000 penguins, a devastating oil spill, and the inspiring story of the world's largest animal rescue. Free Press 2010 307p il map $26   **639.9**
   1. African penguin -- Effect of oil spills on 2. Oil spills 3. Oil spills and wildlife 4. Penguins 5. Wildlife rehabilitation -- South Africa -- Cape Town Region 6. Wildlife rescue -- South Africa -- Cape Town Region
   ISBN 978-1-4391-4817-4; 1-4391-4817-1
                    LC 2010-17156
This "firsthand account of the rescue of the oiled penguins (all of whom fought against their rescuers), repeated washing of each bird, force-feeding, and guano cleanup plunges the reader into the maelstrom of animal rescue and rehabilitation on such a large scale." Booklist
   Includes bibliographical references

Jacobsen, Rowan

The **living** shore; rediscovering a lost world. illustrated by Mary Elder Jacobsen. Bloomsbury 2009 167p il map $20   **639.9**
   1. Commercial fishing 2. Oysters
   ISBN 978-1-59691-684-5; 1-59691-684-2
                    LC 2009-8903
A marine scientist, together with Rowan and a conservancy group interested in habitat restoration, suggests a possible blueprint for cleaning up our oceans by observing an isolated pocket of oysters living on the western side of Vancouver Island.
   "Lovely science writing, and a smart look into where the work of ecological restoration is headed." Kirkus
   Includes bibliographical references

640   Home and family management

Bried, Erin

How to sew a button; and other nifty things your grandmother knew. Ballantine Books 2009 xxii, 278p il pa $15   **640**
   1. Handicraft 2. Home economics 3. Life skills
   ISBN 978-0-345-51875-0; 0-345-51875-6
                LC 2009036046
"These anecdotes and tutorials gleaned from subject experts and grandmothers who were children during the Great Depression cover a broad swath of homemaking skills. Instead of systematic how-tos, Bried presents these lessons as a means to improve the quality of the reader's life. Excellent

information, but definitely written to a female audience." Libr J

Heloise

All-new hints from Heloise; a household guide for the '90s. Putnam 1989 416p il pa $13.95 **640**
   1. Home economics
   ISBN 0-399-51510-0
                  LC 88-33651
The author "offers a mother lode of salient tips on cleaning, child-care, pet care, traveling and much more. . . . She is at her most ingenious and credible in the kitchen and on household maintenance." Publ Wkly

Huff, Darrell

The **complete** how to figure it; {by} Darrell Huff with Kristy Maria Huff; illustrated by Carolyn R. Kinsey; designed by Kristy Maria Huff. Norton 1996 470p il hardcover o.p. pa $17.95   **640**
   1. Mathematics 2. Personal finance
   ISBN 0-393-31924-5 pa
                  LC 95-46480
"This makes an ideal browser on a rainy afternoon, and it is especially friendly to those who can't quite cope with calculators." Booklist

Mendelson, Cheryl

Home comforts; the art and science of keeping house. illustrations by Harry Bates. Scribner 1999 884p il hardcover o.p. pa $21   **640**
   1. Home economics
   ISBN 0-684-81465-X; 0-7432-7286-2 pa
                  LC 99-37555
Mendelson includes "sections on food, clothing, cleanliness, daily life, and safety, with information on negligence, domestic employment laws, insurance, and even the impact of clothing label laws on our laundry. Preferred methods are explained in detail, and some alternatives are offered for those who need to compromise. This is a valuable tool." Libr J
   Includes bibliographical references

Nakone, Lanna

Organizing for your brain type; finding your own solution to managing time, paper, and stuff. St. Martin's Griffin 2005 xlvii, 222p pa $13.95 **640**
   1. Home economics 2. Time management
   ISBN 0-312-33977-1
                  LC 2004-60159
"A quiz at the beginning assigns readers to the maintaining, harmonizing, innovating, or prioritizing style. Nakone then describes the strengths and weaknesses of each type and matches a prescription for how that type can best manage time. . . . This book should do well in most libraries." Libr J
   Includes bibliographical references

Walsh, Peter

How to organize just about everything; more than 500 step-by-step instructions for everything from organizing your closets to planning a wedding to creat-

ing a flawless filing system. Free Press 2005 501p
$25   **640**
   1. Home economics
   ISBN 0-7432-5494-5

                       LC 2004-56277
"Inside the 16 sections are 501 activities, both the usual
and out-of-the-ordinary tasks, from getting organized and
planning a remodeling project to joining the Peace Corps or
becoming an astronaut. Each features the step-by-step procedures, tips, a warning (if necessary), and 'who knew?'—
additional advice designed to make the activity a success.
. . . A great humane reference anytime, anywhere, for any
occasion." Booklist

640.73   Evaluation and purchasing guides

Coyne, Kelly

   Making it; radical home ec for a post-consumer
world. [by] Kelly Coyne and Erik Knutzen. Rodale
2010 310p il pa $19.99   **640.73**
   1. Consumer education 2. Home economics 3.
Simplicity
   ISBN 978-1-60529-462-9; 1-60529-462-4

                       LC 2010023680
"Motivated to reduce household consumption, Coyne
and Knutzen offer 70 projects that reintroduce production-
based homemaking skills. Ranging in difficulty from making cleaning products to building a chicken coop, the projects are parsed into segments of time, giving readers an idea
of how often a project should be repeated during the year."
Libr J

   Includes bibliographical references

Levine, Judith

   Not buying it; my year without shopping. Simon
& Schuster 2006 274p $25   **640.73**
   1. Consumer education 2. Shopping
   ISBN 0-7432-6935-7

                       LC 2005-55517
The author discusses her experiences when she decided
not to buy any nonessential items for a year.
   "This honest and humorous tale of a nonspending year
is well worth putting aside a few hours to read." Christ
Sci Monit

641   Food and drink

Allen, Stewart Lee

   ★ **In** the devil's garden; a sinful history of forbidden food. Ballantine Bks. 2002 315p hardcover
o.p. pa $13.95   **641**
   1. Cookery -- History 2. Cooking 3. Eating customs
4. Food 5. Food habits -- History 6. Gastronomy --
History 7. Menus
   ISBN 0-345-44015-3; 0-345-44016-1 pa

                       LC 2001-43882
"The historical and cultural links between food, sex and
religion make for fascinating reading." Publ Wkly
   Includes bibliographical references

Barlow, John

   Everything but the squeal; eating the whole hog
in northern Spain. Farrar, Straus & Giroux 2008
306p $25   **641**
   1. College teachers 2. Cookery (Pork) 3. Cooking
-- Pork 4. Linguists
   ISBN 978-0-374-15010-5; 0-374-15010-9

                       LC 2008-26051
A "rapturous paean to the pig dishes of northern Spain.
A British writer not so long ago relocated to the Iberian peninsula, Barlow has not just a healthy appetite, but a desire
to travel throughout his pork-obsessed new home and eat—
meal by meal—every single part of the pig. It's a seemingly
simple enough premise, but one that Barlow is able to turn
into a witty and learned appreciation of the unique culture of
Galicia." PopMatters

Bourdain, Anthony

   A **cook's** tour; global adventures in extreme cuisines. Ecco 2002 274p il pa $14.99   **641**
   1. Cooking 2. Food
   ISBN 0-06-001278-1

                       LC 2002-23507
This is an "account of the author's global search for the
'perfect mix of food and context' that takes the reader to
the culinary corners of the earth: from Vietnam (a live cobra
heart) and Japan (poisonous blowfish) to England (roasted
bone marrow) and Scotland (deep-fried Mars bar)." N Y
Times Book Rev

David, Elizabeth

   An **omelette** and a glass of wine. Lyons Press
2010 xxiii, 368p pa $16.95   **641**
   1. Cooking
   ISBN 978-1-59921-860-1

                       LC 2010-6369
A collection of book reviews, restaurant reviews, articles
and recipes that originally appeared in The Spectator, Gourmet magazine, Vogue, and The (London) Sunday Times,
among others.

Davidson, Alan

   The **Oxford** companion to food; edited by Tom
Jaine; illustrations by Soun Vannithone. 2nd ed; Oxford University Press 2006 907p il map $65   **641**
   1. Cookery 2. Food 3. Food -- Encyclopedias 4. Food
habits 5. Reference books
   ISBN 0-19-280681-5; 978-0-19-280681-9

                       LC 2006-48602
"Covering everything from individual ingredients and
cooking techniques to food celebrities and national cuisines,
the authoritative and engaging The Oxford Companion to
Food is one of the best basic culinary reference books available." Libr J
   Includes bibliographical references

Fisher, M. F. K.

   A **stew** or a story; an assortment of short works
by M.F.K. Fisher. gathered and introduced by Joan

Reardon. Shoemaker & Hoard 2006 364p $28; pa $15.95 **641**

1. Authors 2. Cookbook writers 3. Cooking 4. Food 5. Food critics 6. Novelists 7. Travel writers
ISBN 978-1-59376-115-8; 1-59376-115-5; 978-1-59376-165-3 pa; 1-59376-165-1 pa
LC 2006-08708

"Fisher's food writing was ahead of its time; a frequent contributor to Gourmet, Bon App tit, and other publications, Fisher had lived in both France and the California wine country and offered cooking tips that predate the American culinary 'revolution' of the 1960s. As these enjoyable pieces show, she was also a witty writer who offered astute observations along with the occasional recipe. The topics chosen for this collection include coffee making, borscht, olives, picnics, holidays, and places." Libr J

Includes bibliographical references

Herbst, Sharon Tyler

The **deluxe** food lover's companion; [by] Sharon Tyler Herbst and Ron Herbst. Barron's 2009 794p il $29.99 **641**

1. Cooking -- Dictionaries 2. Food -- Dictionaries 3. Reference books
ISBN 978-0-7641-6241-1
LC 2008-938219

This is "an encyclopedia of literally every dish, ingredient and spice imaginable, each featuring cross-references and a pronunciation guide. . . . Quotes from famous chefs, diagrams of meat cuts and sketches on every page make this a solid companion for home cooks." Publ Wkly

Jacobsen, Rowan

American terroir; savoring the flavors of our woods, waters, and fields. Bloomsbury 2010 272p il $25 **641**

1. Cooking 2. Food
ISBN 978-1-59691-648-7
LC 2010-6125

"Jacobsen eases readers into discussions of chemistry, history, geography, and gastronomy with cavalier charm and worldly wit, but his knack for cutting to the core restores exoticism to our backyard. Inspirational and highly engaging." Libr J

Kamp, David

The **United** States of Arugula; how we became a gourmet nation. Broadway Books 2006 392p il $26 **641**

1. Cookery, American 2. Dining 3. Gastronomy
ISBN 0-7679-1579-8
LC 2006-42599

The author "details the development of fine dining in the U.S. and proves healthy, even exotic food movements are having an effect on our diet. . . . This cultural history makes for an engrossing read, documenting the dramas and rivalries of the food industry." Publ Wkly

Includes bibliographical references

Lappé, Anna, 1973-

Diet for a hot planet; the climate crisis at the end of your fork and what you can do about it. with a forward by Bill McKibben. Bloomsbury 2010 xxi, 313p il **641**

1. Eating customs 2. Food industry 3. Food supply 4. Greenhouse effect
ISBN 1-59691-659-1; 978-1-59691-659-3
LC 2010-17363

The author "argues that food is 'the integrating lens' for the innumerable responses to climate change. At three meals or more per day, Lappe writes, we are faced with self-supporting or resisting industrial food production. So-called conventional food production and distribution—ecologically and economically fragile—contributes to nearly one-third of total human-caused global warming and paradoxically creates hunger out of plenty. Organic, local, plant-based foods, on the other hand, have the potential to not only mitigate but ultimately repair this damage. Lappe bolsters her support for a local, organic diet with a substantial bibliography of peer-reviewed science, studies, policies and interviews." Kirkus

Includes bibliographical references

New Yorker (Periodical)

Secret ingredients; the New Yorker book of food and drink. edited by David Remnick. Random House 2007 xv, 582p il $29.95 **641**

1. Cooking 2. Eating customs 3. Food
ISBN 978-1-4000-6547-9
LC 2007-14490

"A wide range of authors are represented, from the familiar A.J. Liebling and M.F.K. Fisher to the piquant Anthony Bourdain and the delightful Calvin Trillin. Those seeking an introduction to fiction and nonfiction food writing would do well to graze this work; seasoned readers will enjoy the nostalgic places and tastes depicted, and the quintessential New Yorker cartoons are a delightful addition." Libr J

Rolland, Jacques L.

The **food** encyclopedia; over 8,000 ingredients, tools, techniques and people. [by] Jacques L. Rolland and Carol Sherman with other contributors. Robert Rose 2006 701p il $49.95 **641**

1. Cookery 2. Cooking 3. Cooking -- Encyclopedias 4. Food 5. Food -- Encyclopedias 6. Reference books
ISBN 978-0-7788-0150-4; 0-7788-0150-0

This encyclopedia "has 8,000 entries, with cross-reference on foods, wines, beverages, cooking methods and techniques, and biographies of prominent people." Publisher's note

Includes bibliographical references

Wright, Clifford A.

A **Mediterranean** feast; the story of the birth of the celebrated cuisines of the Mediterranean, from the Merchants of Venice to the Barbary Corsairs: with more than 500 recipes. Morrow 1999 xxiv, 815p il $35 **641**

1. Cookery, Mediterranean 2. Eating customs 3. Food 4. Mediterranean region -- Social life and customs
ISBN 0-688-15305-4
LC 98-49155

Wright "traces the influences and interconnections among the food and cooking of the diverse cultures that ring the Mediterranean Sea. . . . A unique work, this is recommended for history as well as cookery collections." Libr J

Includes bibliographical references

The backyard homestead; edited by Carleen Madigan. Storey Pub. 2009 367p il pa $18.95 **641**

1. Food -- Preservation 2. Vegetable gardening

ISBN 978-1-60342-138-6

LC 2009-01338

"Madigan presents the information in clear chapters, starting with vegetables, herbs, and fruit and nut trees; moving on through growing grains and grinding them into flour; and then tackling keeping chickens, cows, pigs, and more. The last chapter, 'Food from the Wild,' delves into beekeeping, foraging for berries and mushrooms, and making your own maple syrup. None of the information is particularly in-depth—if you decide to pursue something, you'll likely want to get another book on that one subject. But as an inspiration and an introduction to the various possibilities, it's perfect." Epicurious

Includes bibliographical references

641.2   Beverages (Drinks)

Hopkins, Kate

99 drams of whiskey; the accidental hedonist's quest for the perfect shot and the history of the drink. St. Martin's Press 2009 308p $24.95   **641.2**

1. Whiskey

ISBN 978-0-312-38108-0; 0-312-38108-5

LC 2009-07174

"Kate Hopkins, a popular food blogger and former standup comedian, . . . sets off with her friend Krysta on a ramble through the distilleries of Scotland, Ireland, Canada and the United States in search of the best whiskeys in the world. Hopkins's bits of history go down easy: America's Whiskey Rebellion of 1794; the spread of the Phylloxera vastatrix parasite through French vineyards that wiped out the wine industry and boosted Scotch's popularity; the rivalry between Ireland and Scotland for the best single malts. She also serves up pungent assessments of the spirits she samples." N Y Times Book Rev

Includes bibliographical references.

Kolpan, Steven

Exploring wine; the Culinary Institute of America's complete guide to wines of the world. {by} Steven Kolpan, Brian H. Smith, Michael A. Weiss. 2nd ed; Wiley 2001 820p il maps $65   **641.2**

1. Wine and wine making

ISBN 0-471-35295-0

LC 2001-24345

The authors "cover wine tasting, wine making, and the wines of the world. They provide information about health and pairing wine with food and offer detailed coverage of service, storage, and purchasing, including buying wine at auctions." Booklist

Includes bibliographical references

Peynaud, Emile

The **taste** of wine; the art and science of wine appreciation. {by} Emile Peynaud; with the assistance of Jacques Blouin; translated from the French by Michael Schuster; with a foreword by Michael Broadbent. 2nd ed; Wiley 1996 xxi, 346p il $95   **641.2**

1. Wine and wine making

ISBN 0-471-11376-X

LC 96-24181

"Long considered the definitive tome on winetasting." Libr J

Includes bibliographical references

Wallace, Benjamin

The **billionaire's** vinegar; the mystery of the world's most expensive bottle of wine. Crown Publishers 2008 319p $24.95; pa $14.95   **641.2**

1. Wine and wine making

ISBN 978-0-307-33877-8; 0-307-33877-0; 978-0-307-33878-5 pa; 0-307-33878-9 pa

LC 2007-31645

"This is a gripping story, expertly handled by Benjamin Wallace who writes with wit and verve, drawing the reader into a subculture strewn with eccentrics and monomaniacs. . . . Full of detail that will delight wine lovers. It will also appeal to anyone who merely savours a great tale, well told." Economist

Includes bibliographical references

Wine buyer's guide

Parker's wine buyer's guide; the complete, easy-to-use reference on recent vintages, prices, and ratings for more than 8,000 wines from all the major wine regions. 7th ed.; Simon & Schuster 2008 xxi, 1513p map $65; pa $35   **641.2**

1. Wine and wine making

ISBN 0-7432-7198-X; 978-0-7432-7198-1; 0-7432-7199-8 pa; 978-0-7432-7199-8 pa

LC 2008-1113

This wine guide features "sections for western Europe, North America, and 'The Best of the Rest' (Argentina, Australia, central Europe, Israel, New Zealand, and South America). These sections are divided alphabetically by country or region, with further divisions in the sections for France and Italy. Each treatment begins with a map and an article about the area's wines, followed by ratings for the best wine growers and producers and an alphabetical list of wineries with vintage ratings and brief commentaries. . . . This is a good resource for wine collections in public libraries." Booklist

Includes bibliographical references

Wondrich, David

Punch; the delights (and dangers) of the flowing bowl. Perigee 2010 296p $23.95 **641.2**

1. Punches (Beverages)

ISBN 978-0-399-53616-8; 0-399-53616-7

Wondrich "argues that British sailors, making the best of the ingredients available to them far from home, first improvised Punch using an exotic eastern distillate called arrack, local limes or lemons, sugar, spice and water. In Mr. Wondrich's account, it often seems the main activity at the English East India Company's trading posts in South Asia—

aside from welcoming or sending off the occasional ship—was the making and downing of Punch. The humble quaff soon came to be the drink of the British Empire, beloved not only in India, but in the Caribbean, the American colonies, and of course England herself. As the concept spread, it was adapted to the ingredients at hand. . . . Mr. Wondrich's noble effort to restore Punch's good name offers sound advice on the basics of Punch-making along with a variety of vintage recipes." Wall Street J

Zraly, Kevin

Windows on the World complete wine course; 2010 ed.; Sterling 2009 338p il map $27.95 **641.2**
1. Wine and wine making
ISBN 978-1-4027-6767-8

Looks at how and where wine is made and how this affects its quality and pricing, including information on how the professionals taste and rate wine and a country-by-country tour of the latest vintages.

"The casual browser will find fascinating trivia and facts about wine in numerous sidebars, but may not be able to resist becoming involved in the main text, making this difficult to put down. Highly recommended for all wine connoisseurs." Libr J

Larousse encyclopedia of wine; general editor, Christopher Foulkes. Ed fully updated in 2001 by Larousse; Larousse 2001 624p il maps $45 **641.2**
1. Reference books 2. Wine and wine making
ISBN 2-03-585013-4
LC 2003-269288

This book is a "reference to the world's vineyards and to the enjoyment of wine. . . . Full-color photographs, maps and drawings illustrate the country-by-country, vineyard-by-vineyard descriptions of all the world's wine regions from the United States and Europe to New Zealand and the Orient. . . . The book also details the intricacies of pairing wine with food, wine selection and etiquette, as well as historical and technical information about how wine is made." Publisher's note

★ The Oxford companion to wine; edited by Jancis Robinson. 3rd ed; Oxford University Press 2006 840p il map $65 **641.2**
1. Reference books 2. Wine and wine making
ISBN 0-19-860990-6; 978-0-19-860990-2
LC 2006-50303

The contributors "write with zesty enthusiasm about everything from the different varieties of grapes to the world's greatest wineries and geographic areas of production." Libr J

641.3 Food

Bittman, Mark

The **food** matters cookbook; 500 revolutionary recipes for better living. Simon & Schuster 2010 645p $35; ebook $16.99 **641.3**
1. Cooking 2. Food 3. Health 4. Nutrition
ISBN 978-1-4391-2023-1; 978-1-4391-4123-6 ebook
LC 2010-28623

The author "provides a rational approach to eating that not only improves health but also helps the environment. Extolling the benefits of a plant-heavy diet, Bittman offers more than 500 healthful recipes that feature unprocessed fruits, vegetables, legumes, nuts, and whole grains and reduce all types of meat to backup players. In addition, he shares five basic principles for sane eating that are easy to implement and understand as well as an unusually helpful pantry section and handy charts for substituting produce and seafood by season. . . . Practical and balanced, this collection will shape the way we cook at home for years to come." Publ Wkly

Colquhoun, Kate

Taste: the story of Britain through its cooking. Bloomsbury 2007 460p il $34.95 **641.3**
1. British cooking 2. Eating customs
ISBN 978-1-59691-410-0; 1-59691-410-6

The author offers a culinary history of Great Britain.

"Colquhoun's enthusiasm for her subject leaps from every page." Economist

Includes bibliographical references

Foer, Jonathan Safran

★ **Eating** animals. Little, Brown and Company 2009 341p $25.99; pa $14.99 **641.3**
1. Animal welfare 2. Food industry and trade 3. Slaughtering and slaughter-houses 4. Vegetarianism
ISBN 978-0-316-06990-8; 978-0-316-06988-5 pa
LC 2009-34434

The novelist presents a critique of the food industry and explores arguments in favor of humane agriculture and vegetarianism.

"A blend of solid—and discomforting—reportage with fierce advocacy that will make committed carnivores squeal." Kirkus

Includes bibliographical references

Goldstein, Myrna Chandler

Healthy foods; fact versus fiction. [by] Myrna Chandler Goldstein and Mark A. Goldstein. Greenwood 2010 310p il $55 **641.3**
1. Food 2. Nutrition 3. Reference books
ISBN 978-0-313-38096-9; 0-313-38096-1; 978-0-313-38097-6 ebook; 0-313-38097-X ebook
LC 2010-13684

"This book will appeal to a wide range of health-conscious readers, even those with little time for in-depth study." Libr J

Includes bibliographical references

Gollner, Adam

The **fruit** hunters; a story of nature, adventure, commerce and obsession. [by] Adam Leith Gollner. Scribner 2008 279p il $25 **641.3**
1. Fruit 2. Fruit culture 3. Fruit trade 4. Tropical fruit
ISBN 978-0-7432-9694-6; 0-7432-9694-X
LC 2007-42423

This book is an "account of the world of fruit and fruit fanatics. He's traveled to many countries in search of exotic fruits, and he describes in sensuous detail some of the hundreds of varieties he's sampled. . . . Gollner's passion for fruit is infectious, and his fascinating book is a testament to the fact that there is much more to the world of fruit than the bland varieties on our supermarket shelves." Publ Wkly

Includes bibliographical references

Hill, Tony

The **contemporary** encyclopedia of herbs and spices; seasonings for the global kitchen. J. Wiley 2004 432p il $40   **641.3**
    1. Herbs -- Encyclopedias 2. Reference books 3. Spices -- Encyclopedias
    ISBN 0-471-21423-X

                      LC 2003-007733

The author provides information on some 350 herbs, spices and spice blends and includes history and countries of origin as well as cooking and use guidelines

Masson, J. Moussaieff

The **face** on your plate; the truth about food. W.W. Norton & Co. 2009 288p $24.95   **641.3**
    1. Food of animal origin
    ISBN 978-0-393-06595-4; 0-393-06595-2

                      LC 2008-52733

The author presents "arguments for not eating animal products: the link to global warming, the horrors of factory farming, and the negative influence aquaculture is having on wild fish populations. He concludes that we are in a state of denial about the origins of our food and demonstrates that veganism is not as difficult as it may sound by presenting a day in his life as a vegan. Well footnoted with ample suggestions for further reading." Libr J

McLagan, Jennifer

Odd bits; how to cook the rest of the animal. photography by Leigh Beisch. Ten Speed Press 2011 248p il $35   **641.3**
    1. Cooking -- Meat
    ISBN 978-1-58008-334-8

                      LC 2011-11575

A "unique, informative, and readable cookbook. The ingredients used for the 100 recipes include lungs, necks, spleens, tongues, cheeks, testicles, and feet, as well as a few more common cuts (ribs, brisket, and shanks). In her introduction, McLagan traces the history of eating meat and why in earlier times the odd bits were considered the prime parts. In the last 75 to 100 years, most of these parts have been discarded or used for cat and dog food in the United States. McLagan encourages readers with a detailed and clear discussion of how to choose, prepare, and cook them. She draws the line at eyeballs and notes that lungs are not sold in the United States." Libr J

Norman, Jill

Herbs & spices; photography, Dave King. DK Pub. 2002 336p il $30   **641.3**
    1. Herbs 2. Spices
    ISBN 0-7894-8939-2

                      LC 2003-544667

"Ranging from one to four pages each, the entries for 60 different herbs and 60 different spices include an overview, tasting notes, the parts of the herb or spice used in cooking, buying and storage information, culinary uses, and

some details on cultivation. Separate chapters on preparation, recipes for blending herbs and spices (as in sauces and pastes), recipes that draw on cuisines around the world, and purchasing sources are also included . . . Norman's volume excels at giving the practical details and clear illustrations cooks need when it comes to using these ingredients in the kitchen." Libr J

Includes bibliographical references

Ornelas, Kriemhild Conee

  ★ The **Cambridge** world history of food; editors, Kenneth F. Kiple, Kriemhild Coneè Ornelas. Cambridge Univ. Press 2000 2v set $190   **641.3**
    1. Diseases 2. Edible plants 3. Food -- History 4. Nutrition
    ISBN 0-521-40216-6

                      LC 00-57181

"The two volumes are arranged in eight parts covering the diet of early man, staple foods, dietary liquids, nutrients and food-related disorders, food and drink around the world, nutrition and health, current food-related issues and concluding with a dictionary of plant foods. . . . The Cambridge World History of Food is a thorough study of a topic that is eternally popular. It should become a standard source in reference collections." Booklist

Includes bibliographical references

Parsons, Russ

How to pick a peach; the search for flavor from farm to table. Houghton Mifflin 2007 412p $27   **641.3**
    1. Cooking -- Fruit 2. Cooking -- Vegetables
    ISBN 978-0-618-46348-0; 0-618-46348-8

                      LC 2006-35462

"Equal parts cookbook, agricultural history, chemistry lesson and produce buying guide. . . . [Parsons begins with a] tale of agribusiness trumping our taste buds en route to supplying year-round on-demand produce, and how farmer's markets are bringing back both appreciation of, and access to, local and seasonal foods. He then takes readers on a delectable season-by-season produce tour, from springtime Artichokes Stuffed with Ham and Pine Nuts to midwinter Candied Citrus Peel, and provides readers with the lowdown on where each fruit or vegetable is grown and how to choose, store and prepare it." Publ Wkly

Pierson, Stephanie

The **brisket** book; a love story with recipes. photographs by Roger Sherman. Andrews McMeel Publishing 2011 208p il $29.99   **641.3**
    1. Cooking -- Meat
    ISBN 978-1-4494-0697-4

                      LC 2011-921500

"The book is both humorous and serious: from a section called Found in Translation—how to order brisket in sixteen languages—to The Last Brisket, a joke by David Minkoff. Pierson shares cooking tips, chef interviews, information on beef cuts, different cooking techniques and more than 30 brisket recipes. It took Stephanie a year to select and test the recipes that are included in the book. They come from notable chefs, cookbook authors, cowboys, pit masters and home cooks." KosherEye

Rinzler, Carol Ann

★ The **new** complete book of food; a nutritional, medical, and culinary guide. introduction by Jane E. Brody; foreword by Manfred Kroger. 2nd ed; Facts on File 2009 xxi, 474p $75; pa $19.95 **641.3**

     1. Food 2. Nutrition 3. Reference books

     ISBN 978-0-8160-7710-6; 0-8160-7710-X; 978-0-8160-7711-3 pa; 0-8160-7711-8 pa

LC 2008-29255

The author "describes over 100 foods, some of which constitute a food family; e.g., one entry appears for onions and includes chives, leeks, scallions, and shallots. Each entry of two or more pages includes a nutritional profile, information on buying and storing the food item, cooking tips, and possible health benefits and concerns." Choice

Includes bibliographical references

Rosenblum, Mort

Chocolate: a bittersweet saga of dark and light. North Point Press 2005 290p il $24; pa $14 **641.3**

     1. Chocolate

     ISBN 0-86547-635-7; 0-86547-730-2 pa

LC 2004-54734

The author "unveils chocolate's history and its various incarnations, including in his fresh and insightful discussions the origins of mole; the differences between, say, Hershey's kisses and Valrhona's products; the invention of Nutella; and the small boutique chocolate artisans found nearly everywhere. . . . A compelling and tasty read." Booklist

Wrangham, Richard W.

Catching fire; how cooking made us human. [by] Richard Wrangham. Basic Books 2009 309p $26.95 **641.3**

     1. Cooking 2. Eating customs 3. Fire 4. Fire -- History 5. Food habits -- History 6. Human evolution 7. Prehistoric peoples 8. Prehistoric peoples -- Food 9. Roasting (Cookery)

     ISBN 978-0-465-01362-3

LC 2009-1742

This "is a plainspoken and thoroughly gripping scientific essay that presents nothing less than a new theory of human evolution. . . . [This book] contains serious science yet is related in direct, no-nonsense prose. It is toothsome, skillfully prepared brain food." N Y Times (Late N Y Ed)

Includes bibliographical references

Chilies to chocolate; food the Americas gave the world. edited by Nelson Foster & Linda S. Cordell. University of Ariz. Press 1992 191p hardcover o.p. pa $15.95 **641.3**

     1. Edible plants 2. Farm produce 3. Food 4. International cooking

     ISBN 0-8165-1324-4 pa

LC 92-5243

Essays explore the biological and cultural history of crops cultivated by indigenous peoples of the Americas and trace their dispersion into the fields and kitchens of the Old World.

★ Larousse gastronomique; the world's greatest culinary encyclopedia. with the assistance of the Gastronomic Committee, president Joël Robuchon. Clarkson Potter Publishers 2009 1206p il map $90 **641.3**

     1. Cooking -- Encyclopedias 2. Food -- Encyclopedias 3. French cooking 4. Reference books

     ISBN 978-0-307-46491-0

"The alphabetical entries range in length from a few sentences to several pages. They cover types of food (Apples, Locusts); cooking techniques (Braising, Grilling); famous chefs (Auguste Escoffier, Alice Waters); culinary jobs (Maître d'hôtel, Sommelier); countries (China, Greece); and tools of the trade (Knife, Saucepan). . . . This is an essential resource for most library reference collections as well as a wonderful book to browse." Booklist

★ The Oxford encyclopedia of food and drink in America; Andrew F. Smith, editor in chief. Oxford University Press 2004 2v il set $250 **641.3**

     1. Beverages 2. Cookery, American 3. Food 4. Food -- Encyclopedias 5. Reference books

     ISBN 0-19-515437-1; 978-0-19-515437-5

LC 2003-24873

"Whether readers make a living studying culinary traditions or just enjoy eating, they'll find this book a marvel. . . . For food lovers of all stripes, this work inspires, enlightens and entertains." Publ Wkly

World cheese book; editor-in-chief, Juliet Harbutt; contributors, Martin Aspinwall . . . [et al.] DK 2009 352p il map $25 **641.3**

     1. Cheese

     ISBN 978-0-7566-5442-9

"Harbutt has compiled a comprehensive illustrated guide to more than 750 artisanally and industrially produced cheeses from around the globe. . . . Organized by country, cheeses are listed alphabetically and each has a uniform data table, making information easy to find. Key cheeses such as Parmigiano Reggiano, Stilton, Roquefort, Halloumi, and the like have much longer entries detailing production methods." Booklist

Includes bibliographical references

641.4   Food preservation and storage

Costenbader, Carol W.

★ The **big** book of preserving the harvest; {foreword by Joanne Lamb Hayes} rev ed; Storey Bks. 2002 347p il pa $18.95 **641.4**

     1. Canning and preserving

     ISBN 1-58017-458-2

LC 2002-21172

In addition to recipes this book provides instructions for food preservation techniques, including canning, drying, freezing, the preparation of jams and jellies, pickles, relishes and chutneys, vinegars and seasonings, and cold storage. Includes a section on gift giving, directions on building a food dehydrator, a table of equivalents, and a conversion chart to metric measures.

Mackenzie, Jennifer

The **complete** book of pickling; 250 recipes from pickles & relishes to chutneys & salsas. Robert Rose 2009 335p il pa $24.95   **641.4**
    1. Canning and preserving
    ISBN 978-0-77880216-7; 0-7788-0216-7

This is a "terrific collection of 250 pickles, sauces, chutneys and relishes. . . . Even readers without an appreciation for the tang of a good pickle will appreciate MacKenzie's 50 chutneys, including variations such as Sangria Citrus, classic cranberry and peach, pineapple ginger and spiced tomato; six chili sauces; 18 salsas; and homemade ketchup." Publ Wkly

Ziedrich, Linda

The **joy** of pickling; 250 flavor-packed recipes for vegetables and more from garden or market. foreward by Chuck Williams. Rev. ed.; Harvard Common Press 2009 418p $29.95; pa $18.95   **641.4**
    1. Canning and preserving
    ISBN 978-1-55832-374-2; 978-1-55832-375-9 pa
                        LC 2008-36446

"There are chapters on fresh, sweet, quick, and freezer pickles, as well as cabbage pickles, miso and soy pickles, pickle relishes, and even pickled meat, seafood, and eggs. . . . [It also includes information on] pickling techniques, procedures, safety, and equipment, as well as . . . recipes." Publisher's note

Includes bibliographical references

The Good Housekeeping step-by-step cookbook; edited by Susan Westmoreland with the assistance of Susan Deborah Goldsmith and Elizabeth Brainerd Burge. Hearst Books 2008 576p il $29.95 **641.4**
    1. Cooking
    ISBN 978-1-58816-760-6; 1-58816-760-7

This offers over 1,000 basic recipes illustrated by 1,800 color photographs divided into sections such as appetizers, soups, eggs and cheese, shellfish, poultry, meat, vegetables, pasta, grains and beans, breads, and desserts.

641.5   Cooking

Adrià, Ferran

The **family** meal; home cooking with Ferran Adria. Phaidon Press 2011 383p il $29.95   **641.5**
    ISBN 978-0-7148-6253-8; 0-7148-6253-3

"Even if you're more comfortable navigating cobblestone streets in platforms than wielding a microplane in the kitchen, this book will show even the most harried and clueless of cooks how to prepare a simple dinner at home. And, as an unexpected bonys, it will also be a meal that will forever impress guests." Vogue

Alford, Jeffrey

Beyond the Great Wall; recipes and travels in the other China. [by] Jeffrey Alford and Naomi Duguid; studio photography by Richard Jung; location photographs by Jeffrey Alford and Naomi Duguid. Artisan 2008 376p il map $40   **641.5**
    1. Chinese cooking 2. Cookery, Chinese
    ISBN 978-1-57965-301-9
                        LC 2007-28556

The authors "explore the food and peoples of the outlaying regions of present-day China, historically home to those not ethnically Chinese. Part travel guide and part cookbook, this collection looks at the cultural survival and preservation of food in smaller societies including that of the Tibetan, Mongol, Tuvan and Kirghiz peoples, among others. . . . A handsome and engaging collection suitable for travelers and cooks alike, this book will delight anyone with an interest in this part of the world." Publ Wkly

Includes bibliographical references

America's test kitchen (Television program)

The **America's** test kitchen family cookbook; the editors at America's test kitchen; photography, Daniel J. Van Ackere & Carl Tremblay. Revised ed.; America's Test Kitchen 2006 726p il $34.95 **641.5**
    1. Cooking
    ISBN 978-1-933615-01-1; 1-933615-01-X
                        LC 2007-296245

This volume "offers over 1,200 approachable recipes for a very wide range of dishes-from 'weekday' fare like Creamy Rice Casserole, Cheesy Nachos with Spicy Beef, and Skillet Lasagna, to dressier recipes, including Pan-Seared Lamb Chops with Red Wine Rosemary Sauce, Roasted Trout Stuffed with Bacon and Spinach, and Chocolate Marshmallow Mousse. There are 'specialty' chapters devoted to sandwiches, drinks, and slow cooker and pressure cooker dishes; a grilling section is a tutorial in itself. . . . The book delivers solid, family-friendly dishes with enough fully orchestrated 'how to' to make even novice cooks feel secure when tackling the basics or more ambitious fare." Amazon.com

American Institute for Cancer Research

★ The **new** American plate cookbook; recipes for a healthy weight and a healthy life. American Institute for Cancer Research. University of California Press 2005 306p il $24.95   **641.5**
    1. Cooking
    ISBN 0-520-24234-3
                        LC 2004-17993

The recipes in this book are "built around vegetables and whole grains, with an emphasis on brown rice, wheat pasta, and other healthful foods, rather than protein. . . . Recipes are appealing and easy to make and cover every course of a meal. Well-known dishes are reworked, e.g., New England Clam Chowder, to help with the transition to healthier eating." Libr J

Anderson, Jean

The **food** of Portugal; color photography by the author. Morrow 1986 304p il map hardcover o.p. pa $19.95   **641.5**
    1. Portuguese cooking
    ISBN 0-688-13415-7 pa
                        LC 86-2510

The author "first covers Portugal's geography and touches on distinctive regional cooking styles. The following glossary delineates Portuguese food, drink, and dining terminology. . . . Part 2, . . . is a guide to the country's best food." Booklist

Includes bibliographical references

Anderson, Pam

How to cook without a book; recipes and techniques every cook should know by heart. Broadway Bks. 2000 290p $25　　**641.5**
　1. Cooking 2. Quick and easy cookery
　ISBN 0-7679-0279-3

LC 99-43776

"In chapters organized mostly by course or by technique, Anderson provides basic templates for tossed salads, pasta dishes with vegetables, simple stir-fries, and so forth, with easy suggestions for variations on the theme." Libr J

Perfect recipes for having people over; photographs by Rita Maas. Houghton Mifflin 2005 304p il $35　　**641.5**
　1. Cooking 2. Entertaining
　ISBN 0-618-32972-2

LC 2005-46370

Anderson "offers 200 recipes from entrées to desserts. Most are easy to make; some require guest participation, such as shish kebabs, with a variety of ingredients for all tastes. The book begins with main courses since they will dictate the accompaniments. Each recipe has a question section–e.g., 'Any Shortcuts?' 'What Should I Serve with It?' 'How Far Ahead Can I Make It?' There are many familiar dishes like macaroni and cheese and deviled eggs, but readers will also encounter innovative recipes." Libr J

Andrews, Colman

Country cooking of Ireland; photographs by Christopher Hirsheimer; foreword by Darina Allen. Chronicle 2009 383p il map $50　　**641.5**
　1. Irish cooking
　ISBN 978-0-8118-6670-5

The author "provides new perspectives on the often maligned Irish cuisine. The breathtakingly beautiful photographs are alone enough to convince, but Andrews, calling Irish cuisine one of the most exciting food stories in the world today, lets the dishes make his case. Robust soups such as butternut and apple and roast pork belly start the mouth juices flowing. Andrews offers a culinary feast with everything from nested eggs and steak-and-kidney pie to Arlington chicken liver pâté and battered sausages. . . . Andrews has done the near impossible in elevating a cuisine thought to be humble and drab into tantalizing fare that will have worldwide appeal." Publ Wkly

Includes bibliographical references

Bastianich, Lidia

Lidia cooks from the heart of Italy; by Lidia Matticchio Bastianich and Tanya Bastianich Manuali, with David Nussbaum; full-page photographs by Christopher Hirsheimer; other photographs by Lidia

Matticchio Bastianich. Alfred A. Knopf 2009 411p il $35　　**641.5**
　1. Italian cooking
　ISBN 978-0-307-26751-1; 0-307-26751-2

LC 2009-22021

"Bastianich and daughter Tanya take readers on a culinary tour of Italy's 12 regions. Grouped by those areas, the recipes are simple enough for novice cooks. Included are appetizers, soups, salads and side dishes, condiments, pastas and risottos/rice, vegetarian main courses (aside from pasta), fish and seafood, meat and poultry, and desserts. In addition, there are stories about the history of the dishes." Libr J

Lidia's family table; [by] Lidia Matticchio Bastianich, with David Nussbaum; photographs by Christopher Hirsheimer. Knopf 2004 xxiv, 419p il $35　　**641.5**
　1. Italian cooking
　ISBN 1-4000-4035-3

LC 2004-22411

This cookbook "presents the food Bastianich prepares at home for her large family. . . . The range is impressive, the flavors strong. It's enough to make readers clamor to be adopted into the Bastianich clan." Publ Wkly

Batali, Mario

Italian grill; [by] Mario Batali with Judith Sutton; photography by Beatriz da Costa; art direction by Lisa Eaton and Douglas Riccardi. Ecco 2008 246p il $29.95　　**641.5**
　1. Barbecue cooking 2. Italian cooking
　ISBN 978-0-06-145097-6; 0-06-145097-9

A collection of eighty recipes for grilled Italian food is divided into categories for antipasti, pizza, meat, fish, and vegetables, and includes information on grilling basics, different heat-source options, and differences in grilling equipment.

"This is an essential collection for any serious backyard cook." Publ Wkly

Bayless, Rick

Fiesta at Rick's; fabulous food for great times with friends. [by] Rick Bayless with Deann Groen Bayless; photographs by Paul Elledge. W. W. Norton 2010 348p il $35　　**641.5**
　1. Entertaining 2. Menus 3. Mexican cooking
　ISBN 978-0-393-05899-4

LC 2010-13128

"The book loosely packages recipes around fiestas, from a luxury guacamole and cocktail party for 12 to classic mole for 24, complete with game-plan checklists. . . . The hardest thing about using this book isn't finding the ingredients (today, practically every small town has a great Mexican grocery), it's keeping yourself from eating everything before the guests arrive." N Y Times Book Rev

Beard, James

　★　**James** Beard's American cookery. Little, Brown 1972 877p hardcover o.p. pa $24.95 **641.5**
　1. Cooking
　ISBN 0-316-08566-9 pa

"Comprehensive in scope the cookbook gives eighteenth-and nineteenth-century recipes as well as modern directions for preparation of a full range of U.S. cookery. . . . The format is attractive and the historical data add to the value of an authoritative guide." Booklist

Includes bibliographical references

The **armchair** James Beard; edited by John Ferrone; foreword by Barbara Kafka. Lyons Press 1999 346p $24.95   **641.5**
  1. Cookery 2. Cooking
  ISBN 1-55821-737-1
                                        LC 98-29728
This collection assembles "essays on everything from main courses to condiments; dining in restaurants, hospitals, and al fresco; libations and desserts; and broader philosophical concerns on gastronomy. Each chapter has captured Beard's feeling for food, his wicked sense of humor, his consummate excellence as a writer, and even his love of controversy. . . . The 150 recipes cover the globe and honor the palate." Libr J

The **fireside** cook book; a complete guide to fine cooking for beginner and expert. [by] James A. Beard; illustrated by Alice Provensen and Martin Provensen; foreword by Mark Bittman. Simon & Schuster 2008 336p il $30   **641.5**
  1. Cooking
  ISBN 978-1-4165-8967-9; 1-4165-8967-8
                                        LC 2008-25094
This volume "includes more than 12,000 recipes and variations, with chapters on every course of a meal, as well as 'Outdoor Cookery,' 'Frozen Foods and PickUp Meals,' and more. This 60th-anniversary edition includes the original watercolor illustrations and a brief new foreword by cookbook author Mark Bittman. While some of the information and language is dated, of course, it's amazing how ahead of his time Beard often was. . . . The amount of information the book provides is equally impressive, and Beard's straightforward, opinionated prose remains a delight to read." Libr J

Berley, Peter
  The **modern** vegetarian kitchen; [by] Peter Berley with Melissa Clark. ReganBooks 2000 450p il hardcover o.p. pa $21.99   **641.5**
  1. Cookery -- Psychological aspects 2. Vegetarian cookery 3. Vegetarian cooking
  ISBN 0-06-039295-9; 0-06-098911-4 pa
                                        LC 00-42524
The author "organizes his recipes first by type (e.g., soups, salads, pasta, and beans) and then by season. . . . He also provides lots of background information and recommendations on ingredients, necessary utensils and appliances, and techniques." Libr J

Includes bibliographical references

Bernstein, Richard K.
  The **diabetes** diet; Dr. Bernstein's low-carbohydrate solution. recipes by Marcia Miele. Little, Brown and Co 2005 291p $24.95   **641.5**
  1. Diabetes -- Diet therapy 2. Low-carbohydrate diet
  ISBN 0-316-73784-4
                                        LC 2004-11739
The author offers low-carbohydrate recipes designed "to interrupt the cycle of obesity and insulin resistance and maintain a healthy weight." Publisher's note

Better homes and gardens
  ★ **Better** homes and gardens new cook book; 15th ed.; J. Wiley 2010 660p il $29.95   **641.5**
  1. Cooking
  ISBN 978-0-470-55686-3
                                        LC 2010-25417
"A standard cookbook . . . with staple recipes and types of cooking." N Y Public Libr. Book of How & Where to Look It Up

Bittman, Mark
  How to cook everything; 2,000 simple recipes for great food. illustrations by Alan Witschonke. 2nd ed.; J. Wiley 2008 1044p il $35   **641.5**
  1. Cooking
  ISBN 978-0-76-457865-6; 0-76-457865-0
                                        LC 2008-18984
The author presents "more than 1000 basic recipes and simple and inventive variations. The enormous breadth of recipes along with Bittman's engaging, straightforward prose will appeal to cooks looking for reliable help with kitchen fundamentals." Publ Wkly

Includes bibliographical references

  ★ **How** to cook everything vegetarian; simple meatless recipes for great food. illustrations by Alan Witschonke. Wiley 2007 996p il $35   **641.5**
  1. Vegetarian cooking
  ISBN 978-0-7645-2483-7; 0-7645-2483-6
                                        LC 2006-36937
This vegetarian cookbook "presents more than 2000 recipes and variations. Most of the recipes are quick and easy; prep times are given for each one, and icons indicate those that are especially fast, can be made ahead, and/or are vegan. . . . An essential purchase for all cookery collections." Libr J

  ★ **Mark** Bittman's Kitchen express; 404 inspired seasonal dishes you can make in 20 minutes or less. Simon & Schuster 2009 233p $26   **641.5**
  1. Quick and easy cooking
  ISBN 978-1-4165-7566-5
                                        LC 2008-54823
"Bittman here offers a sampling of 404 inspiring recipes. . . . The no-sweat recipes are divided into four sections: summer, fall, winter and spring, capitalizing on the freshest ingredients of each season while whittling down the prep time of ordinarily elaborate dishes like coq au vin and ricotta cheesecake to 10 minutes or less. The book includes a drill-down of how best to stock your kitchen, and given the

impromptu nature of the book, the substitution grid proves indispensable." Publ Wkly

Bracken, Peg

The **I** hate to cook book; with a new foreword by Jo Bracken; drawings by Hilary Knight. 50th anniversary ed.; Grand Central Pub. 2010 207p $22.99; ebook $10.99   **641.5**
1. Cooking 2. Quick and easy cooking
ISBN 978-0-446-54592-1; 978-0-446-56894-4 ebook
LC 2009-1249

"This book's strident title belies both its usefulness and its popularity. Peg Bracken faced the burden of being a full-time writer, a full-time mother and a full-time housewife. To buy herself a bit more time for other pursuits, she and her friends collected a host of easy, stress-free recipes. What's truly wonderful is Bracken's droll delivery and the more than 200 recipes that run the gamut from appetizers to desserts." Washington Post

Buford, Bill

Heat; an amateur's adventures as kitchen slave, line cook, pasta-maker, and apprentice to a Dante-quoting butcher in Tuscany. Knopf 2006 318p $25.95 **641.5**
1. Cookbook writers 2. Cookery, Italian -- Tuscan style 3. Cooks 4. Food habits -- Italy -- Tuscany 5. Italian cooking 6. Magazine editors 7. Magazine executives 8. Restaurateurs 9. Television personalities
ISBN 1-4000-4120-1; 978-1-4000-4120-6
LC 2005-57868

"Mr Buford also has a biographer's gift of bringing characters to life. . . . [He] fills his book with people as pungent and spicy as the food." Economist

Burke, David

David Burke's new American classics; [by] David Burke and Judith Choate. Knopf 2006 300p il $35   **641.5**
1. Cooking
ISBN 0-375-41231-X
LC 2005-44960

"Burke presents each dish in three separate and distinctive guises: classic, contemporary, and second day (leftovers). This tripartite approach allows him to address cooks possessing different levels of expertise and sophistication. . . . A large number of these recipes require advanced kitchen techniques so that only the most experienced cooks will have the skills to reproduce Burke's results. Color photographs help guide when the instructions alone fail to communicate the chef's intent." Booklist

Chang, David

Momofuku; [by] David Chang and Peter Meehan; photographs by Gabriele Stabile. Clarkson Potter 2009 303p il $40 **641.5**
1. Asian cooking
ISBN 978-0-307-45195-8

"Chang's Virginia upbringing, upscale restaurant experience and love of certain Korean and Japanese flavors result in the kind of dishes that will jam your eyeballs into the back of your head, like brussels sprouts with bacon and kimchi puree. This fawningly produced book . . . is fueled by Chang's hard-core attitude and punctuated with a 'Hell's Kitchen' season's worth of unprintable words. The dude's intense, and he wants you to know it. The food is intense, too, especially as the recipes increase in difficulty as the chapters move up the Momofuku restaurant scale, from Noodle Bar to Ssam Bar to Ko." N Y Times Book Rev

Child, Julia

★ **Mastering** the art of French cooking; by Julia Child, Louisette Bertholle, Simone Beck. updated ed; Knopf 1983 2v il v1 $40; v1 pa $30; v2 $60; v2 pa $30   **641.5**
1. French cooking
ISBN 0-375-41340-5 v1; 0-394-72178-0 v1 pa; 0-394-40152-2 v2; 0-394-72177-2 v2 pa
LC 83-48113

Volume one includes, in addition to usual categories, a chapter dealing with entrees and luncheon dishes, including quiches, pâtés, and crepes, and other cold buffet items. Volume two emphasizes French bread and pastries, with chapters also devoted to soups, meats, chickens, vegetables, and desserts. Appendices discuss stuffings and kitchen equipment.

The **way** to cook; photographs by Brian Leatart and Jim Scherer; food designer, Rosemary Manell. Knopf 1989 511p il $65; pa $39.95 **641.5**
1. Cooking
ISBN 0-394-53264-3; 0-679-74765-6 pa
LC 88-45838

"With her sensible-as-always approach to food, Child has produced a comprehensive cooking bible, filled with stunning photographs and practical illustrations, that will aid the novice {and} inspire the gourmet. . . . A masterwork from a master chef." Libr J

Clark, Melissa

Cook this now; 120 easy and delectable dishes you can't wait to make. Hyperion 2011 396p il $29.99   **641.5**
1. Cooking
ISBN 978-1-4013-2398-1
LC 2011010420

"Clark presents readers with 120 recipes organized by season and month. With a candid opening essay on weekly trips to her local NYC farmers' market in the dead of winter—think frosty fingers, and ice-topped milk—Clark sets the course for this down-to-earth, realistic guide to cooking throughout the year, finding and highlighting seasonal gems in mains, side dishes, and desserts. . . . Even with a multitude of cooking-by-season titles in the marketplace, the author's inspiring use of fresh ingredients and flexible attitude toward cooking make this a solid addition to any kitchen cookbook shelf." Publ Wkly

Cook's illustrated (Periodical)

The **best** International recipe; a home cook's guide to the best recipes in the world. by the editors of Cook's Illustrated. America's Test Kitchen 2007 579p il $35   **641.5**
1. Cooking
ISBN 978-1-933615-17-2; 1-933615-17-6

This volume contains more than 300 recipes from around the world. Each has been tested to ensure success. Includes explanations of ingredients and what to look for, and in some cases, what you can substitute without compromising flavor. Specialty equipment is also discussed. Core techniques are highlighted throughout the book.

The **new** best recipe; by the editors of Cook's illustrated; photography, Carl Tremblay, Daniel J. Van Ackere; illustrations, John Burgoyne. 2nd ed.; America's Test Kitchen 2004 1028p il $35 **641.5**
  1. Cooking
  ISBN 978-0-936184-74-6; 0-936184-74-4

A compendium of more than 1,000 recipes. "Twenty-two chapters cover appetizers to desserts. Even the simplest tasks, such as blanching vegetables or peeling an egg, are explained and illustrated in detail. More involved techniques include brining poultry and roasting a turkey. . . . Well organized and extremely clear." Publ Wkly

Crumpacker, Bunny
  How to slice an onion; cooking basics and beyond--hundreds of tips, techniques, recipes, food facts, and folklore. Thomas Dunne Books 2009 303p il $25.99 **641.5**
  1. Cooking
  ISBN 978-0-312-53718-0

LC 2009-16741
"Beginning with the properly sliced onion, Crumpacker explains the hows of cooking as well as the whys: readers will learn why roasting a chicken upside-down is preferable (it keeps the white meat moist), how you can salvage overcooked scrambled eggs (a little butter or sour cream), and the best way to crush tomatoes for homemade marinara sauce (by hand). These and other tips won't bowl over veteran cooks, but Crumpacker's simple advice will rapidly build cookery confidence in those used to dining on canned or premade products. . . . Though bolstered with recipes, Crumpacker's crisp prose makes this volume a winner—the next best thing to having a chef at your side as you prepare to tackle a new dish." Publ Wkly
  Includes bibliographical references

Culinary Institute of America
  Techniques of healthy cooking; the Culinary Institute of America. John Wiley 2008 578p il $65 **641.5**
  1. Nutrition 2. Quantity cooking
  ISBN 0-470-05232-5; 978-0-470-05232-7

LC 2006-38750
"In addition to offering detailed information on nutrition and diet, this hefty volume provides valuable advice on purchasing and storing healthy foods, menu planning, and cooking techniques that reduce calories while still retaining flavor. From soups to desserts, recipes for 400 different dishes—each of which serves ten or more—are given, with complete nutritional information included for each. . . . An expertly written resource for professional cooks." Libr J
  Includes bibliographical references

David, Elizabeth
  French provincial cooking. Grub Street 2008 519p il $34.95 **641.5**
  1. French cooking
  ISBN 978-1-904943-71-6; 1-904943-71-3

LC 2008-411778
This book "should be approached and read as a series of short stories, as well as written and evocative as the best literature. The voice is highly personal and opinionated, sometimes sharp but always true and always entertaining. This book is a long essay on French cuisine, offering background stories and sketches of recipes very different from the prescriptive type of recipes that most modern readers might be used to today." Living France

  Italian food; rev ed; Penguin Books 1999 xxxiii, 376p pa $16 **641.5**
  1. Italian cooking
  ISBN 978-0-14-118155-4; 0-14-118155-9

LC 99-200031
"David studies and analyzes cooking the way a scholar analyzes literature, and, as a result, her titles are far more than just cookbooks. Along with the recipes, of which there are many, she explains at length the histories of the dishes and offers splendid advice on serving wine with the meals." Libr J
  Includes bibliographical references

  Summer cooking; illustrated by Adrian Daintrey. New York Review Books 2002 234p il pa $12.95 **641.5**
  1. British cooking
  ISBN 978-1-59017-004-5; 1-59017-004-0

LC 2002-744
"Don't let the unsophisticated subject fool you into expecting only cheese sandwiches and potato salads. For all its simplicity, 'Summer Cooking' is a wonderfully subversive volume — every bit as unexpected and enchanting to read today as it must have been 50 years ago, when England was just stirring from its wartime fast and garlic was an ingredient still capable of provoking controversy. . . . David earned her place in gastronomic history by being one of the first writers to suggest that thoughtful food and cooking itself could be a means of escape. Now, 15 years after her death, that voice remains a singular note in the chorus of her contemporaries and acolytes, neither frankly amiable like Julia Child, nor seductively literate like M.F.K. Fisher, nor playfully mod like Nigella Lawson. No matter how trivial the point, David speaks her mind." Salon.com

  A **book** of Mediterranean food; decorated by John Minton. 2nd rev. ed.; New York Review Books 2002 203p il pa $14.95 **641.5**
  1. Mediterranean cooking
  ISBN 978-1-59017-003-8; 1-59017-003-2

LC 2002-749
This is a "mixture of recipes, culinary lore, and frank talk. In bleak postwar Great Britain, when basics were rationed and fresh food a fantasy, David set about to cheer herself—and her audience—up with dishes from the south of France, Italy, Spain, Portugal, Greece, and the Middle East." Publisher's note

DiSpirito, Rocco

Now eat this! 150 of America's favorite comfort foods, all under 350 calories. Ballantine Books 2010 xxiii, 246p il pa $22; ebook $22   **641.5**
1. Cooking 2. Low-calorie diet
ISBN 978-0-345-52090-6 pa; 0-345-52090-4 pa; 978-0-307-76753-0 ebook; 0-307-76753-1 ebook
LC 2009-52470
"Lower-calorie brownies, gravy, spaghetti and meatballs, and beef stroganoff will delight readers who have been avoiding favorite foods." Libr J

Dojny, Brooke

The **New** England cookbook; 350 recipes from town and country, land and sea, hearth and home. illustrations by John MacDonald. Harvard Common Press 1999 652p il $29.95; pa $21.95   **641.5**
1. Cookery, American -- New England style 2. Cooking
ISBN 1-55832-138-1; 1-55832-139-X pa
LC 99-14393
This volume includes traditional dishes as well as "dozens of ethnic specialties from the various immigrant groups who have helped populate New England: Oregano-Scented Greek Lamb Shanks, Portuguese Tuna Escabeche, and Garlicky Mussels, Italian-style, to name a few." Libr J
Includes bibliographical references

Estrine, Darryl

Harvest to heat; cooking with America's best chefs, farmers, and artisans. [by] Darryl Estrine and Kelly Kochendorfer; foreward by Alice Waters. Taunton Press 2010 295p il $40   **641.5**
1. Cooking
ISBN 978-1-60085-254-1
LC 2010-11943
"The authors match farmers and artisans with chefs and restaurants across the country to present 100 original recipes from, e.g., Eric Ripert (Le Bernardin, New York), Paul Kahan (Blackbird, Chicago), and Vitaly Paley (Paley's Place, Portland, OR), for the home cook, for starters and salads, main courses, sides, and desserts. . . . Each recipe is accompanied by a description of the farmer or artisan who provided the main ingredients. Sustainable food is in, and this book will encourage home cooks to follow the tenets of the movement." Libr J

Fairchild, Barbara

The **Bon** Appetit cookbook. Wiley 2006 xxiv, 792p il $34.95   **641.5**
1. Cooking
ISBN 0-7645-9686-1; 978-0-7645-9686-5
LC 2005-5181
"Mirroring the magazine on which it is based, this collection of 1,200 recipes is accessible, applicable to most home cooks' lives and a pleasure to cook from." Publ Wkly

The **Bon** Appetit fast easy fresh cookbook. J. Wiley 2008 xxix, 770p il $34.95   **641.5**
1. Cooking
ISBN 978-0-470-22630-8
LC 2007-44562

This cookbook "presents hundreds of quick and simple recipes from the magazine's popular 'Fast Easy Fresh' feature. An introductory 'Shopping Guide' covers buying and storing produce, meat, and fish, and dozens of sidebars and boxes provide more information on ingredients and techniques. . . . Sure to appeal to any busy cook as well as the magazine's numerous fans, this is highly recommended." Libr J

Fant, Maureen B.

Rome; authentic recipes celebrating the foods of the world. recipes and text Maureen B. Fant; photographs Jean-Blaise Hall; general editor Chuck Williams. Oxmoor House 2005 192p il map $24.95 **641.5**
1. Italian cooking
ISBN 978-0-8487-3006-2
Full-color photographs accompany 45 classic and contemporary recipes, from tonnarelli cacio e pepe and spaghetti alla carbonara to saltimbocca alla Romano and abbacchio alla cacciatora. Seasonal side dishes, wines, and covered. Includes glossary and ingredient sources.

Fearnley-Whittingstall, Hugh

The **River** Cottage cookbook; photography by Simon Wheeler. Ten Speed Press 2008 447p il $35   **641.5**
1. Cooking -- Natural foods 2. English cooking
ISBN 978-1-58008-909-8; 1-58008-909-7
LC 2007-43795
"The author writes with passion and humor, and his unusual book will be useful as both a reference and a cookbook." Libr J
Includes bibliographical references

River Cottage every day; photography by Simon Wheeler. Ten Speed Press 2011 415p il $32.50   **641.5**
1. British cooking 2. Cooking -- Natural foods
ISBN 978-1-60774-098-8
LC 2010-46949
"An advocate of a back-to-basics approach to cooking and sustainable agriculture, . . . [the author] delivers thoughtful insight and colorful narratives that celebrate the joy of good family food, which will inspire and compel readers into the kitchen, book in hand. Simple ingredients become brilliant when combined in fresh and easy recipes like Baked Breakfast Cheesecake, Curried Fish Pie, breads, boxed lunches, and frittatas." Libr J

Flay, Bobby

★ **Bobby** Flay's grilling for life; 75 healthier ideas for big flavor from the fire. [by] Bobby Flay with Stephanie Banyas and Sally Jackson; foreword by Joy Bauer; color photographs by Gentl & Hyers; black-and-white photographs by John Dolan. Scribner 2005 210p il $22   **641.5**
1. Barbecue cooking
ISBN 0-7432-7272-2
LC 2005-45053
The author's "trademark use of bold flavors in dishes like Grilled Red Snapper with Grapefruit-Thyme Mojo, and (skinless) Grilled Duck Breast with Black Pepper-Sweet

Mustard Sauce bring out appealing contrasts and result in food that's satisfying even if it's reduced in calories, carbs or fat." Publ Wkly

Flinn, Kathleen

The **kitchen** counter cooking school; how a few simple lessons transformed nine culinary novices into fearless home cooks. Viking Adult 2011 285p il $26.95 **641.5**
    1. Cooking -- Study and teaching
    ISBN 978-0-670-02300-4

                        LC 2011016222

"A successful, ambitious graduate of Paris' Le Cordon Bleu culinary academy, Flinn scrutinized average American supermarket shoppers and concluded that far too many rely on prepackaged, processed foods. Pressing them about their food choices, she learned that these timid souls simply believed that they lacked the time and certainly the ability to regularly prepare meals for their families from fresh, seasonal ingredients. Flinn eventually recruited nine motivated volunteers who spent time with her to learn how to plan meals confidently, shop effectively, cook thoughtfully, and serve attractively. She taught them such basic techniques as braising as well as simple but important recipes such as roasted chicken. . . . Flinn winningly offers inspiration to anyone who cares about cooking but lacks basic tools and skills." Booklist

    Includes bibliographical references

Food52

The **Food52** cookbook; 140 winning recipes from exceptional home cooks. [by] Amanda Hesser and Merrill Stubbs and the Food52 community; photographs by Sarah Shatz. William Morrow 2011 440p il $35 **641.5**
    1. Cooking
    ISBN 978-0-06-188720-8

                        LC 2010-51727

"Cooks of all skill levels will find plenty of room to stretch." Publ Wkly

Friedman, Andrew

Knives at dawn; the American quest for culinary glory at the legendary Bocuse d'Or competition. Free Press 2009 304p $26 **641.5**
    1. Cooking -- Competitions
    ISBN 978-1-4391-5307-9

                        LC 2009-35271

"A vibrant portrait of the world's most significant cooking competition, the Bocuse d'Or, in Lyon, France. . . . [The author] dynamically illustrates the colorful personalities, ego-battering conflicts, career-defining aspirations, politicking, precision planning, naked missteps and the final judges' decisions regarding the 2009 U.S. team's shot for the culinary gold medal. . . . The book is infused with the muscular, meticulous gusto of a sportswriter covering the Olympics. Edge-of-your-seat food writing of the highest caliber." Kirkus

    Includes bibliographical references

Gand, Gale

Gale Gand's brunch! Clarkson Potter/Publishers 2009 208p il $27.50 **641.5**
    1. Cooking
    ISBN 978-0-307-40698-9

                        LC 2008-36988

Gand "starts with an enticing assortment of drinks (e.g., white hot chocolate and a three-alarm Bloody Mary), then a chapter on brunch's eggy foundations—omelets, stratas, frittatas, quiches and crêpes, each with appetizing variations—that will please any brunch crowd. In subsequent chapters, Gand hits the sweet and savory high points, from pancakes and doughnuts to onion tarts and cheddar grits. . . . Accessible instructions, basic preparation tips and make-ahead hints ensure that both beginners and those who think cooking brunch is too bothersome will find this volume to be inspiring." Publ Wkly

Garten, Ina

Barefoot Contessa family style; easy ideas and recipes that make everyone feel like family. photographs by Maura McEvoy; food styling by Rori Trovato. Potter 2002 240p il $35 **641.5**
    1. Cookery 2. Cooking
    ISBN 0-609-61066-X

                        LC 2002-74979

This is "simple, elegant home cooking with good ingredients and a minimum of fuss. It takes a certain amount of chutzpah to include ordinary chicken noodle soup and mashed potatoes and gravy in a cookbook, but Garten pulls it off with heart and style." Publ Wkly

Gentry, Ann

The **Real** Food Daily cookbook; really fresh, really good, really vegetarian. [by] Ann Gentry with Anthony Head. Ten Speed Press 2005 232p $24.95 **641.5**
    1. Vegetarian cooking
    ISBN 1-58008-618-7

                        LC 2005-16245

The author presents "what she has learned about seasonal, organic, macrobiotic and vegan cooking. Gentry doesn't break new ground—sandwiches made with tempeh instead of meat, and nut cheeses like cashew cheddar will be familiar to most vegans—but she provides clear and comprehensive directions on how to make them more interesting and flavorful. . . . Gentry explains the basics without preaching or condescending to readers, and discusses nutritional benefits without unnecessary jargon." Publ Wkly

Gerson, Fany

My sweet Mexico; recipes for authentic breads, pastries, candies, beverages, and frozen treats. Ten Speed Press 2010 215p il $30 **641.5**
    1. Desserts 2. Mexican cooking
    ISBN 978-1-58008-994-4

                        LC 2010-14469

The author "has dutifully catalogued the confections of her native Mexico. . . . American readers who have only encountered the occasional tres leches cake in a Mexican restaurant will be stunned by the breadth and depth of recipes here, ranging from coffee-flavored corn cookies to guava caramel pecan rolls and hibiscus ice pops, all culled from Gerson's family, friends, and generous strangers. . . . Gerson's vivid descriptions, exacting instruction, and obvious passion for her subject matter make this volume a substantial read about the most tempting indulgences." Publ Wkly

Includes bibliographical references

Good housekeeping (Periodical)

★ The **Good** Housekeeping cookbook; 1,275 recipes from America's favorite test kitchen. edited by Susan Westmoreland. 125th anniversary ed.; Hearst Books 2010 752p il $35   **641.5**

1. Cooking

ISBN 978-1-58816-813-9

LC 2010-18437

Provides over 1,200 traditional and contemporary American recipes and offers information on cooking techniques, tools, ingredients, food handling, nutrition, canning, freezing, and holiday celebrations.

"Quick recipes and simple dessert preparations, like Fire-Roasted Nectarines and Coffee Granita, will please anyone pressed for time, but the encyclopedic inclusion of recipes for everything from Egg Salad, Lobster Bisque, and Chocolate Souffle to Pad Thai, Salmon with Mustard-Dill Sauce, and Muffuletta is its true benefit, making it a cookbook readers will grow with." Publ Wkly

Goodall, Tiffany

★ The **ultimate** student cookbook; from chicken to chili. photography by Claire Peters. Firefly Books 2010 160p il pa $14.95   **641.5**

1. Cooking 2. Quick and easy cooking

ISBN 978-1-55407-602-4

The author "outlines basic kitchen equipment, pantry ingredients, and food hygiene. Writing for the student with no cooking experience, she offers step-by-step photos that will make cooking a breeze. Goodall discusses basics like how to cook noodles, rice, and potatoes and presents dishes like wraps, salads, soups, chili, pizza, kebabs, and cakes. Two alcoholic drinks are included. Highly recommended for the numerous photographs and the variety of recipes." Libr J

Green, Aliza

Starting with ingredients; quintessential recipes for the way we really cook. Running Press 2006 1055p il $39.95   **641.5**

1. Cooking

ISBN 0-7624-2747-7; 978-0-7624-2747-5

LC 2006-921032

This is a "compendium of ingredients from A to Z (with a special chapter on 'X-tras' basic recipes and information). Each chapter opens with an informative and very readable introduction to the featured ingredient, touching on everything from its history to culinary lore . . . to its uses in various cultures around the world. . . . This is an invaluable reference with hundreds of fresh, lively recipes. Essential." Libr J

Greenspan, Dorie

Around my French table; more than 300 recipes from my home to yours. photographs by Alan Richardson. Houghton Mifflin Harcourt 2010 530p il $40   **641.5**

1. French cooking

ISBN 978-0-618-87553-5; 0-618-87553-0

LC 2010-14232

"A part-time Paris resident for more than a decade, Greenspan focuses on what French people really eat at home: easy-to-prepare yet flavorful dishes that are suitable for just about any time of day. From Bacon and Eggs and Asparagus Salad to Chicken in a Pot to Veal Chops with Rosemary Butter, her offerings are hardy, mostly uncomplicated, and superbly appetizing. She also provides sidebars on a wide range of topics, including whether or not to wash raw chicken, several ways of cooking beets, mussels, and more." Publ Wkly

Gur, Janna

The **book** of New Israeli food; a culinary journey. photography, Eilon Paz; contributing writers Rami Hann . . . [et al.] Schocken Books 2008 303p il $35   **641.5**

1. Israeli cooking

ISBN 978-0-8052-1224-2; 0-8052-1224-8

"Beautiful and comprehensive, this book will become an immediate favorite with anyone with even a passing interest in Israeli cuisine." Publ Wkly

Hagman, Bette

★ The **gluten**-free gourmet; living well without wheat. rev ed; Holt & Co. 2000 xx, 330p pa $18   **641.5**

1. Diet in disease 2. Gluten-free diet

ISBN 0-8050-6484-2

LC 00-22448

The recipes "are easy to prepare. Mail-order sources for gluten-free flours will be especially helpful. The . . . accurate information in this makes it a useful purchase for large cookbook collections." Booklist [review of 1990 edition]

Includes bibliographical references

Hair, Jaden

The **steamy** kitchen cookbook; 101 Asian recipes simple enough for tonight's dinner. photography by Jaden Hair. Tuttle Pub. 2009 160p il $27.95 **641.5**

1. Asian cooking

ISBN 978-0-8048-4028-6

LC 2009-17461

The author, a food blogger, "shares recipes drawn from her mother's kitchen, other food bloggers, and her own delightful archives. Her focus is mostly simple Asian dishes (from China, Vietnam, Japan, and Thailand), with several more complicated ones thrown into the mix. . . . For home cooks of all levels of experience seeking to expand their repertoire of Asian recipes, Hair has written an extremely accessible cookbook that blends great recipes with mouthwatering photographs she took." Libr J

Hazan, Marcella

Marcella says . . . Italian cooking wisdom from the legendary teacher's master classes, with more than 120 of her irresistible new recipes. HarperCollins Publishers 2004 390p il $29.95 **641.5**

    1. Italian cooking
    ISBN 0-06-620967-6

                        LC 2004-42892

The author shares lessons in Italian cooking, discussing techniques, ingredients and planning and preparing Italian dishes

Henry, Diana

    Pure simple cooking; effortless meals everyday. photography by Jonathan Lovekin. Ten Speed Press 2009 192p il pa $21.95 **641.5**

    1. Quick and easy cooking
    ISBN 978-1-58008-948-7; 1-58008-948-8

                        LC 2008-35099

This "collection of 150 recipes focuses on simple weeknight dishes, most of which can be prepared in under an hour and with only a handful of ingredients. Strong emphasis is placed on seasonal produce, with vegetable and fruit chapters broken down into 'spring and summer' or 'autumn and winter' categories. . . . Endless variations for savory sauces, poultry stuffing, roasted potatoes and even whipped cream pepper the text, and many of the recipes contain footnotes offering simple substitutions. . . . One hundred sumptuous, full-color photographs serve as both illustration and inspiration." Publ Wkly

    Roast figs, sugar snow; food to warm the soul. photographs by Jason Lowe. Mitchell Beazley 2009 191p il pa $19.99 **641.5**

    1. Cooking
    ISBN 978-1-84533-524-3

This "is an appealing collection of winter dishes from the Northern Hemisphere (including northern Italy, France, Russia, Switzerland, and Vermont), certain to make cooks yearn for a long winter." Libr J

Hesser, Amanda

    ★ The **essential** New York Times cook book; classic recipes for a new century. W.W. Norton 2010 932p il $40 **641.5**

    1. Cookery, American 2. Cooking
    ISBN 978-0-393-06103-1; 0-393-06103-5

                        LC 2010-33311

The author "spent six years combing the Times's vast recipe archive, cooking her way through more than 1000 recipes to assemble this indispensible tome culled from 150 years of the paper's food columns. This daunting compendium features both noteworthy classics (Osso Buco) and modern recipes (Smoked Mashed Potatoes) that have been tested and, in some cases, updated for the contemporary cook. Chapters begin with a time line and are arranged by type of food (e.g., soups, vegetables, cakes) then chronologically within the chapter, making for a fascinating historic overview of the interests of American cooks." Libr J

    Includes bibliographical references

Hyman, Gwen

    Urban Italian; simple recipes and true stories from a life in food. [by] Andrew Carmellini,

and Gwen Hyman; photographs by Quentin Bacon. Bloomsbury 2008 311p il $35 **641.5**

    1. Italian cooking
    ISBN 978-1-59691-470-4

The author "presents spectacular recipes while opening a window onto his life with food, from his Italian-American boyhood and cooking school to revelations while traveling in Italy and being a top New York chef. . . . The recipes, which come from all over Italy and mix regional Italian and American influences, are arranged classically, from antipasti to dolci." Publ Wkly

Iyer, Raghavan

    660 curries; the gateway to the world of Indian cooking. by Raghavan Iyer. Workman Pub. 2008 809p il $32.50; pa $22.95 **641.5**

    1. Cookery (Curry) 2. Cookery, Indic 3. Cooking -- Curry
    ISBN 978-0-7611-4855-5; 0-7611-4855-8; 978-0-7611-3787-0 pa; 0-7611-3787-4 pa

                        LC 2008-1288

"A wide-ranging guide to the curries of the Indian subcontinent, including Pakistan, Nepal, and Sri Lanka. Iyer explains that Indian curries are not based on a can of curry powder and that the term 'curry' refers to any dish simmered in or covered with a fragrant, spicy (though not necessarily hot) sauce or gravy. The hundreds of recipes include appetizer curries such as Skewered Chicken with Creamy Fenugreek Sauce, main-course curries like Yogurt-Marinated Lamb with Ginger and Garlic, and 'contemporary curries' such as Wild Salmon with Chiles, Scallions, and Tomato; there are also recipes for 'curry cohorts'—rice, bread, and other accompaniments." Libr J

Jaffrey, Madhur

    At home with Madhur Jaffrey; simple, delectable dishes from India, Pakistan, Bangladesh, and Sri Lanka. Alfred A. Knopf 2010 301p il $35; ebook $35 **641.5**

    1. Asian cooking
    ISBN 978-0-307-26824-2; 978-0-307-59440-2 ebook
                        LC 2010-19678

This is a "cookbook of easily prepared, thoughtful, and unusual dishes from India, Pakistan, Bangladesh, and Sri Lanka. Anyone looking to explore Indian cooking for the first time will find this volume uniquely helpful." Booklist

Jamison, Cheryl Alters

    The **big** book of outdoor cooking and entertaining; spirited recipes and expert tips for barbecuing, charcoal and gas grilling, rotisserie roasting, smoking, deep-frying, and making merry. [by] Cheryl and Bill Jamison. Morrow 2006 548p $24.95 **641.5**

    1. Barbecue cooking 2. Entertaining
    ISBN 0-06-073784-0; 978-0-06-073784-9

                        LC 2006-41918

This book features "more than 850 recipes and information on every aspect of backyard cooking. There are dozens of 'Party-Time Tips' and other helpful hints, menu suggestions, and sidebars and boxes on techniques, ingredients, and more. . . . New grilling books appear as the season approaches every year, but this one is an essential purchase." Libr J

Jenkins, Nancy Harmon

The **essential** Mediterranean; how regional cooks transform key ingredients into the world's favorite cuisines. HarperCollins Pubs. 2003 436p $29.95 **641.5**

1. Mediterranean cooking

ISBN 0-06-019651-3

LC 2002-69054

"Jenkins's writing experience stands her in good stead in this innovative exploration of this sunny region." Publ Wkly

Includes bibliographical references

The **new** Mediterranean diet cookbook; a delicious alternative for lifelong health. with a foreword by Marion Nestle. Bantam Books 2009 496p $26.95 **641.5**

1. Low-fat diet 2. Mediterranean cooking

ISBN 978-0-553-38509-0; 0-553-38509-7

LC 2008-40982

Jenkins' "knowledge of these cuisines is both personal and informed. . . . An essential purchase." Libr J

Includes bibliographical references

Jones, Judith

The **pleasures** of cooking for one. Alfred A. Knopf 2009 273p il $27.95 **641.5**

1. Cooking

ISBN 978-0-307-27072-6

LC 2009-12307

Counsels readers on how to enjoy a solitary culinary life by preparing meals in accordance with one's own preferences, outlining a range of basic through sophisticated recipes that work in weekly menus and make use of leftovers.

This is a "civilized, unfussy guide to cooking—and cooking well—for solitary diners. . . . [The author] doesn't skip desserts, entertaining or self-indulgence, and best of all, her whole book benefits from the diverse and cumulative gleanings of work with many of the great cooks and cookbook writers (including Julia Child, of course) of the latter half of the 20th century." Publ Wkly

Includes bibliographical references

Kamozawa, Aki

Ideas in food; great recipes and why they work. [by] Aki Kamozawa and H. Alexander Talbot. Clarkson Potter 2010 320p il $25 **641.5**

1. Chemistry 2. Cooking

ISBN 978-0-307-71740-5; 978-0-307-71974-4 ebook

LC 2010-17633

"The authors break down the science behind correctly and deliciously preparing everything from bread, pasta, and eggs (including soft scrambled eggs; hardboiled eggs, and brown butter hollandaise sauce) to homemade butter and yogurt. Most recipes fall into the 'Ideas for Everyone' category, which composes about the first three-quarters of the book; the final section is 'Ideas for Professionals,' which explores trendy molecular gastronomy topics like liquid nitrogen--used to make popcorn gelato--and carbon dioxide, a necessary tool for making coffee onion rings. Straightforward prose and anecdotes with personality keep this from being a dry food science tome. And accessible recipes for such dishes as a simple roast chicken, green beans almon-

dine, and root beer-braised short ribs mean it never gets too lofty." Publ Wkly

Includes bibliographical references

Katz, Rebecca

The **cancer**-fighting kitchen; nourishing big-flavor recipes for cancer treatment and recovery. [by] Rebecca Katz with Mat Edelson. Celestial Arts 2009 222p il $32.50 **641.5**

1. Cancer -- Diet therapy 2. Cooking for the sick

ISBN 978-1-58761-344-9

LC 2009-14359

"Katz's experience with cancer patients and their long, often frustrating recovery lends authority to her wise, common-sense approach, suitable for cooks of all skill levels." Publ Wkly

Includes bibliographical references

Katzen, Mollie

Get cooking; 150 simple recipes to get you started in the kitchen. [by] Mollie Katzen, with photographs by the author. HarperStudio 2009 xx, 268p il pa $24.99 **641.5**

1. Cooking

ISBN 978-0-06-173243-0

LC 2009-32815

This book "offers an invaluable list of equipment and advice (you can never have too many cutting boards), plus an illustrated vegetable-chopping guide. The 150 recipes for such common dishes as chicken noodle soup, potato salad, and spaghetti and meatballs are a good starting place for beginners. The recipes note variations, complementary dishes, and vegan dishes. Highly recommended for new cooks." Libr J

Keller, Thomas

Ad Hoc at home. Artisan Books 2009 359p il $50 **641.5**

1. Cooking

ISBN 978-1-57965-377-4

LC 2009-13258

For this cookbook, the author focuses on "family-style meals for the home cook in this accessible and dazzlingly beautiful book based on the fare served at his Ad Hoc restaurant, in Napa, Calif. . . . [He provides] a thorough primer on the foundations of cooking, offering clear and easy-to-follow instructions on techniques such as butchering and trussing chickens and tying a pork loin. . . . Dishes such as braised beef short ribs, buttermilk fried chicken, and fig-stuffed roast pork loin highlight a vast array of offerings that range from crab cakes to shortbread cookies." Publ Wkly

Kennedy, Diana

From my Mexican kitchen; techniques and ingredients. photographs by Michael Calderwood; and styled by the author. Clarkson Potter 2003 320p il $40 **641.5**

1. Mexican cooking

ISBN 0-609-60700-6

LC 2002-70405

The author "explains how to produce authentic enchiladas, tacos, tamales, sopes, panuchos, and other Mexican classics. Kennedy also provides a guide to wild greens, items rarely seen outside provincial markets. Her advice on freezing excess quantities of cuitlacoche (corn fungus) will reward fans of that uncommon mushroom. This is an indispensable addition to any library cookbook collection." Booklist

Kenney, Matthew

Entertaining in the raw; photographs by Miha Matei. Gibbs Smith 2009 240p il $35   **641.5**
1. Cooking -- Natural foods 2. Entertaining
ISBN 978-1-4236-0208-8; 1-4236-0208-0
LC 2008-30784
"Matthew Kenney has paved the way and taken raw food to new heights in his latest book. . . . The recipes presented in this book are a stellar example of gourmet plant-based raw food." Raw Epicurean

Kiros, Tessa

Food from many Greek kitchens. Andrews McMeel Pub. 2011 333p il $35   **641.5**
1. Greek cooking
ISBN 978-1-4494-0652-3
LC 2010943021
"For each recipe, [the author] gives the title in English and Greek and offers an introduction to the dish and thorough instruction. From Baklava to Keftedes Fried Meatballs to Pita Bread, the accessible dishes are accompanied by beautiful photography. Greek cookbooks written for the beginner are rare, so this book is a gem. It provides a good foundation and is sure to be a gateway to more advanced Greek cooking." Lirb J

Ko, Genevieve

Home cooking with Jean-Georges; [by] Jean-Georges Vongerichten with Genevieve Ko. Clarkson Potter/Publishers 2011 256p il $40   **641.5**
1. Cooking
ISBN 978-0-307-71795-5; 0-307-71795-X
LC 2010-53808
"After working 18-hour days six days a week, Vongerichten buys a weekend country home and rediscovers the joys of unfussy cooking. He shares recipes for the meals he and his family enjoy in this pleasingly accessible volume. Chicken liver and pancetta crostini, swiss chard braised in shiitake butter, shortbread are among the recipes that cover salads, fish and seafood, meat, desserts, and brunch. All focus on flavor yet rely on a minimal number of ingredients that don't take a lot of time and effort to prepare. . . . Dotted with culinary reminiscences both personal and professional, this book shows Vongerichten at his simple best and offers his many fans the opportunity to cook and enjoy his favorite meals without being chained to the kitchen for hours." Publ Wkly

Lagasse, Emeril

From Emeril's kitchens; favorite recipes from Emeril's restaurants. William Morrow/HarperCollins 2003 342p il $27.50   **641.5**
1. Cooking
ISBN 978-0-06-018535-0; 0-06-01853-5
LC 2002-27568
"Spreading his philosophy and history in the introduction, [Emeril] entreats the user not to be put off by the complexity of many of the recipes, but to use the components and mix and match the dishes. The first chapter, 'Basics,' contains the building blocks of many of the dishes, ranging from the customary stocks to Hard Boiled Eggs and Roast Duck. Subsequent chapters are structured in the usual manner ranging from appetizers and first courses through desserts. Each dish is attributed to its restaurant or chef and results in a range of styles and inspirations." Publ Wkly

Lang, Adam Perry

Serious barbecue; smoke, char, baste, and brush your way to great outdoor cooking. [by] Adam Perry Lang, with J.J. Goode and Amy Vogler. Hyperion Books 2009 390p il $35   **641.5**
1. Barbecue cooking
ISBN 978-1-4013-2306-6
LC 2009-1765
The author's "definition of barbecue includes grilling as well as 'low and slow cooking,' and he presents a wide variety of tasty recipes here, along with a detailed introduction to barbecue basics and many useful sidebars on techniques and other tips. Highly recommended for all collections." Libr J

Lawson, Nigella

Feast: food that celebrates life; photographs by James Merrell. Hyperion 2004 472p il $35   **641.5**
1. Cooking
ISBN 1-4013-0136-3
This cookbook "makes the preparation of Thanksgiving, Christmas and other feasts seem so approachable and richly rewarding that it may coax even hardcore cynics or cowards to give roast turkey with all the trimmings a try." Publ Wkly
Includes bibliographical references

Nigella express; good food, fast. photographs by Lis Parsons. Hyperion 2007 390p il $35   **641.5**
1. Cooking
ISBN 978-1-4013-2243-4; 1-4013-2243-3
"Recipes in this book run the gamut from retro crepe suzettes to modern favorites like quesadillas and smoothies; and from orange French toast for breakfast to cocktail nibbles for a party. In the interest of speed Lawson uses prepared ingredients, but they're the ones many of us use already, like mayonnaise from a jar or frozen puff pastry. And if her tastes are sometimes nostalgically British (Eton mess, roly poly pudding) she also has a whole chapter on quick Tex-Mex food." WeightWatchers.com

Lee, Cecilia Hae-Jin

Quick and easy Korean cooking; more than 70 everyday recipes. photographs by Julie Toy and Ce-

cilia Hae-Jin Lee. Chronicle Books 2009 168p il pa
$22.95 **641.5**
1. Korean cooking
ISBN 978-0-8118-6146-5

LC 2008-33629

"Quality, accessible, authentic Korean cookbooks are
hard to come by. Ably filling that gap is [this book]. . . . It's
filled with more than 70 recipes, most of which only call for
about six ingredients. If you're skeptical that such simple
recipes can produce the flavor bombs that are Korean dishes,
know that three recipes were tested, and all worked perfectly
as written. Each one was lively with the flavors of garlic,
chiles, soy sauce, and sesame." Village Voice

Lee, Jennifer 8.
The **fortune** cookie chronicles; adventures in
the world of Chinese food. Twelve 2008 307p hardcover o.p. pa $13 **641.5**
1. Chinese Americans 2. Chinese cooking 3. Cookery,
Chinese 4. Eating customs 5. Food habits -- United
States 6. Restaurants 7. Restaurants -- United States
ISBN 978-0-446-58007-6; 0-446-58007-4; 978-0-446-
69897-9 pa; 0-446-69897-0 pa

LC 2007-33432

"When a large number of Powerball winners in a 2005
drawing revealed that mass-printed paper fortunes were to
blame, the author . . . went in search of the backstory. She
tracked the winners down to Chinese restaurants all over
America, and the paper slips the fortunes are written on back
to a Brooklyn company. This travellike narrative serves as
the spine of her cultural history—not a book on Chinese
cuisine, but the Chinese food of takeout-and-delivery—and
permits her to frequently but safely wander off into various
tangents related to the cookie. . . . Like the numbers on those
lottery fortunes, the book's a winner." Publ Wkly
Includes bibliographical references

Lee, Matthew
The **Lee** Bros. southern cookbook; stories
and recipes for southerners and would-be southerners. [by] Matt Lee and Ted Lee; color photography
by Gentl & Hyers. W.W. Norton 2006 589p il
$35 **641.5**
1. Southern cooking
ISBN 978-0-393-05781-2; 0-393-05781-X

LC 2006-22745

This "cookbook begins with a collection of drink recipes, from sweet tea to potent planters' punch. To accompany
these beverages, the Lee brothers array a long series of snack
and party foods. A section on preserves and pickles documents some rarely seen regional treats, such as Jerusalem
artichoke relish. Meats, seafood, sweets, and breads round
out the book. Every recipe has a story attached, and the large
format makes for easy reading." Booklist

Leite, David
The **new** Portuguese table; exciting flavors from
Europe's western coast. photographs by Nuno Cor-
reia. Clarkson Potter 2009 256p il $32.50 **641.5**
1. Portuguese cooking
ISBN 978-0-307-39441-5; 0-307-39441-7

LC 2008-51283

The author "begins by outlining Portugal's diverse regional cuisines and then describes traditional ingredients.
From there it is a straightforward listing of appetizers,
soups, fish, meat, poultry, vegetable/egg/rice dishes, breads,
sweets, liqueurs, and condiments, with approximately 150
recipes overall. . . . Full of delicious-sounding recipes, this
title is sure to appeal to adventurous cooks wanting to try a
new ethnic cuisine and will also be popular with Portuguese
American communities." Libr J

Lewis, Edna
★ The **taste** of country cooking; [with a foreword by Alice Waters] 30th anniversary ed.; Knopf
2006 xxi, 268p il $22.95 **641.5**
1. Southern cooking
ISBN 0-307-26560-9; 978-0-307-26560-9

"Recipes are categorized by the four seasons and are
ones . . . [the author] grew up with in a small Virginia farming community (personal reminiscences about her family
life appear throughout the text)." Booklist

Link, Donald
Real Cajun; rustic home cooking from Donald
Link's Louisiana. [by] Donald Link with Paula Disbrowe; photographs by Chris Granger. Clarkson Potter Publishers 2009 255p il $35 **641.5**
1. Cooking -- Louisiana
ISBN 978-0-307-39581-8; 0-307-39581-2

LC 2008-36989

"Link shares the fare he ate growing up on the bayou,
as well as what he cooks for family, friends and funerals.
Some recipes are aspirationally insane—fried chicken and
andouille gumbo, or 'game day' choucroute with sausage,
tasso and duck confit—while others I simply aspire to make,
like a fried oyster and bacon sandwich (bacon recipe included), and Link's outstanding boudin, which he also uses as
a heart-stopping beignet filling. The tone is easygoing, the
explanations clear." N Y Times Book Rev

Madison, Deborah
Vegetarian cooking for everyone; 10th anniversary ed; Broadway Books 2007 742p il $40 **641.5**
1. Vegetarian cooking
ISBN 978-0-7679-2747-5; 0-7679-2747-8

LC 2007-10075

Following information on ingredients and techniques,
the recipes focus "mainly on vegetables and grains, aiming
at flavor and variety, both often arrived at via assorted ethnic
approaches." Publ Wkly

Mallmann, Francis
Seven fires; grilling the Argentine way. [by]
Francis Mallmann, with Peter Kaminsky. Artisan
2009 278p il $35 **641.5**
1. Argentine cooking 2. Barbecue cooking 3. Outdoor
cooking
ISBN 978-1-57965-354-5

LC 2008-37367

"Mallmann cooks with the elegant purity achieved only
after attaining a mastery of complicated food. . . . He also
reconnects us to the primal simplicity and visceral pleasure

of cooking over a fire—though his recipes can be made over charcoal or in a grill pan, too." N Y Times Book Rev

Marks, Gil

The **world** of Jewish cooking; more than 500 traditional recipes from Alsace to Yemen. Simon & Schuster 1996 406p il hardcover o.p. pa $17 **641.5**
1. International cooking 2. Jewish cooking
ISBN 0-684-83559-2 pa

LC 96-2848

This cookbook is "loosely arranged by food category, with chapters on appetizers, soups, and main dishes, as well as side items, breads, and desserts. . . . You'll find recipes from India, Africa, even China, here, alongside many dishes that originated in one of the two major Jewish cultural communities, Ashkenazic and Sephardic." Booklist

Moskowitz, Isa Chandra

Vegan pie in the sky; 75 out-of-this-world recipes for pies, tarts, cobblers & more. [by] Isa Chandra Moskowitz & Terry Hope Romero. Da Capo Lifelong 2011 223p il pa $17 **641.5**
1. Pies 2. Vegetarian cooking
ISBN 978-0-7382-1274-6

The authors focus on "dessert in this collection of 75 egg, dairy and animal-free pies, cheesecakes, cobblers and tarts. . . . The duo deserves plaudits for their user-friendly approach as well as their ability to keep scarcer ingredients to a minimum. Bakers who fear they won't be able to recreate these will be happy to discover that once they've mastered a crust or two they'll be able to whip together a Strawberry Field Hand Pie, Chocolate Mousse Tart, or even a Coconut Cream with confidence." Publ Wkly

Nathan, Joan

Jewish cooking in America; expanded ed; Knopf 1998 518p il $35 **641.5**
1. Jewish cooking
ISBN 0-375-40276-4

LC 98-27952

This companion volume to the PBS television series contains nearly 300 recipes. It "is also a history of the Jewish people through their food. Nathan introduces both people and food in a preface that discusses dietary laws, Jewish holidays, Jewish immigration to the U.S., and the impact of Jews—and their food—on American culture. With every recipe comes an original story or a reprint of an article or a personal vignette that intrigues and/or edifies." Booklist
Includes bibliographical references

Quiches, kugels, and couscous; my search for Jewish cooking in France. Alfred A. Knopf 2010 387p il $39.95; ebook $40 **641.5**
1. French cooking 2. Jewish cooking 3. Jews -- France
ISBN 978-0-307-26759-7; 978-0-307-59450-1 ebook

LC 2010-20280

"Nathan's multi-layered, narrative approach makes this treasury of tempting flavors an entertaining and compelling read." Publ Wkly
Includes bibliographical references

Natkin, Michael

Herbivoracious; a flavor revolution with 150 vibrant and original vegetarian recipes. Michael Natkin. Harvard Common Press 2012 367 p. **641.5**
1. Vegetarian cooking
ISBN 1558327452; 9781558327450

LC 2011030819

This vegetarian cookbook offers up 150 . . . recipes. . . . A third of the book is taken up with hearty main courses, ranging from a robust Caribbean Lentil-Stuffed Flatbread across the Atlantic to a comforting Sicilian Spaghetti with Pan-Roasted Cauliflower and around the Cape of Good Hope to a delectable Sichuan Dry-Fried Green Beans and Tofu. An abundance of soups, salads, sauces and condiments, sides, appetizers and small plates, desserts, and breakfasts round out the recipes. [Michael] Natkin . . . provides lots of advice on how to craft vegetarian meals that amply deliver protein and other nutrients, and the . . . menus he presents deliver balanced and complementary flavors. . . . The many dozens of vegan and gluten-free recipes are clearly noted. (Publishers note)

Neely, Pat

Down home with the Neelys; a Southern family cookbook. [by] Patrick Neely and Gina Neely; with Paula Disbrowe. Alfred A. Knopf 2009 278p il $27.95 **641.5**
1. Barbecue cooking 2. Southern cooking
ISBN 978-0-307-26994-2; 0-307-26994-9

LC 2008-54393

This cookbook written by "husband-and-wife television personalities with their own Tennessee chain of barbecue joints . . . [is] full of 120 recipes that pull back the curtain on their award-winning seasonings, sauce, and fixings. Emphasizing their personal story and family recipes, this cookbook is brimming with down-home personality . . . and dishes that are 'simple, stylish, and not too fussy.'" Publ Wkly

New American Heart Association cookbook

★ The **new** American Heart Association cookbook; 8th ed.; Clarkson Potter 2010 xxi, 696p il $35 **641.5**
1. Cooking 2. Heart diseases -- Diet therapy 3. Low-cholesterol diet
ISBN 978-0-307-40757-3

LC 2009-44692

"Each recipe comes with a breakdown of calories, protein content, carbohydrates, cholesterol, fats (broken down by saturated, polyunsaturated and monounsaturated) and sodium content, along with a table of dietary exchange. . . . This book remains a basic in many heart-conscious kitchens." Publ Wkly

Newgent, Jackie

The **all** -natural diabetes cookbook; the whole food approach to great taste and healthy eating. American Diabetes Association 2007 337p il pa $18.95 **641.5**
1. Cooking -- Natural foods 2. Diabetes -- Diet therapy
ISBN 978-1-58040-275-0

LC 2007-11961

The author presents a "cookbook designed to provide diabetes-friendly recipes that emphasize fresh and organically grown produce. . . . A wide variety of food styles are presented, ranging from Southern Black-Eyed Pea Salad to Vietnamese-Style Beef and Soba Noodle Soup. Even desserts are here, with such enticing options as Fudgy Brownies and New Fashioned Oatmeal Cookies. Highly recommended for all cooking collections." Libr J

Newhall, Beaumont

Beaumont's kitchen; lessons on food, life, and photography with Beaumont Newhall. [edited by David Chickey, Darius Himes, Joanna Hurley] Radius Books 2009 169p il $55   641.5

1. Artistic photography 2. Cooking
ISBN 978-1-934435-06-9; 1-934435-06-6

"Often referred to as the 'Father of Photographic History,' the legendary curator and critic Beaumont Newhall was known by his intimate circle—which included Ansel Adams, Edward Weston and Henri Cartier-Bresson, among many others—as a great chef and a gracious host. This beautifully designed volume, with images printed in deluxe duotones, contains a key selection of articles and recipes culled from Epicure Corner, Newhall's weekly column for The Brighton-Pittsford Post, which appeared in the Rochester, New York, newspaper from 1956 to 1969. The columns are accompanied by a selection of photographs by Berenice Abbott, Ansel Adams, Henri Cartier-Bresson, Beaumont Newhall, Janet Russek, Ralph Steiner, Paul Strand, Todd Webb, Edward Weston and Minor White. Essay by David Scheinbaum." Photo-eye

O'Neill, Molly

One big table; a portrait of American cooking 600 recipes from the nation's best home cooks, farmers, fishermen, pit-masters, and chefs. Simon & Schuster 2010 864p il $50; ebook $37.99   641.5

1. Cookery -- United States 2. Cookery, American 3. Cooking
ISBN 978-0-7432-3270-8; 978-1-4516-0977-6 ebook
LC 2010-28841

"This collection celebrates the nation's culinary diversity, both ethnically and agriculturally, and offers a uniquely intimate look at what home cooking in America is truly like today. O'Neill crossed the country, interviewing home cooks and spending time in the kitchens of recent immigrants. The results are enticing recipes that intertwine family stories, personal histories, and food. From stuffed Danish pancakes in Utah to tamales in Santa Fe and Vietnamese shrimp pancakes in Mississippi, this eclectic collection showcases the best this country has to offer." Publ Wkly

Oliver, Jamie

Cook with Jamie; my guide to making you a better cook. photography: David Loftus and Chris Terry. Hyperion 2007 447p il $37.50   641.5

1. Cooking
ISBN 978-1-4013-2233-5; 1-4013-2233-6

"Aiming to educate readers on cooking basics, Oliver offers more than 175 recipes, which emphasize flavor and freshness over labor-intensive preparation. With a conversational style that favors general guidelines over strict instruc-

tions—recipes often call for a 'knob of butter,' a 'handful of shelled peas' or 'a big handful of freshly grated Parmesan'—Oliver's friendly and enthusiastic approach handily deflates new-cook anxiety. Loaded with photos that cover common skills like cleaning and preparing fresh lobster, discerning degrees of doneness in meat and crafting homemade pasta, Oliver's patient explanations leave little room for confusion. His dishes, many of which are updated versions of classics, are impressive and accessible." Publ Wkly

Ong, Julie S.

The **everything** guide to macrobiotics; a practical introduction to the macrobiotic lifestyle--and how it can work for you. [by] Julie S. Ong with Lorena Novak Bull. Adams Media 2010 291p il pa $15.95   641.5

1. Macrobiotic diet 2. Vegetarian cooking
ISBN 978-1-4405-0371-9
LC 2010-283632

The authors introduce "macrobiotics basics, how food affects moods, and the connection between food and nature. . . . This simple, understandable introduction to the macrobiotic lifestyle is highly recommended." Libr J

Includes bibliographical references

Ortega, Simone

★ **1080** recipes; [by] Simone and Ines Ortega; illustrations, Javier Mariscal. Phaidon 2007 975p il $39.95   641.5

1. Spanish cooking
ISBN 978-0-7148-4836-5; 0-7148-4836-0

"Something like the Joy of Cooking for the Spanish home cook, . . . [this book] includes recipes for both traditional regional fare and dishes inspired by a variety of other cuisines. . . . An essential purchase." Libr J

Page, Karen

The **flavor** bible; the essential guide to culinary creativity, based on the wisdom of America's most imaginative chefs. [by] Karen Page and Andrew Dornenburg; photographs by Barry Salzman. Little, Brown and Company 2008 380p il $35   641.5

1. Cooking
ISBN 978-0-316-11840-8; 0-316-11840-0
LC 2007-33064

"The authors first discuss the four basic tastes and the roles played by weather, the season of the year, and other environmental factors in cooking. The rest of the book is an extensive alphabetic guide to different culinary ingredients. . . . . Rather than just another collection of recipes, this is a unique resource that both beginning cooks and serious chefs will find wonderfully inspiring and immensely useful." Libr J

Pascal, Cybele

★ The **whole** foods allergy cookbook; two hundred gourmet & homestyle recipes for the food allergic family. Vital Health Pub. 2006 213p pa $18.95 **641.5**

1. Cooking 2. Diet therapy 3. Food allergy
ISBN 1-890612-45-6; 978-1-890612-45-0

LC 2005-931263

"Each and every dish offered is free of dairy, eggs, wheat, soy, peanuts, tree nuts, fish, and shellfish. . . . [The book includes] recipes for breakfast pancakes, breads, and cereals; lunch soups, salads, spreads, and sandwiches; dinner entrées and side dishes; dessert puddings, cupcakes, cookies, cakes, and pies; and even after-school snacks ranging from trail mix to pizza and pretzels. Included is a resource guide to organizations that can supply information and support, as well as a shopping guide for hard-to-find items." Publisher's note

Includes bibliographical references

Pennington, Amy

Urban pantry; tips & recipes for a thrifty, sustainable & seasonal kitchen. photography by Della Chen. Skipstone 2010 175p il pa $19.95 **641.5**

1. Cooking
ISBN 978-1-59485-346-3

LC 2009049748

"Pennington's tips for stocking and making pantry staples teach readers to use kitchen scraps for stock, stale bread for crumbs, and a variety of leftovers for sauces, giving a solid foundation in kitchen thrift. Recipes for pantry items are accompanied by meal recipes, offering an arsenal of options without running to the store." Libr J

Pepin, Jacques

★ **Essential** Pepin; more than 700 all-time favorites from my life in food. Houghton Mifflin Harcourt 2011 685p il $40 **641.5**

1. French cooking
ISBN 978-0-547-23279-9

LC 2011-16057

Pepin "offers more than 700 of his best French and French-accented dishes from decades of cooking and teaching. They're simple without being dumbed down; approachable yet still adventurous. Whether he's explaining how to make Escoffier quenelles with mushroom sauce; black sea bass gravlax; chicken livers sautéed with vinegar; duck cassoulet; artichoke hearts with tarragon and mushrooms; or tarte tatin, he makes it seem doable and shares tidbits of wisdom to boost confidence and kitchen knowledge. His head notes are brief but informative, warm but not cloying. Pepin's own line drawings accompany the recipes, and they are, appropriately, at once homey and sophisticated. A DVD teaching a variety of cooking techniques accompanies the book, promising to make even the more challenging recipes less intimidating. For serious cooks and beginners alike, this is an instant classic." Publ Wkly

Jacques Pepin celebrates; by Jacques Pépin with Claudine Pépin; photographs by Christopher Hirsheimer; illustrations by Jacques Pépin. Knopf 2001 458p il $40 **641.5**

1. Cookery 2. Cooking 3. Entertaining
ISBN 0-375-41209-3

LC 2001-29929

"In this companion to a new PBS series, Pépin builds on a broad definition of celebrations—encompassing holidays, special occasions, and simply nice weather—to present a collection of typically solid French recipes and numerous useful tips and techniques. . . . More valuable than the recipes . . . are the many notes on chopping, garnishing, carving and so forth." Publ Wkly

The **apprentice**: my life in the kitchen. Houghton Mifflin 2003 318p il $26 **641.5**

1. Cookbook writers 2. Cookery 3. Cooking 4. Cooks 5. Television personalities
ISBN 0-618-19737-0

LC 2002-192158

"Pépin relates how his interest in food and culinary techniques developed into passions for cooking and teaching. He does this deftly, neatly capturing personalities and events with clear, concise writing." Libr J

Perche agli Italiani piace/English

Why Italians love to talk about food; translated from the Italian by Anne Milano Appel. Farrar, Straus and Giroux 2009 xxiii, 449p il map $35 **641.5**

1. Cookery, Italian 2. Eating customs 3. Food habits -- Italy -- History 4. Italian cooking
ISBN 978-0-374-28994-2; 0-374-28994-8

LC 2008-41566

"For readers looking to explore culinary authenticity and origins, this is highly recommended." Libr J

Includes bibliographical references (p. 405-427)

Peterson, James

Cooking. Ten Speed Press 2007 534p il $40 **641.5**

1. Cooking
ISBN 978-1-580-08789-6; 1-580-08789-2

LC 2007-21065

This book "opens with a fairly brief description of ten basic cooking techniques and then moves on to Recipes To Learn By, organized by course or main ingredient. Many of the recipes are traditional French standbys, from Celeriac Rémoulade to Beef à la Mode, although there are dishes inspired by Thai, Mexican, and other cuisines as well. . . . Essentially an intensive course for home cooks in the classic techniques that underlie good cooking, this is recommended for all cookery collections." Libr J

★ **Glorious** French food; a fresh approach to the classics. Wiley 2002 xxv, 742p il map $45 **641.5**

1. French cooking
ISBN 0-471-44276-3

LC 2001-46972

The author presents "50 classic recipes as the starting point for his wide-ranging exploration of French food and techniques; each recipe serves both to demonstrate a variety of techniques and as the inspiration for a diverse collection of other recipes related to it in one way or another. . . . Each chapter includes boxes and charts on improvising with different ingredients and flavors. The suggested variations for individual recipes, often mini-essays in themselves, open up dozens of other possibilities. Peterson is both passionate and knowledgeable about his subject, and his . . . book is an essential purchase." Libr J

Includes bibliographical references

Kitchen simple; essential recipes for everyday cooking. Ten Speed Press 2011 244p il $30 **641.5**

1. Cooking

ISBN 978-1-58008-318-8

LC 2011-04435

"With a solid background in culinary instruction, Peterson easily articulates the basics of cooking and baking the selected recipes for even the most adventurous cook. This diverse assortment of 200 recipes strikes a perfect balance between fundamental and more advanced dishes, making it a useful source for cooks at every level of expertise. The straightforward language and full-color photographs, taken by Peterson himself, combine to create an accessible, well-organized guide to cooking for any occasion." Shelf Awareness

Poses, Steven

The **Frog** Commissary cookbook; by Steven Poses, Anne Clark, and Becky Roller; illustrated by Becky Roller. Camino Books 2002 272p pa $19.95 **641.5**

1. Cooking

ISBN 978-0-940159-73-0; 0-940159-73-2

LC 2001-43691

"Lighthearted, full of ideas. . . . Could inject new life into your dining and entertaining style." Bon Appetit

Prudhomme, Paul

Chef Paul Prudhomme's Louisiana tastes; exciting flavors from the state that cooks. Morrow 2000 347p il $25 **641.5**

1. Cookery, American -- Louisiana style 2. Cooking -- Louisiana

ISBN 0-688-12224-8

LC 99-35611

"Chronicling dishes from his native state, Prudhomme acknowledges that Louisiana home cooks don't normally serve anything so fancy as appetizers, so he offers dozens of ideas for starters that may readily serve as entrees by simply increasing portion size. . . . Each recipe now has its own unique seasoning mix varying from a few to a dozen spices and herbs." Booklist

Psilakis, Michael

How to roast a lamb; new Greek classic cooking. [by] Michael Psilakis with Brigit Binns & Ellen Shapiro; foreword by Barbara Kafka; photography, Christopher Hirsheimer & Melissa Hamilton. Little, Brown and Company 2009 288p il $35 **641.5**

1. Greek cooking 2. Mediterranean cooking

ISBN 978-0-316-04121-8

LC 2008-54932

This "cookbook is an emotional autobiography in narrative and recipe form. It's also an introduction to the marvels of Hellenic cuisine. Psilakis, beginning with childhood favorites, moves from simple home cooking to complex restaurant fare. The bulk of the dishes—precise and lavishly illustrated—are easy enough to replicate (although some of

his Anthos creations require dozens of ingredients and could take all day to make)." Time Out N Y

Puck, Wolfgang

Live, love, eat! the best of Wolfgang Puck. Gramercy Books 2006 243p il $14.99 **641.5**

1. Cooking

ISBN 978-0-517-22868-5; 0-517-22868-8

LC 2006-41232

This volume contains more than 125 recipes for appetizers, a variety of seasonal soups and salads, and, along with pasta and risotto recipes, the California-style pizzas that first made Puck and his original Spago Hollywood a favorite of international celebrities. Puck also serves up all manner of main courses, including seafood recipes, poultry dishes, and meat recipes. To round out the collection, he offers a variety of vegetable and other side-dish recipes, plus desserts. A section covering basics, sauces, and techniques provides guidance for beginning and experienced cooks alike. Illustrated throughout with more than 150 color images of finished dishes and closeup how-to shots demonstrating key techniques and tips.

Quessenberry, Sara

The **good** neighbor cookbook; 125 easy and delicious recipes to surprise and satisfy the new moms, new neighbors, recuperating friends, community-meeting members, book club cohorts, and block party pals in your life! [by] Sara Quessenberry and Suzanne Schlosberg. Andrews McMeel 2011 195p il pa $16.99 **641.5**

1. Cooking

ISBN 978-0-7407-9355-4

Provides 125 recipes for appetizers, soups, salads, entrées, and snacks suitable for a variety of gatherings, including block parties, potluck dinners, book clubs, and recuperating friends.

"This distinctive approach that highlights the communality of cooking is highly recommended." Libr J

Ramineni, Shubhra

Entice with spice; easy Indian recipes for busy people. photography by Masano Kawana; styling by Christina Ong and Magdalene Ong. Tuttle Pub. 2010 160p il map $27.95 **641.5**

1. Indic cooking

ISBN 978-0-8048-4029-3

LC 2009-49092

This is a "cookbook full of traditional Indian recipes adapted for busy American kitchens. Beginning with thorough explanations, from terminology to spice mixtures, she provides time-saving suggestions and tips for preparing ingredients. . . . This may be the Indian cookbook that American foodies have been waiting for." Publ Wkly

Robertson, Robin

Vegan planet; 400 irresistible recipes with fantastic flavors from home and around the world. Harvard Common Press 2003 576p hardcover o.p. pa $21.95 **641.5**

1. Cookery, International 2. Vegan cookery 3.

Vegetarian cooking
ISBN 1-55832-210-8; 1-55832-211-6 pa
LC 2002-7435
The author "offers dozens of imaginative vegan recipes inspired by a wide range of cuisines, from Five-Spiced Portobello Satays and Lebanese Fattoush (bread salad) to Cajun-Style Collards and Moroccan Fava Bean Stew." Libr J

Roden, Claudia

Arabesque: a taste of Morocco, Turkey, and Lebanon. Knopf 2006 341p il $35   **641.5**
1. Lebanese cooking 2. Moroccan cooking 3. Turkish cooking
ISBN 0-307-26498-X; 978-0-307-26498-5
LC 2006-45258
The author "has chosen more than 150 recipes from Morocco, Turkey, and Lebanon, some newly discovered, some variations on more familiar dishes, and a selection of favorite classic dishes. Each section opens with a fascinating insider's guide, providing both cultural and culinary history as well as information on specific ingredients and techniques. . . . An essential purchase." Libr J

Rombauer, Irma von Starkloff

★ **Joy** of cooking; [by] Irma S. Rombauer, Marion Rombauer Becker, Ethan Becker; illustrated by John Norton. 75th anniversary ed.; Scribner 2006 1132p il $30   **641.5**
1. Cooking
ISBN 978-0-7432-4626-2; 0-7432-4626-8
LC 2006-51231
This is the "backbone for any library's cookery reference collection, its nearly 4,000 recipes defining essential American home cooking." Booklist

Ruhlman, Michael

Ratio; the simple codes behind the craft of everyday cooking. Scribner 2009 xxv, 224p il $27 **641.5**
1. Cooking
ISBN 978-1-416-56611-3; 1-416-56611-2
LC 2008-32679
"While Ruhlman was attending the Culinary Institute of America for a book project, a chef showed him a copy of the golden rules, which boiled down the elements of (French) cooking into ratios. . . . [In this volume] Ruhlman guides readers through the ratios for a variety of doughs, batters, stocks, sauces, custards and sausages, explaining their chemical and culinary basis in clear, earnest prose and providing tasteful recipes that lay out the technique for each formula." N Y Times Book Rev

Samuelsson, Marcus

The **soul** of a new cuisine; a discovery of the foods and flavors of Africa. foreword by Desmond Tutu. Wiley 2006 xxii, 344p il map $40   **641.5**
1. African cooking
ISBN 0-7645-6911-2
For this African cookbook, the author "traveled to Africa and even took cooking lessons in Ethiopia, the country of his birth. Samuelsson emphasizes that this is not the definitive cookbook of an area with over 800 languages and dialects, but an overview of what he saw and ate in his travels. . . .

This is a unique cookbook about a little-known cuisine, including travel essays and enhanced by beautiful color photographs that depict the food and the people of Africa. A necessary acquisition for international cookery collections." Libr J
Includes bibliographical references

Scalpi, Gretchen

The **everything** diabetes cookbook; foreword by C. Ranjay Nath. 2nd ed.; Adams Media 2010 289p pa $15.95   **641.5**
1. Diabetes -- Diet therapy
ISBN 978-1-4405-0154-8
The author "discusses types of diabetes, food labels, the Glycemic Index, and shopping. Recipes, which are written for beginners and offer nutritional information (with PCF Ratio), include Southwest Black Bean Burgers, Asian-Style Fish Cakes (which are made with catfish, banana pepper, ginger, lemon juice, and garlic cloves), and Key Lime Pie (using Splenda instead of sugar). . . . Highly recommended for its variety of flavorful recipes and useful resources." Libr J

Silverton, Nancy

A **twist** of the wrist; quick flavorful meals with ingredients from jars, cans, bags, and boxes. [by] Nancy Silverton with Carolynn Carreño; photographs by Amy Neunsinger. Knopf 2007 262p il $29.95   **641.5**
1. Convenience foods 2. Quick and easy cooking
ISBN 978-1-4000-4407-8; 1-4000-4407-3
LC 2006-49557
The author offers recipes requiring "premium prepared ingredients as shortcuts to ease the home cooking time crunch. Most recipes are timed at 30 minutes or less, but the elegance and seeming difficulty of the dishes set them apart from the usual quick-fix crowd pleasers. . . . Cooks looking for upscale yet quick meal ideas, and who will pay extra for pricey exotic items, are sure to appreciate this stylish cheat sheet." Publ Wkly
Includes bibliographical references

Spieler, Marlena

Paris; authentic recipes celebrating the foods of the world. recipes and text Marlena Spieler; photographs Jean-Blaise Hall; general editor Chuck Williams. Oxmoor House 2004 191p il map $24.95 **641.5**
1. French cooking
ISBN 978-0-8487-2854-8
Illustrated with full-color photographs. "Dozens of stories reveal the secrets of making long-cherished foods and profile people, places, and influences that have shaped the Parisian food scene. More than 45 recipes allow you to sample traditional dishes, such as Boeuf en Daube, Steak withe Shallot Sauce, or Raspberry Charlotte, as well as such innovations as Duck Breasts with Port and Figs or Strawberry Soup." Publisher's note

Splendid table (Radio program)

The **Splendid** table's how to eat supper; recipes, stories, and opinions from public radio's award-winning food show. [by] Lynne Rossetto Kasper and

Sally Swift. Clarkson Potter/Publishers 2008 338p il $35 **641.5**

1. Cooking 2. Dining

ISBN 978-0-307-34671-1

LC 2007-24749

"This superb book should grace the shelves of even the most infrequent of cooks." Publ Wkly

Stewart, Martha

Martha Stewart's cooking school; lessons and recipes for the home cook. by Martha Stewart with Sarah Carey; photographs by Marcus Nilsson; portraits by Ditte Isager. Clarkson Potter 2008 504p il $45 **641.5**

1. Cooking 2. Entertaining

ISBN 978-0-307-39644-0; 0-307-39644-4

LC 2008-531117

This "cookbook is the result of what Stewart refers to as her 'mission to teach the methods of home cooking.' Chapters are organized by technique, from 'How To Make White Stock' to 'How To Make Pâte à Choux.' Master recipes are followed by others that build on them, and there are hundreds of color photographs, including many step by steps for essential techniques. The illustrated 'Basics' section that opens the book covers equipment, knife skills, herbs and spices, 'the onion family,' and citrus fruits. Charts, buying guides, and sidebars are featured throughout, along with dozens of tips on ingredients, special techniques, and more." Libr J

Stow, Josie

The **African** kitchen; a day in the life of a safari chef. {by} Josie Stow and Jan Baldwin. Interlink Bks. 1999 144p il hardcover o.p. pa $20 **641.5**

1. African cooking

ISBN 1-56656-354-2; 978-1-56656-580-6 pa; 1-56656-580-4 pa

LC 99-52120

"When Stow first took over the kitchen at a game preserve in South Africa, she found that most such establishments were serving European-style food. Drawing on the knowledge and experience of the cooks working with her, she developed a repertoire of traditional and modern African dishes. . . . Beautiful photographs of African nightcapes, people, and Stow's food illustrate the text." Libr J

Streiff, Fritz

The **art** of simple food; notes, lessons, and recipes from a delicious revolution. [by] Alice Waters, with Patricia Curtan, Kelsie Kerr & Fritz Streiff ; illustrations by Patricia Curtan. Clarkson Potter 2007 405p il $35 **641.5**

1. Quick and easy cooking

ISBN 978-0-307-33679-8; 0-307-33679-4

LC 2007-300393

"After a useful discussion of ingredients and equipment come chapters on techniques, such as making broth and soup. Each of these includes three or four recipes that rely on the technique described. . . . The final third of the book divides many more recipes traditionally into salads, pasta

and so forth. Waters taps an almost endless supply of ideas for appealing and fresh yet low-stress dishes." Publ Wkly

Tanis, David

Heart of the artichoke and other kitchen journeys. Artisan 2010 344p il $35 **641.5**

1. Cooking 2. Entertaining 3. Menus

ISBN 978-1-57965-407-8

LC 2010-4538

The author "begins with 14 'Kitchen Rituals' (ordinary pleasures perfect for one or two people) such as Jalapeño Pancakes and raw artichokes for lunch. Menus are arranged by season and feature, e.g., Fork-Mashed Potatoes and Spring Lamb with Rosemary. There are also menus for a long table (for a large crowd) such as A Perfect Suckling Pig. Simple recipes, eloquent writing, and Tanis's great reputation make this an essential purchase." Libr J

A **platter** of figs and other recipes; foreword by Alice Waters; photographs by Christopher Hirsheimer. Artisan 2008 294p il $35 **641.5**

1. Cooking 2. Entertaining 3. Menus

ISBN 978-1-57965-346-0; 1-57965-346-4

LC 2007-49384

This volume is "both a meditation on the powerful rites of cooking and serving a meal and a gentle but serious education in doing both. . . . With 24 menus distributed over the course of a year, Tanis emphasizes seasonality with ingredients (blueberry-blackberry crumble in summer; celery root mashed potatoes in winter) and with the types of dishes provided for each menu (as with a divine, warming lobster risotto as part of a menu for a cold spring day). Anecdotes from his peripatetic life of enjoying good food around the world, from Venice to Morocco to New Mexico, add another intimate dimension and help the book appear written just for the reader by a kind, patient friend." Publ Wkly

Includes bibliographical references

Tausend, Marilyn

Cocina de la familia; more than 200 authentic recipes from Mexican-American home kitchens. {by} Marilyn Tausend with Miguel Ravago. Simon & Schuster 1997 415p hardcover o.p. pa $20 **641.5**

1. Mexican American cooking

ISBN 0-684-85259-4 pa

LC 97-26979

This cookbook includes recipes for "Green Enchiladas with Spinach and Tofu, Chicken with Spicy Prune Sauce made with Coca-Cola, and Mexican Beef Chow Mein, {as well as} more traditional Mexican fare like Guacamole and Braised Chicken with Rice and Vegetables." Publ Wkly

Includes bibliographical references

Thomas, Anna

Love soup; 160 all-new vegetarian recipes from the author of The Vegetarian Epicure. illustrations by Annika Huett. W. W. Norton & Company 2009 528p il $35; pa $22.95 **641.5**

1. Soups 2. Vegetarian cooking

ISBN 978-0-393-06479-7; 978-0-393-33257-5 pa

LC 2009-19632

The author presents 160 "enticing recipes that may just charm even a die-hard carnivore. Soups are organized by season and range from hearty selections like rustic leek and potato, and minestrone for a crowd, to lighter summer options including tomato and fennel soup with blood orange and sweet corn. . . . Recipes for breads, dips and spreads, salads and a collection of desserts, as well as sample menus at the start of each chapter, make it easy to plan a full meal." Publ Wkly

Thompson, David

Thai food; with photography by Earl Carter. Ten Speed Press 2002 673p $40   **641.5**
    1. Thai cooking
    ISBN 978-1-580-08462-8; 1-580-08462-1
                                                    LC 2002-18117
"The first section of the book provides detailed cultural and social history and a guide to the regions and regional cuisines of Thailand. Then a detailed glossary of ingredients and a guide to techniques introduce the hundreds of recipes. These are grouped into chapters on relishes, soups, curries, salads, and sides, followed by one of menus with recipes. . . . [This] culinary history/cookbook is unique and will be an important purchase for any Asian cookery collection." Libr J
    Includes bibliographical references

Tourles, Stephanie L.

Raw energy; 124 raw food recipes for energy bars, smoothies, and other snacks to supercharge your body. [by] Stephanie Tourles. Storey Pub. 2009 271p il pa $16.95   **641.5**
    1. Cooking -- Natural foods   2. Snack foods   3. Vegetarian cooking
    ISBN 978-1-60342-467-7
                                                    LC 2009-28675
"This delightful addition is easily accessible even to readers looking to make small changes in their diets. . . . [The author] shares a list of ingredients with pictures of each item. A list of kitchen equipment is also provided to accompany these recipes for shakes, bars, and soups, some of which require the use of a juicer or dehydrator. For libraries that don't have any books on the topic, this is an excellent introduction." Libr J
    Includes bibliographical references

Trang, Corinne

Essentials of Asian cuisine; fundamentals and favorite recipes. black-and-white photographs by Corinne Trang; color photographs by Christopher Hirscheimer. Simon & Schuster 2003 592p il hardcover o.p. pa $34.99   **641.5**
    1. Asian cooking   2. Cookery, Asian
    ISBN 0-7432-0312-7; 1-4391-9108-5 pa
                                                    LC 2002-30490
"Authoritative and thoroughly researched, this will be invaluable as both a reference and a cookbook." Libr J
    Includes bibliographical references

Jaffrey, Madhur

Madhur Jaffrey's ultimate curry bible; India, Singapore, Malaysia, Indonesia, Thailand, South Africa, Kenya, Great Britain, Trinidad, Guyana, Japan, USA. Ebury 2003 352p il $51.65   **641.5**
    1. Cooking -- Curry
    ISBN 978-0-09-187415-5; 0-09-187415-7
With over 150 recipes, "Madhur starts with the best curry recipes in India today, moves on to Asian curries, and even includes European curry ideas such as French curry sauces. Some recipes have never before appeared in print, such as fish seasoned with tamarind and coconut and lamb braised with oranges. Also included are Madhur's tips for the best accompanying foods — she gives us ideas for rice, bread, chutneys, relishes and sweets — the perfect complement for any curry." Publisher's note

Tsai, Ming

Blue Ginger; East-meets-West cooking with Ming Tsai. by Ming Tsai and Arthur Boehm. Potter 1999 275p $32.50   **641.5**
    1. Asian cooking   2. Cookery, Asian   3. Cooking
    ISBN 0-609-60530-5
                                                    LC 99-36393
"Chapters divide the 125-plus recipes into soups, dim sum, rice and noodles, poultry, meat, seafood, elaborate side dishes and desserts, with mail-order sources. . . . Instructions are clearly written and often include tips for wine and food pairings and advice on ingredient substitutions and techniques." Publ Wkly

Vetri, Marc

Il viaggio di Vetri; a culinary journey. [by] Marc Vetri with David Joachim; wine notes by Jeff Benjamin; photography by Douglas Takeshi Wolfe. Ten Speed Press 2008 289p il $40   **641.5**
    1. Italian cooking
    ISBN 978-1-58008-888-6; 1-58008-888-0
                                                    LC 2008-21667
"More than a cookbook, this . . . is a guide through the particular Italian cuisine and culture on which . . . [the author] has based his career. . . . Amateur chefs may have only dreamed of having a culinary journey like Vetri's, but with this book he has given them a reliable key to turning dream into reality." Publ Wkly

Vileisis, Ann

Kitchen literacy; how we lost knowledge of where food comes from and why we need to get it back. Island Press/Shearwater Books 2008 332p il $27.95; pa $19.95   **641.5**
    1. Cookery, American -- History   2. Cooking   3. Diet
    4. Diet -- United States -- History   5. Eating customs   6. Food habits -- United States -- History
    ISBN 978-1-59726-144-9; 1-59726-144-0; 978-1-59726-717-5 pa; 1-59726-717-1 pa
                                                    LC 2007-25781
"This book speaks to our increasing lack of knowledge about the food we eat and where it comes from. Historically there was a real knowledge about this topic and the author explains how it has been lost and why it is important to get it back. The book is well written and accessible." Univ Press Books for Public and Second Sch Libr, 2009
    Includes bibliographical references

Waters, Alice

In the green kitchen; techniques to learn by heart. photographs by Hirsheimer & Hamilton. Clarkson Potter/Publishers 2010 151p il $28   **641.5**
1. Cooking -- Natural foods 2. Slow food movement 3. Vegetarian cooking
ISBN 978-0-307-33680-4; 0-307-33680-8
LC 2010-278664

The author "showcases basic cooking techniques every cook can and should master along with recipes using each method in this slim and attractive book. Derived from a Slow Food Nation event she helped organize, where notable chefs and foodies provided demonstrations on foundational procedures, Waters highlights a set of techniques that are universal to all cuisines. She covers the most basic of the basics, from stocking the pantry and washing lettuce to boiling pasta and wilting greens. . . . Ideal for the cooking novice, this gem of a book captures the expertise of world-class chefs in an accessible, straightforward manner." Publ Wkly

Weil, Andrew

The **healthy** kitchen; recipes for a better body, life, and spirit. {by} Andrew Weil and Rosie Daley; photographs by Sang An, Amy Haskell, and Eric Studer. Knopf 2002 xxxvii, 325p il $24.95; pa $16.95   **641.5**
1. Cookery (Natural foods) 2. Cooking 3. Natural foods
ISBN 0-375-41306-5; 0-375-71031-0 pa
LC 2001-50391

This is "a stimulating invitation to healthy, pleasurable eating." Publ Wkly

Weinstein, Bruce

★ **Cooking** know-how; be a better cook with hundreds of easy techniques, step-by-step photos, and ideas for over 500 great meals. [by] Bruce Weinstein & Mark Scarbrough; photography by Lucy Schaeffer. John Wiley 2009 406p il $34.95   **641.5**
1. Cooking
ISBN 978-0-470-18080-8
LC 2008-44375

"The recipes are structured without being fussy and the majority are relatively easy. This is a welcome rarity, imparting a useful, innovative framework as well as the confidence to depart from it." Publ Wkly

Wells, Patricia

Patricia Wells' trattoria; simple and robust fare inspired by the small family restaurants of Italy. William Morrow 2003 338p il pa $18.95   **641.5**
1. Italian cooking
ISBN 978-0-06-093652-5

This "collection of informal, robust recipes, gathered from Italy's small family-run restaurants, should appeal to anyone who appreciates the unmasked flavors of high-quality fresh ingredients, simply but lovingly prepared. Wells's often lengthy headnotes are full of personal reminiscences but also paint a colorful picture of the country's relaxed, generous lifestyle. Wine suggestions follow each recipe, and there are sensible cooking tips throughout." Libr J

The **Provence** cookbook; 175 recipes and a select guide to the markets, shops, & restaurants of France's sunny south. HarperCollins 2004 338p il $29.95   **641.5**
1. French cooking
ISBN 978-0-06-050782-4; 0-06-050782-9
LC 2003-56977

Wells offers "her own recipes, along with some from her butcher, fishmonger, other merchants, neighborhood restaurants, and other sources slightly farther afield. Most of the dishes are simple, allowing the flavors of Provence's wonderfully fresh produce and other ingredients to come through. . . . Wine suggestions are included throughout—sometimes for Wells's own label, since her vineyard is now productive—and she provides addresses and other relevant details about her favorite restaurants and purveyors." Libr J

Wolfert, Paula

The **slow** Mediterranean kitchen; recipes for the passionate cook. Wiley 2003 350p il $34.95 **641.5**
1. Cookery, Mediterranean 2. Mediterranean cooking
ISBN 0-471-26288-9
LC 2002-153265

The author offers "dishes from all the countries of the region: brodetto Pasquale (Italian Easter Lamb Soup), Expatriate Roast Chicken with Lemon and Olives from Morocco, and Catalonian Fall-Apart Lamb Shanks. Although many recipes call for braising, stewing, and other techniques of long cooking, others are not limited to those techniques, for Wolfert's definition of slow cooking also encompasses marinating and similar techniques." Libr J

Worrall-Thompson, Antony

The **essential** diabetes cookbook; good healthy eating from around the world. [by] Anthony Worrall Thompson, with Louise Blair. Kyle: Kyle Cathie 2010 287p il $35   **641.5**
1. Cooking 2. Diabetes -- Diet therapy
ISBN 978-1-906868-15-4
LC 2010-932221

200 recipes for diabetics that take their inspiration from cuisines around the world, including nutritional information for each recipe.

"From fish (Grilled Sea Bass with Spiced Cabbage) to crepes (Asian Surf and Turf Crêpes) to pork (Tofu, Pork, and Shellfish Hot Pot), these dishes bring life back into diabetic cooking. . . . Adventurous cooks will cheer for this diabetes cookbook." Libr J

The 150 best American recipes; edited by Fran McCullough and Molly Stevens; foreword by Rick Bayless; photography by Ben Fink; [selected by the editors of The best American recipes] Houghton Mifflin 2006 352p il $30   **641.5**
1. Cooking
ISBN 978-0-618-71865-8; 0-618-71865-6
LC 2006-5604

The editors "have selected the 'best of the best' recipes from . . . [The Best American Recipes series], choosing from more than 1000 contenders. The recipes come from a variety of sources, from cookbooks to web sites to cooking schools, and the result is a mouthwatering array: Charred Tomatillo Guacamole; Tuscan Pork Roast with Herbed Salt; Mussels with Smoky Bacon, Lime, and Cilantro; and Mocha Fudge Pudding." Libr J

★ American food writing; an anthology with classic recipes. edited by Molly O'Neill. Library of America 2007 753p il $40   **641.5**
1. Cookery 2. Cooking
ISBN 978-1-59853-005-6; 1-59853-005-4

This "collection of essays, anecdotes, and recipes spans three centuries of American food writing, from Meriwether Lewis's account of killing 'two bucks and two buffaloe' during his famous trek across the continent, to Michael Pollan's up-to-the-minute account of the politics of organic food. . . . With so many wonderful ingredients, this rich, delectable treat is a must-have for American foodies." Publ Wkly

Includes bibliographical references

★ Betty Crocker cookbook; everything you need to know to cook today. 10th ed.; Wiley 2005 575p il $29.95; pa $17.95   **641.5**
1. Cooking
ISBN 0-7645-6877-9; 978-0-7645-6877-0; 0-7645-8374-3 pa; 978-0-7645-8374-2 pa

LC 2006-281166

"This book gives easily readable and understandable recipes. Also has a glossary of cooking terms in back, as well as nutritional guidelines and 'special helps.'" N Y Public Libr. Book of How & Where to Look It Up

Betty Crocker's cooking basics; learning to cook with confidence. Macmillan 1998 280p il $19.95   **641.5**
1. Cookery 2. Cooking
ISBN 0-02-862451-3

LC 98-20522

In addition to recipes, this illustrated volume contains tips on food selection, grocery shopping, thawing, and nutrition. Cooking equipment is discussed.

Good Housekeeping great American classics cookbook; edited by Susan Westmoreland. Hearst Communications 2004 336p il $24.95   **641.5**
1. Cookery, American 2. Cooking
ISBN 1-588-16280-X

LC 2004-933

"This volume of American standards offers a . . . snapshot of the state of cooking in the nation's homes at the beginning of the second millennium. . . . Most startling is the European-influenced casual use of wines and spirits in all kinds of appetizers, entrees, and desserts. Current emphasis on food's nutritional value manifests itself in tables enumerating calories, proteins, carbohydrates, and fats appended to each recipe. . . . Brilliant color photos throughout." Booklist

★ Gourmet today; more than 1000 all-new recipes for the contemporary kitchen. edited by Ruth

Reichl. Houghton Mifflin Harcourt 2009 1008p il $40   **641.5**
1. Cooking
ISBN 978-0-618-61018-1

LC 2009-19781

The editor "offers a diverse range of recipes that reflect the ever-changing American palate and the many cultures that have influenced it. Alongside Stilton cheese puff are recipes for babaghanouj, bangers and mash, Armenian lamb pizza, arepas with black beans and feta, and Vietnamese fried spring rolls. Informative sidebars provide details on a huge array of topics, from what salt to use when to preserving fish. . . . Comprehensive, appetizing and thoroughly tested, this mammoth collection is the book no kitchen should be without." Publ Wkly

International dictionary of food & cooking; compiled by Charles G. Sinclair. Fitzroy Dearborn Pubs. 1998 594p $60   **641.5**
1. Cooking -- Dictionaries 2. Food -- Dictionaries 3. Reference books
ISBN 1-57958-057-2

This work contains over "24,000 words and terms that professional chefs and amateur cooks encounter in their kitchens. The entries, varying in length from a few words to a paragraph at most, are arranged alphabetically, with the country of origin for foreign words and phrases indicated within those entries." Libr J

The New York Times Jewish cookbook; more than 825 traditional and contemporary recipes from around the world. edited by Linda Amster; introduction by Mimi Sheraton. St. Martin's Press 2003 xxvi, 614p $35   **641.5**
1. Cookery, Jewish 2. Jewish cooking
ISBN 978-0-312-29093-1; 0-312-29093-4

LC 2002-68358

"Included here are hundreds of recipes from Jewish communities all over the world, reflecting Mimi Sheraton's introductory comment that Jewish food is 'the world's oldest fusion cuisine.' Recipes range from Persian Chicken Soup with Chickpea Dumplings to Alain Ducasse's Rib-Eye Steaks with Peppered Cranberry Marmalade to Fresh Corn and Red Pepper Blini. All the classics are here, too, and there's a separate chapter on 'Trimmings,' including an array of condiments and garnishes. . . . This is an essential purchase." Libr J

The New York Times Passover cookbook; more than 200 holiday recipes from top chefs and writers. edited by Linda Amster. Morrow 1999 xxii, 328p il $25   **641.5**
1. Jewish cooking 2. Passover 3. Passover cookery
ISBN 0-688-15590-1

LC 98-41282

This book's recipes "range from the traditional to the innovative and are drawn from European, Mediterranean and Middle Eastern traditions. . . . Amster has produced what may be the definitive word in Passover cookbooks, from recipes to the feelings evoked by sitting at a beautifully set, bountifully laden table." Publ Wkly

Includes bibliographical references

Recipes from an Italian summer; [translation by Mary Consoni; photographs by Joel Meyerowitz, Andy Sewell; illustrations by Jeffrey Fisher] Phaidon Press Limited 2010 431p il $39.95   **641.5**
1. Italian cooking
ISBN 978-0-714857732

This collection, "from the editors behind The Silver Spoon cookbook, is comprised of a glorious 400+ pages of recipes for picnics, barbecues, light suppers and summer entertaining (with the chapters thus organized, along with chapters on salads, desserts and ice cream/beverages). It's a compilation of dishes from popular Italian vacation regions. . . . The dishes are simple yet glorious in that Italian way (meaning without good ingredients, first press olive oil, farmers market greens, real Parmigiano-Reggiano, there's little point in making many of the recipes)." L A Wkly

The best American recipes 2005-2006; the year's top picks from books, magazines, newspapers, and the Internet. Fran McCullough and Molly Stevens, series editors; with a foreword by Mario Batali. Houghton Mifflin 2004 303p il   **641.5**
1. Cooking
ISBN 978-0-0618-57478-0; 0-618-57478-6

This is a compilation of popular recipes taken from cookbooks, newspapers, magazines, and other sources

The gourmet cookbook; more than 1000 recipes. edited by Ruth Reichl. Houghton Mifflin 2004 1040p $40   **641.5**
1. Cooking
ISBN 0-618-37408-6

LC 2004-47873

Recipes culled from issues of Gourmet magazine include "concoctions like Coq au Vin, Beef Wellington, Coulibiac, Chop Suey, Bananas Foster, and Black Forest Cake. . . . Every chapter begins with an overview of its subject; each recipe has an introduction; and many dishes feature helpful 'cook's notes,' which give tips for food preparation, technique and storage." Publ Wkly

The professional chef; the Culinary Institute of America. 8th ed; Wiley 2006 1215p il map $70   **641.5**
1. Cooking 2. Restaurants
ISBN 978-0-7645-5734-7; 0-7645-5734-3

LC 2004-27110

"The nation's most prestigious training school for food careerists concentrates the essence of its course work within a comprehensive volume that competent students must master. Every aspect of the restaurant business is addressed, from nutrition and portion sizing to fiscal and human resource management. Sections on equipment, from major appliances to handheld tools, show the bond between chef and technology. Chapters on world cooking identify the most typical cooking processes and give examples of commonly appearing ingredients in each style. Recipes record classic preparations that form the foundation for myriad elaborations and personalization to move cooking from mere technique to high art. Although beyond the need of most home cooks, this massive tome is a necessary reference-collection

purchase for any library whose community includes food-service-training programs." Booklist

★ The silver spoon. Phaidon Press 2005 1263p il $39.95   **641.5**
1. Italian cooking
ISBN 978-0-7148-4531-9; 0-7148-4531-0

"The book contains recipes for everything from basic sauces and marinades to salads, game, fish and baked goods, with each section color-coded for easy browsing. Recipes emphasize fresh ingredients and are to-the-point, typically summed up in a paragraph sans photo illustrations. Those who know their way around a kitchen will appreciate the brevity. . . . Almost all of the ingredients called for can be found in a typical supermarket. . . . Globe-trotting gourmands will appreciate the menu and 'signature dish' contributions by famous Italian chefs that round out the book. The most exhaustive Italian cookbook in recent memory, this volume offers something for every cook, regardless of their skill level, and deserves to be a fixture in American kitchens." Publ Wkly

641.59   Cooking characteristic of specific geographic environments, ethnic cooking

Algar, Ayla Esen
Classical Turkish cooking; traditional Turkish food for the American kitchen. {by} Ayla Algar. HarperCollins Pubs. 1991 306p $35; pa $17 **641.59**
1. Turkish cooking
ISBN 0-06-016317-8; 0-06-093163-9 pa

LC 91-55096

"A cuisine that melds the fragrances and flavors of the Far East, Central Asia, Iran, Anatolia, and the Mediterranean is enriched by Algar as she goes well beyond the standard recipes (160 of them) to explain Turkey's historical, cultural, and culinary traditions—and, along the way, to include a glimpse of her personal family heritage." Booklist
Includes bibliographical references

Anderson, Jean
The **new** German cookbook; more than 230 contemporary and traditional recipes. {by} Jean Anderson and Hedy Würz. HarperCollins Pubs. 1993 416p $30   **641.59**
1. German cooking
ISBN 0-06-016202-3

LC 92-56211

"This book should give many cooks a new perspective on German cooking. All of the ingredients traditionally associated with this cuisine appear, but veal, for example, shows up in a Riesling wine sauce as well as in Wiener schnitzel, and dumplings are scented with tarragon and tossed into a clear asparagus soup." Libr J
Includes bibliographical references

Barrenechea, Teresa
The **Basque** table; passionate home cooking from one of Europe's great regional cuisines. {by} Teresa Barrenechea, with Mary Goodbody. Harvard

Common Press 1998 232p il hardcover o.p. pa
$16.95
641.59
1. Basque cooking 2. Cookery, Basque 3. Food habits
-- Spain -- País Vasco
ISBN 1-55832-140-3; 978-1-55832-327-8 pa;
1-55832-327-9 pa

LC 98-29295

The author's "Basque dishes are characterized by fresh,
lively flavors; garlic, hot chilis, and roasted sweet peppers,
fish of all types, and beef and lamb are favorite ingredients.
While home-style dishes are her emphasis here, there are
some entries from nueva cocina as well. A chapter on pin-
chos, the Basque version of tapas, is a highlight, and there
are sidebars on Basque ingredients and traditions throughout." Libr J

Bastianich, Lidia

Lidia's Italian table; edited by Christopher Styler; photography by Christopher Hirscheimer. Morrow 1998 390p il $30
641.59
1. Cookery, Italian 2. Italian cooking
ISBN 0-688-15410-7

LC 98-2949

This book contains recipes that "are unusual, not to be
found in the average Italian cookbook, and Bastianich's considerable knowledge and experience, as well as her enthusiasm, are evident throughout." Libr J

Lidia's Italian-American kitchen; by Lidia
Matticchio Bastianich; photographs by Christopher
Hirsheimer. Knopf 2001 xxvi, 432p il $35 **641.59**
1. Cookery, American 2. Cookery, Italian 3. Italian
cooking
ISBN 0-375-41150-X

LC 2001-45009

"Bastianich has a warm, engaging style, and she's a
teacher as well as a chef: throughout, she provides thoughtful head-notes and sidebars along with useful boxes on
cooking with wine, 'resting' soup, and other such practicalities." Libr J

Bayless, Rick

Rick Bayless's Mexican kitchen; capturing the
vibrant flavors of a world-class cuisine. [by] Rick
Bayless with Deann Groen Bayless and JeanMarie
Brownson; photographs by Maria Robledo; illustrations by John Sandford. Scribner 1996 448p il
$35
641.59
1. Mexican cooking
ISBN 0-684-80006-3

LC 96-218444

This cookbook "includes more than 200 tantalizing recipes and is packed with information on Mexican ingredients
and cooking techniques, regional cuisine, and history. . . .
A serious guide to an often underestimated cuisine, this is
important as both a reference and a cookbook." Libr J
Includes bibliographical references

Child, Julia

Julia and Jacques cooking at home; by Julia
Child and Jacques Pepin, with David Nussbaum.
Knopf 1999 430p il $40
641.59
1. Cookery, French 2. French cooking
ISBN 0-375-40431-7

LC 98-32418

A companion volume to the PBS series. "For each show,
the two chefs started out with ideas and ingredients but no
set recipes, so they improvised as they went along, cooking
a lot of their favorite traditional dishes and coming up with
new ones as well. . . . Dozens of boxes throughout the text
provide information on a wide variety of topics." Libr J

Harris, Jessica B.

The **Africa** cookbook; tastes of a continent. Simon & Schuster 1998 382p il $27
641.59
1. African cooking 2. Cookery, African
ISBN 0-684-80275-9

LC 98-38882

The author begins with an "introductory section that provides history, . . . background on the four general divisions
of the continent, and a very good glossary of ingredients and
equipment. Recipes are organized by course, with country
of origin listed for each, and headnotes offer context as well
as useful tips. Harris writes well, and her accounts of various visits and encounters are particularly readable. With few
other cookbooks available even on specific African cuisines,
her ambitious new book is unique." Libr J
Includes bibliographical references

Hazan, Marcella

★ **Essentials** of classic Italian cooking; illustrated by Karin Kretschmann. Knopf 1992 688p il
$30
641.59
1. Italian cooking
ISBN 0-394-58404-X

LC 92-52954

A guide to the products, techniques and dishes of classic
Italian cooking. Regional specialities are dealt with at length.
This "could readily assume the mantle of the definitive
resource for Italian cuisine." Booklist

Kennedy, Diana

The **essential** cuisines of Mexico. Potter 2000
526p $35
641.59
1. Cookery, Mexican 2. Mexican cooking
ISBN 0-609-60355-8

LC 00-23156

The author has gathered "the recipes from her first cookbook, the groundbreaking Cuisines of Mexico (1972), as
well its two successors, The Tortilla Book (1975) and Mexican Regional Cooking (1978) . . . in this new collection.
She's revised the recipes and simplified some, and there are
also 30 or so new recipes. Kennedy's books became classics
long ago; this compilation of her early works is an essential
purchase." Libr J
Includes bibliographical references

Kochilas, Diane

The **glorious** foods of Greece. Morrow 2000
496p map $40   **641.59**
  1. Cookery, Greek 2. Food habits -- Greece 3. Greek
cooking
  ISBN 0-688-15457-3

LC 00-28158
This cookbook includes over 400 recipes from various
"regions, starting with the Peloponnesus and the Ionian Islands, moving on to Macedonia, the islands of the Aegean,
and Crete, and finishing up in the city of Athens. . . . Kochilas also provides extensive historical background, cultural as
well as culinary, along with detailed descriptions and explanations of ingredients." Libr J
  Includes bibliographical references and index

Lewis, Edna

The **gift** of Southern cooking; recipes and revelations from two great Southern cooks. by Edna
Lewis and Scott Peacock. Knopf 2003   352p il
$29.95   **641.59**
  1. Cookery, American -- Southern style 2. Southern
cooking
  ISBN 0-375-40035-4

LC 2002-73153
"If you care—and I mean really care—about coleslaw,
pan-fried chicken, trout, . . . greens simmered in pork stock
and Southern-style ketchups, relishes and vinegars, this is a
book you shouldn't be without." N Y Times Book Rev

Roden, Claudia

The **new** book of Middle Eastern food; rev ed;
Knopf 2000 513p il $35   **641.59**
  1. Cookery, Middle Eastern 2. Middle Eastern cooking
  ISBN 0-375-40506-2

LC 00-708864
This volume "includes 800 recipes and variations, as
well as historical background, an introduction to essential
ingredients and regional dietary practices, folktales, and a
vast amount of other information." Libr J
  Includes bibliographical references

Shimbo, Hiroko

The **Japanese** kitchen; 250 recipes in a traditional spirit. illustrations by Rodica Prato. Harvard
Common Press 2000 512p il hardcover o.p. pa
$21.95   **641.59**
  1. Cookery, Japanese 2. Japanese cooking
  ISBN 1-55832-176-4; 1-55832-177-2 pa

LC 00-33505
The author provides a "guide to equipment, techniques,
and ingredients, followed by a wide-ranging selection of
recipes of all sorts. There are both the home-style dishes
she grew up on and more elaborate ones for special occasions, as well as the traditional Japanese classics, with her
own touches, of course, and innovative new recipes. . . . An
essential purchase." Libr J

Zanger, Mark H.

The **American** history cookbook. Greenwood
Press 2003 xxiii, 459p il pa $29.95   **641.59**
  1. Cooking
  ISBN 1-57356-376-5

LC 2002-69608
"This book uses historical commentary and recipes to
trace the history of American cooking from the first European contact with Native Americans to the 1970s. Each of 50
chronologically arranged topical chapters contain 500-1,000
words of general commentary followed by descriptions and
. . . step-by-step instructions for 3-4 recipes. The recipes are
drawn from a wide variety of historical cookbooks and other
historical sources." Publisher's note
  Includes bibliographical references

641.6   Cooking specific materials

Aidells, Bruce

The **complete** meat cookbook; a juicy and autho-
rative guide to selecting, seasoning, and cooking today's beef, pork, lamb, and veal. {by} Bruce Aidelle
and Denis Kelly; photographs by Beatriz Da Costa;
illustrations by Mary De Palma. Houghton Mifflin
1998 604p il $35   **641.6**
  1. Cookery (Meat) 2. Cooking -- Meat
  ISBN 0-618-13512-X

LC 98-28216
"More than 230 recipes, many with several variations,
are presented along with charts and illustrations to help the
reader understand different types of meat." Libr J

Brody, Jane E.

★ **Jane** Brody's good seafood book; by Jane E.
Brody with Richard Flaste; illustrations by Pat Stewart. Norton 1994 577p il $27.50   **641.6**
  1. Cooking -- Fish 2. Cooking -- Seafood 3. Low fat
diet 4. Seafood
  ISBN 0-393-03687-1

LC 94-16482
"This is a more than usually comprehensive, conscientious and trustworthy cookbook." Publ Wkly

Cameron, Angus

The **L.L.** Bean game and fish cookbook; by An-
gus Cameron and Judith Jones; illustrations by Bill
Elliott. Random House 1983 475p il $25.95 **641.6**
  1. Cooking -- Fish 2. Cooking -- Game 3. Cooking
-- Game and game birds
  ISBN 0-394-51191-3

LC 82-15089
"With handsome wildlife and botanical drawings by Bill
Elliott, the book was written by two experts and is complete
and comprehensive." Christ Sci Monit

Cole, Tyson

Uchi: the cookbook; by Tyson Cole and Jessica Dupuy; foreword by Lance Armstrong. Umaso Publishing 2011 268p $39.95   **641.6**

1. Cooking -- Seafood 2. Japanese cooking 3. Sushi

ISBN 978-0-292-77129-1; 0-292-77129-0

"Every now and then a cookbook comes along that is such a great read and has such dazzling photography that I can't put it down. Uchi, the Cookbook is one of those." Texas Monthly

Cook's Illustrated (Periodical)

The **best** chicken recipes; by the editors of Cook's illustrated; photography, Keller + Keller, Carl Tremblay, and Daniel J. Van Ackere; illustrations, John Burgoyne. America's Test Kitchen 2008 422p il $35   **641.6**

1. Cooking -- Poultry

ISBN 978-1-933615-23-3; 1-933615-23-0

This volume "offers more than 300 recipes for chicken, along with a primer called 'Chicken 101,' information on techniques (including step-by-step illustrations), and ratings of equipment and ingredients." Libr J

Corson, Trevor

The **zen** of fish; the story of sushi, from Samurai to supermarket. HarperCollins Publishers 2007 372p $24.95   **641.6**

1. Cookery (Fish) 2. Cooking -- Fish 3. Sushi

ISBN 978-0-06-088350-8; 0-06-088350-2

LC 2006-52964

"The book details sushi's origins as a means of preserving old fish, its transformation into a kind of Japanese fast food in the 19th century, and its journey to the U.S. in the mid-20th century. It provides rich details into the science behind everything from the process of making sushi rice to what makes salmon taste so good. It's also a character study of the chefs and chefs-in-training at the California Sushi Academy, the first culinary school in the country devoted solely to sushi. 'Zen' focuses on Kate Murray, a young apprentice learning the traditionally male-dominated trade from some tough teachers. Readers learn the art of sushi right alongside Murray and her fellow students; it's a lot more than just raw fish and rice." Bangor Daily News

Includes bibliographical references

Culinary Institute of America

Vegetables; recipes and techniques from the world's premier culinary college. the Culinary Institute of America; photography by Ben Fink. Lebhar-Friedman Books 2007 293p il $40 **641.6**

1. Cooking -- Vegetables

ISBN 978-0-86730-918-8; 0-8673-0918-0

LC 2007-298057

Includes "over 150 recipes for soups, appetizers, salads, entrees, side dishes, and a chapter devoted to sauces and relishes made from vegetables or perfect to serve with vegetables. Accompanied by 75 full-color photos." Publisher's note

Grescoe, Taras

Bottomfeeder; how to eat ethically in a world of van-

ishing seafood. Bloomsbury USA 2008 327p $24.99; pa $16 **641.6**

1. Conservation of natural resources 2. Cookery (Seafood) 3. Cooking -- Seafood 4. Eating (Philosophy) 5. Marine resources 6. Marine resources conservation 7. Seafood

ISBN 978-1-59691-225-0; 1-59691-225-1; 978-1-59691-625-8 pa; 1-59691-625-7 pa

LC 2007-49843

The author, a food and travel writer, presents an account of his experiences eating fish and seafood around the world and looks at the ecological ramifications of our diet. He argues that we need to redesign our relationship with seafood.

This is "a comprehensive, lively and illuminating guide." Nation

Includes bibliographical references

Issenberg, Sasha

The **sushi** economy; globalization and the making of a modern delicacy. Gotham 2007 xxiv, 323p hardcover o.p. pa $15   **641.6**

1. Cookery (Fish) 2. Cooking -- Fish 3. Sushi

ISBN 978-1-59240-294-6; 1-59240-294-1; 978-1-59240-363-9 pa; 1-59240-363-8 pa

LC 2007-3927

This "book reveals the complex web of commerce, culture, and culinary expertise that hauls fish from the sea, ships it around the world, and delivers it artfully to the plate. Sprinkled throughout with fascinating character studies of the many buyers, importers, sushi chefs, restaurateurs, critics, and diners who make the wheels turn, this work is solidly rooted in place—allowing one to tour four continents slowly. It makes enjoying sushi not only a delight for the palate but also a thought-provoking repast for the mind." Libr J

Includes bibliographical references

Kafka, Barbara

★ **Vegetable** love; a book for cooks. [by] Barbara Kafka with Christopher Styler; photographs by Christina Cornish. Artisan 2005 708p il $35 **641.6**

1. Cooking -- Vegetables 2. Vegetables

ISBN 1-57965-168-2

LC 2005-47818

The author "has triumphed with an outstanding, indispensable cookbook that not only summons the reader to get into the kitchen and cook but also constitutes a valuable and comprehensive reference tool." Booklist

Includes bibliographical references

Lobel, Stanley

The **meat** bible; all you need to know about meat and poultry from America's master butchers. by Stanley Lobel ... [et al.]; with Mary Goodbody and David Whiteman; photographs by Lucy Schaeffer. Chronicle Books 2009 319p il $40   **641.6**

1. Cooking -- Meat 2. Cooking -- Poultry

ISBN 978-0-8118-5826-7; 0-8118-5826-X

LC 2008-33441

"Recipes number 135, well photographed and indexed." Publ Wkly

Moonen, Rick

Fish without a doubt; the cook's essential companion. [by] Rick Moonen and Roy Finamore; photographs by Ben Fink. Houghton Mifflin Co. 2008
496p il $35   **641.6**
   1. Cooking -- Fish 2. Cooking -- Seafood
   ISBN 978-0-618-53119-6; 0-618-53119-X
                       LC 2007-52084
In this cookbook that covers the preparing of sustainable fish, the authors "show how to clean, bone, and portion both finfish and shellfish. Recipes are organized by cooking method—broiling, poaching, roasting, grilling, steaming, [and] frying. . . . Succeeding chapters cover such fish basics as chowders, fish cakes, and salads. . . . Both the book's organization and its comprehensive coverage make this a necessary addition to any cookbook collections." Booklist

Peterson, James

Meat; a kitchen education. Ten Speed Press 2010 326p il $35 **641.6**
   1. Cooking -- Meat
   ISBN 978-1-58008-992-0; 1-58008-992-5
                       LC 2010-21759
"Though his introduction addresses vegans, admonishing all to 'follow your conscience' about the consumption of animals, the rest of [Peterson's] text advocates only the use of the best lamb, rabbit, beef, and chicken available. Thoroughly review the first two chapters; in them Peterson sets forth the proper ways to sauté, grill, braise, and poach (among other methods), illustrates such fundamental preparation methods as julienning a leek and sectioning a turnip, and identifies the flavors associated with different international cuisines. Next, the fun: 175 recipes and, more important, instructions and sidebars to ensure that expensive roasts and whole birds emerge with great taste." Booklist

Schatzker, Mark

Steak; one man's search for the world's tastiest piece of beef. Viking 2010 290p $25.95; ebook $12.99 **641.6**
   1. Beef 2. Cookery (Beef) 3. Cookery, International
   ISBN 978-0-670-02181-9; 0-670-02181-4; 978-1-101-18956-6 ebook
                       LC 2009-50994
"Schatzker allows his obsession with the ideal steak to propel him across the face of the earth in search of that one sizzling slab of perfection. Starting in Texas' ranch country, he looks at cattle production in Scotland, France, Italy, Japan, and Argentina, each of which trumpets the superiority of its particular beef. In order to bring some objectivity to his evaluation, Schatzker devises a detailed, comprehensive list of steak qualities that rivals wine-tasting standards. . . . Meat lovers will learn a lot from this book, which upends a few current beliefs and prejudices." Booklist
   Includes bibliographical references

Schlesinger, Chris

How to cook meat; [by] Chris Schlesinger and John Willoughby. Morrow 2000 466p il hardcover o.p. pa $24.95   **641.6**
   1. Cookery (Meat) 2. Cooking -- Meat
   ISBN 0-06-050771-3 pa
                       LC 00-62482

This cookbook includes 200 recipes for beef, veal, lamb and pork dishes. "Most every recipe is accompanied by useful sidebars that detail the cut of meat to use, offer alternative cuts and even tell you how the dish holds up as a leftover. With humor, clarity and expertise, these two renowned food writers have created a requisite text for any serious meat lover." Publ Wkly

Seaver, Barton

For cod and country. Sterling Epicure 2011 294p il $30   **641.6**
   1. Cooking -- Seafood
   ISBN 978-1-4027-7775-2
A "a user's manual for any seafood lover who wants to eat sustainably—and very well. Seaver's book vibrates with personality, practical advice, photographs (both evocative and how-to), and stovetop wisdom: never be shy about adding butter, but go easy on the black pepper. With the help of step-by-step photographs, he demonstrates seafood-savvy techniques, everything from how to fillet a bass to how to open an oyster without severing one of your arteries. He also provides a list of substitutions for overexploited species: Use Pacific cod in place of Atlantic cod; sablefish instead of Chilean sea bass; squid instead of octopus." Atlantic

Vassallo, Jody

Vegetable basics; 84 recipes illustrated step by step. photographs by Clive Bozzard-Hill. Firefly Books 2010 ca. 300 il pa $24.95   **641.6**
   1. Cooking -- Vegetables
   ISBN 978-1-55407-760-1
"Each recipe is pictured step-by-step with the crisply reductive clarity of a minimalist still life. . . . [The author] identifies all sorts of roots, stalks, leaves, pods, and seeds and serves up a fusion of ethnic recipes, from Onion Flan and Panzanella to Tzatziki and Chocolate Zucchini Cake." Libr J

Vinton, Sherri Brooks

Put 'em up! a comprehensive home preserving guide for the creative cook, from drying and freezing to canning and pickling. Storey Pub. 2010 303p il pa $19.95   **641.6**
   1. Cooking -- Fruit 2. Cooking -- Vegetables 3. Fruit -- Preservation 4. Vegetables -- Preservation
   ISBN 978-1-60342-546-9
                       LC 2010009609
"Vinton provides an excellent introduction to multiple food preservation methods. Organized first by technique, then by fruit or vegetable, this volume contains many easy-to-follow options for prepared and preserved foods." Libr J
   Includes bibliographical references

Wells, Patricia

Vegetable harvest; vegetables at the center of the plate. William Morrow 2007 324p il $34.95 **641.6**
   1. Cooking -- Vegetables
   ISBN 978-0-06-075244-6; 0-06-075244-0
                       LC 2006-43723
"After surveying the bounty of her backyard garden, Wells became inspired to build meals around vegetables rather than starting with meat, fish or poultry. She tripled the

number she served at each meal and tried different cooking methods, looking for the best-tasting, most wholesome ways of cooking each type. She includes nutritional information and an equipment list for each recipe, and selectively offers wine suggestions, translations of French food idioms, and nuggets of folklore connected to the dish or main ingredient. . . . This collection is highly recommended for cooks and gardeners alike." Publ Wkly

Werlin, Laura

Laura Werlin's cheese essentials; an insider's guide to buying and serving cheese: with 50 recipes. photographs by Maren Caruso. Stewart, Tabori & Chang 2007 272p il $24.95 **641.6**
    1. Cheese
    ISBN 978-1-58479-627-5

LC 2007-15459

This is an "introduction to cheese—tasting it, buying it, storing it, and cooking with it. An introductory section describes the basics of cheese making, offers empowering tips for navigating the cheese counter, and lists the basic vocabulary for cheese tasting. The majority of the volume is divided into sections for each of the eight styles of cheese, from mild, fresh cheeses to strong-flavored washed-rind varieties. . . . This well-organized, stylish, timely, and indispensable guide belongs in every cook's library." Booklist

Wisconsin Milk Marketing Board

The **great** big cheese cookbook; foreword by James Robson; Wisconsin Milk Marketing Board. Running Press 2010 480p il $22 **641.6**
    1. Cooking -- Cheese
    ISBN 978-0-7624-3497-8

LC 2008-921274

"Compiled by the Wisconsin Milk Marketing Board, this hefty book includes information on choosing, handling, storing, cutting, and cooking cheese, in addition to more than 300 recipes—like Miami Spice Napoleons with Wisconsin Queso Fresco Cheese and Five Cheese Macaroni—from 60 chefs. A list of cheese substitutes, chosen based on flavors and textures, is provided." Libr J

Wright, Clifford A.

Some like it hot; spicy favorites from the world's hot zones. Harvard Common Press 2005 xxv, 453p $32.95; pa $18.95 **641.6**
    1. Cooking 2. Spices
    ISBN 1-55832-268-X; 1-55832-269-8 pa

LC 2005-4953

The author's "assembly of recipes calling for hot peppers originates from tropical countries, but there are some exceptions to that rule. He inventories Oaxacan mole, Korean kimchi, Thai curries, Louisiana gumbo, Jamaican jerk, Texan chili con carne, African piripiri, and Bengali fish stew. . . . Devotees of spicy cooking will enjoy every fiery mouthful." Booklist

Vegetables from an Italian garden; season-by-season recipes. Phaidon 2011 431p il $39.95 **641.6**
    1. Cooking -- Vegetables 2. Vegetable gardening
    ISBN 978-0-7148-6117-3; 0-7148-6117-0

This book, assembled by the editors at Phaidon Press, "is divided into four chapters, following the four seasons. Each chapter has its own colored ribbon, which makes it easy to go to the season you want to cook from. . . . Each season starts with an explanation of the vegetables available that season. There is a short history of the vegetable, then an explanation of how to select and buy them, along with stunning photos by Andy Sewell. Following this is a description of how and when to plant these vegetables in your own garden. The scrumptious recipes are taken from all parts of Italy. Well written and clear, they let you jump in and start cooking." Super Chef

641.7   Specific cooking processes and techniques

Child, Julia

Baking with Julia; based on the PBS series hosted by Julia Child. written by Dorie Greenspan; photographs by Gentl & Hyers. Morrow 1996 480p il $40 **641.7**
    1. Baking
    ISBN 0-688-14657-0

LC 96-23061

"The 200 recipes are organized as a course in baking, with an early, energetic section on the basic batters and doughs for cakes and pastries. The book moves on to recipes of varying degrees of complexity. . . . But the book's success is due to more than organization: the text never misses a chance to explain, expand and entertain." N Y Times Book Rev

Includes bibliographical references

Cook's Illustrated (Periodical)

Best skillet recipes; a best recipe classic. by the editors of Cook's Illustrated; photography, Keller + Keller, Carl Tremblay, and Daniel J. Van Ackere; illustrations, John Burgoyne. America's Test Kitchen 2009 335p il $35 **641.7**
    1. Cooking
    ISBN 978-1-933615-41-7; 1-933615-41-9

This cookbook celebrates the "versatility of that ordinary workhorse, the 12-inch skillet. An indispensable tool for eggs, pan-seared meats and sautéed vegetables, the skillet can also be used for stovetop-to-oven dishes such as All-American Mini Meatloaves; layered dishes such as tamale pie and Tuscan bean casserole; and even desserts such as hot fudge pudding cake. . . . Whether or not you properly appreciate your skillet, this book will at least teach you to wield it gracefully." Publ Wkly

Farmer, Fannie Merritt

The **Fannie** Farmer baking book; illustrated by Lauren Jarrett. Knopf 1984 624p il hardcover o.p. pa $12.99 **641.7**
    1. Baking
    ISBN 0-517-14829-3

LC 84-47862

"Separate chapters cover pies and tarts, cookies, cakes, yeast breads, quick breads, and crackers in encyclopedic detail with brisk but reassuring professionalism. Many of the 800 recipes are standard favorites." Libr J

Schlesinger, Chris

The **thrill** of the grill; techniques, recipes & down-home barbecue. {by} Chris Schlesinger & John Willoughby, line drawings by Laura Hartman Maestro; photography by Vincent Lee. Morrow 1990 395p il $30; pa $17.95 **641.7**

1. Barbecue cooking
ISBN 0-688-08832-5; 0-06-008449-9 pa
LC 89-77522

The authors present a collection of recipes as well as advice about grilling and barbecuing food.

Schlesinger "favors what he calls 'equatorial cuisine,' and Caribbean, Mexican, and Southeast Asian influences are evident in his recipes. His grilled dishes are full-flavored and often hot and spicy." Libr J

Stevens, Molly

All about roasting; a new approach to a classic art. photographs by Quentin Bacon; wine pairings by Tim Gaiser. W. W. Norton 2011 573p il $35 **641.7**

1. Roasting (Cooking)
ISBN 978-0-393-06526-8
LC 2011022692

The author "begins with a 45-page introduction to the art and science of roasting that should be required reading for anyone in possession of a chunk of meat and an oven. Topics covered include the differences in employing high versus low heat, the reasons to rest meat before carving, the joys of convection ovens, and why fat is always a critical component. Next come 150 recipes divided into chapters on beef, pork, poultry, fish, and vegetables.... [This] is a compelling collection that drives home the difference between a chef merely showing off some recipes and a teacher exploring her craft." Publ Wkly

Includes bibliographical references

641.8 Cooking specific kinds of dishes and preparing beverages

Alexander, William

52 loaves; one man's relentless pursuit of truth, meaning, and a perfect crust. Algonquin Books of Chapel Hill 2010 339p il $23.95 **641.8**

1. Bread
ISBN 978-1-56512-583-4
LC 2009-49656

Charts the author's attempts to bake the perfect loaf of bread, including growing, harvesting, and milling his own wheat.

"Bakers will delight in his often humorous mission as he relates leaving out salt, growing his own wheat, discovering parchment paper, and splashing water into the oven in an effort to create steam.... This humorous memoir is recommended for anyone who has ever tried to bake a loaf." Libr J

Includes bibliographical references

Anderson, Pam

Perfect one-dish dinners; all you need for easy get-togethers. photographs by Judd Pilossof. Houghton Mifflin Harcourt 2010 266p il $32 **641.8**

1. Entertaining 2. One-dish cooking
ISBN 978-0-547-19595-7
LC 2010-21447

This is an "accessible, engaging collection of meals based around a singular dish. Grouped into four sections—summer salads and grilled platters; casseroles; the roasting pan; and stews—Anderson smartly mixes classics like Osso Bucco, Paella, and Lasagna with riffs on standards like Coq Au Vin (here with white wine and spring vegetables) and a Spanish beef stew (with bell peppers, chickpeas, saffron, paprika, and orange).... Whether readers are new to cooking or simply looking for new ideas for meals, Anderson's winning collection is sure to encourage and inspire." Publ Wkly

Andres, Jose

Tapas; a taste of Spain in America. [by] José Andrés with Richard Wolffe. Clarkson Potter 2005 256p il $35 **641.8**

1. Appetizers 2. Spanish cooking
ISBN 1-4000-5359-5
LC 2004-27466

The author presents some of the small-plate dishes "he serves at his tapas restaurants, including traditional favorites recreated with American ingredients.... Recipes are organized by ingredient, from olives and olive oil to citrus to fish, shellfish, and meat, and they are mouth-watering: Oven-Roasted Potatoes and Oyster Mushrooms, for example, or Lobster with Pimentón and Olive Oil." Libr J

Includes bibliographical references

Bauer, Jeni Britton

Jeni's splendid ice creams at home. Artisan 2011 217p il $23.95 **641.8**

1. Ice cream, ices, etc.
ISBN 978-1-57965-436-8; 1-57965-436-3
LC 2010-39453

"This inspiring collection of seasonal ice cream recipes from Ohio-based ice cream whiz Bauer stands apart for its creative, unconventional flavors like Sweet Basil & Honeyed Pine Nut and Sweet Potato with Torched Marshmallows." Libr J

Beard, James

Beard on bread; drawings by Karl Stuecklen. Knopf 1973 230p il hardcover o.p. pa $15 **641.8**

1. Bread
ISBN 0-679-75504-7 pa

"An inclusive guide to the preparation of a variety of breads with recipes for coffee cakes, rolls, flat breads, fried cakes.... The recipes included are those Beard considers the best from around the world which can be made in a U.S. kitchen." Booklist

Beranbaum, Rose Levy

The **cake** bible; edited by Maria D. Guarnaschelli; photographs by Vincent Lee; foreword by Maida Heatter. Morrow 1988 555p il **641.8**

1. Cake

ISBN 0-688-04402-6; 978-0-688-04402-2

LC 8801369

This collection of cake recipes includes "discussions on ingredients and equipment and concludes with a . . . section on the chemistry of cake baking and on making . . . professional wedding cakes." (Libr J) Bibliography. Index.

Black, Keda

Sauce basics; 87 recipes illustrated step by step. photographs by Frédéric Lucano. Firefly Books 2010 87 [i.e. 176] il pa $24.95 **641.8**

1. Sauces

ISBN 978-1-55407-761-8

"Each recipe is pictured step-by-step with the crisply reductive clarity of a minimalist still life. . . . [The author] moves beyond the classic sauces to illustrate prep techniques for salad dressings, condiments, foams, and sweet dessert sauces such as coulis and creams, then puts them to purpose with recipes like Roast Beef with Apple Horseradish Sauce, Whole-Wheat Spaghetti Arrabiata, and Crepes with Caramel and Whipped Cream." Libr J

Blakeslee, Robert L.

Your time to bake; a first cookbook for the novice baker. by Robert L. Blakeslee. Square One Publishers 2012 384 p. (hardback) $29.95 **641.8**

1. Baking

ISBN 9780757003554

LC 2011014622

In this cookbook, [Robert L.] Blakeslee includes [step by step photo instructions, with a finished shot of each recipe. . . . He provides recipes for every simple sweet treat imaginable. . . . Explaining that baking is more about chemistry, "Blakeslee . . . discusses important baking variables and how to control them,i with helpful tips: measuring ingredients exactly and making sure ingredients such as eggs and butter are the correct temperature. Also . . . [included] are sections on essential items needed for baking--such as different flours, sugars, spices and cheeses--important equipment, and baking terms from A to Z. . . . [T]here are more than 150 recipes . . . and a final chapter on decorating cookies, tarts, and cupcakes and making fondant." (Publishers Weekly)

Colicchio, Tom

'wichcraft; craft a sandwich into a meal--and a meal into a sandwich. [by] Tom Colicchio with Sisha Ortúzar; text by Rhona Silverbush; photographs by Bill Bettencourt. Clarkson Potter/Publishers 2009 208p il $27.50 **641.8**

1. Sandwiches

ISBN 978-0-609-61051-0

LC 2008-27803

The authors offer "an entire cookbook featuring the sandwiches served at . . . [their] New York restaurant, 'wichcraft. . . . This book's table of contents alone will have grab-and-go eaters and sophisticated gastronomes alike salivating." Booklist

Corriher, Shirley

BakeWise; the hows and whys of successful baking with over 200 magnificent recipes. [by] Shirley O. Corriher. Scribner 2008 532p $40 **641.8**

1. Baking

ISBN 978-1-4165-6078-4; 1-4165-6078-5

LC 2008-32681

This "collection of more than 200 recipes offers amateur and expert bakers alike clear, numbered steps and a plethora of information on ingredients, equipment and method. Invaluable troubleshooting sections solve pesky problems on everything from pale and crumbly cookies to fallen soufflés. . . . Astute references to a variety of chefs, cookbook authors and restaurants add a knowing punch to this solid collection that's sure to please bakers of all skill levels." Publ Wkly

Crocker, Betty

★ **Betty** Crocker cookie book; rev ed; Wiley 2003 xxix, 322p il $22.95 **641.8**

1. Cookies

ISBN 0-7645-3940-X

LC 2003-270127

This book features "over 240 cookie favorites, from heirloom showstoppers to contemporary treats . . . [including] everything from chocolate chip cookies to brownies, oatmeal cookies to date bars and more." Publisher's note

Daley, Regan

In the sweet kitchen; the definitive baker's companion. Artisan 2001 692p il hardcover o.p. pa $24.95 **641.8**

1. Baking

ISBN 1-57965-208-5; 1-57965-427-4 pa

LC 2001-41289

"While other books include some details on baking ingredients and tools as part of their introduction to the craft, . . . [this] is the definitive guide to all the equipment, techniques, and ingredients a baker uses." Libr J

Includes bibliographical references

DeMasco, Karen

The **craft** of baking; cakes, cookies, & other sweets with ideas for inventing your own. [by] Karen DeMasco & Mindy Fox; photographs by Ellen Silverman. Clarkson Potter Publishers 2009 256p il $35 **641.8**

1. Baking 2. Cake 3. Candy 4. Cookies 5. Desserts

ISBN 978-0-307-40810-5; 0-307-40810-8

"In the first sections, [DeMarco] covers ingredients and techniques accessible even to novice bakers. Then come her 'new modern-day treats,' created with 'traditional recipes and familiar home baking techniques,' e.g., Lemon Olive Cake (an interesting variation on the traditional lemon cake using butter and extra virgin olive oil). Sources are listed for hard-to-find items. Owing to DeMasco's well-respected culinary pedigree, home bakers will want this." Libr J

Desaulniers, Marcel

Death by chocolate cakes; an astonishing array of chocolate enchantment. recipes with Brett Bailey and Kelly Bailey; photography by Duane Winfield. Morrow 2000 216p il $35　　**641.8**

1. Cake 2. Cookery (Chocolate) 3. Cooking -- Chocolate

ISBN 0-688-16297-5

LC 00-56247

This "cookbook features indulgent showstoppers, from Happy All the Time Cakes to Excessively Expressive Espresso Ecstasy, each one shown in a full-page color photograph. Although many of the recipes are complicated, instructions are detailed and clear; there are no headnotes per se to introduce these creations, but 'The Chef's Touch' section at the end of each recipe provides tips and some background." Libr J

Includes bibliographical references

Fowler, Damon Lee

Damon Lee Fowler's new southern baking; classic flavors for today's cook. photographs by Ann Stratton. Simon & Schuster 2005 360p il $26 **641.8**

1. Baking 2. Southern cooking

ISBN 0-7432-5058-3

LC 2005-51591

The author presents an "overview of Southern baking from historical, cultural and social perspectives. . . . Damon traces the influences of Southern mamas; African-American domestic workers and cooks; English, German and French settlers; and Native Americans in his introduction, while his chapter openers delve deeper into specifics, distinguishing between, say, soft winter wheat and red summer wheat and the different flours derived from them. . . . This cookbook is a treat, equally satisfying to cook from or to read." Publ Wkly

Includes bibliographical references

Haedrich, Ken

★ **Pie**: 300 tried-and-true recipes for delicious homemade pie. The Harvard Common Press 2004 639p il $37.95; pa $24.95　　**641.8**

1. Baking

ISBN 1-558-32253-1; 1-558-32254-X pa

LC 2004-3635

Haedrich's "zeal and solid expertise make this book a worthy addition to the baker's bookshelf." Publ Wkly

Heatter, Maida

Maida Heatter's book of great desserts; drawings by Toni Evins. Andrew McMeel 1999 xxxii, 528p il $26.95　　**641.8**

1. Desserts

ISBN 0-8362-7861-5

LC 98-45993

This cookbook features nearly 300 dessert recipes for both light and rich desserts including Queen Mother's Cake, Mushroom Meringues, and East 62nd Street Lemon Cake.

Hensperger, Beth

The **best** quick breads; 150 recipes for muffins, scones, shortcakes, gingerbreads, cornbreads, coffee-

cakes, and more. Beth Hensperger. Harvard Common Press 2000 256p pa $22.95　　**641.8**

1. Bread

ISBN 1-55832-171-3

LC 00-36962

This book includes about 150 recipes. "In addition to quick loaves, both sweet and savory, there are waffles, dumplings, biscuits, popovers, and a variety of other easy baked goods, along with some tasty accompaniments, such as the Fruit Salsa for her Hopi Blue Corn Hotcakes." Libr J

Medrich, Alice

Chewy gooey crispy crunchy melt-in-your-mouth cookies. Artisan Books 2010 384p il $25.95 **641.8**

1. Cookies

ISBN 978-1-57965-397-2

LC 2010-19491

"Medrich presents a compendium of exciting and enticing cookie recipes that reflects every aspect of our widening culinary landscape. . . . The recipes are organized by texture, hence the title, but there's also a section grouping cookies into categories like those containing whole grains, those that keep at least two weeks, ridiculously quick and easy cookies, and cookies to make with kids. This book has redesigned and reframed the often-overlooked cookie and is a boon to the modern, conscious baker." Publ Wkly

Mullins, Paul R.

Glazed America; a history of the doughnut. University Press of Florida 2008 200p il $24.95 **641.8**

1. Doughnuts

ISBN 978-0-8130-3238-2; 0-8130-3238-5

LC 2008-2544

"Mullins' informative and entertaining book discusses the history of doughnut production, marketing and consumption from antiquity to the present day, focusing primarily on how that history reflects many 20th century historical and social patterns. His examination of the relationship between doughnut marketing and demand provides insight into North American culture and society." Univ Press Books for Public and Second Sch Libr, 2009

Includes bibliographical references

Mushet, Cindy

★ The **art** and soul of baking; [by] Sur La Table with Cindy Mushet; foreword by Alice Medrich; photography by Maren Caruso. Andrews McMeel Pub. 2008 454p il $40　　**641.8**

1. Baking

ISBN 978-0-7407-7334-1; 0-7407-7334-8

LC 2008-8232

This guide to baking "covers both sweet and savory baking. . . . Two lengthy introductory chapters cover techniques, equipment, and ingredients, and dozens of sidebars on 'Tips for Success' and 'What the Pros Know' offer further helpful insider advice. . . . Mushet's style is engaging and never intimidating. Essential." Libr J

Pasta, atlante dei prodotti tipici/English

Encyclopedia of pasta; translated by Maureen B. Fant; with a foreword by Carol Field. University of California Press 2009 xxi, 374p il map $29.95 **641.8**
1. Cookery (Pasta) 2. Cookery, Italian 3. Cooking -- Pasta products 4. Pasta products 5. Pasta products -- Encyclopedias 6. Reference books
ISBN 978-0-520-25522-7
LC 2009-10522
This book provides "a complete history of pasta in Italy, showcasing more than 300 types of pasta—from bucatini and gnocchetti to tortellini and ziti. . . . Each entry is nicely displayed in a box and includes an overview of each pasta type: the primary ingredients, preparation techniques, the different names for each kind of pasta, how it is served, the region where it is found, and the author's remarks. . . . This wonderful resource is destined to become the definitive book on pasta. It succeeds both as a scholarly achievement and as an entertaining and authentic overview of Italian history and geography." Libr J
Includes bibliographical references

Patent, Greg

Baking in America; traditional and contemporary favorites from the past 200 years. Houghton Mifflin 2002 552p il $35 **641.8**
1. Baking
ISBN 0-618-04831-6
"Patent's cookbook will be irresistible to anyone interested in the rich traditions and history of American baking." Libr J

Peters, Colette

Colette's cakes; the art of cake decorating. Little, Brown 1991 163p il $35 **641.8**
1. Cake decorating
ISBN 0-316-70205-6
LC 90-24676
"This is not intended as a cookbook, although recipes for a white as well as a chocolate cake precede instructions for basic cake decorating. The bulk of the guide contains step-by-step directions for assembling four fabulous cake designs that range from an impressive seashell cake to multitiered wedding cakes." Booklist
Includes bibliographical references

Peterson, James

Baking. Ten Speed Press 2009 378p il $40 **641.8**
1. Baking
ISBN 978-1-58008-991-3
"This workhorse of a guidebook . . . is a worthy baking school between covers. . . . The work features over 300 recipes, mostly classics based in the French tradition. The five chapters—Cakes; Pies, Tarts and Pastries; Cookies; Breads, Quick Breads, and Bread-based Desserts; and Custards, Soufflés, Fruit Curds and Mousses—include a comprehensive overview, sidebars on techniques and recipes designed to teach techniques that can be used in more than the recipe listed." Publ Wkly

Pillsbury Co.

★ **Pillsbury** best cookies cookbook; favorite recipes from America's most-trusted kitchens. [by] the Pillsbury Company. Wiley Pub 2003 255p il $22.95 **641.8**
1. Cookies
ISBN 0-7645-8854-0; 978-0-7645-8854-9
This "cookbook includes more than 175 recipes for cookies, brownies, and other bars, from old favorites like Chocolate Chips to new ones like Cherry Poppy Seed Twinks. . . . There are also lots of tips and hints, suggestions to 'Make It Special,' and variations, as well as 'real-time' prep times and nutrition analyses for each recipe." Libr J [review of 1997 edition]

Reistad-Long, Sara

The **big** New York sandwich book; 99 delicious creations from the city's greatest restaurants and chefs. [by[Sara Reistad-Long & Jean Tang. Running Press 2011 272p il pa $23 **641.8**
1. Cooking -- New York (N.Y.) 2. Sandwiches
ISBN 978-0-7624-4048-1; 0-7624-4048-1
LC 2010941021
"One city may seem like a relatively small radius for such a universal edible, but there are a mind-boggling number of countries and cultures represented and creatively mashed up within these pages. . . . Recipes are marked for picnic-friendliness, healthfulness, level of difficulty and, when it's required, extra prep time." Wall Street J

Robertson, Chad

Tartine bread; photographs by Eric Wolfinger. Chronicle Books 2010 304p il $40 **641.8**
1. Bread
ISBN 978-0-8118-7041-2
"This 'baker's guidebook' is divided into four parts: Basic Country Bread; Semolina and Whole-Wheat Breads; Baguettes and Enriched Breads; and Day-Old Bread. Robertson's basic recipe is explained in depth with numbered steps, and consists of making a natural leaven and baking in a cast-iron cooker. The author's passionate tone and tales of baking apprenticeships, along with top-notch step-by-step photos, elevate the title from mere manual to enjoyable read." Publ Wkly

Schreiber, Cory

Rustic fruit desserts; crumbles, buckles, cobblers, pandowdies, and more. [by] Cory Schreiber and Julie Richardson; photography by Sara Remington. Ten Speed Press 2009 164p il $22 **641.8**
1. Cooking -- Fruit 2. Desserts
ISBN 978-1-58008-976-0; 1-58008-976-3
LC 2008-49349
"A seasonal mini-bible that goes beyond basics." N Y Times Book Rev

Tornabene, Wanda

100 ways to be pasta; perfect pasta recipes from Gangivecchio. [by] Wanda and Giovanna Tornabene with Carolynn Carreño. Knopf 2005 182p il $24.95   **641.8**

   1. Cooking -- Pasta products

   ISBN 1-400-04104-X

                        LC 2004-48522

The authors "focus on both traditional and contemporary Sicilian ways of dealing with pasta. . . . Cooks everywhere will find inspiring ideas here to feed both families and guests." Booklist

Vollstedt, Maryana

The **big** book of soups & stews; 262 recipes for serious comfort food. Chronicle Bks. 2001 334p pa $19.95   **641.8**

   1. Soups 2. Stews

   ISBN 0-8118-3056-X

                        LC 2001-28034

These recipes range "from a hearty Beef and Chile Stew with Cornmeal Dumplings to a more sophisticated Shrimp and Scallop Chowder; there are many kid-friendly recipes as well, including several hamburger soups. Some of the recipes are staples (such as a classic Irish Stew), but many busy cooks will find it handy to have such favorites gathered in one place." Libr J

Walter, Carole

Great pies & tarts; over 150 recipes to bake, share, and enjoy. foreword by Arthur Schwartz. Gramercy Books 2006 512p $12.99   **641.8**

   1. Baking

   ISBN 978-0-517-22807-4; 0-517-22807-6

                        LC 2006-41104

"Walter begins with an extensive inventorying and analysis of the ingredients that make up today's pies, from crusts' shortening and flour to the various fruits (and vegetables) that fill them. Detailed instructions for preparing piecrust, that touchstone of home kitchen expertise, follow. . . . A glossary, a listing of mail-order sources, and a comprehensive bibliography ensure that no pie-related topic goes unaddressed." Booklist

Includes bibliographical references

Yosses, Bill

★ The **perfect** finish; special desserts for every occasion. [by] Bill Yosses and Melissa Clark; photographs by Marcus Nilsson. W. W. Norton & Company 2010 286p il $35   **641.8**

   1. Desserts

   ISBN 978-0-393-05953-3

                        LC 2010-6891

The authors "showcase elegant, luscious desserts suitable for a variety of occasions from brunch to potlucks to fancy celebrations. Recipes are well-detailed and easy-to-follow, even for the novice, and potentially unfamiliar techniques or temperamental ingredients such as segmenting oranges, varieties of yeast, making great meringue, and how to avoid crystallizing caramel are highlighted. With flat and chewy chocolate chip cookies, blood orange squares, grand old-fashioned blueberry jelly rolls, and orange-scented olive oil cakes with fleur de sel, there is something for every palate. . . . This book is a must-have for all serious bakers and

the only book those with a passing interest in baking will ever need." Publ Wkly

Zabar, Tracey

One sweet cookie; celebrated chefs share favorite recipes. photography by Ellen Silverman. Rizzoli 2011 191p il $30   **641.8**

   1. Cookies

   ISBN 978-0-8478-3666-6

                        LC 2011927545

"When cookie-obsessed baker Zabar couldn't convince friends to participate in a cookie swap, she orchestrated a virtual exchange, the result of which is this outstanding collection of recipes from more than 50 well-known New York City chefs. . . . [It features] contributions from Dorie Greenspan, Michael Laiskonis, Maury Rubin, Laurent Tourondel, and others." Libr J

Includes bibliographical references

The America's test kitchen family baking book; [by] the editors at America's Test Kitchen; photography, Daniel J. Van Ackere, Carl Tremblay, Keller + Keller. America's Test Kitchen 2008 544p il $34.95   **641.8**

   1. Baking

   ISBN 978-1-933615-22-6; 1-933615-22-2

"Expert bakers and novices scared of baking's requisite exactitude can all learn something from this hefty, all-purpose home baking volume." Publ Wkly

★ Baking illustrated; a best recipe classic. by the editors of Cook's illustrated; illustrations, John Burgoyne; photography, Carl Tremblay, Keller + Keller, Daniel Van Ackere. America's Test Kitchen 2004 515p il $35   **641.8**

   1. Baking

   ISBN 0-936184-75-2

"Test kitchen cooks analyzed brand-name baking ingredients and equipment and . . . make 'best buy' recommendations. . . . The test summaries preceding each recipe include both successes and failures; the resulting recipes (more than 350) cover everything from the simplest quick breads to more complex yeast breads and cookies and pastries. . . . This is the best instructional book on baking this reviewer has seen." Libr J

The Complete book of pasta and noodles; by the editors of Cook's illustrated; preface by Christopher Kimball; illustrations by Judy Love; photographs by Daniel J. van Ackere. Potter 2000 483p il hardcover o.p. pa $19.95   **641.8**

   1. Cooking -- Pasta products

   ISBN 0-609-80930-X pa

                        LC 99-40076

This work brings "together information and recipes covering pasta's worldwide range from North America's beloved macaroni and cheese through Italy's sophisticated sauces, across China's exotic rice noodles, and up to Japan's modest Zen noodles in broth. . . . Content and organization combine to make this a superior cooking reference book for libraries." Booklist

The Gourmet cookie book; the single best recipe from each year 1941-2009. Houghton Mifflin Harcourt 2010 161p il $18 **641.8**
1. Cookies
ISBN 978-0-547-32816-4

LC 2010-18882

This cookbook "features one recipe for every year Gourmet magazine was in business. . . . The recipes are grouped by decade, from the ration-era pluck of the 1940s (honey refrigerator cookies and Scotch oat crunchies), when the magazine was published out of a penthouse in the Plaza Hotel, to the twisted classics of the oughts (cranberry turtle bars and glittering lemon sandwich cookies). The wistful headnotes offer historical insight into our past tastes and aspirations." N Y Times Book Rev

Mix shake stir; cocktails for the home bar: recipes from Danny Meyer's acclaimed New York City restaurants. foreword by Danny Meyer. Little, Brown 2009 223p il $29.99 **641.8**
1. Cocktails
ISBN 978-0-316-04512-4; 0-316-04512-8

LC 2008-934947

Restauranteur Meyers "delivers a terrific collection of 140 tempting recipes for cocktails created by bartenders in his award-winning dining establishments. Included are old favorites like the Ritz as well as new classics like the Winter Mojito, and the book's clear instructions and luscious photographs will inspire even nondrinkers to pick up a cocktail shaker. As a bonus, basic tips on mixing drinks, recipes for simple syrups and garnishes, and a concise collection of recipes for bar snacks are offered." Libr J

The best one-dish suppers; a best recipe classic. by the editors of Cook's Illustrated; photography, Keller + Keller, Carl Tremblay, and Daniel J. Van Ackere; illustrations, John Burgoyne. America's Test Kitchen 2011 342p il $35 **641.8**
1. One-dish cooking 2. Quick and easy cooking
ISBN 978-1-933615-81-3

"This volume presents recipes (180 of them, further clarified by 169 illustrations) for supremely simple meals (including many versions of tempting classics) prepared in one cooking vessel. There are dinners that can be made in just a sheet pan, a single pot, a dutch oven, or a slow cooker, plus stews and chilis, casseroles, and stir-frys. . . . This book could easily become a go-to resource for busy home cooks." Publ Wkly

The golden book of desserts; [project director, Anne McRae; introduction, Carla Bardi; texts, Rachel Lane, Carla Bardi] Barron's 2010 608p il $29.99 **641.8**
1. Desserts
ISBN 978-0-7641-6361-6

LC 2009-940366

"With over 250 recipes such as Strawberry Ice Cream Pie and Chocolate Soufflés, you'll have an arsenal of treats to delight family and friends. . . . Each recipe, written for the experienced baker, includes a full-color photograph and difficulty rating." Libr J

642   Meals and table service

Martha Stewart Living (Periodical)

Great parties; recipes, menus, and ideas for perfect gatherings: the best of Martha Stewart Living. Potter 1997 144p il pa $20 **642**
1. Entertaining
ISBN 0-609-80099-X

LC 97-30271

This describes such parties as a Louisiana lunch, a Polynesian fantasy picnic, an East Hampton garden harvest party, a Vietnamese-Thai feast, and a Harlem soul food brunch, including menus, recipes, and table decorations

Stewart, Martha

★ Martha Stewart's menus for entertaining; photographs by Dana Gallagher; design by Robert Valentine Incorporated. Potter 1994 224p il $30; pa $20 **642**
1. Cooking 2. Entertaining 3. Menus
ISBN 0-517-59099-9; 1-4000-4660-2 pa

LC 94-12930

Full-color photographs accompany step-by-step instructions for preparing 20 complete menus for a variety of gatherings. Over 150 recipes are included as well as tips on table settings and flower arrangements.

643   Housing and household equipment

Becker, Norman

The complete book of home inspection; 3rd ed; McGraw-Hill 2002 289p il pa $19.95 **643**
1. Building inspection -- United States 2. Houses -- Inspection 3. Real property surveys
ISBN 0-07-139125-8

LC 2002-27892

The author "provides the novice homebuilder and buyer with inspection information for roofs, exterior landscaping, plumbing, and electrical, as well as tips on searching for insects and rotting materials. Helpful checklists guide readers in inspecting all parts of a home from the exterior walkway to the interior basement." Libr J

Black & Decker Corp.

The complete guide to finishing basements; step-by-step projects for adding living space without adding on. Creative Pub. International 2009 255p il pa $24.99 **643**
1. Basements 2. Houses -- Remodeling
ISBN 978-1-58923-454-3; 1-58923-454-5

LC 2008-45813

"Thorough and filled from beginning to end with handy reference information, this tome more than adequately demostrates how to evaluate, upgrade, and remodel the . . . basement." Booklist

★ The complete photo guide to home improvement; [created by the editors of Creative Publishing International, Inc., in cooperation with Black &

Decker] Creative Pub. International 2009 560p il
$35　　　　　　　　　　　　　　　　　　　**643**
　1. Houses -- Maintenance and repair　2. Houses --
Remodeling
ISBN 978-1-58923-452-9; 1-58923-452-9
　　　　　　　　　　　　　　　　LC 2008-45755
　This home improvement guide covers such topics as
flooring, ceilings and walls, windows and doors, and remodeling different rooms including kitchens, bathrooms,
and basements.
　This "guide is basic, easy to follow, and completely illustrated. The organization is sensible and information easy
to find." Libr J

　The **complete** photo guide to home repair. Creative Pub. International 2008 559p il $35　　**643**
　1. Houses -- Maintenance and repair
　ISBN 978-1-58923-417-8; 1-58923-417-0
　　　　　　　　　　　　　　　　LC 2008-16520
　"Features more than 200 . . . home repair projects, including common wiring, plumbing, interior and exterior repairs." Publisher's note

Bray, Ilona M.
　★　**Nolo's** essential guide to buying your first
home; [by] Ilona Bray, Alayna Schroeder & Marcia
Stewart. 3rd ed.; Nolo 2010 426p il pa $24.99 **643**
　1. Houses -- Buying and selling
　ISBN 978-1-4133-1322-2 pa; 1-4133-1322-1 pa;
　978-1-4133-1348-2 ebook; 1-4133-1348-5 ebook
　　　　　　　　　　　　　　　　LC 2010-31334
　Provides information on selecting the right house, the
right mortgage, the right agent, the right inspections and
more. CD-ROM contains a "Homebuyer's Toolkit" with
forms and other resources.

Bryson, Bill
　At home; a short history of private life. Doubleday 2010 497p il $28.95　　　　　　　　　**643**
　1. Houses 2. Rooms
　ISBN 978-0-7679-1938-8; 0-7679-1938-6
　　　　　　　　　　　　　　　　LC 2010-04008
　The author takes readers on a tour of his house, a rural
English parsonage, showing how each room has figured in
the evolution of private life.
　"It takes a very particular kind of thoughtfulness, as well
as a bold temperament, to stuff all this research into a mattress that's supportive enough to loll about on while pondering the real subject of this book—the development of the
modern world. . . . Bryson is fascinated by everything, and
his curiosity is infectious." N Y Times Book Rev
　Includes bibliographical references

Corbett, Michael
　Before you buy! the homebuyer's handbook
for today's market. Plume 2011 xxiii, 277p il pa
$15　　　　　　　　　　　　　　　　　　**643**
　1. Houses -- Buying and selling　2. Real estate
investment
　ISBN 978-0-452-29680-0
　　　　　　　　　　　　　　　　LC 2010050910

　A real estate developer offers advice on buying a home
during the economic crisis, covering common mistakes
made by buyers and offering advice on how to handle foreclosure, mortgages, inspections, and other issues.

Crook, David
　The **Wall** Street Journal complete home owner's
guidebook; make the most of your biggest asset in
any market. Three Rivers Press 2008 260p il pa
$14.95　　　　　　　　　　　　　　　　**643**
　1. Houses -- Buying and selling　2. Real estate
investment
　ISBN 978-0-307-40592-0; 0-307-40592-3
　　　　　　　　　　　　　　　　LC 2008-25355
　This is a "look at the pros and cons of owning a home—
rather than renting one from a bank via a mortgage—along
with its ultimate costs. . . . For those aspiring to own a home
and those trying to manage the affordability of their biggest
asset, this is a must read." Publ Wkly
　Includes bibliographical references

Family Handyman
　Refresh your home; simple projects and tips
to save money, update, and renovate. editors of the
Family handyman. Reader's Digest 2011 287p il
pa $16.95　　　　　　　　　　　　　　**643**
　1. Houses -- Remodeling
　ISBN 978-1-60652-201-1
　　　　　　　　　　　　　　　　LC 2010029903
　"The coverage of a wealth of home fixes with a dose of
humor makes this DIY guide a delight. . . . There are tips and
insights on every page. New gadgets, considerations for ap-
pliance purchases, and fun little projects populate this book.
The section on power tool safety is important, and 'dos and
don'ts' suggestions are peppered throughout. Even common
goofs are shared with chuckles. A charming and friendly collection of tips and projects." Libr J

German, Roger
　Remodeling a basement; Rev. ed.; Taunton
Press 2010 170p il pa $19.95　　　　　　**643**
　1. Basements 2. Houses -- Remodeling
　ISBN 978-1-60085-292-3
　　　　　　　　　　　　　　　　LC 2009-33545
　"Beginning with solving moisture problems, then renovating space, this book walks the reader through a logical
process for repair and remodeling, with easy-to-follow instruction and illustrations. Design ideas and the latest building code data are also included." Libr J

Home Depot, Inc.
　★　**Home** improvement 1-2-3; 3rd ed., Newly
expanded and rev.; Home Depot Books 2008 607p
il $34.95　　　　　　　　　　　　　　　**643**
　1. Houses -- Maintenance and repair　2. Houses --
Remodeling 3. Interior design
　ISBN 978-0-696-23850-5
　　　　　　　　　　　　　　　　LC 2008-924090
　This book offers illustrated instructions for home remod-
eling, decorating, and repair.

Jackson, Albert

Popular mechanics complete home how-to; [by] Albert Jackson and David Day. Hearst Books 2004 514p il $24.95 **643**

1. Dwellings -- Maintenance and repair -- Amateurs' manuals 2. Houses -- Maintenance and repair
ISBN 1-58816-302-4

LC 2003-56853

"Interior and exterior repairs are included, from simple tasks like replacing an electrical switch to difficult ones like constructing a wall or building a pond, as well as common upgrades. Everything is explained in detail, with a wealth of clear photos and illustrations. A section on skills and tools shows the use of woodworking, building, decorating, plumbing, and electrical equipment, and a reference section describes hardware/materials and defines commonly used terminology. A great general guide to home repairs of all types, this book will see heavy use in most collections." Libr J

Lee, Vinny

Kitchens: a design sourcebook; with photography by James Merrell. This ed published in 2001 and reissued with amendments in 2005; Ryland Peters & Small 2005 192p il pa $19.95 **643**

1. Kitchens
ISBN 1-8417-2885-3; 978-1-8417-2930-5

LC 2004-21090

Over 400 color photos illustrate this guide to remodeling, renovating or building an entirely new kitchen. A resources list is included.

Litchfield, Michael W.

Renovation; [by] Michael Litchfield; Chip Harley, technical editor. 3rd ed, completely rev and updated; Taunton Press 2005 534p il $39.95 **643**

1. Houses -- Remodeling
ISBN 978-1-5615-8588-5; 1-5615-8588-2

LC 2005-110

This "guide covers all aspects of home renovation, including how to assess a house's structure, tools, materials, wiring, plumbing, painting, flooring, etc. Instructions are to the point—there is less hand-holding here than in other titles because some remodeling experience is assumed. A classic." Libr J

Papolos, Janice

The **virgin** homeowner; the essential guide to owning, maintaining, and surviving your first home. Norton 1997 444p il pa $24.95 **643**

1. Houses
ISBN 0-393-04035-6; 978-0-393-33496-8 pa; 0-393-33496-1 pa

LC 96-31304

"Beginning with how to get the most out of the initial home inspection, Papolos takes the reader through a house, describing each system, its quirks, and its potential problems. Later, she covers pest control, security, and safety. This highly readable book will prove useful to both new homeowners and those just thinking of making a purchase,

and veteran homeowners will undoubtedly learn something, too." Libr J

Includes bibliographical references

Reader's Digest Association, Inc.

★ **Complete** do-it-yourself manual; with the editors of Family handyman. rev and updated; Reader's Digest 2005 528p il $35 **643**

1. Houses -- Maintenance and repair
ISBN 0-7621-0579-8

LC 2004-50945

This manual for homeowners covers topics such as power tools, plumbing, landscaping, and storage projects with photos, diagrams and illustrations.

"Intriguing sidebars on wood refinishers (the fastest drying versus the safest), the financial benefits of renting specialty tools for a large drywall project and other subjects round out this must-have guide." Publ Wkly

New fix-it-yourself manual. Reader's Digest Assn. 1996 448p il $35 **643**

1. Furniture -- Repairing 2. Household equipment and supplies -- Maintenance and repair 3. Repairing
ISBN 0-89577-871-8

LC 96-15189

This illustrated book offers instructions for repairing, buying, cleaning and maintaining a wide variety of household items including appliances, furniture, plumbing fixtures, air conditioners, electronic and sports equipment

Solakian, Susan E.

The **homeowner's** guide to managing a renovation; tough-as-nails tactics for getting the most from your money. Sterling 2008 288p il pa $19.95 **643**

1. Houses -- Remodeling
ISBN 978-1-4027-2754-2

LC 2008-03797

"While dollar figures used will quickly be outdated, the principles presented are constant. This is really an underrepresented topic in how-to collections, and Solakian's book is an especially good offering." Libr J

Sussman, Julie

★ **Dare** to repair; a do-it-herself guide to fixing (almost) anything in the home. {by} Julie Sussman and Stephanie Glakas-Tenet; illustrations by Yeorgos Lampathakis. HarperCollins Pubs. 2002 253p il pa $14.95 **643**

1. Houses -- Maintenance and repair
ISBN 0-06-095984-3

LC 2002-27625

The authors "show women how to perform a number of the most common repairs, including unclogging drains and toilets, replacing electrical switches and outlets, leveling appliances, lighting pilot lights, unsticking windows, and installing a door peephole. . . . This is a wonderful book that should be purchased by every public library." Libr J

Williams, Mary Elizabeth

Gimme shelter. Simon & Schuster 2009 320p
$26   **643**
1. Houses -- Buying and selling 2. Real estate
ISBN 978-1-4165-5708-1; 1-4165-5708-3
LC 2008-14169
Williams "provides a blow-by-blow account of the recent inflation of the real estate bubble and its economic--and
emotional--impact on middle-class families like her own.
The author paints a vivid picture of the crisis in New York
City. . . . She provides cogent explanations of the recent financial crisis and foreshadows its still-developing repercussions, given that she is one of the millions who signed onto
an Alt-A (not quite prime) mortgage." Publ Wkly
Includes bibliographical references

Wing, Charlie

How your house works; a visual guide to understanding & maintaining your home. RSMeans 2007
152p il pa $21.95   **643**
1. Houses -- Maintenance and repair
ISBN 978-0-87629-015-6; 0-87629-015-2
This book "teaches the basics of home systems and appliances. Providing clean and detailed diagrams, Wing describes the purpose and function of that system or fixture.
Also accompanying each is a list of tips to use before you
call in a professional. This book is more a 'how' than a 'how-
to' and fills its role quite nicely." Libr J

Do it yourself kitchens; stunning spaces on a shoe-
string budget. Wiley 2011 192p   **643**
1. Kitchens
ISBN 9781118031629
"Ranked by budget, from $1000 up to $10,000, sample
kitchen makeovers showcased here illustrate a range of possibilities. With spending breakdowns, stunning before-and-
after shots, and lots of tips that make big differences, this
book has wide appeal. For each makeover there are detailed
instructions for selected projects, such as installing fixtures,
resurfacing, and tiling. This is not in-depth how-to, but ideas
and inspiration. Each sample kitchen is brimming with creativity and innovation."
"Ranked by budget, from $1000 up to $10,000, sample
kitchen makeovers showcased here illustrate a range of possibilities. With spending breakdowns, stunning before-and-
after shots, and lots of tips that make big differences, this
book has wide appeal. For each makeover there are detailed
instructions for selected projects, such as installing fixtures,
resurfacing, and tiling. This is not in-depth how-to, but ideas
and inspiration. Each sample kitchen is brimming with creativity and innovation." Libr J

Ultimate guide: home repair and improvement;
3rd ed.; Creative Homeowner 2011 607p il
$29.95   **643**
1. Houses -- Maintenance and repair 2. Houses --
Remodeling
ISBN 978-1-58011-528-5
This guide "completely covers the repairs most home
owners need. . . . This strong manual is highly recommended." Libr J

645   Household furnishings

Engelbreit, Mary

Mary Engelbreit's children's companion; the
Mary Engelbreit look and how to get it. illustrations
by Mary Engelbreit; written by Charlotte Lyons; pho-
tographs by Barbara Elliott Martin. Andrews & Mc-
Meel 1997 144p il $24.95   **645**
1. Handicraft 2. Interior design
ISBN 0-8362-3675-0
LC 97-7261
This book offers ideas for designing and decorating chil-
dren's rooms, parties, and backyard and garden play areas.

Montano, Mark

The **big**-ass book of home decor; photographs
by Auxy Espinoza. Stewart, Tabori & Chang 2010
271p il pa $22.50   **645**
1. Interior design
ISBN 978-1-58479-825-5
LC 2009-36376
The author "presents over 100 projects for decorating,
creating, and repurposing furniture and decorative accessories. He offers clearly written instructions illustrated with
color photographs of the steps. The wealth of inspiring projects that require only basic skills—e.g., decoupage, spray
paint, glue gun—will make this a popular choice for both
experienced and inexperienced crafters." Libr J

646.2   Sewing and related operations

Bednar, Nancy

The **encyclopedia** of sewing machine techniques;
[by] Nancy Bednar, JoAnn Pugh-Gannon. Sterling
Pub. 2007 336p il pa $24.95   **646.2**
1. Sewing
ISBN 1-4027-4293-2; 978-1-4027-4293-4
Among the techniques covered in this illustrated step-
by-step guide are beading, fringing, pintucks, and puffing.

Betzina, Sandra

Sandra Betzina sews for your home; {by} Sandra Betzina and Debbie Valentine. Taunton Press
2002 202p il $29.95   **646.2**
1. Household linens 2. Sewing
ISBN 1-56158-446-0
LC 2002-3395
The authors offer ideas and instructions for "sewing accessories for the home. In addition to complete, richly illustrated instructions for dozens of pillows, window treatments,
table coverings, bed linens, and gifts for children and pets,
there are solid sewing instructions that the reader can use in
myriad future sewing projects." Libr J

Cheetham, Kathleen

Singer perfect plus; sew a mix-and-match wardrobe in plus and petite-plus sizes. Quayside Pub. Group 2009 144p il $25 **646.2**

    1. Sewing 2. Tailoring 3. Women's clothing
    ISBN 978-1-58923-394-2; 1-58923-394-8

                      LC 2008-30415

"Cheetham's projects for casual and workplace fashions are accessible for beginning sewers. The mix-and-match tips are reminiscent of fashion magazine features, providing hints for assembling creative outfits. It's refreshing to see the clothes modeled on an actual plus-sized woman (the author herself)." Libr J

Colgrove, Debbie

Teach yourself visually sewing. Wiley 2006 283p il pa $24.99 **646.2**

    1. Sewing
    ISBN 0-471-74991-5; 978-0-471-74991-2

                    LC 2005-939196

This visual guide explains the "basics of hand sewing and sewing with a machine. . . . [It includes] information about tools and fabrics." Publisher's note

Creative Publishing International

The **complete** photo guide to window treatments; [edited by Linda Neubauer] 2nd ed; Creative Publisher International 2011 320p il pa $24.99 **646.2**

    1. Draperies
    ISBN 978-1-58923-607-3

                    LC 2010046925

"Fabric recommendations and materials lists introduce each style of window treatment, with clear, step-by-step instructions. Organization is consistent and well thought out, making this an easy manual to follow." Libr J

Includes bibliographical references

Creative Publishing International, Inc.

★ The **complete** photo guide to sewing; 1200 full-color how-to photos. [created by the editors of Creative Publishing International] Rev. + expanded ed.; Creative Pub. International 2009 352p il pa $24.99 **646.2**

    1. Sewing
    ISBN 978-1-58923-434-5; 1-58923-434-0

                    LC 2008-31264

"Sections include choosing the right tools and notions, using conventional machines and sergers, fashion sewing, tailoring, and home décor projects. Included are step-by-step instructions for basic projects like pillows, tablecloths, and window treatments." Publisher's note

Gardiner, Wendy

The **sewing** machine accessory bible; get the most out of your machine from using basic feet to mastering specialty feet. [by] Wendy Gardiner & Lorna Knight. Griffin: St. Martin's 2011 128p il pa $22.99 **646.2**

    1. Sewing machines
    ISBN 978-0-312-67658-2

This book focuses "on sewing machine accessories—feet, needles, and other attachments. . . . [The authors] briefly cover the basics of sewing machines, but they focus on the specialized feet that come with the machine. A photo of a sewing machine foot is included at the top left corner of each spread, allowing for quick and easy identification. There's also information about how to use each foot—what it's for and how to sew with it. Beginners will find this book especially handy." Libr J

James, Chris

The **complete** serger handbook. Sterling 1997 159p il hardcover o.p. pa $17.95 **646.2**

    1. Sewing 2. Sewing machines
    ISBN 0-8069-9807-5 pa

                    LC 96-39316

This "is a concise guide to the serger and serger techniques. Major sections of the book include identifying the parts of a serger (with photos of each part), serger accessories, types of threads, threading and testing the threading, learning to regulate tension, and techniques." Libr J

Lee, Linda

Sewing edges and corners. Taunton Press 2000 134p il pa $19.95 **646.2**

    1. Sewing
    ISBN 1-56158-418-5

                    LC 00-29919

The author offers about 40 corner and edge techniques for garments and home decorating projects.

"Readers appreciate the clarity of Lee's instructions, since each step is numbered, photographs and other illustrations ease difficult tasks, and sidebars ensure the comfortableness of the sewing." Booklist

Reader's Digest Association, Inc.

New complete guide to sewing; step-by-step techniques for making clothes and home accessories. from the editors at Reader's Digest. Reader's Digest Assn. 2002 384p il $35 **646.2**

    1. Sewing
    ISBN 0-7621-0420-1

                    LC 2002-69944

This illustrated guide begins with an overview of basic equipment and techniques. A discussion of patterns and fabrics is included. The bulk of the book provides step-by-step instructions for making clothes and home furnishings.

★ The new sewing essentials; Updated and rev. ed.; Creative Publishing International 2008 144p il pa $16.99 **646.2**

    1. Sewing
    ISBN 978-1-58923-432-1; 1-58923-432-4

This guide to sewing clothes and other items includes information on equipment, patterns, fabrics, and techniques.

646.4   Clothing and accessories construction

Armstrong, Helen Joseph

Patternmaking for fashion design; technical illustrator, Vincent James Maruzzi; fashion illustrator, Kathryn Hagen. 4th ed; Pearson Prentice Hall 2006 xxi, 805p il $104.40   **646.4**
1. Dressmaking -- Patterns
ISBN 978-0-13-194893-9; 0-13-194893-8
LC 2005-283500
"Covers the three steps in the development of design patterns—dart manipulation, added fullness, and contouring—with a central theme that all designs are based on one, or more of these three major patternmaking and design principles." Publisher's note
Includes bibliographical references

Betzina, Sandra

Power sewing step-by-step. Taunton Press 2000 231p il $34.95; pa $24.95   **646.4**
1. Dressmaking 2. Sewing 3. Tailoring (Women's)
ISBN 1-56158-363-4; 1-56158-572-6 pa
LC 00-23431
"Vests, pants, shirts, dresses, and jackets for women are the focus of this book, with Betzina guiding the reader step by step through her thinking process in planning, constructing, fitting, customizing, and finishing each type of garments. More than 500 color photos illustrate many tricks of the trade, shortcuts, and tips. This will be a core title in any sewing collection." Libr J

Doh, Jenny

Signature styles; 20 stitchers craft their look. Lark Crafts 2011 144p il pa $19.95   **646.4**
1. Dress accessories 2. Dressmaking 3. Sewing
ISBN 978-1-60059-791-6; 1-60059-791-2
LC 2010040531
Reveals how 20 women authors, bloggers, entrepreneurs and more developed their own distinctive looks. Each crafter shares her studio, style, a key technique, and an exclusive project.
This is "a surprisingly varied collection, ranging from costumey retroquirk to urban couture to modern country." Libr J

White, Betz

Sewing green; projects and ideas for stitching with organic, repurposed, and recycled fabrics: plus tips and resources for earth-friendly stitching. Stewart, Tabori & Chang 2009 143p il pa $24.95 **646.4**
1. Clothing and dress 2. Recycling
ISBN 978-1-58479-758-6; 1-58479-758-4
LC 2008023649
"White's collection of green sewing projects features garments and accessories made from thrift-store clothing, scrap fabric, and recycled goods. The looks are contemporary—you won't find any 1970s-era hippie patchwork dresses—and the designer profiles and tips are inspirational. Nicely cutting edge." Libr J

646.7   Management of personal and family life

Begoun, Paula

★ **Don't** go to the cosmetics counter without me; [by] Paula Begoun with Bryan Barron. 8th ed.; Beginning Press; distributed to the U.S. book trade by Publishers Group West 2010 1191p pa $29.95 **646.7**
1. Consumer education 2. Cosmetics 3. Skin -- Care
ISBN 978-1-877988-34-9
"From drugstores and home shopping to department stores and catalogs, Begoun reviews all of the major cosmetic and skin care lines product by product—more than 30,000 in all. . . . Begoun covers product websites, efficacy, and whether claims such as youth extension are accurate. Individual chapters are devoted to best products, a cosmetic ingredients dictionary, and animal testing." Publisher's note

Berg, Rona

Beauty: the new basics; illustrations by Anja Kroencke; photography by Deborah Jaffe. Workman 2001 404p il pa $19.95   **646.7**
1. Beauty, Personal 2. Personal appearance
ISBN 0-7611-0186-1
LC 00-43631
The author discusses "hair and skin care, bath and body, aging, skin cancer, makeup, home spa treatments, aromatherapy, and cosmetic surgery. She includes a directory of day and destination spas and recommended salons. Amusing time lines give thumbnail histories of style and popular products. Essential for small collections in particular." Libr J

Bonner, Lonnice Brittenum

Good hair; for colored girls who've considered weaves when the chemicals became too ruff. Crown Trade Paperbacks 1994 98p il pa $9.95   **646.7**
1. Hair
ISBN 0-517-88151-9
LC 93-42027
The author explains hair "structure and texture while exploring the damaging effects of hot combs and chemical relaxants, in addition to hair care essentials and how to style crimps and corkscrews. Although she doesn't cover a wide range of natural 'dos, her overarching message—that black women should embrace rather than tame their hair—makes this essential." Libr J
Includes bibliographical references

Brandon, Ruth

Ugly beauty; Helena Rubinstein, L'Oreal, and the blemished history of looking good. Harper 2011 290p il $26.99; ebook $21.99   **646.7**
1. Art collectors 2. Biography, Individual 3. Chemists 4. Cosmeticians 5. Cosmetics industry executives 6. Personal appearance
ISBN 978-0-06-174040-4; 0-06-174040-3; 978-0-06-204156-2 ebook; 0-06-204156-8 ebook
LC 2010-24435
"A clearheaded discussion of current beauty standards, vanity, and the gender politics of the modern cosmetic industry rounds out this lively history of the founding of the beauty business as we know it." Publ Wkly
Includes bibliographical references

Brown, Bobbi

Bobbi Brown beauty evolution; a guide to a lifetime of beauty. {by} Bobbi Brown, with Sally Wadyka. HarperCollins Pubs. 2002 211p il $29.95 **646.7**
1. Beauty, Personal 2. Personal appearance 3. Women -- Health and hygiene
ISBN 0-06-008881-8

LC 2002-22988
The author suggests "that readers look beyond the retouched images in magazines to see the possibilities of individual features. Addressing all ages and races, she recommends products that enhance your assets, even during pregnancy and illness. With a chapter on men." Libr J

Cullinane, Jan

The **new** retirement; the ultimate guide to the rest of your life. [by] Jan Cullinane and Cathy Fitzgerald. Rev. and updated ed.; Rodale 2007 484p pa $19.95 **646.7**
1. Retirement
ISBN 978-1-59486-479-7; 1-59486-479-9

LC 2007-15947
This guide provides "information about particular locales, financial planning and tax considerations, lifelong learning opportunities, leisure and volunteer activities, and working after retirement." Publisher's note
Includes bibliographical references

DuPriest, Laura

Natural beauty; pamper yourself with salon secrets at home. Prima Pub. 2002 230p il pa $10.95 **646.7**
1. Beauty, Personal 2. Cosmetics 3. Herbal cosmetics 4. Personal appearance 5. Skin -- Care 6. Skin -- Care and hygiene
ISBN 0-7615-2099-6

LC 2002-72554
The author's "obvious knowledge about everything from waxing to massaging to not being taken in at the cosmetics counter, as well as her inventive concoctions . . . make this a solid beauty resource." Publ Wkly

Fornay, Alfred

The **African** American woman's guide to successful makeup and skincare; rev ed; Wiley 2002 184p il pa $16.95 **646.7**
1. African American women -- Health and hygiene 2. Beauty, Personal 3. Personal appearance 4. Skin -- Care 5. Skin -- Care and hygiene
ISBN 0-471-40278-8

LC 2001-56781
The author "covers basic skin care and types, aging, and special problems such as acne and facial hair. He also provides guidance in selecting colors to complement skin tone and applying makeup to downplay flaws and accentuate good points. With a chapter on skin care for men." Libr J

Gross, Kim Johnson

Woman's face; skin care and makeup. {by Kim Johnson Gross, Jeff Stone; written by Rachel Urquhart} Knopf 1997 190p il $30 **646.7**
1. Cosmetics 2. Face -- Care 3. Personal grooming
ISBN 0-679-44578-1

LC 97-5164
This answers nearly 100 frequently asked questions about make-up and skin care, including advice on the best products, and describing how to accentuate a woman's best features.

Hinden, Stan

How to retire happy; the 12 most important decisions you must make before you retire. [foreword by John C. Bogle] 3rd ed., fully rev. and updated; McGraw-Hill 2010 233p pa $18.95; ebook $18.95 **646.7**
1. Retirement
ISBN 978-0-07-170247-8 pa; 978-0-07-171298-9 ebook
This retirement planning guide covers such topics as Social Security, pension plans, investments after retirement, health insurance, preparing for serious illness, and where to live after retirement.

Kashuk, Sonia

Real beauty; concept by Sonia Kashuk; written with Amie Valentine. Potter 2003 137p il + 1 DVD ROM $27.50 **646.7**
1. Personal appearance 2. Women -- Health and hygiene
ISBN 1-4000-4774-2

LC 2003-535298
The author "showcases women of all ages and ethnic types, covering nutrition and fitness in addition to the usual hair and skin care. The accompanying DVD shows the suggested makeup techniques being performed." Libr J

Kirsch, Melissa

The **girl's** guide to absolutely everything. Workman Pub. 2006 477p il $26.95; pa $15.95 **646.7**
1. Conduct of life 2. Young women
ISBN 978-0-7611-4213-3; 0-7611-4213-4; 978-0-7611-3579-1 pa; 0-7611-3579-0 pa

LC 2006-41840
The author provides "advice for women in their twenties and thirties on everything from body image and friendship to first jobs and money. . . . Her well-designed book is pleasurable to read and encourages healthy, responsible behavior." Libr J
Includes bibliographical references

Lofas, Jeannette

Stepparenting; Rev. and updated.; Citadel Press 2004 241p pa $12.95 **646.7**
1. Parenting 2. Stepchildren 3. Stepparents
ISBN 0-8065-2652-1; 978-0-8065-2652-2

LC 2004-556219
"Acknowledging the difficulty of a stepparent's role, this standout title guides readers through carefully forming a

stepfamily, with straightforward coverage of the usual issues (e.g., etiquette, praising positive behavior)." Libr J

Massey, Lorraine

Curly girl; more than just hair--it's an attitude: a celebration of curls: how to cut them, care for them, love them & set them free. Workman 2001 148p il pa $9.95	**646.7**
1. Hair 2. Hair -- Care and hygiene
ISBN 0-7611-2300-8
LC 2001-26842

This book features "tips on shampoo . . . conditioners . . . drying, combing . . . styling, getting the right cut, and how to Heal Thy Hair after years of strong detergents and damaging blow-dryers. There are before-and-after photographs . . . self-help tests, confessions from curly girls {and} advice." Publisher's note

Price, R. Kevin

The **successful** retirement guide; hundreds of suggestions on how to stay intellectually, socially and physically engaged for the best years of your life. Rainbow Books, Inc. 2009 342p pa $19.95	**646.7**
1. Life skills 2. Retirement
ISBN 978-1-56825-115-8; 1-56825-115-7
LC 2008-19779

"The beauty of retiree Price's book is its simplicity—one can pick a chapter and find a latent interest that could be developed, from building a bird house to quitting smoking. Price gives the reader the opportunity to do that by providing the idea, the opportunity potential, and the resources for getting started. The title doesn't do the book justice; it's an inspirational guide that will provoke people of all ages to engage in new ventures and discover what life can offer." Libr J

Romanowski, Perry

Can you get hooked on lip balm? top cosmetic scientists answer your questions about the lotions, potions, and other beauty products you use every day. [by] Perry Romanowski and the creators of TheBeautyBrains.Com. Harlequin 2011 194p pa $16.95	**646.7**
1. Cosmetics
ISBN 978-0-373-89234-1
LC 2010-44199

"Women who subscribe to such magazines as InStyle and Self will devour this question-and-answer guide to cosmetics, shampoos, and nail polishes." Booklist
Includes bibliographical references

Scott, Susan Craig

★ The **hair** bible; the ultimate guide to healthy, beautiful hair forever. {by} Susan Craig Scott with Karen W. Bressler. Atria Bks. 2003 270p il pa $15	**646.7**
ISBN 0-7434-4260-1
LC 2003-271695

This guide begins with a short history of hair care and treatments and goes on to discuss "the basics of hair care, how to choose the best cut, color and styling products and

how to cope with hair treatments, enhancements and problems. . . . The authors {also} offer home remedies for scalp troubles, discuss female pattern baldness and explore the emotional effects of hair loss. They even cover surgical procedures, such as hair grafts or scalp reductions, that can mitigate hair loss." Publ Wkly
Includes bibliographical references

Spencer, Kit

Pro makeup; salon secrets of the professionals. Firefly Books 2009 255p il $29.95	**646.7**
1. Cosmetics
ISBN 978-1-55407-477-8
LC 2009-279649

This book "provides an organized, attractive overview of makeup application techniques from everyday to costume. The text is enhanced throughout by useful highlights offering tips from professionals on everything from achieving the perfect eyebrow arch to taking the attention away from a wide nose. Bridal and costume party makeup are covered as well. . . . There is a section on developing looks, dealing with skin conditions, choosing equipment, and even applying makeup to men and children." Voice Youth Advocates

Toselli, Leigh

Pro nail care; salon secrets of the professionals. Firefly Books 2009 254p il $29.95	**646.7**
1. Manicuring 2. Personal grooming
ISBN 978-1-55407-478-5
LC 2009-288700

This book "goes well beyond the typical manicure or pedicure. An intriguing history of nail care is provided (who knew they had manicures in ancient Babylon?), as well as a history of nail polish fashion. The anatomy of the hand and foot are examined in detail. Nail diseases and problems are explained with suggested remedies. There are sections on massage, overlay systems, the chemistry of nail products, and a gallery of nail 'looks.' Most interesting is the section on nail art. The looks are explained with step-by-step instructions accompanied by clear photographs." Voice Youth Advocates

Worthington, Charles

The **complete** book of hairstyling. Firefly Bks. 2002 304p il pa $19.95	**646.7**
1. Hair 2. Hair -- Care and hygiene 3. Hairdressing
ISBN 1-55297-576-2
LC 2002-277803

This describes over 100 hairstyles and offers advice on coloring and cutting hair, maintenance of hair style and health, and hair products.

Essence total makeover; body, beauty, spirit. [by the editors of Essence]; Patricia Mignon Hinds, editor; introduction by Susan L. Taylor. Crown 2000 216p il hardcover o.p. pa $18	**646.7**
1. African American women -- Health and hygiene 2. Afro-American women 3. Beauty, Personal 4. Personal appearance
ISBN 0-609-80527-4 pa
LC 99-14442

"Hinds provides practical tips on caring for skin, hair, body, and spirit. Glossy and attractive, this comprehensive volume is aimed at African American women." Libr J

Includes bibliographical references

647 Management of public households (Institutional housekeeping)

Ripert, Eric

On the line; [by] Eric Ripert, Christine Muhlke. Artisan 2008 239p il $35 **647**

1. Restaurants
ISBN 978-1-57965-369-9; 1-57965-369-3

LC 2008-05930

"A behind-the-scenes look at the famed New York restaurant Le Bernardin. . . . Chef Ripert and New York Times writer Muhlke recount the restaurant's history, from its founding in 1986 by Gilbert and Maguy Le Coze, through Ripert's joining the team in 1991, to the present day. This thorough guide to how the restaurant operates teaches about various kitchen stations, tools of the trade, key personnel and their duties, how new dishes are born and what it's like to spend a night 'on the line.' . . . [Some recipes are included.] A huge treat for industry insiders, fans of Le Bernardin and foodies everywhere." Publ Wkly

647.9 Specific kinds of public households and institutions

Schultz, Howard

Onward; how Starbucks fought for its life without losing its soul. [by] Howard Schultz with Joanne Gordon. Rodale 2011 350p il $25.99 **647.9**

1. Coffee industry 2. Leadership
ISBN 978-1-60529-288-5

LC 2011003239

"Throughout this book, readers get a very intimate look at the conviction that drives leaders, the resiliency of employees, the passion that customers feel about a brand, and the global community that one brand can inspire. Whether or not you are a coffee lover or have a fondness for the Starbucks experience, Onward details tremendous leadership lessons from which everyone can learn." T + D

648 Housekeeping

Friedman, Virginia M.

Field guide to stains; how to identify and remove virtually every stain known to man. by Virginia M. Friedman, Melissa Wagner, and Nancy Armstrong. Quirk Bks. 2003 280p il pa $14.95 **648**

1. Cleaning 2. Spotting (Cleaning)
ISBN 1-931686-07-6

LC 2002-104065

This guide to identifying and removing over 100 stains features sections on sauces, fruits and vegetables, office products, and yard and garage stains. It also includes in-

formation on when and where certain stains are most likely to occur.

Platt, Stacey

What's a disorganized person to do? Artisan 2010 277p il pa $16.95 **648**

1. House cleaning 2. Storage in the home
ISBN 978-1-57965-372-9

LC 2009-13493

The author "offers quick tips (e.g., storing sterling silver with chalk to prevent tarnish), instructions (e.g., folding silk scarves correctly), and one-hour projects (e.g., taking back the junk drawer) that anyone can immediately put into practice. Guidelines for organizing office space are designed for those who like to file and those who prefer to pile, and detailed steps for vacation packing and cross-country moving are also included. The employment of one idea alone is worth the price of the book." Libr J

Includes bibliographical references

Consumer Reports how to clean and care for practically anything; [by] the editors of Consumer Reports. Consumer Reports Special Publications 2002 280p il pa $16.95 **648**

1. Cleaning 2. House cleaning
ISBN 978-0-89043-965-4; 0-89043-965-4

LC 2004-297314

This volume offers advice on buying and using cleaning products and appliances and includes a stain removal chart for fabrics.

649 Child rearing; home care of people with disabilities and illnesses

Agnew, Connie L.

Twins! pregnancy, birth, and the first year of life. [by] Connie L. Agnew, Alan H. Klein, and Jill Alison Ganon; illustrations by Victor Robert. 2nd ed.; Collins 2005 360p il pa $18.95 **649**

1. Twins
ISBN 0-06-074219-4; 978-0-06-074219-5

LC 2005-45585

An overview of the physical, medical, emotional, and psychological issues involved in having twins. Fetal and embryonic development, nutrition, and exercise are among the topics covered. Includes interviews with parents of twins.

American Academy of Pediatrics

Caring for your school-age child; ages 5 to 12. editor-in-chief, Edward L. Schor. rev trade pa. ed; Bantam Bks. 1999 xxviii, 624p il pa $19.95 **649**

1. Child care 2. Child development 3. Child rearing 4. School children
ISBN 0-553-37992-5

LC 99-12639

This book "offers comprehensive information about the growth, development, and behavior of children from five to 12 years of age. . . . Bicycle safety, latchkey children, dealing with violence and crime, guns in the home, prejudice, gender identity and sexual orientation, and physical and sexual abuse appear along with the usual information about immunization, diet, school problems, illness, and first aid. The text also offers sound, practical advice about how parents in traditional and nontraditional families can handle a wide variety of situations, stating clearly when they should seek professional help. . . . This book belongs in all parenting and consumer health collections." Libr J {review of 1995 edition}

Ames, Louise Bates

Your eight-year-old; lively and outgoing. by Louise Bates Ames and Carol Chase Haber; illustrated with photographs by Betty David. Delacorte Press 1989 147p il hardcover o.p. pa $12.95   **649**
1. Child rearing
ISBN 0-440-50681-6 pa

                LC 88-31150
A discussion of the basic personality and typical physical and mental development of the eight-year-old.

Your five-year-old; sunny and serene. by Louise Bates Ames and Frances L. Ilg, Gesell Institute of Child Development; illustrated with photographs by Betty David. Delacorte Press 1979 123p il hardcover o.p. pa $12.95   **649**
1. Child rearing
ISBN 0-440-50673-5 pa

                LC 78-11622
Beginning with a description of the general characteristics of the five-year-old, the authors go on to discuss how the child relates to parents and others.

Your four-year-old; wild and wonderful. by Louise Bates Ames and Frances L. Ilg, Gesell Institute of Child Development. Delacorte Press 1976 152p il hardcover o.p. pa $12.95   **649**
1. Child rearing
ISBN 0-440-50675-1 pa
A discussion of the basic personality and typical physical and mental development of the four-year-old.

Your one-year-old; the fun-loving, fussy 12-to-24-month-old. by Louise Bates Ames, Frances L. Ilg, and Carol Chase Haber (Gesell Institute of Child Development); illustrated with photographs by Betty David. Delacorte Press 1982 178p il hardcover o.p. pa $12.95   **649**
1. Child rearing
ISBN 0-440-50672-7 pa

                LC 81-17275
A discussion of the basic personality and typical physical and mental development of the one-year-old.

Your seven-year-old; life in a minor key. by Louise Bates Ames and Carol Chase Haber; illustrated with photographs by Betty David. Delacorte Press 1985 165p il hardcover o.p. pa $12.95   **649**
1. Child rearing
ISBN 0-440-50650-6 pa

                LC 84-15627

A discussion of the basic personality and typical physical and mental development of the seven-year-old.

Your six-year-old; defiant but loving. by Louise Bates Ames and Frances L. Ilg, Gesell Institute of Child Development. Delacorte Press 1976 132p il hardcover o.p. pa $12.95   **649**
1. Child rearing
ISBN 0-440-50674-3 pa
A discussion of the basic personality and typical physical and mental development of the six-year-old.

Your two-year-old; terrible or tender. by Louise Bates Ames, and Frances L. Ilg, Gesell Institute of Child Development. Delacorte Press 1976 149p il hardcover o.p. pa $12.94   **649**
1. Child rearing
ISBN 0-440-50638-7 pa
A discussion of the basic personality and typical physical and mental development of the two-year-old.

Brazelton, T. Berry

Touchpoints birth to 3; your child's emotional and behavioral development. revised with Joshua Sparrow. 2nd ed.; Da Capo Lifelong Books 2006 xxvi, 500p il pa $17.95   **649**
1. Child development 2. Child psychology 3. Child rearing
ISBN 978-0-7382-1049-0; 0-7382-1049-8

                LC 2008-274711
The author "defines 'touchpoints' as the periods of development and regression which every child experiences while growing up. He describes the first six years of life and the touchpoints of that period. . . . Worried new parents will be put at ease after reading this book. Brazelton is knowledgeable, warm, and kind, and his book is a pleasure to read." Libr J
Includes bibliographical references

Brooks, Robert B.

Raising resilient children; fostering strength, hope, and optimism in your child. {by} Robert Brooks, Sam Goldstein. Contemporary Bks. 2001 317p hardcover o.p. pa $14.95   **649**
1. Child rearing 2. Parent and child 3. Parent-child relationship 4. Resilience (Personality trait) in children
ISBN 0-8092-9765-5 pa

                LC 00-60316
The authors "synthesize research on children's coping skills; define and describe resilience (the capacity to cope and feel competent); and offer specific strategies for nurturing resilience in children." Booklist
Includes bibliographical references

Brott, Armin A.

The **expectant** father; facts, tips, and advice for dads-to-be. [by] Armin A. Brott and Jennifer Ash.

3rd ed.; Abbeville Press 2010 373p il $18.95; pa $12.95 **649**

1. Fathers 2. Pregnancy

ISBN 978-0-7892-1079-1; 978-0-7892-1077-7 pa

LC 2010-15973

This book "gives dads-to-be a month-by-month breakdown of what to expect as they prepare to welcome a baby into their family. For each month, Brott and Ash give a rundown of what mothers, babies, and fathers are experiencing physically and emotionally, from moodiness and food cravings (which fathers aren't exempt from) to balancing fatherhood with work. . . . Brott and Ash's measured, experienced tone offers assurance and guidance for those new to the stresses and worries of impending fatherhood, making this a must-have for anyone expecting." Publ Wkly

Includes bibliographical references

Bullard, Sara

Teaching tolerance; raising open-minded empathetic children. Doubleday 1996 235p hardcover o.p. pa $19 **649**

1. Children 2. Parenting 3. Prejudices 4. Toleration

ISBN 0-385-47265-X pa

LC 95-36045

Bullard "states the principles of tolerance adults need to impart to children and provides guidelines for modeling the behavior we want to encourage." Libr J

Cohen, Lawrence J.

Playful parenting; a bold new way to use play in raising your children. Ballantine Bks. 2001 307p $23.95; pa $14 **649**

1. Games 2. Parenting 3. Play

ISBN 0-345-43897-3; 0-345-44286-5 pa

LC 00-66809

"According to Cohen, children of all ages have an ongoing need for connectedness, security and attachment; playful interaction with parents is an important way to develop such bonds. Through play, parents can help their kids develop greater confidence, express bottled up or difficult feelings, recover from daily emotional upheavals, negotiate agreements, express love and—not least—have fun." Publ Wkly

Deak, JoAnn

Girls will be girls; a parent's guide to cultivating confident, competent and connected daughters. by JoAnn Deak with Teresa Barker. Hyperion 2002 287p $23.95; pa $14.95 **649**

1. Child rearing 2. Girls 3. Teenagers

ISBN 0-7868-6768-X; 0-7868-8657-9 pa

LC 2001-39247

"Deak discusses the differences between fathers and daughters and mothers and daughters and also some of the more common problems faced by teens, such as body image and peer pressure." Publ Wkly

Delmolino, Lara

★ **Incentives** for change; motivating people with autism spectrum disorders to learn and gain in-

dependence. [by] Lara Delmolino and Sandra L. Harris. Woodbine House 2004 145p il pa $17.95 **649**

1. Autism 2. Motivation (Psychology)

ISBN 1-89062-760-7

LC 2004-19940

"Easy to follow, this first-rate introduction to ABA [Applied Behavioral Analysis] is accessible to a wide range of audiences." Libr J

Includes bibliographical references

Deutsch, Francine

Halving it all; how equally shared parenting works. Harvard Univ. Press 1999 327p hardcover o.p. pa $14.95 **649**

1. Child rearing 2. Dual-career families 3. Parenting 4. Sex role

ISBN 0-674-36800-2; 0-674-00209-1 pa

LC 98-30738

Based on interviews, Deutsch "describes four groups of working parents: those who share responsibilities and duties equally; those in which one parent, usually the mother, does somewhat more; those in which the mother provides most of the childcare; and parents, primarily blue collar workers, who choose alternate work shifts to share duties." Libr J

Includes bibliographical references

Donovan, Denis M.

What did I just say!?! how new insights into childhood thinking can help you communicate more effectively with your child. {by Denis M. Donovan, Deborah McIntyre} Holt & Co. 1999 230p il hardcover o.p. pa $14 **649**

1. Communication 2. Communication in the family 3. Interpersonal communication in children 4. Parent and child 5. Parent-child relationship

ISBN 0-8050-6502-4 pa

LC 99-11987

"Unless parents state what they want of a child explicitly, literally, logically, and in simple, commonsense terms, what they say and what the child hears and does will rarely be in sync. Donovan and McIntyre scrutinize many phrases . . . through the lens of logic to demonstrate embarrassingly ineffective ways for parents to communicate." Booklist

Includes bibliographical references

Douglas, Ann

The **mother** of all baby books. Hungry Minds 2002 604p pa $15.99 **649**

1. Childbirth 2. Infants -- Care 3. Parenting

ISBN 0-7645-6616-4

Baby care basics covered in this guide include "basic childcare, nutrition, health, and physical, emotional, and social development. [Also discussed are] facts about sleeping patterns, breastfeeding, circumcision, and immunization issues." Publisher's note

Includes bibliographical references

Egan, Amy

Is it a big problem or a little problem? when to worry, when not to worry, and what to do. [by] Amy

Egan . . . [et al.] St. Martin's Press 2007 335p il pa $15.95 **649**

1. Child development 2. Child psychology

ISBN 978-0-312-35412-1

LC 2007-17218

The authors "divide the book into three sections, 'The Basics,' 'Understanding Development,' and 'Where Children Struggle.' Within these, they illustrate specific concerns (e.g., 'She can hear, why doesn't she understand?'), explore the range of normal, and examine signals that indicate a need for professional intervention. . . . Never using an alarmist tone, the authors strike a perfect balance between advocating for early intervention and appreciating the ups and downs of typical childhood behavior." Libr J

Includes bibliographical references

Elias, Maurice J.

Emotionally intelligent parenting; how to raise a self-disciplined, responsible, socially skilled child. {by} Maurice J. Elias, Steven E. Tobias, and Brian S. Friedlander; foreword by Daniel Goleman. Harmony Bks. 1999 246p hardcover o.p. pa $13 **649**

1. Child rearing 2. Parenting

ISBN 0-609-80483-9 pa

LC 98-20835

The authors encourage parents to "try to see things from the child's perspective; stop nagging, threatening and yelling to get your point across; foster positive, and discourage negative, behaviors." Publ Wkly

Elman, Natalie Madorsky

The **unwritten** rules of friendship; simple strategies to help your child make friends. by Natalie Madorsky Elman and Eileen Kennedy-Moore. Little, Brown 2003 340p il pa $14.95 **649**

1. Child rearing 2. Friendship 3. Friendship in children 4. Social skills in children 5. Socialization

ISBN 0-316-91730-3

LC 2002-40611

The authors "formulate nine prototypes of children with friendship problems. These range from passive (e.g., 'sensitive soul') to more aggressive (e.g., 'intimidating' children, 'short-fused' children, and born leaders) personalities. Chapters provide checklists for evaluation, social rules such children need to know, learning activities, and case studies. . . . Colorfully written and practical, Unwritten Rules offers many tips for anxious parents." Libr J

Includes bibliographical references

Faber, Adele

How to talk so kids will listen & listen so kids will talk; [by] Adele Faber and Elaine Mazlish; illustrations by Kimberly Ann Coe. 1st Avon Books rev (20th anniversary) print., 20th anniversary ed updated; Avon Books 1999 286p il pa $13.95 **649**

1. Communication 2. Parenting

ISBN 0-380-81196-0

LC 99-94868

This book designed to facilitate communication between parents and their children discuss how to cope with an unhappy child, resolving family conflicts, and how to set boundaries for a child without damaging goodwill.

Furedi, Frank

Paranoid parenting; why ignoring the experts may be best for your child. Chicago Review Press 2002 233p pa $14.95 **649**

1. Child rearing 2. Parent and child 3. Parent-child relationship 4. Parenting 5. Parents -- Psychology

ISBN 1-55652-464-1

LC 2002-4121

"This book is provocative, well argued, and clearly written, though the rhetoric can be stinging." Libr J

Includes bibliographical references

Garbarino, James

Parents under siege; why you are the solution, not the problem in your child's life. [by] James Garbarino, Claire Bedard. Free Press 2001 246p hardcover o.p. pa $13 **649**

1. Child rearing 2. Interpersonal relations 3. Parent and child 4. Parent-child relationship

ISBN 0-7432-0134-5; 0-7432-2383-7 pa

LC 2001-23692

"This book offers a sound theoretical starting point for parents grappling with a difficult child. It also lists many helpful resources, Web sites and groups, along with suggested further reading." Publ Wkly

Garber, Stephen W.

Monsters under the bed and other childhood fears; helping your child overcome anxieties, fears, and phobias. {by} Stephen W. Garber, Marianne Daniels Garber, and Robyn Freedman Spizman. Villard Bks. 1993 378p hardcover o.p. pa $23 **649**

1. Child rearing 2. Fear

ISBN 0-8129-9222-9 pa

LC 92-56812

"Following opening chapters on understanding and identifying a child's fear and some overall guidelines on teaching basic relaxation techniques, the authors introduce their basic plan for overcoming fear through imagination, information, observation, and exposure. Subsequent chapters apply these four techniques to specific fears." Libr J

Includes bibliographical references

Harris, Sandra L.

Siblings of children with autism; a guide for families. [by] Sandra L. Harris and Beth A. Glasberg. 2nd ed; Woodbine House 2003 180p il pa $16.95 **649**

1. Autism 2. Autistic children -- Family relationships 3. Siblings

ISBN 1-89062-729-1

LC 2003-1239

This "resource for families with autistic children and nonautistic siblings examines the perceptions, needs, compromises, and inevitable stresses that brothers and sisters face." Libr J

Includes bibliographical references

Hewlett, Sylvia Ann

The **war** against parents; what we can do for America's beleaguered moms and dads. {by} Sylvia Ann Hewlett and Cornel West. Houghton Mifflin 1998 302p il hardcover o.p. pa $14   **649**
1. Child welfare -- United States 2. Family 3. Family policy -- United States 4. Parenting 5. Parenting -- United States
ISBN 0-395-95797-4 pa
                              LC 98-5779
The authors contend that "current American political and economic policy, as well as the popular media, discriminate severely against people trying to bring up children. . . . This salutary jeremiad should be required reading in Washington and Hollywood." Publ Wkly
Includes bibliographical references

Hopgood, Mei-Ling

How Eskimos keep their babies warm; Mei-Ling Hopgood. Algonquin Books of Chapel Hill 2012 292 p.   **649**
1. Parent and child -- Cross-cultural studies 2. Parenting -- Cross-cultural studies
ISBN 9781565129580
                              LC 2011036571
The book presents "stories and statistics about how other cultures raise their young. . . . [Author Mei-Ling] Hopgood's first topic is one that many American mothers can relate to: getting their kids to sleep. In Argentina, where Hopgood had her first child, sleep training is not the norm. She writes about one mother who 'often stayed with [her son] — cribs in Argentina are often large enough to fit a small adult — until he fell asleep, usually around 10:00 p.m. or later. . . . [Her] view was that it mattered less where everybody was sleeping, as long as everyone was getting a good night's sleep.'" (Washington Post)

Huggins, Kathleen

★ The **nursing** mother's companion; foreword by Ruth A. Lawrence. 5th ed.; Harvard Common Press 2005 308p il hardcover o.p. pa $14.95 **649**
1. Breast feeding
ISBN 1-55832-303-1; 1-55832-304-X pa
                              LC 2004-21182
This offers advice on preventing and solving breast feeding problems and includes sections on premature babies, babies at risk for underfeeding, and breast pumps, as well as an appendix on drug safety.

Hulbert, Ann

Raising America; experts, parents, and a century of advice about children. Knopf 2003 450p il $27.50; pa $15   **649**
1. Child rearing 2. Parenting
ISBN 0-375-40120-2; 0-375-70122-2 pa
                              LC 2002-73152
This is "an intellectual history of how children and parents have been studied in modern America. Here is the story of how Drs. Hall and Holt begat Drs. Gesell and Watson, who begat Dr. Spock and even Dr. Seuss, and how they in turn spawned an entire mini-industry of parenting experts. .

. . This provocative and informative study is a model of lay scholarship." Publ Wkly
Includes bibliographical references

Ilg, Frances Lillian

Your three-year-old; friend or enemy. by Louise Bates Ames, and Frances L. Ilg, Gesell Institute of Child Development. Delacorte Press 1976 168p il hardcover o.p. pa $12.95   **649**
1. Child rearing
ISBN 0-440-50649-2 pa
A discussion of the basic personality and typical physical and mental development of the three-year-old.

Karp, Harvey

The **happiest** baby on the block; the new way to calm crying and help your baby sleep longer. Bantam Bks. 2002 267p il $21.95; pa $13.95   **649**
1. Child rearing 2. Crying in infants 3. Infants -- Care 4. Infants -- Sleep 5. Parent and child 6. Parent-child relationship
ISBN 0-553-80255-0; 0-553-38146-6 pa
                              LC 2001-56734
To calm a crying baby the author "recommends a series of five steps designed to imitate the uterus. These steps include swaddling, side/stomach position, shhh sounds, swinging and sucking. The book includes detailed advice on the proper way to swaddle a child, the difference between a gentle rocking versus shaking and more." Publ Wkly

La Leche League International

The **Womanly** art of breastfeeding; 7th rev ed; Plume 2004 463p il pa $18   **649**
1. Breast feeding
ISBN 978-0-452-28580-4; 0-452-28580-1
                              LC 2004-557599
This guide explains the benefits of breastfeeding and offers advice on avoiding problems, breastfeeding and working mothers, family life, and weaning.

Leach, Penelope

Your baby & child; from birth to age five. photographs by Jenny Matthews. 3rd ed completely rev; Knopf 1997 559p il $35; pa $20   **649**
1. Child care 2. Child development 3. Infants -- Care
ISBN 0-375-40007-9; 0-375-70000-5 pa
                              LC 97-29325
The author explores the psychosocial needs of children along with their physical growth and progress. Parental concerns are addressed.
"Public and academic libraries would do well to stock . . . this primer on children and their development for circulation as well as for the reference shelf." Libr J

The **essential** first year. DK Publishing 2010 288p il pa $17.95   **649**
1. Child rearing 2. Infants -- Care
ISBN 978-0-7566-5799-4
"Leach empowers parents without overwhelming or guilting them, ultimately making the world a better place for

families and children everywhere. Warning: this will make you want to have babies." Libr J

Includes bibliographical references

Lev, Arlene Istar

The **complete** lesbian & gay parenting guide; Berkeley trade pbk. ed.; Berkley Books 2004 379p pa $17   **649**

1. Gay parents 2. Parenting

ISBN 0-425-19197-4; 978-0-425-19197-2

LC 2004-57080

"This book addresses the concerns of transgendered parents, as well as those of lesbian and gay parents. . . . [The author] knows how to tackle relevant issues, e.g., dealing with the homophobia that children of GLBT parents will inevitably encounter. Humorous and replete with valuable narratives." Libr J

Includes bibliographical references

Lippincott, Jenifer Marshall

7 things your teenager won't tell you; and how to talk about them anyway. [by] Jenifer Marshall Lippincott and Robin M. Deutsch. Ballantine Books 2005 223p pa $14.95   **649**

1. Adolescent psychology 2. Parent-child relationship 3. Parenting 4. Teenagers

ISBN 0-8129-6959-6

LC 2005-297256

"The first section of the book reviews psychological and physiological research on brain development in adolescents. The authors then identify seven important facts to keep in mind, among them: truth is a malleable concept for teens, they suffer from distorted self-images, and they are attracted to risks. . . . Parents of teens will recognize the us-and-them dialogues and will find encouragement and guidance." Booklist

Includes bibliographical references

Mayes, Linda C.

The **Yale** Child Study Center guide to understanding your child; healthy development from birth to adolescence. {by} Linda C. Mayes and Donald J. Cohen with John E. Schowalter and Richard H. Granger; J. L. Bell, editorial consultant; W. Rodney Torbert, illustrator. Little, Brown 2002 548p $40; pa $21.95   **649**

1. Child development 2. Child rearing 3. Parent and child 4. Parent-child relationship

ISBN 0-316-95432-2; 0-316-79432-5 pa

LC 00-39116

"The book offers three perspectives: the scientific, with basic information about meeting a growing child's needs; the emotional, with attention to understanding a child's feelings; and the parental, with emphasis on the feelings and expectations the parent brings to the relationship. . . . The objective is to help parents balance the three perspectives. . . . This approach lends the guide a broad and deep perspective on parenting even as it covers typical issues such as imaginary friends and sibling rivalry." Booklist

Murkoff, Heidi Eisenberg

★ **What** to expect the first year; [by] Heidi Murkoff, Arlene Eisenberg & Sandee Hathaway. 2nd ed, rev and updated; Workman 2003 704p $25.95; pa $15.95   **649**

1. Child rearing 2. Infants 3. Infants -- Care

ISBN 0-7611-3184-1; 0-7611-2958-8 pa

LC 2003-57578

This guide to "taking care of a newborn through the milestone of his or her first birthday . . . [covers] issues such as newborn screening, home births and the resulting at-home newborn care, vitamins and vaccines, milk allergies, causes of colic, sleep problems, SIDS, returning to work, dealing with siblings, weaning, sippy cups, . . . [and] the expanded role of the father." Publisher's note

★ **What** to expect the second year; from 12 to 24 months. [by] Heidi Murkoff and Sharon Mazel; foreword by Mark D. Widome. Workman Pub Co 2011 512p il $24; pa $15.95   **649**

1. Child rearing 2. Toddlers

ISBN 978-0-7611-6364-0; 978-0-7611-5277-4 pa

This is a "look at the toddler from 12 to 24 months. In 15 chapters the authors cover feeding, sleeping, learning, playing, health and safety, injuries and developmental disorders, discipline, and other issues with a meaty center section on behavior. . . . Murkoff offers sound advice and reassurance that will help parent and toddler stay grounded during this whirlwind period of growth and change." Publ Wkly

Nachman, Patricia Ann

You and your only child; the joys, myths, and challenges of raising an only child. {by} Patricia Nachman with Andrea Thompson. HarperCollins Pubs. 1997 244p hardcover o.p. pa $12   **649**

1. Only child 2. Parenting

ISBN 0-06-092896-4 pa

LC 96-32531

The authors discuss social attitudes about only children and offer advice on issues ranging from friendships and stereotyping to the only child and divorce.

Neifert, Marianne R.

Great expectations; the essential guide to breastfeeding. [by] Marianne Neifert. Sterling 2009 312p il pa $14.95   **649**

1. Breast feeding

ISBN 978-1-4027-5817-1

LC 2009-5248

"The author combines detailed, readable medical explanations with practical tips for success and addresses potential challenges honestly rather than glossing over them with bland reassurances. Each chapter seems designed to stand alone, making it easy for time-pressed mothers to find the information they need without reading the entire book." Libr J

Pryor, Gale

★ **Nursing** mother, working mother; the essential guide to breastfeeding your baby before and after you return to work. [by] Gale Pryor and Kathleen

Huggins. 2nd ed.; Harvard Common Press 2006
237p pa $12.95   **649**
1. Breast feeding 2. Mothers
ISBN 1-55832-331-7; 978-1-55832-331-5

LC 2006-26173

This book provides "information on legal rights in the
workplace, breast pumps, and the basics of expressing, storing, and feeding breast milk. Women planning on returning
to paid work will find excellent advice to make breastfeeding a long-term reality even if mother and baby are separated
for many hours of the day." Libr J

Includes bibliographical references

Rosenfeld, Alvin A.

The **over**-scheduled child; avoiding the hyper-
parenting trap. [by] Alvin Rosenfeld and Nicole
Wise; foreword by Robert Coles. St. Martin's Griffin
2001 xxxii, 263p pa $14.95   **649**
1. Child rearing 2. Parenting
ISBN 0-312-26339-2; 978-0-312-26339-3

The author "advocates 'just playing' and just spending
time with one's children rather than living the overbooked
family life of a stereotypical soccer mom. He notes that family schedules are at a breaking point and that parents face a
great deal of guilt and anxiety because they cannot give their
children everything. He promotes the need for more balance
and suggests that parents take to heart Dr. Spock's advice for
parents to trust themselves." Libr J

Includes bibliographical references

Sears, William

The **Baby** book; everything you need to know
about your baby--from birth to age two. {by} William Sears {et al.} 2nd ed. {rev. and updated}; Little,
Brown 2003 769p il pa $21.95   **649**
1. Infants -- Care 2. Infants -- Development
ISBN 0-316-77800-1

LC 2002-016142

"The authors teach new parents how to bond with their
babies through seven fundamental behaviors, including
breastfeeding, 'babywearing' and setting proper boundaries.
. . . From tips for a healthy birth, getting your baby to sleep
and feeding him the 'right fats,' to information about early
health concerns, the major steps in infant development and
troublesome but typical toddler behavior, the authors of this
comprehensive volume . . . are assured and reassuring experts." Publ Wkly

Parenting the fussy baby and high-need child;
everything you need to know--from birth to age five.
{by} William Sears and Martha Sears. Little, Brown
1996 237p il hardcover o.p. pa $12.95   **649**
1. Child psychology 2. Parent and child 3. Parenting
ISBN 0-316-77916-4 pa

LC 95-48381

To cope with a high-need child the authors "recommend
the approach they label attachment parenting; it includes
such techniques as on-demand feeding and weaning; nighttime parenting; sharing sleep; soothing through motion,
sound, visual distraction, and physical contact; and learning
via close study how to anticipate the baby's needs." Booklist

Includes bibliographical references

Shapiro, Lawrence E.

How to raise a child with a high EQ; a parent's
guide to emotional intelligence. HarperCollins Pubs.
1997 256p hardcover o.p. pa $13   **649**
1. Child psychology 2. Child rearing 3. Emotions 4.
Parenting
ISBN 0-06-092891-3 pa

LC 97-5533

"Through games, activities, tricks, skills, and habits,
{this book} guides parents in developing the moral emotions of empathy, honesty, shame, and guilt; thinking skills
such as realism and optimism; resourcefulness; social skills
including conversation, humor, manners, and friendliness;
persistence and motivation; and emotional control." Booklist

Includes bibliographical references

Small, Meredith F.

Our babies, ourselves; how biology and culture
shape the way we parent. Anchor Bks. (NY) 1998
xxii, 292p il hardcover o.p. pa $14.95   **649**
1. Infants -- Care 2. Infants -- Care -- Cross-cultural
studies 3. Infants -- Development 4. Infants --
Development -- Cross-cultural studies 5. Parent
and infant -- Cross-cultural studies 6. Parent-child
relationship
ISBN 0-385-48362-7 pa

LC 97-44348

The author "explores ethnopediatrics, an interdisciplinary science that combines anthropology, pediatrics, and
child development research in order to examine how child-
rearing styles across cultures affect the health and survival of
infants. Small describes the different parenting styles of several cultures, including . . . the nomadic Ache tribe of Para-
guay, the agrarian !Kung San society of the Kalahari Desert
in Africa, and the American industrialized society." Libr J

Includes bibliographical references

Spock, Benjamin

Dr. Spock on parenting; sensible advice from
America's most trusted child care expert. Simon &
Schuster 1988 318p hardcover o.p. pa $16.95 **649**
1. Parenting
ISBN 0-7434-2683-5 pa

LC 88-15792

"The author presents a personal critique on parenting,
often bordering on the autobiographical. . . . He discusses
in depth and with great conviction contemporary and traditional parent concerns, such as divorce, discipline, sex education, and the father's role." Libr J

Dr. Spock's the first two years; the emotional and
physical needs of children from birth to age two. edited by Martin T. Stein. Pocket Bks. 2001 153p pa
$13.95   **649**
1. Child care 2. Child development 3. Child rearing
ISBN 0-7434-1122-6

In these articles culled from Redbook and Parenting
Spock's advice to parents is that they should "trust themselves" and "expands on this idea in his reply to the question, 'What has eroded so many parents' self-asssurance in
asking for reasonably good behavior?'" Libr J

Dr. Spock's the school years; the emotional and social development of children. edited by Martin T. Stein. Pocket Bks. 2001 283p pa $15.95   **649**
1. Child care 2. Child development 3. Child rearing
ISBN 0-7434-1123-4

This volume collects Spock's essays published in Redbook and Parenting. They address "our contemporary culture's tendency to overschedule children." Libr J

White, Burton L.

Raising a happy, unspoiled child. Simon & Schuster 1994 253p il hardcover o.p. pa $13   **649**
1. Child rearing 2. Parenting
ISBN 0-684-80134-5 pa

LC 94-7838

The author argues "that many difficulties—testing parental authority, refusal to share toys with playmates, etc.—can virtually be eliminated if parents are not overly permissive with children of more than five months old." Publ Wkly
Includes bibliographical references

The Nursing mother's problem solver; Claire Martin {with Nancy Funnemark Krebs, editor; foreword by William Sears and Martha Sears} Fireside 2000 336p il pa $13   **649**
1. Breast feeding 2. Breast feeding -- Popular works
ISBN 0-684-85784-7

LC 00-37198

"Based on questions that were asked on the lactation consultant hot-line at the Children's Hospital of Denver, this book addresses common issues of new mothers (e.g., 'latching on', sore nipples, night feedings) as well as less common situations, such as breastfeeding babies with special needs. The scope of the Q&A is wide, providing a wealth of detailed information from a modern-day perspective." Libr J

649.8 Home care of people with disabilities and illnesses

American Cancer Society

★ **Caregiving:** a step-by-step resource for caring for the person with cancer at home; editors, Peter S. Houts, Julia A. Bucher. rev ed; American Cancer Soc. 2003 288p il pa $18.95   **649.8**
1. Cancer 2. Cancer -- Palliative treatment 3. Cancer -- Patients -- Home care 4. Caregivers 5. Home Nursing -- methods 6. Neoplasms -- nursing
ISBN 0-944235-45-X

LC 2003-1115

This book "explains each major kind of cancer treatment, obstacles to recovery, when it is time to call in professional help, plentiful examples of how individuals can help their loved ones, and how to adjust your plan of action as needed. Also addressed are topics such as managing care by involving other family members and using available community resources, emotional conditions such as anxiety or depression, and the most common physical side effects of cancer treatments such as nausea, pain, and fatigue and how to cope with them. A six-step plan successfully solving problems forms the backbone of each chapter. Chockfull of sensible

and reassuring information, this guide is easily accessible to the average reader." Libr J [review of 2000 edition]

Carter, Rosalynn

Helping yourself help others; a book for caregivers. {by} Rosalynn Carter with Susan K. Golant. Times Bks. 1994 278p hardcover o.p. pa $14 **649.8**
1. Caregivers 2. Home care services
ISBN 0-8129-2591-2 pa

LC 94-11924

The authors "describe the stages the caregiver progresses through, from first facing the illness or declining health of a loved one to the 'long-term, hard-work phase of caregiving.' Questions regarding in-home professional care and nursing homes are addressed, and the authors provide information on strategies, support groups, program recommendations, helpful organizations, and books." Booklist

McFarlane, Rodger

The **complete** bedside companion; no-nonsense advice on caring for the seriously ill. {by} Rodger McFarlane, Philip Bashe. Simon & Schuster 1998 544p hardcover o.p. pa $25.95   **649.8**
1. Caregivers 2. Critically ill -- Home care 3. Home nursing 4. Terminal care
ISBN 0-684-84319-6 pa

LC 97-43746

"This primer provides information on general illness and specific diseases, questions to ask the physician, basic nursing skills, making hospital visits, dealing with insurance companies, sources of additional information, and support groups. The authors . . . supplement this material with case studies and personal experiences." Libr J
Includes bibliographical references

650 Management and auxiliary services

Folsom, W. Davis

Understanding American business jargon; a dictionary. W. Davis Folsom. 2nd ed.; Greenwood Press 2005 364p $79.95   **650**
1. Business -- Dictionaries 2. Reference books
ISBN 0-313-33450-1

LC 2005-16817

This book "will help businesspeople, researchers, and students gain understanding of not only the buzzword-laden business-speak but business culture." Am Ref Books Annu, 2006
Includes bibliographical references

Kaufman, Josh

The **personal** MBA; a world-class business education in a single volume. Portfolio Penguin 2010 402p $27.95   **650**
1. Business 2. Commerce 3. Management
ISBN 978-1-59184-352-8

LC 2010-27919

The author "argues that those interested in business would be better served by skipping the M.B.A. and focusing on the critically important concepts that really make or break a business. According to the author, much of what is taught in business schools is outdated; you're better off saving the expense and finding other ways to learn about these core principles—which Kaufman synthesizes—in such areas as value creation, marketing, sales, and finance. . . . While Kaufman's rallying call will not eradicate the need or desire for M.B.A. degrees, he does provide a surprisingly solid alternative full of information that even those already in the workplace will respond to." Publ Wkly

Moss, Rita W.

★ **Strauss's** handbook of business information; a guide for librarians, students, and researchers. 2nd ed; Libraries Unlimited 2003 455p il   **650**
1. Business -- Bibliography 2. Business -- Databases -- Handbooks, manuals, etc 3. Business -- Information services 4. Business -- Reference books -- Bibliography -- Handbooks, manuals, etc 5. Business -- United States -- Electronic information resources -- Handbooks, manuals, etc 6. Business information services -- United States -- Handbooks, manuals, etc 7. Government publications -- United States 8. Government publications -- United States -- Handbooks, manuals, etc 9. Reference books
ISBN 1563085208

LC 2003-54569
This edition "first covers 'formats': directories, periodicals, loose-leaf services, government information services, and electronic sources. References are then organized by 'fields': banking, marketing, accounting, stocks and bonds, etc. Graphics include screen shots of e-sources." Libr J
Includes bibliographical references

Scott, David Logan

★ The **American** Heritage dictionary of business terms; [by] David L. Scott. Houghton Mifflin Harcourt 2009 594p pa $15.95   **650**
1. Business -- Dictionaries 2. Finance -- Dictionaries 3. Reference books
ISBN 978-0-618-75525-7; 0-618-75525-X

LC 2008-42657
"Covering the entire spectrum of business terminology, this A-to-Z contains more than 6000 terms from accounting, economics, finance, and investing to insurance, international business, law, management, marketing, and real estate. . . . This is both a handy and an indispensable reference for business professionals as well as for the general public." Libr J

Business periodicals index. Wilson, H.W.   **650**
1. Business -- Periodicals -- Indexes 2. Reference books
A subject guide to periodicals in accounting, advertising, banking, communications, economics, finance and investments, insurance, management, marketing, taxation, and related fields.

Encyclopedia of business information sources; [project editor], Virgil L. Burton III. 27th ed; Gale, Cengage Learning 2010 2v set $626   **650**
1. Business -- Information services 2. Reference books
ISBN 978-1-4144-4667-7
This is a comprehensive listing of business related finding aids including abstracting and indexing services, alma-

nacs and yearbooks, bibliographies, biographical sources, directories, encyclopedias and dictionaries, financial ratios, handbooks and manuals, online databases, periodicals and newsletters, price sources, research centers and institutes, statistical sources, trade associations and professional societies, and other related sources of information on each topic.

650.1   Personal success in business

Bartiromo, Maria

The **10** laws of enduring success; [by] Maria Bartiromo with Catherine Whitney. Crown Business 2010 293p $26; pa $15; ebook $11.99   **650.1**
1. Self-realization 2. Success
ISBN 978-0-307-45252-8; 978-0-307-45253-5 pa; 978-0-307-45254-2 ebook

LC 2009042267
"The 10 laws the authors present include self-knowledge, vision, initiative, courage, integrity, and resilience. . . . This how-to book is distinguished by presenting Bartiromo's personal and professional experiences and the wisdom she has gleaned from her varied encounters." Booklist

Brzezinski, Mika

Knowing your value; women, money, and getting what you're worth. Weinstein Books 2011 194p $22.95   **650.1**
1. Equal pay for equal work 2. Salaries, wages, etc. 3. Success 4. Women executives
ISBN 978-1-60286-134-3; 1-60286-134-X
Interviews a number of prominent women—including comedian Susie Essman, writer and director Nora Ephron, and TV personality Joy Behar—to reveal how ordinary women can achieve their deserved recognition and financial worth in the modern professional world.
"A thoughtful look at how women can quit getting in their own way." Publ Wkly

Comaford, Christine

Rules for renegades; how to make more money, rock your career, and revel in your individuality. [by] Christine Comaford-Lynch. McGraw-Hill 2007 268p $24.95   **650.1**
1. Business 2. Success
ISBN 978-0-07-148975-1; 0-07-148975-4
The author presents "step-by-step advice for starting a company, making it in a cutthroat environment and reaching life goals in record time, while recounting her entertaining, often hilarious life story. . . . Entrepreneurs and leaders at all levels of their careers will find this inspiring, rags-to-riches story as pleasurable to read as it is thought provoking." Publ Wkly

Felton, Sandra

Organizing your day; time management techniques that will work for you. [by] Sandra Felton and Marsha Sims. Revell 2009 266p pa $13.99 **650.1**
1. Time management
ISBN 978-0-8007-3315-5

LC 2008-52291

"The authors cover all the bases, from discussing personal mental impediments to managing time. The short chapters and interactive text featuring quizzes, bulleted lists, and fill-in charts make the book ideal for time-starved readers looking to get their act together pronto." Libr J

Includes bibliographical references

Godin, Seth

Linchpin; are you indispensible? illustrations by Jessica Hagy and Hugh MacLeod. Portfolio 2010 244p il $26.95 **650.1**

1. Creative thinking 2. Employees 3. Motivation (Psychology)

ISBN 978-1-59184-316-0

LC 2009036957

The author explains why some people make a difference in their professional fields and others do not, and shows readers how to make more meaningful contributions at work.

Goulston, Mark

Just listen; discover the secret to getting through to absolutely anyone. foreword by Keith Ferrazzi. American Management Association 2009 234p il $24.95 **650.1**

1. Business communication 2. Interpersonal relations

ISBN 978-0-8144-1403-3

LC 2009-14386

This is "a primer on dealing with hard-to-reach people in virtually every scenario—defiant executives, angry employees, families in turmoil, warring couples—through use of well-honed psychological techniques. . . . Chapter summaries feature action steps preparing readers to encounter similar scenarios, yielding a guide that is as entertaining as it is useful." Publ Wkly

Graham, Stedman

You can make it happen; a nine-step plan for success. Simon & Schuster 1997 270p il hardcover o.p. pa $13 **650.1**

1. Business 2. Minorities 3. Success

ISBN 0-684-83866-4 pa

LC 96-45457

Graham's "nine-step plan involves increasing self-awareness, creating a vision, developing a plan, understanding and following personal values, taking risks, managing responses to those risks, building a support team, making wise decisions, and forming a total commitment. Although his plan may be most applicable to people focusing on business and career goals, Graham notes that this plan can also be applied to other aspects of life." Libr J

Hawley, Casey Fitts

10 make-or-break career moments; navigate, negotiate, and communicate for success. Ten Speed Press 2010 216p pa $13.99 **650.1**

1. Business communication 2. Success 3. Vocational guidance

ISBN 978-1-58008-723-0

LC 2009-50517

The author "presents and advises on ten career-defining moments, ranging from meeting the CEO to being fired to being asked to commit an ethical violation. Hawley excels at

basic office politics done right, . . . and her chapters—clear, concise, and easy to read, including not just positive strategies, but also pitfalls, such as an early section on 'games NOT to play with an executive'—follow a smooth progression over a typical career arc. The strategies are engaging and relevant." Libr J

Includes bibliographical references

Hill, Napoleon

★ **Think** and grow rich; the landmark bestseller --now revised and updated for the 21st century. rev. and expanded by Arthur R. Pell. 1st Jeremy P. Tarcher/Penguin ed.; Jeremy P. Tarcher/Penguin 2005 302p pa $10 **650.1**

1. Entrepreneurship 2. Success

ISBN 1-585-42433-1

LC 2005-44133

A motivational guide to achieving wealth and success, drawing upon stories of successful millionaires as examples.

Kotter, John P.

Buy-in; saving your good idea from being shot down. [by] John P. Kotter and Lorne A. Whitehead. Harvard Business Review Press 2010 192p **650.1**

1. Creative ability 2. Public relations

ISBN 978-1-4221-5729-9

LC 2010016497

"This book explains how to protect a good idea and win support for it. The authors welcome naysayers, nitpickers, and handwringers into the room during the discussion, because they show you in this book how to respond to the unfair attacks to find success. Readers learn about the four attack strategies—death by delay, confusion, fear mongering, and character assassination—and how to show respect for all and use simple, clear, and common-sense responses. . . . This book helps you gain the upper hand by giving you practical responses to more than 24 generic attacks that people often use to shoot down good ideas." T + D

McCormack, Mark H.

What they don't teach you at Harvard Business School. Bantam Bks. 1984 256p hardcover o.p. pa $16.95 **650.1**

1. Management 2. Success

ISBN 0-553-34583-4 pa

LC 84-45172

McCormack's firm, the International Management Group, merchandises professional sports figures and markets the international television rights to sporting events. In this book, McCormack offers advice on business management.

Patterson, Philana

Black faces in white places; 10 game-changing strategies to achieve success and find greatness. [by] Randal Pinkett and Jeffrey Robinson, with Philana Patterson; foreword by Roland S. Martin. American Management Association 2011 xx, 266p il $24.95 **650.1**

1. African American businesspeople 2. Success

ISBN 978-0-8144-1680-8; 0-8144-1680-2

LC 2010020878

Pinkett "won season four of The Apprentice, the first African American winner. Here he offers ten strategies not simply for successful entrepreneurship but also successful 'intrapreneurship,' gaining success through knowing oneself and the realities of functioning in today's society." Libr J

Includes bibliographical references

Pfeffer, Jeffrey

Power; why some people have it--and others don't. HarperBusiness 2010 273p $27.99; ebook $14.99 **650.1**

1. Management 2. Power (Social sciences) 3. Success

ISBN 978-0-06-178908-3; 978-0-06-201061-2 ebook

LC 2010015280

The author "posits that intelligence, performance, and likeability alone are not the key to moving up in an organization; instead, he asserts, self promotion, building relationships, cultivating a reputation for control and authority, and perfecting a powerful demeanor are vital drivers of advancement and success. . . . Brimming with frank, realistic insights on paths to the top, this book offers unexpected—and aggressive—directions on how to advance and flourish in an evermore competitive workplace." Publ Wkly

Includes bibliographical references

Popcorn, Faith

Clicking; 16 trends to future fit your life, your work, and your business. {by} Faith Popcorn and Lys Marigold; illustrated by Gerti Bierenbroodsot. HarperCollins Pubs. 1996 498p il hardcover o.p. pa $14 **650.1**

1. Forecasting 2. Success

ISBN 0-88730-857-0 pa

LC 96-379

The authors provide tips on how to find one's proper slot in a rapidly changing world. Recognizing and adapting to new trends is discussed. Includes tips on finding a new career.

Spaulding, Tommy

It's not just who you know; transform your life (and your organization) by turning colleagues and contacts into lasting, genuine relationships. Broadway Books 2010 307p $23; ebook $12.99 **650.1**

1. Interpersonal relations 2. Success

ISBN 978-0-307-58913-2; 0-307-58913-7; 978-0-307-58915-6 ebook

LC 2010012355

In this "guide to reaching out to others, Spaulding . . . [discusses] how to create lasting relationships that go well beyond mere superficial contacts and 'second floor' relationships." Publisher's note

Includes bibliographical references

Swanepoel, Stefan

Surviving your Serengeti; 7 skills to master business and life: a fable of self-discovery. Wiley 2011 176p il $21.95; ebook $14.99 **650.1**

1. Industrial efficiency 2. Life skills 3. Success

ISBN 978-0-470-94780-7; 0-470-94780-2; 978-1-1180-0859-1 ebook

LC 2010039905

"In this business fable, Swanepoel offers a . . . tale of life in the Serengeti and what lessons it holds for today's belea-guered workforce. The book follows the story of corporate executive Sean Spencer as he embarks on a three day visit to Africa. Without cell phone coverage or any other form of technology to keep him wired in, Sean is forced to disconnect from the worries of his troubled business thousands of miles away, and instead, he becomes engrossed in the animals that rule this untamed land and the wisdom the Serengeti has to offer." Publisher's note

Syed, Mathew

Bounce; Mozart, Federer, Picasso, Tiger, and the science of success. Harper 2010 312p il $25.99 **650.1**

1. Ability 2. Success

ISBN 978-0-06-172375-9; 0-06-172375-4

LC 2009-48135

"At the age of 24, Syed became the #1 British table tennis player, an achievement he initially attributed to his superior speed and agility. But in retrospect, he realizes that a combination of advantages—a mentor, good facilities nearby, and lots of time to hone his skills—set him up perfectly to become a star performer. . . . He takes on the myth of the child prodigy, emphasizing that Mozart, the Williams sisters, Tiger Woods, and Susan Polgar, the first female grandmaster, all had live-in coaches in the form of supportive parents who put them through a ton of early practice. Cogent discussions of the neuroscience of competition, including the placebo effect of irrational optimism, self-doubt, and superstitions, all lend credence to a compelling narrative." Publ Wkly

Includes bibliographical references

650.14 Success in obtaining jobs and promotions

Asher, Donald

Cracking the hidden job market; how to find opportunity in any economy. Ten Speed Press 2011 198p pa $14.99; ebook $11.99 **650.14**

1. Job hunting 2. Success 3. Vocational guidance

ISBN 978-1-58008-494-9 pa; 978-1-58008-639-4 ebook

LC 2010010857

The author "invites job seekers to develop strategies for finding jobs—before they've been posted. He provides specific rules for figuring out what job is the best fit, and offers templates for structuring informational interviews, e-mail, conversations, and other forms of contact that can be adapted for use according to individual job seeker's needs. . . . Valuable assistance from a leading authority." Publ Wkly

Beatty, Richard H.

175 high-impact cover letters; 3rd ed; Wiley 2002 244p pa $14.95 **650.14**

1. Applications for positions 2. Cover letters 3. Job hunting

ISBN 0-471-21084-6

LC 2001-46963

The **interview** kit; 3rd ed; Wiley 2003 248p pa $14.95 **650.14**

1. Applications for positions 2. Employment

interviewing 3. Interviewing
ISBN 0-471-44925-3

LC 2003-45071

This offers advice for success in job interviews, with answers to 500 questions, strategies for making a good impression, and negotiating salaries and benefits.

Boldt, Laurence G.

Zen and the art of making a living; a practical guide to creative career design. 2010 ed., 3rd rev. ed.; Penguin Books 2009 xxxiii, 569p il pa $22 **650.14**
1. Vocational guidance
ISBN 978-0-14-311459-8

LC 2009-19516

This "career development guide helps the reader identify 'work purpose,' key talents, and objectives. . . . Boldt moves beyond the basics to address unusual practical and psychological issues such as starting a business, freelancing, founding a nonprofit corporation, maintaining a healthy self-esteem, and building marketing strategy." Libr J
Includes bibliographical references

Cohen, Carol Fishman

★ **Back** on the career track; a guide for stay-at-home moms who want to return to work. [by] Carol Fishman Cohen and Vivian Steir Rabin. Warner Books 2007 297p il $24.99 **650.14**
1. Vocational guidance 2. Women -- Employment
ISBN 978-0-446-57820-2; 0-446-57820-7

LC 2006-20986

The authors present a "step-by-step relaunch guide for stay-at-home moms. Both Harvard MBA relaunchers themselves, they explore the role career plays in the quality of life for professional women. . . . A listing of resources, recommended reading, and sample résumés are provided. One of only a few books for the millions of professional women/mothers who are not working for pay; highly recommended for public libraries." Libr J
Includes bibliographical references

Deems, Richard S.

Make job loss work for you; get over it and get your career back on track. [by] Richard S. Deems and Terri A. Deems. JIST Works 2009 194p il pa $12.95 **650.14**
1. Job hunting 2. Unemployment 3. Vocational guidance
ISBN 978-1-59357-740-7

LC 2009-26849

The authors "address the various reactions people have to losing their job. From there, they give a chapter-by-chapter blueprint for getting your next job, covering résumés, interview tips, and networking in detail. . . . Covering all the basics, this work is recommended for job seekers, including those who have been laid off, and is especially appropriate for professionals and management-level workers." Libr J

Enelow, Wendy S.

★ **Cover** letter magic; [by] Wendy S. Enelow [and] Louise Kursmark. 2nd ed.; JIST Works 2004 412p pa $16.95 **650.14**
1. Applications for positions 2. Cover letters 3. Résumés (Employment)
ISBN 1-563-70986-4

LC 2003-23186

This guide to writing cover letters includes "more than 150 . . . cover letters for every profession and situation. Before-and-after transformations . . . tips on resumes, e-mail and scannable cover letters, thank-you letters [and] . . . dozens of sample opening paragraphs [are included.]" Publisher's note

Fry, Ronald W.

Your first resume; for students and anyone preparing to enter today's job market. by Ron Fry. 5th ed; Career Press 2001 188p pa $11.99 **650.14**
1. Résumés (Employment)
ISBN 1-56414-583-2

LC 2001-35875

A step-by-step guide for preparing a successful résumé. Numerous examples accompany the text.

Gardella, Robert

The **Harvard** Business School guide to finding your next job; {by} Robert S. Gardella. Harvard Business School Press 2000 143p pa $16.95 **650.14**
1. Job hunting 2. Job hunting -- United States 3. Vocational guidance -- United States
ISBN 1-57851-223-9

LC 99-58454

"Gardella covers references, résumés, letters, interviews, and negotiation. He also details a strategy for planning and executing a job search campaign, and discusses the emotional aspects of looking for work. Special topics include the 'long-distance' job search, job fairs, and overcoming age discrimination." Booklist
Includes bibliographical references and index

Jackson, Tom

The **perfect** resume; today's ultimate job search tool. Broadway Books 2004 223p pa $12.95 **650.14**
1. Applications for positions 2. Résumés (Employment)
ISBN 0-7679-1623-9

LC 2003-62972

This guide to resumes and job applications emphasizes temporary, freelance, and consulting positions, and offers advice on preparing a capabilities portfolio, on using e-mail, talents banks on the Internet, and electronic job searches.

Laakmann McDowell, Gayle

The **Google** resume; how to prepare for a career and land a job at Apple, Microsoft, Google, or any top tech company. Wiley 2011 280p il $22.95; ebook $14.99 **650.14**
1. Job hunting 2. Résumés (Employment)
ISBN 978-0-470-92762-5; 0-470-92762-3; 978-1-1180-1315-1 ebook

LC 2010039906

This book discusses "how to win a coveted spot at Google, Microsoft, Apple, or other top tech firms. . . . Covers key concerns like what to major in, which extra-curriculars and other experiences look good, how to apply, how to design and tailor your resume, how to prepare for and excel in the interview, and . . . more." Publisher's note

Mackay, Harvey

★ **Use** your head to get your foot in the door; job search secrets no one else will tell you. Portfolio 2010 329p il $25.95; pa $16   **650.14**

1. Job hunting

ISBN 978-1-59184-321-4; 1-59184-321-9; 978-1-59184-343-6 pa; 1-59184-343-X pa

LC 2009039791

"This collection of job search tips by Mackay . . . [comes] complete with humorous examples and 'Quickie' one-page stories that illustrate his main points. Don't let the cover or any worry about his sense of humor dissuade you: this is a very useful book. The short chapters with descriptive titles make it easy to navigate, and Mackay offers tips—from changing your attitude to getting hired—both for those currently employed but wishing to position themselves better in their current companies and for those who are out of work." Libr J

Includes bibliographical references

Martini, Kitty

Thank you for firing me! how to catch the next wave of success after you lose your job. [by] Kitty Martini and Candice Reed. Sterling Publishing Company 2010 232p pa $14.95   **650.14**

1. Career changes 2. Job hunting 3. Vocational guidance

ISBN 978-1-4027-6956-6

LC 2009-34298

"For readers who have lost their jobs, are thinking about venturing forth as freelancers or consultants, or are searching for a new career, this is an invigorating and very helpful book. . . . [The authors'] book is clear, enthusiastic, and, most importantly, loaded with direct, uncluttered advice with tons of specifics. A resource guide in the back lists almost 30 pages' worth of web sites and some print materials, corresponding to the chapter topics, which range from how to develop a support network and how to tune into Gen Y job networking to specifics on global, artistic, and green industries, among others. A great choice for most job hunters." Libr J

Includes bibliographical reference

Mornell, Pierre

Games companies play; the job hunter's guide to playing smart & winning big in the high-stakes hiring game. designed by Kit Hinrichs; illustrations by Regan Dunnick. Ten Speed Press 2000 208p il hardcover o.p. pa $17.95   **650.14**

1. Job hunting

ISBN 1-58008-408-7 pa

LC 00-26736

The author "offers advice on how to ready résumés and recommendations, write eye-catching cover letters, shine in the most difficult interview situation, and finalize job offers.

He includes more than 40 sample interview questions and answers, legal considerations, and a list of important web and print resources." Libr J

Includes bibliographical references

Parker, Yana

The **damn** good resume guide; a crash course in resume writing. 4th ed; Ten Speed Press 2002 73p il pa $9.95   **650.14**

1. Résumés (Employment)

ISBN 1-58008-444-3

LC 2002-9177

This guide offers a ten-step approach to resume writing, providing creative solutions and strategies to various resume problems. Also included are sections on formatting resumes and submitting resumes over the Internet.

Richardson, Bradley G.

Career comeback; 8 steps to getting back on your feet when you're fired, laid off, or your business venture has failed--and finding more job satisfaction than ever. Broadway Bks. 2004 319p pa $14.95   **650.14**

1. Career development 2. Employees -- Dismissal 3. Employees -- Dismissal of 4. Job hunting 5. Vocational guidance

ISBN 0-767-91557-7

LC 2003-56271

"In addition to providing detailed suggestions for sharpening skills—such as resume writing, interviewing, working with recruiters and networking—{the author} addresses the psychological and emotional problems that often accompany the loss of a job. . . . Upbeat and clearly written, Richardson's comeback program will be welcomed by many." Publ Wkly

Includes bibliographical references

Wendleton, Kate

Building a great resume; for job hunters, career changers, consultants, and freelancers. with hints for new grads by Mark Gonska. 2nd ed; Career Press 1999 195p il pa $13.99   **650.14**

1. Career changes 2. Job hunting 3. Résumés (Employment)

ISBN 1-56414-433-X

LC 99-38052

"Creator of the career-counseling network The Five O'Clock Club, Wendleton uses the club's case study approach with before-and-after examples (over 80 industries are featured) to address the entire process of résumé writing for career changers, consultants, freelancers, and job-hunters." Libr J

Yate, Martin John

Knock 'em dead 2011; the ultimate job search guide. [by] Martin Yate. 25th anniversary ed; Adams Media 2010 367p il pa $15.95   **650.14**

1. Applications for positions 2. Interviewing 3. Job hunting

ISBN 978-1-4405-0586-7

"Updated regularly since 1987, Yate's comprehensive how-to covers the entire job search process from résumé writing and interviewing to salary negotiation and psychological and drug testing, with information on recent developments in the job market. Three appendixes address online searching with valuable listings of web sites and resources arranged by subject." Libr J

McGraw-Hill's big red book of resumes; {compiled by Luisa Gerasimo} McGraw-Hill 2002 473p pa $16.95   **650.14**
1. Résumés (Employment)
ISBN 0-07-140195-4
                                                   LC 2002-25523
"Some 300 résumés target a wide variety of jobs, experience, and styles that will prove useful as models." Libr J

651   Auxiliary services

New York Public Library
The **New** York Public Library business desk reference. Wiley 1998 494p il map hardcover o.p. pa $24.95   **651**
1. Office practice -- Handbooks, manuals, etc. 2. Office practice -- United States -- Handbooks, manuals, etc
ISBN 0-471-14442-8; 0-471-32835-9 pa
                                                    LC 97-7408
This work "has sections focusing on information delivery, communications, the office environment, equipment, supplies and systems, human resources, finances, law, public relations, marketing, travel, and information resources. The lists of further information that end each section include organizations, service providers, books, and online resources." Booklist

651.3   Office management

Burton, Sharon
Office procedures for the 21st century; {by} Sharon Burton, Nelda Shelton. 7th ed; Pearson/Prentice-Hall 2008 xxvii, 534p il pa $88   **651.3**
1. Office practice -- Handbooks, manuals, etc. 2. Secretaries -- Handbooks, manuals, etc.
ISBN 978-0-13-234343-5; 0-13-234343-6
This covers business math and language arts skills, the role of office support staff, interpersonal communication, records management, telecommunications, computers and job search skills. Includes application exercises, projects, sample forms and documents.

Stroman, James
★ **Administrative** assistant's and secretary's handbook; by James Stroman, Kevin Wilson, Jennifer Wauson. 3rd ed.; American Management Association 2008 578p il $34.95   **651.3**
1. Office practice -- Handbooks, manuals, etc. 2. Secretaries -- Handbooks, manuals, etc.
ISBN 978-0-8144-0913-8
                                                   LC 2007-20971

This handbook provides information on general procedures and techniques covering such topics as telephone usage, mailing and shipping, office equipment and computers, language usage, financial activities, banking, etc.

651.7   Communication

Lindsell-Roberts, Sheryl
Strategic business letters and e-mail; Sheryl Lindsell-Roberts. Houghton Mifflin 2004 374p il pa $19.95   **651.7**
1. Business letters 2. Electronic mail systems
ISBN 0-618-44833-0
                                                   LC 2004-14030
"This is a book that is not only easy to comprehend but also easy to adapt to one's own business needs." Booklist

Phillips, Ellen Haygood
Shocked, appalled, and dismayed! How to write letters of complaint that get results. Vintage Bks. 1999 333p pa $12   **651.7**
1. Business letters 2. Customer relations
ISBN 0-375-70120-6
                                                   LC 98-13819
A guide to writing effective letters of complaint. Legal advice, illustrative anecdotes, and sample letters are provided. An appendix lists the names and addresses of over 600 major companies, government agencies, and consumer organizations.

651.8   Computer applications

Jaderstrom, Susan
Complete office handbook; the definitive reference for today's electronic office. {by} Susan Jaderstrom, Leonard Kruk, and Joanne Miller; general editor, Susan W. Fenner. 3rd ed; Random House Ref. 2002 596p il maps pa $21.95   **651.8**
1. Office practice -- Automation 2. Office practice -- Handbooks, manuals, etc.
ISBN 0-375-70929-0
                                                  LC 2002-727980
This book "is designed to assist the individual who serves as an administrative assistant, executive assistant, or project manager. . . . It covers, in detail, every facet of office operations, from office supplies and financial record keeping to complex operations, including computers, dictation equipment, and telecommunications equipment. . . . This handbook is just as useful for the entry-level office worker as it is for the professional advancing to the level of executive assistant." Recomm Ref Books for Small & Medium-sized Libr & Media Cent, 2003

652   Processes of written communication

Florey, Kitty Burns

Script and scribble; the rise and fall of handwriting. Melville House 2009 190p $22.95   **652**
1. Graphology 2. Handwriting 3. Penmanship 4. Writing -- Materials and instruments
ISBN 978-1-933633-67-1; 1-933633-67-0
           LC 2008-26964
A "pithy account of the history of handwriting . . . Florey makes a solid case for handwriting as a social indicator, and her affection for its art is thoughtful and aesthetically informed." Bookforum

The book of codes; understanding the world of hidden messages: an illustrated guide to signs, symbols, ciphers, and secret languages. Paul Lunde, general editor. University of California Press 2009 279p il map $29.95   **652**
1. Ciphers
ISBN 978-0-520-26013-9
"Whether or not you're fascinated by the world of Dan Brown's 'The Last Symbol,' there is probably something of interest in this densely researched, beautifully illustrated book. 'The Book of Codes' is so complete — with chapters that include information about everything from religions to body language to digital communication — reading this book won't peg you as a secret-society nut." St. Louis Post-Dispatch

657   Accounting

Siegel, Joel G.

Accounting handbook; [by] Joel G. Siegel, Jae K. Shim. 4th ed; Barron's 2006 993p il $35   **657**
1. Accounting
ISBN 0-7641-5776-0
           LC 2005-45279
This reference includes sections on financial accounting, tax preparation, auditing, personal financial planning, and governmental and nonprofit accounting and includes a dictionary of accounting terms.

658   General management

Bacon, Lauren

The **boss** of you; everything a woman needs to know to start, run, and maintain her own business. [by] Lauren Bacon & Emira Mears. Seal Press 2008 297p pa $15.95   **658**
1. Business enterprises 2. Businesswomen 3. Management
ISBN 978-1-58005-236-8; 1-58005-236-3
           LC 2007-39417
"The authors cover the fundamentals of crafting a mission statement, developing branding, handling finances and legal issues, hiring good employees and expanding your business with admirable clarity, bolstered by success stories, helpful exercises and sample budgets. Women with dreams of owning their own businesses and looking for a place to start will find much to aid them—and much to enjoy—in this thoughtful guide." Publ Wkly
Includes bibliographical references

Barajas, Louis

Small business, big life; five steps to creating a great life with your own small business. Thomas Nelson 2007 xx, 199p il $22.99   **658**
1. Management 2. Small business 3. Success
ISBN 978-1-4016-0336-6; 1-4016-0336-X
           LC 2007-1070
The author "describes his and his father's entrepreneurial paths and suggests an inspirational approach to business that relies on four personal greatness cornerstones—truth, responsibility, awareness, and courage—and on keeping in mind your vision and your team's needs. A new take on how to achieve work/life balance." Libr J
Includes bibliographical references

Bredin, Alice

The **virtual** office survival handbook; what telecommuters and entrepreneurs need to succeed in today's nontraditional workplace. Wiley 1996 259p hardcover o.p. pa $16.95   **658**
1. Home-based business 2. Telecommuting
ISBN 0-471-12059-6 pa
           LC 96-1327
The author "starts by describing the professions and industries most suited to virtual or home offices and the employee personality and temperament that will thrive in the situation. Then she offers first-rate nitty-gritty advice on setting up an office, from choosing computer systems, legal and tax requirements for home business, time management and more." Publ Wkly
Includes bibliographical references

Collins, James C.

Good to great; why some companies make the leap, and others don't. {by} Jim Collins. HarperBusiness 2001 300p il $27.50   **658**
1. Leadership 2. Management 3. Organizational change 4. Strategic planning 5. Technological innovations -- Management
ISBN 0-06-662099-6
           LC 2001-24818
"Starting with every company that ever appeared in the Fortune 500, Collins identifies 11 great ones and looks for similarities among them, and what he finds will both surprise and fascinate anyone involved in management." Booklist
Includes bibliographical references

Connors, Richard J.

★ **Warren** Buffett on business; principles from the sage of Omaha. John Wiley & Sons 2010 259p il $24.95; ebook $16.99   **658**
1. Management
ISBN 978-0-470-50230-3; 978-0-470-57071-5 ebook
           LC 2009024946
Material drawn from Berkshire Hathaway shareholders' letters from 1977–2008, in Warren Buffett's own words.

Drucker, Peter F.

★ The **Drucker** lectures; essential lessons on management, society, and economy. edited and with an introduction by Rick Wartzman. McGraw-Hill 2010 266p $29.95; ebook $29.95   **658**

1. Management

ISBN 978-0-07-170045-0; 0-07-170045-5; 978-0-07-175950-2 ebook; 0-07-175950-6 ebook

LC 2010484567

This book presents thirty-three of Peter F. Drucker's speeches and talks delivered at professional gatherings and in the classroom.

"From his concern with continuous and full employment in the 1950s to globalization, nonprofit management, and the future of the corporation in the early 2000s, these lectures reflect a Drucker that many scholars and practitioners knew, but they also reveal new insights into the currency . . . of his thinking." Choice

Includes bibliographical references

Management challenges for the 21st century; {by} Peter F. Drucker. HarperBusiness 1999 207p $27.50; pa $18   **658**

1. Management 2. Management -- Forecasting 3. Twenty-first century -- Forecasts

ISBN 0-88730-998-4; 0-88730-999-2 pa

LC 99-17087

"Drucker outlines the changing role of management, the new realities of strategy, how to lead in times of great change, how to develop new information sources for effective decision-making, and how individual workers must assume responsibility for managing their own careers." Libr J

Fenn, Donna

Alpha dogs; how your small business can become a leader of the pack. Collins 2005 224p il $24.95; pa $14.95   **658**

1. Businesspeople 2. Entrepreneurship 3. Small business 4. Success

ISBN 0-06-075867-8; 978-0-06-075867-7; 0-06-075868-6 pa; 978-0-06-075868-4 pa

LC 2006-275386

The author "takes us inside the reality of small businesses by showcasing eight successful entrepreneurs who share their stories and strategies. . . . This book offers valuable insight for current and aspiring entrepreneurs." Booklist

Includes bibliographical references

Gerber, Michael E.

The **most** successful small business in the world; the ten principles. John Wiley & Sons 2010 xxv, 162p il $24.95; ebook $16.99   **658**

1. Small business

ISBN 978-0-470-50362-1; 0-470-50362-9; 978-0-470-59432-2 ebook

LC 2009038789

The author presents ten principles toward building and maintaining a successful small business.

Jacobs, Charles S.

Management rewired; why feedback doesn't work and other surprising lessons from the latest brain science. Portfolio 2009 216p $25.95; pa $16 **658**

1. Applied psychology 2. Interpersonal relations 3. Personnel management

ISBN 978-1-59184-262-0; 978-1-59184-337-5 pa

LC 2009-1724

"Well argued and substantiated, this book turns prevalent management theory on its head and will have lasting impact on how it is taught in business schools and implemented in organizations." Publ Wkly

Includes bibliographical references

Kelley, Robert Earl

How to be a star at work; nine breakthrough strategies you need to succeed. Times Business 1998 xxi, 312p il hardcover o.p. pa $13   **658**

1. Leadership 2. Management 3. Office workers 4. Success 5. Success in business 6. Teams in the workplace

ISBN 0-8129-3169-6 pa

LC 97-28117

Kelley's "program is commonsense advice to workers: take initiatives, network for useful information, self-manage, know whom you're trying to please, be a biddable follower when necessary, be a reliable leader when that's called for, work effectively in teams, know your organization and how to present your ideas." Publ Wkly

Includes bibliographical references

Kurtzman, Joel

★ **MBA** in a box; the practical guide to the big ideas of business. [by] Joel Kurtzman with Glenn Rifkin & Victoria Griffith. Crown Business 2004 437p $34.95   **658**

1. Management

ISBN 0-609-61088-0

LC 2003-19647

"This practical guidebook to business concepts is appropriately straightforward in its approach. . . . The book makes for a refreshing and often humorous read." Publ Wkly

Includes bibliographical references

Lonier, Terri

Working solo; the real guide to freedom & financial success with your own business. 2nd ed; Wiley 1998 xxiv, 354p il pa $14.95   **658**

1. Entrepreneurship -- United States 2. One-person corporations 3. Self-employed 4. Self-employed -- Handbooks, manuals, etc 5. Self-employed -- United States -- Handbooks, manuals, etc 6. Small business 7. Small business -- Handbooks, manuals, etc 8. Small business -- United States 9. Sole proprietorship

ISBN 0-471-24713-8

LC 98-10660

This offers advice on starting a small business covering such topics as time management, buying a computer, setting up an office, business planning, low-cost marketing techniques, using technology and the Internet. Includes a resource section on books, on-line services, and software.

Michelli, Joseph A.

The **Starbucks** experience; 5 principles for turning ordinary into extraordinary. McGraw-Hill 2006 208p $21.95 **658**

1. Management 2. Success

ISBN 978-0-07-147784-0; 0-07-147784-5

LC 2006-16788

The author "takes an in-depth look at Starbucks's proven and practical strategies for building a successful, multinational corporation. His chapters illustrate the company's five basic success principles: make it your own, everything matters, surprise and delight, embrace resistance, and leave your mark. Readers will discover a rich mix of ideas and techniques that will help them apply the Starbucks vision, creativity, and leadership to their own careers, workplaces, and companies." Libr J

Includes bibliographical references

Mintzberg, Henry

Managing. Berrett-Koehler Publishers 2009 306p il $26.95 **658**

1. Management

ISBN 978-1-57675-340-8

"This is a great read: a work of rich description and insight rather than a theory of managing, and it will stand the test of time." Management Today

Includes bibliographical references

O'Reilly, Charles A.

Hidden value; how great companies achieve extraordinary results with ordinary people. {by} Charles A. O'Reilly III, Jeffrey Pfeffer. Harvard Business School Press 2000 286p il $29.95 **658**

1. Human capital 2. Human capital -- United States 3. Industrial management -- United States 4. Management

ISBN 0-87584-898-2

LC 00-25016

"Through eight case studies, Hidden Value shows how a firm can use existing talent rather than how firms can attract talent. Smart organizations make it possible for ordinary people to perform as stars by engaging their emotional and intellectual resources." Libr J

Includes bibliographical references

Shipley, David

Send; the essential guide to email for office and home. [by] David Shipley and Will Schwalbe. Alfred A. Knopf 2007 247p hardcover o.p. pa $14.95 **658**

1. Business communication 2. Electronic mail messages 3. Electronic mail systems 4. Interpersonal communication

ISBN 978-0-307-26364-3; 978-0-307-27599-8 pa

LC 2006-35235

A "humorous, pithy, and much-needed guide to the art and science of e-mail. . . . These tutorials are peppered with true tales of e-mail misuse that are both illustrative and amusing. For the more technically inclined, sidebars spell out e-mail's history, . . . briefly explain how it works, and define great moments in e-mail history." Christ Sci Monit

Stephenson, James

Ultimate homebased business handbook; how to start, run and grow your own profitable business. [by] James Stephenson with Rich Mintzer. 2nd ed.; Entrepreneur Press 2008 xxxi, 516p pa $29.95 **658**

1. Business enterprises 2. Home-based business 3. Small business

ISBN 978-1-59918-185-1

LC 2008-4944

"Stephenson's comprehensive publication covers all topics of concern for the would-be side business owner. It is distinguished by comprehensive coverage of marketing, advertising, and PR and a list of business ideas and franchise opportunities." Libr J

Includes bibliographical references

Strauss, Steven D.

★ The **small** business bible; everything you need to know to succeed in your small business. 2nd ed.; Wiley 2008 526p il pa $19.95 **658**

1. Business enterprises 2. Small business

ISBN 978-0-470-26124-8; 0-470-26124-2

LC 2008-12277

"Chapters cover green businesses, online advertising and marketing, emerging technologies, and cutting-edge business building strategies." Libr J

Thompson, Mark

Now, build a great business! 7 ways to maximize your profits in any market. [by] Mark Thompson and Brian Tracy; foreword by Frances Hesselbein. American Management Association 2011 xxii, 228p $24.95 **658**

1. Leadership 2. Marketing

ISBN 978-0-8144-1697-6; 0-8144-1697-7

LC 2010030612

The authors "offer easy, tried-and-true ways to think about and plan organizational growth, especially in tough economic times. In seven steps (with a chapter devoted to each), the authors identify sustainable strategies for attracting customers and recruiting better leaders. They share seven simple questions that leaders ask themselves and provide helpful checklist exercises on a variety of key topics including creating a great business plan, designing an effective marketing plan, and creating a good customer experience." Publ Wkly

Wall Street journal

The **Wall** Street Journal essential guide to management; lasting lessons from the best leadership minds of our time. Harper Business 2010 xxvii, 207p pa $16.99 **658**

1. Management

ISBN 978-0-06-184033-3

LC 2010-2879

The author "lays out in helpful order and understandable prose what he considers the best practices for a good manager to follow; especially instructive are his discussions of 'six different styles that leaders use to motivate others.' . . . For serious consideration for any library business collection." Booklist

Includes bibliographical references

Wooldridge, Adrian

Masters of management; how the business gurus and their ideas have changed the world--for better and for worse. HarperBusiness 2011 446p $29.99 **658**

1. Management

ISBN 978-0-06-177113-2; 9780061771132

LC 2011015690

"The core of the book is a solid examination of the effects of entrepreneurship, globalization, and the free-agency economy on corporate governance. Wooldridge offers a balanced look at how business schools have spawned a guru industry that offers a gamut of theories on learning, innovation, and strategy. Peter Drucker, Tom Peters, and the 'Journo-Gurus' (Thomas Friedman, Malcolm Gladwell, and Chris Anderson) receive focused attention as the main influences in contemporary theory. . . . This is one of the best overviews of management theory in the 20th century. It is written in a clear and accessible style that will appeal to both MBA students and the general reader." Libr J

Business: the ultimate resource; 2nd ed.; Basic Books 2006 liii, 1973p il $59.95 **658**

1. Entrepreneurship 2. Management

ISBN 0-465-00830-5; 978-0-465-00830-8

This book offers "information and insights from experts in the business field and covers a wide array of topics, among them telecommuting, leadership, finance, and biographies of business and management notables. . . . This unique resource offers a huge selection of articles and provides a first step for students and scholars gathering information." Libr J

Includes bibliographical references

Encyclopedia of small business; Arsen J. Darnay, Monique D. Magee, editors. 3rd ed.; Thomson Gale 2007 2v set $550 **658**

1. Reference books 2. Small business -- Encyclopedias

ISBN 0-7876-9112-7; 978-0-7876-9112-7

LC 2006-22623

This reference arranged in A-Z format contains articles and overviews on areas "including financing; financial planning; business plan creation; market analysis; sales strategy; tax planning and more." Publisher's note

Includes bibliographical references

658.1   Organization and financial management

Johnson, Victoria M.

Grant writing 101; everything you need to start raising funds today. McGraw-Hill 2011 269p pa $20; ebook $20 **658.1**

1. Fund raising 2. Grants-in-aid

ISBN 978-0-07-175018-9 pa; 978-0-07-175018-9 ebook

LC 2010039599

This guide to grant writing offers "ten tactics for writing a compelling proposal; tips for finding the best grantor for your needs; important components of various types of grants; [and] next steps for when you're approved." Publisher's note

Judson, Bruce

Go it alone; the secret to building a successful business on your own. Bruce Judson. HarperBusiness 2004 229p $23.95; pa $14.95 **658.1**

1. Business enterprises 2. Entrepreneurship 3. Management 4. Small business

ISBN 0-06-073113-3; 0-06-073114-1 pa

LC 2004-52391

The author "offers sound, cogent advice for budding entrepreneurs in a book that will be of value to all readers thinking about going into business." Booklist

Includes bibliographical references

McGuckin, Frances

★ **Business** for beginners; from research and business plans to money, marketing and the law. Sourcebooks, Inc. 2005 318p il pa $16.95 **658.1**

1. Entrepreneurship 2. Management 3. Small business

ISBN 1-4022-0392-6

LC 2005-3351

This "is the ultimate of primers, starting with a good self-assessment—do you have the skills for success?—and concluding with real-life tales of seven entrepreneurs." Booklist

McKeever, Mike P.

How to write a business plan; by Mike McKeever. 10th ed.; Nolo 2010 273p pa $34.99; ebook $34.99 **658.1**

1. Business enterprises 2. Business planning 3. Small business

ISBN 978-1-4133-1280-5 pa; 1-4133-1280-2 pa; 978-1-4133-1297-3 ebook; 1-4133-1297-7 ebook

LC 2010-21162

"This is an outstanding step-by-step guide to writing a professional and sound business plan. Using examples and worksheets, McKeever helps the reader evaluate the profitability of a business idea, estimate expenses, prepare a cash-flow statement, create profit and loss forecasts, and more." Libr J

Root, Hal

The **small** business start-up guide; a surefire blueprint to successfully launch your own business. [by] Hal Root and Steve Koenig. 4th ed.; Sourcebooks, Inc. 2005 246p il pa $16.95 **658.1**

1. Small business

ISBN 1-4022-0602-X; 978-1-4022-0602-3

LC 2006-279673

This guide covers such topics as finding investors and capital, bank loans, becoming incorporated, and business plans.

Slim, Pamela

Escape from cubicle nation; from corporate prisoner to thriving entrepreneur. Portfolio 2009 340p $25.95; pa $15 **658.1**

1. Business enterprises 2. Entrepreneurship 3. Success

ISBN 978-1-59184-257-6; 1-59184-257-3; 978-0-425-

23284-2 pa; 0-425-23284-0 pa
LC 2008-50022

"Slim shows readers how to navigate the terrifying yet gratifying transition from corporate drone to entrepreneur. . . . What's here is: the nitty-gritty of getting a business off the ground, legal considerations, making the best use of social networking sites, the components of a business model, organized creative brainstorming, financial advice, shopping for self-paid insurance and benefits, and helpful anecdotes of real-life entrepreneurship. With her humorous insights into corporate life and an appealing no-nonsense yet empathic tone, Slim deals swiftly and incisively with anxiety, fear and hesitation. . . . This is a standout in the start-your-own business genre." Publ Wkly

Includes bibliographical references

Small business sourcebook; the entrepreneur's resource. Sonya D. Hill, project editor. 27th ed; Gale Cengage Learning 2010 6v set $649 **658.1**
1. Reference books 2. Small business
ISBN 978-1-4144-4784-1

This "is a standard reference work for identifying information resources for starting, developing, and growing 341 specific small businesses as well as for finding information on general small business topics and sources of assistance at the state and federal levels and by Canadian province. . . . The strength of the reference work lies in its catalog of resources for specific kinds of small businesses as well as the variety of sources covered and the copious annotations. It will aid entrepreneurs who need both general and specific information to help them solve problems." Am Ref Books Annu, 2003

658.3   Personnel management (Human resource management)

Hallowell, Edward M.
Shine; using brain science to get the best from your people. Harvard Business Review Press 2011 197p il $26.95 **658.3**
1. Interpersonal relations 2. Job satisfaction 3. Management 4. Motivation (Psychology)
ISBN 978-1-59139-923-0; 1-59139-923-8
LC 2010024950

"Edward Hallowell draws on brain science, performance research, and his own experience helping people maximize their potential to present a . . . process for getting the best from your people." Publisher's note

Includes bibliographical references

Hewlett, Sylvia Ann
Off-ramps and on-ramps; keeping talented women on the road to success. Harvard Business School Press 2007 299p il $29.95 **658.3**
1. Corporations -- United States 2. Women -- Employment 3. Women -- Employment -- United States 4. Women in the professions -- United States 5. Work and family -- United States
ISBN 978-1-422-10102-5; 1-422-10102-9
LC 2006-38271

The author "examines why many women exit their careers—taking 'off-ramps' (leaving altogether) or 'scenic routes' (opting to work part-time), often during critical, competitive times. She also provides valuable suggestions for companies hoping to retain talented employees of any gender." Libr J

Includes bibliographical references

Kelly, Matthew
The **dream** manager. Hyperion 2007 158p $19.95 **658.3**
1. Employee morale 2. Motivation (Psychology) 3. Personnel management
ISBN 978-1-4013-0370-9; 1-4013-0370-6
LC 2007-13597

This "business fable extols the virtues of helping those working for and with you to achieve their dreams. In this way . . . managers can boost morale and control turnover. . . . This one's sure to appeal to business readers." Libr J

Lancaster, Lynne C.
When generations collide; who they are, why they clash, how to solve the generational puzzle at work. by Lynne C. Lancaster and David Stillman. HarperCollins Pubs. 2002 xxv, 352p $25.95; pa $15.95 **658.3**
1. Conflict of generations 2. Personnel management
ISBN 0-06-662106-2; 0-06-662107-0 pa
LC 2001-39221

The authors address the "ways of attracting and retaining individuals from the four generations that make up the American workforce. . . . Their book is a guide for employers and employees on how to take advantage of generational differences rather than allowing those differences to drain productivity. As with all outstanding business books, this wise and personable one will appeal to a wide range of readers." Booklist

Includes bibliographical references

Tracy, Brian
Full engagement! inspire, motivate, and bring out the best in your people. American Management Association 2011 226p $22 **658.3**
1. Employee morale 2. Motivation (Psychology) 3. Personnel management
ISBN 978-0-8144-1689-1; 0-8144-1689-6
LC 2010048293

The author "shows managers how they can supercharge their employees' efforts." Publisher's note

658.4   Executive management

Batstone, David B.
Saving the corporate soul & (who knows?) maybe your own; eight principles for creating and preserving integrity and profitability without selling

out. {by} David Batstone. Jossey-Bass 2003 270p
$26.95   **658.4**
　　1. Business ethics 2. Leadership
　　ISBN 0-7879-6480-8
　　　　　　　　　　　　　　　　　　　LC 2002-154858
　　The author sends a "message to business leaders that
conscience and profit go hand in hand. He believes principled companies excel financially over the long haul, are
respected more by the public, and are rated as better places
to work." Booklist
　　Includes bibliographical references

Bossidy, Lawrence A.
　　Execution: the discipline of getting things done;
{by} Larry Bossidy & Ram Charan; with Charles
Burck. Crown Business 2002 278p $27.50   **658.4**
　　1. Executive ability 2. Management
　　ISBN 0-609-61057-0
　　　　　　　　　　　　　　　　　　　LC 2002-18743
　　"This is a terrific book that will make smart managers
rethink how business gets done within every level of their
organization or department." Publ Wkly

Bryant, Adam
　　The **corner** office; indispensable and unexpected lessons from CEOs on how to lead and succeed.
Times Books 2011 249p $25; ebook $11.99 **658.4**
　　1. Executive ability 2. Leadership 3. Management
　　ISBN 978-0-8050-9306-3; 0-8050-9306-0; 978-1-
4299-5916-2; 1-4299-5916-9 ebook
　　　　　　　　　　　　　　　　　　　LC 2010042970
　　The author "offers compelling advice for the aspiring
executive. With interviews with more than 75 CEOs and
other top executives at companies of all sizes, he compiles
insights on such questions as what does it take to lead an
organization? what are the keys to achieving the highest levels of success? . . . The conversational format makes these
valuable lessons easy to comprehend and digest, and readers
are left with a new understanding of leadership—why it's
important, how these experts have worked to attain it, and
how they can do the same." Publ Wkly

Byron, Christopher
　　Testosterone inc. tales of CEOs gone wild. Wiley 2004 402p il $27.95; pa $16.95   **658.4**
　　1. Chemical engineers 2. Chief executive officers --
United States -- Case studies 3. Electronics industry
executives 4. Executives 5. Household products
industry executives 6. Machinery industry executives
7. Management consultants
　　ISBN 0-471-42005-0; 0-471-70623-X pa
　　　　　　　　　　　　　　　　　　　LC 2004-3667
　　"This self-described tale of 'CEOs Gone Wild' chronicles four of the best-known businessmen of the 1980s and
1990s, mixing stories of their personal and professional
lives with an emphasis on their marital infidelities and career
power plays. General Electric CEO Jack Welch takes center
stage." Booklist
　　Includes bibliographical references

Camp, Jim
　　Start with no; the negotiating tools that the pros
don't want you to know. Crown Business 2002 271p
$22.95   **658.4**
　　1. Business 2. Management 3. Negotiation 4.
Negotiation in business
　　ISBN 0-609-60800-2
　　　　　　　　　　　　　　　　　　　LC 2001-47742
　　"Camp has developed a system of negotiating that re-
flects the common concept of 'win-win,' and the result is an
excellent book with valuable insights." Booklist

Chan, Ronald W.
　　Behind the Berkshire Hathaway curtain; les-
sons from Warren Buffett's top business leaders.
John Wiley & Sons 2010 178p il $24.95; ebook
$16.99   **658.4**
　　1. Business 2. Executive ability 3. Financiers 4.
Management 5. Success
　　ISBN 978-0-470-56062-4; 0-470-56062-2; 978-0-470-
64297-9 ebook
　　　　　　　　　　　　　　　　　　　LC 2010281776
　　"Chan shares some of the business philosophies, strate-
gies, and mindsets learned from exclusive interviews with
leaders of Buffett's Berkshire Hathaway, including David
Sokol of MidAmerican Energy, Cathy Baron Tamraz of
Business Wire, Brad Kinstler of See's Candies, and Maria
Gottschalk of Pampered Chef. The detailed stories of these
executives' early career decisions bring to life practical lessons for personal and professional success." T + D

Conant, Douglas R.
　　Touchpoints; creating powerful leadership connections
in the smallest of moments. [by] Douglas R. Conant, Mette
Norgaard. Jossey-Bass 2011 xxxi, 173p $26.95; ebook
$12.99 **658.4**
　　1. Leadership
　　ISBN 978-1-1180-0435-7; 978-1-1180-7554-8 ebook
　　　　　　　　　　　　　　　　　　　LC 2011008907
　　"In an engaging personal style, Doug Conant, the CEO
of Campbell Soup Company, discusses a leadership philosophy that he and leadership development expert Mette
Norgaard refer to as 'TouchPoints'—those daily encounters
with staff, co-workers, or colleagues that leaders can use to
'touch' others in meaningful ways, such as influencing, inspiring, or providing clarity. The book highlights ways to
develop that ability and ways to practice leadership in the
moment." T + D

Connors, Roger
　　Change the culture, change the game; the breakthrough strategy for energizing your organization and
creating accountability for results. [by] Roger Connors and Tom Smith. Portfolio Penguin 2011 222p
il $25.95   **658.4**
　　1. Corporate culture -- United States 2. Management
3. Responsibility
　　ISBN 978-1-59184-361-0; 1-59184-361-8
　　　　　　　　　　　　　　　　　　　LC 2010032892
　　"If you don't like the results the company is producing,
take a look at the culture, say [the authors.] . . . The book
describes a 'Results Pyramid,' which presents three critical

components of organizational culture that work together to produce results—experiences, beliefs, and actions. Part one of the book covers how to use each of the elements to help implement the change, and part two provides specific tools and best practices to use throughout the process." T + D

Daniels, Cora

Black Power Inc. the new voice of success. John Wiley & Sons, Inc 2004 xxi, 218p $24.95 **658.4**
1. African American businesspeople 2. African Americans -- Social conditions
ISBN 0-471-47090-2

LC 2003-25143

The author "focuses on black professionals in their mid-30s and younger, including both entrepreneurs and those working in the upper ranks of corporate America, showing how they see themselves working the system to benefit the race." Booklist

Giuliani, Rudolph W.

Leadership; by Rudolph W. Giuliani with Ken Kurson. Miramax Bks. 2002 407p $25.95 **658.4**
1. District attorneys 2. Lawyers 3. Leadership 4. Management 5. Mayors 6. Presidential candidates 7. September 11 terrorist attacks, 2001
ISBN 0-7868-6841-4

This is a "book of guidelines about exemplary management skills {by} New York City's former mayor. . . . {He includes} opening and closing segments about the destruction of the World Trade Center." N Y Times (Late N Y Ed)

Goleman, Daniel

Primal leadership; realizing the power of emotional intelligence. {by} Daniel Goleman, Richard Boyatzis, Annie McKee. Harvard Business School Press 2002 306p $26.95 **658.4**
1. Emotional intelligence 2. Executive ability 3. Leadership 4. Leadership -- Psychological aspects 5. Management 6. Management -- Psychological aspects
ISBN 1-57851-486-X

LC 2001-41207

This "book is well written, intelligent, approachable, and stimulating." Booklist
Includes bibliographical references

Guber, Peter

Tell to win; connect, persuade, and triumph with the hidden power of story. Crown Business 2011 255p $26; ebook $13.99 **658.4**
1. Creative ability 2. Entrepreneurship 3. Storytelling 4. Success
ISBN 978-0-307-58795-4; 0-307-58795-9; 978-0-307-58797-8 ebook

LC 2010019828

The author "offers insight on how to craft and deliver a story that will bring an idea to life. Guber liberally draws on the wealth of stories from his years of experience as a Hollywood studio executive and includes anecdotes from former President Bill Clinton, Michael Jackson, Deepak Chopra, Alice Walker, Gene Simmons, Wolfgang Puck, and dozens of others on how they have used personal stories to motivate." Libr J

Heller, Robert

Essential manager's manual; {by} Robert Heller & Tim Hindle. DK Pub. 1998 864p il $40 **658.4**
1. Communication in management 2. Decision making 3. Decision-making 4. Management 5. Time management
ISBN 0-7894-3519-5

LC 98-6507

The authors "focus on time management, decision making, and communication, but subjects also include successful delegation, interviewing, stress reduction, and managing change. This sturdy manual is well organized and well written, and it has an excellent index." Booklist

Kouzes, James M.

The **truth** about leadership; the no-fads, heart-of-the-matter facts you need to know. [by] James M. Kouzes, Barry Z. Posner. Jossey-Bass 2010 xxv, 197p $24.95; ebook $16.99 **658.4**
1. Executive ability 2. Leadership
ISBN 978-0-470-63354-0; 978-0-470-87243-7 ebook

LC 2010018715

"It's hard to think of a better introduction for a new manager—or back-to-basics review for a veteran." Conference Board Rev
Includes bibliographical references

Krames, Jeffrey A.

The **Rumsfeld** way; leadership wisdom of a battle-hardened maverick. McGraw-Hill 2002 244p il $18.95; pa $12.95 **658.4**
1. Diplomats 2. Electronics industry executives 3. Leadership 4. Members of Congress 5. Pharmaceutical executives 6. Secretaries of defense
ISBN 0-07-140641-7; 0-07-141516-5 pa

LC 2002-523119

This book looks "at the leadership skills, methods, and strategies that have made Secretary of Defense Donald Rumsfeld an accomplished public figure." Libr J
Includes bibliographical references

Magee, David

How Toyota became #1; leadership lessons from the world's greatest car company. Portfolio 2007 239p il $25.95; pa $15 **658.4**
1. Automobile industry 2. Leadership
ISBN 978-1-59184-179-1; 978-1-59184-229-3 pa

LC 2007-18556

The author "presents an insightful history of how Toyota's dynamic organizational culture propelled a small family-run loom company to superstardom as a top-ranked Fortune Global 500 company and automotive-industry leader." Libr J
Includes bibliographical references

Peshawaria, Rajeev

Too many bosses, too few leaders; the art of being a true leader. Free Press 2011 xxii, 222p $26; ebook $12.99 **658.4**
1. Leadership
ISBN 978-1-4391-9774-5; 978-1-4391-9776-9 ebook

"Peshawaria's book ought to become required reading for all business people—from students to executives." Publ Wkly

Includes bibliographical references

Peters, Thomas J.

The **circle** of innovation; you can't shrink your way to greatness. by Tom Peters. Knopf 1997 xxi, 518p il $35; pa $16   **658.4**

1. Creative ability 2. Executive ability 3. Management 4. Organizational change 5. Success

ISBN 0-375-40157-1; 0-679-75765-1 pa

LC 97-74755

The author argues for constant innovation as a survival strategy for both the individual and the organization. Topics discussed include company decentralization, product design, empowering customers, system building, and corporate willingness to experiment

The **little** big things; 163 ways to pursue excellence. [by] Tom Peters. HarperStudio 2010 xxix, 538p $24.99; ebook $11.99   **658.4**

1. Management

ISBN 978-0-06-189408-4; 978-0-06-196350-6 ebook

LC 2009051160

The author "combines observations he has gleaned from his travels, current news items, conversations, and followers of his blog in a compact guide that aims to help readers realize effective projects, customer contentment, employee engagement, and business profitability. No doubt, Peters is on target as he advises readers to appreciate the angry customer, work on their last impressions, make sure that the restroom is clean, and 160 other ways to guarantee success. Each suggestion contains a rationale, example, and method of implementation, all in two pages apiece." Libr J

Pinson, Linda

★ **Anatomy** of a business plan; the step-by-step guide to building your business and securing your company's future. 7th ed.; Out of Your Mind...and Into the Marketplace 2008 356p il pa $22.95 **658.4**

1. Business enterprises 2. Business planning

ISBN 978-0-944205-37-2; 0-944205-37-2

LC 2008-277443

This book "features chapters on financing resources and business planning for nonprofits, as well as a sample restaurant business plan. Blank forms and worksheets help readers write a thoughtful, thorough, and professional business plan." Libr J

Ramsey, Dave

Entreleadership; 20 years of practical business wisdom from the trenches. Howard Books 2011 305p **658.4**

1. Christian life 2. Entrepreneurship 3. Executive ability 4. Leadership 5. Success

ISBN 978-1-4516-1785-6; 978-1-4516-4601-6 ebook

LC 2011016820

"The author 'paid his stupid tax' in his 20s when his successful real-estate investment business failed due to massive debt. Broke and humbled, Ramsey embraced Christian principles in every facet of his life, including his work. This framework would lead to his new venture, a financial con-

sulting firm, which, more than 20 years later, has earned the author tens of millions of dollars in revenues and helped countless others find success as well. Ramsey's faith may serve as his foundation, but any entrepreneur will find inspiration in his nuts-and-bolts advice. He touches on everything from time management and organization to the three things successful businesses never skip: contracts, vendors and collections." Kirkus

Rubinfeld, Arthur

★ **Built** for growth; expanding your business around the corner or across the globe. [by] Arthur Rubinfeld, Collins Hemingway. Wharton School Pub. 2005 xxiv, 343p il map $25.95 **658.4**

1. Management 2. Retail trade

ISBN 0-13-146574-0

LC 20040114697

"The authors intend the book to be 'a valuable primer on all aspects of retail: brand, location, people, finance, property management, expansion strategy and long-term thinking.' . . . An informative read for both beginners and seasoned retailers, this outstanding book abounds with insightful case studies and expert advice that should enhance the success of any retail brand." Libr J

Sawyer, R. Keith

Group genius; the creative power of collaboration. [by] Keith Sawyer. Basic Books 2007 274p il $26.95; pa $16.95   **658.4**

1. Creative thinking 2. Group problem solving

ISBN 978-0-465-07192-0; 0-465-07192-9; 978-0-465-07193-7 pa; 0-465-07193-7 pa

LC 2007-8007

The author "reveals how organizations can foster a spirit of collaboration to encourage creativity and innovation among their constituents. . . . Sawyer demonstrates how breakthroughs frequently grow from discussion, argumentation, and group activities." Libr J

Includes bibliographical references

Sutton, Robert I.

Good boss, bad boss; how to be the best--and learn from the worst. Business Plus 2010 308p $23.99; ebook $10.99   **658.4**

1. Personnel management

ISBN 978-0-446-55608-8; 978-0-446-55847-1 ebook

LC 2009-53414

"With examples from such diverse workplaces as Pixar and Anchor Steam brewery, Sutton reveals how the best bosses take diverse and intertwined steps to create effective and humane workplaces, and offers tips on taking control, getting and giving credit appropriately, taking responsibility, staying in tune with employees, and squelching your potential inner jerk. . . . This entertaining, satisfying guide is a wakeup call for bosses everywhere—and a survival guide for those who work for them." Publ Wkly

Includes bibliographical references

Tarr-Whelan, Linda

Women lead the way; your guide to stepping up to leadership and changing the world. Berrett-Koehler Publishers 2009 213p $24.95 **658.4**

1. Leadership 2. Women executives
ISBN 978-1-60509-135-8; 1-60509-135-9

LC 2009-21826

"Conversational and eye-opening, with many narrative illustrations and concrete advice, Tarr-Whelan's text could prove an important volume for working women looking to advance and enrich their careers." Publ Wkly

Includes bibliographical references

Tatum, Doug

No man's land; what to do when your company is too big to be small but too small to be big. Portfolio 2007 245p il $24.95 **658.4**

1. Management 2. Small business
ISBN 978-1-59184-172-2; 1-59184-172-0

LC 2007-9388

The aim of this guide is to help "companies navigate the fatal trap of 'no man's land,' a perilous zone where they have outgrown the habits and practices that fueled their early growth but have not yet adopted new practices and resources to cope with their new situation and challenges.... Tatum's potent guide communicates the key ideas vividly with engaging stories and evocative writing, and will help leaders identify and survive a key phase in a company's growth." Publ Wkly

Includes bibliographical references

Taylor, William

Practically radical; not-so-crazy ways to transform your company, shake up your industry, and challenge yourself. [by] William C. Taylor. William Morrow 2011 xxi, 293p $27.99; pa $14.99 **658.4**

1. Business enterprises 2. Leadership
ISBN 978-0-06-173461-8; 0-06-173461-6; 978-0-06-203522-6 pa; 0-06-203522-3 pa

LC 2010028021

The author "takes us on an inside look at 25 companies that have grown ever more adaptive to not merely survive but thrive in today's challenging environment.... An engaging and briskly written read, this will captivate and benefit business people interested in change and innovation." Publ Wkly

Includes bibliographical references

Walsh, Bill

The **score** takes care of itself; my philosophy of leadership. [by] Bill Walsh with Steve Jamison and Craig Walsh. Portfolio 2009 251p $25.95 **658.4**

1. Football -- Coaching 2. Leadership 3. Management
ISBN 978-1-59184-266-8

LC 2009-10651

"This posthumous leadership guide by the acclaimed head coach of the San Francisco 49ers is a fascinating compendium of Walsh's philosophy, as compiled by his son and Jamison.... Walsh reveals a simple and strict philosophy that prizes people above all and focuses on core values, principles and ideals.... Enlightening, informative and engag-

ing, this powerful book is a must-read for executives and managers at every level." Publ Wkly

Welch, John F.

Winning; [by] Jack Welch with Suzy Welch. Harper-Business 2005 384p $27.95 **658.4**

1. Business 2. Strategic planning 3. Success 4. Success in business
ISBN 0-06-075394-3

LC 2005-40337

The author offers business advice "from practices he employed at GE (e.g., the much-debated differentiation, which includes winnowing 10% of the workforce at regular intervals), to the personal qualities that lead to success (to Welch, candor is essential), to advice on job hunting and how to work with a bad boss, to ways to maximize the budget process. . . . It's difficult to think of anyone in business who wouldn't benefit from reading this savvy, engaging cubicle-to-boardroom guide to success." Publ Wkly

Encyclopedia of leadership; editors, George R. Goethals, Georgia J. Sorenson, James MacGregor Burns. Sage Publications 2004 4v il map set $595 **658.4**

1. Leadership -- Encyclopedias 2. Reference books
ISBN 0-7619-2597-X

LC 2004-1252

"What is leadership? What is a great leader? What is a great follower? What are the types of leadership? And how does someone become a leader? This set was designed with the needs of several user communities in mind, including students, scholars, and professionals who want to explore such questions." Booklist

Includes bibliographical references

658.5 Management of production

Greene, Jay

Design is how it works; how the smartest companies turn products into icons. Portfolio 2010 231p il $25.95 **658.5**

1. Industrial design 2. Marketing
ISBN 978-1-59184-322-1

LC 2010004030

"Greene introduces us to eight companies (Porsche; Nike; LEGO; OXO, design-centric kitchenware; REI, outdoor outfitter; energy-food company Clif Bar; Ace Hotels; and Virgin Atlantic) of different sizes, in different industries and locations, new and old, publicly traded and privately held to show that design is something in which any company can succeed. Greene provides valuable information and insight for companies in all businesses as he explains the importance of design thinking." Booklist

Includes bibliographical references

658.8   Management of marketing

Anderson, Christopher

The **long** tail; why the future of business is selling less of more. [by] Chris Anderson. Hyperion 2006 238p il $24.95   **658.8**
1. Internet marketing
ISBN 1-4013-0237-8; 978-1-4013-0237-5
LC 2006-43378

This "book does an excellent job of spotting trends and fitting them into an easily accessible theoretical framework that helps explain the changing culture around us." N Y Times (Late N Y Ed)
Includes bibliographical references

Cook, Sarah

Customer care excellence; how to create an effective customer focus. 6th ed.; Kogan Page 2011 278p il pa $39.95; ebook $39.95   **658.8**
1. Customer relations 2. Customer services 3. Quality control
ISBN 978-0-7494-5705-1 pa; 0-7494-5705-8 pa; 978-0-7494-6257-4 ebook
LC 2010023892

"This book explains how to develop and sustain a customer-service focus within a company. Emphasizing both strategic and practical aspects of customer service, the author explains how gaining customer commitment and motivating employees to deliver excellent service can ensure successful results and satisfied customers." Publisher's note
Includes bibliographical references

Gerhards, Paul

How to sell what you make; the business of marketing crafts. rev & updated ed; Stackpole Bks. 1996 151p il pa $12.95   **658.8**
1. Handicraft 2. Selling
ISBN 0-8117-2436-0
LC 95-37330

This offers advice on how to market crafts through fairs, trade shows, and galleries, and includes information on small business management.

Goldman, Aaron

Everything I know about marketing I learned from Google. McGraw-Hill 2011 341p il $26.95; ebook $26.95   **658.8**
1. Google (Web site) 2. Internet marketing 3. Marketing
ISBN 978-0-07-174289-4; 978-0-07-174621-2 ebook
LC 2010025355

The author "outlines 20 lessons that laypeople can use to market their products and services successfully online. Lessons include how to get near the top of search results, keeping marketing simple, and testing and tracking everything you do. . . . Written with humor and frankness, this book is as appealing as a manual for marketing as it is for armchair reading. Anyone interested in the pop culture of Google will appreciate it." Libr J

Handley, Ann

Content rules; how to create killer blogs, podcasts, videos, ebooks, webinars (and more) that engage customers and ignite your business. [by] Ann Handley & C.C. Chapman. Wiley 2011 xxii, 282p il $24.95; ebook $9.99   **658.8**
1. Digital media 2. Internet marketing 3. Web sites -- Design
ISBN 978-0-470-64828-5; 0-470-64828-7; 978-0-470-94872-9 ebook
LC 2011280622

A one-stop source on the art and science of developing marketing content that people care about. This coverage is interwoven with case studies of companies successfully spreading their ideas online—and using them to establish credibility and build a loyal customer base.

Jantsch, John

The **referral** engine; teaching your business how to market itself. Portfolio 2010 243p $25.95 **658.8**
1. Advertising 2. Marketing
ISBN 978-1-59184-311-5
LC 2009-49521

"This practical, smart, and original guide is essential reading for any company looking to grow without a fat marketing budget." EContent

Kawasaki, Guy

★ **Enchantment**; the art of changing hearts, minds, and actions. Portfolio/Penguin 2011 xxiii, 211p il **658.8**
1. Marketing 2. Persuasion (Psychology)
ISBN 978-1-59184-379-5
LC 2010046009

The author discusses "the tricky art of influence and persuasion. Kawasaki . . . transforms the otherwise exhausted and overwrought tropes of how to win friends and influence people with a complete makeover here, whether he's talking about wardrobe choice or tips for effective swearing. . . . Informative, concise guide from one of America's most influential and, yes, enchanting entrepreneurs." Kirkus
Includes bibliographical references

Mainwaring, Simon

We first; how brands and consumers use social media to build a better world. Palgrave Macmillan 2011 250p $26; ebook $12.99   **658.8**
1. Capitalism 2. Digital media 3. Internet marketing 4. Social change 5. Social networking
ISBN 978-0-230-11026-7; 978-0-230-12053-2 ebook
LC 2010048454

"A must-read for those who want to understand and engage the power and potential of social media to promote a healthier, more equitable world." Kirkus
Includes bibliographical references

Moffitt, Sean

Wikibrands; reinventing your company in a customer-driven marketplace. [by] Sean Moffitt and Mike Dover. McGraw-Hill 2011 318p il $28; ebook $28 **658.8**
1. Internet marketing 2. Marketing 3. Wikis (Computer science)
ISBN 978-0-07-174927-5; 0-07-174927-6; 978-0-07-

175235-0 ebook; 0-07-175235-8 ebook

LC 2010029785

"There is a wealth of important information in this broad-based report on the new customer-controlled marketplace; it is an excellent wakeup call, a strategic guide, and an execution road map for business leaders." Booklist

Includes bibliographical references

Resnick, Lynda

Rubies in the orchard; how to uncover the hidden gems in your business. with Francis Wilkinson. Doubleday 2009 xx, 204p il $24.95   **658.8**

1. Advertising 2. Business 3. Marketing
ISBN 978-0-385-52578-7; 0-385-52578-8

LC 2008-23167

"Real-life tales of marketing strategies that rocketed Resnick and her husband to astounding success with companies like Fiji Water, Teleflora, the Franklin Mint and Pom Wonderful, the wildly successful pomegranate juice. The author charms with her winning wit and a self-deprecating tone as she distills the secrets of her extraordinary career into a series of philosophies illustrated through behind-the-scenes looks at various marketing campaigns. . . . A must-read for anyone who aspires to Resnick's level of promotional genius, success or commitment to environmental sustainability." Publ Wkly

Siegel, David

Pull; the power of the Semantic Web to transform your business. Portfolio 2009 270p il $27.95 **658.8**

1. Electronic commerce 2. Information technology 3. Internet marketing
ISBN 978-1-59184-277-4

LC 2009-35779

"This thought-provoking read is sure to spark ideas about what it will take to succeed in tomorrow's marketplace." Publ Wkly

Includes bibliographical references

Underhill, Paco

★ **Why** we buy; the science of shopping. Updated and rev.; Simon & Schuster Pbks. 2009 306p pa $16; ebook $12.99   **658.8**

1. Consumers 2. Marketing 3. Shopping
ISBN 978-1-4165-9524-3 pa; 1-4165-9524-4 pa; 978-1-4165-6174-3 ebook; 1-4165-6174-9 ebook

LC 2010-483248

"Each chapter delves into a particular aspect of a store environment and its interface with customers: the importance of signage and why less is more, how men shop, . . . and clues about waiting time. Throughout, insights are peppered with one or several examples." Booklist [review of 1999 edition]

Walker, Rob

Buying in; the secret dialogue between what we buy and who we are. Random House 2008 xxi, 291p $25   **658.8**

1. Brand name products 2. Brand name products -- Marketing 3. Consumer behavior -- United States 4.

Marketing
ISBN 978-1-4000-6391-8; 1-4000-6391-4

LC 2007-39973

This "is a thoughtful and unhurried investigation into consumerism that pushes the analysis to the maximum and builds a thesis that refutes the myth of the brand-proof consumer." Publ Wkly

Includes bibliographical references

Yellin, Emily

Your call is (not that) important to us; customer service and what it reveals about our world and our lives. Free Press 2009 291p $26   **658.8**

1. Customer relations 2. Customer services
ISBN 978-1-4165-4689-4; 1-4165-4689-8

LC 2009-2468

The author "dives into the often dysfunctional world of customer service, exploring the multimillion-dollar industry from various points of view, interviewing exasperated consumers, displeased CEOs and infuriated customer service reps themselves. . . . While Yellin's study offers more industry anecdotes than concrete solutions, readers will likely look at the industry differently and with more empathy for those who participate in it." Publ Wkly

Includes bibliographical references

Click millionaires; work less, live more with an internet business you love. Scott C. Fox. American Management Association 2012 278 p.   **658.8**

1. Electronic commerce 2. Small business -- Management
ISBN 0814431917; 9780814431917

LC 2012004882

This book offers a guide to escaping the daily grind. . . . [It offers a] program [that] leads readers through every step of the transition from cubicle to home office. . . . [The author] urges readers to create a lifestyle business, in which they prioritize a flexible schedule and independent work over profits and stress, using Web sites, e-commerce, digital publishing, and social media to build businesses that work on their own schedules--first part-time and then developing a niche business online that generates recurring revenues automatically. His comprehensive, pragmatic approach covers online presence, social networking, production and operations, and online advertising, and includes interviews from those whove succeeded. (Publishers Weekly)

658.85   Personal selling

The art of the sale; learning from the masters about the business of life. Philip Delves Broughton. Penguin Press 2012 291 p.   **658.85**

1. Selling
ISBN 1594203326; 9781594203329

LC 2011040209

This book examines the keys to success in sales. Broughton has met with top sellers around the world, traveling to Japan, Morocco and the United Kingdom . . . . In addition to his interview research, he examines academic studies, history, self-help literature, academic research on the psychology of selling and the character attributes of sales people. He explores the differences in theory and practice, and he draws from the history of the field, by way of P.T. Barnum and Joseph Duveen, who brought fine-art sales to the U.S. (Kirkus)

659.1 Advertising

Doucett, Elisabeth
  Creating your library brand; communicating your relevance and value to your patrons. American Library Association 2008 124p il pa $50   **659.1**
  1. Libraries -- Public relations 2. Marketing
  ISBN 978-0-8389-0962-1; 0-8389-0962-0
                          LC 2008-983
  The author "defines marketing and branding and then offers practical advice on the different aspects, from creating a logo to using templates, working with outside help, and creating and evaluating the branding plan. She emphasizes including staff, patrons, and board members in the process and offers helpful examples with which one can follow up online. . . . This type of guide can serve as a useful ready reference, but be forewarned—marking helpful pages will require a book full of tabs." Voice Youth Advocates

Tungate, Mark
  Adland; a global history of advertising. Kogan Page Ltd 2007 278p il $39.95 **659.1**
  1. Advertising -- History
  ISBN 978-0-7494-4837-0; 0-7494-4837-7
                         LC 2007-16432
  "As a definitive record of what happened and why, there is none finer. Whether you're a novice in the industry or . . . a veteran of 25 years, there is much to learn." Management Today
  Includes bibliographical references

The Advertising age encyclopedia of advertising; editors, John McDonough and the Museum of Broadcast Communications, Karen Egolf; illustration editor, Jacqueline V. Reid. Fitzroy Dearborn Pubs. 2003 3v il set $385 **659.1**
  1. Advertising -- Encyclopedias 2. Reference books
  ISBN 1-57958-172-2
                       LC 2003-270744
  "Well-researched, thorough, and fascinating, it belongs in all business collections and most academic and large public libraries." Booklist

★ **The advertising** red books. Advertiser, geographic. LexisNexis 2003   **659.1**
  1. Advertising -- Directories 2. Reference books
  Covers "U.S. corporations, listing advertising budgets, key managment and marketing directors, and company subsidiaries and divisions, and giving addresses and lists of products. Indexed by type of business, personnel, and product trade name." Guide to Ref Books. 11th edition

★ **The advertising** red books. Agencies. LexisNexis 2003 il   **659.1**
  1. Advertising -- Directories 2. Reference books

This periodical lists facts on more than 9,500 advertising agencies in the U.S. Includes people in management, account, and production.

659.2 Public relations

Fertik, Michael
  Wild west 2.0; how to protect and restore your online reputation on the untamed social frontier. [by] Michael Fertik and David Thompson. American Management Association 2010 264p il $24.95 **659.2**
  1. Internet -- Social aspects 2. Public relations 3. Social networking 4. Web 2.0
  ISBN 978-0-8144-1509-2
                        LC 2009-42255
  "Full of invaluable information that readers will be very grateful to have when they need it, this book explains the rules and provides the tools for overcoming online attacks and regaining a positive reputation." Publ Wkly
  Includes bibliographical references

660.6 Biotechnology

Hubbell, Sue
  Shrinking the cat; genetic engineering before we knew about genes. with illustrations by Liddy Hubbell. Houghton Mifflin 2001 175p il $25; pa $13   **660.6**
  1. Apples 2. Breeding 3. Cats 4. Corn 5. Genetic engineering 6. Silk
  ISBN 0-618-04027-7; 0-618-25748-9 pa
                        LC 2001-24547
  "An engaging synthesis of material that will appeal to Hubbell's well-established audience." Booklist
  Includes bibliographical references and index

Kurpinski, Kyle
  How to defeat your own clone; and other tips for surviving the biotech revolution. [by] Kyle Kurpinski and Terry D. Johnson. Bantam Books Trade Paperbacks 2010 180p il pa $14   **660.6**
  1. Biotechnology 2. Cloning 3. Human cloning
  ISBN 978-0-553-38578-6; 0-553-38578-X
                        LC 2009-45899
  "Kurpinski and Johnson have written a science book that is irreverent, timely, accessible, and, best of all, compulsively readable." Publ Wkly

664 Food technology

Adamchak, Raoul W.
  Tomorrow's table; organic farming, genetics, and the future of food. [by] Pamela C. Ronald [and] Raoul W. Adamchak. Oxford University Press 2008 208p il map $29.95   **664**
  1. Food -- Biotechnology 2. Genetic engineering 3.

Genetically modified foods 4. Organic farming
ISBN 9780195301755

LC 2007-7071

"The format is easy to follow and effective at highlighting . . . [the authors'] seemingly adverse positions on the subject. By the book's conclusion, their argument is elegantly presented in a logical fashion." Choice

Includes bibliographical references (p. 179-197)

Winston, Mark L.

Travels in the genetically modified zone. Harvard Univ. Press 2002 280p hardcover o.p. pa $19.50　**664**

1. Agricultural biotechnology 2. Farm produce 3. Food -- Biotechnology 4. Genetically modified foods
ISBN 0-674-00867-7; 978-0-674-01529-6 pa; 0-674-01529-0 pa

LC 2002-17192

The author "first describes the development of hybrid corn, then delves into the use of genetic modifications to combat weeds and diseases. The facets of genetic modification he takes into account include research, industrial processes, growing modified crops, protecting nearby crops, the safety of consumers, and the profits of agribusiness. . . . Winston also fields practical ideas for solving the major problems involved in the rapidly growing field of genetically modified crops. Throughout, however, he maintains a moderate stance on his controversial subject." Booklist

Includes bibliographical references

Winter, Ruth

A **consumer's** dictionary of food additives; 7th ed.; Three Rivers Press 2009 595p pa $17.95; ebook $17.95　**664**

1. Food additives -- Dictionaries 2. Reference books
ISBN 978-0-307-40892-1 pa; 978-0-307-45259-7 ebook

LC 2008-40601

This guide provides "facts about the safety and side effects of more than 12,000 ingredients—such as preservatives, food-tainting pesticides, and animal drugs—that end up in food as a result of processing and curing." Publisher's note

Includes bibliographical references

664.362

Mueller, Tom

Extra virginity; Tom Mueller. 1st ed. W. W. Norton 2011 238 p.　**664.362**

1. Food adulteration and inspection 2. Olive -- Folklore 3. Olive -- History 4. Olive oil -- History 5. Olive oil industry -- Moral and ethical aspects
ISBN 9780393070217

LC 2011041459

In this book, author "Tom Mueller . . . [an] expert on olive oil and olive oil fraud . . . [tells] a story of globalization, deception, and crime in the food industry from ancient times to the present, and a[n] . . . indictment of today's lax protections against fake and even toxic food products in the United States. . . . [The book] is also an . . . account of the artisanal

producers, chemical analysts, chefs, and food activists who are defending the extraordinary oils that truly deserve the name 'extra-virgin.'" (Publisher's note)

666　Ceramic and allied technologies

Garfield, Simon

Mauve; how one man invented a color that changed the world. Norton 2001 222p il hardcover o.p. pa $13.95 **666**

1. Chemists 2. Chemists -- England -- Biography 3. Dye industry -- Great Britain 4. Dyes and dyeing 5. Mauve
ISBN 0-393-32313-7 pa

LC 00-69533

"The text is understandable by the average layman and is enjoyable reading for the scientist and non-scientist alike." Sci Books Films

Includes bibliographical references

Macfarlane, Alan

★ **Glass**: a world history; {by} Alan Macfarlane and Gerry Martin. University of Chicago Press 2002 255p il $27.50　**666**

1. Glass 2. Glass -- History
ISBN 0-226-50028-4

LC 2002-20493

The authors "make the case for the centrality of glass in the artistic renaissance and scientific revolution that took place in Western Europe from the 14th to 17th centuries. They discuss the origins of glass making and trace its development and usage across centuries and multiple cultures (Europe, the Middle East, China, India, and Japan). Their discussion combines cultural, artistic, and aesthetic viewpoints of glass within these cultures with history and developments in science. The result is a thoroughly readable, carefully argued work, filled with delightful surprises. . . . An excellent example of microhistory . . . this is required for history of science collections and recommended for large public and academic collections." Libr J

Includes bibliographical references

667　Cleaning, color, coating, related technologies

Greenfield, Amy Butler

A **perfect** red; empire, espionage, and the quest for the color of desire. Amy Butler Greenfield. 1st ed; HarperCollins 2005 338p il $26.95　**667**

1. Cochineal 2. Dyes and dyeing
ISBN 0-06-052275-5

LC 2004-42376

The author "combines the investigative prowess of a detective with the intellectual reasoning of an academician to create an eminently entertaining and educational read." Booklist

Includes bibliographical references

668 Technology of other organic products

Turin, Luca

The **secret** of scent; adventures in perfume and the science of smell. Ecco 2006 207p il $23.95; pa $13.95   **668**

1. Perfumes 2. Smell

ISBN 0-06-113383-3; 978-0-06-113383-1; 0-06-113384-1 pa; 978-0-06-113384-8 pa

LC 2006-46273

The author "investigates the reason things smell the way they do." N Y Times Book Rev

Includes bibliographical references

Winter, Ruth

A **consumer's** dictionary of cosmetic ingredients; 6th ed., completely rev. and updated; Three Rivers Press 2005 563p pa $16.95   **668**

1. Cosmetics -- Dictionaries 2. Reference books

ISBN 1-4000-5233-5; 978-1-4000-5233-2

LC 2005-273775

This volume describes over 6,000 ingredients used in cosmetics including preservatives, coloring agents, flavorings, fragrances, and preserving agents, their effectiveness and possible toxic and allergic effects.

674 Lumber processing, wood products, cork

Petroski, Henry

The **pencil**; a history of design and circumstance. Knopf 1990 434p il hardcover o.p. pa $20 **674**

1. Pencils

ISBN 0-394-57422-2; 0-679-73415-5 pa

LC 89-45362

The author discusses the manufacture, design, history, and sociological significance of the pencil.

"An incredibly rich and complex history of this entirely unremarkable instrument of communication." SLJ

Includes bibliographical references

The Encyclopedia of wood; a tree-by-tree guide to the world's most versatile resource. general editor, Aidan Walker. Facts on File 2005 192p il map $35   **674**

1. Reference books 2. Wood 3. Wood -- Encyclopedias

ISBN 0-8160-6181-5

LC 2004-60849

"A nice addition to libraries with strong interior design or DIY collections." Libr J

Includes bibliographical references

676 Pulp and paper technology

Grummer, Arnold E.

Trash-to-treasure papermaking. Storey Publishing 2011 207p il pa $16.95   **676**

1. Paper 2. Papermaking

ISBN 978-1-60342-547-6

LC 2010-43056

"Grummer begins with basic papermaking, then progresses to more advanced skills. Ample tips on everything from proper technique to troubleshooting problems with finished paper are included. A gallery of clever projects with directions rounds out this friendly, accessible guide to papermaking." Libr J

Includes bibliographical references

677 Textiles

Schoeser, Mary

★ **World** textiles: a concise history. Thames & Hudson 2003 224p il pa $14.95   **677**

1. Fabrics 2. Textile industry

ISBN 0-500-20369-5

LC 2002-110919

"Arranged roughly into chronological periods, the book . . . details technique, materials, and designs and puts them in historical and cultural context. This is truly a fantastic history of textile arts. . . . The text itself is a delight to read and more comprehensive than in other comparable works." Libr J

Includes bibliographical references

Fairchild's dictionary of textiles; Phyllis G. Tortora, editor; Robert S. Merkel, consulting editor. 7th ed; Fairchild Publications 1995 xx, 662p il $50   **677**

1. Reference books 2. Textile industry -- Dictionaries

ISBN 978-0-87005-707-6; 0-87005-707-3

LC 94-61457

"Reference source for all branches of the industry. Includes entries on fibers, yarns, fabric construction, finishing and sale, inventors and developers, and government standards and regulations. Includes appendix of organizations involved with the textile industry." N Y Public Libr Book of How & Where to Look It Up

Includes bibliographical references

678 Elastomers and elastomer products

Korman, Richard

The **Goodyear** story; an inventor's obsession and the struggle for a rubber monopoly. Encounter Bks. 2002 230p il $25.95; pa $16.95   **678**

1. Inventors 2. Manufacturing executives 3. Rubber

ISBN 1-89355-437-6; 1-89355-482-1 pa

LC 2001-55635

"Charles Goodyear began his obsessive quest to find the recipe for making rubber in the 1830s and ended up becoming an American industrial legend. Besides tracing the life of this inspiring entrepreneur, Korman's social history of factory life and debtors prison in the early to mid-1800s is exceedingly well drawn." Booklist

Includes bibliographical references

Slack, Charles

Noble obsession; Charles Goodyear, Thomas Hancock, and the race to unlock the greatest industrial secret of the nineteenth century. Hyperion 2002 274p il $24.95; pa $14.95 **678**

1. Inventors 2. Manufacturing executives 3. Rubber 4. Rubber -- Technological innovations -- History -- 19th century 5. Rubber industry and trade -- History -- 19th century

ISBN 0-7868-6789-2; 0-7868-8856-3 pa

LC 2002-68932

This is the story of how Charles Goodyear discovered the process of vulcanization of rubber, making possible the manufacture of rubber tires carried out by Thomas Hancock and the company which bears Goodyear's name.

"Slack brings Charles Goodyear back to life and redeems the man who gave up everything to give his gift to the world." Booklist

Includes bibliographical references

681   Precision instruments and other devices

Angel, Solly

The **tale** of the scale; an odyssey of invention. Oxford University Press 2003 304p il $28   **681**

1. College teachers 2. Industrial design 3. Inventions 4. Scales (Weighing instruments) 5. Urban planners

ISBN 0-19-515868-7

LC 2003-48699

This is the "story of one man's attempt to design a novel personal (bathroom) scale. . . . The book is more than simply a narrative of the author's successes and failures; it also contains his musings on topics that should be of interest to scientists and engineers: the . . . scientific method, the relationship between form and function, design theory, and creativity, among others. . . . I highly recommend this very interesting, very entertaining account of how one person went through the product design and development process." Sci Books Films

Includes bibliographical references and index

681.1   Instruments for measuring time, counting and calculating machines and instruments

Marchant, Jo

Decoding the heavens; a 2,000-year-old computer--and the century-long search to discover its secrets. Da Capo Press 2009 328p il $25   **681.1**

1. Astronomical clocks -- History 2. Clocks and watches 3. Technology -- History

ISBN 978-0-306-81742-7; 0-306-81742-X

LC 2008-939733

The author "relates the century-long struggle of competing amateurs and scientists to understand the secrets of a 2000-year-old clock-like mechanism found in 1901 by Greek divers off the coast of Antikythera, a small island near Tunisia. . . . This globe-trotting, era-spanning mystery should absorb armchair scientists of all kinds." Publ Wkly

Includes bibliographical references

682   Small forge work (Blacksmithing)

Parkinson, Peter

The **artist** blacksmith; design and techniques. Crowood Press 2002 160p il $40   **682**

1. Blacksmithing

ISBN 1-86126-428-3

"Parkinson explains the tools, materials, and equipment needed by blacksmiths as well as the most commonly used techniques. Numerous illustrations of beautiful creations (such as gates, sculptures, household items, and furniture) appear throughout this fascinating title." Libr J

684   Furnishings and home workshops

Abram, Norm

Measure twice, cut once; lessons from a master carpenter. Little, Brown 1996 196p il $18.95   **684**

1. Carpentry 2. Woodwork

ISBN 0-316-00494-4

LC 96-7584

In this book about woodwork and carpentry the author "deals mainly with hand tools. Abram covers items such as levels, chalk lines, and plumb-bobs, detailing his experiences with them and his preferences. . . . Even experienced woodworkers will pick up a tip or two from this book." Libr J

Bird, Lonnie

★ **Taunton's** complete illustrated guide to woodworking; [by] Lonnie Bird . . . [et al.]. Taunton Press 2005 311p il $29.95   **684**

1. Woodwork

ISBN 1-56158-769-9

LC 2004-28678

This "guide covers a wide array of woodworking topics. . . . The arrangement is consistent and well thought out, with illustrated referencing at the beginning of each chapter." Libr J

The **complete** illustrated guide to shaping wood. Taunton Press 2001 294p il $39.95   **684**

1. Woodwork

ISBN 1-56158-400-2

LC 2001-27430

This guide shows "the many ways of shaping wood (cutting, edge treatments, decorative techniques, turning, and carving). Techniques of all types and complexity are covered, usually including several means to accomplish each task, such as using hand or power tools. Profusely illustrated with drawings and photos, this book offers something for every woodworker." Libr J

Includes bibliographical references

Davy, Phil

Ultimate woodwork bible; a complete reference with step-by-step techniques. [by] Phil Davy and Ben Plewes. Sterling Pub. Co. 2011 288p il $29.95 **684**

1. Woodwork

ISBN 978-1-84340-574-0; 1-84340-574-1

"A nicely organized manual on a wide range of wood-working basics, from types of tools to techniques. A British book, this guide includes terminology and tool names that may be unfamiliar to U.S. readers. In the large section on tool selection, there are a few items detailed that are not available on this side of the Atlantic. Instructions come with minimal drawings and concise text." Libr J

Hoadley, R. Bruce
Understanding wood; a craftsman's guide to wood technology. 2nd ed; Taunton Press 2000 280p il $39.95   **684**
    1. Wood 2. Woodwork
    ISBN 1-56158-358-8
                    LC 00-44322
This guide "covers the nature of wood and its properties, the basics of wood technology, and the woodworker's raw materials." Publisher's note
    Includes bibliographical references and index

Peters, Rick
Woodworker's guide to wood; softwoods, hardwoods, plywoods, composites, veneers.   Sterling 2000 192p il pa $24.95   **684**
    1. Lumber and lumbering 2. Wood 3. Woodwork
    ISBN 0-8069-3687-8
                    LC 99-86641
Peters' book is "geared toward hobbyist woodworkers. He covers the process of making lumber from start to finish, including how trees grow, their structure, common ways of milling and drying lumber, grading, and possible defects found in wood. One section shows wood samples (both finished and plain) and describes their basic working characteristics." Libr J

Popular woodworking
The **weekend** woodworker's project collection; 40 projects for the time-challenged craftsman. from the editors of Popular Woodworking. Popular Woodworking Books 2010 255p il pa $22.99   **684**
    1. Woodwork
    ISBN 978-1-4403-0888-8
                    LC 2010-15396
"These quick projects for intermediate and advanced woodworkers are quite stylish. From frames and clocks to shelving and boxes, they exhibit enough variety for every taste. Project plans come with exploded views offering dimensions and technique tips. Tool familiarity and woodworking skills are assumed. The photos are attractive and the pieces appealing. . . . [This is] a great addition to any collection." Libr J

Warner, Pat
The **router** book. Taunton Press 2001 185p pa $19.95   **684**
    1. Power tools 2. Routers (Tools) 3. Woodwork
    ISBN 1-56158-423-1
                    LC 2001-27149
"Warner shows readers how to get the most from their router, covering tools, accessories, and its use. Fixed-base, plunge routers, and laminate trimmers are introduced with excellent evaluations of specific models of each type." Libr J

★ **Woodwork**; a step-by-step photographic guide to successful woodworking. [writers, Alan Bridgewater . . . [et al]; illustrator, Simon Rodway] DK Pub. 2010 400p il $40   **684**
    1. Woodwork
    ISBN 978-0-7566-4306-5
                  LC 2010-279214
This book "offers instruction in basic woodworking techniques and pairs profiles of common and exotic woods with great photos. The 25 projects, including furnishings and household products, start from simple and build to complex. While the projects are not particularly distinctive, the supporting materials make this a key purchase for any woodworking collection. Highly recommended." Libr J

684.1   Furniture

Cone, Steve
★ **Singer** upholstery basics plus; complete step-by-step photo guide.   Creative Pub. International 2007 155p il pa $19.95   **684.1**
    1. Upholstery
    ISBN 978-1-58923-329-4; 1-58923-329-8
                  LC 2007-7252
"If there ever was an upholstery bible, this is it." Libr J

Dobson, Cherry
The **complete** guide to upholstery; stuffed with step-by-step techniques for professional results. St. Martin's Griffin 2009 143p il pa $24.95   **684.1**
    1. Furniture -- Repairing 2. Upholstery
    ISBN 978-0-312-38327-5; 0-312-38327-4
"Want to recycle your old furniture with reupholstery? This lovely manual . . . contains fine step-by-step photos and tips on technique. Master upholsterer Dobson easily walks the confident beginner through the basics." Libr J

Hingley, Brian D.
Furniture repair & restoration. Creative Homeowner 2010 175p il pa $14.95   **684.1**
    1. Furniture -- Repairing 2. Furniture finishing
    ISBN 978-1-58011-478-3
"With special sections on evaluation and repair of structural issues, this volume features an array of valuable information on furniture repair and refinishing. . . . Geared toward beginners in wood restoration, the book highlights the author's professional experience, which shows through in the advice and thorough directions." Libr J

Storage & shelving solutions; over 70 projects and ideas that fit your budget, space, and lifestyle. with the editors of The Family Handyman. Reader's Digest Association 2006 255p il $26.95   **684.1**
    1. Cabinetwork 2. Storage in the home
    ISBN 978-0-7621-0636-3; 0-7621-0636-0
                  LC 2005-50772
"These home storage projects are neatly packaged, each accompanied by a box listing skill level, tools needed, and approximate cost (a nice feature) as well as a box with a

shopping and cutting list. . . . This polished book on a great topic is recommended for public libraries." Libr J

686   Printing and related activities

Lee, Marshall

Bookmaking: editing, design, production; technical consultant Joseph Gannon. 3rd ed; Norton 2004 494p il $49.95   **686**
    1. Book industry 2. Books
    ISBN 0-393-73018-2

                                                     LC 2003-59672
This book describes "the business and art of transmitting an author's manuscript to readers by means of a book. The process includes editing, physical and visual design, costing, production planning, scheduling, procurement, and distribution. . . . This timeless classic should be acquired while it is still available." Choice
Includes bibliographical references

686.2   Printing

Garfield, Simon

Just my type; a book about fonts. Gotham Books 2011 356p il $27.50   **686.2**
    1. Fonts 2. Printing 3. Type and type-founding -- History
    ISBN 978-1-59240-652-4

                                                     LC 2011379019
"Conveying the richness and the personality of typefaces with love and passion, this is an accessible and entertaining introduction to the world of lettering." Blueprint
Includes biblliographical references

686.3   Bookbinding

Cambras, Josep

Bookbinding; techniques and projects. [translation from the Spanish, Michael Brunelle and Beatriz Cortabarria] Barron's 2007 143p il pa $26.99 **686.3**
    1. Bookbinding
    ISBN 978-0-7641-6084-4; 0-7641-6084-2

                                                     LC 2007-924989
"Beginning with a historical overview, continuing to an explanation of tools and materials, Cambras showcases his expertise in chapters devoted to half a dozen techniques and the same quantity of paper-painting methods." Booklist

Diehn, Gwen

Real life journals: designing & using handmade books. Lark Books 2010 180p il $24.95   **686.3**
    1. Bookbinding 2. Diaries
    ISBN 978-1-60059-492-2

                                                     LC 2009-32647
"Chapters on tools, covers, paper choices, and bindings are detailed and fully illustrated, but Diehn . . . goes well beyond that, making a point to include information on creating a purposeful design, enriching textual content, and binding the words to the visual elements to reflect a bookmaker's interests and personality. . . [This is] a lovely, helpful volume that will inspire and attract journalers and scrapbookers alike." Booklist

Golden, Alisa

Making handmade books; 100+ bindings, structures & forms. Lark Crafts 2010 256p il pa $19.95   **686.3**
    1. Bookbinding 2. Books
    ISBN 978-1-60059-587-5

                                                     LC 2010-1546
"This volume updates and combines Golden's previous Creating Handmade Books and Unique Handmade Books to provide an introduction to the fascinating world of artists' books. The specimens highlighted are far from your traditional book—they are works of art that will challenge readers' ideas of what books can be. Though there are plenty of inspiring photographs, there is also ample direction to guide readers interested in creating their own books. Golden also intersperses tidbits of bookmaking history and lore throughout, making this guide not only pleasurable and inspiring to look at but fun to read. " Libr J
Includes bibliographical references

690   Construction of buildings

Black & Decker Corp.

The **complete** guide to flooring; updated with new products & techniques. 3rd ed.; Creative Pub. International 2010 271p il $24.99   **690**
    1. Floors
    ISBN 978-1-58923-521-2

                                                     LC 2010-4486
This book covers methods of installing different types of flooring, including "information on renewable flooring materials, such as bamboo, reclaimed floorboards, and natural stone. It also includes . . . techniques for polished and etched concrete flooring. The DVD add-on product includes 50 minutes of real-time demonstration of . . . layout and installation techniques, as well as the entire print edition in electronic form." Publisher's note

The **complete** guide to patios & walkways; money-saving do-it-yourself projects for improving outdoor living space. Creative Pub. International 2010 255p il pa $24.99   **690**
    1. Patios
    ISBN 978-1-58923-481-9

This is a guide to plan, build, repair, and maintain patios and walkways. It "stands out for its detailed photos and step-by-step, logically arranged instructions. . . . There is an original section on drainage options with projects." Libr J

Bollinger, Don

Hardwood floors; laying, sanding and finishing. Taunton Press 1990 137p il pa $19.95   **690**
    1. Floors
    ISBN 0-942391-62-4

                                                     LC 90-11065

The author "addresses the three types of flooring: strip, plank, and parquet—covering such topics as estimating costs; selecting wood types and grades; preparing the underlayment; planning the layout; sanding; and applying various finishes." Libr J

Includes bibliographical references

Cory, Steve

Ultimate guide: porches; building techniques for adding a new porch to your home. Creative Homeowner 2011 191p il pa $16.95 **690**

1. Porches

ISBN 978-1-58011-491-2

LC 2009941175

In this manual, the author "shares numerous, clear illustrations and detailed construction information and techniques. His confident, expert instruction . . . is apparent in the projects presented here. . . . A solid addition to any home improvement collection." Libr J

Gonzalez, Steve

Before you hire a contractor; a construction guidebook for consumers. Consumer's Press 1994 180p il pa $12.95 **690**

1. Consumer education 2. House construction

ISBN 1-8912-6465-6

LC 94-37497

The author "discusses the essentials of selecting a contractor, negotiating contracts, and avoiding scams and provides rudimentary information about liens, insurance, bonding, and consumer rights. . . . The numbers and addresses of consumer protection agencies are listed state by state, as are construction regulatory offices." Libr J

Inwood, Robert

Creative country construction; building & living in harmony with nature. {by} Robert Inwood & Christian Bruyere. Sterling 2000 288p il pa $19.95 **690**

1. House construction

ISBN 0-8069-7115-0

LC 99-86650

This is "a general resource with illustrations depicting various construction practices derived from the building techniques of early American homesteaders. Chapters focus on stone masonry, wood-frame construction, log homes, and post-and-beam construction." Libr J

Kidder, Tracy

House. Houghton Mifflin 1985 341p il hardcover o.p. pa $14 **690**

1. Building 2. House construction 3. Houses

ISBN 0-618-00191-3 pa

LC 85-7630

"The saga of a couple who supervised the building of their house in Massachusetts, this report interweaves the personal lives of those involved in the project with New England history, the sociology of building, popular lore and practical tips for would-be homebuilders." Publ Wkly

Includes bibliographical references

Levy, Matthys

Why buildings fall down; how structures fail. {by} Matthys Levy and Mario Salvadori; illustrations by Kevin Woest. Norton 1992 334p il hardcover o.p. pa $14.95 **690**

1. Building failures 2. Structural failures

ISBN 0-3933-1152-X pa

LC 91-34954

"Two structural engineers examine puzzling structural failures and collapses and the destruction of ancient and modern buildings, bridges, dams, and other constructions. Plenty of illustrations accent the lively text." Booklist

Nash, George

Do-it-yourself housebuilding; the complete handbook. illustrations by Roland Dahlquist. Sterling 1995 704p il pa $24.95 **690**

1. House construction 2. House construction -- Amateurs' manuals

ISBN 0-8069-0424-0

LC 94-2371

This "book covers every step of house construction from site selection to finishing touches. The authors discuss both rough and finish carpentry and show how to install plumbing, and electrical, heating, and air-conditioning systems. The text is supplemented by numerous excellent photographs and illustrations." Libr J

Includes bibliographical references

Peters, Rick

Popular mechanics garage makeovers; adding space without adding on. Hearst Books 2006 192p il pa $17.95 **690**

1. Garages

ISBN 978-1-58816-513-8; 1-58816-513-2

LC 2006-7912

"The book is divided into three main parts: planning, which covers basic construction methods and styles; real-life examples of different projects (including budget estimates); and plans for implementing any or all of the features shown. . . . Peters covers everything from basic construction techniques such as drywalling a ceiling and building walls to installing garage door openers and wall-mounted storage systems. . . . Those considering tackling a garage renovation will find the book's common-sense approach and practical advice invaluable." Publ Wkly

R.S. Means Company, Inc.

★ **Means** illustrated construction dictionary; 3rd ed, unabridged; Means 2000 790p il + 1 computer optical disc $99.95 **690**

1. Building -- Dictionaries 2. Construction industry -- Dictionaries 3. Reference books

ISBN 0-87629-538-3

LC 2001-266365

Over 19,000 definitions of words, terms, and concepts related to the construction industry. Tables of weights, measures, conversions, size determinations, and symbols are included.

"This is an indispensable resource for large do-it-yourself, homeowner, or construction collections. Highly recommended." Libr J

Schoenherr, Matthew

House transformed; getting the home you want --with the house you have. [by] Matthew Schoenherr with Linda Hunter and Wendy Jordan. Taunton Press 2005 186p il $32 **690**
1. Houses -- Remodeling
ISBN 1-56158-711-7

LC 2004-26818

This book outlining projects for home renovation describes "seven keys to a successful remodel, whether you are redoing a kitchen, building an addition, or making over the whole house." Publisher's note

The Art of natural building; design, construction, resources. editors: Joseph F. Kennedy, Michael Smith, Catherine Wanek; illustrated by Joseph F. Kennedy. New Soc. Pubs. 2002 291p il pa $26.95 **690**
1. Building 2. Building materials 3. House construction
ISBN 0-86571-433-9

"The authors, who are practitioners in the natural building movement, introduce a variety of nontraditional construction options, including underground building and building with alternative materials such as adobe, recycled agricultural materials, rammed earth, and straw bale. They also address energy efficiency, design, and the desire to create a healthy environment. The final chapters include case studies." Libr J

Includes bibliographical references

692   Auxiliary construction practices

Architectural graphic standards; authored by the American Institute of Architects; Andrew Pressman, editor-in-chief; Smith Maran Architecture and Interiors, graphics editor; with additional illustrations from the Magnum Group. 11th ed.; Wiley 2007 xxxvi, 1080p il map $250 **692**
1. Architecture -- Details
ISBN 978-0-471-70091-3; 0-471-70091-6

LC 2006-102175

A guide to structural elements and details, types and dimensions of modern building materials, hardware and furniture.

695   Roof covering

Black & Decker Corp.

The **complete** guide to roofing, siding & trim; created by: the editors of Creative Publishing International, Inc., in cooperation with Black & Decker. Updated 2nd ed.; Creative Pub. International 2008 271p il pa $24.99 **695**
1. Roofs 2. Siding (Building materials)
ISBN 978-1-58923-418-5

LC 2008-26823

This guide to installing and maintaining roofing and siding includes a "section on trim work as well as a section on

ecofriendly roofs. . . . The photo gallery is quite attractive and fresh, reflecting current and popular house styles. The evaluation of materials—relating to home style, maintenance, duration, and drawbacks—is particularly nice. Text is matter-of-fact and clear, with no topic overdone. A useful and usable guidebook, this is recommended for all public libraries." Libr J

Kennedy, Terry

★ **Roofing** instant answers. McGraw-Hill 2002 500p il pa $49.95 **695**
1. Roofing 2. Roofs 3. Roofs -- Design and construction
ISBN 0-07-138712-9

LC 2002-284416

This companion volume to Steven Bukowski's Flooring instant answers provides answers to questions about roofing, including more than 300 photos, drawings, tables and checklists.

696   Utilities

Black & Decker Corp.

The **complete** guide to plumbing; modern materials and current codes all new guide to working with gas pipe. Expanded 4th ed.; Creative Pub. International 2008 334p il pa $24.99 **696**
1. Plumbing
ISBN 978-1-58923-378-2; 1-58923-378-6

LC 2008-8636

This guide to plumbing covers fixtures, installations, repairs, materials, tools, and skills.

"The sequential directions for many common household repairs are the real asset here. Excellent photos with simple instruction for each project are also valuable. Includes a DVD with demonstrations of many of the jobs described in the book." Libr J

Ferington, Esther

You can build: plumbing; by Esther Ferington and the editors of Sunset Books. Sunset 2010 239p il pa $24.95 **696**
1. Plumbing
ISBN 978-0-376-01468-9

"Concise and informative, this title offers valuable assistance to homeowners with plumbing problems and no plumbing expertise. Although not extensive, it focuses on proper fixes to common problems and is an excellent money-saving guide. Guidance for minor renovation is also included." Libr J

Henkenius, Merle

★ **Plumbing**: complete projects for the home; New expanded ed.; Creative Homeowner 2006 287p il pa $19.95 **696**
1. Plumbing
ISBN 1-58011-311-7; 978-1-58011-311-3

LC 2006-924699

The author "shows homeowners how to tackle expensive plumbing repairs (e.g., replacing a washer in a leaky faucet). . . . The skill level of each project is rated, and photos walk users step by step through the instructions. . . . Strongly recommended for all collections." Libr J

697   Heating, ventilating, air-conditioning engineering

Ewing, Rex A.

Got sun? go solar; harness nature's free energy to heat and power your grid-tied home. [by] Rex A. Ewing and Doug Pratt. Expanded 2nd ed.; PixyJack Press 2009 191p il map pa $20   **697**

1. Photovoltaic power generation 2. Solar energy 3. Wind power

ISBN 978-0-9773724-6-1

LC 2009-19053

"This is an excellent primer on home application of solar energy. Written in a chatty and amusing style, the book is more informational than mechanical." Libr J

Includes bibliographical references

698   Detail finishing

Garskof, Josh

Tiling; by Josh Garskof and the editors of Sunset Books. Sunset Books 2009 240p il pa $21.95 **698**

1. Tiles

ISBN 978-0-376-01680-5

This book introduces "materials and techniques for tiling various surfaces, both inside and outside the home. Garskof offers great step-by-step instructions for some required basics. A wonderful addition to public library collections." Libr J

Santos, Brian

Painting and wallpapering secrets from Brian Santos, the Wall Wizard. Wiley 2011 240p il pa $21.99   **698**

1. House painting 2. Paperhanging

ISBN 978-0-470-59360-8; 0-470-59360-1

LC 2010-28548

"This guide contains useful information for wall treatments. The practical and reassuring advice includes important directions on what not to do. This is nitty-gritty do-it-yourself, with outstanding prep instruction, tool selection, well-thought-out tips and tricks, and technique photos. While inspirational wall-treatment photo books abound, . . . this is the guide you'll need to achieve those looks." Libr J

700   ARTS

700   The arts

Davenport, Guy

The **Hunter** Gracchus, and other papers on literature and art. Counterpoint 1996 339p il hardcover o.p. pa $19.95   **700**

ISBN 978-1-887178-55-6; 1-887178-55-4

LC 96-43090

The author "announces blithely that this collection of essays and comments 'has for a semblance of unity only their being written on the same typewriter'. . . . Davenport is what the ancient Greek poet Antolochus would call a fox, or one who knows many things, rather than a hedgehog, who has a single central vision. These writings on Kafka, Darwin, Picasso, Shakers, and snake handlers have more in common than their means of production, however, because each is in its own way brilliant, the stylish work of a master stylist." Libr J

Impelluso, Lucia

Gods and heroes in art; edited by Stefano Zuffi; translated by Thomas Michael Hartmann. Getty Mus. 2003 383p il pa $19.95   **700**

1. Art and mythology -- Dictionaries 2. Classical mythology -- Dictionaries 3. Mythology, Classical -- Italian 4. Mythology, Classical, in art -- Italian 5. Reference books

ISBN 0-89236-702-4

LC 2002-13422

The characters of ancient Greek and Roman mythology "are each described in entries summarizing their distinctive stories, their special attributes, and the ways in which artists have depicted them. Each entry is . . . illustrated with reproductions of works of art in which the god or hero is pictured. . . . The book concludes with . . . indexes, including a list of iconographic symbols associated with the subjects, and a bibliography." Publisher's note

Includes bibliographical references

Nelson, Maggie

The **art** of cruelty; Maggie Nelson. W.W. Norton & Co. 2011 288p.   **700**

1. Art -- Moral and ethical aspects 2. Cruelty in art

ISBN 978-0-393-07215-0; 0-393-07215-0

LC 2011001828

This book of "art and cultural criticism takes on . . . representations of violence in art. . . . The pervasiveness of images of torture, horror, and war has all but demolished the twentieth-century hope that such imagery might shock us into a less alienated state, or aid in the creation of a just social order. . . . [A]uthor Maggie Nelson . . . navigates this contemporary predicament, with an eye to the question of whether or not focusing on representations of cruelty makes us cruel. In a journey through high and low culture (Kafka to reality TV), the visual to the verbal (Paul McCarthy to Brian Evenson), and the apolitical to the political (Francis Bacon to Kara Walker), Nelson offers a model of how one might balance strong ethical convictions with an equally strong appreciation for work that tests the limits of taste, taboo, and permissibility." (Publisher's note)

Oakes, Kaya

Slanted and enchanted; the evolution of Indie culture. Henry Holt and Company 2009 256p pa $14   **700**

    1. Arts -- United States
    ISBN 978-0-8050-8852-6; 0-8050-8852-0

                  LC 2008-45286

  "Although the term indie is most associated with rock music, Oakes explores a variety of artists and DIY art forms that operate with some degree of independence from the mainstream. She traces this phenomenon back to the 1950s — to the New York School poets, particularly Frank O'Hara, and the Beats — and from there, she explores a myriad of indie angles: riot-grrrl culture, the crafting world, the growth of underground comics and the music of bands such as Operation Ivy, the Minutemen and Pavement. Oakes is no dry outsider. She believes in what she describes, she contributes to it and she speaks its language. . . . Oakes also shines when she examines an irony of indie life: It often thrives on collaboration and community." Cleveland Plain Dealer

  Includes bibliographical references

Ochoa, George

The **Wilson** chronology of the arts; [by] George Ochoa and Melinda Corey. Wilson, H.W. 1998 476p $115   **700**

    1. Arts -- History 2. Arts -- History -- Chronology
    ISBN 0-8242-0934-6

                 LC 97-23541

  "The authors provide a timeline detailing human creativity that progresses from ca. 43,000 B.C.E. to 1997, with 4,000 entries spread over 13 categories of artistic endeavor. . . . The chronology is global in scope and comprehensive in coverage, emphasizing well-established art forms without neglecting the oral traditions and decorative art forms of nonliterate societies and currently emerging art forms. . . . The straightforward organization of this work makes it suitable for many different uses." Recomm Ref Books for Small & Medium-sized Libr & Media Cent, 1999

Reid, Jane Davidson

★ The **Oxford** guide to classical mythology in the arts, 1300-1990s; [by] Jane Davidson Reid; with the assistance of Chris Rohmann. Oxford Univ. Press 1993 2v set $195   **700**

    1. Arts 2. Classical mythology -- Catalogs 3. Reference books
    ISBN 0-19-504998-5

                 LC 92-35374

  This work catalogs "more than 205 mythological characters and themes as they are represented in the arts from the early Renaissance to the present. More than 30,000 representations, including those from literature, music, dance, and art, are listed. Arranged alphabetically by character or theme, each entry briefly describes the subject and its place in classical mythology, and concludes with a comprehensive bibliography. . . . This is an impressive piece of scholarship that will quickly become a standard reference source." Am Libr

★ Arts and humanities through the eras. Gale 2004 5v il set $450   **700**

    1. Arts -- History 2. Civilization -- History
    ISBN 0-7876-5695-X

                 LC 2004-10243

  "Each volume consists of nine chapters covering the major branches of the humanities: architecture and design, dance, fashion, literature, music, philosophy, religion, theater, and visual arts. . . . This outstanding series offers a wealth of information; the chapters on architecture, dance, and theater alone are worth the price of each volume." Libr J

  Includes bibliographical references

The muses go to school; inspiring stories about the importance of arts in education. edited by Herbert Kohl and Tom Oppenheim. New Press 2012 xxvii, 200 p.p   **700**

    1. Arts -- Study and teaching 2. Education -- Aims and objectives
    ISBN 1595585397; 9781595585394

                 LC 2011042803

  In this book, edited by Herbert Kohl and Tom Oppenheim, autobiographical pieces with well-known artists and performers are paired with . . . essays by . . . educators to produce a . . . case for positioning the arts at the center of primary and secondary school curriculums. Spanning a range of genres from acting and music to literary and visual arts, these . . . voices make surprising connections between the arts and the development of intellect, imagination, spirit, emotional intelligence, self-esteem, and self-discipline of young people. (Publisher's note)

700.92   Biography

Ross, Clifford

The **world** of Edward Gorey; by Clifford Ross and Karen Wilkin. Abrams 1996 190p il hardcover o.p. pa $19.95   **700.92**

    1. Artists 2. Authors 3. Children's authors 4. Illustrators 5. Novelists 6. Set designers
    ISBN 0-8109-9083-0 pa

                 LC 95-47900

  This book includes an "interview with Mr. Ross, {in which} Edward Gorey speaks of his likes and dislikes and aspects of his career. . . . Ms. Wilkin discusses Gorey's work as illustrator, author, stage designer, and miscellaneous creator." Atl Mon

  Includes bibliographical references

701   Philosophy and theory of fine and decorative arts

Dutton, Denis

The **art** instinct; beauty, pleasure, and human evolution. Bloomsbury Press 2009 278p $25   **701**

    1. Aesthetics 2. Art 3. Art -- Philosophy 4. Evolution 5. Evolution (Biology) 6. Instinct
    ISBN 978-1-59691-401-8; 1-59691-401-7

                 LC 2008-28304

"Marshaling intriguing examples and analogies in a co-gent, animated argument destined to provoke debate, Dutton formulates the best answer yet to the question, 'What's art good for?'" Booklist

Includes bibliographical references (p. 259-268)

Higgins, Hannah B.

The **grid** book; [by] Hannah B. Higgins. MIT Press 2009 300p il map pa $24.95   **701**
   1. Design 2. Grids (Crisscross patterns)
   ISBN 978-0-262-51240-4; 0-262-51240-8
                   LC 2008-29430

"Higgins traces the grid from its origins in agriculture and urbanism of 9000 BCE to the developing architectures of digital computers. Indeed, a complete list of the grids she uncovers would mean nothing less than offering a full index of her book, which would include everything from the Code of Hammurabi to meditations on mail-order catalogs and fractal geometry. . . . [The work's] ambition is breathtaking but deftly handled, as Higgins metaphorically detaches the grid off a brick wall, throws it down on city streets, plucks it up into a stave, stretches it into a screen, a net, and finally the web. Though it sounds as if this project would be endless, in fact the book comprises ten intimate and compelling essays, written with a light and playful touch." PopMatters

Includes bibliographical references

Rothenberg, David

Survival of the beautiful; art, science, and evolution. Bloomsbury Press 2011 311p il $30   **701**
   1. Aesthetics 2. Animals in art 3. Art and science 4. Evolution (Biology) 5. Nonfiction
   ISBN 978-1-60819-216-8
                   LC 2011014964

It was the author's intent sto understand why beauty exists in the first place, and what that means to our existence. Evolution and mutation determine what features are passed on in each species, but nature also offers "case after case of wild, untrammeled craziness," patterns, colors, and behavior that are clearly not needed for survival. [David] Rothenberg notes with amusement how Darwin thought ornamentation --colorful feathers, brilliant songs, mating dances--existed to delight the mind of potential mates, throwing evolutionary control into female hands, an idea that didn't sit well with Victorians. Rothenberg goes on to discuss how animal patterns (animal art) have influenced human creativity in cubist and abstract art as well as military camouflage. (Publishers Weekly)

The author "presents a leaps-and-bounds inquiry into the role beauty plays in evolution. . . . Rothenberg argues that to understand nature's 'frills and flourish,' including the wildly impractical peacock's tail, we must look beyond the rigid pragmatism at the core of current evolutionary theory and accept that beauty is not utilitarian. . . . With verve, multidisciplinary fluency, and an encompassing vision, Rothenberg accomplishes his mission to change the way we perceive and understand the intertwining of natural evolution and human cultural evolution, beauty and life, art and science." Booklist

Includes bibliographical references

702 Miscellany of fine and decorative arts

Michels, Caroll

★ **How** to survive and prosper as an artist; selling yourself without selling your soul. 6th ed.; Henry Holt and Co. 2009 381p pa $20   **702**
   1. Art -- Marketing 2. Art -- Vocational guidance
   ISBN 978-0-8050-8848-9; 0-8050-8848-2
                   LC 2008-39615

This is a "guide to taking control of your career and making a good living in the art world . . . [that includes] information on getting into a gallery, being your own PR agent, and negotiating prices, as well as innovative marketing, exhibition, and sales opportunities for various artistic disciplines." Publisher's note

Includes bibliographical references

★ **American** art directory 2009; 63rd ed; National Register Publishing 2008 1035p $297   **702**
   1. American art -- Directories 2. Art -- Directories 3. Canadian art -- Directories 4. Reference books
   ISBN 978-0-87217-755-0; 0-87217-755-6

This book identifies "key characteristics for thousands of art institutions in the U.S. and Canada. This . . . resource provides . . . information on museums, art organizations, art schools, libraries, art editors and critics, scholarships, fellowships, exhibitions and state art councils." Publisher's note

702.8 Auxiliary techniques and procedures; apparatus, equipment, materials

Hoving, Thomas

False impressions; the hunt for big-time art fakes. Simon & Schuster 1996 366p il hardcover o.p. pa $22   **702.8**
   1. Art -- Forgeries 2. Art forgeries
   ISBN 0-684-83148-1 pa
                   LC 95-53800

Hoving "is a magnetic storyteller, achieving just the right blend of humor and mettle." Booklist

Includes bibliographical references

Shay, Bee

Collage lab; experiments, investigations, and exploratory projects. Quarry Books 2010 144p il pa $22.99   **702.8**
   1. Collage
   ISBN 978-1-59253-565-1; 1-59253-565-8
                   LC 2009-22988

"This is a sophisticated and accessible lab manual for all but the complete novice. Shay . . . offers 52 labs that reinforce the basics of art and set the artist on a path to experimental collage with brilliant textures, colors, and images." Libr J

Smith, Ray

★ The **artist's** handbook; [equipment, materials, procedures, techniques] 3rd. ed.; DK Pub. 2009 384p il pa $21.95   **702.8**

1. Art -- Technique 2. Artists' materials

ISBN 978-0-7566-5722-2; 0-7566-5722-9

LC 2010-502586

An illustrated handbook offers step-by-step projects, reproductions of works by master artists, and instruction in creative techniques, covering everything from drawing and painting to printmaking and digital media.

The Grove encyclopedia of materials and techniques in art; edited by Gerald W.R. Ward. Oxford University Press 2008 828p il lib bdg $150 **702.8**

1. Art -- Technique 2. Art -- Technique -- Encyclopedias 3. Artists' materials 4. Artists' materials -- Encyclopedias 5. Reference books

ISBN 978-0-19-531391-8; 0-19-531391-7

LC 2008-2486

Ward "has revised and updated approximately 1440 entries and full-length articles . . . from the venerable 34-volume Grove Dictionary of Art and added some new entries on topics of 'emerging importance' to produce a comprehensive one-volume resource on all aspects of materials and techniques of the fine arts and crafts, from acrylic painting, alabaster, and aquatint to upholstery, varnish, wood-engraving, and zinc. . . . An essential work for artists, historians, and art students and for the libraries that serve them." Libr J

Includes bibliographical references

703   Dictionaries, encyclopedias, concordances of fine and decorative arts

Frazier, Nancy

The **Penguin** concise dictionary of art history. Penguin Ref. 1999 774p hardcover o.p. pa $20 **703**

1. Art -- Dictionaries 2. Art -- History -- Dictionaries 3. Reference books

ISBN 0-14-051420-1 pa

LC 98-56089

"An easy-to-read, scholarly yet not lofty, fascinating, and very well-organized book." Libr J

Includes bibliographical references (p. {731}-736) and index

Langmuir, Erika

Yale dictionary of art and artists; {by} Erika Langmuir and Norbert Lynton. Yale Univ. Press 2000 753p $30; pa $12.95   **703**

1. Art -- Dictionaries 2. Artists -- Dictionaries 3. Reference books

ISBN 0-300-08702-0; 0-300-06458-6 pa

LC 00-25800

"Varying in length from a few lines to several pages for artists such as Leonardo da Vinci, Pablo Picasso, or John Constable, the 3000 entries cover Western art from 1300 until the present. The work covers painters, sculptors, graphic artists, patrons, technical processes, movements, and terminology." Libr J

Lucie-Smith, Edward

★ The **Thames** & Hudson dictionary of art terms; 2nd ed; Thames & Hudson 2004 240p il pa $16.95   **703**

1. Art -- Dictionaries 2. Reference books

ISBN 0-500-20365-2

LC 2003100802

"More than 2,000 entries define and explain terms used to describe painting, sculpture, architecture, graphic arts, decorative and applied arts, and photography, including the terminology of non-Western art. Several entries contain cross-references, and the book's 400 illustrations and diagrams, although reproduced in black and white, help explain the concepts defined. The thorough and clear entries make this volume appropriate for any beginning art history student." Choice

The Concise Oxford dictionary of art and artists; edited by Ian Chilvers. 3rd ed; Oxford University Press 2003 653p pa $14.95   **703**

1. Art -- Dictionaries 2. Artists -- Biography -- Dictionaries 3. Artists -- Dictionaries 4. Reference books

ISBN 0-19-860477-7

LC 2003-278290

This "is an abbreviated lexicon based on 'The Oxford Dictionary of Art'.... It includes western art from the fifth century B.C.E., but has been expanded to include more recent artists born prior to 1965 instead of 1945. Entries include biographies of artists, sculptors, writers, leading collectors and dealers, materials and techniques, and galleries and museums." Am Ref Books Annu, 2004

704   Special topics in fine and decorative arts

Holladay, Wilhelmina Cole

A **museum** of their own; National Museum of Women in the Arts. text contributions by Philip Kopper. Abbeville Press 2008 240p il $50   **704**

1. Women artists

ISBN 978-0-7892-1003-6; 0-7892-1003-7

LC 2008-21646

"The National Museum of Women in the Arts . . . opened in 1987. It changed the status of women artists and the life of its founder, who now tells the museum's fascinating success story in an entertainingly anecdotal, inspiring, and beautifully illustrated [book]. . . . This invaluable work of art history is enlivened by Holladay's encounters with artists . . . and gorgeous reproductions, many of works that will be new to even the most art-expert readers." Booklist

Kort, Carol

A to Z of American women in the visual arts; {by} Carol Kort and Liz Sonneborn. Facts on File 2002 258p il $44 **704**

1. American art -- Dictionaries 2. Art, American -- Dictionaries 3. Reference books 4. Women artists -- Dictionaries 5. Women artists -- United States -- Dictionaries

ISBN 0-8160-4397-3

LC 2001-40231

A "handy, well-written volume. . . . The biographical entries are filled with interesting personal and career details that make for absorbing reading." Voice Youth Advocates

Includes bibliographical references and index

704.03 Ethnic and national groups

Patton, Sharon F.

African-American art. Oxford Univ. Press 1998 319p il maps hardcover o.p. pa $18.95   **704.03**
1. African American art
ISBN 0-19-284213-7 pa

                LC 98-190459

"Comprehensively and with sharp, scholarly accuracy, Patton has closed gaps between the chronological and thematic directions of Black American art and complexities of Euro-American art history." Choice

704.9 Iconography

Bussagli, Marco

Angels. Abrams 2007 780p il $19.95 **704.9**
1. Angels 2. Art and religion
ISBN 978-0-8109-9436-2; 0-8109-9436-4

                LC 2007-010749

"Art historian Marco Bussagli has organized the book by significant Biblical events. . . . Each work of art is accompanied by the Biblical passage it illustrates, along with a commentary exploring its form and meaning." Publisher's note

Includes bibliographical references

705 Serial publications of fine and decorative arts

Art index. Wilson, H.W.   **705**
1. Art -- Bibliography 2. Art -- Periodicals -- Indexes 3. Reference books

An author and subject index to more than 200 periodicals. Subjects covered include advertising art, architecture, art history, crafts, graphic arts, and interior design. Current book reviews are indexed in a separate section.

"The easiest to use of the major indexes to visual arts and a basic tool for arts research." Walford. Guide to Ref Mater. 3d edition

708 Galleries, museums, private collections of fine and decorative arts

Meier, Richard

Building the Getty. University of California Press 1999 204p il pa $25.95   **708**
ISBN 0-520-21730-6; 978-0-520-21730-0

                LC 99-20219

"Charting his involvement in the Getty's construction, Meier recounts in an intriguingly candid, eminently personal style the formidable bureaucratic process entailed upon undertaking to realize this grandiose endeavor. Beginning with the competition itself, Meier's detailed reminiscences offer fascinating insights into the design process and the extraordinarily intricate procedures and systems, as well as endless setbacks, associated with executing a modern-day megalithic structure." Booklist

National Gallery of Art (U.S.)

★ **National** Gallery of Art; [foreword by Earl A. Powell III] 2nd ed.; Thames and Hudson 2006 332p il pa $18.95   **708**
ISBN 0-500-20390-3; 978-0-500-20390-3

                LC 2005-904459

"The collection of the National Gallery of Art in Washington includes works by the greatest masters of Western art from the twelfth century to the present. . . . [In this] look at the National Gallery's masterpieces . . . the works are illustrated in full color, and the curators have written the texts." Publisher's note

708.1 Geographic treatment

Walsh, John

The **J.** Paul Getty Museum and its collections; a museum for the new century. {by} John Walsh, Deborah Gribbon. Getty Mus. 1997 288p hardcover o.p. pa $40   **708.1**
1. Art collectors 2. Energy industry executives 3. Philanthropists
ISBN 0-89236-476-9 pa

                LC 97-12170

This volume is a history of the J. Paul Getty Museum and a guide to its collections.

This is "a lavish visual compendium of J. Paul Getty's amazing art collection; in addition, the text reveals important background details surrounding Getty's life and his passion for art. Walsh and Gribbon communicate just how the magnate's fortunes were put to the test as planned acquisitions of artwork flourished." Booklist

708.13 United States

Loebl, Suzanne

America's art museums; a traveler's guide to great collections large and small. Norton 2002 426p il pa $18.95   **708.13**
1. Art -- United States 2. Art museums 3. Art museums -- United States
ISBN 0-393-32006-5

                LC 2001-44208

This is a "guide to some of America's finest art museums. Not only does it focus on the major and more familiar art museums, it also supplies some much-needed information and marketing for some of the small and little-known, yet important, art galleries in the United States. The book is alphabetically arranged by state and then by city, and provides information on times open, strengths of the museum's collection, activities for children, the museum's history, and Websites." Am Ref Books Annu, 2003

Includes bibliographical references

709   History, geographic treatment, biography

Barnitz, Jacqueline

Twentieth-century art of Latin America. University of Tex. Press 2001 400p il $70; pa $34.95 **709**
1. Art -- 20th century 2. Art, Latin American 3. Art, Modern -- 20th century -- Latin America 4. Latin American art
ISBN 0-292-70857-2; 0-292-70858-0 pa

LC 99-50871

A survey of 20th century Latin American art which includes coverage of regional movements, and discussion of historical, political, and cultural influences.

"Latin American art, the fruit of violent collisions among diverse indigenous, European, and African cultures, is revealed as provocative and vibrant in Barnitz's well-illustrated and groundbreaking overview of its dazzling twentieth-century flowering." Booklist

Includes bibliographical references

Beckett, Wendy

Sister Wendy's American collection; {by} Sister Wendy Beckett. HarperCollins Pubs. 2000 288p il $40 **709**
1. Art -- History 2. Art -- United States 3. Art appreciation
ISBN 0-06-019556-8

LC 00-40953

The author provides a "discussion of works in six of America's renowned art museums. . . . {She} includes a variety of media--paintings, sculpture, decorative arts, armor, and other art objects--and the individual works originate from a dizzying array of time periods and several countries." Libr J

Bramly, Serge

Leonardo; the artist and the man. translated by Sian Reynolds. Penguin Bks. 1994 493p il pa $25 **709**
1. Artists 2. Artists, Italian 3. Painters 4. Scientists 5. Writers on science
ISBN 0-14-023175-7; 978-0-14-023175-5
In this account Bramly "sheds light on the more personal aspects of Leonardo. . . . As he follows da Vinci's often frustrating career and ever-widening sphere of inquiries, inventions, and discoveries, he also patches together overlooked clues about his private life, causing us to marvel anew at Leonardo's fertile and versatile mind while acquiring a sharper image of Leonardo the man. A richly detailed, expansive, and thoroughly enjoyable portrait." Booklist

Includes bibliographical references

Craven, Wayne

American art; history and culture. McGraw-Hill 2003 687p il pa $69 **709**
1. American art
ISBN 978-0-07-282329-5; 0-07-282329-1

LC 2002-035777

The author "establishes seven main stylistic periods—colonial, Federal, romantic, the American Renaissance, early modern, postwar modern, and postmodern—and then goes into great detail within each section, profiling individual artists and discussing the effects of various social, politi-cal, and technological changes on aesthetics and the role of art in daily life. . . . Coverage of American photography and twentieth-century art are particularly dynamic, but his examples and emphases prove to be insightful and creative throughout." Booklist

Includes bibliographical references

Dippie, Brian W.

The **Frederic** Remington Art Museum collection. Abrams 2000 264p il $49.50 **709**
1. Artists 2. Drafters 3. Painters 4. Sculptors 5. West (U.S.) -- In art 6. West (U.S.) in art
ISBN 0-8109-6711-1

LC 00-49339

This biography examines the artist's life and work and follows his evolution from illustrator to artist.

"Photographs and comparative images enhance the author's discussions of Remington himself and of the individual paintings, drawings, and sculptures." Libr J

Includes bibliographical references

Farrington, Lisa E.

★ **Creating** their own image; the history of African-American women artists. Oxford University Press 2005 354p il $55 **709**
1. African American art 2. African American artists 3. African American women 4. African American women artists 5. Women artists
ISBN 0-19-516721-X

LC 2003-66171

"A richly detailed yet fluent work of trailblazing research, fresh interpretations, and cogent argument, Farrington's treatise discusses vital aesthetic as well as social and cultural issues and creates a vibrant context for such seminal artists as Augusta Savage, Faith Ringgold, Barbara Chase-Riboud, Kara Walker, and many more." Booklist

Fenton, James

Leonardo's nephew; essays on art and artists. University of Chicago Press 2000 283p il pa $15 **709**
1. Art -- History
ISBN 0-226-24147-5; 978-0-226-24147-0

LC 99-55666

Fenton presents a collection of fifteen essays on various aspects of art history. Subjects "include Freud's collection of antique statuettes, Egyptian funerary portraits and Joseph Cornell. These essays educate, enlighten, surprise and thrill, unfailingly." N Y Time Book Rev

Includes bibliographical references

FitzGerald, Michael C.

★ **Picasso** and American art; [by] Michael FitzGerald; with a chronology by Julia May Boddewyn. Whitney Museum of American Art; in association with Yale University Press 2006 400p il $65 **709**
1. American art 2. Art, American 3. Artists 4. Avant-garde (Aesthetics) -- United States -- History -- 20th century 5. Painters
ISBN 9780300114522; 0-300-11452-4

LC 2006-1402

A "study of Picasso's influence on some of the most significant American artists of the 20th century. Fitzgerald moves chronologically, from the earliest Americans who engaged cubism in the teens (Max Weber, Mardsen Hartley, Man Ray, Stuart Davis), through the modernist investigations of Arshile Gorky, Willem De Kooning and Jackson Pollack, and winds up with Roy Lichtenstien's pop-art and Jasper Johns' postmodern responses to Picasso. Fitzgerald takes great pains to triangulate exhibition specifics with the work and words of each artist to document the precise nature and extent of the influence in each case. . . . There is a generous supply of images presented with the text, and they are as successful as Fitzgerald's prose in illuminating the complexities of Picasso's influence on these artists." Publ Wkly

Includes bibliographical references

Gardner, Helen

★ **Gardner's** art through the ages; a global history. [revised by] Fred S. Kleiner. Enhanced 13th ed.; Wadsworth, Cengage Learning 2010 1088p il map $165.99　　**709**

1. Art -- History
ISBN 978-0-495-79986-3; 0-495-79986-6

LC 2009-932089

This book surveys world art from prehistoric times to the present day. Painting, sculpture, architecture and some decorative arts are considered. Although the focus is on European art, there are also chapters on ancient Near Eastern, Asian, pre-Columbian, American Indian, African and Oceanic art.

Gombrich, E. H.

★ The **story** of art; 16th ed rev and expanded; Phaidon Press 1995 688p il $49.95; pa $29.95 **709**

1. Art -- History
ISBN 0-7148-3355-X; 0-7148-3247-2 pa

LC 96-140698

This survey of art examines artistic achievements in historical context to consider how prevailing social, political, and economic factors may have influenced the succession and popularity of certain artistic styles.

Hamilton, George Heard

The **art** and architecture of Russia. Yale University Press 1983 482p il map pa $32　　**709**

1. Christian art 2. Church architecture 3. Russian art
ISBN 978-0-300-05327-2; 0-300-05327-4

Hamilton traces the development of Russian art from the height of the Byzantine Empire, through its flowering under Peter the Great, to contemporary work and the influence of Western European culture.

Harclerode, Peter

The **lost** masters; World War II and the looting of Europe's treasurehouses. [by] Peter Harclerode & Brendan Pittaway. Welcome Rain 2000 402p il hardcover o.p. pa $18.95　　**709**

1. Art thefts 2. Art thefts -- Germany -- History -- 20th century 3. Art treasures in war -- Europe -- History -- 20th century 4. World War, 1939-1945 -- Destruction and pillage 5. World War, 1939-1945 -- Destruction and pillage -- Europe

ISBN 1-56649-165-7; 1-56649-253-X pa

LC 00-42867

The authors "trace the elusive web of collaborators, opportunists and dealers who exploited the Third Reich's lust for prestigious trophies. Gripping vignettes and revelatory anecdotes illuminate the fates of specific works of art, including the outstanding story of four paratroopers who contrived to rescue the largest cache of stolen art sequestered by the Nazis." Publ Wkly

Includes bibliographical references

Haskell, Barbara

The **American** century; art and culture. Norton 2000 2v il boxed set $120　　**709**

1. American art 2. Arts -- United States
ISBN 978-0-393-04859-9; 0-393-04859-4

Based on exhibitions at the Whitney Museum, these illustrated volumes cover 20th century American painting, sculpture, printmaking, and photography through political, historical, social, economic, and culture contexts.

Hearn, Maxwell K.

Splendors of Imperial China; treasures from the National Palace Museum, Taipei. Metropolitan Mus. of Art 1996 144p il hardcover o.p. pa $29.95 **709**

1. Chinese art
ISBN 0-87099-766-1 pa

LC 95-46590

Hearn "selected more than 100 works to present here, drawn from an extensive traveling exhibition featuring Neolithic and Bronze Age works, as well as Sung, Ming, and other dynasty masterpieces. This beautifully produced book contains fine quality reproductions that illuminate a splendid collection of rare artwork. . . . The text describes in accessible terms important background information, including cultural climate, historical events, and artistic elements." Booklist

Herrera, Hayden

Frida: a biography of Frida Kahlo. Harper & Row 1983 507p il hardcover o.p. pa $24.95 **709**

1. Artists 2. Artists, Mexican 3. Biography, Individual 4. Painters
ISBN 0-06-008589-4 pa

LC 80-8688

This biography of the Mexican painter and wife of Diego Rivera "is a mesmerizing story of radical art, romantic politics, bizarre loves and physical suffering. . . . Herrera resolves Kahlo the public figure and Kahlo the artist in a perceptive portrait of a woman who rose above a circumscribed content with a grand style." Time

Includes bibliographical references

Hoving, Thomas

Art for dummies; foreword by Andrew Wyeth. IDG Books Worldwide, Inc 1999 382p il $24.99 **709**

1. Art -- History 2. Art appreciation
ISBN 978-0-7645-5104-8; 0-7645-5104-3

LC 99-65838

"In this delightful book, Hoving . . . leads readers gently through thousands of years of art history. . . . His breathless enthusiasm is avuncular, scholarly, and quite infectious—an attitude that happily precludes condescension. . . . A terrific book for students, travelers, tyros, and old hands alike." Libr J

Includes bibliographical references

Hughes, Robert

American visions; the epic history of art in America. Knopf 1997 635p il $65; pa $39.95 **709**
  1. American art
  ISBN 0-679-42627-2; 0-375-70365-9 pa

                        LC 96-45111

"Hughes has orchestrated a spectacular integration of facts, observations, and insights in this ambitious, lively, and gloriously illustrated volume." Booklist

Includes bibliographical references

Janson, H. W.

★ **Janson's** history of art; the western tradition. Penelope J.E. Davies ... [et. al] 8th ed.; Prentice Hall 2011 xxxi, 1152p il map $170.40   **709**
  1. Art -- History
  ISBN 978-0-205-68517-2; 0-205-68517-X

                   LC 2009-22617

A history of art from prehistoric cave paintings to video art. While the focus is primarily on Western art, brief discussions of Oriental, Near Eastern, Islamic, African and Latin American arts are included.

Johnson, Paul

★ **Art**: a new history. HarperCollins Pubs. 2003 777p il $39.95   **709**
  1. Art -- History
  ISBN 0-06-053075-8

"While {Johnson's} narrative is for the most part a conventional journey through the canon, his headlong pace, quirky views and pungent prose make it anything but dull." Publ Wkly

King, Ross

Art: over 2,500 works from cave to contemporary; foreword by Ross King. DK Pub. 2008 612p il $50   **709**
  1. Art -- History 2. Art appreciation 3. Reference books
  ISBN 978-0-7566-3972-3; 0-7566-3972-7

                 LC 2008-301471

Within each time period, provides examples of significant works in painting, sculpture, drawing and other media. Highlights themes that were important at various times such as nudes, landscape, still life, and love. Includes brief biographies of some artists and a "closer look" in depth for the most significant works.

"Easy to read and use, . . . both newcomers to art and art connoisseurs will enjoy this picturesque work." Libr J

Includes glossary

Kirwin, Liza

Lists; to-dos, illustrated inventories, collected thoughts, and other artists' enumerations from the Smithsonian's Archives of American Art. with a foreword by John W. Smith.

Princeton Architectural Press 2010 205p il pa $24.95 **709**
  1. Artists -- United States 2. Lists
  ISBN 978-1-56898-888-7; 1-56898-888-5

               LC 2009-25316

"Collecting work from close to 70 list-makers, including Joseph Cornell, Elaine and Willem de Kooning, Lee Krasner, H.L. Mencken, Pablo Picasso and N.C. Wyeth, Kirwin's beautiful book uses an unusual medium to glimpse into the minds of artists. . . . As an 'entry point', the book seems to presuppose a level of familiarity with the various artists. Fortunately for the unfamiliar (like me), each entry includes a brief bit of text from Kirwin that provides biographical information and analysis of each list. However, with its full-colour reproductions, the book seems more appealing as an unusual, mesmerizing, and intimate collection of outsider-like art." PopMatters

Klein, Stefan

Leonardo's legacy; how Da Vinci reimagined the world. translated by Shelley Frisch. Da Capo Press 2010 291p il $26   **709**
  1. Artists 2. Artists, Italian 3. Biography, Individual 4. Inventors 5. Painters 6. Renaissance -- Italy 7. Scientists 8. Writers on science
  ISBN 978-0-306-81825-7; 0-306-81825-6

               LC 2010-00130

The author "makes a compelling case that DaVinci's ability to trigger an empathetic physical response in the viewer lay in his scientific acumen: the asymmetry of the Mona Lisa's smile, for instance, deliberately reflects the asymmetry of the human brain. While Leonardo is remembered primarily as an artist, his accomplishments as a scientist were at least as important. . . . Including a detailed chronology of the artist's life, this makes an illuminating new look at Leonardo's unique genius." Publ Wkly

Includes bibliographical references

Langdon, Helen

Caravaggio; a life. Westview Press 2000 436p il map pa $22 **709**
  1. Artists 2. Artists, Italian 3. Painters
  ISBN 0-8133-3794-1; 978-0-8133-3794-4

In this study of the Renaissance painter, "Langdon's masterly achievement is to integrate Caravaggio's art and life in a convincing and vividly delineated recreation of his world." Libr J

Includes bibliographical references

Little, Stephen

. . . **isms**: understanding art. Universe 2004 159p il pa $16.95   **709**
  1. Art -- History
  ISBN 0-7893-1209-3

               LC 2004-94996

The author "identifies four types of isms: trends specific to the visual arts (perspectivism), broad cultural trends (romanticism), artist-defined movements (cubism), and retrospectively named movements (mannerism). He then moves forward chronologically, deftly defining more than 50 isms, naming key artists, and showcasing splendid examples." Booklist

Lottman, Herbert R.

Man Ray's Montparnasse. Abrams 2001 261p il $29.95   **709**

1. Artists 2. Artists -- France 3. Painters 4. Photographers 5. Photographers -- France -- Paris

ISBN 0-8109-4333-6

LC 2001-633

Lottman presents a "snapshot of Man Ray between the two world wars, emphasizing the 1920s, with the developing Montparnasse section of Paris as the backdrop. Here are the cutting-edge dadaists and surrealists flanking Man Ray and his unerring camera eye, along with poets and artists, collectors, lovers, and other assorted characters. . . . Lottman's vivid exploration of 20th-century art events will serve the art historian and student of Paris very well in documenting an essential epoch and place." Libr J

Includes bibliographical references

Marin, Cheech

Chicano visions; American painters on the verge. essays by Max Benavidez, Constance Cortez, Tere Tomo. Little, Brown 2002 160p il $35; pa $19.95   **709**

1. American painting 2. Mexican American art -- 20th century 3. Mexican American artists 4. Mexican Americans

ISBN 0-8212-2805-6; 0-8212-2806-4 pa

LC 2002-104645

"Marin's extraordinary collection forms the foundation for this exciting and invaluable showcase . . . {which includes works by} John Valadez, Gronk, Diane Gamboa, Patssi Valdez, Adan Hernandez, and Carlos Almaraz." Booklist

Includes bibliographical references

McPhee, John A.

The **ransom** of Russian art; {by} John McPhee. Farrar, Straus & Giroux 1994 181p il $20; pa $12   **709**

1. Art collectors 2. College teachers 3. Economists 4. Russian art 5. Soviet art

ISBN 0-374-24682-3; 0-374-52450-5 pa

LC 94-14723

"McPhee's engaging narrative sheds light on this suppressed creative milieu." Publ Wkly

Nuland, Sherwin B.

Leonardo da Vinci. Viking 2000 170p il pa $13   **709**

1. Artists 2. Artists -- Italy -- Biography 3. Artists, Italian 4. Painters 5. Scientists 6. Writers on science

ISBN 0-670-89391-9; 978-0-14-303510-7 pa; 0-14-303510-X pa

LC 00-32061

"Nuland . . . elegantly sketches Leonardo's life of constant employment by noblemen eager to enjoy the prestige he reflected on them and of even more constant curiosity, which drove him to become the greatest anatomist before Vasari. . . . A scintillating addition." Booklist

Penrose, Roland

★ **Picasso**: his life and work; 3rd ed; University of Calif. Press 1981 517p il hardcover o.p. pa $21.95   **709**

1. Artists 2. Painters

ISBN 0-520-04207-7 pa

LC 80-54015

The author "has produced a painstaking, comprehensive biography . . . and, what is more, a popular biography, assuming neither knowledge of nor sympathy with twentieth-century art on the part of the reader." Times Lit Suppl {review of 1958 edition}

Includes bibliographical references

Petropoulos, Jonathan

The **Faustian** bargain; the art world in Nazi Germany. Oxford Univ. Press 2000 395p il $42.50 **709**

1. Art and state -- Germany -- History -- 20th century 2. Art thefts 3. National socialism 4. National socialism and art 5. World War, 1939-1945 -- Destruction and pillage

ISBN 0-19-512964-4

LC 99-33372

"Spotlighting five groups--art museum directors, art dealers, art journalists, art historians, and artists--Petropoulos . . . details how each of these groups either directly or indirectly facilitated the theft of countless works of art and legitimized the Nazi regime." Libr J

Includes bibliographical references

Robinson, Roxana

★ **Georgia** O'Keeffe: a life. University Press of New England 1999 639p il pa $22.95   **709**

1. Artists 2. Painters

ISBN 0-87451-906-3

LC 98-30944

"This biography, the first to draw on sources unavailable during O'Keeffe's lifetime—and the first to be granted her family's cooperation—offers a persuasive feminist analysis of the life and work of an iconic figure in American art. . . . [The author's] detailed, sensitive critique of O'Keeffe's work . . . alternates with an absorbing, intimate narrative of O'Keeffe's personal life." Publ Wkly

Includes bibliographical references

Schama, Simon

The **power** of art. Ecco 2006 448p il $50 **709**

1. Art -- History

ISBN 0-06-117610-9; 978-0-06-117610-4

LC 2007-270937

The author "presents eight remarkable artists who created their masterworks against a backdrop of personal and professional distress. From politically charged commentaries (David, Picasso, Turner and Rembrandt) to intensely personal visions of the world (van Gogh and Rothko) and the reinvention of the divine (Bernini and Caravaggio), Schama takes these masters' hallowed works off the museum wall and drags them through the mud and muck that went into their creation." Publ Wkly

Includes bibliographical references

Scott, John F.

Latin American art; ancient to modern. University Press of Fla. 1999 xxiv, 240p il $49.95; pa $29.95 **709**

1. Latin American art

ISBN 0-8130-1645-2; 0-8130-1826-9 pa

LC 98-46535

A study "of Latin American art from pre-Columbian times to the present, encompassing media ranging from sculpture, pottery, and painting to architecture. Scott . . . addresses the major styles and artists that define each period." Libr J

Includes bibliographical references

Tomkins, Calvin

Duchamp; a biography. Holt & Co. 1996 550p il map hardcover o.p. pa $20 **709**

1. Artists 2. Artists, French 3. Biography, Individual 4. Painters

ISBN 0-8050-5789-7

LC 96-3080

"Tomkins organizes the facts of Duchamp's life and work into a sober, coherent whole, and for this alone his book makes valuable reading for anyone seeking to understand how art's cutting edge was honed." New Repub

Includes bibliographical references

Tregear, Mary

Chinese art; rev ed; Thames & Hudson 1997 216p il maps pa $14.95 **709**

1. Chinese art

ISBN 0-500-20299-0

An introduction to major decorative, ceremonial, figurative and narrative aspects of Chinese art. Coverage ranges from works of Neolithic groups and the bronzes of the Shang dynasty to Buddhist sculpture, ceramics, garden design and architecture. Emphasis is also placed on the interaction of poetry, painting and calligraphy.

Verlorene Bilder, Verlorene Leben./English

Lost lives, lost art; Jewish collectors, Nazi art theft, and the quest for justice. [by] Melissa Muller [and] Monika Tatzkow; with contributions from Thomas Blubacher and Gunnar Schnabel; foreword by Ronald S. Lauder. Vendome Press 2010 248p il $40 **709**

1. Art -- Collectors and collecting 2. Art thefts 3. Jews -- Europe 4. World War, 1939-1945 -- Destruction and pillage

ISBN 978-0-8656-5263-7; 0-8656-5263-7

LC 2010-15337

The authors "cover 15 Jewish/possibly Jewish families with vast art collections looted by the Nazis. Jewish collectors either had to sell their treasures for a pittance or had them seized. The Bloch-Bauer family's story is famous, but the unknown histories of other prominent families are compellingly told here, and there is a final historical-legal commentary by expert Gunnar Schnabel on Nazi-looted art and the German laws that perpetuated these crimes. . . . Richly illustrated with excellent art reproductions and family photographs." Libr J

Visona, Monica Blackmun

A **history** of art in Africa; [by] Monica Blackmun Visona, Robin Poynor, Herbert M. Cole; with contributions by Suzanne Preston Blier (introduction), Rowland Abiodun (preface) and Michael D. Harris (chapter 16) 2nd ed; Pearson/Prentice Hall 2007 560p il pa $111 **709**

1. African art 2. Art, African

ISBN 978-0-13-612872-4; 0-13-612872-6

LC 2007-15831

"Treating the subject from an art historical rather than an anthropological perspective, this groundbreaking book is organized geographically to cover the entire continent. Each of the five regional sections focuses on selected major art traditions. . . . Accompanying the text are over 700 photos and scores of maps, plans, drawings, etc." Libr J [review of 2000 edition]

Includes bibliographical references (p. 544-551)

Wittkower, Rudolf

Art and architecture in Italy, 1600-1750; revised by Joseph Connors and Jennifer Montagu. 6th ed; Yale Univ. Press 1999 3v il maps set $160; pa set $80 **709**

1. Baroque art 2. Italian art

ISBN 0-300-07890-0; 0-300-07889-7 pa

LC 98-49066

The author examines works produced during the Early, High, and Late Baroque periods of Italian art, covering such artists as Caravaggio, Bernini, Borromini and Cortona.

★ **Atlas** of world art; edited by John Onians. Oxford University Press 2004 352p il maps $150 **709**

1. Art -- History 2. Art -- History -- Maps 3. Atlases

ISBN 0-19-521583-4

LC 2003-55029

This atlas offers a "framework for coverage of art activity around the world from prehistoric times to 2000. . . . Each of the book's seven parts (each covers a period in art history) includes a brief illustrated introduction followed by a standardized sequence of sections on World, American, European, African, Asian and Pacific Art." Choice

Includes bibliographical references

Contemporary artists; editors, Sara Pendergast and Tom Pendergast; advisers, Jean-Christophe Ammann [et al.] 5th ed; St. James Press 2001 2v il set $265 **709**

1. Artists -- Dictionaries 2. Reference books

ISBN 1-55862-407-4

LC 2001-48443

In this reference "nearly 850 prominent artists (those who have exhibited works in major galleries or museums) are listed. . . . Alphabetic entries provide biographical information (e.g., nationality, education, address), individual and select group exhibitions, collections in which the artist's work is contained, publications by or about the individual, a critical essay or essays, and occasionally a statement by the artist. The essays highlight the artist's achievements and offer insight into their work. . . . As a reference tool, this publication remains a classic, indispensable part of every art library's collection and is highly recommended." Am Ref Books Annu, 2003

Cuba: art and history, from 1868 to today; [edited by Nathalie Bondil; translation, Timothy Bernard et al.] Montreal Museum of Fine Arts 2008 424p il map $85   **709**
1. Cuban art
ISBN 3-7913-4019-0; 978-3-7913-4019-7
LC 2008-396997
"This momentous, dazzling volume interweaves history, biography, and artistic expression to explicate Cuba's distinctive vibrancy and glorious creativity." Booklist
Includes bibliographical references

Encyclopedia of Latin American & Caribbean art; edited by Jane Turner. Oxford University Press 2006 803p il $250   **709**
1. Caribbean art -- Encyclopedias 2. Latin American art -- Encyclopedias 3. Reference books
ISBN 978-0-19-531075-7; 0-19-531075-6
"This work covers the art of every country in Central and South America and the Caribbean, from the colonial period to the present. The entries, expanded and updated from the publisher's mammoth Dictionary of Art, cover countries, artists, and artistic styles, with cross-referencing where appropriate." Libr J [review of 1999 edition]
Includes bibliographical references

Encyclopedia of artists; [consulting editor, William Vaughan; contributors, Christopher Ackroyd, et al.] Oxford Univ. Press 2000 6v il set $195 **709**
1. Art -- Dictionaries 2. Art -- Encyclopedias 3. Artists -- Biography 4. Artists -- Dictionaries 5. Reference books
ISBN 0-19-521572-9
LC 00-27167
"This set is beautifully written and illustrated. It will not only provide reliable information for researchers but will also entertain the interested browser." Am Ref Books Annu, 2001

The Grove encyclopedia of American art; editor in chief, Joan Marter. Oxford University Press 2011 5 v. ill. (some col.), map   **709**
ISBN 9780195335798; 0199739269; 9780199739264; 0195335791
LC 2010030274
This reference book "contains entries . . . that comprise a . . . survey . . . art history. It covers American painting, architecture, sculpture, and photography from the Pre-Columbian sources to the colonial period to the twenty-first century devoting coverage to many previously underrepresented areas of inquiry, including African American artists, Asian American artists, and Native American art, both historical and contemporary. Artists, major movements, institutions, critics, and the architecture found in major cities of the United States are covered, as are new media and methodologies, including digital art, performance art, and installation art. In addition to American artists such as John Singer Sargent, Robert Rauschenberg, Maya Lin, and Kiki Smith, attention is also paid to individuals who have had a significant impact on American art and art history through their activity in the United States, including Marcel Duchamp, Erwin Panofsky, Renzo Piano, and Max Beckmann." (Publisher's note)

North American women artists of the twentieth century; a biographical dictionary. edited by Jules Heller and Nancy G. Heller. Garland 1995 xxii, 612p il hardcover o.p. pa $41.95   **709**
1. Biography, Collective 2. Reference books 3. Women artists -- Biography -- Dictionaries 4. Women artists -- Dictionaries
ISBN 0-8153-2584-3 pa
LC 94-49710
This is a "guide to more than 1500 Canadian, Mexican, and United States women artists born between 1850 and 1960. Artists are listed alphabetically, and each artist . . . is briefly treated in several paragraphs that end with bibliographical citations, often to important journal articles. More than 100 illustrations provide a small sampling of their work. . . . An essential acquisition for all art reference libraries." Libr J

709.01   Periods of development, and arts of nonliterate peoples

Berlo, Janet Catherine
Native North American art; by Janet Catherine Berlo and Ruth B. Phillips. Oxford Univ. Press 1999 291p il map hardcover o.p. pa $24.95   **709.01**
1. Native American art
ISBN 0-19-284218-8 pa
LC 99-177938
This survey covers the "artistic output of most Native American tribes across the northern hemisphere over a period of more than eight centuries. . . . In an introduction that stresses the commonality of themes—cosmology, vision quests, love of ornament, reverence of materials—[the authors] emphasize the importance of today's Native art as a natural extension. Five regional chapters then incorporate history, outstanding crafts and arts, some prominent figures, and social, religious, and cultural aspects." Libr J

709.02   6th-15th centuries, 500-1499

Adams, Laurie
Italian Renaissance art. Westview Press 2001 420p il map $75; pa $65   **709.02**
1. Art -- 15th and 16th centuries 2. Art, Italian 3. Art, Renaissance -- Italy 4. Italian art
ISBN 978-0-8133-3690-9; 0-8133-3690-2; 978-0-8133-3691-6 pa; 0-8133-3691-0 pa
LC 2001-269582
"Adams has produced a near-perfect introduction to the people, places, and events of the Italian Renaissance. . . . The text follows Italian art as it transforms from a highly religious activity into a very human one, and culminates with a focus on the multitalented genius of da Vinci, Raphael, and Michelangelo. . . .The side boxes are helpful and provide further information about the religious figures, ideas, and historical events that directly influenced the era, such as

Dante and the black death. . . . This, along with numerous superb photographs, adds incalculable value to the understanding of the Italian Renaissance." Booklist

Includes bibliographical references

Lowden, John

Early Christian & Byzantine art. Chronicle Bks. 1997 447p il pa $24.95 **709.02**

1. Byzantine art 2. Christian art 3. Christian art and symbolism 4. Medieval art

ISBN 0-7148-3168-9

In this illustrated history of the origins and growth of Christian art Lowden works "deftly through fascinatingly complex and epoch-defining artistic and theological debates, including the so-called Iconoclast Controversy." Booklist

Includes bibliographical references

Snyder, James

★ **Art** of the Middle Ages; [by] James Snyder, Henry Luttikhuizen, Dorothy Verkerk. 2nd ed.; Prentice Hall 2006 530p il map hardcover o.p. pa $134.40 **709.02**

1. Christian art 2. Medieval architecture 3. Medieval art

ISBN 0-13-193825-8; 0-13-192970-4 pa

LC 2004-60135

"Church architecture and decoration receive the bulk of Snyder's attention, with manuscript illumination and sumptuary and secular arts presented rather briefly. The volume is well illustrated, though chiefly in black-and-white photographs." Libr J [review of 1989 edition]

Includes bibliographical references

709.03   Modern period, 1500-

Craske, Matthew

Art in Europe, 1700-1830; a history of the visual arts in an era of unprecedented urban economic growth. Oxford Univ. Press 1997 320p il hardcover o.p. pa $21.50 **709.03**

1. Art -- 19th century 2. European art 3. World history -- 18th century

ISBN 0-19-284206-4 pa

LC 96-37917

This study analyzes "the fundamental historical causes of change that took place from the early 1700s to 1839. . . . Craske . . . provides a series of four stimulating chapters devoted respectively to the function of the artist, art worlds, the appreciation of the visual arts, and evolving ideas of history and civilization. The text is enhanced by 129 high-quality illustrations." Choice

Escritt, Stephen

Art Nouveau. Phaidon 2000 447p il map $24.95 **709.03**

1. Art nouveau 2. Art, Modern -- 19th century 3. Art, Modern -- 20th century

ISBN 0-7148-3822-5; 978-0-7148-3822-9

LC 00-344423

In this book "Stephen Escritt defines Art Nouveau broadly, analyzing the work of such diverse designers as Victor Horta in Belgium, Emile Galle in France, Charles Rennie Mackintosh in Glasgow and Antoni Gaudi in Barcelona." Publisher's note

Includes bibliographical references

709.04   20th century, 1900-1999

Arnason, H. Harvard

★ **History** of modern art; painting, sculpture, architecture, photography. [by] H.H. Arnason, Elizabeth C. Mansfield. 6th ed.; Pearson Prentice Hall 2009 830p il $130.67; pa $122.67 **709.04**

1. Modern art

ISBN 0-205-67367-8; 978-0-205-67367-4; 0-13-606206-7 pa; 978-0-13-606206-6 pa

LC 2009-15436

This covers artists and movements in art from the 19th century to the present, discussing such schools as cubism, surrealism, and abstract impressionism. Video, installation and performance art, sculpture, architecture, and photography are also surveyed.

"An ideal primer on modern art." Libr J

Includes glossary and bibliographical references

Balken, Debra Bricker

Abstract expressionism. Distributed in North America by Harry N. Abrams 2005 80p il $16.50 **709.04**

1. Abstract expressionism 2. American art

ISBN 1-85437-306-4; 978-1-85437-306-9

LC 2004-111326

This book has "60 color illustrations of works created by the artists of the movement . . . [and] examines the critical response to Abstract Expressionism from the time of its heyday up until the present day." Publisher's note

Includes bibliographical references

Brandon, Ruth

Surreal lives; the surrealists, 1917-1945. Grove Press 1999 527p il hardcover o.p. pa $16 **709.04**

1. Arts, Modern -- 20th century 2. Surrealism

ISBN 0-8021-3727-X pa

LC 99-25492

This study of surrealism "gives an account of the school's major practitioners, from Apollinaire to Dali; their flamboyant eccentricities and unconventional sexual entanglements prove a lively and absorbing complement to their work." New Yorker

Includes bibliographical references

Castle, James

James Castle; a retrospective. edited by Ann Percy; essays by Ann Percy . . . [et al.]; interview with Terry Winters by Jeffrey Wolf. Philadelphia Museum

of Art in association with Yale University Press 2008
251p il $60   **709.04**

  1. Outsider art

  ISBN 978-0-300-13730-9; 0-300-13730-3

                       LC 2008-21792

"James Castle (1899-1977), born profoundly deaf, lived
within his own silent world, communicating solely through
his art. . . . [Percy] has brought together an amazing collection of his art as well as scholarly essays and biographical
pieces. Castle used everyday items like soot, swabs, sticks,
and food containers to create intricate constructions, surrealistic images, and collages of words and pictures. . . . The
book also examines Castle's materials and techniques and
his obsession with the ephemera of life around him. A major contribution to the literature of 20th-century art as well
as outsider art; the accompanying DVD features an excellent film, Jeffrey Wolf's James Castle: Portrait of an Artist."
Libr J

  Includes bibliographical references

Dempsey, Amy

  Art in the modern era; a guide to styles, schools
& movements 1860 to the present. Abrams 2002
304p il $55   **709.04**

  1. Art -- 20th century -- Encyclopedias 2. Art
movements -- History -- 20th century -- Encyclopedias
3. Art, Modern -- 20th century -- Encyclopedias 4.
Modern art -- Encyclopedias 5. Reference books

  ISBN 0-8109-4172-4

                       LC 2001-46261

This guide to art from 1860 to the present describes 300
schools and movements and includes a fold-out timeline.

"All major and minor movements are mentioned in this
very comprehensive guide, which could easily become a
standard for modern art survey courses, making it a sensible
purchase for most libraries." Libr J

  Includes bibliographical references

Dickerman, Leah

  ★ Dada; Zurich, Berlin, Hannover, Cologne, New
York, Paris. with essays by Brigid Doherty [et al.] National
Gallery of Art in association with Distributed Art Publishers
2005 519p il $65 **709.04**

  1. Arts, Modern -- 20th century 2. Dadaism

  ISBN 1-933045-20-5

                       LC 2005-17984

"Seven scholars and curators contribute essays that examine each of the various Dada centers in turn. . . . Each
essay examines key locations (e.g., the Cabaret Voltaire),
individuals, publications (including Merz magazine), and
inventions (such as ready-mades and photomontage.) . .
. Its comprehensive scholarship and color illustrations of
many rarely seen works make this book essential for all art
collections." Choice

  Includes bibliographical references

Fineberg, Jonathan David

  Art since 1940; strategies of being. {by} Jonathan Fineberg. 2nd ed; Abrams 2000 528p il
$65   **709.04**

  1. Art -- 20th century 2. Art, American 3. Art,
European 4. Modern art 5. Modernism (Art) -- Europe

6. Modernism (Art) -- United States 7. Postmodernism
-- Europe 8. Postmodernism -- United States

  ISBN 0-18-094209-7

                       LC 99-51584

This surveys American and European art from 1940 to
2000 through a series of biographical profiles of individual
artists linked by discussions of the cultural influences on
their work.

"Fineberg surveys the visual arts in Europe, England,
and North America from 1940 to the present, focusing on
the avant-garde artist in the major Western capitals. . . .
The text is arranged in 15 chapters in chronological order.
Within each chapter the individual artist is discussed, as are
the ideas and events relevant to understanding how cultural
and social situations influenced the artist." Choice {review
of 1995 edition}

  Includes bibliographical references

Hunter, Sam

  Modern art; painting, sculpture, architecture,
photography. [by] Sam Hunter, John Jacobus, Daniel
Wheeler. 3rd ed, rev and expanded; Prentice Hall
2005 472p il hardcover o.p. pa $126.20   **709.04**

  1. Modern art

  ISBN 978-0-13-150519-3; 0-13-150519-X; 978-0-13-
189565-2 pa; 0-13-189565-6 pa

                       LC 2004-46659

This book explains "how European and American vanguard culture created modernist art by heeding the call 'to
make it new.'. . . Coverage ranges across a broad spectrum
of visual arts, from painting, sculpture, and photography to
conceptual forms, installation and video art, and architecture." Publisher's note

  Includes bibliographical references

Livingstone, Marco

  Pop art; a continuing history. 2nd ed. Thames &
Hudson 2000 272p il $29.95   **709.04**

  1. Pop art

  ISBN 978-0-500-28240-3; 0-500-28240-4

                       LC 00-100788

With 300 color plates this volume chronicles the work of
130 artists of the Pop Art movement, including Jasper Johns,
Robert Rauschenberg, Andy Warhol, and Roy Lichtenstein.

"Recommended as the best single historical survey on
Pop Art." Libr J

Lucie-Smith, Edward

  Art today. Phaidon Press 1995 511p il hardcover o.p. pa $45   **709.04**

  1. Art -- 20th century 2. Modern art -- 20th century

  ISBN 0-7148-3888-8 pa

This "survey attempts to essay the scope and aims of the
art of the world over the past 30 years. . . . As well as such
. . . ground as Pop Art, Lucie-Smith covers Conceptual Art,
Installation Art, and Neo-Expressionism. He also covers . . .
artists and works from the former Soviet Union, Africa, the
Far East, and Latin America. Chapters are also included on
'Racial Minorities' and 'Feminist and Gay' art. . . . The book
offers brief biographies of all artists mentioned, a chronology, and bibliography." Libr J

Marquis, Alice Goldfarb

The **pop!** revolution; how an unlikely concatenation of artists, aficionados, businessmen, collectors, critics, curators, dealers, and hangers-on radically transformed the art world. MFA Publications 2010 221p il $29.95 **709.04**
1. American art 2. Pop art
ISBN 978-0-87846-744-0

This volume "will delight both the friends of Pop and its foes, for the book confirms the prejudices of each group. Pop's friends will read it as an account of an aesthetic revolution that displaced the humorless and posturing European-derived formalism of the postwar years. . . and substituted a content-rich art that was deeply engaged with American life and subject matter. . . . Pop's foes, by contrast, will read 'The Pop Revolution' as the saga of a crass commercial enterprise in which a mindless populist fad cut short the career of Abstract Expressionism, America's only meaningful contribution to the world art. . . . Ms. Marquis's principal contribution is that she tells the story of Pop not by profiling the artists themselves, as is usually done, but by tracing the interlocking network of galleries and collectors that sustained them. The result is a Pop social history." Wall Street J

★ Art deco 1910-1939; edited by Charlotte Benton, Tim Benton, and Ghislaine Wood. Bulfinch Press 2003 464p il $65 **709.04**
1. Art deco
ISBN 0-8212-2834-X
LC 2002-113762

This exhibition catalog includes 40 essays about the Art Deco movement and its sources and expression throughout the world in such fields as architecture, ceramics, fashion, jewelry, graphic design, metalwork, glasswork, and film.

Surrealism; edited by Mary Ann Caws. Phaidon 2004 304p il $75 **709.04**
1. Surrealism
ISBN 978-0-7148-4259-2; 0-7148-4259-1

"In this well-organized and nicely illustrated survey of Surrealism, Caws . . . discusses many of the basic ideas and tenets of the movement, emphasizing chance and freedom as the central surrealist concepts." Libr J
Includes bibliographical references

709.05   21st century, 2000-2099

Thornton, Sarah

Seven days in the art world. W.W. Norton 2008 274p il $24.95 **709.05**
1. Art -- Exhibitions 2. Art -- Marketing
ISBN 978-0-393-06722-4; 0-393-06722-X
LC 2008-35056

"The book is cleverly divided into seven day-in-the-life chapters, each focusing on a different facet of the contemporary art world: an auction (at Christie's New York), an art school 'crit' (at the California Institute of the Arts in Valencia), an art fair (Art Basel), an artist's studio (that of the Japanese star Takashi Murakami), a prize (Britain's prestigious Turner Prize), a magazine (Artforum) and a biennale (Venice). Thornton is a smart and savvy guide with a keen

understanding of the subtle power dynamics that animate each of these interconnected milieus." N Y Times Book Rev
Includes bibliographical references

709.1   Areas, regions, places in general

Bloom, Jonathan

The **Grove** encyclopedia of Islamic art and architecture; edited by Jonathan M. Bloom and Sheila S. Blair. Oxford University Press 2009 3v il map set $395 **709.1**
1. Islamic architecture -- Encyclopedias 2. Islamic art -- Encyclopedias 3. Reference books
ISBN 978-0-19-530991-1
LC 2008-28208

This "encyclopedia expands and updates the Islamic art entries from the . . . Grove Dictionary of Art. Rewritten, reedited, and reorganized, these entries amount here to over 1600 A-to-Z articles and over 450 illustrations, drawings, and maps detailing 'the art made by artists and artisans whose religion was Islam, for patrons who lived in predominantly Muslim lands, or for purposes that are restricted or peculiar to a Muslim population or in a Muslim setting.' . . . This volume is everything that one has come to expect from a Grove title: literate, comprehensive, and authoritative." Libr J
Includes bibliographical references

Khalili, Nasser D.

Islamic art and culture; a visual history. Overlook Press 2006 186p il $60 **709.1**
1. Islamic art 2. Islamic civilization
ISBN 1-58567-839-2; 978-1-58567-839-6

This "visual history of Islamic art introduces readers to the diverse peoples, cultures, and styles making up Islam today. Spanning 12 centuries and covering everything from miniature painting to architecture, it shows, e.g., various Qur'ans, coins, armor, and scientific instruments. . . . This is an excellent introduction to the subject that combines aptly chosen and beautifully reproduced photographs with a concise and informative text." Libr J
Includes bibliographical references

O'Kane, Bernard

★ **Treasures** of Islam; artistic glories of the Muslim world. Duncan Baird; Distributed in the USA by Sterling Pub. 2007 224p il map $35 **709.1**
1. Islamic art 2. Islamic civilization
ISBN 978-1-84483-483-9; 1-84483-483-2

The author "combines an overview of Islamic art and architecture with a cursory history of Islam's empires and dynasties. Beginning with a brief discussion of the earliest mosque from the seventh century, and showing how Islamic architects created a distinctive artistic tradition, O'Kane . . . follows architectural and artistic ideas to the 19th century. . . . The wealth of glorious full-color illustrations make this beautifully designed book an excellent introduction to the art of Islam." Publ Wkly
Includes bibliographical references

709.2   Biography

Dictionary of women artists; editor, Delia Gaze; picture editors, Maja Mihajlovic, Leanda Shrimpton. Fitzroy Dearborn Pubs. 1997 2v il set $310   **709.2**
1. Biography, Collective 2. Reference books 3. Women artists -- Biography -- Dictionaries 4. Women artists -- Dictionaries
ISBN 1-88496-421-4
LC 97-206872

"The chronological coverage extends from 975 A.D. to artists born in 1945. Each of the alphabetically arranged entries includes a brief biography, information about the genre of art produced, and an example of the artist's work. These volumes also present 20 introductory surveys on such topics as 'Court Artists' and 'Training and Professionalism,' and include an overview of women's art in the 19th and 20th centuries by country. Together with their chronological list of artists, the volumes include a range of information not ordinarily found in a resource of this type." Am Libr

709.3   Specific continents, countries, localities

Boardman, John
   Greek art; 4th ed, rev and expanded; Thames & Hudson 1996 304p il map pa $16.95   **709.3**
1. Greek art
ISBN 0-500-20292-3
LC 96-60184

Partial contents: The beginnings and geometric Greece; Greece and the arts of the East and Egypt; Archaic Greek art; Classical sculpture and architecture; Hellenistic art; Selected bibliography

"This is a classic in the field made even more readable and useful than before. Highly recommended for all collections." Libr J

Frankfort, Henri
   ★ The **art** and architecture of the ancient Orient; 5th ed; Yale Univ. Press 1996 483p il maps pa $35   **709.3**
1. Ancient art
ISBN 0-300-06470-5
LC 97-224901

This traces the development of art in the Near East from 3500 B.C. to 539 B.C., covering the Sumerians, Assyrians, Babylonians, Hittites, Aramaeans, Levants, and Phoenicians.

Robins, Gay
   The **art** of ancient Egypt; Rev ed; Harvard University Press 2008 271p il map pa $27.95   **709.3**
1. Art, Ancient -- Egypt 2. Art, Egyptian 3. Egyptian art
ISBN 978-0-674-03065-7; 0-674-03065-6
LC 2008-4264

"The first chapter orients the reader in the cultural, technical, and iconographic contexts needed to explore the evolution of the Egyptian artistic tradition in subsequent chapters. Beginning with the predynastic origins (5000 BCE) and concluding in the Ptolemaic Period (304-30 BCE), Robins

traces the development of sculpture, painting, funerary and religious art, and architecture with over 300 illustrations, many in color." Libr J [review of 1997 edition]
Includes bibliographical references (p. 256-266)

Smith, William Stevenson
   ★ The **art** and architecture of ancient Egypt; [by] W. Stevenson Smith. rev with additions; Yale Univ. Press 1998 296p il map hardcover o.p. pa $35   **709.3**
1. Architecture -- Egypt 2. Art, Egyptian 3. Egyptian art
ISBN 0-300-07715-7; 0-300-07747-5 pa
LC 98-24893

"This book shows the tombs at Thebes, including the treasure-filled burial place of Tutankhamen, the temples of Luxor and Karnak, and the palaces of Akhenaten at Tell el Amarna and of Amenhotep III at Thebes. It also presents many revealing portraits depicting a range of subjects from the kings and queens who built the pyramids at Giza and Saqqara to their own civil servants." Publisher's note
Includes bibliographical references

711   Area planning (Civic art)

McGregor, James H.
   ★ **Rome** from the ground up; [by] James H.S. McGregor. Belknap Press of Harvard University Press 2005 344p il map $29.95; pa $18.95   **711**
1. City planning -- Rome
ISBN 0-674-01911-3; 0-674-02263-7 pa
LC 2005-48213

The author "chronologically traces the successive periods of intense architecture and planning that helped Rome achieve strategic greatness, from the Etruscan management of the Tiber Island ford 3,000 years ago, to the city's unparalleled artistic stamp by Bramante and Michelangelo during the Renaissance, to Mussolini's monumental Fascist vision, to the precarious repairs heralding the Jubilee Year of 2000. . . . Here is a walking tour in stately, inviting prose that renders wonderfully manageable a massive history lesson for the intellectually curious and adept." Publ Wkly
Includes bibliographical references

712   Landscape architecture (Landscape design)

Buchanan, Rita
   Taylor's master guide to landscaping. Houghton Mifflin 2000 384p il $40   **712**
1. Landscape gardening
ISBN 0-618-05590-8
LC 99-54110

"Buchanan offers a comprehensive treatment of landscape design, emphasizing designing with plants and including extensive information about choosing and caring for plants, trees, shrubs, vines, and ground covers. . . . A landmark work destined to become a classic." Libr J

Clausen, Ruth Rogers
Dreamscaping; 25 easy designs for home gardens. Hearst Bks. 2002 127p il $30 **712**
1. Garden design 2. Gardens -- Design
ISBN 1-58816-067-X
LC 2001-16928
The author provides "plans, plant lists, and well-illustrated planting directions for all sorts of situations in sun or shade, outdoors and in the home. Tips and reminders are used to address design issues and maintenance, and to point out poisonous species. . . . The book's pretty layout and colorful photographs should entice novices to try something new in the garden." Booklist

Goodwin, Nancy
Montrose; life in a garden. with illustrations by Ippy Patterson; foreword by Maureen Quilligan. Duke University Press 2005 292p il $34.95 **712**
1. Gardening
ISBN 0-8223-3604-9
LC 2005-11387
"Goodwin and her husband, Craufurd, searched for 10 years for a larger piece of property before buying Montrose, a nineteenth-century estate in historic Hillsborough, North Carolina. . . . Godwin taught piano and ran a mail-order nursery before she settled into the full-time gardening . . . that has shaped the rhythm of her life since 1994. This lovely little book, exquisitely illustrated with a friend's penciled and watercolored botanical drawings, chronicles a year in her garden. It's a story of the seasons, the weather, hard work, triumphs, and disappointments. Goodwin's voice, precise and detailed when discussing the differences between various hellebores and snowdrops, remains fondly appreciative of the treasures she grows so lovingly and well." Horticulture

Graham, Wade
American Eden; from Monticello to Central Park to our backyards: what our gardens tell us about who we are. Harper 2011 459p il $35; ebook $27.99 **712**
1. Gardens 2. Landscape architecture
ISBN 978-0-06-158342-1; 978-0-06-207886-5 ebook
LC 2010-24940
"Graham unveils the aesthetic, political, psychological, and ethical dimensions of the American garden. . . . Graham is able to gently mock the fashions of history while astutely observing that we are still as vulnerable to gardening fads today. After more than 250 years, the American gardening tradition has bequeathed to us treasured public parks, suburban sprawl, Kentucky bluegrass lawns in the desert, and kitchen gardens at the White House. Graham's history is a fascinating and illuminating tour of this American landscape." Publ Wkly
Includes bibliographical references

Griswold, Mac K.
The golden age of American gardens; proud owners, private estates, 1890-1940. {by} Mac Griswold, Eleanor Weller; with research assistance by

Helen E. Rollins. Abrams 1991 408p il $75; pa $34.95 **712**
1. Gardens 2. Gardens -- United States
ISBN 0-8109-3358-6; 0-8109-2737-3 pa
LC 91-8283
A "history of owners, designers, and the ultimate country retreats resulting from their collaborations. . . . Weller's compilation of rare, hand-colored lantern slides and hundreds of black-and-white historical photographs of the era are particularly noteworthy." Booklist
Includes bibliographical references

Hayward, Gordon
Stone in the garden; inspiring designs and practical projects. Norton 2001 224p il $39.95 **712**
1. Landscape gardening 2. Stone in landscape gardening
ISBN 0-393-04779-2
LC 00-69945
"The book's first half focuses on the philosophical and design considerations of stone forms as varied as walls, paths, terraces, and even benches. The second half is more practical, covering topics such as estimating the amount of stone needed for a wall, the methods of cutting and laying stone, and building pools and fountains." Libr J
Includes bibliograhical references (p.) and index

Messervy, Julie Moir
Home outside; creating the landscape you love. Taunton Press 2009 249p il $30 **712**
1. Landscape architecture 2. Outdoor living spaces
ISBN 978-1-60085-008-0; 1-60085-008-1
LC 2008-32956
"This book helps home lovers make their outdoor spaces as comfortable and beautiful as their interiors. I like the 'before' and 'after' photos (which I always find more trustworthy in garden design books than drawings.)" Boston Globe
Includes bibliographical references

Miller, Lynden
Parks, plants, and people; beautifying the urban landscape. Norton 2009 206p il $49.95 **712**
1. City planning 2. Landscape gardening 3. Parks
ISBN 978-0-393-73203-0; 0-393-73203-7
LC 2009-04536
This "authoritative book should be required reading for any study of urban planning, but it's equally relevant to the home gardener. It's full of useful design and planting advice, clearly and unpretentiously presented." N Y Times Book Rev
Includes bibliographical references

Nagel, Vanessa Gardner
Understanding garden design; the complete handbook for aspiring designers. Timber Press 2010 235p il $34.95 **712**
1. Garden design
ISBN 978-0-88192-943-0
LC 2009-53692
"Thorough and thoroughly accessible, Nagel's reasoned yet personable approach to an often intimidating subject will benefit both homeowners and design professionals." Booklist
Includes bibliographical references

Newbury, Tim

The **ultimate** garden designer; New ed.; Hamlyn 2009 256p il pa $22.50   **712**

1. Garden design 2. Landscape gardening
ISBN 978-0-600-61987-1

This primer to garden design features design plans for different types of gardens (including family gardens, water gardens, Japanese-style gardens, and roof gardens), information on different types of garden highlights (such as pools, gazebos, fences, and trellises), and a plant directory.

Rybczynski, Witold

A **clearing** in the distance: Frederick Law Olmsted and America in the nineteenth century. Scribner 1999 480p il $28; pa $15.95   **712**

1. Landscape architects 2. Landscape architects -- United States -- Biography 3. Landscape architecture -- United States -- History -- 19th century 4. Travel writers 5. Urban planners
ISBN 0-684-82463-9; 0-684-86575-0 pa

LC 99-18094

"Rybczynski, celebrated for his sparkling prose as well as for his deep knowledge of architectural history, adeptly chronicles the life of the man who 'was a landscape architect before that profession was founded.'" Booklist

Includes bibliographical references

Van Sweden, James A.

★ **Architecture** in the garden; {by} James van Sweden with Thomas Christopher; foreword by Penelope Hobhouse. Random House 2002 264p il $39.95   **712**

1. Garden design 2. Landscape architecture
ISBN 0-375-50154-1

LC 2002-69702

The author attempts "to show that architectural elements are essential in developing a successful garden design. Van Sweden focuses on such components as paths, edgings, fences, walls, water, and artwork, explaining that a garden is not a garden without a sound structural organization that uses these elements. . . . A well-illustrated glossary is included. Recommended for most gardening and landscape architecture collections." Libr J

Includes bibliographical references

Wulf, Andrea

Founding gardeners; the revolutionary generation, nature, and the shaping of the American nation. Knopf 2011 349p il map $30; ebook $14.99   **712**

1. American national characteristics 2. Gardening 3. Gardens 4. Statesmen -- United States
ISBN 978-0-307-26990-4; 0-307-26990-6; 978-0-307-59554-6 ebook

LC 2010-52920

The book discusses how the "leaders of the American Revolution and the early republic were engaged plantation owners keenly interested in scientific agriculture. Andrea Wulf argues that this interest, shared by other Founding Fathers, was no mere sideline activity, but rather something central to their identities as leaders and political thinkers." The author examines "the political role of horticulture/agriculture in the Constitutional Convention and the landmark battle over the Hamilton Bank Bill in 1791 that brought party political differences into the open." (Journal of American History)

The author demonstrates "that the garden, the natural world and the shape of a new nation were, for the men who launched the United States, parts of a whole. The image of the farmer-statesman is an ideal of republican government dating back to Romans. It's no accident that the men who led the Revolution and wrote the Constitution owned plantations and farms. . . . [Wulf is a] writer of considerable grace and breadth of vision, and 'Founding Gardeners' is an excellent portrait of the early years of the federal republic. It will delight the general reader, not just the garden buff. But for the garden enthusiast, this is a book of special interest, reminding us that a garden has a purpose, a character, a soul—that it's an expression of our relationship not just to the soil, but to a vision of the world." Cleveland Plain Dealer

720   Architecture

Altman, Adelaide

Elderhouse: planning your best home ever. Chelsea Green 2002 232p il pa $19.95   **720**

1. Domestic architecture -- Designs and plans 2. Elderly -- Housing
ISBN 1-931498-11-3

LC 2002-31481

"The first section is full of ideas for creating a safe and comfortable home for wheelchair access or for a time in our lives when we are less nimble. The second section addresses the psychology of moving to a new smaller space in the later years of life." Libr J

Includes bibliographical references

Curl, James Stevens

★ A **dictionary** of architecture and landscape architecture; with line-drawings by the author. 2nd ed.; Oxford University Press 2006 xxv, 880p il $45 **720**

1. Architecture -- Dictionaries 2. Landscape architecture -- Dictionaries 3. Reference books
ISBN 978-0-19-280630-7; 0-19-280630-0

LC 2006-40248

For a fuller review, see: Booklist, Nov. 15, 2006

This is a dictionary of the "many stylistic and technical terms used in architecture today. The work covers all periods of Western architectural history in more than 5000 articles." Libr J

Includes bibliographical references

O'Gorman, James F.

ABC of architecture; drawings by Dennis E. McGrath. University of Pa. Press 1997 127p il $35; pa $13.45   **720**

1. Architecture
ISBN 0-8122-3423-5; 0-8122-1631-8 pa

LC 97-22616

The author discusses the history of architecture, types of buildings, advances in technology, and architectural analysis.

This book, "a model of brevity and clarity, may be the best-written work on the subject in English for lay people." N Y Times Book Rev

Includes bibliographical references

Palladio, Andrea

The **four** books on architecture; translated by Robert Tavernor and Richard Schofield. MIT Press 1997 xxxv, 436p il $69.95; pa $24.95   **720**
1. Architecture
ISBN 0-262-16162-1; 0-262-66133-0 pa

LC 96-36406

"Drawing on the monuments of ancient Rome as well as the author's own villas and public works, this philosophical treatise and practical guide served as the pattern book for countless Palladian buildings by other architects around the world. Elegantly translated (in the first new English translation since 1738) and illustrated with the lyrical, rarely seen woodcuts of Palladio's original." N Y Times Book Rev

Includes bibliographical references

★ Dictionary of architecture & construction; edited by Cyril M. Harris. 4th ed.; McGraw-Hill 2005 1089p il $74.95   **720**
1. Architecture -- Dictionaries   2. Building -- Dictionaries 3. Reference books
ISBN 0-07-145237-0

LC 2005-42340

"The handy one-volume format, the reasonable cost, the clarity and accuracy of entries, the legible type and drawings, and the inclusive approach to current developments in the design, building, and scholarly professions related to architecture make this publication a crucial tool." Choice

720.9   History, geographic treatment, biography

Boucher, Bruce

Andrea Palladio; the architect in his time. principal photography by Paolo Marton. 2nd ed; Abbeville Press 2007 324p il pa $39.95   **720.9**
1. Architects 2. Architecture, Renaissance -- Italy
ISBN 978-0-7892-0940-5; 0-7892-0940-3

"In this careful, comprehensive, stunningly illustrated survey, Boucher . . . capably illuminates Palladio's stylistic evolution. . . . Among the 300 plates are more than 100 newly commissioned photographs of building interiors and exteriors, which superbly capture Palladio's distincitve blend of simplicity and grandeur." Publ Wkly

Includes bibliographical references (p. 301-312)

Ching, Frank

A **global** history of architecture; [by] Francis D.K. Ching, Mark Jarzombek, Vikramaditya Prakash. J. Wiley & Sons 2006 800p il map $75   **720.9**
1. Architecture -- History
ISBN 978-0-471-26892-5; 0-471-26892-5

LC 2005-34527

"Ching and colleagues comprehensively look at the history of architecture worldwide from 3500 BCE to CE 1950. . . . The book includes most of the major monuments found in other architectural surveys, plus many more, especially from the non Western world. . . . The book's most informative and attractive feature is its illustrations, hundreds of drawings by Ching, a noted author and architectural illustrator. . . . Includes a portfolio of color photographs, companion Web site, and list of coordinates for Google Earth to provide satellite images of the major monuments." Choice

Includes bibliographical references

Fletcher, Banister Flight

Sir Banister Fletcher's A history of architecture; 20th ed; Architectural Press 1996 xxxviii, 1794p il $145   **720.9**
1. Architecture -- History
ISBN 0-7506-2267-9

LC 96-35511

"Overarching view of architectural history, newly rewritten and expanded to include worldwide coverage. Extensively illustrated, with glossary, index, and bibliographies appended to each chapter. Includes general introductions and background for each chapter." N Y Public Libr Book of How & Where to Look It Up {1987 edition}

Includes bibliographical references

Glancey, Jonathan

The **story** of architecture. Dorling Kindersley 2000 240p il hardcover o.p. pa $25   **720.9**
1. Architecture -- History
ISBN 0-7894-5965-5; 0-7894-9334-9 pa

LC 00-30434

"Devoting nearly half the text to the modern period, Glancey condenses history's panorama into a series of colorful vignettes, each described as having some contemporary relevance. Driven by a contagious enthusiasm, the narrative is enlivened by chatty, sometimes offbeat commentary." Libr J

Hollis, Edward

The **secret** lives of buildings; from the ruins of the Parthenon to the Vegas Strip in thirteen stories. Metropolitan Books 2009 338p il $28   **720.9**
1. Architecture   2. Architecture and history   3. Architecture and society 4. Buildings
ISBN 978-0-8050-8785-7; 0-8050-8785-0

LC 2009-18715

This book is "built around thirteen chapters, each telling the story of a building that changed dramatically over time, either in physical terms (the Parthenon, Gloucester Cathedral) or conceptual ones (the Venetian hotel and casino in Las Vegas, which seeks to capture the image of the Most Serene Republic if not, exactly, the spirit). Hollis's stories are engrossing—his history of the Hulme housing estates in Manchester, and their role as incubator for British post-punk rock, was completely new to me—and his writing is engaging." Bookforum

Includes bibliographical references (p. 315-322)

Mathewson, Casey C. M.

Frank O. Gehry: selected works; 1969 to today. Firefly Books 2007 599p il $69.95   **720.9**
1. Architects
ISBN 978-1-55407-276-7; 1-55407-276-X

LC 2008-271852

"Mathewson reviews Gehry's windows, furniture, and his use of natural light, as well as highlights specific buildings and includes hundreds of artfully composed color photographs of Gehry's interior and exterior projects." Libr J

Ruan Xing

New China architecture; by Xing Ruan; photography by Patrick Bingham-Hall. Periplus Editions 2006 239p il $49.95 **720.9**

    1. Asian architecture

    ISBN 978-0-7946-0389-2; 0-7946-0389-0

"China's remarkable economic boom is generating prodigious architectural and building activity. Ruan . . . offers a sampling by presenting 43 recent and projected buildings or complexes. . . . A diverse parade of designs is featured throughout, including airports, offices, stores, theaters, libraries, museums, villas, and sport showcases for the 2008 Olympic Games. Each rates a brief description and several excellent photographs or artist renderings. Floor plans or sections are often included." Libr J

Rybczynski, Witold

The **perfect** house: a journey with the Renaissance architect Andrea Palladio. Scribner 2002 266p il $25; pa $15 **720.9**

    1. Architects 2. Architects -- Italy -- Biography 3. Architecture -- 15th and 16th centuries 4. Architecture, Renaissance -- Italy

    ISBN 0-7432-0586-3; 0-7432-0587-1 pa

               LC 2002-66838

The author offers a historical and architectural analysis of ten villas attributed to 16th century Italian architect Andrea Palladio.

"With its intriguing biographical detail, precise descriptions of design elements, and engaging insights into daily life in the 16th century, Rybczynski's book is a small but lasting gift to the reader." Libr J

    Includes bibliographical references

Storrer, William Allin

The **Frank** Lloyd Wright companion; Rev ed; University of Chicago Press 2006 492p il $99 **720.9**

    1. Architects 2. Nonfiction writers

    ISBN 0-226-77621-2

               LC 2006-44502

This "volume covers more than 450 buildings designed by master architect Wright between 1886 and 1959. Storrer documents each structure with plans, drawings, photographs, and commentary. Each presentation is both complete and concise, following each stage of Wright's aesthetic development, each leap of his imagination, and each instance of technical innovation." Booklist

Wiseman, Carter

Shaping a nation; twentieth-century American architecture and its makers. Norton 1998 412p il $45 **720.9**

    1. Architects 2. Architects -- United States -- History -- 20th century 3. Architecture -- 20th century 4. Architecture -- United States 5. Architecture, Modern -- 20th century -- United States

    ISBN 0-393-04564-1

               LC 97-9896

In this survey the author is "concerned to trace the ways in which buildings express an American identity. Though his subject is twentieth-century architecture, his search for roots extends back to the colonial vernacular and Thomas Jefferson. . . . Wiseman has written a solid mainstream history in which the look of buildings is seen as important. More significantly, he argues the case for social relevance alongside beauty." Archit J

    Includes bibliographical references

Wolfe, Tom

From Bauhaus to our house. Bantam Books 1999 111p il pa $15 **720.9**

    1. Architecture -- 20th century 2. Architecture -- United States

    ISBN 978-0-553-38063-7; 0-553-38063-X

A humorous history of American architecture in the 20th century.

The Seventy wonders of the modern world; 1500 years of extraordinary feats of engineering and construction. edited by Neil Parkyn. Thames & Hudson 2002 304p il $40 **720.9**

    1. Architecture 2. Building -- History 3. Civil engineering -- History 4. Curiosities and wonders

    ISBN 0-500-51047-4

               LC 2002-100549

"Most of the featured 'wonders' date from the second half of the 20th century. The selections are divided into seven categories: churches, palaces, public buildings, towers and skyscrapers, bridges and railways, canals and dams, and statues. Each entry includes basic information on history, structural and engineering details, innovations, aesthetics, and a sidebar 'fact-file.'" Libr J

    Includes bibliographical references

721 Architectural materials

Maliszewski-Pickart, Margaret

Architecture and ornament; an illustrated dictionary. McFarland & Co. 1998 198p il $35 **721**

    1. Architecture -- Details 2. Architecture -- Directories

    ISBN 0-7864-0383-7

               LC 97-33112

This source pairs a traditional dictionary of architectural elements with a series of illustrations of the same elements. The names located in the numbered illustrations may be found alphabetically in the dictionary; and cross-references in the dictionary refer to specific illustrations. The illustrations are grouped by category: windows and doors; walls; roofs; columns; stairs; ornament and moldings; arches, vaults, and domes.

Rybczynski, Witold

The **look** of architecture. Oxford Univ. Press 2001 130p il hardcover o.p. pa $9.95   **721**
1. Architectural design 2. Architecture 3. Design
ISBN 0-19-513443-5; 0-19-515633-1 pa

LC 00-53077

"The author's deeply informed enthusiasm is infectious, and his removal of architectural writing from an airily theoretical discourse to the realm of practical experience is empowering for the lay reader." Publ Wkly
Includes bibliographical references

★ The elements of style; an encyclopedia of architectural detail. general editor, Stephen Calloway; consultant editor, Elizabeth Cromley. New ed.; Firefly Books 2005 502p il $75   **721**
1. Architecture -- Details 2. Domestic architecture
ISBN 1-55407-079-1

This book "focuses on styles and design elements of British and North American vernacular domestic architecture from 1485 (Tudor) to the present. About half of the book deals with periods and styles before the 20th century. . . . It is an outstanding and economical single-volume resource." Choice
Includes bibliographical references

724   Architecture from 1400

Curtis, William J. R.

Modern architecture since 1900; 3rd ed [rev, expanded, and redesigned]; Phaidon 1996 736p il $59.95; pa $39.95   **724**
1. Architecture -- 20th century
ISBN 978-0-7148-3524-2; 0-7148-3524-2; 978-0-7148-3356-9 pa; 0-7148-3356-8 pa

LC 97-112837

"The volume's well-detailed text is buttressed with 650 color and black-and-white illustrations. This should be a standard volume in all architecture collections." Lib J
Includes bibliographical references

Gropius, Walter

★ The **new** architecture and the Bauhaus; translated from the German by P. Morton Shand; with an introduction by Frank Pick. MIT Press 1965 112p il pa $14.95   **724**
1. Architecture -- 20th century
ISBN 0-262-57006-8

LC 65-10279

The founder of the Dessau Bauhaus describes the work of that institution, and his own architectural theories.

Huxtable, Ada Louise

On architecture; collected reflections on a century of change. Walker 2008 478p il $35   **724**
1. Architectural critics 2. Architecture -- 20th century 3. Architecture, Modern -- 20th century
ISBN 978-0-8027-1707-8; 0-8027-1707-7

The author "presents her penetrating and tough-minded criticism spanning half a century. . . . Centering largely

on modernism, its masters and its discontents, the volume opens with an overview of the past four decades, including startlingly powerful pieces on the late '60s urban decay and the '90s reinvention of architecture." Publ Wkly

726   Buildings for religious and related purposes

Adams, Henry

★ **Mont**-Saint-Michel and Chartres; with an introduction by Ralph Adams Cram. Princeton Univ. Press 1981 401p il hardcover o.p. pa $40   **726**
1. Middle Ages
ISBN 0-691-00335-1 pa

LC 81-47279

"This classic study of medieval civilization is written as the commentary of Henry Adams to an imaginary niece as they tour the Abbey Church at Mont-Saint-Michel and the Chartres Cathedral." Benet's Reader's Ency of Am Lit

King, Ross

Brunelleschi's dome; how a Renaissance genius reinvented architecture. Penguin Books 2001 194p il pa $14   **726**
1. Architects 2. Artists 3. Church buildings 4. Sculptors
ISBN 0-14-200015-9

LC 2001-280068

"King illuminates the mysterious sources of inspiration and the secretive methods of architectural genius Filippo Brunelleschi in a fascinating chronicle of the building of his masterwork, the dome of Santa Maria del Fiore in Florence. A remarkable saga of how one incandescent mind performed the one matchless feat that would forever transform architecture from a mechanical craft into a creative art." Booklist
Includes bibliographical references

728   Residential and related buildings

Cox, Reuben

The **work** of Joe Webb; Appalachian master of rustic architecture. photographs and essay by Reuben Cox. The Jargon Society 2009 116p il $64.95 **728**
1. Log cabins
ISBN 0-912330-85-6

"During the 1920s and 1930s, builder Joe Webb constructed nearly three dozen log homes in the tiny Appalachian town of Highlands, North Carolina. The cabins were built without the aid of power tools—or architectural plans. . . . Using a large-format field camera, Cox has documented all of Webb's extant cabins. . . . [Cox] also includes an essay that places the work within a regional and historical context." Publisher's note

Eck, Jeremiah

★ The **distinctive** home; a vision of timeless design. Taunton Press 2003 234p il $40   **728**
1. Architectural design 2. Building 3. Domestic

architecture -- Designs and plans
ISBN 1-561-58528-9

LC 2002-151820

"Eck firmly believes it is possible to build creative houses without a large budget. He discusses a home's site placement, examines the flow of activity within a modern home, and encourages the reader to think of rooms beyond their traditional uses. Eck's book encourages creativity and provides a series of color photographs for developing sound ideas." Libr J

Friedman, Avi

The **adaptable** house; designing homes for change. McGraw-Hill 2002 271p il $45   **728**
1. Architecture, Domestic 2. Domestic architecture -- Designs and plans 3. Prefabricated houses 4. Room layout (Dwellings)
ISBN 0-07-137746-8

LC 2002-141433

"Friedman urges the reader to reimagine the traditional static home as dynamic space that changes as the needs of the occupants change. A single house, according to the author, should be able to accommodate an individual and/or family throughout their lives. Friedman examines how space functions within a house and the ways a house can be expanded and contracted based on the needs of its owners." Libr J

Includes bibliographical references and index

Jordan, Wendy Adler

Universal design for the home; great looking, great living design for all ages, abilities, and circumstances. Quarry Books 2008 207p il pa $24.99 **728**
1. Domestic architecture -- Designs and plans
ISBN 978-1-59253-381-7; 1-59253-381-7

LC 2007-32663

This book "shows how a home that is accommodating to all can also have a stylish decor. . . . Color photographs and some before-and-after floor plans show how accessibility standards have been incorporated. A list of resources is provided." Libr J

Lind, Carla

The **Wright** style. Simon & Schuster 1992 224p il $50   **728**
1. Architects 2. Domestic architecture 3. Nonfiction writers
ISBN 0-671-74959-5

LC 91-44553

This book "takes us inside dozens of Frank Lloyd Wright's 'organic' houses, including his home and studio in Oak Park, Illinois, and the two Taliesins. . . . Carla Lind's text traces the development and components of Wright's unique, revolutionary aesthetic while 250 color photographs allow readers to appreciate the harmony of Wright's light-filled, graciously rectilinear rooms." Booklist

Includes bibliographical references

Susanka, Sarah

Creating the not so big house; insights and ideas for the new American home. photographs by Grey Crawford. Taunton Press 2000 258p il $34.95; pa $24.95   **728**
1. Architecture -- United States -- 20th century 2. Architecture, Domestic -- United States 3. Domestic architecture 4. Interior architecture -- United States 5. Interior design 6. Space (Architecture)
ISBN 1-56158-377-4; 1-56158-605-6 pa

LC 00-44323

Susanka provides photographs and plans of houses that are designed to look bigger than their actual size.

"Architect Susanka has big ideas about small design. . . . {This book promotes} well-designed, efficient, interesting modest-size homes. . . . {She} includes 25 delightful examples of houses designed by architects from around the country." Booklist

Not so big solutions for your home. Taunton Press 2002 155p il pa $22.95   **728**
1. Architecture, Domestic 2. Domestic architecture -- Designs and plans 3. Interior architecture 4. Interior decoration 5. Interior design
ISBN 1-56158-613-7

LC 2002-7101

The author presents a compilation of 31 essays from her "Drawing Board" column in Fine Homebuilding magazine "that offer a number of solutions to household design problems both big and small. . . . Susanka offers an eclectic mix: tips on site selection, mud room design, planning to fit specific furniture, creating a family room that works, personalizing with tile, and planning window seats, pantries, TV placement, and floor plan changes." Libr J

The **Greenwood** encyclopedia of homes through American history; Thomas W. Paradis, general editor. Greenwood Press 2008 4v il set $399.95   **728**
1. Decorative arts -- Encyclopedias 2. Domestic architecture -- Encyclopedias 3. Reference books
ISBN 978-0-313-33496-2; 0-313-33496-X

LC 2008-2946

"The set covers ten historical eras beginning with the Colonial era and ending with the period 1986 to present. Each era is introduced by a time line and short historical essay. Other essays synthesize research under topics such as building materials, house plans, interior design, and landscaping. . . .The value of the set lies behind the pretty facade of the American home, in the contributors' exploration of the interaction of physical house and family life." Choice

Includes bibliographical references

728.8   Large and elaborate private dwellings

Wiencek, Henry

National Geographic guide to America's great houses; more than 150 outstanding mansions open to the public. by Henry Wiencek and Donna M. Lucey. National Geographic Soc. 1999 320p il pa $25   **728.8**
1. American architecture 2. Architecture -- United

States 3. Domestic architecture
ISBN 0-7922-7424-5

LC 98-53013

Arranged by state, this guide includes information on past owners, furnishings, renovations, room descriptions, and excursion plans for other nearby houses of note. The text is accompanied by 170 full-color photos.

730.9   History, geographic treatment, biography of sculpture and related arts together, of sculpture alone

Manca, Joseph

1000 sculptures of genius; [by] Joseph Manca, Patrick Bade and Sarah Costello. English version; Sirrocco 2007 543p il $24.95   **730.9**
1. Sculpture
ISBN 978-1-84484-215-5; 1-84484-215-0

"This sculpture collection offers a vision of western art. . . . It also includes references, comments on masterworks and biographies." Publisher's note

730.92   Biography

McPhee, Sarah

Bernini's beloved; a portrait of Costanza Picco-lomini. Sarah McPhee. Yale University Press 2012 260p.   **730.92**
1. Art -- Collectors and collecting -- Biography 2. Art -- Collectors and collecting -- Italy -- Rome -- History -- 17th century 3. Marble sculpture, Italian -- Italy -- Rome -- 17th century 4. Mistresses -- Italy -- Biography
ISBN 9780300175271

LC 2011038171

This book is a biography of Costanza Piccolomini, whose marble portrait was [c]arved by sculptor Gianlorenzo Bernini in1636-37.[For centuries Costanza was identified only as Bernini's mistress, who later incited his rage by be-traying him for his brother. Author Sarah McPhee corrects and expands this story . . . [which] sets the bust and Costan-za's own life—her childhood and noble name, her marriage, affair, fall from grace, and recovery—against the backdrop of Baroque Rome." The story expands our understanding of the woman whose intelligence and passion served as inspira-tion for Bernini's celebrated sculpture, and who . . . forged a life for herself in the decades following its creation.' (Pub-lisher s note)

731.4   Techniques and procedures

Belcher, Judy

Polymer clay creative traditions; techniques and projects inspired by the fine and decorative arts. prin-cipal photography by Steve Payne. Watson-Guptill 2006 144p il $21.95   **731.4**
1. Clay 2. Modeling
ISBN 0-8230-4065-8; 978-0-8230-4065-0

LC 2005-927912

"Addressing novices to the medium of polymer clay as well as more advanced crafters in the field, Belcher prepares an attractive handbook on making clay items." Booklist

Butz, Richard

How to carve wood; a book of projects and tech-niques. Taunton Press 1984 215p il pa $19.95 **731.4**
1. Wood carving
ISBN 0-918804-20-5

LC 83-50680

The author introduces "the most common types of carv-ing, whittling, chip carving, relief carving, lettering, and architectural carving. The information on tools and their care is very helpful. This is the best book available on the subject." Libr J
Includes bibliographical references

Hessenberg, Karin

Sculpting basics; everything you need to know to create fantastic three-dimensional artwork. Bar-ron's 2005 128p il $23.99   **731.4**
1. Sculpture -- Technique
ISBN 978-0-7641-5843-8; 0-7641-5843-0

The author "presents a fine overview for beginning sculp-tors. . . . [The book] touches on a wide range of sculptural forms and styles, including the traditional figure, symbolic compositions, and abstract reliefs. . . .For such a slight book, [it] bundles a surprising amount of information." Libr J
Includes bibliographical references

Plowman, John

The **encyclopedia** of sculpting techniques; a comprehensive visual guide to traditional and con-temporary techniques. Sterling 2003 176p il pa $16.95   **731.4**
1. Sculpture -- Technique
ISBN 978-1-4027-0394-2; 1-4027-0394-5

This book on sculpting covers "more than 30 techniques . . . [including] clay, plaster, wood, stone, and papier mâché, as well as . . . aerated concrete block, rubber, and found ob-jects." Publisher's note

736   Other plastic arts

Engel, Peter

10 -fold origami; fabulous paperfolds you can make in just 10 steps! Tuttle 2009 96p il $19.95 **736**
1. Origami
ISBN 978-4-8053-1069-4

LC 2009-920075

This craft book features 26 origami models, all of which can be completed with ten major folds. All models are rated in difficulty from Easy to Advanced.

The author's "art subjects range from the wonderfully whimsical to the eminently practical. . . . Who could re-sist a plateful of sunny-side up eggs and bacon or the stol-idly silent black-and-white penguin? Or not be tempted to use a brightly patterned picture frame or decorative party pinwheels?" Booklist

Hayakawa, Hiroshi

Kirigami menagerie; 38 paper animals to copy, cut & fold. Sterling Pub. 2009 128p il pa $17.95   **736**

1. Animals in art 2. Paper crafts

ISBN 978-1-60059-318-5

LC 2008-50622

The author shows how to cut and fold paper shapes to make 38 different types of animals, including sheep, pandas, and dragons.

Van Sicklen, Margaret

The **joy** of origami. Workman 2005 152p il pa $16.95   **736**

1. Origami

ISBN 0-7611-3988-5; 978-0-7611-3988-1

LC 2005-43687

"The 57 [origami] models [included] range in difficulty from a simple Elephant in Pajamas to a more challenging Tyrannosaurus Rex." Publisher's note

737.4   Coins

Cuhaj, George S.

★ **2012** standard catalog of world coins, 1901-2000; George S. Cuhaj, editor; special contributors: Mahdi Bseiso, Ivan Rakitin, Joeseph Zaffern. 39th ed; Krause Pub. 2011 2345p il map pa $65 **737.4**

1. Coins

ISBN 978-1-4402-1572-8

This illustrated volume covers coins from throughout the world minted 1901-2000. Prices are provided for each coin in up to four grades of preservation. Includes commemorative issues.

Yeoman, R. S.

★ **Handbook** of United States coins 2009; by R. S. Yeoman; edited by Kenneth Bressett. 66th ed; Whitman Publishing 2008 256p il $12.95; pa $9.95   **737.4**

1. Coins

ISBN 978-0-7948-2539-3; 0-7948-2539-7; 978-0-7948-2540-9 pa; 0-7948-2540-0 pa

This companion volume to A Guide book of United States coins gives the wholesale values of U.S. coins from colonial times to the present.

★ A **guide** book of United States coins; [by] R.S. Yeoman; editor, Kenneth Bressett; research editor, Q. David Bowers; valuations editor, Jeff Garrett. 64th ed; Whitman Pub. 2010 429p il $16.95 **737.4**

1. Coins 2. Reference books

ISBN 978-0-7948-3148-6

This guide "known as the 'Red Book' is an outstanding reference on U.S. coins designed for use in identifying and grading coins. All issues from 1616 to the present are covered. The guide provides historical data, statistics, values, and detailed photographs for each coin. Additional sections deal with specialties such as Civil War and Hard Times

tokens, misstruck coins, and uncirculated and proof sets." Nichols. Guide to Ref Books for Sch Media Cent. 4th edition

738   Ceramic arts

Kovel, Ralph M.

Kovels' dictionary of marks: pottery and porcelain; by Ralph M. and Terry H. Kovel. 2nd ed; Crown 1995 278p il $17   **738**

1. Porcelain -- Marks 2. Pottery -- Marks

ISBN 0-517-70137-5

LC 95-3361

This is a guide to identification of American, English, and European pottery and porcelain including an "index of 5,000 marks, listed by prominent features and with a complete cross-reference {showing} at a glance (a) geographical location of mark, (b) factory or family name of manufacturer, (c) type of ware, (d) method of producing the mark on the object, (e) color of the mark, and (f) date when the mark was used. The authors have included a foreword, bibliography, index of manufacturers and a . . . guide to the often misunderstood marks of Delft, Sevres, and England 1842-1883." Publisher's note

Kovels' new dictionary of marks; {by} Ralph and Terry Kovel. Crown 1986 290p il $19   **738**

1. Porcelain -- Marks 2. Pottery -- Marks

ISBN 0-517-55914-5

LC 85-15146

Covering pottery and porcelain from 1850 to the present this volume is regarded as a complimentary volume to the one covering 1650 to 1850.

738.1   Techniques, procedures, apparatus, equipment, materials

Burleson, Mark

The **ceramic** glaze handbook; materials, techniques, formulas. Lark Bks. 2001 144p il hardcover o.p. pa $24.95   **738.1**

1. Glazes 2. Pottery

ISBN 1-57990-439-4 pa

LC 00-63486

"Burleson covers glaze chemistry, application techniques, firing, and problem solving. Color photographs comparing fired samples are particularly good. A collection of formulas by other artists is categorized by type of clay body and firing temperature. Useful for studio potters and hobbyists." Libr J

Hamer, Frank

The **potter's** dictionary of materials and techniques; Frank and Janet Hamer. 5th ed; University of Pa. Press 2004 L 45.00 : CIP entry (Jun.)   **738.1**

1. Ceramics -- Dictionaries 2. Pottery -- Dictionaries 3. Reference books

ISBN 0-8122-3810-9

Articles in this "potter's reference include soda firing, paper clay, computer glaze calculations, and fuming. . . . Alphabetically arranged entries range in length from a brief paragraph or half-page . . . to longer essays on subjects such as formulas, health hazards, and cones. Subject matter ranges widely, covering all the processes and materials involved in pottery formation, decoration, and firing." Am Ref Books Annu, 1998 {entry for 4th edition}

Muller, Kristin

The **potter's** studio handbook; a start-to-finish guide to hand-built and wheel-thrown ceramics. Quarry Books 2007 192p il pa $24.99   **738.1**
   1. Pottery
   ISBN 978-1-59253-373-2; 1-59253-373-6

LC 2007-16693
The author "guides beginners through advanced students in equipping a ceramic studio, handling the design, preparing the clay, constructing slab projects, throwing on a wheel, glazing, and firing. The 16 clay projects featured here include teapots, vases, and dinner plates. Readers can draw inspiration from the creative painting and underglazing examples, as well as the unusual firing techniques for color and texture." Libr J

Nelson, Glenn C.

★ **Ceramics**: a potter's handbook; [by] Glenn C. Nelson, Richard Burkett. 6th ed; Wadsworth/Thomson Learning 2002 439p il pa $90.95   **738.1**
   1. Ceramics 2. Pottery
   ISBN 0-03-028937-8

LC 2001-96329
This manual for beginner to advanced potters presents forming and decorating techniques, body and glaze recipes, and sources for raw materials and equipment.

Otterbein, Kim

Polymer clay 101; [by] Angela Mabray and Kim Otterbein. Creative Pub. International 2011 192p il pa $18.95   **738.1**
   1. Clay 2. Modeling
   ISBN 978-1-58923-470-3

LC 2010-16772
"With the guidance of polymer clay artists Mabray and Otterbein, crafters can get a handle on all of the basics of working with this distinctive medium. The projects are the highlight here—the authors expect readers to learn by doing, and a variety of techniques, including Skinner blends, canes, snakes, mold making, and stamping, are outlined. The DVD features further step-by-step directions for many techniques." Libr J

Pavelka, Lisa

The **complete** book of polymer clay; step-by-step instructions, original projects, inspirational gallery. Taunton Press 2010 221p il pa $24.95 **738.1**
   1. Clay 2. Modeling
   ISBN 978-1-60085-128-5

LC 2009-42430
This book presents projects with complete instructions showing readers how to make pendants, curio boxes, a necklace and a bracelet.

738.4   Specific products and techniques of making them

Darty, Linda

The **art** of enameling; techniques, projects, inspiration. Lark Books 2004 176p il $24.95 **738.4**
   1. Enamel and enameling
   ISBN 1-579-90507-2

LC 2004-5540
This is an "introduction to enameling fundamentals with practice exercises for techniques such as cloisonné and champlevé. There are also a dozen jewelry projects by other artists. This is an excellent and beautifully illustrated summary of a difficult craft." Libr J
Includes bibliographical references

739.2   Work in precious metals

Faber, Toby

Faberge's eggs; the extraordinary story of the masterpieces that outlived an empire. Random House 2008 302p il $30   **739.2**
   1. Artisans 2. Artists 3. Emperors 4. Empresses 5. Jewelers 6. Metalworkers
   ISBN 978-1-4000-6550-9; 1-4000-6550-X

LC 2007-49635
"Faber moves beyond mere description and illustration as he traces the fascinating history and sociology of these turn-of-the-century status symbols." Booklist
Includes bibliographical references

739.27   Jewelry

Codina, Carles

The **complete** book of jewelry making. Lark Bks. 2000 160p il hardcover o.p. pa $19.95 **739.27**
   1. Jewelry 2. Jewelry making
   ISBN 1-57990-188-3; 1-57990-304-5 pa

LC 00-42809
This book covers "the basics, from the ABCs of metallurgy to such complicated techniques as enameling and lacquering. . . . Most of the examples are contemporary, taken from European designers, and all blessed with great color photographs." Booklist

DeCoster, Marcia

★ **Marcia** DeCoster's beaded opulence; elegant jewelry projects with right angle weave. Lark Books 2009 128p il $24.95   **739.27**
   1. Beadwork 2. Jewelry
   ISBN 978-1-60059-292-8

LC 2008-50857
This book features jewelry projects using beading stitches with right-angle weave designs.

Gollberg, Joanna

★ The **art** & craft of making jewelry; a complete guide to essential techniques. Lark Books 2006
176p il $27.95 **739.27**

1. Jewelry

ISBN 978-1-57990-570-5; 1-57990-570-6

LC 2005-34040

"This is an overview of contemporary jewelry-making techniques for studio artists. Individual chapters cover various aspects of metalworking, color addition, and the use of findings, with project instructions and color photographs of finished works by multiple artists supplementing the technical information and practice exercises. This beautifully illustrated book should find a place in public library collections needing additional material on jewelry making." Libr J

Haab, Sherri

The **art** of metal clay; techniques for creating jewelry and decorative objects. Rev. and expanded ed.; Watson-Guptill Publications 2010 160p il pa
$24.99 **739.27**

1. Jewelry 2. Metalwork 3. Precious metal clay

ISBN 978-0-82309-932-0

LC 2009-43781

"An essential project book for anyone interested in learning to work with metal clay. . . . [The projects included involve] bronze and copper metal clays, etching, and enameling. An included DVD has additional projects." Libr J

Miller, Judith

Miller's costume jewelry. Miller's 2010 256p il
$34.99 **739.27**

1. Jewelry

ISBN 978-1-84533-563-2

"The highly informative and entertaining introduction highlights the rise and continued use of costume jewelry from ancient times to the present and features many of the influences that make vintage costume jewelry so popular. The book's remainder is divided into four sections focusing on major designers, classic designers, galleries (special collections), and designers to watch. . . . This delightful book will captivate costume jewelry enthusiasts." Libr J

Young, Anastasia

The **workbench** guide to jewelry techniques. Interweave Press LLC 2009 320p il $34.95 **739.27**

1. Jewelry

ISBN 978-1-59668-169-9

LC 2009-41385

This is a "reference guide for all jewelers, amateur or professional. Includes extensive photographic illustrations of virtually all techniques needed to create quality jewelry. Also has an excellent chapter on design, and additional sections on photographing, exhibiting, marketing, and selling work." Libr J

Includes bibliographical references

741 Drawing and drawings

Barnet, Will

Will Barnet; a sketchbook 1932-1934. with an essay by Robert C. Morgan. George Braziller 2008
90p il $49.95 **741**

1. Figure drawing

ISBN 978-0-807-61597-3; 0-807-61598-6

LC 2008-22376

"Eight decades of American artist Barnet's work have reflected trends from social realism to abstract formalism in prints, drawing, and paintings. Published here is a recently uncovered collection of sketches figurative in their style. Vibrant yet precise, these were executed en plein air in the early 1930s while Barnet was a student at the Art Students League in Manhattan. The drawings evoke the life and vitality of city dwellers in summertime, enjoying New York's Central Park as a communal backyard. The 36 pen-and-ink drawings portray young lovers, sailors and their girlfriends, and mothers with children." Libr J

Includes bibliographical references.

Beever, Julian

Pavement chalk artist; the three-dimensional drawings of Julian Beever. Firefly Books 2010 110p
il $29.95 **741**

1. Street art

ISBN 978-1-55407-661-1

"With these 58 chalk drawings, street artist Beever takes us around the world—to Brussels, Istanbul, London, Tokyo—to the public squares and piazzas where he creates breathtaking colored chalk anamorphic drawings—pictures rendered in perspective and appearing three-dimensional when viewed from a particular angle. The photographs of his immense paintings leap off the page, creating a whimsical wonderland of giant insects and animals, superheroes, gaping chasms, and subterranean waterways that ape and then distort reality. . . . Beever's mastery and unbridled humor are on full display in these dazzling drawings, each accompanied by a description that details artistic techniques, discusses challenges the artist faced, and offers an inside look into his process." Publ Wkly

Delisle, Guy

★ **Pyongyang:** a journey in North Korea; translated by Helge Dascher. Drawn & Quarterly 2005
176p il map hardcover o.p. pa $14.95 **741**

1. Graphic novels

ISBN 1-896597-89-0; 1-897299-21-4 pa

"Pyongyang will appeal to multiple audiences: current events buffs, Persepolis fans and those who just love a good yarn." Publ Wkly

Johnston, Daniel

Daniel Johnston; with contributions by Jad Fair, Phillippe Vergne, Harvey Pekar; and an interview with Daniel Johnston. Rizzoli 2009 147p il $45 **741**

1. Artists 2. Rock musicians 3. Singers 4. Songwriters

ISBN 978-0-8478-3230-9; 0-8478-3230-0

LC 2008-933726

This book features "more than 80 of [Johnston's] pieces, all saturated in color and trippy in content. There are chiseled superheroes, flying ducks, multi-eyed monsters, and a variety of demons floating across the pages. The only thing that punctuates the book are occasional pull-quotes from Johnston, as well as short essays from art curator Philippe Vergne, musician Jad Fair, and comic book writer Harvey Pekar. And unlike some other musicians who pursue success in the visual arts, Johnston's already got the respect of the art world establishment; his work was featured in the 2006 Whitney Biennial. No doubt that with this book, he'll win over the respect of his music fans." Nylon

Satrapi, Marjane

Embroideries. Pantheon Books 2005 134p il $16.95 **741**
1. Graphic novels 2. Sex -- Fiction 3. Women -- Iran -- Graphic novels
ISBN 0-375-42305-2

LC 2004-58660

"Discussions of sex are frank and explicit and laced with high humor. . . . Satrapi's simple black-and-white cartooning style is tremendously effective, expertly portraying emotional nuances with just a few lines." Libr J

Spiegelman, Art

In the shadow of no towers. Pantheon Books 2004 various paging il $19.95 **741**
1. Comic books, strips, etc. 2. Graphic novels 3. September 11 terrorist attacks, 2001 4. September 11 terrorist attacks, 2001 -- Comic books, strips, etc. 5. September 11 terrorist attacks, 2001 -- Graphic novels
ISBN 0-375-42307-9

LC 2004-43870

The author "provides a hair-raising and wry account of his family's frantic efforts to locate one another on September 11 as well as a morbidly funny survey of his trademark sense of existential doom. . . . This is a powerful and quirky work of visual storytelling by a master comics artist." Publ Wkly

741.092 Biography

Lester, Toby

Da Vinci's ghost; genius, obsession, and how Leonardo created the world in his own image. Toby Lester. 1st ed.; Free Press 2012 275 p. **741.092**
ISBN 1439189234; 9781439189238; 9781439189252 (ebook)

LC 2011027966

This book tells "the story of Vitruvian Man: Leonardo da Vincis famous drawing of a man in a circle and a square. Deployed today to celebrate subjects as various as the nature of genius, the beauty of the human form, and the universality of the human spirit . . . it has become the worlds most famous cultural icon, yet almost nobody knows anything about it. . . . Toby Lester weaves together a century-spanning saga of people and ideas. Assembled here is an eclectic cast of . . . characters . . . and, of course, in the starring role, Leonardo himselfwhose ghost Lester resurrects in the . . . unfamiliar context of his own times. (Publisher's note)

741.2 Techniques, procedures, apparatus, equipment, materials

Box, Richard

Drawing step-by-step; [by] Richard Box . . . [et al.] Search Press 2009 144p il pa $19.95 **741.2**
1. Drawing -- Technique
ISBN 978-1-84448-439-3

"This series title is gathered from five previous Search Press books. It features a wide variety of realistic styles and a number of media, including graphite, colored pencils, charcoal, chalks, pastels, water-soluble pencils, and pens." Libr J

Edwards, Betty

The **new** drawing on the right side of the brain; 2nd ed; Jeremy P. Tarcher\Putnam 1999 291p il $27.95; pa $16.95 **741.2**
1. Cerebral dominance 2. Creative ability 3. Drawing -- Technique 4. Visual perception
ISBN 978-0-87477-419-1; 0-87477-419-5; 978-0-87477-424-5 pa; 0-87477-424-1 pa

LC 99-35809

This book describes the author's technique for teaching people how to draw more accurately and creatively by developing the capabilities of the brain's right side, which, according to "split-brain" research, controls the visual and perceptual functions.

Kaupelis, Robert

Experimental drawing; 30th anniversary ed.; Watson-Guptill 2010 192p il pa $22.99 **741.2**
1. Drawing -- Technique
ISBN 978-0-8230-1622-8; 0-8230-1622-6

LC 2009-931354

"This classic work is a perfect next step for artists who have mastered the basics." Libr J
Includes bibliographical references

Lawlor, Veronica

One drawing a day; a 6-week course exploring creativity with illustration and mixed media. Quarry Books 2011 128p il pa $22.99 **741.2**
1. Drawing -- Technique
ISBN 978-1-59253-724-2; 1-59253-724-3

"Each spread in the book features a . . . drawing by one of 8 professional illustrators, with a description and comments by the illustrator as well as a companion exercise. Each exercise includes suggestions for various mediums or mixed-media solutions, advice on how to approach and execute the drawing, as well as professional tips. The book also includes exercises designed to spark new ideas and increase creativity." Publisher's note

Micklewright, Keith

★ **Drawing**: mastering the language of visual expression. Harry N. Abrams 2005 168p il pa $29.95 **741.2**
1. Drawing -- Technique
ISBN 0-8109-9238-8

LC 2005-5862

"Using examples of master artists such as Ingres and Michelangelo as well as more contemporary work of Cezanne, Hockney, and others, different aspects of drawing are examined. Each chapter ends with 'Ideas to Explore,' in which the reader is given suggestions for practice. . . . This book is valuable for those learning the theory behind the elements of drawing and for those looking for practical instruction." Voice Youth Advocates

Includes bibliographical references

Price, Maggie

Painting with pastels; easy techniques to master the medium. North Light Books 2007 128p il pa $24.99   **741.2**
    1. Pastel drawing
    ISBN 978-1-58180-819-3; 1-58180-819-4
                      LC 2006-029048

"This book shows the reader . . . [how] to paint with pastels, from materials and techniques to painting from photographs. . . . Hand-in photos show how to hold and apply the pastel, and the twenty-two step-by-step demonstrations cover . . . preparing your surface, underpainting, figure drawing and more." Publisher's note

741.5   Cartoons, graphic novels, caricatures, comics

Abel, Jessica

Drawing words & writing pictures; making comics: from manga, graphic novels, and beyond. [by] Jessica Abel & Matt Madden. First Second Books 2008 282p il pa $29.95   **741.5**
    1. Cartooning -- Technique 2. Comic books, strips, etc.
    3. Comic books, strips, etc. -- Authorship 4. Drawing
    -- Technique 5. Graphic novels -- Authorship
    ISBN 978-1-59643-131-7; 1-59643-131-8
                      LC 2007-44125

Professional cartoonists Abel and Madden provide a college-level course that takes readers from concept to comic in fifteen lessons. Lessons progress from the basics of defining just what comics are, to single-panel comics, comic strips, panel transitions, pencilling, page composition, lettering, inking, structuring the story, developing characters, panel and title design, world-building, inking with a brush, using scanners and other equipment in reproduction, and creating a 24-hour comic. The first fourteen chapters include homework and extra credit work assignments, and several appendices provide more assignments.

This "book offers step-by-step entry into a complicated series of skills in a nonscary and approachable way." Libr J

Includes bibliographical references

Barry, Lynda

What it is. Drawn & Quarterly 2008 209p il $24.95   **741.5**
    1. Authorship -- Graphic novels 2. Creative writing
    -- Graphic novels
    ISBN 978-1-897299-35-7; 1-897299-35-4
                  LC c2007-9047319

Independent cartoonist Lynda Barry presents an unconventional book that encourages its readers to write by using her colorful art and asking questions such as "How are monsters different? And how are they the same?" "Can/Do images exist without thinking?" "What is the difference between lying and pretending?" Each question appears with illustrated writing prompts and Barry's own ruminations on the topics. It's a workbook of sorts, but it also exists as a book to be read for itself.

"Every so often a book comes along that surpasses expectations, taking readers on an inspirational voyage that they don't want to leave. This is one such book." SLJ

Beatty, Scott

★ The **DC** Comics encyclopedia; the definitive guide to the characters of the DC universe. text by Scott Beatty . . . [et al.]; updated text by Dan Wallace. Updated and expanded; DK Pub. 2008 399p il $40   **741.5**
    1. Comic books, strips, etc. -- Encyclopedias 2.
    Reference books
    ISBN 978-0-7566-4119-1; 0-7566-4119-5
                  LC 2008-300609

The authors "meticulously profile 1000 DC heroes and villains created since DC's 1935 founding. The entries are organized alphabetically, by character name, while introductory insets consistently detail first appearance, hero/villain status, physical statistics, and special powers. A genuinely essential DC character reference." Libr J

Bechdel, Alison

★ **Are** you my mother? a comic drama. Alison Bechdel. Houghton Mifflin Harcourt 2012 286 p.   **741.5**
    1. Cartoonists -- United States -- Comic books, strips, etc 2. Graphic nonfiction 3. Memoirs 4. Mothers & daughters
    ISBN 0618982507; 9780618982509
                  LC 2012010582

In this book, [Alison] Bechdel not only searches for keys to [her relationship with her mother] but perhaps even for surrogate mothers, through therapy, girlfriends and the writing of Virginia Woolf, Adrienne Rich, Alice Miller and others. Yet the primary inspiration in this literary memoir is psychoanalyst Donald Winnicott, whose life and work Bechdel explores along with her own. Incidentally, the narrative also encompasses the writing of and response to Fun Home, a work that changed the author's life and elevated her career to a whole new level. She writes that she agonized over the creation of this follow-up for four years. (Kirkus)

Fun home; a family tragicomic. Houghton Mifflin 2006 232p il $19.95   **741.5**
    1. Artists 2. Authors 3. Autobiographical graphic novels 4. Biography, Individual 5. Cartoonists 6. Comic book writers 7. Essayists 8. Graphic novels 9. Novelists
    ISBN 978-0-618-47794-4; 0-618-47794-2
                  LC 2005-30304

This "is one of the very best graphic novels ever." Booklist

Beland, Tom

True story swear to God archives, vol. 1. Image Comics 2008 528p il pa $19.99   **741.5**
1. Autobiographical graphic novels 2. Cartoonists 3. Graphic novels 4. Romance graphic novels
ISBN 978-1-58240-881-1

They met at a bus stop at Disneyworld, by chance: he was a cartoonist from Napa, California, and she was a radio personality from Puerto Rico. Their chance meeting blossomed into a romance that survived a long-distance separation, a Category 5 hurricane, his leaving home to move to a new world. Tom Beland writes candidly about the ups and downs of his relationship with Lily, with his family, and all the slings and arrows of life one has to deal with daily. He originally self-published these comics, and they were collected in several trade paperbacks from AiT/PlanetLar. The book includes occasional harsh language (including s-bombs and f-bombs), sexual situations, and frank talk about sex.

Brunetti, Ivan

Cartooning; philosophy and practice. Yale University Press 2011 77p il pa $13 **741.5**
1. Cartooning -- Technique
ISBN 978-0-300-17099-3; 0-300-17099-8
LC 2010-940419

"The first half of the book is devoted to the basic terminology and materials of the medium, while the second half is devoted to an intensive and full 15-week comics course. The course should make the non-draftsperson comfortable with drawing and progressively able to translate the panels of the story from head to page. It also breaks down the drawing process so that anyone can draw a couple characters without having to fret about making realistic, Marvel-style, detailed renderings or obsessive crosshatch shading. Cartooning is set to become the next de-facto book for breaking into the comics medium." Molossus

Includes bibliographical references

Daniels, Les

Marvel; five fabulous decades of the world's greatest comics. introduction by Stan Lee. Abrams 1991 287p il hardcover o.p. pa $26.95 **741.5**
1. Comic books, strips, etc.
ISBN 0-8109-2566-4
LC 91-8783

"Daniels' behind-the-scenes look at the development of Marvel, his profiles of the line's foremost heroes and villains, and biographies of leading writers and artists will entice . . . . young fans. . . . But the book's strongest appeal lies in the generous samplings of artwork spread throughout." Booklist

De Haven, Tom

Our hero; Superman on Earth. Yale University Press 2010 224p il $24   **741.5**
1. Superman (Fictitious character)
ISBN 978-0-300-11817-9; 0-300-11817-1
LC 2009-18206

De Haven "offers an extended meditation on the role the flying Krypton orphan has played in comic books, cartoons, movies, and TV. Our Hero: Superman on Earth is part history — a summary of the ways Superman creators Jerry Siegel and Joe Shuster were ripped off will break your heart — and part philosophy. De Haven contends that since his creation

in 1938, Superman has seen many reinventions, but he always represents a uniquely American desire: to have 'the freedom to act in ways that are satisfying to him. It makes him feel good, dammit.' This book will make you feel the same." Entertainment Wkly

Includes bibliographical references

Eisner, Will

★ **Comics** and sequential art; principles and practices from the legendary cartoonist. W.W. Norton 2008 175p il pa $22.95   **741.5**
1. Comic books, strips, etc. -- Authorship 2. Drawing -- Technique 3. Graphic novels -- Authorship
ISBN 978-0-393-33126-4; 0-393-33126-1
LC 2008-20042

This book offers the author's ideas, theories, and advice about graphic storytelling and the uses to which the comic book art form can be applied.

Glidden, Sarah

How to understand Israel in 60 days or less. Vertigo/DC Comics 2010 206p il map $24.99   **741.5**
1. Graphic novels 2. Israel-Arab conflicts -- Graphic novels
ISBN 978-1-4012-2233-8

"Glidden's soft, watercolor palette and realistic art complement without overshadowing this thoughtful exploration of the role that cultural heritage plays in the search for personal identity." SLJ

Goldstein, Nancy

Jackie Ormes; the first African American woman cartoonist. University of Michigan Press 2008 225p il $35   **741.5**
1. African American women -- Biography 2. Biography, Individual 3. Cartooning 4. Cartoonists
ISBN 978-0-472-11624-9; 0-472-11624-X
LC 2007-35395

This book covers the life and career of Jackie Ormes, who was the first African American woman cartoonist. She wrote and drew comic strips that ran in Black newspapers such as the Pittsburgh Courier and the Chicago Defender. She was part of the Black elite in Chicago and knew other luminaries such as singer Eartha Kitt and musician/composer/conductor Duke Ellington. She was also investigated by the FBI because of her Leftist political ideas and activities. While she did such things as create Torchy paper dolls, based on her beautiful and sexy cartoon character, and cute Patty-Jo dolls, Ormes also used her comic strips to put forth her political views. This book reproduces some of her cartoons and comic strips, in both black and white and in color.

Guibert, Emmanuel

Alan's war. First Second 2008 304p il pa $24   **741.5**
1. Biographical graphic novels 2. Graphic novels 3. Soldiers 4. Soldiers -- Graphic novels 5. Veterans 6. World War, 1939-1945 -- Graphic novels
ISBN 978-1-59643-096-9; 1-59643-096-6
LC 2007-46190

French cartoonist Guibert met and became friends with Alan Cope and interviewed him at length to create this book.

It recreates Cope's memories of being an eighteen-year-old G.I. during World War II. Unlike the war movies that focus on battles, this book focuses on more everyday, mundane memories of the day-to-day life of a soldier. Cope frankly describes a bout with crabs (genital lice), matter-of-factly tells of casual man-to-man sexual encounters among the soldiers, and gives the reader a feel for what happened back then. He also talks about postwar relationships and travels.

This is a "poignant and frank graphic memoir of young soldier who was told to serve his country in WWII and how it changed him forever. . . . Cope and Guibert forge a story that resonates with humanity." Publ Wkly

★ The **photographer**; [by] Emmanuel Guibert, Didier Lefèvre and Frédéric Lemercier; translated by Alexis Siegel. First Second 2009 267p il map pa $29.95 **741.5**
  1. Graphic novels 2. Photojournalism -- Graphic novels
  ISBN 978-1-59643-375-5; 1-59643-375-2

"Originally published as three volumes in France from 2003 to 2006, this graphic novel follows photojournalist Didier Lefèvre during his three months in Pakistan and Afghanistan in 1986 as he documented the medical missions of Doctors without Borders. . . . The graphic novel combines traditional comic art with some of the four thousand photographs Lefevre shot while in Afghanistan. . . . Many images will stay with readers as both horrifying and glorious. The Afghan children being treated for burns, bullet wounds, and shrapnel are page by page next to the beauty of the Afghan mountainous landscapes. . . . [This book] has a powerful message and images of a part of the world that should be discussed more often." Voice Youth Advocates

Hajdu, David

The **ten**-cent plague; the great comic-book scare and how it changed America. Farrar, Straus and Giroux 2008 434p $26   **741.5**
  1. Comic books, strips, etc. 2. Comic books, strips, etc. -- Social aspects 3. Comic books, strips, etc. -- United States -- History -- 20th century
  ISBN 978-0-374-18767-5; 0-374-18767-3
                              LC 2007-25024

"Hajdu offers captivating insights into America's early bluestocking-versus-blue-collar culture wars, and the later tensions between wary parents and the first generation of kids with the buying power to mold mass entertainment." Village Voice
  Includes bibliographical references

Hart, Christopher

Cartooning for the beginner. Watson-Guptill 2000 144p il pa $19.95   **741.5**
  1. Cartooning -- Technique 2. Cartoons and caricatures
  ISBN 0-8230-0586-0
                              LC 00-101905

This guide to cartooning techniques "covers the world of cartoon animals, animation, and 'edgy' toons.'" Libr J

Hirschfeld, Al

Hirschfeld on line. Applause Theatre Bk. Pubs. 1998 343p $59.95   **741.5**
  1. Cartoons and caricatures 2. Entertainers
  ISBN 1-55783-356-7

Hirschfeld "is the irreplaceable M.V.P. of the New York theatre world, and this compendium of his drawings amounts to a historic work of droll, generous-minded theatre criticism. The artist himself has annotated the drawings, which cover a range of the performing arts . . . and his comments are as swooping and witty as his lines." New Yorker

Howlett, Mike

The **weird** world of Eerie Publications; comic gore that warped millions of young minds. introduction by Stephen R. Bissett. Feral House 2010 xxv, 310p il $32.95   **741.5**
  1. Comic books, strips, etc.
  ISBN 978-1-932595-87-1; 1-932595-87-2

"Mike Howlett resurrects both Eerie Publications, publisher of many of the post-pulp newsstand magazines, and the grotesque stories and images that filled adolescent minds a decade after the crackdown in 1954, when the Comics Code placed strict puritanical limits on the amount of gore, crime and sex in comic books. Former comic-book publishers took refuge in the unregulated realm of magazines. . . . This colorful book follows the evolution and devolution of these and other horror and novelty magazines and their artists. Even if you're not a fan of this genre, it is a curiously wonderful, weird and eerie tale of magazine history." N Y Times Book Rev

Isabella, Tony

1,000 comic books you must read. Krause Publications 2009 271p il $29.99   **741.5**
  1. Best books 2. Comic books, strips, etc. 3. Comic books, strips, etc. -- Bibliography
  ISBN 978-0-89689-921-6; 0-89689-921-7

Isabella "has the great fortune of not having to decide the thousand finest but rather the thousand that he finds compelling. This lends his hardcover a kaleidoscopic approach to deconstructing the evolution of the American comic rather than focusing on the creme de la creme alone. With its chapters predominantly broken up by decade ('The Fighting Forties,' 'The Fearful Fifties,' etc.), 1000 Comic Books provides short summaries (under 75 words) for each title as well as clear cover scans and creator/ publishing information. A plethora of obscure information is sprinkled through the book. . . . There is no discrimination of subject matter, and even the most ardent comic book reader is bound to learn something new." Cincinnati City Beat

Jacobson, Sidney

The **9** /11 report; a graphic adaptation. by Sid Jacobson and Ernie Colón; [with a foreword by Thomas H. Kean and Lee H. Hamilton] Hill and Wang 2006 133p il $30; pa $16.95   **741.5**
  1. Graphic novels 2. September 11 terrorist attacks, 2001 -- Comic books, strips, etc. 3. September 11 terrorist attacks, 2001 -- Graphic novels
  ISBN 0-8090-5738-7; 978-0-8090-5738-2; 0-8090-5739-5 pa; 978-0-8090-5739-9 pa

"The book aims to make . . . [The 9/11 Commission Report] more accessible to all readers and draw in young adults. . . . This graphic adaptation is an important and necessary part of any collection." Libr J

After 9/11: America's war on terror (2001-) Hill and Wang 2008 149p il map pa $16.95   **741.5**
1. Graphic novels 2. Iraq War, 2003- -- Graphic novels 3. Terrorism -- Graphic novels
ISBN 978-0-8090-2370-7

LC 2008-13298

In 2006, longtime comic book veterans Jacobson and Colon adapted the 9/11 Commission's report into a graphic format that made it a readable, comprehensible work for teens and adults. Now they have used the comic book treatment to cover America's War on Terror since 2001, including the wars in Iraq and in Afghanistan, summarizing events and showing the major players throughout the years. Some images can be disturbing, such as the depiction of prisoner mistreatment at Abu Ghraib and other facilities, as well as depictions of the victims of sectarian violence.

Jones, Gerard
Men of tomorrow; geeks, gangsters and the birth of the comic book. Basic Books 2004 320p il $26; pa $15   **741.5**
1. Cartoonists 2. Cartoonists -- United States -- Biography 3. Comic books, strips, etc -- History and criticism 4. Comic books, strips, etc.
ISBN 0-465-03656-2; 0-465-03657-0 pa

LC 2004-9031

This book tells "the surprising story of the young Jewish misfits, hustlers and nerds who invented the superhero and the comic book industry. . . . Springing unheralded out of working-class Jewish immigrant neighborhoods in the depths of the Depression, these young men transformed an odd mix of geekdom, science fiction, and outsider yearnings into blue-eyed chisel-nosed crime-fighters and adventurers who quickly captured the mainstream imagination. . . . He chronicles how the comics sparked a frightened counterattack that nearly destroyed the industry in the 1950's and how later they surged back at an underground level, to inspire a new generation to transmute those long-ago fantasies into art, literature, blockbuster movies and graphic novels." Publisher's note

Kanfer, Stefan
Serious business; the art and commerce of animation in America from Betty Boop to Toy story. Da Capo Press 2000 256p il pa $17.50   **741.5**
1. Animated films
ISBN 0-306-80918-4; 978-0-306-80918-7

LC 98-50687

"As an art form, animation is magically irresistible; as a reflection of broader American popular culture, it is amazingly on target. . . . Kanfer here shows how the people, politics, prejudices, trends, and technologies of various eras have been so aptly reflected in each set of frames. . . . While Kanfer's humbly stated intention is to augment previous writings on the subject, his work should certainly join the ranks of important literature in the field." Libr J

Kitchen, Denis
The **art** of Harvey Kurtzman; the mad genius of comics. by Denis Kitchen and Paul Buhle; introduction by Art Spiegelman; designed by Kitchen, Lind & Associates. Abrams Comicarts 2009 241p il $40   **741.5**
1. Cartoonists 2. Cartoons and caricatures 3. Comic books, strips, etc. 4. Satire
ISBN 978-0-8109-7296-4; 0-8109-7296-4

LC 2008-04809

"Retrace the strands that led to a lot of current American satire — including The Simpsons, Saturday Night Live and The Daily Show — and sooner or later you end up at Harvey Kurtzman. A comic mastermind who created Mad Magazine and Playboy's 'Little Annie Fanny,' Kurtzman also happened to discover Robert Crumb and gave Gloria Steinem her first job. . . . [This volume] explores the life and art of the famous satirist, weaving together the story of Kurtzman's career with a collection of the artist's images and illustrations." NPR

Kleist, Reinhard
★ **Johnny** Cash; I see a darkness: a graphic novel. [translated from the German edition by Michael Waaler] Abrams ComicArts 2009 221p il pa $17.95   **741.5**
1. Biographical graphic novels 2. Country musicians 3. Country musicians -- Graphic novels 4. Graphic novels 5. Singers 6. Songwriters
ISBN 978-0-8109-8463-9

LC 2010-279149

The author "presents a biography (with seemingly invented dialog that stays true to the facts) focusing on Cash's turning points: from his poor family's 1935 relocation to a New Deal-created cotton farming community, through his troubled first marriage, endless touring, the amphetamine abuse of his early musical career, and climaxing with a famous, highly charged 1968 concert at California's Folsom Prison. Kleist also dramatizes several of Cash's songs and relates the tragic story of Glen Sherley, a Folsom inmate who sent Cash a song he had written hoping Cash would play it in the show. The ruggedness of Kleist's black-and-white illustrations suits their subject, as the stark portrayal of Cash's withdrawal from drugs is inventive and harrowing. . . . This thoughtful and compelling portrait of a towering talent with a tortured soul is recommended for all teen and adult music fans." Libr J

Includes bibliographical references

Lee, Stan
★ **Stan** Lee's How to draw comics; from the legendary co-creator of Spider-Man, the Incredible Hulk, Fantastic Four, X-Men, and Iron Man. Watson-Guptill Publication 2010 224p il pa $24.99 **741.5**
1. Comic books, strips, etc. -- Authorship 2. Drawing -- Technique
ISBN 978-0-8230-0083-8

LC 2010-5781

The author "includes chapters on creating comics with computer programs and online resources and how to get work in the 21st century. The book begins with a brief history of comics, then focuses on action-adventure style, romance, humor, horror, and Japanese manga. This is the one book anyone interested in drawing comics should own." Libr J

Includes bibliographical references

McCloud, Scott

★ **Making** comics; storytelling secrets of comics, manga, and graphic novels. HarperCollins 2006 264p il pa $22.95   **741.5**

1. Comic books, strips, etc. -- Authorship 2. Graphic novels -- Drawing

ISBN 0-06-078094-0; 978-0-06-078094-4

The author "explores practical matters, including comics devices such as panels, word balloons, and sound effects; facial expressions and body language; the creation of convincing and evocative settings; and the different tools artists can use for the job, from pencils to computers. He also delves into the framing of images in panels, the flow of panels on a page, and the relationships between words and pictures in comics. . . . This is thoughtful, fascinating, stimulating, potentially controversial, and inspiring." Libr J

Includes bibliographical references

Reinventing comics; how imagination and technology are revolutionizing an art form. Paradox Press 2000 237p il pa $22.95   **741.5**

1. Cartoons and caricatures 2. Comic books, strips, etc.

ISBN 0-06-095350-0

LC 00-710457

The author maps out "'12 revolutions', which, he believes, need to take place for comics to survive and finally be recognized as a legitimate art form. The topics progress from the oldest of comic-related arguments (seeking respect) to the use of computer technology to renew and expand its audience. These brilliantly presented discussions concern comics as literature, comics as art, creators' rights, industry innovation, and public perception, among other topics." Libr J

Morrison, Grant

Supergods; what masked vigilantes, miraculous mutants, and a sun god from Smallville can teach us about being human. Spiegel & Grau 2011 444p il   **741.5**

1. Comic books, strips, etc. 2. Comic books, strips, etc. -- United States 3. Heroes 4. Superheroes

ISBN 1-4000-6912-2; 978-1-4000-6912-5

LC 2010053712

A graphic novelist presents a history of the superhero in American comic books and movies. Index.

Morrison chronicles the "rise, fall, rise, fall and rise again of comic-book superheroes, from Superman's auspicious beginning as a Depression-era symbol of the power of the individual to Wolverine's rise to prominence in a more morally ambiguous era." Kirkus

Includes bibliographical references

Nadel, Dan

Art in time; unknown comic book adventures 1940-1980. Abrams ComicArts 2010 301p il $40   **741.5**

1. Comic books, strips, etc.

ISBN 978-0-8109-8824-8; 0-8109-8824-0

LC 2009-31672

Nadel "rescues from oblivion an array of fascinatingly offbeat comics in a variety of genres (superhero, thriller, Western). In Art in Time, these meticulously reprinted full-length comic-book stories range from a terrifically sexy noir comic by Harry Lucey, 'The Cutie Killer Caper,' to Matt Fox's 'I Was a Vampire,' whose weirdly wooden art can be downright terrifying. Throughout, Nadel offers plenty of biographical details and brisk art criticism that make these riotous pages even more thrilling to rediscover." Entertainment Wkly

Includes bibliographical references

Neufeld, Josh

A.D. New Orleans after the deluge. Pantheon Books 2009 193p il $24.95 **741.5**

1. Graphic novels 2. Hurricane Katrina, 2005 -- Graphic novels

ISBN 978-0-307-37814-9; 0-307-37814-4

LC 2008-55687

"Graphic artist Neufeld paints an emotive portrait of New Orleans during and after Hurricane Katrina, as seen through the eyes of seven of the city's citizens. The opening panels coalesce into a long cinematic pan, a thrumming set-up for the disaster. The half-page and quarter-page panels— satellite views of weather patterns and close inspections of neighborhoods—are crisp, and the two-page spreads are softly focused. . . . Neufeld's words and images are commensurable and rhythmic, and the vernacular is sharp. Bristling with attitude and pungent with social awareness." Kirkus

O'Neil, Dennis

The **DC** comics guide to writing comics; introduction by Stan Lee. Watson-Guptill 2001 128p il $19.95   **741.5**

1. Comic books, strips, etc. -- Authorship

ISBN 0-8230-1027-9

LC 2001-26101

"O'Neil addresses the universals of writing in a way that makes the book useful to all aspiring scripters, regardless of their knowledge of comics." Booklist

Ottaviani, Jim

Feynman; written by Jim Ottaviani; art by Leland Myrick; coloring by Hilary Sycamore. First Second 2011 262 p. il $29.99 **741.5**

1. Biography, Individual 2. Physicists -- Graphic novels

ISBN 1596432594; 9781596432598

LC 2010036260

Author Jim Ottaviani presents a "graphic novel biography . . . [of] Nobel-winning quantum physicist, adventurer, musician, world-class raconteur, and one of the greatest minds of the twentieth century: Richard Feynman . . . [The book] tells the story of the great mans life from his childhood in Long Island to his work on the Manhattan Project and the Challenger disaster." (Publisher's note)

This is a fascinating look at the life of an eccentric genius, a man who worked on the Manhattan Project, won a Nobel Prize, was the first great physicist to teach freshmen classes, and was the investigator into the cause of the Challenger explosion who discovered the problem was the 0-rings. This work was so entertaining it was difficult to put down. Voice Youth Advocates

Persepolis/English

★ The **complete** Persepolis. Pantheon Books 2007 341p il pa $24.95   **741.5**
1. Artists 2. Authors 3. Autobiographical graphic novels 4. Cartoonists 5. Graphic novels 6. Memoirists 7. Novelists
ISBN 978-0-375-71483-2
          LC 2007-60106
This "is the story of Satrapi's . . . childhood and coming of age within a large and loving family in Tehran during the Islamic Revolution; of the contradictions between private life and public life in a country plagued by political upheaval; of her high school years in Vienna facing the trials of adolescence far from her family; of her homecoming—both sweet and terrible; and, finally, of her self-imposed exile from her beloved homeland." Publisher's note

Rhoades, Shirrel

A **complete** history of American comic books; afterword by Steve Geppi. Peter Lang Publishing Inc. 2008 353p il $119.95; pa $39.95   **741.5**
1. Comic books, strips, etc. -- History and criticism 2. Graphic novels -- History and criticism
ISBN 978-1-4331-0110-6; 1-4331-0110-6; 978-1-4331-0107-6 pa; 1-4331-0107-6 pa
          LC 2007-43460
Rhoades, former publisher of Marvel Comics (after Stan Lee stepped down to move to Hollywood and focus on Marvel Comics in the movies), dates the beginning of the American comic book to the 1930s, when the format was first used. He covers the history of comics from that time to the present, covering all the big names (Will Eisner, Jack Kirby, Stan Lee, etc.). The book is peppered with fun sidebars with such labels as "flashback," "comics trivia," "looking back," "true facts," and so one. These help to make the book fun to read. Rhoades doesn't employ a straight narrative, but includes interviews, the side bars, comics milestones, a list of fanboys who have and had careers in comics, and a comic book quiz.

Rosenkranz, Patrick

Rebel visions: the underground comix revolution, 1963-1975. Fantagraphics Books 2008 292p il pa $34.99   **741.5**
1. Cartoonists 2. Comic books, strips, etc. -- History and criticism 3. Graphic novels
ISBN 978-1-56097-706-3
"The most lasting artistic legacy of the 1960s hippie movement, other than its music, is its eye-poppingly transgressive underground comics—black-and-white pamphlets that spread the counterculture message of sex, drugs, and rebellion to freak and straight alike. Rosenkranz thoroughly documents the phenomenon, providing a year-by-year account of the underground scene, from 1968's Zap #1, which artist R. Crumb sold from a baby carriage on the streets of Haight Ashbury, to its crash in 1973 in the wake of obscenity rulings and a crackdown on head shops. . . . Rosencranz's writing may lack flair, but with personalities this colorful (the artists themselves provide fly-on-the-wall reminiscences) and art this outrageous (reprinted on nearly every page) to write about, who needs it?" Booklist

Santiago, Wilfred

21; Wilfred Santiago. Fantagraphics 2011 148p. chiefly ill. $22.99 **741.5**
1. Autobiographical graphic novels 2. Baseball -- Graphic novels 3. Graphic novels
ISBN 978-1-56097-892-3
This book "is an all-ages graphic biography of baseball star Roberto Clemente: No other baseball player dominated the 1960s like him and no other Latin American player achieved his numbers. '21' chronicles his early days growing up in rural Puerto Rico, the highlights of his career (including the 1960s World Series), the prejudice he faced, his private life and his humanitarian mission." (trplteens.wordpress.com)
"Santiago opens his dazzlingly drawn comics biography of the pioneering Puerto Rican ballplayer on the final game of the 1972 season, with Clemente just one hit shy of joining the 3,000-hit club. Fans will know, of course, that 3,000 would also be his final tally, as he would die in a plane crash delivering relief supplies to the earthquake-rocked Nicaragua that winter. Santiago skitters around formative scenes from Clemente's childhood—striking a complex chord of family, homeland, and a driving passion for baseball—before tracing significant moments from his professional career: staring down racism with the same resolute demeanor with which he faced a high heater, snagging batting championships and fans' hearts many times over, and always looking for ways to honor his heritage." Booklist
Includes bibliographic references.

Satrapi, Marjane

Persepolis. Pantheon Bks. 2003 153p il $17.95; pa $11.95 **741.5**
1. Artists 2. Authors 3. Autobiographical graphic novels 4. Cartoonists 5. Graphic novels 6. Memoirists 7. Novelists
ISBN 0-375-42230-7; 0-375-71457-X pa
          LC 2002-190806
"Satrapi's cursive, geometrical drawing style . . . eloquently conveys her ingenuousness and fervor as a child." Booklist

Persepolis 2; [the story of a return] Pantheon Books 2004 187p il $17.95; pa $12.95   **741.5**
1. Artists 2. Authors 3. Autobiographical graphic novels 4. Cartoonists 5. Graphic novels 6. Memoirists 7. Novelists
ISBN 0-375-42288-9; 0-375-71466-9 pa
          LC 2003-70699
This continuation of Satrapi's memoir-in-comics begins "in the areligious West. There Satrapi endured initiations into sex, drugs, and partying, and travails over peer and love relationships that mirrored those of her Western fellow students. . . . After breaking up with her first love . . . she became homeless for three months and, after hospitalization for exposure, returned to Tehran, where the second half of this book transpires. . . . Satrapi's high-contrast, bold-lined, stencil-ish artwork remains very much at the service of one of the most compelling youth memoirs of recent years." Booklist

Small, David

★ **Stitches**; a memoir. W.W. Norton 2009 329p il

$23.95 **741.5**

1. Art teachers 2. Artists 3. Authors 4. Autobiographical graphic novels 5. Cancer -- Graphic novels 6. Children's authors 7. Comic books, strips, etc. 8. Family life -- Graphic novels 9. Graphic novels 10. Illustrators

ISBN 978-0-393-06857-3; 0-393-06857-9

LC 2009-22526

David Small grew up in a dysfunctional family, with a radiologist father who was distant, an angry mother who expressed her anger in eloquent silences, and an older brother who played drums a lot to express his frustrations. When he was eleven, he had a lump, a growth, on the side of his neck. Nothing was done until he was fourteen. He thought he was going in for a minor surgery to remove the cyst from his neck; instead, there were two surgeries, and when he woke up, he had no voice—a vocal cord was removed. He later learned he had cancer, something his parents refused to discuss. After he finds his mother in bed with another woman and his father confesses that he exposed him to x-rays when he was very young, Small leaves home at age sixteen, with little except his dreams that his art could be his life. In one early scene, Small shows the indignities wrought upon his body by his father, including an enema. In another scene, young Small and his older brother look at their father's medical books and see a woman's breast and a man's penis; towards the end of the book, Small draws his grandmother stripping all her clothes off and dancing wildly after setting her house on fire. Other than these few images, Small's depictions of his horrible childhood and teen years are quiet and low-key.

"Emotionally raw, artistically compelling and psychologically devastating graphic memoir of childhood trauma." Kirkus

Spiegelman, Art

★ **MetaMaus**. Pantheon Books 2011 299p il $35 **741.5**

1. Authors 2. Autobiographical graphic novels 3. Cartoonists 4. Cartoonists -- Graphic novels 5. Graphic novels 6. Holocaust survivors -- Graphic novels 7. Holocaust, 1933-1945 -- Graphic novels 8. Nonfiction writers

ISBN 978-0-375-42394-9

LC 2010052045

The New York cartoonist traces the creative process that went into drawing his Pulitzer Prizewinning classic, revealing the sources of his inspiration and describing his parents' emotional struggles as Holocaust survivors after the end of World War II.

"Informative about everything you may or may not have thought to ask about Maus and the Spiegelmans, this exhaustive purgative has been well organized and packaged and succeeds in being grimly entertaining, indeed almost addictive." Libr J

Steinberg, Saul

Steinberg at the New Yorker; introduction by Ian Frazier. H.N. Abrams 2005 239p il $50   **741.5**

1. Artists 2. Cartoonists 3. Cartoons and caricatures 4. Illustrators

ISBN 0-8109-5901-1

LC 2004-19498

The author "surveys six decades of Steinberg's pieces, including all 89 New Yorker covers (in full color), cartoons, wartime sketches from overseas, evocative (but never literal-minded) illustrations for articles, and unpublished items from the artist's portfolio. The material is arranged thematically, examining such recurring motifs as cats, pedestals and rubber-stamped figures and documenting the turn to visual metaphor in Steinberg's later work. . . . Steinberg's cartoons usually made readers think before they laughed, and so will this splendid memorial to a 20th-century artistic landmark." Publ Wkly

Includes bibliographical references

Torres, Alissa

American widow; illustrated by Sungyoon Choi. Villard Books 2008 209p il $22   **741.5**

1. Autobiographical graphic novels 2. Biography, Individual 3. Educators 4. Graphic novels 5. Memoirists 6. Securities brokers 7. September 11 terrorist attacks, 2001 8. September 11 terrorist attacks, 2001 -- Graphic novels 9. Widows -- Graphic novels

ISBN 978-0-345-50069-4

LC 2008-08396

Alissa Torres' husband Luis had just started his new job in the World Trade Center on September 10, 2001. The next day, he died in the terrorist attacks that destroyed the twin towers. Alissa was more than seven months pregnant. In this book, she recounts the personal struggles she suffered as a pregnant "terror widow," first heaped upon with sympathy, then publicly scorned. She describes the tragedies suffered by all the families who lost loved ones on September 11, 2001 and the frustrations they experienced dealing with bureaucrats as they tried to get even the smallest physical trace of their loved ones.

The author's "tragedy of errors inspires anger on her behalf, although the story is calmly and beautifully told. Choi's simple and attractive line art is set off by turquoise wash, yielding to a full-color photo at the end when Alissa embraces her life anew." Libr J

Tran, G. B.

Vietnamerica; a family's journey. written and illustrated by GB Tran. Villard Books 2010 279 p. chiefly col. ill. $30 **741.5**

1. Artists 2. Cartoonists 3. Graphic novels 4. Illustrators 5. Vietnam War, 1961-1975 -- Graphic novels 6. Vietnamese Americans -- Graphic novels 7. Vietnamese refugees -- Graphic novels

ISBN 0345508726; 9780345508720

LC 2011283144

In this personal memoir, "drawn in the style of a graphic novel, the author tries to make sense of a shattered family history. [G. B.] Tran was born in America shortly after his family fled Vietnam during the fall of Saigon. However, he sees how deeply his parents still feel connected to their homeland, even as they can't fully admit their dismay at being cut off from it. . . . By visiting Vietnam and exploring memories, Tran learns how his grandfather, a lifelong Vietminh supporter, was horrified at the brutal results of the Communist victory and how his father became a glum autocrat after his career as an artist was destroyed. He watches how his parents interact uneasily with the swarm of relatives and friends they left behind." (Publishers Weekly)

"Engaging, challenging, and disturbing, Tran's family memoir belongs in all public and academic libraries; older teens and up for occasionally strong language and violence. The swirly, jagged color art fits the story perfectly." Libr J

Watterson, Bill

The **complete** Calvin and Hobbes. Andrews Mc-Meel Pub. 2005 3v il set $150   **741.5**
1. Comic books, strips, etc.
ISBN 0-7407-4847-5; 978-0-7407-4847-9

LC 2004-62709

This is a collection of the entire run of the comic strip Calvin and Hobbes, which ran from 1985 to 1995.

"This is one of the all-time great comic strips, absolutely essential for every library." Libr J

★ An Anthology of graphic fiction, cartoons, and true stories; edited by Ivan Brunetti. Yale University Press 2006 400p il $28   **741.5**
1. American wit and humor   2. American wit and humor, Pictorial   3. Cartooning -- United States -- History -- 20th century   4. Comic books, strips, etc.   5. Comic books, strips, etc. -- United States -- History -- 20th century
ISBN 978-0-300-11170-5; 0-300-11170-3

LC 2006-14095

Brunetti presents "an overview of the art-comics movement, complete with a handful of the classic newspaper strips that informed today's creators. He finds room for such established veterans as R. Crumb, Lynda Barry, Gilbert and Jaime Hernandez, Daniel Clowes, Gary Panter, and Chester Brown as well as many less-familiar creators. . . . Brunetti admits that his selection criteria are highly personal, but as a cartoonist himself, whose work combines a socially transgressive spirit and impressive formal capability, his idiosyncratic approach is based in professional expertise. If his choices are sometimes arguable, his iconoclasm makes the book livelier and less predictable than such anthologies are wont to be." Booklist

Batman unauthorized; vigilantes, jokers, and heroes in Gotham City. edited by Dennis O'Neil. Benbella Books, Inc. 2008 219p il $17.95   **741.5**
1. Batman (Fictional character)   2. Comic books, strips, etc. -- History and criticism   3. Graphic novels
ISBN 978-1-93377130-4; 1-933771-30-5

LC 2007-46504

Former Batman comics editor and comic book writer O'Neil edits this collection of essays about Batman and his world, written by comics writers, magazine editors, and others. Topics include the cost of being Batman, calculated to the last dollar; why Batman is the most American of superheroes; whether Bruce Wayne might be mentally ill; why Batman needs Robin more than Robin needs Batman; why Arkham Asylum is doing more harm than good for Gotham City; why Batman works better when his world remains closer to reality; and more.

The Horror! The horror! comic books the government didn't want you to read! selected, edited, and with commentary by Jim Trombetta; intro-

duction by R. L. Stine. Abrams ComicArts 2010 304p il $29.95   **741.5**
1. Censorship -- United States   2. Comic books, strips, etc.   3. Horror comic books, strips, etc.
ISBN 0810955954; 9780810955950

LC 2008-54346

The Horror! The Horror! examines "the pre-Code horror comics of the 1950s." (Publisher's note) Index.

"Bonus DVD--Confidential File, a rare 25-minute TV show that first aired on October 9, 1955, about the 'evils'of comic books and their effect on juvenile delinquency is included with the book." Publisher's note

Includes bibliographical references (p. 302) and index.

Humbug; [editor, Harvey Kurtzman; art, Jack Davis . . . [et al.]] Fantagraphics 2009 2v il set $60   **741.5**
1. American wit and humor   2. Comic books, strips, etc.
ISBN 978-1-56097-933-3; 1-56097-933-X

"MAD's early years have been justly lauded for their japing assault on postwar American culture, but this . . . two-volume boxed set reflects the history of comedy in the period after staff stars like Kurtzman jumped ship in 1956. . . . [Humbug's] 11 monthly issues published in 1957 and 1958 are all collected here." Publ Wkly

★ Masters of American comics; essay by John Carlin; with contributions by Stanley Crouch . . . [et al.]; edited by John Carlin, Paul Karasik, and Brian Walker. Yale University Press 2005 316p il $45   **741.5**
1. Cartoonists   2. Comic books, strips, etc.
ISBN 0-300-11317-X

LC 2005-19449

"Hundreds of color reproductions allow the ingenuity of the artists' work to speak for itself." New Yorker

Includes bibliographical references

Newave! the underground mini comix of the 1980s. edited by Michael Dowers. Fantagraphics Books 2010 888p il $24.99   **741.5**
1. Cartoonists   2. Comic books, strips, etc.
ISBN 978-1-60699-313-2; 1-60699-313-5

"In his introduction to this fascinating treasure trove of an anthology, Dower describes drawing, folding, and stapling his first minicomic back in 1982. Many others were doing the same and their combined efforts added up to a do-it-yourself scene in which 'obsessed nutballs' drew like crazy and made trips to the copy shops to get their work out there before the Web. In addition to work by greats like Artie Romero, Rick Geary, and Mary Fleener, and 50 or so others, the book serves as the history of a movement. The Newave Manifesto, written by Clay Geerdes in 1983 starts things off, and introductions and interviews preceding each creator's work puts it in context, while the list of artist Web sites at the end gives readers much more to discover." Publ Wkly

Studio space; the world's greatest comic illustrators at work. Image Comics 2008 318p il $49.99; pa $29.99   **741.5**
1. Cartoonists   2. Comic books, strips, etc.   3. Graphic

novels

ISBN 978-1-58240-909-2; 978-1-58240-908-5 pa

Twenty modern comics artists talk about their careers, their work, and their working methods. Each of them is photographed in his studio, and samples of their artwork are included. The artists are: Brian Bolland, Tim Bradstreet, Howard Chaykin, Steve Dillon, Tommy Lee Edwards, Duncan Fegredo, Dave Gibbons, Adam Hughes, Joe Kubert, Jim Lee, Mike Mignola, Frank Miller, Sean Phillips, George Pratt, Alex Ross, Tim Sale, Walt Simonson, Bryan Talbot, Dave Taylor, and Sergio Toppi.

Wednesday comics. DC Comics 2010 200p il $49.99   **741.5**

1. Comic books, strips, etc. 2. Superhero graphic novels

ISBN 978-1-401227470; 1-401227473

LC 2010-282211

"A must-have book for DC comics fans, fans of any comic art, or even those who used to read comics but haven't done so for years. These classic characters still captivate our imaginations – as they have for decades." Christ Sci Monit

★ **An anthology of graphic fiction, cartoons & true stories, vol. 2;** edited by Ivan Brunetti. Yale University Press 2008 400p il $28   **741.5**

1. American wit and humor 2. Comic books, strips, etc.

ISBN 978-0-300-12671-6; 0-300-12671-9

"Brunetti's second collection of his favorite cartoonists' work is even better than the first—more far-ranging, more personal and eccentric. Clearly a tour of one person's singular tastes, it's arranged in a stream-of-consciousness 'oh, and you have to see this one' sort of way: work by 80-odd cartoonists, mostly from the past few decades, but also incorporating some early-1900s comic strips, a 1940s-vintage Fletcher Hanks story and several circa 1950 Harvey Kurtzman pieces as well as a smattering of previously unpublished gems." Publ Wkly

★ **The complete cartoons of the New Yorker;** edited by Robert Mankoff; foreword by David Remnick. Black Dog & Leventhal 2004 655p il $60 **741.5**

1. Caricatures and cartoons 2. Cartoons and caricatures

ISBN 1-579-12322-8

LC 2004-46371

"Issued as part of the New Yorker's eightieth anniversary celebration, this . . . volume collects, in two formats, the cartoons that have appeared in the pages of that magazine over the course of its distinguished publishing history. . . . The book itself gathers 2,500 of the most representative cartoons for display, but two accompanying CDs contain all the cartoons (68,647, to be exact) ever published in the magazine. Arrangement is by chapter, with each covering a decade of the New Yorker's existence. . . . A testament—a tribute— to the great magazine but also an absolutely special way to spend quality time." Booklist

The psychology of superheroes; an unauthorized exploration. edited by Robin S. Rosenberg with Jennifer Canzoneri. BenBella Books, Inc. 2008 259p bibl f il pa $17.95   **741.5**

1. Conduct of life 2. Superheroes (Fictional characters)

-- Psychology

ISBN 1-933771-31-3; 978-1-933771-31-1

LC 2007-41418

This book collects essays about superheroes from several psychological viewpoints, ranging from the positive moral aspects of superheroes to gender stereotypes, prejudice, anti-heroes, the place of Arkham Asylum (the notorious place where DC super villains get locked up), the role of rage in The Incredible Hulk, and more. Editor Rosenberg is a clinical psychologist, and many of the contributors hold degrees in psychology and have faculty positions at various universities.

741.6   Graphic design, illustration, commercial art

Aldridge, Alan

The **man** with kaleidoscope eyes. Harry N. Abrams 2009 239p il $35   **741.6**

1. Commercial art 2. Graphic arts 3. Posters

ISBN 978-0-8109-0596-2; 0-8109-0596-5

LC 2008-939189

"This book lives up to its title, capturing the lyrical and visual pop of Aldridge's signature psychedelic poster art, which made him a favorite artist among the Beatles, the Who, Cream, Elton John, and Incubus. Readers also get a good sense of the 1960s generation that best defines Aldridge, who is still producing art today. An 'illustrated autobiography,' this work excels at presenting the amusing anecdote and scrapbook aesthetic rather than a historical or critical approach, particularly in terms of other artists working in a similar vein." Libr J

Bowring, Joanna

The **art** of romance; Harlequin Mills & Boon cover designs. [by] Joanna Bowring and Margaret O'Brien. Prestel 2008 253p il pa $25   **741.6**

1. Book covers

ISBN 978-3-791341-22-4; 3-791341-22-7

The authors "trace a century of lovelorn fiction through its covers. Predictably, the formula of a beautiful woman looking longingly at a handsome man has not changed all that much (except now there's more photography). Mills & Boon, Britain's leading publisher of romantic fiction, is 101 years old; Harlequin, which owns the company, is 60. Throughout these years loyal romance readers have been treated to some enduring fantasies—for example, the sheik as hero. . . . Although sheiks have changed, the covers continue to tell the story of undying male and female stereotypes." N Y Times Book Rev

Brower, Steven

Breathless homicidal slime mutants; the art of the paperback. foreword by Steven Heller. Universe 2010 304p il pa $24.95   **741.6**

1. Book covers 2. Paperback books

ISBN 978-0-7893-1804-6; 0-7893-1804-0

"Packed with worthy representatives from numerous genres, Breathless Homicidal Slime Mutants is a visual and visceral feast that provides a compelling introduction to the history of pop art in the 20th century." PopMatters

Crumb, R.

R. Crumb: the complete record cover collection. W. W. Norton & Co. 2011 un il $27.95 **741.6**
1. Popular music 2. Sound recordings -- Album covers
ISBN 978-0-393-08278-4

This volume is "filled with the artist's designs for such ephemera as 'Unknown Detroit Bluesmen' or Cliff Edwards's 'I'm a Bear in a Ladies' Boudoir.' Starting in the 1970s, Mr. Crumb produced covers for reissues from labels like Yazoo, Blue Goose and Barrelhouse Records, and his love for the music is evident—a stippled Robert Johnson stares out in stark black and white, Bessie Smith sings 'Put a Little Sugar in My Bowl' and Charlie Patton gets his own mini-graphic novel. . . . (The biggest act here is Big Brother and the Holding Company, with Janis Joplin done over to fit Crumb's zaftig ideal.) In this journeyman work, however, the discipline of playing second fiddle to his favorite musicians keeps the artist's self-loathing in check without taming the ribald humor that is also a hallmark of the blues. Few Crumb projects seem like so much fun—to read about, to look at or to listen along to." Wall Street J

Donahue, Daniel

Ultraviolet; 69 backlight posters from the Aquarian age and beyond. [by] Dan Donahue. Abrams Image 2009 un il pa $22.50 **741.6**
1. Posters
ISBN 978-0-8109-7999-4; 0-8109-7999-3

The book features posters, "all produced between 1967 and 1972 (apparently—a few don't have years attributed to them), and covering a wide range of subjects. . . . Every page evokes nostalgia, perhaps a flashback, and conveys a strong sense of the wild power and energy of the times. Counterculture historian Dan Donahue compiled the book, and contributed a lucid and thorough essay that covers the development of the oddball art form associated most often with the late '60s." PopMatters

Hayes, Clay

Gig posters volume 1; rock show art of the 21st century. Quirk Books 2009 208p il $40 **741.6**
1. Posters 2. Rock music
ISBN 978-1-59474-326-9; 1-59474-326-6
LC 2008-938830

"There is no single style for gig posters — they are punk, grunge, new wave, neo-modern, comic, retro, parodic and satirical. Some are beautiful, others ugly; some derivative, others novel. Most are eye-catching, and some are memorable. Those that are wheat-pasted on hoardings or taped to lampposts are usually removed within days, so GigPosters has been a terrific archive of the good, the bad and the ugly. But digital versions just don't compare with the printed posters, which is why . . . [this book, compiled by the] founder of GigPosters, is such a useful resource. The book contains posters by leaders of the art form (including Emek, Eleanor Grosch, Lil Tuffy and Luke Drozd), who offer brief commentaries about their work." N Y Times Book Rev

Powell, Aubrey

For the love of vinyl; the album art of Hipgnosis. compiled and written by Aubrey Powell and Storm Thorgerson; designed by Peter Curzon and Storm Thorgerson. PictureBox 2008 232p il $45 **741.6**
1. Sound recordings -- Album covers
ISBN 978-0-98156221-6; 0-98156221-3

"Soon, physical album covers will be as extinct as eight-track tapes. Passionate collectors are hoarding classic record sleeves, some of the most memorable of which were created by a British design firm called Hipgnosis. Founded by Aubrey Powell and Storm Thorgerson in 1968, the firm was known for eerie and erotic staged photography that wed magic realism to Surrealism. Hipgnosis employed comedy, mystery and sexuality (sometimes all at once) in its elaborately composed tableaus. Among the bands branded by its images were Led Zeppelin, Pink Floyd, Black Sabbath, Genesis and Wishbone Ash. Covers for these groups and many more are reproduced in [this volume,] . . . which comes with additional commentary on specific albums by various artists and designers, including Peter Blake and Paula Scher." N Y Times Book Rev

Reaves, Wendy Wick

Ballyhoo! posters as portraiture. National Portrait Gallery, Smithsonian; distributed by the University of Washington Press 2008 159p il pa $19.95 **741.6**
1. Celebrities 2. Posters
ISBN 978-0-295-98862-7; 0-295-98862-2
LC 2008-925960

"The book is a compact historical survey of the medium from its earliest days as a proto-Wanted poster to the massive ad campaigns of today's blockbuster films—from John Wilkes Booth to Johnny Depp, literally. Though the book's subtitle stresses the portraiture aspect, many of the posters reproduced are as much about events as people, with wartime propaganda and social statement mixed in with entertainment. Overall, this is a condensed overview of the cultural landscape, with the 70 or so images serving as telling visible index." PopMatters

Includes bibliographical references

Salisbury, Martin

Illustrating children's books; creating pictures for publication. Barron's Educational Series 2004 144p il pa $22.95 **741.6**
1. Illustration of books 2. Illustrators 3. Picture books for children
ISBN 0-76412-717-9

The author "surveys the genre's distinguished history with examples from Caldecott, Greenaway, N. C. Wyeth, Maxfield Parrish, and Howard Pyle. . . . Through sketches and annotations, Salisbury explains how to create fantasy, fairy tale, realism, and nature drawing. Written for advanced students, the book covers storyboards and layouts, contracts, copyrights, and how to present one's work professionally. Highly recommended for all collections." Libr J

Includes bibliographical references

I heart design; remarkable graphic design selected by designers, illustrators, and critics. [edited by]

Steven Heller. Rockport Publishers 2011 214p il
$45   **741.6**
1. Design 2. Graphic arts
ISBN 978-1-59253-682-5; 1-59253-682-4

LC 2010-41709

Heller "asked 80 experts in the field — including designers, typographers and academics — to each pick an influential example of graphic design that resonates beyond the
context in which it was made and place it within the historical framework of the discipline. Heller also asked each to
explain why that particular piece moves their souls. . . . Selections run the gamut — magazines, logos, posters, maps,
illustrations, architecture, album covers, sculptures, film title
sequences, everyday objects and other ephemera. . . . Some
of the short essays get bogged down by their academic tone,
but in general, readers will enjoy clear discussions of the
ability of the best designs to inform, distill and clarify information and, ultimately, to cut through the visual cacophony
that litters our lives." Los Angeles Times
Includes bibliographical references

The poster; 1,000 posters from Toulouse-Lautrec to
Sagmeister. edited by Cees V. de Jong, Alston W.
Purvis, Martijn F. Le Coultre; text by Alston W.
Ourvis; intorduction by Cees W. de Jong. Abrams
2010 567p il pa $35   **741.6**
1. Posters
ISBN 978-0-8109-9588-8; 0-8109-9588-3

LC 2010-14458

"In the history of art, the poster occupies a strange no-
man's-land, a middle ground at the intersection of design
and commerce. However masterful they might be in terms
of composition and execution, the fact remains that posters
are used to sell something else—a product, an idea, a critical
bit of wartime propaganda. Whether it's cookies or patriotism that is on the block, the purpose of a poster seems to rest
uneasily alongside the artistic spirit that impels it. The Poster
is a book that aims not to apologize for this duality, but to
acknowledge it and then move on. In purely artistic terms,
posters can be marvelous works of skill and imagination—
powerfully designed and skillfully executed. . . . Overall, the
collection succeeds admirably." PopMatters
Includes bibliographical references

741.9   Collections of drawings

Berger, John
Bento's sketchbook; 1st American ed. Pantheon
Books 2011 167p ill. (mostly col.)   **741.9**
1. Art appreciation 2. Berger, John --Themes, motives.
3. Drawing -- Psychological aspects 4. Drawing --
Technique 5. Drawing --Philosophy.
ISBN 9780307379955

LC 2011010841

This is "a meditation, in words and images, on the practice of drawing, by the author of Ways of Seeing (1972)."
(Publisher's note)

743   Drawing and drawings by subject

Robins, Clem
The **art** of figure drawing. North Light Bks.
2003 143p il pa $22.99   **743**
1. Figure drawing 2. Figure drawing -- Technique
ISBN 1-58180-204-8

LC 2002-69598

"Robins' guide considers the elements—line, light and
shade, mass, texture, foreshortening, and more—using basic
geometric shapes to achieve accurate renderings of the nude
human figure. His explanation of equilibrium and center of
gravity as applied to figure drawing is particularly helpful to
the novice exploring this essential foundational skill, and the
index makes for user-friendliness." Booklist

Watson, Lucy
Life drawing class. Watson-Guptill Publications
2003 125p il pa $24.95   **743**
1. Figure drawing
ISBN 0-8230-2767-8

LC 2003-102105

"Watson presents each chapter as a class in which she
introduces basic concepts such as measuring angles, plotting positions, perspective light and tone, and so on. Also
included in each section are suggestions for pose lengths,
lists of materials, and clearly explained, illustrated step-by-
step instructions. Throughout Watson includes examples of
her and other professionals' work in a wide range of styles
and media." Booklist

743.4   Drawing human figures

Hart, Christopher
Human anatomy made amazingly easy. Watson-
Guptill 2000 114p il pa $19.95   **743.4**
1. Anatomy, Artistic 2. Artistic anatomy 3. Drawing
-- Technique 4. Figure drawing 5. Human figure in art
ISBN 0-8230-2497-0

LC 00-43514

In this work for the beginning artist "Hart simplifies the
process in an accessible manual that concentrates on line and
forgoes the complexity of color." Libr J

745   Decorative arts

American Folk Art Museum
★ **Encyclopedia** of American folk art; Gerard
C. Wertkin, editor; Lee Kogan, associate editor; in as-
sociation with the American Folk Art Museum. Rout-
ledge 2004 xxxiii, 612p il $125   **745**
1. American folk art 2. Folk art -- United States --
Encyclopedias
ISBN 0-415-92986-5

LC 2003-18051

This volume "covers more than three centuries of folk
artists and provides information about museum collections,
institutions that collect and sponsor folk art, and subjects
related to the various forms of folk art. Entries tend to be de-

tailed, and in some cases, extensive. . . . The work is heavily and usefully cross-referenced. Most entries end with brief bibliographies. Although not heavily illustrated, the work offers a number of interesting color and black-and-white illustrations keyed to specific entries." Choice

Includes bibliographical references

Lauria, Jo

Craft in America; celebrating two centuries of artists and objects. [by] Jo Lauria and Stephen Fenton; prologue by Jimmy Carter. Clarkson Potter 2007 320p il $60 **745**

1. Decorative arts -- United States

ISBN 978-0-307-34647-6; 0-307-34647-1

LC 2006-34839

This collection of photographs and "prose pays homage to two centuries' worth of baskets, textiles, furniture, pottery, and jewelry from U.S. artisans. . . . Famous artisans, from Revolutionary War silversmith Paul Revere to modern-day jewelers Denise and Sam Wallace, and their works are featured, as are the numerous schools and workshops inspiring those creations and today's student crafts movement. . . . A wondrous companion to read over and over and over again." Booklist

Includes bibliographical references

Tracy, Lisa

Objects of our affection. Bantam Books 2010 233p il $25 **745**

1. Auctions 2. Heirlooms 3. Memoirs 4. Personal belongings 5. Souvenirs (Keepsakes)

ISBN 978-0-553-80726-4; 0-553-80726-9

LC 2009-47841

"Following their mother's death, Tracy and her sister were faced with the daunting task of sifting through her belongings. A military family whose history dated back to the American Revolution, the Tracys had acres of heirlooms, from an elegant, satin-bottomed chair that might have once been occupied by George Washington to a pair of dueling pistols purportedly owned by Aaron Burr. But while these items made for tantalizing stories to be told by the fire, what was their worth if one couldn't establish provenance? When the sisters decide to put selected pieces up for auction, they are both sobered—and occasionally surprised—by the prices they fetch. What they didn't account for was the remorse they would feel after the auction was completed. . . . This will definitely attract the Antiques Roadshow crowd." Booklist

745.1   Antiques

Prisant, Carol

Antiques roadshow primer; the introductory guide to antiques and collectibles from the most-watched show on PBS. Workman 1999 366p il hardcover o.p. pa $19.95 **745.1**

1. Antiques 2. Antiques -- United States 3. Collectibles -- United States

ISBN 0-7611-1624-9 pa

LC 99-29960

"The goal of this volume is to educate collectors about antiques and to help them evaluate pieces they find. . . . It

highlights American antiques, focusing primarily on the types of antiques frequently seen on Roadshow." Libr J

Includes bibliographical references

Miller's antiques encyclopedia; general editor, Judith Miller. new ed.; Distributed in the United States and Canada by Sterling Publ. 2008 592p il $50 **745.1**

1. Antiques -- Encyclopedias 2. Reference books

ISBN 978-1-84533-470-3; 1-84533-470-1

"Richly illustrated with high-quality photos, this volume packs significant amounts of information on what is considered antique or collectible, how various items are manufactured, how to evaluate them, what their current value is, and how to care for them. . . . If you aren't already an antiques fiend, this work is likely to make you one!" Libr J

Includes bibliographical references

★ **Miller's** antiques handbook & price guide; [edited by] Judith Miller. Octopus Books 2011 648p il $45 **745.1**

1. Antiques

ISBN 978-1-84533-638-7

This guide includes photographs, prices and brief descriptions of museum-quality antiques sold at auction or by dealers during the past year.

"Although this is a best-of resource, not covering attic knickknacks, it is an alluring look book with inherent educational value." Libr J

745.4   Pure and applied design and decoration

Albrecht, Donald

The **Work** of Charles and Ray Eames; a legacy of invention. essays by Donald Albrecht . . . {et al.} Abrams 1997 205p il hardcover o.p. pa $24.95 **745.4**

1. Architects 2. Design 3. Exhibit designers 4. Furniture designers 5. Industrial designers 6. Interior designers 7. Motion picture producers

ISBN 0-8109-1799-8; 978-0-8109-9232-0 pa; 0-8109-9232-9 pa

LC 97-4086

This overview of the work of two prominent American postwar designers features "pictures of famous furniture, toys, exhibitions, promotional material, informal snapshots, stills from films, comics, advertisements, exhibitions for the federal government, and much more. The work features six major essays, each with extensive notes, by scholars, designers, academics, and architecture/design writers." Choice

Includes bibliographical references

745.5   Handicrafts

Kilby, Janice Eaton

By hand; 25 beautiful objects to make in the American folk art tradition. [by] Janice Eaton Kilby with the assistance of Veronika Alice Gunter. Lark Bks. 2001 144p il hardcover o.p. pa $17.95 **745.5**

1. Decoration and ornament -- United States 2. Folk art -- United States 3. Handicraft 4. Handicraft -- United States

ISBN 1-57990-376-2 pa

LC 00-54974

This is a "survey collection of two dozen projects for familiar items, such as samplers, decoys, and copper weathervanes, that have been designed by professional artists. Each type of craft has a historic introduction and is illustrated by photographs of museum and gallery pieces. . . . A handy all-in-one source for public libraries." Libr J

Includes bibliographical references

Martha Stewart living

★ **Martha** Stewart's encyclopedia of crafts; an A-to-Z guide with detailed instructions and endless inspiration. [by the editors of Martha Stewart Living] Potter Craft 2009 416p il $35   **745.5**

1. Handicraft

ISBN 978-0-307-45057-9

LC 2008-33415

"In alphabetical order, from albums to wreaths, with intermediate stops at beading, jewelry making, mosaics, quilling, soap making, and more, Stewart presents easily absorbed directions for 200 projects; in each project profile, sumptuous illustrations are partnered with rich, full, stimulating discussion of materials, techniques, and tips. . . . Of primary importance to all crafts collections." Booklist

Tapper, Joan

Craft activism; people, ideas, and projects from the new community of handmade and how you can join in. photography by Gale Zucker; foreword by Faythe Levine. Potter Craft 2011 159p il pa $22.99   **745.5**

1. Handicraft 2. Social movements

ISBN 978-0-307-58662-9; 0-307-58662-6

LC 2011003675

The author, "inspired by a yarn graffiti installation in Washington state, explores the motivations of creative people who use their skills to make public statements about everything from the environment to the role of traditional 'women's work' in contemporary society. . . . The profiles and the projects that follow them are diverse, and readers are bound to find inspiration in this nicely curated volume." Libr J

Includes bibliographical references

Taylor, Terry

Altered art; techniques for creating altered books, boxes, cards & more. Lark Books 2004 144p il $19.95   **745.5**

1. Handicraft

ISBN 1-57990-550-1

LC 2004-5313

Taylor "begins with a brief history of altered art (Joseph Cornell was an early practitioner), discusses copyright issues with regard to borrowed images, then moves straight into techniques, tools, and a . . . gallery of a variety of artists' works. The author includes a few projects with step-by-step

instructions. . . . [This book] is without a doubt one of the finest craft books available." SLJ

Wasinger, Susan

Eco-craft; recycle, recraft, restyle. Lark Books 2009 128p il $24.95   **745.5**

1. Handicraft 2. Interior design 3. Salvage

ISBN 978-1-60059-343-7

LC 2008-31192

The author, a graphic designer, "promotes her own brand of sustainability, starting with the materials (recycled paper with agri-based ink) used to fashion her 30-item craft collection. Everything here is fresh in terms of style, dynamic, and fairly easy to complete, thanks to the step-by-step photographs, well-labeled directions, and notes to ensure a quality finished product." Booklist

Pretty little pincushions; [Susan Brill, ed.] Lark Books 2007 128p il $17.95   **745.5**

1. Pincushions

ISBN 978-1-6005-9144-0; 1-6005-9144-2

LC 2007-18423

"Several crafters submitted designs [for pincushions], which range from a felt beehive complete with miniscule straight-pin bees to tiny cushions to wear on a finger as the needle flies. . . . Front matter provides information on materials, techniques, and project embellishments, including diagrams of several embroidery stitches. . . . Functional, fun, and oh-so-easy, these clever pin holders put the ubiquitous red strawberry in the sewing basket to shame." Booklist

The complete book of home crafts; projects for adventurous beginners. edited by Carine Tracanelli. Skyhorse 2011 352p il $24.95   **745.5**

1. Decoration and ornament 2. Handicraft

ISBN 978-1-61608-322-9

"This extensive collection of projects focuses mainly on home decor, with a brief foray into decorative beadwork. The projects are beginner friendly, and individual steps are illustrated with color photographs, making it easy to follow along. Each section contains a brief introduction, familiarizing crafters with the tools and techniques involved in each type of project. The broad coverage includes picture framing, decorative painting on a variety of different surfaces, decoupage, and tile work." Libr J

745.54   Papers

Helfand, Jessica

Scrapbooks: an American history; A Winterhouse edition; Yale University Press 2008 244p il $45   **745.54**

1. Biography as a literary form 2. Paper crafts 3. Scrapbooks

ISBN 978-0-300-12635-8; 0-300-12635-2

The author "offers both an overview of the history of the creation of scrapbooks and a visual feast for readers via the integration of texts, images, and memorabilia of all types. . . . Helfand has made a brilliant selection of unusual examples by visiting numerous archives, and she weaves a narrative based on examples that she found. . . .The book is sumptuous, a superb marriage in fine design, paper, and print." Choice

Melichson, Henya

The **art** of paper cutting. Quarry Books 2009 128p il pa $19.99   **745.54**
    1. Paper crafts
    ISBN 978-1-59253-525-5
    "Decorative paper cutting using a single sheet of paper produces lacy silhouettes. Melichson's very elaborate designs draw on religious and ethnic motifs from Mediterranean countries and take some practice to draw out and execute. Templates that may be photocopied and traced are provided for less-intricate projects." Libr J

Reeder, Dan

Papier-mache monsters; turn trinkets and trash into magnificent monstrosities. photographs by Julie, Jeff and Dan Reeder. Gibbs Smith 2009 144p il pa $16.99   **745.54**
    1. Monsters in art 2. Paper crafts
    ISBN 978-1-4236-0555-3; 1-4236-0555-1
                       LC 2009-3827
    "For lovers of the truly grotesque, Reeder . . . provides detailed photo instructions for large figures constructed of clothes hangers, newspaper, and glue. Cloth skin, teeth, and slathered-on paint finish them off. The toothy dragons are particularly effective." Libr J

745.55   Shells

Marshall, Marlene Hurley

Shell chic; the ultimate guide to decorating your home with seashells. photographs by Sabine Vollmer von Falken. Storey Bks. 2002 152p il $35   **745.55**
    1. Handicraft 2. Shellcraft 3. Shells
    ISBN 1-58017-440-X
                       LC 2002-1140
    This "contains step-by-step projects for traditional items of shell art such as flower arrangements and shell-encrusted boxes, all interspersed with a colorful running narrative describing decorative uses of shells by contemporary designers." Libr J

745.58   Beads, found and other objects

Benson, Ann

Beading for the first time. Sterling 2000 112p il $19.95   **745.58**
    1. Beadwork
    ISBN 0-8069-6098-1
                       LC 00-48265
    "Step-by-step instructions for jewelry and accessories are accompanied by large color photographs and line drawings. There are sections on materials and equipment with a gallery of the work of several bead artists." Libr J

Fitzgerald, Diane

Diane Fitzgerald's shaped beadwork; dimensional jewelry with peyote stitch. Sterling Pub. Co. 2009 120p il $24.95   **745.58**
    1. Beads 2. Beadwork
    ISBN 978-1-60059-277-5
                    LC 2008-25703
    "Although the majority of the book is devoted to the actual fashioning of . . . [different types of] bead shapes, Fitzgerald adds her personal inspiration by way of a dozen-plus items to make, including a Celtic trefoil, Berber earrings, and a trillium necklace. A true breakthrough in the art of beadwork." Booklist
    Includes bibliographical references

Wells, Carol Wilcox

The **art** & elegance of beadweaving; new jewelry designs with classic stitches. Lark Bks. 2002 160p il hardcover o.p. pa $14.95   **745.58**
    1. Beadwork 2. Jewelry 3. Jewelry -- Design
    ISBN 1-57990-200-6; 1-57990-533-1 pa
                    LC 2001-38958
    Includes instructions for craft projects using beads and five types of weaving stitches.
    What the author "conjures up in more than 30 bracelets, earrings, and necklaces is nothing short of breathtaking." Booklist

745.59   Making specific objects

Heynen, Jennifer

Ceramic bead jewelry; 30 fired & inspired projects. Lark Books 2008 128p il $24.95   **745.59**
    1. Beadwork 2. Ceramics 3. Jewelry
    ISBN 978-1-60059-142-6
                    LC 2007-46536
    "About half of . . . [this] book demonstrates the fundamentals: tools and materials and the making, decorating, and firing (bisque as well as glaze) of beads, along with techniques, like raku, metal clay, and luster, among others. Then on to the 30 projects, ranging from a boyfriend black-and-white bead on a cord necklace to an elaborate autumn-bounty (with acorns and leaves) necklace, with rings, brooches, and bracelets well represented in the projects. Each design includes the requisite list, color photographs, and instructions." Booklist

Michaels, Chris Franchetti

Teach yourself visually jewelry making & beading. Wiley Publishing 2007 290p il pa $24.99   **745.59**
    1. Beads 2. Beadwork 3. Jewelry
    ISBN 978-0-470-10150-6; 0-470-10150-4
    This book explains how "to craft designs that are chic but inexpensive. With hundreds of detailed photos, this book covers tools and supplies, bead stringing and weaving, wire wrapping, and more." Publisher's note

Oppenheimer, Betty

Candlemaker's companion; a complete guide to rolling, pouring, dipping, and decorating your own candles. Completely rev and updated; Storey Bks. 2001 199p il pa $18.95   **745.59**
1. Candles
ISBN 1-58017-366-7
LC 00-53802
This offers a brief history of candles followed by information about wicks, waxes and additives, color and scent, and equipment. Step-by-step instructions on candlemaking techniques and decoration, and a list of suppliers.

Pickering Rothamel, Susan

Encyclopedia of greeting card tools and techniques. Lark Books 2008 304p il $24.95   **745.59**
1. Greeting cards 2. Handicraft
ISBN 978-1-6005-9029-0; 1-6005-9029-2
LC 2007-50641
Rothamel offers "a one-stop annotated and illustrated dictionary of greeting card information, whether the subject is mechanics (accordion fold, wrinkling); how-to's (past paper, thermal embossing); arcane bytes (deltiology is the art of collecting postcards); or relevant tips (the use and safety of craft knives). . . . The author provides a good overview of the craft along with profiles of 14 practitioners, a historical time line, and advice for the wannabe professional (such as card submission and composition guidelines)." Booklist

Wire, CeCe

Creative metal clay jewelry; techniques, projects, inspiration. Lark Bks. 2003 144p il hardcover o.p. pa $14.95   **745.59**
1. Jewelry 2. Precious metal clay
ISBN 1-57990-301-0; 1-60059-182-5 pa
LC 2002-34398
Metal clay "consists of precious metal particles combined with an organic binder and water to make a substance that looks and feels like potters clay. It is worked, dried, and fired like clay. Firing burns off the organic material leaving a fused piece of pure gold or silver. The piece can then be finished like any other metal. Wire . . . gives detailed instructions for using it as a jewelry medium, with step-by-step projects for earrings, bracelets, and other pieces. Contemporary in style, these items tend to resemble cast pieces. This book on an interesting new craft belongs in every crafts collection." Libr J

745.593   Useful objects

Ure, Susan

Scrapbooking your vacations; 200 page designs. Sterling Pub 2004 127p il $24.95   **745.593**
1. Photograph albums 2. Scrapbooks
ISBN 1-402-70819-X
LC 2003-23619
This is a "collection of more than 200 page plans, which brings together designs inspired by choice vacation spots across the globe. Crafters will find great-looking, full-color pages motivated by trips to Asia, Africa, Europe, and more

to copy or adapt as they choose. For each sample scrapbook page, Ure provides a list of the materials used to create it and commentary about the design itself, often including hints that can be applied to other scrapbook projects." Booklist

745.594   Decorative objects

Beaman, Sarah

Ultimate cardmaking; a collection of over 100 techniques and 50 inspirational projects. Collins & Brown; Distributed in the U.S. by Sterling Pub. 2008 192p il $24.95   **745.594**
1. Greeting cards 2. Paper crafts
ISBN 978-1-84340-438-5; 1-84340-438-9
"What distinguishes this from other books on making cards? A clean contemporary-design perspective, with an emphasis on the 'less is more' philosophy; great attention to crafter needs; and quite a few 'fast cards' for those with limited time. Truly timeless and creative ways to invite, thank, and celebrate." Booklist

Deeb, Margie

The **beader's** color palette; 20 creative projects, 220 inspired combinations for beaded and gemstone jewelry. Watson-Guptill 2008 192p il pa $24.95   **745.594**
1. Beadwork 2. Color 3. Jewelry
ISBN 978-0-8230-0474-4; 0-8230-0474-0
LC 2007-936519
The author "provides meticulously worked-out color palettes to capture the essence of period artworks or natural objects. Each palette indicates the proportion of dominant and secondary hues so that the finished piece will reflect the colors of the original period artwork or natural object." Libr J
Includes bibliographical references

Geary, Theresa Flores

The **illustrated** bead bible; terms, tips & techniques. photographs by Debra Whalen. Sterling Pub. 2008 406p il $29.95   **745.594**
1. Beads 2. Beadwork
ISBN 978-1-4027-2353-7; 1-4027-2353-9
LC 2007-026120
"This may be the ultimate bead reference book. The majority of the text is made up of an illustrated alphabetical encyclopedia of beads, broadly defined, and beading terms. Additional chapters include tips and techniques, charts illustrating bead characteristics, and stitch diagrams." Libr J
Includes glossary and bibliographical references

Mann, Elise

★ The **bead** directory; the complete guide to choosing and using more than 600 beautiful beads. Interweave Press 2006 256p il $24.95   **745.594**
1. Beads 2. Beadwork
ISBN 1-59668-002-4; 978-1-59668-002-9
LC 2005-24503
This is a "handbook of currently available beads made of metal, wood, and plastic as well as of the more usual glass,

stone, and clay. Entries for each bead include name, description, suggested use, relative cost, and country of origin and are accompanied by color photos. . . . This resource will prove crucial for public library patrons." Libr J

745.6 Calligraphy, heraldic design, illumination

Gauthier, Jeaneen
  Calligraphy 101; a workshop in a book. Creative Pub. International 2010 240p il $24.99 **745.6**
  1. Calligraphy
  ISBN 978-1-58923-503-8; 1-58923-503-7
                                          LC 2010-16769
  "After introducing a few simple tools and supplies, . . . [the author] teaches the basic strokes and alphabets. Then she presents a full array of tools, methods, and styles with which to create professional-looking cards, invitations, and artists' books. . . . This is a solid manual for beginners." Libr J

Kespersaks, Veiko
  Calligraphy in 24 hours. Barron's 2011 160p il pa $21.99   **745.6**
  1. Calligraphy
  ISBN 978-0-7641-4506-3
  This book "starts with basic instruction and progresses through sessions that challenge readers with projects of increasing difficulty. An opening lesson introduces students to the standard calligraphy tools—pens, inks, and papers. Tutorials that follow go on to teach the basic strokes for constructing 15 different alphabets, letter-by-letter. Timed exercises are presented to help learners build speed and confidence. . . . They will learn how to create professionally designed greeting cards, wall hangings, place settings, wedding invitations, and more." Publisher's note

Shepherd, Margaret
  Learn calligraphy; the complete book of lettering and design. Broadway Bks. 2001 167p il pa $16.95   **745.6**
  1. Calligraphy
  ISBN 0-7679-0732-9
                                          LC 00-53016
  This guide presents historical background, and advice on materials, technique, and workspace organization. Also included are recommended usages for the various alphabets. Step-by-step illustrations are provided

745.7 Decorative coloring

Fresh & fabulous painted furniture. Sterling 2000 128p il hardcover o.p. pa $14.95   **745.7**
  1. Furniture 2. Furniture painting 3. Stencil work
  ISBN 0-8069-7797-3 pa
                                          LC 99-55370
  This describes 25 projects for painting furniture employing techniques such as stenciling, stamping, block-printing, and découpaging.

745.92 Floral arts

Hillier, Malcolm
  Flowers. Dorling Kindersley 2000 516p il $40 **745.92**
  1. Flower arrangement 2. Flowers
  ISBN 0-7894-5954-X
                                          LC 00-29485
  This book "features 150 floral display ideas using fresh and dried flowers. . . . {The author explains} elements of design (color, shape, and texture) and how to create displays for use in the home, for Thanksgiving and Christmas, at weddings, and in churches." Booklist

Packer, Jane
  Jane Packer at home with flowers; beautifully simple arrangements for every room in the house. photography by Catherine Gratwicke. Ryland Peters & Small 2011 144p il $29.95   **745.92**
  1. Flower arrangement 2. Interior design
  ISBN 978-1-84975-119-3; 1-84975-119-6
                                          LC 2010-51126
  Packer "shares her flower design philosophy with photos of floral arrangements throughout the home. The over 100 color photographs are accompanied by Packer's recommendations on color, container, arrangement, and flowers, in contrast to her other recent book, Color, which shows fanciful arrangements grouped by color. A list of resources is given for both UK and U.S. firms as well as instructions on the proper care of cut flowers. Recommended to those looking for contemporary ideas for decorating with flowers, which add natural, seasonal touches to interiors." Libr J

746 Textile arts

Searle, Teresa
  Felt jewelry; 25 pieces to make using a variety of simple felting techniques. St. Martin's Griffin 2008 128p il pa $21.95   **746**
  1. Fabrics 2. Handicraft 3. Jewelry
  ISBN 978-0-312-38356-5; 0-312-38356-8
                                          LC 2008-40066
  "The book is filled with detailed, eye-catching color photographs that will aid beginners and inspire the more accomplished felters." SLJ

Wasinger, Susan
  The **feisty** stitcher; sewing projects with attitude. Lark Books 2009 128p il pa $19.95   **746**
  1. Fabrics 2. Sewing
  ISBN 978-1-60059-465-6
                                          LC 2009-15553
  "In the first chapter, . . . [the author] covers how to finish up with sturdy French seams; the use of grommets, snaps, and closures; how to sew with fat thread and reinforce with X's; and sewing machines that work (that is, those that can sew straight, zigzag, and overcast stitches). Every one of her 30 projects follows a similar offbeat tone—and design. With every item, she features a guide to 'ease level,' time, cost, and unexpected materials—as well as a snappy description for at least one . . . with an immediate segue into a step-by-step narrative and color photographs. Pick among oilcloth

bike bags; an eco-version of Uggs' boots; a see-through punctured lampshade; and a one-day planner fashioned from an inner tube." Booklist

White, Christine

Uniquely felt; dozens of techniques from fulling and shaping to nuno and cobweb: includes 46 creative projects. Storey Pub. 2007 311p il pa $24.95 **746**

1. Fabrics 2. Handicraft

ISBN 978-1-58017-673-6; 1-58017-673-9

LC 2007-23531

The author covers "basic feltmaking techniques as well as needle, nuno, cobweb, 3-D, and carved techniques and featuring 46 projects. . . . What makes this a title of lasting value for libraries is the depth of solid information it offers on the craft and its history, on various artists, and on related topics like setting up a feltmaking studio, teaching felt making, and leading community feltmaking projects." Libr J

Includes bibliographical references

746.1   Products and processes

Dixon, Anne

The **handweaver's** pattern directory; over 600 weaves for 4-shaft looms. Interweave Press 2007 254p il $34.95 **746.1**

1. Weaving

ISBN 978-1-59668-040-1

LC 2007-26351

This "guide to more than 600 different weaving patterns for four-shaft looms divides weaves into basic groups by structure (e.g., basic threadings, block drafts). Each weave is accompanied by warp threading and weaving drafts (the latter, explained in a handy extended flap), a tieup grid, closeup photos of the weave, and color photos of the actual woven fabric. Beginning weavers will appreciate the sections on weaving basics and finishing techniques as well as the glossary of common weaving terms." Libr J

Patrick, Jane

The **weaver's** idea book; creative cloth on a rigid-heddle loom. Interweave Press 2010 239p il $29.95 **746.1**

1. Weaving

ISBN 978-1-59668-175-0

LC 2009-39518

"Patrick's collection of patterns and projects explores the possibilities of weaving on a rigid heddle loom. From basic plain weaves to finger-controlled and pick-up techniques, Patrick guides weavers of all skill levels. . . . This is an excellent addition to any weaving collection." Libr J

Includes bibliographical references

746.2   Laces and related fabrics

Carey, Jacqui

Japanese braiding; the art of Kumihimo. Search Press 2009 96p il pa $21.95 **746.2**

1. Weaving

ISBN 978-1-84448-426-3

"Kumihimo braiding is a traditional craft worked with threads on bobbins strung over a marudai, a donut-shaped disk on four legs. Threads are laid in sequence to form the braid pattern. . . . [This guide is] filled with photos and diagrams showing the sequences for each project." Libr J

746.3   Pictures, hangings, tapestries

Brosens, Koenraad

European tapestries in the Art Institute of Chicago; [by] Koenraad Brosens; with contributions by Pascal-François Bertrand [et al.]; Christa C. Mayer Thurman, general editor. Yale University Press 2008 407p il $75 **746.3**

1. Tapestry 2. Tapestry -- Europe

ISBN 978-0-300-11960-2; 0-300-11960-7

LC 2008-930401

Brosens, "along with a distinguished group of art historians and curators, argues for the historical and artistic importance of tapestry as an art form. Designed to accompany the Art Institute of Chicago's exhibition The Divine Art: Four Centuries of European Tapestries, this is a genuinely unique text. Its pioneering scholarship is both precise in its claims and accessibly written for a wide audience. After introductory essays, the tapestries are arranged by region and then subdivided by chronology. These works range from medieval through baroque art styles. The color illustrations and the essays that analyze each tapestry are exquisite." Libr J

Includes bibliographical references

746.4   Needlework and handwork

Daniel, Nancy Brenan

The **art** of the handmade quilt. Sterling 2008 176p il $24.95 **746.4**

1. Quilting

ISBN 978-1-40273-351-2; 1-40273-351-8

LC 2008-299642

Daniel "focuses on hand quilting in this book of vintage and vintage-inspired quilt patterns. Ranging from a classic nine-patch to a whimsical windblown daisy design, there are plenty of options for beginning and advanced quilters. Daniel includes a difficulty rating for each pattern, as well as directions to guide novice quilters through every step of their project. Colorful piecing diagrams, combined with step-by-step instructions, make construction foolproof, and templates are provided for all pieces and quilting patterns." Libr J

Gordon, Maggi McCormick

The **needlecraft** book; [by] Maggi Gordon, Sally Harding, Ellie Vance. DK 2010 400p il $40 **746.4**
1. Crocheting 2. Needlework 3. Quilting
ISBN 978-0-7566-6170-0

This "compilation of five needlework specialties—knitting, crocheting, embroidery, needlepoint, and quilting/appliqué/patchwork—surveys tools and materials, basic skills, patterns (and how to read/use them), and specifics for each specialty. All projects are brilliantly photographed in color, with good explanations given in just a few choice words, especially when picturing yarns and equipment." Booklist

Includes bibliographical references

746.43   Knitting, crocheting, tatting

Budd, Ann

★ The **knitter's** handy book of patterns; basic designs in multiple sizes and gauges. Interweave Press 2002 112p pa $24.95 **746.43**
1. Knitting 2. Knitting -- Patterns
ISBN 1-931499-04-7

LC 2001-59208

The patterns in this book "allow the knitter to create garments in any size from toddler to extra-large adult in any weight of yarn, from fingering to bulky. The knitter has only to knit a generous swatch with yarn and needles of her/his choice and plug the resulting gauge information into the charted instructions and schematics provided. Highly recommended for all knitting collections." Libr J

Buss, Katharina

Big book of knitting. Sterling 1999 239p il hardcover o.p. pa $19.95 **746.43**
1. Knitting
ISBN 0-8069-6317-4 pa

LC 99-20386

This is an "illustrated knitting reference particularly strong in its coverage of both basic techniques like increasing and decreasing and more advanced techniques like knitting cables without a cable needle, working with charts, and placing sleeve increases in openwork patterns." Libr J

Crowfoot, Jane

Ultimate crochet bible; a complete reference with step-by-step techniques. Collins & Brown; Distributed in the U.S. and Canada by Sterling Pub. 2010 304p il $29.95 **746.43**
1. Crocheting
ISBN 978-1-84340-563-4

This guide begins "with an overview of the craft's origins and its requirements and necessities (for instance, hooks, needles, and knowledge of how to read a chart). Each chapter truly exposes the how-to details, not only in words but also, most important, in oversize illustrations. Included are a well-explained section of basics (for instance, how to differentiate between front and reverse sides and how to work crochet for left-handed crafters) and specific stitch categories: texture and lace, thread, Tunisian entrelac,

color, beads and sequins, edgings, and professional finishing techniques." Booklist

Eckman, Edie

The **crochet** answer book. Storey Pub. 2005 320p il pa $12.95 **746.43**
1. Crocheting
ISBN 1-58017-598-8

LC 2005-16484

This book features "chapters on topics ranging from equipment needs to resources for more information. . . . Appended are standard crochet abbreviations, common crochet terms and phrases, standard body measurements and sizing, suggested sizes for accessories and household items, and yarn care symbols." Booklist

Includes bibliographical references

Epstein, Nicky

Crocheting on the edge; ribs & bobbles, ruffles, flora, fringes, points & scallops: the essential collection of more than 200 decorative borders. Nicky Epstein Books 2008 199p il $29.95 **746.43**
1. Crocheting
ISBN 978-1-9330-2735-7; 1-9330-2735-5

LC 2007-937748

"Starting out with crocheted edges on knitting, Epstein quickly moves on to decorative edgings for crocheted pieces. . . . The edgings are grouped by stitch family . . . The book concludes with a variety of patterns utilizing the decorative edgings presented in the book. An essential addition to any library's collection." Libr J

Hubert, Margaret

The **complete** photo guide to crochet. Creative Pub. International 2010 272p il pa $24.99 **746.43**
1. Crocheting
ISBN 978-1-58923-472-7

LC 2009-31798

"Reference for crocheters; includes instructions and diagrams for 200 stitch patterns, basic information about how to crochet, plus 20 patterns." Publisher's note

Kagan, Sasha

Sasha Kagan's country inspiration; knitwear for all seasons. photographs by Jack Deutsch. Taunton Press 2000 170p il $27.95 **746.43**
1. Knitting 2. Sweaters
ISBN 1-56158-338-3

LC 99-52956

This book features 45 knitting patterns. "Most of the patterns are for sweaters, but there are also throws, caps, and coats. Kagan takes her inspiration from the Welsh countryside where she lives. The knitwear is grouped by topics such as roses, autumn leaves, meadow flowers, and forest fruits." Booklist

Keim, Cecily

Teach yourself visually crochet; [by] Cecily Keim and Kim P. Werker. 2nd ed.; Wiley Publishing, Inc. 2011 333p il pa $24.99   **746.43**

    1. Crocheting

    ISBN 978-0-470-87997-9

                     LC 2010-941213

This guide to crocheting contains techniques, color photos, step-by-step instructions and tips for additional guidance.

Kimmelstiel, Laurie

Exquisite little knits; hand-knitting with luxurious specialty yarns. [by] Laurie Kimmelstiel, Iris Schreier. 1st ed; Lark Books 2004 144p il $19.95   **746.43**

    1. Knitting

    ISBN 1-579-90536-6

                     LC 2004-5314

"The book is divided by both project and type of yarn. Much information is given about each yarn and how it knits up, and several projects are offered for each. There is nothing very complicated among the projects: lots of scarves, shawls, and caps. But by using yarns as varied as lattice, mohair, eyelash, and fur, everything ends up looking great." Booklist

Knight, Erika

Men's knits; 20 new classics. Potter Craft 2009 144p il pa $21.99   **746.43**

    1. Knitting 2. Men's clothing

    ISBN 978-0-307-46049-3

"The first chapter delves into more know-how than how-to's; its contents cover types of yarn and garment care, not casting on and off or the stitches of knitting and purling. The rest of . . . [this] book showcases 25 men and a dog (Rufus) wearing 20 sharp, well-designed knits that will look good no matter the man's age or size. In fact, all patterns—in addition to materials, gauge, and directions—feature full-color finished photographs of the garment worn by different male models. . . . [The garments covered include] an ombre-striped full zip cardigan; a bulked-up collegiate cable sweater; and vests in plain style, argyle, or checkered patterns. Recommended yarns listed." Booklist

Merrick, Kathy

Crochet in color; techniques and designs for playing with color. Interweave Press 2009 127p il pa $22.95   **746.43**

    1. Color 2. Crocheting

    ISBN 978-1-59668-112-5

                     LC 2009-8961

The author "has created a book that veterans and novice stitchers will keep at their immediate beck and call, boasting exquisite patterns, subtle colors, precise directions (in symbols and in words), color photographs that encourage trial and experimentation and tips, and techniques that result in professional garments." Booklist

    Includes bibliographical references

Parkes, Clara

The **knitter's** book of socks; the yarn lover's ultimate guide to creating socks that fit well, feel great, and last a lifetime. Potter Craft 2011 207p il $30   **746.43**

    1. Knitting 2. Socks

    ISBN 978-0-307-58680-3

                     LC 2011002682

"Parkes educates knitters on the ins and outs of fiber and makes minutiae interesting. Here, she describes the qualities that make yarn suitable for sock knitting, explores the different types of fibers that can be used in sock yarn, and analyzes stitches and stitch patterns commonly used in sock knitting. There's also a beautifully curated selection of sock patterns, including new designs by some of the biggest names in the field. Though the instructions are clear, the majority of the patterns are best suited for those with sock-knitting experience. An essential addition." Libr J

Righetti, Maggie

Crocheting in plain English; 2nd ed.; Thomas Dunne Books 2008 268p il pa $16.95   **746.43**

    1. Crocheting

    ISBN 978-0-312-35354-4; 0-312-35354-5

                     LC 2008-43913

This is "one of the most comprehensive and accessible guides to crochet available. This isn't a quick-start guide: Righetti provides an overview of the necessary supplies, a brief history of crochet, and information about gauge before guiding beginners through their first stitch, an ideal approach for readers who wish to understand crochet in-depth." Libr J

    Includes bibliographical references

Silverman, Sharon Hernes

    ★ **Basic** crocheting; all the skills and tools you need to get started. Annie Modesitt, consultant; photographs by Alan Wycheck; illustrations by Marjorie Leggitt. Stackpole Books 2006 112p il pa $19.95   **746.43**

    1. Crocheting

    ISBN 978-0-8117-3316-8; 0-8117-3316-5

                     LC 2005-37862

This book begins with a look at the yarn, hooks, and other tools one needs to get started, and then moves on to cover the fundamental techniques and stitches. Instuctions are provided for creating a wide variety of home accessories and wearables. Skill workshops accompany each project. Instructions for every step of each project are supplemented with photographs and illustrations.

Square, Vicki

    ★ The **knitter's** companion; Expanded and updated, deluxe ed.; Interweave 2010 138p il $24.95   **746.43**

    1. Knitting

    ISBN 978-1-59668-314-3

This is "an excellent ready reference for a variety of knitting techniques, including cast-ons, bind-offs, finishing, and other basics. . . . The demonstrations on the DVDs show knitters exactly what they should be doing. Every knitting collection needs a reference; this one is affordable and accessible." Libr J

Stafford, Jennifer

Domiknitrix; whip your knitting into shape. North Light Books 2007 256p il pa $19.99 **746.43**

1. Knitting

ISBN 978-1-58180-853-7

LC 2006-20117

"Mastering knitting skills requires discipline, attitude, and wit to transform a ho-hum stitcher into a badass knitter—a domiknitrix. Stafford uses the dominatrix language well and with humor in this entertaining, beautifully designed, and instructive book." Booklist

Includes bibliographical references

Stoller, Debbie

★ **Stitch** 'n bitch; the knitter's handbook. illustrations by Adrienne Yan; fashion photography by John Dolan. Workman 2003 248p il hardcover o.p. pa $13.95 **746.43**

1. Knitting

ISBN 0-7611-3258-9; 0-7611-2818-2 pa

LC 2003-53543

"An introduction chronicles the history of knitting from the female perspective, while subsequent chapters cover topics such as yarn type, instruments, stitches, and patterns. Perhaps the most exciting bit is Stoller's 'knit as you learn' technique: with every new stitch, she presents a new pattern, thereby allowing knitters to build on their knowledge. . . . Essential for all crafts collections and perfect for a display." Libr J

Tracy, Gloria

Crochet your way; a learn to crochet afghan, over 40 projects for home and family, easy-to-understand text and symbols, special instructions for left-handers. [by] Gloria Tracy and Susan Levin. Taunton Press 2000 218p il pa $22.95 **746.43**

1. Crocheting

ISBN 1-56158-310-3

LC 99-58398

An explanation of basics "including simple and complex stitches, alternative chain techniques, color tips, and felting instructions." Booklist

Turner, Pauline

★ **How** to crochet; the definitive crochet course, complete with step-by-step techniques, stitch libraries, and projects for your home and family. Collins & Brown 2001 160p il $29.95 **746.43**

1. Crocheting

ISBN 1-85585-827-4

"This is a complete crochet course presented as a series of workshops that cover not only standard crochet but also those varieties of crochet that do not employ a standard crochet hook, such as Tunisian, broomstick, and hairpin crochet. Each workshop features an illustrative project, full-color illustrations of techniques, and step-by-step instructions. . . . Public libraries will want to add this title to their short list of essential crochet books." Libr J

Turner, Sharon

Teach yourself visually knitting; 2nd ed.; Wiley Pub. 2010 339p il pa $22.99 **746.43**

1. Knitting

ISBN 978-0-470-52832-7; 0-470-52832-X

LC 2009-941352

This guide to knitting contains techniques, color photos, step-by-step instructions and tips for additional guidance.

Crochet edgings & trims; 150 stitches. edited by Kate Haxell. Interweave 2009 143p il pa $19.95 **746.43**

1. Crocheting

ISBN 978-1-59668-172-9

This "is a collection of 150 crochet edgings, all geared to turn a plain Jane garment or blanket into a designer-worthy item or gift. The basics are admirably covered, with special attention paid to black-and-white illustrations of stitch how-to's. The stitches follow, each with a close-up color photograph of the finished products along with prose direction and stitch diagrams. . . . A welcome, detail-laden supplement to long-treasured references." Booklist

KnitLit: sweaters and their stories and other writing about knitting; Linda Roghaar & Molly Wolf, editors. Three Rivers Press (NY) 2002 270p pa $13 **746.43**

1. Knitters (Persons) -- Miscellanea 2. Knitting 3. Knitting -- Miscellanea 4. Sweaters

ISBN 0-609-80824-9

LC 2002-5962

This book "is really about what it means to create something. Sometimes, as many knitters know, there is only the dream of what could be, as unused yarn gathers dust. But that's what's so nice about this book of knitters' personal remembrances. . . . People who love to knit will love this book." Booklist

Includes bibliographical references

Vogue knitting stitchionary: cables; the ultimate stitch dictionary. from the editors of Vogue knitting magazine. Sixth & Spring Books 2006 200p il $29.95 **746.43**

1. Knitting

ISBN 978-1-931543-89-7; 1-931543-89-5

This book presents a "collection of cable stitches. . . . The options range from simple to expert level . . . and all the stitches . . . are organized thematically and shown in large, closeup images." Publisher's note

746.44 Embroidery

Kendrick, Helen Winthrope

Stitch-opedia; the only embroidery reference you'll ever need. St. Martin's Griffin 2010 224p il $24.99 **746.44**

1. Embroidery

ISBN 978-0-312-61159-0; 0-312-61159-5

"Following a comprehensive introduction to the basics of embellishing with needle and thread, Kendrick devotes one section to each individual technique, including crewel, Hardanger, stump work, and canvas work. Thirty projects, both practical and decorative, provide practice in each technique, and a full-color stitch dictionary allows novices to compare their work with the examples." Libr J

Prain, Leanne

Hoopla; the art of unexpected embroidery. photography by Jeff Christenson. Arsenal Pulp Press 2011 400p il pa $29.95 **746.44**

1. Embroidery
ISBN 978-1-55152-406-1

"In this combination overview of embroidery and exploration of its current trends, Prain takes a traditional approach, beginning with a cursory look at the craft's history and highlighting practicalities, such as tools and equipment, finishing techniques, and stitching resources. But it is between these lines that the author's true innovation and fun starts: specifically, with interviews with 28 working embroiderers and the same number of unusual projects to complete. . . . Projects don't disappoint, with directions as clear as the designs are funky: handkerchiefs emblazoned with microbes, a modern cuckoo clock stitched on Aida cloth, and knuckle-tattoo church gloves." Booklist
Includes bibliographical references

Reader's Digest Association

The **big** book of cross-stitch designs; over 900 simple-to-stitch decorative motifs. Reader's Digest Association 2007 320p il $29.95 **746.44**

1. Cross-stitch 2. Needlework -- Patterns
ISBN 0-7621-0673-5; 978-0-7621-0673-8

LC 2006-044634

"When editors at Reader's Digest identify a subject to publish, they explore its history, plumb the most popular techniques, then apply those learnings pragmatically. Here, cross-stitching takes on a more artistic bent, starting with the book's layout-big type fonts, step-by-step illustrations with full-color photographs of the projects—and ending with more than 900 designs." Booklist

Van Niekerk, Di

Embroidered alphabets; with ribbon embroidery. Search 2009 128p il pa $25.95 **746.44**

1. Alphabet 2. Embroidery
ISBN 978-1-84448-446-1

Offering 26 "monograms in ribbon embroidery and the instructions for applying them to quilts, toys, journals, cards, and home decor pieces, each step-by-step demonstration in this manual instructs crafters on basic techniques." Publisher's note

★ The encyclopedia of stitches; with 245 stitches illustrated and 24 exquisite projects. edited by Karen Hemingway. New Holland 2005 176p il pa $19.95 **746.44**

1. Embroidery
ISBN 1-84537-203-4; 978-1-84537-203-3

"Each technique is prefaced with history, fabrics, threads, needles, and uses and then segues into the practice. Plus, each is accompanied by, for the most part, a sampler

of stitches with occasional real-life items—like a shisha bag and a Hardanger table mat—to try." Booklist

746.46   Patchwork and quilting

Beyer, Jinny

★ The **quilter's** album of patchwork patterns; more than 4050 pieced blocks for quilters. Breckling Press 2009 488p il $49.95 **746.46**

1. Quilting
ISBN 978-1-933308-08-1

LC 2009-21009

The author "pored through newspapers, catalogs, patterns, and magazines of the 1800s and 1900s to prepare illustrations—along with grids, dates, and multiple names—of more than 4,000 quilting blocks, the foundation of this genre of stitching. Yet providing that resource wasn't enough; Beyer enhances her encyclopedic reference by featuring mini catalogs of like-minded design styles, like bow ties, airplanes, the Red Cross, and kaleidoscope blocks. She also details her sources with commentary and explains how she categorized the blocks. Worthy of any quilting (and quilter's) library." Booklist
Includes bibliographical references

Brackman, Barbara

Facts & fabrications: unraveling the history of quilts and slavery; 8 projects - 20 blocks - first-person accounts. C & T Pub. 2006 110p il $27.95 **746.46**

1. Quilting 2. Slavery -- United States
ISBN 978-1-57120-364-9; 1-57120-364-8

LC 2006-13689

"Enslaved peoples in the American South preserved their memories with quilts. . . . Quilt historian and artist Barbara Brackman guides readers through the stories they told—and lets crafters create quilts and samplers that capture their own memories." Publisher's note
Includes bibliographical references

Causee, Linda

★ **Quilts** A to Z; 26 techniques every quilter should know. Sterling 2006 192p il $24.95 **746.46**

1. Quilting
ISBN 978-1-4027-2318-6; 1-4027-2318-0

LC 2006-42345

"Deciding to arrange techniques and patterns according to the 26 letters of the alphabet, . . . Causee treats readers to some unusual information in her presentation. . . . In addition to the incorporated instructions for 14 techniques, Causee also delights with examples of new-fashioned quilting-stained glass, or a pictorial representation outlined by mini black fabric strips; and watercolor, in which print fabrics are treated as color gradations. For new and experienced stitchers." Booklist

Cox, Meg

★ The **quilter's** catalog; a comprehensive resource guide. Workman Pub. Co. 2007 598p il pa $18.95   **746.46**
1. Quilting 2. Quilts
ISBN 978-0-7611-3881-5; 0-7611-3881-1
LC 2007-36314
"This book is an essential resource for hobbyists and professionals alike, and is sure to be a classic for years to come." Publ Wkly
Includes bibliographical references

Ford, Joan

Scraptherapy cut the scraps! 7 steps to quilting your way through your stash. Taunton Press 2011 202p il pa $24.95   **746.46**
1. Quilts
ISBN 978-1-60085-333-3
LC 2010047873
The author presents "her system for organizing and using scrap fabric—oddly sized pieces too large for a thrifty quilter to throw away but too small to use in most quilts. After a thorough overview of the system, which involves cutting scrap fabric into squares of three specific sizes, Ford offers a variety of patterns that use the scraps. The directions are thorough enough for beginning quilters, and there's intelligent advice throughout. Whether your stash fits in a shoe box or threatens to take over your home, you'll find this book useful." Libr J
Includes bibliographical references

Gaudynski, Diane

Guide to machine quilting. American Quilter's Soc. 2002 143p il pa $24.95   **746.46**
1. Machine quilting 2. Quilting
ISBN 1-57432-796-8
LC 2002-9502
The author "covers every aspect of quilting with a sewing machine, from choosing equipment and supplies to marking and quilting the design and finishing the quilt. Of special note are the sections on free-motion quilting and dealing with the bulk of a quilt in the machine. The text is rounded out by three machine-quilting projects designed to illustrate techniques taught in the book." Libr J
Includes bibliographical references

Hargrave, Harriet

Heirloom machine quilting; comprehensive guide to hand-quilting effects using your sewing machine. 4th ed; C&T Pub 2004 176p il spiral bdg $29.95   **746.46**
1. Machine quilting 2. Quilting
ISBN 1-571-20236-6
LC 2004-781
The author "addresses everything from choosing a chair to selecting thread and batting to marking, basting, and sewing. Exquisite examples of finished quilts will inspire." Libr J
Includes bibliographical references

Kavaya, Karol

Community quilts; how to organize, design, and make a group quilt. by Karol Kavaya and Vicki Skemp. Lark Bks. 2001 136p il $27.95; pa $17.95   **746.46**
1. Bees (Cooperative gatherings) 2. Quilting 3. Quilts
ISBN 1-57990-181-6; 1-57990-377-0 pa
LC 00-46378
This work presents three beginners projects and "a gallery of community quilts that includes background information, full-color photos, and working notes as well as a practical, step by-step method for planning, organizing, and making a group quilt." Libr J
Includes bibliographical references

Michler, J. Marsha

Crazy quilting; the complete guide. Krause Publications 2008 255p il $29.99   **746.46**
1. Needlework -- Patterns 2. Quilting
ISBN 978-0-89689-520-1; 0-89689-520-3
LC 2007-940515
This book contains "methods of patching a crazy quilt, more than 100 embroidery stitches, step-by-step illustrations and how-to directions for finishing a crazy quilt." Publisher's note

The **magic** of crazy quilting; a complete resource for embellished quilting. 2nd ed; Krause Publs. 2004 160p il pa $24.99   **746.46**
1. Crazy quilts 2. Needlework 3. Needlework -- Patterns 4. Patchwork -- Patterns 5. Quilting 6. Quilting -- Patterns
ISBN 0-87349-724-4
"Michler takes the reader step by step through the creation of a crazy quilt and in the process teaches four different piecing methods, 15 embellishments, and more than 1000 embroidery stitch variations. Stitches are divided into broad groups and include stitch diagrams, color photos, and suggestions for use." Libr J
Includes bibliographical references

746.6   Printing, painting, dyeing

Callahan, Gail

Hand dyeing yarn and fleece; dip-dyeing, hand-painting, tie-dyeing, and other creative techniques. photography by John Polak. Storey Pub. 2010 168p il $18.95   **746.6**
1. Dyes and dyeing 2. Wool 3. Yarn
ISBN 978-1-60342-468-4; 1-60342-468-7
LC 2009-28676
This guide to dyeing yarn and fleece "includes instructions for designing self-striping and multicolored yarns with dip-dyeing, tie-dyeing, hand-painting, and other [techniques, as well as] . . . advice on color theory and types of dyes, including food colors and other 'grocery store' dyes." Publisher's note
Includes bibliographical references

746.9 Other textile products

Faerm, Steven

Fashion: design course. Barron's 2010 144p il pa $23.99 **746.9**

1. Fashion design

ISBN 978-0-7641-4423-3

LC 2009-940543

The author "takes readers through a thorough exploration of the fashion industry, from history to inspiration to the design process to landing a job. There are also 14 practical assignments to help budding designers learn more about the industry. Teens exploring careers in fashion will enjoy the practical advice from industry insiders, and fashion-mad readers of all ages will appreciate the information about how fashion design works." Libr J

Webber, Carmen

Chic sweats; 22 ways to transform and restyle your sweatshirts. [by] Carmen Webber and Carmia Marshall. St. Martin's 2009 152p il pa $21.95 **746.9**

1. Sweatshirts

ISBN 978-0-312-37861-5; 0-312-37861-0

LC 2008-37596

Provides step-by-step instructions for transforming sweatshirts and sweatpants into fashionable pieces of clothing and accessories.

"The aesthetic is edgy, hip, and fashion-forward, and readers will be surprised at the imaginative garments that can be made out of humble sweatshirts. Especially outstanding is the introductory material on dressing for your shape." Libr J

747 Interior decoration

Crochet, Treena

Bungalow style; creating classic interiors in your arts and crafts home. Taunton Press 2005 186p il $29.95 **747**

1. Domestic architecture 2. Houses -- Remodeling 3. Interior design

ISBN 978-1-56158-623-3; 1-56158-623-4

LC 2004-9748

This book pictures a "variety of interior details and describes how to add or restore elements that suggest a historic flair while keeping the home comfortable and functional. Common problems such as integrating modern conveniences or gaining needed space are also addressed." Publisher's note

Gillingham-Ryan, Maxwell

Apartment Therapy presents real homes, real people, hundreds of real design solutions; [by] Maxwell Gillingham-Ryan with Jill Slater and Janel Laban. Chronicle Books 2008 264p il $27.50 **747**

1. Apartment houses 2. Interior design

ISBN 978-0-8118-5982-0; 0-8118-5982-7

LC 2007-17179

This "book features 40 homes decorated by real people. Over 400 photos show details of . . . abodes from a tiny rental in Brooklyn to a condo in San Diego to a ranch-style in Miami. Each home profile includes floor plans, . . . resource lists, and 'how I did it' explanations from the renters and owners." Publisher's note

Jordan, Wendy Adler

New kidspace idea book; [by] Wendy A. Jordan. Taunton Press 2005 153p il pa $19.95 **747**

1. Interior design

ISBN 1-56158-694-3

LC 2004-19929

"Jordan believes that functional space should be designed for children and adults throughout the house. Large and colorful photographs illustrate details described in the text. Ideas include creating fun yet safe bathrooms, dynamic and playful bedrooms, and built-in storage space." Libr J [review of 2001 edition]

Sheridan, Judy

How to work with an interior designer. Gibbs Smith, Publisher 2008 134p il pa $24.95 **747**

1. Interior design

ISBN 978-1-4236-0195-1; 1-4236-0195-5

LC 2007-48220

The author "discusses how to find and work with a decorator, including developing a budget and what to do if things go wrong." Libr J

Smith, P. Allen

P. Allen Smith's bringing the garden indoors; containers, crafts, and bouquets for every room. photographs by Jane Colclasure and Kelly Quinn. Clarkson Potter/Publishers 2009 224p il $32.50 **747**

1. Indoor gardening

ISBN 978-0-307-35109-8; 0-307-35109-2

LC 2008-14868

"A fun-filled how-to retort to those who claim they suffer from black-thumb syndrome." Booklist

Includes bibliographical references

748.5 Stained, painted, leaded, mosaic glass

Howell, Karen

Painting on glass & ceramic; [by] Karen Embry. Sterling Pub. 2008 128p il $24.95 **748.5**

1. Ceramics 2. Glass painting and staining 3. Painting -- Technique

ISBN 978-1-4027-5264-3; 1-4027-5264-4

LC 2007-31742

The author "presents not just a helpful rundown of . . . paints and glazes but also descriptions of brushes and other tools and their uses. She provides instructions for how to get started tracing your design onto your piece, as well as details on techniques as varied as sponging, reverse painting, stamping, stenciling, and more, and useful tips about what works well with different surfaces. . . . A truly useful crafting resource." Booklist

Zaccaria, Donatella

Stained glass crafting. Sterling 1998 159p il hardcover o.p. pa $19.95 **748.5**
1. Glass craft 2. Glass painting and staining
ISBN 0-8069-4329-7 pa

LC 98-3575

The author "gears her explanations to both beginners and experienced crafters through step-by-step projects illustrated with photographs. Five patterns . . . become the basis for learning two stained-glass techniques: copper foil with lead and 'straight' lead soldering. Each technique includes excellent closeup photographs of the cutting, trimming, welding, and sealing processes, with enough text to guide unsteady hands." Booklist

749   Furniture and accessories

Kistler, Vivian Carli

The **complete** photo guide to framing & displaying artwork; 500 full-color how-to photos. Creative Pub. International 2009 192p il pa $24.99   **749**
1. Picture frames and framing
ISBN 978-1-58923-422-2; 1-58923-422-7

LC 2008-46612

In this guide, the author "teaches the do-it-yourselfer to frame like a pro. Hundreds of photos illustrate conservation matting, working with premade elements or frame-building from scratch, glazing, and hanging." Libr J

Miller, Judith

Furniture; [world styles from classical to contemporary] [foreword by David Linley] DK Publishing 2005 560p il $60 **749**
1. Furniture
ISBN 0-7566-1340-X

LC 2005-296398

The author "presents a lavish four-color and highly educational book, and the result will never lose its library-patron appeal." Booklist

Includes bibliographical references

751   Techniques, procedures, apparatus, equipment, materials, forms

Ganz, Nicholas

★ **Graffiti** world; street art from five continents. edited by Tristan Manco. Updated ed.; Abrams 2009 391p il $35   **751**
1. Graffiti 2. Mural painting and decoration 3. Street art
ISBN 978-0-8109-8049-5

LC 2009-922509

Ganz's survey of graffiti art includes "upward of 2,000 full-color photographs. . . . An ephemeral, often despised, yet irrefutably powerful mode of expression, graffiti has always been political, and although many of the street artists Ganz succinctly profiles have moved away from illegal spray painting, they have not compromised the inherent subversiveness of their work. . . . Ganz's global array captures

the power and synergy of this vibrant alternative art world in which artists form crews and collectiveness to ensure that their art is seen." Booklist [review of 2004 edition]

Includes bibliographical references

Sanmiguel, David

Complete guide to materials and techniques for drawing and painting; [text, David Sanmiguel; translation, Michael Brunelle and Beatriz Cortabarria] English language ed.;   Barrons Educational Series 2008 239p il $26.99   **751**
1. Artists' materials 2. Drawing -- Technique 3. Painting -- Technique
ISBN 978-0-7641-6111-7; 0-7641-6111-3

LC 2007-931258

"From applicators like pencils and spatulas to auxiliary materials such as fillers and cleaners . . . [this book] covers a variety of artistic media including paint, paper, canvas, and cardboard. . . . The second half of the book describes drawing and painting techniques. . . . Basic enough for a beginning art student and complete enough to hold the interest of practicing artists, this book is a good choice for any collection." Voice Youth Advocates

751.4   Techniques and procedures

Weber, Mark Christopher

Brushwork essentials; how to render expressive form and texture with every stroke. North Light Bks. 2002 143p il $28.99   **751.4**
1. Brushwork 2. Painting -- Technique
ISBN 1-58180-168-8

LC 2001-52162

"Weber writes with humor and confidence, keeping things lighthearted whether he is teaching the mechanics of holding a brush or a wet-into-wet application of paint on canvas." Booklist

★ All about techniques in acrylics; an indispensable manual for artists. {author, Parramón's Editorial Team} Barron's 2004 143p il $26.95   **751.4**
1. Acrylic painting -- Technique
ISBN 0-7641-5710-8

LC 2003-68843

"The book is a delight for anyone interested in acrylics." Voice Youth Advocates

751.42   Use of water-soluble mediums

Bellamy, David

David Bellamy's complete guide to watercolour painting. Search 2009 128p il $29.95; pa $19.95   **751.42**
1. Watercolor painting -- Technique
ISBN 978-1-84448-338-9; 978-1-84448-734-9 pa

"In this short general guide to watercolor painting, Bellamy . . . covers the basics of materials, technique, color, and composition. Advice and suggestions about subject matter are also provided. Bellamy includes numerous sketches, simple step-by-step projects, and diagrammed finished paintings to fully explain the process. Readers will discover the many creative possibilities of this medium, albeit within a traditional figurative framework." Libr J

O'Connor, Birgit

Watercolor essentials; hands-on techniques for exploring watercolor in motion. North Light Books 2009 127p il $29.99   **751.42**

1. Watercolor painting -- Technique

ISBN 978-1-60061-094-3

LC 2008-36576

This guide to watercolor painting covers topics such as types of watercolor paint, painting tools and materials, using color, values, and painting techniques.

"This is an exciting, comprehensive package for the beginning watercolor artist. O'Connor . . . keys her lessons to a 70-minute DVD. Her wet and loose technique and the personal touch of the DVD make this a great choice at a good price." Libr J

751.45   Oil painting

Sanmiguel, David

Oil; text, David Sanmiguel; translated from the Spanish by Michael Brunelle. Sterling Publishing Co. 2008 159p il pa $17.95 **751.45**

1. Painting -- Technique

ISBN 978-1-4027-4913-1

"This unusually good introduction to oil painting is at once practical, approachable, and inspiring. Instructions tell how to mix oil colors, work with solvents and dryers, use brushes and spatulas to shape paint, and execute more advanced techniques like chiaroscuro. Exercises cover the characteristics of warm, cool, and neutral colors and illustrate how to approach figure drawing, still lifes, and landscapes." Libr J

Willenbrink, Mark

Oil painting for the absolute beginner; a clear & easy guide to successful oil painting. by Mark and Mary Willenbrink. North Light Books 2010 127p il pa $24.99   **751.45**

1. Painting -- Technique

ISBN 978-1-60061-784-3

LC 2010-5056

"Unlike less successful art books for beginners, this one starts simply and takes the rank amateur to a satisfying level of accomplishment. . . . The accompanying DVD offers useful demonstrations of two complete paintings." Libr J

751.7   Specific forms

Felisbret, Eric

Graffiti New York; Eric Felisbret DEAL CIA ; contributions by Luke Felisbret SPAR ONE ; foreword by James Prigoff. Abrams 2009 339 p. ill. (chiefly col.)   **751.7**

1. Graffiti -- New York (State) -- New York 2. Mural

painting and decoration, American -- New York (State) -- New York 3. Street art -- New York (State) -- New York

ISBN 0810951460; 9780810951464

LC 2009011736

This book explores the history and influence of New York City as a mecca of graffiti culture. . . . This is the city where it all began, yet few know the back story. mGraffiti New YorkG fills that gap, detailing the concepts, aesthetics, ideals, and social structures that have served as a cultural blueprint for graffiti movements across the world. The book features approximately 1,000 images, complemented by texts by the authors and relevant players in the movement, as well as descriptive graphics and sidebars. [The book describes] . . . the birth of simple signature tags to today s vibrant murals, and covering the ups and downs of the movement, the culturess value system, its social framework, the various forms of graffiti, and significant artists and crews.s (Publisher s Note)

752   Color

Edwards, Betty

Color; a course in mastering the art of mixing colors. Jeremy P. Tarcher/Penguin 2004 206p il $27.95; pa $17.95 **752**

1. Color in art

ISBN 978-1-58542-199-2; 1-58542-199-5; 978-1-58542-219-7 pa; 1-58542-219-3 pa

LC 2003-67215

"This new guide distills the . . . existing knowledge about color theory into a practical method of working with color to produce harmonious combinations. . . . Using techniques tested and honed in her five-day intensive color workshops, Edwards provides a basic understanding of how to see color, how to use it, and—for those involved in art, painting, or design—how to mix and combine hues." Publisher's note

Includes bibliographical references

759   History, geographic treatment, biography

Bailey, Anthony

Velazquez: surrendering at Breda. Holt 2011 264p il $32; ebook $16.99   **759**

1. Artists 2. Artists, Spanish 3. Painters

ISBN 978-0-8050-8835-9; 978-1-4299-7377-9 ebook

LC 2010049809

The author "uses Velázquez's painting of the 1625 surrender of the Dutch town of Breda to Spanish forces as an entry point into a richly detailed portrait of the court of King Philip IV as Spain's Hapsburg empire crumbled around him." Kirkus

Includes bibliographical references

Baillio, Joseph

Claude Monet, 1840-1926; Paris, Galeries nationales, Grand Palais, September 22, 2010-January 24,

2011. [authors of the catalogue, Joseph Baillio . . . [et al.]] Abrams 2010 384p il $65 **759**
1. Artists 2. Impressionism (Art) 3. Painters
ISBN 978-0-8109-9709-7

"In this splendid retrospective catalog for a show at the Galéries Nationales, Grand Palais in Paris through January 2011, Monet's paintings are presented in philosophical, psychological, physical, and personal context in a series of concise, thoughtful, informative, and well-translated essays by noted art historians. . . . This book is what a retrospective catalog should be—expansive and precise, looking over a beloved artist's life and work with many color reproductions." Libr J
Includes bibliographical references

Beckett, Wendy
★ The **story** of painting; contributing consultant, Patricia Wright. 2nd American ed, enhanced & expanded ed; Dorling Kindersley 2000 736p il $40 **759**
1. Painting 2. Painting, American 3. Painting, European
ISBN 0-7894-6805-0
LC 2001-266885
This history of painting over the past 800 years chronicles movements such as Romanticism, Impressionism, Post-Impressionism and Modernism, focusing on 450 masterpieces and including timelines.

Brainard, Joe
The **Nancy** book; essays by Ann Lauterbach [and] Ron Padgett; collaborations with Bill Berkson . . . [et al.] Siglio Press 2008 144p il **759**
1. Artists 2. Authors 3. Cartoonists 4. Nancy (Fictitious character) 5. Poets 6. Set designers
ISBN 097995620X; 9780979956201
From 1963 to 1978 Joe Brainard created some 100 Nancy comic strips. "The Nancy Book includes 78 full page reproductions . . . and features collaborations with poets Bill Berkson, Ted Berrigan, Robert Creeley, Frank Lima, Frank O'Hara, Ron Padgett, and James Schuyler." (Publisher's note)
"The guileless heroine of Ernie Bushmiller's long-running comic strip 'Nancy' is an unlikely icon in contemporary art, recurring in work by postmodern cartoonists like Bill Griffith and Scott McCloud, in an Andy Warhol painting, and in rock posters by Frank Kozik. But no one put her to better use than Joe Brainard, in whose irreverent, effervescent paintings, drawings, and collages (occasionally produced in collaboration with poet friends like Ron Padgett and Frank O'Hara) Nancy appears as an ashtray; a medical illustration; the subject of pieces by de Kooning, Picasso, and Leonardo; and part of Mt. Rushmore. Updating the old 'Tijuana Bibles,' Brainard also gleefully depicts Nancy in flagrante delicto and tripping on hallucinogens. Brash but never bratty, fanciful without descending into preciousness." New Yorker

Brewer, John
The **American** Leonardo; a tale of obsession, art and money. Oxford University Press 2009 310p il $24.95 **759**
1. Art -- 15th and 16th centuries 2. Art -- Collectors and collecting 3. Art -- Expertising 4. Art collections 5. Art collectors 6. Art dealers 7. Artists 8. Painters 9. Painting, Renaissance -- Expertising 10. Patrons of the arts 11. Scientists 12. Writers on science
ISBN 978-0-19-539690-4; 0-19-539690-1
LC 2009008681
"In 1919, a Midwestern auto salesman named Harry Hahn and his French war bride, Andrée, got in touch with Joseph Duveen, the famous New York art dealer, with an offer to sell what they claimed was an original painting by Leonardo da Vinci. Duveen publicly dismissed the work as a fake, and the Hahns, taking him to court for slander, began a decades-long struggle for authentication that scrutinized not only the art world's élitism but the validity of connoisseurship itself. Brewer skillfully outlines the conditions that made America ripe for such an incident and explores how Old Master art became the currency with which the country's new millionaires established their cultural credibility." New Yorker
Includes bibliographical references and index

Brown, David Alan
Leonardo da Vinci; origins of a genius. Yale Univ. Press 1998 240p il $65 **759**
1. Artists 2. Painters 3. Scientists 4. Writers on science
ISBN 0-300-07246-5
LC 98-15164
The author traces the "early influences and the emergence of da Vinci's intense curiosity about nature and ability to re-create it in drawing and painting. The chapter on 'Ginevra de'Benci' is a splendid example of how art history and contemporary scientific techniques can be combined in the examination and attribution of a painting. The excellent full page reproductions and small detail examples are carefully placed within the text for ease of reference." Libr J
Includes bibliographical references (p. 218-235) and index

De Vecchi, Pierluigi
Raphael. Abbeville Press 2002 380p il $125 **759**
1. Architects 2. Artists 3. Painters
ISBN 0-7892-0770-2
LC 2002-23206
This is a survey of the life and work of the Italian Renaissance painter including some 300 illustrations.

Dolnick, Edward
★ The **forger's** spell; a true story of Vermeer, Nazis, and the greatest art hoax of the twentieth century. HarperCollins 2008 349p il $26.95 **759**
1. Art -- Forgeries 2. Art forgers 3. Artists 4. Painters 5. World War, 1939-1945 -- Art and the war
ISBN 978-0-06-082541-6; 0-06-082541-3
LC 2007-36578

This is an account of the Vermeer forgeries done by the Dutch painter Han van Meegeren during the late 1930s and early 1940s.

"Dolnick's zesty, incisive, and entertaining inquiry illuminates the hidden dimensions and explicates the far-reaching implications of this fascinating and provocative collision of art and ambition, deception and war." Booklist

Includes bibliographical references

Graham-Dixon, Andrew

Caravaggio; a life sacred and profane. Andrew Graham-Dixon. Allen Lane 2010 544p **759**

1. Artists 2. Biography, Individual 3. Painters 4. Painting, Italian

ISBN 0713996749; 9780713996746

LC 2010497954

This book presents a biography of "Michelangelo Merisi, known as Caravaggio (1571-1610), . . . contextualizing the artist's early life in the town of Caravaggio and in Milan, a city dominated by Archbishop Carlo Borromeo, whose fearsome doctrine of mass repentance and the selective role of visual spectacle influenced Caravaggio. By the time the artist left Milan for Rome, he had decided to become an artist. The author then chronicles Caravaggio's artistic success in Rome, where, at the age of 24, he found patronage by Cardinal del Monte. He created many masterpieces there, but the rejection of The Death of the Virgin by its ecclesiastical commissioners, the author argues, may have prompted Caravaggio to commit murder. He fled to Naples, then to Malta; he died at age 38, after a troubled and 'disordered' life." (Publishers Weekly)

Hensbergen, Gijs van

Guernica: the biography of a twentieth-century icon. Bloomsbury 2004 373p il $35; pa $16.95 **759**

1. Art -- Political aspects -- Spain 2. Artists 3. Painters

ISBN 1-582-34124-9; 1-582-34606-2 pa

LC 2004-55054

This is a "study of Picasso's antiwar masterpiece, which folds the disciplines of art criticism, political history and biography into a passionate, detailed and well-argued narrative." Publ Wkly

Includes bibliographical references

Kelder, Diane

The **great** book of French impressionism; 2nd Abbeville ed; Abbeville Press 2001 400p il $85 **759**

1. French painting 2. Impressionism (Art)

ISBN 978-0-7892-0688-6; 0-7892-0688-9

LC 2001-266313

This book "traces the development of Impressionism from its roots in landscape and Realist painting through its focus on modern urban life. . . . The works of the major Impressionists and Post Impressionists, Manet, Monet, Renoir, Degas, Toulouse-Lautrec, Seurat, and Cezanne, are featured." Publisher's note

Includes bibliographical references

King, Ross

Michelangelo & the Pope's ceiling. Walker & Co. 2002 371p il hardcover o.p. pa $15 **759**

1. Architects 2. Artists 3. Mural painting and

decoration 4. Mural painting and decoration, Italian 5. Mural painting and decoration, Italian -- Vatican City 6. Mural painting and decoration, Renaissance 7. Mural painting and decoration, Renaissance -- Vatican City 8. Painters 9. Sculptors

ISBN 0-8027-1395-5; 0-14-200369-7 pa

LC 2002-38074

"This engaging narrative sets the record straight on a few points and is highly recommended for most public library collections." Libr J

Includes bibliographical references

The **judgment** of Paris; the revolutionary decade that gave the world impressionism. Walker 2006 448p il $28 **759**

1. Art and society -- France 2. Art and society -- France -- History -- 19th century 3. Artists 4. French art 5. Illustrators 6. Impressionism (Art) 7. Impressionism (Art) -- France 8. Painters 9. Painting, French 10. Sculptors

ISBN 0-8027-1466-8

LC 2005-31089

"The book serves as an entertaining if broad account of a revolutionary transformation in vision—not least of all through art." Libr J

Includes bibliographical references

Leal, Brigitte

The **ultimate** Picasso; {by} Brigitte Léal, Christine Piot, Marie-Laure Bernadac; preface by Jean Leymarie. Abrams 2000 535p il hardcover o.p. pa $ **759**

1. Artists 2. Painters 3. Painters -- Spain 4. Painting, Modern -- 20th century -- Spain 5. Painting, Spanish

ISBN 0-8109-9114-4 pa

These "essays detail events in Picasso's life and the circumstances surrounding the creation of his art, his influences, and world events. This lavish, handsome book contains more than 1200 reproductions, nearly 800 in full color." SLJ

Includes bibliographical references

Museum of Modern Art (New York, N.Y.)

Joan Miro; painting and anti-painting, 1927-1937. edited by Anne Umland. Museum of Modern Art 2008 242p il $50 **759**

1. Artists 2. Painters

ISBN 978-0-87070-734-6; 0-87070-734-5

LC 2008-932020

"Miro's work is presented with concise attention to detail from the artist's passion for painting. Stripped to its essence, this work captures Miro's artistic roughness, while covering most of his best work. His passion for detail in the mediums he chose to present his art is reflected in the Dutch painters as well as those of Salvador Dali and Pablo Picasso. Entirely represented in color, the book's plates aptly represent paintings on all kinds of mediums from unprimed canvas to still life on mesonite backdrops. The book is printed and bound on museum-quality paper, with a multiplicity of color plates representing the artist's work. A must-have for any library collection." Univ Press Books for Public and Second Sch Libr, 2009

Includes bibliographical references

National Gallery of Art (U.S.)

Edouard Vuillard; [by] Guy Cogeval with Kimberly Jones [et al.] National Gallery of Art, in association with Yale University Press 2003 501p il $70 **759**

1. Artists 2. Painters
ISBN 0-300-09737-9

LC 2002-151120

"A superb display of the surprising colors, forceful textures, and mysterious atmosphere of Vuillard's paintings, accompanied by commentaries in which aesthetics, art history, and biography are perfectly balanced." Booklist

Includes bibliographical references

Renoir, Jean

Renoir: my father; introduction by Robert Herbert; translated by Randolph and Dorothy Weaver. New York Review of Bks. 2001 437p il pa $17.95 **759**

1. Artists 2. Painters 3. Painters -- France
ISBN 0-940322-77-3

LC 2001-2539

The author "tells the life story of his father, Pierre Auguste Renoir, the great Impressionist painter. Recounting Pierre-Auguste's extraordinary career, beginning as a painter of fans and porcelain, recording the rules of thumb by which he worked, and capturing his unpretentious and wonderfully engaging talk and personality. . . . {This volume} includes 12 pages of color plates and 18 pages of black and white images." Publisher's note

Robb, Peter

M: the man who became Caravaggio. Holt & Co. 2000 570p il pa $20 **759**

1. Artists 2. Artists, Italian 3. Painters 4. Painters -- Italy -- Biography
ISBN 0-8050-6356-0; 978-0-312-27474-0 pa; 0-312-27474-2 pa

LC 99-43576

The author examines the life and work of the Italian painter.

Robb's "mettlesome assertions regarding M's ruthlessness, 'hairtriggered touchiness,' resiliency, and homosexuality, as well as his confident theories regarding his crimes and punishments, make for great narrative vitality and drama." Booklist

Includes bibliographical references

Roe, Sue

The **private** lives of the impressionists. HarperCollins Publishers 2006 356p il map $29.95 **759**

1. Artists -- Biography 2. Artists, French 3. Impressionism (Art) 4. Impressionism (Art) -- France 5. Impressionist artists
ISBN 0-06-054558-5; 978-0-06-054558-1

LC 2006-43621

This is a "group portrait of the revolutionary artists dubbed the impressionists for their atmospheric landscapes and forthright depictions of everyday life. Here, masterfully set against a panoramic rendering of their turbulent times, are Manet, Pissarro, Degas, Monet, Renoir, Cezanne, Sisley, Morisot, and Cassatt, each incisively defined as an individual and in terms of their complex interactions as they devoted themselves to paintings that met only with derision." Booklist

Includes bibliographical references

Sassoon, Donald

Becoming Mona Lisa; the making of a global icon. Harcourt 2001 337p il $30; pa $16 **759**

1. Artists 2. Painters 3. Scientists 4. Writers on science
ISBN 0-15-100828-0; 0-15-602711-9 pa

LC 2001-24956

This is a history of Leonardo's most famous portrait and its meanings and popularization in the centuries since it was painted.

"Sassoon's knowledge of the minutiae of history and his respect for the image drive the narrative. . . . {This work is} thoroughly researched and highly readable." Libr J

Includes bibliographical references and index

Scotti, R. A.

Vanished smile; the mysterious theft of Mona Lisa. Knopf 2009 241p il map $24.95 **759**

1. Art thefts 2. Art thefts -- France -- History -- 20th century 3. Artists 4. Painters 5. Scientists 6. Thieves 7. Writers on science
ISBN 978-0-307-26580-7; 0-307-26580-3

LC 2008-47851

The author reports on the "1911 theft of Mona Lisa. The lovely woman with the enigmatic smile was simply lifted off the wall and spirited away. The scandal was immense, the investigation feverish, the headlines screaming, and Scotti revels in every turn. Her lively, expert coverage encompasses the fascinating, many-chaptered story of Mona Lisa and ironic revelations about the frenzy among America's robber barons for old masters and the corresponding renaissance in art fraud. . . . Scotti's avid, exciting true-life mystery yields intriguing disclosures and reaffirms Mona Lisa's unique powers." Booklist

Silverman, Debora

Van Gogh and Gauguin; the search for sacred art. Farrar, Straus & Giroux 2000 494p il $60; pa $25 **759**

1. Art and religion 2. Artists 3. Painters 4. Painting, Modern -- France -- 19th century 5. Painting, Modern -- Netherlands -- 19th century
ISBN 0-374-28243-9; 0-374-52932-9 pa

LC 00-37146

"Silverman's scholarship and lucid writing makes this one of the most refreshing and insightful texts on these two artists in years." Libr J

Includes bibliographical references

Thomson, Belinda

Gauguin. Thames & Hudson 1987 215p il pa $14.95 **759**

1. Artists 2. Painters
ISBN 0-500-20220-6

LC 87-50203

This "covers the artist's private life and professional development in great detail and captures the dramatic appeal inherent in both these areas. Some of the controversies of Gauguin's life are also clarified." Booklist

Includes bibliographical references

Wach, Kenneth

Salvador Dali; masterpieces from the collection of the Salvador Dali Museum. Harry N. Abrams, Publishers in association with the Salvador Dali Museum, St. Petersburg, Fla 1996 128p il $35   **759**

1. Artists 2. Painters

ISBN 978-0-8109-3235-7; 0-8109-3235-0

LC 96-3544

"In this slim volume, 40 of the museum's paintings are exquisitely reproduced in full color and accompanied by brief commentaries. . . . A number of Dali's drawings are included in the introduction, and there is an extensive chronology of the artist's life and a bibliography." Publ Wkly

Includes bibliographical references

Dali; curated by Dawn Ades and Michael R. Taylor with the assistance of Montse Aguer. Rizzoli 2004 607p il $75   **759**

1. Artists 2. Painters

ISBN 978-0-8478-2673-5; 0-8478-2673-2

This "retrospective of the artist's work from his early years. . . . [includes] comparative illustrations and photographs." Publisher's note

Includes bibliographic references

759.05   1800-1899

Art Institute of Chicago

Impressionism and post-impressionism in the Art Institute of Chicago; selected by James N. Wood. The Institute 2000 168p il $50   **759.05**

1. Impressionism (Art)

ISBN 978-0-86559-176-9; 0-86559-176-8

LC 99-067929

"The 147 paintings, drawings, prints, and sculptures are presented chronologically and in full color. Brief descriptions by art historians, accompanying each illustration, point out details that may not be obvious to a casual viewer and also concentrate on the influences of other artists as well as interactions among artists. . . . This volume is international in scope, especially with its inclusion of American impressionists, and does provide a good overview." Libr J

759.06   1900-1999

Godfrey, Tony

Painting today. Phaidon Press 2009 448p il $75   **759.06**

1. Painting -- 20th century 2. Painting -- 21st century

ISBN 978-0-7148-4631-6

"Weighing in at over ten pounds, the book is overflowing with gorgeous full-page reproductions of paintings sprinkled with Godfrey's smartly organized commentary. . . . The most exciting part of the book is how the image placement creates a rowdy dialogue between paintings. If this book could

talk, it would roar like a raging party in an echoing art museum." KQED

759.13   United States

Biel, Steven

American Gothic; a life of America's most famous painting. W.W. Norton & Co. 2005 215p il $21.95; pa $13.95   **759.13**

1. Artists 2. Painters

ISBN 0-393-05912-X; 0-393-32855-4 pa

LC 2005-4726

"In this ingenious gem of a book, Stephen Biel . . . weaves together a rich cultural history of this unforgettable picture and asks why it has become, for better or for worse, America's most popular painting." Economist

Includes bibliographical references

Breslin, James E. B.

Mark Rothko; a biography. University of Chicago Press 1993 700p il $45; pa $27.50   **759.13**

1. Artists 2. Biography, Individual 3. Painters

ISBN 0-226-07405-6; 0-226-07406-4 pa

LC 93-14966

This book "is painstakingly researched, fluently written and unfailingly intelligent in tracing the tragic course of its subject's tormented character." N Y Times Book Rev

Includes bibliographical references

Carter, Alice A.

The Red Rose girls; an uncommon story of art and love. Abrams 2000 216p il hardcover o.p. pa $19.95   **759.13**

1. Artists 2. Artists -- United States -- Biography 3. Artists' studios -- Pennsylvania -- Philadelphia Region 4. Illustrators 5. Lesbian artists -- United States -- Biography 6. Painters 7. Women artists -- United States -- Biography

ISBN 0-8109-9068-7 pa

LC 99-39866

"Three of the first American women artists to achieve fame and fortune in the Victorian era—Jessie Willcox Smith, Elizabeth Shippen Green and Violet Oakley—lived unconventional lives marked by a remarkable degree of collaboration. In this . . . study, Carter explores the trio's internecine artistic and romantic relations." Publ Wkly

Includes bibliographical references

Cikovsky, Nicolai

Winslow Homer; {by} Nicolai Cikovsky, Jr., Franklin Kelly; with contributions by Judith Walsh and Charles Brock. National Gallery of Art 1995 420p il $80   **759.13**

1. Artists 2. Painters

ISBN 0-300-06555-8 Yale Univ. Press

LC 95-19025

In this catalog of the American artist's retrospective exhibition, the contributors "present a contextually rich and vibrant analysis of Homer's life and groundbreaking work." Booklist

Includes bibliographical references

Claridge, Laura P.

Norman Rockwell; a life. {by} Laura Claridge. Random House 2001 546p il hardcover o.p. pa $16.95 **759.13**

1. Artists 2. Illustrators 3. Illustrators -- United States -- Biography 4. Painters 5. Painters -- United States -- Biography

ISBN 0-8129-6723-2 pa

LC 2001-19784

The author "isn't overwhelmed by the complexities and contradictions of Rockwell's temperament, relationship, and oeuvre but rather is invigorated by them, and her insightful portrait matches Rockwell's paintings in its judicious detail, layers of perception, delight in discovery, and reflections on 'the slippery nature of truth in art' and life." Booklist

Includes bibliographical references

Cohen-Solal, Annie

★ **Painting** American; the rise of American artists, Paris 1867-New York 1948. translated from the French with Laurie Hurwitz-Attias. Knopf 2001 436p il $30 **759.13**

1. American painting 2. Painting, American -- 19th century 3. Painting, American -- 20th century 4. Painting, French -- Influence

ISBN 0-679-45093-9

LC 2001-32669

"When writing about the founders, trustees, directors and staffs of museums, {the author} is consistently rewarding. . . . Ms Cohen-Solal is at her best when mining the private history of the art trade." Economist

Includes bibliographical references

Elderfield, John

De Kooning: a retrospective; [by] John Elderfield; with Lauren Mahoney [et al.]; edited by David Frankel. Museum of Modern Art 2011 504p il $75 **759.13**

1. Artists 2. Painters

ISBN 978-0-87070-797-1

"A superlative exhibition. (Its catalogue is equally fantastic.)." ARTINFO

Includes bibliographical references

Gerdts, William H.

American impressionism; William H. Gerdts. 2nd ed; Abbeville Press 2001 368p il $85 **759.13**

1. American art 2. Impressionism (Art) 3. Impressionism (Art) -- United States 4. Painting, American 5. Painting, Modern -- 19th century -- United States

ISBN 978-0-7892-0737-1; 0-7892-0737-0

LC 2001-22419

"The best general source available on American Impressionism. . . . [The] book covers the major artists in the movement, including expatriates working in Europe and regional schools throughout the United States during the late 19th and early 20th centuries. . . .The well-chosen illustrations

include many full-page color reproductions as well as photographs of many of the artists." Libr J

Includes bibliographical references

Hennessey, Maureen Hart

Norman Rockwell; pictures for the American people. [by] Maureen Hart Hennessey and Ann Knutson. Abrams 1999 199p il $35 **759.13**

1. Artists 2. Illustrators 3. Painters

ISBN 0-8109-6392-2

LC 99-73071

A catalogue of a traveling exhibition of Rockwell's work. "Colorplates reproduce Rockwell's paintings in . . . detail, and the essays set them in fresh contexts, discussing such themes as Rockwell's urban scenes; the reaction by both black and white Southerners to Rockwell's historic civil rights painting The Problem We All Live With; and Rockwell's role in the development of American illustration." Publisher's note

Includes bibliographical references

Hirshler, Erica E.

Sargent's daughters; the biography of a painting. MFA Publications 2009 262p il $29.95 **759.13**

1. Artists 2. Children in art 3. Painters

ISBN 978-0-87846-742-6; 0-87846-742-4

LC 2009-927634

"This 'life' of Sargent's stirring 'Daughters of Edward Darley Boit' wields a novel's power." N Y Times Book Rev

Includes bibliographical references

Indiana, Gary

Andy Warhol and the can that sold the world. Basic Books 2010 175p $22 **759.13**

1. Artists 2. Avant-garde (Aesthetics) 3. Motion picture directors 4. Pop art

ISBN 9780465002337; 0-465-00233-1

A "look at how Warhol's iconic Soup Cans paintings sparked the Pop Art movement, bringing American artists—Warhol especially—to the forefront of artistic and sociological discourse." Kirkus

Includes bibliographical references

Livingston, Jane

The **paintings** of Joan Mitchell; with essays by Linda Nochlin, Yvette Lee. University of Calif. Press 2002 237p il $65; pa $35 **759.13**

1. Abstract expressionism 2. Abstract expressionism -- United States -- Exhibitions 3. Artists 4. Painters

ISBN 0-520-23568-1; 0-520-23570-3 pa

LC 2001-58514

This is a "vivid portrait of the artist. . . . Mitchell's compositions {are} gorgeously reproduced here in vibrant color." Booklist

Includes bibliographical references

Mathews, Nancy Mowll

Mary Cassatt; a life. Yale Univ. Press 1998 383p il pa $21 **759.13**

1. Artists 2. Artists -- United States 3. Impressionist artists -- United States -- Biography 4. Painters 5. Painters -- United States -- Biography 6. Painting,

American 7. Painting, American -- 20th century 8.
Women painters -- United States -- Biography
ISBN 0-300-07754-8

LC 98-8028

This "is an evenly written, well-documented, and sympathetic—but not patronizing—biography that should be
acquired by most libraries." Libr J

Includes bibliographical references

Philadelphia Museum of Art

Thomas Eakins; organized by Darrel Sewell
with essays by Kathleen A. Foster {et al.}; chronology by Kathleen Brown. Yale Univ. Press 2001 xli,
446p il $75   **759.13**

1. Art teachers 2. Artists 3. Painters 4. Sculptors
ISBN 0-300-09111-7

LC 2001-53142

"This enormous volume accompanies the largest retrospective of {Eakins' work}. . . . {It} includes some 120
photographs as well as examples of his work in watercolor,
drawing, and sculpture. . . . Several lengthy and interesting
biocritical essays, themselves making up 175 pages of text,
separate four sections of color plates. This is clearly the
definitive monograph on one of the most significant artists
America has produced." Libr J

Includes bibliographical references

Vaill, Amanda

Everybody was so young; Gerald and Sara Murphy, a lost generation love story. Broadway Bks.
1999 470p il pa $16.95   **759.13**

1. Artists 2. Artists -- United States 3. Expatriate
painters -- France -- Biography 4. Painters 5. Painters
-- United States -- Biography 6. Painters' spouses --
United States -- Biography 7. Patrons of the arts 8.
Spouses of prominent persons
ISBN 0-7679-0370-6; 978-0-7679-0370-7

LC 99-10416

"Often considered minor Lost Generation celebrities,
the Murphys were in fact much more than legendary party
givers. Vaill's compelling biography unveils their role in the
European avant-garde movement of the 1920s." Libr J

Includes bibliographical references

Wilton, Andrew

American sublime; landscape painting in the
United States, 1820-1880. {by} Andrew Wilton &
Tim Barringer. Princeton Univ. Press 2002 284p il
$49.95; pa $35   **759.13**

1. American painting 2. Landscape painting
ISBN 0-691-09670-8; 0-691-11556-7 pa

"Wilton, of the Tate Gallery, considers the influence of
Edmund Burke's theory of sublimity and the surge in scientific development on American painters, while Barringer . .
. discusses the profound effect on the painters' imaginations
of a pristine land free of Western religious, literary, and historical associations. . . . Wilton and Barringer's commentary
is stimulating and important, and the exceptional plates are
bliss unadulterated." Booklist

Includes bibliographical references

759.2   European painting

Asleson, Robyn

Albert Moore. Phaidon Press 2000 240p il
hardcover o.p. pa $29.95   **759.2**

1. Aesthetic movement (Art) 2. Artists 3. Artists --
England 4. Painters
ISBN 0-7148-3846-2; 978-0-7148-4392-6 pa; 0-7148-
4392-X pa

LC 00-421386

"This book focuses on the artist's interaction with the
Victorian art world as well as his formal pictorial concerns. .
. . In addition, the author looks at the politics of Victorian art
institutions. This is an excellent book filled with gorgeous
color reproductions. Recommended for general collections
as well as libraries that support art programs." Libr J

Includes bibliographical references

759.3   Miscellaneous parts of Europe

O'Connor, Anne-Marie

The **lady** in gold; the extraordinary tale of Gustav Klimt's masterpiece, Portrait of Adele Bloch-
Bauer. by Anne-Marie O'Connor. Knopf 2012 349
p.   **759.3**

ISBN 9780307265647

LC 2011033578

This book explores one of Gustav Klimt's most celebrated paintings. . . . [Anne-Marie] O'Connor traces the multifaceted history of Portrait of Adele Bloch-Bauer (1907).
. . . The [book] . . . evokes the intellectually precocious
and ambitious Adele's rich cultural and social milieu in Vienna, and how she became entwined with the charismatic,
sexually charged, and irreverent Klimt, who may have been
Adele's lover before and also during her marriage. During
WWII, Adele's portrait was renamed by the Nazis as the
Dame in Gold to erase her Jewish identity. O'Connor's final arguments about the tragic yet redemptive symbolism
of Adele's portrait . . . while it represents the failure of the
dream of Jews like Adele to assimilate, through the painting
she achieves her dream of immortality. (Publishers Weekly)

759.4

Bocquet

Kiki de Montparnasse; Catel & Bocquet; [trans-
lated from the Belgian edition by Nora Mahony]
SelfMadeHero 2011 416 p. chiefly ill. (pbk.)
$24.95   **759.4**

1. Artists' models -- France -- Biography -- Comic
books, strips, etc
ISBN 9781906838256

LC 2011431146

This book offers a graphic biography of artist model and
actress Alice Prin, better known as Kiki de Montparnasse.
In bohemian Montparnasse [in Paris, France] of the 1920s,
Kiki escaped poverty to become one of the most charismatic
figures of the avant-garde years between the wars. Partner to
[artist] Man Ray, and one of the first emancipated women of

the 20th century, Kiki made her mark with her freedom of style, word, and thought that could be learned from only one school—the school of life. (Amazon.com)

759.9   Other geographic areas

Bosch, Hieronymus

Hieronymus Bosch; the complete paintings and drawings. {by} Jos Koldeweij, Paul Vandenbroeck, Bernard Vermet. Nai Pubs. 2001 207p il $60 **759.9**
1. Painting -- Netherlands
ISBN 0-8109-6735-9

LC 2001-092544

"As keen as the book's historical and technical sections are, its most enthralling passages contain the authors' insights into Bosch's original and satiric worldview and cosmic iconography." Booklist
Includes bibliographical references

Hamill, Pete

Diego Rivera. Abrams 1999 207p il $49.50; pa $24.95   **759.9**
1. Artists 2. Artists, Mexican 3. Painters 4. Painters -- Mexico -- Biography
ISBN 0-8109-3234-2; 0-8109-9082-2 pa

LC 99-28100

The author examines "Rivera's work and diverse styles. He also describes the pivotal role Rivera's art played in Mexico's development." N Y Times Book Rev
Includes bibliographical references

Liedtke, Walter A.

Vermeer and the Delft school; by Walter Liedtke in collaboration with Michiel C. Plomp and Axel Rüger; with contributions by Reinier Baarsen {et al.} Metropolitan Mus. of Art 2001 626p il $85 **759.9**
1. Artists 2. Dutch painting 3. Painters
ISBN 0-300-08848-5

LC 00-49550

"This is the catalog of an exhibition held at the Metropolitan Museum of Art, New York, N.Y., Mar. 8-May 27, 2001 and at the National Gallery, London, June 20-Sept. 16, 2001. It includes fifteen works by Vermeer and paintings, tapestries and drawings by other Delft artists, including Gerard Houckgeest, Emanuel de Witte, Carel Fabritius, Paulus Potter, Leonaert Bramer, Jan de Bisschop and Pieter de Hooch. . . . Liedtke believes that Vermeer was nurtured and goaded exclusively by Dutch art of his time and by the traditions of his hometown." N Y Rev Books
Includes bibliographical references

Lozano, Luis-Martin

Frida Kahlo. Bulfinch Press 2001 245p il $85   **759.9**
1. Artists 2. Painters
ISBN 0-8212-2766-1

LC 2001-89093

In this "illustrated survey of Frida Kahlo's work Lozano . . . explores her life and paintings in a series of essays that range from a poetic study by noted Mexican cultural critic Carlos Monsiváis to a short, prosaic piece written in 1943 by

her husband, Diego Rivera, to an academic essay by Lozano himself. . . . Lozano uses Kahlo's own stunning images, offering high-quality reproductions of some of Kahlo's most famous works as well as some of her lesser-known pieces. Previously unseen photos of Kahlo at work in her studio are also included. The detail and clarity of the images is incredible." Libr J

Magritte, Rene

The **portable** Magritte; with an essay by Robert Hughes. Universe 2002 438p il $29.95   **759.9**
ISBN 978-0-7893-0665-4; 0-7893-0665-4

LC 2001-095170

"A glossy, compact collection of 400 works spanning the career of the phlegmatic Belgian painter. . . . [This book is] supplemented by lesser known experiments in cubism, impressionism and expressionism." Publ Wkly
Includes bibliographical references

Naifeh, Steven

Van Gogh; [by] Steven Naifeh and Gregory White Smith. Random House 2011 xiii, 953 p.p some colored ill, maps   **759.9**
1. Biography, Individual
ISBN 9780375507489; 0375507485; 9781588360472

LC 2010053005

This book offers a biography of Vincent van Gogh. "Working with the full cooperation of the Van Gogh Museum in Amsterdam, [authors Steven] Naifeh and [Gregory White] Smith have accessed a wealth of previously untapped materials. While drawing . . . from the artist's famously eloquent letters, they have also delved into hundreds of unpublished family correspondences, illuminating . . . the wanderings of Van Gogh's troubled, restless soul. . . . [The book explores] his early struggles to find his place in the world; his intense relationship with his brother Theo; his impetus for turning to brush and canvas; and his move to Provence, where in a brief burst of . . . productivity he painted some of the best-loved works in Western art. The authors also shed . . . light on . . . Van Gogh's inner world: his deep immersion in literature and art; his erratic and tumultuous romantic life; and his bouts of depression and mental illness." (vangoghbiography.com)

Saltzman, Cynthia

Old masters, new world; America's raid on Europe's great pictures, 1880-World War I. Viking 2008 336p il $27.95   **759.9**
1. Art -- Collectors and collecting 2. European painting
ISBN 978-0-670-01831-4; 0-670-01831-7

LC 2008-22141

"The frenzied acquisition of Old Masters by Gilded Age industrialists determined to prove that raw, booming, mercantile America had culture was a blood sport, involving cutthroat competition and calculated deceit. Saltzman . . . draws on both her art history and business backgrounds in this vivacious, anecdotal, and perceptive chronicle of the 'great migration of art' across the Atlantic. Saltzman's close scrutiny of overlooked financial documents led to the resurrection of forgotten players and the exposure of all kinds of shenanigans as tycoons haggled over paintings by such giants as Titian and Rembrandt." Booklist

Includes bibliographical references

Portrait of Dr. Gachet; the story of a van Gogh masterpiece, modernism, money, politics, collectors, dealers, taste, greed, and loss. Viking 1998 xxii, 406p il hardcover o.p. pa $14.95 **759.9**

1. Artists 2. Painters 3. Physicians
ISBN 0-14-025487-0 pa

LC 97-37006

"In van Gogh's portrait of his physician, the painter sought to convey the 'heartbroken expression' of his time; Saltzman has taken up where he left off, charting the portrait's progress through our century. From the Nazis who confiscated it as an example of 'degenerate art,' to the Japanese tycoon who bought it for over eighty million dollars, only to keep it hidden in a Tokyo warehouse, the list of the painting's owners is a who's who of modernity, and touches upon the rise and fall of empires and individuals alike." New Yorker

Includes bibliographical references

Thomson, Belinda
Van Gogh paintings; the masterpieces. Thames & Hudson 2007 190p il $45 **759.9**

1. Artists 2. Painters
ISBN 978-0-500-23838-7; 0-500-23838-3

This book "offers a general survey of Van Gogh's paintings. . . . [and] discusses Van Gogh's paintings in terms of a chronological and biographical progression . . . . Filled with beautifully written descriptive passages of the works and careful analysis of the artist's style. . . . This book is a solid introduction to Van Gogh's paintings." Choice

Includes bibliographical references

760   Printmaking and prints

Caplin, Steve
The **complete** guide to digital illustration; [by] Steve Caplin and Adam Banks; Nigel Holmes, consultant editor. Watson-Guptill 2003 192p il pa $35 **760**

1. Computer art 2. Computer graphics
ISBN 0-8230-0784-7

LC 2002-33190

"This picture-rich resource boasts a glossary, bibliography, and listing of further readings, ensuring that digital designers who are manipulating photos, doing 3D modeling, and exploring the complexities of stacking and layers in illustration will have a wealth of useful instruction and information at hand." Booklist

Includes bibliographical references

Hughes, Robert
★ **Goya**. Knopf 2003 429p il $40 **760**
1. Artists 2. Artists -- Spain -- Biography 3. Etchers 4. Painters 5. Printmakers 6. Women in art
ISBN 0-394-58028-1

LC 2002-43281

This is "a remarkably vital, delectably discursive, and deeply affecting study." Booklist

Includes bibliographical references

Riley, Charles A.
The **art** of Peter Max; by Charles Riley II. Abrams 2002 240p il $49.95 **760**

1. Artists
ISBN 0-8109-3270-9

LC 2002-18229

"Peter Max's gorgeous, technically innovative 1960s rock-music posters and album covers made him an instant success and celebrity. Amid a gallery of brilliant reproductions, Riley charts his life before and after as well as during his star turn." Booklist

760.9   History, geographic treatment, biography

Hammond, Wayne G.
J.R.R. Tolkien, artist & illustrator; {by} Wayne G. Hammond, Christina Scull. Houghton Mifflin 1995 207p il hardcover o.p. pa $25 **760.9**

1. Authors 2. Children's authors 3. Fantasy writers 4. Linguists 5. Novelists 6. Philologists
ISBN 0-618-08361-8 pa

LC 96-105237

Along with biographical material and text describing his artwork, this book reproduces more than 200 drawings, sketches and paintings Tolkien made throughout his life. Included are the "Father Christmas" letters to his children and images created in connection with The Hobbit and The Lord of the Rings.

"The open and inviting format and the reproductions of his art make this a Tolkien lover's dream, and the insightful text will quickly capture attention as well." Booklist

Includes bibliographical references

770   Photography, computer art, cinematography, videography

Adams, Ansel
Ansel Adams, an autobiography; {by} Ansel Adams with Mary Street Alinder. Little, Brown 1985 400p il $65; pa $14.95 **770**

1. Biography, Individual 2. Photographers
ISBN 0-8212-1596-5; 0-8212-2241-4 pa

LC 85-8135

"Consisting of an almost perfect mix of interacting text and images, including some unexpected candid snapshots of Adams himself, this work is an outstanding document of 20th-century American photography." Choice

Includes bibliographical references

Alinder, Mary Street
Ansel Adams; a biography. Holt & Co. 1996 xx, 489p il hardcover o.p. pa $17.95 **770**

1. Biography, Individual 2. Photographers
ISBN 0-8050-5835-4 pa

LC 95-44741

"As Alinder traces the straightforward course of Adams' dazzling career . . . she emphasizes the connection between his stunning landscape photography and his zealous work with the Sierra Club. Alinder is as lucid on the topic of Adams' technical mastery as on his environmentalism and aesthetics, and she also tackles the muddle of his contentious private life with aplomb and candor." Booklist

Includes bibliographical references

Magnum Photos, Inc.

New York September 11; by Magnum photographers; introduction by David Halberstam. Power-House Bks. 2001 140p il $29.95 **770**

1. Documentary photography 2. Terrorism -- New York (State) -- New York 3. World Trade Center terrorist attack, 2001
ISBN 1-57687-130-4

LC 2001-52330

This collection of photographs documents the attack on the World Trade Center on September 11, 2001. The book is organized essentially as a series of picture essays by individual photographers.

Plowden, David

David Plowden: vanishing point; fifty years of photography. foreword by Richard Snow; introduction by Steve Edwards. W.W. Norton 2007 340p il $100 **770**

1. Photography
ISBN 978-0-393-06254-0; 0-393-06254-6

LC 2007-5992

This "book chronicles the American photographer's finest work over a 50-year career that has included some 20 books and numerous exhibits. . . . The breadth, depth, and sheer abundance of Plowden's work over the years are just amazing. Destined to be a classic, this is one of the finest photography books to come along in quite a while." Libr J

Stieglitz, Alfred

★ **Alfred** Stieglitz: the key set; the Alfred Stieglitz collection of photographs. [text by] Sarah Greenough. Abrams 2002 2v il set $150 **770**

1. Art dealers 2. Art museums -- Washington (D.C.) -- Catalogs 3. Photograph collections -- Washington (D.C.) -- Catalogs 4. Photographers 5. Photography, Artistic -- Catalogs
ISBN 0-8109-3533-3

LC 2002-5066

This is a "captioned catalog of 1,642 Stieglitz photographs. . . . It contains 'the finest print of every mounted photograph in Stieglitz's possession at the time of his death.' . . . Greenough's essay examines 'what is and is not in the key set in order to clarify the evolution of Stieglitz's understanding of modernist photography. . . .' The set contains very useful, dense chronologies of Stieglitz's process and techniques (1882-1944) and of exhibitions (1888-1944), a bibliography (1875-2001), and an essay on Stieglitz's concern with reproduction printing and publishing." Choice

Includes bibliographical references

Photos that changed the world; the 20th century. edited by Peter Stepan; with contributions by Claus Biegerd [et al.] Prestel-Verlag 2000 183p il hardcover o.p. pa $19.95 **770**

1. History, Modern -- 20th century 2. Photojournalism
ISBN 3-7913-2395-4; 3-7913-3628-2 pa

Stepan provides "105 images that had the lasting visual power to capture a moment that could be the image of an era held in the instant of a shutter's click for distribution to a generation. . . . The photos are well reproduced and gain from the explanations of time, place, and context included in the excellent short essays that accompany each." Libr J

770.2   Miscellany

Drager, Kerry

Scenic photography 101; a crash course in shooting better pictures outdoors. AMPHOTO 1999 144p il $24.95 **770.2**

1. Landscape photography 2. Outdoor photography
ISBN 0-8174-5819-0

LC 99-29592

This guide discusses equipment, light and color, composition, and how to capture specific details.

McDarrah, Gloria S.

The **photography** encyclopedia; [by] Gloria S. McDarrah, Fred W. McDarrah, and Timothy S. McDarrah. Schirmer Bks. 1999 689p il $125 **770.2**

1. Photography -- Encyclopedias 2. Reference books
ISBN 0-02-865025-5

LC 98-46084

This work "covers all angles of photographers and the tools of their craft. . . . It is filled with carefully selected photographs portraying the irony and beauty of life seen through the camera lens. As a reference work, the photographs are the glue between biographies and terminology. Additional sections list book reviews, films about photographers, and a time line of photography. Additional appendixes include lists of US museums, galleries, manufacturers, booksellers, etc." Choice

770.9   History, geographical treatment, biography

Morris, Errol, 1948-

Believing is seeing; observations on the mysteries of photography. Penguin Press 2011 xxv, 310p il map $40 **770.9**

1. Documentary photography 2. Photography -- History 3. Photography -- Philosophy
ISBN 978-1-59420-301-5; 1-59420-301-6

LC 2011013101

The book "takes the reader on a walking tour of photojournalistic hot spots, from 1855 to 2006 to 2003 to 1936 to 2006 to 1863 , in that order . . . Mostly, Morris tries to clear up unsolved mysteries in the crevices of the history of photography—things like whether Walker Evans moved some knickknacks in a sharecropper's house he photographed; which of two photographs by Roger Fenton, from the Crimean War, was taken first; and how much guilt can be inferred from a digital photo of an American soldier grinning over a dead Iraqi at Abu Ghraib." (Nation)

"Morris' assiduous and profound inquiry into the relationship between reality and photography is eye-opening, mind-expanding, and essential in this age of ubiquitous digital images." Booklist

Includes bibliographical references

Newman, Cathy

Women photographers at National Geographic. National Geographic Soc. 2000 271p il $40; pa $25 **770.9**

1. Photojournalism -- United States 2. Women photographers 3. Women photographers -- Biography

ISBN 0-7922-7689-2; 0-7922-6934-9 pa

LC 00-41575

This look at the life and careers of the photographers "describes their conflicted lives as they balance assignments that took them away from families, homes, and communities for long periods of time. . . . But it is the 144 photographs that attest to the place these women deserve in the history of photography." Libr J

Includes bibliographical references

★ Encyclopedia of nineteenth-century photography; John Hannavy, editor. Taylor & Francis Group 2007 2v il set $545 **770.9**

1. Artistic photography -- Encyclopedias 2. Reference books

ISBN 0-415-97235-3; 978-0-415-97235-2

LC 2007-18144

"These two volumes will no doubt remain the standard reference work for 19th-century photography for many years." Choice

Includes bibliographical references

Photography past forward: Aperture at 50; with a history by R. H. Cravens; and excerpts from Aperture issues 1952-2002; {Melissa Harris, editor} Farrar, Straus & Giroux 2002 239p il $50 **770.9**

1. Artistic photography 2. Photography -- History

ISBN 0-89381-996-4

LC 2002-107716

"Aperture celebrates 50 years as the premier venue for art photography in the United States with a book worthy of its founders' ideals. An anecdotal history lovingly details its transformation from a bright idea for a magazine—conceived by the likes of Minor White and Ansel Adams—to the publisher of hundreds of books, sampled in the accompanying photos, themselves a dizzying display of artistic variety." Libr J

770.92 Biography

Burrows, Larry

Vietnam; introduction by David Halberstam. Knopf 2002 243p il $50 **770.92**

1. Photojournalists 2. Vietnam War, 1961-1975 -- Pictorial works 3. Vietnamese Conflict, 1961-1975 --

Photography 4. War photography -- Vietnam

ISBN 0-375-41102-X

LC 2002-19100

This "confirms that {Burrows} was an artist as well as a journalist, capable of arousing the great tragic emotions, pity and terror." Booklist

Includes bibliographical references

Panzer, Mary

Mathew Brady and the image of history; with an essay by Jeana K. Foley. Smithsonian Institution Press 1997 xxiii, 232p il hardcover o.p. $19.95 **770.92**

1. Photographers 2. Portrait photography 3. United States -- History -- 1861-1865, Civil War -- Art and the war

ISBN 1-56098-793-6; 978-1-58834-143-3 pa; 1-58834-143-7 pa

LC 97-9493

In this reassessment of the life and work of the iconic 19th-century photographer, the author "points out that Brady seldom stood behind the camera, preferring the role of studio chief executive officer and entrepreneur to that of a mere 'operator.' . . . Moreover, Brady was an incompetent businessman, often leaving his creditors in the lurch, and ended his career in bankruptcy. This is enough to make us think twice about Brady, but Panzer's most audacious assertion is that we also need to think twice about the meaning of the pictures attributed to him." N Y Times Book Rev

Includes bibliographical references

Willis, Deborah

Reflections in Black; a history of Black photographers, 1840-1999. Norton 2000 348p il $50; pa $35 **770.92**

1. African American photographers 2. African American photographers -- History -- 19th century 3. African American photographers -- History -- 20th century 4. African Americans in art 5. Photography -- History 6. Photography -- United States -- History -- 19th century 7. Photography -- United States -- History -- 20th century

ISBN 0-393-04880-2; 0-393-32280-7 pa

LC 99-55185

"Willis sketches important figures and traces both developments in photographic techniques and the practice of photography by African Americans. . . . A beautiful and informative album." Booklist

Includes bibliographical references

775 Digital photography

Ang, Tom

★ **Digital** photographer's handbook; Fully updated 4th ed.; Dorling Kindersley 2008 408p il pa $24.95 **775**

1. Digital cameras 2. Digital photography

ISBN 978-0-7566-4310-2

LC 2009-419082

This guide covers topics such as different types of cameras and lenses, scanners, photography techniques, computers, software, digital manipulation, and printing photos.

Digital photography masterclass. DK 2008 360p il $30 **775**
1. Digital photography 2. Photography -- Processing
ISBN 978-0-7566-3672-2; 0-7566-3672-8
LC 2008-299944
The author "teaches how to look at the world with a photographer's eye and offers tutorials, photographic assignments, and step-by-step image-manipulation exercises. Combining technical and artistic aspects of photography, Ang completes the volume with sections on travel, documentary, portrait, nature, sports, and architecture photography. . . . A fine selection for all libraries." Libr J

Freeman, Michael
The **photographer's** mind; creative thinking for better digital photos. Focal Press 2011 192p il pa $29.95 **775**
1. Digital photography
ISBN 978-0-240-81517-6
The author "shares experience he has gained as a professional photographer to improve the quality of the digital pictures nearly everyone is now creating. The content is streamlined into three chapters, on intent, style, and process, that tackle both the practical and the intangible aspects of photography more thoughtfully than many similar books. Freeman is as adept at explaining composition as he is at discussing the problem of cliché or the philosophy of the sublime." Libr J
Includes bibliographical references

Johnson, Dave
★ **How** to do everything: digital camera; 5th ed.; McGraw-Hill 2008 xx, 428p il pa $24.99 **775**
1. Digital cameras 2. Digital photography
ISBN 978-0-07-149580-6
LC 2008-4602
This book teaches "the fundamentals of photography, composition, lighting, and exposure, and . . . techniques for different subjects and situations. The book also explains how to use a variety of photo-editing tools and offers . . . tips for storing, sharing, and printing your photographs." Publisher's note

Ritchin, Fred
After photography. W.W. Norton 2008 199p il $29.95 **775**
1. Digital electronics 2. Digital photography 3. Photography -- Digital techniques 4. Photography -- Social aspects
ISBN 978-0-393-05024-0; 0-393-05024-6
LC 2008-19178
The author "offers a supple, politically astute and fascinating account of the dizzying impact of the digital revolution on the trajectory of the photographic image that, like all new media, changes the world in the very act of observing it. The myth of photographic objectivity has concealed fakery as old as the medium itself, he notes, but in the digital era,

concealment and manipulation come to shape the very experience of the image as sui generis." Publ Wkly

Zuckerman, Jim
Pro secrets to dramatic digital photos. Lark Books 2010 176p il pa $19.95 **775**
1. Composition (Art) 2. Digital photography
ISBN 978-1-60059-638-4
LC 2010-8098
The author "compiles 15 critical steps to achieving great pictures. He covers methods for choosing subjects, the use of color for impact, capturing motion, one-of-a-kind perspectives, and thinking as the lens sees. The book is filled with stunning landscapes, portraits, and abstract images." Libr J

776 Computer art (Digital art)

Ligon, Scott
Digital art revolution; creating fine art with Photoshop. Watson-Guptill 2010 256p il pa $29.99 **776**
1. Adobe Photoshop (Computer program) 2. Computer art 3. Digital art
ISBN 978-0-8230-9536-0
LC 2009-22670
The author "begins with the basics of the Photoshop environment and adds increasingly complex digital techniques, illustrated by 40 noted digital artists. . . . Ligon's book is among the best for beginning and intermediate artists." Libr J
Includes bibliographical references

778 Specific fields and special kinds of photography

Yeros, Dimitris
Shades of love; photographs inspired by the poems of C.P. Cavafy. Insight Editions 2011 168 p. **778**
ISBN 1608870138; 9781608870134
This photography book give[s] visual form to the poems of C.P. Cavafy, the preeminent craftsman of modern Greek verse . . . and one of the twentieth century's earliest lyricists of openly same-sex desire. . . . Mixing genres and sitters, celebrity and anonymity, [Dimitris] Yeros's volume brings to Cavafy's writing a visual range. . . . Cavafy's poem "The Souls of Old Men" is paired with a group portrait of elderly gentleman from a small Greek town. . . . Other juxtapositions are redolent of less specific erotics, setting verse on love and longing next to anonymous nudes. . . . A number of openly gay literati and artworld luminaries sat for Yeros . . . from Gore Vidal and Edmund White, to Edward Lucie-Smith and Edward Albee. . . . But unexpected figures crop up as well, including Chuck Close, Jeff Koons, Naguib Mahfouz, and Gabriel Garcia Marquez. (Afterimage)

778.3   Special kinds of photography

Benson, Michael

Far out; a space-time chronicle. Abrams 2009
328p il $55   **778.3**
1. Space photography
ISBN 978-0-8109-4948-5; 0-8109-4948-2

LC 2009-929096

Presents a collection of photographs depicting various
sections of our solar system as well as of distant galaxies beyond the Milky Way taken by observatories around
the world.

"Here are stars packed like golden sand, gas combed in
delicate blue threads, piled into burgundy thunderheads and
carved into sinuous rilles and ribbons, and galaxies clotted
with star clusters dancing like spiders on the ceiling. . . .
You can sit and look through this book for hours and never
be bored, . . . or you can actually read the accompanying
learned essays. Mr. Benson's prose is up to its visual surroundings, no mean feat." N Y Times (Late N Y Ed)
Includes bibliographical references

Dillard, Ted

Black & white pipeline; converting digital color
into striking grayscale images. Lark Books 2009
240p il pa $29.95   **778.3**
1. Digital photography
ISBN 978-1-60059-400-7; 1-60059-400-X

LC 2009-14894

"Shooting in full color and converting to black and white
. . . [the author] produces a vast range of luminous grays. A
must for serious photographers." Libr J
Includes bibliographical references

778.5   Cinematography and videography

Harryhausen, Ray

The **art** of Ray Harryhausen; [by] Ray Harryhausen & Tony Dalton; with a foreword by Peter
Jackson. Billboard Books 2006 230p il $50 **778.5**
1. Animated films 2. Cinematography
ISBN 0-8230-8400-0

LC 2005-930364

"The text is fun and informative, but the main feast here
is the art, and the reproductions of the concept drawings and
photos of the models are superb." Libr J

Netzley, Patricia D.

The **encyclopedia** of movie special effects. Oryx
Press 2000 291p il $73.95   **778.5**
1. Cinematography 2. Cinematography -- Special
effects -- Encyclopedias
ISBN 1-57356-167-3

LC 99-47733

"This volume provides 366 entries on visual, mechanical, and makeup effects and techniques used in film and includes discussions of every movie to win an Oscar for special effects." Libr J
Includes bibliographical references

Weishar, Peter

Blue Sky; the art of computer animation: featuring Ice Age and Bunny. Abrams 2002 86p il pa
$24.95   **778.5**
1. Computer animation
ISBN 0-8109-9069-5

LC 2001-58988

This goes behind the scenes at "Blue Sky Studios and
uses their . . . film Ice Age to illustrate computer modeling,
rigging, texture mapping, and special effects. Weishar entertainingly details the technological wizardry used to create
3-D animation of everything from storms and smoke to fully
realized film sets and woolly mammoths." Libr J

778.9   Photography of specific subjects

National Audubon Society

National Audubon Society guide to nature photography; Digital ed; Firefly Books 2008 207p il
$24.95   **778.9**
1. Nature photography
ISBN 978-1-5540-7392-4; 1-5540-7392-8

LC 2009-285060

"The author provides practical advice for both the craft
and art of nature photography, beginning with choosing the
right equipment and learning essential skills before moving
on to the specifics of photographing wildlife, landscapes,
and closeup subjects. The final section deals with digital
processing and adjustment of images via such programs as
Photoshop. Although the text assumes that the user has basic knowledge of photographic principles, it will be useful
for just about anyone who wants to move beyond a simple
point-and-shoot camera." Booklist
Includes bibliographical references

Watkins, Carleton Emmons

Carleton Watkins: the complete mammoth photographs; Weston Naef and Christine Hult-Lewis;
with contributions by Michael Hargraves, Jack von
Euw, and Jennifer A. Watts. J. Paul Getty Museum
2011 xxv, 572p il map $195   **778.9**
1. Photography
ISBN 978-1-60606-005-6; 1-60606-005-8

LC 2011-05241

" A monumental achievement in the pictorial historiography of 19th-century America, loaded with new images and
data, this will be an indispensable resource for students of
photography and U.S. history." Libr J
Includes bibliographical references

779   Photographic images

Adams, Robert

Summer nights, walking; along the Colorado
front range, 1976-1982. Aperture; Yale University
Art Gallery 2009 un il $50   **779**
1. Artistic photography
ISBN 978-1-59711-117-1

LC 2009-928119

"The book exalts the aftershocks of twilight in images Adams began making in the 1970s around his hometown of Longmont, Colorado. Snapping away into the night, Adams, the quintessential Western American photographer, produced a body of work in which the illuminative sources—often floodlights and moon glow—become the primary subject matter. In his images, the tactile beauty of a warm summer evening becomes anachronistically more evident when placed against the sad sprawl of ever-looming industry." V

Barnes, Richard

Animal logic; with contributions by Susan Yelavich, Jonathan Rosen, Mark Strand. Princeton Architectural Press 2009 un il $65   **779**
  1. Animals -- Pictorial works 2. Artistic photography
  ISBN 978-1-56898-861-0; 1-56898-861-3
                                          LC 2009-06086
"The first monograph for acclaimed photographer Richard Barnes. Focusing on his work of the past decade, and his 2004 solo exhibition of the same name, the book presents over 100 photographs that explore the collecting and display of animals in natural history museums. His measured, pensive images illustrate the process involved in creating the artificial dioramas and displays." i before e
  Includes bibliographical references

Brandow, Todd

Edward Steichen; lives in photography. [by] Todd Brandow and William A. Ewing. W. W. Norton & Company 2008 355p il $100   **779**
  1. Artistic photography 2. Photographers 3. Photography, Artistic
  ISBN 978-0-393-06626-5
                                          LC 2007-20128
"One of the finest photography books published in many years; highly recommended for all libraries." Libr J
  Includes bibliographical references (p. 309-316)

Burtynsky, Ed

Burtynsky: oil; photographs, Edward Burtynsky; essays, Michael Mitchell, William E. Rees, Paul Roth; [editor, Marcus Schubert] Steidl 2009 215p il $128   **779**
  1. Artistic photography 2. Petroleum industry -- Pictorial works
  ISBN 978-3-86521-943-5; 3-86521-9438
"The extraction, distribution, consumption, and declining availability of petroleum are all explored through [Burtynsky's] large-format photographs. The opening section examines extraction and refinement. The immense size, geometric order and rectilinear shapes of production fields and refineries make for images of striking formal beauty despite the subject matter, all rendered in fine-grained detail. . . . Next is 'Motor Culture,' images of the world oil has made. Aerial shots of geometric highway interchanges, the immensity of exurban sprawl, endless rows of new cars awaiting shipment—even Bike Week in Sturgis, South Dakota, gets the same monumental treatment. Last, and darkest, is 'The End of Oil.' In this section Burtynsky shows us the final result of the process: rusted out, oozing abandoned oil fields, endless ranks of junked cars and airplanes." Online Photographer

Carter, Graydon

Vanity Fair, the portraits; a century of iconic images. by Graydon Carter and the editors of Vanity Fair; foreword by Graydon Carter; essays by Christopher Hitchens, David Friend, and Terence Pepper. Abrams 2008 383p il $65   **779**
  1. Celebrities 2. Portrait photography
  ISBN 978-0-8109-7298-8; 0-8109-7298-0
                                          LC 2008-05033
"Culled from the pages of Vanity Fair magazine by its editor, Graydon Carter, and his staff, and shot by many of the greatest photographers in the history of the medium, these pictures are engrossing less because of the people they portray than because of the breathtaking ingenuity with which each subject is captured. . . . Whether taken by Baron de Meyer, Edward Steichen or Man Ray, or by latter-day geniuses like [Annie] Leibovitz, Helmut Newton or Herb Ritts, these pictures stand as some of the finest examples of photographic craft ever to appear in the mainstream press." N Y Times Book Rev

Coles, Robert

★ **When** they were young; a photographic retrospective of childhood from the Library of Congress. preface by James H. Billington. Kales Press 2002 160p il $39.95   **779**
  1. Artistic photography 2. Children -- Pictorial works
  ISBN 0-9670076-5-8
                                          LC 2002-7177
This is an "illustrated portrayal of early life and the legacies that live on from coming of age. . . . Spanning the history of photography from the daguerreotype to the documentary, each tritone image in this volume is illustrated on a full page. Works by internationally renowned photographers such as Edward Curtis and Dorothea Lange are included." Publisher's note

Eggleston, William

William Eggleston; democratic camera, photographs, and video, 1961-2008. [introduced and edited by] Elisabeth Sussman and Thomas Weski; with contributions by Donna De Salvo, Tina Kukielski, and Stanley Booth. Whitney Museum of American Art 2008 304p il $65   **779**
  1. Artistic photography 2. Photographers 3. Photography, Artistic 4. Videotapes
  ISBN 978-0-300-12621-1; 0-300-12621-2
                                          LC 2008-32248
"Eggleston saturates his extraordinary photographs with light and color, and this makes the banal seem exalted and infused with heightened significance. . . . [He] is a deservedly venerated master, and a full tribute such as this is as compelling as it is overdue." Libr J
  Includes bibliographical references

Elkins, Ken

Picture taker. Univ. of Alabama 2005 120p il $35   **779**
  1. Photojournalism
  ISBN 0-8173-1478-4
                                          LC 2004-25921

A collection of 100 black-and-white photographs taken by the chief photographer of the Anniston Star.

"Elkins is very good at the perfect image caught on the fly. See the picture of a man in a boat who has just paddled it one stroke forward . . . ; a curled ribbon of water is caught leaping from the misted, glassy surface. See the baby crawling on pavement in the driving rain . . . . See the dogs wading in floodwater while fog swallows the whole scene. . . . Perhaps even more than the many exquisitely casual portraits of housedress- and overalls-clad farmers, such visions become engraved in one's memory instantaneously, ineradicably." Booklist

Epstein, Mitch

American power. Steidl 2009 un il $70   779
1. Electric power plants -- Pictorial works   2. Photojournalism
ISBN 978-3-86521-924-4; 3-86521-924-1

"In his ravishing new book, American Power, acclaimed art photographer Mitch Epstein succeeds at both enthralling and horrifying with his 63 images of our widely polluted land. After witnessing the evacuation of an Ohio town in the wake of environmental contamination, he decided to explore the ramifications of American production and consumption of energy. For five years he traveled the country photographing energy production sites, mines, factories, rigs, and deserted gas pumps, as well as the power-related devastation caused by Hurricane Katrina." Artinfo

Haas, Robert B.

Through the eyes of the Vikings; an aerial vision of Arctic lands. Robert B. Haas. Ragged Bears [distributor] 2010 219p il map $50   779
1. Aerial photography 2. Arctic regions -- Pictorial works
ISBN 978-1-4262-0638-2; 1-4262-0638-0
LC 2010549763

Jackson, Bruce

Pictures from a drawer; early 20th century portraits from a Southern prison. Temple University Press 2009 204p il $85; pa $34.95   779
1. Portrait photography 2. Prisoners
ISBN 978-1-59213-948-4; 978-1-59213-949-1 pa
LC 2008-24250

"The book comprises entry and exit photos of prisoners at Cummins in the first half of the 20th century—mugshots that Jackson found, as the title states plainly, in a drawer. These remarkable photos, preserved by Jackson and resurrected through judicious use of Photoshop, are bracketed by an essay on photography and its uses, neatly balanced by Jackson's reflections on the two decades he spent working in prisons, and a convict's first-person account of what Cummins was like in the decades before Jackson first came there in 1971." Artvoice

Includes bibliographical references

Lee, Russell

Russell Lee photographs; images from the Russell Lee photograph collection at the Center for American History. foreword by John Szarkowski; introduction by J. B. Colson; photographs selected

and arranged by Linda Peterson. University of Texas Press 2007 236p il $50   779
1. Documentary photography
ISBN 978-0-292-71499-1; 0-292-71499-8
LC 2006-15020

"Lee's quietly passionate images are masterful works. They set a high standard for a kind of reflective journalism that reminds us that a fine artist may tell you most about himself when first he focuses on others." Texas Observer

Leibovitz, Annie

Annie Leibovitz at work; [Sharon DeLano, editor] Random House 2008 237p il $40   779
1. Celebrities 2. Photographers 3. Photography, Artistic 4. Portrait photography
ISBN 978-0-375-50510-2; 0-375-50510-5
LC 2008-933724

Leibovitz "discusses her personal approaches, trials, and discoveries as a professional photographer, pairing detailed memories and technical discussions with images of her most iconic celebrity portraits (including the Rolling Stones, Demi Moore, John Lennon, and Queen Elizabeth). The book adheres to a chronological format—from Leibovitz's earliest black-and-white photos of the Rolling Stones and John Lennon to her conceptual color portraits from the 1980s. . . . Also included are personal and family photographs as well as her most recent photo shoots for Vanity Fair, including the Obama and Clinton campaigns." Libr J

Women; {photographs by} Annie Leibovitz; {essay by} Susan Sontag. Random House 1999 239p il $75; pa $49.95 779
1. Photography of women 2. Women -- Portraits
ISBN 0-375-50020-0; 0-375-75646-9 pa
LC 99-24968

"Leibovitz greatly increases our lexicon of womanhood with her brilliant photographs of musicians, doctors, teachers, trapeze artists, gangbangers, nude women, a woman in chador, women soldiers, and girls with their Barbies, all commanding attention and respect." Booklist

A **photographer's** life, 1990-2005. Random House 2006 un il $75   779
1. Photographers 2. Portrait photography
ISBN 978-0-375-50509-6; 0-375-50509-1
LC 2006-45765

This is a collection of Leibovitz's "work from 1990-2005. . . . [Portraits of] Johnny Cash, Nicole Kidman, Mikhail Baryshnikov, Keith Richards, Michael Jordan, Joan Didion, R2-D2, Patti Smith, Nelson Mandela, Jack Nicholson, William Burroughs, [and] George W. Bush with members of his Cabinet appear alongside pictures of Leibovitz's family and friends, reportage from the siege of Sarajevo in the early Nineties, and landscapes." Publisher's note

Lyon, Danny

Memories of myself; essays. Phaidon 2009 207p il $90   779
1. Documentary photography
ISBN 978-0-7148-4851-8; 0-7148-4851-4

"What happens when you hang out in brothels, derby pits, and dark alleys for forty years? For starters, you take some damn memorable photos. That's been the path of American photographer Danny Lyon, who, like a Method actor, immersed himself in the subcultures he documented. His iconic work from the '60s (pre–Easy Rider photos of bikers on the road) led to exhibitions in MoMA and the Whitney and two Guggenheim fellowships, and he's credited with pioneering the New Journalism movement in photography. In Memories of Myself . . . he shares 134 mostly unpublished pictures—of Colombian prostitutes in hair curlers, chain-smoking greasers, and Brooklyn teens playing Wiffle Ball—that are so intimate they could have come from the photo albums of the subjects themselves. This is the genius of Lyon's work: He inhabits, rather than invades, the personal space of his subjects." GQ

Maisel, David

Library of dust; essays by Geoff Manaugh, Michael S. Roth, and Terry Toedtemeier. Chronicle Books 2008 un $80   **779**
  1. Artistic photography
  ISBN 978-0-8118-6333-9; 0-8118-6333-6

                        LC 2008-18899
In 2005 Maisel "was immediately intrigued when he read a small news item describing the efforts of the Oregon State Hospital to move the cremated remains of thousands of psychiatric patients who had died between 1913 and 1971. The article hardly suggested an art treasure — except to Maisel, who noticed that the remains were stored in copper canisters, which he guessed had probably turned to dazzling colors over the decades. . . . [In this book] he shows dozens of the canisters in larger-than-life size, their turquoise, pink and gold colors so sumptuous they look more like oil paintings than photographs. . . . The abstract beauty of the canisters is a jolting contrast to their grim origins." Time

McCartney, Linda

Life in photographs; texts by Paul McCartney, Linda McCartney, Annie Leibovitz, Mary McCartney, Martin Harrison, Stella McCartney; edited by Alison Castle. Taschen 2011 un $69.99   **779**
  1. Portrait photography
  ISBN 978-3-8365-2728-6

This volume "offers a portrait of Beatledom from a singularly intimate point of view: that of Paul's wife of nearly three decades, the late Linda McCartney. While the couple's famous friends — Mick Jagger, Steve McQueen, Willem de Kooning — are well represented, the fly-on-the-wall shots of the McCartneys' idyllic intercontinental life . . . are just as enthralling. But the real highlights are the images of Paul with John Lennon, capturing the electric chemistry and childlike joy that informed the Beatles' greatest work." Entertainment Wkly

Mermelstein, Jeff

Twirl/run; text by Robin Hemley. Powerhouse Books 2010 41p $40   **779**
  1. Artistic photography
  ISBN 978-1-57687-518-6; 1-57687-518-0

"Mermelstein sees New York not from the comfort of an office or as a city of interiors, but rather as an organism of millions, all the parts of which intersect in a classic Rube Goldbergian contraption. The pictures shown illustrate

two generic, ubiquitous, nearly involuntary gestures: mostly young women mindlessly twirling their hair as well as the citizens of this hyperactive city – mostly men – running in the street. Mermelstein, a quintessential New Yorker, photographs his hometown and its quirky inhabitants with the eye of a dedicated uncle or an insightful sociologist, schooled in the universities of Garry Winogrand, André Kértész, Robert Frank and Joel Meyerowitz. . . . The power of these pictures, like a good film, is that once entrenched in them, it is impossible not to identify with the characters or see the world in any other way." Art Knowledge News

National Geographic Society (U.S.)

  ★ **In** focus; National Geographic greatest portraits. National Geographic Society 2004 504p il $30   **779**
  1. Portrait photography
  ISBN 0-7922-7363-X

                        LC 2004-44953
"Comprising 280 portraits by 150 of National Geographic's celebrated photographers . . . the book spans over 100 years and covers the entire globe. Organized chronologically as well as thematically and enriched with essays on the development of photographic styles through decades, it is a tasteful celebration of the medium but even more so of human diversity." Libr J

  Through the lens; National Geographic greatest photographs. National Geographic Soc. 2003 504p il $30   **779**
  1. Documentary photography 2. Travel photography
  ISBN 0-7922-6164-X

                        LC 2003-52757
This is a "collection of 250 photos, mostly in color and drawn from the National Geographic Society's archive. . . . The society's signature blend of dramatic, rigorously composed natural shots and 'family of nations'-style culture peeps are backed by broad captions and text. . . . The six sections ('Europe'; 'Asia'; 'Africa & the Middle East'; 'The Americas'; 'Oceans and Isles'; 'The Universe') include the first color underwater photographs, as well as collaborative work with NASA, and prominently credit the 84 photographers whose work is featured." Publ Wkly

Penn, Irving

  Irving Penn: small trades; [text by] Virginia A. Heckert and Anne Lacoste. J. Paul Getty Museum 2009 269p il $64.95   **779**
  1. Artistic photography
  ISBN 978-0-89236-996-6; 0-89236-996-5

                        LC 2009-930114
"The book is a work of art in its own right; both an object of beauty, and a Noah's ark for vanishing trades. Penn may have had an entomologist's eye, but this is no catalogue of specimens; it is an encyclopaedia of humanity." Jewish Chron

  Includes bibliographical references

San Francisco Museum of Modern Art.

  Brought to light; photography and the invisible, 1840-1900. edited by Corey Keller; with essays by Jennifer Tucker, Tom Gunning, Maren Groning. San

Francisco Museum of Modern Art in association with Yale University Press 2008 215p il $50   **779**

1. Photography -- Scientific applications

ISBN 978-0-300-14210-5; 0-300-14210-2

LC 2008-24251

A "collection of scientific photographs taken between 1840 and 1900. From the ornate structure of a tiny mite to the violent splash of stars on an astronomical plate, these pictures document the emergence of the camera as an important scientific tool. Elegant design and thoughtful explanatory text enhance the wonderful, even poignant, power of these images." Entertainment Wkly

Includes bibliographical references

Shaughnessy, Jim

The **call** of trains; railroad photographs of Jim Shaughnessy. text by Jeff Brouws. W.W. Norton 2008 224p il $65   **779**

1. Railroads -- Pictorial works

ISBN 978-0-393-06592-3; 0-393-06592-8

LC 2008-1295

"Shaughnessy began shooting trains in downtown Troy, New York (his hometown), in the middle 1940s. He eventually took lengthy trips, first in New England and Canada, later across the Midwest to the Southwest, to photograph trains. He initially focused on the big engines but quickly extended his purview to include railway workers, railway buildings, and the countrysides through which the trains rolled. A civil engineer rather than a professional photographer, he became as skilled as any pro. . . . Appearing on full pages of this oversize volume, his pictures are engrossing, stunning masterpieces of photodocumentation." Booklist

Includes bibliographical references

Smith, Joel

Edward Steichen: the early years. Princeton Univ. Press 1999 167p il $65   **779**

1. Artistic photography 2. Photographers 3. Photography, Artistic

ISBN 0-691-04873-8

LC 99-26617

Smith examines the photography of Edward Steichen. Alfred Stieglitz was a patron of Steichen's, and Smith discusses "the interrelationship between Steichen's work and Stieglitz's shifting aesthetic interests, as well as the influence of Paris on Steichen's development." N Y Times Book Rev

Includes bibliographical references

Smith, W. Eugene

The **jazz** loft project; photographs and tapes of W. Eugene Smith from 821 Sixth Avenue, 1957-1965. [compiled] by Sam Stephenson. Knopf 2009 268p il $40   **779**

1. Jazz 2. Jazz music 3. Musicians -- Portraits

ISBN 978-0-307-26709-2; 0-307-26709-1

LC 2009-20875

"After having a breakdown in the midst of working on a photo-essay on Pittsburgh in 1957, legendary photographer W. Eugene Smith holed up in a loft in New York's Chelsea, in the Tin Pan Alley area. There, over the next several years, he became deeply embroiled in the New York City jazz scene, opening his home as a practice and performance space for some of the great artists of mid-century jazz, including Thelonious Monk, Zoot Sims and many others. Of course, he took pictures—both of musicians and of a window-size view of mid-century New York—and also wired the place for recording, logging hours and hours of tape, capturing the music and the talk around it. These photos and tapes had been thought lost—the stuff of rumor, buried in Smith's archive—until Stephenson dug them out and culled the best, along with transcriptions of material from the tapes, for this landmark book. . . . This will be an essential book for jazz fans, photography lovers and those interested in the history of New York." Publ Wkly

Sommer, Frederick

★ The **art** of Frederick Sommer; photography, drawing, collage. [essay by Keith F. Davis; interview by Michael Torosian; chronology by April M. Watson] Yale University Press 2005 251p il $65   **779**

1. Artistic photography

ISBN 0-300-10783-8

LC 2004-118000

"The book's sequencing of images wholly succeeds in creating a powerful contemplative experience, and the enticing arguments Davis offers in his introductory remarks incite a hunger for fresh, detailed scholarship about each of Sommer's works." Publ Wkly

Stamolis, Tony

Frezno. Process Media 2008 un $29.95 **779**

ISBN 978-1-934170-04-5; 1-934170-04-6

This book "examines life in California's sixth largest city with vivid, stark and honest imagery. Stamolis captures his hometown, once a beacon of booming surburbia, with a seedy, fluorescent pallor. . . . The downtrodden Fresno that Stamolis depicts is an affectionately upclose look at pure Americana frozen in the frame." Cool Hunting

Stein, Sally

John Gutmann; the photographer at work. foreword by Douglas R. Nickel; with a contribution by Amy Rule. In association with Yale University Press 2009 180p il $50   **779**

1. Art teachers 2. Artists 3. Painters 4. Photographers 5. Photojournalism

ISBN 978-0-300-12331-9; 0-300-12331-0

LC 2009-921441

"Gutmann's camera eye moves with the times themselves in the dynamic America in which he inserted himself, trying to understand but happy to just go. A secondary theme Stein advances concerns the peculiarity of popular English, as on billboards, to a man for whom it is a language acquired as an adult. The photos themselves are exceptionally varied in angle of regard, subject, and place, though all do tend to look caught-on-the-fly and kinetic even when their subjects are stationary. They're so captivating one can't help wishing there were many more than 108 plates in the book." Booklist

Includes bibliographical references

Steinmetz, Mark

Greater Atlanta. Nazraeli Press 2009 85p il $100 **779**

1. Artistic photography
ISBN 978-1-59005-259-4; 1-59005-259-5

LC 2009-504431

"Mark Steinmetz's Greater Atlanta continues this photographer's sexy chronicling of the American South. His photos of junkyards and deserted gas stations exude an Ed Ruscha-like iconicism, yet his strongest pieces remain his photographs of young couples in the awkward blush of adolescence. In these tender, uniquely Southern portraits, you can feel the muggy Georgia air, you can smell the scent of magnolia and mosquito repellent wafting between the girl and boy, the nervous tension and the elixir of estrogen and testosterone searching one another out." Willamette Week

Testino, Mario

Let me in! [photographs by] Mario Testino ; [foreword by Nicole Kidman; essays by Michael Roberts, Mario Testino and Patrick Kinmoth; German translation, Clara Drechsler; French translation, Philippe Safavi] Taschen 2007 il $39.99 **779**

1. Portrait photography
ISBN 978-3-8228-4418-2; 3-8228-4418-7

"It's tough to tell where fashion photography ends and celebrity photography begins but both are getting some respect from the world of high art these days, and nothing proclaims that fact more eloquently than this . . . book of Mario Testino's behind-the-scenes photographs of celebrities in fashionable garb." Miami Herald

Thompson, Michael

Michael Thompson: Portraits; edited by Vince Aletti. Damiani 2011 216p il $65 **779**

1. Artistic photography
ISBN 978-8-86208-156-6; 8-86208-156-1

"There aren't very many successful commercial photographers whose work is considered to be fine art and exhibited in galleries. . . . It's a fine line that one walks to gain that respect, especially for a photographer who specializes in fashion and celebrity. . . . Michael Thompson is one such photographer who has blurred the line and broken the boundary. The memorable portraits in this book of celebrity tell a story of our culture as much as about the person being photographed." Full Frontal Fashion

Towell, Larry

The **world** from my front porch. Chris Boot; Archive of Modern Conflict 2008 224p il $75 **779**

1. Photojournalism
ISBN 978-1-905712-09-0

"Unlike most contemporary photojournalists, who shoot with high-end digital cameras and print their work with ink and paper, Towell only uses traditional black and white film, whether he is in Gaza, Lebanon, or South Africa, or on his own back porch. . . . That Towell is concerned with the poetics of photography should come as no surprise. His meticulously realized compositions are saturated with the history of photography and the history of painting. . . . Towell's work is astounding in its coherence. He treats people facing poverty,

dispossession, and violent conflict in the same spirit as his own family." Walrus

Veasey, Nick

X-ray. Viking Studio 2008 224p il $40 **779**

1. Artistic photography
ISBN 978-0-670-02040-9; 0-670-02040-0

Veasey's "works are beautifully simple, often containing a purpose–to reveal a side never seen before, to evoke emotional response. . . . The images are divided into several categories including humans/animals, objects, nature, abstract, and fashion." Revealed

Wolf, Michael

The **transparent** city. Aperture 2008 111p il $60 **779**

1. Artistic photography
ISBN 978-1-59711-076-1; 1-59711-076-0

"The ground is nowhere in sight in Wolf's dramatically geometric, nearly abstract photographs of Chicago's Loop towers. Shot from strategically selected rooftops and perfectly printed in an aptly large, vertical book, Wolf's subtly modulated color photographs are monumental studies in grays, whites, blacks, golds, and occasional splashes of green and blue. . . . With intimations of surveillance and vulnerability, these intensely beautiful cityscapes seem austere and inhuman until one lands on a magnified picture of a man giving the distant photographer the finger." Booklist

Life: World War 2; history's greatest conflict in pictures. edited by Richard B. Stolley. Little, Brown 2001 351p il hardcover o.p. pa $29.95 **779**

1. World War, 1939-1945 -- Pictorial works 2. World history -- 20th century -- Pictorial works
ISBN 0-8212-2771-8; 0-8212-5713-7 pa

LC 2001-93633

This "album of 665 photographs taken from the archives of Life magazine and other collections begins with the years 1919 to 1939, the two decades leading up to World War II. Editor Stolley then proceeds to chronicle the war, year by year through 1945, and ends with what he calls 'the war's aftermath,' 1946 to 2001. . . . For World War II buffs, the book is a natural treasure." Booklist

The Scurlock Studio and Black Washington; picturing the promise. edited by Paul Gardulo . . . [et al.] National Museum of African American History and Culture: In collaboration with the National Museum o 2009 224p il $35 **779**

1. African Americans -- Pictorial works
ISBN 978-1-58834-262-1; 1-58834-262-X

LC 2008-32847

"In 1911 Addison Scurlock opened a photography studio in Washington, D.C., and went on to chronicle the aspirations and ambitions of the black community into the 1990s. . . . Photographs include the famous (Marian Anderson, Duke Ellington, Ralph Bunche, W. E. B. DuBois, and Muhammad Ali) as well as the influential but perhaps less well known (business owners, churchgoers, civic leaders, members of high society). With more than 100 images, this book is a proud celebration of a vibrant community from the early to the late twentieth century." Booklist

Includes bibliographical references

780　Music

Allman, Gregg

My cross to bear; Gregg Allman with Alan Light. Morrow 2012 390 p. ill. (some col.) $27.99　**780**

1. Allman Brothers Band (Performer) 2. Drug addiction 3. Memoirs 4. Rock musicians -- Sexual behavior 5. Rock musicians -- United States -- Biography

ISBN 0062112031; 9780062112033

LC 2012563465

In "his memoir, . . . Gregg Allman lays bare his soul, carrying us back to his childhood with his older brother, Duane, their days at military school, the first time he picked up a guitar and started making music, the first songs he wrote, his love for Duane, his voracious appetite for drugs and sex, and his countless sexual conquests, his broken relationships and his addictions, and his deep love for music." (Publishers Weekly)

Curtis, Susan

Dancing to a black man's tune: a life of Scott Joplin. University of Mo. Press 1994 xx, 265p il $29.95　**780**

1. Composers 2. Jazz musicians 3. Pianists

ISBN 0-8262-0949-1

LC 93-46116

A "study of the life and world of ragtime creator Scott Joplin (1868-1917). Lapsing only occasionally into academic jargon, the author ably places Joplin in the context of an emerging biracial society and culture as a man who was denied rights because of his color yet applauded as a musician." Publ Wkly

Includes bibliographical references

Glover, Jane

Mozart's women; the man, the music, and the loves of his life. HarperCollins 2006 406p il $27.95; pa $15.95　**780**

1. Biography, Individual 2. Composers

ISBN 0-06-056350-8; 978-0-06-056350-9; 0-06-056351-6 pa; 978-0-06-056351-6 pa

LC 2005-52699

The author "writes perceptively and knowledgeably about the theatrical genius of Mozart's operas, . . . and her expertise contributes significantly to the pleasures afforded by this volume." Christ Sci Monit

Includes bibliographical references

Gutman, Robert W.

Mozart; a cultural biography. Harcourt Brace & Co. 1999 839p hardcover o.p. pa $25 **780**

1. Composers 2. Composers -- Austria -- Biography

ISBN 978-0-15-601171-6 pa; 0-15-601171-9 pa

LC 99-31953

The author interweaves "the chronology of Mozart's life and musical compositions with essays on the social, political, and religious fabrics of the 18th century, offering ex-

tended discourses on the Enlightenment, Sturm und Drang, Freemasonry, and other movements that influenced the composer both personally and in his works." Libr J

Includes bibliographical references

Hoffman, Miles

The **NPR** classical music companion; an essential guide for enlightened listening. Houghton Mifflin 2005 306p pa $15　**780**

1. Music -- Dictionaries 2. Reference books

ISBN 978-0-618-61945-0; 0-618-61945-3

LC 2006-273343

This musical guide includes "entries that are at least a good-size paragraph in length and liable to include, besides technical information, historical and listener's advisory material." Booklist

Holoman, D. Kern

Berlioz. Harvard Univ. Press 1989 687p il $36 **780**

1. Biography, Individual 2. Composers

ISBN 0-674-06778-9

LC 88-35788

This is a biography of the nineteenth-century composer, conductor, and music critic.

"There may be aspects of Berlioz's life which Holoman has not fathomed, but he paints as full a picture as has yet been attempted." New Statesman (1913)

Includes bibliographical references

Hyland, William G.

George Gershwin; a new biography. Praeger Pubs. 2003 312p il $39.95　**780**

1. Biography, Individual 2. Composers

ISBN 0-275-98111-8

LC 2003-46303

"This fresh and well-researched biography of one of America's great composers is highly recommended for all libraries." Libr J

Includes bibliographical references

Joseph, Charles M.

Stravinsky inside out. Yale Univ. Press 2001 xx, 320p il $29.95　**780**

1. Composers

ISBN 0-300-07537-5

LC 2001-913

This study "reveals a . . . flawed and fragile human being, who craved approval, dealt ungenerously with colleagues, loved James Bond movies, and tried hard to further his son's musical career. Although the aged Stravinsky's eagerness to play the role of celebrity composer for the golden age of television . . . was an embarrassment, most of these episodes testify to the protean survival skills of an artist whose sense of identity was always in flux and whose cunning was commensurate with his talent." New Yorker

Includes bibliographical references and index

Mozart, Wolfgang Amadeus

Mozart's letters, Mozart's life; selected letters. edited and newly translated by Robert Spaethling. Norton 2000 479p il $35; pa $19.95 **780**
1. Composers 2. Composers -- Austria -- Correspondence
ISBN 978-0-393-04719-6; 978-0-393-32830-1 pa
LC 00-25530

This is a "wonderful collection that gives Mozart a voice as a son, husband, brother and friend. Mozart's main subjects were his composing and performing, but he usually digresses into love for his parents, his sister and his wife, Constanze. And there was a bawdy side, too, to the composer of such elegant music." N Y Times Book Rev
Includes bibliographical references

Ross, Alex

Listen to this. Farrar, Straus and Giroux 2010 364p il $27; ebook $12.99 **780**
1. Music -- History and criticism 2. Musical criticism
ISBN 978-0-374-18774-3; 0-374-18774-6; 978-1-4299-7761-6 ebook; 1-4299-7761-2 ebook
LC 2010-10283

"Though the bulk of the book examines classical work both historical and contemporary, Ross veers effortlessly from Mozart to Radiohead, from Kurt Cobain to Brahms, bringing a pop fan's enthusiasm to the composers and treating the rock stars seriously as musicians. . . . The triumph of 'Listen to This' is that Ross dusts off music that's centuries old to reval the passion and brilliance that's too often hidden from a contemporary audience. It's a joy for a pop fan or a classical aficionado." N Y Times Book Rev
Includes bibliographical references

Schonberg, Harold C.

★ The **lives** of the great composers; 3rd ed; Norton 1997 653p il $35 **780**
1. Composers
ISBN 0-393-03857-2
LC 96-13308

This book traces the lives of important musical figures from Monteverdi to Ives and includes information on the serialists, minimalist composers and the new tonalists of the 1990s.

"Schonberg writes for the lay reader. His intention is to humanize the composers and the writing, always highly readable, emphasizes biographical information rather than musical analysis." Libr J
Includes bibliographical references

Swafford, Jan

Charles Ives; a life with music. Norton 1996 525p il hardcover o.p. $18.95 **780**
1. Biography, Individual 2. Composers
ISBN 978-0-393-31719-0; 0-393-31719-6
LC 95-22549

"Ives was a professional organist, a successful insurance executive, a political idealist, and an immensely prolific composer. The author believes that Ives's transcendentalism was central to his identity, ceaselessly inspiring him while also spurring him on to an inevitable physical collapse. Swafford—a composer himself—intersperses his biography with valuable 'entr'actes' of approachable musical analysis,

and ends with a ringing endorsement of Ives as an ideal composer for a democratic society." New Yorker
Includes bibliographical references

Johannes Brahms; a biography. Knopf 1997 xxii, 699p il hardcover o.p. $20 **780**
1. Biography, Individual 2. Composers
ISBN 978-0-679-74582-2; 0-679-74582-3
LC 97-29308

"Swafford's study, clearly a labor of profound affection, is a model biography: eloquent, clear-sighted and often moving." Publ Wkly
Includes bibliographical references

Walker-Hill, Helen

From spirituals to symphonies; African-American women composers and their music. Greenwood Press 2002 401p il $94.95 **780**
1. African American women 2. African American women composers 3. African American women composers -- Biography 4. African American women composers -- History and criticism 5. Composers 6. Composers -- United States -- Biography 7. Music -- United States -- History and criticism 8. Poets 9. Singers 10. Teachers 11. Violinists
ISBN 0-313-29947-1
LC 2001-40600

This profiles the lives and works of Undine Smith Moore, Julia Perry, Margaret Bonds, Irene Britton Smith, Dorothy Rudd Moore, Valerie Capers, Mary Watkins, and Regina Harris Baiocchi.

This is "an accessible, thoughtful, and humanist study. . . . Detailed works lists and an appendix enumerating other black women composers add reference value." Libr J
Includes bibliographical references

Wolff, Christoph

Johann Sebastian Bach; the learned musician. Norton 2000 599p il hardcover o.p. $21.95 **780**
1. Composers 2. Composers -- Germany -- Biography
ISBN 9780393322569; 0393322564
LC 99-54364

This work "is likely to be the standard one-volume Bach biography for some time to come. It is a solid, richly informative treatment, presenting the copious details of Bach's life in a coherent, readable narrative." N Y Rev Books
Includes bibliographical references

The Harvard biographical dictionary of music; edited by Don Michael Randel. Belknap Press 1996 1013p il $39.95 **780**
1. Biography, Collective 2. Music -- Bio-bibliography 3. Music -- Bio-bibliography -- Dictionaries 4. Musicians -- Biography -- Dictionaries 5. Reference books
ISBN 0-674-37299-9
LC 96-16456

"International in scope and covering all eras of music from the ancient to the present, this important new reference source has information concerning 5,500 individuals. Most are associated with classical concert music, although prominent jazz, rock, folk, and popular personalities are also represented: Madonna, Mozart, Zoot Sims, Mick Jagger, and Dolly Parton are included. Musicologists, educators, teachers, and reviewers, no matter how influential, are excluded. Entries consist of brief to long paragraphs that may include a bibliography or a list of compositions. . . . This is an authoritative and significant new reference work which all libraries must purchase." Choice

The Harvard concise dictionary of music and musicians; edited by Don Michael Randel. Belknap Press 1999 757p il hardcover o.p. pa $18.95 **780**
   1. Music 2. Music -- Bio-bibliography 3. Music -- Dictionaries 4. Reference books
ISBN 0-674-00084-6; 0-674-00978-9 pa
                              LC 99-40644
"Entries are arranged alphabetically and encompass terms, musical forms and styles, individual works, and instruments, as well as composers, performers, and theorists." Booklist

★ The Harvard dictionary of music; edited by Don Michael Randel. 4th ed; Belknap Press 2003 978p il $39.95   **780**
   1. Music -- Dictionaries 2. Reference books
ISBN 0-674-01163-5
                         LC 2003-58262
This reference "includes entries on all the styles and forms in Western music; . . . articles on the music of Africa, Asia, Latin America, and the Near East; descriptions of instruments . . . {with} historical background, and articles that reflect today's best, including popular music, jazz, and rock." Publisher's note

★ The New Grove dictionary of music and musicians; edited by Stanley Sadie; executive editor, John Tyrrell. 2nd ed; Oxford University Press 2004 29v set $1, 500   **780**
   1. Music -- Bio-bibliography 2. Music -- Dictionaries 3. Music -- Encyclopedias 4. Music -- History and criticism 5. Reference books
ISBN 978-0-19-517067-2
"Grove is not fat, it is limitless. Whether Grove is on the reference shelf or online, teachers, students, researchers, and the common reader will find it an abiding source of satisfaction." Commonweal
Includes bibliographical references

★ The Oxford companion to music; edited by Alison Latham. Oxford Univ. Press 2002 1434p il $65   **780**
   1. Music -- Bio-bibliography 2. Music -- Dictionaries 3. Musicians -- Dictionaries 4. Reference books
ISBN 0-19-866212-2
                        LC 2002-537302
"Among the 8000 entries are articles on composers, theorists, and some performers; instruments, forms, and terms; subjects like electronic music, individual countries, and politics and music; and some pieces (and even some famous arias). Each entry is presented in a dictionary format, with a select index of names appended and sometimes with bibliographic references. . . . The bias is still English, but the book provides cross references to American terms and includes

plenty of American composers and musical subjects. A solid reference with a grand pedigree, usefully improved for home and general library use, this is highly recommended for all public libraries." Libr J
Includes bibliographical references

780.2   Miscellany; texts; treatises on music scores and recordings

Calamar, Gary
   Record store days; from vinyl to digital and back again. [by] Gary Calamar and Phil Gallo. Sterling 2010 238p il $19.95   **780.2**
   1. Music industry 2. Record stores
ISBN 978-1-4027-7232-0
"Packed with quotes from musicians, shop owners, and fans, this volume is a treat for readers, with its inside look at the importance of vinyl in people's lives throughout the 20th century. Major vinyl shops such as Tower Records, Rhino Records, and Bleecker Bob's are profiled. Nearly every page is graced with vintage photographs and interesting sidebars filled with facts, from the format history of recorded music over the century to vinyl oddities. The authors stress the importance of record stores as community meeting places and discuss the demise of the record industry, the rise of digital music, and the comeback of vinyl thanks to bands releasing limited-edition vinyl singles." Libr J

Cutler, David
   The **savvy** musician; building a career, earning a living & making a difference. Helius Press 2009 350p il pa $19.99   **780.2**
   1. Music industry -- Vocational guidance
ISBN 978-0-9823075-0-2
This book "is a guide to the aspiring musician who wants to make their living doing what they love. A . . . blend of music and marketing book, David Cutler encourages musicians to learn how to sell themselves and adapt technology to their approaches, to get themselves out there with a recognizable brand. An honest book about making it in the music industry, 'The Savvy Musician' is a read that can't be missed by music lovers." Midwest Book Rev
Includes bibliographical references

Kot, Greg
  ★ **Ripped**; how the wired generation revolutionized music. Scribner 2009 262p $25; pa $14 **780.2**
   1. Music -- Computer network resources 2. Music -- Internet resources 3. Music industry 4. Music trade -- Computer network resources
ISBN 978-1-4165-4727-3; 1-4165-4727-4; 978-1-4165-4731-0 pa; 1-4165-4731-2 pa
                        LC 2008-40839
The author's "breezy, entertaining, journalistic style and sympathetic tone consistently draw in the reader. Essential for all those interested in the intersection of music and technology." Libr J

780.26   Texts; treatises on music scores and recordings

Day, Timothy

★ A **century** of recorded music; listening to musical history. Yale Univ. Press 2000 306p il $40; pa $19   **780.26**

1. Music -- 20th century -- History and criticism 2. Music -- History and criticism 3. Sound -- Recording and Reproducing -- History 4. Sound recording industry -- History -- 20th century 5. Sound recordings -- History 6. Sound recordings -- History -- 20th century
ISBN 0-300-08442-0; 0-300-09401-9 pa
                    LC 00-43490

This work provides a "narrative of the evolution of recording from cylinders (1887), shellac discs, and acoustic rerecording through the reproducing piano, electrical amplifications (1925), and magnetic tape to the long-playing record (1948) and compact disc of the 1980s. Day also discusses studio practices and the emergence of influential record producers, the role of radio and recordings in creating a mass audience, the expansion of recorded repertoire, and new ways to experience music. Recommended for all music collections." Choice

Includes bibliographical references

780.7   Education, research, related topics; performances

Tunstall, Tricia

Changing lives; Tricia Tunstall. Norton 2012 320 p.   **780.7**

1. Music -- Instruction and study -- United States 2. Music -- Instruction and study -- Venezuela
ISBN 9780393078961
                    LC 2011026504

This book tells the "story of conductor . . . Gustavo Dudamel, and the music education program, El Sistema, that led him to success. When Gustavo Dudamel, at the age of twenty-eight, ascended the podium at the Hollywood Bowl for his inaugural concert as conductor of the Los Angeles Philharmonic, he immediately captivated the hearts of his audience, just as he had the minds of music critics who designated him a modern-day Leonard Bernstein. In 'Changing Lives,' the maestro's story becomes the entry point to an equally captivating subject: El Sistema, the music education program that nurtured his musical talent, first as a young violinist and then as a budding conductor under the mentorship of its founder, José Antonio Abreu. What began in Venezuela has now reached children in Los Angeles, New York City, Baltimore, and cities around the world. No matter the location, the overarching goal of El Sistema is unwavering: to rescue children from the depredations of poverty through music." (Publisher's note)

780.89   Ethnic and national groups

Murray, Albert

The **blue** devils of Nada; a contemporary American approach to aesthetic statement. Pantheon Bks. 1996 238p $23; pa $12   **780.89**

1. African American art 2. African American arts 3. African American music -- History and criticism 4. African American musicians 5. Artists 6. Authors 7. Band leaders 8. Blues music 9. Blues music -- History and criticism 10. Composers 11. Jazz musicians 12. Nobel laureates for literature 13. Novelists 14. Pianists 15. Poets 16. Short story writers 17. Singers 18. Trumpet players
ISBN 0-679-44213-8; 0-679-75859-3 pa
                    LC 95-23331

In these essays Murray "presents Louis Armstrong, Count Basie, Duke Ellington, painter Romare Bearden and Ernest Hemingway as embodying, in their work and their lives, a peculiarly American strain of existential improvisation and epic storytelling. His theme, variously elaborated, is the effort of the engaged artist to document and give shape to the rootlessness and chaos underlying contemporary life in general—and African American life, in particular—in a way that transcends 'agitprop journalism.'" Publ Wkly

780.9   History, geographic treatment, biography

Crawford, Richard

America's musical life; a history. Norton 2000 976p il hardcover o.p. pa $23.95   **780.9**

1. American music -- History and criticism 2. Music -- United States -- History and criticism
ISBN 0-393-04810-1; 978-0-393-32726-7 pa; 0-393-32726-4 pa
                    LC 99-47565

This survey of music in America covers "blues, jazz, swing, pop, rock, hip hop . . . with economics and history as cultural backdrops. Well researched and sensitively constructed, this is highly recommended." Libr J

Includes bibliographical references

Grout, Donald Jay

A **history** of western music; [by] J. Peter Burkholder, Donald Jay Grout, Claude V. Palisca. 8th ed.; W. W. Norton & Company 2010 xxxiv, 986, 129p il $83.12   **780.9**

1. Chants (Plain, Gregorian, etc.) 2. Church music 3. Composers 4. Instrumental music 5. Music -- History and criticism 6. Opera 7. Vocal music
ISBN 978-0-393-93125-9; 0-393-93125-0
                    LC 2008-44302

The authors survey the course of Western music from the ancient world to modern atonalism and dodecaphony. They cover vocal and instrumental forms, notation, performance, music-printing, the development of instruments, and biographical information on composers.

Lang, Paul Henry

   Music in Western civilization; with a new foreword by Leon Botstein. Norton 1997 xxii, 1107p il maps $45   **780.9**

   1. Music -- History and criticism

   ISBN 0-393-04074-7

                           LC 97-5883

   This is a history of Western music from Ancient Greece to the 1920s.

   "Lang's volume has long been hailed as a benchmark in the field." Libr J

   Includes bibliographical references

Mithen, Steven J.

   The **singing** neanderthals; the origins of music, language, mind, and body. [by] Steven Mithen. Harvard University Press 2006 374p il map $25.95; pa $16.95   **780.9**

   1. Evolution 2. Music

   ISBN 0-674-02192-4; 978-0-674-02192-1; 978-0-674-02559-2 pa; 0-674-02559-8 pa

                        LC 2005-30187

   The author argues "that as a species, humans most likely made musical noises that led to language, not the other way around. . . . This book is a rich resource." Choice

   Includes bibliographical references

Rosen, Charles

   The **classical** style; Haydn, Mozart, Beethoven. expanded ed; Norton 1997 xxx, 533p il $35; pa $19.95   **780.9**

   1. Composers 2. Music -- History and criticism

   ISBN 0-393-04020-8; 0-393-31712-9 pa

                        LC 96-27335

   "This remains simply the most important book on the classical style in music." Choice

   Includes bibliographical references

   The **romantic** generation. Harvard Univ. Press 1995 723p il hardcover o.p. pa $18.95   **780.9**

   1. Music -- History and criticism 2. Romanticism

   ISBN 0-674-77934-7 pa

                        LC 94-46239

   The author "explains and describes the first half of the 19th century in conjunction with literature, art, and social changes. . . . Rosen also examines the lives of the composers and pursues some detailed analysis of numerous compositions to make his points. The result is a fresh, challenging, and stimulating view of the society in which Chopin, Liszt, Berlioz, and Schumann flourished." Libr J

Terkel, Studs

   And they all sang; adventures of an eclectic disc jockey. New Press 2005 xxii, 301p $25.95; pa $16.95   **780.9**

   1. Musicians

   ISBN 978-1-59558-003-0; 1-59558-003-4; 978-1-59558-118-1 pa; 1-59558-118-9 pa

                        LC 2005-43866

   In this "collection of 40 interviews, . . . Terkel recalls his venerable radio program, The Wax Museum, which premiered shortly after the end of WWII in 1945, profiling composers, entertainers and impresarios of nearly every type of music. . . . Insightful and daring, Terkel always asks the right questions, whether culturally or musically." Publ Wkly

   Norton anthology of western music; edited by J. Peter Burkholder and Claude V. Palisca. 6th ed; W. W. Norton & Co 2010 3v v1 pa $40; v2 pa $40; v3 pa $40   **780.9**

   1. Music -- History and criticism

   ISBN 978-0-393-93126-6 v1 pa; 978-0-393-93127-3 v2 pa; 978-0-393-93240-9 v3 pa

   This is a collection of musical scores designed to accompany A history of western music by J. Peter Burkholder, Donald J. Grout and Claude V. Palisca.

780.92   Biography

Gilbert, Steven E.

   The **music** of Gershwin. Yale Univ. Press 1995 255p music $47   **780.92**

   1. Composers

   ISBN 0-300-06233-8

                        LC 95-12086

   This book analyzes major musical works of George Gershwin including Rhapsody in Blue, Concerto in F, An American in Paris, Porgy and Bess, and some of his popular songs and lesser known works.

   "With this book, Gershwin's music finally gets the attention it deserves. . . . Gilbert's book is not for the casual reader, since it requires an understanding of music theory and notation." Libr J

   Includes bibliographical references

Lockwood, Lewis

   Beethoven: the music and the life. Norton 2002 604p il music $39.95   **780.92**

   1. Composers

   ISBN 0-393-05081-5

                        LC 2002-75397

   The author "concentrates primarily on his subject's music and development as a composer before dedicating separate chapters to biography and the historical, political, and cultural milieus. . . . All of Lockwood's narrative, including the discussion of specific compositions, will be accessible to serious music lovers with only a modest technical background. This results partly from an interesting innovation . . . 100 additional musical examples are available on a companion web site. . . . Lockwood's study offers a new and authoritative interpretation of a prodigiously gifted and complex man and artist." Libr J

   Includes bibliographical references

Smith, Richard D.

   Can't you hear me callin': the life of Bill Monroe, father of bluegrass. Little, Brown 2000 365p il $25.95   **780.92**

   1. Bluegrass musicians 2. Mandolin players 3. Singers

   ISBN 0-316-80381-2

                        LC 99-54372

The author traces Monroe's "life from a music-rich but isolated childhood in the pastoral backroads of Kentucky to his early years as a struggling professional musician to his well-deserved status as an acclaimed elder statesman and musical ambassador. . . . A sensitive, tasteful, well-balanced portrait of a complicated man." Booklist

Includes discography, videography and bibliographical references

Troupe, Quincy

Miles and me: biography of Miles Davis. University of Calif. Press 2000 189p il $25; pa $12.95 **780.92**
1. African American musicians 2. Band leaders 3. Flugelhornists 4. Jazz musicians 5. Jazz musicians -- United States 6. Trumpet players
ISBN 0-520-21624-5; 0-520-23471-5 pa

LC 99-54370

"In the late 1970s, Troupe met Davis in New York, became friends with him, and eventually collaborated with him on Miles' autobiography. This slim memoir tells the intimate story of their unlikely friendship. . . . This is both a revealing look at a musical genius and a tender, surprisingly sweet remembrance of a good but demanding friend." Booklist

The Norton/Grove dictionary of women composers; edited by Julie Anne Sadie & Rhian Samuel. Norton 1995 xliii, 548p il $45 **780.92**
1. Biography, Collective 2. Music -- Bio-bibliography 3. Reference books 4. Women composers 5. Women composers -- Biography 6. Women composers -- Dictionaries 6. Women composers -- Dictionaries
ISBN 0-393-03487-9
"This important volume does not merely recycle material from the 1980 New Grove but collects 900 newly written articles, the longer ones signed." Libr J

781 Principles, forms, ensembles, voices, instruments

Kennedy, Dan

Rock on. Algonquin Books 2008 224p pa $14.95 **781**
1. Authors 2. Biography, Individual 3. Memoirists 4. Music industry
ISBN 978-1-565-12509-4; 1-565-12509-6

LC 2007-17025

This is a memoir of the author's experiences in the music industry.

"Kennedy's style—hilarious, paranoid and vulnerable—captures wonderfully the absurdity of the corporate music industry." Publ Wkly

Mannes, Elena

The **power** of music; pioneering discoveries in the new science of song. foreword by Dr. Aniruddh Patel. Walker & Company 2011 263p il $26 **781**
1. Music -- Psychological aspects 2. Music and science
ISBN 978-0-8027-1996-6; 0-8027-1996-1

LC 2010-48255

An "investigation of how music affects people and other animals. Detailing a variety of scientific experiments, [the author] shows the effects of sound frequencies and vibrations on body organs and brain waves; her study culminates in documentation supporting music therapy. Mannes's intercontinental explorations range from songbird studies to infants' melodic preferences to the origins of the universe (one topic on which her discussions seem rather far-fetched if fascinating). Interviews with influential musicians such as Bobby McFerrin help lighten an otherwise rather dense text." Libr J

Includes bibliographical references.

781.1 Basic principles of music

Toop, David

Sinister resonance; the mediumship of the listener. Continuum 2010 256p $24.95 **781.1**
1. Music -- Psychological aspects 2. Sound perception
ISBN 978-1-4411-4972-5; 1-4411-4972-4

LC 2009-47734

"An exploration of sound in novels, poems, and paintings from before the era of sound reproduction. . . . Toop doesn't translate mute works into sound by color or verbal line; rather, he uses the aural environments the works themselves depict as jumping-off points to examine both the objects under study and the nature of humanity's relationship to sound itself. . . . Toop's clear sense of mission gives him and his book a firm grip on this slipperiest subject." AV Club

Includes bibliographical references

781.2 Elements of music

Piston, Walter

Counterpoint. Norton 1947 235p music $41.75 **781.2**
1. Counterpoint
ISBN 978-0-393-09728-3; 0-393-09728-5
This work covers the principles and techniques of counterpoint as represented in the works of 18th and 19th century composers.

Harmony; 5th ed; Norton 1987 575p $59.95 **781.2**
1. Harmony
ISBN 0-393-95480-3

LC 86-23901

A presentation of the harmonic structures utilized by composers of the 18th and 19th centuries. Includes examples and exercises.

781.49 Recording of music

Milner, Greg

Perfecting sound forever; an aural history of recorded music. Faber and Faber 2009 416p il $35 **781.49**
1. Music -- Computer programs 2. Musical perception 3. Sound -- Recording and reproducing 4. Sound -- Recording and reproducing -- History 5. Sound

recordings
ISBN 0-571-21165-8; 978-0-571-21165-4
LC 2008-55444

"The author begins in the late 19th century, tracing the evolution from Edison's invention of the phonograph to the contemporary use of digital music files. Broad in scope and steeped in detail, the book strikes a mostly well-maintained balance between the history of the technological development of recordings and the more approachable accounts of the people and events surrounding it." Kirkus

781.6   Traditions of music

Horowitz, Joseph

★ **Classical** music in America; a history of its rise and fall. W. W. Norton & Company 2005 606p il $39.95   **781.6**

1. Music -- United States   2. Music -- United States -- History and criticism
ISBN 0-393-05717-8
LC 2004-27754

"As a comprehensive, convincing analysis of the contemporary dilemma, and a riveting portrait of the century and a half of events and personalities which brought it about, Mr Horowitz's account would be hard to beat." Economist

Includes bibliographical references

Plotkin, Fred

Classical music 101; a complete guide to learning and loving classical music. Hyperion 2002 673p pa $18.95   **781.6**

1. Music -- History and criticism   2. Music appreciation
ISBN 0-7868-8627-7
LC 2002-69075

This introduction to classical music "revolves almost entirely around the orchestra's instruments and the listening experience. {The author} presents material as coursework, and his strictures about really listening (as opposed to mere 'hearing') are well taken and certainly apply to all kinds of music. A valuable feature are the interviews with classical musicians interspersed throughout. . . . Recommended for libraries desiring an up-to-date and informative general introduction to classical music." Libr J

Includes discography and bibliographical references

781.62   Folk music

Sandburg, Carl

The **American** songbag; [compiled by] Carl Sandburg; introduction by Garrison Keillor. Harcourt Brace Jovanovich 1990 xxix, 495p pa $35   **781.62**

1. Folk music -- United States
ISBN 978-0-15-605650-2 pa; 0-15-605650-X pa

"Sandburg was not only a poet but also a noted collector and performer of American folk music. This anthology contains words and music to 290 songs that people have sung in the making of America." Publisher's note

Strom, Yale

The **book** of Klezmer; the history, the music, the folklore. A Cappella Bks. 2002 381p il music $28   **781.62**

1. Jews -- Music -- History and criticism   2. Klezmer music   3. Klezmer music -- History and criticism
ISBN 1-55652-445-5
LC 2002-2701

This history of Klezmer music is divided into "four chapters: 'From King David to Duvid the Klezmer,' 'From the Enlightenment to the Holocaust,' 'Klezmer in the New World, 1880-1960,' and 'From Zev to Zorn: The Masters of the Culture.' The first appendix, 'Klezmer Memories in the Memorial Books,' is one of the most moving sections, featuring a collection of commentaries on klezmer music and musicians from hundreds of memorial books written by Holocaust survivors." Libr J

Includes discography and bibliographical references

Ware, Charles Pickard

Slave songs of the United States; the complete 1867 collection of slave songs. [collected and compiled] by William Francis Allen, Charles Pickard Ware, and Lucy McKim Garrison; piano accompaniments by Irving Schlein; Peter Schlein, editor. Hal Leonard 2007 183p pa $15.95   **781.62**

1. African American music   2. Folk music -- United States   3. Slavery -- United States -- Songs   4. Spirituals (Songs)
ISBN 978-1-42342-262-4 pa; 1-42342-262-7 pa

"One of the first documentary collections of Negro folk songs was compiled in 1867 by William Francis Allen, Charles Pickard Ware and Lucy McKim Garrison. . . . This collection of 136 authentic folk songs of the Negro people revolutionized America's understanding of this music. The book, which contains spirituals, work songs, field hollers, soldier songs of Civil War days, and freedom songs, has become a classic of its kind. . . . In 1965, composer Irving Schlein created . . . piano settings for every song from the original edition. Chords for guitar have also been added to the musical notation." Publisher's note

Young, Rob

Electric Eden; unearthing Britain's visionary music. Faber and Faber 2011 664p il pa $25 **781.62**

1. Folk music -- Great Britain
ISBN 978-0-86547-856-5; 0-86547-856-2
LC 2011-01987

"Young's narrative slips fluidly forward, backward, and through the cracks of canonical music history. And he doesn't just stick to music; like Greil Marcus with a thirst for ancient paganism and postmodern urban theory, Young weaves a poetic, philosophical tapestry as rich and heady as the songs he champions." AV Club

Includes bibliographical references and discography

★ **American** ballads and folk songs; [compiled by] John A. Lomax and Alan Lomax; with a foreword

by George Lyman Kittredge. Dover Publications 1994 xxxix, 625p pa $21.95 **781.62**
1. Ballads 2. Folk music -- United States
ISBN 0-486-28276-7; 978-0-486-28276-3

Treasury of authentic songs, many recorded on location by noted father-and-son folklorists. Music and lyrics for over 200 ballads about the railroads, mountain songs, chain gang songs, creole songs, songs about cocaine and whisky, reels, minstrel songs, songs of childhood and much more. Includes such time-honored favorites as John Henry, Goin Home, Frankie and Albert, Down in the Valley, Little Brown Jug, Alabama-Bound, Shortenin Bread, Skip to My Lou, Frog Went a-Courtin and a host of others. Notes about the origin of each melody, a bibliography and an index are included.

★ Our singing country; folk songs and ballads. collected and compiled by John A. Lomax and Alan Lomax; music editor, Ruth Crawford Seeger; introduction to the Dover edition by Judith Tick; includes bibliography by Harold W. Thompson. Dover 2000 pa $16.95 **781.62**
1. Ballads 2. Folk music -- United States
ISBN 978-0-486-41089-0 pa; 0-486-41089-7 pa

This includes melodies and words for tunes from all parts of the United States. Songs include spirituals, hollers, game songs, lullabies, courting songs, chain-gang work songs, Cajun airs, breakdowns, and many more. Includes over 200 authentic folk songs and ballads.

781.64 Western popular music

Bradley, Andy
House of hits; the story of Houston's Gold Star/SugarHill Recording Studios. by Andy Bradley and Roger Wood. University of Texas Press 2010 334p il $34.95 **781.64**
1. Music industry 2. Popular music
ISBN 978-0-292-71919-4
LC 2009-44441

"A complete and well-annotated history of Gold Star/SugarHill, the oldest continuously operating recording studio in the U.S., the book is a trove of interesting stories and first-person narratives from many of the major players who made the records that are now an indelible part of the lexicon of American music." Houston Press
Includes bibliographical references

Broven, John
Record makers and breakers; voices of the independent rock 'n' roll pioneers. University of Illinois Press 2008 584p il $50 **781.64**
1. Music industry 2. Music trade 3. Popular music 4. Popular music -- History and criticism
ISBN 978-0-252-03290-5; 0-252-03290-X
LC 2008-27204

"The depth of factual detail is incredible, but it's presented in the style of a rich oral history. . . . It's a chronicle of the entrepreneurial American spirit, liberally punctuated

by the creation of some of the most exciting and innovative music of all time." Record Collector
Includes bibliographical references (p. 545-556)

Fletcher, Tony
All hopped up and ready to go; music from the streets of New York, 1927-77. W. W. Norton 2009 476p il pa $18.95 **781.64**
1. Popular music -- History and criticism 2. Popular music -- Social aspects
ISBN 978-0-393-33483-8; 0-393-33483-X
LC 2009-20630

"Anyone interested in popular music and the rich cultural heritage of New York—indeed, all of the U.S.—should read this book." Booklist
Includes bibliographical references

Govenar, Alan B.
Texas blues; the rise of a contemporary sound. [by] Alan Govenar. Texas A&M University Press 2008 599p il $40 **781.64**
1. Blues music 2. Rhythm and blues music
ISBN 978-1-58544-605-6; 1-58544-605-X
LC 2007-39152

As this "study shows, the importance of Texas Blues is demonstrated by the number of musicians who have practiced or are practicing this art. The coverage is expansive, with introductory essays, interviews conducted by Govenar and others, and a wealth of photographs. Govenar . . . manages to profile an amazing number of guitarists, pianists, singers, and others, both well known and obscure, who show how much pioneering blues musicians like T-Bone Walker and Lightnin' Hopkins influenced their own development. The discussion of the role played by tiny establishments, radio stations, country music, and several key record labels is particularly enlightening." Libr J
Includes discography and bibliographical references

Hermes, Will
Love goes to buildings on fire; five years in New York that changed music forever. Faber and Faber 2011 368p il $30 **781.64**
1. Music -- New York (N.Y.) 2. Popular music
ISBN 978-0-86547-980-7
LC 2011-08445

"New York City might have been dead broke, crime-ridden and garbage-infested in the 1970s, but the music sure was great. Bob Marley opened a club date for Bruce Springsteen, Bronx DJs stole power from streetlights to fiddle with turntables in new ways, Philip Glass drove classical purists nuts with his sweeping, hypnotic compositions, and The Fania All Stars remade salsa. Down at CBGB's, the Talking Heads were double-billed with the Ramones. New York City has been pumping out great music from Gershwin to Gaga, but veteran music writer Will Hermes shows in his episodic and idiosyncratic book, 'Love Goes to Buildings on Fire,' how 1973 through 1977 stood out as a time for innovation. Not only did the grimy time plant the seeds of hip-hop, it also fostered the highly influential scenes in jazz, Latino music, punk, disco, new wave and classical." Huffington Post
Includes bibliographical references

Houghton, Mick

Becoming Elektra; the true story of Jac Holzman's visionary record label. Jawbone 2010 304p il pa $29.95 **781.64**

1. Music industry 2. Popular music 3. Recording industry executives

ISBN 978-1-906002-29-9

Includes "full-color reproductions of virtually every title in Elektra's catalog, themselves a revealing portrait of changing tastes and evolving consumer sophistication. Houghton's research is meticulous but he avoids the minutia that clogs many music books." Seattle Post-Intelligencer

Lauterbach, Preston

The **chitlin'** circuit; and the road to rock 'n' roll. W. W. Norton & Company 2011 338p il $26.95 **781.64**

1. African American musicians 2. Jazz music -- History and criticism 3. Rock music -- History and criticism

ISBN 978-0-393-07652-3

LC 2011007209

"The 'chitlin' circuit,' a thriving African American subculture that few outsiders know much about, formed the brash underbelly of the rock 'n' roll story. In this terrific popular history, . . . Lauterbach uncovers a secret world that involves not only music but also racketeering and bribery, bootlegging, and various scandals. Lauterbach focuses on how the chitlin' circuit developed from the late 1930s to the early 1940s, with a particular emphasis on how it nurtured early rock 'n' roll. . . . A major achievement and an important contribution to American musical history." Booklist

Includes bibliographical references

Meltzer, Marisa

Girl power; the nineties revolution in music. Faber and Faber 2010 162p pa $14 **781.64**

1. Riot grrrl movement 2. Women rock musicians

ISBN 978-0-86547-979-1; 0-86547-979-8

LC 2009-25435

"Drawn early to the riot grrrl movement, [Meltzer] subsequently attended Evergreen State College in Olympia, WA, where it flourished and spread. Riot grrrls formed bands, composed and performed their singular brand of punk rock, dressed in girlish outfits and combat boots, spoke openly about politics and gender, and bonded through grassroots fanzines. They defined their own style of music and feminism." Libr J

Includes bibliographical references and filmography

Palmer, Robert

Blues & chaos; the music writing of Robert Palmer. edited by Anthony DeCurtis. Scribner 2009 452p $30 **781.64**

1. Popular music -- History and criticism 2. Rock music -- History and criticism

ISBN 978-1-4165-9974-6; 1-4165-9974-6

LC 2009-14346

A collection of previously published articles and criticism by music critic Robert Palmer.

"The openheartedness of Palmer's writing is refreshing: it addresses different musical styles on their own terms rather than demanding they bend to fit his. His criticism isn't an opportunity for idolatry, but rather for unpacking and understanding. . . . His profiles of the bluesman Muddy Waters and the minimalist composer La Monte Young are riveting and impassioned, seamlessly meshing personal and technical detail." N Y Times Book Rev

Reynolds, Simon

Retromania; pop culture's addiction to its own past. Faber & Faber 2011 458p **781.64**

1. Music literature 2. Musical criticism 3. Popular culture 4. Popular culture -- History 5. Popular music -- History and criticism 6. Popular music -- Social aspects 7. Retro (Style) 8. Rock music

ISBN 978-0-571-23208-6 pa; 0-571-23208-6 pa

LC 2011-930771

In this book, "Simon Reynolds, . . . a prominent journalist of popular music, . . . explores one of the most important facets of contemporary popular culture: the ongoing 'uses and abuses of the pop past.' . . . Reynolds touches on this trend as manifested in various cultural forms--fashion, television, movies, theater--but the spotlight is squarely on music. . . . The various issues explored include those of musical style, . . . recreations, . . . collections, . . . and digital technology." (Notes)

Noting that "there has never been a society in human history so obsessed with the cultural artifacts of its own immediate past, Reynolds . . . offers cogent examples of the lame and shamefull retromania in pop music, including revivals, reissues, reunions, tribute albums, golden oldie shows, boxed sets and music documentaries. Part of a broader societal obsession with nostalgia—e.g., remakes of blockbuster movies, iconic TV shows and vintage fashions—this constant use and abuse of the past prevents the making of groundbreaking music. New styles like hip hop and rave culture can no longer emerge; instead, pop musicians of the 2000s tweak established musical genres and raid archives. Much of Reynolds's absorbing, brightly written and rambling book focuses on the evolution of pop nostalgia. . . . Important—and alarming—reading for pop-music aficionados." Kirkus

Includes bibliographical references

Roden, Steve

. . . i listen to the wind that obliterates my traces; music in vernacular photographs, 1880-1955. Dust-to-Digital 2011 un $50 **781.64**

1. Artistic photography 2. Folk music 3. Musical instruments -- Pictorial works 4. Popular music

ISBN 978-09817342-4-8

This volume is "compiled from the personal collection of interdisciplinary sound and visual artist Steve Roden. It contains a book of photographs of musicians mostly unknown and others related to the hearing of music. This beautifully hardbound book also contains two CDs containing 51 songs recorded between approximately 1914-1955, taken from 78s and acetates. The music ranges from the well known Bradley Kincaid's 1928 recording of 'Froggie Went A-Courtin' and Ukulele Ike's '(I'm Cryin' 'Cause I Know I'm) Losing You' to virtually unknown sides taken from home recordings. This is all annotated by a lengthy poetic essay by Roden that attempts to create a social and poetic context from the ephemeral, and is underscored by epigraphs from writers from James Agee, Joseph Roth, and

William Wordsworth to Pär Lagerqvist and Gerhart Hauptmann." Allmusic.com

Thompson, Gordon

Please please me; change and sixties British
pop. Oxford University Press 2008 340p il $99; pa
$24.95   **781.64**
1. Music industry 2. Popular music 3. Popular music
-- Great Britain -- History and criticism 4. Rock music
5. Sound recording industry -- History
ISBN 978-0-19-533318-3; 978-0-19-533325-1 pa
                                    LC 2007-47545
"As history books go, this one is more engaging than
most. The selected discography is a nice addition, and a song
index (in addition to a general book index) makes it easy to
find passages related to your favorite tunes." Goldmine
Includes discography and bibliographical references (p.
307-314)

Wald, Elijah

How the Beatles destroyed rock 'n' roll; an alternative history of American popular music. Oxford
University Press 2009 323p il $24.95   **781.64**
1. Popular music -- History and criticism 2. Popular
music -- United States -- History and criticism 3. Rock
music -- History and criticism
ISBN 978-0-19-534154-6
                                    LC 2008-42265
"A bracing, inclusive look at the dramatic transformation
in the way music was produced and listened to during the
20th century." Kirkus
Includes bibliographical references (p. 281-289)

Watkins, S. Craig

★ **Hip** hop matters; politics, pop culture, and the
struggle for the soul of a movement. Beacon Press
2005 295p $24.95; pa $16   **781.64**
1. Hip-hop 2. Rap (Music) -- History and criticism 3.
Rap music
ISBN 0-8070-0982-2; 0-8070-0986-5 pa
                                    LC 2004-24187
The author "presents a concise, clear history of the hip-
hop movement in the US and uses it as a springboard for
discussion of contemporary issues of politics, pop culture,
and struggle." Choice
Includes bibliographical references

Westhoff, Ben

Dirty South; Outkast, Lil Wayne, Soulja Boy, and
the Southern rappers who reinvented hip-hop. Chicago Review Press 2011 298p il pa $14.95 **781.64**
1. Rap music
ISBN 978-1-56976-606-4; 1-56976-606-1
                                    LC 2010-53907
An "exploration of the musical and personal terrain of
what has come to be known as the Southern sound of rap
by such artists as Lil Wayne, Young Jeezy, and Ludacris.
Westhoff convincingly details how Southern rap music—
'party music, full of hypnotic hooks and sing-along choruses'—took over from dominant East Coast and West Coast
rap styles by replacing 'normal rap structures and metaphor-
heavy rhymes. . . in favor of chants, grunts and shouts.' In

fact, the beauty of Westhoff's descriptions of the genre as
a whole and various songs in particular will make old fans
as well as newbies want to search out and play classic CDs
such as OutKast's 'Aquemini' and 'Kings of Crunk' by Lil
Jon. And Westhoff's personal trips to the home bases of each
artist he presents show how the personalities of the artists
reinforce their music." Publ Wkly
Includes bibliographical references

★ **Best** music writing 2008; Nelson George, guest
editor; Daphne Carr, series editor. Da Capo Press
2008 337p pa $15.95   **781.64**
1. Popular music -- History and criticism
ISBN 978-0-306-81734-2; 0-306-81734-9
A collection of writings on rock, hip-hop, jazz, pop,
country and other genres.

The **Oxford** American book of great music writing;
edited by Marc Smirnoff; foreword by Van Dyke
Parks. University of Arkansas Press 2008 xxii,
421p il $34.95   **781.64**
1. Popular music -- History and criticism
ISBN 978-1-557-28887-5; 1-557-28887-9
                                    LC 2008-26298
A collection of fifty-five essays taken from Oxford
American magazine's Southern Music Issues from 1996
to 2007.
"With contributions from Nick Tosches, Robert Palmer,
Robert Gordon, and Peter Guralnick, some of the top music writers, Smirnoff reminds us what good music writing
is. This compilation is full of little gems, including Susan
Straight's tender reminiscence of the music of Al Green,
Tom Piazza's harrowing account of his encounter with blue-
grass legend Jimmy Martin, and John Fergus Ryan's report
of his time backstage with Jerry Lee Lewis in 1970. Also
included are Jerry Wexler on Dusty Springfield, Roy Blount
Jr. on Ray Charles, and John Jeremiah Sullivan on Chris Bell
(of Big Star)." Booklist
Includes bibliographical references

781.642   Country music

Carlin, Richard

Country music; a biographical dictionary. Routledge 2003 497p il $125   **781.642**
1. Country music 2. Country music -- Bio-bibliography
-- Dictionaries 3. Country music -- Dictionaries 4.
Reference books
ISBN 0-415-93802-3
                                    LC 2002-3451
The author "presents an authoritative and acerbically
opinionated A-Z guide to 700 country western solo artists
and groups. Each article consists of a brief biography, career
highs and lows, and select discographies." Libr J
Includes bibliographical references

**Country Music Hall of Fame and Museum (Nash-
ville, Tenn.)**

The **Encyclopedia** of country music; the ultimate guide to the music. compiled by the staff of the
Country Music Hall of Fame and Museum; edited by

Paul Kingsbury with the assistance of Laura Garrard, Daniel Cooper, and John Rumble. Oxford Univ. Press 1998 634p il hardcover o.p. pa $39.95 **781.642**
1. Country music -- Encyclopedias 2. Reference books
ISBN 0-19-511671-2; 978-0-19-517608-7 pa; 0-19-517608-1 pa

LC 97-51362

"Interspersed with the biographical entries are historical and sociological essays on the literature of country music, country songwriting, gospel, folk and popular music connections, and even touring and costuming. Thirteen appendixes cover the Country Music Hall of Fame, radio stations, and best-selling country albums." Libr J
Includes bibliographical references

Escott, Colin
The **Grand** ole opry; the making of an American icon. Brenda Colladay, photo editor. Center Street 2006 250p il $24.99   **781.642**
1. Country music
ISBN 978-1-931722-86-5; 1-931722-86-2

LC 2006-7796

"Escott's overview of the long-running Saturday-night performance showcase takes the form of oral history. The preponderance of the text consists of statements by Grand Ole Opry producers, sponsors, and stars, with the older comments drawn from old books and newspaper stories and the newer from Escott's interviews. . . . With decade-by-decade lists of the Opry's members and scads of performance photos, it's a honey of a book for every American library." Booklist

Jennings, Dana Andrew
Sing me back home; love, death, and country music. [by] Dana Jennings. Faber and Faber 2008 257p $24   **781.642**
1. Country music -- History and criticism
ISBN 978-0-86547-960-9; 0-86547-960-7

LC 2007-47955

This "quirky, endearing combination memoir, family history, music criticism, and love-of-place offering, made up of short, punchy chapters and sharp observations about country's appeal and how country has expressed the inchoate emotions of its largely rural following, essentially presents the music as the portrayal of a way of life and a way of being." Booklist
Includes discography and bibliographical references

Kagarise, Leon
Pure country; the Leon Kagarise archives 1961-1971. foreword by Robert Gordon; introduction and text by Eddie Dean. Process Media 2008 191p il $35   **781.642**
1. Country music -- Pictorial works
ISBN 978-1-93417-003-8

"Kagarise was an obsessive fan of 'real' country and bluegrass musics, and he amassed a giant collection of records, live tapes and ephemera, mostly during the 1960s. This volume collects many of the color slides he shot at a couple of outdoor venues in Maryland and Pennsylvania, and the views of this lost scene they provide is unparalleled. Well-known figures like Johnny Cash, George Jones and

Skeeter Davis mix with more legendary unknowns (at least to proles), like the Stoneman family, with whom Kagarise had a special connection, and who he rates far above the Carter family in terms of sheer talent. The main text . . . provides a very boss thumbnail history of country music in the pre-modern era." Arthur

Russell, Tony
Country music originals; the legends & the lost. Oxford University Press 2007 258p il $29.95   **781.642**
1. Country music 2. Country musicians
ISBN 978-0-19-532509-6

LC 2007-8471

"Russell has accomplished a spectacular feat in that he has written a thorough reference book that is as pleasing to read as the best of narrative nonfiction." Publ Wkly
Includes bibliographical references

Zwonitzer, Mark
Will you miss me when I'm gone? the Carter Family and their legacy in American music. [by] Mark Zwonitzer with Charles Hirshberg. Simon & Schuster 2002 417p il hardcover o.p. pa $15   **781.642**
1. Country musicians 2. Country musicians -- United States -- Biography 3. Singers 4. Songwriters
ISBN 0-684-85763-4; 0-7432-4382-X pa

LC 2002-22395

The author "follows the Carter family's history from the 1891 birth of A.P. Carter, the musical founder, up through the late 1970s, offering background on the social, economic and technological developments that spawned American folk, country and rock music. . . . Zwonitzer writes with flair, weaving anecdotes into a compelling study that will intrigue historians and music lovers alike." Publ Wkly

781.643   Blues

Ferris, William
Give my poor heart ease; voices of the Mississippi blues. [interviews by] William Ferris. University of North Carolina Press 2009 302p il $35 **781.643**
1. African Americans -- Mississippi 2. Blues music
ISBN 0-8078-3325-8; 978-0-8078-3325-4

LC 2009-16647

Ferris "presents transcriptions of stories he captured via films and recording devices from the 1960s and 1970s of Mississippi blues practitioners, preachers, and Parchman Prison inmates. The enclosed CD and DVD bring the package together with stories, blues songs, and gospel recordings. B.B. King and Willie Dixon are the most famous artists included, but the stories of desperately poor sharecroppers and ex-inmates are just as engrossing. The comprehensive bibliography is a great resource." Libr J
Includes bibliographical references

Gioia, Ted
Delta blues; the life and times of the Mississippi Masters who revolutionized American music. art-

work by Neil Harpe. W. W. Norton 2008 449p il
$27.95; pa $16.95   **781.643**
1. African American musicians -- Biography 2. Blues
(Music) -- History and criticism 3. Blues (Music) --
Mississippi -- Yazoo River delta 4. Blues music
ISBN 978-0-393-06258-8; 0-393-06258-9; 978-0-393-
33750-1 pa; 0-393-33750-2 pa

LC 2008-09412

Gioia describes the "beginnings of the Delta sound with
Charley Patton and former Parchman inmates Son House
and Bukka White. He relates the stories of such obscure
Delta artists as Tommy Johnson and Big Joe Williams before
delivering the bulk of the book, which describes the lives
and influences of Delta blues icons Robert Johnson, Muddy
Waters, Howlin' Wolf, B.B. King, and John Lee Hooker.
Gioia ends with a chapter about the rediscovery of Delta
legends by rabid blues collectors during the 1960s and then
oddly leaps to 1990s performers such as Chris Thomas King
and Junior Kimbrough in the last few pages. . . . Though presenting little new information and not geared for the blues
fanatic, this is an excellent introduction to Delta blues for the
novice and the general reader." Libr J
Includes bibliographical references

King, B. B.

★ **Blues** all around me; the autobiography of
B.B. King. [by] B.B. King with David Ritz. Avon
Bks. 1996 336p il hardcover o.p. pa $15.99 **781.643**
1. African American musicians 2. Blues music 3.
Blues musicians 4. Guitarists 5. Singers
ISBN 0-380-97318-9; 0-06-206103-8 pa

LC 96-27773

King recounts his humble beginnings and his career as a
prominent blues guitarist.
"This is one of the best recent pop-music bios. King
speaks straight from the soul, it seems, just like he plays the
guitar." Booklist

Lomax, Alan

★ The **land** where the blues began. New Press
2002 539p il pa $21.95   **781.643**
1. African American music 2. African Americans --
Mississippi 3. Blues music
ISBN 1-56584-739-3; 978-1-56584-739-2

LC 2004-268632

This is an account of the folklorist and musicologist's
travels in the Mississippi Delta in the 1940s as he recorded
the work of African American blues musicians.
"If it were a novel, Alan Lomax's long-awaited account
of his adventures in the Mississippi Delta would be called
'sprawling' and a 'must read.' . . . It is as delightful and hard
to put down as any fictional epic." Booklist
Includes bibliographical references, discography and
filmography

Russell, Tony

The **Penguin** guide to blues recordings; [by]
Tony Russell and Chris Smith, with Neil Slaven,
Ricky Russell and Joe Faulkner. Penguin 2006 923p
pa $30   **781.643**
1. Blues music -- Discography 2. Sound recordings

-- Reviews
ISBN 978-0-14-051384-4; 0-14-051384-1
"Listing more than 1000 blues artists in alphabetical
order with a final section for compilations, the editors start
each entry with a brief but adequate biography, following
with the name and date of a recording, the label, and the
musicians on the session. They . . . concentrate on artists
who play primarily acoustic and electric blues, among them
Charley Patton, Bessie Smith, B.B. King, and Buddy Guy.
They critically and carefully rate nearly 6000 CDs on a one
to four-star scale (with a special indicator for essential recordings), applying tongue-in-cheek wit and assigning ratings in a meaningful way to help the discriminating blues listener make a decision about his or her next purchase." Libr J

Nothing but the blues; the music and the musicians.
{edited by} Lawrence Cohn. Abbeville Press
1993 432p il hardcover o.p. pa $39.95 **781.643**
1. Blues music 2. Blues music -- History and criticism
ISBN 0-7892-0607-2 pa

LC 93-2791

This "illustrated compilation of articles by 10 notable
writers examines the origins of blues and the music's various styles and artists, including women." Booklist
Includes discography and bibliographical references

781.644   Soul

Danielsen, Anne

Presence and pleasure; the funk grooves of
James Brown and Parliament. Wesleyan University
Press 2006 262p il $65; pa $24.95   **781.644**
1. Funk (Music) 2. Singers 3. Soul musicians
ISBN 978-0-8195-6822-9; 0-8195-6822-8; 978-0-
8195-6823-6 pa; 0-8195-6823-6 pa

LC 2006-10987

The author "brings a unique perspective to this book. .
. . Her discussion of funk comes from the dual angles of
musicologist and longtime performer." Choice
Includes bibliographical references

781.646   Reggae

Bradley, Lloyd

This is reggae music; the story of Jamaica's mu-
sic. Grove Press 2001 572p il pa $17   **781.646**
1. Jamaicans -- Great Britain 2. Reggae music 3.
Reggae music -- History and criticism 4. Reggae music
-- Jamaica -- History and criticism
ISBN 0-8021-3828-4

LC 2001-33462

Presented "in a witty and engaging manner. . . . For enthusiasts, this book is fabulous." Libr J
Includes bibliographical references and indexes

781.65 Jazz

Armstrong, Louis

Louis Armstrong, in his own words; selected writings. edited and with an introduction by Thomas Brothers; annotated index by Charles Kinzer. Oxford Univ. Press 1999 xxvii, 255p il hardcover o.p. pa $14.95 **781.65**

1. Band leaders 2. Jazz -- History and criticism 3. Jazz musicians 4. Jazz musicians -- United States 5. Singers 6. Trumpet players

ISBN 0-19-514046-X

LC 99-17040

In this collection Armstrong "recounts episodes from his childhood in New Orleans, pays tribute to other musicians, and extolls the virtues of marijuana, laxatives, and rice and beans while speaking candidly about race relations, the music business, and his extramarital affairs. The joy he took in expressing himself on paper is abundantly evident." New Yorker

Includes bibliographical references

Cook, Richard

The **Penguin** guide to jazz recordings; [by] Richard Cook and Brian Morton. 9th ed.; Penguin 2008 pa $37.50 **781.65**

1. Jazz music -- Discography 2. Sound recordings -- Reviews

ISBN 978-0-14-102327-4; 0-14-102327-9

"Entries include very brief descriptions of the artists and a list of their recordings, with reviews and ratings by the authors. The lengths of the CD entries vary from very short (label, catalog number, issue date, and performers) to extensive, multiparagraph descriptions of the album's history, reception, and individual songs. The authors are clearly devout jazz historians, and the character of the entries is as much admiring as it is strictly factual. Their detailed descriptions of albums, songs, and even artists' tone colors and interpretations within specific songs are testament to their expertise." Booklist

Crouch, Stanley

★ **Considering** genius; writings on jazz. Basic Civitas Books 2006 359p $27.50 **781.65**

1. Jazz music 2. Jazz music -- History and criticism

ISBN 0-465-01517-4

LC 2006-2225

"This collection brings together a healthy sampling of [Crouch's] jazz writings dating from 1977 to the present. A long and spirited prologue, 'Jazz Me Blues,' lays out Crouch's jazz aesthetic, but he really shows his stuff in the essays on particular musicians, combining trenchant analysis of the artist with fascinating biographical material and feeling free to speculate at will about the psychology and inner lives of such jazz greats as Miles Davis, Thelonious Monk, and John Coltrane. . . . Essential reading for jazz fans." Booklist

Feather, Leonard

The **biographical** encyclopedia of jazz; [by] Leonard Feather and Ira Gitler, with the assistance of Swing journal, Tokyo. Oxford Univ. Press 1999 xx, 718p hardcover o.p. pa $29.95 **781.65**

1. Jazz 2. Jazz musicians

ISBN 0-19-507418-1; 978-0-19-532000-8 pa; 0-19-532000-X pa

LC 98-15485

This book is based in part on Leonard Feather's Encyclopedia of jazz, The new encyclopedia of jazz, The encyclopedia of jazz in the sixties, and on a subsequent work by Mr. Feather and Ira Gitler, The encyclopedia of jazz in the seventies.

This reference source "is made up of more than 3,000 biographies, listed in alphabetical order. Musicians, singers, songwriters, and producers are included. Each entry begins with birth and death information, instruments played, and music-education information. This is followed by a listing of groups each individual played with for significant periods of time. Concluding each entry are lists of recordings, broadcast appearances, and record labels. . . . An indispensable reference source for its comprehensiveness and quality of scholarship." Booklist

Includes discographies

Friedwald, Will

Jazz singing; America's great voices from Bessie Smith to bebop and beyond. Da Capo Press 1996 505p il pa $18.50 **781.65**

1. Jazz music 2. Jazz vocals -- History and criticism 3. Singers

ISBN 0-306-80712-2

LC 96-23837

"This is an absolutely essential book for anybody who cares in the slightest about adult popular music." Booklist

Includes discography

Giddins, Gary

Jazz; [by] Gary Giddins & Scott DeVeaux. W. W. Norton 2009 704p il $39.95 **781.65**

1. Jazz -- History and criticism 2. Jazz music -- History and criticism

ISBN 978-0-393-06861-0; 0-393-068617

LC 2009-24880

The authors "split duties: DeVeaux provides blow-by-blow, laymen-friendly listening guides to musical examples (there's an accompanying four-CD set, though you have to buy that separately) and Giddins writes the historical narrative. . . . Jazz history for Giddins and DeVeaux isn't a matter of exposition so much as argument, and those arguments — never strident or agenda-driven, but arguments nonetheless — are what provide the 'plot' of this story and carry it through the music's many disparate, colorful characters, styles, and transformations." Boston Phoenix

Includes bibliographical references

Visions of jazz; the first century. Oxford Univ. Press 1998 690p hardcover o.p. pa $18.95 **781.65**

1. Composers -- Biography 2. Jazz -- History and criticism 3. Jazz music 4. Jazz music -- History and criticism 5. Jazz musicians 6. Jazz musicians -- Biography

ISBN 0-19-513241-6 pa

LC 98-12199

"Alongside his virtuoso considerations of Ellington, Monk, Mingus, and the predictable greats, Giddins illuminates the contributions to be found in the likes of Al Jolson's minstrel posing and Stan Kenton's florid kitsch. His writing, like the music he loves, is joyously polyphonic, with history, legend, musicology, biography, and performance all rising out of the mix." New Yorker

Weather bird; jazz at the dawn of its second century. Gary Giddins. Oxford University Press 2004 xxiv, 632p $35   **781.65**
   1. Jazz -- History and criticism 2. Jazz music -- History and criticism 3. Performing arts
   ISBN 0-19-515607-2
                        LC 2004-654
"This book collects more than 140 essays, articles, and reviews that Giddins wrote from 1990 to November 2003. . . . The breadth and depth of his knowledge is extremely impressive, his ear is astounding, and his masterly style routinely achieves the near impossible in writing engagingly about something that inherently eludes description." Libr J

Gioia, Ted
   The **history** of jazz; 2nd ed.; Oxford University Press 2011 444p il pa $19.95   **781.65**
   1. Jazz music -- History and criticism
   ISBN 978-0-19-539970-7; 0-19-539970-6
                    LC 2010-23182
The author "relates the story of African American music from its roots in Africa to the international respect it enjoys today. . . . This well-researched, extensively annotated volume covers the major trends and personalities that have shaped jazz. The excellent bibliography and list of recommended listening make this a valuable purchase for libraries building a jazz collection." Libr J
Includes discography and bibliographical references

Grosse Jazzbuch./English
   The **jazz** book; from ragtime to the 21st century. [by] Joachim-Ernst Berendt and Gunther Huesmann; translated by H. and B. Bredigkeit ... [et al.]. 7th ed., rev. and expanded.; Lawrence Hill Books 2009 754p il $49.95; pa $29.95   **781.65**
   1. Jazz music -- History and criticism
   ISBN 978-1-55652-820-0; 1-55652-820-5; 978-1-55652-823-1 pa; 1-55652-823-X pa
                    LC 2008-53770
"Should this be your first book about jazz? Yes, but you must start with small portions and use the Internet to sample freely as you proceed. The sheer amount of information on offer here makes this most decidedly a Jazz Tome, but one that can be dipped into freely, any time, for any reason." Open Letters
Includes discography

Kahn, Ashley
   The **house** that Trane built; the story of Impulse Records. Norton 2006 338p il $29.95   **781.65**
   1. Jazz -- History and criticism 2. Jazz music 3. Jazz musicians 4. Saxophonists
   ISBN 0-393-05879-4
                 LC 2005-037218

The author "offers a fascinating insider's view of the sessions that produced not only Coltrane's classics but also top-grade albums by both fiery radicals and such timeless stars as Duke Ellington, Coleman Hawkins and Benny Carter." Economist

Lees, Gene
   You can't steal a gift; Dizzy, Clark, Milt, and Nat. foreword by Nat Hentoff. Yale Univ. Press 2001 269p il $27.95   **781.65**
   1. Band leaders 2. Bassists 3. Flugelhornists 4. Jazz musicians 5. Jazz musicians -- United States 6. Photographers 7. Pianists 8. Singers 9. Trumpet players
   ISBN 0-300-08965-1
                    LC 2001-3444
Lees discusses the lives and careers of four jazz musicians: Dizzy Gillespie, Terry Clark, Milt Hinton, and Nat King Cole. A theme of the book is how these artists were affected by race relations in the United States.
The author "has a natural ease with words and a graceful prose style that captures the reader's attention." Booklist

Marsalis, Wynton, 1961-
   Moving to higher ground; how jazz can change your life. [by] Wynton Marsalis with Geoffrey C. Ward. Random House 2008 181p il $26   **781.65**
   1. Jazz music -- History and criticism
   ISBN 978-1-4000-6078-8; 1-4000-6078-8
                    LC 2008-16560
The author "explains in lay readers' terms how jazz works as a diverse musical genre and, more important, how an understanding and appreciation of jazz can enrich one's life. . . . This work is highly recommended." Libr J

Morgenstern, Dan
   Living with jazz; a reader. edited by Sheldon Meyer. Pantheon Books 2004 712p $35   **781.65**
   1. Jazz -- History and criticism 2. Jazz music 3. Jazz music -- History and criticism
   ISBN 0-375-42072-X
                    LC 2004-43432
This is a compilation of "nearly half a century of Morgenstern's profiles, liner notes, record and show reviews and other musings. . . . Morgenstern reminisces about his introduction to jazz in a brief opening memoir, then segues into lengthy sections on his greatest heroes, Louis Armstrong and Duke Ellington. . . . His exuberant characterizations make this monumental volume a stimulating guide to jazz in the second half of the 20th century." Publ Wkly

Paulo, Joaquim
   Jazz covers; ed. Julius Wiedemann; interviews with Bob Ciano . . . [et al.] by Joaquim Paulo; top-10 favorite records lists by jazz DJs Amir Abdullah . . . [et al.] Taschen 2008 494p il pa $39.99   **781.65**
   1. Jazz music 2. Sound recordings -- Album covers
   ISBN 978-3-8228-2366-8; 3-8228-2366-X
This volume "manages to sum up the genre with the thoroughness of a scholarly essay. Vivid photographs are accompanied by pithy back-story writeups of the jazz artists and album designers." Time Out Hong Kong

Ratliff, Ben

Jazz: a critic's guide to the 100 most important recordings. Times Bks. 2002 xx, 250p il pa $16   781.65
1. Jazz music -- Discography
ISBN 0-8050-7068-0

LC 2002-69551

The author "presents essays on what he considers the 100 most important jazz recordings. In each, he discusses a recording's merits and shortcomings and includes a list of its performers. . . . As a guide for the uninitiated it is essential for academic music libraries and public libraries large and small. It would also be most useful for collection development librarians building a well-rounded jazz CD collection." Libr J

The **jazz** ear; conversations over music. Times Books 2008 256p il $25   781.65
1. Jazz music -- History and criticism
ISBN 978-0-8050-8146-6; 0-8050-8146-1

LC 2008-10122

"Originally published as a series in the New York Times, the 15 conversations presented here consist of Ratliff sitting down with such diverse and talented luminaries as Sonny Rollins, Pat Metheny, Paul Motian, and Dianne Reeves. The treasure of these conversations is not just their fluid and intimate manner but their focus on the recordings that had the greatest influence on the artists and their musical paths. . . . An added bonus is the recommended-listening section, in which Ratliff shares his list of his subjects' seminal recordings. Highly recommended." Libr J
Includes bibliographical references

Sandke, Randy

Where the dark and the light folks meet; race and the mythology, politics, and business of jazz. Scarecrow Press 2010 277p $40; ebook $40   781.65
1. Jazz music -- History and criticism
ISBN 978-0-8108-6652-2; 0-8108-6652-8; 978-0-8108-6990-5 ebook; 0-8108-6990-X ebook

LC 2009-37977

The author "tackles a controversial question: Is jazz the product of an insulated African-American environment, shut off from the rest of society by strictures of segregation and discrimination, or is it more properly understood as the juncture of a wide variety of influences under the broader umbrella of American culture?" Publisher's note
Includes bibliographical references

Santoro, Gene

Myself when I am real: the life and music of Charles Mingus. Oxford Univ. Press 2000 452p hardcover o.p. pa $17.95   781.65
1. Bassists 2. Composers 3. Jazz musicians 4. Jazz musicians -- United States
ISBN 0-19-509733-5; 0-19-514711-1 pa

LC 99-46734

The author "has attempted not only to capture the complex, contradictory character of jazz bassist and composer Mingus, but also to assert his music's towering significance in American culture as a whole." Publ Wkly
Includes discography and bibliographical references

Ward, Geoffrey C.

Jazz; a history of America's music. based on a documentary film by Ken Burns written by Geoffrey C. Ward; with a preface by Ken Burns. Knopf 2000 489p il $65; pa $29.95 781.65
1. Jazz -- History and criticism 2. Jazz -- Pictorial works 3. Jazz music
ISBN 0-679-44551-X; 0-679-76539-5 pa

LC 00-22604

The authors "have assembled a comprehensive history with a focus on the musicians and the sociology of jazz. . . . The short articles by Wynton Marsalis, Dan Morgenstern, Gerald Early, Stanley Crouch, and Gary Giddins, which are woven into the text, provide a . . . specific focus on a number of jazz's aspects." Libr J
Includes bibliographical references

Williams, Richard

The **blue** moment; Miles Davis's Kind of blue and the remaking of modern music. W. W. Norton & Company 2010 309p   781.65
1. Band leaders 2. Flugelhornists 3. Jazz music -- History and criticism 4. Jazz musicians 5. Trumpet players
ISBN 978-0-393-07663-9

LC 2009053270

"'Kind of Blue,' the book jacket notes, is the only jazz album many people own. And while that might turn off jazz fans, even purists bow down to the 1959 Miles Davis release. Williams, a writer for The Guardian in Britain, details the recording sessions (it took only nine hours and was recorded in a Manhattan church); the band, which included John Coltrane, Cannonball Adderly and Gil Evans; and the tenor of the times, which helps explain why it's so extraordinary." N Y Post
Includes bibliographical references

★ The **New** Grove dictionary of jazz; edited by Barry Kernfeld. 2nd ed; Grove's Dictionaries Inc. 2002 3v set $295   781.65
1. Jazz -- Bio-bibliography 2. Jazz -- Encyclopedias 3. Jazz music -- Dictionaries 4. Reference books
ISBN 1-56159-284-6

LC 2001-40794

This reference to jazz and jazz musicians includes "more than 7750 entries. . . . [It covers] jazz styles, instruments, record labels, nicknames, guilds and associations, jazz language, libraries and archives, false fingering techniques for horns, festivals, titles of films containing jazz scenes, a list of contrafacts . . . and even biographies of a few jazz writers and critics." Libr J
Includes bibliographical references and discographies

781.66   Rock (Rock 'n' roll)

Almond, Steve

Rock and roll will save your life; a book by and for the fanatics among us (with bitchin' soundtrack) Random House 2010 216p $23   781.66
1. Authors 2. Biography, Individual 3. Humorists 4. Journalists 5. Popular music -- History and criticism 6.

Rock music 7. Rock music -- History and criticism 8. Short story writers
ISBN 978-1-4000-6620-9; 1-4000-6620-4

"As a young writer plagued by self-doubt, Almond reveled in the emotional escape of music; the joy of his fanaticism is conveyed poignantly—and so completely—that we're infected with his touted salvation too. With well-placed 'interludes' or 'reluctant exegeses,' Almond peppers his pages with biting insights and funny vignettes; dismissing, for instance, Toto's 'Africa' as '. . . the lovechild of Muzak and Imperialism.' Though the language feels a bit highbrow, Almond ultimately crafts a playful and intelligent read." Paste

Aronowitz, Nona Willis

★ **Out** of the vinyl deeps; Ellen Willis on rock music. edited by Nona Willis Aronowitz; foreword by Sasha Frere-Jones; afterword by Daphne Carr and Evie Nagy. University of Minnesota Press 2011 232p il $69; pa $22.95 **781.66**
1. Rock music 2. Rock music -- History and criticism
ISBN 978-0-8166-7282-0; 978-0-8166-7283-7 pa
LC 2010-50856

"Willis's work is crystalline enough that reading each essay takes the reader on a trip back to the era when it originally appeared, but it's a testimony to her intellect and talent that those journeys look completely unlike any hagiography you might stumble across." Village Voice
Includes bibliographical references

Bangs, Lester

Mainlines, blood feasts and bad taste; a Lester Bangs reader. edited by John Morthland. Anchor Books 2003 409p pa $15.95 **781.66**
1. Rock music 2. Rock music -- History and criticism 3. Rock musicians
ISBN 978-0375-71367-5; 0-375-71367-0
LC 2003-40392

Mothland includes includes Bangs's "riffs on jazz, heretofore not seen by many eyes. Readers will be reminded of what Bangs . . . should really be famous for: his lust for life and 'soul' music, any tune that hits a nerve and the heart at the same time. Truly, this is a time capsule of when pop music still crackled and people held the stuff to an emotional standard." Libr J

Psychotic reactions and carburetor dung; edited by Greil Marcus. Knopf 1987 386p hardcover o.p. pa $16 **781.66**
1. Rock music -- History and criticism
ISBN 0-394-53896-X; 0-679-72045-6 pa
LC 87-45122

"For rockers whose tastes demand more than Madonna and who remember back before Bruce, this is a gem." Libr J

Blecha, Peter

Sonic boom; the history of Northwest rock, from Louie Louie to Smells like Teen Spirit. Backbeat Books 2009 304p il pa $19.99 **781.66**
1. Rock music
ISBN 978-0-87930-946-6
LC 2008-51529

This book "lends substantial weight to the big fish—long established legends like Jimi Hendrix and Kurt Cobain, as well as newer names like Death Cab for Cutie and Fleet Foxes—but it also pays respect to the lesser known little guys who contributed to 60-plus years of local rock, and as such, . . . does a commendable service to the musical history and the sonic identity of the area and its artists." PopMatters
Includes discography

Browne, David

Fire and rain; the Beatles, Simon & Garfunkel, James Taylor, CSNY, and the lost story of 1970. Da Capo Press 2011 369p il $26 **781.66**
1. Rock music 2. Rock music -- History and criticism 3. Singers 4. Songwriters
ISBN 9780306818509; 0-306-81850-7

"Browne skillfully interleaves the stories of these musicians during this tumultuous year, making room for substantial walk-ons by other significant industry figures like Bill Graham, Peter Yarrow, Phil Spector, Rita Coolidge, Carole King and Joni Mitchell. Intimately familiar with the music, fully comprehending the cross-pollination among the artists, thoroughly awake to the dynamics of the decade's last gasp, the author expertly captures a volatile and hugely interesting moment in rock history." Kirkus
Includes bibliographical references

Buckland, Gail

Who shot rock & roll; a photographic history, 1955 to the present. Alfred A. Knopf 2009 319p il $40 **781.66**
1. Rock music 2. Rock music -- Pictorial works 3. Rock musicians
ISBN 978-0-307-27016-0; 0-307-27016-5
LC 2009-19122

"Here are nearly 300 iconic photographs by those photographers who understood the power of the image in the formation and sustenance of rock-and-roll culture from 1955 onward. The care with which Buckland selects representative photographers and their most significant images is matched by her interpretive prowess. . . . [She] carefully but deliberately argues that the art of rock photography has been sacrificed to the paparazzi and corporate art departments. In light of this inclusive, heady and visceral collection of the genre's best, it would be hard to argue otherwise." Publ Wkly
Includes bibliographical references

Christgau, Robert

Grown up all wrong; 75 great rock and pop artists from vaudeville to techno. Harvard Univ. Press 1998 495p $32.50; pa $18.95 **781.66**
1. Rock groups 2. Rock music -- History and criticism 3. Rock musicians
ISBN 978-0-674-44318-1; 0-674-44318-7; 978-0-674-00382-8 pa; 0-674-00382-9 pa
LC 98-25779

Christgau's subjects "include Elvis Presley, the punk girl band Sleater-Kinney, the rap artist KRS-One, the country singer George Jones and the minstrel singer Emmett Miller, among many, many others. He writes on each with equal erudition, examining the artists and their music as both cultural products and influences." N Y Times Book Rev

Cutler, Sam

You can't always get what you want; my life with the Rolling Stones, the Grateful Dead and other wonderful retrobates. ECW Press 2010 326p il pa $17.95   **781.66**
1. Rock music
ISBN 978-1-55022-932-5

"Effortlessly readable, packed with entertaining, sleazy, behind-the-scenes tales. " Portland Mercury

DeRogatis, Jim

The **Beatles** vs. the Rolling Stones; sound opinions on the great rock 'n' roll rivalry. [by] Jim DeRogatis and Greg Kot. Voyageur Press 2010 191p il $35   **781.66**
1. Rock music
ISBN 978-0-7603-3813-1; 0-7603-3813-2
LC 2010-03192

"The authors' discussion draws from other works in the large canon of Beatles and Rolling Stones literature, debunking some myths and validating others. Some sections are bound to raise a few eyebrows. . . . No doubt most readers will approach 'The Beatles vs. the Rolling Stones' with their own opinions, but even the most steadfast loyalists will appreciate the authors' eloquent and insightful arguments in favor of each act." Boston Globe
Includes bibliographical references

Ellis, Iain

Rebels wit attitude; subversive rock humorists. Soft Skull Press 2008 341p pa $15.95   **781.66**
1. Rock music
ISBN 978-1-59376-206-3; 1-59376-206-2
LC 2008-27013

Ellis "traces the history of humorous rebellion in American rock from the 1950s (Chuck Berry, Little Richard, Screamin' Jay Hawkins) to the 1990s (Eminem, Nirvana, Marilyn Manson), in sections on 'Bawdy Women' (e.g., Big Mama Thornton, Wanda Jackson), rap, and sundry other designations. The anecdotes and insights are rich and plentiful. . . . Madonna, Dylan, the Ramones, and bubblegum as a precursor to punk are among Ellis' other specific subjects. Despite the occasional dreary academic expostulation, good enough for general-interest rock lit collections, excellent for episodic reading." Booklist

Epting, Chris

Led Zeppelin crashed here; the rock and roll landmarks of North America. Santa Monica Press 2007 327p il map pa $16.95   **781.66**
1. Rock music
ISBN 978-1-59580-018-3; 1-59580-018-2
LC 2007-6246

"Discover where Bob Dylan's motorcycle crashed, where Elvis Presley first performed, where Ozzy Osbourne bit the head off a bat and the real location of Bruce Springsteen's E Street. The book includes nearly 600 landmarks along with historical information, trivia, photos and backstage lore. Chapters cover topics such as sex and drugs, live performance locations, recording sites, blues and jazz shrines, places where homicides and suicides occurred, and rock and roll museums. There's also a list of 100 classic road trip songs, 100 road trip albums and 30 great North American music stores. An appendix lists rock and roll landmarks by state." Salt Lake Tribune

German, Bill

Under their thumb; how a nice boy from Brooklyn got mixed up with the Rolling Stones (and lived to tell about it) Villard Books 2009 354p il $25 **781.66**
1. Biography, Individual 2. Magazine editors 3. Memoirists 4. Music critics
ISBN 978-1-4000-6622-3; 1-4000-6622-0
LC 2008-45533

"The epic tale of an obsessive teenager who launched a Rolling Stones fanzine and spent the next two decades capturing the band's whirlwind metamorphosis from behind the scenes. . . . First-rate, firsthand account of the world's greatest rock 'n' roll band, and a disenchanted chronicle of its increasingly crass commercialization." Kirkus

Gruen, Bob

New York Dolls; the photographs of Bob Gruen. introduction by Lenny Kaye; featuring commentary by David Johansen and Sylvain Sylvain and quotes collected by Legs McNeil; afterword by Morrissey. Abrams Image 2008 158p il $24.95   **781.66**
1. Rock musicians
ISBN 978-0-8109-7271-1; 0-8109-7271-9
LC 2008-13074

"Gruen met singer David Johansen, guitarists Johnny Thunders and Sylvain Sylvain, drummer Jerry Nolan and bassist Arthur 'Killer' Kane at the beginning of 1973, months after the untimely death of original drummer Billy Murcia. The book chronicles the glam-rock band's career over 230 photographs, only 30 of which have previously been seen by the public. The last picture in the book is of their 2004 reunion in London. Lenny Kaye wrote the book's foreword and interviewed the group's surviving members, Johansen and Sylvain Sylvain." Rolling Stone

Klosterman, Chuck

Killing yourself to live; 85[percent] of a true story. Scribner 2005 245p hardcover o.p. pa $14   **781.66**
1. Authors 2. Death 3. Motion picture critics 4. Nonfiction writers 5. Novelists 6. Rock music -- History and criticism 7. Rock musicians 8. Rock musicians -- Death 9. Writers on music
ISBN 0-7432-6445-2; 978-0-7432-6445-7; 0-7432-6446-0 pa; 978-0-7432-6446-4 pa
LC 2005-42498

"Klosterman's keen eye for American pop-cultural themes and undercurrents facilitates thoughtful observation, and his prose brings those themes and undercurrents together in strange, fresh ways. A treat for the adventurous." Booklist

Lang, Michael

The **road** to Woodstock; with Holly George-Warren. Ecco 2009 304p il $29.99   **781.66**
ISBN 978-0-06-157655-3; 0-06-157655-7

"The author is a generous raconteur with a good memory for specifics, but what elevates this book above the level of most rock memoirs is the inclusion of voices other than

Lang's—including scenesters and key Woodstock players like Jimi Hendrix, Roger Daltrey, Pete Townshend, Jerry Garcia, Abbie Hoffman, John Sebastian, Greil Marcus and Wavy Gravy. . . . Well-written, informative and tons of fun, Lang's book will be appreciated by rockers and musicologists of all ages." Kirkus

Includes bibliographical references

Marcus, Greil

The **Doors**; a lifetime of listening to five mean years. PublicAffairs 2011 210p $21.99 **781.66**

ISBN 978-1-58648-945-8

LC 2011-27931

"Some of the best passages in The Doors: A Lifetime of Listening to Five Mean Years are the extended descriptions of what Marcus calls 'the drama of a band at war with its audience,' in which lead singer Jim Morrison and listeners exchange taunts that would be unthinkable today at a concert by Usher or Taylor Swift. . . . Like Morrison and the Doors, Marcus likes to set the reader up and then go his own way, and when I say he's a writer's writer, I mean that he has a knack for saying whatever he wants but in a way only he can pull off. Thus in mid-book he riffs on lesser-known bands (Moby Grape) and movies ('Pump Up the Volume') and completely obscure novels (Wayne Wilson's 'Loose Jam'). . . . The thing is, it works. A three-minute song is comforting, and so is a tight prose argument; both distract us briefly, console us, and return us to our everyday lives. Both are escapist, whereas Marcus and his subjects want us to look at life, not avert our glance." Christ Sci Monit

Marcus, Sara

Girls to the front; the true story of the Riot grrrl revolution. HarperPerennial 2010 367p il pa $14.99 **781.66**

1. Feminism 2. Feminism -- United States -- History -- 20th century 3. Riot grrrl movement

ISBN 978-0-06-180636-0; 0-06-180636-6

This book is "a brash, gutsy chronicle of the empowering music and feminist movement of the early 1990s." Publ Wkly

Marshall, Jim

Trust; photographs of Jim Marshall. Omnibus Press 2009 165p il $39.95 **781.66**

1. Rock music -- Pictorial works

ISBN 978-1-84772-110-5; 1-84772-110-9

Jim Marshall "devoted himself to photographing musicians. But more than just taking pictures, Marshall had a knack for capturing moments, snapshots of when the music and the individual collided, which, in turn, revealed something special or private about the artist. His pictures were often windows into the souls of those who were so revered but not always understood. . . . Dr. John sits backstage in full concert regalia, beside him a shrunken human head. Bob Dylan and Johnny Cash casually chat on the set of The Johnny Cash Show. John Coltrane looks contemplative in the backyard of his Queens, NY home. The vast majority of pictures in Trust are split among jazz, blues, and '60s rock and roll. . . . The photographs are paired with short anecdotes about the artists or stories about the images, and in doing this, Marshall lends just enough of his own story to the pictures he presents. But largely, it is Marshall's body of

work that does the talking, and, in that, these photographs are revelatory." Under the Radar

McDermott, John

Ultimate Hendrix; an illustrated encyclopedia of live concerts and sessions. [by] John McDermott with Eddie Kramer and Billy Cox. Backbeat Books 2009 256p il $34.95 **781.66**

1. Guitarists 2. Rock music 3. Rock musicians 4. Singers

ISBN 978-0-87930-938-1; 0-87930-938-5

LC 2008-40226

This survey "begins in 1963, when the guitarist began playing backup for such acts as the Isley Brothers, Curtis Squire, and Little Richard. It wasn't until the summer of 1966, when Hendrix met Animals bassist and future manager Chas Chandler, that things really took off, and at this point the book's broad seasonal headings, such as 'Summer 1965' or 'Fall 65', change to the more consecutive 'Thursday, 13 October 1966 . . . Friday, 14 October 1966 . . . Saturday, 15 October 1966', with rarely a date unfilled. The book's day-to-day entries oscillate between high productivity and very low frustration, with peaks and valleys dictated by Hendrix's fortunes and later his moods. . . . Ultimate Hendrix describes songs being built from the bottom up, listing the many takes and practical procedures behind some of the most familiar, impractical sounds." PopMatters

McMurray, Jacob

Taking punk to the masses; from nowhere to Nevermind; a visual history from the permanent collection of Experience Music Project. Fantagraphics Books 2011 253p il pa $29.99 **781.66**

1. Punk rock music

ISBN 978-1-60699-433-7

This volume "visually documents the explosion of Grunge, the Seattle Sound, within the context of the underground punk subculture that was developing throughout the U.S. in the late 1970s and 1980s. This musical journey is represented entirely through the collection of Experience Music Project, Seattle's museum of music and popular culture . . . . Featuring over 100 key artifacts from EMP's collection, Taking Punk to the Masses illustrates the evolution of punk rock from underground subculture to mainstream embrace." Publisher's note

Miller, Jim

Flowers in the dustbin; the rise of rock and roll, 1947-1977. Simon & Schuster 1999 415p il hardcover o.p. pa $26.95 **781.66**

1. Rock music 2. Rock music -- History and criticism

ISBN 978-0-684-86560-7; 0-684-86560-2 pa

LC 99-21077

Miller "explores the cultural underpinnings of Fifties and Sixties rock'n'roll. In dozens of brief chapters, he identifies turning points in rock history: the rise of jump blues, the introduction of Top 40 radio, Alan Freed's rock'n'roll dances, Dick Clark's American Bandstand, and the payola scandal. Miller pays special attention to Elvis Presley and the Beatles." Libr J

Includes discography

Moore, Thurston

No wave; post-punk, underground, New York, 1976-1980. by Thurston Moore and Byron Coley; introduction by Lydia Lunch. Abrams Image 2008 143p il $24.95   **781.66**

1. Experimental music 2. Punk rock music
ISBN 978-0-8109-9543-7; 0-8109-9543-3
LC 2007-34093

"A treasure trove of rare photographs and oral history of a fleeting moment of New York underground that continues to reverberate 30 years later." Booklist

Russell, Ethan A.

Let it bleed; the Rolling Stones, Altamont, and the end of the sixties. Ethan A. Russell, with Gerard Van der Leun. Springboard Press 2009 239p il $35   **781.66**

ISBN 978-0-446-53904-3
LC 2008-53229

"In 1969, Russell was one of 16 people and the only photographer to join the Rolling Stones on their tour of America. . . . Russell's 200-plus photos, most in stark and clear black and white, range from the band rehearsing and relaxing in a bucolic setting before the tour to Mick Jagger in front of a mirror applying makeup to a closeup of Keith Richards intensely tuning up. Wide onstage shots illustrate the band's relationship with their adoring public. Including interviews and comments from many of the members of the touring group and a haunting narrative of the desolation at Altamont, Russell, with Van Der Leun . . . presents a definitive and authoritative picture of the Stones." Libr J

Smith, Kerry L.

Encyclopedia of indie rock; foreword by Marcus Congleton. Greenwood Press 2008 xxxv, 400p il $75   **781.66**

1. Reference books 2. Rock music -- Encyclopedias
ISBN 978-0-313-34119-9
LC 2008-4529

"The only field-defining encyclopedia to date, this guide defines indie rock practitioners not as a group of unsigned musical artists but as tenacious do-it-yourselfers whose defiant resourcefulness sparked other independent creative movements. . . . Alphabetized entries run several pages and include band photographs whenever possible. Included are indie rock's sub-genres, like shoegazing and sadcore. A time line designates 1952 as indie rock's spiritual inception. Recommended for all musical history collections." Libr J

Includes bibliographical references

Thompson, Dave

I hate new music; the classic rock manifesto. Backbeat Books 2008 225p $24.95   **781.66**

1. Rock music
ISBN 978-0-87930-935-0
LC 2008-39492

"In classic pundit style, [Thompson] tauntingly waves the red flag at the contemporary music scene and counter-intuitively stabs some of rock's greatest icons in the back, before delivering an exquisitely executed coup de grace to the music industry as a whole. . . . The book's subtitle is telling, for this is not a history of classic rock, although it partially works as a potted one, nor a critical analysis of the movement, even though there's a great deal of analysis and criticism found within. Instead, Thompson provides a critique of all that made a specific period of rock classic, explains its eventual destruction, and explores the reasons why rock is unlikely to reach such heady heights again. What makes the book impossible to put down, however, is the author's gonzo approach to the subject — laugh-out-loud funny, peppered with jokes and awash in wry amusement, irony and a touch of biting sarcasm." Goldmine

London's burning; true adventures on the frontlines of punk, 1976-1977. Chicago Review Press 2009 327p il pa $18.95   **781.66**

1. Punk rock music
ISBN 978-1-55652-769-2; 1-55652-769-1
LC 2008-40527

"Thompson, 16 when punk exploded on the London scene in 1976, chronicles that pivotal year month-by-month, starting with American Patti Smith's appearance on BBC-TV's Old Grey Whistle Test. . . . Soon Thompson and friends were wading through a cornucopia of the Ramones, Television, and the rest of the New York punks and New Wavers as well as English acts like the Sex Pistols and the Clash. Reggae surfaced, and the punk and Rasta communities came together after years of violent racial and class strife. It was a heady, creative time, reminiscent of the 'Swingin' London' of Beatlemania days. Excellent anecdotal pop-music history." Booklist

Victor, Adam

The Elvis encyclopedia. Overlook Duckworth 2008 598p il $65   **781.66**

1. Actors 2. Biography, Individual 3. Rock musicians 4. Singers
ISBN 978-1-58567-598-2; 1-58567-598-9

An alphabetical compendium of topics related to Elvis Presley. Includes personal and place names, movie and song titles, events, and general subjects.

"This obsessively detailed and completely entertaining chronicle . . . of every possible aspect of Elvis Preley's life is mesmerizing and deserves a wide audience." Publ Wkly

Waksman, Steve

This ain't the summer of love; conflict and crossover in heavy metal and punk. University of California Press 2009 408p $65; pa $24.95   **781.66**

1. Heavy metal (Music) 2. Punk rock music
ISBN 978-0-520-25310-0; 0-520-25310-8; 978-0-520-25717-7 pa; 0-520-25717-0 pa
LC 2008025957

This survey of heavy metal and punk music "begins on the cusp of the '70s with the colossal arena performances of Grand Funk Railroad, setting up the relationship between performer and (in this case, enormous) audience, which is an ongoing point of reference. From here, Waksman uses subsequent artists to deconstruct the rock concert, moving through the performative stage antics of Alice Cooper and Iggy Pop, to the metal and hardcore bands of the early '80s. . . . The number of fanzines and interviews cited is evidence that this is a comprehensively and enthusiastically researched book. As a critical study it provides an original critique of both the genres involved, and of genre itself; the only flipside is that this ends up playing second fiddle to a damn good story." PopMatters

Includes discography and bibliographical references

Yarm, Mark

Everybody loves our town; an oral history of Grunge. Crown Archetype 2011 567p il $25; ebook $12.99   **781.66**

1. Rock music -- History and criticism

ISBN 978-0-307-46443-9; 978-0-307-46445-3 ebook
LC 2011009192

A tribute to the Pacific Northwest's grunge genre draws on the observations of individuals at the forefront of the movement from Soundgarden and the Melvins to Nirvana and Pearl Jam, citing such influences as the rise of Seattle's Sub Pop record label and the death of Kurt Cobain.

"Yarm's affectionate, gossipy, detailed look at the highs and lows of the contemporary Seattle music scene is one of the most essential rock books of recent years." Kirkus

782   Vocal music

Berger, William

Wagner without fear; learning to love--and even enjoy--opera's most demanding genius. Vintage Bks. 1998 454p maps pa $15.95   **782**

1. Composers 2. Opera

ISBN 978-0-375-70054-5; 0-375-70054-4
LC 98-19825

The author's goal is to make Richard Wagner's operas accessible to the uninitiated. "After a breezy summary of the composer's life, he devotes a chapter to each of his mature works, interspersing plot outlines with chatty commentary. There is a bit of performance history, as well as advice on how to pronounce names, get through the rough spots at the notoriously long performances and when to eat, drink and visit the restroom. . . . Chapters on Wagner CDs and the best books to read on the composer and his operas are useful." Publ Wkly

Robeson, Paul

The **undiscovered** Paul Robeson; the early years (1898-1939) Wiley 2001 383p il $30   **782**

1. Actors 2. Actors -- United States 3. African Americans 4. African Americans -- Biography 5. Civil rights activists 6. Football players 7. Political activists -- United States 8. Singers 9. Singers -- United States

ISBN 0-471-24265-9
LC 2001-17656

This is the first volume of a biography of the African American actor, singer and political activist by his son. It covers the years from Robeson's birth in Princeton, N.J., through the 1930s.

"Extensively illustrated with personal photographs, this is a unique account of a brilliant but troubled man." Libr J

Includes bibliographical references

Sudhalter, Richard

Stardust melody: the life and music of Hoagy Carmichael; [by] Richard M. Sudhalter. Oxford Univ. Press 2002 432p il hardcover o.p. pa $18.95 **782**

1. Actors 2. Composers -- United States 3. Jazz musicians 4. Pianists 5. Singers 6. Songwriters

ISBN 0-19-513120-7; 0-19-516898-4 pa
LC 2001-34612

"Among the legends of American popular music, Carmichael, composer of such standards as 'Star Dust' and 'Skylark,' is not getting his due, argues the author, who intends to rectify this injustice. The result is a thorough and engaging profile of the great American composer and performer." Booklist

Includes bibliographical references

Tosches, Nick

Where dead voices gather. Little, Brown 2001 330p $24.95; pa $14.95   **782**

1. Blackface entertainers -- United States 2. Jazz singers -- United States

ISBN 0-316-89507-5; 0-316-89537-7 pa
LC 2001-18608

"As engrossing as a great mystery novel, this is essential for libraries with a focus on American popular culture." Libr J

The **Cambridge** companion to singing; edited by John Potter. Cambridge Univ. Press 2000 286p il hardcover o.p. pa $24   **782**

1. Performance practice (Music) 2. Singing 3. Singing -- History 4. Vocal music 5. Vocal music -- History and criticism

ISBN 0-521-62225-5; 0-521-62709-5 pa
LC 99-32948

"Articles on popular traditions, including world music, rock, rap, and jazz, describe the major singers and songwriters in each. Then come histories of theatrical singing encompassing twentieth-century stage and screen artists, the beginnings of opera, and grand opera. The growth of choral music and art songs is traced next. . . . The last and largest section concerns performance practices in choral and ensemble singing, medieval singing techniques, singing in the pre-romantic and contemporary periods, teaching singing, children's singing, and vocal production. . . . The guide covers its wide range of topics accessibly as well as thoroughly for a one-volume work." Booklist

Includes bibliographical references

782.1   Vocal forms

Berger, William

Verdi with a vengeance; an energetic guide to the life and complete works of the king of opera. Vintage Bks. 2000 497p il pa $15   **782.1**

1. Composers 2. Composers -- Italy

ISBN 0-375-70518-X
LC 00-42261

The author "provides a brief overview of the composer's life and times and examines the connections between contemporary politics and Verdi's creative output. . . . A glossary and recommended recordings, films, and soundtracks are included. Informative and eminently readable for the novice and scholar alike." Libr J

Includes bibliographical references

Citron, Stephen

Sondheim and Lloyd-Webber; the new musical. Oxford Univ. Press 2001 425p il $39.95 **782.1**

1. Art collectors 2. Composers 3. Composers -- Great Britain -- Biography 4. Composers -- United States -- Biography 5. Lyricists 6. Musicals 7. Musicals -- History and criticism

ISBN 0-19-509601-0

LC 2001-31408

In this volume Citron profiles the two composers, highlighting their personal lives and tracing "their creative development from tentative neophytes to much-feted giants, integrating the various directions that musical theater has taken." Libr J

Includes bibliographical references (p.) and index; Discography

Fiedler, Johanna

Molto agitato; the mayhem behind the music at the Metropolitan Opera. Doubleday 2001 393p il $30; pa $15.95 **782.1**

1. Opera -- New York (State) -- New York -- History and criticism

ISBN 0-385-48187-X; 1-4000-3231-8 pa

LC 2001-27158

This book is about "the business of New York City's Metropolitan Opera and the personalities who have shaped it from its beginnings in the late 19th century to the present day. . . . {The author} spins a fascinating account of strong egos, clashing personalities, power plays, and frequent major disasters. There are enough heroes, villains, and side plots to fill a dozen adventure novels. . . . For those interested in the dirt behind the golden curtain, this will be a feast." Libr J

Gage, Nicholas

Greek fire; the story of Maria Callas and Aristotle Onassis. Knopf 2000 xxi, 422p il $26.95; pa $7.99 **782.1**

1. Opera singers 2. Shipping executives

ISBN 0-375-40244-6; 0-446-61076-3 pa

LC 00-40553

This "biography is perhaps the most understanding of La Callas yet to be published, and its appeal will extend beyond opera lovers to anyone with an interest in the lives of the rich and famous." Booklist

Includes bibliographical references

Ganzl, Kurt

The **musical**; a concise history. Northeastern Univ. Press 1997 432p il $50 **782.1**

1. Musicals 2. Musicals -- History and criticism

ISBN 1-555-53311-6

LC 97-3008

This is a "guidebook to 300 years of musicals, both romantic and comedic, which spans the early 18th to the late 20th centuries, and covers the theatrical scenes in America, Europe and Australia." Publ Wkly

Includes discography

Marmorstein, Gary

A **ship** without a sail; the life of Lorenz Hart. Gary Marmorstein. Simon & Schuster 2012 531p. $30.00 **782.1**

1. Lyricists -- United States -- Biography

ISBN 1416594256; 9781416594253

LC 2011040654

Author Gary Marmorstein offers a biography of Lorenz Hart (1895–1943), the talented, troubled lyricist of film and Broadway fame. . . . Here, the author details Hart's short life, explores his most productive professional partnership with composer Richard Rodgers, chronicles his descent into the alcoholism that killed him, speculates about his sexuality (his colleagues knew he was gay; the public did not), and provides numerous examples of Hart's witty, sometimes risqué lyrics (risqué, of course, by 1940s standards). Hart, whose adult height perhaps touched 5 feet and who seemed always to have a cigar, wrote some 800 songs with Rodgers, many of which are Broadway classics, among them "Manhattan," "My Funny Valentine" and "Where or When.'" (Kirkus)

McBrien, William

Cole Porter; a biography. Knopf 1998 459p il hardcover o.p. $16 **782.1**

1. Composers 2. Composers -- United States -- Biography 3. Lyricists

ISBN 978-0-679-72792-7; 0-679-72792-2

LC 97-46116

In this biography of the American songwriter, the author "weaves a complex and groundbreaking portrait of Porter, interspersed with lyrics and 72 illustrations, recounting his affluent upbringing in Peru, Ind., and his emergence in the 1930s as the musical theater's reigning sophisticate. . . . This astute biography will help to create a standard-setting portrait of Porter as a homosexual artist in a heterosexual world." Publ Wkly

Includes bibliographical references

Schebera, Jurgen

Kurt Weill; an illustrated life. translated by Caroline Murphy. Yale Univ. Press 1995 381p il $55; pa $38 **782.1**

1. Biography, Individual 2. Composers

ISBN 0-300-06055-6; 0-300-07284-8 pa

LC 94-41444

"Schebera makes wonderful use of archival illustrations: concert programs, advertisements, photos, even a few record labels from the Twenties and Thirties. This is a scholarly work, but the appealing subject, complete with the drama of Nazi persecution and flight from prewar Germany, makes it a good choice for most music collections." Libr J

Includes discography and bibliographical references

Scott, Michael

Maria Meneghini Callas. Northeastern Univ. Press 1992 372p il $29.95   **782.1**
1. Biography, Individual 2. Opera singers
ISBN 1-55553-146-6

LC 92-17103

"We come away from this critical biography with a sound understanding of Callas' complicated personal life and her total commitment to her instrument and career." Booklist
Includes bibliographical references

The New Grove dictionary of opera; edited by Stanley Sadie. Grove's Dictionaries of Music 1992 4v il hardcover o.p. pa set $425   **782.1**
1. Opera -- Dictionaries 2. Reference books
ISBN 0-19-522186-9 pa

LC 92-36276

This set "developed from The New Grove Dictionary of Music and Musicians, covers all aspects of the modern Western opera tradition, including composers, performers, directors, companies, stagecraft, theaters, cities, terms, and individual works." Libr J
Includes bibliographical references

The Richard Rodgers reader; edited by Geoffrey Block. Oxford Univ. Press 2002 356p il music $55; pa $38   **782.1**
1. Composers 2. Composers -- United States
ISBN 0-19-513954-2; 0-19-531343-7 pa

LC 2001-37505

"A fine combination of anecdote, music criticism, and biography, this is recommended for all libraries interested in American popular culture and American musical theater." Libr J
Includes bibliographical references

782.109   Biography

Davis, Peter G.

The **American** opera singer; the lives and adventures of America's great singers in opera and concert, from 1825 to the present. Doubleday 1997 626p il hardcover o.p. pa $19.95   **782.109**
1. Biography, Collective 2. Singers 3. Singers -- Biography
ISBN 0-385-42174-5 pa

LC 97-9123

"Davis tells anecdotes and presents essential details of his subjects' personal lives in biographical sketches ranging from a paragraph to several pages in length." Booklist
Includes bibliographical references

782.25   Small-scale vocal forms

★ Encyclopedia of American gospel music; W. K. McNeil, editor. Routledge 2010 488p il pa $57.95   **782.25**
1. Gospel music -- Encyclopedias 2. Reference books
ISBN 978-0-415-87569-1

"Organized alphabetically by surname, title, or term, the entries cover the principal figures, groups, songbooks, publications, companies, and broadcasting outlets that determined the industry's course. . . . [This is] the definitive, wide-angle quick reference for American gospel history." Libr J
Includes discographical and bibliographical references

782.27   Hymns

American hymns old and new; {compiled by} Albert Christ-Janer, Charles W. Hughes, Charles Sprague Smith. Columbia Univ. Press 1980 838p music $104   **782.27**
1. Hymns
ISBN 0-231-03458-X

This is an interdenominational compilation of 625 hymns sung in America since 1615.

782.42   Songs

Foster, Stephen Collins

Stephen Foster & Co. lyrics of America's first great popular songs. edited by Ken Emerson. Library of America 2010 xxii, 182p il $20   **782.42**
1. American songs 2. Popular music
ISBN 978-1-59853-070-4

LC 2009-973459

The editor "introduces and annotates the lyrics to more than thirty of Foster's best and best-known songs. . . . Alongside are fifty other 19th-century American popular songs that influenced Foster or that he in turn influenced, from 'Home! Sweet Home!' in the 1820s to 'Western Home' (the original 'Home on the Range') in the 1870s." Publisher's note
Includes bibliographical references

Gioia, Ted

Work songs; [by] Theodore Gioia. Duke University Press 2006 352p $27.95   **782.42**
1. Folk music 2. Labor -- Songs
ISBN 0-8223-3726-6; 978-0-8223-3726-3

LC 2005026241

Gioia "poignantly tells the story of work songs sung by everyone from prehistoric hunters to today's consumers. His task involved drawing on multilayered and diverse resources that include travel literature, slave narratives, historical accounts and personal journals, myths and legends, biographies, and labor union writings; the focus is on the rhythms, melodies, and lyrics of music that has accompanied such tasks as raising and lowering sails, felling trees, and weaving and sewing garments. . . . This book provides an opportunity to re-experience the history and dignity of our human toils. Highly recommended for public and academic libraries." Libr J
Includes bibliographical references

Gray, Michael

The **Bob** Dylan encyclopedia. Continuum 2006 832p il $40   **782.42**
1. Biography, Individual 2. Folk musicians 3. Singers

4. Songwriters
ISBN 0-82646-933-7; 978-0-82646-933-5

LC 2006-12728

This book "covers many of his songs, albums, and film work, as well as just about every personality associated with the folk singer/rock star. . . . Overall, this is an amazingly well-researched and surprisingly readable work." Libr J

Includes bibliographical references

Guthrie, Woody

The **Woody** Guthrie songbook. Hal Leonard Corporation 2000 61p il pa $10.95   **782.42**

1. Folk music 2. Songs
ISBN 978-0-63402-405-4 pa; 0-63402-405-1 pa

This features 48 of Guthrie's songs along with a bio, introduction, complete lyrics, a discography, photos and sketches. Songs include: Jig Along Home, Roll On, Columbia, Sinking of the Reuben James, This Land Is Your Land, Tom Joad and more.

Hischak, Thomas

The **American** musical film song encyclopedia; {by} Thomas S. Hischak. Greenwood Press 1999 521p $83.95   **782.42**

1. Motion picture music -- Encyclopedias 2. Motion picture music -- United States 3. Reference books 4. Songs, English -- United States
ISBN 0-313-30737-7

LC 98-34723

"Coverage is restricted to songs actually written for film. . . . Entries, arranged by song title, include vocalist, composer, lyricist, and information on the place of the song in the film, as well as recordings by artists other than those in the film. The concise entries combine a wealth of information not found in other sources." Libr J

Includes bibliographical references

The **Tin** Pan Alley song encyclopedia; {by} Thomas S. Hischak. Greenwood Press 2002 530p $74.95   **782.42**

1. Popular music -- Encyclopedias 2. Popular music -- United States 3. Reference books
ISBN 0-313-31992-8

LC 2002-23250

"Tin Pan Alley refers to the American popular music business from the mid-nineteenth through the mid-twentieth centuries, and the songs written for parlor pianos, sing-alongs, dance orchestras, radio broadcasts, etc. This book is an A-Z listing of more than 1,200 popular songs. . . . Each entry includes the year the song was published and highly readable information about its composition and performance history." Booklist

Includes bibliographical references and index

Leadbelly

The **Leadbelly** songbook; the ballads, blues, and folksongs of Huddie Ledbetter. Oak Publications 1962 96p il pa $17.95   **782.42**

1. African American music 2. Folk music -- United States 3. Songs
ISBN 978-0-82560-042-5 pa; 0-82560-042-1 pa

More than 70 songs by Huddie Ledbetter, with chord names, musical transcriptions, and biographical notes. Includes: Midnite Special, Backwater Blues, John Henry, and House Of The Rising Sun.

Lehman, David

A **fine** romance; Jewish songwriters, American songs. Nextbook/Schocken 2009 249p $23 **782.42**

1. Composers 2. Jews -- United States 3. Lyricists 4. Popular music -- History and criticism 5. Songwriters and songwriting
ISBN 978-0-8052-4250-8; 0-8052-4250-3

LC 2009-05942

"Lehman investigates the lasting impact of 20th-century Jewish popular songwriters in America, ranging from Irving Berlin's and Jerome Kern's early efforts in the 1910s through George Gershwin, Harold Arlen, Richard Rodgers, Lorenz Hart, and Oscar Hammerstein II to Leonard Bernstein and the early 1960s. In fluid prose and expert foreshadowing and summations, the author conveys the personality of each musician or writer and recommends selected versions of his favorite songs." Libr J

Includes bibliographical references

Lynskey, Dorian

33 revolutions per minute; a history of protest songs, from Billie Holiday to Green Day. Ecco 2011 660p il pa $19.99   **782.42**

1. Political ballads and songs 2. Popular music -- 20th century 3. Popular music -- 21st century 4. Popular music -- History and criticism 5. Popular music -- Political aspects 6. Protest songs -- History and criticism
ISBN 978-0-06-167015-2 pa; 0-06-167015-4 pa

LC 2010-24247

The author "delves into the protest song movement from 1939 to the present. Dividing the time into discrete sections, he focuses on particular examples but also provides information on related songs. The author traces the historical context, using valuable contemporary sources and quotations from the artists. . . . Lynskey's flowing prose and well-turned phrases bring the times to life. He is especially adept at integrating the songs into the wider social milieu, which extends the appeal to cultural historians as well as music lovers." Libr J

Includes bibliographical references

Marcus, Greil

When that rough god goes riding; listening to Van Morrison. PublicAffairs 2010 195p $22.95 **782.42**

1. Rock music -- History and criticism 2. Rock musicians 3. Singers 4. Songwriters
ISBN 978-1-58648-821-5; 1-58648-821-X

LC 2010-01656

This is a "collection of short 'close listenings'—some as brief as a page or two—concerning performances and recordings from Morrison's 45-year career. The essays are organized by theme rather than chronology, organized as such because Marcus sees Van Morrison's music as 'a story made of fragments', the story of a 'quest', a damned messy epic with ever-changing monsters to slay and enough digressive journeys to rival Don Quixote. This story has no ending, and

Marcus' satisfyingly realistic viewpoint is not, despite its organization, grandly and thematically synoptic." PopMatters
Includes bibliographical references

Porter, Cole

Selected lyrics; Robert Kimball, editor. Library of America 2006 178p $20   **782.42**
1. American songs 2. Musicals -- Excerpts -- Librettos 3. Popular music -- Texts
ISBN 978-1-93108-294-5; 1-93108-294-4
         LC 2006-40809
"For those hankering after a happy medium between American poetry and American Idolatry, Kimball's reading edition affords a golden opportunity to brush up on your Porter—just be sure to listen up, too, if you really want to be wowed." N Y Times Book Rev

Sheed, Wilfrid

★ The **house** that George built; with a little help from Irving, Cole, and a crew of about fifty. Suzanne Slade; illustrated by Rebecca Bond. Charlesbridge 2011 48 p. il (reinforced for library use) $16.95   **782.42**
1. Presidents -- United States -- History -- Juvenile literature
ISBN 1580892620; 9781580892629
         LC 2011025781
This book is a history of the "golden age" of American song. Index.
This book "is a big rich stew of an homage that makes you want to listen to Gershwin and Berlin and Porter and Arlen all over again. Wilfrid Sheed's jazzy prose is a joy to read" N Y Times Book Rev

★ National anthems of the world; edited by Michael Jamieson Bristow. 11th ed.; Weidenfeld & Nicolson 2006 629p $90   **782.42**
1. National songs
ISBN 0-304-36826-1
This volume contains national anthems of about 198 nations, including melody and accompaniment. Words are presented in the native language with transliteration provided where necessary. English translations follow. Brief historical notes on the adoption of each anthem are included
"An essential reference resource for all libraries." Libr J

★ Songwriter's market; Greg Hatfield, editor. 34th annual ed; Writer's Digest 2010 362p il pa $29.99   **782.42**
1. Popular music -- Writing and publishing
ISBN 978-1-58297-954-0
The main section of this guide consists of listings of music publishers, record companies, producers, managers, booking agents, and firms interested in original music. Also included are articles which present an overview of the songwriting field, and listings of resources such as organizations, workshops, and contests.

782.421   Western popular songs

Clarke, Gerald

Get happy: the life of Judy Garland. Random House 2000 510p il hardcover o.p. pa $15.95   **782.421**
1. Actors 2. Singers 3. Singers -- United States -- Biography
ISBN 0-385-33515-6 pa
         LC 99-36285
"This exhaustively researched and illuminating biography . . . is as compassionate as it is wrenching." Publ Wkly
Includes bibliographical references

Dyson, Michael Eric

Holler if you hear me: searching for Tupac Shakur. Basic Bks. 2001 292p il hardcover o.p. pa $15   **782.421**
1. Actors 2. African American musicians 3. Hip-hop 4. Poets 5. Rap music 6. Rap musicians 7. Rap musicians -- United States -- Biography
ISBN 0-465-01755-X; 0-465-01728-2 pa
         LC 2001-36564
"Dyson's discussion goes beyond slogans and poses to the actualities of 'thug life' and the consequences of Shakur's passions and allegiances. Piquant and analytical." Booklist
Includes bibliographical references

Fisher, Eddie

Been there, done that; {by} Eddie Fisher, with David Fisher. St. Martin's Press 1999 341p il $24.95; pa $7.99   **782.421**
1. Singers 2. Singers -- United States -- Biography
ISBN 0-312-20972-X; 0-312-87558-9 pa
         LC 99-27236
"What makes this memoir engaging is Fisher's sharp, often self-deprecating wit and his willingness to dish about his cohorts and conquests." N Y Times Book Rev

Friedwald, Will

★ **Sinatra!** the song is you; a singer's art. Da Capo Press 1997 559p il pa $18.50   **782.421**
1. Actors 2. Singers
ISBN 0-306-80742-4
         LC 96-43855
Friedwald's "commentary is alert and perceptive, and even more valuable is the wealth of pointed reminiscence drawn from interviews he has done with musicians who worked closely with Mr. Sinatra." N Y Times Book Rev
Includes discography and bibliographical references

George, Nelson

Hip hop America. Viking 1998 226p hardcover o.p. pa $15   **782.421**
1. Hip-hop -- United States 2. Music -- Social aspects -- United States 3. Popular culture -- United States 4. Rap (Music) -- History and criticism 5. Rap music
ISBN 0-670-87153-2; 978-0-14-303515-2 pa; 0-14-303515-0 pa
         LC 98-23414

A social and economic history of the rap music industry and hip-hop culture.

"This is an invaluable, entertaining and well written account from one who has not only witnessed the evolution of hip-hop but who, through his own passion and devotion to it as a critic, has had a hand in shaping it as well." N Y Times Book Rev

Includes bibliographical references

Gordon, Robert
Can't be satisfied: the life and times of Muddy Waters. Little, Brown 2002 xx, 408p il $25.95; pa $15.95   **782.421**
1. Blues musicians 2. Blues musicians -- United States -- Biography 3. Guitarists 4. Rhythm and blues music -- History and criticism 5. Singers
ISBN 0-316-32849-9; 0-316-16494-1 pa
LC 2001-50473

In this biography of the blues musician "Gordon details the gritty life reflected in Muddy's lyrics. . . . He makes Muddy the musician, Muddy the man, Muddy the parent, and Muddy the tool of the (not so) sainted Chess brothers come alive. . . . Packed with facts, copiously referenced, and featuring a foreword by . . . Keith Richards, this book is absolutely essential for any popular music collection worthy of the name." Booklist

Includes bibliographical references

Guralnick, Peter
Last train to Memphis: the rise of Elvis Presley. Little, Brown 1994 560p il $27.95; pa $17.95   **782.421**
1. Actors 2. Biography, Individual 3. Rock musicians 4. Singers
ISBN 0-316-33220-8; 0-316-33225-9 pa
LC 94-10763

The author "depicts Elvis as a naive yet extremely talented boy whose dream of stardom came true, leaving him a virtual prisoner of his own success. . . . Taking pains to keep the story fresh and flowing and refraining from foreshadowing and editorializing, Guralnick lets the facts speak for themselves." Booklist

Includes bibliographical references

Hamm, Charles
Irving Berlin; songs from the melting pot: the formative years, 1907-1914. Oxford Univ. Press 1996 292p il $42.50   **782.421**
1. Centenarians 2. Composers 3. Lyricists
ISBN 0-19-507188-3
LC 96-6335

The author "shows an informed sensitivity for the social and historical atmosphere in which these songs were produced, and . . . makes effective use of period recordings . . . in an effort to understand how they were meant to play to their first listeners." N Y Times Book Rev

Includes discography and bibliographical references

Mason, Bobbie Ann
Elvis Presley. Viking 2002 178p hardcover o.p. pa $13   **782.421**
1. Actors 2. Rock musicians 3. Rock musicians --

United States -- Biography 4. Singers
ISBN 0-670-03174-7; 0-14-303889-3 pa
LC 2002-28873

The author "chronicles Elvis' sad story: humble origins, 1954 breakthrough, adoption by 'the Colonel' (manager Tom Parker), early TV appearances, army hitch, the death of his mother, marriage to Priscilla, Hollywood, 1968 'comeback', Las Vegas headliner, prescription drug abuse, meeting with Nixon, and death at 42 in 1977." Booklist

Includes   discography,   filmography   and bibliographical references

McDonough, Jimmy
Shakey: Neil Young's biography. Villard Bks. 2002 786p il $29.95; pa $16.95   **782.421**
1. Guitarists 2. Rock musicians 3. Rock musicians -- Canada -- Biography 4. Singers 5. Songwriters
ISBN 0-679-42772-4; 0-679-75096-7 pa
LC 2001-43528

"When Young talks, the book sparkles and offers a warm, engaging portrait of the man who keeps on rockin' in the free world." Libr J

McNally, Dennis
A long strange trip; the inside history of the Grateful Dead. Broadway Bks. 2002 684p il $30; pa $18.95   **782.421**
1. Rock musicians -- United States -- Biography 2. Rock musicians -- United States -- Interviews
ISBN 0-7679-1185-7; 0-7679-1186-5 pa
LC 2002-25561

A history of the rock music group led by Jerry Garcia which first became popular in the 1960's

"As the Dead's publicist for more than 20 years, McNally packs this . . . full of intimate details otherwise unavailable. . . . The most exhaustively researched book on the band to date." Publ Wkly

Includes bibliographical references

Nicholson, Stuart
Billie Holiday. Northeastern Univ. Press 1995 311p il $42.50; pa $18.95   **782.421**
1. African American singers 2. Biography, Individual 3. Blues musicians 4. Singers
ISBN 1-55553-248-9; 1-55553-303-5 pa
LC 95-16155

"Nicholson's fact-filled biography conveys not only the details of African American jazz singer Holiday's stormy life, but also a sense of the musical and social environments that produced her." Booklist

Includes discography and bibliographical references

Riordan, James
Break on through: the life and death of Jim Morrison; [by] James Riordan and Jerry Prochnicky. Morrow 1991 544p il hardcover o.p. pa $15 **782.421**
1. Biography, Individual 2. Rock musicians 3. Singers 4. Songwriters
ISBN 0-688-11915-8 pa
LC 90-26580

This look at the life and work of Jim Morrison is "well documented and avoids unfounded speculation and unnecessary tales of debauchery common to many other rock 'n' roll biographies. . . . An excellent biography of a true rock icon." Choice

Includes discography and bibliographical references

Sounes, Howard

Down the highway: the life of Bob Dylan. Grove Press 2001 527p il $27.50; pa $16   **782.421**
   1. Folk musicians 2. Rock musicians 3. Singers 4. Singers -- United States -- Biography 5. Songwriters
   ISBN 0-8021-1686-8; 0-8021-3891-8 pa

                 LC 00-69463
"Through extensive interviews Sounes aptly captures the contradictory facets of an American folk legend." Publ Wkly
Includes bibliographical references

White, Charles

The **life** and times of Little Richard; the quasar of rock. Updated ed; Da Capo Press 1994 282p il pa $16   **782.421**
   1. African American musicians 2. Rock musicians 3. Singers
   ISBN 0-306-80552-9; 978-0-306-80552-3

                 LC 93-48054
This biography of the American singer discusses "his flamboyant stage antics; his blatant flaunting of racial taboos; his sexual experiences; his bewildering career that careened between show business and the church; and exactly how he created the music that would become a symbol of rebellion for kids all over the world." Publisher's note
Includes discography and filmography

The Beatles anthology. Chronicle Bks. 2000 367p il $60; pa $35   **782.421**
   1. Drummers 2. Guitarists 3. Rock musicians 4. Rock musicians -- Biography 5. Singers 6. Songwriters
   ISBN 0-8118-2684-8; 0-8118-3636-3 pa

                 LC 00-23685
The story of the Beatles as "told through quotes from John, Paul, George, and Ringo, as well as the group's closest aides: George Martin, Neil Aspinall, and Derek Taylor. . . . The density of the text is daunting, but the book's browsability makes it as appealing to casual readers as it is indispensable to Beatlemaniacs." Libr J
Includes bibliographical references

782.5   Vocal executants

Steinberg, Michael

Choral masterworks; a listener's guide. Michael Steinberg. Oxford University Press 2005 321p $30   **782.5**
   1. Choral music 2. Choral music -- Analysis, appreciation
   ISBN 0-19-512644-0

                 LC 2004-13619
"Well-written, concise introductions that record collectors, concertgoers, and chorus members alike should enjoy." Booklist

784   Instruments and their music

Ewen, David

American songwriters; an H. W. Wilson biographical dictionary. Wilson, H.W. 1987 489p il $105   **784**
   1. Composers -- United States -- Dictionaries 2. Reference books
   ISBN 0-8242-0744-0

                 LC 86-24654
Arranged alphabetically, this reference volume includes 146 biographical entries on American lyricists and composers. Ragtime, minstrel, Tin Pan Alley, Broadway, rock, jazz, blues, folk, country and western, and soul are among the styles represented. Biographies range from Eubie Blake, George Gershwin and George M. Cohan to Chuck Berry, Carole King and Bob Dylan.

Piston, Walter

Orchestration. Norton 1955 477p il music $56.75 **784**
   1. Instrumentation and orchestration 2. Musical instruments
   ISBN 978-0-393-09740-5; 0-393-09740-4
This text on writing for the orchestra begins with a discussion of individual instruments and their playing techniques. The last two sections cover analysis and specific problems of orchestration.

784.2   Full orchestra (Symphony orchestra)

Osborne, Richard

Herbert von Karajan; a life in music. Northeastern Univ. Press 2000 851p il $37.50   **784.2**
   1. Conductors (Music) 2. Conductors (Music) -- Biography
   ISBN 1-55553-425-2

                 LC 99-59108
"Because Karajan's career developed in Nazi Germany, Osborne dwells at length . . . on Karajan's involvement with the regime and his postwar exoneration. Drawing on a vast variety of source materials and quoting some in full, Osborne takes us on the enthralling musical journey that was the life of one of the greatest of conductors." Booklist
Includes bibliographical references

Steinberg, Michael

The **symphony**; a listener's guide. Oxford Univ. Press 1995 678p music $42.50; pa $25 **784.2**
   1. Composers 2. Music appreciation 3. Symphony
   ISBN 0-19-506177-2; 0-19-512665-3 pa

                 LC 95-5568
"Steinberg describes 36 composers and, movement by movement, 118 symphonies, including all the standard repertory . . . as well as a few by less well known composers such as Gorecki, Harbison, Martinu, and Sessions. The writing varies from formal and factual to chatty, with candid asides and stories relevant to the composer, the composition, or an important performance." Libr J
Includes bibliographical references

784.4   Light orchestra

Ritchie, Jean
   Singing family of the Cumberlands. University Press of Ky. 1988 258p il $35; pa $20   **784.4**
   1. Folk music -- United States 2. Folk musicians 3. Singers 4. Songwriters
   ISBN 978-0-8131-1679-2; 0-8131-1679-1; 978-0-8131-0186-6 pa; 0-8131-0186-7 pa
                                    LC 88-17337
   The youngest of the Ritchies, a Cumberland mountain family, whose singing was the order of the day, writes about her own life and that of her family. The Ritchies still sing the songs and ballads brought from Virginia in 1768, by Jean's three times great grandfather. Words and music of 42 songs are included.
   "Ritchie writes as she sings—naturally and with an instinctive sense for rhythms. Her story of her rearing in the hill-circled town of Viper is simple, vivid, and moving. . . . A beautiful story of American living." NY Herald Tribune

785   Ensembles with only one instrument per part

Collier, James Lincoln
   Louis Armstrong, an American genius. Oxford Univ. Press 1983 383p il hardcover o.p. pa $21.50   **785**
   1. Band leaders 2. Biography, Individual 3. Jazz musicians 4. Singers 5. Trumpet players
   ISBN 0-19-503727-8 pa
                                    LC 83-11378
   The author tells the story of Armstrong's life and evaluates his musical contributions
   "Collier's scholarship is impeccable, his note-by-note musical analysis razor sharp, and his conclusions about Armstrong's place in American music expertly defended. In all respects, a biography worthy of its subject." Booklist

Sachs, Harvey
   The **Ninth**; Beethoven and the world in 1824. Random House 2010 225p il **785**
   1. Composers 2. Music -- History and criticism 3. Music -- Political aspects 4. Music -- Social aspects 5. Music -- Social aspects -- Europe -- History 6. Romanticism in music
   ISBN 1-4000-6077-X; 1-58836-981-1 ebook; 978-1-4000-6077-1; 978-1-58836-981-9 ebook
                                    LC 2009-19716
   This analysis of Beethoven's seminal Ninth Symphony identifies it as a key cultural event that reflected major social upheavals, including the emergence of a dynamic Western world and changes in philosophical perspectives on individuality.
   "This discussion of the cornerstone of Romantic music, whose influence extended deep into the twentieth century, is concise, thorough, and written from the heart of a great biographer, musicologist, and lover of fine music." Booklist
   Includes bibliographical references

786.2   Keyboard instruments

Isacoff, Stuart
   A **natural** history of the piano; the instrument, the music, the musicians--from Mozart to modern jazz, and everything in between. Alfred A. Knopf 2011 361p il   **786.2**
   1. Piano music -- History and criticism 2. Pianos
   ISBN 9780307266378; 978030770142-8 ebook
                                    LC 2011011557
   "Isacoff offers an encyclopedic history of the beloved instrument and profiles such masters as Beethoven, Gershwin, and Oscar Peterson in this big slice of heaven for piano lovers." Booklist
   Includes bibliographical references

786.5   Organs

Whitney, Craig R.
   All the stops; the glorious pipe organ and its American masters. Public Affairs 2003 xxv, 323p il $30; pa $17.95   **786.5**
   1. Organ (Musical instrument) -- United States -- History 2. Organ builders -- United States 3. Organs (Musical instruments)
   ISBN 1-586-48173-8; 1-586-48262-9 pa
                                    LC 2002-37025
   "Whitney extolls the organ's eclectic heritage at a time when the instrument seems poised for a return to the mainstream, and his glossary of its colorful terminology will help novices tell a windchest from a bombarde." New Yorker
   Includes bibliographical references

787.3   Violas

Siblin, Eric
   The **cello** suites; J.S. Bach, Pablo Casals, and the search for a Baroque masterpiece. Atlantic Monthly Press 2009 319p $24   **787.3**
   1. Cellists 2. Composers 3. Music appreciation
   ISBN 978-0-8021-1929-2; 0-8021-1929-8
   The author explores the history of Bach's six suites for unaccompanied cello.
   "Siblin's curiosity and passion for his subject is evident throughout, and his method of structuring the story according to the arrangement of the music is inspired. . . . Meticulous in his research, as evidenced by copious notes and resources collected over his travels to several European countries, Siblin makes convincing connections and offers possible answers to the questions surrounding the suites. In the process, he sheds considerable light on the lives of Bach and Casals." Quill Quire
   Includes bibliographical references

787.4 Cellos (Violoncellos)

Wilson, Elizabeth

Jacqueline du Pre; her life, her music, her legend. Arcade Pub. 1999 466p il $27.95; pa $14.95 **787.4**

1. Cellists 2. Classical musicians 3. Violoncellists -- England -- Biography

ISBN 1-55970-490-X; 1-55970-519-1 pa

LC 98-49664

"Wilson, a professional cellist, has given priority to the music. Her method is discreet, methodical, informed and accurate. Above all it is measured in its tone." N Y Times Book Rev

Includes bibliographical references

787.8 Plectral lute family

Seeger, Pete

How to play the 5-string banjo; a manual for beginners. 3rd ed; Oak Publications 2002 72p il pa $16.95 **787.8**

1. Banjos

ISBN 9781597731645 pa; 1597731641 pa

A basic manual for banjo players, with melody line, lyrics, and banjo accompaniment and solos notated in standard form of tablature. Appendix includes material on where to buy a banjo, books on the banjo, books of songs to sing and phonograph records.

787.87 Guitars

Chapman, Richard

The **new** complete guitarist; rev American ed; DK 2003 208p il pa $20 **787.87**

1. Guitars

ISBN 0-7894-9701-8

LC 2004-271630

This work ranges "from fundamentals such as tuning, scales, chords, picking, and strumming, to advanced techniques of various styles such as rock, blues, and jazz. . . . [It also] includes discussions on such topics as sound and amplification, choosing a guitar, studio and home recording, plus care and maintenance of the instrument. An appealing book in the style of the 'Eyewitness' series." SLJ [review of 1993 edition]

Includes bibliographical references

Chappell, Jon

Guitar all-in-one for dummies. Wiley 2009 xxiv, 666p il pa $34.99 **787.87**

1. Guitars

ISBN 978-0-470-48133-2

This conglomeration of eight previously published For Dummies books covers topics such as writing songs and how to play rock and blues guitar.

Murray, Charles Shaar

Crosstown traffic: Jimi Hendrix and the post-war rock'n'roll revolution. St. Martin's Press 1990 247p il hardcover o.p. pa $12 **787.87**

1. Biography, Individual 2. Guitarists 3. Rock musicians 4. Singers

ISBN 0-312-06324-5 pa

LC 89-77681

"This informed, textured account will be irresistible to devotees of Hendrix and psychedelic rock as well as fans of blues, funk, jazz and rock 'n' roll." Booklist

Includes discography and bibliographical references

788 Wind instruments (Aerophones)

Gabbard, Krin

Hotter than that; the trumpet, jazz, and American culture. Faber and Faber 2008 251p il $25 **788**

1. Jazz musicians 2. Jazz musicians -- United States 3. Trumpet 4. Trumpet -- History 5. Trumpet -- Methods (Jazz) 6. Trumpet players

ISBN 9780571211999; 0-571-21199-2

LC 2008-31349

The author "tells the story of how the trumpet came to be the alpha-male instrument of jazz. . . . This engaging and informative book goes well beyond a who's who of jazz trumpet with thought-provoking discussions of jazz trumpet playing as an expression of freedom for African American musicians and as an expression of sexuality." Libr J

Includes bibliographical references

790 Recreational and performing arts

Denmead, Ken

Geek dad; awesomely geeky projects and activities for dads and kids to share. foreword by Chris Anderson. Gotham Books 2010 222p pa $17; ebook $9.99 **790**

1. Amusements 2. Father-son relationship

ISBN 978-1-59240-552-7 pa; 978-1-101-40431-7 ebook

LC 2010-8860

This book contains projects for activities such as creating a customized comic strip, building a lamp with CDs and LEGOs, and launching a video camera with balloons.

790.1 General kinds of recreational activities

Conner, Bobbi

Unplugged play; no batteries, no plugs, pure fun. illustrations by Amy Patacchiola. Workman Pub. 2007 xxv, 401p il $27.95; pa $16.95 **790.1**

1. Games 2. Play

ISBN 978-0-7611-4114-3; 978-0-7611-4390-1 pa

LC 2007-23999

"Conner has compiled more than 710 games and activities sorted by age level. Good old-fashioned play and fun are the motto here with simple props from around the house or just an imagination. The book is separated into three major parts: 'Toddler Play,' 'Preschool Play,' and 'Grade School Play.' Each has a section on solo play, ideas for parent and child, playing with others, and birthday-party activities. Each chapter and section is loaded with ideas and suggestions for simple crafts. There is such a wealth of information in this book." SLJ

791 Public performances

Fine, Marshall
Accidental genius; how John Cassavetes invented the American independent film. Miramax Books 2006 482p il $27.95   **791**
1. Actors 2. Biography, Individual 3. Independent filmmakers -- United States 4. Motion picture directors 5. Motion pictures -- United States
ISBN 1-4013-5249-9
The author "argues that mainstream moviegoers ought to care about maverick director Cassavetes (1929-89) as the progenitor of today's American independent film movement." Booklist

Server, Lee
Ava Gardner; love is nothing. St. Martin's Press 2006 551p il $29.95   **791**
1. Actors 2. Biography, Individual
ISBN 0-312-31209-1; 978-0-312-31209-1
LC 2005-51697
This is a biography of the actress.
"No matter how objective Server tries to appear in detailing the highs and lows of [Gardner's] 67 years—the three marriages, the numerous affairs, the binges, the nightlong cruising of low-life byways and bordellos, the mainly poor movies she was in—he cannot really hide his essential fondness for her. It is the kind of affection virtually every one of the more than 100 people he interviewed felt and spoke of with enthusiasm, the kind a reader too will find hard to resist." N Y Times Book Rev
Includes filmography and bibliographical references

Sonneborn, Liz
A to Z of American women in the performing arts. Facts on File 2001 264p il $44 **791**
1. Entertainers 2. Women -- United States -- Biography 3. Women entertainers -- United States -- Biography 4. Women entertainers -- United States -- Biography -- Dictionaries
ISBN 0-8160-4398-1
LC 2001-23580
This "book profiles 150 female performers, with entries for performing categories that range from actresses, dancers, and singers to circus and Wild West show performers. The book covers women of numerous ethnic groups from the early 1800s to the present. The women are listed alphabetically by their professional names and entries average about a page in length. . . . Each entry concludes with suggestions for further reading and research, and a list of recommended performances available on tape or disc." Book Rep
Includes bibliographical references

Terkel, Studs
The **spectator**. New Press 1999 364p $26.95; pa $16.95 **791**
1. Dramatists 2. Entertainers
ISBN 1-56584-553-6; 1-56584-633-8 pa
LC 99-17129
"Telling portraits of a wide range of artists in conversation with a passionately involved, prodigiously well prepared interlocutor." Booklist

791.3 Circuses

McVicar, Wes
Clown act omnibus; everything you need to know about clowning plus over 200 clown stunts. 2nd ed; Meriwether 1987 184p il pa $14.95 **791.3**
1. Clowns
ISBN 0-916260-41-0
LC 87-42958
This volume covers "the basics of being a clown; clown equipment; walk-ons and walk-arounds; clown acts with special equipment {and includes} over 200 skit ideas, classified." Publisher's note
Includes bibliographical references

Wilkins, Charles
The **circus** at the edge of the earth; travels with the Great Wallenda Circus. McClelland & Stewart 1998 270p il $22.95; pa $15.95   **791.3**
ISBN 0-7710-8847-7; 0-7710-8842-6 pa
LC 99-161790
"Wilkins chronicles a month on the road in his native Canada with the Great Wallenda Circus in the spring of 1997 and, in the process, offers remarkable insight into a subculture—the diverse assortment of gymnasts, animal trainers, daredevils and wanderers who identify themselves as circus folk—that is slowly disappearing from public consciousness." Publ Wkly

791.4 Motion pictures, radio, television

Schickel, Richard
Conversations with Scorsese; Richard Schickel [interviewer] Alfred A. Knopf 2011 423p il **791.4**
1. Motion picture directors 2. Motion picture producers and directors
ISBN 9780307268402; 9780307595461
LC 2010-34250
"Schickel recently sat down with Scorsese for a series of late-night conversations. Stitched together here, they form an illuminating autobiography-cum-film-studies-course from one of the nation's foremost directors. Scorsese speaks candidly about his childhood in Little Italy and his escape into the movies of the 1950s; his pivotal experiences at the NYU film school and his early student efforts; and, of course, his phenomenal filmmaking career, from his 1967 debut, Who's That Knocking at My Door, through . . . Shutter Island. The in-depth treatment provides fascinating insights into Scorsese's films; even his most obsessed fans will discover new revelations, and hearing him discuss his entire

body of work in a single lengthy narrative ties such outliers as The Age of Innocence and Kundun to more-characteristic masterworks like Taxi Driver and Raging Bull." Booklist

Includes filmography and bibliographical references

791.43   Motion pictures

Auiler, Dan

Vertigo; the making of a Hitchcock classic. foreword by Martin Scorsese. St. Martin's Press 1998 220p il hardcover o.p. pa $17.95 **791.43**

1. Motion picture directors

ISBN 0-312-26409-7 pa

LC 97-31654

In this account of the film's production Auiler "reconstructs the sometimes uneasy give-and-take between Hitchcock and his players—actors Jimmy Stewart, Kim Novak and Barbara Bel Geddes; screenwriters Samuel Taylor and Alec Coppel; Robert Burks and his second-unit cameraman who created the now-famous Vertigo effect . . . and Bernard Hermann, who composed the mesmerizing score. Interesting factoids abound." Publ Wkly

Includes bibliographical references

Austerlitz, Saul

Another fine mess; a history of American film comedy. Chicago Review Press 2010 512p il pa $24.95 **791.43**

1. Comedy films 2. Motion pictures -- History and criticism

ISBN 978-1-55652-951-1

LC 2010-9010

"An enthusiastic, well-observed, fresh look at old favorites that makes a compelling case for the genius of American film comedy." Kirkus

Includes bibliographical references

Biskind, Peter

Easy riders, raging bulls; how the sex-drugs-and-rock-'n'-roll generation saved Hollywood. Simon & Schuster 1998 506p il hardcover o.p. pa $15 **791.43**

1. Motion picture producers and directors 2. Motion pictures

ISBN 0-684-85708-1 pa

LC 98-2919

"Biskind does relish the tales of outlandish behaviour. . . . But in kicking over the traces of survivors' more or less reliable memories, he shows that libidinal and pharmaceutical urges were intrinsic to the film-makers' ferocious need to outdo each other as auteurs along the lines of the European greats they studied and worshipped." Sight Sound

Includes filmography and bibliographical references

Bogle, Donald

Bright boulevards, bold dreams; the story of Black Hollywood. One World Ballantine Books 2005 411p il $26.95; pa $15.95 **791.43**

1. African American actors 2. African Americans in motion pictures 3. Blacks in motion pictures 4. Blacks in the motion picture industry 5. Motion picture industry

-- United States -- History

ISBN 0345454189; 0345454197 pa

LC 2004-54781

"Starting with Madame Sul-Te-Wan's work in D.W. Griffith's 1915 The Birth of a Nation and ending with the 1960s deaths of Louise Beavers, Nat 'King' Cole and Dorothy Dandridge, Bogle tells the stories of the stars of Black Hollywood: their outfits, their love affairs and their struggles for better roles. . . . Bogle's lively style . . . and his many anecdotes will entertain and inform film students and black history buffs alike." Publ Wkly

Includes bibliographical references

Bosworth, Patricia

Jane Fonda. Houghton Mifflin Harcourt 2011 596 p. [16] p of plates **791.43**

1. Biography, Individual

ISBN 978-0-547-15257-8; 0-647-15257-4

LC 201109144

'In this book, "[Author Patricia] Bosworth goes behind the image of . . . American . . . [actress] Jane Fonda . . . whose struggles for high achievement, love, and successful motherhood mirror the conflicts of a generation of women. . . . Jane Fonda emerged from a . . . Hollywood family drama to become a 60s onscreen ingénue and then an Oscar-winning actress. At the top of her game she risked all, rising against the Vietnam War and shocking the world with a trip to Hanoi. Later, while becoming one of Hollywood6s most committed feminists, she financed her husband Tom Hayden's political career in the '80s with exercise videos that began a fitness craze and brought in millions of dollars. . . . Fonda's next turn, as a Stepford Wife of the Gulfstream set, [was] marrying Ted Turner and seemingly walking away from her ideals and her career." (Publisher's note)

Marlon Brando. Viking 2001 228p il $21.95 **791.43**

1. Actors

ISBN 0-670-88236-4

LC 00-68591

"Bosworth, a gifted writer, has a clean, spare, but witty style, which helps her pack much more than one might expect into this tiny volume." Booklist

Includes filmography

Chadwick, Bruce

The **reel** Civil War; mythmaking in American film. Knopf 2001 366p il hardcover o.p. pa $15 **791.43**

1. Motion pictures

ISBN 0-375-70832-4 pa

LC 2001-91008

"One-third of 'The Reel Civil War' concentrates on {'The Birth of a Nation' and 'Gone With the Wind'}. Given their prominence, that seems a reasonable balance, and Chadwick's dissection of the myths they helped to foster is superb." N Y Times Book Rev

Includes bibliographical references

Cook, David A.

A **history** of narrative film; 4th ed; W.W. Norton 2004 xxviii, 1120p il pa $78.75 **791.43**

1. Motion pictures -- History and criticism

ISBN 0-393-97868-0; 978-0-393-97868-1

LC 2003-61090

This volume provides discussion and analysis of major films, directors, and national cinemas. In addition to historical and aesthetic concerns, the author explores the technological, social, and economic context of world cinema. Includes in-depth coverage of contemporary filmmaking in Hollywood, the Third World, and the former Soviet Union, as well as an entire chapter on computer-generated imaging.

Davis, Ronald L.

John Ford; Hollywood's old master. University of Okla. Press 1995 383p il hardcover o.p. pa $21.95 **791.43**

1. Biography, Individual 2. Motion picture directors 3. Motion picture producers and directors -- Biography

ISBN 0-8061-2916-6 pa

LC 94-25178

In this study of the influential filmmaker, "Davis draws on the recollections of the actors who worked frequently with Ford, including John Wayne, Henry Fonda and Maureen O'Hara, to document Ford's tyranny on the set, which intimidated his cast but wrung brilliant performances from them." Publ Wkly

Includes bibliographical references

Decharne, Max

Hardboiled Hollywood; the true crime stories behind the classic noir films. Pegasus Books 2010 240p $27.95; pa $14.95 **791.43**

1. Motion pictures 2. Mystery films

ISBN 978-1-60598-076-8; 1-60598-076-5; 978-1-60598-083-6 pa; 1-60598-083-8 pa

"A lively exploration of the origins of some of Hollywood's most vivid plots – not only the reworked novels and screenplays, but real events. Police reports, Mafiosi and serial killers are never far away. Décharné renders an intriguing picture of the powerful place this art form has come to occupy in society, and why." Financial Times

Includes filmography and bibliographical references

Dixon, Wheeler W.

A **short** history of film; [by] Wheeler Winston Dixon & Gwendolyn Audrey Foster. Rutgers University Press 2008 xxxv, 441p il $70; pa $24.95 **791.43**

1. Motion pictures -- History and criticism

ISBN 978-0-8135-4269-0; 0-8135-4269-3; 978-0-8135-4270-6 pa; 0-8135-4270-7 pa

LC 2007-22097

"This excellent introduction stands out in a crowded field with its lively, accessible writing, broad coverage, and particular focus on traditionally marginalized figures in film history." Libr J

Includes bibliographical references

Drazin, Charles

French cinema. Faber and Faber 2011 448p il pa $22 **791.43**

1. Motion pictures -- France

ISBN 978-0-571-21173-9

A "history of French film, from the fanciful, whimsical inventions of pioneer Georges Méliès to the formalist daring and intellectual rigor of contemporary artists like Olivier Assayas and Catherine Breillat. . . . Drazin charts the economic and social conditions that nurtured French film, providing fascinating insights into the pragmatic methods of the Pathé studio, the shift to more escapist, 'Hollywood' style films that characterized the Nazi occupation, the rise of film culture supported by magazines like Cahiers du cinéma and the attendant New Wave spearheaded by directors including François Truffaut and Jean-Luc Godard, and the vital but often uneasy relationship between French and American cinema. Drazin's account is endlessly readable, alternating penetrating analysis of classics like Jean Renoir's La Règle du Jeu with serious appraisals of less well-known figures like Julien Duvivier and Agnès Varda." Kirkus

Includes bibliographical references

Dunne, John Gregory

Monster; living off the big screen. Random House 1997 203p hardcover o.p. pa $12 **791.43**

1. Motion pictures -- Production and direction

ISBN 0-375-75024-X pa

LC 96-26212

The author "traces the life of a screenplay from the first draft to the final wrap. The work in question . . . Up Close & Personal, is the story of two newscasters and was originally intended to follow the life of Jessica Savitch. By the end of the eight years that Dunne and his wife, author Joan Didion, worked on it, however, very little of that germinal plan remained. . . . The account is forthright and written with the wry detachment of true experience." Libr J

Eagan, Daniel

America's film legacy; the authoritative guide to the landmark movies in the National Film Registry. Continuum 2010 xxvii, 818p il $130; pa $39.95 **791.43**

1. Motion pictures -- Catalogs 2. Reference books

ISBN 978-0-826-41849-4; 0-826-41849-X; 978-0-826-42977-3 pa; 0-826-42977-7 pa

LC 2009-42778

The author "chronologically catalogues 500 Registry films, from 1893's 30-second Blacksmithing Scene to 1995's Fargo, jumbling Hollywood classics together with obscure art films, cartoon shorts, documentaries, industrial and student films, newsreel footage from the Hindenburg disaster and the Zapruder film. Each entry includes complete cast and credits lists and an engaging one to two-page historical and interpretive essay. . . . [This is] an erudite, perceptive, always entertaining cinematic encyclopedia." Publ Wkly

Ebert, Roger

★ **Roger** Ebert's movie yearbook 2010. Andrews McMeel Pub. 2010 662p pa $29.99 **791.43**

1. Motion pictures -- Reviews

ISBN 978-0-7407-8536-8

In addition to reviews this volume contains interviews and essays, questions and answers, film festival information, and a rated list of previously reviewed films.

Eyman, Scott

Print the legend; the life and times of John Ford. Johns Hopkins Univ. Press 2000 656p il pa $23.50 **791.43**

1. Motion picture directors 2. Motion picture producers and directors -- Biography 3. Motion picture producers and directors -- United States -- Biography

ISBN 0-8018-6560-3; 978-0-8018-6560-2

LC 00-33044

This is a biography chronicling the life and career of the director of "such classics as The grapes of wrath, The searchers and The man who shot Liberty Valance.... Eyman has written a quietly magnificent biography of an American original who has shaped our perception of movies as serious art." Publ Wkly

Includes bibliographical references

Fagen, Herb

The **encyclopedia** of westerns; foreword by Tom Selleck; preface by Dale Robertson. Checkmark Bks. 2003 xx, 618p il $75; pa $24.95 **791.43**

1. Spaghetti westerns 2. Western films 3. Western films -- United States

ISBN 0-8160-4456-2; 0-8160-4457-0 pa

LC 2002-26355

The author "traces the history of the genre, . . . defining purpose, methodology, and organization. The bulk of the book is made up of more than 3500 film entries, ranging from The Great Train Robbery (1902) to The Quick and the Dead (1995). Typically, entries include title, studio, year, running time, VHS/DVD availability, credits, and annotation. . . . Fagen's knowledge of, and love for, his subject shine through every page of this unique and valuable work." Libr J

Includes bibliographical references

Farber, Manny

★ **Farber** on film; the complete film writings of Manny Farber. edited by Robert Polito. Library of America 2009 824p $40 **791.43**

1. Film criticism 2. Motion pictures -- History and criticism 3. Motion pictures -- Reviews

ISBN 978-1-59853-050-6

LC 2009-928058

"Manny Farber (1917-2008), critic and painter, wrote movie reviews for publications ranging from the starchy New Republic to the raunchy girlie mag Cavalier. This is your first bit of proof that Farber had an itch to get his opinions in print anywhere he could (one measure of a critic who wants to communicate, not just simmer in theory-juice). He never followed the pack, or became part of any 'school' of criticism, or held back a judgment because he thought he'd be jeered at or not allowed at the cool-kids' table. . . . Farber covered movies from 1942 to 1977, which means that in this book he weighs in vividly on everything from Casablanca . . . to Taxi Driver." Entertainment Wkly

Gallagher, Tag

John Ford; the man and his films. University of Calif. Press 1986 572p il $42.50; pa $17.95 **791.43**

1. Motion picture directors 2. Motion pictures

ISBN 0-520-05097-5; 0-520-06334-1 pa

LC 83-18047

"Gallagher's reassessment of John Ford's life and career revels in the complexity of the film director's personality while reconsidering his cinematic achievement. . . . Ford's philosophical and intellectual character is also sketched in this honest yet sympathetic account." Booklist

Includes bibliographical references

Gora, Susannah

You couldn't ignore me if you tried; the Brat Pack, John Hughes, and their impact on a generation. Crown Publishers 2010 367p il $26 **791.43**

1. Motion picture directors 2. Motion picture producers 3. Screenwriters 4. Teenagers in motion pictures

ISBN 978-0-307-40843-3; 0-307-40843-4

"Though Gora discusses the work of Hughes's colleagues, she places the sharpest lens on the godfather of the genre himself. . . . Through extensive research and interviews with insiders, she reveals the romantic undertones in the relationship between the late director and his pouty-lipped muse, Molly Ringwald, 18 years his junior. But, the author argues, perhaps it was his ability to relate to adolescents and his respect for their seemingly insignificant plights that allowed Hughes to capture coming-of-age so candidly. While a long and involved read, Gora's book offers an all-access pass to the Brat Pack, the films they starred in, and those behind the cameras of a movie era that is still relevant today." Paste

Includes bibliographical references

Harris, Mark

★ **Pictures** at a revolution; five movies and the birth of the new Hollywood. Penguin Press 2008 490p il $27.95 **791.43**

1. Academy Awards (Motion pictures) 2. Film criticism 3. Motion picture industry 4. Motion pictures 5. Motion pictures -- History

ISBN 978-1-59420-152-3; 1-59420-152-8

LC 2007-32633

The author examines the five films nominated for the Academy Award for Best Picture in 1967: Bonnie and Clyde, The Graduate, Guess Who's Coming To Dinner, In the Heat of the Night, and Dr. Dolittle.

"Harris gives us a juicy, multilayered chronicle of a turning point in American culture. This is page-turning social history; someone reading this book who didn't live through those days would understand why 'the '60s' had to happen." Newsweek

Includes bibliographical references

Harvey, James

Movie love in the 50's. Da Capo Press 2002 448p il pa $18.95 **791.43**

1. Motion pictures

ISBN 978-0-306-81177-7; 0-306-81177-4

"For every 'sanitized' movie that came out of the Fifties, there were others that shook up old formulas. Critic and essayist Harvey explores—and ultimately eulogizes—Hollywood films of this era, a time of transition when the Production Code was being scrapped and the studio system abandoned. . . . His movie love is inspired and infectious." Libr J

Includes bibliographical references

Haskell, Molly

Frankly, my dear; Gone With the Wind revisited. Yale University Press 2009 244p il **791.43**

1. Authors 2. Motion pictures -- History 3. Novelists

ISBN 978-0-300-11752-3

LC 2008-37296

This book "deals simultaneously with Margaret Mitchell's . . . novel and David Selznick's . . . film version of Gone With the Wind." (Publisher's note) Bibliography. Index.

The author "applies her deep movie knowledge, feminist eye, and Southern roots to Frankly, My Dear, a fiercely smart appreciation of Gone With the Wind. Passionate about the topic since her teens in Richmond, Haskell turns her attention from making-of stories to meaning-of insights, as crisp in her presentation of Hollywood gossip as she is in her scholarly analysis of why the book-turned-movie has such a hold on us." Entertainment Wkly

Includes bibliographical references

Howard, Jean

Jean Howard's Hollywood; a photo memoir. photographs by Jean Howard; text by Jim Watters. Abrams 1989 248p il hardcover o.p. pa $24.95 **791.43**

1. American actors 2. Motion picture industry -- Pictorial works 3. Motion pictures 4. Photographers

ISBN 978-0-8109-2679-0; 0-8109-2679-2

LC 89-264

"Miss Howard has recorded the rarefied behind-the-gates lives of some of the most famous personalities in the history of the motion picture business. No outsider was she, hired for the occasion to 'snap' the swells. Miss Howard is very much one of the swells herself; her pictures are shot from the intimate perspective of the insider, either as a guest at the party or, frequently, as the hostess." N Y Times Book Rev

Jones, G. William

Black cinema treasures; lost and found. foreword by Ossie Davis. University of N. Tex. Press 1991 242p il hardcover o.p. pa $17.95 **791.43**

1. African Americans in motion pictures 2. Blacks in the motion picture industry 3. Motion pictures 4. Motion pictures -- United States

ISBN 1-57441-028-8 pa

LC 91-10882

This book "documents black independent filmmaking from the 1920s to the 1950s, spotlighting sixteen films salvaged from a warehouse in Tyler, Texas, by the author. . . . There are also brief biographies of pioneers such as Oscar Micheaux and Spencer Williams. . . . For anyone with an interest in the social history of the movie industry, this book helps bring to light a much-neglected body of work." San Francisco Rev Books

Includes filmography

Kael, Pauline

The **age** of movies; selected writings of Pauline Kael. edited by Sanford Schwartz. Library of America 2011 xxiv, 828p $40 **791.43**

1. Motion pictures -- Reviews

ISBN 978-1-59853-109-1; 1-59853-109-3

LC 2011-23053

"Spanning 1965 to 1990, the volume holds many sparkling radio essays [Kael] delivered over the East Bay airwaves and had reprinted in places like Film Quarterly before heading east, and a wealth of reviews from magazines, especially from her residency at The New Yorker, where she opined from 1967 to 1991. The full range of Kael's smarts, vision, wit, prejudices, and downright cruelty are on full, wicked display." Millions

Kashner, Sam

The **bad** & the beautiful; Hollywood in the fifties. {by} Sam Kashner and Jennifer MacNair. Norton 2002 380p il $26.95; pa $15.95 **791.43**

1. Motion pictures 2. Motion pictures -- California -- Los Angeles -- History

ISBN 0-393-04321-5; 0-393-32436-2 pa

LC 2002-317

"These accounts, often dipped in acid, will keep readers flipping pages." Publ Wkly

Includes bibliographical references (p. {357}-363) and index

Keaton, Eleanor

Buster Keaton remembered; {by} Eleanor Keaton and Jeffrey Vance; afterword by Kevin Brownlow; Manoah Bowman, photographic editor; photographs from the collection of the Academy of Motion Picture Arts and Sciences. Abrams 2001 238p il $45 **791.43**

1. Actors 2. Motion picture directors

ISBN 0-8109-4227-5

LC 00-61853

A "photographic tribute . . . comprising formal and behind-the-scenes stills, staged publicity shots, and previously unpublished personal photos, this book is the most comprehensive pictorial retrospective on Keaton to date." Libr J

Filmography: p. 219-233; Includes bibliographical references (p. 217-218) and index

Lane, Anthony

Nobody's perfect; writings from the New Yorker. Knopf 2002 xx, 752p $30; pa $16.95 **791.43**

1. Motion pictures -- Reviews

ISBN 0-375-41448-7; 0-375-71434-0 pa

LC 2002-20809

"One of the best aspects of Lane's column, and of this anthology, is that it wanders across cultural and intellectual borders." Libr J

Lanzmann, Claude

The **Patagonian** hare; a memoir. Claude Lanzmann; translated from the French by Frank Wynne. Farrar, Straus & Giroux 2012 x, 528 p.p ill. **791.43**

1. Jews -- France -- Biography 2. Journalists -- France

-- Biography 3. Memoirs 4. Motion picture producers
and directors -- France -- Biography
ISBN 0374230048; 9780374230043

LC 2011048058

This book is the memoir of the journalist and filmmaker
Claude Lanzmann. . . . Raised as a secular Jew in a family
with deep communist sympathies . . . the author served in
the French Resistance and narrowly missed capture by the
Nazis. . . . He became editor of Jean-Paul Sartre's journal Le
Temps Modernes . . . and had an intense seven-year affair
with Sartre's lover, Simone de Beauvoir, who was happy to
take him on as her sixth man. Faithfulness wasn't anyone's
game then, and Lanzmann seemed to seduce nearly every
woman he ever met. He also became deeply immersed in his
own Jewish heritage and documentary filmmaking, ultimately resulting in his nine-hour magnum opus Shoah. (Kirkus)

Lax, Eric
★ **Conversations** with Woody Allen; his films,
the movies, and moviemaking. A.A. Knopf 2007
390p il $30   **791.43**
1. Actors 2. Biography, Individual 3. Film criticism
4. Humorists 5. Motion picture directors 6. Motion
picture producers and directors 7. Motion pictures --
Production and direction 8. Screenwriters
ISBN 978-0-375-41533-3; 0-375-41533-5

LC 2007-06350

This book contains interviews with Woody Allen from
1971 to the present.

"A fine, never-disappointing achievement, this book is in
competition with no other." Choice

Leaming, Barbara
Marilyn Monroe. Crown 1998 464p il hard-
cover o.p. pa $16   **791.43**
1. Actors 2. Motion picture actors and actresses --
United States -- Biography
ISBN 0-609-80553-3 pa

LC 98-18738

Learning "has a sure dramatic instinct for illuminating
overlooked material and re-examining the most interesting
episodes." N Y Times Book Rev

Leider, Emily Wortis
Becoming Mae West. Farrar, Straus & Giroux
1997 431p il hardcover o.p. pa $18.95   **791.43**
1. Actors 2. Authors 3. Biography, Individual 4.
Dramatists 5. Memoirists 6. Novelists 7. Screenwriters
ISBN 978-0-374-10959-2; 978-0-306-80951-4 pa;
0-306-80951-6 pa

LC 96-43803

This exploration of the West persona "focuses on the first
four decades of West's career, up to 1938. Yet Leider's biography is also a portrait of an era: she devotes a great deal
of the book to rendering the historical context, particularly
the moral landscape, of the early 1900's, in order to more
clearlydefine West's place in it and ultimately her mastery of
it." N Y Times Book Rev

Dark lover: the life and death of Rudolph Valentino; [by] Emily W. Leider. Farrar, Straus & Giroux
2003 514p il $35; pa $16 **791.43**
1. Actors
ISBN 0-374-28239-0; 0-571-21114-3 pa

LC 2002-29779

"A comprenhensive . . . portrait of the great screen
lover." Booklist
Includes bibliographical references

Lumet, Sidney
Making movies. Knopf 1995 220p hardcover
o.p. pa $12   **791.43**
1. Motion pictures -- Production and direction
ISBN 0-679-75660-4 pa

LC 94-34449

"A fascinating look at the artist at work." Libr J

Lynn, Kenneth S.
★ **Charlie** Chaplin and his times. Cooper Square
Press 2003 604p il pa $19.95   **791.43**
1. Actors 2. Motion picture directors 3. Motion picture
producers 4. Motion picture producers and directors --
Biography
ISBN 0-8154-1255-X; 978-0-8154-1255-7

LC 2002-31420

The author "interweaves Chaplin's life with the events
and personalities of his era, including British music hall
impresario Fred Karno, silent screen star and pal Douglas
Fairbanks, numerous lovers and wives, brother Sydney, and
Adolf Hitler. . . . Lynn addresses his subject's leftist views
and makes sense of the House Committee on Un-American
Activities investigations of 1947 that led to Chaplin's European exile until 1973. All a biography should be, this is
enthusiastically recommended." Libr J
Includes bibliographical references

Mamet, David
Bambi vs. Godzilla; on the nature, purpose,
and practice of the movie business. Pantheon Books
2007 250p $22   **791.43**
1. Authorship 2. Motion pictures
ISBN 978-0-375-42253-9; 0-375-42253-6

LC 2006-20018

Mamet's "essay collection focuses on the movie industry, and his stance is that of someone who has seen Hollywood's facelift scars and whose advice to eager novices just
off the bus can be summarized thusly: 'Go back.' . . . . He
outlines the Hollywood caste system with a precision that
reflects the bitter experience of the person at the bottom—
the screenwriter. Scorn, betrayal, and subjugation—this is
the lot of the writer, who, according to Mamet, is resented
by nearly everyone in the business. Miraculously, though,
great drama is occasionally realized on the screen, and

Mamet offers writers some guidelines on how to approach it." Booklist

Includes filmography

On directing film. Viking 1991 107p hardcover o.p. pa $14 **791.43**

1. Motion pictures -- Production and direction

ISBN 0-14-012722-4 pa

LC 90-50428

"Noted playwright, screenwriter, and director Mamet offers his views on film directing taken, some in transcript form, from lectures and classes at Columbia. . . . Refreshingly untheoretical, particularly regarding acting technique, this is fitfully interesting stuff." Libr J

Mann, William J.

Behind the screen; how gays and lesbians shaped Hollywood, 1910-1969. Viking 2001 xxiv, 422p il $29.95; pa $16 **791.43**

1. Homosexuality in motion pictures 2. Motion picture industry

ISBN 0-670-03017-1; 0-14-200114-7 pa

LC 2001-17984

In this study "Mann examines how the movie capital of the world was transformed by a host of writers, directors, designers, actors, and producers often at odds with the official codes, and mores of the times. . . . Mann's book is important reading for anyone interested in the history of American film. Essential for all film and gay studies collections." Libr J

Mayer, Geoff

Guide to British cinema. Greenwood Press 2003 440p $99.95 **791.43**

1. Motion pictures -- Great Britain 2. Motion pictures -- Great Britain -- History

ISBN 0-313-30307-X

LC 2002-75325

"Neither a comprehensive guide nor a 'best of' compendium, Mayer's work is nevertheless useful as an introduction to the country's film history." Libr J

Includes bibliographical references

McCann, Graham

Cary Grant; a class apart. Columbia Univ. Press 1997 346p il hardcover o.p. pa $19.95 **791.43**

1. Actors 2. Biography, Individual

ISBN 0-231-10885-0 pa

LC 96-38577

"McCann's biography shows how working-class Archie Leach transformed himself into Cary Grant. Unlike many self-made successes, Grant never renounced his humble origins but incorporated them into his persona. As a result, he became, McCann says, a 'democratic gentleman,' at ease in any element, who shone in both serious dramas and screwball comedies and, unlike most male stars, appealed equally to men and women." Booklist

Includes bibliographical references

McKay, Sinclair

The **man** with the golden touch; how the Bond films conquered the world. Overlook Press 2010 396p il $25.95 **791.43**

1. Bond, James (Fictional character) 2. Motion pictures

ISBN 978-1-59020-298-2

"Not a 'making-of' film book, like so many others, but rather an exploration of the themes and impact of the James Bond movies, this lively volume is sure to appeal to fans of 007. The author, clearly a huge Bond fan himself, writes with a wry tone, but he's brimming with knowledge and insight. He tracks the movies from their origin, as cold-war spy adventures, through their transition to fantastic adventures in supervillainy, to—horror of horrors!—quaint artifacts of a bygone era, and then, inevitably, back around to relevance again. He compares and contrasts the movies to their source material, Ian Fleming's novels and short stories, and he fills the book with delightful Bond arcana." Booklist

Includes bibliographical references

Muir, John Kenneth

The **encyclopedia** of superheroes on film and television; 2nd ed.; McFarland & Co. 2008 696p il $75 **791.43**

1. Reference books 2. Superhero films -- Encyclopedias 3. Superhero television programs -- Encyclopedias

ISBN 978-0-7864-3755-9; 0-7864-3755-3

LC 2008-19724

"Entries start with description and background of the hero. Live-action films are presented with reviewer comments and cast and crew. TV series also present reviewer comments and a description of the series. Episode guides include title, writer and director credits, and air dates as well as episode descriptions and guest casts. . . . A good addition to the pop-culture collection." Booklist

Includes bibliographical references

Muller, Eddie

Dark city; the lost world of film noir. St. Martin's Griffin 1998 206p il pa $22.95 **791.43**

1. Film noir -- United States -- History and criticism 2. Motion pictures

ISBN 0-312-18076-4

LC 98-5677

"There are few fresh insights because the book is essentially a retro trip--and it does succeed in conveying the patina of 40s and 50s crime films pretty magnificently." Sight Sound

Includes bibliographical references

Neupert, Richard

A **history** of the French new wave cinema; [by] Richard Neupert. University of Wis. Press 2002 368p il $50; pa $24.95 **791.43**

1. Motion pictures -- France 2. New wave films -- France

ISBN 0-299-18160-X; 0-299-18164-2 pa

LC 2002-2305

"Refreshingly jargon-free and full of interesting details and anecdotes, this book is a pleasure to read." Libr J

Includes bibliographical references

Osborne, Robert A.

75 years of the Oscar; the official history of the Academy Awards. {by} Robert Osborne. Abbeville Press 2003 416p il $75 **791.43**
1. Academy Awards (Motion pictures)
ISBN 0-7892-0787-7

LC 2003-45311
This includes a history of the Academy of Motion Picture Arts and Sciences, overviews of Academy Award nominees and winners, award ceremonies, and a complete listing of nominees and winners in every category.

Rabin, Nathan

My year of flops; the A.V. Club presents one man's journey deep into the heart of cinematic failure. Scribner 2010 264p il pa $15 **791.43**
1. Film criticism 2. Motion pictures 3. Motion pictures -- Evaluation
ISBN 978-1-4391-5312-3; 1-4391-5312-4

LC 2010-18224
"Follow Nathan Rabin on his quest 'to provide a sympathetic reappraisal of some of the most reviled films of all time,' and what do you learn? 'Pennies From Heaven'and 'Freddy Got Fingered' are better than you might think, and 'Ishtar' offers an 'exquisitely jaundiced take' on American foreign policy. Mostly, though, Mr. Rabin sits slack-jawed watching the everlasting dreadfulness of 'Mame,' 'Battlefield Earth' and 'Exit to Eden' ('the mother of all unsexy sex films'). Always glad to snark it up, Mr. Rabin can also be mournful when reflecting on how worthwhile failures like 'Heaven's Gate' diminished Hollywood's ambitions, then and now. The book, which collects columns that first appeared on The Onion's pop-culture Web site, includes more bad movies and interviews with actors caught up in the cinematic wreckage." N Y Times Book Rev

Reilly, Thomas A.

The **big** picture; filmmaking lessons from a life on the set. St. Martin's Press 2009 239p $25.95 **791.43**
1. Cinematography 2. Motion pictures -- Production and direction
ISBN 978-0-312-38038-0; 0-312-38038-0

LC 2008-44615
The author "has written a valuable guide that film students and novice filmmakers will find illuminating and insightful. In 50 short essays Reilly analyzes the problems that often surface on movie sets, and offers solutions. . . . Reilly opens with film set slang and jargon ('martini' = last shot of the day) and then moves on to cover everything from schedules, blocking actor movements, camera angles and master shots to variables in sunlight and the color palette." Publ Wkly

Richards, Jeffrey

Hollywood's ancient worlds. Continuum 2008 227p il $29.95 **791.43**
1. Epic films 2. History, Ancient 3. Motion pictures
ISBN 978-1-8472-5007-0; 1-8472-5007-6
The author "examines how the ancient world has been presented in the movies, placing particular emphasis on Hollywood films but also including some European films and television productions. He excludes comedies for reasons of

space and authorial preference, but otherwise Hollywood's Ancient Worlds includes consideration of every epic film set in the ancient world which was created between 1916 and 2006. . . . [The book] is packed with information. . . . However, Richards has also produced a jargon-free book which is fun to read and maintains a sense of proportion about the films he discusses." PopMatters

Rough Guides (Firm)

The **Rough** Guide to film; [by] Richard Armstrong . . . [et al.] Distributed by Penguin Putnam 2007 649p il pa $27.99 **791.43**
1. Motion picture producers and directors -- Biography -- Dictionaries 2. Reference books
ISBN 978-1-84353-408-2; 1-84353-408-8

LC 2007-300132
"This volume looks beyond the Hollywood mainstream to provide assistance to anyone who is browsing rental-store shelves or online DVD catalogs in search of something new. More than 800 directors from around the globe are profiled, and more than 2,000 of their most important films are briefly reviewed. . . . If you're in a hurry, you can turn to the various categorized lists of five great directors, five classic films, and five 'lesser-known gems.'" Booklist

Schickel, Richard

Clint Eastwood; a biography. Knopf 1996 557p il hardcover o.p. pa $15 **791.43**
1. Actors 2. Biography, Individual 3. Mayors 4. Motion picture directors
ISBN 0-679-74991-8 pa

LC 96-32836
Schickel examines the life and career of the actor-director.

"No mere celebrity bio, this is a beautifully written, comprehensive and astonishingly insightful study of a man who, seemingly against all odds, has achieved world renown as both a pop culture icon and an accomplished film artist." Publ Wkly

Includes bibliographical references

Scovell, Jane

Oona; living in the shadows: a biography of Oona O'Neill Chaplin. Warner Bks. 1998 354p il hardcover o.p. pa $14.99 **791.43**
1. Actors 2. Comedians -- United States -- Biography 3. Entertainers' spouses -- Biography 4. Motion picture actors and actresses -- United States -- Biography 5. Motion picture directors 6. Motion picture producers 7. Spouses of prominent persons
ISBN 0-446-67541-5 pa

LC 98-21592
A "biography of Oona O'Neill Chaplin, daughter of playwright Eugene O'Neill and wife of film legend Charlie Chaplin." Publ Wkly

Includes bibliographical references

Siegel, Scott

★ The **encyclopedia** of Hollywood; [by] Scott Siegel and Barbara Siegel; revised and updated by

Tom Erskine and James Welsh. Facts on File 2004
548p il $75; pa $24.95   **791.43**
1. Motion picture industry
ISBN 0-8160-4622-0; 0-8160-4623-9 pa
LC 2003-14967

"This encyclopedia offers representative entries on the
American film industry, from the early, pre-Hollywood days
to the present. Entries cover people, including actors, directors, producers, editors, cinematographers, and more; films;
studios; genres . . . [jobs] and terms. . . . [This book] is easy
to use and could be a welcome addition to the circulating as
well as the reference collection." Booklist
Includes bibliographical references

Spacek, Sissy

My extraordinary ordinary life; Sissy Spacek with
Maryanne Vollers. Hyperion 2012 271 p.   **791.43**
1. Motion picture actors and actresses -- United States
-- Biography
ISBN 1401324363; 9781401324360
LC 2011047858

In this memoir, actress Sissy Spacek writes about her
idyllic, barefoot childhood in a small East Texas town. . . .
[S]he describes how she arrived in New York City one starstruck summer as a seventeen-year-old carrying a suitcase
and two guitars; and how she built a career that has spanned
four decades with films such as Carrie, Coal Miners Daughter, 3 Women, and The Help. She details working with some
of the great directors of our time, including Terrence Ma-
lick, Robert Altman, David Lynch, and Brian De Palma. .
. . She also reveals why, at the height of her fame, she and
her family moved away from Los Angeles to a farm in rural
Virginia." (Publishers note)

Spoto, Donald

The **dark** side of genius; the life of Alfred
Hitchcock. {with a new introduction by the author}
Centennial ed; Da Capo Press 1999 594p il pa
$22   **791.43**
1. Motion picture directors 2. Motion picture producers
and directors -- Great Britain -- Biography
ISBN 0-306-80932-X
LC 99-37941

This is a biography of the director of such films as The
man who knew too much, The thirty-nine steps, The lady
vanishes, Rebecca, Spellbound, Strangers on a train, Rear
window, and Psycho.
This "is a vivid and perceptive portrait of a man whose
character was as strange and shadowed as his films. . .
. Hitchcock's final obsession was secretiveness, but he
has been well served by a knowledgeable and revealing
biography." Time
Includes bibliographical references

Thomson, David

The **moment** of Psycho; how Alfred Hitchcock
taught America to love murder. Basic Books 2009
192p $22.95   **791.43**
1. Motion picture directors 2. Motion pictures -- United
States -- History -- 20th century
ISBN 978-0-465-00339-6
LC 2009-30821

"Though readers may not agree with all of Mr. Thomson's arguments here, he makes a powerful—and sometimes
surprising—case for the movie's importance in film and cultural history. Building on the work of Francois Truffaut (who
first helped establish Hitchcock's reputation as an auteur)
and the writings of the critic Robin Wood, Mr. Thomson
does a deft job in this volume of reappraising Hitchcock's
work, even as he deconstructs Psycho and its complex cinematic legacy." N Y Times (Late N Y Ed)
Includes bibliographical references

★ The **whole** equation; a history of Hollywood.
Knopf 2005 402p il hardcover o.p. pa $15 **791.43**
1. Motion picture industry -- California -- Los Angeles
-- History 2. Motion picture industry -- History 3.
Motion pictures -- California -- Los Angeles -- History
4. Motion pictures -- History and criticism
ISBN 0-375-40016-8; 0-375-70154-0 pa
LC 2004-48358

"Peeling back the layers, goring sacred cows, correcting
misconceptions, and revealing truth rather than reprinting
legends, Thomson offers history, yes, but also a philosophical meditation on how the movie industry has inspired and
influenced L.A. and America, and vice versa." Booklist
Includes bibliographical references

Tropiano, Stephen

Obscene, indecent, immoral, and offensive; 100+
years of censored, banned, and controversial films.
Limelight Editions 2009 364p il pa $19.95 **791.43**
1. Motion pictures -- Censorship
ISBN 978-0-87910-359-0
LC 2008-52582

"Though the book is grounded in examples from specific
films, the main issues are not the instances of offensive material within a given film but the ensuing controversies and
attempts to censor it. . . . This book is a quintessential work
for any readers interested in studying issues of censorship in
film . . . . It is written in such a way that the casual movie-
goer is given enough background to understand the issues
and in enough detail that even the most seasoned cinephile is
likely to find new and interesting information." PopMatters

Walker, Alexander

Stanley Kubrick, director; a visual analysis by
Sybil Taylor and Ulrich Ruchti. rev and expanded;
Norton 1999 376p il $35; pa $25   **791.43**
1. Motion picture directors
ISBN 0-393-04601-X; 0-393-32119-3 pa
LC 98-24086

"Walker describes Kubrick as a guarded, suspicious, obsessive, controlling, paranoid workaholic, and makes us feel
that he's bestowing a compliment. Each movie is given a
thorough analysis, reinforced by the extensive use of stills in
each case." Publ Wkly
Includes bibliographical references

Warren, Bill

Keep watching the skies! American science fiction movies of the fifties. research associate, Bill

Thomas; foreword by Howard Waldrop. 21st century ed.; McFarland & Co. 2010 1004p il $99 **791.43**
1. Reference books 2. Science fiction films
ISBN 978-0-7864-4230-0; 0-7864-4230-1

LC 2009-20594

Covers "nearly 300 films released between 1950 and 1962. . . . Although prominent films like Forbidden Planet, Them! The Time Machine, and The Fly receive more extensive coverage, all of the essays . . . include production, cast, and distribution credits; a plot synopsis; production details and fun background facts; discussion of the direction, acting, effects, and other prominent elements of the film; and information about public and critical reaction. Attractive photos accompany most of the essays, and posters for the best-known films are reproduced in 35 color plates. . . . Although the audience for 1950s science fiction may be dwindling, this is the kind of reference that not only informs but also creates new fans." Booklist

Includes bibliographical references

Wasson, Sam
Fifth Avenue, 5 AM; Audrey Hepburn, Breakfast at Tiffany's, and the dawn of the modern woman. HarperStudio 2010 xx, 231p il map $19.99 **791.43**
1. Actors
ISBN 978-0-06-177415-7

LC 2009-52439

The author "presents an irresistibly gossipy account of the production of Breakfast at Tiffany's (1961), charting the transformation of actress Audrey Hepburn into an icon of emerging sexual liberation—the good/bad girl, the lovable 'kook,' independent and sexually experienced but sufficiently charming to bring home to mother. Rich in incident and set among the glitterati of America's most glamorous era, the book reads like a novel." Kirkus

Young, Clive
Homemade Hollywood; fans behind the camera. Continuum 2008 297p il $85; pa $19.95 **791.43**
1. Fan films
ISBN 978-0-8264-2922-3; 0-8264-2922-X; 978-0-8264-2923-0 pa; 0-8264-2923-8 pa

LC 2008-24007

An "overview of the fan-film experience and the renegades who've made the fan film both a refreshing puncture of the movie industry's inflated self-importance and a way to gauge how particular big-budget productions resonate, or fail to resonate, with the moviegoing public. Author Clive Young brings the rigors of a scholar and the inside-baseball of a fan to this well-researched and written survey of how doing it yourself has both helped drive our enduring love of motion pictures and to articulate the populist roots of that obsession." PopMatters

Includes bibliographical references

Zinoman, Jason
Shock value; how a few eccentric outsiders gave us nightmares, conquered Hollywood, and invent-

ed modern horror. Penguin Books 2011 274p il $25.95 **791.43**
1. Horror films 2. Horror films -- History and criticism
ISBN 978-1-59420-302-2; 1-59420-302-4

LC 2010-52279

"Today's filmgoers may think nothing of going to the local multiplex to see the latest incarnation of the Saw franchise, but New York Times theater reporter Zinoman reminds us of a time when such fare was restricted to drive-ins, while 'mainstream' horror consisted of cheesy Vincent Price movies or vampire films from Britain's Hammer studios. The change is attributed to a group of maverick writers and directors including Wes Craven, John Carpenter, Tobe Hooper and George Romero, makers of such films a Night of the Living Dead, The Last House on the Left, The Texas Chainsaw Massacre and Halloween, which created a new type of horror based on reality instead of fantasy. The author investigates the cultural conditions that made the 'New Horror' possible. . . . An engrossing look at an important cultural moment and a valuable addition to the canon of popular film history." Kirkus

Includes bibliographical references

Film noir; the encyclopedia. edited by Alain Silver . . . [et al.]; co-editor: Carl Macek; designed by Bernard Schleifer. [4th ed.]; Overlook Duckworth 2010 511p il **791.43**
1. Motion pictures 2. Mystery films
ISBN 978-1-590201442

An introductory essay "lays out the history and parameters of noir in a succinct but undogmatic way, offering an intro for the new viewer as well as food for thought for the hardboiled fan. Most of the rest of the book consists of synopses of noir films, providing a brief plot summary followed by a paragraph or two detailing key aspects of each film. Important flicks like Kiss Me Deadly and Double Indemnity get a bit more space and consideration, and the authors, for the most part, avoid subjective reviews and concentrate on chasing down each film's address in the naked city of noir. . . . This new edition of the definitive text on film noir is a perfect companion for a foray into the dreamlike world of some of the most dark and mesmerizing movies ever made." PopMatters

International motion picture almanac; 79th ed; Quigley 1225p $195 **791.43**
1. Motion pictures
ISBN 978-0-900610-82-0; 0-900610-82-4

"Includes biographical sketches of movie personalities, lists of services, distributors, film corporations, companies, theaters, suppliers , organizations, markets, and government agencies, primarily in the United States. Lists of films of the previous decade and a review of the previous year in film: awards, polls, and festivals." Ref Sources for Small & Medium-sized Libr. 6th edition

Leonard Maltin's movie guide; edited by Leonard Maltin; managing editor, Darwyn Carson; associate editor, Luke Sader; contributing editors, Mike Clark ... [et al.]; video editor, Casey St. Charnez;

contributors, Jerry Beck, Jessie Maltin. 2011 ed;
Plume 2010 1643p pa $20 **791.43**
1. DVDs 2. Motion pictures 3. Reference books 4.
Videotapes
ISBN 978-0-452-29626-8

"Maltin offers 17,000 summary movie reviews. . . . Also
included are more than 25,000 combined DVD and video
listings. . . . Less commercially familiar works, like foreign
films, indies, and cult classics, are given equal billing. Rated
on a star system, including a category for 'bomb,' paragraph-long reviews contain actor listings and concise narrative synopses, along with incisive critical considerations.
A highly useful, quick reference for film studies and general
collections." Libr J

★ Magill's cinema annual; 2008 edition; Gale
Group 2008 604p $165 **791.43**
1. Motion pictures
ISBN 978-1-5586-2611-9; 1-5586-2611-5

"Each entry includes the movie's tagline (promotional
catch phrases), year-end domestic box office gross, a signed
review and comments on the film's reception, cast/produc-
tion credits, a bibliography of reviews from major newspapers and industry trade papers, memorable dialogue quotes,
a trivia section, and awards and nominations. Reviews average about two pages in length and strive to be both entertaining and analytical. In addition to numerous specialized
indexes (directors, screenwriters, editors, cinematographers,
performers, and subject), the annual also features an obituaries section and a selected list of film books." Am Ref Books
Annu, 2003

791.44   Radio

Dunning, John
★ **On** the air; the encyclopedia of old-time ra-
dio. Oxford Univ. Press 1998 822p $60 **791.44**
1. Radio programs 2. Radio programs -- United States
-- Dictionaries
ISBN 0-19-507678-8
LC 96-41959

Dunning has "compiled and organized a massive amount
of research data on hundreds of radio shows aired from the
1920s through the 1960s. The entries, listed alphabetically
by show title, each contain a treasure trove of information—broadcast dates, casts and personnel, anecdotes, special analyses, and a detailed overview of each show's background, format, and content." Libr J
Includes bibliographical references

Ely, Melvin Patrick
The **adventures** of Amos 'n' Andy; a social his-
tory of an American phenomenon. University Press
of Va. 2001 xxi, 322p il pa $18.50 **791.44**
1. African Americans in television broadcasting 2.
African Americans on television 3. Popular culture --
United States
ISBN 0-8139-2092-2
LC 2001-45538

A "historian examines one of America's greatest cultural
enigmas—the amazing popularity, among blacks as well as

whites, of 'Amos 'n' Andy' on radio for more than 30 years."
N Y Times Book Rev
Includes bibliographical references

Sies, Luther F.
★ **Encyclopedia** of American radio, 1920-1960;
2nd ed.; McFarland & Co. 2008 2v set $195 **791.44**
1. Radio broadcasting -- Encyclopedias 2. Radio
programs -- Encyclopedias 3. Reference books
ISBN 978-0-7864-2942-4; 0-7864-2942-9
LC 2007-36686

The author "attempts to identify as many broadcasters
and their programs as possible. Programs from the early
days of radio reflect the work mainly of individual performers and are entered that way in the encyclopedia. After 1929,
entries are primarily for programs, with individual entries
only for performers whose programs bear their names or for
newscasters, commentators, home economists, DJs, singers,
and vocal and instrumental groups. There are . . . entries on
special topics such as Black radio, Networks, Sports, and
Wartime radio." Booklist
Includes bibliographical references

791.45   Television

Becker, Christine
It's the pictures that got small; Hollywood film
stars on 1950s television. Wesleyan University Press
2008 293p il $70; pa $24.95 **791.45**
1. Actors 2. Television programs
ISBN 0819568937; 0819568945; 9780819568939;
9780819568946
LC 2008-29056

"Based on extensive archival research and amply documented, It's the Pictures That Got Small qualifies both as a
contribution to the scholarly literature and as a general-interest book which is fun to read and would not be out of place
in your beach bag. It includes an extensive bibliography and
endnotes and four appendices documenting the appearances
of established film stars on television programs." PopMatters

Bianculli, David
Dangerously funny; the uncensored story of The
Smothers Brothers Comedy Hour. Simon & Schuster
2009 382p il $24.99 **791.45**
1. Comedians 2. Television personalities 3. Vintners
ISBN 978-1-4391-0116-2; 1-4391-0116-7
LC 2009-36843

"By the time the Smothers got fired in 1969 (they bristle
at the notion that the show was cancelled), Comedy Hour
had become a benchmark for political expression and satire
in prime time. . . . Bianculli devotes the bulk of his work
to the period when Comedy Hour was conceived, produced
and ultimately removed from its Sunday-night slot, leaving
only a few chapters on Tom and Dick Smothers' career before and after the show. This feels right—the best stories are
the increasingly dramatic week-to-week battles between the
idealistic, strong-willed Tom Smothers and CBS censors and
brass." Paste
Includes bibliographical references

Brooks, Tim

★ The **complete** directory to prime time network and cable TV shows, 1946-present; [by] Tim Brooks and Earle Marsh. 9th ed, completely rev and updated; Ballantine Books 2007 xxi, 1832p il pa $29.95   **791.45**
    1. Television programs
    ISBN 978-0-345-49773-4; 0-345-49773-2
"Provides coverage of more than 5,000 nighttime series on commerical networks, with information on the type of show, broadcast history, cast, spin-offs, and plot or format. Index to actors and actresses. Appendixes list each season's prime time schedules, Emmy award winners, long-running and highly rated programs, and spin-offs. Coverage of original cable series began with the sixth edition." Ref Sources for Small & Medium-sized Libr. 6th edition

Davis, Michael

Street gang; the complete history of Sesame Street. Viking 2008 379p il $27.95   **791.45**
    ISBN 978-0-670-01996-0; 0-670-01996-8
                                         LC 2008-35498
This is a history of the children's television series that premiered on November 10, 1969.
"Any grown-up fan will relish this account, gaining an even greater appreciation for the cultural contributions of Kermit, Big Bird, Oscar the Grouch and all their neighbors." Publ Wkly
    Includes bibliographical references

Gervich, Chad

Small screen, big picture; a writer's guide to the TV business. foreword by Howard Gordon. Three Rivers Press 2008 430p pa $15.95   **791.45**
    1. Television authorship
    ISBN 978-0-307-39531-3; 0-307-39531-6
                                         LC 2008-03093
Gervich "concentrates on the mechanics of the industry. He takes a budding scriptwriter through the lengthy, often emotionally draining process of getting a script onto the air, pausing along the way to talk about such fundamental things as pilot season, the way a broadcast day is broken into key segments (called 'dayparts'), how the TV ratings work, the different requirements of specific genres, how to schedule a new series, the syndication process (generally speaking, a show doesn't turn a profit until it's sold into syndication), even the mechanics of filming a television show. . . . It would be difficult to imagine a more engaging, user-friendly, and educational book on the subject." Booklist

Giddins, Gary

Warning shadows; home alone with classic cinema. W. W. Norton & Company 2010 416p pa $18.95   **791.45**
    1. Motion pictures 2. Motion pictures -- History and criticism
    ISBN 978-0-393-33792-1 pa; 0-393-33792-8 pa
                                         LC 2009-49298
Giddins is as much of a fan as a critic, and since he's not a daily film reviewer, he hasn't been beaten down by constant exposure to insufferable movies. It's a mark of his enthusiasm that Warning Shadows makes me want to watch or re-watch nearly every movie he discusses. That includes Disney's insane-sounding 1945 musical The Three Caballeros featuring Donald Duck, Carmen Miranda's sister Aurora and Doa Luz as a disembodied head. The book begins with a new essay tracing, with regret, cinema's century-long migration from Radio City Music Hall to streaming laptops. The rest of the pieces cover directors, stars, genres and individual films. Giddins is especially good at assessing the totality of an artist's work. . . . [His] observations about actors' strengths and significance are consistently keen and often stingingly funny. Los Angeles Times

Harris, Bob

Prisoner of Trebekistan; a decade in Jeopardy! Crown Publishers 2006 339p $23.95   **791.45**
    1. Bloggers 2. Comedians 3. Humorists 4. Political commentators 5. Writers on politics
    ISBN 0-307-33956-4; 978-0-307-33956-0
                                         LC 2006-06267
"Harris' account is a personal story and manages to cram in enough fun facts to keep any trivia nut happy." Booklist
    Includes bibliographical references

Hewitt, Don

Tell me a story; 50 years and 60 minutes in television. PublicAffairs 2001 272p il $26; pa $15   **791.45**
    1. Television producers 2. Television producers and directors -- United States -- Biography
    ISBN 1-58648-017-0; 1-58648-141-X pa
                                         LC 2001-16222
"Hewitt has positive things to say about most of the reporters and anchors he discusses, but his comments about the several generations of CBS executives and owners for whom he has worked are less consistently sunny. At 78, Hewitt remains blunt, opinionated, and full of ideas about where TV news has been and where it's going. His life may be one of the more interesting stories the veteran newsman has ever told." Booklist

Kanfer, Stefan

Ball of fire; the tumultuous life and comic art of Lucille Ball. Knopf 2003 361p il $25.95; pa $15   **791.45**
    1. Actors
    ISBN 0-375-41315-4; 0-375-72771-X pa
                                         LC 2002-43090
This is a biography of the comedian and star of the television shows I Love Lucy, The Lucy Show, and Here's Lucy.
"A fine accumulation of research . . . balanced by Kanfer's insight into what Ball's contribution means in the context of entertainment history, this is the first study to examine all aspects of Ball's life, work, and business acumen." Libr J
    Includes bibliographical references

Larsen, Darl

Monty Python's flying circus; an utterly complete, thoroughly unillustrated, absolutely unauthorized guide to possibly all the references: from Arthur

Two-Sheds Jackson to Zambesi. Scarecrow Press
2008 563p $150   **791.45**
   ISBN 978-0-8108-6131-2; 0-8108-6131-3
                       LC 2007-52082

  "American readers will benefit from definitions of
uniquely British phenomena (e.g., anything associated with
cricket). Along with explication, the essays on occasion look
at the series within the cultural context of the late 1960s,
touching on such topics as its treatment of homosexuality
or women. Larsen . . . is a devoted fan who exhaustively
analyzes the series without ever obscuring its unique brand
of humor." Libr J
  Includes bibliographical references

Miller, James Andrew

  Those guys have all the fun; inside the world
of ESPN. [by] James Andrew Miller and Tom
Shales. Little, Brown and Company 2011 763p il
$27.99   **791.45**
   1. Television broadcasting of sports
   ISBN 978-0-316-04300-7; 0-316-04300-1

  "Compiled from more than 550 interviews, Those Guys
traces ESPN from its birth as an underdog to its current status as a money-printing behemoth. Some of the best sections
deal with the early days of cable, when the network invented
itself through savvy business decisions and slow-pitch-
softball coverage. But it's the big libidos and bigger egos
that will get the most attention. The book is packed with entertaining stories of unpleasant people and awful behavior:
booze-fueled boorishness, absurdly arrogant execs, and the
endlessly fascinating Olbermann. . . . Miller and Shales offer compelling behind-the-scenes tales of many major sports
moments, including the Rush Limbaugh–Donovan McNabb
flap and ESPN's takeover of Monday Night Football."
Entertainment Wkly

Morris, Bruce B.

  Prime time network serials; episode guides,
casts, and credits for 37 continuing television dramas,
1964-1993. with a foreword by Michele Lee. McFarland & Co. 1997 841p il $95   **791.45**
   1. Soap operas 2. Television programs
   ISBN 0-7864-0164-8
                       LC 96-31166

  This volume provides information of thirty-seven serials that aired on the major networks from the 1964 season
through 1992-93.
  This "work belongs in any library collection that serves
a devoted television viewing public." Booklist

Richards, Thomas

  The **meaning** of Star Trek. Doubleday 1997
194p hardcover o.p. pa $15   **791.45**
   ISBN 0-385-48439-9 pa
                       LC 97-6845

  "One of the best recent Star Trek books and also one of
the most cogent, exciting recent literary analyses." Booklist

Terrace, Vincent

  Television sitcom factbook; over 8700 details
from 130 shows, 1985-2000. McFarland & Co. 2000
164p pa $25   **791.45**
   1. Television programs
   ISBN 0-7864-0900-2
                       LC 00-57865

  This volume includes "over 8,700 facts concerning 130
television sitcoms broadcast from 1985 to those still current
in 2000 by ABC, CBS, NBC, Fox, UPN, WB and in syndication." Publisher's note

791.5   Puppetry and toy theaters

Blumenthal, Eileen

  ★ **Puppetry**; a world history. Abrams 2005 272p il
$65 **791.5**
   1. Puppets and puppet plays
   ISBN 0-8109-5587-3
                      LC 2004-29349

  This is a "history of the puppet world, from prehistoric
times to Tony-winning Broadway hit Avenue Q. . . . This
would be a welcome addition to the libraries of performing arts buffs who want to learn more about a lesser known
form." Publ Wkly
  Includes bibliographical references

791.8   Animal performances

Hemingway, Ernest

  ★ **Death** in the afternoon. Scribner 1999 397p
il $35   **791.8**
   1. Bullfights
   ISBN 0-684-85922-X
                       LC 99-231717

  "A loosely organized book on bullfighting in Spain. . . .
Hemingway depicts the bullfight as an emblematic tragedy,
a test of courage, with a bloody and not entirely predictable
end. Throughout, he digresses to philosophize on life and
death in exchanges with a character he calls the Old Lady."
HarperCollins Reader's Ency of Am Lit. 2nd edition

  The **dangerous** summer; introduction by James
A. Michener. Scribner 1985 228p il hardcover o.p.
pa $13   **791.8**
   1. Bullfights 2. Spain -- Description
   ISBN 0-684-83789-7 pa
                       LC 84-27578

  A look at the "personal and professional rivalry of the
two greatest bullfighters since the death of Manolete in
1947: Luis Miguel Dominguín and Antonio Ordóñez. The
Dangerous Summer provides an insider's view based on extensive experience, mingles memory and desire, and is essential reading for anyone interested in the subject or the
author." Natl Rev

Lewine, Edward

Death and the sun; a matador's season in the heart of Spain. Houghton Mifflin 2005 258p map $24 **791.8**

1. Bullfighters 2. Bullfights 3. Bullfights -- Spain
ISBN 0-618-26325-X

LC 2005-40424

This is an account of a year spent observing the Spanish matador Francisco Rivera Ordonez.

"What Lewine has created may be the most in-depth, incisively written literary guide to bullfighting available in English. Every drunken sophomore riding the rails to Pamplona this summer ought to keep a volume in his backpack." N Y Times Book Rev

Includes bibliographical references

Peter, Josh

Fried twinkies, buckle bunnies & bull riders; a year inside the professional bull riders tour. Rodale 2005 246p il $24.95 **791.8**

1. Bull riding
ISBN 1-59486-119-6

LC 2005-17297

"The argument can be made that the Professional Bull Riders Tour may be the most dangerous, least financially rewarding of all sporting endeavors. Skull fractures, punctured lungs, and destroyed knees are all relatively routine injuries. At least now there is a million-dollar payout for the overall champion each season, but even that is in deferred dollars. Peter, a sportswriter for the New Orleans Times-Picayune, spent the 2004 season with the PBR tour and offers a penetrating portrait of a sport that stands at that awkward stage between minor league and national acceptance. . . . Fried Twinkies are a genuine but rare concession delicacy, and buckle bunnies are the young ladies who curry the favor of the young macho men who ride the bulls. This is a tough book to walk away from." Booklist

792 Stage presentations

Adler, Stella

★ **Stella** Adler: the art of acting; compiled and edited by Howard Kissel. Applause Theatre Bk. Pubs. 2000 271p il $25.95 **792**

1. Acting
ISBN 1-55783-373-7

In this collection of Adler's papers Kissel "has taken tapes, transcriptions, notebooks, and other sources to reconstruct an acting course in 22 lessons. . . . The lessons are graduated from very basic matters to quite complex issues of textual analysis and decorum. Though mostly monologs, they include enough exercises and student responses to get the flavor of Adler's work. . . . This is required reading for anyone interested in theater practice." Libr J

Bernhardt, Sarah

My double life: the memoirs of Sarah Bernhardt; translated by Victoria Tietze Larson. State Univ. of N.Y. Press 1999 345p $26.50; pa $25.95 **792**

1. Actors 2. Actors -- France -- Biography
ISBN 0-7914-4053-2; 0-7914-4054-0 pa

LC 98-30036

"The most tempestuous and possibly the most famous actress of her time, Bernhardt . . . is presented as both melodramatic and frustratingly discreet." Publ Wkly

Includes bibliographical references

Bordman, Gerald Martin

★ The **Oxford** companion to American theatre; [by] Gerald Bordman, Thomas S. Hischak. 3rd ed; Oxford University Press 2004 681p $75 **792**

1. American drama -- Dictionaries 2. Reference books 3. Theater -- United States -- Biography -- Dictionaries 4. Theater -- United States -- Dictionaries
ISBN 0-19-516986-7

LC 2003-21367

"Individual entries are packed with detail. . . . Hischak provides ample material for researchers, and should be a mainstay of any performing arts reference collection." Choice

Brestoff, Richard

The **actor's** wheel of connection; how to integrate your skills and refine your performance. Smith and Kraus 2005 160p $16.95 **792**

1. Acting
ISBN 1-57525-391-7

LC 2005-44120

"Brestoff draws on the teachings of the great acting teachers–such as Strasberg, Adler, Meisner, Grotowski, and Stanislavsky–in shaping and explaining his methods. Although probably not appropriate for beginners, his wheel will appeal to actors grappling with disparate techniques." BackStage

Briggs, Jody

★ **Encyclopedia** of stage lighting; foreword by Scott Nolte. McFarland & Co. 2003 334p il $95; pa $49.95 **792**

1. Reference books 2. Stage lighting 3. Stage lighting -- Encyclopedias
ISBN 0-7864-1512-6; 0-7864-4043-0 pa

LC 2003-7619

"Peppered with some 300 simple line drawings and diagrams to illustrate basic concepts, this work emphasizes the principles and practices of the founding fathers of theatrical lighting, among whom are Stanley McCandless, Ariel Davis, Adolphe Appia, and Gordan Craig. . . . This book often goes beyond most encyclopedias, addressing standard lighting procedures and practices, briefly outlining the historical development of theatrical lighting, and providing strategies for dealing with theater directors and other theatrical personalities." Choice

Includes bibliographical references

Brook, Peter

The **empty** space. Atheneum 1968 141p hardcover o.p. pa $11   **792**

1. Drama 2. Theater

ISBN 0-684-82957-6 pa

LC 68-12531

The author "distinguishes four types of theater: the Deadly Theatre (conventional), the Holy Theatre (ritualistic), the Rough Theatre (combative), and the Immediate Theatre (mutative and organic). An impassioned treatise that is also very accessible and direct." Libr J

Chekhov, Michael

To the actor; {rev and expanded ed. by Mala Powers}; Routledge 2002 lii, 222p il $75; pa $19.95   **792**

1. Acting

ISBN 0-415-25875-8; 0-415-25876-6 pa

"Chekhov is among a handful of master acting teachers who have profoundly influenced not only a constellation of famous stars but also shaped an acting style and sensibility. . . . This new edition contains all of Chekhov's brilliant insights, techniques, and exercises, as well as a previously unpublished chapter on the 'Psychological Gesture,' a central precept of his system." Libr J

Includes bibliographical references

Clinton, Catherine

Fanny Kemble's civil wars. Oxford Univ. Press 2001 302p il pa $24   **792**

1. Abolitionists 2. Actors 3. Actors -- Great Britain -- Biography 4. Memoirists 5. Novelists 6. Plantation owners' spouses -- Georgia -- Biography 7. Poets

ISBN 0-19-514815-0

LC 2001-21405

"This biography is every bit as sharp, evocative and eloquent as Kemble's Journal." Publ Wkly

Includes bibliographical references

Corson, Richard

Stage makeup; [by] Richard Corson, Beverly Gore Norcross, James Glavan. 10th ed.; Ally & Bacon/Pearson 2009 xx, 407p il $141.40   **792**

1. Theatrical makeup

ISBN 978-0-205-64454-4

LC 2008-53845

The authors discuss the art and technique of theatrical makeup, covering such topics as facial anatomy, various methods for applying greasepaint and other makeup, and the use of beards, wigs, and prosthetic pieces.

Croall, Jonathan

Gielgud; a theatrical life, 1904-2000. Continuum 2001 579p il $35; pa $24.95 **792**

1. Actors 2. Actors -- Great Britain -- Biography 3. Theatrical directors 4. Theatrical producers

ISBN 0-8264-1333-1; 0-8264-1403-6 pa

LC 2001-28019

Croall examines the life and career of the British actor, director, and producer.

"Witty and well-written as well as well-researched, Croall's fine and complete portrait of the man and his endearing charm often reads more like a novel than like nonfiction." Booklist

Includes bibliographical references and index

Gillette, J. Michael

Designing with light; an introduction to stage lighting. 4th ed; McGraw-Hill 2003 various paging il pa $55.45   **792**

1. Stage lighting

ISBN 0-7674-2733-5

LC 2002-19777

The author "divides his standard text for undergraduate lighting design students into the two constituent elements of his craft—technology and design. He clearly and completely presents both technical and aesthetic design aspects." Libr J

Theatrical design and production; an introduction to scene design and construction, lighting, sound, costume, and makeup. 6th ed; McGraw-Hill Higher Education 2008 613p il $78.20   **792**

1. Theaters -- Stage setting and scenery

ISBN 978-0-07-351419-2; 0-07-351419-5

LC 2007-35218

This is a "survey of the technical and design aspects of play production, including scene design and construction, lighting, sound, costume, and makeup. Health and safety precautions for the backstage crew appear throughout in boxes labeled 'Safety Tips,' and 'Design Inspiration' boxes show how professional designers create the desired look." Publisher's note

Includes bibliographical references

Hagen, Uta

Respect for acting; by Uta Hagen with Haskel Frankel. Macmillan 1973 227p $19.95   **792**

1. Acting

ISBN 0-02-547390-5

This "classic treatise on the process and craft of acting has significantly benefited actors for three decades. Juxtaposed with Hagen's aesthetic is a wealth of practical information, creative ideas, and her uniquely useful object exercises." Libr J

Hodge, Francis

Play directing; analysis, communication, and style. [by] Francis Hodge, Michael McLain. 6th ed; Pearson/Allyn & Bacon 2005 400p il $116.40 **792**

1. Theater -- Production and direction

ISBN 0-205-41923-2

LC 2004-57261

This presents a "methodology for textual analysis, communicative relationships with actors, and understanding and cultivating a sense of interpretive style. All production areas are considered and illustrated with diagrams and photographs. Numerous exercises assist in the explanation of each area." Libr J

Includes bibliographical references

Lewis, Roger

The **real** life of Laurence Olivier. Applause Theatre Bk. Pubs. 1997 272p il $25.95; pa $18.95 **792**
1. Actors 2. Biography, Individual
ISBN 1-55783-298-6; 1-55783-413-X pa

LC 97-31702

This is a life of the English stage and screen actor

"Lewis enjoys exploring the details that make up such a rich life—Olivier seemed to have met everyone, known everyone, and played every major role in existence. The indexing and photographs are quite good." Libr J

Lipton, James

Inside Inside. Dutton 2007 492p il $27.95 **792**
ISBN 978-0-525-95035-6; 0-525-95035-4

LC 2007-12790

This book from the host of the television program Inside The Actors Studio interweaves anecdotal stories from the author's own life with excerpts from interviews with actors given on that program.

"The anecdotes from the fine actors who have appeared on Inside the Actors Studio and the manifold insights into the craftsmanship of acting together justify the purchase of this exemplary book. An unqualified hit among this season's theatrical offerings and a necessary purchase for all performing arts collections." Libr J

Mamet, David

True and false; heresy and common sense for the actor. Pantheon Bks. 1997 127p hardcover o.p. pa $11 **792**
1. Acting
ISBN 0-679-77264-2 pa

LC 97-19336

"Mamet exhorts actors to show up early, have their lines down cold, and have a single objective for each scene. He contends that overthinking and too much emotional interpretation is not the actor's role. Essential reading for theater collections." Libr J

Marasco, Ron

Notes to an actor. Ivan R. Dee 2007 214p $24.95 **792**
1. Acting
ISBN 978-1-56663-757-2; 1-56663-757-0

LC 2007-11653

This is "a compendium of suggestions, inspirations, warnings, and musings about the art of acting. Marasco speaks to actors who already possess at least a basic knowledge of their craft, seeking to heighten their abilities, clarify their artistic choices, eliminate blocks, and make their work more exciting and enriching. . . . This book is truly unique among acting resources. Useful both to those seeking to further their development as actors and to those for whom acting has long been a profession, this is an insightful, invaluable, and definitive work." Choice

Includes bibliographical references

Moore, Sonia

★ The **Stanislavski** system; the professional training of an actor. digested from the teachings of Konstantin S. Stanislavski. 2nd rev ed; Penguin Bks. 1984 96p pa $12.95 **792**
1. Acting 2. Actors 3. Theatrical directors
ISBN 0-14-046660-6

LC 84-2855

This is a concise, simplified guide to the teachings of the great master of the Moscow Art Theater.

Ripken, Cal

The **only** way I know; [by] Cal Ripken, Jr., and Mike Bryan. Viking 1997 326p il hardcover o.p. pa $12.95 **792**
1. Actors 2. Baseball -- Biography 3. Baseball players 4. Biography, Individual
ISBN 0-670-87193-1; 0-14-026626-7 pa

LC 97-9159

"Cal Junior chronicles his moves through the minor leagues and into the majors in great detail, always pointing out what he learned at each step of the journey and who taught it to him. There are some great baseball anecdotes—especially involving fiery Oriole skipper Earl Weaver—and plenty of the behind-the-scenes detail." Booklist

Stanislavsky, Konstantin

Creating a role; [by] Constantin Stanislavski; translated by Elizabeth Reynolds Hapgood; edited by Hermine I. Popper; foreword by Robert Lewis. Routledge 2003 271p pa $19.95 **792**
1. Acting
ISBN 0-87830-981-0

LC 91-228412

"Stanislavski unifies his conceptual canon and applies it to detailed preparatory work for the roles of Othello and Gogol's Inspector General." Libr J

★ An **actor's** work; a student's diary. [by] Konstantin Stanislavski; translated and edited by Jean Benedetti. Routledge 2008 693p $35 **792**
1. Acting 2. Acting -- Psychological aspects 3. Acting -- Study and teaching 4. Acting -- Technique
ISBN 9780415422239; 0-415-42223-X

LC 2007-45357

A combined translation of Stanislavsky's An actor prepares and Building a character, which describe and illustrate the principles of method acting.

This "translation by Benedetti of Stanislavski's famous works . . . will be greeted with excitement by actors everywhere." Libr J

Includes bibliographical references

Thomas, Mike

The **Second** City unscripted; revolution and revelation at the world-famous comedy theater. Villard 2009 272p il $26 **792**
1. Comedians 2. Comedy 3. Comedy -- History and criticism 4. Theater -- Illinois -- Chicago
ISBN 978-0-345-51422-6; 0-345-51422-X

LC 2009-33132

"For 50 years, Chicago's Second City Theater has been the training ground for legendary comedians. From John Belushi to Stephen Colbert, many of America and Canada's finest comic talents have honed their skills on Second City's stage, and this collection of interviews brings together comedians and behind-the-scenes players to bare the secrets of the comedy laboratory where improv was birthed by lesser-known genius Del Close. . . . Though occasionally meandering, Thomas corrals his subjects' testimony in a historical framework paralleling the larger baby boomer narrative, progressing from fringe revolutionaries to institutional stalwarts." Publ Wkly

bibliography: p. 259-264

Tynan, Kenneth

The **diaries** of Kenneth Tynan; edited by John Lahr. Bloomsbury Press 2001 439p il $32.95; pa $16.95   **792**
1. Authors, English -- 20th century -- Diaries 2. Drama critics 3. Theater critics -- Great Britain -- Diaries
ISBN 1-58234-160-5; 1-58234-245-8 pa
LC 2001-35274

Tynan "was one of Britain's foremost drama critics; here, he spent two seasons as theater critic for the New Yorker. Along with Laurence Olivier, he helped found London's National Theater, where he functioned as literary manager for 10 years. Not surprisingly, Tynan dissects theatrical foibles and politicking with a keen inside perspective; he can also discourse on the European common market, Spaniards' attitudes toward homosexuality, cricket, French cuisine, Ethel Merman and much more. . . . Celebrated names are not merely dropped (from Katharine Hepburn and Princess Margaret to W.H. Auden and Jerry Lewis), but integral to his revelatory anecdotes." Publ Wkly

The Cambridge guide to theatre; {edited by} Martin Banham; editorial advisory board, James Brandon {et al.} new ed; Cambridge Univ. Press 1995 1233p il $50   **792**
1. Reference books 2. Theater -- Dictionaries
ISBN 0-521-43437-8
LC 95-1011

"A broad-ranging source of information on individuals, organizations, theatrical forms and movements, individual countries, and a variety of specific topics. Articles are signed; some longer articles have bibliographies. Covers popular theater and entertainments, as well as the legitimate stage. Because of global perspective, especially useful for country surveys of cultures outside the U.S. and Western Europe and entries for forms and individuals associated with those cultures." Guide to Ref Books. 11th edition {1988 edition}

Includes bibliographical references

★ The Oxford companion to theatre and performance; edited by Dennis Kennedy. Oxford University Press 2010 689p $45   **792**
1. Performing arts -- Encyclopedias 2. Reference books 3. Theater -- Encyclopedias
ISBN 978-0-19-957419-3

"This is a one-volume updated version of the two-volume Oxford Encyclopedia of Theatre & Performance published in 2003. Kennedy . . . has succeeded in pulling together 2400 entries intended to educate, delight, and encourage the reader to pursue more in-depth information." Libr J

792.09   History, geographic treatment, biography

Brockett, Oscar G.

History of the theatre; [by] Oscar G. Brockett, Franklin J. Hildy. 10th ed; Pearson 2008 688p il map $113   **792.09**
1. Drama -- History and criticism 2. Theater -- History
ISBN 978-0-205-51186-0
LC 2009-291794

This work traces the development of the theater from primitive times to the present, with an emphasis on European theater.

Sova, Dawn B.

★ **Banned** plays; censorship histories of 125 stage dramas. Facts on File 2003 400p $55; pa $16.95   **792.09**
1. Censorship 2. Drama -- Censorship -- History 3. Drama -- History and criticism 4. Theater -- Censorship -- History
ISBN 0-8160-4018-4; 0-8160-5070-8 pa
LC 2003-63113

The author "has chosen a fine, representative selection of suppressed plays throughout the centuries. . . . This meticulously researched title offers valuable information for both scholars and casual readers." SLJ

Includes bibliographical references

The Oxford illustrated history of theatre; edited by John Russell Brown. Oxford Univ. Press 1995 582p il hardcover o.p. pa $27.50   **792.09**
1. Theater 2. Theater -- History
ISBN 0-19-285442-9
LC 95-231683

Covering theatre history from the ancient Greeks to the 1990s, this "resource provides a wide variety of information from basic theatre chronology to detailed analyses of several well-known and important plays and playwrights. . . . The emphasis is on European and Western theatre, but a chapter provides a concise summary on Southern and Eastern Asian theatre." SLJ

Includes bibliographical references

792.5   Opera

Grout, Donald Jay

★ A **short** history of opera; {by} Donald Jay Grout and Hermine Weigel Williams. 4th ed; Columbia University Press 2003 1030p $65   **792.5**
1. Opera
ISBN 0-231-11958-5
LC 2002-41470

"After surveying anticipations of the operatic form in the lyric theater of the Greeks, medieval dramatic music, and other forerunners, the book reveals the genre's beginnings in the seventeenth century and follows its progress to the present day. . . . The section on twentieth-century opera {is organized} around national operatic traditions, including a chapter devoted solely to opera in the United States that incorporates material on the American musical and ties between classical opera and popular musical theater. A separate section on Chinese opera is also included." Publisher's note

Includes bibliographical references

Osborne, Charles

The **complete** operas of Mozart; a critical guide. Da Capo Press 1986 349p il pa $17.95   **792.5**

1. Composers 2. Opera -- Stories, plots, etc.
ISBN 978-0-306-80190-7; 0-306-80190-6

In this introduction to Mozart's operas, "each opera is treated as a separate chapter. . . . Each chapter begins with a separate page containing the dramatis personae and their voice range . . . the date, place, and cast for the first performance . . . the name of the librettist, and the Kochel number." Choice

The **complete** operas of Puccini; a critical guide. Da Capo Press 1983 279p il pa $9.95   **792.5**

1. Composers 2. Opera -- Stories, plots, etc.
ISBN 0-306-80200-7; 978-0-306-80200-3

LC 83-10142

The author "provides general background information on all 13 Puccini operas. . . . Unencumbered by technical language, this enjoyably written book is accessible to all admirers of one of the most popular opera composers of all time." Choice

Includes bibliographical references

The **complete** operas of Richard Wagner. Da Capo Press 1993 288p il pa $16.95   **792.5**

1. Composers 2. Opera -- Stories, plots, etc.
ISBN 0-306-80522-7; 978-0-306-80522-6

LC 92-34417

In this book, "biography—often in Wagner's own words—combined with criticism by Wagner's contemporaries, literary background, Wagner's librettos, plot summaries, descriptions of musical elements illustrated with musical examples, and Osborne's own insights form a clear picture of Wagner, his world, and the operas." Libr J

Includes bibliographical references

792.6   Musical plays

Bloom, Ken

Broadway musicals; the 101 greatest shows of all time. [by] Ken Bloom & Frank Vlastnik; new preface by Broadway's leading ladies; foreword by Jerry Orbach. Rev. and updated ed.; Black Dog & Leventhal 2010 344p il $40   **792.6**

1. Musicals
ISBN 978-1-57912-849-4

This is a history of Broadway musicals from the past 100 years. Each entry features commentary, photos and brief features on performers and creators.

Boland, Robert

Musicals! directing school and community theatre. {by} Robert Boland and Paul Argentini. Scarecrow Press

1997 xxv, 202p il pa $35 **792.6**

1. Musicals -- Production and direction
ISBN 0-8108-3323-9

LC 97-11996

This is "a handbook for novice directors of the musical. This illustrated nuts-and-bolts compendium includes 22 chapters divided among three major sections addressing preparation, production, and performance. Through accessible prose and a you-can-do-it tone, the authors provide an overview of preproduction planning, auditioning and casting, blocking, stage composition, rehearsals, and choreography, as well as the more technical layers of set design, costumes, and lights." Libr J

Includes bibliographical references

Hischak, Thomas

The **Oxford** companion to the American musical; theatre, film, and television. [by] Thomas S. Hischak. Oxford University Press 2008 923p il $39.95 **792.6**

1. Choreographers 2. Composers 3. Lyricists 4. Musicals -- Dictionaries 5. Musicals -- History and criticism 6. Musicals -- United States 7. Reference books 8. Singers
ISBN 9780195335330

LC 2007-52436

This is an "overview of the American musical theater on the stage, silver screen, and small screen. The 2000-plus entries are brief but detailed accounts of plots; production histories; careers of actors, dancers, musicians, lyricists, composers, choreographers, and directors; organizations; and genres (animated musicals, frontier musicals). . . . This thorough work provides enjoyable reading for anyone interested in American theatrical history in general and musicals in particular." SLJ

Includes discography and bibliographical references (p. 899-902)

Kantor, Michael

★ **Broadway**: the American musical; [by] Michael Kantor; Laurence Maslon. Bulfinch Press 2004 480p il $60   **792.6**

1. Musicals
ISBN 0-8212-2905-2

LC 2003-69715

This companion volume to a PBS documentary includes interviews and photographs of Broadway musicals from 1893 to 2004.

"With its beguiling blend of entertainment and history, this splendid work is a must-have." Publ Wkly

Includes bibliographical references

Norton, Richard C.

★ A **Chronology** of American musical theater. Oxford Univ. Press 2002 3v set $466.50   **792.6**

1. Musicals -- Chronology
ISBN 0-19-508888-3

LC 2001-55710

"The gorgeous illustrations in this season-by-season chronology of every musical comedy, operetta, comic opera, burlesque, and revue performed on a major New York City stage from 1851 through May 2001 might be enticement enough to acquire this set. Entries for more than 3,000 plays include details such as the full cast, crew, production staff, venues, number of performances, creative personnel, and songs, which are listed as they occur within acts when this information is known. Three indexes cover song titles, show names, and names of principal players and famous chorus menbers. Leaving appraisal and plot summaries to other classic references, these volumes are the most in-depth documentary source on the New York musical stage available, with a chapter that carries the timeline for selected plays back to 1750." Am Libr

Includes bibliographical references

Stempel, Larry

Showtime; a history of the Broadway musical theater. W. W. Norton & Company 2010 xx, 826p il $39.95 **792.6**
1. Broadway (New York, N.Y.) 2. Musicals 3. Musicals -- New York (N.Y.)
ISBN 978-0-393-06715-6; 0-393-06715-7
LC 2010-19704

Beginning in the seventeenth-century United States, well before Broadway existed, Stempel presents the multiple theatrical adventures that would lead from various directions to 'West Side Story' (1957) and 'Les Misérables' (1987). He examines not only minstrelsy, vaudeville, and European operetta—the musical's well-known precursors—but also the Astor Place riot of 1849, an event that publicly performed the ever-hardening divisions of class and culture among American audiences. Later, Stempel describes off-Broadway performances . . . beginning with the Works Progress Administration and the Little Theatre movement, progressing to 'Hair' (1968), which eventually transferred to Broadway, and nodding to regional theaters where many shows originated." (Journal of American History)

"Theater buffs will be delighted to find that this scholarly, definitive work is also a hugely entertaining read." Publ Wkly

Includes discography and bibliographical references

792.7 Variety shows and theatrical dancing

Downer, Lesley

Women of the pleasure quarters; the secret history of the geisha. Broadway Bks. 2001 288p il hardcover o.p. pa $14.95 **792.7**
1. Geishas
ISBN 0-7679-0490-7 pa
LC 00-49409

The author "skillfully intertwines her profiles of Kyoto personalities and tea-house customs with a fluidly written geisha history that's unabashedly aimed at a Western audience. . . . Written in dynamic, highly readable prose, the book is supported by exhaustive research and a lengthy bibliography." Publ Wkly

Includes bibliographical references and index

Josephson, Barney

Cafe society; the wrong place for the right people. Barney Josephson; with Terry Trilling-Joseph-

son; foreword by Dan Morgenstern. University of Illinois Press 2009 376p il $32.95 **792.7**
1. Restaurateurs
ISBN 978-0-252-03413-8; 0-252-03413-9
LC 2008-27205

"An epic ode to personal integrity, creative vision and entrepreneurial tenacity, shedding timely light on the germination of the civil-rights movement." Kirkus

Includes bibliographical references

Nachman, Gerald

★ Seriously funny; the rebel comedians of the 1950s and 1960s. Pantheon Bks. 2003 659p il $29.95 **792.7**
1. Comedians 2. Comedians -- United States -- Biography 3. Stand-up comedy -- United States -- History -- 20th century 4. Wit and humor
ISBN 0-375-41030-9
LC 2002-30713

Nachman examines American comedians, including "Mort Sahl, Sid Caesar, Tom Lehrer, Steve Allen, Stan Freberg, Ernie Kovacs, Phyllis Diller, Jonathan Winters, Shelley Berman, Nichols and May, Bob & Ray, Bob Newhart, Lenny Bruce, the Smothers Brothers, Mel Brooks, Dick Gregory, Woody Allen, Bill Cosby, [and] Joan Rivers. . . . 'Taken together, [Nachman writes], they made up the faculty of a new school of vigorous, socially aware satire, a dazzling group of voices that reigned roughly from 1953 to 1965.'" N Y Times Book Rev

Includes bibliographical references

Robinson, Ray

American original: a life of Will Rogers. Oxford Univ. Press 1996 288p il $34 **792.7**
1. Actors 2. Columnists 3. Entertainers 4. Humorists
ISBN 0-19-508693-7
LC 95-31578

In this biography of the American humorist, Robinson attempts "to separate fact from legend and build up a composite portrait of the man. As such, the book is so complete and thorough that until, if ever, new material comes to light, it can scarcely be superseded. Robinson's admiration for Rogers is evident on every page, but that does not blind him to Rogers's faults." Libr J

Trav S. D.

No applause, just throw money; or, The book that made vaudeville famous; a high-class, refined entertainment. Faber and Faber 2005 328p il $25 **792.7**
1. Vaudeville 2. Vaudeville -- United States
ISBN 0-571-21192-5
LC 20050-9787

This book documents the history and legacy of vaudeville in the United States.

"One of the year's best historical performing arts texts; a wonderful story wonderfully told." Libr J

Includes bibliographical references

Vollmann, William T.

Kissing the mask; beauty, understatement, and femininity in Japanese Noh theater: with some thoughts on muses (especially Helga Testorf), trans-

gender women, kabuki goddesses, porn queens, poets, housewives, makeup arti. Ecco 2010 504p il $29.99 **792.7**
1. Feminine beauty (Aesthetics) 2. Femininity 3. Geishas 4. Kabuki 5. No 6. No plays 7. Sex role 8. Transgender people 9. Transgendered people 10. Women -- Psychology 11. Women in the theater -- Japan
ISBN 978-0-06-122848-3; 0-06-122848-6

"Characteristically peripatetic, 'Kissing the Mask' rambles across vast territory in an effort to corral — or at least contemplate — the concept of feminine beauty. Throughout, Vollmann focuses an obsessed and adoring lens on the Noh master Umewaka Rokuro, the Kabuki geishas, and a transgender community in Los Angeles while simultaneously traipsing through Indian, American, European and Norse cultures in an effort to identify what it is (presumption? physiology? carriage?) that makes a woman a woman. Along the way, he pays homage yet again to his pet subject — prostitutes — about whom he has notoriously raved and written throughout his career. Courting controversy, flouting convention, 'Kissing the Mask' is classic Vollmann, right down to the dilettante manner in which he inserts himself directly into his subject." Portland Oregonian

Includes bibliographical references

Yagoda, Ben

Will Rogers; a biography. Knopf 1993 409p il pa $24.95 **792.7**
1. Actors 2. Air pilots 3. Biography, Individual 4. Columnists 5. Entertainers 6. Humorists 7. Theatrical producers
ISBN 0-8061-3238-8

LC 92-40177

This is a biography of "the rope-twirling vaudeville monologist, salty political commentator, silent film actor and New York Times columnist. . . . [This is] a resonant portrait imbued with Rogers's irreverent spirit, yet attuned to both the strengths and limitations of his commonsense, crackerbarrel world view." Publ Wkly

Includes bibliographical references

792.8 Ballet and modern dance

Craine, Debra

★ The **Oxford** dictionary of dance; [by] Debra Craine, Judith Mackrell. 2nd ed.; Oxford University Press 2010 502p il pa $18.95 **792.8**
1. Ballet 2. Dance 3. Dance -- Dictionaries 4. Reference books
ISBN 978-0-19-956344-9; 0-19-956344-6

LC 2010-930321

"The work covers all aspects of the diverse dance world from classical ballet to modern, from flamenco to hip-hop, from tap to South Asian dance forms and includes . . . entries on technical terms, steps, styles, works and countries, in addition to many biographies of dancers, choreographers, and companies." Publisher's note

Includes bibliographical references

Goldner, Nancy

Balanchine variations. University Press of Florida 2008 132p il pa $24.95 **792.8**
1. Ballet 2. Ballet -- History 3. Choreographers 4. Choreography 5. Dancers
ISBN 978-0-8130-3226-9; 0-8130-3226-1

LC 2007-38092

The author discusses twenty-two ballets choreographed by George Balanchine.

"Now at last we can say, 'If you like Balanchine, you must read Nancy Goldner's [book].' Slim enough to fit into a jacket pocket, . . . it's good-humored, enthusiastic and undictatorial; it gives you numerous things to look out for in any performance; and it abounds with insights. . . . 'Balanchine Variations' is in every sense a vade-mecum ('Go with me'): a pocket-size reference book that is also a companion, a guide, a friend." N Y Times (Late N Y Ed)

Includes bibliographical references

Homans, Jennifer

★ **Apollo's** angels. Random House 2010 643p il $35 **792.8**
1. Ballet 2. Ballet -- History 3. Nonfiction 4. Noverre, Jean-Georges 5. Taglioni, Marie, 1804-1884
ISBN 978-1-4000-6060-3; 1-4000-6060-5

LC 201006945

This book places ballet . . . in the larger context of the times and societies in which it evolved, flourished and flagged, only be revitalized by an infusion of fresh ideas. That revitalization could come from a ballet master like Jean-Georges Noverre, presented by Homans as an important Enlightenment figure whose ideas on reforming ballet were consonant with those of Diderot on reforming theater. Renewal came from the genius of dancers like Marie Taglioni, the incarnation of romanticism . . . But in a closing section . . . [the author] sounds a despairing note: "ballet is dying," she declares. Not only is the creative well running dry and performances dull, but more crucially, Homans sees today's values as inimical to those of ballet.p (Publishers Weekly)

"A book of this breadth is going to have its own biorhythms—chapters that engage the author's mind and heart wholly, where everything clicks and the thinking is virtually kinetic, and chapters that don't come as easily. Ms. Homans is at her best when the ideological agenda at hand aspires to discipline, precision and refinement. Her French section is masterful, as are the chapters on the rise of the ballerina, the Danish style, Imperial Russian classicism, and British ballet." Wall Street J

Includes bibliographical references

Kurth, Peter

Isadora; a sensational life. Little, Brown 2001 652p il $29.95; pa $17.95 **792.8**
1. Dancers 2. Dancers -- United States -- Biography
ISBN 0-316-50726-1; 0-316-05713-4 pa

LC 2001-38064

Kurth "diligently tracks Duncan's every triumph and tragedy . . . and sets her entire complex milieu in motion." Booklist

Includes bibliographical references

Reynolds, Nancy

No fixed points; dance in the twentieth century. [by] Nancy Reynolds and Malcolm McCormick. Yale Univ. Press 2003 907p il $50   **792.8**

  1. Ballet 2. Ballet -- History -- 20th century 3. Dance 4. Dance -- History -- 20th century 5. Modern dance

  ISBN 0-300-09366-7

                   LC 2003-10754

"Although everyone will be using the book for reference, Reynolds and McCormick have produced a work that is completely unlike a standard reference book; you don't just look things up in it—you read it. Here is a coherent, reasoned and entertaining chronicle of dance performance in the West over the hundred years that are unquestionably the fullest and most complicated in the long history of this fragmented and elusive art." N Y Times

  Includes bibliographical references

Volynskii, A. L.

Ballet's magic kingdom; selected writings on dance in Russia, 1911-1925. [by] Akim Volynsky; translated and with an introduction and notes by Stanley J. Rabinowitz. Yale University Press 2008 288p il $35   **792.8**

  1. Ballet 2. Ballet -- Russia (Federation) 3. Ballet dancers

  ISBN 978-0-300-12462-0; 0-300-12462-7

                   LC 2008-20365

"The Russian critic Akim Volynsky came late to the art of classical dance but brought to his seat on the aisle a formidable background in philosophy, aesthetics, and polemics. . . . In a sense, editor and translator Stanley J. Rabinowitz, a professor of Russian at Amherst College, has kissed to life one of the most important eras in ballet history—the years when Anna Pavlova and Tamara Karsavina were dancing and when the Imperial classicism of choreographer Marius Petipa was pulled into the twentieth century of Michel Fokine, Sergey Diaghilev, and modernism. How exciting to hear a contemporaneous voice commenting on live performances." Bookforum

  Includes bibliographical references

793 Indoor games and amusements

Lithgow, John

A **Lithgow** palooza! 101 ways to entertain and inspire your kids. Simon & Schuster 2004 351p il pa $15   **793**

  1. Amusements 2. Games 3. Recreation

  ISBN 0-7432-6124-0

                   LC 2004-42820

"One dictionary defines a lollapalooza as 'something outstanding of its kind,' which adequately describes Lithgow's latest book. . . . Essential for all child-rearing collections." Libr J

793.2 Parties and entertainments

Sedaris, Amy

I like you; hospitality under the influence. Warner Books 2006 303p il $27.99   **793.2**

  1. Cooking 2. Entertaining 3. Hospitality 4. Recipes

  ISBN 978-0-446-57884-4; 0-446-57884-3

                   LC 2006-07521

"Novice party-planners will actually find some helpful hints along the way as Sedaris offers instructions and real recipes. . . . [This book] is an outrageous and deadpan delight, greatly enhanced by her deliriously kitschy illustrations and photos." Publ Wkly

793.3 Social, folk, national dancing

Soffee, Anne Thomas

Snake hips; belly dancing and how I found true love. Chicago Review Press 2002 xxii, 262p $22.95   **793.3**

  1. Belly dance -- United States 2. Belly dancing 3. Lebanese Americans -- Virginia -- Richmond -- Biography

  ISBN 1-55652-458-7

                   LC 2002-572

This is the author's story of how she cured a broken heart and changed her life for the better through belly-dancing.

"Soffee's witty, flowing prose draws readers into this unlikely but captivating story." Booklist

  Includes bibliographical references

793.73 Puzzles and puzzle games

Arnot, Michelle

Four-letter words; and other secrets of a crossword insider. Penguin Group 2008 xxi, 214p pa $13.95   **793.73**

  1. Crossword puzzles

  ISBN 978-0-399-53435-5; 0-399-53435-0

                   LC 2008-14260

"The book is full of little-known (to most of us, anyway) nuggets of information: the first crossword puzzle appeared in a New York newspaper on Christmas Day 1913; there are strict rules for composing a puzzle (no more than one-sixth of the spaces can be black, for example); future publishing giant Simon & Schuster's very first book was a collection of crossword puzzles. . . . The book is like a crash course in crossword puzzles and should appeal equally to veteran solvers and novices." Booklist

  Includes bibliographical references

Drabble, Margaret

The **pattern** in the carpet; a personal history with jigsaws. Houghton Mifflin Harcourt 2009 353p $25; pa $14.95   **793.73**

  1. Authors 2. Biography, Individual 3. Dramatists 4. Jigsaw puzzles 5. Novelists

  ISBN 978-0-547-24144-9; 0-547-24144-5; 978-0-547-

38609-6 pa; 0-547-38609-5 pa

LC 2009-12214

"Part memoir, part rigorously researched historical perspective, Drabble's book is a multi-layered look at jigsaw puzzles and their role through the ages for society, individuals, and herself; it's also a charming homage to Drabble's beloved Auntie Phyl, who passed her lifelong love of jigsaws on to Drabble." Publ Wkly

Includes bibliographical references

★ The Official Scrabble players dictionary; 4th ed.; Merriam-Webster 2005 704p $24.95; pa $7.50   **793.73**
   1. Reference books 2. Scrabble (Game) -- Dictionaries
   ISBN 978-0-87779-420-2; 0-87779-420-0; 978-0-87779-929-0 pa; 0-87779-929-6 pa

LC 2005-5110

This is a dictionary of words which can be used in the game of Scrabble including 100,000 2 to 8 letter words.

Random House Webster's crossword puzzle dictionary; 3rd ed; Random House 1998 854p $27.95; pa $18.95   **793.73**
   1. Crossword puzzles -- Dictionaries 2. Crossword puzzles -- Glossaries, vocabularies, etc 3. Reference books
   ISBN 0-679-45856-5; 0-375-70624-0 pa

LC 98-67266

Each entry lists a variety of terms that may be substituted for the entry term. The arrangement within each term listing is alphabetical and by number of letters.

"A useful and entertaining companion for both crossword puzzle and trivia buffs." Ref Sources for Small & Medium-sized Libr. 6th edition

793.74   Mathematical games and recreations

Tahan, Malba

The **man** who counted; a collection of mathematical adventures. illustrated by Patricia Reid Baquero & translated by Leslie Clark and Alastair Reid. Norton 1993 244p il hardcover o.p. pa $15.95 **793.74**
   1. Mathematical recreations
   ISBN 0-393-30934-7 pa

LC 92-18822

"This small book is a joy. . . . These are beautifully expressive tales that find mathematical puzzles and numerical intrigue in human situations and speak not just of solving the problems but of the needs we all have for friendship, love, and beauty." Booklist

793.8   Magic and related activities

Brandon, Ruth

The **life** and many deaths of Harry Houdini. Random House 1994 355p il hardcover o.p. pa $14.95   **793.8**
   1. Biography, Individual 2. Magicians 3. Nonfiction

writers
ISBN 0-8129-7042-X pa

LC 94-4080

The author provides a psychological "portrait of the great and enigmatic escape artist Harry Houdini. She not only reveals Houdini's impressive technical secrets but also identifies the sources of his unabashed melodramatics and puzzling innocence. . . . Houdini was one of the most compelling 'idols of popular culture' in the early years of this mass-appeal century, and he still works his magic through the medium of Brandon's bold and magnetic interpretation." Booklist

Includes bibliographical references

Gardner, Martin

The **colossal** book of short puzzles and problems; combinatorics, probability, algebra, geometry, topology, chess, logic, cryptarithms, wordplay, physics and other topics of recreational mathematics. edited by Dana Richards. Norton 2006 494p il $35   **793.8**
   1. Mathematical recreations 2. Scientific recreations
   ISBN 0-393-06114-0; 978-0-393-06114-7

LC 2005-24080

This is a compilation of puzzles from Martin Gardner's "column, 'Mathematical Games,' which appeared for over 25 years in Scientific American. . . . [The topics] include combinatorics, probability, algebra, plane and solid geometry, topology, games, chess, logic, wordplay, and physics, among others. . . . Anyone interested in recreational mathematics should like this book. The puzzles are fascinating and the book is easily browsed. It can also serve as a good reference for (high school and college) teachers seeking interesting problems to complement routine ones in mathematics texts." Sci Books Films

794   Indoor games of skill

Botermans, Jack

The **book** of games; strategy, tactics & history. [by] Jack Botermans; [translated from the Spanish by Edgar Loy Fankbonner] Sterling 2008 736p il $29.95   **794**
   1. Board games 2. Indoor games
   ISBN 978-1-4027-4221-7; 1-4027-4221-5

LC 2007-10173

"Some 65 international games are described and demonstrated in this colorful book. Ranging from dominoes to mancala and shogi to Yut, each entry highlights the game's origins, versions, and playing rules. . . . Color illustrations and diagrams are used liberally to illustrate strategic moves and the variations of game boards and pieces, while photographs show the games being played. . . . Libraries should consider this for their circulating collections." Booklist

794.1   Chess

Capablanca, Jose Raul
    Chess fundamentals. McKay Co. 1988 246p il
pa $14.95   **794.1**
    1. Chess
    ISBN 978-0-679-14004-7; 0-679-14004-2
    Explains the general principles of chess through eigh-
teen illustrative games, so that, when grounded in these,
the novice may understand the whole elementary science of
the game.

Fischer, Bobby
    Bobby Fischer teaches chess; by Bobby Fisher,
Stuart Margulies, Donn Mosenfelder. Bantam 1972
334p il pa $7.99   **794.1**
    1. Chess
    ISBN 0-553-26315-3; 978-0-553-26315-2
    In this book the authors give specific advice and hints
aimed at both the beginning and advanced player. Each step-
by-step lesson is fully illustrated.

Hallman, J. C.
    The **chess** artist. Thomas Dunne Bks. 2003
334p il map $25.95; pa $13.95   **794.1**
    1. Chess
    ISBN 0-312-27293-6; 0-312-33396-X pa
                        LC 2003-46872
    "Educational, fanciful, entertaining, this is a book that
will make every reader see the game of chess in an entirely
new—if slightly weird—light." Booklist
    Includes bibliographical references

United States Chess Federation
    ★ **U.S.** Chess Federation's official rules of chess;
compiled and sanctioned by the U.S. Chess Federation; Tim Just, chief editor; Daniel B. Burg, editor.
5th ed; Random House Puzzles & Games 2003 xxxvii, 370p il pa $18.95   **794.1**
    1. Chess 2. Chess -- Rules
    ISBN 0-8129-3559-4
                        LC 2003-278349
    This "edition features the latest rules, including guide-
lines for the popular game of speed chess, an updated quick
rating system, and the latest conventions of governing tournaments. It also contains explanations of every legal move,
a guide to calculating lifetime rankings, guidelines for sponsoring and running a tournament, and a lesson on how to
read and write chess notation." Publisher's note

794.7   Ball games

Byrne, Robert
    Byrne's new standard book of pool and billiards.
Harcourt Brace & Co. 1998 xxv, 406p il hardcover
o.p. pa $20   **794.7**
    1. Billiards 2. Pool (Game)
    ISBN 0-15-100325-4; 0-15-600554-9 pa
                        LC 98-14656

The author explains the rules of pool and billiards and
offers advice on strategy with diagrams of various shots.

McCumber, David
    Playing off the rail; a pool hustler's journey.
Avon Books 1997 384p pa $14.95   **794.7**
    1. Pool (Game) 2. Pool players
    ISBN 0-380-72923-7
    A "look at the game of pool, which is a gambling sport
not yet sanitized by what McCumber calls the 'Fellowship
of Christian Athletes types.' He plays financial backer to a
sharp-tongued player named Tony Annigoni, and takes him
on the road across North America in search of highstakes
games. . . . This is a terrific book." New Yorker

794.8   Electronic games

Bissell, Tom
    Extra lives; why video games matter. Pantheon
Books 2010 218p   **794.8**
    1. Video games
    ISBN 0-307-37870-5; 978-0-307-37870-5
                        LC 2009-39602
    This is a volume of essays about video games. Por-
tions of the work originally appeared in The New Yorker,
Tin House, and Kill Screen. Mr Bissell explains: "I wrote
this book as a writer who plays a lot of games, and in these
pages you will find one man's opinions and thoughts on what
playing games feels like, why he plays them, and the questions they make him think about. In the portions of the book
where I address game design and game designers, it is . . .
to a formally explanatory rather than technically informative
end." (Author's note) Index.
    The "first truly indispensable work of literary nonfiction
about society's most lucrative entertainment medium. Bissell's commentary is marvelously astute and his enthusiasm
for games makes even his words on the printed page feel
positively backlit. Any breathless adoration for the medium
he doles out, however, takes on additional weight because of
his willingness to admit when a game falls on its face." Paste

Chatfield, Tom
    Fun Inc. why gaming will dominate the twenty-
first century. Pegasus Books 2010 258p $27.95 **794.8**
    1. Video games
    ISBN 978-1-60598-143-7; 1-60598-143-5
    "A lively, thought-provoking and thoughtful read on an
entertainment juggernaut many of us have failed to properly
recognize. A good book, too, for parents, who might feel far
more comfortably informed about a sector that can come
across as—literally—an alien world their kids inhabit."
Irish Times

Neiburger, Eli
    ★ **Gamers** . . . in the library?! the why, what, and
how of videogame tournaments for all ages. American Library Association 2007 178p pa $42   **794.8**
    1. Computer games 2. Electronic games 3. Video
games 4. Young adults' libraries 5. Young adults'

library services -- Activity projects
ISBN 978-0-8389-0944-7; 0-8389-0944-2
LC 2007-10512
"With the writing as vibrant as its topic, . . . [this book] is a must-read professional tool." Voice Youth Advocates
Includes bibliographical references

Wark, McKenzie
Gamer theory. Harvard University Press 2007 un il $19.95 **794.8**
1. Computer games
ISBN 978-0-674-02519-6; 0-674-02519-9
LC 2006-102852
"For Wark, video games are worth studying because they offer insights into contemporary society and culture. For example, Katamari Damacy exemplifies the way digital technology has altered the experience of space and time; Rez demonstrates how individual identity is now a matter of action not essence, doing not being; Vice City maps out the territory of the new world order of seemingly unending risk and reward. Gamer Theory devotes complete chapters to particular games and the key concepts they clarify. . . . Gamer Theory concerns itself with more than just the interpretation of video games; it's about gaming ambience—that is, gamespace—as the kinetic field within which game players exist." PopMatters
Includes bibliographical references

795.4   Card games

Bellin, Andy
Poker nation; a high stakes, low-life adventure into the heart of a gambling country. HarperCollins Pubs. 2001 258p il hardcover o.p. pa $12.95 **795.4**
1. Card games
ISBN 0-06-095847-2 pa
LC 2001-42409
"Bellin offers the best of both worlds, combining detailed advice on how to play the game with engagingly written, humorous stories about those who play it with passion." Booklist
Includes bibliographical references

Hoyle, Edmond
★ **Hoyle's** rules of games; descriptions of indoor games of skill and chance, with advice on skillful play: based on the foundations laid down by Edmond Hoyle, 1672-1769. edited by Albert H. Morehead and Geoffrey Mott-Smith. 3rd rev. & updated ed.; Plume 2001 362p il pa $14 **795.4**
1. Card games
ISBN 0-452-28313-2
LC 2002-278550
This guide "includes rules, strategies, and playing odds for more than 250 games." Publisher's note
Includes bibliographical references

McManus, James
Cowboys full; the story of poker. Farrar, Straus, and Giroux 2009 516p il $30 **795.4**
1. Poker 2. Poker -- History
ISBN 978-0-374-29924-8; 0-374-29924-2
LC 2009-29533
The story of poker, from its roots in China, the Middle East, and Europe to its ascent as a global—but especially an American—phenomenon, braiding history with poker's relevance to our military, diplomatic, business, and personal affairs.
"The epic story of how poker has grown from disreputable roots to become America's—and the world's—game. . . . A satisfying, useful overview." Kirkus
Includes bibliographical references (p. 471-474)

Positively Fifth Street; murderers, cheetahs, and Binion's World Series of Poker. Farrar, Straus & Giroux 2003 422p il $26 **795.4**
1. Poker
ISBN 0-374-23648-8
LC 2002-33882
"McManus went to Las Vegas in May 2000 on assignment for Harper's to cover the World Series of Poker. . . . He was to throw in coverage of the trial of Sandy Murphy, an ex-stripper, and her boyfriend, Rick Tabish, accused of murdering Ted Binion, the tournament's host. . . . To satisfy his own gambling urge, McManus enter the poker competition and spends 10 days immersed in the culture of Vegas and gambling, rendering a fast-paced, riveting account of his progress through the tournament. . . . A delicious inside look." Booklist
Includes bibliographical references

Scarne, John
Scarne's encyclopedia of card games. Quill 2001 475p il pa $18 **795.4**
1. Card games
ISBN 0-06-273155-6; 978-0-06-273155-5
The material in this book has been excerpted, with alterations and additions, from Scarne's encyclopedia of games (1973).

796   Athletic and outdoor sports and games

Berkow, Ira
The **minority** quarterback, and other lives in sports. Dee, I.R. 2002 307p $26; pa $16.95 **796**
1. Athletes -- United States -- Miscellanea 2. Minorities in sports -- United States -- Miscellanea 3. Sports
ISBN 1-56663-422-9; 1-56663-502-0 pa
LC 2001-47578
"Berkow brings together essays on a theme: athletes overcoming hardships. Whether his subject is minority football players struggling to win recognition as quarterbacks—a position once restricted to whites—or baseball pitcher Jim Abbott working past the handicap of having only one arm, he writes with skill, empathy, and insight." Booklist

Clotfelter, Charles T.

Big-time sports in American universities. Cambridge University Press 2011 313p il $29   **796**

    1. College sports   2. College sports -- United States

    ISBN 1-107-00434-9; 978-1-107-00434-4

                              LC 2010-50331

This book presents "findings about the size, importance and effects of big-time college sports." (Publisher's note) Glossary. Index.

"Clotfelter sets himself an ambitious goal: using an analytical, data-rich approach to the questions of why many leading American universities embrace big-time, commercial athletics (while failing to fully acknowledge the size of its footprint), and whether the marriage is a good one for institutions and society as a whole. . . . He collects information on how much of The New York Times coverage of various universities focuses on their sports programs (much greater at institutions with big-time sports programs than at their peers without them), for instance, and mines a forthcoming study to show that undergraduates at one group of highly selective universities with commercial sports programs spend less time on academics than do their counterparts at institutions without top-level programs. In true economist's fashion, he asks: Do the benefits outweigh the costs? Clotfelter's answers, he acknowledges, are something less than fully satisfactory, and the book uncovers ample evidence for fanatics and haters of big-time sports alike." Inside Higher Ed

    Includes bibliographical references

Dierker, Larry

This ain't brain surgery; how to win the pennant without losing your mind. Simon & Schuster 2003 289p il $25   **796**

    1. Baseball managers   2. Baseball managers -- United States -- Biography   3. Baseball players   4. Baseball players -- United States -- Biography   5. Sportscasters   6. Sportscasters -- United States -- Biography

    ISBN 0-7432-0400-X

                              LC 2003-52809

"Dierker, a pitcher and then radio commentator for the Houston Astros, stepped out of the announcer's booth to become the Astros' manager in 1997. . . . Baseball and the Houston Astros have been Dierker's professional adult life, but unlike many baseball lifers, he has a healthy perspective about the game and his role in it, as reflected in the title of this literate, humorous, and entertaining memoir." Booklist

Fortin, Francois

Sports: the complete visual reference; François Fortin [general editor] Firefly Bks. 2000 372p il $39.95; pa $24.95   **796**

    1. Reference books   2. Sports

    ISBN 1-55209-540-1; 1-55297-807-9 pa

"A sure winner for any sports reference collection." Am Libr

Franck, Irene M.

   ★ **Famous** first facts about sports; {by} Irene M. Franck & David M. Brownstone. Wilson, H.W. 2001 903p $160   **796**

    1. Sports

    ISBN 0-8242-0973-7

                              LC 00-43883

"Franck and Brownstone have compiled 5,415 'firsts' covering more than 110 sports. . . . Arranged alphabetically by sport, the concisely described events are listed in chronological order, with headers for time periods. Entries are given consecutive four-digit numbers, which are cited in the five indexes (subjects, years, days, personal names, and geographical locations). . . . The indexes provide essential access and are easy to use. . . . The depth of coverage is impressive." Choice

    Includes bibliographical references

Guttmann, Allen

Women's sports; a history. Columbia Univ. Press 1991 339p il hardcover o.p. pa $24   **796**

    1. Sports   2. Sports -- History   3. Women athletes

    ISBN 0-231-06957-X pa

                              LC 90-28692

The author explores "the social and cultural contexts of women's athletics in ancient civilizations, the Middle Ages, and the Renaissance. This lays the groundwork for a subsequent discussion of the subject's current state, in which he . . . exposes controversial issues which threaten the development of women's sports." Libr J

    Includes bibliographical references

Halberstam, David

The **teammates**. Hyperion 2003 217p il $22.95 **796**

    1. Baseball -- Biography   2. Baseball managers   3. Baseball players   4. Sportscasters

    ISBN 1-401-30057-X

                              LC 2003-42334

"This account of good people living full lives and appreciating the experience will move readers." Booklist

Haskins, Don

   ★ **Glory** road; my story of the 1966 NCAA basketball championship and how one team triumphed against the odd and changed America forever. [by] Don Haskins with Daniel Wetzel. Hyperion 2006 254p il pa $14.95   **796**

    1. Basketball coaches

    ISBN 1-4013-0791-4

                              LC 2005-50349

"This is one of the best sports autobiographies in many years." Booklist

Kindred, Dave

Sound and fury; two powerful lives, one fateful friendship. Free Press 2006 368p il $27   **796**

    1. Biography, Individual   2. Boxers (Persons)   3. Lawyers   4. Sportscasters   5. Television personalities

    ISBN 0-7432-6211-5; 978-0-7432-6211-8

                              LC 2005-55217

This is an account of the friendship of Muhammad Ali and Howard Cosell.

"Even if the shelves are sagging with books about Ali, room should be made for this approachable, touching, and altogether fascinating buddy comedy." Booklist

Includes bibliographical references

Krantz, Les

Not till the fat lady sings; the most dramatic sports finishes of all time. foreword by Doug Flutie. Triumph Books 2003 148p il $29.95; pa $19.95 **796**

1. Sports

ISBN 1-57243-558-5; 1-57243-767-7 pa

LC 2003-47331

This is "an excellent addition to any sports collection." Booklist

Levine, Peter

Ellis Island to Ebbet's Field; sport and the American-Jewish experience. Oxford Univ. Press 1992 328p il hardcover o.p. pa $38 **796**

1. Jews -- United States 2. Jews -- United States -- History 3. Sports 4. Sports -- United States

ISBN 0-19-505128-9; 0-19-508555-8 pa

LC 91-42016

The author "explores the importance of sport in transforming Jewish immigrants into American Jews. Drawing on interviews with celebrities as well as lesser-known neighborhood stars, Levine vividly recounts the stories of Red Auerbach, Hank Greenberg, Moe Berg, and many others who became Jewish heroes and symbols of the difficult struggle for American success." Univ Press Books for Public and Second Sch Libr

Includes bibliographical references

McDermott, Mickey

A **funny** thing happened on the way to Cooperstown; {by} Mickey McDermott with Howard Eisenberg. Triumph 2003 270p il $24.95 **796**

1. Baseball -- Biography 2. Baseball players 3. Baseball players -- United States -- Biography

ISBN 1-57243-532-1

LC 2002-45573

McDermott "won 18 games for the Boston Red Sox in 1951 and seemed a sure thing, but he finished a lackluster career with 69 wins and 69 losses. . . . After leaving baseball, McDermott struggled at various jobs until, unbelievably, he won $7 million in the Arizona state lottery in 1991. With the help of coauthor Eisenberg, he tells the story of his life and wild times in this thoroughly engaging memoir." Booklist

Miller, Stephen G.

★ **Ancient** Greek athletics. Yale University Press 2004 288p il map $35 **796**

1. Athletics 2. Athletics -- Greece -- History 3. Olympic games 4. Olympic games (Ancient)

ISBN 0-300-10083-3

LC 2003-16875

"Five chapters discuss the origins and history of the [Olympic] games and their sociopolitical significance, but at the core of the book are the 11 chapters that use archaeological and textual evidence . . . to reconstruct the physical reality of Greek athletics. Particularly valuable are the vivid reconstruction of the ancient Olympic program and the lucid

discussion of the evidence for female athletic contests in ancient Greece." Choice

Includes bibliographical references

Rhoden, William C.

$40 million slaves; the rise, fall, and redemption of the Black athlete. Crown Publishers 2006 286p il $23.95 **796**

1. African American athletes 2. Discrimination in sports -- History 3. Race discrimination 4. Sports 5. Sports -- United States -- History

ISBN 0-609-60120-2; 978-0-609-60120-4

LC 2005-34952

"In his provocative, passionate, important and disturbing book—part memoir, part history, part journalism—William Rhoden . . . builds a historic framework that both accounts for the varieties of African-American athletic experience in the past and continues to explain them today." N Y Times Book Rev

Includes bibliographical references

Tuchman, Robert

The **100** sporting events you must see live; an insider's guide to creating the sports experience of a lifetime. BenBella Books 2009 337p pa $17.95 **796**

1. Sports 2. Travel

ISBN 978-1-933771-45-8

LC 2008-45905

The author "gives aficionados of most sports, from golf to baseball, basketball, tennis, hockey, cycling, to football, both American and soccer, a virtual bible of information on the top 100 sporting events worldwide that he recommends traveling to for the live experience. Tuchman presents each sport or event (e.g., the Head of the Charles, the World Cup) with a brief history, followed by specific ticketing information, hotel and restaurant guides, and important phone numbers, i.e, the essentials to plan your trip. . . . Tuchman's book is not only a great resource for vacation planning but also for general sports interest." Libr J

Winston, Wayne L.

Mathletics; how gamblers, managers, and sports enthusiasts use mathematics in baseball, basketball, and football. [by] Wayne Winston. Princeton University Press 2009 358p il $29.95 **796**

1. Mathematics 2. Sports -- Mathematics 3. Sports -- Statistics

ISBN 978-0-691-13913-5; 0-691-13913-X

LC 2008-51678

"Sports fans will learn much from probability theory and statistical models. . . . A rare fusion of sports enthusiasm and numerical acumen." Booklist

Includes bibliographical references (p. 343-352)

★ The Best American sports writing of the century; edited by David Halberstam. Houghton Mifflin 1999 776p $30; pa $18 **796**

1. Sports 2. Sports literature -- United States 3. Sports stories, American

ISBN 0-395-94513-5; 0-395-94514-3 pa

"Although there are pieces about mountain climbing, tennis and chess, fully half of the selections are about two sports: baseball and boxing. The book begins with a Best of the Best section led by Gay Talese's 1966 profile of Joe DiMaggio, 'The Silent Season of a Hero.'. . . The final section is a special six-piece tribute to a man who himself claimed to be the best of the best—Muhammad Ali." Publ Wkly

Rivals; legendary matchups that made sports history. edited by David K. Wiggins and R. Pierre Rodgers. University of Arkansas Press 2010 xx, 465p $75; pa $29.95 **796**
1. Athletes 2. Sports -- History
ISBN 978-1-55728-920-9; 978-1-55728-921-6 pa
LC 2009053650

"In putting together this unique, ambitious volume, Wiggins and Rodgers . . . had four goals: to outline the origin of each rivalry; to uncover the societal conditions that gave rise to it; to reveal the ways the rivalry was maintained; and to discover the meaning of the rivalry for its participants and its fans. They divide the book into three parts, each devoted to a particular type of rivalry. Part 1 covers 'one-on-one' rivalries between two elite athletes; part 2, rivalries between two franchises; and part 3, rivalries between the US and other countries." Choice
Includes bibliographical references

The best American sports writing 2010; edited and with an introduction by Peter Gammons; Glenn Stout, series editor. Houghton Mifflin Harcourt 2010 xxxiv, 411p pa $14.95 **796**
1. Sports
ISBN 978-0-547-15248-6

This is an "annual selection of the best print and web sports pieces. Each of these selections transcends its athletic subject. . . . Even if you aren't emotionally invested in the triumphs and tribulations of today's crop of highly paid professional athletes, this collection is worth acquiring. It will be a hit with both sports fans and those who are simply fans of good nonfiction." Libr J

★ The unlevel playing field; a documentary history of the African American experience in sport. {edited by} David K. Wiggins and Patrick B. Miller. University of Ill. Press 2003 xxi, 493p il hardcover o.p. pa $24.95 **796**
1. African American athletes 2. African American athletes -- History 3. Discrimination in sports -- United States -- History
ISBN 0-252-02820-1; 0-252-07272-3 pa
LC 2002-14269

"This collection contains several of the most significant primary documents tracing the sports experiences of African Americans. Athletes, sports historians, and some of the nation's foremost intellectuals deliver commentaries on a wide range of subjects and athletic events." Libr J
Includes bibliographical references

796.3

Chetwynd, Josh

The **secret** history of balls; Josh Chetwynd; Illustrations by Emily Stackhouse. Perigee Trade 2011 xiv, 221p.p ill. **796.3**
ISBN 9780399536748
LC 2010054221

This book "mines the stories and lore of sports and recreation to offer insight into 60 balls -- whether they're hollow, solid, full of air, or stuffed with twine or made of leather, metal, rubber, plastic, or polyurethane -- that give us joy on playing fields and in every arena from backyards to stadiums around the globe." (Publishers' note)

Riley, Glenda

The **life** and legacy of Annie Oakley. University of Okla. Press 1994 252p il hardcover o.p. pa $19.95 **796.3**
1. Biography, Individual 2. Frontier and pioneer life -- West (U.S.) 3. Marksmen
ISBN 0-8061-2656-6; 978-0-8061-3506-9 pa
LC 94-10260

"To provide a factual and intimate biography of Annie Oakley, the legendary female sharpshooter and star of Buffalo Bill Cody's Wild West Show, Riley attempts to place her seemingly mythical subject firmly into historical, cultural, and sociological contexts. . . . What emerges is a multidimensional portrait of an entertainer and a businesswoman whose enduring fame and popularity both reflected and defied the conventions of her era." Booklist
Includes bibliographical references

796.323   Basketball

Araton, Harvey

When the Garden was Eden; Clyde, the captain, dollar bill, and the glory days of the New York Knicks. photographs by George Kalinsky. Harper 2011 352p il $26.99; ebook $12.99 **796.323**
1. Basketball
ISBN 978-0-06-195623-2; 978-0-06-209705-7 ebook
LC 2011018792

"A warm, accessible celebration of the dynamic early-1970s New York Knicks basketball teams. Populated by such colorful personalities as the flashy but cerebral point guard Walt Frazier, silky-smooth combo guard Earl 'The Pearl' Monroe, hard-nosed forward/center Willis Reed and quirky bench anchor Phil Jackson, this version of the Knicks is near-legendary, even though they were far from a dynasty, only managing a pair of championships (1970 and 1973)." Kirkus
Includes bibliographical references

Barkley, Charles

I may be wrong but I doubt it; edited and with an introduction by Michael Wilbon. Random House 2002 245p $22.95; pa $12.95 **796.323**
1. Basketball players 2. Basketball players -- United

States -- Biography 3. Sportscasters
ISBN 0-375-50883-X; 0-8129-6628-7 pa

LC 2002-29169

The retired NBA champion "explores a wide range of interests. Each chapter has a theme, and Barkley has no problem speaking his mind on any topic, whether it is politics . . . or lack of minority control in sports. . . . In between these chapters are other sections that retell some of the great and not-so-great moments in his career. . . . This is a very entertaining look at one of the most intelligent minds in pro sports, and like Barkley's career, it's bound to produce fierce arguments." Publ Wkly

Blais, Madeleine

In these girls, hope is a muscle. Warner Bks. 1996 266p pa $13.95 **796.323**
1. Basketball
ISBN 0-446-67210-6; 978-0-446-67210-8

"Alternately funny, exciting and moving, the book should be enjoyed not only by girls and women who have played sports but also those who wanted to but let themselves be discouraged." Publ Wkly

Bradley, Bill

Values of the game. Artisan 1998 160p il $30 **796.323**
1. Basketball 2. Sportsmanship
ISBN 1-57965-116-X

LC 98-7280

In this book, the former senator and New York Knick presents a "blend of sports memoir and inspirational advice interspersed with more than 100 dramatic photos of basketball players past and present. . . . While some may dismiss much of his volume as a collection of copybook maxims, the whole is larger than the sum of its parts, not only because it is so personal but because Bradley moves so deftly from the specific to the general." Publ Wkly

Conroy, Pat

My losing season. Talese 2002 402p hardcover o.p. pa $14.95 **796.323**
1. Authors 2. Authors, American 3. Basketball players -- South Carolina -- Charleston 4. Novelists 5. Novelists, American -- 20th century -- Biography
ISBN 0-385-48912-9; 0-553-38190-3 pa

LC 2002-66212

"A wonderfully rich, informative, and well-researched reminiscence." Libr J

D'Orso, Michael

Eagle blue; a team, a tribe, and a high school basketball season in Arctic Alaska. Bloomsbury Pub. 2006 323p il map $23.95 **796.323**
1. Basketball 2. Gwich'in Indians 3. School sports
ISBN 978-1-58234-623-6; 1-58234-623-2

LC 2005-25430

The author "follows the Fort Yukon Eagles through their 2005 season to the state championship, shifting between a mesmerizing narrative and the thoughts of the players, their coach and their fans. What emerges is more than a sports story; it's a striking portrait of a community consisting of a traditional culture bombarded with modernity, where alcoholism, domestic violence and school dropout rates run wild." Publ Wkly

Davis, Seth

When March went mad; the game that transformed basketball. Henry Holt 2009 323p il $26 **796.323**
1. Basketball
ISBN 978-0-8050-8810-6; 0-8050-8810-5

LC 2008-47628

The author "chronicles the 1979 NCAA basketball championship game, which featured two future legends: Earvin 'Magic' Johnson and Larry Bird. The game was a pivotal moment in the development of the sport, leading to an explosion in popularity and a change in the way the game was played and promoted. . . . An essential primer for tournament junkies, and ideal reading material for TV timeouts." Kirkus

Includes bibliographical references

Dohrmann, George

★ **Play** their hearts out; a coach, his star recruit, and the youth basketball machine. Ballantine Books 2010 422p il $26 **796.323**
1. Basketball 2. Basketball -- United States 3. Basketball coaches 4. Basketball players 5. Basketball players -- United States
ISBN 978-0-345-50860-7; 0-345-50860-2

LC 2010-15470

The author "follows California phenom Demetrius Walker through the cycle of Amateur Athletic Union (AAU) summer league hoops, from playing for ambitious hustler and coach Joe Keller to the face of grassroots basketball, longtime coach Pat Barrett. In a constant search for the next Lebron, just as before for the next Michael Jordan, AAU coaches, with support and financing from shoe giants Nike and Adidas, woo youngsters to their summer league basketball teams with gear, shoes, and promises of a college scholarship. . . . [Dohrmann's] insights into the seamy side of youth basketball are investigative journalism at its best." Libr J

Feinstein, John

★ **Last** dance; behind the scenes at the Final Four. John Feinstein. Little, Brown 2006 369p il $25.95 **796.323**
1. Basketball 2. Basketball -- Tournaments -- United States
ISBN 0-316-16030-X

LC 2005-28478

The author "employs the 2005 [Final Four] weekend as the catalyst to discuss the history of the event, the key people, and, most significantly, the effect that involvement in the Final Four has had on participants' lives. . . . The anecdotes are entertaining, and the insights into the tournament's logistics fascinating, but what will linger most are the remembrances of players, especially those who ended up on the losing side." Booklist

A **march** to madness; the view from the floor in the Atlantic Coast Conference. Little, Brown 1997 464p il hardcover o.p. pa $14 **796.323**

1. Baseball teams -- United States 2. Basketball

ISBN 0-316-27740-1; 0-316-27712-6 pa

LC 97-31060

Feinstein "covers one year with all of the teams in the perennially powerful Atlantic Coast Conference. After introducing each of the schools, their teams, their coaches, and their expectations for the 1996/97 basketball season, the book describes their progress week by week, culminating with Dean Smith's run to the NCAA Final Four. Such a detailed accounting of a sports season could seem interminable to readers, but Feinstein has again produced a narrative that is not only interesting but often exciting." Libr J

Kent, Richard G.

Inside women's college basketball; anatomy of a season. {by} Richard Kent. Taylor, W.T. 2000 222p il hardcover o.p. pa $16.95   **796.323**

1. Basketball 2. Basketball for women -- United States

ISBN 0-87833-188-3; 978-0-87833-278-6 pa; 0-87833-278-2 pa

LC 00-42589

"Kent chronicles the 1999-2000 season as experienced by four top women's programs: Tennessee, Connecticut, Rutgers, and Sacred Heart. . . . This is a fine overview for those looking for insights into the women's game." Booklist

Merlino, Doug

The **hustle**; one team and ten lives in Black and White. Bloomsbury USA 2010 309p il $26 **796.323**

1. Basketball 2. School sports

ISBN 978-1-60819-215-1; 1-60819-215-6

LC 2010-23030

"This book, both memoir and social analysis, is an essential read as a recent social history and personal story of America." Libr J

Rosen, Charley

Crazy basketball; a life in and out of bounds. foreword by Phil Jackson. University of Nebraska Press 2011 301p $24.95   **796.323**

1. Authors 2. Basketball -- Biography 3. Basketball coaches 4. Sportswriters

ISBN 978-0-8032-1793-5

LC 2010-26921

The author "recalls his years as a coach in the Continental Basketball Association. . . . The shining star here isn't Rosen or any of the players, it's the game itself. The last half-dozen pages will bring a tear to the eye of anyone for whom the game was or is a passion." Booklist

Simmons, Bill

The **book** of basketball; the NBA according to the sports guy. Ballantine/ESPN Books 2009 715p il $30; pa $18   **796.323**

1. Basketball

ISBN 978-0-345-51176-8; 0-345-51176-X; 978-0-345-52010-4 pa; 0-345-52010-6 pa

LC 2009-36006

The author "summarizes the history of the league, discusses his personal fandom, includes a great 'what if?' chapter (what if Michael Jordan had been drafted second by Portland instead of third by Chicago?), analyzes Most Valuable Player choices through the years, and dissects the careers of the league's all-time best players. The true NBA fan will dive into this hefty volume and won't resurface for about a week, emerging from the man cave unshaven, smelling of beer and pizza, grinning, and armed with NBA history, insight, anecdotes, statistics, and a dozen new examples of Simmons' Unintentional Comedy Scale. This is just plain fun. Expect significant demand from hoops junkies." Booklist

Includes bibliographical references

Swidey, Neil

The **assist**; hoops, hope, and the game of their lives. PublicAffairs 2008 358p il $26 **796.323**

1. Basketball 2. Basketball coaches 3. School sports

ISBN 978-1-58648-469-9; 1-58648-469-9

LC 2007-35826

"This is a prodigiously reported, compulsively readable book that readers (sport fans or not) will savor." Publ Wkly

Wolff, Alexander

Big game, small world; a basketball adventure. Warner Bks. 2002 xxiv, 424p il $24.95; pa $15.95   **796.323**

1. Basketball

ISBN 0-446-52601-0; 0-446-67989-5 pa

"Wolff traveled to 16 countries and 10 states to assess basketball's impact as a global phenomenon. He profiles a cloistered nun who was once a talented hoopster and investigates the origins of the crossover dribble. Wolff's passion for the game burns feverishly throughout." Booklist

FreeDarko presents the macrophenomenal pro basketball almanac; styles, stats and stars in today's game. Bloomsbury USA 2008 219p il $23   **796.323**

1. Basketball

ISBN 978-1-59691-561-9; 1-59691-561-7

"This is a wonderful basketball book that blends a unique perspective, arresting presentation, and superior knowledge of its subject." Booklist

796.332   American football

Anderson, Lars

Carlisle vs. Army; Jim Thorpe, Dwight Eisenhower, Pop Warner, and the forgotten story of football's greatest battle. Random House 2007 349p il $24.95   **796.332**

1. College presidents 2. Decathletes 3. Football 4. Football coaches 5. Generals 6. Olympic athletes 7. Pentathletes 8. Presidents

ISBN 978-1-4000-6600-1; 1-4000-6600-X

LC 2007-8410

"A forgotten football game in 1912, between Carlisle, led by Jim Thorpe and coached by the legendary Pop Warner, and Army, led by Dwight Eisenhower, becomes the launching point for a fascinating look at multiple levels of American popular culture." Booklist

Includes bibliographical references

Billick, Brian

More than a game; the glorious present and uncertain future of the NFL. [by] Brian Billick with Michael MacCambridge. Scribner 2009 229p $26   796.332

1. Football

ISBN 978-1-4391-0918-2

LC 2009-27874

"With provocative ideas and an engaging style, this is essential reading for all football fans." Libr J

Includes bibliographical references

Bissinger, H. G.

★ Friday night lights; a town, a team, and a dream. Da Capo Press 2000 367p il pa $15.95   796.332

1. Football 2. Football -- Social aspects -- Texas -- Odessa

ISBN 0-306-80990-7

LC 00-40510

"It is a tricky balancing act, but Mr. Bissinger carries it off: 'Friday Night Lights' offers a biting indictment of the sports craziness that grips not only Odessa but most of American society, while at the same time providing a moving evocation of its powerful allure." N Y Times Book Rev

Bowden, Mark

The best game ever; Giants vs. Colts, 1958, and the birth of the modern NFL. Atlantic Monthly Press 2008 279p il $35   796.332

1. Football 2. Football -- United States -- History -- 20th century

ISBN 978-0-87113-988-7; 0-87113-988-X

"Bowden dives into the trenches of the 1958 NFL Championship game, where New York and Baltimore waged an overtime battle that wowed TV audiences and ensured the future of pro football. He astutely contrasts Frank Gifford's glamorous Giants with the blue-collar Colts of Johnny Unitas, who moonlighted at a local steel factory, and Raymond Berry, the training-obsessed wide receiver. The mistake-laden title game was hardly the 'best,' but it ushered in an era of riches: While Unitas earned $17,500 in 1958, rookie Joe Namath signed for $200,000 just five years later." Entertainment Wkly

Cosell, Greg

★ The games that changed the game; the evolution of the NFL in seven Sundays. [by] Ron Jaworski, with Greg Cosell and David Plaut. ESPN Books 2010 312p il $26; ebook $26   796.332

1. Football

ISBN 978-0-345-51795-1; 978-0-345-51797-5 ebook

LC 2010-31008

"Filled with anecdotes, player recollections, and other wonderful details, this should be the most popular football book of the season. Terrific reading." Booklist

Curtis, Brian

Every week a season; a journey inside big-time college football. Ballantine Books 2004 299p il $24.95; pa $14.95   796.332

1. College sports 2. Football

ISBN 0-345-47014-1; 0-345-48337-5 pa

LC 2004-303037

Curtis provides "an appreciation for the preparation and emotional investment at the foundation of every college football game. Legions of fans will savor every word." Booklist

Dent, Jim

Courage beyond the game; Jim Dent. Thomas Dunne Books/St. Martins Press 2011 xi, 333 p.p ill.   796.332

1. Football players

ISBN 9780312652852; 9781250007001

LC 2011009348

This book, a 2011 "Kirkus Reviews" Best Nonfiction title, tells the story of "Freddie Steinmark [who] was an under-sized but scrappy young man when he arrived in Austin as a freshman at the University of Texas in 1967. Despite the pronouncement by many coaches that he was too small to play football at the college level, Freddie was a tenacious competitor who vowed to start every game as a varsity Longhorn. By the start of the 1969 season, Freddie was making his mark on the college gridiron and national stage as UTs star safety, but hesd also developed a crippling pain in his thigh that worried his high school sweetheart, Linda. Despite the increasingly debilitating pain, Freddie continued to play throughout the season, helping the Longhorns to rip through opponents like pulpwood. His final game was for the national championship at the end of 1969, when the Longhorns rallied to beat Arkansas in a legendary game that has become known as 'the Game of the Century.' Tragically, bone cancer took Freddie off the field when nothing else could." (Publisher's note)

The Junction boys; how ten days in hell with Bear Bryant forged a champion team. St. Martin's Press 1999 290p il $24.95; pa $13.95   796.332

1. Football 2. Football -- Coaching -- United States 3. Football coaches 4. Football coaches -- United States -- Biography

ISBN 0-312-19293-2; 0-312-26755-X pa

LC 99-22179

"In February 1954, Paul 'Bear' Bryant took the head football coaching position at Texas A & M. The story of his first Aggie team, vividly recounted here by journalist Dent, is a little-known but memorable chapter in the legendary coach's career." Booklist

Resurrection; the miracle season that saved Notre Dame. Thomas Dunne Books 2009 306p il $25.99 796.332

1. Football 2. Football coaches 3. Sportscasters

ISBN 978-0-312-56721-7

LC 2009-16738

"The ubiquitous Notre Dame fan base will seek this [book] out in every corner of the country." Booklist

Includes bibliographical references

The undefeated; the Oklahoma Sooners and the greatest winning streak in college football history. St. Martin's Press 2001 288p il $24.95; pa $14.95 **796.332**

    1. Football

ISBN 0-312-26656-1; 0-312-30326-2 pa

LC 2001-34896

The author recounts how "Oklahoma Sooner football coach Bud Wilkinson won an all-time record 47 straight games over five seasons, which included three undefeated years, from 1954 through 1956. . . . {This} is a fascinating account of an extraordinary athletic achievement that is unlikely to be approached, let alone equaled." Booklist

Includes bibliographical references

Feinstein, John

    Next man up; a year behind the lines in today's NFL. Little, Brown 2005 502p il $25.95　**796.332**

    1. Football

ISBN 0-316-00964-4

Feinstein's look at the current state of the National Football League (NFL) focuses on the 2004 Baltimore Ravens' season.

"Even those who are not fanatical football fans will find that, beyond the information provided on players and coaches, there are two other engaging topics in the book: Feinstein's ruminations on how reporting and writing about football are different from reporting and writing about other sports, and his portrayal of the business side of the game through conversations with Ravens owner Steve Bisciotti. . . . Professional football fans cannot lose by reading this book. As for the rest of us, [it] provides interesting glimpses into a strange but popular cultural realm." Christ Sci Monit

Green, Tim

    The **dark** side of the game; my life in the NFL. Warner Bks. 1996 272p hardcover o.p. pa $7.50　**796.332**

    1. Football

ISBN 0-446-60520-4 pa

LC 95-51000

The author "offers a collection of approximately 70 brief, engagingly written essays on such dark topics as drug use, sex, violence, injuries, cheating, gambling, and money in professional football." Libr J

Lazarus, Adam

    Super Bowl Monday; from the Persian Gulf to the shores of west Florida: the New York Giants, the Buffalo Bills and Super Bowl XXV. Taylor Trade Pub. 2011 325p il $24.95; ebook $11.99　**796.332**

    1. Football 2. Persian Gulf War, 1991 3. Super Bowl Game (Football)

ISBN 978-1-58979-600-3; 978-1-58979-602-7 ebook

LC 2011010710

"This is a wonderful account of a great game and also a look at sports as a diversion from the strife-filled real world. An excellent mix of sports reporting and social history." Booklist

Includes bibliographical references

Miller, John J.

    The **big** scrum; how Teddy Roosevelt saved football. HarperCollins 2011 258p il $25.99; ebook $12.99　**796.332**

    1. College sports 2. College sports -- United States -- History 3. Football 4. Football -- United States -- History 5. Governors 6. Nobel laureates for peace 7. Presidents 8. Vice-presidents

ISBN 978-0-06-174450-1; 0-06-174450-6; 978-0-06-207899-5 ebook; 0-06-207899-2 ebook

LC 2010-32233

"A worthy addendum to the story of football's rise, even though the case for Roosevelt as a cornerstone of its development feels overstated. A good yarn." Kirkus

Includes bibliographical references (p. [227]-245) and index.

Piascik, Andy

    Gridiron gauntlet; the story of the men who integrated pro football, in their own words. Taylor Trade Pub. 2009 258p $24.95　**796.332**

    1. African American athletes 2. Football

ISBN 978-1-58979-442-9

LC 2009-9660

For this history of the integration of professional football, the author "interviewed a dozen black football players who played in the AAFC, the NFL, or the AFL between 1946 and 1961. The players ranged from Hall of Fame fullback Joe Perry and stars George Taliaferro and Bob Mann to lesser lights like Eddie Macon, Eddie Bell, Charlie Powell, and John Brown. . . . The stories they tell are humorous, disturbing, angry, sad, and uplifting. An involving and essential read for anyone interested in football." Libr J

Rielly, Edward J.

    Football; an encyclopedia of popular culture. University of Nebraska Press 2009 439p pa $26.95 **796.332**

    1. Football -- Encyclopedias 2. Reference books

ISBN 978-0-8032-9012-9; 0-8032-9012-8

LC 2009-5245

"Rielly's interest is not so much in football per se as in football as a force in American culture. . . . [This volume offers] short essays arranged alphabetically on topics which the author feels are significant both to football and to American history and culture. Some of the selected topics are expected (Bowl Games, Forward Pass, Television Broadcasting) while others are more surprising (Jewelry, September 11 Terrorist Attacks, Wine). Rielly has a relaxed and informal writing style which practically invites you to pull up a chair and make yourself comfortable while he discourses on his chosen topics." PopMatters

Includes bibliographical references

St. John, Warren

    Rammer jammer yellow hammer; a journey into the heart of fan mania. Crown Publishers 2004 275p $24　**796.332**

    1. Football 2. Football fans -- Southern States -- Social life and customs 3. Recreational vehicles -- Southern states

ISBN 0-609-60708-1

LC 2003-24718

"Wearing a thin veneer of journalistic detachment, St. John followed his beloved Alabama Crimson Tide football team during the 1999 season. The result is a sharp, sneaky-funny, but loving portrait of the team and its incredibly loyal fans." Booklist

796.334   Soccer (Association football)

Dubois, Laurent

Soccer empire; the World Cup and the future of France. University of California Press 2010 xx, 329p il ebook $18.95; $45; pa $18.95   **796.334**
1. Soccer 2. Soccer players 3. World Cup (Soccer)
ISBN 978-0-520-94574-6; 9780520259287; 9780520269781

LC 2009042962
"Laurent Dubois illuminates the connections between empire and sport by tracing the story of World Cup soccer, from the Cup's French origins in the 1930s to Africa and the Caribbean and back again. . . . [He] recounts the lives of two of soccer's most electrifying players, [Zinedine] Zidane and his outspoken teammate, Lilian Thuram." Publisher's note
Includes bibliographical references

Hamm, Mia

Go for the goal; a champion's guide to winning in soccer and life. [by] Mia Hamm with Aaron Heifetz. HarperCollins Pubs. 1999 222p il hardcover o.p. pa $12.95   **796.334**
1. Soccer 2. Soccer -- Psychological aspects 3. Soccer -- Training 4. Success
ISBN 0-06-093159-0 pa

LC 99-19592
Personal anecdotes and both action and instructional photos illustrate soccer skills and techniques.

Hirshey, David

The **ESPN** World Cup companion; everything you need to know about the planet's biggest sporting event. [by] David Hirshey and Roger Bennett; [foreword by Steve Nash] ESPN Books 2010 251p il $30   **796.334**
1. World Cup (Soccer)
ISBN 978-0-345-51792-0

LC 2010-7273
"Arranged chronologically, the guide takes readers through cup competitions of the past 80 years. . . . Unburdened by endless statistics and scores, the guide does include three pages of facts and figures at the end and dozens of photos throughout. An affordable purchase, an enduring value." Libr J
Includes bibliographical references

Kuper, Simon

Soccernomics; why England loses, why Germany and Brazil win, and why the US, Japan, Australia, Turkey--and even Iraq--are destined to become the kings of the world's most popular sport. [by] Simon Kuper and Stefan Szyman-

ski. Nation Books 2009 328p pa $14.95 **796.334**
1. Soccer
ISBN 978-1-56858-425-6

LC 2009-23502
"Whether analyzing the relationship of spending to winning or applying game theory to the penalty kick, the authors' delight in discovery proves both persuasive and contagious. It's a fascinating book with the potential to effect genuine change in the sport." Booklist
Includes bibliographical references

St. John, Warren

Outcasts united; a refugee team, an American town. Spiegel & Grau 2008 307p hardcover o.p. pa $15   **796.334**
1. Maintenance services executives 2. Refugees 3. Soccer 4. Soccer coaches
ISBN 978-0-385-52203-8; 0-385-52203-7; 978-0-385-52204-5 pa; 0-385-52204-5 pa

LC 2008-40697
This is a "book about an unlikely soccer program in the outlying Atlanta burb of Clarkston, Georgia. . . . Clarkston's residents woke up one morning and found that the city's housing projects had become havens of resettlement for refugee families from war-ravaged locales including Liberia, Afghanistan and Bosnia. Soccer is a pastime like sandlot baseball or touch football to the often-traumatized boys on the Fugees, a ramshackle intramural team of nine to 17-year-olds that St. John follows, along with its Jordanian founder Luma Hassan Mufleh, a Smith-educated woman whose role as volunteer coach quickly expands to extended family member and social worker. St. John's aim is to draw a portrait of small-town America in transition, and his eye for detail is compelling from start to finish." Time Out N Y
Includes bibliographical references

796.342   Tennis (Lawn tennis)

Fisher, Marshall

A **terrible** splendor; three extraordinary men, a world poised for war, and the greatest tennis match ever played. [by] Marshall Jon Fisher. Crown Publishers 2009 336p $25   **796.342**
1. Davis cup 2. Gays -- Nazi persecution 3. National socialism 4. Tennis 5. Tennis -- Tournaments 6. Tennis players
ISBN 978-0-307-39394-4; 0-307-39394-1

LC 2008-50527
"Richly detailed . . . the story moves from one nail-biting set to the next against a backdrop of improbably high personal and political stakes." Boston Globe
Includes bibliographical references

McEnroe, John

You cannot be serious; {by} John McEnroe with Jams Kaplan. Putnam 2002 342p il $25.95; pa $14   **796.342**
1. Art dealers 2. Tennis players
ISBN 0-399-14858-2; 0-425-19008-0 pa

LC 2002-23875

Tennis star McEnroe's "recollections fall into three categories: accounts of key matches, life as a jet-setting celebrity, and reflections on the emotional roller coaster that has been his personal life." Booklist

Wertheim, L. Jon

Strokes of genius; Federer, Nadal, and the greatest match ever played. Houghton Mifflin Harcourt 2009 211p $24   **796.342**

1. Tennis 2. Tennis players 3. Wimbledon Championship (Tennis) 4. Wimbledon Tennis Tournament

ISBN 978-0-547-23280-5; 0-547-23280-2

LC 2009-05595

"Wertheim's compelling account of the five-set 2008 Wimbeldon final between Roger Federer and Rafael Nadal captures a classic sports rivalry in its prime." Booklist

796.35   Ball driven by club, mallet, bat

Will, George F.

Men at work; the craft of baseball. HarperPerennial 1991 353p il pa $9.95   **796.35**

1. Baseball 2. Baseball managers 3. Baseball players 4. Sportscasters

ISBN 0-06-097372-2

LC 90-55518

"The author's own devotion to detail in defining the components of the game is sure to instill in readers a greater appreciation of what is required to master the sport at the major league level, thereby providing a deeper understanding of the foundation of the game. Altogether, this is hardcore baseball presented in fluent style." Libr J

796.352   Golf

Chopra, Deepak

Golf for enlightenment; seven lessons for the game of life. Harmony Bks. 2003 200p $21 **796.352**

1. Golf 2. Spiritual life

ISBN 0-609-60390-6

LC 2002-27636

The author tells a story about "Adam, who, on a day particularly productive of shanks and slices, is accosted by an apparition who adjures the despairing soul to consult golf pro Wendy, likewise an ethereal being. In a seven-part 'fable,' Wendy heightens Adams' awareness of 'now,' relieves him of his control compulsions, and restores his golfing life to balance and harmony. The authorial brand and publicity ensure that Chopra's confection will be highly, if transiently, popular." Booklist

Feinstein, John

A **good** walk spoiled; days and nights on the PGA tour. Little, Brown 1995 xx, 475p il hardcover o.p. pa $14.95   **796.352**

1. Golf

ISBN 0-316-27737-1 pa

LC 94-49552

Along with "profiles of the game's big names—Norman, Price, Watson—Feinstein's sojourn through the 1994 PGA tour also offers remarkable glimpses of the marginal players who struggle to first qualify for the tour and then maintain their tenuous places on it. . . . Golfers of all ages simply won't be able to put this book down." Booklist

Frost, Mark

The **greatest** game ever played; Harry Vardon, Francis Ouimet, and the birth of modern golf. Hyperion 2002 488p il $30   **796.352**

1. Golf 2. Golfers

ISBN 0-7868-6920-8

LC 2002-68930

"The climax of the narrative . . . is genuinely exciting, a marvelous re-creation of a signature moment in golf history." Booklist

Nicklaus, Jack

★ **Jack** Nicklaus; my story. with Ken Bowden. Simon & Schuster 1997 505p il $30; pa $24.95   **796.352**

1. Golf 2. Golf -- Personal narratives 3. Golfers

ISBN 0-684-83628-9; 0-684-83870-2 pa

LC 97-3824

"What comes across most forcibly in this fine book is Nicklaus' respect for the complexity of golf and the never-ending challenges it affords players at every level." Booklist

Sampson, Curt

Masters; golf, money, and power in Augusta, Georgia. Villard Bks. 1998 xxxiv, 263p il hardcover o.p. pa $14.95 **796.352**

1. Golf

ISBN 0-375-75337-0 pa

LC 97-49143

This history of one of the PGA's most prestigious events "traces the tournament's history since 1933, revealing both the dramatic moments and the controversial secrets, most notably racism—certainly a book to raise eyebrows at the Augusta National Golf Club." Libr J

796.357   Baseball

Achorn, Edward

Fifty-nine in '84; old Hoss Radbourn, barehanded baseball, and the greatest season a pitcher ever had. Smithsonian Books/HarperCollins 2010 366p il $25.99   **796.357**

1. Baseball 2. Baseball players

ISBN 978-0-06-182586-6; 0-06-182686-7

LC 2009-34296

"This is not just a recitation of barehanded baseball and old-time brawling, but a story that, with its larger-than-life protagonist, numerous exploits, and a love interest, reads like a novel. Hugely appealing for baseball die-hards." Libr J

Angell, Roger

★ **Game** time: a baseball companion; edited by Steve Kettmann. Harcourt 2003 398p hardcover o.p. pa $15   **796.357**
1. Baseball
ISBN 0-15-100824-8; 0-15-601387-8 pa
LC 2002-152611
"Half of the essays in this compilation of highlights from Angell's 40 years of covering baseball for the New Yorker have not previously appeared in book form, and even those that have are well worth revisiting. Angell . . . remains the dean of baseball writers." Booklist

Once more around the park; a baseball reader. Ivan R. Dee 2001 351p pa $16.95   **796.357**
1. Baseball
ISBN 1-566-63371-0; 978-1-566-63371-0
LC 00-50436
A collection of 21 pieces, some from Angell's earlier books and others previously uncollected.
"Outstanding among the choices . . . are visits with Hall of Famer Bob Gibson and then-91-year-old Smoky Joe Wood." Libr J

Barra, Allen

Clearing the bases; the greatest baseball debates of the last century. foreword by Bob Costas. St. Martin's Press 2002 xxi, 261p $23.95; pa $13.95   **796.357**
1. Baseball 2. Baseball -- United States -- History -- 20th century 3. Baseball players -- Rating of -- United States
ISBN 0-312-26556-5; 0-312-30253-3 pa
LC 2001-48992
The author "provides considerable insight into many of the most hotly debated topics of baseball's last 100 years." Booklist

Rickwood Field; a century in America's oldest ballpark. W. W. Norton & Company 2010 367p il $27.95   **796.357**
1. Baseball
ISBN 978-0-393-06933-4; 0-393-06933-8
LC 2010-10896
"Rickwood Field, a covered-grandstand fossil in Birmingham, Ala., turns 100 this season. Named after iron scion Rick Woodward, the stadium — home to the Birmingham Barons — has outlasted Philadelphia's Shibe Park and Pittsburgh's Forbes Field and every other major and minor league ballpark that stood on Aug. 18, 1910, when Birmingham put 57 extra streetcars into service for Opening Day. Barra . . . takes readers far beyond the who's who of baseball legends who visited Rickwood, including Connie Mack, the stadium's design consultant, and Ty Cobb, Babe Ruth, Satchel Paige, Hank Aaron and Reggie Jackson. He spins the thorny racial history of Birmingham through the prism of the old ballpark." Minneapolis Star Tribune
Includes bibliographical references

Barry, Dan

★ **Bottom** of the 33rd; hope and redemption in baseball's longest game. Harper 2011 255p il $26.99   **796.357**
1. Baseball 2. Baseball -- Records 3. Minor league baseball -- United States -- History
ISBN 978-0-06-201448-1; 0-06-201448-X
LC 2010-51656
"On a frigid evening in April 1981, 1,740 Pawtucket, R.I., Red Sox fans settled into their seats for a game with the Rochester Red Wings of the AAA International League. With the score tied 11 at the end of regulation, the teams played on. And on. On past 12:50 a.m., when the curfew provision, mysteriously missing from that year's edition of the rule book, would have suspended the contest; on past the 21st inning, when each team maddeningly scored a run; on past the 29th and record-tying inning; on past 4:00 a.m., the bottom of the 32nd, when the league president was finally reached and ordered the umpires to suspend the contest." Kirkus

Bissinger, H. G.

Three nights in August; strategy, heartbreak, and joy, inside the mind of a manager. [foreword by Tony La Russa] Houghton Mifflin 2005 xxi, 280p $25; pa $13.95   **796.357**
1. Baseball managers 2. Baseball players
ISBN 0-618-40544-5; 0-618-71053-1 pa
LC 2004-65134
For this book, the author "was given complete access to Tony La Russa and his St. Louis Cardinals. . . . La Russa collaborated fully, hid nothing, freely divulged his thoughts, notes, fears. The result is a fascinating look inside the day-to-day, game-by-game, inning by inning managing of a professional baseball team." N Y Times Book Rev
Includes bibliographical references

Boston, Talmage

1939, baseball's tipping point; foreword by John Grisham. Bright Sky Press 2005 288p il $24.95   **796.357**
1. Baseball
ISBN 1-931721-53-X
LC 2004-65046
This is a "terrific collection of stories and profiles of some of the baseball figures that made 1939 one of the most extraordinary years that any sport has ever enjoyed." Newberg Report
Includes bibliographical references

Bradley, Richard

The **greatest** game; the Yankees, the Red Sox, and the playoff of '78. Free Press 2008 286p il hardcover o.p. pa $15   **796.357**
ISBN 978-1-4165-3438-9; 1-4165-3438-5; 978-1-4165-3439-6 pa; 1-4165-3439-3 pa
LC 2007-45382
"In 1978, the American League East division champion was determined by a one-game playoff, a taut battle between the Yankees and the Red Sox at Fenway Park. Bradley gives a pitch-by-pitch breakdown of the Boston loss (a three-run homer by Bucky Dent in the top of the seventh cemented the

Yankees' lead), and an account of the volatile season preceding it. At a time when pro baseball was making the transition from homegrown pastime to big business, emotions ran high and outsized personalities clashed; New York's pugnacious manager, Billy Martin, resigned in tears midseason. Bradley's prosaic style and his penchant for statistics sometimes test the reader's patience, but his portraits of the coaches and players who converged that day in October lend an intimacy and richness to the book." New Yorker

Includes bibliographical references

Bryant, Howard

Shut out; a story of race and baseball in Boston. Routledge 2002 278p il $27.50   **796.357**

1. Baseball 2. Baseball -- Massachusetts -- Boston -- History -- 20th century 3. Discrimination in sports -- Massachusetts -- Boston 4. Race discrimination

ISBN 0-415-92779-X

LC 2002-69950

"Bryant looks at both sides of the race issue, and backs his conclusions with exhaustive research from a variety of sources." Publ Wkly

Includes bibliographical references and index

Costas, Bob

Fair ball; a fan's case for baseball. Broadway Bks. 2000 179p hardcover o.p. pa $12.95 **796.357**

1. Baseball 2. Baseball -- Economic aspects -- United States

ISBN 0-7679-0466-4 pa

LC 99-87992

"The root of baseball's ills, the sports broadcaster Bob Costas argues, lies in how teams like the Yankees and Atlanta Braves, by virtue of vastly higher revenues than franchises like the Montreal Expos or Kansas City Royals, threaten the game's legitimacy by having 'a monopoly on sustained success.' Costas's solution is for team owners to start meaningful revenue sharing and force a salary cap on the intransigent players union, even if it takes another strike or lockout to do it." N Y Times Book Rev

Cramer, Richard Ben

Joe DiMaggio; the hero's life. Simon & Schuster 2000 546p $28; pa $16   **796.357**

1. Baseball players 2. Baseball players -- United States

ISBN 0-684-85391-4; 0-684-86547-5 pa

LC 00-49232

In this biography of the baseball player, "Cramer taps every plank in the wall that DiMaggio erected around himself and that protected him from inquiry. In the wall's hollow spots, Cramer locates the girls, finds the Mob guys, and behind the legend of grace and elegance on and off the field discovers a legend who in reality was more often than not graceless and inelegant." New Yorker

Creamer, Robert W.

Stengel; his life and times. University of Neb. Press 1996 349p il pa $18.95 **796.357**

1. Baseball managers 2. Baseball players

ISBN 0-8032-6367-8

LC 95-40143

"Casey Stengel is remembered as either the shrewd, innovative New York Yankee manager who won 10 pennants and seven World Series from 1949 to 1960 or as the seemingly senile, aged master of malaprop who (mis)-managed the legendarily inept New York Mets in the early 1960s. Creamer . . . dissolves the apparently disparate images and melds them into an inclusive vision of an unexpectedly complex man." Booklist

Dickson, Paul

★ The **Dickson** baseball dictionary; edited and augmented by Skip McAfee. 3rd ed.; Norton 2009 xxiv, 974p il $49.95   **796.357**

1. Baseball -- Dictionaries 2. Reference books

ISBN 978-0-393-06681-4

LC 2008-51238

This dictionary "includes 10,000 terms and 18,000 individual definitions. . . . The book features baseball terminology, slang, team names, and stadiums—but not individuals. Assorted softball terms appear as well. . . . This volume is a fabulous addition for any library and a must-have for any baseball fan's personal library." Choice

Includes bibliographical references

The **hidden** language of baseball; how signs and sign-stealing have influenced the course of our national pastime. Walker & Co 2003 230p il $22 **796.357**

1. Baseball 2. Baseball signs and signals -- United States -- History

ISBN 0-8027-1392-0

LC 2003-41125

"Anyone who has ever played or coached youth baseball or paid close attention to the third-base coach at a big-league game will appreciate the author's guided tour through the history of diamond sign language. Dickson is a fine storyteller, and his latest book is a welcome addition to the rich canon of baseball literature." Booklist

Includes bibliographical references and index

Fleitz, David L.

Shoeless; the life and times of Joe Jackson. McFarland & Co. 2001 314p il pa $29.95 **796.357**

1. Baseball players 2. Baseball players -- United States

ISBN 0-7864-0978-9

LC 2001-18318

"Shoeless Joe Jackson, banned from baseball for his alleged involvement in the 1919 World Series gambling scandal, is viewed by many as an illiterate phenom hustled by city slickers. Fleitz shows it ain't so, Joe, in this provocative biography." Booklist

Includes bibliographical references

Frost, Mark

Game six; Cincinnati, Boston, and the 1975 World Series: the triumph of America's pastime. Hyperion 2009 406p il $26.99; pa $15.99   **796.357**

1. Baseball 2. Baseball -- History 3. World Series (Baseball) 4. World series (Baseball)

ISBN 978-1-4013-2310-3; 1-4013-2310-3; 978-1-4013-1026-4 pa; 1-4013-1026-5 pa

LC 2009-23227

"Game Six of the 1975 World Series between the Boston Red Sox and the Cincinnati Reds has become one of the most storied contests in the history of baseball. . . . [The author] captures all the excitement and tension of the game, and his book reads like a novel, full of suspense and larger-than-life characters." Libr J

Geist, Bill

Little League confidential; one coach's completely unauthorized tale of survival. Dell Pub 1999 217p pa $15　　**796.357**

1. Baseball

ISBN 0-440-50877-0

The author "relates his decade of service as a little-league baseball coach. He admittedly distills his experiences—and those of others—into a season-long 'docudrama' journal. He tells of pompous coaches lecturing their miniplayers on the subtleties of the infield fly rule; he addresses the question of positioning a player with a personal-injury lawyer for a dad. The book is a wonderful effort filled with empathy for kids, impatience for pushy parents, and a good sense of humor." Booklist

Gentile, Derek

★ **Splitters,** squeezes, and steals; the plays, strategies, and rules of baseball. Black Dog & Leventhal 2009 256p il $29.95　　**796.357**

1. Baseball

ISBN 978-1-57912-788-6

LC 2009-00639

This examination of the evolution of the plays, moves, rules, equipment, and strategies that make up baseball "is divided into seven parts: Pitching, Batting, Fielding, Baserunning, Umpires and Management, Equipment, and Ballparks. Chapters include 'The Fastball,' 'The Hit and Run,' 'Stealing Bases,' 'The Hidden Ball Trick,' and more—and each play or move is dissected in detail to reveal its history, its execution, and its greatest innovators." Publisher's note

Includes bibliographical references

Giamatti, A. Bartlett

A **great** and glorious game; baseball writings of A. Bartlett Giamatti. edited by Kenneth S. Robson; foreword by David Halberstam. Algonquin Bks. 1998 121p $15.95　　**796.357**

1. Baseball 2. Baseball -- Social aspects -- United States 3. Baseball -- United States

ISBN 1-56512-192-9

LC 97-32803

Giamatti's "writings make baseball a metaphor for America and Americans. His imagery, in the nine essays in this . . . book, elevates the game from ordinary to beautiful and sometimes humorous." N Y Times Book Rev

Golenbock, Peter

Amazin' the miraculous history of New York's most beloved baseball team. St. Martin's Press 2002 654p il $27.95; pa $18.95　**796.357**

ISBN 0-312-27452-1; 0-312-30992-9 pa

LC 2001-48870

This is a history of the New York Mets baseball team.

"Golenbock combines his own well-researched commentary with the recollections of eyewitnesses. . . . This is a delightful and painstakingly detailed trip down memory lane that Mets fans will cherish." Publ Wkly

Includes bibliographical references

Goodwin, Doris Kearns

Wait till next year; a memoir. Simon & Schuster 1997 261p il hardcover o.p. pa $14　　**796.357**

1. Authors 2. Baseball 3. Biographers 4. Biography, Individual 5. Historians 6. Nonfiction writers 7. Political commentators

ISBN 0-684-84795-7 pa

LC 97-39766

"For self-esteem-building female role models, for baseball lore and inning-by-inning action and for a lively trip into the recent American past, you could hardly do better." N Y Times Book Rev

Gould, Stephen Jay

Triumph and tragedy in Mudville; a lifelong passion for baseball. foreword by David Halberstam. Norton 2003 342p il hardcover o.p. pa $14.95　　**796.357**

1. Baseball 2. Baseball -- Miscellanea 3. Baseball -- United States

ISBN 0-393-05755-0; 978-0-393-32557-7 pa; 0-393-32557-1 pa

LC 2002-155523

This is a collection of Gould's "essays about baseball, written over 20 years and published in venues as divergent as the New York Times and Vanity Fair. . . . The essays are uniformly wonderful. . . . Scientific analysis intersects gently with flat-out fandom. Gould could think, he could write, he was funny, and he loved, loved baseball." Booklist

Gruver, Ed

Koufax; by Edward Gruver. Taylor Pub. Co. 2000 264p il $24.95; pa $16.95 **796.357**

1. Baseball players 2. Baseball players -- United States -- Biography

ISBN 0-87833-157-3; 0-87833-294-4 pa

LC 99-56763

"This is the biography of legendary L.A. Dodgers pitcher Sandy Koufax, who for half a decade mesmerized hitters as few have ever done. . . . Drawing on childhood friends, teammates, opponents, journalists, and Dodger management, Gruver has written a compelling story, complete with appendix of notable statistics." Libr J

Halberstam, David

★ **Summer** of '49. Morrow 1989 304p il hardcover o.p. pa $14.95　　**796.357**

ISBN 978-0-06-088426-0; 0-06-088426-6

LC 89-2886

"This book is ostensibly about the pennant race between the Yankees and Red Sox {in 1949} and the 'rivalry' between Joe DiMaggio and Ted Williams. . . . It is a study of all the elements and personalities that influenced baseball that year and beyond. Halberstam brings them together in such an enjoyable, interesting, and informative manner that a reader needn't be a baseball fan to appreciate the book." Libr J

Hample, Zack

Watching baseball smarter; a professional fan's guide for beginners, semi-experts, and deeply serious geeks. Vintage 2007 254p il pa $13.95   **796.357**

1. Baseball

ISBN 978-0-307-28032-9; 0-307-28032-2

LC 2007-296737

The author "covers basics such as what to watch for in pitchers, catchers, hitters, fielders and base runners; he also provides answers to such nagging questions as why spectators stretch in the seventh inning and why most ballplayers grab their crotches.... Hample hits the equivalent of a reference book home run with his witty and loose style—taking a friendly for-a-fan-by-a-fan approach that doesn't hide his enormous depth of knowledge." Publ Wkly

Hogan, Lawrence D.

★ **Shades** of glory; the Negro Leagues and the story of African-American baseball. with a foreword by Jules Tygiel. National Geographic 2006 422p il $26   **796.357**

1. African American athletes 2. African American baseball players -- History 3. Baseball 4. Negro leagues 5. Negro leagues -- History

ISBN 0-7922-5306-X; 978-0-7922-5306-8

LC 2006-273216

This book "traces the history of black baseball from the 19th century to the first great teams, such as the Cuban Giants, and on to the era of the vibrant barnstorming teams from the East Coast, Chicago, and Cuba." Publisher's note

Jamieson, Dave

Mint condition; how baseball cards became an American obsession. Atlantic Monthly Press 2010 272p il $25   **796.357**

1. Baseball -- History 2. Baseball cards 3. Collectors and collecting

ISBN 978-0-8021-1939-1; 0-8021-1939-5

"For much of his book, Jamieson seems to be saying that greed and grownups have spoiled card collecting forever. But there's comfort in knowing that the cards have always appealed to baseball lovers and bottom-line business types for their own reasons. Even Jamieson holds out hope that they will find their proper place again in American kids' lives even if it's only in their closets." Minneapolis Star Tribune

Includes bibliographical references

Kahn, Roger

Beyond the boys of summer; the very best of Roger Kahn. edited by Rob Miraldi. McGraw-Hill 2005 xxxvi, 364p hardcover o.p. pa $16.95 **796.357**

1. Baseball

ISBN 0-07-144727-X; 0-07-148119-2 pa

LC 2004-24851

"Kahn is a giant among sports journalists, and this is a fine sampling of his most memorable work." Booklist

Includes bibliographical references

October men; Reggie Jackson, George Steinbrenner, Billy Martin, and the Yankees' miraculous finish in 1978. Harcourt 2003 382p il $25 **796.357**

1. Baseball executives 2. Baseball managers 3. Baseball players 4. Shipbuilding executives

ISBN 0-15-100628-8

LC 2003-536

"When it comes to writing about baseball, especially New York City baseball, Kahn is king of the hill." Publ Wkly

The **head** game; baseball seen from the pitcher's mound. Harcourt 2000 xxii, 310p il $25; pa $14   **796.357**

1. Baseball 2. Pitchers (Baseball) 3. Pitching (Baseball)

ISBN 0-15-100441-2; 0-15-601304-5 pa

LC 00-32014

"The title refers to the battle of wits between pitcher and batter, which is the essence of baseball. Kahn sides with pitching, and in a narrative that is both analytical and anecdotal, he rewards the reader with what amounts to a scholarly treatise on the craft. He does so through engrossing portraits of pitching masters, from Candy Cummings, the reputed inventor of the curveball, to Bruce Sutter, the popularizer of the split-finger fastball. Kahn also presents us with Christy Mathewson on the fadeaway, Warren Spahn on the changeup and Don Drysdale on the duster." Sports Illustrated

Includes bibliographical references

Katz, Harry

Baseball Americana; treasures from the Library of Congress. [by] Harry Katz [et al.] Smithsonian Books 2009 240p il $29.99   **796.357**

1. Baseball -- History 2. Baseball -- United States -- History

ISBN 978-0-06-162546-6

LC 2009-13148

"A trove of artifacts and photographs that skillfully conveys the evolution of the game and how it has been chronicled and embraced.... The book spans nearly two centuries: baseball's genesis in the late 1700s; its expansion in the late 19th century; the 'glory years' of the early 20th century; the period between World War I and the Great Depression; and from World War II to the 'wonder years' of the '50s and '60s. Each section is anchored by an essay outlining the period in broad strokes, and copious sidebars help round out the details. The pages are busy, but never scattershot." N Y Times Book Rev

Kelly, Jerry

Bushville; life and time in amateur baseball. McFarland & Co. 2001 202p il pa $21 **796.357**

1. Baseball

ISBN 0-7864-0979-7

LC 01-31264

Kelly's "reflections on what the game has meant to him—from fascination with baseball's special geometry to the sensual pleasure he takes in its textures of leather and wood—

make the perfect antidote to most fans' disgust with the big money and big egos of today's major leaguers." Booklist

Includes bibliographical references

Kurlansky, Mark

The **Eastern** stars; how baseball changed the Dominican town of San Pedro de Macoris. Riverhead Books 2010 272p $25.95   **796.357**

1. Baseball 2. Baseball -- Dominican Republic

ISBN 978-1-59448-750-7; 1-59448-750-2

LC 2009-41036

"In 1956, Ozzie (Osvaldo) Virgil played his first rookie season with the New York Giants, becoming the first Dominican baseball player to enter the major leagues in America. Over the next half a century, 471 Dominicans played in at least one major league game, and one in six of those players have come from the small sugar mill town of San Pedro de Macorís. . . . Kurlansky weaves a chronicle of the history of San Pedro de Macorís with the stories of young men seeking only to play baseball and escape the drudgery of working the sugarcane fields to produce a colorful social history of sport." Publ Wkly

Includes bibliographical references

Leavy, Jane

Sandy Koufax; a lefty's legacy. HarperCollins Pubs. 2002 xxii, 282p $23.95; pa $13.95 **796.357**

1. Baseball players 2. Baseball players -- United States -- Biography

ISBN 0-06-019533-9; 0-06-093329-1 pa

LC 2002-68722

The author "delivers an honest and exquisitely detailed examination of a complex man." Publ Wkly

Leifer, Neil

Neil Leifer: Ballet in the dirt; the golden age of baseball. edited by Eric Kroll; introduction by Ron Shelton; captions by Gabriel Schechter. Taschen 2008 293p il $39.99   **796.357**

1. Baseball -- Pictorial works

ISBN 978-3-8228-4550-9; 3-8228-4550-7

"As a photographer for Sports Illustrated in the 1960s and 1970s, Neil Leifer captured many of baseball's defining moments. But it's the routine, workaday shots he took— Mickey Mantle beating a throw to first, Johnny Bench making a play at the plate or Casey Stengel scolding Yogi Berra during a pitching change—that make this collection fascinating. Here, in gorgeous black and white and Kodachrome color, is the game as it looked before the free-agency craze, before Moneyball, when every player pulled his socks to his knees and performance enhancement meant a big wad to chew." ForbesLife

Includes bibliographical references

Lewis, Michael

★ **Moneyball**; the art of winning an unfair game. Norton 2003 288p $23.95; pa $13.95 **796.357**

1. Baseball 2. Baseball executives

ISBN 0-393-05765-8; 0-393-32481-8 pa

LC 2003-5089

"With so many baseball books to choose from, it is difficult to single out a few as must-haves, but this one comes pretty close." Booklist

Light, Jonathan Fraser

★ The **cultural** encyclopedia of baseball; 2nd ed.; McFarland & Co. 2005 1105p il $75 **796.357**

1. Baseball -- Encyclopedias 2. Reference books

ISBN 0-7864-2087-1

LC 2005-1718

This encyclopedia "profiles every Hall of Fame player, as well as every National and American League club (and predecessors). . . . Statistics play a large role in this resource, which includes facts and figures on just about every conceivable event in the game. Cultural references to baseball are noted throughout in numerous quotations. Some of the more fascinating sections include 'Nicknames,' 'Presidents,' and 'Salaries.' Other entries that make for offbeat perusal include 'Freak Accidents,' 'Sex,' and 'Injuries and Illnesses.'" Choice

Includes bibliographical references

Madden, Bill

Pride of October; what it was to be young and a Yankee. Warner Books 2003 453p il $24.95; pa $14.95   **796.357**

1. Baseball

ISBN 0-446-52932-X; 0-446-69269-7 pa

LC 2002-191063

Madden "has pieced together a loving appreciation of what it means to wear pinstripes. Some of the better profiles are those of lesser lights, like the backup catcher Charlie Silvera and the pitchers Marius Russo and Tommy Byrne." N Y Times Book Rev

Murphy, Cait

★ **Crazy** '08; how a cast of cranks, rogues, boneheads, and magnates created the greatest year in baseball history. Smithsonian/Collins 2007 368p il $24.95   **796.357**

1. Baseball 2. Baseball -- United States -- History -- 20th century

ISBN 978-0-06-088937-1; 0-06-088937-3

LC 2006-50646

This is an account of the 1908 major league baseball season.

"A book that will long claim the attention of serious sports enthusiasts." Booklist

Includes bibliographical references

Pearlman, Jeff

The **bad** guys won; a season of brawling, boozing, bimbo-chasing, and championship baseball with Straw, Doc, Mookie, Nails, the Kid, and the rest of the 1986 Mets, the rowdiest team to put on a New York uniform, and mayb. HarperCollins 2004 287p il $24.95; pa $13.95   **796.357**

1. Baseball

ISBN 0-06-050732-2; 0-06-050733-0 pa

LC 2003-56991

"Baseball aficionados, especially Mets fans, will enjoy this affectionate but critical look at this exciting season." Publ Wkly

Posnanski, Joe

The **soul** of baseball; a road trip through Buck O'Neil's America. Morrow 2007 276p $24.95   **796.357**

1. Baseball 2. Baseball coaches 3. Baseball managers 4. Baseball players

ISBN 978-0-06-085403-4; 0-06-085403-0

An account of how the author "spent a year on the road with the iconic Negro Leagues player and manager Buck O'Neil (1911-2006), recording the magnanimous 94-year-old's encounters with scores of fans and his vast repertoire of entertaining stories." Publ Wkly

Prager, Joshua

★ The **echoing** green; the untold story of Bobby Thomson, Ralph Branca, and the shot heard round the world. Pantheon Books 2006 498p il $26.95   **796.357**

1. Baseball 2. Baseball players

ISBN 0-375-42154-8; 978-0-375-42154-9

LC 2006-43157

The author exposes "multiple layers of fascinating backstory to the drama within a drama, and his psychobiographies of Thomson and especially Branca are unfailingly compelling." Booklist

Includes bibliographical references

Ripken, Cal

Play baseball the Ripken way; the complete illustrated guide to the fundamentals. [by] Cal Ripken, Jr. and Bill Ripken with Larry Burke. Random House 2004 236p il hardcover o.p. pa $15.95   **796.357**

1. Baseball

ISBN 1-4000-6122-9; 0-8129-7050-0 pa

LC 2003-66725

"This book is the next best thing to a personal lesson with the man who broke Lou Gehrig's record of playing in 2,632 consecutive games; it's a comprehensive look at all aspects of how to play baseball that will benefit young players and adult weekend warriors." Publ Wkly

Robinson, Ray

Yankee Stadium; 75 years of drama, glamor, and glory. by Ray Robinson and Christopher Jennison. Penguin Studio 1998 182p il pa $19.95   **796.357**

1. Sports -- New York (State) -- New York -- History

ISBN 0-670-87093-5; 978-0-670-03301-0 pa; 0-670-03301-0 pa

LC 97-48496

"This book is about all the great sporting events—including great boxing matches such as Joe Louis's 1938 demolition of Max Schmeling—and some nonsporting events (such as papal visits and religious revivals) that have occurred at Yankee Stadium over its three-quarters of a century. Baseball does predominate, however, in this tale of 'The House That Ruth Built.' . . . Reminiscences by journal-

ist Pete Hamill, broadcaster Bob Costas, and a few Yankee greats add an extra dimension." Libr J

Ruck, Rob

Raceball; how the Major Leagues colonized the Black and Latin game. Beacon Press 2010 273p il $25.95 **796.357**

1. African American athletes 2. Baseball 3. Hispanic American athletes 4. Race relations

ISBN 978-0-8070-4805-4; 0-8070-4805-4

LC 2010-37079

The book "blends the intertwined histories of African American and Latin baseball, and their usually ill-fated interactions with Major League Baseball (MLB). . . . [It] recasts conventional notions of baseball history by showing how, in the decades before World War I, Havana became the hub of an international baseball culture. . . . Players in the Negro leagues banned from the major leagues commonly played winter ball in the Caribbean . . . until the early 1940s, along with many white big leaguers supplementing their incomes during the off-season. Cuban teams . . . beat the white major leaguers so frequently that MLB banned teams from playing under their own names, to avoid embarrassment." (Journal of American History)

The author "delves deeply into baseball history to explore the inextricable link between the two phenomena, starting with the struggles of black and Latin players in the segregated pre–Jackie Robinson era, continuing through the painful but inspirational period of integration and into the apex of African-American participation in the 1970s (when more than a quarter of players were black), before exploring the current state of a game dominated by Latin Americans. . . . Compellingly weaves together disparate threads of racial and sporting history." Kirkus

Includes bibliographical references

Shapiro, Michael

Bottom of the ninth; Branch Rickey, Casey Stengel, and the daring scheme to save baseball from itself. Times Books 2009 303p il $26   **796.357**

1. Baseball 2. Baseball -- History 3. Baseball -- United States -- History -- 20th century 4. Baseball executives 5. Baseball managers 6. Baseball players

ISBN 978-0-8050-8247-0; 0-8050-8247-6

LC 2008-43582

Shapiro "tells a story of backroom ambitions ultimately defeated by the front offices of the MLB. After the 1958 series, William Shea, Branch Rickey, and Casey Stengel announced their plan to build a third major league, the Continental League; it was fated never to field a team. Shapiro ties the arc of his story to the decline of baseball as America's favorite sport. As much a business history as a baseball story; recommended on both counts." Libr J

bibliography: p. 283-288

The **last** good season; Brooklyn, the Dodgers, and their final pennant race together. Doubleday 2003 356p il $24.95; pa $14.95   **796.357**

1. Baseball 2. Baseball -- New York (N.Y.) -- History

ISBN 0-385-50152-8; 0-767-90688-8 pa

LC 2002-71410

"Equal parts sports, history, politics and sociology, Shapiro's book is reminiscent of the works of Caro, Halbers-

tam and Kahn, and belongs in every sports fan's library."
Publ Wkly

Includes bibliographical references (p.   ) and index

Smith, Red

★ **Red** Smith on baseball; the game's greatest writer on the game's greatest years. with a foreword by Ira Berkow. Dee, I.R. 2000 363p il $24.95; pa $18.95   **796.357**

1. Baseball 2. Baseball -- United States -- History
ISBN 1-56663-289-7; 1-56663-415-6 pa

LC 99-53675

This volume contains columns written from the 1940s to the early 1980s. "Smith's essays on Bobby Thomson's 'shot heard 'round the world,' Mickey Mantle's first game and Don Larsen's no-hit pitching in the 1956 World Series are all worthy of memorization, and his trenchant views on the reserve clause and the night World Series games are strikes down the middle. As a bonus, the collection offers readers a fascinating look at how baseball writing has changed over the years, as have American attitudes." Publ Wkly

Snyder, Brad

Beyond the shadow of the Senators; the untold story of the Homestead Grays and the integration of baseball. Contemporary Books 2003 418p il $24.95; pa $14.95   **796.357**

1. African American baseball players -- History 2. African American baseball players -- Washington (D.C.) -- History -- 20th century 3. Baseball 4. Baseball -- History 5. Baseball -- Washington (D.C.) -- History -- 20th century 6. Discrimination in sports
ISBN 0-07-140820-7; 0-07-143197-7 pa

LC 2002-31335

The author "gives a rich panorama of Washington as it evolved from a Southern provincial town to a large city with a black majority. . . . Snyder's book is not just the history of a team but the tale of one city in all its social complexity." N Y Times Book Rev

Includes bibliographical references

Stout, Glenn

Fenway 1912; the birth of a ballpark, a championship season, and Fenway's remarkable first year. Houghton Mifflin Harcourt 2011 xxii, 392p il $26   **796.357**

ISBN 978-0-547-19562-9

LC 2011016068

"While some sports histories are bone-dry and distant, Stout imbues his account with a unique vibrancy and a razor-sharp intelligence. A wonderful sports book." Booklist

Stump, Al

Cobb; a biography. with a foreword by Jimmie Reese. Algonquin Bks. 1994 436p il hardcover o.p. pa $15.95 **796.357**

1. Baseball players 2. Biography, Individual
ISBN 1-56512-144-9 pa

LC 94-26122

The author, who collaborated with Cobb on his 1961 autobiography (My life in baseball), here presents his own version of the life and times of the baseball player.

"Emphasizing Cobb's bitter final days, Stump's portrait of the splenetic Hall of Famer is both chilling and oddly moving." Am Libr

Includes bibliographical references

Thompson, Teri

★ **American** icon; the fall of Roger Clemens and the rise of steroids in America's pastime. [by] Teri Thompson, Nathaniel Vinton, Michael O'Keeffe, and Christian Red. Alfred A. Knopf 2009 454p $26.95   **796.357**

1. Athletes -- Drug use 2. Baseball 3. Baseball -- Corrupt practices 4. Baseball players 5. Baseball players -- Drug use -- United States 6. Steroids
ISBN 0-307-27180-3; 978-0-307-27180-8

Four sports reporters, who constitute The New York Daily News Sports Investigative Team, examine corruption and the steroids era in American baseball. They discuss the accusations of performance-enhancing drug use that led to the investigation of Yankees' baseball player Roger Clemens by the Justice Department in 2007.

This book "does a nimble job of conjuring up the gym-rat culture in Texas that promoted the use of performance enhancement and anti-aging drugs, and the must-win culture in Major League Baseball that made such drugs appealing to certain players. . . . By focusing on Clemens and the people around him, the authors have turned the sprawling story of steroid-use into a sleek narrative that reads like an investigative thriller, peopled by a Dickensian cast of characters." N Y Times (Late N Y Ed)

Includes bibliographic references

Thorn, John

Baseball in the Garden of Eden; the secret history of the early game. Simon & Schuster 2011 365p il $26; ebook $12.99   **796.357**

1. Baseball 2. Baseball -- United States -- History
ISBN 978-0-7432-9403-4; 0-7432-9403-3; 978-1-4391-7021-2 ebook

LC 2010045155

"Thorn writes with authority, precision and humor." Minneapolis Star Tribune

Includes bibliographical references

Tofel, Richard J.

A **legend** in the making; the New York Yankees in 1939. Dee, I.R. 2002 269p $24.95   **796.357**

1. Baseball
ISBN 1-56663-411-3

LC 2001-40824

This is the "story of the Yankees' 1939 winning season. . . . The casual racism against Italians and the utter dismissal of black baseball are not ignored, and Tofel grounds the year in events outside of baseball: the Wizard of Oz opens, Freud dies, Germany invades Poland. A fine gift for fans." Booklist

Includes bibliographical references

Turbow, Jason

The **baseball** codes; beanballs, sign stealing, and bench-clearing brawls: the unwritten rules of America's pastime. [by] Jason Turbow, with Michael Duca. Pantheon Books 2010 294p $25   **796.357**

1. Baseball 2. Baseball -- Rules

ISBN 978-0-375-42469-4; 0-375-42469-5

LC 2009-22253

"The premise [of this book] is that ballplayers, managers, coaches and various other participants in the culture of baseball are all clued in to a value system, a mode of behavior that defines a gauzy ideal: the right way to play the game. . . . [The authors] have collected dozens of stories from baseball history about situations that are not governed by the rule book but that pertain to the fuzzy notions of rightness and respect and that describe the contours of the so-called baseball codes. . . . The stories the authors have unearthed to illustrate ballpark justice and morality are often delicious." N Y Times Book Rev

Includes bibliographical references

Tygiel, Jules

Baseball's great experiment; Jackie Robinson and his legacy. [with a new afterword] 25th anniversary ed, expanded ed; Oxford University Press 2008 415p il pa $19.95   **796.357**

1. Army officers 2. Baseball 3. Baseball players

ISBN 978-0-19-533928-4; 0-19-533928-2

LC 2008-273059

A history of the segregation and gradual integration of Afro-American athletes into major league baseball. In addition to Jackie Robinson, the author explores the careers of Larry Doby, Luke Easter, Satchel Paige, and others. Tygiel also notes the vast social and demographic changes wrought by WWII that made integration inevitable.

Vecsey, George

Baseball: a history of America's favorite game. Modern Library 2006 252p il $21.95   **796.357**

1. Baseball

ISBN 0-679-64338-9; 978-0-679-64338-8

LC 2006-45033

This history of baseball "unfolds much like a highlights tape, with a breezy background narrative of the game from its pre-Civil War roots to its current drug scandals, structured around set pieces spotlighting the outsized deeds of luminaries like Babe Ruth, Jackie Robinson, Branch Rickey and George Steinbrenner. . . . Vivid, affectionate and clear-eyed, Vecsey's account makes for an engaging sports history." Publ Wkly

Includes bibliographical references

Ward, Geoffrey C.

Baseball: an illustrated history; narrative by Geoffrey C. Ward; based on a documentary filmscript by Geoffrey C. Ward and Ken Burns; preface by Ken Burns and Lynn Novick; with an introduction by Roger Angell; contributions by John Thorn {et al.} Knopf 1994 xxv, 486p il $65; pa $39.95 **796.357**

1. Baseball 2. Baseball -- History

ISBN 0-679-40459-7; 0-679-76541-7 pa

LC 93-39809

"This lavishly produced, gorgeously illustrated history of the game rises far above the often dreary 'companion volume' genre." Booklist

Weber, Bruce

As they see 'em; travels in the land of umpires. Scribner 2009 341p $26   **796.357**

1. Authors 2. Baseball 3. Baseball umpires 4. Editors 5. Sportswriters

ISBN 978-0-7432-9411-9; 0-7432-9411-4

LC 2008-41641

"As a 52-year-old student umpire, the author dons the mask and learns the fundamentals, while spending almost three years visiting baseball venues across the country, as well as interviewing former umpires, players and coaches. . . . Baseball fans will love the insightful, richly textured account of Weber trying to master the plate stance, monitoring each pitch and maintaining a proper strike zone in a physically demanding occupation." Publ Wkly

Includes bibliographical references

Weintraub, Robert

The **house** that Ruth built; a new stadium, the first Yankees championship, and the redemption of 1923. Little, Brown and Co. 2011 421p il $26.99; ebook $12.99   **796.357**

1. Baseball 2. Baseball players

ISBN 978-0-316-08607-3; 978-0-316-17517-3 ebook

LC 2010-48633

The author "examines the 1923 New York Yankees, the team that opened Yankee Stadium and won the first of the Bronx Bombers' record 27 World Series titles. The center of this work is the clash between the Yankees' star, Babe Ruth, with his new 'bashing' style of playing the game, and the classic 'scientific baseball' epitomized by manager John McGraw and his New York Giants." Publ Wkly

Includes bibliographical references

Wendel, Tim

High heat; the secret history of the fastball and the improbable search for the fastest pitcher of all time. Da Capo Press 2010 268p il $25   **796.357**

1. Baseball 2. Baseball -- History 3. Pitchers (Baseball) 4. Pitching (Baseball)

ISBN 978-0-306-81848-6; 0-306-81848-5

LC 2009-53843

"A book like this, so breezy, so informative, so vivid, could only have been written by a true fan of the game. . . . Wendel ends his book by identifying, based on his research, the 12 fastest pitchers in baseball. It's a hard list to argue with. But that doesn't mean some won't. Let the fun continue." PopMatters

Includes bibliographical references

Whitaker, Lang

In the time of Bobby Cox; the Atlanta Braves, their manager, my couch, two decades, and me. Scribner 2011 230p $24   **796.357**

1. Baseball 2. Baseball managers 3. Baseball players

ISBN 978-1-4391-4838-9; 1-4391-4838-4

LC 2010-36177

"In his second incarnation as Atlanta Braves manager, from 1990 through 2010, Bobby Cox, now retired, was so predictably successful—14 straight division titles, 14 seasons of 90 wins or more—as to operate almost under the radar of many baseball fans. Whitaker,. . . pays tribute to

Cox and the teams he managed. There's some analysis here—Whitaker's take on future Hall of Fame pitcher Greg Maddux is especially keen—but readers will more likely appreciate the author's undying connection to his team, which includes an apparently complete, annotated list of every player on the Braves during Cox's second tenure and, more important, the life lessons Whitaker drew from Bobby Cox, among them patience, adaptability, resilience, and a dedication to improving the performance of those he managed. Essential reading for Braves' devotees and a fascinating baseball story for fans of all kinds." Booklist

Williams, Ted

Ted Williams; my life in pictures. {by} Ted Williams with David Pietrusza. Total Sports 2001 201p il $45   **796.357**
   1. Baseball managers 2. Baseball players 3. Baseball players -- United States -- Biography -- Pictorial works
ISBN 1-930844-07-7

LC 2001-23360

Featuring over 300 photographs, this pictorial autobiography recounts Williams's life on and off the field, "many from his personal collection and never before published." Publisher's note

★ Baseball register 2007. Sporting News 712p pa $22.95   **796.357**
   1. Baseball -- Statistics 2. Reference books
ISBN 978-0-89204-866-3; 0-89204-866-2

This book gives information, mostly in tabular form, about active players, managers, coaches and recently retired players in major league baseball. Included are place and date of birth; nicknames; whether right or left-handed; height and weight; hobbies; colleges attended; records and awards; yearly statistics for batting, fielding and pitching in the major and minor leagues and major league career totals; and team records of managers. Includes statistics for play in World Series and All-Star games.

796.4   Weight lifting, track and field, gymnastics

Hoffer, Richard

Something in the air; American passion and defiance in the 1968 Mexico City Olympics. Free Press 2009 258p il $26   **796.4**
   1. Olympic Games (19th: 1968: Mexico City, Mexico) 2. Olympic athletes 3. Olympic games, 1968 (Mexico City, Mex.) 4. Runners (Athletes) 5. Track coaches
ISBN 978-1-4165-8894-8; 1-4165-8894-9

LC 2009-09045

"On Oct. 16, [Tommie] Smith won the gold and [John] Carlos the bronze in the 200-meter race. There they stood on the podium, heads hanging almost humbly and gloved fists raised in a defiant black power salute. Something in the Air, Richard Hoffer's skillfully told tale of the Mexico City Olympics, revolves around this arresting image. . . . There were many other dramas played out in Mexico City—involving George Foreman, the long jumper Bob Beamon and the high jumper Dick Fosbury, among others—and Hoffer gracefully brings them all into the same arena. More important, his jaunty but disciplined prose puts the wind at the

reader's back and shows us how the leaps, lifts and dashes of 1968 made a significant impact on the civil rights movement and raised the political consciousness of athletes." N Y Times Book Rev

Includes bibliographical references

796.42   Track and field

Higdon, Hal

Marathon: the ultimate training guide; 3rd ed; Rodale 2005 369p pa $17.95   **796.42**
   1. Marathon running
ISBN 978-1-59486-199-4; 1-59486-199-4

LC 2005-14083

This "manual includes training schedules designed for busy runners, nutritional information, motivational tips, and race-day guidance to help runners of all experience levels reach the 26.2-mile mark with speed, safety, and great satisfaction." Publisher's note

Joyner-Kersee, Jackie

A kind of grace; the autobiography of the world's greatest female athlete. {by} Jackie Joyner-Kersee with Sonja Steptoe. Warner Bks. 1997 310p il $28   **796.42**
   1. African American athletes 2. Basketball players 3. Child benefactors 4. Heptathletes 5. Olympic athletes
ISBN 0-446-52248-1

LC 97-14966

"A competent account of an admirable life." Booklist

McDougall, Christopher

Born to run; a hidden tribe, superathletes, and the greatest race the world has never seen. Alfred A. Knopf 2009 287p $24.95   **796.42**
   1. Marathon running 2. Tarahumara Indians
ISBN 978-0-307-26630-9; 0-307-26630-3

LC 2009-922861

"Implausibly difficult marathons, hundreds of miles long, and the ultra-elite competitive runners who tackle them for fun. A hidden, almost mythical, tribe in Mexico untouched by modern disease. Shoe manufacturers driven by corporate greed to sustain an industry that has created modern running injuries. An anthropological study of homo sapiens physiology and the course we took to survive while Neanderthals died out. It may seem farfetched, but Born to Run entwines all those strands and even pop-culture references into an engaging and inspirational read." PopMatters

Robbins, Liz

A race like no other; 26.2 miles through the streets of New York. Harper 2008 336p il map $24.99   **796.42**
   1. Marathon running 2. New York City Marathon, New York, N.Y. 3. Runners (Sports) -- Biography
ISBN 978-0-06-137313-8; 0-06-137313-3

LC 2009-275043

A narrative account of the 2007 New York City marathon interweaves the stories of professional and amateur participants, from Great Britain's world-record holder Paula

Radcliffe and Latvian two-time winner Jelena Prokopcuka to South African former champion Hendrick Ramaala and a young cancer survivor running his first race.

The author "allows readers to experience the event without ever putting on a pair of running shoes." Publ Wkly

Includes bibliographical references

Scott, Dagny

Runner's world complete book of women's running; the best advice to get started, stay motivated, lose weight, run injury-free, be safe, and train for any distance. [by] Dagny Scott Barrios. Rev. and updated ed.; Distributed to the trade by Holtzbrinck Publishers 2007 324p il pa $16.95   **796.42**

1. Running

ISBN 978-1-59486-758-3; 1-59486-758-5

LC 2007-30645

Topics covered include racing, nutrition, running during pregnancy, weight loss, and proper clothing.

Runner's world complete book of running; everything you need to run for weight loss, fitness, and competition. edited by Amby Burfoot. Rev. & updated ed.; Rodale; Distributed by Macmillan 2009 312p il $29.95; pa $21.99   **796.42**

1. Running

ISBN 978-1-60529-545-9; 978-1-60529-579-4 pa

LC 2009-33150

Topics covered include: nutrition, injury prevention and treatment, shoe selection, mental readiness, and marathon preparation.

796.48 Olympic games

Guttmann, Allen

The **Olympics,** a history of the modern games; 2nd ed; University of Ill. Press 2002 214p il hardcover o.p. pa $16.95   **796.48**

1. Olympic games 2. Olympics -- History

ISBN 0-252-02725-6; 0-252-07046-1 pa

LC 2001-41383

"Guttmann discusses the intended and actual meaning of the modern Olympic Games, from 1896 to 2000. Recounting the memorable and significant athletic events of the Olympics in terms of their social and political impact, Guttmann . . . [attempts to demonstrate] that the modern games were revived to propagate a political message and continue to serve political purposes." Publisher's note

Includes bibliographical references

Spivey, Nigel Jonathan

★ The **ancient** Olympics; [by] Nigel Spivey. Oxford University Press 2004 xxi, 273p il $28; pa $14.95   **796.48**

1. Olympic games

ISBN 0-19-280433-2; 0-19-280604-1 pa

LC 2004-46147

This book "lets us imagine both the strangeness and the glory that surrounded sports in its infancy." Christ Sci Monit

Includes bibliographical references

796.51   Walking

Hart, John

★ **Walking** softly in the wilderness; the Sierra Club guide to backpacking. 4th ed, complete rev and updated; Sierra Club Books 2005 508p il map pa $16.95   **796.51**

1. Backpacking 2. Wilderness areas

ISBN 1-57805-123-1

LC 2004-56554

This guide for both the novice and experienced hiker reflects the environmental concerns of the Sierra Club. Among topics covered are: clothing and equipment; making and breaking camp; problem animals and plants; hiking and camping with kids. Listings of conservation and wilderness travel organizations, map and equipment sources, land management agencies, and Internet contacts are appended.

Kemsley, William

Backpacker and hiker's handbook. Stackpole Books 2008 290p il map pa $24.95   **796.51**

1. Backpacking 2. Hiking

ISBN 978-0-8117-3462-2; 0-8117-3462-5

LC 2007-21147

This book "tells how to plan and prepare for a backpacking trip and discusses equipment, safety, and the essential trail skills of using a compass, purifying water, cooking, and where and how to set up camp." Publisher's note

Includes bibliographical references

Nicholson, Geoff

The **lost** art of walking; the history, science, philosophy, and literature of pedestrianism. Riverhead Books 2008 276p $24.95   **796.51**

1. Authors 2. Novelists 3. Voyages and travels 4. Walking

ISBN 978-1-59448-998-3; 1-59448-998-X

LC 2008-25182

"Nicholson catalogues every aspect of walking: its origins, its use as a cure for various ills, expert walkers, eccentric walkers, walking songs, spiritual walking, walking on water, walking in prison, and the analysis of perfect and imperfect walks. . . . The book is varied, wide-ranging, and full of a dry and delightful wit. I found myself giggling every few pages. Nicholson's affection for his subjects and his gusto for walking are palpable." Christ Sci Monit

Includes bibliographical references

Solnit, Rebecca

Wanderlust; a history of walking. Viking 2000 326p il hardcover o.p. pa $15 **796.51**

1. Hiking 2. Hiking -- History 3. Voyages and travels 4. Walking 5. Walking -- History

ISBN 0-14-028601-2 pa

LC 99-41153

The author presents a "look at how the act of walking . . . has influenced our history, our science, our literature, and the very way that we see ourselves as human beings. Drawing on a multitude of diverse disciplines, Solnit illustrates that walking has led to some of the best, and worst, incidents in all of history." Booklist

Includes bibliographical references

Tilton, Buck

Hiking & backpacking; a complete illustrated guide. photographs by Stephen Gorman. Knack 2009 244p il map pa $19.95 **796.51**

    1. Backpacking 2. Hiking

    ISBN 978-1-59921-400-9

                   LC 2008-41371

"Colorful, with a graphically driven and accessible approach that covers the full array of topics from gear to where, when, and how to hike and camp. For varying skill levels." Libr J

Includes bibliographical references

796.52 Walking and exploring by kind of terrain

Hurd, Barbara

    ★ **Entering** the stone; on caves and feeling through the dark. Athens 2008 170p pa $16.95 **796.52**

    1. Caves

    ISBN 978-0-8203-3153-9; 0-8203-3153-8

                   LC 2007-44844

The author "uses the sport of caving Maryland's Devil's Hole cave and Oregon's Siskiyous Mountains . . . as the launching point for observations about the ways we 'use landscape and the people in our lives to orient ourselves.' Hurd often weaves resonant parallels between what she sees in the nature of caves and her own life, such as her moving recollections of her father and of a friend dying of cancer." Publ Wkly

Tabor, James M.

    Blind descent; the quest to discover the deepest place on earth. Random House 2010 304p $26; ebook $26 **796.52**

    1. Caves 2. Explorers 3. Spelunkers 4. Structural engineers

    ISBN 978-1-4000-6767-1; 978-1-58836-994-9 ebook

                   LC 2009-33942

"The author examines the two polar opposites at the head of each of two major cave-diving expeditions: the win-at-all-costs, classic alpha-male, American Bill Stone, who led Mexican cave dives in Cheve and Huatula; and mild-mannered organization man, Ukrainian Alexander Klimchouk, who spearheaded the exploration of his country's notorious Krubera cave. Only one of these men came away with the distinction of having descended deeper into the earth's core than anyone else. Tabor expertly fashions a fly-on-the-wall narrative from the firsthand accounts of Stone, Klimchouk and their supporting casts of death-defying followers. . . . A fascinating and informative introduction to the sport of cave diving, as well as a dramatic portrayal of a significant man-vs.-nature conflict." Kirkus

Includes bibliographical references

Taylor, Joseph E.

    Pilgrims of the vertical; Yosemite rock climbers and nature at risk. [by] Joseph E Taylor III. Harvard University Press 2010 368p il map $29.95 **796.52**

    1. Mountaineering

    ISBN 978-0-674-05287-1; 0-674-05287-0

                   LC 2010-21578

Yosemite "has been a climber magnet for decades, and it was here that many of rock climbing's highly ritualized set of norms and mores evolved. . . . [This book] is at once a chronicle of how the sport evolved in Yosemite and a fascinating social history that considers climbing in the larger context of American life. . . . For the general reader, the book makes a fine introduction to the history of climbing and Yosemite's special place in its development. For climbers, 'Pilgrims of the Vertical' offers a somewhat idiosyncratic view of their sport." Wall Street J

Includes bibliographical references

796.522 Mountains, hills, rocks

Blum, Arlene

    Breaking trail; a climbing life. Scribner 2005 313p il map $27.50 **796.522**

    1. Biochemists 2. Biography, Individual 3. Mountaineering 4. Mountaineers

    ISBN 0-7432-5846-0

                   LC 2005-44053

"In hiker's parlance, the person who 'breaks trail' is one who leads others across difficult terrain, creating a path as they go. This aptly describes Blum's role, not only in her experiences as a climber, but also as a scientist doing innovative, groundbreaking work. Blum . . . covers a cross section of her life as a climber, from her first experience, as a college student in 1964, to 1993, when she semiretired. Through climbing, she experiences a wide range of emotions, from exhilaration at success to grief over the death of friends. Interspersed between the climbing stories are scenes from her childhood that do much to explain the person she became. This is an engaging, well-written adventure that also serves as a social history of women's roles." Booklist

Boukreev, Anatoli

    The **climb**; tragic ambitions on Everest. [by] Anatoli Boukreev and G. Weston Dewalt. St. Martin's Press 1997 255p il hardcover o.p. pa $14.95 **796.522**

    1. Mountaineering 2. Mountaineering accidents -- Everest, Mount (China and Nepal) 3. Mountaineering expeditions -- Everest, Mount (China and Nepal)

    ISBN 0-312-20637-2 pa

                   LC 97-23194

"This is a first-person account of the tragic climbing experience in May 1996 on Mount Everest that left eight hikers dead and several others struggling to stay alive. . . . Fast-paced and easy to read, Boukreev's story of adventure and survival will remain in the reader's memory long after the book is finished." Libr J

Coburn, Broughton

    Everest: mountain without mercy; introduction by Tim Cahill, afterword by David Breashears. Na-

tional Geographic Soc. 1997 256p il maps hardcover o.p. pa $24   **796.522**
   1. Mountaineering
   ISBN 0-7922-7014-2; 0-7922-6984-5 pa
                 LC 97-10765

"Bringing an understated yet powerful Buddhist/Sherpa ethical perspective to the tragedy on Everest chronicled in Jon Krakauer's Into Thin Air, Coburn reports on the IMAX film crew who participated in the rescue effort when the May 1996 expeditions led by guides Rob Hall and Scott Fischer ended in death and crippling injury." Publ Wkly

Jamling Tenzing Norgay
   Touching my father's soul; a Sherpa's journey to the top of Everest. [by] Jamling Tenzing Norgay with Broughton Coburn. HarperSanFrancisco 2001 316p il map hardcover o.p. pa $15.95   **796.522**
   1. Mountaineering 2. Mountaineers
   ISBN 0-06-251688-4 pa
                 LC 00-68723

This "work has considerably more depth than an exposition of the climb. . . . The son's climb is a pilgrimage exploring his relationship to his father, his Sherpa culture, and Buddhism. It is also a fascinating look into the world of climbers and their relationship to the Sherpas who risk their lives to assist them." Booklist

Krakauer, Jon
   ★ **Into** thin air; a personal account of the Mount Everest disaster. Villard Bks. 1997 xx, 293p il $25.95; pa $14.95   **796.522**
   1. Mountaineering 2. Mountaineering -- Personal narratives
   ISBN 0-679-45752-6; 0-385-49478-5 pa
                 LC 96-30031

This is an account of the author's May 1996 Mount Everest climbing expedition in which twelve fellow climbers died during a snow storm.
   "This tense, harrowing story is as mesmerizing and hard to put down as any well-written adventure novel." SLJ
   Includes bibliographical references

Trailside (Television program)
   Rock climbing; a trailside guide. illustrations by Ron Hildebrand. Norton 2003 191p il pa $18.95   **796.522**
   1. Mountaineering
   ISBN 0-393-31653-X
                 LC 96-52821

"Designed to be carried on the trail, this will ease beginners into the sport of rock climbing, with step-by-step illustrated tutorials, safety and first-aid tips, and more." Libr J
   Includes bibliographical references

796.54   Camping

Callan, Kevin
   ★ The **happy** camper; an essential guide to life outdoors. Boston Mills Press; distributed by Firefly Books 2005 320p il pa $19.95   **796.54**
   1. Camping
   ISBN 1-55046-450-7; 978-1-55046-450-4
                 LC 2005-415489

"A great all-around guide by a top camping expert for campers of any skill level. [It includes] lots of color photos and accessible tips (how to pick a camping spot, stake a tent, build a fire, etc.)." Libr J
   Includes bibliographical references

   ★   **Guide** to summer camps and summer schools 2008/2009; an objective, comparative reference source for residential summer programs. 31st ed.; Porter Sargent Pub. 2008 862p il $45; pa $27   **796.54**
   1. Camps -- Directories 2. Reference books
   ISBN 978-0-87558-163-7; 0-87558-163-3; 978-0-87558-164-4 pa; 0-87558-164-1 pa

"This reliable comprehensive source of summer academic and tutorial programs, travel programs, specialized study programs, and recreational camps lists about 1,300 such programs in the U.S. and Canada. An extensive table of contents and an index make it possible to access all of this information." Safford. Guide to Ref Materials For Sch Media Cent. 5th edition

796.6   Cycling and related activities

Armstrong, Lance
   Every second counts; [by] Lance Armstrong, with Sally Jenkins. Broadway Books 2003 272p $24.95; pa $14   **796.6**
   1. Athletes 2. Cyclists 3. Olympic athletes
   ISBN 0-385-50871-9; 0-7679-1448-1 pa
                 LC 2003-55580

"The book is the story of a family man, world-class athlete, and cancer survivor who is determined to get every single drop of enjoyment and excitement out of life. It's a joyous, triumphant book, a celebration of all the things that make life good. It's also, for cyclists, a detailed look at the Tour de France, as seen through the eyes of one of its top competitors. Fascinating and inspiring." Booklist

Byrne, David
   Bicycle diaries. Viking 2009 297p il $25.95   **796.6**
   1. Bicycle touring 2. Cycling -- Environmental aspects 3. Rock musicians 4. Singers 5. Songwriters 6. Urban transportation
   ISBN 978-0-670-02114-7; 0-670-02114-8
                 LC 2009-09390

"In these random musings over many years while cycling through such places as Sydney, Australia; Manila, Philippines; San Francisco; or his home of New York, the former Talking Head, artist and author . . . offers his frank views on urban planning, art and postmodern civilization in general. . . . Candid and self-deprecating, Byrne offers a work that is as engaging as it is cerebral and informative." Publ Wkly

Carmichael, Chris

The **ultimate** ride; get fit, get fast, and start winning with the world's top cycling coach. [by] Chris Carmichael with Jim Rutberg. G.P. Putnam's Sons 2003 325p il hardcover o.p. pa $15   **796.6**
  1. Bicycle racing -- Training 2. Cycling 3. Physical fitness
  ISBN 0-399-15071-4; 0-425-19601-1 pa
                                          LC 2003-43214
"This is an excellent guide to obtaining peak performance in cycling competition, but the wealth of training tips and intelligent discussion of nutrition will be almost as valuable to noncompetitive cyclists and even to other athletes serious about conditioning." Booklist

796.7   Driving motor vehicles

Johnson, Wayne

Live to ride; the rumbling, roaring world of speed, escape, and adventure on two wheels. Atria Books 2010 274p $25; ebook $11.99   **796.7**
  1. Motorcycles
  ISBN 978-1-4165-5032-7; 978-1-4391-7715-0 ebook
                                          LC 2009-43983
Shares the author's experiences of pursuing ultimate speeds, performing in high-risk motocross jumps, and joining outlaw motorcycle clubs.
"Johnson captures the obsessive excitement of motorcycle culture with enough verve to make nonriders understand, and jealous, although he doesn't undersell its dangers. Enjoyable and informative—one of the best books on the topic in years." Kirkus

796.72   Automobile racing

Baime, A. J.

Go like hell; Ford, Ferrari, and their battle for speed and glory at Le Mans. Houghton Mifflin Harcourt 2009 304p il map $26   **796.72**
  1. Automobile racing 2. Sports cars
  ISBN 978-0-618-82219-5; 0-618-82219-4
                                          LC 2008-52948
"Baime tells an exciting story at a pace that manages to keep up with the drivers." Libr J
Includes bibliographical references

Bechtel, Mark

He crashed me so I crashed him back; the true story of the year the King, Jaws, Earnhardt, and the rest of NASCAR's feudin', fightin', good ol' boys put stock car racing on the map. Little, Brown and Co. 2010 308p il $25.99   **796.72**
  1. Automobile racing 2. Stock car racing
  ISBN 978-0-316-03402-9; 0-316-03402-9
                                          LC 2009-31952

The story of how Bobby Allison, Donnie Allison, Cale Yarborough, Richard Petty, Dale Earnhardt, Darrell Waltrip, A.J. Foyt, and Kyle Petty came together in an unforgettable season that featured the first nationally televised NASCAR races.
This is "an illuminating, informative, and entertaining read, as the engaging and droll Bechtel is in complete control from start to finish." Publ Wkly
Includes bibliographical references

Hawley, Samuel Jay

Speed duel; the inside story of the land speed record in the sixties. [by] Sam Hawley. Firefly Books 2010 360p il pa $24.95   **796.72**
  1. Automobile racing 2. Automobile racing drivers
  ISBN 978-1-55407-633-8
"Even readers who don't know a spark plug from a gear shift will be transfixed by Hawley's white-knuckled account of the ever-escalating competition to hold the Land Speed Record in the '60s and early '70s. Drawing from countless articles, profiles, documentaries, and interviews with the men and women who were there, Hawley traces the sport's evolution from its first four-wheeled record of 39mph in 1898, to today's jet-propelled 700mph-plus, recounting the creation, testing, and repair of legendary cars like the humble Green Monster and the charismatic Spirit of America." Publ Wkly
Includes filmography and bibliographical references

Menzer, Joe

The **wildest** ride; a history of NASCAR (or, How a bunch of good ol' boys built a billion-dollar industry out of wrecking cars) Simon & Schuster 2001 311p il hardcover o.p. pa $14   **796.72**
  1. Automobile racing
  ISBN 0-7432-0507-3; 0-7432-2625-9 pa
                                          LC 2001-031088
This history focuses on the "legacy of the founding France family, the evolution of the cars from modified stock cars to purpose-built racers, and the fan-base expansion of the 1980s and 1990s. . . . Highly entertaining and full of facts." Libr J
Includes bibliographical references

Waltrip, Michael

In the blink of an eye; Dale, Daytona, and the day that changed everything. by Michael Waltrip and Ellis Henican. Hyperion 2011 223p il $24.99; pa $14.99   **796.72**
  1. Automobile racing 2. Automobile racing drivers
  ISBN 978-1-4013-2431-5; 978-0-7868-9139-9 pa
An account of the colorful NASCAR driver's career describes his hardscrabble upbringing and strained relationship with brother Darrell, while recounting his historic win at the 2001 Daytona 500 and the death of mentor Dale Earnhardt in the same race.
"This is a genuinely heartfelt memoir that is equal parts autobiography and tribute to Earnhardt. . . . Though sadness and loss are a big part of Waltrip's story, he balances them with humor and joy. A really wonderful read for NASCAR fans." Booklist

Wright, James D.

Fixin' to git; one fan's love affair with NAS-CAR's Winston Cup. [by] Jim Wright. Duke Univ. Press 2002 305p il $26.95; pa $18.95   **796.72**
1. Automobile racing 2. Stock car racing -- United States
ISBN 0-8223-2926-3; 0-8223-3220-5 pa
LC 2002-485

"This is the very best book to surface on auto racing in many years. Informative, entertaining, and eye-opening." Booklist

796.8   Combat sports

Cohen, Richard

By the sword; a history of gladiators, musketeers, samurai, swashbucklers, and Olympic champions. Random House 2002 xxiv, 519p il $29.95; pa $15.95   **796.8**
1. Fencing
ISBN 0-375-50417-6; 0-8129-6966-9 pa
LC 2002-21309

This is a worldwide history of sword fighting from Ancient Egypt to the present which considers its role in combat and sports, word origins and customs, and the fencing skills of politicians and actors.

"A fascinating story told with literary verve and the pride of a longtime practitioner; highly recommended." Libr J
Includes bibliographical references

Hauser, Thomas

Boxing is--reflections on the sweet science. The University of Arkansas Press 2010 270p pa $22.50   **796.8**
1. Boxing
ISBN 978-1-55728-942-1
LC 2010-15354

"The collection begins with a detailed biographical examination of the career of Sugar Ray Robinson, considered by many to be the greatest pound-for-pound fighter ever. It's a sadly familiar tale of poverty, ascendancy, fame, and decline, related in a respectful, objective style. The rest of the book is focused on the boxing events of 2009, from the high-profile career of Manny Pacquiao to the progress of several relatively unknown young fighters learning the trade in New York's gyms. Hauser also explores the business end of boxing, especially its painful relationship with television, but above all, he is drawn to the people of the sport: the fighters, trainers, promoters, and hangers-on. Virtually every piece is notable for its carefully drawn characters who will linger on the edges of readers' minds long after the book has been shelved." Booklist
Includes bibliographical references

Kelly, Jason

Shelby's folly; Jack Dempsey, Doc Kearns, and the shakedown of a Montana boomtown. University of Nebraska Press 2010 214p il $26.95   **796.8**
1. Boxers (Persons) 2. Boxing
ISBN 978-0-8032-2655-5; 0-8032-2655-1
LC 2009-40609

"There was a certain nobility in so vast a failure. The men of Shelby had stood fast as the tidal wave of red ink swept over them. Mr. Kelly writes sympathetically, not mockingly, of Shelby, and he has a proper appreciation for the brazen roguery of Doc Kearns, whose greed and manipulativeness made the fight possible—and doomed Shelby's self-promotional hopes." Wall Street J
Includes bibliographical references

Kreidler, Mark

★ **Four** days to glory; wrestling with the soul of the American heartland. HarperCollins Publishers 2007 262p il hardcover o.p. pa $13.99   **796.8**
1. Biography, Individual 2. School sports 3. Wrestlers 4. Wrestling
ISBN 978-0-06-082318-4; 0-06-082318-6; 978-0-06-082319-1 pa; 0-06-082319-4 pa
LC 2007-272997

Jay Borschel and Dan LeClere aspire to be four-time high school wrestling champions in Iowa.

The author's "deftness in 'Four Days' is in turning a niche sport into one as accessible as baseball or basketball." N Y Times Book Rev

Levi, Heather

The **world** of lucha libre; secrets, revelations, and Mexican national identity. Duke University Press 2008 xxii, 265p il $79.95; pa $22.95   **796.8**
1. Wrestling 2. Wrestling -- Mexico
ISBN 978-0-8223-4214-4; 0-8223-4214-6; 978-0-8223-4232-8 pa; 0-8223-4232-4 pa
LC 2008-23166

"A small but fascinating part of Levi's book is the fieldwork she did while preparing the text. While living in Mexico, Levi trained as a luchadora with a former professional wrestler. . . . The experience of training is not the focus of the work, however, but rather a tool the author used to further illuminate her research." PopMatters
Includes bibliographical references

Margolick, David

★ **Beyond** glory; Joe Louis vs. Max Schmeling, and a world on the brink. Knopf 2005 423p il $26.95   **796.8**
1. Boxers (Persons) 2. Boxing 3. Boxing -- History 4. Soldiers
ISBN 0-375-41192-5
LC 2005-45141

The author discusses the historical significance of the fights between Joe Louis and German boxer Max Schmeling in 1936 and 1938.

This book "will be the definitive account of Louis versus Schmeling. And it's a hell of a good read besides." Booklist
Includes bibliographical references

Park, Yeon Hwan

Black belt tae kwon do; the ultimate reference guide to the world's most popular martial art. by Y.H. Park & Jon Gerrard. Facts on File 2000 272p il hardcover o.p. pa $16.95 **796.8**
 1. Tae kwon do
 ISBN 0-8160-4240-3; 0-8160-4241-1 pa

LC 99-57876

Coverage includes practice, warm-up, and advanced techniques and forms, sparring strategies, self-defense, and breaking. Over 700 photographs accompany the text. Appendixes cover official competition rules, weight classes, governing bodies, and international organizations and associations. Includes two glossaries, English to Korean and Korean to English.

Schulberg, Budd

Sparring with Hemingway and other legends of the fight game. Dee, I.R. 1995 256p $25 **796.8**
 1. Boxing
 ISBN 1-56663-080-0

LC 94-49153

This is a collection of the author's articles about boxing, originally published between 1954 and 1994.

"Included are beautifully crafted portraits of legends such as Benny Leonard, Muhammad Ali, and ageless wonder George Foreman. . . . This literate, entertaining collection represents some of the best writing on any sport." Libr J

At the fights; American writers on boxing. edited by George Kimball & John Schulian; foreword by Colum McCann. Library of America 2011 517p $35 **796.8**
 1. Boxers (Sports) 2. Boxing
 ISBN 1-59853-092-5; 978-1-59853-092-6

This collection includes "work by the likes of Pete Hamill, Norman Mailer, Joyce Carol Oates, George Plimpton, David Remnick, Budd Schulberg and Gay Talese." (N Y Times Book Rev) Index.

"The book's editors accomplish several things in 'At the Fights.' They sample the work of devotees such as the incomparable A.J. Liebling and Gene Tunney on his defeat of Jack Dempsey, and of comparative outsiders such as James Baldwin and Joyce Carol Oates, whose novelistic fascination with violence, class and gender inevitably led her to ponder the boxing life. The collection plots a zigzag course through a century of boxing milestones, offering a striking range of approaches to the subject. It also throws open controversies racial, moral, legal and medical that have swirled around the sport since it first attained a sort of legitimacy. . . . [This anthology] presupposes an interest in writing as much as in boxing. Many of its contributors, such as Baldwin, Vic Ziegel, Pete Hamill, Bill Barich and Katherine Dunn, pay as much or more attention to stories tributary to fights as to the ring contests themselves. Observations in many different registers form an engrossing counterpoint as the book proceeds." San Francisco Chron

796.83 Boxing

Anasi, Robert

★ The **gloves;** a boxing chronicle. North Point Press 2002 331p $24; pa $14 **796.83**
 1. Boxing 2. Boxing -- United States 3. Golden Gloves Tournament
 ISBN 0-86547-599-7; 0-86547-652-7 pa

LC 2001-44111

In this "look at the world of amateur boxing, freelance writer Anasi chronicles how jabbing and jump-roping at a grubby gym in San Francisco's Tenderloin district developed into a life-altering quest to compete, in his early 30s, in New York's storied amateur boxing tournament, the Golden Gloves." Publ Wkly

Kram, Mark

The **ghosts** of Manila; the fateful, brutal blood feud between Muhammad Ali and Joe Frazier. HarperCollins Pubs. 2001 232p hardcover o.p. pa $12.95 **796.83**
 1. Boxers (Persons) 2. Boxers (Sports) -- United States -- Biography 3. Boxing
 ISBN 0-06-095480-9 pa

LC 00-53934

This is "a fascinating blend of history and biography." Booklist

796.9 Ice and snow sports

Bennett, Jeff

The **complete** snowboarder; {by} Jeff Bennett, Scott Downey and Charles Arnell. 2nd ed; Ragged Mountain Press 2000 148p il pa $14.95 **796.9**
 1. Snowboarding
 ISBN 0-07-135787-4

LC 00-39059

This offers advice on getting started in snowboarding, equipment, techniques, snowboarding areas and trails, tricks, competitions, safety, and equipment maintenance.

796.962 Ice hockey

Hockey Hall of Fame

Official guide to the players of the Hockey Hall of Fame; Hockey Hall of Fame; compiled by James Duplacey and Eric Zweig. Firefly Books 2010 544p il pa $19.95 **796.962**
 1. Hockey
 ISBN 978-1-55407-662-8

"Hockey fans throughout North America will enjoy this beautiful and richly illustrated record of the lives and careers of the nearly 400 players, builders, and on-ice officials whose signal contributions to hockey, and not merely the National Hockey League, have led to their enshrinement in the Hall of Fame located in Toronto." Libr J

McKinley, Michael

★ **Hockey**: a people's history. McClelland & Stewart 2006 346p il hardcover o.p. pa $37.50   **796.962**

1. Hockey 2. Hockey -- Canada 3. Hockey -- History 4. Hockey players

ISBN 0-7710-5769-5; 978-0-7710-5769-4; 0-7710-5771-7 pa; 978-0-7710-5771-7 pa

This history "chronicles hockey from its genesis as a winter substitute for lacrosse. A companion to a similarly titled CBC TV series, the lavishly illustrated book combines punchy boxed features celebrating individuals and hockey oddments and a detailed tracing of the game's development. . . . Essential for general sports as well as hockey-intensive collections." Booklist

Includes bibliographical references

United States Olympic Committee

A **basic** guide to ice hockey; the U.S. Olympic Committee. Griffin Pub, Distributed by G. Stevens Pub 2002 152p il lib bdg $23.93   **796.962**

1. Hockey

ISBN 0-8368-3103-9

LC 2001-55096

Provides information on such aspects of ice hockey as the history of Olympic competition, game rules and strategies, relevant nutrition, safety and first aid, and more. Describes Olympic and ice hockey organizations.

796.98   Winter Olympic games

Wallechinsky, David

The **complete** book of the Winter Olympics; [by] David Wallechinsky and Jaime Loucky. 2010 ed.; Aurum 2009 322p il pa $24.95   **796.98**

1. Olympic games

ISBN 978-1-84513-491-4

"While the statistics will delight sports geeks, everyone can savor the readable prose accounts that draw out the athletes' character and high points." SLJ

797.1   Aquatic sports

American Canoe Association

★ **Canoeing**; outdoor adventures. editors, Pamela S. Dillon, Jeremy Oyen. Human Kinetics 2008 253p il pa $22.95 **797.1**

1. Canoes and canoeing

ISBN 978-0-7360-6715-7; 0-7360-6715-9

LC 2008-4392

The authors "discuss fitness basics, food and nutrition needs, and gear and equipment—from the canoe itself to life jackets, paddles, and clothing. They then cover . . . safety and survival guidelines, including weather, river hazards, capsizing, cold-water safety, and rescue protocols. . . [The DVD included contains] an introduction to paddle sports and basic safety and paddling techniques." Publisher's note

Kayaking; editors, Pamela S. Dillon, Jeremy Oyen.

Human Kinetics 2009 237p il pa $22.95 **797.1**

1. Canoes and canoeing

ISBN 978-0-7360-6716-4; 0-7360-6716-7

LC 2008-32111

"Part I of Kayaking explains the background knowledge, fitness fundamentals, equipment and gear selection, nutritional needs, and safety and survival skills for a successful adventure. Part II helps build basic techniques, strokes, and maneuvers. . . . [It includes] tips and instruction for the three most popular types of kayaking: sea, river, and whitewater. This book also includes the Quick-Start Your Kayak DVD to reinforce the paddling strokes and safety information found in the book. It features videos of kayaking maneuvers." Publisher's note

Includes bibliographical references

Fredston, Jill A.

Rowing to latitude; journeys along the Arctic's edge. [by] Jill Fredston. North Point Press 2001 289p il hardcover o.p. pa $15   **797.1**

1. Canoeists -- United States -- Biography 2. Canoes and canoeing 3. Canoes and canoeing -- Alaska 4. Women canoeists -- United States -- Biography

ISBN 0-374-28180-7; 0-86547-655-1 pa

LC 2001-30049

The author and her husband, Doug Fesler "canoe the Arctic and sub-Arctic coastlines of Alaska, Canada, Greenland, Norway and Sweden for three months out of each year. . . . Fredston ably describes both the big picture—the coastline, encounters with polar bears, the high-stakes game of second-guessing storms and tides—and the details of their travels. . . . A must-read for armchair travelers, as well as a close and loving look at an intimate relationship." Publ Wkly

Stewart, Chris

Three ways to capsize a boat; an optimist afloat. Broadway Books 2010 178p pa $12.99; ebook $12.99   **797.1**

1. Boats and boating 2. Sailing

ISBN 978-0-307-59237-8 pa; 978-0-307-59238-5 ebook

LC 2009-44105

"This amusing book chronicles . . . [the author's] sailing adventures in the early 1980s, having just turned 30. Despite his lack of experience, a friend recommended him as captain on a sailboat in the Greek islands. He practiced on a boat out of Littlehampton, England, managing to spend hours without moving and then flipping the vessel. His Greek island cruising was punctuated by regular and spectacular engine fires. The final sail he chronicles is a cold and smelly trip from Brighton to Newfoundland (or Vinland), which he spent wearing adventurer Sir Ranulph Fiennes's moleskin trousers. . . . Stewart's eventual love of sailing translates well to landlubbers, while sailors will be glad to have missed the winter storms and sea ice encountered. A funny, appealing read." Libr J

797.2 Swimming and diving

Graver, Dennis

Scuba diving; [by] Dennis K. Graver. 3rd ed; Human Kinetics 2003 209p il pa $23.95 **797.2**
1. Scuba diving
ISBN 0-7360-4539-2

LC 2002-152325

"This colorful beginner's guide is used by many diving classes, including the YMCA Scuba Diving program. All the basics are covered: why dive, equipment, diving science, and what you might see on a dive." Libr J

Includes bibliographical references

Mullen, P. H.

Gold in the water; the true story of ordinary men and their extraordinary dream of Olympic glory. Thomas Dunne Bks. 2001 326p il hardcover o.p. pa $14.95 **797.2**
1. Olympic games, 2000 (Sydney, Australia) 2. Swimmers -- United States -- Biography 3. Swimming 4. Swimming -- Training -- United States
ISBN 0-312-26595-6; 0-312-31116-8 pa

LC 2001-31955

"Mullen chronicles the U.S. Olympic swimming team on its journey to the 2000 Summer Games in Sydney. The text moves back and forth in time, giving a sense of the athletes as people and showing what motivates someone to structure his or her whole life toward a single goal." Booklist

798.4 Horse racing

Clee, Nicholas

Eclipse; Nicholas Clee. Black Swan 2011 352 p. **798.4**
1. Eclipse (Race horse) 2. Horse racing -- Great Britain -- History -- 18th century
ISBN 0552774421; 9780552774420

LC 2011293231

This book presents an account of one of the most famous racehorses in history. Eclipse (1764-89) was a legend in his time and, astonishingly, became the progenitor of all but three of the 50 most recent Kentucky Derby winners. [Nicholas] Clee . . . chronicles both the life of the horse, who started racing at age five, and the Irish gambler Dennis O'Kelly, who purchased him soon thereafter. The author weaves in many other colorful characters who played a part in the story, including Sir Charles Bunbury (founder of the Jockey Club), the Earl of Derby (from whom classic races take their name), and King George IV. . . . For racing fans, Clee also includes histories of famous races, wagers, bloodlines, and the stories of some of Eclipse's most celebrated offspring. (Libr J)

Drape, Joe

The race for the Triple Crown; horses, high stakes, and eternal hope. Atlantic Monthly Press 2001 261p hardcover o.p. pa $14 **798.4**
1. Horse racing 2. Triple Crown (U.S. horse racing)
ISBN 0-8021-3885-3 pa

LC 2001-16044

In this "look at the highest level of horse racing, the author traces the lives of a handful of preeminent horse owners, trainers and jockeys in their preparations for the Kentucky Derby, the Preakness and the Belmont." Publ Wkly

Eisenberg, John

★ The great match race; when North met South in America's first sports spectacle. Houghton Mifflin Co. 2006 258p il $25 **798.4**
1. Horse racing
ISBN 978-0-618-55612-0; 0-618-55612-5

LC 2005-31540

The author "succeeds in creating a gripping yarn of sporting contest, portrayal of a historical moment and smart analysis of a country headed eventually for civil war." Publ Wkly

Includes bibliographical references

Hillenbrand, Laura

★ Seabiscuit; an American legend. Random House 2001 399p il $25.95; pa $15.95 **798.4**
1. Horse racing 2. Seabiscuit (Race horse)
ISBN 0-375-50291-2; 0-449-00561-5 pa

LC 2001-267852

"This is a remarkable tale well told by a writer who deftly blends history and sport." Economist

Includes bibliographical references

Mitchell, Elizabeth

★ Three strides before the wire; the dark and beautiful world of horse racing. Hyperion 2002 403p $24.95; pa $14.95 **798.4**
1. Horse racing 2. Horse racing -- United States -- Anecdotes 3. Horse racing -- United States -- History 4. Horsemen and horsewomen -- United States -- Biography
ISBN 0-7868-6723-X; 0-7868-8622-6 pa

LC 2002-68817

The author "tells the story of Charismatic, who exploded out of the proletarian ranks of claiming horses to come within a stone's throw of sweeping the Triple Crown in 1999 before suffering a career-ending injury in the Belmont Stakes. . . . Mitchell's book possesses an appeal that extends well beyond its subject." Booklist

Ours, Dorothy

Man o' War; a legend like lightning. St Martin's Press 2006 342p il $24.95 **798.4**
1. Horse racing 2. Man o' War (Race horse)
ISBN 0-312-34099-0; 978-0-312-34099-5

LC 2006-41631

This is an account of the thoroughbred racehorse Man o' War, also known as Big Red.

This book "is clearly a labor of love, and it certifies Big Red's claim to immortality." N Y Times Book Rev

Includes bibliographical references

Smiley, Jane

A year at the races; reflections on horses, humans, love, money, and luck. Knopf 2004 287p $22 **798.4**
1. Authors 2. Horse racing 3. Novelists 4. Race

horses 5. Short story writers
ISBN 1-4000-4058-2

LC 2003-65655

"The very qualities of mind that make Smiley such a compelling novelist—her keen attentiveness to the sensuous world, her deep sensitivity to psychological states, and her fascination with life's entwinement of chance and inevitability—enable her to write about horses, both their interior and exterior selves, with extraordinary avidity, empathy, wonder, and gratitude." Booklist

Includes bibliographical references

Squires, James D.

Horse of a different color; a tale of breeding geniuses, dominant females, and the fastest Derby winner since Secretariat. {by} Jim Squires. PublicAffairs 2002 300p il $26; pa $14   **798.4**
1. Horse racing 2. Kentucky Derby 3. Race horses -- Breeding -- Kentucky 4. Race horses -- Kentucky
ISBN 1-58648-117-7; 1-58648-180-0 pa

LC 2001-59602

This is the story of how the author, a former editor of the Chicago Tribune, became a breeder of thoroughbred race horses, including a horse named Monarchos, the champion of the 2001 Kentucky Derby.

This "is fast paced and fun to read. It will appeal not only to horseracing fans but also to people making midlife career changes." Libr J

798.401   Betting

Ainslie, Tom

Ainslie's complete guide to thoroughbred racing; 3rd ed; Simon & Schuster 1986 349p il hardcover o.p. pa $14   **798.401**
1. Gambling 2. Horse racing
ISBN 0-671-65655-4 pa

LC 86-3879

A guide to the fundamentals of handicapping races including such topics as breeding, judging condition of the horses, calculating speed, track ratings and other tips for successful betting.

798.8   Dog racing

Paulsen, Gary

Winterdance; the fine madness of running the Iditarod. Harcourt Brace & Co. 1994 256p il $26; pa $15 **798.8**
1. Authors 2. Children's authors 3. Iditarod Trail Sled Dog Race, Alaska 4. Short story writers 5. Sled dog racers 6. Sled dog racing 7. Sledding 8. Young adult authors
ISBN 0-15-126227-6; 0-15-600145-4 pa

LC 93-42096

"This book is primarily an account of Paulsen's first Iditarod and its frequent life-threatening disasters. . . . However, the book is more than a tabulation of tribulations; it is a meditation on the extraordinary attraction this race holds for some men and women." Libr J

799.1   Fishing

Dorsey, Pat

Fly fishing tailwaters; tactics and patterns for year-round waters. Stackpole Books 2009 198p il $49.95   **799.1**
1. Fly casting
ISBN 978-0-8117-0512-7; 0-8117-0512-9

LC 2008-46861

"No one brings more knowledge or passion to an examination of tailwater trout fishing than Pat Dorsey." Denver Post

Includes bibliographical references

Frazier, Ian

The **fish's** eye; essays about angling and the outdoors. Farrar, Straus & Giroux 2002 163p pa $12; $20   **799.1**
1. Fishing
ISBN 0-312-42169-9 pa; 0-374-15520-8

LC 2001-54451

A compendium of the author's essays written for The New Yorker over the last two decades.

"It's almost impossible to read these heartfelt and lovingly rendered essays without sharing the author's fascination with woods and water and fish." Booklist

Gierach, John

No shortage of good days; illustrations by Glen Wolff. Simon & Schuster 2011 210p il $24; ebook $10.99   **799.1**
1. Fly casting
ISBN 978-0-7432-9175-0; 978-1-4516-1011-6 ebook

LC 2010043739

"The book is a collection of fondly remembered fishing trips and random fishing-related topics, along with miscellaneous other narrative odds and ends thrown in the mix: fishing and firewood, fly-fishing versus bait fishing, fly-fishing's countercultural history, salmon fishing, the experience of fishing with guides and even a random chapter on the perils of combining fishing with the pain-in-the-neck necessity of book tours. The author's strength is his obvious obsessive drive to find the perfect fishing spot and make the perfect cast; his travels take him from his home state of Colorado to Canada, Wisconsin, Washington State and Mexico. . . . Gierach's genial campfire manner and woodsy witticisms should hook more than just the average fishing fanatic." Kirkus

Harrop, Rene

Learning from the water. Stackpole Books 2010 213p il $39.95   **799.1**
1. Fly casting 2. Trout fishing
ISBN 978-0-8117-0579-0; 0-8117-0579-X

LC 2009-50478

"When you see the name Rene Harrop associated with a book on fly fishing you automatically know that you are in for a treat if you are a serious fly fisher." FlyAngles OnLine

Hersey, John

★ **Blues**; with drawings by James Baker. Knopf 1987

205p il hardcover o.p. pa $13 **799.1**
    1. Bluefish 2. Fishing 3. Fishing -- Cape Cod (Mass.)
    ISBN 0-394-75702-5 pa

LC 86-46008

"People who love and care about nature and their place in it, be they fishermen or not, should thoroughly enjoy 'Blues.'" Wilson Libr Bull

Rosenbauer, Tom

The **Orvis** guide to the essential American flies; how to tie the most successful freshwater and saltwater patterns. Universe 2011 208p il $35   **799.1**
    1. Artificial flies 2. Fishing
    ISBN 978-0-7893-2269-2

LC 2011-921540

This "resource features twenty quintessential fly patterns, including the Parachute Adams, Clouser Minnow, and Woolly Bugger. [Includes] detailed chapters exploring the history of and variations on each fly, interviews with fly originators, and step-by-step tying 'recipes' and instructions." Publisher's note

Schullery, Paul

★ The **rise**; streamside observations on trout, flies, and fly fishing. photographs by the author; illustrations by Marsha Karle; with additional illustrations from angling literature. Stackpole Books 2006 194p il $26.95 **799.1**
    1. Artificial flies 2. Trout fishing
    ISBN 978-0-8117-0182-2; 0-8117-0182-4

LC 2005-37913

This work "distills five centuries' worth of angling lore and wisdom about trout feeding behavior and includes a photographic sequence that shows in detail how trout take a fly. . . . [An] examination of flies includes the importance of wings and what they are made of, hooks, soft-hackled flies, and skipping, dapping, and dry-fly techniques." Publisher's note

Includes bibliographical references

Takahashi, Rick

Modern midges; tying & fishing the world's most effective patterns. [by] Rick Takahashi and Jerry Hubka; photos by Brian Yamauchi and Mark Tracy. Headwater Books 2009 282p il $39.95   **799.1**
    1. Fly casting
    ISBN 978-1-934753-00-2; 1-934753-00-9

"Midges may be small, but in many streams and lakes around the world they are the most important year-round food source for trout. . . . Photos and detailed illustrations show the life cycle of the naturals, fishing and rigging techniques for a wide range of waters, and over 1,000 midge patterns." Publisher's note

Tapply, William G.

Every day was special; a fly fisher's lifelong passion. foreword by Nick Lyons. Skyhorse Publishing 2010 186p $26.95   **799.1**
    1. Fly casting
    ISBN 978-1-60239-955-6

LC 2009-45558

This volume collects the late author's pieces on fly-fishing.

"Tapply clearly knows his stuff. His knowledge of royal wulffs, wooly buggers, and Chernobyl ants will demonstrate this to those who share his wisdom. Those who don't can content themselves with his evocative descriptions of summer streams, elusive fish, and the elements of life that gave the author joy. Recommended for all enthusiasts of outdoor writing, whether or not they are fly fishers." Libr J

799.2   Hunting

Jones, Robert F.

The **hunter** in my heart; a sportsman's salmagundi. Lyons Press 2002 268p $24.95   **799.2**
    1. Game and game birds 2. Hunting
    ISBN 1-58574-465-4

This "is a collection of 30 essays and two short stories. . . . Jones not only tells great outdoor stories but also explores his thoughts on hunting and friendship." Libr J

799.3   Shooting other than game

Kasper, Shirl

Annie Oakley. University of Okla. Press 1992 288p il $29.95; pa $19.95   **799.3**
    1. Biography, Individual 2. Frontier and pioneer life -- West (U.S.) 3. Marksmen
    ISBN 0-8061-2418-0; 0-8061-3244-2 pa

LC 91-50864

This biography of the legendary sharpshooter "not only paints a picture of a woman with an unusual occupation for her time; it also colors the whole era of Wild West performers from Buffalo Bill to Will Rogers." Booklist

Includes bibliographical references

800   LITERATURE, RHETORIC & CRITICISM

801   Philosophy and theory

Bloom, Harold, 1930-

The **anatomy** of influence. Yale University Press 2011 357p $32.50   **801**
    1. Authors 2. Authors and readers 3. Biographers 4. College teachers 5. Editors 6. Influence (Literary, artistic, etc.) 7. Literary critics 8. Literature -- Appreciation 9. Literature -- History and criticism 10. Literature -- Philosophy
    ISBN 978-0-300-16760-3; 0-300-16760-1

LC 2010-42456

It was the author's intention to "reveal . . . how writers struggle with the works of those who came before. He cites Shakespeare as the greatest writer in the English language. Moving forward chronologically from the 16th through the 20th centuries, [Harold] Bloom analyzes the works of such giants as John Milton, Samuel Johnson, Percy Bysshe Shelley, and Alfred, Lord Tennyson, illustrating their connections to Shakespeare. Bloom examines Walt Whitman's poetry in depth then considers James Joyce, D.H. Lawrence, Stephen Crane, and Wallace Stevens, as well as contemporary poets, e.g., A.R. Ammons, John Ashbery, and Mark Strand." (Libr J)

"The subtitle of Bloom's new book, 'Literature as a Way of Life,' is not an overstatement. For him, great authors don't merely imitate life or capture facets of being. They create 'heterocosms,' alternative but accessible worlds, open to us all. He had always been an esoteric populist, like his first subjects, Blake and Shelley." N Y Times Book Rev

Includes bibliographical references

Donoghue, Denis

Speaking of beauty. Yale University Press 2003 209p $24.95; pa $15 **801**
1. Aesthetics 2. English literature -- History and criticism
ISBN 0-300-09893-6; 0-300-10593-2 pa
LC 2002-12243

This book "is an eloquent reflection on the language beauty inspires and a careful critique of its place in literary criticism and cultural theory." N Y Times Book Rev

Includes bibliographical references

Garber, Marjorie

The **use** and abuse of literature. Pantheon Books 2011 320p $28.95 **801**
1. Literature -- Appreciation 2. Literature -- Philosophy
ISBN 978-0-375-42434-2; 0-375-42434-2
LC 2010-35417

Garber "examines classic texts like John Donne's 'The Canonization' and Ezra Pound's haiku-like poem 'In a Station of the Metro,' but she is equally happy to devote half a page to listing books with the phrase 'use and abuse' in their titles, and she spends what seems like an inordinate amount of time attacking a 30-year-old book called 'Metaphors We Live By' by George Lakoff and Mark Johnson, for its 'devaluation of the power and nature of words.' This variousness has been a hallmark of Garber's career — she is the author of books on Shakespeare, real estate, bisexuality, and pets — and it enlivens 'The Use and Abuse of Literature' with many incidental insights and pleasures. But the real justification for Garber's method is the way it enacts her central thesis: that literature is not so much a subject as an activity." Boston Globe

Gardner, John

On moral fiction. Basic Bks. 1978 214p hardcover o.p. pa $18 **801**
1. Literature -- Philosophy
ISBN 0-465-05226-6 pa
LC 77-20409

Gardner "submits that contemporary U.S. art, primarily that of fiction, is generally not of high quality because it is not moral, in that it strives to devalue rather than improve life. Furthermore, Gardner charges that critics have lost track of true, moral art and have failed to denounce that which is false or immoral." Booklist

Kermode, Frank

An **appetite** for poetry. Harvard Univ. Press 1989 242p $32 **801**
1. Authors 2. Blind 3. Criticism 4. Dramatists 5. Editors 6. Essayists 7. Insurance executives 8. Lawyers 9. Literary critics 10. Literature -- History and criticism 11. Nobel laureates for literature 12. Poetry -- History and criticism 13. Poets
ISBN 0-674-04093-7
LC 89-31725

This collection contains critical and textual readings of Milton, T. S. Eliot, Wallace Stevens, William Empson and the Bible.

"Kermode is not simply a critic but also an artist. . . . In An Appetite for Poetry we encounter writing of balance and decorum, and reading of unflinching audacity." Commonweal

Includes bibliographical references

Kundera, Milan

★ The **curtain**; an essay in seven parts. translated from the French by Linda Asher. HarperCollins Publishers 2007 168p $22.95 **801**
1. Fiction -- History and criticism 2. Literature -- Philosophy
ISBN 978-0-06-084186-7; 0-06-084186-9
LC 2006-43420

"The immediacy of Kundera's evocative prose and the rich tapestry he weaves compel us to pick up and read, or reread, the bountiful literary treasures of Western literature. This could be a book from which to draw a summer reading list." Libr J

Weinstein, Arnold

A **scream** goes through the house; what literature teaches us about life. Random House 2003 xxxvii, 423p il $29.95; pa $14.95 **801**
1. Literature -- Philosophy 2. Literature, Modern
ISBN 0-375-50624-1; 0-8129-7243-0 pa
LC 2002-31719

"Blending the literary passion of Harold Bloom with the physiological insights of Antonio Damasio, Weinstein offers splendid readings of the creations of James Baldwin, Ingmar Bergman, Edvard Munch, Kafka, Faulkner, William Burroughs, and Toni Morrison." Booklist

Includes bibliographical references

The encyclopedia of literary and cultural theory; general editor: Michael Ryan. Wiley-Blackwell 2011 3 v. **801**
ISBN 9781405183123
LC 2010029411

This reference book "is . . . [a] multi-volume encyclopedia of literary and cultural theory. Arranged in three volumes covering Literary Theory from 1900 to 1966, Literary Theory from 1966 to the Present, and Cultural Theory, this encyclopedia provides . . . entries on the important concepts, theorists and trends in post-1900 literary and cultural theory. . . . [It includes] . . . over 300 entries of 1,000-7,000 words, . . . explanations of complex terms, important theoretical concepts, and tools for critical analysis and summaries of the work and ideas of key figures. (Publisher's note)

803 Dictionaries, encyclopedias, concordances

Abrams, M. H.

★ A **glossary** of literary terms; with contributions by Geoffrey Galt Harpham. 8th ed.; Thomson, Wadsworth 2005 370p pa $34.95   **803**
  1. Literature -- Dictionaries 2. Reference books
  ISBN 1-4130-0218-8; 978-1-4130-0218-8

LC 2004-111345

In a series of essays, the author discusses literary terms and definitions ranging from the traditional to the avant-garde. Subsidiary terms are included under major or generic terms.

Ayto, John

★ **Brewer's** dictionary of modern phrase & fable; by John Ayto & Ian Crofton. 2nd ed.; Chambers Harrap Pub. Ltd. 2010 853p $39.95   **803**
  1. Allusions 2. Literature -- Dictionaries 3. Reference books
  ISBN 978-0550-105-646

"Focusing on the 20th and 21st centuries, . . . [this book covers a] selection of buzzwords, catchphrases, slang, nicknames, fictional characters and . . . cultural phenomena from pop culture to politics, literature to technology." Publisher's note

Cuddon, J. A.

The **Penguin** dictionary of literary terms and literary theory; 4th ed; Penguin 1999 1024p pa $29   **803**
  1. Literature -- Dictionaries 2. Reference books
  ISBN 0-14-051363-9; 978-0-14-051363-9

"Comprehensive dictionary covering all literatures and time periods with basic definitions as currently used. Categories include technical terms, forms, genres, groups, movements, -isms, character types, phrases, motifs or themes, concepts, objects, and styles. Entries often indicate origin and cite examples. Numerous see and see also references." Guide to Ref Books. 11th edition

Dictionary of phrase and fable

★ **Brewer's** dictionary of phrase & fable; edited by Camilla Rockwood. 18th ed.; Brewer's 2009 xxv, 1460p il $49.95   **803**
  1. Allusions 2. English language -- Terms and phrases 3. Literature -- Dictionaries 4. Mythology -- Dictionaries 5. Reference books
  ISBN 978-0-550-10411-3

LC 2009-379960

"Over 15,000 brief entries give the meanings and origins of a broad range of terms, expressions, and names of real, fictitious and mythical characters from world history, science, the arts and literature." N Y Public Libr. Ref Books for Child Collect. 2d edition

★ Benet's reader's encyclopedia; edited by Bruce F. Murphy. 5th ed.; Collins 2008 1210p $60 **803**
  1. Literature -- Dictionaries 2. Reference books
  ISBN 978-0-06-089016-2

LC 2008-31430

This encyclopedia contains over 10,000 entries and covers world literature from early times to the present. Includes entries on authors, literary movements, principal characters, plot synopses, terms, awards, myths and legends, etc.

This is "an edifying staple for any literary library." Libr J

Cyclopedia of literary characters; rev ed; Salem Press 1998 5v set $368   **803**
  1. Characters and characteristics in literature 2. Literature -- Dictionaries 3. Reference books
  ISBN 0-89356-438-9

LC 97-45813

"Entries are arranged alphabetically by the title of the work. . . . {They} begin with the book's title, foreign title if originally published in a language other than English, author's name with birth and death years, date of first publication, genre, locale, time of action, and plot type. Characters are arranged in order of importance; major characters have 100- to 150-word write-ups. Volume 5 contains three indexes: title, author, and character." Booklist

★ Oxford dictionary of phrase and fable; edited by Elizabeth Knowles. 2nd ed.; Oxford University Press 2005 805p $40; pa $18.95   **803**
  1. Allusions 2. Literature -- Dictionaries 3. Reference books
  ISBN 978-0-19-860981-0; 978-0-19-920246-1 pa

This work seeks to define words and phrases of British cultural history.

This "is a highly useful tool to help understand what phrases mean and where they come from and should definitely be added to all reference collections." Booklist

808 Rhetoric and collections of literary texts from more than two literatures

Conway, Jill K.

When memory speaks; reflections on autobiography. [by] Jill Ker Conway. Knopf 1998 205p hardcover o.p. pa $13   **808**
  1. Autobiography 2. Autobiography -- Women authors 3. Biography as a literary form
  ISBN 0-679-76645-6 pa

LC 97-49452

"Conway's small gem is a landmark in eliciting fresh contemplation of the inchoate complexity of memory's manifold voices." Publ Wkly

Includes bibliographical references

Garvey, Mark

Stylized; a slightly obsessive history of Strunk & White's The elements of style. Simon & Schuster 2009 xxv, 208p il **808**
  1. Authors 2. Authorship -- Handbooks, manuals, etc. 3. Authorship -- Style manuals 4. Children's authors 5. College teachers 6. English language -- Rhetoric 7. English language -- Style 8. Essayists 9. Humorists 10. Nonfiction writers 11. Novelists 12. Poets 13. Rhetoric 14. Satirists
  ISBN 1-4165-9092-7; 978-1-4165-9092-7

LC 2009007166

This is a history of the composition and publication of William Strunk and E.B. White's The Elements of Style, which appeared in 1959.

"A fan's meticulously researched, bighearted tribute to a sturdy, perennial writing guide, this history of Elements of Style is complete and unreservedly affectionate." Publ Wkly

Includes bibliographical references

Glenn, Cheryl

Hodges' Harbrace handbook; [by] Cheryl Glenn ... [et al.] 16th ed; Thomson Wadsworth 2007 xxxi, 793p il $81.95   **808**
  1. English language -- Composition and exercises 2. English language -- Grammar
  ISBN 1-4130-1031-8
            LC 2005-937964

A guide to the fundamentals of grammar, composition, and usage

Hooks, Bell

Remembered rapture; the writer at work. Holt & Co. 1999 237p hardcover o.p. pa $13   **808**
  1. American literature -- African American authors 2. American literature -- African American authors -- History and criticism 3. American literature -- Women authors -- History and criticism 4. Authorship
  ISBN 0-8050-5910-5 pa
            LC 98-7998

"The redoubtable Hooks offers a series of essays on writing, focusing on women, black writers (e.g., why there are so many black women novelists and so few in nonfiction), and what it was like to move to writer-saturated New York." Libr J

Jacob, Dianne

Will write for food; the complete guide to writing cookbooks, blogs, reviews, memoir, and more. 2nd ed.; Da Capo Lifelong 2010 342p pa $15.95 **808**
  1. Food writing
  ISBN 978-0-7382-1404-7
            LC 2010-14224

The author "provides detailed, practical advice on such matters as recipe development; how to launch a blog and draw readers, pitch article and book ideas, and refine one's prose style; and where to go to network or study. Also included are writing exercises, extensive suggestions for further reading, lists of publications and websites that accept freelancers, and perspectives drawn from interviews with dozens of well-known food writers such as Mark Bittman, Deborah Madison, and Calvin Trillin. . . . An engaging, informative handbook for hobbyists and aspiring professionals." Libr J

Includes bibliographical references

LaRocque, Paula

The **book** on writing; the ultimate guide to writing well. Marion Street Press 2003 240p pa $18.95   **808**
  1. Authorship
  ISBN 0-9665176-9-5
            LC 2003-13308

The author "organizes her book into three sections: mechanical and structural guidelines (i.e. sharpening accuracy and brevity), creative elements of storytelling (e.g., 'Let the Reader Do Some Work'), and style (grammar, usage and punctuation). LaRocque's advice is sane and sound: avoid pretension and over-complication, and stay away from jargon and clichés. . . . Beginning writers should find clear, useful advice here." Publ Wkly

Modern Language Association of America

★ **MLA** handbook for writers of research papers; 7th ed.; Modern Language Association of America 2009 xxi, 292p il pa $22   **808**
  1. Report writing
  ISBN 978-1-60329-024-1
            LC 2008-47484

This manual discusses research strategies, formatting, documenting sources, writing basics and utilizing electronic sources.

Plotnik, Arthur

Spunk & bite; a writer's guide to punchier, more engaging language & style. Random House 2005 263p hardcover o.p. pa $12.95   **808**
  1. Rhetoric
  ISBN 0-375-72115-0; 0-375-72227-0 pa
            LC 2005-44934

The author "demonstrates how . . . unexpected humor, loquaciousness, and apt description can jolt a writer into engaged authorship. This primer is dotted with illustrative examples that range from Shakespeare and J.K. Rowling to Dave Barry and Maeve Binchy. . . . This is an entertaining and engaging choice for writers." Libr J

Prose, Francine

★ **Reading** like a writer; a guide for people who love books and for those who want to write them. HarperCollins Publishers 2006 273p   **808**
  1. Books and reading 2. Creative writing 3. English language -- Rhetoric 4. Rhetoric
  ISBN 0-06-077704-4; 0-06-077705-2 pa; 978-0-06-077704-3; 978-0-06-077705-0 pa
            LC 2005-58457

The author argues that "would-be writers should turn to the classics for inspiration." (N Y Times Book Rev)

This book "should be greatly appreciated in and out of the classroom. Like the great works of fiction, it's a wise and voluble companion." N Y Times Book Rev

Rabiner, Susan

Thinking like your editor; how to write serious nonfiction--and get it published. by Susan Rabiner and Alfred Fortunato. Norton 2002 284p $26.95; pa $14   **808**
  1. Authorship 2. Authorship -- Marketing 3. Book proposals
  ISBN 0-393-03892-0; 0-393-32461-3 pa
            LC 2001-44551

"In part one, on submissions, the authors discuss how to put together a book proposal and, . . . whether to work through an agent or go solo. In part two, they move to the writing process. . . . Part three discusses how authors and editors (both in-house and freelance) can work together well." Publ Wkly

Siegal, Allan

The **New** York times manual of style and usage; [by] Allan M. Siegal and William G. Connolly. rev and expanded ed; Times Bks. 1999 364p hardcover o.p. pa $15   **808**

    1. Authorship -- Handbooks, manuals, etc.
    ISBN 0-8129-6389-X pa

                     LC 99-10630

Rules and guidelines observed by The New York Times for consistency of spelling, capitalization, punctuation, abbreviation, and preferred usage.

This work "contends with the AP stylebook in authority and usefulness." Columbia J Rev

Stein, Sol

Stein on writing; a master editor of some of the most successful writers of our century shares his craft techniques and strategies. St. Martin's Press 1995 308p $24.95; pa $14.95   **808**

    1. Authorship
    ISBN 0-312-13608-0; 0-312-25421-0 pa

                     LC 95-31793

The author discusses the process of writing "fiction and nonfiction in terms of characterization, pacing, revision, evoking emotion, and 'liposuctioning flab.' Stein's own writing demonstrates the 'resonance' and 'particularities' he discusses, and his original checklists, writing exercises, and numerous examples encourage the reader/writer to see and do the same. A chapter of help sources and a glossary of terms provide the finishing touch." Libr J

Strunk, William

★ The **elements** of style; with revisions, an introduction, and a chapter on writing by E.B. White. 4th ed; Allyn & Bacon 1999 105p $14.95; pa $7.95   **808**

    1. English language -- Rhetoric 2. English language -- Style 3. Report writing 4. Rhetoric
    ISBN 0-205-31342-6; 0-205-30902-X pa

                     LC 99-16419

This work provides guidelines for proper usage and composition. Misused expressions and commonly misspelled words are discussed. Includes examples.

This work is "prescriptive, conservative, and humorous; in sum, it is the best book available on how to write English prose." Nichols. Guide to Ref Books for Sch Media Cent. 4th edition

Turabian, Kate L.

Student's guide to writing college papers; 4th ed; The University of Chicago Press 2010 281p il $39; pa $15; ebook $15   **808**

    1. Academic writing 2. Dissertations 3. Dissertations, Academic -- Handbooks, manuals, etc. 4. Report writing 5. Rhetoric -- Study and teaching
    ISBN 978-0-226-81630-2; 978-0-226-81631-9 pa; 978-0-226-81633-3 ebook

                     LC 2009-31583

This guide covers selecting a topic, collecting material, planning and writing the paper, and preparing footnotes and bibliographies.

★ A **manual** for writers of research papers, theses, and dissertations; Chicago style for students and researchers. revised by Wayne C. Booth, Gregory G. Colomb, Joseph M. Williams, and University of Chicago Press editorial staff. 7th ed.; University of Chicago Press 2007 466p il $35; pa $17   **808**

    1. Dissertations 2. Report writing
    ISBN 978-0-226-82336-2; 0-226-82336-9; 978-0-226-82337-9 pa; 0-226-82337-7 pa

                     LC 2006-25443

Designed to serve as a guide to suitable style in the presentation of formal papers—term papers, reports, articles, theses, dissertations—both in scientific and in nonscientific fields.

United States/Government Printing Office

★ **Style** manual; an official guide to the form and style of Federal Government printing 2008. U.S. Government Printing Office. [30th ed.]; U.S. G.P.O. 2008 453p pa $36   **808**

    1. Authorship -- Handbooks, manuals, etc. 2. Printing -- Style manuals 3. Publishers and publishing -- Handbooks, manuals, etc.
    ISBN 978-0-16-081812-7

                     LC 2009-376600

"A useful and extensive manual giving the practices of the Government Printing Office on copy preparation, with rules for capitalization, punctuation, abbreviations, etc., and information on foreign languages, including alphabets, with pronunciation, special rules, lists of numbers, etc." Guide to Ref Books. 11th edition

Van Wicklen, Janet

The **tech** writer's survival guide; a comprehensive handbook for aspiring technical writers. Facts on File 2001 269p $35; pa $15.95   **808**

    1. Technical writing
    ISBN 0-8160-4038-9; 0-8160-4039-7 pa

                     LC 00-62231

"This guide offers some basic principles of document structure and design for both printed and online media and is full of practical advice on how to glean information from product developers and determine the needs of a document's audience. Van Wicklen draws from her own experience as well as giving testimony from colleagues, demonstrating the wide variability of technical writing jobs. It will be a helpful resource for anyone considering or beginning a career in technical writing." Booklist

Includes bibliographical references

Walker, Janice R.

The **Columbia** guide to online style; [by] Janice R. Walker and Todd Taylor. 2nd ed.; Columbia University Press 2006 xxi, 288p il $45; pa $19.50 **808**

    1. Authorship -- Data processing -- Handbooks, manuals, etc. 2. Bibliographical citations
    ISBN 0-231-13210-7; 978-0-231-13210-7; 0-231-

13211-5 pa; 978-0-231-13211-4 pa

LC 2006-24383

This is a "resource for citing electronic and electronically accessed sources. It is also a . . . style guide for creating documents electronically for submission for print or electronic publication." Publisher's note

Includes bibliographical references

Zinsser, William Knowlton

Writing to learn. Harper & Row 1988 256p
hardcover o.p. pa $145 **808**

1. Rhetoric -- Study and teaching

ISBN 0-06-272040-6 pa

LC 87-45825

"Eschewing theory and philosophical breast-beating, Zinsser uses his own experience to reinforce the fact that clear, eloquent writing can be taught for every subject across the curriculum. A practical manual for teachers and a powerful reminder for everyone that good writing makes possible good thinking." Am Libr

Includes bibliographical referneces

★ 2011 writer's market; edited by Robert Lee Brewer. Writer's Digest 2010 1024p pa $29.99 **808**

1. Authorship -- Handbooks, manuals, etc. 2. Publishers and publishing

ISBN 978-1-58297-948-9

"A guide for freelance writers, covering the practical side of writing for publication, including information about book publishers; consumer magazines; trade, technical and a few professional journals; scriptwriting; syndicates; greeting card and gift markets. Provides extensive lists of contests and awards and of relevant organizations and publications. Subject index of book publishers." Guide to Ref Books. 11th edition

Includes bibliographical references

Black nature; four centuries of African American nature poetry. edited by Camille T. Dungy. University of Georgia Press 2009 xxxv, 387p $69.95; pa $24.95 **808**

1. American poetry -- African American authors 2. Nature poetry

ISBN 978-0-8203-3277-2; 0-8203-3277-1; 978-0-8203-3431-8 pa; 0-8203-3431-6 pa

LC 2009-18528

"Since Bryant, Longfellow, Whitman, and Dickinson, the image of 'nature poetry' has stayed traditionally white. This collection helps complete the picture, by including a people who were chained to a foreign land and yet sustained a love for it." Orion

Includes bibliographical references

★ The Chicago manual of style; 16th ed; The University of Chicago Press 2010 1026p **808**

1. Authorship 2. Authorship -- Handbooks, manuals, etc. 3. Authorship -- Style manuals 4. English language -- Usage 5. Printing -- Style manuals 6. Publishers and publishing 7. Publishers and publishing -- Handbooks, manuals, etc. 8. Writing

ISBN 0226104206; 9780226104201

LC 2009053612

This style manual includes journals and electronic publications, descriptive headings on all numbered paragraphs, and chapters on grammar, usage, and documentation, including guidance on citing electronic sources.

★ Children's writer's & illustrator's market; edited by Alice Pope. Writer's Digest Books il **808**

1. Authorship -- Handbooks, manuals, etc. 2. Publishers and publishing

This reference includes listings of children's book publishers, magazines, agents, art reps, contests, clubs, conferences, awards, and grants with contact information, along with articles and interviews on a variety of subjects relating to children's writing, illustrating, and publishing.

★ MLA style manual and guide to scholarly publishing; 3rd ed.; Modern Language Association of America 2008 xxiv, 336p $32.50 **808**

1. Authorship -- Handbooks, manuals, etc.

ISBN 978-0-87352-297-7; 0-87352-297-4

LC 2008-2894

This book offers "guidance on writing scholarly texts, documenting research sources, submitting manuscripts to publishers, and dealing with legal issues surrounding publication." Publisher's note

Includes bibliographical references

The Writer's digest guide to good writing; edited by Thomas Clark {et al.} Writer's Digest Bks. 1994 338p hardcover o.p. pa $14.99 **808**

1. Authorship 2. Authorship -- Handbooks, manuals, etc. 3. Creative writing

ISBN 1-58297-138-2 pa

LC 93-43554

This collection of articles culled from issues of Writer's Digest magazine contains "essays on how to write with simplicity, plot and pace a story, build suspense, create characters, and tackle certain genres, including mysteries, horror, romance, and various forms of nonfiction. The selections are organized by decades and include essays by Erle Stanley Gardner, Irving Wallace, Louis L'Amour {and} Allen Ginsberg." Booklist

808.06 Rhetoric of specific kinds of writing

Aiken, Joan

The **way** to write for children. St. Martin's Griffin 1999 97p pa $9.95 **808.06**

1. Authorship 2. Children's literature -- Technique

ISBN 0-312-20048-X

LC 99-166931

"In this crisp, informative and often witty survey of 'the market' Aiken is also giving the customers—teachers, librarians, parents, every one concerned with children's literature of quality-a good general idea of what is available already and of what authors are trying to do." Times Lit Suppl

Seuling, Barbara

How to write a children's book and get it published; 3rd ed; Wiley 2005 233p il pa $15.95 **808.06**

1. Authorship 2. Children's literature -- Technique
ISBN 0-471-67619-5

LC 2004-4691

Presents "five essential steps (from researching the current marketplace to submitting your manuscript) to publishing works for children." Libr J

Includes bibliographical references

Shulevitz, Uri

Writing with pictures; how to write and illustrate children's books. Watson-Guptill 1985 271p il hardcover o.p. pa $29.95 **808.06**

1. Children's literature -- Technique 2. Picture books for children
ISBN 0-8230-5935-9 pa

LC 85-15604

"With heavy emphasis on illustration, this detailed book guides aspiring authors/illustrators through telling the story and drawing the pictures to preparing artwork for the printer." Libr J

Includes bibliographical references

808.1 Rhetoric in specific literary forms

Addonizio, Kim

The **poet's** companion; a guide to the pleasures of writing poetry. [by] Kim Addonizio and Dorianne Laux. Norton 1997 284p pa $14.95 **808.1**

1. Poetics
ISBN 0-393-31654-8

LC 96-40451

This work contains "three main sections: 'Subjects for Writing' (e.g. death, the erotic), 'The Poet's Craft' (metaphor, rhyme), and 'The Writing Life' (self-doubt, writer's block); four separate appendixes list other writing texts, anthologies, marketing tips, and electronic resources. . . . Both knowledgeable and practical in their approach, the authors offer everything a poet needs, including . . . a gentle yet insistent lesson on grammar." Libr J

Includes bibliographical references

Deutsch, Babette

Poetry handbook: a dictionary of terms; 4th ed; HarperResource 2002 203p pa $14 **808.1**

1. Poetics -- Dictionaries 2. Poetry -- Terminology 3. Reference books
ISBN 0-06-463548-1

"The craft of verse described in dictionary form. Terms and techniques are defined and illustrated." N Y Public Libr. Ref Books for Child Collect. 2d edition

Higginson, William J.

The **haiku** handbook; how to write, teach, and appreciate haiku. [by] William J. Higginson and Penny Harter; foreword by Jane Reichhold. 25th an-

niversary ed.; Kodansha International 2009 331p pa $18 **808.1**

1. Haiku
ISBN 978-4-770-03113-6; 4-770-03113-0

LC 2009-36628

This book "presents haiku poets writing in English, Spanish, French, German, and five other languages on an equal footing with Japanese poets. Not only are the four great Japanese masters of the haiku represented (Basho, Buson, Issa, and Shiki) but also several major Western authors not commonly known to have written haiku. The book presents a . . . history of the Japanese haiku, including the dynamic changes throughout the twentieth century as the haiku has been adapted to suburban and industrial settings. Full chapters are offered on form, the seasons in haiku, and haiku craft, plus background on the Japanese poetic tradition, and the effect of translation on our understanding of haiku." Publisher's note

Includes bibliographical references

Hirsch, Edward

How to read a poem; and fall in love with poetry. Harcourt Brace & Co. 1999 352p $23; pa $15 **808.1**

1. Poetics 2. Poetry -- Explication 3. Poetry -- History and criticism
ISBN 0-15-100419-6; 0-15-600566-2 pa

LC 98-50065

The author "has gathered an eclectic group of poems from many times and places, with selections as varied as postwar Polish poetry, works by Keats and Christopher Smart, and lyrics from African American work songs. A prolific, award-winning poet in his own right, Hirsch suggests helpful strategies for understanding and appreciating each poem. The book is scholarly but very readable and incorporates interesting anecdotes from the lives of the poets." Libr J

Includes bibliographical references

Kooser, Ted

★ The **poetry** home repair manual; practical advice for beginning poets. University of Nebraska Press 2005 163p $19.95; pa $13.95 **808.1**

1. Poetics
ISBN 0-8032-2769-8; 0-8032-5978-6 pa

LC 2004-24700

"Among the many books offering advice on writing poetry, . . . [this book] stands out for its usefulness and, at the same time, for its inspiring view of the purposes of poetry." Midwest Quarterly

Includes bibliographical references

Oliver, Mary

A **poetry** handbook. Harcourt Brace & Co. 1994 130p pa $13 **808.1**

1. Poetics
ISBN 0-15-672400-6

LC 93-49676

A "handbook for young poets on the formal aspects and structure of poetry. Oliver excels at explaining the sound and sense of poetry—from scansion to imagery, diction to voice. She stresses the importance of reading poetry, since, in order to write well, 'it is entirely necessary to read widely and deeply.' Sage advice is given in an entire chapter dedicated to revision, wherein Oliver urges poets to consider their first draft 'an unfinished piece of work' that can be polished and improved later. Written in a pleasant and lucid style, this book is a wonderful resource." Libr J

★ 2009 poet's market; Nancy Breen, editor. Writer's Digest Bks. 2008 572p pa $27.99   **808.1**
1. Poetry -- Marketing
ISBN 978-1-58297-544-3; 1-58297-544-2

"Useful for those aspiring to publish their poems in literary journals and magazines. . . . Entries include a brief journal profile, submission requirements, and contact information. Offers advice to beginning poets on getting published, brief articles by working poets/editors, grant information, contests and awards, poetry readings, writing colonies, organizations and publications useful to poets. Indexes for chapbook publishers, publishers by subject, publishers by state, and a general index." Guide to Ref Books. 11th edition
Includes bibliographical references

The New Princeton encyclopedia of poetry and poetics; Alex Preminger and T.V.F. Brogan, co-editors; Frank Warnke, O.B. Hardison, Jr., and Earl Miner, associate editors. Princeton Univ. Press 1993 xlvi, 1383p hardcover o.p. pa $45   **808.1**
1. Poetics -- Dictionaries 2. Poetry -- Dictionaries 3. Poetry -- History and criticism 4. Reference books
ISBN 0-691-02123-6 pa

LC 92-41887

This work deals with the history, forms, genres, movements and critical approaches to oral and written verse. It examines issues in such areas as: hermenuetics, feminist poetics, Chicano poetry, deconstruction, poststructuralism and cultural criticism. Non-Western and emergent poetries are featured and 106 national poetries are covered

808.2   Rhetoric of drama

Field, Syd
★ **Screenplay**; the foundations of screenwriting. Rev. ed.; Delta Trade Paperbacks 2005 320p il pa $16 **808.2**
1. Motion picture plays -- Technique
ISBN 0-385-33903-8

LC 2005-48491

This book covers the basics of writing a screenplay, including how to build a character, set up a scene, and what to do after the screenplay is written.

Hauge, Michael
Writing screenplays that sell. HarperPerennial 1991 325p pa $12   **808.2**
1. Motion picture plays -- Technique
ISBN 0-06-272500-9; 978-0-06-272500-4

LC 91-55005

This book provides a "discussion of the craft—characters, story development, etc.—and industry; lays out the all-important details of format; then tells how to market the finished product. Hauge's volume is a detailed manual offering

a step-by-step methodology, a scriptual analysis of a hit film, 'The Karate Kid,' and handy chapter summaries." Libr J
Includes bibliographical references

Now write! screenwriting; exercises by today's best writers and teachers. [by] Sherry Ellis with Laurie Lamson. Jeremy P. Tarcher/Penguin 2011 343p il pa $14.95   **808.2**
1. Motion picture plays -- Technique
ISBN 978-1-58542-851-9

LC 2010-29424

The editors "compile guidelines from successful screenwriters on all of the details of writing a screenplay, from choosing your story to structure to character development. Readers will be interested to hear the opinions of such estimated screenwriters as Linda Seger and Syd Field and their takes on what motivates them to write screenplays and how they cope with writer's block and revisions. . . . This guide stands out from the crowd by incorporating the techniques of a variety of different screenwriters rather than just one professional's approach. Highly recommended for readers interested in writing, screenwriting, film, and storytelling." Libr J

808.3   Rhetoric of fiction

Butler, Robert Olen
From where you dream; the process of writing fiction. edited, with an introduction by Janet Burroway. Grove Press 2005 269p $24; pa $13   **808.3**
1. Authorship 2. Fiction -- Technique
ISBN 0-8021-1795-3; 0-8021-4257-5 pa

LC 2005-40251

This is a collection of lectures the author has given for his creative writing course at Florida State University.

This "is a remarkably candid, clarifying, and profoundly demanding how-to. . . . Incisive and provocative, Butler's tutorials are a must for anyone even thinking about writing fiction, and readers, too, will benefit from his passionate exhortations." Booklist

Eco, Umberto
Confessions of a young novelist. Harvard University Press 2011 231p il $18.95   **808.3**
1. Authors 2. Authorship 3. Biography, Individual 4. College teachers 5. Essayists 6. Fiction -- Authorship 7. Literary critics 8. Novelists 9. Semioticians
ISBN 9780674058699; 0-674-05869-0

LC 2010-33172

"In the first three essays/lectures here, Eco addresses interesting questions: what is the boundary between fiction and nonfiction? How do novelists put together books? Why do we care about wholly fictional characters like Anna Karenina or Emma Bovary? His answer to the second question—on constructing a novel—is that he builds his novels by scrupulous attention to physical detail. The fourth essay, 'My Lists,' original to this collection, was not a lecture. It seems a throwaway but reflects Eco's pleasure in the detailed, serial listing of names as attempts to exhaust the plenitude of qualities and quiddities potentially attributable to any single object. . . . As always, Eco is diverting to read." Libr J
Includes bibliographical references

Gardner, John

On becoming a novelist; foreword by Raymond Carver. W.W. Norton 1999 xxv, 150p pa $14.95 **808.3**
1. Authorship 2. Fiction -- Technique
ISBN 0-393-32003-0
The author "explores the dynamic chemistry at the heart of the writer's creative process. Gardner's book is a superbly written, thoroughly original, eminently useful volume." Choice

The **art** of fiction; notes on craft for young writers. Knopf 1984 224p hardcover o.p. pa $12.95 **808.3**
1. Fiction -- Technique
ISBN 0-679-73403-1 pa
LC 83-47850
"This essay distills the late Gardner's ripest thoughts about what fiction is and how to go about learning to write it. The initial section deals with 'literary-aesthetic theory,' the second with 'the fictional process.' . . . The book concludes with two sets of exercises, one for class use and one for individual use. Recommended for any young writer or writing class, and for all readers who care about the craft of fiction." Booklist

Koch, Stephen

★ The **modern** library writer's workshop; a guide to the craft of fiction. Modern Library 2003 246p pa $12.95 **808.3**
1. Authorship 2. Fiction -- Authorship 3. Fiction -- Technique
ISBN 0-375-75558-6
LC 2002-32593
"Koch's tone is both encouraging and forthright, and his accessible, friendly guide will be essential for aspiring writers." Booklist
Includes bibliographical references

Lukeman, Noah

The **plot** thickens; 8 ways to bring fiction to life. St. Martin's Press 2002 221p $19.95; pa $12.95 **808.3**
1. Fiction -- Technique 2. Plots (Drama, novel, etc.)
ISBN 0-312-28467-5; 0-312-30928-7 pa
LC 2001-58564
"Lukeman focuses on the mechanics of storytelling. He introduces budding writers to the techniques of characterization (ask yourself questions about the people you've created), the various ways of generating suspense (danger, a ticking clock), and the importance of conflict." Booklist

Maass, Donald

Writing the breakout novel; winning advice from a top agent and his bestselling client. foreword by Anne Perry. Writer's Digest Bks. 2001 264p hardcover o.p. pa $16.99 **808.3**
1. Fiction -- Authorship 2. Fiction -- Authorship -- Marketing 3. Fiction -- Technique
ISBN 1-58297-182-X pa
LC 2001-22036

"Using his own clients as case studies, Maass defines the most crucial elements of a breakout novel—a powerful sense of time and place, larger-than-life characters, a high degree of tension, good subplots, and universal themes—and shows the reader how to use these elements efficiently to write a novel that will generate interest and have the potential to hit the best sellers lists. Each section ends with checklists for review." Libr J

Morrell, Jessica Page

Thanks, but this isn't for us; a (sort of) compassionate guide to why your writing is being rejected. Jeremy P. Tarcher-Penguin 2009 357p pa $16.95 **808.3**
1. Authorship
ISBN 978-1-58542-721-5
LC 2009-23252
The author "explores several mistakes new authors make in their manuscripts among them lack of conflict, unbelievable dialogue, and details that lack specific sensory appeal. Each chapter begins with a lively overview of a common problem, then lists what Morrell calls 'deal breakers'—particular habits such as lack of subplots and one-dimensional bad guys—that deter an editor from accepting a manuscript for publication. She concludes each chapter with exercises designed to improve storytelling, and then lists book resources for those wanting to delve more deeply into studies of character, emotion, tension and plot. . . . Emerging and established writers alike will benefit from Morrell's shrewd observations." Writer
Includes bibliographical references

Nabokov, Vladimir Vladimirovich

Lectures on literature; {by} Vladimir Nabokov; edited by Fredson Bowers; introduction by John Updike. Harcourt Brace Jovanovich 1980 xxviii, 385p il hardcover o.p. pa $18 **808.3**
1. Authors 2. Dramatists 3. Essayists 4. Fiction -- History and criticism 5. Literary critics 6. Novelists 7. Poets 8. Short story writers 9. Travel writers
ISBN 978-0-15-602775-5; 0-15-602775-5
LC 79-3690
In the early 1950s, before Nabokov became a famous writer, he taught literature at Wellesley and Cornell. The editor, with the help of Nabokov's wife and son, has collected seven lectures on "Mansfield Park," "Bleak House," "Madame Bovary," "The Strange Case of Dr. Jekyll and Mr. Hyde," "The Walk by Swann's Place," "The Metamorphosis" and "Ulysses." There are two additional lectures on other topics related to literature. The volume includes a sample examination for the course and pages of original manuscripts with maps and diagrams which the author used to illustrate his lectures

Piercy, Marge

So you want to write; how to master the craft of writing fiction and memoir. [by] Marge Piercy and Ira Wood. 2nd ed.; Leapfrog Press 2005 324p pa $16.95 **808.3**
1. Biography as a literary form 2. Fiction -- Technique
ISBN 0-9728984-5-X

This book "uses talks, exercises, anecdotes and examples proven in the classroom, to address: How to begin a piece by seducing your reader, How to create characters that embody the infinite contradictions of human behavior, How to master the elements of plotting fiction, How to create a strategy for telling the story of your life, How to learn to read critically, like a professional writer, How to write about painful personal material without coming off as a victim, [and] How to proceed if your work is continually rejected by publishers." Publisher's note

Includes bibliographical references

Roberts, Gillian

You can write a mystery. Writer's Digest Bks. 1999 124p il pa $12.99   **808.3**

1. Detective and mystery stories -- Authorship 2. Mystery fiction -- Technique

ISBN 0-89879-863-9

LC 99-19316

"Along with analysis of the literary aspects of mystery writing, Roberts also surveys such practical matters as grammar, punctuation, and how to submit the manuscript. If character and setting are what distinguish the best mysteries, failed plot mechanics are invariably what derail the worst. Roberts' basic but too-often-overlooked advice will help keep your story on track." Booklist

Includes bibliographical references

Stein, Sol

How to grow a novel; the most common mistakes writers make and how to overcome them. St. Martin's Press 1999 240p $25.95; pa $14.95   **808.3**

1. Creative writing 2. Fiction -- Authorship 3. Fiction -- Technique

ISBN 0-312-20949-5; 0-312-26749-5 pa

LC 99-36922

"Stein states bluntly right from the beginning that 'liars say they write only for themselves' and that a 'lack of courtesy' toward the reader is one of the chief faults of unsuccessful writing. While this is perhaps a controversial notion, prospective writers will nonetheless be well rewarded by reading this collection of tips, methods, and numerous anecdotes." Libr J

Swain, Dwight V.

Creating characters; how to build story people. Writer's Digest Bks. 1990 195p hardcover o.p. pa $14.99   **808.3**

1. Characters and characteristics in literature 2. Fiction -- Technique

ISBN 0-89879-662-8 pa

LC 90-39640

"Swain talks to his readers in a conversational tone, suggesting techniques, giving examples to illuminate his points, and offering activities for sharpening character development skills. This is a book for those already committed to writing fiction and who want to think about the craft of writing." SLJ

Includes bibliographical references

Techniques of the selling writer. University of Okla. Press 1981 330p $24.95 **808.3**

1. Fiction -- Technique

ISBN 0-8061-1191-7

The author offers practical advice for creating and marketing publishable fiction.

"Often called 'the bible of fiction writing,' this classic is dated slightly by references to such things as 'carbon copies.' But Swain's tried-and-true scene-and-sequel approach has generated many books and workshops." Libr J

Wheat, Carolyn

How to write killer fiction; the funhouse of mystery & the roller coaster of suspense. Perseverance Press 2003 191p il pa $13.95   **808.3**

1. Detective and mystery stories -- Authorship 2. Mystery fiction -- Technique 3. Suspense fiction -- Authorship 4. Suspense fiction -- Technique

ISBN 1-88028-462-6

LC 2002-15588

Wheat begins with a "discussion of the distinction between mystery and suspense . . . and then devotes a section to each genre. She offers up plenty of useful tips, such as how to dispense vital information in subtle ways and how to plant clues without being too obvious about it." Booklist

Includes bibliographical references

Wood, James

★ **How** fiction works. Farrar, Straus and Giroux 2008 265p $24   **808.3**

1. English language -- Writing 2. Fiction 3. Fiction -- Authorship

ISBN 0-374-17340-0; 978-0-374-17340-1

LC 2008-10290

The author addresses such questions as "What is character, point of view, the value of metaphor and simile, and detail? Is it all artifice or realism, or could it be labeled imaginative truth? His engaging discussion covers narration in all its forms, the impersonal author, the tension that exists between an author's and a character's style, flat vs. round characters, irony, and more. Wood uses excerpts from works by notable authors, from Miguel Cervantes and Jane Austen to Saul Bellow and John Updike, to illustrate his statements with pinpoint precision. Whether he is commenting on a work's weakness or strength, he supports his opinion with reasoned scholarship." Libr J

Includes bibliographical references

808.5   Rhetoric of speech

Detz, Joan

★ **How** to write and give a speech; a practical guide for executives, PR people, the military, fundraisers, politicians, educators, and anyone who has to make every word count. 2nd rev ed; St. Martin's Press 2002 xx, 202p pa $12.95   **808.5**

1. Anecdotes 2. Public speaking 3. Quotations

ISBN 0-312-30273-8

LC 2002-67975

Among the various aspects of public speaking discussed are: tips on topic focus, audience assessment, humor, delivery techniques and media coverage.

Flaherty, Francis

The **elements** of story; field notes on nonfiction writing. Harper Collins 2009 xxi, 293p $24.99 **808.5**
1. Rhetoric 2. Storytelling
ISBN 978-0-06-168914-7; 0-06-168914-9
LC 2008-53946

The author offers 50 "tips on the many elements writers can convey in stories. Not a style guide, this is instead a nuts-and-bolts examination of the larger elements of a story. . . . This book can be read in one fell swoop to expose yourself to the full spectrum of story elements—such as theme, motion, artfulness, truth and fairness, leads, and titles—or it can be used as a guide during the process of writing nonfiction. An essential read for both freelance writers and students of journalism." Libr J
Includes bibliographical references

Linklater, Kristin

Freeing the natural voice; drawings by Douglas Florian. Drama Bk. Specialists 1976 210p il hardcover o.p. pa $19.95 **808.5**
1. Voice
ISBN 0-89676-071-5 pa

"Predicated on the basic assumptions that everyone has a voice capable of expressing a full range of emotions within a normal two- to four-octave scale and that daily stress compromises the voice's natural abilities and power {the author} presents a simple and clear narrative, as well as a full set of exercises to cultivate and strengthen the voice." Libr J

Pinsky, Robert

The **sounds** of poetry; a brief guide. Farrar, Straus & Giroux 1998 129p hardcover o.p. pa $13 **808.5**
1. Oral interpretation of poetry 2. Poetry
ISBN 0-374-52617-6
LC 98-18873

"By bringing his passion for the sound of language—so evident in his own poems—to his expert interpretations of the work of others, Pinsky cracks open the glass case that seems to separate poetry from everyday language, allowing the song of each poem to ring bright and clear." Booklist
Includes bibliographical references

808.8   Collections of literary texts from more than two literatures

The **Book** of eulogies; a collection of memorial tributes, poetry, essays, and letters of condolence. edited with commentary by Phyllis Theroux. Scribner 1997 400p $26 **808.8**
1. Bereavement 2. Eulogies 3. Grief
ISBN 0-684-82251-2
LC 97-2197

"Theroux has gathered over 100 eulogies delivered in the form of spoken tributes, editorials, letters of condolence,

essays, and poetry. Many of these testimonials are eloquently penned by the well known to commemorate the well known (e.g., Thomas Merton on Flannery O'Connor, Robert F. Kennedy on Martin Luther King). Others are equally compelling memorials to unknown souls by everyday people. There are helpful commentaries by the author." Libr J

Into the garden; a wedding anthology: poetry and prose on love and marriage. edited by Robert Hass and Stephen Mitchell. HarperCollins Pubs. 1993 193p hardcover o.p. pa $13.95 **808.8**
1. Poetry -- Collections 2. Weddings
ISBN 0-06-092469-1 pa
LC 92-53339

This anthology of readings suitable for wedding ceremonies contains "American Indian, aboriginal Australian, ancient Egyptian, Buddhist, Hindu, and Sufi poetry and prose in addition to . . . biblical, classical Greek and Roman, European, and American passages. . . . {Also included are} traditional or tradition-respecting ceremonies." Booklist

Journalistas; 100 years of the best writing and reporting by women journalists. edited by Eleanor Mills with Kira Cochrane. Carroll & Graf 2005 xx, 364p pa $14.95 **808.8**
1. English literature -- Women authors 2. Literature -- Collections 3. Women journalists
ISBN 0-7867-1667-3

"From Djuna Barnes' 1914 account of being force-fed to end her hunger strike, to Eleanor Roosevelt's 1938 'My Day' column, to Rose George's 2004 article about gang rapes in France, this collection provides a broad and deep look at reporting by women in the past century." Booklist

The **Norton** book of modern war; edited by Paul Fussell. Norton 1991 830p $24.95 **808.8**
1. American literature -- Collections 2. European literature -- Collections 3. Literature -- Collections 4. War in literature 5. War stories
ISBN 0-393-02909-3
LC 90-36495

This anthology of 20th century prose and poetry about war covers World War I, the Spanish Civil War, World War II, the Korean War and Vietnam. Authors represented include Heinrich Böll, Marguerite Duras, Ernest Hemingway, Ron Kovic, Norman Mailer, Wilfred Owen and Siegfried Sassoon.

Nothing makes you free; writings by descendants of Jewish Holocaust survivors. edited by Melvin Jules Bukiet. Norton 2002 394p hardcover o.p. pa $15.95 **808.8**
1. Children of Holocaust survivors 2. Children of Holocaust survivors, Writings of 3. Holocaust survivors 4. Holocaust, 1933-1945, in literature 5. Holocaust, Jewish (1939-1945) 6. Holocaust, Jewish (1939-1945) -- Influence 7. Jewish fiction 8. Literature -- Collections
ISBN 0-393-05046-7; 0-393-32425-7 pa
LC 2001-55863

"Excerpts from the works of 30 writers whose parents survived the Holocaust make up this anthology of fiction and memoirs. . . . In these remarkable pieces issues such as guilt, anger, faith, and accountability are explored. They capture not only the experience of the concentration camps but also its powerful legacy, passed down to a new generation through the bond of love that ties parent and child." Booklist

The Paris review book of heartbreak, madness, sex, love, betrayal, outsiders, intoxication, war, whimsy, horrors, God, death, dinner, baseball, travels, the art of writing, and everything else in the world since 1953; by the editors of the Paris review; with an introduction by George Plimpton. Picador 2003 751p $30; pa $19   **808.8**
1. Literature -- Collections
ISBN 0-312-42238-5; 0-312-42239-3 pa
LC 2003-45971

This anthology includes works by "W.H. Auden, Ernest Hemingway, William Faulkner, Jack Kerouac, Elizabeth Bishop, Truman Capote, William Burroughs, Susan Sontag, Joyce Carol Oates, Toni Morrison, Jonathan Franzen, Ian McEwan and Alice Munro." Publ Wkly

Remembrances and celebrations; a book of eulogies, elegies, letters, and epitaphs. edited by Jill Werman Harris. Pantheon Bks. 1999 xxiii, 308p $25; pa $14   **808.8**
1. Bereavement 2. Eulogies
ISBN 0-375-40123-7; 0-375-70125-7 pa
LC 98-32149

"Comprised of eulogies from the 20th century, as well as, poetic elegies, condolence letters and tombstone epitaphs spanning from the 17th century to the present, this eclectic sourcebook offers inspiration for anyone seeking to memorialize a loved one. Since the mourners and the dead in each instance are well-known writers (Lillian Hellman eulogizes Dashiell Hammett) and public figures (Reverend Jesse Jackson lays Jackie Robinson to rest), the collection is a bonanza for the morbidly minded browser as well." Publ Wkly

808.81   Collections in specific forms

Favorite Poem Project
Americans' favorite poems; the Favorite Poem Project anthology. edited by Robert Pinsky and Maggie Dietz. Norton 1999 327p $27.50   **808.81**
1. Poetry -- Collections
ISBN 0-393-04820-9
LC 99-31979

"People across America, including many teens, share the poetry they love, and talk about what it means in their lives. Their choices—from John Keats to Lucille Clifton—defy stereotypes, and their comments are heartfelt." Booklist

Granger, Edith
★ The **Columbia** Granger's index to poetry in anthologies; edited by Tessa Kale. 13th ed., completely rev., indexing anthologies published through May 31, 2006; Columbia University Press 2007 xxviii, 2376p $295   **808.81**
1. Poetry 2. Poetry -- Indexes 3. Reference books
ISBN 0-231-13988-8; 978-0-231-13988-5
LC 2006-14853

"The 400 total entries are organized alphabetically into three sections: 'Title, First Line, Last Line,' 'Author,' and 'Subject.' The anthologies referenced appear as abbreviations explained in a 14-page introductory list. An essential purchase for literature and poetry collections." Libr J
Includes bibliographical references

Milosz, Czeslaw
A **Book** of lumininous things; an international anthology of poetry. edited and with an introduction by Czeslaw Milosz. Harcourt Brace & Co. 1996 xx, 320p hardcover o.p. pa $15   **808.81**
1. Poetry -- Collections
ISBN 0-15-600574-3
LC 95-38060

"Nobel laureate Milosz states in his introduction that the purpose of this personal and eclectic collection is to present poetry that is 'short, clear, readable, and . . . realistic, that is, loyal toward reality and attempting to describe it as concisely as possible.' . . . Most of the selections are from classical Chinese and 20th-century American and European (primarily Eastern European, Scandinavian, and French) poets." Libr J

University of California (System)
★ **Poems** for the millennium; the University of California book of modern and postmodern poetry. edited by Jerome Rothenberg and Pierre Joris. University of Calif. Press 1995 2v il v1 $70; v1 pa $29.95; v2 pa $29.95   **808.81**
1. Poetry -- Collections
ISBN 0-520-07225-1 v1; 0-520-07227-8 v1 pa; 0-520-20864-1 v2 pa
LC 93-49839

The poetry in this anthology is "often self-referential, certainly aware of its own artistry, embedded in political consciousness, and transgressive. It is the work of more than 100 poets, many little known in the U.S. Rothenberg and Joris see twentieth-century poetics as international and have postwar Japanese poet Fujii Sadakazu rubbing shoulders with Amiri Baraka and Andrei Voznesensky, Tomas Tranströmer and Diane di Prima." Booklist {review of v2}

A Book of love poetry; edited and with an introduction by Jon Stallworthy. Oxford Univ. Press 1974 393p hardcover o.p. pa $18.95   **808.81**
1. Love poetry
ISBN 0-19-504232-8
A collection of poems written during the past 2000 years arranged thematically from young love to the "long look back" of the aged.

City lights pocket poets anthology; edited by Lawrence Ferlinghetti. City Lights Bks. 1995 259p $18.95 **808.81**
1. Poetry -- Collections
ISBN 0-87286-311-5

LC 95-31608

"Drawing from the 52 volumes published in the Pocket Poets series since 1956, this selection provides a handy sampler of many of the prominent avant-garde and leftist poets of the post-WW II era. . . . The series' extensive international scope is highlighted in poems culled from German, Russian, Italian, Dutch, Nicaraguan and Spanish poets." Publ Wkly

★ The Columbia Granger's Index to poetry in collected and selected works; edited by Keith Newton. 2nd ed, completely rev; Columbia Univ. Press 2004 xxi, 1847p $225 **808.81**
1. English poetry -- Indexes 2. Poetry -- Indexes 3. Reference books
ISBN 0-231-12528-3

LC 2003-51469

This "edition includes 315 works, by 266 different poets, locating more than 65,000 poems by title, first line, author, and subject. Included . . . are the works of many of the major American and British poets of the last thirty years, such as Robert Pinsky, Seamus Heaney, and Paul Muldoon; important twentieth-century American poets such as Langston Hughes, Dorothy Parker, and Robert Penn Warren; twentieth-century foreign poets in new translations, such as Eugenio Montale and Paul Celan; and diverse poets from all times and places, collected in new editions, such as Cold Mountain, Jones Very, and Guido Cavalcanti." Publisher's note

The Columbia Granger's dictionary of poetry quotations; edited by Edith P. Hazen. Columbia Univ. Press 1992 1132p $131 **808.81**
1. Quotations 2. Reference books
ISBN 0-231-07546-4

LC 91-42240

This work contains the "most memorable lines written by the greatest poets of English. Quotations are organized alphabetically by poet, and coded so one can find full text in hundreds of current anthologies. With keyword and subject indexing." Univ Press Books for Public and Second Sch Libr

Hagar before the occupation, Hagar after the occupation; poems. by Amal al-Jubouri; translated by Rebecca Gayle Howell with Husam Qaisi. Alice James Books 2011 140 p. **808.81**
1. Poetry -- By individual authors
ISBN 9781882295890

LC 2011015821

This collection of poems depicts the U.S. occupation of Iraq using the Islamic story of Hagar, who is an honored presence, founder of Mecca in her wanderings. Baghdad-born [Amal] al-Jubouri . . . shows us her country before the occupation by U.S. troops and afterward. Though political observation is inevitable (After the occupation, the Tigris escapes// the Green Zone's eyes/ the Palace's eyes/ the invader's grunts), this is . . . a meditation on how a country and its people change after a momentous event, reflected through observation of the physical (photographs, my mouth) and the less tangible (love, freedom, my grave). Loneliness before the occupation arrested our sleep/ our secrets/ our restlessness and afterward escapes from our beds to our bodies." (Libr J)

Holocaust poetry; compiled and introduced by Hilda Schiff. St. Martin's Press 1995 xxiv, 234p hardcover o.p. pa $14.95 **808.81**
1. Holocaust, 1933-1945 -- Poetry 2. Poetry -- Collections
ISBN 0-312-13086-4; 0-312-14357-5 pa

LC 95-2708

"In English and in translation from many languages, more than 80 poets—including Wiesel, Fink, Brecht, Yevtushenko, Auden, and Sachs—give voice to what seems unspeakable. Schiff points out that compelling historical accounts document the facts and numbers, but a poem, like a story, makes us imagine how it felt for one person. These poems are stark and deceptively simple." Booklist
Includes bibliographical references

Index to children's poetry; a title, subject, author, and first line index to poetry in collections for children and youth. compiled by John E. and Sara W. Brewton. Wilson, H.W. 1942 3v $115; first supplement $85; second supplement $85 **808.81**
1. Poetry -- Indexes 2. Reference books
ISBN 0-8242-0021-7; 0-8242-0022-5 first supplement; 0-8242-0023-3 second supplement
The main volume indexes 15,000 poems by 2,500 authors in 130 collections. The two supplements analyze another 15,000 poems by 2700 authors in 151 collections.
"This tool is an invaluable reference source." Peterson. Ref Books for Child

Index to poetry for children and young people; a title, subject, author, and first line index to poetry in collections for children and young people. Wilson, H.W. 1964 6v 1964-1969 $105; 1970-1975 $105; 1976-1981 $105; 1982-1987 $110; 1988-1992 $110; 1993-1997 $115 **808.81**
1. Poetry -- Indexes 2. Reference books
ISBN 0-8242-0435-2 1964-1969; 0-8242-0621-5 1970-1975; 0-8242-0681-9 1976-1981; 0-8242-0773-4 1982-1987; 0-8242-0861-7 1988-1992; 0-8242-0939-7 1993-1997
The volume covering 1964-1969 published 1972 and compiled by John E. and Sara W. Brewton and G. Meredith Blackburn III; 1970-1975 published 1978 compiled by John E. Brewton, G. Meredith Blackburn III and Lorraine A. Blackburn; 1976-1981 published 1984 compiled by John E. Brewton, G. Meredith Blackburn III and Lorraine A. Blackburn; 1982-1987 published 1989 compiled by G. Meredith Blackburn III and Lorraine A. Blackburn; 1988-1992 published 1994 compiled by G. Meredith Blackburn III; 1993-1997 published 1998 compiled by G. Meredith Blackburn III

Language for a new century; contemporary poetry from the Middle East, Asia, and beyond. edited by

Tina Chang, Nathalie Handal, and Ravi Shankar. W.W. Norton 2008 1, 734p il pa $27.95 **808.81**

1. Poetry -- Collections

ISBN 978-0-393-33238-4; 0-393-33238-1

LC 2007-49424

"Even a diligent reader of contemporary poetry will leave this gathering feeling humbled by ignorance of the immense poetic energy of what used to be called the East." Booklist

Includes bibliographical references

Music of a distant drum; classical Arabic, Persian, Turkish, and Hebrew poems. translated and introduced by Bernard Lewis. Princeton Univ. Press 2001 222p il hardcover o.p. pa $17.95 **808.81**

1. Arabic poetry -- Collections 2. Hebrew poetry -- Collections 3. Persian poetry -- Collections 4. Turkish poetry -- Collections

ISBN 0-691-15010-9 pa; 0-691-08928-0

LC 2001-19858

"Lewis, one of the foremost scholars of the Middle East, has devoted much of his career to the history of Islam; this volume collects his translations of poems—nearly all appearing in English for the first time—that span eleven centuries and four major Middle Eastern traditions. Many of the most striking works address, in spare, stirring lines, the twin demands of serving the self and serving God." New Yorker

Includes bibliographical references

The Oxford book of war poetry; chosen and edited by John Stallworthy. Oxford Univ. Press 1984 xxxi, 358p hardcover o.p. pa $19.95 **808.81**

1. Poetry -- Collections 2. War poetry

ISBN 0-19-214125-2; 0-19-955453-6 pa

LC 83-19303

This collection "reminds one of the large numbers and great variety of war poems from many centuries that are very good poems. Mr. Stallworthy's selections include most of the best, at least the best in English." N Y Times Book Rev

Includes bibliographical references

Poems to read; a new favorite poem project anthology. edited by Robert Pinsky and Maggie Dietz. Norton 2002 xxv, 352p $27.95 **808.81**

1. American poetry 2. English poetry 3. Poetry -- Collections 4. Poetry -- Translations into English

ISBN 0-393-01074-0

LC 2002-321

"A graceful, sometimes jubilant, sometimes lyrical, sometimes brooding, but always welcoming and stirring collection." Booklist

Includes bibliographical references

The Poetry of our world; an international anthology of contemporary poetry. edited by Jeffrey Paine. HarperCollins Pubs. 2000 xxviii, 511p hardcover o.p. pa $18.95 **808.81**

1. Poetry -- Collections 2. Poetry, Modern -- 20th century

ISBN 0-06-055369-3; 0-06-095193-1 pa

LC 99-34921

In this global anthology "each section is preceded by a thoughtful introduction of several pages by the selector in

that area. . . . A stunning and highly readable anthology." Libr J

Till I end my song; a gathering of last poems. edited with commentaries by Harold Bloom. Harper 2010 xxviii, 377p $24.99 **808.81**

1. Poetics 2. Poetry -- Collections 3. Poetry -- History and criticism

ISBN 978-0-06-192305-0; 0-06-192305-2

LC 2010-20773

"These are poems that embrace change, time, life, the self, and death. Poems that have lasted and that will 'reverberate into the coming silence.' A collection of surpassing splendor and resonance." Booklist

The Vintage book of contemporary world poetry; edited and with an introduction by J.D. McClatchy. Vintage Bks. 1996 xxviii, 654p pa $16 **808.81**

1. Poetry -- Collections

ISBN 0-679-74115-1

LC 95-50628

A "varied collection of contemporary poetry from Europe, the Middle East, Africa, Asia, Latin America, and the Caribbean. Here readers will find Nobel laureates and other luminaries, such as Joseph Brodsky, Derek Walcott, Czeslaw Milosz, Octavio Paz, Wole Soyinka, Breyten Breytenbach, and Nguyen Chi Thien, as well as less well known poets. Editor McClatchy has chosen well, selecting poems that illuminate the personal as well as the universal." Booklist

Includes bibliographical references

World poetry; an anthology of verse from antiquity to our time. Katharine Washburn and John S. Major, editors; Clifton Fadiman, general editor. Norton 1998 xxii, 1338p $45 **808.81**

1. Poetry -- Collections

ISBN 0-393-04130-1

LC 97-10879

The anthology's "stated aim—'to surprise and delight the common reader'—may seem rather quaint; yet it is a worthy one, and is, on the whole, impressively fulfilled." Times Lit Suppl

Includes bibliographical references

808.82   Collections of drama

★ **2010: the best men's stage monologues and scenes;** edited and foreword by Lawrence Harbison. Smith & Kraus 2010 176p pa $14.95 **808.82**

1. Acting 2. Monologues

ISBN 978-1-57525-773-0

This is a "selection of monologues and scenes from plays that were produced and/or published in the 2009-2010 theatrical season. Most are for younger performers (teens through thirties), but there are also some . . . pieces for men in their forties and fifties, and even a few for older performers. Some are comic (laughs), some are dramatic (generally, no laughs)." Publisher's note

★ **2010: the best women's stage monologues and scenes;** edited and with a foreword by Lawrence

Harbison. Smith & Kraus Book 2010 193p pa
$14.95 **808.82**
1. Acting 2. Monologues
ISBN 978-1-57525-774-7

This is a "selection of monologues and scenes from plays that were produced and/or published in the 2009-2010 theatrical season." Publisher's note

Nine plays of the modern theater; with an introduction by Harold Clurman. Grove Press 1981 896p pa $21 **808.82**
1. Drama -- Collections
ISBN 0-8021-5032-2

LC 79-52121

★ Play index. Wilson, H.W. 1953 11v **808.82**
1. Drama -- Indexes 2. Reference books
Play index indexes plays in collections and single plays; one-act and full-length plays; radio, television, and Broadway plays; plays for amateur production; plays for children, young adults, and adults. It is divided into four parts. Part I is an author, title, and subject index; the author or main entry includes the title of the play, brief synopsis of the plot, number of acts and scenes, size of cast, number of sets, and bibliographic information. Part II is a list of collections indexed, and Part III, a cast analysis, lists plays by the type of cast and number of players required.

"This index is an excellent source for locating published plays." Safford. Guide to Ref Materials for Sch Media Cent. 5th edition

The Ultimate audition book; 222 monologues, 2 minutes & under. edited by Jocelyn A. Beard. Smith & Kraus 1997 2v + v4 ea pa $19.95 **808.82**
1. Acting 2. Auditions 3. Drama -- Collections 4. Monologues
ISBN 1-57525-066-7 v1; 1-57525-270-8 v2; 1-57525-420-4 v4

LC 97-10471

This collection draws "upon lesser-known works from significant writers and those of contemporary favorites and reflects a wide range of tone, age, time period, and voice. Divided among female, male, and unisex categories, all meet the obligatory two minutes or less time limit imposed by most directors and auditions." Libr J [review of volume 2]
Includes bibliographical references

★ The best plays of 2006-2007; edited by Jeffrey Eric Jenkins; illustrated with production photographs. Limelight Eds. 2008 560p il $49.95 **808.82**
1. Drama -- Collections 2. Theater -- United States
ISBN 978-0-8791-0352-1

Some back volumes published by Dodd, Mead available from Applause Theatre Bk. Pubs.; reprints of older annuals available from Ayer; for full information on availability and price contact publishers.

The best stage scenes of 2007; edited by Lawrence Harbison; with a foreword by D.L. Lepidus. Smith & Kraus 2007 202p pa $14.95 **808.82**
1. Acting 2. Drama
ISBN 978-1-57525-588-0; 1-57525-588-X

This title culls "selections from recent plays, divided among scenic groupings for men and women, men, and women. . . . The scenes vary in length and intensity, with each scene providing a setting, description, and the number of needed characters." Libr J

808.83 Collections of fiction

Short story index. Wilson, H.W. **808.83**
1. Short stories -- Indexes

LC 75-649762

This index offers a single-alphabet listing of stories by author, title and subject. The List of collections indexed provides full bibliographic information. Includes a Directory of periodicals.

"These indexes provide valuable access to short stories in collections published since 1900." Ref Sources for Small & Medium-sized Libr. 6th edition

808.84 Collections of essays

Teachers & Writers Collaborative
The **Art** of the personal essay; an anthology from the classical era to the present. selected and with an introduction by Phillip Lopate. Anchor Bks. (NY) 1994 liv, 777p hardcover o.p. pa $17.95 **808.84**
1. Essays 2. Literature -- Collections
ISBN 0-385-42339-X pa

LC 93-29708

"Not only are the selections a veritable feast, but Lopate's genre-defining introduction is not to be missed." Booklist
Includes bibliographical references

★ The Norton book of personal essays; edited by Joseph Epstein. Norton 1997 477p $30 **808.84**
1. Essays
ISBN 0-393-03654-5

LC 96-26975

George Orwell, James Baldwin, Joan Didion, M. F. K. Fisher, Barbara Tuchman and Cynthia Ozick are among the authors chosen by Epstein for inclusion in this collection of "53 personal essays written in English by well-known authors during the past century. They were chosen because he 'found them interesting, touching, pleasing, amusing, delightful—above all, entertaining.' The result is a potpourri of selections that vary widely in subject and style. Topics range from music, racism, and traveling to fathers, children, and childhood." Libr J

808.85 Collections of speeches

Sutton, Roberta Briggs
Speech index; an index to 259 collections of world famous orations and speeches for various occasions. 4th ed rev & enl; Scarecrow Press 1966 947p $85 **808.85**
1. Reference books 2. Speeches -- Indexes
ISBN 0-8108-0138-8

"Speeches are indexed by orator, type of speech, and by subject, with a selected list of titles given in the appendix. Particularly useful for amateur speakers in locating examples to use in preparing a speech and models they can adapt to their needs." Ref Sources for Small & Medium-sized Libr. 6th edition

The World's great speeches; edited by Lewis Copeland, Lawrence W. Lamm, and Stephen J. McKenna. 4th enl 1999 ed; Dover Publs. 1999 xxii, 920p pa $17.95   **808.85**
1. Speeches 2. Speeches, addresses, etc
ISBN 0-486-40903-1
LC 99-32880

An international collection of approximately 300 speeches by over 200 speakers arranged chronologically.

808.86   Collections of letters

Mallon, Thomas
Yours ever; people and their letters. Pantheon Books 2009 338p $26.95   **808.86**
1. Letters
ISBN 978-0-679-44426-8; 0-679-44426-2
LC 2009-06315

This is "an astute, exhilarating tour of the mailbag. . . . [It] is nuanced, informed, full-blooded, a vigorous literary salute." N Y Times Book Rev

Includes bibliographical references (p. 313-320)

808.88   Collections of miscellaneous writings

Bartlett, John
★ Bartlett's familiar quotations; a collection of passages, phrases, and proverbs traced to their sources in ancient and modern literature. Little, Brown 2002 1431p $50   **808.88**
1. Quotations 2. Reference books
ISBN 0-316-08460-3
LC 2003-269668

"Arranged chronologically by author, with exact references. Includes many interesting footnotes, tracing history or usage of analogous thoughts, the circumstances under which a particular remark was made, etc. Author and keyword indexes. One of the best books of quotations with a long history." Guide to Ref Books. 11th edition

Includes bibliographical references

Boller, Paul F.
They never said it; a book of fake quotes, misquotes, and misleading attributions. [by] Paul F. Boller, Jr., and John George. Oxford Univ. Press 1989 xxv, 159p hardcover o.p. pa $15.95   **808.88**
1. Errors 2. Literary forgeries 3. Quotations
ISBN 0-19-506469-0 pa
LC 88-22115

In an alphabetical list of attributees' names or titles the authors expose the truth behind more than 200 phony quotations.

Nowlan, Robert A.
Born this day; a book of birthdays and quotations of prominent people through the centuries. 2nd ed.; McFarland & Co. 2007 511p $55   **808.88**
1. Birthdays 2. Quotations
ISBN 978-0-7864-2935-6; 0-7864-2935-6
LC 2007-3809

"Arranged chronologically by date of the month, the volume offers lists of 12 'significant' people born on each day, with a very brief biography and a representative or telling quotation uttered by the individual. In addition, each date lists the birthdays of a dozen or more lesser-known individuals, noting only name and year. . . . [This is] a fine ready-reference volume offering unique information." Booklist

Lend me your ears; Oxford dictionary of political quotations. edited by Sir Antony Jay. 4th ed; Oxford University Press 2010 xxv, 446p $24.95   **808.88**
1. Political science -- Quotations 2. Reference books
ISBN 978-0-19-957267-0
LC 2010-923325

Entries are organized "by speaker rather than by topic. Don't know the origin of a quotation? Fear not. Turn to the extensive keyword index or the briefer 'selective subject index' in the back of the volume. Helpful also are one-page special category quotes: epitaphs, misquotations, mottoes, slogans, etc. . . . [This is] a great value and an excellent choice for libraries lacking a current work in this area." Libr J

The Oxford book of aphorisms; chosen by John Gross. Oxford University Press 2003 383p pa $19.95   **808.88**
1. Quotations
ISBN 0-19-280456-1
LC 2003-269712

"Contains a well-chosen collection of aphorisms, maxims, quotations, and pensees from ancient times to the present. Entries, arranged under 58 subject sections, are identified with name of aphorist, source, publication date, or approximate date of original statement. Headings include 'nature,' 'good and evil,' 'illusion and reality,' and 'secrets.' An introduction gives definitions of aphorisms and their use throughout history." Wynar. Guide to Ref Books for Sch Media Cent. 3d edition

Includes bibliographical references

The Oxford book of death; chosen and edited by D.J. Enright. Oxford University Press 2008 351p pa $19.95   **808.88**
1. Death -- Quotations
ISBN 978-0-19-955652-6
LC 2008-482099

"Much work has gone into this compilation, and the individual introductions to the component sections are, as we would expect, elegant, modest and very wise." Times Lit Suppl

★ Oxford dictionary of humorous quotations; edited by Ned Sherrin; with a foreword by Alistair Bea-

ton. 4th ed; Oxford University Press 2008 536p
hardcover o.p. pa $24.95 **808.88**
1. Quotations 2. Quotations, English 3. Reference
books 4. Wit and humor
ISBN 978-0-19-923716-6; 0-19-923716-6; 978-0-19-
957006-5 pa; 0-19-957006-X pa
LC 2008-486673
This dictionary "features 5,000 quotations organized
into more than 200 subject categories. Quips are arranged
by broad themes. . . . Coverage spans the centuries, and you
are as likely to find lines by Johnny Depp, Ricky Gervais,
and Eddie Izzard are you are those by Noel Coward, William
Shakespeare, and George Bernard Shaw. . . . An amusing
addition to the reference collection." Booklist

Oxford dictionary of modern quotations; edited by
Elizabeth Knowles. 3rd ed.; Oxford University
Press 2007 479p $39.95; pa $18.95 **808.88**
1. Quotations 2. Reference books
ISBN 978-0-19-920895-1; 0-19-920895-6; 978-0-19-
954746-3 pa; 0-19-954746-7 pa
LC 2007-36871
"Containing more than 5,000 quotations from authors .
. . [such] as Bertolt Brecht, George W. Bush, Homer Simpson, Carl Sagan, William Shatner, and Desmond Tutu, the
dictionary is organized alphabetically by author, with . . .
cross-referencing and keyword and thematic indexes." Publisher's note

★ Oxford dictionary of quotations; edited by Elizabeth Knowles. 7th ed.; Oxford University Press
2009 xxvi, 1155p $50 **808.88**
1. Quotations 2. Reference books
ISBN 978-0-19-923717-3; 0-19-923717-4
LC 2009-464901
Collected here are around 20,000 quotations by nearly
3,500 authors from around the world ranging in time from
the 8th century BC to the present. Arrangement is alphabetical by the names of authors with sections such as Advertising Slogans, Epitaphs, Film Lines, Prayers, etc. included in
the alphabetical order. Indexed by key words.

Toasts; over 1,500 of the best toasts, sentiments,
blessings, and graces. {compiled by} Paul Dickson; illustrated by Rollin McGrail. Crown 1991
256p il $19 **808.88**
1. Toasts 2. Wit and humor
ISBN 0-517-58412-3
LC 91-6967
"Covering traditional occasions such as anniversaries
and weddings as well as a variety of other 'toastable' events,
this book organizes 1,500 toasts under 75 alphabetically
arranged subject headings. Included are ethnic, military,
birthday, and holiday toasts. There are also toasts related
to sports, aging, food, parents, and even cheese and cham-
pagne! The toasts have been gathered from a variety of toast
books, many of which date from the late nineteenth and
early twentieth centuries. An interesting history of toasting
is included." Booklist
Includes bibliographical references

809 History, description, critical appraisal of more than two literatures

Atwood, Margaret
In other worlds; SF and the human imagination.
Nan A. Talese/Doubleday 2011 255p pa $24.95 **809**
1. Science fiction -- Authorship 2. Science fiction --
History and criticism
ISBN 978-0-385-53396-6
LC 2011013776
"Atwood is well known to sf readers for such novels as
The Handmaid's Tale, Oryx and Crake, and The Year of the
Flood. In this collection of essays and short fiction, she fur-
ther explores the genre, beginning with her three previously
unpublished Richard Ellman Lectures in Modern Literature,
which she delivered at Emory University in 2010. . . . A clev-
er, thoughtful investigation that will appeal to science fiction
readers and Atwood's loyal fans." Libr J
Includes bibliographical references

Bentley, Eric
The **life** of the drama. Applause Theatre Bk.
Pubs. 1991 371p pa $12.95 **809**
1. Drama -- History and criticism
ISBN 1-55783-110-6
LC 91-28774
The author discusses plot, character, dialogue, and action
in various theatrical genres. Among the dramatists discussed
are Aeschylus, Beckett, Brecht, Chekhov, Corneille, Goethe,
Ibsen, Ben Jonson, Molière, Pirandello, Racine, Shake-
speare, Shaw, and Sophocles

Bloom, Harold
The **Western** canon; the books and school of the
ages. Riverhead Bks. 1995 546p pa $18 **809**
1. Authors 2. Blind 3. Diplomats 4. Dramatists 5.
Essayists 6. Judges 7. Lexicographers 8. Literary
critics 9. Literature -- History and criticism 10. Nobel
laureates for literature 11. Nobel laureates for peace 12.
Nonfiction writers 13. Novelists 14. Poets 15. Poets
laureate 16. Psychoanalysts 17. Short story writers
18. Translators 19. Writers on medicine 20. Writers
on religion 21. Writers on science
ISBN 1-57322-514-2; 978-1-57322-514-4
The "book succeeds not as a polemic but as a passionate,
erudite and highly idiosyncratic series of essays about the
literature dearest to one of America's most influential academics." Publ Wkly

Boyd, Brian
On the origin of stories; evolution, cognition, and
fiction. Belknap Press of Harvard University Press
2009 540p il $35 **809**
1. Authorship 2. Evolution 3. Fiction -- Authorship 4.
Fiction -- History and criticism
ISBN 978-0-674-03357-3; 0-674-03357-4
LC 2009-07642
The author "has created a compelling, erudite, and thoroughly original work about the nature of humanistic expression in art and literature. Beautifully written and wide-
ranging, the book delves into social science, evolutionary

biology, art, and literature to create a comprehensive account of the evolutionary origins of art and storytelling." Choice

Includes bibliographical references

Calvino, Italo

Why read the classics? translated from the Italian by Martin McLaughlin. Pantheon Bks. 1999 277p hardcover o.p. pa $13 **809**

1. Canon (Literature) 2. Literature -- History and criticism

ISBN 0-679-74349-9 pa

LC 99-21535

"Calvino celebrates a wide range of great thinkers in these provocative essays. Here are writers from the ancient world, the Renaissance and recent times, and from the old and new worlds. . . . [These essays] are a reminder to us that 'rereading' the classics can amuse as well as reward." New Sci

Includes bibliographical references

Damrosch, David

The **buried** book; the loss and rediscovery of the great Epic of Gilgamesh. H. Holt 2007 315p il map hardcover o.p. pa $16.99 **809**

1. Assyriology

ISBN 978-0-8050-8029-2; 0-8050-8029-5; 978-0-8050-8725-3 pa; 0-8050-8725-7 pa

LC 2006-49523

"Combining acuity about cultural contexts with wide-ranging knowledge, Damrosch's account is a superb and engrossing popular presentation." Booklist

Includes bibliographical references

Donoghue, Emma

Inseparable; desire between women in literature. Emma Donoghue. Alfred A. Knopf 2010 x, 271p ill. (hc : alk. paper) $27.95 **809**

1. Desire in literature 2. English literature -- History and criticism 3. French literature -- History and criticism 4. Lesbianism in literature 5. Women in literature

ISBN 9780307270948; 0307270947

LC 2009048368

This book "explores the little-known literary tradition of love between women in Western literature, from Chaucer and Shakespeare to Charlotte Brontë, Dickens, Agatha Christie, and many more. . . . [It] examine[s] how desire between women in English literature has been portrayed, from schoolgirls and vampires to runaway wives, from cross-dressing knights to contemporary murder stories. [Author Emma] Donoghue looks at the work of those writers who have addressed the 'unspeakable subject,' examining whether such desire between women is freakish or omnipresent, holy or evil, heartwarming or ridiculous as she excavates a long-obscured tradition of (inseparable) friendship between women, one that is . . . central to our cultural history." (Publisher's note)

Fraser, Kennedy

Ornament and silence; essays on women's lives. Knopf 1996 247p hardcover o.p. pa $13 **809**

1. Artists 2. Authors 3. Biographers 4. Biography, Collective 5. Botanists 6. College teachers 7.

Dramatists 8. Entomologists 9. Essayists 10. Fashion designers 11. Feminists 12. Literary critics 13. Magazine editors 14. Nonfiction writers 15. Novelists 16. Painters 17. Poets 18. Short story writers 19. Women -- Biography 20. Women authors 21. Writers on politics 22. Writers on science

ISBN 0-375-70112-5 pa

LC 96-11479

A collection of fourteen profiles, personal reminiscences and extended reviews of books.

"A 'daughter of the paternal old NewYorker' in her youth, Fraser . . . has moved on with time, taking for her more mature role models Nina Berberova, Edith Wharton, and Germaine Greer. Fraser's essays are quiet, thorough, and beautifully paced." Libr J

Hollands, Neil

Fellowship in a ring; a guide for science fiction and fantasy book groups. Libraries Unlimited 2010 300p pa $40 **809**

1. Book clubs (Discussion groups) 2. Books and reading 3. Fantasy fiction 4. Fantasy fiction -- Bibliography 5. Fantasy fiction -- History and criticism 6. Science fiction 7. Science fiction -- Bibliography 8. Science fiction -- History and criticism

ISBN 978-1-59158-703-3; 1-59158-703-4

LC 2009-46456

This is "is an excellent resource for both novices looking to initiate groups, and veterans seeking to breathe new life into existing factions. The first chapter delineates the practical building blocks necessary to develop a thriving science fiction/fantasy book group, from suggestions of how to ward off potential problems and keep discussions interesting to creative ideas for preventing meetings from becoming stagnant. . . . Included is a list of fifty recommended science fiction and fantasy novels, with helpful information such as author background, plot summaries, a reading guide, and discussion questions. An especially thorough listing of themes for discussion consists of resources, thematic questions, and suggested works." Voice Youth Advocates

Includes bibliographical references

Isherwood, Christopher, 1904-1986

Liberation; Diaries:1970-1983. HarperCollins 2012 928 p. $39.99 **809**

ISBN 0062084747; 9780062084743

This book is the third and final volume of [Christopher] Isherwood's . . . diaries [and] concludes with a 136-page "glossary" of names . . . . As the 1970 s commence, lover Don Bachardy has just had his screenplay for 'Cabaret' (based on the musical drawn from Isherwood s Goodbye to Berlin) rejected, and the two have begun . . . an unsuccessful stage adaptation of Isherwood's novel, "A Meeting by the River." The last diary entry dates to July 4, 1983, exactly two and a half years before Isherwood's death from cancer. In between, he regales readers with accounts of his collaboration with Bachardy on the screenplay for 'Frankenstein: The True Story," the 1976 publication of "Christopher and His Kind" . . . and nonstop dinners, parties, and foreign travels. (Publishers Weekly)

Iyer, Pico

The **man** within my head; Pico Iyer. Alfred A. Knopf 2012 241 p. **809**

1. Fathers and sons 2. Memoirs 3. Novelists, English -- 20th century -- Biography
ISBN 030726761X; 9780307267610

LC 2011041285

In this book, author Pico "Iyer describes [writer Graham] Greene as constantly in his mind as a kind of imaginative touchstone. . . . Greene . . . edged to the periphery of English life when he became a Roman Catholic in order to marry, and then rapidly steered himself to the periphery of Catholic life when he asserted that belief was irrational and called himself a Catholic atheist. Though an excellent and generous friend to many people, and devoted to a number of women, he lived alone but far from isolated from the world. . . . Mr. Iyer admires all of these characteristics, and the novels too, especially 'The Quiet American,' which tells such a compelling tale of historic disaster and psychological ambivalences. In the second half . . . [Iyer] answers the question he poses in the first half. Why Greene? . . . His answer focuses on the ways that Greene's characters -- Pyle and Fowler in 'The Quiet American,' for example -- have a kind of father-and-son relationship to each other." (Washington Times)

James, Henry

★ **Literary** criticism. Library of Am. 1984 2v v1 ea $50 **809**

1. Literature -- History and criticism
ISBN 0-94050-023-2 v1; 0-94050-22-4 v2

LC 84-11241

"Grouped by nationality, alphabetically by author, and chronologically, the essays provide a kind of critical book within a book on such writers as Balzac, George Eliot, and Hawthorne. These groupings enable the reader to see how James approached a writer and to follow the development of his thinking about particular writers over the years." Publisher's note

Includes bibliographical references

Jarrell, Randall

No other book; selected essays. edited and introduced by Brad Leithauser. HarperCollins Pubs. 1999 xx, 376p hardcover o.p. pa $15 **809**

1. American poetry -- History and criticism 2. American poetry -- History and criticism -- Theory, etc 3. Authors 4. Biographers 5. Books -- Reviews 6. Children's authors 7. College teachers 8. Essayists 9. Insurance executives 10. Lawyers 11. Literature -- History and criticism 12. Literature -- History and criticism -- Theory, etc 13. Memoirists 14. Nobel laureates for literature 15. Novelists 16. Physicians 17. Poets 18. Short story writers 19. Translators
ISBN 0-06-095638-0 pa

LC 98-55353

"Jarrell taught his peers to appreciate first the young Robert Lowell and W. H. Auden, then Marianne Moore, William Carlos Williams, Elizabeth Bishop, Walt Whitman and Robert Frost. . . . The later Jarrell divided his prose between appreciations of poets, digressions on idiosyncratic passions, and funny or sad indictments of 1950s-style popular culture. . . . As a convincing, above all personal, guide to modern poets, and as a captivating writer of criticism Jarrell has no obvious 20th century equal." Publ Wkly

Kundera, Milan

Encounter; translated from the French by Linda Asher. Harper 2010 178p $23.99 **809**

1. Art appreciation 2. Literature -- History and criticism 3. Literature, Modern -- 20th century -- History and criticism 4. Music -- History and criticism 5. Painting -- Appreciation
ISBN 978-0-06-189441-1; 0-06-189441-9

LC 2010-04908

"Of specific interest are chapters comparing Francis Bacon to Samuel Beckett; Kundera's devilish mixing up of Roland Barthes with the dour theologian Karl Barth in a chance conversation; several discussions on the virtues of Rabelais as well as a restoration to prominence of Anatole France, who had been given the French intellectualist bum's rush; a powerful coupling of the bright birth of film with the sad death of Fellini; a scholar's relishing of Bertolt Brecht's body odor; the music of his fellow Czech Leos Janacek. Like the proverbial meal at the Chinese restaurant, the delicious musings of this book are filling at first. Two hours later, one craves more." Publ Wkly

Kurian, George Thomas

★ **Timetables** of world literature. Facts on File 2003 457p $65 **809**

1. Literature -- Chronology
ISBN 0-8160-4197-0

LC 2002-3891

Chronicles world literature from the Classical Age through the twentieth century, discussing literary developments and the relationship between literature and the political and social climate of each historical period.

"This comprehensive reference . . . helps academic researchers place major works of literature from 58 countries in historical and cultural context." Libr J

Includes bibliographical references

Manguel, Alberto

The **dictionary** of imaginary places; {by} Alberto Manguel & Gianni Guadalupi; illustrated by Graham Greenfield; with additional illustrations by Eric Beddows; maps and charts by James Cook. Newly updated and expanded; Harcourt Brace & Co. 1999 755p il maps $40; pa $24 **809**

1. Fantasy fiction -- Dictionaries 2. Geographical myths -- Dictionaries 3. Imaginary places -- Dictionaries 4. Reference books
ISBN 0-15-100541-9; 0-15-600872-6 pa

LC 99-46994

This resource "contains entries for more than 1,200 imaginary places from literature and folklore. Each entry describes the place, its locale, and history and provides citations to the source work or tale. More than 220 maps and illustrations are included." Booklist

Includes bibliographical references

Moore, Steven

The **novel**; an alternative history: beginnings to 1600.

Continuum 2010 698p $39.95 **809**
1. Fiction -- History and criticism
ISBN 9781441177049; 1-4411-7704-3

LC 2010-279268

"Reveling in the most innovative and daring creations, Moore energetically evaluates tales fantastic, chilling, hilarious, erotic, and tragic, comparing centuries-old novels to those of Barth, Gaddis, Pynchon, and Vollmann. Destined for controversy, Moore's erudite, gargantuan, kaleidoscopic, and venturesome alternative history will leave readers feeling as though they've been viewing literature with blinders on." Booklist

Includes bibliographical references

Niebuhr, Gary Warren
  Make mine a mystery; a reader's guide to mystery and detective fiction. Libraries Unlimited 2003 605p $65   **809**
1. Mystery fiction -- Bibliography 2. Mystery fiction -- History and criticism 3. Reference books
ISBN 1-56308-784-7

LC 2003-271056

"The book is divided into two parts. In part 1, 'Introduction to Mystery Fiction,' Niebuhr devotes considerable space to background material: discussion of readers'-advisory service in general and the appeal of mystery fiction in particular and how to build and manage a mystery collection, followed by a history of the genre beginning in 1845. Part 2, 'The Literature,' annotates more than 2,500 titles by more than 200 authors. . . . Among guides to mystery fiction, this one stands out as being thorough and current. Essential for public libraries." Booklist

Ozick, Cynthia
  ★ The **din** in the head; essays. Houghton Mifflin Co. 2006 243p il $24   **809**
1. Literature -- History and criticism 2. Literature, Modern -- 20th century -- History and criticism
ISBN 978-0-618-47050-1; 0-618-47050-6

LC 2005-16102

The author is "not only one of the finest novelists of our time but an essayist of startling spiritual verve and range." Christ Century

Poe, Edgar Allan
  ★ **Essays** and reviews. Library of Am. 1984 1544p $40   **809**
ISBN 0-940450-19-4

LC 83-19923

This volume is divided into six main divisions: Theory of poetry, Reviews of British and Continental authors; Reviews of American authors and American criticism; Magazines and criticism; The literary and social scene; and Articles and marginalia.

Roth, Philip
  Shop talk; a writer and his colleagues and their work. Houghton Mifflin 2001 160p $23   **809**
1. Authors 2. Authors -- Interviews 3. Literature -- History and criticism
ISBN 0-618-15314-4

LC 2001-24523

"In this collection of encounters with distinguished minds—unguarded interviews with Primo Levi and Aharon Appelfeld, among others; an odd exchange of letters with Mary McCarthy; fondly contentious portraits of Bernard Malamud and the painter Philip Guston—Roth manages to tease from his subjects the convictions that fuel their work and the vulnerabilities that make them human." N Y Times Book Rev

Society for the Study of the Short Story
  A **Reader's** companion to the short story in English; edited by Erin Fallon [et al.]; under the auspices of the Society for the Study of the Short Story. Greenwood Press 2001 xxxiv, 432p $105   **809**
1. American fiction -- 20th century 2. Authors, American -- 20th century -- Biography 3. Authors, Commonwealth -- Biography 4. Authors, English -- 20th century -- Biography 5. Commonwealth fiction (English) 6. English fiction -- 20th century 7. Short stories -- History and criticism 8. Short stories, American 9. Short stories, English
ISBN 0-313-29104-7

LC 00-25113

"Although most of the stories covered by Fallon's compilation were written in the later half of the 20th century, the scope is international. . . . Each chapter concisely profiles a writer and contains a biography, a brief review of criticism, a lengthier analysis of specific works, and a bibliography. A section covers the short story genre. This work is extremely important because of the popularity of the genre." Choice

Includes bibliographical references

Symons, Julian
  Bloody murder; from the detective story to the crime novel. 3rd rev ed; Mysterious Press 1993 349p pa $30   **809**
1. Mystery fiction -- History and criticism
ISBN 0-89296-496-0

LC 92-54127

A critical survey of crime fiction, including detective stories, psychological crime stories, thrillers, and espionage, covering authors from Poe to the 1990s.

Yagoda, Ben
  Memoir; a history. Riverhead Books 2009 291p $25.95 **809**
1. Autobiography
ISBN 978-1-59448-886-3; 1-59448-886-X

LC 2009-30859

"With its mixture of literary criticism, cultural history and just enough trivia, Yagoda's survey is sure to appeal to scholars and bibliophiles alike." Publ Wkly

Includes bibliographical references

Beacham's encyclopedia of popular fiction; edited by Kirk H. Beetz. Beacham Pub. 1996 19v **809**
1. Fiction -- Bio-bibliography 2. Reference books
ISBN 0-93383-338-5

LC 96-20771

This reference work consists of a three volume set of Biography series and sixteen volumes of Analyses series. Available separately or in sets. Apply to publisher for price.

Black literature criticism; classic and emerging authors since 1950. Jelena O. Krstovic, project editor; forward by Howard Dodson. 2nd ed.; Gale Cengage Learning 2008 3v il set $459 **809**
1. American literature -- African American authors -- History and criticism 2. Blacks in literature 3. English literature -- Black authors -- History and criticism
ISBN 978-1-4144-3170-3; 1-4144-3170-8
"This work includes African American, Caribbean, and African writers who produce works in English. Authors range from relative newcomers . . . to classic authors. . . . [This is] a worthwhile purchase." Booklist
Includes bibliographical references

Contemporary literary criticism. Gale Res. **809**
1. Literature -- History and criticism
LC 76-38938
"This multivolume, onging series offers significant passages from contemporary criticism on authors who are now living or who have died since December 31, 1959. . . . Brief author sketches are followed by critical excerpts, presented in chronological order. The number of authors covered in each volume has varied over the years." Ref Sources for Small & Medium-sized Libr. 6th edition

★ Critical survey of drama; edited by Carl Rollyson. 2nd rev ed; Salem Press 2003 8v set $499 **809**
1. American drama 2. American drama -- Dictionaries 3. Commonwealth drama (English) 4. Drama 5. Drama -- Dictionaries 6. Drama -- History and criticism 7. English drama 8. English drama -- Dictionaries 9. Reference books
ISBN 1-58765-102-5
LC 2003-2190
This set contains "about 630 essays, of which 570 discuss individual dramatists and 60 cover overview topics. . . Each essay on a dramatist provides . . . material as birth and death dates, lists of the author's major dramatic works (with dates of first production and publication). Each essay opens with a brief survey of the author's publications in literary forms other than drama, a summary of the writer's professional achievements and awards, an extended biographical sketch that centers on the writer's development as a dramatist, and an extensive critical analysis of the writer's major dramatic works. Following this discussion is a list of major publications in fields other than drama and an annotated bibliography of critical works about the author." Publisher's note
Includes bibliographical references

Critical survey of mystery and detective fiction; editor, Carl Rollyson. Rev ed; Salem Press 2008 5v il set $399 **809**
1. Detective and mystery stories 2. Detective and mystery stories -- History and criticism 3. Mystery fiction -- History and criticism
ISBN 978-1-58765-397-1; 1-58765-397-4
LC 2007-40208
This "is the most exhaustive and best-documented account of this genre available." Choice
Includes bibliographical references

★ Cyclopedia of literary places; consulting editor, R. Baird Shuman; editor, R. Kent Rasmussen; introduction by Brian Stableford. Salem Press 2003 3v set $305 **809**
1. Literary landmarks 2. Literature -- Encyclopedias 3. Reference books
ISBN 1-58766-094-0
LC 2002-156159
"This three-volume set completes Salem's trilogy of reference works analyzing stories (Masterplots), characters (Cyclopedia of Literary Characters), and now settings in classic works of literature (mostly novels, though a few plays and poems are included). . . . Literary Places provides details of both real and imaginary geographic places that serve as settings for approximately 1300 titles covered in the previous works. . . . The entries are alphabetized by title, range in length from 300 to 1000 words, and feature author, type of work, type of plot, time of plot, and a brief synopsis. . . . Well written, easy to use, and fun to read, this set . . . is a valuable addition to all libraries." Libr J
Includes bibliographical references

Literary movements for students; presenting analysis, context, and criticism on literary movements. David Galens, project editor. Gale Group 2002 2v il set $185 **809**
1. Literary movements -- Bio-bibliography 2. Literary movements -- History 3. Literature -- History and criticism
ISBN 0-7876-6517-7
LC 2002-10928
Entries provide "historical background information on each movement as well as modern critical interpretation of each movement's characteristic styles and themes. Approximately 25 movements are covered, including absurdism, Greek drama, modernism, science fiction/fantasy, surrealism and many others." Publisher's note
Includes bibliographical references

Literature and its times; profiles of 300 notable literary works and the historical events that influenced them. Gale Res. 1997 5v set $741 **809**
1. Literature -- History and criticism
ISBN 0-7876-0606-5
LC 97-34339
"The editors chose the selections (fiction, poetry, short stories, plays, biographies, and speeches) with the input of public libraries and secondary-school teachers. . . . Each volume covers a time range subdivided by dates and a general description . . . and begins with a brief overview of the historical events of the era, with a time-line providing a synopsis of each period." Libr J

★ Magill's survey of world literature; edited by Steven G. Kellman. Rev ed; Salem Press 2009 6v il set $499 **809**
1. Authors -- Biography 2. Literature -- Bio-bibliography 3. Literature -- History and criticism 4. Reference books
ISBN 978-1-58765-431-2
LC 2008-46042

"A solid choice for anyone in need of an inexpensive, broad biocritical literary reference title on world literature." Libr J

Includes glossary and bibliographical references

Masterpieces of world literature; edited by Frank N. Magill. Harper & Row 1989 957p $55   **809**
1. Best books 2. Literature -- History and criticism 3. Literature -- Stories, plots, etc.
ISBN 0-06-270050-2

LC 89-45052

"The work, arranged alphabetically by title, contains plot summaries, character portrayals, and critical evaluations of 270 classics of world literature (novels, plays, stories, poems, and essays), all reprints from other Magill guides." Nichols. Guide to Ref Books for Sch Media Cent. 4th edition

★ Masterplots II, drama series; editor, Christian H. Moe. rev ed; Salem Press 2003 4v set $404 **809**
1. Drama -- History and criticism 2. Drama -- Stories, plots, etc.
ISBN 1-58765-116-5

LC 2003-12651

"This newest addition to a reference standard belongs in most public, academic, and secondary libraries." Booklist

Mystery and suspense writers; the literature of crime, detection, and espionage. Robin W. Winks, editor in chief; Maureen Corrigan, associate editor. Scribner 1998 2v set $250   **809**
1. Mystery fiction -- Dictionaries 2. Reference books 3. Spies in literature
ISBN 0-684-80521-9

LC 98-36812

"Articles on 68 mystery writers ranging from Edgar Allen Poe to Sarah Paretsky run from ten to 20 pages and include information on the life and works as well as solid bibliographies for each author." Libr J

★ Reference guide to world literature; editors, Sara Pendergast, Tom Pendergast. 3rd ed; St. James Press 2003 2v set $350   **809**
1. Literature 2. Literature -- Bio-bibliography 3. Literature -- History and criticism 4. Reference books
ISBN 1-55862-490-2

LC 2002-15410

This work "contains 1,100 entries, about equally divided between entries on authors and on literary works. Each author entry in volume 1 includes a short biography, a signed critical essay, and selected lists of works by and about the author. Each literary work entry in volume 2 includes the author and date of publication (if known), a signed critical essay, and a selected list of critical studies. The scope of coverage is major works in languages other than English from the earliest known manuscripts to present day writers. . . . Because of its comprehensiveness and authority, this sturdily bound set is recommended for ready reference in libraries with large world literature sections and for smaller libraries needing more information in this area." Am Ref Books Annu, 2003

Includes bibliographical references

Short story criticism; excerpts from criticism of the works of short fiction writers. Gale Res.   **809**
1. Short stories -- History and criticism

This "series presents significant critical excerpts on the most important short story writers of all eras and nationalities. Each entry gives a biographical and critical overview, a list of principal works, excerpts of criticism, and a selected bibliography." Ref Sources for Small & Medium-sized Libr. 6th edition

Short story writers; edited by Charles E. May. Rev. ed.; Salem Press 2008 3v il set $217   **809**
1. Short stories -- History and criticism
ISBN 978-1-58765-389-6

LC 2007-32789

This set "covers writers from Giovanni Boccaccio and Geoffrey Chaucer to Anton Chekhov and Sandra Cisneros. . . . Readers, whether in need of a brief critical overview or in search of what to read next, will find this set extremely useful. Each entry includes a brief biography, a list of principal works, a note on other literary forms the author explored, and a concise list of achievements as well as brief essays . . . on particular stories." SLJ

Includes bibliographical references

★ Supernatural fiction writers; contemporary fantasy and horror. Richard Bleiler, editor. 2nd ed; Scribner 2003 1048p 2v set $250   **809**
1. Authors -- Biography 2. Fantasy fiction -- History and criticism 3. Horror tales -- History and criticism 4. Supernatural in literature
ISBN 0-684-31250-6

LC 2002-11128

This edition "is organized alphabetically by writer. Articles range in length from 5 to 12 pages. There is some biographical information but emphasis is on the works, with analysis of important themes, types of work, and, in many cases, individual series and titles. Each article concludes with a selected bibliography of works by the author under discussion, critical and biographical studies, and Web sites if they are available." Booklist

Includes bibliographical references

★ Twentieth-century literary criticism.   Gale Res.   **809**
1. Literature -- History and criticism

LC 76-46132

"Excerpts from criticism of the works of novelists, poets, playwrights, short story writers, and other creative writers who lived between 1900 and 1999, from the first published critical appraisals to current evaluations." Title page

★ World authors, 1980-1985; editor, Vineta Colby. Wilson, H.W. 1990 938p il $140   **809**
1. Authors -- Dictionaries 2. Literature -- Bio-bibliography 3. Reference books
ISBN 0-8242-0797-1

LC 90-49782

This volume covers 320 contemporary writers

World authors, 1985-1990; a volume in the Wilson authors series. editor, Vineta Colby. Wilson, H.W. 1995 970p il $140 **809**
1. Authors -- Dictionaries 2. Literature -- Bio-bibliography 3. Reference books
ISBN 0-8242-0875-7

LC 95-41656

This volume covers 345 novelists, playwrights, poets, and other authors who have risen to prominence in the late 1980s.

★ World authors, 1990-1995; editor, Clifford Thompson. Wilson, H.W. 1999 863p il $155 **809**
1. Authors -- 20th century -- Biography 2. Authors -- Dictionaries 3. Literature -- Bio-bibliography 4. Reference books
ISBN 0-8242-0956-7

LC 99-48161

The 317 authors treated in this volume include novelists, playwrights, and poets who have published significant work in the early 1990s. Also covers essayists, historians, biographers, critics, philosophers, and social scientists who have made exceptional contributions to the literature of our time.

World authors, 1995-2000; editors, Clifford Thompson, Mari Rich [et. al.] Wilson, H.W. 2003 872p il $160 **809**
1. Authors -- 20th century -- Biography -- Dictionaries 2. Authors -- Dictionaries 3. Literature -- Bio-bibliography 4. Reference books
ISBN 0-8242-1032-8

LC 2003-45062

This reference includes 320 novelists, poets, dramatists, essayists, social scientists, and biographers who have published significant works from 1995 through 2000. Each profile details the author's life and career, the circumstances under which their works were produced, and their literary significance.

The story about the story; great writers explore great literature. edited by J. C. Hallman. Tin House Books 2009 420p pa $18.95 **809**
1. Literature -- History and criticism
ISBN 978-0-9802436-9-7

LC 2009-15717

In his introduction, "editor J.C. Hallman writes about what he calls a 'kind of personal literary analysis, criticism that contemplates rather than analyzes'. He goes on to make the case for writers writing about writing from an individual perspective as his ideal approach to critiquing literature and the inspiration behind his compiling these works by notable writers from Virginia Woolf and D.H. Lawrence to Susan Sontag and Milan Kundera. . . . The selections range from well-known essays like Vladimir Nabokov on The Metamorphosis (he tries to figure out exactly what kind of beetle Gregor Samsa had turned into) to quirkier pleasures like Salman Rushdie on The Wizard of Oz." PopMatters

809.1 Literature in specific forms other than miscellaneous writings

Borges, Jorge Luis

This craft of verse; edited by Calin-Andrei Mihailescu. Harvard Univ. Press 2000 154p il $25; pa $14.95 **809.1**
1. CD-ROMs 2. Poetry -- History and criticism
ISBN 0-674-00290-3; 0-674-00820-0 pa

LC 00-33541

This volume is based on the Argentine writer's "Charles Eliot Norton lectures [delivered] at Harvard in 1967-68. . . . [Borges] discusses some of his favorite texts, conducting a literary journey that began in his father's library in Buenos Aires." N Y Times Book Rev

Includes bibliographical references

Brodsky, Joseph

Less than one; selected essays. Farrar, Straus & Giroux 1986 501p hardcover o.p. pa $18 **809.1**
1. Authors 2. College teachers 3. Essayists 4. Poetry -- History and criticism 5. Poets 6. Russian literature -- History and criticism
ISBN 0-374-52055-0 pa

LC 85-15900

The essays in this volume "begin and end with autobiographical pieces; in between there are alternate homages to favorite poets, both Russian and non-Russian, as well as substantial discussions of such topics as geography and history, political force and ethical choice, and literary tradition." N Y Times Book Rev

Burt, Stephen

Close calls with nonsense; reading new poetry. Graywolf Press 2009 374p bibl f pa $19 **809.1**
1. Poetry -- History and criticism
ISBN 978-1-55597-521-0; 1-55597-521-6

LC 2008-935602

"This collection of 30 essays, many of which began as book reviews, confirms Stephen Burt's reputation as the leading poetry critic of his generation. Informative, matter-of-fact and abounding with an excited spirit more common to film and pop music reviews than to literary criticism, these essays will appeal to the unpracticed reader of contemporary poetry as well as the seasoned reader. . . . Burt comes to the poets he considers—including Rea Armantrout, Juan Felipe Herrera, Paul Muldoon and James Merrill—as both a scholar and a practitioner of the art, but he eschews the specialist's jargon as well as the indulgent lyricality that makes some poets' criticism more dazzling than illuminating." Publ Wkly

Includes bibliographical references

Gioia, Dana

Can poetry matter? essays on poetry and American culture. Dana Gioia. 10th Anniversary ed; Graywolf Press 2002 231p pa $16 **809.1**
1. Artists 2. Authors 3. College teachers 4. Criticism 5. Dramatists 6. Editors 7. Insurance executives 8. Lawyers 9. Literary critics 10. Literature and society -- United States 11. Magazine editors 12. Painters 13. Poetry -- History and criticism 14. Poets 15. Poets

laureate 16. Short story writers 17. Translators 18. Writers on nature

ISBN 1-55597-370-1

LC 2002-102971

In addition to addressing the business of being a poet and the new formalism, the author offers readings of Robinson Jeffers, Weldon Kees, Robert Bly and others.

"Gioia makes his case with erudition and skill, and the best essays bring attention to underappreciated poets like Ted Kooser." Libr J

Hirsch, Edward

Poet's choice; Edward Hirsch. Harcourt 2006 432p $25   **809.1**

1. Poetry -- History and criticism

ISBN 0-15-101356-X; 978-0-15-101356-2

LC 2005-26890

"Hirsch's aesthetic is unerring, and his interpretations are profound as he considers our 'collective destiny' and takes measure of poetry's encompassing vision." Booklist

Iron-Georges, Tracy

Masterplots II, poetry series; rev ed; Salem Press 2002 8v set $499   **809.1**

1. Poetry -- History and criticism 2. Poetry -- Themes, motives

ISBN 1-58765-037-1

LC 2001-55059

"This set supersedes the six-volume Masterplots 2: Poetry Series (1992) and the three-volume Masterplots 2: Poetry Series Supplement (1998). It contains 1,385 signed entries written by scholars on individual poems, arranged alphabetically by poem title and ranging in length from three to five pages apiece." Booklist

Includes bibliographical references

Koch, Kenneth

Making your own days; the pleasures of reading and writing poetry. Simon & Schuster 1999 317p pa $15   **809.1**

1. Poetry -- Collections 2. Poetry -- History and criticism

ISBN 0-684-82438-8

LC 98-115810

"This book is divided into two parts: a series of essays on subjects such as meter, rhyme, and personification and an anthology of favorite poems. Most remarkably, non-English poems often appear with several translations, underscoring the flexibility of poetic language. Making Your Own Days will be most useful to writers already familiar with the basics." Libr J

Orr, David

Beautiful & pointless. HarperCollins 2011 200p $25.99   **809.1**

1. Literary critiques 2. Nonfiction 3. Poetry 4. Poetry -- History and criticism 5. Poetry, Modern 6. Poets, American

ISBN 978-0-06-167345-0; 0-06-167345-5

LC 2011-11599

This book presents a guide and cultural critique of the state of contemporary poetry by David Orr, an attorney, poet,

and poetry reviewer for The New York Times Book Review. "The author looks at themes and influences of various modern poems, including the poem BushBs War,s by Robert Haas. He also explores his own history as an appreciator and writer of poetry. [David Orr] takes a calisthenic view of poetry." (Nation)

What makes this book "different from thousands of other defenses of poetry is that, according to its author, poetry differs from music and stamp collecting in that people's love for poetry is measurably greater than their love for any other activity. Poetry fans don't just love poetry a little; they really love it." N Y Times Book Rev

Paglia, Camille

★ Break, blow, burn; Camille Paglia. Pantheon Books 2005 247p $20; pa $12.95   **809.1**

1. American poetry -- History and criticism 2. English poetry -- History and criticism

ISBN 0-375-42084-3; 0-375-72539-3 pa

LC 2004-56573

This work "is vintage Paglia: bracing, opinionated, and deliciously enjoyable." Natl Rev

Includes bibliographical references

★ Classic writings on poetry; edited by William Harmon. Columbia University Press 2003 538p $79; pa $27.50   **809.1**

1. Poetics 2. Poetry -- History and criticism

ISBN 0-231-12370-1; 0-231-12371-X pa

LC 2003-40917

This anthology contains "writing on poetry by such philosophical royalty as Plato, Aristotle, Milton, Sir Philip Sidney, Wordsworth, and Emily Dickinson. Readers are given a peek through the hole of history's fence into the lives and worlds of our poetic geniuses and reminded of the poem's matchless role in conveying reverence, remembering wars, recording history, entertaining, expressing deep emotion, and above all, allowing the finite mind, for one moment, to contain infinity." Libr J

Includes bibliographical references

★ Poetry in person; twenty-five years of conversation with America's poets. edited and with an introduction by Alexander Neubauer; postscript by Robert Polito. Alfred A. Knopf 2010 343p il $27.95   **809.1**

1. American poetry -- 20th century 2. College teachers 3. Poetics 4. Poetry -- Authorship 5. Poetry -- History and criticism 6. Poets -- Interviews 7. Poets, American

ISBN 978-0-307-26967-6

LC 2009-29277

"For almost 30 years, beginning in 1970, Pearl London taught a course at the New School called Works in Progress, to which she asked famous poets to come with drafts of new poems in hand. This book is a series of transcripts of discussions from those classes, taken from a series of previously unknown recordings found after London's death. . . . Represented in these 23 conversations are such acknowledged masters of late 20th–century poetry as Robert Hass, Lucille Clifton, Amy Clampitt, and Charles Simic." Publ Wkly

810 Literatures of specific languages and language families

Acosta-Belen, Edna

The **Norton** anthology of Latino literature; Ilan Stavans, general editor; [editors], Edna Acosta-Belen [et al.] W.W. Norton & Co. 2010 2489p il map $59.95 **810**

1. American literature -- Hispanic American authors 2. American literature -- Hispanic American authors -- Collections
ISBN 978-0-393-08007-0; 0-393-08007-2
LC 2010-15108

"With a great array of writers celebrated and too little known, and invaluable supporting materials, this grand and affecting treasury of culturally rich and aesthetically dynamic poems, fiction, drama, letters, diaries, and essays illuminates every aspect of Latino life." Booklist

Includes bibliographical references

Bram, Christopher

Eminent outlaws; the gay writers who changed America. Christopher Bram. Twelve 2012 372 p. **810**

1. Authors, American -- 20th century 2. Gay authors -- United States 3. Gays' writings, American -- History and criticism 4. Literature & society -- United States 5. Nonfiction
ISBN 9780446563130
LC 2011029910

This book is a history, literary critique, and collective biography in one. Novelist [Christopher] Bram . . . discusses gay men . . . from Gore Vidal in the early postwar years up through the 1990s and close to the present. His main thesis, that good art can lay the groundwork for social change, is demonstrated and contextualized in dozens of examples of how literature can be not just a reflection of the times but also a catalyst for change; for example, Mart Crowley's 1968 play (made into a 1970 movie), The Boys In the Band is shown to have produced conflicting reactions that spurred the debate of what gay culture should look like. (Libr J)

Cheever, Susan

American Bloomsbury; Louisa May Alcott, Ralph Waldo Emerson, Margaret Fuller, Nathaniel Hawthorne, and Henry David Thoreau: their lives, their loves, their work. Simon & Schuster 2006 223p il $26 **810**

1. American literature -- History and criticism 2. American literature -- Massachusetts -- Concord 3. Authors, American 4. Authors, American -- 19th century -- Biography 5. Biography, Collective
ISBN 0-7432-6461-4; 978-0-7432-6461-7
LC 2006-45015

This book offers a "glimpse into life in Concord, MA, from about 1840 to the mid-1860s, when such luminaries as Louisa May Alcott, Ralph Waldo Emerson, Margaret Fuller, Nathaniel Hawthorne, and Henry David Thoreau lived, worked, and loved. . . . [This] volume examines the dynamic relationships among these remarkable men and women, who constituted what may be considered the first American literary community. . . . Essential reading for anyone with an interest in American letters." Libr J

Includes bibliographical references

Elie, Paul

The **life** you save may be your own; an American pilgrimage. Farrar, Straus and Giroux 2003 554p il hardcover o.p. pa $16 **810**

1. American literature -- 20th century -- History and criticism 2. American literature -- Bio-bibliography 3. American literature -- Catholic authors -- History and criticism 4. American literature -- History and criticism 5. Authors 6. Authors, American -- 20th century -- Biography 7. Catholics -- United States -- Biography 8. Catholics -- United States -- Intellectual life -- 20th century 9. Essayists 10. Journalists 11. Monks 12. Newspaper editors 13. Nonfiction writers 14. Novelists 15. Poets 16. Reference books 17. Short story writers 18. Social reformers 19. Writers on religion
ISBN 0-374-25680-2; 978-0-374-52921-5 pa; 0-374-52921-3 pa
LC 2002-192522

"This thoroughly researched and well-sourced work deserves attention from students of history, literature and religion, but it will be of special significance to Catholic readers interested in the expression of faith in the modern world." Publ Wkly

Facts on File, Inc.

★ **Encyclopedia** of American literature; 2nd ed; Facts on File 2008 4v il set $375 **810**

1. American literature 2. American literature -- Encyclopedias 3. American literature -- History and criticism 4. Reference books
ISBN 978-0-8160-6476-2
LC 2007-25662

Entries in this encyclopedia cover works, writers, movements and other American literature-related topics from colonial times to the present. Each volume includes a chronology.

Hart, James David

★ The **Oxford** companion to American literature; [by] James D. Hart; with revisions and additions by Phillip W. Leininger. 6th ed; Oxford Univ. Press 1995 779p $49.95 **810**

1. American authors -- Biography -- Dictionaries 2. American literature -- Bio-bibliography 3. American literature -- Dictionaries 4. Biography, Collective 5. Reference books
ISBN 0-19-506548-4
LC 94-45727

In addition to over 2000 entries for individual authors and more than 1,100 for important works this reference includes entries for literary movements, awards, magazines, printers, book collectors and newspapers. A chronological index of literary and social history is appended.

Kazin, Alfred

★ An **American** procession. Harvard University Press 1996 408p pa $15.95 **810**

1. American literature -- History and criticism 2.

Authors 3. Dramatists 4. Editors 5. Essayists 6. Historians 7. Humorists 8. Literary critics 9. Memoirists 10. Naturalists 11. Nobel laureates for literature 12. Nonfiction writers 13. Novelists 14. Pacifists 15. Philosophers 16. Poets 17. Satirists 18. Screenwriters 19. Short story writers 20. Travel writers 21. Writers on nature
ISBN 0-674-03143-1

LC 97-220259

"'An American Procession' is a refresher in the best sense: without any fundamental revision of our understanding of our classics, it vivaciously refreshes our awareness of them, and our gratitude for them." New Yorker

Matthiessen, F. O.

★ **American** renaissance; art and expression in the age of Emerson and Whitman. Oxford Univ. Press 1941 xxiv, 678p il hardcover o.p. pa $53 **810**
1. American literature -- History and criticism 2. Artists 3. Authors 4. Essayists 5. Naturalists 6. Nonfiction writers 7. Novelists 8. Pacifists 9. Philosophers 10. Poets 11. Sculptors 12. Short story writers 13. Writers on nature
ISBN 0-19-500759-X pa

A critical study of works by Emerson, Thoreau, Melville, Hawthorne and Whitman and their impact on American intellectual history.

Morgan, Bill

The **typewriter** is holy; the complete, uncensored history of the beat generation. Free Press 2010 291p il $28   **810**
1. American literature -- 20th century -- History and criticism 2. American literature -- History and criticism 3. Beat generation
ISBN 978-1-4165-9242-6; 1-4165-9242-3

LC 2009-42224

"Morgan clearly loves his subjects, but he doesn't gloss over their erratic lifestyle, which involved amazing amounts of drugs and alcohol, and their consummate selfishness. . . . Morgan's own prose is straightforward, even pedestrian, but his ability to draw together so many events and personalities is astonishing." Providence J
Includes bibliographical references

National Story Project (U.S.)

I thought my father was God and other true tales from the National Story Project; edited and introduced by Paul Auster; Nelly Reifler, assistant editor. Holt & Co. 2001 xxi, 383p il hardcover o.p. pa $15   **810**
1. American literature -- Collections
ISBN 0-8050-6714-0; 0-312-42100-1 pa

LC 00-54397

"These are stop-you-in-your-tracks stories about hair-raising coincidences, miracles, tragedies, redemption, and moments of pure hilarity." Booklist

Parini, Jay

Promised land; thirteen books that changed America. Doubleday 2008 385p il $24.95   **810**
1. American literature -- History and criticism 2.

American national characteristics 3. Books and reading -- United States 4. Literature and morals 5. Literature and society -- United States 6. National characteristics, American, in literature
ISBN 978-0-385-52276-2

LC 2008-9990

This is "a mind-expanding book of books guaranteed to provoke discussion and fuel reading groups." Booklist
Includes bibliographical references

Pierpont, Claudia Roth

Passionate minds; women rewriting the world. Knopf 2000 298p il hardcover o.p. pa $13   **810**
1. Actors 2. American literature -- 20th century -- History and criticism 3. American literature -- Women authors -- History and criticism 4. Authors 5. Authors, American -- 20th century -- Biography 6. Authors, English -- 20th century -- Biography 7. College teachers 8. Diarists 9. Dramatists 10. English literature -- 20th century -- History and criticism 11. English literature -- Women authors -- History and criticism 12. Essayists 13. Feminists 14. Folklorists 15. Lawyers 16. Literary critics 17. Memoirists 18. Nobel laureates for literature 19. Nonfiction writers 20. Novelists 21. Philosophers 22. Poets 23. Political and social philosophers 24. Political scientists 25. Screenwriters 26. Short story writers 27. Women and literature -- English-speaking countries -- History -- 20th century 28. Women authors 29. Women authors, American -- Biography 30. Women authors, English -- Biography 31. Writers on politics
ISBN 0-679-43106-3; 0-679-75113-0 pa

LC 99-33349

"A scintillating collection of brief lives of women writers, a book that sparkles with intelligence, wit and human interest. . . . Unfolding with the dramatic élan of a novella, each one is exhaustively researched, sharply focused, convincingly opinionated." N Y Times Book Rev

Salem Press Inc.

★ **Notable** Latino writers; from the editors of Salem Press. Salem Press 2005 3v il set $207 **810**
1. American literature -- Hispanic American authors 2. American literature -- Hispanic American authors -- History and criticism 3. Hispanic Americans -- Intellectual life
ISBN 1-58765-243-9; 978-1-58765-243-1

LC 2005-17567

These volumes feature "122 essays about Latino novelists, short-story writers, poets, and playwrights of the Western Hemisphere who write in English, Spanish, or Portuguese. . . . This set may prove to be a useful research tool for students, teachers, and librarians." Libr J
Includes bibliographical references

Samet, Elizabeth D.

★ **Soldier's** heart; reading literature through peace and war at West Point. Farrar, Straus and Giroux 2007 259p $23   **810**
1. College teachers 2. Literary critics 3. Literature -- Study and teaching 4. Military cadets -- New York (State) -- West Point 5. Philologists 6. Soldiers --

Education, Non-military 7. Soldiers -- United States
ISBN 978-0-374-18063-8; 0-374-18063-6

LC 2007-9159

"Like the best professors, Samet asks tough questions and offers no easy answers. Her book is filled with lively classroom discussions and poignant e-mails from former students now in Iraq, often writing about the books they're reading there. . . . I know of no other new book that's a better choice for any reading group that loves to debate literature and politics." USA Today

Showalter, Elaine

★ A **jury** of her peers; American women writers from Anne Bradstreet to Annie Proulx. Alfred A. Knopf 2009 586p $30   **810**
1. American literature -- Women authors 2. American literature -- Women authors -- Bio-bibliography 3. American literature -- Women authors -- History and criticism 4. Literature -- Women authors 5. Women and literature -- United States -- History 6. Women in literature 7. Women in literature -- United States
ISBN 978-1-4000-4123-7; 1-4000-4123-6

LC 2008-42312

"Showalter's writing is clear, lively, and authoritative; her research is impressive." Libr J
Includes bibliographical references

Taylor, Todd W.

★ The **Companion** to southern literature; themes, genres, places, people, movements, and motifs. edited by Joseph M. Flora and Lucinda H. MacKethan; associate editor, Todd Taylor. Louisiana State Univ. Press 2001 xxvi, 1054p $69.95   **810**
1. American literature -- Southern States 2. American literature -- Southern States -- Encyclopedias 3. Reference books
ISBN 0-8071-2692-6

LC 2001-29959

"This unique compilation [is] . . . an excellent addition to libraries that support studies of Southern literature." Libr J
Includes bibliographical references

Wall, Cheryl A.

Women of the Harlem Renaissance. Indiana Univ. Press 1995 246p il hardcover o.p. pa $14.95   **810**
1. American literature -- African American authors 2. Authors 3. Dramatists 4. Editors 5. Essayists 6. Folklorists 7. Harlem Renaissance 8. Literary critics 9. Memoirists 10. Novelists 11. Nurses 12. Short story writers
ISBN 0-253-20980-3 pa

LC 95-3132

This study of women writers of the Harlem Renaissance begins with an overview: On being young—a woman—and colored, followed by critical and biographical studies of Jessie Redmond Fauset, Nella Larsen, and Zora Neale Hurston.

"Wall offers strong critiques of these women's work, uncovering certain similarities, including, most importantly, the travel motif as not only a reflection of the mass migrations of the day but also a larger dislocation." Publ Wkly
Includes bibliographical references

Wilson, Edmund

Patriotic gore; studies in the literature of the American Civil War. Norton 1994 816p pa $19.95   **810**
1. Abolitionists 2. American literature -- History and criticism 3. Army officers 4. Authors 5. Children's authors 6. Civil rights activists 7. Clergy 8. Diplomats 9. Educators 10. Essayists 11. Flutists 12. Generals 13. Governors 14. Journalists 15. Judges 16. Lawyers 17. Members of Congress 18. Memoirists 19. Nonfiction writers 20. Novelists 21. Novelists, American 22. Pianists 23. Poets 24. Political leaders 25. Presidents 26. Secretaries of war 27. Short story writers 28. Sociologists 29. Spouses of prominent persons 30. State legislators 31. Supreme Court justices 32. White supremacists 33. Writers on politics
ISBN 978-0-393-31256-0; 0-393-31256-9

"A collection of sixteen essays on writing related to the war including the memoirs of Union generals Grant and Sherman and Confederates Mosby and Lee, diaries, political writing, and fiction by writers such as Ambrose Bierce and John De Forest." Benet's Reader's Ency of Am Lit

★ **Baseball**: a literary anthology; edited by Nicholas Dawidoff. Library of Am. 2002 721p $35   **810**
1. American literature -- Collections 2. Baseball
ISBN 1-931082-09-X

LC 2001-38654

"Beginning with Thayer's Casey at the Bat and ending with Buster Olney, there are more than 700 pages of prose and poetry, fiction and sportswriting, writers and players. Scanning the table of contents, it almost seems like everybody wrote about baseball: Damon Runyon, Ring Lardner, James Weldon Johnson, William Carlos Williams, James Thurber. But so did Paul Gallico, Nelson Algren, Tallulah Bankhead, and Jacques Barzun. . . . Ineffable, indispensable, inimitable—just like baseball." Booklist

★ The **Beat** generation; a Gale critical companion. Lynn M. Zott, project editor. Gale 2003 3v set $350   **810**
1. American literature -- History and criticism 2. Beat generation
ISBN 0-7876-7569-5

LC 2002-155786

"Volume 1 gathers a variety of sources that place the movement in cultural context. . . . Volumes 2-3 supply entries for 28 Beat authors. . . . Author entries include a brief biography, notes on major works and critical reception, a list of principal works, a selection of primary sources and secondary criticism, and further readings. . . . The selections include contributions by major Beat Generation scholars and provide a well-balanced, representative view of the Beats." Choice
Includes bibliographical references

Black women writers (1950-1980) a critical evaluation. edited by Mari Evans. Anchor Press 1984 xxviii, 543p hardcover o.p. pa $25   **810**
1. Actors 2. American literature -- African American authors 3. American literature -- History and criticism 4. American literature -- Women authors 5. Authors 6.

Children's authors 7. College teachers 8. Columnists 9. Dramatists 10. Editors 11. Essayists 12. Literary critics 13. Memoirists 14. Motion picture directors 15. Nobel laureates for literature 16. Novelists 17. Poets 18. Short story writers 19. Singers 20. Social activists 21. Theatrical directors 22. Young adult authors
ISBN 0-385-17125-0 pa

LC 81-43914

Critical essays on Maya Angelou, Alice Childress, Toni Morisson, Lucille Clifton, and 11 other post World War II Afro-American women writers.

"This important work, a tribute to the corpus of literature produced by black women, is an indispensable resource for any serious student, scholar or teacher desiring to probe the depths of the Afro-American literary tradition." Freedomways

Includes bibliographical references

The Cambridge handbook of American literature; edited by Jack Salzman. Cambridge Univ. Press 1986 286p $60   **810**
1. American literature -- Bio-bibliography 2. American literature -- Dictionaries 3. Reference books
ISBN 0-521-30703-1

LC 86-2587

This handbook's "750 entries, two thirds of them about authors, briefly describe the contents and contribution of key works, assess the careers of writers, and explain the tenets and characteristics of literary movements." Wilson Libr Bull

The Cambridge history of American literature; general editor, Sacvan Bercovitch; associate editor, Cyrus R.K. Patell. Cambridge Univ. Press 1994 8v set $1,050   **810**
1. American literature -- History and criticism
ISBN 0-521-85760-0

LC 92-42479

Scholars contribute essays assessing major authors, movements and trends in the development of American literature.

★ The Chronology of American literature; America's literary achievements from the colonial era to modern times. edited by Daniel S. Burt. Houghton Mifflin 2004 805p il $40   **810**
1. American literature -- Chronology 2. American literature -- Collections
ISBN 0-618-16821-4

LC 2003-51142

"This chronology includes more than 8,400 literary works by more than 5,000 writers. Sections for each year are grouped in five chapters by period, from 1582 to 1999. Within each year, entries are grouped by genre, such as diaries and other personal writings, fiction, essays, literary criticism and scholarship, nonfiction, poetry, and drama. Within each genre, authors are listed alphabetically, generally with birth and death dates and short descriptions of named works for the year. . . . The Chronology of American Literature is easy to browse and, for book lovers, difficult to put down." Booklist

Includes bibliographical references

Columbia literary history of the United States; Emory Elliott, general editor; associate editors, Martha Banta {et al.}; advisory editors, Houston A. Baker {et al.} Columbia Univ. Press 1988 xxviii, 1263p $119   **810**
1. American literature -- History and criticism
ISBN 0-231-05812-8

LC 87-14672

This anthology "expands the traditional subjects of literary history by incorporating current theoretical ideas and newly discovered writers. Includes treatment of recently explored subjects, such as the role of women and minorities in U.S. literature. No separate bibliography other than what is found in the text." N Y Public Libr Book of How & Where to Look it Up

★ The Continuum encyclopedia of British literature; Steven R. Serafin and Valerie Grosvenor Myer, editors. Continuum 2003 1184p $175   **810**
1. British literature 2. English literature 3. English literature -- Encyclopedias 4. English literature -- Irish authors 5. Reference books
ISBN 0-8264-1456-7

LC 2002-9231

"This reference work provides a fascinating current take on the canon. . . . The historical/literary time line and the lists of prize titles alone will keep researchers happy." SLJ

Includes bibliographical references

Crossing the danger water; three hundred years of African-American writing. edited and with an introduction by Deirdre Mullane. Anchor Bks. (NY) 1993 xxii, 769p pa $20   **810**
1. American literature -- African American authors 2. American literature -- African American authors -- Collections 3. American literature -- Collections
ISBN 0-385-42243-1

LC 93-17194

This anthology "includes fiction, autobiography, poetry, songs, and letters by such writers as Frederick Douglass, Sojourner Truth, W.E.B. Du Bois, Zora Neale Hurston, and Richard Wright. Many topics are covered, from slavery, education, the Civil War, Reconstruction, and political issues to spirituals, songs of the Civil Rights movement, and rap music." Libr J

Includes bibliographical references

Encyclopedia of African-American writing; five centuries of contribution: trials & triumphs of writers, poets, publications and organizations. Shari Dorantes Hatch, editor. 2nd ed.; Grey House Pub. 2009 xxii, 863p il $165   **810**
1. American literature -- African American authors -- Bio-bibliography 2. American literature -- African American authors -- Encyclopedias 3. Reference books
ISBN 978-1-59237-291-1

"This voluminous and inclusive collection consists of 738 entries that cover authors and other topics related to African American writing, such as newspapers, magazines, journals, and publishers and figures such as educators, playwrights, journalists, academics, editors, and librarians from the past 500 years. . . . Although unsigned, the entries are highly accessible, very current, and chock-full of information for a range of audiences." Libr J

Includes bibliographical references

Encyclopedia of American Indian literature; [edited by] Jennifer McClinton-Temple, Alan Velie. Facts on File 2007 466p $75 **810**
1. American literature -- Indian authors 2. American literature -- Indian authors -- History and criticism 3. Native American literature -- Encyclopedias 4. Native Americans in literature -- Encyclopedias 5. Reference books
ISBN 0-8160-5656-0; 978-0-8160-5656-9
LC 2006-23762
"This book brings together solid information from scattered sources, facilitating research on an esoteric subject." Libr J

Includes bibliographical references

★ The Greenwood encyclopedia of African American literature; edited by Hans Ostrom and J. David Macey, Jr. Greenwood Press 2005 5v il set $499.95 **810**
1. American literature -- African American authors -- Encyclopedias 2. Reference books
ISBN 0-313-32972-9
LC 2005-13679
This "set provides coverage of the foundations, development, and proliferation of African American literature, from Colonial times to the present. . . . The depth and breadth of the 1,029 entries make this an invaluable resource." Choice

Includes bibliographical references

★ The Greenwood encyclopedia of multiethnic American literature. Greenwood Press 2005 5v il set $499.95 **810**
1. American literature -- Encyclopedias 2. American literature -- Minority authors -- History and criticism 3. Ethnic groups in literature 4. Minorities -- Encyclopedias 5. Reference books
ISBN 0-313-33059-X
LC 2005-18960
"A comprehensive set unique in its scope, this encyclopedia is an excellent foundational resource that adds much to the growing field of ethnic American literature." Choice

Includes bibliographical references

Jewish American literature; a Norton anthology. [compiled and edited by] Jules Chametzky [et al.] Norton 2000 xxiv, 1221p il $39.95 **810**
1. American literature -- Collections 2. American literature -- Jewish authors 3. Jews -- United States -- Literary collections
ISBN 0-393-04809-8
LC 00-55393
The editors have attempted "to encompass Jewish literature from 1654 to the present in this collection of poems, cartoons, sermons, diaries, letters, stories, speeches, plays, prayers, novel excerpts, and critical writings either translated from Hebrew or Yiddish or written in English. Major sections group the literature chronologically to help identify

large movements. . . . This great anthology is essential for Jewish studies and American literature collections." Libr J

Includes bibliographical references

★ Latino and Latina writers; Alan West-Durán, editor. Charles Scribner's Sons 2004 1072p 2v set $265 **810**
1. American literature -- Hispanic American authors 2. American literature -- Hispanic American authors -- History and criticism 3. Hispanic Americans -- Intellectual life 4. Hispanic Americans in literature
ISBN 0-684-31293-X
LC 2003-15728
This set "begins with five essays of social and historical commentary that focus on key elements of Latino culture in this country. What follows is a series of ten to 20-page biocritical essays on nearly 60 authors (e.g., Gary Soto, Pat Mora, Sandra Cisneros, Victor Villase or, Julia Alvarez, Richard Rodriguez, and Lorna Dee Cervantes). . . . One of the most comprehensive anthologies available of Latino writing in the United States." Libr J

Includes bibliographical references

★ Magill's survey of American literature; edited by Steven G. Kellman. Rev. ed; Salem Press 2007 6v il set $499 **810**
1. American literature 2. American literature -- History and criticism 3. Literature -- Bio-bibliography 4. Literature -- History and criticism 5. Reference books
ISBN 978-1-58765-285-1; 1-58765-285-4
LC 2006-16503
"Examining selected works of 339 U.S. and Canadian writers, from Anne Bradstreet and Benjamin Franklin to Edward Bloor and Octavia E. Butler, this clearly written resource provides sturdy support for assignments, and will also be popular with discussion groups and with general readers of literature." SLJ

Includes bibliographical references

★ Modern American literature; 5th ed; St. James Press 1999 3v set $594 **810**
1. American literature -- 20th century 2. American literature -- 20th century -- History and criticism 3. American literature -- History and criticism
ISBN 1-55862-379-5
LC 98-38952
"This work consists of short excerpts of criticism of 20th-century American authors by important critics writing in newspapers, magazines, scholarly journals, and books. The excerpts (ranging in length from one or two paragraphs to two columns) are allowed to stand on their own without separate plot synopses, summaries, or background information on the authors. The original words of the critics . . . are arranged chronologically to paint a picture of the critical reception of an author over time." Libr J

Includes bibliographical references

Modern American memoirs; selected and edited by Annie Dillard and Cort Conley. HarperCollins Pubs. 1995 449p hardcover o.p. pa $16 **810**
1. American literature -- Collections 2. Authors,

American
ISBN 0-06-092763-1 pa

LC 95-30755

The editors "have collected excerpts from the memoirs of 35 20th-century American authors. The selections represent the best in autobiographical writing published between 1917 and 1992. Included are nine women and 26 men, both black and white, some better known than others, all distinguished writers and wonderful storytellers. . . . The editors precede each entry with a biographical and contextual note. There's an opening essay on the art of the memoirist and an afterword listing additional classics in the genre." Libr J

★ The Norton anthology of African American literature; Henry Louis Gates, Jr., general editor, Nellie Y. McKay, general editor. 2nd ed; Norton 2003 2800p 2 computer laser optical discs pa $70.30 **810**
1. American literature -- African American authors
2. American literature -- African American authors -- Collections
ISBN 0-393-97778-1

LC 2003-66176

"The anthology is divided into seven sections, each with a separate introduction giving the sociopolitical factors that impacted on the material included therein. Featured are 120 writers, 52 of whom are women, richly representing African American vernacular literature, poetry, drama, short stories, novels, slave narratives, and autobiographies." Libr J [review of 1996 edition]
Includes bibliographical references

★ The Norton anthology of American literature; Nina Baym, general editor. Norton 5v 2007 3008p maps **810**
1. American literature -- Collections
An anthology of American prose, poetry and drama dating from 1620 to the late 20th century. Includes essays and introductions to authors and works.

The Oxford book of the American South; testimony, memory, and fiction. edited by Edward L. Ayers, Bradley C. Mittendorf. Oxford Univ. Press 1997 597p hardcover o.p. pa $22 **810**
1. American literature -- Southern States 2. American literature -- Southern States -- Collections
ISBN 0-19-512493-6 pa

LC 96-45135

"Not limiting themselves to fiction (short stories and novels, either in full or in extract), the editors also gather memoirs, diaries, and essays. From both genders and races, from opposite poles on the economic scale, from an eighteenth-century naturalist to a former slave, from Thomas Jefferson to Eudora Welty, these writings give ringing voice to the experiences that have engendered a distinctive southern culture." Booklist

The Oxford book of women's writing in the United States; edited by Linda Wagner-Martin, Cathy N. Davidson. Oxford Univ. Press 1995 596p hardcover o.p. pa $27.50 **810**
1. American literature -- Collections 2. American literature -- Women authors 3. American literature -- Women authors -- Collections
ISBN 0-19-513245-9 pa

LC 95-1499

This anthology provides "samples of the public and private work of 99 women of diverse racial and ethnic backgrounds who write in English and were born in or have lived in the United States over the past four centuries. They include short fiction (almost half of the book), poems, essays, plays, and speeches but have also gone beyond traditional genre categories to include performance pieces, erotica, diaries, letters, and recipes." Libr J

★ The Oxford companion to Canadian literature; general editors, Eugene Benson & William Toye. 2nd ed; Oxford Univ. Press 1997 1199p $75 810
1. Canadian literature -- Dictionaries 2. Reference books
ISBN 0-19-541167-6

LC 98-162071

More than 1100 signed entries cover Québécois, Acadian, and English-Canadian literature.
"The scope of this volume is impressive. It includes not only information about writers and poets but also publishers, publishing houses, themes and symbols in Canadian literature, and essays on individual works that stand out as landmarks in the field. It is the kind of reference work one can 'dip into' for interest or use as a quick reference tool." Booklist

★ The Oxford encyclopedia of American literature; Jay Parini, editor-in-chief. Oxford University Press 2004 4v il set $495 **810**
1. American literature -- Encyclopedias 2. Reference books
ISBN 0-19-515653-6

LC 2002-156325

This set "provides a wealth of reliable information on standard bearers of American literature in an easy-on-the-eyes format for students and general readers." SLJ

The Portable Harlem Renaissance reader; edited and with an introduction by David Levering Lewis. Viking 1994 xlvii, 766p hardcover o.p. pa $18 **810**
1. American literature -- African American authors -- Collections 2. Harlem Renaissance
ISBN 0-14-017036-7

LC 93-30233

"General categories include essay, memoir, fiction, poetry, and drama; specific writers include such expected names as Langston Hughes, Zora Neale Hurston, and Claude McKay, but lesser-known names are also represented. There is anger in these pages and also frustration, pride, pain, and elation, but above all there is incredible talent. Reading the collection straight through would be a wonderful education, but most readers will dip in here and there, and that is edifying, too." Booklist

The Portable Western reader; edited and with an introduction by William Kittredge. Penguin Bks. 1997 xxi, 600p pa $14.95 **810**
1. American literature -- West (U.S.) -- Collections
ISBN 0-14-023026-2

LC 96-47243
"Part 1, 'Ancient Stories,' shows the evolution of Native American storytelling from the early legends to contemporary stories and includes writings by Catherine McClellan, John Graves, and Louise Erdrich. Parts 2 and 3 contrast the mythology of the 19th-century 'Western' with the actual experience of living in the West. Most of these authors, from Walt Whitman to Larry McMurtry, will be familiar to readers. Part 4, 'Brilliant Possibilities,' showcases the new generation of Western writers, including Gretel Ehrlich, Jimmy Santiago Baca, and Sherman Alexie." Libr J

The Portable beat reader; edited by Ann Charters. Viking 1992 xxxvi, 642p hardcover o.p. pa $17 **810**
1. American literature -- Collections 2. Bohemianism
ISBN 0-14-243753-0 pa

LC 91-16155
"Cutting through bohemian posturing and excess, Charters here reprints much of the most vital, readable and relevant material produced by the Beat generation." Publ Wkly
Includes bibliographical references

The Portable sixties reader; edited by Ann Charters. Penguin Bks. 2003 xli, 628p il pa $16 **810**
1. American literature -- 20th century 2. American literature -- Collections
ISBN 0-14-200194-5

LC 2002-32266
This reader includes "essays, poetry, and fiction under thematic subjects, such as civil rights; women's rights; the sexual revolution; environmental issues; the antiwar, free-speech, and black-arts movements; and the use of drugs in pursuit of enlightenment. . . . [Includes works by] James Baldwin, Thomas Merton, Susan Sontag, Gary Snyder, Allen Ginsburg, Rachel Carson, Kate Millett, Nikki Giovanni, and many more." Booklist
Includes bibliographical references

★ Pushcart Prize XXXVI: best of the small presses 2012; edited by Bill Henderson with the Pushcart Prize editors. Pushcart 2011 569p $35; pa $18.95 **810**
1. American literature -- Collections
ISBN 978-1-88888964-2; 978-1-8888864-5 pa
Each volume "consists of short stories, poems and essays; includes the work of established and beginning writers, and has a faintly subversive character. Its audience would seem to be primarily the young, yet among its contributors are many of the best writers in America. . . . Like all interesting literary journals, 'The Pushcart Prize' is eclectic and uneven. . . . The number and diversity of journals represented and the sheer length of it are impressive." Books of the Times
Includes bibliographical references

The Real war will never get in the books; selections from writers during the Civil War. edited by Louis P. Masur. Oxford Univ. Press 1993 301p il hardcover o.p. pa $18.95 **810**
1. American literature -- Collections
ISBN 0-19-509837-4 pa

LC 92-24446
This is a collection of excerpts from letters, journal entries, articles, and speeches written during the American Civil War. The fourteen contributors include such writers as Henry Adams, Louisa May Alcott, Frederick Douglass, Nathaniel Hawthorne, Herman Melville, William Gilmore Simms, Harriet Beecher Stowe, and Walt Whitman.
"This collection makes available to a wide audience some of the best contemporary writing about the conflict." Libr J
Includes bibliographical references

Transcendentalism; a reader. [edited by] Joel Myerson. Oxford Univ. Press 2001 xxxvii, 712p hardcover o.p. pa $32 **810**
1. Transcendentalism -- Collections
ISBN 0-19-512212-7; 0-19-512213-5 pa

LC 00-21484
This reader "draws together in their entirety the essential writings of the Transcendentalist group during its most active period, 1836-1844. It includes the major publications of the Dial, the writings on democratic and social reform, the early poetry, nature writings, and all of Emerson's major essays, as well as an . . . introduction and annotations by Myerson." Publisher's note
Includes bibliographical references

A new literary history of America; edited by Greil Marcus and Werner Sollors. Belknap Press of Harvard University Press 2009 1095p bibl f il $49.95 **810**
1. American literature -- History and criticism
ISBN 978-0-674-03594-2; 0-674-03594-1

LC 2009014255
"This is an adventurous, jazzily choral, and kaleidoscopic book of interpretations, illuminations, and revitalized history." Booklist
Includes bibliographical references and index

811 American poetry

Ackerman, Diane

Origami bridges; poems of psychoanalysis and fire. HarperCollins Pubs. 2002 147p $22.95; pa $11.95 **811**
1. Poetry -- By individual authors 2. Psychoanalysis -- Poetry 3. Psychology -- Poetry 4. Psychotherapist and patient -- Poetry
ISBN 0-06-019988-1; 0-06-055529-7 pa

LC 2002-24685
"Sometimes addressed to herself and her personal history, at least as often addressed to 'Dr. B—,' Ackerman's passionate free verse (short, fluent and adorned by irregular rhyme) describes with nearly unmixed awe the relationship

she created with her analyst, and the personal transformation she achieved." Publ Wkly

Adair, Virginia Hamilton

Ants on the melon; a collection of poems. Random House 1996 158p hardcover o.p. pa $15 **811**

1. Poetry -- By individual authors

ISBN 0-375-75229-3 pa

LC 95-25977

"The appearance of a first collection by a poet now blind and in her 83rd year must be accounted a triumph . . . {Adair} works with equal daring in free verse and more traditional forms; her subjects include social and religious commentary, but her principal theme is ordinary experience and its resistance to facile interpretation." Libr J

Beliefs and blasphemies; a collection of poems. Random House 1998 109p hardcover o.p. pa $15 **811**

1. Poetry -- By individual authors

ISBN 0-8129-9245-8 pa

LC 97-47403

"Adair's searching verses may not always have the ring of the contemporary, and they often stop short here of fully unfurling their insights. But at its best, this collection points the way back to an American tradition of religious poetry understood and cherished by the likes of Elizabeth Bishop and Louise Bogan." Publ Wkly

Adam, Helen

A **Helen** Adam reader; edited, with notes and an introduction by Kristin Prevallet. National Poetry Foundation 2007 492p il $59.95; $29.95 **811**

1. Poetry -- By individual authors

ISBN 978-0-943373-74-4; 0-943373-74-3; 978-0-943373-73-7 pa; 0-943373-73-5 pa

LC 2007-34740

In the Bay Area of the late 1940s Adam "found herself a member—some said godmother, witch or Nurse of Enchantment—of the interlocking Robert Duncan and Jack Spicer poetry circles, which, with the Beats, formed the avant-garde San Francisco Renaissance. . . . Adam combined the narrative economy of ballads—where each line is a discrete unit of information—with the lush sonic tapestry we associate with older Anglo-Saxon and Celtic strains of British verse. . . . On the page, Adam's intricate soundscapes compare with anything by Gerard Manley Hopkins and Dylan Thomas. But to see her sing her ballads—she chants 'Kiltory' on the Reader's accompanying DVD—is to appreciate how the language, trilling and seething by turns, possessed its acolyte." Nation

Includes bibliographical references

Alexander, Elizabeth

Crave radiance; new and selected poems 1990-2010. Graywolf Press 2010 255p $28 **811**

1. Poetry -- By individual authors

ISBN 978-1-55597-568-5

LC 2010-922921

"This potent retrospective collection offers the best of Alexander's five previous books, including selections from her young-adult title, Miss Crandall's School for Young Girls and Little Misses of Color (2007), which hold their own as poems for adults of all ages here. . . . Alexander brings intellectual power, musicality, sensuousness, and vernacular immediacy to her lyrics, which entwine the personal with the social, the tactile with the imaginary, the past with the present." Booklist

Alexie, Sherman

Face. Hanging Loose Press 2009 159p $28; pa $15 **811**

1. Poetry -- By individual authors

ISBN 978-1-931236-71-3; 1-931236-71-2; 978-1-931236-70-6 pa; 1-931236-70-4 pa

LC 2008-46580

The author "has mastered both the metrical dance and fixed forms. A sequence of sonnets finds the Seven Deadly Sins in marriage, for instance; a villanelle begins with Mount Rushmore but eases into a consideration of America's Presidents, complemented by wry and smart footnotes. . . . There are a lot of serious undercurrents in his poetry, and they are always a pleasure to find." Libr J

Altman, Howard

In this house. Turtle Point Press 2010 81p pa $15.95 **811**

1. Poetry -- By individual authors

ISBN 978-1-933527-33-8

LC 2009-929505

A "collection of poems that look at the world with thought-provoking and elegantly bifurcated awareness: 'Inside every man is another man / He would like to leave behind.' At once sturdy and visionary, Altmann's work has won him a variety of fans that include not just poet John Ashbery but also actor Patricia Clarkson." Time Out N Y

Alvarez, Julia

The **woman** I kept to myself; poems. Algonquin Books of Chapel Hill 2004 155p hardcover o.p. pa $14.95 **811**

1. Poetry -- By individual authors 2. Women -- Poetry

ISBN 1-56512-406-5; 1-61620-072-3 pa

LC 2003-70807

This "collection of 75 poems is divided into three sections, and each poem has three stanzas, exactly . . . The poet, who is from the Dominican Republic, writes about being raised with her sisters in New York. The subjects are personal—love, marriage, rejection, divorce, death, religion—but also universal." SLJ

Angelou, Maya

I shall not be moved. Random House 1997 48p $15; pa $9.95 **811**

1. Poetry -- By individual authors

ISBN 0-679-45708-9; 0-553-35458-3 pa

"Angelou's themes include loss of love and youth, human oneness in diversity, the strength of blacks in the face of racism and adversity." Publ Wkly

★ The **complete** collected poems of Maya Angelou. Random House 1994 273p $24.95   **811**
1. Poetry -- By individual authors
ISBN 0-679-42895-X

LC 94-14501

This volume contains all of Angelou's published poems including her inaugural poem On the pulse of morning.

Armantrout, Rae

Versed. Wesleyan University Press 2009 121p $22.95 **811**
1. Poetry -- By individual authors
ISBN 978-0-8195-6879-3; 0-8195-6879-1

LC 2008-43809

This book "book comprises two sequences — 'Versed' and 'Dark Matter'— of loosely interlinked poems dealing with the prolific poet's usual subjects (the body, contemporary society, violence) as well as more personal explorations of illness and mortality, all relayed in Armantrout's concentrated, crystalline voice, with a predilection for skipping some steps along the way to sense." Publ Wkly

Ashbery, John

Collected poems 1956-1987; [edited by Mark Ford] Library of America 2008 1042p $40   **811**
1. Poetry -- By individual authors
ISBN 978-1-59853-028-5

"This major book, the first collection from Library of America by a living poet, offers a view of Ashbery's artistic development over many decades. . . . Watching Ashbery's art grow from the slippery romanticism and verbal hijinks of the early poems through the philosophical, if sideways, inquiry of the '70s, to the chattier, colloquial period inaugurated in the early '80s, is arresting. Though Ashbery has confounded and inspired in seemingly equal measure, he is, according to both his admirers and critics, the towering figure in contemporary American poetry." Publ Wkly

Notes from the air; selected later poems. Ecco 2007 364p $34.95   **811**
1. Poetry -- By individual authors
ISBN 978-0-06-136717-5; 0-06-136717-6

LC 2008-270813

This "volume—beginning with poems from April Galleons (1987) and ending with Where Shall I Wander (2005)—presents . . . [a] panoramic view of Ashbery's second phase, in which he explores, celebrates, sends up and revels in the American vernacular. . . . This is an essential book." Publ Wkly

Planisphere; new poems. Ecco 2009 143p $24.99 **811**
1. Poetry -- By individual authors
ISBN 978-0-06-191521-5; 0-06-191521-1

"In his rendering of American speech, slang, cliché, Ashbery has surpassed most of his contemporaries. But his persistent reach into the 'rut' of tradition should not be forgotten. He could say (with the great Nicaraguan poet Rubén Darío) that he is very 18th century and very archaic and very modern, daring and cosmopolitan. When he becomes most

serious, it is in the presence of either catastrophe or truth. His onslaughts of tragedy, emotional or physical, are of geological force while not relinquishing the vocabulary of iron." N Y Times Book Rev

Selected poems. Viking 1985 349p hardcover o.p. pa $17.95   **811**
1. Poetry -- By individual authors
ISBN 0-14-058553-2 pa

LC 85-40549

"Ashbery's work is seductive precisely because it alludes to shared traditions and assumptions about poetry. His poems attract us with their gestures of 'meaningful' discourse, the meditative pace of their syntax and the memories and expectations of meaningfulness that it evokes, the careful use of qualifiers, and the precisions and surprises of his diction." Benet's Reader's Ency of Am Lit

★ **Where** shall I wander; new poems. J. Ecco 2005 81p $22.95   **811**
1. Poetry -- By individual authors
ISBN 0-06-076529-1

LC 2004-53267

This collection of poetry features the poems "Ignorance of the Law Is No Excuse" and "A Visit to the House of Fools."

"Ashbery expresses a sly playfulness, a tender theatricality, a surreal sensibility, and an urbane wit. . . . Mercurial, elegant, funny, and magical, these mind-bending and beautifully haunting poems are the knowing work of a virtuoso." Booklist

★ A **worldly** country; new poems. Ecco Press 2007 76p $23.95   **811**
1. Poetry -- By individual authors
ISBN 0-06-117383-5; 978-0-06-117383-7

LC 2006-50279

This is a volume of poems by the author of Some Trees (1956); The Tennis Court Oath (1957); Rivers and Mountains (1966); Sunrise in Suburbia (1968); The Double Dream of Spring (1970); Self-portrait in a Convex Mirror (1975); Houseboat Days (1977); As We Know (1979); Shadow Trains (1981); Your Name Here (2000); and Where Shall I Wander (2006).

"Ashbery's syncopated lyrics are sheer pleasure in their music, collaged images, stabbing perceptions. Mysterious and truth-bearing poems that inspire us to 'flame on, flame on.'" Booklist

Auden, W. H.

Collected poems; edited by Edward Mendelson. Vintage Bks. 1991 xxvii, 926p pa $24   **811**
1. Poetry -- By individual authors
ISBN 0-679-73197-0

LC 91-158031

A compilation of all the poems Auden wished to preserve, in his final revisions. Previous collected editions and later shorter poems are included. There is also an absurdist play written 1928: Paid on both sides.

Baca, Jimmy Santiago

Spring poems along the Rio Grande. New Directions Pub. 2007 75p pa $12.95   **811**

1. Poetry -- By individual authors

ISBN 978-0-8112-1685-2; 0-8112-1685-3

LC 2006-101678

"The Rio Grande, as both setting and symbol of freedom and life, meanders through the poems, evoking a natural progression of time and the natural ebb and flow of feelings such as love, hope, and connection. The bosque along the river is home to birds both resident and migratory, trees, fish, bushes, insects, and encroaching urban life represented by power lines and interstate traffic noise. Jogging here, Baca evinces a love of his hometown of Albuquerque but, even more, reveals his well of poetic inspiration: Chicano, Catholic religiosity, Native American symbolism, and universal milestones. . . . With its highly accessible language and thoughtful reflections on the natural world, readers will find Baca's poetry extremely inviting." Booklist

Bang, Mary Jo

Elegy; poems. Graywolf 2007 92p $20 **811**

1. Poetry -- By individual authors

ISBN 978-1-55597-483-1; 1-55597-483-X

LC 2007-924768

The author "captures the complexity and courage of surviving the death of a child, an adult child, an imperfect child. The grief is multilayered, palpable. In this rendition of living in pain, in absence, in an altered reality, the reader never questions the authenticity of the work. . . . This is a book of exceptional grace and strength; it belongs in every library." Libr J

The **bride** of E; poems. Graywolf Press 2009 90p $22   **811**

1. Poetry -- By individual authors

ISBN 978-1-55597-539-5; 1-55597-539-9

LC 2009-926850

"The book takes the form of an abecedarian in which E stands for existence, with the engine of the alphabet overriding the entropy of emptiness, in which 'all action is in the mind, a cluster of notions/ in depravity's head independent of the dreadful/ invention of the magnetic temporary where/ a partition is positioned between right and wrong.' Many of these poems refer to the precariousness of human future, with Bang's medical background contributing convincing detail, and her sharp wit buoys the description with bleak meaning." Libr J

Berkson, Bill

★ **Portrait** and dream; new and selected poems. Coffee House Press 2009 314p pa $22   **811**

1. Poetry -- By individual authors

ISBN 978-1-56689-229-2; 1-56689-206-6

LC 2008-52607

"There was always something of a mythical aura about Berkson, the collaborator of Frank O'Hara and one of the chiefs of the New York School whose friends included painters as well as poets. . . . Berkson's own poetry is subtle and demonstrably abstract in the manner of, let's say, DeKooning: it has an imagistic hardness and lushness that sweeps

aside whatever you might have been thinking before." Exquisite Corpse

Bernstein, Charles

All the whiskey in heaven; selected poems. Farrar, Straus and Giroux 2010 300p $26   **811**

1. Poetry -- By individual authors

ISBN 978-0-374-10344-6; 0-374-10344-5

LC 2009-10187

"Bernstein takes his place in the mainstream of American poetry, the very 'Official Verse Culture' he's attacked entertainingly for years—a fate awaiting all our best outsiders. . . . Early Bernstein can be opaque, annoying those who see difficulty as elitist and who want poetry to be cuddly and educational. But everyone should love the later Bernstein, a writer who is accessible, enormously witty, often joyful— and even more evilly subversive." N Y Times Book Rev

Berry, Wendell

Collected poems, 1957-1982. North Point Press 1985 268p hardcover o.p. pa $17   **811**

1. Poetry -- By individual authors

ISBN 978-0-86547-197-9

LC 84-62305

"As a nature poet Berry has a grass-roots, homespun quality that reminds one of Frost. He moves easily from witty lyrics and graceful elegies to moving love poems, philosophical odes and confessionals." Publ Wkly

Given; new poems. Shoemaker & Hoard 2005 152p $22 **811**

1. Poetry -- By individual authors

ISBN 1-59376-061-2

LC 2005-3762

"The latter half, 'Sabbaths 1998-2004,' . . . [contains] the meditational poems Berry conceives on Sundays alone in the woods on his farm. The other half's three parts contain, respectively, short poems of observation, hortatory poems varying in length from epigram to six-page public epistle, and a brief verse play. . . . For those who believe that life and the world are gifts, this is an invaluable book." Booklist

New collected poems. Counterpoint 2012 391 p. $30.00   **811**

ISBN 1582438153; 9781582438153

This book makes [poet Wendell] Berry's first "Collected [volume] since 1987 and draws on volumes up through 'Leavings.'" It includes a long elegy for Berry's father and a set of haiku-sized poems. Benedictions and prayers coexist with manifestos and georgic, the ancient genre of poems about rural hard work." (Publishers Weekly)

A **timbered** choir; the sabbath poems, 1979-1997. Counterpoint 1998 216p hardcover o.p. pa $14.95   **811**

1. Nature -- Poetry 2. Poetry -- By individual authors 3. Religious poetry, American

ISBN 978-15823-006-5

LC 98-4925

"Berry has continued periodically to write poems out-of-doors on days of little other work. This book reprints Sabbaths, a collection of that writing, adding to it about one and a half times as much new work. . . . Few other poets have such chaste and precise diction or manage line and stanza with such unaffected serenity." Booklist

Berryman, John

★ **Collected** poems, 1937-1971; edited and introduced by Charles Thornbury. Farrar, Straus & Giroux 1989 347p hardcover o.p. pa $25   **811**

  1. Poetry -- By individual authors
    ISBN 978-0-374-52281-0; 0-374-52281-2

LC 89-30944

"Berryman's poetry, sometimes mannered, elliptical, and convoluted, is distinguished by precise technical control and continued experiments with style." Reader's Ency. 4th edition

★ The **dream** songs. Farrar, Straus & Giroux 1969 xx, 427p hardcover o.p. pa $18   **811**

  1. Poetry -- By individual authors
    ISBN 978-0-374-53066-2; 0-374-53066-1

This book contains the author's 385 'dream songs' that originally appeared in various magazines, the Pulitzer Prize winning 77 dream songs (1964) and His toy, his dream, his rest (1968). The poet also provides a brief note about Henry, the poems' central character.

"Berryman makes brilliant use of his speaker's indiscriminately retentive perception—the patter of jukeboxes, of cocktail parties, of the gutter and the cathedral—to drop us dizzily into an original world where life is lived naked and unashamed." Va Q Rev

Bidart, Frank

Star dust. Farrar, Straus and Giroux 2005 84p $20   **811**

  1. Poetry -- By individual authors
    ISBN 0-374-26973-4

LC 2004-56293

This is a collection of poetry by the author of Desire.

"The poems in this collection range from terribly lame confections questioning the appellation of 'poem' itself—to gracefully and powerfully moving lyrics. . . . The more formal Bidart gets, the stronger his work, like a living example of Richard Wilbur's dictum that the genie gains his strength from confinement in the bottle." Am Book Rev

Watching the spring festival. Farrar, Straus & Giroux 2008 61p $25   **811**

  1. Poetry -- By individual authors
    ISBN 978-0-374-28603-3; 0-374-28603-5

LC 2007-40513

This book is "a collection of masterful, carefully modulated lyrics, glimpses of the millennium's turn and dispatches from an ancient world." Antioch Rev

Bishop, Elizabeth

Edgar Allan Poe & the juke-box; uncollected poems, drafts, and fragments. edited and annotated by Alice Quinn. Farrar, Straus, and Giroux 2006 367p $30   **811**

  1. Poetry -- By individual authors
    ISBN 0-374-14645-4

LC 2005-11511

"The publication of 'Edgar Allan Poe & the Juke-Box,' which gathers for the first time Bishop's unpublished material, isn't just a significant event in our poetry; it's part of a continuing alteration in the scale of American life." N Y Times Book Rev

Includes bibliographical references

Blackburn, Paul

The **collected** poems of Paul Blackburn; edited, with an introduction, by Edith Jarolim. Persea Bks. 1985 xxxv, 667p il $55   **811**

  1. Poetry -- By individual authors
    ISBN 978-0-89255-086-9; 0-89255-086-4

LC 85-9309

"Much of Blackburn's poetry is an engaging mix of sharp, allusive adventuring, humor and wordplay, annotated fragments of musical speech, and a moderate but distinctive use of metaphor. Edith Jarolim's introduction provides a concise view of Blackburn's art and life." Choice

Bly, Robert

Eating the honey of words; new and selected poems. HarperFlamingo 1999 270p hardcover o.p. pa $14.95   **811**

  1. Poetry -- By individual authors
    ISBN 0-06-093069-1 pa

LC 98-51152

"Collecting over 200 poems from 1950 to 1998, this volume is an appealing poetic sampler, although the ten new poems are unexciting. The poems celebrating discoveries Bly makes when alone and silent are always striking, and his imaginative prose poems radiate witty delight." Libr J

The **night** Abraham called to the stars; poems. HarperCollins Pubs. 2001 95p hardcover o.p. pa $12.95   **811**

  1. Poetry -- By individual authors
    ISBN 0-06-093444-1 pa

LC 00-66360

"The book's 48 lyrics are written in a single (here terceted) form, the ghazal, used by such great Islamic poets as Ghalib, and harness high points of Western art and literature to draw general, biblically backed conclusions about the human condition out of the mire." Publ Wkly

Booth, Philip

Selves; new poems. by Philip Booth. Viking 1990 75p hardcover o.p. pa $9.95 **811**

  1. Poetry -- By individual authors
    ISBN 0-14-058646-6 pa

LC 89-40317

This collection "features contemplative poems born of the observant patience of North country life. The best are based on concrete observation. . . . Booth's strength is that he speaks of significant issues like the ultimate privacy of suffering, the painful hidden destruction of relationships, the coming of aging and death." Libr J

Bowers, Edgar

Collected poems. Knopf 1997 168p hardcover o.p. pa $15   **811**

1. Poetry -- By individual authors

ISBN 0-679-76607-3 pa

LC 96-38580

"Surety of rhythm, swiftness of thought, and deftness of phrase animate Bowers' triumphant poems about loss and the struggle to be whole. He is, above all, a delineator—vital, ironic, capable of panoramic sweep—of his transfiguring experiences in Germany during and after the Second World War. His roots are deep in Horace and Pindar, but amid all the eloquent austerity there are blessed moments of unexpected Mozartian lilt and wit." New Yorker

Brathwaite, Edward Kamau

Elegguas. Wesleyan University Press 2010 123p il $22.50 **811**

1. Poetry -- By individual authors

ISBN 978-0-8195-6943-1; 0-8195-6943-7

LC 2009-35923

"This is a handsome, thoughtfully produced volume, shaped and sized to respect the poems' requirements for special graphic treatments, page formats, and line lengths. . . . The language varies as much, if not more or more dramatically in many ways, than the graphical treatments, from the intimate and colloquial diction of the work addressed to Zea Mexican [the poet's late wife], to the lyrical conventions of contemporary western poetry, to neologisms and invented forms, to the grammatical constructs of Caribbean speech. Brathwaite is equally adept and comfortable in all of these idioms." NewPages

Includes bibliographical references.

Bronk, William

Selected poems; selected by Henry Weinfield. New Directions 1995 80p pa $8.95   **811**

1. Poetry -- By individual authors

ISBN 978-0-8112-1314-1; 0-8112-1314-5

LC 95-290

"Bronk's poems are almost entirely abstract and disembodied . . . his language desiccated but also conversationally halting and embedded. There is no flesh, no world, precious little metaphor—as though every human attachment is cheating. If anything seems to work—such as cause and effect—it never adds up to anything. . . . Bronk is thinking and thinking, as purely as possible, about how we want—want not to be alone, want things to matter, want to feel that we are connected to reality. His poems are all about wanting and how there is no end to it." Poetry Foundation

Brooks, Gwendolyn

In Montgomery, and other poems. Third World Press 2003 146p $22.95   **811**

1. African Americans -- Poetry 2. Poetry -- By individual authors

ISBN 0-88378-232-4

LC 2003-50749

This is a "posthumous collection consisting primarily of dramatic monologues in a stunning variety of voices, from those of urban children to Winnie Mandela's. Reading the title sequence resembles randomly tuning a radio dial to listen to the diverse voices of Montgomery, Alabama, a city of 'leaning and lostness, glazed paralysis.' . . . Especially moving are the children's monologues. . . . Brooks captures the fierce purity of these children's needs and desires. Her loving witness never sounded more clearly than in these late poems." Booklist

The **essential** Gwendolyn Brooks; Elizabeth Alexander, editor. Library of America 2005 148p il $20   **811**

1. Poetry -- By individual authors

ISBN 978-1-931082-87-7; 1-931082-87-1

LC 2005-44162

"A book like [this] can't make the statement that needs to be made: Gwendolyn Brooks is as important to twentieth-century American poetry as Robert Lowell. . . . Her best poems offer a curative, not only to the narcissistic gloom that we've inherited from the Confessionals, but to Eliot's over-aestheticized visions of social life. That Brooks's purposes were so different from Eliot's only strengthens the connection. It shows the vitality of true poetic inspiration, how it can cut across time, temperament, race, and even the motives of its own practitioners." Poetry (Modern Poetry Association)

Budbill, David

Happy life. Copper Canyon Press 2011 117p pa $16   **811**

1. Poetry -- By individual authors

ISBN 978-1-55659-374-1

LC 2011

The poems evoke "a recognizable immediacy and honesty, accompanied by an endearing wit. . . . Budbill's economical, brush-stroke approach . . . evinces a hard-won clarity, a pure, human tone." Libr J

Bukowski, Charles

★ The **pleasures** of the damned; poems, 1951-1993. edited by John Martin. Ecco 2007 556p $29.95   **811**

1. Poetry -- By individual authors

ISBN 978-0-06-122843-8; 0-06-122843-5

LC 2007-282394

This book is "an insightful walk through the work of a poet by the man who knew him best, and it reveals Bukowski in the many, often conflicting dimensions that make him such a popular, accessible, and, yes, great artist. . . . This extraordinary collection establishes Bukowski as much more than just another West Coast Beat poet." Washington Post

Burnshaw, Stanley

The **collected** poems and selected prose; foreword by Thomas F Stanley. University of Texas Press 2002 487p il $50   **811**

1. Poetry -- By individual authors

ISBN 978-0-292-70909-6; 0-292-70909-9

LC 2001-52226

"Stanley Burnshaw is one of those men of letters who are so variously productive, and for so long, that they can too easily be taken for granted as merely part of the climate. . . . Since any poet considers himself—and deserves to be considered—a poet first of all, it is wonderful news that Burnshaw's work has now been made available for a new generation of readers. The Collected Poems and Selected Prose . . . allows us to see Burnshaw as a genuine and very American heir of the Romantic tradition in poetry, who has pursued the highest themes over his long career." New Republic

Includes bibliographical references

Callow, Philip

From noon to starry night: a life of Walt Whitman. Dee, I.R. 1992 394p il $28.50; pa $14.95 **811**
1. Authors 2. Biography, Individual 3. Essayists 4. Poets
ISBN 0-929587-95-2; 1-56663-133-5 pa
LC 92-5311

"Infused with tenderness and respect, this fine biography deciphers the complexity of Whitman's sexuality and passionate creativity while celebrating his abiding compassion and grandeur of spirit." Booklist

Includes bibliographical references

Carr, Julie

100 notes on violence. Ahsahta Press, Boise State University 2010 109p pa $19 **811**
1. Poetry -- By individual authors 2. Violence -- Poetry
ISBN 978-1-934103-11-1; 1-934103-11-X
LC 2009-26057

"In evocative, powerfully disquieting knife thrusts of verse, Carr examines the human propensity to violence, displayed here in 'notes' that range from personal anecdote to news reports to a lullaby shouted down by the voice of a murderer." Libr J

Includes bibliographical references

Carruth, Hayden

★ **Toward** the distant islands; new & selected poems. edited and with an introduction by Sam Hamill. Copper Canyon Press 2006 181p pa $17 **811**
1. Poetry -- By individual authors
ISBN 1-55659-236-1 pa
LC 2005-28705

Carruth's "books encompass Frostian tales of farm life with New England eccentrics, compilations of haiku, long and unguarded poems of erotic devotion, autobiographical laments, and sensitive odes to jazz greats. . . . All sides of Carruth's oeuvre find a place in this welcome volume. . . . The selection here gives just enough of everything Carruth has learned, and he has learned a lot, especially about the ways and landscapes of New England." Publ Wkly

Carson, Anne

Autobiography of red; a novel in verse. Knopf 1998 149p hardcover o.p. pa $12 **811**
1. Poetry -- By individual authors
ISBN 0-375-70129-X pa
LC 97-49472

"Is it poetry? Is it a novel in verse? A fable? A myth? However you define Carson's distinctive and wildly inventive new work, it is riveting reading. . . . Wistful yet whimsical, offhand yet intense, funky yet erudite . . . this is a reading experience like no other." Libr J

Men in the off hours. Knopf 2000 166p il hardcover o.p. pa $12 **811**
1. Poetry -- By individual authors
ISBN 0-375-70756-5 pa
LC 00-267850

The author "makes bold references to everyone from Oedipus to Akhamatova, but the effect of these astute, gemlike little poems is less a history lesson than a challenging conversation in a sunlit garden." Libr J

The **beauty** of the husband; a fictional essay in 29 tangos. Knopf 2001 147p $24; pa $12 **811**
1. Adultery -- Poetry 2. Marriage -- Poetry 3. Married people -- Poetry 4. Poetry -- By individual authors
ISBN 0-375-40804-5; 0-375-70757-3 pa
LC 00-62002

This poem is "at once the story of a failed marriage and an exploration of Romantic notions of beauty and truth. But Carson's idiosyncratic voice and her punchy declarative style—'You want a clean life I live a dirty one'—quickly make it clear that hers is a thoroughly modern take on the intimate cruelties of married life. And this is the primary pleasure of her writing: it is both entirely new and strangely familiar, like remembering a private language we thought we'd forgotten." New Yorker

Carson, Anne, 1950-

Nox. New Directions 2010 un il $29.95 **811**
1. Poetry -- By individual authors
ISBN 978-0-8112-1870-2; 0-8112-1870-8
LC 2009-01330

This "is an epitaph in the form of a book, a facsimile of a handmade book Carson wrote and created after the death of her brother." (N Y Times Book Rev)

The "book comes in a box the color of a rainy day, with a sliver of a family snapshot on the front. Inside is a Xerox-quality reproduction of a notebook, made after the death of her brother, including text and photographs and letters, pasted-in inkjet printouts, handwriting, paintings and collage. 'Nox' has no page numbers, and it's accordion-folded. It carries a whiff of visual art multiple or gift shop souvenir or 'Griffin & Sabine.' But trust me: it's an Anne Carson book. Maybe her best." N Y Times Book Rev

Carver, Raymond

All of us; the collected poems. Knopf 1998 xxx, 386p hardcover o.p. pa $15 **811**
1. Poetry -- By individual authors
ISBN 978-0-375-70380-5; 0-375-70380-2
LC 98-15880

"The great short story writer's poems are dark and funny, like the stories, and tell of domestic discord, crazy adventures and sweet intimacies, sometimes with sorrow but more often with thankfulness and affection." Booklist

Includes bibliographical references

A **new** path to the waterfall; poems. introduction by Tess Gallagher. Atlantic Monthly Press 1989 xxxi, 126p hardcover o.p. pa $14 **811**
1. Poetry -- By individual authors
ISBN 978-0-87113-374-8 pa; 0-87113-374-1 pa
LC 88-34989

"In her moving introduction, Carver's widow, writer Tess Gallagher, notes how often a particular poem calls to mind a corresponding story, and the reverse is also true. Indeed, to know Carver by his prose is to know him only partially. Master at illuminating those often mundane moments that starkly dramatize entire lives, Carver was also master at creating mood, and many of those poems have a striking lyrical intensity, especially when Carver unflinchingly faces death while celebrating life. A coda to a remarkable literary career." Libr J

Ciardi, John

The **collected** poems of John Ciardi; compiled and edited by Edward M. Cifelli. University of Ark. Press 1997 xxxii, 618p hardcover o.p. pa $34.95 **811**

1. Poetry -- By individual authors
ISBN 978-1-55728-449-5; 1-55728-449-0

LC 96-46331

"This volume supersedes the earlier Selected Poems (1984) providing a vastly more comprehensive sampling of Ciardi's work: 450 poems culled from over 20 individual volumes published between 1940 and 1993. In it we find testimony to Ciardi's desire to achieve not 'a voice,' a style formed to forward an author's individuality, but 'voice'— one that is determined by the externals the poet addresses." Libr J

Clark, Tom

★ **Light** & shade; new and selected poems. introduction by Amy Gerstler. Coffee House Press 2006 338p pa $20 **811**

1. Poetry -- By individual authors
ISBN 1-56689-183-3

LC 2005-35810

"Disarmingly casual yet saturated with loss, Clark's body of work revels in simplicities: lovers, friends, cities and landscapes (New York, Southern California, the Southwest), baseball, basketball, modern painters, sad weather, brief visions and ethereal promises. All make repeat appearances in a poetry rooted at once in spontaneity and in High Romantic aspiration." Publ Wkly

Clifton, Lucille

Mercy; poems. 1st ed; BOA Editions 2004 79p $22; pa $14.95 **811**

1. Poetry -- By individual authors
ISBN 1-929918-54-2; 1-929918-55-0 pa

LC 2004-10396

"These are poems where great restraint mingles with disarming primal imagery to convey poems which hold tremendous emotional weight." Va Q Rev

Cole, Henri

Middle earth; poems. Farrar, Straus & Giroux 2003 55p $23; pa $11 **811**

1. Poetry -- By individual authors
ISBN 0-374-20881-6; 0-374-52928-0 pa

LC 2002-29776

The author "examines the dichotomies between life and death, animal and human, and the lover and the beloved. Many of the poems, including, 'My Tea Ceremony' and 'Self-Portrait at the Red Princess,' show a marked Japanese influence; others record a grown son's grief over the death of his father. . . . Cole writes with clarity and an emotive resonance. These poems succeed as the best poems do: they transport the reader to other worlds, no less beautiful or complicated than our own. Highly recommended." Libr J

Collins, Billy

Nine horses; poems. Random House 2002 120p $21.95; pa $12.95 **811**

1. Poetry -- By individual authors
ISBN 1-4000-6177-6; 0-375-75520-9 pa

LC 2002-24868

Collins is "often able to proceed unburdened by many of the tools—assonance, alliteration, wordplay, complex metrics—that hang from the poet's belt; he makes his way in the world by being funny." N Y Times Book Rev

★ **Sailing** alone around the room; new and selected poems. Random House 2001 171p $21.95; pa $13.95 **811**

1. Poetry -- By individual authors
ISBN 0-375-50380-3; 0-375-75519-5 pa

LC 99-52861

"Collins will tackle any topic: his subject matter varies from snow days to Aristotle to forgetfulness. The results are accessible but not trite, comical but not laughable, and well crafted but not overly flamboyant. Collins relies heavily on imagery, which becomes the cornerstone of the entire volume." Libr J

The **trouble** with poetry and other poems; Billy Collins. Random House 2005 88p $22.95 **811**

1. Poetry -- By individual authors
ISBN 0-375-50382-X

LC 2005-46562

"Skeptical of love and scornful of pretension, Collins is breathtaking in his appreciation of the earth's beauty and the precious daily routines that define life." Booklist

Corbett, William

The **Whalen** poem; drawings by Philip Guston. Hanging Loose Press 2011 61p pa $16 **811**

1. Poetry -- By individual authors
ISBN 978-1-934909-13-3

LC 2010-51639

"Corbett composed this book-length poem, he writes in his introduction, over the summer and autumn of 2007 while in Vermont reading an advanced copy of the collected poems of Philip Whalen (1923-2002). The result is truly a poem for summer, as flighty as a hummingbird, now pausing, now darting too fast to follow to the next luminous blooming. The poem's fluidity offers a delightful ride if one is willing to go along with it. Corbett's economy of language gives him the facility to flit between images, allusions and occurrences, be they personal or seasonal, and his wide ken allows him to track events on several planes at once. . . . Whalen seems to be a spiritual adviser for this poem, a teacher who proved that the paths of the mind, traced mindfully, can be poetry. . . . [The poem] displays an open-ended lyricism that resists closure with the awareness — the insistence — that nothing is ever over, life or a work of literature." Prague Post

Cording, Robert

Walking with Ruskin; poems. CavanKerry Press 2010 93p pa $16 **811**

1. Poetry -- By individual authors

ISBN 978-1-933880-21-1; 1-933880-21-X

LC 2010-13639

These poems combine the "sacred and the mundane in unexpected ways. Even if you don't know much about poetry, Cording's poems tend to be fairly accessible because of their narrative approach, as well as their immersion in the everyday. The poems in this volume take as their subject matter a mother's grief for her child, looking though Czeslaw Milosz's glasses (literally), aging, taking a walk with a dog, and observing woodpeckers, swallows and starlings. . . . Above all, the poems in Walking with Ruskin celebrate the virtue of attentiveness to the created world around us." Christ and Pop Culture

Corso, Gregory

★ **Mindfield**; with foreword by William S. Burroughs & Allan Ginsberg; and drawings by the author. Thunder's Mouth Press 1989 268p il hardcover o.p. pa $13.95 **811**

1. Poetry -- By individual authors

ISBN 0-938410-86-5 pa

LC 89-5152

"This volume includes substantial selections from each of {the author's} six volumes of published poetry and 23 previously unpublished poems. Corso has written a number of the most memorable American poems since WW II. His poetry combines a lyrical directness of speech with a unique blend of surrealism and aphoristic statement." Choice

Crane, Hart

★ **Complete** poems and selected letters. Library of America 2006 849p $40 **811**

1. Authors 2. Biography, Individual 3. Criticism 4. Poetry -- By individual authors 5. Poets 6. Short story writers

ISBN 1-93108-299-5

LC 2006-40922

This volume "gathers all of the author's poetry and collected prose with a large sampling of his letters, some appearing in print for the first time. The correspondents include top writers William Carlos Williams, Marianne Moore, e.e. cummings, and Katherine Anne Porter. A good one-stop resource for Crane." Libr J

Creeley, Robert

★ The **collected** poems of Robert Creeley. University of California Press 1982 2v v1 o.p.; v1 pa $27.50; v2 $60; v2 pa $24.95 **811**

1. Poetry -- By individual authors

ISBN 0-520-04243-3 v1; 978-0-520-24158-9 v1 pa; 978-0-520-24159-6 v2; 978-0-520-25620-0 v2 pa

Creeley's style is "notably spare and laconic; his primary subject is love and the infinite incongruities that characterize love relationships. There is a distinct dearth of imagery in his poetry; the themes are rendered in a cerebral rather than sensual manner. For Creeley, the intent of the poem is definition, not description." Reader's Ency. 4th edition

Cummings, E. E.

★ **Complete** poems, 1904-1962; containing all the published poetry. edited by George J. Firmage. rev corr & expanded ed; Norton 1994 xxxii, 1102p $50 **811**

1. Poetry -- By individual authors

ISBN 978-0-87140-152-6; 0-87140-152-5

LC 91-29158

"This volume has been prepared directly from the poet's original manuscripts, preserving the original typography and format. It includes all the previously published works, from Tulips (1922) to Etcetera (1983), as well as 36 uncollected poems that originally appeared in little magazines or anthologies." Libr J

Cunningham, J. V.

★ The **poems** of J.V. Cunningham; edited with an introduction & commentary by Timothy Steele. Swallow Press 1997 xxxviii, 215p $32.95; pa $19.95 **811**

1. Poetry -- By individual authors

ISBN 0-8040-0997-X; 0-8040-0998-8 pa

LC 97-355

"Cunningham is an austere poet with a passion for exact statement in tightly controlled forms, whose ideal poetic models were those of Roman satire and the conceits of the most formal sixteenth- and seventeenth-century poetry. . . . His chosen form is the classical epigram, his elected idiom the satiric and self-parodic, which allows for the play of wit and irony in his commentary on the absurdity of human life." Oxford Companion to 20th Cent Lit in Engl

Dickinson, Emily

★ The **poems** of Emily Dickinson; edited by R.W. Franklin. Reading ed; Belknap Press 1999 692p $34.50; pa $18.50 **811**

1. Poetry -- By individual authors

ISBN 978-0-674-67624-4; 0-674-67624-6; 978-0-674-01824-2 pa; 0-674-01824-9 pa

LC 99-11821

"Within the guidelines Franklin has set himself, his choices of versions and of alternatives within versions are extremely sensible--and they are efficiently recorded at the end of the volume, making this the first time any volume of Dickinson's poems aimed at a general audience has offered information about the derivation of its texts." Raritan

Dickman, Michael

The **end** of the west. Copper Canyon Press 2009 89p pa $15 **811**

1. Poetry -- By individual authors

ISBN 978-1-55659-289-8; 1-556-59289-2

LC 2008-39990

"Some form of light—sunlight, moonlight, starlight, streetlight— appears in every one of the 18 poems in [this book.] . . . Slight and spare, the poems' frequent recurring themes accumulate beneficially, linking all the individual poems into one, more substantial, piece. Nothing grand takes place in these poems, but the quietness of the language and the creeping, sinister subject matter (heroin addiction, abusive fathers) make this . . . book captivating and very readable." Publ Wkly

Donnelly, Timothy

The **cloud** corporation. Wave Books 2010 153p **811**

1. Poetry -- By individual authors

ISBN 9781933517476

LC 2010-13946

This is a book of poems by the author of Twenty-seven Props for a Production of Eine Lebenszeit (2003).

"Timothy Donnelly pushes abstraction to the limits in this book—anything more, and the book would have collapsed. The book consists mostly of free-flowing tercets, lightly stressed, very much like the light feathery movement of clouds or water. The book is almost a manifesto against the utilization of images and making them the backbone of poetry. . . . This is a very existential, Sartrean project, a constant Sysiphian sifting of indispensable abstract thoughts, and a very challenging book to read." Huffington Post

Dorn, Edward

★ **Way** more West; new and selected poems. introduction by Dale Smith; edited by Michael Rothenberg. Penguin Books 2007 321p $20 **811**

1. Poetry -- By individual authors

ISBN 978-0-14-303869-6

LC 2006-50727

"Throughout his career, he was the least endearing, domesticated or predictable of poets, always determined to go his own way, no matter what anyone thought. And if he hadn't been that way, American poetry would be a lot less vital and interesting." N Y Times Book Rev

Includes bibliographical references

Doty, Mark

Fire to fire; new and selected poems. Harper 2008 336p $22.95; pa $15.95 **811**

1. Poetry -- By individual authors

ISBN 978-0-06-075247-7; 0-06-075247-5; 978-0-06-075251-4 pa; 0-06-075251-3 pa

LC 2007-44646

The author "combines new poems with the best of his previous volumes. His narrative style is expansive, filled with what has been described as a 'lyric glitter' that creates radiance around the ordinary." Libr J

Includes bibliographical references

Dove, Rita

American smooth; poems. W.W. Norton 2004 143p $22.95; pa $13.95 **811**

1. Poetry -- By individual authors

ISBN 0-393-05987-1; 0-393-32744-2 pa

LC 2004-11793

"In these free-verse poems, Dove speaks from her own perspective—as well as from that of biblical characters, black soldiers from World War I, a ten-year-old girl from Harlem, several musicians, and a pair of dancers. The selections work by lists, line breaks where ideas collide, and a juxtaposition of voices. Then using razor-sharp metaphors, Dove goes for the jugular and usually finds it. Although the book's sense of audience seems inconsistent, with some po-

ems suitable for A Child's Garden of Verses and others for The Kama Sutra, the poems are evocative." Libr J

On the bus with Rosa Parks; poems. Norton 1999 95p hardcover o.p. pa $12.95 **811**

1. African American women 2. African American women civil rights workers 3. African Americans -- Civil rights 4. Civil rights movements -- United States 5. Poetry -- By individual authors

ISBN 0-393-32026-X

LC 98-45057

Dove's "poems effortlessly suggest grand narratives and American myths, yet ground themselves tersely in localities, characters, practicalities and particulars. This seventh collection leads off with a Dove specialty, the historical sequence: her 'Cameos' lend broad, social relevance to an intermittently abandoned Depression-era wife and her family." Publ Wkly

Selected poems. Vintage Bks. 1993 xxvi, 210p pa $13 **811**

1. Poetry -- By individual authors

ISBN 0-679-75080-0

LC 93-26112

"This volume places three previous collections under one cover. . . . The selection begins with The Yellow House on the Corner, Dove's first book, most notable for its poems derived from slave narratives. Museum, her second book, offers a potpourri of work that ranges over several continents and many millenia; Dove's tirelessly exact language illuminates the lives of saints, contemporary lifestyles, and Greek myths." Booklist

Downing, Brandon

Lake Antiquity; poems, 1996-2008. Fence Books 2009 184p il pa $40 **811**

1. Poetry -- By individual authors

ISBN 978-1-934200-27-8; 1-934200-27-1

"Drawing on the tradition of fanciful collage practiced by such poets as John Ashbery, David Shapiro, and Joe Brainard, Brandon Downing wields his own scissors to cut a distinctive patch within this New York School specialty. . . . Downing has sequenced his collages with cinematic pacing; you fly through these pages as you might in a dream." Bookforum

Dugan, Alan

★ **Poems** seven; new and complete poetry. Seven Stories Press 2001 422p $35; pa $18.95 **811**

1. Poetry -- By individual authors

ISBN 1-58322-265-0; 1-58322-512-9 pa

LC 2001-41089

This collection documents "Dugan's project of comic, bleak and formally varied commentary on a dirty, terminally frayed and yet attractive America. . . . This carefully constructed, funny and sometimes unvarying volume combines all six of Dugan's previous books with a decade's worth of new verse." Publ Wkly

Duhamel, Denise

Ka-ching! University of Pittsburgh Press 2009 86p il $14.95 **811**
1. Poetry -- By individual authors
ISBN 978-0-8229-6021-8; 0-8229-6021-4 pa

"What better poetry for the current economic period than Denise Duhamel's hymns to money, ATMs, her IRA accounts, the Treasury, gambling. . .and Sean Penn? . . . Using prose poems, sonnets, sestinas, and other forms in Ka-Ching!, Duhamel is a wily technician, a touching humanist, a poet deserving stardom." Entertainment Wkly

Duncan, Robert Edward

Selected poems; [by] Robert Duncan; edited by Robert J. Bertholf. New Directions 1993 147p hardcover o.p. pa $12.95 **811**
1. Poetry -- By individual authors
ISBN 978-0-8112-1227-4; 0-8112-1227-0
LC 92-35812

Duncan "was one of the true masters of contemporary American poetry. His oeuvre is by turns lyrical, experimental, archaic, visionary and political. . . . In Bertholf's brief, insightful introduction, he makes necessary connections between the often-neglected early work and the later masterpieces." Publ Wkly

Dunn, Stephen

Different hours; poems. Norton 2000 121p $22; pa $12.95 **811**
1. Poetry -- By individual authors
ISBN 0-393-04986-8; 0-393-32232-7 pa
LC 00-30556

"Stephen Dunn's poetry is strangely easy to like: philosophical but not arid, lyrical but rarely glib, his storytelling balanced effortlessly between the casual and the vivid. But don't mistake that ease for lack of staying power." N Y Times Book Rev

Local visitations; poems. Norton 2003 96p $21.95 **811**
1. Poetry -- By individual authors
ISBN 0-393-05200-1
LC 2002-14204

"The opening section of poems recasts Dunn's average American as the mythic Sisyphus, imprisoned by repetitive work ('a repetition/which would never mean more/at the end than at the start') and yet bereft without it ('But more often he finds himself dreaming/of his rock, wishing it back, the better/to defend himself against so many hours'). Nearly half the collection transports 19th-century literary figures to contemporary New Jersey towns ('Mary Shelley in Brigantine,' 'Hawthorne in Tuckerton'), a series of poems more attractive in concept than in practice, where the subjects often fail to transcend the contrivance they inhabit." Libr J

Loosestrife. Norton 1996 96p $19; pa $12 **811**
1. Poetry -- By individual authors
ISBN 0-393-03982-X; 0-393-31683-1 pa
LC 96-1238

"Dunn understands that there is sorrow in beauty and a 'strange loneliness' even in pleasure, and he examines these dichotomies in language and form as clear and chilling as ice. We feel knocked off balance by the end of one line, then steadied by the beginning of the next." Booklist

New & selected poems, 1974-1994. Norton 1994 296p hardcover o.p. pa $16.95 **811**
1. Poetry -- By individual authors
ISBN 978-0-393-31300-0; 0-393-31300-X
LC 93-33212

"Dunn might be called a Neo-Horatian poet. He is level-headed, witty, conversational in his diction, and willing to see in domestic life his means for attaining and imparting wisdom. Yet Dunn's variations on Horatian odes and epodes are rarely the drab reportorial missives from the daily grind which are found in so much contemporary poetry. He knows that his first duty is to keep the quotidian life interesting, and this is no mean feat. . . . This is to say that Dunn's a gifted talker, a kind of querulous raconteur, and even his less successful poems are highly readable." Poetry (Modern Poetry Association)

Eady, Cornelius

Brutal imagination; poems. Putnam 2001 108p $24; pa $13 **811**
1. African-Americans -- Poetry 2. Poetry -- By individual authors 3. Race awareness -- Poetry 4. Race relations -- Poetry
ISBN 0-399-14718-7; 0-399-14720-9 pa
LC 00-62674

In this "collection of poetry, Eady invokes a chorus of fictional black characters, from Uncle Tom to the invented criminal whom Susan Smith blamed for the kidnapping of her children. A white woman's 'stray thought,' this man haunts the best of these spare, stirring poems. If the poet's premise—the personification of a black figment of the white imagination—is complex, his verse is unsettingly direct." New Yorker

Edson, Russell

The **rooster's** wife; poems. BOA Editions 2005 91p hardcover o.p. pa $14.95 **811**
1. Poetry -- By individual authors
ISBN 978-1-929918-63-8; 1-929918-63-1
LC 2004-24831

"Edson's prose poems are directly and indirectly concerned with feelings customarily suppressed during wakefulness, whose content is violent, scatological, and, especially, sexual. An Edson prose poem, however amusing and ridiculous—however jokelike—it may be, is disturbing. . . . Laughter never blunts the edges of Edson's elegantly maculate conceptions." Booklist

Eliot, T. S.

★ **Collected** poems, 1909-1962. Harcourt Brace Jovanovich 1963 221p $23 **811**
1. Poetry -- By individual authors
ISBN 0-15-118978-1

This volume contains the complete text of 'Collected poems, 1909-1935,' the 'Four quartets,' and several other poems accompanied by brief prefatory notes.

Inventions of the March Hare; poems 1909-1917. edited by Christopher Ricks. Harcourt Brace & Co. 1997 xlii, 428p $30; pa $15   **811**
    1. Poetry -- By individual authors
    ISBN 0-15-100274-6; 0-15-600587-5 pa
                 LC 96-45399

"Though available in manuscript to scholars since 1968, this is the first appearance—for all but five poems—of Eliot's 'lost' notebook of drafts and fragments. Eliot never intended this unfinished work to see publication, but in page after page his autumnal sensibility, his signature aura of languid urban malaise—however tentative—surfaces unmistakably. . . . For scholars and devotees, Eliot's rehearsals for immortality will yield a cornucopia of delights." Libr J

★ The **complete** poems and plays, 1909-1950. Harcourt Brace & Co. 1952 392p $35   **811**
    1. Poetry -- By individual authors
    ISBN 0-15-121185-X

Ellis, Thomas Sayer

Skin, Inc. identity repair poems. Graywolf Press 2010 181p il $23   **811**
    1. Poetry -- By individual authors
    ISBN 978-1-55597-567-8; 1-55597-567-4
                 LC 2010-922920

This collection of the author's poems "constitutes an impassioned argument for revitalizing America's calcified literary culture ('Flat, fixed and finished'), whose conventional assumptions about the expression of racial identity severely limit the aesthetic choices available to both writers and readers of color. . . . With honesty, eloquence, and precision, Ellis calls for resistance to the outward imposition of social and personal identity while acknowledging the difficulty of the task. . . . Certain to ignite debate on campuses and blogs, this work is the perfectly realized embodiment of its author's intent, likely to inspire poets of all ethnic backgrounds for some time to come." Libr J

Emerson, Ralph Waldo

★ **Collected** poems & translations. Library of Am. 1994 637p $35   **811**
    1. Poetry -- By individual authors
    ISBN 0-940450-28-3
                 LC 93-40245

Contains Emerson's published poetry, plus selections of his unpublished poetry from journals and notebooks, and some of his translations of poetry from other languages, notably Dante's La vita nuova.

Erdrich, Louise

Original fire; selected and new poems. HarperCollins Pubs. 2003 158p $23.95; pa $13.95   **811**
    1. Poetry -- By individual authors
    ISBN 0-06-620986-2; 0-06-093534-0 pa
                 LC 2003-40700

"With this volume, drawn from two previous collections and including 100 pages of new poems, {the author} pres-

ents her first collection in over a decade. . . . Poems from the first collection chronicle her Native American childhood and early schooling, while those from the second rework or invent Native American mythology. The new poems are more rooted in Catholicism and life as a middle-class American. . . . Essential reading for fans of Erdrich's fiction, this volume can be expected to draw poetry readers into the fold." Libr J

Estes, Angie

Tryst. Oberlin College Press 2009 75p pa $15.95 **811**
    1. Poetry -- By individual authors
    ISBN 9780932440358; 0-932440355
                 LC 2008-54661

"Gleeful and gorgeous, delighted by puns and other wordplay (including words from French, Latin and Italian), Estes's fast-paced free verse, rich with internal rhyme, takes rightful pride in the beauties it flaunts and explains. Her fourth collection finds, for recurrent motifs, saints' lives, medieval manuscripts, gold leaf and the alphabet. . . . Each deft poem weaves together multiple topics—some art-historical, others autobiographical—through chains of homonyms and knotty analogies." N Y Times Book Rev

Everson, Landis

Everything preserved: poems, 1955-2005; edited by Ben Mazer. Graywolf Press 2006 106p pa $15   **811**
    1. Poetry -- By individual authors
    ISBN 978-1-55597-453-4; 1-55597-453-8
                 LC 2006-924341

"Everson, who makes his book-length debut in his 70's as winner of the Poetry Foundation's Emily Dickinson first book award, swapped poems with a young Jack Spicer and John Ashbery, then stopped writing for 43 years until a recent creative outburst. This volume—divided into two sections, one for nine poems written between 1955 and 1960, and the other comprising the remaining 66, written since 2003—quickly establishes the charms of the playful early work. . . . The recent work is much more uneven—though much of it has been published in major literary magazines—and there are still plenty of pleasures to be found. Everson evokes the ordinary with a continually surprising touch." Publ Wkly

Fagan, Deirdre

Critical companion to Robert Frost; a literary reference to his life and work. Facts on File 2007 454p il $75   **811**
    1. Authors 2. Poets
    ISBN 0-8160-6182-3; 978-0-8160-6182-2
                 LC 2006-13269

"This encyclopedic guide offers critical entries on each of Frost's published poems, including such classics as 'The Road Not Taken,' 'Stopping By Woods on a Snowy Evening,' and 'The Death of the Hired Man.'" Publisher's note
    Includes bibliographical references

Fay-LeBlanc, Gibson

Death of a ventriloquist; poems. by Gibson Fay-LeBlanc. University of North Texas Press 2012 x,

85 p.p Number 19 in the Vassar Miller prize in poetry series **811**

1. Fatherhood -- Poetry 2. Ventriloquism -- Poetry 3. Ventriloquists -- Poetry

ISBN 157441447X; 9781574414479; 9781574414554

LC 2011042003

In this poetry collection, [Gibson] Fay-LeBlanc's lines . . . lure, guide, and yank us through poems in which a redstart in the boneset and spotted knapweed and eel grass winding your ankles are always waiting to dance upon the tongue. Whether he's overhearing a conversation in a tavern or the music stuck in his head, Fay-LeBlanc uses his ventriloquist to raise important questions about how we perform ourselves through language, creating a voice that locates its source in a Prayer of Glass because it must hide its true source from us. . . . [I]n Notes on Colic, where, in a dream, we suddenly see The foreman of the pity factory,/ where they produce the tiniest/ violins known to man//that guy, /who can't stop itching his welts //does a little jig /to make you feel better. (Publishers Weekly)

Fearing, Kenneth

Selected poems; Robert Polito, editor. Library of America 2004 xxi, 183p $20 **811**

1. Poetry -- By individual authors

ISBN 978-1-931082-57-0; 1-932082-57-X

LC 2003-60482

"Kenneth Fearing writes noir poetry, which is no surprise, considering that he also wrote several noir novels. . . His poems flirt with narrative (but rarely commit), and they're written in a jittery free verse that sounds like the byproduct of a paranoid, slightly strung-out Whitman. . . . There are plenty of people currently writing variations on Fearing (possibly without being aware of it), but it's tough to beat the stylish chill of the original. These poems may be leaves the wind blows from one gutter to another, but sometimes the gutter's the only place to be." Poetry (Modern Poetry Association)

Fenton, James

Selected poems. Farrar, Straus & Giroux 2006 196p pa $14 **811**

1. Poetry -- By individual authors

ISBN 978-0-374-26065-1; 0-374-26065-6

LC 2006-2691

This "collection offers an introduction to the work of a leading British poet and former professor of poetry at Oxford. Love and menace are the principal muses for Fenton's dark wit. Whether describing how an ex is safe because she's no longer loved . . . or narrating war's awful arithmetic . . . the control behind these lines is often terrifying." Publ Wkly

Ferlinghetti, Lawrence

★ **These** are my rivers; new & selected poems, 1955-1993. New Directions 1993 308p il hardcover o.p. pa $13.95 **811**

1. Poetry -- By individual authors

ISBN 0-8112-1273-4

LC 93-10383

"Reading this hefty selection from 12 previous volumes, plus 50 pages of new poems, we realize how accurately the poet described himself in 1979: a man who 'thinks he's

Dylan Thomas and Bob Dylan rolled together with Charlie Chaplin thrown in.' . . . His style is recognizable throughout—phlegmatic poems running several pages, often lacking stanza breaks, with short lines at the left margin or moving across the page as hand follows eye." Libr J

Finney, Nikky

★ **Head** off & split; poems. TriQuarterly Books/ Northwestern University 2011 97p pa $15.95 **811**

1. Poetry -- By individual authors

ISBN 978-0-8101-5216-8; 0-8101-5216-9

LC 2010-28888

"Finney picks through the past selectively, and with flicks of the blade that are personal, political, poetic and always musical, gives us back the present moment with an intensity that makes a reader feel as if, until reading her volume, we have been unfed." Cleveland Plain Dealer

Flynn, Nick

The **captain** asks for a show of hands; poems. Graywolf Press 2011 94p $22 **811**

1. Poetry -- By individual authors

ISBN 978-1-55597-574-6

LC 2010-937512

In this poetry collection, the author "considers the quandary of soldiers trained never to question authority and the profound betrayal of trust encoded in orders to commit torture. His masterfully concise poems deploy lulling meter, evocative images, and shocking disclosures. . . . Each word is a lit match, a thrown stone, a howling blast, a choking torrent. Flynn has forged daringly intimate and clarion poems of conscience." Booklist

Forche, Carolyn

Blue hour. HarperCollins Pubs. 2003 73p hardcover o.p. pa $13.95 **811**

1. Poetry -- By individual authors

ISBN 0-06-009912-7; 978-0-06-009913-8 pa; 0-06-009013-5 pa

LC 2002-27270

This "gathering of elegiac meditations calls up ghostly memories both personal and universal as the poet mourns the terrible death of her grandmother, gives thanks for the blessing of her son's birth, and alludes with few words and deep feelings to the anguish of war and exile." Booklist

Frost, Robert

★ **Collected** poems, prose, & plays. Library of Am. 1995 1036p $35 **811**

1. Dramas 2. Poetry -- By individual authors

ISBN 1-883011-06-X

LC 94-43693

This volume contains "all of the plays, a generous selection of prose, all collected poems, and 94 uncollected poems, as well as 17 poems that were previously unpublished." Libr J

Gallagher, Tess

Dear ghosts, poems. Graywolf Press 2006 140p
$20   **811**

1. Poetry -- By individual authors

ISBN 1-55597-443-0

LC 2005-938149

"So compelling are Gallagher's graceful poems, they
leave the reader feeling 'rearranged from the cells out.'"
Booklist

Galvin, Brendan

★ Habitat; new and selected poems, 1965-2005. Brendan Galvin. Louisiana State University Press 2005 250p
$49.95; pa $26.95 **811**

1. Poetry -- By individual authors

ISBN 0-8071-3046-X; 0-8071-3047-8 pa

LC 2004-22441

"Galvin's work is not only accessible, it turns the commonplace over into something new. A dory, a cormorant, a
pack of dogs, a chickadee—all served up with the eye of
someone who can take you on a trip of rediscovery into your
own backyard." Cape Cod Voice

Gambito, Sarah Verdes

Delivered; poems. [by] Sarah Gambito. Persea Books
2009 64p pa $14 **811**

1. Poetry -- By individual authors

ISBN 978-0-89255-346-4

LC 2008-31269

The poems in this collection "are as much about language as they are about Gambito's Filipina heritage. . . . If
disjunction is a way of talking about or recreating immigrant
experience, these poems 'deliver'—that is, provide and lead
us out of—the incoherences built into cultural transplantation. They are surrealistic, fierce, and playful." Libr J

Gander, Forrest

Core samples from the world; with photographs
by Raymond Meeks, Graciela Iburtide and Lucas
Foglia. New Directions 2011 95p il   **811**

1. Poetry -- By individual authors

ISBN 0-8112-1887-2; 978-0-8112-1887-0

LC 2011-01154

"Gander is an experimental poet in the most literal sense
of the word, in that each of his books attempts things that
haven't been tried before, either by him or others. In this
eighth collection, four sequences of poems respond to pictures by three photographers—Raymond Meeks, Graciela
Iturbide, and Lucas Foglia—making of the images metaphors for people and places that are easy to see but difficult
to penetrate. The poems don't describe the pictures so much
as work in chorus with them. . . . Concluding each section
is a piece of jumpy prose, a kind of lyric essay, narrating one
of four journeys-to Xinjiang, Mexico, Bosnia-Herzegovina,
and Chile. . . . In these pieces, Gander gets as close as one

can to the sensations of being an outsider straining toward
empathy." Publ Wkly

★ Eye against eye; with ten photographs by Sally
Mann. New Directions 2005 80p il pa $14.95 **811**

1. Poetry -- By individual authors

ISBN 0-8112-1635-7

LC 2005-14907

The "opener, 'Burning Towers, Standing Wall,' compares the building of a Mayan wall and its destruction–both
from political and natural forces–to the collapse of the Twin
Towers. In three long poems, linked with pieces that contrast
a couple's relationship with a boy's budding adolescence,
the reader is asked to regard the relationships between words
and subjects. . . . Owing to the poems' placement and the
near absence of punctuation, the reader is propelled through
the verse, left with a sense of urgency and awe." Libr J

Torn awake. New Directions 2001 95p pa
$13.95   **811**

1. Poetry -- By individual authors

ISBN 0-8112-1486-9

LC 2001-32657

"There is no solid ground in the world Forrest Gander
conjures in his new book of poems, yet his tentativeness is
one of this book's essential qualities. . . . The voices vary
throughout this book's six highly speculative sequences, . .
. yet again and again they call from their spectral airiness a
single recurring image, an elemental configuration of man,
woman and child." N Y Times Book Rev

Getty, Sarah

Bring me her heart; poems. Higganum Hill
Books 2006 98p pa $12.95   **811**

1. Poetry -- By individual authors

ISBN 978-0-9741158-8-6; 0-9741158-8-6

LC 2005-23805

The author "makes meter, rhyme, and formal stanzas the
vehicles of winning, natural expression." Booklist

Gibbons, Reginald

Creatures of a day; poems. Louisiana State University Press 2008 79p $45; pa $16.95   **811**

1. Poetry -- By individual authors

ISBN 978-0-8071-3317-0; 978-0-8071-3318-7 pa

LC 2007-34185

The author "presents intense encounters with everyday
people amidst the historical and social contexts of everyday
life. His poems are meditations on memory, obligation, love,
death, celebration, and sorrow." Publisher's note

Includes bibliographical references

It's time: poems. Louisiana State Univ. Press
2002 64p $22.95; pa $15.95   **811**

1. Poetry -- By individual authors

ISBN 0-8071-2814-7; 0-8071-2815-5 pa

LC 2002-73076

"If the thoughtful poems in Gibbons' elegant seventh
collection were pieces of music, they would be measured
piano sonatas, each note, each word, carefully struck, precisely enunciated." Booklist

Gibran, Kahlil

★ The **Prophet**. Knopf 1923 107p il $15 **811**
1. Poetry -- By individual authors
ISBN 0-394-40428-9

A collection of poems by the mystical writer/artist, who was born in Lebanon and died in the United States, in which the prophet Almustafa deals with fundamental aspects of human life such as love, friendship, good and evil, self-knowledge, passion and reason, joy and sorrow, freedom, work, marriage and children, prayer and death.

Gilbert, Jack

★ **Refusing** heaven; poems. Knopf 2005 92p $25 **811**
1. Poetry -- By individual authors
ISBN 1-4000-4365-4

LC 2004-48844

"Jack Gilbert is a poet of reckless charisma and its aftermaths: a catch-as-catch-can Castiglione, consigned by the waywardness of his imagination to write his canon of manners and gestures in lyric poetry. The poems have the quality of brilliant, searching, addled talk after a wild night out. There's a sort of strung-out sprezzatura to this poet, as he bobs and weaves among the memories of old loves in old, European cities. . . . These poems are the stream-of-consciousness work of a consciousness radically narrowed over time, practically armored against new experience. At their best, shuttling associatively between a few old obsessions, they attain claustrophobic beauty that sounds like nobody else." Poetry (Modern Poetry Association)

The **dance** most of all; poems. Alfred A. Knopf 2009 60p $25 **811**
1. Poetry -- By individual authors
ISBN 978-0-307-27076-4; 0-307-27076-9

LC 2008-44670

"These poems are deeply elegiac, looking back over a long life lived in the various modes one comes to associate with Gilbert: desire, love, longing and happiness. In short, Gilbert is as Romantic as ever, but that romance is tinged with a hard grief, a sense of loss, but ultimately one of acceptance. These are the poems of a man who realizes without reserve that his time is coming to an end. Death lingers in the background of these lines, reflected in the landscapes that close readers of Gilbert have come to know: Pittsburgh, Greece, Italy, Paris, the woods of Massachusetts where he now resides." Oregonian

Ginsberg, Allen

★ **Collected** poems, 1947-1997. HarperCollins Publishers 2006 xx, 1189p il hardcover o.p. pa $25.99 **811**
1. Poetry -- By individual authors
ISBN 978-0-06-113974-1; 0-06-113974-2; 978-0-06-113975-8 pa; 0-06-113975-0 pa

LC 2006-41191

This books "reprints the complete text of 1984's Collected Poems 1947-1980, along with the collections that followed: White Shroud, Cosmopolitan Greetings, and Death and Fame, including the original book attributes of each collection. A poet of extremes at times too trusting of his instincts, Ginsberg could be playful, angry, strident, obscene, graceful, and hilarious in the space of a page, and by now his readers know they are likely to encounter as many embarrassing poems as enlightening ones. Still, this compendium provides the most complete edition of Ginsberg available." Libr J

Spontaneous mind; selected interviews, 1958-1996. with a preface by Václav Havel; edited by David Carter. HarperCollins Pubs. 2001 601p hardcover o.p. pa $17.95 **811**
1. Authors 2. Beat generation 3. Poetry -- Authorship 4. Poets 5. Poets, American -- 20th century -- Interviews
ISBN 0-06-093082-9 pa

LC 00-40849

"The bulk of the collection [of interviews] dates from 1965-72, Ginsberg's years as countercultural symbol and spokesman: dialogues at demonstrations and on the road, transcripts from 'Firing Line' and the Chicago Seven trial." N Y Times Book Rev
Includes bibliographical references

Gioia, Dana

Disappearing ink; poetry at the end of print culture. Graywolf Press 2004 271p pa $16 **811**
1. American poetry -- History and criticism 2. Poetry -- By individual authors
ISBN 1-55597-410-4

LC 2004-104190

In this collection of essays, the author discusses the current relevance of poetry and the ways in which it is evolving with the times.
The author "offers accessible, necessary criticism for lay and academic readers of serious poetry." Am Book Rev

Giovanni, Nikki

Bicycles; love poems. William Morrow 2009 109p $16.95 **811**
1. Poetry -- By individual authors
ISBN 978-0-06-172645-3

"Disarming, sly, sensual, and knowing, Giovanni's poems scan like the teasing and wise songs favored by Dinah Washington and Etta James." Booklist

Blues; for all the changes: new poems. Morrow 1999 100p $15 **811**
1. African Americans -- Poetry 2. Poetry -- By individual authors
ISBN 0-688-15698-3

LC 98-50996

"Giovanni never loses sight of the people in her work. In poems built with broken lines and paragraphs of prose, she spars with the ills that confront us, but every struggle has a human face." Libr J

Quilting the black-eyed pea; poems and not quite poems. William Morrow 2002 110p $16.95 **811**
1. Poetry -- By individual authors
ISBN 978-0-06-009952-7; 0-06-009952-6

LC 2002-66025

Giovanni "entwines the political and the personal and celebrates womanhood and black society and culture. Hers is an embracing, uplifting, and sustaining voice, one given to both anger and humor." Booklist

The **collected** poetry of Nikki Giovanni, 1968-1998; chronology and notes by Virginia C. Fowler. William Morrow 2003 xliii, 452p $24.95   **811**
  1. Poetry -- By individual authors
  ISBN 0-06-054133-4
                                              LC 2004-302269
"Giovanni observes and embraces the world like few other poets; seize on these poems spanning three decades, and listen to her sing." Booklist
  Includes bibliographical references

Gluck, Louise
  Averno. Farrar, Straus and Giroux 2006 79p $22 **811**
  1. Poetry -- By individual authors
  ISBN 0-374-10742-4; 978-0-374-10742-0
                                              LC 2005-42658
"Empathic and unforgiving, the voice that unifies Persephone's despondent homelessness, Demeter's rageful mothering and Hades's smitten jealousy is unique in recent poetry, and reveals the flawed humanity of the divine." Publ Wkly

Glück, Louise
  A **village** life. Farrar, Straus, and Giroux 2009 72p $23   **811**
  1. Poetry -- By individual authors
  ISBN 978-0-374-28374-2; 0-374-28374-5
                                              LC 2008-49218
"Glück's achievement in this collection is to show, through the exigencies of the place she has chosen, how interpersonal relationships are formed, shaped and broken by the particular landscape in which they unfurl. Though the poems are intimate and deeply sympathetic, there remains the suggestion of a distance between Glück and the village life she writes about. When she declaims, 'No one really understands/ the savagery of this place,' it feels as though she is speaking less about her chosen subjects than about herself." Publ Wkly

Goldbarth, Albert
  ★ The **kitchen** sink; new and selected poems, 1972-2007. Graywolf Press 2007 345p $26   **811**
  1. Poetry -- By individual authors
  ISBN 978-1-55597-462-6; 1-55597-462-7
                                              LC 2006-929502
"Albert Goldbarth just may be the American poet of his generation for the ages. Often humorous but always serious, Goldbarth combines erudite research, pop-culture fanaticism, and personal anecdote in ways that make his writings among the most stylistically recognizable in the literary world." Georgia Rev

Graber, Kathleen
  The **eternal** city; poems. Princeton University Press 2010 78p $35; pa $16.95   **811**
  1. Poetry -- By individual authors
  ISBN 978-0-691-14609-6; 978-0-691-14610-2 pa
                                              LC 2009-49321
"Graber's lengthy, long-lined, poems take in everything from St. Augustine to Pepperidge Farm Goldfish crackers to

a rash of deaths in the poet's own family, and that's in just one poem. . . . Perhaps half the poems have an epigraph, from the likes of William Blake, Marcus Aurelius and Walter Benjamin. Those sources, as well as Graber's candid tone, set the poems in the midst of an ongoing conversation with the lessons of history and religion. But what makes Graber's poems so fresh and wild are the associative slips that happen between the distant past and the urgent present." Publ Wkly

Graham, Jorie
  Overlord; poems. Ecco 2005 93p $22.95 **811**
  1. Poetry -- By individual authors
  ISBN 0-06-074565-7
                                              LC 2004-53681
"In a distinctly forthright and empathic collection, Graham has constructed poems of lyrical steeliness and cauterizing beauty." Booklist

The **dream** of the unified field; selected poems, 1974-1994. Ecco Press 1995 199p hardcover o.p. pa $15   **811**
  1. Poetry -- By individual authors
  ISBN 0-88001-476-8 pa
                                              LC 95-16572
"Combining great vision like Blake's, a Dickinsonian philosophical introspection, and a richly modern sensuality, this selection demonstrates the full range of Graham's poetic gifts." Booklist

Gregg, Linda
  All of it singing. Graywolf Press 2008 224p $24   **811**
  1. Poetry -- By individual authors
  ISBN 978-1-55597-507-4; 1-55597-507-0
                                              LC 2008-928247
This retrospective "selects from all of Gregg's published books—from her 1981 debut Too Bright to See to 2006's In the Middle Distance—including a group of new poems that show her ongoing investigations into the inner intensities of everyday brutality and grace. . . . The poems travel the globe, set in New England, California, Mexico, Greece and beyond, though wherever her poems go, Gregg never forgets that 'if paradise is to be here/ it will have to include her.' Gregg offers up poems of love lost and won, and of an average life lived with extraordinary force. . . . The poems always rejoice, however dark their subjects, in a powerful sense of simply being alive." Publ Wkly

Grossman, Allen R.
  Descartes' loneliness; [by] Allen Grossman. New Directions 2007 64p il pa $16.95   **811**
  1. Poetry -- By individual authors
  ISBN 978-0-8112-1711-8; 0-8112-1711-6
                                              LC 2007-26896
"Grossman once claimed poetry to be the historical enemy of human forgetfulness. This interest—or better, faith—in poetry's capacity to perform distinctly human acts of preservation has informed Grossman's writing from the beginning. This most recent book showcases some of Grossman's most affecting and memorable lyrics to date." Publ Wkly

Guest, Barbara

The **collected** poems of Barbara Guest; edited by Hadley Haden Guest. Wesleyan University Press 2008 525p $39.95 **811**

1. Authors 2. Poetry -- By individual authors 3. Poets
ISBN 978-0-8195-6860-1; 0-8195-6860-0
LC 2008-20147

"It is impossible for a reader to leave The Collected Poems of Barbara Guest without appreciating the enormous spiritual gift her work has always offered in the form of an aesthetic and philosophical challenge." Boston Rev

Includes index. 'Works by Barbara Guest': p. xxvii-xxix

H. D.

★ **Collected** poems, 1912-1944; edited by Louis L. Martz. New Directions 1983 xxxvi, 629p hardcover o.p. pa $24.95 **811**

1. Poetry -- By individual authors
ISBN 978-0-8112-0971-7; 0-8112-0971-7
LC 83-6380

The editor's textual notes "offer valuable and illuminating scholarly commentary and present the most important of the textual variants. An informative and sensitively written introduction discusses aspects of the interpenetration of H.D.'s biography with her poetic sensibility. This volume is an impressive scholarly work." Choice

Hacker, Marilyn

Selected poems; 1965-1990. Norton 1994 250p $22; pa $13.95 **811**

1. Poetry -- By individual authors
ISBN 0-393-03675-8; 0-393-31349-2 pa
LC 94-27507

"Few poets have been as successful as Hacker in negotiating the boundary of the feminist and lesbian canon while generating a buzz around their early work. Iambic and readable, the pieces in Selected Poems—taken from five previous volumes—use unique inversions to explore self and other through changing situations between friends, lovers, family, and one's surroundings. . . . Often, these are poems of loss, of desire delayed, of pleasure deferred." Libr J

Squares and courtyards. Norton 2000 107p $21; pa $12 **811**

1. Poetry -- By individual authors
ISBN 0-393-04830-6; 0-393-32095-2 pa
LC 99-39110

"With customary fortitude and intelligence, Hacker confronts such sobering subjects as the trauma of her own chemotherapy and the loss of friends, in poems that are at once clear-sighted and emotionally full." New Yorker

Hall, Donald

White apples and the taste of stone; poems, 1946-2006. Houghton Mifflin Co. 2006 431p $30; pa $16.95 **811**

1. Poetry -- By individual authors
ISBN 978-0-618-53721-1; 0-618-53721-X; 978-0-618-91999-4 pa; 0-618-91999-6 pa
LC 2005-20047

"Given to formal short work in the '50s, to lengthy verse essays and verse memoirs later on, Hall shows consistent topics and moods: adult life among New Hampshire's farms and mountains, childhood in the Connecticut suburbs, equanimity and nostalgia, satire and self-satire, middle age and old age, regret and reserve. Most original in his long poems from the '80s and '90s, Hall achieved popular success in recent years,. . . collecting elegies and laments for his late wife, the poet Jane Kenyon." Publ Wkly

The **back** chamber. Houghton Mifflin Harcourt 2011 82p $22 **811**

1. Poetry -- By individual authors
ISBN 978-0-547-64585-8
LC 2011009152

This is "a mix of naughty, funny, sweet, and sad pieces about love, family, death, and the poignancy of things. The old rooms of his grandfather's farmhouse in New Hampshire, where Hall has lived since the 1970s, set the stage for recalled intimacies with his late wife, the poet Jane Kenyon, and recollections of the childhood that first brought him there. . . . Featuring moving, amusing, musical poems about love, aging, and baseball, this work will have broad appeal and is recommended for all collections." Libr J

Harjo, Joy

A **map** to the next world; poetry and tales. Norton 2000 138p hardcover o.p. pa $13.95 **811**

1. Poetry -- By individual authors
ISBN 978-0-393-32096-1; 0-393-32096-0
LC 99-41099

"One of the most significant American Indian poets here expands her poetic practice to include what she calls tales but might as easily be considered prose poems. Harjo's verse has lately taken on a flowing, narrative quality; these tales, by contrast, take an imagistic, stream-of-consciousness form. . . . Written with authority and Harjo's trademark exploratory verve, this is fine, mature work." Booklist

Harrington, Janice N.

Even the hollow my body made is gone; poems. foreword by Elizabeth Spires. BOA Editions, Ltd. 2007 85p pa $15.50 **811**

1. Poetry -- By individual authors
ISBN 978-1-929918-89-8; 1-929918-89-5
LC 2006-30823

The author "sets her first poetry collection mainly in Alabama during the civil-rights era. Her rich, colloquial poems, drawing on both folklore and science, are paeans to a weary but tenacious black family and their journey north through 'a night as wide as the River Jordan.' . . . When the poems themselves seem less pioneering than the spirit they evoke, their scope and empathy largely compensate." New Yorker

Harrison, Jim

In search of small gods. Copper Canyon Press 2009 120p $22 **811**

1. Poetry -- By individual authors
ISBN 978-155659-300-0; 1-55659-300-7
LC 2008-39992

Harrison "writes like a man reconciling the world at large with the natural world he knows well, one that still fascinates and inspires him. Many of his small gods are dogs, and many of them are fish or birds, that is, chickadees and hawks, willow flycatchers and hummingbirds. . . . He looks at them all with awe and ironic amusement. A group of prose poems centers this volume. Whether he imagines an Estonian World War II veteran who is fascinated by light or Vallejo in Paris, collecting empty wine bottles for small change, Harrison is heavily invested in narrative elements that range from the real to the surreal." Libr J

★ The **shape** of the journey; new & collected poems. Copper Canyon Press 1998 463p $30; pa $20　　　　　　　　　　　　　　　　　　**811**
　　1. Poetry -- By individual authors
　　ISBN 1-55659-095-4; 1-55659-149-7 pa
　　　　　　　　　　　　　　　　　LC 98-25501
"This large collection, which also includes a new grab bag of nature verse and prose poems called 'Geo-Bestiary,' has a meandering feel, although Harrison's concerns—aging, women, eating and drinking, hunting, the craft of writing and above all the spirit and rhythms of the natural world—are remarkably constant. . . . Harrison's writing is graceful, direct and muscular, even in those occasional places where the poems feel like dashed-off diary entries or, rarer still, when they hit a mawkish note." N Y Times Book Rev

Harrison, Jim, 1937-
　　Songs of unreason. Copper Canyon Press 2011 143p $22　　　　　　　　　　　　　　　　**811**
　　1. Poetry -- By individual authors
　　ISBN 978-1-55659-389-5
　　　　　　　　　　　　　　　　LC 2011025560
"It wouldn't be a Harrison collection without the poet, novelist, and food critic's reverence for rivers, dogs, and women, but that's not to say Harrison has grown stale or uninteresting in his late poems. Often, as in 'A Part of My History,' which finds the poet tracking the ghost of García Lorca through Granada, his poems stun us simply, with the richness of the clarity, detail, and the immediacy of Harrison's voice. . . . Pushing his formal boundaries, Harrison closes the collection with the meditative 'Suite of Unreason,' a piece that boils down his sharp, epigrammatic lines into a sequence of fist-pumping short poems. But it also wouldn't be a Harrison poem without the hard melancholy that has come to define his voice." Publ Wkly

Hass, Robert
　　Time and materials; poems, 1997-2005. Ecco 2007 88p $22.95　　　　　　　　　　　　　　**811**
　　1. Poetry -- By individual authors
　　ISBN 978-0-06-134960-7; 0-06-134960-7
　　　　　　　　　　　　　　　　LC 2007-30294
This collection of poetry by the former U.S. poet laureate "show a rare internal variety, even as they reflect his constant concerns. One is human impact on the planet at the century's end. . . . Another concern is biography and memory, not so much Hass's own life as the lives of family and friends. . . . Through it all runs a rare skill with long sentences, a light touch, a wish to make claims not just on our ears but on our hearts, and a willingness to wait—few poets wait longer, it seems—for just the right word." Publ Wkly
　　Includes bibliographical references

The **apple** trees at Olema; new and selected poems. Ecco 2010 352p $34.99 **811**
　　1. Poetry -- By individual authors
　　ISBN 978-0-06-192382-1; 0-06-192382-6
This "retrospective collection, drawn from five previous books, beginning with Field Guide (1973), opens with a generous selection of new poems redolent of Whitman and the blues. Narrative poems are droll and astringent in their musings over love's paradoxes and history's shifting claims, children's pleasures, poverty, and danger. . . . Hass distills experiences down to their essence as he limns landscapes, portrays friends and loved ones, and imagines the struggles of strangers. The ordinary is cracked open to reveal metaphysical riddles in poems that feel so natural, their formal complexities nearly elude our detection." Booklist

Haxton, Brooks
　　They lift their wings to cry; poems. Knopf 2008 78p $25　　　　　　　　　　　　　　　　**811**
　　1. Poetry -- By individual authors
　　ISBN 978-0-307-26845-7; 0-307-26845-4
　　　　　　　　　　　　　　　　LC 2008-05766
"You could place Haxton in the Billy Collins school of poetry. His poems read readily, they are funny, smart, and so much more, as their blithe cleverness and charming humility lightly camouflage a spiritual dimension. But Haxton goes his own way, channels his sages of choice, and keeps it low-key, bemused, and philosophical. His emotional palette is warm. His frame of reference encompasses Heraclitus, Ovid, the Bible, a CAT scan. His fascination with the small creatures that make up the bulk of what we call nature—he writes of crickets, moths, birds, a mouse—has a scientific cast even as it springs from a freeflowing empathy with all of life." Booklist

Hayden, Robert Earl
　　★ **Collected** poems; edited by Frederick Glaysher. Liveright 1985 205p hardcover o.p. pa $15 **811**
　　1. Poetry -- By individual authors
　　ISBN 978-0-87140-159-5; 0-87140-159-2
　　　　　　　　　　　　　　　　LC 84-28880
"Hayden's poetry is a blend of unrivaled craftsmanship with a sharp, unrestrained vision. His subjects encompass the whole of human experience, from the extremely personal but never obscure ('Approximations') to the historical but never pedantic ('Belsen, Day of Liberation'). His technique is similarly varied. Hayden is as adept with haiku, imitations of Eskimo song-poems, or sonnets as he is with free verse. A particularly important addition to libraries with black literature collections." Booklist

Hayes, Terrance
　　Lighthead. Penguin Books 2010 95p pa $18 **811**
　　1. Poetry -- By individual authors
　　ISBN 978-0-14-311696-7; 0-14-311696-7
　　　　　　　　　　　　　　　　LC 2009-53319
This collection is a "celebration and castigation of American culture, one worthy of the term 'Americanist.' The title references the light of inspiration and the fire that pours from the heads of two teenage lynching victims in one of the opening poems. The fact that the title can do both inspiration and elegy is indicative of how meaning is contested terrain in Hayes' work. . . . [He] deftly quilts together different

textures of language. Rants move into love poems and biting humor butts up against meditations. . . . Sound is of primary importance to Mr. Hayes. Throughout the book he borrows from hip-hop, jazz, slang, lists, and T-shirt slogans. Content aside, his poems are full of pure pleasure of sound in his startling and sonically dense images." Pittsburgh Post-Gazette

Healey, Steve

10 Mississippi; poems. Coffee House Press 2010 113p pa $16   **811**

1. Poetry -- By individual authors
ISBN 978-1-56689-252-0; 1-56689-252-X
LC 2010-16259

"Steve Healey is one of our most promising young poets, and this collection is full of circumambulations around the same topics, in a skillful takeoff from Gertrude Stein's poetics. Healey quotes from Elizabeth Bishop 'Everything only connected by 'and' and 'and'' and from Steve Reich 'I discovered that the most interesting music of all was made by simply lining the loops up in unison, and letting them slowly shift out of phase with each other.' This seems to be his operative paradigm as well. The whole book is about the mendacity (and utter veracity) of connection; Healey's circling around the dead corpse of false consolations is extremely hypnotic and enchanting. The '10 Mississippi' sequence is particularly effective as a meditation on finality." Huffington Post

Hecht, Anthony

Collected later poems. Knopf 2003 255p hardcover o.p. pa $16.95   **811**

1. Poetry -- By individual authors
ISBN 978-0-375-71030-8; 0-375-71030-2
LC 2003-44601

This volume contains: The transparent man (1990), Flight among the tombs (1996), and The darkness and the light (2001).

"From the outset a fastidious craftsman, Hecht developed out of the legacy of modernism a stately, intricate, rigorously formal poetry that slowly expanded in its range of tones and subject matter." Times Lit Suppl

Hillman, Brenda

Cascadia. Wesleyan Univ. Press 2001 77p $26; pa $13.95 **811**

1. Poetry -- By individual authors
ISBN 0-8195-6491-5; 0-8195-6492-3 pa
LC 2001-35504

"Geologists know 'Cascadia' as the name for the landmass that became the American West Coast: Hillman's serial mix of long and short poems links Californian geology, geography, history (a Gold Rush-era diarist named Shirley), continental philosophy, and personal experience. . . . Some poems are content with their lyrical verbal effects; others play with typography for effects that are energetic, familiar to readers of Susan Howe and Jorie Graham." Publ Wkly

Pieces of air in the epic. Wesleyan Univ. Press 2005 87p $22.95; pa $14.95   **811**

1. Poetry -- By individual authors
ISBN 978-0-8195-6787-1; 0-8195-6787-6; 978-0-8195-6788-8 pa; 0-8195-6788-4 pa
LC 2005-18749

"The second in a tetralogy exploring the four elements, Hillman's expansive new work examines air not just as 'gusts & siroccos, chinooks, hamskin, whooshes' but as voice, song, and spirit. Were it not such a pun, one would be tempted to call this collection literally breathtaking; Hillman has pursued an ambitious program with remarkably fine-tuned language." Libr J

Hirsch, Edward

Earthly measures; poems. Knopf 1994 93p hardcover o.p. pa $18   **811**

1. Poetry -- By individual authors
ISBN 978-0-679-76566-0; 0-679-76566-2
LC 93-26410

"Hirsch contemplates manifestations of the divine in this set of ravishing poems infused with a deeply felt sense of place and history, seeking insights into how instances of spiritual revelation occur in the frequently brutal everyday world." Booklist

On love; poems. Knopf 1998 86p hardcover o.p. pa $15   **811**

1. Poetry -- By individual authors
ISBN 978-0-375-70260-0; 0-375-70260-1
LC 97-49460

"The affirmation of On Love is its language, and the sense it gives that the language of love is inexhaustible. However conversant with the abyss, however true to the devastating logic of desire, the poems ultimately feel triumphant. They are held aloft by nothing but their own joyous artistry." Yale Rev

Special orders; poems. Alfred A. Knopf 2008 64p $25   **811**

1. Poetry -- By individual authors
ISBN 978-0-307-26681-1; 0-307-26681-8
LC 2007-40336

This collection "brings its demotic, heartfelt, autobiographical pieces together to form a picture of Hirsch's whole life, with sadness always visible, but joy in the foreground. He begins with his immigrant 'grandfather,/ an old man from the Old World'; remembers 'the second-story warehouse' where the young poet 'filled orders for the factory downstairs'; and moves on to his own life as a struggling, and then a successful, writer, teacher and father. Jewish and Yiddish heritage, in memory and on canvas (Chaim Soutine, Marc Chagall) pervades the first half of the volume. . . . The second half follows Hirsch as an adult, to Houston (where he taught for many years) and back to New York City, where he now heads the Guggenheim Foundation." Publ Wkly

The **living** fire; new and selected poems, 1975-2010. Alfred A. Knopf 2010 237p $27   **811**

1. Poetry -- By individual authors
ISBN 978-0-375-41522-7; 0-375-41522-X
LC 2009-24452

In Hirsch's work, things are not always what they seem. Certainly, his poems work to dignify the everyday. But they do more than that. What makes Hirsch so singular in American poetry is the balance he strikes between the quotidian and something completely other an irrational counterforce, the living fire that gives its name to his new selected poems.

. . . Literary and allusive, but also domestic and intimate, as it rises toward praise, Hirsch's voice resounds with both force and subtlety. One of the pleasures of reading the new selected poems is the chance to see that voice develop and then range freely and surprisingly. N Y Times Book Rev

Hirshfield, Jane

After; poems. HarperCollins 2006 97p $23.95 **811**

1. Poetry -- By individual authors

ISBN 0-06-077916-0

LC 2005-50260

"These poems' topics range from global warming to insomnia, passion, cheese making, and sneezing. . . . [The author] engages historical figures from Rembrandt, Poe, and Tu Fu to Linnaeus, Roget, and Darwin. The beauty of these historically engaging poems, though, is that they remain firmly tied to our contemporary world." Va Q Rev

Hix, H. L.

First fire, then birds; obsessionals 1985-2010. Etruscan Press 2010 291p $27.95   **811**

1. Poetry -- By individual authors

ISBN 978-0-9819687-4-2; 0-9819687-4-0

"Sometimes achingly beautiful in their accumulated details, sometimes grisly and violent, and sometimes tersely intellectual, Hix's collections have always been hard to forget: since his debut with the sonnets of Perfect Hell (1996), his books have differed greatly one from another, each with its signature long poem or sequence. . . . Formalists cherish Hix's frequent meter and rhyme; devotees of experiment enjoy the bizarre disjunctions and the philosophical demands. This retrospective shuffles individual poems and sequences from his first seven books to good effect, out of chronological order (along with aphorisms from a book of prose). Hix may make new readers' heads spin with his changes of focus, but he also gives them the chance to see his work whole." Publ Wkly

Hoagland, Tony

Unincorporated persons in the late Honda dynasty; poems. Graywolf Press 2010 90p pa $15 **811**

1. Poetry -- By individual authors

ISBN 978-1-55597-549-4; 1-55597-549-6

LC 2009-933818

"There are 15 or 20 better poets in America than Tony Hoagland, but few deliver more pure pleasure. His erudite comic poems are backloaded with heartache and longing, and they function, emotionally, like improvised explosive devices: the pain comes at you from the cruelest angles, on the sunniest of days. . . . On a superficial level Mr. Hoagland's poems — he writes in an alert, caffeinated, lightly accented free verse — resemble those of many writers in what one is tempted to call the Amiable School of American Poets, a group for which Billy Collins serves as both prom king and starting point guard. But Mr. Hoagland's verse is consistently, and crucially, bloodied by a sense of menace and by straight talk." N Y Times (Late N Y Ed)

What narcissism means to me. Graywolf Press 2003 78p pa $14   **811**

1. Poetry -- By individual authors

ISBN 1-55597-386-8 pa

LC 2003-101172

The author's "speaker devotes considerable energy to unmasking . . . {his} vulnerable self, revealing its ugliness, hatred and social sensitivity. . . . In milder poems, which often revolve around eating dinner, drinking wine and hanging out with friends (typically other creative writing professors), he explores a more social self, slipping into a 'he said, she said' mode, and reporting at great length on friends' witticisms." Publ Wkly

Hodgen, John

Heaven & earth holding company. University of Pittsburgh Press 2010 73p pa $14.95   **811**

1. Poetry -- By individual authors

ISBN 978-0-8229-6114-7; 0-8229-6114-8

"Every writer wants to get the strange kaleidoscopic world of ten thousand things into their work; few succeed. But John Hodgen's Heaven and Earth Holding Company delivers that entirely in poem after poem —sun, rain, baseball, Frost and Shakespeare, the birth of a granddaughter, Abraham Lincoln, W.C Fields, saints, dogs, lovers, Viagra, Motel 6, those beeping airport carts. Hodgen's long-lined poems are propulsive, his sentences hypotactic, muscular, alliterative. . . . If these were just playful, wise-cracking poems they would give us pleasure enough; but Hodgen's poems fast-break from humor to sorrow and the mortal coils of our lives." On the Seawall

Hoffman, Daniel

Beyond silence; selected shorter poems, 1948-2003. Louisiana State Univ. Press 2003 226p $49.95; pa $26.95   **811**

1. Poetry -- By individual authors

ISBN 0-8071-2860-0; 0-8071-2861-9 pa

LC 2002-34090

The collection's "organization by theme brings poems from remote parts of his oeuvre into illuminating conversation with one another. And substantial recent poems such as 'Scott Nearing's Ninety-Eighth Year' and 'The Cape Racer' are as strong as anything he's written." NY Times Book Rev

Hollander, John

Figurehead & other poems. Knopf 1999 89p hardcover o.p. pa $15   **811**

1. Poetry -- By individual authors

ISBN 978-0-375-70433-8; 0-375-70433-7

LC 98-14208

Hollander's "justifiably confident in his skills, the solid grace of his constructions, and his ability to make both the light and dark sides of words, thoughts, and even life itself simultaneously visible. It's no wonder that among nimbly philosophic poems about Arachne, Cain, and a painting by Velázquez he disarms, charms, and intrigues his readers with a witty and imaginative tribute to the tabletop sculptures of Saul Steinberg and a bittersweet remembrance of George Moran, an old vaudevillian." Booklist

A draft of light; poems. Alfred A. Knopf 2008 109p $26   **811**

1. Poetry -- By individual authors

ISBN 978-0-307-26911-9; 0-307-26911-6

LC 2008-4751

"As one would expect of a poet whose work has been set to music, Hollander sees poetry as an oral art even though it is first written on paper. What one might not expect from this 78-year-old poet is the wordplay, lighthearted tone, and general mischievousness that seems to come trippingly from his pen. . . . This volume's title poem, for example, ends with a paraphrase of T.S. Eliot's 'Little Gidding.' Other poems paraphrase Percy Bysshe Shelley, Wallace Stevens, and Joyce Kilmer, to say nothing of William Shakespeare. Like Shakespeare, Hollander fuses a somber tone with comic conventions, resulting in the poetic equivalent of the problem play." Libr J

Includes bibliographical references

Howard, Richard

★ **Inner** voices; selected poems, 1963-2003. Farrar, Straus and Giroux 2004 428p $35 **811**
　　1. Poetry -- By individual authors
　　ISBN 0-374-25862-7

　　　　　　　　　　　　　　　　　LC 2004-40464

The author "chooses artists and art as the personae and subjects of many of his poems. . . . Besides artists, Howard often chooses writers as personae, including prominent Victorians (Whitman, Ruskin and Browning); correspondents with other writers and artists; and increasingly, himself as traveler, museumgoer, and engaged reader." Booklist

Without saying; new poems. Turtle Point Press 2008 108p pa $16.95 **811**
　　1. Poetry -- By individual authors
　　ISBN 978-1-933527-14-7 pa; 1-933527-14-5 pa
　　　　　　　　　　　　　　　　　LC 2007-907229

"In this 14th collection of his own verse, [the author] returns to the kinds of poems that made him famous: elaborate dramatic monologues, impersonations and dialogues that are intricately alert to literary history and sexual desire. . . . In these thoughtful new poems, Howard offers, and excels in, sophisticated verbal comedy." Publ Wkly

★ The **silent** treatment; new poems. Turtle Point Press 2005 114p pa $16.95 **811**
　　1. Poetry -- By individual authors
　　ISBN 1-885586-38-3
　　　　　　　　　　　　　　　　　LC 2004-113837

Hannah Arendt, George Eliot, Cosima Wagner, and a boy in a photograph by Arkansas photographer Mike Disfarmer are among the speakers in this collection.

"In characterizing the poems of Richard Howard's latest collection, one is tempted to bypass 'golden' as a description and head straight on to platinum. Now in his eighth decade, Howard has long been–along with the late James Merrill, who jokingly coined the phrase–one of American poetry's 'Great Fancies.'" Wkly Stand

Howe, Susan

Souls of the Labadie tract. New Directions Books 2007 127p pa $16.95 **811**
　　1. Poetry -- By individual authors
　　ISBN 978-0-8112-1718-7; 0-8112-1718-3
　　　　　　　　　　　　　　　　　LC 2007-34255

"In her newest book, Howe stands in thrall to a 17th-century history of Deerfield, Mass., and then chases down an obscure reference to 'Labadist' in Wallace Stevens's family tree, which brings her to the story of a short-lived Utopian 'quietest sect,' followers of Jean de Labadie who established a community in Maryland in 1684 that vanished within 40 years. It is in these vast tracts of time made intimate by texts, by language, that Howe operates. . . . Beginning with a quote from Jonathan Edwards equating the silkworm to 'a type of Christ' and ending with a photograph of a fragment of the silk wedding dress of Edwards's wife, onto which Howe projects a text ('I have already shown that space is God'), this is intense stuff." Publ Wkly

That this. New Directions Pub. 2010 109p il pa $15.95 **811**
　　1. Poetry -- By individual authors
　　ISBN 978-0-8112-1918-1 pa; 0-8112-1918-6 pa
　　　　　　　　　　　　　　　　　LC 2010-41791

"Death is one of the preeminent subjects of poetry, and Howe . . . approaches this topic with the gravitas of one who has endured loss. . . . [This] volume deals chiefly with the death of her husband, Peter Hare. The book juxtaposes Howe's personal recollections with excerpts from an assortment of documents, ranging from 18th-century diaries to an array of half-decayed ephemera, such as bits of Poussin prints and fragments of linguistic sculpture. . . . An intelligent and unorthodox treatment of grief, this title will appeal to poetry and visual arts enthusiasts." Libr J

Howes, Barbara

★ **Collected** poems, 1945-1990. University of Ark. Press 1995 134p hardcover o.p. pa $16 **811**
　　1. Poetry -- By individual authors
　　ISBN 0-679-76592-1 pa
　　　　　　　　　　　　　　　　　LC 94-32343

"How often has a forgotten writer been resurrected, heralded as an important voice, only to end up a disappointment? All too often, alas. Luckily, this is not the case with Barbara Howes, who . . . is as obscure a worthy poet as I can think of. Her book not only exceeds expectations, but exceeds them in ways I never would have guessed. . . . Certainly there is much in this book for lovers of poetic forms: villanelles, sestinas and a 'Near-Pantoum,' as the poet calls it." N Y Times Book Rev

Hughes, Langston

Selected poems of Langston Hughes; drawings by E. McKnight Kauffer. Knopf 1959 297p il hardcover o.p. pa $13.95 **811**
　　1. Poetry -- By individual authors
　　ISBN 0-679-72818-X; 978-0-679-72818-4

This collection represents Langston Hughes' own decisions as to which of his poems he wanted to preserve and reprint.

Hugo, Richard F.

★ **Making** certain it goes on; the collected poems of Richard Hugo. Norton 1983 xxi, 456p hardcover o.p. pa $19.95 **811**
　　1. Poetry -- By individual authors
　　ISBN 978-0-393-30784-9; 0-393-30784-0
　　　　　　　　　　　　　　　　　LC 83-8016

"Though he would never be a serene poet, his collected poems show Hugo turning toward a calm peace that would mark his best work in 'White Center' (1980) and 'The Right Madness On Skye' (1981), and in the 22 new poems in this volume. . . . Among the new poems included [here] Hugo was still driving, looking, and naming. If we had not noticed before that his great gift was the elegy, we see it now." N Y Times Book Rev

Ignatow, David

I have a name. University Press of New England 1996 75p hardcover o.p. pa $13.95   **811**
1. Poetry -- By individual authors
ISBN 978-0-8195-2240-5; 0-8195-2240-6
LC 96-19350

"Ignatow's words are spare and apparently casual, holding us riveted by the force of what is articulated but not spoken. . . . The subjects are timeless: loss, age, death, the joy of fleeting moments." Booklist

Shadowing the ground. Wesleyan Univ. Press 1991 68p hardcover o.p. pa $13.95   **811**
1. Poetry -- By individual authors
ISBN 978-0-8195-1197-3; 0-8195-1197-8
LC 90-20872

"Here are sixty-five short, spare, untitled poems, their uniformity of appearance (two-thirds of them ten lines or fewer) belying the plural perspectives that David Ignatow brings to his considerations of age and death's imminence. . . . Shadowing the Ground celebrates contrary responses to unplanned obsolescence." World Lit Today

Jackson, Major

Holding company. W.W. Norton & Co. 2010 91p $24.95   **811**
1. Poetry -- By individual authors
ISBN 978-0-393-07080-4
LC 2010-17728

"The sonnet sequence has been a staple of love poetry; Major Jackson tries here a sequence of tenline poems, instead of the fourteen of the sonnet, and the form, as always, pressures the poet toward specific meanings. There is greater urgency to get to the point, and it makes the expression of love only more dire, more taut and almost unmanageable. The effect of these poems individually is a certain serenity, a distance toward public turmoil, but cumulatively they amount to a desperate rebellion, a willful declaration of immortality." Huffington Post

Hoops; poems. Norton 2006 125p $23.95 **811**
1. Poetry -- By individual authors
ISBN 0-393-05937-5; 978-0-393-05937-3
LC 2005-33320

The author's "poems are witty, musical, and intelligent; he is equally happy discussing the war on terror . . . or describing early crushes." New Yorker

Jacobsen, Josephine

In the crevice of time; new and collected poems. Johns Hopkins Univ. Press 1995 258p hardcover o.p. pa $25   **811**
1. Poetry -- By individual authors
ISBN 978-0-8018-6339-4; 0-8018-6339-2
LC 95-2798

"In this retrospective spanning nearly six decades of distinguished poetry, the best work comes at the beginning and the end. A contemporary of Robert Penn Warren and Elizabeth Bishop, Jacobsen continues to write stately poems informed by irony, fatalism, and an eloquent appreciation of strength in all its guises, physical and moral. An unabashed formalist, she carefully composes poems that are aggressively metrical . . . and whose surfaces are dense with metaphor, rhyme, assonance, alliteration, and omniscient authority." Libr J

Jarrell, Randall

★ The **complete** poems. Farrar, Straus & Giroux 1969 507p hardcover o.p. pa $22   **811**
1. Poetry -- By individual authors
ISBN 0-374-51305-8 pa

Collected here are the entire contents of three published volumes Selected poems (1955), The woman at the Washington Zoo (1960), and The Lost World (1965) plus poems published from 1934 to 1964 but never collected and some never before published.

Jeffers, Robinson

★ The **collected** poetry of Robinson Jeffers; edited by Tim Hunt. Stanford Univ. Press 1988 5v set $300   **811**
1. Poetry -- By individual authors
ISBN 0-8047-4418-1
LC 87-18083

"Jeffers' strengths and weaknesses as a poet are inextricable, but he wrote nothing trivial. His narratives owe much to the example of Edward Arlington Robinson, but they surpass the model and have not been equaled since. Their plots and characterizations are repetitive and even obsessive, but the narrative pulse of the ten and five stressed lines is both supple and controlled, while the interspersed authorial commentary varies the cadence and lends shrewd perspective. No reevaluation can ignore them. The shorter poems share the same rhythm of lyric thrust checked by terse observation and dicta." Benet's Reader's Ency of Am Lit

The **selected** poetry of Robinson Jeffers; edited by Tim Hunt. Stanford Univ. Press 2001 758p pa $34.95   **811**
1. Poetry -- By individual authors
ISBN 978-0-8047-4108-8; 0-8047-4108-5
LC 00-48490

"Hunt's edition strips the punctuation added by contemporary printers (which 'often obscures the rhythm and pacing of what Jeffers actually wrote, and at points even obscures meaning and nuance') and includes a carefully weighed choice of long and short works, as well as unpublished work. . . . This new selection will get readers closer than ever to the poems as Jeffers himself saw them." Publ Wkly

Johnson, James Weldon

Complete poems; edited with an introduction by Sondra Kathryn Wilson. Penguin Bks. 2000 xxxiii, 202p pa $14 **811**

1. African Americans -- Poetry 2. Poetry -- By individual authors

ISBN 0-14-118545-7

LC 00-39969

This volume contains Fifty years and other poems (1917), God's trombones (1927), Saint Peter relates an incident of the resurrection day (1935), and a number of previously unpublished poems. The editor's introduction considers Johnson's achievements and influence

Johnson, Peter

Rants and raves; selected and new prose poems. White Pine Press 2010 107p pa $16 **811**

1. Poetry -- By individual authors

ISBN 978-1-935210-06-1; 1-935210-06-8

"In the course of reading and rereading his poems one may be reminded of a range of writers, ancient and modern, including Theophrastus, Baudelaire, John Berryman, James Thurber (oh yes!). Peter Johnson represents a big constituency, but always concretely. 'American Male, Acting Up' begins: 'They say your whole life flashes before you when you die, but I'm sure I'll witness the lives of others.' These pages swarm with the lives of others, most particularly 'Peter Johnson,' who rants and raves like any free-mouthed cynic of the good old empire. . . . Savage indignation aside, Johnson is a great poet of friendship and family life. His book brims with wild wisdom, aching longing, tenderness, and most importantly, laughter." Providence J

Johnson, Ronald

The shrubberies; edited by Peter O'Leary. Flood Editions 2001 136p pa $14 **811**

1. Poetry -- By individual authors

ISBN 0-9710059-0-7

LC 2002-279220

This "book consists of a loosely linked sequence written in the last years of the poet's life. With their brevity and almost microscopic wordplay, the poems resemble epigrams. But where epigrams click into place, these poems leave implications floating. . . . The pleasure and insight of these poems come from more than prosodic specifics. Unlike so many 'experimental poets,' Johnson writes from necessity. As Peter O'Leary explains in his eloquent afterword, Johnson had a 'sense that these poems completed his work as a poet.' Several of the poems address mortality with starkness and force." Poetry (Modern Poetry Association)

Johnston, Devin

★ Traveler. Farrar, Straus and Giroux 2011 67p $23 **811**

1. Poetry -- By individual authors

ISBN 978-0-374-27933-2; 0-374-27933-0

LC 2011-08457

This collection brings Johnston's "careful, graceful, almost neoclassical pen to scenes from all over the world—Japan, Shanghai, 'the Mongol steppes,' the Midwest 'when a thunderstorm/ trundles down the Wabash,' and the Scottish holy isle of Iona. . . . Sometimes sublime, more often astringent, Johnston's poems of places and things seen—they

make up most of the volume—should please fans of that older world traveler, August Kleinzahler. Yet Johnston may be most original when his subjects turn up close to home: his cool temperament meets its fruitful complement when he writes of family and children, most of all his young daughter, who in the brief, fine triptych entitled 'Appetites' 'lies awake/ talking in confidential tones/ with one she calls/ my friend who eats me.' It would take a hard heart to resist such humor, such warmth, set amid such control as Johnston shows." Publ Wkly

Jordan, June

★ Directed by desire; the collected poems of June Jordan. edited by Jan Heller Levi and Sara Miles. Copper Canyon Press 2005 649p $40 **811**

1. Poetry -- By individual authors

ISBN 1-55659-228-0

LC 2005-11701

Jordan's poems "consistently display a loving devotion to black English and pride in her femininity, race, and individuality. Directed by Desire is an important addition to African American or feminist poetry collections." Booklist

Justice, Donald Rodney

★ Collected poems. Knopf 2004 288p $25 **811**

1. Poetry -- By individual authors

ISBN 1-4000-4239-9

LC 2003-65735

"Though its primary subject is the past, his work as a whole is more extraordinarily present—more thrillingly contemporary—than most of the styles that have advertised their commitment to 'making it new' over the past half-century." N Y Times Book Rev

Kasischke, Laura

Space, in chains. Copper Canyon Press 2011 113p pa $16 **811**

1. Poetry -- By individual authors

ISBN 978-1-55659-333-8; 1-55659-333-3

LC 2010-40037

"Known for her representations of mothers and teenagers in her poems and in her many novels, Kasischke now takes equal interest in illness and old age: rightly celebrated for her irregular, spiky, and intricately rhyming lines, Kasischke has now extended her interest (begun with her last book, Lilies Without) in the prose poem, using its fragments for recollection. . . . For all its length and all its lists, the volume ends up tightly, almost wrenchingly focused on the omnipresence of suffering, the fact of mortality and the persistence of grief. Some readers might call it melodramatic; many more ought to call it symphonic, perceptive, profound." Publ Wkly

Kelly, Robert

Lapis; poems. Godine 2005 221p pa $18.95 **811**

1. Poetry -- By individual authors

ISBN 1-57423-186-3

LC 2004-16724

This collection "offers dream narratives, elegies, prayers, anecdotes, parables, dialogues, and folktales from a land that may not exist. . . . Kelly has done something remarkable. He has given magic back its dignity, finding it in human warmth." Bookforum

Red actions; selected poems, 1960-1993. Black Sparrow Press 1995 398p hardcover o.p. pa $18.95 **811**

1. Poetry -- By individual authors
ISBN 978-0-87685-977-3; 0-87685-977-5

LC 95-35351

"In more than 35 collections of poetry, Kelly has utterly failed at one thing: to pigeonhole himself into predictability. This rich selection from more than a quarter-century of work contains imagistic bits that seem like fragments of poetic tapestry, long surreal narratives, series poems, and sonorous chants. Whatever the form, they are marked by Kelly's erudition, which covers Greek archaeology as readily as twentieth-century music, Sumerian gods as well as contemporary painting. Yet his work is never merely academic, inspired as it is by a passionate intellect reminiscent of Wallace Stevens. This survey may draw him more of the readers he well deserves." Booklist

Kenner, Hugh

★ The **Pound** era. University of Calif. Press 1971 606p il hardcover o.p. pa $26.95 **811**

1. Authors 2. Literary critics 3. Poetry -- By individual authors 4. Poets
ISBN 978-0-520-02427-4; 0-520-02427-3

"As a reader of Pound, Kenner is superb. He moves with ease and authority through the most tangled passages of allusion, ideogram and fragments of Greek and Latin." N Y Times Book Rev

Includes bibliographical references

Kenyon, Jane

★ **Collected** poems. Graywolf Press 2005 357p $26 **811**

1. Poetry -- By individual authors
ISBN 1-55597-428-7

"This collected edition reproduces verbatim the four books Kenyon saw through to press; the poems from two posthumous collections, Otherwise and A Hundred White Daffodils; Kenyon's translations of Akhmatova; and four previously uncollected poems. . . . Taken as a whole, Kenyon's poems remain a sustaining record of a life staked out in very difficult terrain." Publ Wkly

Kerouac, Jack

Book of blues. Penguin Bks. 1995 273p pa $13.95 **811**

1. Poetry -- By individual authors
ISBN 0-14-058700-4

LC 94-45902

A "set of eight previously unpublished 'blues' poems written between 1954 and 1961. These long poems, series of 'choruses' or sketches, resemble, in form and avidity, Kerouac's amazing verse creation Mexico City Blues (1959).

They are strongly tied to place and are, as the allusion to music implies, boldly improvisational." Booklist

★ **Book** of sketches, 1952-53; introduction by George Condo. Penguin Books 2006 413p pa $18 **811**

1. Poetry -- By individual authors
ISBN 978-0-14-200215-5; 0-14-200215-1

LC 2005-44535

"Somewhere between diary, verbal sketchbook and play-by-play account of whatever passed before his eyes, this collection of poems transcribed from notebooks Kerouac kept in his pocket between 1952 and 1954 turns out to rank with his most interesting work. . . . Kerouac hits all the notes for which he and his fellow beats are known. While not everything here is golden, the immediacy and unpretentiousness of this off-the-cuff writing makes it an intimate glimpse into the consciousness of a man who simply couldn't stop observing." Publ Wkly

Pomes all sizes; introduction by Allen Ginsberg. City Lights Bks. 1992 175p pa $13.95 **811**

1. Poetry -- By individual authors
ISBN 0-87286-269-0

LC 92-1204

"This book, which Kerouac prepared for publication before his death in 1969, collects poems written between 1954 and 1965. Most are playful—comments about friends, variations on the sounds of words. Yet a few extremely sensitive longer pieces appear, including 'Caritas,' in which the poet runs after a barefoot beggar boy to give him money for shoes and then begins to doubt the boy's veracity. Other intriguing poems reflect the poet's religious concerns of the moment, running the gamut of Eastern and Western religions." Libr J

Scattered poems. City Lights Bks. 1971 76p pa $7.95 **811**

1. Poetry -- By individual authors
ISBN 0-87286-064-7

This collection "contains poems that either have previously appeared in periodicals or have not appeared in print at all. The poems are delightfully representative of Kerouac: that free and easy style of writing from the music of the imagination, without a score to follow. Those familiar with the San Francisco school of poetry will readily see Kerouac's affinity in style and content with such writers as Rexroth, Everson, Snyder, Ferlinghetti, Ginsberg, et al. . . . Kerouac sings in the American language to an American tune." Libr J

Kinnell, Galway

Strong is your hold. Houghton Mifflin 2006 69p $25; pa $14.95 **811**

1. Poetry -- By individual authors
ISBN 978-0-618-22497-5; 0-618-22497-1; 978-0-547-05366-0 pa; 0-547-05366-5 pa

LC 2006-11292

"To many readers, the most appealing of these poems will be the half dozen in which the aging poet writes about his wife: cuddling with her in sleep, making love with startling ferocity, waking to find they are holding hands, preparing to say goodbye if one dies before the other. Getting old, as we've heard, is not for sissies. The poet who once chased bears may have slowed a step, but here he's still making like Johnny Cash as he walks the line between sex and death, the odd and the normal, domesticity and wildness, this world and the next. . . . 'Strong Is Your Hold' comes with a CD of Kinnell reading his work in a steady, pleasant voice." N Y Times Book Rev

A **new** selected poems. Houghton Mifflin 2000 173p hardcover o.p. pa $14 **811**
1. Poetry -- By individual authors
ISBN 978-0-618-15445-6; 0-618-15445-0
LC 99-48904
"New England resides in these pages. Kinnell is a native of America's first literary region. Cold snow and clear nights work their way into his poems. The sounds of the woods are everywhere. But these sounds do not echo Emerson. Like any good transcendentalist, Kinnell sees the spiritual in material things." Christ Sci Monit

Kirby, David
Talking about movies with Jesus; poems. Louisiana State University Press 2011 70p $50; pa $17.95 **811**
1. Poetry -- By individual authors
ISBN 978-0-8071-3771-0; 0-8071-3771-5; 978-0-8071-3772-7 pa; 0-8071-3772-3 pa
LC 2010-24229
"David Kirby's poems will put you and your imagination on a jet plane and fly you both around the world. They'll take you to Italy and France or into conversations with Jesus and Elvis. They'll even force all of you serious critics to crack a smile." Flashpoint

Kizer, Carolyn
Cool, calm & collected; poems 1960-2000. Copper Canyon Press 2000 509p $30; pa $20 **811**
1. Poetry -- By individual authors
ISBN 1-55659-146-2; 1-55659-181-0 pa
LC 00-10243
Kizer "covers civil rights, women's rights and almost everything in between, but even when she's writing about more intimate matters, her underlying concern is freedom. . . . Despite her constant railing against the machine, however, Kizer's poetry remains fundamentally optimistic, perhaps because she seems to love existence almost in spite of herself." N Y Times Book Rev

Kleinzahler, August
Sleeping it off in Rapid City; poems, new and selected. Farrar, Straus and Giroux 2008 234p $26 **811**
1. Poetry -- By individual authors
ISBN 978-0-374-26583-0; 0-374-26583-6
LC 2007-41926
This is a collection of poetry by the author of Earthquake Weather (1989), Red Sauce, Whiskey, and Snow (1996), and Live from the Hong Kong Nile Club (2000).
The author "writes most often in a strongly accented free verse that is among the most articulate and alive sounds American poetry is currently making. He plays effortlessly with forms, voices, registers. And his range of cultural refer-

ence—from Catullus to Custer, from Lorca to Eric Dolphy—is wide and artfully deployed. Rarely does high, learned poetic art sound this casual." N Y Times (Late N Y Ed)

Klink, Joanna
Raptus. Penguin Books 2010 60p pa $18 **811**
1. Poetry -- By individual authors
ISBN 978-0-14-311772-8; 0-14-311772-6
LC 2010-08246
"What happens when a relationship fails? Klink gets into the nooks and crannies of that question in her third collection. She sinks into every aspect of the life past and present. . . . She has a rhythmic dedication, a sense that every last emotional corner will be examined in its own time and a keen focus aimed as much at herself as at others. As it cycles through need and loss, this book illuminates just how inextricable experiences can be from the people with whom they are shared." Publ Wkly
Includes bibliographical references

Knott, Bill
The **unsubscriber**. Farrar, Straus and Giroux 2004 122p $20; pa $13 **811**
1. Poetry -- By individual authors
ISBN 978-0-374-26415-4; 0-374-26415-5; 978-0-374-53014-3 pa; 0-374-53014-9 pa
LC 2004-41160
"Knott's talent for compression—his awareness of the physicality of language—has remained undiminished since his youth, surfacing in one poem after another. . . . Like a gifted composer also capable of brilliantly playing every instrument in the orchestra, Knott possesses talent beyond the average allotment. In all fairness, you are not likely to find a more imaginative and provocative book of poetry published in the last year than The Unsubscriber, but neither will you find one that can be more at odds with itself." Am Book Rev

Knox, Jennifer L.
The **mystery** of the hidden driveway. Bloof Books 2010 83p pa $15 **811**
1. Poetry -- By individual authors
ISBN 978-0-9826587-1-0
"If Jennifer L. Knox is a lot of 'fun,' she is also one of the bluntest, most cutting poets in the country. And one of the most consistent — The Mystery of the Hidden Driveway is her best book yet, full of ridiculous characters, speedy narratives of scotch-taped sex and drugs, of emotional instabilities that are likeable and addictive. This is a book of odd and unexpected pleasures, a reminder that if nothing is sacred, everything is." Coldfront

Koch, Kenneth
On the edge; collected long poems. Alfred A. Knopf 2007 411p $35 **811**
1. Poetry -- By individual authors
ISBN 978-0-307-26284-4; 0-307-26284-7
LC 2007-24041
"A principal force behind the New York School of poets that flourished at mid-century, Kenneth Koch never quite won the pride of place occupied by the likes of Frank O'Hara and John Ashbery. This volume compiles Koch's

long poems, making an eloquent argument for his unique stature." New York

★ The **collected** poems of Kenneth Koch. Knopf 2005 761p $40   **811**
1. Poetry -- By individual authors
ISBN 1-4000-4499-5
LC 2004-63827

"The products of a lifetime of continual inventing are beautifully on display in this awe-inspiring banquet of a book." Publ Wkly

Komunyakaa, Yusef
Talking dirty to the gods; poems. Farrar, Straus & Giroux 2000 134p hardcover o.p. pa $13   **811**
1. Poetry -- By individual authors
ISBN 0-374-52793-8 pa
LC 00-21277

"Komunyakaa's mournful surrealism seems to have found a perfect mathematical embodiment in this . . . collection, which comprises a hundred and thirty-two poems of four four-line stanzas. These are poems about the uncontrollable human and natural mysteries, and they are made sharper and more mysterious by the eternal recurrence of the stanzaic structure." New Yorker

Thieves of paradise. University Press of New England 1998 128p $26; pa $14.95   **811**
1. Poetry -- By individual authors
ISBN 0-8195-6330-7; 0-8195-6422-2 pa
LC 97-40294

"The central subjects of Komunyakaa's poetry—his experiences in the Vietnam War and as an African-American male—have always been made compelling in his hands, and equally compelling has been the moodily energetic, jazz-inspired improvisatory technique that he employs with increasing mastery. But what is most gratifying about Komunyakaa's surrealist riffs, with their almost hallucinatory lushness, is their power to convince us that the individual imagination is more than equal to the most excruciating historical burden." New Yorker

Warhorses; poems. Farrar, Straus and Giroux 2008 86p $24 **811**
1. Poetry 2. Poetry -- By individual authors 3. War poetry
ISBN 978-0-3742-8643-9; 0-3742-8643-4
LC 2007-51760

"The poems that comprise [this] new collection provide an astonishingly panoramic view of the totality of war. . . . Strongly recommended." Libr J

The **chameleon** couch; poems. Farrar, Straus and Giroux 2011 115p il $24   **811**
1. Poetry -- By individual authors
ISBN 978-0-374-12038-2; 0-374-12038-2
LC 2010-33148

In this collection, the author "shares unusually personal reflections steeped in his intimacy with ancestors, gods, and monsters. These finely formed lyrics are timeless in their shadows and wounds, and startlingly fresh in mood, metaphor, image, and such pairings as gargoyles and power lines, sugar and salt." Booklist

Kooser, Ted
Delights & shadows; poems. Copper Canyon Press 2004 87p pa $15   **811**
1. Poetry -- By individual authors
ISBN 1-55659-201-9
LC 2003-18447

These "poems reflect a joy for life through powerful human images and intimate observations of everyday things." Booklist

Flying at night; poems, 1965-1985. University of Pittsburgh Press 2005 142p $24.95; pa $14.95 **811**
1. Poetry -- By individual authors
ISBN 0-8229-4258-5; 0-8229-5877-5 pa
LC 2004-28397

"There is a simplicity to these poems, a healthy, peaceful spirit. . . . Kooser is a skilled craftsman, with a sharp eye and fine ear." Libr J

Kumin, Maxine
Connecting the dots; poems. Norton 1996 86p $18.95; pa $11.95   **811**
1. Poetry -- By individual authors
ISBN 0-393-03962-5; 0-393-31695-5 pa
LC 95-44441

"Kumin's is a poetry of wide sympathy and tact in which the ecumenical flavor is dominant, starting with the author's description of herself as a 'Jewish agnostic' educated at a convent school. Here both the odd and the even are at home: New Hampshire farm country as well as cosmopolitan Boston, Heidegger and Berlioz interwoven among depictions of spring training, Bosnia, and a New Year's Eve party. This collection is full of generational severance and renewal." New Yorker

Jack and other new poems. W.W. Norton & Co 2005 112p hardcover o.p. pa $13.95   **811**
1. Poetry -- By individual authors
ISBN 978-0-393-32852-3; 0-393-32852-X
LC 2004-21762

This collection of poetry "focuses on three subjects the poet knows well: first, the fauna (wild and domestic) in and around her New Hampshire farm; second, the troubles and lessons of advancing age; third, large-scale political history, 'this century born in blood and bombs' as this Jewish-American poet has known it. . . . Most of her strongest work (the title poem included) concerns elderly or deceased animals, obvious analogues for Kumin's ill, deceased or grieving human beings." Publ Wkly

Selected poems, 1960-1990. Norton 1997 294p $27.50; pa $17.95   **811**
1. Poetry -- By individual authors
ISBN 0-393-04073-9; 0-393-31836-2 pa
LC 96-42433

"A pastoral poet who was strongly influenced by friend and mentor Anne Sexton, Kumin is quite simply one of the very best poets writing today. The present collection represents a lifetime . . . of Kumin's work and includes selections from all her published volumes." Libr J

The **long** marriage; poems. Norton 2001 118p $21; pa $12 **811**
1. Poetry -- By individual authors
ISBN 0-393-04351-7; 0-393-32437-0 pa
LC 2001-34553
"Although several of the poems treat Kumin's 50-plus year marriage, one feels that the book's title may refer to 'marriage' as a kind of covenant between the poet and her environment. . . . Divided into seven sections, this collection also includes poems about sociopolitical situations (capital punishment, extinct wildlife, revolutions), considerations of aging and rehabilitation, and tributes to Hopkins, Wordsworth, Rukeyser, and Rilke." Libr J

Kunitz, Stanley
★ The **collected** poems. Norton 2000 285p $27.95; pa $15.95 **811**
1. Poetry -- By individual authors
ISBN 0-393-05030-0; 0-393-32294-7 pa
LC 00-41130
"What makes this collection of a lifetime's work so valuable is the way it allows us to perceive the interconnectedness of all Kunitz has written. Each poem stands alone, but each also enriches the others." N Y Times Book Rev
Includes bibliographical references

Kyger, Joanne
About now; collected poems. National Poetry Foundation 2007 798p il $49.95; pa $34.95 **811**
1. Poetry -- By individual authors
ISBN 978-0-943373-72-0; 0-943373-72-7; 978-0-943373-71-3 pa; 0-943373-71-9 pa
LC 2006-48192
This volume "begins with poems of the 1950's, written when Kyger first came to San Francisco and joined the circle of poets around Robert Duncan and Jack Spicer, and ends with Night Palace, poems written in 2003 to 2004. . . . What is exciting about Kyger's poetry is the way she highlights moments which might seem mundane, but under her perceptive eye connect the individual with a greater reality, opening readers' awareness in the process. That immersion in the details of everyday life, quail crossing a yard, a phone call from a friend, or a retelling of last night's dream, is plumbed by Kyger to great depth and is epitomized by the collection's title." Jacket
Includes bibliographical references

Laughlin, James
The **collected** poems of James Laughlin; with an introduction by Hayden Carruth. Moyer Bell 1994 xxxi, 574p il $34.95; pa $19.95 **811**
1. Poetry -- By individual authors
ISBN 978-1-559-21067-6; 1-559-21067-2; 978-1-559-21128-4 pa; 1-559-21128-8 pa
LC 91-32232

"These poems are the work of a man of keen intellectual and moral sophistication, who has read, thought, and lived deeply." Libr J

The **secret** room; poems. New Directions 1997 184p $22.95; pa $14.95 **811**
1. Poetry -- By individual authors
ISBN 0-8112-1343-9; 0-8112-1344-7 pa
LC 96-26188
Laughlin "shares his thoughts with humor and tenderness as he wades in the waters of his golden years. The speaker in many of these poems admires young women and thinks, 'I could see I was entirely out of/my depth.' He realizes he is not as strong as he once was, but he can still 'make old, sick words sound new.'" Libr J

Lauterbach, Ann
Or to begin again. Penguin Books 2009 115p pa $18 **811**
1. Poetry -- By individual authors
ISBN 978-0-14-311520-5; 0-14-311520-0
LC 2008-38414
"Intelligent but no less deeply feeling, this collection confirms Lauterbach's position as one of the most highly principled and tirelessly innovative poets writing today." Publ Wkly

Lax, Robert
Love had a compass; journals and poetry. edited by James J. Uebbing. Grove Press 1996 253p $22 **811**
1. Poetry -- By individual authors
ISBN 978-0-8021-1587-4; 0-8021-1587-X
LC 96-1255
The author has produced "some of the sparest imagist poetry in English with no thought about publishing where the literary high and mighty would read him. Lax dispenses with metaphor and largely with ego . . . to present what he sees with elemental forcefulness, as if in strong Mediterranean sunlight." Booklist

A **thing** that is; new poems. edited by Paul Spaeth. Overlook Press 1997 77p $25; pa $14.95 **811**
1. Poetry -- By individual authors
ISBN 978-0-87951-699-4; 0-8795-1699-2; 978-0-87951-885-1 pa; 0-87951-885-5 pa
LC 96-29264
"Given to short lines arranged in long columns, Lax's poems link the natural and personal in simple, direct, deadpan narration. The simplicity can be misleading, not in its initially unnoticed depth or metaphor but in its very purity, its almost ascetic singleness of purpose. . . . Lax has been working at the margins for a long time and has found a crisp and comfortable way of ordering and exploring his contemplations. This collection is not for everyone, but it is a essential for that special audience for truly avante-garde work." Libr J

Lazarus, Emma

Emma Lazarus; selected poems. John Hollander, editor. Library of America 2005 151p $20 **811**

1. Poetry -- By individual authors

ISBN 978-1-931082-77-8; 1-931082-77-4

LC 2004-61551

"At the age of eighteen [Lazarus] had written an impressive poem titled 'In the Jewish Synagogue at Newport,' which all readers recognized as a response to Longfellow's dignified and respectful poem about the Jewish cemetery there. . . . Lazarus became perhaps the most accomplished American writer of sonnets between the generations of Longfellow and Robert Frost. . . . [Her] remarkable 'Little Poems in Prose,' the title borrowed from Baudelaire, ranged with visionary power across centuries of Jewish experience." N Y Rev Books

Lee, Li-Young

Behind my eyes. W.W. Norton 2008 106p $24.95 **811**

1. Poetry -- By individual authors

ISBN 978-0-393-06542-8; 0-393-06542-1

"In this fourth collection by [the author], timely immigration issues drive such poems as 'Self-Help for Fellow Refugees,' but Lee swiftly folds them into broader inquiries about inheritance, memory and loss. . . . Lee's ringing clarity and his compelling life story have brought him uncommonly loyal readers: this volume should swell their ranks. A CD of Lee reading many of the poems is included." Publ Wkly

Leiter, Sharon

Critical companion to Emily Dickinson; a literary reference to her life and work. Facts on File 2006 448p il $75 **811**

1. Authors 2. Poets

ISBN 0-8160-5448-7; 978-0-8160-5448-0

LC 2005-28123

This book "opens with a foreword by poet and Dickinson scholar Gregory Orr and includes an introduction; an approximately 20-page biography of Dickinson; explications of 150 of her best-known poems (e.g., 'Because I Could Not Stop for Death'); an A-to-Z dictionary of relevant persons, places, and ideas illustrated with black-and-white photos; a chronology; bibliographies; and a comprehensive index." Libr J

Includes bibliographical references

Lerner, Ben

Angle of yaw. Copper Canyon Press 2006 127p pa $15 **811**

1. Poetry -- By individual authors

ISBN 1-55659-246-9

LC 2006-14260

"Employing the language of aphorism, advertising, parable, personal essay, political tirade, journalism and journal, the collage-like poems of Lerner's . . . collection express the ennui of American life in an era when even war feels like a television event." Publ Wkly

Levertov, Denise

Selected poems; with a preface by Robert Creeley; edited and with an afterword by Paul Lacey. New Directions 2002 220p hardcover o.p. pa $14.95 **811**

1. Poetry -- By individual authors

ISBN 978-0-8112-1554-1; 0-8112-1520-2

LC 2002-11891

This volume "endeavors to do what all 'selecteds' do: give readers a chance to see for themselves the development of a poetic sensibility. Editor Paul A. Lacey has brought together poems from nearly every collection of Levertov's oeuvre, producing a catalogue of the wildly diverse subjects that engaged her throughout her long career. Here are poems about love and war, about religion and art, about sorrow and joy, about political resistance and familial intimacy and, perhaps most significantly for Levertov's legacy, numerous poems about the practice of poetry itself." Harvard Rev

Levine, Philip

Breath; poems. Knopf 2004 82p $23 **811**

1. Poetry -- By individual authors

ISBN 1-400-04291-7

LC 2004-40839

The author writes "free verse about American manliness, physical labor, simple pleasures and profound grief, often set in working-class Detroit (where Levine grew up) or in central California (where he now resides), sometimes tinged with reference to his Jewish heritage or to the Spanish poets of rapt simplicity (Machado, Lorca) who remain his most visible influence. Levine's 18th book will neither disappoint his devotees nor silence the doubters." Publ Wkly

New selected poems. Knopf 1991 292p hardcover o.p. pa $20 **811**

1. Poetry -- By individual authors

ISBN 978-0-679-74056-8; 0-679-74056-2

LC 90-53422

This selection contains poems Levine chose for his earlier Selected poems (1984), plus 15 new works.

"This is a monumental work that somehow remains wonderfully accessible, largely because Levine has chosen pieces carefully, favoring shorter works and poems that address his staple themes of family (like 'Uncle' and 'My Son and I') and childhood ('Coming Home'). Many of the poems are powerfully imagistic." Libr J

News of the world; poems. Alfred A Knopf 2009 65p $25 **811**

1. Poetry -- By individual authors

ISBN 978-0-307-27223-2

LC 2009-16517

A volume of prose poems and formal verses includes pieces on breakfasting late-shift Detroit auto workers, a woman who sings with the Spanish dawn, and an Andorran communist black-market supplier.

The author's "flirtations with death in both prose poems and formal verse have a weightiness that remains long after you close the book. . . . These poems exude a certain melancholia, but Levine's ability to examine expertly the beauty in this sadness keeps them from veering toward the unnecessarily depressing. He can paint even the strange with simple, natural language in a way that's subtly moving, and the nostalgic glow he applies to his memories makes this work the perfect addition to the oeuvre that has come to define his life." Libr J

What work is; poems. Knopf 1991 77p hardcover o.p. pa $15 **811**
 1. Poetry -- By individual authors
 ISBN 978-0-679-74058-2; 0-679-74058-9
LC 90-53421
"This collection amounts to a hymn of praise for all the workers of America. These proletarian heroes, with names like Lonnie, Loo, Sweet Pea, and Packy, work the furnaces, forges, slag heaps, assembly lines, and loading docks at places with unglamorous names like Brass Craft or Feinberg and Breslin's First-Rate Plumbing and Plating. . . . But Levine's characters are also significant for their inner lives, not merely their jobs." Libr J

The **mercy**; poems. Knopf 1999 81p hardcover o.p. pa $16 **811**
 1. Poetry -- By individual authors
 ISBN 978-0-375-70135-1; 0-375-70135-4
LC 98-43353
"Levine's poetry has been steadily moving to the front rank of American poetry for three decades. . . . If Walt Whitman's vision contained multitudes, and if Emerson's vision of nature transcended what it saw with its own eyes, Levine's poetic vision, nearly religious, transcends class, transcends natural boundaries, and transcends time." Atl Mon

The **simple** truth; poems. Knopf 1994 69p hardcover o.p. pa $16 **811**
 1. Poetry -- By individual authors
 ISBN 978-0-679-76584-4; 0-679-76584-0
LC 94-14508
This "collection of poetry is largely about the past: friends lost, fates assigned, potatoes eaten, decisions made. . . . Levine's mingling of realism and romanticism, involving many near-meetings between them, produces fascinating, emotionally persuasive shifts and tonal modulations that closely approach a lived truth." Publ Wkly

Lindsay, Sarah
 Twigs & knucklebones. Copper Canyon Press 2008 117p $15 **811**
 1. Poetry -- By individual authors
 ISBN 9781556591648 pa
LC 2008-19578
"Sarah Lindsay uses oddities and 'flukes' as a point of entry to broader questions regarding fate, bygone civilizations, and human nature. Written in finely crafted narrative verse, her poems take place in a diverse set of locales, both ancient and contemporary, and often explore the intersection of the unfamiliar with the everyday. . . . [This] is an enigmatic, evocative, and compelling book." Pedestal

Liu, Xiaobo
 ★ **June** fourth elegies; [Nian nian liu si / Liu Xiaobo]; translated from the Chinese by Jeffrey Yang;

foreword by Dalai Lama. Liu Xiaobo. Jonathan Cape 2012 xxv, 228 p.p **811**
 ISBN 1555976107; 9780224096812
LC 2012427497
This book is the first publication of the poetry of 2010 Nobel Peace Prize Winner Liu Xiaobo . . . [who is] the foremost symbol of the struggle for human rights in China. . . . June Fourth Elegies presents Lius poems written across twenty years in memory of fellow protestors at Tiananmen Square, as well as poems addressed to his wife, Liu Xia. In this bilingual volume, Lius poetry is . . . published . . . in both English translation and in the Chinese original. (Publishers Note) Xiaobo rebukes his nation, used to memorializing tombs as palaces, and his city of near perfect/ shamelessness. He also casts a harsh eye on himself . . . Even if I have the courage/ to be jailed again, Xiaobo writes, it isn't courage enough/ to excavate memories of the dead. (Publishers Weekly)

Logan, William
 Our savage art; poetry and the civil tongue. Columbia University Press 2009 346p bibl $29.50 **811**
 1. American poetry -- 20th century -- History and criticism 2. American poetry -- History and criticism 3. Criticism -- United States -- History
 ISBN 978-0-231-14732-3; 0-231-14732-5
LC 2008-36414
This collection is "the latest installment in William Logan's prolonged and rumbustious assault on the state of American poetry. . . . The most obvious advantage of Logan's Diogenes-like approach to much of the contemporary poetry he writes about is that it transforms the normally rather stultifying genre of the poetry review into something more akin to a blood sport. Logan's hounding and slashing, parodying and chastising, make for what editors call good copy." N Y Times Book Rev
 Includes bibliographical references (p. [341]-344) and index

Longfellow, Henry Wadsworth
 ★ **Poems** and other writings. Library of Am. 2000 854p $35 **811**
 1. Poetry -- By individual authors 2. Short stories -- By individual authors
 ISBN 1-88301-185-X
LC 00-26678
This volume includes "Hiawatha, Evangeline, The Courtship of Miles Standish and 'The Midnight Ride of Paul Revere.' Here, too, are some surprisingly powerful lyric and meditative poems—well made, deeply felt, and not much like the schoolhouse favorites." Publ Wkly
 Includes bibliographical references

Lorde, Audre
 The **collected** poems of Audre Lorde. Norton 1997 489p $35; pa $17.95 **811**
 1. Poetry -- By individual authors
 ISBN 0-393-04090-9; 0-393-31972-5 pa
LC 97-10878
"Since her death in 1992, Lorde's reputation has continued to grow. In life a tough, eloquent crusader who demanded that we honor the varieties of human experience,

she retained her hold on readers despite the unavailability of much of her work. This edition, then, should be welcomed wherever there is interest in women's, minority, and lesbian literature. It includes Lorde's passionately private early work as well as her later, more obviously political work." Booklist

Lowell, Amy

Selected poems; Honor Moore, editor. Library of America 2004 xxxi, 156p $20 **811**

1. Poetry -- By individual authors

ISBN 978-1-93108-270-9; 1-93108-270-7

LC 2004-48505

This volume contains "the 'cadenced verse' of [Lowell's] Imagist . . . works, her experiments in 'polyphonic prose,' her narrative poetry, and her adaptations from the classical Chinese." Publisher's note

Lowell, Robert

★ Collected poems; edited by Frank Bidart and David Gewanter, with the editorial assistance of DeSales Harrison. Farrar, Straus & Giroux 2003 1186p il $45 **811**

1. Authors 2. Poetry -- By individual authors 3. Poets

ISBN 0-374-12617-8

This collection includes "Lowell's first book, Land of Unlikeness (1944); and poems from his 11 ensuing collections, including Life Studies (1959) and The Dolphin (1973). . . . Substantial notes, a chronology, glossary, and critical essays make this an essential title. Readers who think they know Lowell's work will discover new facets, and readers just venturing into Lowell's potently rendered and ceaselessly evocative poetic universe will find much to contemplate." Booklist

Includes bibliographical references

Lucas, Dave

Weather; poems. University of Georgia Press 2011 68p pa $16.95 **811**

1. Poetry -- By individual authors

ISBN 978-0-8203-3882-8; 0-8203-3882-6

LC 2010-44222

"The first thing one notices in 'Weather,' Dave Lucas' first poetry collection, is the almost shocking formality of the language not in vocabulary so much as in a theatrical phrasing no longer so common in poetry. Lucas frequently writes things like 'I am also seething / in my depths,' which might not be so interesting were it not for the fact that the book's main subject is the contemporary Midwest, most often Cleveland and its surrounding environs, which for Lucas, is a landscape as mythic as Troy. . . . If Lucas' almost oracular tone occasionally spills over into melodrama, he makes up for it by the absolute beauty of so many of his lines and descriptions. . . . This is a lovely, promising and powerful first book, even more so for readers who know its landscape." Cleveland Plain Dealer

Includes bibliographical references.

MacGowan, Christopher J.

Twentieth-century American poetry; [by] Christopher MacGowan. Blackwell Pub 2004 331p $66.95; pa $27.95 **811**

1. American poetry -- 20th century -- History and

criticism 2. American poetry -- History and criticism 3. Poetry -- By individual authors

ISBN 0-631-22025-9; 0-631-22026-7 pa

LC 2003-12196

This guide explores the historical and cultural contexts within which twentieth-century American poetry was created and includes a biographical dictionary of such key writers as Robert Frost, Ezra Pound, T. S. Eliot, Langston Hughes, James Dickey, Adrienne Rich, and Rita Dove

MacLeish, Archibald

Collected poems, 1917-1982; with a prefatory note to the newly collected poems by Richard B. McAdoo. Houghton Mifflin 1985 524p hardcover o.p. pa $19 **811**

1. Poetry -- By individual authors

ISBN 0-395-39569-0 pa

LC 85-14392

Collects all the known poetry of the author/public servant. As an expatriate in Paris his early work was heavily influenced by Pound and Eliot. After returning to the States his verse concerned itself more with America's political, social, and cultural heritage.

Mackey, Nathaniel

Splay anthem. New Directions Book 2006 126p pa $15.95 **811**

1. Poetry -- By individual authors

ISBN 0-8112-1652-7

LC 2005-35051

"Often turning adversity to their advantage, the poems sing not of resurrection but repair, and Splay Anthem is the most delicate and delirious installment of Mackey's epic song of salvage. Its poems speak with a torn voice, a rasp punctuated by gasps of anguish and rumbling with the desire for rejuvenation." Nation

Manning, Maurice

The common man. Houghton Mifflin Harcourt 2010 96p $22 **811**

1. Poetry -- By individual authors

ISBN 978-0-547-24961-2; 0-547-24961-6

LC 2009-29080

"The book balances our cynical, back-foot expectations as readers of contemporary poetry with its own unpretentious ambition incredibly well—the natural world becomes strange in Manning's hands, but not unrecognizably so." Sycamore Rev

Mariani, Paul L.

★ Lost puritan: a life of Robert Lowell. Norton 1994 527p il hardcover o.p. pa $15 **811**

1. Authors 2. Biography, Individual 3. Poets

ISBN 0-393-31374-3 pa

LC 93-48018

"Mariani, for all his moment-by-moment acuteness and lucidity, offers no radically new insights into Lowell's life or art, nor does he provide those powerfully developed thematic and narrative lines that distinguish the greatest literary biographies. Still, this remains an impressive piece of writing and documentation." Choice

The **broken** tower: a life of Hart Crane; [by] Paul Mariani. Norton 1999 492p il hardcover o.p. pa $15.95 **811**
    1. Authors 2. Poets 3. Poets, American -- 20th century -- Biography 4. Short story writers
    ISBN 0-393-32041-3 pa

                    LC 98-37726
"Using unpublished letters, manuscripts, and photographs [Mariani] pieces together the life and passions of this brilliant yet tormented man whose creative genius left us 'The Bridge' and whose influence still reverberates among poets today." Libr J
Includes bibliographical references

Matthews, William
    After all; last poems. Houghton Mifflin 1998 55p hardcover o.p. pa $13 **811**
    1. Poetry -- By individual authors
    ISBN 0-618-05685-8 pa

                    LC 98-22909
"Since Matthews was one of the few contemporary poets who really knew how to make the vernacular sing, it's sad to think that these are his last poems. Fittingly, some of them are autumnal, but they range widely and brightly from Prague in 1419 to a Caribbean island in 1967 to Martha Mitchell, Finn sheep, and a poetry reading at West Point. A lovely finale." Libr J

    Selected poems and translations, 1969-1991. Houghton Mifflin 1992 200p hardcover o.p. pa $22.95 **811**
    1. Poetry -- By individual authors
    ISBN 978-0-395-66993-8; 0-395-66993-6

                    LC 91-45716
"Matthews has been widely praised for the solid grounding of his poems, and rightly so. His clear-cut metaphors illuminate the everyday world with the magic of semantic revelation and the grace of othermindedness." Booklist

Mayer, Bernadette
    Scarlet tanager. New Directions 2005 117p pa $14.95 **811**
    1. Poetry -- By individual authors
    ISBN 0-8112-1582-2

                    LC 2005-5539
This collection demonstrates Mayer's "ease in many poetic forms, her attraction to New York City and to the Berkshires (where she now lives), her recovery from a recent stroke and her continued enthusiastic enmeshment with writing itself." Publ Wkly

McClure, Michael
    ★ **Of** indigo and saffron; new and selected poems. edited and with an introduction by Leslie Scalapino. University of California Press 2011 319p **811**
    1. Poetry -- By individual authors
    ISBN 0-520-26287-5; 978-0-520-26287-4

                    LC 2010-32585

"Scalapino includes those parts of McClure's oeuvre that focus on the questioning of identity, the uncertain position of the self, and the irrelevance of the traditional lyric 'I,' the bete noire of language poets. But Scalapino's selections do give a broad taste of McClure's perennial concerns with the body, alternative forms of consciousness and environmentalism. . . . McClure invented a new form for himself: the poem centered in the middle of the page, with occasional lines in capital letters (he has insisted that these are not meant to be shouted), with the phrase or line equivalent to Olson's notion of whatever encompasses a breath. McClure has been able to accommodate every thematic concern, every mood and temperament, within this form's versatile parameters." San Francisco Chron

McGrath, Thomas
    Letter to an imaginary friend. Copper Canyon Press 1997 413p pa $20 **811**
    1. Poetry -- By individual authors
    ISBN 978-1-55659-078-8; 1-55659-078-4

                    LC 97-33929
"Although McGrath, who died in 1990 at 74, published the poem's four parts separately, it appears here complete for the first time. . . . A surprisingly accessible long poem in the Pound tradition of personal epics, Letter arrives 'helved, greaved, and garlanded' and compels our intimate attention." Publ Wkly

McHugh, Heather
    ★ **Upgraded** to serious. Copper Canyon Press 2009 85p $22 **811**
    1. Poetry -- By individual authors
    ISBN 978-1-55659-306-2

                    LC 2009-13347
This collection "offers exactly ravishing poetry that digs deeply into big themes: free will, consciousness, ideas of language. . . . Thinking poems are often poems with lots of moving parts, and when reading (and rereading) this book one notes the elegance with which everything – perception, reflection, feeling – is held in play. And 'play' is the operative word: McHugh's method always involves some winning blend of precision and momentum." Globe and Mail

McLane, Maureen N.
    My poets; Maureen N. McLane. Farrar, Straus and Giroux 2012 273 p. (hc : alk. paper) $25.00 **811**
    1. Bishop, Elizabeth, 1911-1979 2. Chaucer, Geoffrey, d. 1400 3. Poetry -- History and criticism 4. Poetry -- Influence 5. Stein, Gertrude, 1874-1946
    ISBN 0374217491; 9780374217495

                    LC 2011041208
In this book, poet and critic Maureen N. McLane presents an esoteric tour of her personal pantheon, the poets that have shaped her life. "The text is a mixture of prose criticism, memoir, anecdote, and imitative verse written in tribute." The poets discussed include Geoffrey Chaucer, Elizabeth Bishop, and Gertrude Stein. (Publishers Weekly)

McMichael, James

Capacity. Farrar, Straus and Giroux 2006 74p $22 **811**

1. Poetry -- By individual authors

ISBN 978-0-374-11890-7; 0-374-11890-6

LC 2005-51628

"Better known for the infrastructural sweep of his work, McMichael is also a poet of the kind of centripetal force and barely contained emotional heat that we more often associate with the short lyric. What makes him unique in American poetry right now is the strength and subtlety with which he blends conceptual ambition with emotional power. It's very common these days to hear poets talking about their 'projects.' But in James McMichael we actually have a poet whose sustained investigation of a small set of obsessions has produced the most integral and surprising structures." Yale Rev

Melville, Herman

★ The **poems** of Herman Melville; edited by Douglas Robillard. rev ed; Kent State Univ. Press 2000 349p pa $29 **811**

1. Poetry -- By individual authors

ISBN 0-87338-660-4

LC 99-52872

This volume "presents the complete texts of 'Battle-Pieces,' 'John Marr and Other Sailors,' and 'Timoleon,' as well as additional manuscript poems. Also presented are excerpts from the long narrative poem Clarel to give the reader a taste of the style and content of this work. The editor's introduction, as well as his notes at the end of each section, are informative as well as appreciative of Melville's status as a poet." Libr J

Includes bibliographical references

Menashe, Samuel

★ **New** and selected poems; Christopher Ricks, editor. Library of America 2005 191p $20 **811**

1. Poetry -- By individual authors

ISBN 1-931082-85-5

LC 2005-44161

"Menashe is a curious and meticulous writer, whose brief, sparsely punctuated poems depend on difficult rhyme and assonance schemes to relay his observations. A wry but basically optimistic poet, his best writing shows that the stylistic restrictions one selects rapidly cease to be restrictions, even when one identifies them as such." N Y Times Book Rev

Meredith, William

Effort at speech; new and selected poems. TriQuarterly Bks. 1997 231p $46; pa $17.95 **811**

1. Poetry -- By individual authors

ISBN 0-8101-5070-0; 0-8101-5071-9 pa

LC 97-9679

Meredith's early poems "are as subtle as aspirin. So easily digestible in their precise meter and perfectly tuned end-rhyme, their power goes virtually unnoticed until the reader lifts his eyes from the page to find himself moved, affected. In work inspired by the poet's service at sea during WWII, devastation comes on the hushed waves of sonnets. . . . The poems in the book's latter half (1970-1987) find formalism surrendering some ground to free verse as Meredith attempts

to salve not the sharp pains of war but the blunted ache of aging." Publ Wkly

Merrill, James

The **changing** light at Sandover; with the stage adaptation Voices from Sandover. edited by J.D. McClatchy and Stephen Yenser. 2nd Knopf hardcover ed.; Knopf 2006 627p il $40 **811**

1. Poetry -- By individual authors

ISBN 978-0-307-26321-6; 0-307-26321-5

LC 2006-273431

This "is an arduous poem, steep and lofty, more than a little difficult to climb, explore, and comprehend, its intricate faceting of the serious and unserious, sacred and profane, vexing to many a reader; but it has, I believe, one controlling stratagem, Merrill's persistent use of doubling or 'entwinning.'. . . The trilogy (though it goes on far too long, gets periodically dizzy, has too much felix culpa and not enough mea culpa) is, surely, an astonishing performance." N Y Rev Books

★ The **collected** poems of James Merrill; edited by J.D. McClatchy and Stephen Yenser. Knopf 2001 xx, 885p $40; pa $27.50 **811**

1. Poetry -- By individual authors

ISBN 0-375-41139-9; 0-375-70941-X pa

LC 00-40542

"Excluded are some juvenilia and light verse, as well as Merrill's book-length poem The Changing Light at Sandover, in print as a separate volume. Merrill's sonnets, sapphics, longer sequences and sinuous sentences encompass lyric pathos, ebullient comedy, rapt romance and acrid satire. Their formal sophistication can belie their depth of feeling, which is exactly what some readers love best about Merrill's work." Publ Wkly

Merton, Thomas

In the dark before dawn; new selected poems of Thomas Merton. edited with an introduction and notes by Lynn R. Szabo; preface by Kathleen Norris. New Directions 2005 253p pa $16.95 **811**

1. Poetry -- By individual authors

ISBN 978-0-8112-1613-5; 0-8112-1613-6

LC 2004-30957

"Szabo has drawn widely from the furious poetic writing of Merton's final years. This new spectrum of poems helps us tap into the complexity and mystery of Thomas Merton. Readers of Merton's journals will be aware of his shifting attitude to all sorts of things—being an American, being a monk at Gethsemani, being a writer, in particular a poet. Szabo helps us here by assembling the poems in eight thematic sections, so as to display the multiple Mertons. There was the contemplative, drawn to the silent beauties of Gethsemani Abbey, especially at night. There was the stinging and at times declamatory social critic, the admiring and painstaking translator, the avant garde experimentalist and, toward the end, the lovelorn monk." America

Merwin, W. S.

★ **Migration**; new & selected poems. Copper Canyon

Press 2005 545p $40 **811**
1. Poetry -- By individual authors
ISBN 1-55659-218-3

LC 2004-17473

This volume contains poetry from sixteen of Merwin's collections.

"Complex, spiritual, and evocative, Merwin is a major poet, and this is a sublime measure of his achievements." Booklist

Present company. Copper Canyon Press 2005 137p $22 **811**
1. Poetry -- By individual authors
ISBN 1-55659-227-2

LC 2005-08867

"Nearing 80, the Pulitzer Prize winner seems especially mindful of age and mortality, and these poems–like a series of heartfelt thank-you notes–offer homage to the things of this world. In a manner that recalls the cool, spare diction of H.D., Merwin addresses the local and the nondescript . . . as well as the abstract and the universal. . . . The emotional timbre rarely rises above muted melancholy, and Merwin's thoughtful, measured pace never quickens, but the poems are suffused with a warmth and clarity achieved over six decades of disciplined dedication to his art." Libr J

The **shadow** of Sirius. Copper Canyon Press 2008 117p $22 **811**
1. Poetry -- By individual authors
ISBN 978-1-55659-284-3; 1-55659-284-1

LC 2008-14578

Merwin "continues to sing of a disappearing world. At one level these are the Zen-guided, misty disappearances of demarcations. . . . This non-dualist philosophy of Merwin's is perfectly expressed in his smooth, unpunctuated poems, calmly voiced and carefully illuminated with spare, vivid images. There is no overexcited narration (it's tonality rather than personality), no linguistic fireworks to awe the reader. Yet Merwin rarely nods. There is an alert simplicity in nearly every poem." Harvard Rev

Middlebrook, Diane Wood
Anne Sexton; a biography. Vintage Bks. 1992 xxiii, 498p il pa $14 **811**
1. Authors 2. Dramatists 3. Poets 4. Poets, American
ISBN 0-679-74182-8

LC 92-50093

"Ms. Middlebrook has written a wonderful book: just, balanced, insightful, complex in its sympathies and in its judgment of Sexton both as a person and as a writer." NY Times Book Rev

Includes bibliographical references

Millay, Edna St. Vincent
Collected poems; edited by Norma Millay. Harper & Row 1956 xxi, 738p hardcover o.p. pa $22.95 **811**
1. Poetry -- By individual authors
ISBN 0-06-090889-0 pa

The poems in this collection "are divided into two separate sections of lyrics and sonnets, arranged chronologically and printed in groups under the titles of the original

volumes, ranging from 'Renascence' of 1917 to 'Mine the harvest,' published in 1954, four years after the poet's death." Booklist

★ **Selected** poems; J.D. McClatchy, editor. Library of Am. 2003 xxxiii, 231p $20 **811**
1. Poetry -- By individual authors
ISBN 1-931082-35-9

LC 2002-32126

This collection draws from all Millay's "verse books to display her career-long adroitness in her favorite form, the sonnet, and her variety by including even excerpts from an opera libretto. . . . Read occasionally and mixed with her saucy lyrics about erotic love, . . . [her sonnets] reveal their strengths—not of imagery, but of surprising attitudes expressed within strictly observed poetic conventions." Booklist

Mlinko, Ange
Shoulder season; poems. Coffee House Press 2010 81p pa $16 **811**
1. Poetry -- By individual authors
ISBN 978-1-56689-243-8; 1-56689-243-0

LC 2009-51508

This is a book of poems by the author of Matinées (1999) and Starred Wire (2005).

"Pirouetting beyond fields plowed and sown by Frank O'Hara, John Ashbery, James Schuyler, and Alice Notley, Ange Mlinko is creating her own space in the world of poetry and more. To encapsulate her fecund body of work, the word glee keeps coming to mind. And that may be the most American aspect to her work, its joie de vivre. This may be the Shoulder Season, yet no one has to go slumping through it without some ecstasy." Galatea Resurrects

Moore, Marianne
★ The **poems** of Marianne Moore; edited by Grace Schulman. Viking 2003 449p hardcover o.p. pa $18 **811**
1. Poetry -- By individual authors
ISBN 0-14-303908-3 pa

LC 2003-50159

"The great modernist poet finally gets her due with this outstanding compliation." Libr J

Includes bibliographical references

Muldoon, Paul
★ **Moy** sand and gravel. Farrar, Straus & Giroux 2002 107p $22; pa $12 **811**
1. Poetry -- By individual authors
ISBN 0-374-21480-8; 0-374-52884-5 pa

LC 2002-20129

This collection "shimmers with play, the play of mind, the play of recondite information over ordinary experience, the play of observation and sensuous detail, of motion upon custom, of Irish and English languages and landscapes, of meter and rhyme. Sure enough, everything Muldoon thinks of makes him think of something else, and poem after poem takes the form of linked association." N Y Times Book Rev

Murphy, Russell E.

Critical companion to T.S. Eliot; a literary reference to his life and work. [by] Russell Elliott Murphy. Facts on File 2007 614p il $75   **811**

1. Authors 2. Dramatists 3. Editors 4. Essayists 5. Literary critics 6. Nobel laureates for literature 7. Poets
ISBN 978-0-8160-6183-9; 0-8160-6183-1

LC 2006-34076

"This is an excellent and exhaustive resource and a good buy for most libraries." Booklist
Includes bibliographical references

Nadelberg, Amanda

Bright brave phenomena; poems. Amanda Nadelberg. Coffee House Press 2012 118 p.   **811**

ISBN 1566893038; 9781566893039

LC 2011029251

This collection of poetry focus[es] on the ways life itself changes, depending on emotional shadings: I turned into a blanket and went everywhere. With him there was great purpose. . . . A longer segmented poem chronicles various unhappinesses: And when her boyfriend walks to/ her, she looks like death, the/ face of death, big drapes/ in a tall room in France. The boyfriend in this poem is just as mutable, taking the form of a blue door and a French vampire. Nadelberg's ebullient language captures the giddiness of love and youth. . . . But love can also deflate like two people and/ a broken thing/ as a road somewhere. Her perspective is always staunchly feminine, unfolding like a present, her hysteria as a garden, a house/ the colors are beautiful." (Publishers Weekly)

Nemerov, Howard

★ The **selected** poems of Howard Nemerov; edited by Daniel Anderson; foreword by Wyatt Prunty. Swallow Press, Ohio University Press 2003 xxi, 154p $24.95; pa $16.95   **811**

1. Poetry -- By individual authors
ISBN 0-8040-1059-5; 0-8040-1060-9 pa

LC 2003-42380

The selections in this volume span Nemerov's entire poetic output.

This volume "represents the broad spectrum of Nemerov's virtues as a poet—his intelligence, his wit, his compassion, and his irreverence. It stands as the retrospective collection of the best of what Nemerov left behind." Publisher's note

Niedecker, Lorine

Collected works; edited by Jenny Penberthy. University of Calif. Press 2002 xxiii, 471p $55; pa $25.95   **811**

1. Poetry -- By individual authors
ISBN 978-0-520-22433-9; 0-520-22433-7; 978-0-520-22434-6 pa; 0-520-22434-5 pa

LC 2001-5376

Niedecker "is often likened to Emily Dickinson. She, too, remained in the backwater where she was born. Large-scale interest in her work came only years after her death. Her characteristic poems are, like Dickinson's, short or in short stanzas, short-lined, and elliptical. But she wasn't reclusive; she connected with the Objectivists, New York poets 'led'

by Louis Zukofsky. . . . Whereas Dickinson's poetry is metaphysical, Niedecker's mature work is profoundly physical, sparked by wry, class-conscious humor and usually rooted in her Black Lake Island, Wisconsin, neighborhood." Booklist
Includes bibliographical references

Nims, John Frederick

★ The **powers** of heaven and earth; new and selected poems. Louisiana State Univ. Press 2002 247p $36.95; pa $19.95   **811**

1. Poetry -- By individual authors
ISBN 0-8071-2826-0; 0-8071-2827-9 pa

LC 2002-30055

This is a "collection of the work of one of the foremost formalists and classicists among twentieth-century American poets: epigrams, odes, sonnets, shaped verse, and other kinds of poems on life, nature, culture, literature, but first and foremost, on love." Booklist

Norris, Kathleen

Journey: new and selected poems, 1969-1999. University of Pa. 2001 131p hardcover o.p.   pa $16.95   **811**

1. Poetry -- By individual authors
ISBN 0-8229-5761-2 pa

A collection of Norris' "poetry spanning 30 years. Here are poems, arranged chronologically in four sections each beginning with a verse from the Song of Solomon, that tenderly describe an event or scene, examine it, and conclude with a flash of seemingly unrelated insight, leaving profound questions in the reader's heart. . . . Carrying her readers along on her deeply Christian journey, Norris avoids spiritual certainty and preachiness, remaining ever the seeker. Her poems are lyrical, accessible, and hauntingly touching to read and to reread." Libr J

North, Charles

★ **What** it is like; new and selected poems. Turtle Point Press/Hanging Loose Press 2011 302p pa $20   **811**

1. Poetry -- By individual authors
ISBN 978-1-933527-48-2

"North is a younger compatriot of O'Hara and Ashbery, and his nonchalance aspiring to greatness finds the same 'risks inside art' that the other New York School poets found in the city. Juggling a satiric self-consciousness with a 'strange mischief,' North pulls death-defying propositions and playful mockeries from thin air." Publ Wkly

Notley, Alice

★ **Grave** of light; new and selected poems, 1970-2005. Wesleyan University Press 2006 364p $29.95   **811**

1. Poetry -- By individual authors
ISBN 0-8195-6772-8

LC 2006-15712

"Experimental in every sense of the word, Alice Notley has produced an extensive body of work over 30 years in print. This new collection unites previously unpublished poems as well as those from both small-press chapbooks and more widely distributed volumes. Arranged in chronological order while maintaining poetic sequences, Notley's poems tell the story of her artistic development and bear witness to the multitude of styles and influences that Notley has explored. . . . Diversity is Notley's most consistent quality, and this makes her not only somewhat of an enigma aesthetically but also appealing to varying poetic tastes." Booklist

In the pines. Penguin Books 2007 131p pa $18   **811**
1. Poetry -- By individual authors
ISBN 978-0-14-311254-9; 0-14-311254-6

LC 2007-12076

"Notley takes the title of her 30-somethingth collection from a notorious American folk song: a man tries to get his lover to admit she's been unfaithful, asking her where she's slept, and her ambiguous answer—in the pines—only makes things worse. That menacing rhetorical moment informs the whole of this searing collection, which is part autobiography, part riposte to literary culture, and part lyrical reclamation of feminist territory. . . . This master poet continues to inspire and challenge." Publ Wkly

Nye, Naomi Shihab

You & yours: poems. BOA Editions 2005 87p hardcover o.p. pa $15.50   **811**
1. Poetry -- By individual authors
ISBN 1-929918-68-2; 1-929918-69-0 pa

LC 2005-11360

"Tender yet forceful, funny and commonsensical, reflective and empathic, Nye writes radiant poems of nature and piercing poems of war, always touching base with homey details and radiant portraits of family and neighbors." Booklist

O'Brien, Michael

Sleeping and waking. Flood Editions 2007 63p pa $12.95   **811**
1. Poetry -- By individual authors
ISBN 978-0-9787467-2-8 pa; 0-9787467-2-4

"O'Brien is primarily an observer rather than a debater, and the poems here are heavy on isolated images, dream logic, bits of overheard conversation (typically urban conversation) and memories, with larger themes emerging through juxtapositions and repetitions. . . . While O'Brien's technical skills should be crisp enough to please the iciest avant-gardist, he has one virtue more cerebral poets often lack: he isn't afraid to make a plain statement. In other hands, that virtue can become a self-satisfied vice, but here it lends a necessary sharpness to an otherwise fluid and dreamlike collection." N Y Times Book Rev

O'Hara, Frank

Frank O'Hara: selected poems; edited by Mark Ford. Alfred A. Knopf 2008 288p $30   **811**
1. Poetry -- By individual authors
ISBN 978-0-307-26815-0; 0-307-26815-2

LC 2007-42865

"At his strongest O'Hara profoundly affected the development of American poetry. . . . His acute eye and finely tuned ear combined with his breezy idiolect and thoughtful intelligence to create a style expressive of a generation that returned from a brutal war intent on throwing off old conventions and seeking new sensations. If O'Hara's work lacks the gravitas ultimately achieved by Koch and Ashbery,

his clear, youthful voice will nonetheless continue to evoke a heady, hopeful time in our cultural history—before optimism turned to ashes." New Leader

★ The **collected** poems of Frank O'Hara; edited by Donald Allen; with an introduction by John Ashbery. University of Calif. Press 1995 xxix, 586p pa $24.95   **811**
1. Poetry -- By individual authors
ISBN 0-520-20166-3

LC 94-24660

The subjects of this collection "are lunch-time strolls past construction workers and bargains in wrist watches, the lives of artists (whether distant heroes or close friends), the distractions of city life, . . . homosexuality, . . . headlines glimpsed on newstands. . . . Some {are} . . . about friendships, occasional pieces written for a marriage or a departure." Newsweek

Includes bibliographical references

O'Rourke, Meghan

Once; poems. W. W. Norton & Company 2011 89p $24.95 **811**
1. Poetry -- By individual authors
ISBN 978-0-393-08062-9

LC 2011029033

"Capturing a world where the whimsical observations of a child and the agonizing realities of adulthood collide, O'Rourke's poems offer a resonant exploration of relationships with both family and country. Crossing inevitably through the seasons, the collection transitions from summer pools and Popsicles to icy pines and blurred Christmas lights, all the while reverting back to a mother rebelling against a ravenous disease. . . . Bonded by sorrow but never hopeless, the narrator of this powerful collection dives into a gulf of mourning and emerges renewed." Booklist

Olds, Sharon

Blood, tin, straw. Knopf 1999 125p hardcover o.p. pa $16   **811**
1. Poetry -- By individual authors
ISBN 978-0-375-70735-3; 0-375-70735-2

LC 99-15602

"Olds has always been a frank and transcendent poet of the body, and now . . . she expands her profoundly tactile sensibility to embrace the entire cosmos in poems of powerful female eroticism and emotional acuity that celebrate love both earthly and spiritual." Booklist

The **unswept** room. Knopf 2002 96p $25; pa $15   **811**
1. Poetry -- By individual authors
ISBN 0-375-41489-4; 0-375-70998-3 pa

LC 2002-18444

"Organized like her previous works, this work begins with poems about her early life and then moves on to grade school, her marriage, and up to the present day. Throughout, Olds re-creates her life, building a scrapbook through words. Although many of her subjects (family, love, sex) stay the same, her tone has shifted from an angry questioning of fate to a passionate acceptance of her own mortality and the experiences she has had." Libr J

The **wellspring**. Knopf 1996 88p hardcover o.p. pa $16 **811**
1. Poetry -- By individual authors
ISBN 978-0-679-76560-8; 0-679-76560-3
LC 95-15835
This collection "takes the form of an intimate family portrait. Olds begins by imagining her parents making love for the first time. This explicitness informs the entire cycle, from poems about her own birth to snapshots of her youth and early sexual experiences, poems remarkable for their integrity, eroticism, tough humor, and unceasing wonder. . . . Olds continues with a series of strikingly original and profoundly moving poems about her children." Booklist

Oliver, Charles M.

Critical companion to Walt Whitman; a literary reference to his life and work. Facts on File 2005 408p il $65 **811**
1. Authors 2. Essayists 3. Poets
ISBN 0-8160-5768-0
LC 2005-4172
The author "begins this work with a biographical essay that includes several illustrations. A large portion of this book addresses Whitman's works, with entries for the individual poems and for the complete volumes. Each entry describes when and where the book was published and includes a brief account of the poem and its context. The third section of the volume covers people, places, publications, and topics related to Whitman's life and work." Choice
Includes bibliographical references

Oliver, Mary

★ **New** and selected poems. Beacon Press 2005 2v v1 $28.50; v1 pa $16; v2 $24.95; v2 pa $16 **811**
1. Poetry -- By individual authors
ISBN 0-8070-6878-0 v1; 0-8070-6877-2 v1 pa; 0-8070-6886-1 v2; 0-8070-6887-X v2 pa
Volume one contains poems written from 1965 to 1992. Volume two contains poems written from 1994 to 2005.

The **Truro** bear and other adventures; poems and essays. Beacon Press 2008 80p $23; pa $14 **811**
1. Animals -- Poetry 2. Poetry -- By individual authors
ISBN 978-0-8070-6884-7; 0-8070-6884-5; 978-0-8070-6885-4 pa; 0-8070-6885-3 pa
LC 2008-15400
"Oliver's poems hearken back to her 19th-century mentors—particularly Emerson, Thoreau and Whitman—in their attentiveness to the natural world and what it teaches us about ourselves; and yet they are compellingly current, given the fragile condition of the earth and its creatures." America

West wind. Houghton Mifflin 1997 63p hardcover o.p. pa $14 **811**
1. Poetry -- By individual authors
ISBN 0-395-85085-1 pa
LC 97-2986

"Although her papers may scatter as the west wind sweeps through her room, Oliver's house is in order. From the chaos of the world, her poems distill what it means to be human and what is worthwhile about life. Echoing the Romantics and Whitman, she affirms the value of aloneness with nature, of watching and listening—not just to get it down as art but simply to live it." Libr J

Winter hours; prose, prose poems, and poems. Houghton Mifflin 1999 109p $22; pa $14 **811**
1. Poetry -- By individual authors
ISBN 0-395-85084-3; 0-395-85087-8 pa
LC 99-19141
"Oliver has set aside the frames of form and the mask of her poetic persona to share memories and meditations in essays made of both poetry and prose. Writing with the knowingness born of many years of devotion to observation and expression, Oliver declares her unceasing love of nature, the source of her art, and her willingness to embrace what most people resent: the shift in tone and meter age brings." Booklist

The **leaf** and the cloud; a poem. Da Capo Press 2000 55p hardcover o.p. pa $15 **811**
1. Poetry -- By individual authors
ISBN 0-306-81073-5 pa
LC 00-57008
A "book-length poem by a poet devoted to close scrutiny of the natural world and exact, sensuous, and ecstatic description. Lyrical and philosophical in the American transcendental tradition, Oliver addresses her readers directly to ravishing effect." Booklist

Olson, Charles

The **Maximus** poems; edited by George F. Butterick. University of Calif. Press 1985 652p hardcover o.p. pa $42 **811**
1. Poetry -- By individual authors
ISBN 978-520-05595-7; 0-520-05595-0
LC 79-65759
This edition contains the entire sequence of poems set in Gloucester, Massachusetts, whose protagonist is the mythical figure, Maximus.
"It is impossible to describe in this small space the immensity of Charles Olson's achievement—as poet, theoretician and explorer of the 'human universe.' Just as Ezra Pound's writing energized Western poetry in the first half of this century, Olson in the 1950s redefined its direction and inspired the next generation of writers. . . . 'The Maximus Poems' are a complex far-ranging attempt to grasp the history of human thought." Christ Sci Monit

★ The **collected** poems of Charles Olson; excluding the Maximus poems. edited by George F. Butterick. University of Calif. Press 1987 xxxvi, 675p hardcover o.p. pa $45 **811**
1. Poetry -- By individual authors
ISBN 0-520-21231-2
LC 86-14652
"Perhaps the most important American postmodernist poet, Olson was little published during his life. This work, . . . should solidify his reputation. Olson burst into poetry in

his maturity, sure of his instincts. Though his debt to Pound is evident, he went further in exploring both American language and experience. What amazes us now is not just the profundity and erudition of his themes but the variety of ways he expresses his humanity. Ceaselessly experimental, his poems do not lose their intelligence or intelligibility." Libr J

Olstein, Lisa

Lost alphabet. Copper Canyon Press 2009 92p pa $15   **811**
    1. Poetry -- By individual authors
    ISBN 978-1-55659-301-7; 1-55659-301-5
                                    LC 2008-53486
This is a "sequence of prose poems spoken in the voice of a lepidopterist engaged in isolated research on butterflies and moths near a village whose residents reluctantly embrace her presence. Flirting with fiction without quite unfurling a clear narrative, Olstein's speaker finds correlatives for her lonely if exploratory inner life in the insects—living and dead—she is studying." Publ Wkly

Oppen, George

★ **New** collected poems; edited with an introduction and notes by Michael Davidson; preface by Eliot Weinberger. New Directions 2002 xlv, 433p il $37.95   **811**
    1. Poetry -- By individual authors
    ISBN 0-8112-1488-5
                                    LC 2001-44048
"Oppen, a Communist and an objectivist poet deeply influenced by Pound and Williams, believed that there were no ideas except in things, but he also believed, fiercely, that our relationship to things was inherently moral. . . . In 1934, he published a book of stunning, elliptical lyrics about 'big-Business' and American capitalism; he then fell silent for the next twenty-five years, during which he struggled to reconcile his fealty to social causes with the demands of aesthetic originality. The culmination of this struggle was his Pulitzer Prize-winning collection 'Of Being Numerous,' published in 1968, which, to a degree unmatched by any book of American poetry since, movingly portrays the individual in a collective world." New Yorker
    Includes bibliographical references

Orr, Gregory

The **caged** owl; new and selected poems. Copper Canyon Press 2002 235p pa $16   **811**
    1. Poetry -- By individual authors
    ISBN 1-55659-177-2
                                    LC 2001-6504
"The constraints of personal narrative are stretched to their limits in this summation from Orr, . . . as his poems are often based on tragic experiences occurring to those close to him. Orr's archetypal subject in the new poems and selections from six previous collections . . . is fratricide. As a child, Orr accidentally shot and killed his young brother in a hunting accident." Publ Wkly

Ossip, Kathleen

The **cold** war; Kathleen Ossip. 1st ed.; Sarabande Books 2011 77p.   **811**
    ISBN 9781932511956 pa; 1932511954
                                    LC 2010040378
This poetry collection presents a "socio-poetical exploration of post-World War II America, taking as her starting points Karl A. Menninger, who wrote 'The Human Mind'; Vance Packard, author of 'The Status Seekers'; and that scalawag of orgone energy, Wilhelm Reich." (N Y Times) Topics include "confessional writing, social and literary criticism, and history. The book's centerpiece is the traumatized, post-9/11 'Document.'" (Publishers Weekly) "It questions the origins and premises of contemporary American culture." (Publisher's note)

Ostriker, Alicia

No heaven; [by] Alicia Suskin Ostriker. University of Pittsburgh Press 2005 136p pa $12.95 **811**
    1. Poetry -- By individual authors
    ISBN 0-8229-5875-9
In this "collection of clarion poems intimate and worldly, Ostriker writes about her life as a wife, mother, and grandmother with tenderness, but she is also edgy, erotic, funny, and ornery." Booklist

Padgett, Ron

How long. Coffee House Press 2011 88p pa $16   **811**
    1. Poetry -- By individual authors
    ISBN 978-1-56689-256-8
                                    LC 2010-38005
"Padgett's sense of romantic joy is undiminished, as is his thoughtfulness about language and the ways in which time changes meaning, and sense can morph into eloquent absurdity." Entertainment Wkly

How to be perfect. Coffee House Press 2007 114p pa $15   **811**
    1. Poetry -- By individual authors
    ISBN 978-1-56689-203-2; 1-56689-203-1
                                    LC 2007-17772
"Padgett's plainspoken, wry poems deliver their wisdom through a kind of connoisseurship of absurdity. . . . Yet these observational, reminiscent, and prescriptive verses are also informed by a sense of loss—not just for his late mother and for departed comrades like Kenneth Koch but for the bohemian ideal that drew him to New York to begin with. . . . Even so, Padgett's cockeyed humor is ultimately optimistic." New Yorker

You never know; poems. Coffee House Press 2001 84p pa $14.95   **811**
    1. Poetry -- By individual authors
    ISBN 978-1-56689-128-8; 1-56689-128-0
                                    LC 2001-52945
"Padgett is the undisputed Zen master of the chicane, maintaining a perfectly readable and casual tone while turning meanings on a dime, or several dimes, on his way to a reliably radiant and melancholy conclusion. . . . These poems make a go at the epistemological concerns of the title, but like his collaborator Ted Berrigan or his predecessors

James Schuyler and Kenneth Koch, Padgett shines brightest when he interrupts his crazy word combinations to be serious about love and death." Publ Wkly

Page, P. K.

The **hidden** room; collected poems. {by} Patricia Kathleen Page. Porcupine's Quill 1997 2v ea $18.95   **811**

1. Poetry -- By individual authors
ISBN 0-88984-190-X v1; 0-88984-193-4 v2

LC 98-113870

These two volumes incude the majority of all of the poet's works published in volume form, from Unit of five to Hologram, along with some unpublished poems and poems hitherto published only in magazines

Palmer, Michael

Company of moths. New Directions Books 2005 70p pa $16.95   **811**

1. Poetry -- By individual authors
ISBN 0-8112-1623-3

LC 2005-994

Palmer "combines spare lyricism and nocturnal visions ('This writing inside/ the lids of the eyes') in poems that resemble dream notes or lost translations from the French symbolists. They derive their tropes from an evocative if limited palette (owl, star, stone, book, moth) and create a sense of metaphysical unease through rhetorical questioning . . . , repetition, and paradox. . . . Whether or not one is absorbed by Palmer's deep image aesthetic and metanarrative stance, his enigmatic voice continues to fascinate." Libr J

Pankey, Eric

The **pear** as one example; new & selected poems, 1984-2008. Ausable Press 2008 274p pa $16   **811**

1. Poetry -- By individual authors
ISBN 978-1-931337-39-7; 1-931337-39-X

LC 2007-49674

"Fans of an earlier generation of American poets, such as Elizabeth Bishop, A.R. Ammons, and Robert Bly, will find much to enjoy in this large volume of poetry that showcases an acute poetic prowess, capturing a range of heartfelt emotions and experiences. . . . For Pankey, each new dawn presents a multitude of poetic possibilities, and he incorporates both the ugly and the beautiful, pain and pleasure in his aesthetic vision." NewPages

Parini, Jay

★ **Robert** Frost; a life. Holt & Co. 1999 514p il $35; pa $16   **811**

1. Authors 2. Poets 3. Poets, American -- 20th century -- Biography
ISBN 0-8050-3181-2; 0-8050-6341-2 pa

LC 98-26690

"Rarely has Frost's story been told this dexterously, or with a better understanding of the relation of Frost's personal crises to his accomplishment as a poet." Publ Wkly

Includes bibliographical references

Perillo, Lucia

On the spectrum of possible deaths; Lucia Perillo. Copper Canyon Press 2012 81 p.   **811**

1. POETRY -- American -- General
ISBN 155659397X; 9781556593970

LC 2011050110

This book is a poetry collection written by the 2009 Pulitzer Prize finalist author Lucia Perillo. Perillo has long lived with, and written about, her struggle with debilitating multiple sclerosis. Her . . . sixth book of poems, published concurrently with her debut story collection, takes a . . . look at mortality. (Booklist) with subjects ranging from coyotes and Scotch broom to local elections and family history. . . . the mythic and mundane, of media and daily life, as she faces the treachery of illness. (Publishers note)

Perillo, Lucia Maria

Inseminating the elephant; [by] Lucia Perillo. Copper Canyon Press 2009 93p $22   **811**

1. Poetry -- By individual authors
ISBN 978-1-55659-291-1; 1-55659-291-4

LC 2008-44772

Perillo "writes accessible, often funny poems that border on the profane. The title poem of this collection, her fifth, is about just what it says: zoologists tasked with helping impregnate an elephant (it's not easy). There's also an ode to bad smells, a middle-aged narrator's reluctant acceptance of cell phones and a meditation on a Viagra ad. Perillo has another rare power among versifiers: She is able to make dire, life-or-death concerns go down easy. . . . Physical decline is one of Perillo's major themes, one that she tackles with wry humor." Time Out N Y

Phillips, Carl

Double shadow. Farrar, Straus and Giroux 2011 58p $23   **811**

1. Poetry -- By individual authors
ISBN 978-0-374-14157-8; 0-374-14157-6

LC 2010-33097

"In some ways the perpetually shifting textures and shardlike quality of Phillips' language are reminiscent of John Ashbery, that preeminent poet of modern consciousness. But where Ashbery's universe is a theater of nihilistic yet playful hijinks, Phillips' is a somber, autumnal landscape, one that is illuminated by moments of ephemeral, ethereal beauty. The world of 'Double Shadow' is an old world, a faded, tired and depleted world: it is late in the day, the major events have already happened, the light is fading, and darkness will soon be upon us. . . . [Phillips] work is quiet, and at times difficult, but its fragile beauty is unique and at times overwhelming." Chicago Tribune

Rock Harbor. Farrar, Straus & Giroux 2002 110p $20; pa $12   **811**

1. Poetry -- By individual authors
ISBN 0-374-25140-1; 0-374-52885-3 pa

LC 2002-20588

"Phillips reduces lyric poetry to its bare minimum, translating complex states of being into spare and clever syllogisms. His landscapes are stark, singular, and still. The living entities present, be they bird, tree, horse, or man, stand alone in wind and shifting light. Monumental in their carved perfection and deep mystery, they are embodiments of transcendence, objects of desire, instruments of pleasure and pain." Booklist

Speak low. Farrar, Straus & Giroux 2009 68p $23   **811**
  1. Poetry -- By individual authors
  ISBN 978-0-374-26716-2; 0-374-26716-2
                                                                  LC 2008-46000
This book "is a quiet yet wounded reflection on Phillips' signature subjects: relationships, distances, identity, and damage. Phillips' remarkable ability to be clear yet illusive, as well as his dizzying syntax, are ever present as the poems coil into places of confusion." Publ Wkly
  Includes bibliographical references

The **rest** of love. Farrar, Straus and Giroux 2003 70p $20   **811**
  1. Poetry -- By individual authors
  ISBN 0-374-24953-9
                                                                  LC 2003-45213
The author presents a "set of poems on love, sex, masculinity and their classical contours. . . . The result will not only please fans, but will send new readers back to recent books, which may be accumulating more quickly than they can be absorbed." Publ Wkly

Piercy, Marge
  Colors passing through us; poems. Knopf 2003 157p $23; pa $15   **811**
  1. Poetry -- By individual authors
  ISBN 0-375-41537-8; 0-375-71005-1 pa
                                                                  LC 2002-66145
The author "tempers 1960s politics and 1970s feminism with nostalgia for the world of her childhood. . . . Piercy celebrates daily life on Cape Cod, where she and her husband live, with poems about gardening, cats, cooking, canning, and sex after 60. While all of these poems are eminently readable, the best are angry and funny. . . . Piercy fans, of which there are many, will relish this collection." Libr J

Pinsky, Robert
  Democracy, culture, and the voice of poetry. Princeton Univ. Press 2002 96p $29.95; pa $12.95   **811**
  1. American poetry -- 20th century -- History and criticism 2. American poetry -- History and criticism 3. Culture in literature 4. Democracy in literature 5. Poetry 6. Poetry -- By individual authors
  ISBN 0-691-09617-1; 0-691-12263-6 pa
                                                                  LC 2002-25288
This is an "analysis of the way the intimate rhythms of American poetry invoke a social presence. Pinsky, a former poet laureate, passionately argues that American poetry is driven by the anxiety of being forgotten; the solitary poet makes us aware of the presence of others as he yearns for

their approval while striving to preserve his uniqueness." N Y Times Book Rev

★ **Gulf** music. Farrar, Straus and Giroux 2007 83p $22   **811**
  1. Poetry -- By individual authors
  ISBN 978-0-374-16749-3; 0-374-16749-4
                                                                  LC 2007-4325
This collection "presents a carefully tuned yet impassioned vision of a past-haunted present where lessons of history remain unlearned and individuals struggle for comprehension amid atrocities ('In Africa/ The raiders with machetes to cut off hands/ Might make the victim choose, "long sleeve or short"') and contradictions ('Culture the penalty. Culture the escape'). . . . This anthology contains some of Pinsky's most invigorating work." Libr J

Jersey rain. Farrar, Straus & Giroux 2000 52p hardcover o.p. pa $12   **811**
  1. Poetry -- By individual authors
  ISBN 978-0-374-52772-3; 0-374-52772-5
                                                                  LC 99-44209
"The discursive mode suits Pinsky because it allows his mind to range, to consider, to try out images and ideas. The pleasure comes less from the poem's perfection as an artifact than from our sense of the poet's sensitive, inquisitive mind at work." N Y Times Book Rev

The **figured** wheel; new and collected poems, 1966-1996. Farrar, Straus & Giroux 1996 303p hardcover o.p. pa $17   **811**
  1. Poetry -- By individual authors
  ISBN 0-374-52506-4
                                                                  LC 95-47617
"Brought together here are 16 new poems, the work of Pinsky's four original collections and a sampling of his fine translations, including a canto from his well-received version of the Inferno. Taken as a whole, this is the record of a poet who grows from highly competent to near-transcendent." Publ Wkly

Plath, Sylvia
  Ariel; the restored edition. foreword by Frieda Hughes. HarperCollins Publishers 2004 xxi, 211p $24.95 **811**
  1. Poetry -- By individual authors
  ISBN 0-06-073259-8
                                                                  LC 2004-47703
A collection of forty of Plath's poems written between 1960 and her death in 1963, in their original order along with facsimile drafts of the poems included.
  "Readers can see Plath's actual manuscript in this handsome facsimile, which provides a missing piece in the Plath annals and proves that there's nothing like going to the source." Booklist

★ The **collected** poems; edited by Ted Hughes. Harper & Row 1981 351p hardcover o.p. pa $17.95   **811**
  1. Poetry -- By individual authors
  ISBN 0-06-155889-3 pa
"Although her best poems deal with suffering and death, others are exhilarating and affectionate, and her tone is fre-

quently witty as well as disturbing." Concise Oxford Companion to Engl Lit

Poe, Edgar Allan

Complete poems; edited by Thomas Ollive Mabbott. University of Ill. Press 2000 xxx, 627p il pa $25   **811**
  1. Fantasy poetry, American 2. Poetry -- By individual authors
  ISBN 0-252-06921-8
                                                   LC 00-38639
  This book contains 101 poems and their variants. In addition to classic poems such as The raven, The bells, and Annabel Lee, this volume contains previously uncollected poems, fragments, verses published in reviews, and poems attributed to Poe

  ★ **Poems** and poetics; Richard Wilbur, editor. Library of Am. 2003 xxv, 179p $20   **811**
  1. Poetry -- By individual authors
  ISBN 1-931082-51-0
                                                   LC 2003-46637
  "Wilbur wants Poe to be appreciated as a transcendental cosmic theorist and 'the most difficult of the symbolist writers of his century,' and he appends selections from Poe's writings about poetics to help understanding of his cosmology and discusses some of Poe's most intense stories to exemplify his symbolism. The poems, presented chronologically, show again what a young prodigy Poe was, formulating his poetic thought while still in his teens, and what a sonorous Romantic musician he became." Booklist
  Includes bibliographical references

Poems./Selections

  Selected poems; Louis Auchincloss, editor. Library of America 2005 183p $20   **811**
  1. Poetry -- By individual authors
  ISBN 978-1-931082-86-0; 1-931082-86-3
                                                   LC 2005-44163
  "From first to last, poetry was part of Edith Wharton's writing life. . . . Her first models were Romantic, but in the course of her life she absorbed the influences of Symbolism and Modernism; and throughout her poetic career she showed a care for form even in her most private utterances, as in the erotic ode 'Terminus,' never published in her lifetime. This volume collects the bulk of Wharton's significant poetry, including much work previously uncollected or unpublished." Publisher's note

Poems/Selections

  ★ The **collected** poems of Ted Berrigan; edited by Alice Notley, with Anselm Berrigan and Edmund Berrigan; introduction and notes by Alice Notley. University of California Press 2005 749p $60; pa $24.95   **811**
  1. Poetry -- By individual authors
  ISBN 978-0-520-23986-9; 0-520-23986-5; 978-0-520-25155-7 pa; 0-520-25155-5 pa
                                                   LC 2005-42259
  This volume collects the published and unpublished works of a leading figure of the second-generation New York School. Includes the first presentation of the Easter Monday

sequence in the order authorized by Berrigan shortly before his death.
  "More than 20 years in preparation, this is a major volume of 20th-century American poetry. . . . Berrigan was a notoriously charismatic reader, teacher and participant in the community that developed around the Poetry Project at St. Mark's Church; his persona has been cited as often as his poems. This book closes the gap once and for all." Publ Wkly

Ponsot, Marie

  Easy; poems. Alfred A. Knopf 2009 82p $26 **811**
  1. Poetry -- By individual authors
  ISBN 978-0-307-27218-8; 0-307-27218-4
                                                   LC 2009-17488
  "Poetry and old age are difficult human endeavors, yet in her new, aptly titled book of poems, Marie Ponsot makes both look Easy. And who would know better than she? Well into her ninth decade and still evolving as an artist, Ponsot takes her place among a distinguished company of American poets who wrote—and continue to write—into their 80s and beyond. . . . In a youth-obsessed culture like ours, it is exhilarating to read a collection of poems that celebrates the graces of age, the gift of wisdom and the freedom won through endurance." America

  Springing; new and selected poems. Knopf 2002 233p $25; pa $16.95 **811**
  1. Poetry -- By individual authors
  ISBN 0-375-41389-8; 0-375-70987-8 pa
                                                   LC 2001-38432
  "Ponsot's poems are built around . . . unflinching observations of intimate interactions and misfires, whether of familial relations ventriloquized through updated Greek dramatis personae, a French woman's accommodation of her mother's married lover or the self's castings about the natural world." Publ Wkly

Porter, Anne

  ★ **Living** things; collected poems. foreword by David Shapiro. Zoland Books 2006 176p pa $15   **811**
  1. Poetry -- By individual authors
  ISBN 1-58195-216-3
                                                   LC 2005-029944
  Porter "deserves to be called a religious poet, for she sees the world, in all its aspects, as whole within a providential design. In her verse there pulsates a probing, praying spiritual intelligence as well as a poet's sensibility and graceful generosity. . . . Living Things offers over 100 of Porter's poems, all 76 that appeared in An Altogether Different Language (1994) . . . and 39 new poems. The new poems come first. Reading this collection from beginning to end lets the newer work enrich and deepen the older, enhancing the reader's appreciation not for Porter's 'development,' but for discerning and valuing this poet's integrity and vision. The cumulative impact is dazzling." America

Pound, Ezra

  ★ **Poems** and translations. Library of America 2003 1363p $45   **811**
  1. Poetry -- By individual authors
  ISBN 978-1-931082-41-9; 1-931082-41-3
                                                   LC 2003-40142

This volume "offers, in addition to the convenience of having Pound's shorter works compacted into a single volume, a useful chronology of his life and some very helpful, if at times overly terse, annotations to the poems' myriad foreign phrases and proper nouns. Richard Sieburth, an award-winning translator and the author of a previous book on Pound, is clearly at home with the material. . . . More important than all of this, however, what emerges from Poems and Translations is a personality, one of the strongest and strangest in modern poetry." Parnassus: Poetry in Review

★ The **cantos** of Ezra Pound. New Directions 1970 802p $42; pa $22.95 **811**
1. Poetry -- By individual authors
ISBN 0-8112-0350-6; 0-8112-1326-9 pa

"The first sections of the 'Cantos' were published in magazine form as early as 1917. Pound's conception of his epic changed several times during different phases of his life. Originally intended as a didactic treatise for 'philistine' Americans, it combined elements from classical myth, ancient Oriental poetry, Provençal ballads, and modern economic theory, to create a vast disjointed panorama of the growth of civilization. A monumental work of poetic enterprise." Reader's Ency. 4th edition

Powell, D. A.
Chronic. Graywolf Press 2009 79p $20 **811**
1. Poetry -- By individual authors
ISBN 978-1-55597-516-6; 1-55597-516-X
LC 2008-935598

"Richly romantic yet never sentimental, Powell's work in Chronic is often addressed to 'you': a friend, a lover, and you, the reader. It's a lovely, intimate style." Entertainment Wkly

Price, Reynolds
★ The **collected** poems. Scribner 1997 xxiv, 471p $37.50; pa $20 **811**
1. Poetry -- By individual authors
ISBN 0-684-83203-8; 0-684-86002-3 pa
LC 96-53117

"Price has always stood apart from contemporary movements in poetry, and although it is true that he is not a technical innovator, it would be perilous to ignore him: he has a rare facility for making the strange familiar, and the familiar fresh. Compassionate and candid, Price seems likely to reach an audience unusually wide for contemporary poetry with this generous collection." Libr J

Prufer, Kevin
National anthem; poems. Four Way Books 2008 82p pa $15.95 **811**
1. Poetry -- By individual authors
ISBN 978-1-88480-083-2; 1-88480-083-1
LC 2007-37694

This collection "opens with a panoramic vision of the aftermath of apocalypse—'expired' cars, silenced TVs, coffins 'unmoored and happy with the storm'—but ends intimately, with a child's memory of his first encounter with death; the thin wire between political failure and personal grief runs taut throughout. In the eerie centerpiece poem, the suburbs are sealed under an enormous parachute, its nylon shimmering; icicles line the seams and crash into the streets, and the narrator walks for days, never finding the edge." New Yorker

Ramke, Bin
Aerial; Bin Ramke. Omnidawn Pub. 2012 109 p. **811**
ISBN 1890650609; 9781890650605
LC 2011051410

In this book, author Bin Ramke chooses the sky as the guiding figure for his 11th collection of poems. Ramke's sky is something longed for, wished for, and out of reach . . . also representing the ways loved ones are both near and distant at once. Ramke (Theory of Mind) also describes the acts of imagination--dreaming, and of course, writing--letting the sky inspire a wish for openness and lucidity. . . . As in previous books, Ramke delves into the anthropology of words (Art. Article. Articulate. Artifact. Artery. Arthritic) and welcomes the words of other writers, from Weil to Mary Oliver, into his lines. In these poems, Ramke . . . contemplates death, finality, and fear. (Publishers Weekly)

Ras, Barbara
The **last** skin. Penguin Books 2010 63p pa $18 **811**
1. Poetry -- By individual authors
ISBN 978-0-14-311697-4 pa; 0-14-311697-5 pa
LC 2009-53320

Nested in this new book of poems by Barbara Ras, we find an ongoing subtext about the loss of her mother (to whom The Last Skin is dedicated). The title poem holds the one piece of her clothing I'd kept/to bed and bury my face/in her flowered blouse to smell her last skin,/but even from the first it was futile. As direct references to her deceased parents and flowering allusions arise, they reveal the poet's primal experience of losing a parent. But what keeps the poetry from being mere confessional self-pity? First, her loss finds context in our shared mortality but without sentimentality. . . . Second, Ras creates several approaches to the unbearable fragility of life beyond personal loss. . . . Third, there are stunning images about natural phenomena (irises, oceans) and also human objects that subtly suggest grief but do not call its name. San Antonio Express-News

Reed, Ishmael
New and collected poems, 1966-2006. Carroll & Graf 2006 xxi, 482p $25.95; pa $17.95 **811**
1. Poetry -- By individual authors
ISBN 978-0-7867-1788-0; 978-1-56858-341-9 pa
LC 2006-299409

"The mixture of humor and anger is . . . a hallmark of Ishmael Reed, whose strength as an editor, essayist, and novelist (and whose reputation as provocateur) has overshadowed his achievement as a poet. That achievement . . . is based in the vernacular, as well as in his use of folk materials, his fearlessness with form, and his 'irrational' tendency toward the spiritual, which stands as an indictment of the impoverished soul of a bottom-line age." Harvard Review

Rekdal, Paisley

Animal eye; Paisley Rekdal. University of Pittsburgh Press 2012 86 p. Pitt poetry series **811**

1. American poetry
ISBN 0822961792; 9780822961796

LC 2011277541

This book is a collection of poetry from Paisley Rekdal. In poems long and short, Rekdal looks at paintings and wax models . . . , a stuffed fox . . . , a front-yard garden, a bouquet of flowers, all of which become harsh mirrors reflecting the painful lessons of lost love. What's the point of pain if it heals, Rekdal asks, thinking of finding new love after divorce: these poems don't want to be let off easy. Even tango lessons aren't just for fun: The point is not to give yourself away but to connect/ as closely as you are able to// your partner's will in the embrace, so that intent/ slides seamlessly through two// sets of veins. There's a bit of willful masochism in this dance--in any of life's various dances--when the goal is to join two separate hearts." (Publishers Weekly)

Revell, Donald

★ **Pennyweight** windows; new & selected poems. Alice James 2005 220p $26.95; pa $18.95 **811**

1. Poetry -- By individual authors
ISBN 1-882295-51-X; 1-882295-52-8 pa

LC 2004-26191

"Using history, mythology, and contemporary events as a backdrop . . . [the author] tries to balance a public, nearly didactic voice with a personal and revealing one. . . . This readable and well-edited collection—mostly culled from eight previous collections, with some new poems added—is a good representation of Revell's work." Libr J

The **bitter** withy; new poems. Alice James Books 2009 61p pa $15.95 **811**

1. Poetry -- By individual authors
ISBN 978-1-88229-576-0; 1-88229-576-5

LC 2009-25413

This collection features "poetical lexicon (rainbows, flowers, celestial bodies, trees and birds abound) and hymnlike sentiments. . . . Revell's voice has become ecstatic, but it has also remained clear, so his intensely personal, even visionary accounts and meditations are rendered with lucidity and ease." Publ Wkly

A **thief** of strings. Alice James Books 2007 68p pa $14.95 **811**

1. Poetry -- By individual authors
ISBN 978-1-882295-61-6; 1-882295-61-7

LC 2007-1116

"Revell is a post-Romantic, his natural imagery clear and immediate, his feelings never very far from his sleeve, his tone approaching a prayerful devotion that evinces an unshakable love of the real world despite its—or our—compromised state." Libr J

Rexroth, Kenneth

★ The **complete** poems of Kenneth Rexroth; edited by Sam Hamill & Bradford Morrow. Copper Canyon Press 2003 xxxvi, 764p hardcover o.p. pa $24 **811**

1. Poetry -- By individual authors
ISBN 1-55659-217-5 pa

LC 2002-1706

"If you love looking things up and taking reading sidetrips, Rexroth is one of the most readable and rewarding twentieth-century American poets." Booklist

Reznikoff, Charles

Holocaust. David R. Godine 2007 93p pa $15.95 **811**

1. Poetry -- By individual authors
ISBN 978-1-57423-208-0; 1-57423-208-8

LC 2006-33803

"A book-length poem about the Shoah as recounted by witnesses at the Nuremberg Military Tribunal and the trial of Adolf Eichmann, architect of Hitler's 'Final Solution,' held in Jerusalem. From U.S. government transcripts of these trials, [the author] selected and spliced together witness testimonies. . . . Reznikoff's historicism and objectivism are brought together in an ethical and spiritual climax. By using the language of others he attends to the 'object' of genocide without imaginative or philosophical flourish, and by reciting it again in his own rhythm he becomes a second witness to its truth. Ultimately, the reader responds not to the poet but to the testimony itself. . . . It presents a story already told and a story never to be finished. It is neither novel nor revelatory, only horrific; as a piece of art it does not seduce us. But this is precisely its moral power as a document." Boston Rev

★ The **poems** of Charles Reznikoff; 1918-1975. edited by Seamus Cooney. David R. Godine 2005 445p $45; pa $21.95 **811**

1. Poetry -- By individual authors
ISBN 1-57423-204-5; 1-57423-203-7 pa

LC 2005-21218

This collection "of his poems . . . will be welcomed both by old and new readers of his work." Publ Wkly

Includes bibliographical references

Rich, Adrienne

Arts of the possible; essays and conversations. Norton 2001 190p $23.95; pa $13.95 **811**

1. Feminism 2. Poetry 3. Poetry -- Authorship 4. Poets, American -- 20th century
ISBN 0-393-05045-9; 0-393-32312-9 pa

LC 00-51522

This volume "collects Rich's best-known prose from the 1970s and 1980s, with new writing that extends through the 1990s. In letters such as 'Why I Refused the National Medal for the Arts,' and through complaints about feminism as the cult of the personal and a renewed call for a collective global vision, she delights, and is by turns lyrical and polemical." Ms

Collected early poems, 1950-1970. Norton 1993 xxi, 435p hardcover o.p. pa $15 **811**

1. Poetry -- By individual authors
ISBN 0-393-31385-9 pa

LC 92-13150

This collection "contains all of the work included in Rich's first six books, and a few previously uncollected pieces as well. Her poetry of the 1950s stems from a strong, mostly male tradition, obviously and intentionally echoing the work of Frost, Williams, Dickinson and Stevens. . . . The poems written in the 1960s are pervaded by the poet's consciousness of the subversive nature of creativity, especially for women, a gift at risk of being suppressed or curtailed at any moment by the self, family or the male-dominated society. In the last poems of the period, Rich's voice is firm and brave, her language still searingly beautiful and individual. This important volume charts the radical transformation of one of America's most significant poets." Publ Wkly

Fox; poems, 1998-2000. Norton 2001 64p $21; pa $12 **811**

1. Poetry -- By individual authors
ISBN 0-393-04166-2; 0-393-32377-3 pa
LC 2001-31240

"Rich's recent style—developed slowly throughout the 1990s—comes to full fruition here, conveying her familiar attentions to social injustice and intense introspection with and a sometimes harsh, fragmented, versatile line whose sources include George Oppen and Anglo-Saxon accentual verse." Publ Wkly

Midnight salvage; poems, 1995-1998. Norton 1999 75p $22; pa $11 **811**

1. Poetry -- By individual authors
ISBN 0-393-04682-6; 0-393-31984-9 pa
LC 98-19293

Rich's "well-known, fiercely held political ideals—her commitments to economic justice, feminism and gay liberation—manifest themselves, now, in her sense of passing the torch, of trying to show the readers and writers who will come after her what she has learned and how she learned it. Her juxtaposed fragments, self-questionings and self-interruptions, and taut, Anglo-Saxonate verse lines, let her sound accessible, democratic, inspiring, while making us work to discover her poems' formal secrets." Publ Wkly

The **school** among the ruins: poems, 2000-2004. W.W. Norton 2004 113p $22.95 **811**

1. Poetry -- By individual authors
ISBN 0-393-05983-9
LC 2004-8370

"Rich, a clarion poet of conscience, gets the fractured timbre of our times just right in a collection of vigorous lyric poems about cell phones and television, terror and war, commercialization and 'social impotence.'" Booklist

Roberson, Ed

To see the earth before the end of the world. Wesleyan University Press 2010 161p $22.95 **811**

1. Poetry -- By individual authors
ISBN 978-0-8195-6950-9; 0-8195-6950-X
LC 2010-27094

"In poems that proceed snakelike across a page or in traditional flush-left frames, Roberson's images and ideas are startling and complex, often difficult in their dreamlike qualities. His lines have been accurately described as syntactically double-jointed and labyrinthine—and, as with any maze, readers must find a hold, an outside wall to guide them

through Roberson's sometimes surreal vision of the earth." Libr J

Roethke, Theodore

★ The **collected** poems of Theodore Roethke. Doubleday 1966 279p hardcover o.p. pa $14.95 **811**

1. Poetry -- By individual authors
ISBN 0-385-08601-6 pa

Roethke's "refreshingly original rhythms are keenly articulated and often hypnotic. Although his work is uneven and he sometimes gives way to self-indulgence or to surprising naiveté, many of his best poems recreate disconcertingly intense psychic or mystical experience. He also had a flair for the seductively lyrical and the brashly irreverent. He ranks as one of the best poets of the first postmodern generation." Benet's Reader's Ency of Am Lit

Rukeyser, Muriel

Selected poems; Adrienne Rich, editor. Library of America 2004 xxv, 180p $20 **811**

1. Poetry -- By individual authors
ISBN 978-1-931082-58-7; 1-931082-58-8
LC 2003-60484

"Rukeyser was born in 1913, which puts her in the generation of Bishop, Berryman, Lowell, and Jarrell. Her poems range from the sprawling to the epigrammatic; they often have a flat, documentary feel ('The tunnel is part of a huge water power project/begun, latter part of 1929'), and they're formally various (excerpted sections from a single long poem, 'Letter to the Front,' contain both a sonnet and a sestina). . . . At its best, Rukeyser's work can be open, energetic, and well constructed, if a little enamored of its own goody-goodness." Poetry (Modern Poetry Association)

Ryan, Kay

Elephant rocks. Grove Press 1996 84p $18; pa $14 **811**

1. Poetry -- By individual authors
ISBN 978-0-8021-1586-7; 0-8021-1586-1; 978-0-8021-3525-4 pa; 0-8021-3525-0 pa
LC 95-42668

This volume is comprised of "miniature five-paragraph essays, something like those little books the Brontes wrote for their dolls. They're epigrams or digestifs or, better, aphorisms if we remember the source of such things: Hippocrates making little pills of pithiness, haiku with punch lines, prescriptions not meant for the pharmacist. . . . If John Skelton had been Emily Dickinson's tutor instead of Jane Scrope's, these poems would not surprise us. But they do." Antioch Review

The **Niagara** River; poems. Grove Press 2005 72p pa $13 **811**

1. Poetry -- By individual authors
ISBN 0-8021-4222-2
LC 2005-40423

"In two or three shifty sentences per short-lined poem, Ryan brazenly questions the extent to which we are in control of, and thus responsible for, our own and others' suffering. Her work . . . operates in an American tradition stretching from Dickinson through Stevens and Frost to Ammons and Bronk, where fidelity to the natural world works as a scrim for staging such self-exploration. . . . Empathic and wryly unforgiving of the human condition, the poems are equal parts pith and punch. The effect is bracing." Publ Wkly

Say uncle; poems. Grove Press 2000 76p pa $14   **811**
1. Poetry -- By individual authors
ISBN 978-0-8021-3717-3; 0-8021-3717-2
                                                    LC 00-26454
"These precise, epigrammatic poems, which come with hook-and-eye rhymes that click sweetly into place, move deftly and economically. . . . Though they dispose of their subjects wittily and ingeniously, they cannot always suppress a smile of self-satisfaction at having mastered their material; and, like macaroons, they should be taken a few at a time. They are cleverly made. . . . Like cat's cradles, they may be taken in or let out, but at their best they alter the fit of the mind." Atl Mon

The **best** of it; new and selected poems. Grove Press 2010 288p $24   **811**
1. Poetry -- By individual authors
ISBN 978-0-8021-1914-8; 0-8021-1914-X
Ryan's "poems are as slim as runway models, so tiny you could almost tweet them. Their compact refinement, though, does not suggest ease or chic. Her voice is quizzical and impertinent, funny in uncomfortable ways, scuffed by failure and loss. Her mastery, like Emily Dickinson's, has some awkwardness in it, some essential gawkiness that draws you close. . . . [This] is a generous and nearly career-spanning collection of her verse." N Y Times Book Rev

Sandburg, Carl
★ The **complete** poems of Carl Sandburg; rev and expanded ed; Harcourt Brace Jovanovich 1970 xxxi, 797p $40   **811**
1. Poetry -- By individual authors
ISBN 0-15-100996-1
A collection of seven of the author's books: Chicago poems, 1916; Cornhuskers, 1918; Smoke and steel, 1920; Slabs of the sunburnt West, 1922; Good morning, America, 1925; The people, yes, 1936; Honey and salt, 1963.
"Known for his free verse, written under the influence of Walt Whitman and celebrating industrial and agricultural America, American geography and landscape, figures in American history, and the American common people, {Sandburg} frequently makes use of contemporary American slang and colloquialisms." Herzberg. Reader's Ency of Am Lit

Sanders, Ed
Let's not keep fighting the Trojan War; selected poems, 1986-2008. [by] Edward Sanders; introduction by Joanne Kyger. Coffee House Press 2009 245p il pa $20   **811**
1. Poetry -- By individual authors
ISBN 978-1-56689-234-6 pa; 1-56689-234-1 pa
                                                    LC 2009-22843
"Sanders has been an astonishing and fertile presence in our cutlural and political landscape. . . . But it is Sanders's poetry, more than anything else he does, that pulls together

all the varied strands of his interests to weave them into the body of one of our century's most coherent poetics." NPR

Thirsting for peace in a raging century; selected poems, 1961-1985. [by] Edward Sanders. New and rev. ed.; Coffee House Press 2009 260p il pa $20   **811**
1. Poetry -- By individual authors
ISBN 978-1-56689-238-4 pa
                                                    LC 2009-28061
This collection "restores Edward Sanders to his rightful place at the forefront of the poetry of his time, and reminds us that spending one's days in active pursuit of the betterment of all life on the planet isn't necessarily antithetical to the creation of first-rate writing." San Francisco Chron

Sarton, May
Selected poems of May Sarton; edited and with an introduction by Serena Sue Hilsinger and Lois Brynes. Norton 1978 206p hardcover o.p. pa $25   **811**
1. Poetry -- By individual authors
ISBN 978-0-393-04512-3; 0-393-04512-9
                                                    LC 78-14850
"What May Sarton does is to follow the round of a woman's life. Her verse is traditional, warm, ripe with the wisdom of her years as a poet, novelist, autobiographer. She draws on the artifacts of the past for images to live by in the here and now." Christ Sci Monit

Savich, Zach
Annulments. Center for Literary Publishing/Colorado State University 2010 65p pa $16.95 **811**
1. Poetry -- By individual authors
ISBN 978-1-885635-15-0; 1-885635-15-X
                                                    LC 2010-20558
This collection "features poems that communicate what is fragmentary at the expense of the concrete. At once meticulous and vertiginous, these poems are grounded by 'The Mountains Overhead,' a long poem of 113 fragments, in which we find 'Dawn stripping you like a cat/ clawing a band of wallpaper' and horses that 'hold themselves like torches so they/ won't burn like themselves.' The result is a collection that is thrilling and inchoate. . . . In keeping with the trope of annulments, the poems often end suddenly, leaving much to be desired in their genesis and construction. One senses that Savich could go on building his fragmentary mountain forever, not unlike a certain well-known biblical tower whose result was the fragmentation of language itself." Publ Wkly

Scalapino, Leslie
It's go in horizontal; selected poems, 1974-2006. University of California Press 2008 241p il $45; pa $16.95   **811**
ISBN 978-0-520-25461-9; 0-520-25461-9; 978-0-520-25462-6 pa; 0-520-25462-7 pa
                                                    LC 2007-50133
"Most often classified with the language poets, Scalapino is shown in this welcome overview to have developed a distinctive idiom, as fresh and powerful here as when first published in 14 mostly small press editions. Scalapino fuses

a richly detached Buddhist mindfulness with an algorithmically precise disjunctive syntax to explore sex, gender and violence—their politics and their moment-to-moment embodiedness. The longish, serial form that she favors works well in the selected format when the poems are presented in full." Publ Wkly

Schulman, Grace

Days of wonder; new and selected poems. Houghton Mifflin 2002 189p $25; pa $14 **811**
1. Poetry -- By individual authors
ISBN 0-618-08623-4; 0-618-34082-3 pa
LC 2001-39531

"In a characteristic Schulman poem, large, difficult questions resonate in the small, singular moments of appreciation. . . . There are allusions to canonical painters and canonical poems, and a variety of religious references, which engender equal portions of reverence and lament. Many of the poems' small pleasures are found amid sometimes difficult sometimes serene backdrops." Publ Wkly

Schuyler, James

★ **Collected** poems. Farrar, Straus & Giroux 1993 429p hardcover o.p. pa $32 **811**
1. Poetry -- By individual authors
ISBN 978-0-374-52403-6; 0-374-52403-3
LC 92-40977

"Schuyler's subject is his life, and his poems often read like elegant journal entries. The book presents intimate and conversational accounts of life in the Eastern literary landscape—New York City, New England, Long Island. In urbane free verse, the poet recalls and meditates on music and painting, homosexuality, weekends with friends—John Ashbery and Fairfield Porter among them—deaths, a drive to the Hamptons. . . . Rarely has a poet imparted so much of his experience as honestly and engagingly as Schuyler does here." Publ Wkly

Other flowers; uncollected poems. edited by James Meetze and Simon Pettet. Farrar, Straus and Giroux 2010 220p $28 **811**
1. Poetry -- By individual authors
ISBN 978-0-374-53209-3; 0-374-53209-5
LC 2009-31891

"The Velvet Underground, it has been said, did not sell many records, but everyone who bought one went out and started his or her own band. James Schuyler was, perhaps, the Velvet Underground of verse: Almost unknown outside the poetry world, he was massively influential within it. To read Schuyler is, almost inevitably, to be struck with the desire to be a poet. Schuyler's powerful and frequently moving descriptions of nature, of the weather, of domestic engagements — limpid descriptions that lay upon the sensory world like a pellucid dew — have often seemed to constitute the heart of his poetic accomplishment. . . . Such a skill is best showcased by his longer poems, and if the new collection, 'Other Flowers: Uncollected Poems,' feels somewhat slight, it is partly because the recently discovered works gathered here are all short lyrics." Los Angeles Times

Seidel, Frederick

Poems 1959-2009. Farrar, Straus, and Giroux 2009 509p $40 **811**
1. Poetry -- By individual authors
ISBN 978-0-374-12655-1; 0-374-12655-0
LC 2008-47161

"Long regarded as a kind of elegant cult figure in poetry circles, Seidel has a reputation that precedes him into every room: decadent, name-dropper, sexual dalliant, Ducati enthusiast, son of privilege. This runs counter to the man himself. He doesn't do poetry readings and has, for the most part, shunned interviews. There is no doubt that Seidel is one of the best poets alive today, and now, with the release of 'Poems: 1959-2009,' his collected works can be taken at their measure: They are haughty, funny and terrifying, with plenty of delicious contention throughout." Los Angeles Times

Selections.

Selected poems; David Lehman, editor. Library of America 2006 130p $20 **811**
1. Poetry -- By individual authors
ISBN 978-1-931082-93-8; 1-931082-93-6
LC 2006-40807

Ammons "was a difficult figure to pin down. While unassociated with any particular poetic school or group, he picked up threads from Whitman, Williams, Frost and Stevens, weaving them into poetry all his own: equal parts pastoral meditation, philosophical speculation and homespun resignation. In the process, he won nearly every honor a major American poet can. Now, in the first selection to present samplings from the whole of his oeuvre (which ranges from two-line lyrics to book-length sequences), we can survey the extent is his poetic powers." Publ Wkly

Sexton, Anne

The **complete** poems; with a foreword by Maxine Kumin. Houghton Mifflin 1981 xxiv, 622p hardcover o.p. pa $19 **811**
1. Poetry -- By individual authors
ISBN 0-395-95776-1 pa
LC 81-2482

"Even before her death in 1974, Sexton's work was the subject of critical controversy, often dismissed as mere confessionalism. But, as Maxine Kumin observes in an insightful introductory essay, Sexton 'delineated the problematic position of women—the neurotic reality of the time' and in so doing 'earned her place in the canon.'" Choice

Shapiro, David

New and selected poems (1965-2006) Overlook Press 2007 267p $21.95 **811**
1. Poetry -- By individual authors
ISBN 978-1-58567-877-8; 1-58567-877-5
LC 2006-52718

"Shapiro is usually thought of as a New York School poet, but from the evidence of this selection it would probably be more accurate to call him a Greater New York School poet. His metropolis radiates outward to comprehend Weequahic Park and the Palisades, and his aleatory, portentfree sophistication seems confident enough to accommodate primitive, endearing, and frankly tender tropes and situations, as when a poet faces an ailing mother or a growing son. A perennial drama in this volume is that of an erudite and restlessly modernizing mind confronting pains and peculiarities that no amount of urbanity can assuage. . . . The effect is of unforeseen intimacy at the heart of abstraction." New Yorker

Shapiro, Karl Jay

★ **Selected** poems; [by] Karl Shapiro; John Updike, editor. Library of Am. 2003 xxxi, 197p il $20   **811**
   1. Poetry -- By individual authors
   ISBN 1-931082-34-0
                              LC 2002-32123
"Karl Shapiro, one of the more influential voices of the late 20th century, displayed complex and contrary tendencies in both his life and his poetry. Editor Updike notes that Shapiro's experimentation with voices and forms alienated those who admired the metrical dexterity of his early poems." Libr J
   Includes bibliographical references

Shaughnessy, Brenda

Human dark with sugar. Copper Canyon Press 2008 77p pa $15   **811**
   1. Poetry -- By individual authors
   ISBN 978-1-55659-276-8 pa; 1-55659-276-0 pa
                              LC 2007-52225
"The book's three sections contain nine, 11 and 10 poems, respectively, and that off-kilter triangulation . . . proves the right three-cornered lens for looking into the darkest corners of human relationships, including their embodiment. . . . This is a brilliant, beautiful and essential continuation of the metaphysical verse tradition." Publ Wkly

Shockley, Evie

The **new** black; poems. Wesleyan University Press 2011 104p il   **811**
   1. Poetry -- By individual authors
   ISBN 978-0-81957-140-3
                              LC 2010046345
In this book, the author "tells the reader not of some oversimplified and inaccurate version of 'the African-American experience' but of the plethora of experiences that inform the consciousness of one black woman in contemporary America. Shockley's work incorporates elements of myth without being patently 'mythical' and is personal without being self-indulgent, sentimental without being saccharine." Libr J

Simic, Charles

Master of disguises. Houghton Mifflin Harcourt 2010 75p $22   **811**
   1. Poetry -- By individual authors
   ISBN 978-0-547-39709-2; 0-547-39709-7
                              LC 2009-47470

"Simic's edgy, brooding poems are like saxophone solos played under a bridge in the deep, dark hours of the spinning world's bruising insomnia." Booklist

Selected early poems. Braziller 1999 255p $22; pa $14.95   **811**
   1. Poetry -- By individual authors
   ISBN 0-8076-1456-4; 0-8076-1483-1 pa
                              LC 99-34872
"Charles Simic shows that he is among the very few poets for whom surrealism is a genuine vision, a tool of discovery, rather than a collection of abitrary shocks. . . . His skewed vision manages both to capture the alien concreteness of things and to make them reflect his own consciousness. . . . His skill and sure instinct make this book one of the important poetic achievements of our time." N Y Times Book Rev

That little something; poems. Harcourt 2008 73p $23   **811**
   1. Poetry -- By individual authors
   ISBN 978-0-15-101359-3; 0-15-101359-4
                              LC 2007-32812
"Among contemporary poets, Simic, now 70, is not only one of the most prolific but also one of the most distinctive, accessible and enjoyable—the commonplace critique of contemporary poetry as dull, obscure and lacking in individuality definitely does not apply. . . . Just about the only thing critics complain of is that his style has shown relatively little development over the years. That's true, although in the last decade or so his poems seem to me to have become shorter, simpler, less manic." N Y Times Book Rev

★ The **voice** at 3:00 a.m; selected late & new poems. Harcourt 2003 177p $25   **811**
   1. Poetry -- By individual authors
   ISBN 0-15-100842-6
                              LC 2002-38715
"An important purchase for all libraries." Libr J

Simpson, Louis Aston Marantz

★ The **owner** of the house; new collected poems, 1940-2001. [by] Louis Simpson. BOA 2003 407p $30.95; pa $19.95   **811**
   1. Poetry -- By individual authors
   ISBN 1-929918-38-0; 1-929918-39-9 pa
                              LC 2003-45241
The author "opens with 42 new poems and continues with selections from his 11 previous books, ending with There You Are. This work is filled with evocations of places like Jamaica, Manhattan, Paris, and Venice and range over time from tsarist Russia to World War II to the 1960s. Simpson's obsessive theme is the stultifying effect of middle-class suburban life. . . . The result is a collection both timely and accessible. . . . Highly recommended for all poetry collections." Libr J

Smith, Bruce

Devotions. University of Chicago Press 2011 88p pa

$18 **811**

1. Poetry -- By individual authors
ISBN 978-0-226-76435-1; 0-226-76435-4

LC 2010027119

"Devotion is a worn word, an excess of meaning dulling its essence. Yet Smith titled . . . [this] book Devotions, recalling a religious definition, a form of worship, for private use. Smith's poems interrogate the meaning of form, worship, private, use—every crucial word. Nearly all the poems are closely observed blocks of free-associative free verse. . . . Smith riffs on film, cooking, physics, Laundromats, baseball, Rimbaud, and more. His devotions are authoritative and capacious. Neither querulous nor slavish, they give pleasure, which is what we ask of them." Booklist

Smith, Patricia

Blood dazzler; poems. Coffee House Press 2008 77p $16   **811**

1. Hurricane Katrina, 2005 2. Hurricane Katrina, 2005 -- Poetry 3. Poetry -- By individual authors
ISBN 978-1-56689-218-6 pa

LC 2008-12528

"Simultaneously accessible and daring, these short, fiery verses describe with sorrow and passion the Crescent City just before, during and immediately after Katrina. They describe it from startling points of view—one series of poems takes the vantage point of Luther B, a hardy abandoned dog. Another set speaks for the hurricane itself. . . . [The author's] command of the spoken voice gives her work both speed and pathos. She benefits, too, from her range of forms: rhymed sonnet, sestina, alphabet poem, long and short-lined, and fragmentary free verse. This book will stand out among literary records of Katrina's devastation." Publ Wkly

Shoulda been Jimi Savannah; Patricia Smith. Coffee House Press 2012 115 p. (alk. paper) $16.00   **811**

1. Chicago (Ill.) 2. Families in literature 3. Personal names in literature 4. Poems -- Collections 5. Women, Black, in literature
ISBN 1566892996; 9781566892995

LC 2011029282

[Patricia] Smith's mother bestowed on the poet a name fitting for a woman that would 'never idly throat the Lord's name or wear one/ of those thin, sparkled skirts that flirted with her knees./ She'd be a nurse or a third-grade teacher or a postal drone.' . . . But her father, though acquiescing, secretly called her Jimi Savannah, embodying 'the blues-bathed moniker of a ball breaker.' . . . This duality bursts forth in her poems about . . . growing up black and a woman during the 1960s. (Publishers Weekly)

Smith, Tracy K.

Life on Mars. Graywolf Press 2011 75p. pa $15   **811**

1. Poetry -- By individual authors
ISBN 978-1-55597-584-5; 1-55597-584-4

LC 2011920674

"Smith shows herself to be a poet of extraordinary range and ambition. It's not easy to be so convincing in both the grand gesture and the reverent contemplation of a humble plate of eggs, and the early successes of this collection far outweigh its later missteps. As all the best poetry does, 'Life on Mars' first sends us out into the magnificent chill of the imagination and then returns us to ourselves, both changed and consoled." N Y Times Book Rev

Smith, William Jay

★ The **world** below the window; poems, 1937-1997. Johns Hopkins Univ. Press 1998 240p il hardcover o.p. pa $25   **811**

1. Poetry -- By individual authors
ISBN 978-0-8018-6783-5

LC 97-40731

"Excluding Smith's translations, longer poems, poetry for children and much of his light verse, this . . . volume both slims down and augments 1990's Collected Poems. Appearing for the first time, the original, absorbing seven-part series 'Indian Removal' searchingly explores the poet's Choctaw heritage by dramatizing America's shameful past on a hot, tear-laden, swampy Southern stage." Publ Wkly

Snodgrass, W. D.

★ **Not** for specialists; new and selected poems. BOA Editions 2006 251p $27.95; pa $21.95 **811**

1. Poetry -- By individual authors
ISBN 1-92991-877-1; 1-92991-876-3 pa

LC 2005-54846

"If you think that writing primarily in rhyme and meter bespeaks equanimity, or sweetness of character, read Snodgrass. Oh, he mellows out in the face of nature, but he's prickly. . . . His many profoundly bemused and persuasive poems of love's tougher moments, his marvelous angry and denunciatory poems, and the chilling Fuehrer Bunker poems in the voices of the major Nazis during the war's last month—all these might have been impossible if Snodgrass was a nice, easygoing guy. He's not that sort, and his best work seems permanent because he isn't." Booklist

Snyder, Gary

Danger on peaks; poems. Shoemaker & Hoard, Distributed by Publishers Group West 2004 112p il $22; pa $14   **811**

1. Poetry -- By individual authors
ISBN 1-59376-041-8; 1-59376-080-9 pa

LC 2004-11649

This is a collection of poetry by the author of Turtle Island (1975), Axe Handles (1984), No Nature (1992), and The Practice of the Wild (1990).

"From the opening prose-and-verse section on several climbs of Mount St. Helens, through short poems of observation and longer ones on daily life, to more prose-and-verse pieces on journeys near and far, Snyder seems more accepting than ever before. His 1960s eco-Marxist scolding is gone, and he's the wiser for it." Booklist

Includes bibliographical references

Mountains and rivers without end. Counterpoint 1996 165p hardcover o.p. pa $14.50   **811**

1. Poetry -- By individual authors
ISBN 1-887178-57-0 pa

LC 96-26064

"Woven of poems written from 1956 to 1996, this vigorous epic, spanning the landscapes of cities and unsullied nature and covering a period that includes the Beats and their survivors, is rooted in both the American geography and an Eastern spiritual orientation." Publ Wkly

★ **No** nature; new and selected poems. Pantheon Bks. 1992 390p hardcover o.p. pa $16 **811**
1. Poetry -- By individual authors
ISBN 978-0-679-74252-4

LC 92-54110
"There is an understated majesty about the ease with which Mr. Snyder puts the present into perspective." N Y Times Book Rev

Sobin, Gustaf
The **places** as preludes. Talisman House 2005 76p pa $14.95 **811**
1. Poetry -- By individual authors
ISBN 1-58498-040-0
"One of the most significant poets of his generation, the late Gustaf Sobin's verse was enigmatic, unique, thought-provoking, and memorable." Midwest Book Rev

Spicer, Jack
★ **My** vocabulary did this to me; the collected poetry of Jack Spicer. edited by Peter Gizzi and Kevin Killian. Wesleyan University Press 2008 496p il $35 **811**
1. Poetry -- By individual authors
ISBN 978-0-8195-6887-8

LC 2008-24997
"Impeccably edited, this collection gathers the remarkable output of a poet whose writing and person were too counter even for the counterculture of the late '50s and '60s. Spicer's work manages to combine heartbreak, hermeticism, and postwar disquiet in a way both completely of its time and still ahead of ours." Village Voice

Stafford, William Edgar
The **way** it is; new & selected poems. Graywolf Press 1998 xx, 268p $24.95; pa $16 **811**
1. Poetry -- By individual authors
ISBN 1-55597-269-1; 1-55597-284-5 pa

LC 97-80082
"Including 71 previously unpublished new poems, among them the poem Stafford wrote the day he died, this collection fully reacquaints us with a quiet, generous presence on the American poetic landscape." Publ Wkly

Stern, Gerald
This time; new and selected poems. Norton 1998 288p hardcover o.p. pa $15.95 **811**
1. Poetry -- By individual authors
ISBN 0-393-31909-1 pa

LC 97-43670
"At once self-involved and sympathetic, Stern catalogues with wry dexterity a vast range of sensory data and cultural detritus, always united by 'women and men of all sizes and all ages/living together, without satire.' This healthy collection of new poems and selections from his seven previous volumes . . . is remarkable for its generosity of spirit, manifested in a warm surrealism that is often turned with humor toward his own past." Publ Wkly

Stevens, Wallace
★ **Collected** poetry and prose. Library of Am. 1997 xxii, 1032p $35 **811**
1. Poetry -- By individual authors
ISBN 1-88301-145-0

LC 97-7023
Having all of Stevens' "poems—especially all the late poems—in one volume is a great thing (previously, one had to seek them out in three different books); the 'Adagia' and his replies to questionnaires are marvelous; and even in the somewhat turgid prose pieces, he sometimes expresses himself with exemplary force and concision." N Y Times Book Rev

Stone, Ruth
In the dark. Copper Canyon Press 2004 113p $22 **811**
1. Aging -- Poetry 2. Loss (Psychology) -- Poetry 3. People with visual disabilities -- Poetry 4. Poetry -- By individual authors
ISBN 1-55659-210-8

LC 2004-6039
"Stone appeals to the mind's eye and the physical ear, each word tested for ripeness like fruit, each a perfectly held note. Wry animal parables, spare and intense dramas, gorgeous nature lyrics, and bracing metaphysical musings constitute a clarion collection." Booklist

In the next galaxy. Copper Canyon Press 2002 99p $20 **811**
1. Poetry -- By individual authors
ISBN 1-55659-178-0

LC 2001-7424
"Stone writes conversationally, with lyricism, honesty, wit, and plenty of focus on the passage of time. The suicide of her much-loved husband 40 years ago is a frequent theme, as are observations about aging (which she has achieved with great wisdom), the lives of her young students and neighbors, and ecological and political concerns." Libr J

What love comes to; new & selected poems. foreword by Sharon Olds. Copper Canyon Press 2008 359p $32 **811**
1. Poetry -- By individual authors
ISBN 978-1-55659-271-3; 1-55659-271-X

LC 2007045832
"In a field in which collections of selected writings are constantly being released, this book stands out because Stone shows that simplicity can be a deceiving doorway into some of the most challenging poems written by an American poet. Stone's poems blend the personal with dimensions of the larger world in a manner reminiscent of the late William Stafford. Few poets have this gift for taking the workings of ordinary life and fusing them with a poetic process that sustains intense emotion, allowing human experience to be felt through the mysteries of language. . . . Ruth Stone belongs to every generation of poets who have taken the responsibility to give back to the world." Bloomsbury Rev

Strand, Mark

Blizzard of one; poems. Knopf 1998 55p $21;
pa $15   **811**
1. Poetry -- By individual authors
ISBN 0-375-40139-3; 0-375-70137-0 pa
LC 97-49172
"Strand doesn't approach the universal through the particular. He approaches the universal through the universal.
In his masterly new collection, 'Blizzard of One,' even the
single snowflake that gives the volume its title . . . is a kind
of Platonic essence, linked to a continuum of snowflakes out
there in the weather and inside, in the reader's consciousness." N Y Times Book Rev

Man and camel; poems. Knopf 2006 51p
$24   **811**
1. Poetry -- By individual authors
ISBN 0-307-26296-0; 978-0-307-26296-7
LC 2006-40986
The author "writes spare, melancholy, and haunting
poems." Booklist

Swenson, May

Nature; poems old and new. Houghton Mifflin 1994
xxiii, 240p hardcover o.p. pa $15 **811**
1. Poetry -- By individual authors
ISBN 0-618-06408-7 pa
LC 93-45642
This collection of Swenson's poetry "brings together poems from several earlier books, as well as poems published
only in magazines, and introduces us to nine splendid poems published here for the first time. This collection . . . is
brought together with special attention to poems describing
the environment; poems of tides and the sea, of birds and
gardens, of moods and seasons, of self and others. . . . This
is a collection to be treasured; it belongs in all libraries with
even a modest selection of poetry." Libr J

Taggart, John

Is music; selected poems. edited by Peter
O'Leary; foreword, C.D. Wright. Copper Canyon
Press 2010 353p pa $19   **811**
1. Poetry -- By individual authors
ISBN 978-1-55659-304-8 pa; 1-55659-304-X a
LC 2010-04655
"Metaphor, then, is fundamental to Taggart's poetics,
particularly a kind of 'serial metaphor,' a process of making metaphor that is always in motion, like Taggart's musical line, always singing into new meanings, approaching
it, which cannot be said—which is light, which is silence,
which is a poem." Harp & Altar

★ **Pastorelles**. Flood Editions 2004 104p pa
$13.95 **811**
1. Poetry -- By individual authors
ISBN 0-974690-21-X
LC 2004-303826
"Among the small number of poets who have followed
the difficult path of Zukofsky, George Oppen, Lorraine Niedecker, and William Bronk, John Taggart has kept more
closely to the Objectivist trail than most, while at the same
time developing his own signature style and deepening his

explorations into the strata where vision, music, and language converge. Pastorelles may be his most consistent and
fully realized collection, one that maintains and enlivens a
literary movement that, even after decades, has still not been
granted the degree of attention and critical analysis it deserves." Am Book Rev

Tanning, Dorothea

Coming to that; poems. Graywolf Press 2011
55p   **811**
1. Poetry -- By individual authors
ISBN 1555976018 pa; 9781555976019 pa
"Tanning's poems are beautifully created, filled with rich
rhythms and imagery. Mostly, they are made of individual
tableaux and artistic vistas, sometimes filled with flights of
the fantastic. . . . Often ironic and often filled with wisdom
and humor, a Tanning poem asks readers to believe in her
artistic vision. These are poems of beginnings and choices,
of marriage and aging, and of creation—poems still filled
with wondering." Libr J

Tarn, Nathaniel

Selected poems; 1950-2000. Wesleyan Univer-
sity Press 2002 335p $45; pa $19.95   **811**
1. Poetry -- By individual authors
ISBN 978-0-8195-6541-9; 0-8195-6541-5; 978-0-
8195-6542-6 pa; 0-8195-6542-3 pa
LC 2002-1701
"Arranged chronologically, [this volume] has reprints
from nineteen of Tarn's thirty-five books. Here the literary
reader can find reality hybrids and can experience the camaraderie of whole image systems from the twentieth century.
No syllable is lonely or aloof. One is often reminded, by
Tarn's references, his subjects, and his dedications, not only
of Blake but of Yeats, Vallejo, Charles Olson, and Robert
Duncan. Like those writers, his work brings together mythology, Western and Eastern philosophy (including Gnostic thought), political commentary, scientific investigations,
naturalist descriptions and very personal love poetry." Jacket

Tate, James

Selected poems. Wesleyan Univ. Press 1991
239p hardcover o.p. pa $18.95   **811**
1. Poetry -- By individual authors
ISBN 978-0-8195-1192-8; 0-8195-1192-7
LC 90-50918
Tate has "created a voice and a kind of poem that no
one else could have written. His comedy works not only to
entertain, which it does marvelously—he has the rare ability
to be very, very funny on the page—but partly to cover and
partly to reveal underlying disorientation and angst." N Y
Times Book Rev

Shroud of the gnome; poems. Ecco Press 1997
72p hardcover o.p. pa $15   **811**
1. Poetry -- By individual authors
ISBN 0-880015-62-4 pa
LC 97-16224
"The master of our idioms takes us on another dizzy,
dangerous careen through absurd and disintegrating Americana, with his speakers looking on bemusedly as their folk
narratives spin out of control. Tate . . . continues to draw on

small-town kitsch, haywire nature documentaries and 'a gi-antess by the name of Anna Swan' to fuel his often hilarious antistories. The joke has not tired." Publ Wkly

Worshipful Company of Fletchers; poems. Ecco Press 1994 82p hardcover o.p. pa $13   **811**

1. Poetry -- By individual authors
ISBN 0-880014-31-8 pa

LC 94-9821

The author "offers a collection full of confused narra-tive voices, prosaic images made startlingly fresh, and land-scapes that curve at the sides like hallucinations. . . . Tate is at his best when he weaves into his shimmering language such ordinary objects as toy poodles, crayons, Camp Fire Girls, and gum wrappers. In so doing, he solicits the reader with the familiar, then proceeds to act as trail guide to other worlds." Booklist

The **ghost** soldiers; poems. Ecco 2008 217p $22.95   **811**

1. Poetry -- By individual authors
ISBN 978-0-06-143694-9; 0-06-143694-1

LC 2007-29856

"These poems engage everything from war to police-state oppression to romance to small-town family life. Aliens make appearances, as do mythical creatures, talking animals, shadowy government agencies and malevolent cor-porations. Tate is clearly responding to contemporary issues. . . . By locating humor in tragedy, by highlighting the false connections by which we mortals construct daily life, Tate distills the sad little details of existence into a potent elixir, at once pathetic and noble." PopMatters

Toomer, Jean

★ The **collected** poems of Jean Toomer; edited by Robert B. Jones and Margery Toomer Latimer; with an introduction and textual notes by Robert B. Jones. University of N.C. Press 1988 xxxv, 111p hardcover o.p. pa $17.95   **811**

1. Poetry -- By individual authors
ISBN 978-0-8078-4209-6; 0-8078-4209-5

LC 87-19203

"This is the only collected edition of poems by Jean Toomer, the enigmatic Afro-American writer, Gurdjieffian guru, and Quaker convert who is perhaps best known for his 1923 lyrical narrative, Cane. The fifty-five poems here—most of them previously unpublished—chart a fascinating evolution of artistic consciousness." Univ Press Books for Public Libr

Trinidad, David

Dear Prudence; new and selected poems. Turtle Point 2011 493p pa $19   **811**

1. Poetry -- By individual authors
ISBN 978-1-933527-47-5

A collection of poetry from gay poet Trinidad.

The author's "lucid, amusing, and sad journal poems, memoir poems, prose poems, couplets, elegies, sonnets, and impressive pantoums may seem to valorize trash, but that trash sustains a flawed yet invaluable soul aching for loving acceptance." Booklist

Troupe, Quincy

★ **Transcircularities**; new and selected poems. Coffee House Press 2002 368p $30; pa $17 **811**

1. Poetry -- By individual authors
ISBN 1-56689-137-X; 1-56689-135-3 pa

LC 2002-71277

Troupe's "verse returns continually to swing, bebop and free-jazz giants, imitating, commemorating or praising Col-trane, Duke, Bud Powell and others in a series of musicianly poems culminating in the recent 'Back to the Dream Time: Miles Speaks from the Dead.' Troupe's forms, driven by performability, range from ecstatic odes to overtly political expostulations." Publ Wkly

Twichell, Chase

Horses where the answers should have been; new and selected poems. Copper Canyon Press 2010 255p pa $19   **811**

1. Poetry -- By individual authors
ISBN 978-1-55659-318-5; 1-55659-318-X

LC 2009-48885

"To read a well done 'selected poems' is to follow a life, and we find that here as we watch the poet grow from one in love with thought and language to one who quietly yet in-tensely contemplates the world by leaning toward the essen-tial. Hers is a world of wounded beauty which she confronts and records for us." N Y Journal of Books

Includes bibliographical references

Updike, John

Collected poems, 1953-1993. Knopf 1993 xxiv, 387p il hardcover o.p. pa $25   **811**

1. Poetry -- By individual authors
ISBN 978-0-679-76204-1; 0-679-76204-3

LC 92-28957

"From the outset Updike's poems are crisp and exact. There is a mock humbleness, ready wit, and divine concrete-ness to his subjects, an unrelenting curiosity behind his de-scriptions, and a prodding tension between the tactile and the abstract. . . . From the cocky exuberance of 'Midpoint,' a 1968 autobiographical cycle, to the wry, tender mischief of poems about domesticity, marriage, and aging, Updike's thrill over the unending discovery of poetry inspires images and metaphors of time-stopping perfection as well as humor rich in grace and knowingness." Booklist

Includes bibliographical references

Endpoint and other poems. Alfred A. Knopf 2009 97p $25   **811**

1. Poetry -- By individual authors
ISBN 978-0-307-27286-7; 0-307-27286-9

LC 2009-922927

"The heart of 'Endpoint' turns out to be its opening sec-tion, which forms a sequence, beginning with poems writ-ten on the author's recent birthdays, continuing through his bouts with cancer, and ending a month before his death on the North Shore. The poems, often written in a jauntily varied iambic pentameter, read like lineated journal entries, but a feeling of necessity runs beneath each of them. . . . This blend of urgency and poise shows in the language it-self. Line after line, Updike seems driven to get the world, and the word, right. The poems are dignified everywhere by his lucidity of vision and his inventiveness of phrasing." Boston Globe

Valentine, Jean

Door in the mountain; new and collected poems, 1965-2003. Wesleyan University Press 2004 285p $29.95 **811**

1. Poetry -- By individual authors
ISBN 0-8195-6712-4

LC 2004-16019

"The defiant, angular, yet propulsively emotional recent poems that occupy the first and last parts of the book should please both fans of Valentine's earliest poetry and fans of her strongly feminist middle period." Publ Wkly

Includes bibliographical references

Van Duyn, Mona

★ **Selected** poems. Knopf 2002 218p $27.50; pa $16 **811**

1. Poetry -- By individual authors
ISBN 0-375-41369-3; 0-375-70980-0 pa

LC 2001-50672

"Characterized by candor and compassion, Van Duyn's poetry depicts the pleasures and drudgeries of middle-class American life, an approach that at its best becomes an exploration of the spiritual and psychological dimensions of that life. . . . The casually formal surfaces of Van Duyn's poems often resemble those of her model, Elizabeth Bishop, and like Bishop she excels at both formal and free verse." N Y Times Book Rev

Wakoski, Diane

The **diamond** dog. Anhinga Press 2010 110p pa $15 **811**

1. Poetry -- By individual authors
ISBN 978-1-934695-15-9; 1-934695-15-7

Wakoski's "work is often associated with the Deep Image school, with its allegiance to the Jungian imagery said to comprise the collective unconscious, as well as the Confessional and Beat movements in poetry. . . . All of these – the Jungian images, the tendency to confess, the wild leaps and unruly rhythms of the Beat poets, the theme of abandonment – figure in 'The Diamond Dog.' By now, though, Wakoski is able to look back over her 22 books and connect these concerns in the essay called 'Creating a Personal Mythology' that begins the book. Here she provides a career perspective that her fans will welcome. Just as important, she describes a way of writing that young poets will be able to make their own. . . . Wakoski's rhythms are jazzy and easygoing; they're accepting of the world in all its crunchy variety, and they invite the reader to accept as well. The best way to describe her poetics is to say that she asks the reader to go for a walk with her." Christ Sci Monit

Walcott, Derek

★ **Collected** poems, 1948-1984. Farrar, Straus & Giroux 1986 515p hardcover o.p. pa $20 **811**

1. Poetry -- By individual authors
ISBN 0-374-52025-9 pa

LC 85-20688

"It is difficult to think of a poet in our century who— without ever betraying his native sources—has so organi-

cally assimilated the evolution of English literature from the Renaissance to the present, who has absorbed the Classical and Judeo-Christian past, and who has mined the history of Western painting as Walcott has. Throughout his entire body of work he has managed to hold in balance his passionate moral concerns with the ideal of art." Poetry

Includes bibliographical references

★ **Omeros**. Farrar, Straus & Giroux 1990 325p hardcover o.p. pa $16 **811**

1. Poetry -- By individual authors
ISBN 0-374-52350-9 pa

LC 90-33592

"No poet rivals Mr. Walcott in humor, emotional depth, lavish inventiveness in language or in the ability to express the thoughts of his characters and compel the reader to follow the swift mutations of ideas and images in their minds. This wonderful story moves in a spiral, replicating human thought." N Y Times Book Rev

The **prodigal**. Farrar, Straus and Giroux 2004 112p $20 **811**

1. Poetry -- By individual authors
ISBN 0-374-23743-3

LC 2004-5147

"The constants in Nobel laureate Walcott's work are the ravishing beauty of his language, his attunement to the sensuous, his feel for the pulse of history in landscape and seascape, and his despair over the contrast between the glory of European art and the prejudice and brutality that stoked the European conquest of the New World." Booklist

Walcott, Derek, 1930-

White egrets; poems. Farrar, Straus and Giroux 2010 86p $24 **811**

1. Poetry -- By individual authors
ISBN 978-0-374-28929-4; 0-374-28929-8

LC 2009-31895

The author draws the poems in this collection from his Caribbean roots, a love of the Western literary tradition, exotic travel, the wonders of nature, and love, both old and new, as well as the passage of time and the complications that attend age. It is the quest for new love, and the recognition of age, celebrated with grace and wisdom in a delightfully lyrical language, that lie at the heart of this collection. Libr J

Waldman, Anne

In the room of never grieve; new and selected poems, 1985-2003. Coffee House Press 2003 494p il $30 **811**

1. Poetry -- By individual authors
ISBN 978-1-566-89145-5; 1-566-89145-0

LC 2003-55096

"If early work found [Waldman] most engaged with the New York School, these later poems integrate her passions for Buddhism and ethnopoetics into a unique style of vocal, unabashedly current-event-laden, collagistic, wide-ranging work. Waldman's quest to find forms appropriate to her shamanistic, didactic content is particularly compelling in Marriage: A Sentence, with its liquefied gender roles and synthesis of influences ranging from Stein to Corso. . . . Waldman's untiring efforts to link language, ritual and political action come through clearly, urgently and often beautifully." Publ Wkly

Includes bibliographical references and indexes

Waldrop, Keith

   Transcendental studies; a trilogy. University of California Press 2009 201p $50; pa $19.95   **811**

  1. Poetry -- By individual authors

   ISBN 978-0-520-25877-8; 978-0-520-25878-5 pa
                          LC 2008-25958

   "Comprising three sequences—each almost a book in itself—plus an epilogue, it is an extended philosophical meditation on what are, broadly, the major themes of all poetry: perception, the imagination, the body, and how the human inner life interacts with the larger world. In mostly short, jagged free verse pieces, Waldrop goes at these lofty concepts head-on in accessible, if cerebral, language." Publ Wkly

Waldrop, Rosmarie

   Driven to abstraction. New Directions 2010 133p pa $16.95   **811**

  1. Poetry -- By individual authors

   ISBN 978-0-8112-1879-5; 0-8112-1879-1
                          LC 2010-14992

   "Waldrop continues to actualize surprising poems. Language is active and it enacts. In Driven to Abstraction, questions are often answers—'Only God can create out of nothing. But did he use up the void?'— and statements often questions. This specialized form of constructing prose builds many lessons; sidling up against bigger and more layered themes, the book reads like a semester full of engaging seminars." Coldfront

Walker, Alice

   Hard times require furious dancing; new poems. foreword and illustrations by Shiloh McCloud. New World Library 2010 165p il $18   **811**

  1. Poetry -- By individual authors

   ISBN 978-1-57731-930-6
                          LC 2010-29972

   In this poetry collection, the author "writes of loss and disappointment, and the strength that rises from meeting them unflinchingly. . . . These are powerful anthems of womanhood and age, although just as likely to be empowering to men and to the not-yet-old." Booklist

Walsh, Michael

   The **dirt** riddles; poems. University of Arkansas Press 2010 74p pa $16   **811**

  1. Poetry -- By individual authors

   ISBN 9781557289254; 1557289255
                          LC 2009046590

   This poetry "collection depicts childhood on a family farm and a return to the land as an adult. Walsh's love for rural America is palpable in his attention to the senses. . . . Riddles tells an American story—the end of the family farm, a discovery of sexuality in rural America—but also the universal tale of an attempted return to Paradise. Earthy, pared-down, the lyrics comprising Riddles involve little flash, taking instead a tack of honesty and directness." Antioch Rev

Warren, Robert Penn

   ★ The **collected** poems of Robert Penn Warren; edited by John Burt; with a foreword by Harold Bloom. Louisiana State Univ. Press 1998 xxvi, 830p $44.95   **811**

  1. Poetry -- By individual authors

   ISBN 0-8071-2333-1
                          LC 98-26104

   "This immense volume gathers 15 books of poetry—as well as uncollected verse from the beginning and end of his writing life—from a formidable American man of letters and our first poet laureate. . . . Scholars will especially cherish the careful, copious textual and explanatory notes provided by Warren's literary executor Burt . . . and fans of American poetry and literary history alike should welcome this opportunity to explore the prodigious oeuvre of one of the New Criticism's most forceful, convincing proponents." Publ Wkly

Whalen, Philip

   ★ The **collected** poems of Philip Whalen; edited by Michael Rothenberg. Weseleyan University Press 2007 871p $49.95   **811**

  1. Poetry -- By individual authors

   ISBN 978-0-8195-6859-5; 0-8195-6859-7
                          LC 2007-16905

   "Whalen was a Beat writer who read at the famous Six Gallery event at which Ginsberg debuted 'Howl.' He adored Jane Austen and Gertrude Stein, had more than a passing knowledge of several realms of science, read widely in ancient and modern history, and was a thoroughly cultivated gent, 'a Fat and Silly poet' who rarely took himself seriously. He committed the last 35 years of his life to Zen Buddhism. . . . The distinguishing features of Whalen's poetry are its playful freedom, . . . its whizzing momentum, its offhand erudition, its quick eye, its radar ear. But what stands out is his voice. No other American poet sounds like Whalen, though Ginsberg in his less vatic moments and Kerouac in his novels come close." Phoenix

   Includes bibliographical references

Wheatley, Phillis

   ★ The **poems** of Phillis Wheatley; edited with an introduction by Julian D. Mason, Jr. rev & enl ed; University of N.C. Press 1989 235p hardcover o.p. pa $22.95   **811**

  1. Poetry -- By individual authors

   ISBN 0-8078-4245-1 pa
                          LC 88-23280

   This volume contains all of the poems and letters known to have been written by Wheatley, America's first significant black woman writer.

Whitman, Walt

★ **Complete** poetry and collected prose. Library of Am. 1982 1380p $35; pa $17.95 **811**
1. Poetry -- By individual authors
ISBN 0-940450-02-X; 1-883011-35-3 pa
LC 81-20768

★ **Leaves** of grass; edited and with a new afterword by David S. Reynolds. 150th anniversary ed.; Oxford University Press 2005 167p $23 **811**
1. Poetry -- By individual authors
ISBN 0-19-518342-8
LC 2004-26509
"The book, radical in form and content, takes its title from the themes of fertility, universality, and cyclical life. . . . As he revised and added to the original edition, Whitman arranged the poems in a significant autobiographical order." Reader's Ency. 4th edition

★ **Selected** poems; Harold Bloom, editor. Library of Am. 2003 xxxi, 221p $20 **811**
1. Poetry -- By individual authors
ISBN 1-931082-32-4
LC 2002-32124
The editor "is concerned with Whitman's construction of his all-encompassing persona, and he selects with that in mind. . . . Bloom connects Whitman's project to the thesis of his The American Religion (1992) that the tendency of religion in America is to replace God with man, and with the fragments, Bloom presents explicit evidence of the attempt." Booklist
Includes bibliographical references

Whittier, John Greenleaf

Selected poems; Brenda Wineapple, editor. Library of America 2004 xxvii, 187p $20 **811**
1. Poetry -- By individual authors
ISBN 978-1-931082-59-4; 1-931082-59-6
LC 2003-60483
"Touching and effective as [many of] these poems are, there is a longer one that ensures Whittier's place in our canon. Of course I have 'SnowBound' in mind. This poem of over nine hundred lines evokes a rural way of life, already past when it was written, in its memories of a family isolated in their farmhouse for a week by a blizzard. . . . This new selection may not restore Whittier to the schoolroom wall, but surely it will help readers reassess the author of one major long poem and a score of attractive lyrics and narratives that deserve their place in our poetic tradition." Sewanee Rev

Wilbur, Richard

★ **Collected** poems, 1943-2004. Harcourt 2004 608p il $35 **811**
1. Poetry -- By individual authors
ISBN 0-15-101105-2
LC 2004-9228
A comprehensive collection of works written throughout the course of the poet's more than sixty-year career includes "In Trackless Woods" and several new and previously unpublished pieces
"Technically, Wilbur remains assured and impressive; he is the premier American master of formal verse.

His knowledge has expanded with his life, and his wit has grown in humor while mellowing linguistically. . . . He's indispensable." Booklist

Wilbur, Richard, 1921-

Anterooms; new poems and translations. Houghton Mifflin Harcourt 2010 63p $20 **811**
1. Poetry -- By individual authors
ISBN 978-0-547-35811-6; 0-547-35811-3
LC 2010-05772
"The better work in Anterooms, however limited in quantity, is as good as anything Wilbur has ever written, and upholds certain virtues other poets would do well to acknowledge, even if they travel roads different from the relatively straight one Wilbur has followed." N Y Times Book Rev

Williams, C. K.

★ **Collected** poems. Farrar, Straus and Giroux 2006 682p $40 **811**
1. Poetry -- By individual authors
ISBN 978-0-374-12652-0; 0-374-12652-6
LC 2005-51867
"This weighty, even daunting, tome shows new and old readers the long arc of this Pulitzer Prize and National Book Award winner's career, from the morbid sanguinities of his apprentice work to the careful, moving, stanzaic focus evident in 21 new poems." Publ Wkly

On Whitman. Princeton University Press 2010 187p $19.95 **811**
1. Authors 2. Essayists 3. Poets
ISBN 978-0-691-14472-6; 0-691-14472-9
Williams "takes us on a tour of Leaves of Grass as if it were an old, beloved neighborhood. His brief but illuminating chapters cover a range of topics including Whitman's vision, his notebooks, his ever-expanding 'I,' his relationship with Ralph Waldo Emerson, his faith in the imagination, his thematic use of nature, sex, and the body, and his spiritual view of death. To readers already acquainted with Leaves of Grass, these are familiar-enough topics. We know this neighborhood well, especially because Whitman himself spent so much time identifying its key landmarks. But while somewhat predictable in its conception, On Whitman is revelatory when it comes to explaining Whitman's poetic gifts." Philadelphia Inquirer

Wait. Farrar, Straus and Giroux 2010 125p $25; pa $14 **811**
1. Poetry -- By individual authors
ISBN 978-0-374-28591-3; 0-374-28591-8; 978-0-374-53276-5 pa
LC 2009-31893
The author "writes two kinds of poems: proselike pieces that have a narrative drive and tight, short-lined lyrics that seem inspired by haiku. Generally focusing on dramatic situations in which a person—usually an 'I'—muses on his interior life, all of the poems are surprisingly accessible, especially since some of them seem like examinations of conscience. . . . This book belongs on all poetry lovers' shelves." Libr J

Williams, Jonathan

★ **Jubilant** thicket; new & selected poems. Jonathan Williams. Copper Canyon Press 2005 pa $20   **811**

1. Poetry -- By individual authors
ISBN 1-55659-202-7

LC 2004-20436

"Pared down from 1,450 works over 55 years, this selection features jaunty dances through naughty woods . . . , jokes to and about Ezra Pound, selected listings from the Western Carolina Telephone Company phone book, limericks, 'metafours' (poems in which each line has four words), a poem for each Mahler symphony and acrostics using the names of friends like Guy Davenport. . . . By the end of the book, it becomes clear that Williams can make a verse out of whatever's at hand; the result is a kind of commonplace book for a life lived, with wry but inextinguishable enthusiasm, in the company of artists and arts." Publ Wkly

Williams, Miller

Time and the tilting earth; poems. Louisiana State University Press 2008 51p $45; pa $16.95 **811**

1. Poetry -- By individual authors
ISBN 978-0-8071-3352-1; 0-8071-3352-3; 978-0-8071-3353-8 pa; 0-8071-3353-1 pa

LC 2007-47237

This collection "offers many pleasures. Chief among these are Williams's way of entwining the pure earthiness of language as it's spoken with rigorous metrical precision, and, analogously, his affection for the quotidian, with an insistence on confronting unanswerable but unavoidable existential problems. In poem after poem, he mingles the low and the high in both form and content, bringing a sense of cleareyed practicality to life's big questions and a keenly honed poetic technique to the cadences of Arkansas porch talk." N Y Times Book Rev

Williams, Philip Lee

The **flower** seeker; an epic poem of William Bartram. Mercer University Press 2010 454p il $55; pa $25   **811**

1. Poetry -- By individual authors
ISBN 978-0-88146-228-9; 0-88146-228-4; 978-0-88146-221-0 pa; 0-88146-221-7 pa

LC 2010-20190

"Extracts from Bartram's Travels, reworked by Williams (as Ezra Pound reworked the sources for his Cantos), are the underlying strata of this work, which pays homage to the epic tradition in a distinctively American way. Curiosity and delight, beauty and sadness, loss and yearning, and all the 'fragrant disorder of this world' are mingled here in a narrative that suggests the gratuitous abundance of Creation itself. And the physical book has been crafted with an expansive generosity that catches the spirit of the poem." Books and Culture

Williams, Tennessee

The **collected** poems of Tennessee Williams; edited by David Roessel and Nicholas Moschovakis.

New Directions Pub 2002 xxxi, 304p il hardcover o.p. pa $18.95   **811**

1. Poetry -- By individual authors
ISBN 978-0-8112-1691-3; 0-8112-1691-8

LC 2001-55760

"The painful longing and sense of loss that inhabit Williams's plays and stories are no less present in the poems." Oyster Boy Rev

Williams, William Carlos

★ **Paterson**; prepared by Christopher MacGowan. rev ed; New Directions 1992 311p hardcover o.p. pa $15.95 **811**

1. Poetry -- By individual authors
ISBN 978-0-8112-1298-4; 0-8112-1298-X

LC 92-22956

"Set in Paterson, N.J., the poem is a statement on contemporary civilization. Williams uses one dominant metaphor throughout: the city is the human mind beside the river of time; the language of contemporary events (the waterfall) gives the only kind of meaning possible in the flux of time. The poem is composed of lyrics, narrative episodes, prose interludes, bits of letters, etc., to comprise an ecstatic statement on human life." Herzberg. Reader's Ency of Am Lit

★ The **collected** poems of William Carlos Williams. New Directions 1986 2v v1 $40; v1 pa $23.95; v2 $38; v2 pa $22.95   **811**

1. Poetry -- By individual authors
ISBN 0-8112-0999-7 v1; 0-8112-1187-8 v1 pa; 0-8112-1063-4 v2; 0-8112-1188-6 v2 pa

"Williams's poetry is firmly rooted in the commonplace detail of everyday American life. He conceived of the poem as an object: a record of direct experience that deals with the local and the particular. He abandoned conventional rhyme and meter in an effort to reduce the barrier between the reader and his consciousness of his immediate surroundings. . . . Williams's original approach to poetry, his insistence on the importance of the ordinary, and his successful attempts at making his verse as 'tactile' as the spoken word had a far-reaching effect on American poetry." Reader's Ency. 4th edition

Wiman, Christian

Every riven thing. Farrar, Straus and Giroux 2010 93p $24   **811**

1. Poetry -- By individual authors
ISBN 978-0-374-15036-5; 0-374-15036-2

LC 2010-12613

"The work here is searingly honest and beautifully crafted, and it establishes Wiman in his most important public role: a gifted poet whose work cannot be ignored. Wiman's talent is apparent from the opening pages, as are his two central struggles – with illness and faith. . . . [His] ability to love the unconventional or unlovely is one of the qualities that makes his work so memorable and, at times, endearing." Christ Sci Monit

Winters, Yvor

Selected poems; Thom Gunn, editor. Library of America 2003 xxviii, 171p $20   **811**

  1. Poetry -- By individual authors

  ISBN 978-1-93108-250-1; 1-93108-250-2

               LC 2003-46638

A volume of verse by "one of the most famous critics and teachers of his lifetime, whose poetry was then more respected than discussed. Now it seems to be some of the best from his generation of American poets. His early work . . . exemplifies imagism at its best, and it is based in the American West rather than the classical Greece that predominates in the work of H. D., the best imagist, Winters' later, formally precise poetry is elegant, allusive, profound, and rather dour, demanding careful reading and rereading and always repaying the effort. Adding immense value to this edition is the inclusion of an autobiographical story with an eerie account of self-confrontation in which Gunn sees the pivot between Winters' early and late poetic styles." Booklist

Wright, C. D.

One with others; [a little book of her days] Copper Canyon Press 2010 168p pa $18   **811**

  1. African Americans -- Civil rights -- Poetry 2. Poetry -- By individual authors

  ISBN 978-1-55659-324-6; 1-55659-324-4

               LC 2010-16789

"In August, 1969, a Memphis man known as Sweet Willie Wine led a group of black men on a four-day March Against Fear, from West Memphis to Little Rock, passing through the small towns of the Arkansas delta. . . . [This book] tells the story of the march, and of the only outsider to join it, a small-town white woman, Margaret Kaelin McHugh, whom Wright calls V. . . . [It] represents Wright's most audacious experiment yet in loading up lyric with evidentiary fact. . . . An affecting element of this book is the way its elegiac impulses accord with, even as they chafe against, the documentary impulses." New Yorker

★ **Steal** away; selected and new poems. Copper Canyon Press 2002 235p $25; pa $17   **811**

  1. Poetry -- By individual authors

  ISBN 1-55659-172-1; 1-55659-194-2 pa

               LC 2001-7423

Wright's "poems are crazy quilts constructed out of bits of conversation, a to-do list, dreams, a treatment for a harrowing silent film, and a saxophone solo, but Wright also offers sophisticated readings of the routines and cycle of ordinary life, and ponders the amazing persistence of the ever-hungry body and the tricky mind. It's a boon to have such a wealth of her crackling, intelligent, erotic, 'painfully beautiful,' keep-you-on-your-toes poems in one place. New works accompany selections from nine previous, mostly out of print collections, and all are electrifying in their clear-eyed reports on desire, determination, and survival." Booklist

Wright, Charles

Appalachia. Farrar, Straus & Giroux 1998 67p hardcover o.p. pa $12 **811**

  1. Poetry -- By individual authors

  ISBN 978-0-374-52624-5; 0-374-52624-9

               LC 98-16803

Wright's "inquisitive poems reside at the crux of faith and art: the realization that no matter how sincerely one prays, or how devotedly one writes, the universe and the divine force that animates it remain out of reach of language, reason, and imagination. . . . Wright tries to connect with the spiritual by conjuring the ancient beaming of stars, winter's starkness, and the valor of flowers. Finally, in sweet, bemused surrender, he acknowledges both the impossibility of certainty, and our insatiable hunger for it." Booklist

★ **Negative** blue; selected later poems. Farrar, Straus & Giroux 2000 206p $23; pa $15   **811**

  1. Poetry -- By individual authors

  ISBN 0-374-22020-4; 0-374-52773-3 pa

               LC 99-36987

The author "collects a decade's worth of striking description and laid-back meditation in this sample of work from his last three books. . . . Wright's power lies less in whole poems than in lines within them: those linear strenghts owe something to Ezra Pound, and something more to the antiphonal balances of the Psalms. Wright ends the volume with seven new short poems." Publ Wkly

Sestets. Farrar, Straus and Giroux 2009 75p $23 **811**

  1. Poetry -- By individual authors

  ISBN 978-0-374-26115-3; 0-374-26115-6

               LC 2008-33990

"Wright's poems don't bear down toward conclusions, they expand and evanesce as if in a valiant, impossible effort to comprehend and demonstrate Wittgenstein's dictum that 'the world is all that is the case.' Wright's new collection of short poems is less a book unto itself than the next installment in a continuous poem he's been writing for 40-odd years." N Y Times Book Rev

Wright, James Arlington

★ **Above** the river; the complete poems. [by] James Wright; with an introduction by Donald Hall. Farrar, Straus & Giroux 1990 xxxvii, 387p hardcover o.p. pa $20   **811**

  1. Poetry -- By individual authors

  ISBN 978-0-374-52282-7; 0-374-52282-0

               LC 89-16538

"The narrowed range of Wright's characteristic subjects and format, the very delicacy of his instincts, confine him. But his best poems, with their grace and intelligence, not only stand as a rebuke to most of the glib work of his time, but remain among the finest examples of the midcentury American lyric." N Y Times Book Rev

Wright, Jay

★ **Transfigurations**; collected poems. Louisiana State Univ. Press 2000 619p $59.95; pa $24.95 **811**

  1. Poetry -- By individual authors

  ISBN 0-8071-2629-2; 0-8071-2630-6 pa

               LC 00-40560

"Lyric poetry is a way of compressing experience into a heightened moment, but what happens when the experience is one of wanting not to be contained? Wright is an African-American poet who has contended with this dilemma for the last thirty years, and the result is a substantial collection of work. His forcefully musical rhythms drive even poems of everyday experience to a pleasingly contradictory transport. And the later, meditative poems are bound to the world by their attention to the sensual within the spiritual." New Yorker

Youmans, Marly

The **throne** of Psyche. Mercer University Press 2011 106p $30; pa $18 **811**

1. Poetry -- By individual authors

ISBN 978-0-88146-246-3; 978-0-88146-232-6

LC 2011-02079

"Youmans is rather the classicist in outlook; some of her poems actually rhyme. The long title piece is a meditation on the myth of Cupid and Psyche, narrated by some of the characters. . . . Youmans is a nature poet, given to the darker forms of wildness. Her poem 'A Fire in Ice' — a 'riposte' to Billy Collins' 'Taking Off Emily Dickinson's Clothes' — concludes 'Here waits the sphinx whose secret power / In riddles found her finest flower.' Well, someone who likes sphinx riddles can be expected to be a little elusive in meaning, and Youmans can be as slippery as A.R. Ammons sometimes. At other times, though, she's quite accessible." Wilmington Star

Young, Kevin

Ardency; a chronicle of the Amistad rebels. compiled from authentic sources by Kevin Lowell Young. Alfred A. Knopf 2011 249p il map $27.95 **811**

1. Poetry -- By individual authors 2. Slavery -- Poetry

ISBN 978-0-307-26764-1; 0-307-26764-4

LC 2010-30007

This poetry collection "chronicles the slave mutiny aboard the schooner Amistad in 1839. This three-part book focuses on the 53 Africans who rebelled against their would-be slave owners. Young expertly blends cultural and social history as well as religion to dramatize the lives of the rebels. His evocative use of language—punctuated with stunning metaphors—keeps the historical context clear while moving the gripping true story forward." Libr J

Zapruder, Matthew

Come on all you ghosts; Matthew Zapruder. Copper Canyon Press 2010 xi, 111p (alk. paper) $16 **811**

1. American poetry 2. Poetry -- By individual authors

ISBN 1556593228; 9781556593222

LC 2010016787

This book of poetry is written by Matthew Zapruder, the winner of the William Carlos Williams Award. The title poem is an elegy for heroes and mentors—from David Foster Wallace to Zapruder's father—and demonstrates "a[n] . . . expansive range for the poet, highlighting as well a larger body of poetry that . . . wrestles with the desires to live rightly, to make art, and to confront the vast events of the day." (Publisher's note) "Zapruder invokes a variety of second persons: sometimes it's a particular intimate, as in . . . 'Letter to a Lover' or . . . 'Poem for Hannah,' sometimes a recognizable public figure, as in . . . 'Poem for Ferlinghetti.' . . . Greeting and address help the poet to escape the solitary confinement of consciousness." (LA Review of Books)

The poet "speaks 'with a voice that pretends to be shy/ and actually is, always in search of the question/ that might make you ask me one in return.' In his . . . signature, meandering style, he'll often begin with simple, even childlike

observations ('Oh this Diet Coke is really good') that set off associative chains in search of subjects that resonate, psychologically or philosophically, with past personal experiences. . . . Seeming to discover themselves as they go, Zapruder's improvisations (or so they appear) enlist the reader as coexplorer, stumbling into candid self-revelations ('I am also/ always balancing/ on the smooth blade of not/ letting other people down') or surreal quips ('I feel like an elk getting a pelvic exam') with wide-eyed grace." Libr J

Zucker, Rachel

Museum of accidents. Wave Books 2009 78p $14 **811**

1. Poetry -- By individual authors

ISBN 9781933517421 pa

LC 2009-5831

"This is a startling book of poetry about motherhood—not a cooing little picture of mommy love but an effective snapshot of the chaos, emotional and otherwise, that ensues when a child enters your life. . . . Excellent reading for poetry lovers and a good means of persuading others that verse remains engaging and relevant." Libr J

Zukofsky, Louis

Selected poems; Charles Bernstein, editor. Library of America 2006 xxvii, 172p $20 **811**

1. Poetry -- By individual authors

ISBN 978-1-93108-295-2

LC 2006-40808

"Contemporary poet Charles Bernstein uses these pages skillfully to present a compact but diverse selection of Zukofsky's writing, and he supplies a cogent introduction to both the biography and the poetics." Tikkun

180 more; extraordinary poems for every day. selected and with an introduction by Billy Collins. Random House 2005 xxiii, 373p pa $14.95 **811**

1. American poetry 2. American poetry -- Collections 3. Poetry -- Collections

ISBN 0-8129-7296-1

LC 2005-42798

This is a second collection of 180 poems for each day of the school year, designed to expose high school students to poetry.

African-American poetry of the nineteenth century; an anthology. edited by Joan R. Sherman. University of Ill. Press 1992 506p hardcover o.p. pa $26.95 **811**

1. American poetry -- African American authors -- Collections

ISBN 0-252-06246-9 pa

LC 91-41709

"The introduction surveys the historical and cultural values of African American poetry. The poems themselves have historical as well as lyric value; unfamiliar as well as familiar poets are included. Though the poems are formal, the rhymes are generally unforced. . . . This anthology also includes an extensive bibliography to help researchers find other resources." Libr J

★ American poetry, the twentieth century. Library of Am. 2000 2v ea $35 **811**

1. American poetry -- 20th century 2. American poetry -- Collections

ISBN 1-88301-177-9 v1; 1-88301-178-7 v2

LC 99-43721

These volumes represent a "remarkable feat of assemblage, with excellent capsule biographies and explanatory notes at the end of each volume—the biographies, especially, are well worth reading." N Y Times Book Rev

Includes bibliographical references

★ American poetry: the nineteenth century; edited by John Hollander. Library of Am. 1993 2v ea $35 **811**

1. American poetry -- Collections

ISBN 0-940450-60-7 v1; 0-940450-78-X v2

LC 93-10702

An anthology of more than 1,000 poems by nearly 150 poets. Arrangement is chronological by poet's date of birth. Biographical sketches of the poets, a chronology of significant events from 1800 to 1900, and an essay on textual selection are included.

Hollander has compiled "a selection of nineteenth-century American verse so wonderfully catholic that it not just augments but supersedes every other similar collection." Booklist

★ American poetry: the seventeenth and eighteenth centuries; edited by David Shields. Library of America 2007 xxiii, 952p $40 **811**

1. American poetry -- Collections

ISBN 978-1-931082-90-7; 1-931082-90-1

LC 2007-929763

"Besides hefty helpings of the few figures meagerly represented in general American-lit surveys—Anne Bradstreet, Edward Taylor, John Trumbull, Timothy Dwight, Philip Freneau, Phyllis Wheatley—here are poems short and . . . long by dozens of others, most of them obscure to even thoroughgoing, historically minded poetry lovers. . . . The subject matter isn't all religion and politics. Work, family, leisure, and exceptional events and lives (one man recounts escape from the limited slavery that was indenture) are all written up. And, in regular rhymes and meters, it's all quite readable. Early-American history buffs as much as, if not more than, poetry readers may consider the book a gold mine." Booklist

Includes bibliographical references

American religious poems; an anthology by Harold Bloom. Harold Bloom and Jesse Zuba, editors. Library of America 2006 685p $40 **811**

1. American poetry -- Collections 2. Poetry -- Collections 3. Religious poetry 4. Religious poetry, American

ISBN 1-931082-74-X

LC 2006-41031

An anthology of "verse on Christian, Jewish, Islamic, Buddhist, Native American spiritual, Transcendentalist and even agnostic themes, from 17th-century European colonists (one poet is Roger Williams, who founded Rhode Island) to up-and-comers in contemporary verse. Pious readers will have no trouble finding high-quality poetry that confirms

their beliefs—from the monk Thomas Merton, the Anglican T.S. Eliot, the Jewish liturgical poet Esther Schor and the Louisiana-based Christian poet Martha Serpas. Yet from the 19th century to the present, from the decidedly heterodox Emily Dickinson forwards, the anthology often highlights the ways in which American spirituality has challenged all doctrines about who God is and what God does. . . . More than half of the book is taken up by 20th-century poets, who offer varied takes on what religion has come to mean in America." Publ Wkly

★ American war poetry; an anthology. edited by Lorrie Goldensohn. Columbia University Press 2006 413p $27.95 **811**

1. American poetry -- Collections 2. Poetry -- Collections 3. War poetry 4. War poetry, American

ISBN 0-231-13310-3

LC 2005-54762

"Arranged by war, the book begins with the Colonial period and proceeds through Whitman admiring Civil War soldiers crossing a river to end with Brian Turner, who published his first book in 2005, beckoning a bullet in contemporary Iraq. Many voices, by turns elegiac, outraged, rhetorical and ecstatic are represented." Publ Wkly

Includes bibliographical references

American wits; an anthology of light verse. John Hollander, editor. Library of America 2003 xxv, 194p $20 **811**

1. American poetry -- Collections 2. Humorous poetry -- Collections 3. Humorous poetry, American 4. Poetry -- Collections

ISBN 978-1-931082-49-5; 1-931082-49-9

LC 2003-46636

This anthology "offers some exceptionally clever writing, much of which will be unfamiliar to many readers (and therefore all the more amusing). Hollander sensibly allots the most space to Ogden Nash and Dorothy Parker; the selections from both are solid. But Hollander's good judgment is best demonstrated by the third most represented poet here, the screenwriter Samuel Hoffenstein (1890-1947). . . . The poetry world currently has a surplus of writers who are eager, sometimes even desperate, to be funny, but we're suffering from a shortage of genuine wit." Poetry (Modern Poetry Association)

Beat poets; selected and edited by Carmela Ciuraru. Knopf 2002 250p $12.50 **811**

1. American poetry -- Collections 2. Beat generation

ISBN 978-0-375-41332-2; 0-375-41332-4

LC 2002-510236

"The defining work of Allen Ginsberg and Jack Kerouac provides the foundation for this collection, which also features statements on Beat poetics, selections from the alternately ardent, incendiary, and earnest correspondence of Beat Generation writers, and the improvisational verse of such Beat legends as Robert Creeley, Diane Di Prima, Gregory Corso, Denise Levertov, Lawrence Ferlinghetti, Philip Whalen, Bob Kaufman, and Peter Orlovsky, along with the work of other women writers and the lesser-known poets of this school." Publisher's note

Blues poems; selected and edited by Kevin Young.
Knopf 2003 256p $12.50   **811**
1. American poetry -- Collections 2. Blues music --
Poetry
ISBN 978-0-375-41458-9; 0-375-41458-4
LC 2003-53149

A collection of "blues-influenced and blues-inflected poems from, among others, Gwendolyn Brooks, Allen Ginsberg, June Jordan, Richard Wright, Nikki Giovanni, Charles Wright, Yusef Komunyakaa, and Cornelius Eady. And here, too, are classic song lyrics—poems in their own right—from Bessie Smith, Robert Johnson, Ma Rainey, and Muddy Waters." Publisher's note

The Columbia history of American poetry; Jay Parini, editor; Brett C. Millier, associate editor. Columbia Univ. Press 1993 xxxi, 894p $86.50 **811**
1. American poetry -- History and criticism 2. Poetry
-- By individual authors
ISBN 0-231-07836-6
LC 92-29399

"These 31 essays by various experts in the field interrogate, dismantle, and ultimately reassemble the history of poetry in the United States, from the work of the slave George Moses Horton . . . to the writings of Beat, Black Arts, and Marxist-oriented Language Poets of today. The great figures of the past—Whitman, Poe, Eliot, and so on—still loom, yet each time we are made to see them in some new way. . . . An essential volume that shows how poetry intersects with our lives and vice versa." Libr J

Includes bibliographical references

Encyclopedia of American poetry, the twentieth century; edited by Eric L. Haralson. Fitzroy Dearborn Pubs. 2001 846p $125   **811**
1. American poetry -- 20th century 2. American poetry
-- 20th century -- History and criticism 3. American poetry -- Bio-bibliography 4. Poets, American --
Dictionaries 5. Reference books
ISBN 1-57958-240-0

"The volume features more than 400 entries written by academic contributors on individual poets, landmark poems, and major topics. The poet entries are usually 1,000 to 2,000 words long and offer critical treatment of the poet's career and major achievements along with a capsule biography. . . . Approximately one-third of the poet entries include subentries for one or more landmark poems. The 'major topics' entries are longer (around 3,000 words) and include periods or movements (Black Arts movement, Dada), verse traditions (often ethnic, such as Asian American poetry), and styles and themes (Confessional poetry, War and antiwar poetry)." Booklist

Every shut eye ain't asleep; an anthology of poetry by African Americans since 1945. edited by Michael Harper and Anthony Walton. Little, Brown 1994 327p hardcover o.p. pa $19   **811**
1. American poetry -- African American authors
2. American poetry -- African American authors --
Collections 3. American poetry -- Collections
ISBN 0-316-34710-8 pa
LC 93-10788

"Using Robert Hayden and Gwendolyn Brooks's poetry as 'emblematic' successes, this anthology selects 35 African American poets (spanning three generations) who were born between 1913 and 1962 and came of age after 1945. Besides the well-known Imamu Baraka, Lucille Clifton, Rita Dove, and Etheridge Knight, the editors feature little-known or younger poets like Elizabeth Alexander, Gerald Barrax, Jayne Cortex, and Dolores Kendrick." Libr J

From totems to hip-hop; edited by Ishmael Reed.
Thunder's Mouth Press 2003 xxx, 523p $34.95;
pa $17.95   **811**
1. American poetry -- 20th century 2. American poetry
-- Collections
ISBN 1-56025-500-5; 1-56025-458-0 pa
LC 2002-75691

This is "a dynamic and original anthology, an unprecedented amalgam of poets representing many facets of American culture and society." Booklist

Good poems; selected and introduced by Garrison Keillor. Viking 2002 xxvi, 476p $25.95; pa $15   **811**
1. American poetry 2. American poetry -- Collections
3. English poetry 4. English poetry -- Collections
ISBN 0-670-03126-7; 0-14-200344-1 pa
LC 2002-16881

Keillor "has put together a collection of close to 300 poems he has read during . . . [the] PBS broadcast, The Writer's Almanac. . . . Poems are arranged by 19 general themes, such as 'Snow,' 'Failure,' and 'A Good Life.' Authors range from well-known oldies like Emily Dickinson and Robert Frost to unknowns like C.K. Williams. . . . An outstanding feature of this collection is that the selections are all so accessible—even folks who say they don't like poetry can find something here to enjoy." SLJ

Harper's anthology of 20th century Native American poetry; edited by Duane Niatum. Harper & Row 1988 xxxii, 396p hardcover o.p. pa $24.95 **811**
1. American poetry -- Native American authors
ISBN 0-06-250666-8 pa
LC 86-45023

This collection "contains the work of 36 native American poets, with hearty selections from each. Among the 36 are poets near the mainstream (Scott Momaday, James Welch, Louise Erdrich); those in academe (Gerald Vizenor, Linda Hogan, Jim Barnes); those writing in the tribal oral tradition (Barney Bush, Peter Blue Cloud, Wendy Rose); and those working in a modernist voice (Gladys Cardiff, Paula Gunn Allen). This book belongs in every collection that claims to represent the multiple voices of American literature today." Booklist

Includes bibliographical references

Jazz poems. Alfred A. Knopf 2006 256p $12.50 **811**
1. American poetry -- Collections 2. Jazz music --
Poetry
ISBN 978-1-4000-4251-7; 1-4000-4251-8

A collection of poetry inspired by jazz music. Includes poems by Langston Hughes, E. E. Cummings, William Carlos Williams, Frank O'Hara, Gwendolyn Brooks, Yusef Komunyakaa, Charles Simic, Rita Dove, Ntozake Shange, Mark Doty, William Matthews, and C. D. Wright, among others.

★ The Oxford anthology of African-American poetry; edited by Arnold Rampersad; associate editor, Hilary Herbold. Oxford University Press 2006 432p $32.50 **811**
1. African Americans -- Poetry 2. American poetry -- African American authors -- Collections 3. Poetry -- Collections
ISBN 0-19-512563-0; 978-0-19-512563-4
LC 2005-15242
"Predicated on the fact that there is a vast body of poetry written by gifted black poets, this . . . anthology tells the story of African American culture and explicates its crucial role within the larger literary tradition. . . . There is much to admire about the artistry of the poems, and even more to discover about the African American experience." Booklist

★ The Oxford book of American poetry; chosen and edited by David Lehman; associate editor, John Brehm. Oxford University Press 2006 lvii, 1132p $35 **811**
1. American poetry 2. American poetry -- Collections 3. Poetry -- Collections
ISBN 0-19-516251-X; 978-0-19-516251-6
LC 2005-36590
"The book is not only a sound historical survey, but also gives the reader a powerful taste of poetry's impact upon the wider world." Economist
Includes bibliographical references

The Penguin anthology of twentieth-century American poetry; edited with an introduction by Rita Dove. Penguin Books 2011 lii, 599p $40 **811**
1. American poetry -- Collections
ISBN 978-0-14-310643-2
LC 2011036342
"Dove's incisive perception of the role of poetry in cultural and social awakenings infuses this zestful and rigorous gathering of poems both necessary and unexpected by 180 American poets. This landmark anthology will instantly enhance and invigorate every poetry shelf or section." Booklist

Poems from the women's movement; edited by Honor Moore. Library of America 2009 238p $20 **811**
1. American poetry -- Women authors 2. American poetry -- Women authors -- Collections 3. Feminist poetry 4. Women's movement
ISBN 978-1-59853-042-1
This is an anthology of poetry written by women during the women's movement of the late 1960s and 1970s.
"These direct, vibrant, potent, passionate, wild, strong, free, and freeing poems come less like a breath of fresh air than a strong wind." Booklist

Poetry 180; a turning back to poetry. selected and with an introduction by Billy Collins. Random House Trade Paperbacks 2003 xxiv, 323p pa $13.95 **811**
1. American poetry -- 21st century 2. American poetry

-- Collections
ISBN 0-8129-6887-5
LC 2002-36949
The editor "has collected 180 accessible modern poems: one for each day of the school year and together signifying a 180° turning back to poetry. These are poems, he says, you can 'get' the first time around, and he hopes that high schools will expose students to a poem a day via public address system or assemblies. A fine gathering of contemporary poets." Libr J
Includes bibliographical references

The Poetry anthology, 1912-2002; ninety years of America's most distinguished verse magazine. edited by Joseph Parisi & Stephen Young; with an introduction by Joseph Parisi. Ivan R. Dee 2002 lv, 509p $29.95; pa $16.95 **811**
1. American poetry -- 20th century 2. American poetry -- Collections 3. Poetry -- Collections
ISBN 1-56663-468-7; 1-56663-604-3 pa
LC 2002-31178
A collection of 600 poems previously published in Poetry magazine, written by such poets as W.H. Auden, Elizabeth Bishop, Sylvia Plath, James Merrill, and Susan Hahn.
This is a "comprehensive and thrilling anthology, a veritable history of twentieth-century poetry in English." Booklist

Poetry speaks expanded; hear poets from Tennyson to Plath read their own work. Elise Paschen & Rebekah Presson Mosby, editors; Charles Osgood, narrator. [2nd ed.]; Sourcebooks 2007 384p il $49.95 **811**
1. American poetry -- Collections 2. English poetry -- Collections
ISBN 978-1-4022-1062-4; 1-4022-1062-0
LC 2007-37080
"Reluctant poetry readers may find themselves drawn to the printed page by the spoken work, and poetry fans are likely to find much to love here." Publ Wkly

★ Poets of World War II; Harvey Shapiro, editor. Library of Am. 2003 xxxii, 262p $20 **811**
1. American poetry -- 20th century 2. Poetry -- Collections 3. World War, 1939-1945 -- Literature and the war 4. World War, 1939-1945 -- Poetry
ISBN 1-931082-33-2
LC 2002-32125
The editor's "objective is to show that the American poets of the Second World War were as significant as their English counterparts in the first one, if different in tone. Even at their most biting, Siegfried Sassoon and Wilfred Owen struck a heroic note, penning anthems for 'doomed youth' and the destruction of innocence. . . . But those who survived battles of the second conflict to become important poets avoided the attempt to sound noble, or to celebrate fallen comrades. . . . Shapiro, a B-17 gunner, takes pains to show the spectrum of opinion that actually existed and how it evolved." New Leader
Includes bibliographical references

Poets of the Civil War; J.D. McClatchy, editor. Library of America 2005 211p il $20   **811**
1. American poetry -- Collections 2. Poetry -- Collections 3. War poetry, American
ISBN 978-1-93108-276-1; 1-93208-276-6
LC 2004-61552

"The poems wisely selected represent not only the main kinds of responses to the war but also the radically conflicting sympathies of the poets—with the Union cause or with the Confederacy—and the important postwar theme of reconciliation of North and South. McClatchy's selection has not only breadth of representation but fine choices within forms, causes, and poets." Sewanee Rev

Twentieth-century American poetry; edited by Dana Gioia, David Mason, Meg Schoerke. McGraw Hill 2004 xlvi, 1143p il pa $79.69   **811**
1. American poetry -- Collections
ISBN 0-07-240019-6
LC 2003-61449

"The text is divided into sections like 'Realism and Naturalism' and 'The Harlem Renaissance,' with each section prefaced by a penetrating overview and each poet introduced by a biographical essay. Included are poets as diverse as Sherman Alexie, Ezra Pound, and Lucille Clifton, along with Nuyorican poets, New Formalists, Beats, imagists, and surrealists. Make room for this affordable, remarkable volume." Libr J
Includes bibliographical references

The Vintage book of African American poetry; edited and with an introduction by Michael S. Harper and Anthony Walton. Vintage Bks. 2000 xxxiii, 403p pa $14.95   **811**
1. Afro-Americans -- Poetry 2. American poetry -- African American authors -- Collections 3. American poetry -- Afro-American authors
ISBN 0-375-70300-4
LC 99-39428

"Included in chronological order here are over two centuries of poets, from Jupitor Hammon (1720-1800) to Reginald Shepherd (b.1963). . . . The editors' eloquent, outspoken vision provides a springboard for further examination of what constitutes the mainstream of American poetry." Libr J
Includes bibliographical references

Words for the hour; a new anthology of American Civil War poetry. edited by Faith Barrett and Cristanne Miller. University of Massachusetts Press 2005 xxx, 401p il lib bdg $80; pa $27.95 **811**
1. American poetry -- Collections 2. War poetry
ISBN 1-55849-510-X lib bdg; 1-55849-509-6 pa
LC 2005-18477

For this collection, the editors "limit their selection to work written between 1834 and 1891 by poets who lived through and often actively participated in antebellum, wartime, and aftermath events. . . . An interpretational, literary, and documentary monument." Booklist
Includes bibliographical references

The best American poetry 2011. Scribner Poetry 2011 xxvi, 211p $35; pa $16; ebook $9.99 **811**
1. American poetry -- Collections
ISBN 978-1-4391-8150-8; 978-1-4391-8149-2 pa;
978-1-4391-8151-5 ebook

An annual collection of American verse culled from large-circulation magazines and smaller literary reviews.
"There is something for every poetry lover, as well as for readers who might not yet know they love poetry." Publ Wkly
Includes bibliographical references

The complete poems; Philip Larkin; edited by Archie Burnett. Farrar, Straus and Giroux 2012 729 p.   **811**
ISBN 0374126968; 9780374126964
LC 2011945978

This collection edited by Archie Burnett "brings together all of Philip Larkins poems. In addition to those that appear in Collected Poems (1988) and Early Poems and Juvenilia (2005), some unpublished pieces from Larkins typescripts and workbooks are included, as well as verse . . . that had been tucked away in his letters. . . . Larkins poems are [also] given a comprehensive commentary. This . . . covers closely relevant historical contexts, persons and places, allusions and echoes, and linguistic usage. Prominence is given to the poets comments on his own poems, which often outline the circumstances that gave rise to a poem or state what he was trying to achieve." (Publishers note)

The poets laureate anthology; edited and with introductions by Elizabeth Hun Schmidt; foreword by Billy Collins. W.W. Norton & Co. 2010 liii, 762p $39.95   **811**
1. American poetry -- Collections
ISBN 978-0-393-06181-9
LC 2010-21692

Poems by each of the forty-three poets who have been named our nation's Poet Laureate since the post (originally called Consultant in Poetry to the Library of Congress) was established in 1937.
"A hefty and worthy read that everyone will want to savor. Essential for all contemporary poetry collections." Libr J

812   American drama in English

Abbotson, Susan C. W.
Critical companion to Arthur Miller; a literary reference to his life and work. Facts on File 2006 518p il $75   **812**
1. Authors 2. Dramatists 3. Screenwriters
ISBN 0-8160-6194-7; 978-0-8160-6194-5
LC 2006-22902

This book "covers Miller's entire canon, including plays, screenplays, fiction, short stories, and poetry, as well as many of his important essays and critical pieces. Also included are . . . entries on literary, theatrical, and personal figures important to Miller; key terms and topics connected to his work; and various theatrical companies and places with which he has been associated." Publisher's note

Includes bibliographical references

Albee, Edward

★ **Who's** afraid of Virginia Woolf? Scribner Classics 2003 243p $24 **812**
1. College teachers -- Drama 2. Married people -- Drama
ISBN 0-7432-5525-9

LC 2003-54206

Characters: 2 men, 2 women. 3 acts. First produced at the Billy Rose Theatre, New York City, October 13, 1962.

"The play is a virulent unveiling of the relationship between George, a history professor, and his wife, Martha, the college president's daughter. Another couple, Nick and Honey, get caught in the crossfire of George and Martha's verbal and emotional lacerations, and it becomes clear that each character is engaged in an isolated struggle through a personal hell." Reader's Ency. 4th edition

Auburn, David

Proof; a play. Faber & Faber 2001 83p pa $13 **812**
1. Fathers -- Death -- Drama 2. Man-woman relationships -- Drama 3. Mathematicians -- Drama
ISBN 0-571-19997-6

LC 00-50284

Characters: 2 men, 2 women. 2 acts, 9 scenes. First produced by the Manhattan Theatre Club, New York City, May 23, 2000.

"Twenty-five-year-old Catherine, who sacrificed college to care for her mentally ill father (once a brilliant, much-admired mathematician), is left in a kind of limbo after his death. Socially awkward and a bit of a shut-in, she is gruff with Hal, a former student who shows up even before the funeral wanting to root through the countless notebooks her father kept in the years of his decline, hoping to find mathematical gold. On the heels of his arrival comes Claire, Catherine's cosmopolitan, blandly successful, and pushy sister, with plans to sell their father's house and take Catherine . . . with her back to New York." SLJ

Includes bibliographical references and index

Baraka, Imamu Amiri

Dutchman, and The slave; two plays. [by] LeRoi Jones. Morrow 1964 88p hardcover o.p. pa $9.95 **812**
ISBN 978-0-688-21084-7; 0-688-21084-8

In Dutchman Baraka "explores the revolutionary potential of the educated black middle-class intellectual, represented by the protagonist, Clay, a would-be poet. When Clay is exposed as dangerous—that is, as a latent killer—by white society, seductively imaged as a beautiful white woman named Lula, he is summarily executed by that society. The Slave (1964), a fable set in a future of war between the races, continues the theme of black revolutionary militancy." Benet's Reader's Ency of Am Lit

Black, Stephen A.

Eugene O'Neill; beyond mourning and tragedy. Yale Univ. Press 1999 xxiv, 543p $45; pa $17.95 **812**
1. Authors 2. Dramatists 3. Dramatists, American -- 20th century -- Biography 4. Dramatists, American -- 20th century -- Family relationships 5. Dramatists, American -- 20th century -- Psychology 6. Nobel laureates for literature 7. Psychoanalysis and literature -- United States
ISBN 0-300-07676-2; 0-300-09399-3 pa

LC 99-33897

When Black "tracks down correspondences between O'Neill's life and art he adds zip to the life but depersonalizes the art. Still, as he brings the life and the art into apposition, new coloring is cast on a number of the plays. His observations will prove enlightening." New Leader

Includes bibliographical references

Cervantes Saavedra, Miguel de

Man of La Mancha; a musical play. lyrics by Joe Darion; music by Mitch Leigh. Random House 1966 82p il hardcover o.p. pa $9.95 **812**
ISBN 0-394-40621-4; 0-394-40619-2 pa

Characters: 14 men, 5 women, extras. First produced at the ANTA Washington Square Theatre, New York City, November 22, 1965.

Cruz, Nilo

Anna in the tropics. Theatre Communications Group 2003 84p pa $12.95 **812**
1. Cuban Americans -- Drama
ISBN 1-55936-232-4

LC 2003-15859

Characters: 5 men, 3 women. 2 acts, 10 scenes. First produced at the New Theatre, Coral Gables, Florida, October 12, 2002.

"Set in a cigar factory in Tampa, Florida, in 1929, where the Cuban-American employees have just hired a new 'lector' to read novels to them while they work, Anna and the Tropics is written in the lyrical, somewhat formalized parlance of a folktale. The play is both a piece of cultural history and a warm-spirited tribute to the transformative power of art." Time

Dowling, Robert M.

Critical companion to Eugene O'Neill; a literary reference to his life and work. Facts On File 2009 2v il set $150 **812**
1. Authors 2. Dramatists 3. Nobel laureates for literature
ISBN 978-0-8160-6675-9; 0-8160-6675-2

LC 2008-24135

"These volumes are wonderfully organized and very easy to use. . . . Entries are of a length to provide a good background of O'Neill's works and life." Booklist

Includes bibliographical references

Edson, Margaret

Wit; a play. Faber & Faber 1999 85p pa $13 **812**
ISBN 0-571-19877-5

LC 99-11921

Characters: 3 men, 3 women, extras. First produced at Long Wharf Theatre, New Haven, Connecticut, October 31, 1997.

Foote, Horton

Beginnings; a memoir. Scribner 2001 270p il $24; pa $14 **812**

1. Actors 2. Authors 3. Dramatists 4. Dramatists, American -- 20th century -- Biography 5. Novelists 6. Screenwriters 7. Screenwriters -- United States -- Biography 8. Television scriptwriters

ISBN 0-7432-1115-4; 0-7432-1116-2 pa

LC 2001-47088

Foote "chronicled his Wharton, TX, childhood in Farewell. . . . Now he continues his story where he left off, leaving Wharton at 17 to study to become an actor. He travels to theater school in Pasadena but eventually makes it to New York by way of Martha's Vineyard, where he soon discovers his talent for writing and hobnobs with the likes of Martha Graham, Tennessee Williams, and Agnes de Mille." Libr J

Collected plays. v2 Smith & Kraus 1996 216p v2 hardcover o.p. pa $19.95 **812**

ISBN 978-1-57525-019-9; 1-57525-019-5

"Foote's ear for naturalistic dialogue never fails him, and even in the midst of telling an exciting story . . . he never lets the potential for melodrama overwhelm things." Booklist

Gardner, Herb

Herb Gardner: the collected plays and the screenplay Who is Harry Kellerman and why is he saying those terrible things about me? Applause Theatre Bk. Pubs. 2000 489p il $27.95; pa $16.95 **812**

ISBN 1-55783-394-X; 1-55783-466-0 pa

These works "have furnished star actors with some of their most memorable roles and star directors with some of their biggest successes. Those favors are returned by the likes of Jason Robards, Judd Hirsch, Elaine May, Charles Grodin, and Dustin Hoffman, who introduce the plays that brightened their reputations." Booklist

Gibson, William

★ The **miracle** worker. Scribner 2008 112p pa $12.99 **812**

1. Authors 2. Blind 3. Deaf 4. Humanitarians 5. Inspirational writers 6. Memoirists 7. Social welfare leaders 8. Teachers of the blind 9. Teachers of the deaf

ISBN 978-1-4165-9084-2; 1-4165-9084-6

LC 2008-275273

A text of the television play, intended for reading, of Anne Sullivan Macy's attempts to teach her pupil, Helen Keller, to communicate.

"The present text is meant for reading, and differs from the telecast version in that I have restored some passages that read better than they play and others omitted in performance for simple lack of time." Author's note

Goodrich, Frances

The **diary** of Anne Frank; by Frances Goodrich and Albert Hackett; newly adapted by Wendy Kes-

selman. Dramatists Play Service 2000 70p il pa $7.50 **812**

1. World War, 1939-1945 -- Jews -- Drama

ISBN 0-8222-1718-X

LC 2006-455205

Characters: 5 men, 5 women. 2 acts. First produced at the Cort Theatre, New York City, October 5, 1955.

Guare, John

Six degrees of separation; a play. Random House 1990 120p hardcover o.p. pa $12.95 **812**

ISBN 0-679-73481-3 pa

LC 90-53449

Characters: 13 men, 4 women. First produced at the Mitzi Newhouse Theater, New York City, June 1990.

Gurney, A. R.

Love letters and two other plays: The golden age and What I did last summer; with an introduction by the playwright. Penguin Bks. 1990 209p pa $14 **812**

1. American drama -- 20th century

ISBN 978-0-452-26501-1; 0-452-16501-0

LC 90-34177

Love letters dramatizes the 30-year epistolary "exchange between an upper-class man and an upper-upper-class woman. . . . The Golden Age is an updated, romantic-comic variation upon Henry James' Aspern Papers in which a young academic locates an old woman who may possess a missing chapter of The Great Gatsby and schemes to get it from her. What I did Last Summer is about 14-year-old Charlie's bohemian season with Anna, the Pig Woman, who fosters his creativity as she once did his mother's." Booklist

Hansberry, Lorraine

★ A **raisin** in the sun. Modern Lib. 1995 xxvi, 135p $14.95; pa $6.50 **812**

1. African Americans -- Drama

ISBN 0-679-60172-4; 0-679-75533-0 pa

LC 95-16074

Characters: 8 men, 3 women. 6 scenes in 3 acts. First produced at the Ethel Barrymore Theatre, New York City, March 11, 1959.

"Hansberry's drama focuses on the Youngers, a 1950s African-American working-class family in Chicago striving to realize their individual dreams of prosperity and education, and their collective dream of a better life. It was the first play by an African-American woman to be produced on Broadway." Reader's Ency. 4th edition

Hughes, Langston

Five plays; edited with an introduction by Webster Smalley. Indiana Univ. Press 1963 258p hardcover o.p. pa $14.95 **812**

ISBN 0-253-32230-8; 0-253-20121-7 pa

Inge, William

4 plays. Grove Press 1979 304p pa $16 **812**

ISBN 0-8021-3209-X

LC 78-73032

Kaufman, George S.

★ **Kaufman** & Co. Broadway comedies. [by] George S. Kaufman with Edna Ferber [et al.] Library of America 2004 911p $35 **812**
1. Drama
ISBN 1-931082-67-7

LC 2004044200

This compilation includes "Animal Crackers . . . a little-known version that was found among Groucho Marx's personal papers and published here for the first time." Libr J

Kushner, Tony

Angels in America; a gay fantasia on national themes. 1st combined pbk. ed.; Theatre Communications Group 2003 289p pa $15.95 **812**
1. Government officials 2. Lawyers
ISBN 1-55936-231-6

LC 2003-17904

Millennium approaches first presented at the Eureka Theatre Company, San Francisco, May 1991. Perestroika first presented at the Mark Taper Forum, Los Angeles, November 1992.

Lawrence, Jerome

Inherit the wind; [by] Jerome Lawrence and Robert E. Lee. Ballantine Books trade pbk. ed.; Ballantine Books 2007 129p pa $9.95 **812**
1. Evolution -- Study and teaching -- Drama
ISBN 978-0-345-50103-5; 0-345-50103-9

LC 2007-281039

Characters: 23 men, 7 women. 3 acts 5 scenes. First produced at the National Theater, New York City, April 21, 1955.

Mamet, David

Glengarry Glen Ross; a play. Grove Press 1984 108p pa $14 **812**
ISBN 978-0-8021-3091-4; 0-8021-3091-7

LC 83-49380

Characters: 7 men. 2 acts, 4 scenes. First produced at The Cottlesoe Theatre, London, England, September 21, 1983.

A "comedy is about smalltime, cutthroat real esate salesmen trying to grind out a living by pushing plots of land on reluctant buyers in a never-ending scramble for their fair share of the American dream." Publisher's note

Speed-the-plow. Grove Press 1988 82p pa $13 **812**
ISBN 978-0-8021-3046-4; 0-8021-3046-1

LC 87-7252

Characters: 2 men 1 woman. 3 acts. First produced on Broadway at the Royale Theater, May 3, 1988.

"A brilliant black comedy, a dazzling dissection of Hollywood cupidity and another tone poem by our foremost master of the language of moral epilepsy. . . . On its deepest level it belongs with the darker disclosures of movie-biz pathology like Nathanael West's The Day of the Locust and F. Scott Fitzgerald's The Last Tycoon. In a sense Speed-the-Plow distills all of these to a stark quintessence: there's hardly a line in it that isn't somehow insanely funny or scarily insane." Newsweek

McCullers, Carson

★ The **member** of the wedding; a play. an introduction by Dorothy Allison. New Directions 2006 118p pa $11.95 **812**
ISBN 0-8112-1655-1; 978-0-8112-1655-5

LC 2005-36493

Characters: 6 men, 7 women. 3 acts with 3 scenes in the last act. First produced at the Empire Theatre, New York City, January 3, 1950.

Based on the author's book of the same title, this is "a study of the loneliness of an overimaginative young Georgian girl." Saturday Rev

Miller, Arthur

★ **Collected** plays, 1944-1961. Library of America 2006 774p $35 **812**
ISBN 978-1-931082-91-4; 1-931082-91-X

LC 2005-49442

Norman, Marsha

Collected plays. v1 Smith & Kraus 1998 412p v1 pa $19.95 **812**
ISBN 1-57525-029-2

LC 97-7665

Norman's "characters, whether they be performers in a struggling two-bit circus, women in an all-night laundromat, or a Western outlaw, are ones we can easily identify with and understand." Libr J

O'Neil, Eugene

Complete plays; edited by Travis Bogard. Literary Classics of the United States 1988 3v v1 $40; v2 $40; v3 $35 **812**
1. Dramas
ISBN 978-0-940450-48-6 v1; 978-0-940450-49-3 v2; 978-0-940450-50-9 v3

Parks, Suzan-Lori

Topdog/underdog. Theatre Communications Group 2001 110p pa $12.95 **812**
ISBN 1-55936-201-4

LC 2001-27316

Characters: 2 men. 6 scenes. First produced at The Joseph Papp Public Theater/New York Shakespeare Festival, New York City, July 22, 2001.

This is "the story of Lincoln and Booth, two brothers whose names were given to them as a joke foretelling a lifetime of sibling rivalry and resentment. Haunted by the past, the brothers are forced to confront the shattering reality of their future." Publisher's note

Rose, Reginald

Twelve angry men; introduction by David Mamet. Penguin Books 2006 73p pa $11 **812**
ISBN 0-14-310440-3; 978-0-14-310440-7

LC 2006-46006

Characters: 12 men. 3 acts. Original television broadcast on CBS program Studio One, September 20, 1954.

Shepard, Sam

Fool for love, and other plays; introduction by Ross Wetzsteon. Bantam Bks. 1984 307p pa $15 **812**

ISBN 978-0-553-34590-2; 0-553-34129-4

LC 84-45182

"Sam Shepard fills the role of professional playwright as a good ballet dancer or acrobat fulfills his role in performance. That is, he always delivers, he executes feats of dexterity and technical difficulty that an untrained person could not, and makes them seem easy." Village Voice

Sam Shepard; seven plays; introduction by Richard Gilman. Bantam Bks. 1981 337p pa $16 **812**

ISBN 978-0-553-34611-4; 0-553-34611-3

LC 83-100533

The **unseen** hand and other plays. Vintage Bks. 1996 383p pa $14.95 **812**

ISBN 978-0-679-76789-3; 0-679-76789-4

LC 95-47723

Simon, Neil

Brighton Beach memoirs. Plume 1995 130p pa $12 **812**

ISBN 0-452-27528-8

LC 95-21788

"Sex and baseball are the primary preoccupations of 15-year-old Eugene Jerome, narrator of a seriocomic slice of lower-middle-class Jewish family life in Depression-era New York City. The several adolescent characters in the extended family add to the teenage appeal of Simon's . . . play." Booklist

Lost in Yonkers. Plume 1993 120p pa $12 **812**

ISBN 0-452-26883-4

LC 92-29111

Characters: 4 men, 3 women. 2 acts. First presented at the Stevens Center for the Performing Arts, Winston-Salem, December 31, 1990.

This play, "set in 1940s New York, is a sad-funny portrait of a dysfunctional family, headed by a woman who provided for her children but never showed them love." Booklist

Rewrites; a memoir. Simon & Schuster 1996 397p hardcover o.p. pa $14 **812**

1. Authors 2. Biography, Individual 3. Dramatists 4. Screenwriters 5. Television scriptwriters

ISBN 0-684-83562-2 pa

LC 96-13691

This first volume of the dramatist's memoirs focuses on his career as it evolved from writing high school skits to TV programs to Broadway.

"This is a gentleman's autobiography, and Simon never stoops to dishing the dirt on his show biz cronies." Libr J

★ The **collected** plays of Neil Simon; with an introduction by Neil Simon. Random House 1979 4v hardcover o.p. v1-2 each pa $25, v3 o.p., v4 pa $17 **812**

ISBN 978-0-452-25870-9 v1; 978-0-452-26358-1 v2;

978-0-679-40889-5 v3; 978-0-684-84785-6 v4

The **play** goes on; a memoir. Simon & Schuster 1999 348p il hardcover o.p. pa $14 **812**

1. Authors 2. Dramatists 3. Dramatists, American -- 20th century -- Biography 4. Screenwriters 5. Television scriptwriters

ISBN 0-684-86980-2 pa

LC 99-36449

This memoir "recounts the second half of Simon's life, starting with the life-shattering impact of the death of his first wife, Joan, of cancer at 40, and proceeding through the ensuing 30 years, during which Simon had periods of incredible fertility and others in which his creativity dried up and he feared he would never write again." Booklist

Wasserstein, Wendy

An **American** daughter. Harcourt Brace & Co. 1998 105p il hardcover o.p. pa $14 **812**

1. Fathers and daughters -- Drama 2. Women in politics -- Drama

ISBN 0-15-600645-6 pa

LC 97-36079

Characters: 6 men, 4 women. 2 acts, 8 scenes. First produced by the Lincoln Center Theater, New York City, April 13, 1997.

The **Heidi** chronicles and other plays. Vintage Bks. 1991 249p pa $13.95 **812**

ISBN 0-679-73499-6

LC 90-55681

This collection traces "three decades of changing styles, mores, life objectives, and intellectual challenges. Wasserstein examines her characters and their times with great good humor, complexity, depth of feeling, and a firm refusal to accept trite and easy images." Libr J

The **sisters** Rosensweig. 1993 109p il hardcover o.p. pa $11 **812**

ISBN 0-15-600013-X pa

LC 93-224

Characters: 4 men, 4 women. 2 acts 7 scenes. First produced at the Mitzi E. Newhouse Theater, New York City, October 22, 1992.

This is "a domestic, romantic comedy partly about the three middle-aged sisters of the title and their relations with men and careers and partly about how the eldest sister, international banker Sara, in whose London home the play is set, meets a man who comes to dinner and, through not much effort on her part . . . sweeps him off his feet. Wasserstein filled the play with the sharp but poignantly revealing developments and dialogue that she writes so well." Booklist

Wilder, Thornton

Collected plays & writings on theater. Library of America 2007 871p $40 **812**

1. Poetry -- By individual authors

ISBN 978-1-59853-003-2; 1-59853-003-8

LC 2006-48620

"Complementing the selection of plays is [a] . . . group of essays that captures Wilder's reflections on his plays and contains a revealing epistolary account of the film adaptation of Our Town, as well as evaluations of dramatists such as Sophocles, George Bernard Shaw, and the Austrian satirist Johann Nestroy (whose farce Einen Jux will er sich machen Wilder . . . transformed into The Matchmaker)." Publisher's note

★ **Our** town; a play in three acts. foreword by Donald Margulies. HarperCollins Pubs. 2003 xx, 181p $19.95; pa $9.95 **812**

ISBN 0-06-053525-3; 0-06-051263-6 pa

Large mixed cast. First produced at McCarter's Theatre, Princeton, N.J., January 22, 1938.

"Presented without scenery of any kind, utilizing a narrator and loose episodic form, adventurous and imaginative in style, this unique play . . . is one of the most distinguished in the modern repertoire. It deals with the simplest and most touching aspects of life in a small town." HarperCollins Reader's Ency of Am Lit

Williams, Tennessee

★ **Plays,** 1937-1955. Library of America 2000 1054p $40 **812**

ISBN 978-1-883011-86-4; 1-883011-86-4

★ **Plays,** 1957-1980. Library of America 2000 999p $40 **812**

ISBN 978-1-883011-87-1; 1-883011-87-6

★ A **streetcar** named desire; with an introduction by Arthur Miller. New Directions 2004 192p pa $9.95 **812**

ISBN 0-8112-1602-0

LC 2004-11654

Characters: 6 women, 7 men. 11 scenes. First produced at the Barrymore Theatre, New York City, December 3, 1947.

"A study of sexual frustration, violence, and aberration, set in New Orleans, in which Blanche Dubois' fantasies of refinement and grandeur are brutally destroyed by her brother-in-law, Stanley Kowalski, whose animal nature fascinates and repels her." Oxford Companion to Engl Lit. 5th edition

Wilson, August

★ **Fences**; a play. introduction by Lloyd Richards. New Am. Lib. 1986 101p pa $12 **812**

ISBN 978-0-452-26401-4

LC 86-5264

Characters: 5 men, 1 woman, 1 girl. 2 acts, 9 scenes. First produced at the Yale Repertory Theatre, New Haven, Connecticut, April 30, 1985.

Gem of the ocean. Theatre Communications Group 2006 85p $25; pa $13.95 **812**

1. African American neighborhoods -- Drama. 2. African Americans -- Drama. 3. Hill District (Pittsburgh, Pa.) -- Drama. 4. Pittsburgh (Pa.) -- Drama.

ISBN 978-1-55936-281-8; 1-55936-281-2; 978-1-55936-280-1 pa; 1-55936-280-4 pa

LC 2006-7812

Characters: 5 men, 2 women. First produced at the Eugene O'Neill Theater Center, Waterford, Ct., 2002.

"A swelling battle hymn of transporting beauty. Theatergoers who have followed August Wilson's career will find in Gem a touchstone for everything else he has written." N Y Times

Jitney. Overlook Press 2001 96p hardcover o.p. pa $14.95 **812**

1. African American neighborhoods -- Drama 2. African Americans -- Drama

ISBN 978-158567-370-4; 1-58567-370-6

LC 2001-33962

Characters: 8 men, 1 woman. 2 acts, 8 scenes. This is a revised version of a play written 1979.

Joe Turner's come and gone; a play in two acts. New Am. Lib. 1988 94p pa $12 **812**

1. African Americans -- Drama

ISBN 978-0-452-26009-2; 0-452-26009-4

LC 88-1660

Characters: 6 men, 5 women. 2 acts, 10 scenes. 1 setting. First produced at the Yale Repertory Theatre, New Haven, Connecticut, April 29, 1986.

King Hedley II. Theatre Communications Group 2005 103p $27.95; pa $13.95 **812**

1. African American men -- Drama. 2. Ex-convicts -- Drama. 3. Pittsburgh (Pa.) -- Drama.

ISBN 978-1-55936-261-0; 1-55936-261-8; 978-1-55936-260-3 pa; 1-55936-260-X pa

LC 2005-12535

Characters: 4 men, 2 women. First produced at the Seattle Repertory Theatre, Seattle, Wa., 1999.

This is a "big play, filled with big emotions and big speeches. These aria-like monologues are rich in humor, heartbreak and the astonishing details that go into creating real people." Associated Press

Ma Rainey's black bottom; a play in two acts. New Am. Lib. 1985 111p pa $12 **812**

ISBN 978-0-452-26113-6; 0-452-26113-9

LC 84-27156

Characters: 8 men, 2 women. 2 acts. First produced at the Yale Repertory Theatre, New Haven, Connecticut, April 6, 1984.

Radio golf. Theatre Communications Group 2007 81p $25; pa $13.95 **812**

1. African American neighborhoods -- Drama. 2. African Americans -- Drama. 3. Hill District (Pittsburgh, Pa.) -- Drama. 4. Nineteen nineties -- Drama. 5. Real estate development -- Drama.

ISBN 978-1-55936-306-8; 1-55936-306-1; 978-1-55936-308-2 pa; 1-55936-308-8 pa

LC 2007-32541

Characters: 4 men, 1 woman. First produced at the Cort Theatre, New Haven Connecticut, May 8, 2007.

"A play that could well be Mr. Wilson's most provocative." N Y Times

Seven guitars. Dutton 1996 107p hardcover o.p. pa $12   **812**

ISBN 978-0-452-27692-5; 0-452-27692-6 pa

LC 95-50536

Characters: 4 men, 3 women. 2 acts, 9 scenes. First produced at the Goodman Theater, Chicago, January 21, 1995.

"Pittsburgh, summer 1948. Five of his friends gather after the funeral of Floyd Barton, mysteriously murdered at 35, just as his first blues record had become a hit. The sixth play in Wilson's cycle concerned with twentieth-century African American lives is mostly a flashback. We learn what happened to Floyd, but before that horrifying climax, Wilson steeps us in the pathos that Floyd glimpsed a way to escape. . . . As powerful as modern drama gets." Booklist

Two trains running; foreword by Laurence Fishburne. Theatre Communications Group 2007 99p $25   **812**

1. African American neighborhoods -- Drama. 2. African Americans -- Drama. 3. Hill District (Pittsburgh, Pa.) -- Drama. 4. Nineteen sixties -- Drama.

ISBN 978-1-55936-303-7

LC 2007-22095

Characters: 6 men, 1 woman. 2 acts 8 scenes. First produced at the Yale Repertory Theatre, New Haven, Ct., March 27, 1990.

★ The **piano** lesson. New Am. Lib. 1990 108p hardcover o.p. pa $12   **812**

ISBN 978-0-452-26534-9; 0-452-26534-7

LC 90-38734

Characters: 5 men, 3 women. 2 acts, 7 scenes. First presented at the Yale Repertory Theatre, New Haven, November 26, 1987.

Wilson, Lanford

21 short plays. Smith & Kraus 1993 268p pa $19.95   **812**

ISBN 1-880399-31-8

LC 93-34434

"The plays range in form from finely crafted one-act plays to short 'skits' written for various benefits. They are arranged in chronological order and the collection spans the years from 1963 to 1991. Wilson's dramatic style has been characterized by such phrases as 'lyric realism' and 'poetic realism,' but these short plays represent a far greater range of styles." Voice Youth Advocates

★ The **Talley** trilogy. Smith & Kraus 1999 272p hardcover o.p.   **812**

"Wilson didn't begin what became, ultimately, a tetralogy with the idea of creating a play cycle. He just wanted to write a play set in the late 1970s that reflected in some way the post-Vietnam, post-Watergate letdown much of young America was feeling. . . . The resultant four-play cycle captures the Talley's foibles and follies as thoroughly—and as entertainingly—as J.D. Salinger's set of stories and short novels did the Glass family." Booklist

Zindel, Paul

The **effect** of gamma rays on man-in-the-moon marigolds; a drama in two acts. drawings by Dong Kingman. Harper & Row 1971 108p il hardcover o.p. pa $6.99   **812**

ISBN 0-06-075738-8 pa

Characters: 5 women. First produced at the Mercer-O'Casey Theatre, New York City, April 7, 1970.

"The play, in the naturalistic tradition, deals with a widow and her two daughters, the imagination of one of whom has been captured by the atom and the possibilities it offers of producing mutations." McGraw-Hill Ency of World Drama

The Best American short plays; edited by Howard Stein and Glenn Young. Applause Theatre Bk. Pubs.   **812**

1. Drama -- Collections 2. One act plays

In addition to the plays each annual contains brief biographical and bibliographical data about dramatists represented

★ Playwrights at work; Paris review. edited by George Plimpton. Modern Lib. 2000 411p il pa $14.95   **812**

1. Actors 2. American drama -- 20th century -- History and criticism 3. Authors 4. Dramatists 5. Dramatists -- United States -- Interviews 6. Essayists 7. Memoirists 8. Motion picture directors 9. Nobel laureates for literature 10. Novelists 11. Poets 12. Screenwriters 13. Short story writers 14. Television scriptwriters 15. Theatrical directors

ISBN 0-679-64021-5

LC 99-44064

"This is an excellent gathering of brilliant minds in the theater, and these interviews provide significant insight into the works of the writers." Libr J

The play that changed my life; America's foremost playwrights on the plays that influenced them. edited by Ben Hodges. Applause Theatre & Cinema Books 2009 173p il pa $18.99   **812**

1. Authors, American -- 20th century -- Biography 2. Authorship 3. Drama -- History and criticism 4. Drama -- Technique 5. Dramatists, American 6. Dramatists, American -- 20th century

ISBN 978-1-557837-40-0; 1-55783-740-6

LC 2009-32452

"Edited by Hodges, with a foreword by Paula Vogel, the book assembles 19 of the theater's usual suspects, many of them Pulitzer Prize winners, to explain what lured them into their line of work." Arts J

813 American fiction in English

Atlas, James

Bellow; a biography. Random House 2000 686p il hardcover o.p. pa $29 **813**

1. Authors 2. Authors, American 3. Dramatists 4. Nobel laureates for literature 5. Novelists 6. Novelists,

American -- 20th century -- Biography 7. Short story writers
ISBN 0-375-75958-1 pa

LC 00-42529

"Atlas shares his subject's devotion to literature, intimacy with Chicago (the city Bellow immortalized), and Jewishness, and he succeeds brilliantly in chronicling and interpreting Bellow's very full life, difficult personality, and powerful work." Booklist

Includes bibliographical references

Bailey, Blake

A **tragic** honesty: the life and work of Richard Yates. Picador 2003 671p $35; pa $18 **813**
1. Authors 2. Authors, American -- 20th century -- Biography 3. Novelists 4. Short story writers
ISBN 0-312-28721-6; 0-312-42375-6 pa

LC 2002-42525

This biography of the novelist discusses his "unhappy Greenwich Village childhood and his struggles to write while teaching and working as a business writer, Hollywood screenwriter, and speechwriter for Robert Kennedy. As Bailey meticulously and perceptively chronicles Yates' arduous translation of experience into art, he exposes the anguish and transcendence of the writing life and the tragedy of mental illness." Booklist

Boyd, Brian

Stalking Nabokov; selected essays. Columbia University Press 2011 452p $35 **813**
1. Authors 2. College teachers 3. Essayists 4. Literary critics 5. Memoirists 6. Novelists 7. Poets 8. Short story writers 9. Translators
ISBN 978-0-231-15856-5; 0-231-15856-4

LC 2011-08348

This "collection of essays, addresses, and introductions written for an assortment of audiences by a noted Nabokov biographer and scholar is a delight. Boyd . . . does more than an able job of exploring Nabokov's varied intellectual interests—beyond what he could convey in his two-volume biography—from examining Nabokov's lepidopterological pursuits to trenchant assessments of Nabokov as a writer. Boyd dissects several major novels and offers comparisons between Nabokov and writers as diverse as Tolstoy and Machado de Assis." Libr J

Includes bibliographical references

Vladimir Nabokov: the American years. Princeton Univ. Press 1991 783p il hardcover o.p. pa $49 **813**
1. Authors 2. Authors, Russian 3. Biography, Individual 4. College teachers 5. Essayists 6. Literary critics 7. Memoirists 8. Novelists 9. Poets 10. Short story writers 11. Translators
ISBN 0-691-06797-X; 0-691-02471-5 pa

LC 90-26374

This volume, which completes the biography begun with Vladimir Nabokov: The Russian Years (1990), is an ac-

count of the writer's life from 1940, when he arrived in the United States.

Vladimir Nabokov: the Russian years. Princeton Univ. Press 1990 607p il hardcover o.p. pa $49 **813**
1. Authors 2. Authors, Russian 3. Biography, Individual 4. College teachers 5. Essayists 6. Literary critics 7. Memoirists 8. Novelists 9. Poets 10. Short story writers 11. Translators
ISBN 0-691-06794-5; 0-691-02470-7 pa

LC 90-8040

The author aims to "describe the liberal milieu of the aristocratic Nabokovs, their escape from Russia [after the Revolution], Nabokov's education at Cambridge, and the murder of his father in Berlin. Boyd then turns to the years that Nabokov spent, impoverished, in Germany and France, until the coming of Hitler forced him to flee, with wife and son, to the United States." Publisher's note

Includes bibliographical references

Burroughs, Augusten

★ **Running** with scissors; a memoir. St. Martin's Press 2002 304p $23.95; pa $14 **813**
1. Amherst (Mass.) -- Intellectual life 2. Amherst (Mass.) -- Social life and customs 3. Authors 4. Memoirists 5. Novelists 6. Novelists, American -- 20th century -- Biography
ISBN 0-312-28370-9; 0-312-42227-X pa

LC 2001-58857

In this memoir the author recalls his youth with a mentally ill mother, living with his mother's psychiatrist in a chaotic household, and his early homosexual experiences.

"Burroughs tempers the pathos with sharp, riotous humor in stories that are self-deprecating, raunchy, sexually explicit." Booklist

Crane, Stephen

Prose and poetry. Library of Am. 1984 1379p $40; pa $15.95 **813**
1. Short stories
ISBN 0-940450-17-8; 1-883011-39-6 pa

LC 83-19908

"This collection also includes both Crane's collections of epigrammatic free verses—'The Black Riders' and 'War is kind'—and selections from his uncollected poems." Publisher's note

Dearborn, Mary V.

Mailer; a biography. Houghton Mifflin 1999 478p il hardcover o.p. pa $15 **813**
1. Authors 2. Authors, American 3. Authors, American -- 20th century -- Biography 4. Essayists 5. Journalists -- United States -- Biography 6. Novelists
ISBN 0-395-73655-2; 0-618-15460-4 pa

LC 99-32214

"Dearborn supplies a close reading of one of the most controversial American writers of the postwar era. Mailer's body of work, beginning with his career-defining first novel, The Naked and the Dead (1948), is analyzed with remarkable insight. Mailer's notorious personal life is also examined, as Dearborn sorts through the various preoccupations that have obsessed the writer over five decades in the literary spotlight." Booklist

Includes bibliographical references

Doctorow, E. L.

Reporting the universe. Harvard Univ. Press 2003 125p $22.95; pa $13.95   **813**

1. American literature -- History and criticism 2. Authors 3. Novelists

ISBN 0-674-00461-2; 0-674-01628-9 pa

LC 2002-32742

"This potent collection of elegantly distilled essays offers a fresh perspective on our species' capacity for both the sublime and the horrific." Booklist

Facts on File, Inc.

★ The **Facts** on File companion to the American novel; edited by Abby H.P. Werlock; assistant editor, James P. Werlock. Facts on File 2005 3v set $195   **813**

1. American fiction 2. American fiction -- Bio-bibliography 3. American fiction -- Encyclopedias 4. American fiction -- History and criticism 5. Reference books

ISBN 0-8160-4528-3; 978-0-8160-4528-0

LC 2005-12437

"This A-to-Z reference contains 450 biographical overviews of American and foreign-born authors living in the United States and 500 signed analytical essays on their novels. . . . Libraries will value this compact set for including classics as well as hard-to-find contemporary authors." SLJ

Includes bibliographical references

Fargnoli, A. Nicholas

Critical companion to William Faulkner; a literary reference to his life and work. [by] A. Nicholas Fargnoli, Michael Golay, Robert W. Hamblin. Facts On File 2008 562p il $75   **813**

1. Authors 2. Nobel laureates for literature 3. Novelists 4. Screenwriters 5. Short story writers

ISBN 978-0-8160-6432-8

LC 2007-32361

"Coverage includes: Faulkner's major works, including novels, short stories, poetry, and nonfiction; descriptions of characters in Faulkner's fiction, such as Benjy and Quentin from The Sound and the Fury; details about Faulkner's family, friends, colleagues, and critics; real and fictional places important to Faulkner's life and literary development, from Yoknapatawpha County, Mississippi to Hollywood; interviews and speeches given by Faulkner; [and] ideas and events that influenced his life and works, including slavery, the Civil War, World War I, and civil rights." Publisher's note

Includes bibliographical references

Farrell, Susan Elizabeth

Critical companion to Kurt Vonnegut; a literary reference to his life and work. [by] Susan Farrell. Facts On File 2008 532p il $75   **813**

1. Authors 2. Biographers 3. Journalists 4. Novelists 5. Science fiction writers 6. Short story writers

ISBN 978-0-8160-6598-1

LC 2007-37900

This "book covers all his works, including his novels, such as the unforgettable Slaughterhouse-Five; his short stories, such as 'Harrison Bergeron'; and his lectures and essays. . . . Entries on his life, related people, places, and topics are also included." Publisher's note

Includes bibliographical references

Critical companion to Tim O'Brien; a literary reference to his life and work. [by] Susan Farrell. Facts on File 2011 480p $75   **813**

1. Authors 2. Essayists 3. Memoirists 4. Novelists 5. Short story writers

ISBN 978-0-8160-7870-7; 978-1-4381-3661-5 ebook

LC 2010038664

This book features a "biography of O'Brien; entries on all O'Brien's works, including his war novels, Going After Cacciato, The Things They Carried, and In the Lake of the Woods; his memoir, If I Die in a Combat Zone, Box Me Up and Ship Me Home; and all his other published novels and short stories, including The Nuclear Age, July, July, and more; [and] entries on related people, places, and topics, such as Green Berets, Ernest Hemingway, metafiction, and Viet Cong." Publisher's note

Includes bibliographical references

Fitzgerald, F. Scott

A **life** in letters; edited by Matthew J. Bruccoli; with the assistance of Judith S. Baughman. Scribner 1994 xxiii, 503p hardcover o.p. pa $18   **813**

1. Authors 2. Authors, American 3. Biography, Individual 4. Novelists 5. Screenwriters 6. Short story writers

ISBN 0-684-19570-4; 0-684-80153-1 pa

LC 93-31011

"Essential reading for a full understanding of Fitzgerald as an artist and a man." Libr J

Gillespie, Carmen

Critical companion to Alice Walker; a literary reference to her life and work. Facts on File 2011 452p il $75   **813**

1. Authors 2. College teachers 3. Editors 4. Essayists 5. Novelists 6. Poets 7. Short story writers

ISBN 978-0-8160-7530-0; 978-1-4381-3488-8 ebook

LC 2010-18639

This book contains "entries on all of Walker's major works, including such novels as The Color Purple, Meridian, The Third Life of Grange Copeland, and Possessing the Secret of Joy; essay collections and essays, such as 'Beauty: When the Other Dancer Is the Self'; poetry collections and poems; and short stories. Each entry on a major work of fiction contains subentries on the work's main characters." Publisher's note

Includes bibliographical references

Critical companion to Toni Morrison; a literary reference to her life and work. Facts On File 2008 484p il $75   **813**

1. Authors 2. College teachers 3. Dramatists 4. Essayists 5. Literary critics 6. Nobel laureates for

literature 7. Novelists
ISBN 978-0-8160-6276-8

LC 2006-38231

This book "examines Morrison's life and writing, featuring critical analyses of her work and themes, as well as . . . entries on related topics and relevant people, places, and influences." Publisher's note
Includes bibliographical references

Gunn, James E.

Isaac Asimov; the foundations of science fiction. by James Gunn. rev ed; Scarecrow Press 1996 276p hardcover o.p. pa $42   **813**
1. Authors 2. Biochemists 3. Children's authors 4. Novelists 5. Science fiction -- History and criticism 6. Science fiction writers 7. Short story writers 8. Writers on science 9. Young adult authors
ISBN 0-8108-3129-5; 0-8108-5420-1 pa; 978-0-8108-5420-8 pa

LC 96-21068

The author "focuses on Asimov's robots and on the Foundation trilogy, emphasizing throughout Asimov's limited use of background, style, and characterization, and his constantly recurring theme of the rational solution of a problem. The Lucky Starr juveniles get comparatively cursory treatment, but otherwise this is a very fine book indeed—well informed, clearly written, and judicious." Booklist {review of 1982 edition}
Includes bibliographical references

Halpert, Sam

Raymond Carver; an oral biography. University of Iowa Press 1995 196p $32.95; pa $17.95   **813**
1. Authors 2. Poets 3. Short story writers
ISBN 0-87745-502-3; 0-87745-503-1 pa

LC 94-46555

This is a "remembrance of Carver by his family, friends, and fellow writers. . . . These reminiscences include many insights into the sources and literary qualities of his writings. This highly readable oral biography is an expanded and rearranged version of When We Talk About Raymond Carver (Gibbs Smith, 1991)." Libr J

Haralson, Eric L.

Critical companion to Henry James; a literary reference to his life and work. [by] Eric Haralson and Kendall Johnson. Facts On File 2009 516p il $75   **813**
1. Authors 2. Novelists
ISBN 978-0-8160-6886-9

LC 2008-36451

This book "covers the life and works of Henry James as well as the related people, places, and topics that shaped his writing. Other features in this . . . title include a chronology of James's life, bibliographies of his works and of secondary sources, and black-and-white photographs and illustrations." Publisher's note
Includes bibliographical references

Hardwick, Elizabeth

Herman Melville. Viking 2000 161p $19.95 **813**
1. Authors 2. Authors, American 3. Novelists 4.

Novelists, American -- 19th century -- Biography
ISBN 0-670-89158-4

LC 00-36510

"Interweaving critical readings of his fiction and poetry with events in Melville's life, Hardwick offers glimpses into his tortured writing career, his sometimes difficult family life, and his ambivalent relationship with his friend Nathaniel Hawthorne." Libr J
Includes bibliographical references

Harrison, Jim

Off to the side; a memoir. Atlantic Monthly Press 2002 313p $25; pa $14   **813**
1. Authors 2. Authors, American -- 20th century -- Biography 3. Essayists 4. Novelists 5. Poets
ISBN 0-87113-860-3; 0-8021-4030-0 pa

LC 2002-26051

"Harrison reflects on how childhood tragedies and a profound involvement with nature gave rise to . . . [his] passion for writing. . . . A mesmerizing storyteller and down-to-earth philosophizer, Harrison explicates his 'seven obsessions,' which include alcohol, strip clubs, hunting, fishing, and dogs, and offers compelling ruminations on the splendor of nature and the crimes of man, the mysteries of spirit and the revelations of art." Booklist

Harrison, Kathryn

The **kiss**; Kathryn Harrison. Random House 1997 207 p. **813**
1. Authors, American -- Biography 2. Novelists, American -- 20th century -- Biography
ISBN 067944999X; 9780679449997

LC 97153826

In this memoir, Kathryn Harrison here turns an unflinching eye on the episode in her life that has most influenced those books: a secret, sexual affair with her father that began when she was 20. . . . Abandoned by her father as a child, neglected by an emotionally remote and impetuous mother, Harrison is raised by her grandparents. . . . A minister and amateur cameraman, her father visits Harrison after an absence of 10 years, when she is home from college on spring break. The boundary between flirtation and paternal affection is soon blurred. . . . Gradually consenting to his demands for sex, Harrison drops out of college and moves in with her father's new family, extricating herself from the affair only when her mother is stricken with metastatic breast cancer. (Publishers Weekly)

Herbert, Brian

★ **Dreamer** of Dune; the biography of Frank Herbert. TOR Bks. 2003 576p il $27.95; pa $16.95   **813**
1. Authors 2. Novelists 3. Science fiction writers
ISBN 0-7653-0646-8; 0-7653-0647-6 pa

LC 2002-42951

"This moving, sometimes painfully obsessive biography is an impressive testament of family loyalty and love. A must-read for Herbert fans (both senior and junior), it includes family photos and a bibliography." Publ Wkly

Hickam, Homer H.

The **Coalwood** way; by Homer H. Hickam, Jr. Delacorte Press 2000 318p hardcover o.p. pa $6.99   **813**

1. Aerospace engineers 2. Aerospace engineers -- United States -- Biography 3. Authors 4. Authors, American 5. Large print books 6. Memoirists 7. Novelists 8. Novelists, American -- 20th century -- Biography 9. Writers on science

ISBN 0-440-23716-5

LC 00-35884

This sequel to Rocket boys "continues the author's life story with his senior year in high school, 1959, in the declining West Virginia mining town of Coalwood. The rocket club, featured in the last book, is pushed to the periphery, and the focus shifts to Hickam's teenage problems, which include his parents, girls, and a sadness whose cause he cannot divine." Booklist

Hillerman, Tony

Seldom disappointed; a memoir. HarperCollins Pubs. 2001 341p il hardcover o.p. pa $13.95 **813**

1. Authors 2. Authors, American 3. Journalists 4. Large print books 5. Mystery writers 6. Novelists 7. Novelists, American -- 20th century -- Biography

ISBN 0-06-050586-9 pa

LC 2001-24160

In this memoir Hillerman "relates his childhood in Oklahoma during the Depression, his service in World War II, his university education, his career in journalism and academia, and his eventual turn to writing mysteries. The entire book will appeal to his fans, but the first half is intensely gripping." Libr J

Includes bibliographical references

Hiney, Tom

Raymond Chandler; a biography. Atlantic Monthly Press 1997 310p il hardcover o.p. pa $14   **813**

1. Authors 2. Authorship 3. Biography, Individual 4. Mystery writers 5. Novelists 6. Screenwriters

ISBN 0-8021-3637-0 pa

LC 97-264

"Hiney traces the writer's nomadic childhood from pre-Mafia Chicago to pre-telephone Nebraska, from Quaker Ireland and Edwardian England to his education south of London at Dulwich College and his 1913 arrival in the 'mean streets' of Los Angeles, the later setting for his crime fiction. . . . Living at over 100 addresses, he sustained no long friendships, and was 'variously rich, poor, drunk, teetotal, sacked, married and suicidal.'. . . No rough edges have been filed off for this revealing, well-written biography." Publ Wkly

Includes bibliographical references

Jones, Sharon L.

Critical companion to Zora Neale Hurston; a literary reference to her life and work. Facts On File 2008 288p il $75   **813**

1. Authors 2. Dramatists 3. Folklorists 4. Memoirists 5. Novelists 6. Short story writers

ISBN 978-0-8160-6885-2; 0-8160-6885-2

LC 2008-10052

This "covers all her writings, including Their Eyes Were Watching God; her landmark works of folklore and anthropology, such as Mules and Men; and shorter works." Publisher's note

Includes bibliographical references

Kerouac, Jack

Door wide open; a beat love affair in letters, 1957-1958. {by} Jack Kerouac and Joyce Johnson; with introduction and commentary by Joyce Johnson. Viking 2000 xxvi, 182p hardcover o.p. pa $13 **813**

1. Authors 2. Authors, American -- 20th century -- Correspondence 3. Beat generation 4. Editors 5. Love-letters 6. Memoirists 7. Novelists 8. Short story writers

ISBN 0-14-100187-9 pa

LC 99-53219

"In a hip, literate correspondence marked by high diction and '50s slang, 21-year-old Johnson (born Glassman) and 35-year-old Kerouac chart the flowering of the Beats and their complicated love affair." Publ Wkly

Includes bibliographical references and index

Selected letters, 1957-1969; edited with an introduction and commentary by Ann Charters. Viking 1999 xxvii, 514p hardcover o.p. pa $17 **813**

1. Authors 2. Authors, American -- 20th century 3. Beat generation 4. Novelists

ISBN 0-14-029615-8 pa

LC 99-17374

This volume "starts with the publication of On the Road and continues almost to the day Kerouac died. The years 1957-1960, the height of Kerouac's career, occupy more than half the volume. Later letters record his struggle to care for his ailing mother, his efforts to finish his later books and his troubles with money and health. . . . Frequent addressees and subjects include Gary Snyder, Philip Whalen, Lawrence Ferlinghetti, William Burroughs and Allen Ginsberg." Publ Wkly

King, Stephen

On writing; a memoir of the craft. Scribner 2000 288p hardcover o.p. pa $14.95   **813**

1. Authors 2. Authors, American 3. Authors, American -- 20th century -- Biography 4. Authorship 5. Novelists 6. Science fiction writers 7. Short story writers

ISBN 0-684-85352-3; 0-671-02425-6 pa

LC 00-30105

The author recounts "his life from early childhood through the aftermath of the 1999 accident that nearly killed him. Along the way, King touts the writing philosophies of William Strunk and Ernest Hemingway, advocates a healthy appetite for reading, expounds upon the subject of grammar, critiques a number of popular writers, and offers the reader a chance to try out his theories. . . . Recommended for anyone who wants to write and everyone who loves to read." Libr J

Kirk, Connie Ann

Critical companion to Flannery O'Connor. Facts on File 2008 415p il $75   **813**

1. Authors 2. Novelists 3. Short story writers
ISBN 978-0-8160-6417-5

LC 2007-6512

This book examines O'Connor's "life and works, and includes critical analyses of some of the themes in her writing, as well as entries on related topics and relevant people, places, and influences." Publisher's note

Includes bibliographical references

L'Amour, Louis

The **Sackett** companion; a personal guide to the Sackett novels. Bantam Bks. 1988 341p il maps hardcover o.p. pa $14.95   **813**

ISBN 0-553-37102-9 pa

LC 88-47530

"Each individual profile of the 17 Sackett novels contains a map, a cover painting, brief plot synopsis, and an annotated list of characters. Sackett enthusiasts will also welcome the inclusion of a detailed Sackett genealogy and family tree." Booklist

Lardner, Ring

I'd hate myself in the morning; a memoir. {by} Ring Lardner, Jr. Thunder's Mouth Press 2000 198p il $22.95; pa $14.95   **813**

1. Authors, American -- 20th century -- Biography 2. Novelists 3. Screenwriters 4. Screenwriters -- United States -- Biography
ISBN 1-56025-296-0; 1-56025-338-X pa

LC 00-44298

"Of interest to cultural historians as well as general readers, this book belongs in both academic and public libraries." Libr J

McClure, Wendy

The **Wilder** life; my adventures in the lost world of Little house on the prairie. Riverhead Books 2011 336p $25.95   **813**

1. Authors 2. Children's authors 3. Frontier and pioneer life in literature 4. Novelists 5. Western writers 6. Young adult authors
ISBN 978-1-59448-780-4

LC 2010-44960

"Don't worry that McClure's journey . . . is one of those ginned-up-book-proposal-in-hand faux challenges. In Laura World, following Wilder's footsteps turns out to be a surprisingly common rite. McClure is far from alone in her visit to a Laura look-alike contest, or her encounter with pillowy, life-size 'soft sculptures' of the Ingalls family. Her insights and wry honesty elevate the story from gimmickry. Conversational, witty, and questioning, she manages to coexist with her powerful subject." Christ Sci Monit

Includes bibliographical references

Mellow, James R.

Hemingway; a life without consequences. Addison-Wesley 1994 704p il pa $15 **813**

1. Authors 2. Authors, American 3. Journalists 4. Nobel laureates for literature 5. Novelists 6. Poets 7.

Short story writers
ISBN 0-201-62620-9; 978-0-201-62620-9

LC 93-24497

"In sheer number of pages, Mr. Mellow's version of the life is most heavily weighed toward the years 1921 to 1930, when Hemingway lived in Paris during his first two marriages and published the novels and stories that built his early reputation as one of this country's most important writers. Mr. Mellow seems in a hurry to get through the rest of the story, but he does dutifully summarize Hemingway's childhood, adolescence and the major events of the later years. . . . Mr. Mellow takes careful note of Hemingway's publications in the context of his life and gives sensitive readings, both biographical and critical, to them all." N Y Times Book Rev

Includes bibliographical references

Morris, Willie

My dog Skip. Random House 1995 122p il hardcover o.p. pa $10   **813**

1. Authors 2. Biographers 3. Biography, Individual 4. Dogs 5. Essayists 6. Journalists 7. Magazine editors 8. Novelists 9. Short story writers
ISBN 0-679-76722-3 pa

LC 94-41637

"Morris remembers back to the boy-and-his-dog days in his small hometown in the Deep South, where Skip was involved in all of his pranks and escapades. Poignancy rather than humor is the pervading tone of this ode to a steadfast presence." Booklist

Murphy, Mary McDonagh

Scout, Atticus, and Boo; a celebration of fifty years of To kill a mockingbird. Harper 2010 217p il $24.99   **813**

1. Authors 2. Essayists 3. Novelists 4. Short story writers
ISBN 978-0-06-192407-1; 0-06-192407-5

LC 2010-06739

The author tells the story of how the quiet, publicity-shy Southerner Harper Lee came to write her classic. She also conducts interviews (which will later be included in a documentary) with famous folks whose childhoods were transformed by the novel, such as Oprah, Tom Brokaw, and Scott Turow. Lee, now 84, didn't talk—she never does, God bless her—but you come away from Murphy's book with a renewed amazement at what Lee was able to achieve with a single perfect novel. Entertaiment Wkly

Nabokov, Vladimir Vladimirovich

★ **Speak,** memory; an autobiography revisited. {by} Vladimir Nabokov; with an introduction by Brian Boyd. Knopf 1999 xxxv, 268p il map $17; pa $14   **813**

1. Authors 2. Authors, American -- 20th century -- Biography 3. Authors, Russian 4. Authors, Russian -- 20th century -- Biography 5. College teachers 6. Essayists 7. Literary critics 8. Memoirists 9. Novelists 10. Poets 11. Short story writers 12. Translators
ISBN 0-375-40553-4; 0-679-72339-0 pa

LC 98-49237

These recollections of the author's youthful years give an account of a vanishing world. They offer a picture of the author's family, their flight from Russia, education in England, and émigré life in Paris and Berlin.

Nadel, Ira Bruce

Critical companion to Philip Roth; a literary companion to his life and work. [by] Ira B. Nadel. Facts On File, Inc. 2011 356p il $75 **813**

1. Authors 2. Novelists 3. Short story writers
ISBN 978-0-8160-7795-3; 978-1-4381-3555-7 ebook
LC 2010022769

"Coverage includes: a . . . biography of Roth; entries on all of Roth's works; . . . entries on related people, places, and topics, such as anti-Semitism, Claire Bloom, Newark, satire, and . . . more; [and] appendixes, including a chronology, a bibliography of Roth's works, and a secondary-source bibliography." Publisher's note
Includes bibliographical references

Oliver, Charles M.

Critical companion to Ernest Hemingway; a literary reference to his life and work. Facts on File 2006 630p il $75 **813**

1. Authors 2. Nobel laureates for literature 3. Novelists 4. Poets 5. Short story writers
ISBN 0-8160-6418-0; 978-0-8160-6418-2
LC 2006-7970

"This volume features entries on all of Hemingway's major and minor works, places and events related to his works, major figures in his life, and more. Appendixes include a complete list of Hemingway's works; a chronology; a genealogy; a . . . map for readers of Islands in the Stream; a list of film, stage, and radio adaptations; and a bibliography of secondary sources." Publisher's note
Includes filmography and bibliographical references

Parker, Hershel

Herman Melville; v1 a biography. Johns Hopkins Univ. Press 1996 942p v1 il maps $50; pa $29.95 **813**

1. Authors 2. Authors, American 3. Biography, Individual 4. Novelists
ISBN 0-8018-5428-8; 0-8018-8185-4 pa
LC 96-18984

This, the first volume of a two-volume "biography of Melville, ends in 1851, when the author presented to his . . . friend Nathaniel Hawthorne an inscribed pre-publication copy of Moby-Dick." Atl Mon
Includes bibliographical references

Philbrick, Nathaniel

Why read Moby-Dick? Viking 2011 x, 131 p.p (hbk.) $25 **813**

1. Sea stories -- History and criticism
ISBN 0670022993; 9780670022991
LC 2011019766

This book attempts to offer Herman "Melville's [book 'Moby-Dick' a] . . . broad contemporary audience. . . . [Author] Nathaniel Philbrick . . . unpacked the story of the wreck of the whaleship Essex, the real-life incident that inspired Melville to write 'Moby-Dick.' Now, he sets his sights on the fiction itself, offering a . . . tour of . . . [the] novel. . . . Philbrick . . . navigates Melville's world and illuminates

the book's humor and . . . characters-finding the thread that binds Ishmael and Ahab to our own time." (Publisher's note)

"In this cogent and passionate polemic for Melville's masterpiece, Philbrick . . . combines a critical eye and a reader's adoration to make a case for Moby-Dick. The plights of the Pequod, Ishmael and Ahab may seem irrelevant (or worse, quaint) compared to today's troubles, but Philbrick opines that within the pages of this American classic lie timeless archetypes whose relevance stretches across human history. . . . Less lit-crit and more readers' guide, this tome will remind fans why they loved the book in the first place, and whet the appetites of trepid potential readers." Publ Wkly
Includes bibliographical references

Phillips, Julie

James Tiptree, Jr. the double life of Alice B. Sheldon. St. Martin's Press 2006 469p il $27.95 **813**

1. Authors 2. Biography, Individual 3. Science fiction writers
ISBN 0-312-20385-3; 978-0-312-20385-6
LC 2006-40095

This is a biography of the American science fiction writer. The author "has achieved a wonder: an evenhanded, scrupulously documented, objective yet sympathetic portrait of a deliberately elusive personality." Publ Wkly
Includes bibliographical references

Plimpton, George

Truman Capote; in which various friends, enemies, acquaintances, and detractors recall his turbulent career. Talese 1997 498p il hardcover o.p. pa $16.95 **813**

1. Authors 2. Biography, Individual 3. Nonfiction writers 4. Novelists 5. Short story writers
ISBN 0-385-49173-5 pa
LC 97-14792

"The book is an intoxicating swirl of contradictory stories, serious analysis and rumors, adroitly edited in chapters arranged like those of a picaresque novel." Publ Wkly

Pritchard, William H.

Updike. University of Massachusetts Press 2005 350p pa $24.95 **813**

1. Authors 2. Novelists 3. Poets 4. Short story writers
ISBN 978-1-55849-507-4; 1-55849-507-X

"All in all, Pritchard's book is a gentle and intelligent request for a little more thought and a little less cranky let'smoveon speed in judging the work of one of America's pre-eminent writers." N Y Times Book Rev
Includes bibliographical references

Rand, Ayn

Letters of Ayn Rand; edited by Michael S. Berliner; introduction by Leonard Peikoff. Dutton 1995 xxi, 681p il hardcover o.p. pa $20 **813**

1. Authors 2. Biography, Individual 3. Nonfiction writers 4. Novelists 5. Philosophers
ISBN 0-452-27404-4 pa
LC 94-23646

"Imbued with her fiercely held beliefs, the letters most devoted to politics and philosophy fairly blaze off the page. .

.. Regardless of one's opinion of her thinking, her letters add greatly to our understanding of a most exceptional woman of letters." Booklist

Rehak, Melanie

Girl sleuth; Nancy Drew and the women who created her. Harcourt 2005 364p il $25; pa $14 **813**

1. Authors 2. Children's authors 3. Drew, Nancy (Fictitious character) 4. Mystery writers 5. Young adult authors

ISBN 0-15-101041-2; 0-15-603056-X pa

LC 2005-9129

"Packed with revealing anecdotes, Rehak's meticulously researched account of the publishing phenomenon that survived the Depression and WWII . . . will delight fans of the beloved gumshoe whose gumption guaranteed that every reprobate got his due." Booklist

Includes bibliographical references

Reynolds, David S.

Mightier than the sword; Uncle Tom's cabin and the battle for America. W. W. Norton & Co. 2011 351p il $27.95 **813**

1. Abolitionists 2. Authors 3. Children's authors 4. Nonfiction writers 5. Novelists 6. Short story writers

ISBN 978-0-393-08132-9; 0-393-08132-X

LC 2011-00702

"The powerful antislavery message of 'Uncle Tom's Cabin' fueled the flames leading to the Civil War, making it the most influential novel in American history. . . . Stowe claimed the novel came to her in a vision and God was its true author. Accordingly, her book is weighted with religious symbolism, which Reynolds interprets with typical English professor's zeal. He also examines its impacts not just on public attitudes toward slavery, but on women's rights, temperance, capitalism, minstrel shows, sexual customs and other aspects of mid-19th century American life. Reynolds dissects dozens of imitative novels, plays and minstrel shows — some against, others for slavery or segregation — and traces the influence of Stowe's novel into modern times, including film spin-offs. . . .[This is] not easy reading, but it offers virtually everything you ever wanted to know about 'Uncle Tom's Cabin' — and probably a lot more." Seattle Times

Reynolds, Michael S.

Hemingway: the 1930's; [by] Michael Reynolds. Norton 1997 360p il maps hardcover o.p. pa $15.95 **813**

1. Authors 2. Authors, American 3. Biography, Individual 4. Journalists 5. Nobel laureates for literature 6. Novelists 7. Poets 8. Short story writers

ISBN 0-393-04093-3; 0-393-31778-1 pa

LC 96-43113

"Filled with fascinating details and anecdotes, this fine biography illuminates our understanding of this crucial decade." Publ Wkly

Includes bibliographical references

Robertson-Lorant, Laurie

Melville; a biography. University of Massachusetts Press 1998 710p il pa $29.95 **813**

1. Authors 2. Authors, American 3. Novelists 4. Novelists, American -- 19th century -- Biography

ISBN 1-55849-145-7; 978-1-55849-145-8

LC 98-4899

"With access to more than 500 recently discovered Melville family letters, which show Melville to have been a functioning member of a problem-torn extended family, Robertson-Lorant corrects our traditional view of the older Melville as isolato. Instead, he appears here to represent the social consciousness of 19th century America. Together with jargon-free, user-friendly commentary on all Melville's major works. Robertson-Lorant offers an array of historical phenomena . . . that provide an invaluable context for Melville's life and art." Libr J

Includes bibliographical references

Roiphe, Anne Richardson

1185 Park Avenue; a memoir. [by] Anne Roiphe. Free Press 1999 257p il hardcover o.p. pa $14.95 **813**

1. Authors 2. Authors, American 3. Essayists 4. Jewish families -- New York (State) -- New York 5. Jews -- New York (State) -- New York -- Biography 6. Novelists 7. Women novelists, American -- 20th century -- Biography 8. Women novelists, American -- 20th century -- Family relationships

ISBN 0-684-85731-6; 0-684-85732-4 pa

LC 98-51939

"Roiphe's devastating memoir fully engages the reader in her painful story of hatred and betrayal." Publ Wkly

Rollyson, Carl

Critical companion to Herman Melville; a literary reference to his life and work. [by] Carl Rollyson, Lisa Paddock, and April Gentry. Facts on File 2006 394p il $75 **813**

1. Authors 2. Novelists

ISBN 0-8160-6461-X; 978-0-8160-6461-8

LC 2005-36733

Entries in this "volume examine the characters and settings of Melville's novels and short stories, the critics and scholars who commented on his work, and his friends and associates, including such prominent literary figures as Oliver Wendell Holmes and Nathaniel Hawthorne." Publisher's note

Includes bibliographical references

Roth, Philip

Patrimony; a true story. Vintage Bks. 1996 238p pa $12 **813**

1. Authors 2. Insurance agents 3. Novelists 4. Parents of prominent persons 5. Short story writers

ISBN 0-679-75293-5; 978-0-679-75293-6

LC 95-43453

This "ordinary, crucial story is well suited to a comic master, and Mr. Roth brings to the tale his gift for attention, his worldly, vernacular heart and the tremendous inventive force that here he keeps largely in check." N Y Times Book Rev

The **facts**; a novelist's autobiography. Vintage Bks.

1997 195p pa $14 **813**
    1. Authors 2. Authors, American 3. Novelists 4. Short story writers
    ISBN 0-679-74905-5; 978-0-679-74905-9
                      LC 96-28807
"The Facts is a lively and serious version of a novelist's life, but it seems even more interesting as a new way of formulating the questions about the imagination that Roth has been pursuing with increasing complication in the Zuckerman novels." N Y Rev Books

Rowley, Hazel
    Richard Wright; the life and times. Holt & Co. 2001 626p il hardcover o.p. pa $18   **813**
    1. African American authors -- Biography 2. Authors 3. Authors, American -- 20th century -- Biography 4. Dramatists 5. Essayists 6. Nonfiction writers 7. Novelists 8. Short story writers
    ISBN 0-8050-7088-5 pa
                      LC 00-54249
"The strength of {this book} is {the} painstaking research. Rowley . . . has a daunting dedication to primary sources and her documentation is meticulous." N Y Times Book Rev
Includes bibliographical references

Sallis, James
    Chester Himes; a life. Walker & Co. 2000 368p il $28; pa $18.95   **813**
    1. African American novelists -- Biography 2. Authors 3. Mystery writers 4. Novelists 5. Novelists, American -- 20th century -- Biography 6. Short story writers
    ISBN 0-8027-1362-9; 0-8027-7639-6 pa
                      LC 00-63328
This is a biography of the African-American crime novelist. "Sentenced to 25 years in prison for armed robbery when he was 19, he turned to writing while behind bars and, when released after serving eight years, published two novels. Their poor reception by the white establishment only confirmed Himes's beliefs about racism in America. He eventually moved to Paris, spending most of the rest of his life abroad. . . . The author succeeds splendidly in fleshing Himes out in this riveting biography." Libr J
Includes bibliographical references

Salzman, Mark
    Lost in place; growing up absurd in suburbia. Random House 1995 273p hardcover o.p. pa $13   **813**
    1. Asian studies specialists 2. Authors 3. Biography, Individual 4. Memoirists 5. Novelists
    ISBN 0-679-76778-9 pa
                      LC 95-7847
In this "memoir about his 'existential angst' as a slightly off-center teenager, . . . writer Salzman vividly recalls his unconventional friends, frugal parents, and other memorable characters from his freewheeling, Connecticut youth." Booklist

Savigneau, Josyane
    Carson McCullers; a life. translated by Joan E. Howard. Houghton Mifflin 2001 370p il $30 **813**
    1. Authors 2. Authors, American -- 20th century -- Biography 3. Dramatists 4. Novelists 5. Short story writers
    ISBN 0-395-87820-9
                      LC 00-46547
This is a "heartfelt, honest portrait of one of the great novelists of the American South." Libr J
Includes bibliographical references

Schultz, Jeffrey D.
    Critical companion to John Steinbeck; a literary reference to his life and work. [by] Jeffrey Schultz, Luchen Li. Facts on File 2005 406p il $65; pa $19.99   **813**
    1. Authors 2. Nobel laureates for literature 3. Novelists 4. Screenwriters
    ISBN 0-8160-4300-0; 0-8160-4301-9 pa
                      LC 2004-26100
"Useful, succinct, and reasonably priced, it packs an abundance of information into one compact resource." Libr J
Includes bibliographical references

Smiley, Jane
    Thirteen ways of looking at the novel. Knopf 2005 591p $26.95   **813**
    1. Authors 2. Authorship 3. Books and reading 4. Fiction -- History and criticism 5. Novelists 6. Short story writers
    ISBN 1-4000-4059-0
                      LC 2005-45181
"The book is roughly divided into three sections: the first classifies the novel, beginning with the most simple of definitions (e.g., it's long, in prose, has a protagonist), and adds moral and aesthetic complexity as it moves along. The second section consists of a primer for fledgling novelists. . . . The result is a thorough reflection on the art and craft of the novel from one of its best-known contemporary practitioners." Publ Wkly
Includes bibliographical references

Strayed, Cheryl
    Wild; from lost to found on the Pacific Crest Trail. Cheryl Strayed. Alfred A. Knopf 2012 315 p. **813**
    1. Authors, American -- 21st century -- Biography
    ISBN 0307592731; 9780307592736
                      LC 2011033752
The author recounts her experience hiking the Pacific Crest Trail (PCT) in 1995 after her mother's death and her own subsequent divorce. Designated a National Scenic Trail in 1968 but not completed until 1993, the PCT runs from Mexico to Canada, and [Cheryl] Strayed hiked sections of it two summers after it was officially declared finished. She takes readers with her on the trail, and the transformation she experiences on its course is significant: she goes from feeling out of her element with a too-big backpack and too-small boots to finding a sense of home in the wilderness and with the allies she meets along the way. . . . [She includes] descriptions of the natural wonders near the PCT, particularly

Mount Hood, Crater Lake, and the Sierras--what John Muir proclaimed the Range of Light. (Libr J)

Tate, Mary Jo

Critical companion to F. Scott Fitzgerald; a literary reference to his life and work. foreword by Matthew J. Bruccoli. Facts on File 2006 464p il $75
    813

1. Artists 2. Authors 3. Novelists 4. Painters 5. Screenwriters 6. Short story writers 7. Spouses of prominent persons

ISBN 0-8160-6433-4; 978-0-8160-6433-5
    LC 2006-11393

This book "studies the legacy of this writer, highlighting significant themes and historical references of his various works." Publisher's note

Includes bibliographical references

Walker, Alice

The **same** river twice; honoring the difficult: a meditation on life, spirit, art, and the making of the film The color purple, ten years later. Scribner 1996 302p il hardcover o.p. pa $14
    813

1. Authors 2. Biography, Individual 3. College teachers 4. Editors 5. Essayists 6. Novelists 7. Poets 8. Short story writers

ISBN 0-671-00377-1 pa
    LC 95-30056

This "book finds the Pulitzer Prize-winning author still grappling with criticism of the film version of her novel The Color Purple. . . . Walker's memoir pieces together assorted journal entries, magazine clippings, occasional photographs and even her original screenplay to form an intimate scrapbook of the period." Publ Wkly

Includes bibliographical references

White, Edmund

★ **My** lives. Ecco 2006 356p il $25.95 **813**

1. Authors 2. Biographers 3. Memoirists 4. Novelists 5. Short story writers

ISBN 0-06-621397-5; 978-0-06-621397-2
    LC 2005-49506

This is an autobiography by "an award-winning author and leader of the gay liberation movement of the 1960s. . . . The stories of his mother's egotism and incessant chatter, struggle to master the French language, obsession with European culture, literary associates, and work as a novelist, teacher, and essayist are largely overshadowed by graphic and explicit tales of the men in his life. . . . White's writing is amusing, descriptive, shocking, and, ultimately, thought-provoking." Libr J

Wideman, John Edgar

Hoop roots. Houghton Mifflin 2001 242p $24; pa $13
    813

1. African American authors -- Biography 2. Authors 3. Authors, American -- 20th century -- Biography 4. Basketball 5. College teachers 6. Memoirists 7. Nonfiction writers 8. Novelists 9. Short story writers

ISBN 0-395-85731-7; 0-618-25775-6 pa
    LC 2001-26455

Wideman "examines his lifelong relationship with basketball. He argues that basketball first allowed him to set his own standard in a white world that often imposes definitions of success on black people. A poignant, thought-provoking memoir." Booklist

Wiesel, Elie

All rivers run to the sea; memoirs. Knopf 1995 432p il $35; pa $15
    813

1. Authors 2. Biography, Individual 3. Holocaust survivors 4. Holocaust, 1933-1945 -- Personal narratives 5. Human rights activists 6. Journalists 7. Nobel laureates for peace 8. Novelists

ISBN 0-679-43916-1; 0-8052-1028-8 pa
    LC 95-17607

"Wiesel's immensely moving, unforgettable memoir has the searing intensity of his novels and autobiographical tales." Publ Wkly

★ **And** the sea is never full; memoirs, 1969- translated from the French by Marion Wiesel. Knopf 1999 429p hardcover o.p. pa $15
    813

1. Authors 2. Holocaust survivors 3. Holocaust survivors -- Biography 4. Holocaust, 1933-1945 5. Holocaust, 1933-1945 -- Personal narratives 6. Holocaust, Jewish (1939-1945) -- Public opinion 7. Human rights activists 8. Jewish authors -- Biography 9. Jews -- Politics and government -- 1948- 10. Journalists 11. Nobel laureates for peace 12. Novelists

ISBN 0-8052-1029-6 pa
    LC 99-15604

"This concluding volume begins when the author is age 40. He continues his travels . . . and he continues to write, his books including Souls on fire, Four Hasidic Masters, Twilight, and more. . . . Wiesel is the most significant writer to have made the Holocaust the major theme of his work, just as it has been of major importance to his life. The horror of the Holocaust can be felt in this memoir with an intensity beyond words." Booklist

Wright, Sarah Bird

Critical companion to Nathaniel Hawthorne; a literary reference to his life and work. Facts on File 2006 392p il $75
    813

1. Authors 2. Novelists 3. Short story writers

ISBN 0-8160-5583-1; 978-0-8160-5583-8
    LC 2005-34648

This book "offers critical entries on Hawthorne's novels, short stories, travel writing, criticism, and other works, as well as portraits of characters, including Hester Prynne and Roger Chillingworth. This . . . reference also provides entries on Hawthorne's family, friends—ranging from Herman Melville to President Franklin Pierce—publishers, and critics, as well as periodicals that published his work and important places and events in his life." Publisher's note

Includes bibliographical references

Alice Walker; edited and with an introduction by Harold Bloom. New edition; Bloom's Literary Criticism; an imprint of Infobase Publishing 2007 223p $45
    813

1. Authors 2. College teachers 3. Editors 4. Essayists

5. Novelists 6. Poets 7. Short story writers
ISBN 978-0-7910-9611-6
A collection of critical essays discussing the work of The
Color Purple author Alice Walker.

Alice Walker's The color purple; edited and with an
introduction by Harold Bloom. New ed.; Bloom's
Literary Criticism 2008 191p $45 **813**
1. Authors 2. College teachers 3. Editors 4. Essayists
5. Novelists 6. Poets 7. Short story writers
ISBN 978-0-7910-9614-7; 0-7910-9614-9
LC 2008-2775
A collection of ten essays providing international appraisal and interpretation of Walker's novel.

Brave new words; the Oxford dictionary of science
fiction. edited by Jeffrey Prucher; introduction by
Gene Wolfe. Oxford University Press 2007 xxxi,
342p $29.95 **813**
1. Reference books 2. Science fiction -- Dictionaries
ISBN 978-0-19-530567-8; 0-19-530567-1
LC 2006-37280
"This new science fiction lexicon . . . is an important and
entertaining reference source for any science fiction writer,
magazine editor, fan, neophyte reader, or librarian." Choice
Includes bibliographical references

★ The Columbia companion to the twentieth-century American short story; Blanche H. Gelfant,
editor. Columbia Univ. Press 2000 660p $83.50;
pa $24.50 **813**
1. American fiction -- 20th century 2. American fiction
-- 20th century -- History and criticism 3. American
fiction -- Bio-bibliography 4. American fiction --
History and criticism 5. Authors, American -- 20th
century 6. Reference books 7. Short stories -- History
and criticism 8. Short stories, American 9. Short
stories, American -- History and criticism
ISBN 0-231-11098-7; 0-231-11099-5 pa
LC 00-31610
"The first 100 pages are devoted to thematic essays that
focus on the form of the short story, the development of the
genre, several distinct subject types (e.g., short stories of the
Holocaust or of the working class), and four different ethnic
groups (African American, Asian American, Chicano Latino
American, and Native American). . . . The remainder of the
book is devoted to over 100 individual author essays that
focus on reading for pleasure and understanding rather than
critical interpretation. Entries discuss the development of
each author and the content and meaning of his or her major
short stories." Libr J
Includes bibliographical references

Contemporary Jewish-American novelists; a bio-
critical sourcebook. edited by Joel Shatzky and
Michael Taub; with a foreword by Daniel Walden.
Greenwood Press 1997 xxxi, 506p $105 **813**
1. American fiction -- Bio-bibliography 2. American
fiction -- Jewish authors 3. Reference books
ISBN 0-313-29462-3
LC 96-37047

This "reference work 'includes alphabetically arranged
entries for more than 75 Jewish-American novelists whose
major works were largely written after World War II.' While
major canonical figures such as Norman Mailer and Saul Bellow are profiled, lesser-known novelists—including Judith
Katz, Lev Raphael, and Steve Stern—are covered as well.
One of the editors' goals is to show the diversity of Jewish-
American literature. . . . Each entry includes a biographical
section, a cogent discussion of major works and themes, an
overview of each novelist's critical reception, and a bibliography of both primary and secondary sources." Booklist

J.D. Salinger; edited with an introduction by Har-
old Bloom. New ed; Chelsea House 2008 254p
$45 **813**
1. Authors 2. Novelists 3. Short story writers
ISBN 978-0-7910-9813-4
LC 2007-44662
This collection of nine essays provides a view of Salin-
ger's critical reception. Among the contributors are David
Galloway, Anthony Kaufman and Robert Coles.

John Steinbeck; edited and with an introduction by
Harold Bloom. New ed; Bloom's Literary Criticism 2008 176p $45 **813**
1. Authors 2. Nobel laureates for literature 3. Novelists
4. Screenwriters
ISBN 978-0-7910-9787-8; 0-7910-9787-0
LC 2007-38676
A selection of criticism, arranged in chronological order
of publication, devoted to the fiction of John Steinbeck.

★ A Theodore Dreiser encyclopedia; edited by Keith
Newlin. Greenwood Press 2003 xxiii, 431p il
$99.95 **813**
1. Authors 2. Journalists -- United States -- Biography
-- Encyclopedias 3. Novelists 4. Novelists, American
-- 20th century -- Biography -- Encyclopedias
ISBN 0-313-31680-5
LC 2003-40841
This is a "guide to the essential facts surrounding this
prolific author's life and works. Dreiser's novels and short
stories are covered, as are his plays, which are far less
known. Front matter includes a list of entries, a chronology,
and a preface that analyzes prior contributions to Dreiser
scholarship. Alphabetically arranged essays on his books,
short stories, and magazine and newspaper pieces make up
the book's core. . . . The book ends with a bibliography arranged by category (books by Dreiser, critical studies, biographies, etc.). Highly recommended." Choice
Includes bibliographical references and index

William Faulkner; edited and with an introduction by
Harold Bloom. New ed.; Bloom's Literary Criticism 2008 269p $45 **813**
1. Authors 2. Nobel laureates for literature 3. Novelists
4. Screenwriters 5. Short story writers
ISBN 978-0-7910-9786-1
LC 2007-33754
"This volume of . . . critical essays examines The Sound
and the Fury, Light in August, As I Lay Dying, Absalom,

Absalom!, and other key works by this preeminent writer of the twentieth century." Publisher's note

Includes bibliographical references

Zora Neale Hurston; edited and with an introduction by Harold Bloom. New ed; Chelsea House Publishers 2008 238p $45 **813**

1. Authors 2. Dramatists 3. Folklorists 4. Memoirists 5. Novelists 6. Short story writers

ISBN 978-0-7910-9610-9

LC 2007-49161

"Featuring supplemental material such as a chronology, a bibliography, and an index, [this book is a] critical look at Hurston's work and its influence on contemporary themes, such as race and gender in American society." Publisher's note

Includes bibliographical references

814   American essays in English

Aciman, Andre A.

★ **Alibis**; essays on elsewhere. [by] Andre Aciman. Farrar, Straus and Giroux 2011 200p $25 **814**

ISBN 978-0-374-10275-3; 0-374-10275-9

LC 2011-10700

"Many of these essays begin with a city—New York, Barcelona, Rome—before spiraling into images and ideas that connect with other places and times in Aciman's own well-traveled history. Born in Egypt, raised in a French-speaking Jewish family, his complex identity (is he African? French? Jewish?) confronts him with a 'fundamental distortion' that he can make sense of only by the transformative power of art . . . . In a brilliant piece called 'Temporizing,' Aciman examines his own propensity for filtering all experiences through the Egypt in his mind. Writing, even thinking, thus becomes 'an interminable restoration project whose purpose is to prevent all contact with the present.' With his sly self-deprecation and supple, curious mind, Aciman is the perfect guide through the mysteries of time and place." Boston Globe

Angelou, Maya

Even the stars look lonesome. Random House 1997 145p $18; pa $10 **814**

1. African American authors 2. Large print books 3. Meditations 4. Women authors

ISBN 0-375-50031-6; 0-553-37972-0 pa

LC 97-17317

Angelou "touches on a number of topics in this brief collection of essays, including aging, fame, sensuality, art, and violence. Her opening piece, about the ending of a long marriage and the beginning of a new life in a new home, is a winner. Her take on aging is downright amusing; her tribute to sensuality, enlightening; and her salute to black women, a treasure." Libr J

Wouldn't take nothing for my journey now. Random House 1993 141p hardcover o.p. pa $6.99 **814**

1. Meditations

ISBN 0-679-42743-0; 0-553-56907-4 pa

LC 93-5904

The author "shares her thoughts about humankind: how to respect others of different cultures, opinions, and values as taught by universal philosophies. . . . Angelou's prose is brisk, fluid, and entrancing. This work will provide a taste of wisdom to all who read it." Libr J

Atwood, Margaret

Writing with intent; essays, reviews, personal prose, 1983-2005. Carroll & Graf Publishers 2005 427p $26 **814**

ISBN 0-7867-1535-9

LC 2005-42086

In these essays, the author "comments on world events, fellow writers, and her own development. She reviews books by John Updike, Italo Calvino, Antonia Fraser, and Dashiell Hammett, as well as the lesser-known Robert Bringhurst, Hilary Mantel, and H. Rider Haggard. . . . This collection will not disappoint Atwood fans as her analyses both challenge and entertain." Libr J

Includes bibliographical references

Baker, Nicholson, 1957-

The **way** the world works; essays. Nicholson Baker. Simon & Schuster 2012 336 p. (hardcover) $25.00 **814**

ISBN 1416572473; 9781416572473

LC 2011052741

This book is a "collection of essays," in which "[Nicholson] Baker . . . poses important questions about our era of digital readership. As he notes in his essay on the Kindle 2, there is a distinction between a writers work and its presentation in book form. Many essays staunchly defend the reading of print books and newspapers . . . . A proud defender of libraries and newspapers, Baker acknowledges the perception of him as 'a weirdo cultist, a ringleader' for books." (Publishers Weekly)

Baldwin, James

★ **Collected** essays. Library of Am. 1998 869p $35 **814**

ISBN 1-883011-52-3

LC 97-23496

The essays in this volume were selected by Toni Morrison. "Morrison has reprinted all of the material contained in Baldwin's previous collected essays, The Price of the Ticket (1985). She has added eleven pieces, the earliest of which dates from 1947—Baldwin's first published review, of a biography of Frederick Douglass, in the Nation—and the latest from 1984." Times Lit Suppl

Berry, Wendell

Imagination in place; essays. Counterpoint 2010 196p $24 **814**

1. Criticism

ISBN 978-1-58243-562-6; 1-58243-562-6

LC 2009-38104

"For those who've already come to admire Berry's moral clarity and closely argued critiques of contemporary society, 'Imagination in Place' is a welcome chance to continue the conversation." Christ Sci Monit

Includes bibliographical references

Bradbury, Ray

Bradbury speaks; too soon from the cave, too far from the stars. William Morrow 2005 243p hardcover o.p. pa $14.95   **814**

ISBN 0-06-058568-4; 0-06-058569-2 pa

LC 2005-41489

In this collection of essays, the author "weighs in on a medley of topics, including the allure of Paris, his enthusiasm for trains, the genesis of his most popular novels, and his reasons for remaining a diehard optimist. . . . By turns whimsical, insightful, and unabashedly metaphoric, his prose is immediately accessible as well as thought-provoking. Fans and nonfans alike should enjoy." Booklist

Brodsky, Joseph

On grief and reason; essays. Farrar, Straus & Giroux 1996 484p hardcover o.p. pa $18   **814**

ISBN 0-374-52509-9 pa

LC 94-10872

For an "essay on Frost, for an equally probing one on four poems by Thomas Hardy, for an 'Homage to Marcus Aurelius,' for half a hundred pages on an English translation of a poem Rainer Maria Rilke wrote in German 90 years ago, and for many scattered felicities, this collection is occasion for gratitude. It is rare for someone so advantageously situated, within poetry but both within and outside of American speech, culture and experience, to confide in us with such pedagogic confidence." N Y Times Book Rev

Capote, Truman

★ **Portraits** and observations; the essays of Truman Capote. Random House 2007 518p $28.95 **814**

1. Authors 2. Criticism 3. Nonfiction writers 4. Novelists 5. Short story writers 6. Travel writing

ISBN 978-1-4000-6661-2; 1-4000-6661-1

LC 2007-36624

This is a collection of 42 essays written by Capote from 1946 to 1984.

"The featured works cover the artist's interests in travel, celebrities, the arts—both visual and literary—crimes of passion, and himself. . . . This collection offers the highest quality of writing from a genuine American stylist." Libr J

Chabon, Michael

Maps and legends; reading and writing along the borderlands. McSweeney's 2008 222p $24   **814**

1. Authorship 2. Fiction genres 3. Reader-response criticism

ISBN 978-1-932416-89-3; 1-932416-89-7

"In 16 essays, Chabon maps his enthusiasms. . . . Although in part a fragmentary memoir—we receive revealing glimpses of Chabon's family, boyhood home of Columbia, Md., and personal history—'Maps and Legends' is also a manifesto, a declaration of literary principles that asserts the value, even necessity, of genre. Especially in the book's first half, Chabon makes this argument through example, by closely examining and celebrating Arthur Conan Doyle's Sherlock Holmes tales, Philip Pullman's 'His Dark Materials' series, M.R. James' ghost stories, and the comics of Howard Chaykin, Ben Katchor and Will Eisner. . . . However disparately engaging you find the ruminations on other writers, the book's concluding quintet of pieces on the in-

spirations behind Chabon's major work will prove an illuminating delight for those of us who have the same fannish devotion to his work as he does to Conan Doyle's." St. Louis Post-Dispatch

Codrescu, Andrei

New Orleans, mon amour; by Andrei Codrescu. Algonquin Books of Chapel Hill 2006 273p pa $14   **814**

ISBN 1-56512-505-3

LC 2005-53599

In this collection of short essays Codrescu sketches "portraits of a fabled city and its equally fabled inhabitants. The author, who has called the Big Easy home for two decades, shows how, like some gigantic bohemian magnet, New Orleans attracts some of the world's most talented, self-indulgent freaks. Codrescu finds himself quite at home there. He expertly weaves pages of New Orleans history through his stories of personal discovery and debauchery. The last few essays, written post-Katrina, radiate simultaneous anger and clarity. Full of pride and defensiveness, Codrescu closes the collection ruminating about rebuilding the city and his longing to return to its rhythms and eccentricities. Despite Codrescu's frustrations, this collection is, in the end, gentle and sweet." Publ Wkly

Connell, Evan S.

★ The **Aztec** treasure house; new and selected essays. Counterpoint 2001 470p hardcover o.p. pa $17.50   **814**

1. Admirals 2. Alchemists 3. Alchemy 4. Astronomy 5. Cliff dwellers and cliff dwellings 6. Colonial administrators 7. Explorers 8. Government officials 9. Hieroglyphics 10. Incas 11. Kings 12. Northwest Passage 13. Vikings

ISBN 1-58243-253-8 pa

LC 2001-28899

Connell "writes about polar exploration; linguistic research; astronomy; preposterous, unkillable fantasies like El Dorado and Prester John; inspired travelers like Ibn Batuta and Mary Kingsley; the insane and tragic Children's Crusade—any subject that illustrates the human urge to strain against physical and mental boundaries. Connell is skeptical, clearheaded and a sworn enemy of all dogma." N Y Times Book Rev

Includes bibliographical references

Crosley, Sloane

How did you get this number; essays. Riverhead Books 2010 274p il $25.95   **814**

1. American wit and humor

ISBN 978-1-59448-759-0; 1-59448-759-6

LC 2010-07178

"With wit, humor, and a sophistication that more experienced authors would envy, this compilation focuses on Crosley's late twenties. . . . Reading like the diary entries of a thirtysomething, Crosley's essays are brutally honest about her flaws as well as the flaws of others and, as a result, paint a realistic and hilarious portrait of what it's like to be an adult in today's world." Libr J

Davenport, Guy

The **geography** of the imagination; forty essays. 1st Nonpareil ed; David R. Godine 1997 384p pa $19.95 **814**

ISBN 1-567-92080-2

LC 97-17831

In addition to essays on modern and classical literature the author also discusses archaeology, biology, lexicography, music and photography. Among his subjects are: Poe, Agassiz, Pound, Ives, Zukofsky, Meatyard, Tchelitchew and Joyce.

Didion, Joan

We tell ourselves stories in order to live; collected nonfiction. with an introduction by John Leonard. Knopf 2006 1122p $30 **814**

1. Criticism

ISBN 978-0-307-26487-9; 0-307-26487-4

LC 2006-41043

This volume "contains seven books of journalism—all of [Didion's] nonfiction except her 2005 memoir of new widowhood, 'The Year of Magical Thinking.' Didion's writing was from the beginning startlingly individual. . . . Say what you will about her somewhat self-centered style; America needs more courageous thinkers who will write about life as it is lived—not as elites on all sides seek to manufacture it." Nat Rev

Includes bibliographical references

Dirda, Michael

Classics for pleasure. Harcourt 2007 341p $25 **814**

1. Canon (Literature) 2. Literature -- History and criticism

ISBN 978-0-15-101251-0; 0-15-101251-2

LC 2007-03029

This book is "a pleasure to dip into any time. Like the key that opens up the door to The Secret Garden, it provides easy entry to a colorful array of literary gems." America

Doctorow, E. L.

Creationists: selected essays, 1993-2006. Random House 2006 176p $24.95 **814**

1. Creation (Literary, artistic, etc.) 2. Criticism 3. Literature -- History and criticism

ISBN 978-1-4000-6495-3; 1-4000-6495-3

"Doctorow chose his gallery with what may seem a generous dash of whimsy. Many of his writers and other 'creationists' are not exactly habitues of the canon. Standing alongside the likes of Mark Twain, Sinclair Lewis, Scott Fitzgerald and John Dos Passos are Harriet Beecher Stowe; W. G. Sebald; the anonymous translators of Genesis into the King James version; Harpo Marx; Albert Einstein; [and] the makers of the atomic bomb. . . . And yet the writers assembled here efficiently serve the critic's intentions. Each yields in robustly illustrative ways to 'the voice of the book,' a voice more protean than the artist's own; a voice that soars into conjunction with the voice of the region, the nation, the times." N Y Times Book Rev

Du Bois, W. E. B.

★ Writings. Library of Am. 1986 1334p $40; pa

$15.95 **814**

ISBN 0-940450-33-X; 1-883011-31-0 pa

LC 86-10565

Ellison, Ralph

The **collected** essays of Ralph Ellison; edited with an introduction by John F. Callahan; preface by Saul Bellow. Modern Lib. 1995 xxix, 856p hardcover o.p. pa $18 **814**

1. African Americans -- Intellectual life 2. African Americans -- Race identity 3. African Americans in literature 4. Artists 5. Authors 6. Cabinet members 7. Civil rights activists 8. Classical musicians 9. Dramatists 10. Economists 11. Educators 12. Essayists 13. International organization officials 14. Jazz music 15. Jazz music -- History and criticism 16. Journalists 17. Music teachers 18. Newspaper editors 19. Nobel laureates for economic sciences 20. Nonfiction writers 21. Novelists 22. Pianists 23. Screenwriters 24. Short story writers

ISBN 978-0-8129-6826-2 pa; 0-8129-6826-3 pa

LC 95-4719

This book "includes posthumously discovered reviews, criticism, and interviews, as well as the essay collections Shadow and Act (1964) . . . and Going to the Territory (1986), an exploration of literature and folklore, jazz and culture, and the nature and quality of lives that black Americans lead." Publisher's note

Emerson, Ralph Waldo

Essays & lectures. Library of Am. 1983 1321p $35 **814**

ISBN 0-940450-15-1

LC 83-5447

Ephron, Nora, 1941-2012

I feel bad about my neck; and other thoughts on being a woman. Knopf 2006 137p $21.95; pa $12.95 **814**

1. Aging 2. Women

ISBN 0307264556; 0307276821; 9780307264558; 9780307276827

LC 2005-57780

In this collection of essays, Ephron looks "at women who are getting older and dealing with the tribulations of maintenance, menopause, empty nests, and life itself." (Publisher's note)

"While very little in the book is meant to be taken seriously, it is clever enough to qualify as more than just an assemblage of one-liners. Whether you agree with her observations or not, Ephron's perspective as an admittedly high-maintenance, New York-dwelling, successful screenwriter will keep you entertained." Christ Sci Monit

Epstein, Joseph

In a cardboard belt! essays personal, literary, and savage. Houghton Mifflin 2007 xxii, 410p $26 **814**

ISBN 978-0-618-72193-1; 0-618-72193-2

LC 2007-8515

In this compendium Epstein includes "essays on his father's passing, movies, travel, dining, editing, writer's block, and the strangely gratifying unhappiness of academics; there are moving appreciations of W.H. Auden, Marcel Proust, and John Keats, and fierce depreciations of Edmund Wilson, Mortimer Adler, and poetry prizes. The result is an unusually broad portrait of a thinking man doing his stuff. Epstein is one of the handful of writers in America today whom one can pleasurably read both for substance and style. His writing sparkles with observation and humor." Claremont Rev Books

Essays/Selections

The **selected** essays of Gore Vidal; edited by Jay Parini. Doubleday 2008 458p $27.50   **814**

ISBN 978-0-385-52484-1; 0-385-52484-6

LC 2008-13517

"Regardless of what one thinks of Vidal, what Vidal thinks is never in doubt in these 24 essays, divided here into two groups: literary criticism and historical or cultural commentary. His writing is clear, sharp, and disciplined, and his approbation of William Dean Howells and Italo Calvino are as finely tuned as his excoriation of John Updike and Herman Wouk." Libr J

Includes bibliographical references

Fairlie, Henry

Bite the hand that feeds you; essays and provocations. edited and with an introduction by Jeremy McCarter; foreword by Leon Wieseltier. Yale University Press 2009 355p $30   **814**

1. Individualism

ISBN 978-0-300-12383-8; 0-300-12383-3

LC 2008-49888

"A Grub Street transplant, Fairlie brought to America a fluency in history and prose, a jagged wit, a newcomer's affection for the New World, and a set of self-destructive lifestyle habits charming only in hindsight. We could use more of his kind. Fairlie, who had an unmistakable voice—Tory, yet unpredictable—did most of his finest work at The New Republic. This smartly edited collection gets him at his best, a principled conservative with an eye out for the fatuous." New Yorker

Fiedler, Leslie A.

★ **Fiedler** on the roof; essays on literature and Jewish identity. by Leslie Fiedler. Godine 1990 184p $19.95; pa $11.95   **814**

1. Jews in literature 2. Judaism

ISBN 0-87923-859-3; 0-87923-949-2 pa

LC 90-55282

"Disturbing, provocative, and brilliant." Libr J

Franzen, Jonathan

★ **Farther** away; Jonathan Franzen. Farrar, Straus and Giroux 2012 321 p.   **814**

1. Essays 2. Literature -- History & criticism 3. Personality development in literature 4. Storytelling 5. Technology -- Social aspects 6. Wallace, David Foster, 1962-2008

ISBN 0374153574; 9780374153571

LC 2011046067

The author presents "a collection of recent essays, speeches, and reviews, in which he lays out a view of literature in which storytelling and character development trump

lyrical acrobatics, and unearths a few forgotten classics. . . . [Jonathan Franzen discusses] books that revel in the frustrations, despairs, and near-blisses of human relationships. . . . This intimate read is packed with provocative questions about technology, love, and the state of the contemporary novel." (Publishers Weekly)

Gass, William H.

Finding a form: essays. Cornell University Press 1997 354p pa $21   **814**

1. Authors 2. Biography as a literary form 3. Dramatists 4. Editors 5. Essayists 6. Literary critics 7. Logicians 8. Novelists 9. Philosophers 10. Poets 11. Pulitzer Prizes 12. Short story writers

ISBN 0-8014-8489-8

Gass "is 'as obdurate as nails' when it comes to the best possible use of the written word. Each essay in this wide-ranging book (be it titled 'Ezra Pound,' 'Nietzche: The Polemical Philosopher,' 'Robert Walser,' 'Nature, Culture, and Cosmos,' 'Pulitzer, The People Prize,' or 'The Music of Prose') offers evidence for such a conclusion. Gass is concerned with how best to use a phrase or word and believes we should be tough-minded when it comes to reading. He reveals a sardonic sense of humor as well, for example, in discussing the winners of the Pulitzer prize, and he dislikes the fact that anyone would enjoy his/her own writing." Libr J

Ginsberg, Allen

★ **Deliberate** prose; selected essays, 1952-1995. HarperCollins Pubs. 2000 xxiv, 536p hardcover o.p. pa $17   **814**

ISBN 0-06-093081-0 pa

LC 99-41360

This collection of over 100 prose pieces "organizes the material under several general topics: 'Politics and Prophecies,' 'Drug Culture,' 'Manifestations and Spirituality,' 'Censorship and Sex Laws,' 'Autobiographical Fragments,' 'Literary Techniques and the Beat Generation,' 'Writer,' and 'Further Appreciations,' tributes to artistic collaborators and cultural heroes such as Robert Frank, Philip Glass, Andy Warhol, and the Beatles. . . . Taken together, they provide a rare glimpse into Ginsberg's creative practice, a key to sources and influences, and a good overview of his life and art." Libr J

Includes bibliographical references

Gladwell, Malcolm

What the dog saw and other adventures. Little, Brown and Company 2009 410p $27.99   **814**

1. Popular culture -- United States 2. Social values -- United States

ISBN 978-0-316-07584-8; 0-316-07584-1

LC 2009-24010

"An eccentric collection of 19 essays that run the gamut from the trivial (a profile of infomercial maestro Ron Popeil) to the substantial (a less expensive solution for chronic homelessness). What distinguishes each of them is a surprising, often counterintuitive, insight or two, delivered in a no-frills — even formulaic — writing style that could be a flaw in some other context, but here works beautifully, ensuring that the words don't distract from the ideas. . . . Gladwell excels at making unobvious and intriguing connections, as between football and teaching or Enron and antisubmarine warfare, and readers are swept along." PopMatters

Gottlieb, Robert Adams

★ **Lives** and letters. Farrar, Straus and Giroux 2011 426p $30   **814**

ISBN 978-0-374-29882-1; 0-374-29882-3

LC 2010-38530

"Having headed up two formidable cultural institutions, The New Yorker and the Alfred A. Knopf publishing house, Gottlieb is a fairly formidable cultural institution himself. When he passes judgment, we are inclined to listen. Befitting a man of letters, some of the essays meditate on literary figures and questions that attracted Gottlieb's curiosity. In one he examines the unlikely author-editor collaboration between Marjorie Kinnan Rawlings and Maxwell Perkins; in another he ponders how the 'wildly uneven' works of John Steinbeck have all managed to stay in print. The crowd-pleasing portion of the collection is provided by Gottlieb's critical reflections on biographies, many featuring celebrities who soared through life, egos ablaze. Discussing books about prima donnas as diverse as Margot Fonteyn and Judy Garland, Gottlieb is genteelly shocked by salacious revelations he considers an invasion of privacy, though not too shocked to give examples." Boston Globe

Grann, David

The **devil** and Sherlock Holmes; tales of murder, madness, and obsession. Doubleday 2010 304p $26.95   **814**

ISBN 978-0-385-53316-4; 0-385-53316-0

LC 2009-42230

"The real strength of Grann's work isn't earthshaking revelations; it's portraiture. He excels at capturing people and showing what makes them tick. His subjects are always interesting and exceptional, if not always sympathetic. Any appreciator of nonfiction, in fact, may find this book heartbreaking. . . . These pieces are evidence of a great nonfiction writer who has come into his own." Miami Herald

Hampton, Howard

★ **Born** in flames; termite dreams, dialectical fairy tales, and pop apocalypses. Harvard University Press 2007 473p $28.95   **814**

1. Motion pictures 2. Popular culture 3. Rock music

ISBN 978-0-674-02317-8; 0-674-02317-X

LC 2006-43680

"The torrent of allusions presupposes an Olympian level of cultural indoctrination, and some sentences are so dense that they require a little thoughtful chewing, but Hampton offers something that grows scarcer as today's media bombardment grows in volume: fresh thinking. Knee-jerk intellectuals may find it easy to lampoon someone who takes pop this seriously, but Hampton is a writer—possibly the only one—who can analyze Buffy the Vampire Slayer in the context of D. H. Lawrence . . . and make it work." Booklist

Includes bibliographical references

Hitchens, Christopher

Arguably. Twelve 2011 788p $30.00 **814**

1. Authors, English -- 21st century 2. Criticism 3. Essays 4. Hitchens, Christopher, 1949-2011 5.

Journalists 6. Nonfiction

ISBN 085789255X Atlantic Books; 9780857892553 Atlantic Books; 9781455502776; 9781455506781

LC 2011930917

This volume presents collected essays on literature and politics by the author of Orwell's Victory (2002); Blood, Class, and Empire: The Enduring Anglo-American Relationship (2004); God Is Not Great: How Religion Poisons Everything (2007), and Hitch-22: A Memoir (2010). The essays appeared previously in such periodicals as Vanity Fair, Slate and The Atlantic, from 1999-2011.

Goading, brilliant, funny, and caring, Hitchens is a voice of enlightenment in a wilderness of cant. Booklist

Hoagland, Edward

Tigers & ice; reflections on nature and life. Lyons Press 1999 206p $22; pa $16.95   **814**

ISBN 1-55821-742-8; 1-58574-182-5 pa

LC 98-36477

"Edward Hoagland entered his 60's captivated by sight. After three years of legal blindness, a surgeon restored both his vision and his delight for the tableaux of the natural world. . . . In the 11 essays collected in 'Tigers and Ice,' he considers subjects as varied as suicide, friendship, cowardice, man-made ponds, Indian tigers and Antarctic penguins—all colored by his renewed view of the world." N Y Times Book Rev

Johnson, Charles Richard

Turning the wheel; essays on Buddhism and writing. [by] Charles Johnson. Scribner 2003 187p hardcover o.p. pa $15.95   **814**

1. African Americans -- Authorship 2. African Americans in literature 3. Authors 4. Authorship 5. Buddhism 6. College teachers 7. Essayists 8. Novelists 9. Short story writers

ISBN 0-7432-4324-2; 978-1-4165-7243-5; 1-4165-7243-0

LC 2002-44666

"The central leitmotifs of the lucid, fervently reasoned essays collected in 'Turning the Wheel' are 'enlightenment and liberation.'" N Y Times Book Rev

Includes bibliographical references

Kosinski, Jerzy N.

Passing by; selected essays, 1962-1991. [by] Jerzy Kosinski. Grove Press; Distributed by Publishers Group West 1995 256p pa $12   **814**

ISBN 0-8021-3423-8

LC 95-19519

"While the selections would be improved by contextualizing introductions, they portray a man who was impassioned about literature and who saw his role as confronting 'life's threatening encounters.'" Publ Wkly

Includes bibliographical references

Lethem, Jonathan

The **ecstasy** of influence; nonfictions, etc. Doubleday 2011 437p $27.95   **814**

ISBN 978-0-385-53495-6; 9780385534956

LC 2011016248

"Mr. Lethem's crowded pantheon, 'The Ecstasy of Influence' makes clear, includes Marvel comic books and misfit writers like Philip K. Dick, J. G. Ballard, Shirley Jackson and Charles Willeford. It includes improvisational filmmakers like John Cassavetes, little-known bands like the Go-Betweens and rumpled, bohemian critics like Manny Farber. Mr. Lethem is all about the underdogs, and he counts himself snug among their number. 'Most of my heroes,' he declares, 'are partly or entirely out of print.' Mailer gets a hall pass because he is, like Mr. Lethem, from Brooklyn, and because he took a grizzled interest in things like 'graffiti, underground film, marijuana and space travel.' Like almost everything Mr. Lethem has written, 'The Ecstasy of Influence' is a reflection of, and a pixelated homage to, those whose work he fetishizes. If this book has a thesis, it's this: For an artist, influence is everything." N Y Times (Late N Y Ed)

Liebling, A. J.

★ **Just** enough Liebling; classic work by the legendary New Yorker writer. introduction by David Remnick. North Point Press 2004 xxvi, 534p $27.50 **814**

ISBN 0-374-10443-3

LC 2004-50056

"This captivating and appropriately plump . . . collection will bring renewed attention to a master of the man-on-the-street, narrative nonfiction form and celebrate the centenary of Liebling's birth." Booklist

Martin, Steve

Pure drivel. Hyperion 1998 104p $19.95; pa $10.95 **814**

1. Large print books

ISBN 0-7868-6467-2; 0-7868-8505-X pa

LC 98-28739

"The short essays, conversations, and proclamations collected here are relayed in a slyly deadpan Valley voice that belies the coiled craziness of their content. Martin also brings his gift for comedic timing to these creations, setting a quirky beat that perfectly sets off their ironic wiles." Booklist

McPhee, John A.

Silk parachute; [by] John McPhee. Farrar, Straus and Giroux 2010 227p $25 **814**

1. Authors 2. College teachers 3. Journalists 4. Sports journalism 5. Writers on nature

ISBN 978-0-374-26373-7; 0-374-26373-6

LC 2009-31887

"In the age of blogging and tweeting, of writers' near-constant self-promotion, McPhee is an imperative counterweight, a paragon of both sense and civility." N Y Times Book Rev

Miller, Arthur

Echoes down the corridor; collected essays, 1947-1999. edited by Stephen R. Centola. Viking 2000 332p hardcover o.p. pa $15 **814**

ISBN 0-14-200005-1 pa

LC 00-40427

"This collection is not to be missed." Libr J

Oates, Joyce Carol

In rough country; essays and reviews. Ecco 2010 396p pa $14.99 **814**

1. Authors 2. Children's authors 3. Essayists 4. Literature -- History and criticism 5. Novelists 6. Poets 7. Short story writers

ISBN 978-0-06-196398-8; 0-06-196398-4

"Oates explains that in choosing the title for this collection of 28 reviews and reflections, she aimed to describe the 'treacherous geographical/psychological terrains' of her subjects (a list that includes Flannery O'Connor, Jim Crace, Margaret Atwood and Edgar Allan Poe) and of herself after her husband's death. The phrase is almost better as a description of her own criticism. . . . Oates seems to take special, even unusual, pains not to bend her subjects into her own narrative. She is, instead, intensely focused on the books at hand, marking highlights, supplying context, guiding the reader through passage after passage. Her attention, even in a critic's mode, is unfailingly generous." N Y Times Book Rev

Includes bibliographical references

Ozick, Cynthia

★ **Quarrel** & quandary; essays. Knopf 2000 247p hardcover o.p. pa $13 **814**

1. Authors 2. Children 3. Diarists 4. Holocaust victims 5. Literature -- History and criticism 6. Novelists 7. Short story writers

ISBN 0-375-72445-9 pa

LC 99-89889

Among the topics discussed in this collection of personal and literary essays are Henry James, Anne Frank, Kafka, poetry, and public intellectuals.

"All the essays collected here began life elsewhere as reviews and higher journalism. This kind of gathering of literary leftovers is usually not worth reprinting. Ozick's work is an exception. Her pieces have genuine durability. They are great essays." N Y Times Book Rev

Packer, George

Interesting times; writings from a turbulent decade. Farrar, Straus and Giroux 2009 409p $28 **814**

ISBN 978-0-3741-7572-6; 0-3741-7572-1

LC 2009-10186

A collection "essays chronicling global political and cultural tumult between 9/11 and the 2008 presidential election. . . . From Lagos to Myanmar, Tal Afar to Baghdad, the author reports on location and presents on-the-ground particulars that bring robust perspective to issues that are generally broadly reported. . . . In an era marked by the swift decline of well-researched, long-form journalism, these often heart-wrenching essays bring to life social, political and personal elements of far-flung crises in ways that elude more concise mediums." Kirkus

Remnick, David

Reporting; writings from The New Yorker. Knopf 2006 483p $27.95 **814**

1. Authors 2. Boxers (Persons) 3. Cabinet members 4. Computer scientists 5. Conservationists 6. Diplomats 7. Dissenters 8. Dramatists 9. Emperors 10. Empresses 11. Essayists 12. Human rights

activists 13. Hurricane Katrina, 2005 14. Journalism 15. Journalists 16. Mathematicians 17. Members of Congress 18. Members of Parliament 19. Memoirists 20. Newspaper executives 21. Nobel laureates for literature 22. Nobel laureates for peace 23. Nonfiction writers 24. Novelists 25. Poets 26. Political leaders 27. Political prisoners 28. Presidential candidates 29. Presidents 30. Prime ministers 31. Senators 32. Short story writers 33. Sports trainers 34. Translating and interpreting 35. United Nations officials 36. Vice-presidents 37. Writers on politics
ISBN 0-307-26358-4; 978-0-307-26358-2

LC 2005-44709

The author "is an ideal reporter, combining erudition, curiosity, wit, an eye for the telling anecdote and empathy." Publ Wkly

Rich, Adrienne, 1929-2012

A **human** eye. W.W. Norton & Co. 2009 180p $24.95   **814**
1. Art and society 2. Baldwin, James, 1924-1987 3. Essays 4. Jordan, June, 1936-2002 5. Poetry -- History and criticism 6. Rukeyser, Muriel, 1913-1980
ISBN 978-0-393-07006-4; 0-393-07006-9

LC 2008049972

This book collects ten years of [writer Adrienne Rich's] forewords, personal statements and reviews." (London Review of Books). "Strong writing, Rich believes, is about Show we are with each other," and she finds this encompassing theme in the work of Muriel Rukeyser, whom Rich admires for her poetics of historical sensibilityp; James Baldwin, who was "uncanny" in his prescience; and June Jordan, who believed humor and pleasure are essential to social change. Rich deep-reads poetry written in the shadow of AIDS and during tyranny and war in Iraq, and argues that we must all be resistant to dogma.r" (Booklist)

This collection includes a "response to the anthology Iraqi Poetry Today, a critique of three classic socialist manifestos, and a rereading of The Dead Lecturer, an early volume of poems by LeRoi Jones. Rich engages the impulse to make art that both impels toward and interacts with social change, a theme she also traces through the letters of poets Robert Duncan and Denise Levertov, gay and lesbian politics and poetry, and influential texts on Zionism and the Jewish diaspora." Publisher's note

Includes bibliographical references

Richardson, Robert D.

Emerson; the mind on fire: a biography. by Robert D. Richardson, Jr.; with a frontispiece by Barry Moser. University of Calif. Press 1995 671p il $50; pa $21.95 **814**
1. Authors 2. Biography, Individual 3. Essayists 4. Philosophers 5. Poets
ISBN 0-520-08808-5; 0-520-20689-4 pa

LC 94-36008

"Richardson focuses principally on his subject's inner life, the life of his mind and spirit. But in this subtle portrayal of Emerson the thinker, the reader also sees the clearly limned portrait of Emerson the social activist. . . . A masterful work, this biography will attract the attention of scholars and serious general readers for decades." Booklist

Includes bibliographical references

Robinson, Marilynne, 1943-

When I was a child I read books; Marilynne Robinson. Farrar, Straus & Giroux 2012 xvi, 206 p **814**
1. Authors 2. Authorship 3. Calvinism -- United States 4. Essays 5. Philosophy, American 6. Political science -- United States -- Philosophy 7. Religion 8. Religion & science 9. Theology -- United States
ISBN 0374298785; 9780374298784

LC 2011041206

This collection of essays are a continuation of [author Marilynne] Robinson's previous collection 'Absence of Mind' and share the central preoccupation of almost all her work. She is defender-in-chief of the mysteries of humankind. . . . Her enemies are many and varied – militant atheists, scientists, . . . a political system that sees everything in terms of economic value, a government that commits the arch-crimes of closing libraries and filleting universities. . . . She observes that the idea of a public sector is now condemned by many Americans as socialism, a stance at odds with the civic principles on which the country was founded. . . . [The book offers a] close reading of the Bible and a . . . defence of the Old Testament. (New Statesman)

Said, Edward W.

Reflections on exile and other essays. Harvard Univ. Press 2000 xxxv, 617p $36.95; pa $19.95 **814**
1. Authors 2. Criticism 3. Criticism -- Political aspects 4. Literary critics 5. Literature -- History and criticism 6. Literature, Modern -- 20th century -- History and criticism 7. Literature, Modern -- 20th century -- History and criticism -- Theory, etc 8. Motion picture directors 9. Nationalism 10. Novelists 11. Palestinian Arabs 12. Philosophers 13. Politics and culture 14. Politics and literature 15. Politics in literature 16. Psychologists 17. Short story writers
ISBN 0-674-00302-0; 0-674-00997-5 pa

LC 00-44996

"Written between 1967 and the present by a literary critic and advocate for the Palestinian cause, these pieces often deal with the self-deceiving fictions of the colonizers about the people they oppress; others deplore some fashionable critical theories as unengaged with real life and history." N Y Times Book Rev

Includes bibliographical references

Sedaris, David

Dress your family in corduroy and denim. Little, Brown 2004 257p $24.95   **814**
ISBN 0-316-14346-4

LC 2003-65673

The author "has a unique ability to supply exactly the right details to bring every funny, awkward, ludicrous, painful, horrible real-life moment into harrowingly crisp focus." Booklist

Me talk pretty one day. Little, Brown 2000 272p $22.95; pa $14.95   **814**
1. Americans -- France -- Paris -- Humor 2. Large print books 3. Paris (France) -- Humor
ISBN 0-316-77772-2; 0-316-77696-3 pa

LC 00-25052

"In this collection of 27 fairly short essays, some of which appeared in Esquire and The New Yorker, Sedaris gives the impression of ease and naturalness. Whether he is writing about overcoming a lisp, learning to play the guitar, trying to master French, or taking an IQ test, whether the locales are North Carolina, New York, or France, the author is both amused and amusing." Libr J

When you are engulfed in flames. Little, Brown 2008 323p $25.99   **814**
1. Criticism
ISBN 978-0-316-14347-9; 0-316-14347-2
                LC 2007-49021
This collection "gets its title from a booklet with tips for 'Disaster Damage Prevention' that Sedaris found in a Hiroshima hotel room when he moved to Japan for three months to quit smoking. . . . [His stay] provides fresh material aplenty for the longest piece, 'The Smoking Section,' which is destined to become a quit-lit (or quitterature) classic. The draw, as always, is Sedaris's utter lack of sanctimony and his use of humor as a portal to deeper feelings. Instead of insufferably touting his new purity, Sedaris recalls all those nasty habits he's overcome—alcohol, marijuana, cigarettes—with wistful fondness. His honesty is refreshing." Christ Sci Monit

Sontag, Susan

★ **At** the same time; essays and speeches. edited by Paolo Dilonardo and Anne Jump; with a foreword by David Rieff. Farrar, Straus & Giroux 2007 235p $23   **814**
1. Criticism
ISBN 0-374-10072-1; 978-0-374-10072-8
                LC 2006-31179
This is a "collection of 16 essays written toward the end of . . . [Sontag's] life. . . . Every public and academic library should crave to own this." Libr J

★ **Styles** of radical will. Picador USA 2002 274p pa $15   **814**
1. Aesthetics 2. Authors 3. Essayists 4. Motion picture directors 5. Motion pictures 6. Nonfiction writers 7. Philosophers 8. Pornography 9. Silence 10. Theatrical directors 11. Vietnam War, 1961-1975
ISBN 0-312-42021-8
                LC 2001-58071
"The book contains essays, some previously published, arranged in groups. The first group of three is aesthetic and philosophical; three deal with film; and the last set is . . . a reply to a Partisan Review questionnaire about America and an . . . essay on a trip to North Vietnam." Libr J

Where the stress falls; essays. Farrar, Straus & Giroux 2001 351p $25; pa $14   **814**
1. Authors 2. Choreographers 3. College teachers 4. Composers 5. Dancers 6. Dramatists 7. Essayists 8. Journalists 9. Literary critics 10. Nonfiction writers 11. Novelists 12. Poets 13. Short story writers
ISBN 0-374-28917-4; 0-312-42131-1 pa
                LC 2001-33704
The essays in this collection "are organized into three categories. 'Reading' encompasses Sontag's erudite, critical

renderings on autobiography and the works and influence of international literary figures such as Machado de Assis, Roland Barthes, Danilo Kiš, Marina Tsvetaeva, and Robert Walser. In the middle section, 'Seeing,' Sontag is more approachable, expressing her perceptive and provocative opinions on cinema, garden history, photography, painting, opera, drama, and dance. Finally, in 'There and Now,' Sontag recounts her experiences in Sarajevo and her feelings regarding travel, activism, writing, and translations." Libr J

Spiegelman, Willard

Seven pleasures; essays on ordinary happiness. Farrar, Straus, and Giroux 2009 197p $23   **814**
1. Happiness 2. Pleasure 3. Solitude
ISBN 978-0-374-23930-5; 0-374-23930-4
                LC 2008-45049
This book "explores a range of satisfactions to be enjoyed in the everyday life — or, to put it another way, in the no man's land between religion and pharmacology, what Mr. Spiegelman calls the 'twin pillars of the American happiness industry.' Individual chapters focus on his own chief pleasures: reading, walking, looking, dancing, listening, swimming and writing. One theme of his 'book of gerunds' is that ordinariness can yield much more pleasure than is normally assumed. All the striving for happiness in our culture may cause us to overlook the riches of the familiar and near to hand." Wall Street J

Sullivan, John Jeremiah

Pulphead; essays. Farrar, Straus and Giroux 2011 369p il   **814**
1. American literature -- 21st century 2. Essays 3. Popular culture in literature
ISBN 978-0-374-53290-1 pa; 978-1-4299-9504-7 ebook
                LC 2011024875
The book presents a collection of essays reflecting on "our popular, unpopular, and at times completely forgotten culture." (us.macmillan.com) Topics of the essays include "the near-death of his brother . . . the Tennessean writer Andrew Lytle . . . a Christian rock festival called Creation . . . [and] the early-nineteenth-century French explorer and botanist Constantine Samuel Rafinesque." (New Yorker)

"The age-old strangeness of American pop culture gets dissected with hilarious and revelatory precision in these scintillating essays. . . . [The author] surveys 10,000 years of intriguing, inexplicable, and incorrigible socio-aesthetic phenomena, from the ancient Indian cave paintings of Tennessee (and their hillbilly admirers) to the takeover of his Wilmington, N.C., house by the teen soap opera One Tree Hill. Along the way he visits a Christian rock festival brimming with fellowship and frog-devouring savagery; witnesses the collapse of civilization in a post-Katrina gas line; hangs out in the professional-partying demimonde of MTV's Real World; marches with exuberant Tea Partiers; scouts the animal kingdom's gathering war on mankind; and traces the rise of rocker Axl Rose from his origins as a weedy adolescent punk in the small-town void of central Indiana." Publ Wkly

Tan, Amy

The **opposite** of fate; a book of musings. Putnam 2003 398p il $24.95; pa $15   **814**
1. Authors 2. Children's authors 3. Essayists 4. Novelists 5. Short story writers
ISBN 0-399-15074-9; 0-14-200489-8 pa
LC 2003-47190
"No matter how much readers already revere Tan, their appreciation for her will grow tenfold after experiencing these provocative and unforgettable revelations." Booklist

Trillin, Calvin

Too soon to tell. Farrar, Straus & Giroux 1995 292p hardcover o.p. pa $22   **814**
ISBN 0-374-27846-6; 978-0-374-52986-4 pa; 0-374-52986-8 pa
LC 94-24629
"In this collection of nearly 100 syndicated columns, Calvin Trillin holds forth on everything from the animal kingdom . . . to the possibility of being labeled a member of the cultural elite. . . . 'Too Soon to Tell' abounds with Mr. Trillin's self-deprecating humor and slyly acerbic insights, not to mention invaluable homespun wisdom." N Y Times Book Rev

Updike, John

Due considerations; essays and criticism. Alfred A. Knopf 2007 xxii, 703p il $40   **814**
1. Literature, Modern -- History and criticism
ISBN 978-0-307-26640-8; 0-307-26640-0
LC 2007-18665
"A lush book to be savored over a long period of time." Booklist

Vonnegut, Kurt

★ A **man** without a country; edited by Daniel Simon. Seven Stories Press 2005 146p il $23.95 **814**
1. United States -- Politics and government -- 2001-
ISBN 1-58322-713-X
LC 2005-14967
The author discusses politics, human nature, and other topics "in this collection of articles written over the last five years, many from the alternative magazine In These Times." Publ Wkly

Wallace, David Foster

Consider the lobster; and other essays. Little, Brown 2005 343p il $25.95   **814**
1. Criticism
ISBN 0-316-15611-6
LC 2005-10886
"Wallace's complex essays are written, and rightfully so, to be read more than once." Booklist
Includes bibliographical references

White, E. B.

★ **Essays** of E.B. White. Perennial Classics 1999 364p il pa $14.95   **814**
1. Ornithologists
ISBN 0-06-093223-6
LC 98-56019

Most of the essays first appeared in The New Yorker. "They range from a 1934 piece on the St. Nicholas Magazine 'League' and the distinguished writers who were members of it as children, to a 1975 report from Allen Cove, Maine, where White had retreated from the bedlam of the city." Publ Wkly

Williams, Terry Tempest

Finding beauty in a broken world. Pantheon Books 2008 419p $26   **814**
1. Aesthetics
ISBN 978-0-375-42078-8; 0-375-42078-9
LC 2008-7196
The naturalist author of Refuge and An Unspoken Hunger reflects on what it means to be human, the interconnection between the natural and human worlds, and how they combine to produce both tumult and peace, ugliness and beauty.
"Scientific in her exactitude, compassionate in her receptivity, and rhapsodic in expression, Williams has constructed a beautiful mosaic of loss and renewal that affirms, with striking lucidity, the need for reverence for all of life." Booklist
Includes bibliographical references

Williams, William Carlos

In the American grain. New Directions 1956 235p hardcover o.p. pa $13.95   **814**
1. Authors 2. Colonial administrators 3. Diplomats 4. Emperors 5. Essayists 6. Explorers 7. Inventors 8. Members of Congress 9. Missionaries 10. Naval officers 11. Pioneers 12. Poets 13. Scientists 14. Scouts 15. Short story writers 16. Statesmen 17. Vice-presidents 18. Writers on science
ISBN 0-8112-0230-5 pa
LC 56-13360
Williams portrays "the developing American conscience in sketches of such major figures as Columbus, Cotton Mather, Washington, Franklin, and Poe, and such minor ones as Champlain, Thomas Morton, Père Sebastian Rasles, and Jacataqua. He sought the grain of American character especially in homely, rather than heroic, incidents of national history." Benet's Reader's Ency of Am Lit

Wilson, Edmund

Literary essays and reviews of the 1920s & 30s. Library of America 2007 958p $40   **814**
1. Literature -- History and criticism 2. Modernism (Aesthetics)
ISBN 978-1-59853-013-1
LC 2007-928898
This volume collects The Shores of Light (1952), a collection of his early reviews and other writings; and Axel's Castle (1931), a book of literary criticism discussing modernism. It also includes several previously uncollected reviews.
"Anyone wishing to revisit the intellectual and literary passions of the period will be well advised to do so in the company of someone who could be a Virgil as well as recommend the reading of him. Edmund Wilson came as close

as anybody has to making the labor of criticism into an art." Atl Mon

Includes bibliographical references

Literary essays and reviews of the 1930s & 40s; [Lewis M. Dabney, editor] Library of America 2007 979p $40   **814**

1. Literature -- History and criticism 2. Modernism (Aesthetics)

ISBN 978-1-59853-014-8

LC 2007-928899

This volume gathers together The Triple Thinkers (1938, revised 1948), The Wound and The Bow (1941), Classics and Commercials (1950), along with a selection of uncollected reviews.

"This is a required purchase for all libraries, public and academic—even for those collections already having these texts in separate volumes." Libr J

Includes bibliographical references

Wright, Evan

Hella nation; looking for happy meals in Kandahar, rocking the side pipe, wingnut's war against the gap, and other adventures with the totally lost tribes of America. G. P. Putnam's Sons 2009 388p il $25.95   **814**

1. Popular culture -- United States

ISBN 978-0-399-15574-1; 0-399-15574-0

LC 2009-02291

"It's refreshing to read first-person journalism by an unorthodox P.T. Barnum who refuses to put himself at the center of a three-ring circus." Washington Post

★ The Best American essays of the century; Joyce Carol Oates, editor; Robert Atwan, coeditor; with an introduction by Joyce Carol Oates. Houghton Mifflin 2000 596p hardcover o.p. pa $18   **814**

ISBN 0-618-04370-5; 0-618-15587-2 pa

This anthology includes essays "that contemplate diverse worlds, from nature to courtrooms, war and family memories. Race is a pervasive theme, explored with candor and insight by many, including James Baldwin, Zora Neale Hurston, and, in a jolting 1912 condemnation of a Coatesville, Pennsylvania, lynching, John Jay Chapman." Booklist

Includes bibliographical references

Burn this book; PEN writers speak out on the power of the word. edited by Toni Morrison. HarperStudio 2009 118p $16.99   **814**

1. Authorship 2. Censorship 3. Freedom of speech

ISBN 978-0-06-177400-3

"Published in conjunction with the PEN American Center, this slim collection of essays has an amazing list of contributors—Toni Morrison, John Updike, David Grossman, Francine Prose, Pico Iyer, Russell Banks, Paul Auster, Orhan Pamuk, Salman Rushdie, Ed Park, and Nadine Gordimer. . . . [They] discuss the importance of writing from various views, political and social. They illustrate the need for freedom of speech and human rights, and they emphasize the target writers become in a tyranny. . . . This is not an easy

read, but it is a profound, absorbing, and moving collection of work." Libr J

Includes bibliographical references

The Fun of it; stories from The talk of the town, The New Yorker. edited by Lillian Ross; introduction by David Remnick. Modern Lib. 2001 xxi, 478p pa $16.95   **814**

ISBN 0-375-75649-3

LC 00-68237

A "selection of stories from 'Talk' in chronologically arranged sections that begin with the 1920s and end in 2000. Many of the early contributions were unsigned, but through archival research Ross ferrets out and reveals the authors of many of those initial pieces. Included in this lively collection are pieces by writers—some of whom became New Yorker regulars—such as Robert Benchley, James Thurber, E. B. White, A. J. Liebling, John Updike, Garrison Keillor, Ann Beattie, Bill McKibben, Roger Angell, Steve Martin, and Susan Orlean." Libr J

The Inevitable; contemporary writers confront death. edited by David Shields and Bradford Morrow; with an introduction by the editors. W. W. Norton & Co. 2011 332p $17.95   **814**

1. Death

ISBN 9780393339369 pa

LC 2010-43479

"Often poetic and at times funny or gruesome while exposing raw grief, the writers . . . tackle the subject of death with honesty and courage." Publ Wkly

Includes bibliographical references

The beholder's eye; a collection of America's finest personal journalism. edited and with an introduction by Walt Harrington. Grove Press 2005 xxii, 256p pa $14   **814**

ISBN 0-8021-4224-5

LC 2005-46242

"Each writer takes a unique approach to the subject, drawing the reader into the experience of pit-bull fighting or hunting with the Inuit. Among the collection: Harrington, who is married to a black woman, explores his evolving attitudes on race through the lens of his relationship with his in-laws, Pete Earley returns to his hometown in search of the meaning of a sister's death in their youth, Ron Rosenbaum explores his own outlook on life in a philosophical discourse with then-New York governor Mario Cuomo, Davis Miller is unabashedly starstruck in a comfortable and closeup look at Muhammad Ali at the home of Ali's mother, and Stephen S. Hall is personally probing in his exploration, via MRI, of his own brain and its functioning. These stories are amusing, insightful, and touching in a way that only something personal can be." Booklist

★ The best American essays 2010; edited with an introduction by Christopher Hitchens; Robert Atwan, series editor. Houghton Mifflin 2010 xxi, 272p pa $14.95   **814**

ISBN 978-0-547-39451-0

Editors select essays from general interest magazines that touch on topics political, scientific, historical, religious, and sociological, in addition to the personal and literary.

815   American speeches in English

★ American speeches. Library of America 2006 2v ea $35
815
1. American speeches 2. Political oratory -- United States 3. Speeches, addresses, etc., American
ISBN 1-931082-97-9 v1; 1-931082-98-7 v2
LC 2006-40928
This is a collection of over 120 historical speeches delivered between 1761 and 1997.

Representative American speeches. Wilson, H.W.
815
1. American speeches
A compilation containing a selection of speeches of the year made by eminent men and women on major trends and events. Each speech is prefaced by a note about the speaker and the occasion. The appendix in each volume contains biographical notes.

816   American letters in English

Letters of the century; America, 1900-1999. edited by Lisa Grunwald and Stephen J. Adler. Dial Press (NY) 1999 741p il hardcover o.p. pa $18
816
1. American letters
ISBN 0-385-31590-2; 0-385-31593-7 pa
LC 99-16808
Among the letter writers gathered are "Carl Van Doren, Huey Long, Franklin D. Roosevelt, Lillian Hellman and a Vietnam soldier named Dusty. This is one of the most original literary tributes to the closing century." Publ Wkly
Includes bibliographical references

817   American humor and satire in English

Allen, Woody
Side effects. Ballantine 1987 213p pa $6.99 **817**
ISBN 978-0-345-34335-2; 0-345-34335-2
"The sixteen sketches—which are concerned with themes of love and death, angst and despair, bagels and lox—appeared originally in magazines." Commonweal

Without feathers. Ballantine 1983 221p pa $6.99
817
ISBN 0-345-33697-6; 978-0-345-33697-2
A collection of sixteen satirical sketches, most of which previously appeared in The New Yorker and other periodicals, and two one-act plays: God, and Death. The sketches include "takeoffs on other writers (Kafka, Bellow, Strindberg), and several 'intellectual' dissertations on such topics as the Irish genius, the origins of slang, the lesser ballets, psychic phenomena, etc." Libr J

Blount, Roy
Alphabet juice; the energies, gists and spirits of letters, words and combinations thereof: their roots, bones, innards, piths, pips and secret parts, tinctures, tonics and essences: with examples of their usage foul. Farrar, Straus and Giroux 2008 364p $25 **817**
1. Authors 2. English language -- Dictionaries 3. Humorists 4. Nonfiction writers 5. Sportswriters 6. Vocabulary
ISBN 978-0-374-10369-9; 0-374-10369-0
LC 2008-08918
"Laid out in A–Z dictionary format, the book ranges from the pointed critique of conjunction dysfunction to the hilarious diatribe under tump, which finds Blount spending weeks looking for his own name in the new edition of American Heritage Dictionary.... Although some entries are only tangentially connected to his ostensible subject (see TV, on being on), many others provide Blount with ample opportunity to wax eloquent on the joys of language; his perfect parsing of the allure of the phrase 'wonky exegeses' will elicit smiles from fellow language lovers. A knowledgeable handbook that is also chock-full of funny, colorful opinions on marriage, movies, and Monet." Booklist

Carlin, George
Napalm & silly putty. Hyperion 2001 269p $22.95; pa $12.95
817
1. American wit and humor 2. Wit and humor
ISBN 0-7868-6413-3; 0-7868-8758-3 pa
LC 00-54055
The comedian "covers a wide range of issues from rape and religion to the homeless.... And any topic is fair game: abortion, airport security, cars, funerals, language, organ donors, sports, technology, TV and war.... Over 100 scintillating short pieces are interrupted by loony lists and hundreds of clever one-liners." Publ Wkly

Frazier, Ian
Coyote v. Acme. Picador USA 2002 117p pa $11
817
ISBN 0-312-42058-7; 978-0-312-42058-1
LC 2001-50067
"The title essay, with its exposition, in deadly legalese, of one Wile E. Coyote's complaints against a generic purveyor of explosive devices, shows Frazier's great comic range, however trite the subject. Although this book is not Frazier at full-bore, readers of his generation will find an occasional cultural reference long thought lost, and find themselves oddly beholden to a fellow who can resurrect Billy Joe McCallister from beneath the Tallahatchie Bridge." Publ Wkly

Lamentations of the father. Farrar, Straus and Giroux 2008 194p il $22; pa $14 **817**
1. American wit and humor
ISBN 978-0-374-28162-5; 0-374-28162-9; 978-0-312-42835-8 pa; 0-312-42835-9 pa
LC 2008-2137
This is a collection of essays by the American humorist.
"A treat for Frazier fanatics and new readers alike, this compilation from the past 13 years has nary a misstep and begs to be read in one sitting." Publ Wkly

Nilsen, Alleen Pace

Encyclopedia of 20th century American humor; [by] Alleen Pace Nilsen and Don L. F. Nilsen. Oryx Press 2000 360p il $73.95   **817**

1. American wit and humor -- 20th century -- Encyclopedias 2. American wit and humor -- Encyclopedias 3. Reference books
ISBN 1-57356-218-1

LC 99-47257

This "is a 98-entry reference work. A bibliography that includes scholarly works on humor, biographies, and joke books stretches over 20 pages and rounds out the text. Arranged alphabetically, articles vary in length from one to five pages. A few are illustrated with cartoons and photographs. Some longer articles are broken down into subtopics." Booklist

Includes bibliographical references

Peter, Laurence J.

The **Peter** principle; why things always go wrong. [by] Laurence J. Peter and Raymond Hull. 1st Collins Business ed.; Collins Business 2009 xxvi, 161p il $19.99   **817**

1. Management -- Anecdotes
ISBN 978-0-06-169906-1

LC 2008-44122

"In a delightful spoof of administrative inefficiency in both public and private enterprise, the authors expound their theory known as the Peter Principle—'in a hierarchy every employee tends to rise to his level of incompetence.' From this they develop their science of hierarchiology." Cincinnati Public Libr

Includes bibliographical references

Trillin, Calvin

Quite enough of Calvin Trillin; forty years of funny stuff. Random House 2011 340p $27; ebook $12.99   **817**

1. American wit and humor 2. Authors 3. Biography, Individual 4. Essayists 5. Humorists 6. Novelists 7. Poetry -- By individual authors 8. Short story writers
ISBN 978-1-4000-6982-8; 1-4000-6982-3; 978-0-679-60480-8 ebook

LC 2011004050

The author "entertains with this collection of his song lyrics, comic verse, and more than 130 of the brief essays he originally wrote for the New Yorker, the New York Times, the Nation, and his syndicated King Features column. . . . Trillin dances around a subject, examines it from different angles, and often finds fun in the commonplace throughout this huge and hilarious comedic compendium." Publ Wkly

Twain, Mark

Mark Twain's library of humor; illustrated by E.W. Kemble; Steve Martin, series ed.; introduction by Roy Blount. Modern Library 2000 xl, 560p il pa $17   **817**

1. American wit and humor
ISBN 978-0-679-64036-3

LC 00-25971

"Beginning with the piece that made Mark Twain famous—'The Notorious Jumping Frog of Calaveras County'—and ending with his fanciful 'How I Edited an Agricultural Paper,' this . . . anthology, an abridgment of the 1888 original, collects twenty of Twain's own pieces, in addition to tall tales, fables, and satires by forty-three of Twain's contemporaries, including Washington Irving, Harriet Beecher Stowe, Ambrose Bierce, William Dean Howells, Joel Chandler Harris, Artemus Ward, and Bret Harte." Publisher's note

Weingarten, Gene

The **fiddler** in the subway; the true story of what happened when a world-class violinist played for handouts--and other virtuoso performances by America's foremost feature writer. Simon & Schuster 2010 363p il   **817**

1. American wit and humor
ISBN 978-1-4391-8159-1; 978-1-4391-8160-7 ebook

LC 2009-51668

"A sparkling collection of features by the Pulitzer Prize-winning Washington Post columnist. . . . There are plenty of smiles and laughs scattered throughout the uniformly strong pieces assembled here. But the author is about more than grins and giggles. In even the slightest of the essays—seeing his daughter off to college, honoring the memory of his childhood baseball hero—his storytelling, keen observation and deft reporting startle and amaze." Kirkus

Mirth of a nation; the best contemporary humor. edited by Michael J. Rosen. HarperPerennial 2000 619p pa $15.95   **817**

1. American wit and humor
ISBN 0-06-095321-7

LC 99-44293

An anthology of more than 50 contributors, "most represented by two or three short works. Included are veterans like Dave Barry, Roy Blount Jr., and Fran Lebowitz, and rising stars like David Sedaris, Sandra Tsing Loh, Patricia Marx, and David Rakoff. Though many of the pieces have been published or broadcast previously, some appear in this volume for the first time." Booklist

818   American miscellaneous writings in English

Alcott, Louisa May

The **sketches** of Louisa May Alcott; with an introduction by Gregory Eiselein. Ironweed Press 2001 283p pa $22.95   **818**

ISBN 0-9655309-8-1

LC 00-57259

"Grouped into five categories ('Hospital sketches,' 'Letters from the Mountains,' 'Sketches of Europe,' 'Concord, Massachusetts,' and 'From The Youth's Companion and Merry's Museum),' these by turns frank, witty, ironic, charming and pensive pieces were almost all written when Alcott was between the ages of 28 and 43." Publ Wkly

Includes bibliographical references

Angelou, Maya

A **song** flung up to heaven. Random House 2002 212p $23.95; pa $13   **818**
1. Actors 2. African American authors -- Biography 3. Authors, American -- 20th century -- Biography 4. Children's authors 5. Civil rights workers -- United States -- Biography 6. Dramatists 7. Essayists 8. Memoirists 9. Poets 10. Singers
ISBN 0-375-50747-7; 0-553-38203-9 pa
LC 2001-34914
"This sixth installment in Angelou's autobiographical works begins in 1964 as Angelou returned to the U.S. from Ghana. . . . She worked in Watts at the time of the riots, and Malcolm X and Martin Luther King Jr. were both assassinated just before she was to begin working with them. . . . She moved to New York, where she rejoined a vibrant group of famous writers, intellectuals, and friends; worried about her young-adult son; and understood the humor and heartache of a painful love affair. . . . Spiced with her mother's aphorisms, her often-poetic prose is best at the end, as she muses on the condition of black women and sitting at her mother's table, begins to write I Know Why the Caged Bird Sings." Booklist

Auster, Paul, 1947-

★ **Winter** journal; Paul Auster. Henry Holt and Co. 2012 240 p.   **818**
1. Authors, American -- 20th century -- Biography
ISBN 0805095535; 9780805095531
LC 2011039025
This memoir by Paul Auster presents a meditation on death and life. . . . [O]ne by one, they all begin to happen to you, in the same way they happen to everyone else. . . . [T]he stuff of everyday life—the childhood baseball games, the succession of New York and Paris apartments (21 in total), even the women longed for, two of whom became wives—and the events that shook and shaped him. From the vantage point of the winter preceding his 64th birthday, Auster lets his body and its sensations guide his memories. There is no set chronology; time and place [change] from one year to another, between childhood and adulthood. (Publishers Weekly)

Baraka, Imamu Amiri

The **LeRoi** Jones/Amiri Baraka reader; by Amiri Baraka; edited by William Harris in collaboration with Amiri Baraka. 2nd ed; Thunder's Mouth Press 2000 xxxiii, 586p pa $16.95   **818**
1. African American music 2. African Americans -- Literary collections 3. Authors 4. Blues music 5. Civil rights activists 6. Clergy 7. Dramatists 8. Essayists 9. Mayors 10. Members of Parliament 11. Poets 12. Political leaders 13. Presidential candidates 14. Talk show hosts 15. Television personalities
ISBN 1-56025-238-3
LC 99-32364
A collection of Baraka's poems, plays, and other writings. "The selections included are arranged chronologically in four distinct periods: The Beat Period (1957-62), The Transitional Period (1963-65), The Black Nationalist Period (1965-74), and The Third World Marxist Period (1974-present)." Libr J [review of 1991 edition]
Includes bibliographical references

Bishop, Elizabeth

The **collected** prose; edited, with an introduction, by Robert Giroux. Farrar, Straus & Giroux 1984 xxii, 278p hardcover o.p. pa $16   **818**
ISBN 0-374-51855-6 pa
LC 83-16418
A collection of Bishop's autobiographical sketches and short stories.
"Whether she is discussing the sensuous joys and dark fears of childhood or diamond mining and the preparation of food in Brazil, Elizabeth Bishop provides warm, unforced revelations on an array of topics. . . . A book to relish as well as to read." Choice
Includes bibliographical references

Blount, Roy

Alphabetter juice, or, The joy of text; [by] Roy Blount, Jr. Farrar, Straus and Giroux 2011 283p $26; ebook $12.99   **818**
1. American wit and humor 2. English language -- Dictionaries 3. Vocabulary
ISBN 978-0-374-10370-5; 978-1-4299-2278-4 ebook
LC 2010-39937
This book "is almost a subgenre of its own, a reference book from a leading language expert that's also downright funny. . . . Anybody as eclectic as Blount is worth paying attention to; his passion for the sounds and senses of words makes this book infectiously fun reading for word lovers everywhere." Writer

Be sweet; a conditional love story. [by] Roy Blount, Jr. Harcourt Brace & Co. 1999 329p pa $17   **818**
1. Authors 2. Humorists 3. Humorists, American -- 20th century -- Biography -- Humor 4. Nonfiction writers 5. Sportswriters
ISBN 0-15-600682-0; 978-0-15-600682-8
LC 99-15146
"Blount figures that at age 57 he has lived long enough to hunt for life-defining moments among sundry episodes, including his stint as coeditor of his college paper with presidential wanna-be Lamar Alexander, his days smokin' dope with '70s slugger Richie Allen when Blount was a Sports Illustrated reporter, and a slew of childhood memories." Booklist

Bryson, Bill

I'm a stranger here myself; notes on returning to America after 20 years away. Broadway Bks. 1999 288p hardcover o.p. pa $14.95   **818**
1. Large print books
ISBN 0-7679-0382-X pa
LC 99-18074
The author collects "columns on America he wrote weekly, while living in New Hampshire in the mid-to-late 1990s, for a British Sunday newspaper. Although he happily describes himself as dazzled by American ease, friendliness and abundance, Bryson has no trouble finding comic targets, among them fast food, computer efficiency and, ironically, American friendliness and putative convenience." Publ Wkly

Capote, Truman

Music for chameleons; new writing. Random House 1980 262p hardcover o.p. pa $13   **818**

ISBN 0-679-74566-1 pa

LC 79-5532

"There are three sections: one of short stories, or something like; one consisting of the 'In cold blood'-like 'short novel, Handcarved coffins;' and one called 'Conversational portraits,' which is precisely that." Choice

Carson, Anne

Decreation; poetry, essays, opera. Knopf 2005 245p $24.95 **818**

1. Poetry -- By individual authors

ISBN 1-4000-4349-2

LC 2004-63367

"Carson's inquiry into the paradoxical 'decreation' of the self in the quest for the divine exemplifies her gift for joining erudition with feeling, insight with wit, and a sense of cosmic continuity with personal liberation." Booklist

Cather, Willa

★ **Stories,** poems, and other writings. Library of Am. 1992 1039p $35   **818**

ISBN 0-940450-71-2

LC 91-62294

This volume contains the novels Alexander's bridge (1912) and My mortal enemy (1926); the poetry collection April twilights, and other poems (1923); the essay collection Not under forty (1936); and the following short story collections: Youth and the bright Medusa (1920); Obscure destinies (1932); The old beauty, and others (1948); and uncollected stories from 1892-1929.

Dick, Philip K.

The **exegesis** of Philip K. Dick; edited by Pamela Jackson and Jonathan Lethem; Erik Davis, annotations editor. Houghton Mifflin Harcourt 2011 944p $40   **818**

1. Science fiction -- Authorship 2. Technology and civilization

ISBN 978-0-547-54925-5; 0-547-54925-3

LC 2011-28561

"'I sure have odd nights,' wrote Philip K. Dick in a July 1974 letter to a young woman writing her thesis on him. It's a tremendous understatement, and its inclusion in the early pages of The Exegesis — the long-awaited compendium of the sci-fi writer's papers — acts as a palate cleanser, a wry little weigh station wherein Dick pulls back from his own dense, circuitous investigation of his visions; laughs a little at himself; and then dives back in, allowing the reader to do the same. . . . Dick wrote more than eight thousand pages in the eight years leading up to his death in 1982, all in his attempts to decipher a series of visionary, multisensory experiences he had in February and March of '74 ('2-3-74') wherein he glimpsed a vast truth of the world." East Bay Express

Dillard, Annie

★ The **Annie** Dillard reader. HarperCollins Pubs. 1994 455p hardcover o.p. pa $15.95   **818**

ISBN 0-06-092660-0 pa

LC 94-19482

This reader includes Holy the firm; excerpts from Pilgrim at Tinker Creek, An American childhood, and Teaching a stone to talk; and a reworked version of the 1978 short story The living.

"This selection of writings, chosen by Dillard herself, provides a perfect sampling of her incisive, versatile, and impeccable achievements." Booklist

Pilgrim at Tinker Creek. Harper & Row 1974 271p hardcover o.p. pa $14.95   **818**

1. Natural history -- Virginia

ISBN 0-06-123332-3 pa; 978-0-06-123332-6 pa

This work is "in an honored tradition of literature, not quite environmentalism and not the philosophy of science, it is rather the refraction of natural philosophy through the prismatic conscience of art. Highly recommended for the general reader—any general reader, anywhere—who wishes to deepen his awareness of his yard of world and to reflect upon it more profoundly." Choice

Teaching a stone to talk; expeditions and encounters. Harper & Row 1982 177p hardcover o.p. pa $13   **818**

1. Natural history

ISBN 0-06-091541-2 pa

LC 82-47520

"In the fourteen pensées that make up this book {the author} bears witness, reflects on her observations of the order and disorder, the splendor and horror of the natural world." New Yorker

The **writing** life. Harper & Row 1989 111p hardcover o.p. pa $11   **818**

1. Authors 2. Biography, Individual 3. Creation (Literary, artistic, etc.) 4. Essayists 5. Literary critics 6. Poets 7. Writers on nature

ISBN 0-06-091988-4 pa

LC 89-45034

The author "probes the sorcery that levitates her own writing, discussing with clear eye and wry wit how, where and why she writes." Publ Wkly

Eiseley, Loren C.

The **night** country; [by] Loren Eiseley; illustrations by Leonard Everett Fisher; introduction to the Bison Books edition by Gale E. Christianson. University of Nebraska Press 1997 240p il pa $19.95 **818**

ISBN 0-8032-6735-5; 978-0-8032-6735-0

These poetically expressed reflections "evoke a sense of wonder and appreciation of nature and man's place in the universe. The striking black-and-white illustrations preceding each chapter contribute to the mood and tone." Booklist

Includes bibliographical references

The **star** thrower. Harcourt 1979 319p pa $15   **818**

ISBN 978-0-15-684909-8; 0-15-684909-7

"To read this collection is to see the things he points out to us refracted, transmuted, and clarified through the prism of his poetic imagination and literate style." Libr J

Ellison, Ralph

★ **Going** to the territory. Random House 1986 338p hardcover o.p. pa $14.95 **818**
1. Artists 2. Authors 3. Band leaders 4. Composers 5. Dramatists 6. Essayists 7. Jazz musicians 8. Literary critics 9. Nonfiction writers 10. Novelists 11. Short story writers
ISBN 978-0-679-76001-6 pa; 0-679-76001-6 pa
LC 85-28117
"This collection of essays, addresses, and reviews deals with topics in literature, music, and race relations. . . . Ellison tries to view American culture as a cloth of one piece. His analysis of the growth of the culture, and of the dynamic interaction of the diverse elements within it, is perceptive and convincing." Libr J

Franklin, Benjamin

★ **Autobiography,** Poor Richard, and later writings; letters from London, 1757-1775, Paris, 1776-1785, Philadelphia, 1785-1790, Poor Richard's almanack, 1733-1758, The autobiography. Library of America 1997 816p $30 **818**
ISBN 1-883011-53-1
LC 97-21611
"This collection of Franklin's works begins with letters sent from London (1757-1775) describing the events and diplomacy preceding the Revolutionary War. The volume also contains political satires, bagatelles, pamphlets, and letters written in Paris (1776-1785), where he represented the revolutionary United States at the court of Louis XVI, as well as his speeches given in the Constitutional Convention and other works written in Philadelphia (1785-1790), including his last published article, a . . . satire against slavery. Also included are the . . . prefaces to Poor Richard's Almanack (1733-1758). . . . [The] Autobiography, Franklin's last word on his greatest literary creation—his own invented personality—is presented here in a new edition." Publisher's note
Includes bibliographical references

Gibran, Kahlil

The **collected** works; with eighty-four illustrations by the author. Everyman's Library 2007 880p il $27.50 **818**
1. Poetry -- By individual authors 2. Short stories -- By individual authors 3. Spiritual life
ISBN 978-0-307-26707-8; 0-307-26707-5
LC 2007-28736
This anthology of writings by the Syrian poet includes The Madman, The Forerunner, The Prophet, Sand and Foam, Jesus the Son of Man, Earth Gods, The Wanderer, The Garden of the Prophet, Prose Poems, Spirits Rebellious, Nymphs of the Valley, and A Tear and a Smile.

Hearn, Lafcadio

★ **American** writings; [edited by Christopher Benfey] Library of America 2009 848p il $40 **818**
ISBN 978-1-59853-039-1
LC 2008-938732
"Some Chinese Ghosts (1887), a stylized retelling of ancient legends, foreshadows Hearn's later fascination with Asian themes. The . . . novels Chita (1889), about the devastation wrought by a Louisiana hurricane, and Youma (1890),

about a slave rebellion in Martinique, epitomize his writing at its most luxuriantly romantic. . . [His] travel book Two Years in the French West Indies (1890), presented here with the many illustrations from its first edition, provides a richly impressionistic account of his long stay on Martinique and other Caribbean islands. More than two dozen examples of Hearn's journalism from the 1870s and 1880s are also included here." Publisher's note

Hogan, Linda

The **woman** who watches over the world; a native memoir. Norton 2001 224p $24.95; pa $13.95 **818**
1. Authors 2. Authors, American -- 20th century -- Biography 3. Authors, American -- 20th century -- Family relationships 4. Chickasaw Indians -- Biography 5. Dramatists 6. Essayists 7. Indian authors -- Biography 8. Indian women -- Biography 9. Native Americans 10. Novelists 11. Poets 12. Short story writers
ISBN 0-393-05018-1; 0-393-32305-6 pa
LC 00-49005
In this memoir the author chronicles "her difficult childhood, alcoholism, the anguish of her two psychologically damaged adopted children, and struggles with a neuromuscular disease. She also expresses a lacerating yet crucial vision of the tragic legacies of the U.S. government's brutal war on Native Americans." Booklist

Hughes, Langston

★ **I** wonder as I wander; an autobiographical journey. introd. by Arnold Rampersad. 2nd Hill and Wang ed; Hill & Wang 1993 xxii, 405p pa $16 **818**
1. African American authors 2. Authors 3. Dramatists 4. Novelists 5. Poets 6. Poets, American 7. Short story writers 8. Young adult authors
ISBN 0-8090-1550-1
LC 92-39307
Continuing the autobiography begun in The big sea (1940), this volume contains an account of Hughes' journeys through Russia, Spain, China, and Japan, as well as some incidents of his poetry readings in this country.

Jefferson, Thomas

★ **Writings.** Library of Am. 1984 1600p $35 **818**
ISBN 0-940450-16-X
LC 83-19917
This is "the largest and most skillfully edited single-volume Jefferson ever published." N Y Times Book Rev
Includes bibliographical references

Johnson, James Weldon

The **essential** writings of James Weldon Johnson; edited and with an introduction by Rudolph P. Byrd; foreword by Charles Johnson. Modern Library 2008 xxx, 321p pa $15 **818**
ISBN 978-0-8129-7532-1; 0-8129-7532-4
"This collection of poetry, fiction, criticism, autobiography, political writing and two unpublished plays by James Weldon Johnson (1871-1938) spans 60 years of pure triumph over adversity. . . . [Johnson's] nobility, his inspira-

tion shine forth from these pages, setting moral and artistic standards." Los Angeles Times Book Rev

Kaling, Mindy, 1979-

Is everyone hanging out without me? (and other concerns) Mindy Kaling. Crown Archetype 2011 ix, 222 p.p ill **818**

1. American wit and humor

ISBN 9780307886262; 9780307886286

LC 2011033922

'In this book, author "Mindy Kaling . . . [offers thoughts about what she] thinks makes a great best friend (someone who will fill your prescription in the middle of the night), or what makes a great guy (one who is aware of all elderly people in any room at any time and acts accordingly), or what is the perfect amount of fame (so famous you can never get convicted of murder in a court of law), or how to maintain a trim figure (you will not find that information in these pages). . . . Mindy invites readers on a tour of her life and her unscientific observations on romance, friendship, and Hollywood." (Publisher's note)

Kiernan, Frances

Seeing Mary plain: a life of Mary McCarthy. Norton 2000 845p il $35; pa $25 **818**

1. Authors 2. Authors, American -- 20th century 3. Essayists 4. Literary critics 5. Memoirists 6. Novelists 7. Short story writers

ISBN 0-393-03801-7; 0-393-32307-2 pa

LC 99-41098

Kiernan uses "her interviews with more than 200 sources to provide multiple points of view on McCarthy's life and work. McCarthy knew most of her generation's literary leading lights, from the Partisan Review crowd to anti-Vietnam activists. . . . Each chapter includes commentary by McCarthy, friends, ex-lovers, admirers, and adversaries." Booklist

Includes bibliographical references

Kingston, Maxine Hong

The **fifth** book of peace. Knopf 2003 401p $26; pa $14.95 **818**

1. Peace 2. Vietnam War, 1961-1975

ISBN 0-679-44075-5; 0-679-76063-6 pa

LC 2002-34103

When "Kingston embarked on a sequel to her delightful novel 'Tripmaster Monkey,' she called it 'The Fourth Book of Peace,' echoing a half-remembered Chinese legend about Three Books of Peace. But the manuscript was destroyed in a fire—a suggestive occurrence to Kingston, because the books in the legend were also burned. Here she recreates her lost fictional narrative and sets it alongside an account of her life after the fire. . . . The book is rich in empathy and moral conviction." New Yorker

Liebling, A. J.

The **sweet** science and other writings; [edited by Pete Hamill] Library of America 2009 1057p $40 **818**

ISBN 978-1-59853-040-7

"The Sweet Science (1956) offers a lively and idiosyncratic portrait of boxing in the early 1950s that encompasses boastful managers, veteran trainers, wily cornermen, and the fighters themselves: Joe Louis, Rocky Marciano, Sugar Ray Robinson, and Archie Moore. . . . The Earl of Louisiana (1961) is a vivid account of Governor Earl Long's bid for re-election after his release from a mental asylum in 1959—and an insightful look at Southern politics during the civil rights era. The Jollity Building (1962) collects hilarious stories about Manhattan cigar-store owners, nightclub promoters, and the scheming 'Telephone Booth Indians' of Broadway. . . Between Meals: An Appetite for Paris (1962) is a . . . memoir of Liebling's lifelong love for Paris and French food and wine. The Press (1964) brings together the best of Liebling's influential 'Wayward Press' pieces." Publisher's note

Manguel, Alberto

A **reader** on reading. Yale University Press 2010 308p il $27.50 **818**

1. Authors 2. Books and reading 3. Editors 4. Nonfiction writers 5. Novelists 6. Radio scriptwriters 7. Television scriptwriters 8. Translators

ISBN 978-0-300-15982-0; 0-300-15982-X

LC 2009-43719

"Lectures, columns, and other occasional writings are gathered here to form a meditation on 'the art of reading.' Thoughtful interrogations of the value of identity labels like 'Jewish fiction' or 'gay fiction' and the relationship between writers and editors mix with ruminations on the 'ideal reader' and the 'ideal library.' Several autobiographical essays detail a restless life that has taken Manguel from Buenos Aires to Tel Aviv, Canada, and, eventually, France, and an equally restless reading life. Predictable touchstones emerge—Dante and Homer, Shakespeare and Cervantes. Above all, there is Manguel's countryman Borges; he recalls reading aloud to the blind master as a young man in Argentina." New Yorker

Includes bibliographical references

Matthiessen, Peter

The **Peter** Matthiessen reader; nonfiction 1959-1991. edited with an introduction by McKay Jenkins. Vintage Bks. 2000 359p pa $14 **818**

ISBN 0-375-70272-5

LC 99-35246

Excerpts and essays highlighting the spiritual, literary, and political aspects of Matthiessen's work from Wildlife in America to Men's lives.

McMurtry, Larry

Walter Benjamin at the Dairy Queen; reflections at sixty and beyond. Simon & Schuster 1999 204p il hardcover o.p. pa $12 **818**

1. Authors 2. Essayists 3. Large print books 4. Novelists 5. Short story writers

ISBN 0-684-87019-3 pa

LC 99-19346

"When McMurtry recalls reading 'Don Quixote' as a thirteen-year-old on a Texas ranch and imagining himself as a character in the novel, other obsessional readers will immediately feel a kinship with this author. His appealing ruminations about his life and work as a reader, writer, and bookseller explore the differences between 'dense and empty, open and closed, new country and old cities, no society and old society'—the bare land in which he was reared and the crowded universe of literature." New Yorker

Mencken, H. L.

★ **My** life as author and editor; edited and with an introduction by Jonathan Yardley. Knopf 1993 xxi, 449p $30; pa $25 **818**
1. Authors 2. Biography, Individual 3. Essayists 4. Literary critics 5. Newspaper editors 6. Philologists 7. Social critics
ISBN 0-679-41315-4; 0-679-74102-X pa

LC 92-4496
An "absorbing memoir that anyone who cares about modern American literature will want to read." N Y Times Book Rev

A **second** Mencken chrestomathy; a new selection from the writings of America's legendary editor, critic, and wit. selected, revised, and annotated by the author; edited and with an introduction by Terry Teachout. Johns Hopkins University Press 2006 528p pa $35 **818**
ISBN 0-8018-8549-3

LC 2006-11581
"Mencken edited the first Chrestomathy himself in 1948. He called it 'a sort of Mencken Encyclopedia,' but noted that he had 'an excess of copied material about equal in bulk to the matter now in the book.' Mr. Teachout . . . has organized the unused material into discrete sections and provided titles and chapter headings—as well as performing a substantial amount of copy editing." Booklist

Miller, Henry

★ **Henry** Miller on writing; selected by Thomas H. Moore from the published and unpublished works of Henry Miller. New Directions 1964 216p pa $11.95 **818**
ISBN 0-8112-0112-0
The author discusses the art and practice of writing with insights on how he set his goals, how he discovered the excitement of using words, how the books he read influenced him, and how he learned to draw on his own experiences.

Parker, Dorothy

The **portable** Dorothy Parker; with a new introduction by Brendan Gill. rev and enl ed; Viking 1973 xxvii, 610p hardcover o.p. pa $18 **818**
ISBN 978-0-14-303953-2; 0-14-303953-9
This collection contains: thirty-two short stories; poems; drama reviews; book reviews, including the entire text of Constant reader; and miscellaneous articles.
"It is hard to imagine a library that would not want this book." Choice

Percy, Walker

Lost in the cosmos; the last self-help book. Picador 2000 262p pa $14 **818**
1. Self-actualization (Psychology) -- Humor
ISBN 0-312-25399-0

LC 99-87846

"The whole is brought off with that sly humor and intellectual verve that have made the author's novels exceptional." Natl Rev

Signposts in a strange land; edited with an introduction by Patrick Samway. Picador 2000 428p pa $15 **818**
1. Novelists, American -- 20th century -- Interviews
ISBN 0-312-25419-9

LC 99-89573
This collection's "speeches, interviews, and essays (some published for the first time) investigate various aspects of Percy's lifelong interests: the South; science, language, and literature; and morality and religion." Booklist
Includes bibliographical references

Plath, Sylvia

The **unabridged** journals of Sylvia Plath, 1950-1962; edited by Karen V. Kukil. Anchor Press 2000 732p il pa $18 **818**
1. Authors 2. Novelists 3. Poets 4. Poets, American -- 20th century -- Diaries
ISBN 0-385-72025-4

LC 00-42024
"This is essential for anyone engaged in Plath studies." Libr J
Includes bibliographical references

Poe, Edgar Allan

★ **Poetry** and tales. Library of Am. 1984 1408p $37.50 **818**
ISBN 0-940450-18-6

LC 83-19931
This volume contains 70 stories and Poe's poetic work in its entirety.

Rampersad, Arnold

★ The **life** of Langston Hughes Volume II: 1941-1967; I dream a world. 2nd ed; Oxford Univ. Press 2002 576p il hardcover o.p. pa $33 **818**
1. African American authors 2. Authors 3. Dramatists 4. Novelists 5. Poets 6. Poets, American 7. Short story writers 8. Young adult authors
ISBN 0-19-515161-5; 0-19-514643-3 pa

LC 2001-58766
This second volume of a two-volume biography of the Harlem Renaissance poet and author "finds Hughes rooting himself in Harlem, receiving stimulation from his rich cultural surroundings. Here he rethought his view of art and radicalism, and cultivated relationships with younger, more militant writers such as Richard Wright, Ralph Ellison, James Baldwin, and Amiri Bakara." Publisher's note
Includes bibliographical references

Rasmussen, R. Kent

Critical companion to Mark Twain; a literary reference to his life and work. with critical commentary by John H. Davis and Alex Feerst. Rev ed; Facts on File 2007 2v il map set $125 **818**
1. Authors 2. Essayists 3. Humorists 4. Memoirists 5. Novelists 6. Satirists 7. Short story writers 8.

Travel writers
ISBN 0-8160-5398-7; 978-0-8160-5398-8
LC 2004-46910

This companion to the life and works of Mark Twain includes a biography, synopses and critical commentaries on each of his works, discussions about major characters and places in his works, and entries on important people, places, and other aspects of his life.

Rollyson, Carl E.

Susan Sontag; the making of an icon. {by} Carl Rollyson and Lisa Paddock. Norton 2000 370p il $29.95   **818**

1. Authors 2. Essayists 3. Literary critics 4. Novelists 5. Short story writers 6. Women and literature -- United States -- History -- 20th century
ISBN 0-393-04928-0
LC 00-20402

The authors "have unearthed a deluge of information on Sontag's personal life—on her early years and family life, her lesbianism. . . her relationship with son David Rieff and her battles with breast cancer. While the authors provide an intelligent, though not strikingly original, analysis of her work, they are best at detailing how Sontag and her publishers have marketed her image as much as her thought." Publ Wkly

Includes bibliographical references

Silko, Leslie

Storyteller. Arcade Publishing 1989 278p pa $17.95 **818**

ISBN 978-1-55970-005-4; 1-55970-005-X

This "consists of short stories, anecdotes, folktales, poems, historical and autobiographical notes, and photographs." N Y Times Book Rev

Sova, Dawn B.

Critical companion to Edgar Allan Poe; a literary reference to his life and work. Facts on File 2007 458p il $75   **818**

1. Authors 2. Essayists 3. Poets 4. Short story writers
ISBN 0-8160-6408-3; 978-0-8160-6408-3
LC 2006-29466

"Biographical, historical, and critical material on Poe's life and work is presented in alphabetical order in three sections. The entries on Poe's works each provide a synopsis, a publication history, and character descriptions, while major works such as 'The Cask of Amontillado' and 'The Purloined Letter' have . . . [a] commentary and . . . further-reading suggestions." SLJ

Includes bibliographical references

Stein, Gertrude

Writings, 1903-1932. Library of Am. 1998 941p $40   **818**

ISBN 978-1-883011-40-6; 1-883011-40-X
LC 97-28915

In Stein's "early works, she sought a new kind of realism exemplified here by Q.E.D. (written 1903, published posthumously), a novel about lesbian entanglements at college, and the modern classic Three Lives (1909), a set of novellas about the lives of three ordinary women, described in the simplest and most direct of prose. In her . . . abstract 'portraits' Stein uses an extraordinary array of verbal techniques to evoke those friends and collaborators—Matisse, Picasso, Apollinaire, Juan Gris, Satie, Mabel Dodge, Carl Van Vechten, Sherwood Anderson, Virgil Thomson—with whom she shared decades of revolutionary ferment in the arts. Her play Four Saints in Three Acts (1927), which became the basis for an opera by Virgil Thomson, is written for a freewheeling theater of the mind where everything becomes possible. In 'Lifting Belly' and other works she joyously celebrates her lifelong relationship with Alice B. Toklas, one of the most famous domestic partnerships of that century. The Autobiography of Alice B. Toklas (1933), Stein's oblique and playful memoir, became an immediate bestseller and sealed Stein's international celebrity." Publisher's note

★ **Writings,** 1932-1946. Library of Am. 1998 844p $40   **818**

ISBN 1-883011-41-8
LC 97-28916

In addition to theater pieces, fiction, and poetry "memoir, philosophical speculation, literary criticism and theory, all sorts of briefer forms that are hard to account for but easy to marvel at and even to delight in, pack these volumes, and constitute, as the editors surely intended us to discover, the most consistently achieved representation of new ways of responding to life and new possibilities of getting experience into words that American literature has to show." N Y Times Book Rev

Thompson, Hunter S.

The **great** shark hunt; strange tales from a strange time. Summit Bks. 1979 602p hardcover o.p. pa $16   **818**

ISBN 0-7432-5045-1 pa
LC 79-831

"A retrospective in journalistic theater, this gathers together excerpts from Thompson's 'Fear and Loathing in Las Vegas' and 'Fear and Loathing on the Campaign Trail,' plus his reportage from such diverse journals as 'Rolling Stone,' 'Playboy,' 'The New York Times,' etc., going back to 1962." Publ Wkly

Includes bibliographical references

Thoreau, Henry David

★ **Collected** essays and poems. Library of Am. 2001 703p $35   **818**

ISBN 1-883011-95-7
LC 00-46234

Among the 27 essays included are Civil disobedience, Walking, Martyrdom of John Brown, A Yankee in Canada, and Life without principle. Many of the poems were taken from Thoreau's journals and manuscripts.

★ **Walden,** or, Life in the woods; with an introduction by Verlyn Klinkenborg. Knopf 1992 xxxi, 295p $19   **818**

ISBN 0-679-41896-2
LC 92-54444

"Philosophy of life and observations of nature drawn from the author's solitary sojourn of two years in a cabin on Walden Pond near Concord, Massachusetts." Pratt Alcove

Includes bibliographical references

A **week** on the Concord and Merrimack rivers; Walden, or, Life in the woods; The Maine woods; Cape Cod. Library of Am. 1985 1114p il $35 **818**
ISBN 0-940450-27-5

LC 85-5175

"Politically the most conscious of the Transcendentalists, an acute observer of natural and social facts, Thoreau was an outstanding prose stylist." Reader's Ency

Includes bibliographical references

Thursby, Jacqueline S.

Critical companion to Maya Angelou; a literary reference to her life and work. Facts On File 2011 430p il $75 **818**
1. Actors 2. Children's authors 3. Dramatists 4. Essayists 5. Memoirists 6. Poets 7. Singers
ISBN 978-0-8160-8093-9; 978-1-4381-3610-3 ebook

LC 2010032716

Coverage includes a "biography of Angelou; entries on all of Angelou's major works, including all six of her book-length autobiographies, her major poems and poetry collections, her major essays and essay collections, her children's books, and more; entries on the autobiographical works contain subentries on the main figures in the work; entries on related people, places, and topics, such as Harlem, Michelle Obama, racism, San Francisco, and more; [and] appendixes, including chronologies, a bibliography of Angelou's works, and a secondary source bibliography." Publisher's note

Includes bibliographical references

Trethewey, Natasha D., 1966-

Beyond Katrina; a meditation on the Mississippi Gulf Coast. University of Georgia Press 2010 127p il **818**
1. African Americans -- Mississippi 2. Hurricane Katrina, 2005
ISBN 0-8203-3381-6; 978-0-8203-3381-6

LC 2010011417

A collection of essays, poems, and letters, chronicling the effects of Hurricane Katrina on the Mississippi Gulf Coast.

"By looking at the vast devastation with sober and poetic eyes, Trethewey has written a hauntingly beautiful book." Publ Wkly

Twain, Mark

The **wit** and wisdom of Mark Twain; edited by Alex Ayres. Harper & Row 1987 265p hardcover o.p. pa $13.95 **818**
ISBN 978-0-06-075104-3 pa; 0-06-075104-5 pa

LC 87-45020

The editor "provides systematic access to plenty of Twain's bon mots by arranging them in a dictionary of topics from Adam to youth. . . . Where background is needed, Ayres supplies it succinctly and, as an afterword, proffers 'What Mark Twain might say today' on such ponderables as communism, extraterrestrial intelligence, the national debt,

terrorism, and the unborn. Much to Ayres' credit, many of these approximations sound markedly Twainian." Booklist

Includes bibliographical references

Updike, John, 1932-2009

Higher gossip; essays and criticism. edited by Christopher Carduff. Alfred A. Knopf 2011 xxiii, 501p il $40; ebook $21.99 **818**
1. Authors, American 2. Criticism 3. Essays
ISBN 978-0-307-95715-3; 978-0-307-95717-7 ebook

LC 2011013586

This book is a "collection of miscellaneous prose [that] opens with a self-portrait of the writer in winter. . . . It concludes with a . . . meditation on a modern world robbed of imagination--a world without religion, without art--and on the difficulties of faith in a disbelieving age. In between are previously uncollected stories and poems, a pageant of scenes from seventeenth-century Massachusetts, five late 'golf dreams,' and several of Updike's commentaries on his own work. At the heart of the book are his . . . reviews--of John Cheever, Ann Patchett, Toni Morrison, William Maxwell, John le Carré, and essays on Aimee Semple McPherson, Max Factor, and Albert Einstein, among others. Also included are two decades of art criticism--on Chardin, El Greco, Blake, Turner, Van Gogh, Max Ernest, and more." (Publisher's note)

This is a compilation of nearly 100 uncollected pieces by nthe preeminent literary journalist of our times.t Predominantly comprising literary and art criticism from a range of magazines, the volume also embraces poetry, fiction, memoir, and Updike's comments on his own work. Publ Wkly

Von Mehren, Joan

Minerva and the muse: a life of Margaret Fuller. University of Mass. Press 1995 398p il $40; pa $20.95 **818**
1. Biographers 2. Feminists 3. Social reformers
ISBN 0-87023-941-4; 1-55849-015-9 pa

LC 94-18663

"Von Mehren is sympathetic to Fuller's lifelong struggle to achieve fame and public acclamation for her views on Transcendentalism and feminism, but she balances her sympathy with objectivity and distance." Libr J

Includes bibliographical references

Walsh, John Evangelist

Midnight dreary; the mysterious death of Edgar Allan Poe. St. Martin's Minotaur 2000 199p il pa $14.95 **818**
1. Authors 2. Authors, American -- 19th century -- Biography 3. Authors, American -- 19th century -- Death 4. Essayists 5. Poets 6. Short story writers
ISBN 0-312-22732-9; 978-0-312-22732-6

LC 00-25571

Walsh "has undertaken a superbly informed speculation on the week proceeding the mysterious death of Edgar Allan Poe 150 years ago." Libr J

Includes bibliographical references

Wayne, Tiffany K.

Critical companion to Ralph Waldo Emerson; a literary reference to his life and work. Facts On File 2010 444p il $75   **818**

1. Authors 2. Essayists 3. Philosophers 4. Poets

ISBN 978-0-8160-7358-0; 978-1-4381-3048-4 ebook

LC 2009-24809

"This reference book examines the life and works of a central thinker in American history. . . . It begins with Emerson's biography for context. Part 2 focuses on 140 significant (in the view of scholars) individual works, including 60 poems (most with one to three pages of synopses, critical commentary, and further reading). Part 3 covers related people, places, and topics. . . . The final appendixes offer a chronology of Emerson's life and times, bibliographies of both his works and relevant secondary sources." Choice

Includes bibliographical references. 'Bibliography of Emerson's works': p. 406-407. (BLCM)

★ The Oxford companion to Mark Twain; editor, Gregg Camfield. Oxford Univ. Press 2003 xxi, 767p il $75   **818**

1. Authors 2. Authors, American -- 19th century -- Biography -- Handbooks, manuals, etc 3. Essayists 4. Humorists 5. Memoirists 6. Novelists 7. Satirists 8. Short story writers 9. Travel writers

ISBN 0-19-510710-1

LC 2002-151880

This volume "begins with 300 alphabetically arranged entries of varying lengths devoted to all [Twain's] works, places and people related to his life, and analyses of his views on a variety of topics, from animals to spiritualism. Next come a bibliography of his published works collated from other bibliographies, a chronology, and a general index." Choice

Includes bibliographical references

The moment; edited by Larry Smith. Harper Perennial 2012 344p.   **818**

1. American literature -- 21st century 2. Authors, American -- 21st century -- Biography 3. Biography & Autobiography -- Personal Memoirs

ISBN 9780061719653; 9780062099211

LC 2011033766

This book contains "stories of life-changing events from a cadre of ready, self-aware authors, each done in a page or two. A short selection of the contributors: A.J. Jacobs, Melissa Etheridge, Gregory Maguire, Dave Eggers, Elizabeth Gilbert, Jennifer Egan and Judy Collins. There are many 'wake-up calls,' some smiles and plenty of tears in these first-person explorations of a few eternal truths. Each of the 125 participants . . . tell of coming out and hiding, of seeking the light, the path, the truth, the way and/or the writers inner selves. Those goals were achieved by aid of a word, sign, teacher, family road trip, some dope, an inner voice or, more than once, a Eurail pass." (Kirkus)

"Each author's ability to concisely describe such big moments pulls the reader in. Book and writing groups will have a lot to talk about after reading this first-rate collection." (Libr J)

820   English and Old English (Anglo-Saxon) literatures

Coles, Robert

Handing one another along; literature and social reflection. edited by Trevor Hall and Vicki Kennedy. Random House 2010 xxiv, 273p il $27; ebook $27   **820**

1. American literature -- History and criticism 2. English literature -- History and criticism

ISBN 978-1-4000-6203-4; 978-0-679-60403-7 ebook

LC 2009-47337

The author "adapts his undergraduate lectures on literature's contribution to the development of our moral character. . . . While less than comprehensive and eschewing more technical analyses, it delves into a generous handful of writers and artists—perennials like George Orwell, James Agee, Zora Neale Hurston, Tillie Olsen, Ralph Ellison, and Raymond Carver, among others—with uncommon insight and a personal touch, while offering excerpts of poetry and prose that often whet the appetite for more." Publ Wkly

Includes bibliographical references

Greer, Germaine

The **Cambridge** guide to women's writing in English; [edited by] Lorna Sage; advisory editors, Germaine Greer, Elaine Showalter. Cambridge Univ. Press 1999 696p il $80; pa $29   **820**

1. English literature -- Women authors -- Dictionaries 2. Reference books

ISBN 0-521-49525-3; 0-521-66813-1 pa

LC 98-50778

A "guide to women writers in the English language. The coverage is thorough, crossing historical, national, and generic boundaries as it ranges from Julian of Norwich to Terry Macmillan {sic}, from M.F.K. Fisher to Pauline Kael, from Ghanaian playwright Ama Ata Aidoo to Native American writer Mourning Dove. There are also articles on selected titles and themes. The entries, which range from 160 to 500 words, are informative, critical, and jargon-free." Libr J

Lee, Hermione

Virginia Woolf's nose; essays on biography. Princeton University Press 2005 141p $19.95   **820**

1. Authors 2. Authors, English -- Biography 3. Biography as a literary form 4. Diarists 5. Essayists 6. Government officials 7. Members of Parliament 8. Military officials 9. Novelists 10. Poets 11. Short story writers

ISBN 0-691-12032-3

LC 2004-58457

"Lee's immensely enjoyable study will energize debate among thoughtful readers and should become essential reading for aficionados of literary biography." Publ Wkly

Includes bibliographical references

Sanders, Andrew

The **short** Oxford history of English literature; 3rd ed; Oxford University Press 2004 756p pa $45   **820**

1. English literature 2. English literature -- History and

criticism
ISBN 978-0-19-926338-7; 0-19-926338-8

LC 2004-49555

"The History provides detailed discussion of Old and Middle English literature, the Renaissance, Shakespeare, the seventeenth and eighteenth centuries, the Romantics, Victorian and Edwardian literature, Modernism, and postwar writing. Discussions of key writers and works are combined with analysis of the impact on literature of contemporary political, social, and intellectual developments. The book includes Scottish, Irish, and Welsh writers, and it asks about the future of the canon in the light of the fragmented condition of British writing in the post-imperial period." Publisher's note
Includes bibliographical references

Stewart, Bruce

The **Oxford** companion to Irish literature; edited by Robert Welch, assistant editor, Bruce Stewart. Oxford Univ. Press 1996 xxv, 614p maps $55 **820**
1. Irish literature -- Bio-bibliography 2. Irish literature -- Dictionaries 3. Reference books
ISBN 0-19-866158-4

LC 95-44943

Encompassing "Ireland's literary heritage from the bardic poets and Celtic sagas to twentieth-century authors like Brian Friel, Edna O'Brien, and Nuala Ni Dhomhnaill, the more than 2,000 unsigned entries cover writers, titles of major works, literary genres and motifs, folklore, mythology, periodicals, associations, and historical figures and events." Booklist

Vendler, Helen Hennessy

Coming of age as a poet; Milton, Keats, Eliot, Plath. [by] Helen Vendler. Harvard Univ. Press 2003 174p il $22.95 **820**
1. American poetry -- History and criticism 2. Authors 3. Blind 4. Dramatists 5. Editors 6. English poetry -- History and criticism 7. Essayists 8. Literary critics 9. Nobel laureates for literature 10. Novelists 11. Poetry -- History and criticism 12. Poets 13. Writers on medicine
ISBN 0-674-01024-8

LC 2002-27287

Vendler "succeeds in revealing the aesthetic power and technical beauty of great poetry." N Y Times Book Rev
Includes bibliographical references

★ The **Cambridge** guide to literature in English; edited by Dominic Head. 3rd ed; Cambridge University Press 2006 xxiii, 1241p il $50 **820**
1. American literature 2. American literature -- Dictionaries 3. Authors, American -- Biography 4. Authors, Commonwealth -- Biography 5. Authors, English -- Biography 6. Commonwealth literature (English) 7. English literature 8. English literature -- Bio-bibliography 9. English literature -- Dictionaries 10. Reference books
ISBN 978-0-521-83179-6; 0-521-83179-2

LC 2006-271458

"The scope of material covered . . . extends to the literature of the United Kingdom and well beyond: Africa,

Asia, Australia, Canada, the Caribbean, India, New Zealand, and the U.S. are all well represented. . . . Literary terms are explained, literary movements are summarized, and literary magazines are sketched in unsigned entries ranging in length from a few lines to a few paragraphs or more. . . . With its broad coverage, clearly written and accessible text, and relatively modest price, this is a must purchase for most reference collections." Booklist

The **Norton** anthology of English literature; Stephen Greenblatt, general editor; M.H. Abrams, founding editor emeritus. 8th ed.; W.W. Norton 2006 2v il map **820**
1. English literature -- Collections
ISBN 0-393-92713-X v1; 0-393-92531-5 v1 pa; 0-393-92715-6 v2; 0-393-92532-3 v2 pa

LC 2005-52313

Contains representative writings of authors which convey the tone and trends of specific literary movements and periods. Both volumes contain explanatory footnotes, selected bibliographies, notes on literary forms and usage, an author-title index, and marginalia glossaries.

★ The **Oxford** companion to English literature; edited by Dinah Birch. 7th ed; Oxford University Press 2009 1164p $150 **820**
1. American literature -- Bio-bibliography 2. American literature -- Dictionaries 3. American literature -- History and criticism 4. English literature 5. English literature -- Bio-bibliography 6. English literature -- Dictionaries 7. English literature -- History and criticism 8. Reference books
ISBN 978-0-19-280687-1

LC 2009-455948

"The subjects of the entries include literary works, authors, themes, archetypes, journals, and forms. . . . This companion is a highly authoritative resource, with clear, concise, and approachable entries on literary topics of high interest to students and scholars of English literature. An essential reference for most public, high school, and academic libraries." Libr J

★ The **Oxford** guide to literature in English translation; edited by Peter France. Oxford Univ. Press 2000 xxii, 656p hardcover o.p. pa $29.95 **820**
1. Literature -- History and criticism 2. Literature -- Translations into English -- History and criticism 3. Translating and interpreting
ISBN 0-19-924784-6 pa

LC 99-28791

This "guide emphasizes 'high-culture' books in translation that have had the most lasting impact on English-speaking culture since the Middle Ages. . . . The first 116 pages cover translation theory and history, while the heart of this guide is the 17 geographic sections that follow, starting with African languages, moving through Latin, and ending with the West Asian languages. There are excellent bibliographies and an author index." Libr J
Includes bibliographical references

821   English poetry

Adamson, Robert

★ The **goldfinches** of Baghdad. Flood Editions 2006 103p pa $13.95   **821**

1. Poetry -- By individual authors

ISBN 0-9746902-8-7

Adamson "lives on the Hawksbury River in New South Wales. . . . To give an overview of his poetry is difficult, but it is largely concerned with where he is: the river, the natural environment and creatures, his life and history, his neighbours, love and death. It has little of the 'pastoral' feel about it, being obsessively attached to the present condition, and it never gives any sense of a contented settled existence free from urban cares, quite the reverse. There is indication indeed of a quite fraught personal existence, both past and present, without the poetry ever for a moment becoming 'confessional'. It is to objective for that and too poetic." Shearsman

Adcock, Fleur

★ **Poems** 1960-2000. Bloodaxe Books 2000 287p $54.95; pa $24.95   **821**

1. Poetry -- By individual authors

ISBN 1-85224-529-8; 1-85224-530-1 pa

Adcock's "imagination thrives on what threatens her peace of mind, and only when she is unguarded can these threats have their full creative effect. . . . Throughout her writing life, she has made a fine art from holding on to principles of orderliness and good clear sense; but she has made an even finer one from loosening her grip on them." Times Lit Suppl

Auden, W. H.

★ **Collected** poems; edited by Edward Mendelson. Modern Library 2007 928p $40   **821**

1. Poetry -- By individual authors

ISBN 978-0-679-64350-0; 0-679-64350-8

LC 2006-47163

A compilation of all the poems Auden wished to preserve, in his final revisions. Previous collected editions and later shorter poems are included. There is also an absurdist play written in 1928: Paid on both sides.

Bentley, G. E.

The **stranger** from paradise: a biography of William Blake. Yale Univ. Press 2001 xxvii, 532p il maps $39.95; pa $24.95   **821**

1. Artists 2. Artists -- England 3. Authors 4. Engravers 5. Illustrators 6. Poets 7. Poets, English -- 18th century

ISBN 0-300-08939-2; 0-300-10030-2 pa

The author "traces Blake from his natal landscape, youth, marriage, and apprenticeship through to his later years as a working engraver, poet, and radical visionary. Bentley is academic and thorough, and this is more of a straight biography than an analysis." Libr J

Includes bibliographical references

Blake, William

The **complete** poetry and prose of William Blake; edited by David V. Erdman; with a new foreword and commentary by Harold Bloom. Newly rev. ed., 1st

Calif. ed.; University of California Press 2008 xxvi, 990p il $70   **821**

1. Poetry -- By individual authors

ISBN 978-0-520-04473-9

In addition to all of Blake's poetry, this volume also includes miscellaneous prose, marginalia, and letters.

"The crucial preliminary problem [in establishing Blake's text] is simply to make out what Blake wrote. . . . Erdman has used modern aids such as infrared photography and microphotography. . . but his real achievement has been to look at Blake's text more closely and intelligently than any previous editor." N Y Rev Books

Boland, Eavan

New collected poems. W.W. Norton 2008 320p $27.95   **821**

1. Poetry -- By individual authors

ISBN 978-0-393-06579-4; 0-393-06579-0

LC 2007-42554

"Boland's resilient braid of outspoken feminism with Irish identity has given her a following on both sides of the Atlantic. Here is the recent Boland whose rapid verse celebrates women's courage and women's work, both public (several poems acknowledge Mary Robinson, the former president of the Irish Republic) and unsung: the poet remembers herself, when young, asking a statue in Dublin to 'Make me a heroine.' Here is the poet who learned from Adrienne Rich, among others, how to tackle big topics of loyalty, rebellion, descent and dissent." Publ Wkly

Bronte, Emily

★ The **complete** poems of Emily Jane Bronte; edited from the manuscripts by C. W. Hatfield. Columbia Univ. Press 1941 xxi, 262p $65; pa $20 **821**

1. Poetry -- By individual authors

ISBN 0-231-01222-5; 0-231-10347-6 pa

A re-editing of the complete poems of Emily Brontë, based on all the known manuscripts. About half of the 193 poems are those belonging to the so-called Gondal cycle

Brown, Terence

★ The **life** of W.B. Yeats; a critical biography. Blackwell 1999 410p il $66.95; pa $29.95   **821**

1. Authors 2. Dramatists 3. Memoirists 4. Nobel laureates for literature 5. Poets 6. Poets, Irish 7. Poets, Irish -- 20th century

ISBN 0-631-18298-5; 0-631-22851-9 pa

LC 99-28388

In this biography Brown places "Yeats's work as poet and dramatist in its political and social—as well as personal and erotic—context." N Y Times Book Rev

Includes bibliographical references

Browning, Elizabeth Barrett

★ **Sonnets** from the Portuguese; a celebration of love. St. Martin's Press 1986 [63] il $9.95   **821**

1. Poetry -- By individual authors

ISBN 0-312-74501-X

LC 86-13755

A series of sonnets which "were written during a period of seven years and are considered by some scholars to have been inspired by her love for her husband poet Robert Browning." New Century Handb of Engl Lit

Browning, Robert

Robert Browning; the major works. edited with notes by Adam Roberts; with an introduction by Daniel Karlin. Oxford University Press 2005 xxxii, 828p pa $18.95 **821**

    1. Poetry -- By individual authors
    ISBN 978-0-19-280626-0; 0-19-280626-2
                      LC 2006-277696

This "selection includes over eighty of [Browning's] shorter poems, amongst them his most famous and best-loved dramatic monologues, as well as the complete text of many of his longer poems. It contains three books from The Ring and the Book and Browning's critical writing, Essay on Shelley. This edition also selects generously from the love letters between Browning and Elizabeth Barrett." Publisher's note

Includes bibliographical references

★ **Robert** Browning's poetry; authoritative texts, criticism. selected and edited by James F. Loucks and Andrew M. Stauffer. 2nd ed.; W. W. Norton & Co. 2007 689p pa $14.50 **821**

    1. Poetry -- By individual authors
    ISBN 978-0-393-92600-2; 0-393-92600-1
                      LC 2006-47308

This collection of Browning's poetry, which includes Pauline, "reprints the texts of the seventeen-volume 'Fourth and complete edition' (Smith, Elder), of which all but the final volume were approved by Browning before his death. The poems are ordered chronologically according to their first appearance in book form." Publisher's note

Bunting, Basil

Complete poems; associate editor, Richard Caddel. New Directions Books 2003 239p pa $16.95 **821**

    1. Poetry -- By individual authors
    ISBN 978-0-8112-1563-3; 0-8112-1563-6
                      LC 2003-15465

This volume "offers adventure, a confident voice, neat takes on history (both recent and archaic), an attractively careworn secular ethics and an even more attractive combination of archaic and vernacular English models. It also offers superb verbal command, chiseling every stanza to the fewest, densest possible words, giving each an aural shape. Those shapes are not always mellifluous—sometimes they are harsh, a mouthful—but each demonstrates Bunting's mastery, proving itself on the page as well as in the ear, where all good poems find their place." Nation

Burns, Robert

Burns; poems. edited and introduced by Gerard Carruthers. Alfred A. Knopf 2007 255p $12.50 **821**

    1. Poetry -- By individual authors
    ISBN 978-0-307-26616-3; 0-307-26616-8
                      LC 2006-47299

"A pioneer of the Romantic movement, Burns wrote in a light Scots dialect with brio, emotional directness, and wit, drawing on classical and English literary traditions as well as Scottish folklore. . . . All of his most famous lyrics and poems are here, from 'A Red, Red Rose,' 'To a Mouse,' and 'To a Louse' to Tam o'Shanter, 'Holy Willie's Prayer,' and 'Auld Lang Syne.'" Publisher's note

Byron, George Gordon Byron

Selected poetry of Lord Byron; edited by Leslie A. Marchand; introduction by Thomas Disch; notes by Jeffrey Vail. Modern Library 2001 745p pa $16 **821**

    1. Poetry -- By individual authors
    ISBN 978-0-375-75814-0; 0-375-75814-3
                      LC 2001-42771

"From 'Manfred,' with its evocation of the figure that came to be called the 'Byronic hero,' to the melancholy 'Childe Harold,' to the satirical masterpiece 'Don Juan' (presented here in judiciously selected form), this . . . [selection seeks to include] the essential Byron." Publisher's note

Chaucer, Geoffrey

★ The **complete** poetry and prose of Geoffrey Chaucer; edited by John H. Fisher. 2nd ed; Harcourt Brace & Co. 1989 1040p il $105.95 **821**

    1. Poetry -- By individual authors
    ISBN 0-03-028612-3
                      LC 88-29400

Coleridge, Samuel Taylor

The **complete** poems; edited by William Keach. Penguin 1997 xxx, 626p pa $18 **821**

    1. Poetry -- By individual authors
    ISBN 978-0-14-042353-2

This edition "contains the final texts of all the poems published in the poet's lifetime, together with a substantial selection from the verse still in manuscript on his death. William Keach's notes draw attention to significant variants, and important earlier versions of 'Monody on the Death of Chatterton', 'The Eolian Harp', 'The Rime of the Ancient Mariner' and 'Dejection: An Ode' are included in full. The poems are arranged in chronological order of composition." Publisher's note

Constantine, David

Collected poems. Bloodaxe Books 2005 384p pa $31.95 **821**

    1. Poetry -- By individual authors
    ISBN 1-85224-667-7

"From the first line on this book's first page ('As our bloods separate the clock resumes') to the first sentence on its last ('When the kingfisher flitted/ Under the hazels I entered again into boyhood') Constantine declares himself a Romantic, in almost all the loaded, unfashionable and daring senses that once-omnipresent term can bear. In his elaborate lines, intelligence and strong emotion are collaborators, not competitors; he knows how to let them spur each other on." Times Lit Suppl

Davie, Donald

Collected poems; edited by Neil Powell. Carcanet 2002 xxi, 634p $49.95; pa $24.95 **821**

    1. English poetry -- 20th century 2. Poetry -- By

individual authors

ISBN 978-1-85754-579-1; 1-85754-579-6; 978-1-85754-406-0; 1-85754-406-4 pa

"Davie's poetic output, which abundantly stretches from Hardyesque lyrics ('Bride of Reason,' 'A Winter Talent,' 'The Battered Wife') to cognitively powerful long poems ('Six Epistles to Eva Hesse,' 'The Forests of Lithuania'), from translations of Pasternak and Mandelstam to lyrically brutal political commentary ('August, 1968'), evinces a kind of wide sweep and committed imagination that doesn't necessarily close itself off to confrontation and experiential risk, nor resign itself to failure as the phenomenological and lyrical refusal of further inquiry. In this sense, Davie has always seemed to be a poet working in the very high art of his eighteenth-century forebears." Jacket

Davis, Dick

Belonging; poems. Swallow Press 2002 54p $24.95; pa $14.95 **821**

1. Poetry -- By individual authors

ISBN 0-8040-1042-0; 0-8040-1043-9 pa

LC 2002-17749

Davis' "poems are full of fine emotion, intelligence, wit, and multinational culture. He lithely celebrates the legendary rake Casanova; poignantly conjures 'Kipling's Kim, Thirty Years On'; economically reports a father's aching futility in comforting his child ('A Bit of Paternity'); deftly valorizes the power of art ('Just So'); and often muses on the shortness of life and the limitations of being human, so cogently that a single quatrain can take one's breath away." Booklist

Day Lewis, C.

The **complete** poems of C. Day Lewis; [edited by] Jill Balcon. Stanford Univ. Press 1992 745p hardcover o.p. pa $32.95 **821**

1. Poetry -- By individual authors

ISBN 978-0-8047-2585-9; 0-8047-2585-3

LC 91-68076

"The still lively fascination of his verse seems to depend on the variety of tones [Day Lewis] could pick up, change, and discard at will. . . . His modesty was genuine and profound, giving his verse texture its winning versatility, its air that 'tenure is not for me.' . . . Nothing that Day Lewis wrote is lacking its own sort of ephemeral though rediscoverable effectiveness. He was well aware of this, and it was a part of his modesty, as Jill Balcon points out in her thoughtful and sensitive introduction. . . . For anyone who likes poetry there is real interest here in [this] complete record." N Y Rev Books

Donne, John

★ The **complete** poetry and selected prose of John Donne; edited by Charles M. Coffin; introduction by Denis Donoghue; notes by W. T. Chmielewski. Modern Lib. 2001 xxxii, 697p pa $14.95 **821**

1. Poetry -- By individual authors

ISBN 0-375-75734-1

LC 2001-30077

This volume contains Donne's love poetry, satires, epigrams, verse letters and holy sonnets. Also includes selected prose and a sampling of private letters.

Feinstein, Elaine

Ted Hughes; the life of a poet. Norton 2001 273p il $29.95; pa $15.95 **821**

1. Authors 2. Poets 3. Poets laureate 4. Poets, English -- 20th century -- Biography

ISBN 0-393-04967-1; 0-393-32362-5 pa

LC 2001-44925

This biography of the English poet examines Hughes's relationship with "his first wife, Sylvia Plath, who committed suicide in 1963 during the acrimonious breakup of their marriage, . . . {and with} Assia Wevill, the woman for whom Hughes left Plath, and who later killed herself and their child." Economist

Includes bibliographical references

Fisher, Roy

★ **Selected** poems; edited by August Kleinzahler. Flood Editions 2011 158p pa $15.95 **821**

1. Poetry -- By individual authors

ISBN 978-0-9819520-6-2

"Fisher's texts have never been as well served on the page as they are here. The poems are given real space and the movement of Fisher's breath, rhythm and cadence is as clear as it possibly could be." Manchester Rev

Foster, R. F.

W.B. Yeats: a life. v1 Oxford Univ. Press 1997 xxxi, 640p v1 il hardcover o.p. pa $29.95 **821**

1. Authors 2. Biography, Individual 3. Dramatists 4. Memoirists 5. Nobel laureates for literature 6. Poets 7. Poets, Irish

ISBN 0-19-211735-1; 0-19-288085-3 pa

LC 96-31671

This is the first installment of a two-volume biography of the Irish poet.

Foulds, Adam

The **broken** word; an epic poem of the British Empire in Kenya, and the Mau Mau uprising against it. Penguin 2011 60p pa $16 **821**

ISBN 978-0-14-311809-1

Offers a lyrical poem about Tom, a young man who gets caught up in the violent 1950s Mau Mau Uprising in Kenya protesting the British colonial control of that country.

"A tour de force of a long narrative poem, rare in contemporary English poetry." Libr J

Gunn, Thom

Boss Cupid. Farrar, Straus & Giroux 2000 111p hardcover o.p. pa $13 **821**

1. Poetry -- By individual authors

ISBN 0-374-52771-7 pa

LC 99-57739

"Boss Cupid offers a splendid introduction for the uninitiated. Almost all of Gunn's virtues are on display here: his playful, metrical dexterity, his unflinching celebration both of beauty and of transience. . . . Advancing age and the AIDS-related deaths of friends—'my everpresent dead'—

figure prominently in these poems, but so does Gunn's humorous touch." Time

Collected poems. Farrar, Straus & Giroux 1994
495p pa $20 **821**
1. Poetry -- By individual authors
ISBN 978-0-374-52433-3; 0-374-52433-5
LC 93-74183
There is a "a unity of purpose that extends throughout the work, from the watchful early metrics through the syllabics, the reach and skill of the free verse and, in much of the latest work, a return to strong form that might be termed triumphant had it not been called into the service of matter so saddening." Times Lit Suppl

Heaney, Seamus

District and circle. Farrar, Straus and Giroux 2006 78p $20 **821**
1. Poetry -- By individual authors
ISBN 0-374-14092-8; 978-0-374-14092-2
LC 2005-44687
This "collection of robust lyrics celebrates work, memory, and the physicality of existence. Brimming with anvils, hammers, shovels, and pumps, these poems are scored into the page with Heaney's signature accentual and alliterative force." Libr J

Electric light. Farrar, Straus & Giroux 2001 98p hardcover o.p. pa $13 **821**
1. Poetry -- By individual authors
ISBN 0-374-14683-7; 0-374-52841-1 pa
LC 00-67278
Heaney's "book of poems is a compendium of poetic genres set in an array of forms and tuned to many kinds of experience, the work of a mature poet and world citizen, aware of his cultural authority as a public man and of the rights and responsibilities that go with it." N Y Times Book Rev

★ **Finders** keepers; selected prose 1971-2001.
Farrar, Straus & Giroux 2002 452p $30; pa $15 **821**
1. Authors 2. College teachers 3. Dramatists 4. Editors 5. Essayists 6. Librarians 7. Literary critics 8. Memoirists 9. Nobel laureates for literature 10. Novelists 11. Poetry -- History and criticism 12. Poets 13. Poets laureate 14. Translators
ISBN 0-374-15496-1; 0-374-52878-0 pa
This collection "gathers Heaney's occasional prose from four decades, much of it meditating upon other poets who have moved him, including familiar members of the canon, such as Eliot and Yeats and Auden, and lesser-known and newer moderns, such as Hugh MacDiarmid, Thomas Kinsella, and Norman MacCaig, whose work draws his interest. Not surprisingly for a poet from a war-wracked land, Heaney comes back again and again to the question of how poetry can matter against human savagery." Booklist

Human chain. Farrar, Straus and Giroux 2010 85p $24 **821**
1. Poetry -- By individual authors
ISBN 978-0-374-17351-7
LC 2010-10274

"Nostalgia and memory, numinous visions and the earthy music of compound adjectives together control the short poems and sequences of the Irish Nobel laureate's 14th collection of verse. . . . Old teachers, schoolmates, farmhands, and even the employees of an 'Eelworks' arrive transfigured through Heaney's command of sound. . . . For all the variety of Heaney's framed glimpses, though, the standout poems grow from occasions neither trivial nor topical: Heaney in 2006 had a minor stroke, and the discreet analogies and glimpsed moments in poems such as 'Chanson d'Aventure' (about a ride in an ambulance) and 'In the Attic' ('As I age and blank on names') bring his characteristic warmth and subtlety to mortality, rehabilitation, recent trauma, and old age." Publ Wkly

Opened ground; selected poems, 1966-1996.
Farrar, Straus & Giroux 1998 443p hardcover o.p. pa $16 **821**
1. Poetry -- By individual authors
ISBN 0-374-52678-8 pa
LC 98-4331
"The best of nobel laureate Heaney's poems, gathered from 12 previous collections, create a substantial volume that charts the course of one man's thoroughly examined personal life and reflects a volatile era in the life of his troubled country, Northern Ireland, though the particulars Heaney renders so vibrantly become archetypal and unbounded in their tragedy and bliss." Booklist

Herbert, George

Herbert: poems. Alfred A. Knopf 2004 253p $12.50 **821**
1. Christian poetry, English -- Early modern, 1500-1700. 2. Poetry -- By individual authors
ISBN 978-1-4000-4329-3; 1-4000-4329-8
LC 2005-273574
Herbert experimented with a variety of forms, "from hymns and sonnets to 'pattern poems,' the shape of which reveal their subjects. Such technical agility never seems ostentatious, however, for precision of language and expression of genuine feeling were the primary concerns of this poet who admonished his readers to 'dare to be true.' An Anglican priest who took his calling with deep seriousness, he brought to his work a religious reverence richly allied with a playful wit and with literary and musical gifts of the highest order." Publisher's note

Hill, Geoffrey

Selected poems. Yale University Press 2009 276p **821**
1. Poetry -- By individual authors
ISBN 978-0-300-12156-8
LC 2008-930384
"After four decades with just five books, the past 10 years have seen Hill offer six more, including a trio of long works some liken to Dante and Blake. This first selected since 1994 . . . should get instant critical attention (and sustained academic adoption) even though it contains no new work. Here, entire, is Mercian Hymns, with its gorgeously medievalized evocation of a rural English upbringing. Here, complete, are all three recent long poems, with their erudite mix of elegy and jeremiad. . . . Here, too, are the descriptive

beauties that sparkle through even Hill's most rebarbative works." Publ Wkly

Without title. Yale University Press 2007 81p $26; pa $16   821
1. Poetry -- By individual authors
ISBN 978-0-300-12176-6; 0-300-12176-8; 0-300-12157-1 pa; 978-0-300-12157-5 pa
LC 2006-926124

"For much of Hill's five-decade career, his forbiddingly allusive and elliptical style, his sometimes peevish tone, his interest in English church history, and his rapt pastoralism have made him an unfashionable figure, but also a highly individual one. His latest collection exhibits typical erudition: who else would name-drop the Jesuit theologian Karl Rahner or describe Jimi Hendrix as an 'exquisite player of neumes' ('neumes' being an archaic form of musical notation)? Though the method is a magpie one, the impression that emerges is of absolute control and single-mindedness. And while Hill's outlook can seem willfully bleak . . . there is genuine grace in his descriptions of natural beauty." New Yorker

★ The **orchards** of Syon. Counterpoint 2002 72p $24   821
1. Christian poetry, English 2. Poetry -- By individual authors
ISBN 1-58243-166-3
LC 2001-47245

"Cast as a sequence of 72 uniform blank-verse soliloquies compounded out of a dissonant amalgam of demotic jabber and oracular utterance, 'The Orchards of Syon' confirms that Hill, for all his newfound volubility, can be as refractory as ever. . . . But for readers with the patience and stamina to stick with it, Hill's brooding meditations on his ancestral countryside's 'wintry swamp-thickets, brush-heaps of burnt light' or 'the burring air of the fell' carry the haunting force of a last will and testament." N Y Times Book Rev

The **triumph** of love. Houghton Mifflin 1998 82p hardcover o.p. pa $13   821
1. Poetry -- By individual authors
ISBN 0-618-00183-2 pa
LC 98-19502

This book-length poem "ends up so much more satisfying than much of Hill's recent work because there is so much more of Hill in it. . . . When we have read [the book] a few times (no one should read it just once) we know, more than we could from his previous work, what vexes and distresses, what heartens and cheers Hill, what gives him his grim satisfactions and how." Yale Rev

Hollis, Matthew

Now all roads lead to France; the last years of Edward Thomas. Matthew Hollis. Faber & Faber 2011 416 p. ill., maps $29.95   821
1. Authors 2. Biography, Individual 3. Essayists 4. Nonfiction 5. Poets 6. Writers on nature
ISBN 9780571245987
LC 2011505697

This book presents a study of [poet Edward] Thomas' life and work from (roughly) the winter of 1913 onwards,

with a strong emphasis on his poetic aspirations. (Times Literary Supplement). [Matthew] Hollis gives a portrait of the artist as a man at work: shaping, revising, making poems. The biography . . . [is] a story of . . . the last four years of his life, during which he developed a close friendship with Robert Frost, decided to enlist in the army and fight in the First World War, and turned himself into a poet. (New Statesman)

Hopkins, Gerard Manley

Poems and prose. Alfred A. Knopf 1995 256p $13.50   821
1. Poetry -- By individual authors
ISBN 978-0-679-44469-5; 0-679-44469-6
LC 95-15331

This volume "contains a full selection of Hopkins's work, including selected verse, prose, and letters, and an index of first lines." Publisher's note

Housman, A. E.

★ The **collected** poems of A. E. Housman. Holt & Co. 1965 254p pa $16   821
1. Poetry -- By individual authors
ISBN 0-8050-0547-1

This anthology "constitutes the authorized canon of A. E. Housman's verse as established in 1939." Note on the text

Hughes, Ted

Collected poems; edited by Paul Keegan. Farrar, Straus and Giroux 2003 1376p $50; pa $25   821
1. Poetry -- By individual authors
ISBN 978-0-374-12538-7; 0-374-12538-4; 978-0-374-52965-9 pa; 0-374-52965-5 pa
LC 2003-59938

"Paul Keegan has taken Hughes's New Selected Poems of 1995 as his model, and intercalated the expected and familiar Faber texts with uncollected or small press works like a Viennese layer cake—in astonishing quantity and quality." Poetry (Modern Poetry Association)

Johnston, Kenneth R.

The **hidden** Wordsworth; poet, lover, rebel, spy. Norton 1998 965p il $45; pa $24.95   821
1. Authors 2. Poets 3. Poets laureate 4. Poets, English -- 19th century -- Biography 5. Revolutionaries -- Great Britain -- Biography 6. Spies -- Great Britain -- Biography
ISBN 0-393-04623-0; 0-393-32159-2 pa
LC 97-40317

This "volume focuses on the poet's first thirty-six years, the tumultuous decades immortalized in 'The Prelude.' Johnston's spacious, absorbing argument—that Wordsworth's moments of emotion recollected in tranquillity were themselves rather less than tranquil—is amply supported by a thorough documentation of the multifarious life and times of the young poet, at Hawkshead, at Cambridge, in Grasmere, and abroad." New Yorker

Bibliography: p927-933. - Includes index

Jonson, Ben

The **complete** poems; edited by George Parfitt. Penguin Books 1988 634p pa $17   **821**

1. Poetry -- By individual authors

ISBN 978-0-14-042277-1; 0-14-042277-3

LC 88-196178

"As well as the entire body of Jonson's nondramatic verse, extensively annotated, this edition contains many of the songs from his plays and masques and his translation of 'Horace, of the Art of Poetry'. His 'Conversations with Drummond', which adds much to our sense of the man, appears as an Appendix, as does 'Discoveries'; together they shed valuable light on Jonson's poetic theory and practice." Publisher's note

Keats, John

Poems. Knopf 1994 253p $12.50 **821**

1. Poetry -- By individual authors

ISBN 0-679-43319-8

LC 94-2495

A representative collection by the influential English romantic.

★ The **complete** poems of John Keats. Modern Lib. 1994 398p $19.95   **821**

1. Poetry -- By individual authors

ISBN 0-679-60108-2

LC 94-4339

The works in this compilation include Lamia, Isabella, The Eve of St. Agnes', Endymion, and La Belle Dame sans Merci.

Kipling, Rudyard

★ **Complete** verse; definitive edition. Doubleday 1989 850p hardcover o.p. pa $20   **821**

1. Poetry -- By individual authors

ISBN 0-385-26089-X pa

LC 88-7364

This edition includes all of Kipling's published poetry and, in addition, more than 20 poems which have not previously appeared in the inclusive edition of his verse.

Langland, William

Piers Plowman; the Donaldson translation, Middle English text, sources and backgrounds, criticism. edited by Elizabeth Robertson and Stephen H.A. Shepherd. Norton 2006 xxviii, 644p pa $15   **821**

1. Poetry -- By individual authors

ISBN 978-0-393-97559-8; 0-393-97559-2

LC 2004-57578

This Middle English poem is "written in 'Alliterative Verse' like Old English poetry and uses a deliberately rustic and archaic dialect. It is an allegorical moral and social satire, written as a 'vision' of the common medieval type." Reader's Ency. 4th edition

Larkin, Philip

★ **Collected** poems; edited with an introduction by Anthony Thwaite. Farrar, Straus & Giroux 1989 330p hardcover o.p. pa $15   **821**

1. Poetry -- By individual authors

ISBN 978-0-374-52920-8 pa; 0-374-52920-5 pa

LC 88-83528

"'Larkin's poetry is a bit too easily resigned to grimness don't you think?' Elizabeth Bishop once wrote to Robert Lowell. It is true that his range is narrow, but within its confines is a beguiling variety of tones and forms. He never repeats himself to make the same point, and his poems are more readily memorized than those of almost any other postwar poet. . . . And when most of the flashier, more blustery contemporary literature has passed away, his poetry—ghostly, heartbreaking, exhilarating—will continue to haunt." N Y Times Book Rev

Lawrence, D. H.

The **complete** poems; collected and edited with an introduction and notes by Vivian de Sola Pinto and Warren Roberts. Penguin Books 1993 1079p pa $24.95   **821**

1. Poetry -- By individual authors

ISBN 978-0-14-018657-4; 0-14-018657-3

This "collection of Lawrence's poems, with appendices containing juvenilia, variants, and early drafts, and Lawrence's own critical introductions to his poems, also includes full textual and explanatory notes, glossary, and index." Publisher's note

Lear, Edward

The **complete** verse and other nonsense; compiled and edited with an introduction and notes by Vivien Noakes. Penguin Bks. 2002 566p il pa $18   **821**

1. Nonsense literature, English 2. Nonsense verses 3. Nonsense verses, English 4. Poetry -- By individual authors

ISBN 0-14-200227-5

LC 2002-28998

This volume "presents all of Lear's verse and other nonsense writings, including stories, letters, and illustrated alphabets, as well as previously unpublished material, line drawings, and . . . [an] introduction by scholar Vivien Noakes." Publisher's note

Includes bibliographical references

MacDiarmid, Hugh

Selected poetry; introduction by Eliot Weinberger; edited by Alan Riach & Michael Grieve. New Directions 1993 289p $30.95   **821**

1. Poetry -- By individual authors

ISBN 978-0-8112-1248-9; 0-8112-1248-3

LC 93-5312

"The preface by the poet's son Michael Grieve, 'Recalling Hugh MacDiarmid,' includes major biographical facts which shaped the poet's work. . . . Alan Riach's 'Reading Hugh MacDiarmid' provides a scholarly look at MacDiarmid's importance to the Scottish Renaissance and the themes that informed his poetry. . . . In addition to the two introductory essays, the volume also contains a chronology of Mac-Diarmid's life, illustrating both his private maturation and the public events that influenced him. The real reason to purchase the volume, however, is for the exceptional overview and easy accessibility it provides to a major poetic voice not only in Scotland but in the world." World Lit Today

Marvell, Andrew

Poems; [selected by Peter Washington] A. A. Knopf 2004 256p $12.50 **821**

1. Poetry -- By individual authors

ISBN 978-1-4000-4252-4; 1-4000-4252-6

The "metaphysical poet Andrew Marvell was one of the chief wits and satirists of his time as well as a passionate defender of individual liberty. Today, however, he is known chiefly for his brilliant lyric poems, including 'The Garden,' 'The Definition of Love,' 'Bermudas,' 'To His Coy Mistress,' and the 'Horatian Ode' to Cromwell." Publisher's note

Motion, Andrew

Keats. University of Chicago Press 1999 636p il pa $18 **821**

1. Authors 2. Poets 3. Poets, English 4. Poets, English -- 19th century -- Biography 5. Writers on medicine

ISBN 0-226-54240-8; 978-0-226-54240-9

LC 98-41014

"Motion emphasizes that Keats was no otherworldly creature of exquisite sensibilities but a man whose liberal politics and commitment to medicine animated his aesthetics and enlightened his poetry." Booklist

Includes bibliographical references

Muldoon, Paul

★ Horse latitudes. Farrar, Straus and Giroux 2006 107p $22 **821**

1. Poetry -- By individual authors

ISBN 978-0-374-17305-0; 0-374-17305-2

LC 2006-306

"Beginning with a sequence of sonnets whose titles start with the letter B, to a series of instant messages formatted as haiku, to an ending that tributes rocker Warren Zevon, readers are in for a lively ride." Libr J

Maggot; poems. Farrar, Straus and Giroux 2010 134p $24 **821**

1. Poetry -- By individual authors

ISBN 978-0-374-20032-9; 0-374-20032-7

LC 2010-05700

"The play on the word maggot, which can also mean a whim or extravagant notion as well as the larva, tells us all we need to know about Paul Muldoon's poetics. So comfortable is he in both worlds, the debased and the ecstatic, that critics often willfully misunderstand him.... Everywhere in 'Maggot,' Mr. Muldoon chafes at the bit, belatedly, against duty and responsibility. He is most susceptible to the charge of triviality in his longer poems, and often in 'Maggot,' he does indeed flirt too closely with absurdity.... [He] barely squeaks by on the side of seriousness, but just barely! Credit

him with continuing to walk that trapeze, with no net underneath him." Pittsburgh Post-Gazette

★ Poems, 1968-1998. Farrar, Straus & Giroux 2001 479p $35; pa $19   **821**

1. Poetry -- By individual authors

ISBN 0-374-12543-0; 0-374-52844-6 pa

LC 00-45607

"Language is heightened, experimental, and also utterly mundane, even coarse. His subjects match the language, what with trips on mescaline chockablock with bucolic landscapes. The luck of this collection is that it is long and dense enough to show the poet wrestling not only with craft—his intricate and often hidden rhymes show, right from the start, his obsession with form—but also with the reason for poetry in a technological age." Booklist

Murray, Les A.

★ Conscious and verbal; [by] Les Murray. Farrar, Straus & Giroux 2001 94p $23; pa $13   **821**

1. Poetry -- By individual authors

ISBN 0-374-12882-0; 0-374-52860-8 pa

LC 2001-40222

"The poet became a minor celebrity when he awoke from a three-week coma and was pronounced 'conscious and verbal,' but this new volume is more concerned with his familiar Australian topography: dead dogs, the 'Internationale,' oysters, soil, the color yellow. Murray sticks to the cheerfully formal lines that distinguish his work while letting his voice shift between chestnuts of local dialect and a brawny but humble standard English." New Yorker

Poems the size of photographs; [by] Les Murray. Farrar, Straus & Giroux 2003 128p $20   **821**

1. Poetry -- By individual authors

ISBN 0-374-23520-1

LC 2002-192520

"Murray concentrates his muscular style, passion for landscape, and satirical humor into short and pithy poems. Tightly framed, most can be taken in at a glance, and yet, like developing photographs, they fully disclose their finer details and nuances more slowly. Murray begins with a mischievous tribute to the 'new hieroglyphics,' the international symbols of airports and restaurants, pictographs of the forbidden and the required. The contrasts between words and images intrigue Murray and inform his sly, sometimes startling, always colorful and animated lyrics, yarns, and epigrams." Booklist

The biplane houses. Farrar, Straus and Giroux 2007 99p $23   **821**

1. Poetry -- By individual authors

ISBN 978-0-374-11548-7; 0-374-11548-6

LC 2006-31763

"Murray's poems, never exactly intimate and often patrolled by details and place-names nearly indecipherable to an outsider, reflect a life lived self-consciously and rather flamboyantly off the beaten track.... Pastoral is a sophisticated game pitting poets against earlier poets, like a chess match played across time. No poet writing about the natural world entirely opts out of the game, but Murray's poetry of elk and emus, bougainvillea and turmeric dust, comes close." New Yorker

Murray, Les, 1938-
Taller when prone; poems. [by] Les Murray. Farrar, Straus and Giroux 2011 82p $24   **821**
1. Poetry -- By individual authors
ISBN 978-0-374-27237-1
LC 2010033150
This "is Les Murray's first volume of new poems since The Biplane Houses, published five years ago." (Publisher's note)

The title of Murray's collection "plays with the notion of cutting self down to size. He uses humour to restore perspective (although the punchline to the wonderful and ludicrous 'A Frequent Flyer Proposes a Name', in which he suggests a name for a new London airport, does not qualify as a deflationary joke). There are many more serious and ambitious pieces here, too. There are elegies in the tradition of Gerard Manley Hopkins's 'Felix Randal' – 'Rugby Wheels', about a disabled rugby player, and 'Double Diamond', about a gauche octogenarian soldier at his wife's funeral. It is a collection filled with celebrations of ordinary people, extraordinary Australian birds and open endings. Murray has a gentle way with his poems, letting them go, never forcing a conclusion. One of his great gifts is that he is noninterventionist, never blocks a view – art in apparent artlessness." Guardian (UK)

O'Driscoll, Dennis
Stepping stones; interviews with Seamus Heaney. Farrar, Straus, and Giroux 2008 xxx, 552p il map $32   **821**
1. Authors 2. Biography, Individual 3. Essayists 4. Nobel laureates for literature 5. Poetry -- History and criticism 6. Poets 7. Translators
ISBN 978-0-374-26983-8; 0-374-26983-1
LC 2008-41252
"The book is a collection of questions and answers, compiled, largely by correspondence, over a period of some seven years. The compiler, Dennis O'Driscolla poet, senior tax inspector and strict questioner—persuades you that there will be no tolerance of arrears for Heaney here. The replies are tantamount to, while not pre-empting an autobiography, by someone who says he 'inclines to discretion' but is not a 'self-concealing person'. This is a forthright though not a confessional book, inclined both to 'elevated stuff' and to jokes." Times Lit Suppl
Includes bibliographical references

Paterson, Don
Rain. Farrar, Straus, and Giroux 2010 61p $24; pa $13 **821**
1. Poetry -- By individual authors
ISBN 978-0-374-24629-7; 978-0-374-53268-0 pa
LC 2009-938696
"There's something of the shadow puppeteer in Don Paterson — reading his poems, you don't know what's real and what's illusion; they play with the reader's perceptions and sense of perspective, so that you aren't quite sure whether what you're looking are the moving figures themselves or the backlit projection screen. At their best, this gives them a curiously disorienting quality, like looking at a photographic negative, in which the world or its representation has been turned inside out." Guardian (London)

Pickard, Tom
★ **Hole** in the wall; new & selected poems. Flood Editions 2004 139p pa $15   **821**
1. Poetry -- By individual authors
ISBN 0-9710059-3-1
"In the Objectivist tradition, paring words down to broaden their sound and register meaning, Pickard's work here is of compact, dazzling, Bunting-esque musicality. It also bursts with a fluid sensual appeal reminiscent of D.H. Lawrence." Skanky Possum

Poems
All the poems of Muriel Spark. New Directions 2004 130p pa $13.95   **821**
1. Poetry -- By individual authors
ISBN 978-0-8112-1576-3; 0-8112-1576-8
LC 2004-948
"As one might expect from a novelist who has always made use of the full range of fictional genres and devices, All the Poems does not come in a straightforward, chronological package or arrangement; from the outset, the book, like so much else written by Spark, is amusingly perverse. Beginning with 'A Tour of London' (c1950-51), it then immediately skips, in terms of both time and place, to 'The Dark Music of the Rue du Cherche-Midi' (2000), comes right up to date with 'The Creative Writing Class' (2003), travels back to 'The Victoria Falls' (c1948) and 'Shipton-under-Wychwood' (c1950), before regressing finally to a series of translations from Latin (c1949). The reader is therefore encouraged to search for the persistent themes and obvious connections. There is clearly a concern and interest in certain technical forms; there is a ballad, an ode, a couple of villanelles. There's the sharp intelligence and wry wit demonstrated in poems that function mainly as conundrums, unanswered questions and, possibly, as skipping rhymes.... But the most memorable parts of the book are those that give some clue to Spark's lifelong determination and dedication to her craft." Guardian (UK)

Poems. Knopf 1993 250p $12.50 **821**
1. Poetry -- By individual authors
ISBN 978-0-679-42909-8; 0-679-42909-3
LC 93-78335
"Among the English Romantics, [Shelley] has recovered his position as an undoubted major figure: the poet of volcanic hope for a better world, of fiery inspirations shot upward through bitter gloom." Oxford Companion to Engl Lit. 6th edition rev.

Poems and prose. A.A. Knopf 1995 256p $12.50   **821**
1. Poetry -- By individual authors
ISBN 978-0-679-44467-1; 0-679-44467-X
LC 95-15330
"Contains Songs and Sonnets, Letters to the Countess of Bedford, The First Anniversary, Holy Sonnets, Divine Poems, excerpts from Paradoxes and Problems, Ignatius His

Conclave, The Sermons, Essays and Devotions, and an index of first lines." Publisher's note

Thomas Hardy; the complete poems. edited by James Gibson. Palgrave 2001 xxxvi, 1003p il pa $33.95   **821**
1. Poetry -- By individual authors
ISBN 978-0-333-94929-0; 0-333-94929-3
LC 2001-32732
This collection "includes Hardy's more than 900 poems, complemented by detailed notes. Collected here are his eight books of verse, all the uncollected poems, Domicilium, and the songs from The Dynasts. This edition contains an additional poem, The Sound of Her." Publisher's note
Includes bibliographical references

Poems./Selections
Selected poetry; edited with an introduction and notes by Pat Rogers. Oxford University Press 1998 xxiii, 226p pa $12.95   **821**
1. Poetry -- By individual authors 2. Verse satire, English.
ISBN 978-0-19-283494-2; 0-19-283494-0
LC 98-230887
Pope achieved "success with his first published work at the age of twenty-one. A succession of brilliant poems followed, including An Essay on Criticism (1711), Windsor Forest (1715), and his masterpiece, The Rape of the Lock. A second period of great poetry was begun in 1728 with the appearance of the first Dunciad. All these works . . . are included in this selection of his poetry." Publisher's note
Includes bibliographical references

Pope, Alexander
★ **Selected** poetry; edited with an introduction and notes by Pat Rogers. Oxford Univ. Press 1998 xxiii, 226p pa $11.95   **821**
1. Poetry -- By individual authors
ISBN 0-19-283494-0
LC 98-230887
The works in this compilation of poems by the 18th century satirist include The Rape of the Lock, An Essay on Criticism, Windsor Forest, and The Dunciad.

Presley, Frances
Myne; new & selected poems and prose 1976-2005. Shearsman Books 2006 199p $20 **821**
1. Poetry -- By individual authors
ISBN 0-907562-87-6 pa
"Myne is a survey of Frances Presley's career to date, as well as a new collection of her poems. It begins with two recent cycles: the title sequence inspired by the Somerset landscape, and 'Stone Settings' which retraces the enigmatic patterns of prehistoric stones on Exmoor. Also here are the entire Somerset Letters, and Linocut, both originally published by Oasis Books, plus substantial selections from the author's first two books, The Sex of Art and Hula Hoop." Publisher's note

Raine, Kathleen
The **collected** poems of Kathleen Raine. Counterpoint 2001 368p $30   **821**
1. Imagination -- Poetry 2. Poetry -- By individual authors
ISBN 978-1-58243-135-2; 1-58243-135-3
LC 00-64448
"Here is a signature collection of [Raine's] work that will delight many and introduce her to many others. She deserves a very wide audience, as she has much to teach us. . . . Her personal religious journey was from a strict Protestant upbringing through conversion to Roman Catholicism to Eastern Vedic belief. From first to last, her poetry is unified by a tone of transcendental belief in visions, presence, angels, and oracles rooted in her Scottish mother's experience of nature." World Lit Today

Robinson, Edwin Arlington
Poems; selected and edited by Scott Donaldson. A. A. Knopf 2007 553p $12.50 **821**
1. Poetry -- By individual authors
ISBN 978-0-307-26576-0; 0-307-26576-5
LC 2006-48269
"Wisely concentrating on poems of short and middling length, Donaldson . . . admits extracts only from Captain Craig and the ending of Lancelot. . . . [He] gives us whole texts of 'Rembrandt to Rembrandt,' 'Isaac and Archibald,' 'Aunt Imogen,' 'John Brown,' and 'Ben Jonson Entertains a Man from Stratford'— major poems all. For texts, he draws entirely from the Collected Poems, save for 'Romance' and four poems given as they appeared in magazines." New Criterion

Ross, David A.
Critical companion to William Butler Yeats; a literary reference to his life and work. Facts On File 2008 652p il $75   **821**
1. Authors 2. Dramatists 3. Memoirists 4. Nobel laureates for literature 5. Poets
ISBN 978-0-8160-5895-2
LC 2008-13642
"Coverage includes: all of Yeats's . . . poems, as well as all his volumes of poetry; all his plays and important drama-related topics, including Dublin's Abbey Theatre, which he helped establish; his critical and other nonfiction writing, including his . . . autobiographies; important themes in his work; [and] friends and literary influences, including Maud Gonne and James Joyce." Publisher's note
Includes bibliographical references

Rossetti, Christina Georgina
Christina Rossetti; the complete poems. text [edited] by R.W. Crump; notes and introduction by Betty S. Flowers. Penguin 2001 lv, 1221p pa $20   **821**
1. Poetry -- By individual authors
ISBN 978-0-14-042366-2; 0-14-042366-4
LC 2002-281810
This "fully annotated collection, based on the definitive texts, brings together fantasy poems such as 'Goblin Market,' terrifyingly vivid verses for children, love lyrics, sonnets, hymns, and ballads, as well as the vast body of her

devotional poetry. . . . [This edition] incorporates contextual notes as well as notes on the text and language, an introduction, and a chronology of Rossetti's life and work." Publisher's note

Includes bibliographical references

Rossignol, Rosalyn

Critical companion to Chaucer; a literary reference to his life and work. Facts on File 2006 648p il $85 **821**

1. Authors 2. Poets

ISBN 0-8160-6193-9; 978-0-8160-6193-8

LC 2006-99

This book on the works of Chaucer includes a biography of Chaucer, synopses and critical commentary on his works (including the Canterbury Tales), and lists of related people, places and topics.

Schmidt, Michael

★ **Lives** of the poets. Knopf 1999 975p hardcover o.p. pa $20 **821**

1. American poetry -- History and criticism 2. English poetry -- History and criticism 3. Poetry -- By individual authors 4. Poets, English -- Biography

ISBN 0-375-70604-6 pa

LC 98-51913

In this "survey of poetry in English, Schmidt . . . enthuses about more than 250 poets whose work dates from the 14th century to 1998. More than a critical essay, this friendly and accessible history embodies the life of poetry and conveys its changeable, subjective beauty." Libr J

Includes bibliographical references

Selections.

John Dryden; the major works. edited with an introduction and notes by Keith Walker. Oxford University Press 2003 xviii, 967p pa $18.95 **821**

1. Poetry -- By individual authors

ISBN 978-0-19-284077-6; 0-19-284077-0

LC 2003-270051

This "edition brings together a unique combination of Dryden's poetry and prose—all the major poems in full, literary criticism, and translations—to give the essence of his work and thinking. The collection includes the poems, MacFlecknoe and Absalom and Achitophel as well as Dryden's classical translations; his versions of Homer, Horace, and Ovid are reproduced in full. There are also substantial selections from Dryden's Virgil, Juvenal, and other classical writers. Fables, Ancient and Modern, taken from Chaucer, Ovid, Boccaccio, and Homer, his last and possibly greatest work, also appears in full." Publisher's note

Includes bibliographical references

Shelley, Percy Bysshe

Shelley's poetry and prose; authoritative texts, criticism. selected and edited by Donald H. Reiman and Neil Fraistat. 2nd ed; Norton 2002 xxii, 786p il pa $18.75 **821**

1. Poetry -- By individual authors

ISBN 0-393-97752-8

LC 2001-30903

"This edition includes all of Shelley's greatest poetry and other poems frequently taught or discussed . . . as well as three of his most important prose works." Preface

Includes bibliographical references (p. 775-783) and index

Sisson, C. H.

Selected poems; foreword by M.L. Rosenthal. New Directions 1996 94p pa $9.95 **821**

1. Poetry -- By individual authors

ISBN 978-0-8112-1327-1; 0-8112-1327-7

LC 95-47599

"C.H. Sisson's Christianity is an austere, rural form that forbids pity for a newborn duckling that will obviously not survive. Yet Sisson, like Frost, sees death and old age as part of a design, not so much insidious as inexorable and thus no occasion for tears. Like Donne, whom he commemorates in 'A Letter to John Donne,' Sisson understands probably better than any contemporary poet the struggle between the call of the flesh and the love of God, and he knows, like Donne, that their reconciliation can only occur in art. . . . The poems [collected here] are sardonic, elegiac, but not despairing." World Lit Today

Smith, Stevie

★ **Collected** poems; edited with a preface by James MacGibbon. New Directions 1983 591p il pa $19.95 **821**

1. Poetry -- By individual authors

ISBN 0-8112-0882-6

LC 83-43008

Smith "wrote three novels, but has been more widely recognized for her witty, caustic, and enigmatic verse, much of it illustrated by her own comic drawings." Concise Oxford Companion to Engl Lit

Spencer, Bernard, 1909-1963

Complete poetry: translations & selected prose; edited by Peter Robinson. Bloodaxe Books 2011 351p pa $33.95 **821**

1. Poetry -- By individual authors

ISBN 978-1-85224-891-8 pa; 1-85224-891-2 pa

Spencer "was not a natural self-promoter, publishing sparely and modestly; moreover, his semi-expatriate status and the adventurousness of his reading all but excluded him from narrower and more familiar English traditions. . . . This new edition by Peter Robinson, who has worked extensively with the Spencer archive at Reading University, is the first to appear since Roger Bowen's Collected Poems of 1981, and aims to stir new interest in the work. As well as Spencer's two published collections, Aegean Islands and Other Poems (1946) and With Luck Lasting (1963), and the later poems collected by Bowen, Robinson includes previously uncollected and unpublished drafts, prose drawn from interviews, lectures and notes, and Spencer's pioneering translations of George Seferis, Odysseus Elytis and Eugenio Montale. Reading these alongside his own poems, it becomes clearer than ever how much Spencer drew on Greek and Latin traditions, blending them with the green-grass Englishness of Edward Thomas, and the civilised anguish of MacNeice to make what Robinson's excellent introduction calls 'a European poetry in English'." Guardian (UK)

Spenser, Edmund

★ The **faerie** queene; edited by Thomas P. Roche, Jr., with the assistance of C. Patrick O'Donnell, Jr. Penguin Books 1987 1246p pa $20 **821**

1. Poetry -- By individual authors

ISBN 978-0-14-043307-8; 0-14-042207-2

"The greatest work of Spenser, of which the first three books were entrusted to the printer in Nov. 1589, and the second three were published in 1596." Oxford Companion to Engl Lit

Stevenson, Anne

★ **Poems,** 1955-2005. Bloodaxe Books 2005 413p $64.95; pa $29.95 **821**

1. Poetry -- By individual authors

ISBN 1-85224-721-5; 1-85224-699-5 pa

"While Anne Stevenson is most certainly, and rightly, regarded as one of the major poets of our period, it has never been by virtue of this or that much anthologised poem, but by the work or mind as a whole. It is not so much a matter of the odd lightning-struck tree as of an entire landscape, and that landscape is always humane, intelligent and sane, composed of both natural and rational elements, and amply furnished with patches of wit and fury, which only serve to bring out the humanity." London Magazine

Swift, Daniel

Bomber County; the poetry of a lost pilot's war. Farrar, Straus and Giroux 2010 269p il $26 **821**

1. English poetry -- 20th century -- History and criticism 2. English poetry -- History and criticism 3. War poetry, English -- History and criticism 4. World War, 1939-1945 -- Great Britain -- Literature and the war 5. World War, 1939-1945 -- Literature and the war 6. World War, 1939-1945 -- Poetry

ISBN 0374273316; 9780374273316

LC 2010-23402

'Bomber County' narrates the story of Daniel Swift's grandfather, "a pilot with the 83rd Squadron of the Royal Air Force, who on June 12, 1943, climbed aboard a Lancaster bomber, along with six other men for a raid on Münster, Germany. His plane never returned." (N Y Times (Late N Y Ed))

"Swift has found an ingeniously oblique way to throw fresh light on history. His main achievement here is not new facts but what is done with them, in a subtle exercise in traversing genres." Times Lit Suppl

Includes bibliographical references

Tennyson, Alfred Tennyson

Poems. A. A. Knopf 2004 255p $12.50 **821**

1. Poetry -- By individual authors

ISBN 978-1-4000-4187-9; 1-4000-4187-2

LC 2003-49505

"This collection includes such famous poems as 'The Lady of Shalott' and 'The Charge of the Light Brigade.' There are extracts from all the major masterpieces—Idylls of the King, The Princess, In Memoriam—and several complete long poems, such as 'Ulysses' and 'Demeter and Persephone,' that demonstrate his narrative grace. Finally, there are many of the short lyrical poems, such as 'Come into the Garden, Maud' and 'Break, Break, Break,' for which he is justly celebrated." Publisher's note

Thomas, Dylan

The **poems** of Dylan Thomas; edited with an introduction and notes by Daniel Jones; with a preface by Dylan Thomas. rev ed; New Directions 2003 xxix, 320p il $34.95 **821**

1. Poetry -- By individual authors

ISBN 978-0-8112-1541-1; 0-8112-1541-5

LC 2002-155790

"To the 90 poems Thomas published in Collected Poems, 1934-1952 Jones has added 102 and placed the total, as far as he could determine, in the chronological order of their composition. Some of the poems were still in manuscript form when Thomas died; others had been published in periodicals and anthologies. In an appendix, Jones offers Thomas' early poems—including one written when the poet was 12." Libr J [review of 1971 edition]

Includes bibliographical references

Tomlinson, Charles

Selected poems; 1955-1997. New Directions 1997 226p pa $13.95 **821**

1. Poetry -- By individual authors

ISBN 978-0-8112-1369-1; 0-8112-1369-2

LC 97-25373

"These poems are a fine achievement; they are the work of a consciousness mostly at ease with its dwelling in this world, and unabashed by a lack of inclination to dwell unduly on shadows rather than light. The sunniness of disposition, both geographically and psychologically, combined with Tomlinson's canny ability to metrically heighten what still sounds to the ear like the language of common day, give a tone that might be rationally described as Tomlinsonian. This . . . [is] a book essential to any collection of the best poetry of the postwar years." Am Book Rev

Skywriting and other poems. Ivan R. Dee 2003 96p $18.95 **821**

1. Poetry -- By individual authors

ISBN 978-1-566-63541-7; 1-556-63541-1

LC 2003-55504

"Mr Tomlinson is an eloquent poet of place—in this collection he moves through Mexico, Italy, Japan, and his home county of Gloucestershire—whose work combines visual exactitude with an uncommon gracefulness of expression." Economist

Turnbull, Gael

★ **There** are words; collected poems. Shearsman Books 2006 495p pa $30 **821**

1. Poetry -- By individual authors

ISBN 0-90756-289-2

"Restlessly experimental—but never for its own sake—Turnbull was constantly doing what Ezra Pound asked of poets at the beginning of the twentieth century, namely to make it new. His range is very wide. He employed the long line before C.K. Williams or Ciaran Carson; he experimented with prose-poems, found-poems; he wrote ballads, poems meant to be read out loud, poems that deftly rhyme and ones that deftly don't; he shaped poems on the page with varying line-lengths and indentings; he used the spaces between lines and verses functionally; the touch is sometimes light, sometimes profoundly earnest. . . . In the almost 500pp of this superb

Collected Poems there isn't one dud piece, one poem that doesn't have genuine poetic power and resonance." Stride (UK)

West, Richard

Chaucer, 1340-1400; the life and times of the first English poet. Carroll & Graf Pubs. 2000 302p il map hardcover o.p. pa $14 **821**
1. Authors 2. Poets
ISBN 0-7867-0925-1 pa

LC 00-712752

West's biography "combines history and literary criticism. He places Chaucer within his historical context and examines his life and writings." Libr J

Wordsworth, William

★ **Selected** poetry of William Wordsworth; edited by Mark Van Doren; introduction by David Bromwich. Modern Lib. 2001 xxii, 687p $24.95; pa $11.95 **821**
1. Poetry -- By individual authors
ISBN 0-679-64224-2; 0-375-75941-7 pa

LC 00-66444

This collection "represents Wordsworth's prolific output, from the poems first published in Lyrical Ballads in 1798 . . . to the late 'Yarrow Revisited.' Wordsworth's poetry is celebrated for its deep feeling, its use of ordinary speech, the love of nature it expresses, and its representation of commonplace things and events." Publisher's note

Yeats, W. B.

The **collected** poems of W.B. Yeats; edited by Richard J. Finneran. Rev. 2nd ed.; Scribner Paperback Poetry 1996 xxv, 544p pa $20 **821**
1. Poetry -- By individual authors
ISBN 978-0-684-80731-7; 0-684-80731-9

LC 96-23314

This volume "includes all of the poems authorized by Yeats for inclusion in his standard canon. . . . Revised and corrected, this edition includes Yeats's own notes on his poetry, complemented by explanatory notes from . . .Yeats scholar Richard J. Finneran." Publisher's note

★ 100 essential modern poems; selected and introduced by Joseph Parisi. Ivan R. Dee 2005 305p $24.95 **821**
1. American poetry -- Collections 2. English poetry -- Collections
ISBN 1-56663-612-4

LC 2005-9897

"Preceded by wonderfully conversational and expertly appreciative biocritical essays about each poet, his choices are superb as he lingers over Yeats and Stevens and includes often-overlooked witty and satirical poets, among them Dorothy Parker, Ogden Nash, Kay Ryan, Frank O'Hara, and Billy Collins." Booklist

★ 100 great poems of the twentieth century; [edited by] Mark Strand. Norton 2005 320p $24.95 **821**
1. American poetry -- Collections 2. English poetry

-- Collections
ISBN 0-393-05894-8

LC 2005-2150

The editor "has selected works by poets of Europe and North and South America, and because there are so many gifted American poets, he restricted himself to those born before 1927. The result is a marvelously graceful, shimmering cosmos of poems by the likes of Anna Akhmatova, A. R. Ammons, Amy Clampit, Robert Desnos, Robert Frost, Nazim Hikmet, Kenneth Koch, Edna St. Vincent Millay, Gabriela Mistral, Eugenio Montale, Octavio Paz, and Derek Walcott." Booklist

★ The Best poems of the English language; from Chaucer through Robert Frost. selected and with commentary by Harold Bloom. HarperCollins Publishers 2004 xxviii, 972p $34.95; pa $19.95 **821**
1. American poetry 2. American poetry -- Collections 3. English poetry 4. English poetry -- Collections
ISBN 0-06-054041-9; 0-06-054042-7 pa

LC 2003-51104

"Arranged chronologically by author, the poems are preceded by commentaries that extol their specific virtues and place them in historical context. Taken together, they provide an overview of Bloom's own theories of writing, such as his notion that the greatest poems manifest an 'inevitability' of phrasing . . . Bloom rarely bores, and at his best he achieves a cogency . . . worthy of the poets he so deeply admires." Libr J
Includes bibliographical references

British women poets of the Romantic era; an anthology. edited by Paula R. Feldman. Johns Hopkins Univ. Press 1997 xxxvi, 879p hardcover o.p. pa $29.95 **821**
1. English poetry -- Women authors 2. English poetry -- Women authors -- Collections 3. Romanticism
ISBN 0-8018-6640-5 pa

LC 96-47417

An "anthology of works by 62 British women poets writing between 1770 and 1840. . . . The poets are presented in alphabetical order, with each entry including a brief biography with birth and death dates, sample poems, major works, selected works, and the source of the poetry. The result is a singular resource providing information found in no other reference work." Libr J
Includes bibliographical references

Christmas poems; selected and edited by John Hollander and J.D. McClatchy. Knopf 1999 254p $12.50 **821**
1. American poetry -- Collections 2. Christmas -- Poetry 3. English poetry -- Collections
ISBN 0-375-40789-8

LC 99-36265

Contributors to this collection of Christmas poetry include Milton, Tennyson, Rossetti, Thackeray, Eliot, McGinley, Morris, Bishop and Geoffrey Hill

The Columbia anthology of British poetry; edited by Carl Woodring and James Shapiro. Columbia Univ. Press 1995 xxxi, 891p $41   **821**

1. English poetry -- Collections

ISBN 0-231-10180-5

LC 94-46333

This anthology "contains major British poetry from Beowulf to the present day. Poets receive a short biographical introduction along with their poetry. . . . It includes more female poets than most comparable anthologies, and is conducive to browsing. Major poems such as Coleridge's 'Rime of the Ancient Mariner,' Britain's best-loved poems, and newly rediscovered poems are part of this collection." SLJ

★ Contemporary poets; editor, Thomas Riggs; with a preface by Diane Wakoski. 7th ed; St. James Press 2001 xxiii, 1443p $230   **821**

1. American poetry -- 20th century 2. American poetry -- 20th century -- History and criticism 3. American poetry -- Bio-bibliography 4. English poetry -- 20th century 5. English poetry -- 20th century -- History and criticism 6. Poets, American -- 20th century 7. Poets, American -- Dictionaries 8. Poets, English -- 20th century 9. Poets, English -- Dictionaries 10. Reference books

ISBN 1-55862-349-3

LC 00-45882

"A biographical handbook of contemporary poets, arranged alphabetically. Entries consist of a short biography, full bibliography, comments by many of the poets, and a signed critical essay." Ref Sources for Small & Medium-sized Libr. 6th edition

Includes bibliographical references

Geoffrey Chaucer's The Canterbury tales; edited and with an introduction by Harold Bloom. New ed; Chelsea House 2008 286p $45   **821**

1. Authors 2. Poetry -- By individual authors 3. Poets

ISBN 978-0-7910-9618-5

LC 2007-49158

A collection of eleven critical essays on Chaucer's well-known work, arranged in chronological order of their original publication.

The Making of a poem; a Norton anthology of poetic forms. edited by Mark Strand and Eavan Boland. Norton 2000 xxxi, 366p hardcover o.p. pa $15.95   **821**

1. American poetry 2. American poetry -- Collections 3. English poetry 4. English poetry -- Collections 5. Literary form

ISBN 0-393-32178-9 pa

LC 99-55233

A "collection of villanelles, sestinas, sonnets, elegies, pastorals, ballads, pantoums, odes, and other familiar structures that have shaped English poetry since Beowulf. Each chapter focuses on a single form. . . . Most useful are the selections themselves, which illustrate how particular forms have been employed over time, from canonical classics by Chaucer, Shelley, and Elizabeth Bishop through newer piec-

es by Hayden Carruth, Michael Palmer, and Thylias Moss." Libr J

Includes bibliographical references

★ The New Oxford book of Irish verse; edited, with translations, by Thomas Kinsella. Oxford Univ. Press 2001 xxx, 423p pa $16.95   **821**

1. English poetry -- Irish authors 2. Irish poetry 3. Irish poetry -- Collections

ISBN 0-19-280192-9

LC 2001-278442

"This selection is divided into three parts. Book I opens with the earliest pre-Christian poetry in Old Irish and ends in the fourteenth century with the first Irish poetry in the English language. Book II covers the fourteenth to the eighteenth centuries and Book III the nineteenth and twentieth centuries." Publisher's note

★ The New Oxford book of Victorian verse. Oxford Univ. Press 1987 xxxiv, 654p hardcover o.p. pa $25.95   **821**

1. English poetry -- Collections

ISBN 978-0-19-955631-1 pa

LC 86-23701

An anthology of 19th century English poetry. Among the poets prominently featured are: Clough, Morris, Arnold, the Decadents, Emily Brontë, Clare, Barnes, and Christina Rossetti.

"While general collections should all add Ricks, those retaining [the Quiller-Couch edition] should dust him off and keep him available in order to represent fully Victorian verse and changing attitudes toward it." Libr J

★ The Norton anthology of modern and contemporary poetry; edited by Jahan Ramazani, Richard Ellmann, Robert O'Clair. 3rd ed; Norton 2003 2v pa set $75   **821**

1. American poetry -- Collections 2. English poetry -- Collections 3. Poetry -- Collections

ISBN 0-393-32429-X

LC 2002-37990

This volume includes "1596 poems by 195 poets. . . . The anthology includes the works of such masters as Walt Whitman, Ezra Pound, Dylan Thomas, Langston Hughes, Gertrude Stein, Lucille Clifton, Louise Erdrich, and Allen Ginsberg. . . . Extensive, and beautifully composed introductions provide insight, observations, and historical context for the selections. . . . This ambitious, highly successful work is a veritable tribute to the enduring power of literature and language." SLJ

Includes bibliographical references

★ The Oxford book of English verse; edited by Christopher Ricks. Oxford Univ. Press 1999 xxxii, 690p $39.95   **821**

1. English poetry 2. English poetry -- Collections

ISBN 0-19-214182-1

LC 99-20831

This collection "starts with anonymous 13th-century lyric and ends with Seamus Heaney; in between are seven centuries' worth of poems in English from Britain and Ireland. . . . Ricks brings in plenty of dialect verse, excerpts from long

poems and verse plays, and a few translations into English. .
. . Long after reviewers stop debating how Ricks chose each
item, readers will keep returning to these pages to find yet
another good poem they've not before seen." Publ Wkly

★ The Oxford book of comic verse; edited by John
   Gross. Oxford University Press 2009 xxxiv,
   512p pa $19.95   **821**
1. American poetry -- Collections 2. English poetry --
Collections 3. Humorous poetry -- Collections
ISBN 978-0-19-956161-2

              LC 2009-291577
The editor "defines comic verse as primarily meant to
amuse. From this bland definition he delves his principles
of inclusion: funny poems that do not exceed the boundaries
of good taste. No bawdy lyrics, no skewering satire here.
Within these limits, he surveys the field from Chaucer to
Glyn Maxwell (1962)." Publ Wkly
   Includes bibliographical references

The Oxford book of sonnets; edited by John Fuller.
   Oxford Univ. Press 2000 xxxiv, 362p $25; pa
   $15.95   **821**
1. American poetry -- Collections 2. English poetry --
Collections 3. Sonnets, American 4. Sonnets, English
ISBN 0-19-214267-4; 0-19-280389-1 pa

              LC 00-36757
"Indisputable masterpieces appear plentifully, but Fuller's determination to present a large number of distinguished
practitioners assures that there are also many superb poems
by virtual unknowns. And Fuller's introduction is a sharp-
witted miracle of concise comprehensiveness." Booklist
   Includes bibliographical references

The Oxford companion to Chaucer; edited by Douglas Gray. Oxford University Press 2003 xxiii,
   526p il map $95   **821**
1. Authors 2. Poetry -- By individual authors 3. Poets
4. Poets, English -- Middle English, 1100-1500 --
Biography -- Encyclopedias
ISBN 0-19-811765-5

            LC 2004-270323
This reference includes "more than 2,000 signed entries
on various aspects of Chaucer and his works as well as their
larger cultural and literary context." Choice
   Includes bibliographical references

The Penguin book of the sonnet; 500 years of a clas-
   sic tradition in English. edited by Phillis Levin.
   Penguin Bks. 2001 419p pa $18   **821**
1. American poetry -- Collections 2. English poetry
-- Collections 3. Sonnets, English
ISBN 0-14-058929-5

            LC 00-62350
In an introductory essay, Levin "discusses the sonnet's
origins, history, traditions, and possibilities. . . . Interwoven
with the history are approaches to interpreting and criticizing this poetic form. The bulk of the text is an anthology of
over 600 sonnets composed by more than 230 poets. Over
150 of the poets represented wrote during the 20th century."
Libr J

   Includes bibliographical references

An anthology of modern Irish poetry; edited by Wes
   Davis. Belknap Press of Harvard University Press
   2010 976p $35   **821**
1. English poetry -- Irish authors 2. Irish poetry -- 20th
century 3. Irish poetry -- Collections
ISBN 9780674049512; 0-674-04951-9

            LC 2009-37231
This volume, "running to almost a thousand pages,
comes from a country with a population roughly equal to
that of Tennessee. The book includes upwards of 50 poets—
and there's not a dull page in it. Editor Wes Davis's selection
is judicious, while his introduction and notes are as informative as they are brief." Wall Street J

822   English drama

Behan, Brendan
   ★ The **complete** plays; introduced by Alan
Simpson; with a bibliography by E. H. Mikhail.
Grove Weidenfeld 1991 384p pa $15   **822**
   ISBN 0-8021-3070-4

            LC 78-53931

Bennett, Alan
   The **history** boys. Faber and Faber 2006 xxvii,
109p pa $13   **822**
1. Boarding schools -- Drama. 2. Education -- Drama.
3. England -- Drama. 4. Teacher-student relationships
-- Drama.
ISBN 978-0-571-22464-7; 0-571-22464-4

            LC 2005-936593
Characters: 11 men, 1 woman extras. First produced at
the Lyttleton Theatre, London, May 18, 2004.
   "Nothing could diminish the incendiary achievement of
this subtle, deep-wrought and immensely funny play about
the value and meaning of education. . . . In short, a superb,
life-enhancing play." Guardian

Bolt, Robert
   ★ A **man** for all seasons; a play in two acts.
Random House 1962 xxv, 163p il hardcover o.p. pa
$9.50   **822**
1. Authors 2. Saints 3. Statesmen 4. Writers on law
5. Writers on religion
ISBN 0-679-72822-8 pa
   Characters: 11 men, 2 women. First produced in the
United States at the ANTA Theatre, New York City, Novem-
ber 22, 1961.

Christie, Agatha
   The **mousetrap** and other plays. New American
Library 2000 742p hardcover o.p. pa $7.99   **822**
1. English drama -- Collections
ISBN 0-451-20118-3; 0-451-20114-0 pa

            LC 00-64727
"The noted mystery writer composed adaptations of sev-
en novels and stories into arresting plays as well as creating
one original theater piece ('Verdict'). . . . All are as delightful
to read for pleasure as Christie's mystery novels, especially

since some that earlier appeared in the latter form have been intriguingly altered." Booklist

Churchill, Caryl

Mad forest; a play from Romania. Theatre Communications Group 1996 87p pa $13.95   **822**

ISBN 1-55936-114-X; 978-1-55936-114-9

LC 96-12875

Large mixed cast. 3 acts. First performed at the New York Theater Workshop, New York, December 4, 1991.

This play "explores the reactions of two ordinary families to the confused events of the Romanian revolution: the dreadful damage done to people's lives by years of repression, and the painful difficulties of sudden but lasting change." Publisher's note

Coward, Noel

★ **Three** plays; Blithe spirit, Hay fever, Private lives. introduction by Philip Hoare. Vintage Bks. 1999 254p pa $13   **822**

ISBN 0-679-78179-X

LC 98-47414

Dryden, John

★ **All** for love; edited by David M. Vieth. University of Neb. Press 1972 xxxiv, 146p hardcover o.p. pa $24.95   **822**

1. Queens

ISBN 0-8032-5379-6 pa

An English Restoration tragedy which is an adaptation of Shakespeare's "Antony and Cleopatra" done in blank verse.

Fugard, Athol

Blood knot and other plays. Theatre Communications Group 1991 202p hardcover o.p. pa $15 **822**

ISBN 978-1-55936-019-7; 1-55936-019-4

LC 90-29029

"The brothers of Blood Knot—one dark-skinned, one light—betray their dream of a better future with the impossible wish of passing for white. In Hello and Goodbye, a poor white brother and sister churn through their once-promising past to comprehend their bleak present. Boesman and Lena, black husband and wife, tramp homelessly through a severe and unforgiving landscape, discovering strength and delivering devotion through an encounter with a mysterious old African." Publisher's note

★ **Master** Harold-- and the boys. Vintage Books 2009 60p pa $12.95   **822**

ISBN 978-0-307-47520-6; 0-307-47520-4

LC 2010-292381

Characters: 3 men. 1 act. First produced at the Yale Repertory theatre, New Haven, Connecticut, 1982.

Gay, John

The **beggar's** opera; edited by Edgar V. Roberts; music edited by Edward Smith. University of Neb. Press 1969 xxix, 238p music hardcover o.p. pa $21.95   **822**

ISBN 978-0-8032-5361-2 pa; 0-8032-5361-3 pa

A ballad opera, this is a rogues' comedy satirizing corrupt politics in 18th century England.

Heaney, Seamus

The **burial** at Thebes; a version of Sophocles' Antigone. Farrar, Straus and Giroux 2004 79p $18   **822**

1. Antigone (Greek mythology) 2. Greek drama (Tragedy)

ISBN 0-374-11721-7

LC 2004-43986

"There are many translations of Sophocles' Antigone but few with the understated power and spare beauty of . . . Heaney's version. . . . Written in a muscular but lively style, the translation, like Heaney's best poetry, finds music in the language of the streets and reveals the raw, primal power in the most carefully constructed rhetorical tropes." Booklist

Jonson, Ben

Volpone and other plays; edited by Michael Jamieson. Penguin 2004 496p pa $12   **822**

ISBN 978-0-14-144118-4; 0-14-144118-6

LC 2004-275516

"Ben Jonson created in Volpone and The Alchemist hilarious portraits of cupidity and chicanery, while in Bartholomew Fair he portrays his fellow Londoners at their most festive—and most bawdy." Publisher's note

Osborne, John

★ **Look** back in anger. Penguin 1982 96p pa $12   **822**

ISBN 0-14-048-175-3; 978-0-14-048-175-4

LC 82-9144

Characters: 3 men, 2 women. First produced at the Royal Court Theatre, London, May 8, 1956.

This play "introduced a new strain of realism to British theatre and set the tone for the generation of anti-Establishment writers who became known as the Angry Young Men. Osborne described his own parents as 'impoverished middle class,' but his play deals with the frustrations, crude language, and squalid conditions of working-class life." Reader's Ency. 4th edition

Peters, Sally

Bernard Shaw; the ascent of the superman. Yale Univ. Press 1996 328p il hardcover o.p. pa $22 **822**

1. Authors 2. Biography, Individual 3. Dramatists 4. Dramatists, English 5. Essayists 6. Nobel laureates for literature 7. Nonfiction writers 8. Novelists

ISBN 0-300-06097-1; 0-300-07500-6 pa

LC 95-37248

An "exploration of the ambiguities and passions that formed this great playwright and thinker. Shaw's sexuality, always a good topic of speculation, is studied here, but one wishes for more insights and in-depth analysis. Peters does devote a chapter to Shaw's close relationship with the actor and playwright Harley Granville Barker, mainly from Shaw's point of view. One may not agree with Peter's conclusions, but they will prove to be of interest to anyone studying Shaw." Libr J

Includes bibliographical references

Pinter, Harold

Complete works; with an introduction, Writing for the theatre. Grove Weidenfeld 1990 4v v1 pa $14.50; v2 pa $13.50; v3 pa $14; v4 pa $13.50 **822**
ISBN 0-8021-5096-9 v1; 0-8021-3237-5 v2; 0-8021-5049-7 v3; 0-8021-5050-0 v4
LC 90-13933

Plays

The **complete** plays; introduced by John Lahr. Grove Weidenfeld 1990 448p pa $15 **822**
ISBN 978-0-8021-3215-4
LC 90-3069

Shaffer, Peter

★ **Equus**. Scribner 2005 112p pa $12 **822**
ISBN 0-7432-8730-4; 978-0-7432-8730-2
LC 2005-51600
Characters: 5 men, 4 women. 1 act, 35 scenes. First produced by the National Theater, London, July 26, 1973.

Drama about "a jolting confrontation between a psychiatrist and a 17-year-old boy who has blinded six horses from the stable where he is employed. As the probe into the boy's attitudes and behavior deepens, this criminal act is revealed to have been a result of his notions of a sexual/religious spirit in horses." Booklist

★ **Peter** Shaffer's Amadeus; with an introduction by the director Sir Peter Hall and a wholly new preface by the author. Perennial Bks. 2001 xxxiv, 124p pa $15 **822**
1. Composers
ISBN 0-06-093549-9
LC 2001-278382
Characters: 9 men, 1 woman, extras. 2 acts. First produced at the National Theater of Great Britain, November 1979.

Shaw, Bernard

Arms and the man; a pleasant play. [by] Bernard Shaw; introduction by Rodelle Weintraub; definitive text under the editorial supervision of Dan H. Laurence. Penguin Books 2006 xxvi 73 pa $9 **822**
ISBN 978-0-14-303976-1; 0-14-303976-8
LC 2005-56724
First produced 1894. Comedy set in Bulgaria satirizing romantic attitudes about war.

Heartbreak House; a fantasia in the Russian manner on English themes. definitive text under the editorial supervision of Dan H. Laurence; with an introduction by David Hare. Penguin Books 2000 160p il pa $10 **822**
ISBN 978-0-14-043787-4; 0-14-043787-8
LC 2001-266517
"A complex allegorical work in which Shaw indicts apathy, confusion, and lack of purpose as the causes of the world's problems. The characters—all larger than life and with symbolic names—are gathered at the home of an eccentric sea captain; they each represent an evil in the modern world. Into their midst comes young Ellie Dunn, whose

search for a husband Shaw treats as a new generation searching for a way of life." Benet's Reader's Ency. 4th edition
Includes bibliographical references

Major Barbara; definitive text under the editorial supervision of Dan H. Laurence; with an introduction by Margery Morgan. Penguin Books 2000 156p pa $11 **822**
1. Crime 2. Father-daughter relationship
ISBN 978-0-14-043790-4; 0-14-043790-8
LC 2002-275028
In this "comedy, originally staged in 1905, Andrew Undershaft, a millionaire armaments dealer, loves money and despises poverty. His energetic daughter Barbara, however, is a devout major in the Salvation Army. She sees her father as just another soul to be saved. But when the Salvation Army needs funds to keep going, it is Undershaft who saves the day." Publisher's note

Man and Superman; a comedy and a philosophy. definitive text under the editorial supervision of Dan H. Laurence; introduced by Stanley Weintraub. Penguin 2000 264p pa $11 **822**
ISBN 978-0-14-043788-1; 0-14-043788-6
"In Man and Superman, Shaw combined seriousness with comedy to create a satirical and buoyant exposé of the eternal struggle between the sexes. . . . This volume includes Shaw's Preface of 1903 and his appendix, 'The Revolutionist's Handbook', the cast list from the first production of Man and Superman and a list of his principal works." Publisher's note

★ **Pygmalion** . . . and My fair lady; [Pygmalion] by George Bernard Shaw; and My fair lady/based on Shaw's Pygmalion; adaptation and lyrics by Alan Jay Lerner; music by Frederick Loewe. 50th anniversary ed.; Signet Classic 2006 219p pa $5.95 **822**
ISBN 0-451-53009-8
This volume includes the complete texts of Shaw's Pygmalion and Lerner's musical adaptation My fair lady.

Saint Joan; a chronicle play in six scenes and an epilogue. definitive text under the editorial supervision of Dan H. Laurence; with 'On playing Joan' by Imogen Stubbs; and an introduction by Joley Wood. Penguin 2003 xx, 168p pa $12 **822**
1. Saints
ISBN 978-0-14-043791-6; 0-14-04379-1
Chronicle play in "which Joan of Arc, the young girl who led France to victory over the English, emerges as an unlettered country girl gifted with masterful will and innate intelligence." McGraw-Hill Ency World Drama

Sheridan, Richard Brinsley

The **school** for scandal and other plays; edited with an introduction by Eric S. Rump. New ed; Penguin 2004 288p pa $12 **822**
ISBN 978-0-14-043240-4
"In The Rivals, Captain Absolute becomes his own rival for the hand of Lydia Languish wooing her under another name, while her aunt, the verbally inept Mrs Malaprop,

wishes her to marry the real Captain. The Critic, featuring the pompous Puff and the arrogant Sneer, is a mocking depiction of the theatre, playwrights and, of course, critics. And The School for Scandal continues the theme of imposture when Sir Oliver Surface tests his nephews by appearing before them in disguise, and learns that reputation and the approval of society are of little value. In his introduction, Eric S. Rump places the plays in their historical and dramatic context and examines their enduring popularity." Publisher's note

Stoppard, Tom
★ **Arcadia**. Faber & Faber 1993 97p hardcover o.p. pa $14 **822**

    ISBN 0-571-16934-1 pa
                LC 94-103754

    Characters: 8 men, 3 women. 2 acts, 7 scenes. First produced at the Royal National Theatre, London, 1993. In the U.S., first produced at the Lincoln Center Theater, New York City, March 30, 1995.

★ **Rosencrantz** and Guildenstern are dead. Grove Press 1967 126p hardcover o.p. pa $12 **822**

    1. Authors 2. Dramatists 3. Poets
    ISBN 0-8021-3275-8 pa

    Characters: 13 men, 2 women, extras. First produced in this form April 11, 1967 in London

    This play "took the theatre world on both sides of the Atlantic by storm. The originality of the idea which put Hamlet's two insignificant friends centerstage was matched by the brilliance of the dialogue between these bewildered nonentities." Reader's Ency. 4th edition

★ **Travesties**. Grove Press 1975 99p pa $13 **822**

    ISBN 0-8021-5089-6

    Characters: 5 men, 2 women. Prologue, 2 acts. First produced at the Aldwych Theatre, London, June 10, 1974

The **invention** of love. Grove Press 1998 102p pa $12   **822**

    1. Authors 2. Poets
    ISBN 0-8021-3581-1
                LC 98-28331

    Characters: 19 men, 1 woman, extras. 2 acts. First performed at the American Conservatory Theater, San Francisco, January 14, 2000.

Synge, J. M.
★ The **complete** plays. Vintage Bks. 1960 268p pa $10   **822**

    ISBN 0-394-70178-X

Thomas, Dylan
★ **Under** milk wood; a play for voices. New Directions 1954 107p music pa $8.95   **822**

    ISBN 0-8112-0209-7

    "A radio play for voices. Written in poetic, inventive prose, this play is full of humor, a joyful sense of the goodness of life and love, and a strong Welsh flavor. It is an impression of a spring day in the lives of the people of Llareggub, a Welsh village situated under Milk Wood. It has no plot, but a wealth of characters who dream aloud, converse with one another, and speak in choruses of alternating voices." Reader's Ency. 4th edition

Wilde, Oscar
★ The **importance** of being earnest and other plays; introduction by Terrence McNally; notes by Michael F. Davis. Modern Library 2003 257p pa $9.95   **822**

    ISBN 0-8129-6714-3
               LC 2003-44566

    The title play, written in 1895, is a drawing room comedy exposing quirks and foibles of Victorian society with plot revolving around amorous pursuits of two men who face social obstacles when they woo young ladies of quality. The book also features Lady Windermere's fan (1893), a four act comedy about a woman who has an affair when she suspects her husband of adultery, and An ideal husband (1895), a comedy about a blackmail scheme involving a lord's investment in the Suez Canal days before the British government's purchase of it, and his wife's reaction to her husband's past misdeeds.

★ Everyman, and medieval miracle plays; edited by A. C. Cawley; with a new preface and bibliography by Anne Rooney. Tuttle 1993 256p hardcover o.p. pa $6.95   **822**

    1. Mysteries and miracle plays
    ISBN 0-460-87280-X pa

    In addition to Everyman, this collection includes plays from the Towneley, Coventry, York and Chester cycles.

822.3   Drama of Elizabethan period, 1558-1625

Bate, Jonathan
Soul of the age; a biography of the mind of William Shakespeare. Random House 2009 471p il map $35   **822.3**

    1. Authors 2. Dramatists 3. Poets
    ISBN 978-1-4000-6206-5
               LC 2008-16561

    In this biography of Shakespeare, the author uses "the Bard's own 'Seven Ages of Man' speech from As You Like It to envision him as an infant, a school boy, a lover, a soldier, a justice, a pantaloon, and an old man entering 'oblivion.' The result is a fresh new way to look at Shakespeare and a welcome reminder of what literary biography can still do." Libr J

    Includes bibliographical references

Bloom, Harold
Hamlet: poem unlimited. Riverhead Bks. 2003 154p hardcover o.p. pa $13   **822.3**

    1. Authors 2. Dramatists 3. Poets
    ISBN 1-57322-233-X; 1-57322-377-8 pa
              LC 2002-31691

"Far superior to existing theories of performance and worth yards of criticism for each well-wrought page." Libr J

Shakespeare: the invention of the human. Riverhead Bks. 1998 xx, 745p hardcover o.p. pa $18 **822.3**
1. Authors 2. Characters and characteristics in literature 3. Drama -- Psychological aspects 4. Dramatists 5. Humanism in literature 6. Personality in literature 7. Poets
ISBN 1-57322-751-X pa

LC 98-21325
"The passion and obsessiveness of Bloom's approach are its greatest recommendation." N Y Rev Books

Boyce, Charles
Critical companion to William Shakespeare; a literary reference to his life and work. Rev. ed; Facts on File 2005 2v il set $104.50 **822.3**
1. Authors 2. Dramatists 3. Poets
ISBN 0-8160-5373-1

LC 2004-25769
"The first two-thirds [of this set] covers the plays. Arranged alphabetically by title, the 3000 entries generally consist of a scene-by-scene summary, a commentary, sources, theatrical history, and character sketches. The last one-third features entries for actors, composers, musicians, places that figured in the plays, and miscellaneous items." Libr J
Includes bibliographical references

Bryson, Bill
Shakespeare; the world as stage. Atlas Books/HarperCollins 2007 199p $19.95 **822.3**
1. Authors 2. Biography, Individual 3. Dramatists 4. Poets
ISBN 978-0-06-074022-1; 0-06-074022-1

LC 2007-21647
In this biography, the author marshals "the usual little facts that others might overlook—for example, that in Shakespeare's day perhaps 40% of women were pregnant when they got married—to paint a portrait of the world in which the Bard lived and prospered. . . . Bryson is a pleasant and funny guide to a subject at once overexposed and elusive—as Bryson puts it, he is a kind of literary equivalent of an electron—forever there and not there." Publ Wkly
Includes bibliographical references

Butler, Colin
The **practical** Shakespeare; the plays in practice and on the page. Ohio University Press 2005 205p $39.95; pa $19.95 **822.3**
1. Authors 2. Dramatists 3. Poets
ISBN 0-8214-1621-9; 0-8214-1622-7 pa

LC 2004-30580
"Notes on staging, acting behaviors, scenes not shown, entrances, exits, characterizations, prologues, choruses, and staging are each featured in the text. References to specific scenes in the plays are used to illustrate and support the material. Any group preparing a production of one of the plays should find this a useful reference." Univ Press Books for Public and Second Sch Libr, 2006
Includes bibliographical references

Collins, Paul
★ The **book** of William; how Shakespeare's first folio conquered the world. Bloomsbury 2009 246p $25 **822.3**
1. Authors 2. Dramatists 3. Early printed books -- 17th century 4. Early printed books -- Great Britain -- 17th century 5. Poets 6. Rare books
ISBN 978-1-59691-195-6; 1-59691-195-6

LC 2009-6722
"Witty, detailed, and highly entertaining, . . . [this book] will be appreciated by fans of Shakespeare, history, or human folly." Libr J
Includes bibliographical references

Frye, Northrop
Northrop Frye on Shakespeare; edited by Robert Sandler. Yale Univ. Press 1986 186p hardcover o.p. pa $17 **822.3**
1. Authors 2. Dramatists 3. Poets
ISBN 0-300-04208-6 pa

LC 86-50485
Shakespeare scholar Frye provides in-depth analyses of ten plays.
"Frye's work is completely accessible, its style crisp and engaging. Most of all, it is full of basic 'good sense' about our most abused literary figure." Libr J

Garber, Marjorie
Shakespeare after all. Pantheon Books 2004 989p hardcover o.p. pa $20 **822.3**
1. Authors 2. Dramatists 3. Poets
ISBN 0-375-42190-4; 0-385-72214-1 pa

LC 2004-40063
The author "provides a handbook on Shakespeare's plays. After an introduction supplying standard overviews of the Renaissance theater and Shakespeare's life, she offers a critical essay on each play, complete with bibliographies and filmographies. The strength of this work is that Garber shows how the plays are interrelated by recurring language, characters, and themes, how each era has interpreted Shakespeare for itself, and how Shakespeare continues to shape today's culture." Libr J
Includes bibliographical references

Shakespeare and modern culture. Pantheon Books 2008 326p il $30 **822.3**
1. Authors 2. Dramatists 3. Poets
ISBN 978-0-307-37767-8; 0-307-37767-9

LC 2008-26802
"Writing on ten plays, [Garber] offers examples of their 'uncanny' anticipation of present-day phenomena and our own appropriations of them, as in the now fashionable use of 'Henry V' as a blueprint for success in business. (She quotes one manual that calls Bardolph's hanging the 'ultimate pink slip.') Garber's approach is eclectic, spanning Freud and evolutionary biology; occasionally, she gets caught up in secondary concerns, but she is an inspiring reader." New Yorker
Includes bibliographical references

Greenblatt, Stephen J.

Will in the world; how Shakespeare became Shakespeare. [by] Stephen Greenblatt. Norton 2004 430p il $26.95   **822.3**

    1. Authors 2. Dramatists 3. Poets

    ISBN 0-393-05057-2

                     LC 2004-11512

    "Greenblatt is at his best when he merges his gifts as a literary critic and scholar with his instincts as a biographer. He writes with real subtlety and skill about the sonnets. . . . He also writes very well about the climate of fear and the use of public punishment and torture in Elizabethan and early Jacobean England, and how this enters into the very spirit of Shakespeare's work." N Y Times Book Rev

    Includes bibliographical references

Heylin, Clinton

So long as men can breathe; the untold story of Shakespeare's Sonnets. Da Capo Press 2009 280p $24   **822.3**

    1. Authors 2. Dramatists 3. Poets

    ISBN 978-0-306-81805-9; 0-306-81805-1

                     LC 2009-08999

    An account of the publication of Shakespeare's Sonnets. The author "introduces us to the 'unholy alliance' involved in this precarious enterprise: Thomas Thorpe, the publisher, a self-described 'well wishing adventurer;' George Eld, the printer, heavily embroiled in large-scale pirating; William Aspley, the prestigious bookseller, who mysteriously ended his association with Thorpe soon after. Leaving the calamitous world of Elizabethan publishing, Heylin goes on to chart the many editions of the Sonnets through the years and the editorial decisions that led to their present configuration." Publisher's note

    Includes bibliographical references

Kermode, Frank

Shakespeare's language. Farrar, Straus & Giroux 2000 324p hardcover o.p. pa $15   **822.3**

    1. Authors 2. Dramatists 3. English language -- Early modern, 1500-1700 -- Style 4. English language -- Early modern, 1500-1700 -- Versification 5. Poets

    ISBN 0-374-52774-1 pa

                     LC 99-55846

    Kermode "devotes particular attention to the four great tragedies written at the height of Shakespeare's powers: Hamlet, Othello, King Lear and Macbeth. While Kermode's concern is with the Bard's verse, he betrays no simplistic notions about literary language operating in a vacuum. A careful, close analysis of passages in each play is informed by a breathtaking knowledge of Elizabethan history and culture, as well as by the entire history of Shakespeare criticism from Coleridge to Eliot and the new historicists." Publ Wkly

    Includes bibliographical references

Lamb, Charles

Tales from Shakespeare; by Charles & Mary Lamb; with an introduction by Marina Warner. Penguin Books 2007 304p pa $12   **822.3**

    1. Authors 2. Dramatists 3. Poets

    ISBN 978-0-14-144162-7; 0-14-144162-3

    A now classic collection of twenty plays by Shakespeare adapted as prose stories—the comedies by Mary Lamb, the tragedies by Charles Lamb.

    "The Tales were the first version of 'Shakespeare' to be published specifically for children. They are written in a clear, vigorous style, not often encumbered by the attempt to make the language resemble that of the original. A lot is left out. . . . But the literary quality of the Tales makes them outshine almost every other English children's book of this period, and they proved an immediate and lasting success." Oxford Companion to Child Lit

Norwich, John Julius

Shakespeare's kings; the great plays and the history of England in the Middle Ages, 1337-1485. Scribner 2000 401p il hardcover o.p. pa $16 **822.3**

    1. Authors 2. Dramatists 3. Great Britain -- History -- Medieval period, 1066-1485 -- Historiography 4. Historical drama, English -- History and criticism 5. Kings and rulers in literature 6. Middle Ages in literature 7. Poets

    ISBN 0-7432-0031-4 pa

                     LC 99-58271

    The author offers "overviews of Edward III; Richard II; Henry IV, parts 1 and 2; Henry V; Henry VI, parts 1, 2, and 3; and Richard III, examining each play through the lens of history. In addition to providing the necessary historical commentary, he also fills in the gaps between the plays, enabling readers to thoroughly comprehend the entire series in the proper historical context." Booklist

Nuttall, A. D.

Shakespeare the thinker. Yale University Press 2007 428p $30   **822.3**

    ISBN 978-0-300-11928-2; 0-300-11928-3

                     LC 2006-35179

    The author "traces ideas about motivation, identity, speech, and symbol in Shakespeare's plays. His study is rich in unexpected juxtapositions: Hippolyta, of 'A Midsummer Night's Dream,' finds herself in casual conversation with David Hume, and Titus Andronicus is seen in the context of 'Goodfellas.' The analysis never pulls too far away from the action onstage; indeed, Nuttall painstakingly shows Shakespeare's skill at negotiating abstract ideas through suspense, conflict, and character." New Yorker

    Includes bibliographical references

Olsen, Kirstin

All things Shakespeare; an encyclopedia of Shakespeare's world. Greenwood Press 2002 2v il maps set $150   **822.3**

    1. Authors 2. Dramatists 3. Poets 4. Reference books

    ISBN 0-313-31503-5

                     LC 2002-69732

    This "encyclopedia describes Shakespeare's physical environment, including common objects, daily activities, and popular beliefs and attitudes. Information is grouped into general topic clusters such as 'Behavior,' 'Clothing and Dress,' 'Furniture,' 'Fire,' and 'War and Peace.' . . . Within the 200-plus entries, references are made to the play, act, and scene in which Shakespeare mentions the item or activity being discussed." Libr J

Rasmussen, Eric

The **Shakespeare** thefts; in search of the first folios. Palgrave Macmillan 2011 212p il **822.3**
1. Authors 2. Book collecting 3. Dramatists 4. Early printed books 5. Poets 6. Rare books 7. Shakespeare, William, 1564-1616 -- Bibliography -- Folios 8. Theft
ISBN 9780230109414; 9780230341203 ebook

LC 2011028287

This book discusses "the known surviving copies of the 1623 First Folio, which published 36 of [William] Shakespeare's plays. Of the 232 recorded surviving copies, the majority are in public institutions rather than private hands. [Eric] Rasmussen . . . and his team of researchers were part of the global quest to catalog every extant copy." (Library Journal)

Part literary history and part detective story, this is an engaging book about the known surviving copies of the 1623 First Folio, which published 36 of Shakespeare's plays. Of the 232 recorded surviving copies, the majority are in public institutions rather than private hands. Rasmussen . . . and his team of researchers were part of the global quest to catalog every extant copy. Rasmussen uses a lively, nonacademic style and engrossing anecdotes to tell us about one of history's most fascinating books.P Libr J

Includes bibliographical references

Rosenbaum, Ron

The **Shakespeare** wars; clashing scholars, public fiascoes, palace coups. Random House 2006 601p $35 **822.3**
1. Authors 2. Dramatists 3. Poets
ISBN 0-375-50339-0; 978-0-375-50339-9

LC 2006-42541

The author "conveys the impassioned arguments of leading directors and scholars concerning how Shakespeare should be printed and performed. . . . Balancing academic reportage with his own lively observations, Rosenbaum wrestles with the weightiest issues of Shakespeare studies in a down-to-earth manner that readers will applaud." Publ Wkly

Includes bibliographical references

Shakespeare, William

★ The **Columbia** dictionary of quotations from Shakespeare; [selected by] Mary and Reginald Foakes. Columbia Univ. Press 1998 516p $63 **822.3**
1. Authors 2. Dramatists 3. Poets 4. Quotations
ISBN 0-231-10434-0

LC 97-44894

"The book is organized by topics ('Age,' 'Duplicity,' 'Fish'), followed by passages of about five or six lines. After each selection, the citation, the character, and usually the context of the lines are given. If a reference is obscure, the explanation is more elaborate. Indexes provide access by play and poem, by character, and by keyword." SLJ

★ The **complete** works; general editors, Stanley Wells and Gary Taylor; editors, Stanley Wells . . . [et al.]; with introductions by Stanley Wells. 2nd ed.; Clarendon Press; Oxford University Press 2005 lxxv, 1344p il $40 **822.3**
1. Authors 2. Dramatists 3. Poets
ISBN 0-19-926717-0

LC 2005-47272

This anthology "features a brief introduction to each work as well as [a] General Introduction. . . . [The volume includes] essay on language, a list of contemporary allusions to Shakespeare, an index of Shakespearean characters, a glossary, a consolidated bibliography, and an index of first lines of the Sonnets." Publisher's note

Shapiro, James

Contested Will; who wrote Shakespeare? James Shapiro. Simon & Schuster 2010 339 p. $26 **822.3**
1. Authors 2. Dramatists 3. Poets
ISBN 978-1-4165-4162-2; 1-4165-4162-4; 1416541624; 9781416541622

LC 2009032710

"A thorough, engaging work whose arguments would prove more persuasive were we not living in an era of such fierce anti-intellectualism and pervasive conspiracy theory." Kirkus

Includes bibliographical references and index

A **year** in the life of William Shakespeare, 1599. HarperCollins Publishers 2005 394p il map $27.95 **822.3**
1. Authors 2. Biography, Individual 3. Dramatists 4. Poets
ISBN 0-571-21448-0

LC 2005-43342

The author "offers a critical examination of four plays Shakespeare wrote in the seminal year of 1599—Henry V, Julius Caesar, As You Like It, and Hamlet—and of the events that influenced the Bard at the time of their writing. . . . This work gives the reader a realistic sense of the multilayered and complex political, social, and literary pressures that influenced Shakespeare as a citizen of England, as a business partner in the Globe Theatre, and as a writer." Libr J

Includes bibliographical references

Wells, Stanley W.

★ **Shakespeare**: for all time; [by] Stanley Wells. Oxford Univ. Press 2003 xxi, 442p il $40 **822.3**
1. Authors 2. Dramatists 3. Poets
ISBN 0-19-516093-2

LC 2002-27412

"Chapters on Shakespeare's life in Stratford and in London offer a . . . view of the development of the writer's career and personality. At the core of the book lies a . . . study of the writings themselves—how Shakespeare set about writing a play, his relationships with the company of actors with whom he worked, his developing mastery of the literary and rhetorical skills that he learned at the Stratford grammar school, the essentially theatrical quality of the structure and language of his plays. Subsequent chapters trace the fluctuating fortunes of his reputation and influence." Publisher's note

Includes bibliographical references

Wills, Garry

Verdi's Shakespeare; man of the theater. Viking 2011 220p $25.95   **822.3**
1. Authors 2. Composers 3. Dramatists 4. Italy -- History -- 19th century 5. Opera 6. Poets
ISBN 978-0-670-02304-2

LC 2011019768

Yoshino, Kenji

A **thousand** times more fair; what Shakespeare can teach us about justice. Ecco 2011 305p $26.99; ebook $12.99   **822.3**
1. Authors 2. Dramatists 3. Law in literature 4. Poets
ISBN 978-0-06-176910-8; 0-06-176910-X; 978-0-06-208772-0 ebook; 0-06-208772-X ebook

Looks at the roles of justice and law in the lives of modern-day people through the lens of Shakespeare's plays.

"Readers will find Yoshino provocative, often controversial, and Shakespeare, as always, entertaining." Publ Wkly
Includes bibliographical references

★ The **Greenwood** companion to Shakespeare; a comprehensive guide to students. edited by Joseph Rosenblum. Greenwood Press 2005 4v set $299.95   **822.3**
1. Authors 2. Dramatists 3. Poets
ISBN 0-313-32779-3

LC 2004-28690

"Each of the set's four volumes relates to a specific genre—Overviews and the History Plays (Vol. 1), The Comedies (Vol. 2), The Tragedies (Vol. 3), and The Romances and Poetry (Vol. 4)—and is organized in 'Cliff Notes' fashion, devoting each entry to a single play, long poem, sonnet, or sonnet pair. . . . A great introduction to the Bard." Libr J
Includes bibliographical references

★ The **Oxford** companion to Shakespeare; general editor, Michael Dobson; associate general editor, Stanley Wells. Oxford Univ. Press 2001 xxix, 541p il maps hardcover o.p. pa $39.95   **822.3**
1. Authors 2. Dramatists 3. Poets 4. Reference books
ISBN 0-19-811735-3; 0-19-280614-9 pa

LC 2001-277478

This volume "illuminates not only Shakespeare's life and works but also the many forms that interpretation of Shakespeare has taken in the centuries since his death." Booklist
Includes bibliographical references

823   English fiction

Achebe, Chinua

Home and exile. Anchor Bks. 2001 115p pa $11   **823**
1. Authors 2. Authors, Nigerian -- 20th century -- Biography 3. Essayists 4. Novelists 5. Poets 6. Short story writers
ISBN 978-0-385-72133-2; 0-385-72133-1

LC 2001-22599

"This slim volume—told in Achebe's subtle, witty and gracious style—is one of those small gems of literary and historical analysis that readers will treasure and reread over the years." Publ Wkly
Includes bibliographical references

Baker, William

Critical companion to Jane Austen; a literary reference to her life and work. Facts on File 2008 644p il $75   **823**
1. Authors 2. Novelists
ISBN 978-0-8160-6416-8

LC 2006-102848

This book examines Jane Austen's "life and works, and includes critical analyses of the themes within her writing, as well as entries on related topics and relevant people, places, and influences." Publisher's note
Includes bibliographical references

Bayley, John

Elegy for Iris. St. Martin's Press 1999 275p il hardcover o.p. pa $13   **823**
1. Alzheimer's disease 2. Alzheimer's disease -- Patients -- Biography 3. Authors 4. College teachers 5. College teachers -- Great Britain -- Biography 6. Critics -- Great Britain -- Biography 7. Essayists 8. Literary critics 9. Married people -- Great Britain -- Biography 10. Novelists 11. Novelists, English -- 20th century -- Biography 12. Philosophers 13. Philosophers -- Great Britain -- Biography
ISBN 0-312-42111-7 pa

LC 98-40895

"This splendid book enlarges our imagination of the range and possibilities of love." N Y Times Book Rev

Bowker, Gordon, 1934-

★ **James** Joyce; a new biography. Gordon Bowker. Farrar, Straus and Giroux 2012 608 p. ill. (hbk. : alk. paper) $35.00   **823**
1. Authors, Irish -- 20th century -- Biography 2. Authorship 3. Biographies 4. Joyce, James, 1882-1941 -- Health
ISBN 0374178720; 9780374178727

LC 2011045954

This biography of James Joyce "show[s] the complexities and contradictions of the man. . . . The author charts . . . his struggle to survive in the early days of his adulthood and marriage, the sad madness of his daughter, . . . and his difficulty finding publishers for 'Dubliners' and the more controversial works that followed. . . . We see Joyce, too, as a prodigious worker who labored for endless hours, completing not just the shelf- and mind-bending novels 'Ulysses' and 'Finnegan's Wake' but a play, stories and essays." (Kirkus Reviews)

Conradi, Peter

Iris Murdoch; a life. {by} Peter J. Conradi. Norton 2001 xxix, 706p il $35; pa $19.95   **823**
1. Authors 2. Essayists 3. Novelists 4. Novelists, English -- 20th century -- Biography 5. Philosophers 6. Philosophers -- Great Britain -- Biography
ISBN 0-393-04875-6; 0-393-32401-X pa

LC 2001-32972

"Rich footnoting leads the reader to expansions on the narrative as well as to the authority behind the biographer's statements. Scholars need this text, but it will also intrigue lay readers." Libr J

Includes bibliographical references

Davis, Paul B.

★ **Critical** companion to Charles Dickens; a literary reference to his life and work. Rev ed; Facts on File 2007 676p il $75   **823**
  1. Authors 2. Novelists
  ISBN 0-8160-6407-5; 978-0-8160-6407-6
                        LC 2006-3026
This "reference contains entries on this writer's works, including the characters in each work, . . . historical and thematic information, and critical discussion. It also includes entries on related people, places, themes, topics, and influences. Additional features include 116 illustrations, a chronology, a bibliography of primary and secondary sources, and much more." Publisher's note

Includes bibliographical references

Dirda, Michael

On Conan Doyle; or, The whole art of storytelling. Princeton University Press 2011 210p $19.95   **823**
  1. Authors 2. Mystery writers 3. Novelists
  ISBN 978-0-691-15135-9; 0-691-15135-0
                        LC 2011-20674
"Dirda is at his best in his sensitive appreciation of Doyle's style, direct, fluent, and surprisingly flexible as he moves from genre to genre, and in his account of manly civic inspiration as the value Doyle aimed above all to inculcate in his writing . . . . An endearing, well-balanced introduction to a writer the Strand Magazine called 'the greatest natural storyteller of his age.'" Kirkus

Includes bibliographical references

Fargnoli, A. Nicholas

Critical companion to James Joyce; a literary companion to his life and work. [by] A. Nicholas Fargnoli, Michael Patrick Gillespie. Rev ed; Facts On File 2006 450p il $65; pa $19.95   **823**
  1. Authors 2. Dramatists 3. Novelists 4. Poets 5. Short story writers
  ISBN 0-8160-6232-3; 978-0-8160-6232-4; 0-8160-6689-2 pa; 978-0-8160-6689-6 pa
                        LC 2005-15721
The authors "divide this reference to the writer's life and work into four parts. Part 1 is a brief biography. Part 2 focuses on individual works (e.g., Dubliners), including its publication date, a brief history, a synopsis, early critical reception, contemporary perspectives, and one or two recommended titles for further reading. The entries in Part 3 cover people (including friends and relatives), places, and ideas related to Joyce. Part 4 contains an appendix, a bibliography of the writer's work, a bibliography of secondary sources, chronologies, family trees, and more. . . . [This is] a great primer for those needing a detailed introduction into Joyce's world." Libr J

Includes bibliographical references

Ford, Paul F.

Companion to Narnia; a complete guide to the magical world of C.S. Lewis's The chronicles of Narnia. foreword by Madeleine L'Engle; illustrated by Lorinda Bryan Cauley. Rev and expanded; HarperSanFrancisco 2005 xxvi, 530p il map pa $16.95 **823**
  1. Authors 2. Children's authors 3. Essayists 4. Literary critics 5. Novelists 6. Satirists 7. Theologians
  ISBN 0-06-079127-6
C. S. Lewis wrote seven books of fantasy that are collectively called The Chronicles of Narnia. This book "is an encyclopedia of Narnian names and terms and related matters, with . . . footnoted articles, page references to American and British hardcover editions, cross-references, and a running footline for quick location of materials in the alphabet." Choice

Includes bibliographical references

Gordimer, Nadine

Conversations with Nadine Gordimer; edited by Nancy Topping Bazin and Marilyn Dallman Seymour. University Press of Miss. 1990 xxiv, 321p $46   **823**
  1. Authors 2. Dramatists 3. Essayists 4. Nobel laureates for literature 5. Novelists 6. Short story writers
  ISBN 0-87805-444-8
                        LC 90-12556
This is a collection of interviews in which Gordimer talks "about her life as a white South African, about her fiction, and about writers she admires." Booklist

Includes bibliographical references

Head, Dominic

★ The **Cambridge** introduction to modern British fiction, 1950-2000. Cambridge Univ. Press 2002 307p $65; pa $22   **823**
  1. English fiction -- 20th century -- History and criticism
  2. English fiction -- History and criticism
  ISBN 0-521-66014-9; 0-521-66966-9 pa
                        LC 2001-43261
"Anyone with an interest in the contemporary novel, not just British fiction, will appreciate this outstanding survey and analysis. . . . The quality of discussion is admirably consistent within and between each chapter, the prose as carefully crafted as the judgments are measured. . . . This book should become a standard reference work for its subject." Choice

Includes bibliographical references

Hughes, Kathryn

George Eliot; the last Victorian. Cooper Square Press 2001 383p il pa $19.95   **823**
  1. Authors 2. Authors, English 3. Essayists 4. Novelists 5. Novelists, English -- 19th century -- Biography
  ISBN 0-8154-1121-9; 978-0-8154-1121-5
                        LC 2001-28024
In this biography Hughes "shows how George Eliot (nee Mary Anne Evans, 1819-80), in spite of her outwardly anti-Victorian lifestyle, was in fact a true Victorian. . . . A soli-

tary, ascetic child and young woman, she was raised in an upwardly mobile country family. . . . In 1852 she met the married writer and editor George Henry Lewes, with whom she lived until his death in 1878." Libr J

Includes bibliographical references

James, P. D.

Talking about detective fiction. Alfred A. Knopf 2009 198p il $22   **823**

1. Detective and mystery stories, English -- History and criticism 2. Mystery fiction -- History and criticism

ISBN 978-0-307-59282-8

LC 2009-38501

"For crime fiction fans, this master class from one of the leading practitioners of the art will be a real treat." Publ Wkly

Includes bibliographical references

Time to be in earnest; a fragment of autobiography. Knopf 2000 269p hardcover o.p. pa $12.95   **823**

1. Authors 2. Detective and mystery stories -- Authorship 3. Mystery writers 4. Novelists 5. Novelists, English -- 20th century -- Diaries

ISBN 0-345-44212-1 pa

LC 99-57603

"In 1997, on the eve of her 77th birthday noted mystery novelist James . . . decided to keep a diary for the first time ever, recording one year in her life. The result is this 'fragment of autobiography,' a mix of memoir, ruminations on everything from her writing career to Princess Diana's death, and literary criticism." Libr J

Kermode, Frank

Concerning E.M. Forster. Farrar, Straus and Giroux 2009 180p $24   **823**

1. Authors 2. Essayists 3. Literary critics 4. Novelists 5. Short story writers

ISBN 978-0-374-29899-9; 0-374-29899-8

LC 2009-39143

"Overall, Kermode's occasional exasperation with his subject enlivens rather than distorts his eminently fair assessment. Like all good criticism, Concerning EM Forster makes one want to read the books under discussion once more, and it ends on an appropriately affectionate note." Times (London)

Includes bibliographical references

Kiberd, Declan

Ulysses and us; the art of everyday life in Joyce's masterpiece. W.W. Norton & Co. 2009 399p $28.95   **823**

1. Authors 2. Dramatists 3. Novelists 4. Poets 5. Short story writers

ISBN 978-0-393-07099-6; 0-393-07099-9

LC 2009014101

This "is an ideal introduction [to Ulysses] for the uninitiated—accessible, richly argued, funny and, in a kind of devil's advocacy fashion, begging for rebuttal." Publ Wkly

Includes bibliographical references

King, Dean

Patrick O'Brian; a life revealed. Holt & Co. 2000 397p il hardcover o.p. pa $15   **823**

1. Authors 2. Biographers 3. Historical fiction -- Authorship 4. Novelists 5. Novelists, English -- 20th century -- Biography 6. Sea stories -- Authorship 7. Short story writers 8. Writers on the sea

ISBN 0-8050-5977-6 pa

LC 99-48495

"This is exactly the sort of literary biography that O'Brian, the author of the celebrated Aubrey/Maturin naval novels, hoped to avoid. Reluctant to provide facts about himself, and often untruthful when he did so, O'Brian . . . had much in his past that he wanted buried. He walked away from his first marriage, changed his name from Russ to O'Brian, and pretended Anglo-Irish ancestry. King's diligent research yields pleasing details." New Yorker

Includes bibliographical references

Lee, Hermione

★ **Virginia** Woolf. Knopf 1997 893p il hardcover o.p. pa $20   **823**

1. Authors 2. Authors, English 3. Biography, Individual 4. Essayists 5. Novelists 6. Short story writers 7. Women authors

ISBN 0-375-70136-2 pa

LC 97-71155

Lee "re-creates the world Woolf was born into in 1882, a maze of formalities and reticences, and then leads us through changes that, slow in coming but shocking in effect, made all that seem light-years away by the time Woolf was 50. She convinces us that Woolf, contrary to previous assumptions, reveled in a deep intimacy with her husband, Leonard. Finally, she makes a persuasive case for the underlying sanity of this woman as she battled her own madness and shows the brilliant literary uses she made of her instability." N Y Times Book Rev

Includes bibliographical references

Maunder, Andrew

The **Facts** on File companion to the British short story. Facts on File 2006 528p $75   **823**

1. Short stories -- History and criticism 2. Short stories, English 3. Short stories, English -- History and criticism

ISBN 0-8160-5990-X; 978-0-8160-5990-4

LC 2006-6897

More than 450 alphabetically arranged entries cover authors, characters, and major short stories. Literary terms, themes, and motifs are covered. Winners of prizes and awards are noted.

Miller, Laura

The **magician's** book; a skeptic's adventures in Narnia. Little, Brown and Co. 2008 311p $25.99 **823**

1. Authors 2. Children's authors 3. Children's literature -- History and criticism 4. Essayists 5. Literary critics 6. Novelists 7. Satirists 8. Theologians

ISBN 978-0-316-01763-3; 0-316-01763-9

LC 2008-20629

The author explores the meaning and influence of C.S. Lewis' Chronicles of Narnia series while revealing how

Lewis's troubled childhood, unconventional love life, and friendship with J. R. R. Tolkien affected his writing.

"Miller's book is itself a welcome bit of magic: part reader's log, part biography, part literary criticism." N Y Times Book Rev

Naipaul, V. S.

Between father and son; selected correspondence of V.S. Naipaul and his family, 1949-1953. edited by Gillon Aitken. Knopf 2000 297p $26; pa $13 **823**
1. Authors 2. Authors, Trinidadian -- 20th century -- Correspondence 3. Authors, Trinidadian -- 20th century -- Family relationships 4. Essayists 5. Fathers and sons -- Trinidad 6. Journalists 7. Nobel laureates for literature 8. Nonfiction writers 9. Novelists 10. Radio reporters 11. Short story writers 12. Travel writers
ISBN 0-375-40730-8; 0-375-70726-3 pa
LC 99-31089
"In 1950, at the age of 17, famous-writer-in-the-making V. S. Naipaul ventured to Oxford University in England on a scholarship supplied by the government of his native Trinidad. He and his father maintained a rich, full correspondence during his time away, and these letters fortunately have been gathered into book form." Booklist
Include bibliographical references

Nokes, David

Jane Austen; a life. University of Calif. Press 1998 577p il pa $24.95 **823**
1. Authors 2. Authors, English 3. Novelists 4. Novelists, English -- 19th century -- Biography 5. Women authors
ISBN 0-520-21606-7; 978-0-520-21606-8
LC 98-15785
"Eschewing the biographer's usual perspective of omniscient foreknowledge in favor of a novelistic perspective of ambiguous immediacy, Nokes allows us to see Austen's talent as a mystery unfolding, not a fact explained. We thus witness the emergence of a personality sufficiently subtle and complex to produce Sense and Sensibility, Pride and Prejudice, and Emma. Readers of Austen's fiction will rejoice at having a biography so carefully nuanced, so refreshingly candid." Booklist
Includes bibliographical references

O'Brien, Edna

★ **James** Joyce. Viking 1999 179p $19.95 **823**
1. Authors 2. Dramatists 3. Novelists 4. Novelists, Irish -- 20th century -- Biography 5. Poets 6. Short story writers
ISBN 0-670-88230-5
LC 99-23214
O'Brien "tells the story of the aspiring young writer and his downwardly mobile family, his escape to Europe, the constant struggle to scrape together enough money to live on, and finally his relative comfort, thanks to patrons, once Ulysses was published. She also provides thoughtful appreciations of Joyce's major works." Booklist
Includes bibliographical references

Olsen, Kirstin

All things Austen; an encyclopedia of Austen's world. Greenwood Press 2005 2v il maps set $157.95 **823**
1. Authors 2. Novelists 3. Reference books
ISBN 0-313-33032-8
LC 2004-28664
"This well-written and meticulously researched work provides a convenient means for general readers, students, and scholars to gain a better understanding of the social, cultural, and political climate of Austen's time." Booklist

Shakespeare, Nicholas

Bruce Chatwin. Talese 2000 618p il $35; pa $18 **823**
1. Authors 2. Authors, English -- 20th century -- Biography 3. Memoirists 4. Novelists 5. Travel writers 6. Travelers -- Great Britain -- Biography
ISBN 0-385-49829-2; 0-385-49830-6 pa
LC 99-36474
"This life of the author of 'The Songlines', who died of AIDS in 1989, portrays a man, beset with an almost biological lust for loneliness, whose singular genius was for passionate transitory connection." N Y Times Book Rev
Includes bibliographical references

Shields, Carol

Jane Austen. Viking 2001 185p hardcover o.p. pa $13 **823**
1. Authors 2. Authors, English 3. Large print books 4. Novelists 5. Novelists, English -- 19th century -- Biography 6. Women authors
ISBN 0-670-89488-5; 0-14-303516-9 pa
LC 00-43807
"In chronicling her subject's life and personality, Shields emphasizes Austen's keen ability to listen, observe, and capture clearly the social mores of her time and explore human nature in her writing. Shields contends that historical references are behind many of the scenes and characters in Austen's novels, and as a way of more clearly personalizing Austen's experiences or feelings, she interjects commentary regarding writing and publishing that is presumably based on personal experience." Libr J

Smiley, Jane

Charles Dickens. Viking 2002 212p $19.95 **823**
1. Authors 2. Authors, English 3. Large print books 4. Novelists 5. Novelists, English -- 19th century -- Biography
ISBN 0-670-03077-5
LC 2001-45607
This "biography examines Dickens' life through his work, starting not with his birth but rather the beginnings of his literary career. After writing short essays for a monthly magazine, Dickens began the serialization of his first novel, The Pickwick Papers. Dickens quickly became both a best-selling novelist and a famous man, who had to contend with both the envy of other authors and, much later on, the very public dissolution of his marriage. . . . Smiley's superb and thoughtful analysis should appeal to anyone familiar with the great author's work." Booklist

Sunstein, Emily W.

Mary Shelley; romance and reality. Johns Hopkins Univ. Press 1991 478p il pa $20.95 **823**
1. Authors 2. Authors, English 3. Novelists 4. Women authors
ISBN 0-8018-4218-2; 978-0-8018-4218-4
LC 90-23541

A "revisionist account of a woman who 'literally embodies the English Romantic movement'.... Sunstein provides substantial documentation of the breadth of Shelley's education and the extent of her writing.... Most rewarding, perhaps, are Sunstein's astute insights into Shelley's emotional life." Choice

Includes bibliographical references

Swift, Jonathan

A **tale** of a tub, and other work; edited with an introduction by Angus Ross and David Woolley. Oxford Univ. Press 1986 xxviii, 237p pa $8.95 **823**
ISBN 0-19-283593-9
LC 85-5072

A tale of a tub, The battle of the books, and A discourse concerning the mechanical operation of the spirit, were first published together in 1704. The first is an allegorical satire ridiculing the corruptions of religion and learning by extremists and pedants. The second is a mock heroic satire on squabbles concerning the relative merits of ancient and modern authors presented as an account of the battle between ancient and modern books in St James Library. The third ridicules the manner of worship and preaching of religious enthusiasts of the period

Tomalin, Claire

Jane Austen; a life. Knopf 1997 341p il hardcover o.p. pa $14 **823**
1. Authors 2. Authors, English 3. Biography, Individual 4. Novelists 5. Women authors
ISBN 0-679-76676-6 pa
LC 97-36887

The author "has produced a portrait of remarkable subtlety. The light Ms. Tomalin casts on her subject is strong but oblique: the profile of the novelist appears surrounded by her friends and neighbours and by her energetic and beloved family." Economist

Wainaina, Binyavanga

One day I will write about this place. Graywolf Press 2011 256p **823**
1. Authors 2. Biography, Individual 3. College teachers 4. Journalists 5. Novelists 6. Short story writers
ISBN 1555975917; 9781555975913
LC 2011923190

In this memoir, the Kenyan writer describes "his school days, his mother's religious period, his failed attempt to study in South Africa as a computer programmer, a moving family reunion in Uganda, and his travels around Kenya. The landscape in front of him always claims his main attention, but he also evokes the shifting political scene that unsettles his views on family, tribe, and nationhood. Throughout, reading is his refuge and his solace. And when, in 2002, a writing prize comes through, the door is opened for him

to pursue the career that perhaps had been beckoning all along." (Publisher's note)

Weldon, Fay

Auto da Fay. Grove Press 2003 366p il $25; pa $14 **823**
1. Authors 2. Authors, English -- 20th century -- Biography 3. Dramatists 4. New Zealanders -- Great Britain -- Biography 5. Novelists 6. Short story writers
ISBN 0-8021-1750-3; 0-8021-4142-0 pa
LC 2002-44685

This "autobiography primarily focuses on her peripatetic childhood and difficult years of single parenthood, concluding in the 1960s with her second marriage and the beginning of her writing career.... Filled with warmth, wit, and her trademark irreverence, Weldon's memoir is a vivid and engaging account of a brave and brainy 'lost girl' who found her way." Booklist

Wilson, A. N.

C.S. Lewis; a biography. Norton 1990 334p il hardcover o.p. pa $15.95 **823**
1. Authors 2. Biography, Individual 3. Children's authors 4. Essayists 5. Literary critics 6. Novelists 7. Satirists 8. Theologians
ISBN 0-393-32340-4 pa
LC 89-27361

"The mixture presented in Wilson's biography of the life of learning, the college life at Magdalen where he taught, of domestic drama and bad temper, religion, and sex, is irresistible." N Y Rev Books

Includes bibliographical references

Woolf, Virginia

Moments of being; edited, with an introduction and notes, by Jeanne Schulkind. 2nd ed; Harcourt Brace Jovanovich 1985 230p pa $14 **823**
1. Authors 2. Authors, English 3. Essayists 4. Novelists 5. Short story writers 6. Women authors
ISBN 0-15-661918-0
LC 85-8521

This volume consists of unpublished autobiographical writings, including several "Reminiscences" written at the start of Woolf's career, a piece entitled "A sketch of the past" written shortly before her suicide, and papers read to the Memoir Club.

The Cambridge companion to Jane Austen; edited by Edward Copeland and Juliet McMaster. Cambridge Univ. Press 1997 251p **823**
1. Authors 2. Novelists
ISBN 0-521-49517-2; 0-521-49867-8 pa
LC 96-23387

This volume contains a selection of critical essays on the English novelist. "Deirdre Le Faye provides an Austen chronology; Jan Fergus outlines the situation of professional women writers; other essays deal with the novels and letters, and with . . . 'themes' (class, money, religion and politics)." (Times Lit Suppl) Bibliography. Index.

Scholars assess "Jane Austen's works in the contexts of her contemporary world, and of present-day critical discourse. Besides discussions of Austen's novels and letters, there are essays on religion, politics, class consciousness, publishing practices, domestic economy, style in the novels and the significance of her juvenile works. A chronology provides biographical information." Publisher's note

The Columbia history of the British novel; John Richetti, editor; John Bender, Deirdre David, Michael Seidel, associate editors. Columbia Univ. Press 1994 xxix, 1064p $95 **823**
1. English fiction -- History and criticism
ISBN 0-231-07858-7

LC 92-35749
In this chronologically arranged volume, scholars provide 39 essays surveying the history of the British novel. "Some essays are devoted to individual authors (e.g., Austen, Dickens), others to several authors (e.g., Amis, Snow, and Wilson), and still others to such topics as 'The Gothic Novel, 1764-1824.' Each essay has a brief selected bibliography; an appendix includes thumbnail sketches of 100 of the British novelists discussed." Libr J

★ The Facts on File companion to the British novel. Facts on File 2005 2v set $140 **823**
1. English fiction -- History and criticism
ISBN 0-8160-6377-X; 978-0-8160-6377-2

LC 2004-20914
"With more than one thousand entries, each with a selected bibliography and a set of very usable appendixes, this work accomplishes much in a compact set." Ref & User Services Quarterly
Includes bibliographical references

★ Horror: another 100 best books; edited by Stephen Jones and Kim Newman; with a foreword by Peter Straub. Carroll & Graf Publishers 2005 456p pa $16.95 **823**
1. Best books 2. Horror fiction -- History and criticism
ISBN 0-7867-1577-4
"Horror fans seeking what to read next will not only find out here; they'll also have their taste and appreciative capacity refined by the intelligent, passionate commentary of the 100 writers who selected these 100 books." Booklist

A truth universally acknowledged; 33 great writers on why we read Jane Austen. edited by Susannah Carson; foreword by Harold Bloom. Random House 2009 295p $25 **823**
1. Authors 2. Novelists 3. Novelists, English -- 19th century
ISBN 978-1-4000-6805-0; 1-4000-6805-3

LC 2009-12904
"A collection for both newcomers to the charms of Jane Austen and those longtime 'Janeites'. . . . The writers in this volume explain their own relationship with Austen and together are a kind of invitation for us, whether we're Janeites or not, to understand why we are so in her thrall." Chicago Trib
Includes bibliographical references

823.914

McWilliam, Candia
What to look for in winter. HarperCollins 2012 464p **823.914**
ISBN 0062094505; 9780062094506
This book is a memoir of "novelist Candia McWilliam [who] began losing her sight, a gradual onset of blindness that seemed like an assault cruelly tailored for someone whose life consisted of reading and writing. Propelled to look inward and into the past, McWilliam embarked on a painful personal voyage through a waste of snows punctuated by shards of ice as she attempted to write her life back. What followed was a flow of memory: her childhood in Edinburgh, her devastating alcoholism, finding and losing her bearings in Cambridge and London, her marriages, her children, and, overshadowing it all, her mother's suicide." (Publisher's note)

824   English essays

Carlyle, Thomas
★ **Sartor** resartus; edited with an introduction and notes by Kerry McSweeney and Peter Sabor. Oxford Univ. Press 1987 xlii, 273p pa $11.95 **824**
ISBN 0-19-283673-0

LC 87-5753
First published 1833-1834, Sartor resartus contains the germ of Carlyle's philosophy. It purports to be an interpretation of the work of an erudite German professor but is really the story of Carlyle's own fierce spiritual conflict between doubt and faith. It presents a philosophy of clothes, or the outward forms of things

De Quincey, Thomas
The **confessions** of an English opium-eater and other writings. Penguin Books 2003 xliv, 296p pa $14 **824**
1. Drug abuse
ISBN 978-0-14-043901-4; 0-14-043901-3
"Confessions forged a link between artistic self-expression and addiction, paving the way for later generations of literary drug-users from Baudelaire to Burroughs, and anticipating psychoanalysis with its insights into the subconscious. This edition is based on the original serial version of 1821, and reproduces the two 'sequels', 'Suspiria de Profundis' (1845) and 'The English Mail-Coach' (1849). It also includes a critical introduction discussing the romantic figure of the addict and the tradition of confessional literature, and an appendix on opium in the nineteenth century." Publisher's note

Dyer, Geoff
Otherwise known as the human condition; selected essays and reviews, 1989-2010. Graywolf Press 2011 421p il **824**
1. Authors 2. Criticism 3. Essays 4. Literature -- History & criticism 5. Photographic criticism
ISBN 1-555-97579-8; 978-1-55597-579-1

LC 2010-937517

This book of essays covers a broad territory stretching from photographers such as Richard Avedon and William Gedney . . . ; musicians Miles Davis and Def Leppard; writers like D.H. Lawrence, Ian McEwan, and Richard Ford; as well as personal ruminations on, say, reader's block. (Publishers Weekly)

A grab-bag of critical essays, reportage and personal stories from the irrepressibly curious Dyer. . . . The title of this hefty tome, featuring pieces published in two United Kingdom–only collections, suggests ponderous philosophizing. But though Dyer takes his art seriously, his prose is as relaxed and self-effacing as it is informed. . . . Though the book is wide-ranging, his command is consistent, whether he's writing about Richard Avedon or model airplanes. Kirkus

Includes bibliographical references

Hazlitt, William

Selected writings; edited with an introduction and notes by Jon Cook. Oxford University Press 1998 xlvi, 423p pa $13.95   **824**

ISBN 978-0-19-283800-1; 0-19-283800-1

Hazlitt "developed a variety of identities as a writer: essayist, philosopher, critic of literature, drama and art, biographer, political commentator, and polemicist. Praised for his eloquence, he was also reviled by conservatives for his radical politics. This edition, thematically organized for ease of access, contains some of his best-known essays, such as 'The Indian Jugglers' and 'The Fight,' as well as more obscure pieces on politics, philosophy, and culture." Publisher's note

James, Clive

As of this writing; the essential essays, 1968-2002. Norton 2003 619p $35   **824**

1. Literature -- History and criticism

ISBN 0-393-05180-3

"James writes with fluent wit, remarkable warmth, deep knowledge, and an exhilarating sense of mission." Booklist

Kermode, Frank

★ **Pieces** of my mind; essays and criticism, 1958-2002. Farrar, Straus & Giroux 2003 466p $26; pa $16   **824**

ISBN 0-8090-7601-2; 0-374-52936-1 pa

LC 2003-54727

The author "parses complicated, even esoteric aspects of story and text, metaphysics and poetry, and the link between social change and the evolution of the novel, yet he is unfailingly clear and cheerfully engaging, classy, and stimulating." Booklist

Includes bibliographical references

O'Faolain, Nuala

A **radiant** life; Nuala O'Faolain; [introduction by Fintan O'Toole; note by Sheridan Hay]. Abrams Image 2011 302p pa $18.95   **824**

ISBN 978-0-8109-9806-3; 0-8109-9806-8

LC 2010-37687

"The collection spans two decades and runs the gamut, from feminism to social justice, from pop culture to the elusive fruits of progress. It makes little difference that they

spring from a quintessentially Irish voice; they are universal in their appeal. Read more: Book review: Nuala O'Faolain's Irish prose holds universal appeal." Denver Post

Orwell, George

Essays; selected and introduced by John Carey. Alfred A. Knopf 2002 xlv, 1369p $35   **824**

ISBN 978-0-375-41503-6; 0-375-41503-3

"The real reason we read Orwell is because his own fault-line, his fundamental schism, his hybridity, left him exceptionally sensitive to the fissure—which is everywhere apparent–between what ought to be the case and what actually is the case. He says the unsayable." Financial Times

Smith, Zadie

Changing my mind; occasional essays. Penguin Press 2009 306p $26.95   **824**

1. Authors 2. Criticism 3. Novelists 4. Short story writers

ISBN 978-1-59420-237-7; 1-59420-237-0

LC 2009-23419

The author has organized this collection of "essays into sections on reading, being, seeing, feeling, and remembering to create a strong and piquant collection. As the title implies, Smith's thinking evolves before our eyes as she articulates her responses to art and life. . . . Smith is a superb essayist of skill, candor, and caring." Booklist

Includes bibliographical references

Wilde, Oscar

The **artist** as critic; critical writings of Oscar Wilde. edited by Richard Ellmann. University of Chicago Press 1982 xxviii, 446p pa $36.50   **824**

1. Criticism 2. Literature -- History and criticism

ISBN 978-0-226-89764-6; 0-226-89764-8

LC 82-13361

Wilde's "book reviews and occasional pieces prove that while Wilde could be superbly malicious with fatheads, he was a generous and painstaking critic, quick to find merit and delighted to announce the discovery. It is easy to damn a book amusingly. Wilde could praise amusingly, a rare and difficult trick." Atlantic

826   English letters

★ The Oxford book of letters; edited by Frank and Anita Kermode. Oxford Univ. Press 1995 559p hardcover o.p. pa $16.95   **826**

1. American letters 2. English letters

ISBN 0-19-280490-1 pa

LC 94-36412

"This volume includes more than 300 letters that document the concerns of writers, political leaders, and ordinary citizens over the period 1535-1985. Each letter is accompanied by an explanatory note identifying the writer and establishing the context. The correspondents, some more skilled than others, pursue a range of topics, including an account of a public execution, gossip about friends and relatives, and the hardships of moving to a new land in search of a better life." Libr J

827 English humor and satire

★ The Oxford book of humorous prose; William Caxton to P.G. Wodehouse: a conducted tour. [chosen and edited] by Frank Muir. Oxford Univ. Press 1990 xxxiv, 1162p hardcover o.p. pa $21.50 **827**
1. American wit and humor 2. English wit and humor
ISBN 0-19-280379-4 pa

LC 89-9242

"Selections are generally very short, with bridges, often fairly humorous of themselves, by Muir. The humor ranges from the broad to the subtle and, in fact, in any other way that humor might range; there's something in here for everyone." Libr J

828 English miscellaneous writings

Bradford, Richard
Lucky him: the life of Kingsley Amis. Owen, P. 2001 432p il $44.95 **828**
1. Authors 2. Essayists 3. Humorists 4. Literary critics 5. Novelists 6. Novelists, English -- 20th century 7. Poets 8. Short story writers
ISBN 0-7206-1117-2

LC 2001-431013

This is a biography of the English novelist, best known for such works as Lucky Jim, The old devils, and Difficulties with girls.

"The writing is consistently clear and the insights—literary and biographical—are formidable." Publ Wkly

Includes bibliographical references

DeGategno, Paul J.
Critical companion to Jonathan Swift; a literary reference to his life and works. [by] Paul J. DeGategno, R. Jay Stubblefield. Facts on File 2006 474p il $75 **828**
1. Authors 2. Clergy 3. Pamphleteers 4. Poets 5. Satirists 6. Writers on politics
ISBN 0-8160-5093-7; 978-0-8160-5093-2

LC 2005-25470

This "work is divided into five parts. These parts consist of a ten-page biography of satirist Jonathan Swift (1667-1745); a 'Works A-Z' section that includes synopses and commentaries that generally run to several hundred words on virtually all of Swift's poems, essays, and books; a 'Related Entries' section with similar brief articles on persons, topics, and places relevant to Swift studies; appendixes that include a chronology of Swift's life; a . . . bibliography of primary and secondary works; and an index." Libr J

Includes bibliographical references

Huxley, Elspeth
The **flame** trees of Thika; memories of an African childhood. Penguin Bks. 2000 280p pa $15 **828**
1. Authors 2. Authors, English -- 20th century -- Biography 3. Memoirists 4. Novelists
ISBN 0-14-118378-0; 978-0-14-118378-7

LC 99-47965

This is an account of the author's childhood on a coffee plantation in Kenya. She describes the landscape, the Kikuya peoples, the European settlers and the difficulties her parents faced adjusting to life in the bush.

Johnson, Samuel
Samuel Johnson; the major works. edited with an introduction and notes by Donald Greene. Oxford University Press 2000 xxvii, 840p pa $18.95 **828**
ISBN 978-0-19-284042-4; 0-19-284042-8

LC 83-17280

"This volume celebrates Johnson's astonishing talent by selecting widely across the full range of his work. It includes 'London' and 'The Vanity of Human Wishes' among other poems, and many of his essays for the Rambler and Idler. The prefaces to his edition of Shakespeare and his famous Dictionary, together with samples from the texts, are given, as well as selections from A Journey to the Western Islands of Scotland, the Lives of the Poets, and Rasselas in its entirety. There is also a substantial representation of lesser-known prose, and of his poetry, letters, and journals." Publisher's note

Includes bibliographical references

Martin, Peter
★ A **life** of James Boswell. Yale Univ. Press 2000 613p $35; pa $18.95 **828**
1. Authors 2. Authors, Scottish -- 18th century -- Biography 3. Biographers 4. Biographers -- Great Britain -- Biography 5. Lawyers
ISBN 0-300-08489-7; 0-300-09312-8 pa

This is a biography of the diarist and author of The life of Samuel Johnson.

"Martin has written the best biography of the greatest biographer in the English language. . . . One of the many virtues of Martin's work is his successful synthesis of Boswell's life story with a keen analysis of Boswell's artistry." Atl Mon

Includes bibliographical references

Meyers, Jeffrey
Orwell; wintry conscience of a generation. Norton 2000 380p il maps hardcover o.p. pa $16.95 **828**
1. Authors 2. Authors, English -- 20th century -- Biography 3. Essayists 4. Journalists -- Great Britain -- Biography 5. Literature and society -- England -- History -- 20th century 6. Novelists 7. Politics and literature -- Great Britain -- History -- 20th century
ISBN 0-393-32263-7 pa

LC 00-38020

"With wit and acumen, Meyers portrays a complex, eccentric, intelligent, and unbending man hard on family and friends, a writer of singular gifts, and a 'prophetic moralist' whose vision continues to illuminate society's dark side." Booklist

Includes bibliographical references

Quinn, Edward

Critical companion to George Orwell; a literary reference to his life and work. Facts On File 2009 450p il $75   **828**

1. Authors 2. Essayists 3. Novelists
ISBN 978-0-8160-7091-6

LC 2008-26727

This volume provides a "review of Orwell's life and covers all his novels, nonfiction, and other writings. . . . It is a superb resource for those desiring an introduction to George Orwell, the man and the writer." Booklist

Includes bibliographical references

Sisman, Adam

Boswell's presumptuous task; the making of the life of Dr. Johnson. Penguin 2002 351p il pa $15   **828**

1. Authors 2. Biographers 3. Lawyers
ISBN 978-0-14-200175-2; 0-14-200175-9

James Boswell's The Life of Samuel Johnson was published in 1791, six years after the death of its subject. In this book, Sisman chronicles Boswell's motives for writing his biography and the techniques he adopted.

"Mr. Sisman's book is illuminating both of Boswell's character and of all aspects of his authorship." Economist

Includes bibliographical references

Swift, Graham

Making an elephant; writing from within. Alfred A. Knopf 2009 400p il $26.95   **828**

ISBN 978-0-307-27099-3

LC 2009-14052

"Out from behind the scrim of fiction, Swift is highly entertaining, at once welcoming and teasing, clever and probing." Booklist

Includes bibliographical references

Thomas, Dylan

A **child's** Christmas in Wales; with woodcuts by Ellen Raskin. New Directions 2007 51p il pa $9.95   **828**

1. Christmas -- Wales
ISBN 978-0-8112-1731-6; 0-8112-1731-0

LC 2007-24727

The Welsh poet Dylan Thomas recalls the celebration of Christmas with his family and the feelings it evoked in him as a child.

For any season of the year "the language is enchanting and the poetry shines with an unearthly radiance." N Y Times Book Rev

Woolf, Virginia

The **Virginia** Woolf reader; edited by Mitchell A. Leaska. Harcourt Brace Jovanovich 1984 371p hardcover o.p. pa $16   **828**

ISBN 0-15-693590-2 pa

LC 84-4478

Excerpts from Woolf's "novels form less than 20 percent of a reader whose selections of short stories, essays, letters, and diary entries are excellent. This collection will be useful to those already familiar with Woolf's novels and seeking an introductory selection of her other writings." Libr J

★ The New Oxford book of literary anecdotes. Oxford University Press 2006 385p il hardcover o.p. pa $16.95   **828**

1. Anecdotes 2. Authors, American -- Anecdotes 3. Authors, English 4. Authors, English -- Anecdotes 5. English literature 6. English literature -- Anecdotes
ISBN 0-19-280468-5; 978-0-19-280468-6; 0-19-954341-0 pa; 978-0-19-954341-0 pa

LC 2005-33698

The editor "has compiled more than 700 anecdotes about English-language writers, from Geoffrey Chaucer to J.K. Rowling. The brief, chronologically-arranged (by subject's birth date) entries offer a glimpse into the personalities and times of these authors." Libr J

Includes bibliographical references

830   German literature and literatures of related languages

Garland, Henry B.

★ The **Oxford** companion to German literature; by Henry and Mary Garland. 3rd ed; Oxford Univ. Press 1997 951p maps $95   **830**

1. German literature -- Bio-bibliography 2. German literature -- Dictionaries 3. Reference books
ISBN 0-19-815896-3

LC 96-53309

Entries include biographies, synopses of important works, literary terms and movements, historical events and figures, and material relevant to the social and intellectual background of German literature from the earliest records to the present.

★ The Cambridge history of German literature; edited by Helen Watanabe-O'Kelly. Cambridge Univ. Press 1997 613p $90; pa $32   **830**

1. German literature -- History and criticism
ISBN 0-521-43417-3; 0-521-78573-1 pa

LC 95-52412

A "briskly written survey of German literature that grounds literary practice in the social and historical context of each period and yet does not shortchange the aesthetic qualities of the representative works discussed." Choice

★ Encyclopedia of German literature; Matthias Konzett, editor. Fitzroy Dearborn Pubs. 2000 2v set $175   **830**

1. German literature 2. German literature -- Bio-bibliography 3. German literature -- Encyclopedias 4. Reference books
ISBN 1-57958-138-2

"Essay-like entries cover three main categories: authors, works (novels, books of poetry, and essays), and topics, the last encompassing everything from literary terms and movements, artistic forums, cities, and historical eras to the key legacy of the Frankfurt School and its members. Rather lengthy lists for further reading are provided with each essay." Libr J

Includes bibliographical references

831   German poetry

Celan, Paul

★ **Poems** of Paul Celan; translated by Michael Hamburger. Rev and expanded; Persea Bks. 2002 xxxiv, 366p $35; pa $18.95   **831**

1. Bilingual books -- English-German 2. Poetry -- By individual authors

ISBN 0-89255-275-1; 0-89255-276-X pa

LC 2001-59341

"This bilingual German-English selection culled from [the poet's] nine collections reveals that his is a poetry of darkness: anguish over what life offers and denies; the ever-present shadow of death that shades each breath. . . . Yet it also expresses an undefined, perhaps undefinable, joy." Booklist [review of 1989 edition]

Goethe, Johann Wolfgang von

Selected poetry; translated with an introduction and notes by David Luke. Penguin Books 2005 xliv, 283p pa $16   **831**

1. Poetry -- By individual authors

ISBN 978-0-14-042456-0; 0-14-042456-3

"The introduction gives a thoughtful summary of Goethe's fascinating and problematic life. . . . What Luke triumphantly does is not only to stay close to the original, but also to create a total structure that gives a convincing sense of the overall movement of the poem. . . . Goethe made no secret of his huge debt to Shakespeare; perhaps the English tradition might celebrate the new millennium by learning something from him in return. David Luke's selection makes an excellent starting point." Times Lit Suppl

Maxwell, Glyn, 1962-

One thousand nights and counting; selected poems. Farrar, Straus and Giroux 2011 239p   **831**

1. Poetry -- By individual authors

ISBN 9780374226480

LC 2011005176

"The British poet Maxwell's first U.S. selected presents a conversational style that is a constant throughout, as is the setting of England and New England; otherwise, these often surreal and opaque poems range across moods and subjects. The best moments occur when readers can lose themselves in the very long poems, in particular the inventive re-imagining of the story of Noah's Ark, 'Out of the Rain,' and the elegiac 'Letters to Edward Thomas,' in which the speaker waits for a friend who never arrives. . . . Maxwell's poetry can be playful and inventive, beautiful and melancholic, but can also be self-aggrandizing . . . and even pretentious. . . . Yet Maxwell is one of stars of poetry across the pond and a rising presence here; this book should win him new fans." Publ Wkly

Morike, Eduard Friedrich

Mozart's journey to Prague and a selection of poems; [by] Eduard Mörike; translated and with an introduction and notes by David Luke; Scots translations by Gilbert McKay. rev ed; Penguin Books 2003 xl, 216p pa $14   **831**

1. Poetry -- By individual authors

ISBN 978-0-14-044737-8; 0-14-044737-7

LC 2004-298957

A selection of Mörike's most popular romantic and classical folk and fairy-tale poems. Also includes the 1855 novella Mozart's journey to Prague, an imaginary recreation of the journey Mozart made from Vienna to Prague in 1787 to conduct the first performance of Don Giovanni.

Rilke, Rainer Maria

★ **Duino** elegies; translated by David Young; with an introduction and commentary. W. W. Norton 2006 202p pa $13.95   **831**

1. Poetry -- By individual authors

ISBN 978-0-393-32884-4; 0-393-32884-8

LC 2006-9872

"These elegies, the last great work of the poet, were named for the castle of Duino on the Adriatic, where they were first conceived." New Statesman (1913)

New poems; selected and translated by Edward Snow. rev bilingual ed; North Point Press 2001 329p pa $15   **831**

1. Bilingual books -- English-German 2. Poetry -- By individual authors

ISBN 0-86547-612-8

LC 2001-42714

In this "translation, Edward Snow renders into believable English the complete text of Rilke's work of early maturity. . . Maintaining fidelity to Rilke's idiosyncratic and problematic German, Snow does not reproduce his formal structures but does capture the rhythms, tone shifts, and overall feel of the poems to an admirable degree. Bilingual edition." Booklist [review of 1984 edition of New poems (1907)]

★ **Sonnets** to Orpheus; translated by M.D. Herter Norton. W. W. Norton 2006 160p pa $13.95 **831**

1. Poetry -- By individual authors

ISBN 0-393-32885-6

"Deeply rooted in the symbolist tradition, the 'Sonnets' collapse the barriers that exist between the inner and the outer world and celebrate the inherently musical quality of language. In his masterful translation of the 'Sonnets', Young captures the fluidity of the original with sensitivity and precision." Libr J

Uncollected poems; selected and translated by Edward Snow. Bilingual ed; North Point Press 1995 265p hardcover o.p. pa $15   **831**

1. Poetry -- By individual authors

ISBN 0-86547-513-X pa

LC 94-24438

"Snow is particularly adept at capturing what one might call the non-Orphic side of Rilke's voice. Even in the most complex and rhetorically charged pieces, however, Snow is careful never to simplify Rilke. . . . Most important of all, these translations . . . let us get beyond the simplifications of the Rilke legend with its cycles of transcendent inspiration and imaginative paralysis." New Repub

Sebald, Winfried Georg, 1944-2001

Across the land and the water; new and selected poems, 1964-2001. W.G. Sebald; [translated from the German by Iain Galbraith] Random House 2012 166 p.   **831**

1. Authors, German 2. Poems -- Collections 3. Poets, German

ISBN 9781400068906

LC 2011025272

The book "compiles [W. G. Sebald's] . . . poetic output from his student days through to the last years of his life. . . . Sebald's poems engage . . . with the private archives of Germany's memory of the war. In an age of distrust for abstruseness or overabundance in poetry, the force of suggestion in the seeming simplicity of his word-choice and phraseology contrasts with many modern poetic idioms, which aim to be instantly accessible. . . . Each poem, in its way, reaches towards the irreducible truth of a large number of individuals, Jewish and non-Jewish, brutally transported from home and out of recognition and existence." (New Statesman)

832   German drama

Durrenmatt, Friedrich

★ The **visit**; a tragi-comedy. translated from the German by Patrick Bowles. Grove Press 1962 109p pa $12 **832**

ISBN 0-8021-3066-6

Characters: 28 men, 6 women, extras. 3 acts. First produced in the United States at the Lunt-Fontaine Theatre, New York City, May 5, 1958.

This play "concerns millionaire Claire Zachanassian's return to her small home town where, in her youth, she was seduced and abandoned by III. She seeks revenge and, to get it, she bribes the entire population: every man, woman and child will be rich for the rest of their lives if they agree to put III to death. After a feeble moral struggle and a travesty of a trial, the people of Güllen condemn and execute the erstwhile lover. In so doing they condemn themselves and Dürrenmatt condemns society as a whole." Cambridge Guide to World Theatre

Goethe, Johann Wolfgang von

★ **Goethe's** Faust; the original German and a new tr. and introduction by Walter Kaufmann; part one and sections from part two. Anchor Books 1962 503p pa $10.95   **832**

ISBN 978-0-385-03114-1; 0-385-03114-9

In this epic drama "Mephistopheles makes a bargain with the aged Faust. If Faust is granted one moment of complete contentment, he loses his soul. Faust regains his youth and with Mephistopheles he travels about enjoying every form of earthly pleasure." Haydn. Thesaurus of Book Dig

Lessing, Gotthold Ephraim

Nathan the Wise, Minna von Barnhelm, and other plays and writings; edited by Peter Demetz; fore-word by Hannah Arendt. Continuum 1991 xxvii, 335p hardcover o.p. pa $29.95   **832**

ISBN 0-8264-0706-4; 0-8264-0707-2 pa

LC 91-19344

Schiller, Friedrich

Don Carlos and Mary Stuart; translated with notes by Hilary Collier Sy-Quia; adapted in verse drama by Peter Oswald; with an introduction by Lesley Sharpe. Oxford University Press 2008 xxx, 359p il pa $13.95   **832**

1. Princes 2. Queens

ISBN 978-0-19-954074-7

LC 2008-275155

This volume contains Don Carlos and Mary Stuart, two German historical dramas. "Dating from 1787 and 1800 respectively, one play was written immediately before the French Revolution, the other in its aftermath. These new translations into blank verse are accurate, elegant, and playable. The Introduction, Notes, and Chronology set the plays in their cultural and intellectual background, while a family tree explains the historical relationship between Don Carlos and Mary Stuart." Publisher's note

Includes bibliographical references

The **robbers** [and] Wallenstein; translated with an introduction by F. J. Lamport. Penguin Books 1979 472p pa $16   **832**

ISBN 978-0-14-044368-4; 0-14-044368-1

In The robbers (1782) a man, cheated out of his inheritance by his brother, forms a band of thieves. The Wallenstein trilogy, based on the fall of the German general Count Albrecht von Wallenstein, is comprised of: Wallenstein's camp (1798), The Piccolominis (1799), and Wallenstein's death (1799).

833   German fiction

Sebald, Winfried Georg

★ **On** the natural history of destruction; with essays on Alfred Andersch, Jean Amery, and Peter Weiss. {by} W.G. Sebald; translated by Anthea Bell. Random House 2003 202p $23.95; pa $12.95 **833**

1. Artists 2. Authors 3. Bombing, Aerial -- Germany 4. Dramatists 5. Essayists 6. German literature -- 20th century -- History and criticism 7. German literature -- History and criticism 8. Nonfiction writers 9. Novelists 10. Painters 11. Philosophers 12. Short story writers 13. World War, 1939-1945 -- Destruction and pillage -- Germany 14. World War, 1939-1945 -- Literature and the war

ISBN 0-375-50484-2; 0-375-75657-4 pa

LC 2002-75187

838 German miscellaneous writings

Kleist, Heinrich von

Selected writings; edited and translated by David Constantine. Hackett Pub. 2004 xxvii, 442p $44; pa $14.95 **838**

ISBN 978-0-87220-744-8; 0-87220-744-7; 978-0-87220-743-1 pa; 0-87220-743-9 pa

LC 2004-54378

"This volume includes the majority of Kleist's writings in English translation. An outstanding representation of his work, this selection offers three plays, eight short stories, five anecdotes, and three essays. Kleist's dramas and stories resonate with complex circumstances and obscure consequences that the characters struggle to sail through. Things are not always what they seem to be; intriguingly, the guilty can look innocent and the innocent guilty. The play The Broken Jug, as well as the stories 'Michael Kohlhaas' and 'The Chilean Earthquake,' depict predicaments of the falsely accused who are denied justice. Constantine . . . does an outstanding job of conveying the beauty of Kleist's literary style while allowing himself some liberties in translation." Libr J

Includes bibliographical references

839 Other Germanic literatures

Singer, Isaac Bashevis

More stories from my father's court; translated by Curt Leviant. Farrar, Straus & Giroux 2000 216p hardcover o.p. pa $12 **839**

1. Authors 2. Children's authors 3. Essayists 4. Jews -- Poland 5. Journalists 6. Nobel laureates for literature 7. Novelists 8. Rabbinical courts -- Poland -- Warsaw 9. Short story writers

ISBN 0-374-52798-9 pa

LC 00-37583

These autobiographical sketches depict the workings of the beth din, the rabbinical court that met in the Singer's Warsaw home.

"This book is a portrait of the artist as a voyeuristic yeshiva boy, someone who assimilated into his soul the weird contradictions of modern Jewish life and, half chronicler and half creator, spun them into lasting stories." N Y Times Book Rev

★ The Sagas of Icelanders; a selection. preface by Jane Smiley; introduction by Robert Kellogg. Viking 2000 lxvi, 782p il maps hardcover o.p. pa $20 **839**

1. Old Norse literature 2. Old Norse literature -- Translations into English 3. Sagas 4. Sagas -- Translations into English

ISBN 0-14-100003-1 pa

LC 99-44111

"The Icelandic Sagas are among the masterpieces of world literature whose composition stretches from about the year 1000 to 1500. Presenting the adventures of Norse and Viking heroes, the sagas are told with ritual simplicity and a realism that anticipate the modern novel." Libr J

Includes bibliographical references

839.3 Netherlandish literatures

Prose, Francine

Anne Frank; the book, the life, the afterlife. HarperCollins 2009 322p $24.99 **839.3**

1. Children 2. Creative writing 3. Diarists 4. Holocaust victims 5. Holocaust, 1933-1945 -- Personal narratives 6. Holocaust, Jewish (1939-1945) -- Personal narratives -- History and criticism

ISBN 978-0-06-143079-4; 0-06-143079-X

LC 2009-17703

"In this definitive, deeply moving inquiry into the life of the young, imperiled artist, and masterful literary exegesis of The Diary of a Young Girl, Prose tells the crushing story of the Frank family, performs a revelatory analysis of Anne's exacting revision of her coming-of-age memoir, and assesses her father's editorial decisions as he edited his murdered daughter's manuscript for publication. . . . Extraordinary testimony to the power of literature and compassion." Booklist

Includes bibliographical references

839.7 Swedish literature

Hammarskjold, Dag

Markings; translated from the Swedish by Leif Sjöberg & W. H. Auden; with a foreword by W. H. Auden. Knopf 1964 xxiii, 221p hardcover o.p. pa $13.95 **839.7**

1. Spiritual life

ISBN 0-394-43532-X; 0-307-27742-9 pa; 978-0-307-27742-8 pa

The author described this account as a sort of white book concerning his negotiations with himself and with God. A record of his inner life, it opens with a poem he wrote around 1925; most of the entries were made during the nineteen forties and fifties—and the book ends with a poem written only a few weeks before his plane crashed.

Strindberg, August

Strindberg: five plays; translated, with an introduction by Harry G. Carlson. University of Calif. Press 1983 297p hardcover o.p. pa $21.95 **839.7**

ISBN 978-0-520-04698-6 pa

LC 82-15882

Tranströmer, Tomas, 1931-

The great enigma. New Directions 2006 xxi, 262p pa $16.95 **839.7**

1. Landscapes in literature 2. Memoirs 3. Poems -- Collections 4. Poets in literature 5. Sweden

ISBN 978-0-8112-1672-2; 0-8112-1672-1

LC 2006-22551

This volume "offers the most generous collection of Tranströmer's poems to date. . . . Lean and uncluttered, Fulton's translations in The Great Enigma neither preach nor moralize. They refuse staged psychology and let interiority take shape as mysterious judgments, made by the selection of detail and the juxtaposition of things and times and experiences." Boston Rev

839.8   Danish and Norwegian literatures

Ibsen, Henrik

★ The **complete** major prose plays; translated [from the Norwegian] and introduced by Rolf Fjelde. New American Library 1978 1143p pa $28   **839.8**
ISBN 978-0-452-26205-8; 0-452-26205-4
LC 78-50714

Jacobsen, Rolf

The **roads** have come to an end now; selected and last poems of Rolf Jacobsen. translated by Robert Bly, Roger Greenwald, and Robert Hedin. Copper Canyon Press 2001 168p pa $16   **839.8**
1. Bilingual books -- English-Norwegian
ISBN 1-55659-165-9
LC 2001-4488

"This bilingual (Norwegian-English) edition of 73 poems demonstrates a poet whose vision of the natural world and humanity's place in it is cosmically penetrative. Jacobsen regards the world as filled with an essential energy, animated by what must be God, and reading his work induces a certain calm ecstasy about everyday existence." Booklist

Wullschlager, Jackie

Hans Christian Andersen; the life of a story teller. University of Chicago Press 2002 489p il map pa $19   **839.8**
1. Authors 2. Authors, Danish 3. Authors, Danish -- 19th century 4. Children's authors 5. Dramatists 6. Novelists 7. Short story writers
ISBN 0-226-91747-9; 978-0-226-91747-4
LC 2002-18010

"Wullschlager succeeds brilliantly at portraying Andersens inner mind and uncovering his hopes and fears and details the historical context that served to produce such a grand body of literature. . . . [This biography] will be a standard study for years to come." Libr J

Includes bibliographical references

840   French literature and literatures of related Romance languages

★ The New Oxford companion to literature in French; edited by Peter France. Oxford Univ. Press 1995 li, 865p maps $80   **840**
1. French literature -- Bio-bibliography 2. French literature -- Dictionaries 3. Reference books
ISBN 0-19-866125-8

"This work views literature from the perspective of its greater cultural context. Accordingly, topics discussed go beyond the poets, novelists, and dramatists of the traditional French canon, and include philosophy, science, art, history, linguistics, and cinema. Even strip cartoons and pamphlets are treated. . . . The more than 3,000 entries are written by approximately 130 international experts. In addition to brief entries, there are long articles on general topics, such as Québec, feminism, Occitan literature, and the history of the French language." Am Ref Books Annu, 1996

841   French poetry

Baudelaire, Charles

Les fleurs du mal; the complete text of The flowers of evil. in a new translation by Richard Howard; illustrated with nine original monotypes by Michael Mazur. Godine 1982 xxxii, 365p il hardcover o.p. pa $18.95   **841**
1. Poetry -- By individual authors
ISBN 978-0-87923-462-1 pa; 0-87923-462-8 pa
LC 81-13283

"Howard puts the original's rhymed alexandrines primarily into iambic pentameter blank verse, which allows him to capture the immediate, concrete, visceral quality of Baudelaire's imagery." Choice

★ **Poems.** Knopf 1993 256p $12.50 **841**
1. Poetry -- By individual authors
ISBN 0-679-42910-7
LC 93-14363

A representative selection of poetry by the French symbolist.

Beckett, Samuel

★ **Collected** poems in English and French. Grove Press 1977 147p hardcover o.p. pa $13.95   **841**
1. Poetry -- By individual authors
ISBN 978-0-8021-3096-9 pa
LC 77-77855

This work contains poems written by Beckett in English and French along with his translations and bilingual versions of poems by Eluard, Rimbaud, Apollinaire, and Chamfort.

Chanson de Roland

★ The **song** of Roland; translated, with an introduction, by W.S. Merwin. Modern Library 2001 137p pa $11.95   **841**
1. Roland (Legendary character) 2. Roland (Legendary character) -- Fiction
ISBN 0-375-75711-2
LC 00-48989

"This heroic poem celebrates the mighty feats of Roland, the great French hero in the time of Charlemagne. The medieval legend has replaced and transformed the actual facts of history to a great extent but the epic poem has continued in popularity." Bookman's Manual

Includes bibliographical references

Mallarme, Stephane

Collected poems and other verse; translated with notes by E.H. and A.M. Blackmore; with an introduction by Elizabeth McCombie. Oxford University Press 2006 xxxvii, 282p pa $15.95   **841**
1. Poetry -- By individual authors
ISBN 978-0-19-280362-7; 0-19-280362-X

This collection presents Mallarme's "Poesies in the last arrangement known to have been approved by the author. Prose poems, uncollected verse, and the unique, unclassifiable Un Coup de des. . . (A Dice Throw. . .) are also present, including over 20 items that have never previously been translated. Original spelling, punctuation, and lineation have been preserved throughout." Publisher's note

Rimbaud, Arthur

Poems; [selected by Peter Washington] Knopf 1994 288p $12.50 **841**

1. Poetry -- By individual authors
ISBN 978-0-679-43321-7; 0-679-43321-X

LC 94-2496

A collection of work by the French Symbolist known for his daring images and pioneering prose poems.

Verlaine, Paul

★ **Selected** poems; translated by C. F. Mac Intyre. University of Calif. Press 1948 xx, 228p il pa $15.95 **841**

1. Poetry -- By individual authors
ISBN 0-520-01298-4

Eighty poems, chosen from Verlaine's first six books. French originals and translations are on facing pages. Contains a preface by the translator.

The translator "has done Verlaine a gracious courtesy, and American readers a great kindness. The charm, verbal fireworks, sympathy and nostalgia of this major French poet are Englished with color and convictions." Chicago Sunday Trib

Includes bibliographical references

French poetry, 1820-1950, with prose translations; selected, translated, and introduced by William Rees. Penguin Books 1994 xli, 854p pa $22 **841**

1. French poetry -- Collections
ISBN 978-0-14-042385-3; 0-14-042385-0

LC 91-127343

"While this anthology contains . . . generous selections from the established giants—Baudelaire, Rimbaud, Mallarmé, Valéry, Apollinaire, Michaux—it also draws attention to interesting 'minor' poets, such as Claudel or Cendrars, whose writing has been vital to the evolution of poetry in France. William Rees gives us an introduction to each poet, his or her life, affinities and aesthetics, and the significant literary movements Romanticism, the Parnassian Movement, Symbolism, Cubism, Surrealism and 'Négritude' are signposted and discussed." Publisher's note

The Random House book of twentieth-century French poetry; with translations by American and British poets; edited by Paul Auster. Random House 1982 xlix, 635p hardcover o.p. pa $26 **841**

1. French poetry -- Collections
ISBN 978-0-394-71748-7; 0-394-71748-1 pa

LC 82-280

This bilingual edition collects the verse of forty-eight poets as translated by eighty-four poets. The volume opens with a section of poems by Guillaume Apollinaire and closes with a group of poems by Philippe Denis. The original and translation appear on facing pages.

"This excellent anthology undertakes a double task: to provide a comprehensive view of French poetry in the twentieth century and to show, in the range of translators it offers, the influences of that poetry on American and British poets.

. . . Paul Auster has done an excellent job of matching poets and translators." Nation

Includes bibliographical references

842 French drama

Beckett, Samuel

Dramatic works; Paul Auster, series editor; introduction by Edward Albee. Grove Press 2006 509p $24.95 **842**

ISBN 978-0-8021-1819-0; 0-8021-1819-4

LC 2005-55078

Camus, Albert

★ **Caligula** & three other plays; translated from the French by Stuart Gilbert; with a preface written specially for this edition and translated by Justin O'Brien. Knopf 1958 302p hardcover o.p. pa $13 **842**

ISBN 978-0-394-70207-0 pa; 0-394-70207-7 pa

"Four of the author's best-known plays, written between 1938 and 1950. 'Caligula,' about the infamous emperor's self-destroying rebellion against fate; 'The Misunderstanding,' about the murder of a man by his ghoulish mother and sister,' 'The Just Assassins,' on the self-questionings of terrorists; and 'State of Siege,' an allegory about the refusal of one individual in a plague-stricken city to compromise with evil." Publ Wkly

Genet, Jean

★ **The blacks**: a clown show; translated from the French by Bernard Frechtman. Grove Press 1960 128p pa $13 **842**

ISBN 0-8021-5028-4

"Drama in which a group of bizarrely dressed Negroes give a performance for another group of Negroes who wear white masks and represent the major figures of white society's established authority." McGraw-Hill Ency of World Drama

★ **The maids** [and] Deathwatch; two plays. with an introduction by Jean-Paul Sartre; translated from the French by Bernard Frechtman. Grove Press 1954 166p hardcover o.p. pa $14 **842**

ISBN 978-0-8021-5056-1 pa; 0-8021-5056-X pa

Deathwatch, a one-act play written 1947 and first produced 1949 "deals with an insignificant criminal who tries to assume the highly desirable and prestigious role of murderer. . . . In 'The Maids (Les bonnes),' produced in 1947, . . . two servant girls have created an elaborate ritual in which they impersonate their mistress and finally murder her symbolically." McGraw-Hill Ency of World Drama

Ionesco, Eugene

★ **Rhinoceros,** and other plays; translated by Derek Prouse. Grove Press 1960 141p pa $10 **842**

ISBN 0-8021-3098-4

Three satirical comedies by a leading dramatist of the "theater of the absurd." In Rhinoceros, one man resists the pressure to conform as everyone about him accepts their transformation into rhinoceroses and he finds himself socially isolated. In The future is in eggs, a couple must produce eggs destined to become intellectuals. The leader is a satire on the mass adulation of political figures in which the leader turns out to be a headless figure.

Moliere

★ **Tartuffe** and other plays. Signet Classics 2007 xxiv, 408p pa $7.95 **842**
  ISBN 978-0-451-53033-2
  LC 2007-275593

The **misanthrope** and other plays. Signet Classics 2005 524p pa $7.95 **842**
  ISBN 0-451-52987-1; 978-0-451-52987-9
  LC 2006-276841

Rostand, Edmond

Cyrano de Bergerac; translated and adapted for the modern stage by Anthony Burgess. Applause Theatre & Cinema Bks. 1998 175p pa $6.95 **842**
  1. Authors 2. Authors, French -- 17th century -- Drama 3. Poets 4. Soldiers
  ISBN 1-55783-230-7
  LC 96-2545

This version was commissioned for production at the Tyrone Guthrie Theater in Minneapolis. It is adapted and translated from the French play originally produced in 1897. Cyrano, the hero, a Gascon poet and swordsman notorious for his long nose, is in love with Roxana.

Sartre, Jean Paul

★ **No** exit, and three other plays. Vintage Bks. 1989 275p pa $12 **842**
  ISBN 0-679-72516-4
  LC 89-40097

No exit is a modern morality play; The flies is a reworking of the Orestes-Electra story. The third play concerns a young Communist intellectual's attempt to maintain his integrity as party line changes and personal relationships alter perceptions of his murder of a party boss who had fallen out of favor, but whose memory is later rehabilitated. The last play concerns a prostitute's involvement in false charges of rape against a murdered black man and his companion in a town in the American South.

Samuel Beckett's Waiting for Godot; edited and with an introduction by Harold Bloom. New ed; Chelsea House 2008 172p $45 **842**
  1. Authors 2. Dramatists 3. Nobel laureates for literature 4. Novelists 5. Poets 6. Short story writers
  ISBN 978-0-7910-9793-9
  LC 2007-49864

Critical interpretations of Beckett's classic tragicomedy illustrating the apparent meaninglessness of life.

843 French fiction

Carter, William C.

Marcel Proust; a life. Yale Univ. Press 2000 946p $45; pa $18.95 **843**
  1. Authors 2. Essayists 3. Literary critics 4. Novelists 5. Novelists, French -- 20th century
  ISBN 0-300-08145-6; 0-300-09400-0 pa
  LC 99-53701

"Excavating biographic details out of such material as untranslated memoirs and recently collected letters, Carter . . . accounts for the daily affairs of this social butterfly-turned-hypochondriac and shut-in. Proust's romances and infatuations, his political action during the Dreyfus affair, and his literary runs-ins with Anatole France and André Gide, as well as larger issues such as his homosexuality, all receive lengthy treatment." Publ Wkly
  Includes bibliographical references

Jack, Belinda Elizabeth

George Sand; a woman's life writ large. {by} Belinda Jack. Knopf 2000 395p il hardcover o.p. pa $16 **843**
  1. Authors 2. Dramatists 3. Novelists 4. Novelists, French -- 19th century -- Biography 5. Women novelists, French -- 19th century -- Biography
  ISBN 0-679-77918-3 pa
  LC 99-40857

"Prodigious author, cross-dresser, lover of Chopin and Alfred de Musset, intimate of (among others) Liszt, Balzac, Dumas (père and fils), Turgenev, and Flaubert (who cried twice at her funeral), Sand was both before her time and quintessentially of it. Jack's nuanced, moving assessment of the writer's early years . . . is the strongest section of this packed life. When Sand moves onto a larger stage, Jack's style becomes breathless, as if she could barely keep up with her flamboyant subject." New Yorker

Severson, Marilyn S.

★ **Masterpieces** of French literature. Greenwood Press 2004 186p $45 **843**
  1. French fiction -- 19th century -- History and criticism 2. French fiction -- 20th century -- History and criticism 3. French literature -- History and criticism
  ISBN 0-313-31484-5
  LC 2003-59635

Among the novels discussed are Albert Camus's The stranger and The plague, Gustave Flaubert's Madame Bovary, Victor Hugo's The hunchback of Notre Dame and Les Miserables, and Alexander Dumas's The three musketeers.

"Students and general readers seeking a thorough understanding of these influential novels will benefit greatly from this outstanding guide." Libr J
  Includes bibliographical references

Shattuck, Roger

Proust's way; a field guide to In search of lost time. Norton 2000 xxiv, 290p hardcover o.p. pa $16.95 **843**
  1. Authors 2. Essayists 3. Literary critics 4. Novelists
  ISBN 0-393-32180-0 pa
  LC 99-58472

Shattuck "explains the major settings of the work, summarizes character and plot, and discusses central themes. Shattuck acknowledges that there is no one right interpretation of In Search of Lost Time but succeeds in providing a framework to help readers get through it. He addresses readers coming to the work for the first time." Libr J

Includes bibliographical references

844   French essays

Camus, Albert

Resistance, rebellion, and death; translated from the French and with an introduction by Justin O'Brien. Knopf 1961 271p hardcover o.p. pa $13.95   **844**
ISBN 978-0-679-76401-4 pa; 0679764011 pa

"A selection of forthright essays on contemporary world politics, on capital punishment and the relations of the state and the individual, and on art, chosen from the three volumes of 'Actuelles,' published in France between 1950 and 1958." Publ Wkly

★ The **myth** of Sisyphus, and other essays; translated from the French by Justin O'Brien. Knopf 1955 212p hardcover o.p. pa $12.95   **844**
ISBN 0-679-73373-6 pa

Personal reflections on the meaning of life and the philosophical questions surrounding suicide.

Frampton, Saul

When I am playing with my cat, how do I know she is not playing with me? Montaigne and being in touch with life. Pantheon Books 2011 300p $26; ebook $12.99   **844**
1. Authors 2. Essayists 3. Judges
ISBN 978-0-375-42471-7; 978-0-307-37959-7 ebook
LC 2010-43642

The author "renders a rigorous history of ideas in this engaging account of the life and the work of Michel de Montaigne (1533–1592). . . . Frampton tucks a good deal of biography into his tour of the evolution of the essays and the events that inspired them—but his extraordinary achievement is in conveying—and inviting the reader to commune with—Montaigne's unique sensibility and his take on death, sex, travel, friendship, kidney stones, the human thumb, and above all, 'the power of the ordinary and the unremarkable, the value of the here-and-now.' This scholarly romp through the Renaissance is a jewel." Publ Wkly

Includes bibliographical references

848   French miscellaneous writings

Bair, Deirdre

Simone de Beauvoir; a biography. Summit Bks. 1990 718p il hardcover o.p. pa $31.95   **848**
1. Authors 2. Biographers 3. Biography, Individual 4. Dramatists 5. Essayists 6. Feminists 7. Nobel laureates for literature 8. Nonfiction writers 9. Novelists 10.

Philosophers 11. Short story writers
ISBN 0-671-74180-2 pa
LC 89-22029

"Bair's biography of the French author, philosopher, and feminist aims to restore the balance between interest in de Beauvoir's personal life—as the lifelong companion of Jean-Paul Sartre and sometime lover of Nelson Algren—and the question of her achievements as a writer and thinker." Booklist

Includes bibliographical references

Damrosch, Leo

★ **Jean**-Jacques Rousseau; restless genius. Leo Damrosch. Houghton Mifflin Co. 2005 x, 566 p.p ill., map o.p.; (pbk.) $12.00; o.p.   **848**
1. Authors 2. Biography, Individual 3. Memoirists 4. Novelists 5. Political and social philosophers
ISBN 9780618446964; 9780618872022; 0618446966
LC 2005013579

This book "is [a] . . . single-volume biography of [Jean-Jacques] Rousseau, . . . published in English for the general reader. It . . . illuminate[s] the last decade of his life, a time when his psychological complexity and strangeness came to the fore yet his intellect and creative powers triumphed over his difficult, paranoid temperament. During those ten years, he finished the 'Confessions,' wrote the 'Dialogues,' or 'Rousseau Judge of Jean-Jacques,' which he tried in vain to place in the Notre-Dame cathedral for safekeeping, and began writing 'Reveries of the Solitary Walker.'" (Publisher's note)

"A delight to read, Damrosch comes as close to Rousseau's authentic self as we are likely to get." N Y Times Book Rev

Includes bibliographical references (p. [499]-549) and index.

Gordon, Lois G.

The **world** of Samuel Beckett, 1906-1946; {by} Lois Gordon. Yale Univ. Press 1996 250p il $50; pa $16.95   **848**
1. Authors 2. Biography, Individual 3. Dramatists 4. Nobel laureates for literature 5. Novelists 6. Poets 7. Short story writers
ISBN 0-300-06409-8; 0-300-07495-6 pa
LC 95-22851

Gordon "examines the first 40 years of the playwright/novelist's 83-year life, which includes periods in Ireland, where he was born; in Paris, where he spent much of his life; and in London, Germany, and other parts of France. . . . Gordon has been thorough in her research and careful in her presentation." Choice

Includes bibliographical references

Kaplan, Alice Yaeger

The **collaborator**: the trial & execution of Robert Brasillach; {by} Alice Kaplan. University of Chicago Press 2000 308p $25; pa $15   **848**
1. Authors 2. Authors, French -- 20th century -- Biography 3. Collaborationists 4. Fascism -- France 5. Fascism and literature -- France -- History -- 20th century 6. Intellectuals -- France -- Political activity 7. Journalists 8. Novelists 9. World War, 1939-1945 --

Collaborationists -- France 10. World War, 1939-1945 -- France

ISBN 0-226-42414-6; 0-226-42415-4 pa

LC 99-48291

Kaplan details "the life of Robert Brasillach, a prolific and controversial French critic who was executed for treason, at age 35, after France's liberation from the Nazis. A fascist-leaning writer known for his defense of Nazi crimes . . . Brasillach was the only distinguished writer put to death by the postwar French government." Publ Wkly

Includes bibliographical references

Rimbaud, Arthur

Rimbaud; complete works, selected letters: a bilingual edition. translated with an introduction and notes by Wallace Fowlie; updated, revised and with a foreword by Seth Whidden. University of Chicago Press 2005 xxxvi, 458p il $50; pa $19 **848**

ISBN 978-0-226-71976-4; 0-226-71976-6; 978-0-226-71977-1 pa; 0226719774 pa

LC 2005-41859

In this bilingual edition of Rimbaud's work the original French texts are accompanied by English prose translations. In addition to the complete poetic works there are two prose fragments, a short story in the form of a seminarian's journal, and a selection of letters chosen to illustrate biographical details and Rimbaud's credo as a poet.

Todd, Olivier

Albert Camus; a life. translated by Benjamin Ivry. abr & ed English version; Knopf 1997 434p il $30 **848**

1. Authors 2. Authors, French 3. Biography, Individual 4. Dramatists 5. Essayists 6. Nobel laureates for literature 7. Novelists

ISBN 0-679-42855-0

LC 97-2991

This is a biography of the French novelist, playwright, literary editor, and philosopher.

"Todd's exhaustive biography, which aims—and succeeds—in presenting 'the man' and not just the writer, has been shortened for its English translation, which refers readers to the French edition for notes, sources and bibliography." Publ Wkly

Valery, Paul

★ **Selected** writings. New Directions 1950 256p hardcover o.p. pa $12.95 **848**

ISBN 0-8112-0213-5 pa

"Seventeen poems are translated by eighteen translators, including Denis Devlin, Léonie Adams, and C. Day Lewis. . . . The rest of the book is composed of the French love miscellanies, essays, dialogues, and critiques." New Yorker

Voltaire

★ The **portable** Voltaire; edited, and with an introduction by Ben Ray Redmen. Viking 1949 569p hardcover o.p. pa $17 **848**

ISBN 0-14-015041-2 pa

The selections from Voltaire's works include: Candide, part one; Three stories: Zadig, Micromegas, and Story of a good Brahmin; Letters, and selections from the Philosophi-

cal Dictionary and other works. The editor's introduction gives a biographical sketch of Voltaire.

850   Literatures of Italian, Dalmatian, Romanian, Rhaetian, Sardinian, Corsican languages

Ruud, Jay

Critical companion to Dante; a literary reference to his life and work. Facts on File 2008 566p il $75 **850**

1. Authors 2. Poets

ISBN 978-0-8160-6521-9

LC 2007-33473

This title covers the works of Dante, including The Divine Comedy, La Vita Nuova, and his philosophical works.

"Ruud has written a useful introductory resource that students and lay readers alike can enjoy." Booklist

Includes bibliographical references

The **Cambridge** history of Italian literature; edited by Peter Brand and Lino Pertile. rev ed; Cambridge Univ. Press 1999 xxii, 699p map pa $33 **850**

1. Italian literature -- History and criticism

ISBN 0-521-66622-8

LC 00-265436

Scholars analyze and describe the works of writers who have added to Italy's literary tradition from its origins to today. The editors provide translations, maps, bibliographies, and chronological charts.

"Contemporary readers will no doubt be delighted to learn more about such topics as the evolution of opera, compositions by Italian women writers, and the development of feminism." Choice

★ The **Oxford** companion to Italian literature; edited by Peter Hainsworth and David Robey. Oxford Univ. Press 2002 xli, 644p maps $95 **850**

1. Authors, Italian 2. Italian literature 3. Italian literature -- Bio-bibliography 4. Italian literature -- Dictionaries 5. Reference books

ISBN 0-19-818332-1

LC 2001-59301

"A magisterial addition to the Oxford companions to literature, this volume goes far beyond its core subject of Italian literature to cover its substrate and context. . . . An excellent ready-reference companion for readers seeking less an introduction to the summits of the literature . . . but a reminder of relevant details." Choice

Includes bibliographical references

851   Italian poetry

Ariosto, Lodovico

Orlando Furioso/The frenzy of Orlando, part 1; a romantic epic. by Ludovico Ariosto; translated with

an introduction by Barbara Reynolds. Penguin Books 1975 827p map pa $18   **851**
1. Poetry -- By individual authors
ISBN 978-0-14-044311-0; 0-14-044311-8
LC 75-327748
An English verse translation in the original meter of the epic poem by the sixteenth-century Italian poet, courtier, and statesman, which is based on the adventures of Roland and other knights of Charlemagne in the wars against the Saracens.

This translation is "lucid, lively, and eminently readable. . . . The first volume contains one-half (23) of the cantos plus invaluable aids for the reader: a lengthy, informative introduction, a list of characters and devices, maps and genealogical tables, notes for each canto and an index of proper names." Choice

Orlando Furioso/The frenzy of Orlando, part 2; a romantic epic. [by] Ludovico Ariosto; translated with an introduction by Barbara Reynolds. Penguin Books 1977 794p pa $18   **851**
1. Poetry -- By individual authors
ISBN 978-0-14-044310-3; 0-14-044310-X
"The value of this faithful translation is primarily that it helps you with the Italian. It lets you make your way painlessly into the poem. . . . It does not . . . draw attention to itself. Modestly, it points across, to the things going on in the original." Times Lit Suppl

Dante Alighieri

The **Inferno**; translated by Robert Hollander and Jean Hollander; introduction & notes by Robert Hollander. Doubleday 2000 704p hardcover o.p. pa $16.95 **851**
1. Poetry -- By individual authors
ISBN 978-0-385-49698-8 pa; 0-385-49698-2 pa
LC 00-34531
A translation of Dante's poem, in which the Roman poet Virgil guides Dante through the underworld.

"The heart of the Hollanders' edition is the translation itself, which nicely balances the precision required for a much-interpreted allegory and the poetic qualities that draw most readers to the work. The result is a terse, lean Dante with its own kind of beauty. . . . The Hollanders' lines will satisfy both the poetry lover and scholar; they are at once literary, accessible and possessed of the seeming transparence that often characterizes great translations. The Italian text is included on the facing page for easy reference, along with notes drawing on some 60 Dante scholars, several indexes, a list of works cited and an introduction by Robert Hollander." Publ Wkly
Includes bibliographical references

Paradiso; a verse translation by Robert & Jean Hollander; introduction & notes by Robert Hollander. Doubleday 2007 915p $40; pa $19.95 **851**
1. Italian poetry -- Translations into English 2. Poetry -- By individual authors
ISBN 978-0-385-50678-6; 0-385-50678-3; 978-1-4000-3115-3 pa; 1-4000-3115-X pa
LC 2007-18070
This is a verse translation of the third volume of Dante's Divine Comedy with the original Italian text on facing pages and an introduction and notes.

"Dante's terza rima is impossible to recreate satisfactorily in English, but the Hollanders have produced a fine verse substitute. . . . Splendid as this new translation is, the endlessly valuable notes are what make this edition supplant all others. The commentary here has evolved not only from extensive research but also from the famous Dante Seminar Hollander has taught at Princeton for many years." Natl Rev

Purgatorio; a verse translation by Jean and Robert Hollander; introduction and notes by Robert Hollander. Doubleday 2003 xxiv, 742p hardcover o.p. pa $18.95 **851**
1. Poetry -- By individual authors
ISBN 978-0-385-49700-8 pa
LC 2002-67100
"To enter Dante's Purgatorio is to step into a charmed world, balanced by the rhythmic interplay of sleep, dreams, light, shadows, smiles, tears, and the reverberations of both solo and choral song. This is the most aesthetically vibrant of Dante's three realms, the one in which the artisanal gestures of poet, painter, and musician prevail. . . . The Hollanders have rendered both the supple lyricism and the rich imagery of the Purgatorio with an admirably informed expertise, preserving the stately economy of Dante's Italian throughout." Literary Rev (Madison, N. J.)
Includes bibliographical references

★ The **divine** comedy; translated by Allen Mandelbaum; with an introduction by Eugenio Montale; and notes by Peter Armour. Alfred A. Knopf 1995 798p il $25   **851**
1. Poetry -- By individual authors
ISBN 978-0-679-43313-2; 0-679-43313-9
LC 95-75206
An epic poem, completed in 1321, in which the poet describes his visionary spiritual journey through Hell, Purgatory and Paradise—guided first by the classical poet Vergil and then by his beloved Beatrice—which results in a purification of his religious faith.

The **portable** Dante; translated, edited, and with an introduction and notes by Mark Musa. Penguin Bks. 1995 xliii, 654p pa $17   **851**
1. Poetry -- By individual authors
ISBN 0-14-243754-9
LC 94-15988
Contains complete verse translations of The Divine comedy and La vita nuova.

This book "contains complete verse translations of Dante's two masterworks, The Divine Comedy and La Vita Nuova, as well as a bibliography, notes, and an introduction by . . . Mark Musa." Publisher's note
Includes bibliographical references

Montale, Eugenio

★ **Collected** poems, 1920-1954; translated and annotated by Jonathan Galassi. rev ed; Farrar, Straus & Giroux 2000 625p pa $18   **851**
1. Poetry -- By individual authors
ISBN 0-374-52625-7
LC 00-35456
"It is generally agreed that the core of Montale's work consists of three major collections: Cuttlefish Bones (1925),

The Occasions (1939), and The Storm, etc. (1956). Galassi chooses to publish all three together, separating them from a body of work of almost equal length that came later. He defends this decision in a brilliant afterword that offers the best short account I have yet come across of the nature, import, and elusive content of Montale's work." N Y Rev Books {review of 1997 edition}

Includes bibliographical references

The **collected** poems of Eugenio Montale 1925-1977; translated by William Arrowsmith; edited by Rosanna Warren. W. W. Norton & Co. 2012 793 p.   **851**

ISBN 0393080633; 9780393080636

LC 2011034993

This poetry collection features works of the 20th-century Nobel Prize-winning writer Eugenio Montale, edited by Rosanna Warren and translated by William Arrowsmith. Hailed as one of the key poets of the modern era, Eugenio Montale . . . helped to create international Modernism. . . . His poems chart [a] . . . response to the shocks of modernity, fascism, and two world wars. . . . [This collection] presents . . . translations of Poetic Diary 1971, 1972, and the Poetic Notebook, as well as his previously published translations of four volumes: Cuttlefish Bones, The Occasions, The Storm and Other Things, and Satura. (Publishers note)

Saba, Umberto

Songbook; the selected poems of Umberto Saba. translated by George Hochfield and Leonard Nathan; introduction, notes, and commentary by George Hochfield. Yale University Press 2009 562p $35 **851**

1. Poetry -- By individual authors

ISBN 978-0-300-13603-6; 0-300-13603-X

LC 2008-17685

"The author of more than fifteen individual books of poetry and a thousand pages of prose, Saba is best known for his Il Canzoniere (The Songbook), a continually revised and augmented collection in poems of his life's work. . . . [This volume] has been handsomely produced by Yale University Press; not among the least of its attractions is how well it fits in the hand. The edition includes, among other work, a generous number of Saba's earliest poems; all fifteen sonnets of his important Autobiografia (1924); several of his experimental works of 1928-29, titled Preludes and Fugues; and a sampling of his late-life poems, including his beautiful sequence Uccelli (Birds) from 1948. . . . Clearly a labor of love, these collaborative versions, presented with the Italian on facing pages, occupied Hochfield and Nathan for more than a decade." Nation

854   Italian essays

Eco, Umberto

How to travel with a salmon & other essays; translated from the Italian by William Weaver. Harcourt Brace & Co. 1994 248p il hardcover o.p. pa $15   **854**

ISBN 978-0-15-600125-0 pa; 0-15-600125-X pa

LC 94-10340

"In this collection of parodies, satires and whimsical mini-essays written over the last 30 years, Italian novelist/critic Eco . . . takes readers on a delightful romp through the absurdities of modern life." Publ Wkly

860   Literatures of Spanish, Portuguese, Galician languages

Gonzalez Echevarria, Roberto

The **Cambridge** history of Latin American literature; edited by Roberto González Echevarría and Enrique Pupo-Walker. Cambridge Univ. Press 1996 3v ea $180   **860**

1. Latin American literature -- History and criticism

ISBN 0-521-34069-1 v1; 0-521-34070-5 v2; 0-521-41035-5 v3

LC 93-37750

"The editors have added an interdisciplinary dimension to their work by incorporating the materials and methodologies proper to history. . . . [This] will become a classic in the field." Choice

★ The Cambridge history of Spanish literature; edited by David T. Gies. Cambridge University Press 2004 863p $160   **860**

1. Spanish literature -- History and criticism

ISBN 0-521-80618-6

LC 2004-45601

"The classics of the canon of eleven centuries of Spanish literature are covered, from Berceo, Cervantes and Calderón to García Lorca and Martín Gaite, but attention is also paid to lesser-known writers and works. . . . The volume concludes with a consideration of the influences of film and new media on modern Spanish literature." Publisher's note

Includes bibliographical references

★ Concise encyclopedia of Latin American literature; editor, Verity Smith. Fitzroy Dearborn Pubs. 2000 xxi, 678p $75   **860**

1. Latin American literature 2. Latin American literature -- Bio-bibliography 3. Latin American literature -- Encyclopedias 4. Reference books

ISBN 1-57958-252-4

Contains entries on 50 leading writers and 50 important works of Latin American and Caribbean literature. Also includes survey articles on the literature of individual countries and topical essays. Bibliographies of primary and secondary sources are listed

861   Spanish poetry

Aleixandre, Vicente

A **longing** for the light; selected poems of Vicente Aleixandre. edited by Lewis Hyde. 2nd ed; Copper Canyon Press 2007 xxi, 279p pa $18 **861**

1. Poetry -- By individual authors

ISBN 978-1-55659-254-6; 1-55659-254-X

LC 2007-992

This "is the only available bilingual Spanish-English translation of the poetry of Nobel Laureate Vicente Aleixandre. The collection spans the entirety of Aleixandre's career—from early surrealist work to his complex and fascinating 'dialogues.' It also contains prose interludes, an introduction by editor Lewis Hyde, and a descriptive bibliography." Publisher's note

Borges, Jorge Luis

★ **Selected** poems; edited by Alexander Coleman. Viking 1999 477p hardcover o.p. pa $20 **861**
1. Poetry -- By individual authors
ISBN 0-14-058721-7 pa

LC 99-10318

"Poetry is the heart of Borges' metaphysical, mythical, and cosmopolitan oeuvre. . . . Editor Coleman commissioned a wealth of new translations for this unprecedented and invaluable collection, and the roster of translators includes such luminaries as Robert S. Fitzgerald, W.S. Merwin, Mark Strand, and John Updike." Booklist

Cardenal, Ernesto

Pluriverse; new and selected poems. edited by Jonathan Cohen; with a foreword by Lawrence Ferlinghetti; translations from the Spanish by Jonathan Cohen [et al.] New Directions Pub. 2009 249p pa $17.95 **861**
1. Poetry -- By individual authors
ISBN 978-0-8112-1809-2 pa; 0-8112-1809-0 pa

LC 2008-40582

"Cardenal, now in his 80s, is a Roman Catholic priest and was a leading light of the Nicaraguan Sandinistas. One of his country's most revered figures, Cardenal is these days being persecuted by President Daniel Ortega, the leader whose legend Cardenal did much to create and who has slid now into authoritarian rule. Such tends to be the fate of the revolutionary writer. Cardenal is political, of course, and much of the work presented here (translated by many illustrious hands, including Jonathan Cohen, Thomas Merton and Kenneth Rexroth) deals with the struggle and history of his country and Latin America at large. But he can sing lyrically too. . . . Beautiful." Los Angeles Times Book Rev

Cid

★ The **poem** of the Cid; translated by Rita Hamilton and Janet Perry; with an introduction and notes by Ian Michael. Penguin 1984 242p map pa $14 **861**
1. Poetry -- By individual authors
ISBN 0-14-044446-7

"The poem is based on the exploits of Rodrigo or Ruy Diaz de Bivar (c.1043-1099), who was known as 'el Cid.' . . . Similar in form to the 'Chanson de Roland,' the poem is notable for its simplicity and directness and for its exact, picturesque detail. Despite the inclusion of much legendary material, the figure of the Cid who is depicted as the model Castilian warrior, is not idealized to an extravagant degree." Reader's Ency. 4th edition

Garcia Lorca, Federico

Collected poems; edited and with an introduction and notes by Christopher Maurer; translated by Fran-

cisco Aragon [et al.] Farrar, Straus & Giroux 1991 893p hardcover o.p. pa $25 **861**
1. Poetry -- By individual authors
ISBN 978-0-374-52691-7; 0-374-52691-5 pa

This bilingual edition of Garcia Lorca's poetry, "which modestly claims not to be 'definitive,' includes every poem written by the acclaimed Spanish poet except Poet in New York. Assembled in the light of recent scholarship, its contents have been rendered into English by newer translators such as Alan S. Trueblood, Catherine Brown, Will Kirkland, and Greg Simon; older translators such as Stephen Spender, Langston Hughes, and Ben Belitt are not represented. Generally, rhyme and assonance are sacrificed to the 'silent counterpoint of poetic meaning,' and old-fashioned diction is avoided." Libr J

Poet in New York; edited and with an introduction and notes by Christopher Maurer; translated by Greg Simon and Steven F. White. Farrar, Straus & Giroux 1988 xxx, 275p il pa $18 **861**
1. Poetry -- By individual authors
ISBN 978-0-374-52540-8; 0-374-52083-4

LC 87-33154

This "is one of the perplexing classics of twentieth-century poetry. It is a difficult, sometimes bewildered, often hermetic work. It is elusive and enigmatic, mysterious, tortured—a book, to borrow one of the poet's own phrases, 'that can baptize in dark water all who look at it.' Reading it in [this] convincing new translation, . . . one feels the anguished authority and the demonic force and impact of the original. For all its strangeness, Lorca's testament may well be one of the greatest books of poems ever written about New York City." New Yorker
Includes bibliographical references

Juana Ines de la Cruz

★ A **Sor** Juana anthology; translated by Alan S. Trueblood; with a foreword by Octavio Paz. Harvard Univ. Press 1988 248p hardcover o.p. pa $23 **861**
1. Poetry -- By individual authors
ISBN 0-674-82121-1 pa

LC 87-27693

This volume "offers a useful sampling and English rendition of Sor Juana's work. Poetry predominates among the selections. . . . Given the difficulty of Mr. Trueblood's task—attempting to capture in English the voice of a poet who herself mastered many poetic languages—his translations are admirable." N Y Times Book Rev
Includes bibliographical references

Neruda, Pablo

★ The **poetry** of Pablo Neruda; edited and with an introduction by Ilan Stavans. Farrar, Straus and Giroux 2003 996p hardcover o.p. pa $20 **861**
1. Authors 2. Diplomats 3. Nobel laureates for literature 4. Nobel laureates for peace 5. Novelists 6. Poetry -- By individual authors 7. Poets
ISBN 0-374-29995-1; 0-374-52960-4 pa

LC 2002-32548

"Stavans has assembled the most complete anthology of Neruda yet available in English, drawing evenhandedly from the various stages of the poet's long and complex career. Neruda was, it seems, at least half a dozen poets, many of them in competition with the others. Needless to say, there are wonders in these pages that will delight readers unfamiliar with the tumultuously varied planet known as Neruda." Nation

Includes bibliographical references

Paz, Octavio

★ The **collected** poems of Octavio Paz, 1957-1987; edited & translated by Eliot Weinberger; with additional translations by Elizabeth Bishop [et al.] New Directions 1987 669p il hardcover o.p. pa $26.95 **861**

1. Poetry -- By individual authors
ISBN 978-0-8112-1173-4 pa; 0-8112-1173-8 pa
LC 87-23989

"Dense, weighty, and miraculous, this bilingual edition compresses into one volume all the poems published in book form since 1957. Nearly 200 poems, some newly translated, many new to an English-language edition, conclusively demonstrate Paz's power." Libr J

Includes bibliographical references

Torre, Monica de la

Reversible monuments; contemporary Mexican poetry. edited by Mónica de la Torre and Michael Wiegers. Copper Canyon Press 2002 675p pa $20 **861**

1. Mexican poetry -- 20th century 2. Mexican poetry -- 20th century -- Translations into English 3. Mexican poetry -- Collections
ISBN 1-55659-159-4
LC 2002-6189

This bilingual anthology includes 31 contributors, "most writing in Spanish but some in indigenous languages. Spacious and accommodating, this work presents a generous number of gracefully translated poems by each poet, a felicitous in-depth approach that makes this much more than a sampler, and a sound decision given the poet's propensity for long, dreamy poems. Sensuality is ever-present, as is an intimate connection with nature. . . . This is without doubt a landmark volume." Booklist

The Penguin book of Spanish verse; introduced and edited by J.M. Cohen; with plain prose translations of each poem. 3rd ed; Penguin 1988 xliii, 596p pa $18 **861**

1. Spanish poetry -- Collections
ISBN 978-0-14-058570-4; 0-14-058570-2
LC 88-166999

More than 300 works by 100 poets reflect nine centuries of poetry in Spain.

Twentieth century Latin American poetry; a bilingual anthology. edited by Stephen Tapscott. University of Tex. Press 1996 xxii, 418p il hardcover o.p. pa $26.95 **861**

1. Latin American poetry -- Collections
ISBN 0-292-78140-7 pa
LC 95-40288

This anthology "samples the works of more than 75 poets, including such giants as Neruda, Dario, Reyes, Vallejo, Borges and Paz. With original-language versions and translations set side by side, the collection is arranged in order of the poets' dates of birth from José Marti, born in Cuba in 1853, to Marjorie Agosin, born in the U.S. 102 years later. Tapscott's well-conceived and lucid introduction is expanded in concise individual introductions that provide basic information and some evaluation." Publ Wkly

Includes bibliographical references

862   Spanish drama

Calderon de la Barca, Pedro

Life's a dream; a prose translation and critical introduction by Michael Kidd. University Press of Colorado 2004 159p hardcover o.p. pa $13.95 **862**

ISBN 978-0-87081-777-9 pa
LC 2004-10260

17th century Spanish verse play in prose translation. King of Poland tests son, imprisoned from birth because of prophecy, to see if he will become tyrant. Savage at first, Prince later shows true nobility, exposing actual meaning of prophecy.

"Michael Kidd advances the work of two often-exclusive camps of comediantes: scholarship and performance. While his introduction provides ample criticism for the scholar, he successfully presents an accessible script for theatre practitioners looking to enact the story of the play." Bulletin of Hispanic Studies

Includes bibliographical references

Garcia Lorca, Federico

Four major plays; translated by John Edmunds; introduction by Nicholas Round; notes by Ann MacLaren. Oxford University Press 1999 xli, 234p pa $11.95 **862**

ISBN 978-0-19-283938-1
LC 00-703215

Edmunds's "versions are accurate . . . faithful . . . fluent and idiomatic; they look like utterances of English. . . . Readers can be sure that the texts will not lead them astray, but they will also be grateful for the quite excellent introductory essay by Nick Round. This is a characteristically gritty display of erudition and common sense." Times Lit Suppl

Includes bibliographical references

Vega, Lope de

Three major plays; translated with an introduction and notes by Gwynne Edwards. Oxford University Press 2008 xli, 300p pa $14.95 **862**

ISBN 978-0-19-954017-4; 0-19-954017-9
LC 98-26991

"Fuente Ovejuna, based on Spanish history, and revealing how tyranny leads to rebellion, is perhaps [Vega's] best-known play. The Knight from Olmedo is a moving dramatization of impetuous and youthful passion which ends in death. Punishment without Revenge, Lope's most powerful tragedy, centres on the illicit relationship of a young wife with her stepson and the revenge of a dishonoured husband." Publisher's note

Includes bibliographical references

863   Spanish fiction

Allende, Isabel

My invented country; a nostalgic journey through Chile. translated from the Spanish by Margaret Sayers Peden. HarperCollins Pubs. 2003 199p map $23.95; pa $13.95   863

1. Authors 2. Authors, Chilean 3. Authors, Chilean -- 20th century -- Biography 4. Children's authors 5. Dramatists 6. Journalists 7. Novelists

ISBN 0-06-054564-X; 0-06-054567-4 pa

LC 2002-191267

"In this memoir-cum-study of her 'home ground,' the author delves into the history, social mores and idiosyncrasies of Chile, where she was raised, showing, in the process, how that land has served as her muse. . . . This is a reflective book, lacking the pull of Allende's fiction but unearthing intriguing elements of the author's captivating history." Publ Wkly

864   Spanish essays

Borges, Jorge Luis

★ Selected non-fictions; edited by Eliot Weinberger; translated by Esther Allen, Suzanne Jill Levine & Eliot Weinberger. Viking 1999 559p hardcover o.p. pa $20   864

ISBN 978-0-14-029011-0 pa; 0-14-029011-7 pa

LC 99-12386

"Shifting effortlessly from Homer to Hitler, from Kafka to King Kong, these hundred and sixty-one essays, appreciations, prologues, and philosophical investigations are dizzying in scope and dazzling in execution. But it is Borges's dogged pursuit of familiar themes—infinity and eternity, reflexivity and recurrence—which gives this collection its unusual unity and depth." New Yorker

Includes bibliographical references

Fuentes, Carlos

Myself with others; selected essays. Farrar, Straus & Giroux 1988 214p $19.95; pa $18   864

ISBN 0-374-21750-5; 0-374-52237-5 pa

LC 87-7448

Essays by the Mexican writer on subjects ranging from the cinema of Buñuel to the literary output of Cervantes, Borges and Garcia Marquez.

Paz, Octavio

★ The labyrinth of solitude; The other Mexico, Return to the labyrinth of solitude, Mexico and the United States, The philanthropic ogre. Grove Press 1985 398p hardcover o.p. pa $14.50   864

1. Mexican national characteristics

ISBN 978-0-8021-5042-4 pa; 0-8021-5042-X pa

LC 82-47999

In this collection of essays and one interview, Paz explorers the cultural and historical influences on the social behavior of his countrymen.

Vargas Llosa, Mario

The language of passion; translated by Natasha Wimmer. Farrar, Straus & Giroux 2003 292p $24; pa $14   864

ISBN 0-374-18326-0; 0-312-42254-7 pa

LC 2002-37909

"This collection focuses on the essays that appeared during the 1990s, most of which are imbued with a wit and an intellect that make them instantly engaging." Libr J

Includes bibliographical references

868   Spanish miscellaneous writings

Abad, Hector

Oblivion; a memoir. Héctor Abad; translated from the Spanish by Anne McLean and Rosalind Harvey. Farrar, Straus and Giroux 2012 263 p.   868

1. Authors, Colombian -- 20th century -- Biography 2. Biography & Autobiography -- Literary 3. Biography & Autobiography -- Political 4. Physicians -- Colombia -- Biography 5. Political activists -- Colombia -- Biography 6. Political activists -- Crimes against

ISBN 0374223971; 9780374223977

LC 2011045885

This memoir by Héctor Abad describes the life and work of the authors father Héctor Abad Gómez, a professor and doctor devoted to his family, moved to tearsby poetry and music, and committed to a better Colombia. The latter aspiration cost him his life when he was assassinated in 1987, and his son began writing this book five years later. Abad spends much of the book expressing his love for his father, . . . but also discusses Gómez's public health and human rights projectssuch as founding the Colombian Institute of Family Wellbeing, which built aqueducts and sewer systems in villages, rural districts, and cities." (Publishers Weekly)

869   Literatures of Portuguese and Galician languages

Antunes, Antonio Lobo

The fat man and infinity; and other writings. translated with an introduction by Margaret Jull Costa. W. W. Norton & Company 2009 396p il $26.95   869

1. Authors 2. Biography, Individual 3. Novelists 4. Short stories -- By individual authors

ISBN 978-0-393-06198-7; 0-393-06198-1

LC 2008-41551

This volume "collects the short, impressionistic newspaper columns, or 'cronicas,' that [Antunes] has written for various publications, notably the Portuguese newspaper O Público. Mr. Antunes has played down these columns, referring to them as 'divertissments' written to earn pocket money. But as this book's translator, Margaret Jull Costa, points out, in Portugal these collections 'have enjoyed the kind of popular success his novels never have.' (This book also contains a selection of Mr. Antunes's short stories. . .). Mr. Antunes makes for an unusual newspaper columnist. Jimmy Breslin he's not. His bite-size essays contain no political ruminations and almost nothing about sports, or popular culture, or literary criticism or run-ins with the great and good. Instead they are interior diaries of a kind, most of them imbued with a deep nostalgia for the author's youth." N Y Times Book Rev

Camoes, Luis de
★ **Selected** sonnets; edited and translated by William Baer. Bilingual ed; University of Chicago Press 2005 199p il $26   **869**
  1. Poetry -- By individual authors
  ISBN 0-226-09266-6
                  LC 2004-58521
Camões "is Portugal's great sonneteer. He published only one sonnet in his lifetime, and many of doubtful authorship crept into the canon during their first century of great popularity. Baer presents 70 in Portuguese and his own English versions, formally faithful to the originals except that in the octaves Baer uses four (abba, cddc) rather than Camoes' two (abba, abba) rhymes. A sketch of Camoes' amazingly adventurous and colorful life, his works, and his reputation precedes the poems." Booklist

Lispector, Clarice
★ **Selected** cronicas; translated by Giovanni Pontiero. New Directions 1996 212p pa $12.95 **869**
  ISBN 0-8112-1340-4
                  LC 96-23768
"In these crônicas—part anecdote, memoir, observation, essay—the late avante-garde writer shows herself to have been as adept at short nonfiction as she was at short fiction. Based on a column she began writing at the behest of Brazil's leading newspaper in 1967, these pieces bring together the lyricism of poetry to everyday reality." Publ Wkly

Pessoa, Fernando
★ **Fernando** Pessoa & Co. selected poems. edited and translated from the Portuguese by Richard Zenith. Grove Press 1998 290p hardcover o.p. pa $14   **869**
  1. Poetry -- By individual authors
  ISBN 978-0-8021-3627-5 pa; 0-8021-3627-3 pa
                  LC 97-50201
"Pessoa developed his poetic opus through the mouthpieces of distinct and separate literary personalities called heteronyms. . . . This collection includes selections from three of those alter egos—the bucolic pagan Caeiro, the Epicurean classicist Reis, and the sensational modernist Campos—plus the 'real' Pessoa." Libr J
Includes bibliographical references

870   Latin literature and literatures of related Italic languages

★ The **Portable** Roman reader; edited, and with an introduction by Basil Davenport. Viking 1951 656p hardcover o.p. pa $18   **870**
  1. Latin literature -- Collections
  ISBN 0-14-015056-0 pa
This anthology includes selections from Plautus, Terence, Caesar, Virgil, Seneca, Juvenal as well as complete plays by Plautus and Terence and the anonymous poem Vigil of Venus.

871   Latin poetry

Horace
The **epistles** of Horace; [translated by] David Ferry. Farrar, Straus, and Giroux 2001 203p hardcover o.p. pa $19   **871**
  1. Poetry -- By individual authors
  ISBN 978-0-374-52852-7 pa; 0-374-52852-7 pa
                  LC 00-52746
"Ferry takes his bearings from the great blank verse poets of the last two hundred years, especially Frost, and while he manages to be faithful to the meaning, substance and shades, of the Latin original, Ferry achieves through his historical, cultural, and linguistic cross-pollination something more important and lasting than mere translation: he brings to life new as well as old possibilities for poetry in America now." Harvard Rev
Includes bibliographical references

Virgil
The **eclogues** of Virgil; a translation by David Ferry. Farrar, Straus & Giroux 1999 101p hardcover o.p. pa $14   **871**
  1. Country life -- Rome -- Poetry 2. Pastoral poetry, Latin -- Translations into English 3. Poetry -- By individual authors
  ISBN 978-0-374-52696-2 pa; 0-374-52696-6 pa
                  LC 98-52547
The Eclogues "comprise not much more than 800 lines in total, but they may be the most influential collection of short poems by one author ever written. . . . It is a conspicuous merit of Ferry's translations that they have a kind of transparency; he does not intrude his style or his personality between the reader and himself. His versions are rather plain, unfussy, and usually of a quiet dignity." New Republic

★ The **Roman** poets; selected and edited by Peter Washington. Knopf 1997 253p il $12.50 **871**
  1. Latin poetry -- Collections
  ISBN 0-375-40071-0
                  LC 98-124022
A representative selection of classical Latin verse.

872 Latin dramatic poetry and drama

Plautus, Titus Maccius

The **pot** of gold, and other plays; [by] Plautus; tr. by E. F. Watling. Penguin Books 1965 267p pa $12 **872**

ISBN 978-0-14-044149-9; 0-14-044149-2

LC 65-8577

Plautus "romanized many of the plots and characters of New Greek Comedy. Through his plays, he introduced to the non-Greek world characters which have since become part of traditional western European comedy, among them the braggard soldier (in his Miles Gloriosus) and the sly servant (in his Pseudolus)." Benet's Reader's Ency. 4th edition

The **rope,** and other plays; [by] Plautus; tr. by E. F. Watling. Penguin Books 1964 284p pa $12 **872**

ISBN 978-0-14-044136-9; 0-14-044136-0

LC 63-2117

Terence

Terence, the comedies; translations by Palmer Bovie, Constance Carrier, and Douglass Parker; edited by Palmer Bovie. Johns Hopkins Univ. Press 1992 xxi, 398p hardcover o.p. pa $25 **872**

ISBN 978-0-8018-4354-9 pa; 0-8018-4354-5 pa

LC 91-33984

Virgil

The **Georgics** of Virgil; a translation. a translation [translated] by David Ferry. Farrar, Straus and Giroux 2005 xx, 202p hardcover o.p. pa $14 **872**

ISBN 978-0-374-16131-0; 0-374-16131-9 pa

LC 2004-20023

"Ferry shows tremendous skill with his taut yet pliant pentameter. He also employs demotic and high lyrical diction with equal finesse. His version contains all the freshness of American speech and all the classical poise of the original: it comes across neither as a curatorial act of conservation nor as a modish remake. . . . This is the best poetry of Ancient Rome, rendered by the best translator of modern America." Poetry (Modern Poetry Association)

873 Latin epic poetry and fiction

Aeneid

The **Aeneid**; translated by Robert Fitzgerald. Knopf 1992 xxvii, 483 $20 **873**

1. Poetry -- By individual authors

ISBN 978-0-679-41335-6; 0-679-41335-9

LC 91-58698

"Fitzgerald's is so decisively the best modern Aeneid that it is unthinkable anyone will want to use any other version for a long time to come. Latinists, as they read it, will be led to consider their original afresh. Those without Latin are going to find, to their surprise, and I hope their pleasure, that the poem is still as good as anyone ever said it was." N Y Rev Books

Ovid

★ **Metamorphoses**; [by] Ovid; translated and with notes by Charles Martin; introduction by Bernard Knox. W.W. Norton & Co 2004 xxvi, 597p $57; pa $17.95 **873**

ISBN 0-393-05810-7; 0-393-32642-X pa

LC 2003-14491

"A series of tales in Latin verse. . . . Dealing with mythological, legendary, and historical figures, they are written in hexameters, in fifteen books, beginning with the creation of the world and ending with the deification of Caesar and the reign of Augustus." Reader's Ency. 4th edition

Includes bibliographical references

★ **Tales** from Ovid; [translated by] Ted Hughes. Farrar, Straus & Giroux 1997 257p hardcover o.p. pa $14 **873**

1. Poetry -- By individual authors

ISBN 0-374-52587-0 pa

LC 97-36061

Hughes retells 24 Greco-Roman myths from Ovid's Latin epic Metamorphoses.

This is "an inspired act of translation that stands as vigorous poetry in its own right." N Y Times Book Rev

Includes bibliographical references

874 Latin lyric poetry

Catullus, Gaius Valerius

The **poems** of Catullus; translated by Charles Martin. Johns Hopkins Univ. Press 1990 181p hardcover o.p. pa $19.95 **874**

1. Poetry -- By individual authors

ISBN 978-0-8018-3926-9 pa; 0-8018-3926-2 pa

LC 89-45486

"The introduction ranges through Martin's observations on Catullus' place among Roman lyricists, his virtuosity, acuity, irony, and appeal to modern poets. The translations themselves, while open to inevitable quibbling among Latinists, are remarkably true to the versification, denotations, and connotations of the original texts. Martin is particularly adept at shaping the English into approximations of the Latin meters." Choice

Horace

The **odes** of Horace; a translation by David Ferry. Farrar, Straus & Giroux 1997 343p hardcover o.p. pa $28 **874**

1. Poetry -- By individual authors

ISBN 978-0-374-52572-9 pa; 0-374-52572-2 pa

LC 97-9483

Ferry "wisely does not try to reproduce Horace's meters in English. . . . And he often rearranges Horace's material to fit the run of his own verse, sometimes to stunning effect. . . . This is a Horace for our times." N Y Rev Books

875   Latin speeches

Cicero, Marcus Tullius

  Political speeches; [by] Cicero; translated with introductions and notes by D.H. Berry. Oxford University Press 2006 xl, 345p map pa $13.95   **875**
  1. Speeches
  ISBN 978-0-19-283266-5; 0-19-283266-2
                          LC 2005-20919

  "Cicero (106-43 BC) was the greatest orator of the ancient world and a leading politician of the closing era of the Roman republic. This book presents nine speeches which reflect the development, variety, and drama of his political career,among them two speeches from his prosecution of Verres, a corrupt and cruel governor of Sicily; four speeches against the conspirator Catiline; and the Second Philippic, the famous denunciation of Mark Antony which cost Cicero his life. Also included are On the Command of Gnaeus Pompeius , in which he praises the military successes of Pompey, and For Marcellus , a panegyric in praise of the dictator Julius Caesar." Publisher's note
  Includes bibliographical references

877   Latin humor and satire

Erasmus, Desiderius

  ★ **Praise** of folly; and, Letter to Maarten Van Dorp, 1515. [by] Erasmus of Rotterdam; translated by Betty Radice; with an introduction and notes by A.H.T. Levi. Penguin Books 1993 lvi, 188p pa $13   **877**
  ISBN 978-014-044608-1; 0-14-044608-7
                        LC 94-142502

  A "satirical monologue in Latin. . . . Folly praises herself and proclaims her superiority over Wisdom. The author's argument, of course, is 'that it is folly not to see things as they really are; scholars should not abandon ideals just because they cannot be fully realized but should apply their learning and reason as best they can to daily living.'" Reader's Adviser

Juvenal

  ★ The **sixteen** satires; translated with an introduction and notes by Peter Green. 3rd ed; Penguin Books 1999 lxviii, 252p pa $13   **877**
  ISBN 978-0-14-044704-0; 0-14-044704-0
                        LC 99-987049

  "The sixteen 'Satires' of Juvenal, which contain a vivid picture of contemporary Rome under the Empire, have seldom been equalled as biting diatribes. . . . Juvenal's invectives in powerful hexameters, exact and epigrammatic, were aimed at lax and luxurious society, tyranny, criminal excesses, and the immorality of women." Reader's Adviser

878   Latin miscellaneous writings

Caesar, Julius

  ★ The **Gallic** War; with an English translation by H. J. Edwards. Harvard Univ. Press 1958 xxii, 616p il maps $21.50   **878**
  ISBN 0-674-99080-3

  Caesar's account of his campaign (58-50 B.C.) to bring the province of Gaul (France) under his control.

Cicero, Marcus Tullius

  On the good life; translated with an introduction by Michael Grant. Penguin Books 1971 382p map pa $16   **878**
  1. Ethics
  ISBN 978-0-14-044244-1; 0-14-044244-8
                        LC 77-30399

  For "Roman orator and statesman Cicero, 'the good life' was at once a life of contentment and one of moral virtue and the two were inescapably intertwined. This volume brings together a wide range of his reflections upon the importance of moral integrity in the search for happiness. . . . Cicero presents his views upon the significance of friendship and duty to state and family, and outlines a clear system of practical ethics." Publisher's note

Martial

  Epigrams; selected and translated by James Michie; introduction by Shadi Bartsch. Modern Library 2002 xxxiv, 199p pa $14.95 **878**
  1. Epigrams
  ISBN 978-0-375-76042-6; 0-375-76042-3
                        LC 2002-22343

  Michie "has translated a selection of the epigrams— about one tenth of what Martial wrote. He has the text on the facing page—a great advantage if you can read Latin—an Introduction [and] Notes. . . . [He] uses rhyme, and makes his Martial much more like the English idea of an epigram than like the epigrams in the Greek Anthology. There isn't much pure humor in Latin literature (as opposed to waspishness and scurrility) but Martial is often very funny." Encounter (London, England)
  Includes bibliographical references

Suetonius Tranquillus, C.

  ★ The **twelve** Caesars; {by} Gaius Suetonius Tranquillus; translated by Robert Graves; revised with an introduction by Michael Grant. Penguin Bks. 2003 363p maps pa $14   **878**
  1. Emperors 2. Emperors -- Rome
  ISBN 0-14-044921-3
                        LC 2003-267782

  "A detailed account of the life and times of the first twelve emperors from Caesar to Domitian." Reader's Ency. 4th edition
  Includes bibliographical references

Tacitus, Cornelius

  ★ **Complete** works of Tacitus; translated from the Latin by Alfred John Church and William Jackson

Brodribb; edited and with an introduction by Moses Hadas. McGraw-Hill 1964 773p il pa $14.75 **878**

1. Colonial administrators 2. Generals

ISBN 0-07-553639-0; 978-0-07-553639-0

880 Classical Greek literature and literatures of related Hellenic languages

Thorburn, John E.

★ The **Facts** on File companion to classical drama. Facts on File 2005 680p map $71.50 **880**

1. Classical drama 2. Classical drama -- Encyclopedias 3. Reference books

ISBN 0-8160-5202-6

LC 2004-16803

"It is difficult to think of any other resource quite this thorough that combines all of Greek and Roman drama into a convenient single-volume publication." Libr J

Includes bibliographical references

★ The Norton book of classical literature; edited by Bernard Knox. Norton 1993 866p $29.95 **880**

1. Classical literature -- Collections 2. Greek literature -- Collections

ISBN 0-393-03426-7

LC 92-10378

"A comprehensive volume of more than 300 pieces of classical literature, primarily Greek but also some Roman." Booklist

★ The Oxford companion to classical literature; edited by M.C. Howatson. 3rd ed.; Oxford University Press 2011 un map $65 **880**

1. Classical literature -- Dictionaries 2. Reference books

ISBN 978-0-19-954854-5

This work "covers classical literature from the appearance of the Greeks, around 2200 B.C., to the close of the Athenian philosophy schools in A.D. 529. It includes articles on authors, major works, historical notables, mythological figures, and topics of literary significance. Short summaries of major works, chronologies, charts, and maps are special features." Nichols. Guide to Ref Books for Sch Media Cent. 4th edition

★ The classical Greek reader; edited by Kenneth J. Atchity; associate editor, Rosemary McKenna. Oxford University Press 1998 xxxiv, 442p il pa $24.95 **880**

1. Greek literature -- Collections

ISBN 0-19-512303-4

LC 98-12978

This reader provides excerpts from the works of classical Greek writers.

"Across the centuries, ranging from the Homeric poets to Graeco-Roman writers of the third century A.D., we find ourselves in the company of physicians and storytellers, herbalists and romance writers—and women. Atchity is mining a tradition of inexhaustible riches: the voices we encounter here offer passage to the literary, artistic, social,

political, religious, scientific and philosophical texts that underlie Western intellectual tradition." Smithsonian

Includes bibliographical references

881 Classical Greek poetry

Apollonius

The **voyage** of Argo: the Argonautica; translated with an introd. by E.V. Rieu. 2nd ed; Penguin Books 1971 213p map pa $14 **881**

1. Argonauts (Greek mythology) 2. Poetry -- By individual authors

ISBN 978-0-14-044085-0; 0-14-044085-0

An epic account of Jason's voyage in quest of the Golden Fleece written in the third century B.C.

Hesiod

Works and days; and Theogony; translated by Stanley Lombardo; with introduction, notes, and glossary by Robert Lamberton. Hackett 1993 128p hardcover o.p. pa $10.95 **881**

1. Poetry -- By individual authors

ISBN 978-0-87220-179-8 pa; 0-87220-179-1 pa

LC 93-24545

This is a translation of two ancient Greek poems. "Theogony is a genealogy of the Greek gods and some of their myths, and the Works and Days is a meditation on work, justice, and the gods, together with a farmer's almanac of the ancient agricultural year.... For a literal rendition of the Greek, readers should turn elsewhere, but those who want a translation that captures something of the spirit of an ancient Greek poetic voice and its cultural milieu and transmits it in an appealing, lively, and accessible style will now turn to Lombardo." Choice

7 Greeks; translations by Guy Davenport. New Directions 1995 241p pa $16.95 **881**

1. Greek literature -- Collections

ISBN 978-0-8112-1288-5; 0-8112-1288-2

LC 95-4227

Davenport has translated a sampling of seventh- to third-century B.C.E. Greek poetry. "Included among the poems and fragments are lyrics by Archilochos, Sappho, Alkman, and Anakreon; philosophical verse by Herakleitos and Diogenes; and comic dramatic verse by Herondas. Arguing that no translation is final and occasionally offering several versions of the same work, Davenport attempts to capture the tone of the original rather than offering a literal or formal rendition." Libr J

★ The Oxford book of classical verse in translation; edited by Adrian Poole and Jeremy Maule. Oxford University Press 1995 xlix, 606p $45 **881**

1. Classical literature -- Collections 2. Classical poetry -- Collections

ISBN 0-19-214209-7

A "collection of classical verse from Homer to Boethius. Translations, modern and older, are brought together in a rich blending of Greek and Latin writings. Some of the greatest poets in the English language—Dryden, Pope, Tennyson, Poe, Byron, Yeats, Browning, Houseman, Wilde,

Shelley, and Pound are among the translators. They emphasize the debt English poetry owes to the classics." SLJ

882   Classical Greek dramatic poetry and drama

Aeschylus

Aeschylus; edited by David Grene and Richmond Lattimore. University of Chicago Press 1992 352p $55 **882**
  ISBN 978-0-226-30764-0; 0-226-30764-6

The **Oresteia**; translated by Alan Shapiro and Peter Bu-
rian. Oxford University Press 2003 285p hardcover o.p.
pa $11.95 **882**
  ISBN 978-0-19-513592-3 pa; 0-19-513592-X pa
                                            LC 2002-66272
"The collaboration of poet and scholar . . . produces a
language that is easy to read and easy to speak." Libr J
  Includes bibliographical references

Aristophanes

The **complete** plays; the new translations by
Paul Roche. New American Library 2005 715p pa
$17   **882**
  1. Athens (Greece) -- Drama.
  ISBN 978-0-451-21409-6; 0-451-21409-9
                                            LC 2004-56681

Euripides

Euripides; edited by David Grene and Richmond Lattimore. University of Chicago Press 1992 665p $65 **882**
  ISBN 978-0-226-30766-4; 0-226-30766-2

Euripides [2] edited by David Grene and Richmond Lattimore. University of Chicago Press 1992
314p $44   **882**
  ISBN 978-0-226-30767-1; 0-226-30767-0

Selections./English

The **Theban** plays of Sophocles; translated by
David R. Slavitt. Yale University Press 2007 237p
$28   **882**
  ISBN 978-0-300-11776-9; 0-300-11776-0
                                            LC 2006-26965
"This version is meant to be an updated one, and the easy
currency of its diction is a great virtue. The natural cadences
of its free verse slide smoothly and sometimes beautifully
into the ear." Claremont Rev Books
  Includes bibliographical references

Seneca, Lucius Annaeus

Four tragedies, and Octavia; [by] Seneca; tr.
with an introduction by E. F. Watling. Penguin Books
1966 318p pa $14   **882**
  ISBN 978-0-14-044174-1; 0-12-044174-3
                                            LC 66-8618
"Although their themes are borrowed from Greek drama,
these exuberant and often macabre plays focus on action
rather than moral concerns and are strikingly different in
style from Seneca's prose writing." Publisher's note

Sophocles

Sophocles; edited by David Grene and Richmond Lattimore. University of Chicago Press 1992 466p $50 **882**
  ISBN 978-0-226-30765-7; 0-226-30765-4

883   Classical Greek epic poetry and fiction

Alexander, Caroline

The **war** that killed Achilles; the true story of
Homer's Iliad and the Trojan War. Viking 2009 296p
map $26.95   **883**
  1. Achilles (Greek mythology) 2. Authors 3. Poets 4.
  Trojan War 5. Trojan War -- Literature and the war 6.
  War in literature
  ISBN 978-0-670-02112-3; 0-670-02112-1
                                            LC 2009-20160
"In its bones and sinews, the book is a nobly bold, even
rousing, venture, a read-through of the 'Iliad,' from beginning to end, always with a sharp eye to half a century of revealing scholarship, by great Hellenists like Gregory Nagy,
Jasper Griffin, M.L. West and many others. The book's best
ideas won't be new to readers versed in this work, but it
would be hard to find a faster, livelier, more compact introduction to such a great range of recent Iliadic explorations."
N Y Times Book Rev
  Includes bibliographical references

Homer

The **Iliad**; translated by Robert Fagles; introduction
and notes by Bernard Knox. Viking 1990 683p $40; pa
$15.95 **883**
  1. Poetry -- By individual authors 2. Trojan War
  ISBN 978-0-670-83510-2; 978-0-14-027536-0 pa
                                            LC 89-70695
Homer's epic of the Trojan War.
"Fagles gives us a stark and terrible poem, an Iliad about,
as its first word announces, rage. He conveys, far better than
either Lattimore or Fitzgerald, the psychological experience
of combat and war." Classical World

Iliad; translated by Stanley Lombardo; introduction
by Sheila Murnaghan. Hackett 1997 516p $37.95; pa
$12.95 **883**
  1. Poetry -- By individual authors
  ISBN 978-0-87220-353-2; 0-87220-353-0; 978-0-
  87220-352-5 pa; 0-87220-352-2 pa
                                            LC 96-53368
This is a translation from the Greek of the epic poem on
the Trojan War.
"Lombardo manages to be respectful of Homer's dire
spirit while providing on nearly every page some wonderfully fresh refashioning of his Greek. The result is a vivid
and sometimes disarmingly hard-bitten reworking of a great
classic. . . . Not all of Lombardo's gambles pay off, and his
attention-grabbing colloquialisms sometimes undermine
the force of the original. . . . Still, the success of so many
of Lombardo's choices more than makes up for the false
notes." N Y Times Book Rev

The **Iliad**; translated by Robert Fitzgerald. Knopf

1992 xxi, 594p $22 **883**
1. Poetry -- By individual authors
ISBN 978-0-679-41075-1; 0-679-41075-9

LC 91-53222

Homer's epic of the Trojan War in blank verse.

"Fitzgerald has solved virtually every problem that has plagued translators of Homer. The narrative runs, the dialogue speaks, the military action is clear, and the repetitive epithets become useful text rather than exotic relics. Aside from the ability to write poetry, which is basic to the undertaking, Mr. Fitzgerald's success derives from the use of a predominantly Anglo-Saxon vocabulary, a concentration on specific meanings, and an occasional arbitrary, but highly effective, substitution of implication for literal sense." Atlantic

Odyssey; translated by Stanley Lombardo; introduction by Sheila Murnaghan. Hackett 2000 414p il $37.95; pa $12.95 **883**
1. Epic poetry, Greek -- Translations into English 2. Odysseus (Greek mythology) -- Poetry 3. Poetry -- By individual authors
ISBN 978-0-87220-485-0; 0-87220-485-5; 978-0-87220-484-3 pa; 0-87220-484-7 pa

LC 99-54175

A retelling of Homer's epic that describes the wanderings of Odysseus after the fall of Troy.

Lombardo "has brought his laconic wit and love of the ribald, as well as his clever use of idiomatic American slang, to his version of the 'Odyssey.' His carefully honed syntax gives the narrative energy and a whirlwind pace. The lines, rhythmic and clipped, have the tautness and force of Odysseus' bow." N Y Times Book Rev

Includes bibliographical references

Manguel, Alberto

Homer's The Iliad and The Odyssey; a biography. Atlantic Monthly Press 2008 285p $19.95 **883**
1. Authors 2. Epic poetry 3. Epic poetry, Greek 4. Odysseus (Greek mythology) 5. Poets 6. Trojan War -- Literature and the war
ISBN 978-0-87113-976-4; 0-87113-976-6

A "study of the influence of The Iliad and The Odyssey on Western literature. First describing the two epics and the Homer question, Manguel then compares various translations in English, Spanish, French, and German, a move that brings out the complexities and richness of Homer's language. Does the poet sing of the rage, wrath, anger, rancor, or mania of Achilles? Then, following a more or less chronological progression, Manguel surveys the various shifting interpretations of the epics from Plato and Virgil to the present, including extended discussions of Derek Walcott, Timothy Findley, and Jorge Luis Borges. Highly recommended for general readers." Libr J

Odyssey

The **Odyssey**; translated by Robert Fagles; introduction and notes by Bernard Knox. Viking 1996 541p $35; pa $16 **883**
1. Poetry -- By individual authors
ISBN 978-0-670-82162-4; 978-0-14-026886-7 pa

LC 96-17280

This is a verse translation of Homer's epic poem.

"Fagles' Odyssey is the one to put into the hands of younger, first-time readers, not least because of its paucity of notes, which, though sometimes frustrating, is a sign that translation has been used to do the work of explanation. Altogether, an outstanding piece of work." Booklist

Includes bibliographical references

884 Classical Greek lyric poetry

Pindar

★ The **complete** odes of Pindar; translated by Anthony Verity; with an introduction and notes by Stephen Instone. Oxford University Press 2007 xxvii, 186p pa $15.95 **884**
1. Poetry -- By individual authors
ISBN 978-0-19-280553-9; 0-19-280553-3

LC 2006-39673

The Odes (Epinicia) celebrated victories in the great national games, and were accompanied by music, which is lost to us. The fragments represent almost every kind of lyric poem.

"Since Pindar's Epinicia are generally concerned with mythical subjects, reserving praise of the mortal victor for the end of the ode, his works are a fine source of legend." Reader's Ency. 4th edition

Sappho

★ **If** not, winter; fragments of Sappho. translated by Anne Carson. Knopf 2002 397p $27.50; pa $14 **884**
1. Lesbos Island (Greece) -- Poetry 2. Poetry -- By individual authors 3. Women -- Greece -- Poetry
ISBN 0-375-41067-8; 0-375-72451-6 pa

LC 2001-50247

"Carson's translation follows Sappho's diction and form . . . closely and includes the Greek original on the facing page. Much of what survives of Sappho are fragments, often just a stray word, phrase, or even a few letters. Like many modern poets, Carson deploys these on the blank page, letting their suggestiveness fill the gaps and create whole lyrics in the imagination of the readers." Libr J

Includes bibliographical references

888 Classical Greek miscellaneous writings

Aristotle

★ The **basic** works of Aristotle; edited, and with an introduction by Richard McKeon. Random House 1941 xxxix, 1487p $49.95; pa $19.95 **888**
ISBN 0-394-41610-4; 0-375-75799-6 pa

Contains entire texts of the following: Physica; De generatione et corruptione; De anima; Parva naturalia; Metaphysica; Ethica Nicomachea; Politica; De poetica

Plato

The **collected** dialogues of Plato, including the letters; edited by Edith Hamilton and Huntington

Cairns. With introd. and prefatory notes. Princeton University Press 1961 xxv, 1743p $49.50   **888**

ISBN 978-0-691-09718-3; 0-691-09718-6

"This elegant edition contains many of the best and most readable English translations of the Dialogues and Letters. . . . Judiciously edited, beautifully printed." Rev of Metaphysics

The **republic**; edited by G.R.F. Ferrari; translated by Tom Griffith. Cambridge Univ. Press 2000 xlviii, 382p $38; pa $11 **888**

1. Political science 2. Utopias

ISBN 0-521-48173-2; 0-521-48443-X pa

LC 00-24471

Griffith's "aim was to translate the Greek text as if it were a conversation, and he has succeeded admirably. The text does indeed flow like a conversation, with the entire back-and-forth interaction that such exchanges involve. . . . [He] has also written a very useful introduction that places the work in a historical context and provides a glossary that will help readers identify individuals and places mentioned in the work." Libr J

Includes bibliographical references

889   Modern Greek literature

Cavafy, Constantine P.

★ **Collected** poems; [by] C.P. Cavafy; translated, with introduction and commentary, by Daniel Mendelsohn. Alfred A. Knopf 2009 547p $35 **889**

1. Poetry -- By individual authors

ISBN 978-0-375-40096-4; 0-375-40096-6

LC 2008-34718

"Mendelsohn drew together his interests in ancient history, literature, gay life and culture, and beautiful language to produce the finest, most readable version of the modern Greek poet Cavafy (1863-1933) to come along in decades." Publ Wkly

★ The **unfinished** poems; [by] C.P. Cavafy; the first English translation, with introduction and commentary, by Daniel Mendelsohn. Alfred A. Knopf 2009 121p $30 **889**

1. Poetry -- By individual authors

ISBN 978-0-307-26546-3; 0-307-26546-3

LC 2008-34717

This book "contains the first English versions of 30 poems that Cavafy had not finished entirely to his satisfaction when he died. All are in his most developed manner, in which apprehension of the past is so rich and powerful as to expunge mere nostalgia. They are historical vignettes of the declines of Alexander's Hellenistic hegemony, imperial Rome, and the Byzantine Empire; and glowing memories, triggered by news items, drink, or moonlight, of decades-old homosexual rapture. . . . One could become well informed about centuries of seldom-taught history just by reading the notes, though yet more so by absorbing the poems, as well." Booklist

Elytes, Odysseus

The **collected** poems of Odysseus Elytis; translated by Jeffrey Carson and Nikos Sarris; introduction and notes by Jeffrey Carson. Rev and expanded ed; Johns Hopkins University Press 2005 $60 **889**

1. Poetry -- By individual authors

ISBN 0-8018-8045-9

LC 2004-13496

"The work of 1979 Nobel Prize winner Elytis (1911-96) has the quality of a cathedral or epic—vast in scope yet richly decorated. This excellent 'complete' collected edition (it omits unpublished poems) testifies to the bountiful, sincere nature of Elytis's voice as patriot and poet. . . . Containing informative annotations, a chronology, an autobiographical essay, and the author's Nobel address, this work is a valuable resource on international poetry." Libr J

Includes bibliographical references

Seferis, George

★ **Collected** poems; translated, edited, and introduced by Edmund Keeley and Philip Sherrard. rev ed; Princeton Univ. Press 1995 296p hardcover o.p. pa $24.95 **889**

ISBN 978-0-691-01491-3 pa; 0-691-01491-4 pa

LC 92-10552

Nobel laurete Seferis' "verse is spare, hernetic, and characterized by a profound knowledge of Greek history and classical mythology and a deep understanding of Greece's past and its relevance to her present and future." Reader's Ency. 4th edition

Includes bibliographical references

891   East Indo-European and Celtic literatures

Divan-i Shams-i Tabrizi./English./Selections

Rumi: the big red book; the great masterpiece celebrating mystical love and friendship. the collected translations of Coleman Barks, based on the work of John Moyne ... [et al.] HarperOne 2010 492p $29.95; ebook $14.99 **891**

1. Poetry -- By individual authors

ISBN 978-0-06-190582-7; 978-0-06-202078-9 ebook

LC 2010-7895

This is "a vast collection centering on Shams Tabrizi, a wandering mystic who transformed Rumi's life. Rumi was already renowned when Shams arrived in Konya, in today's Turkey, having wandered for years searching for someone with a soul as profound as his own with whom to share 'sobbet,' a mystical conversation about God and love. Rumi and Shams inspired each other for several years, until Shams mysteriously disappeared. He lives on in Rumi's searching poems. . . . Richly sensual yet never flowery, Barks' language emphasizes Rumi's embodied spirituality in a book to savor." Booklist

Includes bibliographical references

Firdawsi

★ **Shahnameh**; the Persian book of kings. [by] Abolqasem Ferdowsi; translated by Dick Davis; with a fore-

word by Azar Nafisi. Viking 2006 xxxvii, 886p il $45 **891**
ISBN 0-670-03485-1

LC 2005-42352

"Unlike Western epics that grasp the events of a single generation, whether of men or angels, Persia's Book of Kings encompasses whole ages of the world, chronicling the stratagems of Kings and heroes as real as Alexander the Great and as legendary as Rostam. . . . Action, myth, and history fairly fly off the page, for Davis renders Ferdowsi's 50,000 sesquipedalian lines of poetry as a prose narrative that here and there erupts into sonnet-sized snatches of verse. The scheme works brilliantly. Repeated for pages on end, Ferdowsi's lines, each longer than an heroic couplet, breed longueurs, but Davis's carefully rendered snatches of the best classic Farsi poetry illuminate the English text like so many Persian miniatures." New Criterion

Frank, Joseph

Dostoevsky. v4 Princeton Univ. Press 1995 523p v4 il hardcover o.p. pa $24.95 **891**
1. Authors 2. Authors, Russian 3. Biography, Individual 4. Novelists 5. Short story writers
ISBN 0-691-04364-7; 0-691-01587-2 pa

LC 94-43403

"This fourth installment in Frank's acclaimed . . . five-volume biography presents an astonishingly vivid, uncanny portrait of Dostoevsky's spiritual, emotional and artistic development during his crucial years abroad." Publ Wkly
Includes bibliographical references

Hafiz

The **gift**; poems by the great Sufi master. translated by Daniel James Ladinsky. Penguin/Arkana 1999 333p pa $16 **891**
1. Poetry -- By individual authors
ISBN 978-0-14-019581-1; 0-14-019581-5

LC 99-10920

"Less well known in the U.S. than his Sufi predecessor, Rumi, Hafiz (Shams-ud-din Muhammad) is also worthy of attention, and Ladinsky's free translations should help see that he gets it. Hafiz is so beloved in Iran that he outsells the Koran. Many know his verses by heart and recite them with gusto. And gusto is appropriate to this passionate, earthy poet who melds mind, spirit, and body in each of his usually brief pensees. Ladinsky has deliberately chosen a loose and colloquial tone for this collection, which might grate on the nerves of purists but makes Hafiz come vividly alive for the average reader." Booklist

Narayan, R. K.

★ The **Ramayana**; a shortened modern prose version of the Indian epic (suggested by the Tamil version of Kamban) introduction by Pankaj Mishra. Penguin Books 2006 157p pa $13 **891**
ISBN 0-14-303967-9

LC 2006-45201

A retelling of Prince Rama's courtship of the fourteen-year-old Sita, their exile, Sita's abduction, the search, and the great battle with her abductor Ravana, involving a pantheon of gods, heroes, and evil spirits.

Selections/English

The **essential** Rumi; translated by Coleman Barks, with John Moyne, A.A. Arberry, Reynold Nicholson. Harper 1995 302p $23.95; pa $14.95 **891**
1. Poetry -- By individual authors
ISBN 978-0-06-250958-1; 0-06-250958-6; 978-0-06-250959-8 pa; 0-06-250959-4 pa

LC 94-44995

A collection of ecstatic verse by the 13th-century Sufi mystic.

Tagore, Rabindranath

Selected poems; translated by William Radice. Penguin Books 2005 202p pa $14 **891**
1. Poetry -- By individual authors
ISBN 978-0-14-044988-4

"This collection offers a wide array of Tagore's poems from 1882 to 1941, plus textual notes and other scholarly extras." Libr J

Persian poets; selected and edited by Peter Washington. Knopf 2000 254p $12.50 **891**
1. Persian poetry -- Collections
ISBN 978-0-375-41126-7

Includes works by Omar, Sanai, Attar, Rumi, Saadi, Hafez, and Jami.

891.6   Celtic literatures

Tain bo Cuailnge

The **Tain**; translated from the Irish epic Tain Bo Cuailnge. [translated] by Thomas Kinsella; with brush drawings by Louis le Brocquy. Oxford University Press 2002 282p il map pa $19.95 **891.6**
ISBN 0-19-280373-5

LC 2002-726950

This Irish epic is the "centerpiece of the eighth-century Ulster cycle of heroic tales. . . . [This] translation is based on the partial texts in two medieval manuscripts, with elements from other versions. This edition includes a group of related stories which prepare for the action of the Tain." Publisher's note
Includes bibliographical references

891.7   Russian literature and related East Slavic literatures

Bartlett, Rosamund

★ **Tolstoy**; 1st U.S. ed. Houghton Mifflin Harcourt 2011 544 p. **891.7**
1. Authors 2. Biography, Individual 3. Dramatists 4. Novelists 5. Short story writers 6. Writers on religion
ISBN 9781846681387 Profile Books; 1846681383 Profile Books; 9780151014385

LC 2010050015

This book presents a biography of writer Leo Tolstoy which draws primarily upon Russian scholarship, as well as Tolstoy's "memoirs and correspondences," to narrate his life. As a cultural historian, Bartlett strives to place the man within his time and milieu. Her Tolstoy in his incarnations as aristocrat, muzhik, czar and other roles is thoroughly Russian, and she uses him to introduce her anglophone readers to sometimes exotic details of Russian life and history. . . . She offers, for instance, a brief history of the family of TolstoyAs wife, the Behrses, who came from a different order of Russian society than the counts and princes from whom Tolstoy descended. . . . There are similar . . . digressions about the Caucasus, Russian Orthodoxy, peasant life, Tolstoyans and other matters." (The Globe and Mail)

Batuman, Elif
The **possessed**; adventures with Russian books and the people who read them. Farrar, Straus and Giroux 2010 296p pa $15 **891.7**
1. Russian literature -- Appreciation 2. Russian literature -- History and criticism
ISBN 978-0-374-53218-5; 0-374-53218-4
LC 2009-25416
In this book, the author "makes you look at Russian literature from a fresh perspective, using an unusual blend of memoir and travelogue as she delves into the lives and personalities of such Russian literary giants as Isaac Babel, Fyodor Dostoevsky and Leo Tolstoy. Many of the chapters are extensions of pieces Batuman first wrote for The New Yorker and n+1 and range geographically from Palo Alto, Calif., where Batuman managed to lose one of Babel's daughters at the local airport, to Uzbekistan, where Batuman spent a few months studying Uzbek. In a sense, the details of Batuman's essays are less significant than the tone. She cruises through minor crises with an air of detached amusement, eye focused on the little absurdities that make travel—and people—fun." Cleveland Plain Dealer
Includes bibliographical references

Brodsky, Joseph
★ **Collected** poems in English, 1972-1999; edited by Ann Kjellberg. Farrar, Straus & Giroux 2000 539p $30; pa $18   **891.7**
1. Poetry -- By individual authors
ISBN 0-374-12545-7; 0-374-52838-1 pa
LC 00-21059
This volume "gathers all the poetry in English Brodsky originally saw through to press in books (or had earmarked for eventual publication), including Russian poems he translated or co-translated. Originally Russian verse from the '60s and '70s gives way to the later, sometimes lighter, work of his last two decades, when he found a second home in the speech of his adoptive country." Publ Wkly

Callow, Philip
Chekhov, the hidden ground; a biography. Dee, I.R. 1998 428p il $30; pa $18.95   **891.7**
1. Authors 2. Authors, Russian -- 19th century -- Biography 3. Dramatists 4. Physicians 5. Short story writers
ISBN 1-56663-187-4; 1-56663-395-8 pa
LC 97-46679
"Callow sees Chekhov as distant in virtually all his relationships, with romantic disillusionment and the search for intimacy recurring themes in his writing. He argues persuasively that while Chekhov's art is resplendent with human

emotion, his own life was strangely cold and remote. . . . Not strictly a literary biography, this book is particularly effective in discussing Chekhov's work as it relates to his life." Libr J
Includes bibliographical references

Chekhov, Anton Pavlovich
Chekhov; the four major plays. in new translations by Curt Columbus. Ivan R. Dee 2005 294p pa $15.95 **891.7**
ISBN 978-1-56663-626-1; 1-56663-626-4
LC 2004-48612
"Columbus's translation triumphs through its clarity and consistent use of the active voice." Chicago Reader

The **complete** plays; [by] Anton Chekhov; translated, edited, and annotated by Laurence Senelick. W. W. Norton 2006 lx, 1060p pa $22.95   **891.7**
ISBN 978-0-393-04885-8; 0-393-04885-3; 978-0-393-33069-4 pa; 0-393-33069-9 pa
LC 2005-24362
"This volume contains work never previously translated, including the newly discovered farce The Power of Hypnotism, the first version of Ivanov, Chekhov's early humorous dialogues, and a description of lost plays and those Chekhov intended to write but never did." Publisher's note

The **portable** Chekhov; edited and with an introduction by Avrahm Yarmolinsky. Viking 1947 631p hardcover o.p. pa $17   **891.7**
ISBN 0-14-015035-8 pa
This collection contains "two plays, 'The Cherry Orchard' and 'The Boor,' 28 short stories and selections from Chekhov's letters." Publ Wkly

Frank, Joseph
Dostoevsky. v3 Princeton Univ. Press 1986 395p v3 il hardcover o.p. pa $24.95 **891.7**
1. Authors 2. Authors, Russian 3. Biography, Individual 4. Novelists 5. Short story writers
ISBN 0-691-06652-3; 0-691-01452-3 pa
LC 85-43280
In this third volume of a five-volume biography of the writer, Frank "describes the influence of the social and political background of Dostoyevsky's Russia on his intellectual and artistic development." Natl Rev
Includes bibliographical references

Malcolm, Janet
Reading Chekhov; a critical journey. Random House 2001 209p hardcover o.p. pa $13.95 **891.7**
1. Authors 2. Dramatists 3. Physicians 4. Short story writers
ISBN 0-375-50668-3; 0-375-76106-3 pa
LC 2001-19585
"The author's pilgrimage to Chekhov's Russia—Moscow, St. Petersburg, the gardens of his villa in Yalta—is a reunion with this most reticent of literary fathers. Malcolm analyzes the transformations that Chekhov grants his redeemable roués and guileless heroines, and illuminates the hidden surreality and waywardness of his realism." New Yorker
Includes bibliographical references

Mandelstam, Osip

The **selected** poems of Osip Mandelstam; translated by Clarence Brown and W.S. Merwin. New York Review Books 2004 167p pa $14.95 **891.7**
1. Poetry -- By individual authors
ISBN 978-1-59017-091-1; 1-59017-091-1
LC 2004-14656

"The Brown/Merwin versions represent a sensitive and sensible selection of Mandelstam's poetry. The translations do not attempt to imitate Mandelstam's fluid syntax or subtle sound play. But they are honest representations of Mandelstam's themes and recurrent imagery and many of them, particularly certain of the poems in the section 'Poems of the Thirties,' come across as fine English poems." Libr J

Mayakovsky, Vladimir

Listen! early poems. translated by Maria Enzensberger; with a foreward [sic] by Elaine Feinstein. City Lights Bks. 1991 60p pa $9.95 **891.7**
1. Poetry -- By individual authors
ISBN 978-0-87286-255-5; 0-87286-255-0
LC 91-10330

This collection of the Russian poet's early work has parallel text in Russian and English and is illustrated with some of Mayakovsky's art.

Nabokov, Vladimir Vladimirovich

Lectures on Russian literature; edited with an introduction by Fredson Bowers. Harcourt Brace Jovanovich 1981 324p il hardcover o.p. pa $16 **891.7**
1. Authors 2. Communism and literature 3. Dramatists 4. Memoirists 5. Novelists 6. Physicians 7. Russian literature -- History and criticism 8. Short story writers 9. Writers on religion
ISBN 0-15-602776-3 pa

This book is "derived from notes Nabokov made for his literature classes at Wellesley and Cornell. Included are chapters on Gogol, Turgenev, Dostoevsky, Tolstoy, Chekhov, and Gorki, as well as several miscellaneous essays on censorship and the art of translation." Libr J

Pushkin, Aleksandr Sergeevich

Eugene Onegin and other poems; translated by Charles Johnston. Knopf 1999 240p $12.50 **891.7**
1. Poetry -- By individual authors
ISBN 978-0-375-40672-0; 0-375-40672-7

Tale in verse of a rich, bored young man who rather offhandedly destroys his chance at love by killing a friend in a duel and alienating his would-be beloved.

Selections./English.

Poems; [by] Akhmatova; translated by D.M. Thomas. New expanded ed.; Knopf 2006 6p $12.50 **891.7**
1. Poetry -- By individual authors
ISBN 978-0-307-26424-4; 0-307-26424-6
LC 2006-297217

A representative selection of material from all her major works—including "Requiem" commemorating the victims of Stalin's terror.

Terras, Victor

A **history** of Russian literature. Yale Univ. Press 1991 654p $37 **891.7**
1. Russian literature -- History and criticism
ISBN 978-0-300-04971-8; 0-300-04971-4
LC 91-13337

This history of Russian literature begins with a chapter on folklore and then presents a chronological account covering Old Russian literature (eleventh to sixteenth centuries); the seventeenth century; the eighteenth century; the Romantic period; the age of the novel; the Silver Age, and the Soviet period.

"The book's minor shortcomings are overshadowed by its numerous merits; its accuracy, keenness of observation, subtle comments, vivid quotations, erudition. . . . Almost every page of the book invites one to read and re-read Russian literature." Times Lit Suppl

Includes bibliographical references

Tolstaia, Tat'iana

Pushkin's children; writings on Russia and Russians. [by] Tatyana Tolstaya; translated by Jamey Gambrell. Houghton Mifflin 2003 242p pa $15 **891.7**
1. Authors 2. Cabinet members 3. Communist leaders 4. Nobel laureates for literature 5. Nobel laureates for peace 6. Nonfiction writers 7. Novelists 8. Poets 9. Political prisoners 10. Presidents 11. Prime ministers 12. Short story writers 13. Writers on politics
ISBN 0-618-12500-0
LC 2002-27610

"Tolstaya's essays in this compact, historically significant volume offer a fascinating, highly intelligent analysis of Russian society and politics." Publ Wkly

Tsvetaeva, Marina Ivanovna

Selected poems; [by] Marina Tsvetayeva; translated and introduced by Elaine Feinstein; with literal versions provided by Angela Livingstone . . . [et al.] Penguin Books 1994 131p pa $15 **891.7**
ISBN 978-0-14-018759-5; 0-14-018759-6

"As a poet Tsvetayeva impresses with her psychic energy, she is on fire with poetry, and nothing is put in perspective, everything is immediate, emotional in the best sense." N Y Times Book Rev

Volkov, Solomon

Romanov riches; Russian writers and artists under the tsars. translated from the Russian by Antonina W. Bouis. Alfred A. Knopf 2011 285p il $30 **891.7**
1. Artists -- Russia 2. Arts, Russian 3. Authors, Russian 4. Composers -- Russia 5. Emperors 6. Empresses 7. Russian arts 8. Russian literature -- History and criticism
ISBN 0-307-27063-7; 978-0-307-27063-4
LC 2010-45132

This is a "cultural history of Russia from the rise of the house of Romanov in 1613 to its downfall at the hands of the Bolsheviks in 1917." (Publisher's note) Index

"Volkov revitalizes our understanding of rebellious poet Pushkin and offers fresh insights into Tchaikovsky, Dostoevsky, and Turgenev. A thrillingly anecdotal and incisive look at the paradigmatic and paradoxical Romanov world of politics, patronage, and the quest for artistic freedom." Booklist

Includes bibliographical references

Yevtushenko, Yevgeny Aleksandrovich

Selected poems; [by] Yevgeni Yevtushenko; translated by Robin Milner-Gulland and Peter Levi; with an introduction by Robin Milner-Gulland. Penguin Books 2008 90p il pa $14   **891.7**

1. Poetry -- By individual authors

ISBN 978-0-14-042477-5; 0-14-042477-6

"These poems beat and tumble and thrash with life." Daily Telegraph

The Cambridge history of Russian literature; edited by Charles A. Moser. rev ed; Cambridge Univ. Press 1992 709p hardcover o.p. pa $55 **891.7**

1. Russian literature -- History and criticism

ISBN 0-521-42567-0 pa

LC 91-38275

This volume presents "a survey of Russian literature from the beginnings to this decade, in sufficient but not overwhelming detail.' Ten chapters by specialists elucidate this history from 988 to approximately 1980, with a lengthy bibliography at the end of the volume." Sheehy. Guide to Ref Books. 10th edition. suppl

Reference guide to Russian literature; editor, Neil Cornwell; associate editor, Nicole Christian. Fitzroy Dearborn Pubs. 1998 xl, 972p $160 **891.7**

1. Reference books 2. Russian literature -- Biobibliogaphy -- Dictionaries 3. Russian literature -- Bio-bibliography 4. Russian literature -- Dictionaries

ISBN 1-88496-410-9

LC 97-169924

A guide to approximately 270 writers and their works "author entries include telegraphic biographical sketches, detailed bibliographies of Russian- and English-language sources and critical studies and, in many cases, 1000-word entries for specific novels, plays, and stories. There are alphabetical and chronological lists, 13 introductory essays on various aspects of Russian literature, and a Russian/English title index." Libr J

Includes bibliographical references

891.71   Russian poetry

Akhmatova, Anna Andreevna

★ The **complete** poems of Anna Akhmatova; {by} Anna Akhmatova; translated by Judith Hemschemeyer; edited and with an introduction by Roberta Reeder. Zephyr Press (Somerville) 1990 2v il hardcover o.p. pa $29   **891.71**

1. Poetry -- By individual authors

ISBN 0-939010-27-5 pa

LC 88-51831

"Anna Akhmatova—the high priestess of Russian poetry—saw her husband shot, her son imprisoned twice by Stalin, her work banned in the 1930's and late 40's. . . .

Sonorous, calm, deliberate in movement, her Russian has no English equivalent, but in this admirably restrained and accurate translation, sense and message strike with all the weight of the original." N Y Times Book Rev

Mandelstam, Nadezhda

Hope against hope; a memoir. translated from the Russian by Max Hayward; with an introduction by Clarence Brown and: Nadezhda Mandelstaum (1899-1980): an obituary, by Joseph Brodsky. Modern Lib. 1999 442p pa $23   **891.71**

1. Authors 2. Memoirists 3. Poets 4. Poets, Russian -- 20th century -- Biography 5. Translators

ISBN 978-0-375-75316-9; 0-375-75316-8

LC 98-47833

"Mandelstam tells the story of her family's experiences of hardship in Soviet Russia under Stalin. What is remarkable about the book is not just its content but also its authorial voice, which, in Max Hayward's deft translation, is so unique and consistent that the reader can get a sense of it by opening the book at random and reading almost any paragraph. Although Hope Against Hope is a painful book to read, one of the things that makes it bearable, apart from its sheer beauty, is a kind of unquenchable spirit and optimism that keeps rising to the surface, compounding the more mysterious consolations of art." Harper's

891.8   Slavic (Slavonic) literatures

Capek, Karel

★ **R.U.R.** and The insect play; by the Brothers Capek. Oxford Univ. Press 1961 179p pa $15.95   **891.8**

ISBN 0-19-281010-3

"R.U.R." is a fantasy in which robots revolt against their human masters. In "The insect play," a dying tramp dreams about insect life.

Dimkovska, Lidija

PH neutral history; Lidija Dimkovska; translated from the Macedonian by Ljubica Arsovska and Peggy Reid. Copper Canyon Press 2012 120 p. (pbk. : alk. paper) $16.00   **891.8**

ISBN 1556593759; 9781556593758

LC 2011044017

In this, the "sixth collection of poetry" by "Macedonian poet and novelist Lidija Dimkovska," the author "scrutinizes lifes customary and trivial details in a quest for greater meaning." Topics referenced include "religious tenents," "native folklore," and "nostalgia for her youth." Her brotherss suicide offers her "reflections on death and its neutralization: life." (Publisher's note)

Herbert, Zbigniew

The **collected** poems, 1956-1998; translated and edited by Alissa Valles; with additional translations by Czesław Miłosz and Peter Dale Scott; introduction by Adam Zagajewski. Ecco Press 2007 600p $34.95   **891.8**

1. Poetry -- By individual authors 2. Polish poetry --

Translations into English
ISBN 978-0-06-078390-7; 0-06-078390-7
LC 2006-40856

Herbert is a "titan of not only Polish poetry, but of twentieth-century European poetry. His celebrated alter ego, Mr. Cogito, ranks as the one of the most original characters in modern poetry. . . . Herbert lived through the Nazi occupation of 1941 and the Soviet occupations of 1939 and 1944 and was an active member of Poland's underground resistance. Decades later, after marshal law was declared in Poland in 1981, Herbert supported the underground opposition to communism and was an important figure in the Solidarity movement. . . . If Herbert is a political poet, he's political in the way Don Quixote is political. He doesn't make us more aware. He makes us more human." Brooklyn Rail

Milosz, Czeslaw

Legends of modernity; essays and letters from occupied Poland, 1942-1943. translated from the Polish by Madeline G. Levine; introduction by Jaroslaw Anders. Farrar, Straus and Giroux 2005 266p $25 **891.8**
  1. Authors 2. Biography, Individual 3. Essayists 4. Literary critics 5. Nobel laureates for literature 6. Novelists 7. Poets 8. Polish literature 9. Short story writers
  ISBN 0-374-18499-2
LC 2005-40950

"Written to the young intellectual Jerzy Andrejewski, the letters reveal Milosz's concern about the political climate of the era and the deterioration of religious influence owing to the chaos all across Europe and the rest of the world. . . . The essays explore the ideas of William James, André Gide, Stendhal (Henri Beyle), Honoré de Balzac, and others as they relate to religious faith, reason and rationalism, contradictions, doubting, and believing in a civilized world and its religious institutions. . . . Reading Milosz is a demanding, rewarding, and ultimately powerful experience for the mind and the soul." Libr J

★ **Milosz's** ABCs; translated from the Polish by Madeline G. Levine. Farrar, Straus & Giroux 2001 313p hardcover o.p. pa $14 **891.8**
  ISBN 0-374-52795-4 pa
LC 00-42176

"The short prose entries in this quiet book take note of some of the people and places and ideas that contributed to the making of Milosz. The subjects of his sketches range from Alchemy and Curiosity to Rimbaud and Whitman, from childhood friends to Polish intellectuals little known in the West. But what could have been no more than a light memory work becomes almost a registry of gratitude: a meditation on the obligations of having lived a life and the responsibilities inherent in its particulars." New Yorker
  Includes bibliographical references

★ **New** and collected poems 1931-2001. HarperCollins Pubs. 2001 xxi, 776p $45; pa $19.95 **891.8**
  1. Poetry -- By individual authors
  ISBN 0-06-019667-X; 0-06-051448-5 pa
LC 2001-50123

"Milosz has stated repeatedly in his poems his belief in the power of language to rescue from the void all he has seen and all the people he has known in a long life. But beneath this belief, it now appears, was the deeper belief that none of this was possible because of the inadequacy of language to capture reality, though he maintains this always has to be the poet's goal. . . . Throughout his career and throughout this vast collection, Milosz argues with himself about his poetics." N Y Times Book Rev

To begin where I am; selected essays. edited and with an introduction by Bogdana Carpenter and Madeline G. Levine. Farrar, Straus & Giroux 2001 462p hardcover o.p. pa $15 **891.8**
  1. Authors 2. College teachers 3. Dramatists 4. Editors 5. Essayists 6. Literary critics 7. Nobel laureates for literature 8. Novelists 9. Philosophers 10. Poets 11. Political and social philosophers 12. Political prisoners 13. Short story writers 14. Translators
  ISBN 0-374-52859-4 pa
LC 2001-33356

A retrospective of Milosz's "prose works, in which he weaves autobiography and portraits of people, famous and otherwise, who have influenced him into graceful and provocative musings on time, history, religion, science, and art." Booklist
  Includes bibliographical references

★ A **roadside** dog. Farrar, Straus & Giroux 1998 208p hardcover o.p. pa $14 **891.8**
  1. Poetry -- By individual authors
  ISBN 0-374-52623-0 pa
LC 98-14026

"Milosz makes a wise, wryly humane fin de siècle companion." Publ Wkly

Plays/English

The **garden** party and other plays. Grove Press 1993 273p $13.00; pa $14 **891.8**
  ISBN 978-0-8021-3307-6; 0-8021-3307-X
LC 93-8656

"Gathered together here for the first time are seven plays that span Havel's career from his early days at the Theater of the Balustrade through the Prague Spring, Charter 77, and the repeated imprisonments that made Havel's name into a rallying cry and propelled him to the leadership of his country." Publisher's note

Poems./English./Selections

Lodgings; selected poems, 1987-2010. translated from the Polish by Benjamin Paloff. Open Letter 2011 163p pa $13.95 **891.8**
  1. Poetry -- By individual authors
  ISBN 978-1-934824-32-0; 1-934824-32-1
LC 2010-52054

With this volume, "translator Benjamin Paloff has made an important contribution to the body of Polish poetry currently available to readers in English. Complete with a translator's note, a conversation between Sosnowski and Paloff, and poems that span Sosnowski's entire career to date (1987-2010), Lodgings offers an unusual glimpse into a polyphonous, expansive, and chameleonic strain of Polish poetry. The poems included are pulled from nine of Sosnowski's collections . . . , and they are presented, with two exceptions, in their original order." Words without Borders

Szymborska, Wislawa

★ **Monologue** of a dog; new poems. translated from the Polish by Clare Cavanagh and Stanislaw Baranczak; [foreword by Billy Collins] Harcourt 2005 96p $22   **891.8**
    1. Poetry -- By individual authors
    ISBN 0-15-101220-2
                           LC 2005-16084
In this volume, Nobel laureate Szymborska "invites readers to linger over moments small, earthly, and sometimes life-altering. With characteristically simple language and imagery, wit and irony, she shows us how life can change at any moment. Hers are the politics of the everyday, little observations on the value of life." Libr J

★ **Poems,** new and collected, 1957-1997; translated from the Polish by Stanislaw Baranczak and Clare Cavanagh. Harcourt Brace & Co. 1998 273p $27; pa $17   **891.8**
    ISBN 0-15-100353-X; 0-15-601146-8 pa
                            LC 97-32277
This career-spanning collection by the 1996 Nobel Prize winner includes her Nobel lecture.
Szymborska's "work is ultimately wisdom literature, written in a first person that expresses a universal humanity that American poets—lockstep individualists all—haven't dared essay since early in this century." Booklist

View with a grain of sand; selected poems. translated from the Polish by Stanislaw Baranczak and Clare Cavanagh. Harcourt Brace & Co. 1995 214p $20; pa $14   **891.8**
    1. Poetry -- By individual authors
    ISBN 0-15-100153-7; 0-15-600216-7 pa
                            LC 94-36112
This collection by Poland's Nobel laureate "selects work from seven volumes of poetry that span nearly 40 years. Her eye is sharp and her wit wonderfully wicked. . . . It is about time more readers found the poetry of Szymborska, and this collection gives them the opportunity." Libr J

Zagajewski, Adam

★ **Without** end; new and selected poems. translations by Clare Cavanagh [et al.] Farrar, Straus & Giroux 2002 285p $30; pa $15   **891.8**
    ISBN 0-374-22096-4; 0-374-52861-6 pa
                           LC 2001-40252
"Zagajewski's poetic evolution is clearly charted in 'Without End,' a new anthology of his work that is made up of his three English-language collections—'Tremor' (1985), 'Canvas' (1991) and 'Mysticism for Beginners' (1997)—as well as his most recent work and new translations of some early poems. . . . Zagajewski's poems pull us from whatever routine threatens to dull our senses, from whatever might lull us into mere existence. This is an astonishing book." N Y Times Book Rev

Zagajewski, Adam, 1945-

Eternal enemies; translated from the Polish by Clare Cavanagh. Farrar, Straus and Giroux 2008 116p   **891.8**
    1. Poetry -- By individual authors
    ISBN 0-374-21634-7; 978-0-374-21634-4
                           LC 2007-42855
This is a collection of poetry by the author of Two Cities (1995), Without End (2002), and A Defense of Ardor (2004).
"Cavanagh's supple translations let the verse sing in American English without making this Polish poet sound too American." Publ Wkly

Unseen hand; translated from the Polish by Clare Cavanagh. Farrar, Straus and Giroux 2011 107p $23   **891.8**
    1. Poetry -- By individual authors 2. Polish poetry 3. Travel
    ISBN 978-0-374-28089-5; 0-374-28089-4
                           LC 2010-46274
The book "is Adam Zagajewski's sixth book of poetry translated into English. . . . If Szymborska is a poet of imaginary journeys, Zagajewski is a real traveler with a ticket and a suitcase. He even has a poem called 'Self-Portrait in an Airplane.' Many of his poems are about towns and cities in Europe and the United States that he had either lived in or visited. Poetry and travel are allied, Czeslaw Milosz once claimed, since poetry is an expression of wondering at things, landscapes, people, their habits and mores. . . . He compares the impassive river Garonne, flowing in silence, to an Indian brave in plumes of sun; a plane taking off from an airport to a zealous pupil who believes what the old masters told him; the light bulbs hissing in gray hallways at night to the signals of sinking ships." (New York Review of Books)
"The collective calm of these poems creates an odd tension: Within [Zagajewski's] clear, contemplative lines, the indifference of time can always be felt drifting unstoppably by, even as we attempt to scaffold it with history or cage it with memory. . . . [The poems,] translated by the admirably consistent Clare Cavanagh, move through the various locales of Zagajewski's life; from his Polish upbringing in Lvov and the provincial garrison town of Gliwice (to which his family was forced to move shortly after his birth in 1945), to various stints in Krakow, Paris, and Chicago. Markers of place and time are everywhere, but Zagajewski is especially perceptive of the ways the past is channeled through the present — his 'now' tends to carry the authority of an 'always.'" Boston Globe

892   Afro-Asiatic literatures

Amichai, Yehuda

Poems of Jerusalem; and, Love poems; a bilingual edition. Sheep Meadow Press 1992 265p pa $16.95   **892**
    1. Love poetry 2. Poetry -- By individual authors
    ISBN 1-87881-819-8
                           LC 92-31558
This work is "actually drawn from eight previous works and boasts an even larger array of translators (including Stephen Mitchell, David Rosenberg, Ted Hughes, and the poet

himself). The thematic arrangement deftly emphasizes the Israeli poet's constant preoccupation with both Jerusalem and love." Libr J

The **selected** poetry of Yehuda Amichai; edited and translated from the Hebrew by Chana Bloch and Stephen Mitchell. newly rev & expanded ed; University of Calif. Press 1996 195p pa $16.95 **892**
1. Poetry -- By individual authors
ISBN 0-520-20538-3

LC 96-18580

"Although much of Amichai's poetry focuses on war, he is able to describe its horrors by maintaining a clear distance between himself and his subject. The result is a finely controlled emotional pitch that allows the poet to convey his sense of pain and outrage without pathos or sentimentality. He writes colloquially, in language that is always commensurate with emotional experience." Reader's Ency. 4th edition

Gilgamesh
★ **Gilgamesh**; a new English version [by] Stephen Mitchell. Free Press 2004 290p $25; pa $14 **892**
1. Poetry -- By individual authors
ISBN 0-7432-6164-X; 0-7432-6169-0 pa

LC 2004-50072

"Relying on existing translations (and in places where there are gaps, on his own imagination), Mitchell seeks language that is as swift and strong as the story itself. . . . This wonderful new version of the story of Gilgamesh shows how the story came to achieve literary immortality—not because it is a rare ancient artifact, but because reading it can make people in the here and now feel more completely alive." Publ Wkly
Includes bibliographical references

892.4   Hebrew literature

Amichai, Yehuda
Open closed open; poems. translated from the Hebrew by Chana Bloch and Chana Kronfeld. Harcourt Brace & Co. 2000 184p $25 **892.4**
1. Poetry -- By individual authors
ISBN 0-15-100378-5

LC 00-23537

Amichai "writes with the casual wisdom and generous humor of a master." Booklist

Poems./English./Selections
War & love, love & war; new and selected poems. translated by Peter Cole. New Directions 2010 175p pa $15.95 **892.4**
1. Poetry -- By individual authors
ISBN 978-0-8112-1890-0; 0-8112-1890-2

LC 2010-10440

"Gritty, controversial and intensely lyrical, this is an excellent collection from one of Israel's most important contemporary poets. Spanning more than three-and-a-half decades of writing, it exhibits a wealth of experimentation with various styles, and a multitude of yearnings and obsessions. As the title implies, engagement with the Israeli-Palestinian

conflict is one of the book's chief subjects. The real gem, though, is the closing cycle of poems, which mourns the passing of Shabtai's wife, Tanya Reinhart." Forward
Includes bibliographical references

892.7   Arabic and Maltese literatures

Darwish, Mahmud
If I were another; translated from the Arabic by Fady Joudah. Farrar, Straus and Giroux 2009 201p $28 **892.7**
1. Poetry -- By individual authors
ISBN 978-0-374-17429-3; 0-374-17429-6

LC 2009-11521

This volume "comprises four nonconsecutive books of longer poems spanning 1990 to 2005. These works follow Darwish's poetic development from a historically focused middle period to the devastatingly personal lyric-epic of his late style. Formally varied—Rubaiyats alternate with sprawling freeform poems, in which prose paragraphs meet both long and short verse lines—Darwish's Sufi-inspired poetry probes, admires, describes, longs for and questions." Publ Wkly
Includes bibliographical references

Anthology of modern Palestinian literature; edited and introduced by Salma Khadra Jayyusi. Columbia Univ. Press 1992 xxxiii, 744p hardcover o.p. pa $30.50 **892.7**
1. Arabic literature -- Collections   2. Palestine in literature
ISBN 0-231-07508-1; 0-231-07509-X pa

LC 92-5189

"Presented here are translations of poems, stories, and excerpts from novels, as well as works by Palestinian poets who write in English. Also included are personal narratives by Palestinian writers depicting the varied aspects of Palestinian life from the turn of the century to the present. . . . Biographical sketches introduce the authors, and a chronology of modern Palestinian history provides background for some of the events and places referred to in the selections. The introduction by the editor provides a concise but comprehensive political history of Palestinian literature during the twentieth century." Publisher's note
Includes bibliographical references

Night and horses and the desert; an anthology of classical Arabic literature. edited by Robert Irwin. Anchor Books 2001 462p pa $16 **892.7**
1. Arabic literature -- Collections   2. Arabic literature -- History and criticism
ISBN 0-385-72155-2

LC 2001-53721

"The chapter on the Qur'an is perhaps the most essential as it examines just how vital the dogma of Islam has been for the Arabic understanding of culture and art. . . . This persuasive work will surely fill in the gap in the study of Arabic literature in this country." Publ Wkly
Includes bibliographical references

The Poetry of Arab women; a contemporary anthology. edited by Nathalie Handal. Interlink Bks. 2000 xxi, 355p pa $22 **892.7**
1. Arabic poetry -- 20th century -- Translations into English 2. Arabic poetry -- Collections 3. Arabic poetry -- Women authors -- Translations into English 4. Poetry -- Arab authors
ISBN 978-1-56656-374-1; 1-56656-374-7
LC 00-58054
"Handal deserves high praise for producing an anthology that mirrors faithfully Arab women's creative role throughout the last century." Multicultural Rev

894 Literatures of Altaic, Uralic, Hyperborean, Dravidian languages; literatures of miscellaneous languages of south Asia

Pamuk, Orhan
Other colors; essays and a story. translated from the Turkish by Maureen Freely. Alfred A. Knopf 2007 433p il $27.95 **894**
1. Authors 2. Literature -- History and criticism 3. Nobel laureates for literature 4. Novelists
ISBN 978-0-307-26675-0; 0-307-26675-3
LC 2007-21132
"Whether he's writing wistfully about Andre Gide as the hero of Turkish intellectuals . . . or recalling how he used to collect Coca-Cola cans as a boy, from the trash cans of expat Americans, Pamuk is taking the world we thought we knew and making it fresh and alive." N Y Times Book Rev

895.1 Chinese literature

An Anthology of Chinese literature; beginnings to 1911. edited and translated by Stephen Owen. Norton 1996 xlviii, 1212p hardcover o.p. pa $59.65 **895.1**
1. Chinese literature -- Collections
ISBN 0-393-97106-6 pa
LC 95-11409
"In a book that moves roughly chronologically through the tradition, Owen gathers texts according to genres, themes, forms, and other groupings to show the way essential texts build off each other and how the tradition echoes itself. Included are a range of forms . . . presented . . . {with} commentary to provide a . . . view of the interplay between Chinese literature, culture, and history." Publisher's note
Includes bibliographical references

Anthology of modern Chinese poetry; edited and translated by Michelle Yeh. Yale Univ. Press 1993 245p hardcover o.p. pa $21 **895.1**
1. Chinese poetry -- Collections
ISBN 0-300-05947-7 pa
LC 92-16322
"Arranged chronologically, this selection of twentieth-century poetry from China and Taiwan offers a few poems by each of 67 poets born between 1891 and 1963. Its scope is enormous, its range impressive. Editor Yeh's translations are accessible and fluid; her introduction and notes are helpful without being overbearingly scholarly." Booklist
Includes bibliographical references

The Columbia book of Chinese poetry; from early times to the thirteenth century. translated and edited by Burton Watson. Columbia Univ. Press 1984 385p il $69; pa $27 **895.1**
1. Chinese poetry -- Collections
ISBN 0-231-05682-6; 0-231-05683-4 pa
LC 83-26182
This anthology's "arrangement is historical, beginning with selections from a first millenium BC collection of Chinese verse (the Shih ching), and ending with tz'u lyrics from the Sung period (AD 960-1279). The 12 selections [are] each prefaced with a two- or three-page introduction." Choice
Includes bibliographical references

The Columbia history of Chinese literature; Victor H. Mair, editor. Columbia Univ. Press 2001 xx, 1342p $78 **895.1**
1. Chinese literature -- History and criticism
ISBN 0-231-10984-9
LC 2001-28236
This "history explores a wide range of Chinese literature, from the classics to humor to folk tales to oral traditions, and moves from ancient times to the end of the 20th century. . . . Mair has overseen a host of excellent scholars writing on a vast subject." Libr J
Includes bibliographical references

Mountain home; the wilderness poetry of ancient China. selected and translated by David Hinton. New Directions Pub. 2005 xxi, 295p map pa $17.95 **895.1**
1. Chinese poetry -- Collections
ISBN 978-0-8112-1624-1
LC 2005-869
"Translator and scholar Hinton ensures that Western readers will experience this supreme collection of Chinese rivers-and-mountains (shan-shui) poetry at the deepest possible level by succinctly explaining the cosmology inherent in this vital and profoundly influential tradition. The keys to understanding the elegant poetry of such masters as T'ao Ch'ien (365-427), Li Po (701-762), and Lu Yu (1125-1210) are realizing that they perceive no divide between the human and what we call nature, or between being and nonbeing. . . . Oneness with life at its purest is the desired mode for these thoughtful, yet often playful, poets, and dwelling within these meditative pages is the first step on the way there." Booklist

The New Directions anthology of classical chinese poetry; edited by Eliot Weinberger; translations by William Carlos Williams . . . [et al.] New Directions 2003 xxvii, 242p $24.95; pa $16.95 **895.1**
1. Chinese poetry -- Collections
ISBN 978-0-8112-1540-4; 0-8112-1540-7; 978-0-8112-1605-0 pa; 0-8112-1605-5 pa
LC 2002-156731

The poems are "translated into English by four of the best-known American poets of the 20th century—Ezra Pound, William Carlos Williams, Kenneth Rexroth and Gary Snyder—and an academic scholar/translator called David Hinton, who deserves to be as well known as the others. It is not often that an anthology really demands attention. . . . This poetry means what it says. It feels companionable, and even sexy. It is not excessively—or confusingly—metaphorical. It is not foggy with abstract philosophising. It lacks the shriek of rhetoric; it seems to move, so often, at an agreeable walking pace. It feels spacious. In fact, there seems to be space between the words themselves. It mixes the high and the low with seeming ease. Its temper suggests that there is no unsuitable subject matter for poetry at all." New Statesman

The Shorter Columbia anthology of traditional Chinese literature; Victor H. Mair, editor. Columbia Univ. Press 2000 xxx, 741p map $65; pa $26 **895.1**
1. Chinese literature 2. Chinese literature -- Collections
ISBN 0-231-11998-4; 0-231-11999-2 pa
LC 00-35878
This "abridged volume, which, like the original includes selections of Chinese literature from the beginnings to 1919 . . . retains the characteristics of the original in that it is arranged according to genre rather than chronology and interprets 'literature' very broadly to include not just literary fiction, poetry, and drama, but folk and popular literature, lyrics and arias, elegies and rhapsodies, biographies, autobiographies and memoirs, letters, criticism and theory, and travelogues and jokes. It also contains fresh translations by newer voices in the field." Publisher's note
Includes bibliographical references

895.6   Japanese literature

Keene, Donald
Five modern Japanese novelists. Columbia Univ. Press 2002 113p $26 **895.6**
1. Authors 2. Authors, Japanese -- 20th century 3. Dramatists 4. Essayists 5. Japanese fiction -- 20th century 6. Japanese fiction -- 20th century -- History and criticism 7. Japanese literature -- History and criticism 8. Nobel laureates for literature 9. Novelists 10. Short story writers
ISBN 0-231-12610-7
LC 2002-73412
The author's essays, "part memoir and part literary evaluation, are ideal introductions to their subjects." Booklist
Includes bibliographical references

Seeds in the heart; Japanese literature from earliest times to the late sixteenth century. with a new preface by the author, Donald Keene. Columbia University Press 1999 1265p pa $37 **895.6**
1. Japanese literature -- History and criticism
ISBN 0-231-11441-9
LC 99-25990

This volume completes the author's history of Japanese literature begun with: World within walls (1977) and Dawn to the West (1984).

"The first half of 'Seeds in the Heart' encompasses everything from the myths, legends, songs and poems of the eighth-century 'Kojiki' ('Record of Ancient Matters') and 'Manyoshu,' a collection of 4,500 poems, to the 'The Tale of Genji' and later works of fiction. . . . During Japan's middle ages (1185-1600), Buddhism and popular (rather than aristocratic) forms of storytelling and theater generated a repertory of characters and genres that would eventually form the country's first broadly based, national culture. The literature of these centuries has rarely attracted the scholarly attention paid to the earlier 'high' classical tradition. So Mr. Keene's attention to this period makes the second half of 'Seeds in the Heart' especially valuable." N Y Times Book Rev
Includes bibliographical references

The **pleasures** of Japanese literature. Columbia Univ. Press 1988 133p il $60; pa $19.50 **895.6**
1. Aesthetics 2. Japanese literature -- History and criticism 3. Theater -- Japan
ISBN 0-231-06736-4; 0-231-06737-2 pa
LC 88-18069
The author discusses Japanese aesthetics, poetry, fiction and drama, focusing on works of the premodern period.

"If your library has no other introduction to the Japanese classics, nor any need for another, this is the one it ought to include." Booklist
Includes bibliographical references

Waley, Arthur
The **No** plays of Japan; an anthology. Dover Publications 1998 270p pa $12.95 **895.6**
1. No plays 2. No plays -- Translations into English
ISBN 978-0-486-40156-0
LC 97-46053
Contains translation of 20 No plays and summaries of 16 more. In his introduction Mr. Waley gives a brief history of the No drama, its origin, the text of the plays, and the chief playwrights. He also tells about the stage settings, costumes and properties used in the production of these plays. The greatest representation is given to the works of Seami and Zenchiku Ujinobu.

Haiku before haiku; from the Renga masters to Basho. translated, with an introduction, by Steven D. Carter. Columbia University Press 2011 163p $69.50; pa $22.50; ebook $9.99 **895.6**
1. Haiku 2. Japanese poetry 3. Renga
ISBN 978-0-231-15648-6; 978-0-231-15647-9 pa; 978-0-231-52706-4 ebook
LC 2010-37030
"While the rise of the charmingly simple, brilliantly evocative haiku is often associated with the seventeenth-century Japanese poet Matsuo Basho, the form had already flourished for more than four hundred years before Basho even began to write. These early poems, known as hokku, are identical to haiku in syllable count and structure but function differently as a genre. Whereas each haiku is its own constellation of image and meaning, a hokku opens a series of linked, collaborative stanzas in a sequence called renga. .

. . [This anthology] presents 320 hokku composed between the thirteenth and early eighteenth centuries, from the poems of the courtier Nijo Yoshimoto to those of the genre's first 'professional' master, Sogi, and his disciples. It features 20 masterpieces by Basho himself." Publisher's note

Includes bibliographical references

Modern Japanese literature; an anthology. compiled and edited by Donald Keene. Grove Press 1960 440p hardcover o.p. pa $15.95   **895.6**
1. Japanese literature -- Collections
ISBN 0-8021-5095-0 pa

"The selections give a representative sampling of the poetry, prose, and drama from the 1870's through the 1940's. Short enlightening notes on the writers or background for the text are added unobtrusively." Booklist

Modern Japanese writers; Jay Rubin, editor. Scribner 2000 434p $130   **895.6**
1. Authors, Japanese   2. Authors, Japanese -- 20th century   3. Authors, Japanese -- 20th century -- Biography   4. Japanese literature -- 20th century -- History and criticism   5. Japanese literature -- History and criticism
ISBN 0-684-80598-7
LC 00-63505

"This handbook is a collection of alphabetically arranged articles on 23 twentieth-century Japanese writers and one literary genre, written by noted scholars in the field. Entries are generally around 18 pages in length. Each author entry treats a writer's life and work and is accompanied by a selected bibliography of primary and secondary sources. Most of the writers included have been translated into English, and two of them, Kawabata Yasunari and Oe Kenzaburo, are Nobel Prize winners." Booklist

Includes bibliographical references

One hundred poems from the Japanese; {edited and translated} by Kenneth Rexroth. New Directions 1956 143p hardcover o.p. pa $11.95   **895.6**
1. Japanese poetry -- Collections
ISBN 0-8112-0181-3 pa

A bilingual collection of poems drawn chiefly from the traditional Manÿoshu, Kokinshu, and Hyakunin Isshu collections and also containing examples of haiku and other later forms. The translator's introduction provides background information on the history and nature of Japanese poetry.

896   African literatures

★ The New African poetry; an anthology. edited by Tanure Ojaide, Tijan M. Sallah. Lynne Rienner Pubs. 1999 253p hardcover o.p. pa $19.95 **896**
1. African poetry   2. African poetry (English)   3. African poetry -- Collections
ISBN 978-0-89410-891-4; 0-89410-891-3
LC 99-29889

In this anthology the editors "group poets by region. . . Most of these 62 well-educated postcolonial poets more willingly embrace the ancestral 'oratory' tradition of the African continent than poets with a Western literary ori-

entation of the era of Leopold Senghor and Wole Soyinka. Instead of anti-colonialism, these poets focus on women's roles, rural life, and the need for creativity despite economic hardships. Realistic criticism of patriarchies and traditional taboos arises from a strong attachment to homeland. Overall, regional diversity seems to have replaced defensiveness of Pan-African unity." Libr J

The Penguin book of modern African poetry; edited by Gerald Moore and Ulli Beier. 4th ed.; Penguin Books 2007 xxvi, 448p pa $17   **896**
1. African poetry -- Collections
ISBN 978-0-14-042472-0; 0-14-042472-5

This anthology includes over 200 poems by 67 poets from 23 countries.

897   Literatures of North American native languages

The Cambridge companion to Native American literature; edited by Joy Porter and Kenneth M. Roemer. Cambridge University Press 2005 343p il map hardcover o.p. pa $26.95   **897**
1. American literature -- Indian authors -- History and criticism   2. Indians of North America -- Intellectual life   3. Native American literature -- History and criticism
ISBN 978-0-521-52979-2 pa; 0-521-52979-4 pa
LC 2005-44298

Essays organized "by historical and cultural context, by genre, and according to individual authors. Particularly insightful and informative are the tightly written essays on the eight currently best-known Indian writers. Also included are maps, a time line, suggested readings, and a brief series of 40 biobibliographies of notable Native American writers. . . . Readers of this volume should probably already have a working knowledge of the main figures in this increasingly important and respected segment of American literature." Libr J

900   HISTORY

900   History, geography, and auxiliary disciplines

Báez, Fernando
A **universal** history of the destruction of books; from ancient Sumer to modern-day Iraq. translated by Alfred MacAdam. Atlas & Co. 2008 354p il map $25   **900**
1. Books -- Censorship   2. Books and reading -- History   3. Censorship   4. Libraries -- Destruction and pillage
ISBN 978-1-934633-01-4
LC 2008-932321

This is a "horrific chronicle of the centuries-long assault on human memory. . . . A sobering reminder of just how deep-seated is the instinct to destroy other people's truths." Kirkus

Includes bibliographical references

901　Philosophy and theory of history

Hobsbawm, E. J.

On history. New Press (NY) 1997 305p $25; pa
$15.95　　　　　　　　　　　　　　　　**901**
1. Historiography 2. History -- Philosophy
ISBN 1-56584-393-2; 1-56584-468-8 pa

"In these collected pieces—articles, lectures and reviews—Eric Hobsbawm surveys the writings of modern historians with the magisterial gaze of a man who has seen both
the rise of Hitler and the fall of Communism. He notes how
the discipline has changed in the last century: how social
history and economic history have come of age, how modern historians speak of change and forces where Victorians
spoke of ideas and progress. He rejects postmodernist claims
that history can be freely revised because all facts are merely
intellectual constructions." N Y Times Book Rev

MacMillan, Margaret

Dangerous games; the uses and abuses of history. Modern Library 2009 188p $22　　　**901**
1. Decision making 2. Historiography 3. History --
Errors, inventions, etc. 4. History -- Philosophy
ISBN 978-0-679-64358-6; 0-679-64358-3

Explores the ways in which history has been used to
influence people and government, focusing on how reportage of past events has been manipulated to justify religious
movements and political campaigns. Based on the Joanne
Goodman lecture series of the University of Western Ontario.

"This is a must read for anyone who wants to under-
stand the importance of correctly understanding the past."
Publ Wkly
Includes bibliographical references

Ortega y Gasset, Jose

The **revolt** of the masses; translated, annotated,
and with an introduction by Anthony Kerrigan; edited
by Kenneth Moore; with a foreword by Saul Bellow.
University of Notre Dame Press 1985 xxxi, 192p
hardcover o.p. pa $13.95　　　　　　　**901**
1. Civilization 2. Proletariat
ISBN 0-393-31095-7

LC 81-40457
A collection of essays by the Spanish intellectual in
which he analyzes the dangers of control of government by
the masses. He sees Bolshevism and Fascism as particularly
threatening to civilization.

Spengler, Oswald

The **decline** of the West, volume one; Form
and actuality. authorized translation with notes by
Charles Frances Atkinson. A. Knopf 1996 various
paging $45　　　　　　　　　　　　　　**901**
1. Civilization -- History 2. History -- Philosophy
ISBN 0-394-42179-5

The first volume of a work that "reflects the pessimistic
atmosphere in Germany after World War I. Spengler maintained that history has a natural development, in which every
culture is a distinct organic form that grows, matures, and
decays." Reader's Ency. 4th edition
Includes bibliographical references

902　Miscellany of history

Grafton, Anthony

Cartographies of time; a history of the timeline.
[by] Daniel Rosenberg and Anthony Grafton. Princeton Architectural Press 2010 272p il $50　　**902**
1. Historical chronology 2. History -- Philosophy
ISBN 978-1-56898-763-7; 1-56898-763-3

LC 2008-52892
The authors "aim to provide the first full account of the
development of the modern timeline, from its inauspicious
beginnings in crude lists and tables, to the glorious, colorful
artworks that convey the sweep of time with arresting visual drama. There's more to this story, however. The story of
the timeline is also the story of how humanity's perception
of time has evolved, and how the various representations
of time can tell us much about the personality and procliv-
ity of the era in which it was designed. . . . Rosenberg and
Grafton's text is crisp and informative, but the true stars of
Cartographies of Time are the numerous illustrations and
photographs of the chronologies themselves." PopMatters
Includes bibliographical references.

Grun, Bernard

★ The **timetables** of history; a historical linkage of people and events. 4th ed.; Simon & Schuster
2005 835p $25　　　　　　　　　　　　**902**
1. Historical chronology
ISBN 0-7432-7003-7; 978-0-7432-7003-8

LC 2005-49766
This chronology "includes material from 4500 BCE to
2004. . . . The information is listed by year in seven columns
labeled 'History, Politics', 'Literature, Theater', 'Religion,
Philosophy, Learning', 'Visual Arts', 'Music', 'Science,
Technology, Growth', and 'Daily Life.' . . . This work is
an excellent chronological tool, and should be found in all
libraries." Choice

Steinberg, S. H.

The **Wilson** calendar of world history; edited by
John Paxton and Edward W. Knappman; contributors:
Rodney Carlisle [et al.] Wilson, H.W. 1999 460p il
$100　　　　　　　　　　　　　　　　　**902**
1. Calendars 2. Chronology, Historical 3. Historical
chronology
ISBN 0-8242-0937-0

LC 98-50998
This successor to Steinberg's chronology reports on
25,000 historical events and includes expanded coverage
of the arts and sciences as well as events in Latin America,
Asia, and Africa. Includes index for people, places, events,
concepts, inventions, discoveries, and titles of works.

★ National Geographic concise history of the world;
an illustrated timeline. edited by Neil Kagan.
National Geographic Society 2005 416p il map
$40　　　　　　　　　　　　　　　　　　**902**
1. Historical chronology
ISBN 0-792-28364-3

LC 2005-52248

This history is organized in time line format and broken up into eight historical eras. Includes maps, sidebars, and illustrations.

The timetables of American history; Laurence Urdang, editor; with an introduction by Henry Steele Commager and a new foreword by Arthur Schlesinger, Jr. Simon & Schuster 2001 534p il pa $24   **902**
1. Historical chronology
ISBN 0-7432-0261-9
Presents information chronologically in tabular form. Each double-page spread has columns for history and politics, the arts, science and technology, and miscellaneous.

902.2   Illustrations, models, miniatures

National Geographic Society (U.S.)
   National Geographic visual history of the world; [authors, Klaus Berndl . . . et al.]. National Geographic Society 2005 656p il $35   **902.2**
1. World history
ISBN 0-7922-3695-5
                    LC 2005-541553
"Over 4,000 illustrations and photographs cover individuals and events from prehistory (the beginning to ca. 4000 BCE) to the contemporary world (1945 to the present). . . . This educational and entertaining volume of social, cultural, and military history will appeal to a wide readership." Choice

903   Dictionaries, encyclopedias, concordances of history

Berkshire encyclopedia of world history; William H. McNeill, Jerry H. Bentley [and] David Christian, editors. 2nd ed.; Berkshire Pub. Group 2010 6v il map set $875   **903**
1. Reference books 2. World history -- Encyclopedias
ISBN 978-1-933782-65-2
                    LC 2010021635
"To cover 250,000 years of human history, knowledge from various disciplines is synthesized, summarized, and presented in an easy-to-read fashion. Emphasis is placed on social change and cultural contact over time and place." Booklist
Includes bibliographical references

904   Collected accounts of events

Davis, Lee Allyn
   Man-made catastrophes; [by] Lee Davis. rev ed; Facts on File 2002 402p il $60   **904**
1. Disasters
ISBN 0-8160-4418-X
                    LC 2001-54324
This describes man-made disasters "from the burning of Babylon in 538B.C. to the 2001 terrorist attack on the World Trade Center in New York City. . . . [The entries]

are organized by disaster type: air crashes, civil unrest and terrorism, explosions, maritime disasters, nuclear and industrial accidents, railway disasters, and space disasters." Publisher's note
Includes bibliographical references

Hanson, Victor Davis
   Carnage and culture; landmark battles in the rise of Western power. Doubleday 2001 492p il hardcover o.p. pa $16   **904**
1. Battles 2. Military history
ISBN 0-385-72038-6 pa
                    LC 00-65582
"This provocative work is likely to engender controversy." Booklist
Includes bibliographical references

907   Education, research, related topics of history

Hamilton, Nigel
   ★ **Biography**; a brief history. Harvard University Press 2007 345p il $21.95 **907**
1. Biography as a literary form
ISBN 978-0-674-02466-3; 0-674-02466-4
                    LC 2006-51132
"Hamilton has given readers a thoughtprovoking look at biography in its various forms; a fascinating and handy reference book for anyone wishing to know more about the history and art of biography." Libr J
Includes bibliographical references (p. 315-21)

Mills, Elizabeth S.
   Evidence explained; citing history sources from artifacts to cyberspace. [by] Elizabeth Shown Mills. 2nd ed; Genealogical Pub. Co. 2009 885p $59.95   **907**
1. History -- Research 2. History -- Sources
ISBN 978-0-8063-1806-6
                    LC 2009-934128
This resource is "indispensable for scholars and accessible enough to meet the needs of amateur genealogists and students." Libr J
Includes bibliographical references

Tuchman, Barbara Wertheim
   Practicing history; selected essays. by Barbara W. Tuchman. Knopf 1981 306p hardcover o.p. pa $14.95   **907**
1. College presidents 2. Diplomats 3. Executive power 4. Financiers 5. Governors 6. Historiography 7. Modern history 8. Nobel laureates for peace 9. Presidents 10. Vietnam War, 1961-1975 11. World War, 1914-1918 -- United States
ISBN 0-345-30363-6 pa
                    LC 81-47509
A collection of essays on the nature, methodology and writing of history.

908　History with respect to groups of people

Murray, Charles A.

Human accomplishment; the pursuit of excellence in the arts and sciences, 800 B.C. to 1950. [by] Charles Murray. HarperCollins Pubs. 2003 xx, 668p il map pa $24.95　　**908**
　　1. Civilization -- History　2. Genius　3. Genius -- Case studies　4. Gifted persons -- Case studies　5. History -- Psychological aspects
　　ISBN 0-06-019247-X; 978-0-06-092964-0 pa; 0-06-092964-2 pa

　　　　　　　　　　　　　　LC 2003-47820
　　This is an "account of human excellence, from the age of Homer to our own time. . . . Murray compiles inventories of the people who have been [considered] essential to the stories of literature, music, art, philosophy, and the sciences—a total of 4,002 men and women from around the world, ranked according to their eminence. The heart of [the book] is a series of . . . descriptive chapters: on the giants in the arts and what sets them apart from the merely great; on the differences between great achievement in the arts and in the sciences; on the meta-inventions, 14 crucial leaps in human capacity to create great art and science; and on the patterns and trajectories of accomplishment across time and geography." Publisher's note
　　Includes bibliographical references

909　World history

Ariès, Philippe

A **History** of private life; v2 [Philippe Ariès and Georges Duby, general editors; translated by] Arthur Goldhammer. Belknap Press 1988 650p v2 il hardcover o.p. pa $28　　**909**
　　1. Family life　2. Manners and customs　3. Medieval civilization
　　ISBN 0-674-40001-1

　　　　　　　　　　　　　　LC 86-18286
　　"Spanning the period from the 11th century to the Renaissance and focusing on France and Tuscan Italy, this [second volume] continues the . . . five-volume history of private life from the Roman world to the present. 'Private' is here defined as what medieval people considered intimate, familial, domestic." Libr J
　　Includes bibliographical references

Boorstin, Daniel J.

The **creators**. Random House 1992 811p il hardcover o.p. pa $18.95 **909**
　　1. Arts　2. Civilization　3. Creation (Literary, artistic, etc.)
　　ISBN 0-394-54395-5; 0-679-74375-8 pa

　　　　　　　　　　　　　　LC 91-39948
　　In this volume "Boorstin undertakes an interpretive history of creativity in Western civilization. Packed with shrewd, entertaining profiles of Dante, Goethe, Benjamin Franklin and dozens of others, this stimulating synthesis sets the achievements of individual geniuses into a coherent narrative of humanity's advance from ignorance." Publ Wkly
　　Includes bibliographical references

Brendon, Piers

★　The **decline** and fall of the British Empire, 1781-1997. Alfred A. Knopf 2008 xxii, 786p il map $37.50　　**909**
　　ISBN 978-0-307-26829-7; 0-307-26829-2

　　　　　　　　　　　　　　LC 2008-14192
　　"A richly detailed, lucid account of how the British Empire grew and grew—and then, not quite inexorably, fell apart." Kirkus
　　Includes bibliographical references

Brenner, Frederic

Diaspora: homelands in exile.　HarperCollins 2003　2v il map set $100　　**909**
　　1. Jewish diaspora　2. Jews -- Pictorial works
　　ISBN 0-06-008778-1

　　　　　　　　　　　　　　LC 2003-42328
　　This is a "collection of photographs, taken over the course of 25 years, chronicling Jewish lives, often in declining communities, in every corner of the world, from Azerbaijan and Uzbekistan to Ethiopia and Las Vegas. For anyone, Jewish or otherwise, who generally thinks of Jews in terms of Israel and the United States, the book will be a revelation." Publ Wkly
　　Includes bibliographical references

Brown, Cynthia Stokes

A **big** history; from the Big Bang to the present. Distributed by W.W. Norton 2007 288p il map $25.95　　**909**
　　1. Human ecology　2. World history
　　ISBN 978-1-59558-196-9; 1-59558-196-0

　　　　　　　　　　　　　　LC 2007-6741
　　"In a multidisciplinary narrative subtly emphasizing the mutual impact of people and planet, Brown covers Earth's history from the big bang through the development of life and the growth of civilization. . . . This exciting saga crosses space and time to illustrate how humans, born of stardust, were shaped—and how they in turn shaped the world we know today." Publ Wkly

Cahill, Thomas

Sailing the wine-dark sea; why the Greeks matter. Talese 2003 304p $27.50; pa $14.95　　**909**
　　1. Civilization, Classical　2. Civilization, Western -- Greek influences
　　ISBN 0-385-49553-6; 0-385-49554-4 pa

　　　　　　　　　　　　　　LC 2003-50725
　　This author "begins with a discussion of Homer's Iliad and Odyssey and how these two epic poems relate to the history of Greece. He then focuses on such themes as the Greek alphabet, literature, and political system, and its playwrights, philosophers, and artists. A final chapter examines

the effects that Greco-Roman and Judeo-Christian traditions had on each other." Booklist

Includes bibliographical references

The **gifts** of the Jews; how a tribe of desert nomads changed the way everyone thinks and feels. Talese 1998 291p $23.50; pa $14   **909**

1. Jews -- History 2. Judaism -- History

ISBN 0-385-48248-5; 0-385-48249-3 pa

LC 97-45139

In this colloquial look at the influence of the Hebrew Bible on civilization, the author gives "the Jews credit for revolutionizing the concepts of democracy, universal law, monotheism, linear time, personal vocation, destiny, self-improvement and the belief in the equality of all humans. He stumbles on the odd aside and occasionally is surprisingly insensitive. . . Still, his passion and breadth of knowledge are admirable." N Y Times Book Rev

Includes bibliographical references

Cliff, Nigel

Holy war. Harper 2011 x, 547 p col. ill., maps (chiefly col)   **909**

ISBN 978-0-06-173512-7

LC 2011021331

This book presents an historical "interpretation of Vasco da Gama's groundbreaking voyages, seen as a turning point in the struggle between Christianity and Islam." It was the author's intent to demonstrate "that both Vasco da Gama and his archrival, Christopher Columbus, set sail with the clear purpose of launching a Crusade whose objective was to reach the Indies; seize control of its markets in spices, silks, and precious gems from Muslim traders; and claim for Portugal or Spain, respectively, all the territories they discovered. Vasco da Gama triumphed in his mission and drew a dividing line between the Muslim and Christian eras of history -- what we in the West call the medieval and the modern ages." (Publisher's note)

Fargues, Philippe

The **atlas** of the Arab world; [by] Philippe Fargues & Rafic Boustani. Facts on File 1991 144p il maps $55   **909**

ISBN 0-8160-2346-8

LC 89-675447

"A wealth of information presented in colorful maps, graphs, diagrams, and charts. Arranged by broad cultural topics such as ethnic groups and religions, society, cities, oil and industry, facts not readily available in standard resources are presented and compared." SLJ

Includes bibliographical references

Ferguson, Niall

Empire: the rise and demise of the British world order and the lessons for global power. Basic Books 2003 392p il map hardcover o.p. pa $17.95   **909**

1. Civilization, Modern -- British influences 2. Imperialism

ISBN 0-465-02329-0 pa

LC 2003-41469

This book "is ambitious, provocative, and entertaining—a rare hat trick in the genre of historical writing—in its me-ticulous charting of the rise and fall of the world's largest empire. . . . Ferguson makes a subtle, but impressive, argument that free trade, the English language, and superior education helped improve the lot of those under colonial rule." Natl Rev

Includes bibliographical references

Freeman, Charles

★ **Egypt,** Greece, and Rome; civilizations of the ancient Mediterranean. 2nd ed; Oxford Univ. Press 2004 688p $29.95   **909**

1. Civilization, Ancient 2. Civilization, Classical 3. Mediterranean civilization

ISBN 0-19-926364-7

LC 2004-41505

Freeman's "introduction to the ancient Mediterranean adds Egypt to the standard Greco-Roman nexus. Covering an immense variety of material with competence and sensitivity to nuance, Freeman relates the familiar parts of the classical story, but his is no mere rehash of the Persian War or the fall of the Roman Republic. He analytically recounts political events, religious movements, and society, with steady awareness of the fragmented character of the surviving evidence." Booklist [review of 1996 edition]

Includes bibliographical references

Galeano, Eduardo H.

Mirrors; stories of almost everyone. [by] Eduardo Galeano; English translation by Mark Fried. Nation Books 2009 391p il $26.95 **909**

1. History 2. History -- Miscellanea

ISBN 978-1-56858-423-2; 1-56858-423-7

LC 2009-004518

This book contains some 600 meditations on events or persons in history.

"Each entry is an avatar of outrage over the depredations of power against its multifarious victims, those rendered helpless by poverty, religion, race, sexual identity or—as in the vignettes about Galileo and Isaac Babel—the simple accident of being right when the truth defined by the prevailing authority was wrong. . . . As in his previous books, [Galeano] succeeds in capturing the bottomless horror of the state's capacity to inflict pain on the individual, offering as effective an act of political dissent as exists anywhere in contemporary literature." N Y Times Book Rev

Hourani, Albert Habib

A **history** of the Arab peoples; with a new afterword by Malise Ruthven. 2nd ed; Belknap Press 2002 xx, 565p il maps hardcover o.p. pa $18.95 **909**

1. Arab civilization

ISBN 0-674-01017-5; 0-674-05819-4 pa

LC 2003-269357

This history of the Arab peoples is divided into five parts: The making of a world (seventh-tenth century); Arab Muslim societies (eleventh-fifteenth century); The Ottoman age (sixteenth-eighteenth century); The age of European empires (1800-1939); The age of nation-states (since 1939). Includes a 2002 afterword, genealogies and dynasties

Johnson, Paul

A **history** of the Jews. Harper & Row 1987 644p hardcover o.p. pa $17 **909**
1. Jews -- History
ISBN 0-06-091533-1 pa

LC 85-42575

This "is an absorbing, provocative, well-written, often moving book, an insightful and impassioned blend of history and myth, story and interpretation." Christ Sci Monit
Includes bibliographical references

Kennedy, Hugh

★ The **great** Arab conquests; how the spread of Islam changed the world we live in. Da Capo 2007 421p $27.95 **909**
1. Arabs -- History 2. Islam -- History 3. Islamic civilization
ISBN 0-306-81585-0; 978-0-306-81585-0

LC 2008-297360

The author "has produced an extremely readable work chronicling the early Arab conquests to 750 CE. In the flowing narrative style for which he has become known, Kennedy brings together Arab, Byzantine, Armenian, Coptic, and Persian histories, legends, and anecdotes related to Arab expansion into the lands stretching from the Iberian Peninsula to the Sind. . . . Each chapter details the conquest of a given region, intertwining historic reality with legendary tales to provide for very colorful reading." Choice
Includes bibliographical references

Lamb, David

★ The **Arabs**; journeys beyond the mirage. 2nd Vintage Books ed, rev and updated; Vintage Bks. 2002 348p map pa $15 **909**
ISBN 1-4000-3041-2

LC 2002-524048

"Intelligent and incisive . . . Mr. Lamb has the first-rate reporter's tools, and he uses them to relate, with compelling detail, who the Arabs are." N Y Times Book Rev
Includes bibliographical references

Mann, Charles C.

1493; uncovering the new world Columbus created. Knopf 2011 535p il map $30.50; ebook $14.99 **909**
1. Agriculture -- History 2. Commerce -- History 3. Ecology -- History 4. Economic conditions 5. Economic history 6. Explorers 7. History, Modern 8. Industrial revolution 9. Modern history
ISBN 978-0-307-26572-2; 0-307-26572-2; 978-0-307-59672-7 ebook

LC 2011003408

"Mann traces the subtle, epochal influences of the intercontinental 'Columbian Exchange' of flora, fauna, commodities, and peoples, showing how European honeybees and earthworms remade New World landscapes; how New World corn, potatoes, and fertilizer ignited Eurasian population booms; how Old World diseases prompted an eruption of slavery in the Western Hemisphere; . . . how Latin American silver undermined China's Ming Dynasty; and how the decimation of Indian peoples changed the world's climate. . . . Brilliantly assembling colorful details into big-picture

insights, Mann's fresh, challenge to Eurocentric histories puts interdependence at the origin of modernity." Publ Wkly
Includes bibliographical references

Morris, Ian

Why the West rules--for now; the patterns of history, and what they reveal about the future. Farrar, Straus and Giroux 2010 750p il map **909**
1. Civilization, Modern 2. Civilization, Western 3. Comparative civilization 4. East and West 5. Modern civilization 6. Western civilization
ISBN 0374290024; 9780374290023

LC 2010005702

Morris argues that Western dominance is largely "the result of geography on the everyday efforts of ordinary people as they deal with crises of resources, disease, migration, and climate." (Publisher's note) Bibliography. Index.

"It may seem at first sight a little odd to recommend a history book as a guide to the future. But Morris' new book illustrates perfectly why one really scholarly book about the past is worth a hundred fanciful works of futurology." Foreign Affairs
Includes bibliographical references

Pagden, Anthony

★ **Peoples** and empires; a short history of European migration, exploration, and conquest from Greece to the present. Modern library ed; Modern Lib. 2001 xxv, 206p hardcover o.p. pa $10.95 **909**
1. Colonies 2. Emigration and immigration -- History 3. Germanic peoples 4. Immigration and emigration 5. Migration of nations 6. World history
ISBN 0-679-64096-7; 0-8129-6761-5 pa

LC 00-66204

This "overview of European empire building and colonization commences with the diffusion of Greek civilization and traces the subsequent evolution of the ensuing Roman, Spanish, French, and British empires. More interesting than how those empires physically expanded is the insightful discussion on what motivated individual men and entire nations to migrate and conquer." Booklist
Includes bibliographical references

Roberts, Callum

The **unnatural** history of the sea. Island Press/ Shearwater Books 2007 435p il map $28 **909**
1. Commercial fishing 2. Human influence on nature 3. Ocean
ISBN 978-1-59726-102-9; 1-59726-102-5

LC 2007-1841

"Starting with the eighteenth-century voyages of Vitus Bering, Roberts leads the reader through a wealth of maritime history revealing countless examples of overfishing. . . . Thoughtful, inspiring, devastating, and powerful, Roberts' comprehensive, welcoming, and compelling approach to an urgent subject conveys large problems in a succinct and involving manner. Readers won't be able to put it down." Booklist
Includes bibliographical references

Roberts, J. M.

The **new** history of the world; 4th rev ed; Oxford Univ. Press 2003 1232p il map $40   **909**

1. World history
ISBN 0-19-521927-9

LC 2003-270110

This overview of history from prehistoric times to the effects of the September 11, 2001 attacks is divided into eight sections: Before history--beginnings; The first civilizations; The classical Mediterranean; The age of diverging traditions; The making of the European age; The great acceleration; The end of the Europeans' world; The latest age.

Rogan, Eugene

The **Arabs**; a history. Basic Books 2009 553p il map **909**

1. Arab civilization 2. Imperialism -- History 3. Nationalism -- Arab countries -- History
ISBN 0465071007; 9780465071005

LC 2009-28575

"Eugene Rogan traces five centuries of Arab history, from the Ottoman conquests through the British and French colonial periods and up to the present age." (Publisher's note) Index.

This "is not a particularly happy story, but it is a fascinating one, and exceedingly well told. [Eugene] Rogan manoeuvres with skilful assurance, maintaining a steady pace through time, and keeping the wider horizon in view even as he makes use of a broad range of judiciously chosen primary sources to enrich the narrative." Economist

Includes bibliographical references

Sachar, Howard Morley

A **history** of the Jews in the modern world; [by] Howard M. Sachar. Knopf 2005 831p hardcover o.p. pa $23   **909**

1. Jews -- History 2. Jews -- History -- 1789-1945 3. Jews -- History -- 17th century 4. Jews -- History -- 18th century 5. Jews -- History -- 1945-
ISBN 0-375-41497-5; 1-4000-3097-8 pa

LC 2004-48814

This book "relates an immensely complex story with precision and learning." N Y Times Book Rev

Includes bibliographical references

Tinniswood, Adrian

Pirates of Barbary; corsairs, conquests, and captivity in the seventeenth-century Mediterranean. Riverhead Books 2010 xx, 343p il map $26.95   **909**

1. Pirates
ISBN 978-1-59448-774-3

LC 2010-23421

Tinniswood "demonstrates an excellent grasp of obscure sources in crafting a comprehensive synthesis. . . . Throughout, the writing is precise and mordant but also witty, allowing the reader to feel empathy for the rough and absurd lives of these long-ago mariners, and agree with the author's conclusion that whatever the corsairs' faults, a lack of courage was not among them." Kirkus

Includes bibliographical references

★ **Africana**: the encyclopedia of the African and African American experience; editors, Kwame Anthony Appiah, Henry Louis Gates, Jr. 2nd ed; Oxford University Press 2005 5v set $550 **909**

1. African Americans 2. African Americans -- Encyclopedias 3. African diaspora 4. African diaspora -- Encyclopedias 5. Blacks 6. Blacks -- Encyclopedias 7. Reference books
ISBN 978-0-19-517055-9; 0-19-517055-5

LC 2004-20222

This encyclopedia covers "prominent individuals, events, trends, places, political movements, art forms, business and trade, religions, ethnic groups, organizations, and countries on both sides of the ocean. . . . There are articles on contemporary nations of sub-Saharan Africa, ethnic groups from various regions of Africa, African American Academy award winners, Caribbean musical styles, African religions in Brazil, and European colonial powers." Booklist [review of 1999 edition]

Includes bibliographical references

The **Cambridge** illustrated history of the Islamic world; edited by Francis Robinson. Cambridge Univ. Press 1996 xxiii, 328p map hardcover o.p. pa $36.99   **909**

ISBN 0-521-43510-2; 0-521-66993-6 pa

LC 95-37562

"Facts about Islam's history and practice are presented, along with its economic, societal, and intellectual structures. Excellent graphics support the text. Maps are extensive and exact." SLJ

Includes bibliographical references

★ **Cultures** of the Jews; a new history. edited with an introduction by David Biale. Schocken Bks. 2002 xxxiii, 1196p il $45   **909**

1. Jewish civilization 2. Jews -- Civilization 3. Jews -- History 4. Judaism -- History
ISBN 0-8052-4131-0

LC 2002-23008

"The book is truly one of the most important works on the subject ever published." Booklist

Includes bibliographical references

Daily life through world history in primary documents; Lawrence Morris, general editor. Greenwood Press 2009 3v il set $299.95 **909**

1. Civilization -- History -- Sources 2. Manners and customs -- History -- Sources 3. Reference books 4. Social history -- Sources
ISBN 978-0-313-33898-4

LC 2008-8925

"Each of the three volumes . . . begins with a chronology of the era covered as well as a clear, concise historical overview that provides readers with core knowledge of the cultures discussed. The more than 530 entries are grouped into seven categories: domestic, economic, intellectual, material, political, recreational, and religious life." Booklist

Includes bibliographical references

Encyclopedia of Islam and the Muslim world; edited by Richard C. Martin. Macmillan Reference USA 2004 2v il map set $295 **909**
1. Islam 2. Islam -- Encyclopedias 3. Reference books
ISBN 0-02-865603-2

LC 2003-9964

"A solid choice for libraries needing a general treatment of Islam in sufficient detail." Choice

Includes bibliographical references

Encyclopedia of the developing world; Thomas M. Leonard, editor. Routledge 2005 3v set $625 **909**
1. Reference books
ISBN 1-57958-388-1

LC 2005-49976

The entries "detail developments from 1945 forward. In addition to basic statistical and geographical information, country-focused entries detail history, economy, and political situation. Thematic entries cover people (e.g., Jomo Kenyatta), historical topics (e.g., colonialism), economic and government models (e.g., communism), the environment (e.g., water) and organizations (e.g., WTO)." Libr J

Includes bibliographical references

Great events from history, The 17th century, 1601-1700; editor, Larissa Juliet Taylor. Salem Press 2005 2v il map set $160 **909**
1. Reference books 2. World history -- 17th century
ISBN 1-58765-225-0; 978-1-58765-225-7

LC 2005-17362

This set "offers two to three-page essays that detail the major milestones of the century as well as social developments that were reflective of daily life during the period. The perspective here is international and spans a variety of categories, including religion and theology, cultural and intellectual history, expansion and land acquisition, and natural disasters. A list of key figures involved in each event is provided." SLJ

Includes bibliographical references

Great events from history, The Renaissance & early modern era, 1454-1600; editor, Christina J. Moose. Salem Press 2005 2v il map set $160 **909**
1. Fifteenth century 2. History, Modern -- 16th century 3. Reference books 4. Renaissance 5. Sixteenth century 6. World history -- 15th century 7. World history -- 16th century
ISBN 1-58765-214-5; 978-1-58765-214-1

LC 2004-28878

This collection of essays covers events in the scientific, intellectual, literary, sociological, political and military disciplines that happened worldwide during the Renaissance.

★ A Historical atlas of the Jewish people; from the time of the patriarchs to the present. general editor, Eli Barnavi; English edition editor, Miriam Eliav-Feldon; cartography, Michel Opatowski;

new edition revised by Denis Charbit. new ed; Schocken Bks. 2002 321p il maps $45 **909**
1. Jews -- History -- Maps
ISBN 0-8052-4226-0

LC 2003-279553

"Covering three millennia of Jewish history and culture through a combination of concise text, accurate and well-drawn maps, and a sumptuous array of photographs, diagrams, and reproductions of paintings, this atlas succeeds in covering all the main themes of the Jewish experience. The material is arranged chronologically and systematically. . . . The result is a reference that will profit both scholars and lay readers." Libr J [review of 1992 edition]

909.07 General historical periods

Andrea, Alfred J.
Encyclopedia of the crusades. Greenwood Press 2003 xxiii, 356p il, maps $75 **909.07**
1. Crusades 2. Crusades -- Encyclopedias 3. Reference books
ISBN 0-313-31659-7

LC 2003-48544

This encyclopedia includes "more than 200 entries, each one between approximately 10 lines and four pages in length. . . . The introduction gives the entries some historical context and defines the term crusade for the reader. The entries are in alphabetical order and include cross-references in bold type to other entries in the book. Many entries also include suggested readings, both primary sources and historical studies. At the end of the work, the author has included a chronology of important dates and events, a 'Basic Crusade Library' of further readings in bibliographic essay style, and a general index. . . . This encyclopedia is recommended for high-school, undergraduate, and public libraries." Booklist

Includes bibliographical references

Asbridge, Thomas
★ The **crusades**; the authoritative history of the war for the Holy Land. [by] Thomas Asbridge. Ecco Press 2010 767p il map **909.07**
1. Christianity and other religions 2. Church history -- 600-1500, Middle Ages 3. Crusades 4. Medieval civilization 5. Religion and civilization
ISBN 9780060787288

Asbridge sets out to "uncover what drove Muslims and Christians alike to embrace the ideals of 'jihad' and crusade, and considers how these holy wars reshaped the medieval world and why they continue to influence events today." (Publisher's note) Index.

"Covering the 200-year period of the Crusades in a single volume is a monumental task, but Asbridge . . . handles it well, presenting an evenhanded view of the actions of Christian and Muslim forces and paying particular attention to the larger-than-life figures of Richard the Lionheart and Saladin. In addition to relating the facts of the expeditions, he explores both the motivations of the Crusaders . . . and the reasons that Christians eventually failed to retain any hold on conquered territory." Libr J

Includes bibliographical references

Burns, Thomas S.

A **history** of the Ostrogoths. Indiana Univ. Press
1984 299p il hardcover o.p. pa $19.95   **909.07**
1. Medieval civilization 2. Teutonic peoples
ISBN 0-253-20600-6 pa

LC 83-49286

This "study of the Ostrogoths . . . explores the interaction
between Rome and her eastern Germanic neighbors with the
focus on the Ostrogothic experience. Traditional literary
sources are looked at with a fresh eye, and new archaeological materials are thoroughly explored." Libr J

Includes bibliographical references

Phillips, Jonathan

Holy warriors; a modern history of the Crusades.
Random House 2010 434p il map $30   **909.07**
1. Church history -- 600-1500, Middle Ages 2. Crusades
3. Religion and civilization
ISBN 978-1-4000-6580-6; 1-4000-6580-1

LC 2009-33153

The author "superbly condenses the four centuries of the
Crusades into a single, easily accessible volume. . . . The
narrative weaves a tragic tapestry, beginning with the blood-
ily successful First Crusade, through the establishment of
the Crusader states, to the failure of subsequent Crusades,
the victories of the Muslim 'counter-Crusade,' and the continuing legacy of religious and cultural hatred that permeates
the Holy Land. . . . This is an outstanding summary of centuries of religious strife." Publ Wkly

Includes bibliographical references

★   The Crusades; an encyclopedia. Alan V. Murray, editor. ABC-CLIO 2006 4v il map set
$385   **909.07**
1. Crusades 2. Crusades -- Encyclopedias 3. Reference
books
ISBN 1-57607-862-0; 978-1-57607-862-4

LC 2006-19410

This encyclopedia "surveys all aspects of the crusading
movement from its origins in the 11th century to its decline
in the 16th century." Publisher's note

Includes bibliographical references

★   Dictionary of the Middle Ages; Joseph R. Strayer,
editor in chief. Scribner 1982 12v + index il
maps set $1,625   **909.07**
1. Middle Ages -- Dictionaries 2. Reference books
ISBN 0-684-19073-7

LC 82-5904

"Authoritative and modern, this interdisciplinary dictionary spans the years from A.D. 500 to 1500, taking cog-
nizance of the Byzantine, Islamic, and Jewish contributions
to medieval life as well as the European. . . . The contents
are in alphabetical sequence, some articles providing brief
definitions or identifications, others offering extensive background and analysis." Ref Sources: a brief guide

Great events from history, The Middle Ages, 477-
1453; editor, Brian A. Pavlac; consulting editors,
Byron Cannon, . . . [et al.] Salem Press 2005 2v
il map set $160   **909.07**
1. Civilization, Medieval 2. Medieval civilization 3.

Middle Ages 4. Middle Ages -- History 5. Reference
books
ISBN 1-58765-167-X; 978-1-58765-167-0

LC 2004-16640

This set "offers 322 essays, beginning with Confucianism arrives in Japan (fifth or sixth century) and ending with
Fall of Constantinople (May 29, 1453)." Booklist

Includes bibliographical references

The Oxford illustrated history of the Crusades; edited by Jonathan Riley-Smith. Oxford Univ.
Press 1995 436p il maps hardcover o.p. pa
$26.50   **909.07**
1. Crusades
ISBN 0-19-820435-3; 0-19-285428-3 pa

LC 94-24229

Scholars explore the complex religious, economic, and
military aspects of the Crusades.

909.08   Modern history, 1450/1500-

Aaronovitch, David

Voodoo histories; the role of the conspiracy theory in shaping modern history. Riverhead Books 2010
388p il $26.95   **909.08**
1. Conspiracies
ISBN 978-1-59448-895-5

LC 2009-37018

"The book is an evenhanded, lively, and fascinating look
not just at the people who believe these theories but also at
the people who promote them: the evidence manipulators,
the liars, the con artists, and the almost pathetically gullible
and uninformed." Booklist

Includes bibliographical references

Garton Ash, Timothy

★   **Free** world; America, Europe, and the surprising future of the West. Random House 2004 286p il
map $24.95; pa $14.95   **909.08**
1. World politics -- 1991-
ISBN 1-400-06219-5; 1-400-07646-3 pa

LC 2004-53862

The author "traces the gradual unravelling of the Atlantic
alliance back through the destruction of the Twin Towers in
2001, America's 9/11, to the fall of the Berlin Wall on November 9, 1989, Europe's 9/11. He writes with great insight,
balance and yet with passion, too." Times Lit Suppl

Includes bibliographical references

Herman, Arthur

The **idea** of decline in Western history. Free
Press 1996 521p pa $23.95   **909.08**
1. Historians 2. History -- Philosophy 3. Philosophers
4. Western civilization
ISBN 0-684-82791-3; 978-1-4165-7633-4 pa; 1-4165-
7633-9 pa

LC 96-36285

"Herman recaps the two-century-long tradition of criticism of Western civilization. . . . He covers two historians
most closely identified with predicting decline, Oswald
Spengler and Arnold Toynbee, and also brings forth less fa-

mous prognosticators of the doom of the West. . . . An accessible survey for the serious nonacademic." Booklist

Includes bibliographical references

Jasanoff, Maya

Edge of empire; lives, culture, and conquest in the East, 1750-1850. Knopf 2005 404p il $27.95 **909.08**

1. Collectors and collecting 2. Collectors and collecting -- History 3. Material culture -- Great Britain

ISBN 1-4000-4167-8

LC 2004-60221

"In graceful prose and with evocative illustrations, Jasanoff scores her points about conquest, collecting, and cultural crossing, offering a thoughtful and highly subtle study." Libr J

Includes bibliographical references

Kennedy, Paul M., 1945-

The **rise** and fall of the great powers; economic change and military conflict from 1500 to 2000. by Paul Kennedy. Vintage Books 1989 xxv, 677 p.p hardcover o.p. pa $17 **909.08**

1. Balance of power 2. Economic conditions 3. Economic history 4. Military history, Modern 5. Military readiness -- Economic aspects 6. Modern history

ISBN 0-679-72019-7 pa; 0679720197 pa

LC 88040123

"Kennedy's great achievement is that he makes us see our current international problems against a background of empires that have gone under because they were unable to sustain the material cost of greatness; and he does so in a universal historical perspective." N Y Rev Books

Bibliography: p. 625-662

Tuchman, Barbara Wertheim

★ The **march** of folly; from Troy to Vietnam. [by] Barbara W. Tuchman. Knopf 1984 447p il hardcover o.p. pa $16.95 **909.08**

1. Modern history 2. Popes 3. Reformation 4. Trojan War 5. Vietnam War, 1961-1975

ISBN 0-345-30823-9 pa

LC 83-22206

The author analyzes examples of governmental bumbling including the Trojan horse, the U.S. involvement in Vietnam, and the British loss of the American colonies.

909.7   Specific historical periods since 1700

Winik, Jay

★ The **great** upheaval; America and the birth of the modern world, 1788-1800. Harper 2007 xx, 659p il map $29.95; pa $17.95 **909.7**

1. Modern civilization 2. Modern history

ISBN 0-06-008313-1; 978-0-06-008313-7; 0-06-008314-X pa; 978-0-06-008314-4 pa

"An outstandingly wide-ranging account of this vital era in world history." Booklist

Includes bibliographical references

Great events from history, The 18th century, 1701-1800; editor John Powell. Salem Press 2006 2v il map set $160 **909.7**

1. Reference books 2. World history -- 18th century

ISBN 978-1-58765-279-0; 1-58765-279-X

LC 2006-5406

"Topics include geopolitical events, social and intellectual issues, scientific developments, philosophy, and the arts. The global coverage emphasizes turning points that redirected and shaped history and helped create the modem world. Essays have an average length of 1600 words. Each one begins with a short summary of the topic and includes dates, locales, categories, key figures, text, significance, further reading, see-also references, and cross-referencing to other essays in this set and in the rest of the series. . . . An informative resource." SLJ

Includes bibliographical references

909.8   1800-

Getty Images Inc.

History of the world in photographs; [by] Getty Images; Encyclopedia Britannica. Black Dog & Leventhal 2008 559p il $50 **909.8**

1. Modern history -- Pictorial works

ISBN 978-1-57912-583-7; 1-57912-583-2

This "volume would entice just about anyone to learn about history." Libr J

909.81   19th century, 1800-1899

Great events from history, The 19th century, 1801-1900; editor, John Powell. Salem Press 2006 4v il map set $360 **909.81**

1. Reference books 2. World history -- 19th century

ISBN 978-1-58765-297-4; 1-58765-297-8

LC 2006-19789

"These volumes cover the world's most important events and developments from 1801 through 1900. . . . Essays address important social and cultural developments in daily life: major literary movements, significant developments in art and music, trends in immigration, and progressive social legislation." Publisher's note

Includes bibliographical references

909.82   20th century, 1900-1999

Dallek, Robert

The **lost** peace; leadership in a time of horror and hope, 1945-1953. Harper 2010 420p il $28.99; ebook $22.99 **909.82**

1. Cold War 2. Cold war 3. World War, 1939-1945 -- Peace 4. World politics -- 1945- 5. World politics, 1945-1989

ISBN 978-0-06-162866-5; 978-0-06-201671-3 ebook

LC 2010-05727

The author's "interpretation of the thinking and actions of American, Chinese, European, and Soviet leaders is worth the book's reasonable price. This is solid historical scholarship from a master." Libr J

Includes bibliographical references

Gilbert, Martin

History of the twentieth century. Morrow 2001 783p maps hardcover o.p. pa $19.95   **909.82**
1. World history -- 20th century
ISBN 0-06-050594-X pa

LC 2001-32612

The author "chronicles world events year by year, from the dawn of aviation to the flourishing technology age, taking us through World War I to the inauguration of Franklin Roosevelt as president of the United States and Hitler as chancellor of Germany. He continues on to document wars in South Africa, China, Ethiopia, Spain, Korea, Vietnam, and Bosnia, as well as apartheid, the arms race, the moon landing, and the beginnings of the computer age, while interspersing the influence of art, literature, music, and religion." Publisher's note

Hillstrom, Kevin

★ The **Cold** War; foreword by Christian Ostermann. Omnigraphics 2006 xx, 536p il $65 **909.82**
1. Cold War -- Sources 2. Cold war 3. World politics -- 1945-1991 4. World politics, 1945-1989 -- Sources 5. World politics, 1985-1995 -- Sources
ISBN 0-7808-0934-3; 978-0-7808-0934-5

LC 2006-15330

"The wide-ranging scope of documents compiled in this volume will provide AP history and social studies classes with a wealth of information for research and analysis." Libr Media Connect

Includes glossary and bibliographical references

Huntington, Samuel P.

The **clash** of civilizations and the remaking of world order. Simon & Schuster 1996 367p il maps hardcover o.p. pa $17   **909.82**
1. Modern civilization -- 1950- 2. World politics -- 1965-
ISBN 0-684-84441-9 pa

LC 96-31492

"The Huntington argument that the West should stop intervening in civilizational conflicts it doesn't understand makes a powerful claim that internationalists cannot easily ignore." N Y Times Book Rev

Judt, Tony

Reappraisals; reflections on the forgotten twentieth century. Penguin Press 2008 448p bibl f $29.95 **909.82**
1. History, Modern -- 20th century 2. Modern history 3. Twentieth century 4. World history -- 20th century
ISBN 978-1-59420-136-3; 1-59420-136-6

LC 2007-30297

The author "writes informatively about Manes Sperber, tenderly about Primo Levi, enthusiastically about Hannah Arendt. . . . [Tony Judt is] not only a historian of the first rank but (in a word we need an equivalent for) a politicologue who gives engagement a good name." N Y Times Book Rev

Includes bibliographical references and index

Junger, Sebastian

Fire. Norton 2001 224p $24.95 **909.82**
1. Disasters 2. Low-intensity conflicts (Military science) 3. Terrorism 4. Urban warfare 5. War 6. World politics -- 1989- 7. World politics -- 1991-
ISBN 0-393-01046-5

LC 2001-45236

The stories are "all told with Junger's unfailing eye for detail, which often lends the pieces a disturbing authenticity." Libr J

Kurlansky, Mark

1968; the year that rocked the world. Ballantine 2004 xx, 441p il $26.95 **909.82**
1. History, Modern -- 1945-1989 2. Insurgency 3. Insurgency -- History 4. Nineteen sixty-eight, A.D. 5. Political violence -- History 6. Radicalism 7. Radicalism -- History 8. World history -- 1945-
ISBN 0-345-45581-9

LC 2004-299128

This is an account "of the global, social, and political upheaval, warfare, and assassinations that define one year in a tumultuous decade." Booklist

Includes bibliographical references

Milo, Paul

Your flying car awaits; robot butlers, lunar vacations, and other dead-wrong predictions from the twentieth century. Harper 2009 280p pa $14.99   **909.82**
1. Forecasting 2. Modern civilization
ISBN 978-0-06-172460-2

LC 2009-19710

"The book is broken into little sections that are quick and concise but never lacking in detail or depth." PopMatters

National Geographic Society (U.S.)

National Geographic eyewitness to the 20th century. National Geographic Soc. 1998 400p il hardcover o.p. pa $22.95   **909.82**
1. Discoveries in geography 2. History, Modern -- 20th century 3. Natural history 4. Science -- History -- 20th century 5. World history -- 20th century
ISBN 0-7922-8063-6 pa

LC 98-22756

"Chapters are arranged thematically by decade and open with a six-page essay discussing each era. . . . Most useful of all are the double-page spreads for each year presenting events, people, and themes in short paragraph entries. Brief trends and trivia are listed vertically. A time line appears along the bottom of the pages. Photographs bring the discussions to life and sidebars present interesting developments and people." SLJ

Reynolds, David

One world divisible; a global history since 1945. Norton 2000 861p il $35; pa $19.95   **909.82**
1. History, Modern -- 1945- 2. World history -- 1945-
ISBN 0-393-04821-7; 0-393-32108-8 pa

LC 99-33903

This world history focuses on the "concept of statebuilding, within the contexts of the competing trends of globalization and fragmentation. Writing with great economy but without compromising essential insights, Reynolds brings forth the forces at work—as often as not determined or fanatical individuals—in shaping a country's government and foreign policy. Whether assessing Nasser in Egypt, Jinnah in Pakistan, or Mao in China, Reynolds injects the account with fresh explanations of events." Booklist

Includes bibliographical references

Summits; six meetings that shaped the twentieth century. Basic Books 2007 544p il map $35 **909.82**
1. Diplomacy 2. World history -- 20th century 3. World politics
ISBN 978-0-465-06904-0; 0-465-06904-5
"The author's thorough mastery of his subject is reflected in the fluency and assurance of the writing." Publ Wkly
Includes bibliographical references

Schwartz, Richard Alan
The **1990s**; [by] Richard A. Schwartz. Facts on File 2006 496p il $75 **909.82**
ISBN 0-8160-5696-X
LC 2004-28884
This book "provides hundreds of firsthand accounts of the 1990s—including diary entries, letters, speeches, and newspaper accounts—that illustrate how historical events appeared to those who lived through them. Each chapter provides an introductory essay and a chronology of events." Publisher's note
Includes bibliographical references

Tuchman, Barbara Wertheim
The **proud** tower; a portrait of the world before the war, 1890-1914. [by] Barbara W. Tuchman. 1st Ballantine Books ed; Ballantine Books 1996 528p il pa $15.95 **909.82**
1. Anarchism and anarchists 2. Army officers 3. Composers 4. Socialism 5. World history -- 19th century 6. World history -- 20th century
ISBN 0-345-40501-3
LC 96-96511
The author describes prewar social conditions in the U.S., France, England and Germany.

The Columbia history of the 20th century; {edited by} Richard W. Bulliet. Columbia Univ. Press 1998 651p $62; pa $29 **909.82**
1. History, Modern -- 20th century 2. World history -- 20th century
ISBN 0-231-07628-2; 0-231-07629-0 pa
LC 97-39426
Scholars contribute chapters on topics ranging "from 'Ethnicity and Racism,' to 'Nationalism,' 'Communications,' 'Industry and Business,' and others. The idea is for readers to peruse those chapters that appeal to them. Articles average under 25 pages, so content is quite broad. While the level of scholarship varies a bit, overall quality is good." Libr J
Includes bibliographical references

Encyclopedia of conflicts since World War II; edited by James Ciment. 2nd ed; M.E. Sharpe 2007 4v set $439 **909.82**
1. International relations -- History -- 20th century 2. Military history, Modern -- 20th century 3. Reference books 4. War -- History -- 20th century 5. World politics -- 1945- 6. World politics -- 1945- -- Encyclopedias
ISBN 978-0-7656-8005-1; 0-7656-8005-X
LC 2006-14011
"The illustrations are strong and the maps helpful, and the thumbnail biographies and glossary are useful. A valuable resource for most school and public libraries." SLJ
Includes bibliographical references

Encyclopedia of the Cold War; a political, social, and military history. Spencer C. Tucker, editor. ABC-CLIO 2007 5v il map set $495 **909.82**
1. Cold war -- Encyclopedias 2. Reference books 3. World politics -- 1945- -- Encyclopedias
ISBN 978-1-85109-701-2
LC 2007-9681
"The content gives a broad global view of an anxious period and provides useful background for some of today's conflicts." Booklist
Includes bibliographical references

Great events from history: The 20th century, 1901-1940; editor, Robert F. Gorman. Salem Press 2007 6v il map set $495 **909.82**
1. Reference books 2. World history -- 20th century
ISBN 978-1-58765-324-7; 1-58765-324-9
LC 2007-1930
This work "identifies key events that helped to shape the course of the history of the world from 1901 to 1940. In more than 1,000 essays, a plethora of topics are presented, including Canada claiming the Arctic Islands (1901); the plague killing 1.2 million in India (1907); Gertrude Ederle swimming the English Channel (1926); Stalin beginning the Purge Trials (1934); and Germany hosting the 1936 Olympics." Booklist
Includes bibliographical references

Great events from history: The 20th century, 1941-1970; editor, Robert F. Gorman. Salem Press 2008 6v il map set $495 **909.82**
1. Reference books 2. World history -- 20th century
ISBN 978-1-58765-331-5; 1-58765-331-1
LC 2007-37204
The articles in this set "cover everything from the bombing of Pearl Harbor to the celebration of the First Earth Day. Each article lists a locale, key figures, categories, and a summary of events; readers can search for additional information based on categories or key figures. The sixth volume contains a bibliography, personage, subject, category, and geographical indexes and a chronological list of entries. . . . An excellent cross-reference tool." Libr J
Includes bibliographical references

Great events from history: The 20th century, 1971-
2000; editor, Robert F. Gorman. Salem Press
2008 6v il map set $495   **909.82**
1. Reference books 2. World history -- 20th century
ISBN 978-1-58765-338-4; 1-58765-338-9
                                    LC 2007-51351
This set "provides extended coverage of 1,083 major
events between 1971 and 2000." Publisher's note
Includes bibliographical references

The Oxford history of the twentieth century; edited
by Michael Howard and Wm. Roger Louis. Oxford Univ. Press 1998 xxii, 458p il hardcover
o.p. pa $26.50   **909.82**
1. History, Modern -- 20th century 2. Twentieth century
3. World history 4. World history -- 20th century
ISBN 978-0-19-280378-8 pa; 0-19-280378-6 pa
                                    LC 98-12861
"Besides global wars hot and cold, population explosion and urbanization impacted the entire century, as one
of 27 articles in Twentieth Century underscores. Embracing nonpolitical topics in areas such as physics, modernism
in art, and international economics, this work exposes the
interested reader to developments that have affected most
people." Booklist
Includes bibliographical references

909.83   21st century, 2000-2099

Bergen, Peter L.
The **longest** war; the enduring conflict between
America and al-Qaeda. Free Press 2011 xx, 473p il
map $28; ebook $12.99   **909.83**
1. Iraq War, 2003- 2. Terrorism 3. Terrorism -- United
States -- Prevention 4. War on Terrorism, 2001- 5. War
on terrorism
ISBN 978-0-7432-7893-5; 0-7432-7893-3; 978-1-
4391-6059-6 ebook; 1-4391-6059-7 ebook
                                    LC 2010-15268
This is "a broad, almost stereoscopic account that brings
an array of sources together into an illuminating synthesis. .
. . If you want a solid, readable history of the Long War, this
is a great place to start." Washington Monthly
Includes bibliographical references

Khan, Mahvish Rukhsana
My Guantanamo diary; the detainees and the
stories they told me. Public Affairs 2008 302p il
$25.95   **909.83**
1. Afghan War, 2001- 2. Lawyers 3. Prisoners of
war 4. Prisoners of war -- United States 5. War on
Terrorism, 2001- 6. War on terrorism
ISBN 978-1-58648-498-9
                                    LC 2008-274233
This book "provides a valuable account of what we can
now recognize as one of the most shameful episodes in the
war on terror. It is hard to read this book without a growing sense of embarrassment and indignation." N Y Times
Book Rev
Includes bibliographical references

Mueller, Andrew
I wouldn't start from here; the 21st century and
where it all went wrong. Soft Skull Press 2009 464p
pa $16.95   **909.83**
1. Modern history 2. Social conflict 3. War 4. World
politics
ISBN 978-1-59376-218-6
                                    LC 2008-44091
"An erstwhile rock critic, Mueller took the leap into battlefield journalism to investigate the ways in which a chaotic
and tenacious concept of nationality can infuse a country's
individual citizens with the fervor to kill or die in its defense.
Having been wounded and imprisoned in pursuit of this underlying truth through 70 of the world's most volatile regimes, Mueller examines the daily lives of both a new breed
of revolutionary and an old guard whose rhetoric is steeped
in centuries-old traditions. Peppered with trenchant observations that reflect a nimble, cut-to-the-chase practicality,
Mueller's interviews with everyone from terrorist warlords
to international peacemakers are refreshingly irreverent yet
astute." Booklist
Includes bibliographical references

The 21st century; edited by Hilary D. Claggett. Wilson, H.W. 1999 185p pa $50   **909.83**
1. Forecasting 2. Millennium 3. Reference shelf 4.
Social prediction 5. Twenty-first century 6. Twenty-
first century -- Forecasts 7. Two thousand, A.D
ISBN 0-8242-0966-4
                                    LC 99-462343
A collection of articles focusing on the millenial years
1000 and 2000. The Y2K scare is discussed and contributors
speculate on the future of the planet

Reuters; our world now. Reuters. 5th ed. Thames &
Hudson 2012 352 p. col. ill. (pbk.) $24.95 **909.83**
1. Civilization, Modern -- 21st century -- Pictorial
works 2. History, Modern -- 21st century -- Pictorial
works 3. Photojournalism
ISBN 0500289867 2012 edition; 9780500289860
2012 edition
                                    LC 2011933209
This fifth volume in the Our World series from news
agency Reuters "captures 2011 in over 350 powerful photos
covering the full range of news reporting – politics, commerce, conflict, accidents and disasters, the environment,
faith and festivities, entertainment, celebrity and lifestyle. . .
. [C]aptions summarize the story behind each image." (Publisher s note)

910   Geography and travel

Allaby, Michael
The **encyclopedia** of Earth; a complete visual
guide. [authors, Michael Allaby ... [et al.]] University of California Press 2008 608p il map $39.95 **910**
1. Earth sciences -- Encyclopedias 2. Reference books
ISBN 978-0-520-25471-8; 0-520-25471-6
                                    LC 2008-6956
This "source includes six main sections. 'Birth' is an
overview of Earth's history and evolution; 'Fire' covers

its inner workings, structure, and landscape; 'Land' covers rocks, minerals, and habitats; 'Air' covers weather; 'Water' includes information on oceans, rivers, and lakes; and 'Humans' is about humankind's relationship with Earth, including management of its resources. . . . This is a stunning, reasonably priced resource, especially useful for those in need of illustrations or a visual representation of a phenomenon or concept." Choice

Thomas, Nicholas

Cook; the extraordinary voyages of Captain James Cook. Walker & Company 2003 xxxvii, 467p il map $28; pa $18.95 **910**

1. Biography, Individual 2. Explorers 3. Naval officers 4. Travel writers

ISBN 0-8027-1412-9; 0-8027-7711-2 pa

LC 2003-57648

"Rich, vivid and deeply provocative, Thomas's work combines premiere adventure story with thorough history and intensive sociology." Publ Wkly

Includes bibliographical references

United States/Central Intelligence Agency

The **CIA** world factbook 2011. Skyhorse Pub. 2010 xxvi, 837p map pa $14.95 **910**

1. Geography -- Handbooks, manuals, etc. 2. Political science -- Handbooks, manuals, etc. 3. World politics -- Handbooks, manuals, etc.

ISBN 978-1-61608-047-1

Provides information on such topics as politics, military expenditures, and economics, and shares comprehensive, country-by-country statistical and rate information.

Points unknown; a century of great exploration. edited by David Roberts. Norton 2000 608p $29.95 **910**

1. Adventure and adventurers 2. Explorers 3. Voyages and travels

ISBN 0-393-05000-9

LC 00-32915

"A mesmerizing display of the pull adventure exerts." Booklist

910.2 Miscellany

Lopes, Rosaly M. C.

The **volcano** adventure guide; [by] Rosaly Lopes. Cambridge University Press 2005 352p il map $55 **910.2**

1. Travel 2. Volcanoes

ISBN 0-521-55453-5; 978-0-521-55453-4

This is a travel "guide to world-class volcanoes. Readers are first introduced to the different types of volcanoes and the various dynamic processes and eruption styles that produce them. . . . The second part of the book is packed with information and guidance to 20 select examples of volcanoes from around the world, coupled with more information on additional volcanoes in each area that could easily be visited. . . . Spectacular color photos, geologic and geographic

maps, and schematic interpretive illustrations provide excellent support for a beautifully written text." Choice

Includes bibliographical references

Stellin, Susan

How to travel practically anywhere; the ultimate travel guide. Houghton Mifflin Co. 2006 321p pa $15.95 **910.2**

1. Travel

ISBN 978-0-618-60753-2; 0-618-60753-6

LC 2005-22728

This "guide to travel planning that covers the ins and outs (and ups and downs) of do-it-yourself travel. . . . [The author] offers information and advice on topics that traditional travel guides discuss only minimally: solo travel, travel insurance, last-minute planning, government travel advisories, web fares, home-exchange information, and more; she also includes a helpful section on what to do in an emergency—when you need a doctor or have lost your passport. . . . This comprehensive and well-researched guide is useful for both new and seasoned travelers and is highly recommended for all libraries with travel collections." Libr J

Unesco

World heritage sites; a complete guide to 911 UNESCO world heritage sites. Rev. and updated; Firefly Books 2011 856p il map pa $29.95 **910.2**

1. Historic buildings 2. Historic sites 3. Reference books

ISBN 978-1-55407-827-1; 1-55407-827-X

LC 2010-671075

Each site has an entry explaining its historical and cultural significance, with a description and location map.

"UNESCO's World Heritage mission is to encourage the identification, protection, and preservation of cultural and natural heritage around the world considered to be of outstanding value to humanity. This treasure trove of a book reinforces that mission and, through spectacular photographs, shows how remarkable and beautiful our planet truly is. An excellent (and affordable) addition to any library." Libr J

910.3 Dictionaries, encyclopedias, concordances, gazetteers

Waldman, Carl

Encyclopedia of exploration; [by] Carl Waldman and Alan Wexler. Facts on File 2004 2v il map set $225 **910.3**

1. Discoveries in geography -- Encyclopedias 2. Exploration 3. Explorers 4. Explorers -- Biography -- Encyclopedias 5. Voyages and travels 6. Voyages and travels -- Encyclopedias

ISBN 0-8160-4678-6

LC 2004-10625

"The first volume is all biographical entries with accompanying appendixes that list explorers by occupation, area(s) explored, chronology, and the respective explorers' nationality. The second volume has topical entries about all things related to exploration, such as specific areas, technologies, and routes." Am Ref Books Annu, 2005

Includes bibliographical references

★ The Columbia gazetteer of the world; edited by
Saul B. Cohen. 2nd ed.; Columbia University
Press 2008 3v set $595   **910.3**
1. Gazetteers 2. Reference books
ISBN 978-0-231-14554-1
                LC 2008-9181
"The 170,000-plus entries cover political, physical, and
special places, including monuments and historic sites. . . .
Historically accurate, this title can be considered a reference
standard." Libr J

Merriam-Webster's geographical dictionary; 3rd
ed; Merriam-Webster 1997 1361p maps
$32.95   **910.3**
1. Gazetteers 2. Geography -- Dictionaries 3.
Reference books
ISBN 0-87779-546-0
                LC 96-52365
This guide contains data about countries, cities, and
physical features. More than 48,000 entries and over 250
maps provide population, size, economic data and historical notes. Pronunciations are included and a table of foreign
terms used in English is provided.

The Oxford companion to world exploration; David Buisseret, editor in chief. Oxford University
Press 2007 2v il map set $250   **910.3**
1. Discoveries in geography 2. Exploration
ISBN 0-19-514922-X; 978-0-19-514922-7
                LC 2006-27968
"The entries are presented in alphabetical order and cover not only individual explorers, but also some geographic
regions, wars, commercial operations, and religious organizations. . . . This work will become the first stop for students
and general readers who seek either basic information or a
starting point for further reading." Sci Books Films
    Includes bibliographical references

910.4   Accounts of travel and facilities for travelers

Baggett, Jennifer
    The **lost** girls; three friends, four continents,
one unconventional detour around the world. [by]
Jennifer Baggett, Holly C. Corbett, Amanda Pressner. HarperCollins 2010 542p map $24.99; ebook
$11.99   **910.4**
1. Backpacking 2. Broadcasting executives 3.
Magazine editors 4. Marketing executives 5. Travel
writers 6. Voyages and travels 7. Women -- Travel
ISBN 978-0-06-168906-2; 978-0-06-199347-3 ebook
                LC 2009-54294
"Friends Pressner, Baggett, and Corbett were all busy
climbing the corporate ladder of Manhattan media when
they realized that, in their late twenties, they weren't sure
they wanted the golden handcuffs of New York success. Re-
prioritizing, they decide on a rebellious, extreme course of
action: quit their jobs, abandon their boyfriends, and take a
yearlong trip around the world. In this group memoir, the
three take turns chronicling a journey from Peru to Kenya to

Vietnam to Australia, and everywhere in between. . . . [The
authors] provide passionate, vivid descriptions of their far-
flung travels, bolstered by thoughtful insights and genuine
intentions, making this an intensely enjoyable read for fans
of travel writing." Publ Wkly

Bathurst, Bella
    The **wreckers**; a story of killing seas and plundered
shipwrecks, from the eighteenth century to the present day.
Houghton Mifflin 2005 326p il maps $25 **910.4**
1. Shipwrecks 2. Shipwrecks -- Great Britain 3.
Shipwrecks -- Great Britain -- History 4. Wreckers (of
ships)
ISBN 0-618-41677-3
                LC 2005-45951
The author "explains that 'wreckers' were people who
watched for a ship in distress and stole everything on board
of any value, sometimes also drowning the crew and burning
the boats. . . . Bathurst traveled to eight wrecking 'hot spots'
in Britain in researching the history of wrecking over the last
300 years, its heyday occurring in the eighteenth and nineteenth centuries. . . . The result is an exceptional chronicle
of knavery." Booklist
    Includes bibliographical references (p. 309-19)

Bellec, Francois
    Unknown lands; the log books of the great ex-
plorers. translated by Lisa Davidson and Elizabeth
Ayre. Overlook Press 2002 213p il map $55 **910.4**
1. Discoveries in geography -- History 2. Explorers
3. Explorers -- History 4. Navigation -- History 5.
Voyages and travels 6. Voyages and travels -- History
ISBN 1-58567-201-7
                LC 2001-36800
"Weaving together logs, correspondence, and stories
of the 'ordinary and extraordinary men' who explored the
oceans and unknown lands over five centuries, Bellec offers
a . . . snapshot of the cultural and political circumstances
that set the stage for maritime adventures and New World
discoveries. Eyewitness accounts retold alongside maps and
drawings contribute to an enlightening view of the minds,
hearts, and talents of adventurers such as Columbus, Vasco
de Gama, and James Cook. . . . This is simply a stunning
book." Libr J
    Includes bibliographical references

Bergreen, Laurence
    Over the edge of the world; Magellan's terrifying
circumnavigation of the globe. Morrow 2003 458p
il maps hardcover o.p. pa $15.95   **910.4**
1. Explorers 2. Voyages around the world
ISBN 0-06-621173-5; 0-06-093638-X pa; 978-0-06-
093638-9 pa
                LC 2003-50143
The author "tells a well-rounded story of Magellan, not
just that of the romanticized hero but also that of the explorer's darker side. . . . Fascinating reading for history buffs, and
a great story that rivals any seagoing adventure." Booklist
    Includes bibliographical references

Brandt, Anthony

The **man** who ate his boots; the tragic history of the search for the Northwest Passage. Alfred A. Knopf 2010 441p il map $28.95 **910.4**

1. Explorers 2. Naval officers 3. Northwest Passage 4. Travel writers

ISBN 978-0-307-26392-6; 0-307-26392-4

LC 2009-38835

The author tells the story of the search for the Northwest Passage, from its beginnings early in the age of exploration through its development into a British national obsession to the final sordid, terrible descent into scurvy, starvation, and cannibalism.

"Often witty in his approach, Brandt makes the absurdity of Arctic exploration and the quest for the Northwest Passage entertaining for the general reader. Highly recommended for fans of British or Arctic exploration history." Libr J

Includes bibliographical references

Cordingly, David

Under the black flag; the romance and the reality of life among the pirates. Random House 1996 296p maps hardcover o.p. pa $15 **910.4**

1. Pirates

ISBN 0-679-42560-8; 978-0-8129-7722-6 pa; 0-8129-7722-X pa

LC 95-41414

"This succinct history is full of unexpected revelations about the facts and myths of piracy; a typical seventeenth-century Western pirate vessel, for example, was run democratically long before the French Revolution, and one of the most successful pirates of all time was a nineteenth-century Chinese woman who controlled some fifty thousand seagoing outlaws." New Yorker

Includes bibliographical references

Women sailors and sailors' women; an untold maritime history. Random House 2001 286p il hardcover o.p. pa $14.95 **910.4**

1. Adventure and adventurers 2. Voyages and travels 3. Women 4. Women and the sea

ISBN 0-375-75872-0 pa

LC 00-62762

A look at "the lives of the intrepid women who went to sea during the great age of sail. Countless females set sail for reasons of adventure, romance, or duty in the seventeenth, eighteenth, and nineteenth centuries. Included among their numbers were the wives or mistresses of ships' officers, prostitutes, female pirates, and women disguised as male sailors. . . . A significant contribution to both women's history and maritime scholarship." Booklist

Includes bibliographical references

Dana, Richard Henry

★ **Two** years before the mast; a personal narrative of life at sea. introduction by Gary Kinder; notes by Duncan Hasell. Modern Library 2001 xxiv, 516p il pa $12.95 **910.4**

1. Seafaring life 2. Voyages and travels

ISBN 0-375-75794-5

LC 2001-31243

The author "shipped out of Boston in 1834 on the Pilgrim and sailed around the Horn to California on a hide-trading expedition. The book is based on the journal he kept during the voyage. Horrified by the brutal captain's mistreatment of the sailors, and shocked by their lack of legal redress, Dana wrote with a burning indignation that did much to rouse the public to the mariners' plight." HarperCollins Reader's Ency of Am Lit. 2d edition

Garcia Marquez, Gabriel

The **story** of a shipwrecked sailor; who drifted on a life raft for ten days without food or water, was proclaimed a national hero, kissed by beauty queens, made rich through publicity, and then spurned by the government and forgotten for all time. Translated from the Spanish by Randolph Hogan. Knopf 1986 106p hardcover o.p. pa $11 **910.4**

1. Survival after airplane accidents, shipwrecks, etc.

ISBN 0-679-72205-X pa

LC 85-45673

"In 1955 Garcia Marquez was working as a reporter in Colombia. One of his stories was a serialized account of a sailor who was swept overboard with seven other crew members of a Colombian destroyer and who was the only one to survive. This book presents Garcia Marquez' version of the sailor's first-person narrative." Booklist

Heyerdahl, Thor

Kon-Tiki; across the Pacific by raft. translated by F.H. Lyon. Washington Square Press 1984 240p map pa $5.99 **910.4**

1. Ethnology -- Polynesia

ISBN 0-671-72652-8

LC 84-42785

The "story of the six men who crossed the Pacific from Peru to the Polynesians on a primitive balsa-log raft such as Peruvian natives of the fifth century used, to prove that it was possible that the legendary race that came to Easter Island and the Polynesians could have come from Peru." Wis Libr Bull

Hoffman, Carl

The **lunatic** express; discovering the world -- via its most dangerous buses, boats, trains, and planes. Broadway Books 2010 286p map $24.99 **910.4**

1. Transportation 2. Voyages and travels

ISBN 0-7679-2980-2; 978-0-7679-2980-6

LC 2009-21477

Hoffman "manages to be both brave and compassionate as he lurches on his near-interminable journey from his home turf in the Adams Morgan neighborhood of Washington to the Gobi Desert and back again. He learns enough about himself en route to satisfy the travel-writing theorists, true, and this can be a little tedious. But—more important—he learns along the way a great deal about the habits of the world's peripatetic poor, and he writes about both the process and the people with verve and charity, making this book both extraordinary and extraordinarily valuable." Wall Street J

Jacobson, Mark

12,000 miles in the nick of time; a semi-dysfunctional family circumnavigates the globe. with additional commentary by Rae Jacobson. Atlantic Monthly Press 2003 271p il maps hardcover o.p. pa $13   **910.4**

1. Voyages around the world
ISBN 0-8021-4138-2 pa

                LC 2003-41821

"The book is very funny—the trip doesn't go exactly as the parents plan—but it is also hugely educational, history presented as a grand adventure. The kids learned a lot, and so do we." Booklist
Includes bibliographical references

Junger, Sebastian

★ The **perfect** storm; a true story of men against the sea. Norton 1997 226p il map $23.95; pa $14.95   **910.4**

1. Shipwrecks 2. Storms 3. Storms -- New England
ISBN 0-393-04016-X; 0-393-33701-4 pa

                LC 96-42412

"With waves as high as a hundred feet and winds so strong that anemometers were torn from their moorings, the storm of the title struck unsuspecting mariners off the coast of Nova Scotia in October, 1991. Junger traces the last voyage of the Andrea Gail—a commercial swordfishing boat that was lost, with all six hands, in the storm—and his account is relentlessly suspenseful." New Yorker

Konstam, Angus

The **history** of pirates. Lyons Press 1999 192p il maps hardcover o.p. pa $19.95   **910.4**

1. Pirates
ISBN 1-58574-516-2 pa

The author "chronicles the evolution of piracy from antiquity to the present. . . . Konstam profiles individual pirates, explores infamous vessels, and compares and contrasts various pirate regions and eras. He does a commendable job of separating fact from fiction." Booklist

Lord, Walter

★ A **night** to remember. Holt & Co. 1955 209p il hardcover o.p. pa $14   **910.4**

1. Shipwrecks
ISBN 0-03-027615-2; 0-8050-7764-2 pa

A detailed account of "the tragic drama of that terrible night—April 4, 1912—when the 'Titanic,' the unsinkable ship, struck an iceberg and went down in the icy waters of the Atlantic." Libr J

Macleod, Alasdair

Explorers; great tales of adventure and endurance. Royal Geographical Society; [written by Alasdair Macleod] DK in association with the Smithsonian Institution 2010 360p il $40 **910.4**

1. Exploration 2. Explorers
ISBN 978-0-7566-6737-5

"The book covers the history of exploration from the discovery of the ancient Egyptians in Nubia to the exploration of space by the Soviet Union and the United States in the 20th century. . . . [It] is a wonderful introduction to the

various personalities who, over a period of several thousand years, devoted themselves, to studying the world and revealing its fascinatingly diverse landscapes, conditions, and cultures." Sci Books Films

Mancall, Peter C.

Fatal journey; the final expedition of Henry Hudson-- a tale of mutiny and murder in the Arctic. Basic Books 2009 303p il map $26.95   **910.4**

1. Explorers
ISBN 978-0-465-00511-6; 0-465-00511-X

                LC 2009-03072

Mancall "vividly recreates the eager anticipation of the voyage, the lust for conquest and for spices, the voyage's risks and the joy and terrors that Hudson and his crew faced." Publ Wkly
Includes bibliographical references

McPhee, John A.

Looking for a ship. Farrar, Straus & Giroux 1990 241p $18.95; pa $15   **910.4**

1. Merchant marine -- United States 2. Seafaring life
ISBN 0-374-19077-1; 0-374-52319-3 pa

                LC 90-3311

In this book McPhee focuses on the "plight of the U.S. merchant marine. Accompanying Second Mate Andy Chase on a 42-day run down the west coast of South America aboard the S.S. Stella Lykes, McPhee provides the reader with stories and tales of modern seafaring life and the problems of making a living as a merchant mariner. . . . An engrossing tale of the sea, with excellent detail and humanity." Libr J

Morris, Jan

Contact! a book of encounters. W. W. Norton & Co. 2010 202p $23.95 **910.4**

1. Authors 2. Journalists 3. Travel writers 4. Voyages and travels
ISBN 978-0-393-07640-0

                LC 2009-52193

The author "collects vignettes of encounters with and observations of people from her numerous adventures and assignments. Varying from a few sentences to a few paragraphs, each vignette paints a picture or tells a story that brings a personal touch to the narrative of Morris's life and travels. They range from the humorous to the enchanting and tell us as much about Morris as she tells us of people around the world. This is not a typical travelog that one reads essay by essay but something to pick up and put down as time allows. Readers will appreciate the diversity of the people, from the famous to the relatively unremarkable, from six continents." Libr J

Netzley, Patricia D.

Encyclopedia of women's travel and exploration. Oryx Press 2000 259p il $88.95   **910.4**

1. Reference books 2. Voyages and travels 3. Voyages and travels -- Encyclopedias 4. Women -- Travel -- Encyclopedias 5. Women travelers
ISBN 1-573-56238-6; 978-1-57356-238-6

                LC 00-10720

"The 315 entries, arranged alphabetically, focus on a wide variety of women explorers, adventurers, and travelers throughout history and across continents. Most entries are biographical, but some examine related topics such as accommodations, solo travel, guide books, and mountaineering, occasionally offering perceptive insights into women's travel experiences and motivations." Choice

Includes bibliographical references

Nooteboom, Cees

Nomad's hotel; travels in time and space. translated from the Dutch by Ann Kelland; [introduction by Alberto Manguel] Houghton Mifflin Harcourt 2009 242p il pa $13.95   **910.4**
  1. Voyages and travels
  ISBN 978-0-15-603535-4
                                        LC 2008-20813

The author "surrounds his reader with the sounds, sights, and smells of his wanderings in this lyrical collection written over three decades. From the bone-chilling dampness of winter in the Aran Islands and the insistent bells marking time in the labyrinth of Venice to the endless dry and empty lands of Gambia and Mali, whose people struggle to find their future, Nooteboom weaves a compelling, perceptive, and yet wondering view of the places he visits. . . . Armchair traveling at its best." Libr J

Read, Piers Paul

★ **Alive**; sixteen men, seventy-two days, and insurmountable odds--the classic adventure of survival in the Andes. Harper Perennial 2005 398p il pa $13.95 **910.4**
  1. Survival after airplane accidents, shipwrecks, etc.
  ISBN 0-06-077866-0

The author describes the extraordinary hardships endured by the survivors of a horrific plane crash in the Andes.

Theroux, Paul

The **tao** of travel; enlightenments from lives on the road. Houghton Mifflin Harcourt 2011 285p il $25; ebook $25   **910.4**
  1. Travel 2. Travelers 3. Voyages and travels
  ISBN 978-0-547-33691-6; 0-547-33691-8; 978-0-547-54919-4 ebook; 0-547-54919-9 ebook
                                        LC 2010-42022

A collection of writings from Paul Theroux's fifty years of travel. Included are writings from other travelers such as Charles Dickens, Eudora Welty, Anton Chekhov, Ernest Hemingway and many others.

"Unfailingly quotable throughout, this is partly an elegy for a golden age of travel . . . and partly a vade mecum crammed with good advice, such as that guns are more trouble than they're worth, especially 'when armed dudes find you're packing'." Geographical

Includes bibliographical references

Turner, Steve

The **band** that played on; the extraordinary story of the 8 musicians who went down with the Titanic. Thomas Nelson 2011 259p $24.99   **910.4**
  1. Musicians -- Biography
  ISBN 978-1-59555-219-8; 1-59555-219-7
                                        LC 2010-47182

This is the "first book since the great ship went down to examine the lives of the eight musicians who were employed by the Titanic. What these men did – standing calmly on deck playing throughout the disaster – achieved global recognition. But their individual stories, until now, have been largely unknown. What Turner has uncovered is a narrow but unique slice of history – one more chapter of compelling Titanic lore." Christ Sci Monit

Includes bibliographical references

Wheeler, Sara

The **magnetic** north; notes from the Arctic circle. Farrar, Straus and Giroux 2011 315p il map $26; ebook $12.99   **910.4**
  ISBN 9780374200138; 0374200130; 9781429991940 ebook
                                        LC 2010-14576

"With wry humor and extensive research, Wheeler captures a swiftly transforming region with which we all have a symbiotic relationship." N Y Times Book Rev

Includes bibliographical references (p. [297]-302) and index.

Williams, Glyn

Voyages of delusion; the quest for the Northwest Passage. Yale Univ. Press 2003 xx, 467p il maps $29.95   **910.4**
  1. Northwest Passage
  ISBN 0-300-09866-9
                                        LC 2002-109284

"Students of maritime exploration and 18th-century British politics will find this work engrossing, especially the detailed notes on sources." Publ Wkly

Williams, Glyndwr

★ **Arctic** labyrinth; the quest for the Northwest Passage. [by] Glyn Williams. University of California Press 2010 439p il map $34.95   **910.4**
  1. Explorers 2. Northwest Passage
  ISBN 978-0-5202-6627-8
                                        LC 2009-35546

"If you read one book on the history of the mythic Northwest Passage, read this one. . . . Williams deftly weaves together explorers' logbooks and diaries (published and unpublished) with a lifetime of research, and the result is a masterpiece." Libr J

Includes bibliographical references

Literature of travel and exploration; an encyclopedia. Jennifer Speake, editor. Fitzroy Dearborn 2003 3v il map set $495   **910.4**
  1. Voyages and travels
  ISBN 1-57958-247-8
                                        LC 2003-5352

"This is a rich introduction to primary sources . . . and an excellent source for further research." Booklist

Includes bibliographical references

910.91 Geography of and travel in areas, regions, places in general

Wilkinson, Alec

The **ice** balloon; S.A. Andrée and the heroic age of arctic exploration. by Alec Wilkinson. Alfred A. Knopf 2011 239 p. **910.91**

    1. Balloon ascensions -- Arctic regions 2. Explorers -- Sweden -- Biography

    ISBN 9780307594808

                 LC 2011025434

This book explores a 1897 voyage, when Swedish national S.A. Andrée and a crew of two attempted to fly from Spitsbergen to the North Pole and back via hydrogen balloon. [Alec] Wilkinson . . . describes this little-known Arctic expedition and provides details about late 19th-century ballooning. After being aloft for nearly 66 hours while traveling 517 miles, the balloon landed 300 miles short of the pole. Thus Andrée, Nils Strindberg, and Knut Fraenkel began the hard work of crossing the Arctic to find land. . . . Andrée's journal abruptly ends with his landing on White Island after nearly three months of sledging. No one knows exactly how or when the men died, a fact that lends greater mystery to this unusual Arctic expedition. (Libr J)

911 Historical geography

Beck, Warren A.

Historical atlas of the American West; by Warren A. Beck and Ynez D. Haase. University of Okla. Press 1989 xlii, 78p maps hardcover o.p. pa $24.95 **911**

    1. Historical atlases 2. Reference books

    ISBN 0-8061-2456-3

                 LC 88-40540

"Defining the West as that part of the United States lying west of the 100th meridian, Beck and Haase provide a cartographic survey of the history of the region. In addition to maps illustrating such standard themes as natural resources, exploration and travel routes, the growth of the transportation network, and Indian tribal lands, the authors have included detailed maps on such topics as the Spanish-Mexican land grants and the Mt. St. Helens's eruption. . . . This atlas is an essential purchase for most libraries." Libr J

Hayes, Derek

  ★ **Historical** atlas of the American West; with original maps. University of California Press 2009 288p il map **911**

    1. Historical atlases 2. Reference books

    ISBN 978-0-520-25652-1

              LC 20090279536

"The West, for the purpose of this atlas, is defined as the Dakotas, Nebraska, Kansas, Oklahoma, Texas, and all states west of them, including Alaska, but not Hawai'i. More than 600 maps have been carefully selected and beautifully reproduced in full color. They provide the primary-source documentation for the historical narrative, written for the general reader, tracing the development of the Western United States from its indigenous inhabitants to European exploration, the migration of settlers, and 20th-century events. . . . A high quality publication at an amazingly low price, this atlas is highly recommended for all public and academic libraries, history buffs, and map enthusiasts." Libr J

  Includes bibliographical references

Historical atlas of the United States; with original maps. University of California Press 2007 280p il map $45 **911**

    1. Atlases 2. Reference books

    ISBN 978-0-520-25036-9; 0-520-25036-2

             LC 2006-42405

"Hayes has produced an excellent visual history of the land that became the US. The work includes 535 maps gathered from a variety of international collections, coupled with more than 60 other illustrations to chronicle the expansion and development of the nation over the last 500 years." Choice

  Includes bibliographical references

Hellmann, Paul T.

  ★ **Historical** gazetteer of the United States. Routledge 2005 865p $150 **911**

    1. Reference books

    ISBN 0-415-93948-8

             LC 2004-11421

This reference provides "historical records of U.S. cities and towns. Arrangement is alphabetical by state, including the District of Columbia. Each state chapter contains a brief description of major cities, date of incorporation into the U.S., the number of counties, and a rough breakdown of how the state categorizes municipalities, towns, townships, and cities. This is followed by alphabetical entries for significant places. Inclusion is determined more by historical importance (national or regional) than by population. All county seats are included. Entries are in paragraph form and typically begin by noting the country and the part of the state in which the place is located as well as its approximate distance from the state's most important city. Events are listed chronologically ." Booklist

Magocsi, Paul R.

Historical atlas of Central Europe; [by] Paul Robert Magocsi. rev and expanded ed; University of Wash. Press 2002 274p maps hardcover o.p. pa $45 **911**

    1. Atlases 2. Reference books

    ISBN 0-295-98146-6

             LC 2001-27907

"The volume is arranged chronologically, with coverage beginning about A.D. 400 (roughly the time of the demise of the Roman Empire) and continuing through the end of the 20th century. The maps and tables provide information on military affairs; population and population movements; economy; ethnolinguistic distributions; and religious, cultural, and educational institutions. All are extremely well done." SLJ

Thubron, Colin

  Shadow of the Silk Road. Harper Collins 2007 363p map $25.95 **911**

    ISBN 978-0-06-123172-8; 0-06-123172-X

             LC 2006-52142

"An illuminating account of a breathtaking journey." Booklist

Atlas of exploration; cartography by Philip's; foreword by John Hemming. Oxford University Press 2008 256p il map $50 **911**
1. Exploration -- Atlases 2. Reference books
ISBN 978-0-19-534318-2

LC 2008-626565

"This atlas describes many of the explorations and participants that changed history and enhanced man's knowledge and perception of the world. . . . The volume is a visual delight, festooned with more than 100 specially drawn maps and 300 b&w and color photographs, period paintings, and illustrations on the various explorations." Libr Media Connect

912 Graphic representations of surface of earth and of extraterrestrial worlds

Aczel, Amir D.
The **riddle** of the compass; the invention that changed the world. Harcourt 2001 178p il maps hardcover o.p. pa $13 **912**
1. Compass 2. Compass -- History
ISBN 0-15-100506-0; 0-15-600753-3 pa

LC 00-47153

This book tracks "down the roots of the compass and tells the story of navigation through the ages." Publisher's note
Includes bibliographical references

Lavin, Stephen J.
Atlas of the great plains; Stephen J. Lavin, Fred M. Shelley, and J. Clark Archer; foreword by David J. Wishart; introduction by John C. Hudson. University of Nebraska Press 2011 335p il $39.95 **912**
1. Atlases 2. Great Plains -- History -- Maps 3. Reference books
ISBN 978-0-8032-1536-8

Lester, Toby
The **fourth** part of the world; the race to the ends of the Earth, and the epic story of the map that gave America its name. Free Press 2009 462p il map $30 **912**
1. Cartographers 2. Cartography -- History 3. Discoveries in geography -- History 4. Map drawing 5. Voyages and travels -- History 6. World maps
ISBN 9781416535317; 1-416-53531-4

LC 2009-1230

"In 2003, the Library of Congress paid $10 million for a 1507 map of the world that first used the name 'America' for lands in the New World. It was touted as America's birth certificate. Lester . . . traces the fascinating background to the creation of this map, as Europeans tried to assimilate the discoveries of Columbus, Vespucci, and other explorers into their worldview. . . . Lester provides an engrossing adventure for both general and informed lay readers." Libr J
Includes bibliographical references

★ Hammond world atlas; 5th ed.; Hammond World Atlas Corporation 2008 346p il map $59.95 **912**
1. Atlases 2. Reference books
ISBN 978-0-8437-0967-4; 0-8437-0967-7

This atlas includes an "illustrated 64-page 'Thematic Section,' a 48-page 'Satellite Section' with more than 40 color photos and a commentary, and 228 pages of . . . full-color physical and political maps representing the world, continents, and regions with detailed . . . computer-generated terrain modeling." Libr J

★ National Geographic atlas of the world; 9th ed.; National Geographic Society 2010 153p il $175 **912**
1. Atlases 2. Reference books
ISBN 978-1-4262-0634-4

"The National Geographic Society presents more than 80 large-format color maps grouped by continent portraying the world with detailed, digitally painted terrain modeling. Each continent is introduced by satellite, political, and physical maps. Political maps for regions and specific countries follow." Libr J

★ National Geographic visual atlas of the world. National Geographic Society 2009 416p il map $100 **912**
1. Atlases 2. Reference books
ISBN 978-1-4262-0332-9

LC 2008-627044

This atlas "has the usual atlas features but emphasizes the more than 850 UNESCO World Heritage Sites. . . . Double-page spreads of regional maps are framed with four to six color photographs of the heritage sites that are indicated on the map. . . . Beautiful color photography and clear topical material combined with detailed maps of areas not covered as well in other world atlases make the Visual Atlas a recommended purchase. This is a first choice for any library needing a new medium-priced atlas." Booklist
Includes bibliographical references

★ Oxford atlas of the world; [cartography by Philip's] 17th ed; Oxford University Press 2010 448p il map $80 **912**
1. Atlases 2. Reference books
ISBN 978-0-19-975128-0

LC 20100594813

Provides maps and satellite photography that reflect the most recent political, economic, and demographic statistics, and presents articles addressing the environment and population matters in major cities of the world.

Times comprehensive atlas of the world; 12th ed.; Times Books 2008 various paging il map $285 **912**
1. Atlases 2. Reference books
ISBN 978-0-06-146450-8

"The classic atlas. Very detailed with listings for most geographic and urban locations. Index gives longitude and latitude as well as map reference. Contains . . . [125] plates and . . . [an] index-gazetteer." Ref Sources for Small & Medium-sized Libr. 6th edition
Includes glossary

The new atlas of the Arab world. American University in Cairo Press 2010 144p il map $39.50 **912**
1. Atlases 2. Reference books
ISBN 978-977-416-419-4

This atlas contains maps of the Arab world "showing physical features, political boundaries, towns, and communication networks. In addition, each of the twenty-two countries is the subject of an illustrated essay, with notes and . . . statistics on the geography, population, history and politics, and economy of the country. The countries covered are: Algeria, Bahrain, Comoros, Djibouti, Egypt, Iraq, Jordan, Kuwait, Lebanon, Libya, Mauritania, Morocco, Oman, Palestine, Qatar, Saudi Arabia, Somalia, Sudan, Syria, Tunisia, United Arab Emirates, Yemen." Publisher's note

913   Geography of and travel in specific continents, countries, localities; extraterrestrial worlds

Grant, Michael
A **guide** to the ancient world; a dictionary of classical place names. Wilson, H.W. 1986 728p maps $105   **913**
1. Classical dictionaries 2. Mediterranean region -- Gazetteers 3. Reference books
ISBN 0-8242-0742-4
LC 86-15785

"This dictionary provides background for about nine hundred places important to an understanding of the cultures of the ancient Greeks, Etruscans, and Romans. . . . The time period covered is from the first millennium B.C. until the fall of the Roman empire in the fifth century A.D. Depending on the subject, a typical entry includes information about history, geography, archaeology, and sometimes art and mythology." Am Ref Books Annu, 1987

914   Geography of and travel in Europe

Baxter, John
The **most** beautiful walk in the world; a pedestrian in Paris. Harper Perennial 2011 298p il pa $14.99   **914**
1. Walking
ISBN 978-0-06-199854-6; 0-06-199854-0
LC 2010-46259

The author "knows Paris, both the modern, cosmopolitan city of today as well as the 1920s cultural mecca of expat American authors like Ernest Hemingway and F. Scott Fitzgerald. Baxter, in fact, lives in the same Paris building that once was a Jazz Age hangout for literary greats like James Joyce, Ezra Pound, Hemingway, and others. It's also the site of Sylvia Beach's famous bookstore, Shakespeare and Company. . . . [He] takes us on a tour of the city's outdoor cafes, amazing restaurants, cabarets, and gorgeous architecture; he tells us about its history and its unique passion for art. Baxter gives us a Paris that is not just a place but an idea." Boston Globe

Boswell, James
The **journal** of a tour to the Hebrides with Samuel Johnson. Kessinger Publishing 2004 277p pa $28.95   **914**
1. Lexicographers 2. Literary critics
ISBN 978-1-4191-6794-2; 1-4191-6794-4

The renowned biographer here recounts the daily events of a tour which he took in 1773 with Johnson.

Bryson, Bill
Notes from a small island. Morrow 1996 324p hardcover o.p. pa $14   **914**
ISBN 0-380-72750-1 pa
LC 95-43437

"Before his return to the U.S. after a 20-year residence in England, journalist Bryson . . . embarked on a farewell tour of his adopted homeland. His trenchant, witty and detailed observations of life in a variety of towns and villages will delight Anglophiles." Publ Wkly

Caro, Ina
Paris to the past; traveling through French history by train. W.W. Norton & Co. 2011 381p map $27.95   **914**
1. Historic sites 2. Railroads -- France
ISBN 978-0-393-07894-7; 0-393-07894-9
LC 2011-03060

"One single Paris Metro line can take you through a dazzling panoply of history: the Chateau de Vincennes, Charles V's 14th-century fortress; Francis I's Hotel de Ville; the Place de la Concorde, constructed by Louis V in the mid-18th century; the Palais-Royal, fashioned by Philippe Egalite in the late 18th century; and the 21st-century neighborhood of La Defense. Take another Metro line, Caro discovered gleefully, and you can descend to the period of the Romans, on the Ile-de-la-Cite, then arrive glamorously in the 19th century, at the Opera Garnier. Moreover, you can manage day trips to sites as far away as Tours (90 minutes by TGV) in one day, returning to Paris. In this cheerful, logical, easy-to-follow narrative (which includes favorite restaurants and hotels), Caro builds on previous trips to France and presents her timeline through history chronologically, from the 12th-century Basilica of Saint-Denis, where nearly all of the French kings and queen are buried, to the Gare d'Orsay, now fabulously converted into a museum of 19th-century art." Kirkus
Includes bibliographical references

Ich bin dann mal weg./English
I'm off then; my journey along the Camino de Santiago. translated from the German by Shelley Frisch. Free Press 2009 333p il pa $15   **914**
ISBN 978-1-416-55387-8; 1-416-55387-8
LC 2008-51464

"Hape Kerkeling, a popular TV talk-show host and cabaret star in his native Germany, cuts loose from the comforts of Düsseldorf and sets off on a hike across the Pyrenees to the grave of St. James at the Cathedral of Santiago de Compostela. Searching for spiritual meaning, this self-described 'couch potato' follows a 1,000-year-old pilgrimage route that lures 100,000 trekkers each year, experiencing almost insufferable heat and physical agony in the process. . . . He skips some of the hardest stretches to hitch rides with local farmers or hop aboard trains, and he avoids fetid pilgrims' hostels whenever possible in favor of the best hotel in town (often not much better). Despite such tactics, this gregarious traveler soon gets into the spirit of things, and his encounters with fellow pilgrims, including a Peruvian shaman with a creepy fondness for 'Mein Kampf,' can be both funny and moving." N Y Times Book Rev

Macfarlane, Robert

The **wild** places. Penguin Books 2008 340p map pa $15   **914**

1. Wilderness areas

ISBN 978-0-14-311393-5; 0-14-311393-3

LC 2008-17162

"Evocative and well-written, a delight for nature and travel buffs." Kirkus

Includes bibliographical references

Mayes, Frances

A **year** in the world; journeys of a passionate traveller. Broadway Books 2006 xx, 420p map hardcover o.p. pa $15   **914**

ISBN 0-7679-1005-2; 978-0-7679-1005-7; 978-0-7679-1006-4 pa; 0-7679-1006-0 pa

LC 2005-50831

"Befitting her gifts as a poet, Mayes' prose shines with evocative imagery, bringing life to every subject she encounters across her peripatetic year." Booklist

Includes bibliographical references

McGregor, James H. S.

Paris from the ground up. Belknap Press of Harvard University Press 2009 327p il map $29.95 **914**

ISBN 978-0-674-03316-0; 0-674-03316-7

LC 2008-43696

"Readers can use this as a well-researched but accessible history of Paris, tracing the story of the City of Light from its earliest residents, the Gauls and the Parisii, to the present day. Travelers will use chapters on churches, cathedrals, museums, and neighborhoods; those interested in the history of a particular area or landmark will find the index excellent. The many illustrations enhance the text, and the ten historical and contemporary maps help pinpoint attractions both ancient and modern." Libr J

Includes bibliographical references

Starr, William W.

Whisky, kilts, and the Loch Ness Monster; traveling through Scotland with Boswell and Johnson. University of South Carolina Press 2011 223p map $29.95   **914**

1. Authors   2.   Biographers   3.   Lawyers   4. Lexicographers 5. Literary critics

ISBN 978-1-57003-948-5

LC 2010020165

The author "is a Samuel Johnson and James Boswell fanatic. He here relates meeting Scots along his travels who drew a blank when asked about Johnson and Boswell, despite the men's whirlwind journey through Scotland in 1773. . . . Starr traces their trek in reverse via car, using their own words as guides and inspiration as he tours the great Scot-

tish sites (and partakes in the great Scottish beverage). . . . Scottish history and travel buffs and Johnson and Boswell enthusiasts will find this fun and inspiring." Libr J

Includes bibliographical references

915   Geography of and travel in Asia

Belliveau, Denis

In the footsteps of Marco Polo; [by] Denis Belliveau and Francis O'Donnell. Rowman & Littlefield Publishers 2008 280p il map $29.95   **915**

1. Travel writers 2. Travelers

ISBN 978-0-7425-5683-6; 0-7425-5683-2

LC 2008-23411

"The stunning photographs in this elegant book should please even the most casual reader, while the authors' unpretentious observations will satisfy those who want to know more about a still alien world. A travel/adventure book rather than a study of Marco Polo the man or a history of his travels, this volume deserves many readers. Warmly recommended." Libr J

Includes bibliographical references

Elliot, Jason

Mirrors of the unseen; journeys in Iran. St. Martin's Press 2006 415p il $26.95   **915**

ISBN 978-0-312-30191-0; 0-312-30191-X

LC 2006-42918

The author discusses his travels in Iran.

"With Iran so central in the news, this is a good read for the armchair traveler and amateur geopolitical strategist alike." Publ Wkly

Feiler, Bruce S.

Walking the Bible; a journey by land through the five books of Moses. by Bruce Feiler. Morrow 2001 451p $26; pa $14.95   **915**

1. Middle East -- Description

ISBN 0-380-97775-3; 0-380-80731-9 pa

LC 00-56076

"Determined to connect more deeply with his religious roots, Feiler joined an archaeologist in a trek through the Middle East, visiting the sites mentioned in the Pentateuch, the first five books of the Hebrew Bible. A book full of wonder and awe and personal enlightenment." Booklist

Includes bibliographical references

Gargan, Edward A.

A **river's** tale; a year on the Mekong. Knopf 2002 332p il maps hardcover o.p. pa $14.95 **915**

ISBN 0-375-70559-7 pa

LC 2001-38056

"A chronicle of a year-long journey along the nearly 3,000 miles of the Mekong River as it descends from the Tibetan plateau through southern Asia, Gargan's book is a vivid look at the disparate peoples [that] settled the length of the river's path." Publ Wkly

Includes bibliographical references

Grange, Kevin

Beneath blossom rain; discovering Bhutan on the toughest trek in the world. University of Nebraska Press 2011 336p il map pa $19.95   **915**
1. Mountaineering
ISBN 978-0-8032-3433-8; 0-8032-3433-3
LC 2010-28970
"For the armchair traveler, Grange does a fine job of showing readers the nature, history, and landscape of Bhutan, as well as taking us to remote villages and monasteries. . . He is equally open about what is essentially a personal search for meaning." Seattle Post-Intelligencer
Includes bibliographical references.

Horwitz, Tony

Baghdad without a map, and other misadventures in Arabia. Dutton 1991 276p map hardcover o.p. pa $16   **915**
ISBN 0-452-26745-5 pa
LC 90-46653
"Horwitz mixes insight and humor in these observations that illustrate on an everyday level both the contradictions and the idiosyncrasies of the Arab world." Booklist

Jubber, Nicholas

Drinking arak off an ayatollah's beard; a journey through the inside-out worlds of Iran and Afghanistan. Da Capo Press 2010 327p il map pa $15.95   **915**
ISBN 978-0-306-81884-4
LC 2009-48191
"Jubber's account offers a full and satisfying panorama of the region with its rich paradoxes and complexities intact." Publ Wkly
Includes bibliographical references

MacLean, Rory

Magic bus; on the hippie trail from Istanbul to India. Ig Pub. 2009 280p pa $14.95   **915**
1. Hippies
ISBN 978-0-9788431-9-9; 0-9788431-9-3
LC 2008-45918
"For a certain breed of independent travelers in the 1960s and '70s, Asia was the Promised Land. For nearly 20 years during those iconic decades, flower children, beat philosophers, and Western wanderers took to the road for the roughly 6,000-mile journey from Turkey to India. Hundreds of thousands may have made the trek, though no one has an exact count. For years after, the trip was nearly impossible to make through this war-torn area — especially for Westerners. So after parts of the trail reopened in 2002, UK-based Canadian travel writer Rory MacLean set his sights east. . . . He recounts his eight-month journey along this epic route. The book strings together a series of vignettes from his trip that en masse form a well-rounded and insightful look into the region." Boston Globe

Matthiessen, Peter

The **snow** leopard. Viking 1978 338p hardcover o.p. pa $15   **915**
1. Himalaya Mountains -- Description 2. Natural history -- Himalaya Mountains 3. Zen Buddhism
ISBN 0-14-025508-7 pa
LC 78-5
This book "is based on the journal Matthiessen kept during his trek with the field biologist George Schaller to the Crystal Mountain, in upper Nepal, in 1973. The trek took them 250 miles to the Land of Dolpo, on the Tibetan plateau. . . . The purpose: to observe the November rut of the Himalayan blue sheep in order to determine whether this little-known species is related to the extinct common ancestor of the goat and the sheep." Saturday Rev
Includes bibliographical references

Morris-Suzuki, Tessa

To the Diamond Mountains; a hundred-year journey through China and Korea. Rowman & Littlefield Publishers 2010 201p il map $34.95   **915**
1. Adventurers 2. Artists 3. Authors
ISBN 978-1-4422-0503-1; 978-1-4422-0505-5 ebook
LC 2010023685
"Morris-Suzuki, an Australian professor, recently traveled through northeast China and the two Koreas; she was retracing the route of Emily Kemp, an extraordinary writer, artist, and intrepid adventurer who wrote about her experiences a century ago. Morris-Suzuki, like her predecessor, is a keen observer and a fine writer; she has combined the disciplines of history and travel writing in an absorbing analysis of the past, present, and future of this volatile region." Booklist
Includes bibliographical references

Rose, Daniel Asa

Larry's kidney; being the true story of how I found myself in China with my black sheep cousin and his mail-order bride, skirting the law to get him a transplant and save his life. William Morrow 2009 305p $25.99   **915**
1. Kidneys 2. Transplantation of organs, tissues, etc.
ISBN 978-0-06-170870-1
LC 2009-517312
"A satisfying, hysterical page-turner, this will captivate fans of travel writing and family narratives, with special interest for anyone who's helped a love one through serious illness." Publ Wkly

Theroux, Paul

Riding the iron rooster; by train through China. Paul Theroux. 1st Mariner Books ed.; Houghton Mifflin 2006 480p map pa $7.50   **915**
1. Railroads
ISBN 978-0-6186-5897-8
LC 2006028745
This is an account of the author's yearlong rail journey through China. "For Theroux, traveling is both about people—their thoughts, customs, and peculiarities-and a form of autobiography, and here we learn as much about his own

quirks and fancies as we do about the intriguing world of contemporary China." Libr J

The **great** railway bazaar; by train through Asia. Houghton Mifflin 1975 342p hardcover o.p. pa $14.95   **915**
1. Railroads -- Asia
ISBN 0-618-65894-7 pa
The author "took a four-month solitary lecture tour of Asia in 1973, traveling by train wherever possible. His route was through Turkey, Iran, India, Southeast Asia, Japan, and back to London via the Soviet Union. He writes of conversations and impressions of the people encountered." Libr J

Thubron, Colin
To a mountain in Tibet. Harper 2011 227p map $24.99; ebook $19.99   **915**
1. Authors 2. Novelists 3. Travel writers
ISBN 978-0-06-176826-2; 978-0-06-206605-3 ebook
LC 2010-43013
"Emotional subtlety and vivid evocations of the people and places are only part of what makes the book so enjoyable. The present-tense narration allows readers make discoveries alongside Thubron, which adds immeasurably to the intimacy and immediacy of the reading experience. A powerful and hauntingly elegiac hybrid of travelogue and memoir." Kirkus

916   Geography of and travel in Africa

Benanav, Michael
Men of salt; across the Sahara with the caravan of white gold. Lyons Press 2006 220p il map $23.95   **916**
1. Salt
ISBN 1-59228-772-7; 978-1-59228-772-7
LC 2005-23205
"Even if readers don't find the idea of spending 40 harrowing days with a caravan crossing some of the world's most unforgiving desert as enticing as Benanav does, that doesn't mean they won't quickly devour his thrilling account of that otherworldly journey." Publ Wkly
Includes bibliographical references

Butcher, Tim
Chasing the Devil; a journey through sub-Saharan Africa in the footsteps of Graham Greene. Atlas & Co. 2011 325p il map $26.95   **916**
1. Authors 2. Essayists 3. Motion picture critics 4. Novelists 5. Short story writers 6. Travel writers
ISBN 978-1-935633-29-7; 1-935633-29-5
"Butcher used Graham Greene's little-known 1935 travel book, Journey Without Maps, as his guide on the 350-mile trek from Freetown, on the coast of Sierra Leone, to the coast of Liberia." Publ Wkly
Includes bibliographical references

Campbell, James T.
Middle passages; African American journeys to Africa, 1787-2005. [by] James Campbell. Penguin Press 2006 513p il $29.95   **916**
1. African Americans -- Travel
ISBN 1-59420-083-1; 978-1-59420-083-0
LC 2005-58672
"From the repatriation of former slaves in the early years of the United States to the recent heritage tourism featuring Goree Island and other slave-trading sites, Campbell provides an artful reconstruction of the often bittersweet experience of return and reunion." N Y Times Book Rev

Grant, Richard
Crazy river; a journey to the source of the Nile. Free Press 2011 336p pa $15; ebook $9.99   **916**
1. Asian studies specialists 2. Explorers 3. Middle Eastern studies specialists 4. Travel writers
ISBN 978-1-4391-5414-4 pa; 978-1-4391-5764-0 ebook
LC 2011012168
"The Malagarasi River in Tanzania had not been fully traveled by either Westerners or Africans. So, the tradition of 19th-century British explorers, first and foremost Richard Burton, who became his spectral travel companion, Grant set out to do so. But his adventures on the river—disease and disappointment, danger from crocs, hippos and bandits—became but part of his larger story about what Africa is and how to make sense of it. . . . Dyspeptic, disturbing and brilliantly realized, Grant's account of Africa is literally unforgettable." Kirkus

Langewiesche, William
Sahara unveiled; a journey across the desert. Pantheon Bks. 1996 301p il hardcover o.p. pa $14   **916**
1. Sahara -- Description
ISBN 0-679-75006-1 pa
LC 95-48864
"Besides evoking the Sahara's power, majesty, emptiness, heat, beauty and terrors and describing its ecology and meteorology, Langewiesche adds details that may astonish armchair travelers who still think of the desert as populated by camels and Bedouins. . . . He is knowledgeable about the imprint of French colonialism on North African economy and politics, and about Muslim beliefs in practice. Throughout this vivid account, he scatters many charming native folktales." Publ Wkly

Matthiessen, Peter
★ **African** silences. Random House 1991 225p maps hardcover o.p. pa $13   **916**
1. Africa -- Description 2. Natural history -- Africa
ISBN 0-679-73102-4 pa
LC 90-52893
"In this account of three trips to Central and Western Africa, Matthiessen reports on the almost total devastation of wildlife in Senegal, Gambia, and the Ivory Coast and describes an expedition searching for the rare Congo peacock and gorillas in the Virunga Mountains of Zaire." Libr J

Tayler, Jeffrey

Angry wind; through Muslim Black Africa by truck, bus, boat, and camel. Houghton Mifflin 2005 252p map $25　　　　　**916**

ISBN 0-618-33467-X

LC 2004-54066

"This substantial and informative work is no mere travel tale—it is a firsthand account of the author's deeply personal quest for knowledge and understanding of a people and a region that continues to struggle with extreme poverty and unrest." Libr J

Theroux, Paul

Dark star safari; overland from Cairo to Cape Town. Houghton Mifflin 2003 472p maps $28 **916**

1. Authors 2. Novelists 3. Short story writers 4. Travel writers

ISBN 0-618-13424-7

LC 2002-32710

"Where Theroux sees Africa uncluttered by preconceived notions, his writing can be brilliant. . . . But where Theroux has traveled before—40 years ago, as first a Peace Corps teacher, then a lecturer at Uganda's Makerere University in the golden years just after the country's independence—he sees Africa not for what it is, but for what it might have been." Christ Sci Monit

917　Geography of and travel in North America

Ambrose, Stephen E.

Undaunted courage; Meriwether Lewis, Thomas Jefferson, and the opening of the American West. Simon & Schuster 1996 511p il maps $30; pa $17　　　　　**917**

1. Biography, Individual 2. Explorers 3. Territorial governors

ISBN 0-684-81107-3; 0-684-82697-6 pa

LC 95-37146

This treatment of the Lewis and Clark Expedition "is essentially a biography of Lewis, although the bulk of it is a lively retelling of the journey of the two captains—together with their party of soldiers and frontiersmen, Clark's black slave, York, and the legendary Shoshone Indian woman, Sacagawea, and her infant son—conveyed with passionate enthusiasm by Mr. Ambrose and sprinkled liberally with some of the most famous and vivid passages from the travelers' journals." N Y Times Book Rev

Includes bibliographical references

Beatty, Michael A.

County name origins of the United States. McFarland & Co. 2001 665p $195　　　　　**917**

1. Geographic names -- United States 2. Names, Geographical -- United States

ISBN 0-7864-1025-6

LC 2001-18034

Arranged alphabetically by state, this study shows "how each county in the United States was named. Dates and circumstances under which counties were named or renamed are provided, including brief biographical, geographical, and other relevant historical information. In cases where name derivations are unknown or disputed, an informed discussion gives probable origins." Libr J

Includes bibliographical references

Bryson, Bill

A walk in the woods; rediscovering America on the Appalachian Trail. Broadway Bks. 1998 276p hardcover o.p. pa $14.95　　　　　**917**

ISBN 0-7679-0251-3; 0-7679-0252-1 pa

LC 97-32627

"Bryson's breezy, self-mocking tone may turn off readers who hanker for another 'Into Thin Air' or 'Seven Years in Tibet.' Others, however, may find themselves turning the pages with increasing amusement and anticipation as they discover that they're in the hands of a satirist of the first rank, one who writes (and walks) with Chaucerian brio." N Y Times Book Rev

Includes bibliographical references

Cronkite, Walter

Around America; a tour of our magnificent coastline. drawings by David Canright. Norton 2001 211p il maps $23.95; pa $13.95　　　　　**917**

ISBN 0-393-04083-6; 0-393-32335-8 pa

LC 00-69563

In this "rumination on the people and places along America's seashores, Cronkite shows his reverence for the country's coastal means of travel. Starting in the Northeast, working south, then circling around to the West Coast, the book reads like a lively but laid-back cruise." Publ Wkly

Curtis, Nancy C.

Black heritage sites; an African American odyssey and finder's guide. American Lib. Assn. 1996 677p il $75　　　　　**917**

1. African Americans -- History 2. Historic sites 3. Historic sites -- United States 4. Historic sites -- United States -- Directories

ISBN 0-8389-0643-5

LC 95-5788

This "guide locates significant places in African-American history and supplies . . . recent addresses, phone numbers, and visitors' information. . . . Organized by region, a historical essay introduces each section, presenting the culture and history in that area." Publisher's note

Duncan, Dayton

Lewis & Clark; the journey of the Corps of Discovery. based on a documentary film by Ken Burns, written by Dayton Duncan; with a preface by Ken Burns and conributions by Stephen E. Ambrose, Erica Funkhouser, William Least Heat-Moon. Knopf 1997 248p il maps $45　　　　　**917**

1. West (U.S.) -- Exploration

ISBN 0-679-45450-0

LC 97-73823

This is a companion volume to PBS television film "Lewis and Clark: The journey of the Corps of Discovery," by Ken Burns.

An "attractive book with a well-written text and an excellent presentation of historic paintings, photographs, maps, and original quotations from various of Lewis and Clark's journals." Sci Books Films

Ferris, Gary W.

Presidential places; a guide to the historic sites of U.S. presidents. [by] Gary Ferris. Blair 1999 284p il pa $15.95 **917**

1. Historic sites 2. Historic sites -- United States -- Guidebooks 3. Presidents -- United States -- Homes 4. Presidents -- United States -- Homes and haunts -- Guidebooks

ISBN 0-89587-176-9

LC 98-50395

This is a "guide to historic places of interest relating to all the American presidents. Included are, among other things, presidential birthplaces, where they lived, where they went to school, the churches they attended, where they are buried, and the monuments, museums, and libraries dedicated to their lives and administrations." Libr J

Includes bibliographical references

Fletcher, Colin

The **man** who walked through time. Vintage Bks. 1989 247p il pa $14.95 **917**

1. Authors 2. Hikers 3. Travel writers

ISBN 0-679-72306-4; 978-0-679-72306-6

LC 72-4082

An account of the author's journey on foot through the Grand Canyon National Park.

Frazier, Ian

Great Plains. Farrar, Straus & Giroux 1989 290p il maps hardcover o.p. pa $13 **917**

1. Great Plains -- Description 2. West (U.S.) -- Description 3. West (U.S.) -- Social life and customs

ISBN 0-312-27850-0 pa

LC 88-31106

The author recounts his experiences and observations traveling in the Western United States.

"This is a colorful and engaging blend of travelogue, local color, geography and folklore." Publ Wkly

Gimlette, John

Theatre of fish; travels through Newfoundland and Labrador. Alfred A. Knopf 2005 xxii, 360p il map $25 **917**

1. Authors 2. Lawyers 3. Travel writers

ISBN 1-4000-4322-0

LC 2005-44149

"Readers will be fascinated by Newfoundland's and Labrador's bizarre, often tragic pasts and equally strange presents, and they will be glad it was the eloquent Gimlette who made the trip so they don't have to." Publ Wkly

Includes bibliographical references

Heat Moon, William Least

Blue highways; a journey into America. photographs by the author; with a new afterword by the author. Back Bay Bks. 1999 429p il $29.95; pa $14.95 **917**

ISBN 0-316-35391-4; 0-316-35329-9 pa

LC 00-265444

An account of the author's journey across the U.S. in a van taking only secondary roads.

Roads to Quoz; an American mosey. Little, Brown and Co. 2008 581p il map $27.99 **917**

1. Authors 2. Essayists 3. Travel writers 4. Writers on nature

ISBN 978-0-316-11025-9; 0-316-11025-6

LC 2008-19375

The author's "journey is as meandering as the Ouachita itself, and readers will relish the experiences he and . . . [his wife] describe along their trip." Libr J

Jenkins, Peter

A **walk** across America. Morrow 1979 288p il maps hardcover o.p. pa $6.99 **917**

ISBN 0-06-095955-X pa

LC 78-10320

This book chronicles the author's journey with his dog from New York to the Gulf of Mexico.

Levy, Bernard Henri

American vertigo; traveling America in the footsteps of Tocqueville. [by] Bernard-Henri Lévy; translated by Charlotte Mandell. Random House 2006 308p $24.95 **917**

1. American national characteristics 2. National characteristics, American 3. Nonfiction writers 4. Philosophers 5. Political scientists 6. Statesmen 7. Travel writers 8. Writers on politics

ISBN 1-4000-6434-1

LC 2005-44782

This is "an engaging but often-disturbing portrait of our nation from an eloquent, brutally honest foreigner who wishes our country well." Booklist

McMurtry, Larry

Roads; driving America's great highways. Simon & Schuster 2000 206p hardcover o.p. pa $13 **917**

1. Large print books 2. Roads 3. Roads -- United States

ISBN 0-684-86885-7 pa

LC 00-27889

In this volume McMurtry provides "reminiscence and commentary on whatever pops up in the windows or in his mind as he crisscrosses the country: enigmatic glances at the Western past, salutes to hundreds of literary and historical figures." N Y Times Book Rev

National Geographic Society (U.S.)

★ **National** Geographic guide to the national parks of the United States; [project manger, Caroline Hickey] 6th ed.; National Geographic 2009 480p il pa $26 **917**

1. National parks and reserves -- United States

ISBN 978-1-4262-0393-0

This guide provides information on each of the fifty-eight national parks, including things to do, campgrounds and accommodations, and facilities for the disabled.

"You can't do better than this guide. . . . Highly detailed and beautiful, this one is a must for all collections." Libr J

National Geographic guide to the state parks of the United States; 3rd ed.; National Geographic 2008 384p il pa $25   **917**
1. Parks -- United States
ISBN 978-1-4262-0251-3

A guide to more than 200 parks in all 50 states. Each entry provides information on: outstanding scenery and nature; historic and cultural sites; recreational activities; wildlife watching; camping and lodging. 32 maps and 250 color photographs accompany the text.

Sandoval-Strausz, A. K.
  ★ **Hotel**; an American history. Yale University Press 2007 375p il map $37.50 **917**
1. Hotels -- Social aspects 2. Hotels -- United States -- History 3. Hotels and motels
ISBN 978-0-300-10616-9; 0-300-10616-5
                            LC 2007-10239
The author "develops social, moral, economic, legal and political connections with originality and insight. His impassioned reading of our 'built environment' is fascinating, his research prodigious. And the subject merits his talent as a historian." N Y Times Book Rev
Includes bibliographical references

Stone, Nathaniel
  On the water; discovering America in a rowboat. illustrations by Elizabeth Stone. Broadway Bks. 2002 323p il $21.95; pa $12.95   **917**
1. Boats and boating 2. Boats and boating -- United States
ISBN 0-7679-0841-4; 0-7679-0842-2 pa
                            LC 2002-18489
"Pushing off from New York City's Hudson River, {the author} rowed to the Erie Canal, down to Ohio, onward to the Mississippi, across the Gulf to Key West, and back up along the coastline of the Atlantic to Maine. It was a 6,000-mile journey, and it took him 10 months to complete. This is the chronicle of his adventure, his voyage into and around America, the story of the people he met and the places he saw. . . . It's a straightforward, crisply written memoir." Booklist

Thoreau, Henry David
  ★ **Cape** Cod; photographs by Scot Miller. Ill. ed. of the American classic.; Houghton Mifflin Co. 2008 255p il $35   **917**
ISBN 978-0-618-75845-6; 0-618-75845-3
                            LC 2007-42952
This "account is based on the author's experiences during the three short visits to Cape Cod (Oct. 1849; June 1850; July 1855), and includes ten essays on the history and character of the inhabitants, 'The Highland Light,' Nantucket,

the sea, the beach, and other aspects of the Cape." Oxford Companion to Am Lit

  The **Maine** woods; introduction by Edward Hoagland. Penguin Books 1988 xxxiii, 442p pa $16   **917**
ISBN 0-14-017013-8
                            LC 88-3644
This account of the author's rambles around the lakes and woods of Maine "records three different excursions: Thoreau's trip to Mount Katahdin (which he called 'Ktaadn'), published in the 'Union Magazine' in 1848; 'Chesuncook,' which appeared in the 'Atlantic Monthly' in the same year; and 'The Allegash and the East Branch,' which is a marvel of precise observation." Herzberg. Reader's Ency of Am Lit

Wallis, Michael
  Route 66: the mother road. St. Martin's Griffin 2001 276p il maps $35; pa $19.95   **917**
ISBN 0-312-28167-6; 0-312-28161-7 pa
                            LC 2001-31944
The author examines the highway's history, roadside diners, towns, motels, and people.

Woodger, Elin
  Encyclopedia of the Lewis and Clark Expedition; [by] Elin Woodger, Brandon Toropov; foreword by Ned Blackhawk. Facts on File 2004 xxv, 438p il $65.00; pa $21.95   **917**
ISBN 0-8160-4781-2; 0-8160-4782-0 pa
                            LC 2003-6120
"This is a complete, authoritative overview of a fascinating landmark in American history and will be a first purchase for most libraries." SLJ
  Includes bibliographical references

The Columbia gazetteer of North America; edited by Saul B. Cohen. Columbia Univ. Press 2000 1157p il $156   **917**
ISBN 0-231-11990-9
                            LC 00-27512
"This work includes more than 50,000 entries covering every incorporated place and country in the United States, along with many unincorporated places and physical features throughout North America. Arranged alphabetically, each entry includes a pronunciation guide, location information, and longitude and latitude where appropriate. If the listing is a municipality, brief population figures are provided as well. . . . Color maps of the physical regions of North America, along with political maps of the region, are included as reference points." Am Ref Books Annu, 2001

Home ground; language for an American landscape. Barry Lopez, editor; Debra Gwartney, managing editor. Trinity University Press 2006 xxiv, 449p il $29.95   **917**
1. Americanisms -- Encyclopedias 2. Geographic names -- Encyclopedias 3. Geography -- Terminology 4. Landscape in literature 5. Names, Geographical --

United States 6. Reference books
ISBN 978-1-59534-024-5; 1-59534-024-6

LC 2006-19942

This is a "collection of geographical terms from every region of the United States. The 45 contributors, among them Jon Krakauer and Barbara Kingsolver, chose words that Americans use to describe landscape features where they live, then enriched their definitions with literary quotes, comments, irony, and humor. The result is a readable A-to-Z geological and geographical dictionary that surpasses other dictionaries in both scope and coverage." Libr J

Includes bibliographical references

The official guide to America's national parks; editor: Molly Moker. 13th ed; Fodors Travel Pub. 2009 xxxix, 488p il map pa $18.95   **917**
1. National parks and reserves -- United States
ISBN 978-1-4000-1628-0

This park visitors' guide also covers national monuments, military parks, seashores and lakeshores, historic sites, and battlefields. Entries are listed by State, and include contact information, activities and facilities, travel directories, and nearby attractions and points of interest.

918   Geography of and travel in South America

Chatwin, Bruce

In Patagonia; introduction by Nicholas Shakespeare. Penguin Books 2003 204p il map pa $15   **918**
ISBN 0-14-243719-0; 978-0-14-243719-3

LC 2002-45038

This travelogue "captures the exotic characters and scenery Chatwin encountered in the southern tip of South America on a search for an important prehistoric artifact." Booklist

Grann, David

The **lost** city of Z; a tale of deadly obsession in the Amazon. Doubleday 2009 339p il map $27.50   **918**
1. El Dorado 2. Explorers
ISBN 978-0-385-51353-1; 0-385-51353-4

LC 2008-17432

Interweaves the story of British explorer Percy Fawcett, who vanished during a 1925 expedition into the Amazon, with the author's own quest to uncover the mysteries surrounding Fawcett's final journey and the secrets of what lies deep in the Amazon jungle.

"A colorful tale of true adventure, marked by satisfyingly unexpected twists, turns and plenty of dark portents." Kirkus

Includes bibliographical references (p. 315-326)

Theroux, Paul

The **old** Patagonian express; by train through the Americas. Houghton Mifflin 1979 404p hardcover o.p. pa $15   **918**
1. America -- Description 2. Railroads -- Latin America
ISBN 0-395-52105-X pa

LC 79-15353

The author describes his journey from Boston to Patagonia by train.

919   Geography of and travel in Australasia, Pacific Ocean islands, Atlantic Ocean islands, Arctic islands, Antarctica and on extraterrestrial worlds

Bryson, Bill

In a sunburned country. Broadway Bks. 2000 307p il maps hardcover o.p. pa $14.95   **919**
1. Large print books
ISBN 0-7679-0386-2 pa

LC 00-25566

In this book, Bryson "chronicles his exploration of Australia, he introduces us to a town that went without electricity until the early 1990s, a former high-ranking politician who hawks his own autobiography to passersby, an assortment of coffee shops and restaurants, . . . a type of giant worm, and the world's most poisonous creature, the box jellyfish." Booklist

Includes bibliographical references

Chatwin, Bruce

The **songlines**. Viking 1987 293p hardcover o.p. pa $13.95 **919**
1. Australia -- Description 2. Australian aborigines
ISBN 0-14-009429-6 pa

LC 86-40512

"This is an important book and a challenging one. . . . It is full of odd characters, bizarre incidents, moments of poetry—some of them comic—that spring as much from the writer's own generosity of spirit as from the richness of things." Times Lit Suppl

Cookman, Scott

★ **Ice** blink; the mysterious fate of Sir John Franklin's lost polar expedition. Wiley 2000 244p il maps $24.95; pa $15.95   **919**
1. Explorers 2. Naval officers 3. Northwest Passage 4. Travel writers
ISBN 0-471-37790-2; 0-471-40420-9 pa

LC 99-47620

In this "account of the fabled 1845 Franklin expedition in search of the Northwest Passage, Cookman inculpates a novel malefactor in the tragedy: botulism. In the 1980s, three frozen corpses of expedition members were found and exhumed. . . . Autopsies revealed lead, fingering lead-soldered cans from the provisions. . . . Adventure readers will flock to this fine regaling of the enduring mystery surrounding the best-known disaster in Arctic exploration." Booklist

Includes bibliographical references

Fleming, Fergus

Ninety degrees North; the quest for the North Pole. Grove Press 2002 xxi, 470p il maps $26; pa $15   **919**
ISBN 0-8021-1725-2; 0-8021-4036-X pa

LC 2002-21469

"The book is fascinating for how Fleming renders the haughty, post-Enlightenment brio of the principal adventurers and the extreme, often fatal ends toward which it pushed them." Publ Wkly

Includes bibliographical references

Preston, Diana

A **first** rate tragedy; Robert Falcon Scott and the race to the South Pole. Houghton Mifflin 1998 269p il map hardcover o.p. pa $14 **919**

1. Explorers 2. Explorers -- Great Britain -- Biography
ISBN 0-618-00201-4 pa

LC 98-47411

"A whole generation was brought up on the legend of Scott of the Antarctic. Diana Preston successfully explains why and how this came about. . . . {She} has written a first-rate book retelling the familiar tale in compulsive terms and adding a thoughtful twist of her own." Times Lit Suppl

Includes bibliographical references

Pyne, Stephen J.

★ **Voyager**; seeking newer worlds in the third great age of discovery. Viking 2010 444p il $29.95 **919**

1. Aeronautics -- United States -- History 2. Astronautics -- United States 3. Astronautics -- United States -- History 4. Planets -- Exploration 5. Project Voyager
ISBN 978-0-670-02183-3; 0-670-02183-0

LC 2009-46305

"By looking at the mission of Voyager 1 and Voyager 2 and comparing it with past voyages of discovery on Earth, Pyne offers a unique and engrossing history of the Western world's love affair with such journeys. . . . [The author] calls the Voyager mission the hallmark of a 'Third Great Age of Discovery,' similar to ambitious seagoing expeditions in the 16th and 18th centuries. . . . Pyne captures the Western passion for exploration and the lure of the unknown, while relating the fascinating story of two fragile spacecraft continuing after three decades their brave quest across space and time." Publ Wkly

Includes bibliographical references

Solomon, Susan

The **coldest** March. Yale Univ. Press 2001 xxii, 383p il maps hardcover o.p. pa $16.95 **919**

1. Antarctica -- Discovery and exploration 2. Explorers
ISBN 0-300-08967-8; 0-300-09921-5 pa

LC 00-54996

"In November 1911, Capt. Robert Falcon Scott and his British team set out to be the first to reach the South Pole. Battling the brutal weather of Antarctica, they reached the pole in January 1912 only to discover that a Norwegian team had beat them there by nearly a month. On their return from the Pole, Scott and four of his companions died in harsh conditions. Ever since, history has not known whether to label them heroes or bunglers. Solomon . . . analyzes all the factors present during Scott's expedition in an attempt to explain that his failure was due not to incompetence but to a combination of unpredictable weather, erroneous choices and bad luck." Libr J

Includes bibliographical references

Theroux, Paul

The **happy** isles of Oceania; paddling the Pacific. Houghton Mifflin Co. 2006 528p map pa $15.95 **919**

ISBN 978-0-618-65898-5; 0-618-65898-X

LC 2006-28742

The author "spent 18 months in a one-man collapsible kayak exploring such exotic Pacific islands as New Zealand, Australia, the Soloman and Cook Islands, Fiji, Samoa, Tahiti, Easter Island, and Hawaii. . . . A brilliant storyteller with an eye for the absurd, Theroux takes the reader to little-known places where time seems to have stood still and people lead simple lives totally unrelated to 20th-century America." Libr J

920 Biography, genealogy, insignia

Abdul-Jabbar, Kareem

Black profiles in courage; a legacy of African American achievement. [by] Kareem Abdul-Jabbar and Alan Steinberg; foreword by Henry Louis Gates, Jr. Morrow 1996 xxiv, 232p il hardcover o.p. pa $13 **920**

1. Abolitionists 2. African Americans -- Biography 3. African Americans -- History 4. Authors 5. Children 6. Civil rights activists 7. Colonists 8. Dissenters 9. Explorers 10. Inventors 11. Memoirists 12. Murder victims 13. Revolutionaries 14. Sheriffs 15. Slaves 16. Writers on science
ISBN 0-688-13097-6; 0-380-81341-6 pa

LC 96-26245

The authors have provided "interesting and nuanced accounts of heroic African Americans whose accomplishments changed U.S. history. . . . Although Abdul-Jabbar is highly critical of past and present racism in the U.S., he gives credit to the abolitionist movement and leaders such as William Lloyd Garrison for their efforts toward ending slavery." Publ Wkly

Includes bibliographical references

Acocella, Joan Ross

Twenty-eight artists and two saints; essays. [by] Joan Acocella. Pantheon Books 2007 524p il $30 **920**

1. Art -- 20th century 2. Artists 3. Artists -- Psychology 4. Arts, Modern -- 20th century
ISBN 978-0-375-42416-8; 0-375-42416-4

LC 2006-47266

"Like every great critic, Acocella is subjective, uncompromising. She has a distinct point of view, a refreshingly not-fashionable one—she salutes Sunday-school virtues!—and writes from her conviction that beneath its hectic, irresponsible, even intoxicated surface, art makes singularly unglamorous demands: integrity, sacrifice, discipline." N Y Times Book Rev

Adams, Maureen B.

Shaggy muses; the dogs who inspired Virginia Woolf, Emily Dickinson, Edith Wharton, Elizabeth Barrett Browning, and Emily Bronte. Ballantine Books 2007 299p il $24.95 **920**

1. Authors 2. Biography, Collective 3. Dogs 4. Essayists 5. Nonfiction writers 6. Novelists 7. Poets 8. Short story writers 9. Women authors, American -- Biography 10. Women authors, English -- Biography

11. Women dog owners
ISBN 978-0-345-48406-2; 0-345-48406-1

LC 2006-101291

"Despite their different personalities and backgrounds, these writers all had in common dogs that provided stability and consistency in their lives. Each chapter is a minibiography of an author emphasizing and offering anecdotes about the deep bond she shared with her dog. By using diaries, letters, illustrations, and sometimes passages from these women's writings, Adams provides a unique perspective of her subjects as pet owners. A recurrent theme is the comfort the dogs provided. . . . From this unusual vantage point, Adams succeeds in linking these writers' lives in various ways." Libr J

Includes bibliographical references

Angelo, Bonnie

★ **First** families; the impact of the White House on their lives. Morrow 2005 336p il hardcover o.p. pa $15.95 **920**

1. Presidents -- United States -- Family
ISBN 0-06-056356-7; 0-06-056358-3 pa

LC 2005-41474

"Relying heavily on the recollections and memoirs of presidential family members, White House staff, and D.C. journalists, this chatty slice of Americana is chock-full of fun First Family facts." Booklist

Includes bibliographical references

Anthony, Carl Sferrazza

America's first families; an inside view of 200 years of private life in the White House. Touchstone 2000 411p il hardcover o.p. pa $18 **920**

1. Presidents -- United States -- Family
ISBN 0-684-86442-8 pa

LC 00-64936

"This close-up look at the lives of White House residents offers an intimate and objective perspective on the fish-bowl life most First Families have experienced." Libr J

Includes bibliographical references

Baker, John F.

The **Washingtons** of Wessyngton Plantation; stories of my family's generational journey to freedom. Atria 2009 419p il $26 **920**

1. Plantation life 2. Slavery
ISBN 978-1-4165-6740-0; 1-4165-6740-2

LC 2008-18742

"When Baker was in a seventh-grade social studies class, he saw a photograph of four African Americans in a textbook. Baker later learned from his grandmother that the three men and one woman were ancestors, former slaves of the Washington family of Tennessee. . . . Based on the papers of the Washington family, U.S. census records, period newspaper accounts, interviews with 11 family members, and DNA evidence, Baker's book traces his family from its origin in West Africa through enslavement in Virginia and Tennessee, the Civil War, emancipation and sharecropping, and departure from the rural South for the urban North. He also provides a detailed account of life on the Wessyngton Plantation, once the largest tobacco plantation in the United States. Historians will find this book useful for its examina-

tion of rural life in the 19th-century South, and general readers will find a moving story of a family achieving freedom." Libr J

Includes bibliographical references

Ball, Edward

The **sweet** hell inside; the rise of an elite Black family in the segregated South. Perennial 2002 384p il pa $13.95 **920**

1. African Americans -- Biography
ISBN 978-0-06-050590-5; 0-06-050590-7

"The Harlestons of South Carolina were descended from a slave woman and her master, the start of a line of fair-skinned blacks who rose to prominence in the state through commerce, social service, and the arts. . . . [The author] was approached by Edwina Harleston Whitlock, a distant black relative (a sixth cousin, twice removed), to take a storehouse of genealogical material she had about her family and to write its history. The result is a stunning look at a fascinating family and the history of blacks in the U.S. from the 1800s to the 1960s." Booklist

Includes bibliographical references

Bell, Eric Temple

★ **Men** of mathematics; [by] E. T. Bell. Simon & Schuster 1937 xxi, 592p il hardcover o.p. pa $18 **920**

1. Astronomers 2. Authors 3. College teachers 4. Essayists 5. Logicians 6. Mathematicians 7. Memoirists 8. Philosophers 9. Physicists 10. Theologians 11. Writers on religion 12. Writers on science
ISBN 0-671-62818-6 pa

This volume looks at the lives and contributions of 35 pioneers of modern mathematics.

Benfey, Christopher E. G.

A **summer** of hummingbirds; love, art, and scandal in the intersecting worlds of Emily Dickinson, Mark Twain, Harriet Beecher Stowe, and Martin Johnson Heade. [by] Christopher Benfey. Penguin Press 2008 287p il $25.95 **920**

1. Abolitionists 2. American literature -- History and criticism 3. Artists 4. Authors 5. Children's authors 6. Essayists 7. Humorists 8. Literature and history -- United States -- History -- 19th century 9. Literature and society -- United States -- History -- 19th century 10. Memoirists 11. Nonfiction writers 12. Novelists 13. Painters 14. Poets 15. Satirists 16. Short story writers 17. Travel writers 18. Women and literature -- United States -- History -- 19th century 19. Women in literature
ISBN 978-1-594-20160-8; 1-594-20160-9

LC 2007-36512

"Benfey's subtitle neatly conveys the fascinating and sometimes tortuous complexities of this literary/historical snapshot of post–Civil War America. . . . Benfey finds a common connection among these diverse characters through, improbably, hummingbirds, an intense interest in which seems to have taken hold of artists and writers throughout the late nineteenth century. Benfey's eclectic and original approach brings this period and these personalities vividly to life. He presents sensitive critiques of literature and art alongside tales of illicit love and broken, bent, or triumphant lives, all of which makes for compelling reading for specialist and nonspecialist alike." Booklist

Berkin, Carol

Civil War wives; the lives and times of Angelina Grimke Weld, Varina Howell Davis, and Julia Dent Grant. Alfred A. Knopf 2009 361p il $28.95   **920**
  1. Abolitionists 2. Authors 3. Feminists 4. Married women -- United States -- History 5. Nonfiction writers 6. Spouses of presidents 7. Spouses of prominent persons 8. Women -- United States -- Biography 9. Women -- United States -- Social conditions -- 19th century
  ISBN 978-1-4000-4446-7
                                              LC 2009-19476
"This finely nuanced, absorbing account makes an important contribution to both Civil War literature and the history of American women." Booklist
  Includes bibliographical references (p. 317-345)

Boller, Paul F.

Presidential wives; {by} Paul F. Boller, Jr. 2nd, rev ed; Oxford Univ. Press 1998 553p pa $17.95   **920**
  1. Presidents' spouses -- United States 2. Presidents' spouses -- United States -- Anecdotes
  ISBN 0-19-512142-2
                                              LC 98-3480
This collection covers every First Lady from Martha Washington to Hillary Rodham Clinton. The author devotes a chapter to each of his subjects featuring a biographical essay followed by anecdotes

Bond, Jenny

Who the hell is Pansy O'Hara? the fascinating stories behind 50 of the world's best-loved books. [by] Jenny Bond & Chris Sheedy. Penguin Books 2008 318p pa $13   **920**
  1. Authors, American 2. Authors, English 3. Authorship
  ISBN 978-0-14-311364-5; 0-14-311364-X
                                              LC 2007-39840
"From Stephen King's childhood fascination with gruesome comics to the famous family name behind Peter Benchley, . . . Bond and Sheedy light up some intriguing angles on many popular authors. Journalists in Australia, the authors deliver their 50 profiles with reportorial vigor, moving quickly through each profile while highlighting the salient and salacious details of, for example, the role played by Mary Shelley's literary legacy (daughter of two leading British writers) and her free-love husband (poet Percy Shelley) in the genesis of Frankenstein. . . . Between the engaging information and the range of popular texts (Pride and Prejudice, The Origin of Species, The War of the Worlds, In Cold Blood, Lolita, Roots, The Cat in the Hat, The Da Vinci Code), this affectionate literary history should appeal to many readers." Publ Wkly
  Includes bibliographical references

Booknotes (Television program)

Booknotes: life stories; notable biographers on the people who shaped America. {complied by} Bri-

an Lamb. Times Bks. 1999 xxiii, 471p il hardcover o.p. pa $16.95   **920**
  1. Biography
  ISBN 0-8129-3339-7 pa
                                              LC 98-41374
"Lamb, host of C-SPAN's Booknotes, has compiled an anthology of interviews focusing on the lives of 75 prominent people from the 1700s to the present. The result is chatty and informal." Libr J

Brightman, Carol

Sweet chaos; the Grateful Dead's American adventure. Pocket 1999 356p il pa $17   **920**
  1. Guitarists 2. Rock musicians 3. Singers
  ISBN 0-671-01117-0
"Brightman's is an engrossing treatment of the Dead and their times. . . . She offers fresh perspectives and insights and captures the flavor of the band." Booklist
  Includes bibliographical references

Brighton, Terry

Patton, Montgomery, Rommel; masters of war. Crown Forum 2009 426p il map $30   **920**
  1. Army officers 2. Generals 3. Marshals 4. World War, 1939-1945 -- Biography
  ISBN 978-0-307-46154-4
"Brighton shows how during the period between the wars, each refined his skills, which included reading one another's published treatises on the subject of mobile warfare. The author pulls no punches in revealing their flaws as well. Very highly recommended." Libr J
  Includes bibliographical references

Brynner, Rock

★ Empire & odyssey; the Brynners in Far East Russia and beyond. Steerforth Press 2006 331p il map $29.95   **920**
  1. Actors 2. Industrialists
  ISBN 1-58642-102-6; 978-1-58642-102-1
                                              LC 2005-36507
The author "chronicles the lives of four generations of his own family, beginning with his great-grandfather, Jules Bryner, a Swiss who eventually settled in Vladivostok, where he was greatly responsible for establishing its importance in the Russian Far East. Next, he covers Jules's son Boris, a major industrialist, and then Boris's son, the author's father, actor Yul Brynner. He concludes, full circle, with his own odyssey to Vladivostok in 2003. . . . [This is] a fascinating tale of a fascinating family." Libr J
  Includes bibliographical references

Cannon, John

The kings & queens of Britain; [by] John Cannon and Anne Hargreaves. 2nd ed., rev; Oxford University Press 2009 404p il map pa $19.99   **920**
  1. Reference books
  ISBN 978-0-19-955922-0; 0-19-955922-8
                                              LC 2009-278738
This book "details the pedigree, birth order, and political legacies of 600 English, Irish, and Welsh regents. . . . Studded with informative black-and-white artifact illustrations,

maps, portraits, and family trees, this [is an] extensive quick-reference " Libr J

Includes bibliographical references

Carey, Charles W.

American inventors, entrepreneurs & business visionaries; [by] Charles W. Carey, Jr. Rev. ed; Facts On File 2010 xxi, 455p il $95 **920**

1. Businesspeople 2. Inventors 3. Reference books

ISBN 978-0-8160-8146-2; 978-1-4381-3336-2 ebook

LC 2009-54269

"This biographical dictionary includes profiles of more than 300 individuals who have made significant and lasting contributions to American industry dating from the Colonial era to the present. Each entry addresses the subject chronologically through his or her life, focusing on major professional achievements as well as personal triumphs and tragedies. . . . The book paints a fascinating portrait of American ingenuity. A well-written biographical dictionary that will appeal to anyone interested in the history of American invention and entrepreneurialism." Libr J

Includes bibliographical references

Caroli, Betty Boyd

First ladies; from Martha Washington to Michelle Obama. Rev. and updated ed.; Oxford University Press 2010 xxii, 437p il pa $17.95 **920**

1. Presidents' spouses -- United States

ISBN 978-0-19-539285-2; 0-19-539285-X

LC 2010-14673

In addition to profiling each woman who has served as First Lady the author examines the ways the role has evolved over the years.

Carr, Jonathan

The **Wagner** clan; the saga of Germany's most illustrious and infamous family. Grove Atlantic 2007 409p $27.50; pa $16.95 **920**

1. Biography, Individual 2. Composers 3. Music -- Germany -- 20th century

ISBN 978-0-87113-975-7; 0-87113-975-8; 978-0-8021-4399-0 pa; 0-8021-4399-7 pa

"Carr's sprightly, fluent narrative places the family in its historical and intellectual context without reducing it to the symbolic effigy it has often become." Publ Wkly

Includes bibliographical references

Castor, Helen

She-wolves; the women who ruled England before Elizabeth. Harper/Collins 2011 480p il map $27.99; ebook $19.99 **920**

1. Monarchy -- Great Britain -- History 2. Queens

ISBN 978-0-06-143076-3; 978-0-06-206578-0 ebook

LC 2010013263

The author "recounts the lives of six women who exercised—or tried to exercise—political power in England prior to Elizabeth I: Matilda, granddaughter of William the Conqueror; Eleanor of Aquitaine; Isabella of France; Margaret of Anjou; Jane Grey; and Mary Tudor. . . . Readers of popular history of British royals will enjoy their immensely

human stories and applaud the indomitable will of these strong protofeminists." Libr J

Includes bibliographical references

Chernow, Ron

The **Warburgs**; the twentieth-century odyssey of a remarkable Jewish family. Random House 1993 820p il hardcover o.p. pa $21 **920**

1. Bankers

ISBN 0-679-74359-6 pa

LC 93-16599

The author "chronicles the saga of {one} of the world's most powerful and oldest banking families. In telling this monumental tale of the Warburgs, Chernow offers a panoramic view of nearly 500 years of world history, concentrating on the role of Jews in German business, culture, and politics from the time of Kaiser Wilhelm to that of Adolf Hitler. He also explains how the Warburgs extended their influence to America by marrying into two influential families." Booklist

Includes bibliographical references

Chick, Steve

Spray paint the walls; the story of Black Flag. IPG/PM 2011 403p il pa $19.95 **920**

1. Punk rock music

ISBN 978-1-60486-418-2

This is a history of seminal punk band Black Flag.

"For a plunge into SST lore, this is the book to grab for summer's enervating heat. Don't expect newfound testimonies that will upset the Black Flag brand, but do expect a fascinating and eventful journey into the heart of damaged territory." PopMatters

Includes discography and bibliographical references

Clay, Catrine

King, Kaiser, Tsar; three royal cousins who led the world to war. Walker & Company 2007 416p il $26.95; pa $16.99 **920**

1. Biography, Individual 2. Emperors 3. Kings 4. Kings and rulers 5. World War, 1914-1918 6. World War, 1914-1918 -- Causes

ISBN 0-8027-1623-7; 978-0-8027-1623-1; 0-8027-1677-6 pa; 978-0-8027-1677-4 pa

This is a "biography of not one but three significant men. King George V of England, Kaiser Wilhelm II of Germany, and Tsar Nicholas II of Russia (familiarly known as Georgie, Willy, and Nicky) were more than just the leaders of three of the most powerful countries in the world in the early 20th century—they were cousins who had grown up together, played together, and attended family functions together. . . . [The author] provides an intimate look inside the lives of these boys as they grew into manhood and became king, kaiser, and tsar, bringing new pleasures and details to a well-known subject." Libr J

Includes bibliographical references

Cohen, Rich

Sweet and low; a family story. Farrar, Straus and Giroux 2006 272p il $25 **920**

1. Biography, Individual 2. Food industry executives

3. Sugar substitutes
ISBN 0-374-27229-8; 978-0-374-27229-6

LC 2005-15730

This "is a story peopled with eccentrics and naifs and scoundrels, and a story recounted with uncommon acuity and wit." N Y Times (Late N Y Ed)

Coll, Steve

The **Bin** Ladens; an Arabian family in the American century. Penguin Press 2008 671p il $35 **920**
1. Biography, Individual 2. Terrorists
ISBN 978-1-59420-164-6

LC 2007-42748

This "book not only gives us the most psychologically detailed portrait of the brutal 9/11 mastermind yet, but in telling the epic story of Osama bin Laden's extended family, it also reveals the crucial role that his relatives and their relationship with the royal house of Saud played in shaping his thinking, his ambitions, his technological expertise and his tactics." N Y Times (Late N Y Ed)
Includes bibliographical references

Dance, Stanley

The **world** of Count Basie. Da Capo Press 1985 xxi, 399p il pa $18 **920**
1. Band leaders 2. Clarinetists 3. Drummers 4. Flutists 5. Guitarists 6. Jazz musicians 7. Pianists 8. Saxophonists 9. Singers 10. Trombonists 11. Trumpet players
ISBN 0-306-80245-7

LC 85-12901

This book "consists of numerous tape-recorded and edited interviews with musicians and vocalists associated with Basie, and each gets to tell his own story. Many overlap and there are interesting confirmations and disputes over details. The language has been polished (and no doubt in some cases cleaned up), but Dance does not noticeably impose his own views on others. There are good photographs." Choice
Includes discography and bibliographical references

De Lisle, Leanda

The **sisters** who would be queen; Mary, Katherine, and Lady Jane Grey: a Tudor tragedy. Ballantine Books 2009 xxx, 350p il $30 **920**
1. Courtiers 2. Queens
ISBN 978-0-345-49135-0

LC 2009-31074

This is a biography of the Grey sisters, "who were victimized in the notoriously vicious Tudor power struggle and whose heirs would otherwise probably be ruling England today." Publisher's note
Includes bibliographical references

De Waal, Edmund

The **hare** with amber eyes; a family's century of art and loss. Farrar, Straus and Giroux 2010 354p il map $26 **920**
1. Art collections 2. Art collectors 3. Bankers 4. Magazine executives 5. Patrons of the arts
ISBN 978-0-374-10597-6

LC 2010-25539

"From a hard and vast archival mass of journals, memoirs, newspaper clippings and art-history books, Mr de Waal has fashioned, stroke by minuscule stroke, a book as fresh with detail as if it had been written from life, and as full of beauty and whimsy as a netsuke from the hands of a master carver." Economist

Denlinger, Elizabeth Campbell

Before Victoria; extraordinary women of the British Romantic era. by Elizabeth Campbell Denlinger; foreword by Lyndall Gordon. Columbia University Press 2005 188p il $41.50 **920**
1. Women -- Great Britain
ISBN 0-231-13630-7

LC 2004-59267

This book "offers portraits of a group of women who were scientists, artists, writers, poets, philanthropists and reformers during the Romantic Era and details how their accomplishments changed the social and economic landscape for women." Univ Press Books for Public and Second Sch Libr, 2006
Includes bibliographical references

Dinnage, Rosemary

★ **Alone!** alone!: lives of some outsider women. New York Review Books 2004 296p $24.95 **920**
1. Biography, Collective 2. Women -- Biography 3. Women authors 4. Women authors -- Biography
ISBN 1-590-17069-5

LC 2003-27805

The subjects of this volume of biographical essays include: Gwen John, Stevie Smith, Barbara Pym, Simone Weil, Clementine Churchill, Ottoline Morrell, Dora Russell, Giuseppina Verdi, Olive Schreiner, Helena Blavatsky and Annie Besant; Marie Stopes, Enid Blyton, Angela Brazil, Isak Dinesen, Rebecca West, Margaret Oliphant, Alice James and Katherine Mansfield.
"The book is dutifully footnoted and academically solid yet is also beautifully written, marked with great feeling and vivid flashes of insight. It cannot fail to enrich a collection." Libr J

Dray, Philip

Capitol men; the epic story of Reconstruction through the lives of the first Black congressmen. Houghton Mifflin Co. 2008 463p il $30 **920**
1. African American legislators 2. African Americans -- Biography 3. Reconstruction (1865-1876) 4. Reconstruction (U.S. history, 1865-1877)
ISBN 978-0-618-56370-8; 0-618-56370-9

LC 2008-11292

"A welcome addition to the literature of the Civil War and Reconstruction Era, and important for students of the civil-rights movement and its origins." Kirkus
Includes bibliographical references

Englehart, Murray

AC/DC; maximum rock and roll. [by] Murray Engleheart with Arnaud Durieux. Morrow 2007 488p il $25.95　　　　**920**

1. Rock musicians

ISBN 0-06-113391-4; 978-0-06-113391-6

LC 2007-295661

This is a "biography of the wildly successful Australian rockers. Covering everything from guitarist Angus Young's first record purchase (Club A Go-Go by the Yardbirds) to the band's induction into the Rock and Roll Hall of Fame and all points in between, this book is a godsend for fans." Publ Wkly

Includes discography

Evans, Harold

They made America; [by] Harold Evans, with Gail Buckland and David Lefer. Little, Brown 2004 496p $40; pa $18.95　　　　**920**

1. Inventions 2. Inventors

ISBN 0-316-27766-5; 0-316-01385-4 pa

LC 2003-65954

The author "profiles 70 of America's leading inventors, entrepreneurs and innovators, some better known than others. Along with such obvious choices as Henry Ford, Thomas Edison and the Wright brothers, Evans profiles Lewis Tappan (an abolitionist who dreamed up the idea of credit ratings), Gen. Georges Doriot (pioneer of venture capital) and Joan Ganz Cooney, of the Children's Television Workshop." Publ Wkly

Farris, Scott

Almost president; the men who lost the race but changed the nation. Lyons Press 2012 339p il $24.95　　　　**920**

1. Presidents -- United States -- Election

ISBN 978-0-7627-6378-8

LC 2011033001

When the author "lost a 1998 race for Wyoming's at-large congressional district, he was prompted to examine the role losers play in democracy. Farris notes that some unsuccessful White House aspirants have had a far greater impact on American history than many who became president. . . . Moving chronologically through 184 years, he finds past/present linkages as he profiles Henry Clay, Stephen Douglas, William Jennings Bryan, Al Smith, Thomas E. Dewey, Barry Goldwater, George McGovern, Ross Perot, Al Gore, John Kerry, and John McCain. . . . Documenting changes in the face of America and the impact of such issues as race, religion, and workplace reform on elections, Farris writes with a lively flair, skillfully illustrating his solid historical research with revelatory anecdotes and facts." Publ Wkly

Includes bibliographical references

Feather, Leonard

From Satchmo to Miles; new foreword by the author. Da Capo Press 1984 258p il hardcover o.p. pa $16　　　　**920**

1. African American musicians 2. Band leaders 3. Blind 4. Blues musicians 5. Composers 6. Flugelhornists 7. Jazz musicians 8. Pianists 9. Pop musicians 10. Recording producers 11. Saxophonists 12. Singers 13.

Trumpet players

ISBN 0-306-80302-X pa

LC 83-15223

A collection of profiles of jazz musicians including Count Basie, Lester Young, Oscar Peterson, Ray Charles, Don Ellis, Duke Ellington, Billie Holiday, Ella Fitzgerald, Louis Armstrong, Dizzy Gillespie, Norman Granz, Miles Davis and Charlie Parker.

Feldman, Burton

112 Mercer Street; Einstein, Russell, Godel, Pauli, and the end of innocence in science. edited and completed by Katherine Williams. Arcade Pub. 2007 243p $26　　　　**920**

1. Biography, Collective 2. Essayists 3. Logicians 4. Mathematicians 5. Nobel laureates for literature 6. Nobel laureates for physics 7. Nonfiction writers 8. Philosophers 9. Physicists 10. Science -- History 11. Scientists

ISBN 978-1-55970-704-6; 1-55970-704-6

LC 2007-1194

"During the winter of 1943–1944, Albert Einstein met weekly with three other aging geniuses—philosopher Bertrand Russell, mathematician Kurt Gödel and physicist Wolfgang Pauli—in the study of his home at 112 Mercer Street in Princeton, N.J. . . . What the authors present are illuminating biographical sketches of these men and their earlier, groundbreaking work." Publ Wkly

Includes bibliographical references

Feldman, Noah

Scorpions; the battles and triumphs of FDR's great Supreme Court justices. Twelve 2010 513p il $30　　　　**920**

1. Attorneys general 2. Biography, Collective 3. Government officials 4. Governors 5. Handicapped 6. Judges 7. Judges -- United States 8. Lawyers 9. Philatelists 10. Presidential advisers 11. Presidents 12. Regulatory agency officials 13. Senators 14. Supreme Court justice 15. Supreme Court justices

ISBN 978-0-446-58057-1; 0-446-58057-0

LC 2010-07788

The book discusses the period of U.S. Supreme Court history in which "FDR had promised the next Supreme Court seat to Joe Robinson, the Senate majority leader who led the fight for the court-packing bill in Congress. As the plan was collapsing in the Senate, the exhausted Robinson died of a heart attack. Roosevelt nominated Senator Hugo Black for the seat. He was able to appoint eight more justices, including Felix Frankfurter, William O. Douglas, and Robert Jackson, who with Black are generally recognized to be among the Court's greatest judges. These four are the subjects of Noah Feldman's 'Scorpions.' . . . Feldman's . . . book is . . . focused on the members of the Court and their decisions; . . . but also takes more time to explain each judge's distinctive theories of the Constitution and the role of judges in interpreting it." (New York Review of Books)

The author argues "that the 'distinctive constitutional theories' of Roosevelt's four greatest justices, all of whom began as New Deal liberals—Hugo Black, William O. Douglas, Felix Frankfurter, and Robert Jackson—have continued to 'cover the whole field of constitutional thought' up to the present day. . . . This is a first-rate work of narrative history that succeeds in bringing the intellectual and political battles of the post-Roosevelt Court vividly to life." Publ Wkly

Includes bibliographical references

Finkbeiner, Ann K.

The **Jasons**; the secret history of science's post-war elite. [by] Ann Finkbeiner. Viking 2006 304p hardcover o.p. pa $15   **920**

1. Biography, Collective 2. Physicists 3. Physicists -- United States -- Biography 4. Research -- United States -- History -- 20th century 5. Scientists 6. Scientists -- United States -- Biography

ISBN 978-0-670-03489-5; 0-670-03489-4; 978-0-14-303847-4 pa; 0-14-303847-8 pa

LC 2005-43471

"The Jasons is a small and elite group of scientists—once consisting almost exclusively of physicists, but now more ecumenical—who since 1960 have helped the government find solutions to particularly difficult technical problems, mostly having to do with defense. During the Cold War, the Jasons were a hush-hush organization, much like the National Security Agency. Today, they labor not so much in secret as in obscurity—which, one learns from Finkbeiner's book, is the way most Jasons prefer it. . . . By focusing on some of the more colorful Jasons, Finkbeiner shines a spotlight on the activities of the group as a whole." American Scientist

Flanders, Judith

A **circle** of sisters; Alice Kipling, Georgiana Burne-Jones, Agnes Poynter and Louisa Baldwin. W.W. Norton & Co. 2005 xxiii, 392p $27.95   **920**

1. Authors 2. Novelists 3. Parents of prominent persons 4. Poets 5. Short story writers 6. Spouses of prominent persons

ISBN 0-393-05210-9

LC 2004-65415

This is a collective biography of the McDonald sisters, two of whom grew up to marry Edward Burne-Jones and Edward Poynter, while the other two became the mothers of Rudyard Kipling and prime minister Stanley Baldwin.

"Offering perceptive commentary on the prescribed role of women in Victorian society to be mere helpmeets, Flanders' attentive, scholarly accuracy is enhanced by piquant observations that demonstrate both her professional talent and personal take on the lives of these remarkable, but unremarked upon, women." Booklist

Includes bibliographical references

Fraser, Antonia

The **wives** of Henry VIII. Knopf 1993 479p il hardcover o.p. pa $18.95   **920**

1. Kings 2. Queens

ISBN 978-0-394-58538-3; 978-0-679-73001-9 pa; 0-679-73001-X pa

LC 92-52950

This work examines the lives of the six women—Catherine of Aragon, Anne Boleyn, Jane Seymour, Anna of Cleves, Katherine Howard, and Catherine Parr—who became Queens of England between 1509 and 1547. The author discusses their marriages to Henry VIII.

"Fraser's readable style, empathy for her subjects, and piquant use of historical details and anecdotes make this a satisfying addition to the history shelves." Libr J

Includes bibliographical references

Fraser, Flora

Princesses; the six daughters of George III. Knopf 2005 478p il hardcover o.p. pa $16.95 **920**

1. Biography, Collective 2. Kings 3. Princesses 4. Queens

ISBN 0-679-45118-8; 1-4000-9669-5 pa

This "is a rich and richly hued Regency tale. . . . Fraser is splendidly at home in the 18th century, adroit at teasing history out from between guarded lines." N Y Times Book Rev

Includes bibliographical references

Gigante, Denise

The **Keats** brothers; Denise Gigante. Belknap Press of Harvard University Press 2011 ix, 499p.p ill., maps   **920**

ISBN 9780674048560

LC 2011014487

This book examines the impact of "George [Keats's] 1818 move to the western frontier of the United States, an imaginative leap across four thousand miles onto the tabula rasa of the American dream, created in John [Keats] an abysm of alienation and loneliness that would inspire the poet's most plangent and sublime poetry. [Author] Denise Gigantess account of this emigration places John's life and work in a transatlantic context that has eluded his previous biographers, while revealing the emotional turmoil at the heart of some of the most lasting verse in English." (Publisher's note)

Gordon-Reed, Annette

★ The **Hemingses** of Monticello; an American family. W.W. Norton & Co. 2008 798p il map $35   **920**

1. African Americans -- Biography 2. Architects 3. Biography, Individual 4. Essayists 5. Mistresses 6. Presidents 7. Slaves 8. Vice-presidents

ISBN 978-0-393-06477-3

LC 2008-14642

The author tells the story of the Hemingses, an American slave family and their close blood ties to Thomas Jefferson.

"This is a masterpiece brimming with decades of dedicated research and dexterous writing." Libr J

Includes bibliographical references

Gould, Jonathan

Can't buy me love; the Beatles, Britain, and America. Harmony Books 2007 661p il $27.50 **920**

1. Rock musicians

ISBN 978-0-307-35337-5; 0-307-35337-0

LC 2007-13240

"Gould's combination group biography, cultural history, and musical criticism artfully places the Beatles in their time and social context while examining with great skill how they became an international phenomenon comparable only to themselves." Booklist

Includes bibliographical references

Grant, Colin

The **natural** mystics; Marley, Tosh, and Wailer. W. W. Norton 2011 305p il $26.95 **920**

1. Percussionists 2. Reggae music 3. Reggae musicians 4. Singers 5. Songwriters

ISBN 978-0-393-08117-6; 0-393-08117-6

LC 2011-12323

"This history of the Wailers, among the first acts to bring reggae to a worldwide audience in the 1970s, doesn't function like most music biographies. Grant . . . resists assembling detailed family trees for the band's prime movers, Bob Marley, Peter Tosh and Bunny Wailer. Nor does he obsess over discography or even dwell much on the musical shifts the trio made as it evolved from playful, syncopated ska to emotionally intense Rastafarian reggae. Instead of writing from a critical remove, Grant freely injects the story with first-person asides about his experiences with interviewees. All these tactics are assets, because they help the author avoid stock band-history patter and instead drill into the broader cultural life of 20th-century Jamaica." Kirkus

Includes bibliographical references

Grant, Gail Milissa

At the elbows of my elders; one family's journey toward civil rights. Missouri History Museum 2008 251p il $24.95 **920**

1. African Americans -- Biography 2. African Americans -- Civil rights 3. Art historians 4. Blacks -- History 5. Civil rights -- History 6. Diplomats 7. Lecturers 8. Memoirists 9. Race discrimination -- Missouri 10. Undertakers

ISBN 978-1-8839-8266-9; 1-8839-8266-9

LC 2008-24219

"Grant's father, a lawyer and civil rights activist in St. Louis in the 1950s, was among the less well known resisters of segregation, eventually working with more prominent figures, from Thurgood Marshall to Ralph Bunche and A. Phillip Randolph, to fight racial inequities in St. Louis. Grant recalls a long line of family resisters, middle-class business owners who were always on the forefront of the racial divide, challenging Jim Crow laws and practices while sustaining the social and economic underpinnings of the segregated black community. . . . This is a fascinating look at the struggles of one black family that mirrored the national struggle for civil rights." Booklist

Includes bibliographical references

Green, Stanley

The **world** of musical comedy; the story of the American musical stage as told through the careers of its foremost composers and lyricists. 4th ed rev and enl; Da Capo Press 1984 480p il pa $35 **920**

1. Actors 2. Authors 3. Centenarians 4. Composers 5. Composers -- United States 6. Conductors (Music) 7. Dramatists 8. Librettists 9. Lyricists 10. Musicals 11. Screenwriters 12. Songwriters 13. Theatrical directors 14. Theatrical producers

ISBN 0-306-80207-4

LC 83-26340

"From Victor Herbert to Marvin Hamlisch, Green gives us a classic history of the genre. . . . Thirty-one chapters tell the tale of some 70 individuals or teams that have had a lasting effect on the musical theater. . . . The appendix gives the vitals on every major production of the past 85 years." Booklist

Greenstein, George

Portraits of discovery; profiles in scientific genius. Wiley 1997 232p il $24.95 **920**

1. Astronomers 2. Astrophysicists 3. Authors 4. College teachers 5. Curators 6. Deaf 7. Nobel laureates for physics 8. Physicists 9. Scientists 10. Writers on science

ISBN 0-471-19138-8

LC 97-6048

The author examines the interaction between the personal and professional in the lives of: Annie Jump Cannon, Cecilia Helena Payne Gaposchkin, Ludwig Boltzman, George Gamow, Homi Jehangir Bhaba, Luis W. Alvarez, Richard Phillips Feynman, Martin L. Perl, Margaret J. Geller, and John Huchra.

Greenstein's "portraits are at least as interesting in what they reveal about the blemishes on the face of great scientists: The eccentricities and idiosyncrasies that energize many scientists' work also may accentuate their human flaws." Sci Books & Film

Includes bibliographical references

Gross, Michael

Rogues' gallery; the secret history of the moguls and the money that made the Metropolitan Museum. Broadway Books 2009 545p $29.95 **920**

1. Art -- Collectors and collecting 2. Art -- Collectors and collecting -- United States

ISBN 978-0-7679-2488-7; 0-76792488-6

LC 2008-41480

"A deft rendering of the down-and-dirty politics of the art world." Kirkus

Includes bibliographical references

Haley, Alex

★ **Roots**; the saga of an American family: the 30th anniversary edition. Vanguard Books 2007 899p pa $15.95 **920**

1. African American families. 2. African Americans -- Biography.

ISBN 978-1-59315-449-3; 1-59315-449-6

LC 2007-8822

This book details Haley's "search for the genealogical history of his family. He describes his trip to Gambia, the African homeland of his ancestors, and recounts the lives of his forebears." Benet's Reader's Ency of Am Lit

Hardesty, Von

Black wings; courageous stories of African Americans in aviation and space history. HarperCollins Publishers 2007 180p il $21.95 **920**

1. African American astronauts 2. African American pilots

ISBN 978-0-06-126138-1

LC 2007-21270

"This book companion to the Smithsonian National Air and Space Museum exhibit of the same name offers a look at the little-known and long-neglected history of black pioneers in aviation. . . . [Along with] the Tuskegee Airmen, Hardesty profiles barnstormers, including the Blackbirds; William J. Powell, founder of an aviation club; military flyers, including Benjamin O. Davis Jr.; and astronauts Guy Bluford, Ronald McNair, and Mae Jemison. This is an inspiring look at the adventurous individuals who pushed against the limits of racial discrimination to realize their passion for flying." Booklist

Includes bibliographical references

Hargittai, Istvan

The **Martians** of science; five physicists who changed the twentieth century. Oxford University Press 2006 xxiv, 313p il map $34.50   **920**

1. Aeronautical engineers 2. Biography, Collective 3. College teachers 4. Hungarians -- Biography 5. Mathematicians 6. Mathematics teachers 7. Nobel laureates for physics 8. Nuclear weapons -- Research 9. Physicists 10. Physicists -- Biography 11. Physicists -- United States -- Biography 12. Writers on science
ISBN 978-0-19-517845-6; 0-19-517845-9

LC 2005-29427

This is a "presentation of the lives of five scientists (physicists and engineers) from Hungary who went to Germany and then to the United States. They . . . [are] Theodore von Karman, Leo Szilard, Eugene P. Wigner, John von Neumann, and Edward Teller. . . . [This book is an] extremely valuable account of the lives of these five brilliant and interesting Hungarian physicists." Sci Books Films

Includes bibliographical references

Haskins, James

African American religious leaders; [by] Jim Haskins and Kathleen Benson. Wiley 2008 162p il lib bdg $24.95   **920**

1. African Americans -- Biography 2. African Americans -- Religion
ISBN 978-0-471-73632-5; 0-471-73632-5

LC 2007-27347

"It's great to have all these figures between two covers, and even a sampling of the entries captures the importance of religion, and its leaders, in African American life." Booklist

Includes bibliographical references

Heller, Nancy

Women artists; an illustrated history. 4th ed.; Abbeville Press 2003 312p il $39.95   **920**

1. Women artists
ISBN 978-0-7892-0768-5; 0-7892-0768-0

LC 2004-269241

"Organized in six chapters by century, the survey provides brief biographical information, some critical analysis and context, and at least one color plate of the work of 125 women artists who lived and worked in Europe or North America. . . . An excellent resource." SLJ

Includes bibliographical references

Hibbert, Christopher

The **House** of Medici; its rise and fall. Morrow 1975 364p il maps hardcover o.p. pa $16   **920**

1. Bankers 2. Political leaders
ISBN 0-688-05339-4 pa

This book is concerned with "heads of the Medici family {who} directed the government of the Florentine state from 1434, with Cosimo's return from exile, until the death of the Grand Duke Giovanni Gastone in 1737." Times Lit Suppl

Includes bibliographical references

Hutchison, Kay Bailey

American heroines; the spirited women who shaped our country. 1st ed; William Morrow 2004 384p il $24.95; pa $14.95   **920**

1. Women -- United States -- Biography
ISBN 0-06-056635-3; 0-06-056636-1 pa

LC 2004-56677

"Hutchinson's lively, personal writing makes this an accessible and important volume." Booklist

James, Clive

Cultural amnesia; necessary memories from history and the arts. W.W. Norton & Co. 2007 xxxii, 876p il $35   **920**

1. Artists 2. Artists -- Biography 3. Civilization, Western 4. Humanism -- History -- 20th century 5. Intellectual life 6. Intellectual life -- History -- 20th century 7. Intellectuals 8. Memory -- Social aspects 9. Musicians 10. Musicians -- Biography 11. Philosophers 12. Philosophers -- Biography 13. Western civilization
ISBN 978-0-393-06116-1; 0-393-06116-7

LC 2006-36398

The author "not only preserves culture and nurtures humanism but also revitalizes the beauty and power of the English language." Booklist

Kennedy, John F.

★ **Profiles** in courage. HarperCollins Pubs. 2003 xxii, 245p $19.95; pa $13.95   **920**

1. Army officers 2. Courage 3. Governors 4. Judges 5. Lawyers 6. Legislators -- United States -- Biography 7. Members of Congress 8. Newspaper executives 9. Political leaders 10. Politicians -- United States 11. Presidential candidates 12. Presidents 13. Secretaries of state 14. Secretaries of the interior 15. Senators 16. State legislators 17. Statesmen 18. Supreme Court justices 19. Territorial governors
ISBN 0-06-053062-6; 0-06-085493-6 pa

LC 2003-40676

This series of profiles of Americans who took courageous stands at crucial moments in public life includes John Quincy Adams, Daniel Webster, Thomas Hart Benton, Sam Houston, Edmund G. Ross, Lucius Q. C. Lamar, George Norris, Robert A. Taft and others.

Kimball, George

Four kings; Leonard, Hagler, Hearns, Duran, and the last great era of boxing. [foreword by Pete Hamill] McBooks Press 2008 339p il $22.95; pa $16.95   **920**

1. Boxers (Persons) 2. Boxing -- Biography 3. Olympic athletes
ISBN 978-1-59013-162-6; 1-59013-162-2; 978-1-59013-238-8 pa; 1-59013-238-6 pa

LC 2008-13825

The author "resurrects Sugar Ray Leonard, Marvin Hagler, Thomas Hearns, and Roberto Duran from the mists of memory, re-creating the nine bouts the middleweights fought against one another in the 1980s. A great boxing book." Booklist

Includes bibliographical references

Kingston, Maxine Hong

China men. Knopf 1980 308p hardcover o.p. pa $13.95   **920**
1. Chinese Americans -- Biography
ISBN 0-679-72328-5 pa
LC 79-3469

This book "paints a rich picture of the writer's male family members, but those portraits of her grandfathers, father, and brothers are interspersed with fascinating bits of historical data. . . . The whole is held together by pieces of folklore that one feels compelled to go back to and reread." Libr J

Kreisler, Harry

Political awakenings; conversations with history. New Press; distributed by Perseus Distribution 2010 286p pa $17.95   **920**
1. Political activists 2. World history -- 1945- 3. World politics -- 1945-
ISBN 978-1-59558-340-6
LC 2009-36808

"As the director of the Institute of International Studies at the University of California at Berkeley, Kreisler has spent 25 years interviewing hundreds of well-regarded economists, politicians, activists, and artists. In this fascinating collection, he offers 20 of those interviews, focusing on the common theme of how their ideas and perspectives were formulated. . . . Interviews are organized under topical headings, including protest and change, environmental issues, imperialism, resistance through the arts, and human rights." Booklist

Laskin, David

The **long** way home; an American journey from Ellis Island to the Great War. Harper 2010 xxiv, 386p il $26.99   **920**
1. Immigrants -- United States 2. Soldiers -- United States 3. World War, 1914-1918 -- Biography
ISBN 978-0-06-123333-3
LC 2009-28191

The author follows "the lives of 12 American doughboys who had been born in Europe and who then returned there to fight for their adopted country in World War I. It's an imaginative concept, and Laskin mines family legends and official documents to tell the stories of these ordinary foot soldiers from Italy and Ireland, Poland and Russia, Slovakia and Norway." Washington Post

Includes bibliographical references

Lattin, Don

The **Harvard** Psychedelic Club; how Timothy Leary, Ram Dass, Huston Smith, and Andrew Weil killed the fifties and ushered in a new age for America. HarperCollins Publishers 2010 256p il $24.99   **920**
1. Alternative medicine practitioners 2. College teachers

3. Counter culture 4. Counterculture -- United States 5. Hallucinogenic drugs -- Research 6. Hallucinogens 7. Nonfiction writers 8. Physicians 9. Psychologists 10. Religion and sociology -- United States 11. Religious scholars 12. Social reformers 13. Writers on medicine 14. Writers on religion 15. Yogis
ISBN 978-0-06-165593-7; 0-06-165593-7
LC 2009-26323

"Mr. Lattin does a lovely, gently humorous job of setting the scene and bringing these men together. . . . This groovy story unfurls . . . like a ready-made treatment for a sprawling, elegiac and crisply comic movie, let's say Robert Altman by way of Wes Anderson." N Y Times (Late N Y Ed)

Includes bibliographical references

Leamer, Laurence

The **Kennedy** men; 1901-1963: the laws of the father. Perennial 2002 882p il pa $19.95   **920**
1. Diplomats 2. Financiers 3. Members of Congress 4. Parents of presidents 5. Political leaders 6. Presidents 7. Regulatory agency officials 8. Senators
ISBN 978-0-06-050288-1; 0-06-050288-6

This is a biography of Joseph P. Kennedy and his sons from the beginning of the last century through the assassination of John F. Kennedy.

"Leamer's writing is impressive throughout, regularly catching the reader up with a felicitous phrase or a surprising insight." Booklist

Includes bibliographical references

Louvin, Charlie, 1927-2011

Satan is real; the ballad of the Louvin Brothers. Charlie Louvin and Benjamin Whitmer. itBooks 2012 297 p. $22.99   **920**
ISBN 0062069039; 9780062069030

This book tells "[t]he tempestuous history of country musics Louvin Brothers, recalled by the younger musical sibling [Charlie]. . . . Here, Charlie . . . recounts the twosomess rise from hardscrabble beginnings in Alabamass cotton country to national fame. Basically self-taught, the brothers were reared on church singing before they launched an uphill professional career in the s40s. Louvin maps the pair4s arduous journey through small-town radio gigs and endless regional touring." (Kirkus)

Louvish, Simon

Monkey business; the lives and legends of the Marx brothers: Groucho, Chico, Harpo, Zeppo with added Gummo. St. Martin's Press 2000 471p il hardcover o.p. pa $13.95   **920**
1. Comedians
ISBN 0-312-28382-2 pa
LC 00-302623

In addition to Groucho, the author "expands the canvas to appraise the contributions of the other brothers, plus Margaret Dumont, a regular target of the brothers' mayhem. . . . Louvish does a solid job of separating fact from fiction and includes a family tree and a discussion of the FBI's file on the group." Libr J

Maki, Allan

Football's greatest stars; additional research and writing by George Johnson; with a foreword by Thurman Thomas. Firefly Books 2008 216p il $35 **920**

    1. Athletes 2. Football -- Biography

    ISBN 978-1-55407-389-4; 1-55407-389-8

    "This book attempts to profile the top 50 stars of the last 50 years of professional football. . . . The 50 selections are divided into two sections, Top 20 and Next 30, and are arranged alphabetically within those groupings. . . . The profiles themselves are knowledgably written but take a back seat to the well-chosen illustrations—135 color photographs mixed with scores of black-and-white ones in a very striking layout. . . . In short, a beautiful if not essential book that would be at home in any public library." Libr J

    Includes bibliographical references

Malone, John Williams

It doesn't take a rocket scientist; great amateurs of science. {by} John Malone. Wiley 2002 232p $24.95 **920**

    1. Architects 2. Astronomers 3. Authors 4. Chemists 5. Clergy 6. Essayists 7. Geneticists 8. Microbiologists 9. Novelists 10. Photometrists 11. Physicists 12. Presidents 13. Science fiction writers 14. Scientists 15. Short story writers 16. Vice-presidents 17. Writers on science

    ISBN 0-471-41431-X

               LC 2003-269159

    This examines the lives and work of ten amateur scientists, including Gregor Mendel, David H. Levy, Henrietta Swan Leavitt, Joseph Priestley, Michael Faraday, Grote Reber, Arthur C. Clarke, Thomas Jefferson, Susan Hendrickson, and Felix d'Herelle.

Marias, Javier

★ **Written** lives; translated from the Spanish by Margaret Jull Costa. New Directions 2006 200p il $22.95 **920**

    1. Authors 2. Authors -- Biography 3. Biography, Collective

    ISBN 0-8112-1611-X

               LC 2005-15033

    This book features "portraits of Rimbaud, Turgenev, Rilke, Giuseppe Tomasi di Lampedusa, Robert Louis Stevenson, Isak Dinesen, Djuna Barnes and a dozen other literary eminences. . . . [Though the author] acknowledges the artistic greatness of his chosen writers, he prefers to point out and relish their personal oddities, all those quirks, eccentricities and obsessions that make them neurotically and sometimes pitiably human. . . . This is a delightful volume." Washington Post Book World

Marton, Kati

Hidden power; presidential marriages that shaped our recent history. Pantheon Bks. 2001 414p il hardcover o.p. pa $14 **920**

    1. Biography, Collective 2. Presidents -- United States 3. Presidents' spouses -- United States

    ISBN 0-385-72188-9 pa

    This book provides a "survey of a dozen First Couples, from Edith and Woodrow Wilson to Laura and George Bush.

Marton mixes some good history with a lot of pop marriage psychology to show the part that patience, tolerance, insight, determination, sex and occasionally even love have played in the pursuit and exercise of presidential power." Time

    Includes bibliographical references

The great escape; nine Jews who fled Hitler and changed the world. Simon & Schuster 2006 271p il $27 **920**

    1. Authors 2. Biography, Collective 3. College teachers 4. Essayists 5. Exiles -- Hungary -- History -- 20th century 6. Jewish refugees 7. Jews -- Hungary 8. Jews -- Hungary -- Budapest 9. Jews, Hungarian 10. Journalists 11. Mathematicians 12. Mathematics teachers 13. Motion picture directors 14. Motion picture producers 15. Nobel laureates for physics 16. Novelists 17. Photographers 18. Photojournalists 19. Physicists 20. Writers on science

    ISBN 978-0-7432-6115-9; 0-7432-6115-1

               LC 2006-49162

    "By looking at these nine lives—salvaged, and crucial—Marton provides a moving measure of how much was lost." New Yorker

    Includes bibliographical references

Matteson, John

The lives of Margaret Fuller; John Matteson. W. W. Norton & Co. 2012 384p. **920**

    1. Biographies 2. Feminists -- United States -- Biography 3. Transcendentalism (New England) 4. Women authors, American -- 19th century -- Biography

    ISBN 9780393068054

               LC 2011040432

    This book offers a biography of "writer and a fiery social critic, Margaret Fuller (1810–1850) [who] was perhaps the most famous American woman of her generation. Outspoken and quick-witted, idealistic and adventurous, she became the leading female figure in the transcendentalist movement, wrote a celebrated column of literary and social commentary for Horace Greeley's newspaper, and served as the first foreign correspondent for an American newspaper. While living in Europe she fell in love with an Italian nobleman, with whom she became pregnant out of wedlock. In 1848 she joined the fight for Italian independence and, the following year, reported on the struggle while nursing the wounded within range of enemy cannons." (Publisher's note)

Matuz, Roger

Reconstruction era: biographies; Lawrence W. Baker, project editor. UXL 2004 xxiv, 246p il $60 **920**

    1. Reconstruction (1865-1876)

    ISBN 0-7876-9218-2

               LC 2004-17300

    This "volume covers political and military leaders as well as activists, artists, writers, and more. Among them are Louisa May Alcott, Frederick Douglass, Ulysses S. Grant, and Zebulon Vance. Within each biographical entry are cross-references to other individuals covered in this volume." Booklist

    Includes bibliographical references

McBrien, Richard P.

Lives of the popes; the pontiffs from St. Peter to John Paul II. HarperOne 2006 522p il pa $19.95   **920**
1. Papacy 2. Popes
ISBN 978-0-06-087807-8; 0-06-087807-X
McBrien offers "plenty of historical facts and sobering, valuable judgments." N Y Times Book Rev
Includes bibliographical references

Morgan, Edmund Sears

★ **American** heroes; profiles of men and women who shaped early America. [by] Edmund S. Morgan. W.W. Norton & Co. 2009 278p il $27.95   **920**
1. Biography, Collective 2. Heroes and heroines
ISBN 978-0-393-07010-1; 0-393-07010-7
                                             LC 2009-714
"This book is a perfect gem. . . . Both specialists and general readers will find this book both authoritative and fun to read." Libr J

Morgan, Robert, 1944-

Lions of the West; heroes and villains of the westward expansion. Algonquin Books of Chapel Hill 2011 xxiii, 497p il map $29.95; ebook $28.95 **920**
ISBN 978-1-56512-626-8; 978-1-61620-119-7 ebook
                                             LC 2011023832
This is a "collection of biographical sketches of 10 men largely limited to the pivotal roles each played in America's westward expansion. Included are four U.S. presidents, Thomas Jefferson, Andrew Jackson, James K. Polk, and John Quincy Adams; orchardist and naturalist John 'Johnny Appleseed' Chapman; frontier legends Davy Crockett and Kit Carson; statesmen Sam Houston and Nicholas Trist; and General Winfield Scott. . . . This collective biography provides a digestible introduction to American expansion, Manifest Destiny, and the larger-than-life men who led the inexorable charge westward." Booklist
Includes bibliographical references

Morris, Charles R.

The **surgeons**; life and death in a top heart center. W.W. Norton 2007 317p $24.95; pa $15.95   **920**
1. Heart -- Surgery
ISBN 978-0-393-06562-6; 0-393-06562-6; 978-0-393-33400-5 pa; 0-393-33400-7 pa
                                             LC 2007-24227
Morris "embedded himself for six months in the elite cardiac surgery center at Columbia-Presbyterian hospital in New York City. Unlike some noncardiac surgeries where music blares in the operating room, an aortic valve replacement for a retired pharmacy executive, says Morris, is a solemn affair, the calm briefly interrupted only when the patient fibrillates, his heart muscle fibers fluttering irregularly. . . . The reserved Craig Smith, the unit's head, who gained national fame when he performed a quadruple bypass on former President Clinton, impresses readers with his skill and deep concern for his patients. From detailing the workings of the heart's chambers and valves to the bald economics of cardiac surgery—including Smith's income ($1.5 million in 2004), the hospital's billing and collection procedures and forecasts on universal health insurance—Morris masterfully

breaks down complex jargon, procedures and policies for a lay audience." Publ Wkly
Includes bibliographical references

Morrow, Lance

The **best** year of their lives; Kennedy, Johnson, and Nixon in 1948: learning the secrets of power. Basic Books 2005 xl, 312p $26   **920**
1. Biography, Individual 2. Members of Congress 3. Nonfiction writers 4. Presidents 5. Senators 6. Vice-presidents
ISBN 0-465-04723-8
                                             LC 2005-1836
"The book succeeds in drawing together three fascinating characters into an illuminating historical intersection. You don't have to agree with all of Morrow's interpretations to be entertained by his lively treatment of three crucial figures during an important time in American history." N Y Times Book Rev
Includes bibliographical references

Mortimer, Gavin

The **great** swim. Walker & Company 2008 325p il map $24.95   **920**
1. Marathon swimming 2. Women athletes
ISBN 978-0-8027-1595-1; 0-8027-1595-8
                                             LC 2008-256
Draws on primary sources, diaries, and family interviews to document the story of four American athletes who in 1926 became the first women to swim the English Channel, in an account that also cites the media frenzy that surrounded their achievement.
"The book can be read as the story of a sporting competition or as an exploration of our timeless fascination with celebrity. Either way, it's an absorbing and inspirational saga in the Seabiscuit mold." Booklist
Includes bibliographical references

Nelson, James Carl

The **remains** of Company D; a story of the Great War. St. Martin's Press 2009 363p il map $25.99   **920**
1. Argonne, Battle of the, 1918 2. Cantigny (France), Battle of, 1918 3. Centenarians 4. Soldiers 5. Soldiers -- United States 6. Veterans 7. World War, 1914-1918 -- Campaigns -- France 8. World War, 1914-1918 -- Personal narratives 9. World War, 1914-1918 -- Personal narratives, American 10. World War, 1914-1918 -- Regimental histories -- United States
ISBN 978-0-312-55100-1; 0-312-55100-2
                                             LC 2009-16931
"This outstanding book paints the portrait of a small military unit, in this case, Company D of the Twenty-eighth Infantry Regiment in World War I. . . . Nelson orients the narrative around his grandfather, who lived to 101 despite serious wounds and awakened Nelson's interest in WWI by what he did not say about his experiences. Nelson set out to tell the Company D story from official records and the documents and reminiscences left behind by dozens of other veterans. . . . [The author] writes so clearly about the background, especially trench warfare, that even readers

with minimal WWI knowledge will feel educated as well as fascinated." Booklist

Includes bibliographical references

O'Brien, Geoffrey

The **fall** of the house of Walworth; a tale of madness and murder in gilded age America. Henry Holt and Co. 2010 337p il $30   **920**

1. Authors 2. Biography, Collective 3. Historic preservationists 4. Homicide 5. Lawyers 6. Mental illness 7. Murder victims 8. Murderers 9. Novelists

ISBN 978-0-8050-8115-2; 0-8050-8115-1

LC 2010-00394

The author "turns a telescopic lens on the moral and economic collapse of the Walworths, a socially prominent Saratoga Springs, New York, clan. While tracing the rise and fall of the Walworths over the course of the nineteenth century, he also exposes signs of insanity festering in various family members across several generations. The downward spiral of this once-proud family culminates in 1873 when 18-year-old Frank Walworth calmly and deliberately shot and killed his father. O'Brien makes the most of this gripping saga by steeping the narrative in descriptive Gilded Age details." Booklist

Includes bibliographical references

Persico, Joseph E.

Franklin and Lucy; President Roosevelt, Mrs. Rutherfurd, and the other remarkable women in his life. Random House 2008 443p il $28; pa $18 **920**

1. Archivists 2. Biography, Individual 3. Columnists 4. Diplomats 5. Governors 6. Handicapped 7. Humanitarians 8. Parents of presidents 9. Philatelists 10. Presidents 11. Presidents -- United States 12. Presidents' spouses -- United States 13. Private secretaries 14. Social activists 15. Spouses of presidents 16. Spouses of prominent persons 17. United Nations officials

ISBN 978-1-4000-6442-7; 1-4000-6442-2; 978-0-8129-7496-6 pa; 0-8129-7496-4 pa

LC 2007-36851

The author "engagingly and eloquently narrates the tangled relationships between Franklin and the various women to whom he became close.... Persico offers what will prove an important, lasting addition to the literature of the Roosevelts." Publ Wkly

Includes bibliographical references

Plutarch

Plutarch: the lives of the noble Grecians and Romans; the Dryden translation; edited and revised by Arthur Hugh Clough. Modern Lib. 1992 2v ea $23.95   **920**

ISBN 0-679-60008-6 v1; 0-679-60009-4 v2

LC 92-50223

This work is "arranged mainly in pairs in which a Greek and a Roman are contrasted. His subjects, who include Demosthenes and Cicero, were statesmen or generals. In the process of writing about them, he invents dialogue and describes the emotions of the personages involved." Reader's Ency. 4th edition

Povey, Glenn

Echoes: the complete history of Pink Floyd. Chicago Review Press 2010 388p il $39.95   **920**

1. Rock musicians

ISBN 978-1-56976-313-1; 1-56976-313-5

"Long time fans will find Echoes a pleasure to read as well as to look at. For the most part, the book has the knowing and reverential feeling of liner notes. But occasionally some mordant humor comes through.... A congenital defect of tribute volumes is that they tend to recite band lore that you already know about. For the most part, Povey avoids this tendency and digs up some of the strange bypaths of the band's long history." PopMatters

Includes discography and bibliographical references

Ritter, Lawrence S.

The **glory** of their times; the story of the early days of baseball told by the men who played it. new enl ed; Morrow 1984 360p il hardcover o.p. pa $14.95   **920**

1. Baseball -- Biography

ISBN 0688112730 pa

LC 84-221549

A collection of 26 oral histories of baseball's early days by veteran players.

Roberts, Cokie

★ **Founding** mothers; the women who raised our nation. William Morrow 2004 xx, 359p il $24.95; pa $14.95   **920**

1. Women -- United States -- History

ISBN 0-06-009025-1; 0-06-009026-X pa

LC 2004-042873

"In addition to telling wonderful stories, Roberts also presents a very readable, serviceable account of politics—male and female—in early America. If only our standard history textbooks were written with such flair!" Publ Wkly

Ladies of liberty; the women who shaped our nation. William Morrow 2008 481p il $26.95; pa $15.99   **920**

1. Women -- United States -- Biography 2. Women -- United States -- History

ISBN 978-0-06-078234-4; 0-06-078234-X; 978-0-06-078235-1 pa; 0-06-078235-8 pa

"While Roberts' aim is to see the period from her subjects' point of view, she is not uncritical; for instance, Roberts casts blame on Mrs. Adams's uncompromising partisanship 'in the undoing of her husband.' With a little-seen perspective and fascinating insight into the culture of the day, this is popular history done right." Publ Wkly

Roiphe, Katie

Uncommon arrangements; seven portraits of married life in London literary circles, 1910-1939. Dial Press 2007 343p il $26   **920**

1. Authors, English 2. Authors, English -- 20th century -- Biography 3. Authors, English -- Relations with women 4. Biography, Collective 5. Man-woman relationships 6. Marriage 7. Women authors 8.

Women authors -- Relations with men
ISBN 978-0-385-33937-7; 0-385-33937-2

LC 2007-11798

"Roiphe is at her most insightful—and funniest—in showing us where the declared credo of her characters collides with reality. . . . Often these unorthodox unions endured only because someone was willing to knuckle under." N Y Times Book Rev

Rubin, Louis Decimus

My father's people; a family of Southern Jews. {by} Louis D. Rubin Jr. Louisiana State Univ. Press 2002 139p il $22.50 **920**
1. Biography, Individual 2. College teachers 3. Jews -- South Carolina -- Charleston 4. Literary critics 5. Publishing executives
ISBN 0-8071-2808-2

LC 2002-454

The author "tells the stories of Hyman and Fannie Rubin, his grandparents, and their seven children. . . . Rubin's descriptions are affectionate, yet he doesn't gloss over their flaws, and as a result, those he knows best come alive for readers." Publ Wkly

Salley, Columbus

The black 100; a ranking of the most influential African-Americans, past and present. Columbus Salley. rev ed; Kensington Publishing Corp. 1999 384p il pa $18.95 **920**
1. African Americans -- Biography
ISBN 978-0-8065-1550-2; 0-8065-1550-3

LC 98-47713

The author profiles 100 black men and women and ranks them, based upon his subjective evaluation of their contributions to black American society. They include Dr. Martin Luther King, Jr., Malcolm X, Zora Neale Hurston, Paul Robeson, Muhammad Ali, Arthur Ashe, Toni Morrison, Oprah Winfrey, and August Wilson.

Schiff, Karenna Gore

Lighting the way; nine women who changed modern America. Miramax Books/Hyperion 2006 528p il $25.95; pa $17.95 **920**
1. Biography, Collective 2. Social reformers -- United States -- Biography 3. Women -- United States -- Biography
ISBN 1-4013-5218-9; 1-4013-6015-7 pa

LC 2005-56247

"This is an inspirational collection of biographies of women of various social, ethnic, and racial backgrounds fighting for social justice." Booklist
Includes bibliographical references

Schonberg, Harold C.

The great pianists; rev and updated; Simon & Schuster 1987 525p il hardcover o.p. pa $18 **920**
1. Classical musicians 2. Composers 3. Conductors (Music) 4. Musicians 5. Pianists 6. Prime ministers 7. Statesmen
ISBN 0-671-63837-8 pa

LC 87-341

Beginning with the Bach family, the author describes the personal lives and careers of outstanding pianists from the eighteenth century to the present

Scott-Heron, Gil, 1949-2011

The last holiday; Gil Scott Heron. Grove Press 2012 384p. **920**
1. African American musicians 2. Civil rights movements -- United States -- History -- 20th century 3. Memoirs 4. Music industry -- United States 5. Southern States -- In literature

LC 97808802129017

"This [book, a posthumously published memoir,] is a . . . testament to the career and achievements of [African-American musician and writer] Gil Scott-Heron. But it is also a . . . personal account of his growing up in the South, a . . . portrait of Stevie Wonder, and a . . . narrative vehicle for Scott-Herons . . . insights into the music industry, the civil rights movement, modern America, governmental hypocrisy, and our wider place in the world." (Publisher's note)

Singer, Mark

Character studies; encounters with the curiously obsessed. Houghton Mifflin 2005 256p hardcover o.p. pa $13.95 **920**
1. Actors 2. Airline executives 3. Biography, Collective 4. Book collectors 5. Characters and characteristics 6. Collectors 7. Construction industry executives 8. Eccentrics and eccentricities 9. Eccentrics and eccentricities -- United States 10. Educators 11. Hotel executives 12. Magicians 13. Motion picture directors 14. Purchasing managers 15. Real estate developers
ISBN 0-618-77363-0 pa

LC 2004-62757

This is a "mix of . . . [the author's] portraits from The New Yorker, gathered in book form for the first time. In the essays he trains his skills on the likes of Martin Scorsese and Donald Trump; The Wednesday Group, the self-selected intelligentsia of El Paso; well-known bibliophile Michael Zinman; high-powered women who decide to quit the fast track; and Richard Seiverling, a Tom Mix fan determined to preserve the memory of the movie cowboy. It's quite a cast of characters, and Singer lavishly gives them all their due." Libr J

Smith, Andrew

Moondust; in search of the men who fell to earth. Fourth Estate 2005 372p il $24.95; pa $14.95 **920**
1. Apollo project 2. Astronauts 3. Astronauts -- United States 4. Biography, Collective
ISBN 0-00-71554-17; 978-0-00-715541-5; 0-00-715542-5 pa; 978-0-00-715542-2 pa

LC 2005-40081

This book describes the lives of nine astronauts after they walked on the moon.
"In an artful blend of memoir and popular history, Smith makes flesh-and-blood people out of icons and reveals the tenderness of his own heart." Publ Wkly
Includes bibliographical references

Spera, Keith

Groove interrupted; loss, renewal, and the music of New Orleans. St. Martin's Press 2011 260p $26.99 **920**

1. Hurricane Katrina, 2005 2. Music -- New Orleans (La.) 3. Musicians

ISBN 978-0-312-55225-1; 0-312-55225-4

LC 2011-10122

This look at the music community "of New Orleans is a collection of profiles of individual musicians who all had their ability to make music threatened after Hurricane Katrina in 2005. . . . many of the stories presented here had their origin in Spera's articles written before and after Katrina. All of them show how artists as varied as blues guitarist Clarence 'Gatemouth' Brown, jazz trumpeter Terence Blanchard, heavy metal singer Phil Anselmo of Pantera, and New Orleans legends Fats Domino and Allen Toussaint tried 'to make sense of the storm through music, comforting themselves and uplifting those around them.' Some of the finest profiles—and there is no weak one in the book—detail a combination of sadness and joy, such as Aaron Neville's triumphant return to the city after the death of his wife to close out the 2008 New Orleans Jazz & Heritage Festival." Publ Wkly

Spitz, Bob

★ The **Beatles**: the biography. Little, Brown 2005 983p il hardcover o.p. pa $17.99 **920**

1. Biography, Individual 2. Drummers 3. Guitarists 4. Rock musicians 5. Singers 6. Songwriters

ISBN 0-316-80352-9; 0-316-01331-5 pa

LC 2005-3838

This "beautifully written chronicle breathes new life into the familiar story of the Liverpool boys who conquered the world and became . . . the most influential entertainers of the past century. The author's passion for his subject, and for every nuance of every scene, electrifies even the most familiar moments in the legend." N Y Times Book Rev

Includes discography and bibliographical references

Stark, Steven D.

Meet the Beatles; a cultural history of the band that shook youth, gender, and the world. HarperEntertainment 2005 344p il $26.95; pa $14.95 **920**

1. Rock musicians

ISBN 0-06-000892-X; 0-06-000893-8 pa

LC 2004-59794

In this biography of the Beatles, the author focuses "as much on the cultural trends that produced the Beatles—and the trends they created—as on the Fab Four themselves. . . . Throughout, Stark is sharp and insightful, even when he wades into the psychoanalytic waters of the John/Yoko and Paul/Linda relationships." Publ Wkly

Strathern, Paul

The **artist**, the philosopher, and the warrior; the intersecting lives of da Vinci, Machiavelli, and Borgia and the world they shaped. Bantam Books 2009 xxiii, 456p il map $30 **920**

1. Artists 2. Authors 3. Dramatists 4. Heads of state 5. Painters 6. Political and social philosophers 7. Renaissance 8. Scientists 9. Statesmen 10. Writers on politics 11. Writers on science

ISBN 978-0-553-80752-3

LC 2009-6950

Strathern "does for Machiavelli and da Vinci what he does for Borgia: creates a flesh-and-blood portrait for each that defies historical stereotype. Using his novelist's eye and a historian's sweep, Strathern conveys the emotional subtleties that animated their lives. It's no small feat that he makes you care deeply for these complex figures who lived half a millennium ago." Washington Post

Includes bibliographical references

Strauss, Neil

Everyone loves you when you're dead; journeys into fame and madness. It Books 2011 507p il pa $16.99 **920**

1. Celebrities 2. Rock musicians

ISBN 978-0-06-154367-8

LC 2010-52255

"By his own count, the author has conducted some 3,000 interviews with the famous, not-so-famous, used-to-be-famous and ought-to-be-famous denizens of popular culture. Here he brings together the best of these interviews in loosely and at times bizarrely connected chapters. All the well-knowns are here, including Madonna, Lady Gaga, David Bowie, The Who, Kenny G, Led Zeppelin, Puffy Combs and Bo Diddley. . . . Gonzo interviewing at its best." Kirkus

Terkel, Studs

★ My American century. New Press 1997 xxiii, 532p hardcover o.p. pa $14.95 **920**

1. American national characteristics

ISBN 1-56584-469-6 pa

LC 96-52779

This volume gathers "the introductions Terkel wrote for his eight oral-history books (and the fiftieth anniversary edition of Steinbeck's The Grapes of Wrath) with 40-odd interviews: Terkel's conversations with gangsters and grandmothers, authors and executives, photographers and farmers, cabbies and crusaders. . . . A superb introduction to Terkel's work (or to oral history) and a trip down memory lane for his fans." Booklist

Thomas, Robert McG.

52 McGs; the best obituaries from legendary New York Times writer Robert McG. Thomas Jr. edited by Chris Calhoun; foreword by Thomas Mallon. Scribner 2001 192p il hardcover o.p. pa $14.95 **920**

1. Biography -- 20th century 2. Celebrities -- Biography 3. Obituaries

ISBN 1-4165-9827-8 pa

LC 2001-42952

"This highly browsable collection of 52 obits shows Thomas at his deadline best." Publ Wkly

Tillyard, Stella K.

A **royal** affair; George III and his scandalous siblings. [by] Stella Tillyard. Random House 2006 xxiv, 352p il $26.95 **920**

1. Kings

ISBN 978-1-4000-6371-0; 1-4000-6371-X

LC 2006-45130

This biography examines the life of King George III of Great Britain and his siblings.

"This riveting account reminds us that in the past, the misdemeanors of royals had serious, not simply gossip-rag, implications." Booklist

Includes bibliographical references

Tinniswood, Adrian

The **Verneys**; a true story of love, war, and madness in seventeenth-century England. Riverhead Books 2007 569p il map $35   **920**

1. Biography, Collective

ISBN 978-1-59448-948-8; 1-59448-948-3

LC 2007-911

"The letters of the Verney family survive as the largest and most continuous collection of personal correspondence from seventeenth-century Britain, and Tinniswood draws on them to produce a lively, almost novelistic account of an aristocratic family. . . Their stories range from the outrageous—Sir Francis Verney, who 'turned Turk' and became a pirate along the Barbary Coast; 'Mad' Mary Verney, whose husband's philandering drove her to zelotypia, or morbid jealousy—to the more familiar and heartrending: a father and son separated by political allegiances during civil war; a patriarch who worries about his children's financial security. Tinniswood's portraits are intimate, compelling, and deftly situated within the broader historical period, so that the turbulence of the seventeenth century is rendered as a human drama." New Yorker

Includes bibliographical references

Tomkins, Calvin

Lives of the artists. Henry Holt 2008 254p $26   **920**

1. Art -- 20th century 2. Art, Modern -- 20th century 3. Artists -- Biography 4. Biography, Collective

ISBN 978-0-8050-8872-4; 0-8050-8872-5

LC 2008-13121

"Tomkins is a ruthless observer. . . . Books that trade on content that originally appeared in the New Yorker have become a small industry, but not all are as intimate as this one." Publ Wkly

Unferth, Deb Olin

Revolution; Deb Olin Unferth. Henry Holt 2011 208p   **920**

1. Authors 2. Biography, Individual 3. College teachers 4. Novelists 5. Short story writers

ISBN 978-0-8050-9323-0; 0-8050-9323-0

LC 201023471

The author writes about "the year she ran away from college with her . . . boyfriend and followed him to Nicaragua to join the Sandinistas." (Publisher's note)

Vowell, Sarah

Assassination vacation. Simon & Schuster 2005 258p il hardcover o.p. pa $14   **920**

1. Assassins -- United States -- History -- 19th century 2. Authors 3. Essayists 4. Historic sites -- United States 5. Nonfiction writers 6. Presidents -- United

States -- Assassination 7. Radio personalities

ISBN 0-7432-6003-1; 0-7432-6004-X pa

LC 2004-59134

"[Vowell] has done her homework, providing lucid descriptions of the murders and agile summations of the scholarly assessments of each era." America

Waller, Maureen

Sovereign ladies; the six reigning queens of England. St. Martin's Press 2007 554p il $29.95; pa $19.95   **920**

1. Queens

ISBN 978-0-312-33801-5; 0-312-33801-5; 978-0-312-38608-5 pa; 0-312-38608-7 pa

LC 2007-16181

This is a "glossy, deeply detailed . . . comparative examination of the six queens who have ruled England in their own right." Kirkus

Includes bibliographical references

Walsh, Jim

The **Replacements**: all over but the shouting; an oral history. MBI Pub. Co. and Voyageur Press 2007 304p il $21.95   **920**

1. Rock musicians

ISBN 978-0-7603-3062-3; 0-7603-3062-X

LC 2007-22576

"In this loving, appropriately ramshackle tribute to one of the most beloved rock-and-roll bands of the 1980s, Walsh gives his subjects the oral history treatment, assembling a wide range of associates, friends and famous fans to put their memories on the record." Publ Wkly

Includes bibliographical references

Ward-Royster, Willa

How I got over; Clara Ward and the world-famous Ward Singers. {by} Willa Ward-Royster; as told to Toni Rose; foreword by Horace Clarence Boyer. Temple Univ. Press 1997 263p hardcover o.p. pa $24.95   **920**

1. Gospel music

ISBN 1-56639-489-9; 978-1-56639-490-1 pa; 1-56639-490-2 pa

LC 96-5943

"Ward-Royster relates the rise of her family's world-renowned gospel group, formed by her mother and headlined by her sister. . . . The book contains details on everything from successful performances on the stage of the Apollo, major TV variety shows, and international tours to top sales of hit recordings and friendships with such luminaries as Mahalia Jackson." Libr J

Warner, Ezra J.

★ **Generals** in blue; lives of the Union commanders. Louisiana State Univ. Press 1964 xxiv, 679p il $39.95   **920**

1. Generals

ISBN 0-8071-0822-7

This book contains biographical sketches of the 583 men who attained the rank of general during the Civil War years. A photograph of each man is also included

Generals in gray; lives of the Confederate commanders. Louisiana State Univ. Press 1959 xxvii, 420p il $39.95   **920**
1. Confederate States of America -- Biography 2. Generals
ISBN 0-8071-0823-5
"Biographical sketches of the Confederate generals; concise outlines of their military careers, also giving dates of birth and death and places of burial. The product of ten years of research, much of it done in interviews with descendants. Illustrated with 425 portraits." Publ Wkly
Includes bibliographical references

Waugh, Alexander
Fathers and sons; the autobiography of a family. Nan A. Talese 2007 472p il $27.50   **920**
1. Authors 2. Authors, English
ISBN 978-0-385-52150-5; 0-385-52150-2
    LC 2007-5239
"The scion of an illustrious—and fabulously eccentric—English literary dynasty referees four generations of father-son antagonisms in this scintillating family memoir. Waugh . . . focuses on the fraught relationship between his great-grandfather, prominent critic and publisher Arthur Waugh, and Arthur's son, the famous novelist Evelyn. . . . If this tome were merely an excuse to reprint some of Evelyn's hilarious jottings, it would be well worth the price, but it's also an absorbing study of how writers process their most painfully formative experiences." Publ Wkly
Includes bibliographical references

The **House** of Wittgenstein; a family at war. Doubleday 2009 333p il $28.95   **920**
1. Biography, Individual 2. Logicians 3. Metal industry executives 4. Philosophers
ISBN 978-0-385-52060-7; 0-385-52060-3
    LC 2008-33312
Waugh "tells the story of the downfall of the wealthy Wittgenstein family. He follows the intellectually and musically gifted Wittgenstein children as history conspires to rob them of one of Europe's largest fortunes. Waugh weaves the family's story around that of the fourth son, Paul: losing his arm in the Great War, Paul gained international acclaim as a left-handed concert pianist; at that time, his brother Ludwig's notoriety was limited to a small circle at Cambridge. With the rise of the Nazis, the Wittgenstein siblings were declared racially Jewish and held hostage for their wealth—a peril that ratchets up the book's tension and contributes to the already tragic atmosphere haunting the family. Waugh sifted through letters and journals held in archives and private collections for this masterfully researched work that brings the characters of this previously untold story to life. He moves seamlessly among historical circumstance, personal relations, and the world of classical composition and performance." Libr J
Includes bibliographical references (p. 315-21)

Waxman, Sharon
Rebels on the backlot; six maverick directors and how they conquered the Hollywood studio system. 1st ed; W. Morrow 2005 386p il $25.95; pa $14.95   **920**
1. Actors 2. Biography, Collective 3. Motion picture directors 4. Motion picture producers and directors -- Biography 5. Motion pictures -- Production and direction 6. Screenwriters 7. Video directors
ISBN 0-06-054017-6; 0-06-054018-4 pa
    LC 2004-59269
This is the author's "study of six boundary-breaking young directors who revolutionized 1990s filmmaking and still represent a refreshing alternative to 'cookie cutter scripts and cheap MTV imagery.' Her full-blooded profiles introduce Quentin Tarantino (Pulp Fiction), Paul Thomas Anderson (Boogie Nights), David Fincher (Fight Club), Steven Soderbergh (Traffic), David O. Russell (Three Kings) and Spike Jonze (Being John Malkovich). . . . Their stories make for compelling reading." Publ Wkly
Includes bibliographical references

Weber, Nicholas Fox, 1947-
The **Bauhaus** group; six masters of modernism. Alfred A. Knopf 2009 521p il $40   **920**
1. Architects 2. Art teachers 3. Artists 4. Artists, German 5. Avant-garde (Aesthetics) 6. Avant-garde (Aesthetics) -- Germany -- History -- 20th century 7. Biography, Collective 8. Furniture designers 9. Painters 10. Printmakers 11. Textile artists 12. Weavers
ISBN 978-0-307-26836-5; 0-307-26836-5
    LC 2009-28729
"A rigorously researched and often fascinating history that morphs into memoir." Kirkus
Includes bibliographical references

Weintraub, Stanley
15 stars; Eisenhower, MacArthur, Marshall: three generals who saved the American century. Free Press 2007 541p il $30   **920**
1. Biography, Individual 2. College presidents 3. Generals 4. Nobel laureates for peace 5. Presidents 6. Secretaries of defense 7. Secretaries of state 8. Statesmen 9. World War, 1939-1945 -- Campaigns
ISBN 978-0-7432-7527-9; 0-7432-7527-6
    LC 2007-16018
The author "provides a detailed and absorbing gloss on the relationships among three extraordinary leaders." Libr J
Includes bibliographical references

Weller, Sheila
Girls like us; Carole King, Joni Mitchell, and Carly Simon--and the journey of a generation. Atria Books 2008 584p il $27.95; pa $17   **920**
1. Biography, Individual 2. Folk musicians 3. Rock musicians 4. Singers 5. Songwriters 6. Women musicians
ISBN 978-0-743-49147-1; 0-743-49147-5; 978-0-743-49148-8 pa; 0-743-49148-3 pa
    LC 2007-43445
This is a biography of the singer-songwriters Carole King, Joni Mitchell, and Carly Simon.

"A must-read for any fan of these artists, this bio will prove an absorbing, eye-opening tour of rock (and American) history for anyone who's appreciated a female musician in the past thirty years." Publ Wkly

Wiencek, Henry

The **Hairstons**; an American family in black and white. St. Martin's Press 1999 xx, 361p il map hardcover o.p. pa $14.95 **920**

1. African American families -- Southern States -- Biography 2. African Americans -- Southern States 3. Slavery -- United States

ISBN 0-312-25393-1 pa

LC 98-44014

Wiencek tells the "story of the Hairston family, the largest slaveholders in the South and one of the wealthiest families in the U.S. Wiencek details the race mixing that occured between master and slave and the family's efforts to keep its dark-skinned members enslaved and to maintain wealth only for its white members. A fascinating book that explores the complexity of family and racial relationships in the U.S." Booklist

Includes bibliographical references

Wolff, Daniel

★ **How** Lincoln learned to read; twelve great Americans and the educations that made them. Bloomsbury 2009 345p $26 **920**

1. Education -- United States -- History

ISBN 978-1-59691-290-8; 1-59691-290-1

LC 2008-24695

"This provocative book is not only an important addition to the history of education in America, but also a valuable contribution to the history and understanding of the country's ideas and culture." SLJ

Includes bibliographical references

Xinran

China witness; voices from a silent generation. translated from Chinese by Nicky Harman, Julia Lovell and Esther Tyldesley. Pantheon Books 2009 434p il map $28.95 **920**

1. Biography, Collective

ISBN 978-0-375-42547-9; 0-375-42547-0

LC 2008-35840

The author, "traveling across the expanse of the Chinese Republic over the years, sought out those who had witnessed the rise of communism more than half a century ago. The result is this stirring, startlingly honest account of life under Chairman Mao and the current reformers revamping the socialist state." Publ Wkly

African American lives; edited by Henry Louis Gates, Jr. and Evelyn Brooks Higginbotham. Oxford University Press 2004 xxvi, 1025p $55 **920**

1. African Americans -- Biography

ISBN 0-19-516024-X

LC 2003-23640

"This work opens multiple fresh vistas on proper African American history. . . . Essential for any serious African American collection." Libr J

Includes bibliographical references

Biography index; a cumulative index to biographical material in books and magazines. Wilson, H.W. **920**

1. Biography -- Bibliography 2. Biography -- Indexes

"Indexes biographical articles published in . . . periodicals, current books of individual and collected biography, obituaries, letters, diaries, memoirs, and incidental biographical material in otherwise nonbiographical books. Includes an index by professions and occupations. Annual and three-year cumulations." Ref Sources for Small & Medium-sized Libr. 6th edition

Contemporary black biography, v68; profiles from the international black community. Gale Res. 2008 275p il $124 **920**

1. African Americans -- Biography

ISBN 978-1-4144-3275-5; 1-4144-3275-5

"Included in each volume are biographies of innovators in the black global community who are currently living and/or who have had a lasting impact on society. Every field of endeavor imaginable is represented, from science, politics, and creative arts to sports. . . . This . . . title will be useful for its coverage of current people in the news who are not as easy to find elsewhere." Booklist

★ Facts about the presidents; a compilation of biographical and historical information. Joseph Nathan Kane, Janet Podell [editors] 8th ed; Wilson, H.W. 2009 720p $125 **920**

1. Presidents -- United States 2. Reference books

ISBN 978-0-8242-1087-8; 0-8242-1087-8

LC 2008056016

The main part of this work provides an individual chapter on each President, from Washington through Barack Obama, presenting such information as family, education, election, Vice President, main events and accomplishments of his administration, and First Lady. Part two contains tables and lists presenting comparative data on all the Presidents

The Grove book of opera singers; edited by Laura Macy. Oxford University Press 2008 626p il $39.95 **920**

1. Opera 2. Singers

ISBN 978-0-19-533765-5; 0-19-533765-4

LC 2008-17065

"A useful and comprehensive tool for novice and experienced opera researchers alike." Libr J

Life stories; profiles from The New Yorker. edited by David Remnick. Random House 2000 480p hardcover o.p. pa $15.95 **920**

1. Actors 2. Advice columnists 3. Authors 4. Ballet dancers 5. Baseball players 6. Biography -- 20th century 7. Boxers (Persons) 8. Children's authors 9. Choreographers 10. College teachers 11. Comedians 12. Dancers 13. Essayists 14. Game show hosts 15. Homemakers 16. Journalists 17. Literary critics 18. Magazine editors 19. Magazine executives 20. Mathematicians 21. Memoirists 22. Mystery writers 23. Nobel laureates for literature 24. Novelists 25. Poets 26. Screenwriters 27. Short story writers 28. Sportscasters 29. Spouses of prominent persons 30.

Talk show hosts 31. Television personalities 32. Television producers 33. Television scriptwriters 34. Writers on crime

ISBN 0-375-50355-2; 0-375-75751-1 pa

LC 99-53712

An assemblage of 25 biographical profiles spanning the years 1927 to 1999 "with subjects ranging from Ernest Hemingway and Marlon Brando to a fake prince, a pair of eccentric mathematicians, and Biff the show dog." Booklist

The Mitfords; letters between six sisters. edited by Charlotte Mosley. Harper 2007 xxi, 834p il $39.95   **920**

1. Eccentrics

ISBN 978-0-06-137364-0; 0-06-137364-8

"The lost art of letter writing is splendidly portrayed in this massive volume of correspondence among the six Mitford sisters: Nancy, Pamela, Diana, Unity, Jessica, and Deborah. . . . Arranged chronologically covering the years 1925-2002, they include footnotes identifying people, places, and activities. In introductions to each of the nine sections of letters, Mosley provides a synopsis of the major events in each sister's life as well as thoughtful commentary and analysis." Libr J

Includes bibliographical references

★   The Norton book of American autobiography; edited and introduced by Jay Parini and with a preface by Gore Vidal. Norton 1999 711p $32.50   **920**

1. Autobiographies -- United States 2. Autobiography

ISBN 0-393-04677-X

LC 98-43398

"Parini has compiled over 60 selections from autobiographies and memoirs published since the 17th century. . . . {He} includes works by such diverse writers as Henry David Thoreau, U.S. Grant, Gertrude Stein, Malcom X, Mary McCarthy, and Richard Rodriguez. . . . The selections are arranged chronologically, and each is prefaced by an introduction on its author and its merit." Libr J

Includes bibliographical references

Sifters: Native American women's lives; edited by Theda Perdue. Oxford Univ. Press 2001 260p $55; pa $19.95   **920**

1. Indian women -- United States 2. Native American women

ISBN 0-19-513080-4; 0-19-513081-2 pa

LC 00-39950

"From Pocahontas, a Powhatan woman of the seventeenth century, to Ada Deer, the Menominee woman who headed the Bureau of Indian Affairs in the 1990s, the essays span four centuries. Each one recounts the experiences of women from vastly different cultural traditions. . . . Contributors focus on the ways in which different women have fashioned lives that remain firmly rooted in their identity as Native women." Publisher's note

Includes bibliographical references

Stolen voices; young people's war diaries from World War I to Iraq. edited with commentaries by Zlata Filipovic and Melanie Challenger; foreword

by Olara A. Otunnu. Penguin 2007 xxiii, 293p il pa $14   **920**

1. Children and war

ISBN 978-0-14-303871-9; 0-14-303871-0

The editors have "compiled 14 diaries that were kept by children during wartime, from World War I to Iraq. Their poignant voices will break your heart." Libr J

920.003   Dictionaries, encyclopedias, concordances of biography as a discipline

American Council of Learned Societies

★   **American** national biography; general editors, John A. Garraty, Mark C. Carnes. Oxford Univ. Press 1999 24v set $2,095   **920.003**

1. Reference books 2. United States -- Biography -- Dictionaries

ISBN 0-19-520635-5

LC 98-20826

"ANB defines 'American' broadly as a person whose significance, achievement, fame, or influence occurred during residence within what is now the US, or whose life or career directly influenced the course of US history. Subjects must have died before 1996. . . . Subjects are arranged alphabetically. The typical entry, 750 to 7,500 words in length, proceeds chronologically, following the major personal and professional events of the subject's life, birth to death. The concluding paragraph attempts to assess the subject's contributions from today's perspective. A brief bibliography after each entry, not meant to be comprehensive, lists major sources, including locations of archives and collections of personal papers." Choice

Includes bibliographical references

Ancell, R. Manning

The **biographical** dictionary of World War II generals and flag officers; the U.S. Armed Forces. {by} R. Manning Ancell with Christine M. Miller. Greenwood Press 1996 706p $130.95   **920.003**

1. Admirals -- Biography -- Dictionaries 2. Biography, Collective 3. Generals -- Biography -- Dictionaries 4. World War, 1939-1945 -- Biography 5. World War, 1939-1945 -- Biography -- Dictionaries

ISBN 0-313-29546-8

LC 95-50450

"The nearly 2,400 entries, which, according to the preface, represent 99 percent of the total number who served, are listed in alphabetical order in six chapters: 'Army,' 'Army Air Force,' 'National Guard,' 'Navy,' 'Marine Corps,' and 'Coast Guard.' . . . The volume concludes with two appendixes (state-by-state and service-by-service summary of birthplaces and birth dates; generals and flag officers who died during World War II) and an alphabetical index to all biographees." Booklist

Includes bibliographical references

Attwater, Donald

The **Penguin** dictionary of saints; {by} Donald Attwater, with Catherine Rachel John. 3rd ed; Penguin Bks. 1995 381p pa $15.95   **920.003**
  1. Christian saints -- Dictionaries 2. Reference books
  ISBN 0-14-051312-4

                    LC 96-165638
"Information includes classification of saints (martyr, confessor, and so on); date of existence; their circumstances in becoming a saint; and their feast day. It also provides a glossary and lists of further reading, some patron saints, some emblems that identify specific saints, and feast days in the order that they arrive within the calendar year." Am Ref Books Annu, 1997

Bader, Philip

  ★ **African**-American writers; revised by Catherine Reef. Rev. ed; Facts On File 2010 340p il $49.50   **920.003**
  1. African American authors -- Dictionaries 2. African Americans in literature 3. American literature -- African American authors 4. American literature -- African American authors -- Bio-bibliography 5. American literature -- African American authors -- History and criticism 6. Reference books
  ISBN 978-0-8160-8141-7

                    LC 2010-05463
This book "profiles popular and prominent African-American writers across many genres of literature. Each entry in this . . . resource provides a biographical profile, concentrating on the major literary works and accomplishments of each author as well as an outline of his or her contributions to American literature." Publisher's note
  Includes bibliographical references

Baile de Laperriere, Charles

  Who's who in art; Charles Baile de Laperrière, editor. 33rd ed; Hilmarton Manor Press 2008 1128p $175   **920.003**
  1. Artists, British -- Dictionaries 2. Reference books
  ISBN 978-0-9047-2242-0; 0-9047-2242-2

"Includes primarily British artists, designers, craftsmen, critics, writers, teachers, collectors, and curators, with appendixes of monograms and signatures, and obituary, and acronyms. Includes a list of academies, groups, and societies." Guide to Ref Books. 11th edition

Butler, Alban

  ★ **Butler's** Lives of the saints. Christian Classics 1956 4v set $149.95; pa set $109.95 **920.003**
  1. Christian saints -- Dictionaries 2. Reference books
  ISBN 0-87061-045-7; 0-87061-137-2 pa

"The biographies of the saints and beati are arranged by their feast days with each of the four volumes containing three months. . . . Each volume has a table of contents arranged by the days of the month with a list of the feasts for each day." Booklist

Drew, Bernard A.

  100 most popular nonfiction authors; biographical sketches and bibliographies. Libraries Unlimited 2007 438p il $65   **920.003**
  1. American prose literature -- 20th century 2. American prose literature -- 20th century -- History and criticism 3. Authors -- Dictionaries 4. Authors, American -- 20th century -- Biography 5. Literature -- Bio-bibliography 6. Non-fiction 7. Popular literature -- United States 8. Popular literature -- United States -- History and criticism 9. Reference books
  ISBN 978-1-59158-487-2

                    LC 2007-19949
"The authors, chosen by means of consultations with librarians, are those whose impact has been seen mostly in the last half century, among them Diane Ackerman, John Krakauer, David McCullough, and Cornel West. Entries are headed by author's birth year and birthplace, and, if applicable, date of death, and by signature work and primary genres." Booklist
  Includes bibliographical references

Farmer, David Hugh

The **Oxford** dictionary of saints; 5th ed; Oxford University Press 2004 xxiv, 579p map pa $16.95   **920.003**
  1. Christian saints -- Dictionaries 2. Reference books
  ISBN 978-0-19-860949-0; 0-19-860949-3 pa

                    LC 2005-272790
This biographical dictionary profiles the lives, cults, and artistic associations of over 1,000 saints, from the famous to the obscure. An appendix on pilgrimage sights in Europe is also included.
  "Even those who do not believe in the saints . . . will be able to enjoy and to profit from this splendid book." Economist
  Includes bibliographical references

Friedman, Ian C.

  Latino athletes. Facts on File 2007 278p il $44   **920.003**
  1. Athletes -- Dictionaries 2. Hispanic Americans -- Dictionaries 3. Reference books
  ISBN 978-0-8160-6384-0; 0-8160-6384-2

                    LC 2006-16901
"Gymnast Trent Dimas, mountain biker Juli Furtado, and speed skater Derek Parra are among the 176 athletes profiled in this volume. . . . Following the entries, athletes are listed by sport, year of birth, and ethnicity or country of origin." Booklist
  Includes bibliographical references

Friedwald, Will

A **biographical** guide to the great jazz and pop singers. Pantheon Books 2010 811p $45 **920.003**
  1. Biography, Collective 2. Jazz music -- Bio-bibliography 3. Jazz music -- Dictionaries 4. Jazz singers 5. Popular music -- Bio-bibliography 6. Popular music -- Dictionaries 7. Popular music -- United States 8. Reference books 9. Singers 10.

Singers -- Dictionaries
ISBN 978-0-375-42149-5; 0-375-42149-1
LC 2009-44405

The author "celebrates 200-odd performers of jazz and pop standards, from the mid-20th-century titans—Louis Armstrong, Bing Crosby, Ella Fitzgerald, Frank Sinatra—to latter-day acolytes like Diana Krall and Harry Connick Jr., with a raft of unjustly obscure singers in between. . . . Friedwald is all about the music; he primly shies away from his subjects' scandal-prone personal lives, but accords each a substantial career retrospective, selected discography and wonderfully pithy interpretive essay. . . . Friedwald's exuberant medley is that rarest of things: music criticism that actually makes you sit up and listen." Publ Wkly

Gates, Alexander E.

A to Z of earth scientists. Facts on File 2002 336p il $45   **920.003**
1. Earth sciences 2. Earth scientists 3. Reference books 4. Scientists -- Dictionaries
ISBN 0-8160-4580-1
LC 2002-14616

This "profiles the lives of 192 people who devoted their careers to the disciplines and subdisciplines of the earth sciences during the 18th century to the present. . . . Entries appear in alphabetic order under the name by which the scientist is most commonly known. Also included are birth date, date of death (if applicable), nationality, and earth science specialty. An essay containing more personal data, including an emphasis on the scientist's main work and contributions to the field follows this information." Am Ref Books Annu, 2003
Includes bibliographical references

Genovese, Michael A.

Encyclopedia of the American presidency; Rev. ed; Facts on File 2010 606p il $95   **920.003**
1. Presidents -- United States 2. Presidents -- United States -- Biography 3. Presidents -- United States -- Encyclopedias 4. Reference books
ISBN 978-0-8160-7366-5
LC 2008-54208

"Birth and death dates, major public acts, family life, and other particulars give a concise but well-rounded view of each Chief Executive as man and as man of the people. . . . An altogether excellent introduction to the study of the presidency of the United States; articles are informative without being pedantic and interesting while remaining pertinent and to the point." Libr J
Includes bibliographical references

Grant, Michael

★ **Greek** and Latin authors, 800 B.C.-A.D. 1000; a biographical dictionary. Wilson, H.W. 1980 490p il $105   **920.003**
1. Authors, Greek -- Dictionaries 2. Authors, Latin -- Dictionaries 3. Classical literature -- Dictionaries 4. Reference books
ISBN 0-8242-0640-1
LC 79-27446

Covers more than 370 classical authors. Each entry includes "the pronunciation of the author's name, biographical background, an overview of major works with critical commentary on the nature and quality of those works, and, where relevant, a brief discussion of the influence of the author's works on later literature." Ref Sources for Small & Medium-sized Libr. 5th edition

Great lives from history

Great lives from history, The 18th century, 1701-1800; editor, John Powell; editor, first edition, Frank N. Magill. Salem Press 2006 2v il map set $160   **920.003**
1. Biography -- Dictionaries 2. Reference books 3. World history -- 18th century
ISBN 978-1-58765-276-9; 1-58765-276-5
LC 2006-5336

"The alphabetically listed subjects encompass 36 areas of expertise and include John Newbery, Pontiac, Qianlong, Hannah More, Pius IV, Paul Revere, and Shah Wali Allah, among others. Each article is approximately three pages long and lists the subject's major accomplishments, important dates, and areas of achievement. . . . A well-written, useful set." SLJ
Includes bibliographical references

Hamilton, Neil A.

Presidents; a biographical dictionary. Ian C. Friedman, reviser. 3rd ed; Facts on File 2010 496p il $85; pa $19.95   **920.003**
1. Presidents -- United States 2. Presidents -- United States -- Dictionaries 3. Reference books
ISBN 978-0-8160-7708-3; 978-0-8160-8247-6 pa
LC 2009-10191

This book "contains biographies and portraits of all presidents, a . . . chronology of the life of each president, and suggested further reading about each president." Publisher's note
Includes bibliographical references

Havlice, Patricia Pate

Index to artistic biography. Scarecrow Press 1973 2v set $135   **920.003**
1. Artists -- Biography 2. Biography -- Indexes 3. Reference books
ISBN 0-8108-0540-5

The first two volumes list some 70,000 artists' biographies found in sixty-four reference works. The first supplement covers seventy titles and lists around 47,000 names. The second supplement covers 131 titles published from 1980 through 1999

Jaques Cattell Press

Who's who in American politics 2007-2008; [prepared by Marquis Who's Who] 21st ed.; Marquis Who's Who 2007 xxxvi, 1960p $314.10   **920.003**
1. Politicians -- United States -- Dictionaries 2. Reference books
ISBN 978-0-8379-6918-3

"Biographical directory of political leaders in the Congress, the executive branch of the federal government, state legislatures, state executive branches, mayors of cities with populations over 50,000, national and state party chairs, national party committee members, county chairs, and state supreme court justices. Entries are arranged by state, then alphabetically by name. Indexed by name." Ref Sources for Small & Medium-sized Libr. 6th edition

Kelly, J. N. D.

The **Oxford** dictionary of Popes; with new material by Michael Walsh. Updated [ed]; Oxford University Press 2006 349p pa $21.43　　**920.003**
1. Popes -- Dictionaries 2. Reference books
ISBN 978-0-19-861433-3; 0-19-861433-0
LC 2006-277841

"An excellent source of information, arranged chronologically with an alphabetical index. Includes popes, antipopes, and an appendix on Pope Joan." Ref Sources for Small & Medium-sized Libr. 6th edition
Includes bibliographical references

Krismann, Carol

★ **Encyclopedia** of American women in business; from colonial times to the present. [by] Carol H. Krisman. Greenwood Press 2004 692p 2v set $175　　**920.003**
1. Businesswomen -- Encyclopedias 2. Reference books 3. Women executives -- Encyclopedias
ISBN 0-313-32757-2
LC 2004-56065

The author "presents the stories of 327 businesswomen who have succeeded as entrepreneurs, executives, or business owners in profit-making enterprises from Colonial times to this day. . . . In addition to the biographies, the book contains entries for work-related issues like old-boys network, office romance, and diversity as well as profiles of agencies related to women. . . . This excellent reference book is wonderfully readable and should encourage readers to conduct further research of the women profiled." Libr J
Includes bibliographical references

Kuhlman, Erika A.

A to Z of women in world history; [by] Erika Kuhlman. Facts on File 2002 452p il $49.50 **920.003**
1. Reference books 2. Women -- Biography 3. Women -- Biography -- Dictionaries
ISBN 0-8160-4334-5
LC 2001-54327

"The 260 women who are profiled here have not only made a mark on their own cultures but have also 'influenced other women from diverse cultures and different historical periods pursuing the same goals.'. . . Entries are organized first under 14 areas of accomplishment, from 'Adventurers and Athletes' to 'Writers.'. . . Entries are generally around two pages in length, and each offers suggestions for further reading. . . . A to Z of Women in World History is a good place to start for researchers who are taking a sphere-of-activity approach to women's history. This highly readable volume is recommended." Booklist
Includes bibliographical references

Kunitz, Stanley

★ **World** authors, 1970-1975; editor, John Wakeman; editorial consultant, Stanley J. Kunitz. Wilson, H.W. 1980 894p il $140　　**920.003**
1. Authors -- Dictionaries 2. Literature -- Bio-

bibliography 3. Reference books
ISBN 0-8242-0641-X
LC 79-21874

This volume provides biographical or autobiographical sketches for 348 of the most influential and popular men and women of letters who have come into prominence between 1970 and 1975.

Mandel, David

Who's who in the Jewish Bible. Jewish Publication Society 2007 xx, 422p pa $30　　**920.003**
1. Reference books
ISBN 978-0-8276-0863-4; 0-8276-0863-2
LC 2007-27288

"Using only the Bible as its basis, this encyclopedia catalogues 3,000 characters from A to Z. General readers and students interested in past Jewish life will find this work most useful as a quick reference for information and a starting point for research." Booklist
Includes bibliographical references

Martinez Wood, Jamie

Latino writers and journalists. Facts on File 2007 294p il $44　　**920.003**
1. American literature -- Hispanic American authors -- Bio-bibliography 2. Hispanic Americans -- Dictionaries 3. Reference books
ISBN 0-8160-6422-9; 978-0-8160-6422-9
LC 2006-17394

This book "brings together 150 writers identified as Latino Americans. Approximately one-third of the profiles are accompanied by photographs." Booklist
Includes bibliographical references

Millar, David

★ The **Cambridge** dictionary of scientists; [by] David Millar [et al.] 2nd ed; Cambridge Univ. Press 2002 464p il hardcover o.p. $99; pa $34.99 **920.003**
1. Reference books 2. Science -- History 3. Scientists 4. Scientists -- Dictionaries
ISBN 0-521-80602-X; 0-521-00062-9 pa
LC 2002-512240

"The alphabetically organized, illustrated biographical dictionary . . . [covers] over 1,500 key scientists . . . from 40 countries. Physics, chemistry, biology, geology, astronomy, mathematics, medicine, meteorology and technology are all represented and special attention is paid to pioneer women." Publisher's note

Monush, Barry

★ **Screen** world presents the encyclopedia of Hollywood film actors; v1 edited by Barry Monush. Applause Theatre and Cinema Bks. 2003 1200p v1 il $35　　**920.003**
1. Actors -- Dictionaries 2. Motion pictures -- Biography -- Dictionaries 3. Reference books
ISBN 1-557-83551-9
LC 2002-152728

"The first of a projected two-volume set, this encyclopedia provides biographical profiles of actors who worked in Hollywood between 1915 and 1965 . . . . [The author] includes all Oscar-winning actors as well as performers who became prominent in film before the late 1960s. . . . Entries are arranged in alphabetical order (Bud Abbott and Lou Costello to George Zucco), include vital statistics, and note any higher-education institution the actor attended. . . . This is an item that academic libraries and specialized film libraries will want to add. It would also no doubt find an audience in public libraries." Booklist

Newton, David E.

Latinos in science, math, and professions. Facts on File 2007 274p il $44   **920.003**

1. Hispanic Americans -- Dictionaries 2. Mathematicians -- Dictionaries 3. Reference books 4. Scientists -- Dictionaries

ISBN 978-0-8160-6385-7; 0-8160-6385-0

LC 2006-16769

Among the figures profiled in this biographical dictionary "are sociology expert Maxine Baca Zinn; Ellen Ochoa, the first Latina in space; and research entomologist Fernando E. Vega." Libr J

Includes bibliographical references

Oakes, Elizabeth H.

★ **A to Z of chemists**. Facts on File 2002 276p il $45   **920.003**

1. Chemists 2. Reference books 3. Scientists -- Dictionaries

ISBN 0-8160-4579-8

LC 2002-68685

"This title includes 152 biographies of chemists, including 23 women. . . . The entries run between 750 and 1200 words (one to one and one-half pages apiece). They all begin with a summary of the subject's major contribution, followed by a chronological biography of their personal and professional life. Appendixes list the birthplace and country of activity of the chemists as well as a chart of their life spans." Libr J

Includes bibliographical references

American writers. Facts on File 2004 430p il $65   **920.003**

1.   American literature -- Bio-bibliography   2. American literature -- Bio-bibliography -- Dictionaries 3. American literature -- Dictionaries 4. Authors, American -- Biography -- Dictionaries 5. Authors, American -- Dictionaries 6. Reference books

ISBN 0-8160-5158-5

LC 2003-15743

"The volume has alphabetically arranged entries for approximately 260 authors from a variety of genres—poetry, fiction, drama, essay, and autobiography. Each . . . entry contains a short biography, critical analysis, and a bibliography of works about the author in both printed and Web formats. . . . [This book] offers a convenient introduction and is a worthwhile purchase." Booklist

Includes bibliographical references

Otfinoski, Steven

Latinos in the arts. Facts on File 2007 277p il $44   **920.003**

1. Actors -- Dictionaries 2. Artists -- Dictionaries 3. Hispanic Americans -- Dictionaries 4. Musicians --

Dictionaries 5. Reference books

ISBN 978-0-8160-6394-9; 0-8160-6394-X

LC 2006-16900

"This volume profiles more than 178 individuals in the performing and visual arts 'who were born in the United States or who settled here permanently,' among them Marc Anthony, Cameron Diaz, Carmen Miranda, Tito Punete, and Shakira. Each entry concludes with a list of 'Further Reading' . . . and, in many cases, 'Further Listening' and 'Further Viewing.'" Booklist

Includes bibliographical references

Pendergast, Tom

★ U-X-L graphic novelists; [by] Tom Pendergast and Sara Pendergast; Sarah Hermsen, project editor. U-X-L/Thomson Gale 2007 lxii, 634p 3v il set $181   **920.003**

1. Authors -- Dictionaries 2. Cartoonists -- Dictionaries 3. Comic books, strips, etc. 4. Graphic novels 5. Graphic novels -- Dictionaries   6.   Illustrators -- Dictionaries 7. Reference books

ISBN 1-4144-0440-9; 978-1-4144-0440-0

LC 2006-13711

The three volumes include 75 alphabetically-arranged articles that profile authors, illustrators, and author-illustrators, and include European, American, and Japanese creators. The introduction provides some history of graphic novels, and there is a separate essay on manga.

"This accessible and readable survey of a timely topic should generate considerable attention in school library media center and public library collections. Well researched and documented, with subject and language appropriate for its intended audience, this set is highly recommended." Booklist

Includes bibliographical references

Radcliffe Institute for Advanced Study

Notable American women; a biographical dictionary completing the twentieth century. Susan Ware, editor; Stacy Braukman, assistant editor. Belknap Press 2004 xxx, 729p $45   **920.003**

1. Reference books 2. Women -- United States -- Biography

ISBN 0-674-01488-X

LC 2004-48859

This volume includes "stars of the golden ages of radio, film, dance, and television; scientists and scholars; politicians and entrepreneurs; authors and aviators; civil rights activists and religious leaders; Native American craftspeople and world-renowned artists. Women from a broad spectrum of ethnic, class, political, religious, and sexual identities are all acknowledged." Publisher's note

Includes bibliographical references

Schneider, Dorothy

★ **First** ladies; a biographical dictionary. [by] Dorothy Schneider, Carl J. Schneider. 3rd ed; Facts on File 2010 436p il $85   **920.003**

1. Presidents' spouses -- United States 2. Presidents' spouses -- United States -- Dictionaries 3. Reference books

ISBN 978-0-8160-7724-3

LC 2009-9047

This book "covers all the women who have held this esteemed 'office' since the founding of the United States. . . . Arranged chronologically by term of presidency, each biographical entry includes a . . . biography emphasizing each first lady's life during the presidency, as well as a chronology, appendixes, and suggestions for further reading." Publisher's note

Includes bibliographical references

Shipp, Steve

   Latin American and Caribbean artists of the modern era; a biographical dictionary of more than 12,700 persons. McFarland & Co 2002 864p il $115 **920.003**
   1. Artists -- Dictionaries 2. Latin American art 3. Reference books
   ISBN 0-7864-1057-4

LC 2002-13828

"All entries include expected information such as birth date and place and artist's medium, and longer entries also feature biographical sketches, including education and influences, as well as lists of collections, exhibits, and titles. . . . A good starting point for further research." Libr J

   Includes bibliographical references

Waldrup, Carole Chandler

   The **vice** presidents; biographies of the 45 men who have held the second highest office in the United States. McFarland & Co. 1996 271p il hardcover o.p. pa $39.95 **920.003**
   1. Biography, Collective 2. Vice-Presidents -- United States -- Biography 3. Vice-presidents -- United States
   ISBN 0-7864-0179-6; 978-0-7864-2611-9 pa; 0-7864-2611-X pa

LC 96-30538

"Well-written with clear, precise language and vocabulary, this informative book will be useful in either the reference section or with the collective biographies." Book Rep

   Includes bibliographical references

Yount, Lisa

   ★ **A to Z of biologists**. Facts on File 2003 390p il $45 **920.003**
   1. Biologists 2. Reference books 3. Scientists -- Dictionaries
   ISBN 0-8160-4541-0

LC 2002-13816

"Each profile focuses on a particular biologist's research and contributions to the field and his or her effect on scientists whose work followed. Their lives and personalities are also discussed through incidents, quotations, and photographs. The profiles are culturally inclusive and span a range of biologists from ancient times to the present day." Publisher's note

   Includes bibliographical references

   ★ The African American national biography; editors in chief, Henry Louis Gates, Jr., Evelyn Brooks-Higginbotham. Oxford University Press 2008 8v il set $995 **920.003**
   1. African Americans -- Biography -- Dictionaries 2.

Reference books
ISBN 978-0-19-516019-2

LC 2007-44671

"A supplement to the 24-volume American National Biography . . . [this biographical encyclopedia] records the contributions of more than 4,000 African Americans—slaves, architects, entertainers, dentists, political leaders, artists, poets, and activists. . . . [This] is a major . . . standard reference work that most libraries of any size will want to have." Booklist

   Includes bibliographical references

   American authors, 1600-1900; a biographical dictionary of American literature. edited by Stanley J. Kunitz and Howard Haycraft. Wilson, H.W. 1938 846p il $120 **920.003**
   1. American literature -- Bio-bibliography 2. Authors, American -- Dictionaries 3. Reference books
   ISBN 0-8242-0001-2

"This volume contains biographies of 1,300 authors who contributed to the development of American literature, from the founding of Jamestown (1607) to the end of the nineteenth century. Each essay describes the author's life, discusses past and present significance, and evaluates principal works." Safford. Guide to Ref Materials for Sch Media Cent. 5th edition

   American men & women of science; a biographical directory of today's leaders in physical, biological and related sciences. 25th ed; Gale Group 2008 8v set$1530.75 **920.003**
   1. Reference books 2. Scientists -- Dictionaries
   ISBN 1-4144-3291-7; 978-1-4144-3291-5

"Brief biographical sketches of . . . scientists and engineers active in the United States and Canada. Arranged alphabetically, with discipline index." Ref Sources for Small & Medium-sized Libr. 6th edition

   American statesmen; secretaries of state from John Jay to Colin Powell. edited by Edward S. Mihalkanin. Greenwood Press 2004 xxxv, 571p $99.95 **920.003**
   1. Cabinet officers -- United States 2. Reference books 3. Statesmen -- United States 4. Statesmen -- United States -- Dictionaries
   ISBN 0-313-30828-4

LC 2004-10871

For a fuller review, see: Booklist, Feb. 15, 2005

This biographical dictionary features "65 biographical essays on each of the secretaries of state plus two important interim secretaries. . . . Each essay blends biographical information, early life, education, and influences; career information, appointment, and relations with the president and Congress; and a review of the major issues and accomplishments during the secretary's tenure in office." Am Ref Books Annu, 2005

   Includes bibliographical references

   American writers; a collection of literary biographies. Leonard Unger, editor in chief. Scribner 1974 4v + supplement I-IV set $1845 **920.003**
   1. American literature -- History and criticism 2.

Authors, American -- Dictionaries 3. Reference books
ISBN 0-684-80586-3

"Signed essays on the life and works of selected American authors; selective bibliographies by and about each author. The basic set (1974. 4 v.) contains 97 essays originally published in the University of Minnesota pamphlets on American writers series; some have been revised and updated. Each of the 2-v. supplements covers 29 writers not included in the parent series; the supplements give greater attention to women and minorities." Guide to Ref Books. 11th edition

★ Biographical encyclopedia of artists; Sir Lawrence Gowing, general editor. Facts on File 2005
4v il set $260   **920.003**
1. Artists -- Biography -- Encyclopedias 2. Reference books
ISBN 0-8160-5803-2
                                          LC 2005-40500

"The artists covered include Laurie Anderson, Frank Gehry, Anselm Kiefer, Jan Vermeer, and Andy Warhol. . . . A visual chronology of artists by country and era functions as an index to artists, and an alphabetical artist/subject index concludes the work." Libr J
Includes bibliographical references

★ Black women in America; Darlene Clark Hine, editor in chief. 2nd ed; Oxford University Press
2005 3v il set $325   **920.003**
1. African American women -- Dictionaries 2. Reference books
ISBN 0-19-515677-3
                                          LC 2005-1532

"The essays offer fascinating glimpses into black women's economic, social, and political contributions, even at the grassroots level, and explore issues such as spirituality, domestic servitude, and mixed-race identity in terms of how they have shaped history." SLJ
Includes bibliographical references

British authors of the nineteenth century; edited by Stanley J. Kunitz; associate editor: Howard Haycraft; complete in one volume with 1000 biographies and 350 portraits. Wilson, H.W. 1936 677p
il $105   **920.003**
1. Authors, English -- Dictionaries 2. English literature -- Bio-bibliography 3. Reference books
ISBN 0-8242-0007-1

Contemporary women artists; editors, Laurie Collier Hillstrom, Kevin Hillstrom; with a preface by Lucy R. Lippard. St. James Press 1999 760p
$175   **920.003**
1. Reference books 2. Women artists -- Dictionaries
ISBN 1-558-62372-8
                                          LC 99-10053

This work "covers 350 women artists, mostly US painters and sculptors. Entries are helpfully indexed by nationality and medium and include photographers, performance and video artists, ceramicists, filmmakers, textile artists, and

weavers from countries in Latin America and western and eastern Europe." Choice
Includes bibliographical references

Current biography yearbook, 2010; editor, Clifford Thompson; senior editors, Miriam Helbok, Mari Rich. Wilson, H.W. 2011 738p il $185 **920.003**
1. Biography -- Periodicals
ISBN 978-0-8242-1113-4

"Biographies of prominent people written in lively, popular prose. Emphasis is on entertainers, star athletes, politicians, and other celebrities. Series is cumulative, with biographies revised and updated occasionally. Each volume has seven-year index." N Y Public Libr Book of How & Where to Look It Up

Encyclopedia of women's autobiography; edited by Victoria Boynton and Jo Malin; Emmanuel S. Nelson, advisory editor. Greenwood Press 2005
2v set $249.95   **920.003**
1. Autobiography 2. Reference books 3. Women -- Biography -- Encyclopedias
ISBN 0-313-32737-8
                                          LC 2005-8526

This set's "encyclopedic and culturally diverse nature should appeal to a wide audience and provide a valuable starting point for further research." Libr J
Includes bibliographical references

★ Encyclopedia of world biography; 2nd ed; Gale Res. 1998 17v il set $1787   **920.003**
1. Biography -- Dictionaries 2. Biography -- Encyclopedias 3. Reference books
ISBN 0-7876-2221-4
                                          LC 97-42327

Presents brief biographical sketches which provide vital statistics as well as information on the importance of the person listed. Volumes 1-16 are arranged alphabetically; volume 17 is the index.

European authors, 1000-1900; a biographical dictionary of European literature. edited by Stanley J. Kunitz and Vineta Colby; complete in one volume with 967 biographies and 309 portraits. Wilson, H.W. 1967 1016p il $115   **920.003**
1. Authors, European -- Dictionaries 2. Literature -- Bio-bibliography 3. Reference books
ISBN 0-8242-0013-6

Includes continental European writers born after the year 1000 and dead before 1925. Nearly a thousand major and minor contributors to thirty-one different literatures are discussed.

"These biographies provide quick, satisfactory introductions to a staggering variety of authors and literatures." Choice

Great lives from history, The 17th century, 1601-1700; editor, Larissa Juliet Taylor. Salem Press 2005 2v il set $160   **920.003**
1. Biography -- Dictionaries 2. Reference books 3.

World history -- 17th century
ISBN 1-58765-222-6; 978-1-58765-222-6
LC 2005-17804

This "is a collection of biographical essays, ranging from three to five pages in length and documenting the lives of those individuals who helped to shape the history of the 17th century. The coverage is also global and includes both well-known and lesser-known figures." SLJ
Includes bibliographical references

Great lives from history, The 19th century, 1801-1900; editor, John Powell. Salem Press 2006 4v il map set $360 **920.003**
1. Biography -- Dictionaries 2. Reference books 3. World history -- 19th century
ISBN 978-1-58765-292-9; 1-58765-292-7
LC 2006-20187

"A total of 737 essays covering 757 major figures including 123 on women make up the set. . . . Major world leaders appear here, as well as the giants of religious faith who dominated the century: monarchs, presidents, popes, philosophers, writers, social reformers, educators, and military leaders who left their imprint on political as well as spiritual institutions." Publisher's note
Includes bibliographical references

Great lives from history, The ancient world, prehistory-476 C.E; editor, Christina A. Salowey. Salem Press 2004 2v il, maps set $160 **920.003**
1. Ancient history 2. Biography -- Dictionaries 3. History, Ancient 4. Reference books
ISBN 1-587-65152-1; 978-1-58765-164-9
LC 2004-705

This "set provides three-to-six-page biographies on major personages from the ancient world. Arranged alphabetically, each article gives basic information such as when and where the individual was born and also where and when he or she died, a description of his or her early life and life's work, the significance of the individual, an annotated bibliography, and related entries in both this set and in the . . . [Great events from history] set." Ref & User Services Quarterly
Includes bibliographical references

Great lives from history, the Middle Ages, 477-1453; editor, Shelley Wolbrink. Salem Press 2005 2v il map set $160 **920.003**
1. Biography -- Dictionaries 2. Middle Ages -- History 3. Middle ages -- Biography 4. Reference books
ISBN 1-58765-164-5; 978-1-58765-164-9
LC 2004-16696

These "volumes focus on the people throughout the world from after the Fall of Rome, in 476 C.E., to 1453. Coverage is worldwide. . . . Each entry begins with ready-reference information, followed by a summary of the person's life, a paragraph or two on 'Significance,' a list of further readings, and cross-references to entries both within the set and within the [Great events in history] companion set." Booklist
Includes bibliographical references

Great lives from history, the Renaissance & early modern era, 1454-1600; editor, Christina J. Moose. Salem Press 2005 2v il map set $160 **920.003**
1. Biography -- Dictionaries 2. Reference books 3. Renaissance
ISBN 1-58765-211-0; 978-1-58765-211-0
LC 2004-28875

"This two-volume work offers biographies of 338 historical figures in entries that range from two to five pages in length. A publisher's note in volume 1 explains the set's format and use. All the biographies include name, nationality or ethnicity, historical role, dates, and area(s) of achievement; description of early life, work, and significance; an annotated bibliography; and cross-references." Choice
Includes bibliographical references

Great lives from history: Notorious lives; editor, Carl L. Bankston III. Salem Press 2007 3v il set $252 **920.003**
1. Biography 2. Biography -- Dictionaries 3. Crime 4. Criminals 5. Dictators 6. Political corruption 7. Reference books 8. Terrorism 9. Terrorists 10. War crimes 11. War criminals
ISBN 978-1-58765-320-9
LC 2006-32935

"The scope and depth of coverage make it a valuable resource for not just biographies but for criminal justice and popular culture as well." Booklist
Includes bibliographical references

Great lives from history: the 20th century, 1901-2000; editor, Robert F. Gorman. Salem Press 2008 10v il set $795 **920.003**
1. Biography 2. Biography -- Dictionaries 3. History, Modern -- 20th century 4. Reference books 5. World history -- 20th century
ISBN 978-1-58765-345-2
LC 2008-17125

"This ten-volume set offers 1,330 . . . biographies of major personages in world history (many still living) from 1901-2000. . . . The personages covered are identified with one or more of the following regions: Africa, Asia, Australia, Caribbean, Europe, Latin America, Middle East, North America, South America, and Southeast Asia." Publisher's note
Includes bibliographical references

★ Holy people of the world; a cross-cultural encyclopedia. Phyllis G. Jestice, editor. ABC-CLIO 2004 3v il set $285 **920.003**
1. Reference books 2. Religious biography 3. Religious biography -- Encyclopedias
ISBN 1-576-07355-6
LC 2004-22606

"This edition deserves to become well-worn by the time a second appears." Libr J
Includes bibliographical references

The International who's who; 71st ed; Europa Publs. 2460p $650   **920.003**
1. Biography -- Dictionaries 2. Reference books
ISBN 978-1-85743-415-6; 1-85743-415-3
"Offers brief biographical data on prominent persons throughout the world." Guide to Ref Books. 11th edition

Jewish women in America; an historical encyclopedia. edited by Paula E. Hyman and Deborah Dash Moore. Routledge 1997 xxxi, 1770p 2v set $275   **920.003**
1. Biography, Collective 2. Jewish women -- Biography 3. Jewish women -- Dictionaries 4. Jews -- United States 5. Reference books
ISBN 0-415-91936-3
LC 97-26842
This work contains 800 "biographies and 110 topical essays on subjects ranging from cookbooks to vaudeville. . . . [It provides] encyclopedic coverage of the many varied roles that Jewish women have occupied in America, from the earliest days until the present. All articles are signed and written with attention to detail by noted scholars; 500 period photographs are well-chosen and supplement the text." Am Libr

Musicians & composers of the 20th century; editor Alfred W. Cramer. Salem Press 2009 5v il set $399   **920.003**
1. Music -- Bio-bibliography 2. Musicians -- Dictionaries 3. Reference books
ISBN 978-1-58765-512-8
LC 2009-2980
"The work covers 614 composers, performers, and teachers, chosen for musical influence as well as fame. All major genres are covered, from classical to rap, along with many subgenres, such as rockabilly, atonal, and funk. . . . This work provides valuable, basic information on the topic as well as multiple, easy-access routes to it. Highly recommended." Libr J
Includes bibliographical references

Musicians since 1900; performers in concert and opera. compiled and edited by David Ewen. Wilson, H.W. 1978 974p il $120   **920.003**
1. Musicians -- Dictionaries 2. Reference books
ISBN 0-8242-0565-0
LC 78-12727
"Replaces 'Living musicians' and its supplement (1940-57). Gives 'detailed biographical, critical and personal information about 432 of the most distinguished performing musicians in concert and opera since 1900.'—Introd.' . . . A few bibliographical references are given at the end of each biography; a classified list of musicians concludes the volume." Sheehy. Guide to Ref Books. 10th edition

New dictionary of scientific biography; Noretta Koertge, editor in chief. Scribner's 2008 8v il set $995   **920.003**
1. Reference books 2. Scientists -- Dictionaries
ISBN 978-0-684-31320-7
LC 2007-31384

This biographical dictionary "contains thousands of biographies of mathematicians and natural scientists from all countries and from all historical periods." Publisher's note
Includes bibliographical references

Notable American women: the modern period; a biographical dictionary. edited by Barbara Sicherman {et al.} Harvard Univ. Press 1980 xxii, 773p hardcover o.p. pa $41.50   **920.003**
1. Reference books 2. Women -- United States -- Biography
ISBN 0-674-62733-4 pa
LC 80-18402
This set provides "1 1/2- to 2-page biographies and references for 442 American women. Women were chosen from science, business, and engineering as well as from such traditional fields as education, entertainment, and social work, with a wide variety of 'career patterns, philosophical outlooks and personal styles' represented. . . . Entries describe the life and personality of the individual, evaluate her career, and place it in an historical context. Special emphasis is given to the conflicting demands of her public and personal lives." Choice

Notable black American men, book I; Jessie Carney Smith, editor. Gale Res. 1998 xxxiv, 1365p il $150   **920.003**
1. African American men -- Biography -- Dictionaries 2. African Americans -- Biography -- Dictionaries 3. Reference books
ISBN 0-7876-0763-0
LC 98-38166
This work, the first volume of a two-volume biographical dictionary, "profiles 500 men, from poet Jupiter Hammon (b. 1711) to Tiger Woods. . . . Each entry begins with birth and death dates and a few words describing the subject's major fields of endeavor, followed by a biographical essay, a list of references, and, in some cases, a note on collections of source material." Booklist
Includes bibliographical references

Notable black American men, book II; Jessie Carney Smith, editor. Thomson Gale 2007 xxiv, 827p il $193   **920.003**
1. African Americans -- Biography -- Dictionaries 2. Reference books
ISBN 0-7876-6493-6; 978-0-7876-6493-0
LC 2006-21193
Covering "prominent newsmakers as well as lesser-known individuals, . . . [this second volume of a two-volume work] offers full biographical entries, portraits, addresses for living listees and recommended sources for further study." Publisher's note
Includes bibliographical references

Notable black American women, Book III; Jessie Carney Smith, editor. Gale 2003 lxxviii, 881p il $165   **920.003**
1. African American women -- Dictionaries 2. Reference books
ISBN 0-7876-6494-4

In this third volume of a three-volume biographical dictionary, "narrative biographical essays . . . discuss each woman's significant achievements and the public response to those achievements. . . . [This book] features 300 contemporary and historical women, including Sarah Allen, Alicia Keys, Ruth Simmons and . . . more." Publisher's note
Includes bibliographical references

Notable black American women, book I; Jessie Carney Smith, editor. Gale Res. 1992 xlvii, 1334p il $203 **920.003**
1. African American women -- Dictionaries 2. Reference books
ISBN 0-8103-4749-0

LC 91-35074
This first volume of a three-volume biographical encyclopedia "documents the achievements of 500 African-American women who have made significant contributions to American culture from the colonial era to the present. . . . Subjects include women active in all fields of endeavor, from education, science, and the arts, to business, law and politics. . . . Authoritative and entertaining at the same time." Am Libr

Notable mathematicians; from ancient times to the present. Robyn V. Young, editor; Zoran Minderovic, associate editor. Gale Res. 1998 xxi, 612p il $120 **920.003**
1. Mathematicians -- Dictionaries 2. Reference books
ISBN 0-7876-3071-3

LC 97-33662
This work profiles "300 mathematicians chosen for their historical importance, discoveries, familiarity to the public, awards and prizes, and involvement in mathematics education. . . . Female and minority mathematicians have been expressly represented." Libr J
Includes bibliographical references

Notable native Americans; Sharon Malinowski, editor; George H.J. Abrams, consulting editor and author of foreword. Gale Res. 1995 xliv, 492p il $105 **920.003**
1. Indians of North America -- Biography 2. Native Americans -- Dictionaries 3. Reference books
ISBN 0-8103-9638-6

LC 94-36202
This is a "compilation of biographical and bibliographical information on more than two hundred and sixty-five notable Native North American men and women throughout history, from all fields of endeavor. . . . Approximately thirty percent of the entries focus on historical figures and seventy percent on contemporary or twentieth-century individuals. Signed narrative essays, ranging from one to three pages in length, include Indian names and their English translations as well as name variants." Preface

The Scribner encyclopedia of American lives; Kenneth T. Jackson, editor in chief; Karen Markoe,

general editor; Arnold Markoe, executive editor. Scribner 1998 8v il set $768 **920.003**
1. Reference books
ISBN 0-684-31292-1

LC 98-33793
"Scribner envisions SEAL as the continuation of the Dictionary of American Biography (DAB). . . . Selection criteria are that the biographees made significant contributions to American life and culture. . . . An appreciable number of women and people of color are recognized. All biographies are signed contributions by 332 scholars." Libr J [review of first two volumes]

The Scribner encyclopedia of American lives, The 1960s; William L. O'Neill, volume editor. Scribner 2003 2v il set $250 **920.003**
1. Biography -- 20th century 2. Reference books
ISBN 0-684-80666-5

LC 2002-12581
"The two alphabetically arranged volumes in SEAL 1960s contain biographical sketches, usually between 1,000 and 2,000 words, of 647 figures who 'defined the decade, or who were influential at the time.' Americans from different races, socioeconomic groups, classes, and regions of the U.S. are included, along with the occasional person of another nationality who had long periods of residence in the U.S. and was an influence on American culture. The signed entries, written by scholars, begin with a brief summary of the person's chronology and important accomplishments. This is followed by a narrative of the subject's life. . . . In many cases, a black-and-white photograph accompanies the narrative, which concludes with an assessment of the subject's overall contribution and a brief bibliography listing a few key sources. . . . Recommended for all high-school, public, and academic libraries wanting complete SEAL coverage or libraries wanting to supplement their collection of 1960s resources with a purely biographical approach." Booklist
Includes bibliographical references

St. James guide to Hispanic artists; profiles of Latino and Latin American artists. editor, Thomas Riggs. St. James Press 2002 xx, 682p il $195 **920.003**
1. Artists -- United States 2. Hispanic American art 3. Hispanic American art -- 20th century 4. Hispanic American artists
ISBN 1-55862-470-8

LC 2001-41935
This "guide profiles some 375 of the most prominent Hispanic artists of the past century. The entries include basic biographical information, critical commentary, and lists of exhibitions, publications, and collections holding their works." Libr J
Includes bibliographical references and indexes

The Supreme Court justices: a biographical dictionary; edited by Melvin I. Urofsky. Garland 1994 570p il $85 **920.003**
1. Judges -- Dictionaries 2. Reference books
ISBN 0-8153-1176-1

LC 94-10028
"Alphabetically arranged, each entry begins with life dates, the date of nomination to the Court, the name of the

president who nominated the justice, and the date he or she was seated. The contributors . . . provide facts and context along with analysis of the important cases in the individual justice's career." Libr J

Who was who in America; with world notables. Marquis Who's Who 1942 23v set $999.95 **920.003**
1. Reference books
ISBN 978-0-8379-0282-1
"Includes sketches removed from 'Who's who in America' because of death of the biographee; date of death and, often, interment location is added." Guide to Ref Books. 11th edition

★ Who's who 2008; an annual biographical dictionary. 160th ed.; A. & C. Black 2007 2574p $325 **920.003**
1. Reference books
ISBN 978-0-7136-8555-8; 0-7136-8555-7
"The pioneer work of the who's who type and still one of the most important. Until 1897, it was the handbook of titled and official classes and included lists of names rather than biographical sketches. . . . It is principally British, but a few prominent names of other nationalities are included. Biographies are reliable and fairly detailed; they give main facts, addresses, often telephone numbers and in case of authors, lists of works." Guide to Ref Books. 11th edition

Who's who among African Americans; 21st ed.; Gale Res. 2008 1477p $275 **920.003**
1. African Americans -- Biography -- Dictionaries 2. Reference books
ISBN 978-1-4144-0020-4; 1-4144-0020-9
"Short entries focusing on career achievements and positions. Indexes list entries by place of birth and profession." N Y Public Libr Book of How & Where to Look It Up

Who's who in America, 2008; 62nd ed.; Marquis Who's Who 2007 2v set $710.10 **920.003**
1. Reference books
ISBN 978-0-8379-7011-0; 0-8379-7011-3
"The standard dictionary of contemporary biography, containing concise biographical data, prepared according to established practices, with addresses and, in the case of authors, lists of works. . . . Each edition is thoroughly revised, new biographies added, and others dropped. For names of persons dropped because of death, see 'Who was who in America'." Guide to Ref Books. 11th edition

★ Who's who in American art, 2008; 28th ed.; Marquis Who's Who 2007 1550p $267.30 **920.003**
1. Artists -- United States -- Dictionaries 2. Reference books
ISBN 978-0-8379-6307-5; 0-8379-6307-9
"Profiles representatives of all segments of the art world including artists, administrators, and librarians. Entries give vital statistics, professional education and training, commissions and exhibitions, and membership in art societies. Includes geographic and professional classification indexes and cumulative necrology." N Y Public Libr Book of How & Where to Look It Up

Who's who in British history; beginnings to 1901. general editor, Geoffrey Treasure; authors and contributors, Ian Dawson {et al.} Fitzroy Dearborn Pubs. 1998 2v maps set $325 **920.003**
1. Reference books
ISBN 1-884964-90-7
"The length of entries varies from many pages (Henry VIII) to a column for most persons. . . . The choice of entries (ending with 1901) reflects the traditional emphasis of history teaching, with heavy representation of statemen, royalty, military persons, diplomats, major writers, and leading ladies of the stage and aristocracy." Choice
Includes bibliographical references

★ Who's who in finance and business 2008-2009; 36th ed; Marquis Who's Who 2007 1,100 $349 **920.003**
1. Business -- Biography -- Dictionaries 2. Reference books
ISBN 978-0-8379-0356-9
"Gives international coverage of businessmen. Includes index of firms with references to personnel for whom sketches are included." Guide to Ref Books. 11th edition

★ Who's who of American women 2007; 26th ed; Marquis Who's Who 2006 1,700 $305 **920.003**
1. Reference books 2. Women -- United States -- Biography
ISBN 0-8379-0434-X
"This title provides information on women who are successful in a variety of professions, including business, government, education, art and culture, and those who have received prestigious honors or have been selected for honorary institutions. The biographical data are provided by the women themselves so the quality varies. In general it includes name, occupation, birth date, education, career history, publications, professional activities, awards, and home and office addresses. This has long been a standard source in many public and academic libraries." Am Ref Books Annu, 2003

Women in world history; a biographical encyclopedia. Anne Commire, editor, Deborah Klezmer, associate editor. Gale Res. 1999 17v set $1,495 **920.003**
1. Reference books 2. Women -- Biography 3. Women -- Biography -- Encyclopedias 4. Women -- History -- Encyclopedias
ISBN 0-7876-3736-X

LC 99-24692
"The editors researched wives, daughters, mothers, and other women who were not documented in traditional, male-oriented sources, especially history books. . . . Some entries are only a sentence or two because of lack of information, but the majority include most or all of the following: dates, if known, or time of flourishing; an identifying summary of life and achievements; a personal profile with vital statistics and names of family members; events in the life of the biographee; vitae listing such things as works for authors or winning records for athletes; a quotation by or about the individual; and bibliographical references." Booklist
Includes bibliographical references

World artists, 1950-1980; an H.W. Wilson biographical dictionary. {edited} by Claude Marks. Wilson, H.W. 1984 912p il $130 **920.003**
1. Artists -- Biography 2. Artists -- Dictionaries 3. Biography, Collective 4. Modern art -- 20th century -- Biography 5. Reference books
ISBN 0-8242-0707-6

LC 84-13152
"The 312 painters, sculptors, and graphic artists in this biographical dictionary were selected from the outstanding artistic figures in the US, Europe, and Latin America. . . . The biographical information includes family, working background, and aesthetic beliefs. There are many quotations from the artist and from critics. Also included is a list of significant collections and a bibliography." Choice

★ World artists, 1980-1990; an H.W. Wilson biographical dictionary. edited by Claude Marks. Wilson, H.W. 1991 413p il $95 **920.003**
1. Artists -- Dictionaries 2. Reference books
ISBN 0-8242-0827-7

LC 91-13183
This volume contains brief biographies of 118 artists from around the world who have been influential in the 1980's

World authors, 1950-1970; a companion volume to Twentieth century authors. edited by John Wakeman; editorial consultant: Stanley J. Kunitz. Wilson, H.W. 1975 1594p il $160 **920.003**
1. Authors -- Dictionaries 2. Literature -- Bio-bibliography 3. Reference books
ISBN 0-8242-0419-0

This volume includes 959 "authors who came into prominence between 1950 and 1970. . . . Authors were chosen for literary importance or outstanding popularity." Wilson Libr Bull

World authors, 1975-1980; editor, Vineta Colby. Wilson, H.W. 1985 829p il $140 **920.003**
1. Authors -- Dictionaries 2. Literature -- Bio-bibliography 3. Reference books
ISBN 0-8242-0715-7

LC 85-10045
This work profiles the lives and works of 379 writers.

★ World authors, 2000-2005; editors, Jennifer Curry, David Ramm, Mari Rich, Albert Rolls. Wilson, H. W. 2007 800p il $170 **920.003**
1. Authors 2. Authors -- Dictionaries 3. Literature 4. Literature -- Bio-bibliography 5. Literature -- History and criticism 6. Reference books
ISBN 978-0-8242-1077-9

This book "covers some 300 novelists, poets, dramatists, essayists, scientists, biographers, and other authors whose books [were] published 2000 through 2005." Publisher's note

World explorers and discoverers; editor, Richard E. Bohlander; consultants, John L. Allen {et al.} Macmillan 1991 531p il maps $110 **920.003**
1. Biography, Collective 2. Explorers -- Biography 3.

Explorers -- Dictionaries 4. Reference books
ISBN 978-0-02-897445-3; 0-02-897445-X

LC 91-23156
"Over 300 explorers and discoverers are featured in this attractive compilation that covers exploration from ancient times to the present and includes such notable moderns as Jacques Cousteau and Edmund Hillary." Am Libr

World musicians; edited by Clifford Thompson; staff contributors: Denise Bonilla [et al.]; consultants: Justin Dello Joio, Lewis Porter. Wilson, H.W. 1999 1181p il $115 **920.003**
1. Musicians -- Dictionaries 2. Reference books
ISBN 0-8242-0940-0

LC 98-29205
International in coverage, this volume profiles "contemporary musicians whose specialties range from classical to pop, opera to rap, bluegrass to rock. . . . Written in a lively style and ranging in length from 500 to 3,500 words, the articles cover each musician's personal and professional life and are frequently spiced with quotations from published interviews with the subject and excerpts from critical commentary. Many entries include a black-and-white photo of the musician, and all conclude with a selected bibliography of additional publications and recordings." Booklist

920.009 History and geographic treatment of biography as a discipline; general collections of biography by period, region, group

McCullough, David G., 1933-
★ The **greater** journey; [by] David McCullough. Simon & Schuster 2011 558p. ill. (some col.), maps $37.50; ebook $19.99 **920.009**
1. Americans -- France 2. Americans -- France -- Paris -- History -- 19th century 3. Artists 4. Authors, American 5. Biography, Collective
ISBN 978-1-4165-7176-6; 1-4165-7176-0; 978-1-4165-7689-1 ebook; 9781416571766; 9781416576891; 1416576894

LC 2010053001
In this book, "award-winning historian [David] McCullough . . . [tells the story of] a cluster of aspiring young people such as portraitist George Healy and lawyer Charles Sumner, eager to expand their horizons [in Paris] in the 1830s. . . . [The book] include[s] numerous other visitors over an entire eventful century. . . . [N]ovelist James Fenimore Cooper, widowed schoolteacher Emma Hart Willard and young medical student Oliver Wendell Holmes Sr. all knew their education was not complete without a stint in the medieval capital. For many of these American rubes, exposure to the fine arts, old-world architecture, fashion, fine dining, museums and teaching hospitals proved transformative, and the knowledge they gained would define their professional lives back in America." (Kirkus)

"An account of young Americans, driven by wanderlust, setting out in search of greener Parisian pastures. Well-known figures such as James Fenimore Cooper, Oliver Wendell Holmes Sr., and Mary Cassat, and long-forgotten entities like Elizabeth Blackwell and William Wells Brown, all walked along the Avenue des Champs-Élysées, went to the Musée du Louvre, ate wonderful meals, and became inspired. Their life-changing adventures played a vital role in transforming the course of US history." Christ Sci Monit

Includes bibliographical references (p. 519-537) and index.

920.71   Men

Gates, Henry Louis

Thirteen ways of looking at a black man. Random House 1997 xxvii, 226p hardcover o.p. pa $12   **920.71**

1. Actors 2. African American men -- Biography 3. African Americans -- Biography 4. Authors 5. Biography, Collective 6. Black Muslim leaders 7. Choreographers 8. Dancers 9. Dramatists 10. Essayists 11. Football players 12. Generals 13. Literary critics 14. Memoirists 15. Music historians 16. Novelists 17. Screenwriters 18. Secretaries of state 19. Short story writers 20. Singers 21. Social activists 22. Sportscasters 23. Young adult authors

ISBN 0-679-77666-4 pa

LC 96-33138

"Mr. Gates's strong suit is finding the common man in uncommon figures, without losing sight of the ways in which race, class and personal experience have shaped each life." N Y Times Book Rev

920.72   Women

Ware, Susan

Letter to the world; seven women who shaped the American century. Norton 1998 xxiv, 344p il $25.95   **920.72**

1. Actors 2. Anthropologists 3. Biography -- 20th century 4. Choreographers 5. Columnists 6. Curators 7. Dance teachers 8. Dancers 9. Diplomats 10. Golfers 11. High jumpers 12. Humanitarians 13. Hurdlers 14. Javelin throwers 15. Journalists 16. Olympic athletes 17. Opera singers 18. Social activists 19. Spouses of presidents 20. United Nations officials 21. Women -- Biography 22. Women -- United States -- Biography 23. Writers on science

ISBN 0-393-04652-4

LC 97-45923

The author "considers the lives of seven women who had an exceptional impact on 20th-century American culture and society's perception of the role of women: Eleanor Roosevelt, Dorothy Thompson, Margaret Mead, Katharine Hepburn, Babe Didrikson Zaharias, Martha Graham, and Marian Anderson. In addition to focusing on outstanding achievements in their chosen fields, Ware looks at their often unconventional private lives." Libr J

Includes bibliographical references

92

Abbott, Karen

American rose; a nation laid bare: the life and times of Gypsy Rose Lee. Random House 2010 422p il $26; ebook $12.99   **92**

1. Actors 2. Biography, Individual 3. Burlesque (Theater) -- History 4. Novelists 5. Striptease 6. Stripteasers

ISBN 978-1-4000-6691-9; 978-0-679-60456-3 ebook

LC 2010-15081

"Imaginative and engaging, Abbott's biography of the celebrated stripper, who died in 1970 at age 59, also proves a well-informed look at the evolution of musical theater in the early 20th century." Publ Wkly

Includes bibliographical references

Abdul-Jabbar, Kareem

★ On the shoulders of giants; my journey through the Harlem Renaissance. [by] Kareem Abdul-Jabbar with Raymond Obstfeld. Simon & Schuster 2007 274p il hardcover o.p. pa $18.99   **92**

1. African Americans -- Biography 2. Basketball players 3. Harlem Renaissance 4. Nonfiction writers

ISBN 1-4165-3488-1; 978-1-4165-3488-4; 1-4165-3489-X pa; 978-1-4165-3489-1 pa

LC 2006-51776

"By mixing personal anecdotes with traditional research and reporting, . . . [Abdul-Jabbar] acts as a knowledgeable, passionate tour guide through the artistic and social history of one America's most dynamic creative eras." N Y Times Book Rev

Includes bibliographical references

Achebe, Chinua, 1930-

The education of a British-protected child; essays. A.A. Knopf 2009 172p $24.95   **92**

1. African literature -- History and criticism 2. Authors 3. Authors, Nigerian 4. Essayists 5. Novelists 6. Poets 7. Racism 8. Short story writers

ISBN 978-0-3072-7255-3

LC 2009017480

This is a collection of essays by the author of Things Fall Apart. In the title piece, Achebe discusses "growing up in colonial Nigeria and inhabiting its 'middle ground,' recalling both his happy memories of reading novels in secondary school and the harsher truths of colonial rule. . . . Politics and history figure in 'What Is Nigeria to Me?,' 'Africa's Tarnished Name,' and 'Politics of the Politicians of Language.' And Achebe's . . . family comes into view in 'My Dad and Me' and 'My Daughters.'" (Publisher's note)

"Humane and carefully argued responses to events of recent years, coupled with a long look back at the African past." Kirkus

Includes bibliographical references

Ackroyd, Peter

Chaucer; Peter Ackroyd. 1st ed in the U.S.A; Nan A. Talese/Doubleday 2005 188p il $19.95 **92**

1. Authors 2. Poets 3. Poets, English -- Middle

English, 1100-1500 -- Biography
ISBN 0-385-50797-6

LC 2004-49796

This "account of the life of Geoffrey Chaucer (1343?-1400) [is also] a consideration of his role in shaping England's national identity. The poet is hailed as the 'progenitor of a national style,' and deft literary analysis explicates Chaucer's innovations while acknowledging the influence of other poets. . . . Much is made of Chaucer's position in the royal court, which provided the financial means to live comfortably while writing his verse." Publ Wkly

Includes bibliographical references

Poe; a life cut short. Nan A. Talese/Doubleday 2008
205p il $21.95 **92**
1. Authors 2. Authors, American 3. Essayists 4. Poets
5. Short story writers
ISBN 978-0-385-50800-1; 0-385-50800-X

LC 2008-18244

Explores Poe's literary accomplishments and legacy against the background of his erratic, dramatic, and sometimes sordid life, including his marriage to his thirteen-year-old cousin and his much-written-about problems with gambling and alcohol.

This "readable account should appeal to Poe devotees and newcomers alike." Publ Wkly

Includes bibliographical references

Adams, Henry

Tom and Jack; the intertwined lives of Thomas Hart Benton and Jackson Pollock. Bloomsbury Press 2009 405p il $35 **92**
1. Artists 2. Artists -- United States 3. Biography, Individual 4. Illustrators 5. Lithographers 6. Painters
ISBN 1-59691-420-3; 978-1-59691-420-9

LC 2009-12309

"In this absorbing, carefully reasoned inquiry into a profound relationship between two painters, Adams reclaims the wrongfully maligned Benton and recalibrates our perception of Pollock and his masterpieces." Booklist

Includes bibliographical references (p. 375-390)

The **education** of Henry Adams; an autobiography. with a new introduction by Donald Hall. Houghton Mifflin 2000 517p pa $12 **92**
1. Authors 2. Essayists 3. Historians 4. Novelists
ISBN 0-618-05666-1

LC 00-26235

"The book omits any mention of the thirteen years of Adams's marriage and the seven years following his wife's suicide. It does, however, present a vivid picture of the people and places the author knew." Reader's Ency. 4th edition

Adams, John

Hallelujah junction; composing an American life. Farrar, Straus and Giroux 2008 340p il $26 **92**
1. Biography, Individual 2. Composers 3. Minimal music
ISBN 978-0-374-28115-1; 0-374-28115-7

LC 2008-17922

An eminent composer shares the story of his life, from his childhood and early studies in classical composition to his minimalist and "docu-opera" achievements, in an account that evaluates his professional relationships and the social movements that inspired his creative process.

"Readers will enjoy the candor and completeness of the book, which serves as a gateway to an accomplished body of work. Like the author's music: carefully considered, deliberate and often exciting, gathering together many disparate elements of American life." Kirkus

★ **My** dearest friend; letters of Abigail and John Adams. edited by Margaret A. Hogan and C. James Taylor. Belknap Press of Harvard University Press 2007 508p il map $35 **92**
1. Biography, Individual 2. Parents of presidents 3. Presidents 4. Presidents -- United States 5. Presidents' spouses -- United States 6. Spouses of presidents 7. Vice-presidents
ISBN 978-0-674-02606-3; 0-674-02606-3

LC 2007-4380

This collection of correspondence between John and Abigail Adams includes "selection from the entire body of the Adams' correspondence, from their courtship . . . until Abigail left the White House near the end of John's presidential term, reminding him, 'I want to see the list of judges.' . . . This is a treasure, for general readers and scholars alike." Booklist

Adams, Mark

Mister America; how muscular millionaire Bernarr Macfadden transformed the nation through sex, salad, and the ultimate starvation diet. Harper 2009 292p il $25.99 **92**
1. Bodybuilding 2. Fitness experts 3. Magazine executives 4. Physical fitness
ISBN 978-0-06-059475-6

LC 2008-18705

This is a "biography of pioneering health-and-fitness guru Bernarr Macfadden. . . . A funny, informative history of a true American eccentric and the national preoccupation with health and fitness." Kirkus

Adler, William M.

The **man** who never died; the life, times, and legacy of Joe Hill, American labor icon. Bloomsbury 2011 435p il $30 **92**
1. Authors 2. Biography, Individual 3. Folk musicians 4. Poets 5. Revolutionaries 6. Songwriters
ISBN 978-1-59691-696-8; 1-59691-696-6

LC 2011009821

This is a biography of the poet, songwriter and labor activist who was executed in 1915. Index.

"Presenting Hill as man and symbol, Adler contributes vitally to labor history." Booklist

Includes bibliographical references

Agassi, Andre

Open; an autobiography. A. Knopf 2009 385p il $28.95 **92**
1. Biography, Individual 2. Tennis 3. Tennis -- Biography 4. Tennis players
ISBN 978-0-307-26819-8; 0-307-26819-5

LC 2009-24004

This is a memoir by the eight-time Grand Slam championship winner who founded the Andre Agassi Charitable Foundation and the Andre Agassi College Preparatory Academy for underprivileged children in Las Vegas.

"By sharing an unvarnished, at times inspiring story in an arresting, muscular style, Agassi may have just penned one of the best sports autobiographies of all time. Check— it's one of the better memoirs out there, period. . . . Fans will devour Agassi's juicy revelations about both himself and other tennis luminaries." Time

Al Jundi, Sami

The **hour** of sunlight; one Palestinian's journey from prisoner to peacemaker. by Sami al Jundi and Jen Marlowe. Nation Books 2010 344p il pa $16.99   **92**

1. Israel-Arab conflicts 2. Pacifists 3. Palestinian Arabs 4. Prisoners
ISBN 978-1-56858-448-5

LC 2010-29340

The authors "trace al Jundi's evolution from Palestinian militant to peacemaker. As teenagers, al Jundi and two friends joined the PLO, but when a bomb exploded as they were building it, one boy was killed, and the other two badly injured—and on the receiving end of Israeli interrogations and torture. Sentenced to a decade in prison, al Jundi dedicates himself to an extensive education program maintained by the prisoners themselves, ultimately committing himself to nonviolence and to bridging the Israeli-Palestinian divide." Publ Wkly

Includes bibliographical references

Albers, Patricia

Joan Mitchell; lady painter: a life. Alfred A. Knopf 2011 xxi, 514p il $40; ebook $21.99   **92**

1. Abstract expressionism 2. Artists 3. Artists -- United States 4. Biography, Individual 5. Painters 6. Women artists
ISBN 978-0-375-41437-4; 978-0-307-59598-0 ebook

LC 2011-00457

This is a "biography of Joan Mitchell (1925–92), a major 20th-century American artist. . . . This significant biography covers all aspects of Mitchell's life, including her synesthesia, eidetic memory, alcoholism, troubled relationships, and art. Filled with intimate details of her complex personality and unconventional lifestyle, this is a conscientiously objective yet sympathetic portrait of the 'lady painter' and the social and cultural contexts in which she became a successful artist in the male-dominated Parisian and New York art worlds." Libr J

Includes bibliographical references

Alexander, Kelly

Hometown appetites; the story of Clementine Paddleford, the forgotten food writer who chronicled how America ate. by Kelly Alexander and Cynthia Harris; foreward by Coleman Andrews. Gotham Books 2008 318p il $27.50   **92**

1. Columnists 2. Food critics 3. Magazine editors
ISBN 978-1-592-40389-9; 1-592-40389-1

LC 2008-15264

This biography explores "Paddleford's career as food writer from 1936 to 1966 at the New York Herald Tribune. . . . The authors make an upbeat case for reconsidering Paddleford's achievement in this enjoyable read, and include a slew of her comfort recipes." Publ Wkly

Includes bibliographical references

Alexander, Larry

Biggest brother; the life of Major D. Winters, the man who led the Band of Brothers. NAL Caliber 2005 287p il $24.95   **92**

1. Army officers 2. Biography, Individual 3. Veterans 4. World War, 1939-1945 5. World War, 1939-1945 -- Campaigns -- Western Front 6. World War, 1939-1945 -- Regimental histories -- United States
ISBN 0-451-21510-9

LC 2004-27330

This is "the story of what distinguished Easy Company from other first-class field units: its leadership, in the person of Major Richard Winters, its commander. . . . Alexander is especially good at showing how Winters' sense of responsibility developed as a student, an enlistee, in OCS, and as an officer. He also gives a detailed picture of the army of 60-plus years ago, and the process that turned thousands of young civilians into the men who beat the Germans." Booklist

Alexander, Paul

Boulevard of broken dreams; the life, times, and legend of James Dean. Plume 1997 312p il pa $16   **92**

1. Actors
ISBN 978-0-452-27840-0; 0-452-27840-6

"The interesting thing about James Dean is the fact that, almost 40 years after his death, he remains an icon of American pop culture. In the last chapter of this tell-all biography, Alexander takes a stab at accounting for Dean's continuing popularity, but his real interest throughout the book is in the actor's sex life. Although he devotes some attention to Dean's work as an actor and to his heterosexual liaisons, Alexander's contribution to the Dean legend is to label him as homosexual." Booklist

Ali, Khaliah

Fighting weight; how I achieved healthy weight loss with banding, a new procedure that eliminates hunger--forever. [by] Khaliah Ali; George Fielding, Christine Ren, Lawrence Lindner. HarperCollins 2007 241p il $22.95   **92**

1. Children of prominent persons 2. Fashion designers 3. Memoirists 4. Models (Persons) 5. Stomach -- Surgery 6. Talk show hosts 7. Weight loss
ISBN 0-06-117094-1; 978-0-06-117094-2

LC 2007-60870

The author "describes her own lifelong battle with obesity and the effect of her own gastric-banding surgery. . . . Co-author George Fielding, M.D., who performed Ali's surgery, explains the process and how it differs from other bariatric surgeries. . . . A good combination of scientific information and personal narrative, this title belongs in all public libraries." Libr J

Ali, Nujood

I am Nujood, age 10 and divorced; [by] Nujood Ali, with Delphine Minoui; translated by Linda Coverdale. Three Rivers Press 2010 188p pa $12

92

1. Abused persons 2. Child marriage 3. Children
ISBN 978-0-307-58967-5; 0-307-58967-6

LC 2009-33063

"One of 16 children living in squalor in Yemen, Nujood was married off at about age 10. Though her husband vowed he'd wait for sex until she reached puberty, he rapes her on their first night together. After months of abuse, Nujood goes to the courthouse, where with heartbreaking naiveté, she tells a judge she wants a divorce. Supported by the legal system, Nujood gets her wish." People

Includes bibliographical references

Alison, Jane

The **sisters** antipodes. Houghton Mifflin Harcourt 2009 276p $23

92

1. Authors 2. Biography, Individual 3. Novelists
ISBN 978-0-15-101280-0; 0-15-101280-6

LC 2008-14747

The author describes "the strangely definitive reconfiguration of her family when her parents broke up and switched partners and children with another couple they met in Australia. . . . [This is] a truly unusual, harrowing journey of identity." Publ Wkly

Allende, Isabel

★ **Paula**; translated from the Spanish by Margaret Sayers Peden. HarperPerennial 2008 330, 23p pa $14.99 **92**

1. Authors 2. Authors, Chilean 3. Children's authors
4. Dramatists 5. Journalists 6. Novelists
ISBN 978-0-06-156490-1

Allende "interweaves the story of her own life with the slow dying of her 28-year-old daughter, Paula." Publ Wkly

The **sum** of our days; translated from the Spanish by Margaret Sayers Peden. HarperCollins 2008 320p $26.95

92

1. Authors 2. Authors, Chilean 3. Biography, Individual 4. Children's authors 5. Dramatists 6. Journalists 7. Novelists
ISBN 978-0-06-155183-3; 0-06-155183-X

LC 2007-33251

"In this sequel to her memoir Paula (1995), about the yearlong coma suffered by her daughter, Chilean novelist Allende tells of the difficult years following Paula's death. . . . Surprisingly candid, frequently funny, and highly aware of her own failings, Allende is a person fully engaged in life, and readers will find her eloquent memoir inspirational reading." Booklist

Alter, Jonathan

The **promise**; President Obama, year one. Simon & Schuster 2010 458p il $28; ebook $12.99 **92**

1. Lawyers 2. Nobel laureates for peace 3. Presidents 4. Presidents -- United States 5. Senators 6. State legislators
ISBN 978-1-4391-0119-3; 978-1-4391-5408-3 ebook

LC 2010-20438

"Alter's writing is sharp. His tone is breezy and engaging but appropriate to the subject matter. No deep, dark secrets are revealed, but readers will come away from this book with a good idea of how the Obama administration understands itself." Commonweal

Includes bibliographical references

Ambrose, Stephen E.

Eisenhower; soldier and president. Simon & Schuster 1990 635p il hardcover o.p. pa $18 **92**

1. College presidents 2. Generals 3. Presidents 4. Presidents -- United States
ISBN 0-671-74758-4 pa

LC 90-9701

"Tracing Eisenhower's family background, education, military and political careers, and influence as elder statesman, the author chronicles Eisenhower's triumphs and failures and at the same time provides a vivid picture of the off-duty Ike. . . . This is the definitive one-volume biography of Eisenhower." Publ Wkly

Includes bibliographical references

Amis, Martin

Experience. Hyperion 2000 406p il $23.95; pa $14 **92**

1. Authors 2. Essayists 3. Humorists 4. Literary critics 5. Novelists 6. Poets 7. Short story writers
ISBN 0-7868-6652-7; 0-375-72683-7 pa

LC 00-699777

This is a "portmanteau of personal history, ancestor worship and promiscuous opinionizing, and a piñata of literary gossip that Amis beats with a stick, causing many names to drop. . . . And if we stay put till the last 100 pages, it will break our heart." N Y Times Book Rev

Andelman, Bob

Will Eisner, a spirited life. M Press 2005 375p il pa $14.95 **92**

1. Authors 2. Cartoonists 3. Comic book writers 4. Publishing executives
ISBN 1-59582-011-6

LC 2005-26326

This is a biography of the American cartoonist and comic book publisher.

"Besides verifying Eisner's impact on nearly every artist who drew comics in his wake, Andelman shows that Eisner's influence extends to such film directors as Spielberg and Tarantino." Booklist

Andersen, Jens

Hans Christian Andersen: a new life; translated from the Danish by Tiina Nunnally. Overlook Press 2005 624p il hardcover o.p. pa $22.95 **92**

1. Authors 2. Authors, Danish 3. Children's authors 4. Dramatists 5. Novelists 6. Short story writers
ISBN 1-58567-642-X; 1-58567-737-X pa

LC 2004-65985

The author examines Andersen's "considerable gifts as an oral storyteller; his eccentric, often annoying public habits; his ambivalent sexuality; his bouts of narcissism; his painfully slow transformation from rough-hewn provincial and awkward melodramatist into brilliant, internationally famous writer-celebrity. The biography is best and most moving when it is frank about formerly suppressed aspects of Andersen's life." Booklist

Includes bibliographical references

Anderson, Jon Lee

Che Guevara; a revolutionary life. Grove Press 1997 814p il maps hardcover o.p. pa $20   **92**

1. Physicians 2. Revolutionaries

ISBN 0-8021-3558-7 pa

LC 97-3993

This is a "biography of the life and death of the larger-than-life revolutionary Ernesto 'Che' Guevara, the Argentine doctor who joined with Castro to overturn Fulgencio Batista's reign in Cuba. . . . This book, with its 89 photographs, will be an invaluable addition to the literature of American revolutionaries." Booklist

Includes bibliographical references

Anderson, William T.

Laura Ingalls Wilder country; text by William Anderson; color photography by Leslie A. Kelly. HarperPerennial 1990 119p il hardcover o.p. pa $24.95   **92**

1. Authors 2. Children's authors 3. Literary landmarks -- United States 4. Novelists 5. Western writers 6. Young adult authors

ISBN 0-06-097346-3 pa

LC 89-46512

"Contemporary and period photographs of the places in the Laura Ingalls Wilder books have been combined with a narrative about the actual historical settings." Horn Book

Andoe, Joe

Jubilee city; a memoir at full speed. William Morrow 2007 207p il $22.95   **92**

1. Artists 2. Biography, Individual 3. Painters

ISBN 978-0-06-124031-7; 0-06-124031-1

In this "memoir, Andoe narrates his journey from his Tulsa childhood through redneck, hard-partying teen years to a highly successful career as a (hard-partying redneck) painter in New York City. While Andoe may not be a professional writer, his humor and offbeat artistic sensibility make up for any lack of prose-writing chops. Through discrete anecdotes that seldom run longer than two pages, Andoe assembles vivid portraits of his family and friends and of the various environments he inhabited-the working-class Tulsa neighborhoods of the 1960s, the high school and college drug culture at the end of the hippie era, and the New York art scene of the 1980s." Publ Wkly

Andrews, Julie

Home; a memoir of my early years. Hyperion 2008 339p il $26.95 **92**

1. Actors 2. Children's authors 3. Singers

ISBN 978-0-7868-6565-9; 0-7868-6565-2

LC 2007-48830

"Spanning events from her 1935 birth to the early 1960s, . . . [the author] covers her rise to fame and ends with Walt Disney casting her in Mary Poppins (1963). . . . The heart of her book documents the rehearsals, tryouts and smash 1956 opening of My Fair Lady. Readers will rejoice, since Andrews is an accomplished writer who holds back nothing

while adding a patina of poetry to the antics and anecdotes throughout this memoir of bittersweet backstage encounters and theatrical triumphs." Publ Wkly

Angelou, Maya

★ **I** know why the caged bird sings. Random House 2002 281p $21.95   **92**

1. Actors 2. African American authors 3. Children's authors 4. Dramatists 5. Essayists 6. Memoirists 7. Poets 8. Singers 9. Women authors

ISBN 0-375-50789-2

LC 2001-41914

The first volume in the author's autobiographical series covers her childhood and adolescence in rural Arkansas, St. Louis, and San Francisco.

"Angelou is a skillful writer; her language ranges from beautifully lyrical prose to earthy metaphor, and her descriptions have power and sensitivity." Libr J

Angelou, Maya, 1928-

Letter to my daughter. Random House 2008 166p $25   **92**

1. Actors 2. African American authors 3. Children's authors 4. Dramatists 5. Essayists 6. Memoirists 7. Poets 8. Singers 9. Women authors

ISBN 978-1-4000-6612-4

LC 2008-28843

"A slim volume packed with nourishing nuggets of wisdom." Kirkus

Angier, Carole

The **double** bond: Primo Levi, a biography. Farrar, Straus & Giroux 2002 xxvi, 898p il $40; pa $20   **92**

1. Authors 2. Chemists 3. Essayists 4. Holocaust survivors 5. Memoirists 6. Novelists 7. Poets 8. Short story writers

ISBN 0-374-11315-7; 0-374-52898-5 pa

This is a biography of the Italian Jewish chemist and writer. Levi was the author of The Periodic Table, Survival in Auschwitz, The Drowned and the Saved and Other People's Trades.

"Angier's long, gripping narrative of Levi's time in Auschwitz synthesizes the best of his memoirs, poetry, fiction, essays, and scientific writing. . . . A compelling biography and a must for all Holocaust collections." Booklist

Includes bibliographical references

Anissimov, Myriam

Primo Levi; tragedy of an optimist. Overlook Press 1998 452p il $37.95; pa $18.95   **92**

1. Authors 2. Chemists 3. Essayists 4. Holocaust survivors 5. Memoirists 6. Novelists 7. Poets 8. Short story writers

ISBN 0-87951-806-5; 1-58567-020-0 pa

LC 97-9904

"A serious, lively, conscientiously researched biography of the distinguished Italian writer whose optimism and rationalism were not totally suppressed by his experience as an inmate of Auschwitz." N Y Times Book Rev

Includes bibliographical references

Anthony, Carl Sferrazza

Nellie Taft; the unconventional first lady of the ragtime era. 1st ed; William Morrow 2005 534p il $29.95; pa $15.95 **92**
1. Spouses of presidents
ISBN 0-06-051382-9; 0-06-051383-7 pa

LC 2004-52553

"This lively biography provides an illuminating glimpse into the life of an until-now underappreciated First Lady." Booklist

Includes bibliographical references

Anthony, Susan B.

★ **Failure** is impossible; Susan B. Anthony in her own words. [edited by] Lynn Sherr. Times Bks. 1995 xxviii, 384p il hardcover o.p. pa $23 **92**
1. Abolitionists 2. Feminism 3. Suffragists
ISBN 0-8129-2718-4

LC 94-29913

This is a collection of Susan B. Anthony's journal entries, correspondence, speeches, interviews, and published writings. The author has arranged the selections by topic and chronologically within topics

Applegate, Debby

★ The **most** famous man in America; the biography of Henry Ward Beecher. Doubleday 2006 529p il map $27.95 **92**
1. Biography, Individual 2. Clergy 3. Nonfiction writers
ISBN 0-385-51396-8; 978-0-385-51396-8

LC 2005-54842

This is a biography of the American clergyman.
"By illuminating Beecher's position in history, Applegate has produced a biography worthy of its subject." N Y Times Book Rev

Includes bibliographical references

Aquino, Lucia

Leonardo Da Vinci; preface by Mario Pomilio; [translation, Miriam Hurley] Rizzoli 2005 173p il pa $9.95 **92**
1. Artists 2. Artists, Italian 3. Painters 4. Scientists 5. Writers on science
ISBN 978-0-8478-2677-3; 0-8478-2677-5

LC 2004-099908

This book "features a literary introduction and . . . description of a selection of the artist's masterpieces. . . . [It also includes] a visual chart with captions as to the whereabouts of each painting and a . . . bibliography." Publisher's note

Includes bibliographical references

Arana, Marie

American chica; two worlds, one childhood. Dial Press (NY) 2001 309p hardcover o.p. pa $12.95 **92**
1. Authors 2. Editors 3. Hispanic American journalists -- United States -- Biography 4. Journalists -- United States -- Biography 5. Literary critics 6. Memoirists

7. Novelists
ISBN 0-385-31963-0 pa

LC 00-47529

The author, born to a Peruvian father and an American mother, writes of her childhood in Peru.

Arana "blends a journalist's dedication to research with a style that sings with humor. Her memoir is an outstanding contribution to the growing shelf of Latina literature." Publ Wkly

Ardizzone, Heidi

An **illuminated** life; Belle da Costa Greene's journey from prejudice to privilege. W. W. Norton & Co. 2007 580p il $35 **92**
1. African American librarians 2. African American women 3. Bibliographers 4. Biography, Individual 5. Librarians
ISBN 978-0-393-05104-9; 0-393-05104-8

LC 2007-04967

This is a biography of the first director of the Morgan Library.

"Ardizzone more than succeeds in portraying a vivid figure who rose to the top in a segregated, paternalistic world yet suffered loneliness and was haunted by personal demons. A valuable work for students of early 20th-century culture as well as for librarians, feminists, and students of race relations." Libr J

Includes bibliographical references

Arkin, Alan

An **improvised** life; a memoir. Da Capo Press 2011 201p $17 **92**
1. Actors 2. Theatrical directors
ISBN 978-0-306-81966-7

LC 2010-45034

"Arkin looks back on his career as an actor, but this memoir forgoes the backstage gossip and star-studded anecdotes readers might expect. In fact, the author largely ignores his accomplishments in favor of charting his inner evolution as an artist, focusing on intellectual and spiritual epiphanies that have shaped his approach to acting. . . . Earnest, intelligent and well-observed—less a celebrity memoir than a serious consideration of the principles of acting and improvisation. " Kirkus

Armstrong, John

Love, life, Goethe; lessons of the imagination from the great German poet. 1st American ed.; Farrar, Straus and Giroux 2007 482p il $30 **92**
1. Authors 2. Dramatists 3. Essayists 4. Nonfiction writers 5. Novelists 6. Poets 7. Writers on science
ISBN 978-0-374-29968-2; 0-374-29968-4

LC 2006-34072

"Armstrong's thoughtful analysis of Goethe's life and works enables readers to fully appreciate the great German poet as an eminently human genius striving for growth and wholeness." Booklist

Includes bibliographical references

Armstrong, Karen

The **spiral** staircase; my climb out of darkness. Knopf 2004 xxii, 305p hardcover o.p. pa $14 **92**

1. Nuns 2. Religious scholars

ISBN 0-375-41318-9; 0-385-72127-7 pa

LC 2003-47550

This "is the story of Armstrong's personal spiritual quest, which led her at age 17 to join a convent. However, she found that her own skeptical nature and the physical constraints of convent life crippled her intellectually and spiritually. . . . After seven years, Armstrong left the convent." SLJ

Armstrong, Lance

★ **It's** not about the bike; my journey back to life. [by] Lance Armstrong with Sally Jenkins. Putnam 2000 275p il hardcover o.p. pa $14 **92**

1. Athletes 2. Cancer patients -- United States -- Biography 3. Cyclists 4. Cyclists -- United States -- Biography 5. Olympic athletes

ISBN 0-399-14611-3; 0-425-17961-3 pa

LC 00-35612

Armstrong describes his early years growing up in Plano, Texas, his rise through the sports world as a champion American cyclist, his diagnosis and recovery from testicular cancer and his triumph in the 1999 Tour de France.

"Readers will respond to the inspirational recovery story, and they will appreciate the behind-the-scenes cycling information." Booklist

Aron, Wendy

Hide & seek; how I laughed at depression, conquered my fears and found happiness. Kunati 2008 235p pa $14.95 **92**

1. Authors 2. Depression (Psychology) 3. Dramatists 4. Journalists 5. Memoirists 6. Television scriptwriters

ISBN 978-1-60164-158-8

LC 2008-14008

"In her efforts to subdue raging depression, TV and stage writer Aron tried to no avail virtually every mainstream and alternative remedy. Her adventures among the lunatic fringe are laugh-out-loud funny. . . . Anyone who has overcome recurring bouts with the blues will relish this comic self-help tale." Libr J

Includes bibliographical references

Ashton, Nigel John

King Hussein of Jordan; a political life. [by] Nigel Ashton. Yale University Press 2008 431p il map $35 **92**

1. Biography, Individual 2. Kings

ISBN 978-0-300-09167-0; 0-300-09167-2

LC 2008-10803

With "unprecedented access to the late king's entire correspondence and more than two dozen interviews . . . Ashton reveals Hussein's longstanding covert contact with Israel and his clandestine communications with Israelis in the immediate aftermath of the 1967 war to suggest the possibilities and missed opportunities (including by the U.S.) for a peaceful settlement in the Palestinian-Israeli conflict." Publ Wkly

Includes bibliographical references (p. 371-378)

Athill, Diana

Somewhere towards the end. W.W. Norton 2009 182p $24.95; pa $13.95 **92**

1. Aging 2. Authors 3. Biography, Individual 4. Editors 5. Memoirists 6. Old age 7. Short story writers 8. Translators

ISBN 978-0-393-06770-5; 0-393-06770-X; 978-0-393-33800-3 pa; 0-393-33800-2 pa

LC 2008-41533

The author "offers a spry dispatch on the condition of being elderly. . . . Her perspective is both remorseless and tender as she considers the waning of her sexual desire, the sharpening of her atheist resolve, her increasing preference for nonfiction rather than novels . . . and the truth that, even in her advanced state, much of her time is taken up with caring for those still older. The achievement of Athill's work is its refusal to reduce the specificities of her captivating life to homilies about wisdom." New Yorker

Atlas, Teddy

Atlas; from the streets to the ring: a son's struggle to become a man. [by] Teddy Atlas and Peter Alson. Ecco 2006 278p il $24.95 **92**

1. Biography, Individual 2. Sports trainers

ISBN 0-06-054240-3; 978-0-06-054240-5

LC 2005-52104

The author "traces his circuitous route from Staten Island street thug, emotionally ignored by his doctor father, to renowned [boxing] trainer. . . . It's all here—the good, the bad and the ugly of Teddy Atlas, often rendered in a crude but convincing street language, captured so faithfully and so forcefully by his collaborator, Peter Alson." N Y Times Book Rev

Auletta, Ken

Media man; Ted Turner's improbable empire. Norton 2004 205p il $22.95 **92**

1. Baseball executives 2. Boat racers 3. Broadcasting executives 4. Philanthropists

ISBN 0-393-05168-4

LC 2004-12215

The author "describes how Turner's upbringing by a domineering father and his marriage to and later divorce from actress and radical Jane Fonda influenced his life and career. He also shows how Turner revolutionized TV by turning a tiny Atlanta station into a national cable powerhouse." Libr J

Includes bibliographical references

Avery, Kevin

Everything is an afterthought; the life and writings of Paul Nelson. Fantagraphics Books 2011 xxvi, 497p il $29.99 **92**

1. Journalists 2. Music critics 3. Rock music -- History and criticism 4. Writers on music

ISBN 978-1-60699-475-7

"Seamlessly incorporating the perspectives of Nick Tosches, Robert Christgau, and Jann Wenner, Avery has crafted both a cautionary tale and a celebration of a noir-influenced writer who deserves a place alongside Lester Bangs for his ability to live, always, in the music. Devotees of folk, establishment rock 'n' roll, and pulp fiction will rue not having discovered Nelson sooner." Libr J

Includes bibliographical references

Bacall, Lauren

By myself and then some. HarperEntertainment 2005 506p il $26.95   **92**
1. Actors
ISBN 0-06-075535-0

LC 2005-40256

In this memoir, the actress describes how she got her start in acting and her relationships with other actors, including Humphrey Bogart.

"Certainly more intelligently written than your average celebrity autobiography, this memoir tells a fascinating story of one woman's journey through life with an intimacy that's sure to engage legions of readers." Booklist

Bach, Steven

Dazzler; the life and times of Moss Hart. Da Capo 2002 462p il pa $20 **92**
1. Authors 2. Dramatists 3. Dramatists, American
ISBN 0-306-81135-9; 978-0-306-81135-7

"In narrating its subject's life, Dazzler is both gossipy and credible, a relatively rare and laudable combination." New Leader

Includes bibliographical references

Leni: the life and work of Leni Riefenstahl. A.A. Knopf 2007 368p il $30   **92**
1. Actors 2. Centenarians 3. Motion picture directors 4. Motion picture producers
ISBN 978-0-375-40400-9; 0-375-40400-7

LC 2006-49323

This is a biography of the filmmaker.

This "is a lively, incisive look at a compelling and somewhat appalling figure who demonstrated that beauty isn't always truth." Publ Wkly

Includes bibliographical references

Bailey, Blake

Cheever; a life. Alfred A. Knopf 2009 770p il $35 **92**
1. Authors 2. Authors, American 3. Biography, Individual 4. Novelists 5. Short story writers
ISBN 978-1-4000-4394-1; 1-4000-4394-8

LC 2008-42277

The author "plunges deeply into the murky, sometimes fetid stew of John Cheever's life (1912-82). Beginning with his 1982 appearance at Carnegie Hall to receive the National Medal for Literature (more details appear some 650 pages later), the author proceeds in chronological fashion to tell the story of a deeply needy, difficult man. . . . [This is a] superb work that shows Cheever wrestling with dark angels, but wresting from those encounters some celestial prose." Kirkus

Includes bibliographical references

Bailey, Elisabeth Tova

The **sound** of a wild snail eating. Algonquin Books of Chapel Hill 2010 190p il $18.95   **92**
1. Authors 2. Biography, Individual 3. Essayists 4.

Short story writers 5. Snails
ISBN 978-1-56512-606-0

LC 2010-18603

"A small, short book filled with an enormous amount of natural history and science about snails; also, an acknowledgment of an individual's determination to recover and regain life with humor and insight. Highly recommended." Libr J

Includes bibliographical references

Bainton, Roland Herbert

Here I stand: a life of Martin Luther. Abingdon Press 1950 422p il music hardcover o.p. pa $7 **92**
1. Reformation 2. Religious leaders 3. Social reformers 4. Theologians 5. Writers on religion
ISBN 0-687-16895-3 pa

This biography of Martin Luther interprets his work, writings, and lasting contributions. It recreates the spiritual setting of the sixteenth century and shows Luther's place within it.

Baker, Deborah

The **convert**; a tale of exile and extremism. Graywolf Press 2011 246p il $23 **92**
1. Biography, Individual 2. Converts 3. Muslim women
ISBN 978-1-55597-582-1; 1-55597-582-8

This "is a cogent, thought-provoking look at a radical life and its rippling consequences." Publ Wkly

Includes bibliographical references

Baker, Jean H.

Margaret Sanger. Hill and Wang 2011 349p il $35   **92**
1. Biographies 2. Birth control 3. Essayists 4. Family planning advocates 5. Feminists 6. Memoirists 7. Nurses 8. Social activists 9. Women's rights
ISBN 978-0-8090-9498-1

LC 2011008439

This biography of Margaret Sanger seeks to clear the noted birth-control pioneerss name of the charges of elitism and racism, which have darkened her reputation in recent years. . . . Born to a large, poor Irish family, Sanger transformed herself from middle-class housewife to internationally renowned sex educator. . . . It was the death of a young woman from a self-induced abortion that impelled her to take up the cause of women's rights to contraception. . . . [The author] acknowledges Sanger's support of eugenics but asserts that Sanger was being pragmatic, requiring allies and finding many in the then-popular eugenics movement. [Jean H.] Baker also asserts that to label her as racist is an unjust tactic of pro-life groups and that, in her day, Sanger, who opposed segregation, was more racially tolerant than most Americans. (Kirkus)

"Baker relates Sanger's crusade with unfailing precision as she recounts Singer's years as a nurse, when she mended the damage caused by self-induced abortions and listened to the pitiful plights of young women enchained by the relentless cycle of childbirth. Sanger distributed pamphlets on contraception, risking imprisonment on account of their legally designated obscenity; opened the first legal family planning clinic in 1940; and at the culmination of her career, in the 1960s, promoted use of the birth control pill.

Connecting the details of each battle Sanger won and lost, Baker recreates the train of events in an arduous, iconic, and controversial journey. A moving biography chronicling the hard-fought struggle for women to gain control of their reproductive destiny." Booklist

Mary Todd Lincoln; a biography. Norton 1987 429p il hardcover o.p. pa $17.95   **92**
1. Spouses of presidents 2. Spouses of the presidents
ISBN 0-393-30586-4 pa
LC 86-23757
The author "portrays Mrs. Lincoln as a woman tortured by a series of family bereavements and thwarted from developing her natural talents by a patriarchal society that branded as 'unwomanly' her involvement in her husband's political career. Ms. Baker establishes her first argument with a lengthy investigation of Mary Todd's early family history in Lexington, Ky., and sustains the second by enlarging upon such topics as 19th-century domesticity, childbirth, mourning customs, spiritualism and America's deplorable insanity laws." NY Times Book Rev
Includes bibliographical references

Baker, Russell
Growing up. New American Library 1983 278p pa $15   **92**
1. Authors 2. Essayists 3. Humorists 4. Journalists 5. Memoirists 6. Satirists
ISBN 0-452-25550-3
This book "recounts the first 24 years of [Baker's] life as the son of an independent and deep-rooted Virginian family." Natl Rev

Bakewell, Sarah
How to live, or, A life of Montaigne in one question and twenty attempts at an answer. Other Press 2010 389p il map $25; ebook $19.99   **92**
1. Authors 2. Authors, French 3. Essayists 4. Judges
ISBN 978-1-59051-425-2; 978-1-59051-426-9 ebook
LC 2010-26896
"In a wide-ranging intellectual career, Michel de Montaigne found no knowledge so hard to acquire as the knowledge of how to live this life well. By casting her biography of the writer as 20 chapters, each focused on a different answer to the question How to live? Bakewell limns Montaigne's ceaseless pursuit of this most elusive knowledge. Embedded in the 20 life-knowledge responses, readers will find essential facts—when and where Montaigne was born, how and whom he married, how he became mayor of Bordeaux, how he managed a public life in a time of lethal religious and political passions. . . . Because Montaigne's capacious mirror still captivates many, this insightful life study will win high praise from both scholars and general readers." Booklist
Includes bibliographical references

Balbirer, Nancy
Take your shirt off and cry; a memoir of near-fame experiences. Bloomsbury 2009 231p pa $16   **92**
1. Actors 2. Memoirists
ISBN 978-1-59691-478-0; 1-59691-478-5
LC 2008-45397

"It is a fact of life seldom discussed in our celebrity-mad media: most actors do not become either rich or famous. Balbirer revels in her failure in this witty, poignant, exceedingly well-written memoir chronicling the ups and downs (mostly downs) of a trained, hardworking actress who always seems on the cusp of greatness but who nevertheless always fails to make the grade." Booklist

Balf, Todd
Major; a Black athlete, a White era, and the fight to be the world's fastest human being. Crown Publishers 2008 306p il $24; pa $13.95 **92**
1. African American athletes 2. Bicycle racing 3. Cyclists
ISBN 978-0-307-23658-6; 0-307-23658-7; 978-0-307-23659-3 pa; 0-307-23659-5 pa
LC 2007-20747
The author "chronicles the life of the unlikeliest of stars in the early years of cycling: Marshall 'Major' Taylor. Taylor was an incomparable athlete, poet and celebrity, but he was also a black man living during a time when the scars of the Civil War and slavery were still fresh in the minds of Americans. Balf . . . does great work presenting the complex nature of Taylor's life, including his upbringing in poverty in Indianapolis, the years he was treated as a son by a rich white family, the fans who both worshipped and vilified him and his close relationships with his white trainer and promoter." Publ Wkly
Includes bibliographical references

Balsamo, William
Young Al Capone; the untold story of Scarface in New York, 1899-1925. [by] William Balsamo and John Balsamo. Skyhorse Pub. 2010 270p il $24.95   **92**
1. Bootleggers 2. Criminals 3. Mafia 4. Mobsters
ISBN 978-1-616-08085-3
LC 2010-34682
"Before he became the mythical untouchable 'Scarface,' Alphonse Capone (1899-1947) was a young, cunningly brutal thug schooled by hardboiled criminal minds in pre-Depression Brooklyn, N.Y. . . . [The authors] revisit Capone's apprenticeship years in the violent Brooklyn Navy Yard street gangs and his transformation from a wayward youth to polished, cold-blooded gangster under the tutelage of two master mobsters, Johnny Torrio and 'Frankie Yale' Ioele. . . . With insider facts and spare narrative, the authors show us not only how Capone got his scarred face; they deliver a scathing portrait of a power-mad predator coming up through the criminal ranks." Publ Wkly

Bard, Elizabeth
Lunch in Paris; a love story, with recipes. Little, Brown and Co. 2010 324p $23.99   **92**
1. Americans -- France 2. Art historians 3. French cooking 4. Journalists
ISBN 978-0-316-04279-6; 0-316-04279-X
LC 2009-22064
"Falling in love with a Frenchman was not in Elizabeth Bard's master plan, but then he took her to a local canteen: 'Not to minimize Gwendal's many charms, but he was halfway to home base as soon as I cut into that marvelous steak,' she writes. Culture shock set in as she learned to shop and

cook in Paris, standing in line here for the best green beans, going there for the best walnuts. I thought the recipes were a cutesy touch until I made a few of them: chicken tagine with two kinds of lemon, spiced apricots, chouquettes. Forget the narrative — you could just buy this as a cookbook." Entertainment Wkly

Barnes, Julian
    Nothing to be frightened of. Alfred A. Knopf 2008 243p $24   **92**
        1. Authors 2. Authors, English 3. Death 4. Essayists 5. Novelists 6. Short story writers 7. Television critics
        ISBN 978-0-307-26963-8; 0-307-26963-9
                                                        LC 2008-19603
    This is "an elegant memoir and meditation, a deep seismic tremor of a book that keeps rumbling and grumbling in the mind for weeks thereafter." N Y Times Book Rev

Barr, Nevada
    Seeking enlightenment--hat by hat; a skeptic's path to religion. Putnam 2003 222p $21.95; pa $13   **92**
        1. Authors 2. Mystery writers 3. Park rangers
        ISBN 0-399-15057-9; 0-425-19603-8 pa
                                                        LC 2003-43101
    The author "charts the course of her spiritual evolution, how she sought to understand the many aspects of spiritual life, from forgiveness ('a sigh of relief on which the memory of evil is breathed out') to pain ('it is a duty to relieve our own pain') to commitment ('not a contract with the world but with the self'). Barr's account of her transformation from nonbeliever to committed churchgoer—but one who maintains a healthy sense of doubt even as she prays and attends Bible studies—is moving but never saccharine." Booklist

Barra, Allen
    Inventing Wyatt Earp; his life and many legends. Carroll & Graf Pubs. 1998 432p hardcover o.p. pa $15.95   **92**
        1. Peace officers -- West (U.S.) -- Biography 2. Sheriffs
        ISBN 0-7867-0685-6 pa
    "Barra is at his best in describing the efforts of assorted Hollywood icons, including John Ford, John Sturges, and Kevin Costner, to depict the 'real' Earp." Booklist

    ★ **Yogi** Berra; eternal Yankee. W. W. Norton & Co. 2009 451p il $27.95   **92**
        1. Baseball -- Biography 2. Baseball coaches 3. Baseball managers 4. Baseball players 5. Biography, Individual
        ISBN 978-0-393-06233-5; 0-393-06233-3
                                                        LC 2008-45799
    "Barra brings to his sporting version of the Everyman story an encyclopedic knowledge and warm understanding of the game of baseball; meticulous research into business,

sociology, and history; and a fluid writing style. . . . Baseball biography taken to a higher level." Booklist
    Includes bibliographical references

    The last coach: a life of Paul Bear Bryant. W. W. Norton & Co. 2005 xxix, 546p il $26.95   **92**
        1. Football 2. Football coaches
        ISBN 0-393-05982-0
                                                        LC 2005-14609
    "Readers will experience an array of emotions—humor, sadness, inspiration, awe—as Barra reveals his subject's contributions to college football and ability to touch and inspire people long after their associations with Bryant ended." Libr J
    Includes bibliographical references

Bartlett, Allison Hoover
    The man who loved books too much; the true story of a thief, a detective, and a world of literary obsession. Riverhead Books 2009 274p $24.95 **92**
        1. Bibliomania 2. Book collecting 3. Book thefts 4. Thieves
        ISBN 978-1-59448-891-7; 1-59448-891-6
                                                        LC 2009-21324
    "This excellent tale of people's intimate, complex, and sometimes dangerous relationships to books will be relished by readers, writers, and collectors who are passionate about books as well as fans of true crime stories." Libr J

Bartok, Mira
    ★ The **memory** palace; by Mira Bartok. Free Press 2011 305p. ill. $25; ebook $11.99   **92**
        1. Artists 2. Authors 3. Biography, Individual 4. Children's authors 5. Essayists 6. Homeless 7. Memoirists 8. Mentally ill 9. Pianists 10. Schizophrenia 11. Schizophrenics
        ISBN 978-1-4391-8331-1; 1-4391-8331-7; 978-1-4391-8333-5 ebook; 1-4391-8333-3 ebook
                                                        LC 201008399
    Bartók is a painter and the author of children's books. "'The Memory Palace' begins in the final days of her mother's life, when Bartók finds out that the woman she has not seen in 17 years is dying and decides to go to her." (N Y Times Book Rev)
    This is "personal narrative about growing up with a brilliant but schizophrenic mother. The book is comprised of two intertwining narratives. One concerns artist Bartók's mother, Norma Herr, and her struggle with mental illness. The other examines the author's midlife struggle with a traumatic brain injury. . . . Richly textured, compassionate and heartbreaking." Kirkus

Basie, Count
    Good morning blues: the autobiography of Count Basie; as told to Albert Murray. Da Capo Press 1995 399p il pa $17.95   **92**
        1. African American musicians 2. Band leaders 3. Jazz musicians 4. Pianists
        ISBN 0-306-81107-3
                                                        LC 94-44697
    "Basie pays tribute to his colleagues and managers (and to John Hammond for 'discovering' him), but does not hesi-

tate to discuss their weaknesses and short-comings; his language is direct and earthy. Although some of the book reads more like a catalogue or itinerary than an autobiography, it will have strong appeal for jazz buffs and fans of the late bandleader." Publ Wkly

Bass, Rick

Why I came West. Houghton Mifflin Co. 2008 238p $24; pa $14.95   **92**

1. Authors 2. Authors, American 3. Biography, Individual 4. Conservationists 5. Essayists 6. Geologists 7. Literary landmarks 8. Nature conservation -- Montana -- Yaak Valley 9. Novelists 10. Short story writers 11. Writers on nature
ISBN 978-0-618-59675-1; 0-618-59675-5; 978-0-5472-3771-8 pa; 0-5472-3771-5 pa
LC 2007-30660

Bass "tells the tale of his apprenticeship to literature and the place that has defined his life for the past two decades, Montana's Yaak Valley. Bass looks back to his Houston childhood, Utah college years, and work as an oil geologist in Mississippi, searching for clues to his love-at-first sight response to the Yaak. As he describes his deep immersion in this bountiful land as a hunter, hiker, artist, and environmentalist, he . . . shares his anguish over the clear-cutting of woods, and chronicles the hard work of wilderness advocacy and the virulent hatred it arouses. Versed in paradox, Bass is bracing in his candor about how difficult it will be to change our destructive ways, and incandescent in his reasoned call to preserve the few remaining unspoiled places." Booklist

Baszile, Jennifer

The **Black** girl next door; a memoir. Simon & Schuster 2009 310p il $25   **92**

1. African Americans -- Social conditions 2. Biography, Individual 3. College teachers 4. Historians 5. Memoirists
ISBN 978-1-4165-4327-5; 1-4165-4327-9
LC 2008-12867

"The Baszile family's move to an exclusive white suburb in Palos Verde, California, was the culmination of the parents' striving for a racially integrated, middle-class life. For their daughters, it meant isolation and coping with the occasional racial slurs that went along with the advantages of suburban life. Their parents veered between an aggressive integration strategy and an equally aggressive strategy to keep their daughters socially connected to other black teens. . . . This is an absorbing look behind the facade of one black family's striving for integration and the American dream." Booklist

Bate, Jonathan

John Clare: a biography. Farrar, Straus & Giroux 2003 648p il map $40   **92**

1. Authors 2. Poets
ISBN 0-374-17990-5
LC 2003-44063

This biography "succeeds splendidly . . . not only making generous use of Clare's own wonderful prose and verse but adding historical perspective and a constant, intelligent probing which amount almost to a dialogue with Clare's view of himself." Times Lit Suppl

Includes bibliographical references

Beah, Ishmael

★ A **long** way gone; memoirs of a boy soldier. Farrar, Straus & Giroux 2007 229p map $22; pa $12   **92**

1. Children and war 2. Memoirists 3. Refugees 4. Social activists 5. Soldiers
ISBN 978-0-374-10523-5; 0-374-95191-8; 978-0-374-53126-3 pa; 0-374-53126-9 pa
LC 2006-17101

"In 1993, when the author was twelve, rebel forces attacked his home town, in Sierra Leone, and he was separated from his parents. For months, he straggled through the war-torn countryside, starving and terrified, until he was taken under the wing of a Shakespeare-spouting lieutenant in the government army. Soon, he was being fed amphetamines and trained to shoot an AK-47. . . . Beah's memoir documents his transformation from a child into a hardened, brutally efficient soldier who high-fived his fellow-recruits after they slaughtered their enemies—often boys their own age—and who 'felt no pity for anyone.'" New Yorker

Beasley, Sandra

Don't kill the birthday girl; tales from an allergic life. Crown Publishers 2011 229p il $23; ebook $11.99   **92**

1. Authors 2. Food allergy 3. Poets
ISBN 978-0-307-58811-1; 978-0-307-58813-5 ebook
LC 2010043724

"If you didn't have sympathy for this relatively new generation of sufferers, you will after Beasley's book. . . . The emotional stuff is the best—from worrying about kissing boys who may have eaten forbidden foods, to considering the implications of having kids who'll have to wash their hands before hugging their mother." Maclean's

Becker, Suzy

I had brain surgery, what's your excuse? an illustrated memoir. Workman Pub 2003 282p il $19.95   **92**

1. AIDS activists 2. Authors 3. Brain -- Surgery -- Patients -- Biography 4. Brain -- Surgery -- Patients -- Caricatures and cartoons 5. Brain -- Surgery -- Patients -- Humor 6. Cartoonists 7. Humorists 8. Illustrators 9. Memoirists 10. Nonfiction writers 11. Social activists
ISBN 0-7611-2478-0
LC 2003-60039

Becker "was suffering seizures but didn't tell anyone until a friend witnessed an incident. Eventually, she was scheduled for brain surgery to remove a tumor. Writing with the dry sense of humor that some of us rely on to make it through situations, Becker recalls her reactions to her medical problems, from liking the first doctor who gave her no bad news ('just stress') to the terror of the eventual diagnosis. Her descriptions of the surgery and its dreadful, but temporary, effects on her ability to speak, read, write, and draw make for especially compelling reading. . . . Becker has turned one person's experience into a universal story of family, healing, and the return to creativity." Libr J

Belafonte, Harry

My song; a memoir. with Michael Shnayerson. Alfred A. Knopf 2011 469p il   **92**

1. Actors 2. African American singers 3. Singers 4. Social activists

ISBN 9780307272263; 9780307700483

LC 2011014602

The popular singer and former UNICEF Goodwill Ambassador shares the story of his life and career, from his impoverished childhood in Harlem and Jamaica and his racial barrier-breaking career to his commitment to numerous civil causes.

The author "covers his public career as an American entertainment icon (which solidified with his 1956 album, Calypso) and his interactions with many politicians and celebrities, e.g., Paul Robeson, Poitier, Marlon Brando, and Robert Kennedy, among many others. How these different strands interweave—the anger generated by the poverty and racial discrimination of his early years, the socially conscious reformer, and the well-respected entertainer—make for a potent memoir of our times." Libr J

Bell, Laura

Claiming ground. Alfred A. Knopf 2010 241p $24.95   **92**

1. Conservationists 2. Memoirists 3. Ranch life 4. Shepherds

ISBN 978-0-307-27288-1

LC 2009-29644

"After college, a Kentucky girl spends a summer in Wyoming to find herself and regroup. Thirty years later, she's still there. In this memoir, Bell vividly depicts her life out West, starting with her first job herding sheep—an occupation usually done by men. She goes on to write about her life as a ranch hand, masseuse, housewife, stepmother, and forest ranger, mixing work experiences with touching and poignant accounts of family and friends. . . . Bell here turns in satisfying reading for ranching enthusiasts, memoir fanatics, and anyone who likes to get lost in stories about rural life and nature's beauty." Libr J

Bell, Madison Smartt

★ **Toussaint** Louverture; a biography. Pantheon Books 2007 333p map $27   **92**

1. Biography, Individual 2. Generals 3. Revolutionaries

ISBN 978-0-375-42337-6; 0-375-42337-0

LC 2006-45848

This is a biography of the Haitian leader.

"This is the best biography of Toussaint yet, in large part because Bell does not shy away from the man's contradictions." N Y Times Book Rev

Includes bibliographical references

Bellow, Saul

Saul Bellow; letters. edited by Benjamin Taylor. Viking 2010 571p il $35   **92**

1. Authors 2. Authors, American 3. Biography, Individual 4. Dramatists 5. Nobel laureates for literature 6. Novelists 7. Short story writers

ISBN 978-0-670-02221-2; 0-670-02221-7

LC 2010-22395

"Collected for the first time, Bellow's letters offer an alluring backstory to the Chicago-bred imagination that created The Adventures of Augie March, Herzog, Humboldt's Gift and won the Nobel Prize. Like the fiction, the missives can be brilliant, glistening, scathing, boring, funny, generous, probing and always genuinely human. . . . The correspondents throughout are friends, lovers, wives, agents and publishers. Among the dozens of major literary figures with whom Bellow corresponded were William Faulkner, Bernard Malamud, Edmund Wilson, John Berryman, Ralph Ellison, Robert Penn Warren, Philip Roth and Martin Amis. While nothing can substitute for a Bellow novel, Letters offers a strong salve to those who miss his familiar voice. The range of interests, battles fought and art created reflected here is Olympian. Yet the cauldron for much of it was the everyday streets of Chicago." Chicago Sun-Times

Berg, A. Scott

Kate remembered. Putnam 2003 370p il $25.95; pa $15   **92**

1. Actors

ISBN 0-399-15164-8; 0-425-19909-6 pa

LC 2003-545232

In this posthumous biography, the author reveals "details about such pivotal events as the death of her brother by hanging, her relationships with powerful men like Howard Hughes and John Ford, and her slow, sad decline. . . . Berg's writing is so intimate that readers may feel they are hiding behind a curtain as they listen to the stories he elicits from his subject. Kate herself comes across pretty much the way she did on screen: bossy, courageous, and self-involved." Booklist

Berger, William

Puccini without excuses; a refreshing reassessment of the world's most popular composer. Vintage Books 2005 471p pa $16   **92**

1. Composers 2. Opera

ISBN 978-1-4000-7778-6; 1-4000-7778-8

LC 2005-46157

The author "sets Puccini within his times before discussing the circumstances of each opera's premiere and famous interpreters of the roles, providing character lists and synopses and fleshing all this out with musical commentary. Chapters on opera production and the genre's relation to film are useful. . . Berger's lucid yet hardly dispassionate views are designed to elicit strong reactions, so this is not the first place one should go for an unbiased introduction to the composer's oeuvre. But the author's grounding information is helpful for the novice, and he refers to some of the current authoritative sources." Libr J

Bergreen, Laurence

Marco Polo; from Venice to Xanadu. Knopf 2007 415p il map $28.95; pa $16.95   **92**

1. Biography, Individual 2. Explorers 3. Mongols -- History 4. Travel writers 5. Travelers 6. Voyages and travels

ISBN 978-1-4000-4345-3; 1-4000-4345-3; 978-1-4000-7880-6 pa; 1-4000-7880-6 pa

LC 2007-21860

This is a biography of the Venetian explorer.

The author "gives a full-blooded rendition of Polo's astonishing journey. It is richly researched and vividly conveyed." Washington Post Book World

Includes bibliographical references (p. 383-391)

Berlin, Edward A.

King of ragtime: Scott Joplin and his era. Oxford Univ. Press 1994 334p il hardcover o.p. pa $21.50 **92**

1. Composers 2. Jazz musicians 3. Pianists

ISBN 0-19-510108-1 pa

LC 93-28318

"Essential in any library concerned with American music." Booklist

Includes bibliographical references

Bernstein, Burton

★ **Leonard** Bernstein; American original; how a modern renaissance man transformed music and the world during his New York Philharmonic years, 1943-1976. [by] Burton Bernstein and Barbara B. Haws. HarperCollins 2008 223p il $29.95 **92**

1. Composers 2. Composers -- United States 3. Conductors (Music) 4. Musicians

ISBN 978-0-06-153786-8; 0-06-153786-1

LC 2008-13702

"A flat-out wonderful book." Booklist

Bernstein, Carl

A **woman** in charge; the life of Hillary Rodham Clinton. Alfred A. Knopf 2007 628p il $27.95 **92**

1. Biography, Individual 2. Lawyers 3. Presidential candidates 4. Secretaries of state 5. Senators 6. Spouses of presidents

ISBN 978-0-375-40766-6; 0-375-40766-9

LC 2007-17472

The author "offers a three-dimensional portrait of a person with enduring strengths (discipline, tenacity, a sustaining religious faith) and weaknesses (excessive secrecy, a tendency to self-righteousness and a habit of nursing grudges). . . . Bernstein almost always finds new facts and telling details. [His] account benefits enormously from remarkably candid on-the-record assessments of both Clintons by intimates such as close friend Jim Blair and Betsey Wright, Clinton's gubernatorial chief of staff in Arkansas." Los Angeles Times Book Rev

Includes bibliographical references

Bernstein, Richard B.

Thomas Jefferson; [by] R.B. Bernstein. Oxford University Press 2003 253p il hardcover o.p. pa $15.95 **92**

1. Architects 2. Essayists 3. Presidents 4. Presidents -- United States 5. Vice-presidents

ISBN 0-19-516911-5; 978-0-19-518130-2 pa; 0-19-518130-1 pa

LC 2003-5556

The author "provides a . . . view not of Jefferson the politician, but of the man whose ideas changed the world and provided the US with a sense of purpose. This short biography provides a judicious synthesis of the prevailing scholarship on the third president and explores more deeply

his views on government and union, slavery (revealing what is known about the Sally Hemings affair and what cannot yet be determined), and debt. . . . Its concise form, limited notes, and evenhanded style will appeal to general readers seeking insight into an incredibly complex historical figure." Choice

Includes bibliographical references

Berr, Helene

The **journal** of Helene Berr; translated from the French by David Bellos, with an introduction and an essay by David Bellos, and afterword by Mariette Job. Weinstein Books 2008 307p il map $24.95 **92**

1. Diarists 2. Holocaust victims 3. Holocaust, 1933-1945 -- Personal narratives 4. Jews -- France

ISBN 978-1-60286-064-3; 1-60286-064-5

This diary of a young Sorbonne graduate who died at Bergen-Belsen "recounts the experiences and private thoughts of the 21-year-old daughter of a prominent Jewish family as she and those she loved suffered the indignities of life under the Occupation prior to their arrest and ultimate deportation and death. . . . The volume includes useful annotations as well as a postscript that places the plight of French Jewry within historical context." Libr J

Includes bibliographical references

Berrigan, Ted

Dear Sandy, hello; letters from Ted to Sandy Berrigan. edited by Sandy Berrigan and Ron Padgett. Coffee House Press 2010 310p il pa $19.95 **92**

1. Authors 2. Biography, Individual 3. Poets 4. Poets, American

ISBN 978-1-56689-249-0; 1-56689-249-X

LC 2010-16258

"In addition to the letters, this collection contains never-before-published reproductions from A Book of Poetry for Sandy, featuring Berrigan's cutouts, drawings, photographs of fellow poets and artists, and excerpts from poems that eventually became The Sonnets." Publisher's note

Beyer, Kurt W.

★ **Grace** Hopper and the invention of the information age. MIT Press 2009 398p il $27.95 **92**

1. Admirals 2. Biography, Individual 3. COBOL (Computer program language) 4. Computer programming 5. Computer scientists

ISBN 978-0-262-01310-9

LC 2008-44229

This is a biography of the computer programmer who "abandoned academia to serve her country in the Navy after Pearl Harbor. . . . Hopper made herself 'one of the boys' in Howard Aiken's wartime Computation Laboratory at Harvard, then moved on to the Eckert and Mauchly Computer Corporation. . . . . Hopper's greatest technical achievement was to create the tools that would allow humans to communicate with computers in terms other than ones and zeroes." (Publisher's note) Index.

"In Beyer's fascinating mix of biography and technological history, Grace Hopper comes vividly to life as a navy admiral who launched the art of computer programming." Booklist

Includes bibliographical references

Bhutto, Benazir

★ **Reconciliation**; Islam, democracy, and the West. HarperCollins 2008 328p $27.95   **92**
1. Biography, Individual 2. Islam -- Middle East 3. Islam and politics 4. Political leaders 5. Prime ministers 6. Prime ministers -- Pakistan
ISBN 978-0-06-156758-2; 0-06-156758-2

This "is a book of enormous intelligence, courage and clarity. . . . Washington should arrange to have the portions of the book about Islam republished as a separate volume and translated into several languages. It would do more to win the battle of ideas within Islam than anything an American president could ever say." N Y Times Book Rev

Includes bibliographical references

Biddle, Daniel R.

Tasting freedom; Octavius Catto and the battle for equality in Civil War America. [by] Daniel R. Biddle [and] Murray Dubin. Temple University Press 2010 616p il $35; e-book $35   **92**
1. African American athletes 2. African American educators 3. African Americans -- Biography 4. African Americans -- Civil rights -- Pennsylvania -- Philadelphia 5. Baseball -- Biography 6. Biography, Individual 7. Civil rights movements -- Pennsylvania -- Philadelphia 8. Political activists
ISBN 978-1-59213-465-6; 978-1-59213-467-0 e-book
LC 2009049276

This is a biography of 19th-century civil rights activist and baseball player "Octavius Catto of Philadelphia. Catto was a part of the city's black intelligentsia and a vigorous proponent of equal rights. . . . Catto became a martyr to his cause when, at age 32, he was gunned down in Philadelphia's 1871 election-day riot. . . . [The authors] present a clear and compelling portrait of this significant early civil rights activist; they also present a thoughtful assessment of how Catto's efforts relate to the modern black civil rights movement." Choice

Includes bibliographical references

Biddle, Wayne

Dark side of the moon; Wernher von Braun, the Third Reich, and the space race. W.W. Norton 2009 220p il map $25.95   **92**
1. Aerospace engineers 2. Biography, Individual 3. NASA officials 4. Rocketry 5. Scientists 6. Space race 7. Space vehicles -- Design 8. World War, 1939-1945 -- Science -- Germany
ISBN 978-0-393-05910-6; 0-393-05910-3
LC 2009-15572

"A stern, prosecutorial portrait of the famous German American rocketeer." Booklist

Includes bibliographical references

Bigsby, Christopher

Arthur Miller; 1915-1962. [by] Christopher Bigsby. Harvard University Press 2009 739p il $35   **92**
1. Authors 2. Dramatists 3. Dramatists, American 4. Screenwriters
ISBN 978-0-674-03505-8; 0-674-03505-4
LC 2009-2489

This is a biography of the American playwright.

"A richly detailed, revealing look at the making of a playwright and a man." Kirkus

Includes bibliographical references

Bilal, Wafaa

Shoot an Iraqi; art, life and resistance under the gun. by Wafaa Bilal and Kari Lydersen. City Lights 2008 177p il pa $16.95   **92**
1. Artists 2. Iraq War, 2003- -- Art and the war 3. Performance artists 4. Video artists
ISBN 978-0-8728-6491-7; 0-8728-6491-X
LC 2008-20487

The creator of 'Domestic Tension,' an unsettling interactive performance piece that speaks to the horrors of life in a conflict zone, reveals his experiences growing up under Saddam Hussein's rule.

"A powerful and demanding read, that is, frankly, a literary punch to the gut." Booklist

Binyon, T. J.

★ **Pushkin**: a biography. Knopf 2003 xxix, 727p il maps $35; pa $20   **92**
1. Authors 2. Novelists 3. Poets 4. Short story writers
ISBN 1-4000-4110-4; 1-4000-7652-8 pa
LC 2003-112113

The author argues that Pushkin's "political views and rebellious temper were a continual source of trouble, inviting criticism and condemnation his entire life and eventually ending it in 1837 when he was fatally wounded in a duel with George D'Anthes. . . . A stunning achievement, this thorough biography is sure to become the definitive account of Pushkin's life for years to come and will appeal to the scholar and general reader alike." Libr J

Includes bibliographical references

Bird, Kai

★ **American** Prometheus; the triumph and tragedy of J. Robert Oppenheimer. [by] Kai Bird and Martin J. Sherwin. Knopf 2005 721p il hardcover o.p. pa $18.95   **92**
1. Biography, Individual 2. College teachers 3. Government officials 4. Physicists
ISBN 0-375-41202-6; 0-375-72626-8 pa
LC 2004-61535

The authors explore Oppenheimer's life "from his youth as a child prodigy through his radical political activities in the 1930s, and on to the Manhattan Project and its political fallout. The humanity of the troubled man behind the porkpie hat emerges on every page of this unquestionably definitive account." Booklist

Includes bibliographical references

Biskind, Peter

Star; how Warren Beatty seduced America. Simon & Schuster 2010 627p il $30   **92**
1. Actors 2. Biography, Individual 3. Motion picture directors 4. Motion picture industry -- United States 5. Motion picture producers
ISBN 978-0-7432-4658-3; 0-7432-4658--6
LC 2009-22225

"Biskind brings his historian's acumen to bear on the production of era-defining triumphs like Bonnie and Clyde (1967), Shampoo (1975) and Reds (1981), as well as notorious flops like Ishtar (1987), Love Affair (1994) and Town & Country (2001), and his accounts are full of juicy gossip and intriguing insights into the actor's psychology. . . . A gripping portrait of a difficult talent." Kirkus

Includes bibliographical references

Biskupic, Joan

Sandra Day O'Connor; how the first woman on the Supreme Court became its most influential justice. Ecco 2005 419p il $26.95   **92**

1. Biography, Individual 2. Supreme Court justices

ISBN 0-06-059018-1

LC 2005-52103

The author "offers an insightful biography of perhaps the most influential associate justice in recent history." Libr J

Includes bibliographical references

Bix, Herbert P.

★ **Hirohito** and the making of modern Japan. HarperCollins Pubs. 2000 800p il maps hardcover o.p. pa $18   **92**

1. Emperors 2. Emperors -- Japan -- Biography

ISBN 0-06-093130-2 pa

LC 99-89427

"In 1945, fearing that the Japanese would resist American occupation unless the Emperor ordered them to obey, General MacArthur colluded with Hirohito in maintaining that the sovereign had been powerless to control Japan's military leaders. . . . {Bix}, uses newly available sources to argue that Hirohito was a war criminal. An imperialist whose policies reflected his belief in the racial superiority of the Japanese, Hirohito governed by manipulation for almost two decades, and used the threat of Soviet Communism to justify domestic repression and soaring military budgets. The author's virtuoso scholarship and accessible narrative invite us into Hirohito's world." New Yorker

Includes bibliographical references

Bjork, Daniel W.

B.F. Skinner; a life. American Psychological Assn. 1997 298p il pa $19.95   **92**

1. Psychologists

ISBN 1-55798-416-6

LC 96-40385

This is a biography of the psychologist known for his utopian novel Walden Two, his book Beyond freedom and dignity, and his behaviorist theories

"Bjork places Skinner squarely in the context of the US social, technological, and political history. . . . Although heavily documented, Bjork's book is very readable because documentation is in endnotes. A handsome, well-indexed work, with an excellent bibliography." Choice

Black Elk

Black Elk speaks; being the life story of a holy man of the Oglala Sioux. [as told through] John G. Neihardt; foreword by Vine Deloria, Jr.; with illustrations by Standing Bear; essays by Alexis N. Petri

and Lori Utecht. University of Nebraska Press 2004 xxix, 270p il map pa $14.95   **92**

1. Indian leaders 2. Native Americans -- Biography 3. Oglala Indians 4. Shamans

ISBN 0-8032-8385-7

LC 2004-12692

The Indian whose life story this is, was born in 1863. He was a famous warrior and hunter in his youth, and became a practicing medicine man among his people. Of him Neihardt says, "As an indubitable seer, he seemed to represent the consciousness of the Plains Indian more fully than any other I had ever known."

This "is about as near as you can get to seeing life and death, war and religion, through an Indian's eyes." Outlook

Black, Conrad M.

Richard M. Nixon; a life in full. [by] Conrad Black. PublicAffairs 2007 1152p il $40   **92**

1. Members of Congress 2. Nonfiction writers 3. Presidents 4. Presidents -- United States 5. Senators 6. Vice-presidents

ISBN 978-1-58648-519-1; 1-58648-519-9

LC 2007-34530

This is a biography of the thirty-seventh president.

"Black's superb volume, incorporating much new research, is an important and worthy addition to the literature." Publ Wkly

Includes bibliographical references

Blackburn, Julia

Old man Goya. Pantheon Bks. 2002 239p il $23; pa $13   **92**

1. Artists 2. Artists -- Spain -- Biography 3. Etchers 4. Painters 5. Printmakers

ISBN 0-375-40611-5; 0-375-70579-1 pa

LC 2002-280534

The author "focuses on the second half of Goya's long and amazingly productive life, beginning with the devastating illness that left him deaf at age 47. . . . {She} not only empathetically imagines the sea change caused by Goya's abrupt sensory loss, and convincingly assesses its impact on his work, she also conjures up the artists's mise-en-scène, from the frenetic streets of Madrid to the sanctuary of the studio, the bizarreness of the court of Charles IV, the horrors of famine and war, Goya's long marriage, and, after his wife's death, late-life relationship with a much younger woman. . . . {This is a} vital, inventively participatory portrait of a master portraitist and observer of life." Booklist

Includes bibliographical references

★ **With** Billie. Pantheon Books 2005 354p $25   **92**

1. African American singers 2. Biography, Individual 3. Blues musicians 4. Singers

ISBN 0-375-40610-7

LC 2004-58661

This "oral biography of Billie Holiday is based on interviews that researcher Linda Kuehl did in the late 1970s with more than 150 people who knew and worked with the singer. . . . Rather than her recordings, the emphasis is on the events and issues surrounding the music. . . . This is in many

ways a joyful portrait of a woman determined to go her own way but, in the end, unable to fulfill her own dreams." Libr J
Includes bibliographical references

The **three** of us; a family story. Pantheon Books 2008 313p il $26 **92**
1. Artists 2. Authors 3. Biographers 4. Biography, Individual 5. Essayists 6. Family life 7. Novelists 8. Painters 9. Parents 10. Poets
ISBN 978-0-375-42474-8; 0-375-42474-1
LC 2007-50147
This is a "strangely compelling memoir." Publ Wkly

Blainey, Geoffrey
Sea of dangers; Captain Cook and his rivals in the South Pacific. Ivan R. Dee 2009 322p il map $27.50 **92**
1. Explorers 2. Naval officers 3. Ship captains 4. Travel writers 5. Voyages around the world
ISBN 978-1-56663-825-8; 1-56663-825-9
LC 2008-52623
"An excellent work of popular history that recounts the exploits of men who dramatically expanded our knowledge of the globe." Booklist
Includes bibliographical references

Blair, Tony
A **journey**; my political life. Alfred A. Knopf 2010 699p il $35; ebook $35 **92**
1. Biography, Individual 2. Members of Parliament 3. Political leaders 4. Prime ministers 5. Prime ministers -- Great Britain
ISBN 978-0-307-26983-6; 978-0-307-59487-7 ebook
LC 2010-28262
These are the memoirs of the British Labour Party politician who served as the prime minister of the United Kingdom from 1997 to 2007.
"Without delving too deeply into his personal life, . . . [Blair] gives the reader a good sense of his role not just as a public figure but also as a son, husband, and father. . . . Particulars of British party politics might elude some American readers, but the narrative keeps flowing. Essential for readers of current British politics." Libr J
Includes bibliographical references

Bloom, John
There you have it; the life, legacy, and legend of Howard Cosell. University of Massachusetts Press 2010 220p il $80; pa $24.95 **92**
1. Lawyers 2. Sportscasters 3. Television broadcasting of sports 4. Television personalities
ISBN 978-1-55849-836-5; 1-55849-836-2; 978-1-55849-837-2 pa; 1-55849-837-0 pa
LC 2010037284
"Many of the contradictions of his character and the finer intricacies of his legacy are teased out in this carefully observed portrait." Publ Wkly
Includes bibliographical references

Blunt, Judy
Breaking clean. Knopf 2002 303p hardcover o.p. pa $13 **92**
1. Authors 2. Memoirists 3. Ranch life -- Montana 4. Ranchers 5. Women ranchers -- Montana -- Biography
ISBN 0-375-70130-3 pa
LC 2001-29861
The author chronicles the hardships she endured as a ranch wife, mother, and laborer in rural Montana, and how she left it all, including her marriage, to get herself a college education and become a writer.
Blunt has a "keen and poetic awareness, steely candor, and commanding storytelling skills." Booklist

Blunt, Wilfrid
Linnaeus, the compleat naturalist; with an introduction by William T. Stearn. Princeton Univ. Press 2002 264p il maps $35 **92**
1. Botanists 2. Botany -- Sweden 3. Writers on science
ISBN 0-691-09636-8
This biography traces the Swedish scientist's life from his days as a poor student at Lund University through his scientific achievements and academic career at Uppsala.

Bogle, Donald
Heat wave; the life and career of Ethel Waters. HarperCollins 2011 624p il $26.99 **92**
1. Actors 2. African American singers 3. Biography, Individual 4. Singers
ISBN 978-0-06-124173-4; 0-06-124173-3
LC 2010-29230
"In this powerful biography, Bogle recovers the rich fullness of singer Ethel Waters's life (1896–1977). In vivid though often exhausting detail, Bogle traces Waters's rise from the poverty of her surroundings in Chester, Pa., through her early musical successes in Harlem in the 1920s and 1930s to her film and Broadway career and her later religious conversion as her health declined." Publ Wkly
Includes bibliographical references

Bolkovac, Kathryn
The **whistleblower**; sex trafficking, military contractors, and one woman's fight for justice. [by] Kathryn Bolkovac with Cari Lynn. Palgrave Macmillan 2011 240p il map $25; pa $16; ebook $11.99 **92**
1. Human rights activists 2. Juvenile prostitution 3. United Nations employees 4. Whistle blowing
ISBN 978-0-230-10802-8; 978-0-230-11522-4 pa; 978-0-230-11563-7 ebook
LC 2010-23196
This story "bristles with disturbing details and heartfelt compassion." Publ Wkly

Bolt, Rodney
The **librettist** of Venice; the remarkable life of Lorenzo Da Ponte, Mozart's poet, Casanova's friend, and Italian opera's impresario in America. Bloomsbury Pub. 2006 428p il $29.95 **92**
1. Authors 2. Biography, Individual 3. Librettists 4.

Poets
ISBN 1-59691-118-2

LC 2006-5713

"Reading Bolt's lively narrative of Da Ponte's life from the ghetto of Venice to the sparkling opera houses of Europe is pure pleasure." Publ Wkly

Borneman, Walter R.

Polk; the man who transformed the presidency and America. Random House 2008 422p il map $30 **92**

1. Governors 2. Members of Congress 3. Presidents 4. Presidents -- United States 5. Speakers of the House
ISBN 978-1-4000-6560-8

LC 2007-14040

The author "presents a birth-death biography of Polk. . . . Borneman has a pleasing style and makes fine use of primary sources that all demonstrate why Polk is habitually ranked as one of the ten best presidents by historians." Libr J

Includes bibliographical references

Bostridge, Mark

Florence Nightingale; the making of an icon. Farrar, Straus and Giroux 2008 646p il $35 **92**

1. Nonfiction writers 2. Nurses
ISBN 978-0-374-15665-7; 0-374-15665-4

LC 2008-31424

Bostridge presents a "well-researched, and comprehensive biography of Nightingale, drawing heavily on letters, diaries, and other primary sources in a successful effort to create a balanced and authentic portrait of the woman, not the myth. Beginning with moving depictions of Nightingale's struggles to be allowed to pursue her calling despite her family's objections, Bostridge skillfully illuminates the spiritual and philosophical motivations that drove Nightingale's impassioned and lifelong dedication to the causes of nursing and public health reform." Libr J

Includes bibliographical references

Boswell, James

The life of Samuel Johnson; with an introduction by Claude Rawson. Random House 1992 liii, 127p il $30 **92**

1. Lexicographers 2. Literary critics
ISBN 0-679-41717-6

LC 92-52915

"The most famous biography in the English language. It is an intimate and minute delineation of the great lexicographer's life, character and person, enlivened with small-talk, gossip and bits of familiar correspondence. It is also an admirable portrayal of the society of which Johnson was the outstanding figure." Pratt Alcove

Includes bibliographical references

Bourdain, Anthony

Kitchen confidential; adventures in the culinary underbelly. Updated ed; Harper Perennial 2007 312, 22p pa $15.99 **92**

1. Authors 2. Cooks 3. Memoirists 4. Novelists 5. Television personalities
ISBN 978-0-06-089922-6; 0-06-089922-0

LC 2007-280057

"This is one bitter, nasty, searing, hard-to-swallow piece of work. But if you can choke the thing down, you'll probably wake up grinning in the middle of the night. . . . In a style partaking of Hunter S. Thompson, Iggy Pop and a little Jonathan Swift, Bourdain gleefully rips through the scenery to reveal private backstage horrors little dreamed of by the trusting public. . . . To a world infested with synthesized romance, candlelit illusions and sentimental piety, 'Kitchen Confidential' offers a nice palate-clearing taste of poison." N Y Times Book Rev

Medium raw; a bloody valentine to the world of food and the people who cook. Ecco Press 2010 281p $26.99 **92**

1. Authors 2. Cooks 3. Gastronomy 4. Memoirists 5. Novelists 6. Television personalities
ISBN 978-0-06-171894-6; 0-06-171894-7

This book mixes personal memoir with travelogues and ruminations on such matters as the degradation of the American hamburger, the dumbing down of the Food Network, the tedium of multicourse tasting menus and the rise of food gurus such as David Chang. . . . Mr. Bourdain is a vivid, bawdy and often foul-mouthed writer. He thrills in the attack, but he is also an enthusiast who writes well about things he holds dear. His detailed reporting on the backroom lives of restaurant employees is terrific. Wall Street J

Bowles, Hamish

Jacqueline Kennedy; the White House Years: selections from the John F. Kennedy Library and Museum. {compiled and edited by} Hamish Bowles; with essays by Arthur Schlesinger, Jr., Hamish Bowles, and James Wagner. Bulfinch Press 2001 198p il $50 **92**

1. Editors 2. Socialites 3. Spouses of presidents
ISBN 0-8212-2745-9

LC 00-66237

The selections "examine in detail different aspects of Jackie's life, including the inauguration, her White House style, her travels, and her hats, as well as other topics. . . . Viewers can expect a sense of nostalgia, a swelling of pride, and a tightening of the throat. A time line of Jackie's life is appended." Booklist

Boyd, Gerald M.

My Times in black and white; race and power at the New York Times. [by] Gerald M. Boyd; afterword by Robin D. Stone. Lawrence Hill Books 2010 402p il **92**

1. Biography, Individual 2. Journalists 3. Newspaper editors
ISBN 1-55652-952-X; 978-1-55652-952-8

LC 2009-35506

This is a memoir of Boyd's experiences as a reporter and editor at The St. Louis Post-Dispatch and The New York Times. Index.

The author "has written a good book filled with ill feeling toward the Times, many of its editors, and a variety of colleagues who turned against him under pressure or simply because they wanted him to fail and be damned. . . . Lovers of newspaper gossip will find it delightfully indiscreet about self-serving treacheries hatched in the newsroom by people simultaneously engaged in high-minded pursuit of all the news that's fit to print." N Y Rev Books

Boyd, Valerie

Wrapped in rainbows; the life of Zora Neale Hurston. Scribner 2003 527p il $30   **92**
1. African American authors 2. African American women -- Biography 3. Authors 4. Dramatists 5. Folklorists 6. Memoirists 7. Novelists 8. Short story writers
ISBN 0-684-84230-0

LC 2002-17011

This is a biography of the folklorist and author of Their Eyes Were Watching God (1937), Tell My Horse (1938), Dust Tracks on a Road (1942) and Seraph on the Suwanee (1948).

"As the author adeptly and passionately analyzes Hurston's revolutionary books, intense spirituality, and myriad adventures, Hurston emerges in all her splendor—not only smarter, tougher, and more dazzlingly alive than most people but also freer." Booklist

Includes bibliographical references

Boylan, Jennifer Finney

I'm looking through you; growing up haunted. Broadway Books 2008 270p il $23.95   **92**
1. Authors 2. Authors, American 3. Ghosts 4. Novelists 5. Short story writers 6. Transsexualism 7. Transsexuals 8. Young adult authors
ISBN 978-0-7679-2174-9; 0-7679-2174-7

LC 2007-19199

The author, a male-to-female transgendered person, "uses the metaphor of 'being haunted' throughout to illustrate not only her boyhood experiences but also the memories that have shaped her as a person as she struggled with her gender identity throughout most of her life. . . . Her writing style is witty, self-deprecating, entertaining, and often poignant, especially when describing family and friends who have passed away. An adventure to read, this is highly recommended for all libraries." Libr J

Bozza, Anthony

Whatever you say I am; the life and times of Eminem. Crown Pubs. 2003 278p il $23; pa $12.95   **92**
1. Actors 2. Rap music 3. Rap musicians 4. Recording producers 5. Songwriters
ISBN 1-400-05059-6; 1-400-05380-3 pa

LC 2003-8923

"It is Bozza's relationship with Eminem that lends credibility to this bio, as well as his ability to fold personal reminiscence into longer analytical sections on Eminem's life, the Detroit rap scene and pop culture. Bozza's unprecedented access to Mathers then and now has given rise to one of the only fully honest accounts of the now brilliant star." Publ Wkly

Includes bibliographical references

Brackett, Elizabeth

Pay to play; how Rod Blagojevich turned political corruption into a national sideshow. Ivan R. Dee 2009 247p il $24.95   **92**
1. Governors 2. Members of Congress 3. Political corruption 4. State legislators
ISBN 978-1-56663-834-0

LC 2009-10566

"Blagojevich, the well-coiffed, Elvis-loving former Illinois governor, gained national disrepute for his alleged attempts to sell the vacated U.S. Senate seat of President Barack Obama. . . . Brackett details the long and rocky road that brought Blagojevich to infamy. . . . A thorough and concise look at political corruption and the brazen man behind the scandal." Booklist

Bradford, Sarah

Lucrezia Borgia; life, love, and death in Renaissance Italy. Viking 2004 xxiv, 421p il map $27.95; pa $16   **92**
1. Patrons of the arts
ISBN 0-670-03353-7; 0-14-303595-9 pa

LC 2004-54881

The author "presents Lucrezia as an intelligent noblewoman, powerless to defy her family's patriarchal order, yet an enlightened ruler in her own right as Duchess of Ferrara. . . . As a project designed to distinguish the historical Lucrezia Borgia from the legend, Bradford's readable biography resoundingly succeeds." Publ Wkly

Includes bibliographical references

Brady, Frank

Endgame; Bobby Fischer's remarkable rise and fall--from America's brightest prodigy to the edge of madness. Crown 2010 402p il $25.99   **92**
1. Biography, Individual 2. Chess 3. Chess players
ISBN 978-0-307-46390-6; 0-307-46390-7

LC 2010-33840

"Brady's insightful biography of the legendary chess player focuses more on Fischer's life as a chess champion than on his much-publicized legal troubles and alleged psychological breakdowns. Brady first became friends with Fischer at a chess tournament when they were both children, and he combines a traditional biography with a personal memoir. . . . Brady is uniquely qualified to write this book. Not only is he a seasoned biographer and someone who knew Fischer on a personal level; he's also an accomplished chess player himself, able to convey the game's intricacies to the reader in a clear, uncomplicated manner." Booklist

Brady, Patricia

Martha Washington; an American life. Viking 2005 276p il $24.95; pa $15   **92**
1. Biography, Individual 2. Presidents' spouses -- United States 3. Spouses of presidents
ISBN 0-670-03430-4; 0-14-303713-7 pa

LC 2004-61242

"Brady's splendid biography offers a compelling new portrait of this passionate, committed founding mother who has unjustly been obscured by others, such as Abigail Adams." Publ Wkly

Includes bibliographical references

Bragg, Rick

The **prince** of Frogtown. Alfred A. Knopf 2008
255p $24   **92**
1. Authors 2. Biography, Individual 3. Father-son
relationship 4. Journalists 5. Memoirists 6. Stepfathers
ISBN 978-1-4000-4040-7; 1-4000-4040-X
LC 2007-38884

The author "merges his father's history of severe hardships and simple joys with a tale from the present: his own
relationship with his 10-year-old stepson. . . . [This book] is
lush with narratives about manhood, fathers and sons, families and the changing face of the rural South." Publ Wkly

Branch, Taylor

The **Clinton** tapes; wrestling history with the
president. Simon & Schuster 2009 707p $35; pa
$20   **92**
1. Biography, Individual 2. Governors 3. Presidents 4.
Presidents -- United States
ISBN 978-1-4165-4333-6; 1-4165-4333-3; 978-1-
4165-4334-3 pa; 1-4165-4334-1 pa

"Not everyone who begins it will finish Branch's book,
yet Clinton's remarks . . . contribute critically to the historical record and accordingly merit a place in most library
collections." Booklist

Brands, H. W.

★ **Andrew** Jackson; his life and times. Double-
day 2005 620p il map $35   **92**
1. Biography, Individual 2. Generals 3. Presidents 4.
Presidents -- United States
ISBN 0-385-50738-0; 978-0-385-50738-7
LC 2005-42178

This is a biography of the seventh president of the
United States.

This book "is a bracing, human portrait of both a remarkable man and of American democracy as it was transformed
from a 'government of the people' into a 'government by the
people.'" Publ Wkly
Includes bibliographical references

Traitor to his class; the privileged life and radical
presidency of Franklin Delano Roosevelt. Doubleday
2008 888p il $35   **92**
1. Biography, Individual 2. Columnists 3. Diplomats
4. Governors 5. Handicapped 6. Humanitarians 7.
New Deal, 1933-1939 8. Philatelists 9. Presidents
10. Presidents -- United States 11. Social activists 12.
Spouses of presidents 13. United Nations officials 14.
World War, 1939-1945 -- United States
ISBN 978-0-385-51958-8; 0-385-51958-3
LC 2008-15164

This is a study of Franklin D. Roosevelt's life and career.
"A thoroughly readable, scrupulously fair assessment
of the one president who could inspire a Mt. Rushmore
makeover." Kirkus
Includes bibliographical references

The **first** American: the life and times of Benjamin Franklin. Doubleday 2000 759p hardcover o.p.
pa $17   **92**
1. Authors 2. Diplomats 3. Inventors 4. Members

of Congress 5. Scientists 6. Statesmen 7. Statesmen
-- United States 8. Writers on science
ISBN 0-385-49540-4 pa
LC 00-27930

"Brands fills in disparate pockets of history (the importance of Cotton Mather in Boston, the intellectual enthusiasms of the Royal Society in London) with readable, unobtrusive scholarship. Perhaps he took as his model his unassuming subject, who treated his extraordinary achievements
in fields as diverse as science and diplomacy as if they were
ordinary. Franklin emerges as a man with a passion to add to
human happiness." New Yorker
Includes bibliographical references

Breitman, Richard

The **architect** of genocide; Himmler and the final solution. University Press of New England 1992
335p pa $30   **92**
1. Heads of state 2. National socialism 3. Nazi leaders
ISBN 0-87451-596-3; 978-0-87451-596-1
LC 92-53857

"This engrossing, detailed study constitutes a powerful refutation of revisionist scholars who claim that Hitler
did not plan the Final Solution in advance but instead improvised it out of either military or political frustration."
Publ Wkly
Includes bibliographical references

Brenner, Marie

Apples and oranges; my brother and me, lost and
found. Farrar, Straus & Giroux 2008 268p il $24;
pa $15   **92**
1. Biography, Individual 2. Cancer 3. Fruit growers 4.
Journalists 5. Lawyers
ISBN 978-0-374-17352-4; 0-374-17352-4; 978-0-312-
42880-8 pa; 0-312-42880-4 pa
LC 2008-08929

"In this elegiac memoir, the author, a reporter, applies
the same investigative skills that led to her exposé of the
tobacco industry and Enron to a more intimate subject: her
contentious relationship with her late brother. From an eccentric Jewish Texan family of compulsive record keepers—
their father maintained a four-page list of his life's achievements—Marie became a New York liberal, Carl a diehard
conservative who abandoned a legal career to farm apples.
As a teenager, he smashed his sister's Joan Baez records; as
an adult, given a diagnosis of terminal cancer, he informed
her via FedEx. Her attempts to smooth over their differences
by mastering the language of fruit (Carl often started conversations, 'I am going to give you a quiz') are at once comic
and tinged with regret." New Yorker

Breslin, Ed

Drinking with Miss Dutchie; a memoir. Thomas
Dunne Books 2011 274p $23.99   **92**
1. Alcoholism 2. Dogs 3. Editors 4. Memoirists 5.
Publishing executives
ISBN 978-0-312-61975-6
LC 2010-39302

"Breslin writes about the death of his cherished dog,
Miss Dutchie, and how, with her help, he succeeded in overcoming alcoholism. While not a dog-lover himself, in 1994

he bought Dutchie sight-unseen, as a surprise birthday gift for his wife. However, he freely admits that his motives were not entirely pure. 'I got Miss Dutchie to get Lynn off my back about my drinking,' he writes. Breslin had recently quit a decades-long career in publishing in an attempt to write a novel, and he did not expect to be spending his valuable time with a dog. . . . The story revolves around the dog who became the center of the childless couple's life, but the author also writes affectingly about his efforts to overcome addiction to alcohol and nicotine." Kirkus

Breslin, Jimmy

Branch Rickey. Viking 2010 147p $19.95 **92**
1. Baseball -- Biography 2. Baseball executives 3. Baseball managers 4. Biography, Individual
ISBN 978-0-670-02249-6; 0-670-02249-7
LC 2010-35008
"Breslin reveals much about the development of baseball, the Dodgers' last years in Brooklyn, and the struggle to overcome the national pastime's racism while tracing the life, deeds, and some (but not all) of Branch Rickey's warts. A breezy read, this 'Penguin Life' is nonetheless insightful, humorous, and biting at times as it traces how the man dubbed 'the Mahatma' by sportswriters emerged from obscurity as an Idaho lawyer to develop the baseball farm system, multiple MLB winners, Vero Beach spring training, the scientific teaching of skills, and the MLB expansion that brought New York the Mets." Libr J
Includes bibliographical references

I want to thank my brain for remembering me; a memoir. Little, Brown 1996 219p hardcover o.p. pa $12.95 **92**
1. Authors 2. Columnists 3. Nonfiction writers 4. Novelists
ISBN 0-316-11879-6 pa
LC 96-10488
"Confronting the possibility of death just past age 65 . . . Breslin memory-surfs through a troubled childhood and a lifetime in various journalistic trenches, from copyboy to columnist. . . . The book is full of family stories, political stories, and classic Breslin street stories, plus lots of details about brain operations from both patient's and surgeon's point of view." Booklist

Brian, Denis

The **Curies**; a biography of the most controversial family in science. Wiley 2005 438p il $30 **92**
1. Chemists 2. Nobel laureates for physics 3. Physicists
ISBN 0-471-27391-0
LC 2005-7001
This book "follows five generations of the Sklodowska-Curie-Joliot family. Beginning before Marie Sklodowska and Pierre Curie meet, Brian details their courtship and 11-year marriage, bringing the reader to the Curie dinner table and into the converted garden shed (replete with a leaking roof) where the Curies' work on polonium and radium transformed physics and won them two Nobel prizes. . . . Extremely well-done and highly recommended." Publ Wkly
Includes bibliographical references

Briggs, Julia

Virginia Woolf: an inner life. Harcourt 2005 527p il $30 **92**
1. Authors 2. Authors, English 3. Essayists 4. Novelists 5. Short story writers 6. Women authors
ISBN 0-15-101143-5
LC 2005-16048
"That this book is a must for Woolf fans goes without saying, but it is also a must for anyone interested in the nature of female consciousness at its most self-aware and the workings of artistic sensibility at their most illuminating." Publ Wkly
Includes bibliographical references

Brinkley, Alan

★ The **publisher**; Henry Luce and his American century. Alfred A. Knopf 2010 531p il $35 **92**
1. Biography, Individual 2. Journalism -- United States -- History -- 20th century 3. Journalists 4. Magazine editors 5. Magazine executives 6. Publishers and publishing
ISBN 978-0-679-41444-5; 0-679-41444-4
LC 2009-38834
"In this superb biography Alan Brinkley . . . has told the curiously depressing story of a brilliant man who got everything wrong, including so many of the things that mattered most to him. Mr Brinkley has an eye for both the telling detail and the broad sweep of Luce's role as the man who saw the need for a national news magazine and foresaw the American century." Economist
Includes bibliographical references

Brinkley, Douglas

The **wilderness** warrior; Theodore Roosevelt and the crusade for America. Harper 2009 940p il map $34.99 **92**
1. Biography, Individual 2. Conservation of natural resources 3. Conservation of natural resources -- United States -- History -- 20th century 4. Nature conservation 5. Presidents -- United States 6. Wilderness areas -- United States
ISBN 978-0-06-056528-2; 0-06-056528-4
This biography of the 26th president of the United States focuses on his interests and activities on behalf of conservation and nature.
The author "has absorbed a huge amount of research, but encyclopedic inclusiveness and repetition occasionally mar narrative movement. . . . But this book has Rooseveltian energy. It is largehearted, full of the vitality of its subject and a palpable love for the landscape it describes." N Y Times Book Rev
Includes bibliographical references

Broadwater, Jeff

★ **George** Mason, forgotten founder. University of North Carolina Press 2006 329p il $34.95 **92**
1. Biography, Individual 2. Colonial leaders 3. Constitutional history 4. Essayists 5. Plantation owners 6. Statesmen
ISBN 978-0-8078-3053-6; 0-8078-3053-4
LC 2006-10729

"Because Mason left little evidence of his private life, there are blurred edges in the portrait that Broadwater paints, but overall this is an exemplary biography: sympathetic but dispassionate, thorough but not cluttered, convincing in its interpretations and arguments. It leaves no doubt that Mason deserves to be returned to the esteem and reputation he enjoyed during his lifetime, but in no way is it hagiography." Washington Post Book World

Includes bibliographical references

Brock, Pope

Charlatan; America's most dangerous huckster, the man who pursued him, and the age of flimflam. Crown Publishers 2008 324p il   **92**

1. Biography, Individual 2. Broadcasters 3. Physicians 4. Quacks and quackery 5. Quacks and quackery -- United States 6. Swindlers

ISBN 0307339882; 9780307339881

LC 2007-10074

This is a biography of John Richard Brinkley. In 1917, Brinkley arrived in "Milford, Kansas. He set up a medical practice and introduced . . . [a] surgical method of using goat glands to restore the fading virility of local farmers. . . . Thousands of paying customers quickly turned 'Dr.' Brinkley into America's richest and most famous surgeon." (Publisher's note)

"Presentation is everything in telling this elaborate, many-faceted story. And Mr. Brock's has three outstanding virtues. First of all, he has a terrific ear for singling out quotations. . . . Second, he is selective. This fast-moving, light-stepping book takes care not to throw in extraneous detail. Third, his own voice is wry enough to compete with the actual Brinkley material, which is saying a great deal." N Y Times (Late N Y Ed)

Includes bibliographical references

Brodie, Fawn McKay

No man knows my history: the life of Joseph Smith, the Mormon prophet; by Fawn M. Brodie. 2nd ed rev and enl; Knopf 1971 499, xxp il hardcover o.p. pa $18   **92**

1. Mormon leaders 2. Mormons

ISBN 0-679-73054-0 pa

Taking as her title a phrase from a sermon by Joseph Smith himself, the author has attempted to discover as much of the truth concerning Joseph Smith and the beginnings of Mormonism, as can be found in an intensive research into documents, diaries, unpublished manuscripts, etc.

Brombert, Beth Archer

Edouard Manet; rebel in a frock coat. University of Chicago Press 1997 505p il pa $19.95   **92**

1. Artists 2. Artists, French 3. Painters

ISBN 0-226-07544-3; 978-0-226-07544-0

LC 97-3321

"To recount Manet's life, as Brombert has done in this elegant biography, is to tell the story of an enormously influential artist struggling to paint what he called 'the spirit of contemporaneity' while remaining committed to the conservative institutions of civil life—the very same institutions that shunned him." New Yorker

Includes bibliographical references

Brookhiser, Richard

Alexander Hamilton, American. Free Press 1999 240p il hardcover o.p. pa $14   **92**

1. Secretaries of the treasury 2. Statesmen

ISBN 0-684-86331-6 pa

LC 98-46846

This is a biography of the Secretary of the Treasury. Brookhiser discusses Hamilton's life, from his "teenage years in St. Croix and youth in Manhattan, through his formative years as Washington's aide during the Revolutionary War, to his role in the writing of the Constitution and the Federalist Papers, to his later careers as Secretary of the Treasury, lawyer, politician, and journalist." Natl Rev

Includes bibliographical references

Founding father: rediscovering George Washington. Free Press 1996 230p hardcover o.p. pa $14   **92**

1. Generals 2. Presidents 3. Presidents -- United States

ISBN 0-684-83142-2 pa

LC 95-50650

"Brookhiser's slim, graceful volume is readable in one sitting. His style is muscular and discursive, yet unaffectedly erudite." Christ Sci Monit

Includes bibliographical references

Right time, right place; coming of age with William F. Buckley, Jr. and the conservative movement. Basic Books 2009 262p $27.50   **92**

1. Authors 2. Biographers 3. Biography, Individual 4. Columnists 5. Conservatism 6. Conservatism -- United States 7. Historians 8. Journalists 9. Magazine editors 10. Novelists

ISBN 978-0-465-01355-5; 0-465-01355-4

LC 2009-03073

"Think of a cause you care about deeply. Who's the figure you most admire in that movement? Now picture that person taking you to lunch, when you're 23, and declaring that you – you! – will be his successor. Such was the fantasy that Richard Brookhiser lived as a protégé of National Review editor William F. Buckley Jr., conservatism's standard-bearer for a half-century. Brookhiser was, to put it mildly, a prodigy. He wrote his first magazine cover story at 14. Steep falls often follow such precocious rises. But when Buckley changed his mind and sought a different heir, Brookhiser didn't self-destruct; he just rejiggered his career. Such equanimity means Right Time, Right Place is refreshingly free of spicy score settling and juicy revelations. Instead, readers get tasty morsels of candor caramelized in the searing heat of self-reflection. The result is a psychologically rich personal narrative." Christ Sci Monit

Brown, Carolyn

★ **Chance** and circumstance; twenty years with Cage and Cunningham. Alfred A. Knopf 2007 645p il $37.50   **92**

1. Authors 2. Choreographers 3. Composers 4. Dancers 5. Essayists 6. Poets

ISBN 978-0-394-40191-1; 0-394-40191-3

LC 2006-48799

The author "traces the trajectory of her modern dance career with that organization during its crawling stages in the

1950s and 1960s, when composer John Cage was musical director and artist Robert Rauschenberg was set and costume designer. Brown documents the company's early struggles for acceptance (it was considered avant-garde), various tours, and eventual world recognition. . . . This book will appeal to modern dance buffs and memoir readers." Libr J

Brown, Claude

Manchild in the promised land. Touchstone 1999 415p pa $14.95   **92**

1. African Americans -- Biography   2. African Americans -- Harlem (New York, N.Y.)   3. Authors   4. Essayists   5. Journalists   6. Memoirists

ISBN 0-684-86418-5

This is "the autobiography of a young black man raised in Harlem. It is a realistic description of life in the ghetto. . . . The core of the book concerns the 'plague' of heroin addiction that swept through Harlem in the 1950s taking the lives of many of Brown's contemporaries." Publ Wkly

Brown, Daniel

The **indifferent** stars above; the harrowing saga of a Donner Party bride. [by] Daniel James Brown. William Morrow 2009 337p il $25.99   **92**

1. Donner Party   2. Donner party   3. Frontier and pioneer life -- California   4. Overland journeys to the Pacific   5. Pioneers

ISBN 978-0-06-134810-5; 0-06-134810-4

LC 2008-40646

"In April 1846, as young newlywed Sarah Graves departed her Illinois home on a journey to California, she could not foresee the misery and horror that awaited her. After numerous delays on their difficult westward path, she and her family found themselves dangerously behind schedule as winter loomed, and they decided to join an ill-fated wagon train under the leadership of George Donner. Ending up snowbound and starving in the Sierra Nevada range, the Donner party descended into cannibalism. . . . Never melodramatic or maudlin, Brown's work gracefully balances graphic depictions of extreme privation with humanizing glimpses of the emigrants' everyday hopes and fears." Libr J

Includes bibliographical references

Brown, Frederick

Flaubert; a biography. Little, Brown 2006 628p il $35   **92**

1. Authors   2. Biography, Individual   3. Novelists   4. Short story writers

ISBN 0-316-11878-8

LC 2005-17036

This is a biography of the nineteenth-century French novelist.

The author "has put together a judicious work that sticks to the record and relies on expertly chosen passages from Flaubert's brilliant letters and the works of his contemporaries to develop a convincing portrait, brushstroke by brushstroke." N Y Times (Late N Y Ed)

Includes bibliographical references

Brown, James

James Brown, the godfather of soul; by James Brown with Bruce Tucker; new introduction by Bruce

Tucker; epilogue by Dave Marsh. Thunder's Mouth Press 1997 352p il pa $14.95   **92**

1. African American singers   2. Singers   3. Soul musicians

ISBN 978-1-56025-115-6; 1-56025-115-8

LC 90-31961

This "is a solid, informative autobiography, and fans will welcome its vast discography." N Y Times Book Rev

Includes discography

The **Los** Angeles diaries; a memoir. Morrow 2003 200p $21.95; pa $12.95   **92**

1. Authors   2. Novelists   3. Short story writers

ISBN 0-06-052151-1; 0-06-052152-X pa

LC 2003-48779

"Brown's revelations have no smugness or self-congratulation; they reek of remorse and desire, passion and futility. . . . The result is a grimly exquisite memoir that reads like a noir novel but grips unrelentingly like the hand of a homeless drunk begging for help." Publ Wkly

Brown, Judith M.

Nehru: a political life. Yale University Press 2003 407p il $35   **92**

1. Biography, Individual   2. Nonfiction writers   3. Prime ministers   4. Prime ministers -- India

ISBN 0-300-09279-2

LC 2003-5807

"This compelling biography, the most complete and penetrating account of Nehru yet written, casts new light on both the public and private man. It also offers insights into the history of India's nationalist movement and the complexities of constructing a new nation state in the aftermath of imperial rule." Univ Press Books for Public and Second Sch Libr, 2004

Includes bibliographical references

Brown, Malcolm

★ **T.E.** Lawrence. New York University Press 2003 160p il map $21.95   **92**

1. Archaeologists   2. Authors   3. Orientalists -- Great Britain -- Biography   4. Soldiers   5. Soldiers -- Great Britain -- Biography   6. Travel writers

ISBN 0-8147-9920-5

LC 2003-51387

"The book is a major literary work." Publ Wkly

Includes bibliographical references

Brown, Mick

★ **Tearing** down the wall of sound; the rise and fall of Phil Spector. Knopf 2007 452p il $26.95; pa $16.95   **92**

1. Biography, Individual   2. Music arrangers   3. Record producers   4. Recording producers   5. Songwriters

ISBN 978-1-4000-4219-7; 1-400-04219-4; 978-1-4000-7661-1 pa; 1-4000-7661-7 pa

LC 2007-4819

This is a biography of the record producer and songwriter.

"Stacked with incredible anecdotes, Brown's entertaining and nuanced portrait lifts the fog of myth and outright falsehood (including Spector's own) that have obscured the celebrity producer (like an enormous, gravity-defying wig) through the years." Publ Wkly

Includes bibliographical references

Brown, Nancy Marie

The **abacus** and the cross; the story of the pope who brought the light of science to the Dark Ages. Basic Books 2010 310p il map $27.95 **92**

1. Biography, Individual 2. Popes 3. Religion and science

ISBN 9780465009503; 0465009506

LC 2010-36361

"As readably knowledgeable about Gerbert's political fortunes as about his intellectual influence, Brown is a lively narrator and interesting interpreter of Gerbert's life and world. This portrait gives both the science and the history audiences something to talk about." Booklist

Includes bibliographical references and index.

Brown, Tina

★ The **Diana** chronicles. Doubleday 2007 542p $27.50 **92**

1. Biography, Individual 2. Princesses

ISBN 978-0-385-51708-9; 0-385-51708-4

This is a biography of Diana, Princess of Wales.

"Like scraping barnacles off an old hulk, Tina Brown has taken the story of Princess Diana, hosed off layers of hearsay and myth, sifted through tons of accumulated legend, and presented us with a fresh and vividly perceptive portrait." Times Lit Suppl

Includes bibliographical references

Browne, Janet

Charles Darwin. v2 Knopf 2002 591p v2 il $37.50 **92**

1. Naturalists 2. Travel writers 3. Writers on science

ISBN 0-679-42932-8

This second volume of Browne's biography of Darwin begins "a year before the publication of On the Origin of Species, with the arrival of a package from Alfred Russel Wallace, whose own ideas on natural selection virtually mirrored Darwin's, forcing him to go public. . . . Browne's subject is monumental, but her writing style is never overburdened by the weight. Rather, her prose is elegant in its clarity of thought, her craftsmanship impeccable in the way it weaves a coherent whole from the innumerable threads of thought, experience and persona that comprised this colossal life." Publ Wkly

Includes bibliographical references

Brownfield, Christopher J.

My nuclear family; a coming-of-age in America's twenty-first century military. Alfred A. Knopf 2010 314p il $26.95; ebook $26.95 **92**

1. Iraq War, 2003- -- Personal narratives 2. Memoirists 3. Naval officers 4. Nuclear submarines 5. Political scientists

ISBN 978-0-307-27169-3; 978-0-307-59428-0 ebook

LC 2010-11833

This "is not the best book written by an insider about America's post-9/11 military, but it's certainly the most entertaining. It's got a cocky, star-spangled, wide-angle feel, as if a subversive young novelist had decided to rewrite a Tom Clancy thriller after first piloting some nuclear submarines as a gonzo practice drill. . . . This is a book that's going to rattle some cages." N Y Times Book Rev

Includes bibliographical references

Bruni, Frank

Born round; the secret history of a full-time eater. Penguin Press 2009 354p il $25.95; pa $16 **92**

1. Biography, Individual 2. Dinners and dining 3. Food critics 4. Obesity

ISBN 978-1-59420-231-5; 1-59420-231-1; 978-0-14-311767-4 pa; 0-14-311767-X pa

LC 2009-09532

"The book does not contain paeans to the glories of locavorism. It's not a tale of bawdy kitchen exploits, or of finding your true self over a bowl of pasta in Rome . . . His memoir tells a story of food addiction, eating disorders, and a lifelong struggle with his voracious appetite . . . Born Round makes for a breezy read. Even at its darkest, it goes down easy." Village Voice

Bryant, Howard

The **last** hero; a life of Henry Aaron. Pantheon Books 2010 600p il $29.95 **92**

1. African American athletes 2. Baseball -- Biography 3. Baseball players

ISBN 978-0-375-42485-4; 0-375-42485-7

LC 2009-40573

This biography of the baseball player "reveals a multifaceted man, a great American, and an accomplished athlete, in that order. . . . Bryant evokes the apparently distant world marked by cruel segregation, racism, and poverty of the soul, as well as reliving some of the greatest moments of baseball. A most welcome book, most highly recommended." Libr J

Includes bibliographical references

Bryson, Bill

The **life** and times of the thunderbolt kid; a memoir. Broadway Books 2006 270p il $25 **92**

1. Authors 2. Biography, Individual 3. Essayists 4. Journalists 5. Lexicographers 6. Linguists 7. Nonfiction writers 8. Travel writers

ISBN 0-7679-1936-X; 978-0-7679-1936-4

LC 2006-43859

"This affectionate portrait wistfully recalls the bygone days of Burns and Allen and downtown department stores but with a good-natured elbow poke to the ribs." Booklist

Includes bibliographical references

Buckley, Christopher Taylor

Losing Mum and Pup; a memoir. [by] Christopher Buckley. Twelve 2009 251p il $24.99; pa $13.99 **92**

1. Authors 2. Authors, American 3. Biography, Individual 4. Columnists 5. Humorists 6. Magazine editors 7. Novelists 8. Philanthropists 9. Socialites 10. Speechwriters 11. Spouses of prominent persons

ISBN 978-0-446-54094-0; 0-446-54094-3; 978-0-446-54095-7 pa; 0-446-54095-1 pa

LC 2008-43532

"Christopher Buckley has not written a 'Mommie Dearest' for the Evelyn Waugh set. 'Losing Mum and Pup' is a subtle, fond and, above all, honest chronicle of his celebrated parents. . . . Buckley has pulled off what eludes many writers: he has written candidly but not unkindly about people whose vices and virtues he sees clearly." Newsweek

Buckley, William F.

Miles gone by; a literary autobiography. [by] William F. Buckley Jr. Regnery Pub. 2004 594p il $29.95; pa $18.95   **92**

1. Authors 2. Biography, Individual 3. Columnists 4. Magazine editors 5. Novelists

ISBN 0-89526-089-1; 0-89526-004-2 pa

LC 2004-7170

This "is an elegant book, one of Buckley's best, and the man the reader meets in these pages is the Platonic ideal of a dinner companion, a raconteur whose pomposity is calculated and whose self-deprecation charms." N Y Times Book Rev

The **Reagan** I knew; [by] William F. Buckley, Jr. Basic Books 2008 279p il $25   **92**

1. Actors 2. Authors 3. Biography, Individual 4. Columnists 5. Governors 6. Magazine editors 7. Novelists 8. Presidents 9. Presidents -- United States 10. Spouses of presidents

ISBN 978-0-465-00926-8; 0-465-00926-3

LC 2008-32557

"The correspondence, which spans the period 1965–98 (with one final letter, written in 2005), seems on the surface to be concerned almost entirely with mundane matters: thank-you letters written after a get-together, apologies for missed birthdays, etc. But look beneath the surface, and you'll find a revealing portrait of two men: Reagan, a driven political contender who never gave up his decency or his sense of family, and Buckley, a tireless Reagan booster who used his many public forums to promote Reagan's political agenda." Booklist

Buford, Kate

Burt Lancaster; an American life. Da Capo Press 2001 447p il pa $20   **92**

1. Actors 2. Motion picture producers

ISBN 978-0-306-81019-0; 0-306-81019-0

"Lancaster's decades-long political involvement with liberal causes (and his constant run-ins with the House Un-American Activities Committee in the 1950s) are a central theme in this well-researched and engaging biography, which also details the artist's acting career, his turns as a producer and his personal life." Publ Wkly

Includes filmography and bibliographical references

Native American son; the life and sporting legend of Jim Thorpe. Alfred A. Knopf 2010 479p il $35   **92**

1. Athletes 2. Biography, Individual 3. Native Americans -- Biography

ISBN 978-0-375-41324-7; 0-375-41324-3

LC 2010012815

This biography of the Native American athlete covers topics ranging "from the disastrous divvying up of Native

American land that young Jim witnessed in 1890s Oklahoma; to Thorpe's stellar performances in football, baseball, and track and field; to the stripping of his 1912 Olympics medals because he was paid to play baseball for two summers; and, finally, to the makeshift life he cobbled together after his playing days ended. Buford imparts a sense of the incandescent skills Thorpe applied to his sports, and the discrimination and self-destruction that shadowed him throughout his life." Booklist

Includes bibliographical references

Buk-Swienty, Tom

The **other** half; the life of Jacob Riis and the world of immigrant America. translated from the Danish by Annette Buk-Swienty. W.W. Norton & Co. 2008 331p il $27.95   **92**

1. Biography, Individual 2. Journalists 3. Memoirists 4. Photojournalists 5. Social reformers

ISBN 978-0-393-06023-2; 0-393-06023-3

LC 2008-22853

This "biography is superb—not only as an instructive tale for today's journalists, but as a remarkable immigrant saga for readers from all vocations." Columbia J Rev

Includes bibliographical references and index

Bullock, Alan

Hitler and Stalin; parallel lives. Knopf 1992 1081p il maps hardcover o.p. pa $25   **92**

1. Communist leaders 2. Heads of state 3. Nazi leaders 4. Political leaders

ISBN 0-679-72994-1 pa

LC 91-52711

"The twentieth century cannot be understood without close examination of the work of Stalin and Hitler. It is particularly important to note what their regimes and aims had in common and where they differed. Alan Bullock has put us all in his debt by placing their actions side by side, in enormous detail, and in chronological sequence to make the comparison easy." Times Lit Suppl

Includes bibliographical references

Bullock-Prado, Gesine

Confections of a closet master baker; one woman's sweet journey from unhappy Hollywood executive to contented country baker. illustrations by Raymond G. Prado. Broadway Books 2009 226p il $24   **92**

1. Bakers 2. Baking 3. Motion picture executives

ISBN 978-0-7679-3268-4

LC 2009-945

The author "chronicles her career change from schmoozing Hollywood production company executive to running a bakery in Montpelier, VT. . . . Memoir lovers will find this a lighthearted, entertaining read filled with humor and acerbic wit; foodies will enjoy the insider's view of running a bakery." Libr J

Bunting, Josiah

Ulysses S. Grant; [by] Josiah Bunting III. Times Books 2004 xx, 180p $20   **92**

1. Generals 2. Presidents 3. Presidents -- United States

-- Biography
ISBN 0-8050-6949-6

LC 2004-47889

"This superb book should support those who are gradually moving Grant from the lower to the upper half of rankings of chief executives." Publ Wkly

Includes bibliographical references

Burana, Lily

I love a man in uniform; a memoir of love, war and other battles. Weinstein Books 2009 352p $23.95 **92**

1. Authors 2. Editors 3. Essayists 4. Memoirists 5. Military spouses 6. Stripteasers
ISBN 978-1-60286-083-4; 1-60286-083-1

This "is a humorous, moving and surprising account of married life in today's military." N Y Times Book Rev

Burke, Carolyn

★ **Lee** Miller; a life. Knopf 2005 426p il $35 **92**

1. Biography, Individual 2. Models (Persons) 3. Photographers
ISBN 0-375-40147-4

LC 2004-43844

This is a biography of the model and photographer.

This "sympathetic tribute sheds further light on the lives of this highly original, often misunderstood woman." Economist

Includes bibliographical references

No regrets; the life of Edith Piaf. Alfred A. Knopf 2011 282p il $27.95 **92**

1. Biography, Individual 2. Singers
ISBN 978-0-307-26801-3; 0-307-26801-2

LC 2010-35229

The author "focuses on the internationally renowned French vocalist and lyricist best known for the song 'La Vie en Rose.' Piaf is commonly associated with la chanson réaliste, realistic songs that speak to the underprivileged. . . . Burke's contextual detail and attention to research will appeal to scholars, and her masterful storytelling will engage readers." Libr J

Includes bibliographical references

Burlingame, Michael

Abraham Lincoln; a life. Johns Hopkins University Press 2008 2v il set $125 **92**

1. Biography, Individual 2. Lawyers 3. Members of Congress 4. Presidents 5. Presidents -- United States 6. State legislators
ISBN 978-0-8018-8993-6; 0-8018-8993-6

LC 2007-52919

This is a biography of the 16th president of the United States.

The author "has produced the finest Lincoln biography in more than 60 years. . . . Future Lincoln books cannot be written without it, and from no other book can a general reader learn so much about Abraham Lincoln." Publ Wkly

Includes bibliographical references

Burns, Rebecca

Burial for a King; Martin Luther King Jr.'s funeral and the week that transformed Atlanta and rocked the nation. Scribner 2011 244p il $25; ebook $11.99 **92**

1. Civil rights activists 2. Clergy 3. Nobel laureates for peace 4. Nonfiction writers
ISBN 978-1-4391-3054-4; 978-1-4391-4309-4 ebook

LC 2010-29980

This is a "recreation of the aftermath of Martin Luther King Jr.'s assassination. . . . [The author] provides a snapshot of a still-segregated nation poised between uneasy reconciliation and violent chaos. Using terse language and precise, straightforward descriptions . . . she views the crisis and aftermath of King's death in Memphis through multiple points of view, beginning with the traumatic center of his family and closest associates in Atlanta. . . . A pertinent, you-are-there historical page-turner with a strong moral message." Kirkus

Burstein, Andrew

The **passions** of Andrew Jackson. Knopf 2003 xxi, 292p il map $25; pa $15 **92**

1. Generals 2. Presidents 3. Presidents -- United States
ISBN 0-375-41428-2; 0-375-71404-9 pa

LC 2002-16258

Burstein "explains his subject's imperious personality in relation to the uncertainties of frontier life in the Old Southwest and guides the reader through the 'politics of memory,' or what people have chosen to remember. The author succeeds in illuminating the strengths and weakness of his subject, whose forceful, at times bullying personality represented the temperament of many early 19th-century Americans. This captivating, richly documented work fills a niche even within the crowded field of Jackson studies. A worthwhile purchase for academic and large public libraries." Libr J

Includes bibliographical references

Bush, Barbara

Barbara Bush; a memoir. Scribner 1994 575p il $25; pa $16 **92**

1. Diplomats 2. Members of Congress 3. Parents of presidents 4. Presidents 5. Spouses of presidents 6. United Nations officials 7. Vice-presidents
ISBN 0-02-519635-9; 0-7432-5447-3 pa

LC 94-13829

The former "First Lady, one of the most popular in modern history, gives the reader a tour through her life story and the parallel universe of the political spouse." NY Times Book Rev

Bush, George

All the best, George Bush; my life in letters and other writings. Scribner 1999 640p il $30; pa $16 **92**

1. Diplomats 2. Members of Congress 3. Parents of presidents 4. Presidents 5. Presidents -- United States 6. United Nations officials 7. Vice-presidents
ISBN 0-684-83958-X; 0-7432-0041-1 pa

LC 99-40440

The former president presents his autobiography in the form of annotated letters, memos, journal entries, and speeches written between 1942 and March 1999.

This work "is refreshing and, in many ways, will shed more light on the man's personal character and public persona than any memoir or biography could. It offers an intriguing picture of a man who takes fierce pride in his modesty." Publ Wkly

Bush, George W. (George Walker), 1946-

Decision points. Crown Publishers 2010 497p il $35; ebook $14.99   **92**
1. Baseball executives 2. Biography, Individual 3. Children of presidents 4. Energy industry executives 5. Governors 6. Presidents 7. Presidents -- United States
ISBN 978-0-307-59061-9; 0-307-59061-5; 978-0-307-59062-6 ebook

"Critics on both the left and right are challenged to walk in his shoes, and may come away with a new view of the former president—or at least an appreciation of the hard and often ambiguous choices he was forced to make. . . . Honest, of course, but also surprisingly approachable and engaging." Kirkus

Bush, Laura

★ **Spoken** from the heart. Scribner 2010 456p il $30; ebook $12.99   **92**
1. Biography, Individual 2. Librarians 3. Presidents' spouses -- United States 4. Spouses of presidents 5. Teachers
ISBN 978-1-439-15520-2; 1-439-15520-8; 978-1-439-16034-3 ebook; 1-439-16034-1 ebook
                  LC 2010-13701

This book "reveals Laura Welch Bush to be a beautiful writer, a keen observer and a tender soul who drew on her roots to live a life in the public eye with compassion and grace." Wall Street J

Includes bibliographical references

Bushman, Richard L.

Joseph Smith; rough stone rolling. [by] Richard Lyman Bushman, with the assistance of Jed Woodworth. Knopf 2005 740p il map $35; pa $18.95 **92**
1. Biography, Individual 2. Mormon Church -- United States -- History 3. Mormon leaders 4. Mormons
ISBN 1-4000-4270-4; 1-4000-7753-2 pa
                  LC 2004-61613

In this biography of the founder of the Mormon church, the author "stresses the boy seer's thoroughly ordinary origins—born to a hard-pressed New England farm family and denied all but the rudiments of a formal education—to emphasize the marvel of the religious revolution he brought about. . . . A deft portrait of a deeply controversial figure." Booklist

Includes bibliographical references

Cadillac Man

Land of the lost souls; my life on the streets. Bloomsbury 2009 288p $25   **92**
1. Biography, Individual 2. Homeless 3. Homeless persons 4. Homeless persons -- New York (N.Y.) 5.

Veterans
ISBN 978-1-596-914063; 1-596-91406-8
                  LC 2008-41111

Memoir of a man who became homeless at age 44. Describes his adventures and daily experiences that he recorded in a series of spiral notebooks over fourteen years. He writes about the "indelible characters" who share his New York City streets, including Penny, a young runaway whom he eventually reunites with her family.

"A surprising find, Cadillac lets readers in on a rarely seen community, revealing the compassionate hearts that beat even in the most despairing circumstances." Publ Wkly

Caldwell, Gail

★ **Let's** take the long way home; a memoir of friendship. Random House 2010 190p $23   **92**
1. Biography, Individual 2. Columnists 3. Friendship 4. Journalists 5. Literary critics 6. Memoirists
ISBN 978-1-4000-6738-1; 1-4000-6738-3
                  LC 2009-29384

"This is a book you'll want to share with your own 'necessary pillars of life,' as Caldwell refers to her nearest and dearest. . . . Her memoir, a tribute to the enduring power of friendship, is a lovely gift to readers." Washington Post

Calhoun, Charles W.

Benjamin Harrison. Times Books 2005 206p il $20   **92**
1. Presidents 2. Presidents -- United States 3. Senators
ISBN 0-8050-6952-6; 978-0-8050-6952-5
                  LC 2004-63778

The author "dusts off an almost thoroughly forgotten chief executive, known primarily for serving between Cleveland's two terms, to disclose a harbinger of the modern, activist president. . . . One of the most revelatory entries in the American Presidents series." Booklist

Includes bibliographical references

Callahan, Tom

In search of Tiger; a journey through golf with Tiger Woods. Crown 2003 245p il $23.95; pa $14   **92**
1. Golfers
ISBN 0-609-60943-2; 1-4000-5140-1 pa
                  LC 2002-11350

The author "examines Tiger's early years, how he got to the top of his game and his vision for the future. Anecdotes and insider insights highlight portraits of major Tiger victories. . . . This is a comprehensive examination of the man, his talent, his competition and the world of professional golf, a must-read for fans and players alike." Publ Wkly

Campbell, Gordon

John Milton; life, work, and thought. [by] Gordon Campbell [and] Thomas N. Corns. Oxford University Press 2008 488p il map $39.95   **92**
1. Authors 2. Biography, Individual 3. Blind 4. English poetry -- 17th century -- History and criticism 5. Essayists 6. Poets
ISBN 978-0-19-928984-4; 0-19-928984-0
                  LC 2008-300712

This biography "draws chiefly on documentary evidence and an easy familiarity with the 17th-century English scene. As a prodigy scholar, pamphleteer, government translator on the international stage and the blind . . . bard of the Bible, Milton found himself astride a world of hardening views, as it spiraled in political and spiritual transition. . . . The authors set Milton's imaginative life against this backdrop, stretching from Shakespeare, to whom Milton's father may have been loosely connected, to Dryden's ingenious staging of Paradise Lost in couplets. With nearly 100 pages of notes and bibliography, this is a no-nonsense contribution to our understanding of a genius who, in many ways, is hardly remote from our times." Publ Wkly

Includes bibliographical references (p. 446-472)

Cannadine, David

★ **Mellon**; an American life. A.A. Knopf 2006 779p il $35 **92**

1. Art collectors 2. Biography, Individual 3. Financiers 4. Philanthropists 5. Secretaries of the treasury

ISBN 0-679-45032-7; 978-0-679-45032-0

LC 2006-45116

This is a "biography of Andrew Mellon, the powerful American financier, secretary of the treasury, and art collector. . . . Cannadine's recounting of Mellon's public career make this a worthy contribution to our understanding of the man and his era." Booklist

Includes bibliographical references

Capote, Truman

★ **Too** brief a treat; the letters of Truman Capote. edited by Gerald Clarke. Random House 2004 487p il $27.95; pa $16 **92**

1. Authors 2. Biography, Individual 3. Nonfiction writers 4. Novelists 5. Short story writers

ISBN 0-375-50133-9; 0-375-70241-5 pa

LC 2004-50313

"Capote's untrammeled personality fairly falls off the pages of these letters, and rather than being irritating, his disregard of reticence is especially poignant in this day of sterile e-mailing. Ideal for devotees to dip into here and there instead of reading from start to finish." Booklist

Includes bibliographical references

Carlo, Philip

Gaspipe; confessions of a Mafia boss. William Morrow 2008 346p il $25.95 **92**

1. Criminals 2. Informers 3. Mafia 4. Mobsters 5. Organized crime

ISBN 978-0-06-142984-2

LC 2008-2683

"This powerful story is required reading for anyone with a yen for the Mafia, the criminal underworld and a law enforcement system struggling to keep up." Publ Wkly

Caro, Robert A.

Master of the senate. Knopf 2002 xxiv, 1167p il $35; pa $19.95 **92**

1. Members of Congress 2. Politics 3. Presidents 4. Presidents -- United States 5. Senators 6. Vice-presidents

ISBN 0-394-52836-0; 0-394-72095-4 pa

LC 2002-282796

The third entry in Mr. Caro's multi-volume biography of the thirty-sixth president of the United States, this installment covers Johnson's Senate career.

"Mr. Caro has written a panoramic study of how power plays out in the legislative arena. Combining the best techniques of investigative reporting with majestic storytelling ability, he has created a vivid, revelatory institutional history as well as a rich hologram of Johnson's character." N Y Times (Late N Y Ed)

Includes bibliographical references

Means of ascent. Knopf 1990 xxxiv, 506p il $45; pa $20 **92**

1. Members of Congress 2. Presidents 3. Presidents -- United States 4. Senators 5. Vice-presidents

ISBN 0-394-52835-2; 0-679-73371-X pa

LC 90-201544

"Caro has written a brilliant but disturbing book that Johnson admirers will intensely dislike. It throws a merciless spotlight on its subject. Readers are asked to reexamine the distinction between political means and ends. Caro examines what he perceives to be Johnson's deepest weaknesses: his lust for power and wealth; his mean spiritedness; his perversity to exploit the difficulties of others and then revel in his own brazen dishonesty. One looks in vain for a redeeming sign of decency in the LBJ of this volume." Christ Sci Monit

Includes bibliographical references

The **power** broker: Robert Moses and the fall of New York. Knopf 1974 1246, xxxivp il $50; pa $21.95 **92**

1. Local government officials 2. State government officials 3. Urban planners

ISBN 0-394-48076-7; 0-394-72024-5 pa

This is a biographical critique of the man who in four decades as a public official "built most of the parks, bridges and highways in and around New York City." Newsweek

Includes bibliographical references

Carr, David

The **night** of the gun; a reporter investigates the darkest story of his life, his own. Simon & Schuster 2008 389p il $26; pa $15 **92**

1. Biography, Individual 2. Columnists 3. Drug addicts 4. Journalists 5. Memoirists

ISBN 978-1-4165-4152-3; 1-4165-4152-7; 978-1-4165-4153-0 pa; 1-4165-4153-5 pa

LC 2008-12178

Carr "takes a detailed inventory of his years of drug addiction, chronicling the slide from drinking and marijuana use during his teen years in Minneapolis to shooting cocaine and smoking crack while trying to maintain his life as a reporter and the father of twin girls. Carr is meticulous in the investigation of his past, reconstructing events with the aid of police reports, magazine rejection letters, and more than sixty interviews with friends, former dealers, and fellow-addicts. His journalistic skills are on full display as he works to excavate the truth from his often hazy memories. He evinces genuine remorse for his frequently reprehensible behavior and succeeds in creating something more than merely another entry in what he terms the 'growing pile of junkie memoirs.'" New Yorker

Carretta, Vincent

★ **Equiano,** the African; biography of a self-made man. University of Georgia Press 2005 xxiv, 436p il map $29.95   **92**
1. Abolitionists 2. Biography, Individual 3. Memoirists 4. Slaves
ISBN 0-8203-2571-6

LC 2005-11898

"This is a thoroughly rich, engrossing, and well-researched portrait of an exceptional man and the cause he championed." Booklist
Includes bibliographical references

Carroll, Diahann

The **legs** are the last to go; aging, acting, marrying, and other things I learned the hard way. Amistad 2008 271p il $24.95   **92**
1. Actors 2. African American actors 3. African American singers 4. Singers
ISBN 978-0-06-076326-8; 0-06-076326-4

"Carroll looks back on a groundbreaking career: the first black actress to star in her own television show and, more recently, the first black actress to play the role of Norma Desmond in Sunset Boulevard. In between, Carroll has racked up a breathtaking list of achievements on stage, in film, and on television. She's also racked up four failed marriages and a life full of the kind of mistakes a driven woman will make climbing to the top of a show-business career during a period when women and African Americans had few opportunities. Carroll is candid about the trials and tribulations—as well as the joys and triumphs—in her public and private life." Booklist

Carroll, James

Practicing Catholic. Houghton Mifflin Harcourt 2009 385p $28   **92**
1. Authors 2. Biography, Individual 3. Catholic Church 4. Catholic Church -- Doctrines 5. Catholic Church -- United States 6. Memoirists 7. Novelists 8. Priests
ISBN 978-0-618-67018-5; 0-618-67018-1

LC 2008-37386

"This book is both a memoir of former priest and writer Carroll's life and a keen analysis of American Catholicism in the late 20th century.... Brilliant prose, historically insightful, and sincere passion remain hallmarks of the author's work." Libr J
Includes bibliographical references

Carson, Clayborne

Malcolm X: the FBI file; introduction by Spike Lee; edited by David Gallen. Carroll & Graf Pubs. 1991 514p il hardcover o.p. pa $13.95   **92**
1. Black Muslim leaders 2. Civil rights activists
ISBN 0-88184-758-5 pa

LC 91-26697

"This is a collection of declassified documents from the FBI surveillance of the orator and religious (later political) leader that, with historian Carson's studious commentary, focuses less on Malcolm's relation to the FBI and more on that to the larger civil rights movement. These excerpts . . . follow his travels and speeches, media interviews and FBI interviews, oftentimes including transcripts as written or summarized by Gallen and Carson." Booklist

Carter, Jimmy

Everything to gain; making the most of the rest of your life. [by] Jimmy and Rosalynn Carter. University of Arkansas Press 1995 176p pa $21.95 **92**
1. Governors 2. Nobel laureates for peace 3. Presidents 4. Presidents -- United States
ISBN 978-1-55728-388-7; 1-55728-388-5

"The former president and First Lady alternate first-person reminiscences with sections written jointly to tell the story of their lives after leaving the White House in 1980. Frankly acknowledging the trauma of the lost election, the Carters record their efforts to overcome the difficulties of making a fresh start while deeply in debt, adjusting to life in a small house in Plains, Ga., and other challenges." Publ Wkly

Keeping faith: memoirs of a president. University of Ark. Press 1995 633p il pa $34.95   **92**
1. Governors 2. Nobel laureates for peace 3. Presidents 4. Presidents -- United States
ISBN 1-55728-330-3

LC 95-9691

These memoirs treat such matters as "improving relations with China; enacting energy legislation; negotiating the second Strategic Arms Limitation treaty (SALT II); concluding the Panama Canal treaties; and convincing Menachem Begin and Anwar Sadat to reach agreement at Camp David. Carter also devotes more than a quarter of the book to the frustrations arising from the capture of hostages in Tehran." N Y Rev Books

Sharing good times. Simon & Schuster 2004 174p $21; pa $13   **92**
1. Governors 2. Nobel laureates for peace 3. Presidents 4. Presidents -- United States
ISBN 0-7432-7033-9; 0-7432-7068-1 pa

LC 2004-51351

The author "recalls various occasions in his life that became 'lasting sources of pleasure.' . . . [These remembrances] include his personal reasons for seeing his father as a hero, watching minor and major-league baseball games growing up, his days in the navy, road trips with his wife and children, his entry into politics, taking vacations while in the White House, his famous volunteer work, and even his hobbies." Booklist

Carter, Jimmy, 1924-

White House diary. Farrar, Straus and Giroux 2010 570p il $30; ebook $14.99   **92**
1. Biography, Individual 2. Presidents -- United States
ISBN 978-0-374-28099-4; 978-1-4299-9065-3 ebook

LC 2010-15544

Jimmy Carter, the 39th president of the United States, presents an edited and annotated version of a diary he kept during his term in office.

"That the language is blunt and occasionally a little un-Christian may come as a surprise. . . . But the writings here reflect the Mr. Carter we know: boastful and painfully confessional, sanctimonious and callous, insightful and un-self-aware. These are the thoughts of a secular preacher and calculating politician, surrounded by friends and yet often alone." N Y Times (Late N Y Ed)

Carter, Miranda

Anthony Blunt: his lives. Farrar, Straus & Giroux 2001 590p il $30; pa $18   92
1. Art historians 2. Museum administrators 3. Spies
ISBN 0-374-10531-6; 0-312-42146-X pa
LC 2001-50135
"Thoroughly researched and carefully crafted, this is sure to be the definitive biography." Publ Wkly

Carwardine, Richard

Lincoln: a life of purpose and power.   Knopf 2006 394p il map $27.50   92
1. Biography, Individual 2. Lawyers 3. Members of Congress 4. Presidents 5. Presidents -- United States 6. State legislators
ISBN 1-4000-4456-1
LC 2005047230
This book "is not only analytical and smart, it's also delightfully readable—and it will surely emerge as one of the most important Lincoln books to be published this decade." Publ Wkly
Includes bibliographical references

Cash, Jean W.

Flannery O'Connor: a life. University of Tenn. Press 2002 356p il $30; pa $24.95   92
1. Authors 2. Novelists 3. Short story writers
ISBN 1-572-33192-5; 1-572-33305-7 pa
LC 2002-250
"Cash analyzes the woman behind the myth, introducing an extraordinarily intelligent human being noted for her keen sense of humor, intellectual versatility, and tremendous capacity for friendship. This intimate chronicle of a major literary talent will appeal to both students and scholars." Booklist
Includes bibliographical references

Cash, Rosanne

★ **Composed**; a memoir. Viking 2010 343p $26.95   92
1. Biography, Individual 2. Country music 3. Country musicians 4. Singers 5. Songwriters
ISBN 978-0-670-02196-3
LC 2010-10327
"The moving chapters about Roseanne Cash's glorious career—and the moments of great tenderness and tension with her legendary family—are like exquisite album tracks: Individually they are great reads, but together they add up to something cohesive and powerful. Composed provides no bombshell confessions about her failed marriage to Rodney Crowell or her wonderfully complicated relationship with

her dad, Johnny. (Though she does dismiss the biopic Walk the Line as 'an egregious oversimplification of our family's private pain.') Instead, Cash delivers writerly meditations on what it means to be an artist and a public person and, yes, a daughter. Rare is the celebrity memoir that is so full of self-awareness and dignity." Entertainment Wkly

Cassidy, David C.

Beyond uncertainty; Heisenberg, quantum physics, and the bomb. David C. Cassidy. Bellevue Literary Press 2009 480 p. $27   92
1. Atomic bomb -- Germany -- History -- 20th century 2. Biography, Individual 3. Nobel laureates for physics 4. Physicists 5. Physicists -- Germany -- Biography 6. World War, 1939-1945 -- Science -- Germany
ISBN 978-1-934137-13-0; 1-934137-13-8; 1934137138; 9781934137130
LC 2008039885
This is a biography "of the German wunderkind Werner Heisenberg (1901–1976), who won the 1932 Nobel Prize in physics for revolutionizing the nascent field of quantum physics, first with his matrix interpretation of quantum mechanics, then with his famous uncertainty principle. . . . Exhaustively detailed yet eminently readable, this is an important book." Publ Wkly
Includes bibliographical references (p. [411]-456) and index

Castro, Fidel

★ **Fidel** Castro: my life; a spoken autobiography. [by] Fidel Castro and Ignacio Ramonet; translated by Andrew Hurley. Scribner 2008 723p il map $40   92
1. Communist leaders 2. Presidents
ISBN 978-1-4165-5328-1; 1-4165-5328-2
Ramonet "sat down with Castro over the course of many hours, engaging him in long, involved discussions about his revolutionary life (and little about his personal life). The result is, in the words of the interviewer, Castro's 'political testament, an oral summoning-up of Fidel Castro's life by Fidel himself at almost eighty.' That rather simple description does not begin to cover the magnitude and significance of this major document. . . . By itself an incomplete history of the Cuban Revolution, to be sure, but an important—the ultimate insider view—contribution to the complete picture." Booklist
Includes bibliographical references

Catherine

★ The **memoirs** of Catherine the Great; a new translation by Mark Cruse and Hilde Hoogenboom. Modern Library 2005 xc, 247p il map $26.95   92
1. Empresses
ISBN 0-679-64299-4
LC 2004-61107
This is "a source of major importance and every serious library should own it." Choice

Catton, Bruce

★ **Grant** moves south; with maps by Samuel H. Bryant. Little, Brown 1960 564p maps hardcover o.p. pa $24.99   **92**

1. Generals 2. Presidents
ISBN 0-316-13244-6 pa

"Grant's development as a man and leader is brilliantly shown in this reconstruction of his Mississippi campaign." Booklist

Includes bibliographical references

Grant takes command; with maps by Samuel H. Bryant. Little, Brown 1969 556p maps hardcover o.p. pa $24.99   **92**

1. Generals 2. Presidents
ISBN 0-316-13240-3 pa

This sequel to Grant moves south "takes up Ulysses S. Grant's career just after his capture of Vicksburg in 1863. . . . It carries the action right up to Richmond and Lee's surrender at Appomattox." Publ Wkly

Includes bibliographical references

Century, Douglas

Barney Ross. Schocken Books 2006 215p il $19.95   **92**

1. Biography, Individual 2. Boxers (Persons)
ISBN 0-8052-4223-6; 978-0-8052-4223-2
LC 2005-49939

This is a biography of the American boxer.

"This is an excellent story of a man and his times. And proof positive that time does not relinquish its hold over men or monuments." N Y Times Book Rev

Includes bibliographical references

Chabon, Michael

Manhood for amateurs; the pleasures and regrets of a husband, father, and son. Harper 2009 306p $25.99   **92**

1. Authors 2. Biography, Individual 3. Fathers 4. Men -- Psychology 5. Novelists 6. Short story writers
ISBN 978-0-06-149018-7; 0-06-149018-0
LC 2009-4749

"For the most part in these pages [Chabon] manages to write about himself, his family and his generation with humor and introspective wisdom. As in his novels, he shifts gears easily between the comic and the melancholy, the whimsical and the serious, demonstrating once again his ability to write about the big subjects of love and memory and regret without falling prey to the Scylla and Charybdis of cynicism and sentimentality." N Y Times (Late N Y Ed)

Chace, James

Acheson; the Secretary of State who created the American world. Simon & Schuster 1998 512p hardcover o.p. pa $20   **92**

1. Authors 2. Nonfiction writers 3. Secretaries of state
ISBN 978-1-416-54865-2; 1-416-54865-3
LC 98-3801

"Dean Acheson was Truman's Secretary of State from 1949 to 1953, and today's world, as Chace shows in this lu-cid biography, was shaped in no small degree by his efforts." New Yorker

Includes bibliographical references

Chambers, Whittaker

Witness; forewords by William F. Buckley and Robert D. Novak. 50th annivesay ed; Regnery Pub. 2001 808p pa $19.95   **92**

1. Authors 2. Communism -- United States 3. Journalists 4. Memoirists
ISBN 978-0-89526-789-4; 0-89526-789-6

Whittaker Chambers' own account of his life, his connection with the Communist Party and his repudiation of it, and his role in the Hiss-Chambers trial.

Chandler, Charlotte

It's only a movie; Alfred Hitchcock, a personal biography. Simon & Schuster 2005 349p il $26 **92**

1. Motion picture directors
ISBN 0-7432-4508-3
LC 2004-52559

The author reveals "several insights into Hitchcock's technical genius, creative worldview and personality. . . . Chandler allows her sources to reminisce at great length, and they tend to tell fascinating stories." Publ Wkly

Includes filmography

Chang, Jung

Mao: the unknown story; [by] Jung Chang, Jon Halliday. Knopf 2005 814p il $35   **92**

1. Biography, Individual 2. Communist leaders 3. Heads of state 4. Political leaders
ISBN 0-679-42271-4
LC 2004-63826

"This is a magisterial work. . . . This biography supplies substantial . . . information and presents it all in a stylish way that will put it on bedside tables around the world." N Y Times Book Rev

Includes bibliographical references

Chatwin, Bruce

Under the sun; the letters of Bruce Chatwin. selected and edited by Elizabeth Chatwin and Nicholas Shakespeare. Viking 2011 554p il $35   **92**

1. Authors 2. Authors, English 3. Biography, Individual 4. Memoirists 5. Novelists 6. Travel writers
ISBN 978-0-670-02246-5; 0-670-02246-2
LC 2010-33591

"Chatwin's many appreciators will see the compilation in its overall significance as a personal visit with one of their literary heroes, as much as that is possible now." Booklist

Chekhov, Anton Pavlovich

Anton Chekhov's life and thought; selected letters and commentary. translated from the Russian by Michael Henry Heim, in collaboration with Simon Karlinsky; selection, introduction, and commentary by Simon Karlinsky. Northwestern Univ. Press 1997 494p pa $39.95   **92**

1. Authors 2. Dramatists 3. Physicians 4. Short story

writers
ISBN 978-0-8101-1460-9; 0-8101-1460-7

LC 96-41240

"Karlinsky's extended commentary and detailed notes amount to a first-rate critical biography, with much unfamiliar information and arrows pointing us toward further investigation." Newsweek

Chen, Da

Colors of the mountain. Random House 1999 310p hardcover o.p. pa $13   **92**

1. Calligraphers 2. Lawyers 3. Linguists
ISBN 0-385-72060-2 pa

"Despite the devastating circumstances of his childhood and adolescence, Chen recounts his coming of age with arresting simplicity." Publ Wkly

Chen, Pauline W.

★ Final exam; a surgeon's reflections on mortality. Alfred A. Knopf 2007 267p $23.95   **92**

1. Death 2. Physicians (General practice) -- Training of 3. Surgeons 4. Terminal care -- Ethical aspects
ISBN 978-0-307-26353-7; 0-307-26353-3

LC 2006-49361

"A graceful, precise, and empathetic writer enthralled by her work, Chen imparts much about medical schooling and surgery, too." Booklist
Includes bibliographical references

Cheng, Nien

Life and death in Shanghai. Grove Press 1987 547p hardcover o.p. pa $16   **92**

1. Memoirists 2. Political prisoners
ISBN 0-14-010870-X pa

LC 86-45254

This "is a volume that belongs on the shelf alongside the writings of Primo Levi, Elie Wiesel, Dith Pran, and other chroniclers of ideological fanaticism, its dehumanizing consequences, and its all too rare resisters." Christ Sci Monit

Chernow, Ron

★ Alexander Hamilton. Penguin Press 2004 818p il $35   **92**

1. Biography, Individual 2. Secretaries of the treasury 3. Statesmen
ISBN 1-594-20009-2

LC 2003-65641

"Chernow makes fresh contributions to Hamiltoniana: no one has discovered so much about Hamilton's illegitimate origins and harrowed youth; few have been so taken by Hamilton's long-suffering, loving wife, Eliza. . . . This is a fine work that captures Hamilton's life with judiciousness and verve." Publ Wkly
Includes bibliographical references

Titan: the life of John D. Rockefeller, Sr. Random House 1998 xxii, 774p il $30; pa $18   **92**

1. Energy industry executives 2. Philanthropists
ISBN 0-679-43808-4; 0-679-75703-1 pa

LC 97-33117

"This book is a triumph of the art of biography. Unflaggingly interesting, it brings John D. Rockefeller Sr. . . to life

through sustained narrative portraiture of the large-scale, 19th-century kind." N Y Times Book Rev
Includes bibliographical references

Washington; a life. Penguin Press 2010 xxi, 904p il $40   **92**

1. Biography, Individual 2. Presidents -- United States
ISBN 978-1-59420-266-7

LC 2010-19154

Chernow "has done justice to the solid flesh, the human frailty and the dental miseries of his subject—and also to his immense historical importance. . . . This is a magnificently fair, full-scale biography. Its judgments are lapidary." Economist
Includes bibliographical references

Chiger, Krystyna

The **girl** in the green sweater; a life in Holocaust's shadow. [by] Krystyna Chiger with Daniel Paisner. St. Martin's Press 2008 272p il $24.95 **92**

1. Dentists 2. Holocaust survivors 3. Holocaust, 1933-1945 -- Personal narratives 4. Jews -- Ukraine 5. Memoirists
ISBN 978-0-312-37656-7; 0-312-37656-1

LC 2008-22521

In 1943, with Lvov's 150,000 Jews having been killed, exiled, or forced into ghettos, a group of Polish Jews daringly sought refuge in the city's sewer system. Chiger, the last surviving member of this group, shares one of the most intimate, harrowing, and ultimately triumphant tales of survival to emerge from the Holocaust.

"With a powerful story and a keen voice, Chiger's Holocaust survivor's tale is a worthy and memorable addition to the canon." Publ Wkly

Child, Julia

As always, Julia; the letters of Julia Child and Avis DeVoto: food, friendship, and the making of a masterpiece. selected and edited by Joan Reardon. Houghton Mifflin Harcourt Pub. Co. 2010 416p il $26   **92**

1. Biography, Individual 2. Cookbook writers 3. Cooks 4. Editors 5. Literary critics 6. Television personalities
ISBN 9780547417714

LC 2010-25840

Presents more than 200 letters exchanged between Julia and Avis DeVoto, her friend and unofficial literary agent.

"Their letters span a wide range of topics, from cookbooks, menus, recipes, and restaurants to Balzac, sex, goose stuffing, gardening, learning languages, the political climate, Sunday afternoon cocktail parties, and proofreading. Witty, enlightening and entertaining." Publ Wkly

My life in France; [by] Julia Child with Alex Prud'homme. Knopf 2006 317p il $25.95   **92**

1. Cookbook writers 2. Cooks 3. Television personalities
ISBN 1-4000-4346-8; 978-1-4000-4346-0

LC 2005-44727

This is a "memoir of the famous chef's first, formative sojourn in France with her new husband, Paul Child, in 1949. . . . This is a valuable record of gorgeous meals in bygone Parisian restaurants, and the secret arts of a culinary genius." Publ Wkly

Ciezadlo, Annia

Day of honey; a memoir of food, love, and war. Free Press 2011 382p $26; pa $12.99 **92**

1. Food -- Social aspects 2. Journalists 3. Memoirists 4. Women journalists

ISBN 978-1-4165-8393-6; 1-4165-8393-9; 978-1-4165-8422-3 pa; 1-4165-8422-6 pa

LC 2010-19739

"There are many good reasons to read 'Day of Honey.' It's a carefully researched tour through the history of Middle Eastern food. It's filled with adrenalized scenes from war zones, scenes of narrow escapes and clandestine phone calls and frightening cultural misunderstandings. . . . These things wouldn't matter much, though, if her sentences didn't make such a sensual, smart, wired-up sound on the page." N Y Times Book Rev

Includes bibliographical references

Clapton, Eric, 1945-

Clapton; the autobiography. Broadway Books 2007 343p il $26 **92**

1. Biography, Individual 2. Guitarists 3. Rock musicians 4. Singers

ISBN 978-0-385-51851-2; 0-385-51851-X

LC 2007-15482

"As he retraces every step of his career, from the early stints with the Yardbirds and Cream to his solo successes, Clapton also devotes copious detail to his drug and alcohol addictions, particularly how they intersected with his romantic obsession with Pattie Boyd. . . . Both the youthful excesses and the current calm state are narrated with an engaging tone that nudges Clapton's story ahead of other rock 'n' roll memoirs." Publ Wkly

Clark, Ella Elizabeth

★ **Sacagawea** of the Lewis and Clark expedition; {by} Ella E. Clark and Margot Edmonds. University of Calif. Press 1979 171p il hardcover o.p. pa $16.95 **92**

1. Guides (Persons) 2. Interpreters

ISBN 0-520-05060-6 pa

LC 78-65466

"Sacagawea, the Shoshone Indian woman who accompanied the Lewis and Clark expedition, has been a regional heroine and a feminist celebrity for most of this century. But, as these writers show, her role as 'the guide' was more fictive than actual. . . . Based on careful interpretation of the explorer's journals, this revisionist study does a good job of redefining her actual contributions." Booklist

Includes bibliographical references

Clarke, Donald

Billie Holiday; wishing on the moon. Da Capo 2002 468p il pa $21 **92**

1. African American singers 2. Blues musicians 3. Singers

ISBN 0-306-81136-7; 978-0-306-81136-4

This biography "not only chronicles every phase of Holiday's ascent from the streets of Baltimore to the stages of New York's hottest nightclubs and most prestigious concert halls, but also documents every significant recording session, performance, and tour. . . . Clarke's portrait embraces every facet of Holiday's paradoxical nature, from her fierceness to her vulnerability, her childlikeness to her innate elegance and amazing strength." Booklist

Clarke, Thurston

The **last** campaign; Robert F. Kennedy and 82 days that inspired America. Thurston Clarke. Henry Holt 2008 321p il $25; pa $15 **92**

1. Attorneys general 2. Presidential candidates 3. Senators 4. Siblings of presidents

ISBN 978-0-8050-7792-6; 0-8050-7792-8; 978-0-8050-9022-2 pa; 0-8050-9022-3 pa

LC 2007-45880

In this account of Robert F. Kennedy's run for president, Clarke "follows on Bobby's heels as he plunged headlong into his campaign, from Kansas and Indiana to Oregon and California, throwing off his brother's mantle and becoming at last his own man. He spoke passionately, almost recklessly, inciting crowds to frenzy with his idealistic speeches about the moral shame of Vietnam, the needs of the poor and minorities and the responsibility of each American. Incorporating accounts by a gamut of reporters, politicians, family and 'Honorary Kennedys,' as well as extracts from Bobby's own stunning stump speeches, Clarke compellingly recreates this 'huge, joyous adenture.'" Kirkus

Includes bibliographical references

Clary, David A.

★ **Rocket** man; Robert H. Goddard and the birth of the space age. Hyperion 2003 324p il $24.95 **92**

1. Aeronautical engineers 2. Aerospace engineers 3. Physicists 4. Rocketry 5. Rocketry -- United States

ISBN 0-7868-6817-1

LC 2002-27321

In this biography Goddard emerges "as a paradoxical man who relentlessly promoted his work, winning hundreds of thousands of dollars in Guggenheim grants, while shunning offers to collaborate with other scientists. Clary presents a clear and relatively straightforward narrative of his subject's life. . . . Readers who come to this generally well-written biography with some knowledge of Goddard's significance will find much of interest to fill out their knowledge of this complex and fascinating scientist for whom NASA's Goddard Space Center is named." Publ Wkly

Includes bibliographical references

Clavin, Thomas

Roger Maris; baseball's reluctant hero. [by] Tom Clavin and Danny Peary. Simon & Schuster 2010 422p il $26.99 **92**

1. Baseball -- Biography 2. Baseball -- History 3. Baseball players

ISBN 978-1-4165-8928-0; 1-4165-8928-7

LC 2009-39722

The authors "trace the dramatic arc of Maris's life, from his boyhood in Fargo through his early pro career in the Cleveland Indians farm program, to his World Series championship years in New York and beyond. At the center is the exciting story of the 1961 season and the ordeal Maris endured as an outsider in Yankee pinstripes, unloved by fans who compared him unfavorably to their heroes Ruth and Mantle, relentlessly attacked by an aggressive press corps who found him cold and inaccessible, and treated miserably by the organization." Publisher's note

Includes bibliographical references

Cleland, Max

Heart of a patriot; how I found the courage to survive Vietnam, Walter Reed and Karl Rove. [by] Max Cleland, with Ben Raines. Simon & Schuster 2009 259p il $26   **92**
1. Amputees 2. Government officials 3. Senators 4. State government officials 5. Veterans 6. Veterans -- United States
ISBN 978-1-4391-2605-9

LC 2009-11620

"This heartrending memoir is aimed at former soldiers who have struggled with the trauma of war and at those of us who haven't served in the military but need to understand the personal cost to those who have." Booklist

Includes bibliographical references

Clinton, Bill

My life. Knopf 2004 957p il $35   **92**
1. Biography, Individual 2. Governors 3. Presidents 4. Presidents -- United States 5. United States -- Politics and government -- 1993-
ISBN 0-375-41457-6

LC 2004-107564

In this memoir the former president traces his life from his childhood in Arkansas through his time as governor of Arkansas and then focuses on his White House years.

"Clinton's memoir has the raw material for a blockbuster book." Publ Wkly

Clinton, Catherine

Mrs. Lincoln; a life. HarperCollins 2009 415p il $26.99   **92**
1. Biography, Individual 2. Lawyers 3. Members of Congress 4. Presidents 5. Presidents' spouses -- United States 6. Spouses of presidents 7. State legislators
ISBN 978-0-06-076040-3; 0-06-076040-0

The author "sifts through the many criticisms of Mary Lincoln to offer a sensitive reassessment that debunks unjust attacks and reveals Mrs. Lincoln's many strengths—charitableness, devotion to family and nation, unwavering love and encouragement for her beleaguered husband—alongside the mental illness and flaws of temperament for which she is better known. . . . Written in a style that will appeal to the general reader, Clinton's book features sufficient nuance to satisfy scholars looking for a greater interpretation of the life of this controversial historical figure." Libr J

Includes bibliographical references

Coates, Ta-Nehisi

The **beautiful** struggle. Spiegel & Grau 2008 223p map $22.95; pa $14   **92**
1. African Americans -- Social conditions 2. Essayists

3. Father-son relationship
ISBN 978-0-3855-2036-2; 0-3855-2036-0; 978-0-3855-2746-0 pa; 0-3855-2746-2 pa

LC 2007-52166

"Coates grew up in a tough Baltimore neighborhood, subject to the same temptations as other young black boys. But he had a father in the household, a man steeped in race consciousness and willing to go to any lengths—including beatings—to keep his sons on the right path. With sharp cultural observations and emotional depth, Coates recalls an adolescence of surreptitiously standing on corners eying girls, drinking fifths, and earning reps, mindful of his father's admonition about the Knowledge. . . . A beautifully written, loving portrait of a strong father bringing his sons to manhood." Booklist

Cockburn, Henry

Henry's demons; living with schizophrenia: a father and son's story. [by] Patrick Cockburn and Henry Cockburn. Scribner 2011 238p il $25; ebook $11.99   **92**
1. Artists 2. Father-son relationship 3. Painters 4. Schizophrenia 5. Schizophrenics
ISBN 978-1-4391-5470-0; 1-4391-5470-8; 978-1-4391-6035-0 ebook; 1-4391-6035-X ebook

LC 2010-17760

"This straightforward, unsentimental book, is a bold plea for more research and cutting-edge therapies to combat mental illness." Publ Wkly

Cohen, Morton Norton

★ **Lewis** Carroll; a biography. by Morton N. Cohen. Knopf 1995 xxiii, 577p il hardcover o.p. pa $14.36   **92**
1. Authors 2. Children's authors 3. Mathematicians 4. Novelists 5. Writers on science
ISBN 0-679-74562-9 pa

LC 95-2663

"Delightfully illustrated with photographs and Carroll's drawings woven throughout, this extraordinary, meticulous biography gives us a sharper and deeper picture of Carroll than any before, presenting a many-sided man." Publ Wkly

Cohen-Solal, Annie

Leo & his circle; the life of Leo Castelli. Alfred A. Knopf 2010 540p il $35   **92**
1. Art dealers 2. Biography, Individual
ISBN 978-1-4000-4427-6; 1-4000-4427-8

LC 2009-34454

This is a biography of the art dealer from Trieste who came to New York in 1941 and opened his first New York gallery in 1957. Castelli displayed early work by Andy Warhol, Jasper Johns, Roy Lichtenstein, and Cy Twombly.

This "biography fleshes out not only a fascinating portrait of Castelli but also the excitement of the developing American art world to which he was so central." Publ Wkly

Includes bibliographical references

Cohodas, Nadine

Princess Noire; the tumultuous reign of Nina Simone. Pantheon Books 2010 449p il $30   **92**
1. African American musicians 2. African American

singers 3. Biography, Individual 4. Jazz musicians 5. Pianists 6. Singers 7. Songwriters 8. Soul musicians
ISBN 0-307-37899-3 ebook; 0-375-42401-6; 978-0-307-37899-6 ebook; 978-0-375-42401-4

LC 2009-22252

This is a biography of the singer. Discography. Bibliography. Index.

"Looking at every aspect of Simone's work, from stage decorum to audience interaction, the author offers many rich insights into her subject's conflicted emotional world. Throughout, she nurtures the reader's empathy for the artist but takes care to avoid unfounded speculation on racism or gender bias. In fact, this is a 360-degree profile of Simone, offering solid critical insights at every turn." Choice

Includes discography and bibliographical references

Cole, K. C.

Something incredibly wonderful happens; Frank Oppenheimer and the world he made up. Houghton Mifflin Harcourt 2009 396p il $27   **92**

1. Biography, Individual 2. College teachers 3. Museum administrators 4. Physicists
ISBN 978-0-15-100822-3; 0-15-100822-1

LC 2008052954

This is a biography of the physicist and young brother of J. Robert Oppenheimer.

"In a thought-provoking and pleasant manner, Cole's much-welcomed book shines a new light on a remarkable man and scientist. Readers interested in good popular science biographies will enjoy this." Libr J

Includes bibliographical references

Cole, Natalie

Angel on my shoulder; an autobiography. written with Digby Diehl. Warner Bks. 2000 353p il $38   **92**

1. Pop musicians 2. Singers 3. Singers -- United States -- Biography 4. Women singers -- United States -- Biography
ISBN 978-0-446-52746-0; 0-446-52746-7

LC 00-61455

In this memoir by the daughter of the late Nat King Cole, the Grammy Award-winning songstress recalls her childhood, her personal battle and victory over drugs and alcohol, and the legal battles with her mother and siblings over her father's estate

"Although she concentrates mostly on the good times, Cole isn't shy about the bad times, which makes this intriguing, engaging, and inspirational life story worthy of attention." Booklist

Coleman, Melissa

This life is in your hands; one dream, sixty acres, and a family undone. HarperCollins 2011 325p il map $25.99; ebook $12.99   **92**

1. Authors 2. Biography, Individual 3. Columnists 4. Death 5. Farm life -- Maine 6. Farm life -- Maine -- Penobscot Bay region 7. Farmers 8. Gardeners 9. Loss (Psychology) 10. Memoirists
ISBN 978-0-06-195832-8; 978-0-06-208735-5 ebook

LC 2010-24942

"Especially pertinent to those with an interest in self-sufficiency and the locavore movement, this book is packed with historical information beyond the family story. Ultimately, a complex tale of a noble pursuit with tragic consequences." Libr J

Coleman, Rick

Blue Monday; Fats Domino and the lost dawn of rock 'n' roll. Da Capo 2006 364p il map hardcover o.p. pa $15.95   **92**

1. African American musicians 2. Pianists 3. Rock musicians 4. Singers
ISBN 0-306-81491-9; 978-0-306-81531-7 pa; 0-306-81531-1 pa

Coleman has crafted a "biography of Fats Domino, drawing on new interviews with the pianist himself. From his childhood in New Orleans through the early days of rock'n'roll, when he endured travel difficulties in the segregated South and frequent riots at his concerts, Fats remained a shy but demanding performer and personality. A homesick father who seemed to cherish his family, Fats was also a hard-drinking womanizer, and Coleman tells his story with compassion and honesty up to Fats's survival of Hurricane Katrina in his Ninth Ward home. His argument that rock'n'roll sprung from Fats and the New Orleans sound is hard to dispute, as Fats was playing long before others now credited with starting the revolution. Despite the occasional slips into fandom, this is an essential purchase for any library collecting the history of rock'n'roll." Libr J

Includes bibliographical references

Collins, Paul

The **trouble** with Tom: the strange afterlife and times of Thomas Paine. Bloomsbury 2005 278p map hardcover o.p. pa $15   **92**

1. Essayists 2. Pamphleteers 3. Political and social philosophers 4. Writers on politics 5. Writers on religion
ISBN 1-58234-502-3; 1-58234-613-5 pa

LC 2005-45240

The author "traces the bizarre story of Thomas Paine's remains through nearly two centuries of American and English history. . . . Part travelogue, part memoir and part historical mystery, this book reads like a wry, witty novel and offers a delicious twist at the end." Publ Wkly

Includes bibliographical references

Coltman, Leycester

The **real** Fidel Castro; with a foreword by Julia E. Sweig. Yale Univ. Press 2003 335p il map $30; pa $20   **92**

1. Biography, Individual 2. Communist leaders 3. Presidents
ISBN 0-300-10188-0; 0-300-10760-9 pa

LC 2003-12942

This biography "offers a fresh assessment of the revolutionary leader. . . . It chronicles the events of Castro's extraordinary life and explores the contradiction between the private character and the public reputation." Univ Press Books for Public and Second Sch Libr, 2004

Includes bibliographical references

Common

One day it'll all make sense; a memoir. by Common with Adam Bradley. 1st Atria Books hardcover ed.; Atria Books 2011 305 p. ill. (chiefly col.) $25   **92**

1. Rap musicians -- United States -- Biography
ISBN 9781451625875; 9781451625882 pa; 9781451625905

LC 2011021691

The author of the book, the hip-hop musician Common, discusses fame and the deeper meanings of his life. . . . He portrays himself as an openhearted, curious kid, trying to understand the tumult of Chicago's African-American South Side. . . . Common writes frankly about his youthful involvement with gang culture, portrayed as an inevitable rite of passage that became increasingly violent. . . . By 1989, his early demos as Common Sense were drawing industry attention, and he dropped out of college to pursue this calling, over his mother's objections. Much of what follows is a . . . showbiz narrative, moving from hip-hop to film acting. (Kirkus)

Connolly, Kevin Michael

Double take; a memoir. HarperStudio 2009 227p il $19.99; pa $14.99   **92**

1. Athletes 2. Handicapped 3. Photographers 4. Physically handicapped athletes 5. Skateboarding 6. Skiers 7. Skiing
ISBN 978-0-06-179153-6; 978-0-06-179152-9 pa

LC 2009-30496

"An X Games competitive skier and photographer recounts an extraordinary life spent overcoming immense physical limitations. Connolly was born without legs in the summer of 1985, in Helena, Mont. . . . A courageous, immensely rewarding chronicle expressed in arresting words and pictures." Kirkus

Connor, James A.

Pascal's wager; the man who played dice with God. HarperSanFrancisco 2006 224p il $24.95 **92**

1. Mathematicians 2. Theologians 3. Writers on religion
ISBN 978-0-06-076691-7; 0-06-076691-3

LC 2006-43489

This biography of the mathematician and theologian focuses on his Jansenist religious beliefs.

This book "should interest readers drawn to the crossroads of religion and science." Booklist
Includes bibliographical references

Conquest, Robert

Stalin; breaker of nations. Viking 1991 346p il hardcover o.p. pa $14.95   **92**

1. Communist leaders 2. Dictators 3. Heads of state 4. Political leaders
ISBN 0-14-016953-9 pa

LC 91-28782

"Intended for the general reader, [this work] provides a superb portrait of the man who terrorized his country for 30 years. . . . Briskly written, authoritative yet not pedantic,

filled with interesting incidents and anecdotes, [it] makes for fascinating reading." N Y Times Book Rev
Includes bibliographical references

Conway, J. North

The big policeman; the rise and fall of America's first, most ruthless, and greatest detective. Lyons Press 2010 323p il $24.95   **92**

1. Detectives 2. Police -- New York (N.Y.) 3. Police officials
ISBN 978-1-59921-965-3

This is a biography of "Thomas Byrnes, a New York City law enforcer whose career peaked in the 1890s as superintendent of the police force. Impressed by Byrnes' ascent, which began with street-patrol courageousness in the city's 1863 antidraft, antiblack riots, Conway proceeds to Byrnes' successes as a detective, which form the core of the biography. Going case-by-case, . . . Conway combines narrative with explanation of Byrnes' methods of investigation and interrogation. . . . Creating period atmosphere by quoting extensively from newspaper accounts of the sensational crimes Byrnes solved, Conway portrays his subject's cleverness and excesses with a flawed-hero flavor that should draw in true-crime fans." Booklist
Includes bibliographical references

Conway, Jill K.

True north; a memoir. Knopf 1994 250p hardcover o.p. pa $13   **92**

1. College presidents 2. College teachers 3. Historians
ISBN 0-679-74461-4 pa

LC 93-45302

"Conway analyzes her own experiences in the U.S. and Canada just as thoughtfully and penetratingly as her academic work investigates the lives of several previous generations of American women." Booklist

Cook, Blanche Wiesen

Eleanor Roosevelt. v2 Viking 1999 686p v2 hardcover o.p. pa $20   **92**

1. Biography, Individual 2. Columnists 3. Diplomats 4. Humanitarians 5. Presidents' spouses -- United States 6. Social activists 7. Spouses of presidents 8. United Nations officials
ISBN 0-14-017894-5 pa

"Cook is unafraid to take on difficult issues . . . thus rendering the biography not simply a riveting read but also a profoundly moving and wise account of how history has been shaped by the intricacies of the human heart, mind and spirit." Publ Wkly
Includes bibliographical references

Cook, Kevin

Tommy's honor; the story of old Tom Morris and young Tom Morris, golf's founding father and son. Gotham Books 2007 327p il $27.50   **92**

1. Golf 2. Golfers
ISBN 978-1-59240-297-7; 1-59240-297-6

LC 2007-8165

"In Cook's telling, the story of Tom Morris, winner of golf's first Open Championship in 1860, and his son, Tom-

my, who won the Open three years in a row, becomes a compelling saga of near-Homeric proportions." Booklist
Includes bibliographical references

Cook, Richard

It's about that time; Miles Davis on and off record. Oxford University Press 2007 373p il $27 **92**
1. African American musicians 2. Band leaders 3. Flugelhornists 4. Jazz musicians 5. Trumpet players
ISBN 978-0-19-532266-8; 0-19-532266-5

LC 2006-50694

"Cook's thoughtful, illuminating criticism and boundless knowledge of his subject make this a rich and satisfying read for jazz aficionados and novices alike." Publ Wkly
Includes discography and bibliographical references

Cook, Richard M.

Alfred Kazin's journals; selected and edited by Richard M. Cook. Yale University Press 2011 598p $45 **92**
1. Biography, Individual
ISBN 978-0-300-14203-7; 0-300-14203-X

LC 2010-45254

The literary critic's "passions — for sex, for novels, for ideas, for talk, for city life — spill from 'Alfred Kazin's Journals,' edited by his biographer, Richard M. Cook. This is a remarkable book, easily one of the great diaries and moral documents of the past American century. What it lacks in cohesiveness it makes up in its frankness, its quick-pivoting angularities. Kazin dismisses his journal at one point as a 'disorderly pile of shavings.' That disorder only adds to its amplitude." N Y Times Book Rev
Includes bibliographical references

Cooper, Helene

The **house** at Sugar Beach; in search of a lost African childhood. Simon & Schuster 2008 354p il map $25 **92**
1. Biography, Individual 2. Journalists
ISBN 0-7432-6624-2; 978-0-7432-6624-6

The author traces her childhood in wartorn Liberia and her reunion with a foster sister who had been left behind when her family fled the region.

"A coming-of-age story told with unremitting honesty. With her pedigree and her freedom from internalized racism, Cooper is liberated to enjoy a social universe that is a fluid mix of all things American and African. . . . While Cooper's memoir is mesmerizing in its portrayal of a Liberia rarely witnessed, its description of the psychological devastation—and coping mechanisms—brought on by profound loss is equally captivating." N Y Times Book Rev

Cooper, John Milton

Woodrow Wilson; a biography. Alfred A. Knopf 2009 702p il $35 **92**
1. Biography, Individual 2. College presidents 3. Governors 4. Nobel laureates for peace 5. Presidents 6. Presidents -- United States
ISBN 978-0-307-26541-8

LC 2009-19097

This is a biography of the twenty-eighth president of the United States. Index.

"Cooper exhibits complete command of his materials, a sure knowledge of the man and a nuanced understanding of a presidency almost Shakespearean in its dimensions." Kirkus
Includes bibliographical references (p. [601]-668) and index.

The **warrior** and the priest: Woodrow Wilson and Theodore Roosevelt; [by] John Milton Cooper, Jr. Belknap Press 1983 442p il hardcover o.p. pa $20.95 **92**
1. College presidents 2. Governors 3. Nobel laureates for peace 4. Presidents 5. Presidents -- United States 6. Vice-presidents
ISBN 0-674-94751-7 pa

LC 83-6021

The author's "distinctions are sharp, his insights original, his judgments balanced and his narrative unfailingly graceful." N Y Times Book Rev
Includes bibliographical references

Cordery, Stacy A.

Alice; Alice Roosevelt Longworth, from White House princess to Washington power broker. Viking 2007 590p il $32.95 **92**
1. Biography, Individual 2. Children of presidents 3. Governors 4. Nobel laureates for peace 5. Presidents 6. Socialites 7. Vice-presidents
ISBN 978-0-670-01833-8

LC 2006-103087

This is a biography of Alice Roosevelt Longworth, the Washington hostess and author of Crowded Hours (1933).

The author "pens an authoritative, intriguing portrait of a first daughter who broke the mold." Publ Wkly
Includes bibliographical references (p. [555]-572) and index.

Cornwell, John

Hitler's pope: the secret history of Pius XII. Viking 1999 430p il hardcover o.p. pa $15 **92**
1. Heads of state 2. Nazi leaders 3. Popes 4. World War, 1939-1945 -- Catholic Church
ISBN 0-14-029627-1 pa

LC 99-28311

"Relying on exclusive access to Vatican and Jesuit archives, . . . {the author} argues that through a 1933 Concordat with Hitler, Pope Pius XII facilitated the dictator's rise—and, ultimately, the Holocaust." Libr J
Includes bibliographical references

The **pontiff** in winter; triumph and conflict in the reign of John Paul II. Doubleday 2004 336p il $24.95; pa $14.95 **92**
1. Biography, Individual 2. Catholic Church 3. Popes
ISBN 0-385-51484-0; 0-385-51485-9 pa

LC 2004-58306

The author "argues that John Paul's mystical view of history and conviction that his mission has been divinely established are central to understanding his pontificate." Publisher's note
Includes bibliographical references

Corrigan, Kelly

The **middle** place. Voice/Hyperion 2008 266p il $23.95; pa $14.95   **92**

1. Breast cancer 2. Cancer patients 3. Columnists

ISBN 978-1-4013-0336-5; 978-1-4013-4093-3 pa

LC 2007-15316

The author "was a happily married mother of two young daughters when she discovered a cancerous lump in her breast. She was still undergoing treatment when she learned that her beloved father, who'd already survived prostate cancer, now had bladder cancer. Corrigan's story could have been unbearably depressing had she not made it clear from the start that she came from sturdy stock. . . . Those learning to accept their own adulthood might find strength—and humor—in Corrigan's feisty memoir." Publ Wkly

Coupland, Douglas

Marshall McLuhan; you know nothing of my work! Atlas & Co. 2010 216p $24   **92**

1. Authors 2. Literary critics 3. Mass media 4. Nonfiction writers 5. Sociologists 6. Television critics

ISBN 978-1-935633-16-7

This is a biography of the Canadian mass media specialist.

"The book rewards by refusing to slip into the numbing vortex of academic discourse, taking a fizzy, pop-culture approach to explaining a deep thinker, one who ended up popularized almost in spite of himself." N Y Times Book Rev

Cox, Lynne

Swimming to Antarctica; tales of a long-distance swimmer. Knopf 2004 323p $24.95   **92**

1. Biography, Individual 2. Long distance swimming 3. Swimmers 4. Women athletes

ISBN 0-375-41507-6

LC 2003-47577

"Cox is a pleasure. . . . Many passages are grip-the-page exciting, whether she's dodging Antarctic icebergs or Nile River sewage." Booklist

Coyle, Daniel

Lance Armstrong's war; one man's battle against fate, fame, love, death, scandal, and a few other rivals on the road to the Tour de France. HarperCollins Publishers 2005 326p il $25.95   **92**

1. Athletes 2. Biography, Individual 3. Cyclists 4. Olympic athletes

ISBN 0-06-073497-3

LC 2005-279702

This biography focuses particular attention on the American cyclist's preparation for and participation in the 2004 Tour de France, an event that Armstrong won for the sixth time in as many years.

"This work is honest, personal and passionate, with plenty to chew on for fans and novices alike." Publ Wkly

Crais, Clifton C.

Sara Baartman and the Hottentot Venus; a ghost story and a biography. [by] Clifton Crais and Pamela Scully. Princeton University Press 2009 232p il map $29.95   **92**

1. Biography, Individual 2. Museum exhibits -- Moral and ethical aspects 3. Racism in museum exhibits

ISBN 9780691135809; 0-691-13580-0

LC 2008-14918

"A member of a small indigenous tribe of herdsmen dubbed the Hottentots by Dutch colonists (but known today by their name Khoikhoi), Baartman was captured in the course of ongoing colonial warfare that effected a genocidal destruction of this peaceful people. Having been enslaved, she was taken to Europe by a member of the family that 'owned' and exhibited her much as an exotic animal might be. . . . [The authors] have done an excellent job not only of telling this rebarbative story but of putting it into the context of its time. This enables them to explain what permitted such an exhibition while at the same time viewing it through our (thankfully) more humane and enlightened lens." Los Angeles Times Book Rev

Includes bibliographical references

Crane, Kathleen

Sea legs; tales of a woman oceanographer. Westview Press 2003 318p il map hardcover o.p. pa $16   **92**

1. Oceanographers 2. Oceanography 3. Oceanography -- History 4. Women scientists

ISBN 0-8133-4004-7; 0-8133-4285-6 pa

LC 2003-1690

"Crane chronicles the relentless adversity she faced in becoming a world-class oceanographer with a modest matter-of-factness that almost camouflages the high caliber of her achievements. . . . She was the first to postulate the existence of the now famous deep-sea hot springs. . . . Crane's experiences are diverse, dramatic, and important; her understanding of international affairs and environmental realities laudable and moving; and her triumphs over personal sorrows and illness impressive and inspiring." Booklist

Includes bibliographical references

Cranston, Maurice

Jean-Jacques: the early life and work of Jean-Jacques Rousseau, 1712-1754. University of Chicago Press 1991 382p il map pa $23   **92**

1. Authors 2. Memoirists 3. Novelists 4. Political and social philosophers

ISBN 0-226-11862-2

LC 90-45994

"Cranston presents Rousseau's work in the context of his life. He proceeds impartially but not dispassionately; his scholarship is impeccable but not obtrusive. The result is a most readable narrative that has something for readers at all levels of sophistication." Choice

Includes bibliographical references

The **noble** savage: Jean-Jacques Rousseau, 1754-1762. University of Chicago Press 1991 399p il $45; pa $20   **92**

1. Authors 2. Memoirists 3. Novelists 4. Political and social philosophers

ISBN 0-226-11863-0; 0-226-11864-9 pa

LC 90-28111

"Cranston offers the finest and most richly detailed portrait ever assembled of these vagabond years." New Statesman Soc

Includes bibliographical references

The **solitary** self: Jean-Jacques Rousseau in exile and adversity; with a foreword by Sanford Lakoff. University of Chicago Press 1997 247p il $35; pa $20   **92**
1. Authors 2. Memoirists 3. Novelists 4. Political and social philosophers
ISBN 0-226-11865-7; 0-226-11866-5 pa
LC 96-12922
"This final volume in Cranston's definitive trilogy chronicles Rousseau's last turbulent years as an outcast in England and Neuchatel, after the burning of "Emile" and the order for his arrest. . . . This is a scholarly yet ingratiating portrayal of a man whose last years found him battling sciatica and Voltaire, enjoying botany and Boswell. Cranston's authoritative work has given us an invaluable account of the paradoxical life of an emotionally devoted yet tactlessly demanding man." Booklist
Includes bibliographical references

Crapol, Edward P.
★ **John** Tyler; the accidental president. University of North Carolina Press 2006 332p il map $37.50   **92**
1. Biography, Individual 2. Governors 3. History 4. Members of Congress 5. Presidents 6. Senators 7. Vice-presidents
ISBN 978-0-8078-3041-3; 0-8078-3041-0
LC 2005-37963
In this biography of the former U.S. president, the author "argues that Tyler was in fact a terrifically strong president who helped strengthen the executive branch. . . . This balanced, fascinating volume will introduce a new generation of readers to an oft-ignored president." Publ Wkly
Includes bibliographical references

Crawford, Bill
★ **All** American; the rise and fall of Jim Thorpe. John Wiley & Sons, Inc 2004 284p il $24.95   **92**
1. Athletes 2. Decathletes 3. Native Americans -- Biography 4. Olympic athletes 5. Pentathletes
ISBN 0-471-55732-3
LC 2004-14376
This "terse, punchy biography of sports legend Thorpe (1888–1953) illuminates the current debate over the exploitation of unpaid college athletes by moneymaking, headline-grabbing educational institutions." Publ Wkly
Includes bibliographical references

Crawford, Robert
The **bard**; Robert Burns, a biography. Princeton University Press 2009 465p $35   **92**
1. Authors 2. Poets
ISBN 978-0-691-14171-8; 0-691-14171-1
LC 2008-937561
"Crawford's Burns, merrily mixing high and low culture, seems eerily contemporary. He shares with great hip-hop artists a genius for catchy, sexy, and memorable rhymes

gloriously liberated from the hegemony of standard English." New Yorker
Includes bibliographical references

Creamer, Robert W.
Babe; the legend comes to life. Simon & Schuster 1974 443p il hardcover o.p. pa $14   **92**
1. Baseball -- Biography 2. Baseball players
ISBN 0-671-76070-X pa
This biography covers Babe Ruth's personal life and his sports career.

Cross, Charles R.
Heavier than heaven: a biography of Kurt Cobain. Hyperion 2001 381p il $24.95; pa $14.95 **92**
1. Guitarists 2. Rock musicians 3. Singers
ISBN 0-7868-6505-9; 0-7868-8402-9 pa
LC 2001-24187
This is a biography of Kurt Cobain, the lead singer of the rock group Nirvana, who committed suicide in 1994 at the age of 27.
"Cross followed the Nirvana juggernaut from the beginning, and though he nearly bludgeons the reader with tales of Cobain's debauched excesses, one is still drawn to the artist's forceful personality." Libr J

★ **Room** full of mirrors; a biography of Jimi Hendrix. Hyperion 2005 384p il $24.95; pa $15.99   **92**
1. Biography, Individual 2. Guitarists 3. Rock musicians 4. Singers
ISBN 1-401-30028-6; 0-7868-8841-5 pa
LC 2005-46362
"Admirably comprehensive and well referenced, this is the Hendrix biography to acquire if you can acquire only one." Booklist
Includes bibliographical references

Crowe, David
Oskar Schindler; the untold account of his life, wartime activities, and the true story behind the list. [by] David M. Crowe. Westview Press 2004 766p il $30   **92**
1. Biography, Individual 2. Humanitarians 3. Manufacturing executives
ISBN 0-8133-3375-X
LC 2004-13879
This book "is essential in understanding one of the most extraordinary figures from the Holocaust." Booklist
Includes bibliographical references

Crowell, Rodney
★ **Chinaberry** sidewalks. Alfred A. Knopf 2011 259p il $24.95   **92**
1. Biography, Individual 2. Country musicians 3. Singers 4. Songwriters
ISBN 978-0-307-59420-4
LC 2010-35996
"Crowell is among the best storytellers to emerge from Nashville. Up to now, he told his stories in song, but with this heartfelt memoir, he can now be called a writer of the first order. Houston, where Crowell grew up in the 1950s and

early 1960s, was a city full of characters found in stereotypical country songs: hard-drinking fathers and longsuffering mothers singing along to the beer-soaked ballads of Hank Williams. But this is not fiction; Crowell actually lived the life, soaking up its exhilarating and disturbing atmosphere. Crowell is unsparingly honest, yet there is an admirable restraint here, too." Booklist

Culkin, Jennifer

A **final** arc of sky; a memoir of critical care. Beacon Press 2009 237p $24.95   92
1. Authors 2. Essayists 3. Nurses 4. Nursing
ISBN 978-0-8070-7285-1
LC 2008-46810

"It's clear that Culkin has little use for cheap sentiment. However, this memoir time and again shares with us her efforts to make meaning of the pain and fear and loss that is intrinsic to her line of work. . . . The author gets even more personal when she shares stories from her own family. With unflinching honesty, she talks about how she coped with the decline of her father's health; what she did at the deathbed of her mother; and how she came to terms with her own MS diagnosis. 'A Final Arc of Sky' tackles that toughest of subjects—our own mortality—with grit, compassion, and humor." Bellingham Herald
Includes bibliographical references

Curtis, James

Spencer Tracy; a biography. Alfred A. Knopf 2011 1001p il $39.95; ebook $19.99   92
1. Actors 2. Biography, Individual
ISBN 978-0-307-26289-9; 978-0-307-59522-5 ebook
LC 2011014719

The author "presents an exhaustive and exhausting biography of the legendary Hollywood star, famed for his uncanny naturalism and authority on camera and best remembered for the series of films he made with longtime companion Katharine Hepburn. . . . A monumental, definitive biography of one the finest film actors in the history of the medium." Kirkus
Includes bibliographical references and index

D'Antonio, Michael

Forever blue; the true story of Walter O'Malley, baseball's most controversial owner, and the Dodgers of Brooklyn and Los Angeles. Riverhead Books 2009 355p il $25.95   92
1. Baseball -- Biography 2. Baseball executives 3. Biography, Individual
ISBN 978-1-59448-856-6; 1-59448-856-8
LC 2008-46311

"This is a wonderfully readable, insightful, and—for anyone interested in baseball history—important biography

of the man who forever changed the course of the game in America." Booklist
Includes bibliographical references

Hershey; Milton S. Hershey's extraordinary life of wealth, empire, and utopian dreams. Simon & Schuster 2006 305p il hardcover o.p. pa $15   92
1. Biography, Individual 2. Food industry executives
ISBN 0-7432-6409-6; 0-7432-6410-X pa
LC 2005-51581

"While some look at Hershey and see either a beneficent angel or a willful tyrant, it is the great charm of D'Antonio's book that he will not plunk entirely for one judgment or the other. It's the man he's after, not the god." N Y Times Book Rev
Includes bibliographical references

D'Este, Carlo

Patton; a genius for war. HarperCollins Pubs. 1995 977p il maps hardcover o.p. pa $21   92
1. Army officers 2. Generals
ISBN 0-06-092762-3 pa
LC 95-38433

In this biography of the World War II general the author "provides new information from family archives and other sources about Patton's ancestry, childhood and pre-WW II military career. . . . The account of Patton's campaigns from North Africa through Sicily, Normandy and the Ardennes enables the reader to understand why the general is regarded as one of the great military leaders. This is a major biography of a major American military figure." Publ Wkly
Includes bibliographical references

Warlord; a life of Winston Churchill at war, 1874-1945. Harper 2008 845p il map $39.95   92
1. Biography, Individual 2. Cabinet members 3. Historians 4. Members of Parliament 5. Memoirists 6. Nobel laureates for literature 7. Prime ministers 8. Prime ministers -- Great Britain 9. Statesmen 10. Strategy 11. World War, 1914-1918 -- Campaigns 12. World War, 1939-1945 -- Campaigns 13. World war, 1939-1945 -- Great Britain
ISBN 978-0-06-057573-1; 0-06-057573-5
LC 2008-9272

A biography of Winston Churchill's military career from his youth through World War II.

"D'Este has produced an outstanding work that should take its rightful place alongside the dozens of other studies of this most remarkable statesman." Libr J
Includes bibliographical references

Dalai Lama

★ **Freedom** in exile; the autobiography of the Dalai Lama. HarperCollins Pubs. 1990 288p il maps hardcover o.p. pa $15   92
1. Buddhism 2. Buddhist leaders 3. Nobel laureates for peace 4. Political leaders
ISBN 0-06-098701-4
LC 89-46523

"The Dalai Lama's story is, in part, a chapter in the 2,500-year history of Buddhism as well as a testament to the 'mendacity and barbarity' of Communist China. He shares the details of his amazing life, a glimpse at some of the mysteries of Tibetan Buddhism, and his unshakable belief in the basic good of humanity." Booklist

Dallek, Robert

Harry S. Truman; 1945-1953. Times Books 2008 183p $22 **92**

1. Presidents 2. Presidents -- United States 3. Senators 4. Vice-presidents

ISBN 978-0-8050-6938-9

LC 2008-10193

This is a biography of the 33rd president.

This book is "the best starting point for knowledge of Truman's life and for an astute assessment of his career." Publ Wkly

Includes bibliographical references

Let every nation know; John F. Kennedy in his own words. [by] Robert Dallek and Terry Golway. Sourcebooks MediaFusion 2006 289p il $29.95; pa $19.95 **92**

1. Biography, Individual 2. Members of Congress 3. Presidents 4. Presidents -- United States 5. Senators

ISBN 1-4022-0647-X; 978-1-4022-0647-4; 1-4022-0922-3 pa; 978-1-4022-0922-2 pa

LC 2005-37973

This book gives "brief analyses of 31 of JFK's speeches and debates, presented in audio selections on the accompanying CD-ROM. The results reveal Kennedy's eloquence, humor, and grace under pressure. . . . This work illuminates the importance of public address to the success and reputation of presidents and shows that Kennedy mastered this art." Libr J

Includes bibliographical references

Nixon and Kissinger; partners in power. HarperCollins Publishers 2007 740p il $32.50 **92**

1. Biography, Individual 2. College teachers 3. International relations specialists 4. Members of Congress 5. Nobel laureates for peace 6. Nonfiction writers 7. Presidential advisers 8. Presidents 9. Secretaries of state 10. Senators 11. Vice-presidents 12. Writers on politics

ISBN 978-0-06-072230-2; 0-06-072230-4

LC 2006-52100

A look "behind the scenes at this quintessential pair of power brokers and their lasting influence, for good and ill, on the political stage." Bookmarks Magazine

Includes bibliographical references

Danticat, Edwidge

★ Brother, I'm dying. Alfred A. Knopf 2007 272p hardcover o.p. pa $15 **92**

1. Authors 2. Biography, Individual 3. Children's authors 4. Dramatists 5. Editors 6. Essayists 7. Novelists 8. Short story writers 9. Women authors

ISBN 978-1-4000-4115-2; 1-4000-4115-5; 978-1-4000-3430-7 pa; 1-4000-3430-2 pa

LC 2007-06887

The author "has written a fierce, haunting book about exile and loss and family love, and how that love can survive

distance and separation, loss and abandonment and somehow endure, undented and robust." N Y Times (Late NY Ed)

Create dangerously; the immigrant artist at work. Princeton University Press 2010 189p $19.95 **92**

1. Authors 2. Biography, Individual 3. Children's authors 4. Dramatists 5. Editors 6. Essayists 7. Novelists 8. Short story writers 9. Women authors

ISBN 978-0-691-14018-6; 0-691-14018-9

LC 2010-10302

This "tender . . . book about loss and the unquenchable passion for homeland makes us remember the powerful material from which most fiction is wrought: it comes from childhood, and place. No matter her geographic and temporal distance from these, Danticat writes about them with the immediacy of love." N Y Times Book Rev

Includes bibliographical references

Darling, Ron

The complete game; reflections on baseball, pitching, and life on the mound. by Ron Darling, with Daniel Paisner. Alfred A. Knopf 2009 272p $24.95 **92**

1. Baseball -- Biography 2. Baseball players 3. Pitching (Baseball)

ISBN 978-0-307-26984-3; 0-307-26984-1

LC 2008-55706

Darling, "the stalwart ex-Mets starter and incumbent Mets broadcaster . . . offers pitches and outcomes (but no box scores) from ten selected games in his career, including a successful World Series start against the Red Sox at Fenway Park in 1986, a gruesome windy-day thumping suffered at Wrigley Field, and his celebrated extra-inning near-no-hitter back when he was pitching for Yale. Among them are enough oddities and thrilling turns of baseball to make a reader glad to be here and—well, not out there." New Yorker

Darnton, John

Almost a family; a memoir. Alfred A. Knopf 2011 347p il $27.95; ebook $13.99 **92**

1. Authors 2. Authors, American 3. Biography, Individual 4. Father-son relationship 5. Journalists

ISBN 978-0-307-26617-0; 978-0-307-59524-9 ebook

LC 2010-16835

"In this unsentimental narrative, Darnton vividly chronicles the high-water era of classic journalism and his stints as a Times correspondent in Africa and Solidarity-era Poland, but what drives his memoir are the pursuit of the fullest possible picture of his father's death, the story of his mother's alcoholism and sobriety, and most of all, the quest for deeply buried facts about his parents and their relationship." Publ Wkly

Darst, Jeanne

Fiction ruined my family. Riverhead Hardcover 2011 303p $25.95 **92**

1. Authors 2. Novelists, American 3. Performance artists

ISBN 978-1-59448-814-6

LC 2011027830

"Perfectly balanced in tone, this is one of the few truly funny memoirs that can also talk about the love, frustration, and deep despair that only relatives can bring out. With highly quotable moments; a keeper." Libr J

Daugherty, Tracy

Hiding man; a biography of Donald Barthelme. St. Martin's Press 2008 581p il $35   **92**

1. Authors 2. Authors, American 3. Biography, Individual 4. Novelists 5. Short story writers

ISBN 978-0-312-37868-4; 0-312-37868-8

LC 2008-29881

"Not dwelling on Barthelme's dark soul or his uneven work, Daugherty has created a convincing narrative from a life that was engaged, passionate and maybe even fulfilled." N Y Times Book Rev

Includes bibliographical references (p. 549-556)

Just one catch; a biography of Joseph Heller. St. Martin's Press 2011 548p il $35   **92**

1. Authors 2. Authors, American 3. Biography, Individual 4. Novelists 5. Short story writers

ISBN 978-0-312-59685-9; 0-312-59685-5

LC 2011-20749

This biography offers "countless insightful, amusing anecdotes from Heller's childhood, military service and postpublication notoriety as a celebrated literary figure. But the writing, publishing and ensuing aftermath of Catch-22 is the clear focal point of Daugherty's book. Lacking the self-assured swagger of Norman Mailer and the countercultural sway of the Beats, Heller was a long-frustrated and surprising emergent on the literary scene. A reluctant participant in the burgeoning Madison Avenue advertising world of the 1950s, Heller seemed a figure unlikely to publish a work of such unimpeachable influence. Published when Heller was 39, Catch-22 represents the high-water mark of his career and to some extent his personal life—it is as if everything prepublication was prologue and everything that followed was postscript. Heller wrote copiously throughout the remainder of his life but never attained those heights again, critically or commercially. Nonetheless, Daugherty persuasively endorses the view of Heller as a pivotal figure in American letters." Time Out N Y

Includes bibliographical references

Davis, Jack E.

An **Everglades** providence; Marjory Stoneman Douglas and the American environmental century. University of Georgia Press 2009 758p il map $34.95   **92**

1. Authors 2. Biography, Individual 3. Centenarians 4. Conservationists 5. Nature conservation 6. Novelists 7. Short story writers 8. Writers on nature

ISBN 978-0-8203-3071-6; 0-8203-3071-X

LC 2008-49073

This is "both a portrait of one of the 20th century's most important environmental figures and a history of Florida's Everglades. The long-lived Douglas (1890-1998) is best known for the classic The Everglades: River of Grass and her tireless efforts to preserve that region. But she was also a lifelong feminist and social activist who worked to advance human rights. . . . In addition to the rich detail and documentation of Douglas's life, Davis offers an impressive look at America during Douglas's lifetime and the growth of America's environmental movement." Libr J

Includes bibliographical references

Davis, John H.

Jacqueline Bouvier; an intimate memoir. [by] John Davis. Wiley 1996 208p il $24.95; pa $14.95   **92**

1. Biography, Individual 2. Editors 3. Socialites 4. Spouses of presidents

ISBN 0-471-12945-3; 0-471-24944-0 pa

LC 96-4332

"Davis is an engaging writer, and although many of the facts of his story will be known by Kennedy aficionados, there is a wistful sweetness to his writing that captures both the woman and the era of privileged upbringings." Booklist

Davis, Miles

Miles, the autobiography; {by} Miles Davis with Quincy Troupe. Simon & Schuster 1989 431p il hardcover o.p. pa $15   **92**

1. African American musicians 2. Band leaders 3. Flugelhornists 4. Jazz musicians 5. Trumpet players

ISBN 0-671-72582-3 pa

LC 89-19652

"The legendary jazz musician Miles Davis . . . takes us on a historical journey that begins with his growing up in the mid-1920s in East St. Louis, then moves on to New York City in the 1940s, where he was a student at the Julliard School of Music, and to his encounters with other jazz greats like Charlie Parker, Dizzy Gillespie, Billie Holiday, Herbie Hancock, and George Duke." Libr J

Davis, William C.

The **pirates** Laffite; the treacherous world of the corsairs of the Gulf. Harcourt 2005 706p il map $28   **92**

1. Pirates 2. Pirates -- History

ISBN 0-15-100403-X

LC 2004-29150

"This is an excellent examination of interesting, tough men who knew how to survive in an interesting, tough age." Booklist

Includes bibliographical references

Dawidoff, Nicholas

The **crowd** sounds happy; a story of love, madness, and baseball. Pantheon Books 2008 271p $24.95   **92**

1. Authors 2. Baseball -- Biography 3. Biography, Individual 4. Nonfiction writers 5. Sportswriters

ISBN 978-0-375-40028-5; 0-375-40028-1

LC 2007-30525

In this memoir, the author describes how his love of baseball helped him through rough periods of his youth, including his father descent into mental illness.

"Essential reading for anyone who wishes a balm for heartbreaks in youth, torn family life, love, and seventh-game losses." Libr J

De Madariaga, Isabel

Ivan the Terrible; first tsar of Russia. Yale University Press 2005 xxi, 484p il map $35   **92**
1. Emperors
ISBN 0-300-09757-3
LC 2004-29807
This is a biography of the Russian tsar.
This "is a persuasively argued, widely researched and impressively authoritative work that casts new light on the Tsar, his reign, and Russia in the sixteenth century." Times Lit Suppl
Includes bibliographical references

De Young, Karen

Soldier: the life of Colin Powell. Knopf 2006 610p il $28.95   **92**
1. Biography, Individual 2. Generals 3. Secretaries of state 4. Statesmen -- United States
ISBN 1-400-04170-8
LC 2006-45288
This is a "diligent, sympathetic, but not uncritical full-scale biography." N Y Rev Books
Includes bibliographical references

DePastino, Todd

Bill Mauldin; a life up front. W.W. Norton 2008 370p il $27.95   **92**
1. Biography, Individual 2. Cartoonists
ISBN 978-0-393-06183-3; 0-393-06183-3
LC 2007-40494
This is a biography of the author of What's Got Your Back Up? (1961), I've Decided I Want My Seat Back (1965), and The Brass Ring (1971). During World War II, Mauldin was a cartoonist who depicted the daily lives of soldiers for the G.I. newspaper Stars and Stripes.
"Thoroughly researched and sprightly written, DePastino's balanced biography is a solid introduction to an American original. Classic Mauldin cartoons are an entertaining bonus." Publ Wkly
Includes bibliographical references

Debo, Angie

Geronimo; the man, his time, his place. University of Okla. Press 1976 xx, 480p il maps hardcover o.p. pa $24.95   **92**
1. Apache Indians 2. Indian chiefs
ISBN 0-8061-1333-2; 0-8061-1828-8 pa
LC 76-13858
The author "interviewed people who knew Geronimo, who fought with him and lived with him in captivity. She has written a colorful narrative of revenge and raids, of escape, pursuit and surrender. . . . Her portrait of Geronimo the old celebrity is touching, and a tribute to an exceptional leader." Publ Wkly
Includes bibliographical references

Deen, Paula H.

Paula Deen; it ain't all about the cookin' [by] Paula Deen, with Sherry Suib Cohen. Simon & Schuster 2007 287p il $25; pa $14   **92**
1. Cookbook writers 2. Cooks 3. Restaurateurs 4. Southern cooking 5. Television personalities
ISBN 978-0-7432-9285-6; 0-7432-9285-5; 978-1-4391-6335-1 pa; 1-4391-6335-9 pa
LC 2006-53501
"Deen talks about everything from her decades-long battle with agoraphobia and her troubled first marriage to the hard work that went into building her first business, The Bag Lady, and the professional and personal successes that followed. A few of Deen's recipes . . . are sprinkled among her stories, which offer a sample of the distinctively Southern cooking that is the foundation of Deen's life and career. This wonderfully nourishing book will have readers laughing, crying, and hungry for more." Libr J

Delany, Sadie

Having our say; the Delany sisters' first 100 years. [by] Sarah and A. Elizabeth Delany; with Amy Hill Hearth. Kodansha Int. 1993 210p il $20   **92**
1. African American women -- Biography 2. Biography, Individual 3. Centenarians 4. Dentists 5. Nonfiction writers 6. Science teachers
ISBN 1-56836-010-X
LC 93-23890
"The combination of the two voices, beautifully blended by Ms. Hearth, evokes an epic history, often cruel and brutal, but always deeply humane in their spirited telling of it." N Y Times Book Rev

Delbanco, Andrew

Melville; his world and work. Knopf 2005 xxiii, 415p il map $30   **92**
1. Authors 2. Authors, American 3. Biography, Individual 4. Novelists
ISBN 0-375-40314-0
LC 2005-40919
"This is sure to elicit new appreciation for Melville's work and could well be the best one-volume biography for some time to come." Libr J
Includes bibliographical references

Delbridge, Melissa J.

Family Bible. University of Iowa Press 2008 143p $23.95   **92**
1. Authors 2. Biography, Individual 3. Memoirists 4. Short story writers
ISBN 978-1-58729-651-2; 1-58729-651-9
LC 2007-43968
A collection of autobiographical essays about growing up in 1960s Tuscaloosa, Alabama.
"Melissa's daddy was a charmer, a Kirk Douglas look-alike who loved to fish and hunt and to go away for the weekend pretending to be fishing and hunting at the 'River Bend Hunting Club' while actually seeing other women. This naturally drove Momma crazy and, sadly, she took it out on Melissa. Momma took her kids from the house in the middle of the night, moved across town, and, when she left Melissa's father for good, 'remarried fast enough to cause a lot of high talk.' . . . The relationship between Delbridge's parents and then the toxic mess that constituted her home with her stepdad, identified as a local exterminator magnate and ex-Marine, are staples in memoir, but the story is gracefully told, without self-pity. . . . Much of this volume is, as

one might expect, about Delbridge's own sexual awakening, and you know it will be out of the ordinary, even melodramatic." Tuscaloosa News

Denton, Sally

The **pink** lady; the many lives of Helen Gahagan Douglas. Bloomsbury Press 2009 240p il $26   **92**

1. Actors 2. Biography, Individual 3. Members of Congress 4. Singers

ISBN 978-1-59691-480-3; 1-59691-480-7

LC 2009-08148

This is a "biography of the Broadway star turned California Democratic Congresswoman. . . . [The author] does a handsome job exploring Helen Gahagan's early life as an actress and singer as well as her later political activism . . . [and] displays a solid grasp of the ignominious politics of McCarthy-era America. Eye-opening, entertaining portrait of a fascinating proto-feminist." Kirkus

Includes bibliographical references (p. [215]-223) and index.

Desmond, Adrian J.

Darwin; [by] Adrian Desmond & James Moore. W.W. Norton & Co. 1994 808p il pa $23.95   **92**

1. Naturalists 2. Travel writers 3. Writers on science

ISBN 0-393-31150-3; 978-0-393-31150-1

"No other biography of Darwin has anywhere near the density of detail this book has. This rich tapestry, supplemented with 91 fine illustrations, is intended to provide the basis for relating Darwin the creative scientist to his social and political milieu." N Y Times Book Rev

Includes bibliographical references

Darwin's sacred cause; how a hatred of slavery shaped Darwin's views on human evolution. [by] Adrian Desmond & James Moore. Houghton Mifflin Harcourt 2009 484p il map $30   **92**

1. Abolitionists -- Great Britain -- History -- 19th century 2. Biography, Individual 3. Evolution 4. Evolution (Biology) -- History 5. Naturalists 6. Slavery 7. Travel writers 8. Writers on science

ISBN 978-0-547-05526-8; 0-547-05526-9

LC 2008-43482

This "book reinterprets much of . . . [Darwin's] life work as having been motivated by an altruistic humanitarian vision and an equally intense abhorrence of slavery. . . . Well researched, likely to be controversial (some will call it revisionist history), this book provides another enlightening glimpse into a life of seemingly infinite complexity." Libr J

Includes bibliographical references

DiSilvestro, Roger L.

Theodore Roosevelt in the Badlands; a young politician's quest for recovery in the American West. Walker & Co. 2011 352p il map $27   **92**

1. Frontier and pioneer life -- North Dakota 2. Governors 3. Nobel laureates for peace 4. Presidents 5. Presidents -- United States 6. Ranch life 7. Vice-presidents

ISBN 978-0-8027-1721-4

LC 2010-44297

"Focused on TR in his twenties, DiSilvestro's work elaborates on the future president's days devoted to hunting and ranching in the Dakota Territory. . . . With its sources fully researched and capably integrated, DiSilvestro's account definitively fills in this part of TR's story." Booklist

Includes bibliographical references

Dickinson, Amy

The **mighty** queens of Freeville; a mother, a daughter, and the town that raised them. Hyperion Books 2009 225p $22.99   **92**

1. Advice columnists 2. Authors 3. Journalists

ISBN 978-1-4013-2285-4; 1-4013-2285-9

LC 2008-26525

"In the summertime of 2002, after spending months living off of her credit cards between freelance writing jobs, Dickinson sent in an audition column to the Chicago Tribune and became the paper's replacement for the late Ann Landers. Here, Dickinson traces her own personal history, as well as the history of her mother's family whose members make up the Mighty Queens of Freeville, N.Y., the small town where Dickinson was raised, and where she raised her own daughter between stints in London; New York City; Washington, D.C.; and Chicago. Dickinson writes with an honesty that is at once folksy and intelligent, and brings to life all of the struggles of raising a child (Dickinson was a single mother) and the challenges and rewards of having a supportive extended family." Publ Wkly

Didion, Joan

★ The **year** of magical thinking. Knopf 2005 227p $23.95   **92**

1. Authors 2. Biography, Individual 3. Essayists 4. Journalists 5. Nonfiction writers 6. Novelists 7. Screenwriters

ISBN 1-4000-4314-X

LC 2005-45132

The author "chronicles the year following the death of her husband, fellow writer John Gregory Dunne, from a massive heart attack on December 30, 2003, while the couple's only daughter, Quintana, lay unconscious in a nearby hospital suffering from pneumonia and septic shock. . . . This is an indispensable addition to Didion's body of work and a lyrical, disciplined entry in the annals of mourning literature." Publ Wkly

Didion, Joan, 1934-

Blue nights. Alfred A. Knopf 2011 188p $25; ebook $12.99   **92**

1. Biography, Individual 2. Fear of death 3. Grief in women 4. Memoirs 5. Michael, Quintana Roo Dunne, d. 2005 6. Mothers & daughters 7. Novelists, American

ISBN 978-0-307-26767-2; 0-307-26767-9; 978-0-307-70051-3 ebook

LC 2011013582

"In December 2003, Didion's husband, fellow writer John Gregory Dunne, died of a heart attack while only daughter Quintana Roo lay hospitalized with a bout of pneumonia that had led to septic shock. Quintana recovered to attend the services but died of a hematoma in 2005. . . . Here, Didion focuses on her daughter, recalling Quintana's life while asking herself the questions parents inevitably ask about what they did wrong and what important clues they missed." Libr J

Dillard, Annie

An **American** childhood. Harper & Row 1987 255p hardcover o.p. pa $14   **92**
1. Authors 2. Essayists 3. Literary critics 4. Poets 5. Writers on nature
ISBN 0-06-091518-8 pa

LC 87-45042

In this autobiography, Dillard presents as account of her life from her childhood in Pittsburgh until her entrance into college.

"Dillard's luminous prose painlessly captures the pain of growing up in this wonderful evocation of childhood. . . . The events of childhood often loom larger than life; the magic of Dillard's writing is that she sets down typical childhood happenings with their original immediacy and force." Publ Wkly

Diller, Phyllis

Like a lampshade in a whorehouse; my life in comedy. [by] Phyllis Diller with Richard Buskin. J.P. TarcherPenguin 2005 266p il $24.95; pa $14.95 **92**
1. Biography, Individual 2. Comedians
ISBN 1-585-42396-3; 1-585-42476-5 pa

LC 2004-58520

This is an autobiography by the American comedian.

"Brash comedy and a surprising bitterness fuel this unsparing account of Diller's drive to make it big." Publ Wkly

Diski, Jenny

The **Sixties**. Picador 2009 148p pa $14   **92**
1. Authors 2. Authors, English 3. Counter culture 4. Nineteen sixties 5. Novelists
ISBN 978-0-312-42721-4; 0-312-42721-2

The author "recalls (sometimes hilariously) her experience of the '60s, but her emphasis is on the culture's ideas—about drugs, sex, education, mental illness and, to a lesser extent, politics. Very little of what she says is new, but she says it with intelligence, wit, an eye for detail and an extraordinary ability to laugh at her young self while respecting that self's hopes and efforts. . . . She leaves you with plenty to think about, and wanting more." N Y Times Book Rev

Donald, David Herbert

Lincoln. Simon & Schuster 1995 714p il maps hardcover o.p. pa $20   **92**
1. Lawyers 2. Members of Congress 3. Presidents 4. Presidents -- United States 5. State legislators
ISBN 0-684-80846-3; 0-684-82535-X pa

LC 95-4782

This biography examines: "Lincoln's relationship with his father; his romance with Ann Rutledge; his bouts of 'hypo,' which amounted at times almost to clinical depression; his marriage; his political ambition; his attitudes toward slavery and black people; his relations with radical Republicans during the Civil War; the mistakes and successes of his wartime leadership." Atl Mon

Includes bibliographical references

Donaldson, Ross I.

The **Lassa** ward; one man's fight against one of the world's deadliest diseases. St. Martin's Press 2009 270p $24.95; pa $14.99   **92**
1. Lassa fever 2. Physicians 3. Textbook writers
ISBN 978-0-312-37700-7; 0-312-37700-2; 978-0-312-37701-4 pa; 0-312-37701-0 pa

LC 2008-43923

"This book is a wild and extraordinary memoir of . . . [the author's] 2003 summer in Sierra Leone as a naïve medical student studying Lassa fever (a close cousin of the Ebola virus). Donaldson gives passionate and powerful reportage on a struggling clinic treating villagers and refugees from neighboring war-torn Liberia suffering from the devastating and often fatal illness." Publ Wkly

Donovan, Brian

Hard driving: the Wendell Scott story; the odyssey of NASCAR'S first Black driver. Steerfort Press 2008 311p il hardcover o.p. pa $16.99   **92**
1. African American athletes 2. Automobile racing 3. Automobile racing drivers
ISBN 978-1-58642-144-1; 978-1-58642-160-1 pa

LC 2008-24287

For this biography, the author "interviewed Scott extensively over the last 14 months of his life. He also interviewed more than 200 other individuals, including Scott's widow and children. The result is the gripping story of a fascinating, brave man who deserves serious recognition for his solitary accomplishment. . . . A must-read for NASCAR fans." Booklist

Includes bibliographical references

Dornstein, Ken

The **boy** who fell out of the sky; a true story. Random House 2006 304p il $23.95; pa $13.95 **92**
1. Murder victims 2. Pan Am Flight 103 Bombing Incident, 1988 3. Travelers 4. Victims of terrorism -- Scotland -- Lockerbie
ISBN 0-375-50359-5; 0-375-70769-7 pa

LC 2005-42683

"Dornstein's account of his relationship with his brother and of his own self-examination is a startlingly honest, completely absorbing look at loss and brotherly love." Booklist

Includes bibliographical references

Doty, Mark

Dog years; a memoir. HarperCollins Publishers 2007 215p $23.95   **92**
1. Authors 2. Dogs 3. Essayists 4. Poets
ISBN 0-06-117100-X; 978-0-06-117100-0

LC 2006-46491

The author "celebrates the 16 lovely years his two beloved 70-pound Labs, Beau and Arden, gave him. . . . Against a backdrop of devastating human loss, both personal (the death of his partner) and public (9/11), Doty bears witness to the inexorable decline of his beloved retrievers. . . . Poignant, intelligent, and quite simply superb." Libr J

Dougherty, David C.

Shouting down the silence: a biography of Stanley Elkin. University of Illinois Press 2010 281p il $40   **92**

1. Authors 2. Authors, American 3. Novelists 4. Short story writers

ISBN 978-0-252-03508-1; 0-252-03508-9

LC 2009-24341

"The life of a writer often celebrated by critics and admired by fellow novelists but who never achieved the popular acclaim and wealth he felt he deserved. . . . Elkin stayed married to the same woman, remained a professor at the same school—Washington University in St. Louis, though he had numerous visiting gigs elsewhere—stayed devoted to his early literary mentors and to his craft, continuing to labor on his fiction and essays until multiple sclerosis and a troubled heart finally felled him. Dougherty proceeds in traditional fashion. After mentioning each new major work, he pauses for summary and analysis. . . . Though sometimes admiring rather than analytical, a thoroughly reliable portrait of a neglected novelist." Kirkus

Douglas-Fairhurst, Robert

Becoming Dickens; the invention of a novelist. Belknap Press of Harvard University Press 2011 389p il $29.95   **92**

1. Authors 2. Biography, Individual 3. Novelists 4. Novelists, English

ISBN 978-0-674-05003-7; 0-674-05003-7

LC 2011004219

This "is an ingenious, playful and often brilliant analysis as much as it is a narrative." Economist

Includes bibliographical references

Douglass, Frederick

Narrative of the life of Frederick Douglass, an American slave; written by himself; edited with an introduction by Houston A. Baker, Jr. Penguin Bks 1982 159p il pa $10   **92**

1. Abolitionists 2. African Americans -- Biography 3. Authors 4. Memoirists 5. Slaves

ISBN 0-14-039012-X

LC 82-5371

"Frederick Douglass became famous as a slave who escaped to the North and spent his lifetime in the abolitionist movement. His 'Narrative,' one of three autobiographical works written by the self-taught slave, is the story of his life up to his escape to freedom." Libr J

Includes bibliographical references

Downey, Kirstin

The **woman** behind the New Deal; the life of Frances Perkins, FDR's Secretary of Labor and his moral conscience. Nan A. Talese 2009 458p il $35   **92**

1. Biography, Individual 2. Cabinet officers 3. College teachers 4. New Deal, 1933-1939 5. Secretaries of labor 6. State government officials

ISBN 978-0-385-51365-4; 0-385-51365-8

LC 2008-23208

A biography of "one of FDR's confidants and the first female secretary of labor in U.S. history. . . . Like many biographers, Downey . . . is enamored of her subject. But her fascination serves her well, allowing her to construct an intriguing catalog of Perkins's achievements and explore the influences that held sway in her life, a psychological approach lacking in previous Perkins biographies. Here Perkins's triumphs and tragedies are compiled into a compelling narrative that never loses its scholarly touch." Libr J

Includes bibliographical references

Doyle, Arthur Conan

★ **Arthur** Conan Doyle; his life in letters. edited by Jon Lellenberg, Daniel Stashower & Charles Foley. Harper Press 2007 706p il $37.95   **92**

1. Authors 2. Authors, Scottish 3. Biography, Individual 4. Mystery writers 5. Novelists

ISBN 978-1-59420-135-6; 1-59420-135-8

LC 2007-14692

This volume presents the selected correspondence of the British author at various points during his life.

"This will be essential reading for all fans of Conan Doyle and his sleuth." Publ Wkly

Draitser, Emil

Stalin's Romeo spy; the meteoric rise and fall of the KGB's most daring operative: the true life of Dmitri Bystrolyotov. Northwestern University Press 2010 420p il map $35   **92**

1. Intelligence service -- Soviet Union -- History 2. Novelists 3. Political prisoners -- Soviet Union 4. Russian espionage 5. Spies 6. Translators

ISBN 978-0-8101-2664-0; 0-8101-2664-8

LC 2009-44637

"This book, undertaken after much international research, is [the author's] effort to show a daring professional at work and to counter Russian efforts to whitewash their history. The details of espionage work and of Soviet life are fascinating. This amazing story should be read by those interested in espionage, Soviet affairs, and European history." Libr J

Includes bibliographical references (p. 407-412) and index.

Drape, Joe

Black maestro; the epic life of an American legend. Morrow 2006 280p il $24.95   **92**

1. Biography, Individual 2. Jockeys

ISBN 0-06-053729-9; 978-0-06-053759-6

LC 2006-41939

This is a biography of "Jimmy Winkfield, the last black jockey to win the Kentucky Derby. . . . This well-researched biography of Jimmy Winkfield and the larger chapter of America his life highlights is a valuable and entertaining read." Publ Wkly

Dregni, Michael

Django: the life and music of a Gypsy legend. Oxford University Press 2004 326p il $35; pa $16.95 **92**

1. Biography, Individual 2. Guitarists 3. Jazz musicians
ISBN 0-19-516752-X; 0-19-530448-9 pa

LC 2004-6214

This "biography does its complex subject justice. And even when Dregni dallies overlong on some byways, his immersion in the period's history enriches his storytelling and our understanding. The panoramic results present Django Reinhardt as he has never been seen." N Y Times Book Rev

Includes bibliographical references

Drohojowska-Philp, Hunter

Full bloom; the art and life of Georgia O'Keeffe. W.W. Norton 2004 630p hardcover o.p. pa $21.95 **92**

1. Artists 2. Biography, Individual 3. Painters
ISBN 0-393-05853-0; 0-393-32741-8 pa

LC 2003-26071

This is a biography of the American painter.

"O'Keeffe lived a long, adventurous, and profoundly productive life, and Drohojowska-Philp charts her triumphs over adversity in an involving, revelatory biography that attains the grand scope and depth her subject deserves." Booklist

Includes bibliographical references

Dry, Sarah

Curie; with an essay by Sabine Seifert. Haus 2003 170p il pa $15.95 **92**

1. Chemists 2. Chemists -- France 3. Chemists -- Poland 4. Nobel laureates for physics 5. Physicists 6. Women chemists -- France 7. Women chemists -- Poland 8. Women scientists
ISBN 1-904341-29-2

This is a biography of the first woman to win two Nobel Prizes, one for physics and the other for chemistry.

"Concise and engaging, this amply illustrated history of Madame Curie . . . makes an excellent introduction to the feminist icon and scientific pioneer. Dry does an excellent job of delineating the major events of Curie's life, including her early education in the underground schools of the 19th-century Polish resistance movement, her heady intellectual courtship with Pierre Curie in France, and later their discovery of radioactivity in 1898. Sidebars on topics such as the invention of the laboratory, and the inclusion of Seifert's essay on Irène Joliot-Curie, Marie Curie's less famous daughter and co-worker, make this pocket sized book especially comprehensive, and a wonderful introduction to a fascinating and inspiring career." Publ Wkly

Includes bibliographical references

Duberman, Martin B.

A **saving** remnant; the radical lives of Barbara Deming and David McReynolds. New Press 2011 298p il $27.95 **92**

1. Authors 2. Biography, Individual 3. Essayists 4. Feminism 5. Pacifists 6. Peace movements -- United States -- History -- 20th century 7. Poets 8. Political activists 9. Political leaders 10. Political prisoners 11. Radicalism 12. Social justice -- United States -- History 13. Socialist leaders
ISBN 978-1-59558-323-9; 1-59558-323-8

LC 2010-45060

"As radical left-wing writers and activists, Deming and McReynolds were immersed in the issues of nonviolence, nuclear disarmament, civil rights and the Vietnam War. Both remained dedicated to peaceful protest, even in the face of legal repercussions. Though naturally frail, Deming picketed and marched her way through the 1960s, and was frequently imprisoned. In 1963, several weeks after taking part in the March on Washington, McReynolds was thrown into a North Carolina jail for eating at a whites-only restaurant with black acquaintants. Two years later, he was one of the first men in the nation to publicly burn his draft card. Duberman . . . tells us that the two were friends and 'often worked together politically,' though we rarely see them interact. The book's parallel narratives intersect in a meaningful way only when its subjects disagree, most notably on the issues of a gay rights movement and feminism. . . . The author makes use of letters, private papers, diaries and recent interviews with McReynolds. (Deming died of ovarian cancer in 1984.) The result is an intimate study, written in straightforward prose." N Y Times Book Rev

Includes bibliographical references

Dubus, Andre, 1959-

Townie; a memoir. [by] Andre Dubus III. W. W. Norton & Co. 2011 387p $25.95 **92**

1. Authors 2. Authors, American 3. Biography, Individual 4. Novelists 5. Short story writers
ISBN 978-0-393-06466-7; 0-393-06466-2

LC 2010038029

This is a memoir by the author of Bluesman (1993) and The Garden of Last Days (2008). "Young Andre and his siblings, two sisters and a brother, grew up in a series of Massachusetts mill towns after their father left their mother for one of his . . . young students." (N Y Times (Late N Y Ed))

"The author grew up poor in Massachusetts mill towns, the oldest of four children of the celebrated short-story writer Andre Dubus (1936–1999), who abandoned the family in 1968 to pursue a young student. Beautifully written and bursting with life, the book tells the story of a boy struggling to express his 'hurt and rage,' first through violence aimed at school and barroom bullies and ultimately through the power of words." Kirkus

Dukakis, Olympia

Ask me again tomorrow; a life in progress. [by] Olympia Dukakis with Emily Heckman. HarperCollins Pubs. 2003 211p il $25.95; pa $13.95 **92**

1. Actors
ISBN 0-06-018821-9; 0-06-093409-3 pa

LC 2003-49909

"Students of the theater will be interested in her views on acting. All in all, this is a satisfying look into the personal and professional life of a theater actor." Libr J

Includes bibliographical references

Dunaway, David King

★ **How** can I keep from singing? the ballad of Pete Seeger. Trade paperback ed.; Villard 2008 xxx, 512p il pa $18 **92**
1. Folk musicians 2. Singers 3. Songwriters
ISBN 978-0-345-50608-5

LC 2007-41814

"The focus of Seeger's life has been on using music as a force for social change. . . . But he is perhaps best known as the major banjo-playing folksinger who pioneered the folk music revival that flowered in the 1960s. This excellent book provides a well-written and extensively researched account, not only of Seeger's life, but also of the social and political movements of the times in which he lived. An extensive bibliography and discography add to the book's usefulness." Libr J

Includes discography and bibliographical references

Dylan, Bob

Chronicles. v1 Simon & Schuster 2004 293p v1 il $24 **92**
1. Biography, Individual 2. Folk musicians 3. Rock musicians 4. Singers 5. Songwriters
ISBN 0-7432-2815-4

LC 2004-564

This is the first installment of a projected three-volume autobiography by the American singer and songwriter.

"This book will stand as a record of a young man's self-education, as contagious in its frank excitement as the letters of John Keats and as sincere in its ramble as Jack Kerouac's On the Road, to which Dylan frequently refers. A person of Dylan's stature could have gotten away with far less; that he has been so thoughtful in the creation of this book is a measure of his talents, and a gift to his fans." Publ Wkly

Ebadi, Shirin

Iran awakening; a memoir of revolution and hope. [by] Shirin Ebadi with Azedeh Moaveni. Random House 2006 232p il map hardcover o.p. pa $14.95 **92**
1. Biography, Individual 2. Human rights activists 3. Islam and politics -- Iran 4. Law -- Iran 5. Lawyers 6. Nobel laureates for peace
ISBN 1-4000-6470-8; 978-1-4000-6470-0; 978-0-8129-7528-4 pa; 0-8129-7528-6 pa

LC 2005-55255

This is a memoir by the Iranian lawyer and human right activist.

This book "offers the chance to understand Iran's tumultuous recent history, seen through the eyes of a supremely courageous Islamic woman." Christ Sci Monit

Includes bibliographical references

Ebenstein, Alan O.

Milton Friedman; a biography. [by] Lanny Ebenstein. Palgrave Macmillan 2007 286p $27.95 **92**
1. Biography, Individual 2. College teachers 3. Economic history -- 20th century 4. Economists 5. Nobel laureates for economic sciences
ISBN 1-4039-7627-9; 978-1-4039-7627-7

LC 2006-52023

The author "creates a picture of Milton Friedman, one of the leading economists and political philosophers of the twentieth century, as not just a revered economic theorist but also a public intellectual. Ebenstein begins with Friedman's childhood and early career, moving through his long tenure as an economist at the University of Chicago, and completes the book with a picture of Friedman as a renowned public figure. . . . Ebenstein's attention to detail and copious quotes from others who knew Friedman well make for an engaging picture of one of America's most important economic theorists." Booklist

Includes bibliographical references

Ebert, Roger, 1942-

Life itself; a memoir. Grand Central Pub. 2011 436p il $27.99; ebook $12.99 **92**
1. Motion picture critics 2. Motion pictures -- History and criticism 3. Writers on film
ISBN 978-0-446-58497-5; 978-0-446-58498-2 ebook

LC 2011022442

The book presents an autobiography by newspaper film reviewer Roger Ebert. It is "an episodic tour of Ebert's memory cabinet, one three-or-four page jot at a time, from his upbringing and his college opportunities to his days as a cub reporter in Chicago, his decision to quit drinking and join AA in 1979, [and] his screenwriting with Russ Meyer. . . . [Ebert] spends many chapters recalling the dinners and interviews he had with Martin Scorsese, Werner Horzog, Robert Mitchum, Woody Allen etc. Naturally, he also ruminates at length about his testy relationship with TV co-host Gene Siskel." (Sight & Sound)

"Ebert illuminates and assesses his life with the same insight and clarity that mark his acclaimed movie reviews." Booklist

Edelman, Marian Wright

Lanterns; a memoir of mentors. HarperPerennial 2000 xxi, 208p il pa $14 **92**
1. Children's rights advocates 2. Mentoring 3. Social welfare leaders
ISBN 0-06-095859-6

LC 00-33430

"Throughout this absorbing memoir, Edelman's voice resounds with spirituality, a reliance on her faith, and a belief in equality." Booklist

Includes bibliographical references

Edwards, Bob

Edward R. Murrow and the birth of broadcast journalism; {by} Robert A. Edwards. Wiley 2004 174p $19.95 **92**
1. Government officials 2. Journalists 3. Radio reporters 4. Television news anchors 5. Television reporters
ISBN 0-471-47753-2

LC 2003-21223

"The author chronicles Murrow's innovations in radio and television broadcasting, including live radio reports of the war in progress in Europe in 1940; exposure of the despotism of Senator Joseph McCarthy on CBS in 1953; the powerful television documentary Harvest of Shame on the deplorable conditions of migrant workers in the U.S.; and

the first in-depth television news program, See It Now. . . . Edwards brings to life the early days of radio and television and the innovations that Murrow sparked. . . . Readers interested in journalism will enjoy this slim book." Booklist
Includes bibliographical references

Eggers, Dave, 1970-
Zeitoun. McSweeney's 2009 351p il $24 **92**
1. Arab Americans -- Social conditions 2. Contractors 3. House painters 4. Hurricane Katrina, 2005 5. Hurricane Katrina, 2005 -- Social aspects 6. Muslims -- United States
ISBN 978-1-934781-63-0; 1-934781-63-0
This book is a more powerful indictment of America's dystopia in the Bush era than any number of well-written polemics. N Y Times Book Rev
Includes bibliographical references

Eig, Jonathan
Get Capone; the real story of America's legendary gangster. Simon & Schuster 2010 468p il $28 **92**
1. Biography, Individual 2. Bootleggers 3. Criminals 4. Gangsters -- United States -- History -- 20th century 5. Mobsters 6. Organized crime 7. Organized crime investigation -- United States -- History -- 20th century
ISBN 978-1-4165-8059-1; 1-4165-8059-X
LC 2009-33949
The author "rescues the narrative of Al Capone from the realm of pop melodrama, offering vibrant historical storytelling and a nuanced, enigmatic portrait of Capone and his Chicago milieu. . . . An impressive, accessible history of a troubled time." Kirkus
Includes bibliographical references

Luckiest man; the life and death of Lou Gehrig. Simon & Schuster 2005 420p il $26; pa $15 **92**
1. Baseball -- Biography 2. Baseball players 3. Biography, Individual
ISBN 0-7432-4591-1; 0-7432-6893-8 pa
LC 2004-59137
This is a biography of the first baseman for the New York Yankees.
The author "has done a superb job of digging out the real Gehrig from behind the legend, and the mask of his own modesty." N Y Times Book Rev
Includes bibliographical references

Einstein, Albert
Einstein on politics; his private thoughts and public stands on nationalism, Zionism, war, peace, and the bomb. edited by David E. Rowe and Robert Schulmann. Princeton University Press 2007 xxxiv, 523p il $29.95 **92**
1. Nobel laureates for physics 2. Physicists 3. Political science 4. Politics
ISBN 978-0-691-12094-2; 0-691-12094-3
LC 2006-100303
This is a collection of excerpts from Albert Einstein's writings on politics and other social topics.

"Powerful in its personal and political disclosures, this is an essential primary source." Booklist
Includes bibliographical references

Einstein, Alfred
Mozart; his character, his work. translated by Arthur Mendel and Nathan Broder. Oxford Univ. Press 1945 492p il music hardcover o.p. pa $22.50 **92**
1. Composers
ISBN 0-19-500732-8 pa
The author's "examination of the events of Mozart's life in relation to his character, and even more, his analysis of the sources, models, and methods of the musician's creative processes are penetrating and illuminating." Christ Sci Monit

Eire, Carlos M. N.
Learning to die in Miami; confessions of a refugee boy. [by] Carlos Eire. Free Press 2010 307p $26 **92**
1. Biography, Individual 2. College teachers 3. Cuban Americans 4. Cuban refugees 5. Memoirists 6. Religious scholars 7. Writers on religion
ISBN 978-1-4391-8190-4; 1-4391-8190-X
LC 2009052286
The author, a professor of history and religious studies at Yale, continues the memoir begun with Waiting for Snow in Havana (2003). In the present volume he writes about his introduction to America in 1962, when he was eleven.
The author "takes readers on his personal journey, beginning in 1962 when he and his brother arrived in Florida as part of Operation Peter Pan—an evacuation of 14,000 Cuban children whose parents arranged for their relocation to the United States, away from Castro. Eire's prose engages us throughout as we learn of the challenges he faced as he assimilated to his new world. . . . Readers of memoir and immigrant stories will appreciate Eire's journey and celebrate his accomplishments." Libr J

Waiting for snow in Havana; confessions of a Cuban boy. {by} Carlos Eire. Free Press 2003 383p il hardcover o.p. pa $15 **92**
1. College teachers 2. Cuban Americans -- Biography 3. Memoirists 4. Refugee children -- United States -- Biography 5. Religious scholars 6. Writers on religion
ISBN 0-7432-1965-1; 978-0-7432-4641-5; 0-7432-4641-1 pa
LC 2002-73875
"From 1960 through 1962, some fourteen thousand Cuban children were airlifted—unaccompanied—to the United States by Operation Pedro (Peter) Pan. Once here, they were farmed out to CIA-funded refugee camps, then to foster homes. Many never saw their island parents again. Carlos Eire, now a Yale professor of history and religious studies, was a Peter Pan. {This memoir} tells mostly of Eire's privileged boyhood during the pre-Castro 1950s." Commonweal

Eisenhower, David
Going home to glory; a memoir of life with Dwight D. Eisenhower, 1961-1969. [by] David Eisenhower with Julie Nixon Eisenhower. Simon & Schuster 2010 323p il $28; ebook $14.99 **92**
1. College presidents 2. Generals 3. Presidents 4.

Presidents -- United States
ISBN 978-1-4391-9090-6; 1-4391-9090-9; 978-1-4391-9095-1 ebook; 1-4391-9095-X ebook

LC 2010-27707

The authors "present an amiable and insightful memoir of the ex-president's retirement years. . . . [David Eisenhower's] mixture of personal memories and research produces a fine addition to the history of both Eisenhower and the '60s." Kirkus

Includes bibliographical references

Eisler, Benita

Byron--child of passion, fool of fame. Knopf 1999 837p il hardcover o.p. pa $18 **92**

1. Authors 2. Poets
ISBN 0-679-74085-6 pa

LC 98-35261

"This is a splendidly readable biography of a perpetually fascinating genius." Atl Mon

Includes bibliographical references

Chopin's funeral. Knopf 2003 230p il $23; pa $13.95 **92**

1. Authors 2. Classical musicians 3. Composers 4. Dramatists 5. Novelists 6. Pianists
ISBN 0-375-40945-9; 0-375-70868-5 pa

LC 2002-73097

"Eisler is a compelling storyteller, sweeping the reader into the exhilarating milieu of Paris in the 1820s and 1830s." Libr J

Includes bibliographical references

Naked in the marketplace; the lives of George Sand. Counterpoint 2006 308p $26.95 **92**

1. Authors 2. Biography, Individual 3. Dramatists 4. Novelists
ISBN 978-1-58243-349-3; 1-58243-349-6

LC 2006-21684

This is a biography of the French writer.

"Eisler's portrait of this woman of many firsts brings Sand and her boldly improvised life forward more vividly than ever before." Booklist

Includes bibliographical references

El-Hai, Jack

★ The **lobotomist**; a maverick medical genius and his tragic quest to rid the world of mental illness. J. Wiley 2005 362p il $27.95; pa $16.95 **92**

1. Biography, Individual 2. Brain -- Surgery 3. College teachers 4. Neurologists
ISBN 0-471-23292-0; 0-470-09830-9 pa

LC 2004-14946

El-Hai chronicles the life and professional career of the American neuroscientist who pioneered the use of lobotomy in the treatment of mental illness.

"This is a well-written, thoroughly researched book, a fascinating story that deserves to be considered as the definitive biography of a physician who went from fame to infamy as 'the most scorned physician of the twentieth century.'" Sci Books Films

Includes bibliographical references

Elledge, Scott

E. B. White; a biography. Norton 1984 400p il hardcover o.p. pa $21.95 **92**

1. Authors 2. Authors, American 3. Children's authors 4. Essayists 5. Humorists 6. Novelists 7. Poets 8. Satirists
ISBN 0-393-30305-5 pa

LC 83-4032

The author is "fair, respectful, thorough, entertaining, skillful and unpedantic. He has performed a splendid exercise in scholarship and literary analysis, and the result is fun." N Y Times Book Rev

Includes bibliographical references

Eller, Jonathan R.

Becoming Ray Bradbury. University of Illinois Press 2011 324p il $34.95 **92**

1. Authors 2. Authors, American 3. Children's authors 4. Novelists 5. Science fiction writers 6. Screenwriters 7. Short story writers
ISBN 978-0-252-03629-3

LC 2011008562

The author "provides a detailed account of the experiences that shaped Ray Bradbury's life and writing career from his childhood until he embarked on the screenplay for John Huston's Moby Dick in late 1953. . . . Eller's work is thorough and enlightening on the subject of one of science fiction's greatest minds. Highly recommended not just for Bradbury fans but for all students of science fiction." Libr J

Includes bibliographical references

Ellis, Joseph J.

★ **His** Excellency; George Washington. Knopf 2004 320p il hardcover o.p. pa $15 **92**

1. Generals 2. Presidents 3. Presidents -- United States
ISBN 1-4000-4031-0; 1-4000-3253-9 pa

LC 2004-46576

The author "offers a magisterial account of the life and times of George Washington, celebrating the heroic image of the president whom peers like Jefferson and Madison recognized as 'their unquestioned superior' while acknowledging his all-too-human qualities." Publ Wkly

Includes bibliographical references

Ellmann, Richard

James Joyce; new and rev ed; Oxford Univ. Press 1982 887p il hardcover o.p. pa $27.50 **92**

1. Authors 2. Dramatists 3. Novelists 4. Poets 5. Short story writers
ISBN 0-19-503381-7 pa

LC 81-22455

This "is a vast undertaking and continuing achievement—massive, masterly, and definitive, rich in anecdote and detail. It is also extremely readable; the easy, often sympathetic style communicates gracefully not only facts but analysis." Choice

Includes bibliographical references

Oscar Wilde. Knopf 1988 680p il hardcover o.p. pa $19.95 **92**

1. Authors 2. Dramatists 3. Lecturers 4. Novelists

5. Poets
ISBN 0-394-75984-2 pa

LC 87-45354

"Wilde's life epitomizes the classic formula for a tragic history, the man who, by hubris, falls from greatness. In Mr. Ellmann's hands, the story becomes as compelling as fiction while never deviating from the facts. Humour and elegance illuminate the accounts of Wilde's family, his friends and the enemies he earned." Economist

Includes bibliographical references

Emerson, Ken

Doo-dah!: Stephen Foster and the rise of American popular culture. Da Capo Press 1998 400p il pa $16.50   **92**

1. Composers 2. Songwriters
ISBN 0-306-80852-8

LC 98-15480

The author "explores the roots of early popular music while tracing the tragic life of composer Stephen Collins Foster. . . . He also aims his spotlight at other musical personalities of the period, and provides further illumination of how Foster's songs have been incorporated into popular contemporary melodies. . . . Emerson's exhaustive research . . . has been meticulously worked into a vivid portrait of 19th-century America." Publ Wkly

Includes discography and bibliographical references

English, Bella

Last lion; the fall and rise of Ted Kennedy. Simon & Schuster 2009 464p il $28   **92**

1. Presidential candidates 2. Senators 3. Siblings of presidents
ISBN 978-1-4391-3817-5; 1-4391-3817-6

LC 2008-50491

"A respectful but not stuffy . . . [biography] of Edward Kennedy, the playboy of legendary appetites turned senior statesman. . . . A balanced, nuanced, warts-and-all portrait." Kirkus

Includes bibliographical references

Epstein, Daniel Mark

★ **Nat** King Cole. Northeastern University Press 2000 437p il pa $20   **92**

1. African American singers 2. Jazz musicians 3. Pianists 4. Singers
ISBN 1-555-53469-4; 978-1-555-53469-1

LC 00-42727

"The biographer sometimes digs too deep into esoterica, spending pages analyzing the lyrics of Straighten Up and Fly Right, for example. But when he recounts the singer's personal struggles, including a shocking 1956 onstage kidnapping attempt by Alabama racists, the human drama is, well unforgettable." Time

Includes bibliographical references

Sister Aimee: the life of Aimee Semple McPherson. 1993 475p il hardcover o.p. pa $18   **92**

1. Evangelists
ISBN 0-15-600093-8 pa

LC 92-23324

This is a biography of the American evangelist and faith healer.

"Any secular treatment of a subject who claims divine inspiration must sooner or later confront The Question: did God actually speak to her? Epstein's hedge is that Sister Aimee believed He did. . . . On the whole, however, the book is a lively read. That it is neither hagiography nor exposé is its strength as well as its weakness. Sister Aimee emerges as an unlikely yet compelling heroine." Natl Rev

Includes bibliographical references

The **ballad** of Bob Dylan; a portrait. Harper 2011 496p il $27.99   **92**

1. Biography, Individual 2. Folk musicians 3. Singers 4. Songwriters
ISBN 978-0-06-180732-9; 0-06-180732-X

LC 2011-282607

The author "tells the songwriter's story through a series of concerts and albums, beginning with an appearance in Washington, D.C., in 1963. He cleverly pits the young Mr. Dylan's self-styled orphan-hobo persona against the real-life son of middle-class Jewish parents from Hibbing, Minn. When a Newsweek article in 1963 spills the beans about his actual origins, the fiction and the reality collide, and Mr. Dylan is devastated, railing at his managers for talking to the press. . . . [The author] is one of the better stylists to tackle the Dylan story. Still, like many intellectuals who write about Mr. Dylan, he errs on the side of idolatry. . . . Mr. Epstein takes us next to concerts at Madison Square Garden in 1974, Tanglewood in 1997 and Aberdeen in 2009. His meticulous set lists chart Mr. Dylan's changes from folk, to electric, to Christian and trace the high and low points of the Rolling Thunder Review (which featured Joan Baez, Ramblin' Jack Elliott and others in 1975-76) and the Never-Ending Tour (that is, Mr. Dylan's crowded performance schedule since 1988)." Wall Street J

Epstein, Edward Jay

Dossier; the secret history of Armand Hammer. Carroll & Graf 1999 418p il pa $15.95   **92**

1. Art collectors 2. Art dealers 3. Energy industry executives
ISBN 978-0-7867-0677-8; 0-7867-0677-5

The author employs a "wealth of primary sources he tapped in Soviet archives and elsewhere. . . . It is hard to imagine a sharper picture of how a tycoon is both born and made and how the power game is played." N Y Times Book Rev

Includes bibliographical references

Epstein, Joseph

Alexis De Tocqueville; democracy's guide. Atlas Books 2006 208p $21.95   **92**

1. Biography, Individual 2. Political scientists 3. Statesmen 4. Writers on politics
ISBN 0-06-059898-0; 978-0-06-059898-3

LC 2006-47175

The author provides an "examination of the man, his works, his influence, his times and what we can learn from Democracy in America. . . . As an introduction to the man and a primer for his works, Epstein's book is admirable." Publ Wkly

Erdrich, Louise

Books and islands in Ojibwe country. National Geographic Soc. 2003 143p il map $20 **92**

1. Authors 2. Children's authors 3. Essayists 4. Novelists 5. Ojibwa Indians 6. Poets 7. Short story writers

ISBN 0-7922-5719-7

LC 2003-45906

"Fans of Erdrich's bestselling fiction will recognize her signature combination of the sacred and the ordinary in this lively traveler's memoir, and many will enjoy the rare glimpse of her personal life as well as the physical facts of her journey from her home in Minneapolis to the lakes and islands of her Ojibwe ancestors in Ontario and Minnesota." Booklist

Erickson, Carolly

Her little majesty: the life of Queen Victoria. Simon & Schuster 1997 304p il hardcover o.p. pa $19.95 **92**

1. Queens

ISBN 0-7432-3657-2 pa

LC 96-35041

This is a biography of the British monarch.

"Erickson has a knack for plucking pithy quotes, and the essentials of the queen's life are often deftly set out." Publ Wkly

Includes bibliographical references

Erikson, Erik H.

Young man Luther; a study in psychoanalysis and history. Norton 1958 288p hardcover o.p. pa $13.95 **92**

1. Reformation 2. Religious leaders 3. Social reformers 4. Theologians 5. Writers on religion

ISBN 0-393-31036-1 pa

"This study of Martin Luther as a young man was planned as a chapter in a book on emotional crises in late adolescence and early adulthood. But Luther proved too bulky a man to be merely a chapter." Preface

Escott, Colin

Hank Williams; the biography. {by} Colin Escott with George Merritt and William MacEwen. Little, Brown 1994 307p il hardcover o.p. pa $19.99 **92**

1. Country musicians 2. Singers 3. Songwriters

ISBN 0-316-24938-6 pa

LC 93-48092

A look at the career of the influential country singer/songwriter. Williams' self-destructive behavior and turbulent personal life are also examined

Esfandiari, Haleh

My prison, my home; one woman's story of captivity in Iran. Ecco/HarperCollins 2009 230p il $25.99 **92**

1. Biography, Individual 2. Intelligence service -- Iran 3. Islam and politics -- Iran 4. Middle Eastern studies specialists 5. Political prisoners

ISBN 978-0-06-158327-8; 0-06-158327-8

"Esfandiari, born in Tehran in 1940, had been living in the U.S. with her Jewish husband since 1980 when she returned to Tehran in December 2006 to visit her aging mother. On the eve of her departure for the U.S. she was picked up for interrogation—and ended up spending four months in solitary confinement in the dreaded Evin Prison, drawing worldwide attention. In her remarkable memoir, Esfandiari tells the story of her education, her evolution from an apolitical student to an ardent feminist and staunch supporter for the rights of Iranian women, and her many accomplishments, including serving as director of the Woodrow Wilson Center's Middle East Program." Booklist

Eteraz, Ali

Children of dust; a memoir of Pakistan. HarperOne 2009 337p $25.99 **92**

1. Bloggers 2. Islamic fundamentalism 3. Journalists 4. Memoirists 5. Muslims 6. Radicalism 7. Writers on politics 8. Writers on religion

ISBN 978-0-06-156708-7

LC 2009-9666

The author "opens his memoir with a vivid description of his father promising Allah that if God bestowed him with a son, that boy 'will become a great leader and servant of Islam.' The rest of the book finds Eteraz, whose given name is Abir ul Islam (which translates as 'Perfume of Islam') trying to come to terms with his father's mannat, or covenant, and understand the role that Islam will play in his life as well as the role he will play for Islam. . . . A gifted writer and scholar, Eteraz is able to create a true-life Islamic bildungsroman as he effortlessly conveys his coming-of-age tale while educating the reader. When his religious awakening finally occurs, his catharsis transcends the page." Publ Wkly

Evans, Harold

My paper chase; true stories of vanished times: an autobiography. Little, Brown and Co. 2009 515p il $27.99 **92**

1. Biography, Individual 2. Journalism -- Great Britain -- History 3. Journalists 4. Magazine editors 5. Newspaper editors 6. Publishing executives

ISBN 978-0-316-03142-4

LC 2009-15541

This is a memoir by the British journalist. Evans discusses his early life in Manchester, his National Service tour of duty in the R.A.F, his editorships at the Northern Echo and subsequently at the Sunday Times, where he campaigned to win compensation for the victims of Thalidomide, his relationship with Rupert Murdoch, and his second career in American publishing.

This "refreshing memoir . . . jettisons hand-wringing over the 'vanished times' of its melancholy subtitle for one man's unquenchable enthusiasm. . . . [This] is the Gospel of Evans, and the gospel makes juicy copy." Christ Sci Monit

Includes bibliographical references

Evans, R. Tripp

Grant Wood; a life. Alfred A. Knopf 2010 402p il $37.50; ebook $37.50 **92**

1. Artists 2. Artists -- United States 3. Biography,

Individual 4. Painters
ISBN 978-0-307-26629-3; 978-0-307-59433-4 ebook
LC 2010-18019
"Evans transforms our view of painter Grant Wood and his all-American paintings, including American Gothic, in a revelatory and heartrending biography of an artist forced to conceal his homosexuality." Booklist
Includes bibliographical references

Everitt, Anthony

★ **Augustus**; the life of Rome's first emperor. Random House 2006 377p il map $26.95   **92**
  1. Biography, Individual 2. Emperors
ISBN 1-4000-6128-8; 978-1-4000-6128-0
LC 2006-41735
The author's "writing is so crisp and so lively he brings both Rome and Augustus to life in this magnificent work, a must-read for anyone interested in classical times." Booklist
Includes bibliographical references

Cicero; the life and times of Rome's greatest politician. Random House 2002 359p il maps hardcover o.p. pa $14.95   **92**
  1. Orators 2. Orators -- Rome -- Biography 3. Philosophers 4. Statesmen 5. Statesmen -- Rome -- Biography
ISBN 0-375-75895-X pa
LC 2001-48531
This "masterful biography draws on Cicero's letters to his friend Atticus to give a clear picture of the famous Roman orator, noting both his brilliance and his faults." Booklist
Includes bibliographical references

Hadrian and the triumph of Rome. Random House 2009 xxix, 392p il map $30   **92**
  1. Emperors 2. Emperors -- Rome
ISBN 978-1-4000-6662-9; 1-4000-6662-X
LC 2009-05683
"Emperor from 117 to 138 A.D., Hadrian styled himself princeps, or first among equals, and his reversal of his predecessors' expansionist policies contributed to an era of prosperity and relative calm. He was unapologetically Hellenic, a poet and a dabbler in magic, and he kept in his retinue a young male lover whom he later deified. If Hadrian is indeed an enigma, it's because so few accounts of his life have survived, and this is where Everitt—whose books rely heavily on primary sources—runs into difficulty. One gets a clear and compelling sense of Hadrian's times, but the Emperor himself remains tantalizingly unknowable." New Yorker
Includes bibliographical references

Evers, Medgar Wiley

The **autobiography** of Medgar Evers: a hero's life and legacy revealed through his writings, letters, and speeches; edited by Myrlie Evers-Williams and Manning Marable. Basic Civitas Books 2005 xxiv, 352p il $26; pa $14   **92**
  1. African Americans -- Mississippi 2. Civil rights activists 3. Civil rights workers -- Mississippi
ISBN 0-465-02177-8; 0-465-02178-6 pa
LC 2006-296327

This is a collection of "Evers's unpublished papers and personal collections as well as [his widow] Evers-Williams's recollections. The resulting text resurrects the life, intellectual output, and creative legacy of the slain civil rights hero." Libr J
Includes bibliographical references

Ewing, Heather P.

The **lost** world of James Smithson; science, revolution, and the birth of the Smithsonian. [by] Heather Ewing. Bloomsbury 2007 432p il map $29.95   **92**
  1. Biography, Individual 2. Chemists 3. Geologists 4. Philanthropists 5. Science -- United States -- History 6. Scientists
ISBN 978-1-59691-029-4; 1-59691-029-1
This is a biography of the British chemist who founded the Smithsonian Institution in Washington, DC.
The author "provides a readable and informative perspective on late Enlightenment chemistry, backing it up with extensive archival research and forays into secondary literature on science." Times Lit Suppl
Includes bibliographical references

Eyman, Scott

★ **Empire** of dreams; the epic life of Cecil B. DeMille. Simon & Schuster 2010 579p il $35; ebook $16.99   **92**
  1. Biography, Individual 2. Motion picture directors 3. Motion picture industry -- California -- Los Angeles -- History 4. Motion picture producers 5. Motion picture producers and directors
ISBN 978-0-7432-8955-9; 0-7432-8955-2; 978-1-4391-8041-9 ebook; 1-4391-8041-5 ebook
LC 2010-27710
This is a biography of the film director and producer Cecil B. DeMille, whose movies include King of Kings and The Ten Commandments.
"Eyman's evocative prose and exhaustive research makes this an engaging and authoritative biography." Publ Wkly
Includes bibliographical references

★ **Lion** of Hollywood; the life and legend of Louis B. Mayer. Simon & Schuster 2005 596p il $35   **92**
  1. Biography, Individual 2. Motion picture executives
ISBN 0-7432-0481-6
LC 2005-42472
"Eyman's extensive knowledge of old Hollywood, his scrupulous research and his refusal to indict the often-pilloried Mayer make this biography an often revelatory delight." Publ Wkly
Includes bibliographical references

Falkner, David

★ **Great** time coming: the life of Jackie Robinson, from baseball to Birmingham. Simon & Schuster 1995 382p il hardcover o.p. pa $18.95   **92**
  1. Army officers 2. Baseball players
ISBN 0-684-82348-9 pa
LC 94-44876

This is a biography of the baseball player and civil rights activist. In addition to covering Robinson's professional career, the book focuses attention on his life after baseball.

"Falkner has written a very balanced account—neither muckraking nor fawning—of a fascinating and complex figure, one whose importance and interest reaches well beyond his exploits as an athlete." Christ Sci Monit

Includes bibliographical references

Fara, Patricia

Newton: the making of genius. Columbia Univ. Press 2002 347p il $83.50; pa $23   **92**
1. Mathematicians 2. Physicists 3. Scientists 4. Writers on science
ISBN 0-231-12806-1; 0-231-12807-X pa
LC 2003-265510

This "social history examines the reasons behind Isaac Newton's canonization as scientific genius. . . . Fara contributes to Newton's biography by focusing on the roots of Newton's apotheosis. She examines how idealized portraits propagated Newton's public image, and how the marketing of Newtonian images outside academic circles commercialized science in the same way Einstein's face sells today. Throughout, Fara, . . . effectively employs the words and imagery of religious discourse to characterize the idealization and commercialization of Newton in the service of emerging secular politics and culture." Publ Wkly

Includes bibliographical references

Faragher, John Mack

Daniel Boone; the life and legend of an American pioneer. Holt & Co. 1992 429p il maps hardcover o.p. pa $18   **92**
1. Frontier and pioneer life 2. Pioneers 3. Scouts
ISBN 0-8050-3007-7 pa
LC 92-21873

"The popular image of Daniel Boone is that of an unlettered backwoodsman, skilled hunter and Indian fighter. But evidence argues that he was reasonably well educated for his time and place, that he was a landowner, businessman and a respected leader of frontier society. Faragher . . . has sifted through folklore and fact to reconstruct a realistic portrait of Boone and the expanding frontier. . . . Faragher has written an absorbing, definitive biography." Publ Wkly

Includes bibliographical references

Farmelo, Graham

★ The strangest man; the hidden life of Paul Dirac, mystic of the atom. Basic Books 2009 539p il $29.95   **92**
1. Nobel laureates for physics 2. Physicists 3. Quantum theory
ISBN 978-0-465-01827-7

This is a biography of the British theoretical physicist Paul Dirac.

"This biography is a gift. It is both wonderfully written . . . and a thought-provoking meditation on human achievement, limitations and the relations between the two." N Y Times Book Rev

Includes bibliographical references (p. 439-508)

Farrell, John A.

Clarence Darrow; attorney for the damned. Doubleday 2011 561p il $32.50; ebook $15.99 **92**
1. Lawyers 2. Memoirists 3. State legislators 4. Writers on law
ISBN 978-0-385-52258-8; 0-385-52258-4; 978-0-385-53451-2 ebook
LC 2010-46273

This is a biography of the American lawyer who defended John Scopes, Nathan Leopold and Richard Loeb.

"Farrell gleans from previously undisclosed material to offer a completely engaging portrait of a flawed man of noble ideals." Booklist

Includes bibliographical references

Farrington, Tim

A hell of mercy; a meditation on depression and the dark night of the soul. HarperOne 2009 117p pa $18.95   **92**
1. Authors 2. Biography, Individual 3. Depression (Psychology) 4. Depression, Mental -- Religious aspects -- Christianity 5. Mysticism 6. Novelists
ISBN 978-0-06-082518-8; 0-06-082518-9

The author "offers a wry, almost stream-of-consciousness musing about his struggles with depression throughout a large part of his life. Bordering on a devotional of sorts, the book includes frequent quotations from John of the Cross and many other spiritual writers. Farrington also fills his book with funny anecdotes and jokes that illustrate points he is making. Ultimately, this is a personal diary of one man's journey to the other side of the black chasm of depression." Libr J

Fatsis, Stefan

A few seconds of panic; a 5-foot-8, 170-pound, 43-year-old sportswriter plays in the NFL. Penguin Press 2008 340p il hardcover o.p. pa $16   **92**
1. Football -- Biography 2. Football players -- United States 3. Journalists 4. Nonfiction writers
ISBN 978-1-59420-178-3; 978-0-14-311547-2 pa
LC 2008-2919

For this book, the author attended "the Denver Broncos' training camp in hopes of learning 'one very specific athletic skill'—that is, placekicking—and not to become an NFL-caliber kicker, but to become a 'credible one.' . . . It's an incredibly fascinating read for football fans, squashing the notion that the life of an NFL player is always glamorous." Publ Wkly

Includes bibliographical references

Federico, Meg

Welcome to the departure lounge; adventures in mothering mother. Random House 2009 191p $25   **92**
1. Aging parents 2. Aging parents -- Care 3. Biography, Individual 4. Caregivers 5. Humorists 6. Mother-daughter relationship 7. Mothers and daughters
ISBN 978-1-4000-6795-4; 1-4000-6795-2

One can read Meg Federico's "account of caring for her difficult mother, Addie (and her mother's beyond-difficult new husband, Walter) during Addie's last 18 months, and laugh all the way through in a there-but-for-the-grace-of-

God way. From its opening, when Addie, 81 and unconscious on a hospital gurney, wakes up long enough to yell, 'I demand an autopsy,' to 82-year-old Walter's fascination with mail-order sex aids, the book reads like a geriatric version of a 1930s screwball comedy. Federico is a humour columnist, and her story is skilfully told, but in the end (no pun intended), it's no laughing matter. Flowing not very far beneath the surface humour, and made palatable by the laughs, are some dead serious issues that, one way or another, most of us will someday face." Macleans

Feiffer, Jules

Backing into forward; a memoir. Nan A. Talese-Doubleday 2010 440p il $30   **92**
1. Artists   2. Authors   3. Authors, American   4. Biography, Individual   5. Cartoonists   6. Children's authors   7. Dramatists   8. Illustrators   9. Novelists   10. Satirists
ISBN 978-0-385-53158-0

LC 2009-21933
This is an autobiography by the American syndicated cartoonist.
"Feiffer is masterful at self-analyzing the skinny Jewish kid from the Bronx who grew up during the Depression, whose sister was a Communist, and whose distant cousin Roy Cohn was a Red-baiter, while he himself was full of insecurities but fortunate enough to 'luck into the zeitgeist.' . . . He offers social commentary and memorable moments from career and family life as he moved from cartooning to screen and playwriting, to authoring children's books, all the while maintaining a wry perspective that shows in the cartoons interspersed throughout this wonderful memoir." Booklist

Feinstein, Adam

★ **Pablo** Neruda; a passion for life. Bloomsbury 2004 497p il $32.50; pa $18.95   **92**
1. Authors   2. Biography, Individual   3. Diplomats   4. Nobel laureates for literature   5. Nobel laureates for peace   6. Novelists   7. Poets
ISBN 1-582-34410-8; 1-582-34594-5 pa

LC 2004-715
"Feinstein undoubtedly researched every existent source and found new ones, and the result is a detailed and accurate biography. . . . This is a necessary book, with many beautiful photos." Publ Wkly
Includes bibliographical references

Feinstein, Elaine

★ **Anna** of all the Russias; the life of Anna Akhmatova. Knopf 2006 331p il $27.50   **92**
1. Authors   2. Poets
ISBN 1-4000-4089-2; 978-1-4000-4089-6

LC 2005-44542
"In her superb and concise biography, Feinstein brings to life the complex interplay between poetic truth and the ordinary truth of experience in the poet's life and work. . . . Feinstein's poetic sensibility gives her book a distinctive quality, setting it apart from previous biographies." N Y Rev Books
Includes bibliographical references

Feinstein, John

Living on the black; two pitchers, two teams, one season to remember. Little, Brown 2008 525p il $26.99   **92**
1. Baseball -- Biography   2. Baseball players   3. Biography, Individual   4. Pitchers (Baseball)   5. Pitching (Baseball)
ISBN 978-0-316-11391-5; 0-316-11391-3

LC 2007-50618
The author presents a yearlong look at the lives of pitchers Mike Mussina of the New York Yankees and Tom Glavine of the New York Mets during the 2007 MLB season.
"Feinstein achieves a double play fans should savor for its scrupulous look at what life is like for the 21st-century major leaguer." Christ Sci Monit

Fellman, Michael

Citizen Sherman; a life of William Tecumseh Sherman. University Press of Kansas 1997 486p il pa $19.95   **92**
1. Generals   2. Memoirists   3. Secretaries of war
ISBN 978-0-7006-0840-9; 0-7006-0840-0
"This superb biography gives as full a portrait of nineteenth-century family dynamics as of the dynamics of the battlefield. Fellman's Sherman is not a lovable man, but he is a complete one." New Yorker
Includes bibliographical references

Felsenthal, Carol

Clinton in exile; a president out of the White House. William Morrow 2008 386p il $25.95   **92**
1. Biography, Individual   2. Governors   3. Presidents   4. Presidents -- United States
ISBN 978-0-06-123159-9; 0-06-123159-2
"Anyone curious, but especially those who remain fans, will enjoy Felsenthal's look at Clinton's post-presidency." Publ Wkly

Fenster, J. M.

FDR's shadow; Louis Howe, the force that shaped Franklin and Eleanor Roosevelt. [by] Julie M. Fenster. Palgrave Macmillan 2009 248p il $27 **92**
1. Columnists   2. Diplomats   3. Government officials   4. Governors   5. Handicapped   6. Humanitarians   7. Philatelists   8. Presidential advisers   9. Presidents   10. Social activists   11. Spouses of presidents   12. United Nations officials
ISBN 0-230-60910-4; 978-0-230-60910-5

LC 2009-39965
This is a "portrait of a once-famous, now nearly forgotten figure in 20th-century American politics. Louis Howe (1871-1936) met Franklin Roosevelt in 1911, when Howe was a newspaper reporter and FDR a freshly minted New York state senator. They became fast friends, and Howe proved to be a pivotal figure in Roosevelt's life and career. . . . An insightful look at a complex relationship that has been largely lost to history." Kirkus
Includes bibliographical references

Ferguson, Niall

High financier; the lives and time of Siegmund Warburg. Penguin Press 2010 548p il pa $22; $35 **92**

1. Bankers 2. Banks and banking 3. Banks and banking -- Great Britain -- History -- 20th century 4. Biography, Individual

ISBN 978-0-14-311940-1 pa; 978-1-59420-246-9

LC 2010-18353

This is a biography of the founder of the investment bank S. G. Warburg and Company. Index.

"Ferguson draws a richly vivid portrait of this unusual banker, an intellectual who read the Latin and Greek classics in the original and preferred Nietzsche to newspapers." N Y Times Book Rev

Includes bibliographical references

Fernandez-Armesto, Felipe

★ **Amerigo**; the man who gave his name to America. Random House 2007 231p il map $24.95; pa $15 **92**

1. Explorers

ISBN 978-1-4000-6281-2; 1-4000-6281-0; 978-0-8129-7298-6 pa; 0-8129-7298-8 pa

LC 2006-51739

The author chronicles the life and times of the explorer and navigator Amerigo Vespucci.

"A well-connected Florentine wheeler-dealer who settled in Seville, Vespucci began by outfitting Columbus's ships and later made voyages of his own. . . . Fernandez-Armesto accepts that Amerigo Vespucci made two voyages to north eastern South America, one in 1499 and another in 1501-02. But the evidence is maddeningly vague on exactly where he went, what he did, and even in what capacity he served (he is unlikely to have been the commander, as he claimed). Faced by such unreliable sources, Fernandez-Armesto sticks to what can be said of Vespucci with confidence, and wisely opts to paint a rich portrait of the times rather than speculate about details that may never be known." Times Lit Suppl

Includes bibliographical references

Ferro, Marc

Nicholas II; the last of the tsars. translated by Brian Pearce. Oxford Univ. Press 1993 305p il map hardcover o.p. pa $19.95 **92**

1. Emperors

ISBN 0-19-509382-8 pa

LC 92-41440

"The last Tsar, as this fluently written biography makes abundantly clear, was largely to blame for the demise of the monarchy. Ferro is concerned to illuminate the personality of the Tsar, his relationship with his wife and Rasputin and to look again at the circumstances surrounding his death." Hist Today

Includes bibliographical references

Fest, Joachim C.

Speer: the final verdict; {by} Joachim Fest; translated from the German by Ewald Osers and Alexandra Dring. Harcourt 2002 419p il $30; pa $15 **92**

1. Architects 2. Architecture -- Germany 3. Memoirists

4. National socialism 5. Nazi leaders 6. War criminals

ISBN 0-15-100556-7; 0-15-602874-3 pa

LC 2002-6074

"This is a valuable, important biography, but perhaps it is an effort to explain the unexplainable." Booklist

Includes bibliographical references

Fey, Tina, 1970-

Bossypants. Little, Brown and Co. 2011 277p il $26.99 **92**

1. Actors 2. American wit and humor 3. Biography, Individual 4. Comedians 5. Screenwriters 6. Television scriptwriters

ISBN 978-0-316-05686-1

LC 2011002415

In this book, comedian "Tina Fey's story can be told. From her youthful days as a vicious nerd to her tour of duty on 'Saturday Night Live'; from her passionately halfhearted pursuit of physical beauty to her life as a mother eating things off the floor; from her one-sided college romance to her nearly fatal honeymoon -- from the beginning of this paragraph to this final sentence. Tina Fey reveals all, and proves what we've all suspected: you're no one until someone calls you bossy." (Publisher's note)

"Perhaps best known to mass audiences for her writing and performances on Saturday Night Live, Fey's most inventive work is likely her writing for the critically acclaimed TV show 30 Rock, in which she stars alongside Alec Baldwin and fellow SNL alum Tracy Morgan. In typical self-deprecating style, the author traces her awkward childhood and adolescence, rise within the improv ranks of Second City and career on the sets of SNL and 30 Rock." Kirkus

Finan, Christopher M.

Alfred E. Smith, the happy warrior. Hill & Wang 2002 396p il $26; pa $16 **92**

1. Governors 2. Political leaders 3. Presidential candidates 4. State legislators

ISBN 0-8090-3033-0; 0-8090-1632-X pa

LC 2002-19476

"Finan writes well, but for an occasional lapse into anachronism." NY Times Book Rev

Includes bibliographical references

Finch, Christopher

Chuck Close; life. Prestel 2010 350p il $34.95 **92**

1. Artists 2. Artists -- United States 3. Painters

ISBN 978-3-7913-3677-0

"Focusing on Close's paradigm-altering approaches to portraiture, the author offers an astounding and inspiring story of an artist of uncommon powers." Booklist

Includes bibliographical references

Finkelman, Paul

Millard Fillmore. Times Books 2011 171p $23; ebook $10.99 **92**

1. Members of Congress 2. Presidents 3. Presidents -- United States 4. Vice-presidents

ISBN 978-0-8050-8715-4; 978-1-4299-2301-9 ebook

LC 2010-47174

The author "describes Millard Fillmore's nearly forgotten presidency by rigidly contrasting him with Abraham Lincoln, another self-made man who wrestled with racial and regional tensions as president. . . . This book is an enlightening view into the often overlooked beginnings of the Civil War, which history buffs and students alike will find enjoyable." Publ Wkly

Includes bibliographical references

Fischer, David Hackett

★ **Champlain's** dream. Simon & Schuster 2008 834p il map $40   **92**

1. Biography, Individual 2. Explorers

ISBN 978-1-4165-9332-4; 1-4165-9332-2

LC 2008-16286

The author "offers the definitive biography of an extraordinary and flawed man: Samuel de Champlain (1567-1635): spy, explorer, courtier, soldier and founder and governor of New France (today's Quebec)." Publ Wkly

Includes bibliographical references

Fisher, Carrie

Wishful drinking. Simon & Schuster 2008 163p il $21   **92**

1. Actors 2. Authors 3. Biography, Individual 4. Memoirists 5. Novelists 6. Short story writers

ISBN 978-1-439-10225-1; 1-439-10225-2

In this "memoir, Carrie Fisher—actress, novelist and self-described daughter of 'Hollywood inbreeding'—writes about her tumultuous life as showbiz royalty. In Wishful Drinking, Fisher discusses her bipolar disorder, addictions and divorce—and still manages to laugh." NPR

Fitch, Noel Riley

Appetite for life; the biography of Julia Child. Doubleday 1997 569p il hardcover o.p. pa $16.95   **92**

1. Biography, Individual 2. Cookbook writers 3. Cooks 4. Television personalities

ISBN 0-385-49383-5 pa

LC 97-11061

This biography details the private life and professional career of PBS' The French chef, whose Mastering the art of French cooking (1961) revolutionized the American kitchen.

"Fitch not only richly details Child's personal life but also effectively places her writing and television shows within the context of work by other cooking luminaries of the time. Entertaining and informative." Libr J

Includes bibliographical references

Fletcher, Joann

Cleopatra the great; the woman behind the legend. Harpercollins 2011 454p map $27.99   **92**

1. Queens

ISBN 978-0-06-058558-7

In this biography, the author "argues that Cleopatra's genius as a strategist, which allowed her to restore a fading Egypt to its former glory, is what makes her the 'true heir' to her ancestor Alexander the Great. . . . Those interested in Cleopatra, ancient history, or a well-written and academically sound biography will enjoy this authentic look at a queen of Egypt who managed to be all things to all people—mother, queen, goddess, and whore." Libr J

Includes bibliographical references

Flexner, James Thomas

George Washington and the new nation, 1783-1793. Little, Brown 1969 466p il map $42   **92**

1. Generals 2. Presidents 3. Presidents -- United States

ISBN 0-316-28600-1

LC 78-117042

This third volume of a four-volume biography of Washington focuses on the period between the end of the Revolutionary War through his first term as president.

George Washington: anguish and farewell 1793-1799. Little, Brown 1972 554p il $45   **92**

1. Generals 2. Presidents 3. Presidents -- United States

ISBN 0-316-28602-8

LC 72-6875

This final volume of a four-volume biography of Washington covers his second term as president, his retirement, and death.

George Washington: the forge of experience, 1732-1775. Little 1965 390p il map $40   **92**

1. Generals 2. Presidents 3. Presidents -- United States

ISBN 0-316-28597-8

LC 65-21361

The author "covers forty-three years of Washington's life in this volume, the first in a series of four . . . [that carries] Washington through the Revolutionary War and on to the end of his life." Publisher's note

Includes bibliographical references

Flinn, Caryl

Brass diva; the life and legends of Ethel Merman. University of California Press 2007 542p il $34.95; pa $18.95   **92**

1. Actors 2. Biography, Individual 3. Singers

ISBN 978-0-520-22942-6; 0-520-22942-8; 978-0-520-26022-1 pa; 0-520-26022-8 pa

LC 2007-29515

This is a biography of the singer and musical comedy star who appeared in the shows Girl Crazy (1930), Annie Get Your Gun (1946), and Gypsy (1959).

"A definitive all-inclusive piece of work that has been masterfully put together." Univ Press Books for Public and Second Sch Libr, 2008

Includes bibliographical references, discography, and filmography

Flood, Charles Bracelen

Grant and Sherman; the friendship that won the Civil War. Farrar, Straus and Giroux 2005 460p il map $27   **92**

1. Biography, Individual 2. Generals 3. Memoirists 4. Presidents 5. Secretaries of war

ISBN 0-374-16600-5

LC 2005-04170

The author "underscores the powerful bond formed between Ulysses S. Grant and William Tecumseh Sherman and tells the story of a friendship that would influence both the politics and the military operations of the Civil War. . . . One of the big-profile history books of the season and highly recommended for all history-minded readers." Booklist

Includes bibliographical references

Grant's final victory; Ulysses S. Grant's heroic last year. Da Capo Press 2011 288p il $27.50   **92**
1. Generals 2. Presidents 3. Presidents -- United States
ISBN 978-0-306-82028-1; 978-0-306-82056-4 ebook
LC 2011020263
The author "writes movingly of the last months of Ulysses S. Grant's life, 1884–85, when, in the wake of financial ruin from a failed investment and suffering from terminal throat cancer, he labored to complete his memoirs (which would be published by Mark Twain) so that his family might once again prosper after his death. . . . Those who like presidential or post-Civil War history will especially enjoy this book, aimed at general readers, with its compelling portrait of a well-known historical figure." Libr J

Includes bibliographical references

Flynn, Nick
Another bullshit night in Suck City; a memoir. W.W. Norton & Co 2004 347p il $23.95   **92**
1. Authors 2. Biography, Individual 3. Poets
ISBN 0-393-05139-0
LC 2004-11796
This "memoir describes the years poet Flynn . . . spent, in his late 20s, working at one of the city's homeless shelters, where his path crisscrossed with his down-and-out father's. . . . Although it's depressing, the book never seems hopeless, because readers know the author has succeeded at doing what his father only pretended to do: write, and write well." Publ Wkly

Flynn, Raymond
John Paul II; a personal portrait of the pope and the man. St. Martin's Press 2001 204p il hardcover o.p. pa $14.95   **92**
1. Papacy -- History -- 20th century 2. Popes
ISBN 0-312-28328-8 pa
LC 00-45965
Flynn, the "former mayor of Boston and ex-ambassador to the Vatican, tells us . . . what his book is not: It is not a biography, or an analysis. . . . Flynn views it, rather, as a profile based on his own experiences with Pope John Paul II, dating back to a 1969 visit to Boston of then-Cardinal Karol Wojtyla." Natl Rev

Foner, Moe
Not for bread alone; a memoir. by Moe Foner with Dan North; foreword by Ossie Davis. Cornell Univ. Press 2002 142p $25   **92**
1. Health care personnel 2. Hospitals -- Staff -- Labor unions -- New York (State) -- History 3. Labor leaders 4. Labor leaders -- New York (State) -- Biography
ISBN 0-8014-4061-0
LC 2002-5100
Foner's "memoir is a unique window into the evolution of 1199 SEIU from its origins as a tiny conglomeration of

drugstore employees into the country's largest healthcare union." Libr J

Includes bibliographical references and index

Fowler, Ruth
No man's land; a memoir. Viking Penguin 2008 265p $24.95   **92**
1. Journalists 2. Memoirists 3. Striptease
ISBN 978-0-670-01939-7; 0-670-01939-9
LC 2007-40509
"Eyebrow-raising revelations about the sex industry abound in this sharp, racy, and relentlessly candid tale." Booklist

Fox, Michael J.
Always looking up; the adventures of an incurable optimist. Hyperion 2009 279p il $25.99   **92**
1. Actors 2. Parkinson's disease -- Personal narratives
ISBN 978-1-4013-0338-9
LC 2008-55129
An autobiography of the actor and Parkinson's disease sufferer.

Lucky man; a memoir. Hyperion 2002 304p $22.95; pa $12.95   **92**
1. Actors 2. Parkinson's disease -- Personal narratives
ISBN 0-7868-6764-7; 0-7868-8874-1 pa
In this autobiography the actor discusses his professional career in feature films and television. He also "writes of the last 10 years, during which--with the unswerving support of his wife, family, and friends--he has dealt with his illness. He talks about what Parkinson's has given him: the chance to appreciate a wonderful life and career, and the opportunity to help search for a cure and spread public awareness of the disease." Publisher's note

Fox, William Price
Satchel Paige's America. University of Alabama Press 2005 142p pa $16.95   **92**
1. Baseball -- Biography 2. Baseball players
ISBN 0-8173-5189-2
LC 2004-18911
This biography is based upon the author's conversations with the legendary baseball pitcher as he spent a week following him around Kansas City, MO, in 1970.
This is "a lively, moving, and often hilarious tale of an encounter 30 years ago and of a life richly led." Libr J

Fragoso, Margaux
Tiger, tiger; a memoir. Farrar, Straus and Giroux 2011 322p $26   **92**
1. Adult child sexual abuse victims 2. Authors 3. Child sexual abuse 4. Memoirists 5. Poets 6. Short story writers
ISBN 978-0-374-27762-8; 0-374-27762-1
LC 2010-39058
"In this gut-wrenching memoir of sexual abuse, Fragoso . . . explores with unflinching honesty the ways in which pedophiles can manipulate their way into the lives of children. Fragoso met Peter Curran at a public pool in Union City, N.J., in 1985 when she was seven and he was 51. He seemed harmless, and invited Fragoso and her mother back to his

house. This marked the beginning of Curran and Fragoso's 15-year relationship, which ended when Curran committed suicide at age 66. . . . Using her own diaries and the myriad letters, diaries, and photographs Curran left behind, Fragoso eloquently depicts psychological and sexual abuse in disturbing detail." Publ Wkly

Frank, Joseph
Dostoevsky. v1 Princeton University Press 1976 401p v1 il hardcover o.p. pa $24.95 **92**
1. Authors 2. Authors, Russian 3. Novelists 4. Short story writers
ISBN 0-691-06260-9; 0-691-01355-1 pa
This first volume of a five volume biography of Dostoyevsky traces his life from his boyhood to 1849. His writings are discussed in relation to influences and themes which recur in his greatest works.

Frank, Josh
In heaven everything is fine; the unsolved life of Peter Ivers and the lost history of New wave theatre. [by] Josh Frank with Charlie Buckholtz. Free Press 2008 327p il $25 **92**
1. Comedians 2. Rock musicians 3. Songwriters 4. Television personalities
ISBN 978-1-4165-5120-1; 1-4165-5120-4
LC 2008-2943
In this chronicle of Ivers' life, the authors examine his influence upon "such contemporaries and friends . . . as National Lampoon cofounder Doug Kenney, John Belushi, and David Lynch. . . . An appreciative look at a figure peripheral to a clutch of now-aging major stars." Booklist
Includes bibliographical references

Frank, Richard B.
MacArthur; foreword by Wesley K. Clark. Palgrave Macmillan 2007 224p hardcover o.p. pa $12.95 **92**
1. Generals
ISBN 1-4039-7658-9; 978-1-4039-7658-1; 0-230-61397-7 pa; 978-0-230-61397-3 pa
This biography of the World War II general is an "assessment of both the man and the soldier, covering the failures and triumphs in an assured and dispassionate tone. . . . A good starting point for generalists." Libr J

Frankl, Viktor E.
★ **Man's** search for meaning; part one translated by Ilse Lasch; foreword by Harold S. Kushner; afterword by William J. Winslade. Beacon Press 2006 165p pa $13 **92**
1. Holocaust, 1933-1945 -- Personal narratives 2. Psychologists
ISBN 0-8070-1427-3; 978-0-8070-1427-1
LC 2006-287144
"Between 1942 and 1945 Frankl labored in four different camps, including Auschwitz, while his parents, brother, and pregnant wife perished. Based on his own experience and the experiences of others he treated later in his practice, Frankl argues that we cannot avoid suffering but we can choose how to cope with it, find meaning in it, and move forward with renewed purpose. Frankl's theory—known as

logotherapy, from the Greek word logos ('meaning')—holds that our primary drive in life is not pleasure, as Freud maintained, but the discovery and pursuit of what we personally find meaningful." Publisher's note

Franklin, Benjamin
★ **Not** your usual founding father; selected readings from Benjamin Franklin. edited by Edmund S. Morgan. Yale University Press 2006 303p il map hardcover o.p. pa $16 **92**
1. Authors 2. Diplomats 3. Inventors 4. Members of Congress 5. Scientists 6. Statesmen 7. Statesmen -- United States 8. Writers on science
ISBN 0-300-11394-3; 978-0-300-11394-5; 0-300-12688-3 pa; 978-0-300-126884 pa
LC 2006-45706
The editor "explains that this anthology differs from the typical selections of writings by founders, which showcase themes of revolution, war, and political philosophy. Here Morgan pursues the man himself, particularly Franklin's fascination with the curiosities of human behavior. . . . Franklin's humane solicitude and observational acuity surface in varied places (on ship, in Parisian salons) and in varied formats (personal letters, published satires) in such a way that readers encounter directly Franklin's seeming simplicity, which actually masked a deep complexity and which continually makes him the most interesting founder." Booklist

★ The **autobiography** of Benjamin Franklin; introduction by Lewis Leary. Simon & Schuster 2004 143p pa $10.95 **92**
1. Authors 2. Diplomats 3. Inventors 4. Members of Congress 5. Scientists 6. Statesmen 7. Statesmen -- United States 8. Writers on science
ISBN 0-7432-5506-2
LC 2003-54477
"Franklin's account of his life, written for his son William. . . . During the Revolutionary War, the manuscript was put aside. . . . Franklin later more than doubled the length . . . but still took the story only to 1757-1759, ending before the period of his greatest public service. Still, the book remains the first undisputed classic of American literature and one of the most interesting autobiographies in English." Benet's Reader's Ency of Am Lit

Franklin, Wayne
James Fenimore Cooper; the early years. Yale University Press 2007 708p il map $40 **92**
1. Authors 2. Authors, American 3. Biography, Individual 4. Novelists
ISBN 978-0-300-10805-7; 0-300-10805-2
LC 2006-31247
"This volume profoundly enriches our understanding of how the young writer helped forge our national mythology in works such as The Last of The Mohicans and The Pioneers." Booklist
Includes bibliographical references

Franzen, Jonathan

The **discomfort** zone; a personal history. Farrar, Straus & Giroux 2006 195p $22 **92**

1. Authors 2. Biography, Individual 3. Novelists

ISBN 978-0-374-29919-4; 0-374-29919-6

LC 2006-2700

This is a memoir by the author of The Corrections.

"For those who admire the razor-sharp jabs Franzen makes at himself and anyone else standing too close, 'The Discomfort Zone' is both a delicious read and a clever showcase for Franzen's talents." Christ Sci Monit

Fraser, Antonia

Love and Louis XIV; the women in the life of the Sun King. Nan A. Talese/Doubleday 2006 xxviii, 388p il $32.50 **92**

1. Biography, Individual 2. Kings

ISBN 978-0-38550984-8; 0-385-50984-7

LC 2006-44674

This is an account of Louis XIV's relationships with his wife and his mistresses.

"One of the most enveloping popular histories of the current publishing season." Booklist

Includes bibliographical references

Mary Queen of Scots; illustrated abridged ed; Delacorte Press 1978 208p il hardcover o.p. pa $19.95 **92**

1. Queens

ISBN 0-380-31129-X pa

LC 78-703

A look at the tragic life of Mary Stuart, the 16th century Catholic ruler of Protestant Scotland, and her incessant struggle with political and religious opponents.

Must you go? my life with Harold Pinter. Nan A. Talese/Doubleday 2010 328p il $28.95; ebook $28.95 **92**

1. Authors 2. Authors, English 3. Dramatists 4. Dramatists, English 5. Nobel laureates for literature 6. Screenwriters

ISBN 978-0-385-53250-1; 978-0-385-53251-8 ebook

LC 2010-7374

Harold Pinter's widow, the biographer, historian and novelist Antonia Fraser, recalls their years together from 1975 until the playwright's death of cancer on Christmas Eve in 2008.

The author "simultaneously creates a tender portrait of an exciting marriage, and a deliciously detailed account of living in the thick of creativity and fame." Entertainment Wkly

Fraser, David

Knight's cross: a life of Field Marshal Erwin Rommel. HarperCollins Pubs. 1994 601p il maps hardcover o.p. pa $21.95 **92**

1. Marshals

ISBN 0-06-092597-3 pa

LC 93-43832

This is a biography of the general who commanded German troops in World War II.

"Fraser presents what definitely will become the standard biography . . . as the author astutely traces the qualities of leadership which Rommel embodied." Booklist

Includes bibliographical references

Fraser, Flora

Pauline Bonaparte; Venus of Empire. Alfred A. Knopf 2009 287p il $28.95 **92**

1. Biography, Individual 2. Patrons of the arts 3. Princesses

ISBN 978-0-307-26544-9; 0-307-26544-7

LC 2008-28639

This "narrative by British biographer Fraser . . . fleshes out the privileged and politically unstable world of Pauline, who both commissioned and modeled nearly nude for Canova's symbolic marble statue Venus Victorious as a testament to herself. Pauline's raison d'être was the joyful pursuit of astonishing variety in her love affairs, which Fraser asserts may have been a source of her invalidism throughout her adult life. But her life showcased the dangers in Napoleonic France as well as its pleasures: she faced death from yellow fever and insurrection in French colonial Haiti. Fraser's narrative provides insight into the permissive culture of the French Empire and glimpses into Napoleon as a protective and exasperated older brother while simultaneously engaged in politics, invasions and his eventual fall from power." Publ Wkly

Includes bibliographical references

Fraser, Laura

All over the map. Harmony Books 2010 271p $24; ebook $24 **92**

1. Journalists 2. Single women 3. Women authors

ISBN 978-0-307-45063-0; 0-307-45063-5; 978-0-307-45091-3 ebook; 0-307-45091-0 ebook

LC 2009-45251

"The title is an apt description of both Fraser's travels—which include jaunts to Italy, Provence, and Rwanda described in evocative, lush prose—and her frame of mind over the course of the eight years that her winning coming-of-middle-age memoir spans." Booklist

French, Francis

Falling to Earth; an Apollo 15 astronaut's journey. [by] Al Worden with Francis French. Smithsonian Books 2011 300p il **92**

1. Air force officers 2. Apollo project 3. Astronauts 4. Biography, Individual 5. Space flight to the moon

ISBN 1-58834-309-X; 978-1-58834-309-3

LC 2011003440

"Worden is eloquent, witty, and brutally honest, still in awe of the company he kept and the history he belongs to. A solid addition to space-literature collections."

"Worden is eloquent, witty, and brutally honest, still in awe of the company he kept and the history he belongs to. A solid addition to space-literature collections." Booklist

Includes bibliographical references

French, Patrick

The **world** is what it is; the authorized biography of V.S. Naipaul. Knopf 2008 554p il $30 **92**

1. Authors 2. Biography, Individual 3. Essayists

4. Journalists 5. Nobel laureates for literature 6. Nonfiction writers 7. Novelists 8. Radio reporters 9. Short story writers 10. Travel writers

ISBN 978-1-4000-4405-4; 1-4000-4405-7

LC 2008-6988

This authorized study of Nobel laureate V.S. Naipaul examines his difficult early life as a child of Indian parents in colonial Trinidad, his Oxford education, the depression that marked his life in England, his complex personal life and romantic relationships, and his pursuit of becoming a great writer.

This book "is a prodigious achievement, a wonderful biography, a justification for the art of biography itself." Times Lit Suppl

Includes bibliographical references

Frey, Julia

Toulouse-Lautrec; a life. Phoenix 1995 597p il pa $27.50
92

1. Artists 2. Artists, French 3. Lithographers 4. Painters

ISBN 1-85799-363-2; 978-1-85799-363-9

"The author chronicles Toulouse-Lautrec's transformation from a pampered invalid into one of the most radical of the fin de siecle artists. . . . Her sensitive, eloquent, and richly illustrated biography has brought the real Toulouse-Lautrec out from behind the scrim of myth." Booklist

Includes bibliographical references

Fried, Albert

F.D.R. and his enemies. St. Martin's Press 1999 261p hardcover o.p. pa $15.95
92

1. Governors 2. Handicapped 3. Philatelists 4. Presidents 5. Presidents -- United States

ISBN 0-312-23827-4 pa

LC 98-56141

The author "examines Roosevelt's conflict with and victory over varied critics, including Al Smith, Huey Long, Charles Lindbergh, and Charles Coughlin. Fried convincingly asserts that Roosevelt defeated his critics primarily because he was a superb pragmatist who refused to be hindered by an ideological straightjacket." Booklist

Includes bibliographical references

Fried, Stephen

Appetite for America; how visionary businessman Fred Harvey built a railroad hospitality empire that civilized the Wild West. Bantam Books 2010 518p il map $27
92

1. Biography, Individual 2. Cookery, American 3. Railroads -- Western States -- History 4. Restaurants 5. Restaurateurs

ISBN 978-0-553-80437-9; 0-553-80437-5

LC 2009-47790

This is a biography of Fred Harvey, whose Harvey House restaurants were located at railroad depots across America. Bibliography. Index.

"A sturdy, detailed work of history that will appeal to business readers as well as aficionados of railroading and the Old West." Kirkus

Includes bibliographical references (p. 483-488)

Friedman, Lawrence Jacob

Identity's architect; a biography of Erik H. Erikson. Harvard University Press 2000 592p il pa $19.95
92

1. Authors 2. Essayists 3. Psychoanalysts

ISBN 978-0-674-00437-5; 0-674-00437-X

"Friedman's biography is lucidly written, extensively researched and covers both Erikson's rise to celebrity in the 1950s and 1960s and the attacks on his reputation from feminist and New Left critics in the 1970s." Publ Wkly

Includes bibliographical references

Friedman, Maurice S.

Encounter on the narrow ridge: a life of Martin Buber; {by} Maurice Friedman. Paragon House 1991 496p il $22.95; pa $18.95
92

1. Authors 2. Essayists 3. Jewish philosophy 4. Novelists 5. Philosophers 6. Translators 7. Writers on religion 8. Zionism

ISBN 1-55778-453-1; 1-55778-596-1 pa

LC 90-44502

This biography (based on the author's three volume Martin Buber's life and work) "traces Buber's career showing the pivotal events in his life as well as the influences of Judaism, Christianity, general philosophical thought, and linguistics on his writings and lectures. Friedman analyzes succinctly, but with great care, Buber's responses to the important events of the 20th century." Libr J

Includes bibliographical references

Fuegi, John

Brecht and company; sex, politics, and the making of the modern drama. Grove Press 1994 xx, 732p il hardcover o.p. pa $20
92

1. Authors 2. Dramatists 3. Novelists 4. Poets 5. Theatrical directors

ISBN 0-8021-3910-8 pa

LC 93-23051

The author "believes Brecht wrote very little in the dramas that made him famous; rather, he systematically plagiarized and 'collaborated' with lovers and colleagues by signing his name to plays they essentially wrote. . . . Fuegi's massive effort examines every aspect of Brecht's career and personality, and ranges from his childhood in Augsburg through his early successes and his exile to his return to East Germany." Booklist

Includes bibliographical references

Fuller, Alexandra

Don't let's go to the dogs tonight; an African childhood. Random House 2002 301p il hardcover o.p. pa $13.95
92

1. Authors 2. Memoirists

ISBN 0-375-50750-7; 0-375-75899-2 pa

LC 2001-41752

"Fuller grew up in Rhodesia (now Zimbabwe) during the civil war, and she watched her parents fight against the local Africans to keep their farm. In a memoir powerful in its frank straightforwardness, she neither apologizes for nor champions her family's views and actions. Instead she gives us an honest, moving portrait of one family struggling to survive tumultuous times." Booklist

Furmansky, Dyana Z.

Rosalie Edge, hawk of mercy; the activist who saved nature from the conservationists. [by] Dyana Z. Furmansky; with a foreword by Bill McKibben & an afterword by Roland C. Clement. University of Georgia Press 2009 312p il $28.95 **92**

1. Conservationists 2. Feminists 3. Suffragists
ISBN 978-0-8203-3341-0; 0-8203-3341-7

LC 2009-8551

The book discusses "Mabel Rosalie Barrow Edge (1877–1962) [who was] . . . a conservation activist . . . [and t]he founder of the Emergency Conservation Committee (ECC). . . . Using previously unavailable primary sources, Dyana Z. Furmansky offers an engaging portrait of Edge as activist while piecing together the story of Edge as a daughter, wife, mother, friend, and colleague. . . . Furmansky notes that Edge's writings, public testimony, and sometimes-assertive personal style inspired others to see and care about nature as she did. Furmansky looks for clues to Edge's commitment to nature in her privileged New York childhood, in her experiences abroad, and in her engagement with the suffrage movement. Edge's activism began after she read a 1929 pamphlet called 'Crisis in Conservation,' written in part by Willard Van Name, who would become Edge's mentor and financial backer. This pamphlet inspired Edge to found the ECC." (Journal of American History)

A biography of the conservationist and suffragette who "founded the Hawk Mountain Sanctuary and fought hard for the Olympic National Park. Clearly relishing every moment of Edge's remarkable life, Furmansky vividly enriches environmental history with her inspiring portrait of this indomitable champion of the wild." Booklist

Includes bibliographical references

Gabriel, Mary

Love and capital; Karl and Jennie Marx and the birth of a revolution. Little, Brown and Company 2011 lviii, 707p il **92**

1. Marxism 2. Political and social philosophers 3. Spouses of prominent persons 4. Writers on politics
ISBN 0-316-06611-7; 978-0-316-06611-2

LC 2010-44021

An "account of the lives of Karl Marx and his wife, Jenny von Westphalen. . . . Tracing their tumultuous lives from Prussia, via Paris to Brussels and finally London, Gabriel tells the story of a woman who forswore the comforts of her noble upbringing to raise a family in often very straitened circumstances with a man committed in both his life and letters to social justice and the emancipation of the working class. Equally at home with the details of Marxist theory and revolutionary Europe as she is with the private lives of Karl and Jenny, the author dazzles most with her fascinating accounts of the lives of the Marx children." Publ Wkly

Includes bibliographical references

Gabriel, Sarah

Eating pomegranates; a memoir of mothers, daughters, and the BRCA gene. Scribner 2010 259p $25 **92**

1. Breast -- Cancer 2. Breast cancer 3. Journalists
ISBN 978-1-4391-4819-8; 1-4391-4819-8

LC 2009-49524

"Gabriel shares an estimable gift for memoir and introspection in this forceful account of the breast cancer caused by a potentially fatal inheritance, the BRCA Gene, from her mother and her mother's mother before her and so on. . . . Raw grace is in evidence here as Gabriel lives to speak to realities to which all too many women can relate." Booklist

Gage, Nicholas

★ **Eleni**. Random House 1983 470p hardcover o.p. pa $14.95 **92**

1. Biography, Individual 2. Greece -- History -- 1453- 3. Greece -- History -- 1900-1999 (20th century) 4. Martyrs 5. Murder victims 6. Parents of prominent persons
ISBN 0-394-52093-9; 978-0-345-41043-6 pa; 0-345-41043-2 pa

LC 82-42803

"The separate strands lead to an intensely moving climax, making Eleni one of the rare books in which the power of art re-creates the full historical truth." NY Rev Books

Gaines, James R.

For liberty and glory; Washington, Lafayette, and their revolutions. W.W. Norton & Co. 2007 533p il map $29.95 **92**

1. Generals 2. Presidents 3. Statesmen
ISBN 0-393-06138-8; 978-0-393-06138-3

LC 2007-22449

Gaines examines the relationship between George Washington and the Marquis de Lafayette.

This is a "fresh and engaging new look at the pair. . . . Gaines has a dry sense of humor and an appreciation for human foibles. . . . The American founding fathers, in particular, come across as extraordinary men with ordinary obsessions and—surprise!—senses of humor." Christ Sci Monit

Includes bibliographical references

Garcia Marquez, Gabriel

Living to tell the tale; translated by Edith Grossman. Knopf 2003 483p maps $26.95; pa $14.95 **92**

1. Authors 2. Authors, Colombian -- 20th century -- Biography 3. Journalists 4. Nobel laureates for literature 5. Novelists 6. Short story writers
ISBN 1-4000-4134-1; 1-4000-3454-X pa

LC 2003-58924

"Garcia Márquez tells the entrancing story of his remarkable family, chronicles the turbulence of his troubled country, Colombia, and offers a piquant portrait of himself as a struggling young writer. A resplendent memoir written with compassion and artistry." Booklist

Gardner, Chris

The **pursuit** of happyness; [by] Chris Gardner with Quincy Troupe and Mim Eichler Rivas. Amistad 2006 302p il map $25.95 **92**

1. Securities brokers
ISBN 978-0-06-074486-1; 0-06-074486-3

LC 2005-57203

The author "recounts his 'long walk to Wall Street,' a journey that took him from a childhood in the ghettos of Milwaukee to an enormously successful career as a stockbroker in New York city." Libr J

Gardner, Mark L.

To hell on a fast horse; Billy the Kid, Pat Garrett, and the epic chase to justice in the Old West. William Morrow 2010 325p il $26.99　　　**92**

1. Outlaws 2. Sheriffs

ISBN 978-0-06-136827-1; 0-06-136827-X

LC 2009025467

A "double biography of the iconic western outlaw Billy the Kid and Sheriff Pat Garrett. Maintaining an objective perspective on both men in a narrative closely tied to historic source materials, Gardner's quick-moving story follows events of the civil war in Lincoln County, New Mexico Territory in 1877–78, and the Kid's death-by-shooting at the hands of Garrett in 1881. . . . The final chapters describing Garrett as an old-style lawman in a postfrontier society, with interactions with President Theodore Roosevelt, serve to distinguish this book from other recent Kid biographies." Libr J

Includes bibligraphical references

Gaskell, Elizabeth Cleghorn

The **life** of Charlotte Bronte; [by] Elizabeth Gaskell; edited with an introduction and notes by Angus Eason. Oxford University Press 2001 xxxvi, 587p pa $13.95　　　**92**

1. Authors 2. Authors, English 3. Novelists 4. Poets 5. Women authors

ISBN 0-19-283805-9

"Mrs. Gaskell was herself a popular novelist, who commanded a very wide audience. She brought to bear upon the biography of Charlotte Bronte all those literary gifts which had made the charm of her seven volumes of romance. . . . It is quite certain that Charlotte Bronte would not stand on so splendid a pedestal today but for the single-minded devotion of her accomplished biographer." Clement K. Shorter

Includes bibliographical references

Gates, Henry Louis

Colored people; a memoir. [by] Henry Louis Gates, Jr. Knopf 1994 216p hardcover o.p. pa $13　　　**92**

1. Authors 2. College teachers 3. Literary critics 4. Nonfiction writers 5. Philologists 6. Social scientists

ISBN 0-679-73919-X pa

LC 93-12256

"As Gates traces his evolution from 'Negro' to Afro-wearing 'black,' he also traces the evolution of Piedmont (and, by extension, of much of America) at a time when the relationship between the races was being redefined." Newsweek

Gaustad, Edwin Scott

Roger Williams; [by] Edwin S. Gaustad. Oxford University Press 2005 150p il $17.95　　　**92**

1. Biography, Individual 2. Clergy 3. Colonial leaders 4. Puritans 5. Writers on religion

ISBN 0-19-518369-X

LC 2004-25246

The author "provides not just an excellent introduction to the man but a deep analysis of his largely unacknowledged influence on our political and cultural life." Reason

Gavin, James

Stormy weather; the life of Lena Horne. Atria 2009 598p il $27; pa $16　　　**92**

1. Actors 2. African American singers 3. African American women 4. Biography, Individual 5. Singers

ISBN 978-0-7432-7143-1; 0-7432-7143-2; 978-0-7432-7144-8 pa; 0-7432-7144-0 pa

LC 2009-08170

This is a biography of the American singer who has appeared in the films Stormy Weather and Cabin in the Sky (both 1943) and on Broadway in Jamaica (1957) and The Lady and Her Music (1981).

Horne "has had a life so rich in ups and downs as to make page after page eventful and suspenseful. This all the more so since the book is also two books in one: a thorough and fluent biography and a history of the slow social rise of black people despite crippling discrimination and stinging humiliations—a history in which Horne's story is embedded." N Y Times Book Rev

Includes discography, filmography, and bibliographic references

Gay, Peter

Freud; a life for our time. with a new foreword. Norton 2006 810p il pa $21.95　　　**92**

1. Psychoanalysts 2. Writers on medicine

ISBN 0-393-32861-9

LC 2006-283026

"The book is beautifully written. Gay's approach is to try to understand Freud and his alliances and environment rather than to worship or challenge him." Choice

Includes bibliographical references

Gay, Timothy M.

Tris Speaker; the rough-and-tumble life of a baseball legend. University of Nebraska Press 2005 314p il $27.95　　　**92**

1. Baseball managers 2. Baseball players

ISBN 0-8032-2206-8

LC 2005-16975

This is a "look at the Hall of Fame center fielder, whose colorful personality and remarkable talent were overshadowed by contemporaries like Ty Cobb and Cy Young. . . . Gay has insured the righting of history with this biography. A worthwhile read for any sports fan." Publ Wkly

Gayford, Martin

The **yellow** house; Van Gogh, Gauguin, and nine turbulent weeks in Arles. Little, Brown and Co. 2006 339p il $24.99　　　**92**

1. Artists 2. Painters

ISBN 978-0-316-76901-3; 0-316-76901-0

LC 2006-10538

"Though it is impossible to entirely understand what motivated these two great artists during their weeks together in Arles, these pages deliver as close and vivid an image as may be possible." Publ Wkly

Includes bibliographical references

Geck, Martin

★ **Johann** Sebastian Bach; life and work. translated from the German by John Hargraves. Harcourt 2006 738p il $40   **92**

1. Biography, Individual 2. Composers
ISBN 978-0-15-100648-9; 0-15-100648-2

LC 2006-12390

This book "adds original scholarship to an exhaustive study of other studies of Bach. And although it is often dense with information, it is just as often entertaining: rich in anecdotes and scintillating in its conjectures." N Y Times (Late N Y Ed)

Includes bibliographical references

Gehring, Wes D.

★ **James** Dean: rebel with a cause. Indiana Historical Society Press 2005 303p il $19.95   **92**

1. Actors
ISBN 0-87195-181-9

LC 2005-41440

This is a "study of Dean's entire life and an appreciation of his rightful place in film history. Gehring makes the point that audiences have confused the actor with his troubled-teenager roles, and he counters that misimpression with a fuller portrait." Booklist

Includes filmography and bibliographical references

Geiringer, Karl

Haydn: a creative life in music; by Karl Geiringer in collaboration with Irene Geiringer. 3rd rev & enl ed; University of Calif. Press 1982 403p il hardcover o.p. pa $21.95   **92**

1. Composers
ISBN 0-520-04317-0 pa

LC 82-2821

The author is "one of the few scholars who have devoted themselves almost exclusively to the study of this great master. He has not only collected all the new data that have cast light on Haydn research . . . he has also contributed many valuable observations and ideas." Saturday Rev

Includes bibliographical references

Gelb, Arthur

City room. Putnam 2003 664p $29.95; pa $17.95   **92**

1. Newspaper editors
ISBN 0-399-15075-7; 0-425-19831-6 pa

LC 2003-43154

This is a "memoir of life at The New York Times by one who spent nearly 50 years there, rising from copy boy to managing editor; {the author} has the power to evoke whole generations of change in the news business, reaching back to the glorious postwar years of manual typewriters, chain smokers, and all-nighters." N Y Times Book Rev

Gentile, Olivia

★ **Life** list; a woman's quest for the world's most amazing birds. Bloomsbury USA 2008 345p il $26   **92**

1. Biography, Individual 2. Bird watchers 3. Bird watching

ISBN 978-1-59691-169-7; 1-59691-169-7

LC 2008-27036

Gentile describes Phoebe Snetsinger as a "frustrated stay-at-home wife and mother during the 1950s and 1960s who began birding to escape the boredom of suburban life. When she was diagnosed with terminal cancer at age 49, she decided to travel the world in search of birds while her health allowed. Each trip became a short-term goal for Phoebe and let her focus on birds instead of the cancer. She did this for 18 years, traveling between two and ten months a year, despite two cancer recurrences, injuries, assaults, kidnapping, and other difficulties. Phoebe eventually amassed a life list of 8,674 species, or 85 percent of living birds then known." Libr J

Includes bibliographical references

George-Warren, Holly

Public cowboy no. 1; the life and times of Gene Autry. Oxford University Press 2007 406p il $28 **92**

1. Actors 2. Baseball executives 3. Biography, Individual 4. Broadcasting executives 5. Country musicians 6. Cowboys 7. Singers
ISBN 978-0-19-517746-6; 0-19-517746-0

LC 2006-36369

This is a biography of the radio performer, singer and actor who performed in rodeos and appeared in such movies as Public Cowboy No.1 (1937) and The Phantom Empire (1935).

"This colorful study is much more than a biography of Autry; it also tells the story of country-western music, singing cowboys, radio and early television, and celebrity." Choice

Includes filmography, discography, and bibliographical references

Gessen, Masha

Perfect rigor; a genius and the mathematical breakthrough of the century. Houghton Mifflin Harcourt 2009 242p $26   **92**

1. Biography, Individual 2. Mathematicians 3. Poincaré series
ISBN 978-0-15-101406-4; 0-15-101406-X

LC 2009-14742

"The story of Russian mathematical prodigy Grigory Perelman, who solved a problem that had stumped everyone for a century—then walked away from his chosen field. . . . [The author] paints a fascinating picture of the Soviet math establishment and of the mind of one of its most singular products. An engrossing examination of an enigmatic genius." Kirkus

Includes bibliographical references

Gevisser, Mark

A **legacy** of liberation; Thabo Mbeki and the future of the South African dream. Palgrave Macmillan 2009 376p il $29.95   **92**

1. Biography, Individual 2. Blacks -- South Africa -- Social conditions 3. Government officials 4. Political leaders 5. Presidents
ISBN 978-0-230-61100-9; 0-230-61100-1

LC 2008-50763

This is a biography of South Africa's second president. Gevisser "traces Mbeki's family back several generations, from colonial dispossession through the struggle for liberation. . . . Mbeki's life story has the makings of a gripping tale. . . . Gevisser writes well, particularly when he is witness to an event, when his narrative leaps off the page." N Y Times Book Rev

Includes bibliographical references (p. [346]-365) and index

Ghahramani, Zarah

My life as a traitor; [by] Zarah Ghahramani, with Robert Hillman. Farrar, Straus and Giroux 2008 242p $23   **92**
1. Biography, Individual 2. Dissenters 3. Memoirists 4. Political prisoners 5. Women -- Iran
ISBN 978-0-374-21730-3; 0-374-21730-0

LC 2007-17983

"This compelling book is a coming-of-age story in which the author examines her beliefs and emotions while she tells of a country in turmoil." SLJ

Ghiglione, Loren

CBS's Don Hollenbeck; an honest reporter in the age of McCarthyism. Columbia University Press 2008 330p il $29.95   **92**
1. Journalism 2. Journalists 3. Radio reporters 4. Television broadcasting of news 5. Television reporters
ISBN 978-0-231-14496-4; 0-231-14496-2

LC 2008-10686

"Ghiglione's attention to detail and use of numerous personal interviews make this both a compelling biography and a rich contextual history of the McCarthy era." Libr J

Includes bibliographical references (p. 289-316)

Gibson, Ian

Federico Garcia Lorca: a life. Pantheon Bks. 1989 xxii, 551p il hardcover o.p. pa $18   **92**
1. Authors 2. Dramatists 3. Poets 4. Theatrical directors
ISBN 0-679-77401-7 pa

LC 88-28871

This is a biography of the Spanish writer who was assassinated during the Spanish Civil War.

"Gibson's sense of place is equalled by his sense of person. His re-creation of the teeming artistic talent and the café life of Spain in the 1930s is superb. So effective is Gibson's account of Lorca's vitality and fecundity that along with admiration for the poet's opulent talent, he provokes a fierce outrage at his ultimate fate." Times Lit Suppl

Includes bibliographical references

Giddings, Paula

★ **Ida**: a sword among lions; Ida B. Wells and the campaign against lynching. Amistad 2008 800p il $35   **92**
1. African American women -- Biography 2. African Americans -- Civil rights 3. Authors 4. Biography, Individual 5. Civil rights activists 6. Essayists 7. Journalists 8. Lynching 9. Newspaper executives 10. Nonfiction writers 11. Women political activists
ISBN 978-0-06-051921-6; 0-06-051921-5

"An iconic figure in American history, Wells was not always celebrated by her contemporaries for her groundbreaking activism because of her assertive politics and difficult personality. . . . Giddings offers a look at how Wells' own self-assertion affected her relationships with family, friends, colleagues, and the broader American public as she evolved as a woman and an activist. . . . With meticulous research, including Wells' own diary, Giddings brings to life one of the most fascinating women in American history, giving readers a real feel for the texture and context of Wells' life." Booklist

Includes bibliographical references

Giddins, Gary

Bing Crosby: a pocketful of dreams: the early years, 1903-1940. Little, Brown 2001 728p il $30; pa $17.95   **92**
1. Actors 2. Singers
ISBN 0-316-88188-0; 0-316-88645-9 pa

LC 00-44403

"Giddins has contributed a landmark study of popular singing in the first half of the twentieth century." Booklist

Includes bibliographical references

Gielgud, John

An **actor** and his time. Applause Theatre Bk. Pubs. 1997 333p $21.95; pa $16.95   **92**
1. Actors 2. Theatrical directors 3. Theatrical producers
ISBN 1-55783-299-4; 1-55783-415-6 pa

LC 97-31701

This autobiography chronicles Gielgud's work in the theatre and motion pictures. Includes his personal reminiscences of Ellen Terry, Sarah Bernhardt, Mrs. Patrick Campbell, Bernard Shaw and Ralph Richardson, among others.

Gielgud "proves himself to be a storyteller of the highest order, making this essential reading for theater lovers." Libr J

Giffels, David

All the way home; building a family in a falling-down house. William Morrow 2008 314p $25.95 **92**
1. Authors 2. Columnists 3. Essayists 4. Houses 5. Memoirists 6. Television scriptwriters
ISBN 978-0-06-136286-6; 0-06-136286-7

LC 2007-39267

Journalist Giffels "settles on a rundown, soon to be condemned early–20th century mansion, but when he arrives at the mansion to begin his work—aided eventually by scores of workers—he finds leaks in several areas of the roof, crumbling brick, dry-rotted wood, warped floors, vermin droppings and nests, as well as a beautiful old staircase, a fireplace in the bedroom and gorgeous brass hinges and other fixtures. Convinced that he can recover the former glory of this house with a little elbow grease and perseverance, Giffels sets out on his mission—fueled by the strains of R.E.M. and the Clash—to renovate the house one room at a time. . . . Sometimes humorous, Giffels's memoir comments sadly on one man's stubbornness and selfishness (even his wife's miscarriages don't stop him from his work) in his quest to make a house a home." Publ Wkly

Gifford, Bill

Ledyard; in search of the first American explorer. Harcourt 2007 331p il map $25   **92**

1. Biography, Individual 2. Explorers 3. Travel writers

ISBN 978-0-15-101218-3; 0-15-101218-0

LC 2006-17064

This book "makes an important contribution to the existing literature through its personal approach to Ledyard's life. Few of Ledyard's letters and journals remain . . . but, by using most of what's available and tracking down details through his own travels, the author paints a fascinating portrait of the man he calls the 'archetype of the restless American wanderer.'" N Y Times Book Rev

Gilbert, Elizabeth

Eat, pray, love; one woman's search for everything across Italy, India and Indonesia. Viking 2006 334p $24.95   **92**

1. Authors 2. Biography, Individual 3. Journalists 4. Novelists 5. Short story writers

ISBN 0-670-03471-1

LC 2005-42435

"A probing, thoughtful title with a free and easy style, this work seamlessly blends history and travel for a very enjoyable read." Libr J

Gill, Anton

★ Art lover; a biography of Peggy Guggenheim. HarperCollins Pubs. 2002 480p il $29.95; pa $15.95   **92**

1. Art collectors 2. Art, Modern 3. Patrons of the arts

ISBN 0-06-019697-1; 0-06-095681-X pa

LC 2001-51731

Guggenheim "was known as much for her sexual exploits as for her championing of modern art, a fact Gill . . . examines with candor, sensitivity, and mellifluous grace." Booklist

Includes bibliographical references

Gillespie, Marcia Ann

Maya Angelou; a glorious celebration. [by] Marcia Ann Gillespie, Rosa Johnson Butler and Richard A. Long; foreword by Oprah Winfrey. Doubleday 2008 191p il $30   **92**

1. Actors 2. African American authors 3. Children's authors 4. Dramatists 5. Essayists 6. Memoirists 7. Poets 8. Singers 9. Women authors

ISBN 978-0-385-51108-7

LC 2007-31301

This look at Maya Angelou's life as well as her myriad interests and accomplishments by the people who know her best (longtime friends Marcia Ann Gillespie and Richard Long and niece Rosa Johnson Butler) features over 150 sepia portraits, family photographs, and letters. Includes a bibliography of her works.

"A loving tribute to one of the most renowned authors today, this work is highly recommended." Libr J

Gillies, Isabel

Happens every day; an all-too-true story. Scribner 2009 261p il $25   **92**

1. Actors

ISBN 978-1-4391-1007-2; 1-4391-1007-7

LC 2008-51362

Gillies "has created an evenhanded account of a horribly difficult time in her life, which she has probed for meaning and mined for a great story." Libr J

Gilmour, David

The long recessional: the imperial life of Rudyard Kipling. Farrar, Straus & Giroux 2002 351p il maps $26; pa $15   **92**

1. Authors 2. Children's authors 3. Memoirists 4. Nobel laureates for literature 5. Novelists 6. Poets 7. Short story writers

ISBN 0-374-18702-9; 0-374-52896-9 pa

LC 2002-100585

This biography focuses on Kipling's social and political views in relation to the British Empire, especially as expressed in his fiction and poetry.

The author "offers a brief, sympathetic, well-informed, and highly readable account of Kipling." Libr J

Includes bibliographical references

Ginsberg, Allen

The letters of Allen Ginsberg; edited by Bill Morgan. DaCapo Press 2008 468p $30   **92**

1. Authors 2. Biography, Individual 3. Poets 4. Poets, American

ISBN 978-0-30681-463-1; 0-30681-463-3

LC 2008-11054

"Morgan, Ginsberg's biographer (I Celebrate Myself) and archivist, studied 3700 letters left behind by the poet, selecting 165 of the most significant for this edition; over 125 appear here for the first time. Always intelligent, sometimes gossipy, and occasionally cranky and impatient, Ginsberg is accurately reflected in these letters taken together. Correspondents include Ginsberg's father, Louis, and brother, Eugene; the poet's longtime companion, Peter Orlovsky; fellow Beat writers Jack Kerouac, William Burroughs, and Gregory Corso; and a host of friends and acquaintances." Libr J

Includes bibliographical references

Ginzberg, Lori D.

Elizabeth Cady Stanton; an American life. Hill and Wang 2009 254p il $25   **92**

1. Biography, Individual 2. Feminism 3. Suffragists 4. Women -- Suffrage 5. Women -- Suffrage -- History

ISBN 978-0-8090-9493-6; 0-8090-9493-2

LC 2008-54395

The author "makes a convincing case for Stanton as the founding philosopher of the American women's rights movement in a lively voice that enhances her eccentric subject. . . . Ginzberg has created a vibrant portrait of a key, often misrepresented figure in American history." Am Hist

Includes bibliographical references

Gleick, James

Genius: the life and science of Richard Feynman. Pantheon Bks. 1992 532p hardcover o.p. pa $16 **92**

   1. Authors 2. Nobel laureates for physics 3. Physicists 4. Writers on science

   ISBN 0-679-74704-4 pa

LC 92-6577

"Although it would be hard to relate personal stories about Feynman more engagingly than Feynman himself did in What Do You Care What Other People Think? the late Nobelist could not hope for better than his biographer here delivers—a portrait in which the physicist remains a person and is not reduced to an icon of science." Publ Wkly

   Includes bibliographical references

Glendinning, Victoria

   ★ **Leonard** Woolf; a biography. Simon & Schuster 2006 498p il $30 **92**

   1. Authors 2. Biography, Individual 3. Editors 4. Essayists 5. Memoirists 6. Publishing executives 7. Writers on politics

   ISBN 978-0-7432-4653-8; 0-7432-4653-5

LC 2006-49784

This is a biography of the publisher and author of Empire and Commerce in Africa (1920), Village in the Jungle (1926), After the Deluge (1931), Quack, Quack! (1935), Barbarians Within and Without (1939), Sowing (1960), Growing (1961), Beginning Again (1964), Downhill All the Way (1967), and The Journey Not the Arrival Matters (1969).

"Glendinning's generous biography does not ignore that Woolf could be grumpy and was too often cheeseparing, but her account does justice to his range of passions, his literary and political contributions and, above all, his human goodness—he was a man who knew how to live." New Statesman

   Includes bibliographical references

Glines, Carroll V.

   I could never be so lucky again; an autobiography. by General James H. "Jimmy" Doolittle, with Carroll V. Glines. Bantam Bks. 1991 574p il hardcover o.p. pa $7.99 **92**

   1. Air force officers 2. Air pilots 3. Generals

   ISBN 0-553-07807-0; 0-553-58464-2 pa

LC 91-3353

"The book recalls vividly Doolittle's days as an aviation pioneer—and retells the exciting story of the Tokyo raid." Publ Wkly

   Includes bibliographical references

Godwin, Gail

   The **making** of a writer; journals, 1961-1963. edited by Rob Neufeld. Random House 2006 333p hardcover o.p. pa $16.95 **92**

   1. Authors 2. Authors, American 3. Biography, Individual 4. Nonfiction writers 5. Novelists 6. Short story writers

   ISBN 1-4000-6432-5; 0-8129-7469-7 pa

LC 2005-44929

"The text begins in 1961 after Godwin, 24, has departed North Carolina for a job at the Miami Herald—a job from which she is soon fired. At the same time, she is married and divorced. She records her relationships and observations throughout with humor and humility, which results in a vivid portrait of Godwin's daily life and her relentless pursuit of a career as a writer." Libr J

   Includes bibliographical references

Godwin, Peter

   When a crocodile eats the sun; a memoir of Africa. Little, Brown and Co. 2007 344p il map $24.99 **92**

   1. Biography, Individual 2. Journalists

   ISBN 978-0-316-15894-7; 0-316-15894-1

LC 2006-27973

"In 1996 when his father suffers a heart attack, Godwin returns to Africa and sparks the central revelation of the book—the father is Jewish and has hidden it from Godwin and his siblings. As his father's health deteriorates, so does Zimbabwe. [Robert] Mugabe, self-proclaimed president for life, institutes a series of ill-conceived land reforms that throw the white farmers off the land they've cultivated for generations and consequently throws the country's economy into free fall. . . . This is a tour de force of personal journalism and not to be missed." Publ Wkly

   Includes bibliographical references

Goldberg, Jeffrey

   ★ **Prisoners**; a Muslim and a Jew across the Middle East divide. Knopf 2006 316p $25 **92**

   1. Arab-Israeli conflict 2. Biography, Individual 3. Israel-Arab conflicts 4. Journalists 5. Political leaders

   ISBN 0-375-41234-4; 978-0-375-41234-9

LC 2006-41026

This is a "memoir of the author, an American-bred Zionist, and his 15-year relationship with a Palestinian insurgent. . . . Goldberg lived in Israel as a college student, sharpening the contradictory emotions shared by many of his American peers and eventually watching his former certainty crumble under the weight of military service at Ketziot, an Israeli prison. Grounded in his relationship with a prisoner, Goldberg's book travels from Long Island to Afghanistan as he struggles to understand Israeli-Palestinian violence. . . . Like the warring nationalisms it presents, his book is complex and deeply affecting." Publ Wkly

Goldsmith, Barbara

   Other powers; the age of suffrage, spiritualism, and the scandalous Victoria Woodhull. HarperPerennial 1999 531p il pa $16 **92**

   1. Feminism 2. Feminists 3. Presidential candidates 4. Spiritualism 5. Suffragists 6. Women -- Suffrage

   ISBN 0-06-095332-2

LC 98-33315

"Victoria Woodhull was a charismatic and notorious figure in the struggle for women's rights in the years following the Civil War. She was the first woman to address Congress and the first woman to run for president. Goldsmith . . . has successfully woven together a history of Woodhull's life with the lives of the powerful she touched." Libr J

   Includes bibliographical references

Goldstein, Rebecca

Incompleteness; the proof and paradox of Kurt Godel. Rebecca Goldstein. W.W. Norton 2005 296p il $22.95   **92**

1. Biography, Individual 2. Mathematicians

ISBN 0-393-05169-2

LC 2004-23052

This "is a stimulating exploration of both the power and the limitations of the human intellect." Publ Wkly

Includes bibliographical references

Goldstein, Warren

★ **For** the love of physics; from the end of the rainbow to the edge of time--a journey through the wonders of physics. [by] Walter Lewin and Warren Goldstein. Free Press 2011 302p il $26; ebook $12.99   **92**

1. Colleges and universities -- Faculty 2. Physicists 3. Physics -- Study and teaching

ISBN 978-1-4391-0827-7; 978-1-4391-2354-6 ebook

LC 2010-47737

"MIT's Lewin is deservedly popular for his memorable physics lectures . . . and this quick-paced autobiography-cum-physics intro fully captures his candor and lively teaching style. . . . [This text] glows with energy and should please a wide range of readers." Publ Wkly

Goldsworthy, Adrian Keith

Antony and Cleopatra; [by] Adrian Goldsworthy. Yale University Press 2010 470p il map $35   **92**

1. Biography, Individual 2. Generals 3. Orators 4. Queens 5. Statesmen

ISBN 978-0-300-16534-0

LC 2010-929122

"Narrating [Antony] and Cleopatra's parts in the tumultuous end of the Roman Republic, Goldsworthy skillfully integrates the partial and partisan source material into an accessible presentation of a classic tale from classical times." Booklist

Includes bibliographical references

★ **Caesar**; life of a colossus. [by] Adrian Goldsworthy. Yale University Press 2006 583p il map $35   **92**

1. Biography, Individual 2. Historians 3. Statesmen

ISBN 978-0-300-12048-6; 0-300-12048-6

LC 2006-922060

This biography draws "together Julius Caesar's personal, political, and military history into a single volume. . . . This is an engaging and well-drawn resource for those who wish to be introduced to the man who was Caesar." Libr J

Includes bibliographical references

Gooch, Brad

★ **Flannery**; a life of Flannery O'Connor. Little, Brown and Co. 2009 448p il $30   **92**

1. Authors 2. Authors, American 3. Biography, Individual 4. Novelists 5. Short story writers 6. Women authors

ISBN 978-0-316-00066-6; 0-316-00066-3

LC 2008-28504

This is a biography of the author of Wise Blood (1952), A Good Man Is Hard to Find (1955), The Violent Bear It Away (1960), and Everything That Rises Must Converge (1965).

"Gooch comfortably traces her fiction to its real-life roots in a meticulous yet seemingly effortless writing style, resulting in the definitive biography as well as providing the impetus for general readers to return to O'Connor's timeless fiction." Booklist

Includes bibliographical references

Goodall, Jane

★ **Beyond** innocence; an autobiography in letters: the later years. edited by Dale Peterson. Houghton Mifflin 2001 418p il $28; pa $15   **92**

1. Nonfiction writers 2. Primatologists 3. Primatologists -- Correspondence 4. Women scientists 5. Writers on nature

ISBN 0-618-12520-5; 0-618-25734-9 pa

LC 00-54124

In this "volume of Goodall's letters, a lively portrait is formed through her missives as the young woman rose to the height of her scientific contributions and fame. She became a mother, divorced her first husband, married her second, and lost him to cancer. She was also the first to observe cannibalism in chimps, lost many of her study troop during a polio epidemic, and weathered the kidnapping of a group of her students. . . . This illuminating glimpse into the mind, emotions, and philosophy of an important scientist who also happens to be a celebrated figure will be requested in all libraries." Booklist

Reason for hope; a spiritual journey. {by} Jane Goodall with Phillip Berman. Warner Bks. 1999 282p $26.95; pa $14.95   **92**

1. Nonfiction writers 2. Primatologists 3. Women scientists 4. Writers on nature

ISBN 0-446-52225-2; 0-446-67613-6 pa

LC 99-25611

Primatologist Goodall "offers this autobiography as a meditation on how her spiritual beliefs evolved in response to major events of her lifetime, including her childhood in World War II-era England; early days at Gombe with the chimpanzees; rearing her only child, Grub; divorce, remarriage, and the loss of her second husband to cancer, and the turning point in her career when she dedicated herself to the plight of chimpanzees held in captivity for biomedical research." Libr J

Goodchild, Peter

★ **Edward** Teller, the real Dr Strangelove. Harvard University Press 2004 xxv, 469p il $29.95 **92**

1. Physicists 2. Writers on science

ISBN 0-674-01669-6

LC 2004-54257

This is a biography of "the 'father of the hydrogen bomb,' a witness against J. Robert Oppenheimer in the latter's security hearing, and, finally, an ardent promoter of the Cold War arms race. . . . {The author} studied a wide range of primary and secondary sources and interviewed many people on both sides of the controversies that swirled around

Teller. The result is a remarkably well-balanced study of a notoriously prickly and opinionated person." Libr J
Includes bibliographical references

Goodwin, Doris Kearns

★ **No** ordinary time; Franklin and Eleanor Roosevelt: the home front in World War II. Simon & Schuster 1994 759p il hardcover o.p. pa $18   **92**
1. Columnists   2. Diplomats   3. Governors   4. Handicapped   5. Humanitarians   6. Philatelists   7. Presidents   8. Social activists   9. Spouses of presidents   10. United Nations officials   11. World War, 1939-1945 -- United States
ISBN 0-684-80448-4 pa

LC 94-28565

"This is a nearly day-by-day account of the doings of Franklin and Eleanor Roosevelt during the Second World War. While Eleanor was championing the rights of female munitions workers and of Negroes in segregated Army barracks, her husband was making and breaking policy." New Yorker
Includes bibliographical references

★ **Team** of rivals; the political genius of Abraham Lincoln. Simon & Schuster 2005 916p il map $35   **92**
1. Attorneys general   2. Biography, Individual   3. Governors   4. Lawyers   5. Members of Congress   6. Presidential candidates   7. Presidents   8. Presidents -- United States   9. Secretaries of state   10. Secretaries of the treasury   11. Senators   12. State legislators   13. Supreme Court justices
ISBN 0-684-82490-6

LC 2005-44615

"The knowledge gained here about these three significant figures who well attended Lincoln gain for the reader an even keener appreciation of the rare individual that he was." Booklist
Includes bibliographical references

Gordin, Michael D.

★ A **well**-ordered thing: Dmitrii Mendeleev and the shadow of the periodic table. Basic Books 2004 364p il $30   **92**
1. Chemists   2. Periodic law
ISBN 0-465-02775-X

LC 2003-25533

"This is not a chronological biography of the man; rather, it is a work that shows Mendeleev as an important part of the changes that occurred in Russia during the days between the freeing of the serfs in 1861 and the crumbling of tsarist power in 1905." Sci Books & Films
Includes bibliographical references

Gordon, Charlotte

Mistress Bradstreet; the untold life of America's first poet. Little, Brown and Co. 2005 337p il map $27.95   **92**
1. Authors   2. Biography, Individual   3. Colonists   4. Poets   5. Women poets
ISBN 0-316-16904-8

LC 2004-22702

This is a biography of the colonial poet.
"Written with maximal clarity and communicativeness, this is a vibrant, engaging, realistic portrayal of early colonial Massachusetts and of its fascinating biographical subject." Booklist
Includes bibliographical references

Gordon, Linda

Dorothea Lange; a life beyond limits. W.W. Norton 2009 xxiii, 536p il $35   **92**
1. Biography, Individual   2. Photography -- History -- United States   3. Women photographers
ISBN 978-0-393-05730-0; 0-393-05730-5

LC 2009-19639

This is a biography of the American photographer who worked for the Historical Section of the Farm Security Administration (FSA) during the Depression.
"Gordon's elegant biography is testament to Lange's gift for challenging her country to open its eyes." N Y Times Book Rev
Includes bibliographical references

Gordon, Lyndall

Charlotte Bronte; a passionate life. Norton 1995 418p il hardcover o.p. pa $17   **92**
1. Authors   2. Authors, English   3. Novelists   4. Poets   5. Women authors
ISBN 0-393-31448-0 pa

The author "dismantles once and for all the image of Charlotte Brontë as a figure of pathos and presents, instead, a courageous survivor, a determined writer, and a woman of volcanic emotion. . . . Gordon, as skilled at literary analysis as at chronicling a life, approaches Brontë's tragic and enduringly relevant story from several angles, carefully identifying all the autobiographical elements of her novels and contrasting her commitment to writing and her independent spirit to her era's strict and pitiless code of behavior for women." Booklist
Includes bibliographical references

★ **Lives** like loaded guns; Emily Dickinson and her family's feuds. Viking 2010 491p il $32.95 **92**
1. Authors   2. Biography, Individual   3. Editors   4. Poets   5. Poets, American   6. Travel writers   7. Writers on nature
ISBN 978-0-670-02193-2; 0-670-02193-8

LC 2009-46311

The author argues that "it wasn't heartbreak that kept the poet sequestered, . . . it was epilepsy, a then-uncontrollable and shameful malady. With one stroke, Gordon recasts Dickinson's entire oeuvre. She then reveals the outrageous treachery of the poet's esteemed brother, Austin, who held his unmarried sisters, wife Susan, and their children hostage to his passion for his ambitious mistress, Mabel Loomis Todd, whose scheming husband encouraged the affair. . . . A jolting and utterly intriguing watershed achievement." Booklist
Includes bibliographical references

★ **T.S.** Eliot; an imperfect life. Norton 1999 721p $35; pa $18.95   **92**
1. Authors   2. Critics -- Great Britain -- Biography   3. Dramatists   4. Editors   5. Essayists   6. Literary critics

7. Nobel laureates for literature 8. Poets 9. Poets, American -- 20th century -- Biography
ISBN 0-393-04728-8; 0-393-32093-6 pa

LC 98-46864

"Gordon's book is the most authoritative life of Eliot thus far, and is certain to spark new controversies." Publ Wkly
Includes bibliographical references

Vindication; a life of Mary Wollstonecraft. HarperCollins 2005 562p il $29.95   **92**
1. Authors 2. Biography, Individual 3. Essayists 4. Feminists 5. Novelists 6. Writers on politics
ISBN 0-06-019802-8

LC 2005-40237

The author "tackles this formidable woman with grace, clarity and much new research. . . . Gordon relates Wollstonecraft's story with the same potent mixture of passion and reason her subject personified." N Y Times Book Rev
Includes bibliographical references

Virginia Woolf, a writer's life. Norton 1985 341p il hardcover o.p. pa $14.95   **92**
1. Authors 2. Authors, English 3. Essayists 4. Novelists 5. Short story writers 6. Women authors
ISBN 0-393-32205-X pa

LC 84-25424

"Gordon combines literary criticism with biographical investigation in her life of Virginia Woolf. . . . Using the major novels To the Lighthouse and The Waves, Gordon explores in detail the autobiographical ramifications of these works as she traces Woolf's childhood, marriage, and literary career." Booklist
Includes bibliographical references

Gordon, Mary

Circling my mother. Pantheon Books 2007 254p $24   **92**
1. Authors 2. Authors, American 3. Biography, Individual 4. Legal secretaries 5. Novelists 6. Parents of prominent persons 7. Short story writers
ISBN 978-0-375-42456-4; 0-375-42456-3

LC 2006-102286

This is "is a moving, affecting work on the tug-of-war between mother and daughter, between women and the changing world around them." Publ Wkly

Gordon-Reed, Annette

Andrew Johnson. Times Books/Henry Holt and Company 2011 166p il $23   **92**
1. Governors 2. Members of Congress 3. Presidents 4. Presidents -- United States 5. Vice-presidents
ISBN 978-0-8050-6948-8

LC 2010-32595

"Andrew Johnson rose from humble beginnings in the South to serve as Lincoln's second vice president, thus becoming President just as the Civil War was ending. He showed none of his predecessor's political finesse and is often viewed as among the worst to hold the office. . . . [The author] argues that the nation went from the best President to the worst during this most crucial period of its history. This slim study does cover Johnson from birth to death (1808–75), but the focus is assuredly on his presidency." Libr J
Includes bibliographical references

Gorn, Elliott J.

Dillinger's wild ride; the year that made America's public enemy number one. Oxford University Press 2009 268p il $24.95   **92**
1. Biography, Individual 2. Crime -- United States -- History -- 20th century 3. Criminals
ISBN 978-0-19-530483-1; 0-19-530483-7

LC 2008-48150

"A solid, unromanticized account. . . . [The author] relies on newspaper accounts and government documents (and, thankfully, no reconstructed dialogue) to plot the movements of a criminal who, 75 years after his death, still reverberates in the American consciousness." Publ Wkly
Includes bibliographical references

Gorokhova, Elena

A **mountain** of crumbs; a memoir. Simon & Schuster 2010 308p il $26   **92**
1. Biography, Individual 2. College teachers 3. Linguists 4. Memoirists
ISBN 978-1-4391-2567-0; 1-4391-2567-8

LC 2009-474

In this memoir, Elena Gorokhova discusses growing up in Leningrad, her love of languages and her eventual move to the United States.

"Gorokhova vividly evokes the bleak years of the latter half of the 20th century in Russia, when the Great Patriotic War was followed by the Cold War and food shortages were the norm. . . . Articulate, touching and hopeful." Kirkus

Gortemaker, Heike B.

Eva Braun; life with Hitler. by Heike B. Görtemaker; translated from the German by Damion Searls. Alfred A. Knopf 2011 324 p. $27.95; ebook $13.99   **92**
1. Mistresses -- Germany -- Biography 2. Spouses of heads of state -- Germany -- Biography 3. Women -- Germany -- Biography
ISBN 978-0-307-59582-9; 978-0-307-70139-8 ebook; 9780307595829

LC 2011009551

This book offers a biography of Adolf Hilters mistress Eva Braun. "Although by the early-to-mid-Thirties Eva Braun thought that her relationship with Hitler was now on a more established footing, she was soon disillusioned by even longer absences." . . . Görtemaker writes of Eva Braun's "practically unassailable position at Hitler's side, even if in the dangerous and byzantine world of the Nazi hierarchy nothing was guaranteed. . . . Hitler . . . appreciate[d] her unquestioning loyalty. . . . Eva Braun . . . probably knew little of the sadism, the squalor, and the horror of the camps. As an impressionable young woman, she had been molded in her opinions during her time in Hitler's presence. (New York Review of Books)

The author "coaxes from history's shadows the woman who for 14 years was the companion, lover and, near the end, wife of Adolf Hitler." Kirkus
Includes bibliographical references

Gottfried, Martin

Arthur Miller; his life and work. Da Capo Press 2003 484p il hardcover o.p. pa $18   **92**
1. Authors 2. Dramatists 3. Screenwriters
ISBN 0-306812-14-2; 0-306813-77-7 pa
LC 2004-298989
This is "an uncomfortable, challenging work, forbidding us any bien-pensant ease, and we should be grateful for it." Times Lit Suppl
Includes bibliographical references

Gottlieb, Robert Adams

George Balanchine: the ballet maker. HarperCollins\Atlas Books 2004 224p $19.95   **92**
1. Ballet 2. Choreographers 3. Dancers
ISBN 0-06-075070-7
LC 2004-48856
"This loving tribute captures Balanchine's legacy: his energy, confidence, lack of pretension and, most important, his joy in creation." Publ Wkly
Includes bibliographical references

Goudsouzian, Aram

Sidney Poitier; man, actor, icon. University of North Carolina Press 2004 480p il $29.95   **92**
1. Actors 2. Biography, Individual 3. Motion picture directors
ISBN 0-8078-2843-2
LC 2003-19372
The author "traces Poitier's journey from life as the son of a poor Bahamian farmer to celebrity status in the States as a trailblazing actor who has received as much criticism as praise for his portrayal of dignified and stoical black men." Booklist
Includes bibliographical references

Govenar, Alan B.

Lightnin' Hopkins; his life and blues. Chicago Review Press 2010 334p il $28.95   **92**
1. African American musicians 2. Blues music 3. Blues musicians 4. Guitarists 5. Singers 6. Songwriters
ISBN 978-1-55652-962-7
LC 2009-48798
In this "biography of the prolific and influential blues icon Sam 'Lightnin' Hopkins, . . . [the author] presents important new research and employs neglected primary sources to offer an accessible critical analysis of Hopkins's artistic achievement buttressed by generous quotations from his lyrics. . . . [This] biography of an important figure in blues history is an essential purchase for anyone interested in American popular music or African American culture." Libr J
Includes discography and bibliographical references

Graham, Billy

Just as I am; the autobiography of Billy Graham. HarperSanFrancisco 1997 xxiii, 760p il maps hardcover o.p. pa $18   **92**
1. Clergy 2. Evangelists 3. Inspirational writers
ISBN 0-06-063387-5; 0-06-063392-1 pa
LC 97-605

"In this memoir, Graham looks back at age 78 on his lifetime of personal relationships, ministry, leadership, and experiences. He chronicles such events and stories as his boyhood in North Carolina, his first steps in ministry, details of evangelistic trips and revivals, and meetings with world and local leaders. . . . All libraries would do well to stock this readable title by an important national figure." Libr J

Grandmaster Flash

The **adventures** of Grandmaster Flash; my life, my beats. by Grandmaster Flash with David Ritz. Broadway Books 2008 258p il $22.95   **92**
1. Disc jockeys (Club) 2. Hip-hop 3. Musicians 4. Rap musicians
ISBN 978-0-7679-2475-7; 0-7679-2475-4
LC 2007-48224
"Grandmaster Flash is best known in conjunction with the Furious Five, the first hip-hop artists inducted into the Rock and Roll Hall of Fame. But before the fame, Joseph Robert Saddler was born into an abusive family in the Bronx. His evolution from a kid spinning records in the streets to hip-hop stardom is an inspiring story filled with heartbreak, determination, and perseverance." Libr J
Includes discography and bibliographical references

Grant, James

★ **John** Adams; party of one. [by] James L. Grant. Farrar, Straus and Giroux 2005 530p il $30   **92**
1. Biography, Individual 2. Presidents 3. Presidents -- United States 4. Vice-presidents
ISBN 0-374-11314-9
LC 2004-10863
The author "is excellent at developing Adams' devotion to liberty, honed by British policies that affronted him and turned him into a revolutionary. In Grant's fine synthesis, Adams on the page is the pious, ambitious, and loving man he was in life." Booklist
Includes bibliographical references

Gray, Charlotte

★ **Reluctant** genius; Alexander Graham Bell and the passion for invention. Arcade Pub. 2006 466p il map $29.95   **92**
1. Biography, Individual 2. Inventors 3. Teachers of the deaf 4. Telecommunications executives
ISBN 1-55970-809-3; 978-1-55970-809-8
LC 2005-29609
The author "recounts both the inventor of the telephone's creation of the device and the projects he pursued once his future was secured. . . . Combining the household history of the Bells with that of Alexander's successive enthusiasms (Helen Keller, kites, airplanes, hydrocraft), Gray fairly portrays the attractions and exasperations of Bell's life." Booklist
Includes bibliographical references

Gray, Michael

Hand me my travelin' shoes; in search of Blind Willie McTell. Chicago Review Press 2009 432p il $26.95   **92**
1. Blind 2. Blues music 3. Blues musicians 4.

Guitarists 5. Singers 6. Songwriters

ISBN 978-1-55652-975-7

LC 2009-22329

"Less a conventional biography than a mixture of history, travelogue and detective story, Gray paints an evocative portrait of an artist who defied blues stereotypes." Kirkus

Includes bibliographical references

Grayling, A. C.

Descartes: the life and times of a genius. Walker 2006 303p il map $27 **92**

1. Authors 2. Mathematicians 3. Philosophers

ISBN 978-0-8027-1501-2; 0-8027-1501-X

"As Newton was to physics, so Descartes was to philosophy, moving it from superstition and religion to science and reason. They are the founding fathers of the modern world. Grayling's life of Descartes is set firmly in the age of the Counter-Reformation and the Thirty Years War, which are evoked in a lively, almost novelistic style of which Descartes would certainly have approved. This propels the narrative forward and illuminates the philosophy for a lay readership." Times (London)

Greenberg, Keith Elliot

December 8, 1980; the day John Lennon died. Backbeat Books 2010 240p il $24.99 **92**

1. Rock musicians 2. Singers 3. Songwriters

ISBN 978-0-87930-963-3

LC 2010-31425

"Greenberg's definitive and unforgettable inquiry into John Lennon's death illuminates the cruel mysteries of madness, and, more resonantly, all the qualities that made Lennon such an exceptional and compelling artist." Booklist

Includes bibliographical references

Greenberg, Michael

Beg, borrow, steal; a writer's life. Other Press 2009 217p $19.95 **92**

1. Authors 2. Biography, Individual 3. Columnists 4. Essayists 5. Journalists 6. Literary critics 7. Memoirists 8. Short story writers

ISBN 978-1-59051-341-5

LC 2009-17790

"The short pieces in 'Beg, Borrow, Steal' are in the tradition of the literary-journalistic essays that Europeans call feuilletons. Although flexible, this form requires skill and concision, and Michael Greenberg uses it brilliantly. Personal experience is at the center of each piece, but none is solipsistic; the tone is understated and ironic, and every essay contains a hard-won glimmer of insight." Washington Post Book World

Hurry down sunshine. Other Press 2008 234p $22 **92**

1. Authors 2. Biography, Individual 3. Columnists 4. Essayists 5. Literary critics 6. Manic-depressive illness 7. Manic-depressive illness in adolescence 8. Memoirists 9. Mentally ill 10. Parents of mentally ill children 11. Short story writers

ISBN 978-1-59051-191-6; 1-59051-191-3

LC 2008-2674

Greenberg presents a memoir of his daughter Sally, who began experiencing psychiatric problems at the age of fifteen.

"In its detail, depth, richness, and sheer intelligence, Hurry Down Sunshine will be recognized as a classic of its kind." New York Rev Books

Greene, Graham

Graham Greene; a life in letters. edited by Richard Greene. W. W. Norton & Company 2008 446p il $35 **92**

1. Authors 2. Essayists 3. Motion picture critics 4. Novelists 5. Short story writers 6. Travel writers

ISBN 978-0-393-06642-5; 0-393-06642-8

LC 2008-40452

"Greene is presented in these letters through the five main preoccupations of his life: Roman Catholicism, politics, love, travel and . . . the processes of writing and publishing. . . . This well-thought-out collection newly reveals a remarkable activist-writer." Publ Wkly

Includes bibliographical references

Greene, Melissa Fay

There is no me without you; one woman's odyssey to rescue Africa's children. Bloomsbury Pub. 2006 472p il $25.95 **92**

1. AIDS (Disease) 2. AIDS (Disease) -- Africa 3. AIDS (Disease) in children 4. Child benefactors 5. Orphans 6. Relief workers

ISBN 978-1-59691-116-1; 1-59691-116-6

LC 2006-14088

This book chronicles "the odyssey of Haregewoin Teferra, who took in AIDS orphans. . . . In telling her story, journalist Greene who had adopted two Ethiopian children before meeting Teferra, juggles political history, medical reportage and personal memoir. . . . Greene takes a very close look at what appears to be the fringe of an important social event and illuminates the entire subject." Publ Wkly

Includes bibliographical references

Greenfield, Robert

Timothy Leary; a biography. Harcourt, Inc. 2006 689p il $28 **92**

1. Biography, Individual 2. College teachers 3. Psychologists 4. Social reformers

ISBN 0-15-100500-1; 978-0-15-100500-0

LC 2005-30154

This is a biography of LSD guru and counterculture icon Timothy Leary.

"A veritable who's who of the age of Aquarius and a real page-turner, Greenfield's cornerstone portrait of the acidhead who would be king brilliantly illuminates the paradoxes of the psychedelic age." Booklist

The last sultan; the life and times of Ahmet Ertegun. Simon & Schuster 2011 429p il map $30; ebook $14.99 **92**

1. Music industry 2. Recording industry executives 3. Soccer executives 4. Sound recordings

ISBN 978-1-4165-5838-5; 1-4165-5838-1; 978-1-4391-9862-9 ebook; 1-4391-9862-4 ebook

LC 2011-28507

"The eternal music-biz question—what exactly do record-label executives do?—is explored in this sprightly bio of the legendary Atlantic Records cofounder. Journalist Greenfield . . . finds Mephistophelian traits in the Turkish-American impresario—a preternaturally suave, persuasive schmoozer, Ertegun commits his share of cheats, betrayals and payola—but Greenfield credits him with creative mid-wifery of the rock 'n' roll revolution. We see Ertegun scouting R&B pioneers, spotting potential hits amid the dross, singing backup on the pathbreaking 'Shake, Rattle and Roll,' matchmaking super-group Crosby, Stills, Nash, and Young, and introducing Bianca and Mick. . . . A vivid saga of the an industry in its salad days, and of the unholy but fertile union of money and music." Publ Wkly

Includes bibliographical references

Greenhouse, Linda

Becoming Justice Blackmun; Harry Blackmun's Supreme Court journey. Times Books 2005 268p il $25   **92**
1. Biography, Individual 2. Constitutional history -- United States 3. Government officials 4. Judges 5. Supreme Court justices 6. Supreme Court justices -- History
ISBN 0-8050-7791-X
            LC 2004-63772
The author's "achievement in her meticulous narrative history is to provide new ammunition for Justice Black-mun's critics as well as his admirers. And readers who are unfamiliar with the inner workings of the court could not hope for a more engrossing introduction." N Y Times (Late N Y Ed)

Greenlaw, Lavinia

The **importance** of music to girls. Farrar, Straus and Giroux 2008 195p $23; pa $15   **92**
1. Authors 2. Biography, Individual 3. Music appreciation 4. Novelists 5. Poets 6. Women authors
ISBN 978-0-374-17454-5; 978-0-312-42837-2 pa
            LC 2008-925188
The author "brings her youth to life in this book. And whether it's madrigal singers rehearsing in the living room or metal blasting from the radio in a car full of partying teen-agers, readers will hear the accompanying soundtrack waft-ing off the pages." Washington Post

Greenspan, Alan

The **age** of turbulence; adventures in a new world. Penguin Press 2007 531p il $35   **92**
1. Bankers 2. Biography, Individual 3. Economists 4. Government officials 5. Presidential advisers 6. Regulatory agency officials
ISBN 978-1-59420-131-8
            LC 2007-13169
"The former U. S. Federal Reserve Board chair relates his life story, focusing on lessons learned in government ser-vice, particularly post-9/11. He also includes political anec-dotes, asserts his faith in market capitalism, and shares his predictions for the world of 2030." Libr J

Includes bibliographical references

Greenspan, Nancy Thorndike

The **end** of the certain world; the Nobel physicist who ignited the quantum revolution. Basic Books 2005 374p il $26.95   **92**
1. Biography, Individual 2. Nobel laureates for physics 3. Physicists
ISBN 0-7382-0693-8
            LC 2004-21809
"This empathetic work . . . lifts a deserving figure out of semi-obscurity and adds a valuable perspective on the origin of modern physics." Publ Wkly

Includes bibliographical references

Grennan, Conor

Little princes; one man's promise to bring home the lost children of Nepal. Willliam Morrow 2011 294p il map $25.99; ebook $20.99   **92**
1. Child benefactors 2. Orphanages
ISBN 978-0-06-193005-8; 0-06-193005-9; 978-0-06-204243-9 ebook; 0-06-204243-2 ebook
Describes how the author's three-month service as a volunteer at the Little Princes Orphanage in wartorn Nepal became a commitment for advocacy and reform when he discovered that many of his young charges were victims res-cued from human traffickers.

"If you've never believed in miracles, this book could convince you otherwise. . . . Like the children he writes about, Grennan has boundless resilience and determination, in addition to self-effacing humor and tunnel-vision devo-tion. He's also a good writer." Christ Sci Monit

Griffin, Farah Jasmine

If you can't be free, be a mystery; in search of Billie Holiday. Ballantine Books 2002 240p il pa $14.95   **92**
1. African American singers 2. Blues musicians 3. Singers
ISBN 978-0-345-44973-3; 0-345-44973-8
"While Griffin's book isn't the last word on Holiday, it does prove to be an excellent antidote to the often ridicu-lous material that has been written about Lady Day over the years." Libr J

Includes bibliographical references

Grimes, Tom

Mentor; a memoir. Tin House Books 2010 242p $24.95; pa $16.95   **92**
1. Authors 2. Authors, American 3. Authorship 4. Biographers 5. Creative writing 6. Dramatists 7. Memoirists 8. Mentoring 9. Novelists 10. Short story writers
ISBN 978-0-9825048-8-8; 978-0-9825048-9-5 pa
            LC 2010-7124
"Anyone who dreams of becoming a novelist will need to read Tom Grimes's brutally honest and wonderful Men-tor. While there have been plenty of books on how to write, or how to get published, or how to promote your work, as well as a number of triumphalist accounts of 'making it,' this is a story of what it's like to just miss succeeding." Washington Post

Includes bibliographical references

Grogan, John

The **longest** trip home; a memoir. William Morrow 2008 334p il $25.95   **92**

1. Biography, Individual 2. Journalists 3. Memoirists

ISBN 978-0-06-171324-8; 0-06-171324-4

LC 2008-25913

This is the author's "hilarious and touching memoir of his childhood in suburban Detroit." Publ Wkly

Groom, Kelle

I wore the ocean in the shape of a girl; a memoir. Free Press 2011 238p $23   **92**

1. Alcoholism 2. Authors 3. Bereavement 4. Essayists 5. Magazine editors 6. Memoirists 7. Poets 8. Poets, American 9. Short story writers

ISBN 978-1-4516-1668-2

LC 2010048931

"Groom's stunning memoir reads more like poetry than prose and leaves the 'brain singing with neurons like a city at night.' Precise diction and punchy syntax coupled with raw subject matter give birth to an intense narrative containing some matter-of-fact passages almost too grueling to accept." Booklist

Includes bibliographical references

Gubar, Susan

★ **Judas**; a biography. W. W. Norton & Co. 2009 453p il $27.95   **92**

1. Apostles 2. Biography, Individual 3. Church history -- Primitive and early church, ca. 30-600

ISBN 978-0-393-06483-4; 0-393-06483-2

LC 2008-42967

An account of the story of the New Testament's archvillain and his history over the past 2000 years in which Gubar links Christian anti-Semitism with Christianity's attempt to grapple with transcendent evil.

"An exhaustive, beautifully written cultural history of our favorite wrongdoer, Gubar's work is an immensely rewarding and crucially important book." Libr J

Includes bibliographical references

Gunther, John

★ **Death** be not proud; a memoir. Harper & Row 1949 261p il hardcover o.p. pa $13.95   **92**

1. Brain -- Tumors 2. Cancer 3. Sick

ISBN 0-06-123097-9

A memoir of John Gunther's seventeen-year-old son, who died after a series of operations for a brain tumor. Not only a tribute to a remarkable boy but an account of a brave fight against disease

Guralnick, Peter

★ **Careless** love: the unmaking of Elvis Presley. Little, Brown 1999 767p il $27.95; pa $17.95 **92**

1. Actors 2. Rock musicians 3. Singers

ISBN 0-316-33222-4; 0-316-33297-6 pa

LC 98-25778

This second and concluding volume of Guralnick's biography of the rock star covers "Elvis's hitch in the army through his death in 1977. . . . The breadth of Guralnick's research is nothing short of amazing, and his lyrical narrative presents an empathetic portrait of a man struggling with

drugs, sex, family, personal eccentricities, money, and the delicate web of relationships surrounding any famous figure." Libr J

Includes bibliographical references

★ **Dream** boogie; the triumph of Sam Cooke. Little, Brown 2005 750p il $27.95   **92**

1. Biography, Individual 2. Singers 3. Soul musicians

ISBN 0-316-37794-5

LC 2005-77

This is a biography of the American singer.

"For those who only know the singer through his pop hits—'You Send Me'; 'Twistin' the Night Away'—the extensive account of his childhood background in gospel music will prove fascinating, and the evocation of the harsh realities faced by African-American musicians touring the South a powerful reminder of just how explosive this music could be." Publ Wkly

Includes discography and bibliographical references

Gussow, Mel

Edward Albee; a singular journey: a biography. Applause 2001 448p il pa $16.95   **92**

1. Authors 2. Dramatists 3. Dramatists, American

ISBN 978-1-55783-447-8; 1-55783-447-4

"Albee regained his position as one of America's greatest playwrights with the 1994 production of 'Three Tall Women,' achieving a level of theatrical mastery and critical acclaim that he hadn't seen since 'Who's Afraid of Virginia Woolf' and 'A Delicate Balance,' almost two decades earlier. The years in between were marked by excessive drinking, outrageous behavior, inferior work, and a diminished career, but Gussow, with a light and generous touch, shows us the strengths of an artist whose core of resilience ultimately insured his survival." New Yorker

Includes bibliographical references

Guttenplan, D. D.

American radical; the life and times of I. F. Stone. Farrar, Straus and Giroux 2009 570p il $35   **92**

1. Authors 2. Biography, Individual 3. Journalists 4. Magazine editors

ISBN 978-0-374-18393-6; 0-374-18393-7

LC 2009-09667

This is a biography of the American journalist who published I.F. Stone's Weekly from 1953 until 1971.

"Guttenplan's lively biography brings back to life a man whose work has often been forgotten but whose writing and life provide a model for the kind of freethinking journalism missing in society today." Publ Wkly

Includes bibliographical references (p. [483]-538) and index. (BLCM)

Gwynne, S. C.

Empire of the summer moon; Quanah Parker and the rise and fall of the Comanches, the most powerful Indian tribe in American history. Scribner 2010 371p il map $27.50   **92**

1. Comanche Indians 2. Comanche Indians -- History 3. Comanche Indians -- Wars 4. Frontier and pioneer life -- West (U.S.) 5. Frontier and pioneer life -- Western

States 6. Indian chiefs
ISBN 978-1-4165-9105-4; 1-4165-9105-2

LC 2009049747

"A welcome contribution to the history of Texas, Westward expansion and Native America." Kirkus
Includes bibliographical references

Habegger, Alfred

My wars are laid away in books; the life of Emily Dickinson. Random House 2001 764p il hardcover o.p. pa $16.95　　**92**
1. Authors 2. Poets
ISBN 0-8129-6601-5 pa

LC 2001-19429

"Weaving together a chronologically integrated reading of Emily Dickinson's poetry and correspondence, Habegger has written the most complete and satisfying biography to date of a poet long shrouded in myth and illusion." Booklist
Includes bibliographical references

Hafner, Katie

A **romance** on three legs; Glenn Gould's obsessive quest for the perfect piano. Bloomsbury 2008 259p il $24.99; pa $16　　**92**
1. Composers 2. Pianists 3. Piano -- Construction 4. Pianos 5. Steinway piano
ISBN 978-1-59691-524-4; 1-59691-524-2; 978-1-59691-525-1 pa; 1-59691-525-0 pa

LC 2007-48808

"When Gould was paired with the right composer, Bach especially, he could make you wonder if he was altogether human. And reading Hafner on Gould is sometimes as much fun as listening to him play. And that's saying a lot." Newsweek
Includes bibliographical references

Hager, Thomas

The **alchemy** of air; a Jewish genius, a doomed tycoon, and the scientific discovery that fed the world but fueled the rise of Hitler. Harmony Books 2008 316p $24.95; pa $15　　**92**
1. Biography, Individual 2. Chemists 3. Fertilizers 4. Nitrogen fertilizers 5. Nobel laureates for chemistry
ISBN 978-0-307-35178-4; 0-307-35178-5; 978-0-307-35179-1 pa; 0-307-35179-3 pa

LC 2008-3192

"A fast-paced account of the early-20th-century quest to develop synthetic fertilizer. . . . Science writing of the first order." Kirkus
Includes bibliographical references

Hague, William Jefferson

William Wilberforce; the life of the great antislave trade campaigner. HarperCollins 2008 582p il $35　　**92**
1. Abolitionists 2. Antislavery movements -- History 3. Biography, Individual 4. Essayists 5. Members of Parliament 6. Philanthropists 7. Writers on religion
ISBN 978-0-15-101267-1; 0-15-101267-9

LC 2007-45981

Hague describes how Wilberforce, "dedicating his political life to moral causes . . . decided on two: 'the reformation

of manners,' as he confided to his diary, and the abolition of African slavery. Wilberforce's campaign against vice had scant historical effect, but that against slavery in British realms arguably prodded the Western world toward abolition. Why Wilberforce's effort (trade in slaves was banned in 1807; abolition occurred in 1834) followed a tortuous path becomes understandable as Hague explains the parliamentary practicalities that Wilberforce faced. Incorporating Wilberforce's domestic life, Hague's effort is a well-rounded portrait of the pioneering British abolitionist." Booklist

Hair, William Ivy

The **Kingfish** and his realm: the life and times of Huey P. Long. Louisiana State Univ. Press 1991 406p il map hardcover o.p. pa $21.95　　**92**
1. Governors 2. Senators 3. State government officials
ISBN 0-8071-2124-X pa

LC 91-18546

This is a biography of the man who was governor of Louisiana from 1928 to 1932 and senator from 1932 until his assassination in 1935.

"Written with passion and mordant wit, the book is literally hard to put down; the Kingfish seems to stimulate good writing. Overall, {this} is one of the more convincing negative biographies of recent years." Rev Am Hist
Includes bibliographical references

Hajratwala, Minal

Leaving India; my family's journey from five villages to five continents. Houghton Mifflin Harcourt 2009 430p il $26　　**92**
1. Authors 2. Children of immigrants 3. East Indians 4. Gujarati Americans 5. Immigration and emigration 6. Journalists 7. Performance artists 8. Poets
ISBN 978-0-618-25129-2; 0-618-25129-4

LC 2008-36079

"At times the writer's many threads are confusing, and the narrative could have been more tightly edited; nevertheless, 'Leaving India' is a rich, entertaining and illuminating story." San Francisco Chron
Includes bibliographical references

Halberstadt, Alex E.

Lonely avenue; the unlikely life and times of Doc Pomus. Da Capo Press 2007 254p il $26　　**92**
1. Biography, Individual 2. Blues musicians 3. Singers 4. Songwriters
ISBN 978-0-306-81300-9; 0-306-81300-9

"Throughout this book Halberstadt sketches a broad canvas of characters, Pomus's friends and enemies along with a gallery of rogues, malcontents, hustlers, knaves, acquaintances, colleagues, and hangers-on. . . . There's some guesswork here; Halberstadt had access to Pomus' notebooks and done interviews with some of Doc's contemporaries, but there are also moments of revelation and introspection that can only be ventured. Halberstadt exercises this license faithfully and believably." PopMatters

Halberstam, David

Playing for keeps: Michael Jordan and the world he made. Random House 1999 426p hardcover o.p. pa $16.95   **92**
   1. African American athletes 2. Baseball players 3. Basketball -- Biography 4. Basketball players 5. Olympic athletes
ISBN 0-7679-0444-3 pa
                    LC 98-49964
Halberstam presents a biography of basketball player Michael Jordan.

   "What's particularly effective about Halberstam's storytelling is that he follows Jordan's athletic trajectory, not in chronological order but through juxtaposed images of a hot-blooded college player with an as-yet unpolished game and an even-tempered 30-year-old at the height of his career. Jordan was not born a flawless pro, but developed his gifts by working tirelessly and intensely." Natl Rev

Hall, Meredith

Without a map; a memoir. Beacon Press 2007 221p $24.95   **92**
   1. Authors 2. Authors, American 3. College teachers 4. Essayists 5. Memoirists
ISBN 978-0-8070-7273-8; 0-8070-7273-7
                LC 2006-27507
   "The year: 1965. The place: a small, insular New Hampshire community where church and home life are dominant forces. When Hall becomes pregnant at 16, she is shunned by family members and friends she's known throughout her school years. After traveling to the Middle East and suffering the indignities of loneliness and poverty, which include selling her own blood, she returns to the United States and creates a new life out of her still-palpable grief. . . . The message of redemptive compassion makes this a worthwhile and moving read." Libr J

Hamilton, Gabrielle

Blood, bones & butter; the inadvertent education of a reluctant chef. Random House 2011 291p $26   **92**
   1. Biography, Individual 2. Cooks 3. Restaurateurs
ISBN 978-1-4000-6872-2; 1-4000-6872-X; 978-1-58836-931-4 ebook; 1-58836-931-5 ebook
                LC 2010-17518
This is a memoir by the chef who owns the Prune restaurant in New York.

   Though this book "is rhapsodic about food—in every variety, from the humble egg-on-a-roll sandwich served by Greek delis in New York to more esoteric things like 'fried zucchini agrodolce with fresh mint and hot chili flakes'— the book is hardly just for foodies. Ms. Hamilton . . . is as evocative writing about people and places as she is at writing about cooking." N Y Times (Late N Y Ed)

Hansberry, Lorraine

To be young, gifted, and Black; Lorraine Hansberry in her own words. adapted by Robert Nemiroff; with drawings and art by Lorraine Hansberry; introduction by James Baldwin; and a new preface by

Jewell Handy Gresham Nemiroff. 1st Vintage Books ed; Vintage Books 1995 xxx, 261p il pa $13.95 **92**
   1. African American women -- Biography 2. Authors 3. Dramatists 4. Dramatists, American 5. Essayists 6. Newspaper editors 7. Nonfiction writers
ISBN 0-679-76415-1
               LC 96-119999
   Work on this book and on the script for the play of the same title, which was presented at New York's Cherry Lane Theatre in 1969, "proceeded concurrently, each drawing upon the experiences and creative discoveries of the other, but ultimately diverging quite drastically." Postscript

Hari, Daoud

The translator; a tribesman's memoir of Darfur. Random House 2008 204p hardcover o.p. pa $13   **92**
   1. Biography, Individual 2. Guides (Persons) 3. Memoirists 4. Refugees
ISBN 978-1-4000-6744-2; 1-4000-6744-8; 978-0-8129-7917-6 pa; 0-8129-7917-6 pa
                LC 2007-42308
   In this memoir, the author recounts his life in Darfur, Sudan before and after the conflict in 2003.

   "Those with the courage to join Hari's odyssey may find this a life-changing read." Publ Wkly

Harlan, Elizabeth

George Sand. Yale University Press 2004 376p il $35   **92**
   1. Authors 2. Biography, Individual 3. Dramatists 4. Novelists
ISBN 0-300-10417-0
                LC 2004-10315
   "Sand, née, Aurore Dupin, left her husband and two children in provincial France and successfully launched herself as a self-supporting writer in Paris, donning men's clothing to ease passage into the professional world and taking a pseudonym to protect her aristocratic family's name. Sand took on many lovers, among them poet Alfred de Musset and composer Frédéric Chopin. Yet despite Sand's outward daring, as Harlan shows, she obsessed over her identity, as both a woman and an aristocrat. . . . Harlan sensitively analyzes the gaps and idiosyncrasies in her subject's heavily self-edited correspondence, autobiography and novels to uncover a fresh portrait of this volatile, imaginative woman of letters." Publ Wkly

   Includes bibliographical references

Harlan, Louis R.

Booker T. Washington: the making of a black leader, 1856-1901. Oxford Univ. Press 1972 379p il hardcover o.p. pa $21.50   **92**
   1. African American educators 2. African Americans -- Biography 3. Authors 4. Civil rights activists 5. Educators 6. Memoirists 7. Nonfiction writers 8. Slaves
ISBN 0-19-501915-6 pa
   This book "covers Washington's life from his birth as a slave in western Virginia up to [the year 1901, when he dined] with Theodore Roosevelt at the White House, an event signifying white recognition of Washington as the

chief spokesman for black interests in the period before World War I." Libr J

Booker T. Washington: the wizard of Tuskegee, 1901-1915. Oxford Univ. Press 1983 548p il hardcover o.p. pa $24.95   **92**
1. African American educators 2. African Americans -- Biography 3. Authors 4. Civil rights activists 5. Educators 6. Memoirists 7. Nonfiction writers 8. Slaves
ISBN 0-19-504229-8 pa
LC 82-14547
This is the second and concluding volume of a life of the black educator and founder of Tuskegee Institute.
"Having avoided the pitfalls of white guilt and black rage and the temptation to judge the past by standards of the present, Mr. Harlan deserves honors for his remarkable achievement." N Y Times Book Rev
Includes bibliographical references

Harman, Claire
Jane's fame; how Jane Austen conquered the world. Henry Holt and Co. 2010 277p il $26   **92**
1. Authors 2. Authors, English 3. Novelists 4. Women authors
ISBN 978-0-8050-8258-6; 0-8050-8258-1
LC 2009-22291
"Engagingly written and full of fascinating bits of information as well as valuable insights, this is a must for any serious Austen reader." Booklist
Includes bibliographical references

Harman, Oren Solomon
The **price** of altruism; George Price and the search for the origins of kindness. W.W. Norton 2010 451p il $27.95   **92**
1. Altruism 2. Altruistic behavior in animals 3. Biography, Individual 4. Geneticists 5. Genetics 6. Population genetics 7. Scientists
ISBN 978-0-393-06778-1; 0-393-06778-5
LC 2010-11934
This book "puts Price's work into a wide scientific and social context, showing real insight into its importance and genuine sympathy for the tale of his life." New Sci
Includes bibliographical references

Harris, David
The **genius**; how Bill Walsh reinvented football and created an NFL dynasty. Random House 2008 385p il $26   **92**
1. Biography, Individual 2. Football -- Biography 3. Football coaches
ISBN 978-1-4000-6665-0; 1-4000-6665-4
LC 2008-16566
"Walsh was one of the NFL's greatest coaches, and Harris' book does him justice." Booklist
Includes bibliographical references

Harris, J. William
The **hanging** of Thomas Jeremiah; a free Black man's encounter with liberty. Yale University Press 2009 223p il map $27.50   **92**
1. African Americans -- Social conditions 2. Biography, Individual 3. Colonial administrators 4. Colonial leaders 5. Diplomats 6. Government officials 7. Merchants 8. Plantation owners 9. Ship captains 10. Slavery -- United States
ISBN 978-0-300-15214-2; 0-300-15214-0
LC 2009-15233
This is an "account of nebulous historical figure Thomas Jeremiah. . . . Owner of a fishing company and worth $200,000 in 2009 dollars, . . . [Jeremiah] was probably the richest black man in North America; he was also a slave owner. That didn't stop him from becoming a scapegoat, accused by patriot leader Henry Laurens—a wealthy plantation owner with hundreds of slaves—of secretly leading a British-sponsored slave insurrection. Though Governor William Campbell, aggrieved by the unlawfulness of Jeremiah's trial, interceded, it didn't stop those determined to hang Jeremiah. . . . Readers will learn much about the darker side of American institutions; students of American history and civil rights will appreciate Harris's impassive approach and thorough standards." Publ Wkly
Includes bibliographical references

Harvey, Miles
Painter in a savage land; the strange saga of the first European artist in North America. Random House 2008 xx, 338p il map $27   **92**
1. Artists 2. Artists, French
ISBN 978-1-4000-6120-4; 1-4000-6120-2
LC 2007-39105
"This book doubles as a narrative of Harvey's own expedition to discover more about his subject and the story of Le Moyne's works in the centuries after his death—and their sad fate at the hands of a New York antiquities dealer. Harvey's volume hits the sweet spot for both adventure buffs and history fans." Publ Wkly
Includes bibliographical references

Hastings, Selina
The **secret** lives of Somerset Maugham; a biography. Random House 2010 626p il   **92**
1. Authors 2. Authors, English 3. Biography, Individual 4. Dramatists 5. Novelists 6. Short story writers 7. Travel writers
ISBN 978-1-4000-6141-9
LC 2009-35797
This is a biography of the English novelist and playwright.
"This steady-eyed biography of an extraordinary, extravagant, generous and bitter artist will not only fascinate its readers but encourage some to go to his work for the first time." Times Lit Suppl
Includes bibliographical references (p. 599-602)

Hauerwas, Stanley, 1940-
Hannah's child; a theologian's memoir. W.B. Eerdmans Pub. Co. 2010 287p $24.99   **92**
1. Authors 2. Biography, Individual 3. College

teachers 4. Theologians 5. Writers on religion
ISBN 978-0-8028-6487-1; 0-8028-6487-2

LC 2009-44729

This is an autobiography by the son of a Texas bricklayer who now teaches theological ethics at Duke University's Divinity School. His title refers to the Biblical Hannah, mother of Samuel, who promised God that if He allowed her to conceive a son in her old age, the child would be dedicated to God's service.

"Fans of Christian memoirs will be pleased with Hauerwas's frank yet poignant style, and those who are simply fans of the memoir genre will find the book's careful blend of faith and scholarship easily accessible and far from didactic." Publ Wkly

Havel, Vaclav

To the castle and back; translated from the Czech by Paul Wilson. Knopf 2007 383p $27.95; pa $15.95   92
1. Authors 2. Biography, Individual 3. Dissenters 4. Dramatists 5. Essayists 6. Presidents
ISBN 978-0-307-26641-5; 0-307-26641-9; 978-0-307-33845-2 pa; 0-307-38845-X pa

LC 2007-4413

The book "gives Havel's account of his journey from dissident-in-chief to head of state during the Velvet Revolution of 1989—and the turmoil that followed. Hardly a conventional memoir, its three intermixed narratives are at first as disorienting as his role reversal—which dismayed his wife Olga as much as himself. . . . These selections are by turns obscure, funny, insightful, poignant, and peevish. . . . Living in truth was what [Havel] preached as a dissident, and it is what he preached as president. . . . Whatever his political shortcomings in office, at least in this, the Czechs were privileged to have Havel as president." Commonweal

Hawkes, David

John Milton; a hero for our time. Counterpoint 2010 354p $28   92
1. Authors 2. Blind 3. Essayists 4. Poets 5. Poets, English
ISBN 978-1-58243-437-7; 1-58243-437-9

LC 2009-53998

"Hawkes writes with little academic jargon, and his style is lively and entertaining. Political and religious history enthusiasts will find this excellent and challenging." Libr J
Includes bibliographical references

Haygood, Wil

★ **Sweet** thunder; the life and times of Sugar Ray Robinson. Alfred A. Knopf 2009 461p il $27.95   92
1. Biography, Individual 2. Boxers (Persons) 3. Boxing -- Biography
ISBN 978-1-4000-4497-9

LC 2009-5534

This "book is certainly one of the best biographies of a boxer ever written . . . [and] an important contribution to both sports literature and African American studies." Washington Post Book World
Includes bibliographical references

Hazan, Marcella

Amarcord, Marcella remembers; the remarkable life story of the woman who started out teaching science in a small town in Italy, but ended up teaching America how to cook Italian. Gotham Books 2008 307p il $27.50   92
1. Biography, Individual 2. Cookbook writers 3. Cookery, Italian 4. Cooking teachers 5. Cooks 6. Copywriters 7. Fashion designers 8. Food critics 9. Italian cooking
ISBN 978-1-59240-388-2; 1-59240-388-3

LC 2007-46197

This is a memoir by the author of The Classic Italian Cook Book (1973) and More Classic Italian Cooking (1978).

"Hazan has selected the best stories from her own life to present Amarcord with all the warmth and humor of a long meal in famiglia made from the choicest ingredients. . . . If you've never been [to] Italy, the time spent with Hazan will have you planning your next vacation faster than you can say manicotti." Christ Sci Monit

Hazleton, Lesley

Mary: a flesh-and-blood biography of the Virgin Mother. Bloomsbury 2004 246p $24.95   92
1. Saints
ISBN 1-582-34236-9

LC 2003-17403

Hazleton "takes readers through an impressive array of historical, cultural, literary, and spiritual topics. . . . This book is an easy read, and Hazleton's stream-of-consciousness style is intriguing." Libr J
Includes bibliographical references

Heaney, Christopher

Cradle of gold; the story of Hiram Bingham, a real-life Indiana Jones, and the search for Machu Picchu. Palgrave Macmillan 2010 285p il $27   92
1. Explorers 2. Governors 3. Historians 4. Incas 5. Senators
ISBN 978-0-230-61169-6; 0-230-61169-9

LC 2009-38535

"On an archaeological trip to Peru on July 24, 1911, Hiram Bingham, an American explorer and history professor at Yale, happened upon the ruins of the Inca city of Machu Picchu. Although the site was already known to the local native people, Bingham made the Machu Picchu ruins famous and received acclaim as their 'discoverer.' Heaney presents a well-researched and very readable biography of Bingham from his childhood in Hawaii as the son of missionaries, through his education and careers as historian, educator, explorer, and finally politician. He probes the depths of Bingham's work and character, examining setbacks, scandals, and achievements and skillfully unraveling Bingham's role in the controversy that still exists today between the government of Peru and Yale University over the ownership of the Machu Picchu burials and artifacts." Libr J
Includes bibliographical references

Hedrick, Joan D.

Harriet Beecher Stowe; a life. Oxford Univ. Press 1994 507p il hardcover o.p. pa $19.95   92
1. Abolitionists 2. Authors 3. Children's authors 4.

Nonfiction writers 5. Novelists 6. Short story writers
ISBN 0-19-509639-8 pa

LC 93-16610

This biography "brings to life not just the complex and fascinating woman and writer but also the 19th-century America that shaped her and was in turn shaped by her. Hedrick manages to weave into his immensely readable biography a history teeming with the domestic detail of the famous Beecher clan, the settling of the West, and the impact of the Civil War and the abolition movement." Libr J

Includes bibliographical references

Hefez, Nir

Ariel Sharon; a life. [by] Nir Hefez and Gadi Bloom; translated from the Hebrew by Mitch Ginsburg. Random House 2006 490p il $29.95 **92**

1. Biography, Individual 2. Cabinet members 3. Generals 4. Political leaders 5. Prime ministers
ISBN 1-4000-6587-9; 978-1-4000-6587-5

LC 2006-49144

This is a biography of the Israeli prime minister.

"This revealing and engrossing biography adds a great deal to our understanding of the man." Booklist

Includes bibliographical references

Heidler, David Stephen

Henry Clay; the essential American. [by] David S. Heidler and Jeanne T. Heidler. Random House 2010 595p il $30 **92**

1. Biography, Individual 2. Members of Congress 3. Secretaries of state 4. Senators 5. Speakers of the House 6. Statesmen 7. Statesmen -- United States
ISBN 978-1-4000-6726-8; 1-4000-6726-X

LC 2009-27872

"Anyone wanting to understand political, economic, and social life in the early republic will appreciate the Heidlers' command of sources and balanced treatment of a man too long in the shadow of Andrew Jackson and very much a metaphor for his era." Libr J

Includes bibliographical references

Heilbron, J. L.

Galileo. Oxford University Press 2010 508p il $34.95 **92**

1. Astronomers 2. Astronomy -- History 3. Biography, Individual 4. Science -- Italy -- History 5. Writers on science
ISBN 978-0-19-958352-2; 0-19-958352-8

This "will no doubt become the standard, comprehensive biography. . . . In one of his most inventive sections, [Heilbron] creates a Galilean dialogue on issues of algebra and geometry. Though not easy to read, it brilliantly expresses the ambiguities and blind alleys as Galileo wrestled with the conceptual difficulty of introducing a nongeometrical quantity—time itself—into the proportions." N Y Times Book Rev

Includes bibliographical references

Heilbrun, Carolyn G.

The **education** of a woman; the life of Gloria Steinem. Ballantine Books 1996 450p il pa $23 **92**

1. Authors 2. Feminism 3. Feminists 4. Journalists 5.

Magazine editors 6. Memoirists
ISBN 0-345-40621-4; 978-0-345-40621-7

"The portrait that results is nuanced and thoughtful. . . . Heilbrun's goal is at once to understand how Steinem became the woman she is, and what her life can teach us about childhood and family, self and society. Slow at the start, but Heilbrun soon captures readers' interest and imagination." Booklist

Includes bibliographical references

Heilpern, John

John Osborne; the many lives of the angry young man. Alfred A. Knopf 2007 527p il $35 **92**

1. Authors 2. Dramatists
ISBN 978-0-375-40315-6; 0-375-40315-9

LC 2006-46575

"Heilpern draws on Osborne's bleak private notebooks to generate acute readings of his often autobiographical plays. Sympathy for the man and admiration for the work don't blind Heilpern to his subject's outsized flaws. Osborne had a talent for invective and could be cruelly intolerant in matters large and small. He threatened theatre critics with physical violence by way of anonymous seaside postcards. Stung by his teenage daughter's indifference to high culture, he damned her as 'criminally commonplace' and never spoke to her again. Without excusing such 'breathtaking abuse,' Heilpern makes a compelling case for Osborne as a necessary 'truthteller' and 'unyielding advocate of individualism in conformist times.'" New Yorker

Includes bibliographical references

Heller, Anne Conover

Ayn Rand and the world she made; [by] Anne C. Heller. Nan A. Talese/Doubleday 2008 567p il $35 **92**

1. Authors 2. Authors, American 3. Biography, Individual 4. Nonfiction writers 5. Novelists 6. Objectivism (Philosophy) 7. Philosophers 8. Women authors
ISBN 978-0-385-51399-9

LC 2008-27638

This is a biography of the author of Atlas Shrugged and The Fountainhead.

The author "has delivered a thoughtful, flesh-and-blood portrait of an extremely complicated and self-contradictory woman, coupling this character study with literary analysis and plumbing the quirkier depths of Rand's prodigious imagination." N Y Times (Late N Y Ed)

Includes bibliographical references

Heller, Erica

Yossarian slept here; when Joseph Heller was dad, the Apthorp was home, and life was a catch-22. Simon & Schuster 2011 272p il $25; ebook $11.99 **92**

1. Authors 2. Biography, Individual 3. Children of prominent persons 4. Copywriters 5. Journalists 6. Novelists 7. Novelists, American 8. Short story writers
ISBN 978-1-4391-9768-4; 1-4391-9768-7; 978-1-4391-9770-7 ebook; 1-4391-9770-9 ebook

LC 2011-08283

The daughter of author Joseph Heller shares the story of her childhood, marked by her father's fame, her parents' acrimonious divorce, and their unconventional parenting choices.

"An affectionate family scrapbook crafted with a bittersweet blend of humor and pathos." Kirkus

Hellman, Lillian

Pentimento. Little, Brown 1973 297p hardcover o.p. pa $14.95   **92**

1. Authors 2. Dramatists 3. Dramatists, American 4. Memoirists

ISBN 0-316-35288-8 pa

This continuation of An unfinished woman—a memoir (1969) offers sketches of events and people from the author's past. She reminisces about her childhood in the South, some of her eccentric relatives including Cousin Bethe and Uncle Willy, Julia, her childhood friend who was trapped by the Nazis, Dashiell Hammett, who was her lover, and her experiences in the theater

"Pentimento is valuable as a picture of a woman and writer in the making." New Repub

Helm, Sarah

A **life** in secrets; Vera Atkins and the missing agents of WWII. Nan A. Talese 2006 493p il map hardcover o.p. pa $16   **92**

1. Intelligence service agents 2. World War, 1939-1945 -- Secret service

ISBN 0-385-50845-X; 978-1-4000-3140-5 pa; 1-4000-3140-0 pa

LC 2005-56870

This is a biography of "the highest-ranking female official in the French section of a WWII British intelligence unit that aided the resistance. Atkins sent 400 agents into France, including 39 women she'd personally recruited and supervised. . . . Helm has produced a memorable portrait of a woman who knowingly sent other women to their deaths and a searing history of female courage and suffering during WWII." Publ Wkly

Includes bibliographical references

Hemphill, Paul

★ **Lovesick** blues; the life of Hank Williams. Viking 2005 207p $23.95   **92**

1. Biography, Individual 2. Country musicians 3. Singers 4. Songwriters

ISBN 0-670-03414-2

LC 2004-65113

This is a biography of the country singer.

"This is the finest work of literature about Williams yet written." Booklist

Henderson, Bill

★ **All** my dogs; a life. drawings by leslie Moore. David R. Godine 2011 145p $19.95   **92**

1. Authors 2. Dogs 3. Editors 4. Memoirists 5. Novelists 6. Publishing executives

ISBN 978-1-56792-435-0; 1-56792-435-2

LC 2010-49824

"This is a lovely little volume, gentle in tone and a bit artless, telling the story of a life through the dogs who at-

tended it. Bill Henderson, the founder of Pushcart Press and its better-known progeny, the annual Pushcart Prize, hasn't written his account as an instructional, or a confessional, or even a celebration. Rather, it's a meditation on the grace notes both dogs and people bring to a life—a hybrid 'mutt memoir,' as he calls it. . . . This small, kind book is steeped with an earnest sort of fondness all the way through—the back matter even points out that it's set in Minion, which means 'faithful companion.' The accompanying line drawings by Leslie Moore, appealing portraits of each dog recreated from photos and Henderson's desriptions, add a nice touch." Open Letters Monthly

Hendrickson, Paul

★ **Hemingway's** boat; everything he loved in life, and lost, 1934-1961. Alfred A. Knopf 2011 531p il $30; ebook $14.99   **92**

1. Authors 2. Authors, American 3. Biography, Individual 4. Journalists 5. Nobel laureates for literature 6. Novelists 7. Poets 8. Short story writers

ISBN 9781400041626; 1400041627; 9780307700537 ebook

LC 2011003398

The author frames "the last 27 years of Hemingway's over-dissected life with his yacht, Pilar. Outlasting marriages and relationships with friends and family, the 38' Brooklyn-built fishing machine was the lasting love of his life. Hendrickson has come neither to praise nor to bury his subject, but to give him a fair shot. . . . Hendrickson brings fresh meat to the table, delivering one of the most satisfying Hemingway assessments in many years. A delight for Ernesto's numerous fans." Libr J

Includes bibliographical references and index.

Hennessey, Patrick

The **Junior** Officers' Reading Club; killing time and fighting wars. Riverhead Books 2010 310p il map pa $16   **92**

1. Afghan War, 2001- -- Personal narratives 2. Army officers 3. Iraq War, 2003- -- Personal narratives 4. Soldiers -- Great Britain

ISBN 978-1-59448-479-7; 1-59448-479-1

LC 2010-17134

"Oxford graduate Hennessey decided he wanted to do something exciting, so he went to Sandhurst, England's Royal Military Academy, and then to Bosnia, Iraq, and, ultimately, Afghanistan as a lieutenant and platoon leader in the Grenadier Guards. There he found what he was looking for, and this voluble, kinetic, and often funny book recounts his experiences. . . . The book's pace, never leisurely, accelerates in Afghanistan, as Hennessey vividly describes near-constant battle with Taliban fighters and confronts his reactions: exhaustion, fear, grief, fellowship, confusion, and what he calls the 'rapture' of war. All wars generate fine books. This may be one of the best to come out of the war in Afghanistan." Booklist

Hensley, William L.

Fifty miles from tomorrow; a memoir of Alaska and the real people. [by] William L. Iggiagruk Hens-

ley. Farrar, Straus and Giroux 2008 256p il map
$24
92
1. Biography, Individual 2. Eskimo leaders 3. Inuit
-- Alaska 4. Inupiat 5. State legislators
ISBN 978-0-374-15484-4; 0-374-15484-8
LC 2008-31409
The author "manages to make fresh an old narrative of
people who arise just as their culture is being erased—be
they 'Braveheart' Scotsmen or outback Aborigines. His
book is also bright and detailed, moving along at a clip most
sled dogs would have trouble keeping up with." N Y Times
Book Rev

Hepburn, Katharine
Me; stories of my life. Knopf 1991 420p il
hardcover o.p. pa $15.95
92
1. Actors 2. Biography, Individual 3. Large print books
ISBN 0-345-41009-2
LC 90-50805
This book "sounds just like its author—lots of cropped
sentences, dashes, Hepburnian phrasing. But it's not a full-
dress autobiography; as the subtitle proclaims, this is a collection of stories. . . . Still, fans will not be disappointed.
Beginning with her early years . . . and concluding with
her relationship with Tracy, Hepburn delivers all kinds of
wry moments and, of course, a most interesting cast of
characters." Booklist

Herlihy, David V.
The **lost** cyclist; the epic tale of an American
adventurer and his mysterious disappearance. [by]
David V. Herlihy. Houghton Mifflin Harcourt 2010
326p il map
92
1. Biography, Individual 2. Cycling 3. Cyclists 4.
Murder victims 5. Photographers 6. Retail personnel
ISBN 0-547-19557-5; 0-547-52198-7 pa; 978-0-547-
19557-5; 978-0-547-52198-5 pa
LC 2009-28857
This is a biography of "Frank Lenz, a 24-year-old wheel-
man [who] departed New York in 1892 to round the globe.
. . . [Lenz disappeared in] eastern Turkey, in the midst of a
Turkish and Kurdish campaign that would kill some 10,000
Armenian civilians." (N Y Times Book Rev) Index.
"This well-researched and stylishly written book puts
Lenz back in the public eye as well as offering readers a look
at the very early days of modern cycling." Booklist

Herman, Arthur
Gandhi and Churchill; the epic rivalry that destroyed an empire and forged our age. Bantam Book
2008 721p il map $30
92
1. Authors 2. Cabinet members 3. Essayists 4.
Historians 5. Journalists 6. Members of Parliament 7.
Memoirists 8. Nobel laureates for literature 9. Pacifists
10. Political leaders 11. Prime ministers 12. Statesmen
13. Writers on politics
ISBN 978-0-553-80463-8; 0-553-80463-4
LC 2008-149
"A well-wrought historical narrative that adds significantly to our understanding of both figures." Kirkus
Includes bibliographical references (p. 673-85)

Herriot, James
All creatures great and small; 20th anniversary ed; St. Martin's Press 1992 442p $21.95; pa
$13.95
92
1. Authors 2. Memoirists 3. Veterinarians 4.
Veterinary medicine
ISBN 0-312-08498-6; 0-312-33085-5 pa
LC 92-18975
The first volume of Herriot's autobiographical account
of the practice of veterinary medicine in Yorkshire, England
in the 1930s.

Herrmann, Dorothy
Helen Keller; a life. University of Chicago Press
1999 394p il pa $22
92
1. Authors 2. Blind 3. Deaf 4. Humanitarians 5.
Inspirational writers 6. Memoirists 7. Social welfare
leaders
ISBN 0-226-32763-9; 978-0-226-32763-1
LC 99-23242
The author "takes us beyond the image of Helen Keller
portrayed in The Miracle Worker to unearth a passionate, politically radical woman whose inspiration and teacher, Annie
Sullivan, is equally fiery and brilliant. Herrmann brings us
into the every day lives of the famous pair, but the story is
hardly mundane. . . . Herrmann gives us fascinating details
via archives and unpublished memoirs to show how society's view of disabled people was greatly shaped by Keller
and Sullivan." Libr J
Includes bibliographical references

Hertog, Susan
Anne Morrow Lindbergh; a biography. Talese
1999 561p il hardcover o.p. pa $17
92
1. Air pilots' spouses -- United States -- Biography
2. Authors 3. Authors, American -- 20th century --
Biography 4. Diarists 5. Essayists 6. Memoirists 7.
Novelists 8. Poets 9. Spouses of prominent persons
10. Women air pilots -- United States -- Biography
ISBN 0-385-72007-6 pa
LC 99-28759
After her marriage to Charles Lindbergh, Anne Morrow "soon recognized the difficulty of reconciling her literary ambitions with accompanying her husband as copilot,
navigator and radio operator. After the tragic kidnapping
and death of their first child, which they blamed in part on
dogged press coverage of their personal life, the Lindberghs
moved abroad. They became embroiled with the leaders of
Nazi Germany, according to Hertog, because Charles believed that the democratic system was weak and ineffectual.
. . . This sympathetic portrayal of Anne as a wife, mother,
poet and feminist may well find a readership more interested
in a talented woman's creative struggle than in the oft-told
Lindbergh story." Publ Wkly
Includes bibliographical references

Hibbert, Christopher
Nelson; a personal history. Addison-Wesley
1994 472p il hardcover o.p. pa $22
92
1. Admirals
ISBN 0-201-40800-7 pa
LC 94-39545

The book "succeeds admirably in presenting a vivid and intimate picture of Nelson and Lady Hamilton together, helped by numerous and apt illustrations, half of them in colour. . . . The result is essentially a book of domestic detail, told with charm and perception." Times Lit Suppl

Includes bibliographical references

Queen Victoria; a personal history. Basic Bks. 2000 557p il hardcover o.p. pa $21   **92**
1. Queens
ISBN 0-306-81085-9 pa
LC 2001-269136

Hibbert explores the life and reign of the British monarch based on "primary sources, particularly the 60 million words of Victoria's letters and journals. As a result, he renders Victoria and her familial and political relationships with deliciously gossipy and often touching intimacy." N Y Times Book Rev

Includes bibliographical references

★ **Wellington**; a personal history. Perseus Books 1999 460p il map pa $22   **92**
1. Generals 2. Prime ministers 3. Statesmen
ISBN 0-7382-0148-0; 978-0-7382-0148-1

"Altogether, Wellington does not quite pass the 'niceness' test. . . . He was a difficult man, a major military figure, a minor Prime Minister and in sum a historically important legend. Hibbert skillfully brings out all these characteristics." N Y Times Book Rev

Includes bibliographical references

The **virgin** queen: Elizabeth I, genius of the Golden Age. Perseus Books 1992 287p il map pa $22   **92**
1. Queens
ISBN 978-0-201-60817-5; 0-201-60817-0

This "biography is essentially personal rather than political history. . . . There are many biographies of Elizabeth, and more than a few good ones, but Hibbert's is solid and sure to charm. . . . A reliable and highly readable choice." Libr J

Includes bibliographical references

Hikayati sharhun yatul./English
The **locust** and the bird; my mother's story. translated from the Arabic by Roger Allen. Pantheon Books 2009 302p il $24.95   **92**
1. Muslim women 2. Parents of prominent persons
ISBN 978-0-307-37820-0; 0-307-37820-9
LC 2008-54683

"Al-Shaykh's poignant family history, narrated in the voice of her mother, Kamila, transports us to Beirut in the nineteen-thirties. At eleven, the beautiful and strong-willed Kamila is illiterate, her family penniless. She falls in love with the handsome Muhammad, but at fourteen is married off to an older man. . . . Later, Kamila runs away with Muhammad, abandoning her daughters. Al-Shaykh writes in the prologue that this book is largely an attempt to come to terms with that decision. Through telling her mother's story, she learns to appreciate the sacrifices demanded of so many Arab women in their bid for freedom." New Yorker

Hilburn, Robert
Cornflakes with John Lennon; and other tales from a rock 'n' roll life. Rodale 2009 208p il $24.99   **92**
1. Journalists 2. Music critics 3. Rock musicians -- Anecdotes
ISBN 978-1-59486-921-1; 1-59486-921-9
LC 2009-26604

"Fans of Springsteen, Dylan and U2 will be thrilled to find multiple chapters devoted to their idols, who are clearly Hilburn's favorites as well. . . . The most intriguing sections, however, are the glimpses into the private lives of a who's who of popular music in the 20th century. . . . A must-read for pop-music lovers." Kirkus

Hinton, Milt
Playing the changes; Milt Hinton's life in stories and photographs. [by] Milt Hinton, David G. Berger, and Holly Maxson; foreword by Clint Eastwood; preface by Dan Morganstern. Vanderbilt University Press 2008 364p il $75   **92**
1. Bassists 2. Jazz musicians 3. Photographers
ISBN 978-0-8265-1574-2; 0-8265-1574-6
LC 2007-30389

"More than just a biography and more than a photography book. This is an excellent selection for any library music collection. It opens up the world of jazz as well as a time in African-American history that isn't always pleasant to remember." Univ Press Books for Public and Second Sch Libr, 2009

Includes   discography,   filmography,   and bibliographical references

Hirsch, James S.
Willie Mays; the life, the legend. authorized by Willie Mays. Scribner 2010 628p il $30   **92**
1. Baseball -- Biography 2. Baseball -- History 3. Baseball players 4. Biography, Individual
ISBN 978-1-4165-4790-7; 1-4165-4790-8
LC 2009-49214

"This is a superb baseball book, but it's also a riveting narrative of Mays' life and times, ranging from his penchant for fancy suits to urban development in New York City to the giddy cult of celebrity. In the mid-1950s, Willie Mays was as famous as anyone in the country, gracing the cover of Time and other magazines and appearing on numerous television shows. More impressive — and what distinguishes this book from the run-of-the-mill sports biography — is Hirsch's extensive and cogent take on race relations and the civil-rights movement both within and outside of baseball." Seattle Times

Includes bibliographical references

Hirshfeld, Alan
Eureka man; the life and legacy of Archimedes. Walker 2009 242p il map $26   **92**
1. Biography, Individual 2. Mathematicians 3. Science -- Greece -- History 4. Scientists 5. Writers on science
ISBN 978-0-8027-1618-7; 0-8027-1618-0
LC 2009-05608

"Thoroughly enjoyable look at the tumultuous life and resounding influence of a genius of antiquity. . . . Hirshfeld

writes clearly and with enthusiasm, navigating even the occasional dense mathematical concept with easy-to-understand language and accompanying diagrams." Kirkus
Includes bibliographical references

Hirsi Ali, Ayaan

Infidel. Free Press 2007 353p il $26; pa $15 **92**
1. Biography, Individual 2. Feminists 3. Members of Parliament 4. Memoirists 5. Muslim women 6. Refugees
ISBN 0-7432-8968-4; 978-0-7432-8968-9; 0-7432-8969-2 pa; 978-0-7432-8969-6 pa

LC 2006-49762

"A Somali by birth and a recently elected member of the Dutch Parliament, Ms. Hirsi Ali had waged a personal crusade to improve the lot of Muslim women. Her warnings about the dangers posed to the Netherlands by unassimilated Muslims made her Public Enemy No. 1 for Muslim extremists, a feminist counterpart to Salman Rushdie. The circuitous, violence-filled path that led Ms. Hirsi Ali from Somalia to the Netherlands is the subject of 'Infidel,' her brave, inspiring and beautifully written memoir." N Y Times (Late N Y Ed)

Hitchens, Christopher

Thomas Jefferson: author of America. HarperCollins Publishers 2005 188p $19.95 **92**
1. Architects 2. Essayists 3. Presidents 4. Presidents -- United States 5. Vice-presidents
ISBN 0-06-059896-4

LC 2005-296593

"Beginning with his aristocratic upbringing, . . . this biography explores both the private and public aspects of Jefferson's life, from his political philosophies to his affair with his slave Sally Hemings. . . . This opinionated, lively narrative sheds light not only on Jefferson's complex personality but on the politics of his time, making it both a fascinating character study and an excellent review of early American history." Publ Wkly

Hitchens, Christopher, 1949-2011

Hitch-22; a memoir. Twelve 2010 435p il $26.99 **92**
1. Authors 2. Biography, Individual 3. Essayists 4. Journalists 5. Writers on politics
ISBN 978-0-446-54033-9

LC 2009051959

This is an autobiography by the British journalist. Christopher Hitchens is the author of For the Sake of Argument: Essays and Minority Reports (1993); Blood, Class, and Nostalgia (1990); Blood, Class, and Empire (2004), and God is Not Great (2007). Index.

Few authors can rile as easily as Hitchens does, but even his detractors might find it difficult to put down a book so witty, so piercing, so spoiling for a fight. He makes you want to be as good a reader as he is a writer. Booklist

Hitler, Adolf

★ **Mein** Kampf; translated by Ralph Manheim. Houghton Mifflin 1943 xxi, 694p $40; pa $22 **92**
1. Heads of state 2. National socialism 3. Nazi leaders
ISBN 0-395-95105-4; 0-395-92503-7 pa

"Hitler's steady rise to power was interrupted only by the Beer Hall Putsch (1923), an unsuccessful attempt to overthrow the Weimar Republic. . . . During the nine months of imprisonment that followed he wrote 'Mein Kampf' (1924; tr. 'My struggle,' 1940). This book contained autobiographical and reflective passages, rife with hysterical anti-Semitism and paranoia, as well as the program he intended to implement; for the West it was a warning that went unheeded." Reader's Ency. 3d edition

Hoban, Phoebe

Alice Neel; the art of not sitting pretty. St. Martin's Press 2010 500p il $35 **92**
1. Artists 2. Biography, Individual 3. Painters 4. Women artists
ISBN 978-0-312-60748-7; 0-312-60748-7

LC 2010-35781

"Judicious and ardent, Hoban has created a galvanizing portrait of a 'rebel artist' who remained true to her humanist convictions." Booklist
Includes bibliographical references

Hoffman, Adina

★ **My** happiness bears no relation to happiness; a poet's life in the Palestinian century. Yale University Press 2009 454p il map $27.50 **92**
1. Arabic poetry -- 20th century -- History and criticism 2. Authors 3. Biography, Individual 4. Poets
ISBN 978-0-300-14150-4

LC 2008-37298

"An exceptional introduction to a literary world that has, until now, been little known to English-language readers, this is highly recommended for all libraries." Libr J
Includes bibliographical references

Hogwood, Christopher

Handel; chronological table by Anthony Hicks. Rev ed; Thames & Hudson 2007 324p map pa $21.95 **92**
1. Composers
ISBN 978-0-500-28681-4; 0-500-28681-7

LC 2006-909559

The author "addresses his book to the serious layman. The composer's comings and goings are documented as accurately as possible, and Mr. Hogwood has added terse critical commentary about the music in sophisticated language but without musical examples." N Y Times Book Rev
Includes bibliographical references

Holiday, Billie

★ **Lady** sings the blues; [Billie Holiday with William Dufty] 50th anniversary ed.; Harlem Moon 2006 231p il pa $15.95 **92**
1. African American singers 2. Blues musicians 3. Singers
ISBN 978-0-7679-2386-6; 0-7679-2386-3

LC 2007-271682

"A hard, bitter and unsentimental book, written with brutal honesty and having much to say not only about Billie Holiday, the person, but about what it means to be poor and black in America." N Y Her Trib Books
Includes discography

Holmes, Rachel

★ **African** queen; the real life of the Hottentot Venus. Random House 2007 161p il $23.95 **92**

1. Biography, Individual 2. Entertainers

ISBN 978-1-4000-6136-5; 1-4000-6136-9

LC 2006-45166

"This is a probing look at historical racism and sexual exploitation presented through the life of an extraordinary woman." Booklist

Includes bibliographical references

Holroyd, Michael

A **strange** eventful history; the dramatic lives of Ellen Terry, Henry Irving and their remarkable families. Farrar Straus Giroux 2009 620p $40 **92**

1. Actors 2. Biography, Collective 3. Set designers 4. Theater -- Great Britain -- History -- 19th century 5. Theater -- Great Britain -- History -- 20th century 6. Theatrical directors 7. Theatrical producers 8. Writers on theater

ISBN 978-0-374-27080-3; 0-374-27080-5

LC 2008-48330

"Holroyd's sweeping group biography traces the lives of Ellen Terry and Henry Irving, two stars of the Victorian theatre, and their descendants. Terry was 'embodied sunshine,' beloved for her naturalness and grace onstage. In 1878, when she was thirty-one, she began a professional (and perhaps amorous) partnership with Irving, the despotic actor-manager of the Lyceum Theatre, in London. . . . The pair rose to international fame performing melodramas and Shakespeare abridgments. Both had children who attempted careers in the theatre, and the second half of the book dwells on their struggles amid their parents' decline." New Yorker

Holton, Woody

Abigail Adams; a life. Free Press 2009 483p il map $30 **92**

1. Biography, Individual 2. Parents of presidents 3. Presidents 4. Presidents' spouses -- United States 5. Spouses of presidents 6. Vice-presidents 7. Women in politics -- United States -- History -- 18th century

ISBN 978-1-4165-4680-1; 1-4165-4680-4

LC 2009016288

This is a "reinterpretation of Adams's life story and of women's roles in the creation of the republic." (Publisher's note) Index.

"Holton's superb biography shows us a three-dimensional Adams as a forward-thinking woman with a mind of her own." Publ Wkly

Includes bibliographical references

Holzer, Harold

Lincoln president-elect; Abraham Lincoln and the great secession winter 1860-1861. Simon & Schuster 2008 623p il $30 **92**

1. Biography, Individual 2. Lawyers 3. Members of Congress 4. Presidents 5. Presidents -- United States 6. State legislators

ISBN 978-0-7432-8947-4; 0-7432-8947-1

LC 2008-21520

"This excellent study fills a gap about which not much has been written in Lincoln's presidential career." Choice

Includes bibliographical references

Homes, A. M.

The **mistress's** daughter. Viking 2007 238p il $24.95 **92**

1. Authors 2. Biography, Individual 3. Novelists 4. Short story writers

ISBN 978-0-670-03838-1; 0-670-03838-5

LC 2006-41354

"Though the quest seems, at times, overwrought as Homes searches for meaning and connection where there may not be any, the writing is consistently controlled and knowing. . . . Though Homes gives away some of her mystery with this book, she will gain further respect as a writer." Seattle Times

Honan, Park

★ **Christopher** Marlowe; poet & spy. Oxford University Press 2005 421p il $32.50 **92**

1. Authors 2. Biography, Individual 3. Dramatists 4. Dramatists, English

ISBN 0-19-818695-9

LC 2005-19761

This is a biography of the sixteenth-century English dramatist.

The author "sheds light on the much-speculated (and previously erroneously reported) aspects of Marlowe's life without neglecting its more ordinary features (his stable two-parent upbringing, his diligent scholarship at Cambridge) or destroying the poet's aura of intrigue." Publ Wkly

Includes bibliographical references

Honig, Donald

The **fifth** season; tales of my life in baseball. Ivan R. Dee 2009 287p $26.95 **92**

1. Authors 2. Baseball -- Biography 3. Historians 4. Mystery writers 5. Novelists 6. Short story writers 7. Sportswriters

ISBN 978-1-56663-810-4; 1-56663-810-0

LC 2008-36471

"Honig gives us a lyrical account of growing up in New York City besotted with baseball, his own abbreviated pitching career, and his passion for the greats and near-greats of the game. This nuanced, pitch-perfect memoir will make readers appreciate the nuances and permutations of the game itself. Stats, salary statistics, and free-agent greed are (thankfully) absent, replaced by warm recitations of bygone games and now-departed characters both on the field and off." Libr J

Hood, Ann

Comfort; a journey through grief. W. W. Norton & Co. 2008 188p $19.95 **92**

1. Authors 2. Bereavement 3. Death 4. Loss (Psychology) 5. Novelists 6. Short story writers

ISBN 978-0-393-06456-8

LC 2008-1310

"Ann Hood has written about her little girl's death. Grace died on April 18, 2002, from a virulent form of strep. She was 5 years old. One morning she was there and the next she was gone, leaving her tights on the floor and her leopard-print rain boots in the hall and her hat with the pompom on a hook by the door. . . . What makes this book so different from other such memoirs is that it seems to be taking place in real time. Hood doesn't cut us any slack. Even Joan Didion, grieving the loss of her husband and her daughter's illness in 'The Year of Magical Thinking,' held back from the brink, retreated into her vast intellect. Hood will not retreat." Los Angeles Times Book Rev

Hooks, Bell
Belonging; a culture of place. Routledge 2008 230p $95; pa $19.95   **92**
1. African American authors 2. African American farmers -- History 3. African Americans -- Social conditions 4. Authors 5. Children's authors 6. College teachers 7. Country life -- Kentucky 8. Dramatists 9. Essayists 10. Feminists 11. Home 12. Memoirists 13. Nonfiction writers 14. Poets 15. Social critics 16. Women authors
ISBN 978-0-415-96815-7; 978-0-415-96816-4 pa
LC 2008-21846
The author "writes about the solace she found as a girl in the hills of Kentucky, her long years away, and her return, which has inspired a fresh look at the self-reliant communities of black Appalachians and their nurturing connection to the land." Booklist
Includes bibliographical references

Wounds of passion; a writing life. Holt & Co. 1997 xxiii, 260p hardcover o.p. pa $13   **92**
1. Authors 2. Biography, Individual 3. Children's authors 4. College teachers 5. Dramatists 6. Essayists 7. Feminists 8. Memoirists 9. Nonfiction writers 10. Poets 11. Social critics
ISBN 0-8050-5722-6 pa
LC 97-23506
In this continuation of the author's autobiography, Hooks chronicles "her rigorous education, both in a long, complicated relationship with a fellow writer and as a college and graduate student, experiences that led her away from poetry (her first literary love) to groundbreaking prose that expressed her feminist convictions and views on the status of black women in America." Booklist

Hopkins, Jerry
No one here gets out alive; by Jerry Hopkins and Daniel Sugerman. Warner Bks. 1980 387p il hardcover o.p. pa $7.99   **92**
1. Rock musicians 2. Singers 3. Songwriters
ISBN 0-446-60228-0 pa
LC 79-26611
This biography of rock musician Jim Morrison gives "an idea of how profoundly Morrison, as lyricist and lead singer of the Doors, affected the youth of America in the late 1960s. . . . The book includes a list of the Doors' records, books, and films." Booklist

Horwitz, Tony
★ **Midnight** rising; John Brown and raid that sparked the Civil War. Henry Holt and Co. 2011 365p il map $29; ebook $12.99   **92**
1. Abolitionists 2. Pioneers
ISBN 978-0-8050-9153-3; 0-8050-9153-X; 978-1-4299-9698-3 ebook; 1-4299-9698-6 ebook
LC 2011015659
The author presents a "narrative of Brown and the raid on Harpers Ferry that in many ways set the stage for Southern secession and civil war. . . . Horwitz's Brown did not die in vain. By recalling the drama that fired the imagination and fears of Brown's time, Midnight Rising calls readers to account for complacency about social injustices today. This is a book for our time." Libr J
Includes bibliographical references

Hoskyns, Barney
Lowside of the road; a life of Tom Waits. Broadway Books 2009 xxix, 609p il $29.95   **92**
1. Actors 2. Biography, Individual 3. Blues musicians 4. Rock musicians 5. Singers 6. Songwriters
ISBN 978-0-7679-2708-6; 0-7679-2708-7
This "book lights up and whirls like one of the greasy carnival rides in Mr. Waits's own sprawling oeuvre . . . Mr. Hoskyns rummaged through Mr. Waits's interviews, pored through the historical record and talked to those who were willing to speak. Thus his unauthorized biography mirrors, in some ways, Mr. Waits's own junkyard aesthetic. Mr. Hoskyns picks up what shards of Mr. Waits's life he can find and holds them to the light, turning them eagerly in his hands." N Y Times Book Rev

Hough, Richard Alexander
Captain James Cook; {by} Richard Hough. Norton 1995 398p il hardcover o.p. pa $18.95 **92**
1. Explorers 2. Naval officers 3. Travel writers
ISBN 0-393-31519-3 pa
LC 94-35998
"Hough's easygoing, thorough treatment . . . spotlights a proud, determined man." Booklist
Includes bibliographical references

Hough, Susan Elizabeth
Richter's scale; measure of an earthquake, measure of a man. Princeton University Press 2007 335p il $27.95   **92**
1. Biography, Individual 2. College teachers 3. Earthquakes 4. Richter scale 5. Scientists 6. Seismologists 7. Seismology
ISBN 978-0-691-12807-8; 0-691-12807-3
LC 2006-16480
"The discussions of the effects of earthquakes on land, structures, and people and the intense search for an understanding of the complex, underlying science will be of interest to many. Readers with substantially different levels of scientific knowledge will find the book comprehensible and interesting." Sci Books Films
Includes bibliographical references (p. 231-240)

Houze, David

★ **Twilight** people; one man's journey to find his roots. University of California Press 2006 329p il $24.95 **92**

1. African Americans -- Civil rights 2. Apartheid 3. Journalists 4. Memoirists

ISBN 0-520-24398-6; 978-0-520-24398-9

LC 2005-35322

This "graceful memoir is a sensitive look into racial history in Africa and America, as well as a riveting personal narrative." Publ Wkly

Includes bibliographical references

Howard, Johnette

The **rivals**; Chris Evert vs. Martina Navratilova: their epic duels and extraordinary friendship. Broadway Books 2005 296p il $24.95 **92**

1. Biography, Individual 2. Tennis -- Biography 3. Tennis players

ISBN 0-7679-1884-3

LC 2004-61918

"This work makes a fine contribution to the history of women in sports." Publ Wkly

Howe, Ben Ryder

My **Korean** deli; risking it all for a convenience store. Henry Holt and Co. 2010 304p $25 **92**

1. Biography, Individual 2. Convenience stores 3. Convenience stores -- New York (N.Y.) 4. Editors 5. Korean Americans 6. Small business owners

ISBN 978-0-8050-9343-8; 0-8050-9343-5

LC 2010-24962

The author's "wife Gab bought (with the money the couple had saved for a down payment on their first house) her hardworking Korean parents a deli in Brooklyn as a gesture of thanks for all their self-sacrifice. What follows is a series of both comic and tragic vignettes that will leave the reader as surprised as the author about how emotionally invested you can get in a deli. . . . [Howe] delivers a smartly written narrative about love, literature, and the lengths one goes to for family, which turns out to be epically far." Maclean's

Howell, Georgina

Gertrude Bell; queen of the desert, shaper of nations. Farrar, Straus and Giroux 2007 481p il map hardcover o.p. pa $16 **92**

1. Archaeologists 2. Archeologists 3. Biography, Individual 4. Explorers 5. Travelers 6. Women -- Travel

ISBN 978-0-374-16162-0; 0-374-16162-3; 978-0-374-53135-5 pa; 0-374-53135-8 pa

LC 2006-29994

This is a biography of the British archaeologist and author of Desert and the Sown (1907) and Persian Pictures (1928).

"Bell's role in the creation of Iraq and the placement of Faisal upon the throne, is fully detailed. . . . But the strength and delight of Howell's superb biography is in the fullness with which Bell's character is drawn." Publ Wkly

Includes bibliographical references

Hudson, Mark

Titian; the last days. Walker 2009 304p il $27 **92**

1. Artists 2. Artists, French 3. Painters 4. Painting, Italian

ISBN 978-0-8027-1076-5; 0-8027-1076-X

"At the time of his death—from plague, in Venice in 1576—Titian had been one of the most celebrated artists in Europe for most of the century, the revered portrait painter of popes, emperors, and kings. But in his final works, as plague swept Venice, Titian, then in his mid-eighties, began confronting darker themes, including his own mortality. Hudson focusses his book on this group of paintings, now largely lost, and discusses Titian's career with humor, enlivening a potentially staid subject." New Yorker

Hughes, Bettany

★ The **hemlock** cup; Socrates, Athens, and the search for the good life. Alfred A. Knopf 2011 484p il map $35 **92**

1. Biography, Individual 2. Philosophers

ISBN 978-1-4000-4179-4; 1-4000-4179-1

LC 2010-45486

"For decades, while his city underwent war and hardship and defeat and civil war and political restructuring, Socrates settled himself in the agora and talked of inner things, the essence of things. Some of his words were taken down by acolytes such as Plato and Xenophon; some of his mannerisms were mocked by playwrights such as Aristophanes; the master himself, a man Hughes claims 'we can all benefit from getting to know a little better,' wrote nothing, but his recorded dialogues, his 'Socratic method' of relentless questioning, have become indispensable pieces of our Western mental furniture. Hughes revisits all of this with the panache of a born explainer, enthusiastically filling out the world of ancient Athens. . . . She takes readers through the torturous birth and early crises of Athenian democracy, and she's refreshingly evenhanded about the resentment such a democracy might feel toward somebody like Socrates." Washington Post

Includes bibliographical (p. 438-472) references

Hughes, Robert

★ **Things** I didn't know; a memoir. Knopf 2006 395p $27.95 **92**

1. Art critics 2. Biography, Individual 3. Nonfiction writers

ISBN 1-4000-4444-8; 978-1-4000-4444-3

LC 2006-40968

This is a memoir by the author of Heaven and Hell in Western Art (1968), The Shock of the New, and The Culture of Complaint (1993).

"Hughes's vivid ruminations and sharp-eyed insights combine in bold, definitive strokes to yield a rich portrait of the art expert." Publ Wkly

Humbert, Agnes

Resistance; a woman's journal of struggle and defiance in occupied France. Bloomsbury 2008 370p il $26 **92**

1. Art historians 2. Underground leaders 3. World War, 1939-1945 -- Personal narratives 4. World War, 1939-

1945 -- Prisoners and prisons 5. World War, 1939-1945
-- Underground movements
ISBN 978-1-59691-559-6; 1-59691-559-5

LC 2008-16603

"Humbert's firsthand account of her work for the resistance in occupied Paris and her subsequent arrest and deportation to a forced-labor camp in Germany is an invaluable addition to works highlighting the role of women during wartime." Publ Wkly

Includes bibliographical references

Humez, Jean McMahon

Harriet Tubman; the life and the life stories. [by] Jean M. Humez. University of Wisconsin Press 2004 471p il hardcover o.p. pa $21.95 **92**
1. Abolitionists 2. African American women 3. African American women -- Biography 4. African Americans -- History 5. Underground railroad
ISBN 0-299-19120-6; 0-299-19124-9 pa

LC 2003-5676

In this volume the author "includes a collection of Tubman's autobiographical stories culled from rare early publications and manuscript sources. This book will become an important resource for scholars, historians, and general readers interested in slavery, the Underground Railroad, the Civil War, and African American women." Univ Press Books for Public and Second Sch Libr, 2004

Includes bibliographical references

Hunt, Tristram

Marx's general; the revolutionary life of Friedrich Engels. Metropolitan Books 2009 430p il $32 **92**
1. Biography, Individual 2. Political and social philosophers
ISBN 978-0-8050-8025-4; 0-8050-8025-2

LC 2009-03845

"A useful and well-done study of Engels and the radical epoch he helped create." Booklist

Includes bibliographical references

Hunter, Michael

Boyle; between God and science. Yale University Press 2009 366p il **92**
1. Biography, Individual 2. Chemists 3. Nonfiction writers 4. Physicists 5. Religion and science 6. Religion and science -- England -- History -- 17th century 7. Scientists 8. Writers on science
ISBN 0-300-12381-7; 9780300123814

LC 2009-13997

This is a biography of the seventeenth-century natural philosopher and scientist. Index.

"This painstakingly researched biography of the seventeenth-century scientist Robert Boyle outlines a life in which 'science and theology were truly complementary' but not always in harmony. Best known for Boyle's law, which established a constant relationship between air's volume and its pressure, Boyle was a moralist from a privileged upbringing whose conception of science—both of its empirical basis and of its transformative potential for mankind—was far ahead of its time." New Yorker

Includes bibliographical references

Hurston, Zora Neale

★ **Dust** tracks on a road; an autobiography. with a foreword by Maya Angelou. 1st Harper Perennial Modern Classic ed; Harper Perennial Modern Classics 2006 308p il pa $13.95 **92**
1. African American authors 2. African American women -- Biography 3. Authors 4. Dramatists 5. Folklorists 6. Memoirists 7. Novelists 8. Short story writers
ISBN 0-06-085408-1; 978-0-06-085408-9

LC 2005-52616

The author describes her wanderings in and out of schools and jobs as a young girl, finishing her course work at Barnard, and beginning her life's work.

Zora Neale Hurston: a life in letters; collected and edited by Carla Kaplan. Doubleday 2002 880p il $40; pa $19.95 **92**
1. African American authors 2. African American women -- Biography 3. Authors 4. Dramatists 5. Folklorists 6. Memoirists 7. Novelists 8. Short story writers
ISBN 0-385-49035-6; 0-385-49036-4 pa

LC 00-65671

A collection of over 500 letters by the Harlem Renaissance author.

These letters reveal "a gifted yet complex personality at once humorous, cynical, and analytical." Libr J

Includes bibliographical references

Hustvedt, Siri

The **shaking** woman; or, A history of my nerves. Henry Holt 2010 224p $23 **92**
1. Authors 2. Biography, Individual 3. Convulsions -- Diagnosis 4. Novelists
ISBN 978-0-8050-9169-4; 0-8050-9169-6

LC 2009-15385

Hustvedt "investigates the reason(s) she suddenly began shuddering violently while delivering a memorial talk about her father, more than two years after his death. The author pursues her symptoms with Javertian devotion. . . She read voraciously, attended lectures on brain science, visited a variety of medical and psychological specialists, underwent examinations and MRIs and took drugs. She also ruminated excessively. The result is a narrative that is alternately transparent and scientifically dense, frustrating and satisfying, conclusive and vague. . . . Self-absorption can be grating in memoirs by lesser writers; in Hustvedt's capable hands, it opens a door to revelation." Kirkus

Hutchinson, George

In search of Nella Larsen; a biography of the color line. Belknap Press of Harvard University Press 2006 611p il $39.95 **92**
1. Authors 2. Biography, Individual 3. Novelists 4. Nurses 5. Short story writers
ISBN 0-674-02180-0; 978-0-674-02180-8

LC 2005-58129

This is a biography of the author of Quicksand (1928) and Passing (1929).

The author "has produced what must be the definitive biography of Larsen. It's hard to think of a stone he hasn't looked under in his quest to establish the facts, correct mistakes and trace her private life. But Hutchinson's biography also manages to be an insightful reconsideration of a much-studied period in American literature and black cultural history." Nation

Includes bibliographical references

Huxtable, Ada Louise

★ **Frank** Lloyd Wright. Lipper\Viking 2004 251p il $19.95 **92**

1. Architects 2. Biography, Individual 3. Nonfiction writers

ISBN 0-670-03342-1

LC 2004-46477

"The eventfulness of the extraordinary life and the refreshing intelligence and craft of the author make this book a pleasure to read. That I found myself on occasion arguing with the text only proves the provocative quality of Huxtable's exploration." N Y Times Book Rev

Ian, Janis

Society's child; my autobiography. Jeremy P. Tarcher/Penguin 2008 xxii, 361p il $26.95 **92**

1. Singers

ISBN 978-1-58542-675-1

LC 2008-17130

This is a memoir by the American folk singer.

"Fans will love the book, of course, but many nonfans, too, should find this painfully candid memoir hard to put down." Booklist

Includes bibliographical references

Ice-T

Ice; a memoir of gangster life and redemption --from South Central to Hollywood. [by] Ice-T and Douglas Century. One World Books 2011 251p il $25; ebook $12.99 **92**

1. Actors 2. African American musicians 3. Biography, Individual 4. Rap music 5. Rap musicians

ISBN 978-0-345-52328-0; 978-0-345-52330-3 ebook

LC 2010-41069

"A fascinating and inspiring story about an African American orphan who beat the odds to become successful, this memoir will appeal to fans of hip-hop and popular culture." Booklist

Imber, Gerald

Genius on the edge; the bizarre story of William Stewart Halsted, the father of modern surgery. Kaplan Pub. 2010 389p il $25.95 **92**

1. Biography, Individual 2. Drug abuse 3. Surgeons 4. Writers on medicine

ISBN 978-1-60714-627-8; 1-60714-627-4

LC 2009-35525

This biography of William Halsted is in "many ways . . . a history of medicine/surgery in America. Halsted was very influential in bringing aseptic techniques to surgery and introduced the residency training system. He used his knowledge of anatomy to improve surgical technique. He performed the first successful hernia repair and radical mastectomy for breast cancer. Early in his career Halsted became addicted to cocaine while experimenting with the

drug for use as a local anesthetic. Treatment at the time, involved substituting morphine for cocaine. Halsted spent 40 years of his life struggling with his addiction to both cocaine and morphine. . . . You don't need to be a surgeon to appreciate this book. You only need to have a love of history." Better Health

Inaba, Mitsutoshi

Willie Dixon; preacher of the blues. Scarecrow Press 2011 xxxi, 445p il $55; ebook $57.99 **92**

1. African American musicians 2. Blues music -- History and criticism 3. Blues musicians 4. Singers

ISBN 978-0-8108-6993-6; 978-0-8108-6994-3 ebook

LC 2009033237

"This exhaustive biography and analysis of Dixon's music, the most comprehensive study of Dixon's life and work available, features extensive references, many details drawn from interviews, an analysis of Dixon's composition and studio methods, and a complete discography. Inaba . . . tells the story of Dixon's life, from his 1915 birth in Vicksburg, Mississippi, through his childhood in an impoverished area blemished further by racism, to his adulthood in Chicago as a boxer and musician. . . . From the Big Three Trio to Dixon's highly productive years with Chess Records to finally, his own Blues Factory studio, Inaba traces and comments on the significance of Dixon's lasting imprint on music." Publ Wkly

Includes discography and bibliographical references

Isaacson, Walter

Benjamin Franklin; an American life. Simon & Schuster 2003 590p il $30; pa $16.95 **92**

1. Authors 2. Diplomats 3. Inventors 4. Members of Congress 5. Scientists 6. Statesmen 7. Statesmen -- United States 8. Writers on science

ISBN 0-684-80761-0; 0-7432-5807-X pa

LC 2003-50463

This "is a thoroughly researched, crisply written, convincingly argued chronicle that is also studded with little nuggets of fresh information." N Y Times Book Rev

Includes bibliographical references

★ **Einstein** : his life and universe. Simon & Schuster 2007 xxii, 675p il hardcover o.p. pa $17.95 **92**

1. Nobel laureates for physics 2. Physicists

ISBN 978-0-7432-6473-0; 0-7432-6473-8; 978-0-7432-6474-7 pa; 0-7432-6474-6 pa

LC 2006-51264

This book tells the story of the German-American physicist's life.

"This is a warm, insightful, affectionate portrait with a human and immensely charming Einstein at its core." N Y Times (Late N Y Ed)

Includes bibliographical references

Isenberg, Barbara

Conversations with Frank Gehry. Alfred A. Knopf 2009 290p il map $40 **92**

1. Architects 2. Biography, Individual

ISBN 978-0-307-26800-6; 0-307-26800-4

LC 2008-47616

This book "brings together in one book a series of candid interviews that the accomplished Isenberg recorded between 2004 and 2008, embracing Gehry's entire life and career, comprising a kind of verbal autobiography. . . . This very accessible, readable volume will be a gold mine for scholars and the general public for generations." Libr J

Israel, Paul

★ **Edison**; a life of invention. Wiley 1998 552p il $50; pa $18.95 **92**
1. Inventors
ISBN 0-471-52942-7; 0-471-36270-0 pa
LC 98-10105
This biography focuses on Edison's technical work, experiments, and business dealings.

"Dozens of facsimiles of his original drawings are reproduced, which fortify the impression of Edison's meticulousness, as do Israel's accounts of his business ventures." Booklist
Includes bibliographical references

Iyer, Pico

★ The **open** road; the global journey of the fourteenth Dalai Lama. Bloomsbury 2008 288p $24 **92**
1. Biography, Individual 2. Buddhist leaders 3. Nobel laureates for peace 4. Political leaders
ISBN 978-0-307-26760-3; 0-307-26760-1
LC 2007-43991
"The combination of Iyer's exacting observations, incisive analysis, and frank respect for the unknowable results in a uniquely internalized, even empathic portrait of one of the world's most embraced and least understood guiding lights." Booklist
Includes bibliographical references

Jackson, Blair

Garcia; an American life. Viking 1999 497p hardcover o.p. $18 **92**
1. Guitarists 2. Rock musicians 3. Rock musicians -- United States -- Biography 4. Singers
ISBN 978-0-14-029199-5; 0-14-029199-7
LC 99-28775
"Jackson has written a wonderful account of the beginnings of the band . . . in the mid-1960's, their relationship with Ken Kesey and his Merry Pranksters, their embrace of psychedelic drugs and the adoration and obsession of Deadheads throughout the country." N Y Times Book Rev
Includes bibliographical references

Jackson, Carlton

Hattie: the life of Hattie McDaniel. Madison Bks. 1989 220p il hardcover o.p. pa $12.95 **92**
1. Actors
ISBN 1-56833-004-9 pa
LC 89-30903
"For those of us who knew her only as 'Mammy' in Gone with the Wind, Hattie McDaniel's life story holds lots of surprises. She was also a singer, songwriter, and radio, stage, and TV performer. With an anecdotal style, the author clears up a lot of errors concerning her career." Booklist
Includes bibliographical references

Jackson, Troy

Becoming King; Martin Luther King, Jr. and the making of a national leader. introduction by Clayborne Carson. University Press of Kentucky 2008 248p $35 **92**
1. African Americans -- Civil rights 2. African Americans -- Civil rights -- Alabama 3. African Americans -- Civil rights -- Alabama -- Montgomery 4. Biography, Individual 5. Civil rights activists 6. Civil rights movements -- Alabama -- Montgomery -- History -- 20th century 7. Clergy 8. Nobel laureates for peace 9. Nonfiction writers 10. Segregation in transportation -- Alabama -- Montgomery -- History -- 20th century
ISBN 978-0-8131-2520-6; 0-8131-2520-0
LC 2008-25041
"The author's comprehensive analysis of King's sermons before, during and after the boycott artfully depicts a man in transition, from naive do-gooder to world-changer. Jackson's treatment of Montgomery in the post-boycott era offers new insight into the void in leadership and the fractious infighting among the movement's luminaries after King departed the scene. An informed investigation of the struggles that defined a time and place--and the man who gave them a voice." Kirkus
Includes bibliographical references (p. 229-239) and index.

Jacob, Kathryn Allamong

King of the lobby; the life and times of Sam Ward, man-about-Washington in the Gilded Age. Johns Hopkins University Press 2010 212p il $40 **92**
1. Lobbying 2. Lobbyists
ISBN 978-0-8018-9397-1; 0-8018-9397-6
LC 2009-9807
The author's "trim and surprising biography of Sam Ward . . . will not change most people's view of what is essentially a hustler's profession. But she brilliantly shows how, in the hands of a master, lobbying can be lifted to the level of art." Wall Street J
Includes bibliographical references

Jacobson, Sidney

Anne Frank; the Anne Frank House authorized graphic biography. [by] Sid Jacobson and Ernie Colón. Hill and Wang 2010 152p il $30; pa $16.95 **92**
1. Biographical graphic novels 2. Children 3. Diarists 4. Graphic novels 5. Holocaust victims 6. Holocaust, 1933-1945 -- Graphic novels 7. Jews -- Netherlands -- Graphic novels 8. World War, 1939-1945 -- Jews -- Graphic novels
ISBN 978-0-8090-2684-5; 978-0-8090-2685-2 pa
LC 2010-5776
"Panel arrangements effectively show simultaneous events happening in the life of the family and in the world, while brief 'snapshots' provide enough historical information to make motives, fears, and expectations sensible to anyone unfamiliar with the Holocaust's machinery. More than simply poignant, this biography elucidates the complex emotional aspects of living a sequestered adolescence as a brilliant, budding writer." Booklist
Includes bibliographical references

Jaffrey, Madhur

Climbing the mango trees; a memoir of a child-hood in India. Knopf 2006 297p il $25   **92**
1. Actors 2. Biography, Individual 3. Cookbook writers
ISBN 1-4000-4295-X; 978-1-4000-4295-1
LC 2006-45255

This is the memoir by the Indian actress and cookbook author.

The author's "taste memories sparkle with enthusiasm, and her talent for conveying them makes the book relentlessly appetizing." N Y Times Book Rev

James, Eloisa

★ **Paris** in love; a memoir. Eloisa James. Random House 2012 x, 260 p.p   **92**
1. Americans -- France -- Paris -- Biography 2. Authors, American -- Biography 3. Cancer -- Patients -- Biography 4. Life change events 5. Quality of life -- France -- Paris 6. Self-actualization (Psychology) 7. Women authors, American -- Biography
ISBN 9780679604440; 9781400069569; 0679604448; 1400069564
LC 2011040662

This expatriate memoir by Eloisa James tells how in 2009, [the] . . . author . . . sold her house, took a sabbatical from her job as a Shakespeare professor, and moved her family to Paris. [The story} chronicles her joyful year . . . [w]ith no classes to teach, no committee meetings to attend, no lawn to mow or cars to park, Eloisa revels in the ordinary pleasures of life . . . She copes with her Italian husband's notions of quality time; her two hilarious children, ages eleven and fifteen, as they navigate schools—not to mention puberty—in a foreign language; and her mother-in-law Marina's raised eyebrow in the kitchen (even as Marina overfeeds Milo, the family dog). (Publishers note)

James, Etta

Rage to survive; the Etta James story. [by] Etta James with David Ritz. Da Capo Press 2003 288p il pa $18   **92**
1. Blues musicians 2. Singers 3. Singers -- United States 4. Songwriters 5. Soul musicians
ISBN 0-306-81262-2; 978-0-306-81262-0

"With a supporting cast resembling the roster of the Rock Hall of Fame, this autobiography reads as its author sings-rough, gritty, and brutally honest." Libr J
Discography

James, Jamie

The **snake** charmer; a life and death in pursuit of knowledge. Hyperion 2008 260p il $24.95   **92**
1. Biography, Individual 2. Curators 3. Herpetologists 4. Herpetology 5. Snakes
ISBN 978-1-4013-0213-9; 1-4013-0213-0
LC 2007-48987

James recounts "the gritty and sad story of Joe Slowinski, a flamboyant and well-known herpetologist who died in Burma in 2001, aged 38, from the poisonous bite of a krait snake. . . . This book is both a tribute to Slowinski's spirit and scientific accomplishments, and a cautionary tale about the dangers of an overly passionate ambition." Publ Wkly

Jamison, Kay R.

Nothing was the same; a memoir. by Kay Redfield Jamison. Alfred A. Knopf 2009 208p $25   **92**
1. Bereavement 2. Biography, Individual 3. College teachers 4. Hodgkin's disease 5. Manic-depressive illness 6. Psychiatrists 7. Psychologists
ISBN 978-0-307-26537-1; 0-307-26537-4
LC 2009-11096

"The great gift Jamison offers here, beyond her honesty and the beauty of her writing, is perspective: a clear-eyed view of illness and death, sanity and insanity, love and grief. . . . Jamison seems to be telling the truth, no matter how difficult it may be, in a way that avoids self-pity and inspires courage." Washington Post Book World

Jeal, Tim

Stanley; the impossible life of Africa's greatest explorer. Yale University Press 2007 570p il map $38   **92**
1. Explorers 2. Journalists 3. Travel writers
ISBN 978-0-300-12625-9; 0-300-12625-5
LC 2007-923548

This is a biography of the explorer.

"There have been many biographies of Stanley, but Jeal's is the most felicitous, the best informed, the most complete and readable and exhaustive." N Y Times Book Rev
Includes bibliographical references

Jenkins, Charles Robert

The **reluctant** communist; my desertion, court-martial, and forty-year imprisonment in North Korea. with Jim Frederick. University of California Press 2008 xxxvi, 192p il $24.95; pa $15.95   **92**
1. Defectors 2. Military deserters 3. Military desertion -- United States
ISBN 978-0-520-25333-9; 0-520-25333-7; 978-0-520-25999-7 pa; 0-520-25999-8 pa
LC 2007-33315

This "book is one of the most important and devastating accounts of life inside a totalitarian society to appear in many years." Commentary

Johnson, George

Miss Leavitt's stars; the untold story of the woman who discovered how to measure the universe. W. W. Norton 2005 162p il $22.95   **92**
1. Astronomers 2. Biography, Individual 3. Photometrists
ISBN 0-393-05128-5
LC 2005-02823

This is a biography of the American astronomer whose research concerned the measuring of distance in space.

This book is "a fine tribute to a remarkable woman of science." Publ Wkly
Includes bibliographical references

Johnson, Harriet McBryde

Too late to die young; nearly true tales from a life. Henry Holt and Co. 2005 261p $23; pa $14 **92**
1. Human rights activists 2. Lawyers
ISBN 0-8050-7594-1; 0-312-42571-6 pa
LC 2004-54007

In this memoir, the wheelchair-bound lawyer and activist describes her battles for disability rights.

"From her first demonstration against the MDA telethon to her celebrated debate with Peter Singer of Harvard, who has stated that killing a disabled infant is not morally equivalent to killing a person, this lady pulls no punches. An entertaining look at an activist who insists on living life her way, disability or no." Libr J

Johnson, Paul

Churchill. Viking 2009 181p il $24.95 **92**
1. Biography, Individual 2. Cabinet members 3. Historians 4. Members of Parliament 5. Memoirists 6. Nobel laureates for literature 7. Prime ministers 8. Prime ministers -- Great Britain 9. Statesmen 10. World war, 1939-1945 -- Great Britain
ISBN 978-0-670-02105-5; 0-670-02105-9
LC 2009-08326

"From his beginnings as a youthful war correspondent, to his mature political career, to his hobbies of landscape painting and bricklaying, no aspect of Churchill's life is ignored. . . . An overview of Churchill's life that instructs rather than awes is Johnson's great achievement." New Criterion
Includes bibliographical references

George Washington: the Founding Father. HarperCollins Publishers 2005 126p $19.95 **92**
1. Generals 2. Presidents 3. Presidents -- United States
ISBN 0-06-075365-X
LC 2004-52907

This is a biography of the first president of the United States.

The author "submits a beautifully cogent, enthrallingly perceptive, and . . . startlingly fresh take on the ultimate American icon." Booklist
Includes bibliographical references

Johnson, Paul, 1928-

Socrates; a man for our times. Viking 2011 208p $25.95 **92**
1. Philosophers
ISBN 978-0-670-02303-5
LC 2011019767

"A succinct, useful exploration of life in ancient Athens and of the great philosopher's essential beliefs." Kirkus
Includes bibliographical references

Johnson, Steven

The **invention** of air; a story of science, faith, revolution, and the birth of America. Riverhead Books 2008 254p il $25.95 **92**
1. Biography, Individual 2. Chemists 3. Clergy 4. Scientists 5. Writers on science
ISBN 978-1-59448-852-8; 1-59448-852-5
LC 2008-46101

"What enlivens the book is that Johnson does not simply describe the system within which Priestley and his contemporaries hashed out the features of classical science; he sets it against other, later systems for comprehending physical reality, showing laymen how far we have come from the classical age of science." N Y Times Book Rev
Includes bibliographical references

Johnson-Sirleaf, Ellen

This child will be great; memoir of a remarkable life by Africa's first woman president. HarperCollins 2009 353p il $26.99 **92**
1. Biography, Individual 2. Cabinet members 3. Economists 4. Nobel laureates for peace 5. Political leaders 6. Presidents 7. Presidents -- Liberia
ISBN 978-0-06-135347-5

"An inspiring inside look at a nation struggling to rebuild itself and the woman now behind those efforts." Booklist
Includes bibliographical references

Jones, Judith

The **tenth** muse; my life in food. Alfred A. Knopf 2007 290p il $24.95 **92**
1. Cooks 2. Editors
ISBN 0-307-26495-5; 978-0-307-26495-4
LC 2007-6789

The author "recounts experiences that food and book lovers will admire and envy." Booklist
Includes bibliographical references

Jones, Malcolm

Little boy blues; a crash course in growing up. Pantheon Books 2010 228p il map $24.95 **92**
1. Biography, Individual 2. Journalists 3. Magazine editors
ISBN 978-0-307-37772-2; 0-307-37772-5
LC 2009-17838

"In the background of this memoir, the South also complicates the child's horizon, with its own coded vocabulary, reprimanding glances and generations clinging to a crumbling way of life. . . . With all the hype, marketing and lying that the genre's been subjected to in recent years, I had forgotten that it is also the most vulnerable, intimate form a writer can employ. Often, this gets covered over in support-speak: the way a writer's memories turn into a way to help alleviate the pain of others suffering from similar memories. Jones is far too good a writer to indulge in messianic messages." PopMatters

Jones, Quincy

Q: the autobiography of Quincy Jones. Doubleday 2001 412p il $26; pa $15.95 **92**
1. Composers 2. Conductors (Music) 3. Music arrangers 4. Recording producers
ISBN 0-385-48896-3; 0-7679-0510-5 pa
LC 2001-28151

"With some chapters written by Jones, and others by his family and friends . . . this (auto)biography full of behind-the-scenes anecdotes has an improvisational feel that suits its subject: a jazz musician and superstar composer. . . .

Jones has composed a life story that gives much more than the typical celebrity memoir." Publ Wkly

Includes discography and filmography

Jordan, Mary

The **prison** angel; Mother Antonia's journey from Beverly Hills to a life of service in a Mexican jail. [by] Mary Jordan and Kevin Sullivan. Penguin Press 2005 237p il $24.95   **92**

1. Nuns

ISBN 1-59420-056-4

LC 2004-60238

The authors describe the "journey of a woman who, at the age of 50, left the comforts of suburban L.A. to begin a charity mission in Mexico. . . . This is an inspiring story of one woman's compassion and her own journey of spiritual growth." Booklist

Judt, Tony, 1948-2010

The **memory** chalet. Penguin Press 2010 226p $25.95   **92**

1. Authors, English 2. College teachers 3. Historians 4. Modern civilization 5. Nonfiction writers 6. World history -- 20th century

ISBN 978-1-59420-289-6; 1-59420-289-3

LC 2010-283600

The book "is a memoir . . . [consisting of] essay[s that] bring . . . the smallest details of personal experience into the larger frame of history. Judt's youthful love of a London bus route becomes a reflection on public civility. . . . Judt takes us from the postwar London of his childhood through Paris, Prague, and points east to New York, where he found his home. Judt [discusses] . . . everything from fast cars to radical politics and, finally, the devastating illness that took his life. This book, composed when Judt was paralyzed and unable physically to write, found its shape in the ordered rooms of a Swiss Chalet of the mind: a warm refuge in the closing darkness of his final years." (Publisher's note)

This "is a book that stands above the gimmickry and canned nostalgia of most memoirs both in its authenticity and its urgency. Writing literally kept Judt alive: The Memory Chalet was an effort to get everything onto the page before dying. It is a beautiful book that invites the reader into the most intimate spaces of his mind, which chugged briskly along even as his body was a train lifting slowly off the tracks." Washington Monthly

Jurgensen, Dalia

Spiced; a pastry chef's true stories of trials by fire, afterhours exploits, and what really goes on in the kitchen. Putnam 2009 274p il $24.95   **92**

1. Cooks

ISBN 978-0-399-15561-1; 0-399-15561-9

LC 2008-46364

Jurgensen's "book takes readers on a culinary adventure through her rise as a pastry chef at New York's best restaurants while attending culinary school. The highlights include her experiences at Martha Stewart Living Television, when she accidentally melted her glasses while making macaroons. A quick read, this book will appeal to those interested in chef stories and what happens behind the scenes in the kitchen." Libr J

Kafka, die Jahre der Entscheidungen/English

★ **Kafka,** the decisive years; the decisive years. translated from the German by Shelley Frisch. 1st U.S. ed.; Harcourt 2005 581p il $35   **92**

1. Authors 2. Biography, Individual 3. Novelists 4. Poets 5. Short story writers

ISBN 0-15-100752-7

LC 2005-14554

This first of a projected three-volume biography focuses on Kafka's life from 1910 to 1915, during which he wrote "The Metamorphosis" and The Trial.

"Essential reading for all Kafka devotees." Booklist

Includes bibliographical references

Kahlo, Frida

The **diary** of Frida Kahlo; an intimate self-portrait. introduction by Carlos Fuentes; essay and commentaries by Sarah M. Lowe; [project director, Claudia Madrazo; editor, Phyllis Freeman; translators, Barbara Crow de Toledo and Ricardo Pohlenz] 2005 ed.; Harry N. Abrams 2005 295p il $24.95 **92**

1. Artists 2. Artists, Mexican 3. Painters

ISBN 0-8109-5954-2

LC 2006-284768

"Sprinkled with irony, black humor, even gaiety . . . this volume is a testament to Kahlo's resilience and courage." Publ Wkly

Includes bibliographical references

Kahn, Roger

A **flame** of pure fire: Jack Dempsey and the roaring '20s. Harcourt Brace & Co. 1999 474p il hardcover o.p. pa $15   **92**

1. Boxers (Persons)

ISBN 0-15-601414-9 pa

LC 99-15382

This biography details the life and career of heavyweight boxer William Harrison "Jack" Dempsey.

"In graceful and fluid prose, Kahn presents the con men, gangsters, prostitutes and starlets who inhabited the turbulent, Prohibition-era story of Jack Dempsey." Publ Wkly

Includes bibliographical references

Kambalu, Samson

The **jive** talker; an artist's genesis: a memoir. Free Press 2008 320p $24   **92**

1. Artists 2. Biography, Individual

ISBN 978-1-4165-5931-3; 1-4165-5931-0

LC 2008-26784

"Artist Kambalu recounts his long journey from poverty in Malawi to fame in the London art world. The 'jive talker' was his father, a hospital administrator whose career ups and downs set the mood for the entire family even as they endured the political fortunes of Malawi under Life President Hastings Banda. Kambalu senior died of AIDS in 1995, bequeathing his family memories of his odd assortment of books and love of words." Booklist

Kamkwamba, William

The **boy** who harnessed the wind; [by] William Kamkwamba and Bryan Mealer. William Morrow 2009 273 p. (hbk.) $25.99; pa $14.99 **92**
1. Electric power production -- Malawi 2. Mechanical engineers -- Malawi -- Biography 3. Rural electrification -- Malawi 4. Water-supply, Rural -- Malawi 5. Windmills -- Malawi
ISBN 978-0-06-173032-0; 0-06-173032-7; 978-0-06-173033-7 pa; 0-06-173033-5 pa; 0061730327; 9780061730320
LC 2010275963
Autobiography of a teenager in Malawi who builds a windmill and brings electricity to his village.

"This exquisite tale strips life down to its barest essentials, and once there finds reason for hopes and dreams, and is especially resonant for Americans given the economy and increasingly heated debates over health care and energy policy." Publ Wkly

Kanfer, Stefan

Groucho: the life and times of Julius Henry Marx. Knopf 2000 465p il hardcover o.p. pa $15 **92**
1. Comedians 2. Game show hosts 3. Television personalities
ISBN 0-375-70207-5 pa
LC 99-54002
"Plagued by nagging financial insecurities, partly realized literary ambitions, and difficult, unsatisfying relations with his wives, lovers, and daughters, Groucho was a 'depressive clown,' notes Kanter. . . . The book also details Groucho's ambivalent relations with his son, Arthur; his brothers; New Deal liberals; intellectuals and collaborators like S. J. Perelman; and his custodian, Erin Fleming." Libr J
Includes bibliographical references

Kantner, Seth

Shopping for porcupine; a life in arctic Alaska. Milkweed Editions 2008 240p il $28; pa $18 **92**
1. Authors 2. Authors, American 3. Fishermen 4. Novelists 5. Photographers 6. Trappers 7. Young adult authors
ISBN 978-1-57131-301-0; 978-1-57131-311-9 pa
LC 2007-46477
"Crafted with the precision and verve acquired by living off the land, this is a powerful and important book of remembrance, protest, and warning." Booklist

Kaplan, James

Frank; the voice. Doubleday 2010 786p il $35; ebook $35 **92**
1. Actors 2. Biography, Individual 3. Singers
ISBN 978-0-385-51804-8; 0-385-51804-8; 978-0-385-53364-5 ebook; 0-385-53364-0 ebook
LC 2009-31046
This biography covers the life of the American singer and actor from his birth in 1915 to his comeback in 1954 in the film From Here to Eternity.
"Kaplan's enthralling tale of an American icon serves as an introduction of 'old blue eyes' to a new generation of listeners while winning the hearts of Sinatra's diehard fans." Publ Wkly
Includes bibliographical references

Karp, Brianna

The **girl's** guide to homelessness; a memoir. Harlequin 2011 344p pa $16.95 **92**
1. Homeless 2. Homeless persons 3. Office workers
ISBN 978-0-373-89235-8
LC 2010044201
"Sexually and emotionally abused by her parents, Karp left home ASAP. Self-sufficiency delighted her; she adored her job and beach cottage. She lost both to the recession and moved into a trailer she parked in a Walmart lot while using free Starbucks wi-fi and her laptop to apply for jobs. She began blogging about her situation, documenting her struggles with homelessness and trying to regain stability. Candidly humorous, Karp's memoir is sharp and insightful, reminding readers just how perilous the security of a permanent address can be and offering tips on what to do if it is lost." Libr J

Karr, Mary

Lit; a memoir. Harper 2009 386p $25.99; pa $14.95 **92**
1. Alcoholics 2. Authors 3. Biography, Individual 4. College teachers 5. Essayists 6. Memoirists 7. Poets 8. Poets, American
ISBN 978-0-06-059698-9; 0-06-059698-8; 978-0-06-059699-6 pa; 0-06-059699-6 pa
LC 2009-24810
The author reveals how, shortly after giving birth to a child she adored, she drank herself into the same numbness that nearly devoured her charismatic but troubled mother, reaching the brink of suicide before a spiritual awakening led her to sobriety.
Karr "has written a book that lassos you, hogties your emotions and won't let you go. It's a memoir that . . . explores the subjectivity of memory even as it chronicles with searching intelligence, humor and grace the author's slow, sometimes exhilarating, sometimes painful discovery of her vocation." N Y Times (Late N Y Ed)

Kashner, Sam

Furious love; Elizabeth Taylor, Richard Burton, and the marriage of the century. [by] Sam Kashner and Nancy Schoenberger. Harper 2010 500p il $27.99 **92**
1. Actors 2. Biography, Individual
ISBN 978-0-06-156284-6; 0-06-156284-X
LC 2010-06732
"In this dual biography of the two legendary film stars, the authors draw upon new information, including interviews with Elizabeth Taylor and with the Burton family, to capture the famously passionate and tumultuous relationship between the legendary couple. . . . It's a mesmerizing tale, but it's also sad, and sometimes ugly, as the two stars engaged in vicious fights, nursed their jealousies and insecurities, and descended into alcoholism while outwardly living a life of glamour and sophistication." Booklist
Includes bibliographical references

Kastin, David

Nica's dream; the life and legend of the jazz baroness. W. W. Norton 2011 336p il $26.95   **92**
1. Jazz music -- History and criticism 2. Patrons of the arts
ISBN 978-0-393-06940-2

                  LC 2011013213

"Kastin succeeds in bringing the surprisingly selfeffacing Nica to blazing life while also capturing the transcendent synergy among now-iconic jazz musicians, beat writers, and abstract painters, a creative cosmos profoundly enriched by the passion, largesse, and daring of the incomparable baroness." Booklist
Includes discography and bibliographical references

Kauffman, Bill

Forgotten founder, drunken prophet; the life of Luther Martin. ISI Books 2008 202p $25   **92**
1. Law enforcement officials 2. Lawyers 3. Members of Congress 4. State government officials
ISBN 978-1-933859-73-6; 1-933859-73-3

                  LC 2008-928223

Kauffman "tells the story of Luther Martin, one of America's less-remembered founding fathers. A livid Anti-Federalist, Martin has gone down in the annals of 18th century America as little more than a footnote. He was accused of being an absolute boor, drinking to excess, rambling in speech with incessant monotony, and having an altogether prickly disposition. Kauffman takes up the cross of giving Martin a fair shake, not by defending the man but just by telling his story. . . . Never the explicit apologist, Kauffman delicately and humorously weaves a more complete portrait of Martin. Furthermore, Kauffman's writing is well-founded upon a towering bibliography that Kauffman adroitly parses." PopMatters
Includes bibliographical references

Kaufman, David

Doris Day; the untold story of the girl next door. Virgin Books 2008 626p il $29.95; pa $19.95 **92**
1. Actors 2. Biography, Individual 3. Singers
ISBN 978-1-90526-430-8; 1-90526-430-5; 978-0-75351-809-0 pa; 0-75351-809-0 pa

                  LC 2008-9410

This is a biography of the actor who starred in such films as Love Me or Leave Me (1955), The Man Who Knew Too Much (1956), and Pillow Talk (1959).
"Readers, especially fans of the star, will thoroughly enjoy this meaty, well-written, entertaining look at the surprisingly tumultuous life of an American icon." Booklist
Includes bibliographical references

Kavanagh, Julie

★ **Nureyev**; the life. Pantheon Books 2007 782p il $37.50   **92**
1. Ballet dancers
ISBN 978-0-375-40513-6; 0-375-40513-5

                  LC 2006-38137

In this biography of the Russian ballet dancer, the author "chronicles Nureyev's many tempestuous relationships, including his legendary work with Margot Fonteyn and his formative affair with the outstanding Danish dancer Erik Bruhn. . . . Kavanagh's consummate biography will stand as a pillar in dance history." Booklist
Includes bibliographical references

Kazin, Michael

A **godly** hero; the life of William Jennings Bryan. Knopf 2006 374p il hardcover o.p. pa $16.95 **92**
1. Authors 2. Biography, Individual 3. Lawyers 4. Political leaders 5. Presidential candidates 6. Secretaries of state
ISBN 0-375-41135-6; 978-0-385-72056-4 pa; 0-385-72056-4 pa

                  LC 2005-44105

"Kazin is not the first biographer to tackle the Great Commoner, but he is definitely the best writer among them. 'A Godly Hero' is a richly textured narrative with an excellent pace." Christ Sci Monit
Includes bibliographical references

Keiler, Allan

Marian Anderson; a singer's journey. University of Illinois Press 2002 447p hardcover o.p. pa $21.95   **92**
1. African American singers 2. African American women -- Biography 3. Opera singers
ISBN 0-684-80711-4; 0-252-07067-4 pa

                  LC 99-43319

The author's "clear, succinct prose, initially lacking narrative coherence, gains strength and momentum as his subject matures from a young and struggling artist into one of the enduring voices of our century." Publ Wkly
Includes discography and bibliographical references

Keller, Helen

Helen Keller: selected writings; edited by Kim E. Nielsen; consulting editor, Harvey J. Kaye. New York University Press 2005 317p il $35   **92**
1. Authors 2. Blind 3. Deaf 4. Humanitarians 5. Inspirational writers 6. Memoirists 7. Social welfare leaders
ISBN 0-8147-5829-0

                  LC 2004-28974

This is a collection "of Keller's personal letters, political writings, speeches, and excerpts of her published materials from 1887 to 1968." Univ Press Books for Public and Second Sch Libr, 2006
Includes bibliographical references

★ The **story** of my life; edited and with a preface by James Berger. The restored ed.; Modern Library 2003 xlvi, 343p il hardcover o.p. pa $9.95 **92**
1. Authors 2. Blind 3. Blind women -- United States -- Biography 4. Deaf 5. Deaf women -- United States -- Biography 6. Humanitarians 7. Inspirational writers 8. Memoirists 9. People with disabilities -- Education -- United States 10. Social welfare leaders
ISBN 0-679-64287-0; 0-8129-6886-7 pa

                  LC 2002-40971

This biography of the inspirational Keller contains accounts of her home life and her relationship with her devoted teacher Anne Sullivan.

Kelley, Robin D. G.

★ **Thelonious** Monk; the life and times of an American original. Free Press 2009 588p il $30 **92**
1. African American musicians 2. Biography, Individual 3. Jazz 4. Jazz musicians 5. Pianists
ISBN 978-0-684-83190-9; 0-684-83190-2
LC 2009-08526
This is a biography of the jazz musician and composer.
The author "knows music, especially Monk's music, and his descriptions of assorted studio and live dates, along with what Monk is up to musically throughout, are handled expertly. . . . Likewise, the characters in Monk's life and career are well served. . . . The 'genius of modern music' has gotten the passionate, and compassionate, advocate he deserves." N Y Times Book Rev
Includes discography, videography, and bibliographical references

Kellman, Steven G.

Redemption: the life of Henry Roth. W.W. Norton 2005 371p il $25.95 **92**
1. Authors 2. Biography, Individual 3. Essayists 4. Novelists 5. Short story writers
ISBN 0-393-05779-8
LC 2005-11979
The author "traces Roth's fascinating career from his birth in Galicia, Austria-Hungary, to his final years in New Mexico. He focuses on his experience of New York's Lower East Side and Jewish and Irish Harlem. . . . This biography should be included in all public library and academic collections." Libr J
Includes bibliographical references

Kellow, Brian

Pauline Kael; a life in the dark. Viking 2011 417p il $27.95 **92**
1. Motion picture critics 2. Motion pictures 3. Writers on film
ISBN 978-0-670-02312-7; 0-670-02312-4
LC 2011-21798
"During her glory years at The New Yorker from 1968 to 1991, Pauline Kael enlivened the quiet art of analyzing movies with a lusty noise that echoes in certain movie-festival hallways a decade after her death. . . . [Kellow] brings two unassailable strengths to a bio that's bound to be catnip for both Kael's fans and her naysayers. First, he is impressively thorough in his research. He ferrets out illuminating information about Kael's childhood as the daughter of Polish Jewish chicken farmers in California, her never-quite-satisfactory romantic relationships with men, her dependence on the daughter she raised as a single mother, her financial struggles, and (most juicily) her oil-and-water clashes with The New Yorker's painfully genteel editor William Shawn. As for Kellow's second strength, it's an elegantly simple one: He's a movie lover but not a professional critic. Kael had many axes to grind, but Kellow appears to have none." Entertainment Wkly

Kelly, Christopher

The **end** of empire; Attila the Hun and the fall of Rome. W.W. Norton 2009 350p il map $26.95 **92**
1. Huns 2. Tribal leaders
ISBN 978-0-393-06196-3
LC 2009-009072
The author "paints an engaging portrait of Attila the Hun's rise to prominence and places the feared warlord in the context of his own time." Libr J
Includes bibliographical references

Keneally, Thomas

Abraham Lincoln. Viking 2003 183p hardcover o.p. pa $14 **92**
1. Lawyers 2. Members of Congress 3. Presidents 4. Presidents -- United States 5. State legislators
ISBN 0-670-03175-5; 0-14-311475-1 pa
LC 2003-268078
"Keneally's Lincoln is a self-actuated farm boy made good by self-discipline, savvy instincts, wit, the wisdom acquired from courtrooms, friendships, and political huckstering—and luck . . . [The author] recounts Lincoln's early missteps in romance, business, and politics and his self-doubts and depression as his star dimmed several times, and he concedes Lincoln's erratic course toward emancipation and a successful strategy for Union victory during the Civil War . . . This is an epic compressed into a tightly written biography that all Americans might read with profit. Keneally's occasional tendency to let folklore stand as fact notwithstanding, there is no better brief introduction to Lincoln and his American dream." Libr J

★ **American** scoundrel: the life of the notorious Civil War General Dan Sickles. Talese 2002 397p $27.50; pa $15 **92**
1. Diplomats 2. Generals 3. Members of Congress
ISBN 0-385-50139-0; 0-385-72225-7 pa
LC 2001-43078
"A frequently spellbinding recitation of the career of a totally awful politician, crook, adulterer and murderer who was no good as a general either." N Y Times Book Rev

Kennan, George Frost

Sketches from a life. W. W. Norton 2000 365p pa $14.95 **92**
1. Authors 2. Centenarians 3. Diplomats 4. Historians 5. Nonfiction writers
ISBN 978-0-393-32139-5; 0-393-32139-8
"This is a collection of very private reflections spanning some 60 years of foreign service in Nazi Germany, the Baltic states, the Low Countries, the Soviet Union, as well as nonofficial travels covering the entire globe. Kennan has marvelous insight into his ever-changing surroundings—an insight that is always sharp, sometimes melancholy, and punctuated frequently by dry, Midwestern wit." Libr J
Includes bibliographical references

Kennedy, Edward Moore

★ **True** compass; a memoir. [by] Edward M. Kennedy. Twelve 2009 532p il $35 **92**
1. Biography, Individual 2. Presidential candidates 3.

Senators 4. Siblings of presidents
ISBN 978-0-446-53925-8; 0-446-53925-2
This autobiography by the former senator from Massachusetts was published posthumously.

"Mr. Kennedy's conversational gifts as a storyteller and his sense of humor . . . shine through here, as does his old-school sense of public service and his hard-won knowledge, in his son Teddy Jr.'s words, that 'even our most profound losses are survivable.'" N Y Times (Late N Y Ed)
Includes bibliographical references

Kennedy, Kostya

56; Joe DiMaggio and the last magic number in sports. Sports Illustrated Books 2011 367p il por $26.95   **92**
1. Baseball -- Biography 2. Baseball -- History 3. Baseball players 4. Batting (Baseball)
ISBN 9781603201773; 1603201777
Recounts Joe DiMaggio's streak during the summer of 1941 and how it found its way into countless lives.

"From the private world inhabited only by DiMaggio and his new bride to Newark barbershops, the playgrounds of Queens, and the streets of DiMaggio's hometown, San Francisco, Kennedy humanizes an immortal accomplishment." Publ Wkly
Includes bibliographical references (p. 351-357) and index.

Kenney, David Ngaruri

Asylum denied; a refugee's struggle for safety in America. [by] David Ngaruri Kenney and Philip G. Schrag. University of California Press 2008 352p il map $40; pa $17.95   **92**
1. Biography, Individual 2. Civil rights 3. Defectors 4. Immigrants -- Government policy -- United States 5. Immigrants -- United States 6. Immigration policy 7. Political refugees 8. Political refugees -- Legal status, laws, etc. -- United States -- Cases 9. Refugees
ISBN 978-0-520-25510-4; 0-520-25510-0; 978-0-520-26159-4 pa; 0-520-26159-3 pa
                   LC 2007-48703
"One cannot read this book without experiencing rage, disbelief, and an overwhelming sense of sadness over the inhumanity Kenney suffered, both in Kenya and in this country. Still, it is also an inspiring story of human courage, heartfelt friendships, and unrelenting devotion to fighting the good fight. . . . This account should be required reading for anyone who has contact with immigrants in America. It should also be on the reading list of anyone who cares about the preservation of human rights and human dignity in our world." Calif Lawyer
Includes bibliographical references

Kerouac, Jack

★ **Jack** Kerouac and Allen Ginsberg; the letters. edited by Bill Morgan and David Stanford. Viking 2010 500p $35   **92**
1. Authors 2. Beat generation 3. Biography, Individual 4. Novelists 5. Poets
ISBN 978-0-670-02194-9; 0-670-02194-6
                   LC 2010-03213

"At times loving, at others blistering, sarcastic, often uncomfortably self-lacerating and intimate, these 200 letters, collected in a heroic editorial effort by Ginsberg biographer Morgan and independent editor Stanford, cover the years 1944-1963, the most fertile in the creative lives of Kerouac and Ginsberg. . . . Throughout, the sometimes sporadic letter writing is filled with fragments of works in progress and pungent observations on the authors and publishing people who influenced them, from Dante and Gide to Malcolm Cowley and Sterling Lord. There also is plenty of gossip about Peter Orlovsky, William Burroughs, and others in the circle." Publ Wkly

Selected letters, 1940-1956; edited with an introduction and commentary by Ann Charters. Viking 1995 xxvi, 629p hardcover o.p. pa $16.95   **92**
1. Authors 2. Novelists
ISBN 0-14-023444-6 pa
                   LC 94-12911
The editor "made two very wise decisions here: she supplied continuity and context for the letters, and she included significant letters from the correspondents. The frustration of the long-rejected writer is doubly felt by the reader, since this selection ends on the eve of the big Beat breakthrough." Choice
Includes bibliographical references

Kershaw, Ian

Hitler; a biography. W.W. Norton 2008 1029p il map $39.95   **92**
1. Heads of state 2. Nazi leaders
ISBN 978-0-393-06757-6; 0-393-06757-2
                   LC 2008-37294
This abridgment of the author's two-volume biography on Hitler "retains two themes of Kershaw's full-scale original: analyzing the political support the demagogue mustered from the populace and key institutional centers of Germany on his ascent to and exercise of power; and the decisive personal role of Hitler in instigating World War II and genocide. The narrative Kershaw constructs on this foundation is a superb organization and expression of Hitler's chronological arc that plummeted the world into catastrophe and moral trauma, a trajectory informed by Kershaw's attention to rationalizations by which people in and outside Germany, whether leaders or led, buried doubts about Hitler until his power was unrestrained, impossible to stop but by war or assassination. Manifestly, Kershaw constitutes core-collection material." Booklist
Includes bibliographical references

Hitler, 1889-1936: hubris. Norton 1999 xxx, 845p il $35; pa $21.95   **92**
1. Heads of state 2. Nazi leaders
ISBN 0-393-04671-0; 0-393-32035-9 pa
                   LC 98-29569
"Kershaw provides an examination based on a number of archival sources not used by previous biographers. . . . More than a chronicle of Hitler's life, this is an analysis of the major historiographical issues, the circumstances that shaped his personality, and the historical events that enabled Hitler to rise to power." Libr J
Includes bibliographical references

Kersten, Jason

The **art** of making money; the story of a master counterfeiter. Gotham Books 2009 292p $26   **92**

1. Counterfeiters 2. Counterfeits and counterfeiting 3. Criminals

ISBN 978-1-59240-446-9

LC 2009-9407

This "absorbing account reads like crime fiction, offering an understanding of modern counterfeiting that will appeal to readers of that genre as well as those who like true crime." Libr J

Kessner, Thomas

The **flight** of the century; Charles Lindbergh & the rise of American aviation. Oxford University Press 2010 313p il map   **92**

1. Aeronautics -- United States -- History 2. Air force officers 3. Air pilots 4. Biography, Individual 5. Generals 6. Memoirists

ISBN 978-0-19-532019-0; 0-19-532019-0

LC 2010-06082

"In May 1927 at the age of 25, the 'Lone Eagle' flew from New York to Paris, a startling accomplishment that made the awkward, reticent aviator the world's best-known person. But Lindbergh lived until 1974, and two elements were added to his legacy — he was the father whose tiny son was kidnapped and slain by Bruno Hauptmann, and, much worse for his reputation, he was the fascist-tinged advocate of U.S. neutrality before World War II. . . . [Kessner's book] aims to balance the equation. His book recaps Lindbergh's epochal flight and carries it forward, discussing his subsequent role in the aviation boom that followed. While there is nothing particularly earth-shattering about what he has written, Kessner's fresh perspective breathes new life into Lindbergh's tale." Philadelphia Inquirer

Includes bibliographical references and index

Kidder, Tracy

Mountains beyond mountains. Random House 2003 336p hardcover o.p. pa $14.95   **92**

1. Humanitarians 2. Organization officials 3. Physicians 4. Social activists 5. Writers on medicine

ISBN 0-375-50616-0; 0-8129-7301-1 pa

LC 2003-41253

"This story is remarkable, and Kidder's skill in sequencing both dramatic and understated elements into a reflective commentary is unsurpassed." SLJ

Includes bibliographical references

Strength in what remains. Random House 2009 277p $26; pa $16   **92**

1. Genocide 2. Genocide -- Burundi 3. Immigrants -- New York (N.Y.) 4. Immigrants -- United States 5. Medical students -- United States 6. Refugees 7. Refugees -- Burundi 8. Students

ISBN 978-1-4000-6621-6; 1-4000-6621-2; 978-0-8129-7761-5 pa; 0-8121-7761-0 pa

LC 2008-44865

"This profoundly gripping, hopeful and crucial testament is a work of the utmost skill, sympathy and moral clarity." Publ Wkly

Includes bibliographical references

Kimball, Kristin

The **dirty** life; on farming, food, and love. Scribner 2010 276p $25; ebook $11.99   **92**

1. Authors 2. Farm life -- New York (State) 3. Farmers 4. Journalists 5. Organic farming

ISBN 978-1-4165-5160-7; 978-1-4391-8714-2 ebook

"A hearty, chromatic account of a meaningful accomplishment in farming, 'that dirty concupiscent art.'" Kirkus

King, James

Farley: the life of Farley Mowat. Steerforth Press 2002 397p il $27.95   **92**

1. Authors 2. Children's authors 3. Ethnologists 4. Historians 5. Nonfiction writers

ISBN 1-58642-055-0

LC 2002-151149

The author "recounts Mowat's life from his experience in college to his service in World War II and his work in the Northwest Territories as a student biologist. The emerging portrait is of a man whose evolution as both an environmentalist and an artist was profound, an activist who has never backed away from a controversy. The exploration of Mowat's life is detailed but never boring." Libr J

Includes bibliographical references

Kinkade, Thomas

The **Thomas** Kinkade story; a 20-year chronology of the artist. [by] Thomas Kinkade; text by Rick Barnett. Bulfinch Press 2003 224p il $24.95   **92**

1. Artists 2. Artists -- United States 3. Nonfiction writers 4. Painters

ISBN 978-0-8212-6179-8; 0-8212-6179-7

LC 2003-052256

This book provides a "look at the artist's life and work. Each period in Kinkade's career is examined." Publisher's note

Kirkpatrick, Sidney

Edgar Cayce; an American prophet. Riverhead Bks. 2000 564p il hardcover o.p. pa $16   **92**

1. Psychics 2. Psychics -- United States -- Biography

ISBN 1-57322-896-6 pa

LC 00-27975

This is a "fair, fascinating, and well-researched biography of one of 20th-century America's most famous psychics." Libr J

The **revenge** of Thomas Eakins; [by] Sidney D. Kirkpatrick. Yale University Press 2006 565p il $39.95   **92**

1. Art teachers 2. Artists 3. Biography, Individual 4. Painters 5. Sculptors

ISBN 0-300-10855-9

LC 2005-27935

This is a "portrait of Thomas Eakins, the controversial Philadelphia portrait artist whose 'failure to abide by the artistic trends that defined his times' resulted in work that was richly interesting and highly controversial. . . . Kirkpatrick gives Eakins convincing depth that reminds readers of the ways biography can enhance appreciation of art." Publ Wkly

Includes bibliographical references

Kirshenblatt, Mayer

They called me Mayer July; painted memories of a Jewish childhood in Poland before the Holocaust. [by] Mayer Kirshenblatt, Barbara Kirshenblatt-Gimblett. University of California Press 2007 411p il $39.95   **92**
    1. Artists 2. Holocaust survivors 3. Jews -- Poland 4. Memoirists 5. Painters
    ISBN 978-0-520-24961-5
                        LC 2006-36182
"Kirshenblatt's illustrated memoir of growing up as a Jew in pre-World War II Poland reads like an episodic novel as he introduces the reader to village life and the myriad of unusual and interesting characters." Univ Press Books for Public and Second Sch Libr, 2008
    Includes bibliographical references

Kirtzman, Andrew

Rudy Giuliani; emperor of the city. Morrow 2000 333p il hardcover o.p. pa $13.95   **92**
    1. District attorneys 2. Lawyers 3. Mayors 4. Presidential candidates
    ISBN 0-06-009389-7 pa
This political biography follows Giuliani from 1989 when he first set out to capture New York's City's mayoralty to his withdrawal from the 2000 senate race for medical and personal reasons.

Klein, Joe

Woody Guthrie; a life. Knopf 1980 475p il pa $17   **92**
    1. Folk musicians 2. Memoirists 3. Musicians -- United States 4. Singers 5. Songwriters
    ISBN 0-385-33385-4 pa
                        LC 80-7634
"The author incorporates into his text a great deal of information sifted from Guthrie's voluminous unpublished writings. . . . He also uses information from historical sources, published works, and hundreds of interviews to place Guthrie in a social and historical perspective. The result of all this research is . . . a very interesting and personal biography." Libr J

Kluger, Jeffrey

Splendid solution: Jonas Salk and the conquest of polio. G.P. Putnam's Sons 2004 373p il hardcover o.p. pa $15   **92**
    1. Biography, Individual 2. Microbiologists 3. Physicians 4. Poliomyelitis 5. Writers on medicine
    ISBN 0-399-15216-4; 0-425-20570-3 pa
                   LC 2004-50527
"Can't-put-it-down medical-science history." Booklist
    Includes bibliographical references

Knight, Bobby

Knight: my story; [by] Bob Knight with Bob Hammel. Thomas Dunne Bks. 2002 387p il $25.95; pa $14.95   **92**
    1. Basketball -- Biography 2. Basketball coaches
    ISBN 0-312-28257-5; 0-312-31117-6 pa
                   LC 2001-48990

"College hoops fans can learn more about the game from this book than from most instructional guides." Publ Wkly

Knight, Louise W.

Jane Addams; spirit in action. W. W. Norton 2010 334p il $28.95   **92**
    1. Authors 2. Essayists 3. Nobel laureates for peace 4. Pacifists 5. Philanthropists 6. Social welfare leaders
    ISBN 978-0-393-07165-8
                  LC 2010-20648
In this "biography of social reformer and peace activist Jane Addams (1860–1935) . . . [the author] begins with a speech the 72-year-old Addams, by then a Nobel laureate, made in 1933, which urged her audience to break free from conventional thinking. Knight uses Addams's thesis as the key to understanding her life. . . . A sympathetic portrait of—and tribute to—a brave and committed human being." Kirkus
    Includes bibliographical references

Korda, Michael

Hero; the life and legend of Lawrence of Arabia. Harper 2010 762p il map $34.99   **92**
    1. Archaeologists 2. Authors 3. Biography, Individual 4. Soldiers 5. Soldiers -- Great Britain 6. Travel writers 7. World War, 1914-1918 -- Campaigns -- Middle East 8. World War, 1914-1918 -- Campaigns -- Turkey 9. World War, 1914-1918 -- Middle East
    ISBN 978-0-06-171261-6
                  LC 2010-33189
This is a biography of T. E. Lawrence, the "British scholar, adventurer, soldier, and hero who became a myth in his lifetime." (Publisher's note) Index.
    "This magisterial biography of British soldier and adventurer T.E. Lawrence celebrates a life spent subverting authority in the most glamorous—and bizarre—ways. . . . [The author] gives a rousing, lucid account of Lawrence's leadership of the Arab revolt against the Ottoman Empire during WWI and his diplomatic championing of Arab nationalism. But it's Lawrence's artistic bent . . . and his magnetic but tortured soul that take center stage." Publ Wkly
    Includes bibliographical references

Ike; an American hero. HarperCollins 2007 779p il map $34.95   **92**
    1. Biography, Individual 2. College presidents 3. Generals 4. Presidents 5. Presidents -- United States 6. World War, 1939-1945
    ISBN 978-0-06-075665-9; 0-06-075665-9
                  LC 2006-52856
This is a biography of the American president and World War II general.
    "With a sure touch on Ike's Kansas boyhood, marriage to Mamie, and prewar army mentors, Korda . . . successfully reintroduces the Eisenhower personality that was so popular privately, militarily, and politically." Booklist
    Includes bibliographical references

Ulysses S. Grant: the unlikely hero. Atlas Books\ HarperCollins 2004 161p $19.95   **92**
    1. Children of presidents 2. Generals 3. Lawyers 4.

Presidents 5. Real estate developers
ISBN 0-06-059015-7

LC 2004-46125

The author "freshly characterizes his man without psychologizing an unpromising subject. . . . This is a highly readable, accurate study of the man." Publ Wkly

Includes bibliographical references

Kramer, Clara

Clara's war; one girl's story of survival. [by] Clara Kramer with Stephen Glantz. Ecco 2009 339p il $25.99   92
1. Holocaust survivors 2. Holocaust, 1933-1945 -- Personal narratives 3. Jews -- Poland 4. Memoirists
ISBN 978-0-06-172860-0; 0-06-172860-8

"Based on her wartime diary, which she kept while hiding in a basement in Poland, Kramer's book vividly recalls the tensions within her hidden community after the Nazis overtook the town of Zolkiew in 1942. Of particular interest are revelations about the family who hid the Kramers, particularly how an anti-Semitic Polish householder demonstrated great courage in shielding Jews in his basement." Libr J

Krauss, Lawrence Maxwell

Quantum man; Richard Feynman's life in science. [by] Lawrence M. Krauss. W.W. Norton 2011 350p il $24.95   92
1. Authors 2. Biography, Individual 3. Nobel laureates for physics 4. Physicists 5. Writers on science
ISBN 978-0-393-06471-1; 0-393-06471-9

LC 2010-45512

"This book is highly recommended for readers who want to get to know one of the preeminent scientists of the 20th century." Publ Wkly

Includes bibliographical references

Kriegel, Mark

★ Pistol; the life of Pete Maravich. Free Press 2007 381p il $27; pa $15   92
1. Basketball players
ISBN 978-0-7432-8497-4; 0-7432-8497-6; 978-0-7432-8498-1 pa; 0-7432-8498-4 pa

LC 2006-51526

This is a biography of the basketball player who played at Louisiana State University before joining the N.B.A.

The author "skillfully pulls off the balancing act required of good sports biography. It plays large historical forces (segregation, the rise of televised sports) against the individual magic of its subject." New York

Includes bibliographical references

Kroeber, Theodora

★ Ishi in two worlds; a biography of the last wild Indian in North America. University of Calif. Press 1976 262p il $50; pa $16.95   92
1. Linguistic informants 2. Yana Indians
ISBN 0-520-00674-7; 0-520-22940-1 pa

An account "of the life of the sole survivor of a California Indian tribe. The author, wife of the famed anthropologist, reconstructs the decimation of Ishi's {Yana} people and his reluctant entry in 1911 into the world of his conquerors." Booklist

Kruth, John

To live's to fly; the ballad of the late, great Townes Van Zandt. Da Capo 2007 326p il $26 92
1. Country musicians 2. Folk musicians 3. Guitarists 4. Singers 5. Songwriters
ISBN 978-0-306-81553-9; 0-306-81553-2

This is "the first biography of legendary Texas singer/songwriter Townes Van Zandt (1944-97). In his struggle for recognition among a wider public, Van Zandt wrestled for years with depression and alcoholism while writing songs— e.g., 'Pancho and Lefty' and 'Be Here To Love Me'—that today are revered by the elite of Texas and Nashville songwriters as well as by a cult group of fans. Through access to Van Zandt's friends, family members, and fellow musicians, Kruth provides an intimate and unflinching look at the singer's life." Libr J

Kuipers, Dean

Operation Bite Back; Rod Coronado's war to save American wilderness. Bloomsbury 2009 309p il $25   92
1. Animal rights activists 2. Animal rights movement 3. Environmentalists
ISBN 1-59691-458-0; 978-1-59691-458-2

LC 2009-6600

This "account of animal rights activist Rod Coronado follows the charismatic Coronado from his introduction to animal protection in the 1980s to his campaign of sabotage against the fur industry, his life in the underground and on reservations among fellow Native Americans, and ultimately his arrests and incarcerations. . . . An important book that will appeal to readers interested in environmental and social issues." Libr J

Kunhardt, Philip B.

Looking for Lincoln; the making of an American icon. [by] Philip B. Kunhardt III, Peter W. Kunhardt and Peter W. Kunhardt, Jr.; foreword by David Herbert Donald; introduction by Doris Kearns Goodwin. Alfred A. Knopf 2008 494p il $50   92
1. Lawyers 2. Members of Congress 3. Popular culture -- Political aspects -- United States 4. Presidents 5. Presidents -- United States 6. Public opinion -- United States 7. State legislators
ISBN 978-0-307-26713-9; 0-307-26713-X

LC 2008-14193

"The Kunhardts' book represents a visual and literary feast for all devotees of the sacred national idol that is Lincoln." Publ Wkly

Includes bibliographical references

Kurosawa, Akira

Something like an autobiography; translated by Audie E. Bock. Knopf 1982 205p il hardcover o.p. pa $15   92
1. Motion picture directors 2. Motion picture industry
ISBN 0-394-71439-3 pa

LC 81-48100

These are the memoirs of the Japanese filmmaker, covering his life up to 1951-52, when his film Rashomon won international awards.

This "is a fascinating, moving record of one man's pursuit of excellence in a single art." N Y Times Book Rev

Kurson, Robert

Crashing through; a story of risk, adventure, and the man who dared to see. Random House 2007 306p il $25.95 **92**

1. Authors 2. Blind 3. Blind -- Biography 4. Blind -- Rehabilitation 5. Eye -- Surgery -- Patients 6. Journalists 7. Manufacturing executives 8. Nonfiction writers 9. Skiers
ISBN 978-1-4000-6335-2; 1-4000-6335-3
LC 2007-3092

The book "becomes most interesting when the flaws in Mr. May's new eyesight become apparent. He makes wondrous discoveries of things blind people never hear about—shadows, freckles, the movement and transparency of running water—but has more difficulty with the cognitive aspects of pattern recognition. He can see facial features but cannot decipher facial expressions. . . . Eventually the joy of sight fades for him and the investigatory challenges begin." N Y Times (Late N Y Ed)

Kurzke, Hermann

Thomas Mann; life as a work of art: a biography. translated by Leslie Willson. Princeton Univ. Press 2002 581p il $35 **92**

1. Authors 2. Essayists 3. Nobel laureates for literature 4. Novelists 5. Novelists, German -- 20th century -- Biography 6. Short story writers
ISBN 0-691-07069-5
LC 2002-23665

"A major achievement in literary biography." Booklist

LaPlante, Eve

Salem witch judge; the life and repentance of Samuel Sewall. HarperSanFrancisco 2007 352p il map $25.95 **92**

1. Biography, Individual 2. Colonial leaders 3. Diarists 4. Judges
ISBN 978-0-06-078661-8; 0-06-078661-2
LC 2007-18392

"In 1692, Salem magistrate Samuel Sewall (1652-1730), along with several others, presided over the conviction and execution of 20 people accused of witchcraft. Five years and much soul-searching later, Sewall publicly repented of his part in the witch trials. . . . [The author] richly narrates his life in its cultural and religious setting." Publ Wkly
Includes bibliographical references

Landon, Margaret

Anna and the King of Siam; illustrated by Margaret Ayer. Harper & Row 1944 391p il map hardcover o.p. pa $14.95 **92**

1. Governesses 2. Kings
ISBN 0-06-095488-4 pa

Anna Leonowens' experiences at the Siamese court in the 1860's. From her experiences she wrote two books, "The English governess at the Siamese court," and "The romance of the harem." The author has put these two books into one story with additions to make a complete tale.

Lang, Lang

Journey of a thousand miles; my story. [by] Lang Lang with David Ritz. Spiegel & Grau 2008 239p il $24.95 **92**

1. Classical musicians 2. Pianists
ISBN 978-0-385-52456-8
LC 2008-732

An autobiography of the Chinese classical piano prodigy.
"Lang tells the story of his childhood without self-pity or bitterness, making his success, and the book itself, all the more satisfying." N Y Times Book Rev

Larson, Erik

In the garden of beasts; love, terror, and an American family in Hitler's Berlin. Crown 2011 448p il map $26 **92**

1. Diplomats 2. Historians 3. National socialism 4. National socialism -- Germany
ISBN 978-0-307-40884-6; 0-307-40884-1
LC 2010045402

This is an account of the experiences of William Dodd and his family in Berlin. Dodd, formerly a professor of history, served as the American ambassador to Germany from 1933 to 1937. Index.

Larson describes the "experiences of U.S. ambassador to Germany William E. Dodd and his family in Berlin in the early years of Hitler's rule. Dodd had been teaching history at the University of Chicago when he was summoned by FDR to the German ambassadorship. Larson, using lots of archival as well as secondary-source research, focuses on Dodd's first year in Berlin and, using Dodd's diary, chillingly portrays the terror and oppression that slowly settled over Germany in 1933. Dodd quickly realized the Nazis' evil intentions; his daughter Martha, in her mid-20s, was initially smitten by the courteous SS soldiers surrounding her family, but over time she, too, became disenchanted with the brutality of the regime. Along the way Larson provides portraits based on primary-source impressions of Hermann Göring, Joseph Goebbels, Heinrich Himmler, and Hitler himself. He also traces the Dodds' lives after their time in Germany." Libr J
Includes bibliographical references

Larson, Kate Clifford

Bound for the promised land; Harriet Tubman, portrait of an American hero. Ballantine Bks. 2003 xxi, 402p il map $26.95; pa $14.95 **92**

1. Abolitionists 2. African American women -- Biography 3. Underground railroad
ISBN 0-345-45627-0; 0-345-45628-9 pa
LC 2004-297886

"Using a clear writing style, Larson does an excellent job of placing Tubman in the context of her times." SLJ
Includes bibliographical references

Latus, Janine

If I am missing or dead. Simon & Schuster 2007 309p il $25 **92**

1. Abused persons 2. Abused women 3. Journalists 4. Memoirists 5. Murder victims 6. Social activists
ISBN 978-0-7432-9653-3; 0-7432-9653-2
LC 2006-52313

"When journalist Latus's younger sister Amy vanishes at age 37 in 2002, authorities find a chiller of a note in Amy's desk: 'If I am missing or dead . . . question Ron.' Ron Ball is Amy's ex-con boyfriend, and when Amy's body is found, something shatters in Latus. A victim of abuse herself, Latus tunnels back to her difficult suburban childhood to decode why two smart, talented sisters might be so starving for love that they would risk their lives to get it. Latus's book unfolds like a gripping novel, getting at the brutal heart of darkness that underscores domestic violence." People

Lawday, David

The **giant** of the French Revolution; Danton, a life. Grove Press 2010 294p il map $27.50   **92**
1. Revolutionaries
ISBN 978-0-8021-1933-9

"This is the best biography of Danton to be written since Hilaire Belloc's over 100 years ago. Both the scholar and the general reader will find this biography an informative and lively read." Libr J

Includes bibliographical references

Lawrence, Sarahlee

River house; a memoir. Tin House Books 2010 272p pa $16.95   **92**
1. Adventure and adventurers 2. Farmers 3. Rafting (Sports)
ISBN 978-0-9825691-3-9

LC 2010-7702

"Handy with tools and rafts, a good neighbor, and a mighty fine horsewoman, Lawrence is also adept with language, writing with arresting lucidity and a driving need to understand her father, her legacy, the land, community, work, and herself. A true adventure story of rare dimension." Booklist

Lazenby, Roland

Jerry West; the life and legend of a basketball icon. ESPN Books; Ballantine Books 2010 xxi, 422p il $28   **92**
1. Basketball -- Biography 2. Basketball executives 3. Basketball players
ISBN 978-0-345-51083-9; 0-345-51083-6

LC 2009-43777

The life of the basketball great from his hardscrabble West Virginia youth to his pro career with the Los Angeles Lakers from 1960 to 1974.

"Sports biographies tend to career between breathless hagiography and the slyly salacious. Lazenby . . . has produced something of a different order — a first-rate piece of narrative nonfiction whose subject happens to be a star athlete. His biography of West is, by turns, smart, beautifully reported, well-written and psychologically shrewd. It also manages to put both the NBA and individual players in a telling social and historical context without straying into didacticism." PopMatters

Includes bibliographical references

LeMieux, Richard

Breakfast at Sally's; one homeless man's inspirational journey. Skyhorse 2008 433p il $24.95 **92**
1. Homeless 2. Homeless persons 3. Memoirists
ISBN 978-1-60239-293-9; 1-60239-293-5

LC 2008-24420

"Former successful businessman Richard LeMieux has lived better than the average American, but descended, through economic and personal failures, to homelessness for almost two years. Writing of life on the streets with his dog, Willow, he introduces a cast of characters from his experiences. . . . This inspirational political and social memoir can offer readers hope for a renewal of faith—in God and humanity. All public libraries will want this book for their collections." Libr J

Leader, Zachary

The **life** of Kingsley Amis. Pantheon Books 2007 996p $39.95   **92**
1. Authors 2. Essayists 3. Humorists 4. Literary critics 5. Novelists 6. Poets 7. Short story writers
ISBN 978-0-375-42498-4; 0-375-42498-9

LC 2006-35012

The "great virtue of Leader's biography of Amis is that you do not have to share his high opinion of the subject to benefit from the book's prodigious research and wealth of information so well presented." San Francisco Chronicle

Includes bibliographical references

Leaming, Barbara

Katharine Hepburn. Limelight Eds. 2000 549p il $23.95   **92**
1. Actors
ISBN 0-87910-293-4

LC 00-25227

This biography begins with a "portrait of the entire Hepburn clan, stressing the effect of the suicides that ran through Kate's maternal and paternal families. This is, in fact, a family biography, with at least half the book devoted to Hepburn's grandmother and mother. . . . By the time Kate enters the story, readers will be thoroughly caught up in a tale that already has delivered a full measure of intrigue, romance, and scandal. The book has been prodigiously researched (Leaming's source notes make fascinating reading on their own), and her access to various, previously unavailable papers not only makes possible the family history, but also paves the way for startling new revelations about Hepburn's life." Booklist {review of 1995 edition}

Lear, Linda J.

★ **Beatrix** Potter; a life in nature. [by] Linda Lear. Allen Lane/Penguin 2007 583p il $30   **92**
1. Artists 2. Authors 3. Biography, Individual 4. Children's authors 5. Illustrators
ISBN 9780312369347; 0-312-36934-4

LC 2006-51245

This is a biography of the children's author.

This "is a meticulously researched and brilliantly recreated life that . . . is endlessly fascinating and often illuminating. It is altogether a remarkable achievement." Booklist

Includes bibliographical references (p. 541-544)

Leavitt, David

The **man** who knew too much; Alan Turing and the invention of the computer. W. W. Norton 2006 319p il $22.95   **92**

1. Biography, Individual 2. Mathematicians

ISBN 0-393-05236-2

LC 2005-18034

This is a biography of the British mathematician.

The author "succeeds in drawing a wonderfully vivid picture of his shy, dry, brilliant hero." Natl Rev

Includes bibliographical references

Leavy, Jane

★ The **last** boy; Mickey Mantle and the end of America's childhood. HarperCollins Publishers 2010 456p il $27.99   **92**

1. Baseball -- Biography 2. Baseball -- History 3. Baseball players 4. Biography, Individual

ISBN 978-0-06-088352-2; 0-06-088352-9

This is a biography of the New York Yankees center fielder. Bibliography. Index.

"This is unlike any biography on the sports shelf. Leavy, in exploring her own ambivalent feelings toward Mantle, permits readers to experience the same confusing emotions that many of those around him felt: proud to bask in his reflected glory but too intimidated to confront him. . . . A masterpiece of sports biography." Booklist

Lebrecht, Norman

Why Mahler? how one man and ten symphonies changed our world. Pantheon Books 2010 326p $27.95   **92**

1. Biography, Individual 2. Composers 3. Conductors (Music)

ISBN 978-0-375-42381-9; 0-375-42381-8

LC 2010-06034

"This is music history, criticism, and biography at its best. A treasure trove for Mahler fans, this is also likely to convert even the most obstinate detractor. Highly recommended for all music lovers." Libr J

Includes bibliographical references

Lee, Carol Ann

The **hidden** life of Otto Frank. Morrow 2003 411p il hardcover o.p. pa $13.95   **92**

1. Amsterdam (Netherlands) -- Biography 2. Holocaust survivors 3. Holocaust, 1933-1945 4. Holocaust, Jewish (1939-1945) -- Netherlands -- Amsterdam 5. Jews -- Germany -- Biography 6. Jews, German -- Netherlands -- Amsterdam -- Biography 7. Parents of prominent persons 8. World War, 1939-1945 -- Collaborationists -- Netherlands -- Amsterdam

ISBN 0-06-052083-3 pa

LC 2002-38941

Lee offers a portrait of Anne Frank's father and seeks to settle the question of who betrayed the Frank family to the Nazis.

Lee, Hermione

★ **Edith** Wharton. Alfred A. Knopf 2007 869p il $35   **92**

1. Authors 2. Nonfiction writers 3. Novelists 4. Short story writers

ISBN 978-0-375-40004-9; 0-375-40004-4

LC 2006-48795

"Marked by an elegant literary style that does justice to its subject and a clear, compassionate eye for detail, [this] is not only the best book on its subject, but one of the finest literary biographies to appear in recent years." Atlanta Journal-Constitution

Includes bibliographical references

Willa Cather; double lives. Pantheon Bks. 1989 410p il hardcover o.p. pa $23 **92**

1. Authors 2. Novelists 3. Short story writers 4. Western writers

ISBN 0-679-73649-2 pa

LC 89-43233

The author's "discussion of Cather's 12 novels and numerous stories is so absorbing that it provokes a rereading of the work, which makes it a valuable critical study." N Y Times Book Rev

Includes bibliographical references

Leiber, Jerry

Hound dog; the Leiber & Stoller autobiography. [by] Jerry Leiber and Mike Stoller with David Ritz. Simon & Schuster 2009 322p il $25   **92**

1. Biography, Individual 2. Composers 3. Lyricists 4. Rock music -- History and criticism 5. Songwriters

ISBN 978-1-4165-5938-2; 1-4165-5938-8

LC 2008-47821

"Collaboration is a messy business. So is autobiography. But it shouldn't be forgotten that Leiber and Stoller were among the pioneers who helped bring black and white musical forms together. It has been a historically fraught process, but the collision of cultures is probably what has given such energy and tension to American music. Hound Dog is an important part of that story." N Y Times Book Rev

Includes bibliographical references

Leibowitz, Herbert A.

Something urgent I have to say to you: the life and works of William Carlos Williams; [by] Herbert Leibowitz. Farrar, Straus and Giroux 2011 496p il $40   **92**

1. Authors 2. Biography, Individual 3. Essayists 4. Physicians 5. Poets 6. Short story writers

ISBN 978-0-374-11329-2; 0-374-11329-7

LC 2010-46548

"In the 50s when Williams first became popular, convention said critics did not cross boundaries to conjecture on psychological motivations. This book is very much a product of a new century where all is transparent; and if Williams broke taboos in writing, Leibowitz does in reporting. . . . Leibowitz is quick to attribute Williams's writing to his tortured sexuality. The poet's pull between duty and a libidinous fantasy world is well known but never before used so relentlessly as capital. This also makes the book as readable as fiction, something bound to get it off the shelf and into the reader's hands. Leibowitz tackles the poetry through the man, not the other way around. . . . In the second half of the book, Leibowitz's comparison of Williams's book Spring and All to T.S. Eliot's The Waste Land is a brilliant analysis. Also, the careful reasoning behind Williams's In the American Grain is a contribution to literary thought. Another real bonus is that this biography tracks the Little Magazine movement in America nicely." Washington Independent Rev of Books

Includes bibliographical references

Leider, Emily W.

Myrna Loy; the only good girl in Hollywood. [by] Emily W. Leider. University of California Press 2011 411p il $34.95 **92**
1. Actors
ISBN 978-0-520-25320-9; 0-520-25320-5
LC 2011-11571

"Loy's gifts are easy to enjoy, hard to describe. She's been lucky in attracting an even-tempered sympathetic biographer like Ms. Leider, whose book, like the best of its genre, sends you back to the films." Wall Street J

Includes bibliographical references

Lelyveld, Joseph

Great soul; Mahatma Gandhi and his struggle with India. Alfred A. Knopf 2011 425p il map $28.95; ebook $14.99 **92**
1. Authors 2. Biography, Individual 3. Essayists 4. Journalists 5. Memoirists 6. Pacifists 7. Political leaders 8. Statesmen -- India 9. Writers on politics
ISBN 978-0-307-26958-4; 978-0-307-59536-2 ebook
LC 2010-34252

"Mr. Lelyveld has restored human depth to the Mahatma, the plaster saint, allowing his flawed human readers to feel a little closer to his lofty ideals of nonviolence and universal brotherhood." N Y Times (Late N Y Ed)

Includes bibliographical references

Omaha blues; a memory loop. Farrar, Straus and Giroux 2005 226p il $22; pa $14 **92**
1. Biography, Individual 2. Newspaper editors 3. Nonfiction writers
ISBN 0-374-22590-7; 0-312-42510-4 pa
LC 2004-12362

In this autobiographical narrative, the American newspaper editor reflects on his childhood.

This "is a worldly, graceful book; there is a great deal to admire in it and to be moved by." New Leader

Lemmon, Gayle Tzemach

The **dressmaker** of Khair Khana; five sisters, one remarkable family, and the woman who risked everything to keep them safe. Harper 2011 256p **92**
1. Businesswomen 2. Dressmakers 3. Dressmaking
ISBN 978-0-06-173237-9
LC 2010-20774

This book "is a fascinating window on Afghan life under the Taliban and a celebration of women the world over who support their loved ones with tenacity, inventiveness and sheer guts." People

Includes bibliographical references

Lemon, Alex

Happy; a memoir. Scribner 2010 292p $25 **92**
1. Authors 2. Biography, Individual 3. Brain -- Diseases 4. Poets 5. Poets, American
ISBN 978-1-4165-5023-5; 1-4165-5023-2
LC 2009-27293

The author, a poet, "was a carefree, hard partying, baseball-playing college student at Macalester College in Minnesota in 1997 when he suffered a stroke and later two brain bleeds. Readers are swept along on his rough ride during the next two years, through his nasty travails of frenetic drug and alcohol use, terribly misguided attempts to cope with his deteriorating and frightening condition. . . . Lemon offers a raw and honest narration of his college life, his relationships with girlfriends and family members, especially his loving and quirky mother. . . . [This] is a voltaic narrative that is alternately horrifying and touching." Publ Wkly

Lemonick, Michael D.

The **Georgian** star; how William and Caroline Herschel revolutionized our understanding of the cosmos. W.W. Norton 2009 199p il map $23.95; pa $14.95 **92**
1. Astronomers
ISBN 978-0-393-06574-9; 0-393-06574-X; 978-0-393-33709-9 pa; 0-393-33709-X pa
LC 2008-29820

A tribute to the scientific contributions of William Herschel and his pioneering sister, Caroline, describes their establishment of surveying techniques that are still in use, Caroline's cataloging of nebulae, and William's discovery of infrared radiation.

"A rewarding account of two scientists who not only made great discoveries but enjoyed world recognition during their long, eventful lives." Kirkus

Includes bibliographical references

Lessing, Doris May

★ **Under** my skin; volume one of my autobiography, to 1949. {by} Doris Lessing. HarperCollins Pubs. 1994 419p il hardcover o.p. pa $15 **92**
1. Authors 2. Dramatists 3. Essayists 4. Nobel laureates for literature 5. Novelists 6. Short story writers
ISBN 0-06-092664-3 pa
LC 94-20051

"In this immediate, vivid, beautifully paced memoir, Doris Lessing sets the individual against history, the personal against the general, and shows, by the example of her own life set down honestly, how biography and fiction mesh, how fiction transmutes the personal to the general, how the particular experience illuminates the universe." London Rev Books

Leuchtenburg, William Edward

Herbert Hoover; [by] William E. Leuchtenburg. Times Books 2009 186p $22 **92**
1. Biography, Individual 2. Depressions -- 1929 -- United States 3. Philanthropists 4. Presidents 5. Presidents -- United States 6. Secretaries of commerce
ISBN 978-0-8050-6958-7; 0-8050-6958-5
LC 2008-26456

This is a biography of the American president.

"A veteran historian of this period, Leuchtenburg brings vivid prose and strong opinions to this richly insightful biography of a president whose impressive business acumen served him poorly." Publ Wkly

Includes bibliographical references (p. 167-172)

Levenson, Thomas

Newton and the counterfeiter; the unknown detective career of the world's greatest scientist. Houghton Mifflin Harcourt 2009 318p $25; pa $14.95 **92**

1. Biography, Individual 2. Counterfeiters 3. Counterfeits and counterfeiting 4. Mathematicians 5. Physicists 6. Writers on science

ISBN 978-0-15-101278-7; 0-15-101278-4; 978-0-547-33604-6 pa; 0-547-33604-7 pa

LC 2008-53511

"Levenson demonstrates a surpassing felicity in his brisk treatment of this late-17th-century true-crime adventure. . . . Swift, agile treatment of a little known but highly entertaining episode in a legendary life." Kirkus

Includes bibliographical references

Lever, Evelyne

Marie Antoinette; the last queen of France. translated from the French by Catherine Temerson. Farrar, Straus & Giroux 2000 357p il hardcover o.p. pa $16.95 **92**

1. Queens

ISBN 0-312-28333-4 pa

LC 00-28763

The author examines "the opulent Versailles subculture and the queen whose royal excesses served as a major catalyst for the revolutionary upheaval of 1789. Through the skillful use of memoirs and other primary documents, Lever creates an empathic picture of Louis XVI's headstrong wife." Libr J

Includes bibliographical references

Lever, Maurice

Beaumarchais; a biography. Farrar, Straus and Giroux 2008 411p $35 **92**

1. Authors 2. Biography, Individual 3. Dramatists 4. Dramatists, French

ISBN 9780374113285; 0-374-11328-9

LC 2008-55449

"Best known as the author of the comedies that became Mozart's 'The Marriage of Figaro' and Rossini's 'The Barber of Seville,' Beaumarchais was a high-spirited adventurer for whom writing plays was only an 'honest relaxation.' This erudite and wry biography covers the full range of his occupations, including watchmaking, espionage, pamphleteering, and transatlantic trade." New Yorker

Includes bibliographical references

Leverich, Lyle

Tom; the unknown Tennessee Williams. Norton 2007 644p il pa $35 **92**

1. Authors 2. Dramatists 3. Dramatists, American 4. Novelists 5. Short story writers

ISBN 978-0-393-31663-6; 0-393-31663-7

This is the first installment of a projected two-volume biography of the American dramatist. Coverage begins with Williams' birth in 1911 and extends to the opening of The Glass Menagerie in 1945.

"The book is a tremendous accomplishment, and Leverich is an appealing biographer: modest, thorough, balanced, and passionate. In prose that is clear—if not scintillating—he bushwhacks a path through a morass of gossip and myth, and prepares the way for a more subtle interpretation of the man and his plays." New Yorker

Levi, Primo, 1919-1987

The **periodic** table; translated from the Italian by Raymond Rosenthal. Schocken Bks. 1984 233p hardcover o.p. pa $12 **92**

1. Authors 2. Chemists 3. Essayists 4. Holocaust survivors 5. Memoirists 6. Novelists 7. Poets 8. Short story writers

ISBN 0805210415 pa; 0-8052-1041-5 pa

LC 84-5453

"This curious memoir, organized in 21 chapters from Argon to Zinc, ransacks the periodic table of the elements for strained metaphors as it traces one adolescent's search for identity. Levi ironically portrays himself as a young aspiring chemist eager to fathom nature's secrets." Publ Wkly

Levin, Gail

Lee Krasner; a biography. William Morrow 2011 546p il $30; ebook $23.99 **92**

1. Artists 2. Artists -- United States 3. Biography, Individual 4. Painters 5. Women artists

ISBN 978-0-06-184525-3; 0-06-184525-6; 978-0-06-207462-1 ebook; 0-06-207462-8 ebook

LC 2010-46347

This is a "full-length treatment of the talented and tenacious painter. . . . Levin piles up adequate evidence to assure Krasner's place in the American abstract expressionist pantheon. Detailed and meticulously researched, this is essential reading for those who want to know more about protofeminist artist Krasner, New York-based action/abstract expressionist painting, and the postwar NYC art scene." Libr J

Levy, Alan Howard

Floyd Patterson; a boxer and a gentleman. [by] Alan H. Levy. McFarland & Co. 2008 289p il pa $35 **92**

1. African American athletes 2. Boxers (Persons) 3. Boxing -- Biography

ISBN 978-0-7864-3950-8; 0-7864-3950-5

LC 2008-32250

This is a "biography of the man who was the youngest world heavyweight champion in boxing history as well as the first boxer to regain the championship after losing it. . . . This book is not only an excellent study of Patterson but a superior source on professional boxing from the mid-1950s through the mid-1970s." Libr J

Includes bibliographical references

Levy, Andrew

The **first** emancipator; the forgotten story of Robert Carter, the founding father who freed his

slaves. Random House 2005 310p hardcover o.p.
pa $15.95   **92**
1. Biography, Individual 2. Plantation owners 3.
Slavery -- United States
ISBN 0-375-50865-1; 0-375-76104-7 pa
LC 2004-54054
"This well-written and thoroughly engaging book will
certainly appeal to readers interested in the history of 18th-
and 19th-century Virginia, but also to those interested in the
history of slavery and racism in America and in historical
biography." Publ Wkly
Includes bibliographical references

Levy, Emanuel
Vincente Minnelli; Hollywood's dark dreamer.
St. Martin's Press 2009 448p il $35   **92**
1. Biography, Individual 2. Motion picture directors
3. Motion picture producers and directors 4. Motion
pictures -- History
ISBN 978-0-312-32925-9; 0-312-32925-3
LC 2008-28751
"Relying mostly on secondary sources, Levy traces
[Minnelli's] career from early days as a stage designer in
New York to arrival at MGM and his most fruitful period,
the 1950s, when his films were box office and critical successes, to his frustrating final decades after the collapse of
the studio system. . . . Levy provides some valuable insight
into the life of a genuine artist who struggled—frequently
successfully—to inject a higher aesthetic into popular
entertainment." Booklist
Includes bibliographical references

Levy, Shawn
Paul Newman; a life. Harmony Books 2009
490p il $29.99; pa $16   **92**
1. Actors 2. Automobile racing drivers 3. Motion
picture directors
ISBN 978-0-307-35375-7; 0-307-35375-3; 978-0-307-
35376-4 pa; 0-307-35376-1 pa
LC 2009-11220
This is a behind-the-scenes examination of the actor's
life, from his merry pranks on the set to his lasting romance
with Joanne Woodward to the devastating impact of his
son's death from a drug overdose.
"An illuminating look at one of the true greats, full of humor and intelligent analysis—highly recommended." Kirkus
Includes bibliographical references

Lewis, David Levering
★ **W.E.B.** Du Bois; a biography. Henry Holt
and Co. 2009 893p hardcover o.p. pa $25   **92**
1. African Americans -- Biography 2. African
Americans -- Civil rights 3. Authors 4. Civil rights
activists 5. Editors 6. Essayists 7. Historians 8.
Nonfiction writers 9. Novelists 10. Sociologists
ISBN 978-0-8050-8769-7; 0-8050-8769-9; 978-0-
8050-8805-2 pa; 0-8050-8805-9 pa
LC 2008-696
This is a biography of the African American scholar who
helped bring forth the civil rights movement.

Lewis, Jerry
Dean & me; a love story. Doubleday 2005 340p
il $26.95   **92**
1. Actors 2. Comedians 3. Motion picture directors 4.
Singers 5. Television personalities
ISBN 0-7679-2086-4
LC 2005-49682
"This is a wild, joyous book, but also a heartbreaking
one." N Y Times Book Rev

Lewis, Michael
★ The **blind** side; evolution of a game. W.W.
Norton 2006 299p $24.95   **92**
1. Biography, Individual 2. College sports 3. College
sports -- United States 4. Football -- Biography 5.
Football players
ISBN 978-0-393-06123-9; 0-393-06123-X
LC 2006-23509
The author "describes the NFL's ever-growing obsession
with left tackles as a means to counter defenders who seem
to grow bigger, stronger, and more vicious each season. He
juxtaposes that narrative with the unlikely story of [football
player] Michael Oher. . . . The book works on three levels.
First as a shrewd analysis of the NFL; second, as an expose
of the insanity of big-time college football recruiting; and,
third, as a moving portrait of the positive effect that love,
family, and education can have in reversing the path of a life
that was destined to be lived unhappily and, most likely, end
badly." Booklist

Li, Charles N.
The **bitter** sea; coming of age in a China before
Mao. HarperCollins Publishers 2008 283p il hardcover o.p. pa $14.99   **92**
1. Anthropologists 2. Biography, Individual 3. College
teachers 4. Linguists
ISBN 978-0-06-134664-4; 0-06-134664-0; 978-0-06-
170954-8 pa; 0-06-170954-9 pa
LC 2007-25697
The author, "who had an extraordinary life growing up
in pre-Communist China, shares his story of betrayal, loss,
hope, and triumph in this lyrical account. . . . This brilliant
memoir is as much about modern Chinese history as it is
about familial relationships." Libr J

Li, Laura Tyson
Madame Chiang Kai-Shek; China's eternal first
lady. Atlantic Monthly 2006 557p il map $30 **92**
1. Spouses of presidents
ISBN 0-87113-933-2; 978-0-87113-933-7
LC 2005-58858
This is a biography of the wife of former Chinese presi-
dent Chiang Kai-Shek.
"With access to newly opened files, fluent insights into
China's convulsive transformation, and a phenomenal gift
for elucidating intricate politics and complicated psyches,
Li brilliantly analyzes a fearless and profoundly conflicted
woman of extraordinary force." Booklist
Includes bibliographical references

Li, Leslie

Daughter of heaven; a memoir with earthly recipes. Arcade Pub. 2005 274p $25; pa $13.95   **92**
1. Chinese cooking
ISBN 1-55970-768-2; 1-55970-800-X pa
LC 2004-23452
The book centers on the author's "relationship with both
her father and Nai-nai, her grandmother, who lands in New
York City for an extended visit. . . . In stories and in the nearly
20 recipes (including Drunken Chicken and Cantonese Fried
Rice), Li reveals the tale of an Asian woman caught between
many different worlds and times and places." Booklist

Lind, Michael

What Lincoln believed; the values and convic-
tions of America's greatest president. Doubleday
2005 358p $27.95   **92**
1. Lawyers 2. Members of Congress 3. Presidents 4.
Presidents -- United States 5. State legislators
ISBN 0-385-50739-9
LC 2004-41333
"Some readers may not recognize their own cherished
Lincoln in Lind's well-researched and reasoned book. Yet
it adds a valuable perspective to the vast arena of Lincoln
scholarship." Christ Sci Monit
Includes bibliographical references

Lindbergh, Reeve

Under a wing; a memoir. Delta Trade Paper-
backs 1999 223p il pa $15   **92**
1. Air force officers 2. Air pilots 3. Authors 4.
Children of prominent persons 5. Children's authors 6.
Diarists 7. Essayists 8. Generals 9. Memoirists 10.
Novelists 11. Poets 12. Spouses of prominent persons
ISBN 978-0-385-33444-0; 0-385-33444-3
"A rare memoir whose goal is not to expose but finally
to understand." Libr J

Linklater, Andro

An **artist** in treason; the extraordinary double
life of General James Wilkinson. Walker 2009 392p
il map $27   **92**
1. Biography, Individual 2. Generals 3. Spies 4.
Territorial governors
ISBN 978-0-8027-1720-7
LC 2009-19184
A profile of the Continental Army general explores his
career with the Spanish secret service, his protection by four
presidents in spite of his treasonous acts, and his role in foil-
ing Aaron Burr's conspiracy to break up the Union.
The author "lucidly details the general's often tangled
affairs, but he also uses his story to illuminate the personal
feuds, political struggles, and international entanglements
that helped shape the young United States. He manages to
tell this story of skullduggery and self-interest without wag-
ging his finger in high moral dudgeon at Wilkinson's betrayals. In fact, at times the wily double-crosser almost comes
across as sympathetic—but never as someone to trust."
Am Heritage
Includes bibliographical references and index.

Linn, Edward

Hitter: the life and turmoils of Ted Williams;
{by} Ed Linn. 1993 437p il hardcover o.p. pa
$16   **92**
1. Baseball managers 2. Baseball players
ISBN 0-15-600091-1 pa
LC 92-41870
"Linn's book is not a typical game-by-game baseball
biography, but a series of snapshots of Williams's career.
The {author} . . . touches on the many high points, but does
not neglect Williams's warts, including his constant battle
with Boston baseball writers. The product of an unhappy
childhood, Williams formed close friendships with the 'underdogs,' and gave unsparingly of himself to a charity for
combatting cancer in children." Libr J

Lithgow, John, 1945-

Drama; an actor's education. John Lithgow.
Harper 2011 p. cm. $26.99; $12.99   **92**
1. Actors -- United States -- Biography 2. Biography &
Autobiography -- Entertainment & Performing Arts 3.
Biography & Autobiography -- Personal Memoirs
ISBN 978-0-06-173497-7; 978-0-06-209773-6 ebook;
9780061734977
LC 2011008172
"More than the run-of-the-mill 'And then I met . . . And
then I was in . . . ' actor's autobiography, this is both a mem-
oir full of emotion and a cautionary tale." Libr J

Lively, Penelope

A **house** unlocked. Grove Press 2002 225p il
$23; pa $13   **92**
1. Authors 2. Children's authors 3. Novelists 4. Short
story writers
ISBN 0-8021-1712-0; 0-8021-4007-6 pa
LC 2001-55745
"The British novelist Penelope Lively spent her early
childhood in Egypt, but it was her school holidays at Gol-
soncott—a manor house that her grandparents bought in
the wilds of Somerset, in 1923—that shaped her life. In
this slim, beguiling book, Lively describes the contents
and customs of the house. . . . By meticulously tracing the
provenance of these objects, she re-creates the life they once
furnished." New Yorker
Includes bibliographical references

LoBrutto, Vincent

Stanley Kubrick; a biography. Da Capo Press
1999 579p pa $20   **92**
1. Motion picture directors 2. Motion picture producers
and directors -- Biography
ISBN 0-306-80906-0
LC 98-47434
"For the true film buff, there's an astonishing amount of
technical information, but there's also a good deal of illuminating backstage human interest." Publ Wkly
Includes filmography and bibliographical references

Lobdell, William

Losing my religion; how I lost my faith reporting on religion in America--and found unexpected peace. Collins 2009 291p $25.99   **92**
1. Bloggers 2. Journalists
ISBN 978-0-06-162681-4; 0-06-162681-3

LC 2008-24010

"Lobdell's spiritual journey fascinates, not least on account of the irony of his trajectory from agnosticism to belief to atheism while covering religion. It's a story that may raise eyebrows among believers and nonbelievers alike." Booklist
Includes bibliographical references

Long, Robert Emmet

Truman Capote, enfant terrible.   Continuum 2008 130p $24.95   **92**
1. Authors 2. Authors, American 3. Nonfiction writers 4. Novelists 5. Short story writers
ISBN 978-0-8264-2763-2; 0-8264-2763-4

LC 2008-4957

Long recounts "Capote's early life, highlighting his tragic childhood and the relationships the eccentric author maintained with various members of New York's elite. Long draws heavily from Capote's unpublished papers and from Gerald Clarke's Capote: A Biography. This brief sketch, however, sets the stage for a compelling analysis of the effect of the author's tragic life on the gothic nature of his prose. Long brilliantly places each piece in the context of the author's life and of the culture at the time of its release. The book ends with a retrospective contemplation of Capote's influence and place in American letters. Each chapter represents a cogent and concise snapshot of Capote's genius in a specific period, while the entire book becomes a journey through Capote's life, work, and demons placed within the context of American literary culture." Libr J
Includes bibliographical references

Lopez, Steve

★ The **soloist**; a lost dream, an unlikely friendship, and the redemptive power of music. G. P. Putnam's Sons 2008 273p hardcover o.p. pa $15   **92**
1. Biography, Individual 2. Homeless 3. Homeless persons 4. Music therapy 5. Schizophrenics 6. Street entertainers 7. Violinists
ISBN 978-0-399-15506-2; 0-399-15506-6; 978-0-425-23836-3 pa; 0-425-23836-9 pa

LC 2007-46314

The true story of Nathaniel Ayers, a musician who becomes schizophrenic and homeless, and his friendship with Steve Lopez, the Los Angeles columnist who discovers and writes about him in the newspaper.

"With self-effacing humor, fast-paced yet elegant prose and unsparing honesty, Lopez tells an inspiring story of heartbreak and hope." Publ Wkly

Lorance, Loretta

Becoming Bucky Fuller. MIT Press 2009 284p il $29.95   **92**
1. Architects 2. Engineers 3. Inventors 4. Mechanical engineers 5. Writers on science
ISBN 978-0-262-12302-0; 0-262-12302-9

LC 2008-29418

The author is the "first to compare systematically the authorized biography with the actual documents in Fuller's scrapbooks. Her focus is the critical interlude between 1927 and 1930, when Fuller conceived the Dymaxion House and first presented it to the public. Her chief insight is that if Fuller was a futurist prophet, it was only inadvertently. He should rather be seen as a failed entrepreneur who recast himself as a bold visionary only after the Dymaxion project collapsed ignominiously. . . . In the end, her revisionist Fuller is not terribly different from the one we have always had before us—a vivid example of the inventor/salesman/messiah type that America seems to produce every generation or so." Wall Street J
Includes bibliographical references

Love, Robert

The **Great** Oom; the improbable birth of yoga in America. Viking 2010 402p il   **92**
1. Yoga 2. Yogis
ISBN 067002175X; 9780670021758

LC 2009044784

This book focuses on Pierre Bernard's involvement in the popularization of Yoga in the United States. Bibliography. Index.

A "history of yoga's early days in America. The spiritual discipline that has colonized America's gyms and trendy loft spaces was once a fringe practice, its advocates treated as charlatans and, occasionally, criminals. Yoga's cultural rise is a story of scandal, financial shenanigans, bodily discipline, oversize egos and bizarre love triangles, with a few performing elephants thrown in for good measure. Mr. Love tells his story through the life of one of yoga's earliest promoters, Pierre Bernard—known as the 'Great Oom'—a zany man whose talent for self-invention rivaled that of P.T. Barnum." Wall Street J
Includes bibliographical references

Lovell, Mary S.

A **rage** to live: a biography of Richard and Isabel Burton. Norton 1998 910p il hardcover o.p. pa $19.95   **92**
1. Asian studies specialists 2. Authors 3. Explorers 4. Middle Eastern studies specialists 5. Travel writers
ISBN 0-393-32039-1 pa

LC 98-29886

This is "a readable narrative of great verve and passion." N Y Rev Books
Includes bibliographical references

Loving, Jerome

Mark Twain; the adventures of Samuel L. Clemens. University of California Press 2010 491p il $34.95   **92**
1. Authors 2. Authors, American 3. Biography, Individual 4. Essayists 5. Humorists 6. Memoirists 7. Novelists 8. Satirists 9. Short story writers 10. Travel writers
ISBN 978-0-520-25257-8

LC 2009-15366

The author "serves up a balanced literary biography of a crowded life—'to renew our acquaintance with this familiar stranger in our literature and culture.' Many of the best chapters include sensitive appraisals of The Adventures of Huckleberry Finn, The Tragedy of Pudd'nhead Wilson, and the anonymously published Personal Recollections of Joan of Arc, with The Adventures of Tom Sawyer put in a different context as possibly the most overrated work of American fiction when considered as adult literature. . . . [This] is a solid contribution to literary interpretation of the man who infused American literature with what has been called 'tragic laughter.'" Publ Wkly

Includes bibliographical references

Lowe, Jaime

Digging for dirt; the life and death of ODB. Faber and Faber 2008 273p $25   **92**

1. African American musicians 2. Rap music 3. Rap musicians

ISBN 978-0-8654-7969-2; 0-8654-7969-0

LC 2008-29144

"As one of Wu Tang Clan, Russell Jones became known for his off-kilter raps and odd stage mannerisms. Like bandmates Method Man and Ghostface Killah, he also had a solo career as Ol' Dirty Bastard (ODB) that placed two number-one albums on the rap charts, and his duet with Mariah Carey, 'Fantasy,' brought mainstream success. Simply put, life was good. As time went by, though, he devolved into a more and more disturbed state, and some of his entertaining traits came to suggest mental-health issues. . . . Seemingly unable to avoid incarceration for a variety of offenses, he died of 'heart failure after cerebral hemorrhaging,' arguably caused by years of drug and other abuse. Lowe tells ODB's tale admirably thoroughly, making this a must-have profile of a singular personality and another sad casualty in rap history." Booklist

Lukas, Christopher

Blue genes; a memoir of loss and survival. Doubleday 2008 248p il $24.95   **92**

1. Authors 2. Biography, Individual 3. Depression (Psychology) 4. Journalists 5. Manic-depressive illness 6. Television directors 7. Television producers 8. Television scriptwriters

ISBN 978-0-385-52520-6; 0-385-52520-6

LC 2008-6648

In this memoir, "Lukas shatters the silence surrounding the long history of suicide in his Hungarian-German-Jewish family, especially that of his older brother, J. Anthony Lukas (Tony). Depression and what is now diagnosed as bipolar disorder hounded various family members, most notably the brothers' beautiful college-educated actress mother, Elizabeth, whose deepening depression . . . led her to cut her own throat in 1941, when the boys were just six and eight. Lukas writes with the reassuring sagacity of hindsight, knowing the negative long-term effects of his mother's mental illness on his brother especially. . . . In clear, forceful prose, the author attempts to make sense of these calamities and assert a life-affirming purpose." Publ Wkly

Luxenberg, Steve

Annie's ghosts; a journey into a family secret. Hyperion Books 2009 401p il $24.99   **92**

1. Newspaper editors

ISBN 978-1-4013-2247-2; 1-4013-2247-6

LC 2008-55661

"Part memoir, part mystery, part history of the mental-health movement, . . . [this] is a fascinating account of a life lived in the shadows." Booklist

Includes bibliographical references

Lycett, Andrew

Dylan Thomas: a new life. Overlook Press 2004 434p il $35   **92**

1. Authors 2. Poets

ISBN 1-58567-541-5

"Other biographies . . . have ably recounted the essential details of Thomas's life, but Lycett here provides a wealth of useful detail, bringing the Welsh poet's life story up to date." Libr J

Includes bibliographical references

Lynn, Kenneth S.

Hemingway. Harvard University Press 1995 702p il pa $27   **92**

1. Authors 2. Authors, American 3. Journalists 4. Nobel laureates for literature 5. Novelists 6. Poets 7. Short story writers

ISBN 0-674-38732-5; 978-0-674-38732-4

LC 95-129513

"Taking as his premise Hemingway's glib assertion that the only analyst he relied upon was his 'portable Corona Number 3,' Lynn tracks the exploration of a disordered inner world as Hemingway sought to find some sort of resolution to the agony of his personal conflicts through 'his cunningly wrought fiction.' The man who emerges from Lynn's biography is a vastly more complex and compelling figure than the white-bearded, pontificating 'Papa' of myth." Publ Wkly

Includes bibliographical references

Lynn, Loretta

Still woman enough; a memoir. {by} Loretta Lynn with Patsi Bale Cox. Hyperion 2002 244p il $24.95; pa $7.99   **92**

1. Country musicians 2. Singers 3. Songwriters

ISBN 0-7868-6650-0; 0-7868-8987-X pa

In this sequel to Coal miner's daughter, "Lynn mostly focuses on her marriage and the trials and pleasures of Nashville stardom, including fond recollections of friends like Conway Twitty and Tammy Wynette. . . . Though her grammar may make purists flinch . . . Lynn's literary voice is as natural and endearing as her songs." Publ Wkly

Lytle, Mark H.

The **gentle** subversive; Rachel Carson, Silent spring, and the rise of the environmental movement. Oxford University Press 2007 277p il $23; $12.95   **92**

1. Authors 2. Biography, Individual 3. College teachers 4. Conservationists 5. Environmental movement 6. Environmentalism -- History 7. Marine biologists 8. Writers on nature 9. Writers on science

ISBN 978-0-19-517246-1; 0-19-517246-9; 978-0-19-517247-8 pa; 0-19-517247-7 pa

LC 2006-49350

The author "examines the life of Rachel Carson, founder of today's environmental movement and antithesis of the stereotypical 1950s woman. Carson was educated in the sciences, worked full time, and was her family's primary provider and caregiver. Genteel in appearance, she was firmly committed to her goal of preserving nature. Using a lyrical, narrative style, Lytle probes Carson's interests and her purposes in writing a series of well-known books that include The Sea Around Us—and her most famous, Silent Spring." Libr J

Includes bibliographical references

Maathai, Wangari

Unbowed; a memoir. [by] Wangari Muta Maathai. Knopf 2006 314p il hardcover o.p. pa $15   **92**
1. Biography, Individual 2. Biologists 3. Conservationists 4. Environmentalists 5. Forest conservation -- Kenya 6. Nobel laureates for peace
ISBN 0-307-26348-7; 978-0-307-26348-3; 0-307-27520-5 pa; 978-0-307-27520-2 pa
    LC 2006-44729
"Nobel Peace Prize winner Maathai tells the unforgettable story of her Kenya girlhood, struggles as a biologist and professor, and founding of the Green Belt Movement to restore Kenya's decimated forests and provide women with work." Booklist

MacLeish, Archibald

Archibald MacLeish: reflections; edited by Bernard A. Drabeck and Helen E. Ellis; foreword by Richard Wilbur. University of Mass. Press 1986 291p il $40; pa $18.95   **92**
1. Authors 2. Biography, Individual 3. Essayists 4. Librarians of Congress 5. Poets
ISBN 0-87023-511-7; 0-87023-623-7 pa
    LC 85-28912
"In this genial, relaxed book we have a golden view of the candidly retrospective statesman-poet in his old age as he really was, with most pretension and all rhetoric abandoned." N Y Times Book Rev

Includes bibliographical references

MacPherson, Myra

★ All governments lie; the life and times of rebel journalist I.F. Stone. Scribner 2006 564p il hardcover o.p. pa $20   **92**
1. Authors 2. Biography, Individual 3. Journalists 4. Magazine editors
ISBN 978-0-684-80713-3; 0-684-80713-0; 978-1-4165-5679-4 pa; 1-4165-5679-6 pa
    LC 2006-42389
"This biography interweaves his life and journalism within the context of the social and political era, providing an engaging overview of a complex man who challenged his contemporaries. Many of the political issues Stone confronted will resonate with today's readers." Libr J

Includes bibliographical references

Macintyre, Ben

Agent Zigzag; a true story of Nazi espionage, love, and betrayal. Harmony Books 2007 364p il $25.95   **92**
1. Intelligence service agents 2. Thieves 3. World War,

1939-1945 -- Secret service
ISBN 978-0-307-35340-5
    LC 2006-101603
This is a biography of Eddie Chapman, a British double agent during World War II.
"Meticulously researched—relying extensively on recently released wartime files of Britain's Secret Intelligence Service—Macintyre's biography often reads like a spy thriller." Publ Wkly

Includes bibliographical references

Maddox, Brenda

Rosalind Franklin: the dark lady of DNA. HarperCollins Pubs. 2002 380p il $29.95; pa $15.95 **92**
1. Biologists 2. Chemists 3. DNA 4. Geochemists
ISBN 0-06-018407-8; 0-06-098508-9 pa
    LC 2002-68898
The author "does an excellent job of revisiting Franklin's scientific contributions . . . while revealing Franklin's complicated personality." Libr J

Includes bibliographical references

Magueijo, Joao

A brilliant darkness; the extraordinary life and disappearance of Ettore Majorana, the troubled genius of the nuclear age. Basic Books 2009 280p il $27.50   **92**
1. Biography, Individual 2. Neutrinos 3. Nuclear physics 4. Nuclear physics -- History 5. Physicists
ISBN 978-0-465-00903-9; 0-465-00903-4
    LC 2009-37678
The author "paints the life of a twenty something math prodigy who joined Enrico Fermi, Emilio Segre, and the other 'Via Panisperna Boys' who in 1934 discovered nuclear fusion. The author could have easily fallen into the jargon of his profession to describe the work of a fellow scientist, but he does not. His clear explanation of Majorana's insight into nuclear physics, often accompanied with drawings and illustrations, will appeal to a wide audience." Libr J

Includes bibliographical references

Maguire, James

Impresario; the life and times of Ed Sullivan. Billboard Books 2006 344p il $24.95   **92**
1. Biography, Individual 2. Columnists 3. Television personalities
ISBN 0-8230-7962-7; 978-0-8230-7962-9 ISBN-13
The author "has written a fascinating biography and meticulously recorded the birth of TV, the heyday of newspaper columnists and the glamour of New York." Publ Wkly

Mahoney, Richard D.

Sons and brothers: the days of Jack and Bobby Kennedy. Arcade Pub. 1999 441p il $27.95; pa $14.95   **92**
1. Attorneys general 2. Diplomats 3. Financiers 4. Members of Congress 5. Parents of presidents 6. Presidential candidates 7. Presidents 8. Regulatory agency officials 9. Senators 10. Siblings of presidents
ISBN 1-55970-480-2; 1-55970-534-5 pa
    LC 99-25681

"Writing in a steady, almost relentlessly elegiac tone, Mahoney proves that the lives and deaths of John F. and Robert F. Kennedy remain as compelling now as they were throughout the turbulent 1960s." Publ Wkly

Includes bibliographical references

Mailer, Norris Church

A **ticket** to the circus; a memoir. Random House 2010 416p il $26 **92**

1. Artists 2. Authors 3. Authors, American 4. Biography, Individual 5. Essayists 6. Novelists 7. Spouses of prominent persons

ISBN 978-1-4000-6794-7; 1-4000-6794-4

LC 2009-33941

This memoir by Norris Church Mailer focuses on her marriage of thirty-three years to Norman Mailer.

The author adds "a fat new sheaf to the public dossier on her late husband, Norman Mailer, and tells an involving coming-of-age story to boot. . . . The book will be of interest to anyone who works in a university marriage lab. It also shows that Norman wasn't the only talented raconteur in the family." N Y Times Book Rev

Malcolm X

★ The **autobiography** of Malcolm X; with the assistance of Alex Haley; introduction by M. S. Handler; epilogue by Alex Haley; afterword by Ossie Davis. Ballantine Bks. 1992 500p $25; pa $15 **92**

1. African Americans -- Biography 2. Black Muslim leaders 3. Black Muslims 4. Civil rights activists

ISBN 0-345-37975-6; 0-345-37671-4 pa

LC 92-52659

Based on tape-recorded conversations with Alex Haley, this account of the life of the Black Muslim leader was completed shortly before his murder.

Alex Haley "did his job with sensitivity and with devotion. . . . {The book} will have a permanent place in the literature of the Afro-American struggle." N Y Rev Books

Malcolm, Janet

Two lives; Gertrude and Alice. Yale University Press 2007 229p il $25 **92**

1. Authors 2. Authors, American 3. Biography, Individual 4. Essayists 5. Literary critics 6. Memoirists 7. Novelists 8. Poets 9. Private secretaries

ISBN 978-0-300-12551-1; 0-300-12551-8

LC 2007-12085

"This is a vital addition to Stein criticism as well as an important work that critiques the political responsibility of the artist (even a genius) to the larger world." Publ Wkly

Includes bibliographical references

Mandela, Nelson

Long walk to freedom: the autobiography of Nelson Mandela. Little, Brown 1994 558p il hardcover o.p. pa $16.95 **92**

1. Human rights activists 2. Nobel laureates for peace 3. Political leaders 4. Political prisoners 5. Presidents

ISBN 0-316-54818-9 pa

LC 94-79980

This book "provides important new evidence to the forty-year story of apartheid, as seen by its most formidable opponent. And there is enough candour to provide insights into the nature of leadership." Times Lit Suppl

Mandela, Nelson, 1918-

Conversations with myself. Farrar Straus & Giroux 2010 454p il map $28 **92**

1. Apartheid -- South Africa 2. Biography, Individual 3. Human rights activists 4. Nobel laureates for peace 5. Political leaders 6. Political prisoners 7. Presidents 8. Presidents -- South Africa

ISBN 978-0-374-12895-1; 0-374-12895-2

LC 2010-933174

This "is a moving account of Mandela's struggle and a testament to his triumph." Publ Wkly

Includes bibliographical references

In his own words; edited by Kader Asmal, David Chidester, [and] Wilmot James. Little, Brown 2003 558p il $28.95 **92**

1. Human rights activists 2. Nobel laureates for peace 3. Political leaders 4. Political prisoners 5. Presidents

ISBN 0-316-11019-1

LC 2004-107807

"This collection of Mandela's speeches shows why he remains a universal hero. . . . This volume will be in great demand for the personal drama, the history, and, yes, for the inspiring moral values." Booklist

Mankiller, Wilma

Mankiller: a chief and her people; {by} Wilma Mankiller and Michael Wallis. St. Martin's Press 1993 xxiv, 292p il hardcover o.p. pa $14.95 **92**

1. Cherokee Indians 2. Indian chiefs

ISBN 0-312-20662-3 pa

LC 93-25698

"A must-read for everyone interested in, specifically, the history of Native Americans and women and, in general, tales of exceptional people." Booklist

Mann, William J.

Kate: the woman who was Hepburn. H. Holt 2006 xxviii, 621p il $30 **92**

1. Actors 2. Biography, Individual

ISBN 978-0-8050-7625-7; 0-8050-7625-5

This is a biography of the American actress.

"This will surely be the definitive version of Hepburn's life for decades to come, as it is an outstanding example of painstaking research matched with splendid writing." Publ Wkly

Includes bibliographical references

Marable, Manning

Malcolm X. Viking 2011 594p. ill. $30 **92**

1. African Americans -- Biography 2. African Americans -- Civil rights 3. Biography, Individual 4. Black Muslim leaders 5. Black Muslims 6. Black Muslims -- United States -- History 7. Black nationalism -- United States -- History 8. Civil rights activists

ISBN 978-0-670-02220-5; 0-670-02220-9

LC 2010025768

This "biography of Malcolm X draws on new research to trace his life from his troubled youth through his involvement in the Nation of Islam, his activism in the world of Black Nationalism, and his assassination." (Publisher's note) Glossary. Bibliography. Index.

"This superbly perceptive and resolutely honest book will long endure as a definitive treatment of Malcolm's life." Wilson Quarterly

Maraniss, David

Clemente; the passion and grace of baseball's last hero. Simon & Schuster 2006 401p il maps hardcover o.p. pa $15   92

1. Baseball -- Biography 2. Baseball players 3. Biography, Individual

ISBN 0-7432-1781-0; 978-0-7432-1781-1; 0-7432-9999-X; 978-0-7432-9999-2 pa

LC 2006-42235

The author "has produced a baseball-savvy book sensitive to the social context that made Clemente, a black Puerto Rican, a leading indicator of baseball's future." N Y Times Book Rev

Includes bibliographical references

★ First in his class: a biography of Bill Clinton. Simon & Schuster 1995 512p il hardcover o.p. pa $15   92

1. Governors 2. Presidents 3. Presidents -- United States

ISBN 0-684-81890-6 pa

LC 94-48245

The author "offers a heavily documented (nearly 400 interviews), unauthorized biography that ends with Clinton's announcement for the presidency. Maraniss writes, 'My goal was for this book to be neither pathography nor hagiography, but a fair-minded examination of a complicated human being and the forces that shaped him and his generation.' He has achieved his goal. . . . All in all, First in His Class is solid journalism that thoughtfully evokes the tumultuous times—desegregation, assassinations, Vietnam—that shaped Clinton." Booklist

Includes bibliographical references

Into the story; a writer's journey through life, politics, sports and loss. Simon & Schuster 2010 283p il $26   92

1. Biographers 2. Journalists 3. Sports -- United States

ISBN 978-1-4391-6002-2; 1-4391-6002-3

LC 2009-42338

"In this collection of previously published articles and excerpts from his books, . . . [the author] ranges over topics from the death of his sister and the deaths of strangers on September 11 to the political fortunes of Barack Obama, Bill Clinton, and Al Gore and the timeless contributions to sports of legendary figures like Vince Lombardi, Muhammad Ali, and Roberto Clemente. . . . Maraniss's lively sketches illuminate the lives of significant cultural and political figures and intimately capture various moments that define modern American cultural history." Publ Wkly

When pride still mattered: a life of Vince Lombardi. Simon & Schuster 1999 541p il hardcover o.p. pa $16   92

1. Football coaches 2. Football coaches -- United States

-- Biography

ISBN 0-684-77018-5 pa

LC 99-37859

"From Lombardi's formative years as a player and coach at Fordham University through assistantships with West Point and the Giants and, finally, to his tenure as head coach of the Packers, Maraniss presents a portrait of a complicated human being who was a great teacher but a mediocre listener, an effective psychologist despite being rife with flaws." Publ Wkly

Includes bibliographical references

Margolick, David

Elizabeth and Hazel; two women of Little Rock. Yale University Press 2011 310p il $26   92

1. School integration 2. School integration -- Arkansas -- Little Rock -- History -- 20th century

ISBN 978-0-300-14193-1; 0-300-14193-9

LC 2011-14101

"When Elizabeth Eckford braved the gauntlet of white hecklers leading to the newly desegregated Central High School in Little Rock, Arkansas, in 1957, photographers captured her image and that of the angry young white woman behind her. Elizabeth, the stoic, and Hazel Bryan, the tormentor, were frozen as icons. Elizabeth was part of the Little Rock Nine, the black teens who became the targets of race hatred as well as national and international inspirations. . . . Margolick draws on interviews and press reports of the time to present a very nuanced analysis of how Elizabeth and Hazel were affected by the scene that made them famous. . . . A complex look at two women at the center of a historic moment." Booklist

Includes bibliographical references

Marion, Robert

Genetic rounds; a doctor's encounters in the field that has revolutionized medicine. Kaplan Pub. 2009 275p $24.95   92

1. Medical genetics 2. Pediatricians 3. Physicians

ISBN 978-1-60714-460-1

LC 2009-19110

This is "a straightforward, and often poignant, collection of true stories. Particularly compelling are several stories that describe the pain and pathos of life for some individuals with genetic disorders." Am J Human Genetics

Marnham, Patrick

Dreaming with his eyes open; a life of Diego Rivera. University of California Press 2000 350p il pa $29.95   92

1. Artists 2. Artists, Mexican 3. Painters

ISBN 0-520-22408-6; 978-0-520-22408-7

LC 99-44964

"For the browsing public as well as specialists in European, Latin American, and American modern art, this book is not to be overlooked." Libr J

Includes bibliographical references

Marrs, Suzanne

Eudora Welty: a biography. Harcourt 2005 652p il $28   92

1. Authors 2. Authors, American 3. Biography,

Individual 4. Novelists 5. Short story writers
ISBN 0-15-100914-7

LC 2004-30490

This book "belongs on the shelf beside its subject's own work. Neither hagiography nor pathography, it is, you feel, the thoroughly respectful and straightforward biography its honest, modest, intensely private subject would have wanted." N Y Times Book Rev

Includes bibliographical references

Marsden, George M.

Jonathan Edwards; a life. Yale Univ. Press 2003 xx, 615p $35; pa $19.95   **92**

1. Clergy 2. College presidents 3. Congregationalism 4. Theologians 5. Writers on religion
ISBN 0-300-09693-3; 0-300-10596-7 pa

LC 2002-013611

"Clearly sympathetic to his subject without ever becoming an outright apologist for either his character or his theology, Marsden . . . writes with such verve that he has given us not only the definitive biography but also a narrative that reads like a novel—that most appropriate art form for examining the interior drama of the soul." Commonweal

Includes bibliographical references

Marshall, Leslie

Every step you take; a memoir. with Leslie Marshall. Harper 2011 271p il $24.99; ebook $11.99   **92**

1. Ballet dancers
ISBN 978-0-06-173238-6; 978-0-06-209798-9 ebook

LC 2011012725

"Acclaimed dancer Soto—a principal for the New York City Ballet for 20 years (1985–2005)—writes about his career, his Native American heritage, his homosexuality, his passion for cooking, his struggles to find a family and his discovery of love. . . . A powerful story, affectionately told, about the demands and dimensions of personal and professional success." Kirkus

Marshall, Paule

Triangular road; a memoir. BasicCivitas Books 2009 165p il $23   **92**

1. African American authors 2. African Americans -- Intellectual life 3. Authors 4. Biography, Individual 5. Dramatists 6. Essayists 7. Novelists 8. Poets 9. Short story writers 10. Young adult authors
ISBN 978-0-465-01359-3

LC 2008-36671

This is a memoir by the author of Praisesong for the widow (1983).

"Though fiction may have pride of place in . . . [the author's] heart, 'Triangular Road' reveals a strong gift for self-scrutiny made all the more revealing by quiet humor and what appears to be complete honesty." Washington Post

Martin, Gerald

★ **Gabriel** Garcia Marquez; a life. Alfred A. Knopf 2009 642p il map   **92**

1. Authors 2. Authors, Colombian 3. Journalists 4. Nobel laureates for literature 5. Novelists 6. Short

story writers
ISBN 978-0-307-27177-8

LC 200903806

This is a biography of the Colombian novelist and author of One Hundred Years of Solitude (1967) and Love in the Time of Cholera (1985).

"This superbly researched biography is nothing short of a tour de force. . . . This work not only details the life of a great writer but also provides considerable insight into life in Latin America." Libr J

Includes bibliographical references

Martin, Justin

Greenspan; the man behind money. Perseus Bks. 2000 284p il hardcover o.p. pa $17.50   **92**

1. Bankers 2. Economists 3. Government officials 4. Presidential advisers 5. Regulatory agency officials
ISBN 0-7382-0524-9 pa

In this biography the author "shows how Alan Greenspan's early experiences have shaped his tenure as chairman of the Federal Reserve Board." N Y Times Book Rev

Includes bibliographical references

Martin, Peter

Samuel Johnson; a biography. Harvard University Press 2008 608p il $35   **92**

1. Biography, Individual 2. English literature -- 18th century -- History and criticism 3. Lexicographers 4. Literary critics
ISBN 978-0-674-03160-9; 0-674-03160-1

LC 2008-11327

This "biography of the English essayist, lexicographer, and literary personality . . . emphasizes aspects of Johnson not covered by any previously published biographies . . . notably Johnson's deep depressions; his liberal views on women writers, slavery, and poverty (he was not the complete Tory that others have painted him); and Johnson as a writer whose works deserve to be better known by the general public. Martin covers all the well-known facts and accomplishments of Johnson's life, and he emphasizes the turbulent times in which Johnson lived and the intriguing people he knew. Scholarly but written in an engaging manner and featuring many quotations from Johnson and his friends and acquaintances, this [is a] new portrait of a complex, multifaceted writer and thinker." Libr J

Includes bibliographical references (p. 565-572)

Martin, Roger H.

Racing Odysseus; a college president becomes a freshman again. University of California Press 2008 262p $24.95   **92**

1. Biography, Individual 2. Education, Higher -- United States 3. Higher education
ISBN 978-0-520-25541-8; 0-520-25541-0

LC 2007-51017

Martin "examines a number of experiences uncommon to 61-year-old college presidents. On a sabbatical after horrific treatments for cancer, he enrolled as a freshman at St. John's College in Maryland, studied classics, joined the crew team, prepared for a major race, and learned to connect with his 18-year-old classmates. He notes the follies of the students, as well as his own, and offers perceptive and affectionate insights into the challenges of growing up in today's complicated world. Education is his profession, and as he carefully observes the impact of the Great Books curriculum at St. John's, he sees the relevance of the Greek classics to our own time." Libr J

Includes bibliographical references

Martin, Steve

Born standing up; a comic's life. Scribner 2007 209p il $25   **92**

1. Actors 2. Biography, Individual 3. Comedians 4. Dramatists 5. Memoirists 6. Novelists 7. Screenwriters
ISBN 978-1-4165-5364-9; 1-4165-5364-9

LC 2007-27143

This is an autobiography by the comedian and author of Shopgirl (2000).

This book "does a sharp-witted job of breaking down the step-by-step process that brought [the author] from Disneyland, where he spent his version of a Dickensian childhood as a schoolboy employee, to both the pinnacle of stardom and the brink of disaster. . . . Even for readers already familiar with Mr. Martin's solemn side, [this] is a surprising book: smart, serious, heartfelt and confessional without being maudlin." N Y Times (Late NY Ed)

Martin, Valerie

Salvation: scenes from the life of St. Francis. Knopf 2001 268p hardcover o.p. pa $13   **92**

1. Saints 2. Writers on religion
ISBN 0-375-70883-9 pa

LC 00-44361

"This portrait will be most interesting to readers who are already familiar with the basic facts of Francis's life and remain open to exploring a new, gritty interpretation of them." Publ Wkly

Includes bibliographical references

Martines, Lauro

Fire in the city; Savonarola and the struggle for Renaissance Florence. Oxford University Press 2006 336p il map $30   **92**

1. Martyrs 2. Monks 3. Writers on religion
ISBN 0-19-517748-7; 978-0-19-517748-0

LC 2005-31802

"This absorbing account . . . captures Savonarola's brilliance as well as the exciting and dangerous days of Renaissance Florence." Publ Wkly

Includes bibliographical references

Martinson, Deborah

Lillian Hellman; a life with foxes and scoundrels. Counterpoint 2005 448p il $27.95   **92**

1. Authors 2. Biography, Individual 3. Dramatists 4. Dramatists, American 5. Memoirists
ISBN 1-58243-315-1

LC 2005-16616

This is "a richly thorough, sometimes somber, and fairly objective portrait of an enigmatic individual." Libr J

Includes bibliographical references

Marton, Kati

Enemies of the people; my family's journey to America. Simon & Schuster 2009 272p il $26   **92**

1. Authors 2. Biography, Individual 3. Journalists 4. Nonfiction writers 5. Political prisoners 6. Political prisoners -- Hungary
ISBN 978-1-4165-8612-8; 1-4165-8612-1

LC 2009-14480

"An American journalist trolls the archives of the Hungarian secret police (AVO) to piece together her parents' imprisonment in and flight from Hungary in the mid-1950s. . . . The author's probing work effectively renders an enormously unsettled, painful time of shifting allegiances and political treachery. . . . A dark, compelling narrative of secrecy and betrayal." Kirkus

Includes bibliographical references

Massie, Robert K.

Nicholas and Alexandra. Ballantine Books 2000 613p il map pa $18.95   **92**

1. Courtiers 2. Emperors 3. Empresses 4. Monks
ISBN 0-345-43831-0; 978-0-345-43831-7

LC 99-91507

This study provides an intimate account of the Romanov family and the coming of the Russian Revolution. Kerensky, Lenin and Rasputin are among the personalities profiled.

This book, "solid with research, reads as lightly as a novel, as authoritatively as a textbook. Dialogue and lively description lend a sense of immediacy, but his notes, discreetly relegated to the back of the book, show how carefully he has avoided slipping into fiction." Christ Sci Monit

Includes bibliographical references

Masters, Jarvis

That bird has my wings; the autobiography of an innocent man on death row. [by] Jarvis Jay Masters. HarperOne 2009 281p $24.99   **92**

1. African Americans -- Biography 2. Prisoners
ISBN 978-0-06-173045-0; 0-06-173045-9

LC 2009-22124

"A heartbreaking memoir; the brutal conditions of Masters's boyhood will be difficult for some readers to take, but his ultimate message of hope and reconciliation is moving and inspiring." Libr J

Matsen, Bradford

Jacques Cousteau; the sea king. [by] Brad Matsen. Pantheon Books 2009 296p il $27.95   **92**

1. Authors 2. Biography, Individual 3. Divers 4. Naval officers 5. Nonfiction writers 6. Oceanographers 7. Oceanography
ISBN 978-0-375-42413-7; 0-375-42413-X

LC 2009-11640

This biography "places Cousteau's films, books, and fame into the context of the rest of his life—ambitions, childhood, family relationships, friendships, and disagreements. . . . Readers who dive, who are interested in ecology or the oceans, or who simply recognize the name Cousteau, will want to read this full, well-rounded portrait of one of the world's greatest explorers and conservationists. Highly recommended." Libr J

Includes bibliographical references

Matteson, John

   Eden's outcasts; the story of Louisa May Alcott and her father. W.W. Norton 2007 497p il $29.95 **92**

   1. Authors 2. Authors, American 3. Biography, Individual 4. Educators 5. Nonfiction writers 6. Novelists 7. Philosophers 8. Young adult authors

   ISBN 978-0-393-05964-9

                       LC 2007-13707

   "Matteson's lucid, commanding biography casts new light on an unusual father-daughter bond and a new land at war with itself." Booklist

   Includes bibliographical references

May, Gary

   John Tyler. Times Books/Henry Holt and Co. 2008 183p $22   **92**

   1. Governors 2. Members of Congress 3. Presidents 4. Presidents -- United States 5. Senators 6. Vice-presidents

   ISBN 978-0-8050-8238-8; 0-8050-8238-7

                       LC 2008-18131

   This biography of the American president focuses on "Tyler's controversial presidency, which saw him set aside his dedication to the Constitution to gain his two great ambitions: Texas and a place in history." Publisher's note

   Includes bibliographical references

Mayor, Adrienne

   The **Poison** King; the life and legend of Mithridates, Rome's deadliest enemy. Princeton University Press 2009 448p il map $29.95   **92**

   1. Biography, Individual 2. Kings 3. Kings and rulers

   ISBN 9780691126838

                       LC 2009-15050

   This is "a reappraisal of Mithradates's character and a detailed account of his scientific pursuits, notably his in-depth studies of poison. . . . [The author places] him in his proper context as a Greco-Persian ruler following in the footsteps of his purported ancestor Alexander the Great. The most compelling aspect of this book is Mayor's engaging style. A true storyteller, she makes Mithradates's world come alive." Libr J

   Includes bibliographical references

Mazor, Barry

   Meeting Jimmie Rodgers; how America's original roots music hero changed the pop sounds of a century. Oxford University Press 2009 376p il $27.95   **92**

   1. Country music -- History and criticism 2. Country musicians 3. Singers 4. Songwriters

   ISBN 978-0-19-532762-5

                       LC 2008-41924

   "This is a fine addition to the literature on Rodgers. . . . [The author] traces Rodgers's influence through the 20th century and into the 21st not only on country music but also on popular music of many other genres and on media such as film. Whereas Rodgers's influence on country artists could be expected, his influence on people as diverse as Rick Nelson, George Harrison, and Louis Armstrong might not. A book for both music researchers and fans." Choice

   · Includes bibliographical references

McBride, James

   The **color** of water; a black man's tribute to his white mother. Riverhead Bks. 1996 228p il pa $14; $23.95   **92**

   1. Authors 2. Biography, Individual 3. Journalists 4. Memoirists 5. Novelists 6. Parents of prominent persons

   ISBN 1-57322-578-9 pa; 1-57322-022-1

                       LC 95-37243

   "Told with humor and clear-eyed grace, McBride's memoir is not only a terrific story, it's a subtle contribution to the current debates on race and identity. . . . The sheer strength of spirit, pain and humor of McBride and his mother as they wrestled with different aspects of race and identity is vividly told." Nation

McCabe, John

   Cagney. Carroll & Graf Pub. 1999 439p il pa $18.95   **92**

   1. Actors

   ISBN 978-0-7867-0580-1; 0-7867-0580-9

   This work "exceeds the typical standards of celebrity biography because McCabe is fully attentive to the many dimensions of his subject's artistry." Commonweal

   Includes filmography and bibliographical references

McCain, John S.

   Faith of my fathers; {by} John McCain with Mark Salter. Random House 1999 349p $25   **92**

   1. Members of Congress 2. Presidential candidates 3. Prisoners of war 4. Senators

   ISBN 0-375-50191-6

                       LC 99-13496

   This is a "serious, utterly engrossing account of faith, fathers and military tradition." Publ Wkly

McCourt, Alphie

   A **long** stone's throw. Sterling & Ross Publishers 2008 267p $24.95   **92**

   1. Business managers 2. Immigrants -- United States 3. Irish Americans 4. Memoirists 5. Restaurateurs

   ISBN 978-0-9814535-5-2; 0-9814535-5-4

                       LC 2008-32672

   "Alphie is the youngest of the four McCourt brothers and the third—after Frank and Malachy—to pen a memoir about his life in Ireland and the U.S. . . . McCourt always finds irony in life and his tales of the bar and restaurant business and its clientele are laugh-out-loud funny. Sensitive, lyrical, funny, stubborn, impetuous, McCourt writes with a steady hand, a joyful heart, and an Irishman's sense of life's absurdities." Publ WKly

McCourt, Frank

   Teacher man; a memoir. Scribner 2005 258p $26   **92**

   1. Authors 2. Biography, Individual 3. High school teachers 4. Irish Americans 5. Memoirists

   ISBN 0-7432-4377-3

                       LC 2005-54113

   "Full of gritty specifics, never preachy, often hilarious, McCourt's . . . book thrusts you right into the hormones-and-catcalls chaos of the classroom—where learning is not just a mystery but a flat-out miracle." Newsweek

'Tis; a memoir. Scribner 1999 367p hardcover o.p. pa $14 **92**
1. Authors 2. High school teachers 3. Irish Americans 4. Memoirists
ISBN 0-684-86574-2 pa
LC 99-31280
This volume "takes McCourt from his arrival in America and subsequent service in the Korean War through the mid-1980s. . . . This memoir features a mesmerizing narrative fraught with sufferings. It triumphs by effecting a genuinely comic meditation upon human frailty, grace and possibility." Publ Wkly

McCracken, Elizabeth
An **exact** replica of a figment of my imagination; a memoir. Little, Brown and Co. 2008 184p $19.99 **92**
1. Authors 2. Bereavement 3. Biography, Individual 4. Essayists 5. Librarians 6. Miscarriage 7. Novelists 8. Short story writers
ISBN 978-0-316-02767-0; 0-316-02767-7
LC 2008-5032
This is a memoir by the American novelist. "Two years ago [Elizabeth McCracken] was living in a remote part of France, working on her novel, and waiting for the birth of her first child. This book is about what happened next. In her ninth month of pregnancy, she learned that her baby boy had died. How do you deal with and recover from this kind of loss? . . . McCracken considers the nature of love and grief [here]." (Publisher's note)
"McCracken has succeeded in writing a beautiful, precise and heartbreaking account without sentimentality or pity." Publ Wkly

McCrum, Robert
Wodehouse; a life. Norton 2004 530p il $27.95 **92**
1. Authors 2. Dramatists 3. Humorists 4. Novelists 5. Short story writers
ISBN 0-393-05159-5
LC 2004-18562
The author "takes the reader from Wodehouse's school days at Dulwich to his successful work as a Broadway lyricist and a master storyteller of Edwardian times who gave us Bertie Wooster and Jeeves to his darkest hour during World War II and final years of semi-exile in America. He offers his most spirited and convincing analysis in countering accusations that Wodehouse knowingly collaborated with the Nazis. . . . This work is thoroughly researched and well written; it will please Wodehouse aficionados and general readers alike." Libr J
Includes bibliographical references

McCullough, David G.
Mornings on horseback; {by} David McCullough. Simon & Schuster 1981 445p il hardcover o.p. pa $16 **92**
1. Governors 2. Nobel laureates for peace 3. Presidents

4. Presidents -- United States 5. Vice-presidents
ISBN 0-671-44754-8 pa
LC 81-1697
This biography follows Theodore Roosevelt from his childhood to his defeat for mayor of New York and marriage to Edith Carow in 1886.
"Based on diligent and thorough research, with emphasis on family, physical ailments, and friends, and written with verve and color, this is a stimulating book that will appeal to the general reader." Libr J
Includes bibliographical references

McDonough, Jimmy
Tammy Wynette; tragic country queen. Viking 2010 432p il $27.95 **92**
1. Country musicians 2. Singers
ISBN 978-0-670-02153-6; 0-670-02153-9
LC 2009-42565
"Mr. McDonough is crazy about Wynette but also detached enough to see her clearly, writing with obvious respect for both her life and art. . . . You 'bookish types,' as Mr. McDonough describes his readers, will surely want to listen to her sing on the basis of this book's recommendations. With an emphatic sense of her place in country music—at the top of the heap, casting a shadow big enough to obscure today's woefully synthetic assembly-line singers—he combines a love of her overlooked and minor classics with a compelling big-picture life story. His opinions are often corroborated by the colorfully authentic voices of those who knew her well and marveled at her moxie." N Y Times (Late N Y Ed)
Includes bibliographical references

McGilligan, Patrick
Oscar Micheaux; the great and only; the life of America's first great Black filmmaker. HarperCollins Publishers 2007 402p il $29.95 **92**
1. Authors 2. Biography, Individual 3. Motion picture directors 4. Novelists 5. Screenwriters
ISBN 978-0-06-073139-7; 0-06-073130-7
LC 2007-60735
"One of the fascinating side streets in American film is the history of 'race pictures,' celluloid productions by black artists for black audiences during those decades when Jim Crow laws enforced segregation. The mainstay of race pictures was Oscar Micheaux (18841951), an intrepid filmmaker-novelist-entrepreneur whose career spanned four decades and who made more than 40 movies. . . . McGilligan's prose style may be pedestrian, but he organizes his biographical materials into a lively, readable tale." N Y Times Book Rev

McGoogan, Kenneth
Race to the Polar Sea; the heroic adventures of Elisha Kent Kane. [by] Ken McGoogan. Counterpoint 2008 380p il map $28 **92**
1. Biography, Individual 2. Eskimos -- Social life and customs 3. Explorers 4. Physicians 5. Travel writers
ISBN 978-1-58243-440-7; 1-58243-440-9
LC 2008-12045
This is a biography of the American explorer who discovered the Humboldt Glacier.

"With his access to previously unknown Kane logbooks, McGoogan makes an impressive case for the bravery and importance of the explorer who first identified the Greenland ice sheet." Publ Wkly

Includes bibliographical references

McKeen, William

Outlaw journalist; the life and times of Hunter S. Thompson. W. W. Norton 2008 428p il $27.95; pa $16.95   **92**

1. Authors 2. Biography, Individual 3. Columnists 4. Journalists 5. Nonfiction writers 6. Novelists 7. Satirists

ISBN 978-0-393-06192-5; 0-393-06192-2; 978-0-393-33545-3 pa; 0-393-33545-3 pa

LC 2008-13214

This is a biography of the journalist and author of Hell's Angels (1967), Fear and Loathing in Las Vegas (1972), The Great Shark Hunt (1979) and Generation of Swine (1988).

"The book does justice to the legend that was Thompson. The thorough reporting lends insight to a writer who was as much a personality as a scribe." Am Journalism

Includes bibliographical references

McMurtry, Larry

Books; a memoir. Simon & Schuster 2008 259p $24   **92**

1. Antiquarian booksellers 2. Authors 3. Authors, American 4. Biography, Individual 5. Booksellers and bookselling 6. Essayists 7. Novelists 8. Short story writers

ISBN 978-1-416-58334-9; 1-416-58334-3

LC 2008-10565

"A pleasant amble in Bookland and a treat for the bookishly inclined." Kirkus

Crazy Horse. Viking 1999 148p hardcover o.p. pa $14   **92**

1. Indian chiefs 2. Large print books 3. Native Americans -- Biography 4. Oglala Indians

ISBN 0-670-88234-8; 0-14-303480-4 pa

LC 98-26644

"Though essentially a loner and devoid of political ambition, Crazy Horse was a respected military tactician, equally feared and admired for the strength and the intensity of his convictions. Rather than merely attempting to sort out fact from fiction, McMurtry incorporates conjecture and legend into this philosophical portrait of both the man and the myth." Booklist

McPherson, James M.

★ **Abraham** Lincoln. Oxford University Press 2009 79p $12.95   **92**

1. Lawyers 2. Members of Congress 3. Presidents 4. Presidents -- United States 5. State legislators

ISBN 978-0-19-537452-0; 0-19-537452-5

LC 2008-35623

"McPherson, America's leading authority on Lincoln and his times, demonstrates his complete command of his subject in this concise but remarkably rich and perceptive

biography. . . . This little book is bigger than its pages and should be in every library, schoolhouse, and home." Libr J

Includes bibliographical references

★ **Tried** by war; Abraham Lincoln as commander in chief. Penguin Press 2008 329p il map hardcover o.p. pa $17   **92**

1. Executive power -- United States -- History 2. Lawyers 3. Members of Congress 4. Presidents 5. Presidents -- United States 6. State legislators

ISBN 978-1-594-20191-2; 1-594-20191-9; 978-0-14-311614-1 pa; 0-14-311614-2 pa

LC 2008-25229

Evaluates Lincoln's talents as a commander in chief in spite of limited military experience, tracing the ways in which he worked with, or against, his senior commanders to defeat the Confederacy and reshape the presidential role.

This book "is a perfect primer, not just for Civil War buffs or fans of Abraham Lincoln, but for anyone who wishes to understand the evolution of the president's role as commander in chief." N Y Times Book Rev

Includes bibliographical references

McRae, Donald

The **last** trials of Clarence Darrow. William Morrow 2009 422p il $26.99   **92**

1. Lawyers 2. Memoirists 3. State legislators 4. Writers on law

ISBN 978-0-06-116149-0; 0-06-116149-7

LC 2008-51237

"Darrow's long affair with journalist Mary Field Parton frames a vivid retelling of his three most famous court cases: defending an evolutionist against the church; a black physician accused of killing a member of a lynch mob; and Leopold and Loeb, two wealthy teenagers who killed a younger boy for fun. Viewed through Field Parton's eyes, Darrow's flawed brilliance is compelling." Guardian

Includes bibliographical references

Meacham, Jon

American lion; Andrew Jackson in the White House. Random House 2008 483p il $30   **92**

1. Biography, Individual 2. Generals 3. Presidents 4. Presidents -- United States

ISBN 978-1-4000-6325-3; 1-4000-6325-6

LC 2008-23466

The author "looks past the theatrics and posturing to the essential elements of Jackson's many showdowns. Mr. Meacham . . . dispenses with the usual view of Jackson as a Tennessee hothead and instead sees a cannily ambitious figure determined to reshape the power of the presidency during his time in office (1829 to 1837). Case by case, Mr. Meacham dissects Jackson's battles and reinterprets them in a revealing new light." N Y Times (Late N Y Ed)

Includes bibliographical references

Mead, Margaret

Blackberry winter; my earlier years. with a new introduction by Nancy Lutkehaus. Kodansha International 1995 305p il pa $15 **92**
1. Anthropologists 2. Curators 3. Writers on science
ISBN 1-568-36069-X; 978-1-568-36069-0
LC 95-13302
"About one-third of Mead's autobiography covers the years before she became an anthropologist and another third her field work in Samoa, in New Guinea, among the Omaha Indians, and in Bali. . . . The concluding chapters . . . describe in subjective detail her role as mother and grandmother." Choice
Includes bibliographical references

Meade, Marion

Buster Keaton; cut to the chase. 1st Da Capo Press ed.; Da Capo Press 1997 440p il pa $18 **92**
1. Actors 2. Motion picture directors
ISBN 0-306-80802-1
LC 97-17745
The author "paints a moving and loving portrait of a comic genius, mechanical thinker, and superb athlete. The book provides the context of family and friends, (including Charlie Chaplin and Fatty Arbuckle) behind Keaton's career, and in doing so adds flesh and humanity to the funny bones and gags that have entertained and marveled audiences for decades. A remarkably gentle and insightful story of a silent comic riddle." Choice
Includes filmography and bibliographical references

Dorothy Parker; what fresh hell is this? Penguin 1989 459p il pa $20 **92**
1. Authors 2. Authors, American 3. Dramatists 4. Essayists 5. Humorists 6. Poets 7. Screenwriters 8. Short story writers
ISBN 0-14-011616-8; 978-0-14-011616-8
LC 88-23782
"The author has written a disturbing story of a writer whose life was marked by endless disturbances and self-depreciation, and who left behind no correspondence, manuscripts, or private papers. Under the circumstances, Ms. Meade has brilliantly reconstructed her subject's life. . . . The book is a tribute to a woman who left her mark on the literary history of her times and whose coruscating wit is still remembered." West Coast Rev Books
Includes bibliographical references

Lonelyhearts; the screwball world of Nathanael West and Eileen McKenney. Houghton Mifflin Harcourt 2010 392p il map $28 **92**
1. Authors 2. Authors, American 3. Biography, Individual 4. Novelists 5. Screenwriters 6. Spouses of prominent persons
ISBN 978-0-15-101149-0
LC 2009-13285
"West and McKenney died young in a car crash in 1940—too soon for him to know that his lacerating novels, especially The Day of the Locust (1939), would become American classics; too soon for his new wife, Eileen, to claim her life for her own after her sister, Ruth, co-opted it to write her best-seller, My Sister Eileen (1938). . . . [The author] tells the trenchant and secret-laden life stories of West (born Nathan Weinstein in New York) and Ohioan McKenney in a ravishingly atmospheric yet propulsive narrative." Booklist
Includes bibliographical references

Means, Howard B.

Johnny Appleseed; the man, the myth, the American story. [by] Howard Means. Simon & Schuster 2011 320p il map $26; ebook $12.99 **92**
1. Apples 2. Frontier and pioneer life 3. Fruit growers 4. Pioneers
ISBN 978-1-4391-7825-6; 978-1-4391-7827-0 ebook
LC 2011-665
"Delightfully wry and perceptive, Means' quest to understand Chapman/Appleseed is a captivating achievement in Americana." Booklist

Meeink, Frank

Autobiography of a recovering skinhead; Frank Meeink's story. as told to Jody M. Roy. Hawthorne Books 2010 350p pa $10 **92**
1. Gang members 2. Memoirists 3. Motivational speakers 4. Social activists 5. White supremacists 6. White supremacy movements
ISBN 978-0-9790188-2-4
LC 2009-27527
"Before he was out of his teens, Meeink, a member of a group of white supremacists, was behind prison bars. But by the time he was released on parole, he was a changed man, having cast off his hatred; he became a public speaker, sharing his experiences, helping others to understand the nature of hatred and to find ways to combat it. . . . Stories of personal redemption don't get much more interesting than this one, and the gritty first-person narrative . . . draws the reader into Meeink's story, giving it an immediacy and a visceral intensity that makes us feel as though we've lived a bit of his life. Readers should be warned that the book is unflinchingly straightforward: some of the language is quite raw, and some of the imagery quite graphic." Booklist

Mendell, David

Obama; from promise to power. Amistad 2007 406p il $25.95; pa $14.95 **92**
1. African Americans -- Biography 2. Biography, Individual 3. Lawyers 4. Nobel laureates for peace 5. Presidents 6. Presidents -- United States 7. Racially mixed people 8. Senators 9. State legislators 10. United States -- Politics and government -- 2001-
ISBN 978-0-06-085820-9; 0-06-085820-6; 978-0-06-085821-6 pa; 0-06-085821-4 pa
This is a biography of President Barack Obama.
The author "draws on interviews with Obama, his wife, family, friends, aides, and rivals, as well as his own extensive coverage since Obama's days in the Illinois Senate, to offer a nuanced, compelling look at a man of idealism and ambition intent on making history." Booklist
Includes bibliographical references

Mendelsohn, Daniel

The **lost**; a search for six of six million. photographs by Matt Mendelsohn. HarperCollins Publishers 2006 512p il $27.95 **92**

1. Classicists 2. College teachers 3. Holocaust, 1933-1945 4. Holocaust, Jewish (1939-1945) -- Poland 5. Journalists 6. Literary critics
ISBN 0-06-054297-7

LC 2006-41096

The author describes his efforts to find out what happened to his uncle Shmiel Jager, his wife and four daughters, who lived in the Polish town of Bolechow, and perished during the Holocaust.

"Mr. Mendelsohn, an evocative, ruminative writer, brings to life the vanished world not just of prewar Poland but also of his childhood and his extended family." N Y Times (Late N Y Ed)

Mercer-Taylor, Peter Jameson

The **life** of Mendelssohn; [by] Peter Mercer-Taylor. Cambridge Univ. Press 2000 238p il hardcover o.p. pa $34.99 **92**

1. Composers 2. Composers -- Germany
ISBN 0-521-63025-8; 0-521-63972-7 pa

LC 99-58441

"The book is well written, carefully produced, and a pleasure to read." Choice

Merry, Robert W.

A **country** of vast designs; James K. Polk, the Mexican War, and the conquest of the American continent. Simon & Schuster 2009 576p il map **92**

1. Biography, Individual 2. Governors 3. Members of Congress 4. Presidents 5. Presidents -- United States 6. Speakers of the House
ISBN 0743297431; 9780743297431

LC 2009024131

This is a biography of the eleventh president of the United States. Bibliography. Index.

"Merry's chronicle is filled with excellent insights into the critical events and fine portrayals of a cast of statesmen, warriors, and scheming rogues. . . . [This is] an outstanding addition to American history collections." Booklist

Includes bibliographical references (p. 543-550)

Merton, Thomas

★ The **seven** storey mountain; Fiftieth anniversary edition; Harcourt Brace & Co. 1998 467p $35; pa $16 **92**

1. Authors 2. Monks 3. Nonfiction writers 4. Poets 5. Writers on religion
ISBN 0-15-100413-7; 0-15-601086-0 pa

LC 98-198169

"The autobiography of a poet who became a convert to Catholicism and at the age of 26 after a full and traveled world career as student and teacher, entered a Trappist monastery." Publ Wkly

Messick, Kendall

The **projectionist**. Princeton Architectural Press 2010 159p il $40 **92**

1. Motion picture projectionists 2. Motion picture theaters
ISBN 978-1-56898-933-4

LC 2010-08864

"Marveling at this amazing creation, Kendall knew that he had to photograph not only the theater, but the theater's owner and creator. And fortunately, the timing was perfect. Mr. Brinckle, a very elderly man, was extremely concerned about what would happen to his masterpiece after his passing. Their collaboration has resulted into something quite remarkable." Lenscratch

Metaxas, Eric

Bonhoeffer; pastor, martyr, prophet, spy: a Righteous Gentile vs. the Third Reich. Thomas Nelson 2010 591p il **92**

1. Biography, Individual 2. Clergy 3. Dissenters 4. Spies 5. Theologians 6. Writers on religion
ISBN 1-59555-138-7; 1-59555-246-4 pa; 978-1-59555-138-2; 978-1-59555-246-4 pa

LC 2009013944

This is a biography of the German Lutheran pastor and theologian executed by the Nazis for plotting to overthrow Hitler.

"Insightful and illuminating, this tome makes a powerful contribution to biography, history and theology." Publ Wkly

Includes bibliographical references

Meyers, Jeffrey

John Huston; courage and art. Crown Archetype 2011 475p il $30; ebook $14.99 **92**

1. Motion picture directors 2. Motion picture producers and directors 3. Screenwriters
ISBN 978-0-307-59067-1; 978-0-307-59069-5 ebook

LC 2010047642

"By balancing the flamboyant life with the landmark works of legendary movie director John Huston, . . . Meyers reveals how a flawed man produced nearly flawless and indelible films." Booklist

Includes filmography and bibliographical references

Samuel Johnson; the struggle. Basic Books 2008 528p il $35 **92**

1. Authors, English 2. Biography, Individual 3. English literature -- 18th century -- History and criticism 4. Lexicographers 5. Literary critics
ISBN 978-0-465-04571-6; 0-465-04571-5

LC 2008-12302

This biography "departs from a strict chronology to narrate significant events and their meaning for Johnson. A central concern involves one of Johnson's darkest secrets, which Meyers says other biographers have evaded: his masochistic sexuality at the hands of his confidante Mrs. Hester Thrale. The biography also speculates on other aspects of Johnson's sex life, both during his marriage to a much older woman and after her death. But Meyers's book is balanced and accomplishes much else." Publ Wkly

Includes bibliographical references

Michaelis, David

N.C. Wyeth; a biography. Perennial 2003 555p il pa $27.95 **92**

1. Artists 2. Artists -- United States 3. Illustrators 4. Painters

ISBN 0-06-008926-1; 978-0-06-008926-9

LC 2003-42876

"Michaelis's work is an outstanding example of the biographer's art. Integrating Wyeth's complex personal and psychological life with his artistic oeuvre, Michaelis creates a portrait of both the artist and the man." Libr J

Includes bibliographical references

★ Schulz and Peanuts; a biography. Harper 2007 655p il $34.95 **92**

1. Biography, Individual 2. Cartoonists

ISBN 978-0-06-621393-4; 0-06-621393-2

This is a biography of the cartoonist and author of Happiness is a Warm Puppy (1962), The Charlie Brown Dictionary (1973), Peanuts Jubilee (1975), Snoopy's Tennis Book (1979), and Things I Learned After It Was Too Late (1981).

"It is Mr. Michaelis's achievement in these pages that he leaves us with both a shrewd appreciation of Schulz's minimalist art and a sympathetic understanding of Schulz the man." N Y Times (Late N Y Ed)

Includes bibliographical references

Milford, Nancy

Savage beauty: the life of Edna St. Vincent Millay. Random House 2001 550p il $29.95; pa $14.95 **92**

1. Authors 2. Dramatists 3. Large print books 4. Poets

ISBN 0-394-57589-X; 0-375-76081-4 pa

LC 2001-18598

"In 1923, Edna St. Vincent Millay became the first woman to win the Pulitzer Prize for poetry. To write her biography, Milford . . . persuaded Millay's younger sister and sole heir, Norma, to give her access to hundreds of Millay's personal papers, letters, and notebooks. Selecting from 'this extraordinary collection,' Milford meticulously integrates Millay's major poems, letters received and sent, reactions of friends, and comments from extensive interviews with Norma into an orderly and affecting narrative." Libr J

Includes bibliographical references

Mill, John Stuart

★ Autobiography; edited with an introduction by John M. Robson. Penguin Bks. 1989 234p pa $8.95 **92**

1. Economists 2. Essayists 3. Philosophers 4. Writers on politics

ISBN 0-14-043316-3

LC 91-103446

"A human document of unusual interest. Mill, a noble spirit educated by a narrow-minded pedant, shut off from all normal contact, developed an egotism that makes this book so completely an autobiography that besides his father and [his] wife he seems to exist alone in a world of which he has both center and circumference." Pratt Alcove

Includes bibliographical references

Miller, Edwin Haviland

Salem is my dwelling place: a life of Nathaniel Hawthorne. University of Iowa Press 1991 596p il hardcover o.p. pa $24.95 **92**

1. Authors 2. Novelists 3. Short story writers

ISBN 0-87745-332-2; 0-87745-381-0 pa

LC 91-14543

This is a biography of the 19th century American novelist.

"Psychologically probing (but free of all jargon), Miller's elegantly written study gives us a fresh, sympathetic picture of an immensely complex, repressed man. . . . A masterful work, wholly satisfying." Libr J

Includes bibliographical references

Miller, Marta R.

Betsy Ross and the making of America. Henry Holt 2010 467p il map $30 **92**

1. Biography, Individual 2. Dressmakers 3. Flags -- United States 4. Needleworkers

ISBN 978-0-8050-8297-5; 0-8050-8297-2

LC 2009-35385

"This first-rate biography of Ross (1752–1836) is authoritative and engrossing and goes a long way toward recovering the history of early American women and work." Publ Wkly

Includes bibliographical references

Miller, Sue

The story of my father; a memoir. Knopf 2003 173p il $22.50; pa $12.95 **92**

1. Authors 2. Memoirists 3. Novelists 4. Short story writers

ISBN 0-375-41479-7; 0-345-45544-4 pa

LC 2002-69460

"A familiar but still touching story of a parent's descent into Alzheimer's disease; the deeper Miller's father sinks into confusion, the more powerfully candid her writing becomes." N Y Times Book Rev

Millner, Caille

The golden road; notes on my gentrification. Penguin Press 2007 248p $22.95 **92**

1. Journalists

ISBN 978-1-59420-109-7; 1-59420-109-9

LC 2006-51010

The author "uses her own story to explore geographic and personal notions of place and the effects of change on both. The product of a troubled family and raised in Latino and Caucasian neighborhoods, she searches for her identity as a black woman, a search complicated by her parents' efforts to succeed in white America and their determination that their children do the same. . . . In quietly mesmerizing prose informed throughout by an attitude of wry objectivity, Millner makes her life thus far compelling reading and an outstanding addition to a crowded field." Libr J

Milner, Clyde A.

As big as the West; the pioneer life of Granville Stuart. [by] Clyde A. Milner II and Carol A.

O'Connor. Oxford University Press 2009 430p il map $34.95 **92**

1. Biography, Individual 2. Diplomats 3. Frontier and pioneer life 4. Frontier and pioneer life -- Montana 5. Merchants 6. Miners 7. Pioneers 8. Ranchers

ISBN 978-0-19-512709-6; 0-19-512709-9

"In fully revealing Stuart's fascinating and complex life, Milner and O'Connor illuminate the conflicting realities of the frontier." Libr J

Includes bibliographical references and index

Min, Anchee

Red Azalea. Anchor Books 2006 306p pa $13 **92**

1. Actors 2. Artists 3. Authors 4. Memoirists 5. Novelists 6. Photographers

ISBN 978-1-4000-9698-5; 1-4000-9698-7

LC 2006-271433

"In this memoir of growing up in China during the Cultural Revolution, sexual freedom becomes a powerful political as well as literary statement." N Y Times Book Rev

Minutaglio, Bill

First son: George W. Bush and the Bush family dynasty. Times Bks. 1999 371p il hardcover o.p. pa $14 **92**

1. Baseball executives 2. Children of presidents 3. Energy industry executives 4. Governors 5. Presidents 6. Presidents -- United States

ISBN 0-609-80867-2 pa

LC 99-16462

In this political biography the "author traces the Bush family history from Prescott to George to First Son. This family dynasty has been of great assistance to George W. as he is called, in his rise in business and politics. While giving surprisingly little attention to George W.'s performance as governor of Texas . . . the author focuses on his development as a young man and emergence into the national political limelight." Libr J

Mitchell, Andrea

Talking back--to presidents, dictators, and assorted scoundrels. Viking 2005 414p il $25.95 **92**

1. Spouses of prominent persons 2. Television reporters

ISBN 0-670-03403-7

LC 2005-42279

This "is a collection of good stories, inside dope and real-life quandaries, all from someone still eager enough to compare herself to Nancy Drew and Brenda Starr." Am Journalism Rev

Mitton, Simon

Conflict in the cosmos; Fred Hoyle's life in science. Joseph Henry Press 2005 401p il $27.95 **92**

1. Astronomers 2. Authors 3. Biography, Individual 4. Novelists 5. Science fiction writers 6. Writers on science

ISBN 0-309-09313-9

LC 2004-30638

The author "sheds light on both the scientist and the science through research and his own experiences with Hoyle's colleagues, students, and the man himself. . . . This excellent biography brings Hoyle to life while explaining, in language clear enough for the amateur enthusiast, the work that made him great." Libr J

Includes bibliographical references

Mlodinow, Leonard

Feynman's rainbow; a search for beauty in physics and life. Warner Bks. 2003 171p il $21; pa $13.95 **92**

1. Authors 2. Nobel laureates for physics 3. Physicists 4. Physicists -- United States -- Biography 5. Writers on science

ISBN 0-446-53045-X; 0-446-69251-4 pa

LC 2002-31137

In this memoir "of a stint as a postdoctoral colleague of Feynman's at Caltech, the aging physicist . . . cracks wise, crashes parties, works on his physics at a strip joint and needles stuffed-shirt academics. . . . Mlodinow's accessible style manages to convey Feynman's cantankerous appeal as well as some of the weirdness of theoretical physics without overtaxing lay readers." Publ Wkly

Moaveni, Azadeh

Honeymoon in Tehran; two years of love and danger in Iran. Random House 2009 340p $26 **92**

1. Authors 2. Biography, Individual 3. Iranian Americans 4. Journalists 5. Memoirists 6. Women journalists

ISBN 978-1-4000-6645-2; 1-4000-6645-X

The Iranian-American author describes her return to Iran as a reporter for 'Time' magazine, her marriage to an Iranian man, the repressive Iranian society and its impact, and her family's decision to leave Iran.

"This perfect blend of political commentary and social observation is an excellent choice for readers interested in going beyond the headlines to gain an in-depth understanding of twenty-first-century Iran." Booklist

Includes bibliographical references

Lipstick jihad; a memoir of growing up Iranian in America and American in Iran. Public Affairs 2005 249p $25; pa $13 **92**

1. Authors 2. Biography, Individual 3. Journalists 4. Memoirists

ISBN 1-58648-193-2; 1-58648-378-1 pa

LC 2004-43184

"Moaveni, an Iranian-American who grew up in California, decided to embark on a journey in spring 2000 to rediscover her Iranian heritage. In this account, she . . . conveys the tensions she observed between the fundamentalist mullahs and younger Iranians, who are pushing for a more Westernized, modern Iran. . . . A charming and informative memoir." Libr J

Moffat, Wendy

A **great** unrecorded history; a new life of E.M. Forster. Farrar, Straus and Giroux 2010 480p il $32.50 **92**

1. Authors 2. Authors, English 3. Biography, Individual 4. Essayists 5. Literary critics 6. Novelists

7. Short story writers
ISBN 978-0-374-16678-6; 0-374-16678-1
LC 2009-29504

In this "well-written, intelligent and perceptive biography of Forster . . . [the author attempts] to draw a picture of a figure who was sensitive, sensuous and kind, an artist who possessed a keen, plain sort of wisdom and lightness of touch that make him, to this day, an immensely influential novelist, almost a prophet. She uses the sources for our knowledge of Forster's sexuality, including letters and diaries, without reducing the mystery and sheer individuality of Forster, without making his sexuality explain everything." N Y Times Book Rev

Includes bibliographical references

Mohandas

Gandhi; the man, his people, and the empire. University of California Press 2008 xv, 738p il map $34.95 **92**
1. Authors 2. Essayists 3. Journalists 4. Memoirists 5. Pacifists 6. Political leaders 7. Writers on politics
ISBN 978-0-520-25570-8; 0-520-25570-4
LC 2007-40986

The author exhibits a deep "understanding of the social and political landscape of India, of the cleavages of caste and religion, and of the dynamics of the dominant Congress Party (to which Gandhi had a lifelong allegiance). Rajmohan takes us at a leisurely pace through the broad sweep of Gandhi's personal and public life." Times Lit Suppl

Includes bibliographical references (p. 703-708)

Molesworth, Charles

Marianne Moore; a literary life. Northeastern University Press 1991 xxii, 472p il pa $16.95 **92**
1. Authors 2. Essayists 3. Poets 4. Poets, American
ISBN 1-555-53115-6
LC 91-13570

"Molesworth charts the growth of a major modernist through careful critical readings of her poetry and prose, her work as an editor of the Dial, and an examination of Moore as an active, social New York literary figure whose colleagues and admirers included T.S. Eliot and Ezra Pound." Publ Wkly

Includes bibliographical references

Monninger, Joseph

Two Ton; one fight, one night: Tony Galento vs. Joe Louis. Steerforth Press 2006 208p il $19.95 **92**
1. Boxers (Persons)
ISBN 978-1-58642-115-1; 1-58642-115-8
LC 2006-12828

Th author offers a detailed "description of the 1939 heavyweight title fight between Joe Louis and Orange, New Jersey native 'Two Ton' Tony Galento. Monninger's real achievement is not the tale of the fight itself, but rather of the circumstances that lead up to it, and its explanation of how one chunky, heavyset bartender with a far-from-average left hook could rise to fight for the world championship." BrickCityBoxing.com

Montefiore, Sebag

★ **Stalin**: the court of the red tsar; by Simon Sebag Montefiore. Knopf 2004 xxvii, 785p il map $30 **92**
1. Communist leaders 2. Dictators 3. Heads of state 4. Heads of state -- Soviet Union -- Biography 5. Political leaders
ISBN 1-400-04230-5
LC 2003-27390

"In the relentless detail, the mood-setting descriptions of the leader's surroundings, the sketches of the people around him and in Stalin's own words, pranks and tempers, Montefiore gives us not only the most intimate view of the general secretary that we have to date but a rounded and complex portrait of a man who could go from charming to lethal in the space of a few seconds." Nation

Includes bibliographical references

★ **Young** Stalin; [by] Simon Sebag Montefiore. Knopf 2007 xxxii, 460p il map $30 **92**
1. Biography, Individual 2. Communist leaders 3. Dictators 4. Heads of state 5. Political leaders
ISBN 1-4000-4465-0; 978-1-4000-4465-8
LC 2007-29220

Stalin "is brilliantly brought to life in this superb biography." Hist Today

Includes bibliographical references

Mooney, Jonathan

The **short** bus; a journey beyond normal. H. Holt 2007 272p hardcover o.p. pa $14.99 **92**
1. Handicapped students 2. Memoirists 3. Motivational speakers 4. Social activists
ISBN 978-0-8050-7427-7; 0-8050-7427-9; 978-0-8050-8804-5 pa; 0-8050-8804-0 pa
LC 2006-52588

The author's "target audience is not policy makers but his fellow misfits, and his boundless empathy will surely console those who also face the worst that cruel schoolchildren and the educational bureaucracy have to offer." N Y Times Book Rev

Mooney, Paul

Black is the new white; a memoir. Simon Spotlight Entertainment 2009 264p il $24.99 **92**
1. Actors 2. Comedians 3. Screenwriters 4. Television scriptwriters
ISBN 978-1-4165-8795-8; 1-4165-8795-0
LC 2009-19572

"Paul Mooney recalls the day he became Richard Pryor's shadow partner. It was 1968, and the two young comics were sitting in a Hollywood greasy spoon, with Pryor nursing another hangover, so Mooney lightened the mood with an off-the-cuff, X-rated one-liner that made his buddy convulse. . . . [This book] is Mooney's unvarnished memoir of that friendship. At a time when comedians—even African American icons such as Bill Cosby—never talked about race, Pryor (aided and abetted by Mooney) dared to confront the elephant in the room. Mooney, who has also written for 'In Living Color' and 'Chappelle's Show,' also traces his own path from humble Deep South roots to a comedy elder statesman known for his incisive riffs on racism." Los Angeles Times book Rev

Moore, Honor

The **bishop's** daughter; a memoir. W. W. Norton & Co. 2008 365p il $25.95; pa $16.95   **92**

  1. Authors 2. Biography, Individual 3. Bishops 4. Dramatists 5. Episcopal Church 6. Essayists 7. Literary critics 8. Memoirists 9. Poets

ISBN 978-0-393-05984-7; 978-0-393-33536-1 pa

LC 2008-01337

This is "a generous and thought-provoking chronicle of public altruism and private betrayal, high ideals and forbidden desire, love and forgiveness." Booklist

Includes bibliographical references

Moore, Mary Tyler

Growing up again; life, love, and oh yeah, diabetes. St. Martin's Press 2009 216p il $24.95   **92**

  1. Actors 2. Diabetes

ISBN 978-0-312-37631-4; 0-312-37631-6

LC 2008-37579

"While working on The Dick Van Dyke Show, . . . [the author] was diagnosed with juvenile (Type 1) diabetes and quickly discovered that managing the disease is a full-time job. . . . Moore details the daily challenges she faces to maintain healthy blood sugar levels. . . . Moore's humor, authoritative information, and honest evaluation of her own experiences with diabetes make this work essential for diabetes and consumer health collections." Libr J

Moore, Wes

The **other** Wes Moore; the story of one name and two fates. [by] Wes Moore; afterword by Tavis Smiley. Spiegel & Grau 2010 233p il $25   **92**

  1. African Americans -- Biography 2. Army officers 3. Memoirists 4. Murderers 5. Prisoners

ISBN 978-0-385-52819-1

LC 2009-41663

"In 2000, Wes Moore had recently been named a Rhodes Scholar in his final year of college at Johns Hopkins University when he read a newspaper article about another Wes Moore who was on his way to prison. It turned out that the two of them had much in common, both young black men raised in inner-city neighborhoods by single mothers. Stunned by the similarities in their names and backgrounds and the differences in their ultimate fates, the author eventually contacted the other Wes Moore and began a long relationship. . . . The author examines eight years in the lives of both Wes Moores to explore the factors and choices that led one to a Rhodes scholarship, military service, and a White House fellowship, and the other to drug dealing, prison, and eventual conversion to the Muslim faith, with both sharing a gritty sense of realism about their pasts." Booklist

Moorehead, Caroline

Dancing to the precipice: Lucie de la Tour du Pin and the French Revolution. HarperCollins 2009 480p il $27.99   **92**

  1. Biography, Individual 2. Memoirists

ISBN 978-0-7011-7904-5; 0-7011-7904-X

"In 1820, at the age of forty-nine, Lucie Dillon, the Marquise de la Tour du Pin, started writing her memoirs, an endeavor that went on for thirty years and produced one of the great monuments of French history. Lucie began life as an aristocrat, débuting at Versailles at the age of eleven; at the beginning of the Terror, as friends and relatives fell to the guillotine, she fled France with her husband and children. Resilient and resourceful, the family thrived on a farm in upstate New York, where Lucie churned butter, traded with Indians, and played hostess to Talleyrand. A return to France brought Lucie and her husband into Napoleon's inner circle; in later years, following an exile in London, they found favor with the restored Bourbon monarchy. Moorehead's biography, drawing on a trove of previously unpublished correspondence, captures the rhythm of the radical contrasts in her subject's life." New Yorker

Includes bibliographical references

Mordden, Ethan

Ziegfeld; the man who invented show business. St. Martin's Press 2008 335p il   **92**

  1. Biography, Individual 2. Theatrical producers 3. Theatrical producers and directors

ISBN 0312375433; 9780312375430

LC 2008028746

This is a biography of the impresario whose Ziegfeld Follies showcased such performers as Fanny Brice, Will Rogers, Eddie Cantor, W.C. Fields, and Marilyn Miller. Index.

"In his witty, well-researched biography of the great producer Florenz Ziegfeld, Mordden discusses Ziegfeld's extraordinary eye for talent and transforming approach to staging musicals." Booklist

Includes bibliographical references

Morgan, Bill

I celebrate myself; the somewhat private life of Allen Ginsberg. Viking 2006 702p il $29.95   **92**

  1. Authors 2. Beat generation 3. Biography, Individual 4. Poets

ISBN 0-670-03796-6

LC 2006-50045

"Relying heavily on Ginsberg's journals and letters, as well as interviews with close friends, [Morgan] creates here a detailed, revealing portrait of Ginsberg as a gifted poet and flawed human being driven by a fierce hunger for love and an insatiable thirst for fame. This most exhaustive biography to date chronicles Ginsberg's life from cradle to grave, but a major theme is Ginsberg's love life especially his relationship with Peter Orlovsky. Although he became an icon for gay liberation, Ginsberg tended to fall in love with straight men like Jack Kerouac, Neal Cassady, and Orlovsky, which, of course, led to a good deal of rejection and frustration. Morgan's is the first life of Ginsberg to explore this curious paradox in any depth. Cleverly designed, his book includes marginal references to the poems Ginsberg was working on at the time. A monumental work." Libr J

Morgan, Edmund Sears

Benjamin Franklin; {by} Edmund S. Morgan. Yale Univ. Press 2002 339p il $24.95; pa $16 **92**

  1. Authors 2. Diplomats 3. Inventors 4. Large print books 5. Members of Congress 6. Scientists 7. Statesmen 8. Statesmen -- United States 9. Writers

on science
ISBN 0-300-09532-5; 0-300-10162-7 pa

LC 2002-1143

"The general reader will find this book to be a well-written, thoughtful appreciation of one of the Founding Fathers who did the most to shape his era and our own." Libr J

Includes bibliographical references

Morgan, Judith

★ **Dr.** Seuss & Mr. Geisel; a biography. [by] Judith & Neil Morgan. Da Capo Press 1996 345p il pa $18.50   **92**

1. Artists 2. Authors 3. Authors, American 4. Children's authors 5. Humorists 6. Illustrators
ISBN 0-306-80736-X; 978-0-306-80736-7

LC 96-19313

"Fans of The Cat in the Hat, The Grinch Who Stole Christmas and other classics may be surprised to learn that Dr. Seuss was terrified of children and had none of his own, and that writing verse was a supreme effort for him. While children's literature is Ted Geisel's principal claim to fame, his creative life was multifarious, including an apprenticeship with film director and army major Frank Capra during WWII and stints in advertising. The authors deftly evoke the settings where Geisel lived and worked." Publ Wkly

Morgan, Robert

Boone; a biography. Algonquin Books of Chapel Hill 2007 538p il map $29.95   **92**

1. Biography, Individual 2. Frontier and pioneer life 3. Frontier and pioneer life -- Kentucky 4. Pioneers 5. Scouts
ISBN 978-1-56512-455-4; 1-56512-455-3

LC 2007-14204

A biography of the American pioneer scout.

This is an "absorbing and stirring chronicle of the great frontiersman." Booklist

Includes bibliographical references

Morison, Samuel Eliot

Admiral of the ocean sea: a life of Christopher Columbus; maps by Erwin Raisz; drawings by Bertram Greene. Little, Brown 1942 xx, 680p il maps hardcover o.p. pa $28.99   **92**

1. Explorers
ISBN 0-316-58478-9 pa

"An authoritative . . . biography of Columbus which is also decidedly original in its emphasis on the ability of Columbus as seaman and navigator and in the amount of space given to tracing the routes of the voyages and landings." Libr J

John Paul Jones; a sailor's biography. with an introduction by James C. Bradford; charts and diagrams by Erwin Raisz. Naval Inst. Press 1989 xxvi, 537p il hardcover o.p. pa $24.95   **92**

1. Naval officers
ISBN 1-55750-410-5 pa

LC 89-13423

"Morison has destroyed the myth of John Paul Jones but has left us a more human, more understandable character." Best Sellers

Includes bibliographical references

Mormando, Franco

Bernini; his life and his Rome. University of Chicago Press 2011 429p il map pa $35   **92**

1. Architects 2. Artists 3. Artists, Italian 4. Sculptors
ISBN 978-0-226-53852-5; 0-226-53852-4

LC 2011023774

In this biography "of Baroque sculptor Gian Lorenzo Bernini since his death in 1680, . . . Mormando constructs a comprehensive, extraordinarily vivid portrait of the sculptor known as 'the Michelangelo of his age.' . . . Of great interest to general readers seeking a well-researched, highly readable portrait of the sculptor and those interested in the cultural history of baroque Rome." Publ Wkly

Includes bibliographical references

Morris, Edmund

Beethoven: the universal composer. HarperCollins Publishers 2005 243p $21.95   **92**

1. Composers
ISBN 0-06-075974-7; 978-0-06-075974-2

LC 2006-274925

This is a biography of the German composer.

The author "clearly admires his subject not only for the work but also for his constant fight against the odds, and he has written an ideal biography for the general reader." Publ Wkly

Includes bibliographical references

★ The **rise** of Theodore Roosevelt; Modern Library pa. ed; Modern Lib. 2001 xxxiv, 920p il pa $17.95   **92**

1. Governors 2. Nobel laureates for peace 3. Presidents 4. Presidents -- United States 5. Vice-presidents
ISBN 0-375-75678-7

LC 2001-30520

This first volume of a three volume study of the life and times of Theodore Roosevelt "covers Roosevelt's life up to the age of 42, when an assassin's bullet elected him the youngest president in the nation's history." Booklist

Includes bibliographical references

Morris, Edmund, 1940-

★ **Colonel** Roosevelt. Random House 2010 766p il map $35; ebook $35   **92**

1. Biography, Individual 2. Presidents -- United States
ISBN 978-0-375-50487-7; 0-375-50487-7; 978-0-679-60415-0 ebook; 0-679-60415-4 ebook

LC 2010-5890

"Mr. Morris has addressed the toughest and most frustrating part of Roosevelt's life with the same care and precision that he brought to the two earlier installments. And if this story of a lifetime is his own life's work, he has reason to be immensely proud." N Y Times (Late N Y Ed)

Includes bibliographical references

Morris, James McGrath

Pulitzer; a life in politics, print, and power.
Harper 2010 558p il $29.99   **92**
    1. Biography, Individual 2. Journalism -- United States
-- History 3. Journalists 4. Members of Congress 5.
Newspaper executives
    ISBN 978-0-06-079869-7; 0-06-079869-6
                        LC 2009-27501
    This is an "excellent book: a thorough, possibly defini-
tive biography of the man who shaped the modern newspa-
per more than anyone else." Washington Post
    Includes bibliographical references

Morris, Roy

Ambrose Bierce; alone in bad company. Oxford
University Press 1998 306p il $19.95   **92**
    1. Authors 2. Authors, American 3. Essayists 4.
Journalists 5. Short story writers
    ISBN 0-19-512628-9
                        LC 98-33467
    "Mr. Morris's disturbing, vividly realized biography
brings to life a haunted writer whose private torments mirrored a turbulent era." NY Times Book Rev
    Includes bibliographical references

Morris, Sylvia Jukes

Rage for fame: the ascent of Clare Boothe Luce.
Random House 1997 561p il hardcover o.p. pa
$27   **92**
    1. Authors 2. Diplomats 3. Dramatists 4. Members of
Congress 5. Writers on politics
    ISBN 0-8129-9249-0 pa
                        LC 96-43084
    This first of a projected two-volume biography "de-
scribes how the future congresswoman and second wife of
Time magazine founder Henry Luce, bedded her way upward while career-climbing in New York journalism and
writing a stage mega-hit, The Women. . . . By 1942—at age
39—she turned to politics and was elected a Republican representative from Connecticut." Publ Wkly
    Includes bibliographical references

Moser, Benjamin

Why this world; a biography of Clarice Lispector.
Oxford University Press 2009 479p il $29.95   **92**
    1. Authors 2. Biography, Individual 3. Journalists 4.
Novelists 5. Short story writers 6. Women authors
    ISBN 978-0-19-538556-4; 0-19-538556-X
                        LC 2008-55639
    This is a biography of the Brazilian novelist.
    "Lispector makes a difficult, often lurid subject, and
Moser's account of her life is riveting—he draws extensively on previously untranslated letters and criticism (he
does the translations himself, from Yiddish, German, French
and Portuguese); at times the book reads like a gothic horror
story." Nation
    Includes bibliographical references

Mowat, Farley

Born naked. Houghton Mifflin 1994 256p il
maps hardcover o.p. pa $13   **92**
    1. Authors 2. Authors, Canadian 3. Children's

authors 4. Ethnologists 5. Historians 6. Naturalists 7.
Nonfiction writers
    ISBN 0-395-73528-9
                        LC 93-23702
    "There are no dull pages here; every man, woman, child,
and animal mentioned even casually makes an impression.
. . . Highly recommended to all those who like good writing." Libr J

Moyers, William C.

Broken: my story of addiction and redemption;
[by] William Cope Moyers with Katherine Ketcham.
Viking 2006 372p il $25.95   **92**
    1. Journalists
    ISBN 0-670-03789-3; 978-0-670-03789-6
                        LC 2006-41378
    The author's "gripping account of his struggles with al-
cohol and crack addiction will have readers rooting for him
from the very beginning." Libr J

Muir, John

The **story** of my boyhood and youth; with a foreword by Vernon Carstensen. University of Wisconsin
Press 1965 227p hardcover o.p. pa $17.95   **92**
    1. Authors 2. Naturalists 3. Writers on nature
    ISBN 0-299-03654-5 pa
                        LC 65-14539
    "The naturalist's childhood in a strict Presbyterian home
in Scotland, his boyhood experiences of the privations and
out-of-door delights of pioneer life on a Wisconsin farm, and
his shifts and contrivances while earning his way through
the state university." Cleveland Public Libr

Murphy, Terry Weible

Life in rewind; the story of a young courageous
man who persevered over OCD and the Harvard doctor who broke all the rules to help him. with Michael
A. Jenike and Edward E. Zine. HarperCollins 2009
242p il $24.99   **92**
    1. College teachers 2. Mentally ill 3. Obsessive-
compulsive disorder 4. Psychiatrists
    ISBN 978-0-06-156153-5; 0-06-156153-3
                        LC 2008-51240
    "Murphy, mother of an OCD patient, recounts the . . .
tale of Ed Zine, a man so mired in obsessive-compulsive
behavior that he was trapped for six years in his squalid
basement, compelled to perform an endless series of rituals
meant to stop time and the inevitability of death. . . . Murphy
traces Zine's illness from its roots in childhood trauma (his
mother's death from cancer) through its full flower, shortly
after high school graduation, when it began to take over his
life. Unable to get Zine out of his house, leading OCD expert Jenike made the three-hour trip from his Boston office
to Zine's Cape Cod home once a week. The bond between
them developed slowly and with difficulty, but ultimately
proved deeper than either suspected. . . . A passionate, faithful narrative from a reporter who understands the stakes and
the people behind them, this is a fascinating, hopeful read."
Publ Wkly

Murray, Liz

Breaking night; a memoir of forgiveness, survival, and my journey from homeless to Harvard. Hyperion 2010 334p il $24.99   **92**
1. Biography, Individual 2. Children of drug addicts 3. Homeless 4. Homeless persons 5. Motivational speakers 6. Students
ISBN 978-0-7868-6891-9; 0-7868-6891-0
LC 2010-13679
"Neither sensationalizing nor soliciting pity, Murray's generous account of and caring attitude toward her past are not only uplifting, but also a fascinating lesson in the value of dedication." Booklist

Murray, Nicholas

Kafka. Yale University Press 2004 440p il $30   **92**
1. Authors 2. Novelists 3. Poets 4. Short story writers
ISBN 0-300-10631-9
LC 2004-107048
This biography "relates Kafka's brief life, trying valiantly to depict a more normal Kafka, a man who lived in society with good friends, enjoyed sex, had wide-ranging intellectual interests and became enamored of Judaism. In Murray's account, Kafka's employer valued him highly, and under the imprint of no less a figure than Kurt Wolff, he experienced some literary success. Despite Murray's best efforts to contain Kafka's idiosyncrasies, though, the writer remains the tormented soul who created out of his personal anxieties and agonies some of the most acclaimed works of the 20th century." Publ Wkly
Includes bibliographical references

Nafisi, Azar

Reading Lolita in Tehran; a memoir in books. Random House 2003 347p $23.95; pa $11.16 **92**
1. Books and reading 2. College teachers 3. Literary critics 4. Memoirists 5. Women -- Iran
ISBN 0-375-50490-7; 0-8129-7106-X pa
LC 2002-36724
"In 1997 Iran, Nafisi formed an illicit book group whose syllabus provided the perfect framework for appraising life before and after the Islamic Revolution—and afforded her female students what little freedom they knew. Through impassioned discussions of Nabokov, James, and Fitzgerald, she details her teaching career and the obstacles her students faced. Her seamless blend of literary criticism and memoir begets a whole new genre." Libr J

★ **Things** I've been silent about; memories. Random House 2008 336p il $27   **92**
1. Biography, Individual 2. College teachers 3. Literary critics 4. Memoirists 5. Women -- Iran
ISBN 978-1-4000-6361-1; 1-4000-6361-2
LC 2008-482096
This is the author's "account of growing up under a chilly, tyrannical parent in a changing Iran. . . . An immensely rewarding and beautifully written act of courage, by turns amusing, tender and obsessively dogged." Kirkus

Nagel, Paul C.

John Quincy Adams; a public life, a private life. Harvard University Press 1999 432p il map pa $18.95   **92**
1. Members of Congress 2. Presidents 3. Presidents -- United States 4. Secretaries of state 5. Senators
ISBN 0-674-47940-8
The author traces the life and career of the sixth president of the United States "utilizing diary entries to provide keen insight into this extraordinary man, who often suffered from severe depression. The result is a fascinating psychobiography." Libr J
Includes bibliographical references

Naipaul, V. S.

Reading & writing; a personal account. New York Review of Bks. 2000 64p $16.95   **92**
1. Authors 2. Authors, Trinidadian -- 20th century 3. Authorship 4. Books and reading 5. East Indians -- Trinidad -- Social life and customs 6. Essayists 7. Journalists 8. Nobel laureates for literature 9. Nonfiction writers 10. Novelists 11. Radio reporters 12. Short story writers 13. Travel writers 14. Trinidadians -- England
ISBN 0-940322-38-2
LC 99-49615
Naipaul writes about his experiences growing up as an Indian living in Trinidad, his travels in India, his education at Oxford, and his struggles as a young writer in London.
The author "elegantly expresses hard-earned wisdom about literature and culture, the political stakes of history and the relationship between the writer and the world." N Y Times Book Rev

Nasaw, David

Andrew Carnegie. Penguin Press 2006 878p il $35; pa $20   **92**
1. Biography, Individual 2. Metal industry executives 3. Philanthropists
ISBN 1-59420-104-8; 0-14-311244-9 pa
LC 2006-44840
This is a biography of the Scottish-born businessman and philanthropist. Carnegie was the founder of the Carnegie Steel Company which later became U.S. Steel.
"Highly readable despite it's length, 'Andrew Carnegie' shows signs of prodigious original research on almost every page." N Y Times (Late N Y Ed)
Includes bibliographical references

Nathan, Debbie

Sybil exposed; the extraordinary story behind the famous multiple personality case. Free Press 2011 xxi, 297p il $26; ebook $12.99   **92**
1. Artists 2. Mentally ill 3. Multiple personality 4. Painters
ISBN 978-1-4391-6827-1; 978-1-4391-6829-5 ebook
LC 2011009164
The author "claims that the subject of the 1973 international bestseller, Sybil by Flora Schreiber, and the blockbuster film that followed, was a deliberate fabrication that not only fooled a mass popular audience but shaped the practice of psychiatry, opening the door to mass hysteria and

misdiagnosis. . . . A nuanced, not-entirely-unsympathetic account of the women who perpetrated a sensational literary fraud." Kirkus

Includes bibliographical references

Navasky, Victor S.

A **matter** of opinion. Farrar, Straus and Giroux 2005 458p $27 **92**

1. Authors 2. Journalists 3. Magazine editors

ISBN 0-374-29997-8

LC 2004-59395

"Anybody who has ever dreamed of starting a magazine, or worried that the country is losing the ability to speak seriously to itself, should read 'A Matter of Opinion.'" N Y Times Book Rev

Nemat, Marina

Prisoner of Tehran; a memoir. Free Press 2007 306p $26 **92**

1. Biography, Individual 2. Memoirists 3. Political prisoners

ISBN 1-4165-3742-2; 978-1-4165-3742-7

LC 2006-50191

Nemat was sixteen when she was arrested in Iran in early 1982 for political protests against the new fundamentalist regime. This is an account of her prison experiences.

The author's "story is not so much a political history lesson than it is a memoir of faith and love, a protest against violence that cannot be silenced. . . . Her persistence in standing for goodness is a lesson for us all." Christ Sci Monit

Neufeld, Michael J.

★ **Von** Braun; dreamer of space, engineer of war. A.A. Knopf 2007 587p il $35; pa $19.95 **92**

1. Aerospace engineers 2. Biography, Individual 3. NASA officials 4. Rocketry 5. Scientists 6. Space sciences -- History

ISBN 978-0-307-26292-9; 0-307-26292-8; 978-0-307-38937-4 pa; 0-307-38937-5 pa

LC 2007-5711

This "is a meticulously researched and technically accurate biography of von Braun." N Y Rev Books

Includes bibliographical references

Newman, Richard S.

Freedom's prophet; Bishop Richard Allen, the AME Church, and the Black founding fathers. New York University Press 2008 359p il $34.95 **92**

1. African Methodist Episcopal Church -- History 2. Biography, Individual 3. Bishops 4. Slaves

ISBN 978-0-8147-5826-7; 0-8147-5826-6

LC 2007-43259

"Newman's beautifully written study is not only a first-rate social history of the early Republic and African-American culture and religion, it provides a detailed sketch of Allen that is sure to become the definitive biography of the leader." Publ Wkly

Includes bibliographical references

Nice, David

★ **Prokofiev**: from Russia to the West, 1891-1935. Yale Univ. Press 2003 390p il music $35 **92**

1. Composers

ISBN 0-300-09914-2

"Part 1 chronicles Prokofiev's childhood, family relationships, and training at the St. Petersburg Conservatoire, while Part 2 covers his concert tours in America, France, and Germany and prodigious compositional output, beginning with the fairy tale opera, The Love of Three Oranges. . . . Nice embeds many musical examples in the body of the text and writes cogently about them. . . . Overall, the writing is fluid and unencumbered by excessive analytical detail, and at times witty. . . . Throughout, the composer's outsized personality and compositional brilliance shine through." Libr J

Includes discography and bibliographical references

Nicholl, Charles

The **reckoning**; the murder of Christopher Marlowe. University of Chicago Press 1995 413p il pa $33 **92**

1. Authors 2. Dramatists 3. Dramatists, English

ISBN 0-226-58024-5; 978-0-226-58024-1

The author argues that the Elizabethan playwright, who is believed to have been stabbed in a dispute over the bill ('recknynge') at Eleanor Bull's victualling house in 1593, was in fact murdered with government complicity as part of a plot against Sir Walter Raleigh.

"A remarkable piece of scholarship, this work carefully reconstructs the events leading up to the murder with all the excitement and suspense of a modern mystery novel; at the same time it vividly conveys the energy and color of Elizabethan England." Libr J

Includes bibliographical references

Nissenson, Marilyn

The **lady** upstairs; Dorothy Schiff and the New York Post. St. Martin's Press 2007 500p il $29.95 **92**

1. Biography, Individual 2. Newspaper executives

ISBN 978-0-312-31310-4; 0-312-31310-1

LC 2006-53087

This "is Marilyn Nissenson's carefully documented and revealing account of Schiff's nearly four decades of ownership. It's an admiring but not uncritical story of a woman who at her best 'was feisty rather than cowed, personally diffident but professionally forceful,' and who, although married four times, ended up wedded mainly to the paper itself." Columbia J Rev

Includes bibliographical references

Niven, Jennifer

Ada Blackjack; a true story of survival in the Arctic. Hyperion 2003 431p il map $24.95 **92**

1. Explorers 2. Inuit women 3. Women explorers

ISBN 0-7868-6863-5

LC 2003-50826

The book "is exhilarating reading." Booklist

Includes bibliographical references

Nolan, Tom

Three chords for beauty's sake: the life of Artie Shaw. W.W. Norton 2010 430p il $29.95 **92**
1. Band leaders 2. Biography, Individual 3. Clarinetists 4. Jazz musicians
ISBN 978-0-393-06201-4; 0-393-06201-5
LC 2010-06301
In this biography of the swing clarinetist-bandleader Nolan, "who interviewed Shaw and many of his band mates and intimates, appraises his difficult subject with a cool eye. His briskly written work lauds the musician's instrumental virtuosity and ambitious conceptions, but the author cuts Shaw no slack about his many personal failings—his arrogance, anger, selfishness, egocentricity and his horrific relationships with parents, wives and children. It's a multidimensional portrait of a brilliant yet self-absorbed autodidact who could never find happiness or satisfaction, even when his greatest fantasies of fame and success were realized. An exemplary work of jazz biography." Kirkus
Includes bibliographical references

Norgren, Jill

Belva Lockwood; the woman who would be president. New York University Press 2007 311p il $40; pa $22 **92**
1. Biography, Individual 2. Lawyers 3. Lecturers 4. Presidential candidates 5. Suffragists 6. Women in politics -- United States
ISBN 978-0-8147-5834-2; 0-8147-5834-7; 978-0-8147-5851-9 pa; 0-8147-5851-7 pa
LC 2006-34486
"Those with interests in women's, political, social, and cultural history will enjoy Lockwood." Choice
Includes bibliographical references

Norman, Philip

John Lennon; the life. Ecco HarperCollins 2008 851p il $34.95; pa $19.99 **92**
1. Artists 2. Biography, Individual 3. Rock music -- History and criticism 4. Rock musicians 5. Singers 6. Songwriters
ISBN 978-0-06-075401-3; 0-06-075401-X; 978-0-06-075402-0 pa; 0-06-075402-8 pa
LC 2008-4684
This is a biography of the singer-songwriter and author of In His Own Write (1964), A Spaniard in the Works (1965), and Lennon Remembers (1971).
This work's "ambitious range proves to be its strength, enveloping you in ways that a quicker read could not. . . . [This] is a gift of a book, heartfelt and heart-rending." Christ Sci Monit

Norrell, Robert J.

Up from history; the life of Booker T. Washington. Belknap Press of Harvard University Press 2009 508p il $35 **92**
1. African American educators 2. African Americans -- Biography 3. Authors 4. Biography, Individual 5. Civil rights activists 6. Educators 7. Memoirists 8. Nonfiction writers 9. Race discrimination -- History 10. Slaves
ISBN 067403211X; 9780674032118; 978-0-674-

03211-8; 0-674-03211-X
LC 2008-32599
This is a biography of the educator who founded the Tuskegee Institute and wrote the memoir Up From Slavery (1901). Index.
This "is in all respects an exemplary book, scrupulously fair to its subject and thus to the reader as well." Washington Post Book World
Includes bibliographical references

Norris, Kathleen

Acedia & me; a marriage, monks, and a writer's life. Riverhead Books 2008 334p $25.95 **92**
1. Apathy 2. Authors 3. Biography, Individual 4. Despair -- Religious aspects -- Christianity 5. Hope -- Religious aspects -- Christianity 6. Inspirational writers 7. Melancholy 8. Monasticism and religious orders 9. Poets 10. Spiritual life
ISBN 978-1-59448-996-9
LC 2008-10150
"The result of Norris's decades-long meditation on acedia is peaceful, graceful prose, amplified by word histories and gentle humor." Christ Today
Includes bibliographical references

Norris, Michele

The grace of silence; a memoir. Pantheon Books 2010 185p il $24.95; ebook $24.95 **92**
1. African American women -- Biography 2. Biography, Individual 3. Journalists 4. Radio reporters 5. Television reporters 6. Women journalists
ISBN 978-0-307-37876-7; 978-0-307-37946-7 ebook
LC 2010-19285
"In examining her personal roots for this memoir, African American Norris . . . found some skeletons in her family's closet. For example, she discovered that in the early 20th century her grandmother had dressed as Aunt Jemima to pitch pancake flour to the wives of white farmers in the Midwest. Using her skills as an investigative reporter, Norris also pieces together details of an incident in 1946 when her father was shot by a white policeman in Birmingham, AL. . . . Norris's family history offers Americans of all races a moving and revealing account of the obstacles facing several generations of middle-class African Americans in the pre-Civil Rights era." Libr J
Includes bibliographical references

Norris, Robert S.

Racing for the bomb: General Leslie R. Groves, the Manhattan Project's indispensable man. Steerforth Press 2002 xxi, 722p hardcover o.p. pa $24.95 **92**
1. Computer industry executives 2. Generals
ISBN 1-58642-067-4 pa
LC 2001-57629
This is a biography of the military engineer in charge of the Manhattan Project, which developed the atomic bomb.
This "work will not only serve scholars and general readers equally well but also take its place among the handful of best books about the birth of the atomic age." Booklist
Includes bibliographical references

Novacek, Michael J.

Time traveler; in search of dinosaurs and ancient mammals from Montana to Mongolia. {by} Michael Novacek. Farrar, Straus & Giroux 2002 368p il $26; pa $15   **92**

1. Curators 2. Paleontologists 3. Paleontologists -- United States 4. Paleontology

ISBN 0-374-27880-6; 0-374-52876-4 pa

LC 2001-40438

"The author first describes the youthful experiences that inspired him to become a paleontologist. . . . Then Novacek launches into his various expeditions. . . . Interweaving his adventures with explanations of where his finds fit into the geologic past, Novacek has combined the comedic with the informative in this entertaining survey of his career." Booklist

Includes bibliographical references

Nuland, Sherwin B.

Lost in America; a journey with my father. Knopf 2003 209p $24; pa $12   **92**

1. Authors 2. Factory workers 3. Surgeons 4. Writers on medicine

ISBN 0-375-41294-8; 0-375-75722-1 pa

LC 2002-40795

"Written with enormous empathy, yet without a hint of sentimentality, Nuland's memoir is both heartbreaking and breathtaking." Publ Wkly

The **doctors'** plague; germs, childbed fever, and the strange story of Ignac Semmelweis. Norton 2003 191p il $21.95; pa $13.95   **92**

1. Physicians 2. Puerperal septicemia 3. Writers on medicine

ISBN 0-393-05299-0; 0-393-32625-X pa

LC 2003-11412

This is an account of the work of the 19th-century obstetrician Ignas Semmelweis. "Semmelweis is remembered for the now-commonplace notion that doctors must wash their hands before examining patients. . . . With deaths from childbed fever exploding, Semmelweis discovered that doctors themselves were spreading the disease." Publisher's note

Includes bibliographical references

Nusseibeh, Sari

Once upon a country; a Palestinian life. [by] Sari Nusseibeh, with Anthony David. Farrar, Straus and Giroux 2007 542p il $27.50   **92**

1. Biography, Individual 2. College presidents 3. Israel-Arab conflicts 4. Palestinian Arabs 5. Philosophers 6. Political leaders

ISBN 978-0-374-29950-7; 0-374-29950-1

LC 2006-13272

"This is a rare book, one written by a partisan in the struggle over Palestine who nevertheless recognizes—and bravely records—the moral and political failures of his own people." Los Angeles Times

Includes bibliographical references

O'Connor, Flannery

The **habit** of being; letters. edited and with an introduction by Sally Fitzgerald. Farrar, Straus & Giroux 1979 617p hardcover o.p. pa $20   **92**

1. Authors 2. Novelists 3. Short story writers

ISBN 0-374-52104-2 pa

LC 78-11559

This collection includes letters to friends in the literary establishment: Robert Lowell and Elizabeth Hardwick, Caroline Gordon Tate, Robert and Sally Fitzgerald and others.

O'Connor, Garry

Universal Father: a life of John Paul II. Bloomsbury 2005 436p il map $24.95   **92**

1. Biography, Individual 2. Popes

ISBN 1-59691-096-8

"The text is divided into four distinct phases of Pope John Paul II's life: '1920-1946,' '1946-1978,' '1978-1990,' and '1990-2005.' Each phase balances fact with anecdotal evidence, which lends the biography both credibility and charm. . . . This timely and remarkable biography will be sought after by serious readers." Libr J

O'Dell, Chris

Miss O'Dell; my hard days and long nights with the Beatles, the Stones, Bob Dylan, Eric Clapton, and the women they loved. [by] Chris O'Dell with Katherine Ketcham. Touchstone 2009 403p il $26   **92**

1. Biography, Individual 2. Drug abuse counselors 3. Hypnotists 4. Memoirists 5. Music industry 6. Rock musicians 7. Rock musicians -- Anecdotes

ISBN 978-1-416-59093-4; 1-416-59093-5

LC 2009-14555

"An irresistible memoir of one of the lesser lights of a major constellation of rock stars and their satellites." Kirkus

O'Meally, Robert G.

Lady Day; the many faces of Billie Holiday. [by] Robert O'Meally; produced by Toby Byron/Multiprises. Da Capo Press 1991 207p il pa $20   **92**

1. African American singers 2. Blues musicians 3. Singers

ISBN 978-0-306-80959-0; 0-306-80959-1

"Narcotics, jail, sexual abuse, and prejudice are often our first associations concerning the life of the great jazz singer, but this biography recalls only Holiday as artist. O'Meally . . . puts her tragedy and talent into perspective, and what emerges is a critique of a singer. The book's first section is outstanding in this regard, employing stories, quotes, and interviews in describing Holiday's technique." Libr J

Includes discography and bibliographical references

O'Reilly, Bill

A **bold** fresh piece of humanity. Broadway Books 2008 256p il $26   **92**

1. Biography, Individual 2. Journalists 3. Talk show hosts 4. Television moderators 5. Television reporters

ISBN 978-0-7679-2882-3; 0-7679-2882-2

LC 2008-25510

This is a memoir by the broadcaster and author of The O'Reilly Factor (2000), The No Spin Zone (2001), and Who's Looking Out For You? (2003).

O'Rourke, Meghan

The **long** goodbye; a memoir. Riverhead Books 2011 306p $25.95   **92**

1. Authors 2. Bereavement 3. Biography, Individual 4. Cancer patients 5. Essayists 6. Magazine editors 7. Mother-daughter relationship 8. Mothers and daughters 9. Poets 10. Poets, American

ISBN 978-1-59448-798-9

LC 2010047948

"The raw feelings, the inevitable self-pity over each person's own loss, and their futile wishes to somehow make Mother's last days not be her last days will likely feel all too close to home for many who have suffered similarly. . . . Every tear-stained page is not a road map, but rather a lovely gift from a fellow traveler." Booklist

Includes bibliographical references

O'Shea, James

The **deal** from hell; how moguls and Wall Street plundered great American newspapers. PublicAffairs 2011 395p $28.99   **92**

1. Cooperative organization administrators 2. Journalists 3. Newspaper editors 4. Newspaper executives 5. Newspapers -- United States

ISBN 978-1-58648-791-1; 978-1-58648-865-9 ebook

LC 2011009204

The author "recounts the events leading to the dissolution of several major American newspapers in this gripping story of a troubled industry. Told from the 'front-row,' O'Shea shows how ill-advised mergers, mismanagement, acquisitive Wall Street execs, and the Tribune Company's eventual bankruptcy filing crippled an industry. . . . For those who want an inside look at what makes American journalism work (and not work), O'Shea offers a unique and valuable perspective." Publ Wkly

Includes bibliographical references

O'Toole, Patricia

When trumpets call; Theodore Roosevelt after the White House. Simon & Schuster 2005 494p il hardcover o.p. pa $16   **92**

1. Biography, Individual 2. Governors 3. Nobel laureates for peace 4. Presidents 5. Presidents -- United States 6. Vice-presidents

ISBN 0-684-86477-0; 0-684-86478-9 pa

LC 2004-62590

The author "adeptly revisits this story, uncovering previously unexploited material and presenting a fuller and more sympathetic account. . . . O'Toole has written the definitive account of TR's postpresidential years." Libr J

Includes bibliographical references

Oates, Joyce Carol

★ The **journal** of Joyce Carol Oates: 1973-1982; edited by Greg Johnson. Ecco 2007 509p il $29.95   **92**

1. Authors 2. Authors, American 3. Children's authors 4. Essayists 5. Novelists 6. Poets 7. Short story

writers 8. Women authors

ISBN 978-0-06-122798-1; 0-06-122798-6

LC 2007-29378

This is a collection of diaries from the period when Oates published Do With Me What You Will (1973), Bellefleur (1980), and other works.

"This journal immerses the reader in a complex, searching, imaginative personality—an artist who continues to refine her search for literary expression." Publ Wkly

Includes bibliographical references

A **widow's** story; a memoir. Ecco 2011 415p il $27.99   **92**

1. Authors 2. Authors, American 3. Bereavement 4. Biographers 5. Biography, Individual 6. Children's authors 7. Essayists 8. Loss (Psychology) 9. Magazine editors 10. Novelists 11. Poets 12. Short story writers 13. Spouses of prominent persons 14. Widows

ISBN 978-0-06-201553-2

"In a narrative as searing as the best of her fiction, Oates describes the aftermath of her husband Ray's unexpected death from pneumonia. Scattershot moments stand out — the day she cancels their 30-year subscription to The New York Times, unable to bear the sight of his favorite paper; her fury at the tulips, harbingers of spring, pushing through the snow ('Too soon! This is too soon!'); the night she weans herself from Lorazepam. A Widow's Story is the painful, scorchingly angry journey of a woman struggling to live in a house 'from which meaning has departed, like air leaking from a balloon.' " Entertainment Wkly

Oates, Stephen B.

A **woman** of valor: Clara Barton and the Civil War. Free Press 1994 527p il map hardcover o.p. pa $16.95   **92**

1. Nurses 2. Red Cross officials 3. Social welfare leaders

ISBN 0-02-923405-0; 0-02-874012-2 pa

LC 93-38830

"This is a carefully written and researched work that brings to life both the Civil War and a period of Barton's life that was to affect her forever." Libr J

Includes bibliographical references

Obama, Barack

★ **Dreams** from my father; a story of race and inheritance. Crown Publishers 2007 442p $25.95 **92**

1. African Americans -- Biography 2. Lawyers 3. Nobel laureates for peace 4. Presidents 5. Presidents -- United States 6. Racially mixed people 7. Senators 8. State legislators

ISBN 978-0-307-38341-9

LC 2007-271892

This is the autobiography of the Illinois senator who would later become the 44th president of the United States.

The author "offers an account of his life's journey that reflects brilliantly on the power of race consciousness in America. . . . Obama writes well; his account is sensitive, probing, and compelling." Choice [review of 1995 edition]

Oberman, Heiko Augustinus

Luther: man between God and the Devil; {by} Heiko A. Oberman; translated by Eileen Walliser-Schwarzbart. Yale Univ. Press 1990 xx, 380p il hardcover o.p. pa $20 **92**
1. Reformation 2. Religious leaders 3. Social reformers 4. Theologians 5. Writers on religion
ISBN 978-0-300-10313-7 pa; 0-300-10313-1 pa
LC 89-5747

The author "posits that to understand Luther the reformer is to first realize he was a medieval man for whom Satan was as real as God and human. By placing Luther back into the context of his own age, Oberman strips away any simplistic, post-Enlightenment notions of Luther as the savior of humanity from the darkest obscurantism of the Catholic Church. . . . A triumph of scholarship that brings Luther to life in all of his furious, outspoken, and violent passion." Booklist
Includes bibliographical references

Offit, Paul A.

Vaccinated; one man's quest to defeat the world's deadliest diseases. Smithsonian Books/Collins 2007 254p $26.95 **92**
1. Biologists 2. Microbiologists 3. Vaccination
ISBN 978-0-06-122795-0; 0-06-122795-1
LC 2006-53054

"This book leaves one with a great appreciation for the work of the Salks and Sabins of the world, and it makes one want to lead a movement to enshrine Maurice Hilleman in the pantheon of American pop heroes." Choice
Includes bibliographical references

Ollestad, Norman

Crazy for the storm; a memoir of survival. Ecco 2009 272p il $25.99 **92**
1. Aircraft accidents 2. Biography, Individual 3. Father-son relationship 4. Memoirists
ISBN 978-0-06-176672-5; 0-061-76672-0
LC 2008-53675

"In the winter of 1979, the 11-year-old Ollestad survived a plane crash in which his father and his father's girlfriend were killed. Alternating with young Norman's nine-hour trek to safety are scenes from the year preceding the crash, when the boy took a surfing trip with his father through the jungle along Mexico's Pacific coast. The flashbacks sections are the most fascinating parts of the book, and Ollestad ably captures the contrast between his charismatically cool father, Norman Sr., and his bullying stepfather-to-be, Nick. . . . [He] presents a captivating account of high-altitude disaster that nicely dovetails with his coming-of-age story in '70s California. Deep and resonant." Kirkus

Osbourne, Ozzy

I am Ozzy; [by] Ozzy Osbourne with Chris Ayres. Grand Central Publishing 2010 391p $26.99 **92**
1. Rock musicians 2. Singers
ISBN 978-0-446-56989-7
LC 2009-937230

"Osbourne offers the most detail about growing up and the Black Sabbath years – no surprise as you'd expect decades of drug use have nearly wiped clean those later years.

He discusses his youth in England, his brief stint in jail, how a flier posted in a music store – 'Ozzy Zig Needs a Gig' – led to the eventual formation of Black Sabbath, his relationship with his wives and children, his own health scares, and The Osbournes television show. The book is written with Osbourne's wit and sense of humor as he shares laugh-out-loud tales of practical jokes while touring around the world and recording inside a castle. There's even a look at the sensitive side when he discusses the death of guitarist Randy Rhodes and his wife's (Sharon's) battle with cancer." Creative Loafing

Oz, Amos

A **tale** of love and darkness; translated from the Hebrew by Nicholas de Lange. Harcourt 2004 538p $26 **92**
1. Authors 2. Authors, Israeli -- Biography 3. Essayists 4. Novelists 5. Short story writers
ISBN 0-15-100878-7
LC 2004-7302

"A powerful story of the making of a writer . . . Oz's panoramic memoir enhances the history of literature and of Israel, and the literature of examined lives." Booklist

Pakula, Hannah

The **last** empress; Madame Chiang Kai-Shek and the birth of modern China. Simon & Schuster 2009 787p il map $35 **92**
1. Biography, Individual 2. Generals 3. Presidents 4. Spouses of presidents
ISBN 978-1-4391-4893-8; 1-4391-4893-7
LC 2009-17576

This is a biography of Soong Mei-ling, who became the wife of the Chinese Nationalist leader Chiang Kai-shek.

"A winning combination of measured, balanced research and critical evaluation—the definitive account of an important figure in 20th-century Chinese politics." Kirkus
Includes bibliographical references

Palin, Michael

Halfway to Hollywood; diaries 1980-1988. Thomas Dunne Books 2011 622p il $32.50 **92**
1. Actors 2. Authors 3. Biography, Individual 4. Comedians 5. Humorists 6. Screenwriters 7. Television scriptwriters
ISBN 978-0-312-68202-6; 0-312-68202-6

Palmer, Arnold

A **golfer's** life; {by} Arnold Palmer with James Dodson. Ballantine Bks. 1999 420p il hardcover o.p. pa $15 **92**
1. Golfers 2. Large print books
ISBN 0-345-41482-9 pa
LC 98-51681

Palmer's "immense popularity is widely credited with rescuing professional golf in the late 1950s and 1960s. Written with humor and candor, the book recounts Palmer's friendships and rivalries with the greats of the game, his enduring marriage to Winnie Palmer, his legendary triumphs and disasters, and his battle against cancer." Libr J

Palmer, James

The **bloody** white baron; the extraordinary story of the Russian nobleman who became the last khan of Mongolia. Basic Books 2009 274p $26.95   **92**

1. Generals

ISBN 978-0-465-01448-4; 0-465-01448-8

LC 2008-937254

"What makes 'The Bloody White Baron' so exceptional is Palmer's lucid scholarship, his ability to make perfect sense of the maelstrom of a forgotten war. This is a brilliant book." N Y Times Book Rev

Includes bibliographical references

Parini, Jay

★ **One** matchless time; a life of William Faulkner. HarperCollins Publishers 2004 492p il $29.95; pa $14.95   **92**

1. Authors 2. Biography, Individual 3. Nobel laureates for literature 4. Novelists 5. Screenwriters 6. Short story writers

ISBN 0-06-621072-0; 0-06-093555-3 pa

LC 2004-42891

The author "offers a portrait of a man always trying to invent a new mask for himself as well as the portrait of an artist consumed by a desire to tell about the South and its class struggles, its depravity, and its captivity to the double bonds of land and history. Parini examines each of Faulkner's novels, from Soldier's Pay to The Reivers, and connects the Snopses, Sutpens, and Compsons of Faulkner's mythic Yoknapatawpha County foibles, his insecurities, and his inestimable literary achievement." Libr J

Includes bibliographical references

Parker, Douglas M.

Ogden Nash; the life and work of America's laureate of light verse. with a foreword by Dana Gioia. Ivan R. Dee 2005 316p il $27.50   **92**

1. Authors 2. Biography, Individual 3. Children's authors 4. Humorists 5. Poets

ISBN 1-566-63637-X

LC 2004-59912

"Parker's is a useful, highly readable biography of one of America's best-loved poets." Publ Wkly

Includes bibliographical references

Partnoy, Frank

The **match** king; Ivar Kreuger, the financial genius behind a century of Wall Street scandals. PubliCAffairs 2009 272p $26.95; pa $15.95   **92**

1. Biography, Individual 2. Capitalists and financiers 3. Financiers 4. International finance -- Corrupt practices 5. Manufacturing executives 6. Swindlers and swindling

ISBN 978-1-58648-743-0; 1-58648-743-4; 978-1-58648-812-3 pa; 1-58648-812-0 pa

The author "delivers a thrilling account of the grandfather of all Ponzi and Madoff schemes—Ivar Kreuger (1880-1932), who made his fortune in the 1920s by raising money from American investors to lend to European governments in exchange for match monopolies. . . . A fascinating depiction of a man and his era." Publ Wkly

Includes bibliographical references (p. 230-235)

Patchett, Ann

Truth & beauty; a friendship. HarperCollins Publishers 2004 257p hardcover o.p. pa $13.95 **92**

1. Authors 2. Biography, Individual 3. Memoirists 4. Novelists 5. Poets 6. Women authors

ISBN 0-06-057214-0; 0-06-057215-9 pa

LC 2003-67586

"As young writers. Patchett and Lucy Grealy began an intense friendship that lasted until Grealy's tragic death. With intimacy, grace, and humor, Patchett's memoir captures Lucy's exuberance and her roller-coaster struggles with disfigurement and depression." Booklist

Patel, Eboo

Acts of faith; the story of an American Muslim, the struggle for the soul of a generation. Beacon Press 2010 195p pa $14   **92**

1. Multiculturalism 2. Muslims -- United States 3. Organization officials 4. Religious leaders 5. Sociologists 6. Writers on religion 7. Youth leaders

ISBN 978-0-8070-0622-1; 0-8070-0622-X

LC 2010-537438

The author, "a founder of the Interfaith Youth Core, traces the personal journey that led to the group's formation and introduces readers to its philosophy." Kirkus

Includes bibliographical references

Patoski, Joe Nick

★ **Willie** Nelson; an epic life. Little, Brown 2008 567p il $27.99; pa $16.99   **92**

1. Biography, Individual 2. Country musicians 3. Singers 4. Songwriters

ISBN 978-0-316-01778-7; 0-316-01778-7; 978-0-316-01779-4 pa; 0-316-01779-5 pa

LC 2007-44984

A biography of the country music singer and songwriter.

"This impressive, entertaining chronicle of Willie Nelson's life is replete with exactly what you'd expect—honky-tonk, long nights on the open road, whiskey, womanizing and weed—but . . . [the author] looks beyond country music trappings to find the funny, talented, determined man who became an unlikely icon." Publ Wkly

Includes discography and bibliographical references

Paul, Alan

Big in China; my unlikely adventures raising a family, playing the blues, and becoming a star in Beijing. HarperCollins Pub. 2011 282p $25.99; ebook $20.99   **92**

1. Bloggers 2. Blues musicians 3. Columnists 4. Journalists 5. Memoirists

ISBN 978-0-06-199315-2; 978-0-06-206582-7 ebook

"A rollicking, inspiring narrative with plenty of memorable characters and scenes." Libr J

Pauly, Thomas H.

Zane Grey; his life, his adventures, his women. University of Illinois Press 2005 385p il map $34.95   **92**

1. Authors 2. Biography, Individual 3. Novelists 4.

Western writers
ISBN 978-0-252-03044-4; 0-252-03044-3

LC 2005-9413

The author "offers an honest exploration of the complex author. . . . A solid, entertaining read." Choice
Includes bibliographical references

Peacock, Molly, 1947-

The **paper** garden; an artist begins her life's work at 72. Bloomsbury USA 2010 397p il $30 **92**
1. Artists 2. Artists, British 3. Biography, Individual 4. Collage 5. Creation (Literary, artistic, etc.) 6. Creative ability in old age 7. Flowers in art 8. Women artists
ISBN 978-1-60819-523-7; 1-60819-523-6

"The author entwines the story of Delany with private reflections on her own life as an artist and a woman. As Peacock undertook her eccentric quest to discover the life of the woman who created the beautiful paper mosaics that she so admired, she discovered resonant parallels. . . . A lyrical, meditative rumination on art and the blossoming beauty of self that can be the gift of age and love." Kirkus
Includes bibliographical references

Pearson, Roger

★ **Voltaire** almighty; a life in pursuit of freedom. Bloomsbury 2005 xxxii, 447p il $35 **92**
1. Authors 2. Biography, Individual 3. Dramatists 4. Essayists 5. Novelists 6. Philosophers 7. Poets
ISBN 978-1-58234-630-4; 1-58234-630-5

LC 2005-53027

This is a biography of the French philosopher.
The author "has composed a lively and thorough account of the illustrious philosophe's chaotic life." Choice
Includes bibliographical references

Pelosi, Nancy

Know your power; a message to America's daughters. with Amy Hill Hearth. Doubleday 2008 180p $23.95; pa $14.95 **92**
1. Members of Congress 2. Politicians -- United States 3. Speakers of the House 4. Women politicians
ISBN 978-0-385-52586-2; 0-385-52586-9; 978-0-7679-2944-8 pa; 0-7679-2944-6 pa

LC 2008-20607

"In this graceful personal and political history, Pelosi describes growing up as the daughter of a congressman in an Italian-American Catholic world . . . and her burgeoning political interest. . . . Pelosi's book is a simply crafted acknowledgment of the support of her family, mentors and helpful colleagues without rhetorical flourishes, insider scandal or intimate revelations—a gentle account from a tough politician." Publ Wkly

Pendle, George

Strange angel; the otherworldly life of rocket scientist John Whiteside Parsons. Harcourt 2005 350p il $25; pa $15 **92**
1. Biography, Individual 2. Scientists
ISBN 0-15-100997-X; 0-15-603179-5 pa

LC 2004-10666

"Marshaling a cast of characters ranging from Robert Millikan to L. Ron Hubbard, Pendle offers a fascinating glimpse into a world long past, a story that would make a compelling work of fiction if it weren't so astonishingly true." Publ Wkly
Includes bibliographical references

Pernoud, Regine

Joan of Arc: her story; Régine Pernoud, Marie-Véronique Clin; translated and revised by Jeremy duQuesnay Adams; edited by Bonnie Wheeler. St. Martin's Griffin 1999 xxii, 304p il map hardcover o.p. pa $16.95 **92**
1. Christian saints 2. Saints
ISBN 0-312-21442-1; 0-312-22730-2 pa

LC 98-45059

This work "traces the appearance of Joan as a documented historical character rather than adhering to a standard chronological sequence. Informing the narrative is a novel interpretation of Joan as a political prisoner. Moving beyond the narrative, the American translator . . . has added a series of appendixes containing valuable contextual material. . . . These materials discuss key historical events, provide biographical information on Joan's contemporaries, and discuss Joan's afterlife in history, literature, folklore, art, and iconography." Libr J
Includes bibliographical references

Perry, Bruce

Malcolm; the life of a man who changed black America. Station Hill Press 1991 542p il hardcover o.p. pa $14.95 **92**
1. Black Muslim leaders 2. Civil rights activists
ISBN 0-88268-121-4 pa

LC 90-23350

"Perry traces Malcolm X's footsteps from birth in 1925 to death in 1965, using several hundred interviews to fill in detail and correct the autobiography Alex Haley edited. Probing what he labels as the deep-seated and hidden causes that made Malcolm who and what he was, Perry produces a portrait of an emotionally abused and abandoned boy who grew to manipulate his fearful helplessness into emotional and political power." Libr J
Includes bibliographical references

Perry, Michael

Coop; a year of poultry, pigs, and parenting. Harper 2009 352p il $25.99 **92**
1. Authors 2. Biography, Individual 3. Essayists 4. Farm life 5. Farmers 6. Humorists 7. Marketing executives 8. Memoirists
ISBN 978-0-06-124043-0

LC 2008-43832

The author's "essays chronicle a year on 37 acres of land with his wife, daughters and titular menagerie of livestock. . . . But these luminous pieces meander back to his childhood on the hardscrabble Wisconsin dairy farm where his parents, members of a tiny fundamentalist Christian sect, raised him and dozens of siblings and foster-siblings, many of them disabled. . . . Perry writes vividly about rural life; peck at any sentence . . . and you'll find a poetic evocation of barnyard grace." Publ Wkly

Peter, Jason

Hero of the underground; a memoir. [by] Jason Peter with Tony O'Neill. St. Martin's Press 2008 289p $24.95; pa $14.95 **92**
1. Drug abuse 2. Football -- Biography 3. Football players 4. Heroin
ISBN 978-0-312-37576-8; 0-312-37576-X; 978-0-312-56103-1 pa; 0-312-56103-2 pa
LC 2008-12364
A former NFL player traces his journey from professional athlete to drug addict after injuries ended his career, describing the range of physical, psychological, and legal dilemmas that affected his perception of reality and nearly ended his life.
"Avoiding self-help urgings and self-congratulations, Peter (who is now clean) and O'Neill have crafted an unflinching look at the dark side of a life devoted to pleasure." Publ Wkly

Peters, Charles

Lyndon B. Johnson. Times Books 2010 199p $23 **92**
1. Members of Congress 2. Presidents 3. Presidents -- United States 4. Senators 5. Vice-presidents
ISBN 978-0-8050-8239-5
LC 2009-45612
"Peters describes Johnson's Texas childhood, his years in Congress, his frustrating years as Kennedy's vice president, and the triumphs and failures of his presidency (1963-68). . . . This book is aimed at general readers who want a brief account of this controversial President. . . . Its intended audience will not be disappointed with this fast-moving story." Libr J
Includes bibliographical references

Peterson, Dale

Jane Goodall: the woman who redefined man. Houghton Mifflin 2006 740p il $24.95; pa $17.95 **92**
1. Nonfiction writers 2. Primatologists 3. Women scientists 4. Writers on nature
ISBN 978-0-395-85405-1; 0-395-85405-9; 978-0-547-05356-1 pa; 0-547-05356-8 pa
LC 2006-6050
Peterson "vividly and significantly enriches our understanding of Goodall as a scientist, spiritual thinker, and humanist." Booklist
Includes bibliographical references

Pham, Andrew X.

★ The eaves of heaven; a life in three wars. by Andrew X. Pham, on behalf of my father, Thong Van Pham. Harmony Books 2008 301p $24.95 **92**
1. Biography, Individual 2. Refugees 3. Vietnamese Americans
ISBN 978-0-307-38120-0; 0-307-38120-X
LC 2007-33894
"In a narrative set between the years of 1940 and 1976, Pham . . . recounts the story of his once wealthy father, Thong Van Pham, who lived through the French occupation of Indochina, the Japanese invasion during WWII, and the Vietnam War. . . . For those not familiar with Vietnam-ese history, Pham does an admirable job of recounting the complex cast of characters and the political machinations of the various groups vying for power over the years. In the end, he also gracefully delivers a heartfelt family history." Publ Wkly
Includes bibliographical references

Phillips, Kevin P.

★ William McKinley; {by} Kevin Phillips. Times Bks. 2003 188p $20 **92**
1. Governors 2. Members of Congress 3. Presidents
ISBN 0-8050-6953-4
LC 2003-50701
"This little work of rehabilitation should help set McKinley's reputation right." Publ Wkly
Includes bibliographical references

Pimlott, Ben

The Queen: a biography of Elizabeth II. Wiley 1997 651p il hardcover o.p. pa $24.95 **92**
1. Queens
ISBN 0-471-28330-4 pa
LC 97-21270
The author explores "the role of the queen and how the events of the past few decades have changed it. Is the monarch just a figurehead, or are there specific governmental actions she can take? How did the royal family lose its privacy, along with much public respect? Pimlott tackles these questions and other historical, psychological, and sociological issues surrounding the queen and her family." Libr J
Includes bibliographical references

Pinsker, Matthew

Lincoln's sanctuary; Abraham Lincoln and the Soldiers' Home. Oxford University Press 2003 256p il maps hardcover o.p. pa $17.95 **92**
1. Biography, Individual 2. Lawyers 3. Members of Congress 4. Presidents 5. Presidents -- United States 6. State legislators
ISBN 0-19-516206-4; 978-0-19-517985-9 pa; 0-19-517985-4 pa
LC 2003-1215
The author "follows the War President to his 'retreat' at the Soldiers' Home away from the daily noise, posturing, and politicking of the capital and finds there a serenity that allowed Lincoln to relax with his family, think through issues, conduct secret meetings with allies and enemies, and reinvigorate his resolve. . . . Through Pinsker's probing inquiry into sources heretofore surprisingly underused, the ever elusive private Lincoln comes into new light. A book for our time and for all libraries." Libr J

Pinsky, Robert

The life of David. Schocken 2005 209p $19.95 **92**
1. Biography, Individual 2. Kings
ISBN 0-8052-4203-1
LC 2005-41696
The author "considers the peculiarities, paradoxes, and timeless significance of David's often baffling story from his golden days as a handsome upstart confronting King Saul in 'gangsterish' encounters to David's wild years as a desert

Robin Hood and ascension to the throne. . . . Witty, frank, skeptical, and clearly moved by mercurial David's chutzpah and losses, Pinsky brings remarkable lucidity, depth, and creativity to his dynamic and poetic reading of a legendary figure who has become emblematic of both destructive and heroic aspects of human nature." Booklist

Pirsig, Robert M.

Zen and the art of motorcycle maintenance; an inquiry into values. Morrow 1974 412p $26; pa $13.95 **92**

1. Authors 2. Essayists 3. Novelists
ISBN 0-688-00230-7; 0-06-083987-2 pa

A collection of the author's philosophical musings inspired by a motorcycle trip with his son

Plummer, Christopher

In spite of myself; a memoir. Knopf 2009 648p il $29.95 **92**

1. Actors 2. Biography, Individual
ISBN 978-0-679-42162-7; 0-679-42162-9
LC 2008-31229

The author is "an enchanting observer of the showbiz cavalcade, drawing vivid thumbnails of everyone from Laurence Olivier to Lenny Bruce and tossing off witty anecdotes . . . like the most effortless ad libs. The result is a sparkling star turn from a born raconteur for whom all the world is indeed a stage." Publ Wkly

Poitier, Sidney

★ The **measure** of a man; a spiritual autobiography. HarperSanFrancisco 2007 299p il $25.95; pa $14.95 **92**

1. Actors 2. Actors -- United States -- Biography 3. Motion picture directors
ISBN 978-0-06-135791-6; 0-06-135791-X; 978-0-06-135790-9 pa; 0-06-135790-1 pa

"Poitier attempts to unravel for himself his own remarkable life story, looking at early life experiences, his family, and various themes that he believes have contributed to his success. Measure is not a chronological autobiography; the book emphasizes themes that have shaped his life. . . . Poitier's tale is an affirmation of the value of morality and personal integrity in leading a successful, fulfilling life." Booklist

Pollack, Howard

★ **George** Gershwin; his life and work. University of California Press 2006 884p il $39.95 **92**

1. Biography, Individual 2. Composers
ISBN 978-0-520-24864-9; 0-520-24864-3
LC 2006-17926

"This engaging biography is also a tour de force of scholarship." Booklist
Includes bibliographical references

Pomper, Philip

Lenin's brother; the origins of the October Revolution. W.W. Norton & Co. 2010 276p il $24.95 **92**

1. Communist leaders 2. Heads of state 3. Political

leaders 4. Revolutionaries
ISBN 978-0-393-07079-8
LC 2009-27390

"In 1887, the future leader of the Russian revolution, Vladimir Ulyanov (later Lenin), was 17 when his 21-year-old brother was hanged for his role in a bungled attempt to assassinate Czar Alexander III. Historians consider this the seminal event that launched Lenin's career as a revolutionary. . . . [The author] delivers an absorbing and surprisingly detailed account of Alexander Ulyanov's short life and even shorter career (four months) as a terrorist." Publ Wkly
Includes bibliographical references

Porter, Linda

Katherine the queen; the remarkable life of Katherine Parr, the last wife of Henry VIII. St. Martin's Press 2010 383p il $27.99 **92**

1. Biography, Individual 2. Queens
ISBN 9780312384388
LC 2010035251

In this biography of Katherine Parr, Porter argues that "Henry VIII's last queen was a more human, complex and modern figure than has hitherto been realized." (Publisher's note) Index.

"Although often depicted by the Victorians as a matronly nurse to an elderly king, Katherine Parr (1512–1548), according to Porter, was a stylish trendsetter of 30, sensual, confident, dynamic, exceptionally educated and cultured, and able to perform with aplomb on both an English and international stage. . . . Rich, perceptive, nuanced and creative, this first full-scale biography gives one of Britain's best but least-known queens her due." Publ Wkly
Includes bibliographical references

Powell, Colin L.

My American journey; [by] Colin L. Powell, with Joseph E. Persico. Random House 1995 643p il $26.95; pa $14.95 **92**

1. Generals 2. Secretaries of state 3. Statesmen -- United States
ISBN 0-679-43296-5; 0-345-46641-1 pa
LC 95-17119

This "is an endearing and well-written book. It will make you like Colin Powell." N Y Times Book Rev

Power, Samantha

Chasing the flame; Sergio Vieira de Mello and the fight to save the world. Penguin Press 2008 622p il $32.95 **92**

1. Biography, Individual 2. Diplomats 3. Iraq War, 2003- 4. Peace-building 5. United Nations officials
ISBN 978-1-594-20128-8
LC 2007-30978

"Strongly argued, lacerating, and utterly human, this invaluable history will be a catalyst for soul searching and debate." Booklist
Includes bibliographical references

Powers, Ron

Mark Twain; a life. Free Press 2005 722p il $35 **92**

1. Authors 2. Biography, Individual 3. Essayists 4.

Humorists 5. Memoirists 6. Novelists 7. Satirists 8. Short story writers 9. Travel writers
ISBN 0-7432-4899-6

LC 2005-48816

"A masterful biography of interest to both general readers and academics." Booklist
Includes bibliographical references

Powers, Thomas

The **killing** of Crazy Horse. Alfred A. Knopf 2010 568p il map $30   **92**
1. Biography, Individual 2. Dakota Indians -- Wars 3. Indian chiefs 4. Oglala Indians
ISBN 978-0-375-41446-6; 0-375-41446-0

LC 2010-16842

"With the Great Sioux War as background and context, . . . Powers recounts the final months and days of Crazy Horse's life." (Publisher's note) Bibliography. Index.

"Despite the title, this beautifully written and absorbing work is less about the death of Crazy Horse and more about the personality and life of the Native American icon. It is also an insightful and scrupulously fair examination of the culture of Plains Indian bands and their interaction with advancing white civilization in the nineteenth century." Booklist
Includes bibliographical references

Preston, Diana

A **pirate** of exquisite mind: explorer, naturalist, and buccaneer: the life of William Dampier; {by} Diana and Michael Preston. Walker & Company 2004 372p il map $27   **92**
1. Explorers 2. Naval officers 3. Travel writers 4. Voyages around the world
ISBN 0-8027-1425-0

LC 2003-62197

"Dampier's adventures and observations ignited the imagination of a generation, but today his name is largely unknown. This exhaustive biography . . . won't make Dampier famous again, but it will give readers a clear understanding of one of the most well-traveled men in history." Publ Wkly
Includes bibliographical references

Preston, Paul

Juan Carlos; steering Spain from dictatorship to democracy. W. W. Norton 2004 608p $35   **92**
1. Kings
ISBN 0-393-05804-2

LC 2004-47435

This biography explores the life of the Spanish monarch
Preston "supplies a much-needed, serious, comprehensive, and absolutely dynamic biography of el rey, impressively researched and deeply probing." Booklist
Includes bibliographical references

Prial, Dunstan

The **producer**; John Hammond and the soul of American music. Farrar, Straus and Giroux 2006 347p il $27   **92**
1. Biography, Individual 2. Recording industry

executives
ISBN 978-0-374-11304-9; 0-374-11304-1

LC 2005-12666

The author "brings Hammond to life in clear, insightful prose and places him and figures such as Dylan, Franklin, and Springsteen in the proper historical context." Libr J
Includes discography and bibliographical references

Price, Reynolds

Ardent spirits; leaving home, coming back. Scribner 2009 408p il $35   **92**
1. Authors 2. Biography, Individual 3. College teachers 4. Essayists 5. Novelists 6. Short story writers
ISBN 978-0-7432-9189-7; 0-7432-9189-1

LC 2009-2376

In this memoir, Price "takes up where his 1989 Clear Pictures left off—with a young Price heading for England on a Rhodes scholarship, a young man lighting into new and unfamiliar territories and the lessons he learns about literature, life and love. Covering the years 1955 to 1961, Price chronicles the challenges of living in a strange place, his emotional insecurities and his anxieties about his ability to complete the thesis on Milton, his adventures in Europe with a close friend and his eventual return to his alma mater, Duke University, to teach writing and literature. Along the way, Price recalls his friendships with Stephen Spender, Cyril Connolly, W.H. Auden and his brief encounters with Jean-Paul Sartre and J.R.R. Tolkien. . . . [Price] powerfully articulates the strength of memory in shaping our lives and gracefully draws us into a literary life lived fully." Publ Wkly

Prideaux, Sue

Edvard Munch; behind the Scream. Yale University Press 2005 391p il map $35   **92**
1. Artists 2. Painters
ISBN 0-300-11024-3

LC 2005-12040

Prideaux's "treatment is very effective and her writing, cohesive, clear, and often compelling." Libr J
Includes bibliographical references

Pringle, Peter

The **murder** of Nikolai Vavilov; the story of Stalin's persecution of one of the great scientists of the twentieth century. Simon & Schuster 2008 370p il $26   **92**
1. Biography, Individual 2. Botanists 3. Communist leaders 4. Heads of state 5. Plant geneticists 6. Political crimes and offenses -- Soviet Union -- History 7. Political leaders
ISBN 978-0-7432-6498-3; 0-7432-6498-3

LC 2008-03510

This is a biography of the Russian botanist and geneticist who was starved to death in a Soviet prison in 1943.

This "is a must-read to grasp the ultimate, disasterous effect of politics trumping science." Sci Books Films
Includes bibliographical references

Prophet, Erin L.

  Prophet's daughter; my life with Elizabeth Clare Prophet inside the Church Universal and Triumphant. Lyons Press 2009 286p il $24.95   **92**

  1. Religious leaders 2. Writers on religion

  ISBN 978-1-5992-1425-2; 1-5992-1425-3

               LC 2008-33760

  "Prophet pulls the curtain back on the highest levels of life inside a cult, documenting her life inside as the daughter of cult leader Elizabeth Clare Prophet, of the Church Universal and Triumphant, from her birth through 1990, when the Church's long-awaited apocalypse failed to materialize. Without judgment or reservation, but a remarkably clear-eyed view built on more than 10 years on the outside, Prophet's account reveals cult life through the complex relationship with her charismatic, manipulative mother—a figure of equal reverence and alarm. . . . Prophet's intense tale is sure to stick with readers long after they make it through." Publ Wkly

Prose, Francine

  Caravaggio; painter of miracles. Atlas Books/ HarperCollins 2005 149p il $21.95   **92**

  1. Artists 2. Artists, Italian 3. Biography, Individual 4. Painters

  ISBN 0-06-057560-3

               LC 2005-40203

  "A contemporary of Shakespeare, Caravaggio was 'belligerent, contemptuous, and competitive,' a revered artist and a notorious street fighter wanted for murder who died at 39 under tragic circumstances. Much has been written about Caravaggio and his dramatic paintings, especially his daringly earthy depictions of biblical scenes, but somehow Prose's concentrated interpretation has a stronger impact. Not only does she cover all the biographical essentials but she also more clearly and descriptively explicates the pioneering painter's unique perception of the miraculous in everyday life. Prose also reveals, with both subtlety and flourish, how Caravaggio's frank interpretations of violence and pain, fear and grief, dignity and transcendence are matched with a brilliant subversion of our sense of reality." Booklist

Proulx, Annie

  Bird cloud; a memoir. Scribner 2011 234p il map $26; ebook $12.99   **92**

  1. Authors 2. Biography, Individual 3. Editors 4. Journalists 5. Natural history -- Wyoming 6. Nonfiction writers 7. Novelists 8. Short story writers 9. Women authors

  ISBN 978-0-7432-8880-4; 978-1-4391-7171-4 ebook

  "Proulx bought a 640-acre nature preserve by the North Platte River in Wyoming and started building her dream house, a project that took years and went hundreds of thousands of dollars over budget. In her bustling account, Proulx salivates over the prospect of a Japanese soak tub, polished concrete floor, solar panels, and luxe furnishings that often turn into pricey engineering fiascoes. . . . [This] is a fine evocation of place that becomes a meditation on the importance of a home, however harsh and evanescent." Publ Wkly

  Includes bibliographical references

Pugliese, Stanislao G.

  Bitter spring; a life of Ignazio Silone. Farrar, Straus and Giroux 2009 426p il $35   **92**

  1. Anti-fascist movements -- Italy 2. Authors 3. Authors, Italian 4. Biography, Individual 5. Essayists 6. Novelists

  ISBN 978-0-374-11348-3; 0-374-11348-3

               LC 2008-50410

  The author a mature account of a life that produced some of the twentieth century's most powerful and widely translated literary art and political commentary. . . . A much-needed work of literary and political scholarship. Booklist

  Includes bibliographical references (p. 387-397)

Putin, Vladimir

  First person: an astonishingly frank self-portrait; by Russia's president Vladimir Putin with Nataliya Gevorkyan, Natalya Timakova, and Andrei Kolesnikov; translated by Catherine A. Fitzpatrick. PublicAffairs 2000 206p il pa $15   **92**

  1. Presidents 2. Prime ministers

  ISBN 1-58648-018-9

               LC 00-132549

  This volume is "the product of some 24 hours of interviews with Putin conducted by three Russian journalists, with brief comments from other sources, including Putin's family, friends, teachers, and some associates. . . . The approach is chronological , describing Putin as son, schoolboy, university student, young intelligence specialist, spy, democrat, bureaucrat, family man, and politician." Booklist

Qazwini, Hassan

  American crescent; A Muslim cleric on the power of his faith, the struggle against prejudice, and the future of Islam and America. Random House 2007 282p il $26.95   **92**

  1. Biography, Individual 2. Islamic leaders 3. Muslims -- United States

  ISBN 978-1-4000-6454-0; 1-4000-6454-0

               LC 2007-10345

  This is "a useful book, especially for American readers who are unfamiliar with Islam or who wonder how Muslim Americans and Arab-Americans can be integrated into American life." N Y Times Book Rev

  Includes bibliographical references

Quammen, David

  ★ The **reluctant** Mr. Darwin; an intimate portrait of Charles Darwin and the making of his theory of evolution. Atlas Books/Norton 2006 304p hardcover o.p. pa $14.95   **92**

  1. Biography, Individual 2. Naturalists 3. Travel writers 4. Writers on science

  ISBN 0-393-05981-2; 978-0-393-05981-6; 0-393-32995-X pa; 978-0-393-32995-7 pa

               LC 2006-9864

  "This often slyly witty book stands out among the flood of books being published for Darwin's bicentenary." Publ Wkly

  Includes bibliographical references

Quasthoff, Thomas

The **voice**; a memoir. recorded by Michael Quasthoff; translated from the German by Kirsten Stoldt Wittenborn. Pantheon 2008 241p $24.95   **92**
1. Biography, Individual 2. Classical musicians 3. Singers
ISBN 978-0-375-42406-9; 0-375-42406-7
LC 2007-39089
"Bass-baritone Quasthoff recounts his remarkable experience overcoming severe physical disability to become one of the world's most celebrated classical singers. . . . Playful and humorous in tone, this inspirational story prompts admiration for the author's intellect and integrity, rather than facile tears for his condition." Kirkus
Includes discography

Queenan, Joe

Closing time; a memoir. Viking 2009 338p $26.95   **92**
1. Adult children of alcoholics 2. Authors 3. Authors, American 4. Biography, Individual 5. Essayists 6. Father-son relationship 7. Irish American families -- Pennsylvania -- Philadelphia 8. Motion picture critics 9. Satirists 10. Social critics
ISBN 978-0-670-02063-8; 0-670-02063-X
LC 2008-34567
"Unsentimental and brutally honest, Queenan's memoir captures the pathos of growing up in a difficult family and somehow getting beyond it." Publ Wkly

Queller, Jessica

Pretty is what changes; impossible choices, the breast cancer gene, and how I defied my destiny. Spiegel & Grau 2008 247p $24.95   **92**
1. Breast cancer 2. Cancer -- Genetic aspects 3. Surgical patients 4. Television scriptwriters
ISBN 978-0-385-52040-9; 0-385-52040-9
LC 2008-4303
The author tells her story—from her mother's death from ovarian cancer and her positive testing for the breast cancer gene BRCA-1 to her decision to have a double mastectomy and remove her ovaries.
This "story is seamless and gripping; readers will be rooting for Queller and her heroic decision to confront her genetic destiny." Publ Wkly

Quirk, Lawrence J.

Bob Hope: the road well-traveled. Applause Theatre Bk. Pubs. 1998 327p il hardcover o.p. pa $14.95   **92**
1. Actors 2. Comedians 3. Large print books
ISBN 1-55783-353-2; 1-55783-450-4 pa
LC 98-87957
"Quirk recaps Hope's life and surveys his relationships with myriad entertainment personalities. . . . This is a good, solid Hollywood bio by a veteran Tinseltown observer." Booklist
Includes filmography and bibliographical references

Quiñones-Hinojosa, Alfredo

Becoming Dr. Q; my journey from migrant farm worker to brain surgeon. with Mim Eichler Rivas. University of California Press 2011 317p il $27.50   **92**
1. Mexican Americans 2. Migrant labor 3. Neurologists 4. Neurosurgeons 5. Surgeons
ISBN 978-0-520-27118-0; 0-520-27118-1
LC 2011011531
"When the callow Quiñones-Hinojosa, or Dr. Q, made up his mind to pursue a better life and, especially, an education in the U.S., no border or barrier could have kept him from his destiny: a fate that led eventually to his becoming a Johns Hopkins University neurosurgeon, professor, and brain-cancer research scientist. Indeed, the brash teenager left all that was familiar in his native Mexico and, with less than $70 in his pocket, climbed the fence. In fact, he scaled it twice because he was caught the first time and sent back. . . . Quiñones-Hinojosa's story is gripping, inspiring, and just plain awesome." Booklist

Radzinsky, Edvard

Stalin; the first in-depth biography based on explosive new documents from Russia's secret archives. translated by H.T. Willetts. Doubleday 1996 607p il hardcover o.p. pa $16.95   **92**
1. Communist leaders 2. Dictators 3. Heads of state 4. Political leaders
ISBN 0-385-47954-9 pa
LC 95-4495
For this biography of the Soviet ruler the author "has examined mountains of rare archival sources and interviewed many who lived through decades of Stalinist (mis)rule. The result is the best general biography of Stalin to date. Radzinsky strips away layer after layer of myth, falsehood, and enigma to produce a riveting portrait of a man whose primary role model was Ivan the Terrible." Libr J
Includes bibliographical references

Rampersad, Arnold

★ **Ralph** Ellison; a biography. Alfred A. Knopf 2007 657p il $35   **92**
1. Authors 2. Biography, Individual 3. Essayists 4. Literary critics 5. Novelists 6. Short story writers
ISBN 978-0-375-40827-4; 0-375-40827-4
LC 2006-26464
"As the first scholar granted complete access to the Ellison papers, Rampersad introduces us to people and places that reveal the total range of Ellison's sensibilities. . . . Through elegant and lively prose, Rampersad reveals sides of Ellison that are disturbing and instructive." Charlotte Observer
Includes bibliographical references

The **life** of Langston Hughes Volume I: 1902-1941; I, too, sing America. 2nd ed; Oxford University Press 2002 478p il hardcover o.p. pa $33   **92**
1. African American authors 2. Authors 3. Dramatists 4. Novelists 5. Poets 6. Poets, American 7. Short story writers 8. Young adult authors
ISBN 0-19-515160-7; 0-19-514642-5 pa

This is the first volume of a two-volume set chronicling the life of the Harlem Renaissance poet and author.

Rand, Ayn

Journals of Ayn Rand; edited by David Harriman; foreword by Leonard Peikoff. Dutton 1997 727p il hardcover o.p. pa $22   **92**
1. Authors 2. Biography, Individual 3. Nonfiction writers 4. Novelists 5. Philosophers
ISBN 0-452-27887-2 pa
LC 97-12737

"This work offers almost everything the author ever wrote to herself. As intriguing yet sometimes numbing as her fiction, the book, which covers the years from 1927 to the mid-1970s, contains her first philosophical stabs, notes on her novels, HUAC testimony against alleged Hollywood communists, and her unfinished projects." Publ Wkly

Randal, Jonathan C.

Osama: the making of a terrorist; {by} Jonathan Randal. Knopf 2004 339p $26.95   **92**
1. Terrorism 2. Terrorists
ISBN 0-375-40901-7
LC 2004-46522

The author's "meticulous account of the emergence and spread of the terror virus is less a biography of the strange, desiccated Saudi Arabian terrorist who heads Al Qaeda than a map of the world that produced him and his fellow Islamists. This is the biography of a hatred: deep, detailed, and depressing." N Y Times Book Rev
Includes bibliographical references

Randall, Willard Sterne

Alexander Hamilton; a life. HarperCollins Pubs. 2003 476p il map $32.50; pa $15.95   **92**
1. Secretaries of the treasury 2. Statesmen
ISBN 0-06-019549-5; 0-06-095466-3 pa
LC 2002-68674

The author focuses on "Hamilton's fortune-marked rise to fame, which was sealed when the ambitious aide-de-camp of Washington pleaded for, and got, the assignment to lead the final assault at the Battle of Yorktown. . . . Randall's vigorous prose captures shows the compass of Hamilton's life and his role in making the U.S. a going concern." Booklist
Includes bibliographical references

Thomas Jefferson; a life. HarperPerennial 1994 708p pa $20   **92**
1. Architects 2. Essayists 3. Presidents 4. Presidents -- United States 5. Vice-presidents
ISBN 0-06-097617-9
LC 94-14363

"Randall's substantial, balanced biography will be valuable for general readers who seek a one-volume work on one of the leading Founding Fathers." Libr J
Includes bibliographical references

Rao, Cheeni

In Hanuman's hands; a memoir of recovery and redemption. HarperOne 2009 399p $25.99   **92**
1. Authors 2. Dramatists 3. Drug addicts 4. East Indian Americans 5. Editors 6. Memoirists 7. Short story writers
ISBN 978-0-06-073662-0; 0-06-073662-3
LC 2008-55421

"It is the rapture of . . . [the author's] language; his hallucinatory, world-bridging storytelling; and his high-wire variations on the timeless struggles between truth and deception, good and evil, that make this journey to hell and back all-consuming and profound." Booklist

Rapoport, Roger

Citizen Moore; the life and times of an American iconoclast. RDR 2006 310p il $15.95   **92**
1. Biography, Individual 2. Magazine editors 3. Motion picture directors 4. Motion picture producers and directors -- Biography 5. Nonfiction writers 6. Screenwriters 7. Social critics
ISBN 1-57143-163-2; 9781571431639 pa

In this biography of the controversial filmmaker, the author "compares Moore to Upton Sinclair and Ralph Nader, chronicling the filmmaker's early activism, community organizing, radio and theater career, and involvement in alternative journalism. . . . In this engaging profile, Rapoport portrays the quirks and complexities of a man whose life is as fascinating as his films." Booklist

Rathbone, Belinda

Walker Evans; a biography. Houghton Mifflin 1995 358p il hardcover o.p. pa $15   **92**
1. Photographers
ISBN 0-6180-5672-6 pa
LC 95-3711

"Rathbone does a superb job of describing Evans' elusive personality and unique vision." Booklist
Includes bibliographical references

Rathbone, John Paul

The **sugar** king of Havana; the rise and fall of Julio Lobo, Cuba's last tycoon. Penguin Press 2010 304p il map $27.95   **92**
1. Agribusiness executives 2. Biography, Individual 3. Businessmen 4. Sugar 5. Sugar trade -- Cuba -- History
ISBN 978-1-59420-258-2; 1594202583
LC 2010-13790

"An exceptionally rich portrait not only of an empire and its progenitor but Cuba itself, and the economic legacy of Castro's revolution, the loss of capital, and the end of Cuba's 'great age of sugar.'" Publ Wkly
Includes bibliographical references

Ratliff, Ben

Coltrane; the story of a sound. Farrar, Straus & Giroux 2007 xxi, 250p il hardcover o.p. pa $16 **92**
1. African American musicians 2. Biography, Individual 3. Jazz musicians 4. Saxophonists
ISBN 978-0-374-12606-3; 0-374-12606-2; 978-0-312-42778-8 pa; 0-312-42778-6 pa
LC 2007-4362

This is a biography of the jazz musician.
This is an "engaging study of the jazz saxophonist's artistic influence. . . . Ratliff patiently explicates Coltrane's legend, writing in short, aphoristic bursts, often as ellipti-

cally as his subject played tenor saxophone, but never less than lucidly." N Y Times Book Rev

Includes bibliographical references

Reagan, Ron

My father at 100. Viking 2011 228p il $25.95 **92**
1. Actors 2. Biography, Individual 3. Governors 4. Presidents 5. Presidents -- United States
ISBN 978-0-670-02259-5; 0-670-02259-4

LC 2010-45833

The son of Ronald and Nancy Reagan presents an assessment of his father's life that features his childhood observations of the qualities that rendered the future fortieth president a powerful leader.

A "nuanced and satisfying portrait is provided by Ron Reagan in My Father at 100. . . . [This work] is most poignant in its description of the author's search for his father's approval, forever just out of reach." Time

Reagan, Ronald

★ **Reagan**; a life in letters. edited, with an introduction and commentary by Kiron K. Skinner, Annelise Anderson, {and} Martin Anderson; with a foreword by George P. Shultz. Free Press 2003 934p $35; pa $18.95 **92**
1. Actors 2. Governors 3. Presidents 4. Presidents -- United States 5. Presidents -- United States -- Correspondence
ISBN 0-7432-1966-X; 0-7432-1967-8 pa

LC 2003-49249

"This volume consists of a sampling of the former president's copious outpouring of personal letters, from his childhood to the onset of Alzheimer's after the presidency. The editors . . . arrange the letters thematically, introduce each chapter with a brief commentary, and introduce each letter with a sentence or two of explanation. The editors have done an admirable job in compiling these documents. Their commentary is exactly as it might have been had Ronald Reagan been able to produce this volume himself." Choice

Includes bibliographical references

Reagan, Ronald, 1911-2004

The **Reagan** diaries; edited by Douglas Brinkley. HarperCollins 2007 767p il $35; pa $19.99 **92**
1. Biography, Individual 2. Presidents -- United States
ISBN 978-0-06-087600-5; 0-06-087600-X; 978-0-06-155833-7 pa; 0-06-155833-8 pa

"There is a kind of touching banality to many of the entries, as though Reagan were just another CEO writing about corporate life at the top, albeit corporate life that revolved around nuclear and hostage negotiations. Edited by Douglas Brinkley . . . , the book shows a Reagan almost sweetly amazed by small trappings of office. . . . Reading these diaries, Americans will find it easier to understand how Reagan did what he did for so long: by steady work, and a steadfast commitment to the job at hand." Newsweek

Reesman, Jeanne Campbell

Jack London, photographer; [by] Jeanne Campbell Reesman, Sara S. Hodson, & Philip Adam. University of Georgia Press 2010 271p il $49.95 **92**
1. Authors 2. Authors, American 3. Novelists 4.

Photographers 5. Short story writers
ISBN 978-0-8203-2967-3

LC 2010005973

"This book will be of great appeal to a broad range of audiences interested in history, American literature, and photography." Libr J

Includes bibliographical references

Reeve, Christopher

Still me. Random House 1998 309p il hardcover o.p. pa $7.99 **92**
1. Actors 2. Handicapped 3. Large print books 4. Physically handicapped
ISBN 0-345-43241-X pa

LC 98-10223

This autobiography begins with Reeve's "riding accident and relates in almost slow-motion detail what happened before and after the near-fatal spill in 1995. His remembrances then move back and forth in time. Reeve's early life, his complex relationships, and his career are juxtaposed against the life he leads now as filmmaker, husband and father, and spokesman for those with spinal-cord injuries." Booklist

Reeves, Richard

A **force** of nature; the frontier genius of Ernest Rutherford. W. W. Norton & Co. 2008 207p il $23.95 **92**
1. Nobel laureates for chemistry 2. Physicists
ISBN 978-0-393-05750-8; 0-393-05750-X

LC 2007-33184

The author "re-introduces Ernest Rutherford, one of the founding geniuses of nuclear physics. . . . This biography does an outstanding job of capturing the excitement and almost breathless pace of physics research in the 20th century's first four decades." Publ Wkly

Includes bibliographical references

Reich, Eugenie Samuel

Plastic fantastic; how the biggest fraud in physics shook the scientific world. Palgrave Macmillan 2009 266p $26.95 **92**
1. Biography, Individual 2. Fraud in science 3. Physicists
ISBN 0230224679; 9780230224674; 0-230-22467-9; 978-0-230-22467-4

LC 2008-51801

This is the story of Bell Laboratories "physicist Jan Henrik Schön who faked the discovery of a new superconductor made from plastic." (Publisher's note) Index.

"A compelling look inside big science at one of its least admirable moments." Kirkus

Includes bibliographical references

Reichl, Ruth

Comfort me with apples; more adventures at the table. Random House 2001 302p $24.95; pa $13.95 **92**
1. Cookery 2. Food critics 3. Magazine editors 4. Memoirists 5. Women food writers -- United States -- Biography
ISBN 0-375-50195-9; 0-375-75873-9 pa

LC 00-53355

"In this second installment of her memoirs, {Reichl} retraces her route from married life on a commune in late-seventies Berkeley to her first job as a food critic, dining at expensive restaurants in Los Angeles with her glamorous editor.... Reichl writes with gusto, and her story has all the ingredients of a modern fairy tale: hard work, weird food, and endless curiosity." New Yorker

Garlic and sapphires. Penguin Press 2005 333p $24.95   **92**
1. Biography, Individual 2. Food critics 3. Magazine editors 4. Memoirists
ISBN 1-594-20031-9
LC 2004-51362
"Reichl's ability to experience meals in such a dramatic way brings an infectious passion to her memoir. Reading this work . . . ensures that the next time readers sit down in a restaurant, they'll notice things they've never noticed before." Publ Wkly

Reiner, Jon
The **man** who couldn't eat; a memoir. Gallery 2011 313p $25; ebook $11.99   **92**
1. Inflammatory bowel diseases 2. Sick
ISBN 978-1-4391-9246-7; 1-4391-9246-4; 978-1-4391-9254-2 ebook; 1-4391-9254-5 ebook
LC 2011005441
"Reiner's self-pitiless account stands out for the irony of a foodie being unable to eat, the sheer magnitude of the torment endured, the courage to stare down unrelenting pain, the honest introspection into how suffering made the author insufferable and rocked his family and, above all, his refreshingly snide attitude toward his disease.... An inspiring, incredible tale. " Kirkus

Reisen, Harriet
Louisa May Alcott; the woman behind Little women. Henry Holt 2009 362p $26   **92**
1. Authors 2. Authors, American 3. Novelists 4. Young adult authors
ISBN 978-0-8050-8299-9; 0-8050-8299-9
LC 2009-10637
In this biography of the American author, "Reisen analyzes Louisa's great pleasure in writing lucrative pulp fiction, her sacrifices, adventures, and brilliant career. Here . . . is Alcott whole, a trailblazing woman grasping freedom in a time of sexual inequality and war, a survivor of cruel tragedies, a quintessential American writer." Booklist
Includes bibliographical references

Reiss, Tom
The **Orientalist**; solving the mystery of a strange and a dangerous life. Random House 2005 xxvii, 433p il $25.95; pa $14.95   **92**
1. Authors 2. Biographers 3. Biography, Individual 4. Historians 5. Novelists
ISBN 1-4000-6265-9; 0-8129-7276-7 pa
LC 2004-50928
This is a biography of Lev Nussimbaum, a Jew from Baku who wrote in Germany under the pseudonyms Essad Bey and Kurban Said.

The author "takes the reader through his own search for the truth; through the twists of 20th-century history in Russia and Germany, and hence though the life-story itself. This would be hard work if the interweaving of biography, investigation and geopolitics were not so elegant." Economist
Includes bibliographical references

Remini, Robert Vincent
Andrew Jackson; [by] Robert V. Remini; foreword by General Wesley K. Clark. Palgrave Macmillan 2008 204p il map $21.95   **92**
1. Biography, Individual 2. Generals 3. Indians of North America -- Wars 4. Presidents 5. Presidents -- United States
ISBN 0-230-60015-8; 978-0-230-60015-7
LC 2008-394
This is a "study of Jackson from a military perspective. Remini maintains a birth-to-death narrative while keeping the focus on Jackson's fundamental existence as a soldier. The result is a fine introduction based on years of advanced knowledge on the subject, distilled by Remini into a very good read." Libr J
Includes bibliographical references

Remnick, David
King of the world: Muhammad Ali and the rise of an American hero. Random House 1998 326p il hardcover o.p. pa $14   **92**
1. African American athletes 2. Boxers (Persons)
ISBN 0-375-50065-0; 0-375-70229-6 pa
LC 98-24539
"This is the best book ever on Muhammad Ali and one of the best on America in the 1960s." Booklist
Includes bibliographical references

Remnick, David, 1958-
★ The **bridge**; the life and rise of Barack Obama. Alfred A. Knopf 2010 656p il $29.95   **92**
1. African Americans -- Biography 2. Biography, Individual 3. Lawyers 4. Nobel laureates for peace 5. Presidents 6. Presidents -- United States 7. Racially mixed people 8. Senators 9. State legislators
ISBN 978-1-4000-4360-6; 1-4000-4360-3
LC 2010-922697
This is a biography of the 44th president of the United States.
Writing with emotional precision and a sure knowledge of politics, Mr. Remnick situates Mr. Obama's career firmly within a historical context. He puts Mr. Obama's life and political philosophy in perspective with the civil rights movement that shaped his imagination, as well as the power politics of Chicago, and the politics of race as it has been played out, often nastily, on the state and national stages. N Y Times (Late N Y Ed)
Includes bibliographical references (p. [617]-623) and index

Renehan, Edward J.
Commodore; the life of Cornelius Vanderbilt. [by] Edward J. Renehan Jr. Basic Books 2007 xx, 364p il $27.50   **92**
1. Businessmen 2. Financiers 3. Railroad executives

4. Shipping executives
ISBN 978-0-465-00255-9; 0-465-00255-2
LC 2007-22392
"A warts and more warts portrait of a brilliantly success-ful, genuinely despicable man." Kirkus
Includes bibliographical references

Repcheck, Jack
Copernicus' secret; how the scientific revolution began. Simon & Schuster 2007 239p il map $25 **92**
1. Astronomers 2. Biography, Individual
ISBN 978-0-7432-8951-1; 0-7432-8951-X
LC 2007-24649
"The book is fascinating reading, even to those who may be familiar with much of its contents." Choice
Includes bibliographical references

Reynolds, David S.
John Brown, abolitionist; the man who killed slavery, sparked the Civil War, and seeded civil rights. Alfred A. Knopf 2005 578p il $35 **92**
1. Abolitionists 2. Biography, Individual
ISBN 0-375-41188-7
LC 2004-48864
"Almost every page forces you to think hard, and in new ways, about American violence, American history, and what used to be called the American character." New Yorker
Includes bibliographical references

Reynolds, Michael S.
Hemingway: the Paris years; [by] Michael Reyn-olds. W.W. Norton 1999 402p il map pa $18.95 **92**
1. Authors 2. Authors, American 3. Journalists 4. Nobel laureates for literature 5. Novelists 6. Poets 7. Short story writers
ISBN 0-393-31879-6
In this second volume of a five-volume biography of Hemingway begun with The young Hemingway (1998), the author "locates Hemingway in an American sociocultural context wherein he rejects middle-class restraints and as-pires to identity as hero and self-reliant frontiersman (sol-dier, bullfighter, hunter, lover). The genius of the book lies in a graceful and informative linkage between literary creation and biographical incident." Libr J
Includes bibliographical references

Hemingway: the homecoming; [by] Michael Reynolds. W.W. Norton 1999 xxiii, 264p il map pa $14.95 **92**
1. Authors 2. Authors, American 3. Journalists 4. Nobel laureates for literature 5. Novelists 6. Poets 7. Short story writers
ISBN 0-393-31981-4
This third volume of a five-volume study of Heming-way's life begun with The young Hemingway (1998) and Hemingway: the Paris years (1999) "covers 1926-29, a tran-sitional period that marked the conclusion of Hemingway's artistic apprenticeship and the cooling of many literary friendships; the end of one marriage and the beginning of another; the suicide of his father; and the writing of The Sun

Also Rises, Men Without Women, A Farewell to Arms, and an ultimately abandoned novel." Libr J
Includes bibliographical references

The **young** Hemingway; [by] Michael Reynolds. W. W. Norton 1998 291p il pa $15.95 **92**
1. Authors 2. Authors, American 3. Journalists 4. Nobel laureates for literature 5. Novelists 6. Poets 7. Short story writers
ISBN 0-393-31776-5
"This incisive, well-written biography . . . will prove useful at almost every readership level, from general reader to scholar." Choice
Includes bibliographical references

Rhodes, Richard
Hedy's folly; the life and breakthrough inven-tions of Hedy Lamarr, the most beautiful woman in the world. Doubleday 2011 261p il $26.95; ebook $13.99 **92**
1. Actors 2. Inventors
ISBN 978-0-385-53438-3; 978-0-385-53439-0 ebook
LC 2011021746
"Here's a recipe that might surprise you: take a silver-screen sex goddess (Hedy Lamarr), an avant-garde com-poser (George Antheil), a Hollywood friendship, and mutual technological curiosity, and mix well. What results is a pat-ent for spread-spectrum radio, which has impacted the de-velopment of everything from torpedoes to cell phones and GPS technologies. This surprising and long-forgotten story is brought to life . . . [by Rhodes,] who deftly moves between Nazi secrets, scandalous films, engineering breakthroughs, and musical flops to weave a taut story that straddles two very different worlds—the entertainment industry and war-time weaponry—and yet somehow manages to remain a de-lectable read." Libr J
Includes bibliographical references

John James Audubon; the making of an Ameri-can. Knopf 2004 528p il $30; pa $16 **92**
1. Artists 2. Artists -- United States 3. Biography, Individual 4. Naturalists 5. Ornithologists 6. Painters 7. Writers on science
ISBN 0-375-41412-6; 0-375-71393-X pa
LC 2003-69489
The author "chronicles Audubon's ineluctable sense of mission, phenomenal skills, and triumph over adversity. . . . Rhodes sets Audubon's engrossing tale within the context of the War of 1812, the Louisiana Purchase, the wars against Native Americans (whom Audubon profoundly admired), and the rapid decimation of the American wilderness. . . . Full of passion and discovery, hardship and transcendence, Audubon's story is at once intimate and mythic, and Rhodes' fresh, comprehensive biography will capture the imagina-tion of readers everywhere." Booklist
Includes bibliographical references

Rhodes, William R.
Banker to the world; leadership lessons from the front lines of global finance. [by] William R. Rhodes. McGraw-Hill 2011 xxxiii, 249p $25; ebook $25 **92**
1. Bankers 2. Banks and banking 3. Banks and

banking, International 4. Biography, Individual 5. Decision making 6. International finance 7. Leadership
ISBN 978-0-07-170425-0; 0-07-170425-6; 978-0-07-170424-3 ebook; 0-07-170424-8 ebook

LC 2010032040

This book "should be required reading not only for other bankers, but also for Washington's would-be reformers of Wall Street, and most of all for the ordinary lay citizen dismayed by the persisting panic that has gripped us since 2007." Am Spectator

Includes bibliographical references

Ribowsky, Mark

Howard Cosell. W.W. Norton & Co. 2011 477p il $29.95 **92**
1. Ali, Muhammad, 1942- 2. Announcers 3. Biographies 4. Cosell, Howard 5. Lawyers 6. Popular culture -- United States -- History -- 20th century 7. Sports 8. Sports journalism 9. Sportscasters 10. Television broadcasting of sports -- History 11. Television personalities
ISBN 978-0-393-08017-9; 0-393-08017-X

LC 2011-27501

This book offers a biography of Howard Cosell, of ABC, who died in 1995, [and] was [a] . . . famous television sports announcer. . . . He was a star for three decades, and during his early-1970s heyday, which coincided with the maximum reach of network television, he was a ubiquitous figure in American culture. . . . [The book attempts to elucidate] the interplay among Cosell's life story, the stories he covered, and the institutional rise of televised sports . . . [and larger claims] about American culture. . . . [The author examines how] Cosell became a star by covering a bigger star, Muhammad Ali, the great heavyweight boxer, [as well as other aspects of his career.]H (N Y Review of Books)

"The sportscaster Howard Cosell erupted onto the national stage in the 1960s and quickly became a pop-culture icon. His raspy, heavily New York-accented voice, a sharp mind, an expansive vocabulary and a photographic memory were packaged into a larger-than-life and sometimes abrasive figure. Whether his audience loved him, hated him or loved to hate him, they tuned in, and he turned them on. He was impossible to ignore. . . . Mr. Ribowsky's book is an entertaining read and a thought-provoking portrayal of the multifaceted Howard Cosell in all his glory and enmity. It is based on voluminous, well-sourced research into print and electronic material, coupled with numerous interviews with Cosell's contemporaries." Wall Street J

Includes bibliographical references

Rice, Anne

Called out of darkness; a spiritual confession. Alfred A. Knopf 2008 245p $24 **92**
1. Authors 2. Authors, American 3. Biography, Individual 4. Catholic Church 5. Catholics -- United States 6. Novelists 7. Spiritual life 8. Spiritual life -- Catholic Church 9. Women authors
ISBN 0-307-26827-6; 978-0-307-26827-3

LC 2008-20192

This memoir by the author of Interview With the Vampire (1976) focuses on Rice's return to Catholicism.

"As plainly written as a Quaker spiritual journal, Rice's confession of faith will impress many who wouldn't think of reading vampire romances—and possibly many who read little else." Booklist

Includes bibliographical references

Rice, Condoleezza, 1954-

Extraordinary, ordinary people; a memoir of family. Crown Publishers 2010 342p il **92**
1. African American women -- Biography 2. Biography, Individual 3. College administrators 4. College teachers 5. Government officials 6. Political scientists 7. Presidential advisers 8. Secretaries of state 9. Statesmen -- United States
ISBN 978-0-307-58787-9; 978-0-307-71960-7 ebook

LC 2010-21645

"The personal story of the former Secretary of State traces her childhood in segregated Alabama, describes the influence of people who shaped her life, and pays tribute to her parents' characters and sacrifices." (Publisher's note) Index.

"Rice's graceful memoir is a personal, multigenerational look into her own, and our country's, past. With vivid and heartfelt writing, Rice, U.S. secretary of state under George W. Bush, looks back on her grandparents and parents, then moves forward through her own life up to the 2000 election. . . . Readers will perceive Rice's emotion in relating her story, yet her portrayal seems fair and unbiased." Libr J

Richard, Mark, 1955-

House of prayer no. 2; a writer's journey home. Nan A. Talese/Doubleday 2011 201p $23.95 **92**
1. Authors 2. Authors, American 3. Authorship 4. Biography, Individual 5. Novelists 6. Short story writers
ISBN 0-385-51302-X; 978-0-385-51302-9

LC 2010-06317

An "account of growing up in the 1960s South, living with a disability, becoming a writer and finding faith. Richard's book attests to the power of words (and the Word) in shaping a life, while at the same time challenging some dearly held beliefs about memoir as a genre." N Y Times Book Rev

Richards, Keith

★ **Life**; [by] Keith Richards with James Fox. Little, Brown 2010 564p il $29.99; ebook $14.99 **92**
1. Guitarists 2. Rock musicians
ISBN 978-0-316-03438-8; 978-0-316-12856-8 ebook

This autobiography of the Rolling Stones guitarist "is way more than a revealing showbiz memoir. It is also a high-def, high-velocity portrait of the era when rock 'n' roll came of age, a raw report from deep inside the counterculture maelstrom of how that music swept like a tsunami over Britain and the United States. It's an eye-opening all-nighter in the studio with a master craftsman disclosing the alchemical secrets of his art. And it's the intimate and moving story of one man's long strange trip over the decades, told in dead-on, visceral prose without any of the pretense, caution or self-consciousness that usually attend great artists sitting for their self-portraits." N Y Times Book Rev

Richardson, John

The **sorcerer's** apprentice; Picasso, Provence, and Douglas Cooper. University of Chicago Press 2001 318p il pa $17   **92**
1. Art critics 2. Art historians 3. Biographers
ISBN 0-226-71245-1

Picasso biographer John Richardson "has written a concise account of the first half of his own life and notably of his long relationship as a young man with the Cubist art historian and collector Douglas Cooper. The account concentrates on the dozen years, from early 1949 to the end of 1960, when Richardson lived with Cooper, visiting museums and monuments all over Europe, meeting the great artists and other personalities of the day, and restoring the colonnaded Chateau de Castille in the south of France." NY Times Book Rev
Includes bibliographical references

Richardson, Robert D.

William James; in the maelstrom of American modernism: a biography. Houghton Mifflin 2006 622p il $30   **92**
1. Biography, Individual 2. Philosophers 3. Psychologists 4. Writers on science
ISBN 978-0-618-43325-4; 0-618-43325-2
        LC 2005-37776
This is a biography of the psychologist and philosopher. The author's "enthusiasm for what he calls 'the matchless incandescent spirit' of William James is contagious." Publ Wkly
Includes bibliographical references (p. 586-9)

Ricketts, Harry

Rudyard Kipling; a life. Carroll & Graf Pubs. 2000 434p il hardcover o.p. pa $16   **92**
1. Authors 2. Children's authors 3. Memoirists 4. Nobel laureates for literature 5. Novelists 6. Poets 7. Short story writers
ISBN 0-7867-0830-1 pa
This work "succeeds in disentangling some of the political muddle of Kipling's life. Ricketts' literary analysis is competent, if unsophisticated. Most valuably, he traces the debt to Browning and the many other resonant literary allusions in Kipling's work, thus undermining the charges of philistinism . . . levelled against it." New Statesman (Engl)

Rickford, Russell John

Betty Shabazz: a remarkable story of survival and faith before and after Malcolm X; foreword by Myrlie Evers-Williams. Sourcebooks 2003 xxii, 633p il $35   **92**
1. African Americans -- Civil rights 2. Civil rights activists 3. Spouses of prominent persons
ISBN 1-4022-0171-0
        LC 2002-003447
"Just as the achievements of her husband, Malcolm X, were overshadowed by those of Martin Luther King Jr., Betty Shabazz's accomplishments have been overshadowed by those of King's widow. {The author} corrects that imbalance with this penetrating biography." Booklist
Includes bibliographical references

Rideau, Wilbert

In the place of justice; a story of punishment and deliverance. Alfred A. Knopf 2010 366p il map $26.95   **92**
1. Biography, Individual 2. Criminal justice, Administration of -- Louisiana 3. Journalists 4. Murderers 5. Prisoners 6. Thieves
ISBN 978-0-307-26481-7; 0-307-26481-5
        LC 2009038526
"In 1961, after a bungled bank robbery, Rideau was convicted of murder at the age of 19 and received a death sentence that was later commuted to life in prison at Louisiana's Angola penitentiary, then the most violent in the nation. Against all expectations, his own included, he turned his up-to-then cursed life around, becoming editor of the prison newsmagazine, the Angolite, and an NPR correspondent who published nationally acclaimed articles on prison violence, rape and sexual slavery, and the cruelty of the electric chair. Rideau frames his 44-year fight to get his conviction reduced to manslaughter and win parole (he succeeded in 2005) as a black man's struggle against a racist criminal justice establishment. . . . Rideau's story is a compelling reminder that rehabilitation should be the focus of a penal system." Publ Wkly

Ridley, Glynis

The **discovery** of Jeanne Baret; a story of science, the high seas, and the first woman to circumnavigate the globe. Crown Publishers 2010 288p il $25; ebook $25   **92**
1. Botanists 2. Explorers 3. Voyages around the world 4. Women scientists
ISBN 978-0-307-46352-4; 978-0-307-46354-8 ebook
        LC 2010-16778
This is a biography "of Jeanne Baret. Born in 1740 in France's Loire valley, Baret became an expert 'herb woman' who proved to be indispensable to the ambitious botanist Philibert Commerson, accompanying him as his assistant when Commerson was appointed naturalist for France's first expedition to circumnavigate the globe. But women were forbidden, so Baret dressed as a man. . . . Woven throughout this gripping story are Ridley's piquant insights into eighteenth-century exploration, botany, taxonomy, biopiracy, and sexism. Baret could not have asked for a more exacting and expressive champion. Ridley is incandescent in her passion for the truth." Booklist
Includes bibliographical references

Ridley, Matt

Francis Crick; discoverer of the genetic code. Atlas Books 2006 213p $19.95   **92**
1. Biochemists 2. Biography, Individual 3. Genetics 4. Nobel laureates for physiology or medicine 5. Scientists
ISBN 0-06-082333-X; 978-0-06-082333-7
        LC 2005-55878
"A briskly written essential for the DNA shelf." Booklist
Includes bibliographical references

Riley, Tim

Lennon; the man, the myth, the music--the definitive life. Hyperion 2011 765p il $35   **92**
1. Biography, Individual 2. Rock musicians 3. Singers

4. Songwriters
ISBN 978-1-4013-2452-0; 1-4013-2452-5
LC 2011-15657

"Here is Lennon in the fullness of his diffracted personality, across the spectrum of his phases and faces. Leather
John, mugging sailors in Hamburg — 'A Lennon punch
felled him to his knees' — is superseded by Beatle John,
mugging for the world's press. . . . Beatle John contains
both 'Ed Sullivan' John, yodeling harmonies and bending
his knees in awkward demi-pliés, and 'Revolver' John, acidhead, sleepyhead, drug dormouse, singing in that cold little
cocoon voice (Riley calls it 'timefrozen') about floating
downstream and not wanting to be woken up. Then there's
'Imagine' John, the drooping sage. And finally, of course,
John the martyr." N Y Times Book Rev
Includes bibliographical references and discography

Rilke, Rainer Maria

Diaries of a young poet; translated and annotated
by Edward Snow and Michael Winkler. Norton 1997
xxi, 306p il hardcover o.p. pa $15.95   **92**
1. Authors 2. Novelists 3. Poets 4. Short story writers
ISBN 0-393-31850-8 pa

"Three diaries reveal three Rilkes. The Florence Diary,
which he began at twenty-two, is a kind of open letter to his
then love, Lou Andreas-Salomé, full of youthful ardor and
sublime observations of art and nature. . . . The Schmargen-
dorf Diary reveals the virtuoso at play, with slender fragments of stories, fairy tales, and poems following each other
in dazzling succession. The last diary, written during his
stay in Worpswede, is the most rewarding, for the chance to
watch Rilke's rich friendships with other artists ripen alongside the growing authority of his poetic voice." New Yorker

Robb, Graham

Balzac; a life. Norton 1994 521p il hardcover
o.p. pa $15   **92**
1. Authors 2. Novelists 3. Short story writers
ISBN 0-393-31387-5 pa
LC 94-18614

"Balzac's life was more cause for incredulity than anything he wrote, and Robb compellingly sets out the docu-
mentable facts against and within the world Balzac created
from them. . . . The result is nearly a novel, although Robb
does not fictionalize with re-created dialogs and hypothetical events. He has in fact produced an extensive traditional
biography . . . not a critical reassessment." Libr J
Includes bibliographical references

Roberts, Jason

A **sense** of the world; how a blind man became
history's greatest traveler. HarperCollins Publishers
2006 382p il $26.95; pa $14.95   **92**
1. Biography, Individual 2. Blind 3. Naval officers 4.
Travel writers
ISBN 0-00-716106-9; 978-0-00-716106-5; 0-00-
716126-3 pa; 978-0-00-716126-3 pa
LC 2005-58166

The author "narrates the life of a 19th-century British
naval officer who was mysteriously blinded at 25, but nevertheless became the greatest traveler of his time. . . . Roberts

does Holman justice, evoking with grace and wit the tale of
this man once lionized as 'The Blind Traveler.'" Publ Wkly
Includes bibliographical references

Roberts, Randy

Joe Louis; hard times man. Yale University
Press 2010 308p il $27.50   **92**
1. African American athletes 2. Biography, Individual
3. Boxing -- Biography 4. Boxing -- History
ISBN 978-0-300-12222-0
LC 2010-15422

In this biography of the American boxer, "Roberts
handles the boxing action with professional aplomb, and he
knows when to cut away to tell us something of consequence
and when to return to the ring. The author ably chronicles
Louis's rise from Alabama cotton fields to the cavernous
Yankee Stadium, where celebrities glittered in the ringside
seats for his big fights; the development of the mass media
(boxing was enormously popular on radio); Louis's career
in the U.S. Army; and his sad decline, amid unpayable debts
and mental illness. All legendary athletes should hope for
treatment by such capable, compassionate hands." Kirkus
Includes bibliographical references and index

Roberts, Siobhan

★ **King** of infinite space; Donald Coxeter, the
man who saved geometry. Walker & Co. 2006 399p
il $27.95   **92**
1. Biography, Individual 2. College teachers 3.
Mathematicians
ISBN 0-8027-1499-4; 978-0-8027-1499-2
LC 2006-497355

This is the story of geometer H. S. M. "Donald" Coxeter's "life, his work, and his interactions with mathematicians, scientists, and artists of his time. . . . The author carefully weaves a lot of mathematical details into her work, but
not so much that it becomes burdensome to the historical
focus of the book." Sci Books Films
Includes bibliographical references

Robertson, David

W.C. Handy; the life and times of the man who
made the blues. Alfred A. Knopf 2009 286p il
$27.95   **92**
1. Biography, Individual 2. Blues music 3. Blues
musicians 4. Composers 5. Music publishers
ISBN 978-0-307-26609-5; 0-307-26609-5
LC 2008-45983

The author "casts overdue light on Handy's essential role
in establishing the blues as a popular art, and he does this,
much to his credit, without resorting to dubious claims that
Handy was the first or the best of the blues' multiple pro-
genitors. A mark of both the evenhandedness of his scholarship and the delicacy of his writing is Robertson's resistance
to the idea of Handy as the Father of the Blues — a notion
that Handy himself advanced and exploited deftly during his
lifetime." N Y Times Book Rev
Includes bibliographical references

Robeson, Paul

Here I stand; with a preface by Lloyd L. Brown and a new introduction by Sterling Stuckey. Beacon Press 1988 xxxvi, 121p hardcover o.p. pa $14 **92**

1. Actors 2. African Americans -- Civil rights 3. Civil rights activists 4. Football players 5. Singers
ISBN 0-8070-6445-9 pa

LC 87-47882

"Combining a narrative of his life and travels with commentary on history and the events of his time, [the author] relates the fight against segregation to social progress for all Americans, white and black, claiming that 'white supremacy' disenfranchises and impoverishes white workers and white farmers as well as black." Libr J

Robinson, Ray

Iron horse: Lou Gehrig in his time. Norton 1990 300p il pa $14.95 **92**

1. Baseball -- Biography 2. Baseball players
ISBN 978-0-393-32882-0 pa; 0-393-32882-1 pa

LC 89-29272

"Playing in the considerable shadow of Babe Ruth, Lou Gehrig's accomplishments as baseball's 'Iron Horse' include a legendary record of 2,130 consecutive games played. . . . Robinson's narrative not only traces Gehrig's life and career but also provides an insightful look at baseball in the 1920s and the Depression years." Libr J

Rockne of Notre Dame; the making of a football legend. Oxford Univ. Press 1999 290p il hardcover o.p. pa $16.95 **92**

1. Football coaches 2. Football coaches -- United States -- Biography
ISBN 0-19-515792-3 pa

LC 99-13712

"After a childhood sketch, Robinson briefly touches on Rockne's playing career before devoting most of the book to a game-by-game description of Rockne's 12 years as coach, during which his Notre Dame teams, with the help of Rockne's motivational techniques and coaching tactics, won an astounding 105 games while losing only 12. To Robinson's credit, the book is cleanly written and mainly free of sports jargon." Publ Wkly

Robison, John Elder

Look me in the eye; my life with Asperger's. Crown Publishers 2007 288p $25.95 **92**

1. Asperger's syndrome 2. Mechanics (Persons) 3. Memoirists 4. Photographers 5. Restorers
ISBN 978-0-307-39598-6; 0-307-39598-7

LC 2007-13139

In this memoir, the author describes growing up with Asperger's syndrome (which went undiagnosed until he was 40 years old), dealing with an alcoholic father and a mentally unstable mother, and developing an affinity for machines that would eventually lead him to a career restoring classic cars.

"Robison's memoir is must reading for its unblinking (as only an Aspergian can) glimpse into the life of a person who had to wait decades for the medical community to catch up with him." Booklist

Includes bibliographical references

Rodgers, Marion Elizabeth

Mencken; the American iconoclast. Oxford University Press 2005 662p il $35 **92**

1. Authors 2. Biography, Individual 3. Essayists 4. Literary critics 5. Newspaper editors 6. Philologists 7. Social critics
ISBN 0-19-507238-3

LC 2005-47786

"This is a meticulous portrait of one of the most original and complicated men in American letters." Publ Wkly
Includes bibliographical references

Rodriguez, Richard

Hunger of memory; the education of Richard Rodriguez: an autobiography. Bantam trade pbk. ed.; Bantam Books 2004 212p pa $15 **92**

1. Authors 2. Essayists 3. Memoirists 4. Mexican Americans -- Biography 5. Poets 6. Television personalities
ISBN 0-553-38251-9

LC 2004-269979

An account "of the coming of age of a person of Mexican descent and culture in American society and the inevitable transition in the private life of his family. Rodriguez focuses on his educational experiences, from his parochial elementary school . . . to his university years and subsequent experience as an educator." Libr J

Rogovoy, Seth

Bob Dylan; prophet, mystic, poet. Scribner 2009 324p $26 **92**

1. Folk musicians 2. Popular music -- Religious aspects 3. Rock musicians 4. Singers 5. Songwriters
ISBN 978-1-4165-5915-3; 1-4165-5915-9

The author "explores the influence of the Bible, the Talmud, and the Kabbalah on Dylan's songwriting, uncovering references to these texts in each of Dylan's 33 studio albums, up through 2009's Together Through Life. Rogovoy's research adds fresh insight into iconic songs such as 'Blowin' in the Wind,' 'Like a Rolling Stone,' and 'Forever Young,' providing a deeper understanding of Dylan's Jewish influences. Chronological album-by-album and song-by-song analyses make up the book's core, and Rogovoy gives just enough biographical context to argue convincingly that Judaism strongly influences Dylan's life and lyrics." Libr J
Includes bibliographical references (p. 291-296)

Roiphe, Anne Richardson

Art and madness; a memoir of lust without reason. [by] Anne Roiphe. Nan A. Talese/Doubleday 2011 220p il $24.95 **92**

1. Authors 2. Authors, American 3. Biography, Individual 4. Essayists 5. Novelists 6. Women authors
ISBN 9780385531641

LC 2010-28051

The book is a memoir of author Anne Roiphe that describes a "second-wave feminist, . . . once a shy Jewish girl who worked at a public relations firm and happily typed the manuscripts of her playwright husband. . . . Complementing . . . [her story] is the time and place, the New York publishing world of the 1950s and '60s, when 'editors and writers went out to three-martini lunches' and 'absurdity was very fashionable.' On the inner-workings of the literary myth machine, Roiphe delivers, explaining how a scuffle between Norman Mailer and Doc Humes became legend in the span of a smoked cigarette: 'constellations in the sky were named after the encounter.'" (Nation)

"Roiphe's narrative moves in punchy, spare episodes, nonchronologically and erratically, veering from past to present tense, and requiring effort on the part of the reader. Yet she is a masterly writer: her work presents vivid, priceless snapshots of the roiling era of Communist hysteria, faddish homosexuality, male privilege, and the heartbreaking fragility of talented men and their dreams of fame." Publ Wkly

Epilogue; a memoir. [by] Anne Roiphe. Harper 2008 214p il $24.95   **92**
1. Authors 2. Authors, American 3. Bereavement 4. Biography, Individual 5. Essayists 6. Novelists 7. Widows 8. Women authors
ISBN 978-0-06-125462-8; 0-06-125462-2
                                            LC 2008-34530
The author "tells an unflinching and unsentimental story of widowhood's stupefying disquiet, of surviving love and living on." Publ Wkly

Roller, Duane W.
Cleopatra; a biography. Oxford University Press 2010 252p il map $24.95   **92**
1. Biography, Individual 2. Queens
ISBN 978-0-19-536553-5; 0-19-536553-4
                                            LC 2009-24061
"Basing this chronicle exclusively on primary sources culled from classical antiquity, the author painstakingly separates myth from reality, discounting . . . [Cleopatra's] undeserved reputation as a seductress and concentrating on her impressive—but often overlooked or minimized—political, military, and administrative achievements. This revisionist portrait of one of the most powerful women in the ancient world adds substance and heft to her exotic legacy." Booklist
Includes bibliographical references

Romm, Robin
The **mercy** papers; a memoir of three weeks. Scribner 2009 213p $22   **92**
1. Authors 2. Biography, Individual 3. Breast -- Cancer -- Patients 4. College teachers 5. Hospices 6. Mother-daughter relationship 7. Short story writers 8. Terminally ill
ISBN 978-1-4165-6788-2; 1-4165-6788-7
                                            LC 2008-10601
In this book Robin Romm focuses on the final weeks of her mother Jackie's life.
"A piercing, heartbreaking reminder that 'loss doesn't end.'" Kirkus

Roosevelt, Curtis
Too close to the sun; growing up in the shadow of my grandparents, Franklin and Eleanor. PublicAffairs 2008 302p il $29.95   **92**
1. College administrators 2. Columnists 3. Diplomats 4. Governors 5. Grandparent-grandchild relationship 6. Handicapped 7. Humanitarians 8. Philatelists

9. Presidents 10. Presidents -- United States 11. Presidents' spouses -- United States 12. Social activists 13. Spouses of presidents 14. United Nations officials
ISBN 978-1-5864-8554-2; 1-5864-8554-2
                                            LC 2008-33994
Offers a portrait of this celebrated president and his wife as experienced by the grandson of FDR, who recounts what it was like to come of age under constant media attention and public scrutiny in their formidable shadows.
"No one alive today knew Franklin and Eleanor quite as well as Curtis, their eldest grandson, and his sister. Thus this splendid, intimate memoir represents an invaluable addition to the literature of the Roosevelt era." Publ Wkly
Includes bibliographical references

Rosenblatt, Roger
Making toast; a family story. Ecco 2010 166p $21.99   **92**
1. Authors 2. Authors, American 3. Bereavement 4. Essayists 5. Grandparent and child 6. Grandparent-grandchild relationship 7. Grandparents as parents 8. Journalists 9. Nonfiction writers 10. Parenting 11. Political commentators
ISBN 978-0-06-182593-4; 0-06-182593-X
"A 38-year-old pediatrician named Amy Solomon collapsed on her treadmill at home. She died of what was discovered to be a rare, undiagnosed heart defect. The day she died, Amy's parents—Roger and Ginny Rosenblatt—drove from their house on Long Island to their daughter's home in Bethesda, Md. The Rosenblatts have been there ever since, helping their son-in-law take care of three children, who were 6, 4, and 1 when their mother died. Now, Roger Rosenblatt has written about this reconfigured family in an exquisite, restrained little memoir filled with both hurt and humor." NPR

Roth, Joseph, 1894-1939
Joseph Roth; Joseph Roth; translated and edited by Michael Hofmann. W. W. Norton 2012 xvii, 551p $39.95   **92**
1. Authors 2. Authors -- Correspondence 3. Authors, Austrian 4. Journalists 5. Novelists 6. Short story writers
ISBN 978-0-393-06064-5
                                            LC 2011032677
This book "contains 457 letters [by writer Joseph Roth], only a small number of which are to family or close friends or comment on his novels as he was writing them. Most are to fellow writers . . . or to translators and colleagues at The Frankfurter Zeitung and other newspapers for which Roth wrote essays, reviews, and sketches." He discusses "his personal affairs, . . . his health, his squabbles with editors, the shabby hotels where he lived, the bad translations of his work, his problems with women, and, most of all, his unending financial woes, some of them self-inflicted by the penchant for drink that contributed to his death." Other topics include "Nazism, . . . Jewishness, . . . [and] the Soviet Union." (N Y Times)

Rounding, Virginia

Catherine the Great; love, sex and power. St. Martin's Press 2007 566p il $29.95   **92**
1. Empresses
ISBN 978-0-312-32887-0; 0-312-32887-7
LC 2006-47084
The author "relies on memoirs, private letters and previous monographs as she details how, after dissolution of the unhappy marriage that brought Catherine (1729-1798) to Russia from Germany, the empress juggled her relationships with men as she attempted to thrust Russia into the modern era and make it a European power. . . . [This] work will appeal to Catherine-philes and those interested in women's history." Publ Wkly
Includes bibliographical references

Rousseau, Jean-Jacques

Confessions; edited and introduced by P. N. Furbank. Knopf 1992 2v in 1 $20   **92**
1. Authors 2. Memoirists 3. Novelists 4. Political and social philosophers
ISBN 0-679-40998-X
LC 91-53194
"An autobiography by Jean-Jacques Rousseau. The twelve volumes, written between 1766 and 1770, were published posthumously (I-VI, 1781; VII-XII, 1788). In this work, Rousseau 'frankly and sincerely' reveals the details of his erratic and rebellious life. Scholars find, however, that his unconscious motivation was to justify himself in the eyes of his supposedly numerous persecutors." Reader's Ency. 4th edition

Rowan, Carl Thomas

Dream makers, dream breakers; the world of Justice Thurgood Marshall. [by] Carl T. Rowan. Welcome Rain 2002 475p il pa $18.95   **92**
1. Civil rights activists 2. Judges 3. Lawyers 4. Solicitors general 5. Supreme Court justices
ISBN 978-1-56649-235-5; 1-56649-235-1
The author "offers a no-holds barred account of one of the most influential and controversial figures in American law and jurisprudence of this century. His work brings to life Marshall, the Surpreme Court, U.S. law and modern America itself. Particularly effective is Rowan's account of the innovative legal arguments Marshall and his colleagues employed to win the now-famous Brown v. Board of Education case of 1954." Libr J
Includes bibliographical references

Rudd, Mark

Underground; my life with SDS and the Weathermen. William Morrow 2009 324p il map $25.99 **92**
1. Biography, Individual 2. Radicalism 3. Revolutionaries 4. Teachers 5. Youth leaders
ISBN 978-0-06-147275-6; 0-06-147275-1
"Even those who condemn Rudd's work in history can be grateful for Rudd's work of history. 'Underground' is honest and funny, passionate and contrite, meticulously researched and deeply philosophical: an essential document on the '60s." Washington Post Book World

Rudnick, Paul

I shudder; and other reactions to life, death, and New Jersey. Harper 2009 318p $23.99   **92**
1. Authors 2. Biography, Individual 3. Dramatists 4. Dramatists, American 5. Humorists 6. Novelists 7. Screenwriters
ISBN 978-0-06-178018-9; 0-06-178018-9
LC 2009-36459
This is the author's "collection of uproariously self-deprecating essays about being gay and Jewish in suburban New Jersey and downtown Manhattan, and about his career as a playwright and script doctor in Hollywood and on Broadway." N Y Times Book Rev

Rule, Ann

The **stranger** beside me; Updated 20th anniversary ed; Signet 2001 548p il pa $7.99   **92**
1. Criminals 2. Murderers
ISBN 0-451-20326-7; 978-0-451-20326-7
This is a biography of Ted Bundy, written by someone who "worked a suicide hotline in Seattle with Ted Bundy, not knowing he was a serial killer." Libr J

Russell, Thaddeus

Out of the jungle; Jimmy Hoffa and the remaking of the American working class. Temple University Press 2003 272p il pa $21.95   **92**
1. Labor leaders 2. Labor unions -- United States -- Officials and employees -- Biography 3. Missing persons 4. Trucking executives
ISBN 1-592-13027-5; 978-1-592-13027-6
LC 2002-43556
"Russell makes good use of a range of primary-source materials plus period newspaper accounts and other materials to highlight this story." Libr J
Includes bibliographical references

Ryan, Donald P.

Beneath the sands of Egypt; adventures of an unconventional archaeologist. William Morrow 2010 286p il $26.99; ebook $12.99   **92**
1. Archaeologists 2. Archeologists 3. College teachers 4. Excavations (Archeology) -- Egypt 5. Queens
ISBN 978-0-06-173282-9; 0-06-173282-6; 978-0-06-200280-8 ebook; 0-06-200280-5 ebook
LC 2010-20355
"Ryan, the archaeologist who rediscovered tomb KV 60 in the Valley of the Kings (later identified as the final resting place of the pharoah Hatshepsut), takes us through his life, career, and numerous expeditions. It's a thrilling book, not because it's full of Indiana Jones heroics but because Ryan's enthusiasm for what he does (more dirt-sifting than bullwhip-wielding) is manifested on every page; and . . . he catches us up in his excitement, makes us wish we weren't just reading about this stuff but were actually doing it. . . . This wonderful adventure story should be must reading for anyone aspiring to become an archaeologist, but even those of us who harbor no such dreams will be aching to get a little dirt under our fingernails." Booklist

Ryan, Mark

Hornet's sting; the amazing untold story of World War II spy Thomas Sneum. Skyhorse Pub. 2009 386p il map $24.95   **92**

1. Spies 2. World War, 1939-1945 -- Secret service

ISBN 978-1-6023-9710-1

LC 2009-6210

Sneum's "real-life exploits include all the key elements of any good spy story: sex, danger, and intrigue. . . . Readers will find the book hard to put down." Libr J

Includes bibliographical references

Sabbag, Robert

Down around midnight; a memoir of crash and survival. Viking 2009 214p $25.95   **92**

1. Aircraft accidents 2. Authors, American 3. Biography, Individual 4. Journalists 5. Survival after airplane accidents, shipwrecks, etc.

ISBN 978-0-670-02102-4

LC 2008-46688

"A remarkably powerful, human story not merely of a plane crash but of the impact that one brief moment can have on an entire life." Booklist

Saldana, Stephanie

The **bread** of angels; a journey to love and faith. Doubleday 2010 309p $24.95; pa $15   **92**

1. Biography, Individual 2. Christianity and other religions 3. Christianity and other religions -- Islam 4. Islam -- Relations -- Christianity 5. Spiritual biography

ISBN 978-0-385-52200-7; 0-385-52200-2; 978-0-307-28046-6 pa; 0-307-28046-2 pa

LC 2009-16852

This book "operates on several levels: as a spiritual testament and journey of faith; as a Western woman's positive encounter with Islam; as a writer's successful quest to find poetry and beauty even in the midst of war; and as a love story, told with novelistic suspense and a refreshing humor that keeps the romanticism of her story as grounded in reality as possible. . . . This is the type of memoir, recounting a journey to the depths of the soul, that makes the personal universal." America

Salisbury, Laney

Provenance; how a con man and a forger rewrote the history of modern art. [by] Laney Salisbury and Aly Sujo. Penguin Press 2009 327p $26.95; pa $16   **92**

1. Art -- Forgeries 2. Art -- Provenance 3. Art dealers 4. Art forgers 5. Arts -- Forgeries 6. Biography, Individual 7. Criminals 8. Impostors and imposture 9. Painters 10. Swindlers

ISBN 978-1-59420-220-9; 978-0-14-311740-7 pa

LC 2009-3552

"Tautly written and assiduously researched . . . [this book] has the pace and suspense of a good thriller, and a colorful international cast." Wall Street J

Includes bibliographical references

Sampson, Anthony

Nelson Mandela; the authorized biography. Knopf 1999 xxvi, 672p hardcover o.p. pa $19   **92**

1. Human rights activists 2. Nobel laureates for peace 3. Political leaders 4. Political prisoners 5. Presidents

ISBN 0-679-78178-1 pa

LC 99-18498

"While not neglecting the personality of the man, Mr. Sampson has concentrated on the politics, and, for an authorised life, it can be treated as definitive." Economist

Includes bibliographical references

Sandburg, Carl

Abraham Lincoln: The prairie years and The war years; illustrated ed; Harcourt Brace Jovanovich 1970 640p il maps hardcover o.p. pa $26   **92**

1. Frontier and pioneer life 2. Lawyers 3. Members of Congress 4. Presidents 5. Presidents -- United States 6. State legislators

ISBN 0-15-602752-6 pa

A condensation of the two volumes of "The prairie years" (1926) and the four volumes of "The war years" (1939). The author has taken advantage of material made available since the original volumes were published to include in this edition of his lifetime study of Lincoln.

"A biography that as a whole is superior to the longer life. This one volume has a form which the six lacked. It is a tighter and tidier book. It retains the superb qualities of the original work without the faults of the latter." Saturday Rev

Includes bibliographical references

Sanders, Scott R.

A **private** history of awe; [by] Scott Russell Sanders. North Point Press 2006 322p hardcover o.p. pa $15   **92**

1. Authors 2. Children's authors 3. College teachers 4. Essayists 5. Novelists 6. Short story writers

ISBN 0-86547-693-4; 978-0-86547-693-6; 978-0-86547-734-6 pa; 0-86547-734-5 pa

LC 2005-14236

The author "uses autobiography as a vehicle for far-reaching reflections on nature and humankind. . . . Sanders' thoughtful reflections on the cycles of life, the flashpoints of awe, and our quest for meaning are quietly revelatory." Booklist

Includes bibliographical references

Sandison, David

★ **Neal** Cassady; the fast life of a beat hero. [by] David Sandison and Graham Vickers. Chicago Review Press 2006 340p il $24.95   **92**

1. Authors 2. Beat generation 3. Biography, Individual 4. Memoirists

ISBN 978-1-55652-615-2; 1-55652-615-6

LC 2006-9112

"Drawing on Cassady's correspondence, interviews with those who knew him, and previous works by memoirist Carolyn Cassady (the subject's widow), biographer Tom Christopher, and others, Sandison and Vickers portray Cassady as all too human—a desperate, lost soul who was plagued by contradictions and sought personal fulfillment and spiritual salvation. Debunking the mythology that grew up around

Cassady as a result of his appearance in works by Kerouac, Ken Kesey, and Tom Wolfe, the authors attempt to separate the life from the legend. They present Cassady as someone who wanted to be a good husband and father but was unable to conquer his demons, which included sex, drugs, gambling, and an innate restlessness. Ironically, it was these very demons that ensured Cassady's place in American literature." Libr J

Includes bibliographical references

Sandweiss, Martha A.

Passing strange; a Gilded Age tale of love and deception across the color line. Penguin Press 2009 370p il $27.95   **92**
1. African Americans -- Race identity 2. Biography, Individual 3. Geologists 4. Government officials 5. Passing (Identity) 6. Racially mixed people -- Race identity 7. Travel writers 8. Writers on science
ISBN 978-1-59420-200-1

LC 2008-34886

The book tells the story of "Clarence King (1842–1901), the eminent nineteenth-century geologist . . . [and] mapper of the American West . . . [who] successfully avoided military service in the Civil War and chose instead to cultivate his manliness in the rugged life of a western explorer." In particular the book looks at his travels across the color line in the U.S. and how "for the last thirteen years of his life he led a double life in Brooklyn as James Todd, a light-skinned African American Pullman porter." (Journal of American History)

Sandweiss's "great accomplishment is to have explored not only how the 19th-century explorer and scientist Clarence King reinvented himself but also why that reinvention was so singularly American. Best of all are Ms. Sandweiss's insights into what King's deception and its consequences really mean." N Y Times (Late N Y Ed)

Includes bibliographical references

Santopietro, Tom

Sinatra in Hollywood. Thomas Dunne Books 2008 530p il $29.95   **92**
1. Actors 2. Singers
ISBN 978-0-312-36226-3; 0-312-36226-9

LC 2008-24941

"Striving for honest critiques and a witty, encyclopedic coverage, Santopietro begins with Sinatra's 1935 short subjects; dances through the grandiose 1940s MGM musicals; documents Sinatra's professional and personal despair and decline in such giant turkey disasters as The Kissing Bandit (1948); and analyzes his Oscar-winning comeback in From Here to Eternity (1953). . . . This mammoth movie compendium, filled with forgotten facts, 53 b&w photos and a detailed filmography, is certain to satisfy Sinatra's legions of fans." Publ Wkly

Includes bibliographical references

Sartre, Jean Paul

The **words**; translated from the French by Bernard Frechtman. Vintage 1981 255p pa $11.95 **92**
1. Authors 2. Authors, French 3. Dramatists 4. Essayists 5. Nobel laureates for literature 6. Nonfiction writers 7. Novelists 8. Philosophers 9. Short story

writers
ISBN 0-394-74709-7; 978-0-394-74709-5

The French existentialist writer "examines the formation of his character during his childhood years, which were passed in a completely adult world between his widowed mother and her parents. The central event of his childhood was the discovery of the world of words, of language." Libr J

Sawyer-Laucanno, Christopher

★ **E.E.** Cummings; a biography. Sourcebooks 2004 606p il $29.95; pa $16.95   **92**
1. Authors 2. Biography, Individual 3. Poets
ISBN 1-570-71775-3; 1-4022-0594-5 pa

LC 2004-12234

This biography of poet and artist e.e. cummings draws parallels between cummings' private life and his work.

This "is a responsible, adept, and necessary contribution to the body of secondary work about one of America's greatest poets." Christ Sci Monit

Sayrafiezadeh, Said

When skateboards will be free; a memoir of a political childhood. Dial Press 2009 287p $22; pa $15   **92**
1. Authors 2. Biography, Individual 3. Dramatists 4. Memoirists 5. Socialism
ISBN 978-0-385-34068-7; 0-385-34068-0; 978-0-385-34069-4 pa; 0-385-34069-9 pa

LC 2008-51096

The author presents a memoir "of growing up with (and without) his parents, ardent members of the Socialist Workers Party." N Y Times (Late N Y Ed)

Scammell, Michael

Koestler; the literary and political odyssey of a twentieth-century skeptic. Random House 2009 xxi, 689p il   **92**
1. Authors 2. Authors, English 3. Essayists 4. Journalists 5. Novelists
ISBN 0-394-57630-6; 978-0-394-57630-5

LC 2008-51108

"Although he wrote more than 30 books, Koestler is today known primarily, perhaps exclusively, as the author of 'Darkness at Noon,' his gripping short novel of Stalinist coercion. The biographer Michael Scammell wants to put Koestler's multifaceted intelligence back on display and to show that something more than frivolity or opportunism lay behind his ever-shifting preoccupations and allegiances. As a source of information, 'Koestler,' the work of two decades, will never be surpassed. As an argument for the man's importance, however, it must contend with the eccentricity of Koestler's preoccupations and—although Scammell does not always seem to realize it—his vices." N Y Times Book Rev

Includes bibliographical references

Scanlon, Jennifer

Bad girls go everywhere: the life of Helen Gurley Brown. Oxford University Press 2009 270p il $27.95   **92**
1. Biography, Individual 2. Columnists 3. Feminism

4. Magazine editors 5. Nonfiction writers
ISBN 978-0-19-534205-5; 0-19-534205-4

LC 2008-30466

This is a biography of Helen Gurley Brown, former editor of Cosmopolitan magazine and author of Sex and the Single Girl (1962), Sex and the Office (1964), and Single Girl's Cookbook (1969).

"Jennifer Scanlon delivers Helen Gurley Brown's 'delightfully knotty life story' in a neat and satisfying package. . . . This is not chick lit but cultural history, the first serious biography of the woman who, in Scanlon's view, 'ushered in and has long continued to define the feminist mainstream.'" Natl Rev

Includes bibliographical references

Schaap, Jeremy

Cinderella Man; James J. Braddock, Max Baer, and the greatest upset in boxing history. Houghton Mifflin 2005 324p il hardcover o.p. pa $13.95 **92**
1. Boxers (Persons) 2. Boxing -- Biography
ISBN 0-618-55117-4; 0-618-71190-2 pa

LC 2004-66085

The author goes into "detail on the brawny, reserved Braddock, who, at his lowest moments, was reduced to living off government relief and doing grueling work on the Hoboken, N.J., docks. But the story is as much about Max Baer, the lovably clownish and handsome heavyweight Braddock defeated as a 10-to-one underdog. . . . Boxing enthusiasts will be more than satisfied by Schaap's meticulous account, which includes round-by-round details of the fight, as well as profiles of other fighters of the era." Publ Wkly

Includes bibliographical references

Triumph; the untold story of Jesse Owens and Hitler's Olympics. Houghton Mifflin 2007 272p il $24; pa $14.95 **92**
1. African American athletes 2. Olympic athletes 3. Olympic games, 1936 (Berlin, Ger.) 4. Runners (Athletes)
ISBN 978-0-618-68822-7; 0-618-68822-6; 978-0-618-91910-9 pa; 0-618-91910-4 pa

LC 2006-26926

"Schaap's chronicle of Jesse Owens's journey to and glorious triumph at the 1936 Berlin Olympics is snappy and dramatic, with an eye for the rousing climax." Publ Wkly

Includes bibliographical references

Schama, Chloe

Wild romance; a Victorian story of a marriage, a trial, and a self-made woman. Walker & Co. 2010 249p il map $24 **92**
1. Army officers 2. Authors 3. Novelists
ISBN 978-0-8027-1736-8; 0-8027-1736-5

LC 2009-44758

Schama details the "bigamy trial of William Charles Yelverton, which dominated the front pages of Irish, Scottish, and British newspapers in 1861. Although the story of Yelverton and his first wife, Theresa Longworth, practically tells itself through court documents, letters, and public opinion, Schama adds a journalist's touch in her story development. The latter part of the book deals with Theresa's later

life in America as a self-made woman still haunted by her past." Libr J

Includes bibliographical references

Schama, Simon

Rembrandt's eyes. Knopf 1999 640p il $50; pa $35 **92**
1. Artists 2. Drafters 3. Etchers 4. Painters
ISBN 0-679-40256-X; 0-375-70981-9 pa

LC 99-19971

Schama's prose unfurls the life of Rembrandt in all its pathos. From prodigy to pauper, the troubled genius of 17th century Dutch painting is intricately conceived as he rises and falls in a world of war, plague and stolid bourgeois comfort. . . . Schama's book is a marvel of storytelling: sometimes heart pounding, always sympathetic and coolly reasoned. Seamlessly joining social history and art, what a triumph of scholarship and imagination." Time

Scheeres, Julia

Jesus land; a memoir. Counterpoint 2005 356p $23; pa $14 **92**
1. Adoption 2. Biography, Individual 3. Child abuse 4. Christian life 5. Journalists 6. Memoirists 7. Siblings
ISBN 1-58243-338-0; 1-58243-354-2 pa

LC 2005-14816

"Tinged with sadness yet pervaded by a sense of triumph, Scheeres's book is a crisply written and earnest examination of the meaning of family and Christian values." Publ Wkly

Scheijen, Sjeng

Diaghilev; a life. translated by Jane Hedley-Prôle and S.J. Leinbach. Oxford University Press 2010 552p il **92**
1. Ballet dancers 2. Biography, Individual 3. Theatrical producers
ISBN 0199751498; 9780199751495

LC 2010-02205

This is a "biography of Serge Diaghilev, founder and impresario of the Ballets Russes." (Publisher's note) Bibliography. Index.

"The parade of great dancers, composers, and artists through Diaghilev's life give this book the sweep of a Russian novel with a fascinating, brilliant, and complex protagonist who, according to the author, lived a very public life, but kept his most intimate feelings hidden." Publ Wkly

Includes bibliographical references

Schenkar, Joan

The **talented** Miss Highsmith; the secret life and serious art of Patricia Highsmith. St. Martin's Press 2009 684p il $40 **92**
1. Authors 2. Authors, American 3. Biography, Individual 4. Mystery writers 5. Novelists
ISBN 978-0-312-30375-4

LC 2009-18363

"It is hard to imagine a more thoroughly fact-filled or energetic biography than 'The Talented Miss Highsmith' or one more determined to examine the deepest recesses of its complicated subject. Ms. Schenkar's presentation is cubist, off-putting at first, featuring separated essays that isolate various topics. The dislocation can be confusing, yet one soon comes to accept the method as a way of mining the many veins of a very strange life." Wall Street J

Includes bibliographical references

Scherman, Tony

★ **Pop**; the genius of Andy Warhol. [by] Tony Scherman and David Dalton. HarperCollins 2009 509p il $40 **92**

1. Artists 2. Artists -- United States 3. Biography, Individual 4. Motion picture directors 5. Pop art

ISBN 978-0-06-621243-2; 0-06-621243-X

LC 2009-24815

This biography covers the artist's career and personal life through 1968.

"Not only is . . . [this book] well written and researched, it manages to unearth details that reframe the debate about Warhol's real importance as an artist." Bookforum

Includes bibliographical references

Scheuer, Michael

Osama bin Laden; [by] Michael Scheuer. Oxford University Press 2011 278p $19.95 **92**

1. Biography, Individual 2. Terrorists

ISBN 978-0-19-973866-3; 0-19-973866-1

LC 2010-21715

The author "offers a serious and nonideological treatment and analysis of bin Laden's thinking. Unlike many Western analysts who dismiss bin Laden as simplistic, uncouth, and incompetent, Scheuer portrays him as a patient, devout, and talented, albeit ruthless, leader who remains a formidable enemy of the West. . . . This informative book is one of the most detailed biographical sketches of bin Laden available in the West and is useful for both the general public and specialists." Libr J

Includes bibliographical references

Schiavi, Michael R.

Celluloid activist; the life and times of Vito Russo. [by] Michael Schiavi. University of Wisconsin Press 2011 361p il $29.95; e-book $14.95 **92**

1. Film historians 2. Gay activists 3. Gay rights activists 4. Homosexuality in motion pictures 5. Motion picture critics

ISBN 978-0-299-28230-1; 978-0-299-28233-2 e-book

LC 2010-44627

"Conventionally academic but complex portrait of an undeservedly obscure gay author and activist." Kirkus

Includes bibliographical references

Schickel, Richard

Elia Kazan; a biography. HarperCollins 2005 xxxi, 510p il $29.95 **92**

1. Authors 2. Biography, Individual 3. Memoirists 4. Motion picture directors 5. Novelists 6. Theatrical directors

ISBN 0-06-019579-7

LC 2005-43344

This is "the life story of the distinguished stage and screen director. No mere page turner, this is a page devourer, generating the kind of suspense that is usually the province of the playwright or novelist." N Y Times Book Rev

Includes bibliographical references

Schiff, Stacy

★ **Cleopatra**; a life. Little, Brown and Co. 2010 368p il map $29.99; ebook $14.99 **92**

1. Biography, Individual 2. Queens

ISBN 978-0-316-00192-2; 0-316-00192-9; 978-0-316-12180-4 ebook

LC 2010-06988

"It's dizzying to contemplate the thicket of prejudices, personalities and propaganda Schiff penetrated to reconstruct a woman whose style, ambition and audacity make her a subject worthy of her latest biographer. After all, Stacy Schiff's writing is distinguished by those very same virtues." N Y Times Book Rev

Includes bibliographical references

Schlesinger, Arthur M.

Journals: 1952-2000; edited by Andrew Schlesinger and Stephen Schlesinger. Penguin Press 2007 894p $40 **92**

1. Authors 2. Biographers 3. Biography, Individual 4. Government officials 5. Historians 6. Historians -- United States 7. Nonfiction writers

ISBN 978-1-594-20142-4

The distinguished political historian's journals provide an intimate history of postwar America, the writer's contributions to multiple presidential administrations, and his relationships with numerous cultural and intellectual figures.

This book "contains juicy morsels on every one of its [pages]. . . . The book contains not just his witty apercus, but those of hundreds of A-list friends, some of whom are still alive and will blanch at seeing private lunches in print. The presidential scuttlebutt is prime. . . . The private score-settling is fun reading." Newsweek

Robert Kennedy and his times; {by} Arthur M. Schlesinger, Jr. Houghton Mifflin 1978 1066p il hardcover o.p. pa $17.95 **92**

1. Attorneys general 2. Presidential candidates 3. Senators 4. Siblings of presidents

ISBN 978-0-618-21928-5 pa; 0-618-21928-5 pa

LC 78-8469

"A highly sympathetic and readable political biography covering in depth Robert Kennedy's tenure in public life. At times extremely partisan, at times dispassionate, Schlesinger's study effectively captures Kennedy's impact on national politics and the main currents of American politics during the 1950s and 1960s." Choice

Includes bibliographical references

Schmidt, Leigh Eric

Heaven's bride; the unprintable life of Ida C. Craddock, American mystic, scholar, sexologist, martyr, and madwoman. Basic Books 2010 335p il **92**

1. Biography, Individual 2. Mysticism 3. Occultists 4. Sex researchers

ISBN 9780465002986

LC 2010-929343

This is a biography of the American freethinker. Index.

The author "delineates the life of Philadelphia-born self-styled religion scholar and sexologist Ida Craddock (1857–1902), who navigated two important currents in late-19th-century America: the campaign for 'moral purity' waged by a righteous Protestant majority, and a spirit of liberalism and spiritualism as advocated by women's-rights activists, intellectuals and free-thinkers. . . . A colorful contextual study of Craddock and her teeming era." Kirkus

Includes bibliographical references

Schom, Alan

Napoleon Bonaparte; a life. HarperCollins Pubs. 1997 xxii, 888p hardcover o.p. pa $23.95   **92**

1. Emperors 2. Emperors -- France -- Biography

ISBN 0-06-092958-8 pa

LC 97-5805

"Schom's judgments have all the more impact for being brief and infrequent. What really interests him is telling the story of the man who made universal rules for others but recognized none for himself. He tells it straightforwardly and well; and not, thankfully, at the multi-volume length he believes the subject still really requires." Times Lit Suppl

Includes bibliographical references

Schroeder, Alice D.

The **snowball**: Warren Buffett and the business of life; [by] Alice Schroeder. Bantam Books 2008 960p il $35   **92**

1. Biography, Individual 2. Capitalists and financiers 3. Financiers

ISBN 978-0-553-80509-3; 0-553-80509-6

LC 2008-17338

A portrait of the life and career of investment guru Warren Buffett.

"In a book that is dominated by unstinting descriptions of Buffett's appetites—for profit, women (particularly nurturing maternal types), food (Buffett maintained his and his family's weight by 'dangling money')—it is refreshing that Schroeder keeps her tone free of judgment or awe; Buffett's plain-speaking suffuses the book and renders his public and private successes and failures wonderfully human and universal. . . . Inspiring managerial advice abounds and competes with gossip tidbits . . . in this rich, surprisingly affecting biography." Publ Wkly

Includes bibliographical references

Schroth, Raymond A.

Bob Drinan; the controversial life of the first Catholic priest elected to Congress. Fordham University Press 2011 393p il   **92**

1. Biography, Individual 2. Catholic Church -- Clergy 3. Catholic Church -- United States -- History 4. College deans 5. College teachers 6. Lawyers 7. Members of Congress 8. Priests

ISBN 9780823233045; 9780823233069

LC 2010033726

This is a biography of the Jesuit priest and law professor who served as Democratic congressman from Massachusetts for ten years. Father Drinan demonstrated against the Vietnam War and ran as an anti-war candidate, called for the impeachment of Richard Nixon, and was a strong supporter of the civil rights movement. He believed that abortion was morally wrong but should not be illegal. Father Drinan withdrew his candidacy for Congress in 1980 when Pope John Paul II requested it, based on the principle that priests should not hold political office. Bibliography. Index.

"In 1970, the Jesuit priest Robert Drinan was elected to Congress after famously running as an antiwar candidate; he served for a decade, opposing the encroachment of U.S. military forces into Cambodia and actively calling for President Nixon's impeachment. Schroth's . . . biography carefully and lovingly chronicles Drinan's life and work, from his childhood and youth in Massachusetts through his development into a passionate advocate for civil rights and ecumenical dialogue, especially between Christians and Jews, and as a moral architect for change in America. . . . Schroth's loving tribute to Drinan restores the late priest-legislator's thoughtful and forceful voice to contemporary religious life." Publ Wkly

Includes bibliographical references

Schultz, Philip

My dyslexia. W. W. Norton & Co. 2011 120p $21.95   **92**

1. Authors 2. College teachers 3. Dyslexia 4. Poets 5. Poets, American

ISBN 978-0-393-07964-7

LC 2011015859

The author "tackles his struggle with dyslexia—a condition he only learned he had when his son was diagnosed. Schultz paints a precise and compelling picture of how his brain works, how he sees himself, and how he thinks others have seen him throughout his life. . . . His affecting prose will inspire compassion and leave readers with an understanding not only of dyslexia, but of the lifelong challenges that someone with disabilities may face." Publ Wkly

Schumacher, Michael

Crossroads; the life and music of Eric Clapton. Citadel Press 2003 420p il pa $15.95   **92**

1. Guitarists 2. Rock musicians 3. Singers

ISBN 978-0-8065-2466-5; 0-8065-2466-9

The author "chronicles the life and career of the reclusive British blues performer. . . . Schumacher covers a tale of unhappy personal relationships, a failed marriage, drug and alcohol addiction and the tragic death of the performer's infant son, while giving full account of Clapton's significant accomplishments as guitarist and vocalist, his forays into rock and his performances and recordings." Publ Wkly

Will Eisner; a dreamer's life in comics. Bloomsbury 2010 359p il $28   **92**

1. Authors 2. Cartoonists 3. Comic book writers 4. Publishing executives

ISBN 978-1-60819-013-3

LC 2010-11283

"Born in 1917, Will Eisner, now known as the father of the graphic novel, grew up in the Bronx poor but resourceful. . . . [The author] zeroes in on the essence of Eisner's success: his rare ability to unite art (he inherited his phenomenal gift for drawing from his immigrant artist father) with practicality (his mother's specialty). . . . Propelled by Eisner's geyserlike energy and output, Schumacher keenly chronicles Eisner's brilliant career within a lively history of American comics and creates an inspiring portrait of a perpetually diligent and innovative artist whose belief in comics as fine art fueled a new and fertile creative universe." Booklist

Includes bibliographical references

Schwarzkopf, H. Norman

It doesn't take a hero: General H. Norman Schwarzkopf; the autobiography. written with Peter Petre. Bantam Bks. 1992 530p il maps hardcover o.p. pa $7.99 **92**

1. Generals 2. Persian Gulf War, 1991
ISBN 0-553-56338-6 pa

LC 92-20762

"The whole book is a description of General Schwarz-kopf's relations with people. It is remarkably emotional. To an unusual degree he sees events as secondary to the personalities he has been affected by. He emphasizes his sensitive side. . . . 'It Doesn't Take a Hero' is not a military record. . . . It covers the gulf war, of course, but General Schwarzkopf devotes so much space to his life before that event that he has produced two books in one." N Y Times Book Rev
Includes bibliographical references

Scurr, Ruth

Fatal purity; Robespierre and the French Revolution. Metropolitan Books 2006 408p il map $30 **92**
1. Biography, Individual 2. Political leaders 3. Revolutionaries
ISBN 978-0-8050-7987-6; 0-8050-7987-4

LC 2005-57694

This is a biography of the French revolutionary.

This "is quite the calmest and least abusive history of the Revolution you will ever read. It works well as a general history of the years 1789-94, besides being a succinct guide to one of its dominant figures." London Rev Books
Includes bibliographical references

Seal, Mark

Wildflower; a story of love, murder, and the woman who tried to save Kenya. Random House 2009 232p il $26 **92**
1. Conservationists 2. Motion picture producers
ISBN 978-1-4000-6736-7; 1-4000-6736-7

LC 2008-51106

"This is a great story built from many interviews of friends and family and from Root's extensive diaries and letters. What an adventure! What an example!" Libr J

Sears, Stephen W.

George B. McClellan; the young Napoleon. Da Capo Press 1999 482p il map pa $16.95 **92**
1. Generals 2. Governors 3. Presidential candidates
ISBN 0-306-80913-3

LC 98-33277

This biography of the Civil War general "covers both the awkward character traits that led to McClellan's incompetence and the battlefield actions that he regularly bungled. In addition to its merit as Civil War history, the book is of great interest as the portrait of an intelligent man working at what he failed to realize was the wrong profession." Atlantic
Includes bibliographical references

Secrest, Meryle

Frank Lloyd Wright; a biography. University of Chicago Press 1998 634p il pa $20 **92**
1. Architects 2. Architects -- United States -- Biography

3. Nonfiction writers
ISBN 0-226-74414-0

LC 97-51590

A portrait of a "complex, often contradictory architect. . . . Secrest writes with authority and compassion about Wright's long and turbulent career. Her exhaustive scholarship provides fresh insights into Wright's personality." Libr J
Includes bibliographical references

Modigliani; a life.

Alfred A. Knopf 2011 387p il $35; ebook $17.99 **92**
1. Artists, Italian 2. Biography, Individual
ISBN 978-0-307-26368-1; 978-0-307-59547-8 ebook

LC 2010-45357

This "is an enjoyable read for all, and a most welcome contribution to Modigliani scholarship." Publ Wkly

Segev, Tom

Simon Wiesenthal; the life and legends. Doubleday 2010 482p il $35; ebook $35 **92**
1. Architects 2. Authors 3. Biography, Individual 4. Essayists 5. Holocaust survivors 6. Jewish leaders 7. Jews -- Austria 8. Memoirists 9. Nazi 10. Nazi hunters
ISBN 978-0-385-51946-5; 978-0-385-53371-3 ebook

LC 2009-53480

The book is a biography about "Simon Wiesenthal, . . . the survivor of a succession of concentration camps, . . . [and] the Nazi hunter who tracked down Adolf Eichmann and brought to justice such [war criminals] . . . as Franz Stangl, the commandant of Treblinka, . . . and Hermine Braunsteiner." The author recounts how Wiesenthal "talked his way into jobs with the American military—an army war crimes unit and the local bureau of the counterintelligence corps—and became the head of local refugee groups, . . . as well as a representative of the Joint Distribution Committee, a Jewish relief organization working with DPs. The American connection, which involved identifying and apprehending war criminals, led directly to his life's work: creating a database of Nazi criminals, tracking them down, and bringing them to justice." (New York Review of Books)

"The man who emerges from this text is ultimately more complex, and indeed likable, than the mythologized figure. Segev's study should be the standard for many years." Libr J
Includes bibliographical references

Senna, Danzy

Where did you sleep last night? a personal history. Farrar, Straus and Giroux 2009 200p il $23 **92**
1. Authors 2. Authors, American 3. Biography, Individual 4. Novelists 5. Racially mixed people
ISBN 978-0-374-28915-7; 0-374-28915-8

LC 2008-43413

This "is a haunting, introspective meditation on race and family ties that tackles the tricky questions involved in constructing identity." Publ Wkly

Sereny, Gitta

Albert Speer; his battle with truth. Knopf 1995 757p il hardcover o.p. pa $25 **92**
1. Architects 2. Memoirists 3. National socialism 4.

Nazi leaders 5. War criminals
ISBN 0-679-76812-2 pa

LC 94-19764

The author of this biography of the Nazi war criminal "conducted intensive and protracted interviews with Speer . . . and many of the people who were close to him. Along with the interviews and analysis are good descriptions of what was happening in Germany throughout the Third Reich. Sereny's clear and concise prose makes this book suitable for both the scholar and the lay reader. She has produced what will become one of the standard works in Holocaust studies." Libr J

Includes bibliographical references

Servadio, Gaia

Rossini; a life. Carroll & Graf Publishers 2003 244p il $26 **92**

1. Composers 2. Composers -- Italy -- Biography
ISBN 0-7867-1195-7

LC 2003-43563

"This is a deeply rewarding book, written with real personality and much scholarship." Publ Wkly

Includes bibliographical references

Service, Robert

Stalin; a biography. Belknap Press of Harvard University Press 2005 715p il map $29.95 **92**

1. Communist leaders 2. Dictators 3. Heads of state 4. Political leaders
ISBN 0-674-01697-1

LC 2004-61115

This book covers Stalin's life "from his early, troubled years in a small town in Georgia to the pinnacle of power in the Kremlin. . . . By providing such a rich and complex portrait of the dictator and the Soviet system, Service humanizes Stalin without ever diminishing the extent of the atrocities he unleashed upon the Soviet population." Publ Wkly

Includes bibliographical references

★ **Trotsky**; a biography. Belknap Press of Harvard University Press 2009 600p il map $35 **92**

1. Biography, Individual 2. Communism -- Soviet Union 3. Communist leaders 4. Nonfiction writers 5. Political leaders 6. Revolutionaries
ISBN 978-0-674-03615-4; 0-674-03615-8

LC 2009-25417

"Thick and intensely researched but a pleasure to read, . . . [this] should remain the definitive work for some time. . . . This is a thoughtful, rewarding and essential contribution to 20th-century history." Publ Wkly

Includes bibliographical references

Seth, Vikram, 1952-

★ **Two** lives; Vikram Seth. HarperCollins 2005 503p ill. (pbk.) $15.95; o.p. **92**

1. Authors 2. Authors, English -- 20th century -- Biography 3. Authors, Indic -- Homes and haunts -- England -- London 4. Biography, Individual 5. Children's authors 6. Dentists 7. East Indians -- England -- London 8. Interracial marriage -- England -- London 9. Novelists 10. Poets 11. Translators 12.

Travel writers
ISBN 9780060599676; 0060599669

LC 2005052694

"In this book, the author presents biographies of his Shanti Uncle and Aunty Henny. . . . Shanti was Seth's grandfather's brother, a dentist who studied in Berlin, lodging with Fau Caro, whose daughter, Henny was in love with someone else. He left for Britain in 1936. . . . [I]n 1940, as war broke out, he enlisted, served throughout and lost his right arm in combat. . . . Meanwhile, Henny, a German Jew, arrived in Britain weeks before war was declared, leaving her beloved mother and sister behind to death camp murder. . . . Part two of his narrative focuses on Shanti. Part three, Henny's story . . . is based on a trove of remarkable letters she received and wrote. . . . Part four examines their marriage (they didn't marry until seven years after the war), and part five details a family mystery about Shanti's will and Seth's . . . research into these lives. (Publishers Weekly)

"In clear and elegant writing, Seth explores the macrocosm through the microcosm, resulting in a most unusual, worthwhile book." Publ Wkly

Seymour, Miranda

Mary Shelley. Grove Press 2001 655p il $35; pa $20 **92**

1. Authors 2. Authors, English 3. Novelists 4. Women authors
ISBN 0-8021-1702-3; 0-8021-3948-5 pa

LC 2001-35094

"A convincing and memorable portrait." Booklist

Includes bibliographical references

Shalev, Meir

My Russian grandmother and her American vacuum cleaner; a memoir. translated from the Hebrew by Evan Fallenberg. Schocken Books 2011 $25.95 **92**

1. Authors, Israeli
ISBN 978-0-8052-4287-4

"Shalev delivers a punchy family memoir that examines his relationship with his grandmother. Grandma Tonia, who, as a young woman immigrated to Israel and married, is obsessed with cleanliness. When her husband's oldest brother sends an American vacuum cleaner from Los Angeles, however, she locks it in the bathroom, where it lives 'in dark and lonely confinement wrapped in its white shroud and as clean as the day it was born, untainted by dust.' . . . This memoir composed of a series of engaging anecdotes, mostly about Shalev's training in 'Grandma Tonia's University of Cleaning,' grants readers a glimpse into the zany aspects of immigrant culture and acclimation." Booklist

Shawn, Allen

Wish I could be there; notes from a phobic life. Viking 2007 267p $24.95 **92**

1. Agoraphobia 2. Biography, Individual 3. Composers 4. Phobias
ISBN 0-670-03842-3; 978-0-670-03842-8

LC 2006-41368

The author "probes the causes of his long struggle with agoraphobia—a fear of certain spaces which makes it difficult to 'move forward in the world without knowing already what lies ahead'—in this vividly written combination of memoir and scientific inquiry." New Yorker

Includes bibliographical references

Shea, William R.

Galileo in Rome; the rise and fall of a troublesome genius. [by] William R. Shea and Mariano Artigas. Oxford University Press 2003 226p il hardcover o.p. pa $15.95   92

1. Astronomers 2. Biography, Individual 3. Religion and science 4. Religion and science -- History -- 16th century 5. Writers on science

ISBN 0-19-516598-5; 0-19-517758-4 pa

LC 2003-4247

In recounting the story of Galileo's conflict with the Roman Catholic Church over his heliocentric theory, this book "promotes the idea that Galileo himself contributed to his fate. . . . Structuring their narrative around the several journeys Galileo made from Florence to Rome, Shea and Artigas identify numerous friendly suggestions given to him by supporters to tone things down. . . . In recounting the actual people with whom Galileo fenced, as well as the theological doctrines involved, the authors demythologize the man. Their criticism makes Galileo as interesting a figure as ever." Booklist

Includes bibliographical references

Shearer, Stephen Michael

Beautiful; the life of Hedy Lamarr. Thomas Dunne Books 2010 464p il $29.99   92

1. Actors 2. Biography, Individual

ISBN 978-0-312-55098-1; 0-312-55098-7

LC 2010-13058

This biography chronicles "the life of Hollywood legend Hedy Lamarr, from her cosseted childhood in an assimilated Jewish family in Austria to her early breaks in Max Reinhardt's internationally famous theater company; her scandalous, career-launching nude scene in the Czech film Ecstasy; her tortured first marriage to Jewish Nazi arms manufacturer Friedrich Mandl (dubbed an 'honorary Aryan' by the Third Reich); and her daring escape from the sadistic Mandl and Nazi Germany to Los Angeles and MGM. . . . One finishes the book feeling that one has read a complete portrait of Hedy Lamarr, actor and inventor, a biography that reveals, with drama and wit, how much more there was to this complex, brilliant woman than her ethereal natural beauty." Booklist

Includes bibliographical references

Sheehan, Jason

★ **Cooking** dirty; a story of life, sex, love and death in the kitchen. Farrar, Straus and Giroux 2009 355p $26; pa $15   92

1. Cooks 2. Food critics

ISBN 978-0-374-28921-8; 0-374-28921-2; 978-0-374-53227-7 pa; 0-374-53227-3 pa

LC 2008-47158

"Sheehan's memoir is emphatically not about 'the glam end of cooking' or celebrity chefs, but about 'a straight blue-collar gig,' where the kitchens are staffed by the kind of guys who get off on the fact that the work is insanely grueling. . . . The war stories are as profane and outrageous as you'd expect, and Sheehan finds just the right balance between bravado and humility." Publ Wkly

Sheehan, Neil

A **fiery** peace in a cold war; Bernard Schriever and the ultimate weapon. Random House 2009 534p il $32   92

1. Aeronautics, Military -- Research 2. Aeronautics, Military -- United States -- History 3. Air force officers 4. Astronautics -- United States -- History 5. Ballistic missiles 6. Biography, Individual 7. Cold War 8. Cold war 9. Generals 10. Intercontinental ballistic missiles 11. Nuclear weapons 12. Nuclear weapons -- United States -- History

ISBN 978-0-679-42284-6

LC 2009-02247

The author "has written the best kind of biography, one that tells history through a central character. . . . The real story is of the bureaucratic hand-to-hand combat that let to . . . [the ICBM] finally taking flight. . . . Crafting an engrossing five-hundred-page account of a bureaucratic tussle is no easy task. Yet Sheehan makes it work." Columbia J Rev

Includes bibliographical references (p. [501]-509) and index.

Shelden, Michael

Mark Twain; man in white: the grand adventure of his final years. Random House 2010 xxxix, 484p il $30   92

1. Authors 2. Authors, American 3. Biography, Individual 4. Essayists 5. Humorists 6. Memoirists 7. Novelists 8. Satirists 9. Short story writers 10. Travel writers

ISBN 978-0-679-44800-6; 0-679-44800-4

LC 2009-19719

The author "tells the story of Twain's last 40 months, richly detailing fresh facts new to most readers and fleshing out the conventional Twain biography to make the man's life complete. . . . This superb biography, told in a nonacademic tone, is saturated with sadness, but every reader will be grateful that, finally, Mark Twain appears before us, warts and all." Libr J

Includes bibliographical references

Shen, Aisling Juanjuan

A **tiger's** heart; the story of a modern Chinese woman. Soho Press 2009 309p $24   92

1. Chinese Americans -- Biography 2. Financial analysts 3. Immigrants -- United States 4. Memoirists

ISBN 978-1-56947-586-7; 1-56947-586-5

LC 2009-5426

"Like a suspense novel, this book is impossible to put down. All readers interested in China, as well as memoir fans (especially of success stories), must read this astonishing title." Libr J

Shenk, Joshua Wolf

Lincoln's melancholy; how depression challenged a president and fueled his greatness. Houghton Mifflin 2005 350p $25   92

1. Biography, Individual 2. Lawyers 3. Members of Congress 4. Presidents 5. Presidents -- United States

6. State legislators
ISBN 0-618-55116-6

LC 2005-9653

"An estimable contribution to the Lincoln literature." Booklist

Includes bibliographical references

Shepard, Sadia

The **girl** from foreign; a search for shipwrecked ancestors, forgotten histories, and a sense of home. Penguin Press 2008 364p il map $25.95; pa $16 **92**

1. Jews -- India 2. Memoirists 3. Motion picture directors
ISBN 978-1-59420-151-6; 978-0-14-311577-9 pa

LC 2008-3912

A young Muslim-Christian woman travels to an insular Jewish community in India to unlock her family's secret history.

"A readable account that gives a vivid taste of life in present-day India as well as a poignant glimpse of complicated family relations." Kirkus

Includes bibliographical references

Sherry, Norman

The **life** of Graham Greene. v3 Viking 2004 800p v3 $39.95 **92**

1. Authors 2. Essayists 3. Motion picture critics 4. Novelists 5. Short story writers 6. Travel writers
ISBN 0-670-0342-9

"In the final volume of this definitive life of Greene . . . {Sherry} chronicles years during which Greene turned almost everything—politics, romance, literature, and religion—into reasons for conflict. . . . Nor did Greene's religious faith—eaten away by doubt and self-accusation—provide much late-life serenity or assurance. In narrating Greene's unending struggles, Sherry candidly confronts the author's deplorable lapses in craft and judgment. But, in the end, he delivers a writer who triumphed in his truth-seeking artistry and who even experienced the unexpected final beauty of peace on his Swiss deathbed. Greene's many readers will cherish this poignant and detailed concluding volume to a masterful portrait." Booklist

Shields, Charles J.

And so it goes: Kurt Vonnegut: a life. Henry Holt and Co. 2011 513p il $30 **92**

1. Authors 2. Authors, American 3. Biographers 4. Journalists 5. Novelists 6. Science fiction writers 7. Short story writers
ISBN 978-0-8050-8693-5

LC 2010-45173

"Kurt Vonnegut had a chip on his shoulder when it came to the critics. Despite being one of the most popular writers of his generation, he routinely complained that his work was overlooked, or miscast as high-concept, middle-brow fiction. The publication of Charles J. Shields's fascinating new biography . . . probably won't put this beef to rest, at least among his loyalists. But it does provide a definitive and disturbing account of the late author, whose ambition and talent transformed him from an obscure science fiction writer to a countercultural icon." Boston Globe

Includes bibliographical references

Showalter, Dennis E.

★ **Patton** and Rommel; men of war in the twentieth century. [by] Dennis Showalter. Berkley Caliber 2005 441p $24.95 **92**

1. Army officers 2. Generals 3. Marshals 4. World War, 1939-1945
ISBN 0-425-19346-2

LC 2004-57464

This is a "parallel biography of George Patton and Erwin Rommel. The research is thorough, the quality of the writing superb. . . . [The author] ranks as a scholar who has done them justice, making two complex men and a vast panorama of military history remarkably accessible for experts and lay readers alike." Publ Wkly

Shulman, Alix Kates

To love what is; a marriage transformed. Farrar, Straus and Giroux 2008 160p $22 **92**

1. Authors 2. Biography, Individual 3. Brain damage -- Patients -- Care 4. Feminists 5. Love 6. Marriage 7. Novelists
ISBN 978-0-374-27815-1; 0-374-27815-6

LC 2008-21504

"A fall from a loft bed left author Shulman's 75-year-old husband with traumatic brain injury and utterly dependent on his wife, as she recounts in this deeply affecting memoir of their ordeal together. . . . Carving out time for herself and her writing kept her from having a nervous breakdown, and while her hope at times flagged, Shulman's devotion never faltered, as demonstrated by her candid account." Publ Wkly

Siegel, Frederick F.

The **prince** of the city; Giuliani, New York, and the genius of American life. [by] Fred Siegel, with Harry Siegel. Encounter Books 2005 386p $26.95 **92**

1. Biography, Individual 2. District attorneys 3. Lawyers 4. Mayors 5. Presidential candidates
ISBN 1-594-03084-7

LC 2005-40127

This is a "narrative of Giuliani's eight years (1994-2001) as New York's chief elected executive. The account engagingly portrays how Giuliani made things happen, ranging from Giuliani the man to Giuliani the politician to Giuliani the policy innovator." Choice

Includes bibliographical references

Sielski, Mike

Fading echoes; a true story of rivalry and brotherhood from the football field to the fields of honor. Berkley Books 2009 342p il $24.95 **92**

1. Army officers 2. Football -- Biography 3. Iraq War, 2003- 4. Marines 5. School sports 6. Soldiers -- United States
ISBN 978-0-425-22974-3

LC 2009-17001

"Bryan Buckley was the captain of Central Bucks West and [Colby] Umbrell was one of the leaders of Central Bucks East when their teams clashed in their senior year of 1998. Eight years later, both were officers leading men in combat in Iraq, Buckley as a marine and Umbrell as an army ranger. Both were proudly fighting for ideals in which they believed, and only one would come home alive. Sielski . . . chronicles the lives of these two athletes and illustrates how their personalities and values were formed from interactions with family, friends, coaches, and community. In the process, he writes of much broader topics in contemporary American life: dreams, competition, resolve, war, honor, sacrifice, and true heartbreak." Libr J

Includes bibliographical references

Sikov, Ed

On Sunset Boulevard: the life and times of Billy Wilder. Hyperion 1998 675p il hardcover o.p. pa $17.95 **92**

1. Motion picture directors 2. Screenwriters
ISBN 0-7868-8503-3 pa

LC 98-23504

"Sikov has painted as good a portrait of Billy Wilder, the man, the artist, the showman, the self-promoter, the profitably prescient art collector and the successful businessman, as we are likely to get from the outside." N Y Times Book Rev

Includes filmography

Silko, Leslie

The **turquoise** ledge; [by] Leslie Marmon Silko. Viking 2010 319p $25.95 **92**

1. Authors 2. Authors, American 3. Biography, Individual 4. College teachers 5. Novelists 6. Poets 7. Short story writers 8. Women authors
ISBN 978-0-670-02211-3; 0-670-02211-X

LC 2010-12128

"Silko draws on her Laguna Pueblo, Cherokee, Mexican, and European ancestry and extended family in this richly veined eco-memoir of desert life, spiritual forces, close bonds with animals, and environmental destruction." Booklist

Silverman, Kenneth

Begin again; a biography of John Cage. Alfred A. Knopf 2010 483p il $40 **92**

1. Authors 2. Biography, Individual 3. Composers 4. Essayists 5. Poets
ISBN 1-4000-4437-5; 978-1-4000-4437-5

LC 2010-09525

This is a biography of the American "musician, inventor, composer, poet." (Publisher's note) Index.

In this biography of "one of the most influential composers of the 20th century . . . [the author traces Cage's] innovations chronologically—his breakthrough years as a composer of experimental dance and percussion music, his definitive decade inventing chance-derived music as a member of the New York School of artists and musicians in the '50s, and his later development of indeterminate music, the content of which could be created by the performer. . . . Not

just an exemplary biography, but a significant contribution to the cultural history of American music." Kirkus

Includes bibliographical references

Edgar A. Poe; mournful and never-ending remembrance. HarperCollins Pubs. 1991 564p il hardcover o.p. pa $18 **92**

1. Authors 2. Essayists 3. Poets 4. Short story writers
ISBN 0-06-092331-8 pa

LC 90-56397

The author explains "how Poe's early life influenced his work. He details Poe's turbulent career as poet, short story writer, and editor . . . and traces his literary development through bouts of alcoholism and hallucinations and disputes with literary rivals. An excellent addition to the literature that furthers understanding of America's gothic tale-teller." Libr J

Includes bibliographical references

Sklenicka, Carol

Raymond Carver; a writer's life. Scribner 2009 578p il $35 **92**

1. Authors 2. Authors, American 3. Biography, Individual 4. Poets 5. Short story writers
ISBN 978-0-7432-6245-3; 0-7432-6245-X

LC 2009-27291

This is a biography of the American short-story writer and poet.

The author "spoke with nearly everyone in Carver's orbit, making the book a kind ofhistory of American fiction in the '70s and '80s, capturing the crucial writers (Richard Ford, Tobias Wolff, John Cheever) and sea changes in the publishing industry that made Carver such a powerful influence on writers today. The epic biography that Carver deserves." Kirkus

Includes bibliographical references

Skloot, Floyd

The **wink** of the zenith; the shaping of a writer's life. University of Nebraska Press 2008 231p $24.95 **92**

1. Authors 2. Essayists 3. Novelists 4. Poets
ISBN 978-0-8032-1119-3; 0-8032-1119-8

LC 2008-3674

"Novelist and poet Skloot was struck by a brain virus in 1988, which left him unable to write novels. The memoir form 'saved' him, and in his latest he ponders the proclivities and circumstances that led him to become a writer. . . . [This book is] wise, thoughtful, and gently humorous." Booklist

Skloot, Rebecca

★ The **immortal** life of Henrietta Lacks. Crown Publishers 2010 369p il $26 **92**

1. African American women -- Biography 2. Cancer 3. Cancer patients 4. Homemakers 5. Human experimentation in medicine
ISBN 978-1-4000-5217-2

LC 2009-31785

"A thorny and provocative book about cancer, racism, scientific ethics and crippling poverty, 'The Immortal Life of Henrietta Lacks' also floods over you like a narrative dam break, as if someone had managed to distill and purify the more addictive qualities of 'Erin Brockovich,' 'Midnight in the Garden of Good and Evil' and 'The Andromeda Strain.' More than 10 years in the making, it feels like the book Ms. Skloot was born to write." N Y Times Book Rev

Includes bibliographical references

Slater, Michael

★ **Charles** Dickens. Yale University Press 2009 696p il $35   **92**
1. Authors 2. Authors, English 3. Biography, Individual 4. Novelists
ISBN 978-0-300-11207-8; 0-300-11207-6
LC 2009-26834

This "biography actually feels somewhat austere: Slater sticks to the known Gradgrindian facts, emphasizes the writing and public performances, seldom goes in for much scene-painting or gratuitous anecdote, and refuses to speculate unduly without evidence. . . . For anybody who wants to know more about this dynamo of Victorian letters, Michael Slater's superb biography is the one to read." Washington Post Book World

Includes bibliographical references (p. 624-626)

Slater, Robert

No such thing as over-exposure; inside the life and celebrity of Donald Trump. Prentice Hall 2005 xxiv, 247p $24.95   **92**
1. Airline executives 2. Construction industry executives 3. Hotel executives 4. Real estate developers
ISBN 0-13-149734-0
LC 2004-116294

Donald Trump "is not so easily understood, but this book goes a long way toward defining him." Booklist

Includes bibliographical references

Slaughter, Thomas P.

The **beautiful** soul of John Woolman, apostle of abolition. Hill and Wang 2008 464p il map   **92**
1. Abolitionists 2. Authors 3. Biography, Individual 4. Clergy 5. Diarists 6. Essayists 7. Quaker leaders 8. Slavery and the church -- Society of Friends
ISBN 0-8090-9514-9; 978-0-8090-9514-8
LC 2008-22765

This is a biography of the New Jersey Quaker abolitionist. Index.

"Any understanding of the history of social reform in America begins with Woolman, and understanding Woolman begins here." Kirkus

Includes bibliographical references and index

Slawenski, Kenneth

★ **J.D.** Salinger; a life. Random House 2011 450p il $27; ebook $27   **92**
1. Authors 2. Authors, American 3. Novelists 4. Short story writers
ISBN 978-1-4000-6951-4; 978-0-679-60479-2 ebook
LC 201008926

This biography is "a highly informative effort to assess the arc of Salinger's career, the themes of his fiction, and his influence on 20th-century American literature. . . . Slawenski describes Salinger's three marriages, records his contentious relationships with his publishers, his special re-

lationship with the New Yorker, and Slawenski's assiduous research allows him to identify and assess many obscure and unpublished stories. In total, an invaluable work that sheds fascinating light on the willfully elusive author." Publ Wkly

Includes bibliographical references

Slotten, Ross A.

The **heretic** in Darwin's court; the life of Alfred Russel Wallace. Columbia University Press 2004 602p il maps $77.50; pa $25   **92**
1. Biography, Individual 2. Naturalists 3. Writers on science
ISBN 0-231-13010-4; 0-231-13011-2 pa
LC 2003-68833

"With a narrative of almost 500 pages, the biography was clearly a labor of love for the author, who is a medical doctor and a Wallace enthusiast. Although some readers may find the amount of material overwhelming, it is quite accessible to general audiences." Sci Books Films

Includes bibliographical references

Smardz Frost, Karolyn

★ **I've** got a home in glory land; a lost tale of the Underground Railroad. Farrar, Straus & Giroux 2006 450p il map $30   **92**
1. Biography, Individual 2. Coach drivers 3. Slaves 4. Underground railroad
ISBN 978-0-374-16481-2; 0-374-16481-9
LC 2006-64

The author's "fascination with her subject and love of detailed historical documentation are evident in this engrossing look at a couple who defied slavery with their escape and their assistance to other fugitive slaves." Booklist

Includes bibliographical references

Smiley, Jane

The **man** who invented the computer; the biography of John Atanasoff, digital pioneer. Doubleday 2010 246p il $25.95   **92**
1. Biography, Individual 2. Computer scientists 3. Inventors 4. Mathematicians 5. Physicists
ISBN 978-0-385-52713-2; 0-385-52713-6
LC 2010-18887

"Engrossing. Smiley takes science history and injects it with a touch of noir and an exciting clash of vanities." Kirkus

Includes bibliographical references

Smith, David James

Young Mandela. Little, Brown 2010 405p il **92**
1. Anti-apartheid movement 2. Apartheid 3. Biography, Individual 4. Human rights activists 5. Nobel laureates for peace 6. Political leaders 7. Political prisoners 8. Presidents
ISBN 0-316-03548-3; 978-0-316-03548-4
LC 2010-31883

This is an account of Mandela's life from boyhood through the early 1960s. Bibliography. Index.

"No hagiography, Smith's measured study qualifies, lends nuance to, and even contradicts the mythology around Mandela's background and formative influences." Publ Wkly

Includes bibliographical references

Smith, Jane S.

The **garden** of invention; Luther Burbank and the business of breeding plants. Penguin Press 2009 354p il $25.95 **92**

1. Biography, Individual 2. Horticulturists 3. Plant breeding 4. Plant breeding -- United States -- History

ISBN 978-1-59420-209-4

LC 2009-1822

"An accessible introduction to an agricultural innovator that gives equal weight to his life of experimentation and what it has meant for society." Kirkus

Includes bibliographical references

Smith, Janna Malamud

My father is a book; a memoir of Bernard Malamud. Houghton Mifflin 2006 292p $24 **92**

1. Authors 2. Biography, Individual 3. Novelists 4. Short story writers

ISBN 0-618-69166-9; 978-0-618-69166-1

LC 2005-24736

"Analytical without being acrimonious, honest without wallowing in self-preening exposure, this is a wise, generous book full of insights on what it's like to be a writer and to be a writer's daughter." Christ Sci Monit

Includes bibliographical references

Smith, Jean Edward

FDR. Random House 2007 858p il $35 **92**

1. Biography, Individual 2. Governors 3. Handicapped 4. Philatelists 5. Presidents 6. Presidents -- United States

ISBN 978-1-4000-6121-1; 1-4000-6121-0

LC 2006-43087

Smith's "FDR is at once a careful, intelligent synopsis of the existing Roosevelt scholarship (the sheer bulk of which is huge) and a meticulous reinterpretation of the man and his record. Smith pays more attention to Roosevelt's personal life than have most previous biographers. He is openly sympathetic yet ready to criticize when that is warranted, and to do so in sharp terms; he conveys the full flavor and import of Roosevelt's career without ever bogging down in detail." Washington Post Book World

Includes bibliographical references

Smith, Patti, 1946-

★ **Just** kids. Ecco 2010 278p il $27; pa $16 **92**

1. Biography, Individual 2. Poets, American 3. Rock musicians

ISBN 978-0-06-621131-2; 0-06-621131-X; 978-0-06-093622-8 pa; 0-06-093622-3 pa

The author writes about her relationship with the photographer Robert Mapplethorpe in the late 1960s and 1970s.

This "is one of the best books ever written on becoming an artist—not the race for online celebrity and corporate sponsorship that often passes for artistic success these days, but the far more powerful, often difficult journey toward the ecstatic experience of capturing radiance of imagination on a page or stage or photographic paper." Washington Post

Smock, Raymond W.

Booker T. Washington; black leadership in the age of Jim Crow. [by] Raymond W. Smock. Ivan R. Dee 2009 223p il $26 **92**

1. African American educators 2. African Americans -- Biography 3. Authors 4. Civil rights activists 5. Educators 6. Memoirists 7. Nonfiction writers 8. Slaves

ISBN 978-1-56663-725-1; 1-56663-725-2

LC 2009-3277

The author "examines Washington's legacy and how he came to be alternately lauded and lambasted for his practical approach to racism following Reconstruction: to build a school to prepare blacks to occupy the unchallenged place set aside for them in the Jim Crow South. . . . This is a nuanced portrait of an enigmatic man of enduring contribution to black leadership." Booklist

Includes bibliographical references

Snyder, Timothy

The **Red** Prince; the secret lives of a Habsburg archduke. Basic Books 2008 344p il map $27.95 **92**

1. Biography, Individual 2. Communism -- Soviet Union -- History 3. Emperors 4. Empresses 5. Princes 6. Spies

ISBN 978-0-465-00237-5; 0-465-00237-4

LC 2008-2783

"As a scion of the Austrian imperial family, [Wilhelm von Habsburg] had many of the predictable aristocratic attributes, including a grasp of several languages, skill at swordplay, and a sense that he was entitled to command and rule others. Yet he turned his back on his family and a life of comfortable exile to engage in a series of dangerous escapades until his death, in a Soviet prison hospital in 1948. Along the way, von Habsburg led Ukrainian nationalists in a futile fight to establish an independent state, fought the Nazis, plotted against the Soviets, and managed to acquire a diverse collection of sexual conquests. Snyder portrays him as a restless spirit with dreams of grandeur who was attractive, even charismatic, without being particularly admirable." Booklist

Includes bibliographical references

Sobel, Dava

Galileo's daughter; a historical memoir of science, faith, and love. Walker & Co. 1999 420p $27 **92**

1. Astronomers 2. Astronomers -- Italy -- Biography 3. Children of prominent persons 4. Nuns 5. Writers on science

ISBN 0-8027-1343-2

LC 99-23885

"Sobel has a remarkable ability to explain technical subjects without being simplistic or pedantic. There is a tremendous amount of fascinating detail in this work, and yet it reads as smoothly and compellingly as fiction." Libr J

Includes bibliographical references

Solomon, Deborah

Jackson Pollock; a biography. Cooper Square Press 2001 287p il pa $17.95 **92**

1. Abstract expressionism 2. Artists 3. Artists -- United

States 4. Painters

ISBN 978-0-8154-1182-6; 0-8154-1182-0

LC 2001-28915

A biography of the American abstract expressionist painter.

"A concisely written biography; the footnotes indicate solid research." Libr J

Includes bibliographical references

Solomon, Dorothy Allred

Predators, prey, and other kinfolk; growing up in polygamy. Norton 2003 399p $24.95   **92**

1. Memoirists 2. Mormons 3. Polygamy 4. Teachers

ISBN 0-393-04946-9

LC 2003-1044

The author "provides a remarkably balanced account of the contradictions and pressures she experienced both from within her family and from the surrounding culture." Libr J

Includes bibliographical references

Solomon, Maynard

Beethoven; 2nd rev ed; Schirmer Bks. 1998 554p hardcover o.p. pa $19.95   **92**

1. Composers

ISBN 978-0-8256-7268-2 pa; 0-8256-7268-6 pa

LC 97-51363

In this revision, "Solomon approaches his subject from myriad different angles—historical, psychological, sociological, and aesthetic—to treat the reader to a view of Beethoven, his music, and his era that answers long-standing questions and reveals new ways of considering the composer, his works, and his motivation." Libr J

Mozart; a life. HarperCollins Pubs. 1995 640p il hardcover o.p. pa $22.95   **92**

1. Composers

ISBN 0-06-019046-9; 978-0-06-088344-7 pa; 0-06-088344-8 pa

LC 94-42277

"The author explores Mozart's life and works with a wealth of facts that were culled from 18th-century sources as well as from the most recent scholarship. Mozart and his family emerge in a new light from this mass of well-chosen detail through Solomon's own convincing interpretation of events and relationships. Appropriate musical and pictorial examples, which will appeal to both scholarly and casual readers, accompany the text." Libr J

Includes bibliographical references

Sondheim, Stephen

Finishing the hat; collected lyrics (1954-1981) with attendant comments, principles, heresies, grudges, whines and anecdotes. Knopf 2010 445p il $39.95   **92**

1. Biography, Individual 2. Composers 3. Lyricists 4. Musical theater -- History 5. Musicals 6. Popular music -- Writing and publishing 7. Songs

ISBN 978-0-679-43907-3; 0-679-43907-2

LC 2010-11056

"There's so much more to 'Finishing the Hat' than witty, profound and groundbreaking lyrics. In chapters and annotations every budding lyricist and musical fan will relish,

Sondheim covers everything from the history of musical theater and views of major lyricists to stories about the making of his shows and lessons in the craft of lyric writing. . . . The 80-year-old Sondheim, not surprisingly, turns out to be a remarkable writer, even when no rhymes are in sight. He's at turns funny and poignant, ornery and instructive. His honesty often stings, especially in analytical sidebars that detail the varied flaws of such heralded lyric-writing comrades as Noel Coward, Ira Gershwin, Lorenz Hart, Alan Jay Lerner and (heresy!) even Oscar Hammerstein II, his mentor." Cleveland Plain Dealer

Includes bibliographical references

Sonnenberg, Susanna

Her last death; a memoir. Scribner 2008 273p $24   **92**

1. Authors 2. Biography, Individual 3. Columnists 4. Journalists

ISBN 978-0-7432-9108-8; 0-7432-9108-5

LC 2007-3515

Sonnenberg's memoir illuminates her resolve to forge her independence, to become a woman capable of trust and to be a good mother to her own children after being raised by a mother who was a compulsive liar and a drug user.

"A heartbreaking yet wickedly entertaining portrait of a magically seductive, immensely flawed mother who fails dramatically as a parent and of a daughter who learns to trust and love others despite an orphanlike upbringing marked by disillusion." Libr J

Sontag, Susan

Reborn; journals and notebooks, 1947-1963. edited by David Rieff. Farrar, Straus and Giroux 2008 318p $24   **92**

1. Authors 2. Authors, American 3. Biography, Individual 4. Essayists 5. Literary critics 6. Novelists 7. Short story writers 8. Women authors

ISBN 978-0-374-10074-2; 0-374-10074-8

LC 2008-34247

"As a psychic collage, Reborn is far more fascinating than the sum of its parts: lists of errands, scraps of dialogue, notes on the breakup of a marriage. An essential tension animates almost every page. Sontag's theoretical mind always wants to be totalizing—to sum up, distill, command. But journal entries are, like the lives they document, provisional, incomplete, ragged. The resulting clash—with its canceled insights, non sequiturs, and self-critical marginalia—often reads like a brilliant pomo bildungsroman: A Portrait of the Theorist As a Young Woman," New York

Sorensen, Theodore C.

Counselor; a life at the edge of history. [by] Ted Sorensen. HarperCollins 2008 556p il $27.95   **92**

1. Biography, Individual 2. Government officials 3. Lawyers 4. Members of Congress 5. Presidential advisers 6. Presidents 7. Senators

ISBN 978-0-06-079871-0; 0-06-079871-8

LC 2007-47328

This is a memoir by President Kennedy's advisor and speechwriter.

"This book is instantly essential for any student of the period. It fills gaps in the historical record; it vividly conveys life inside the administration; and it generously dishes anecdotes." Washington Post Book World

Soskice, Janet Martin

The **sisters** of Sinai; how two lady adventurers discovered the hidden Gospels. [by] Janet Soskice. Alfred A. Knopf 2009 316p $27.95   **92**
    1. Biblical scholars 2. Biography, Individual 3. Travelers 4. Twins
    ISBN 978-1-4000-4133-6; 1-4000-4133-3; 1400041333; 9781400041336

            LC 2009011098

This is a biography of Agnes and Margaret Smith, sisters "whose travels to St. Catherine's Monastery in the Sinai desert resulted in the . . . discovery of one of the oldest manuscripts of the Gospels ever found. . . . The Sinai Palimpsest, or Lewis Codex, as it came to be called, would prove to date to the late fourth century; the translation it preserved . . . [dated] from the late second century A.D." (N Y Times Book Rev) Bibliography. Index.

This book "is by turns a rattling adventure yarn—thick with roving Bedouin and ancient tombs—and a testament to the power of perseverance." Washington Post Book World
Includes bibliographical references

Sounes, Howard

Fab; an intimate life of Paul McCartney. Da Capo Press 2010 634p il $29.95   **92**
    1. Rock musicians 2. Singers 3. Songwriters
    ISBN 978-0-306-81783-0

            LC 2010-936124

"Divided into two equally large sections—'With the Beatles' and 'After the Beatles'—Fab covers all the highlights of McCartney's life and long career: his early days in Liverpool; his meeting with John Lennon; the craziness of Beatlemania; his solo albums; the creation and collapse of his post-Beatles band, Wings; his marriage to Linda Eastman; his last meetings with Lennon; his drug bust in Japan; his forays into classical music; his disastrous second marriage to Heather Mills. . . . Sounes is often brutally honest, offering a full portrait—warts and all—of one of the most famous men of the modern era. A must for Beatles and McCartney fans." Booklist
Includes bibliographical references

Soyinka, Wole

★ **You** must set forth at dawn; a memoir. Random House 2006 499p map $26.95   **92**
    1. Authors 2. Biography, Individual 3. Dramatists 4. Essayists 5. Memoirists 6. Nobel laureates for literature 7. Novelists 8. Poets
    ISBN 0-375-50365-X; 978-0-375-50365-8

"By turns panoramic and intimate, ruminative and politically resolute, Soyinka's memoir is a dense but intriguing conversation between a writer and his times." Publ Wkly

Spencer, Charles Edward Maurice Spencer

Prince Rupert; the last cavalier. [by] Charles Spencer. Weidenfeld and Nicolson 2007 430p il $37.95; pa $19.95   **92**
    1. Admirals 2. Biography, Individual 3. Generals 4.

Princes
    ISBN 978-0-297-84610-9; 0-297-84610-8; 978-0-7538-2401-6 pa; 0-7538-2401-9 pa

"This delightful book could change the nonspecialist reader's perception of the English Civil War era as tedious while impressing those already familiar with it. . . . highly recommended for any college, high school, or public library." Libr J
Includes bibliographical references

Spender, Matthew

From a high place; a life of Arshile Gorky. University of California Press 2000 417p il pa $21.95   **92**
    1. Artists 2. Artists -- United States 3. Painters
    ISBN 0-520-22548-1; 978-0-520-22548-0

            LC 00-28715

"Spender, a sculptor and writer and the husband of Gorky's daughter, provides a personal and intimate biography of the Armenian American abstract expressionist." Libr J
Includes bibliographical references

Sperber, Ann M.

Murrow, his life and times; {by} A. M. Sperber; with a preface by Neil Hickey. Fordham Univ. Press 1998 xxvi, 795p il $35; pa $25   **92**
    1. Government officials 2. Journalists 3. Journalists -- United States -- Biography 4. Radio reporters 5. Television news anchors 6. Television reporters
    ISBN 0-8232-1881-3; 0-8232-1882-1 pa

            LC 98-52507

This "ambitious exploration of Murrow's life places his story in the foreground of what is, as well, a panorama of the years 1935-65." N Y Times Book Rev
Includes bibliographical references

Spitz, Bob

Dylan; a biography. with a discography by Jeff Friedman. Norton 1991 664p il pa $19.95   **92**
    1. Folk musicians 2. Rock musicians 3. Singers 4. Songwriters
    ISBN 0-393-30769-7

            LC 88-12912

"Lamenting the impenetrable mythology that surrounds singer/songwriter Bob Dylan . . . Spitz accomplishes his demystification through a sometimes fanciful reconstruction of Dylan's life, replete with sordid examples of his reputedly capricious personality. Although the relevance of such treatment is questionable and his often lurid prose will be objectionable to some, Spitz gives a fascinating portrayal of one of the most influential and complex figures in popular music." Choice
Includes discography and bibliographical references

Spitz, Marc

Bowie; a biography. Crown 2009 429p il $26.99   **92**
    1. Actors 2. Rock musicians 3. Singers 4. Songwriters
    ISBN 978-0-307-39396-8

            LC 2009-16806

For this biography, the author "concentrates on the complex evolution of Bowie's music to deliver an evenhanded, critically thorough, while still reverential life of the Thin White Duke." Publ Wkly

Includes bibliographical references

Spoto, Donald

Notorious; the life of Ingrid Bergman. Da Capo Press 2001 474p il pa $22 **92**

1. Actors

ISBN 978-0-306-81030-5; 0-306-81030-1

The author's "perceptions about Bergman personally and professionally are keen, and the narrative reads like a full-bodied story, not just a listing of professional credits and personal landmarks." Booklist

Includes bibliographical references

Spellbound by beauty; Alfred Hitchcock and his leading ladies. Harmony Books 2008 xxiii, 324p il $25.95 **92**

1. Biography, Individual 2. Motion picture actors and actresses -- United States -- Biography 3. Motion picture directors 4. Motion picture producers and directors

ISBN 978-0-307-35130-2; 0-307-35130-0

LC 2008-08922

The third volume in a trilogy exploring the life and work of the legendary director examines Hitchcock's life in terms of his relationships with the actresses in his films, including Ingrid Bergman, Grace Kelly, Kim Novak, and Tippi Hedren, in a study of his films, rise to fame and power, artistic legacy, unconventional marriage, and obsessions.

"Relying on hours of personal interviews with both Hitchcock and his various players, Spoto shines an admiring yet unflinching light on one of the most celebrated directors in history." Publ Wkly

Includes bibliographical references

The **kindness** of strangers: the life of Tennessee Williams. Da Capo Press 1997 409p il pa $18.50 **92**

1. Authors 2. Dramatists 3. Novelists 4. Short story writers

ISBN 0-306-80805-6

LC 97-8428

"Based on hundreds of interviews with those who knew him and on other previously unpublished material, {the author} presents a portrait of Tennessee Williams which is both respectful and sensitive." Wilson Libr Bull

Includes bibliographical references

Spring, Justin

Secret historian; the life and times of Samuel Steward, professor, tattoo artist, and sexual renegade. Farrar, Straus and Giroux 2010 478p il $32.50; ebook $16.99 **92**

1. Authors 2. Authors, American 3. Biography, Individual 4. College teachers 5. Novelists 6. Short story writers 7. Tattoo artists

ISBN 978-0-374-28134-2; 0-374-28134-3; 978-1-4299-3294-3 ebook; 1-4299-3294-5 ebook

LC 2009-43086

"This is a rich and exuberant biography of a man who deserves to be better known, as well as a rare window on gay life in an era known mostly for its furtiveness and repression." Economist

Includes bibliographical references

Spurling, Hilary

Matisse the master; a life of Henri Matisse, the conquest of colour, 1909-1954. Knopf 2005 xxi, 511p il $40 **92**

1. Artists 2. Painters

ISBN 0-679-43429-1

LC 2004-51074

"Spurling's rich, flexible style is well attuned to the rigors and flights of Matisse's creative life." Publ Wkly

Includes bibliographical references

Pearl Buck in China; journey to The Good Earth. Simon & Schuster 2010 304p il map $27; ebook $12.99 **92**

1. Authors 2. Authors, American 3. Biographers 4. Biography, Individual 5. Essayists 6. Memoirists 7. Nobel laureates for literature 8. Novelists 9. Short

ISBN 978-1-4165-4042-7; 1-4165-4042-3; 978-1-4391-8044-0 ebook; 1-4391-8044-X ebook

LC 2010-07712

This is a biography of the American author of The Good Earth (1931).

The author's "account of Buck's 'rootless and fractured existence' provides a fascinating dissection of the tortured relationships between a man of God, the hapless wife sucked into supporting his mission and their increasingly sceptical daughter, Pearl, who, in 1933, publicly turned her back on her late father's church. It is also just as revealing about the no less tortured relationship between the West and China in the early part of the last century." Economist

Includes bibliographical references

The **unknown** Matisse; v1 a life of Henri Matisse. Knopf 1998 xxv, 480p v1 il $40 **92**

1. Artists 2. Painters

ISBN 0-679-43428-3

LC 97-46816

In this first volume of the author's biography of the French artist, Spurling focuses on Matisse's training as an art student in Paris.

This volume "makes for a gripping read and reveals much about the artist's early development." Publ Wkly

Includes bibliographical references

Sragow, Michael

Victor Fleming; an American movie master. Pantheon 2008 645p il $40 **92**

1. Biography, Individual 2. Motion picture directors 3. Motion picture producers and directors -- Biography 4. Motion pictures -- United States -- History

ISBN 978-0-375-40748-2; 0-375-40748-0

LC 2008-15255

Fleming "was the director MGM tapped to take over two thorny, unwieldy and expensive projects—'The Wizard of Oz' and 'Gone With the Wind'—and make them into enormous successes. Had he never completed those two epics, Fleming's other cinematic triumphs had already sealed his reputation. They included 'The Virginian,' 'Red Dust,' 'Mantrap,' 'Bombshell' and 'Captains Courageous.' . . . Mr. Sragow deftly takes us through the twists and turns of Fleming's life, with a vital sense of time and place. We learn much not only about Fleming, but also about his contemporaries and the Hollywood they lived in." Washington Times

Includes bibliographical references and filmography

Stanley, Ralph

Man of constant sorrow; my life and times. [by] Ralph Stanley with Eddie Dean. Gotham Books 2009 452p $27.50   **92**
1. Banjo players 2. Bluegrass music 3. Bluegrass musicians
ISBN 978-1-592-40425-4

LC 2009-21920

A memoir by the bluegrass singer and banjo player.

"Unashamedly old-fashioned, opinionated and prickly, . . . [the author is] at his best recalling his backwoods upbringing, the vicissitudes of the bluegrass road, the murder of one of his lead singers, regional Democratic politics, the power of gospel music and old-time religion and the fast-vanishing South of his boyhood. An often tart yet affecting music memoir." Kirkus

Stannard, Martin

Muriel Spark; the biography. W.W. Norton & Co. 2010 xxvi, 627p il $35   **92**
1. Authors 2. Authors, Scottish 3. Biographers 4. Novelists 5. Short story writers 6. Women authors
ISBN 978-0-393-05174-2

LC 2009-47982

This is "among the richest and most satisfying literary biographies of our time: not only a portrait of the artist herself but also a rendering of her literary and social context and a judicious examination of her works." Wall Street J

Includes bibliographical references

Stanton, Tom

Road to Cooperstown; a father, two sons, and the journey of a lifetime. Thomas Dunne Bks. 2003 260p il $24.95; pa $13.95   **92**
1. Artists 2. Baseball -- Biography 3. Painters
ISBN 0-312-30350-5; 0-312-33118-5 pa

LC 2003-40862

The author "examines family, fatherhood, life and, of course, baseball while on a road trip that was a lifetime in the making." Publ Wkly

Stashower, Daniel

Teller of tales: the life of Arthur Conan Doyle. Holt & Co. 1999 472p il hardcover o.p. pa $16 **92**
1. Authors 2. Authors, Scottish 3. Mystery writers 4. Novelists
ISBN 0-8050-6684-5 pa

LC 98-35059

"Stashower has done an admirable job in creating both a general, well-researched biography of a complex literary giant and in providing insights into the origins and apparent contradictions of his later beliefs." Publ Wkly

Includes bibliographical references

Steavenson, Wendell

The **weight** of a mustard seed; the intimate story of an Iraqi General and his family during thirty years of tyranny. Collins Pub. Group 2009 288p $24.99   **92**
1. Biography, Individual 2. Generals
ISBN 978-0-06-172178-6; 0-06-172178-6

LC 2008-24402

This is "a masterly and elegantly told story that weaves together the Iraqi past and present." N Y Times Book Rev

Steffens, Lincoln

The **autobiography** of Lincoln Steffens; foreword by Thomas C. Leonard. Heyday Books 2005 882p il pa $21.95   **92**
1. Authors 2. Biographers 3. Essayists 4. Journalists 5. Social reformers 6. Writers on politics
ISBN 1-59714-016-3

LC 2005-27009

The life of an American reporter, journalist, student of ethics and politics.

"Here is a textbook on journalism; a treasure house for the historian of that wave of social idealism that shook the United States from 1900 to 1917; a casebook for the psychologist of political types. Above all it is the vivid diary of a bold and humane pilgrim." Survey

Stein, Gertrude

The **autobiography** of Alice B. Toklas. Modern Lib. 1993 342p hardcover o.p. pa $13   **92**
1. Authors 2. Authors, American 3. Essayists 4. Literary critics 5. Memoirists 6. Novelists 7. Poets 8. Private secretaries
ISBN 0-679-60081-7; 0-679-72463-X pa

LC 93-15339

"The book is really Stein's autobiography, presented as though written by her secretary, Alice Toklas. The book provoked a rejoinder from various Parisian artists and writers, Testimony Against Gertrude Stein (1935). . . . For the average reader, however, Stein's book holds much fascination in its views of Parisian life and personalities, and the whole is offered in a genuinely witty style." Benet's Reader's Ency of Am Lit

Steinberg, Jonathan

Bismarck; Jonathan Steinberg. Oxford University Press 2011 x, 577 p., [16] p. of platesp $34.95 **92**
1. Biographies 2. Statesmen -- Germany -- Biography 3. William II, German Emperor, 1859-1941
ISBN 978-0-19-978252-9; 0-19-978252-0; 9780199782529

LC 2010045387

The author of this biography of German Chancellor Otto von Bismarck argues that his subject remains rthe most remarkable and complex political leader of the nineteenth century' . . . [Jonathan] Steinberg sets out to understand how the man with 'an extraordinary, gigantic selft did it. He reminds readers that Bismarck succeeded only as long as he was indispensable to his royal master and ultimately he fell when Wilhelm II had had enough. Prof. Steinberg also uses his knowledge of nineteenth-century European history . . . to describe the stage on which Bismarck acted. In addition he pays great attention to original sources and Bismarck's collected works. (Contemporary Review) Index.

"This is a beautifully written book that provides a stimulating and enjoyable introduction to the history of modern Europe." New Statesman

Includes bibliographical references (p. [528]-537) and index

Steinberg, Neil

Drunkard; a hard-drinking life. Dutton 2008 270p $24.95; pa $15   **92**
1. Alcoholics -- Rehabilitation 2. Journalists 3. Nonfiction writers
ISBN 978-0-5259-5065-3; 0-5259-5065-6; 978-0-4522-9543-8 pa
LC 2007-51603

"Forced by the court into rehab, Steinberg chronicles his journey to sobriety, following a circuitous route that included plenty of stops in local watering holes along the way. . . . Frank, funny, and insightful, Steinberg writes the book of his life." Booklist

Steinke, Darcey

Easter everywhere; a memoir. Bloomsbury USA 2007 225p $24.95   **92**
1. Authors 2. Biography, Individual 3. College teachers 4. Novelists 5. Spiritual life
ISBN 978-1-582-34530-7; 1-582-34530-9
LC 2006-31637

"This book is an excellent account of a writer going head-to-head with the divine and finding some inner quiet—even in the darkest corners of her imagination." Time Out New York

Steinmeyer, Jim

Charles Fort; the man who invented the supernatural. J. P. Tarcher/Penguin 2008 332p il $24.95   **92**
1. Curiosities and wonders 2. Parapsychologists 3. Parapsychology 4. Supernatural 5. Writers on science
ISBN 978-1-58542-640-9; 1-58542-640-7
LC 2008-5961

"Steinmeyer is an elegant and unobtrusive author who shows us an entirely fascinating, shy, and witty man. . . . This book is not to be missed." Libr J

Includes bibliographical references

The **last** greatest magician in the world; Howard Thurston versus Houdini & the battles of the American wizards. Jeremy P. Tarcher/Penguin, a member of Penguin Group 2011 377p il $26.95   **92**
1. Magicians 2. Nonfiction writers
ISBN 978-1-58542-845-8
LC 2010-35384

This is a "an engaging full-length biography of the man Orson Welles called 'the master.' . . . Tracing the magician's rise to fame, this volume neatly juggles his marriages and his magic with his triumphs, travails, showmanship, and marketing ballyhoo." Publ Wkly

Stern, Jessica

Denial; a memoir of terror. Ecco Press 2010 300p $24.99; ebook $11.99   **92**
1. Biography, Individual 2. Chemists 3. College teachers 4. International relations specialists 5. Rape victims
ISBN 978-0-06-162665-4; 978-0-06-200011-8 ebook

A scientist and expert on terrorism and post-traumatic stress disorder describes her own journey through trauma and its lingering effects after repressing and disassociating her own ordeal as the victim of an unsolved sexual assault as a teenager.

"Though the narrative continually threatens to spiral into stream-of-consciousness ramblings, Stern always manages to hold it together, thus lending a sense of the floating dissociation she often feels while still holding the narrative together as a cohesive whole. She successfully unearths difficult emotional terrain without sinking into utter subjectivity and maintains an orderly progression without becoming clinical. A disturbing, captivating memoir." Kirkus

Includes bibliographical references

Stiles, T. J.

★ The **first** tycoon; the epic life of Cornelius Vanderbilt. Alfred A. Knopf 2009 719p $37.50 **92**
1. Biography, Individual 2. Businessmen 3. Railroads -- History 4. Steamboats -- History
ISBN 978-0-375-41542-5; 0-375-41542-4
LC 2008-47879

This is a biography of the American steamship and railroad magnate.

"This is a mighty—and mighty confident—work, one that moves with force and conviction and imperious wit through Vanderbilt's noisy life and times. . . . This is state-of-the-art biography, crisper and more piquant than a 600-page book has any right to be." N Y Times (Late N Y Ed)

Includes bibliographical references

Stone, Robert

Prime green; remembering the sixties. Ecco 2007 229p il $25.95   **92**
1. Authors 2. Biography, Individual 3. Nineteen sixties 4. Novelists 5. Screenwriters
ISBN 0-06-019816-8; 978-0-06-019816-9
LC 2006-46351

The author "is a born storyteller, with a wonderful feel for place and character that vividly evokes the cultural gulf America crossed in that decade." Publ Wkly

Strachey, Lytton

Elizabeth and Essex; a tragic history. Harcourt Brace & Co. 1928 296p il hardcover o.p. pa $14 **92**
1. Conspirators 2. Courtiers 3. Generals 4. Queens 5. Royal favorites
ISBN 0-15-602761-5 pa

The story "begins where the conventional biography recedes, when the queen at fifty-three falls in love with a lad of twenty—a favorite whom she forgives again and again and sends at last to the scaffold." Chicago Public Libr

Includes bibliographical references

Streb, Elizabeth

Streb; how to become an extreme action hero. foreword by Anna Deavere Smith & introduction by Peggy Phelan. Feminist Press 2010 201p il pa $18.95   **92**
1. Biography, Individual 2. Choreographers 3. Dance 4. Dancers 5. Human beings -- Attitude and movement 6. Human locomotion 7. Movement, Psychology of
ISBN 978-1-55861-656-1

        LC 2009-52614

"In this dizzying, inspirational self-help memoir, choreographer and performer Streb details her lifelong exploration of movement, the body, and time while providing brief lessons in math and practical philosophy. . . . In her explanations and experiments, including an unprotected and unrehearsed dive through glass, Streb gives readers news ways to consider the body and its movement, from 'the mechanical measurement of the legs, arms, torso, neck, hips, feet, shoulders, ankles, and knees' to 'the alchemetic processes of the neurological systems.' Accompanied by full-color and black-and-white photographs, Streb's riveting prose should provoke and inspire philosophy students, dancers, and athletes of all kinds." Publ Wkly

Includes bibliographical references

Streissguth, Michael

Johnny Cash; the biography. Da Capo Press 2006 334p il hardcover o.p. pa $15.95   **92**
1. Biography, Individual 2. Country musicians 3. Singers 4. Songwriters
ISBN 0-306-81368-8; 0-306-81565-6 pa

        LC 2006-101191

This is a biography of the country singer and songwriter. The author "leaves us mightily impressed with the volume of Cash's work and the convictions that animate it, and perhaps even more impressed by Cash's endurance of his own self-destructiveness. . . . Streissguth gives everyone interested in Cash a very satisfying book about him." Booklist

Includes bibliographical references

Strickland, Bill

Tour de Lance; the extraordinary story of Lance Armstrong's fight to reclaim the Tour De France. Harmony Books 2010 300p il map $25.99   **92**
1. Athletes 2. Cyclists 3. Olympic athletes
ISBN 978-0-307-58984-2

        LC 2010-4504

This is "the story of Lance Armstrong's return in 2009, after a three-year absence, to the Tour de France. . . . Strickland, who had access to Armstrong's inner circle, enhances it with an eye for detail and an understanding of its importance in the context of cycling's own physical demands and singular history. He reminds readers, as if they need it, of Armstrong's supremacy and laser dedication in the sport. . . . An irresistible account of a story that needed telling." Booklist

Stringer, Caverly

Sleepaway school; stories from a boy's life. [by] Lee Stringer. A Seven Stories Press 1st ed; Seven Stories Press 2004 227p $21.95; pa $13.95   **92**
1. African Americans -- Biography 2. Authors 3.

Homeless 4. Memoirists
ISBN 1-58322-478-5; 1-58322-701-6 pa

        LC 2004-3610

The author "deftly tells a believable, candid and vivid tale of a person scarred by his past." Publ Wkly

Strouse, Charles

Put on a happy face; a Broadway memoir. Union Square Press 2008 326p il $19.95   **92**
1. Composers 2. Composers -- United States 3. Musicians
ISBN 978-1-4027-5889-8; 1-4027-5889-8

        LC 2008-300247

"Three-time Tony Award–winning composer Strouse is best known for the musical Annie and his All in the Family theme, 'Those Were the Days.' While wary of the ghosts that appear, he summons up memories of a career that spans decades, beginning with his Manhattan boyhood, study at Rochester's Eastman School of Music, touring the South with Butterfly McQueen and early collaborations with lyricist Lee Adams. . . . Although he covers his film scores and music for TV commercials, the book's best chapters center on the staging struggles of Annie and Applause, plus breaking racial barriers with Sammy Davis Jr. in Golden Boy. . . . Detailing desperate rewrites, insecurities of theater people, footlight failures and humiliations, as well as theatrical triumphs, Strouse's superb backstage memoir deserves a standing ovation." Publ Wkly

Strouse, Jean

Morgan; American financier. HarperPerennial 2000 796p il pa $18   **92**
1. Art -- Collectors and collecting -- United States -- Biography 2. Bankers 3. Bankers -- United States -- Biography 4. Book collectors 5. Businesspeople 6. Capitalists and financiers -- United States -- Biography 7. Financiers
ISBN 0-06-095589-9; 978-0-06-095589-2

        LC 99-87598

"Strouse is in full command of Pierpont Morgan's personal life, his financial operations, his collecting, and his benefactions, and presents a rich, vivid picture of the background against which they took place. . . . She has written a magnificent biography, which illuminates her subject and his world." N Y Rev Books

Includes bibliographical references

Sturrock, Donald

Storyteller; the authorized biography of Roald Dahl. Simon & Schuster 2010 655p il $30   **92**
1. Authors 2. Authors, English 3. Biography, Individual 4. Children's authors 5. Short story writers
ISBN 978-1-4165-5082-2; 1-4165-5082-8

        LC 2010-07175

The author "first examines incidents and figures in Dahl's ancestry that he judges significant, then retraces his subject's schooling, exploits as an RAF pilot, suave diplomatic attaché and (as a friend puts it) 'one of the biggest cocksmen in Washington,' and finally follows his progress from moderately successful writer of comically macabre short stories for adults to renowned creator of outrageously edgy fantasies for younger readers. . . . Bearing lightly its torrents of references, this examination of the character and career of the iconoclastic writer is as perceptive as it is dishy and exciting." Kirkus

Includes bibliographical references

Sugden, John

Nelson: a dream of glory, 1758-1797. Henry Holt 2004 943p il map $35   **92**

1. Admirals
ISBN 0-8050-7757-X

LC 2004-54057

"This first of a projected two-volume study covers the least familiar period of Nelson's life, from childhood through his rise to international fame in 1797. . . . Sugden's account of Nelson's early career certainly bids fair to fill the gaps, ranging from the future admiral's first years to the disastrous action off Tenerife. . . . Sugden has done well here." Libr J

Includes bibliographical references (p. 883-906)

Sullivan, James

The **hardest** working man; how James Brown saved the soul of America: live at the Boston Garden, 1968. Gotham Books 2008 244p il $25   **92**

1. African American singers 2. Singers 3. Soul musicians
ISBN 978-1-592-40390-5; 1-592-40390-5

LC 2008-13670

"Sullivan examines James Brown's role in saving Boston from the fires and riots that swept the U.S. after Martin Luther King Jr.'s assassination. Booked into Boston Garden the night of April 5, 1968, Brown agreed to put the show on live local TV to give would-be rioters reason to stay home. Garden management wanted to cancel, doubtless to avoid rioting in the Garden, but Brown and Boston's first black city councillor interceded with Mayor Kevin White to prevent cancellation. Sullivan goes further in crediting Brown for keeping the peace than others have, and so doing, he also examines the Godfather of Soul's life and career in the context of the Civil Rights movement. . . . A good record of a pivotal event and a serviceable Brown bio, to boot." Booklist

Includes bibliographical references

Sullivan, Robert

The **Thoreau** you don't know; what the prophet of environmentalism really meant. Collins 2009 354p $25.99   **92**

1. Authors 2. Authors, American 3. Biography, Individual 4. Environmentalism -- United States -- History 5. Essayists 6. Naturalists 7. Nature study 8. Nonfiction writers 9. Pacifists 10. Writers on nature
ISBN 978-0-06-171031-5; 0-06-171031-8

LC 2008-34495

The author "endeavors to free Henry David Thoreau from his calcified reputation as a cantankerous hermit and nature worshipper. Sounding like your favorite teacher who manages to make history fun and relevant, Sullivan vibrantly portrays the sage of Walden as a geeky, curious, compassionate fellow of high intelligence and deep feelings who loved company, music, and long walks." Booklist

Sutherland, John

Stephen Spender; a literary life. Oxford University Press 2005 627p il $40   **92**

1. Authors 2. Biographers 3. Biography, Individual 4. Essayists 5. Literary critics 6. Memoirists 7. Novelists 8. Poets 9. Short story writers
ISBN 0-19517-816-5

LC 2004-09727

"Stephen Spender was one of a generation of Oxford-educated English writers, including W. H. Auden and Christopher Isherwood, who sought to revolutionize literature in the 1930s. In this official account of his life . . . emphasis is appropriately placed on the 1930s, when Spender came to prominence writing prose, short stories, criticism, and journalism in addition to his politically charged poetry. He was as experimental in life as in art, as evidenced by his bisexuality and his loyalty to left-wing Socialist causes." Libr J

Swan, Annalyn

De Kooning: an American master; [by] Mark Stevens and Annalyn Swan. Knopf 2004 731p il $35   **92**

1. Artists 2. Biography, Individual 3. Painters
ISBN 1-4000-4175-9

LC 2004-48297

This is a biography of the twentieth-century painter and a study of his work

This is a "sweeping, authoritative biography. . . . The elusiveness of its subject makes the achievements of 'De Kooning' that much more dazzling. This is a book that traces de Kooning's history, puts him on Freud's couch, plumbs the mysteries of his cryptic and ever-changing work and follows the arc of modern art through much of the 20th century, fusing all these elements into a remarkably lucid narrative." N Y Times (Late N Y ed)

Includes bibliographical references

Symonds, Craig L.

Lincoln and his admirals; Abraham Lincoln, the U.S. Navy, and the Civil War. Oxford University Press 2008 430p il $27.95   **92**

1. Biography, Individual 2. Government officials 3. Lawyers 4. Members of Congress 5. Military officials 6. Newspaper executives 7. Presidents 8. Presidents -- United States 9. Secretaries of the navy 10. State government officials 11. State legislators
ISBN 978-0-19-531022-1; 0-19-531022-5

LC 2008-4251

"For scholars and the general reader alike, an insightful and highly readable treatment of a neglected dimension of Lincoln's wartime leadership." Kirkus

Includes bibliographical references (p. 407-416)

Sypeck, Jeff

Becoming Charlemagne; Europe, Baghdad, and the empires of 800 A.D. ECCO 2006 284p il map $25.95   **92**

1. Emperors 2. Kings and rulers
ISBN 978-0-060-79706-5; 0-06-079706-1

LC 2006-46460

"An inspired, instantly readable work of popular history." Booklist

Includes bibliographical references (p. 249-67)

Szulc, Tad

Fidel; a critical portrait. Post Road Press 2000 703p map pa $18.95   **92**

1. Communist leaders 2. Presidents

ISBN 978-0-380-80888-5; 0-380-80888-9

The author "devotes the greater part of this book to Castro's early, formative years and the forging and triumph of his revolutionary movement. The years of Castro's rule after the Bay of Pigs invasion receive briefer treatment. Well written and very readable." Choice

Includes bibliographical references

Szwed, John F.

Alan Lomax; the man who recorded the world. Viking 2010 438p $29.95   **92**

1. Authors 2. Biography, Individual 3. Folk music 4. Folklorists 5. Musicologists 6. Writers on music

ISBN 978-0-670-02199-4

LC 2010-15332

This is a biography of the American folklorist and ethnomusicologist.

This "biography is a worthy testament to Lomax's passions and ideals, which gifted the world some of the most important American recordings ever made." New Statesman

Includes bibliographical references

Tallchief, Maria

Maria Tallchief; America's prima ballerina. [by] Maria Tallchief with Larry Kaplan. University Press of Florida 2005 368p pa $19.95   **92**

1. Ballerinas -- United States -- Biography. 2. Ballet dancers 3. Dance teachers 4. Indian ballerinas -- United States -- Biography. 5. Osage Indians -- United States -- Biography.

ISBN 0-8130-2846-9; 978-0-8130-2846-0

LC 2005-42211

In this memoir Tallchief focuses "on her remembrances of her years with choreographer George Balanchine. . . . She met Balanchine at the start of her career, when she was with the Ballet Russe de Monte Carlo and Balanchine was about to form a company that would become a precursor to the New York City Ballet. Tallchief subsequently became Balanchine's wife, muse, and prima ballerina, and, though the marriage was short-lived, their artistic partnership endures in Balanchine's works created for Tallchief. She also writes about other stars, but the memoir sparkles when she recalls the subtlety and detail of a movement or the beauty of a musical phrase." Libr J

Talty, Stephan

Escape from the land of snows; the young Dalai Lama's harrowing flight to freedom and the making of a spiritual hero. Crown Publishers 2010 320p map $26; ebook $26   **92**

1. Buddhist leaders 2. Escapes 3. Nobel laureates for peace 4. Political leaders

ISBN 978-0-307-46095-0; 978-0-307-46097-4 ebook

LC 2010-19827

This is a "narrative about the current Dalai Lama's 14-day escape from Chinese-occupied Tibet in 1959. . . . [The author] uses this remarkable historical event to tell the greater story of Tibet's transformation from a veiled kingdom to a world cause, and the Dalai Lama's coming of age from a teenage king and living god to an international spiritual leader. The author effectively gives the reader an introductory lesson in Tibetan history and a sense of the Tibetan people while maintaining the pace of an adventure tale." Kirkus

Includes bibliographical references

Tammet, Daniel

Born on a blue day; inside the extraordinary mind of an autistic savant: a memoir. Free Press 2007 226p il $24; pa $14   **92**

1. Asperger's syndrome 2. Autism 3. Mental calculators 4. Savants (Savant syndrome)

ISBN 1-4165-3507-1; 978-1-4165-3507-2; 1-4165-4901-3 pa; 978-1-4165-4901-7 pa

LC 2006-41331

This "autobiography is as fascinating as Benjamin Franklin's and John Stuart Mill's, both of which are, like his, about the growth of a mind." Booklist

Tankard, Judith B.

Beatrix Farrand; private gardens, public landscapes. Monacelli Press 2009 240p il $60   **92**

1. Garden design 2. Landscape architects 3. Landscape architecture

ISBN 978-1-58093-227-1; 1-58093-227-4

LC 2009-17705

"This book brings to life the gardens of a nascent and grand American landscape style, influenced by European gardens, modified for the nouveaux riches. You might want to get out a magnifying glass to view Farrand's meticulous plans, a trove of inspiration." N Y Times Book Rev

Includes bibliographical references

Taraborrelli, J. Randy

★ The secret life of Marilyn Monroe. Grand Central Pub. 2009 560p il $26.99   **92**

1. Actors 2. Biography, Individual

ISBN 978-0-446-58082-3

LC 2008-44704

For this biography, the author "delves beneath the legend of Marilyn Monroe to uncover the stark facts of the life and times of a singularly vulnerable woman woefully unequipped to deal with the quotidian business of 'normal' life, much less the pressures of a Hollywood career and international celebrity. . . . A painful and engrossing account of the profoundly damaged personality at the heart of the world's greatest sex symbol." Kirkus

Includes filmography

Taubman, William

Khrushchev; the man and his era. Norton 2003 p. cm   **92**

1. Communist leaders 2. Heads of state 3. Heads of state -- Soviet Union -- Biography 4. Political leaders

ISBN 0-393-05144-7

LC 2002-26404

Taylor, Barbara Brown

An **altar** in the world; a geography of faith. HarperOne 2008 216p $24.99   **92**

1. Biography, Individual 2. Clergy 3. Religious scholars 4. Spiritual life 5. Spiritual life -- Christianity 6. Writers on religion

ISBN 978-0-06-137046-5

LC 2008-18303

"Taylor is one of those rare people who truly can see the holy in everything. Since everyone should know such a person, those who don't can—no, must—read this book, with its friendly reminders of everyday sacred." Publ Wkly

Taylor, David J.

★ **Orwell**: the life; {by} D.J. Taylor. Holt & Co. 2003 466p il $30; pa $17   **92**

1. Authors 2. Essayists 3. Novelists

ISBN 0-8050-7473-2; 0-8050-7693-X pa

LC 2003-41747

"Starting with a . . . description of Orwell's funeral in 1950, Taylor . . . presents the years in India, the 'down and out' adventures, fighting in Spain, Orwell's work with the BBC during the war, and his final great novels. Taylor breaks the chronological flow with nine brief, interpretive essays (e.g., on Orwell's face, voice, and paranoia). . . . Taylor's book is a fresh and compelling life of the man he calls 'a light glinting in the darkness.'" Libr J

Includes bibliographical references

Taylor, Jay

The **generalissimo**; Chiang Kai-shek and the struggle for modern China. Belknap Press of Harvard University Press 2009 722p il map $35   **92**

1. Biography, Individual 2. Generals 3. Presidents 4. Presidents -- China 5. Presidents -- Taiwan

ISBN 978-0-674-03338-2

LC 2008-40492

This is a biography of the Chinese president who was forced into exile in Taiwan in 1949.

"Taylor's fact-based chronological presentation of Chiang should temper the preexisting opinions of him that history readers may take into reading the book. . . . An important biography, essential to the Chinese history shelves." Booklist

Includes bibliographical references

Teachout, Terry

★ **All** in the dances: a brief life of George Balanchine. Harcourt 2004 208p $22   **92**

1. Ballet 2. Choreographers 3. Dancers

ISBN 0-15-101088-9

LC 2004-9226

"Balanchine's ballets are modern masterpieces, and Teachout, moving chronologically from work to work, uses them as stepping stones to tell Balanchine's own story. This is highly recommended as a first book on the life and art of George Balanchine for students and the general reader." Publ Wkly

Includes bibliographical references

Pops; a life of Louis Armstrong. Houghton Mifflin Harcourt 2009 475p il $30   **92**

1. Biography, Individual 2. Jazz -- History and criticism

3. Jazz musicians

ISBN 978-0-15-101089-9; 0-15-101089-7

LC 2009-6035

"The author makes an eloquent case for Armstrong's status as a pioneer, not just in jazz but in the broader context of 20th-century art. A rewarding jazz biography and a revealing look at a broad swath of American cultural history." Kirkus

Includes discography and bibliographical references

The **skeptic**: the life of H.L. Mencken. HarperCollins Pubs. 2002 410p il $29.95; pa $15.95   **92**

1. Authors 2. Essayists 3. Literary critics 4. Newspaper editors 5. Philologists 6. Social critics

ISBN 0-06-050528-1; 0-06-050529-X pa

LC 2002-24953

This is "an engrossing, sympathetic biography." Booklist

Includes bibliograpical references

Tedlow, Richard S.

Andy Grove; the life and times of an American. Portfolio 2006 512p $29.95   **92**

1. Biography, Individual 2. College teachers 3. Electronics industry executives

ISBN 978-1-591-84139-5; 1-591-84139-9

LC 2006-49829

The author "presents the story of Andy Grove, a penniless Hungarian immigrant who became an icon of twentieth-century corporate America. Grove joined Intel in 1968 at its founding, and while he was CEO from 1987 to 1998, 'market capitalization increased from $4.3 billion to $197.6 billion, a compound annual growth rate of 42% and a total increase of almost 4,500%.' Grove led the company with Intel's 386 microprocessor, which became the industry standard. Tedlow describes Grove, Time magazine's 1997 man of the year, as an extraordinary manager, author, and significant player in the fights against prostate cancer and Parkinson's disease. With unique access to Grove and Intel's internal resources and documents, Tedlow claims objectivity, telling the truth as he sees it in this laudatory narrative, although he also confirms his close ties to the subject." Booklist

Tefertiller, Casey

Wyatt Earp; the life behind the legend. Wiley 1997 403p $45; pa $19.95   **92**

1. Biography, Individual 2. Sheriffs

ISBN 0-471-18967-7; 0-471-28362-2 pa

LC 97-2932

"An engrossing, satisfying inspection of a quintessential figure in American popular culture." Booklist

Includes bibliographical references

Teller, Edward

Memoirs; a twentieth-century journey in science and politics. {by} Edward Teller with Judith Shoolery. Perseus Bks. 2001 628p il hardcover o.p. pa $18.95   **92**

1. Physicists 2. Physicists -- United States 3. Writers on science

ISBN 0-7382-0778-0 pa

This memoir, by the nuclear physicist who worked to develop the hydrogen bomb, recounts his origins in the scientific community in Germany prior to the Nazi takeover and describes his "work on safe proliferation of nuclear energy, the so-called Stars Wars defense system and the early detection of earth-crossing objects. . . . Readers can enjoy these panoramic and beautifully written recollections of one of the great scientific, if controversial, figures of all time." Publ Wkly

Includes bibliographical references

Terkel, Studs

Touch and go; a memoir. [by] Studs Terkel, with Sydney Lewis. New Press 2007 269p il $24.95 **92**
1. Authors 2. Authors, American 3. Biography, Individual 4. Historians 5. Talk show hosts 6. Television moderators
ISBN 978-1-59558-043-6; 1-59558-043-3

LC 2007-18673

"Terkel's memoir is . . . a medley of all the extraordinary characters he's encountered through his career, from the adult loners of his youth in Chicago's Wells-Grand Hotel, to New Deal politicians. Terkel details his long journey through law school, the air force, theater, radio, early television, sports commentary, jazz criticism and oral history. . . . Americans might get to know their collective past a lot better if all history lessons were as absorbing and entertaining as this one." Publ Wkly

Thomas, Abigail

A **three** dog life. Harcourt 2006 182p $22 **92**
1. Authors 2. Novelists 3. Short story writers
ISBN 978-0-15-101211-4; 0-15-101211-3

LC 2005-33782

"Thomas has elevated what could be, at best, an overemotional sermon or, at worst, a grim romp in self-pity to a high plain of true inspiration." Booklist

Thompson, Nicholas

The **hawk** and the dove; Paul Nitze, George Kennan, and the history of the Cold War. Henry Holt 2009 403p il $27.50 **92**
1. Anti-communist movements -- United States -- History -- 20th century 2. Authors 3. Biography, Individual 4. Centenarians 5. Cold war 6. Diplomats 7. Government officials 8. Historians 9. National security -- United States -- History -- 20th century 10. Nonfiction writers 11. Secretaries of the navy 12. Statesmen
ISBN 0805081429; 9780805081428

LC 2009-09225

This biography of Nitze and Kennan focuses on their "careers as statesmen, policy makers and public intellectuals." (N Y Times Book Rev) Index.

This book "does an inspired job of telling the story of the Cold War through the careers of two of its most interesting and important figures." Washington Monthly

Includes bibliographical references

Thomson, David

Bette Davis; photo research by Lucy Gray. Faber and Faber 2010 128p il pa $14 **92**
1. Actors
ISBN 978-0-86547-931-9

LC 2009-41760

"Chronicling Davis' life and evolution in Hollywood, Thomson illustrates how changes in her often-disappointing private life (she had a habit of marrying the wrong men) influenced and often deepened her onscreen persona. Reading of how Davis bounced from one bad movie to the next in the early years of her career, it's hard not to share Thomson's enthusiasm for her talent, drive, and will. And it is hard not to feel Thomson's disappointment when Davis' major, artistic breakthroughs (The Little Foxes, All About Eve) are followed by lapses into forgettable mediocrity (The Man Who Came to Dinner, Payment on Demand)." Booklist

Includes filmography and bibliographical references

Gary Cooper; photo research by Lucy Gray. Faber and Faber 2010 129p il pa $14 **92**
1. Actors
ISBN 978-0-86547-932-6

LC 2009-41759

In this biography of the actor, "Cooper is presented as a hapless, weak-willed adulterer whose lean body, rugged handsomeness and preternatural stillness translated on camera as a quintessentially American rectitude and heroic stoicism. . . . Thomson is wickedly funny and startlingly poetic in his observations." Kirkus

Humphrey Bogart; photo research by Lucy Gray. Faber and Faber, Inc. 2010 127p il pa $14 **92**
1. Actors
ISBN 978-0-86547-933-3

LC 2009-41758

In this biography, the author "focuses on how long it took the well-bred and educated Bogart to develop his trademark style as the rough-hewn, disillusioned, world-weary, wisecracking, fallen romantic of Casablanca and The Maltese Falcon. He charts Bogart's progress from New York stage performer to featured player in 1930s Hollywood, where he was often cast as a certain kind of feral street rat, to star." Booklist

Ingrid Bergman; photo research by Lucy Gray. Faber and Faber, Inc. 2010 113p il pa $14 **92**
1. Actors
ISBN 978-0-86547-934-0

LC 2009-41757

In this biography, the author describes Bergman's "Hollywood-like rise, seemingly both unexpected and preordained, from talented Swedish actress to Hollywood goddess. . . . He reserves his harshest criticism not for her increasingly chaotic private life but for how, after her brilliance in the 1940s—Casablanca, Gaslight, and the Hitchcock masterpieces Spellbound and Notorious, and more—she settled into a kind of unsatisfying mediocrity in the 1950s and 1960s. Thomson speculates that her fortunes faded with her legendary beauty." Booklist

Rosebud: the story of Orson Welles. Knopf 1996 463p il hardcover o.p. pa $16 **92**
1. Actors 2. Motion picture directors 3. Motion picture producers 4. Radio directors 5. Theatrical directors 6. Theatrical producers
ISBN 0-679-77283-9 pa

LC 95-44216

In this examination of Welles, "Thomson trots out the myths and reinterprets them in Welles' favor, which he fits into his ingenious conceit of Welles as the antihero Kane. . . . Throughout, Thomson is engaging and humorous, particularly in working with another masterful conceit. On a controversial interpretation or on an exquisite insight, the publisher enters the narrative and converses with the author. Prettily done. Thomson summarizes that Welles was, at once, 'magnificent and a poor bastard.' And this is, at once, a brilliant and maddening inquiry." Booklist

Includes bibliographical references

Try to tell the story; a memoir. Alfred A. Knopf 2009 214p $23.95   **92**
1. Authors 2. Biographers 3. Biography, Individual 4. Father-son relationship 5. Film historians 6. Novelists 7. World War, 1939-1945 -- Personal narratives
ISBN 978-0-375-41213-4; 0-375-41213-1
   LC 2008-19605

"In the heart of this haunting, eloquent memoir, as might be expected, [Thomson] gets rhapsodic when recalling the films that left an indelible impression on him: Red River, Meet Me in St. Louis, Citizen Kane, East of Eden. While following a film critic in the making, we also see the changing cultural landscape of the 1940s and 1950s through his eyes." Publ Wkly

Thomson, Graeme

The **resurrection** of Johnny Cash; hurt, redemption, and American Recordings. Jawbone 2011 254p il pa $19.95   **92**
1. Country musicians 2. Singers 3. Songwriters
ISBN 978-1-906002-36-7

This "book focuses on what is, without question, the most spectacular musical comeback of the last 20 years. Cash had been all but dismissed by an increasingly corporate and shallow Nashville, before the unlikely figure of Rick Rubin masterminded a series of stripped-down intimate albums that reestablished his legendary status. It was a rebirth of almost Biblical proportions, the forgotten man in black newly feted by future generations, with the likes of Nick Cave, Trent Reznor, U2, Depeche Mode and Elvis Costello queuing up to have their songs given a fresh lick of statesmanlike paint. . . . One of the difficulties of writing a music biography in modern times is that the internet age makes available all manner of nuts and bolts to fans of any given artist, but though Thomson might not uncover much in the way of previously unknown information his always eloquent writing fills the pages with atmosphere and keen critical assessment." Record Collector

Includes bibliographical references

Thomson, Keith Stewart

The **young** Charles Darwin; [by] Keith Thomson. Yale University Press 2009 276p il $28   **92**
1. Biography, Individual 2. Naturalists 3. Travel writers 4. Writers on science
ISBN 978-0-300-13608-1; 0-300-13608-0

"Thomson's writing style is fluid and engaging and his grasp of the Darwinian literature encyclopedic. His scholar-

ly thoroughness is balanced by his very human appreciation for a very human scientist." Choice

Includes bibliographical references

Thorndike, John

The **last** of his mind; a year in the shadow of Alzheimer's. Swallow Press 2009 243p il $24.95   **92**
1. Alzheimer's disease 2. Alzheimer's disease -- Patients -- Family relationships 3. Authors 4. Biography, Individual 5. Magazine editors
ISBN 978-0-8040-1122-8; 0-8040-1122-2
   LC 2009-26118

"A brave, moving story of a son's devotion to his dying father. . . . Thorndike's prose is serenely beautiful and his patience in caring for an Alzheimer's patient is extremely admirable. An affecting work of emotional honesty and forgiveness." Kirkus

Thurman, Judith

★ **Isak** Dinesen; the life of a storyteller. St. Martin's Press 1982 495p il hardcover o.p. pa $18   **92**
1. Authors 2. Memoirists 3. Novelists 4. Short story writers
ISBN 0-312-13525-4 pa
   LC 82-5573

This biography traces Dinesen's life from her childhood in Denmark through her years in Kenya and her return to Denmark to focus on her literary career.

"With great insight and a novelist's gift for nuance and narrative sweep, Thurman shows the extraordinary degree to which Dinesen's life and art meshed. In addition, Thurman's sensitive criticism of Dinesen's work reveals exceptional artistry in its own right." Booklist

Includes bibliographical references

Secrets of the flesh: a life of Colette. Knopf 1999 592p il hardcover o.p. pa $18.95   **92**
1. Authors 2. Biographers 3. Novelists
ISBN 0-345-37103-8 pa
   LC 99-18959

Thurman focuses on the "morally subversive Colette in the social milieu of early-20th-century Paris. . . . {She} does not hesitate to expose the dishonest, selfish, exploitive facets of the feminist icon who wrote articles for Occupation newspapers and sometimes behaved heartlessly toward lovers. Nevertheless, her Colette comes off as an appealing, even heroic, figure." Publ Wkly

Includes bibliographical references

Timerman, Jacobo

Prisoner without a name, cell without a number; translated from the Spanish by Toby Talbot. University of Wisconsin Press 2002 164p pa $17.95   **92**
1. Journalists 2. Newspaper executives 3. Political prisoners
ISBN 978-0-299-18244-1; 0-299-18244-4

The author, "an outspoken Zionist and formerly a newspaper publisher in Buenos Aires, relates his 30-month political incarceration—torture and isolation in a clandestine prison, then detention in an official penal institution—which preceded his expulsion from Argentina in 1979." Publ Wkly

Tingey, John

The **Englishman** who posted himself and other curious objects. Princeton Architectural Press 2010 175p il $24.95 **92**
1. Autographs 2. Collectors 3. Eccentrics 4. Postal service -- Great Britain
ISBN 978-1-56898-872-6

LC 2009-48612

"The disposition of Bray's collection and how Tingey discovered it add further interest to an already fascinating account. Equally engaging as the narrative are the illustrations." Fine Books & Collections

Includes bibliographical references.

Tirone Smith, Mary-Ann

★ **Girls** of tender age; a memoir. Free Press 2006 285p il map $24 **92**
1. Authors 2. Biography, Individual 3. Memoirists 4. Novelists 5. Young adult authors
ISBN 0-7432-7977-8

LC 2005-51376

This memoir, an "unsentimental view of life in a post-World War II working-class family, is interspersed with the story of Bob Malm, a serial pedophile who brutally murdered a fifth-grade classmate of hers in December 1953. . . . This poignant memoir belongs in all collections." Libr J

Includes bibliographical references

Tofel, Richard J.

Restless genius; Barney Kilgore, The Wall Street journal, and the invention of modern journalism. St. Martin's Press 2009 271p il $25.95 **92**
1. Journalists 2. Newspaper executives
ISBN 978-0-312-53674-9; 0-312-53674-7

LC 2008-29880

"What makes this work especially appealing is the incorporation of the many letters Kilgore wrote to his father, giving the reader a glimpse into this esteemed newsman's way of thinking about his newspaper and the news of the day." Libr J

Includes bibliographical references

Toland, John

Adolf Hitler. Anchor Bks. (NY) 1992 xx, 1035p il pa $24 **92**
1. Heads of state 2. National socialism 3. Nazi leaders
ISBN 0-385-42053-6

LC 91-31242

This biography is based on more than 250 interviews with people acquainted with Hitler and materials from U.S. and British archives.

"In the course of detailed and painstaking investigations {Toland} has disposed of a number of myths." N Y Times Book Rev

Includes bibliographical references

Tomalin, Claire

Charles Dickens. Penguin Press 2011 $35 **92**
1. Authors, English -- 19th century -- Biography 2. Biographies 3. Books & reading -- Great Britain -- History -- 19th century 4. Dickens, Charles, 1812-1870

5. English male authors 6. Judge, Rick
ISBN 978-1-59420-309-1; 1-59420-309-1

LC 2011031466

The book presents a biography of author Charles Dickens, with topics including "the familiar story of the idyllic childhood years in Kent . . . the terrible experience of being forced to work in a blacking factory rather than go to school . . . a rapid, improbable journey from obscure clerk to diligent reporter and sketch-writer . . . Tomalin shows how Dickens' extravagant plots and unlikely endings owe much to the popular culture of penny dreadfuls and melodrama in which the author was steeped. . . She agrees with those who feel he cannot write effectively about women and . . . how he had tremendous imaginative affinity for the lot of the small man or indeed woman or child, the individuals who were trampled over by the great march of 19th-century progress. . . . She . . . chronicles Dickens' moral and physical decline as he abandoned his wife, home and many family members and friends to pursue and ultimately seduce [actress Nelly Ternan]." (History Today)

The author "tells a story. Clear-eyed, sympathetic and scholarly, she spreads the whole canvas, alive with incident and detail, with places and people. She writes of publishers, illustrators, collaborators and all Dickens's intersecting circles of friends and family. It is wonderfully done." Economist

Thomas Hardy. Penguin Group 2006 xxv, 486p il map $35 **92**
1. Authors 2. Biography, Individual 3. Novelists 4. Poets 5. Short story writers
ISBN 1-59420-118-8; 978-1-59420-118-9

LC 2007-295886

"A priceless resource for the general reader and the Victorian scholar." Booklist

Includes bibliographical references

Torre, Joe

The **Yankee** years; [by] Joe Torre and Tom Verducci. Doubleday 2009 502p il $26.95 **92**
1. Baseball -- Biography 2. Baseball managers 3. Baseball players
ISBN 978-0-385-52740-8; 0-385-52740-3

LC 2008-52628

Joe Torre, who was manager of the New York Yankees from 1996 to 2007, focuses on the team's circumstances beginning with their loss of the seventh game of the 2001 World Series.

"This is an interesting and fast read and, for those who are not aficionados of baseball, the clash of powerful personalities and drama are more than sufficient to merit attention. Baseball enthusiasts, while undoubtedly familiar with the characters and events, will find the quick review of 12 years of Yankee history enjoyable for its details, particularly as the men's words flesh out the drama behind the sports pages." USA Today

Toye, Richard

Churchill's empire; the world that made him and the world he made. Henry Holt 2010 xx, 423p il $32 **92**
1. Cabinet members 2. Historians 3. Members of

Parliament 4. Memoirists 5. Nobel laureates for literature 6. Prime ministers 7. Prime ministers -- Great Britain 8. Statesmen

ISBN 978-0-8050-8795-6

LC 2010-1427

In this biography, the author "stresses that Churchill (1874-1965), a Victorian aristocrat, assumed white superiority but regularly proclaimed that nonwhites deserved equal rights and, eventually, independence once they discarded their primitive ways and achieved European levels of culture. . . . This work is a valuable contribution to greater understanding of a historical icon." Booklist

Includes bibliographical reference

Treglown, Jeremy

V.S. Pritchett: a working life. Random House 2005 334p $25.95 **92**

1. Authors 2. Literary critics 3. Novelists 4. Short story writers

ISBN 0-375-50853-8

LC 2004-53857

This biography follows the life and career of the English writer, who for most of the century ennobled the ordinary and whose two tumultuous marriages fueled his art

"Treglown's genial and sympathetic biography effectively expands . . . awareness of the life and career of this greatly accessible and warmhearted writer of fiction, travel literature, and criticism. . . . This is a biography as open-minded and unpretentious as Pritchett's own writing." Booklist

Includes bibliographical references

Trillin, Calvin

About Alice. Random House 2007 78p $14.95 **92**

1. Authors 2. Biography, Individual 3. Essayists 4. Humorists 5. Novelists 6. Short story writers 7. Television producers

ISBN 1-4000-6615-8; 978-1-4000-6615-5

LC 2006-45573

"This succinct account of Alice's upbringing, their meeting, their romance, their family, and her career beyond that of Trillin's helpmeet, offers glimpses into a multifaceted character." Booklist

Trimborn, Jurgen

Leni Riefenstahl; translated from the German by Edna McCown. Faber & Faber 2007 351p il $30 **92**

1. Actors 2. Biography, Individual 3. Centenarians 4. Motion picture directors 5. Motion picture producers

ISBN 978-0-374-18493-3; 0-374-18493-3

LC 2006-13263

This is a biography of the German filmmaker whose work includes Triumph of the Will, a propaganda film for Hitler, and Ölympia, a documentary of the 1936 Olympics in Berlin.

Trimborn "interviewed Riefenstahl in 1997, when he was twenty-five, having already spent six years of 'intensive labor' on the project, and he briefly entertained the quixotic hope of writing a definitive book with her blessing and collaboration. Unwilling to misrepresent himself as a hagiographer, he was doomed to fail, though his disappointment does not seem to have warped his fair-mindedness. . . . [The author's] aim was to correct the murky published record and

the 'attitudes' of his compatriots. One has to admire the sniperlike precision with which he takes out fugitive falsehoods that have lived under cover for a century." New Yorker

Troyat, Henri

Catherine the Great; translated by Joan Pinkham. Dutton 1980 377p il hardcover o.p. pa $16.95 **92**

1. Empresses

ISBN 0-452-01120-5 pa

LC 79-25613

"Relying heavily on Catherine's own memoirs, plus her correspondence with her Western idolaters-publicists, such as Friedrich Grimm, Voltaire and Diderot, Troyat gives us a portrait the Empress herself might have decreed for posterity." Publ Wkly

Includes bibliographical references

Trynka, Paul

Iggy Pop; open up and bleed. Broadway Books 2007 371p il $23.95; pa $14.95 **92**

1. Punk rock music 2. Rock musicians 3. Singers 4. Songwriters

ISBN 978-0-7679-2319-4; 978-0-7679-2320-0 pa

LC 2006-30216

"Drawing from original interviews with Iggy (né James Newell Osterberg Jr.) and his countless accomplices over the years, Trynka . . . has constructed a comprehensive portrait of the seemingly indestructible rock provocateur, one that touches all the familiar bases in recounting Iggy's riotous ascent from suburban Michigan schoolboy to frontman of the Stooges to solo artist with an intermittently transcendent career to composer of a drug-inspired hit song that became the jingle for a luxury cruise line." N Y Times Book Rev

Includes bibliographical references

Tuck, Lily

Woman of Rome: a life of Elsa Morante. HarperCollins 2008 263p il $25.95 **92**

1. Authors 2. Authors, Italian 3. Biography, Individual 4. Novelists 5. Poets 6. Short story writers 7. Women authors

ISBN 978-0-06-147256-5; 0-06-147256-5

LC 2007-44647

"Written with a charming personal touch . . . that warms the narrative to a fine glow, this is a vital biography bringing to American audiences a writer most will have previously known little about." Booklist

Includes bibliographical references (p. 245-246)

Turan, Kenneth

★ **Free** for all; Joe Papp, the Public, and the greatest theater story ever told. [by] Kenneth Turan and Joseph Papp; with the assistance of Gail Merrifield Papp. Doubleday 2009 592p il $39.95 **92**

1. Actors -- United States 2. Biography, Individual 3. Theater -- New York (N.Y.) -- History -- 20th century 4. Theatrical directors 5. Theatrical producers 6. Theatrical producers and directors

ISBN 978-0-7679-3168-7

LC 2008-50887

"A wonderful book that clearly and powerfully shows that Papp's story was the most enduring drama he ever produced." Kirkus

Turner, Tina

    I, Tina; {by} Tina Turner, with Kurt Loder. Morrow 1986 236p il pa $6.99   **92**
    1. Rhythm and blues musicians 2. Singers
    ISBN 0-380-70097-2 pa

    LC 86-16455
    "Kurt Loder has edited I, Tina nicely, letting {Turner's} narrative take center stage, punctuating it with the voices of friends, colleagues, and family." Nation

Twain, Mark

    The **autobiography** of Mark Twain; as arranged and edited with an introduction and notes, by Charles Neider. Harper & Row 1959 xxvi, 388p il hardcover o.p. pa $15   **92**
    1. Authors 2. Authors, American 3. Essayists 4. Humorists 5. Memoirists 6. Novelists 7. Satirists 8. Short story writers 9. Travel writers
    ISBN 0-06-095542-2 pa
    The editor "has arranged the selections in coordinated chronological order, ending with the death of Clemens' daughter Jean in December, 1909." Booklist

Twain, Mark, 1835-1910

    ★ **Autobiography** of Mark Twain; v1 the complete and authoritative edition. Harriet Elinor Smith, editor; associate editors: Benjamin Griffin, Victor Fischer, Michael B. Frank, Sharon K. Goetz, Leslie Myrick. University of California Press 2010 736p il $34.95; ebook $28   **92**
    1. Authors 2. Authors, American 3. Biography, Individual 4. Essayists 5. Humorists 6. Memoirists 7. Novelists 8. Satirists 9. Short story writers 10. Travel writers
    ISBN 9780520267190; 9780520946996; 978-0-520-26719-0; 978-0-520-94699-6 ebook

    LC 2009-47700
    This is the first volume of the American author's autobiography, including texts that were not to be published until the 100th anniversary of Twain's death.
    "Twain's memoirs are a pointillist masterpiece from which his vision of America—half paradise, half swindle—emerges with indelible force." Publ Wkly
    Includes bibliographical references

Tye, Diane

    Baking as biography; a life story in recipes. McGill-Queen's University Press 2010 268p il   **92**
    1. Baking 2. Biography, Individual 3. Eating customs 4. Food -- Social aspects 5. Homemakers 6. Women -- Canada
    ISBN 978-0-7735-3724-8; 978-0-7735-3725-5 pa
    Diane Tye uses her mother's recipe collection as a focus for this memoir and study of Maritime culture. Index
    "Using her mother's recipes as a framework, Tye . . . explores Canadian women's roles from 1930 to 1980. She recalls her mother as a minister's wife who didn't care for bak-

ing yet consistently produced an abundance of sweets for her family, church, and community. Her succinct recipes range from simple (biscuits and oatcakes) to 'exotic' (anything involving JELL-O, Dream Whip, or canned pie filling). . . . Because this book blends memoir, biography, culinary history, and research, it should appeal to both scholars and readers who enjoy historical or intellectual food writing." Libr J
    Includes bibliographical references

Tye, Larry

    Satchel; the life and times of an American legend. Random House 2009 392p il   **92**
    1. African American athletes 2. Baseball -- Biography 3. Baseball players 4. Biography, Individual 5. Negro leagues -- History
    ISBN 0812977971; 1400066514; 9780812977974; 9781400066513

    LC 2008-44858
    A biography of the Negro League pitcher Satchel Paige "evaluates the role of discrimination in limiting his career, covering such topics as his near-defeat of a young Joe DiMaggio, the Jim Crow biases that prevented his signing with the big leagues until he was in his forties, and his [legacy]." (Publisher's note)
    This is a "discerning, empathetic and hype-free [biography]. . . . While Paige's life has become the stuff of legend, its particulars are not easily verified. . . . Yet 'Satchel' makes a cool, clear, tenacious effort to find the real Paige behind all [the] hyperbole." N Y Times (Late N Y Ed)
    Includes bibliographical references

Tyldesley, Joyce A.

    Cleopatra; last queen of Egypt. [by] Joyce Tyldesley. Basic Books 2008 290p il map $27.50 **92**
    1. Queens
    ISBN 978-0-465-00940-4; 0-465-00940-9

    LC 2008-921307
    The author "unscrambles a slew of Ptolemys and Cleopatras who ruled wealthy Egypt from 332 to 30 BCE to tell the story of the dynasty's last and best-remembered queen, Cleopatra VII (c.70-30 BCE). . . . This fascinating and scholarly book belongs in all libraries." Libr J
    Includes bibliographical references

Tytell, John

    Ezra Pound; the solitary volcano. Anchor Press 1987 368p il hardcover o.p. pa $19   **92**
    1. Authors 2. Literary critics 3. Poets
    ISBN 0-385-19870-1 pa

    LC 86-25912
    "In this incisive interpretative biography, based on interviews with those who knew him and a mass of published and unpublished Poundiana, Tytell examines the circumstances behind the poems and thereby generates new understanding of the man." Publ Wkly
    Includes bibliographical references

Uglow, Jennifer S.

Nature's engraver; a life of Thomas Bewick. Farrar, Straus and Giroux 2007 458p il map $30 **92**

1. Artists 2. Illustrators 3. Woodcut artists 4. Woodcuts
ISBN 978-0-374-11236-3; 0-374-11236-3

LC 2006-31878

"Biographies rarely afford a glimpse behind the office door, and it is the image of Bewick at work that is so valuable here. . . . It is hard to imagine a better biographer for this subject than Uglow, with her background in publishing and her knowledge of the North of England and the eighteenth century. It is also hard to imagine a more beautifully produced and illustrated book: scores of Bewick's frameless vignettes float frame-free and captionless throughout, appearing as they would have done in his own time, tale pieces every one." Times Lit Suppl

Includes bibliographical references

A **gambling** man; Charles II's Restoration game. [by] Jenny Uglow. Farrar, Straus and Giroux 2009 580p il map $35 **92**

1. Biography, Individual 2. Kings
ISBN 978-0-374-28137-3; 0-374-28137-8

LC 2009-25469

"When Charles II became King of England, in 1660, his task was daunting: to restore the authority of the monarchy while courting a fractious parliament. Uglow's vivid history of the first decade of his reign shows how boldly Charles embraced the openness and experimentation of the Age of Reason." New Yorker

Includes bibliographical references

Uhlberg, Myron

Hands of my father; a hearing boy, his deaf parents, and the language of love. Bantam Books 2009 232p il $23 **92**

1. American Sign Language 2. Authors 3. Biography, Individual 4. Children of deaf parents 5. Children's authors 6. Deaf
ISBN 978-0-553-80688-5; 0-553-80688-2

LC 2008-25628

A memoir about growing up the son of deaf parents in 1940s Brooklyn.

"Uhlberg's emotions toward his family, and especially his father, run the gamut from embarrassment to anger to a deep and abiding love. Sections titled 'Memorabilia' pepper the narrative, and many black-and-white photographs are scattered throughout this rich, textured portrait of the deaf community on Coney Island at a turbulent time in U.S. history." SLJ

Umrigar, Thrity N.

First darling of the morning; selected memories of an Indian childhood. Harper Perennial 2008 294, 18p pa $14.95 **92**

1. Authors 2. Authors, American 3. Essayists 4. Journalists 5. Literary critics 6. Novelists
ISBN 978-0-06-145161-4; 0-06-145161-4

In this memoir, the author "alternates between sweet and biting accounts of her middle-class Parsi upbringing in 1960s and 1970s Bombay. With a mixture of rawness and warmth, she recalls moments from her tumultuous child-

hood through her teenage years, and finally into her early 20s when she leaves India for the U.S. . . . Umrigar's memoir is colorful and moving." Publ Wkly

Ung, Loung

★ **Lucky** child; a daughter of Cambodia reunites with the sister she left behind. HarperCollins Publishers 2005 268p il $24.95; pa $13.95 **92**

1. Cambodian Americans 2. Homemakers 3. Memoirists 4. Social activists
ISBN 0-06-073394-2; 0-06-073395-0 pa

LC 2004-54346

In this "memoir, Ung picks up where her first . . . left off, with the author escaping a devastated Cambodia in 1980 at age 10 and flying to her new home in Vermont. . . . She and her eldest brother, with whom she escaped, left behind their three other siblings. This book is alternately heart-wrenching and heartwarming, as it follows the parallel lives of Loung Ung and her closest sister, Chou, during the 15 years it took for them to reunite." Publ Wkly

Includes bibliographical references

Unger, Harlow G.

The **last** founding father; James Monroe and a nation's call to greatness. [by] Harlow Giles Unger. Da Capo Press 2009 388p il map $26 **92**

1. Architects 2. Essayists 3. Generals 4. Members of Congress 5. Presidents 6. Presidents -- United States 7. Presidents -- United States -- Biography 8. Secretaries of state 9. Vice-presidents
ISBN 978-0-306-81808-0

LC 2009-26195

"A worthy attempt to rescue Monroe from obscurity for a mainstream audience." Kirkus

Includes bibliographical references (p. 371-376)

Urofsky, Melvin I.

Louis D. Brandeis; a life. Pantheon Books 2009 955p il **92**

1. Biography, Individual 2. Judges 3. Law -- United States -- History 4. Lawyers 5. Supreme Court justices
ISBN 9780375423666

LC 200903992

This is a biography of the American lawyer who was nominated to the Supreme Court in 1916 and served as a justice until his retirement in 1939. Index.

This is a "monumental, authoritative and appreciative biography of the man Franklin D. Roosevelt called 'Isaiah.'" N Y Times Book Rev

Includes bibliographical references

Urrutia, Matilde

My life with Pablo Neruda; {translated by} Alexandria Giardino. Stanford University Press 2004 318p $27.95 **92**

1. Authors 2. Diplomats 3. Nobel laureates for literature 4. Nobel laureates for peace 5. Novelists 6. Poets 7. Poets, Chilean -- 20th century -- Biography 8. Spouses of prominent persons
ISBN 0-8047-5009-2

LC 2004-8535

"Urrutia, Neruda's third wife, provides a . . . biography from her particular vantage. Her purpose is twofold: to present her Pablo as the exuberant, warm, and loving individual he was and to inform readers of the menace imposed by Chilean dictator Pinochet, who was responsible for the assassination of elected president Allende, Neruda's close friend. Urrutia's account is highly selective but well worth reading for another perspective on this great man." Libr J

Utley, Robert Marshall

Sitting Bull: the life and times of an American patriot; by Robert M. Utley. Henry Holt 2008 464p il pa $18   **92**
1. Indian chiefs
ISBN 978-0-8050-8830-4; 0-8050-8830-X
"This book is well written, strongly documented, and fairly reasoned to satisfy even specialists within the field. It surpasses all previous biographies of Sitting Bull." Choice
Includes bibliographical references

Vaill, Amanda

★ **Somewhere**; the life of Jerome Robbins. Broadway Books 2006 675p il $40   **92**
1. Biography, Individual 2. Choreographers 3. Dance -- History 4. Dancers 5. Theatrical directors
ISBN 0-7679-0420-6; 978-0-7679-0420-9
LC 2006-48960
This is a biography of the choreographer of such works as Afternoon of a Faun, On the Town, Gypsy, West Side Story, and Fiddler on the Roof.
"The book is essential reading for lovers of theater and dance." Publ Wkly
Includes bibliographical references

VanderVelde, Lea

Mrs. Dred Scott; a life on slavery's frontier. Oxford University Press 2009 480p il map $34.95 **92**
1. Biography, Individual 2. Slavery -- United States 3. Slaves 4. Slaves -- Legal status, laws, etc. 5. Slaves -- United States -- Biography 6. Spouses of prominent persons
ISBN 978-0-19-536656-3; 0-19-536656-5
LC 2008-27920
"Through Harriet Scott's life, the author is able to create a valuable portrait of the development of slavery on the U.S. frontier during an era in which that scourge was leading the country toward civil war. Despite the wealth of historical knowledge presented, the heart of this well-researched work is the tragic tale of how a loving family's effort to gain their freedom was brutally rejected by Supreme Court justices bent on maintaining the institution of slavery at all costs." Libr J
Includes bibliographical references (p. 443-466)

Varmus, Harold

The **art** and politics of science. W.W. Norton 2009 315p il $24.95   **92**
1. Biography, Individual 2. Cancer -- Research 3. College teachers 4. Genetics -- Research 5. Government officials 6. Microbiologists 7. Nobel Prizes 8. Nobel laureates for physiology or medicine 9. Public health officials 10. Scientists
ISBN 978-0-393-06128-4; 0-393-06128-0
LC 2008-42963
"Varmus offers a plain-spoken and fascinating story of his path from graduate student in English literature to the forefront of biomedical research. His journey to the highest echelons of the scientific establishment is as interesting for its incidental details as for its glimpse into the process of modern biomedical science." Washington Post
Includes bibliographical references

Vaughan, Hal

Sleeping with the enemy; Coco Chanel's secret war. Knopf 2011 279p il $27.95; ebook $13.99 **92**
1. Biography, Individual 2. Cosmetics industry executives 3. Fashion designers 4. German espionage 5. Perfumers 6. World War, 1939-1945 -- Secret service
ISBN 978-0-307-59263-7; 978-0-307-95703-0 ebook; 0-7011-8500-7 Chatto & Windus; 978-0-7011-8500-8 Chatto & Windus
LC 2011020430
The author argues "that there were two sides to the elegant Coco Chanel. Using information from French counterintelligence sources as well as other documents hidden for years in French, German, Italian, Soviet, and U.S. archives, he unmasks her activities during the war years; she embarked on a romance with a senior German officer in occupied Paris and cooperated with German military intelligence agents. . . . Engrossing and accessible, this is recommended for general readers interested in fashion celebrity, espionage, or World War II." Libr J
Includes bibliographical references and index

Vidal, Gore

Point to point navigation; a memoir, 1964 to 2006. Doubleday 2006 277p il $26   **92**
1. Authors 2. Biography, Individual 3. Dramatists 4. Essayists 5. Novelists 6. Screenwriters
ISBN 0-385-51721-1; 978-0-385-51721-8
LC 2006-11644
"The memoir is a perfect encapsulation of Vidal's outsized personality—and readers' reactions will be determined by how they already feel about him." Publ Wkly

Viroli, Maurizio

Niccolo's smile: a biography of Machiavelli; translated from the Italian by Antony Shugaar. Farrar, Straus & Giroux 2000 271p maps hardcover o.p. pa $13   **92**
1. Authors 2. Dramatists 3. Political and social philosophers 4. Statesmen 5. Writers on politics
ISBN 0-374-52800-4 pa
LC 00-29380
This biography of the Italian political philosopher traces his life "from respected secretary of the Florentine republic, dispatched on crucial diplomatic missions to Europe's most illustrious courts, to forgotten commoner. . . . Viroli provides a detailed, historical background for Machiavelli's personal triumphs and woes. But the strength of this work lies in his ceaseless concentration on Machiavelli the man, who comes alive on each page." Publ Wkly
Includes bibliographical references

Vollmann, William T.

Uncentering the Earth; Copernicus and The Revolutions of the Heavenly Spheres. Norton 2006 295p il $22.95 **92**

1. Astronomers 2. Astronomy -- Early works to 1800 3. Solar system -- Early works to 1800

ISBN 0-393-05969-3

LC 2005-25864

"Readers who want to understand the significance of Copernicus's book in both his own time and ours will find this the next best thing to reading it." Publ Wkly

Volpe, Joseph

The **toughest** show on earth; my rise and reign at the Metropolitan Opera. [by] Joseph Volpe with Charles Michener. Knopf 2006 304p il $25.95 **92**

1. Biography, Individual 2. Music administrators

ISBN 0-307-26285-5; 978-0-307-26285-1

LC 2005-57932

This is a memoir by the "general manager of New York's Metropolitan Opera since 1990. . . . This enthralling book provides an insider's view of a complex and fascinating institution." Libr J

Includes bibliographical references

Wagner-Martin, Linda

Sylvia Plath; a literary life. St. Martin's Press 1999 172p $45; pa $19.95 **92**

1. Authors 2. Novelists 3. Poets

ISBN 0-312-22323-4; 1-40391-653-5 pa

LC 99-12184

The author "begins by summarizing Plath's childhood, which was marked by her educator parents' deep involvement with books, and her father's unexpected death when she was eight. . . . Wagner-Martin works strictly by the light of Plath's writings as she spins the oft-told tale of Plath's blazing creativity and fatal despair, and what emerges is a tragic tale of an artist envied and mistreated by those closest to her, and of a poet far more artistic than her reputation for being confessional implies." Booklist

Includes bibliographical references

Wald, Elijah

★ **Escaping** the delta; Robert Johnson and the invention of the blues. Amistad 2004 342p $24.95; pa $14.95 **92**

1. African American musicians 2. Biography, Individual 3. Blues (Music) -- History and criticism 4. Blues music 5. Blues musicians 6. Guitarists 7. Singers 8. Songwriters

ISBN 0-06-052423-5; 0-06-052427-8 pa

LC 2003-52287

The author "writes better than anyone else ever has about the blues. If you read only one book about blues—maybe ever—read this one." Booklist

Includes bibliographical references

Waldron, Ann

Eudora; a writer's life. Doubleday 1998 398p il hardcover o.p. pa $23 **92**

1. Authors 2. Authors, American 3. Novelists 4. Short story writers

ISBN 0-385-47648-5 pa

LC 98-5708

This is a biography of the writer from Mississippi

"Waldron's biography of Welty is the first to be written and, until the definitive treatment arrives, will satisfy readers curious to know details about the life of this much loved figure." Booklist

Includes bibliographical references

Walker, Alexander

Audrey; her real story. St. Martin's Press 1995 319p il hardcover o.p. pa $16.95 **92**

1. Actors

ISBN 0-312-18046-2 pa

LC 94-33716

The author "recounts his subject's childhood in war-torn Europe and her early stage and film career. . . . Both the narrative and the writing itself become more lively as he discusses the heyday of her career, her sometimes turbulent love life and her work with Third World children for UNICEF." Publ Wkly

Wallace, Danny

Friends like these; my worldwide quest to find my best childhood friends, knock on their doors, and ask them to come out and play. with illustrations by Daniel Wallace. Little, Brown 2009 402p il $24.99 **92**

1. Friendship 2. Humorists 3. Television producers 4. Television scriptwriters

ISBN 978-0-316-04277-2

LC 2009-6616

The author "describes how impending adulthood—he was about to turn 30—made him wonder what had happened to the friends he hung out with years ago. He did what any impulsive fella would do: he hauled out an old address book and started making calls. . . . A well-told, often laugh-out-loud-funny story that will ring true for anyone who's stared an approaching birthday in the face and not liked what they saw." Booklist

Wallach, Eli

The **good**, the bad, and me; in my anecdotage. Harcourt 2005 312p il $25; pa $16 **92**

1. Actors

ISBN 0-15-101189-3; 0-15-603169-8 pa

LC 2004-23121

The author "tells his story, from a Brooklyn childhood as the only Jew in an Italian neighborhood, through Actors Studio days with Brando and others, and on to his long and illustrious career on both stage and screen. . . . This compelling memoir shows the full range of a remarkable actor's life." Booklist

Wallis, Michael

★ **Billy** the Kid; the endless ride. W.W. Norton & Co. 2007 328p il map $25.95 **92**

1. Biography, Individual 2. Outlaws

ISBN 978-0-393-06068-3; 0-393-06068-3

LC 2006-101364

"Drawing on archival sources and interviews as well as documents and secondary works, Wallis digs beneath the surface, clearly identifying what is known or probable and presenting the reasonable alternatives for what is conjecture." Libr J

Includes bibliographical references

Walls, Jeannette

★ The **glass** castle; a memoir. Scribner 2005 288p $25; pa $14 **92**

1. Authors 2. Gossip columnists 3. Memoirists 4. Novelists

ISBN 0-7432-4753-1; 0-7432-4754-X pa

LC 2004-58907

"Shocking, sad, and occasionally bitter, this gracefully written account speaks candidly, yet with surprising affection, about parents and about the strength of family ties—for both good and ill." Booklist

Walsh, Stephen

Stravinsky: a creative spring; Russia and France, 1882-1934. University of California Press 2002 698p il pa $25.95 **92**

1. Composers

ISBN 978-0-520-22749-1; 0-520-22749-2

LC 2002-23256

"In this reference-oriented biography, Walsh uses diaries, press clippings, and other materials to probe in detail the life of a man kept very busy with effectively dividing his time between performance, composition, family, and mistress." Booklist

Includes bibliographical references

Stravinsky: the second exile; France and America, 1934-1971. Stephen Walsh. Alfred A. Knopf 2006 709p il $40 **92**

1. Biography, Individual 2. Composers

ISBN 0-375-40752-9

LC 2005-47231

"This is essential reading for musicologists and other music enthusiasts who wish to delve into the life and mind of perhaps the greatest composer of the 20th century." Libr J

Includes bibliographical references

Walters, Barbara

Audition; a memoir. Alfred A. Knopf 2008 612p il $29.95 **92**

1. Biography, Individual 2. Broadcast journalism 3. Talk show hosts 4. Television news anchors 5. Women journalists

ISBN 978-0-307-26646-0; 0-307-26646-X

LC 2008-05843

This is a memoir by the television newscaster.

"Alternating between tales of her personal struggles, professional achievements and insider anecdotes about the celebrities and world leaders she's interviewed, this mammoth memoir's energy never flags." Publ Wkly

Walton, Sam

Sam Walton, made in America; my story. by Sam Walton with John Huey. Bantam Books 1992 346p il pa $7.99 **92**

1. Businessmen 2. Retail executives

ISBN 0-553-56283-5; 978-0-553-56283-5

The founder of Wal-Mart Stores, the largest retail chain in the world, recounts how he made his fortune.

"Readers will enjoy the folksy narrative of the small-town millionaire who revolutionized retail distribution. . . . Coauthor Huey does a fine job of incorporating candid testimonials from family members and associates." Libr J

Ward, Geoffrey C.

★ **Unforgivable** blackness; the rise and fall of Jack Johnson. Knopf 2004 492p il $26.95 **92**

1. Biography, Individual 2. Boxers (Persons)

ISBN 0-375-41532-7

LC 2004-48524

The author "brings us back into Johnson's life and times with exquisitely rendered details, and the fight scenes themselves are gripping: fights so bloody that referees have to change shirts midbout, for instance, and a manager who pulls a gun on his fighter to keep him from quitting. The authoritative biography of Johnson for sure, but also one of the best boxing books in recent memory." Booklist

Includes bibliographical references

Ward, Martha Coonfield

Voodoo queen; the spirited lives of Marie Laveau. by Martha Ward. University Press of Mississippi 2004 246p il map $26 **92**

1. Voodooism 2. Witches

ISBN 1-578-06629-8

LC 2003-18292

"Spiritual leaders Marie Laveau, mother and daughter, reigned in New Orleans between the 1820s and 1880s. Through their story, Ward offers fresh perspective on Creole culture and voodoo." Booklist

Including bibliographical references

Wareham, Dean

Black postcards; a rock & roll romance. Penguin Press 2008 324p il $25.95 **92**

1. Biography, Individual 2. Guitarists 3. Rock musicians 4. Singers

ISBN 978-1-59420-155-4; 1-59420-155-2

LC 2007-35280

"In this collection of over 50 sequential autobiographical essays, . . . [the author] takes us from his childhood in New Zealand, through his formative years exploring New York City's punk scene, to his adult life in Cambridge, MA, where he becomes a notable figure in the alternative music scene. Wareham documents in great detail the history of his two bands, Galaxy 500 and Luna. . . . Fans of Wareham's bands and such bands as Bongwater, Cocteau Twins, R.E.M., and the Velvet Underground, as well as anyone with an interest in American and European alternative music, will find this to be an insightful and entertaining read." Libr J

Warren, Louis S.

Buffalo Bill's America; William Cody and the Wild West Show. Alfred A. Knopf 2005 652p il $30   **92**

1. Biography, Individual 2. Circus executives 3. Circus performers 4. Entertainers 5. Frontier and pioneer life 6. Frontier and pioneer life -- Western States 7. Hunters 8. Scouts 9. Wild west shows
ISBN 0-375-41216-6

LC 2004-63280

This is a biography of the American showman.

This book "is well written and exhaustively researched, the weightiest and surely the most ambitious book ever published about Cody and his times." N Y Times Book Rev

Includes bibliographical references

Washington, Booker T.

★ **Up** from slavery; edited with an introduction and notes by William L. Andrews. Oxford University Press 2008 xxvii, 196p pa $9.95   **92**

1. African American educators 2. African Americans -- Biography 3. Authors 4. Civil rights activists 5. Educators 6. Memoirists 7. Nonfiction writers 8. Slaves
ISBN 978-0-19-955239-9

LC 2008-279129

"The classic autobiography of the man who, though born in slavery, educated himself and went on to found Tuskegee Institute." N Y Public Libr

Includes bibliographical references

Waters, John

Role models. Farrar, Straus and Giroux 2010 304p il $25   **92**

1. Biography, Individual 2. Motion picture directors 3. Motion picture producers and directors 4. Screenwriters
ISBN 978-0-374-25147-5; 0-374-25147-9

LC 2009-42211

"The famed cult-film director recalls the famous—and not-so-famous—people he has idolized over the years. . . . In this consistently charming and witty collection of essays, he fondly remembers the many artists he has admired throughout his life, from stars, such as Little Richard, to such near-unknown figures as the 1960s Baltimore stripper Lady Zorro. . . . An impressive, heartfelt collection by a true American iconoclast." Kirkus

Includes bibliographical references

Watson, James D.

Avoid boring people; lessons from a life in science. Alfred A. Knopf 2007 347p il $26.95   **92**

1. Biography, Individual 2. College teachers 3. Molecular biologists 4. Nobel laureates for physiology or medicine 5. Scientists
ISBN 978-0-375-41284-4; 0-375-41284-0

LC 2007-15675

"In this memoir, Watson shows by example how to get to the top and stay there. Spanning his boyhood interest in birds to his resignation from Harvard University in 1976 to his leadership of Cold Spring Harbor Laboratory, Watson's reminiscences encompass his claim to fame—cocredit for deducing DNA's structure in 1953—but focus on his am-

bition and his conduct of academic politics. . . . In angular and opinionated prose, Watson proves as engaging as ever." Booklist

Includes bibliographical references

Genes, girls, and Gamow; after the double helix. Knopf 2002 xxix, 259p il $26; pa $14   **92**

1. College teachers 2. Molecular biologists 3. Molecular biologists -- United States -- Biography 4. Nobel laureates for physiology or medicine
ISBN 0-375-41283-2; 0-375-72715-9 pa

LC 2001-38543

"In 1953, Watson, then 25, and colleague Francis Crick discovered the structure of DNA. . . . Here Watson . . . gives a detailed, journal-writer's account of the aftermath, recalling . . . his younger self's professional and—equally pressing—amorous ambitions. . . . Reading Watson is a delight, an opportunity to breathe the rarefied air of his generation's greatest scientists and to crash a faculty cocktail party or two along the way." Publ Wkly

Watson, Richard A.

★ **Cogito** ergo sum: the life of Rene Descartes; {by} Richard Watson. Godine 2002 375p $35   **92**

1. Authors 2. Mathematicians 3. Philosophers 4. Philosophers -- France -- Biography
ISBN 1-56792-184-1

LC 2001-40858

"For all of his puckish delight in a juicy anecdote, Watson recognizes and carefully explicates the cultural centrality of Descartes' intellectual legacy. That legacy ensures numerous readers sure to praise a biographer who delivers both the philosopher's cerebral doctrines and his unmistakably human conduct." Booklist

Includes bibliographical references

Watts, Jill

Hattie McDaniel; black ambition, white Hollywood. Amistad 2005 352p il hardcover o.p. pa $14.95   **92**

1. Actors 2. Biography, Individual
ISBN 0-06-051490-6; 0-06-051491-4 pa

LC 2005-42126

"Watts is both sympathetic and honest: we pity McDaniel and her unenviable position, but at the same time, see how her intense careerism drove her often to accommodate rather than challenge film industry racism. . . . Watts' research is extensive, her writing clear and accessible, and her book a thorough, engaging, intelligent piece of historical scholarship." Women's Rev of Books

Watts, Steven

Mr. Playboy; Hugh Hefner and the American dream. Wiley 2008 529p il $29.95   **92**

1. Biography, Individual 2. Magazine executives
ISBN 9780471690597; 0-4716-9059-7

LC 2008-9572

"This is not a gossip book but a well-documented biography written with access to Hefner's over 1800 scrapbooks, the company archives, and interviews. Watts finds Hefner comparable to the subjects of his other books about Henry

Ford and Walt Disney in that all were major contributors to aspects of the American dream." Libr J

Includes bibliographical references

The **people's** tycoon; Henry Ford and the American century. Knopf 2005 614p il $30 **92**
1. Antisemitism 2. Automobile executives 3. Automobile industry and trade -- United States -- History 4. Biography, Individual 5. Philanthropists
ISBN 0-375-40735-9

LC 2004-48594

"Steven Watts is intelligent, thorough and engaging . . . in telling the story of an American who not only was influential but remains unavoidable to this day." N Y Times Book Rev

Includes bibliographical references

Webster, Charles

Paracelsus; medicine, magic and mission at the end of time. Yale University Press 2008 326p il $40 **92**
1. Alchemists 2. Alchemy 3. Physicians 4. Writers on science
ISBN 978-0-300-13911-2; 0-300-13911-X

LC 2008-27973

In this consideration of the "Renaissance doctor, alchemist, and theologian, Webster draws on nonscientific writings by Paracelsus that have been made widely available only in the past few decades. . . . [Paracelsus] orbited a wealthy and powerful class of physicians, but his unorthodox views made him a virtual 'vagrant' among his peers. He broke from the millennia-old theory of the humors, developing new medical theories based upon a mystical vision of man as a microcosm of the universe, and an alchemically informed notion of the intrinsic properties of certain metals. Webster paints Paracelsus as a 'religious and social controversialist,' and argues that the diverse strands of his thought were unified by his belief that the end of time was near, when, he imagined, the demise of physical suffering would obviate the need for medical intervention." New Yorker

Includes bibliographical references and index.

Weigel, George

Witness to hope: the biography of Pope John Paul II. Cliff St. Bks. 1999 992p il $35; pa $20 **92**
1. Popes
ISBN 0-06-018793-X; 0-06-093286-4 pa

LC 99-26340

Weigel "focuses on John Paul's trademark ideas: Christian humanism, the inner connection between freedom and truth, and culture as the driving force of history. As a guide to the pope's thought, Witness to Hope is invaluable." Publ Wkly

Includes bibliographical references

Weintraub, Stanley

Charlotte and Lionel; a Rothschild love story. Free Press 2003 316p il hardcover o.p. pa $22.95 **92**
1. Bankers 2. Bankers -- Great Britain -- Biography 3. Banks and banking -- Great Britain -- History 4. Jewish bankers 5. Jewish bankers -- Great Britain -- Biography

6. Members of Parliament 7. Spouses of prominent persons
ISBN 0-7432-2686-0; 978-1-4165-7332-6; 1-4165-7332-1 pa

LC 2002-29994

The author profiles one of the Victorian era's "oddly (given their Jewishness and British anti-Semitism) quintessential couples. Lionel Rothschild, scion of the British branch of the famed banking family, married his beautiful German wife, Charlotte, in 1836, when she was 16 (he was a decade older). The bride was, following family custom, also Lionel's cousin and would mature into a sparkling saloniste and hostess whose dinner invitations, Weintraub notes, were preferred over those from Buckingham Palace. . . . Weintraub offers an enticing inside look at a storied family that played a central public role in Victorian England." Publ Wkly

Includes bibliographical references

Weir, Alison

Mary, Queen of Scots, and the murder of Lord Darnley. Ballantine Bks. 2003 670p il map $27.95; pa $16.95 **92**
1. Princes 2. Queens
ISBN 0-345-43658-X; 0-8129-7151-5 pa

LC 2002-34467

"No stone is left unturned in {Weir's} investigation, and despite its detail, her book is as dramatic as witnessing firsthand the most riveting court case." Booklist

The **lady** in the tower; the fall of Anne Boleyn. Ballantine Books 2009 434p il $28 **92**
1. Biography, Individual 2. Kings 3. Queens
ISBN 978-0-345-45321-1; 0-345-45321-2

LC 2009-42748

Historian Weir is "well equipped to parse the evidence, ferret out the misconceptions and arrive at sturdy hypotheses about what actually befell Anne. Her command of minutiae is impressive, as is her enthusiasm for even the most minor aspects of Anne's frequently distorted story." N Y Times Book Rev

Includes bibliographical references

Weisskopf, Michael

Blood brothers; among the soldiers of Ward 57. H. Holt 2006 301p il hardcover o.p. pa $15 **92**
1. Iraq War, 2003 -- Personal narratives 2. Iraq War, 2003- -- Personal narratives 3. Journalists
ISBN 978-0-8050-7860-2; 0-8050-7860-6; 978-0-8050-8660-7 pa; 0-8050-8660-9 pa

LC 2006-43382

"Weisskopf recognizes his own experience in that of the soldiers, making for a wonderful story of tragedy and recovery." Libr J

Includes bibliographical references

Weller, Sam

The **Bradbury** chronicles; the life of Ray Bradbury. William Morrow 2005 384p il $26.95; pa $15.95 **92**
1. Authors 2. Authors, American 3. Biography, Individual 4. Children's authors 5. Novelists 6.

Science fiction writers 7. Screenwriters 8. Short story writers
ISBN 0-06-054581-X; 0-06-054584-4 pa
LC 2004-59491

"Weller's research—based on interviews with Bradbury as well as family members and colleagues—is almost exhaustive in its detail, and he does a fine job of presenting the facts of his subject's unique life. The lively, conversational prose brings out the writer's winning personality and turns his struggles and successes into a highly readable story." SLJ

Includes bibliographical references

Welty, Eudora

One writer's beginnings. Harvard Univ. Press 1984 104p il hardcover o.p. pa $12   **92**
1. Authors 2. Authors, American 3. Biography, Individual 4. Novelists 5. Short story writers
ISBN 0-674-63925-1; 0-674-63927-8 pa
LC 83-18638

A series of lectures in which the author reflects on her Southern heritage and her early artistic influences.

Wenner, Jann S.

★ **Gonzo**; the life of Hunter S. Thompson. by Jann S. Wenner & Corey Seymour; introduction by Johnny Depp. Little, Brown 2007 467p il $28.99 **92**
1. Authors 2. Biography, Individual 3. Columnists 4. Journalists 5. Nonfiction writers 6. Novelists 7. Satirists
ISBN 978-0-316-00527-2; 0-316-00527-4
LC 2007-11693

This oral biography is a "look at the turbulent life of Gonzo journalism pioneer Hunter S. Thompson (1937-2005). . . . This fine, fond biography amuses, inspires, outrages and haunts at all the right moments—and sometimes all at once." Publ Wkly

Wert, Jeffry D.

Cavalryman of the lost cause; a biography of J.E.B. Stuart. Simon & Schuster 2008 496p il map $32; pa $18   **92**
1. Generals
ISBN 978-0-7432-7819-5; 0-7432-7819-4; 978-0-7432-7824-9 pa; 0-7432-7824-0 pa
LC 2007-51552

This is a chronicle of the life of "the controversial cavalry leader of the Army of Northern Virginia until his death in combat in 1864. Wert's thoughtful account of Stuart's role at Gettysburg eventuates in a balanced analysis of a well-conceived reconnaissance-in-force. . . . This is a portrait of a Stuart more complex and, indeed, more attractive than either his friends or his enemies have painted in at least a generation." Booklist

Includes bibliographical references

Wertheim, L. Jon

Blood in the cage; mixed martial arts, Pat Miletich, and the furious rise of the UFC. Houghton Mifflin Harcourt 2009 251p il $25   **92**
1. Martial arts 2. Sportswriters
ISBN 978-0-618-98261-5; 0-618-98261-2
LC 2008-36764

"MMA has yet to find its great scribe, its Liebling, Pierce Egan or Norman Mailer, but it is young. Until that new bard of bloodshed comes along, 'Blood in the Cage' will stand as a worthy introduction to the birth of something both awful and beautiful." Salon

White, Bill

Uppity; my untold story about the games people play. [by] Bill White with Gordon Dillow; foreword by Willie Mays. Grand Central Pub. 2011 303p il $26.99   **92**
1. African American athletes 2. Baseball -- Biography 3. Baseball executives 4. Baseball players 5. Biography, Individual 6. Sport association executives 7. Sportscasters
ISBN 9780446555258; 0446555258
LC 2010-38025

"During his 13 years as a player, [Bill White] won All-Star recognition and frequent Gold Gloves as a slick-fielding, power-hitting first baseman, though he was never the flamboyant type who would call attention to himself. Then he embarked on an 18-year career as a broadcaster, memorably providing a balance to the more unpredictable Phil Rizzuto as announcers for the New York Yankees. He capped his career by serving five years as president of the National League. . . . Whatever his level of involvement, White approached baseball as a career through which he made his living rather than a sport he loved, an attitude that is likely to ruffle sentimentalists. . . . He describes the abuse he took from redneck fans during minor league days when he was one of the few black players on a team, through his battles with the white tycoons who exerted increasing control over the industry before he resigned as league president. Yet his account is otherwise color blind as it separates the heroes of White's life (Willie Mays, Bing Devine, Johnny Keane and others in addition to Rizzuto) from the villains." Kirkus

White, E. B.

Letters of E.B. White; originally collected and edited by Dorothy Lobrano Guth. Rev. ed.; Harper Collins 2006 713p il $35   **92**
1. Authors 2. Authors, American 3. Children's authors 4. Essayists 5. Humorists 6. Novelists 7. Poets 8. Satirists
ISBN 978-0-06-075708-3; 0-06-075708-6
LC 2006-43490

This collection of letters by the essayist, poet, novelist and author of several classic children's books is chronologically arranged. Written between the years 1908 when White was nine and 1985 when he died, they concern his relationships with his wife, Katherine White and his family and friends, which include Harold Ross, James Thurber, Robert Benchley, Alexander Woollcott and others.

White, Edmund

City boy; my life in New York during the 1960s and 70s. Bloomsbury USA 2009 297p $26   **92**
1. Authors 2. Authors, American 3. Biographers 4. Biography, Individual 5. Gay men 6. Memoirists 7. Novelists 8. Short story writers
ISBN 978-1-596-91402-5; 1-596-91402-5
LC 2009-12493

The author "weaves erotic encounters and long-ago lite-rati into a vast tapestry of Manhattan memories. . . . This is a brilliant recreation of an era, rich in revels, revolutions and 'leather boys leading the human tidal wave.'" Publ Wkly

Rimbaud; the double life of a rebel. Atlas & Company 2008 192p $24   **92**
1. Authors 2. Biography, Individual 3. Poets 4. Poets, French
ISBN 978-1-934633-15-1
"Included in this literary biography are White's superb translations of works he is discussing. . . . This is a disturbing and original portrait of a man White sees as a fallen angel who misbehaved even in hell." Publ Wkly

White, Michael
Leonardo; the first scientist. St. Martin's Press 2000 370p il $27.95; pa $16.95   **92**
1. Artists 2. Artists, Italian 3. Painters 4. Scientists 5. Writers on science
ISBN 0-312-20333-0; 0-312-27026-7 pa
The author "focuses on the scientific creations of da Vinci, emphasizing his notebooks, which had been lost for 200 years and only portions of which have been recovered. White describes how da Vinci's personal life affected his sci-entific discoveries and predictions, and vice versa." Booklist

White, Ronald C.
A. Lincoln; a biography. Random House Pub. Group 2009 796p il map $35   **92**
1. Biography, Individual 2. Lawyers 3. Members of Congress 4. Presidents 5. Presidents -- United States 6. State legislators
ISBN 978-1-4000-6499-1

LC 2008-28840
In this biography, the author "follows the familiar trajec-tory of the 16th President's life; what's unique is his insight into the moral and intellectual framework of Lincoln's think-ing. . . . An exceptional work that belongs in every public and academic library." Libr J
Includes bibliographical references (p. [745]-764) and index.

The **eloquent** president: a portrait of Lincoln through his words; [by] Ronald C. White, Jr. Random House 2005 xxiii, 448p il $26.95; pa $15.95 **92**
1. Lawyers 2. Members of Congress 3. Presidents 4. Presidents -- United States 5. State legislators
ISBN 1-400-06119-9; 0-8129-7046-2 pa

LC 2004-50766
The author "traces Lincoln's evolving rhetoric over the course of his presidency in a series of highly detailed critical essays. He follows Lincoln from the cautious, lawyerly text of the First Inaugural to the soaring, triumphant poetics of the Gettysburg Address." Publ Wkly
Includes bibliographical references

Whitehouse, Beth
The **match**; savior siblings and one family's bat-tle to heal their daughter. Beacon Press 2010 255p $24.95; pa $16   **92**
1. Bone marrow -- Transplantation 2. Fertilization in

vitro 3. Procurement of organs, tissues, etc. 4. Sick
ISBN 978-0-8070-7286-8; 0-8070-7286-9; 978-0-8070-0121-9 pa; 0-8070-0121-X pa

LC 2009035949
The author "tracks Stacy and Steve Trebing and their decision to create a baby boy selected as an embryo as a genetic match for a sister suffering from Diamond-Blackfan anemia, a rare and fatal disease." Publ Wkly

Whitfield, Eileen
Pickford; the woman who made Hollywood. University Press of Ky. 1997 441p il $27.50   **92**
1. Actors 2. Biography, Individual
ISBN 0-8131-2045-4

LC 97-29312
"Silent screen star Mary Pickford was 'America's Sweetheart,' capturing the imagination of the public as 'Lit-tle Mary,' the adolescent with spunk. She married swash-buckler Douglas Fairbanks, and with Charlie Chaplin and D.W. Griffith they formed United Artists, the first production company run by people who acted and directed. . . . Though it does include delicious anecdotes from those who were there, this is not simply a typical celebrity biography but a 'biography' of the times." Libr J
Includes bibliographical references

Whyte, Kenneth
The **uncrowned** king; the sensational rise of William Randolph Hearst. Counterpoint 2009 546p il $30   **92**
1. Biography, Individual 2. Journalism -- United States -- History 3. Newspaper editors 4. Newspaper executives 5. Publishers and publishing
ISBN 978-1-58243-467-4; 1-58243-467-0

LC 2008-47442
"A very worthwhile reexamination of the rise of a flawed but accomplished man." Booklist
Includes bibliographical references (p. 505-511)

Widmer, Edward L.
Martin Van Buren; [by] Ted Widmer. Times Bks. 2005 189p $20   **92**
1. Biography, Individual 2. Presidents 3. Presidents -- United States 4. Secretaries of state 5. Vice-presidents
ISBN 0-8050-6922-4

LC 2004-53652
The author "keenly evokes the environment that enabled Van Buren to thrive. . . . Widmer also lends a certain dignity to Van Buren's post-presidential attempts to resolve the sec-tional crisis." N Y Times Book Rev
Includes bibliographical references

Wilentz, Sean
Andrew Jackson. Times Books 2005 195p $20   **92**
1. Generals 2. Presidents 3. Presidents -- United States
ISBN 0-8050-6925-9

LC 2005-52857
The author "shows that our complicated seventh presi-dent was a central figure in the development of American de-

mocracy.... It is rare that historians manage both Wilentz's deep interpretation and lively narrative." Publ Wkly

Includes bibliographical references

Bob Dylan in America. Doubleday 2010 400p il $28.95 **92**

1. Folk musicians 2. Popular culture -- United States 3. Popular music -- United States -- History and criticism 4. Singers 5. Songwriters

ISBN 978-0-385-52988-4; 0-385-52988-0

LC 2009-47636

"Dylan, of course, has been the subject of other biographies and has published the first book in what he intends as a multi-volume autobiography. Wilentz's book stands apart from these in the lucidity of its prose, the rigor of its research and convincing originality of the place he assigns his subject in the context of American cultural history. Fans looking for a recording-by-recording, concert-by-concert account of the singer and songwriter's career would do better looking elsewhere, though there's plenty of truly fine analysis of the most significant songs and recordings. Where Wilentz excels is in teasing out the origins of Dylan's artistic impulses, the context in which they arose and flowered, the multiple sources of his art." Los Angeles Times

Includes bibliographical references

Wilkinson, Alec

The **protest** singer; an intimate portrait of Pete Seeger. Alfred A. Knopf 2009 151p il $22.95; pa $14 **92**

1. Biography, Individual 2. Folk musicians 3. Singers 4. Songwriters

ISBN 978-0-307-26995-9; 978-0-307-39098-1 pa

LC 2008-54387

The author "draws on interviews with Seeger and others to present a seamless chronicle of his life and music, vivifying his passion for humanity, love of the environment, and deep curiosity about music." Libr J

Williams, Kate

Becoming Queen Victoria; the tragic death of Princess Charlotte and the unexpected rise of Britain's greatest monarch. Ballantine Books 2010 448p il $30; ebook $30 **92**

1. Princesses 2. Queens

ISBN 978-0-345-46195-7; 978-0-345-52193-4 ebook

LC 2010-13227

"A lively, juicy read, full of the sordid details of the debauched rule of kings and princes that led to the moralistic rule of a queen focused on creating a royal family that embodied the ideals of a nation. Perfect for fans of royal histories and historical television shows or armchair historians interested in a swift and enjoyable read." Libr J

Includes bibliographical references

Williamson, Edwin

Borges, a life. Viking 2004 416p $34.95 **92**

1. Authors 2. Biography, Individual 3. Essayists 4. Literary critics 5. Novelists 6. Poets 7. Short story writers 8. Translators

ISBN 0-670-88579-7

LC 2004-41290

This "is a richly psychological, dynamically intellectual, and deeply affecting portrait of an often anguished and inhibited man who, through heroic perserverance and spiritual conviction, found salvation in writing and transformed literature for all time." Booklist

Includes bibliographical references

Wills, Garry

Outside looking in; adventures of an observer. Viking 2010 195p $25.95 **92**

1. Authors 2. Biography, Individual 3. College teachers 4. Essayists 5. Historians 6. Journalists 7. Social critics

ISBN 978-0-670-02214-4

LC 2010-05323

"Wills's curiosity and personal integrity shine through this intellectual memoir that is both intimate and journalistic. Readers who have followed Wills's writing career will welcome these reflections on his life and the world around him." Libr J

Includes bibliographical references

Wilson, A. N.

Betjeman; a life. Farrar, Straus & Giroux 2006 375p il $27 **92**

1. Architectural historians 2. Authors 3. Historic preservationists 4. Poets 5. Poets laureate 6. Satirists

ISBN 978-0-374-11198-4; 0-374-11198-7

LC 2006-930677

Wilson's biography of the British Poet Laureate "is a sharp-edged triumph of honest hero worship. Amazingly, he has found a real-life character whom he can love and admire.... Brushing aside hundreds of chatty anecdotes and conversations that might have happened, Wilson has tied his primary source material around a subtle analysis of the ultimate first sources, the poems themselves. This, it is safe to say, should be the final biography." Times Lit Suppl

Wilson, Derek A.

Charlemagne. Doubleday 2006 226p il map $26; pa $14.95 **92**

1. Emperors 2. Kings and rulers

ISBN 0-385-51670-3; 0-307-27480-2 pa

LC 2005-48483

The author "writes with clarity and passion, and his thesis is food for thought for both general readers and students." Libr J

Includes bibliographical references

Out of the storm; the life and legacy of Martin Luther. [by] Derek Wilson. St. Martin's Press 2008 399p il $29.95 **92**

1. Reformation 2. Religious leaders 3. Social reformers 4. Theologians 5. Writers on religion

ISBN 978-0-312-37588-1; 0-312-37588-3

LC 2007-39331

"A nuanced portrait of a perplexing titan." Booklist

Includes bibliographical references

Wilson, Diane

Holy roller; growing up in the church of knock down drag out, or, How I stopped loving a blue-eyed

Jesus: a childhood memoir. Chelsea Green Pub. 2008 210p il $24.95 **92**

1. Conservationists 2. Environmentalists 3. Fishermen

ISBN 978-1-933392-82-0; 1-933392-82-7

LC 2008-21199

"Churchgoing was more than an occasional Sunday morning outing; it was a 24/7 occupation overseen by a grandmother who judged every aspect of life according to a strict and literal interpretation of the scriptures. In Wilson's provocative memoir of life in the Texas Bible Belt of the 1950s, snake-handling preachers, fitful parishioners speaking in tongues, and money-hungry radio evangelists share equal billing with corrupt game wardens, outlaw fishermen, and less-than-devout male relatives whose 'backsliding' ways give their womenfolk immense cause for concern. Through a vividly kaleidoscopic voice that captures the intensity of fanatical religious rapture with pitch-perfect accuracy, Wilson exuberantly animates a feverish time, a frenetic place, and its fiery people." Booklist

An **unreasonable** woman; a true story of shrimpers, politicos, polluters and the fight for Seadrift, Texas. foreword by Kenny Ausubel. Chelsea Green 2005 400p map $27.50; pa $18 **92**

1. Biography, Individual 2. Chemical industry -- Waste disposal 3. Conservationists 4. Environmental protection 5. Environmental protection -- Texas 6. Fishermen

ISBN 1-931498-88-1; 978-1-931498-88-3; 1-933392-27-4 pa; 978-1-933392-27-1 pa

LC 2005-9894

"With the discovery that her 'piddlin' little county on the Gulf Coast' led the nation in toxic emissions, shrimper Wilson, a mother of five, found herself embarking on a voyage of discovery and activism that would strain her marriage and stretch her horizons. A David up against big-time chemical Goliaths, Wilson is a gifted storyteller, rendering dialogue and pacing plot turns as a novelist might." Publ Wkly

Wilson, Frances

The **ballad** of Dorothy Wordsworth; a life. Farrar, Straus and Giroux 2009 316p il map $30 **92**

1. Authors 2. Authors, English 3. Diarists 4. Poets 5. Poets laureate 6. Travel writers

ISBN 978-0-374-10867-0; 0-374-10867-6

LC 2008-41263

"Ms. Wilson focuses primarily on the years 1800-3, when Dorothy, then in her late 20s and early 30s, lived with her brother in the Lake District of England and kept her famous Grasmere Journals, which were not published in full until 1958. They were crucial years, not just for her but also for her brother, who was still writing some of his most important poems, and for Samuel Coleridge, who moves in and out of this book like the third magpie in a bustling nest. Ms. Wilson's decision to limit her scope was a small bit of genius. She's written a succinct yet roomy book, one that moves along with novelistic buoyancy and grace." N Y Times Book Rev

Includes bibliographical references

Winchester, Simon

★ The **man** who loved China; the fantastic story of the eccentric scientist who unlocked the mysteries of the Middle Kingdom. HarperCollins Publishers 2008 316p il map $27.95 **92**

1. Biochemists 2. Biography, Individual 3. Science -- China -- History 4. Science historians 5. Scientists 6. Writers on science

ISBN 978-0-06-088459-8; 0-06-088459-2

LC 2007-40516

The author "explores Needham's fascinating and sometimes controversial personal life, his travels to China, and especially the significance and topicality of his scholarship on the early accomplishments of Chinese science and technology. . . . Essential for all libraries." Libr J

Includes bibliographical references

Wineapple, Brenda

Hawthorne: a life. Alfred A. Knopf 2003 509p il $30 **92**

1. Authors 2. Novelists 3. Short story writers

ISBN 0-375-40044-3

LC 2002-192485

In this biography Wineapple discusses the "public controversies that shaped [Hawthorne's] world: the Whig triumphs that cost him his customhouse job and forced him into writing; the critical exchanges that heartened him with praise for his work . . . and wounded him with disparagement; and the Civil War battles that drove him to despair— and into political disrepute as a copperhead." Booklist

Includes bibliographical references

White heat; the friendship of Emily Dickinson and Thomas Wentworth Higginson. Alfred A. Knopf 2008 416p il $27.95 **92**

1. Authors 2. Biography, Individual 3. Clergy 4. Memoirists 5. Poets 6. Poets, American 7. Social reformers

ISBN 1-4000-4401-4; 978-1-4000-4401-6

LC 2008-11770

This is an account of the friendship between the poet Emily Dickinson and the reformer Thomas Wentworth Higginson, author of Army Life in a Black Regiment (1869).

"A moving portrait of two unalike but kindred spirits who did indeed 'Dare [to] see a Soul at the "White Heat."'" Kirkus

Includes bibliographical references

Winters, Kathleen C.

Amelia Earhart; the turbulent life of an American icon. Palgrave Macmillan 2010 242p il map $25 **92**

1. Air pilots 2. Biography, Individual 3. Memoirists 4. Missing persons 5. Women air pilots

ISBN 978-0-230-61669-1

LC 2010-20026

"With erudite analysis of everything from Earhart's flying to her marriage and longtime financial support of her parents and sister, Winters proves there is still much to learn about this American icon." Booklist

Includes bibliographical references

Anne Morrow Lindbergh; first lady of the air. Palgrave Macmillan 2006 241p il map $24.95   **92**

1. Authors 2. Biography, Individual 3. Diarists 4. Essayists 5. Memoirists 6. Novelists 7. Poets 8. Spouses of prominent persons

ISBN 978-1-4039-6932-3; 1-4039-6932-9

LC 2006-43290

This book focuses on Anne Morrow Lindbergh's career as an aviator. "She was one of the earliest female pilots, as well as the first American female glider pilot, and a radio operator. . . . Winters shows in great detail that Lindbergh accomplished this under the glare of an unremitting spotlight, and in the company of an often-demanding spouse. That the author is able to bring something new to the Lindbergh story is impressive, and she does it through both technical explanations of Lindbergh's accomplishments and Anne's own words about her flying exploits, marriage, and writing." Booklist

Includes bibliographical references

Wintle, Justin

Perfect hostage; a life of Aung San Suu Kyi, Burma's prisoner of conscience. Skyhorse Pub. 2008 464p il map $27.95   **92**

1. Dissenters 2. Human rights activists 3. Nobel laureates for peace 4. Nonfiction writers 5. Political leaders 6. Political prisoners 7. Women political activists

ISBN 978-1-60239-266-3; 1-60239-266-8

LC 2007-51031

This is a biography of the Burmese human rights activist.

The author "writes with a snarling wit, firm grasp of Burma's horrors, and penetrating respect for this tenacious and composed prisoner of conscience, detailing her genius for connecting with people, the threats against her life, and her devotion to peace." Booklist

Includes bibliographical references (p. 432-9)

Wizenberg, Molly

A **homemade** life; stories and recipes from my kitchen table. illustrations by Camilla Engman. Simon & Schuster 2009 320p il $25   **92**

1. Bloggers 2. Cookery 3. Cooking 4. Food critics 5. Women authors

ISBN 978-1-4165-5105-8; 1-4165-5105-0

LC 2008-36430

This "delightful . . . book will undoubtedly be gobbled up like a tin of Christmas cookies." Libr J

Wolfe, Charles K.

The **life** and legend of Leadbelly; [by] Charles Wolfe and Kip Lornell. Da Capo Press 1999 333p il pa $16.95   **92**

1. Accordionists 2. African American musicians 3. Blues music 4. Guitarists 5. Singers 6. Songwriters

ISBN 978-0-306-80896-8; 0-306-80896-X

"Drawing on a variety of primary and secondary sources, including numerous interviews, Wolfe and Lornell attempt

to separate fact from fiction. . . . Photographs, informative notes, and a full discography are valuable additions." Choice

Includes discography and bibliographical references

Wolff, Michael

The **man** who owns the news; inside the secret world of Rupert Murdoch. Broadway Books 2008 446p $29.95   **92**

1. Biography, Individual 2. Broadcasting executives 3. Businessmen 4. Mass media 5. Mass media -- Australia 6. Motion picture executives 7. Newspaper executives 8. Publishing executives

ISBN 978-0-385-52612-8; 0-385-52612-1

LC 2008-37414

This biography of the Australian media entrepreneur describes how Rupert Murdoch came to own various companies, including The Wall Street Journal as well as its parent company, Dow Jones.

"There's lots of good material. . . . Perhaps most instructive, Wolff has melded interview and observation into what might be called a plausible theory of Murdoch." LA Times

Includes bibliographical references (p. 430-434)

Wolff, Tobias

★ **This** boy's life: a memoir. Atlantic Monthly Press 1989 288p hardcover o.p. pa $14   **92**

1. Authors 2. Authors, American 3. College teachers 4. Memoirists 5. Nonfiction writers 6. Novelists 7. Short story writers

ISBN 0-871-13248-6; 0-8021-3668-0 pa

LC 88-17600

The novelist and short story writer "offers an engrossing and candid look into his childhood and adolescence in his first book of nonfiction. In unaffected prose he recreates scenes from his life that sparkle with the immediacy of narrative fiction. The result is an intriguingly guileless book, distinct from the usual reflective commentary of autobiography." Libr J

Woo, Ilyon

The **great** divorce; a nineteenth-century mother's extraordinary fight against her husband, the Shakers, and her times. Atlantic Monthly Press 2010 404p $25   **92**

1. Abusive persons 2. Child custody 3. Converts 4. Divorce 5. Feminists 6. Parental kidnapping 7. Shakers 8. Shakers -- New York (State)

ISBN 978-0-8021-1946-9; 0-8021-1946-8

"Both Eunice's struggle and the Shakers' story fascinate equally while dispelling romanticized myths of utopian societies in the tumultuous postrevolutionary period." Publ Wkly

Includes bibliographical references

Woodress, James Leslie

Willa Cather; a literary life. {by} James Woodress. University of Neb. Press 1987 xx, 583p il hardcover o.p. pa $29.95   **92**

1. Authors 2. Novelists 3. Short story writers 4. Western writers

ISBN 0-8032-9708-4 pa

LC 86-30894

The author "does a fine job of describing Willa Cather's colorful public life and of piecing together the puzzle of her unconventional private life. . . . Mr. Woodress does not try to superimpose on Cather's life any theories—feminist, Freudian, Lacanian, or otherwise. Instead, he recounts in straightforward and lively prose the life of a remarkable woman." N Y Times Book Rev

Includes bibliographical references

Woods, Randall Bennett

LBJ; architect of American ambition. [by] Randall B. Woods. Free Press 2006 1007p il $35   **92**
1. Biography, Individual 2. Members of Congress 3. Presidents 4. Presidents -- United States 5. Senators 6. Vice-presidents
ISBN 978-0-684-83458-0; 0-684-83458-8
                  LC 2006-41259
This is a biography of the 36th president of the United States.
The author "has produced an excellent biography that fully deserves a place alongside the best of the Johnson studies yet to appear." N Y Times Book Rev
Includes bibliographical references

Woodworth, Steven E.

Sherman; [foreword by Wesley K. Clark] Palgrave Macmillan 2009 198p il map $21.95   **92**
1. Generals 2. Memoirists 3. Secretaries of war
ISBN 0-230-61024-2; 978-0-230-61024-8
                  LC 2008-22060
This is a biography of the Civil War general.
"An excellent brief life of a major and controversial figure." Booklist
Includes bibliographical references

Woolf, Virginia

A **moment's** liberty: the shorter diary; abridged and edited by Anne Olivier Bell; introduction by Quentin Bell. Harcourt Brace Jovanovich 1990 516p hardcover o.p. pa $20   **92**
1. Authors 2. Authors, English 3. Essayists 4. Novelists 5. Short story writers
ISBN 0-15-161894-1; 0-15-661912-1 pa
                  LC 90-33428
"The diaries here may appeal to a larger audience, not least because each year represented is prefaced by a wonderfully succinct overview. Here are Woolf's superbly drawn portraits of Max Beerbohm, T.S. Eliot, John Maynard Keynes, Katherine Mansfield—and her occasionally acerbic remarks on what they said and did. But the diaries are also a repository for luminous thoughts on birds and weather, the pleasures of walking or listening to music." Publ Wkly

Worster, Donald

A **passion** for nature; the life of John Muir. Oxford University Press 2008 535p il map $34.95 **92**
1. Authors 2. Biography, Individual 3. Naturalists 4. Nature conservation -- United States -- History 5. Writers on nature
ISBN 978-0-19-516682-8; 0-19-516682-5
                  LC 2008-1441

The author "draws on John Muir's (1838-1914) correspondence and writings to offer an enlightening biography of the influential naturalist. . . . Competently documented, this all-inclusive biography explains the life and times of a figure known to all who love nature and will appeal to general readers and anyone interested in the early roots of today's green movement and its founding fathers." Libr J

Includes bibliographical references (p. 494-508)

Worthen, John

D.H. Lawrence; the life of an outsider. Counterpoint 2005 xxvi, 518p il $29.95   **92**
1. Authors 2. Dramatists 3. Essayists 4. Novelists 5. Poets 6. Short story writers
ISBN 1-58243-341-0
"Using as a unifying theme Lawrence's perpetual status as an outsider, both in working-class Nottinghamshire and in the English literary world, Worthen gives us the full sweep of this groundbreaking writer's utterly unconventional, often torturous, and occasionally rhapsodic life." Booklist
Includes bibliographical references

D.H. Lawrence, the early years, 1885-1912. Cambridge Univ. Press 1991 626p il hardcover o.p. pa $30   **92**
1. Authors 2. Dramatists 3. Essayists 4. Novelists 5. Poets 6. Short story writers
ISBN 0-521-43772-5 pa
                  LC 90-23423
This "first volume of Cambridge's three-volume life of Lawrence, . . . takes the young writer through his elopement with Frieda. . . . This persuasive biography is compulsive good reading from cover to cover. A major event in modern literary studies." Libr J
Includes bibliographical references

Wranovics, John

Chaplin and Agee; the untold story of the tramp, the writer, and the lost screenplay. Palgrave Macmillan 2005 256p il $24.95   **92**
1. Actors 2. Authors 3. Biography, Individual 4. Motion picture critics 5. Motion picture directors 6. Motion picture producers 7. Nonfiction writers 8. Novelists 9. Poets 10. Screenwriters
ISBN 1-403-96866-7
                  LC 2004-62807
A "double biography of two of the 20th century's most talented artists. Wranovic's hook is a lost screenplay titled The Tramp's New World, which Agee wrote for Chaplin after the detonation of the atomic bomb over Hiroshima. . . . Using personal correspondence and critical reviews, Wranovics re-creates the fascinating historical backdrop of the Agee/Chaplin friendship, interweaving into the stunning tapestry the colorful lives of such luminaries as Brecht, Auden, Ed Sullivan, and John Huston." Choice

Wright, Orville

How we invented the airplane; an illustrated history. edited with an introduction and commentary by Fred C. Kelly; additional text by Alan Weissman. Dover Publs. 1988 87p il pa $9.95   **92**
1. Aeronautics -- History 2. Aircraft industry executives

3. Airplanes 4. Inventors
ISBN 0-486-25662-6

LC 87-33037

This "account by the two inventors . . . covers experiments, discovery of aeronautical principles, construction of planes and motors, first flights, and much more. Also included is a later account written by both brothers." Publisher's note

Includes bibliographical references

Wright, Richard

★ **Black** boy; (American hunger): a record of childhood and youth. foreword by Edward P. Jones. 60th anniversary ed., 1st ed.; HarperCollinsPublishers 2005 419p $24.95; pa $14.95   **92**

1. African American authors 2. African Americans -- Social conditions 3. Authors 4. Dramatists 5. Essayists 6. Nonfiction writers 7. Novelists 8. Short story writers

ISBN 0-06-083400-5; 978-0-06-083400-5; 0-06-113024-9 pa; 978-0-06-113024-3 pa

LC 2005-52698

This autobiographical work concludes with Wright "newly arrived in Chicago in 1927 as a fugitive from the white South that never knew him. [It] relates his nomadic life in Tennessee, Arkansas, and Mississippi, abandoned by his father and with his mother working at menial jobs or incapacitated by illness." Benet's Reader's Ency of Am Lit

Includes bibliographical references

Wullschlager, Jackie

★ **Chagall**; a biography. Alfred A. Knopf 2008 582p il $40   **92**

1. Art, Russian -- 20th century 2. Artists 3. Artists, Russian 4. Biography, Individual 5. Painters

ISBN 978-0-375-41455-8; 0-375-41455-X

LC 2008-6162

This is a biography of the Russian artist and author of Lithographs (1960), My Life (1960), and The Jerusalem Windows (1962).

"This biography presents Chagall's moving portraits of a vanished age in colors as glowing and haunting as his own canvases." Washington Post Book World

Includes bibliographical references

Wyeth, Andrew

Andrew Wyeth; autobiography. [by] Andrew Wyeth and Thomas Hoving. Bulfinch Press 1999 168p il $29.99   **92**

1. Artists 2. Artists -- United States 3. Painters

ISBN 978-0-8212-2569-1; 0-8212-2569-3

"Each painting is accompanied by commentary from the artist that lends insight into his life and character. Several nude studies are included." Booklist [review of 1995 edition]

Includes bibliographical references

Yaffe, David

Bob Dylan; like a complete unknown. Yale University Press 2011 171p il $19.95   **92**

1. Biography, Individual 2. Folk musicians 3. Singers

4. Songwriters
ISBN 978-0-300-12457-6; 0-300-12457-0

LC 2011-920627

"Not for the neophyte, but fascinating for obsessives who think they know everything and want to know more." Kirkus

Includes bibliographical references

Yang, Kao Kalia

The **latehomecomer**; a Hmong family memoir. Coffee House Press 2008 277p il pa $14.95   **92**

1. Authors 2. Hmong Americans 3. Memoirists 4. Refugees

ISBN 978-1-56689-208-7

LC 2007-46386

"By the end of this moving, unforgettable book . . . readers will delight at how intimately they have become part of this formerly strange culture." Publ Wkly

Yellin, Jean Fagan

Harriet Jacobs: a life. Basic Civitas Books 2004 394p il map $27.50; pa $16.95   **92**

1. Authors 2. Biography, Individual 3. Domestics 4. Memoirists 5. Slaves

ISBN 0-465-09288-8; 0-465-09289-6 pa

LC 2003-17256

"This scholarly account, woven in a reader friendly fashion, restores 'an heroic woman who lived in an heroic time' to history and to us." Publ Wkly

Includes bibliographical references

Yenne, Bill

Sitting Bull. Westholme 2008 379p il map $29.95   **92**

1. Dakota Indians 2. Indian chiefs

ISBN 978-1-59416-060-8; 1-59416-060-0

In this biography, the author "captures the extraordinary life of Plains Indian leader Sitting Bull while providing new insight into the nomadic culture of the Lakota." Publ Wkly

Includes bibliographical references

Young, Alfred Fabian

★ **Masquerade**: the life and times of Deborah Sampson, Continental soldier; [by] Alfred F. Young. Knopf 2004 417p il map $26.95; pa $16   **92**

1. Biography, Individual 2. Memoirists 3. Soldiers 4. Women soldiers

ISBN 0-679-44165-4; 0-679-76185-3 pa

LC 2003-47549

This book "makes a valuable contribution to American women's history. It offers nuggets of insight about an array of historical topics. . . . What's more, it tells a terrific story." Rev Am Hist

Includes bibliographical references

Young, Andrew

An **easy** burden; the civil rights movement and the transformation of America. foreword by Quincy Jones. Baylor University Press 2008 550p il pa $29.95   **92**

1. African Americans -- Civil rights 2. Civil rights activists 3. Clergy 4. Mayors 5. Members of Congress 6. Nobel laureates for peace 7. Nonfiction writers 8.

United Nations officials
ISBN 978-1-602580-73-2

LC 2007-49679

This memoir focuses on Young's early life as a middle-class African American growing up in segregated New Orleans, his call to the ministry, and his years working with Dr. King and the Southern Christian Leadership Conference.

Yunte Huang

Charlie Chan; the untold story of the honorable detective and his rendezvous with American history. W.W. Norton 2010 354p il map **92**
1. Biography, Individual 2. Chan, Charlie (Fictional character) 3. Chan, Charlie (Fictitious character) 4. Detectives
ISBN 0393069621; 9780393069624

LC 2010016653

This is a history of Charlie Chan, the detective feaured in six novels and 47 movies. Huang contends that Charlie Chan is based upon Chang Apana, a real-life Chinese detective on the Honolulu police force. Bibliography. Index.

This "is a terrifically enjoyable and informative book, one that should appeal to both students of racial history and to fans of one of cinema's greatest detectives." Washington Post Book World

Includes bibliographical references

Zamora, Martha

★ **Frida** Kahlo; the brush of anguish. abridged and translated by Marilyn Sode Smith. Chronicle Bks. 1990 143p il hardcover o.p. pa $24.95 **92**
1. Artists 2. Artists, Mexican 3. Biography, Individual 4. Painters
ISBN 0-8118-0485-2 pa

LC 90-33874

Most "important here is the collection of 75 color plates of the artist's original works. Of interest to the initiated because they comprise largely seldom-seen works in various Mexican collections, these plates represent the best collection now available of Kahlo's work." Libr J

Includes bibliographical references

Zappa, Frank

The **real** Frank Zappa book; [by] Frank Zappa, with Peter Occhiogrosso. Poseidon Press 1989 352p il hardcover o.p. pa $14 **92**
1. Composers 2. Guitarists 3. Recording producers 4. Rock musicians 5. Songwriters
ISBN 0-671-70572-5 pa

LC 89-3470

"The outspoken Zappa, one of the most inventive and controversial artists of the past 20 years, is frank, often disgusting, and always entertaining in describing his life. . . . Zappa also relates his opinions about the music performing and recording industries, but then rattles on about a myriad of things: church, drugs, yuppies, politics." Libr J

Zelizer, Julian E.

Jimmy Carter. Times Books 2010 183p il $23; ebook $10.99 **92**
1. Governors 2. Nobel laureates for peace 3. Presidents

4. Presidents -- United States
ISBN 978-0-8050-8957-8; 978-1-4299-5075-6 ebook

LC 2010-16818

"For general readers, this work offers a fine analysis of the man and his career." Booklist

Includes bibliographical references

Zellner, Robert

The **wrong** side of Murder Creek; a White southerner in the freedom movement. [by] Bob Zellner, with Constance Curry; foreword by Julian Bond. NewSouth Books 2008 351p il $27.95 **92**
1. Civil rights activists 2. Civil rights demonstrations 3. College teachers 4. Historians
ISBN 978-1-58838-222-1; 1-58838-222-2

LC 2008-25962

"Zellner's memoir focuses on his experiences as a civil rights activist from 1960 to 1967. He tells a story that is sometimes horrific, always interesting, and ultimately inspirational about a white Southerner's commitment to racial justice. . . . This powerful portrait of a courageous man is highly recommended." Libr J

Zelnick, Bob

Gore: a political life. Regnery Pub. 1999 384p $29.95; pa $16.95 **92**
1. Conservationists 2. Members of Congress 3. Nobel laureates for peace 4. Presidential candidates 5. Senators 6. Vice-presidents
ISBN 0-89526-326-2; 0-89526-241-X pa

LC 99-194035

Zelnick examines the life and career of Al Gore, the former senator from Tennessee and Vice President of the United States.

The author provides "a useful and comprehensive survey of the highs and lows of Gore's political career." NY Times Book Rev

Zevon, Crystal

I'll sleep when I'm dead; the dirty life and times of Warren Zevon. foreword by Carl Hiassen. Ecco Press 2007 452p il $26.95; pa $15.95 **92**
1. Biography, Individual 2. Rock music -- History and criticism 3. Rock musicians 4. Singers 5. Songwriters
ISBN 978-0-06-076345-9; 0-06-076345-0; 978-0-06-076349-7 pa; 0-06-076349-3 pa

LC 2006-52138

"Interweaving the remembrances of Zevon's many friends with entries from his own journals, Crystal, his widow, presents an intimate look at Zevon's wild life of drugs, women, and music. Among others, Jackson Browne, Linda Ronstadt, Bruce Springsteen, Carl Hiaasen, Stephen King, and the Everly Brothers, with whom Zevon got his start, share reminiscences. . . . All pop music collections need this book." Libr J

Zhao Ziyang

Prisoner of the state; the secret journal of premier Zhao Ziyang. translated and edited by Bao Pu, Renee Chiang and Adi Ignatius; foreword by Roder-

ick MacFarquhar. Simon and Schuster 2009 306p il
$26   **92**
　　1. Biography, Individual　2.　Cabinet members　3.
Communist leaders　4.　Prime ministers
　　ISBN 978-1-4391-4938-6; 1-4391-4938-0
　　"Until the appearance of this posthumous work, not a
single voice of dissent had ever emerged from the [Chinese
Communist] party's inner circle . . . . Fascinating." Economist

Zuckoff, Mitchell
　　Robert Altman; the oral biography. Alfred A.
Knopf 2009 560p il   **92**
　　1. Biography, Individual　2. Motion picture directors　3.
Motion picture producers　4.　Motion picture producers
and directors　5.　Television directors
　　ISBN 0-307-26768-7; 978-0-307-26768-9
　　　　　　　　　　　　　　　　　　LC 2009-19847
　　This is a biography of the director of such films as
MASH (1970), Nashville (1975), The Player (1992), and
Gosford Park (2001). Filmography. Index.
　　This "is a smart, amusing, lively book, full of anecdotes
and a generous step toward perceiving the glorious and per-
verse ways of Altman himself." New Repub
　　Includes filmography

George, being George; George Plimpton's life as told,
　　admired, deplored, and envied by 200 friends,
　　relatives, lovers, acquaintances, rivals, and a few
　　unappreciative observers. edited by Nelson W.
　　Aldrich, Jr. Random House 2008 423p il $30 **92**
　　1.　Authors　2.　Biography, Individual　3.　Essayists　4.
Journalists　5.　Magazine editors　6.　Sportswriters
　　ISBN 978-1-4000-6398-7; 1-4000-6398-1
　　　　　　　　　　　　　　　　　　LC 2007-46215
　　"George Plimpton (1927–2003) wore many hats: writer, Paris Review editor, actor, boxing fanatic, toastmaster,
prankster, fireworks enthusiast, urban cyclist. In the oral
history George, Being George, Nelson W. Aldrich Jr. skillfully weaves together more than 200 voices into a coherent
account of Plimpton's prismatic existence. . . . The contributors—who include literary luminaries Norman Mailer, Gore
Vidal and Peter Matthiessen—report on Plimpton's life with
varying degrees of grandiosity and nuance." Time Out N Y

Haydn; edited by David Wyn Jones; consultant edi-
　　tor Otto Biba.　Oxford Univ. Press　2002　xxi,
　　515p il map $75   **92**
　　1. Composers
　　ISBN 0-19-866216-5
　　　　　　　　　　　　　　　　　　LC 2002-510033
　　"This volume will be useful to persons who need quick,
specific information about Haydn, his works, and 18th-cen-
tury style." Choice

The Lincoln anthology; great writers on his life and
　　legacy from 1860 to now. edited by Harold Hol-
　　zer. Library of America 2009 964p il $40　**92**
　　1.　Biography, Individual　2.　Lawyers　3.　Members of
Congress　4.　Presidents　5.　Presidents -- United States
6.　State legislators
　　ISBN 978-1-59853-033-9; 1-59853-033-X
　　　　　　　　　　　　　　　　　　LC 2008-934337

　　This "is a solid compilation of work on Abraham Lincoln from a diverse selection of writers in various genres,
celebrating his extensive legacy and providing insight from
a number of angles and time periods." Publ Wkly
　　Includes bibliographical references

Night wraps the sky; writings by and about Maya-
　　kovsky. edited by Michael Almereyda.　Farrar,
　　Straus and Giroux 2008 xxvii, 272p il $27　**92**
　　1.　Authors　2.　Biography, Individual　3.　Dramatists　4.
Poetry -- By individual authors　5.　Poets
　　ISBN 978-0-374-28135-9; 0-374-28135-1
　　　　　　　　　　　　　　　　　　LC 2007-46662
　　"The book further explores Mayakovsky's relationships
with Lili Brik and Tatiana Yakovleva, explains his propaganda work, and addresses his mixture of the surreal, the
lyric, and the sarcastic; the text is generously illustrated with
photographs of Mayakovsky's friends and contemporaries
and artworks of the times." Libr J

Nikita Khrushchev; edited by William Taubman,
　　Sergei Khrushchev, and Abbott Gleason; translat-
　　ed by David Gehrenbeck, Eileen Kane, and Alla
　　Bashenko. Yale Univ. Press 2000 391p $45　**92**
　　1.　Communist leaders　2.　Heads of state　3.　Heads of
state -- Soviet Union　4.　Political leaders
　　ISBN 0-300-07635-6
　　　　　　　　　　　　　　　　　　LC 99-51323
　　A collection of essays re-evaluating aspects of Khrushchev's political career. Topics include his rise to power and
his domestic, foreign, and military policy. Two essays compare Khrushchev and Gorbachev

★ Our Lincoln; new perspectives on Lincoln and his
　　world. edited by Eric Foner. W.W. Norton 2008
　　336p il   **92**
　　1.　Lawyers　2.　Members of Congress　3.　Presidents　4.
Presidents -- United States　5.　State legislators
　　ISBN 0-393-06756-4; 9780393067569
　　　　　　　　　　　　　　　　　　LC 2008-17096
　　"Twelve essays present the ideas of recent historians on
Lincoln's evolving views on race, religion, and civil liberties, his military leadership, his family, photographs and
portraits of Lincoln, and the use of his memory in the 21st
century." (Publisher's note) Index.
　　Historians "collectively situate Lincoln's ideas, interests,
and policies and the meanings various people from abolitionists to neo-Confederates have found in Lincoln, from
the microscopic to a wider historical context of politics, culture, and memory. Essays explore such topics as presidential
leadership, civil liberties, citizenship and rights, democratic
politics, mass-produced imagery, African colonization, antislavery, race, religion, family life, writing sensibilities and
style, and the need to claim Lincoln for one's own cause.
The eloquent and compelling results show how and why
Lincoln was both a man of his time and a man for all time."
Libr J
　　Includes bibliographical references

Shalom, friend: the life and legacy of Yitzhak Rabin;
　　the Jerusalem Report staff; edited by David Horo-

vitz; prologue by Hirsch Goodman. Newmarket Press 1996 314p il maps $24.95　**92**
1. Cabinet members　2. Nobel laureates for peace　3. Political leaders　4. Prime ministers
ISBN 1-55704-287-X

LC 96-5146

"This is a collaborative effort by more than a dozen writers and editors of the Jerusalem Report, a prestigious Israeli newsmagazine, all of whom had close personal and professional knowledge of the former prime minister, assassinated in November 1995. Their views are supplemented by numerous, interviews with knowledgeable people." Libr J
Includes bibliographical references

What there is to say we have said; the correspondence of Eudora Welty and William Maxwell. edited by Suzanne Marrs. Houghton Mifflin Harcourt 2011 499p il $35　**92**
1. Authors　2. Magazine editors　3. Novelists　4. Short story writers
ISBN 0547376499; 9780547376493; 978-0-547-37649-3; 0-547-37649-9

LC 2010-42105

"Letters between writers often have a lot of shop talk of interest to other writers and literary cultists, but this collection yields broader pleasures, too. In addition to being stellar writers, Welty and Maxwell were also accomplished critics, and one of the joys of the book is eavesdropping on their assessments of authors as varied as John Updike and Virginia Woolf, Anton Chekhov and Charles Dickens, William Faulkner and E. M. Forster. Welty and Maxwell also shared an intense love of gardening – so much so that Marrs was forced, in the book's index, to include an extensive listing of various varieties of roses. . . . As these letters show, Welty and Maxwell regarded domestic life not as a tedious distraction from the writing desk, but as a crucial source of insight. . . . The title of the collection comes from Maxwell's conclusion, as he and Welty faced their mortality, that 'what there is to say we have said, in one way or the other. You know how much we love you.' That love, a source of sustenance and strength between two great writers, is also a bright tonic for the readers of this volume." Christ Sci Monit
Includes bibliographical references

The essential Chaplin; perspectives on the life and art of the great comedian. edited with an introduction by Richard Schickel. I.R. Dee 2006 315p $27.50; pa $16.95　**92**
1. Actors　2. Motion picture directors　3. Motion picture producers　4. Motion picture producers and directors -- Biography
ISBN 978-1-56663-682-7; 1-56663-682-5; 978-1-56663-701-5 pa; 1-56663-701-5 pa

LC 2005-37250

"The book's best feature is its organized cacophony, its trace of this astonishingly long and rich body of work and personal travail . . . in some several dozen voices of fading or lasting memory, and with countless aesthetic and ideological grudges beyond the narrow province of the movies. There is much to savor in these essays; and the book might also serve as a worthy companion to a reader's return to Chaplin's films themselves." Va Q Rev

The letters of Sylvia Beach; edited by Keri Walsh; with a foreword by Noël Riley Fitch. Columbia University Press 2010 347p il $29.95　**92**
1. Booksellers　2. Booksellers and bookselling　3. Booksellers and bookselling -- France -- Paris　4. Memoirists
ISBN 978-0-231-14536-7; 0-231-14535-5

LC 2009-45434

"Beach's story has been told before. . . . [But these letters] have an unvarnished charm all their own. Written to friends, writers, customers and family members, they depict a witty and resourceful woman struggling to keep her business, her writers and her precarious existence afloat." N Y Times Book Rev
Includes bibliographical references

929　Genealogy, names, insignia

Baxter, Angus
In search of your European roots; a complete guide to tracing your ancestors in every country in Europe. 3rd ed; Genealogical 2001 315p pa $18.95　**929**
1. European Americans -- Genealogy -- Handbooks, manuals, etc　2. Genealogy
ISBN 0-8063-1657-8

LC 00-136383

This work covers the various types of genealogical records available in approximately 30 European countries. Archival resources from the national to local level are described. Also included are telephone numbers, e-mail addresses, fax numbers, and URL's for various European archives and organizations.

Bentley, Elizabeth Petty
Directory of family associations; {by} Elizabeth Petty Bentley, & Deborah Ann Carl. 4th ed; Genealogical 2001 320p $34.95　**929**
1. Genealogy
ISBN 0-8063-1679-9

LC 2001-131456

Contains information on approximately 6,000 family name associations in the United States; lists addresses, phone numbers, contact persons, and publications (if any).

★ The **genealogist's** address book; state and local resources: with special resources including ethnic and religious organizations. 6th ed.; Genealogical Pub. Co. 2009 799p $69.95　**929**
1. Genealogy
ISBN 978-0-8063-1796-0

This is a source for "fax, phone, web addresses, and contact names for genealogical, historical, and religious societies across the United States. Bentley . . . judiciously divides contact information into three subject segments. The first organizes genealogical and historical associations alphabetically, initially by state, then county, and finally by society name. Essential for genealogists and regional historians." Libr J

Croom, Emily Anne

The **genealogist's** companion and sourcebook; 2nd ed; Betterway Bks. 2003 454p il map pa $19.99 **929**

1. Genealogy

ISBN 1-55870-651-8

LC 2003-50017

This how-to genealogy handbook seeks to explore "collections and libraries within the U.S. and the records that may be found within them. . . . In addition to covering government records, cemetery records, newspapers, city directories, and other sources, there are chapters of African American and Native American genealogy. . . . Because the volume is easy reading and instructive at the same time, it will be a very popular choice for public libraries." Booklist {review of 1994 edition}

Includes bibliographical references

Franklin, John Hope

★ **In** search of the promised land; a Black family and the Old South. [by] John Hope Franklin, Loren Schweninger. Oxford University Press 2005 286p il map $23; pa $13.95 **929**

1. African Americans -- Southern States 2. Slavery -- United States

ISBN 0-19-516087-8; 0-19-516088-6 pa

LC 2004-61666

The authors trace "the history, of the Thomas-Rapier family during the antebellum and Civil War eras. Starting with matriarch Sally Thomas, born a slave in 1787, the book enables readers to distinguish the various complex modes within which slavery operated. The resulting family history also traces the evolution of race relations in diverse locations from New Orleans to New York City, Canada, Minnesota, and the Caribbean." Libr J

Includes bibliographical references

Greenwood, Val D.

The **researcher's** guide to American genealogy; 3rd ed; Genealogical 2000 662p il $29.95 **929**

1. Archives -- United States 2. Genealogy

ISBN 0-8063-1621-7

LC 99-73349

"This classic textbook for the more experienced researcher gives detailed answers to questions about primary records, including vital, census, probate, land, court (including adoption), church, military, cemetery, and wills. Completely updated, it remains the outstanding text and reference book in American genealogy and the benchmark against which others must be judged." Libr J {review of 1990 edition}

Includes bibliographical references and index

Kemp, Thomas Jay

International vital records handbook; 5th ed.; Genealogical Publishing Co. 2009 587p pa $49.95 **929**

1. Registers of births, etc.

ISBN 978-0-8063-1793-9

LC 2008-940022

"The book is divided into these three major segments. The first offers approved-form facsimiles for the request of U.S. state-issued documents. The second segment covers request forms issued in U.S. Territories. The third details various procedures and forms necessary to attain official documents in foreign countries. . . . A crucial, time-saving resource." Libr J

Includes bibliographical references

Virtual roots 2.0; a guide to genealogy and local history on the World Wide Web. rev and updated; Scholarly Resources 2003 311p $75; pa $29.95 **929**

1. Genealogy 2. World Wide Web

ISBN 0-8420-2922-2; 0-8420-2923-0 pa

LC 2002-154366

The more than 1,000 "Web sites in this directory are arranged into four primary categories—general subjects, U.S., international, and family associations—each of which is further subdivided by topic, state, country, or family name. Web site entries include organization name, address, telephone number(s), Internet and e-mail addresses, and, where appropriate, other Web links that open even more doorways." Booklist {review of 1997 edition}

Includes bibliographical references

Kovacs, Diane K.

Genealogical research on the Web. Neal-Schuman 2002 194p pa $59.95 **929**

1. Genealogy -- Internet resources

ISBN 1-55570-430-1

LC 2001-59644

"The first section of this book . . . addresses the basics of using the Internet for genealogical research. Next is a discussion of the top 10 genealogical tools on the Internet, followed by a chapter on networking with other genealogists. . . . Each chapter ends with a tutorial composed of several activities, typically involving visits to Web sites. . . . This is one work that serves a variety of users as well as uses and should be of interest wherever genealogists are to be found." Booklist

Includes bibliographical references

McCourt, Frank

★ **Angela's** ashes; a memoir. Scribner 1996 364p il $25; pa $14 **929**

1. Authors 2. Biography, Individual 3. High school teachers 4. Irish Americans 5. Memoirists

ISBN 0-684-87435-0; 0-684-84267-X pa

LC 96-5335

"Frank McCourt, a teacher, grandfather and occasional actor, was born in New York City, but grew up in the Irish town of Limerick during the grim 1930's and 40's before he came back here as a teen-ager. His recollections of childhood are mournful and humorous, angry and forgiving." N Y Times Book Rev

Melnyk, Marcia Yannizze

Family history 101; a beginner's guide to finding your ancestors. [by] Marcia D. Yannizze Melnyk. Family Tree Books 2005 138p il pa $16.99 **929**

1. Genealogy

ISBN 1-558-70706-9

LC 2004-58111

"The author provides information on recording data, surfing the Web in search of relevant information, separating facts from fiction, and accessing the most likely places to locate records. . . . Novices wondering where and how to undertake the task will appreciate having the fundamentals succinctly laid out for them." Booklist

Includes bibliographical references

Moore, Dahrl Elizabeth

The **librarian's** genealogy notebook; a guide to resources. American Lib. Assn. 1998 142p il map pa $35   **929**

1. Genealogy

ISBN 0-8389-0744-X

LC 98-19110

"Moore shows librarians how to mine their own libraries for reference sources that might already be available, offers useful advice on obtaining information from external sources, and also includes general sources to which libraries may want to provide access or own." Publisher's note

Includes bibliographical references

Roberts, Ralph

Genealogy via the Internet; tracing your family roots quickly and easily: computerized genealogy in plain English. 2nd ed; Alexander Bks. 2003 288p il $24.95   **929**

1. Genealogy -- Internet resources

ISBN 1-57090-129-5

The author "explains about personal computers, the basics of genealogy and how to go about combining the two for online searching. He provides several pages of possible web sites a searcher might explore, and an index for easy location of topics." Book Rep {review of 1998 edition}

Includes bibliographical references

929.4   Personal names

Ciuraru, Carmela

Nom de plume; a (secret) history of pseudonyms. Harper 2011 xxiv, 343p $24.99   **929.4**

1. Authors 2. Pseudonyms

ISBN 978-0-06-173526-4

LC 2010-53603

The author "tells the stories of some of literature's most famous pen names by weaving in details about these secretive, often eccentric writers' lives and works to examine their decision to use pen names. From Lewis Carroll (born Charles Dodgson) to Mark Twain (Samuel Clemens) and Victoria Lucas (Sylvia Plath), one chapter is devoted to each with so much detail that the authors under discussion seem to become characters in Ciuraru's book. . . . For anyone who creates — writers, artists and performers — the book will enthrall. It's as much a meditation on the creative process as it is a tell-all about their names and the intrigue, branding or mind games that created them." Associated Press

Includes bibliographical references

Delahunty, Andrew

Oxford dictionary of nicknames. Oxford University Press 2003 229p $29.95; pa $24   **929.4**

1. Nicknames

ISBN 0-19-860539-0; 0-19-860948-5 pa

LC 2004-273526

"This volume is a treasure trove of popular linguistic creativity. From the Hanging Judge to Hanoi Jane, and from Queen Dick to the Queen of Hearts, it makes for delightful bathroom browsing with just a dab of history and culture." Publ Wkly

Latham, Edward

A **dictionary** of names, nicknames, and surnames of persons, places, and things. Omnigraphics 1990 334p $48   **929.4**

1. Names -- Dictionaries 2. Nicknames 3. Personal names -- Dictionaries 4. Reference books

ISBN 1-55888-901-9

LC 89-26513

Compiled as a supplement to the "ordinary dictionaries of biography, geography, mythology, etc. {wherein} a person or place is often alluded to by means of a surname or nickname without any clue being given to the reader, who does not happen to be aware of the actual name of the person or place." Preface

Shankle, George Earlie

American nicknames; their origin and significance. 2nd ed; Wilson, H.W. 1955 524p $85 **929.4**

1. Geographic names -- United States 2. Nicknames 3. Personal names -- United States

ISBN 0-8242-0004-7

"Not limited to nicknames of persons, but includes also those applied to places, institutions, or objects, arranged by real names with cross-references from nicknames. Information under the real names includes some explanation of the nicknames and their origin, and gives references to sources of information in footnotes." Guide to Ref Books. 11th edition

★ **Dictionary** of American family names; Patrick Hanks, editor. Oxford Univ. Press 2003 3v set $295   **929.4**

1. Names, Personal -- United States -- Dictionaries 2. Personal names -- United States

ISBN 0-19-508137-4

LC 2003-3844

"This set will be useful for genealogists, historians, and others curious about their family roots." SLJ

Includes bibliographical references

Twentieth century American nicknames; edited by Laurence Urdang; compiled by Walter C. Kidney and George C. Kohn; with a foreword by Leslie Alan Dunkling. Wilson, H.W. 1979 398p $70   **929.4**

1. Geographic names -- United States 2. Nicknames 3. Personal names -- United States

ISBN 0-8242-0642-8

LC 79-23390

"Nicknames and the real names of persons, places, etc., are listed in a single alphabet. Includes variant nicknames. Editor attempted to avoid duplication of nicknames appearing in Shankle's American nicknames." Ref Sources for Small & Medium-sized Libr. 5th edition

929.9   Forms of insignia and identification

Leepson, Marc

Flag: an American biography. Thomas Dunne Books/St. Martin's Press 2005 334p il $24.95; pa $14.95   **929.9**
1. Flags -- United States
ISBN 978-0-312-32308-0; 0-312-32308-5; 978-0-312-32309-7 pa; 0-312-32309-3 pa

LC 2004-65920

"From reverence to kitsch, Americans' attitudes to their flag and its mythology have changed over the years, and Leepson does a creditable job of recounting those changes." Publ Wkly

Includes bibliographical references

Minahan, James

The **complete** guide to national symbols and emblems. Greenwood Press 2010 2v il set $180 **929.9**
1. National characteristics -- Encyclopedias 2. National emblems -- Encyclopedias 3. Reference books 4. Signs and symbols
ISBN 978-0-313-34496-1; 978-0-313-34497-8 ebook

LC 2009-36963

"This set is an impressive compilation of material that should be quite useful for anyone looking for current information about flags, anthems, athletic teams, cuisines, and such. The 200-plus entries cover independent nations of the world and some dependent states and territories that seek greater visibility, such as Wallonia (an autonomous region within Belgium) and Puerto Rico. Volume 1 covers Asia and Oceania, Central and South America, and Europe. Volume 2 covers the Middle East and North Africa, North America and the Caribbean, and sub-Saharan Africa. National flags and coats of arms are shown in color." Booklist

Includes bibliographical references

Shearer, Benjamin F.

State names, seals, flags, and symbols; a historical guide. [by] Benjamin F. Shearer and Barbara S. Shearer. 3rd ed, rev and expanded; Greenwood Press 2001 495p il $73.95   **929.9**
1. Flags -- United States 2. Geographic names -- United States 3. Reference books 4. Seals (Numismatics)
ISBN 0-313-31534-5

LC 2001-23525

"Chapters on mottoes, flowers, trees, birds, songs, holidays, and license plates are just a sampling of what is covered, and the format is such that the concisely written material can be found as expeditiously as possible. Even though the book is touted predominantly as a reference tool, the information provided makes fascinating and enlightening reading." Libr J [review of 1994 edition]

Includes bibliographical references

Testi, Arnaldo

Capture the flag; the Stars and Stripes in American history. translated by Noor Giovanni Mazhar. New York University Press 2010 165p il $22.95   **929.9**
1. American national characteristics 2. Flags -- United States 3. Flags -- United States -- History 4. Patriotism
ISBN 978-0-8147-83221; 0-8147-8322-8

LC 2009-39278

"From our July 4th celebrations to the iconic images from 9/11, the American flag is an all-pervasive, definitive symbol of American national identity. . . . [Testi] provides readers with an engaging and fresh perspective that can only be provided by an outsider standing above the fray. Whether discussing the evolution of flag etiquette or its relationship to the U.S. Constitution, Testi deftly explores the shifting cultural meanings of the American symbol, from 1776 through the growth of the American empire to the contentious debates occurring today." Libr J

Includes bibliographical references

930   History of specific continents, countries, localities; extraterrestrial worlds

Cantor, Norman F.

Antiquity: the civilization of the ancient world. HarperCollins Pubs. 2003 240p map $24.95; pa $13.95   **930**
1. Ancient civilization
ISBN 0-06-017409-9; 0-06-093098-5 pa

LC 2003-42317

"Cantor's work provides the beginning classicist with an enticing yet sturdy foundation for further exploration." Booklist

Includes bibliographical references

Felch, Jason

Chasing Aphrodite; the hunt for looted antiquities at the world's richest museum. [by] Jason Felch and Ralph Frammolino. Houghton Mifflin Harcourt 2011 375p il $28   **930**
1. Archaeological thefts 2. Classical antiquities 3. Classical antiquities -- Destruction and pillage 4. Classical antiquities -- Italy 5. Cultural property 6. Cultural property -- Repatriation -- Italy
ISBN 978-0-15-101501-6; 0-15-101501-5

LC 2010-25835

In 1976 "oil billionaire J. Paul Getty left his estate to the museum that bears his name, which was suddenly the wealthiest collecting institution in the world—one whose problem was how to spend rather than raise money. The founder's narrow interests had determined the museum's collecting areas, one of which was Greek and Roman art. The stage was set for trouble, and the trouble is described in fascinating detail in 'Chasing Aphrodite,' an account of the Getty's travails in collection-building by Los Angeles Times reporters Jason Felch and Ralph Frammolino. In 2005, longtime Getty curator Marion True would be indicted by authorities in Rome for traffic in illicit antiquities; not long after, in a related controversy, she was forced to resign. The reporters

covered these events, as well as the museum's agreements to repatriate works acquired before and during Ms. True's tenure. They were given access by unidentified sources to the museum's archives, and in this book they document a museum administration often motivated by ambition but eventually also by stirrings of conscience." Wall Street J
Includes bibliographical references and index

Kapuscinski, Ryszard

Travels with Herodotus; translated from the Polish by Klara Glowczewska. Alfred A. Knopf 2007 275p $25   **930**
  1. Authors 2. Biographers 3. Historians 4. Journalists 5. Nonfiction writers 6. Voyages and travels
ISBN 9781400043385; 1-400-04338-5
              LC 2006-39565
"A work of art: so eloquent, so simple, that you find yourself marveling at its prose, its gentle observation and the rhythm of the words. And you find yourself applauding such good translation as well." Washington Post Book World

The Cambridge ancient history. Cambridge Univ. Press 1970 il maps set $3500   **930**
  1. Ancient history
ISBN 978-0-521-85073-5
"An excellent reference history. Each chapter has been written by a specialist, with full bibliographies at the end of each volume." Guide to Ref Books. 11th edition

★ Encyclopedia of the ancient world; editor, Thomas J. Sienkewicz. Salem Press 2002 3v il maps set $341   **930**
  1. Ancient civilization -- Encyclopedias 2. Civilization, Ancient -- Encyclopedias 3. Reference books
ISBN 0-89356-038-3
              LC 2001-49896
This reference work encompasses "not only Greece and Rome but also 'the civilizations, cultures, traditions, monuments and artifacts, significant wars and battles, and important personages of the rest of the world: Europe (outside Greece and Rome), Africa, the Americas, Asia, and Oceania.' The time span is from prehistory to approximately 700 C.E." Booklist
Includes bibliographical references

Great events from history, The ancient world, prehistory-476 C.E. editor, Mark W. Chavalas; consulting editors, Mark S. Aldenderfer . . . [et al.] Salem Press 2004 2v il map set $160   **930**
  1. Ancient history 2. History, Ancient 3. Reference books
ISBN 1-58765-155-6; 978-1-58765-155-7
              LC 2004-1360
"Articles are arranged chronologically, beginning around 25,000 B.C.E. with the San Peoples, who created the first discernible art in Africa, and ends on September 4, 476 C.E. with the fall of Rome, when the last Roman emperor, Romulus Augustulus, was deposed. Articles cover the entire world, with special attention paid to non-European areas. . . . All articles maintain the same structure and give the locale of the event, its category, a summary of the event, its

significance, an annotated list of further readings, and cross references to related events." Ref & User Services Quarterly
Includes bibliographical references

930.1   Archaeology

Ceram, C. W.

Gods, graves, and scholars; the story of archaeology. translated from the German by E. B. Garside and Sophie Wilkins. 2nd rev and substantially enl ed; Knopf 1967 441p il maps hardcover o.p. pa $11.16   **930.1**
  1. Archeology 2. Aztecs 3. Babel, Tower of 4. Cuneiform inscriptions 5. Hieroglyphics 6. Kings 7. Mayas 8. Rosetta stone inscription
ISBN 0-394-74319-9 pa
"The story of Champollion and the reading of the Rosetta Stone, the decipherment of the inscriptions on the monument of Darius the Great, Leonard Woolley's famous excavations at Ur, and John Lloyd Stephens' discovery of the ruins of a great Mayan city are . . . told in this book." Doors to More Mature Read
Includes bibliographical references

Childs, Craig Leland

Finders keepers; a tale of archaeological plunder and obsession. Little, Brown and Co. 2010 274p $24.99   **930.1**
  1. Antiquities -- Collection and preservation -- Moral and ethical aspects 2. Archaeologists -- Professional ethics 3. Archaeology -- Moral and ethical aspects 4. Archeologists -- Ethics 5. Cultural property -- Moral and ethical aspects
ISBN 978-0-316-06642-6; 0-316-06642-7
              LC 2009-51921
"Childs treks the canyon-incised Colorado Plateau in search of pre-Columbian artifacts. Their legal regulation collides with collectors' obsessions to possess them. Childs, though, does not remove what he finds, an ethic that vies with other precepts for the proper preservation of antiquities. For every stand he takes on archaeological morality in this narrative mix of his backcountry experiences and conversations with collectors, curators, dealers, and an occasional looter, Childs engages their justifications for taking custody of ancient objects. . . . Alternating romantic and practical moods, Childs hunts virtue as much as baskets in this engaging discourse." Booklist
Includes bibliographical references

Hunt, Patrick

Ten discoveries that rewrote history. Plume 2007 226p pa $27.95   **930.1**
  1. Ancient civilization 2. Antiquities 3. Archaeology -- History 4. Archeology -- History 5. Civilization, Ancient 6. Excavations (Archaeology) 7. Extinct cities 8. Historic sites
ISBN 978-0-452-28877-5; 0-452-28877-0
              LC 2007-19808
The author "has produced a wonderful volume of archaeological history. In doing so, he has provided a seldom

seen look at some of the most important scientific developments in the field." Sci Books Films

Includes bibliographical references

Ryan, William B. F.

Noah's flood; the new scientific discoveries about the event that changed history. [by] William Ryan and Walter Pitman; illustrations by Anastasia Sotiropoulos; maps by William Haxby. Simon & Schuster 1999 319p il maps hardcover o.p. pa $14   **930.1**

1. Floods

ISBN 0-684-81052-2; 0-684-85920-3 pa

LC 98-45384

This is "an interesting and provocative story . . . that incorporates archeology, oceanography, biblical studies, anthropology (not to mention archeobotany, paleopathology and archeozoology) and, one must conclude, a healthy portion of imagination." N Y Times Book Rev

Includes bibliographical references

Van Tilburg, JoAnne

Among stone giants; the life of Katherine Routledge and her remarkable expedition to Easter Island. foreword by Andrew Tatham. Scribner 2003 351p il $26   **930.1**

1. Antiquities, Prehistoric -- Easter Island 2. Archaeologists 3. Sculpture, Prehistoric -- Easter Island 4. Women archaeologists -- Easter Island -- Biography

ISBN 0-7432-4480-X

LC 2002-42751

This is a "biography of Katherine Routledge, an Englishwoman who was the first to attempt a methodical archaeological study of Easter Island." N Y Times Book Rev

Includes bibliographical references

Beneath the seven seas; adventures with the Intitute of Nautical Archaeology. edited by George F. Bass. Thames & Hudson 2005 256p il maps $39.95   **930.1**

1. Archeology 2. Shipwrecks 3. Underwater archaeology 4. Underwater exploration

ISBN 978-0-500-05136-8; 0-500-05136-4

LC 2005-900862

This book features "accounts by many distinguished archaeologists associated with the INA [Institute of Nautical Archaeology]. They tell of the discovery, excavation, and preservation of more than 40 shipwrecks—and one sunken city—the world over, from ancient times through the Byzantine, medieval, and Renaissance eras and on through World War II. . . . This book will appeal to general readers and specialists alike in nautical archaeology." Libr J

Includes bibliographical references

The Oxford companion to archaeology; editor in chief, Brian M. Fagan; editors, Charlotte Beck [et al.] Oxford Univ. Press 1996 xx, 844p il maps $75   **930.1**

1. Archeology -- Dictionaries 2. Reference books

ISBN 0-19-507618-4

LC 96-30792

"In addition to broad discussions of specific civilizations such as Islamic, Olmec, and African, there are entries on theories (post processual), ethics, processes (lithics), dating techniques, pop culture (archaeology in film and television), specific sites and site management, plantation archaeology, and human evolution." Booklist

932   Egypt to 640

Aldred, Cyril

Akhenaten: King of Egypt. Thames & Hudson 1988 320p il hardcover o.p. pa $26.95   **932**

1. Kings

ISBN 0-500-27621-8 pa

LC 87-51153

Aldred "ranges over archaeology, art-history, morbid pathology, social and political history and the evolution of ideas. This is a book to which one will return, and gain each time one does so." Times Lit Suppl

Includes bibliographical references

Brier, Bob

The **murder** of Tutankhamen; a true story. Berkley Books 2005 xx, 264p il pa $14   **932**

1. Kings

ISBN 0-425-20690-4; 978-0-425-20690-4

LC 2005-41085

"Brier obviously knows his subject and is impassioned by it. Readers who enjoy history or true-crime stories will be intrigued by this work." SLJ

Includes bibliographical references

Bunson, Margaret R.

Encyclopedia of ancient Egypt; rev ed; Facts on File 2002 462p il maps $70   **932**

1. Reference books

ISBN 0-8160-4563-1

LC 2002-3550

This work consists of "alphabetically arranged entries covering Egypt from around 3200 B.C. to the fall of the New Kingdom in 1070 B.C. There are several broad entries such as Egypt, Agriculture, and Religion. The bulk of the book, however, consists of specific entries for kings and queens, gods and goddesses, cities, important documents, etc." Booklist [review of 1991 edition]

David, A. Rosalie

Handbook to life in ancient Egypt; [by] Rosalie David. rev ed; Facts on File 2003 417p il map $50   **932**

ISBN 0-8160-5034-1

LC 2002-35229

This covers such topics as the geography of Ancient Egypt, society and government, religion, funerary beliefs and customs, architecture, trade and transport, the army and navy, economy and industry, and everyday life.

Dreyfus, Renee

Hatshepsut: from queen to Pharaoh; edited by Catharine H. Roehrig with Renée Dreyfus and Cathleen A. Keller. Yale University Press 2005 339p il map $65   **932**

1. Queens

ISBN 0-300-11139-8

LC 2005-20286

The editors "offer a magnificent portrait of this remarkable woman and all aspects of Egyptian life in the 18th Dynasty, from religion and politics to art and jewelry." Publ Wkly

Includes bibliographical references

Hawass, Zahi A.

Hidden treasures of ancient Egypt; unearthing the masterpieces of Egyptian history. [by] Zahi Hawass; photographs by Kenneth Garrett. National Geographic Society 2004 256p il $35   **932**

1. Egyptian art 2. Excavations (Archaeology) -- Egypt 3. Excavations (Archeology) -- Egypt

ISBN 0-7922-6319-7

LC 2004-44845

The author "narrates the past 150 years of excavation, from the colonial period—when Westerners overwhelmed the ranks of those recovering the nation's treasures—through Egypt's independence and the present era of international cooperation. . . . This breathtaking glimpse at the country's archeological wealth should excite curious and adventurous minds worldwide." Publ Wkly

★ **Tutankhamun** and the golden age of the pharaohs; [by] Zahi Hawass; photographs by Kenneth Garrett. National Geographic Books 2005 285p il map $35   **932**

1. Kings

ISBN 0-7922-3873-7

LC 2005-41678

This companion to an exhibition displaying about 130 items found in the tombs of Tutankhamun and other kings from the same dynasty "describes the physical and symbolic attributes of each object and explains its purpose in the afterlife. . . . An arrestingly visual album destined for high demand." Booklist

Includes bibliographical references

Lepre, J. P.

The **Egyptian** pyramids; a comprehensive, illustrated reference. McFarland & Co. 1990 341p il hardcover o.p. pa $35   **932**

1. Pyramids

ISBN 0-89950-461-2; 0-7864-2955-0 pa

LC 89-43623

This "study of the pyramids built during the reigns of 42 different pharaohs, incorporates details pertaining to the history of each of the pharaohs who constructed a pyramid, concise chronological listings of the pyramids, relevant textual studies from the ancient Egyptian sources, and a review of the material remains associated with the pyramids." Choice

Includes bibliographical references

Mertz, Barbara

Temples, tombs, & hieroglyphs; a popular history of ancient Egypt. 2nd ed., 1st William Mor-

row ed.; William Morrow 2007 xxvi, 324p il map $26.95   **932**

1. Egyptian language 2. Hieroglyphics 3. Kings 4. Queens

ISBN 978-0-06-125276-1; 0-06-125276-X

LC 2007-29118

This is an "introduction to the history of ancient Egypt and Egyptology. . . . Mertz gives special attention to such topics as the kingship (yes) of Queen Hatshepsut, the exploits of Thutmose III, and the Amarna Period with its intriguing players Akhenaten, Nefertiti, and Tutankhamen. Presenting both pros and cons of current theories, Mertz also explains in simple language archaeological techniques such as carbon 14 dating and historical chronology. . . . [This is] an excellent introduction for patrons interested in the land of the pharaohs." Libr J

Tyldesley, Joyce A.

Nefertiti; Egypt's sun queen. {by} Joyce Tyldesley. Viking 1999 232p il $27.95; pa $14.95   **932**

1. Queens

ISBN 0-670-86998-8; 0-14-025820-5 pa

LC 98-35469

"Born in approximately 1350 B.C., Nefertiti was the wife of Akhenaten, an eighteenth-dynasty pharaoh who initiated a radical religious revolution in his kingdom. . . . Adored by the masses, Nefertiti was elevated to semidivine status and adopted a dynamic political and cultural role. . . . Tyldesley manages to do an admirable job re-creating the exquisite opulence of palace life and piecing together Nefertiti's early public years." Booklist

Includes bibliographical references

Verner, Miroslav

The **pyramids**; the mystery, culture, and science of Egypt's great monuments. translated from the German by Steven Rendall. Grove Press 2001 495p il map hardcover o.p. pa $17.50   **932**

1. Pyramids 2. Pyramids -- Egypt

ISBN 0-8021-3935-3 pa

LC 2001-35084

In this study, the author "focuses on research of the last decade and excavations over the past 20 years. Verner divides his book into chapters according to pharaonic dynasty, spotlighting individual pharaohs' pyramids. He not only explains the layout of each pyramid but also presents various theories on how each pyramid was built and tells stories about the people that were buried there." Booklist

Includes bibliographical references

Wilkinson, Toby

★ The **rise** and fall of ancient Egypt; [by] Toby Wilkinson. Random House 2011 611p il map $35   **932**

ISBN 978-0-553-80553-6; 0-553-80553-3

LC 2009-47322

The author "offers a revisionist view of the ugly life hidden by the splendors and dazzling treasures of pharaonic Egypt. He shows in rich detail that it was a brutal society where life was cheap, royal power absolute and established through fear and coercion. . . . This is a penetrating and authoritative overview of a violent ancient civilization of-

ten revered by contemporary scholars and enthusiasts."
Publ Wkly

Includes bibliographical references

The Oxford encyclopedia of ancient Egypt; Donald
B. Redford, editor in chief. Oxford Univ. Press
2001 3v set $450   **932**
1. Reference books
ISBN 0-19-510234-7

LC 99-54801

This reference work covers "archaeology, biography,
history, language, social history, and more. . . . [It features]
essays from more than 250 contributors from various countries and scholarly pursuits, all with solid academic credentials. . . . One is not likely to encounter another work of this
magnitude on a subject of such universal interest for some
time." Booklist

Includes bibliographical references

933   Palestine to 70

Burleigh, Nina
Unholy business; a true tale of faith, greed, and
forgery in the holy land. Smithsonian Books 2008
271p $27.50   **933**
1. Antiquarians 2. Engineers 3. Entrepreneurs 4.
Forgery
ISBN 978-0-06-145845-3

LC 2008-23425

"In 2002, the James Ossuary, an ancient limestone box
for bones with an inscription on it that said 'James, son of Joseph, brother of Jesus' was publicized as the first real physical evidence of Jesus Christ's existence. The plot thickened
when the ossuary went on tour, creating lots of publicity, a
book by advocate Hershel Shanks, and a Discovery Channel
documentary. Then the ossuary's owner, Oded Golan, and
his antique-dealer associates were charged with forgery. . . .
Whether or not readers believe the ossuary is authentic, they
will thoroughly enjoy this book." Libr J

Goodman, Martin
Rome and Jerusalem; the clash of ancient civili-
zations. Alfred A. Knopf 2007 598p il map $35 **933**
1. Jerusalem in Christianity 2. Jews -- History 3. Jews
-- Rome
ISBN 978-0-375-41185-4; 0-375-41185-2

LC 2007-5267

"For scholars of Roman and Jewish history as well as
well-informed general readers, this work provides a definitive account." Booklist

Includes bibliographical references

Korb, Scott
Life in year one; what the world was like in
first-century Palestine. Riverhead Books 2010 241p
$25.95   **933**
1. Jews -- History
ISBN 978-1-59448-899-3

LC 2010-146

The author "calls his retrospective 'a lively romp through
the land of Palestine,' circa 5 B.C.E.–70 C.E., but the picture

he draws from archeology, ancient historical accounts, and
religious texts is anything but lighthearted. . . . Korb's vivid,
breezy prose makes accessible a mountain of scholarship
that illuminates the past." Publ Wkly

Includes bibliographical references

935   Mesopotamia to 637 and Iranian Plateau
to 637

Kriwaczek, Paul
Babylon; Mesopotamia and the birth of civili-
zation. Paul Kriwaczek. Thomas Dunne Books/St.
Martin's Press 2012 310 p.   **935**
ISBN 9781250000071; 9781429941068

LC 2012003104

This book is an overview of the rich, ancient civilizations that flourished in the land between the two rivers. . . .
The ancient simmering conflict of the Fertile Crescent boils
down to the question: Should the Tigris-Euphrates Valley be
mastered from the west or the east? . . .. The need to organize
systems of irrigation in Eridu . . . spawned an urban revolution, with the invention of cities and all that came with them:
division of labor, social classes, engineering, the arts, education, numbers and law, to mention a few. . . . The author
keeps close to biblical readings for comparative accounts of
the Flood and the succession of kings of the city-states to the
founder of the first true empire, Sargon. (Kirkus)

936   Europe north and west of Italian Peninsula
to ca. 499

Cunliffe, Barry
The **ancient** Celts. Penguin Books 1999 324p
il map pa $21.95   **936**
1. Celts
ISBN 0-14-025422-6

This is a "survey of the origins of the Celts and their
expansion during the Iron Age through their largely successful subjection by the Romans. . . . [Cunliffe] has written a
readable and informative book with many attractive illustrations." Libr J

Includes bibliographical references

Hill, Rosemary
Stonehenge. Harvard University Press 2008
242p il map $19.95   **936**
1. Megalithic monuments -- England 2. Megalithic
monuments -- Great Britain
ISBN 9780674031326; 0674031326

LC 2008-12024

Hill's "book is a treasure: stylish, thoughtful, miraculously condensed, and as full of knowledge as a megalith is
full of megalith." Sunday Times (London)

Includes bibliographical references (p. 211-222)

★ Ancient Europe 8000 B.C.-A.D. 1000; encyclopedia of the Barbarian world. Peter Bogucki &

Pam J. Crabtree, editors-in-chief. Thomson/Gale 2004 2v il, maps set $280 **936**
1. Ancient history 2. Reference books
ISBN 0-684-80668-1

LC 2003-15251

"Any public and academic library that has a clientele interested in European archeology or the featured historical period covered will find this a valuable purchase." Booklist

Includes bibliographical references

937 Italian Peninsula to 476 and adjacent territories to 476

Allan, Tony

Life, myth, and art in Ancient Rome. J. Paul Getty Museum 2005 144p il pa $19.95 **937**
1. Roman art 2. Roman mythology
ISBN 0-89236-821-7

LC 2004-114326

This is an "illustrated guide to the cultural and political heritage of ancient Rome, including the enduring legacy of its art and architecture, the engineering innovations of its vast system of roads and aqueducts, the . . . myths of its gods and goddesses, and the power of its emperors and legions." Publisher's note

Includes bibliographical references

Beard, Mary

The **fires** of Vesuvius; Pompeii lost and found. Belknap Press of Harvard University Press 2008 360p il map $26.95; pa $17.95 **937**
ISBN 978-0-674-02976-7; 0-674-02976-3; 978-0-674-04586-6 pa; 0-674-04586-6 pa

LC 2008-27513

"The eruption of Mt. Vesuvius in 79 A.D. preserved a uniquely rich sample of Roman life. Buried among the ruins of Pompeii are frescoes, graffiti ('Atimetus got me pregnant'), campaign ads, and housewares; the victims themselves left hollows in the lava that, when cast in plaster, yield details as fine as the imprint of one man's eyebrows. In this lively survey, Beard, a classicist at Cambridge, tempers erudition with a skepticism toward interpretive overreach. " New Yorker

Includes bibliographical references

Berry, Joanne

The **complete** Pompeii. Thames & Hudson 2007 256p il map $40 **937**
ISBN 978-0-500-05150-4; 0-500-05150-X

LC 2007-922095

This book "covers the origins and evolution of the city, the daily life of its residents, the geography of the region, and the eruption of Mt. Vesuvius, as well as a history of the excavation of the site. Easy to read and with full color pictures of the excavation, along with maps, time lines, diagrams, and vivid art reproductions, this book gives a broad and comprehensive introduction to the Pompeian world. . . . High school libraries should be advised that there is a section on eroticism that contains visually and verbally explicit sexual material." Libr J

Includes bibliographical references

Bunson, Matthew

Encyclopedia of the Roman Empire; rev ed; Facts on File 2002 636p il maps $75 **937**
1. Reference books
ISBN 0-8160-4562-3

LC 2001-53253

This reference work provides information on the key places, people, events, and culture of Roman history, from the reign of Julius Caesar to the fall of the last Roman emperor in 476 A.D.

"An excellent ready-reference source." Booklist [review of 1994 edition]

Includes bibliographical references

Fowler, Brenda

Iceman; uncovering the life and times of a prehistoric man found in an alpine glacier. University of Chicago Press ed; University of Chicago Press 2001 315p il pa $15 **937**
1. Mummies 2. Prehistoric peoples
ISBN 0-226-25823-8

LC 2001-27805

"In September 1991, hikers in the Alps discovered a well-preserved frozen corpse; nearby lay a stone ax and swatches of leather and fur. The man turned out to have died in the early Bronze Age, making him an incalculable treasure for students of early human beings. Fowler . . . offers a brisk and easy-to-follow narrative, first of the great discovery, then of the personal and political struggles for control of the frozen body." Publ Wkly

Includes bibliographical references

Freisenbruch, Annelise

Caesars' wives; sex, power, and politics in the Roman Empire. Free Press 2010 xxvi, 337p il $28; ebook $14.99 **937**
1. Empresses 2. Women -- Rome
ISBN 978-1-4165-8303-5; 1-4165-8303-3; 978-1-4165-8357-8 ebook; 1-4165-8357-2 ebook

LC 2010-19368

"Providing well-chosen, scintillating details—e.g., enemies being boiled alive, familial bonds savagely snapped in an instant—alongside careful historical analysis, the author breathes new life into these overlooked subjects. . . . A captivating look at imperial Rome's roots in the making of the modern stateswoman " Kirkus

Includes bibliographical references

Gibbon, Edward

★ The **decline** and fall of the Roman empire; Edward Gibbon; edited, abridged, and with a critical introduction by Hans-Friedrich Mueller; introduction by Daniel J. Boorstin; illustrations by Giovanni Battista Piranesi. Modern Library paperback ed.; Modern Library 2003 xxxvii, 1258p il map pa $15.95 **937**
ISBN 0-375-75811-9

LC 2002-32585

"In this substantial history of the Roman Empire, Gibbon bridges the abyss between the ancient and the modern world. It is the one historical work of the eighteenth century that is still accepted as authoritative. It covers thirteen centuries of history, during which time paganism was breaking down and Christianity was taking its place." Reader's Adviser

Includes bibliographical references

Goldsworthy, Adrian Keith

How Rome fell; death of a superpower. [by] Adrian Goldsworthy. Yale University Press 2009 531p il map $32.50   **937**

ISBN 978-0-300-13719-4; 0-300-13719-2

"This richly rewarding work will serve as an introduction to Roman history, but will also provide plenty of depth to satisfy the educated reader." Publ Wkly

Includes bibliographical references

Grant, Michael

Collapse and recovery of the Roman Empire. Routledge 1999 123p $34.95   **937**

1. Emperors -- Rome

ISBN 0-415-17323-X

LC 98-8222

"Grant examines the causes for the near disintegration of the empire in the mid-third century A.D., including the problems of imperial succession, Germanic encroachments on the frontiers, and chronic conflicts with the Persians in the East. . . . This work is a worthy and necessary addition to both academic and public library collections on classical history." Booklist

Includes bibliographical references

O'Connell, Robert L.

The **ghosts** of Cannae; Hannibal and the darkest hour of the Roman republic. Random House 2010 310p map $27   **937**

1. Cannae, Battle of, 216 B.C. 2. Generals 3. Punic War, 2nd, 218-201 B.C. 4. Punic Wars, 264-146 B.C.

ISBN 978-1-4000-6702-2; 1-4000-6702-2

LC 2009-40006

"The distinctive edge of The Ghosts of Cannae is Robert L. O'Connell's consistently professional instinct for the behavior of men and units on the battlefield. He is able to put himself and his reader on the ground at Cannae, gagging in the heat of a southern Italian midsummer, assailed by an overload from every one of the five senses." N Y Times Book Rev

Includes bibliographical references

Pellegrino, Charles R.

★ **Ghosts** of Vesuvius; a new look at the last days of Pompeii, how the towers fell, and other strange connections. [by] Charles Pellegrino. 1st ed; W. Morrow 2004 489p il map $25.95; pa $15.95   **937**

1. Excavations (Archeology) -- Italy

ISBN 0-380-97310-3; 0-06-075100-2 pa

LC 2003-71055

"In August A.D. 79, Mt. Vesuvius erupted and famously buried the city of Pompeii and, less famously, the city of Herculaneum. From this node of history, Pellegrino goes off on a . . . search for the connections and ruptures that have shaped not only human civilization but the very course of life on Earth and the universe at large. . . . This is a book to

be savored, reread and passed along to future generations." Publ Wkly

Includes bibliographical references

The **Cambridge** illustrated history of the Roman world; edited by Greg Woolf. Cambridge University Press 2003 384p il map $45   **937**

ISBN 0-521-82775-2

LC 2004-298480

This book explores such topics as "religion, Rome's relationship with Greece, warfare and Empire, and science and culture." Publisher's note

Includes bibliographical references

The **Oxford** history of the Roman world; edited by John Boardman, Jasper Griffin, Oswyn Murray. Oxford Univ. Press 1991 518p il maps hardcover o.p. pa $17.95   **937**

ISBN 0-19-280203-8

LC 91-11763

This "work tells the story of the rise of Rome from its origins as a cluster of villages to the foundation of the Roman Empire by Augustus, to its consolidation in the first two centuries CE. It also discusses aspects of the later Empire and its influence on Western civilization." Publisher's note

Includes bibliographical references

938   Greece to 323

Adkins, Lesley

Handbook to life in ancient Greece; [by] Lesley Adkins and Roy A. Adkins. Updated ed; Facts on File 2005 514p il map $70   **938**

ISBN 0-8160-5659-5

LC 2004-47105

This book covers "all aspects of ancient Greek life—from the beginnings of the Minoan civilization in Crete to the final defeat by the Roman world in 30 BCE." Publisher's note

Includes bibliographical references

Burckhardt, Jacob

The **Greeks** and Greek civilization; translated by Sheila Stern; edited with an introduction by Oswyn Murray. St. Martin's Press 1998 449p hardcover o.p. pa $16.95   **938**

1. Greece -- Civilization -- To 146 B.C

ISBN 0-312-24447-9 pa

LC 98-30107

"These lectures provide not only a rich overview of Burckhardt's learning but a precious glimpse into the intellectual world of the late nineteenth century. . . . Here his topics range from the importance of the 'agon' in forging individualism to the pessimism and violence that underlay much of Greek culture." New Yorker

Includes bibliographical references

Cartledge, Paul

Ancient Greece; a history in eleven cities. Oxford University Press 2009 261p il map $19.95 **938**
ISBN 978-0-19-923338-0

LC 2009-26999

"Aiming for a general audience, Cartledge achieves a fast-paced, highly engaging romp through ancient Greece. An excellent choice for anyone seeking an introduction to the topic; for all its readability, this book doesn't skimp on the research." Libr J

Includes bibliographical references

Green, Peter

The Hellenistic age; a history. Modern Library 2007 xxxiii, 199p map hardcover o.p. pa $14 **938**
1. Hellenism
ISBN 978-0-679-64279-4; 0-679-64279-X; 978-0-8129-6740-1 pa; 0-8129-6740-2 pa

LC 2006-46657

This study "traces the unfolding of Hellenistic civilization in a linear fashion, while at the same time drawing connections between successive alterations in the political, economic and social landscape of the Hellenistic East and the appearance of new cultural and intellectual perspectives. . . . [The book] provides an interesting and well-written overview of a historical period that Green aptly describes as covering 'some of the most crucial and transformational history of the ancient world. . . . The changes are lasting and fundamental.' If only for this, students of world history are in Green's debt." Philadelphia Inquirer

Includes bibliographical references

Herodotus, ca. 484-425 B.C.

★ The landmark Herodotus; the Histories: a new translation. a new translation by Andrea L. Purvis with maps, annotations, appendices, and encyclopedic index; edited by Robert B. Strassler; with an introduction by Rosalind Thomas. Pantheon Books 2007 lxiv, 953p $45 **938**
1. History, Ancient
ISBN 978-0-375-42109-9; 0-375-42109-2; 0375421092; 9780375421099

LC 2007024149

This is a new translation of Herodotus' Histories. Indexes.

"A major theme of the Histories is the way in which time can effect surprising changes in the fortunes and reputations of empires, cities, and men; all the more appropriate, then, that Herodotus' reputation has once again been riding very high. In the academy, his technique, once derided as haphazard, has earned newfound respect, while his popularity among ordinary readers will likely get a boost from the publication of perhaps the most densely annotated, richly illustrated, and user-friendly edition of his Histories ever to appear: 'The Landmark Herodotus,' edited by Robert B. Strassler and bristling with appendices, by a phalanx of experts, on everything from the design of Athenian warships to ancient units of liquid measure." New Yorker

Includes bibliographical references

Higgins, Charlotte

It's all Greek to me; from Homer to the Hippocratic Oath, how ancient Greece has shaped our world. Harper 2010 229p il map $16.99 **938**
ISBN 978-0-06-180400-7; 0-06-180400-2

LC 2010-06737

"The book has plenty of useful aspects, perhaps most notably in the rich back matter, comprising an alphabet, map, timeline, key to important Greek gods and notables and a sampling of Greek sayings and words (and root words) that still inhabit our language (tantalizing, Draconian). Anyone reading The Iliad or any other of the Greek classic texts for the first time would do well to keep the section bookmarked. Higgins covers Homer, the playwrights, the historians, the nascent scientists and the philosophers, and she gives special attention to the warriors, wars and other aspects of the ancient world that continue to make us uncomfortable—e.g., homosexuality, women's rights, slavery. Periodically, she pauses to offer mini-disquisitions on topics as varied as the plots of The Iliad and The Odyssey, the architecture of the Parthenon and the uneven verisimilitude of the 2007 film 300." Kirkus

Includes bibliographical references

Kagan, Donald

The Peloponnesian War. Viking 2003 xxvii, 511p il map $29.95; pa $15 **938**
ISBN 0-670-03211-5; 0-14-200437-5 pa

LC 2002-193377

This is a study of "the conflict between Athens and Sparta in the fifth century B.C.E. . . . {Kagan's} primary source is, of course, Thucydides' epic history, but {he} draws on Aristotle, Xenophon, and others to provide an objective, nuanced perspective on the military drama. And it's quite a drama: the clash of democracy and oligarchy, the testing of great leaders, the innovative military tactics, and the unprecedented human cost." Booklist

Includes bibliographical references

Thucydides; the reinvention of history. Viking 2009 257p map $26.95 **938**
1. Historians 2. Historiography
ISBN 0670921296; 9780670021291

LC 2009-08368

Kagan argues that "The Peloponnesian War differs significantly from other accounts offered by Thucydides' contemporaries and stands as the first modern work of political history." (Publisher's note) Index.

"Kagan's utter mastery is on display in this vigorous, elegantly written, provocative book." PopMatters

Includes bibliographical references

Lane Fox, Robin

The classical world; an epic history from Homer to Hadrian. Basic Books 2006 656p il map $35 **938**
1. Classical civilization
ISBN 978-0-465-02496-4; 0-465-02496-3

LC 2006-20247

A "portrait of Greek and Roman culture over a period of roughly 900 years. Although he utilizes a broadly chronological approach, Fox goes well beyond the usual, dreary narrative of battles, dynastic changes, and political conflicts that often characterize surveys of the period. Instead, Fox focuses on the gradual development and transformation of various cultural aspects of Greek and Roman societies, and he discusses in often fascinating detail topics that are normally given short shrift in general histories." Booklist

Sacks, David

Encyclopedia of the ancient Greek world; editorial consultant, Oswyn Murray; revised by Lisa R. Brody. Rev ed; Facts on File 2005 xx, 412p il map $75   **938**

1. Reference books
ISBN 0-8160-5722-2

LC 2004-56429

This encyclopedia covers "ancient Greece, from the dawning of Minoan civilization to the conquest of Rome—2000 years of a remarkable civilization that left an indelible imprint on human history. . . . This is a first-rate purchase for libraries on a topic of endless inquiry and fascination." SLJ

Includes bibliographical references

Thucydides

The **history** of the Peloponnesian War; Rev ed; Penguin Group 1954 648p map pa $15   **938**

ISBN 978-0-14-044039-3; 0-14-044039-9

Thucydides' "chosen subject was the Peloponnesian War, which covered 27 years of his own lifetime, 431-404 B.C., and in which he fought as a commander of the Athenian troops in Thrace. His ideal of history is said to have been first accuracy, and then relevancy. . . . He rarely digressed. His history is unfinished, breaking off in the middle of the year 411 B.C." Reader's Adviser

The **landmark** Thucydides; a comprehensive guide to the Peloponnesian War. edited by Robert B. Strassler; introduction by Victor Davis Hanson. A newly revised edition of the Richard Crawley translation with maps, annotations, appendices, and e Free Press 1996 xxxiii,713 $45; pa $25   **938**

ISBN 978-1-416-59087-3; 0-684-82790-5

LC 96-24555

"Strassler, an unaffiliated scholar of classical studies, has remedied many of the flaws of Richard Crawley's 1874 translation of The Peloponnesian War. He has added descriptive paragraph-by-paragraph synopses, topic headers on every page, numerous maps keyed to the adjoining text, explanatory footnotes, an extensive index, an excellent introduction by Victor Davis Hanson . . . , and 11 appendixes (by various scholars) on politics, warfare, and society in the Greece of the fifth century B.C.E." Libr J

★ Ancient Greece; edited by Thomas J. Sienkewicz. Salem Press 2007 3v il map set $207   **938**

1. Reference books
ISBN 1-58765-281-1; 978-1-58765-281-3

LC 2006-16525

This is a "comprehensive examination of Greek civilization and its impact on Western history, 'from its earliest archaeological remains until the Battle of Actium in 31 B.C.E.' . . . [The essays included] cover art, daily life and customs, government, literature, medicine and science, war, the role of women, and mythology. Biographical entries pro-

file statesmen, artists, writers, scientists, and philosophers, and relevant entries probe battles, philosophical movements, and types of literature." SLJ

Includes bibliographical references

★ The Cambridge dictionary of classical civilization; edited by Graham Shipley . . . [et al.] Cambridge University Press 2006 xliv, 966p il map $180   **938**

1. Classical civilization -- Dictionaries 2. Reference books
ISBN 0-521-48313-1; 978-0-521-48313-1

LC 2006-299203

The "entries and more than 500 illustrations focus on social, economic, and cultural aspects of these civilizations from the mid-eighth century BCE to the end of the fifth century." Booklist

Includes bibliographical references

Great moments in Greek archaeology; academic coordinator, Panos Valavanis; translated by David Hardy; foreword by Angelos Delivorrias; essays by George F. Bass . . . [et al.] The J. Paul Getty Museum 2007 379p il $75   **938**

1. Excavations (Archaeology) -- Greece 2. Excavations (Archeology) -- Greece
ISBN 978-0-89236-910-2; 0-89236-910-8

LC 2007-16609

"This magnificently illustrated book with essays by leading scholars—frequently the excavators themselves—tells the story of Greek archaeological discoveries, capturing the excitement and rendering details accessible to a wide audience." Libr J

Includes bibliographical references

★ The Landmark Xenophon's Hellenika; a new translation. translation by John Marincola; with maps, annotations, appendices, and encyclopedic index edited by Robert B. Strassler; with an introduction by David Thomas. Pantheon Books 2009 lxxxii, 579p il map $40   **938**

ISBN 9780375422553

LC 2009-20970

This is a new translation "of the Hellenika, the major primary source for the events of the final seven years and aftermath of the Peloponnesian War. Hellenika covers the years between 411 and 362 B.C.E.." (Publisher's note) Glossary. Bibliography. Index.

"The Hellenika is often messy: Athens and Sparta are the primary players, but Corinth and Thebes constantly jump into the fray, and Persia, Sparta's sometime ally, is always lurking at the periphery. All this can be confusing, and one of the more impressive things about the Landmark edition is how much it tries—and succeeds—in making the texts of ancient Greece accessible to contemporary audiences. The extensive footnotes are both informative and readable. . . . Side notes, meanwhile, offer a running plot summary, in case the casual reader neglects to follow, say, the hostilities between Agesilaos and Phleious. The maps generously sprinkled across these pages are uniformly clear, showing both battle maneuvers and shifting geopolitical alliances.

And the appendix is a veritable treasure trove of secondary material." New Criterion

Includes bibliographical references and index

The Oxford classical dictionary; edited by Simon Hornblower and Antony Spawforth. 3rd rev ed; Oxford Univ. Press 2003 lv, 1640p $110 **938**
1. Classical dictionaries 2. Reference books
ISBN 0-19-860641-9

This reference includes over 6,000 entries about the ancient Greco-Roman world, covering such topics as politics, government and economy, religion and mythology, law and philosophy, science and geography, languages, literature, art and architecture, archeology, historical writing, military history, social history, sex, and gender.

"This is a work that makes a fascinating world of learning accessible to a broad audience." Booklist

Includes bibliographical references

939   Other parts of ancient world

Wood, Michael
In search of the Trojan War. University of Calif. Press 1998 288p il pa $19.95 **939**
1. Bronze Age 2. Trojan War 3. Turkey -- Antiquities
ISBN 0-520-21599-0

LC 98-4958

"This is a first-rate book. . . . The book makes a readable and clear approach to some of the knottiest problems of Bronze Age archaeology." Choice [review of 1985 edition]

Includes bibliographical references

★ Civilizations of the Ancient Near East; Jack M. Sasson, editor in chief; John Baines, Gary Beckman, Karen S. Rubinson, associate editors. Hendrickson Publishers 2000 4v in 2 il map set $169.95 **939**
ISBN 1-56563-607-4

LC 00-63144

This "work concentrates on the Near East, broadly defined to include a region from Northeast Africa to India, Pakistan, and Burma, with principal focus on the core areas of Egypt, Syro-Palestine, Mesopotamia, and Anatolia. The time span ranges from the third millennium B.C.E., when writing was invented, to 330 B.C.E., when Alexander triumphed over the Persian Empire. The 189 contributors from five continents and 16 countries include some of the world's finest scholars." Libr J [review of 1995 edition]

Includes bibliographical references

940   History of specific continents, countries, localities in modern world; extraterrestrial worlds

Sachar, Howard Morley
Dreamland; Europeans and Jews in the aftermath of the Great War. {by} Howard M. Sachar. Knopf 2002 385p map hardcover o.p. pa $15 **940**
1. Jews -- Europe 2. Jews -- Europe -- History -- 20th

century 3. Jews -- Europe -- Social conditions -- 20th century
ISBN 0-375-70829-4 pa

LC 2001-38471

An overview of Jewish life in Europe during the three decades before the Holocaust.

"This scholarly analysis provides a completely original slant on the much-studied interwar period." Booklist

Includes bibliographical references

Eastern Europe; an introduction to the people, lands, and culture. edited by Richard Frucht. ABC-CLIO 2004 3v set $285 **940**
ISBN 1-57607-800-0

LC 2004-22300

For a review see: Booklist, March 15, 2005

940.1   Early history to 1453

English, Edward D.
Encyclopedia of the medieval world. Facts on File 2004 2v il map set $150 **940.1**
1. Middle Ages -- Encyclopedias 2. Reference books
ISBN 0-8160-4690-5

LC 2003-27825

This encyclopedia "covers the time period from the late antique world to about 1500 C.E and includes events, people, institutions, and culture in western and eastern Europe, Scandinavia, North Africa, Byzantium, and the Near East. The 2,000 entries discuss significant people, art, politics, literature, religion, economics, law, science, and warfare in an A-Z format." Booklist

Includes bibliographical references

Freeman, Charles
The **closing** of the Western mind; the rise of faith and the fall of reason. Knopf 2003 xxiii, 432p il map $32.50; pa $16.95 **940.1**
1. Church and state -- Europe -- History 2. Church history -- 30-600, Early church 3. Civilization, Western 4. Hellenism 5. Western civilization
ISBN 1-400-04085-X; 1-400-03380-2 pa

LC 2002-44821

"This is one of the best books to date on the development of Christianity. . . . Beautifully written and impressively annotated, this is an indispensable read for anyone interested in the roots of Christianity and its implications for our modern worldview." Choice

Includes bibliographical references

Gies, Frances
★ **Life** in a medieval village; [by] Frances and Joseph Gies. Harper & Row 1990 257p il maps hardcover o.p. pa $14.95 **940.1**
1. Medieval civilization 2. Middle Ages
ISBN 0-06-016215-5; 0-06-092046-7 pa

LC 89-33759

"Elton, England, is the focal point of the authors' efforts to portray the everyday life and social structure of the High Middle Ages. After giving a brief summary of Elton's origins and development in the Roman and Anglo-Saxon periods, the book examines just how the residents lived and worked within the feudal structure at the beginning of the fourteenth century." Booklist

Includes bibliographical references

Gies, Joseph

Life in a medieval city; [by] Joseph and Frances Gies. HarperPerennial 1981 274p il map pa $13.95   **940.1**

1. Medieval civilization 2. Middle Ages
ISBN 0-06-090880-7

"A portrait of a medieval city [Troyes], a flourishing settlement of a type not known in Europe before the Middle Ages." Cincinnati Public Libr

Includes bibliographical references

Herlihy, David

The **black** death and the transformation of the west; edited and with an introduction by Samuel K. Cohn, Jr. Harvard Univ. Press 1997 117p hardcover o.p. pa $12   **940.1**

1. Medieval civilization 2. Plague 3. Renaissance
ISBN 0-674-07613-3 pa

LC 96-54637

These "essays redefine the historical study of the Black Death. . . . Herlihy's contention is that we can learn from this 'devastating natural disaster': for example, parallels can be drawn to today's pandemic of AIDS, especially in the resultant bigotries that both engendered. Cohn introduces the lectures, admirably setting the scene. This book, which opens a new chapter on the history and implications of the plague, is essential for all readers of medieval history." Libr J

Includes bibliographical references

Reston, James

The **last** apocalypse; Europe at the year 1000 A.D. Doubleday 1998 299p il map hardcover o.p. pa $14.95   **940.1**

ISBN 0-385-48336-8 pa

LC 97-18812

"Reston's seemingly encyclopedic knowledge of the tenth century, combined with his disarming interpretations of the period's events, makes for fascinating reading." Booklist

Includes bibliographical references

Slotkin, Richard

Lost battalions; the Great War and the crisis of American nationality. Richard Slotkin. H. Holt 2005 639p il maps   **940.1**

1. African American soldiers 2. African American soldiers -- History 3. Minorities -- United States 4. World War, 1914-1918 -- Participation, African American 5. World War, 1914-1918 -- Regimental histories 6. World War, 1914-1918 -- Regimental histories -- United States 7. World War, 1914-1918 -- United States
ISBN 0-8050-4124-9

LC 2005-46312

This is a "history of the African-American 369th Infantry, known as the 'Harlem Hellfighters,' and the 77th Division, dubbed the 'Melting Pot' for its ranks of Italians, Jews and other eastern Europeans. . . . Slotkin smoothly

telescopes from the trenches to the political and social implications for decades to come in this insightful, valuable account." Publ Wkly

Wickham, Chris

★ The **inheritance** of Rome; a history of Europe from 400 to 1000. Viking 2009 650p il map $35   **940.1**

1. Medieval civilization 2. Middle Ages
ISBN 978-0-670-02098-0

LC 2009-15169

"Wickham's achievement contributes richly to our picture of this often narrowly understood period." Publ Wkly

Includes bibliographical references

Knights; in history and in legend. chief consultant Constance Brittain Bouchard. Firefly Books 2009 304p il map $40   **940.1**

1. Knights and knighthood 2. Military art and science -- History
ISBN 978-1-55407-480-8

The history of knights, from their everyday lives to their clothing, training, heraldry and orders, as well as their role in literature and film, and the decline of traditional knighthood.

"Aimed at history and art history lovers, this work would be excellent reading for medieval history enthusiasts and should be welcomed as a library reference resource." Libr J

Includes bibliographical references

The **New Cambridge** medieval history; edited by Paul Fouracre . . . [et al.] Cambridge Univ. Press 2005 7v in 8 il maps set $1600   **940.1**

1. Medieval civilization 2. Middle Ages
ISBN 978-0-521-85360-6; 0-521-85360-5

"An excellent reference history, written by specialists, with full bibliographies at the end of each volume." Guide to Ref Books. 11th edition [entry for Cambridge medieval history]

★ The **Oxford** history of medieval Europe; edited by George Holmes. Oxford Univ. Press 2001 395p il maps pa $16.95   **940.1**

ISBN 0-19-280133-3

LC 2002-281715

This compact edition covers such subjects as the chivalric code of knights, popular festivals, new art forms, the Black Death, the fall of Rome, and the emergence of the Reformation

940.2   -1453

Adkin, Mark

The **Trafalgar** companion; a guide to history's most famous sea battle and the life of Admiral Lord Nelson. Aurum Press 2005 560p il map $75 **940.2**

1. Admirals 2. Trafalgar (Spain), Battle of, 1805
ISBN 1-84513-018-9

"Beginning with a prologue that describes the wounding and death of Vice-Admiral Horatio Nelson, the book introduces readers to the history of the campaign from 1802 to

1805 and to . . . information about the men and ships of the Royal Navy, in alternate chapters. . . . It will long stand as the definitive one-volume study of Great Britain's foremost naval hero and his times." Choice

Includes bibliographical references

Barbero, Alessandro

The **Battle**; a new history of Waterloo. Walker & Company 2005 340p il map $28; pa $16   **940.2**
1. Napoleonic Wars, 1800-1815 -- Campaigns -- Belgium 2. Waterloo, Battle of, 1815
ISBN 0-8027-1453-6; 978-0-8027-1453-4; 0-8027-1500-1 pa; 978-0-8027-1500-5 pa

The author's "narrative flows smoothly, making readers feel part of the battle's events. The chapters are short—never more than a few pages—and they pull the reader along with the action." Choice

Includes bibliographical references (p. 318-324)

Barzun, Jacques

From dawn to decadence; 500 years of Western cultural life, 1500 to the present. HarperCollins Pubs. 2000 877p hardcover o.p. pa $20   **940.2**
1. Civilization, Western 2. Western civilization
ISBN 0-06-092883-2 pa

LC 99-16194

"Encyclopedic without being discontinuous, the book hardly seems as long, as carefully constructed or as densely packed as it is. Though the ideas it explains are often complicated, the explanations it offers are limpidly clear, sparkling with biographical anecdote and counter-canonical observations." N Y Times Book Rev

Includes bibliographical references

Blanning, T. C. W.

★ The **pursuit** of glory; Europe, 1648-1815. [by] Tim Blanning. Viking 2007 xxvii, 707p il map $39.95   **940.2**
ISBN 978-0-670-06320-8; 0-670-06320-7

LC 2006-37324

The author "thoroughly covers the politics and endless wars of the period. . . . 'The Pursuit of Glory' is history writing at its glorious best." N Y Times (Late N Y Ed)

Includes bibliographical references

Blom, Philipp

The **vertigo** years; Europe 1900-1914. Basic Books 2008 466p il $29.95   **940.2**
ISBN 0-465-01116-0; 978-0-465-01116-2

LC 2008-935053

Blom examines the period between 1900 and the outbreak of the First World War, as cities grew, "education changed the outlook of millions; mass-produced items transformed daily life; industrial laborers demanded a share of political power; and women sought to change their place in society." (Publisher's note) Bibliography. Index.

"Blom's engrossing history begins with an invitation: 'Imagine yourself looking at the years 1900 to 1914 without the long shadows of the future darkening their historical present.' His imaginative recreation of this period argues that speed—both literal and figurative—came to typify and, ultimately, define modern life. This was the age that gave

rise not only to Futurism and Vorticism but also to car racing and the electric chair. Precipitate change also ushered in an age of uncertainty and attraction to the seeming stability of the past. The book's strength is also its charm—a multifaceted, panoramic approach animated by vivacious narration of individual stories." New Yorker

Includes bibliographical references

Coote, Stephen

Napoleon and the Hundred Days. DaCapo Press 2005 308p il $27.50   **940.2**
1. Emperors
ISBN 0-306-81408-0

LC 2004-65505

This history "of the 100 days between Napoleon's escape from Elba and his capitulation after Waterloo uses the period as a lens through which to examine his character in general. . . . This accessible work is reminiscent of the finest classical Roman histories and biographies." Publ Wkly

Includes bibliographical references

Esdaile, Charles J.

Napoleon's wars; an international history, 1803-1815. [by] Charles Esdaile. Viking 2008 621p il map $35   **940.2**
1. Emperors 2. Napoleonic Wars, 1800-1815
ISBN 978-0-670-02030-0; 0-670-02030-3

"Recapturing the flux of international diplomacy and Napoléon's congenital rejection of compromise, Esdaile persuasively places the diplomatic foundation to popular military histories about the Napoleonic wars." Booklist

Includes bibliographical references (p. 567-602)

Gies, Joseph

Life in a medieval castle; [by] Joseph and Frances Gies. Harper & Row 1979 272p il pa $14.95 **940.2**
1. Castles 2. Feudalism 3. Hunting -- Great Britain 4. Knights and knighthood 5. Middle Ages
ISBN 0-06-090674-X

LC 79-103901

Using Chepstow Castle on the Welsh border as a model, the authors provide "descriptions of the medieval world where the castle was household, feudal center, and military target, and by concentrating on Anglo-Norman examples illustrate what existence was like as the dark ages began to brighten." Booklist

Includes glossary and bibliographical references

Greenblatt, Stephen J.

★ The **swerve**; [by] Stephen Greenblatt. W.W. Norton 2011 356p il $26.95   **940.2**
1. Civilization, Modern 2. Modern civilization 3. Philosophers 4. Philosophy, Renaissance 5. Poets 6. Renaissance 7. Science, Renaissance
ISBN 0393064476; 9780393064476

LC 2011019765

The book presents a history of the "ancient Roman philosophical epic, On the Nature of Things, by Lucretius - a beautiful poem of the most dangerous ideas: that the universe functioned without the aid of gods, that religious fear was damaging to human life, and that matter was made up of very small particles in eternal motion, colliding and swerving in new directions." According to the author, "the copying and translation of this ancient book -- the greatest discovery of the greatest book-hunter of his age -- fueled the Renaissance, inspiring artists such as Botticelli and thinkers such as Giordano Bruno; shaped the thought of Galileo and Freud, Darwin and Einstein; and had a revolutionary influence on writers such as Montaigne and Shakespeare and even Thomas Jefferson." (books.wwnorton.com)

"A fascinating, intelligent look at what may well be the most historically resonant book-hunt of all time." Booklist

Includes bibliographical references (p. [309]-335) and index.

Hobsbawm, E. J.

The **age** of revolution 1789-1848. Vintage Books 1996 356p il map pa $15.95   940.2
1. Industries -- History
ISBN 978-0-679-77253-8; 0-679-77253-7

"This book traces the transformation of the world between 1789 and 1848 insofar as it was due to what is here called the 'dual revolution'—the French Revolution of 1789 and the contemporaneous (British) Industrial Revolution." Preface

Includes bibliographical references

King, David

Vienna, 1814; how the conquerors of Napoleon made love, war, and peace at the Congress of Vienna. Harmony Books 2008 434p il $27.50   940.2
ISBN 978-0-307-33716-0; 0-307-33716-2
LC 2007-24680

"The conquerors of Napoleon were in a festive mood when they met in Vienna in the fall of 1814 to decide the fate of Europe.... [The author] does a superb job of evoking the bedazzling social scene that served as the backdrop to the Congress of Vienna. His characterizations of such luminaries as Czar Alexander, Metternich, Talleyrand, and Castlereagh are lucid and thoroughly grounded in primary sources.... This is a worthy contribution to the study of a critical historical event long neglected by historians." Libr J

Includes bibliographical references

Lieven, D. C. B.

Russia against Napoleon; the true story of the campaigns of War and Peace. [by] Dominic Lieven. Viking 2010 617p il map $35.95   940.2
1. Emperors 2. Napoleonic Wars, 1800-1815 -- Campaigns -- Russia
ISBN 978-0-670-02157-4
LC 2009-42564

"Lieven's book is lucid, engaging and reflects his deep love for Russia. This is a fascinating, exhaustively researched work, an elegant handling of a welter of confusing sources and a vital account of Russia from 1807 to 1814 that is unlikely to be bettered." Hist Today

Includes bibliographical references

Manchester, William

A **world** lit only by fire; the medieval mind and the Renaissance: portrait of an age. Little, Brown 1992 318p il maps hardcover o.p. pa $15.95 **940.2**
1. Explorers 2. Renaissance
ISBN 0-316-54556-2 pa
LC 91-39928

The author covers "the tumultuous span from the Dark Ages to the dawn of the Renaissance. He delineates an age when invisible spirits infested the air, when tolerance was seen as treachery and 'a mafia of profane popes desecrated Christianity.' Besides re-creating the arduous lives of ordinary people, ... {Manchester} peoples his tapestry with such figures as Leonardo, Machiavelli, Lucrezia Borgia, Erasmus, Luther, Henry VIII and Anne Boleyn." Publ Wkly

Includes bibliographical references

Mostert, Noel

The **line** upon a wind; the great war at sea, 1793-1815. W.W. Norton & Co. 2008 xxv, 774p il map $35   **940.2**
1. Anglo-French War, 1793-1802 -- Naval operations
2. Napoleonic Wars, 1800-1815 -- Naval operations 3. Naval history 4. Seafaring life
ISBN 978-0-393-06653-1; 0-393-06653-3
LC 2007-39313

"This is a vast, fast-moving chronicle that ranges across great distances while examining a host of characters, both well known and relatively obscure. Mostert does justifiably place great emphasis on Admiral Nelson and the critical battle at Trafalgar. He also offers useful and interesting descriptions of less-prominent aspects of the wars, including conflicts with the Barbary pirates and the British struggles against the rise of American naval power. This is an outstanding survey of a prolonged struggle that helped shape world history." Booklist

Includes bibliographical references (p. 748-752)

O'Brien, Michael

Mrs. Adams in winter; a journey in the last days of Napoleon. Farrar, Straus and Giroux 2010 364p il map $27   **940.2**
1. Members of Congress 2. Presidents 3. Secretaries of state 4. Senators 5. Spouses of presidents
ISBN 978-0-374-21581-1; 0-374-21581-2
LC 2009-25437

The author "pursues Louisa Adams's 40-day trek through a Europe in the process of transformation. The Mrs. Adams in question is not to be confused with Abigail Adams, the Colonial matriarch and wife of the second president. Rather, Louisa Catherine Adams was her London-born daughter-in-law, the wife to Abigail's son John Quincy Adams.... O'Brien's narrative is richly contextual, encompassing not only the great personalities of the age, whom Mrs. Adams met, but penetrating the secrets of a complicated marriage. A wide-sweeping historical survey and original intellectual journey." Kirkus

Includes bibliographical references

Pocock, Tom

The **terror** before Trafalgar; Nelson, Napoleon and the secret war. Naval Institute Press 2005 255p il map pa $16.95   **940.2**
  1. Admirals 2. Emperors
  ISBN 978-1-5911-4681-0; 1-5911-4681-X
             LC 2004-58185
The author "retells the story of the four years in which the French confidently prepared to invade Britain, overrun its army, take out its armaments and replace the government with something easier to control. . . . Pocock's little book . . . gives a chilling insight into ineffectual undercover operations and groundbreaking weaponry: rockets, torpedos, submarines, airships and the construction of an undersea tunnel, all so far ahead of their time that none turned out in the end to be much use in practical terms to either side." N Y Times Book Rev
  Includes bibliographical references

Pope, Stephen

★ **Dictionary** of the Napoleonic wars. Facts on File 2000 572p $71.50   **940.2**
  1. Europe -- History -- 1789-1815 -- Dictionaries
  2. Napoleonic Wars, 1800-1815 -- Dictionaries 3. Reference books
  ISBN 0-8160-4243-8
             LC 99-48829
Pope "has produced more than 1000 alphabetical entries, supplemented by 30 maps, detailing nearly every aspect of Napoleonic warfare. From broad subjects such as strategy, tactics, diplomacy, and propaganda to specific battles, treaties, weapons, naval warfare, and myriad colorful personalities, the book offers a wealth of succinct information." Libr J

Renaissance Society of America

★ **Encyclopedia** of the Renaissance; Paul F. Grendler, editor in chief. Scribner 1999 6v set $750   **940.2**
  1. Reference books 2. Renaissance -- Encyclopedias
  ISBN 0-684-80514-6
             LC 99-48290
This set covers "aspects of the Renaissance from the origins of humanism in Italy (ca. 1350) through 1750. . . . The encyclopedia's strength lies in its scholarship and in the comprehensiveness and diversity of its scope." Booklist

Reston, James

Defenders of the faith; Charles V, Suleyman the Magnificent, and the battle for Europe, 1520-1536. Penguin Press 2009 xxi, 407p il map $29.95 **940.2**
  1. Emperors 2. Holy Roman Empire 3. Sultans
  ISBN 978-1-59420-225-4
             LC 2008-54655
"Fast-paced and engaging, this is excellent reading for popular audiences." Libr J
  Includes bibliographical references

Roberts, Andrew

Waterloo: June 18, 1815; the battle for modern Europe. HarperCollins 2005 143p il maps $21.95; pa $12.95   **940.2**
  1. Waterloo, Battle of, 1815
  ISBN 0-06-008866-4; 0-06-076215-2 pa
             LC 2005-282517
This is a study of the defeat of Napoleon's army at the Battle of Waterloo in June, 1815.
  The author "instills an appreciation for Waterloo as a horrific experience saturated with alternative possible outcomes. A must for the military shelf." Booklist
  Includes bibliographical references (p. 135-136)

Talty, Stephan

The **illustrious** dead; the terrifying story of how typhus killed Napoleon's greatest army. Crown Publishers 2009 315p map $27   **940.2**
  1. Emperors 2. Typhus
  ISBN 978-0-307-39404-0
             LC 2008-50646
"Talty delivers a breezy, popular account of a gruesome campaign, emphasizing the equally gruesome epidemic that accompanied it." Publ Wkly
  Includes bibliographical references

Vincent, Edgar

Nelson; love & fame. Yale Univ. Press 2003 640p il map $35; pa $19.95   **940.2**
  1. Admirals 2. Admirals -- Great Britain -- Biography
  3. Spouses of prominent persons
  ISBN 0-300-09797-2; 0-300-10260-7 pa
             LC 2002-14566
"Nelson is a masterly biography, cool and sharp in long shots, intimately persuasive in close focus, at all times difficult to put down and as timely as it is suggestive in its implications." N Y Times Book Rev
  Includes bibliographical references

Wells, C. M.

Sailing from Byzantium; how a lost empire shaped the world. Colin Wells. Delacorte Press 2006 xxx, 335p map $22   **940.2**
  1. Civilization, Islamic -- Byzantine influences 2. Civilization, Slavic -- Byzantine influences
  ISBN 0-553-80381-6
             LC 2006-42665
The author "considers how Byzantium, the Eastern, Greek-language Roman Empire of the Middle Ages, influenced three successor civilizations Western Europe, Islam, and the eastern Slavic world of the Balkans and Russia. . . . This history is a needed reminder of the debt that three of our major civilizations owe to Byzantium." Libr J
  Includes bibliographical references

Wilson, Ellen Judy

★ **Encyclopedia** of the Enlightenment; Peter Hanns Reill, consulting editor; Ellen Judy Wilson, principal author. rev ed; Facts on File 2004 670p $75   **940.2**
  1. Enlightenment 2. Enlightenment -- Encyclopedias

3. Philosophy 4. Philosophy -- Encyclopedias 5. Reference books

ISBN 0-8160-5335-9

LC 2003-22973

This reference provides a "review of the important ideas, people, and events that shaped the world during the Enlightenment. [It] covers the major changes in science, education, philosophy, art and architecture, and politics which took place during the 17th and 18th centuries and led to the birth of the modern era. . . . The biographical entries cover such notables as Robespierre, Schiller, Fielding, Kant, and Voltaire. . . . Larger public, school, and academic libraries looking for a comprehensive overview of the subject for the student or interested reader will find this a valuable and accessible resource." Libr J

Includes bibliographical references

Wilson, Peter H.

The **Thirty** Years War; Europe's tragedy. Belknap Press of Harvard University Press 2009 xxii, 996p il map $35   **940.2**

1. Thirty Years' War, 1618-1648

ISBN 978-0-674-03634-5

LC 2009-11266

This "is a history of prodigious erudition that manages to corral the byzantine complexity of the Thirty Years War into a coherent narrative." Wall Street J

Includes bibliographical references

Zamoyski, Adam

Rites of peace; the fall of Napoleon and the Congress of Vienna. HarperColins 2007 634p il map $29.95   **940.2**

1. Napoleonic Wars, 1800-1815 -- Diplomatic history 2. Napoleonic Wars, 1800-1815 -- Peace

ISBN 0-06-077518-1; 978-0-06-077518-6

This "book is old-fashioned, impressively detailed diplomatic history." Economist

Includes bibliographical references

Europe 1789 to 1914; encyclopedia of the age of industry and empire. Merriman and Jay Winter, editors in chief. Charles Scribner's Sons 2006 5v il map set $595   **940.2**

1. Reference books

ISBN 0-684-31359-6; 978-0-684-31359-7

LC 2006-7335

This encyclopedia covers "the time period between the onset of the French Revolution to the outbreak of World War I." Publisher's note

Includes bibliographical references

The Renaissance; an encyclopedia for students. [edited by] Paul F. Grendler. Charles Scribner's Sons 2003 4v set $395   **940.2**

1. Reference books 2. Renaissance 3. Renaissance -- Encyclopedias

ISBN 0-684-31281-6

LC 2003-15672

This encyclopedia includes articles on various aspects of social, cultural, and political history such as literature, government, warfare, and technology, plus maps, charts, definitions, and chronology.

"Researchers should find their needs more than satisfied by this appealing and student-friendly resource." SLJ

940.3   World War I, 1914-1918

Audoin-Rouzeau, Stephane

14-18, understanding the Great War; {by} Stéphane Audoin-Rouzeau and Annette Becker; translated from the French by Catherine Temerson. Hill & Wang 2002 280p $24; pa $14   **940.3**

1. World War, 1914-1918

ISBN 0-8090-4642-3; 0-8090-4643-1 pa

LC 2002-111422

"The authors take an anthropological approach to the cataclysm that engulfed Europe in 1914 and examine three significant aspects of the war: violence, crusade, and mourning. . . . Supported by contemporary documentation, this unique work will become a classic study." Libr J

Includes bibliographical references

Burg, David F.

Almanac of World War I; [by] David F. Burg and L. Edward Purcell; introduction by William Manchester. University Press of Ky. 1998 320p il maps hardcover o.p. pa $22   **940.3**

1. Military biography 2. World War, 1914-1918 3. World War, 1914-1918 -- Biography 4. World War, 1914-1918 -- Chronology

ISBN 0-8131-2072-1; 0-8131-9087-8 pa

LC 98-26625

"The bulk of the text is arranged chronologically by year and date, listing almost daily occurrences from 1914 through 1918. . . . The work is international in scope, covering political and military happenings from around the world. . . . There is really nothing comparable to this volume." Booklist

Includes bibliographical references

Carter, Miranda

George, Nicholas, and Wilhelm; three royal cousins and the road to World War I. Alfred A. Knopf 2010 498p il map $30   **940.3**

1. Biography, Individual 2. Emperors 3. Kings 4. World War, 1914-1918 -- Causes

ISBN 978-1-4000-4363-7; 1-4000-4363-8

LC 2009-37690

In the years before World War I, the great European powers were ruled by three first cousins: King George V, Kaiser Wilhelm II, and Tsar Nicholas II. Carter uses the cousins' correspondence and a host of historical sources to tell their tragicomic stories.

The author "writes with lusty humour at times, has a fresh clarifying intelligence when unravelling knotty problems of ancien régime life and a sharp eye for telling details about people's gestures, temper, appearance and attitudes. . . . This is traditional narrative history with a 21st-century zing—a real corker of a book." Hist Today

Includes bibliographical references

Englund, Peter

★ The **beauty** and the sorrow; an intimate history of the First World War. translated by Peter Graves. Alfred A. Knopf 2011 540p il $35   **940.3**

1. World War, 1914-1918 -- Personal narratives
ISBN 978-0-307-59386-3; 0-307-59386-X
LC 2011-20828

This work "threads together the wartime experiences of 20 more or less unremarkable men and women, on both sides of the war, from schoolgirls and botanists to mountain climbers, doctors, ambulance drivers and clerks. A few of these people will become heroes. A few will become prisoners of war, or lose limbs, go mad or die. . . . Mr. Englund's book is a deviation from standard history books. It is a corrective too to the notion that World War I was only about the dire trench warfare on the Western Front. . . . [It] expertly pans across other theaters of war: the Alps, the Balkans, the Eastern Front, Mesopotamia, East Africa." N Y Times Book Rev

Includes bibliographical references

Gilbert, Martin

The **First** World War; a complete history. Holt & Co. 1994 xxiv, 615p il maps hardcover o.p. pa $25   **940.3**

1. World War, 1914-1918
ISBN 0-8050-1540-X; 0-8050-7617-4 pa
LC 94-27268

"What Mr. Gilbert seeks to do, and frequently succeeds in doing, is to humanize, indeed to personalize, World War I. His effort and accomplishment make this a rewarding and significant book." N Y Times Book Rev

Includes bibliographical references

Hochschild, Adam

To end all wars; a story of loyalty and rebellion, 1914-1918. Houghton Mifflin Harcourt 2011 xx, 448p map $28; ebook $28   **940.3**

1. Pacifism 2. Soldiers -- Great Britain 3. World War, 1914-1918 -- Conscientious objectors 4. World War, 1914-1918 -- Great Britain 5. World War, 1914-1918 -- Psychological aspects 6. World War, 1914-1918 -- Social aspects
ISBN 978-0-618-75828-9; 0-618-75828-3; 978-0-54754-921-7 ebook; 0-54754-921-0 ebook
LC 2010-25836

"An ambitious narrative that presents a teeming world-view through intimate, human portraits." Kirkus

Includes bibliographical references

MacMillan, Margaret

Paris 1919; six months that changed the world. Random House 2002 560p $35; pa $16.95   **940.3**

1. College presidents 2. Governors 3. Nobel laureates for peace 4. Presidents 5. World War, 1914-1918 -- Peace
ISBN 0-375-50826-0; 0-375-76052-0 pa
LC 2002-23707

"MacMillan's lucid prose brings her participants to colorful and quotable life, and the grand sweep of her narra-

tive encompasses all the continents the peacemakers vainly carved up." Publ Wkly

Includes bibliographical references

McMeekin, Sean

★ The **Berlin**-Baghdad express; the Ottoman Empire and Germany's bid for world power. The Belknap Press of Harvard University Press 2010 460p il map   **940.3**

1. Geopolitics 2. Jihad 3. Railroads 4. World War, 1914-1918
ISBN 0-0674-05739-2; 978-0-674-05739-5
LC 2010019199

"Germany saw the ambitious Berlin-to-Baghdad railway as a powerful tool to win World War I. But the doomed project wasn't completed until 1940. The railway debacle provides a colorful backdrop for historian McMeekin's look at the Great War from the German-Turk perspective; as a cast of ruthless characters illustrate Germany's attempt to topple what was then the largest Middle East power: the British Empire." N Y Post

Includes bibliographical references

Stone, Norman

★ **World** War One. Basic Books 2009 226p il map $25   **940.3**

1. World War, 1914-1918
ISBN 978-0-465-01368-5; 0-465-01368-6

The author presents a narrative history of the First World War.

"Stone is as unconventional as he is brilliant, and this provocative interpretation of the Great War combines impressive command of the literature with a telling eye for relevant facts and a sensitive ear for telling epigrams." Publ Wkly

Includes bibliographical references

Strachan, Hew

The **First** World War. Viking 2004 364p il maps hardcover o.p. pa $16   **940.3**

1. World War, 1914-1918
ISBN 0-670-03295-6; 0-14-303518-5 pa
LC 2003-62191

"Readers already familiar with the sequence of events in strict order will benefit most. But all readers will eventually be gripped, and even the most seasoned ones will praise the insights and the original choice of illustrations." Publ Wkly

Includes bibliographical references

Tuchman, Barbara Wertheim

The **Zimmermann** telegram. Ballantine Books 1985 244p il pa $14   **940.3**

1. World War, 1914-1918 -- Causes
ISBN 0-345-32425-0
LC 84-91737

The author discusses the German plan to induce Mexico to attack the U.S. during World War I.

★ The **guns** of August; [by] Barbara W. Tuchman; [with a new foreword by Robert K. Massie] 1st

Ballantine Books ed; Ballantine 1994 xxiv, 511p il, maps pa $14   **940.3**
1. World War, 1914-1918
ISBN 0-345-38623-X

LC 93-90461

A history of the negotiations that preceded World War I and the course of the war's first month.

Woodward, David R.
World War I almanac. Facts On File 2009 554p il map $95   **940.3**
1. Almanacs 2. Reference books 3. World War, 1914-1918
ISBN 978-0-8160-7134-0; 978-1-4381-1896-3 ebook

LC 2008-41575

This book "would be a welcome addition to public, school, and academic libraries where a student needs to find basic information quickly." Booklist
Includes glossary and bibliographical references

The Encyclopedia of World War I; a political, social, and military history. ABC-CLIO 2005 5v il map set $485   **940.3**
1. Reference books 2. World War, 1914-1918 -- Encyclopedias
ISBN 1-85109-420-2

LC 2005-22937

This set opens with "four essays discussing the origins, outbreak, overview, and legacy of the war. They are followed by alphabetical entries on virtually every aspect of the conflict, including battles, people, military equipment and strategies, and social and political changes associated with it." SLJ
Includes bibliographical references

The United States in the First World War; an encyclopedia. editor, Anne Cipriano Venzon; consulting editor, Paul L. Miles. Garland 1995 xx, 830p maps $155; pa $45   **940.3**
1. Reference books 2. World War, 1914-1918 3. World War, 1914-1918 -- Encyclopedias
ISBN 0-8240-7055-0; 0-8153-3353-6 pa

LC 95-1782

"Biography, economics, civil rights, women's issues, foreign relations, battles, armaments, and conferences are among the topics included. Arrangement is alphabetical, and most articles are brief—between one column and a page. . . . Most articles include brief bibliographies. There are six maps, but no other illustrations." Libr J

World War I; a history. edited by Hew Strachan. Oxford Univ. Press 1999 356p il maps hardcover o.p. pa $28.95   **940.3**
1. World War, 1914-1918
ISBN 0-19-820614-3; 978-0-19-289325-3 pa; 0-19-289325-4 pa

LC 97-44997

"Strachan has commissioned 20 historians to summarize present thought about the July 1914 crisis, the military course of the war, the social and economic strains it exerted in all the belligerents, and its conclusion in revolutions and treaties. . . . Readers will find this comprehensive work a captivating introduction to the Great War." Booklist
Includes bibliographical references

940.4   Military history of World War I

Bloody victory
Three armies on the Somme; the first battle of the twentieth century. [by] William Philpott. Alfred A. Knopf 2010 631p il map $35; ebook $35 **940.4**
1. World War, 1914-1918 -- Campaigns -- France
ISBN 978-0-307-26585-2; 978-0-307-59372-6 ebook

LC 2010-4070

"The Battle of the Somme is branded in British memory as the exemplar of WWI: a months-long cataclysm that, at the cost of monumental casualties, repelled the Germans from a few square miles of shell-blasted French countryside. This account by a descendant of an artillerist in the battle has two aims: to narrate the battle from its initial strategic concept to its sputtering-out in late 1916 and to refute historical and popular opinion about the battle. . . . Comprehensive research and convention-bucking argument qualify Philpott for the WWI shelf." Booklist
Includes bibliographical references

Dallas, Gregor
1918: war and peace. Overlook Press 2001 616p $40; pa $19.95   **940.4**
1. World War, 1914-1918 -- Armistices 2. World War, 1914-1918 -- Peace
ISBN 1-58567-157-6; 1-58567-319-6 pa

LC 2001-21104

Dallas "provides a meticulously detailed and intensive study of the years 1918-1919." Publ Wkly
Includes bibliographical references

Dyer, Geoff
The **missing** of the Somme; Geoff Dyer. Vintage Books 2011 176p.   **940.4**
ISBN 9780307742971; 9780307743237

LC 2002327412

This book offers an "exploration of the meaning and formal remembrance of British participation in World War I. . . . [Author Geoff] Dyer argues that our perceptions of the WWI are shaped by impressions of the war presented through the literature and public statuary (and, to a lesser degree, photography) produced within 15 years of the Armistice. The dominant theme of these cultural works is . . . sacrifice as a virtue in itself and its formal remembrance, and he believes this was evident even in works produced at the very beginning of the war. . . . Dyer intertwines the story of his travels with two friends to visit monuments and military cemeteries of the Western Front with . . . observations on statuary by Charles Sargeant Jagger, the poetry of Wilfred Owen and the literary criticism of Paul Fussell, among others." (Kirkus)

Eisenhower, John S. D.
Yanks: the epic story of the American Army in World War I; {by} John S. D. Eisenhower with

Joanne Thompson Eisenhower. Free Press 2001 353p il maps hardcover o.p. pa $16 **940.4**
  1. World War, 1914-1918 -- Campaigns 2. World War, 1914-1918 -- Campaigns -- Western Front
ISBN 0-684-86304-9; 0-7432-2385-3 pa
                      LC 2001-23124
  "This is an important work that should help alter the historical picture of the American role in the conflict." Booklist
Includes bibliographical references

Farwell, Byron

  Over there; the United States in the Great War, 1917-1918. Norton 1999 336p $27.95; pa $15.95 **940.4**
  1. World War, 1914-1918 -- United States
ISBN 0-393-04698-2; 0-393-32028-6 pa
                      LC 98-35705
  This history of American intervention in World War I focuses primarily on the military aspects of the war but also discusses its social and economic impact.
  "This title does provide good coverage on the intervention in Russia and the role of women in the war, notably the 'Hello Girls.' " Libr J
Includes bibliographical references

Harries, Meirion

  The **last** days of innocence; America at war, 1917-1918. {by} Meirion and Susie Harries. Random House 1997 573p il hardcover o.p. pa $16 **940.4**
  1. World War, 1914-1918 -- United States
ISBN 0-679-74376-6 pa
                      LC 96-21756
  "This is an excellent study of US participation in WWI. The research is in far greater depth than the usual 'popular history,' the analysis is sharp and informative, and the writing is clear and a pleasure to read. The authors strike an even balance between necessity for condensation and the accuracy that comes from detailed treatment." Choice
Includes bibliographical references

Hart, Peter

  The **Somme**; the darkest hour on the Western Front. Pegasus Books 2008 589p il map $35; pa $17.95 **940.4**
  1. World War, 1914-1918 -- Campaigns -- France
ISBN 978-1-60598-016-4; 1-60598-016-1; 978-1-60598-081-2 pa; 1-60598-081-1 pa
  This is an "account of the Somme offensive. . . . [The author evokes] the horrors of combat on the western front, skillfully blending these personal accounts with strategic considerations of a battle that slaughtered nearly a million French, German, and British soldiers. . . . Military history at its best." Libr J
Includes bibliographical references

Herwig, Holger H.

  The **Marne**, 1914; the opening of World War I and the battle that changed the world. Random House 2009 391p il map $28 **940.4**
  1. Marne (France), Battle of the, 1914 2. World War,

1914-1918 -- Campaigns -- France
ISBN 9781400066711; 1-4000-6671-9
                      LC 2009-5687
  This fine history of World War I's opening battle argues persuasively that it was decisive in setting the pattern for the war, a pattern that made World War II inevitable. . . . Herwig's research has been exhaustive, including of archives long since thought destroyed that help him fill in a great many details about the German side. . . . As fine an addition to scholarly World War I literature as has been seen in some time. Booklist
Includes bibliographical references

Lawrence, T. E.

  Seven pillars of wisdom; a triumph. Doubleday 1935 672p il maps hardcover o.p. pa $19.95 **940.4**
  1. Arabs 2. Bedouins 3. Wahhabis 4. World War, 1914-1918 -- Middle East
ISBN 0-385-41895-7 pa
  "Not only a history of the Arab revolt during the {First} World War, but a commentary on the national characteristics, and political policies of Arabs, Turks and British." Cleveland Public Libr

Liddell Hart, Basil Henry

  The **real** war, 1914-1918; with twenty-five maps. by B. H. Liddell Hart. Little, Brown 1930 508p maps hardcover o.p. pa $23.99 **940.4**
  1. World War, 1914-1918
ISBN 0-316-52505-7 pa
  A short history of World War I in which the action of the book ranges wherever Germany and the Allies locked in combat: Poland, Mesopotamia, Gallipoli, Caporetto, Baghdad, the North Sea, and the Mediterranean.

Massie, Robert K.

  Castles of steel; Britain, Germany, and the winning of the Great War at sea. Random House 2003 865p il map $35; pa $17.95 **940.4**
  1. World War, 1914-1918 -- Naval operations 2. World War, 1914-1918 -- Naval operations, British 3. World War, 1914-1918 -- Naval operations, German
ISBN 0-679-45671-6; 0-345-40878-0 pa
                      LC 2003-41373
  The author "makes a coherent if long narrative out of a sequence of events familiar to students of naval history but probably not to many other potential readers." Publ Wkly

Millman, Chad

  The **detonators**; the secret plot to destroy America and an epic hunt for justice. Little, Brown 2006 330p il map $24.99 **940.4**
  1. Bankers 2. Espionage, German -- United States -- History -- 20th century 3. Government officials 4. International organization officials 5. Lawyers 6. Presidential advisers 7. Sabotage 8. Sabotage -- United States -- History -- 20th century 9. World War, 1914-1918 -- New Jersey 10. World War, 1914-1918 -- United States
ISBN 978-0-316-73496-7; 0-316-73496-9
                      LC 2005-24401

"With its obvious contemporary resonance, Millman's able account of an earlier foreign attack on America should draw the espionage audience and more." Booklist

Includes bibliographical references

Mosier, John

The **myth** of the Great War; a new military history of World War I. HarperCollins Pubs. 2001 381p il hardcover o.p. pa $14.95   **940.4**

1. World War, 1914-1918 -- Campaigns

ISBN 0-06-019676-9; 0-06-008433-2 pa

LC 00-46103

"After dissecting the major campaigns on the western front, Mosier concludes that Germany's ultimate defeat was the direct result of the influx of American soldiers into France in 1917 and 1918. . . . This is revisionist history that convincingly smashes the myths that Allied governments, leaders, and propagandists worked so hard to promulgate. Mosier's masterful account is a welcome addition." Booklist

Includes bibliographical references

Neiberg, Michael

★ **Fighting** the Great War; a global history. [by] Michael S. Neiberg. Harvard University Press 2005 xx, 395p il map $27.95   **940.4**

1. World War, 1914-1918

ISBN 0-674-01696-3

LC 2004-54330

"Readers interested in a general overview of WW I can do no better than Neiberg's excellent account." Choice

Includes bibliographical references

Ousby, Ian

The **road** to Verdun; World War I's most momentous battle and the folly of nationalism. Doubleday 2002 393p il maps $30; pa $16   **940.4**

1. Nationalism -- Europe -- History -- 20th century 2. Verdun, Battle of, 1916 3. World War, 1914-1918 -- Campaigns 4. World War, 1914-1918 -- Campaigns -- France

ISBN 0-385-50393-8; 0-385-72173-0 pa

LC 2002-19475

This is a study of the Battle of Verdun which "killed 700,000 French and German soldiers, 10% of all those killed in the war. Yet a sense of glory was maintained, however inappropriately, amid the gore: the road leading to the battlefield was called the Sacred Way, and the French General Neville gained immortality by his brave statement, 'They {the Germans} shall not pass.'" Publ Wkly

Paice, Edward

World War I: the African Front. Pegasus 2008 xxxix, 488p il map $35   **940.4**

1. World War, 1914-1918 -- Campaigns -- East Africa

ISBN 978-1-933648-90-3

"An authoritative summing-up of a grim, complex and little-known part of World War I." Kirkus

Includes bibliographical references

Thompson, Mark

The **white** war; life and death on the Italian front, 1915-1919. Basic Books 2009 454p il map $30   **940.4**

1. World War, 1914-1918 -- Campaigns -- Italy

ISBN 978-0-465-01329-6; 0-465-01329-5

"Penetrating study of one of the forgotten fronts of the Great War. . . . A much-needed addition to the literature of World War I." Kirkus

Includes bibliographical references

Weber, Thomas

Hitler's first war; Adolf Hitler, the men of the List Regiment, and the First World War. Oxford University Press 2010 450p il $34.95   **940.4**

1. Biography, Individual 2. Heads of state 3. Nazi leaders 4. Soldiers -- Germany 5. World War, 1914-1918 6. World War, 1914-1918 -- Campaigns 7. World War, 1914-1918 -- Germany

ISBN 9780199233205; 0-19-923320-9

"A triumph of original research in a very stony field. The conclusion that might be drawn is that Hitler was far more of the opportunist than is generally supposed. He made things up as he went along, including his own past." Wall Street J

Includes bibliographical references

940.5 -1918

Linenthal, Edward Tabor

Preserving memory; the struggle to create America's Holocaust Museum. [by] Edward T. Linenthal. Columbia University Press 2001 xxiv, 336p il pa $18.50   **940.5**

1. Holocaust, 1933-1945

ISBN 0-231-12407-4

LC 2001-37168

The author "describes the 15-year effort to create a national museum commemorating the Holocaust. He begins with the creation in May 1978 of the President's Commission on the Holocaust during the Carter administration. He then covers issues related to the location, design, and construction of the museum building. Linenthal's most significant contribution is the chapter on defining and representing the horror of the Holocaust." Libr J

Includes bibliographical references

Mak, Geert

★ **In** Europe; travels through the twentieth century. translated from the Dutch by Sam Garrett. Pantheon 2007 876p map $35   **940.5**

1. Political culture -- Europe -- History -- 20th century

ISBN 0-375-42495-4; 978-0-375-42495-3

LC 2007-9260

This book recounts the author's travels through Europe and examines the history of European countries, particularly focusing on the the the effects of the Treaty of Rome.

"Mak's brilliant compendium is difficult to define—is it a history book, a travelogue, a memoir?—but stands out as a remarkable, insightful, exhilarating exposition on that peculiar continent across the Atlantic." Publ Wkly

Talty, Stephan

Agent Garbo; the brilliant, eccentric secret agent who tricked Hitler and saved D-Day. Stephan Talty. Houghton Mifflin Harcourt 2012 301 p.   **940.5**

1. Spies -- Great Britain -- Biography 2. World War, 1939-1945 -- Secret service -- Great Britain

ISBN 0547614810; 9780547614816

LC 2012005470

This book tells the story of a young Spanish spy who managed to become Britain's most effective tool in deceiving Hitler. The mammoth concerted effort to trick the Germans into believing that the D-Day invasion was not really landing at Normandy but at Calais . . . required months of careful planning and streams of deceptive information fed to the Germans by agents like Juan Pujol, aka Garbo. . . . Pujol grew to hate the Germans after witnessing the mechanized violence of the Spanish Civil War and concocted imaginative scenarios to help the Allies by initially offering himself as a spy for Germany. Once he convinced the British he was for real, he was used to feed the Nazis a steady mixture of truth and falsehood to establish his trustworthiness. (Kirkus)

Europe since 1914; encyclopedia of the age of war and reconstruction. John Merriman and Jay Winter, editors in chief. Charles Scribner's Sons/Thomson Gale 2006 5v il map set $595 **940.5**

1. Reference books

ISBN 0-684-31365-0; 978-0-684-31365-8

LC 2006-14427

This encyclopedia "details European history from the Bolshevik Revolution to the European Union, linking it to the history of the rest of the world." Publisher's note

Includes bibliographical references

940.53   World War II, 1939-1945

Ackerman, Diane

★ The zookeeper's wife. W.W. Norton 2007 368p il $24.95   **940.53**

1. Holocaust, 1933-1945 2. Holocaust, Jewish (1939-1945) -- Poland -- Warsaw 3. Jews -- Poland 4. Jews -- Poland -- Warsaw 5. Righteous Gentiles in the Holocaust 6. World War, 1939-1945 -- Jews -- Rescue 7. World War, 1939-1945 -- Jews -- Rescue -- Poland 8. Zoos

ISBN 978-0-393-06172-7; 0-393-06172-8

LC 2007-12635

This is an account of how the director of the Warsaw Zoo and his wife, Jan and Antonina Zabinski, respectively, saved 300 Jews during World War II.

"An exemplary work of scholarship and an 'ecstasy of imagining,' Ackerman's affecting telling of the heroic Zabinskis' dramatic story illuminates the profound connection between humankind and nature, and celebrates life's beauty, mystery, and tenacity." Booklist

Includes bibliographical references

Allied Forces/Supreme Headquarters/Psychological Warfare Division/Intelligence Team

The Buchenwald report; translated, edited, and with an introduction by David A. Hackett; foreword by Frederick A. Praeger. Westview Press 1995 397p map hardcover o.p. pa $29   **940.53**

1. Buchenwald (Germany: Concentration camp) 2. Holocaust, 1933-1945 -- Personal narratives 3. Holocaust, 1933-1945 -- Sources

ISBN 0-8133-1777-0; 0-8133-3363-6 pa

LC 94-39714

"This seminal document, published here in its entirety for the first time, is a report compiled for the Allied Army from interviews with the inmates of the Buchenwald concentration camp, located near Weimar, Germany in April 1945, shortly after the camp's liberation. . . . It is immediate, direct, and, as the product of the testimony of many people, more inclusive and wide-ranging than any single individual's personal testament. A classic of Holocaust literature that should be in any library that covers European history." Libr J

Includes bibliographical references

Arrington, Leonard J.

Japanese Americans, from relocation to redress; edited by Roger Daniels, Sandra C. Taylor, Harry H.L. Kitano; contributions by Leonard J. Arrington {et al.} rev & updated ed; University of Wash. Press 1991 xxi, 242p il pa $25   **940.53**

1. Japanese Americans -- Evacuation and relocation, 1942-1945 2. World War, 1939-1945 -- Reparations

ISBN 0-295-97117-7

LC 91-2892

A collection of essays on Japanese Americans focusing on their wartime relocation and their efforts to seek reparations.

Berenbaum, Michael

The world must know; the history of the Holocaust as told in the United States Holocaust Memorial Museum. Arnold Kramer, editor of photographs. 2nd ed; United States Holocaust Memorial Museum 2006 xxi, 250p il pa $29.95   **940.53**

1. Holocaust, 1933-1945 2. Holocaust, Jewish (1939-1945)

ISBN 0-8018-8358-X

"Visually evocative and unsettling, the book, supplemented with a useful bibliography, is an excellent choice for those with little acquaintance of the subject or those needing a concise synopsis." Libr J [review of 1993 edition]

Includes bibliographical references

Berthon, Simon

Warlords; an extraordinary recreation of World War II through the eyes and minds of Hitler, Roosevelt, Churchill, and Stalin. [by] Simon Berthon and Joanna Potts. Da Capo Press 2006 358p il $24.95   **940.53**

1. Cabinet members 2. Communist leaders 3. Governors 4. Handicapped 5. Heads of state 6. Historians 7. Members of Parliament 8. Memoirists 9. Nazi leaders 10. Nobel laureates for literature 11. Philatelists 12. Political leaders 13. Political leadership 14. Presidents 15. Prime ministers 16. Statesmen 17.

World War, 1939-1945 -- Diplomatic history
ISBN 0-306-81467-6

LC 2005-432583

This book focuses "on the day-to-day actions of Hitler, Stalin, Churchill, and Roosevelt as they grapple with the war's events and plot strategy. . . . For anyone interested in how these four leaders engaged in the war, here is a great place to start." Libr J

Includes bibliographical references

Beschloss, Michael R.

★ The **conquerors**: Roosevelt, Truman, and the destruction of Hitler's Germany, 1941-1945; {by} Michael Beschloss. Simon & Schuster 2002 377p il maps $26.95; pa $15   **940.53**

1. Government officials 2. Governors 3. Handicapped 4. Philatelists 5. Presidents 6. Reconstruction (1939-1951) 7. Reconstruction (1939-1951) -- Germany 8. Secretaries of the treasury 9. Senators 10. Vice-presidents 11. World War, 1939-1945 -- Diplomatic history 12. World War, 1939-1945 -- Germany

ISBN 0-684-81027-1; 0-7432-4454-0 pa

LC 2002-30331

"As German forces were driven back in 1943-45, American leaders were anxious that in 20 years, just as it had done after its defeat in 1918, a vengeful Germany would start another world war. To prevent this, two schools of thought flowed through DC's salons of power: punishment or rehabilitation. . . . Beschloss covers the meeting-by-meeting, memo-by-memo political battle between the two approaches. . . . Beschloss' comprehensive research and narration into every nuance opens a significant perspective on bureaucratic politics' effect on the Germany that eventually formed in the early cold war." Booklist

Includes bibliographical references

Carley, Michael Jabara

1939; the alliance that never was and the coming of World War II. Dee, I.R. 1999 xxv, 321p maps $28.95   **940.53**

1. World War, 1939-1945 -- Causes 2. World War, 1939-1945 -- Diplomatic history

ISBN 1-56663-252-8

LC 99-24873

The author "provides a detailed and fascinating perspective on one of the major causes of World War II." Libr J

Includes bibliographical references

Churchill, Winston

Closing the ring. Houghton Mifflin 1951 749p maps hardcover o.p. pa $18   **940.53**

1. World War, 1939-1945 2. World War, 1939-1945 -- Great Britain

ISBN 0-395-41059-2 pa

"'Closing the Ring' sets forth the year of conflict from June 1943 to June 1944. Aided by the command of the oceans, the mastery of the U-boats, and our ever growing superiority in the air, the Western Allies were able to conquer Sicily and invade Italy, with the result that Mussolini

was overthrown and the Italian nation came over to our side." Preface

Their finest hour. Houghton Mifflin 1949 751p maps hardcover o.p. pa $19   **940.53**

1. World War, 1939-1945 2. World War, 1939-1945 -- Great Britain

ISBN 0-395-41056-8 pa

This volume starts with the problems confronting Churchill as he assumed the office of Prime Minister in 1940 and continues with accounts of the Battle of Britain, the Battle of France and Dunkirk

Triumph and tragedy. Houghton Mifflin 1953 800p maps hardcover o.p. pa $18   **940.53**

1. World War, 1939-1945 2. World War, 1939-1945 -- Great Britain

ISBN 0-395-41060-6 pa

The concluding volume of Churchill's history of World War II begins with D-Day and covers campaigns leading to the defeat of Germany and Japan.

The **gathering** storm. Houghton Mifflin 1948 784p maps hardcover o.p. pa $19   **940.53**

1. World War, 1939-1945 2. World War, 1939-1945 -- Great Britain

ISBN 0-395-41055-X pa

The first volume of Churchill's monumental history of the Second World War describes the days between the false peace and Hitler's near-victory just before Dunkirk.

The **grand** alliance. Houghton Mifflin 1950 903p maps hardcover o.p. pa $18   **940.53**

1. World War, 1939-1945 2. World War, 1939-1945 -- Great Britain

ISBN 0-395-41057-6 pa

This volume begins with the German drive in the East, covers the War in Africa and describes the entrance into the war of Russia and, after Pearl Harbor, the United States.

The **hinge** of fate. Houghton Mifflin 1950 1000p maps hardcover o.p. pa $18   **940.53**

1. World War, 1939-1945 2. World War, 1939-1945 -- Great Britain

ISBN 0-395-41058-4 pa

Describing events leading to the invasion of Sicily, warfare in Africa, the discouragingly slow job of reconquest in Europe, meetings with Roosevelt, and efforts at collaboration with Stalin, this volume covers the period from January 1942 to May 1943.

Clendinnen, Inga

Reading the Holocaust. Cambridge Univ. Press 1999 227p il map $69; pa $19.99   **940.53**

1. Holocaust, 1933-1945 -- Historiography 2. Holocaust, Jewish (1939-1945) -- Historiography 3. Holocaust, Jewish (1939-1945) -- History and criticism 4. Holocaust, Jewish (1939-1945), in literature

ISBN 0-521-64174-8; 0-521-01269-4 pa

LC 98-53636

In this reexamination of the Holocaust Clendinnen "first considers the problematic nature of eyewitness accounts, then turns to an unflinching inquiry into the Nazi mentality and finally takes on the tough question of artistic representation. . . . This slim, powerful book forces a reader to re-examine almost all the assumptions we've accepted since the Holocaust occurred." N Y Times Book Rev

Includes bibliographical references

Cohen, Rich

The **avengers**. Knopf 2000 261p il hardcover o.p. pa $13   **940.53**
1. Authors 2. Holocaust, 1933-1945 3. Holocaust, Jewish (1939-1945) -- Biography 4. Poets 5. Underground leaders 6. World War, 1939-1945 -- Jewish resistance 7. World War, 1939-1945 -- Underground movements
ISBN 0-375-70529-5 pa

LC 00-21062

Cohen chronicles the resistance efforts of a small group of European Jews during the Second World War. Attention is focused primarily on the activities of three individuals: Rozka Korczak, Vitka Kempner, and Abba Kovner.

"Cohen is a skilled writer. His language is spare and muscular, his descriptions evocative, his technique suspenseful." N Y Times Book Rev

Cooke, Alistair

American home front, 1941-1942. Atlantic Monthly 2006 xx, 327p il $24   **940.53**
1. World War, 1939-1945 -- United States
ISBN 978-0-87113-939-9; 0-87113-939-1

LC 2005-58860

"Crisscrossing the American continent from east to west and north to south, stopping in diners and bus stations and newly humming industrial plants, Mr. Cooke brings to life an America stepping into the unknown, committing its muscle and blood to an enterprise that most citizens could barely articulate, in places most of them had never heard of." N Y Times (Late N Y Ed)

Dallas, Gregor

1945; the war that never ended. Yale University Press 2005 xx, 739p il map $40; pa $22   **940.53**
1. World War, 1939-1945
ISBN 0-300-10980-6; 978-0-300-10980-1; 0-300-11988-7 pa; 978-0-300-11988-6 pa

LC 2005-926051

"The book begins with the death of Adolf Hitler, followed by a history of WW II in Europe, omitting the struggle in Asia. The author argues that the movement of armies determined European life for the next two generations. . . . Dallas's history is not for beginners, but it will be a very important addition to every collection on WW II in Europe." Choice

Includes bibliographical references

Daniels, Roger

Prisoners without trial; Japanese Americans in World War II. Rev. ed.; Hill and Wang 2004 162p il pa $12   **940.53**
1. Japanese Americans -- Evacuation and relocation,

1942-1945 2. World War, 1939-1945 -- United States
ISBN 0-8090-7896-1

LC 2004-47328

An account of "the relocation of Japanese Americans during World War II, an injustice prompted not by military necessity but by political and racial motivations. The purpose of this volume is to tell the story in light of the redress legislation enacted in 1988." Libr J [review of 1993 edition]

Includes bibliographical references

Dawidowicz, Lucy S.

The **war** against the Jews, 1933-1945; 10th anniversary ed; Bantam Books 1986 xxxx, 466p il pa $19   **940.53**
1. Holocaust, 1933-1945 2. Jews -- Europe
ISBN 978-0-553-34532-2; 0-553-34532-X

LC 85-48051

"One of the best histories of the mass murder of Jews in World War II. Argues for the centrality of anti-Semitism in Hitler's program." Reader's Adviser

Includes bibliographical references

Dower, John W.

★ **Ways** of forgetting, ways of remembering; Japan in the modern world. John W. Dower. New Press 2012 336 p. (hardcover : alk. paper) $26.95 **940.53**
1. Collective memory -- Japan -- History -- 20th century 2. Social change -- Japan -- History -- 20th century 3. World War, 1939-1945 -- Influence 4. World War, 1939-1945 -- Japan 5. World War, 1939-1945 -- Japan -- Historiography 6. World War, 1939-1945 -- Social aspects -- Japan
ISBN 1595586180; 9781595586186

LC 2011033861

This book brings together a number of [John W. Dowerbs] essays written between 1993 and 2007. . . . Most deal with Japan since WWII, although Dower . . . invokes much earlier history.s Particular focus is given to national hypocrisy and the misuses of history and memory, American as well as Japanese. His topics include Japanese racism along with the enthusiasm with which Japan went to war. He shows, through analyses of such cultural products as comics, playing cards, art, and clothing, how the Japanese themselves could ridicule as well as praise their leaders even in the midst of warfare's horrors and atomic catastrophe. . . . [E]ssays on Hiroshima round out the volume. Dower also tries to apply his knowledge to current policy issues, especially American ease in going to war.n (Publishers Weekly)

Dwork, Deborah

★ **Holocaust**: a history; {by} Deborah Dwork, Robert Jan Van Pelt. Norton 2002 xx, 444p il $27.95; pa $15.95   **940.53**
1. Holocaust, 1933-1945 2. Holocaust, Jewish (1939-1945) -- Causes 3. Holocaust, Jewish (1939-1945) -- Moral and ethical aspects 4. Jews -- Germany 5. Jews -- Persecutions -- Germany
ISBN 0-393-05188-9; 0-393-32524-5 pa

LC 2002-23565

"The authors examine such issues as the historic relationship between Jews, gentiles, and Germans; World War I and its consequences; National Socialism in the Weimar

Republic; the Third Reich and its anti-Semitic measures; worldwide refugee policies that became a disaster for the Jews; and Jewish and gentile life under German occupation. They also examine the efforts by Allied nations to help the Jews. . . . This is a monumental work of impeccable scholarship." Booklist

Includes bibliographical references

Epstein, Eric Joseph

Dictionary of the Holocaust; biography, geography, and terminology. [by] Eric Joseph Epstein and Philip Rosen; foreword by Henry R. Huttenbach. Greenwood Press 1997 416p $67.95   **940.53**

1. Holocaust, 1933-1945 -- Dictionaries   2. Reference books

ISBN 0-313-30355-X

LC 97-8779

The nearly 2,000 alphabetically arranged entries cover people, places and events related to the Holocaust. "Among the personalities profiled here are Dietrich Bonhoeffer, Anne Frank, Primo Levi, Oskar Schindler, Harry S. Truman, and Elie Wiesel. Place entries include references to well-known locations, the number of prewar Jewish inhabitants, the date of liberation, and the number of Jews left after liberation. Entries dealing with concentration camps are generally the longest and identify camps by location, type, when opened and liberated, nationalities incarcerated, numbers murdered, other victimization, and camp commandants. Among the terms that are defined are many foreign expressions." Booklist

Evans, Richard J.

Lying about Hitler; history, Holocaust, and the David Irving trial. [by] Richard Evans. Basic Bks. 2001 318p hardcover o.p. pa $16.95   **940.53**

1. College teachers   2. Historians   3. Holocaust denial literature -- Great Britain   4. Holocaust, 1933-1945 -- Historiography   5. Holocaust, Jewish (1939-1945) -- Historiography   6. Trials   7. Trials (Libel) -- England -- London

ISBN 0-465-02152-2; 0-465-02153-0 pa

LC 00-140130

Evans's "superb [book], . . . is never less than absorbing. A sure-footed writer, he allows the story to tell itself, eschewing rhetorical flourishes in favor of a clinical dissection of Irving's works and statements." Natl Rev

Includes bibliographical references

★ The **Third** Reich at war. Penguin Press 2009 926p il map $40   **940.53**

1. World War, 1939-1945 -- Germany

ISBN 978-1-59420-206-3

LC 2008-44765

This is a "very readable, well-paced account that is fully familiar with the huge amount of specialist scholarship in this field but never gets bogged down by excessive detail." Hist Today

Includes bibliographical references

Faber, David

Munich, 1938; appeasement and World War II. Simon & Schuster 2009 520p il $30   **940.53**

1. World War, 1939-1945 -- Causes   2. World War,

1939-1945 -- Diplomatic history

ISBN 978-1-4391-3233-3

LC 2008-44896

"The 1938 Munich Conference has been referred to as the Great Betrayal, virtually guaranteeing the start of war in Europe the following year. In return for Hitler's empty promises of peace, the British and French governments acquiesced to his demand to annex the Sudetenland, a largely German-speaking region of Czechoslovakia. The appeasement emboldened Hitler and led directly to the German-Soviet nonaggression pact and their joint invasion of Poland. Faber's account of the preparation for and actual unfolding of the conference is comprehensive, engrossing, and depressing, like viewing a slow-motion train wreck. . . . He does a masterful job of recounting the political maneuvers and infighting within both the British and German camps." Booklist

Includes bibliographical references

Fortunoff Video Archive for Holocaust Testimonies

Witness; voices from the Holocaust. edited by Joshua M. Greene and Shiva Kumar in consultation with Joanne Weiner Rudof; foreword by Lawrence L. Langer; in association with the Fortunoff Video Archive for Holocaust Testimonies, Yale University. Free Press 2000 xxx, 270p il $26; pa $15   **940.53**

1. Holocaust, 1933-1945 -- Personal narratives   2. Holocaust, Jewish (1939-1945) -- Personal narratives

ISBN 0-684-86525-4; 0-684-86526-2 pa

LC 99-58401

In this companion to the PBS series the editors "have woven together the testimonies of 27 individuals into an unforgettable narrative of the Holocaust: starting with pre-WWII Jewish life, they go on to describe the war's outbreak, ghettos, resistance and hiding, death camps, death marches, liberation and life after the Holocaust." Publ Wkly

Includes bibliographical references

Frank, Anne

The **diary** of Anne Frank: the critical edition; rev Critical ed; Doubleday 2003 851p il $75   **940.53**

1. Children   2. Diarists   3. Holocaust victims   4. Holocaust, 1933-1945   5. Holocaust, Jewish (1939-1945) -- Netherlands -- Amsterdam -- Personal narratives   6. Jews -- Netherlands   7. Jews -- Persecutions -- Netherlands -- Amsterdam   8. World War, 1939-1945 -- Jews

ISBN 0-385-50847-6

LC 2003-269527

This volume brings together "the three known versions of Frank's diary—the original, a self-edited version . . . {and} another edited by her father. It also contains . . . handwriting and paper analyses, new documentation regarding the Frank family's arrest, and . . . information about the diary's troubled publication history." Libr J {review of 1989 edition}

Includes bibliographical references

★ The **diary** of a young girl: the definitive edition; edited by Otto H. Frank and Mirjam Pressler;

translated by Susan Massotty. Doubleday 1995 340p
$29.95; pa $6.99 **940.53**
  1. Biography, Individual 2. Children 3. Diarists 4.
  Holocaust victims 5. Holocaust, 1933-1945 6. Jews
  -- Netherlands 7. World War, 1939-1945 -- Jews
  ISBN 0-385-47378-8; 0-553-57712-3 pa
    LC 94-41379
"This new translation of Frank's famous diary includes
material about her emerging sexuality and her relationship
with her mother that was originally excised by Frank's father, the only family member to survive the Holocaust."
Libr J

Friedlander, Saul
  Nazi Germany and the Jews. v1 HarperCollins
Pubs. 1997 436p v1 hardcover o.p. pa $19.95 **940.53**
  1. Holocaust, 1933-1945 2. Jews -- Germany 3. Jews
  -- Persecutions
  ISBN 0-06-019042-6; 0-06-092878-6 pa
    LC 96-21915
"Not the least impressive aspect of Friedländer's book is
the skill with which he juxtaposes different levels of reality
within an overall chronological frame, moving from high-
level Nazi debates on Jewish policy to the routine brutalities
of the SA and SS, and from the perceptions of the average
German citizen to those of the victims." N Y Rev Books
  Includes bibliographical references

  The **years** of extermination; Nazi Germany and
the Jews, 1939-1945. HarperCollins Publishers 2007
xxvi, 870p $39.95 **940.53**
  1. Holocaust, 1933-1945 2. Holocaust, Jewish (1939-
  1945) 3. Jews -- Germany 4. Jews -- Persecutions
  ISBN 0-06-019043-4; 978-0-06-019043-9
    LC 2006-48982
"This is a masterful synthesis that draws on a lifetime of
learning and research." Publ Wkly
  Includes bibliographic references

Gies, Miep
  Anne Frank remembered; the story of the woman
who helped to hide the Frank family. [by] Miep Gies
and Alison Leslie Gold. Simon & Schuster trade pbk.
ed.; Simon and Schuster Paperbacks 2009 264p il
pa $15 **940.53**
  1. Holocaust, 1933-1945
  ISBN 978-1-4165-9885-5; 1-4165-9885-5
    LC 2009294295
"A memoir by the courageous Dutch woman who helped
hide the Frank family, this book augments the Anne Frank
story. Perceptive characterizations, with insight into life in
Amsterdam during the Nazi occupation." SLJ

Gilbert, Martin
  Holocaust journey; traveling in search of the
past. Columbia Univ. Press 1997 480p il $60; pa
$20.95 **940.53**
  1. Concentration camps 2. Holocaust, 1933-1945 3.
  Jews -- Europe
  ISBN 0-231-10964-4; 0-231-10965-2 pa
    LC 97-15895

The author chronicles "a tour of Holocaust sites that
he conducted with a dozen students and friends; the text of
documents they studied at each stop is included. Gilbert not
only describes their itinerary and the problems of conducting
a tour but integrates the history of European Jewry into his
narrative. He then details the specific events of the Holocaust associated with each location." Libr J
  Includes bibliographical references

  Kristallnacht; prelude to destruction. Harper-
Collins Publishers 2006 314p il map hardcover o.p.
pa $14.99 **940.53**
  1. Antisemitism -- Germany -- History 2. Jews --
  Germany -- History 3. Jews -- Persecutions 4. Jews
  -- Persecutions -- Germany
  ISBN 0-06-057083-0; 978-0-06-057083-5; 0-06-
  112135-5 pa; 978-0-06-112135-7 pa
    LC 2005-58169
This is "an account of the Night of Broken Glass, which
was unleashed against the Jewish communities across Germany on November 10, 1938. . . . A powerful account of the
helplessness of the Jews." Booklist
  Includes bibliographical references

  ★ The **Routledge** atlas of the Holocaust; 4th ed.;
Routledge 2009 286p map $120; pa $30.95 **940.53**
  1. Atlases 2. Holocaust, 1933-1945 -- Maps 3.
  Reference books
  ISBN 978-0-415-48481-7; 0-415-48481-2; 978-0-415-
  48486-2 pa; 0-415-48486-3 pa
    LC 2008-43844
The author uses "maps, text, and photographs to document Hitler's attempt to destroy Europe's Jews. . . . Commentary offers statistical information, historical background,
and something about the people of the area. Archival photographs bring the events to life. . . . This small but effective work demonstrates the magnitude of the Nazi terror by
bringing it down to a personal level." Am Ref Books Annu,
2003 [review of 2002 edition]
  Includes bibliographical references

  The **Second** World War; a complete history.
Holt & Co. 1989 846p il maps hardcover o.p. pa
$25 **940.53**
  1. World War, 1939-1945
  ISBN 0-8050-1788-7 pa
    LC 89-11129
The author begins this study "with the invasion of Poland. Gilbert's flowing narrative is spiced with anecdotal
details culled from diaries, memoirs and official documents.
He is especially skillful at interweaving summaries of military strategy with vignettes of civilian suffering—the genocide of the Jews is never far from view." Newsweek
  Includes bibliographical references

Glass, James M.
  Life unworthy of life; racial phobia and mass
murder in Hitler's Germany. Basic Bks. 1997 252p
hardcover o.p. pa $23 **940.53**
  1. Antisemitism 2. Eugenics 3. Holocaust, 1933-1945
  ISBN 0-465-09846-0 pa
    LC 97-20118

"Forcefully argued and well documented, this work is a must for any Holocaust collection." Booklist

Includes bibliographical references

Goldhagen, Daniel

Hitler's willing executioners; ordinary Germans and the Holocaust. [by] Daniel Jonah Goldhagen. Knopf 1996 622p il maps hardcover o.p. pa $16   **940.53**
1. Antisemitism 2. Holocaust, 1933-1945 3. National socialism 4. World War, 1939-1945 -- Germany
ISBN 0-679-44695-8; 0-679-77268-5 pa
LC 95-38591

The author "endeavors to show that the common apologia for the Germans—that Hitler 'brainwashed' them—is nonsense and that most Germans gave their active assent to genocide. An ordinary German commander, for example, might feel himself bound by a strict code of conduct yet not be at all averse to murdering Jews. The book ends with a detailed notes section and an appendix that explains the correct methodology for studying the Nazi period." Libr J

A **moral** reckoning; the role of the Catholic Church in the Holocaust and its unfulfilled duty of repair. [by] Daniel Jonah Goldhagen. Knopf 2002 362p il hardcover o.p. pa $16   **940.53**
1. Antisemitism 2. Catholic Church -- Relations -- Judaism 3. Christianity and antisemitism -- History -- 20th century 4. Holocaust, 1933-1945 5. Holocaust, Jewish (1939-1945) 6. Judaism -- Relations -- Christianity 7. Popes 8. World War, 1939-1945 -- Religious aspects -- Catholic Church
ISBN 0-375-41434-7; 0-375-71417-0 pa
LC 2002-16264

This is "a landmark work. . . . This volume is recommended for all libraries and essential for those supporting a Holocaust studies program." Libr J

Includes bibliographical references

Goldsmith, Martin

The **inextinguishable** symphony; a true story of music and love in Nazi Germany. Wiley 2000 346p il hardcover o.p. pa $15.95   **940.53**
1. Drummers 2. Holocaust, 1933-1945 3. Holocaust, Jewish (1939-1945) 4. Jewish musicians -- Germany 5. Jews -- Germany
ISBN 0-471-35097-4; 0-471-07864-6 pa
LC 00-25955

Goldsmith's "weaving together of cultural and personal history constitutes a gripping tale of persecution, intrigue, and love and an insider's—or two insiders'—view of a dark time." Booklist

Includes bibliographical references

Groom, Winston

★ **1942**; the year that tried men's souls. Atlantic Monthly Press 2005 459p il maps $27.50   **940.53**
1. World War, 1939-1945
ISBN 0-8711-3889-1
LC 2004-62779

In this military history of one year during World War II, the author "delivers the traditional worshipful portrait of

General MacArthur while admitting he made several key blunders that doomed the Philippines in the year's early months. . . . He adds that brains and luck win more battles than courage, providing a perfect illustration in Midway, fought in June 1942. . . . Groom has written a page-turner; readers needing an introduction will love it." Publ Wkly

Includes bibliographical references

Guttenplan, D. D.

The **Holocaust** on trial. Norton 2001 328p il hardcover o.p. pa $15.95   **940.53**
1. College teachers 2. Historians 3. Holocaust denial -- Great Britain 4. Holocaust, 1933-1945 -- Historiography 5. Holocaust, Jewish (1939-1945) -- Historiography 6. Trials 7. Trials (Libel) -- England -- London
ISBN 0-393-32292-0 pa
LC 2001-30370

The author chronicles the "libel trial in Britain brought by historian David Irving. Irving, widely viewed as an apologist for Hitler, sued American scholar Deborah Lipstadt, whose Denying the Holocaust (1993) had labeled Irving as a right-wing extremist. . . . Interspersing essayistic diversions, the author presents a thoughtful work as well as a courtroom thriller." Booklist

Includes bibliographical references

Herman, Arthur

Freedom's forge; how American business produced victory in World War II. Arthur Herman. Random House 2012 xiv, 413 p.p   **940.53**
1. Industrial management -- United States -- History -- 20th century 2. Industrial mobilization -- United States -- History -- 20th century 3. Manufacturing industries -- Military aspects -- United States -- History -- 20th century 4. Nonfiction 5. World War, 1939-1945 -- Economic aspects -- United States
ISBN 1400069645; 9780679604631; 9781400069644
LC 2011040661

In this book, the author argues . . . against the conventional wisdom that America's rearmament [during World War II] took place under the guidance of a competent federal government. . . . [T]he production of the flood of war materiel that drowned the Axis was achieved by the voluntary cooperation of businesses driven as much by the profit motive as by patriotism, solving problems through their own ingenuity rather than waiting for government directives. (Kirkus Reviews)

Hoffman, Eva

After such knowledge; memory, history and the legacy of the Holocaust. Public Affairs 2004 301p $25; pa $14   **940.53**
1. Holocaust, 1933-1945 2. Holocaust, Jewish (1939-1945) -- Historiography 3. Holocaust, Jewish (1939-1945) -- Psychological aspects 4. Memory
ISBN 1-586-48046-4; 0-586-48304-8 pa
LC 2003-66443

The author "focuses on the consciousness and experience of the Holocaust's second generation—the children of survivors. . . . The book considers such diverse concepts as how the 'trauma' of the Holocaust is constructed, the role of emigration and national identity in shaping the second generation's narratives of their lives. . . . Hoffman writes with a subdued but vibrant passion." Publ Wkly

Includes bibliographical references

Horwitz, Gordon J.

Ghettostadt; Lodz and the making of a Nazi city. The Belknap Press of Harvard University Press 2008 395p il map **940.53**

1. Holocaust, 1933-1945 2. Holocaust, Jewish (1939-1945) -- Poland -- Łódz 3. Jews -- Persecutions 4. Jews -- Persecutions -- Poland -- Łódz -- History

ISBN 0-674-02799-X; 978-0-674-02799-2

LC 2007-50934

The author discusses how the Nazis transformed Lodz, whose population was more than one-third Jewish, into a new German city called Litzmannstadt. Index.

"The Nazis' use of bureaucracy to achieve their genocidal aims comes through clearly in this historical tour de force. The Nazis attempted to 're-engineer' the Polish city of Lodz, home to more than 230,000 Jews (one-third of the city's population) before the war, into a model—and Judenfrei—German city embodying health and beauty they called Litzmannstadt. This required forcing the Jews into a ghetto with the help of Jewish leaders, especially the . . . reportedly lascivious industrialist Chaim Rumkowski. . . . With a graceful style rare in academic history, Horwitz . . . marshals a host of primary sources to highlight the gradual destruction of the ghetto." Publ Wkly

Includes bibliographical references

Huchthausen, Peter A.

Shadow voyage; the extraordinary wartime escape of the legendary SS Bremen. Wiley 2005 260p il $24.95 **940.53**

1. World War, 1939-1945 -- Naval operations

ISBN 0-471-45758-2

LC 2004-14948

"This book will interest not only World War II buffs but also anyone drawn to tales of the sea." Libr J

Includes bibliographical references

Keegan, John

The **Second** World War. Penguin Books 2005 608p il map pa $22 **940.53**

1. World War, 1939-1945

ISBN 0-14-303573-8; 978-0-14-303573-2

LC 2005-274899

This military and stategic history contains sections covering the Eastern and Western fronts and the war in the Pacific.

"Keegan accompanies his narrative with a series of set battlepieces, of strategic analyses, and of 'themes of war'. . . . The book is beautifully ordered and . . . a pleasure to read." New Statesman Soc

Includes bibliographical references

Kershaw, Ian

Hitler, the Germans, and the final solution. Yale University Press 2008 394p $35; pa $22 **940.53**

1. Heads of state 2. Holocaust, 1933-1945 3. Holocaust, Jewish (1939-1945) 4. National socialism

5. Nazi leaders

ISBN 978-0-300-12427-9; 978-0-300-15127-5 pa

LC 2007-940635

This "history of Hitler's rise to power—14 essays arranged in four sections—offers a comprehensive view of the destructive force of the Nazi leadership and of the attitudes and behavior of Germans in the persecution of the Jews. . . . This is a precise and sensitive account of an aspect of the Holocaust." Booklist

Includes bibliographical references

Kruk, Herman

The **last** days of the Jerusalem of Lithuania; chronicles from the Vilna ghetto and the camps, 1939-1944. edited and introduced by Benjamin Harshav; translated by Barbara Harshav. Yivo Inst. for Jewish Res. 2002 732p il maps $45 **940.53**

1. Holocaust, 1933-1945 2. Holocaust, Jewish (1939-1945) -- Lithuania -- Vilnius 3. Jews -- Lithuania 4. Jews -- Persecution -- Lithuania -- Vilnius 5. World War, 1939-1945 -- Jewish resistance -- Lithuania -- Vilnius 6. World War, 1939-1945 -- Underground movements

ISBN 0-300-04494-1

LC 2002-16736

This a collection of Kruk's journals and other writings from the Jewish ghetto of Vilna and a labor camp in Estonia.

This "is a major addition to Holocaust literature and Jewish history. In 1961 a Yiddish edition of the Vilna diaries was published. This larger new edition has been painstakingly assembled from those diaries and other documents and writings by Kruk that were widely scattered and only found since the 1961 edition; Harshav has also added a wealth of new footnotes." Publ Wkly

Includes bibliographical references

Langer, Lawrence L.

Admitting the Holocaust; collected essays. Oxford Univ. Press 1995 202p hardcover o.p. pa $14.95 **940.53**

1. Authors 2. Dramatists 3. Essayists 4. Holocaust, 1933-1945 5. Holocaust, 1933-1945 -- Ethical aspects 6. Holocaust, 1933-1945 -- Historiography 7. Holocaust, 1933-1945, in literature 8. Holocaust, 1933-1945, in motion pictures 9. Nobel laureates for literature 10. Novelists 11. Poets 12. Short story writers

ISBN 0-19-510648-2 pa

LC 94-13368

"A horribly bleak, undeniably important book." Booklist

Includes bibliographical references

Lewy, Guenter

★ The **Nazi** persecution of the gypsies. Oxford Univ. Press 2000 306p il hardcover o.p. pa $24.95 **940.53**

1. Gypsies 2. National socialism 3. Romanies -- Germany -- History -- 20th century 4. Romanies -- Nazi persecution 5. World War, 1939-1945 -- Atrocities

ISBN 0-19-512556-8; 0-19-514240-3 pa

LC 98-52545

The author "begins with a brief history of the maltreatment of Gypsies all over Europe, from the fifteenth century onward; then, by dint of exhaustive research, Lewy documents the horrors of their expulsions, detentions, deportations, and deaths during the systematic madness of the Holocaust." Booklist

Includes bibliographical references

Lifton, Robert Jay

The **Nazi** doctors; medical killing and the psychology of genocide. Basic Bks. 1986 561p hardcover o.p. pa $23   **940.53**

   1. Concentration camps 2. Holocaust, 1933-1945
3. Murderers 4. Nazi leaders 5. Physicians 6. War criminals 7. World War, 1939-1945 -- Atrocities

ISBN 0-465-04905-2 pa

                        LC 85-73874

"How could German physicians trained as scientist-healers carry out Nazi orders for mass killings? . . . Lifton, an American Jewish physician, seeks answers through interviews with surviving doctors, family members, and victims and by painstakingly gleaning Holocaust archives." Sci Books Films

Includes bibliographical references

Lipstadt, Deborah E.

Denying the Holocaust; the growing assault on truth and memory. with a new preface by the author. Plume 1994 278p pa $16   **940.53**

   1. Antisemitism 2. Holocaust, 1933-1945 -- Historiography

ISBN 0-452-27274-2; 978-0-452-27274-3

                        LC 93-45586

"Lipstadt has written a disturbing book that deserves a wide readership." Libr J

Includes bibliographical references

★ **History** on trial; my day in court with David Irving. Ecco 2005 xxi, 346p il $25.95; pa $14.95   **940.53**

   1. Historians 2. Holocaust, 1933-1945 -- Historiography
3. Trials

ISBN 0-06-059376-8; 0-06-059377-6 pa

                        LC 2004-57533

"No one who cares about historical truth, freedom of speech or the Holocaust will avoid a sense of triumph from Gray's decision—or a sense of dismay that British libel laws allowed such intimidation by Irving of a historian and a publisher in the first place." Publ Wkly

Includes bibliographical references

Lukacs, John

Five days in London, May 1940. Yale Univ. Press 1999 236p $19.95; pa $11.95   **940.53**

   1. Cabinet members 2. Colonial administrators 3. Diplomats 4. Government officials 5. Historians 6. Members of Parliament 7. Memoirists 8. Nobel laureates for literature 9. Prime ministers 10. Statesmen 11. World War, 1939-1945 -- Diplomatic history 12. World War, 1939-1945 -- Great Britain 13. World war, 1939-1945 -- Great Britain

ISBN 0-300-08030-1; 0-300-08466-8 pa

                        LC 99-27583

This work focuses on the "chaotic few days during which, according to the author, Hitler came closest to winning the war. . . . Lukacs concentrates on the struggle within the British War Cabinet, which pitted the Prime Minister, Winston Churchill, against the Foreign Secretary, Lord Halifax, a Tory idol and a friend of the King. The point of contention was Halifax's belief that England should attempt to negotiate a general European settlement with Hitler. Churchill's stubborn refusal won out. The author's equally stubborn digging uncovered a stunning amount of defeatism and intrigue against Churchill by contemporary statesmen." New Yorker

Includes bibliographical references

Maitland, Leslie

Crossing the borders of time; a true story of war, exile, and love reclaimed. Leslie Maitland. Other Press 2012 494 p.   **940.53**

   1. Biographies 2. First loves -- France -- Biography
3. Immigrants -- United States 4. Jewish refugees -- United States -- Biography 5. World War, 1939-1945 -- Jews -- France -- Biography 6. World War, 1939-1945 -- Refugees -- France -- Biography

ISBN 1590514963; 9781590514962

                        LC 2011047110

This book focuses on love lost in Alsace during World War II, rediscovered 50 years later in New Jersey. . . . [Author Leslie] Maitland's mother Janine, along with her German-speaking parents, sister and brother, originally fled in 1938 from Freiburg, having lost everything they owned. . . . The family then landed in Lyon, where Janine . . . reignited a friendship with a dashing Catholic law student, Roland Arcieri. After falling in love during their brief time together, Janine was yanked away again with her family. . . . Janine did not stop grieving for her first love, and Arcieri apparently tried to find her. However, Janine's father, who wanted her to have a fresh start in America, intercepted his letters. . . . Once her father died, she tracked down Arcieri, who was then living in Montreal. (Kirkus)

Mazower, Mark

Hitler's empire; how the Nazis ruled Europe. Penguin Press 2008 xl, 725p il map   **940.53**

   1. National socialism 2. World War, 1939-1945 -- Germany

ISBN 1-594-20188-9; 978-1-594-20188-2

                        LC 2008-26997

This is an account of how the Nazis designed, maintained, and ultimately lost their European empire. (Publisher's note) Index.

The author's compelling analysis of the contradictions underpinning the Nazis' dream of Lebensraum impressively demonstrates that the Nazis were destined to lose World War II. But he soberly reminds us that, inefficient as the Nazis may have been at running an empire, they were brutally effective at suppressing resistance to it. New Leader

Includes bibliographical references

Mortimer, Gavin

The **longest** night; the bombing of London on May 10, 1941. Berkley Caliber 2005 356p il $24.95   **940.53**

   1. World War, 1939-1945 -- Aerial operations 2. World

War, 1939-1945 -- Great Britain
ISBN 0-425-20557-6

LC 2005-45281

"This account is given special power and poignancy by using the recollections of surviving men and women who endured that terrible night. An outstanding addition to World War II collections." Booklist

Ng, Wendy L.

Japanese American internment during World War II; a history and reference guide. [by] Wendy Ng. Greenwood Press 2002 xxvi, 204p $45 **940.53**
1. Japanese Americans -- Evacuation and relocation, 1942-1945
ISBN 0-313-31375-X

LC 00-69128

"The combination of historical facts as presented in the essays and the ideas and sentiments expressed in the primary documents gives readers a vivid sense of this period in history. This readable book would be a solid addition to high school, public, and academic libraries." Voice Youth Advocates
Includes bibliographical references

Nicholas, Lynn H.

★ **Cruel** world; the children of Europe in the Nazi web. A.A. Knopf 2005 632p il maps $35; pa $17.95 **940.53**
1. Children -- Europe -- History 2. Children -- Europe -- History -- 20th century 3. Children and war 4. Holocaust, 1933-1945 5. Jewish children in the Holocaust 6. National socialism and youth 7. World War, 1939-1945 -- Children 8. World War, 1939-1945 -- Children -- Europe 9. World War, 1939-1945 -- Sources
ISBN 0-679-45464-0; 0-679-77663-X pa

LC 2004-57745

This is an account of the lives of children in Europe during the Holocaust and World War II.
The author "has put together a well-written, compelling history that makes us look at the war era anew." Publ Wkly
Includes bibliographical references

Nossiter, Adam

★ The **Algeria** Hotel; France, memory, and the Second World War. Houghton Mifflin 2001 302p il maps $26 **940.53**
1. Holocaust, Jewish (1939-1945) -- France -- Public opinion 2. Jews -- Persecutions -- France -- Public opinion 3. Public opinion -- France 4. World War, 1939-1945 -- Collaborationists -- France -- Public opinion 5. World War, 1939-1945 -- France
ISBN 0-395-90245-2

LC 00-69458

"The rationalizations that let the French dispose of the past are the subject of this sensitive book, which covers the trial of a former cabinet minister, the Vichy memory hole and the interpretation of a Nazi atrocity." N Y Times Book Rev
Includes bibliographical references

Overy, R. J.

Why the Allies won; {by} Richard Overy. Norton 1996 396p il maps hardcover o.p. pa $17.95 **940.53**
1. Strategy 2. World War, 1939-1945
ISBN 0-393-31619-X pa

LC 95-52444

"Eschewing the belief that the Allies won solely because of their prodigious production of weapons and equipment, Mr. Overy points out that in the early stages of the war, before the Allies were fully mobilized, the Axis countries held the production advantage, yet failed to achieve victory because Germany's management of supply logistics was far inferior to that of the Allies—frequently as a result of Hitler's wrongheaded interference. . . . Assiduously researched and concisely written, this is a highly perceptive study." N Y Times Book Rev
Includes bibliographical references

Pick, Hella

Simon Wiesenthal; a life in search of justice. Northeastern Univ. Press 1996 349p il $35 **940.53**
1. Architects 2. Authors 3. Biography, Individual 4. Essayists 5. Holocaust survivors 6. Jewish leaders 7. Memoirists 8. Nazi hunters
ISBN 1-55553-273-X

LC 96-11808

This biography "has interesting things to say about forgiveness, including an extraordinary hallucinogenic encounter with a dying SS officer, and conveys a broadly sympathetic picture of a man capable of distinguishing between individuals and their political rhetoric." Times Lit Suppl
Includes bibliographical references

Plokhy, S. M.

Yalta; the price of peace. [by] S.M. Plokhy. Viking 2010 xxviii, 451p il map **940.53**
1. World War, 1939-1945 -- Diplomatic history 2. World War, 1939-1945 -- Peace 3. World politics -- 1945-1991
ISBN 978-0-670-02141-3

LC 2009-26833

Plokhy "has produced a colorful and gripping portrait of the three aging leaders at their historic encounter." Wall Street J
Includes bibliographical references

Rees, Laurence

Auschwitz: a new history; Laurence Rees. Public Affairs 2005 xxii, 327p il $30; pa $16 **940.53**
1. Holocaust, 1933-1945
ISBN 1-586-48303-X; 1-586-48357-9 pa

LC 2004-43196

For this history of the concentration camp, the author "interviewed 100 former Nazi perpetrators and survivors from the camp and drew on hundreds of interviews conducted for his previous research on the Third Reich, many with former members of the Nazi Party. . . . This is a significant contribution to our understanding of the intricacies of Nazi racial and ethnic policy that resulted in this ultimate abomination." Booklist
Includes bibliographical references

Reynolds, David

In command of history; Churchill fighting and writing the Second World War. by David Reynolds. Random House 2005 xxiv, 631p il $35   **940.53**
1. Cabinet members 2. Historians 3. Members of Parliament 4. Memoirists 5. Nobel laureates for literature 6. Prime ministers 7. Statesmen 8. World War, 1939-1945 -- Historiography
ISBN 0-679-45743-7
LC 2004-51087

"Packed with detail and vivid characterizations . . . [this book is] a different take on one of the few men capable of both making history and writing it." Publ Wkly

Includes bibliographical references

Rosenfeld, Oskar

In the beginning was the ghetto; 890 days in Lodz. edited and with an introduction by Hanno Loewy; translated from the German by Brigitte M. Goldstein. Northwestern Univ. Press 2002 xxxviii, 313p $40   **940.53**
1. Holocaust, 1933-1945 -- Personal narratives 2. Holocaust, Jewish (1939-1945) -- Poland -- Łódz 3. Jews -- Poland 4. Jews -- Poland -- Łódz
ISBN 0-8101-1488-7
LC 2001-6691

These entries from Rosenfeld's diary "contain vivid descriptions of daily life in the ghetto, including details about deportations, forced labor, hunger, diseases, cold, terror, and the struggle to maintain human dignity. . . . This book is one of the most important and lasting works documenting the horrors of the Holocaust." Booklist

Includes bibliographical references

Rosenzveig, Charles H.

★ The **World** reacts to the Holocaust; David S. Wyman, editor; Charles H. Rosenzveig, project director. Johns Hopkins Univ. Press 1996 xxiii, 981p $80   **940.53**
1. Antisemitism 2. Holocaust, 1933-1945
ISBN 0-8018-4969-1
LC 96-15395

This is a "country-by-country chronicle of the impact of the Holocaust on world history. Covering 22 countries and the United Nations, the volume carefully traces the contentions and controversies involved in coming to terms with the events leading up to the Holocaust, from prewar attitudes and perceptions to the political, economic, and cultural legacies in the 1990s." Univ Press Books for Public and Second Sch Libr

Includes bibliographical references

Shephard, Ben

The **long** road home; the aftermath of the Second World War. Alfred A. Knopf 2011 489p map $35; ebook $35   **940.53**
1. World War, 1939-1945 -- Forced repatriation 2. World War, 1939-1945 -- Refugees
ISBN 978-1-4000-4068-1; 978-1-4000-4068-1 ebook
LC 2010-23894

The book examines the experience of "roughly eleven million foreigners stranded in Germany [after World War II], often in ghastly conditions, after surviving years of hard labor and imprisonment in labor camps, concentration camps, death camps, and POW camps. . . . The Allied armies, chiefly the Americans, Soviets, and British, were faced with the kind of catastrophe left in the wake of most wars, but the scale in 1945 was unprecedented. . . . Shephard describes . . . the . . . confrontation of well-fed people from a relatively secure world with human beings who had indeed been reduced to a state that seemed lower than animals." (New York Review of Books)

"Ben Shephard's account of this demanding and important subject is a triumph. He has unearthed new and moving testimony by former DPs and has burrowed into official and personal papers without ever letting his deep scholarship get in the way of the riveting story he has to tell." Hist Today

Includes bibliographical references

Smith, Lyn

Remembering, voices of the holocaust; a new history in the words of the men and women who survived. [foreword by Laurence Rees] Carroll & Graf 2006 351p il map $27   **940.53**
1. Holocaust, 1933-1945 -- Personal narratives
ISBN 0-7867-1640-1
LC 2006-284769

The author, "who has recorded the experiences of survivors for London's Imperial War Museum, weaves together more than 100 accounts to construct a narrative of Nazi persecutions from the first anti-Semitic measures in 1933 through the liberation of the concentration camps. . . . This is an extraordinary work of scholarship and a reminder of the power of individual stories, which can bring home the horrors of WWII more forcefully than abstract numbers." Publ Wkly

Includes bibliographical references

Spiegelman, Art

Maus; a survivor's tale. Pantheon Bks. 1996 2v in 1 il $35   **940.53**
1. Biographical graphic novels 2. Graphic novels 3. Holocaust, 1933-1945 -- Comic books, strips, etc. 4. Holocaust, 1933-1945 -- Graphic novels
ISBN 0-679-40641-7
LC 96-32796

In this work "Spiegelman takes the comic book to a new level of seriousness, portraying Jews as mice and Nazis as cats. Depicting himself being told about the Holocaust by his Polish survivor father, Spiegelman not only explores the concentration-camp experience, but also the guilt, love, and anger between father and son." Rochman. Against borders

Stargardt, Nicholas

Witnesses of war; children's lives under the Nazis. Distributed by Random House 2006 493p il map $30; pa $16.95   **940.53**
1. World War, 1939-1945 -- Children
ISBN 1-4000-4088-4; 978-1-4000-4088-9; 1-4000-3379-9 pa; 978-1-4000-3379-9 pa
LC 2005-50409

This is "a sharp and taut account of misery." Publ Wkly
Includes bibliographical references

Takaki, Ronald T.
Double victory; a multicultural history of America in World War II. [by] Ronald Takaki. Little, Brown 2000 282p il hardcover o.p. pa $19.99   **940.53**
  1. Racism -- United States 2. World War, 1939-1945 -- United States
  ISBN 0-316-83155-7; 0-316-83156-5 pa
               LC 99-40374
"Takaki discusses the experiences of African Americans, Indians, Chicanos, Asian Americans from several nations, German and Italian Americans, and Jewish Americans. . . . Despite Jim Crow, internment camps, neglected slums, barrios, reservations, and rejection of Jewish refugees, the nation's not-quite-Americans fought bravely in World War II." Booklist
Includes bibliographical references

United States Holocaust Memorial Museum
  The **Holocaust** and history; the known, the unknown, the disputed, and the reexamined. edited by Michael Berenbaum and Abraham J. Peck. Indiana Univ. Press 1998 836p $58.71; pa $35   **940.53**
  1. Holocaust, 1933-1945
  ISBN 0-253-33374-1; 0-253-21529-3 pa
               LC 97-40030
"Papers collected here originated at a 1993 conference organized by the US Holocaust Memorial Museum's Research Institute. . . . The 50 contributors treat the subject from every conceivable angle: the role of antisemitism and racism; the politics of 'racial hygiene'; Nazi leadership and bureaucracy; the complicity of 'ordinary' people; the experiences of Gypsies, homosexuals, and blacks; the concentration camps; the Holocaust as reflected in international relations; the response of Jews, rescuers, and survivors. Recognizing the passionately controversial nature of the field, the editors have opted for variety over unanimity." Choice

Weinberg, Gerhard L.
  ★ A **world** at arms; a global history of World War II. 2nd ed; Cambridge University Press 2005 xxix, 1178p map $65; pa $25.99   **940.53**
  1. World War, 1939-1945
  ISBN 0-521-85316-8; 978-0-521-85316-3; 0-521-61826-6 pa; 978-0-521-61826-7 pa
               LC 2005-41954
"Weinberg's unrivaled command of archival sources combine with a smooth writing style to produce a definitive one-volume history of World War II." Libr J [review of 1994 edition]
Includes bibliographical references

Weller, George
  Weller's war; a legendary foreign correspondent's saga of World War II on five continents. edited by Anthony Weller. Crown Publishers 2009 644p il map $30   **940.53**
  1. World War, 1939-1945 -- Campaigns 2. World War,

1939-1945 -- Personal narratives
  ISBN 978-0-307-40655-2; 0-307-40655-5
The author "wrote for the Chicago Daily News for 35 years, achieving fame for his widely ranging dispatches from the many fronts of World War II. He was captured by the Gestapo in Greece, escaped from Java on a boat strafed by Japanese fighters, marched with Belgian colonial troops fighting Italian colonial troops in Ethiopia, and slogged through swamps with Americans and Australians locked in grim struggles in New Guinea. Weller's war reporting won him the Pulitzer Prize in 1943. Here, his son assembles many of his dispatches, which add tremendously to our understanding of the war at ground level, the people's war." Libr J

Weyr, Thomas
  The **setting** of the pearl; Vienna under Hitler. by Thomas Weyr. Oxford University Press 2005 352p il map $30   **940.53**
  1. National socialism -- Austria 2. World War, 1939-1945 -- Austria 3. World War, 1939-1945 -- Austria -- Vienna
  ISBN 0-19-514679-4
               LC 2004-18295
"This is a superbly written work and an excellent addition to World War II collections." Booklist
Includes bibliographical references

Yellin, Emily
  Our mothers' war; American women at home and at the Front during World War II. Free Press 2004 447p il hardcover o.p. pa $14   **940.53**
  1. World War, 1939-1945 -- Women 2. World War, 1939-1945 -- Women -- United States
  ISBN 0-7432-4514-8; 0-7432-4516-4 pa
               LC 2004-40496
"Yellin reveals all of the responsibilities held by women, including helping to manufacture aircraft, ships, and other munitions; and, in the process, outproducing all of America's allies and enemies, by far. Readers see war brides who worked hard to maintain the morale of their husbands while surviving long separation, fear, and shortages of virtually everything necessary to support a family. . . . [This book] is an important book because the role played by women in World War II has been regularly ignored." SLJ
Includes bibliographical references

Zuccotti, Susan
  Under his very windows; the Vatican and the Holocaust in Italy. Yale Univ. Press 2000 408p il $29.95; pa $16.95   **940.53**
  1. Antisemitism -- Italy 2. Catholic Church -- Relations -- Judaism 3. Holocaust, 1933-1945 4. Holocaust, Jewish (1939-1945) -- Italy 5. Jews -- Italy 6. Jews -- Persecutions -- Italy 7. Judaism -- Relations -- Catholic Church 8. Popes 9. World War, 1939-1945 -- Religious aspects -- Catholic Church
  ISBN 0-300-08487-0; 0-300-09310-1 pa
               LC 00-43307
Zuccotti's "aim is to show that whatever help was given to the Jews by the Catholic Church during the war resulted almost entirely from spontaneous acts by courageous individuals—priests, monks and nuns, and occasionally prel-

ates—and not from any interventions by the Vatican. . . . Zuccotti makes her case strongly. . . . This is a serious and well-researched book." N Y Times Book Rev

Includes bibliographical references (p.) and index

Encyclopedia of Jewish life before and during the Holocaust; edited by Shmuel Spector and Geoffrey Wigoder. New York Univ. Press 2001 3v il maps set $99   **940.53**
1. Holocaust, 1933-1945 -- Encyclopedias 2. Jews -- Europe 3. Reference books
ISBN 0-8147-9356-8

"Each entry provides vital information on the town's Jewish inhabitants on the eve of German occupation, gives the dates of Jewish roundups and mass executions and estimates how many Jews from that community survived the war." Publ Wkly

★ Encyclopedia of World War II; a political, social and military history. Spencer C. Tucker, editor, Priscilla Mary Roberts, editor volume 5. ABC-CLIO 2004 5v il map set $485   **940.53**
1. History, Modern -- 20th century 2. Reference books 3. World War, 1939-1945 4. World War, 1939-1945 -- Encyclopedias
ISBN 1-576-07999-6

LC 2004-23745

"The 1,465 alphabetically arranged articles provide an international perspective on people; key battles, campaigns, and events; military equipment and strategy; countries; and other relevant topics. . . . Country entries not only cover the main Allied and Axis powers but also such countries as Afghanistan, Brazil, Estonia, Iraq, Mexico, New Zealand, and Somalia as well as world regions. . . . An excellent resource for high-school, public, and academic libraries." Booklist

Includes bibliographical references

Encyclopedia of the Holocaust; Schmuel Spector, Robert Rozett, editors. Facts on File 2000 528p il $93.50   **940.53**
1. Holocaust, 1933-1945 -- Encyclopedias 2. Holocaust, Jewish (1939-1945) 3. Holocaust, Jewish (1939-1945) -- Encyclopedias 4. Reference books
ISBN 0-8160-4333-7

LC 00-30917

Following several introductory essays are "alphabetical entries on people, places, events, organizations, laws, and concepts. The language is clear, but more important is the authenticity of the information and the refusal to surrender to a simplification of issues. There are ample good-quality, black-and-white photographs, some unfamiliar, and also maps and tables. A detailed chronology and a thematic bibliography conclude the volume." SLJ

Includes bibliographical references

The Holocaust encyclopedia; Walter Laqueur, editor; Judith Tydor Baumel, associate editor. Yale Univ. Press 2001 xxxix, 765p il maps $60   **940.53**
1. Holocaust, 1933-1945 -- Encyclopedias 2. Holocaust, Jewish (1939-1945) 3. Reference books
ISBN 0-300-08432-3

LC 00-106567

This "encyclopedia provides fresh and lengthy articles on such topics as antisemitism, historiography, Jewish women, memorials, and resistance, just to brush the surface." Choice

Includes bibliographical references

Reporting World War II. Library of Am. 1995 2v ea $35   **940.53**
1. Reporters and reporting 2. World War, 1939-1945 3. World War, 1939-1945 -- Journalists
ISBN 1-883011-04-3 v1; 1-883011-05-1 v2

LC 94-45463

This "collection of some 200 entries by nearly 90 writers, drawn from newspapers, magazine articles, broadcast transcripts and book excerpts, recalls WW II campaigns and battles in all theaters but pays attention to the home front as well. It begins with an excerpt from William L. Shirer's Berlin Diary and ends with one from John Hersey's Hiroshima. . . . This is a treasure trove of war reporting, featuring writing of the highest order." Publ Wkly

World War II; an encyclopedia of quotations. compiled and edited by Howard J. Langer. Greenwood Press 1999 449p il $83.95   **940.53**
1. Quotations 2. World War, 1939-1945 -- Quotations
ISBN 0-313-30018-6

LC 98-26436

This is a collection of 1,554 "quotations dealing with World War II. . . . The first 12 chapters are arranged by type of person quoted . . . and then alphabetically by name. A typical entry has a short introductory paragraph providing biographical and historical information including birth and death years of persons. The remaining chapters cover other sources, including movies and songs." Booklist

A woman in Berlin; eight weeks in the conquered city: a diary. by Anonymous; translated by Philip Boehm. Metropolitan Books/Henry Holt 2005 261p $23   **940.53**
1. Berlin, Battle of, 1945 2. World War, 1939-1945 -- Atrocities 3. World War, 1939-1945 -- Germany -- Berlin 4. World War, 1939-1945 -- Personal narratives 5. World War, 1939-1945 -- Personal narratives, German 6. World War, 1939-1945 -- Women
ISBN 0-8050-7540-2

LC 2005-41984

This "is one of the most important documents to emerge from World War II." N Y Times Book Rev

940.54   Military history of World War II

Alperovitz, Gar
The **decision** to use the atomic bomb and the architecture of an American myth; {by} Gar Alperovitz with the assistance of Sanho Tree {et al.} Knopf 1995 843p hardcover o.p. pa $18   **940.54**
1. World War, 1939-1945 -- Japan 2. World War, 1939-1945 -- United States
ISBN 0-679-76285-X pa

LC 95-8778

"Alperovitz is the dean of revisionist scholars who argue that the nuclear bombing of Japan was unnecessary and that America bears a hefty responsibility for the cold war. . . . His main and probably most controversial contention is that certain documents pertaining to the decision were doctored, some by none other than Truman himself. Further, Alperovitz sees James Byrnes, Truman's Mephistophelian secretary of state, as a furtive player who nixed such alternative plans as modifying the unconditional-surrender demand and encouraging a Russian declaration of war." Booklist

Includes bibliographical references

Ambrose, Stephen E.

★ **Band** of brothers; E Company, 506th Regiment, 101st Airborne from Normandy to Hitler's Eagle's Nest. [by] Stephen Ambrose. Simon & Schuster 2001 333p il maps $25; pa $16   **940.54**
1. World War, 1939-1945 -- Campaigns -- Western Front 2. World War, 1939-1945 -- Europe 3. World War, 1939-1945 -- Regimental histories -- United States
ISBN 0-7432-1638-5; 0-7432-2454-X pa

LC 2001-20134

"Moving, poignant, and uplifting, this book is highly recommended for medium and large World War II collections." Booklist

Includes bibliographical references

Citizen soldiers; the U.S. Army from the Normandy beaches to the Bulge to the surrender of Germany, June 7, 1944-May 7, 1945. Simon & Schuster 1997 512p il maps hardcover o.p. pa $17   **940.54**
1. Soldiers -- United States -- Biography 2. World War, 1939-1945 -- Campaigns -- Europe 3. World War, 1939-1945 -- Campaigns -- France 4. World War, 1939-1945 -- Personal narratives, American
ISBN 0-684-84801-5 pa

LC 97-23876

This continuation of D-Day focuses on the front-line experiences of American soldiers who fought in northwestern Europe in the war's last years.

"These events have all been well documented, but in Ambrose's capable hands, the bloody and dramatic battles fought in northwest Europe in 1944-45 come alive as never before." N Y Times Book Rev

Includes bibliographical references

D-Day, June 6, 1944; the climactic battle of World War II. Simon & Schuster 1994 655p il maps $30; pa $17   **940.54**
1. Normandy (France), Attack on, 1944 2. World War, 1939-1945 -- Campaigns -- France
ISBN 0-671-88403-4; 0-684-80137-X pa

LC 93-40353

"Mr. Ambrose wonderfully illuminates the mind of the very young soldier of any nation anywhere who has never been in fighting before." N Y Times Book Rev

Includes bibliographical references

The **victors**; Eisenhower and his boys, the men of World War II. Simon & Schuster 1998 396p hardcover o.p. pa $16   **940.54**
1. College presidents 2. Generals 3. Presidents 4.

World War, 1939-1945 -- Campaigns 5. World War, 1939-1945 -- Campaigns -- Europe
ISBN 0-684-85629-8 pa

LC 98-37808

"The author is a master of letting his subjects tell the story, of standing back and allowing the large lessons to unfold. The result is history with lasting impact." SLJ

Includes bibliographical references

The **wild** blue; the men and boys who flew the B-24s over Germany 1944-45. Simon & Schuster 2001 299p il $26; pa $16   **940.54**
1. Air pilots 2. B-24 bomber 3. Bomber pilots -- United States 4. Flight crews -- United States 5. Government officials 6. Members of Congress 7. Presidential candidates 8. Senators 9. World War, 1939-1945 -- Aerial operations 10. World War, 1939-1945 -- Aerial operations, American
ISBN 0-7432-0339-9; 0-7432-2309-8 pa

LC 2001-20563

Ambrose presents profiles of American pilots who flew B-24 bombers focusing on the Dakota Queen piloted by future senator and presidential candidate George McGovern.

"Ambrose's narrative flows smoothly, even as he manages to cover each man's story." Libr J

Includes bibliographical references

Atkinson, Rick

★ An **army** at dawn; the war in North Africa, 1942-1943. Holt & Co. 2002 681p il maps $30; pa $16   **940.54**
1. World War, 1939-1945 -- Campaigns -- Africa, North 2. World War, 1939-1945 -- Campaigns -- North Africa 3. World War, 1939-1945 -- North Africa
ISBN 0-8050-6288-2; 0-8050-7448-1 pa

LC 2002-24130

This is the first volume of a projected World War II trilogy.

This "volume covers the conception of Operation Torch through the German surrender in Tunisia in May 1943. . . . An exemplary work that feeds anticipation of the succeeding volumes." Booklist

Includes bibliographical references

★ The **day** of battle; the war in Sicily and Italy, 1943-1944. H. Holt 2007 791p il map $35; pa $17   **940.54**
1. World War, 1939-1945 -- Campaigns -- Italy 2. World War, 1939-1945 -- Campaigns -- Italy -- Sicily
ISBN 978-0-8050-6289-2; 0-805-06289-0; 978-0-8050-8861-8 pa; 0-8050-8861-X pa

LC 2007-7653

"The second volume of . . . [the author's] 'Liberation' trilogy, which began with the Pulitzer Prizewinning An Army at Dawn: The War in North Africa, 1942–1943, this is probably the most eagerly awaited World War II book of the year. Atkinson's clear prose, perceptive analysis, and grasp of the personalities and nuances of the campaigns make his book an essential purchase." Libr J

Includes bibliographical references

Ballard, Robert D.

Return to Midway; {by} Robert D. Ballard and Rick Archbold; principal photography by David Doubilet. . . . National Geographic Soc. 1999 191p il maps $40 **940.54**

1. Midway, Battle of, 1942 2. Shipwrecks 3. Shipwrecks -- Pacific Ocean 4. World War, 1939-1945 -- Naval operations 5. World War, 1939-1945 -- Naval operations, American

ISBN 0-7922-7500-4

LC 99-10831

In this narrative, Ballard "intersperses chapters on the Battle of Midway with a fascinating account of his search for the U.S.S. Yorktown, which was sunk by a Japanese destroyer on June 7, 1942. Period photographs from the battle are combined with those of the Yorktown as she rests today, and paintings by marine artist Ken Marschall add detail to complete the record. The lively narrative is punctuated with two Japanese and two American oral history accounts of the battle." Libr J

Includes bibliographical references

Bayly, C. A.

Forgotten armies; the fall of British Asia, 1941-1945. [by] Christopher Bayly and Tim Harper. Belknap Press of Harvard University Press 2005 xxxiii, 555p il maps $29.95; pa $18.95 **940.54**

1. World War, 1939-1945 -- Asia 2. World War, 1939-1945 -- Southeast Asia

ISBN 0-674-01748-X; 0-674-02219-X pa

LC 2004-54300

This "study is by far the most comprehensive to date, an excellent survey for those interested in both WW II and the denouement of British imperialism in Asia." Choice

Includes bibliographical references

Beevor, Antony

D-day; the Battle for Normandy. Viking 2009 591p il map $32.95 **940.54**

1. Normandy (France), Attack on, 1944 2. World War, 1939-1945 -- Campaigns -- Normandy 3. World War, 1939-1945 -- France -- Normandy

ISBN 978-0-670-02119-2

LC 2009-23574

This "is a vibrant work of history that honors the sacrifice of tens of thousands of men and women." Time

Includes bibliographical references

The **Second** World War; Antony Beevor. Little, Brown & Co 2012 xii, 863 p.p **940.54**

1. Geopolitics 2. Historical literature 3. World War, 1939-1945 4. World War, 1939-1945 -- Atrocities 5. World War, 1939-1945 -- Campaigns

ISBN 0316023744; 9780316023740

LC 2012007028

This book on World War II by Anthony Beevor presents . . . a warning not to become overwhelmed by statistics and abstractions or by the notion that historical events are predetermined. WWII was an amalgamation of conflicts dating back as far as WWI and structured by a cycle of resentments. But the war was set in motion by a single person--Adolf Hitler--and its extension reflected specific decisions by specific people, and its course changed lives across the globe in ways impossible to predict. . . . And from heads of state to frontline riflemen, from field marshals to teenaged girls, Beevor's protagonists exercise choice in the context of the greatest man-made disaster in history. (Publishers Weekly)

The **fall** of Berlin 1945. Viking 2002 xxxvii, 489p il maps $29.95; pa $16 **940.54**

1. Berlin, Battle of, 1945 2. Berlin, Battle of, Berlin, Germany, 1945 3. World War, 1939-1945 -- Destruction and pillage -- Germany -- Berlin 4. World War, 1939-1945 -- Germany 5. World War, 1939-1945 -- Germany -- Berlin

ISBN 0-670-03041-4; 0-14-200280-1 pa

LC 2002-510674

The author "relies on material from American, German, British, French, and Swedish archives and documents from former Soviet files, making the book an invaluable and meticulous account." Booklist

Includes bibliographical references (p. 466-475) and index

Blair, Clay

Hitler's U-boat war; the hunted, 1942-1945. Random House 1998 xxviii, 909p 2v il map hardcover o.p. pa $19.95 **940.54**

1. World War, 1939-1945 -- Atlantic Ocean 2. World War, 1939-1945 -- Campaigns -- Atlantic Ocean 3. World War, 1939-1945 -- Naval operations -- Submarine

ISBN 0-6794-5742-9

LC 96-2275

This is a history of the German submarine campaign against Allied forces during the Second World War.

This is "the most thorough study of the U-Boat campaign available; it includes a massive amount of detailed statistics." Libr J {review of volume 1}

Includes bibliographical references

Bradley, James

Flags of our fathers; [by] James Bradley with Ron Powers. Bantam Bks. 2000 376p $24.95; pa $14 **940.54**

1. Iwo Jima, Battle of, 1945 2. Iwo Jima, Battle of, 1945 -- Pictorial works 3. Photographs -- History -- 20th century 4. Photojournalists

ISBN 0-553-11133-7; 0-553-38415-5 pa

LC 00-25803

This is the "story of the most famous photograph to come out of World War II, the flag-raising on Mount Suribachi during the Battle of Iwo Jima in February 1945. Bradley is the son of one of the six men immortalized in that remarkable photo, and his gripping narrative, vivid descriptions, and heartfelt style make this a powerful story of courage, humility, and tragedy." Libr J

Includes bibliographical references

Breitman, Richard

Official secrets; what the Nazis planned, what the British and Americans knew. Hill & Wang 1998 325p hardcover o.p. pa $22 **940.54**

1. Genocide -- Germany 2. Holocaust, 1933-1945 3. Holocaust, Jewish (1939-1945) 4. World War, 1939

1945 -- Atrocities
ISBN 0-8090-3819-6; 0-8090-0184-5 pa
LC 98-7997
This "is a remarkable study, concise yet carefully nuanced." N Y Times Book Rev
Includes bibliographical references

Brokaw, Tom
An **album** of memories; personal histories from the greatest generation. Random House 2001 314p il maps $29.95; pa $14.95 **940.54**
1. Large print books 2. World War, 1939-1945 3. World War, 1939-1945 -- Participation, American 4. World War, 1939-1945 -- Personal narratives
ISBN 0-375-50581-4; 0-375-76041-5 pa
LC 2001-273436
This volume "gathers letters written to Brokaw by Americans who lived through the Depression and World War II and, in some cases, letters written by their children. Brokaw provides a brief introduction and a time line for each chapter; these cover the Depression, the war in Europe and in the Pacific, and the wartime 'home front,' closing with 'Reflections.' The book is lavishly illustrated with reproductions of photographs, drawings, documents, and other memorabilia of the era." Booklist

Burgin, R. V.
Islands of the damned; a Marine at war in the Pacific. [by] R.V. Burgin with William Marvel. New American Library 2010 296p il $24.95 **940.54**
1. Marines 2. Veterans 3. World War, 1939-1945 -- Pacific Ocean 4. World War, 1939-1945 -- Personal narratives
ISBN 978-0-451-22990-8
LC 2009-40454
"As this well-written, excellently detailed personal narrative makes clear, some Marines who fought alongside him did not make it home alive. They and thousands more died amid war's confusing and unspeakable horrors. Sometimes they were killed by the enemy, sometimes by friendly fire, sometimes by accidents, and sometimes by shocking, split-second decisions where one life was sacrificed to save others. . . . Time is thinning the ranks of America's Pacific War veterans. But Islands of the Damned is a taut, engrossing, haunting book that will help keep their accomplishments and enormous sacrifices alive." Dallas Morning News

Burleigh, Michael
Moral combat; good and evil in World War II. Harper 2011 xxi, 650p il map $29.95 **940.54**
1. World War, 1939-1945 -- Ethical aspects
ISBN 978-0-06-058097-1; 0-06-058097-6
"No-one with an interest in the Second World War should be without this book; and indeed nor should anyone who cares about how our world has come about." Daily Telegraph
Includes bibliographical references

Conant, Jennet
A **covert** affair; Julia Child and Paul Child in the OSS. Simon & Schuster 2011 395p il $28 **940.54**
1. Anti-communist movements -- United States --

History -- 20th century 2. Anticommunist movements 3. Artists 4. Cookbook writers 5. Cooks 6. Diplomats 7. Intelligence service 8. Senators 9. Spouses of prominent persons 10. Television personalities 11. World War, 1939-1945 -- Secret service 12. World War, 1939-1945 -- Secret service -- United States
ISBN 978-1-4391-6352-8; 978-1-4391-6850-9 ebook
LC 2011-02875
"Paul and Julia Child are merely supporting players in this book about the Office of Strategic Services in World War II and the McCarthy witch hunts that followed. Despite this blatant marketing ploy, the book is a well-researched and well-written account of this period in American history." Seattle Times
Includes bibliographical references

The **irregulars**; Roald Dahl and the British spy ring in wartime Washington. Simon & Schuster 2008 xx, 393p il $27.95 **940.54**
1. Authors 2. Biography, Individual 3. Children's authors 4. Intelligence service -- Great Britain 5. Short story writers 6. World War, 1939-1945 -- Propaganda 7. World War, 1939-1945 -- Secret service 8. World War, 1939-1945 -- Secret service -- Great Britain 9. World War, 1939-1945 -- Secret service -- United States
ISBN 978-0-7432-9458-4; 0-7432-9458-0
LC 2008-12483
Conant tells the story of young writer Roald Dahl who is assigned by His Majesty's Government to Washington, D.C. as a diplomat to gather intelligence about America's isolationist circles. In the course of his "spying," he meets or works closely with David Ogilvy, Ian Fleming, and the great spymaster William Stephenson (aka Intrepid).
"Entertaining social history that also reveals a little-known aspect of an important literary figure's life." Kirkus
Includes bibliographical references

Costello, John
The **Pacific** War. Quill 1982 742p il $21.95 **940.54**
1. World War, 1939-1945 -- Pacific Ocean
ISBN 0-688-01620-0; 978-0-688-01620-3
LC 82-15054
A "history of World War II as it was played out in the Pacific theater. . . . Emphasizing the role played by Allied intelligence sources during the early period of the war, Costello analyzes the actual battles from Pearl Harbor to the atomic bombing of Japan." Booklist
Includes bibliographical references

Daws, Gavan
★ **Prisoners** of the Japanese; POWs of World War II in the Pacific. Morrow 1994 462p il map hardcover o.p. pa $19.95 **940.54**
1. Prisoners of war 2. World War, 1939-1945 -- Japan 3. World War, 1939-1945 -- Pacific Ocean 4. World War, 1939-1945 -- Prisoners and prisons
ISBN 0-688-11812-7; 0-688-14370-9 pa
LC 93-49363

"Daws offers a well-written thoroughly researched account of these POWs. . . . An exceptionally worthwhile addition to the literature on the war in the Pacific." Booklist

Includes bibliographical references

Dunnigan, James F.

The **Pacific** War encyclopedia; {by} James F. Dunnigan and Albert A. Nofi. Facts on File 1998 2v il maps set $137.50   **940.54**

1. Reference books 2. World War, 1939-1945 -- Encyclopedias

ISBN 0-8160-3439-7

LC 97-15634

This work "is lively as well as informative, and . . . will be attractive to military buffs while still useful to more serious researchers." Libr J

Frank, Richard B.

★ **Downfall**; the end of the Imperial Japanese Empire. Penguin 2001 484p il map pa $18 **940.54**

1. World War, 1939-1945 -- Aerial operations 2. World War, 1939-1945 -- Japan

ISBN 0-14-100146-1

"Weaving together the strands of military and diplomatic events, Frank contends that absent the bombings of Hiroshima and Nagasaki the war would have continued for at least several more months, at a cost in Japanese and Allied civilian and combatant lives far in excess of the admittedly awful toll that the atomic bombs exacted. A powerful work of history." Libr J

Includes bibliographical references

Fussell, Paul

Wartime: understanding and behavior in the Second World War. Oxford Univ. Press 1989 330p il $35; pa $16.95   **940.54**

1. World War, 1939-1945 -- Great Britain 2. World War, 1939-1945 -- Propaganda 3. World War, 1939-1945 -- United States

ISBN 0-19-503797-9; 0-19-506577-8 pa

LC 89-2875

"Fussell's version of the war doesn't, perhaps, exactly 'balance the scales,' but it is a useful corrective. Nobody who reads it will come away thinking about the war complacently." New Repub

Includes bibliographical references

Giangreco, D. M.

Hell to pay; Operation Downfall and the invasion of Japan, 1945-47. Naval Institute Press 2009 xxiii, 362p il map $36.95   **940.54**

1. World War, 1939-1945 -- Campaigns -- Japan

ISBN 978-1-59114-316-1

LC 2009-27766

"Illustrative of just how much the war with Japan was a close-run thing, this is essential reading." Libr J

Includes bibliographical references

Grayling, A. C.

Among the dead cities; the history and moral legacy of the WWII bombing of civilians in Germa-

ny and Japan. Walker & Co. 2006 361p il maps $25.95   **940.54**

1. World War, 1939-1945 -- Aerial operations 2. World War, 1939-1945 -- Aerial operations, American 3. World War, 1939-1945 -- Aerial operations, British 4. World War, 1939-1945 -- Ethical aspects 5. World War, 1939-1945 -- Moral and ethical aspects

ISBN 0-8027-1471-4

LC 2005-58597

"Was it wrong for the Allies to bomb German and Japanese civilians in World War II? In this book, . . . [the author] attends to one of the twentieth-century's largest unexploded moral conundrums. . . . Grayling's book builds careful, generous cases for and against the bombing, admitting as evidence both the experience of the bombed as well as the bombers." Booklist

Includes bibliographical references

Hastings, Max

Armageddon: the battle for Germany, 1944-45. A.A. Knopf 2004 584p il maps $30   **940.54**

1. World War, 1939-1945 2. World War, 1939-1945 -- Campaigns -- Western Front

ISBN 0-375-41433-9

LC 2004-46468

The author "tells the grim tale of the final collapse of the Third Reich. It does so from the viewpoints of the upper millstone (the Western Allies), the lower millstone (the Russians) and the grain being ground in between (the Germans). The research includes previously untapped Russian archives (particularly in the accounts of Soviet veterans) and leads to a gripping and horrifying story that serious students of military history will find almost impossible to put down." Publ Wkly

Includes bibliographical references

Inferno; by Max Hastings. Alfred A. Knopf 2011 xx, 729 p.p [48] p. of plates ill maps   **940.54**

ISBN 9780307273598

LC 2011013890

'This book "offers an account of the [Second World] war that concentrates on the lived experience of the men and women who took part in it. On almost every page there is . . . material from interviews, diaries, letters, memoirs and personal documents of many kinds. . . . This is at its core very much a military history, despite the space devoted to the experiences of civilians. . . . [Author Max] Hastings argues that the navies of the United Kingdom and the United States were their best fighting forces; he thinks the armies of the two Allied powers were mostly no match for the ruthless fighting prowess of the Germans and Japanese, whose willingness to sacrifice themselves contrasted with the care taken by Allied generals to minimize casualties among their own men. Red Army troops behaved in a manner not unlike that of the Germans, their reckless disregard for their own safety driven on by the knowledge that the Soviet secret police would shoot them if they hesitated." (N Y Times)

Retribution; the battle for Japan, 1944-45. Alfred A. Knopf 2008 615p il map $35   **940.54**

1. World War, 1939-1945 -- Campaigns -- Pacific region

2. World War, 1939-1945 -- Japan
ISBN 978-0-307-26351-3; 0-307-26351-7

LC 2007-34202

This chronicle of the final year of the Pacific war discusses such topics as the events leading to Allied victory, Japan's war against China, and the decision to bomb Hiroshima and Nagasaki.

"Encompassing the British, Chinese, and Soviet roles in vanquishing Japan, Hastings is both comprehensive and finely acute in this masterful interpretive narrative." Booklist

Includes bibliographical references

Haynes, Fred

The **lions** of Iwo Jima; [by] Fred Haynes and James A. Warren. Henry Holt 2008 272p il map $26; pa $17 **940.54**
1. Iwo Jima, Battle of, 1945 2. World War, 1939-1945 -- Personal narratives
ISBN 978-0-8050-8325-5; 0-8050-8325-1; 978-0-8050-9017-8 pa; 0-8050-9017-7 pa

LC 2007-42245

"The account focuses on the experience of Combat Team 28, a unit of 4,500 marines; their best-known accomplishment was the raising of the flag atop Mount Suribachi. However, that event, immortalized by the classic photograph, occurred only four days into the monthlong battle. Ahead lay a cauldron of merciless slaughter, with marines inching forward against Japanese troops entrenched in a series of interlocking caves and tunnels. The authors capture the horror of their advance as close-range combat in confined areas became the norm. This is a disturbing, sometimes sickening chronicle, but the harsh face of war in the Pacific theater has rarely been portrayed so effectively." Booklist

Includes bibliographical references

Hersey, John

Hiroshima; a new edition with a final chapter written forty years after the explosion. Knopf 1985 196p il $26; pa $6.50 **940.54**
1. Atomic bomb 2. Atomic bomb -- Physiological effect 3. Hiroshima (Japan) -- Bombardment, 1945 4. World War, 1939-1945 5. World War, 1939-1945 -- Japan
ISBN 0-394-54844-2; 0-679-72103-7 pa

LC 85-40346

An account of the aftermath of the first atomic bomb as reflected in the lives of six survivors.

Hicks, George

★ The **comfort** women; Japan's brutal regime of enforced prostitution in the Second World War. Norton 1995 303p il maps hardcover o.p. pa $14.95 **940.54**
1. Comfort women 2. Draft 3. Prostitution 4. Sino-Japanese Conflict, 1937-1945 5. Sino-Japanese Conflict, 1937-1945 -- Personal narratives 6. Women -- Asia 7. World War, 1939-1945 -- Atrocities 8. World War, 1939-1945 -- Women
ISBN 0-393-03807-6; 0-393-31694-7 pa

LC 95-2162

The author begins his "report with a historical survey of wartime sexual exploitation of women, then narrows the focus to the 'comfort women' system developed by the Japanese. The copious testimony of victims is shockingly graphic. . . . This significant addition to 'the poor record of mankind to womankind, especially in war,' properly approaches the subject as a human-rights issue tied to the rise of feminism in Asia." Publ Wkly

Includes bibliographical references

Hillenbrand, Laura

Unbroken. Random House 2010 473p il map $27; ebook $27 **940.54**
1. Air force officers 2. Biography, Individual 3. Evangelists 4. Olympic athletes 5. Prisoners of war 6. Runners (Athletes) 7. Veterans 8. World War, 1939-1945 -- Aerial operations 9. World War, 1939-1945 -- Prisoners and prisons
ISBN 978-1-4000-6416-8; 1-4000-6416-3; 978-0-679-60375-7 ebook; 0-679-60375-1 ebook

LC 2010017517

This is an account of Army Air Force bomber Louis Zamperini's plane crash in 1943 and his abuse as a Japanese prisoner of war.

"Hillenbrand's triumph is that in telling Louie's story . . . she tells the stories of thousands whose suffering has been mostly forgotten. She restores to our collective memory this tale of heroism, cruelty, life, death, joy, suffering, remorselessness, and redemption." Publ Wkly

Includes bibliographical references

Holland, James

Battle of Britain; five months that changed history, May-October 1940. St. Martin's Press 2011 677p il map $40; ebook $19.99 **940.54**
1. Britain, Battle of, 1940
ISBN 978-0-312-67500-4; 978-1-4299-1941-8 ebook

LC 2010-40646

"This massive volume is informative, enthralling, and moving—often all three at once. It effectively combines narrative and analysis to tell the story of the confrontation between the Luftwaffe and RAF Fighter Command from May through October 1940." Booklist

Includes bibliographical references

Hornfischer, James D.

Ship of ghosts; the story of the USS Houston, FDR's legendary lost cruiser, and the epic saga of her survivors. Bantam Books 2006 530p il map $26 **940.54**
1. World War, 1939-1945 -- Naval operations
ISBN 0-553-80390-5; 978-0-553-80390-7

LC 2006-47530

This book "recounts the exploits of the Houston, mainstay of the skimpy Allied fleet opposing the Japanese onslaught in the war's early days, until her sinking in a desperate battle with overwhelming Japanese forces in the Java Sea in 1942. . . . The narrative then shifts gears to follow the Houston's several hundred survivors through Japanese POW camps in Southeast Asia, focusing on the labor camps on the Burma-Thailand railway (glamorized in the movie Bridge on the River Kwai). . . . [This is] a gripping, well-told memorial to Greatest Generation martyrdom." Publ Wkly

Includes bibliographical references

Jones, Michael K.

The **retreat**; Hitler's first defeat. [by] Michael Jones. Thomas Dunne Books/St. Martin's Press 2010 xxi, 328p il map $27.99   **940.54**

1. World War, 1939-1945 -- Campaigns -- Soviet Union
ISBN 978-0-312-62819-2

LC 2010-34784

"Fluently written with good sourcing, this book covers both sides of a vast conflict that dwarfed any other in Western Europe." Libr J

Includes bibliographical references

Jordan, Jonathan W.

Brothers, rivals, victors; Eisenhower, Patton, Bradley, and the partnership that drove the Allied conquest in Europe. New American Library 2011 654p il map $28.95   **940.54**

1. Army officers 2. College presidents 3. Generals 4. Presidents 5. World War, 1939-1945 -- Campaigns -- Europe 6. World War, 1939-1945 -- Europe
ISBN 0451232127; 9780451232120

LC 2010-34841

This book explores the "relationships of Dwight Eisenhower, George Patton, and Omar Bradley." (N Y Times Book Rev) Glossary. Bibliography. Index.

"Dwight D. Eisenhower, George S. Patton and Omar N. Bradley, the three outstanding American commanders in North Africa and Europe from 1942 to 1945, were, if not exactly 'brothers in arms,' at least friends, even if their friendship was often disrupted by envy, backbiting and disagreements over strategy. . . . This is not really a work of military history. Readers who want a rounded description of the war in Europe should look elsewhere. What Jordan gives us is the war as Eisenhower, Bradley and Patton saw it. Indeed, German generals and a whole range of major Allied figures, including Alan Brooke and Harold Alexander, get limited treatment. At his worst, Jordan can sound parochial. . . . Where Jordan does excel is in his diligent use of quotations to capture exactly what the three men thought of one another, and to show how each went out of his way to strike the image of a 'fighting general.' " N Y Times Book Rev

Includes bibliographical references

Kaplan, Alice Yaeger

The **interpreter**; [by] Alice Kaplan. University of Chicago Press 2007 240p il map pa $15 **940.54**

1. African American soldiers 2. Army officers 3. Authors 4. Novelists 5. Trials (Homicide) 6. Veterans 7. World War, 1939-1945 -- African Americans
ISBN 978-0-226-42425-5; 0-226-42425-1

LC 2006-35822

This is an "account of the trials of two American soldiers accused of murdering French citizens in the waning days of World War II. One of the accused soldiers, a black man named James Hendricks, was sentenced to death, while the other, George Whittington, a white who had been proclaimed a war hero, was acquitted. French political novelist Louis Guilloux served as an interpreter at these trials, and Kaplan draws from Guilloux's diaries as well as from a novel he based upon the trials. . . . Inventive, moving, and

beautifully written, this is a major contribution to investigative history." Libr J

Includes bibliographical references

Katz, Robert

The **battle** for Rome; the Germans, the allies, the partisans and the Pope, September 1943-June 1944. Simon & Schuster 2003 418p il map $28; pa $16   **940.54**

1. World War, 1939-1945 -- Italy 2. World War, 1939-1945 -- Italy -- Rome
ISBN 0-7432-1642-3; 0-7432-5808-8 pa

LC 2003-45677

"This narrative history describes the Eternal City at a key time of struggle—the dark year of German occupation between the overthrow of Mussolini in 1943 and liberation by the Allies in 1944. Four parties wrestle for Rome: the ruthless yet wary German occupiers, the Holy See in self-preservation mode, a gutsy band of patriotic students with homemade explosives, and the U.S. Fifth Army under Mark Clark. . . . This is challenging research presented fluidly, and Katz's fascination with a key moment for a fascinating city shines through." Booklist

Includes bibliographical references

Kershaw, Alex

Escape from the deep; the epic story of a legendary submarine and her courageous crew. Da Capo Press 2008 270p il map $26; pa $15.95 **940.54**

1. World War, 1939-1945 -- Naval operations 2. World War, 1939-1945 -- Pacific Ocean 3. World War, 1939-1945 -- Prisoners and prisons
ISBN 978-0-306-81519-5; 0-306-81519-2; 978-0-306-81790-8 pa; 0-306-81790-X pa

LC 2008-298762

Details the history of the U.S. Navy submarine Tang in the Pacific theater of World War II, the explosion that led to its sinking, the ordeal of its surviving crew members and their capture by the Japanese, followed by months of brutal captivity.

The author "has researched exhaustively, including interviewing the last two living survivors, and written compactly the portrait of nine Americans who rose to heroism and of a ship that well deserved its status . . . as a legend in the naval history of World War II." Booklist

Includes bibliographical references

Keuning-Tichelaar, An

Passing on the comfort; the war, the quilts, and the women who made a difference. [by] An Keuning-Tichelaar and Lynn Kaplanian-Buller. Good Books 2005 186p il pa $14.95   **940.54**

1. Quilts 2. World War, 1939-1945 -- Personal narratives
ISBN 1-561484-82-2

LC 2005-01932

This is the "narrative of a Dutch resistance operation during WWII conducted by Keuning-Tichelaar and her husband, Herman, a Mennonite minister. With the support of their townspeople, the two young newlyweds sheltered and saved the lives of Jewish adults and children, and others in danger from the Nazis. As part of a relief effort, quilts were created by women in North American Mennonite circles and sent to the Netherlands. Beautifully illustrated with 19 color photographs of the quilts, this book describes in an understated voice the harrowing events and the daily acts of courage that Keuning-Tichelaar undertook. When, decades later, coauthor Kaplanian-Buller, a U.S. citizen living in Amsterdam, found the old quilts, she persuaded An to share her story." Publ Wkly

Includes bibliographical references

Korda, Michael

With wings like eagles; a history of the Battle of Britain. Harper 2009 322p il map $25.95　**940.54**
　1. Britain, Battle of, 1940　2. Cabinet members　3. Historians　4. Members of Parliament　5. Memoirists　6. Nobel laureates for literature　7. Prime ministers　8. Statesmen　9. World War, 1939-1945 -- Aerial operations　10. World War, 1939-1945 -- Aerial operations, British　11. World War, 1939-1945 -- Aerial operations, German
　ISBN 978-0-06-112535-5; 0-06-112535-0
LC 2008-09293

This "is a skillful, absorbing, often moving contribution to the popular understanding of one of the few episodes in history to live on untarnished and undiminished in the collective memory and to deserve the description 'heroic.'" Washington Post

Includes bibliographical references (p. 303-305)

Leckie, Robert

Okinawa; the last battle of World War II. Viking 1995 220p il hardcover o.p. pa $13.95　**940.54**
　1. Okinawa, Battle of, 1945　2. World War, 1939-1945 -- Campaigns -- Okinawa Island
　ISBN 0-670-84716-X; 0-14-017389-7 pa
LC 94-39145

In this history of the Battle of Okinawa "Leckie supplies an accessible historical overview of a perplexing war tactic, the kamikaze attack." Booklist

Lee, Bruce

Marching orders; the untold story of World War II. Da Capo Press 2001 608p map pa $24　**940.54**
　1. Cryptography　2. World War, 1939-1945 -- Japan　3. World War, 1939-1945 -- Secret service
　ISBN 978-0-306-81036-7; 0-306-81036-0

"Many of the mysteries that have eluded historians since the end of the war are much clarified. . . . This is the most significant publication about World War II since the recent series of books on the Ultra revelations and should be purchased by all libraries." Libr J

Includes bibliographical references

Liebling, A. J.

World War II writings. Library of America 2008 1089p map $40　**940.54**
　1. World War, 1939-1945 -- Campaigns　2. World War, 1939-1945 -- Personal narratives
　ISBN 978-1-59853-018-6
LC 2007-938791

"The war brought out the best in [Liebling]. Here he . . relied on straightforward observation, delivered in a style less mannered than Hemingway's, less sentimental than Ernie Pyle's, less excitable than Michael Herr's. It's the kind of writing that looks easy, except that very few war correspondents have ever done it so well." N Y Times Book Rev

Includes bibliographical references

Lifton, Robert Jay

Hiroshima in America; a half century of denial. [by] Robert Jay Lifton & Greg Mitchell; with a new afterword by the authors. Avon Books 1996 427p il pa $18.95　**940.54**
　1. Atomic bomb
　ISBN 978-0-380-72764-3; 0-380-72764-1

Lifton and Mitchell examine "the reaction of the American people to the bombing of Hiroshima in 1945 and its domestic aftermath. The authors examine what they perceive to be a conspiracy by the government to mislead and suppress information about the actual bombing, Truman's decision to drop the bomb, and the birth and mismanagement of the beginning of the nuclear age." Libr J

Includes bibliographical references

Lukacs, John D.

Escape from Davao; the forgotten story of the most daring prison break of the Pacific war. Simon & Schuster 2010 xiii, 433p il $27.99　**940.54**
　1. Soldiers -- United States　2. World War, 1939-1945 -- Philippines　3. World War, 1939-1945 -- Prisoners and prisons　4. World War, 1939-1945 -- Underground movements
　ISBN 978-0-7432-6278-1; 0-7432-6278-6
LC 2010-03238

The author "is a gifted stylist and storyteller. He doesn't flinch at the grim or the gruesome. . . . At bottom, 'Escape From Davao' is a morality tale, not unlike the war movies of the 1940s and '50s, about pluck, luck, courage, comradeship, Yankee humor, ingenuity, and religious faith." Pittsburgh Post-Gazette

Includes bibliographical references

Macintyre, Ben

Operation Mincemeat; how a dead man and a bizarre plan fooled the Nazis and assured an allied victory. Harmony Books 2010 400p il $25.99　**940.54**
　1. Intelligence service agents　2. Lawyers　3. World War, 1939-1945 -- Secret service
　ISBN 978-0-307-45327-3; 0-307-45327-8
LC 2009-47562

A "true WWII tale that reads like something by Ian Fleming. In fact, two of Fleming's fellow British intelligence officers hatched the title operation. They dressed a corpse in uniform and arranged for it to wash up on a Nazi-friendly stretch of the Spanish coast bearing a suitcase with false war plans. Against all odds, Operation Mincemeat succeeded — and helped convince the Germans that the Allies planned to invade Sardinia and Greece in 1943 instead of their real target, Sicily. Relying on a cache of once-classified documents, Macintyre provides the fullest account yet of this curious episode and enlivens his yarn with quirky details." Entertainment Wkly

Includes bibliographical references

Macintyre, Ben, 1963-

Double cross; the true story of the D-day spies. Ben Macintyre. Crown 2012 399 p. ill., maps   **940.54**

1. Deception (Military science) -- History -- 20th century 2. Espionage -- Europe -- History -- 20th century 3. Spies -- Europe -- Biography 4. World War, 1939-1945 -- Deception 5. World War, 1939-1945 -- Military intelligence 6. World War, 1939-1945 -- Secret service
ISBN 9780307888754; 9780307888761

LC 2012003089

"This book looks at the deceit operation [that] was aimed at convincing the Nazis that Calais and Norway, not Normandy, were the targets of the 150,000-strong [D-Day] invasion force. The deception involved every branch of Allied wartime intelligence -- the Bletchley Park code-breakers, MI5, MI6, SOE, Scientific Intelligence, the FBI and the French Resistance. But at its heart was the 'Double Cross System', a team of double agents controlled by the secret 'Twenty Committee.' The squad comprised a bisexual Peruvian playgirl, a tiny Polish fighter pilot, a Serbian seducer, a wildly imaginative Spaniard with a diploma in chicken farming, and a hysterical Frenchwoman whose obsessive love for her pet dog very nearly wrecked the entire deception, a as well as a sixth spy." (Publisher s note)

Manchester, William

Goodbye, darkness; a memoir of the Pacific War. Little, Brown 1980 401p il hardcover o.p. pa $16.95   **940.54**

1. World War, 1939-1945 -- Pacific Ocean 2. World War, 1939-1945 -- Personal narratives
ISBN 0-316-50111-5 pa

LC 80-17310

This memoir arises from a 1978 trip the author made "to Pacific battlefields, seeking to exorcise three decades of nightmares dating to wartime days as a Marine Corps sergeant. . . . First tracing his family background, youth, enlistment, training, and embarkation from San Diego, Manchester unravels a memoir featuring historical reconstruction, disjointed flash-forwards, shocking vignettes, {and} redoubtable vocabulary." Choice

Megellas, James

All the way to Berlin; a paratrooper at war in Europe. Presidio Press 2003 xxi, 309p il maps $25.95   **940.54**

1. World War, 1939-1945 -- Campaigns 2. World War, 1939-1945 -- Europe 3. World War, 1939-1945 -- Personal narratives
ISBN 0-89141-784-2

LC 2002-192563

This is the author's account of "the September 1944 assault across the Waal River. . . . The attrition Megellas witnessed over months on the front line, at Anzio and in the Battle of the Bulge, shapes his narrative, but his observations about the craft of killing lend it a distinctive tone. . . . Strongly put and unsentimental, this memoir is a must for the World War II collection." Booklist

Merridale, Catherine

★ Ivan's war; life and death in the Red Army, 1939-1945. Metropolitan Books 2006 426p il map $30   **940.54**

1. Soldiers -- Soviet Union 2. World War, 1939-1945 -- Campaigns -- Eastern Front 3. World War, 1939-1945 -- Soviet Union
ISBN 0-8050-7455-4

LC 2005-50457

The author discusses the life of the ordinary Russian soldier during World War II.

Merridale "succeeds admirably in fashioning a compelling portrait, helped immensely by her talent as a writer." Foreign Affairs

Includes bibliographical references

Miller, Nathan

War at sea; a naval history of World War II. Oxford University Press 1996 592p il map pa $29.95   **940.54**

1. World War, 1939-1945 -- Naval operations
ISBN 0-19-511038-2

LC 96-31787

"Miller's research—primarily on the Royal Navy—and a reading of hundreds of pertinent monographs has enabled him to fashion a briskly paced narrative that will both inform and entertain." Choice

Includes bibliographical references

Moses, Sam

At all costs; how a crippled ship and two American merchant mariners turned the tide of World War II. Random House 2006 335p il $25.95   **940.54**

1. World War, 1939-1945 -- Mediterranean Sea 2. World War, 1939-1945 -- Naval operations
ISBN 1-4000-6318-3

LC 2006-40425

"The remarkable heroism that won the day, as well as Moses' thorough retelling, makes this an exciting, imperative read for anyone interested in WWII." Publ Wkly

Includes bibliographical references

Murphy, David E.

What Stalin knew; the enigma of Barbarossa. Yale University Press 2005 xxii, 310p il maps $30; pa $18   **940.54**

1. Communist leaders 2. Heads of state 3. Political leaders 4. World War, 1939-1945 -- Campaigns -- Eastern Front 5. World War, 1939-1945 -- Campaigns -- Soviet Union
ISBN 0-300-10780-3; 0-300-11981-X pa

LC 2004-65916

This is an account of Soviet intelligence regarding the German invasion in 1941.

"Murphy's well-researched account offers both a meticulous reconstruction of an intelligence epic and a window into the tragedy of Stalin's despotism." Publ Wkly

Includes bibliographical references

Nelson, Craig

The **first** heroes; the extraordinary story of the Doolittle Raid--America's first World War II victory. Viking 2002 430p il $27.95; pa $15   **940.54**
1. Air force officers 2. Bombing, Aerial -- Japan -- Tokyo 3. Generals 4. World War, 1939-1945 -- Aerial operations 5. World War, 1939-1945 -- Aerial operations, American 6. World War, 1939-1945 -- Japan
ISBN 0-670-03087-2; 0-14-200341-7 pa

LC 2002-28092

"The most interesting part of the book is the harrowing story of survival as crew members are forced to ditch their planes on the Asian mainland. This is a thrilling real-life saga that both informs and inspires." Booklist

Includes bibliographical references (p. {403}-415) and index

Norman, Michael

★ **Tears** in the darkness; the story of the Bataan Death March and its aftermath. [by] Michael Norman and Elizabeth M. Norman. Farrar, Straus, and Giroux 2009 463p il $30   **940.54**
1. Prisoners of war 2. Prisoners of war -- Philippines -- Bataan (Province) 3. World War, 1939-1945 -- Atrocities 4. World War, 1939-1945 -- Campaigns -- Philippines 5. World War, 1939-1945 -- Prisoners and prisons 6. World War, 1939-1945 -- Prisoners and prisons, Japanese
ISBN 978-0-374-27260-9; 0-374-27260-3

LC 2008-47163

This book "is authoritative history. Ten years in the making, it is based on hundreds of interviews with American, Filipino and Japanese combatants. But it is also a narrative achievement. The book seamlessly blends a wide-angle view with the stories of many individual participants." N Y Times (Late N Y Ed)

Includes bibliographical references

Olson, Lynne

Citizens of London; the Americans who stood with Britain in its darkest, finest hour.   Random House 2010 471p il $28   **940.54**
1. Diplomats 2. Government officials 3. Governors 4. Radio reporters 5. Television news anchors 6. Television reporters 7. World War, 1939-1945 -- Diplomatic history
ISBN 978-1-4000-6758-9

The story of how the United States forged its wartime alliance with Britain, told from the perspective of three key American players in London: Edward R. Murrow, Averell Harriman, and John Gilbert Winant.

A nuanced history that captures the intensity of life in a period when victory was not a foregone conclusion. Kirkus

Includes bibliographical references

Patton, George S.

War as I knew it; by George S. Patton, Jr.; annotated by Paul D. Harkins. Houghton Mifflin 1947 425p il maps hardcover o.p. pa $18   **940.54**
1. World War, 1939-1945 -- Campaigns
ISBN 0-395-73529-7 pa

An account of the General's WWII European campaigns from the fight for Sicily to the conquest of Germany based on a series of "open letters" written to his wife.

Pleshakov, Konstantin

★ **Stalin's** folly; the tragic first ten days of World War II on the Eastern Front. [by] Constantine Pleshakov. Houghton Mifflin 2005 326p il map $26   **940.54**
1. Communist leaders 2. Heads of state 3. Political leaders 4. World War, 1939-1945 -- Campaigns -- Eastern Front 5. World War, 1939-1945 -- Europe
ISBN 0-618-36701-2

LC 2004-65133

This is an account of the German invasion of the Soviet Union in 1941.

This book "belongs in every World War II collection." Libr J

Includes bibliographical references

Prange, Gordon William

At dawn we slept; the untold story of Pearl Harbor. {by} Gordon W. Prange in collaboration with Donald M. Goldstein and Katherine V. Dillon. Viking 1991 889p il hardcover o.p.   **940.54**
1. Pearl Harbor (Oahu, Hawaii), Attack on, 1941

LC 91-50176

The author "offers a comprehensive account of Japanese preparations for the attack, the origins and extent of American unpreparedness, and the aftermath of the attack on both sides." Booklist

Includes bibliographical references

Read, Anthony

The **fall** of Berlin; [by] Anthony Read and David Fisher. Da Capo Press 1995 513p il map pa $18.50   **940.54**
1. Berlin, Battle of, 1945 2. World War, 1939-1945 -- Germany
ISBN 0-306-80619-3; 978-0-306-80619-3

LC 94-47998

A description of "the bombing of Berlin by the British and Americans and how the Russian Army fought its way toward and through Berlin in 1945. The authors intend no startling new interpretations or profound analysis. Instead, they offer vignettes, often based on diaries, to describe life in Berlin late in the war. They also retell the story of fanatical Nazi leaders and of the Wehrmacht's desperate efforts to defend the city. The result is a highly readable and, at the same time, sophisticated and reliable narrative history." Libr J

Includes bibliographical references

Roberts, Andrew

Masters and commanders; how four titans won the war in the West, 1941-1945. HarperCollins 2009 xl, 673p il map $35   **940.54**
1. Cabinet members 2. Generals 3. Governors 4. Handicapped 5. Historians 6. Marshals 7. Members of Parliament 8. Memoirists 9. Nobel laureates for literature 10. Nobel laureates for peace 11. Philatelists 12. Presidents 13. Prime ministers 14. Secretaries of

defense 15. Secretaries of state 16. Statesmen 17. Strategy -- History -- 20th century 18. World War, 1939-1945 -- Campaigns 19. World War, 1939-1945 -- Military intelligence 20. World War, 1939-1945 -- Personal narratives, American 21. World War, 1939-1945 -- Personal narratives, British

ISBN 978-0-06-122857-5; 0-06-122857-5

Roberts examines the "history of the four men responsible for final decisions: FDR, Churchill, and their top military advisors, George Marshall and Alan Brooke, respectively. Both to humanize the pressure on figures now memorialized in bronze and to serve as Clio's arbiter of impassioned disagreements over the optimal strategy to defeat Nazi Germany, Roberts examines how arguments played out amongst the quartet and those in their orbit. . . . Roberts reinforces his reputation for high-quality military history with this comprehensive synthesis of primary sources about the fundamental strategic decisions of WWII." Booklist

The **storm** of war; a new history of the Second World War. HarperCollins 2011 lvi, 712p il map $29.99   **940.54**
    1. World War, 1939-1945
    ISBN 978-0-06-122859-9; 0-06-122859-1

"In general, histories of the Second World War in the English language can be divided sharply into those written by Americans, which downplay the British role in the war, and those written by British historians, which downplay the role of the Americans (and also give less space and attention to the Pacific theater than the European theater). Roberts has managed to write a book that both strives and succeeds in giving more or less equal time to both, and also manages to include enough about events in China and the war on the Eastern Front to give the reader a well-balanced and excitingly written account of the whole war. . . . His scholarship is superb, and the 'packaging' of the book, with very good illustrations and ample first-class maps, makes it a real pleasure to read." Daily Beast

Includes bibliographical references

Rooney, Andrew A.
    My war; [by] Andy Rooney. PublicAffairs 2000 333p il $20; pa $14   **940.54**
    1. Authors 2. Humorists 3. Journalists 4. World War, 1939-1945 5. World War, 1939-1945 -- Personal narratives
    ISBN 1-58648-010-3; 1-58648-159-2 pa
                    LC 00-59228

The author "relates how he became a notable combat journalist in WW II, a war he calls 'the ultimate experience for anyone in it.' For the Army newspaper Stars and Stripes, he covered the air war over Germany, the D-Day invasion of Normandy and the Allied drive into Germany. Rooney's simple, ruminative style . . . grips the reader as he describes famous events of the war." Publ Wkly

Scott-Clark, Cathy
    The **Amber** Room; the fate of the world's greatest lost treasure. [by] Catherine Scott-Clark & Adrian Levy. Walker & Co. 2004 386p il $26   **940.54**
    1. Amber art objects 2. Amber art objects -- Russia 3. Art thefts 4. Art treasures in war -- Russia (Federation)

5. World War, 1939-1945 -- Art and the war 6. World War, 1939-1945 -- Destruction and pillage
    ISBN 0-8027-1424-2
                    LC 2004-49625

The authors "tell an exciting, intense, and surprising story. It is filled with episodes of cold-war intrigue, cynicism, amoral betrayal, and bureaucratic stalling that degenerates into absurdity." Booklist

Includes bibliographical references

Sebag-Montefiore, Hugh
    Enigma: the battle for the code. Wiley 2000 422p il hardcover o.p. pa $16.95   **940.54**
    1. Cryptography 2. Enigma cipher system -- History 3. World War, 1939-1945 -- Cryptography 4. World War, 1939-1945 -- Secret service
    ISBN 0-471-40738-0; 0-471-49035-0 pa
                    LC 00-43920

This is the story of the German Enigma code.

"Describing the breaking of the German naval code during World War II, is both engrossing and exciting. Much of the information presented here is based on recently declassified documents." Booklist

Includes bibliographical references

Sheftall, Mordecai G.
    Blossoms in the wind; the human legacy of the Kamikaze. [by] M.G. Sheftall. NAL Caliber 2005 480p il $24.95   **940.54**
    1. Kamikaze airplanes 2. World War, 1939-1945 -- Aerial operations
    ISBN 0-451-21487-0
                    LC 2004-27356

This account of the "design, training, and execution [of Japanese suicide missions] includes interviews with the families of dead pilots and, harder to reach, pilots who survived the missions." Booklist

Includes bibliographical references

Sides, Hampton
    Ghost soldiers; the forgotten epic story of World War II's most dramatic mission. Doubleday 2001 342p il maps $24.95   **940.54**
    1. Cabanatuan (Philippines) -- History, Military -- 20th century 2. Large print books 3. World War, 1939-1945 -- Campaigns -- Philippines 4. World War, 1939-1945 -- Campaigns -- Philippines -- Cabanatuan 5. World War, 1939-1945 -- Prisoners and prisons
    ISBN 0-385-49564-1
                    LC 2001-17337

"The author's excellent grasp of human emotions and bravery makes this a compelling book hard to put down." Publ Wkly

Smyth, Denis
    Deathly deception; the real story of Operation Mincemeat. Oxford University Press 2010 xx, 367p il   **940.54**
    1. Intelligence service agents 2. Lawyers 3. World War, 1939-1945 -- Secret service
    ISBN 978-0-19-923398-4
                    LC 2010-923437

"When the Allies decided to invade Sicily in summer 1943, they floated the body of a British military officer ashore in German-friendly Spain with the hope that the documents he carried would influence the Germans to believe that the Greek islands or Sardinia would be the Allies' actual target—and the ruse appeared to work. . . . [This is an] administrative history of both sides."

"This superlative and almost unexpurgated account of Operation Mincemeat will enthrall serious students of WWII." Booklist

Includes bibliographical references

Snyder, Timothy

Bloodlands; Europe between Hitler and Stalin. Basic Books 2010 524p map $29.95   **940.54**
1. Communist leaders 2. Genocide 3. Genocide -- Europe 4. Heads of state 5. Holocaust, 1933-1945 6. Holocaust, Jewish (1939-1945) 7. Massacres 8. Nazi leaders 9. Political leaders 10. World War, 1939-1945 -- Atrocities
ISBN 978-0-465-00239-9; 0-465-00239-0
                      LC 2010-16816
The book "tr[ies] to explain mass violence in parts of Eastern Europe in the twentieth century. . . . Snyder deals with territories that were ruled for some time by both Nazi Germany and the USSR from 1930 to 1953. He covers most of today's Poland and Ukraine (the focus of his interest), Belarus, the three Baltic countries, and the most western strip of Russia. . . . Snyder gives a[n] . . . account of political history. . . . [He] places . . . emphasis on the exploitation of the countryside and enforced hunger, which claimed half of the fourteen million victims in the 'bloodlands.' Economically speaking, he emphasizes the extraction of resources by imperialists as the cause of mass starvation." (American Historical Review)

"Mr. Snyder's book is revisionist history of the best kind: in spare, closely argued prose, with meticulous use of statistics, he makes the reader rethink some of the best-known episodes in Europe's modern history." Economist

Includes bibliographical references

Spector, Ronald

Eagle against the sun; the American war with Japan. {by} Ronald H. Spector. Free Press 1985 589p il hardcover o.p. pa $18   **940.54**
1. World War, 1939-1945 -- Campaigns -- Pacific Ocean 2. World War, 1939-1945 -- Japan 3. World War, 1939-1945 -- United States
ISBN 0-394-74101-3 pa
                      LC 84-47888
While "policy, strategy and military operations are emphasized . . . Mr. Spector makes a real attempt to give readers some idea of what the war was like for the men and women who fought it. It is here that the book is at its best." N Y Times Book Rev

Includes bibliographical references

Stinnett, Robert B.

Day of deceit; the truth about FDR and Pearl Harbor. Free Press 1999 386p il maps hardcover o.p. pa $16   **940.54**
1. Governors 2. Handicapped 3. Intelligence service -- United States 4. Pearl Harbor (Hawaii), Attack on, 1941 5. Pearl Harbor (Oahu, Hawaii), Attack on, 1941 6. Philatelists 7. Presidents
ISBN 0-7432-0129-9 pa
                      LC 99-38402
The author addresses the question of whether the U.S. had knowledge of the impending Japanese attack on Pearl Harbor.

"Although Stinnett's accusatory light doesn't definitively fall on FDR, it illuminates fishy aspects of the case. . . . Whether the result of simple dereliction or sinister dereliction of duty, Pearl Harbor holds fewer secrets because of Stinnett's research." Booklist

Includes bibliographical references

Takaki, Ronald T.

Hiroshima; why America dropped the atomic bomb. [by] Ronald Takaki. Little, Brown 1995 193p il $28; pa $14.95   **940.54**
1. Atomic bomb 2. Hiroshima (Japan) -- Bombardment, 1945 3. World War, 1939-1945 -- United States
ISBN 0-316-83122-0; 0-316-83124-7 pa
                      LC 95-13546
This study of the bombings of Hiroshima and Nagasaki focuses on the psychological motivations of the American decision-makers, especially Harry Truman.

"Right or wrong, the study is a provocative addition to the unresolved debate over the dropping of the atomic bombs." Publ Wkly

Includes bibliographical references

Thomas, Evan

★ **Sea** of thunder; four commanders and the last great naval campaign, 1941-1945. Simon & Schuster 2006 415p il map $27   **940.54**
1. World War, 1939-1945 -- Campaigns -- Pacific Ocean 2. World War, 1939-1945 -- Naval operations 3. World War, 1939-1945 -- Naval operations, American 4. World War, 1939-1945 -- Naval operations, Japanese
ISBN 978-0-7432-5221-8; 0-7432-5221-7
                      LC 2006-47511
This is an "account of the Battle of Leyte Gulf, October 1944, one of history's largest naval battles, where Admiral William 'Bull' Halsey, the commander of the U.S. Third Fleet, and his commander, Ernest Evans, met the forces of Japanese admirals Takeo Kurita and Matome Ugaki. . . . Thomas paints compelling portraits of these men, offering insight into their characters and actions throughout the war in the Pacific." Libr J

Includes bibliographical references

Toll, Ian W.

Pacific crucible; war at sea in the Pacific, 1941-1942. W.W. Norton 2011 xxxvi, 597p il map $35   **940.54**
1. World War, 1939-1945 -- Campaigns -- Pacific Ocean 2. World War, 1939-1945 -- Naval operations
ISBN 978-0-393-06813-9; 0-393-06813-7
                      LC 2011028907
In this book, "[p]rize-winning freelance naval historian [Ian W.] Toll . . . chronicles one of the U.S. Navy's finest performances of WWII in this . . . narrative of the months

following the . . . attacks on Pearl Harbor. Eyewitness accounts and . . . research in American and Japanese print and archival sources" form the book's basis. (Publishers Weekly)

The author makes vast quantities of technological and tactical concepts intelligible to all but the rankest beginner—for whom this book is not remotely suitable. A particular gift of the author is intelligent character portraits: Yamamoto, MacArthur, Halsey, and Nimitz (clearly one of the author's favorites). Add to all these other attributes a thorough scholarly apparatus, and it is difficult to think of a recent book on this subject that is of such consistently outstanding value. Booklist

Includes bibliographical references

Zuckoff, Mitchell

Lost in Shangri-la. HarperCollins 2011 xii, 384.p.p ill. $26.99   **940.54**
1. Aircraft accidents -- New Guinea 2. Primitive societies 3. Primitive societies -- New Guinea 4. Survival after airplane accidents, shipwrecks, etc. 5. World War, 1939-1945 -- Aerial operations, American 6. World War, 1939-1945 -- Missing in action 7. World War, 1939-1945 -- Search and rescue operations
ISBN 978-0-06-198834-9; 0-06-198834-0
LC 201034508
This book describes "how three World War II sightseers survived a crash in remote New Guinea." (N Y Times Book Rev) Bibliography. Index.

"On May 13, 1945, an American transport plane carrying 24 servicemen and women crashed into a mountain in the tropical jungles of Dutch New Guinea (now Papua), leaving three survivors. Learning about the event while researching another subject, the author recognized the ingredients of a terrific tale: a beautiful young WAC, a hidden valley reminiscent of the Shangri-La in James Hilton's Lost Horizon, primitive tribal people and a daring air rescue. In this well-crafted book, Zuckoff turns the long-forgotten episode into an unusually exciting narrative. Drawing on the young WAC survivor Margaret Hastings' diary as well as journals and interviews, the author hones in on life at the U.S. military base in Hollandia, on the northern coast of uncharted New Guinea; a soldier's chance discovery a year earlier of Baliem Valley, a verdant area about 150 miles into the interior, with its hundreds of native villages surrounded by gardens; and the doomed flight of officers and enlisted personnel out on a joy ride to view this much-talked-about land of Stone Age people from the air." Kirkus

Includes bibliographical references and index.

Iwo Jima; World War II veterans remember the greatest battle of the Pacific. [edited by] Larry Smith. W.W. Norton 2008 xxiv, 345p il map $26.95; pa $17.95   **940.54**
1. Iwo Jima, Battle of, 1945 2. World War, 1939-1945 -- Personal narratives
ISBN 978-0-393-06234-2; 0-393-06234-1; 978-0-393-33491-3 pa; 0-393-33491-0 pa
LC 2008-1301
This is "a superb collection of 22 oral histories from Iwo Jima veterans, including two Medal of Honor winners, a Navajo 'Code-Talker,' the last surviving flag raiser from the first flag raising on Mount Suribachi, a war correspondent,

and an African American marine who served in an ammo company." Libr J

The Pacific War; from Pearl Harbor to Hiroshima. editor, Daniel Marston. Pbk. ed.; Osprey Pub. 2010 272p il map pa $19.95   **940.54**
1. World War, 1939-1945 -- Campaigns -- Pacific Ocean
ISBN 978-1-84908-382-9
LC 2010-292672
"These essays on the Pacific theater of WW II, written by a group of international scholars representing Australia, Great Britain, Japan, and the US, cover the wellknown events at Pearl Harbor, the Coral Sea, and Midway; MacArthur's push to the Philippines; Nimitz's island campaign in the central Pacific; Okinawa; and the dropping of the atomic bomb on Hiroshima and Nagasaki. . . . A chronology, detailed maps, and photographs greatly enhance this excellent volume on the Pacific phase of WW II." Choice

Includes bibliographical references

The good war; an oral history of World War Two. [edited by] Studs Terkel. New Press 1997 589p pa $16.95   **940.54**
1. World War, 1939-1945 -- Personal narratives
ISBN 1-56584-343-6
LC 2003-389322
In a series of interviews Terkel depicts how WWII affected the lives of average Americans.

940.55   1945-1999

Judt, Tony

Postwar; a history of Europe since 1945. Penguin Press 2005 878p il maps $39.95   **940.55**
ISBN 1-59420-065-3
LC 2005-52126
"This is the best history we have of Europe in the postwar period and not likely to be surpassed for many years." Publ Wkly

Includes bibliographical references

Mazower, Mark

Dark continent: Europe's twentieth century. Knopf 1999 487p il maps hardcover o.p. pa $16   **940.55**
ISBN 0-679-75704-X pa
LC 98-15886
The author's "relative unconcern with international and great-power politics probably accounts for a rather intra-European perspective . . . just as it contributes to some exaggeration of the points of comparison and convergence in East and West European economic history. . . . But these are minor defects, the price to be paid for a confident and unconventional work of historical interpretation." N Y Times Book Rev

Includes bibliographical references

941   British Isles

Burns, William E.
A **brief** history of Great Britain. Facts On File
2010 xxiv, 296p il map $49.50; pa $19.95   **941**
ISBN 978-0-8160-7728-1; 978-0-8160-8124-0 pa
LC 2009-8217
This book "narrates the history of Great Britain from
the earliest times to the 21st century, covering the entire
island—England, Wales, and Scotland—as well as associated archipelagos such as the Channel Islands, the Orkneys,
and Ireland as they have influenced British history. The central story of this volume is the development of the British
kingdom, including its rise and decline on the world stage."
Publisher's note
Includes bibliographical references

Farquhar, Michael
Behind the palace doors; five centuries of sex,
adventure, vice, treachery, and folly from royal Britain. Random House Trade Paperbacks 2011 307p
pa $15; ebook $11.99   **941**
ISBN 978-0-8129-7904-6 pa; 978-0-679-60453-2
ebook
LC 2010-21116
The author "probes 500 years of monarchical mishaps
and misdeeds, screaming headlines and gleeful attacks by
cartoonists. He uncloaks secrets, schemes, scandals, blood-
soaked sheets, public humiliations, intrigues, and adultery.
Illustrated with lineage charts and chronologically organized, chapters cover the houses of Tudor, Stuart, Hanover,
Saxe-Coburg-Gotha, and Windsor. . . . [His] style is a breezy
pleasure throughout." Publ Wkly
Includes bibliographical references.

Fraser, Rebecca
★ The **story** of Britain; from the Romans to the
present: a narrative history. Norton 2005 829p il
map $35   **941**
ISBN 0-393-06010-1
LC 2004-26049
The author's "narrative advances with the emphasis on
the roles of a litany of historical icons, from Queen Boudica
to Margaret Thatcher. For those readers who are primarily
interested in the 'who, what, when, where, why' of British
history, this is a valuable general study." Booklist
Includes bibliographical references

Lacey, Robert
Great tales from English history; the truth about
King Arthur, Lady Godiva, Richard the Lionheart,
and more. Little, Brown and Co. 2004 254p maps
$22.95   **941**
ISBN 0-316-10910-X
LC 2003-115660

"This volume begins in 7150 BC with the life and death
of Cheddar Man and ends in 1381 with Wat Tyler and the
Peasants' Revolt." Publisher's note
Includes bibliographical references

Great tales from English history [2] Joan of Arc,
the princes in the Tower, Bloody Mary, Oliver Cromwell, Sir Isaac Newton, and more. Little, Brown and
Co. 2005 271p il map $23.95   **941**
ISBN 0-316-10924-X
LC 2004-63351
The author's "second volume on English history opens
in 1348, the year of the Black Plague, which wiped out half
of England's five million people, and proceeds through the
astonishing scientific discoveries of Sir Isaac Newton in
1687. . . . Lacey's animated prose, energetic storytelling and
spirited approach to British history bring the past to life."
Publ Wkly
Includes bibliographical references

★ **Great** tales from English history [3] Captain
Cook, Samuel Johnson, Queen Victoria, Charles Darwin, Edward the Abdicator, and more. Little, Brown
and Co. 2006 305p $23.99   **941**
ISBN 978-0-316-11459-2; 0-316-11459-6
LC 2006-931723
"The third volume in Lacey's series of edifying and
entertaining stories from English history abounds in fasci-
nating profiles. Industrial and agricultural pioneers such as
Jethro Tull, James Hargreaves and Isambard Kingdom Bru-
nel abide alongside human rights protestors such as Thomas
Clarkson, who founded the British antislavery movement;
feminist philosopher Mary Wollstonecraft; and journalist
Annie Besant, who initiated a successful 1888 match girls'
strike." Publ Wkly
Includes bibliographical references

Schama, Simon
A **history** of Britain. Hyperion 2000 3v ea
$40   **941**
ISBN 0-7868-6675-6 v1; 0-7868-6752-3 v2; 0-7868-
6899-6 v3
LC 00-61442
Schama "writes wonderfully, in an easygoing yet el-
egant manner, with an eye for the telling aesthetic detail, and
throughout brimming with intelligence and passion." N Y
Times Book Rev
Includes bibliographical references

Tompson, Richard S.
★ **Great** Britain: a reference guide from the Renaissance to the present. Facts on File 2003 552p il
$85   **941**
ISBN 0-8160-4474-0
LC 200219
This guide contains "an introductory overview of British history, Renaissance to the present; a narrative history; a
historical dictionary, topical and biographical; a chronology;
appendixes (maps, genealogies of English royal houses, lists
of English sovereigns from 899, and prime ministers from
1721). The work concludes with an unannotated bibliogra-

phy, arranged in sections for bibliogaphies, dictionaries and encyclopedias, general works, surveys, and topics." Choice

The Columbia companion to British history; edited by Juliet Gardiner & Neil Wenborn. Columbia Univ. Press 1997 840p maps $63 **941**
1. Reference books
ISBN 0-231-10792-7

LC 96-23774

This reference work contains "more than 4,500 dictionary entries that not only cover political and constitutional history, but also provide information on social, economic, religious, military, naval, legal, and cultural history. . . . The entries . . . {cover topics such as} blasphemy, divorce, and homosexuality, as well as the historical events and rulers that are standard for any encyclopedia. In addition, the encyclopedia seems to be strong on entries for Scotland and Ireland." Booklist

The Oxford history of Britain; edited by Kenneth O. Morgan. Rev ed, New ed; Oxford University Press 2010 821p map pa $18.95 **941**
ISBN 978-0-19-957925-9; 0-19-957925-3

LC 2010279308

This "volume tells the story of Britain and its people over two thousand years, from the coming of the Roman legions to the present day." Publisher's note
Includes bibliographical references

941.06 House of Stuart and Commonwealth periods, 1603-1714

Long, James
The **plot** against Pepys; [by] James Long & Ben Long. Overlook Press 2008 322p il $27.95 **941.06**
1. Diarists 2. Government officials 3. Members of Parliament 4. Military officials 5. Trials
ISBN 978-1-59020-069-8; 1-59020-069-1

"The book is packed with marvellous asides that add colour to an already kaleidoscopic cavalcade of crass credulousness, court drama and crookery. . . . I couldn't put it down, and there aren't many books on the seventeenth century you can say that about." Hist Today
Includes bibliographical references

Pepys, Samuel
★ The **diary** of Samuel Pepys; edited and with a preface by Richard Le Gallienne; introduction by Robert Louis Stevenson. Modern Lib. 2001 xxxv, 310p $22; pa $15.95 **941.06**
1. Authors, English -- Early modern, 1500-1700 2. Diarists 3. Government officials 4. Members of Parliament 5. Military officials
ISBN 0-679-64221-8; 0-8129-7071-3 pa

LC 00-54817

An abridged edition of Pepys' eleven-volume diary, originally written between 1660 and 1669.

Tomalin, Claire
Samuel Pepys; the unequalled self. Knopf 2002 xxiii, 470p il $30; pa $16.95 **941.06**
1. Cabinet officers -- Great Britain -- Biography 2. Diarists 3. Diarists -- Great Britain -- Biography 4. English diaries -- History and criticism 5. Government officials 6. Great Britain -- History -- Stuarts, 1603-1714 -- Biography 7. Members of Parliament 8. Military officials
ISBN 0-375-41143-7; 0-375-72553-9 pa

LC 2002-75701

"Tomalin mines the diary, and she also expands upon the characters and events, great and small, that affected Pepys' life and livelihood to bring the man and his milieu to life— pungently as well as vibrantly." Booklist
Includes bibliographical references

941.07 Period of House of Hanover, 1714-1837

Brewer, John
The **pleasures** of the imagination; English culture in the eighteenth century. University of Chicago Press 2000 721p il pa $20 **941.07**
ISBN 0-226-07419-6; 978-0-226-07419-1

LC 99-57059

"A remarkable feat of scholarship, this volume will quickly establish itself as an indispensable reference." Booklist
Includes bibliographical references

Foreman, Amanda
Georgiana, Duchess of Devonshire. Random House 2000 454p hardcover o.p. pa $15.95 **941.07**
1. Nobility -- Great Britain -- Biography 2. Socialites 3. Spouses of prominent persons 4. Women politicians -- Great Britain -- Biography
ISBN 0-375-75383-4 pa

LC 99-23580

Georgiana "was the society leader of her day. Daughter of the fabulously wealthy Earl Spencer (and ancestor of the late princess of Wales) and married to the even more wealthy duke of Devonshire, Georgiana was watched, adored, and imitated. But she evolved herself into more than just a fashionable hostess; she got involved in Whig politics, to an extent unprecedented for women. . . . The tenor of the subject's time and place—in this instance, aristocratic Britain in the late 1700s and early 1800s—is both colorfully and meaningfully realized." Booklist
Includes bibliographical references

McLynn, Frank
1759: the year Britain became master of the world. Atlantic Monthly Press 2004 422p il map $26 **941.07**
1. Seven Years' War, 1756-1763
ISBN 0-87113-881-6

LC 2004-57397

1759 "was the fourth [year] in the Seven Years War, a struggle between France and England for global dominance that was fought worldwide. McLynn focuses on the deadly conflict, contrasting the two nations' differing wartime policies and showing how the combination of Britain's maritime prowess and sheer good luck helped it emerge triumphant, albeit by a narrow margin. . . . Splendidly narrated, with balanced insights into the Native American aspect of the French and Indian Wars, McLynn's book will enthrall all lovers of history told well." Publ Wkly

Includes bibliographical references

941.08   Period of Victoria and House of Windsor, 1837-

McKillop, A. B.

The **spinster** & the prophet; H.G. Wells, Florence Deeks, and the case of the plagiarized text. Four Walls Eight Windows 2002 477p il $26.95 **941.08**

1. Authors 2. Feminists 3. Historians 4. Historiography 5. Novelists 6. Plagiarism 7. Plagiarism -- Great Britain -- History -- 20th century 8. Science fiction writers 9. World history 10. Writers on politics 11. Writers on science

ISBN 1-56858-236-6

LC 2002-71292

"When, in 1920, Florence Deeks finally received her rejected manuscript—a feminist history of the world—from Macmillan after eight months, she couldn't understand why it appeared in such bad condition. . . . Later that year, when she read H.G. Wells's new book, The Outline of History, published by Macmillan, she felt a chill. There were so many similarities to her own work: shared themes, organization, word choice, even the same mistakes. Florence made a dramatic decision—she would sue Wells and his publisher for plagiarism. . . . The author handles the dual story line brilliantly, weaving together two opposing characters into one altogether gripping tale of literary theft." Publ Wkly

Includes bibliographical references

Vallone, Lynne

Becoming Victoria. Yale Univ. Press 2001 256p il $26.95 **941.08**

1. Queens 2. Queens -- Great Britain

ISBN 0-300-08950-3

LC 00-68561

"Analyzing Victoria's girlhood diaries, drawings and fiction, as well as records of her education and scores of accounts of her childhood, Valone . . . constructs a revisionist account of the princess's youthful persona but also traces the process by which Victoria was molded into the 'right' kind of adult: capable of assuming the throne and also a clear embodiment of all that was womanly and pure. . . . Well-researched, and with sophisticated cultural criticism, this sound scholarship will engage the interest of academics and nonacademics alike." Publ Wkly

Includes bibliographical references

★ The Cambridge illustrated history of the British Empire; edited by P.J. Marshall. Cambridge Univ. Press 1996 400p il maps $55; pa $35 **941.08**

1. Imperialism

ISBN 0-521-43211-1; 0-521-00254-0 pa

LC 95-14535

"This book examines the experience of colonialism in North America, India, Africa, Australia and the Caribbean,

giving a brief history of the British imperial territories and looking at slavery, trade, religion, art, transportation, and the development of new ideas." Book Rep

Includes bibliographical references

941.081   Reign of Victoria, 1837-1901

Jenkins, Roy

Gladstone; a biography. Random House 1997 xxvii, 698p il hardcover o.p. pa $16.95 **941.081**

1. Biography, Individual 2. Prime ministers 3. Statesmen

ISBN 0-8129-6641-4 pa

LC 96-49632

This "book is a very decent try at an immensely difficult subject, encompassing an enormous amount of material. Lord Jenkins goes through the sources with commendable zeal. He also writes well." N Y Times Book Rev

Includes bibliographical references

Wilson, A. N.

The **Victorians**. Norton 2003 724p il $35; pa $17.95 **941.081**

ISBN 0-393-04974-4; 0-393-32543-1 pa

LC 2002-33809

"Even to fastidious readers, Wilson's failings are minor, and the colorful tapestry he presents of a smoky world peopled with the likes of Carlyle, Mill, Marx, Ruskin, and Darwin can hardly fail to enthrall. Both professional scholars and laypeople will love to relax with this book, although some knowledge of the age is a must." Choice

Includes bibliographical references

Encyclopedia of the Victorian era; James Eli Adams, editor in chief; Tom Pendergast, Sara Pendergast, editors. Grolier Academic Reference 2004 4v il map set $499 **941.081**

ISBN 0-7172-5860-2

LC 2003-57101

"Entries ranging in length from a few paragraphs to several pages are written by experts, treat topics from William Acton to zoological gardens, and seek to encompass the important issues, people, and events of the Victorian era. . . . While predictable figures such as Queen Victoria and Benjamin Disraeli appear, so too do social history topics such as the sporting life, penny dreadfuls, and cholera." Choice

Includes bibliographical references

941.084   1936-1945

Manchester, William

The **last** lion, Winston Spencer Churchill; visions of glory, 1874-1932. Little, Brown 1983 973p il maps $50 **941.084**

1. Biography, Individual 2. Cabinet members 3. Historians 4. Members of Parliament 5. Memoirists 6. Nobel laureates for literature 7. Prime ministers 8.

Prime ministers -- Great Britain 9. Statesmen
ISBN 0-316-54503-1

LC 82-24972

This first volume of a projected three-volume biography of Churchill covers the life of the British statesman from his birth up to his split with the Conservative party over its policy regarding Indian self-rule.

941.085   1945-1999

Junor, Penny
The **Firm**: the troubled life of the House of Windsor. Thomas Dunne Books 2005 xxi, 442p il $25.95   **941.085**
1. Kings 2. Queens
ISBN 0-312-35274-3

LC 2005-45528

"Readers of this interesting and occasionally jaw-dropping look at the world's most famous dysfunctional family will find plenty to engage them." Libr J
Includes bibliographical references

Kynaston, David
Austerity Britain; 1945-51. Walker & Co. 2008 692p il $45   **941.085**
ISBN 978-0-8027-1693-4; 0-8027-1693-8
"Drawing on a remarkable array of diaries, letters, memoirs, and surveys, Kynaston assembles a polyphonic history of a pivotal time." New Yorker
Includes bibliographic references

Family Britain, 1951-1957. Walker & Co 2010 776p il $47.50   **941.085**
ISBN 978-0-8027-1797-9
"Picking up where the much-lauded Austerity Britain, 1945-1951 (2008) left off, Kynaston's latest presents a panoramic view of a transformative period. . . . Leading us on an immersive tour of headlines and correspondence, diaries and sociological studies, Kynaston narrates moments and motifs both great and small, among them the Festival of Britain, Council housing, the queen's coronation, pub culture, Kingsley Amis, smog, labor strikes, skiffle, the 'colour bar,' grammar schools, football, the Suez Crisis, young Mick Jagger, and the BBC." Booklist
Includes bibliographical references

941.1   Scotland

Devine, T. M.
The **Scottish** nation 1700-2000. Viking 1999 xxiii, 695p il maps hardcover o.p. pa $20   **941.1**
ISBN 0-14-100234-4 pa

LC 99-29866

"The author divides the book into chronological periods to cover Scottish economic, military, and social history; regional differences in the Highlands and Lowlands; and the development of Scottish identity." Libr J
Includes bibliographical references

Herman, Arthur
How the Scots invented the modern world; the true story of how western Europe's poorest nation created our world & everything in it. Crown 2001 392p $25.95; pa $14.95   **941.1**
1. Civilization, Modern -- Scottish influences 2. National characteristics, Scottish 3. Scottish national characteristics
ISBN 0-609-60635-2; 0-609-80999-7 pa

LC 2001-28951

"This is a worthwhile book for the general reader." Publ Wkly
Includes bibliographical references

Nicolson, Adam
Sea room: an island life in the Hebrides. North Point Press 2002 391p il maps $27; pa $14 **941.1**
1. Hebrides (Scotland) -- Social life and customs
ISBN 0-86547-636-5; 0-86547-667-5 pa

LC 2002-19816

"Magnificent and poetic, this is a literary and ecological masterpiece." Booklist
Includes bibliographical references

941.5   Ireland

Ferriter, Diarmaid
The **transformation** of Ireland. Overlook Press 2005 884p $37.50   **941.5**
ISBN 1-58567-681-0

LC 2005-49849

"This book isn't a political history of 20th-century Ireland; it's more a chronicle of the social reaction to the events that shaped that century. . . . [The author] has written an informative, funny, at times derisive book that takes a fresh approach to 20th-century Ireland." Publ Wkly
Includes bibliographical references

State, Paul F.
A **brief** history of Ireland. Facts On File 2009 xxiv, 408p il map $49.50; pa $19.95   **941.5**
ISBN 978-0-8160-7516-4; 0-8160-7516-6; 978-0-8160-7517-1 pa; 0-8160-7517-4 pa

LC 2008-29243

The author "opens this vibrant reference with an introduction to Ireland's landscape, people, economics, natural resources, and current government. Following this essay-style overview are 11 chronologically organized chapters. Each is devoted to a significant historical watershed, tracing events from Ireland's prehistory to its contemporary prosperity. Appendixes provide at-a-glance portraits of Northern Ireland and the Irish Republic, including a list of presidents, prime ministers, and a time line of notable dates." Libr J
Includes bibliographical references

The Encyclopedia of Ireland; edited by Brian Lalor; foreword by Frank McCourt. Yale University Press 2003 xxxvii, 1218p il map $65   **941.5**
1. Reference books
ISBN 0-300-09442-6
                   LC 2003-103834
This encyclopedia contains alphabetically arranged entries from Abbey Theatre to Zozimus, a nineteenth-century balladeer. Coverage includes art, cinema, current events, fashion, food, history, Irish language, literature, music, politics, religion, sports, and biographies of a wide range of famous people of Irish descent, including St. Brigid, Éamon de Valera, John F. Kennedy, Bono, Eugene O'Neill, Mary Robinson, and William Butler Yeats.
"This wonderful reference work will delight researchers and lovers of Ireland and the Irish." Choice

★ Encyclopedia of Irish history and culture; James S. Donnelly Jr., editor in chief; Karl S. Bottigheimer . . . [et al.], associate editors. Macmillan Reference USA 2004 2v il map set $270   **941.5**
1. Reference books
ISBN 0-02-865902-3
                   LC 2004-5353
"The A-Z entries are preceded by a chronology and followed by a selection of almost 150 primary documents ranging from the Confession of St. Patrick (c. 450) to the Belfast/Good Friday Agreement (1998). . . . Providing the latest in scholarship, entries are well written and cover the gamut of historical, social, and cultural topics." Booklist
Includes bibliographical references

The Oxford illustrated history of Ireland; edited by R.F. Foster. Oxford University Press 2001 382p il map pa $29.95   **941.5**
ISBN 0-19-289323-8
This illustrated history includes "six essays by Irish scholars, five covering chronological periods in Irish history and the sixth a . . . discussion of the interplay between Irish literature and history." Libr J
Includes bibliographical references

941.501   Early history to 1086

Cahill, Thomas
  How the Irish saved civilization; the untold story of Ireland's heroic role from the fall of Rome to the rise of medieval Europe. {by} Thomas Cahill. Talese 1995 246p il maps $27.50; pa $12.95   **941.501**
1. Learning and scholarship 2. Medieval civilization 3. Western civilization
ISBN 0-385-41848-5; 0-385-41849-3 pa
                   LC 94-28130
"Highly literate and affectionate, if somewhat rambling and indulgent. . . . As a freewheeling, witty popular history of Irish Christianity in the Dark Ages, this will amuse and enlighten." Libr J
Includes bibliographical references

941.6   Northern Ireland; Donegal, Monaghan, Cavan counties of Republic of Ireland

Campbell, Julieann
  Setting the truth free; the inside story of the Bloody Sunday Justice Campaign. Julieann Campbell. Liberties Press 2012 219 p. ill. (some col.) (pbk.) $24.95   **941.6**
1. Bloody Sunday, Derry, Northern Ireland, 1972 2. Massacres -- Northern Ireland -- Londonderry -- History -- 20th century 3. Nonfiction
ISBN 1907593373; 9781907593376
                 LC 2012379691
In this book about the "1972 Bloody Sunday massacre during a peaceful civil rights march in Derry, Northern Ireland .. . . [Julieann] Campbell, an Irish journalist . . . niece of the first person slain on that tragic day . . . [and] the press officer for the campaign to find justice for those killed and wounded, not only tells the tale of her murdered 17-year-old uncle, Jackie Duddy, but also details the planning of the march, the . . . slaughter by the British troops, and the traumatic remembrances of the survivors. . . . A need to seek justice, as Campbell writes, motivated the Irish community to protest and pressure the British government to launch a real inquiry into the shootings." (Publishers Weekly)

Coogan, Tim Pat
  The **troubles**; Ireland's ordeal, 1966-1996, and the search for peace. Palgrave 2002 589p il map pa $22.95   **941.6**
  ISBN 978-0-312-29418-2; 0-312-29418-2
In this political history the author "examines all parties to the struggle. . . . He reconstructs the past 30 years, from the 1969 marching and riots to the H-Block protests, the MacBride Principles, the Anglo-Irish agreement, and the recent paramilitary cease-fire. Coogan traces the current peace process, stalled by Great Britain's insistence that the IRA hand in its weapons, to the 1979 visit of Pope John Paul II." Libr J
Includes bibliographical references

942   England and Wales

Ackroyd, Peter
  London: the biography. Talese 2001 xxvi, 801p il $45; pa $18.95   **942**
  ISBN 0-385-49770-9; 0-385-49771-7 pa
                 LC 2001-27153
"A sweeping, highly readable account of London's colorful and complicated history." Libr J
Includes bibliographical references

  Thames; the biography. Nan A. Talese/Doubleday 2008 481p il map $40   **942**
  ISBN 978-0-385-52623-4; 0-385-52623-7
                 LC 2008-02864
"Eschewing standard organization, Ackroyd jumps from today's posh London banks to Roger Bacon's observatory at Grandpont to Dickens's 'deathlike and mysterious' waterway. We learn about the riverbank's many species of willow

(white, weeping, crack, cane osier), and about the Retribution and the Belliqueux, eighteenth-century prison boats that each held hundreds of men. . . . A survey of the many ways in which the river can kill notes that most Thames suicides remain 'anonymous and unlamented.' Not every tidbit will appeal to every reader, but the book demands to be read as it was written, according to one's fancy." New Yorker

Includes bibliographical references

Cartwright, Justin

Oxford revisited. Bloomsbury 2009 223p pa $18   **942**

ISBN 978-1-59691-093-5; 1-59691-093-3

"A South African-born novelist who graduated from Oxford University in the 1960s, Cartwright returns to the medieval campus nearly four decades later on a combination nostalgic tour and journalistic inquiry. Seeking to define the university's greatness, Cartwright offers erudite meditations on everything from the solidity of its buildings . . . to the fiercely individualistic lives of its students. . . . He offers sharply observed homages to the thinkers and writers—Isaiah Berlin, J. R. R. Tolkien, Charles Dodgson—who shaped Oxford's discourse, and maps out the university's peculiar mix of silly rituals and sublime intellectual life. In addition, the book retraces Cartwright's own journey from callow teenager to confident young scholar-athlete." N Y Times Book Rev

Hollis, Leo

London rising; the men who made modern London. Walker & Co. 2008 390p il map $27.99   **942**

1. Architects 2. Authors 3. Biographers 4. College teachers 5. Diarists 6. Economists 7. Essayists 8. Members of Parliament 9. Philosophers 10. Physicians 11. Physicists 12. Political and social philosophers

ISBN 978-0-8027-1632-3; 0-8027-1632-6

LC 2008-000179

"London in the mid-17th century remained a medieval city. The civil war, a plague that claimed 100,000 lives and the Great Fire of 1666 would have been sufficient to send it back to the Dark Ages. Instead, London was transformed into a modern metropolis. . . . Hollis controls the narrative by focusing on the five figures who best represent the spirit of the age. John Locke, the philosopher, outlined a daring theory of universal natural rights; social observer John Evelyn grappled with the specific meaning of Englishness; real estate developer and speculator Nicholas Barbon rebuilt the center of London (with designs by the scientific polymath Robert Hooke); and lastly, Christopher Wren, who created St. Paul's Cathedral, eternal symbol of the glittering city." Publ Wkly

Includes bibliographical references

Nicolson, Juliet

The perfect summer; England 1911, just before the storm. Grove Press 2007 290p il $25; pa $15   **942**

1. Social classes -- Great Britain -- History -- 20th century 2. Social structure -- Great Britain

ISBN 0-8021-1846-1; 978-0-8021-1846-2; 0-8021-4367-9 pa; 978-0-8021-4367-9 pa

LC 2006-48854

"With her sparkling social history about Edwardian society on the brink of World War I, Nicolson has created the perfect beach reading for Anglophiles." Christ Sci Monit

Includes bibliographical references

Taylor, A. J. P.

★ English history, 1914-1945. Oxford Univ. Press 1965 xxvii, 708p maps $194.50   **942**

1. World War, 1914-1918 -- Great Britain 2. World War, 1939-1945 -- Great Britain

ISBN 0-19-821715-3

A study of the political, economic, and social changes in England over a thirty year span.

Medieval England; an encyclopedia. editors: Paul E. Szarmach, M. Teresa Tavormina, Joel T. Rosentha. Garland 1998 lxiv, 882p il maps $155 **942**

1. Medieval civilization -- Encyclopedias 2. Reference books

ISBN 0-8240-5786-4

LC 97-35523

"Containing more than 700 entries by more than 300 international scholars, the volume encompasses the fields of Old English and Middle English language and literature, music and liturgy, history, and history of art. . . . The A-Z entries are supported by lists of kings and queens of England, archbishops of Canterbury and York, and popes, 590-1502, as well as a glossary of musical and liturgical terms." Booklist

942.01   Historical periods of England and Wales together, of England alone

Goodrich, Norma Lorre

King Arthur. Harper & Row 1989 406p il map pa $17   **942.01**

1. Kings

ISBN 0-06-097182-7; 978-0-06-097182-3

LC 85-22558

The author examines historical and literary materials relating to Arthur as both an actual and legendary figure.

King Arthur in legend and history; edited by Richard White; foreword by Allan Massie. Routledge 1998 xxv, 570p il maps hardcover o.p. pa $34.95   **942.01**

1. Kings

ISBN 0-415-92063-9 pa

LC 97-47726

"This book is a compilation of source material excerpted primarily from longer works. . . . The documents themselves are arranged in roughly chronological and geographical order, ranging from Gildas (c. 548) to The Buik of the Chronicles of Scotland (1535). The anthology presents both historical and literary works and draws from French and German as well as English sources." Libr J

Includes bibliographical references

942.03 Period of House of Plantagenet, 1154-1399

Weir, Alison
  Eleanor of Aquitaine; a life. Ballantine Bks.
2000 xxi, 441p il maps $28; pa $15.95   **942.03**
  1. Great Britain -- History -- Henry II, 1154-1189 --
Biography 2. Queens 3. Queens -- France -- Biography
4. Queens -- Great Britain -- Biography
  ISBN 0-345-40540-4; 0-345-43487-0 pa
LC 99-54785
  A biography of the twelfth-century queen, first of France,
then of England, the consort of Henry II and mother of Richard the Lionhearted.
  "In approaching as complex a subject as feudalism, Weir
wears her learning lightly and has a pleasant habit of anticipating all the questions of a curious reader." Publ Wkly
  Includes bibliographical references

Thomas Becket; warrior, priest, rebel : a nine-hun-
  dred-year-old story retold. John Guy. Random
  House 2011 424 p.   **942.03**
  1. Christian martyrs -- England -- Biography 2.
Christian saints -- England -- Biography 3. Statesmen
-- Great Britain -- Biography
  ISBN 1400069076; 9780679603412; 9781400069071
LC 2011042794
  This book by John Guy presents a biography of Thomas
Becket (1118-1170), the man who refused to subordinate the
power of the church to the power of the state, and was martyred for it. . . . Distilling and disputing materials from several previous Becket biographies, Guy traces his subject's
development from a handsome, superficial, and socially ambitious youth to a mature man who rose intellectually, morally, and politically to become lord chancellor to Henry II. In
1162, he was named archbishop of Canterbury, a position he
accepted reluctantly, knowing that his honest exercise of the
office as a defender of liberty and as one who would assert
the church's power to cancel unjust state laws would bring
him into conflict with Henry. (Publishers Weekly)

942.04 Period of Houses of Lancaster and York, 1399-1485

Weir, Alison
  The **Wars** of the Roses. Ballantine Bks. 1995
462p il hardcover o.p. pa $15.95   **942.04**
  1. Great Britain -- History -- 1455-1485, Wars of the
Roses
  ISBN 0-345-39117-9; 0-345-40433-5 pa
  "No history collection should do without this perfectly
focused and beautifully unfolded account." Booklist

942.05 Period of House of Tudor, 1485-1603

Meyer, G. J.
  The **Tudors**; the complete story of England's
most notorious dynasty. Delacorte Press 2010 xxvi,
612p il map $30   **942.05**
  1. Kings 2. Queens
  ISBN 978-0-385-34076-2
LC 2009-40032
  "History buffs will savor Meyer's cheeky, nuanced, and
authoritative perspective on an entire dynasty, and his study
brims with enriching background discussions, ranging from
class structure and the medieval Catholic Church to the Tudor connection to Spanish royalty." Publ Wkly
  Includes bibliographical references

Starkey, David
  Six wives: the queens of Henry VIII. HarperCol-
lins Pubs. 2003 xxvii, 852p il hardcover o.p. pa
$16.95   **942.05**
  1. Kings 2. Queens 3. Queens -- Great Britain --
Biography
  ISBN 0-694-01043-X; 0-06-000550-5 pa
  "Solidly researched and delightfully told, this is highly
recommended." Libr J
  Includes bibliographical references

Weir, Alison
  Henry VIII; the king and his court. Ballantine
Bks. 2001 632p il $28; pa $16.95   **942.05**
  1. Kings
  ISBN 0-345-43659-8; 0-345-43708-X pa
LC 2001-116042
  In this biography of the Tudor king, the author "examines the minutiae of his daily life and gives prominence
to the background players of his court. . . . At times, the
weighty detail and numerous characters will make the work
inaccessible; however, as a scholarly study it is a significant
achievement." Libr J
  Includes bibliographical references

The **life** of Elizabeth I. Ballantine Bks. 1998
532p il hardcover o.p. pa $15.95   **942.05**
  1. Queens 2. Queens -- Great Britain -- Biography
  ISBN 0-345-42550-2 pa
LC 98-34917
  "Weir brings a fine sense of selection and consider-
able zest to her portrait of the self-styled Virgin Queen."
Publ Wkly
  Includes bibliographical references

The **six** wives of Henry VIII. Grove Weidenfeld
1992 643p il hardcover o.p. pa $15   **942.05**
  1. Biography, Collective 2. Great Britain -- History --
1485-1603, Tudors 3. Kings 4. Queens -- Great Britain
  ISBN 0-8021-3683-4 pa
LC 91-29522
  This is a collective biography of the wives of the Tudor
king of England.

"Wonderfully detailed, extensively researched. . . . The narrative is free flowing, humorous, informative, and readable." SLJ

Includes bibliographical references

942.06   House of Stuart and Commonwealth periods to present, 1603-

Fraser, Antonia

★ **Faith** and treason; the story of the Gunpowder Plot. Doubleday 1996 xxxv, 347p il hardcover o.p. pa $16   **942.06**

1. Conspirators   2.   Gunpowder Plot, 1605   3. Gunpowder plot, 1605   4. Revolutionaries

ISBN 0-385-47190-4 pa

LC 96-21709

"A small group of Roman Catholics planned to blow up Parliament on its opening day in 1605, when the Protestant King James and his older son would be present, and to proclaim the nine-year-old princess Elizabeth queen, raise her as a Catholic, and so restore Catholicism as the state religion. . . . The Gunpowder Plot was both cruel and crackpot, but Fraser does a wonderful job of conveying to the modern reader just why a few Catholics felt that it was justified and also was likely to succeed." New Yorker

Includes bibliographical references

Trevelyan, George Macaulay

The **English** Revolution, 1688-1689; [by] G. M. Trevelyan. Oxford University Press 1965 136p pa $30   **942.06**

ISBN 978-0-19-500263-8; 0-19-500263-6

This study covers not only the revolution itself but also the events of the reign of James II, which led up to it and the political changes which followed.

942.9   Wales

Morris, Jan

A **writer's** house in Wales. National Geographic Soc. 2002 143p $25   **942.9**

1. Wales, North -- Civilization   2. Wales, North -- Description and travel

ISBN 0-7922-6523-8

LC 2001-44731

The author "reflects on her home in Wales, its beautiful setting and the nature of being Welsh. . . . This slim and charming volume offers a crisp account of the turbulent history of the Welsh and their battle to maintain their language and culture in the shadow of their more powerful neighbor." Publ Wkly

943   Germany and neighboring central European countries

Coy, Jason Philip

A **brief** history of Germany; [by] Jason P. Coy. Facts on File 2011 288p il map $49.50; pa $19.95   **943**

ISBN 978-0-8160-8142-4; 978-0-8160-8329-9 pa

LC 2010-23139

This book provides an "account of the events, people, and special customs and traditions that have shaped Germany from ancient times to the present." Publisher's note

Includes bibliographical references

Craig, Gordon Alexander

The **Germans**; [by] Gordon A. Craig. Meridian 1991 361p il pa $18   **943**

1. Antisemitism 2. Heads of state 3. Nazi leaders

ISBN 0-452-01085-3; 978-0-452-01085-7

LC 91-12814

This work examining the social history of Germany contains "chapters on religion, money, Germans and Jews, women, professors and students, romantics, literature and society, soldiers, Berlin—and an appendix called 'The Awful German Language.'" Publisher's note

Includes bibliographical references

Fulbrook, Mary

★ A **concise** history of Germany; 2nd ed; Cambridge University Press 2004 277p il, maps hardcover o.p. pa $22   **943**

1. Heads of state 2. National socialism 3. Nazi leaders 4. Prime ministers 5. Princes 6. Statesmen

ISBN 0-521-83320-5; 0-521-54071-2 pa

LC 2004-271599

This history of Germany "spans the early Middle Ages to the present day. . . . Mary Fulbrook explores the interrelationships between social, political and cultural factors in the light of the latest scholarly controversies." Publ Wkly

Includes bibliographical references

Gay, Peter

My German question; growing up in Nazi Berlin. Yale Univ. Press 1998 208p il $40; pa $11.95 **943**

1. College teachers 2. Historians 3. Jews -- Germany 4. Jews -- Germany -- Biography 5. Jews -- Persecutions 6. National socialism 7. Nonfiction writers

ISBN 0-300-07670-3; 0-300-08070-0 pa

LC 98-26686

"A searching, sensitive portrait of Gay's youth, as crystalline as memory can be made." Booklist

Gay, Ruth

The **Jews** of Germany; a historical portrait. with an introduction by Peter Gay. Yale Univ. Press 1992 297p il maps hardcover o.p. pa $35   **943**

1. Jews -- Germany

ISBN 0-300-05155-7; 0-300-06052-1 pa

LC 91-30235

This is a history of Germany's Jews from the first century to the Holocaust.

"Illustrated sumptuously with paintings, photographs and excerpts from letters and historical documents, . . . this affirming history survives the sad end of the centuries-old German Jewish way of life." N Y Times Book Rev

Gorra, Michael Edward

The **bells** in their silence; travels through Germany. {by} Michael Gorra. Princeton University Press 2004 211p $24.95   **943**
ISBN 0-691-11765-9

Gorra's "account of his travels through Germany is shaped—perhaps even haunted—by figures from the past: historical, literary, personal. A captivating, unique work of synthesis." Booklist
Includes bibliographical references

MacDonogh, Giles

Frederick the Great; a life in deed and letters. St. Martin's Press 2000 436p il hardcover o.p. pa $16.95   **943**
1. Kings 2. Prussia (Germany) -- History -- Frederick II, 1740-1786 3. Prussia (Germany) -- Kings and rulers -- Biography
ISBN 0-312-27266-9 pa
       LC 00-24799

"Both general readers and those with a strong background in European history will find great value in this outstanding biography." Booklist
Includes bibliographical references

Moorhouse, Roger

Berlin at war. Basic Books 2010 432p il $29.95   **943**
1. World War, 1939-1945 -- Germany
ISBN 978-0-465-00533-8
       LC 2010-907169

"Election results in the fading days of the Weimar Republic indicate that Berliners were not particularly sympathetic to Hitler or his movement. Yet Berlin endured horrible physical destruction, deprivation, and death. This included intense Allied bombings by day and night, and a siege and eventual ravaging by the Russian army. . . . [Moorhouse] begins with an almost idyllic scene as huge crowds in Berlin witness the celebration of Hitler's birthday in April 1939; at the time, of course, Germany seemed to have achieved its foreign-policy goals without firing a shot. As the fortunes of Germany and Berlin deteriorate, Moorhouse uses the testimonies of a variety of Berliners to describe some memorable scenes and struggles.This is a hard, unrelenting saga of the effects of total warfare on citizens just hoping to survive." Booklist
Includes bibliographical references

Schulze, Hagen

Germany; a new history. translated by Deborah Lucas Schneider. Harvard Univ. Press 1998 356p il maps hardcover o.p. pa $16.95   **943**
ISBN 0-674-00545-7 pa
       LC 98-23629

Schulze provides "a concise overview of 2,000 years of German history. . . . This is a fast-moving survey that manages to touch most of the critical bases—from Charlemagne

to Frederick the Great to Hitler—without concentrating on any one particular historical era." Booklist
Includes bibliographical references

Watson, Peter

The **German** genius; Europe's third renaissance, the second scientific revolution, and the twentieth century. Harper 2010 964p il $35   **943**
ISBN 0060760222; 9780060760229
       LC 2010-06738

This is a "cultural history of German ideas and influence, from 1750 to the present day." (Publisher's note) Index.

This is "a panoramic review of German cultural and intellectual development from 1750 to the present. Examining the contributions of literally hundreds of German thinkers and doers and mapping the conceptual connections between them, the author demonstrates the breadth, volume, and influence of German output in philosophy, science, industry, art, literature, and all forms of scholarly activity. But Watson's true focus is the cultural crucible, forged in the eighteenth and nineteenth centuries and informed by notions of Bildung and inwardness, that gave rise to such accomplishments but also set the stage for the evil actions of the Third Reich. To some extent an effort to untether our understanding of German history from the conflicts of the twentieth century, this study is also a reminder that our modern Western worldview has deep German roots." Booklist
Includes bibliographical references

943.08   Germany since 1866

Craig, Gordon Alexander

Germany, 1866-1945; by Gordon A. Craig. Oxford Univ. Press 1978 825p hardcover o.p. pa $41.95   **943.08**
ISBN 0-19-502724-8 pa
       LC 78-58471

"An impressive . . . survey of modern German history, this book is an indispensable reference." New Statesman (1913)
Includes bibliographical references

Evans, Richard J.

★ The **coming** of the Third Reich; a history. Penguin Press 2004 622p il map hardcover o.p. pa $18   **943.08**
1. National socialism 2. National socialism -- History
ISBN 1-594-20004-1; 0-14-303469-3 pa
       LC 2003-63205

"This is a first-rate narrative history that informs and educates and may inspire readers to delve even deeper into the subject." Booklist
Includes bibliographical references

Stern, Fritz Richard

Five Germanys I have known; [by] Fritz Stern. Farrar, Straus & Giroux 2006 546p il map $30   **943.08**

1. College teachers 2. Historians
ISBN 978-0-374-15540-7; 0-374-15540-2

LC 2006-60

In this "memoir, Stern looks back over the 'five Germanys' his generation has seen—the Weimar Republic, Nazi tyranny, the post-1945 Federal Republic, the Soviet-controlled German Democratic Republic and, lastly, the reunited Germany of the present—and explains how he came to reconcile himself with his birth country (which his Jewish family fled in 1938) as it has come to terms with its new place in today's more cohesive and peaceful Europe. . . . The book's intriguing structure makes it a wonderful combination of history, memoir, analysis and even poetry." Publ Wkly

943.085   Period of Weimar Republic, 1918-1933

Haffner, Sebastian

Defying Hitler; a memoir. translated from the German by Oliver Pretzel. Farrar, Straus & Giroux 2002 309p il $24; pa $14   **943.085**

1. Historians -- Germany -- Biography
ISBN 0-374-16157-7; 0-312-42113-3 pa

LC 2002-17058

"In August 1938 a young German lawyer and journalist with the . . . name of Raimund Pretzel arrived in England. . . . Pretzel, a non-Jew, was fleeing to join and marry a Jewish woman pregnant with their first child. . . . Choosing a new name—Sebastian Haffner—to keep the Nazis from retaliating against his relatives, he went on to a . . . career as a journalist and historian in England, where he died in 1999. Afterward, while perusing his father's papers, Oliver Pretzel . . . found a . . . typescript in German. It was Haffner's unfinished memoir about his early years, begun in 1939, that sought through autobiography to understand how Hitler came to power." New Leader

943.086   Period of Third Reich, 1933-1945

Aycoberry, Pierre

The **social** history of the Third Reich; 1933-1945. translated from the French by Janet Lloyd. New Press 2000 380p $30; pa $15.95   **943.086**

1. Germany -- Social conditions 2. National socialism
ISBN 1-56584-549-8; 1-56584-635-4 pa

LC 99-14059

"In examining the actions of individuals and social groups, {the author} illustrates that German citizens' response to the Nazi regime varied wildly. Some resisted bravely; others saw an opportunity for advancement. Most people sought merely to survive. In fact, what is extremely unsettling is how so many could maintain a semblance of normalcy in their lives. Aycoberry does not attempt to answer the unanswerable questions posed by the Nazi era, but

his disturbing, brutally honest, and scrupulously fair work may be a landmark in the field." Booklist

Includes bibliographical references

Bascomb, Neal

Hunting Eichmann; how a band of survivors and a young spy agency chased down the world's most notorious Nazi. Houghton Mifflin Harcourt 2009 390p il map $26   **943.086**

1. Nazi leaders 2. Secret service -- Israel 3. War criminals 4. War criminals -- Germany
ISBN 978-0-618-85867-5; 0-618-85867-9

LC 2008-35757

The author recounts the pursuit, capture, and abduction of Nazi war criminal Adolf Eichmann. "Bascomb spread a wide net in researching the 15-year hunt, and he fills his book with previously unknown or neglected details, utilizing the remembrances of former Mossad agents, German and American intelligence operatives, and Argentine Nazi sympathizers who tried to find Eichmann after his seizure. . . . This is an outstanding account of a sustained and worthy manhunt." Booklist

Includes bibliographical references

Burleigh, Michael

The **Third** Reich; a new history. Hill & Wang 2000 xxv, 965p il maps hardcover o.p. pa $18   **943.086**

ISBN 0-8090-9326-X pa

LC 00-31838

"This brilliant and unique view of a great tyranny is an important addition to our understanding of the first half of the twentieth century." Booklist

Includes bibliographical references

Evans, Richard J.

★ The **Third** Reich in power, 1933-1939. Penguin Press 2005 941p il map hardcover o.p. pa $20   **943.086**

1. National socialism 2. National socialism -- History
ISBN 1-594-20074-2; 0-14-303790-0 pa

LC 2005-52128

This "is a major achievement. No other recent synthetic history has quite the range and narrative power of Evans's work." Publ Wkly

Includes bibliographical references

Fischer, Klaus P.

Nazi Germany; a new history. Continuum 1995 734p il hardcover o.p. pa $32.95   **943.086**

1. Heads of state 2. National socialism 3. Nazi leaders
ISBN 0-8264-0906-7 pa

LC 94-41796

"An indispensable, compellingly readable political, military and social history of the Third Reich." Publ Wkly

Includes bibliographical references

Fleming, Gerald

Hitler and the final solution; with an introduction by Saul Friedlander. University of Calif. Press 1984 xxxvi, 219p il hardcover o.p. pa $18.95 **943.086**
1. Heads of state 2. Holocaust, 1933-1945 3. Nazi leaders
ISBN 0-520-06022-9 pa

LC 83-24352

This work attempts to prove "that the Final Solution was deliberately designed and personally willed and ordered by Hitler. Fleming reveals the elaborate precautions taken not only to disguise the nature of the operation but also to ensure that it could not be connected with Hitler." Publisher's note
Includes bibliographical references

Fritzsche, Peter

Life and death in the Third Reich. Belknap Press of Harvard University Press 2008 368p **943.086**
1. Collective memory -- Germany 2. Holocaust, 1933-1945 3. Holocaust, Jewish (1939-1945) 4. Holocaust, Jewish (1939-1945) -- Germany 5. National socialism
ISBN 0-674-02793-0; 0-674-03465-1 pa; 978-0-674-02793-0; 978-0-674-03465-5 pa

LC 2007-40552

This is a sequel to the author's Germans into Nazis (1998). In this study, Fritzsche seeks to explain the success of the ideology of Nazism. He argues that "its basic appeal lay in the Volksgemeinschaft—a 'people's community' that appealed to Germans to be part of a great project to redress the wrongs of the Versailles treaty, make the country strong and vital, and rid the body politic of unhealthy elements. The goal was to create a new national and racial self-consciousness among Germans. For Germany to live, others—especially Jews—had to die. . . . Fritzsche examines the efforts of Germans to adjust to new racial identities, to believe in the necessity of war, to accept the dynamic of unconditional destruction—in short, to become Nazis." (Publisher's note) Index.

"This book combines a compelling historical narrative with a thought-provoking analysis and will be of much interest to scholars in the field as well as a more general readership." Times Higher Ed
Includes bibliographical references

Johnson, Eric A.

What we knew; terror, mass murder and everyday life in Nazi Germany: an oral history. [by] Eric A. Johnson and Karl-Heinz Reuband. Basic Books 2005 xxiii, 434p $27.50 **943.086**
1. Holocaust, 1933-1945
ISBN 0-465-08571-7

"The authors posit that 'far from living in a state of constant fear and discontent, most Germans led happy and even normal lives in Nazi Germany.' They believe that the Holocaust could not have been possible without the complicity of the majority of the German population. . . . This scholarly work is a major contribution to the understanding of life in Nazi Germany and a compelling narrative that is certain to be the standard work on the subject." Booklist
Includes bibliographical references

Kershaw, Ian

Hitler, 1936-1945: nemesis. Norton 2000 832p hardcover o.p. pa $25 **943.086**
1. Biography, Individual 2. Dictators 3. Heads of state 4. National socialism 5. Nazi leaders
ISBN 0-393-04994-9; 0-393-32252-1 pa

"The second volume of Kershaw's biography of Hitler covers the period from the Anschluss with Austria to 1945. . . . By 1938, Hitler's word was the equivalent of written law. After 1936, Hitler also came to believe his own propaganda. . . . Without any reasonable restraint, he led Germany inexorably to destruction. . . . Kershaw's two volumes will probably be the standard source for many years." Libr J

Klemperer, Victor

★ **I** will bear witness; a diary of the Nazi years, 1933-1941. translated by Martin Chalmers. Random House 1998 556p hardcover o.p. pa $15.95 **943.086**
1. Diarists 2. Holocaust survivors 3. Jews -- Germany -- History -- 1933-1945
ISBN 0-375-75378-8 pa

LC 98-15429

"Never has the isolation of living in a world that wishes one's people dead been rendered with greater pathos. Every act of cruelty as well as every gesture of kindness is scrupulously recorded." Nation

Nelson, Anne

Red Orchestra; the story of the Berlin underground and the circle of friends who resisted Hitler. Random House 2009 388p il $27 **943.086**
1. Anti-Nazi movement -- Germany -- Berlin 2. National socialism 3. World War, 1939-1945 -- Underground movements 4. World War, 1939-1945 -- Underground movements -- Germany
ISBN 978-1-4000-6000-9; 1-4000-6000-1

LC 2008-23465

The author "documents the wartime journey of Greta Kuckhoff, a young German, and her valiant colleagues who formed a potent resistance to the Hitler regime in its glory days. . . . Nelson's riveting book speaks proudly of Greta . . . and all of the nearly three million Germans who resisted Hitler's iron will, and gives the reader a somber view of hell from the inside." Publ Wkly
Includes bibliographical references

Parssinen, Terry M.

The **Oster** conspiracy of 1938; the unknown story of the military plot to kill Hitler and avert World War II. {by} Terry Parssinen. HarperCollins Pubs. 2003 xxii, 232p il map $27.95; pa $13.95 **943.086**
1. Generals 2. Heads of state 3. Nazi leaders 4. Underground leaders
ISBN 0-06-019587-8; 0-06-095525-2 pa

LC 2002-68896

"A fascinating, blow-by-blow account of a seemingly feasible but failed attempt to prevent World War II. . . . Even knowing the outcome, readers feel suspense and hope as events unfold; alternate history buffs and history students alike will gain new insight into the past and into human character from this tragic story." SLJ
Includes bibliographical references

Pool, James

Hitler and his secret partners; contributions, loot and rewards, 1933-1945. Pocket Bks. 1997 415p il hardcover o.p. pa $14   **943.086**
1. Heads of state 2. Nazi leaders 3. World War, 1939-1945 -- Destruction and pillage
ISBN 0-671-76082-3 pa
LC 97-15506

The author examines the way German industrialists and financiers backed Hitler and how the Nazis received material support from abroad. Pool alleges that Henry Ford, Edward VIII and Joe Kennedy assisted the Nazi regime.

This book "is a reminder that the worst-kept secret of WWII is that so many malefactors emerged little the worse." Publ Wkly
Includes bibliographical references

Rempel, Gerhard

★ Hitler's children; the Hitler youth and the SS. University of N.C. Press 1989 354p il hardcover o.p. pa $24.95   **943.086**
1. National socialism
ISBN 0-8078-4299-0 pa
LC 88-28036

The author examines the alliance between the Nazi SS and the Hitler Youth.

"Rempel's objective work brings into focus one aspect of the sordid history of the Third Reich." Booklist
Includes bibliographical references

Rosenbaum, Ron

Explaining Hitler; the search for the origins of his evil. HarperPerennial 1999 444p pa $16 **943.086**
1. Heads of state 2. National socialism 3. Nazi leaders
ISBN 0-06-095339-X; 978-0-06-095339-3
LC 99-25965

This book examines interpretations of Hitler made by his contemporaries and by historians.

"In this brilliantly skeptical inventory of the world's Hitler-thinking, Rosenbaum analyzes not only the multiple Hitler theories but also the agendas and fantasies that the theorizers bring to their subject." Time
Includes bibliographical references

Shirer, William L.

The rise and fall of the Third Reich; a history of Nazi Germany. with a new afterword by the author. Simon & Schuster 1990 1249p hardcover o.p. pa $25   **943.086**
1. Heads of state 2. Nazi leaders 3. World War, 1939-1945 -- Germany
ISBN 0-671-72868-7 pa
LC 90-221762

This is a comprehensive, documented history of Germany from the beginning of the Nazi party in 1918 to the World War II defeat of Germany in 1945. Here is a detailed account of the events, and the leading figures of the Nazi era, especially Adolf Hitler.

Speer, Albert

★ Inside the Third Reich; memoirs. translated from the German by Richard and Clara Winston; introduction by Eugene Davidson. Simon & Schuster 1997 596p il pa $18   **943.086**
1. Heads of state 2. Nazi leaders 3. World War, 1939-1945 -- Germany
ISBN 0-684-82949-5; 978-0-684-82949-4

The author, Hitler's "architect and later his armaments minister, was in the dictator's inner circle for almost 12 years. . . . After the war Speer used the enforced leisure of his 20 prison years as a war criminal to plan and write these memoirs." Libr J
Includes bibliographical references

Tubach, Frederic C.

German voices; memories of life during Hitler's Third Reich. [by] Frederic C. Tubach with Sally Patterson Tubach. University of California Press 2011 273p il $26.95   **943.086**
1. National socialism 2. World War, 1939-1945 -- Germany
ISBN 978-0-520-26964-4; 0-520-26964-0
LC 2010-51218

"Tubach approaches his mission with a nice, unobtrusive blend of sympathetic warmth and scholarly detachment. . . . The best recommendation I can make—and it is a warm one—is that readers go into German Voices prepared to treat it as one facet of a larger investigation into the phenomenon that was the Third Reich—as a uniquely accessible, honest and frequently thought-provoking window enabling some valuable ground-level insight into the much larger evil behavior that prevailed—until it imploded." PopMatters
Includes bibliographical references

Turner, Henry Ashby

Hitler's thirty days to power; January 1933. {by} Henry Ashby Turner, Jr. Addison-Wesley 1996 255p il hardcover o.p. pa $16   **943.086**
1. Heads of state 2. National socialism 3. Nazi leaders
ISBN 0-201-32800-3 pa
LC 96-20012

The author explores "the fateful 30 days before Hitler became chancellor of Germany in January 1933. Although many of the facts are known, this study reveals that the Nazi dictator did not come to power as the result of 'impersonal forces.' The slender, analytical volume indicates that rather, at a time of mortal peril for Germany—and the world—intrigue was the order of the day in Berlin. . . . Students of German history and extremist movements should enjoy this fast-paced narrative." Publ Wkly
Includes bibliographical references

Album of the damned; snapshots from the Third Reich. Academy Chicago Publishers 2008 408p il $50   **943.086**
1. World War, 1939-1945 2. World War, 1939-1945 -- Pictorial works
ISBN 978-0-89733-576-8; 0-89733-576-7

"Photographed almost exclusively by amateurs — both soldiers and civilians — the pictures in Album of the Damned center on the daily life within the Third Reich, both at home and on the battlefield. . . . Garson assembled the exclusively black-and-white photos from private collections around the world, including many captured by the Soviets that only became available after the fall of the Soviet Union. . . . Critics might maintain that by focusing on showing how Nazis were 'human,' attention is diverted from their crimes against humanity. But it's impossible to thumb through the book on any page and not see the ghosts of the six million floating around every photo. A narrative that snakes through the book provides an overview of the time period and background on what's taking place in the photos." Jerusalem Post

943.087   1945-1990

Bessel, Richard
   Germany 1945; from war to peace. HarperCollins 2009 522p il map $28.99   **943.087**
   1. Reconstruction (1939-1951) 2. Reconstruction (1939-1951) -- Germany 3. World War, 1939-1945 -- Germany 4. World War, 1939-1945 -- Peace
   ISBN 978-0-06-054036-4; 0-06-054036-2
   This is an account of the German home front during the last months of the war. Bessel also writes about the country's path to economic recovery in the second half of 1945.
   The author "does an excellent job of evoking the blasted landscape of a conquered Germany—the homelessness and the hunger, the rubble and the mass rape." New Yorker
   Includes bibliographical references

Brenner, Michael
   After the Holocaust; rebuilding Jewish lives in postwar Germany. translated from the German by Barbara Harshav. Princeton Univ. Press 1997 196p il $47.50; pa $19.95   **943.087**
   1. Holocaust survivors 2. Jews -- Germany
   ISBN 0-691-02665-3; 0-691-00679-2 pa
                                  LC 97-1149
   This introduction to German Jewry since 1945 consists of two essays by Brenner and 15 short autobiographical statements by Jewish communal, religious, and cultural leaders.
   "If the middle section of interviews seems redundant, it is only because Brenner has covered the material so well and so succinctly elsewhere." Publ Wkly
   Includes bibliographical references

Darnton, Robert
   Berlin journal, 1989-1990. Norton 1991 352p il hardcover o.p. pa $12.95   **943.087**
   ISBN 0-393-31018-3 pa
                                  LC 90-19745
   "Darnton spent parts of 1989 and 1990 in Germany, witnessing the end of that country's division into East and West as the Berlin Wall fell. . . . {He} focuses more on events and aftereffects in East Germany as experienced by ordinary citizens, rather than trying to write a definitive study. Darnton talks with workers, bureaucrats, and government officials and describes what was happening and what the people understood about these momentous events." Booklist

Reeves, Richard
   Daring young men; the heroism and triumph of the Berlin Airlift, June 1948-May 1949. Simon & Schuster 2010 316p il map $28   **943.087**
   1. Air pilots 2. Air pilots -- Biography 3. Air pilots, Military -- History
   ISBN 978-1-4165-4119-6; 1-4165-4119-5
                                  LC 2009-15333
   "'The American people will not allow the German people to starve,' Colonel Frank Howley, one of the top American commanders in Berlin, said in June, 1948, after the Soviets cut off all supply routes except an air corridor to the Western sectors of the city. But when the blockade began, as Reeves notes in his appealing account, almost no one believed that food and fuel for an urban population of more than two million could be delivered by air, and many American officials thought the question was how Berlin could be abandoned with the least embarrassment. Ten and a half months and a quarter-million American and British flights later—an unmatched act of politico-logistical bravado—the Soviets abandoned their blockade." New Yorker
   Includes bibliographical references

Taylor, Fred
   Exorcising Hitler; the occupation and denazification of Germany. [by] Frederick Taylor. Bloomsbury Press 2011 xxxvii, 438p il $30   **943.087**
   1. Denazification 2. Heads of state 3. Nazi leaders 4. Reconstruction (1939-1951) -- Germany
   ISBN 978-1-59691-536-7; 1-59691-536-6
                                  LC 2010-46282
   "Filled with quotable quotes and memorable anecdotes, . . . [this book] presents a vivid portrait of life in Germany at and just after the end of the war. And there is enough analysis here to give the reader a clear view of what motivated Allied conduct and of how and why it changed over time. Taylor's book is popular history at its best, essential reading for anyone who is interested in the Nazis and wants to know what happened next." New Statesman
   Includes bibliographical references

943.71   Czech Republic

Albright, Madeleine Korbel, 1937-
   Prague winter; a personal story of remembrance and war, 1937-1948. Madeleine Albright with Bill Woodward. HarperCollins 2012 x, 467 p.p $29.99   **943.71**
   1. Biography & autobiography -- Personal Memoirs 2. History -- General 3. Jewish families -- Czech Republic -- Prague -- Biography 4. Jews -- Czechoslovakia 5. Memoirs 6. World War, 1939-1945 -- Czech Republic -- Prague 7. World War, 1939-1945 -- Czechoslovakia
   ISBN 0062030310; 9780062030313
                                  LC 2011049416
   This book by Madeleine Albright chronicles her personal "experiences, and those of her family . . . [during] the years of 1937 to 1948. . . . The book takes readers from the Bohemian capital . . . to the bomb shelters of London, from the desolate prison ghetto of Terezin to the highest councils of European and American government. Albright reflects on

her discovery of her family's Jewish heritage many decades after the war, [and] on her Czech homeland's tangled history." (Publisher's note)

Demetz, Peter

   Prague in black and gold; scenes from the life of a European city. Hill & Wang 1997 411p maps hardcover o.p. pa $15   **943.71**
   1. Prague (Czech Republic) -- History
   ISBN 0-8090-1609-5 pa
                                LC 96-52216
   The author presents an "account of the city's history and culture by focusing on epic events as well as heroes, villains and martyrs throughout the millennia of its existence. . . . A highly literate panorama of a focal point of European culture." Publ Wkly
   Includes bibliographical references

943.8   Poland

The Chronicle of the Lodz ghetto, 1941-1944; edited by Lucjan Dobroszycki; translated by Richard Lourie {et al.} Yale Univ. Press 1984 lxviii, 551p il hardcover o.p. pa $37   **943.8**
   1. Holocaust, 1933-1945 2. Jews -- Poland
   ISBN 0-300-03924-7 pa
                                  LC 84-3614
   "The record is made more profoundly melancholic by the restrained archivist style employed by the chroniclers." New Statesman (1913)

943.9   Hungary

Michener, James A.

   The **bridge** at Andau. Fawcett Crest 1983 277p pa $6.99   **943.9**
   1. Hungarian refugees
   ISBN 978-0-449-21050-5; 0-449-21050-2
   "The heroism, horror and tragedy of the 1956 Hungarian revolt is revealed through interviews with many refugees who crossed the bridge at Andau to freedom." Cleveland Public Libr

944   France and Monaco

Baldwin, Rosecrans

   Paris, I love you but you're bringing me down; Rosecrans Baldwin. Farrar, Straus and Giroux 2012 286 p.   **944**
   1. Aliens (Persons) -- France 2. Americans -- France -- Paris -- Biography 3. Couples -- France -- Paris -- Biography 4. Memoirs
   ISBN 0374146683; 9780374146689
                              LC 2011045886
   This expatriate memoir by Rosecrans Baldwin presents an account of his time living in Paris, France. Baldwin discovered some very French things about office life in Paris: You have to eat lunch, because the company docks a portion of your pay and returns it to you as meal coupons. . . . It's virtually impossible to get fired. . . . The author also discovered that French banks seem never to have heard of credit cards, and although he and wife qualified as legal residents for health-insurance coverage, the cards permitting them to actually use the insurance didn't arrive until a month before they left. Nonetheless, despite tight finances and loud construction work around their apartment, Baldwin fell in love just like everyone else. (Kirkus)

Buckley, Veronica

   The **secret** wife of Louis XIV; Francoise d'Aubigne, Madame de Maintenon. Farrar, Straus and Giroux 2009 498p il map $35   **944**
   1. Biography, Individual 2. Kings 3. Royal favorites
   ISBN 978-0-374-15830-9; 0-374-15830-4
                          LC 2008-16210
   This is "a lively, sympathetic portrayal of the woman who, against all odds, succeeded in taming the royal tomcat." N Y Times Book Rev
   Includes bibliographical references

Fraser, Antonia

   Marie Antoinette; the journey. Talese 2001 xxii, 512p il $35; pa $16.95   **944**
   1. Large print books 2. Queens 3. Queens -- France -- Biography
   ISBN 0-385-48948-X; 0-385-48949-8 pa
                          LC 2001-23493
   "A well-researched biography that may cause one to rethink the role in which history has cast Marie Antoinette." Libr J
   Includes bibliographical references

Gordon, Mary

   ★ **Joan** of Arc. Viking 2000 xxv, 180p $19.95   **944**
   1. Christian saints 2. Christian women saints -- France -- Biography 3. Saints
   ISBN 0-670-88537-1
                          LC 99-55678
   "This biography rehearses the well-known highlights in Joan's short life: the voices she heard who charged her with the mission to save France, her participation in the Battle of Orléans and the coronation of King Charles VII; her trial by an ecclesiastical court, where she was charged with witchcraft, heresy and idolatry. . . . The strength of this 'biographical meditation' lies in the penultimate chapter, in which Gordon investigates the numerous re-creations of Joan on stage and screen." Publ Wkly
   Includes bibliographical references

Horne, Alistair

   ★ **La** belle France; a short history. Knopf 2005 485p il map $30   **944**
   ISBN 1-4000-4140-6
                          LC 2004-42329

"This compelling narrative belongs in any public library needing an excellent, current one-volume history of France." Booklist

Includes bibliographical references

Seven ages of Paris. Knopf 2002 448p $35; pa $16 **944**

ISBN 0-679-45481-0; 1-4000-3446-9 pa

LC 2002-29653

The author traces "the history of Paris through seven periods, beginning in the 12th century and ending with the death of Charles de Gaulle in 1969. . . . Each section includes fascinating insights into the social and cultural life of the age, fashions in clothing, architectural developments, leading personalities, and lifestyles of rich and poor alike. With the verve of a master storyteller, Horne captures Parisians' 'zest for living.'" Libr J

Includes bibliographical references

Jones, Colin

Paris; biography of a city. Colin Jones. Viking 2005 xxv, 566p il map $29.95 **944**

ISBN 0-670-03393-6

LC 2004-53608

"Moving from prehistoric tribal habitation through Roman times, medieval uncertainty and splendor, early modern religious wars, Enlightenment, revolution, and two world wars, Jones examines how rulers, economy, religion and violence have shaped the city. . . . Anyone who loves Paris will find connections and revelations here, a Paris of the mind that resonates through the centuries." Publ Wkly

Includes bibliographical references

Jonnes, Jill

Eiffel's tower; and the World's Fair where Buffalo Bill beguiled Paris, the artists quarreled, and Thomas Edison became a count. Viking 2009 354p il map $27.95 **944**

1. Structural engineers

ISBN 978-0-670-02060-7; 0-670-02060-5

LC 2008-49839

"Not long after Gustave Eiffel, an engineer and builder of railway bridges, won the contract to build a centerpiece attraction for the 1889 World's Fair, he faced a barrage of criticism of its design as well as financial, architectural, mechanical, and political obstacles to its construction. Jonnes . . . captures the verve and personality of the Belle Epoque as Paris struggled to show the world its glory. . . . [She also] details the iconic figures who added to the allure of the fair—James McNeill Whistler, Paul Gauguin, Thomas Edison, Annie Oakley, and Buffalo Bill—and the excitement and ambitions of the era." Booklist

Includes bibliographical references

Kaplan, Alice

Dreaming in French; the Paris years of Jacqueline Bouvier Kennedy, Susan Sontag, and Angela Davis. Alice Kaplan. University of Chicago Press 2012 x, 289 p.p **944**

1. Students, Foreign -- France -- Paris -- Biography 2. Women -- United States -- Biography 3. Women

-- United States -- Intellectual life

ISBN 0226424383; 9780226424385

LC 2011026598

This book looks at the reciprocal effects that student and place can have on each other. . . . [S]he notes that each of their experiences helps to illuminate a moment in French or U.S. history: Jacqueline Bouvier's [visit was part of] . . . one of the first post-World War II student-abroad programs; Susan Sontag arrived in Paris in the late 1950s . . . as France grappled with the Algerian independence movement; Angela Davis was the sole black student in her study-abroad cohort in the early 1960s, while the U.S. civil rights movement gained momentum. Kaplan . . . describ[es] the long-term impact that French culture had on the woman in question. She relies as much as possible on the women's own words to detail their experiences, filling in with compatriot students' diaries, letters, and interviews as necessary. (Libr J)

Karnow, Stanley

Paris in the fifties; illustrations by Annette Karnow. Times Bks. 1997 352p il hardcover o.p. pa $14 **944**

1. Biography, Individual 2. French national characteristics 3. Paris (France) -- Social life and customs

ISBN 0-8129-3137-8 pa

LC 97-18521

"Not content with simply ensconcing himself in the Time bureau offices, . . . Karnow created a personal life for himself and took in all that Paris and the provinces had to offer. And now he offers this succulent book, which Francophiles will devour." Booklist

Lever, Evelyne

Madame de Pompadour; translated from the French by Catherine Temerson. Farrar, Straus & Giroux 2002 310p il $26; pa $16.95 **944**

1. Favorites, Royal -- France -- Biography 2. France -- Kings and rulers -- Mistresses -- Biography 3. Kings 4. Royal favorites

ISBN 0-374-11308-4; 0-312-31050-1 pa

LC 2002-22811

"Lever has crafted a detailed and fascinating portrait of the woman who pretty well ran France from 1745 to 1764." Publ Wkly

Includes bibliographical references

Riding, Alan

And the show went on; cultural life in Nazi-occcupied Paris. Alfred A. Knopf 2010 399p il map $28.95 **944**

1. Popular culture -- France 2. Popular culture -- France -- Paris 3. World War, 1939-1945 -- France 4. World War, 1939-1945 -- France -- Paris

ISBN 978-0-307-26897-6; 0-307-26897-7

LC 2010-16841

"This engrossing work, rich in detail, should appeal to French historians and serious readers interested in 20th-century cultural history." Libr J

Includes bibliographical references

Robb, Graham

Parisians; an adventure history of Paris. W.W. Norton & Co. 2010 475p il map $28.95   **944**

    ISBN 978-0-393-06724-8; 0-393-06724-6

                               LC 2009-54279

    Part history, part travelog, part Ripley's Believe It or Not!, this creative historical geography takes us on a tour of Paris via a series of chronologically arranged vignettes stretching from the eve of the Revolution of 1789 to the present. . . . The book records a series of moments and meetings when characters both obscure and famous interacted with key landmarks like the Palais Royal, Notre Dame, or Place de la Concorde. Robb . . . recreates the drama and turmoil of key events like the bloody horrors of the Commune, De Gaulle's triumphant 1944 entry into Paris, or the tumultuous student demonstrations of May 1968. Libr J

    Includes bibliographical references

Tuchman, Barbara Wertheim

A **distant** mirror; the calamitous 14th century. {by} Barbara W. Tuchman. Knopf 1978 xx, 677p il maps hardcover o.p. pa $17.95   **944**

    1. Church history -- 600-1500, Middle Ages 2. Crusades 3. Medieval civilization 4. Plague 5. Women -- Europe 6. World history -- 14th century

    ISBN 0-345-34957-1 pa

                                 LC 78-5985

    The author traces the history of the fourteenth century by following the career of a "feudal lord, Enguerrand de Coucy VII, the seigneur of some 150 towns and villages in Picardy. He was born in 1340, and he died in captivity in 1397, having been made a prisoner by the Turks." Time

    Includes bibliographical references

Williams, Charles

The **last** great Frenchman; a life of General de Gaulle. Wiley 1995 544p il $30; pa $19.95   **944**

    1. Generals 2. Presidents 3. Presidents -- France -- Biography 4. Prime ministers 5. Statesmen

    ISBN 0-471-11711-0; 0-471-18071-8 pa

                                LC 94-42881

    The author offers "appraisals of de Gaulle's career as soldier, politician and head of state. Williams contrasts the infuriatingly obstinate public figure with the private man, emotional and affectionate in the bosom of his family. Especially interesting is the account of de Gaulle's tender relationship with his retarded daughter. . . . The author also sheds light on de Gaulle's determined anti-Americanism during his final years." Publ Wkly

    Includes bibliographical references

Yalom, Marilyn

How the French invented love; nine hundred years of passion and romance. HarperCollins 2012 416 p. $15.99   **944**

    ISBN 0062048317; 9780062048318

    This book offers author Marilyn Yalom's investigation, through literature, into "how the French manage their romances, marriages, affairs, and obsession with love and sex.h She argues that itas not only gender-specific traits and roles that are socially constructed, but love, too. For example, 'Les liaisons dangereuses' . . . is still on the list of required reading in French high schools. She draws analytical connections . . . to the love lives of [French] writers (gay, straight, or just plain neurotic)." (Publishers Weekly)

Paris was ours; thirty-two writers reflect on the City of Light. edited by Penelope Rowlands. Algonquin Books of Chapel Hill 2011 279p pa $15.95   **944**

    ISBN 978-1-56512-953-5; 1-56512-953-9

                                 LC 2010-30560

    In this anthology "Penelope Rowlands culled 32 essays, stories and poems, some original, some previously published, from writers who include professors, single mothers, gay men, a homeless woman, a wealthy Iranian and a poor young Cuban. The collection takes some of the shine off Paris but not the allure — not unlike the pull of a troubled but passionate lover who could never be more than a fling. . . . Ultimately, the writers fall in love with Paris, a city that embraces sorrow, depression, snarkiness, human frailty and living in the moment no matter the menial task that entails. In dismantling the dream of Paris, they reveal an infinitely more complex city and people." Minneapolis Star Tribune

944.04   France since 1789

Burke, Edmund

★ **Reflections** on the Revolution in France; edited by J.C.D. Clark. Stanford Univ. Press 2001 446p $65; pa $29.95   **944.04**

    1. Public opinion -- Great Britain -- History -- 18th century

    ISBN 0-8047-3923-4; 978-0-8047-3923-8; 0-8047-4205-7 pa; 0-8047-4205-4 pa

                                 LC 00-63732

    "A treatise by Edmund Burke, written in the form of a letter to a Frenchman. It attacks the leaders and principles of the French Revolution for their violence and excesses, and urges reform, rather than rebellion, as a means of correcting social and political abuses." Benet's Reader's Ency. 4th edition

    Includes bibliographical references

Lefebvre, Georges

The **French** Revolution. Columbia Univ. Press 1962 2v hardcover o.p. v1 pa $32; v2 pa $32 **944.04**

    ISBN 0-231-08598-2 v1 pa; 0-231-08599-0 v2 pa

    An account of the political, military, social, economic and intellectual aspects of the French Revolution.

944.05   Period of First Empire, 1804-1815

Johnson, Paul

★ **Napoleon**. Viking 2002 190p hardcover o.p. pa $13   **944.05**

    1. Emperors 2. Emperors -- France -- Biography 3. Large print books

    ISBN 0-670-03078-3; 0-14-303745-5 pa

                                 LC 2001-45605

Johnson "presents a concise appraisal of Napoleon's career and a precise understanding of his enigmatic character. The author views Napoleon, not as an 'idea man' whose ideology was the ladder by which he propelled himself to heights of power, but as an opportunist who took advantage of a series of events and situations he could manipulate into achieving supreme control." Booklist

Includes bibliographical references

Schom, Alan

One hundred days; Napoleon's road to Waterloo. Oxford University Press 1993 398p pa $45 **944.05**
1. Emperors 2. Waterloo, Battle of, 1815
ISBN 978-0-19-508177-0; 0-19-508177-3

LC 93-11787

This is an account of "Napoleon's escape from Elba in February 1815 and his return . . . to France. Rallying the nation behind him, he mustered his army and marched off to meet Wellington at Waterloo. . . . This is a first-class reconstruction of Napoleon's final campaign." Publ Wkly

Includes bibliographical references

944.081   Period of Third Republic, 1870-1945

Bredin, Jean-Denis

The **affair**; the case of Alfred Dreyfus. translated from the French by Jeffrey Mehlman. Braziller 1986 628p il hardcover o.p. pa $19.95   **944.081**
1. Antisemitism 2. Army officers 3. Trials
ISBN 0-8076-1175-1 pa

LC 85-22374

"That Bredin manages to be both passionate and exact is his first outstanding virtue. He is admirably free of the baroque conspiracy theories that sprout so luxuriantly on both sides of this case." N Y Rev Books

Includes bibliographical references

Brown, Frederick

For the soul of France; culture wars in the age of Dreyfus. Alfred A. Knopf 2010 304p il $28.95   **944.081**
1. Church and state -- France -- History -- 19th century 2. French national characteristics 3. National characteristics, French 4. Nationalism -- France 5. Nationalism -- France -- History -- 19th century
ISBN 978-0-307-26631-6; 0-307-26631-1

LC 2009-30912

"Brown recounts the history of France, following its 1789 revolution, as an ongoing contest between the champions and foes of the Enlightenment. . . . The humiliating defeat of the Franco-Prussian War of 1870-71 was followed by the economic crash of 1882 and the Panama Company bribery scandal of 1893, both of which were reputedly executed by Jewish masters. . . . In 1894, an opportunity for revenge presented itself in the person of Alfred Dreyfus, a 34-year-old Jewish army officer. Accused of espionage on the flimsiest of evidence—fabrications, and forgeries—Dreyfus was twice tried and convicted. Dreyfus was eventually freed in 1906, one year after a law requiring the separation of church and state had passed. Secularism seemed to hold sway. But, as Brown demonstrates in his brilliant study, religious fervor

and bellicose patriotism combined in World War I to shift the balance yet again." Boston Globe

Includes bibliographical references

Derfler, Leslie

★ The **Dreyfus** affair. Greenwood Press 2002 xxii, 167p il $44.95   **944.081**
1. Antisemitism 2. Army officers
ISBN 0-313-31791-7

LC 2001-38365

"Following a chronology is a 'Historical Overview' containing several chapters of background and analysis. These chapters provide context for what is commonly known as the Dreyfus affair, discuss how anti-Semitism and socialism played into and were affected by the affair, and summarize how the affair has been viewed through history. The next section is an A-Z collection of biographies of almost 20 key individuals. . . . Primary documents comprise the next chapter and most documents are accompanied by short explanations. . . . This guide is useful for researchers who need more information than they can find in an encyclopedia." Booklist

Includes bibliographical references

Glass, Charles

Americans in Paris; life and death under Nazi occupation. Penguin Press 2010 524p il map $32.95   **944.081**
1. Americans -- France 2. World War, 1939-1945 -- France
ISBN 978-1-59420-242-1; 1-59420-242-7

LC 2009-39650

"Despite occasional excesses of detail, Americans in Paris is a much richer book than its title suggests, and for anyone interested in France during this period it is a fascinating treat." Telegraph (London)

Includes bibliographical references

Read, Piers Paul, 1941-

The **Dreyfus** affair; the scandal that tore France in two. Piers Paul Read. Bloomsbury Press 2012 408 p.   **944.081**
1. Antisemitism -- France -- History -- 19th century 2. Religion and politics -- France -- History -- 19th century 3. Scandals -- France -- History -- 19th century 4. Trials (Treason) -- Political aspects -- France
ISBN 1608194329; 9781608194322

LC 2011034456

This historical work by Piers Paul Read reviews the Dreyfus Affair. Captain Alfred Dreyfus was a rising star in the French artillery command. . . . However, Dreyfus had enemies as a result of his ambition. . . . On the basis of flimsy evidence, Dreyfus was placed under arrest for the crime of high treason. Not long afterward, he was sentenced to spend the rest of his life on the legendary, lethal Devil's Island. The saga of Dreyfus's many trials . . . the fight to free him, and the intrigues on both sides, is a . . . story rife with heroes and villains. . . . The anti-Semitism and deceit on display in the Dreyfus case was an ominous prelude to the Holocaust and the long, bloody twentieth century to come. (Publisher's note)

944.083   Period of Fifth Republic, 1958-

Mayle, Peter

Encore Provence; new adventures in the south of France. Knopf 1999 226p $23; pa $12   **944.083**
1. Authors 2. Children's authors 3. Humorists 4. Nonfiction writers
ISBN 0-679-44124-7; 0-679-76269-8 pa
LC 99-62335

Mayle's "book is all about the renewal of his acquaintance with the land he so loves. Essays range widely over Provençal life. . . . His observations and commentaries are laced with humor but encompass true respect and admiration for his adopted homeland." Booklist

White, Edmund

The flaneur; a stroll through the paradoxes of Paris. Bloomsbury Pub. 2001 211p maps $16.95   **944.083**
1. Authors 2. Biographers 3. Large print books 4. Memoirists 5. Novelists 6. Short story writers
ISBN 1-58234-135-4
LC 00-46812

"White is richly informed, and his evocative writing should appeal to both armchair travelers and visitors to Paris." Libr J

945   Italy, San Marino, Vatican City, Malta

Berendt, John

The city of falling angels; a Venice story. Penguin Press 2005 414p $25.95; pa $15   **945**
ISBN 1-59420-058-0; 1-59420-061-0 pa
LC 2005-47661

The author describes some of his encounters with contemporary Venetians. The starting point for his travels was the investigation of the fire which destroyed La Fenice opera house in 1996.

Berendt "delivers an urbane, beautifully fashioned book with much exotic charm. . . . [The author] makes erudite, inquisitive, nicely skeptical company as he leads the reader through the shadows of what was heretofore better known as a tourist attraction." N Y Times (Late N Y Ed)

Bosworth, R. J. B.

Mussolini's Italy; life under the dictatorship, 1915-1945. Penguin 2006 xxvi, 692p il map $35   **945**
1. Fascism -- Italy 2. Heads of state
ISBN 1-59420-078-5
LC 2005-52127

Bosworth "combines prodigious research with a clear writing style that will appeal to all readers interested in the Italy of Il Duce." Libr J
Includes bibliographical references

Clark, Robert

Dark water; flood and redemption in the city of masterpieces. Doubleday 2008 354p il $26   **945**
1. Art -- Conservation and restoration -- Italy --

Florence 2. Art, Italian -- Italy -- Florence 3. Floods 4. Volunteers -- Italy
ISBN 978-0-7679-2648-5; 0-7679-2648-X
LC 2008-1695

This is an account of the Florence flood of 1966.
The author "tells an enthralling true story in a way that makes it read like a novel." Economist
Includes bibliographical references

Hazzard, Shirley

The ancient shore; dispatches from Naples. [by] Shirley Hazzard and Francis Steegmuller. University of Chicago Press 2008 129p il $18; pa $13   **945**
1. Authors 2. Novelists 3. Short story writers
ISBN 978-0-2263-2201-8; 0-2263-2201-7; 978-0-226-32202-5 pa; 0-226-32202-5 pa
LC 2008-15420

"Much larger than all its parts, this book does full justice to a place, and a time, where 'nothing was pristine, except the light.'" Bookforum

Hibbert, Christopher

The Borgias and their enemies; 1431-1519. Harcourt, Inc. 2008 328p $26   **945**
1. Kings
ISBN 978-0-15-101033-2; 0-15-101033-1
LC 2008-03076

"Lucrezia Borgia, on hearing that her father, Pope Alexander VI, was choosing her third husband, noted that her first two had been 'very unlucky.' Luck had little to do with it, as Hibbert shows in this vivid chronicle of the notoriously corrupt Renaissance family. One husband was killed on the orders of her brother Cesare, whose ruthlessness made him the model for Machiavelli's 'The Prince'; the other was discarded after ceasing to be politically useful to the Pope. Hibbert ably traces the web of alliances through which the Spanish-born Alexander hoped to secure his hold on Italy and his family's place in power." New Yorker
Includes bibliographical references

Hughes, Robert

Rome; a cultural, visual, and personal history. Alfred A. Knopf 2011 498p il $35   **945**
ISBN 978-0-307-26844-0; 0-307-26844-6
LC 2011-14600

The author "gives us a guided tour through the city in its many incarnations, excavating the geologic layers of its cultural past and creating an indelible portrait of a city in love with spectacle and power . . . The reader need not agree with Mr. Hughes's acerbic assessments or even be interested in Rome as a destination on the map to relish this volume, so captivating is his narrative. Although his book is a biography of Rome, it is also an acutely written historical essay informed by his wide-ranging knowledge of art, architecture and classical literature, and a thought-provoking meditation on how gifted artists (like Bernini and Michelangelo) and powerful politicians and church leaders (like Augustus, Mussolini and Pope Sixtus V) can reshape the map and mood of a city." N Y Times Book Rev
Includes bibliographical references

Keahey, John

Seeking Sicily; a cultural journey through myth and reality in the heart of the Mediterranean. Thomas Dunne Books/St. Martin's Press 2011 312p il $27.99; ebook $14.99 **945**

ISBN 978-0-312-59705-4; 978-1-4299-9067-7 ebook

LC 2011026786

The author "takes a meandering and inspiring tour through the history, culture, and landscape of Sicily, an island that has been a crossroads for the various peoples of the Mediterranean for millennia. . . . Keahey's thoroughly researched book will inspire any traveler to look past the Sicily of the traditional tourist's guide and appreciate its diverse, layered, and sometimes dark history." Libr J

Includes bibliographical references

Levey, Michael

Florence; a portrait. Harvard Univ. Press 1996 xxix, 498p il hardcover o.p. pa $22.95 **945**

1. Italian art

ISBN 0-674-30658-9 pa

LC 95-31215

"If at times the detail overwhelms the big picture, the 150 illustrations (50 in color) and Levey's excellent artistic counsel make this a worthy guide for anyone seriously seeking Florence." Publ Wkly

Includes bibliographical references

Mayes, Frances

★ **Under** the Tuscan sun; at home in Italy. Chronicle Bks. 1996 280p $22.95 **945**

1. Authors 2. Houses -- Remodeling 3. Italian cooking 4. Memoirists 5. Poets 6. Tuscany (Italy) -- Description

ISBN 0-8118-0842-4

LC 96-15137

"Casual and conversational, {Ms. Mayes's} chapters are filled with craftsmen and cooks, with exploratory jaunts into the countryside—but what they all boil down to is an intense celebration of what she calls 'the voluptuousness of Italian life.' Occasionally, this leads to the sort of gushy observations you might expect from a besotted lover. But more often it produces an appealing and very vivid snapshot imagery." N Y Times Book Rev

Taylor, Benjamin

Naples declared; a walk around the bay. Benjamin Taylor. G.P. Putnam's Sons 2012 240 p. **945**

1. City and town life -- Italy -- Naples

ISBN 0399159177; 9780399159176

LC 2011049450

This book by Benjamin Taylor provides a description of Naples, Italy with discussions of history, philosophy, religion, art, culture, literature, [and] customs. The book meanders between past and present, wanders in stream-of-thought fashion through the Naples streets, delves . . . into the citys stories, lives, and lore, and drops in for conversations with locals . . . (Library Journal) [including] present-day encounters with a fervently communist doctor, with a chain-smoking student of Faulkner, and with novelist Shirley Hazzard. (Kirkus)

945.091 Reign of Victor Emmanuel III, 1900-1946

Bosworth, R. J. B.

Mussolini. Oxford Univ. Press 2002 584p il hardcover o.p. pa $14.95 **945.091**

1. Fascism 2. Fascism -- Italy 3. Fascism -- Italy -- History 4. Heads of state 5. Heads of state -- Italy -- Biography

ISBN 0-340-73144-3; 0-340-80988-4 pa

LC 2002-283267

This is "the definitive study of the Italian dictator and belongs in every public and academic library with a strong European history collection." Libr J

Includes bibliographical references

946 Spain, Andorra, Gibraltar, Portugal

Kamen, Henry

Philip of Spain. Yale Univ. Press 1997 384p il maps hardcover o.p. pa $18.95 **946**

1. Biography, Individual 2. Kings

ISBN 0-300-07081-0; 0-300-07800-5 pa

LC 96-52421

"Kamen's prose is lucid, succinct, and thorough. . . . In humanizing a man too often viewed as a cardboard tyrant, Kamen has made a valuable contribution to European historiography." Booklist

Includes bibliographical references

Kurlansky, Mark

The **Basque** history of the world. Penguin 2001 387p il map pa $15 **946**

ISBN 978-0-14-029851-2; 0-14-029851-7

"This book traces the history of the Basques from their mysterious origins to their politically fraught existence in this century. . . . Kurlansky shows how Basques, famed for their geographic and linguistic isolation, have played significant roles in world history--as mercenaries in ancient Greece, whalers in the Middle Ages, explorers in the Americas, and even cautious supporters of modern European integration." New Yorker

Lowney, Chris

A **vanished** world; medieval Spain's golden age of enlightenment. Free Press 2005 320p il map $26 **946**

1. Religion and politics -- Spain -- History

ISBN 0-7432-4359-5

LC 2004-56362

This is a history of Spain between the Muslim conquest in 711 and the driving of Muslims from Iberia in 1492, during which the author argues there was a tentative peace between Christians, Muslims, and Jews.

The author "successfully brings the story of medieval Spain to a wider audience and draws out of this rich history important lessons for the post-9/11 world." Christ Sci Monit

Includes bibliographical references

Tremlett, Giles

Ghosts of Spain; travels through Spain and its secret past. Walker 2007 386p $26.95   **946**

ISBN 0-8027-1574-5; 978-0-8027-1574-6

An "examination of the Franco years and their legacy make a somber backdrop for an otherwise cheery tale. Having summoned the ghosts, [the author] moves along to offer a guided tour of modern Spain, making stops at the usual journalistic destinations. The educational system, politics, health care, child rearing and the national character are dealt with in well-organized chapters that move the reader briskly along. . . . A highly informative, well-written introduction to post-Franco Spain." N Y Times (Late N Y Ed)

Spain: a history; edited by Raymond Carr. Oxford Univ. Press 2000 318p il hardcover o.p. pa $19.95   **946**

ISBN 0-19-820619-4; 978-0-19-280236-1 pa; 0-19-280236-4 pa

LC 99-42639

The essays in this volume present a journey through Spain's "entire history: from its prehistoric settlement through Roman, Visigothic, and Islamic rule, and from its golden age of exploration to the Spanish Civil War in the 1930s, Franco's resulting rule, the monarchy's reestablishment, Basque separatists, and modern Spain's political unrest." Booklist

Includes bibliographical references

946.081   Period of Second Republic, 1931-1939

Lewis, Norman

The **tomb** in Seville; crossing Spain on the brink of civil war. introduction by Julian Evans. Carroll & Graf 2005 150p $20; pa $14.95   **946.081**

ISBN 0-7867-1439-5; 0-7867-1687-8 pa

"Reading the author's account of his travels in a country on the brink of war is almost as satisfying as being there." Booklist

946.083   Reign of Juan Carlos I, 1975-

Stewart, Chris

Driving over lemons; an optimist in Andalucia. Pantheon Bks. 2000 248p il maps hardcover o.p. pa $13.95   **946.083**

1. Spain -- Description
ISBN 978-0-375-41028-4; 978-0-375-70915-9 pa; 0-375-70915-0 pa

LC 99-56675

"The ability to write hilarious travelogues featuring excruciating scenes of discomfort may well be a {British} national characteristic. It's certainly possessed by Chris Stewart." N Y Times Book Rev

947   Russia and neighboring east European countries

Borrero, Mauricio

★ **Russia**: a reference guide from the Renaissance to the present. Facts on File 2004 497p il map $85   **947**

1. Reference books
ISBN 0-8160-4454-6

LC 2003-60547

Alphabetically arranged entries cover "influential individuals, significant places, important policies . . . {and} various moments that have profoundly impacted the historical development of the country and its people." Publisher's note

Includes bibliographical references

Drakulic, Slavenka

Cafe Europa; life after communism. Penguin Books 1999 213p pa $14   **947**

ISBN 978-0-14-027772-2; 0-14-027772-2

The author of these pieces is "at once critical of a culture that remains bleakly conformist in the aftermath of Communist rule and empathetic for its having known nothing else. With consistent equanimity, she examines the frustrating plight of the novice Balkan democracies. On a more quotidian level, too, she finds that much is wanting, measured against Western standards of richesse, congeniality, and even taxi service. Owing largely to Drakulic's knack for drawing humor from an abundance of anecdotes—whether about a toothpaste monopoly or the bureaucratic cartwheels required to purchase a vacuum cleaner—these essays read like stories." New Yorker

Erickson, Carolly

Great Catherine. St. Martin's Griffin 1995 392p pa $18.95   **947**

1. Empresses
ISBN 0-312-13503-3

LC 95-22619

"Erickson's fluid, captivating portrait of Catherine the Great reads like a first-rate historical novel." Booklist

Figes, Orlando

The **Crimean** War; a history. Metropolitan Books 2010 576p il map $35; e-book $16.99 **947**

1. Crimean War, 1853-1856
ISBN 978-0-8050-7460-4; 0-8050-7460-0; 978-1-4299-9724-9 e-book; 1-4299-9724-9 e-book

LC 2010-23152

This "is a complex tale, told vividly by Mr Figes. Perhaps it should serve as a healthy cold shower for any modern civilisational warrior who sets out to present the course of history as a simple tug-of-war between Christianity and Islam." Economist

Includes bibliographical references

Hosking, Geoffrey A.

★ **Russia** and the Russians; a history. {by} Geoffrey Hosking. Belknap Press 2001 718p il map $35; pa $18.95 **947**

ISBN 0-674-00473-6; 0-674-01114-7 pa

LC 00-65085

"This is a high-quality overview, suitable for all libraries." Booklist

Russia: people and empire, 1552-1917; {by} Geoffrey Hosking. Harvard Univ. Press 1997 548p maps $33; pa $15.16 **947**

1. Russian national characteristics

ISBN 0-674-78118-X; 0-674-78119-8 pa

LC 97-5069

The author explores the question "of how and why the Russians never developed a sense of nation. He argues that the Russian monarchy and aristocracy were always more interested in building an expansive empire than in promoting the belief in nationhood, something understood by the powerless peasantry. The expensive and inefficient bureaucracy that emerged over the centuries weighed against any possibility of community, and in the end this tottering edifice was unable to withstand the cataclysm of World War I. Hosking has brought a powerful intellect and great erudition to this work." Libr J

Includes bibliographical references

King, David

Red star over Russia; a visual history of the Soviet Union from the revolution to the death of Stalin: posters, photographs and graphics from the David King collection. Abrams 2009 345p il $50 **947**

1. Russian art

ISBN 978-0-8109-8279-6; 0-8109-8279-X

In this survey "the graphics used to promote the workers' paradise deserve admiration. But the rest of this extraordinarily illustrated book provides witness to the corrosive effects of ham-handed propaganda, and to the role of state-sanctioned imagery in demeaning and subjugating the arts. Red Star Over Russia is a mammoth collection of rare Soviet applied art and photographs . . . organized not into individual chapters, but into pages and spreads devoted to a range of themes addressed in graphic and photographic materials, including 'Political Abstraction,' 'Urban Proletariat' and 'Workers of the World, Unite.' Prominent artists like El Lissitzky and Gustav Klutsis are featured." N Y Times Book Rev

Kotkin, Stephen

Uncivil society; 1989 and the implosion of the communist establishment. with a contribution by Jan T. Gross. Modern Library 2009 197p il map $24 **947**

1. Civil society -- Eastern Europe 2. Civil society -- Soviet Union 3. Social change -- Eastern Europe 4. Social change -- Soviet Union

ISBN 978-0-679-64276-3; 0-679-64276-5

LC 2009-12903

"Combining scholarship with sparkling prose, the authors recount a thoroughly satisfying historical struggle in which the good guys won." Publ Wkly

Includes bibliographical references

Massie, Robert K.

Catherine the Great; portrait of a woman. Robert K. Massie. Random House 2011 xiii, 625p ill. (some col.), maps **947**

1. Empresses

ISBN 9780679456728; 9781588360441

LC 2011015279

Presents a reconstruction of the eighteenth-century empress's life that covers her efforts to engage Russia in the cultural life of Europe, her creation of the Hermitage, and her numerous scandal-free romantic affairs.

"Massie delivers a fascinating account of dog-eat-dog politics in 18th-century Europe and the larger-than-life Russian empress who gave as good as she got." Kirkus

Includes bibliographical references

Massie, Suzanne

Land of the firebird; the beauty of old Russia. Hearttree 1980 493p il pa $32 **947**

1. Russian art

ISBN 978-0-9644184-1-7; 0-9644184-1-X

The author's intent "is to give 'a sense of the whole, now-vanished culture of old Russia . . . to describe that beauty which the Russians once knew how to create, what they loved, and admired and how they once lived and rejoiced.'" N Y Times Book Rev

Includes bibliographical references

Milner-Gulland, R. R.

Cultural atlas of Russia and the former Soviet Union; by Robin Milner-Gulland with Nikolai Dejevsky. rev ed; Checkmark Bks. 1998 240p il maps $50 **947**

ISBN 0-8160-3815-5

LC 98-29263

This survey of the civilizations of Russia and the former Soviet republics is divided into three parts: The geographical background, History, and Regions and countries of the former Soviet Union.

"Aimed at the general reader, the atlas is easy to use, informative, and entertaining." Choice {review of 1989 edition}

Includes bibliographical references

Pleshakov, Konstantin

There is no freedom without bread! 1989 and the civil war that brought down communism. [by] Constantine Pleshakov. Farrar, Straus, and Giroux 2009 289p $26 **947**

1. Anti-communist movements -- Eastern Europe 2. Anti-communist movements -- Soviet Union 3. Berlin Wall, Berlin, Germany, 1961-1989 4. Communism 5. Communism -- Eastern Europe 6. Communism -- Soviet Union

ISBN 978-0-374-28902-7; 0-374-28902-6

LC 2009-10185

The author's "explanation of the 1989 collapse respects the complexity of Eastern Europe, yet his account is both clear and beautifully lyrical. His greatest strength lies in not being burdened by doctrine; he finds worth in communists and in Reagan. . . . Pleshakov writes history with a human face." Washington Post Book World

Includes bibliographical references

Polonsky, Rachel

Molotov's magic lantern; travels in Russian history. Farrar, Straus and Giroux 2011 390p map $27; ebook $14.99   **947**

1. Authors, Russian   2. Cabinet members   3. Communism and literature   4. Communist leaders   5. Diplomats

ISBN 978-0-374-21197-4; 978-1-4299-7490-5 ebook
LC 2010-23037

Polonsky "has produced a spectacular and enjoyable display of intellectual fireworks for the general reader. . . . Her finely drawn literary travelogues on Taganrog, Murmansk, Vologda, Irkutsk and other places depict squalor, pomp, misery, exhilaration, heroism and brutishness, each cameo framed in its historical, cultural and physical context. . . . She has a knack for putting herself into other people's shoes with empathy and skill. . . . The author has grit, charm and style—and a gift for traveller's tales." Economist

Riasanovsky, Nicholas V.

A **history** of Russia; 8th ed; Oxford University Press 2011 various paging il map pa $64.95   **947**

ISBN 978-0-19-534197-3
LC 2010-23174

This narrative history includes discussions of economics, social organization, religion, and culture.

Sebestyen, Victor

Revolution 1989; the fall of the Soviet empire. Pantheon Books 2009 xxi, 451p il $30   **947**

ISBN 978-0-375-42532-5; 0-375-42532-2
LC 2009-23045

"Numerous books have come out that attempt to synthesize the compelling story of the fall of communism, but Revolution 1989 comes closest to being the essential volume. Sebestyen's elegant narrative lays out in crisp episodes what was happening in Russia, Bulgaria, East Germany, Hungary, Czechoslovakia, and Afghanistan throughout the tumultuous 1980s. His portrait of Gorbachev is particularly sharp—and asks us to reconsider the Soviet leader's surprising role 20 years ago. As a refugee from Hungary in 1956, Sebestyen brings a personal touch to these historic moments." Daily Beast

Includes bibliographical references

Volkov, Solomon

St. Petersburg; a cultural history. translated by Antonina W. Bouis. Free Press 1995 598p il hardcover o.p. pa $26.50   **947**

1. Authors   2. Choreographers   3. Composers   4. Dancers   5. Dramatists   6. Essayists   7. Nobel laureates for literature   8. Poets   9. Saint Petersburg (Russia) --

History
ISBN 0-684-83296-8 pa
LC 95-24116

Four of Volkov's "six very long chapters revolve around figures representative of certain periods or trends in the evolution of the St. Petersburg myth: Akhmatova, Balanchine, Shostakovich and Brodsky. Aspects of these central biographical and cultural portraits lead him . . . into countless mini-biographies of related figures." N Y Times Book Rev

Warnes, David

Chronicle of the Russian tsars; the reign-by-reign record of the rulers of imperial Russia. Thames & Hudson 1999 224p il $34.95   **947**

ISBN 0-500-05093-7
LC 98-61289

The introduction provides a "historical overview of how Tsarism came into being. The succeeding chapters are divided by major political events and social upheaval. . . . The reign of each tsar is analyzed within this framework, highlighting major events, but also giving abundant personal details such as marriages, children, etc." SLJ

Includes bibliographical references (p. 218-219) and index

947.08   Russia since 1855

Kurth, Peter

Tsar: the lost world of Nicholas and Alexandra; photographs by Peter Christopher. Little, Brown 1995 229p il hardcover o.p. pa $29.95   **947.08**

1. Biography, Individual   2. Emperors   3. Empresses
ISBN 0-316-50787-3; 0-316-55788-9 pa
LC 95-12820

In text and photographs, this volume examines the lives of Tsar Nicholas II, the Empress Alexandra, and the Russian Imperial family.

"A large format and a profusion of illustrations ostensibly mark it a picture book; instead it is a remarkably comprehensive overview of the reign of the last czar and his consort. . . . Kurth sensitively documents the imperial family's suffering as prisoners of the Bolsheviks and their eventual execution." Booklist

Includes bibliographical references

Massie, Robert K.

★ The **Romanovs**; the final chapter. Random House 1995 308p il hardcover o.p. pa $14.95 **947.08**

1. Emperors   2. Empresses   3. Forensic anthropology   4. Impostors   5. Royal pretenders
ISBN 0-394-58048-6; 0-345-40640-0 pa
LC 95-4718

This book "is divided into three major parts. The first segment—by far the most fascinating and original—focuses on the complex scientific process used in identifying the Romanovs' remains. . . . The second part concerns the various impostors who have claimed to be members of the Russian imperial family. . . . [The] third segment [is] a report on those Romanov émigrés—close relatives of the Czar's—who survived the Bolsheviks' persecution." N Y Times Book Rev

Includes bibliographical references

Pipes, Richard

The **Russian** Revolution. Knopf 1990 xxiv, 944p il maps hardcover o.p. pa $25   **947.08**
ISBN 0-679-73660-3 pa

LC 89-35129

This is a "massive, wonderfully vivid, gripping chronicle. . . . No other book so brilliantly clarifies the inner dynamics of the Russian Revolution." Publ Wkly

Includes bibliographical references

947.084   1917-1991

Amis, Martin

Koba the dread; laughter and the twenty million. Hyperion 2002 306p il $24.95   **947.084**
1. Communist leaders 2. Heads of state 3. Political leaders 4. Political persecution -- Soviet Union 5. Terrorism -- Soviet Union
ISBN 0-7868-6876-7

"Amis create{s} a compelling narrative, summarizing vast amounts of information and presenting it in a lucid, accessible form." New York Times

Brent, Jonathan

Stalin's last crime; the plot against the Jewish doctors, 1948-1953. {by} Jonathan Brent and Vladimir P. Naumov. HarperCollins 2003 399p $26.95; pa $14.95   **947.084**
1. Communist leaders 2. Heads of state 3. Jewish physicians -- Soviet Union 4. Jews -- Persecutions 5. Jews -- Persecutions -- Soviet Union 6. Jews -- Soviet Union 7. Political leaders
ISBN 0-06-019524-X; 0-06-093310-0 pa

LC 2002-191930

"This book points out suspicious inconsistencies in official accounts of Stalin's death and fingers chief of secret police Beria as a likely assassin. . . . Brent and Naumov link Stalin's famously anti-Semitic 'Doctors' Plot,' in which Jewish doctors were unjustly accused of conspiring to murder important politicians, to the ridiculous 'plan of the internal blow,' another alleged conspiracy of officials supposedly aiding an American plan to nuke the Kremlin itself. The authors argue that these Stalin-engineered plots were to be used by the paranoid dictator as justification for nuclear war. Tales of Stalin's paranoia are nothing new, but rarely are his subtle, yet relentless, machinations laid out in such intricate detail." Booklist

Includes bibliographical references

Figes, Orlando

A **people's** tragedy; the Russian Revolution, 1891-1924. Viking 1997 xx, 923p hardcover o.p. pa $25   **947.084**
ISBN 0-14-024364-X pa

LC 96-36761

The author has "produced an engagingly written and well-researched book that will leave few readers with any doubts that the Bolsheviks, and especially their leader, Lenin, were ruthless killers, willing to sacrifice millions of lives for the sake of power and their own personal ambitions." N Y Times Book Rev

Includes bibliographical references

★ The **whisperers**; private life in Stalin's Russia. Metropolitan Books 2007 xxxviii, 739p il map $35   **947.084**
1. Communism -- Soviet Union 2. Communism -- Soviet Union -- History
ISBN 978-0-8050-7461-1; 0-8050-7461-9

LC 2007-24223

"This is a humbling monument to the evil and endurance of Russia's Soviet past and, implicitly, a guide to its present." Economist

Includes bibliographical references

Hochschild, Adam

The **unquiet** ghost; Russians remember Stalin. Houghton Mifflin 2003 304p il map pa $14.95   **947.084**
1. Communist leaders 2. Heads of state 3. Political leaders
ISBN 978-0-618-25747-8; 0-618-25747-0

In this look at Stalin's legacy the author "visits the ruins of the old prison camps of Kazakhstan and Kolyma, digs through the K.G.B. archives and spends a night at Stalin's seaside retreat. Most important, he interviews camp survivors, camp guards and the children of both. The questions he asks are of universal significance. . . . By asking these questions while traveling through today's Russia, Mr. Hochschild effectively places Stalinism in a modern context." N Y Times Book Rev

Includes bibliographical references

McMeekin, Sean

History's greatest heist; the looting of Russia by the Bolsheviks. Yale University Press 2009 302p il $38   **947.084**
1. Finance, Public -- Soviet Union -- History 2. Pillage -- Soviet Union -- History 3. Public finance
ISBN 9780300135589

LC 2008-22100

"After the October Revolution, the Bolsheviks were enmeshed in a civil war and desperate for funds for everything from guns and boots for soldiers to a luxury car for Lenin. In theory, they had at their disposal the riches of the deposed Tsar, including one of the world's great reserves of gold. But the gold was the security for Russia's national debt, and most of Europe didn't recognize the new regime or its right to the treasury anyway. . . . What followed, McMeekin writes, was a 'gold-laundering boom,' involving art-thieving commissars, double-dealing smugglers, and a surprisingly nefarious cast of Swedes." New Yorker

Includes bibliographical references

Medvedev, Roy Aleksandrovich

★ **Let** history judge; the origins and consequences of Stalinism. {by} Roy Medvedev. rev and expanded ed; Columbia Univ. Press 1989 xxi, 903p $104; pa $35   **947.084**
1. Communist leaders 2. Heads of state 3. Political crimes and offenses 4. Political leaders 5. Soviet

Union -- Politics and government -- 1925-1953

ISBN 0-231-06350-4; 0-231-06351-2 pa

LC 89-758

"Never have Stalin's crimes against humanity been more forcefully or more thoroughly documented than in . . . {this book, which} distills firsthand testimonies of the mass arrests, torture, imprisonment and executions that befell millions of innocent Soviet citizens." Publ Wkly

Includes bibliographical references

Pipes, Richard

Russia under the Bolshevik regime. Vintage Books 1995 587p il map pa $21   **947.084**

1. Communist leaders 2. Heads of state 3. Political leaders 4. Revolutionaries

ISBN 978-0-679-76184-6; 0-679-76184-5

"In this sequel to The Russian Revolution Pipes persuasively argues that Lenin's one-party dictatorship, through its terrorizing, suppression of the press, censorship and monopolistic control of cultural organizations, set the stage for Stalin's genocidal totalitarianism. . . . Pipes shows how both Hitler and Mussolini drew on Lenin's tyrannical methods, and he perceptively analyzes the mindset of Western fellow-travelers who wove fantasies of the U.S.S.R. as an egalitarian Eden while rationalizing its evils." Publ Wkly

Includes bibliographical references

A **concise** history of the Russian Revolution. Knopf 1995 431p il maps hardcover o.p. pa $16   **947.084**

ISBN 0-679-74544-0 pa

LC 95-3127

"Forcefully showing why the 70-year-old Communist experiment failed {Pipes} provides the nonacademic reader with accurate historical events in a highly readable format." Libr J

Includes bibliographical references

Reed, John

Ten days that shook the world. Penguin Books 2007 368p pa $12   **947.084**

ISBN 978-0-14-144212-9; 0-14-144212-3

"A reportorial, firsthand, and sympathetic account of the November Revolution in Russia (1917). . . . After prefatory explanation of political groups and other organizations, and of the background of the uprising, the work tells with graphic detail of the fall of the provisional government, the revolution and counterrevolution, the solidifying of power, and the resultant congress." Oxford Companion to Am Lit. 5th edition

Service, Robert

Lenin--a biography. Harvard Univ. Press 2000 xxv, 561p il maps $38.95; pa $19.95   **947.084**

1. Communist leaders 2. Heads of state 3. Heads of state -- Soviet Union -- Biography 4. Political leaders 5. Revolutionaries 6. Revolutionaries -- Russia -- Biography

ISBN 0-674-00330-6; 0-674-00828-6 pa

LC 00-21394

This biography focuses "on Lenin the man. It draws on a wealth of new material to provide a subtle and complex

portrait. . . . In particular, Service's account adds much to our knowledge of Lenin's early years and his final years as a man cut down by a series of strokes. . . . It is lucidly written, sharply observed, full of good sense, packed with vivid anecdote and, above all, succeeds—where so many have failed—in creating a Lenin who is believably human." Hist Today

Includes bibliographical references

A **history** of twentieth-century Russia. Harvard Univ. Press 1998 xxxiii, 653p il maps $32.50; pa $20.95   **947.084**

1. Russia (Federation) -- History 2. Soviet Union -- History -- 20th century

ISBN 0-674-40347-9; 0-674-40348-7 pa

LC 97-37440

"A perceptive, judicious appraisal." Booklist

Includes bibliographical references

Volkogonov, Dmitrii Antonovich

Lenin; a new biography. {by} Dmitri Volkogonov; translated and edited by Harold Shukman. Free Press 1994 xxxix, 529p il $30   **947.084**

1. Biography, Individual 2. Communist leaders 3. Heads of state 4. Political leaders 5. Revolutionaries

ISBN 0-02-933435-7

LC 94-31752

"The author draws heavily on newly declassified KGB archives that he oversees as special assistant to President Boris Yeltsin. . . . Volkogonov's narrative is indispensable for understanding the Bolshevik coup, their crushing of the democratic opposition and the tragic aftermath." Publ Wkly

Includes bibliographical references

Competing voices from the Russian Revolution; edited by Michael C. Hickey. Greenwood 2011 xiii, 599p ill. Fighting Words (alk. paper) $65.00   **947.084**

1. Social conflict -- Soviet Union -- History -- Sources

ISBN 9780313385230; 0313385238; 9780313385247; 0313385246

LC 2010039676

This book presents documents that underscore the . . . public discussion about key events and issues during the 1917 Russian Revolution, one of the pivotal events in modern history. . . . [T]he documents . . . clarify the issues while revealing the broad range of ways in which Russians understood the events unfolding around them. Focusing on public rhetoric and debate in Russia from the outbreak of World War I in 1914 through the dissolution of the Constituent Assembly in January 1918, the documents present the views not only of key political figures, but also of ordinary men and women—mothers, soldiers, factory workers, peasants, students, businesspeople, and educated professionals.m (Publisher s note)

947.085   1953-1991

Carlson, Peter
K blows top; a Cold War comic interlude starring Nikita Khrushchev, America's most unlikely tourist. PublicAffairs 2009 327p il $26.95   **947.085**
   1. Cold War 2. Cold war 3. Communist leaders 4. Heads of state 5. Political leaders
   ISBN 9781586484972; 1-58648-497-4
               LC 2008-39090
Recounts Khrushchev's 1959 trip across America against the backdrop of the Cold War and a capitalist America living under the shadow of the hydrogen bomb.

"Drawing on contemporary news reports, modern interviews, and memoirs written by some of the participants, [this is] . . . a story about a poorly educated but extraordinarily powerful man who became, for a brief time, a pop-culture icon. . . . A fine example of popular history at its most engaging—anecdotal but informative and written with great feeling for the comedic side of current events." Booklist
Includes bibliographical references

Gorbachev, Mikhail
On my country and the world; {by} Gorbachev. Columbia Univ. Press 1999 300p $50; pa $17.95   **947.085**
   1. World politics -- 1965-
   ISBN 0-231-11514-8; 0-231-11515-6 pa
               LC 99-31273
The former Soviet leader presents an analysis of his country's Communist past and an account of his role in government in the 1980s. Gorbachev also includes ideas for political change.

Gorbachev is "fresh and candid in its initial section on the pluses and minuses of the Revolution of 1917." Nation

Remnick, David
★ **Lenin's** tomb; Russia and the fall of Communism. Random House 1993 576p hardcover o.p. pa $15.95   **947.085**
   ISBN 0-679-75125-4 pa
               LC 92-56841
"This book is a record of almost four years beginning in 1988 when David Remnick, a Washington Post reporter, was assigned to Moscow. . . . He argues convincingly that what did in the old Soviet leadership, right down through Mikhail Gorbachev, was its unending assault not only on people but on memory. By making a secret of history, it made its people increasingly distracted, and desperate, until they overthrew it." N Y Times Book Rev

Satter, David
Age of delirium; the decline and fall of the Soviet Union. Yale University Press 2001 424p pa $30   **947.085**
   ISBN 0-300-08705-5; 978-0-300-08705-5
The author "appraises the Russians by writing about the travails of average people in the last decade of Soviet rule. Objects of the Communist ideology's enforced unanimity, his subjects include dissidents sent to psychiatric wards, persecuted religious people, a TASS journalist learning how to write the party line, and miners exploited by the work-

ers' state. . . . An insightful from-the-ground-up view of typical Russians whom the top-down politicians are now courting." Booklist

Stokes, Gale
The **walls** came tumbling down; the collapse of communism in Eastern Europe. Oxford Univ. Press 1993 319p hardcover o.p. pa $31.95   **947.085**
   1. Communism 2. Communism -- Eastern Europe
   ISBN 0-19-506644-8; 0-19-506645-6 pa
               LC 92-44862
This book "can be recommended as a coherent, well-written history that defines its time frame well, provides sound coverage, makes prudent judgments, and wears its analysis lightly. . . . Stokes's overview traces the ebb and flow of personalities and events in a manner that is both accessible to lay readers and informative to scholars." Libr J

947.086   -1991

Baker, Peter
Kremlin rising; Vladimir Putin's Russia and the end of revolution. [by] Peter Baker and Susan Glasser. Scribner 2005 453p il $27.50   **947.086**
   1. Presidents 2. Prime ministers
   ISBN 0-743-26431-2
               LC 2005-44157
The authors chronicle the transformation of contemporary Russia under President Vladimir Putin.

"Well written, well reported and well organized, the book consists of freestanding chapters that touch on the most important events and trends in contemporary Russia, from the war in Chechnya to the spread of AIDS and the dire state of the Russian judicial system." N Y Times (Late N Y Ed)
Includes bibliographical references

Brent, Jonathan
Inside the Stalin archives; discovering the new Russia. Atlas & Company 2008 335p il $26 **947.086**
   1. Archives -- Soviet Union 2. Communist leaders 3. Heads of state 4. Political leaders 5. Publishing executives
   ISBN 978-0-9777-4333-9; 0-9777-4333-0
This work, which draws upon the author's fifteen years of unprecedented access to high-level Soviet Archives, "reveals as much about the grim realities of post-Soviet life and bureaucracy as it does about the archives themselves. Equipped with little Russian and few contacts, but with an almost palpable sense of decency and honest intentions that illuminate his book, Brent explains for the general reader as well as for specialists how he went about his work in the new Russia." N Y Times Book Rev

Lieven, Anatol
Chechnya; tombstone of Russian power. with photographs by Heidi Bradner. Yale Univ. Press 1998 436p il $55; pa $28   **947.086**
   ISBN 0-300-07398-4; 0-300-07881-1 pa
               LC 98-84479

"The book is a great, ostentatiously erudite festival of ideas, sometimes brilliant, sometimes dubious, but never less than interesting." N Y Times Book Rev

Meier, Andrew

Black earth; a journey through Russia after the fall. Norton 2003 511p il map $28.95; pa $15.95   **947.086**
1. Journalists 2. Post-communism -- Russia (Federation)
ISBN 0-393-05178-1; 0-393-32641-1 pa
LC 2003-6562
"After talking to scores of people—from survivors of the Aldy massacre to a harrowed Russian lieutenant colonel who runs the body-collection point closest to the Chechen battleground—Meier paints in this heartbreaking book a devastating picture of contemporary life in a country where, as one man put it, people have 'lived like the lowest dogs for more than eighty years.'" Publ Wkly
Includes bibliographical references

Politkovskaya, Anna

A **Russian** diary; a journalist's final account of life, corruption, and death in Putin's Russia. translated by Arch Tait; foreword by Scott Simon. Random House 2007 369p map $25.95   **947.086**
1. Biography, Individual 2. Journalists 3. Presidents 4. Prime ministers
ISBN 1-4000-6682-4; 978-1-4000-6682-7
LC 2007-296943
These are the journals kept by the Russian journalist who was killed in Moscow in 2006.
This is a "brilliant . . . portrayal of Russian life during the middle years of Putin's rule." New York Rev Books

Remnick, David

★ **Resurrection**; the struggle for a new Russia. Random House 1997 398p hardcover o.p. pa $15   **947.086**
ISBN 0-375-75023-1 pa
LC 96-47360
In this companion volume to Lenin's tomb, "Remnick concentrates on the post-Soviet scene and its prospects. . . . Chaotic uncertainty, massive corruption, and crime are notoriously present, yet the possibility of a different, better life also beckons. . . . This is an interesting, highly informative portrait of a country struggling toward a fateful future." Libr J
Includes bibliographical references

Richards, Susan

Lost and found in Russia; lives in a post-Soviet landscape. Other Press 2010 544p pa $15.95; ebook $15.95   **947.086**
ISBN 978-1-59051-348-4 pa; 978-1-59051-369-9 ebook
"During many trips from 1992 to 1998, Richards . . . traveled to visit friends in Russia, particularly in the southwestern towns of Saratov and Marx. . . . She fashions the narrative around the friends she met and lived with closely. Vera, follower of the Vissarion cult, was an inhabitant of Saratov, once called the Athens of the Volga, now a forsaken place closed to foreigners because of its military industry

(presently defunct). In Marx, once the nexus of the Russian Germans, Richards stayed with Anna, a tensely coiled journalist—a pravednik, or 'truth bearer'—who had been punished for her honest writing; the volatile couple Natasha and Igor, lured to the dead-end town by Gorbachev's promise of a German homeland, now mostly unemployed and alcoholic; and the couple Misha and Tatiana, marooned in Marx after their engineering training, who became thriving entrepreneurs and part of the rising Russian middle class. . . . Other trips took her through Siberia and the Crimea to view the residues of Russian Orthodoxy, the Old Believers and folksy spiritualism. A patiently crafted glimpse 'through a crack in the wardrobe' of the devastation wrought on Russian society during the turbulent post-Communist '90s." Kirkus

Treisman, Daniel

The **return**; Russia's journey from Gorbachev to Medvedev. Free Press 2011 523p il $30; ebook $14.99   **947.086**
ISBN 978-1-4165-6071-5; 1-4165-6071-8; 978-1-4516-0574-7 ebook; 1-4516-0574-9 ebook; 1416560718; 1451605749 ebook; 978141656071-5; 9781451605747 ebook
LC 2010011520
"The politics and economics of post-Communist Russia occupy this survey of the past two decades. Treisman . . . works commentary about Russia's successive leaders—Gorbachev, Yeltsin, Putin, and Medvedev—into the problems they confronted. . . . Encompassing foreign policy and Russian public opinion, Treisman's knowledgeable presentation is a reliable current-affairs source for Russia's economic revival and reassertion in international affairs." Booklist

947.5   Caucasus

Baiev, Khassan

The **Oath**; a surgeon under fire. [by] Khassan Baiev; with Ruth and Nicholas Daniloff. Walker & Co. 2003 376p il $26   **947.5**
1. Chechnia (Russia) -- History -- Civil War, 1994- -- Personal narratives, Chechen 2. Human rights activists 3. Memoirists 4. Surgeons 5. Surgeons -- Russia (Federation) -- Chechnia (Russia) -- Biography
ISBN 0-8027-1404-8
LC 2003-52502
The author "is modest, which only adds to his heroism. But more than that, he has humanized the Chechens, whom others have portrayed as terrorists. Russian president Vladimir Putin has tried to equate Russia's fight against the Chechens with the U.S. battle against al-Qaida. Those who read this stirring memoir will be hard-pressed to see the situation so simply." Publ Wkly

Seierstad, Asne

The **angel** of Grozny; orphans of a forgotten war. translated by Nadia Christensen. Basic Books 2008 340p $25.95   **947.5**
1. Journalists
ISBN 978-0-465-01122-3; 0-465-01122-5
LC 2008-925222

In the early hours of New Year's 1994, Russian troops invaded the Republic of Chechnya, plunging the country into a prolonged and bloody conflict that continues to this day. A foreign correspondent in Moscow at the time, Asne Seierstad traveled regularly to Chechnya to report on the war, describing its affects on those trying to live their daily lives amidst violence.

"Seierstad's searing, evocative recounting brings Chechnya to life, especially the unimaginable suffering and strength of the Chechen people. Powerful, painful, and raw, . . . [this] is essential reading." Booklist

947.7 Ukraine

King, Charles

Odessa; genius and death in a city of dreams. W.W. Norton & Co. 2011 336p il map $27.95 **947.7**
1. Jews -- Ukraine 2. Jews -- Ukraine -- Odessa -- History
ISBN 9780393070842; 0-393-07084-0

LC 2010-38000

This is a "finely written and evocative portrait of the city. . . . [Its] detail, coupled with a fine feel for the sweep of history . . . makes this book a worthy tribute to one of Europe's greatest and least-known cities." Economist
Includes bibliographical references

947.98 Estonia

Theroux, Alexander

Estonia: a ramble through the periphery. Fantagraphics Books 2011 351p il $29.99 **947.98**
ISBN 978-1-60699-465-8; 1-60699-465-4

Theroux "follows his wife, Sarah, to [Estonia] in 2008, where she paints on her Fulbright grant scenes of its stolid towns. Brother of the equally waspish travel writer Paul, Alexander Theroux, meanwhile, skulks, fulminates, studies, and walks wherever he can, soaking up the frigid atmosphere of its people. . . . He deploys bombast, overkill, and ridicule to pepper his perennial pop-up targets of greed, lassitude, and stupidity. He includes here his caustic if characteristic habit of lists, ruminations, and rants. For all his predilection for careful observation of how people look, sound, and move, he inflates, if maybe in sly self-deprecation, the impact others have on him—rather than vice versa. . . . Full of endnotes, translating many phrases he quotes in their original languages, and graced by a few of the couple's photos and Sarahs plein air oil paintings, this provides a suitably quirky introduction to Theroux as an essayist and critic." PopMatters

948 Scandinavia

Ferguson, Robert

The **Vikings**; a history. Viking 2009 450p il map **948**
1. Vikings
ISBN 978-0-670-02079-9

LC 2009-26818

"Ferguson's scholarly study requires close attention, but the intellectual rewards are plentiful. Provides a significant deepening of our knowledge of the Vikings." Kirkus
Includes bibliographical references

Roesdahl, Else

The **Vikings**; translated by Susan M. Margeson and Kirsten Williams. 2nd ed; Penguin Books 1998 324p il map pa $17 **948**
1. Vikings
ISBN 0-14-025282-7; 978-0-14-025282-8

A survey of Viking civilization from c.750-c.1050.

"About one-third of the book deals with Viking expansion into Russia, Normandy, the British Isles, Iceland, Greenland, etc. . . . Most of the book surveys the geography, people, society, religion, art, etc., of the Vikings' Scandinavian homelands." Libr J
Includes bibliographical references

The **Oxford illustrated history of the Vikings**; edited by Peter Sawyer. Oxford Univ. Press 1997 298p il maps hardcover o.p. pa $27.50 **948**
1. Vikings
ISBN 0-19-820526-0; 0-19-285434-8 pa

LC 97-16649

This illustrated collection of articles includes discussion of the Vikings' impact on England, Iceland, Greenland, Russia, and the Frankish and Danish Empires; Viking ships and ship-building; Viking religion; and the ways in which Vikings have been portrayed throughout history. Significant archaeological finds are featured.

948.97 Finland

Beach, Hugh

A **year** in Lapland; guest of the reindeer herders. with a new afterword by the author. University of Washington Press 2001 242p il map pa $25 **948.97**
1. Sami (European people)
ISBN 0-295-98037-0; 978-0-295-98037-9

LC 00-47936

The author "tells of his first year among the Saami reindeer herders of Swedish Lapland. His narrative interweaves adventure, descriptions of the harsh beauty of the landscape, supernatural tales and ancient myths. Beach also explores topics of change in the lives of the herders brought on by laws requiring village groups to move and by adaptations to new items such as rubber boots, seaplanes, and appliances." Libr J

Edwards, Robert

The **Winter** War; Russia's invasion of Finland, 1939-1940. Pegasus Books 2008 319p il map $27.95 **948.97**
1. Russo-Finnish War, 1939-1940 2. World War, 1939-1945 -- Finland
ISBN 978-1-933648-50-7

"A brisk, efficient account of one of the most overlooked episodes of World War II. . . . Highly readable and informative." Kirkus
Includes bibliographical references

949.2   Netherlands

Schama, Simon

The **embarrassment** of riches; an interpretation of Dutch culture in the Golden Age. Knopf 1987 698p il maps hardcover o.p. pa $23   **949.2**
    ISBN 0-679-78124-2 pa

                        LC 86-45418

"Delving into customs, beliefs, popular art and quirks of behavior, Schama has fashioned a tour de force, a profound, unconventional and rewarding portrait of a people." Publ Wkly

    Includes bibliographical references

949.5   Greece

Brownworth, Lars

    Lost to the West; the forgotten Byzantine Empire that rescued Western civilization. Crown Publishers 2009 329p map $26; pa $15   **949.5**
    ISBN 978-0-307-40795-5; 978-0-307-40796-2 pa

    "Brownworth delivers just enough of the big picture for interested readers to pursue specific events in greater detail. An energetic look at a still-misunderstood period in late antiquity." Kirkus

    Includes bibliographical references

Clogg, Richard

    A **concise** history of Greece; 2nd ed; Cambridge Univ. Press 2002 291p il maps $53; pa $19 **949.5**
    ISBN 0-521-80872-3; 0-521-00479-9 pa

                        LC 2002-725551

    This is an illustrated introduction to the history of modern Greece from the late eighteenth century to the present.

Mazower, Mark

    Salonica, city of ghosts; Christians, Muslims, and Jews, 1430-1950. Knopf 2005 490p il maps $35   **949.5**
    ISBN 0-375-41298-0

                        LC 2004-57690

    This is a history of the Greek city.

    The author's "graceful, evocative prose, his deft attention to details and his empathetic presentation of all sides of the story add up to a magnificent tale of this unique city." Publ Wkly

    Includes bibliographical references

Norwich, John Julius

    Byzantium: the apogee. Knopf 1991 xxiv, 389p il map $49.95   **949.5**
    ISBN 0-394-53779-3

                        LC 91-53119

    This is the second volume of a three-volume narrative history of the Byzantine Empire. "Beginning with Charlemagne's coronation in 800 A.D. and the resulting split in the Christian world, Norwich traces the return of iconoclasm, political intrigues, military campaigns, atrocities, and alliances, ending with the fateful battle at Nanzikert from

which the Empire never recovered. . . . [The author] deftly brings to life the frozen icons of the history books." Libr J

    Includes bibliographical references

    Byzantium: the decline and fall. Knopf 1995 xxxvii, 488p il maps $49.95   **949.5**
    ISBN 0-679-41650-1

    This final volume of the author's three volume narrative history chronicles the last four centuries of the Byzantine Empire.

    Byzantium: the early centuries. Knopf 1989 407p il $49.95   **949.5**
    ISBN 0-394-53778-5

                        LC 88-45508

    This is the first of a three-volume narrative history of the Byzantine Empire. It traces Byzantium's history "from the birth of Constantine c.274 to the coronation of Charlemagne on Christmas Day 800." Libr J

    Includes bibliographical references

    ★ A **short** history of Byzantium. Knopf 1997 430p il maps hardcover o.p. pa $17.95   **949.5**
    ISBN 0-679-77269-3 pa

                        LC 96-44458

    "In his shorter telling of the history between the founding of Constantinople in 330 and its fall in 1453, Lord Norwich has sacrificed none of the virtues of the longer work: lively narration and a taste for the eccentric anecodote and revelatory detail." N Y Times Book Rev

949.6   Balkan Peninsula

Pamuk, Orhan

    Istanbul; memories and the city. translated from the Turkish by Maureen Freely. Knopf 2005 384p il $26.95   **949.6**
    1. Authors 2. Nobel laureates for literature 3. Novelists
    ISBN 1-400-04095-7

                        LC 2004-61537

    The novelist writes about his life as a resident of Istanbul.

    "The author mingles 'personal memoir with cultural history', and a fascinating read it is too for anyone who has even the slightest acquaintance with this fabled bridge between east and west." Economist

949.7   Serbia, Croatia, Slovenia, Bosnia and Hercegovina, Montenegro, Macedonia

Di Giovanni, Janine

    Madness visible; a memoir of war. Knopf 2003 285p map hardcover o.p. pa $14   **949.7**
    1. Journalists 2. Kosovo (Serbia) -- History -- Civil War, 1998- 3. War -- Psychological aspects
    ISBN 0-375-41073-2; 978-0-375-72455-8 pa; 0-375-72455-9 pa

                        LC 2002-44820

    This "narrative of the 1999 war in Kosovo, NATO's campaign against Serbia, and the ouster of Milosevic offers an unbiased view of the enormous suffering of Yugoslav Albanians and Serbs following the genocidal rage of the Belgrade regime against the Kosovo Liberation Army's (KLA) drive for an independent Kosovo. . . . This exciting work is highly recommended for all libraries." Libr J

Includes bibliographical references

Rieff, David
Slaughterhouse; Bosnia and the failure of the West. Simon & Schuster 1995 240p hardcover o.p. pa $18.95　　**949.7**
　1. Yugoslav War, 1991-1995
　ISBN 0-684-81903-1 pa

　　　　　　　　　　　　LC 94-40148
This account of the war in the former Yugoslavia grew out of Rieff's travels in the region from 1992 through 1994.

"Slaughterhouse is perhaps the most powerful, passionate, and penetrating dissection of a Westerner of the ongoing Bosnian tragedy." Booklist

Rohde, David
Endgame; the betrayal and fall of Srebrenica, Europe's worst massacre since World War II. Westview Press 1998 450p il pa $20　　**949.7**
　1. Yugoslav War, 1991-1995
　ISBN 0-8133-3533-7; 978-0-8133-3533-9

　　　　　　　　　　　　LC 98-26127
"Rohde argues that the fall of Srebrenica could have been prevented, but he is ultimately unable to explain the 'collective failure' of the United States, the United Nations, and NATO in stopping the massacre. His investigation is carefully documented by over 300 footnotes. This is an important and revealing book." Libr J

Includes bibliographical references

Silber, Laura
★ **Yugoslavia;** death of a nation. {by} Laura Silber and Allan Little. rev and updated ed; Penguin Bks. 1997 403p il maps pa $15　　**949.7**
　1. Yugoslav War, 1991-1995
　ISBN 0-14-026263-6

　　　　　　　　　　　　LC 96-36086
This book, a companion volume to a BBC television series called The Death of Yugoslavia, chronicles the disintegration of the Socialist Federal Republic of Yugoslavia in 1991 and charts the development of the ensuing conflict.

This is "an impressive achievement. Strong on characters, regional nuances, and the 'inner' diplomatic game, 'Yugoslavia' is a work of depth and breadth that will be hard to eclipse. It answers many perplexities left from five years of Balkan intrigues and war." Christ Sci Monit {review of 1996 edition}

West, Richard
Tito; and the rise and fall of Yugoslavia. Carroll & Graf Pubs. 1995 436p il hardcover o.p. pa $15.95　　**949.7**
　1. Biography, Individual 2. Communist leaders 3. Heads of state 4. Political leaders
　ISBN 0-7867-0332-6 pa

　　　　　　　　　　　　LC 95-10404

This biography "describes Tito's rise to power, his creation of the Partisan Army during the Axis occupation, his consolidation of southern Slavs after the war and establishment of a Communist Yugoslavia, the break with Stalin in 1948, Tito's subsequent rivalry with the Soviet bloc and his leadership of nonaligned states. . . . The book also clarifies the present three-way conflict among Serbs, Croats and Muslims." Publ Wkly

Includes bibliographical references

949.702　Yugoslavia, 1918-1991

Maass, Peter
Love thy neighbor; a story of war. Knopf 1996 305p hardcover o.p. pa $14　　**949.702**
　1. Yugoslav War, 1991-1995
　ISBN 0-679-76389-9 pa

　　　　　　　　　　　　LC 95-39250
This book on the Yugoslav conflict is based on Maass's experiences as the Washington Post's reporter in Bosnia.

"Maass was only in Bosnia for about a year, from 1992 to 1993, but he saw a great deal. And he displays extraordinary sensitivity to the ambiguities of his position." Nation

Includes bibliographical references

949.703　Period as sovereign nations, 1991-

Clark, Wesley K.
★ **Waging** modern war; Bosnia, Kosovo, and the future of combat. PublicAffairs 2001 xxxi, 479p il map hardcover o.p. pa $18　　**949.703**
　1. Kosovo (Serbia) -- History 2. Kosovo (Serbia) -- History -- Civil War, 1998-1999 -- Personal narratives, American 3. Yugoslav War, 1991-1995 4. Yugoslav War, 1991-1995 -- Bosnia and Hercegovina 5. Yugoslav War, 1991-1995 -- Personal narratives, American
　ISBN 1-58648-139-8 pa

　　　　　　　　　　　　LC 01-19717
This is an account of the former Supreme Allied Commander's experiences during the Kosovo crises. "Clark tells a story of frustration with NATO allies, who had to approve each operation and target selection, and with U.S. policymakers as he tried to formulate a strategy that would achieve his military goals." Libr J

949.71　Serbia

McAllester, Matthew
Beyond the Mountains of the Damned; the war inside Kosovo. New York Univ. Press 2002 227p il $30; pa $17.95　　**949.71**
　1. Kosovo (Serbia) -- History 2. Pec (Serbia) -- History, Military -- 20th century
　ISBN 0-8147-5660-3; 0-8147-5661-1 pa

　　　　　　　　　　　　LC 2001-4370

"McAllester's spare, understated prose . . . is potent, as is his exploration of the human side of geopolitics and war." Publ Wkly

Includes bibliographical references

950 History of Asia

Fallows, James M.

Looking at the sun; {by} James Fallows. Pantheon Bks. 1994 517p hardcover o.p. pa $15 **950**

ISBN 0-679-76162-4 pa

LC 93-38367

"A fascinating, fresh, and potentially controversial contemplation of the global market." Booklist

Higham, Charles

Encyclopedia of ancient Asian civilizations; [by] Charles F.W. Higham. Facts on File 2004 xxi, 440p il map $85 **950**

1. Asia -- Civilization -- Encyclopedias 2. Reference books

ISBN 0-8160-4640-9

LC 2003-48513

"This is a good beginning point for research, especially in regard to archaeological excavations." Booklist

Includes bibliographical references

Levinson, David

Encyclopedia of modern Asia; {by} David Levinson, Karen Christensen. Scribner 2002 6v il maps set $695 **950**

1. Asia -- Encyclopedias 2. Reference books

ISBN 0-684-80617-7

LC 2002-8712

This "set is alphabetically arranged by topic. Volume 6 provides the index for the set. . . . The topics cover the 33 Asian countries' geography, economics, politics, human rights, cultures and languages, and biographies. Sidebars derived from primary source materials and black-and-white illustrations are interspersed throughout the text." Am Ref Books Annu, 2003

Includes bibliographical references

951 China and adjacent areas

Atwood, Christopher Pratt

Encyclopedia of Mongolia and the Mongol empire; [by] Christopher P. Atwood. Facts on File 2004 678p il map $85 **951**

ISBN 0-8160-4671-9

LC 2003-61696

"Coverage is good for all time periods, and the encyclopedia as a whole makes a sound case for the enormous influence of Mongolian civilization on the history of the Far East, the Indian subcontinent, and Eastern Europe." Booklist

Includes bibliographical references

Chetham, Deirdre

Before the deluge; the vanishing world of the Yangtze's Three Gorges. Palgrave 2002 xxiii, 296p il map hardcover o.p. pa $17.95 **951**

ISBN 1-4039-6428-9 pa

LC 2002-16939

The author "paints a pulsating picture of the great river, the countryside, the people and their occupations, the amazingly fluid political philosophies and the sheer endurance of all parties, past and present, involved with the overwhelming project." Publ Wkly

Includes bibliographical references

Dalai Lama

My Tibet; text by His Holiness the fourteenth Dalai Lama of Tibet; photographs and introduction by Galen Rowell. University of Calif. Press 1990 162p il hardcover o.p. pa $34.95 **951**

1. Buddhism 2. Tibet (China) -- Pictorial works

ISBN 0-520-08948-0 pa

LC 90-10868

This is "a volume of photographs taken in recent years by Galen Rowell, with a text drawn from interviews with the Dalai Lama or essays written previously by him." N Y Times Book Rev

Dalle, Eric

Facts about China; edited by Xiao-bin Ji; contributors, Eric Dalle. Wilson, H.W. 2003 751p map $105 **951**

ISBN 0-8242-0961-3

LC 2001-45510

This "reference source covers all major topics regarding the People's Republic of China. Part 1 includes chapters on its geography and climate, peoples and language, systems of thought and belief, health and medicine, arts, entertainment and sports, literature, science and technology, economy and trade, and institutions (government and other) of Chinese society. Part 2 provides a chronology of important events in Chinese history; part 3, an alphabetical list of common Chinese concepts, important figures and events; and part 4, information and advice for future travelers." Choice

Includes bibliographical references

DeWoskin, Rachel

Foreign babes in Beijing; behind the scenes of a new China. W. W. Norton 2005 332p $24.95; pa $13.95 **951**

ISBN 0-393-05902-2; 0-393-32859-7 pa

LC 2005-939

The author recounts her experiences living in China in the 1990s, where she had a starring role in the soap opera "Foreign Babes in Beijing."

"Ms DeWoskin's portrait of the complexities of urban China is not uncritical. But her book is written with enormous warmth for its people. And it is all the better for avoiding neat conclusions." Economist

Dong, Stella

Shanghai, 1842-1949; the rise and fall of a decadent city. Morrow 2000 318p il hardcover o.p. pa $15 **951**
ISBN 0-06-093481-6 pa
LC 99-41902

An "account of a city legendary for decadence, violence, and greedy imperialism. Dong meticulously details the European commercial interests that deliberately promoted opium trafficking and exploited the land and people of Shanghai with every conceivable vice for nearly 100 years." Booklist

Fairbank, John King

★ **China**; a new history. [by] John King Fairbank and Merle Goldman. 2nd enl. ed.; Belknap Press of Harvard University Press 2006 560p il map pa $24 **951**
ISBN 0-674-01828-1; 978-0-674-01828-0
LC 2005-53695

Fairbank covers the history of China from paleolithic cultures of 400,000 B.C. up to 1989. Goldman adds a chapter on events in the post-Mao period and an epilogue on China at the beginning of the 21st century.

The **great** Chinese revolution: 1800-1985. Harper & Row 1986 396p maps hardcover o.p. pa $16 **951**
ISBN 0-06-039057-3; 0-06-039076-X pa
LC 86-665

"The book is never pedantic, but gathers together a lifetime of scholarship plus a true gift for presentation of complex issues and a fine eye for telling illustration." Libr J

Includes bibliographical references

Hessler, Peter

★ **Oracle** bones; a journey between China's past and present. HarperCollins 2006 491p il $26.95; pa $15.99 **951**
ISBN 0-06-082658-4; 0-06-082659-2 pa
LC 2005-52607

The author "has a marvelous sense of the intonations and gestures that give life to the moment; he knows when to join in the action and when simply to wait for things to happen. Today's China could have been made for him." N Y Times Book Rev

Includes bibliographical references

Meyer, Michael J.

The **last** days of old Beijing; life in the vanishing backstreets of a city transformed. [by] Michael Meyer. Walker & Company 2008 355p il map $25.99; pa $16 **951**
1. Urban renewal -- China -- Beijing
ISBN 978-0-8027-1652-1; 0-8027-1652-0; 978-0-8027-1750-4 pa; 0-8027-1750-4 pa
LC 2008-15546

This is a "revealing portrait of urban change, and the consequences of China's unquenchable thirst for modernization." Kirkus

Includes bibliographical references

Palmer, James

Heaven cracks, earth shakes; James Palmer. Basic Books, a member of the Perseus Books Group 2012 ix, 273p.p ill. **951**
ISBN 9780465014781; 9780465023493
LC 2011934180

In this book, "Beijing-based author [James] Palmer . . . lays out the devastation wrought by 10 years of the Cultural Revolution, and how over the space of a few months the Chinese people managed to rebound and move forward. The year was scarred irrevocably by three events: the death in January of the people's beloved prime minister Zhou Enlai; the earthquake in Tangshan, which had been predicted several days before yet warnings ignored, flattening the coal-mining town in the space of 23 seconds and killing more than 650,000 people; and Mao's death in September, which set off a power struggle between the Gang of Four, led by Mao's widow, Jiang Qing, and the supporters of Deng Xiaoping." (Kirkus)

Platt, Stephen R.

Autumn in the Heavenly Kingdom; China, the West, and the epic story of the Taiping Civil War. by Stephen R. Platt. Alfred A. Knopf 2012 468 p. **951**
1. Americans -- China -- History -- 19th century
2. Ethnic conflict -- China -- History -- 19th century
3. Europeans -- China -- History -- 19th century 4. Manchus -- History -- 19th century 5. Visitors, Foreign -- China -- History -- 19th century
ISBN 9780307271730
LC 2011035137

The book is author Stephen R. Platt's account of [t]he cataclysmic Taiping rebellion. . . . In 1837 a peasant named Hong Xiuquan announced that he was Jesus' younger brother, sent to rid China of devils including its weak, corrupt, ethnically foreign Manchu rulers. His charisma attracted a vast following that by the 1850s had conquered a large area, the Taiping Heavenly Kingdom, with a capital at Nanjing. . . . [M]any Christian missionaries . . . supported the Taipings, but could not win over their governments, who were preoccupied with pugnacious efforts to extract trading concessions from the enfeebled central government. Crushed with immense bloodshed, the rebellion left the Manchu dynasty even weaker, although it limped on for 50 more years. (Publishers Wkly)

Prager, Emily

Wuhu diary; on taking my adopted daughter back to her hometown in China. Random House 2001 238p il hardcover o.p. pa $13 **951**
1. Adoption
ISBN 0-385-72199-4 pa
LC 2001-19104

"For anyone considering multicultural adoption or already involved in one, this compelling work offers encouragement and an example of how to help an adopted child get acquainted with her roots and build her sense of self. For others, it provides a wonderful view of a part of China seldom written about." Libr J

Preston, Diana

The **Boxer** Rebellion; the dramatic story of China's war on foreigners that shook the world in the summer of 1900. Walker & Co. 2000 xxvii, 436p il maps $28   **951**

ISBN 0-8027-1361-0

LC 00-39243

"Preston's account, compiled from the many letters, diaries, and memoirs by European survivors of the siege, captures an odd strain of mordant humor." N Y Times Book Rev

Includes bibliographical references and index

Schell, Orville

Virtual Tibet; searching for Shangri-la from the Himalayas to Hollywood. Metropolitan Bks. 2000 340p $26; pa $15   **951**

1. Tibet (China) -- Foreign public opinion 2. Tibet (China) -- In motion pictures

ISBN 0-8050-4381-0; 0-8050-4382-9 pa

LC 99-88146

Schell examines romanticized visions of Tibet in Western travel accounts and films.

The author is a "seasoned traveler in China, . . . and his book has the bracing air about it of disenchantment. The fact that he was a bit of a seeker once himself, mesmerized by the idea of Tibet, and of Communist China, makes him the perfect chronicler of such afflictions in others." N Y Rev Books

Spence, Jonathan D.

The **Chan's** great continent; China in Western minds. Norton 1998 279p hardcover o.p. pa $14.95   **951**

ISBN 0-393-31989-X pa

LC 98-10823

"Spence's book will appeal not only to those interested in history and literature, but to anyone looking for a perspective on contemporary discourse about China." Publ Wkly

Includes bibliographical references

God's Chinese son; the Taiping Heavenly Kingdom of Hong Xiuquan. Norton 1996 400p il maps hardcover o.p. pa $15.95   **951**

1. Religious leaders 2. Revolutionaries

ISBN 0-393-31556-8 pa

LC 95-17245

"In 1836, twenty-two-year-old Hong Xiuquan failed the civil-service examinations in Canton and came across some Christian tracts. When he later fell sick and had visions, he became convinced that he was the Christian God's second son, destined to rule a 'heavenly kingdom' on earth. Many were attracted to Hong's egalitarian policies—despite his enforced separation of the sexes—and his sect prospered. But its attempts to overthrow the Qing dynasty resulted in unprecedented bloodshed: twenty million people died before

the uprising was defeated, in 1864. Spence's present-tense narrative is riveting." New Yorker

Includes bibliographical references

Treason by the book; {by} Jonathan Spence. Viking 2001 300p map $24.95; pa $14   **951**

1. Revolutionaries -- China -- Biography

ISBN 0-670-89292-0; 0-14-200041-8 pa

LC 00-43805

"Spence's story of emperor, officials, and conspirators is both rousingly unlikely and highly informative." Libr J

The **search** for modern China. Norton 1990 xxv, 876p il maps hardcover o.p. pa $27.70   **951**

ISBN 0-393-30780-8 pa

LC 89-9241

Spence's "own sense of China's past is so vivid, his understanding so sure and his writer's skill so powerful that the reader apprehends distant events as if they were contemporary." New Statesman (1913)

Includes bibliographical references

Tsering Shakya

The **dragon** in the land of snows; a history of modern Tibet since 1947. Columbia Univ. Press 1999 574p il $32.50   **951**

ISBN 0-231-11814-7

LC 99-14020

"Drawing on Tibetan, Chinese, British, Indian and American sources, Shakya weaves an authoritative and easily readable narrative. 'The Dragon in the Land of Snows' is likely to be the definitive history of modern Tibet for a generation or more." N Y Times Book Rev

Includes bibliographical references

Berkshire encyclopedia of China; modern and historic views of the world's newest and oldest global power. Berkshire Pub. Group 2009 5v il map set $675   **951**

1. Reference books

ISBN 978-0-9770159-4-8; 0-9770159-4-7

LC 2009-7589

"Arranged alphabetically, the nearly 1000 articles cover an . . . array of subjects as they relate to China. Among those explored are the country's history (both ancient and modern), politicians, architecture, food, international relations, and medicine." Libr J

Includes bibliographical references

★ The Cambridge history of China; general editors, Denis Twitchett and John K. Fairbank. Cambridge Univ. Press 1978 12v v1 $205; v3 $205; v6 $178; v7 $205; v8 $178; v9 $178; v10 $195; v11 $205; v12 $205; v13 $205; v14 $180; v15 $195   **951**

ISBN 0-521-24327-0 v1; 0-521-21446-7 v3; 0-521-24331-9 v6; 0-521-24332-7 v7; 0-521-24333-5 v8; 0-521-24334-3 v9; 0-521-21447-5 v10; 0-521-22029-7 v11; 0-521-23541-3 v12; 0-521-24338-6 v13; 0-521-24336-X v14; 0-521-24337-8 v15

LC 76-29852

"An important series for scholars, this is also a valuable reference tool for general collections." Libr J

Includes bibliographical references

Encyclopedia of modern China; David Pong, editor in chief. Charles Scribner's Sons/Gale, Cengage Learning 2009 4v il map set $520 **951**
1. Reference books
ISBN 978-0-684-31566-9; 978-0-684-31571-3 ebook
LC 2009-3279

"Covering the period 1800 to the present, this attractive and authoritative set includes 936 entries and sidebars by nearly 500 authors. . . . There are main entries for each province (including a map and a box containing key data), major cities, important people, Chinese relations with countries from Australia to Vietnam, and hundreds of miscellaneous subjects." Booklist

Includes bibliographical references

951.04   Period of Republic, 1912-1949

Chang, Iris

★ The **rape** of Nanking; the forgotten holocaust of World War II. Penguin 1998 290p il pa $16 **951.04**
1. Nanjing (Jiangsu Province, China) massacre, 1937 2. Sino-Japanese Conflict, 1937-1945
ISBN 0-14-027744-7; 978-0-14-027744-9
LC 97-24137

"Chang's book is a memorial to the victims of Nanking, a damning indictment of Japanese political historiography, a valuable addition to Pacific war literature, and a literary model of how to speak about the unspeakable." Booklist

Includes bibliographical references

Sun Shuyun

The **Long** March; the true history of Communist China's founding myth. Doubleday 2007 270p il map $26 **951.04**
1. Communist leaders 2. Heads of state 3. Political leaders 4. Soldiers -- China
ISBN 978-0-385-52024-9; 0-385-52024-7

"In 1934, surrounded by Chiang Kai-shek's forces in the south, Mao's Red Army marched more than eight thousand miles to a new base, in the northwest. The march, completed by only a fifth of the original army, was a defeat in all ways but one: it returned Mao from the political wilderness to power. Mao transformed the march into the founding myth of modern China and, in doing so, created a new narrative around victories that never happened. Shuyun, a Chinese-born BBC documentary producer, retraces the route and interviews the few remaining survivors, in an account that shows the human cost of Mao's revisionism." New Yorker

951.05   Period of People's Republic, 1949-

August, Oliver

Inside the red mansion; on the trail of China's most wanted man. Houghton Mifflin Company 2007 268p map $26 **951.05**
1. Commercial agents 2. Smugglers
ISBN 978-0-618-71498-8; 0-618-71498-7
LC 2006-26930

"In 1999, China's Public Enemy No. 1 was 'Fatty' Lai Changxing, an illiterate rice farmer turned real-estate and shipping mogul who fled the country, accused of heading a multibillion-dollar smuggling ring. This account . . . casts Lai's rise and fall as a cautionary tale of boomtown China. The author tours the remains of Lai's empire—a film studio built as a replica of the Forbidden City; a posh brothel where he bribed Party officials with the company of 'Miss Temporarys'—but he reserves his most vivid prose for the 'fakers and fortune seekers, oddballs and outlaws' he meets along the way." New Yorker

Becker, Jasper

The **Chinese**. Oxford University Press 2002 493p il map pa $21.95 **951.05**
ISBN 0-19-514940-8

This "is a captivating and enlightening read for anyone interested in Asian or cultural studies." Booklist [review of 2000 edition]

Includes bibliographical references

Buruma, Ian

Bad elements; Chinese rebels from Los Angeles to Beijing. Random House 2001 xxv, 367p hardcover o.p. pa $15 **951.05**
1. Dissent 2. Dissenters -- China 3. Human rights 4. Human rights -- China
ISBN 0-679-78136-6 pa
LC 2001-19365

The author interviews Chinese dissidents in the United States, Asia, and Europe "to find out what happened to them and how they feel about the future of human rights in China. Buruma's study is both engaging and deeply informed." Libr J

Includes bibliographical references

Chang, Jung

Wild swans; three daughters of China. Simon & Schuster 1991 524p il hardcover o.p. pa $15 **951.05**
1. Women -- China
ISBN 0-7432-4698-5 pa
LC 91-20696

The author "tells the harrowing life stories of her maternal grandmother, her mother, and herself. Their tales span a period of radical change in China that has touched every aspect of life." Booklist

Chen, Da

Sounds of the river; a memoir. HarperCollins Pubs. 2002 307p hardcover o.p. pa $12.95 **951.05**
1. Calligraphers 2. Lawyers 3. Linguists
ISBN 0-06-095872-3 pa
LC 2001-39215

"Da Chen once again describes his past with fondness and buoyancy." N Y Times Book Rev

Dikötter, Frank

Mao's great famine; the history of China's most devastating catastrophe, 1958-1962. Walker & Co. 2010 420p il map $30   **951.05**
1. Communist leaders 2. Economic policy -- China 3. Famines -- China 4. Food supply 5. Food supply -- China 6. Heads of state 7. Political leaders
ISBN 978-0-8027-7768-3; 0-8027-7768-6
LC 2010-13141

This is an account of the "famine brought about by the Great Leap Forward (GLF) of 1958-1960." (N Y Rev Books) Chronology. Annotated bibliography. Bibliography. Index.

This book "is a masterpiece of historical investigation into one of the world's greatest crimes. Writing throughout in a sober and restrained style that only highlights the horror of the events it records, Dikötter shows in rigorous detail how responsibility for the disaster must be traced back directly to Mao.... Uncovering the magnitude of this terrible crime, Dikötter has produced one of the few books that anyone who wants to understand the 20th century simply must read." New Statesman

Includes bibliographical references and index

Fallows, James M.

Postcards from Tomorrow Square; reports from China. [by] James Fallows. Vintage Books 2009 262p pa $14.95   **951.05**
ISBN 978-0-307-45624-3; 0-307-45624-2
LC 2008-28083

"In this series of articles, Fallows reports on interesting trends and personalities in China—ambitious entrepreneurs and the rise in popularity of reality shows on state-run television. Despite the Western view of a powerful, single-minded China, Fallows presents a portrait of a huge and complex nation with such a vast range of ages and regional, geographic, and cultural differences that it defies simple definition." Booklist

Fang Lizhi

Bringing down the Great Wall; writings on science, culture, and democracy in China. introduction by Orville Schell; editor and principal translator, James H. Williams. Norton 1992 336p pa $10.95   **951.05**
1. Human rights
ISBN 0-393-30885-5; 978-0-393-30885-3
LC 90-53064

"A comprehensive selection of the written (and spoken) words of the witty, passionate, tenacious and articulate Chinese scientist and dissident who at present is living in the United States." N Y Times Book Rev

Includes bibliographical references

Kemenade, Willem van

China, Hong Kong, Taiwan, Inc. translated from the Dutch by Diane Webb. Knopf 1997 444p hardcover o.p. pa $16   **951.05**
ISBN 0-679-77756-3 pa
LC 97-71923

This is an "analysis of China's recent past and reflections on its future direction. Van Kemenade explores the anticipated political and economic fallout from the mainland's absorption of capitalist Hong Kong . . . and the possibility of its eventual takeover of Taiwan. He projects a foreseeable confrontation with Japan over Asian hegemony, ethnic and economic upheavals on China's 'wild' western border that abuts former Soviet republics and a political backlash from the fast-growing middle class, which in its pursuit of wealth seems no longer loyal to socialist ideals." Publ Wkly

Leibovitz, Liel

Fortunate sons; the 120 Chinese boys who came to America, went to school, and revolutionized an ancient civilization. [by] Liel Leibovitz & Matthew Miller. W.W. Norton 2011 319p il $26.95   **951.05**
1. Chinese students -- United States -- History 2. Education -- China 3. Educators
ISBN 978-0-393-07004-0; 0-393-07004-2
LC 2010-37724

"A curious, little-known episode of Sino-American history vividly told." Kirkus

Includes bibliographical references

Lord, Bette Bao

Legacies: a Chinese mosaic. Knopf 1990 245p hardcover o.p. pa $19   **951.05**
ISBN 0-449-90620-5 pa
LC 89-43452

The author lived in China from 1985 to 1989. Her book is based on interviews with Chinese people, including an actress, a teacher, a veteran of the Long March, an artist, a journalist, a peasant, an entrepreneur and a Communist Party cadre, who recount their experiences of persecution during the Cultural Revolution. The author also describes her own experiences and her family history.

"A vivid and startling mosaic of the political struggles that foreshadowed the Tiananmen Square uprising." Time

Ma Jian

Red dust; a path through China. translated from the Chinese by Flora Drew. Pantheon Bks. 2001 324p maps hardcover o.p. pa $14   **951.05**
ISBN 0-385-72023-8 pa
LC 2001-21575

"Faced with imprisonment, Jian fled to the Chinese countryside, eventually making his way to Tibet. His journey is presented as a combination travelogue and a narrative of sheer poetry and spirituality." Booklist

Mexico, Zachary

China underground. Soft Skull Press 2009 306p pa $16.95   **951.05**
ISBN 978-1-59376-223-0; 1-59376-223-2
LC 2008-45319

"Through encounters with sundry artists, musicians, students, bar owners, gangsters, prostitutes, and slackers, Mexico assembles a compelling portrait of China's contemporary youth culture and the limits of Communist control. The book's subjects include a twenty-seven-year-old self-taught disaster photographer from the coal country in Shenyang; a twenty-nine-year-old mobster in Qingdao; a twenty-two-year-old Hendrixian Uighur guitar player making a splash in Shanghai; a Beijing university student who wishes that the system encouraged less rote memorization and more original thought; and an investigative journalist who no longer publishes himself, instead leading Western reporters to controversial stories." New Yorker

Pan, Philip P.

★ **Out** of Mao's shadow; the struggle for the soul of a new China. Simon & Schuster 2008 349p il map $28; pa $16 **951.05**
ISBN 978-1-4165-3705-2; 1-4165-3705-8; 978-1-4165-3706-9 pa; 1-4165-3706-6 pa
LC 2008-11550
This is "one of the most revealing books about China since it opened up to the outside world in the 1970s." N Y Rev Books
Includes bibliographical references

Pomfret, John

Chinese lessons; five classmates and the story of the new China. H. Holt 2006 315p il map $26 **951.05**
1. Poets
ISBN 978-0-8050-7615-8; 0-8050-7615-8
LC 2006-41211
This "is a highly personal, honest, funny and well-informed account of China's hyperactive effort to forget its past and reinvent its future." N Y Times Book Rev

Salzman, Mark

Iron & silk. Random House 1987 211p hardcover o.p. pa $12.95 **951.05**
1. Martial arts
ISBN 0-394-55156-7; 0-394-75511-1 pa
LC 86-11846
The author tells of his two years teaching English to medical students in China's Hunan Province following his graduation from Yale University in 1982.
This book is "not so much a treatise on modern Chinese mores as a series of telling vignettes. . . . [The author] describes his encounter with Pan Qingfu, the country's foremost master of wushu, the traditional Chinese martial art." Time

Schoppa, R. Keith

The **Columbia** guide to modern Chinese history. Columbia Univ. Press 2000 356p il map $49 **951.05**
ISBN 0-231-11276-9
LC 99-53420
This narrative overview of Chinese history focuses on five areas: domestic politics, society, the economy, culture, and relations with the outside world. Contains approximately 500 annotated entries for further research in English as well as electronic resources and films. A chronology, ex-

cerpts from primary documents, and numerous graphs and tables are appended

Short, Philip

Mao; a life. Holt & Co. 2000 782p il maps hardcover o.p. pa $20 **951.05**
1. Communist leaders 2. Heads of state 3. Heads of state -- China -- Biography 4. Political leaders
ISBN 0-8050-6638-1 pa
LC 99-41839
This biography "takes Mao from his 1893 birth in the village of Shaoshan to school in Changsha, where he trained to be a teacher, and then into revolutionary activity, the long fight with Chiang Kai-shek, and leadership of the most populous nation on Earth." Booklist
Includes bibliographical references

Spence, Jonathan D.

Mao Zedong; {by} Jonathan Spence. Viking 1999 188p map $19.95 **951.05**
1. Communist leaders 2. Heads of state 3. Heads of state -- China -- Biography 4. Political leaders
ISBN 0-670-88669-6
LC 99-27739
"This specialist's book for nonspecialists concisely recounts the life of the Communist leader who revolutionized China. Ideas travel fast: Mao, a peasant son born in 1893, was able to read Darwin and Marx in translation and add Western ideas to his heritage of classical Chinese thought, and Spence helps us understand why he eventually embraced Communism. What is less clear is why a gifted, high-minded youth became a ruthless, crackpot tyrant." New Yorker
Includes bibliographical references

Vogel, Ezra F.

Deng Xiaoping and the transformation of China; Ezra F. Vogel. Belknap Press of Harvard University Press 2011 xxiv, 876p ill. **951.05**
1. Biography, Individual 2. China -- Economic conditions -- 1949- 3. China -- Politics & government -- 20th century 4. Statesmen -- China -- Biography
ISBN 978-0-674-05544-5; 0-674-05544-6; 9780674062832
LC 2011006925
This book, a 2012 Lionel Gelber Prize winner, offers a biography of Chinese politician Deng Xiaoping. "Deng was the pragmatic yet disciplined driving force behind China's radical transformation in the late twentieth century. He confronted the damage wrought by the Cultural Revolution, dissolved Mao's cult of personality, and loosened the economic and social policies that had stunted China's growth. Obsessed with modernization and technology, Deng opened trade relations with the West, which lifted hundreds of millions of his countrymen out of poverty. Yet at the same time he answered to his authoritarian roots, most notably when he ordered the crackdown in June 1989 at Tiananmen Square. . . . In the fifty years of his tumultuous rise to power, he endured accusations, purges, and even exile before becoming China's preeminent leader from 1978 to 1989 and again in 1992. When he reached the top, Deng saw an opportunity to creatively destroy much of the economic system he had

helped build for five decades as a loyal follower of Mao—and he did not hesitate." (Publisher's note)

Wong, Jan

A **comrade** lost and found; a Beijing story. Houghton Mifflin Harcourt 2009 322p map $25   **951.05**

1. Journalists
ISBN 978-0-15-101342-5; 0-15-101342-X
LC 2008-23788

Wong spent a year in Beijing on a foreign exchange program during the cultural revolution. In this "book, she recounts her return to the city in an effort to find a former classmate she betrayed with grave consequences. . . . Wong is a gifted storyteller, and hers is a deeply personal and richly detailed eyewitness account of China's journey to glossy modernity." Booklist

Wu, Harry

Bitter winds; a memoir of my years in China's Gulag. {by} Harry Wu and Carolyn Wakeman. Wiley 1993 290p il $35; pa $19.95   **951.05**

1. Human rights activists 2. Political prisoners 3. Prisons -- China
ISBN 0-471-55645-9; 0-471-11425-1 pa
LC 93-15799

In this "memoir, Wu recalls his 19 years in Chinese labor camps. Though a middle-class college student, he was initially a patriotic Communist, but he soon ran afoul of the thought police. Hoping to flee the country in 1959, he was denounced as an 'enemy of the revolution.' The book . . . focuses primarily on Wu's first decade as a prisoner struggling against starvation, seeing others succumb and learning a brutal survival ethic from fellow inmates. It is an intimate story of bravery and tragedy." Publ Wkly

Troublemaker; one man's crusade against China's cruelty. [by] Harry Wu, with George Vecsey. NewsMax.com Book 2002 326p il pa $24.95 **951.05**

1. Human rights 2. Political prisoners
ISBN 0-9704029-9-6; 978-0-9704029-9-8
LC 2004-273145

"Denounced in China as a 'traitor' and 'spy,' Wu is hailed as a hero in the West and has received many human rights awards. This book meticulously unveils the dramatic story of his 'crusade' against the Chinese government. . . . An interesting but disturbing book." Libr J

951.9 Korea

Brady, James

The **coldest** war; a memoir of Korea. St. Martin's Griffin 2000 248p il map pa $15.95   **951.9**

1. Korean War, 1950-1953 -- Personal narratives
ISBN 978-0-312-26511-3; 0-312-26511-5

"From November 1951 to July 1952, the author was a marine lieutenant who frequently found himself called upon to fight and kill Chinese and North Korean soldiers on the battlefields of Korea. His memoir of that experience is a well-crafted piece told in a voice that skillfully mixes the sardonic insight of an older man looking back on a highly

extraordinary episode of his past with the naivete of the young warrior he once was." Booklist

Breen, Michael

The **Koreans**; who they are, what they want, where their future lies. St. Martin's Press 1999 276p hardcover o.p. pa $14.95   **951.9**

1. Korean national characteristics
ISBN 0-312-32609-2 pa
LC 99-45599

In this survey of Korea's culture, the author "probes such diverse topics as the status of civil liberties, generational social strains within families, and the massive corruption that permeates Korean society. He writes with a snappy, readable style." Booklist
Includes bibliographical references

Cumings, Bruce

★ **Korea's** place in the sun; a modern history. Updated ed; W. W. Norton 2005 542p il map pa $16.95   **951.9**

ISBN 0-393-32702-7; 0-393-31681-5
LC 2006-276040

This history of Korea from 1860 focuses primarily on the post-1945 period.
"Mr. Cumings has pored over the historical documents and he argues intelligently. His book is important precisely because he marshals considerable evidence to challenge conventional understanding." N Y Times Book Rev
Includes bibliographical references

Cumings, Bruce, 1943-

The **Korean** War; a history. Modern Library 2010 288p il map   **951.9**

1. Korean War, 1950-1953 2. Korean War, 1950-1953 -- United States
ISBN 0-679-64357-5; 978-0-679-64357-9
LC 2010005629

This is a "revisionist history of America's intervention in Korea." (N Y Times (Late N Y Ed)) Index.
A "revisionist history of America's intervention in Korea. Beneath its bland title, Mr. Cumings's book is a squirm-inducing assault on America's moral behavior during the Korean War, a conflict that he says is misremembered when it is remembered at all. It's a book that puts the reflexive anti-Americanism of North Korea's leaders into sympathetic historical context. . . . [Cumings] mows down a host of myths about the war in his short new book, which is a distillation of his own scholarship and that of many other historians." N Y Times (Late N Y Ed)
Includes bibliographical references

Edwards, Paul M.

Korean War almanac. Facts on File 2006 592p il map $85   **951.9**

1. Korean War, 1950-1953
ISBN 0-8160-6037-1
LC 2005-9374

This book "contains a day-by-day chronology of the events and the people involved in this important war." Publisher's note
Includes bibliographical references

Halberstam, David

★ The **coldest** winter; America and the Korean War. Hyperion 2007 719p map $35   **951.9**
1. Korean War, 1950-1953 2. Korean War, 1950-1953 -- Campaigns 3. Korean War, 1950-1953 -- United States
ISBN 1-401-30052-9; 978-1-401-30052-4
          LC 2007-1635
"Alive with the voices of the men who fought, Halberstam's telling is a virtuoso work of history." Publ Wkly
Includes bibliographical references

Oberdorfer, Don

The **two** Koreas; a contemporary history. New ed; Basic Bks. 2001 521p il map pa $21   **951.9**
ISBN 0-465-05162-6
          LC 2001-43486
This is a study of North and South Korean politics and an analysis of U.S. policy from the 1970s to the present.

Peterson, Mark

A **brief** history of Korea; [by] Mark Peterson with Phillip Margulies. Facts On File 2010 328p il map $49.50   **951.9**
ISBN 978-0-8160-5085-7
          LC 2009-18889
This book "covers the history of Korea from the origins of the Korean people in prehistoric times to the economic and political situation in North and South Korea today." Publisher's note
Includes bibliographical references

The encyclopedia of the Korean War; a political, social, and military history. Spencer C. Tucker, volume editor; Paul G. Pierpaoli, Jr., associate editor and editor, documents volume; Jinwung Kim, Xiaobing Li, James I. Matray, assistant editors. 2nd ed.; ABC-CLIO 2010 3v il map set $295   **951.9**
1. Korean War, 1950-1953 -- Encyclopedias 2. Reference books
ISBN 978-1-85109-849-1; 1-85109-849-6; 978-1-85109-850-7 ebook; 1-85109-850-X ebook
          LC 2010-681
A resource on the confrontation that became the first shooting war of the Cold War, the first limited conflict of the Atomic Age, and the war that led to a dramatic escalation of the national security state while foreshadowing U.S. involvement in Vietnam.
"This is an excellent source for high-school, academic, and public libraries." Booklist
Includes glossary and bibliographical references

951.904   1945-1999

Hickey, Michael

The **Korean** War; the West confronts communism. Overlook Press 2000 397p il maps $35   **951.904**
1. Korean War, 1950-1953
ISBN 1-58567-035-9
          LC 00-27692
An "analysis of both the military and political factors that caused the war and the conduct on all sides. . . . The author does not mince words when criticizing General MacArthur and other UN commanders. Using declassified documents as well as regimental and personal diaries, he wades through political intrigue and military disasters and triumphs to give us a memorable account." Libr J
Includes bibliographical references

951.93   North Korea (People's Democratic Republic of Korea)

Demick, Barbara

Nothing to envy; ordinary lives in North Korea. Spiegel & Grau 2009 314p il map   **951.93**
1. Koreans
ISBN 0-385-52390-4; 978-0-385-52390-5
          LC 2009-22420
This book "follows the lives of six ordinary North Koreans, including a female doctor, a pair of star-crossed lovers, a factory worker and an orphan." (N Y Times (Late N Y Ed))
"A fascinating and deeply personal look at the lives of six defectors from the repressive totalitarian regime of the Republic of North Korea, in which Demick . . . draws out details of daily life that would not otherwise be known to Western eyes because of the near-complete media censorship north of the arbitrary border drawn after Japan's surrender ending WWII." Publ Wkly
Includes bibliographical references

Hassig, Ralph

The **hidden** people of North Korea; everyday life in the hermit kingdom. [by] Ralph Hassig and Kongdan Oh. Rowman & Littlefield Publishers 2009 300p il $39.95   **951.93**
1. Communist leaders 2. Heads of state 3. Political culture -- Korea (North)
ISBN 978-0-7425-6718-4; 0-7425-6718-4
          LC 2009-29786
The authors "gather behind-the-curtain research to expose day-to-day life, and the powers that control it, in North Korea, a developed nation where meat is a luxury and the Internet doesn't exist for anyone but the dictator. . . . The uninformed will find much that's fascinating and shocking: a nation of castes and concentration camps, replete with a politics of fear that rivals the worst Orwell could imagine." Publ Wkly
Includes bibliographical references

952   Japan

Jansen, Marius B.
★ The **making** of modern Japan. Belknap Press
2000 871p il maps $35; pa $18.95   **952**
ISBN 0-674-00334-9; 0-674-00991-6 pa

LC 00-41352

"Jansen has produced what is sure to become the standard narrative history of modern Japan. . . . In every way
this is a remarkable book . . . and no reference collection on
Japan can pretend to be complete without it." Choice

Includes bibliographical references

McClain, James L.
Japan, a modern history. Norton 2001 632p il
maps $35; pa $31.25   **952**
ISBN 0-393-04156-5; 0-393-97720-X pa

LC 2001-34545

"This is a well-written, well-researched, and easily readable survey of the modern history of a fascinating and important nation." Booklist

Includes bibliographical references

Perez, Louis G.
The **history** of Japan; 2nd ed.; Greenwood Press
2009 266p map $49.95   **952**
1. Reference books
ISBN 978-0-313-36442-6

LC 2008-52242

This history covers prehistoric and early feudal Japan to
the 21st Century. Cultural aspects examined include theater
and cinema, marriage customs, and youth culture as well as
the women's movement and political scandals.

"With its essential chronology, term glossary, and premier list, the volume serves as both engaging read and
quick-reference." Libr J

Includes bibliographical references

Reischauer, Edwin O.
Japan; the story of a nation. 4th ed.; McGraw-
Hill 1990 401p il map pa $68.75   **952**
ISBN 0-07-557074-2; 978-0-07-557074-5

LC 89-12418

This history of the Japanese people from their origins
to the present examines their civilization, cultural heritage,
militarism, and economy.

The **Japanese** today; change and continuity. Belknap Press 1988 426p il maps $25; pa
$12.50   **952**
1. Agriculture -- Japan 2. Education -- Japan 3.
Feudalism
ISBN 0-674-47181-4; 0-674-47182-2 pa

LC 87-14904

The author "shows how change within continuity has
been the most enduring characteristic of the Japanese experience—throughout the nation's history. He analyzes and
explains in detail the government, education, business, and
social structure of the country in modern times." Christ
Sci Monit

Includes bibliography

Smith, Patrick L.
Japan; a reinterpretation. Pantheon Bks. 1997
385p hardcover o.p. pa $14   **952**
ISBN 0-679-74511-4 pa

LC 96-39220

This study focuses on events after World War II. Smith
examines the U.S. role in post-war Japan, and the social
structure of Japanese society.

"In his sweeping analysis of the country's history,
economy, politics and culture, Smith has produced a new
startlingly clear-sighted vision of the often misunderstood
Japanese." Publ Wkly

Includes bibliographical references

The **Cambridge** encyclopedia of Japan;   editors,
Richard Bowring, Peter Kornicki.   Cambridge
Univ. Press 1993 400p il maps $70   **952**
1. Reference books
ISBN 0-521-40352-9

LC 92-8167

This volume is divided "into eight categories: geography, history, language, thought and religion, arts and crafts,
society, politics, and the economy. Each of these categories
is further divided into 7-11 subjects that deal with numerous
topics, such as the physical structure of the country, climate,
education, family, judicial system, cinema, products, foreign
policy, and important historical figures." Am Ref Books
Annu, 1994

952.03   1868-1945

Buruma, Ian
Inventing Japan, 1853-1964. Modern Lib. 2003
194p hardcover o.p. pa $12.95   **952.03**
ISBN 0-679-64085-1; 0-8129-7286-4 pa

LC 2002-26346

"Buruma traces the remarkable metamorphosis that
transformed an isolated island shogunate into an expansive
military empire and then into a pacified and prosperous democracy. . . . An excellent introductory study." Booklist

Includes bibliographical references

Gordon, Andrew
The **modern** history of Japan. Oxford University
Press 2003 384p il $35; pa $29.95   **952.03**
ISBN 0-19-511060-9; 0-19-511061-7 pa

LC 2002-70916

The author examines "Japan's political, economic, social, and cultural inventions of its modernity in evolving
international contexts, incorporating inside viewpoints and
debates. Beyond identifying the national stages (feudalism,
militarism, democracy), the author innovatively emphasizes
how labor unions, cultural figures, and groups in society
(especially women) have been affected over time and have
responded." Libr J

Includes bibliographical references and index

Keene, Donald

Emperor of Japan: Meiji and His world, 1852-1912. Columbia Univ. Press 2002 922p il $82.50; pa $27.95 **952.03**
1. Emperors
ISBN 0-231-12340-X; 0-231-12341-8 pa
LC 2001-28826

This is a "biography-cum-history of Emperor Meiji and his times. . . . Meiji's reign saw Japan become fully industrialized under a brand new constitution, and with new economic and educational systems adopted. Despite the book's massive scale, Keene's graceful writing holds the reader's interest throughout." Booklist
Includes bibliographical references

Pleshakov, Konstantin

The **Tsar's** last armada; the epic journey to the Battle of Tsushima. {by} Constantine Pleshakov. Basic Bks. 2002 xx, 396p il maps hardcover o.p. pa $17.50 **952.03**
1. Russo-Japanese War, 1904-1905 2. Tsushima, Battle of, 1905
ISBN 0-465-05792-6 pa
LC 2001-52532

This is an account of events leading to the Russo-Japanese War and the defeat of the Russian fleet in the Tsushima Straits in 1905.
"A compulsively readable account told from the Russian viewpoint." Booklist
Includes bibliographical references

Seagrave, Sterling

The **Yamato** dynasty; the secret history of Japan's Imperial family. Broadway Bks. 2000 394p il hardcover o.p. pa $23 **952.03**
1. Emperors 2. Emperors -- Japan -- Biography
ISBN 0-7679-0497-4 pa
LC 99-49888

This "history of Japan from the mid-19th century to the present weaves together an iconoclastic historical narrative with a mostly caustic view of Japan's imperial family. The Seagraves depict modern Japan as a country consistently dominated by a closed financial oligarchy in league with politicians, bureaucrats, the imperial family, and underworld bosses." Libr J
Includes bibliographical references

952.04   1945-1999

Dower, John W.

Embracing defeat; Japan in the wake of World War II. by John Dower. Norton 1999 676p il $29.95; pa $17.95 **952.04**
ISBN 0-393-04686-9; 0-393-32027-8 pa
LC 98-22133

"Dower demonstrates an impressive mastery of voluminous sources, both American and Japanese, and he deftly situates the political story within a rich cultural context." Publ Wkly
Includes bibliographical references

Richie, Donald

The **Japan** journals, 1947-2004; edited by Leza Lowitz. Stone Bridge Press 2004 494p il $29.95 **952.04**
1. Art critics 2. Biography, Individual 3. Literary critics 4. Motion picture critics
ISBN 1-88065-691-4
LC 2004-16239

"The material in this volume was extracted and organized by Lowitz from previously unpublished sporadic diaries and jottings. They give a running commentary on Japan's rise from wartime destitution into the rich society of the 1980s boom, then its development into overbuilt and washed out postmodern complacency. There is some personal trivia, but most entries are alert and sometimes surprising glimpses of modern Japanese writers and filmmakers." Libr J

★ **Encyclopedia** of contemporary Japanese culture; edited by Sandra Buckley. Routledge 2001 xxix, 634p $315; pa $80 **952.04**
1. Reference books
ISBN 0-415-14344-6; 0-415-48152-X pa
LC 2001-19655

This reference includes "more than 750 topical and biographical entries exploring the 'lived experience of everyday Japanese life' for the postwar period. . . . [It includes] articles on minorities in Japan and the Japanese Diaspora in the Americas. Most notably . . . [this] features excellent coverage of Japanese women and consistently introduces critical feminist perspectives that are rarely seen in other reference works on Japan. . . . [This] is eminently readable . . . an ideal reference tool." Am Ref Books Annu, 2003
Includes bibliographical references

953   Arabian Peninsula and adjacent areas

Krane, Jim

City of gold; Dubai and the dream of capitalism. St. Martin's Press 2009 356p il map $27.99 **953**
ISBN 9780312535742
LC 2009-13188

The author "traces the historical roots and economic and political changes of 'a small Arab village that grew into a big city' and profiles the members of the ruling royal family—Sheikh Rashid, Sheikh Zayed, and Sheikh Mohammed—whose vision brought Dubai to where it is today. . . . This landmark work is recommended to those interested in the history, politics, and economics of the Middle East; an excellent choice for anyone who wishes to learn more about Dubai." Libr J
Includes bibliographical references

Theroux, Peter

Sandstorms: days and nights in Arabia. Norton 1990 281p hardcover o.p. pa $13.95 **953**
1. Arab civilization 2. Arab countries -- Description
ISBN 0-393-30797-2 pa
LC 89-28609

The author "recounts his experiences in the Middle East of the 1980s. The author went to Egypt to teach English and wound up chronicling the disappearance of Lebanon's Shia

Iman Moussa Sadr. But Sandstorms is the human side of an American in Arabia. . . . Theroux's Arabia is rough but undeniably real, poignant and elemental." Libr J

953.8   Saudi Arabia

Lacey, Robert

Inside the Kingdom; kings, clerics, modernists, terrorists, and the struggle for Saudi Arabia. Viking 2009 404p il map $27.95   **953.8**

ISBN 978-0-670-02118-5; 0-670-02118-0

LC 2009-08367

The author's "eye for sweeping trends and the telling detail combined with the depth, breadth and evenhandedness of his research makes for an indispensable guide." Publ Wkly

Includes bibliographical references

Wynbrandt, James

A **brief** history of Saudi Arabia; foreword by Fawaz A. Gerges. 2nd ed; Facts On File 2010 364p il map $49.50; pa $19.95   **953.8**

ISBN 978-0-8160-7876-9; 978-0-8160-8250-6 pa

LC 2010-5466

This history of Saudi Arabia covers "pre-Islamic Arabia; Bedouin society and culture; the birth and spread of Islam; the development of and philosophy behind Wahhabism; the origins of House Saud; Saudi Arabia's role in the Middle East; Saudi Arabia's relationship to the United States; the battle between conservative and progressive elements in the monarchy today; [and] the reign of King Abdullah." Publisher's note

Includes glossary and bibliographical references

954   India and neighboring south Asian countries

Dalrymple, William

White Mughals; love and betrayal in the eighteenth-century India. Viking 2003 xlvii, 459p il map $34.95; pa $16   **954**

1. British -- India 2. British -- India -- History

ISBN 0-670-03184-4; 0-14-200412-X pa

LC 2002-191082

James Kirkpatrick was the Resident of the East India Company in Hyderabad. This book documents his marriage to Khair-un-Nissa, a Mughal aristocrat.

This "book, ambitious in scope and rich in detail, demonstrates that a century before Kipling's 'never the twain'—and two centuries before neocons and radical Islamists trumpeted the clash of civilizations—the story of the Westerner in Muslim India was one not of conquest but of appreciation, adaptation, and seduction." New Yorker

Includes bibliographical references

Hardy, Justine

In the valley of mist; Kashmir: one family in a changing world. Free Press 2009 209p il map $25   **954**

1. Journalists 2. Merchants

ISBN 978-1-4391-0289-3; 1-4391-0289-9

LC 2008-55093

The author "channels the story of Kashmir's dark transformation from an idyllic place . . . of beauty and freedom to a realm of chaos and bloodshed through the lives of one family, the Dars. . . . Hardy's intimate and dramatic chronicle clarifies and humanizes Kashmir's torments, which are of grave global consequence." Booklist

Lapierre, Dominique

The **City** of Joy. Warner Books 1991 528p il pa $7.99   **954**

ISBN 0-446-35556-9

An account of life in the most squalid of Calcutta's slums, Anand Nagar (The City of Joy). The author focuses on the lives of a rickshaw driver, a Polish Catholic priest, an American doctor and an Assamese nurse.

McLeod, John

The **history** of India. Greenwood Press 2002 xx, 223p $39.95   **954**

1. Mogul Empire

ISBN 0-313-31459-4

LC 2002-276829

The author presents "in broad outlines some of the major events and episodes that make up India's history. . . . This is a useful compilation of important facts relating to Indian history. Its strength lies primarily in the last six chapters in which brief narratives of the struggle for independence and post-independence India down to the close of the twentieth century are nicely presented. All in all, this is a book that all libraries should have." Recomm Ref Books for Small & Medium-sized Libr & Media Cent, 2003

Includes bibliographical references

Mehta, Suketu

★ **Maximum** city; Bombay lost and found. Alfred A. Knopf 2004 542p $27.95   **954**

ISBN 0-375-40372-8

LC 2004-48969

The author "explores various aspects of Bombay life, from setting up residence to exploring the hugely successful domestic film industry; from detailing Bombay's sex industry to profiling the reasons behind India's own 'September 11,' the 1993 riots and bombings that exposed a vast enmity between extremist Hindus and Muslims. . . . Mehta delivers a fresh and unblinking look at contemporary Bombay." Booklist

Miller, Sam

Delhi; adventures in a megacity. St. Martin's Press 2010 291p il map $25.99   **954**

ISBN 978-0-312-61237-5

LC 2010-13043

The author "presents a highly entertaining and witty account of a walking tour of Delhi. He describes 12 walks that begin in the center of the city and proceed outward to the satellite towns at the outskirts. Miller's portrayal of the changing landscape and street life is engrossing." Libr J

Rashid, Ahmed

Descent into chaos; the US and the failure of nation building in Pakistan, Afghanistan, and Central Asia. Viking 2008 lviii, 484p il map $27.95; pa $18   **954**
ISBN 978-0-670-01970-0; 0-670-01970-4; 978-0-14-311557-1 pa; 0-14-311557-X pa
LC 2008-02949
This is a "lucid, insightful, and highly readable tome on the existent and emergent threats in Central Asia." Choice
Includes bibliographical references

Roy, Arundhati

Walking with the comrades. Penguin Books 2011 220p il map pa $15   **954**
1. Atrocities 2. Guerrillas 3. Social conflict 4. Terrorism
ISBN 978-0-14-312059-9
LC 2011039307
The author "exposes the violent contradictions of India's economic miracle in this blistering critique of the Indian government's campaign against the Maoist insurgents in the country's central tribal lands encompassing several states. Roy, who recounts time spent on the move with a cadre of rebels, argues forcefully that Operation Green Hunt—launched by the state under the rubric of the threat of terrorism—is an all-out war to remove indigenous communities from lands already promised to corporations eager to exploit their extremely valuable resources. . . . Informed, impassioned, at times strident, and fleet and fascinating when describing life on the ground among the rebels, Roy's prose will both rouse and ruffle." Publ Wkly
Includes bibliographical references

Sen, Amartya Kumar

The argumentative Indian; writings on Indian history, culture, and identity. [by] Amartya Sen. Farrar, Straus and Giroux 2006 xx, 409p il   **954**
ISBN 0-374-10583-9
LC 2005-49460
"Sen's lucid reasoning and thoroughgoing humanism . . . ensure a lively and commanding defense of diversity and dialogue." Publ Wkly
Includes bibliographical references

Walsh, Judith E.

A brief history of India; 2nd ed.; Facts On File, Inc. 2010 414p il map $49.50; pa $19.95   **954**
ISBN 978-0-8160-8143-1; 978-0-8160-8362-6 pa
LC 2010-26316

Wolpert, Stanley A.

A new history of India; 7th ed; Oxford University Press 2004 530p il map $63.95; pa $43   **954**
1. Mogul Empire
ISBN 0-19-516677-9; 0-19-516678-7 pa
LC 2003-53589
A comprehensive survey of Indian history from its early beginnings to the present. Includes discussion of the assas-

sination of Rajiv Gandhi; violence in Kashmir, Punjab, and Assam; and the effects of rural development.

954.03   Period of British rule, 1785-1947

Chadha, Yogesh

Gandhi; a life. Wiley 1998 546p il hardcover o.p. pa $19.95   **954.03**
1. Authors 2. Biography, Individual 3. Essayists 4. Journalists 5. Memoirists 6. Pacifists 7. Political leaders 8. Writers on politics
ISBN 0-471-35062-1 pa
LC 97-37406
"Chadha reexamines Gandhi's life with an eye to restoring its complications and contradictions, noting that 'to suppress his weaknesses would be to undermine his strengths.' And he succeeds in his mission, presenting the great leader not as a holy man but as a humanist and politician." Booklist
Includes bibliographical references

Wolpert, Stanley A.

★ Gandhi's passion; the life and legacy of Mahatma Gandhi. [by] Stanley Wolpert. Oxford Univ. Press 2001 308p il hardcover o.p. pa $17.95 **954.03**
1. Authors 2. Essayists 3. Journalists 4. Memoirists 5. Nationalists -- India 6. Pacifists 7. Political leaders 8. Statesmen -- India 9. Writers on politics
ISBN 0-19-513060-X; 0-19-515634-X pa
LC 00-45298
"From his pampered childhood to his ascetic final years, the text follows the Mahatma ('Great Soul') on a paradoxical pilgrimage in which the deliberate acceptance of suffering endowed him with the power he needed to challenge the leading politicians of Europe, Africa, and Asia." Booklist
Includes bibliographical references

954.04   1947-1971

French, Patrick

India; a portrait. Alfred A. Knopf 2011 398p il $30   **954.04**
ISBN 978-0-307-27243-0; 0-307-27243-5
LC 2011-03921
This work "combines deep research about the country's history with a series of vignettes culled from French's street-level reporting. Taken together, his reading of seminal texts and his interviews with politicians, pimps, businessmen, laborers, farmers, scholars and people from all levels of India's caste system result in a fittingly vigorous and colorful book about what it means to live in India six decades after the nation freed itself from British rule." San Francisco Chron
Includes bibliographical references

Guha, Ramachandra

India after Gandhi; the history of the world's largest democracy. Ecco 2007 893p il map $34.95   **954.04**
ISBN 978-0-06-019881-7; 0-06-019881-8
LC 2006-52180

This book documents India's transformation from a colonial state to independence.

The author "builds his story by making us witnesses of events as they occur, drawing on contemporary accounts. His voluminous account may seem daunting, but it is crucial for the understanding of modern India. . . . Guha is patient in his approach, gentle in his criticism, exasperated by what he does not like, and eclectic in drawing on evidence that supports his argument." New Statesman

Includes bibliographical references

Tharoor, Shashi

India; from midnight to the millennium. Arcade Pub. 1997 392p map hardcover o.p. pa $15.95   **954.04**
    ISBN 1-55970-384-9; 978-1-55970-803-6 pa;
    1-55970-803-4 pa
        LC 97-8376
"Each telling anecdote illuminates some aspect of Indian culture, from politics to religion, creating a mosaic that reflects India's endless variations on the theme of life." Booklist

Nehru: the invention of India. Arcade Pub 2003 282p $24.95; pa $13.95   **954.04**
    1. Biography, Individual 2. Nonfiction writers 3. Prime ministers 4. Prime ministers -- India
    ISBN 1-559-70697-X; 1-559-70737-2 pa
        LC 2003-58274
The author touches "on key points in Nehru's life: his English education, the importance of guidance he received from his father and Gandhi, his prison years during the drive for independence, and his administration of the new Indian republic. He neatly pulls together the essence of Nehru's beliefs in democratic institution building, pan-Indian secularism, Socialist democratic economy, and the foreign policy of nonalignment. . . . If readers could choose only one narrative about Nehru, this would suffice." Libr J

Includes bibliographical references

954.05   -1971

Deb, Siddhartha

The **beautiful** and the damned; Siddhartha Deb. Faber and Faber, Inc. 2011 253p.   **954.05**
    ISBN 9780865478732; 0865478627; 9780865478626
        LC 2011024408
This book "examines India's many contradictions through various individual . . . perspectives. . . . [Author Siddhartha] Deb introduces the reader to an unforgettable group of Indians, including a Gatsby-like mogul in Delhi whose hobby is producing big-budget gangster films that no one sees; a wiry, dusty farmer named Gopeti whose village is plagued by suicides and was the epicenter of a riot; and a sad-eyed waitress named Esther who has set aside her dual degrees in biochemistry and botany to serve Coca-Cola to arms dealers at an upscale hotel called Shangri La." (Publisher's note)

Giridharadas, Anand

India calling; an intimate portrait of a nation's remaking. Times Books/Henry Holt and Co. 2011 273p $25; ebook $11.99   **954.05**
    1. Journalists 2. National characteristics, East Indian 3. Social change -- India
    ISBN 0-8050-9177-7; 1-4299-5062-5 ebook; 978-0-8050-9177-9; 978-1-4299-5062-6 pa
        LC 2010-18447
The author, who is "an American, traces his parents' journey from India." (N Y Times Book Rev) Index.

This "is a fine book, elegant, self-aware and unafraid of contradictions and complexity. Giridharadas captures fundamental changes in the nature of family and class relationships and the very idea of what it means to be an Indian." N Y Times Book Rev

Mishra, Pankaj

★ **Temptations** of the West; how to be modern in India, Pakistan, Tibet, and beyond. Farrar, Straus & Giroux 2006 323p $25   **954.05**
    ISBN 0-374-17321-4; 978-0-374-17321-0
        LC 2006-11987
"It is impossible in a short form to do justice to the density and complexity of . . . [the author's] arguments, to his comprehensive illustrations, to his scathing demolition of the comfort zones of both East and West, and to the intrepid and endlessly questioning spirit which lies behind his book." N Y Rev Books

954.9   Other jurisdictions

Napoli, Lisa

Radio Shangri-La; what I learned in the happiest kingdom on earth. Crown Publishers 2010 xx, 277p $25   **954.9**
    ISBN 978-0-307-45302-0; 978-0-307-45304-4 ebook
        LC 2009-49176
"The author provides a readable account of her life-changing decision to leave the comforts of her cosmopolitan Los Angeles life and serve as a volunteer at Kuzoo FM 90, a radio station for young people in the remote Himalayan kingdom of Bhutan. Disillusioned with her love life and fed up with her job as a public-radio commentator, Napoli took a chance on a mysterious stranger's offer of unpaid work in a country where '[b]eing, not having' and '[h]appiness above wealth' were the prevailing national philosophies. . . . The author's authentic voice and light, pleasant cultural insights make for a refreshingly uplifting book." Kirkus

Includes bibliographical references

954.91   Pakistan

Gull, Imtiaz

The **most** dangerous place; Pakistan's lawless frontier. Viking 2010 xxx, 282p map   **954.91**
    1. Terrorism
    ISBN 0-670-02225-X; 978-0-670-02225-0
        LC 2010-01898

Gul "tracks the Taliban and al-Qaeda insurgents into the mountainous tribal regions to investigate the tangle of perilous allegiances. The destabilized Afghanistan-Pakistan border region is constantly in the news as the Obama administration attempts to flush out the militants using the area as a base to train soldiers and launch terrorist attacks. In a dense, timely study, the author investigates the complicated makeup of these groups. . . . Informational rather than didactic, Gul's insider take will serve as an excellent resource." Kirkus

Includes bibliographical references

Inskeep, Steve

Instant city; life and death in Karachi. Penguin Press 2011 284p il map $27.95   **954.91**

ISBN 978-1-59420-315-2; 1-59420-315-6

LC 2011020673

Analyzes the growing metropolis of Karachi, Pakistan, including the importance of regional stability to American security interests, the terrorist bombing of a Shia religious procession, and the challenging religious, ethnic, and political divides.

"This is an intimate book about a megacity, and Inskeep succeeds by keeping his ambitions modest. By trying to understand the horrific event of one particular day, he keeps his narrative well paced and full of small surprises. The book sparkles when Inskeep takes an unexpected turn and follows a stranger, or when he tracks down a new trend to illuminate a new facet of the city." Publ Wkly

Includes bibliographical references

Lieven, Anatol

Pakistan; a hard country. PublicAffairs 2011 558p il $35   **954.91**

ISBN 978-1-61039-021-7; 1-61039-021-0

LC 2011-921821

"Lieven breaks down his study by specific region; considers the structures of justice, religion, the military and politics in turn; and, finally, in a skillful, insightful synthesis, addresses the history of and issues concerning the Taliban, both Pakistani and Afghani. A well-reasoned, welcome resource for Western 'experts' and lay readers alike." Kirkus

Schmidle, Nicholas

To live or to perish forever; two tumultuous years in Pakistan. Henry Holt and Co. 2009 254p il map $25   **954.91**

1. Journalists

ISBN 978-0-8050-8938-7; 0-8050-8938-1

LC 2008-48373

"Schmidle offers a gripping, grim account of his two years as a journalism fellow in Pakistan, where his travels took him into the most isolated and unfriendly provinces, and into the thick of interests and beliefs that impede that nation's peace and progress. . . . Schmidle has, with this effort, established himself as a fresh, eloquent and informed contributor to the ongoing dialogue regarding Pakistan, terrorism and the strategic importance of engaging Central Asia in efforts toward peace and stability." Publ Wkly

955 Iran

Follett, Ken

On wings of eagles. New American Library 1984 415p il pa $7.99   **955**

1. Iran hostage crisis, 1979-1981

ISBN 0-451-16353-2; 978-0-451-16353-0

The author "recounts the efforts of successful Texas industrialist Ross Perot to rescue from a Teheran jail two senior corporate executives arrested during the anti-American and revolutionary period in Iran in 1979." Libr J

Housden, Roger

Saved by beauty; an American romantic in Iran. Broadway Books 2011 290p map $24; ebook $11.99   **955**

1. Iran -- Social life and customs

ISBN 978-0-307-58773-2; 978-0-307-58775-6 ebook

LC 2011003323

The author "documents his travels to Iran in late 2008 and early 2009. The narrative flows seamlessly as the author visits Tehran, paradise gardens in Shiraz, the Pasargadae archaeological site where Cyrus the Great is buried, Persepolis, the Jewish quarter in Yazd, Esfaha-n, Sanandaj, Mashhad, Neysha-bur, Tu-s, Kermanshah, Ahvaz, and Turkey's Bursa and Konya, as well as surrounding settlements, plains, deserts, and mountainous areas. . . . Poetry lovers and adventurers alike will appreciate this work." Libr J

Mackey, Sandra

The **Iranians**; Persia, Islam, and the soul of a nation. W. Scott Harrop, research assistant. Dutton 1996 xxii, 426p maps hardcover o.p. pa $15.95 **955**

ISBN 04-522-7563-6 pa

LC 95-44135

The author presents "information on Iranian civilization from Cyrus the Great to the present. Throughout this turbulent history of invasions and conquerors, the Persian soul, with its foundations in the Zoroastrian concept of justice overlaid with Shia Islam, has steadfastly endured. Since many Westerners had little familiarity with Iran until the overthrow of the Shah in 1979, this very readable book provides a perspective on what led up to those events, what is happening in Iran today, and how the current situation is likely to affect the future of Iran and its relationship with the West." Libr J

Majd, Hooman

The **Ayatollah** begs to differ; the paradox of modern Iran. Doubleday 2008 272p il $24.95 **955**

1. Authors 2. Journalists 3. National characteristics, Iranian 4. Nonfiction writers 5. Translators

ISBN 978-0-385-52334-9; 0-385-52334-3

LC 2008-4648

The son of an Iranian diplomat and the grandson of an ayatollah grew up in exile, yet he also remained closely attached to his homeland. Majd's reports on his travels throughout Iran try to explain the economic, political, and social forces that lie at its heart, and to show the paradoxes of the Iranian character that have baffled Americans.

The author's "witty and captivating book makes it possible for a nonexpert to appreciate the multiple layers of sociocultural factors that define today's Iran." Libr J

Includes bibliographical references

Peterson, Scott

Let the swords encircle me; Iran--a journey behind the headlines. Simon & Schuster 2010 732p il $32; ebook $16.99   **955**

1. Iranians -- Ethnic identity
ISBN 978-1-4165-9728-5; 978-1-4165-9739-1 ebook

LC 2010-17761

"Reading 'Let the Swords Encircle Me' is like taking a seminar on modern Iran with a patient guide who knows and loves both Iran and the US, and wants only for them to reconcile. The book's deep understanding of the nuances and many shades of Iran are valuable." Christ Sci Monit

Includes bibliographical references

Wright, Robert A.

Our man in Tehran; the true story behind the secret mission to save six Americans during the Iran Hostage Crisis and the foreign ambassador who worked with the CIA to bring them home. [by] Robert Wright. Other Press ed.; Other Press 2011 xxvi, 406p il $25.95; ebook $25.95   **955**

1. Diplomats 2. Escapes 3. Iran hostage crisis, 1979-1981
ISBN 978-1-59051-413-9; 978-1-59051-414-6 ebook

LC 2010-20376

"Much of Iran's relationship with the West—and their mutual antipathy—stems from the muddled events of a single day: November 4, 1979, when Iranian militants overran the U.S. embassy in Tehran, launching a 444-daylong hostage drama. What's often forgotten is that six Americans evaded their would-be captors and were protected and eventually extracted from Iran by Canadian diplomats. In this fascinating account of spycraft and compassion, Wright . . . puts newly unclassified documents to excellent use in recounting how Canadian ambassador Ken Taylor hid the Americans who had slipped out a side door and gathered intelligence for the U.S. government." Publ Wkly

Includes bibliographical references

955.05   1906-2005

Wright, Robin

The **last** great revolution; turmoil and transformation in Iran. Knopf 2000 xxiv, 339p il hardcover o.p. pa $14   **955.05**

ISBN 0-375-40639-5; 0-375-70630-5 pa

LC 99-27798

The author "talks to journalists, educators, politicians, entertainers, and others to present a picture of the cultural and political changes in Iran: the softening of cultural restrictions, the empowerment of women, and the modernization of industry and the economy." Booklist

Includes bibliographical references

956   Middle East (Near East)

Barr, James

A **line** in the sand. W. W. Norton & Co. 2012 xii, 450 p ill. 12 p. of plates   **956**

1. Diplomats 2. Historical literature 3. World War, 1914-1918 -- Middle East
ISBN 1-84737-453-0 Simon & Schuster; 978-1-84737-453-0 Simon & Schuster; 9780393070651 W.W. Norton & Co. 2012; 0393070654 W.W. Norton & Co., 2012

LC 2011038037

"In 1916, in the middle of the First World War, two men secretly agreed to divide the Middle East between them. Sir Mark Sykes was a visionary politician; François Georges-Picot a diplomat with a grudge. The deal they struck, which was designed to relieve tensions that threatened to engulf the Entente Cordiale, drew a line in the sand from the Mediterranean to the Persian frontier. Territory north of that stark line would go to France; land south of it, to Britain. . . . Their pact survived the war to form the basis for the postwar division of the region into five new countries Britain and France would rule. The creation of Britain's mandates of Palestine, Transjordan and Iraq, and France's in Lebanon and Syria, made the two powers uneasy neighbours for the following thirty years. . . . [This book] tells the story of the . . . era when Britain and France ruled the Middle East. It [aims to] explain . . . how the old antagonism between these two powers inflamed the . . . modern rivalry between the Arabs and the Jews, and ultimately led to war between the British and the French in 1941 and between the Arabs and the Jews in 1948." (Publisher's note)

Churchill, Buntzie Ellis

Notes on a century; reflections of a Middle East historian. Bernard Lewis; with Buntzie Ellis Churchill. Viking 2012 388 p.   **956**

1. Middle East specialists -- Great Britain -- Biography 2. Nonfiction
ISBN 0670023531; 9780670023530

LC 2011049267

This memoir by political consultant and historian Bernard Lewis provides the author's personal reflections on his international career and his views on the major themes of world politics spanning 'World War II, up through the Arab Spring. . . . Lewis . . . was the first to warn of a coming 'clash of civilizations,' a term he coined in 1957, and has led [a] life, as much a political actor as a scholar of the Middle East." (Publisher's note)

Congressional Quarterly, Inc.

★ The **Middle** East; 11th ed; CQ Press 2007 xix, 663p il map $70; pa $46.95   **956**

ISBN 978-0-87289-368-9; 0-87289-368-5; 978-0-87289-369-6 pa; 0-87289-369-3 pa

LC 2007-19956

Covers topics such as oil, Islam, the Arab-Israeli conflict, the Persian Gulf, and the arms trade in the Middle East. Also presents profiles of Middle Eastern nations and twentieth-century leaders and includes documents such as UN resolutions and peace treaties

Finkel, Caroline

★ **Osman's** dream; the story of the Ottoman Empire, 1300-1923. Basic Books 2006 660p il map **956**

ISBN 0465023967; 9780465023967

This is a history "of the Ottoman Empire from its origins in the thirteenth century through its destruction on the battlefields of World War I." Publisher's note

Includes bibliographical references

Friedman, Thomas L.

From Beirut to Jerusalem. Farrar, Straus & Giroux 541p il maps $32 **956**

1. Jewish-Arab relations

ISBN 0-374-15895-9

LC 92-148666

The author presents an account of the political situation in the Middle East as he witnessed it in his years as a reporter in Lebanon and Jerusalem.

"When recounting his frequently harrowing experiences in that troubled region, Friedman can be absolutely riveting; similarly, his historical insights, his explanation of the root causes of the Arab-Israeli conflict, and his impressions of people and places in the Holy Land never fail to fascinate." Booklist

Herzog, Chaim

The **Arab**-Israeli wars; war and peace in the Middle East from the 1948 War of Independence to the present. updated by Shlomo Gazit; introduction by Isaac Herzog and Michael Herzog. 2nd ed, rev and updated; Vintage Books 2005 476p il pa $16.95 **956**

1. Jewish-Arab relations

ISBN 1-4000-7963-2

LC 2005-280207

This book traces "the Arab-Israeli wars and military conflicts from the 1948 War of Independence through the 1973 Yom Kippur War." Libr J

Includes bibliographic references

Hiro, Dilip

The **essential** Middle East; a comprehensive guide. Dilip Hiro. 1st Carroll & Graf ed.; Carroll & Graf 2003 639p il map pa $17.95 **956**

ISBN 0786712694

LC 2003055293

"In more than 1,000 alphabetically arranged entries, varying in length from a few lines to a few pages, Hiro covers more than 150 personalities in politics, business, culture, and religion; places of religious and cultural significance; oil and other minerals; political and religious sects; economic infrastructure; and political and religious ideologies." Booklist

Lewis, Bernard

The **Middle** East; a brief history of the last 2,000 years. Scribner 1995 433p il hardcover o.p. pa $16 **956**

ISBN 0-684-80712-2; 0-684-83280-1 pa

LC 96-4384

"Lewis has chosen to accentuate the social, economic, and cultural changes that have occurred over 20 centuries. He ranges from seemingly trivial concerns (changes in dress and manners in an Arab coffeehouse) to earth-shaking events (the Mongol conquest of Mesopotamia) in painting a rich, varied, and fascinating portrait of a region that is steeped in traditionalism while often forced by geography and politics to accept change." Booklist

Includes bibliographical references

What went wrong? Western impact and Middle Eastern response. Oxford Univ. Press 2002 180p il $23 **956**

ISBN 0-19-514420-1

LC 2001-36214

"Like many of Lewis's previous writings on this subject . . . this book will undoubtedly generate significant debate and disagreement among scholars regarding the author's analysis of Islamic responses to modernity and Westernization." Libr J

Includes bibliographical references

Meyer, Karl E.

Kingmakers; the invention of the modern Middle East. [by] Karl E. Meyer and Shareen Blair Brysac. Norton 2008 507p il map $27.95 **956**

ISBN 978-0-393-06199-4; 0-393-06199-X

LC 2008-07378

The authors "have written a timely and engrossing study of the men and women who were instrumental in giving birth to some of the nations, institutions, and chronic problems of the area." Booklist

Includes bibliographical references

Morris, Benny

Righteous victims; a history of the Zionist-Arab conflict, 1881-1998. Knopf 1999 751p hardcover o.p. pa $18 **956**

1. Arab-Israeli conflict 2. Arab-Israeli conflict -- 1993- -- Peace 3. Israel-Arab conflicts 4. Jewish-Arab relations 5. Jewish-Arab relations -- History -- 1917-1948

ISBN 0-679-74475-4 pa

LC 98-42774

Morris traces the history of Arab-Israeli conflicts and examines major events and their aftereffects.

"The author displays a remarkable grasp of the history of the Zionist-Arab conflict and an analytical style that is devoid of the polemics that have characterized so many books on this subject." Libr J

Includes bibliographical references

Palakean, Grigoris

Armenian Golgotha; translated by Peter Balakian with Aris Sevag. Alfred A. Knopf 2009 509p il map $35 **956**

1. Armenian massacres, 1915-1923 2. Armenian massacres, 1915-1923 -- Personal narratives 3. Biography, Individual 4. Genocide 5. Genocide -- Turkey 6. Priests

ISBN 978-0-307-26288-2; 0-307-26288-X

LC 2008-39957

"On the night of April 24, 1915, Grigoris Balakian, an Armenian priest, and more than two hundred other Armenian politicians and intellectuals were arrested in Constantinople. Soon, Armenians across Turkey were massacred or forced to join a death march to the desert of Der Zor. Balakian walked among the displaced for months before he fled, disguising himself variously as a German engineer, a soldier, and a worker in the vineyards; he began this book while in hiding. (It was published in Armenian in 1922 and in 1959; the translator is Balakian's great-nephew.) Both a memoir and an attempt at a history of the genocide, it assumes considerable familiarity with Ottoman politics, but remains fascinating firsthand testimony to a monumental crime." New Yorker
Includes bibliographical references

Wallach, Janet
Desert queen; the extraordinary life of Gertrude Bell: adventurer, adviser to kings, ally of Lawrence of Arabia. Talese 1996 xxv, 419p hardcover o.p. pa $15.95 **956**
1. Archaeologists 2. Archeologists 3. Biography, Individual 4. Explorers 5. Travelers 6. Women -- Travel
ISBN 0-385-47408-3; 978-1-4000-9619-0 pa; 1-4000-9619-7 pa
LC 95-44868
"High-spirited, outspoken, and self-reliant, . . . {Bell} was the first woman to earn a degree in history at Oxford, a skilled mountain climber and equestrienne, and an avid and fearless traveler who found her spiritual home in the deserts of Iraq and Arabia. . . . Fluent in Arabic and on good terms with powerful men, Bell became an invaluable asset to British intelligence and was drafted as a spy during World War I. . . . Wallach . . . brings the resolute Bell and her complex world vividly to life." Booklist
Includes bibliographical references

de Bellaigue, Christopher
Rebel land; unraveling the riddle of history in a Turkish town. Penguin Press 2010 270p il map $25.95 **956**
1. Armenian massacres, 1915-1923 2. Genocide
ISBN 978-1-59420-252-0; 1-59420-252-4
This is "a revealing and stunning examination of Turkey's past and present that also poses interesting questions about ethnic and national identity." Booklist
Includes bibliographical references

The Continuum political encyclopedia of the Middle East; Avraham Sela, editor. rev and updated ed; Continuum 2002 944p maps $175 **956**
ISBN 0-8264-1413-3
LC 2001-8542
This "contains entries on countries ranging from Afghanistan to Yemen; political movements and leaders; major foreign nations that impact this area, such as the United States and Russia; religions and religious movements; and regional topics of concern including 'Oil,' 'Terrorism,' 'Water Politics,' and 'Women, Gender and Politics.'. . . Alphabetical entries range from a few paragraphs to lengthy commentary. . . . Large libraries serving older students will find

this a useful . . . source of objective information on the history and issues affecting the contemporary Middle East." SLJ
Includes bibliographical references

Encyclopedia of the modern Middle East & North Africa; Philip Mattar, editor in chief. 2nd ed; Macmillan Reference USA 2004 4v il map set $475 **956**
1. Reference books
ISBN 0-02-865769-1
LC 2004-5650
"For current, accurate, and non-partisan information on the Middle East and North Africa, this excellent reference set . . . will answer basic questions and serve as a starting point for research on the region." Libr Media Connect
Includes bibliographical references

956.04 1945-1980

MacFarquhar, Neil
The **media** relations department of Hizbollah wishes you a happy birthday; unexpected encounters in the changing Middle East. PublicAffairs 2009 387p il map $26.95; pa $15.95 **956.04**
1. Authors 2. Journalists 3. Novelists
ISBN 978-1-58648-635-8; 978-1-58648-811-6 pa
LC 2009-2004
The author "offers something fresh and unexpected for readers steeped in a decade of news reports about suicide bombers, absolutist imams and tyrannical despots. . . . [This book] is MacFarquhar's effort to write a funny (yet penetrating) account about real Arabs—and a few Persians—struggling against long odds to bring their societies into the modern age. . . . For those who care about the Middle East and want to start listening to weak but growing voices calling for reform and modernization on local rather than Western terms, MacFarquhar's account is a fine place to begin." N Y Times Book Rev
Includes bibliographical references

Oren, Michael
Six days of war; June 1967 and the making of the modern Middle East. {by} Michael B. Oren. Oxford Univ. Press 2002 446p il $30 **956.04**
1. Israel-Arab War, 1967
ISBN 0-19-515174-7
LC 2001-58823
This is a history of the June 1967 Arab-Israeli War.
"What makes this book important is the breadth and depth of the research. Oren draws on archives, newly declassified documents, memoirs and interviews from Israel, America, Britain and what was then the Soviet Union." N Y Times Book Rev
Includes bibliographical references and index

Sacco, Joe
Footnotes in Gaza. Metropolitan Books 2009 418p il $29.95 **956.04**
1. Arab-Israeli conflict -- 1948-1967 2. Graphic novels 3. Israel-Arab conflicts -- Graphic novels 4.

Massacres -- Gaza Strip 5. Massacres -- Graphic novels 6. Violence -- Gaza Strip
ISBN 978-0-8050-7347-8; 0-8050-7347-7

LC 2009-28433

"Cartoonist and journalist Joe Sacco is the world's foremost creator of 'comics journalism'—a contemporary field he basically invented. . . . [This] book, whose 'footnotes' refer both to facts and metaphorically to history's forgotten people, is about two massacres of Palestinians in the Gaza Strip in November 1956. . . . Very little has been written about either event. Sacco conducted extensive research of U.N. documents and other materials, and additionally set out to interview as many eyewitnesses as he could track down. This is really the heart of this moving, precisely drawn work." Time Out N Y

Includes bibliographical references

Shlaim, Avi

Israel and Palestine; reappraisals, revisions, refutations. Verso 2009 392p map $34.95   **956.04**
1. Arab-Israeli conflict 2. Israel-Arab conflicts 3. Palestinian Arabs
ISBN 978-1-84467-366-7

LC 2009-455813

The author, "an Israeli army veteran and international relations professor at Oxford University, offers a penetrating critique of Zionism in these reviews and essays collected from the last 30 years. He focuses on the three main watersheds—Israel's establishment, the Six Day War of 1967 and the Oslo Accords of 1993 and offers valuable commentary on current scholarship." Publ Wkly

Includes bibliographical references

The **iron** wall; Israel and the Arab world since 1948. Norton 1999 704p il hardcover o.p. pa $17.95   **956.04**
1. Arab-Israeli conflict 2. Israel-Arab conflicts 3. Jewish-Arab relations
ISBN 0-393-32112-6 pa

LC 99-23121

"A thorough analysis of Israel's relationships with the West as well as its neighbors from a controversial but thoughtful point of view." Booklist

Includes bibliographical references

956.05   -1980

Hider, James

The **spiders** of Allah; travels of an unbeliever on the frontline of holy war. St. Martin's Griffin 2009 323p pa $14.95   **956.05**
1. Religion and politics 2. Religious fundamentalism 3. Terrorism -- Religious aspects
ISBN 978-0-312-56585-5; 0-312-56585-2

LC 2009-7378

"A British journalist's firsthand account of fanaticism and bloodshed in the Middle East. . . . [The author] loosely examines the ways in which radical Islam and fundamentalist Christianity have continually warped and damaged an already difficult situation. . . . The author's dense, vivid descriptions, frequently steeped in irony and humor, make for a slow but powerful read." Kirkus

Miller, Aaron David

The **much** too promised land; America's elusive search for Arab-Israeli peace. Bantam Books 2008 407p $26; pa $16   **956.05**
1. Israel-Arab conflicts
ISBN 978-0-553-80490-4; 0-553-80490-1; 978-0-553-38414-7 pa; 0-553-38414-7 pa

LC 2007-38982

The author presents advice on Mideast policy after having been a participant in diplomatic efforts made by the administrations of Presidents Carter, Clinton, and George W. Bush.

This is "an indispensable guide to the recent history of American peacemaking efforts in the defining conflict of the Middle East." Bookforum

Includes bibliographical references

Pope, Hugh

Dining with al-Qaeda; three decades exploring the many worlds of the Middle East. Thomas Dunne Books/St. Martin's Press 2010 332p il map $26.99   **956.05**
ISBN 978-0-312-38313-8

Pope's "criticisms of the invasion and of Israel may grate some readers, but those interested in the interpersonal rather than the international will enjoy Pope's bold curiosity in meeting people all over the Middle East." Booklist

Sadat, Jehan

My hope for peace. Free Press 2009 208p map $25   **956.05**
1. Islam and politics 2. Israel-Arab conflicts 3. Nobel laureates for peace 4. Presidents
ISBN 978-1-4165-9219-8; 1-4165-9219-9

LC 2008-32100

"Widow of the assassinated Egyptian president Anwar Sadat, Jehan Sadat . . . fashions a gracious plea for better understanding between the East and West, especially in terms of the fundamentals of Islam and the derailed Middle East peace process. . . . Sadat provides an important, insistent voice for continued advancement in peace and social justice." Publ Wkly

Includes bibliographical references

Said, Edward W.

The **end** of the peace process; Oslo and after. Pantheon Bks. 2000 345p $27.50; pa $14   **956.05**
1. Arab-Israeli conflict -- 1993- -- Peace 2. Israel-Arab conflicts 3. Jewish-Arab relations
ISBN 0-375-40930-0; 0-375-72574-1 pa

LC 99-44765

The author provides "analysis of the pitfalls of the Oslo agreement. Most of the essays in this collection have appeared in Cairo's al-Ahram Weekly and al-Hayat, London's Arabic-language daily. Each essay is Said's reflection on a dimension of the Palestinian predicament. . . . He is as critical of the corruption, incompetence, and authoritarianism of the Palestinian Authority as he is of American and Israeli postures." Libr J

Stack, Megan

Every man in this village is a liar; an education in war. [by] Megan K. Stack. Doubleday 2010 257p $26.95   **956.05**
  1. Journalists 2. Terrorism -- Middle East 3. War and civilization 4. War and society -- Middle East 5. War on Terrorism, 2001- 6. War on terrorism
  ISBN 978-0-385-52716-3; 0-385-52716-0
                                                LC 2009-34473
  "As a 25-year-old correspondent for the Los Angeles Times, Stack covered Afghanistan in the days immediately following 9/11, then traveled to other outposts in the war on terror, from Iraq to Iran, Libya, and Lebanon. In a disquieting series of essays, Stack now takes readers deep into the carnage where she was exposed to the insanity, innocence, and inhumanity of wars with no beginning, middle, or end. Her soaring imagery sears itself into the brain, in acute and accurate tales that should never be forgotten by the wider world, and yet always are." Booklist

Wright, Robin

Dreams and shadows; the future of the Middle East. Penguin Press 2008 464p map $26.95 **956.05**
  ISBN 1-59420-111-0; 978-1-59420-111-0
                                                LC 2007-46267
  "Absorbing accounts of brave activists are interwoven with relevant context and history in clear, vivid language. These elements make the book an engaging read, and a useful one for people who want to better understand this important part of the world." Christ Sci Monit
  Includes bibliographical reference

956.1   Turkey

Goodwin, Jason

Lords of the horizons; a history of the Ottoman Empire. Holt & Co. 1999 351p il map hardcover o.p. pa $15   **956.1**
  ISBN 0-312-42066-8 pa
                                                LC 98-41601
  "A history of distinctive originality, Goodwin's account imbibes deeply of traveler's impressions and seeks to see and describe, rather than explain and judge. A valuable synthesis." Booklist
  Includes bibliographical references

Kinzer, Stephen

Crescent and star; Turkey between two worlds. Farrar, Straus & Giroux 2001 252p hardcover o.p. pa $14   **956.1**
  1. Civil society -- Turkey -- History -- 20th century 2. Turkey -- Ethnic relations -- History -- 20th century
  ISBN 0-374-52866-7 pa
                                                LC 2001-23298
  The author "gives a concise introduction to Turkey: Kemal Atatürk's post-WWI establishment of the modern secular Turkish state; the odd makeup of contemporary society, in which the military enforces Atatürk's reforms. In stylized but substantive prose, he devotes chapters to the problems he sees plaguing Turkish society: Islamic fundamentalism,

frictions regarding the large Kurdish minority and the lack of democratic freedoms." Publ Wkly

Mango, Andrew

The **Turks** today; Andrew Mango. 1st ed; Overlook Press 2004 292p map $29.95; pa $17.95 **956.1**
  ISBN 1-585-67615-2; 1-585-67756-6 pa
                                                LC 2004-58339
  "This fascinating and timely survey is both a political history and a cultural examination of a diverse, dynamic society." Booklist
  Includes bibliographical references

Pope, Hugh

Turkey unveiled; a history of modern Turkey. {by} Hugh and Nicole Pope. Overlook Press 1998 373p il maps $29.95; pa $16.95   **956.1**
  ISBN 0-87951-898-7; 1-58567-096-0 pa
                                                LC 98-16616
  "The Popes have written a deeply revealing guide to modern Turkish culture and politics that fills a wide gap in our cultural knowledge." N Y Times Book Rev
  Includes bibliographical references p. ({363}-366) and index

956.6   Eastern Turkey

Akcam, Taner

A **shameful** act; the Armenian genocide and the question of Turkish responsibility. translated by Paul Bessemer. Metropolitan Books 2006 483p map $30   **956.6**
  1. Armenian massacres, 1915-1923 2. Genocide 3. War crimes
  ISBN 0-8050-7932-7; 978-0-8050-7932-6
                                                LC 2005-58401
  "This groundbreaking and lucid account by a prominent Turkish scholar speaks forcefully to all." Publ Wkly
  Includes bibliographical references

Balakian, Peter

★ The **burning** Tigris; the Armenian genocide and America's response. HarperCollins 2003 xx, 475p il $26.95; pa $14.95   **956.6**
  1. Armenian massacres, 1915-1923 2. Genocide 3. Genocide -- Turkey 4. Human rights
  ISBN 0-06-019840-0; 0-06-055870-9 pa
                                                LC 2003-44986
  "The book's real power derives from the eyewitness accounts of the genocide itself. The sheer volume of outsiders' testimony that Balakian compiles, and the horrifying similarity of their observations of men, women and children beaten, tortured, burned to death in churches or sent out into the desert to starve, is an overwhelmingly convincing retort to genocide deniers." N Y Times Book Rev
  Includes bibliographical references

956.7 Iraq

Allawi, Ali A.

The **occupation** of Iraq; winning the war, losing the peace. Yale University Press 2007 xxiv, 518p il map $28 **956.7**

1. Iraq War, 2003 2. Iraq War, 2003- 3. Military occupation

ISBN 978-0-300-11015-9; 0-300-11015-4

LC 2006-39445

This "scholarly yet immensely readable exposition of Iraqi society and politics will likely become the standard reference on post-9/11 Iraq." Publ Wkly

Includes bibliographical references

Atkinson, Rick

Crusade; the untold story of the Persian Gulf War. Houghton Mifflin 1993 575p il maps hardcover o.p. pa $17 **956.7**

1. Persian Gulf War, 1991

ISBN 0-395-71083-9 pa

LC 93-14388

The author provides an "account of the actions and utterances of those who directed and fought in the Persian Gulf War. He also provides a thorough analysis of diplomatic and political aspects of the conflict. Rich in pertinent details, the powerful narrative leaps nimbly from Washington to Riyadh, from Baghdad to Kuwait City, and to various battle sites across the sands. Expectedly, the book's dominant personality is General H. Norman Schwarzkopf." Publ Wkly

Includes bibliographical references

In the company of soldiers; a chronicle of combat. H. Holt 2004 319p il maps $25; pa $14 **956.7**

1. Iraq War, 2003 2. Iraq War, 2003-

ISBN 0-8050-7561-5; 0-8050-7773-1 pa

LC 2003-67607

This is an eyewitness account of the war in Iraq. "In the spring of 2003, the author accompanied combat units to Iraq. He spent two months embedded with the 101st Airborne Division's headquarters staff, sharing their daily experiences from initial deployment out of Fort Campbell, KY, to overseas staging areas in Kuwait, and ultimately bearing witness to the unit's march on Baghdad. His view of the war was from a vantage point that permitted scrutiny of strategy, planning, and decision making at the senior command level." SLJ

Baker, James A.

★ The **Iraq** Study Group report; James A. Baker, III, and Lee H. Hamilton, co-chairs; [by] Lawrence S. Eagleburger . . . [et al.] Vintage Books 2006 142p map pa $10.95 **956.7**

1. Iraq War, 2003 2. Iraq War, 2003- 3. Military policy -- United States 4. Terrorism -- Government policy -- United States 5. United States -- Foreign relations -- 2001- 6. War on terrorism

ISBN 0-307-38656-2; 978-0-307-38656-4

LC 2006-474152

This book was "delivered by the Iraq Study Group to the Bush administration and simultaneously and inexpensively published for the general public. And there is no excuse for any public library, large or small, not to own a copy." Booklist

Bogdanos, Matthew

Thieves of Baghdad; one marine's passion for ancient civilizations and the journey to recover the world's greatest stolen treasures. [by] Matthew Bogdanos with William Patrick. Bloomsbury 2005 302p il map $25.95; pa $15.95 **956.7**

1. District attorneys 2. Iraq War, 2003 -- Destruction and pillage 3. Iraq War, 2003- -- Destruction and pillage 4. Iraq War, 2003- -- Personal narratives 5. Marine corps officers

ISBN 1-58234-645-3; 1-59691-146-8 pa

LC 2005-27652

Bogdanos "cuts through politics and hyperbole to tell an engrossing story abundant with history, colored by stories of brave Iraqis and Americans, and shaded with hope for the future." Publ Wkly

Includes bibliographical references

Campbell, Donovan

Joker one; a Marine platoon's story of courage, sacrifice, and brotherhood. Random House 2009 313p map hardcover o.p. pa $16 **956.7**

1. Beverage industry executives 2. Iraq War, 2003- -- Campaigns 3. Iraq War, 2003- -- Personal narratives 4. Marine corps officers 5. Memoirists

ISBN 978-1-4000-6773-2; 1-4000-6773-1; 978-0-8129-7956-5 pa; 0-8129-7956-7 pa

LC 2008-23896

This is "a harrowing narrative of [the author's] time as an infantry officer in Ramadi from March to September of 2004. . . . Campbell is a gifted writer who describes his own marines with deep care and attention." Washington Post

Chatterjee, Pratap

Halliburton's army; how a well-connected Texas oil company revolutionized the way America makes war. Nation Books 2009 284p $26.95 **956.7**

ISBN 978-1-56858-392-1

LC 2008-45876

This book "delves into the nebulous world of the Houston-based Halliburton corporation, tracing the company to its roots. . . . The author details the military contracting that largely funded the company through WWII and into the present-day war in Iraq, intertwining the company's history with the biographies of Dick Cheney, Donald Rumsfeld and other officials in the Bush administration. . . . Chatterjee keeps the pace of the narrative at a quick clip and nimbly marshals his extensive evidence to reveal—without sanctimony or stridency—Halliburton's record of corruption, political manipulation and human rights abuses." Publ Wkly

Includes bibliographical references

Cockburn, Patrick

The **occupation**. Norton 2006 229p map $24.95; pa $16.95 **956.7**

1. Iraq War, 2003 2. Iraq War, 2003-

ISBN 1-84467-100-3; 978-1-84467-100-7; 1-84467-164-X pa; 978-1-84467-164-9 pa

LC 2006-19472

The author "takes the reader through the often bewildering array of forces and personalities that are shaping developments in post-Saddam Iraq and makes them comprehensible to Western readers. . . . Cockburn's account of the evolving conflict, the emergence of the resistance movement, the increasingly sectarian nature of the conflict, and the jockeying for power among the Shia, Sunni, and Kurdish communities is informed by his keen personal observations and understanding of the complexities and horrors of daily life in Iraq." Libr J

Includes bibliographical references

Danner, Mark

Torture and truth; America, Abu Ghraib, and the war on terror. New York Review Books 2004 580p il pa $19.95   **956.7**
1. Iraq War, 2003 2. Iraq War, 2003 -- Atrocities 3. Iraq War, 2003- 4. Political prisoners 5. Prisoners of war -- Iraq 6. Torture
ISBN 1-590-17152-7

LC 2004-22408

This is "a book of permanent value for the study of the Iraq war and of how apparently reasonable policies can be swept away by intense pressure, political or military, to produce a particular result." Publ Wkly

Etherington, Mark

Revolt on the Tigris; the Al-Sadr uprising and the governing of Iraq. Cornell University Press 2005 252p il maps $25   **956.7**
1. Clergy 2. Counterinsurgency -- Iraq 3. Insurgency -- Iraq 4. Iraq War, 2003 5. Iraq War, 2003 -- Reconstruction 6. Iraq War, 2003- 7. Iraq War, 2003- -- Reconstruction 8. Islamic leaders
ISBN 0-8014-4451-9

LC 2005-49675

"Anyone seriously interested either in the future of that beleaguered nation or the possibilities of intelligent diplomacy would do well to read this firsthand account." Publ Wkly

Includes bibliographical references

Feuer, Alan

Over there; from the Bronx to Baghdad. Counterpoint 2005 283p $24   **956.7**
1. Iraq War, 2003 -- Personal narratives 2. Iraq War, 2003- -- Personal narratives
ISBN 1-58243-327-5; 978-1-58243-327-1

LC 2004-27149

The author describes the events that occured after he "was bustled off to the Middle East to cover the invasion of Iraq. . . . This is one war memoir that demands to be read." Booklist

Filkins, Dexter

★ The **forever** war. Alfred A. Knopf 2008 368p il $25   **956.7**
1. Iraq War, 2003- 2. Iraq War, 2003- -- Personal narratives 3. Journalists 4. War on Terrorism, 2001-
ISBN 0-307-26639-7; 978-0-307-26639-2

LC 2008-11761

An account of the wars in Afghanistan and Iraq since the 1990s.

This is "wonderfully written and carefully researched [book]. . . . Filkins's gripping account gives readers a clear, though disturbing, view of what's happening on the ground in Iraq. And he has put himself in the middle of this madness to deliver a stunning and illuminating story." Christ Sci Monit

Includes bibliographical references

Finkel, David

The **good** soldiers. Sarah Crichton Books 2009 287p il $26   **956.7**
1. Counterinsurgency -- Iraq 2. Iraq War, 2003- 3. Iraq War, 2003- -- Campaigns 4. Soldiers -- United States 5. Soldiers -- United States -- Biography
ISBN 978-0-374-16573-4; 0-374-16573-4

LC 2009-19391

"Finkel's keen firsthand reportage, its grit and impact only heightened by the literary polish of his prose, gives us one of the best accounts yet of the American experience in Iraq." Publ Wkly

Frederick, Jim

Black hearts; one platoon's descent into madness in Iraq's triangle of death. Harmony Books 2010 439p il map $26   **956.7**
1. Iraq War, 2003- -- Atrocities 2. War crimes
ISBN 978-0-307-45075-3; 0-307-45075-9

LC 2009-35537

"Frederick recounts the events leading up to and following the murder of 14-year-old Iraqi Abeer al-Janabi and the subsequent murder of her family—parents Qassim and Fakhriah and six-year-old sister Hadeel—committed by members of one U.S. Army deployment in Iraq's 'Triangle of Death.'" Publ Wkly

Includes bibliographical references

Ghareeb, Edmund

Historical dictionary of Iraq; [by] Edmund A. Ghareeb; with the assistance of Beth K. Dougherty. Scarecrow Press 2004 lxxvi, 459p map $85 **956.7**
ISBN 0-8108-4330-7

LC 2003-11526

"This work should be a required purchase in academic, public, and even some high-school libraries." Booklist

Includes bibliographical references

Gordon, Michael R.

The **generals'** war; the inside story of the conflict in the Gulf. by Michael R. Gordon and Bernard E. Trainor. Little, Brown 1994 551p il map hardcover o.p. pa $18.95   **956.7**
1. Persian Gulf War, 1991
ISBN 0-316-32100-1 pa

LC 94-27144

"This cogent analysis provides several disturbing answers worthy of our attention." Libr J

Includes bibliographical references

Gourevitch, Philip

Standard operating procedure; [by] Philip Gourevitch and Errol Morris. Penguin Press 2008 286p il $25.95 **956.7**
1. Iraq War, 2003- 2. Prisoners of war 3. Prisoners of war -- Abuse of 4. Prisoners of war -- Iraq
ISBN 978-1-59420-132-5

LC 2008-10215

"This deft piece of reportage will stir readers' anger, at both the actions and the consequences. . . . A thorough, terrifying account of an American-made 'bedlam.'" Publ Wkly

Haass, Richard

War of necessity: war of choice; a memoir of two Iraq wars. by Richard N. Haass. Simon & Schuster 2009 336 p. $27 **956.7**
1. Iraq War, 2003- -- Causes 2. Iraq War, 2003- -- Political aspects 3. Persian Gulf War, 1991 -- Causes 4. Persian Gulf War, 1991 -- Political aspects
ISBN 978-1-4165-4902-4; 1-4165-4902-1; 1416549021; 9781416549024

LC 2009004495

"A unique perspective on how war policy was formed by two very different presidents." Kirkus
Includes bibliographical references and index

Kelly, Michael

Martyrs' Day; chronicle of a small war. 2nd Vintage Books ed; Vintage Bks. 2001 365p pa $14 **956.7**
1. Persian Gulf War, 1991 -- Personal narratives
ISBN 1-4000-3036-6

LC 2002-524049

"This eyewitness account differs from the many other books on the Persian Gulf War in that it deals primarily with the human-interest elements rather than military matters. Kelly, a journalist who traveled extensively in the countries that were affected by the Gulf conflict, chronicles the vagaries of the war and its impact on the lives of the people in a revealing and disturbing text." Libr J

Kennedy, Hugh

When Baghdad ruled the Muslim world; the rise and fall of Islam's greatest dynasty. Da Capo Press 2005 xxv, 326p il map hardcover o.p. pa $18.95 **956.7**
1. Islamic civilization
ISBN 0-306-81435-8; 978-0-306-81435-8; 0-306-81480-3 pa; 978-0-306-81480-8 pa

LC 2006-295518

The author "has written an informative and sobering lesson for those who idolize the past." Choice
Includes bibliographical references

Mansoor, Peter R.

Baghdad at sunrise; a Brigade Commander's war in Iraq. foreword by Donald Kagan and Frederick Kagan. Yale University Press 2008 xxvii, 376p il map $28 **956.7**
1. Army officers 2. Iraq War, 2003- -- Personal

narratives 3. Military historians
ISBN 978-0-300-14069-9; 0-300-14069-X

LC 2008-07366

"This is a unique contribution to the burgeoning literature on the Iraq war. . . . The critique is balanced, perceptive and merciless." Publ Wkly
Includes bibliographical references

Miller, T. Christian

Blood money; wasted billions, lost lives, and corporate greed in Iraq. Little, Brown 2006 334p il map $24.99; pa $14.99 **956.7**
1. Baseball executives 2. Children of presidents 3. Energy industry executives 4. Governors 5. Iraq War, 2003 6. Iraq War, 2003- 7. Presidents
ISBN 0-316-16627-8; 978-0-316-16627-0; 0-316-16628-6 pa; 978-0-316-16628-7 pa

LC 2006-15074

This is an "account of how the Bush administration has mismanaged the Iraq war and reconstruction. Miller focuses on the bungling of government spending and private contracts, some $30 billion committed to rebuilding Iraq, a greater sum than for the Marshall Plan. . . . Readers interested in understanding the political and economic dynamics behind the faltering campaign in Iraq will appreciate this investigation." Booklist
Includes bibliographical references

Mills, Dan

Sniper one; on scope and under siege with a sniper team in Iraq. St. Martin's Press 2008 xxvi, 349p il map $26.95 **956.7**
1. Iraq War, 2003- -- Personal narratives 2. Soldiers
ISBN 978-0-312-53126-3; 0-312-53126-5

LC 2008-20438

"When a battalion of the Prince of Wales' Royal Regiment landed in Iraq in 2004, Mills commanded the 18 men of the sniper platoon. His gripping combat narrative covers how the platoon did more than its share of the fighting during the months when the Iraqis virtually besieged the battalion." Booklist

Murray, Williamson

The **Iraq** war; a military history. by Williamson Murray and Robert H. Scales, Jr. Belknap Press of Harvard University Press 2003 312p il map $29.95; pa $20 **956.7**
1. Iraq War, 2003 2. Iraq War, 2003-
ISBN 0-674-01280-1; 0-674-01968-7 pa

This is a military history of the 2003 American-led war against Iraq.

"Williamson Murray and Robert Scales, both American military academics, have produced a superlative record of the invasion—part history, part critique and part doctrinal template for the future. Technical and operational aspects are explained clearly without losing the depth required to make this a serious study." Economist
Includes bibliographical references

Packer, George

The **assassins'** gate; America in Iraq. Farrar, Straus & Giroux 2005 467p hardcover o.p. pa $15 **956.7**

1. Iraq War, 2003 2. Iraq War, 2003-
ISBN 0-374-29963-3; 0-374-53055-6 pa
LC 2005-11521

This "book rests on three main pillars: analysis of the intellectual origins of the Iraq war, summary of the political argument that preceded and then led to it, and firsthand description of the consequences on the ground. . . . The Iraq debate has long needed someone who is both tough-minded enough, and sufficiently sensitive, to register all its complexities. In George Packer's work, this need is answered." Publ Wkly

Includes bibliographical references

Polk, William Roe

★ **Understanding** Iraq; the whole sweep of Iraqi history, from Genghis Khan's Mongols to the Ottoman Turks to the British mandate to the American occupation. [by] William R. Polk. HarperCollins 2005 221p map $22.95; pa $13.95 **956.7**

ISBN 0-06-076468-6; 0-06-076469-4 pa
LC 2005-281319

The author presents an account of the history of Iraq, from the Dark Ages to the American occupation that began in 2003.

This is "a sober and informed account of Iraq's history, culminating in a compelling critique of the U.S. intervention there." Foreign Affairs

Includes bibliographical references

Raddatz, Martha

The **long** road home; a story of war and family. Putnam 2007 310p il map hardcover o.p. pa $15 **956.7**

1. Biography, Collective 2. Iraq War, 2003- --- Personal narratives 3. Soldiers -- Biography 4. Soldiers -- United States 5. Television reporters
ISBN 0-399-15382-9; 978-0-399-15382-2; 0-425-21934-8 pa; 978-0-425-21934-8 pa
LC 2006-37332

This "account has grit and high drama. . . . Sometimes the level of detail is astonishing." N Y Times (Late N Y Ed)

Rosen, Nir

Aftermath; following the bloodshed of America's wars in the Muslim world. Nation Books 2010 587p map $35 **956.7**

1. Iraq War, 2003- 2. Islam and politics
ISBN 978-1-56858-401-0; 9781568584010
LC 2010023467

This is "a scathing study of U.S. policy in the region—with a focus on the 2003 invasion of Iraq and its aftermath. Rosen argues that the 'brutal' occupation inflicted daily violence and humiliation on civilians, 'divided Iraqis against one another,' catalyzed a devastating civil war, and reinvigorated regional sectarianism. . . . [This book is] a pro-

vocative indictment of American policy and policy makers." Publ Wkly

Includes bibliographical references

Seierstad, Asne

A **hundred** and one days; a Baghdad journal. translated by Ingrid Christophersen. Basic Books 2005 321p il maps hardcover o.p. pa $14 **956.7**

1. Iraq War, 2003 2. Iraq War, 2003- -- Personal narratives 3. Journalists
ISBN 0-465-07600-9; 0-465-07601-7 pa

The author "writes about her stay as a reporter for Scandinavian, Dutch, and German media in Baghdad in the days before the war in Iraq through the fall of Baghdad. . . . Seierstad puts a human face to and provides insight into the mosaic of the people of Iraq, the Bath party supporters, the dissidents, and the average person caught in the nightmare of the Saddam regime and the horrors of war." SLJ

Shadid, Anthony

Night draws near; Iraq's people in the shadow of America's war. Picador 2006 507p map pa $15 **956.7**

1. Iraq War, 2003-
ISBN 978-0-312-42603-3; 0-312-42603-8

"Evenhanded and keenly observed, containing just enough (and no more) of the author to suggest a decent man worthy of our trust, . . . [this book] is written for the inexpert but has fresh material for scholars." Economist

Includes bibliographical references

Sheeler, Jim

Final salute; a story of unfinished lives. Penguin Press 2008 280p il $25.95 **956.7**

1. Bereavement 2. Death 3. Death -- Psychological aspects 4. Death notification -- United States 5. Families of military personnel -- United States 6. Iraq War, 2003- 7. Iraq War, 2003- -- Casualties 8. Military personnel -- United States
ISBN 978-1-59420-165-3; 1-59420-165-X
LC 2007-44130

This is a "tribute to the soldiers who have died in Iraq and their devastated families. The author spent two years shadowing Maj. Steve Beck, a marine in charge of casualty notification, as he delivered the news of battlefield death to families. Sheeler puts readers in Beck's shoes as he walks up to houses, delivers the knock on the door so dreaded by military families and tries to comfort distraught spouses and parents. . . . Sheeler's book is a devastating account of the sacrifices military families make and should be required reading for all Americans." Publ Wkly

Skiba, Katherine M.

Sister in the Band of Brothers; embedded with the 101st Airborne in Iraq. University Press of Kansas 2005 257p il $29.95 **956.7**

1. Iraq War, 2003 -- Personal narratives 2. Iraq War, 2003- -- Personal narratives
ISBN 0-7006-1382-X
LC 2004-26475

The author "was the only woman embedded with the 101st Airborne when the United States invaded Iraq in 2003.

She has written a fascinating memoir of her time within the training with other reporters, waiting to invade Iraq and spending the first few months of the war with soldiers in Iraq." Univ Press Books for Public and Second Sch Libr, 2006

Stewart, Rory

★ The **prince** of the marshes; and other occupational hazards of a year in Iraq. Harcourt, Inc. 2006 396p il $25 **956.7**
1. Diplomats 2. Nonfiction writers
ISBN 978-0-15-101235-0; 0-15-101235-0
LC 2006-06905

"In 2003, Stewart, a former British diplomat, joined the Coalition Provisional Authority in Iraq and was posted to the southern province of Maysan, where he found himself the de-facto governor of a restive populace whose allegiances were split among fifty-four political parties, twenty major tribes, and numerous militias. Stewart's account of his attempts to placate the various local figures who continually threaten to kill each other, or him, is both shrewd and self-deprecating." New Yorker

Tripp, Charles

A **history** of Iraq; 3rd ed.; Cambridge University Press 2007 xxiii, 357p il map $70; pa $24.99 **956.7**
ISBN 978-0-521-87823-4; 978-0-521-70247-8 pa
LC 2007-282451

This book traces the political history of Iraq from the Ottoman Empire to the fall of Saddam Hussein and the American occupation.

Woodward, Bob

★ **Plan** of attack. Simon & Schuster 2004 467p il map hardcover o.p. pa $14 **956.7**
1. Baseball executives 2. Children of presidents 3. Energy industry executives 4. Governors 5. Iraq War, 2003 6. Iraq War, 2003- 7. Presidents 8. United States -- Politics and government -- 2001-
ISBN 0-7432-5547-X; 0-7432-5548-8 pa
LC 2004-351204

The author "delivers an engrossing blow-by-blow of the run-up to war in Iraq. . . . With this book, Woodward . . . has delivered his most important and impressive work in years. Ultimately, this first-class work of contemporary history will be remembered for shedding needed light on the Iraq War." Publ Wkly

Wright, Evan

Generation kill; Devil Dogs, Iceman, Captain America, and the new face of American war. G.P. Putnam's Sons 2004 354p il maps hardcover o.p. pa $15 **956.7**
1. Iraq War, 2003 2. Iraq War, 2003- -- Personal narratives
ISBN 0-399-15193-1; 0-425-20040-X pa
LC 2004-44682

The author discusses his experiences when embedded with the First Marine Division in Iraq. This book is based on a series of articles that originally appeared in Rolling Stone.

This "account is a personality-driven, readable and insightful look at the Iraq War's first month from the Marine grunt's point of view." Publ Wkly

Operation homecoming; Iraq, Afghanistan, and the Home Front, in the words of U.S. troops and their families. preface by Dana Gioia; edited by Andrew Carroll. Updated ed.; University of Chicago Press 2008 xxviii, 408p il pa $16 **956.7**
1. Afghan War, 2001- -- Personal narratives 2. Iraq War, 2003- -- Personal narratives
ISBN 978-0-226-09499-1; 0-226-09499-5
LC 2007-48835

This book was created as part of a National Endowment for the Arts-funded project that "brought together some of the nation's most distinguished writers, including Tobias Wolff and Marilyn Nelson, and the men and women (and their spouses) fighting in the Middle East. The result is an incredibly wide range of opinions and emotions about U.S. policy in the Middle East, the war on terrorism, and the duties and responsibilities of citizens and the military. In 100 pieces of poetry, essays, letters, e-mails, plays, and journal entries, soldiers recall the awful thrill in the threat of killing or being killed, the deaths of buddies, and the cultural and psychological adjustments to a strange land." Booklist

What was asked of us; an oral history of the Iraq War by the soldiers who fought it. [compiled by] Trish Wood. Little, Brown and Co. 2006 309p il map pa $14.99 **956.7**
1. Iraq War, 2003 -- Personal narratives 2. Iraq War, 2003- -- Personal narratives 3. Soldiers -- United States
ISBN 978-0-316-01670-4; 0-316-01670-5; 978-0-316-01671-1 pa; 0-316-01671-3 pa
LC 2006-930963

"Colloquial, coarse and compelling, these narratives flash with humor, horror, nihilism and poesy." Publ Wkly

956.704   -1979

Castner, Brian

The **long** walk; a story of war and the life that follows. Brian Castner. Doubleday 2012 222 p. **956.704**
1. Iraq War, 2003-2011 -- Personal narratives, American 2. Iraq War, 2003-2011 -- Veterans -- United States -- Biography 3. Ordnance disposal units -- Iraq 4. Ordnance disposal units -- United States
ISBN 0385536208; 9780385536202
LC 2011052419

This memoir by Brian Castner describes his life during and after the Iraq War. [A]s the commander of an Explosive Ordnance Disposal unit in Iraq . . . [d]ays and nights he and his team . . . would venture forth in heavily armed convoys from their Forward Operating Base to engage in . . . disarming the deadly improvised explosive devices that had been discovered. . . . They relied on an army of remote-controlled cameras and robots, but if that technology failed, a technician would have to don the eighty-pound Kevlar suit, take the Long Walk up to the bomb, and disarm it by hand. . . . When Castner returned home to his wife and family, he began a struggle with . . . an unshakable feeling of fear and confusion and survivors guilt that he terms The Crazy. (Publishers note)

Chandrasekaran, Rajiv
Imperial life in the emerald city; inside Iraq's green zone. Rajiv Chandrasekaran. Alfred A. Knopf 2006 x, 320p maps (alk. paper) $25.95   **956.704**
1. Iraq War, 2003- 2. Political corruption 3. Postwar reconstruction -- Iraq
ISBN 1400044871; 9781400044870
LC 2006041014
This book discusses "the Green Zone in Baghdad, headquarters for the American occupation in Iraq, . . . [and provides a] portrait of the Green Zone and the Coalition Provisional Authority (which ran Iraqs government from April 2003 to June 2004) that becomes a metaphor for the [U.S.] administrationss larger failings in Iraq. An insular, often blinkered approach to decision making; a reluctance to listen to experts; Pollyannaish expectations leading to inadequate allocations of resources and staff; a willful ignorance of Iraqi culture and history; and an obliviousness to realities on the ground: all are on unfortunate display in the Emerald City." (New York Times)
"This is a clearly written, blessedly undidactic book. It should be read by anyone who wants to understand how things went so badly wrong in Iraq." N Y Times Book Rev
Includes bibliographical references (p. [303]-306) and index.

Clancy, Tom
Into the storm; a study in command. {by} Tom Clancy with Fred Franks, Jr. Putnam 1997 531p il maps hardcover o.p. pa $16.95   **956.704**
1. Persian Gulf War, 1991
ISBN 0-425-16308-3 pa
LC 96-38068
This history of the Persian Gulf War focuses on the command of General Frederick M. Banks.

Mackey, Sandra
The **reckoning**; Iraq and the legacy of Saddam Hussein. Norton 2002 415p il maps $27.95; pa $16.95   **956.704**
1. Iraq -- Politics and government -- 1958- 2. Presidents
ISBN 0-393-05141-2; 0-393-32428-1 pa
LC 2002-16611
The author offers a "history of Iraq and its early Mesopotamian civilization with . . . biographies of all of its historical figures through the ages, shedding perspective on the current regime of Saddam Hussein and looking ahead to what an Iraq without Hussein might resemble. . . . An extremely thorough appraisal." Booklist
Includes bibliographical references

Maraniss, David
They marched into sunlight; war and peace in Vietnam and America, October 1967. Simon

& Schuster 2003 592p il map hardcover o.p. pa $16   **956.704**
1. Vietnam War, 1961-1975
ISBN 0-7432-1780-2; 0-7432-6104-6 pa
LC 2003-52885
This is a "narrative by a reporter who juxtaposes a ghastly little battle in Vietnam with an antiwar and anti-Dow demonstration at the University of Wisconsin, Madison, on the same day; it captures moral ambiguity everywhere, without stereotyping or condescension." N Y Times Book Rev
Includes bibliographical references

Newell, Clayton R.
Historical dictionary of the Persian Gulf War, 1990-1991. Scarecrow Press 1998 lix, 363p maps $65   **956.704**
1. Persian Gulf War, 1991
ISBN 0-8108-3511-8
LC 98-18944
The author attempts "to help the reader understand the Gulf War and its background. He includes several pages of abbreviations and acronyms along with pages of maps, all . . . describing what happened and why during the 1991 conflict. There is . . . a 30-page introduction that describes the political developments that led up to the war and a much-needed chronology of events. . . . The dictionary entries average about a paragraph and cover the war's personalities as well as its combat equipment." Libr J

Ricks, Thomas E.
Fiasco: the American military adventure in Iraq. Penguin Press 2006 482p il map hardcover o.p. pa $16   **956.704**
1. Iraq War, 2003 2. Iraq War, 2003-
ISBN 1-59420-103-X; 978-1-59420-103-5; 0-14-303891-5 pa; 978-0-14-303891-7 pa
LC 2006-45357
This book is "not a political rant nor is it shrill. But in its low-key, extraordinarily well-sourced, highly-detailed portrait of the run-up to and conduct of the war it is devastating." Christ Sci Monit
Includes bibliographical references

Schwartz, Richard Alan
Encyclopedia of the Persian Gulf War. McFarland & Co. 1998 216p il maps hardcover o.p. pa $45   **956.704**
1. Air force officers 2. Army officers 3. Diplomats 4. Energy industry executives 5. Generals 6. Marine corps officers 7. Members of Congress 8. Parents of presidents 9. Persian Gulf War, 1991 10. Persian Gulf War, 1991 -- Encyclopedias 11. Presidents 12. Reference books 13. Secretaries of defense 14. Secretaries of state 15. United Nations officials 16. Vice-presidents
ISBN 0-7864-0451-5; 0-7864-4103-8 pa
LC 97-51886
"Beginning with a seven-page overview, this encyclopedia presents alphabetically arranged entries that describe the conflict, including key figures, places, battles, diplomacy, and more." SLJ
Includes bibliographical references

Swofford, Anthony

Jarhead: a Marine's chronicle of the Gulf War and other battles. Scribner 2003 260p hardcover o.p. pa $15   **956.704**
  1. Marines 2. Memoirists 3. Persian Gulf War, 1991 -- Personal narratives 4. Persian Gulf War, 1991 -- Personal narratives, American
  ISBN 0-7432-3535-5; 0-7432-8721-5 pa
                         LC 2002-30866
This book offers "an unflinching portrayal of the loneliness and brutality of modern warfare and sophisticated analyses of—and visceral reactions to—its politics." Publ Wkly

956.94   Palestine; Israel

Armstrong, Karen

Jerusalem; one city, three faiths. Knopf 1996 xxi, 471p il maps hardcover o.p. pa $17.95 **956.94**
  1. Jerusalem -- History
  ISBN 0-679-43596-4; 0-345-39168-3 pa
                         LC 96-75888
Armstrong's "overarching theme, that Jerusalem has been central to the experience and 'sacred geography' of Jews, Muslims and Christians and thus has led to deadly struggles for dominance, is a familiar one, yet she brings to her sweeping, profusely illustrated narrative a grasp of sociopolitical conditions seldom found in other books." Publ Wkly

Bregman, Ahron

A **history** of Israel. Palgrave Macmillan 2002 xx, 320p map $70; pa $21.95   **956.94**
  ISBN 0-333-67631-9; 0-333-67632-7 pa
                         LC 2002-72304
"Bregman takes into account all the major issues involving Israel's history." Booklist
  Includes bibliographical references and index

Carroll, James

Jerusalem, Jerusalem; how the ancient city ignited our modern world. Houghton Mifflin Harcourt 2011 418p $20   **956.94**
  ISBN 978-0-547-19561-2; 0-547-19561-3
                         LC 2010-43034
"Carroll examines the enigma that is Jerusalem—the holiest and most blood-soaked spot on earth. . . . While various religions flourished all over the ancient world, it was in Jerusalem that God emerged. Not just a god, but God, one who recognizes how both the need for violence and the hatred of violence reside within the human spirit. These conflicting impulses are the subthemes that propel Carroll's story across the ages, through Jerusalem's wreckages and rebirths, as the three Abrahamic religions claim the city as its own. Carroll's writing is so compelling, so beautifully constructed, that, ironically, the book can be a very slow read. There is something on almost every page that makes the reader want to stop and contemplate." Booklist
  Includes bibliographical references

Cesarani, David

Major Farran's hat; the untold story of the struggle to establish the Jewish state. Da Capo Press 2009 290p il map $26   **956.94**
  1. Army officers 2. Government officials 3. Kidnap victims 4. Murder victims 5. Newspaper executives 6. Political leaders 7. Revolutionaries 8. Terrorism
  ISBN 978-0-306-81845-5
This book "provides a neat, if briskly presented, history of British involvement in Palestine and the international power politics involved. . . . [It] is a piece of contemporary history with bite and verve." Times Higher Ed
  Includes bibliographical references

Cohen, Rich

Israel is real. Farrar, Straus, and Giroux 2009 383p map $27; pa $16   **956.94**
  1. Jews -- History
  ISBN 978-0-374-17778-2; 0-374-17778-3; 978-0-312-42976-8 pa; 0-312-42976-2 pa
                         LC 2008-49223
The author explains "the history of a people and its religion from the time Zealots revolted against their Roman occupiers to the rise of the Zionists, who helped build the current republic. . . . A must-read for those who want to understand the context of the modern Jewish state." Kirkus
  Includes bibliographical references

Collins, Larry

O Jerusalem! {by} Larry Collins and Dominique Lapierre. Simon & Schuster 1972 637p il maps hardcover o.p. pa $17   **956.94**
  1. Israel-Arab War, 1948-1949
  ISBN 0-671-66241-4 pa
This is an account of the struggle for the city of Jerusalem during the Israel-Arab War of 1948.

Farsoun, Samih K.

Palestine and the Palestinians; {by} Samih K. Farsoun with Christina E. Zacharia. Westview Press 1997 375p maps hardcover o.p. pa $29   **956.94**
  1. Israel-Arab conflicts 2. Palestinian Arabs
  ISBN 0-8133-2773-3 pa
                         LC 97-21954
This study of the Palestinian peoples covers their economic and social conditions, their political activity and national aspirations.
  "This is an excellent introduction to the modern history of the Palestinians, the transformations of their troubled land, and the prospects of both." Choice
  Includes bibliographical references

Gilbert, Martin

Jerusalem in the twentieth century. Wiley 1996 412p il maps $30; pa $16.95   **956.94**
  1. Palestine -- History
  ISBN 0-471-16308-2; 0-471-28328-2 pa
                         LC 96-18458
"Gilbert's history is heavily Zionist. . . . Nonetheless, despite his tilt, Gilbert is well worth reading. He has an unrivalled ability to tell a story through the eyes of (some of)

those taking part and his book is good popular history." London Rev Books

Includes bibliographical references

Gorenberg, Gershom

The **accidental** empire; Israel and the birth of the settlements, 1967-1977. Times Books 2006 454p il map $30   **956.94**

1. Jews -- Colonization -- Palestine 2. Land settlement -- Palestine

ISBN 0-8050-7564-X; 978-0-8050-7564-9

LC 2005-52988

This is an account of the settler movement in Israel, beginning with the aftermath of the 1967 war.

This is "an absorbing narrative with extensive references to archives, private papers, oral histories, books and articles." Nation

Includes bibliographical references

Laqueur, Walter

A **history** of Zionism; with a new preface by the author. Schocken Bks. 1989 xxii, 639p il hardcover o.p. pa $16.95   **956.94**

1. Zionism

ISBN 0-8052-1149-7 pa

LC 88-38221

The author examines the history of Zionism over the past three centuries from its European roots to the establishment of the state of Israel.

LeBor, Adam

City of oranges; an intimate history of Arabs and Jews in Jaffa. W.W. Norton 2007 xxxviii, 424p il map pa $14.95   **956.94**

1. Israel-Arab conflicts 2. Jews -- Israel -- Social conditions 3. Palestinian Arabs -- Israel -- Social conditions

ISBN 0-393-32984-4; 978-0-393-32984-1

LC 2007-2389

LeBor presents interviews with Arab and Jewish families in Jaffa, Israel.

"Those looking for a well-rounded and truly human insight into the conflict will enjoy this account." Publ Wkly

Includes bibliographical references

Miller, Jennifer

★ **Inheriting** the Holy Land; an American's search for hope in the Middle East. Ballantine Books 2005 xxxiii, 261p map $24.95; pa $14.95 **956.94**

1. Israel-Arab conflicts

ISBN 0-345-46924-0; 978-0-345-46924-3; 0-345-46925-9 pa; 978-0-345-46925-0 pa

LC 2004-66349

The author "is the daughter of one of the chief American negotiators in the Israeli-Palestinian conflict and a longtime participant in the Seeds of Peace program, bringing together Israeli and Palestinian children. Using the many contacts that she has made, from the highest leaders to the children on the street, Miller explores . . . the many different viewpoints and preconceptions of the people involved in the conflict,

not excluding her own. . . . This is a superb book on a crucial issue of our time." SLJ

Includes bibliographical references

Montefiore, Sebag

Jerusalem; the biography. [by] Simon Sebag Montefiore. Knopf 2011 638p il map $35 **956.94**

1. Biography, Collective 2. Jerusalem -- History

ISBN 978-0-307-26651-4; 0-307-26651-6

Sachar, Howard Morley

A **history** of Israel; from the rise of Zionism to our time. [by] Howard M. Sachar. 3rd ed, rev and updated; Knopf 2007 xxii, 1270p map pa $39.95   **956.94**

1. Zionism

ISBN 978-0-375-71132-9; 0-375-71132-5

LC 2006-101970

This is a history of the state of Israel. "When first published in 1976, this truly monumental history was hailed as a definitive work. . . . As extraordinarily stimulating as the first edition." Booklist

Includes bibliographical references

Shipler, David K.

Arab and Jew; wounded spirits in a promised land. rev ed; Penguin Bks. 2002 xxxix, 565p maps pa $17   **956.94**

1. Arab-Israeli conflict 2. Israel -- Social conditions 3. Israel-Arab conflicts 4. Jewish-Arab relations 5. Palestinian Arabs

ISBN 0-14-200229-1

LC 2001-54862

The author examines the stereotypes that Arabs and Jews have of one another and "the origins of the prejudices that have been intensified by war, terrorism, and nationalism. . . . Shipler examines the process of indoctrination that begins in schools; he discusses the far-ranging effects of socioeconomic differences, historical conflicts between Islam and Judaism, attitudes about the Holocaust, and much more." Publisher's note

Includes bibliographical references and index

Timmerman, Kenneth R.

Preachers of hate; Islam and the war on America. Crown Publishers 2003 370p $25.95; pa $14.95   **956.94**

1. Israel-Arab conflicts

ISBN 1-4000-4901-6; 1-4000-5373-0 pa

LC 2003-11455

The author "examines the politics that demonize Israel—and, increasingly, the U.S.—for failures of domestic policy in many Arab nations." Booklist

Includes bibliographical references

Tolan, Sandy

The **lemon** tree; an Arab, a Jew, and the heart of the Middle East. Bloomsbury Pub. 2006 362p $24.95   **956.94**

1. Arab-Israeli conflict 2. Biography, Individual 3. Israel-Arab conflicts 4. Kindergarten teachers 5.

Refugees
ISBN 1-58234-343-8; 978-1-58234-343-3
LC 2005-30360
The author "captures the Arab-Israeli struggle in this story of a house and the two families, first Palestinian and then Jewish, who successively lived in it. . . . This wonderful human story vividly depicts the depths of attachment to contested ground." Libr J

★ How Israelis and Palestinians negotiate; a cross-cultural analysis of the Oslo peace process. edited by Tamara Cofman Wittes. United States Institute of Peace Press 2005 160p $40; pa $12 **956.94**
1. Cross-cultural studies 2. Israel-Arab conflicts 3. Israeli national characteristics 4. Palestinian Arabs
ISBN 1-929223-64-1; 1-929223-63-3 pa
LC 2004-65759
"Five essays by leading scholars focus on the concept of culture and the role it plays in the success and failure of the Middle East peace process. Both Israeli and Palestinian cultures are assessed and explained as a context to understand snags and successes from Oslo II to the Camp David accords. This small volume is very accessible to high school readers and should generate interest in understanding the larger issues which continue to add to the instability of the region." Univ Press Books for Public and Second Sch Libr, 2006
Includes bibliographical references

956.940 -1948

Horovitz, David Phillip
A **little** too close to God; the thrills and panic of a life in Israel. {by} David Horovitz. Knopf 2000 311p $27.50   **956.940**
1. Israel -- Social conditions 2. Israeli national characteristics
ISBN 0-375-40381-7
The author, editor of the Jerusalem Report, argues "that in recent years the conservative Netanyahu government and the continued influence of extreme Orthodox Jews have done little except complicate daily life in Israel and prevent serious peace negotiations from taking place. He presents a highly informative history and current-events narrative in a manner that makes it personal and relevant to Jews and non-Jews alike." Libr J

La Guardia, Anton
War without end; Israelis, Palestinians, and the struggle for a promised land. St. Martin's Griffin 2003 xxii, 436p il map pa $16.95 **956.940**
1. Arab-Israeli conflict 2. Arab-Israeli conflict -- 1993- -- Influence 3. Israel-Arab conflicts 4. Israeli national characteristics 5. Jews -- Israel -- Identity 6. National characteristics, Israeli 7. Palestinian Arabs 8. Palestinian Arabs -- Ethnic identity 9. Zionism
ISBN 0-312-31633-X
LC 2003-41288
"This is fundamentally an examination of two wounded peoples, neither of whom seems capable of surmounting national myths and past hatreds to forge a new future. La

Guardia is evenhanded in his criticism of both Israeli and Palestinian leaders, but he does not spare ordinary people. . . . This is an absorbing but heartbreaking examination of a seemingly endless tragedy that continues to unfold before our eyes." Booklist [review of 2002 edition]
Includes bibliographical references

Lozowick, Yaacov
Right to exist; a moral defense of Israel's wars. Doubleday 2003 326p map $26; pa $15 **956.940**
1. Arab-Israeli conflict 2. Israel-Arab conflicts
ISBN 0-385-50905-7; 1-4000-3243-1 pa
LC 2003-48477
The author "asserts that Israel is now, as before, struggling against opponents whose goal is the eventual destruction of the Jewish state. In examining the entire history of the Zionist enterprise, he illustrates both the moral justification of that enterprise and of the wars Israelis have been compelled to fight to preserve their independence. . . . {This} is an eloquent and necessary justification of Israel's right to defend itself." Booklist

956.95   Jordan and West Bank

Grossman, David
The **yellow** wind; translated from the Hebrew by Haim Watzman; {with a new afterword by the author} Picador 2002 222p map pa $13   **956.95**
1. Arab-Israeli conflict -- 1973-1993 2. Jewish-Arab relations 3. Palestinian Arabs
ISBN 0-312-42098-6
LC 2002-67325
"Grossman was assigned to report for a weekly newspaper on life for both occupied and occupier on the West Bank during the 20th anniversary of its conquest. With an eye and ear for revealing detail, he argues that the Jews are now doing to Palestinians what has been done to them through the ages." Libr J

Shehadeh, Raja
Palestinian walks; forays into a vanishing landscape. Scribner 2008 xxii, 200p il map pa $15   **956.95**
1. Israel-Arab conflicts
ISBN 978-1-4165-6966-4; 1-4165-6966-9
The author "spent most of his adult life as a lawyer trying to prevent Jewish settlement development in the West Bank. In this work, he recounts his thoughts during six walks into the surrounding Ramallah wilderness between 1978 and 2006. . . . He reveals his anger and pain as he muses on history, his life, his failures, political turmoil, and the unique natural beauty of a beloved land that is succumbing to development and access restrictions. . . . This compelling but unsettling story, which provides insight into the endless woes of a troubled region, is highly recommended for general libraries and Middle Eastern collections." Libr J

Winslow, Philip C.

Victory for us is to see you suffer; in the West Bank with the Palestinians and the Israelis. Beacon Press 2007 xxiii, 224p map $24.95   **956.95**

1. Israel-Arab conflicts

ISBN 978-0-8070-6906-6; 0-8070-6906-X

LC 2007-13411

The author "depicts the universal cost of Israel's occupation of Palestinian lands in excruciatingly human terms in a memoir detailing 30 months spent on the West Bank with the United Nations Relief and Works Agency (UNRWA)." Publ Wkly

Includes bibliographical references

957   Siberia (Asiatic Russia)

Frazier, Ian

Travels in Siberia. Farrar, Straus and Giroux 2010 529p il map $30   **957**

1. Authors 2. Essayists 3. Humorists 4. Nonfiction writers

ISBN 978-0-374-27872-4; 0-374-27872-4

LC 2010-05784

"Frazier records several visits [to Siberia]: a summer's trip via cantankerous automobile across the entire region, in the company of a couple of local companions; a winter's journey by train and car, during which the car sometimes used frozen waterways for roads; and a return visit to see the effects of the emerging Russian energy industry. . . . The contrasts are stark—one day, he walked through the ruins of a remote, frozen Soviet-era prison camp and later saw a ballet in St. Petersburg—and the writing is consistently rich. A dense, challenging, dazzling work that will leave readers exhausted but yearning for more." Kirkus

Includes bibliographical references

Thubron, Colin

In Siberia. HarperCollins Pubs. 2000 287p hardcover o.p. pa $14   **957**

ISBN 0-06-095373-X pa

LC 99-41346

"Thubron elegantly encompasses both awe-inspiring landscapes and their dark histories as well as immersing himself in local eccentricities." Times Lit Suppl

958   Central Asia

Hanks, Reuel R.

★ **Central** Asia; a global studies handbook. ABC-CLIO 2005 xvii, 467p il map $55   **958**

ISBN 1-85109-656-6

LC 2005-14716

"The superb text makes accessible, whether for reports or general reading, former Silk Road lands that may play increasingly important roles—think of oil-rich Kazakhstan—in the world's economy." SLJ

Includes bibliographical references

958.1   Afghanistan

Ansary, Mir Tamim

West of Kabul, East of New York; an Afghan American story. Farrar, Straus & Giroux 2002 292p hardcover o.p. pa $13   **958.1**

1. Afghan Americans -- Biography 2. Islamic civilization

ISBN 0-374-28757-0; 0-312-42151-6 pa

The author, an Afghan American, reflects on his dual heritage. In light of the events of September 11, he focuses particular attention on the relationship between Islam and the West.

"While Ansary's political insights can be detached or perhaps purposefully aloof his descriptions of having lived in and identified alternately with the West and the Islamic world are utterly compelling." Publ Wkly

Chayes, Sarah

★ The **punishment** of virtue; inside Afghanistan after the Taliban. Penguin Press 2006 386p il map hardcover o.p. pa $16   **958.1**

1. Afghan War, 2001- 2. Afghanistan -- History 3. Radio reporters

ISBN 1-59420-096-3; 978-0-14-311206-8 pa; 0-14-311206-6 pa

LC 2006-43499

The author's "hands-on experience as a deeply immersed reporter and activist gives her lucid analysis and prescriptions a practical scope and persuasive authority." Publ Wkly

Includes bibliographical references

Coll, Steve

Ghost wars; the secret history of the CIA, Afghanistan, and bin Laden, from the Soviet invasion to September 10, 2001. Penguin Press 2004 695p maps $29.95; pa $16   **958.1**

1. Afghanistan -- History 2. Terrorists

ISBN 1-594-20007-6; 0-14-303466-9 pa

LC 2003-58593

The author "has given us what is certainly the finest historical narrative so far on the origins of Al Qaeda in the post-Soviet rubble of Afghanistan." N Y Times Book Rev

Includes bibliographical references

Elliot, Jason

An **unexpected** light; travels in Afghanistan. St. Martin's Press 2001 473p map hardcover o.p. pa $18   **958.1**

ISBN 0-312-28846-8 pa

LC 2001-50036

This "is an account of Elliot's two visits to Afghanistan. The first occurred when he joined the mujaheddin circa 1979 and was smuggled into Soviet-occupied Afghanistan; the second happened nearly ten years later, when he returned to the still war-torn land. The skirmishes that Elliot painstakingly describes here took place between the Taliban and the government of Gen. Ahmad Shah Massoud in Kabul. . . . Elliot traveled widely in the hinterland, visiting Faizabad in the north and Herat in the west. The result is some of the finest travel writing in recent years." Libr J

Ewans, Martin

Afghanistan; a short history of its people and politics. HarperCollins Pubs. 2002 244p il maps hardcover o.p. pa $13.95   **958.1**
ISBN 0-06-050508-7 pa

LC 2002-17342

"This is a fascinating story and the best book-length examination of Afghanistan's history we're likely to have for some time." Booklist

Includes bibliographical references

Feifer, Gregory

The **great** gamble; the Soviet war in Afghanistan. Harper 2009 326p il map $27.99   **958.1**
1. Soldiers -- Soviet Union
ISBN 978-0-06-114318-2; 0-06-114318-9

LC 2008-22594

This is a history of the Soviet Union's 1979-1989 war in Afghanistan. "Taking advantage of his skills, experience, and contacts . . . as a foreign correspondent, Feifer's narrative relies greatly on the experiences of those involved on all sides of the conflict—from Soviet political and military insiders to various participants in the mujahideen resistance and even former CIA operatives—but he leans most heavily on the poignant stories of Soviet veterans. Fortunately for the reader, Feifer's research also includes a prudent mix of combat analyses, contemporary reports, and historical studies that inform a balanced treatment of his complex subject." Open Letters

Includes bibliographical references

Fitzgerald, Paul

Invisible history; Afghanistan's untold story. by Paul Fitzgerald and Elizabeth Gould. City Lights Books 2009 389p map pa $18.95   **958.1**
ISBN 978-0-87286-494-8; 0-87286-494-4

LC 2008-20486

The authors "seek to clarify and contextualize the current situation in conflict-torn Afghanistan with this comprehensive history. The material covers events starting in ancient antiquity, but puts a heavy emphasis on the second half of the 20th century through the end of 2007. The work concludes with analysis and strategy recommendations for the incoming American President and is supplemented by an appendix of historical maps." Middle East Journal

Includes bibliographical references

Junger, Sebastian

War. Twelve 2010 287p map $26.99   **958.1**
1. Afghan War, 2001- -- Personal narratives
ISBN 978-0-446-55624-8

LC 2009-49493

"The war in Afghanistan contains brutal trauma but also transcendent purpose in this riveting combat narrative. Junger spent 14 months in 2007-2008 intermittently embedded with a platoon of the 173rd Airborne brigade in Afghanistan's Korengal Valley, one of the bloodiest corners of the conflict. . . . Junger experiences everything they do—nerve-racking patrols, terrifying roadside bombings and ambushes, stultifying weeks in camp when they long for a firefight to relieve the tedium. . . . The result is an unforgettable portrait of men under fire." Publ Wkly

Includes bibliographical references

Rashid, Ahmed

Taliban; militant Islam, oil and fundamentalism in Central Asia. 2nd ed; Yale University Press 2010 319p map pa $17.95   **958.1**
1. Islam and politics 2. Islam and state -- Afghanistan 3. Islamic fundamentalism
ISBN 978-0-300-16368-1; 0-300-16368-1

LC 2009-938249

The author explains "the Taliban's rise to power, its impact on Afghanistan and the region, its role in oil and gas company decisions, and the effects of changing American attitudes toward the Taliban. He also describes the new face of Islamic fundamentalism and explains why Afghanistan has become the world center for international terrorism." Publisher's note

Includes bibliographical references

Schroen, Gary C.

First in; an insider's account of how the CIA spearheaded the war on terror in Afghanistan. Presidio Press/Ballantine Books 2005 $25.95; pa $14.95   **958.1**
1. Intelligence service agents 2. Nonfiction writers 3. War on Terrorism, 2001-
ISBN 0-89141-872-5; 0-89141-875-X pa

LC 2005-43171

The author describes his experiences after he "was tapped to lead the effort to establish contact with the Northern Alliance in the days following 9/11; the 35-year CIA veteran commanded the first American team on the ground in Afghanistan. . . . Schroen delivers what he advertises: a powerful account that takes the reader inside war councils and 19th-century-style cavalry charges in the months just after 9/11." Publ Wkly

Seierstad, Asne

The **bookseller** of Kabul; translated by Ingrid Christophersen. Little, Brown 2003 287p $19.95; pa $12.95   **958.1**
1. Women -- Afghanistan
ISBN 0-316-73450-0; 0-316-15941-7 pa

LC 2003-54643

The author "entered Kabul with Northern Alliance soldiers after they ousted the Taliban. She took the rare opportunity to live with and write a book about the extended family of Sultan Khan, bookseller and entrepreneur. The result, organized around events in the lives of individual members of Khan's large clan . . . provides appropriate information about recent Afghani history, a glimpse from the inside at an Islamic family, and an understanding of the harshness and difficulty of the daily grind in Afghanistan—both under the Taliban and after the U.S. antiterrorist campaign." Booklist

Shah, Saira

The **storyteller's** daughter. Knopf 2003 253p $24; pa $13.95   **958.1**
ISBN 0-375-41531-9; 1-4000-3147-8 pa

LC 2004-295126

The author "weaves oral traditions with history to describe life as an Afghani raised in the West but with solid roots in the East. . . . We learn about Shah's documentary work in Afghanistan, the power of myth through which Afghanistan's tradition is born, the brave work of peoples and organizations such as the Revolutionary Association of the Women of Afghanistan (RAWA), and the West's (and even East's) misconceptions regarding Muslim teachings. . . . This rare personal and historic account of the region is a great addition to public and academic libraries." Libr J

Wahab, Shaista

★ A **brief** history of Afghanistan; [by] Shaista Wahab and Barry Youngerman. 2nd ed; Facts on File 2010 354p il map $49.50; pa $19.95   **958.1**
> ISBN 978-0-8160-8218-6; 978-0-8160-8219-3 pa; 978-1-4381-0819-3 ebook
>
>   LC 2010-19656

This history of Afghanistan "examines this country's isolation and how it found itself involved in 30 years of war and anarchy. . . . [It] explores the culture and politics of the Pashtun tribes whose homeland extends across much of Afghanistan and northern Pakistan, as well as the Taliban insurgency and the relationship between local leaders and the central government in Kabul." Publisher's note
> Includes bibliographical references

West, Bing

The **wrong** war; grit, strategy, and the way out of Afghanistan. [by] Bing West. Random House 2011 307p il map $28   **958.1**
> 1. Afghan War, 2001-
> ISBN 978-1-4000-6873-9; 1-4000-6873-8
>
>   LC 2010043107

West argues that "the central premise of counterinsurgency doctrine holds that if the Americans sacrifice on behalf of the Afghan government, then the Afghan people will risk their lives for that same government in return. They will fight the Taliban. . . . This isn't happening. . . . [The author contends that] the Afghans are waiting to see who prevails, but prevailing is impossible without their help." (N Y Times Book Rev) Bibliography. Index.

This is "a crushing and seemingly irrefutable critique of the American plan in Afghanistan. It should be read by anyone who wants to understand why the war there is so hard." N Y Times Book Rev
> Includes bibliographical references

Zoya

Zoya's story; an Afghan woman's struggle for freedom. {by} Zoya with John Follain and Rita Cristofari. HarperCollins Pubs. 2002 239p $24.95; pa $12.95   **958.1**
> 1. Women -- Afghanistan
> ISBN 0-06-009782-5; 0-06-009783-3 pa

"After both her parents were killed by the Mujahideen, Zoya took up her mother's work in the Revolutionary Association of the Women of Afghanistan and, with her grandmother, journeyed to Pakistan, where she could receive an education. A few years later, Zoya returned to Afghanistan, where she witnessed public executions but also saw heartening displays of courage. A stirring memoir by an uncompromisingly brave woman." Booklist

958.104   -1919

Anderson, Jon Lee

The **lion's** grave; dispatches from Afghanistan. photographs by Thomas Dworzak. Grove Press 2002 244p il $23; pa $13   **958.104**
> 1. Authors 2. Journalists
> ISBN 0-8021-1723-6; 0-8021-4025-4 pa
>
>   LC 2002-70659

In this "account, which includes his diary entries. Anderson recounts the arduous task of developing sources and reporting on the complexities of a nation caught up in its own ethnic and religious conflicts and its place in the new war on terrorism." Booklist

Chandrasekaran, Rajiv

Little America; the war within the war for Afghanistan. Rajiv Chandrasekaran. Alfred A. Knopf 2012 368 p. ill., maps $27.95   **958.104**
> 1. Afghan War, 2001- -- Political aspects -- United States 2. Internal security -- Afghanistan
> ISBN 0307957144; 9780307957146
>
>   LC 2012010354

This book offers journalist Rajiv Chandrasekarans coverage of the U.S. surge in Afghanistan. 'He found the effort sabotaged not only by Afghan and Pakistani malfeasance but by infighting and incompetence within the American government . . . . In one . . . scene after another, Chandrasekaran follows American efforts to reclaim the . . . territory from the Taliban. Along the way, we meet an Army general whose experience as the top military officer in charge of Iraq's Green Zone couldn't prepare him for the bureaucratic knots of Afghanistan, a Marine commander whose desire to charge into remote hamlets conflicted with civilian priorities, and a war-seasoned diplomat frustrated in his push for a scaled-down but long-term American commitment. (Publisher s note)

Corwin, Phillip

Doomed in Afghanistan; a UN officer's memoir of the fall of Kabul and Najibullah's escape, 1992. Rutgers Univ. Press 2003 xx, 241p il $28 **958.104**
> 1. Communist leaders 2. Presidents
> ISBN 0-8135-3171-3
>
>   LC 2002-24831

This book "focuses on the period after the Soviets left the country in 1988, when the UN was given the task of establishing a broad-based regime that would have included the communists. Thanks to the intrigues of the US and its clients, Pakistan and Saudi Arabia, the UN team, of which the author was a member, failed to effect the escape of Najibullah, the leftist president of Afghanistan, from Kabul. As a result, there could be no broad-based coalition that might have prevented the rise of the Taliban and the country's decline into barbarism. . . . This engaging and sympathetic essay enables readers to understand the country's tragic recent past and the failure of diplomacy . . . which paved the way for civil war and the rise of 'Islamic fundamentalism.'" Choice
> Includes bibliographical references and index

958.4 Turkestan

Girardet, Edward
   Killing the cranes; Edward Girardet. Chelsea
Green Pub. Co. 2011 xiv, 417p.p   **958.4**
   ISBN 9781603583428

   LC 2011014661
   This book presents a "personal account of Afghanistan
and its people from 1979 to the present. . . . During his long
career, Girardet has met, befriended and been threatened by
many key figures in Afghanistan's recent history, including
Gulbuddin Hekmatyar, Ahmed Shah Massoud and even the
recently assassinated Osama bin Ladin. . . . The author is
concerned that corruption, criminality and religious fundamentalism have undermined the country's potential, especially since the 1990s. With a long-view perspective, Girardet puts forward a view of a culture based on generosity and
openness, a culture which he thinks has been wronged by
misguided association with the fighting qualities of guerrillas and terrorists." (Kirkus)

Robbins, Christopher
   Apples are from Kazakhstan; the land that disap-
peared. Atlas Books 2008 296p il map $24   **958.4**
   ISBN 0-9777433-8-1; 978-0-9777433-8-4

   LC 2008-299516
   A "delightful and masterful travelog reveals . . . a country rich in history, natural beauty, and, perhaps most important, tolerance. . . . [The author] manages to make this an
overall hopeful book by combining grave topics with less
grave ones and adding a good dose of wit." Libr J

959   Southeast Asia

Somers Heidhues, Mary F.
   Southeast Asia: a concise history. Thames &
Hudson 2000 192p il maps hardcover o.p. pa
$18.95   **959**
   ISBN 0-500-28303-6 pa

   LC 99-66014
   This "history ranges from Southeast Asia's prehistoric
times to the most recent political developments in Indonesia. Heidhues . . . divides her study into seven well-balanced
chapters, touching on the political history, economics, society, and culture of Burma, Thailand, Cambodia, Vietnam,
Malaysia, Singapore, Brunei, Indonesia, and the Philippines." Libr J

★ Southeast Asia; a historical encyclopedia from
Angkor Wat to East Timor. edited by Ooi Keat
Gin. ABC-CLIO 2004 3v il map set $285 **959**
   ISBN 1-576-07770-5

   LC 2004-4813
   The countries covered in this book include "Myanmar
(Burma), Thailand (Siam), Laos, Cambodia, Vietnam, Malaysia, Singapore, the Philippines, Indonesia, and
East Timor. This A-Z aims to help students and researchers
grasp the fragmented region through 800 detailed articles on
archaeology, politics, culture, economic transformation, and
more." Libr J

   Includes bibliographical references

959.1   Myanmar

Aung San Suu Kyi
   Freedom from fear, and other writings; edited
with an introduction by Michael Aris; foreword to the
first edition by Vaclav Havel, foreword to the second
edition by Archbishop Desmond Tutu. rev ed; Penguin Bks. 1995 xxxi, 374p il pa $14.95   **959.1**
   ISBN 0-14-025317-3

   LC 96-902734
   This is a collection of essays, letters, speeches, and other
writings by the Burmese opposition leader, Winner of the
1991 Nobel Peace Prize.
   "Mrs. Aung San Suu Kyi's excellent book offers inspiration to many other peoples in the region as much as it reflects
Myanmar's own desire for change." N Y Times Book Rev
{review of 1991 edition}
   Includes bibliographical references

Larkin, Emma
   Everything is broken; a tale of catastrophe in
Burma. Penguin Press 2010 271p map $25.95 **959.1**
   1. Cyclones 2. Disaster relief
   ISBN 978-1-59420-257-5; 1-59420-257-5

   LC 2010-04029
   "Larkin is such a facile observer and writer, she tempts
comparisons to Orwell, and certainly ranks with Ryszard
Kapuscinski as a lyric writer of reportage." Cleveland
Plain Dealer

Thant Myint-U
   Where China meets India; Burma and the new
crossroads of Asia. Farrar, Straus and Giroux 2011
361p map $27   **959.1**
   ISBN 978-0-374-29907-1; 0-374-29907-2

   LC 2011024406
   In the book, "Thant Myint-U advances the . . . argument
for changing Western policy [regarding Burma]: isolation is
useless because Burma is . . . becoming a bridge between
two rising global giants. Writing of his travels through the
borderlands of China, India and Burma, Thant Myint-U
hopes to demonstrate how this region of Asia, home to more
than 600 million people, is integrating, and how Burma will
be at the center of it. If the West does not join Asian nations in aiding, investing in and interacting with the Burmese
government, he argues, the power of Burma's leaders will
remain undiminished and the West will be hampered strategically. It will lose access to . . . sources of petroleum, and it
will lack leverage over Burma's government, which has the
second-biggest army in Southeast Asia, a . . . close relationship with North Korea and, possibly, nuclear ambitions. But
if Western nations do engage with Burma, they can benefit
from the new Asian trade, aid and investment flowing into
Burma, and help ensure that it benefits the Burmese people
rather than only their rulers." (Nation)
   Focusing "on his home country of Burma, and the area
encompassed by a diameter of 1,000 miles drawn from the
city of Mandalay on the edge of the Shan Plateau, Thant
suggests that this corner of the world (with a population of
600 million) is destined to become a bridge between Bengal,

Bangladesh, India's North Eastern Provinces, and China's Yunnan province." Publ Wkly

Includes bibliographical references

The **river** of lost footsteps; histories of Burma. Farrar, Straus & Giroux 2006 361p il map $25; pa $15   **959.1**

ISBN 978-0-374-16342-6; 0-374-16342-1; 978-0-374-53116-4 pa; 0-374-53116-1 pa

LC 2006-09199

"This readable, reflective history will support revived interest in Burma." Booklist

Includes bibliographical references

959.3   Thailand

Krauss, Erich

Wave of destruction; the stories of four families and history's deadliest tsunami. Rodale 2006 244p il map $24.95   **959.3**

1. Survival after airplane accidents, shipwrecks, etc. 2. Tsunamis

ISBN 1-59486-378-4

LC 2005-24531

The author provides an "account of four families in a Thai village devastated by the tsunami of December 26, 2004. . . . Passionately told, this tragic story portrays the full human cost of natural devastation." Publ Wkly

Osborne, Lawrence

Bangkok days. North Point Press 2009 271p il $25   **959.3**

1. Authors 2. Biography, Individual 3. Memoirists 4. Novelists 5. Travel writers

ISBN 978-0-86547-732-2; 0-86547-732-9

LC 2008-44741

Osborne "provides a raunchy account of the nightlife and bars and bargirls of Thailand's capital. In particular, he delves into the lives of a motley band of aging, libertine Westerners (Farangs) living in his apartment complex and explores the city in their company. Their tragicomic lives are compelling, and Osborne provides some extraordinary anecdotes." Libr J

Wyatt, David K.

★ **Thailand**: a short history; 2nd ed; Yale Univ. Press 2003 352p il maps pa $20   **959.3**

ISBN 0-3000-8475-7

This volume provides a general history of Thailand beginning with the migrations of the Tai peoples from southern China, examining the social and economic changes to the present.

959.6   Cambodia

Brinkley, Joel

Cambodia's curse; the modern history of a troubled land. PublicAffairs 2011 386p il $27.99 **959.6**

1. Communist leaders 2. Democracy -- Cambodia 3.

Heads of state 4. Political leaders

ISBN 978-1-58648-787-4; 1-58648-787-6

LC 2010-44806

"Brinkley cuts a clear narrative path through the bewildering, cynical politics and violent social life of one of the worlds most brutalized and hard-up countries." Foreign Affairs

Includes bibliographical references

Dunlop, Nic

The **lost** executioner; a journey to the heart of the killing fields. Walker & Co. 2006 326p il map $24   **959.6**

1. Evangelists 2. Executioners 3. Murderers

ISBN 0-8027-1472-2

This is an "account of the Khmer Rouge, the Cambodian Communist regime responsible for more than two million deaths between 1975 and 1979. Armed with a black-and-white photograph of Comrade Duch—Pol Pot's chief executioner—Dunlop traveled to the war-ravaged country to probe the dark depths of a once-studious young boy and dedicated teacher who became one of the twentieth-century's most notorious mass murderers. . . . Dunlop's interviews with former Khmer Rouge members are both wrenching and revelatory." Booklist

Includes bibliographical references

Kiernan, Ben

The **Pol** Pot regime; race, power, and genocide in Cambodia under the Khmer Rouge, 1975-79. 2nd ed; Yale Univ. Press 2002 xxiii, 477p il map pa $19.95   **959.6**

1. Atrocities 2. Communism -- Cambodia

ISBN 0-300-09649-6

LC 2002-100979

This is an account of "the Cambodian catastrophe; the significant internal resistance to the Khmer Rouge; and the racialist and totalitarian attitudes by which Pol Pot's regime justified the death, by starvation and disease as well as torture and murder, of some 1.5 million of their 8 million countrymen." Booklist {review of 1996 edition}

Includes bibliographical references

Ung, Loung

First they killed my father; a daughter of Cambodia remembers. HarperCollins Pubs. 2000 240p il hardcover o.p. pa $13.95   **959.6**

1. Political atrocities -- Cambodia

ISBN 0-06-019332-8; 0-06-085626-2 pa

LC 99-34707

The author's father was a "high-ranking government official in Phnom Penh. She was only five when the Khmer Rouge stormed the city and her family was forced to flee. They sought refuge in various camps, hiding their wealth and education, always on the move and ever fearful of being betrayed. After 20 months, Ung's father was taken away, never to be seen again. Her story of starvation, forced labor, beatings, attempted rape, separations, and the deaths of her family members is one of horror and brutality." SLJ

959.604   -1949

Bizot, Francois

The **gate**; translated from the French by Euan Cameron; with a preface by John Le Carré. Knopf 2003 275p $24; pa $14   **959.604**
1. Atrocities 2. Communism -- Cambodia 3. Political atrocities -- Cambodia
ISBN 0-375-41293-X; 0-375-72723-X pa
                                    LC 2002-69428
Bizot's "tale of his experiences, both in the camp and as translator at the gate of the French embassy, leaves readers with haunting images of the doomed." Booklist

Him, Chanrithy

When broken glass floats; growing up under the Khmer Rouge. Norton 2000 330p il map hardcover o.p. pa $13.95   **959.604**
1. Interpreters 2. Memoirists 3. Political atrocities -- Cambodia 4. Political refugees -- Cambodia 5. Political refugees -- United States 6. Refugees
ISBN 0-393-32210-6 pa
                                    LC 99-58417
Him "was 10 in 1975 when the Khmer Rouge overtook her country in what she calls the time of broken glass. Feeling a survivor's responsibility to do so, Him vividly recalls the brutality of the camps, the strict social control, and alienation from family that the Khmer Rouge enforced." Booklist

Kamm, Henry

Cambodia: report from a stricken land. Arcade Pub. 1998 xxiv, 262p il maps $25.95   **959.604**
ISBN 1-55970-433-0
                                    LC 98-22707
"Sober yet passionate, Kamm's well-informed survey is an excellent introduction to a country that the world has all but abandoned." Libr J

959.7   Vietnam

Sachs, Dana

The **house** on Dream Street; memoir of an American woman in Vietnam. Seal Press 2003 357p pa $15.95   **959.7**
ISBN 1-580-05100-6
                                    LC 2003-57299
This is an American journalist's account of her visits to Vietnam. "Her memoir covers the time from her initial plunge into the country, as a touring backpacker in 1989, to her triumphant return in 1998 with . . '. [her] husband and son." Publ Wkly

959.704   -1945

Anderson, David L.

★ The **Columbia** guide to the Vietnam War. Columbia Univ. Press 2002 308p maps $47; pa $22.50   **959.704**
1. Vietnam War, 1961-1975 2. Vietnamese Conflict, 1961-1975
ISBN 0-231-11492-3; 0-231-11493-1 pa
                                    LC 2002-20143
"Anderson's guide successfully compresses the copiously documented, labyrinthine history of the Vietnamese conflict into a single economical volume. In five parts, the guide's narrative and encyclopedia sections provide a fascinating survey of the war, while the remaining elements of the work link modern researchers to a host of richly documented resources. . . . The guide will become an important resource for those seeking a historical overview as well as direction for further research. Strongly recommended." Choice
Includes bibliographical references

Berman, Larry

No peace, no honor; Nixon, Kissinger, and betrayal in Vietnam. Free Press 2001 334p $27.50; pa $14   **959.704**
1. College teachers 2. International relations specialists 3. Members of Congress 4. Nobel laureates for peace 5. Nonfiction writers 6. Presidential advisers 7. Presidents 8. Secretaries of state 9. Senators 10. Vice-presidents 11. Vietnam War, 1961-1975 12. Vietnamese conflict, 1961-1975 -- United States 13. Writers on politics
ISBN 0-684-84968-2; 0-7432-2349-7 pa
                                    LC 2001-23904
"In the endless flow of assessments, reassessments and re-reassessments of the war in Vietnam, a study occasionally appears that goes beyond a rehash of the polemics that have marked that tragic experience. Larry Berman's 'No Peace, No Honor' belongs in that select category." N Y Times Book Rev
Includes bibliographical references

Bissell, Tom

The **father** of all things; a Marine, his son, and the legacy of Vietnam. Pantheon Books 2007 407p il $25   **959.704**
1. Authors 2. Essayists 3. Marine corps officers 4. Nonfiction writers 5. Short story writers 6. Veterans 7. Vietnam War, 1961-1975 8. Vietnamese Conflict, 1961-1975
ISBN 978-0-375-42265-2; 0-375-42265-X
                                    LC 2006-49427
"In 2003, Bissell travelled to Vietnam with his father, who had fought there nearly four decades before. Their relationship was uneasy: as a child, Bissell once reported his father to an abuse hotline (after an unusually physical game of rock, paper, scissors), and, at the age of twenty-nine, he still felt 'diminished' in the man's presence; meanwhile, his father, only half joking, called him a Communist. In this ambitious, uneven book, Bissell chronicles their pilgrimage to former battlefields and seeks to reconcile his personal 'mythology,' as the son of a Vietnam veteran, with the larger context of 'the only war in which the United States failed to enact its will.' Bissell writes with conviction, and his prose, if sometimes swashbuckling, has moments of startling beauty." New Yorker
Includes bibliographical references

Caputo, Philip

★ A **rumor** of war; with a twentieth anniversary postscript by the author. Henry Holt and Co. 1996 xxi, 356p pa $15   **959.704**

1. Vietnam War, 1961-1975 -- Personal narratives
ISBN 0-8050-4695-X

LC 96-19314

These are "the combat recollections of a very young Marine officer in Vietnam in 1965-1966. Caputo later became a newspaperman. . . . He remembers himself as a patriotic youngster, eager to prove his manhood, and then . . . he takes us through his step-by-step discovery that war and manhood and their interrelation are more complicated than he had dreamed." New Yorker

Duiker, William J.

Ho Chi Minh; by William Duiker. Hyperion 2000 695p il maps $35; pa $16.95   **959.704**

1. Communist leaders 2. Heads of state 3. Political leaders 4. Presidents -- Vietnam (Democratic Republic) -- Biography
ISBN 0-7868-6387-0; 0-7868-8701-X pa

LC 00-26757

In this biography the author "examines Ho's life primarily in the context of his political activity in Paris, Moscow, southern China, and Vietnam, occasionally spiced with anecdotes of Ho's highly secretive personal life. . . . Duiker handles the complicated political and diplomatic issues with ease, and his narrative, though it sometimes strays from Ho's life to fill in the bigger picture, never bogs down." Booklist

Includes bibliographical references

Ellsberg, Daniel

Secrets: a memoir of Vietnam and the Pentagon papers. Viking 2002 498p il $29.95; pa $16   **959.704**

1. Dissenters 2. Government officials 3. Nonfiction writers 4. Pacifists 5. Vietnam War, 1961-1975 6. Vietnamese conflict, 1961-1975 -- United States
ISBN 0-670-03030-9; 0-14-200342-5 pa

LC 2002-16874

Ellsberg recalls how he leaked "the Pentagon Papers, which documented U.S. foreign-policy failures and deceit in Vietnam from 1945 to 1968. . . . Ellsberg's autobiographical account provides insight into the disturbing abuses of presidential power that plagued the Vietnam/Watergate era." Libr J

Includes bibliographical references

FitzGerald, Frances

Fire in the lake; the Vietnamese and the Americans in Vietnam. Little, Brown 1972 491p maps hardcover o.p. pa $16.95   **959.704**

1. Vietnam War, 1961-1975
ISBN 0-316-15919-0 pa

This book looks at the effects American intervention had on the Vietnamese social and intellectual landscape.

Frankum, Ronald B.

Historical dictionary of the war in Vietnam; Ronald B. Frankum, Jr. Scarecrow Press 2011 672p $99; ebook $99   **959.704**

1. Vietnamese Conflict, 1961-1975
ISBN 978-0-8108-6796-3; 978-0-8108-7956-0 ebook; 9780810867963 (cloth : alk. paper); 9780810879560 (ebook)

LC 2010052321

This book "contains approximately 700 entries that provide a balanced view, beginning with the start of the First Indochina War, in 1946, through the fall of Saigon, in 1975. The main portion of the book is, appropriately, the dictionary entry section. From one or two-paragraph definitions for terms such as Napalm, Nixon Doctrine, and Viet Cong to multipage descriptions for entries such as Air war, Ho Chi Minh, and Tet Offensive, 1968, Frankum's writing is consistently straightforward and accurate, and the topics he includes are appropriate." Booklist

Includes bibliographical references.

Glasser, Ronald J.

365 days. Braziller 1971 292p hardcover o.p. pa $14.95   **959.704**

1. Vietnam War, 1961-1975 -- Medical care 2. Vietnam War, 1961-1975 -- Personal narratives
ISBN 0-8076-1527-7 pa

The author, a military doctor who was stationed in Japan, recounts his experiences treating wounded American military personnel during the Vietnam War.

Goldstein, Donald M.

The **Vietnam** War: the story and photographs; by Donald M. Goldstein, Katherine V. Dillon, and J. Michael Wenger. Brassey's 1997 179p il maps hardcover o.p. pa $19.95   **959.704**

1. Vietnam War, 1961-1975
ISBN 1-57488-210-4 pa

LC 97-11574

This history of the Vietnam War "proceeds both chronologically and thematically, beginning with the French colonial era and the Indochina War, then covering successive stages of the U.S. involvement. The text is sufficiently detailed, clear, and balanced to serve as a narrative introduction to the subject, but the real strength lies in the photographs. They cover the subject with admirable thoroughness. . . . They do not include too many chestnuts, and they adequately cover the Vietnamese, the navy, and other subjects relatively neglected in the literature thus far." Booklist

Includes bibliographical references

Hendrickson, Paul

The **living** and the dead; Robert McNamara and five lives of a lost war. Knopf 1996 427p il hardcover o.p. pa $15   **959.704**

1. Bankers 2. International organization officials 3. Secretaries of defense 4. Vietnam War, 1961-1975 5. Vietnam War, 1961-1975 -- United States
ISBN 0-679-7811-X pa

LC 96-7445

"Exhaustively researched, probing, important contribution to the annals of American history." Publ Wkly

Includes bibliographical references

Isaacs, Arnold R.

Vietnam shadows; the war, its ghosts, and its legacy. Johns Hopkins Univ. Press 1997 236p hardcover o.p. pa $19.95   **959.704**

1. Vietnam War, 1961-1975

ISBN 0-8018-6344-9 pa

LC 97-10823

This overview of the Vietnam War explores the political, social, cultural and military dimensions of the conflict.

The author's "range is impressive. He comments on everything from the moral opacity of Robert McNamara to American 'escape-goating'—his neologism for the impulse to produce counterfactual histories in which we win the war after all. Isaacs's basic judgments are sound, and his exquisite nose for detecting self-deception leads him to some awkward truths about the wartime mythologies that have become encased in middle-aged amber." NY Times Book Rev

Includes bibliographical references

Kaiser, David E.

American tragedy; Kennedy, Johnson, and the origins of the Vietnam War. {by} David Kaiser. Harvard Univ. Press 2000 566p il $36; pa $18.95   **959.704**

1. Members of Congress 2. Presidents 3. Senators 4. Vice-presidents 5. Vietnam War, 1961-1975 6. Vietnamese Conflict, 1961-1975 -- United States

ISBN 0-674-00225-3; 0-674-00672-0 pa

LC 99-52925

"The first-rate research is complemented by an intriguing model of intergenerational policy-making." Libr J

Includes bibliographical references and index

Karnow, Stanley

Vietnam; a history. 2nd rev & updated ed; Penguin Bks. 1997 768p il maps pa $17.95   **959.704**

1. Vietnam War, 1961-1975

ISBN 0-14-026547-3

A summation "of over two centuries of conflict in Indochina. Chronicling a tragic history, Karnow presents a balanced and sympathetic view of Vietnamese aspirations and the mishaps that led to American involvement in a 'war nobody won.'" Voice Youth Advocates [review of 1983 edition]

Includes bibliographical references

Kissinger, Henry

Ending the Vietnam War; a history of America's involvement in and extrication from the Vietnam War. Touchstone 2002 640p map pa $18   **959.704**

1. Vietnam War, 1961-1975 2. Vietnamese Conflict, 1961-1975 -- Diplomatic history 3. Vietnamese conflict, 1961-1975 -- United States

ISBN 0-7432-1532-X

LC 2002-17996

"Readers interested in the Vietnam period but unfamiliar with Kissinger's previous books will find this new volume worthwhile. . . . Kissinger's account of America's venture in Vietnam and his role in that shipwreck is factually accurate, eminently informed and masterfully crafted." Publ Wkly

Includes bibliographical references

Langguth, A. J.

Our Vietnam; the war, 1954-1975. Simon & Schuster 2000 766p il maps hardcover o.p. pa $20   **959.704**

1. Vietnam War, 1961-1975 2. Vietnamese Conflict, 1961-1975 -- United States

ISBN 0-7432-1231-2 pa

LC 00-57384

This book "is unique in its perspective of the major players on both sides." Booklist

Includes bibliographical references

Lind, Michael

Vietnam, the necessary war; a reinterpretation of America's most disastrous military conflict. Free Press 1999 314p $25; pa $14   **959.704**

1. Politics and war 2. Vietnam War, 1961-1975 3. Vietnamese Conflict, 1961-1975

ISBN 0-684-84254-8; 0-684-87027-4 pa

LC 99-28449

"Lind's arguments, if not always persuasive, are always provocative." Publ Wkly

Includes bibliographical references and index

Logevall, Fredrik

Embers of War; The Fall of an Empire and the Making of America's Vietnam. Fredrik Logevall. Random House 2012   **959.704**

ISBN 0375504427; 9780375504426

This book presents the [Vietnam] war's roots in the U.S. reaction to the French colonial experience. And that experience was inextricably linked to the global changes wrought by WWII, the beginning of the cold war, and America's new role as the pre-eminent power in Asian and world affairs. Without neglecting the military aspects of the Franco-Indochina War and its aftermath, [Fredrik] Logevall concentrates on political and diplomatic aspects. . . . Logevall makes a detailed case that America's Vietnam involvement replicated the French experience: the U.S. was fighting against an anticolonialist revolution and giving the Democratic Republic of Vietnam legitimacy that would be neither discredited nor defeated in 10 more years of war. (Publishers Weekly)

Mann, Robert

A grand delusion; America's descent into Vietnam. Basic Bks. 2000 821p il $35; pa $22 **959.704**

1. Vietnam War, 1961-1975 2. Vietnamese Conflict, 1961-1975 -- United States

ISBN 0-465-04369-0; 0-465-04370-4 pa

LC 00-49824

This account of the United States involvement in the Vietnam War focuses on the political causes and "collision of personalities throughout the White House, Congress, and elsewhere during that era. Mann's history concentrates on seven American leaders in the halls of power rather than on the battlefield." Libr J

Includes bibliographical references and index

McCloud, Bill

What should we tell our children about Vietnam? University of Okla. Press 1989 155p hardcover o.p. pa $14.95   **959.704**

1. Vietnam War, 1961-1975

ISBN 0-8061-3240-X pa

LC 89-40218

"President Bush, William Westmoreland, Gary Trudeau, and Philip Caputo are among some of the best known of 128 individuals who gave their views when McCloud, a junior high school teacher and veteran, wrote to ask them what young people should understand about the war." Booklist

Includes bibliographical references

McNamara, Robert S.

In retrospect; the tragedy and lessons of Vietnam. Vintage Bks. 1996 518p il map pa $16.95 **959.704**

1. Vietnam War, 1961-1975

ISBN 0-679-76749-5; 978-0-679-76749-7

"Former defense secretary McNamara seeks 'to put Vietnam in context' and counter 'the cynicism and even contempt with which so many people view our political institutions and leaders.' . . . He identifies 'eleven major causes for our disaster in Vietnam' and six points when the U.S. could legitimately have withdrawn. Certainly not the last word on this still-controversial subject but an essential acquisition for most libraries." Booklist

Includes bibliographical references

Moore, Harold G.

We are soldiers still; a journey back to the battlefields of Vietnam. [by] Harold G. Moore and Joseph L. Galloway. Harper 2008 248p il $24.95; pa $14.99   **959.704**

1. Generals 2. Ia Drang Valley (Vietnam), Battle of, 1965 3. Journalists 4. Vietnam War, 1961-1975 -- Personal narratives 5. Vietnamese Conflict, 1961-1975 -- Personal narratives

ISBN 978-0-06-114776-0; 0-06-114776-1; 978-0-06-114777-7 pa; 0-06-114777-X pa

LC 2008-11034

"A worthy and wise successor to one of the best books ever about combat in Vietnam." Kirkus

We were soldiers once--and young; Ia Drang: the battle that changed the war in Vietnam. [by] Harold G. Moore and Joseph L. Galloway. Random House 1992 412p il maps $26.95; pa $7.50   **959.704**

1. Ia Drang Valley (Vietnam), Battle of, 1965 2. Vietnam War, 1961-1975 -- Personal narratives

ISBN 0-679-41158-5; 0-345-47264-0 pa

LC 92-53642

"On Nov. 14, 1965, the 1st Battalion of the 7th Cavalry, commanded by Col. Moore and accompanied by UPI reporter Galloway, helicoptered into Vietnam's remote Ia Drang Valley and found itself surrounded by a numerically superior force of North Vietnamese regulars. Moore and Galloway here offer a detailed account, based on interviews with participants and on their own recollections, of what happened during the four-day battle." Publ Wkly

Includes bibliographical references

Morgan, Ted

Valley of death; the tragedy at Dien Bien Phu that led America into the Vietnam War. Random House 2010 722p il map $35   **959.704**

1. Dien Bien Phu, Battle of, 1954 2. Indochinese War, 1946-1954 3. Điện Biên Phu (Vietnam), Battle of, 1954

ISBN 978-1-4000-6664-3

LC 2009-19714

"This absorbing account of the prelude, battle, and aftermath that ended the 'first Viet Nam War' is a sad tale of misconception, missed opportunities, and massive blunders by French and even American military and civilian officials. . . . This is a superb chronicle of a sad and avoidable conflict that led to an even more destructive one." Booklist

Includes bibliographical references

Prochnau, William W.

Once upon a distant war. Vintage Bks. 1996 546p il pa $15   **959.704**

1. Authors 2. Historians 3. Journalists 4. Nonfiction writers 5. Novelists 6. Vietnam War, 1961-1975 -- Journalists

ISBN 0-679-77265-0

This is a study of American journalists who reported on the Vietnam War, focusing on the years between 1961 and 1963. The author discusses the activities of reporters and photographers such as Peter Arnett, Homer Bigart, Malcolm Browne, Horst Fass, David Halberstam, Marguerite Higgins, Charley Mohr, and Neil Sheehan.

Prochnau's "thesis is hardly new—Vietnam has long been seen as the lesson that taught reporters to stop automatically believing government handout—but Prochnau illustrates it in fresh, interesting ways." Time

Sallah, Michael

Tiger Force; a true story of men and war. [by] Michael Sallah and Mitch Weiss. Little, Brown 2006 403p il map $25.95   **959.704**

1. Vietnam War, 1961-1975

ISBN 0-316-15997-2; 978-0-316-15997-5

LC 2005-20921

"In 1967, the Tiger Force platoon of the 101st Airborne went on a seven-month-long rampage through South Vietnam's central highlands that left dead more than 325 civilians, mostly children, women, and old men. . . . [This] is a searing narrative, difficult to read yet difficult to put down, about Tiger Force's descent into a leaderless and ruthless unit, in which, as one of the ex-soldiers puts it to the authors, the objective was to 'kill anything that moves.'" Libr J

Includes bibliographical references

Sheehan, Neil

A **bright** shining lie: John Paul Vann and America in Vietnam. Random House 1988 861p il hardcover o.p. pa $18   **959.704**

1. Army officers 2. Vietnam War, 1961-1975

ISBN 0-679-72414-1 pa

LC 87-43330

The author "tells the story of the war through the focus of John Paul Vann, an army officer who faced down South Vietnamese politicians and American generals to expose the corruption that undermined our efforts and later was President Nixon's civilian adviser in Vietnam until he was killed in a helicopter crash in 1972. It is a dramatic device that lets Mr. Sheehan bring the very palpable feel of the war to us with passionate power." N Y Times Book Rev

Includes bibliographical references

Shultz, Richard H.

The **secret** war against Hanoi; Kennedy and Johnson's use of spies, saboteurs, and covert warriors in North Vietnam. {by} Richard H. Shultz, Jr. HarperCollins Pubs. 1999 408p il hardcover o.p. pa $15   **959.704**
1. Subversive activities 2. Vietnam War, 1961-1975 -- Secret service
ISBN 0-06-093253-8 pa

LC 99-44524

"Organized in a military entity euphemistically named the Studies and Observation Group (SOG), the covert war, it was hoped, would annoy Hanoi enough to force it to scale back its war in the south. . . . Schultz was given access to SOG archives and veterans and has produced a professional volume on how SOG originated and operated over its eight-year existence." Booklist

Includes bibliographical references

Willbanks, James H.

Vietnam War almanac. Facts On File 2008 590p il map $95   **959.704**
1. Reference books 2. Vietnam War, 1961-1975 3. Vietnamese Conflict, 1961-1975
ISBN 978-0-8160-7102-9; 0-8160-7102-0

LC 2008-6881

Contains a "day-by-day chronology of the events and people involved in the Vietnam War . . . [and] also features an A-to-Z biographical dictionary of the key figures involved in the conflict." Publisher's note

Includes bibliographical references

Inside the Pentagon papers; edited by John Prados and Margaret Pratt Porter. University Press of Kansas 2004 248p $29.95   **959.704**
1. Vietnam War, 1961-1975 2. Vietnamese Conflict, 1961-1975 3. Vietnamese Conflict, 1961-1975 -- Congresses
ISBN 0-7006-1325-0

LC 2004-1961

The editors "reexamine the secret government papers that blew the whistle on the Vietnam War, led to the federal attempts to restrain the press and ultimately resulted in President Richard Nixon's resignation. . . . Volumes about these issues abound, but Prados and Porter offer a concise look at those pivotal events and their long-term effects." Publ Wkly

Includes bibliographical references

The Vietnam War; editor, Mark Lawrence; introduction by David K. Shipler. Fitzroy Dearborn Pubs. 2001 2v il maps set $150   **959.704**
1. Vietnam War, 1961-1975 2. Vietnamese Conflict, 1961-1975 -- History
ISBN 1-57958-368-7

LC 2002-726953

"A must-have for all libraries." Recomm Ref Books for Small & Medium-sized Libr & Media Cent, 2003

The encyclopedia of the Vietnam War; a political, social, and military history. Spencer C. Tucker, editor. 2nd ed.; ABC-CLIO 2011 4v il map set $395   **959.704**
1. Reference books 2. Vietnam War, 1961-1975 -- Encyclopedias
ISBN 978-1-85109-960-3; 978-1-85109-961-0 ebook

LC 2011007604

"Written to provide multidimensional perspectives into the conflict, . . . [this encyclopedia] covers not only the American experience in Vietnam, but also the entire scope of Vietnamese history, including the French experience and the Indochina War, as well as the origins of the conflict, how the United States became involved, and the extensive aftermath of this prolonged war." Publisher's note

Includes bibliographical references

959.8   Indonesia and East Timor

Taylor, Jean Gelman

★ **Indonesia**: peoples and histories. Yale University Press 2003 420p il maps hardcover o.p. pa $24   **959.8**
ISBN 0-300-09709-3; 0-300-10518-5 pa

LC 2002-152348

This is "an account of Indonesia from the earliest migrations and settlements in the archipelago to the collapse of yet another government just a few years ago. While basically historical in design, this is no ordinary history. The book is one great historical essay . . . that allows the historian's search for the past to wander into social, religious, artistic, and anthropological byways." Choice

Includes bibliographical references

959.9   Philippines

Karnow, Stanley

In our image; America's empire in the Philippines. Random House 1989 494p il maps hardcover o.p. pa $27   **959.9**
1. Philippines -- History
ISBN 0-345-32816-7 pa

LC 88-42676

A history of American involvement in the Philippines from 1898 to the present.

The author's "treatment of the indecisiveness of President McKinley over the issue of empire and of the egotistical General MacArthur make the work a definite purchase for libraries. . . . Those who love swashbuckling history will enjoy this work." Libr J

Includes bibliographical references

960   History of Africa

Falola, Toyin
★ **Key** events in African history; a reference guide. Greenwood Press 2002 xxiii, 347p il maps $64.95; pa $25   **960**
ISBN 0-313-31323-7; 0-313-36122-3 pa
LC 2001-58644

"Falola surveys the . . . history of the African continent by focusing on 36 pivotal events that either caused or led to significant changes and developments in African social, political, and cultural life from around 40,000 B.C.E. to the collapse of apartheid in the 1990s. . . . Following a detailed time line of historical events, each topic is highlighted in an individual chapter including cross-references, historical and political maps, illustrations, a notes section, and a suggested list for further reading." Booklist
Includes bibliographical references

Gates, Henry Louis
Wonders of the African world; [by] Henry Louis Gates, Jr. Knopf 1999 275p il map hardcover o.p. pa $24.95   **960**
ISBN 0-375-40235-7; 0-375-70948-7 pa
LC 99-18496

"Gates writes with concentration and clarity, and anticipates the questions that arise in the wary reader's mind, delivering the answers at just the right time." N Y Times Book Rev
Includes bibliographical references

Lefkowitz, Mary R.
Not out of Africa; how Afrocentrism became an excuse to teach myth as history. [by] Mary Lefkowitz. Basic Bks. 1996 222p il map hardcover o.p. pa $19   **960**
1. History -- Study and teaching
ISBN 0-465-09837-1; 0-465-09838-X pa
LC 95-49109

"The book is a case study in historical methods, the value and limits of scholarship, and the preciousness of hardbitten reason and objectivity. The book is also lucid and accessible." Christ Sci Monit
Includes bibliographical references

Meredith, Martin
Born in Africa; by Martin Meredith. 1st ed.; PublicAffairs 2011 xxiv, 230p ill.   **960**
ISBN 9781586486631 pa; 9781610391054
LC 2010043985

This book presents an "account of human evolution and the fiercely competitive anthropologists who are unearthing our ancestors' remains and arguing over what they mean. . . . [It] describ[es] the nuts-and-bolts of field research, the meaning of the often headline-producing findings and the ever-changing variety of species who split off from the common ancestors of chimpanzees and hominids." (Kirkus)
"Scientists . . . have firmly established Africa as the birthplace not only of humankind but of modern humans. They have revealed how early technology, language ability, and artistic endeavour all originated in Africa; and they have shown how small groups of Africans spread out from Africa

in an exodus sixty thousand years ago to populate the rest of the world." (Publisher's note)

Pakenham, Thomas
The **scramble** for Africa; the White man's conquest of the dark continent from 1876 to 1912. Avon 1992 xxv, 738p il map pa $22.95   **960**
ISBN 0-380-71999-1

This book is an account of the colonization and conquest of Africa by five European nations—Great Britain, France, Belgium, Germany, and Italy.

This is a "sweeping narrative, refreshingly old fashioned in its appreciation of the fact that imperialism did have some virtues, which offers as good an introduction to the 'scramble' as has ever been written." Libr J
Includes bibliographical references

Africa: an encyclopedia for students; John Middleton, editor. Scribner 2002 4v il maps set $395   **960**
1. Reference books
ISBN 0-684-80650-9
LC 2001-49348

A comprehensive look at the continent of Africa and the countries that comprise it, including peoples and cultures, the land and its history, art and architecture, and daily life.

Encyclopedia of African history; Kevin Shillington, editor. Fitzroy Dearborn 2004 3v il map set $395   **960**
1. Reference books
ISBN 1-579-58245-1
LC 2004-16779

"The scope of the coverage encompasses the entire continent, including North Africa, and features all historical periods, with special attention to recent events. Most entries are given 1000 words, though major topics, such as regional surveys, stretch to 3000-4000 words. Topics range from art to anthropology to economics, but emphasis is placed on biographies and country studies, both pre- and postcolonial. . . . Simply put, this is an essential reference resource for students of African history." Libr J
Includes bibliographical references

★ **Encyclopedia of African history and culture;** Willie F. Page, editor. rev ed; Facts on File 2005 5v il map set $425   **960**
1. Reference books
ISBN 0-8160-5199-2
LC 2004-22929

This set "fulfills its information and education goals and is highly recommended for high-school, public, and academic libraries." Booklist
Includes bibliographical references

New encyclopedia of Africa; John Middleton, editor in chief; Joseph C. Miller, editor. Charles Scribner's Sons 2008 5v il map set $625   **960**
1. Reference books
ISBN 978-0-684-31454-9
LC 2007-21746

This encyclopedia "covers the entire continent, from the Europe-facing shores of the Mediterranean to the commercial bustle of Cape Town. The set addresses the . . . history of African cultures from the pharaohs and the ancient civilizations of the south through the colonial era to the emergence of 53 independent countries." Publisher's note

Includes bibliographical references

962   Egypt, Sudan, South Sudan

Goldschmidt, Arthur

A **brief** history of Egypt. Facts on File 2008 294p il map $45; pa $19.95   **962**
    ISBN 978-0-8160-6672-8; 0-8160-6672-8; 978-0-8160-7333-7 pa; 0-8160-7333-3 pa

LC 2007-7374

The author "explores Egypt's broad political, economic, social, and cultural developments, covering roughly 6,000 years of history." Publisher's note

Includes glossary and bibliographical references

Jeal, Tim

Explorers of the Nile; the triumph and tragedy of a great Victorian adventure. Yale 2011 510p il map $32.50   **962**
    1. Explorers 2. Nonfiction
    ISBN 978-0-300-14935-7

LC 2011933872

In this book on Victorian efforts to find the source of the [Nile River], the author focuses on a quintet of great Victorian explorers, namely David Livingstone, Henry Morton Stanley, John Hanning Speke, Richard Burton, and Samuel Baker. He recreates the mosquito-infested journeys and reveals the complex personal relationships, as Livingstone's early ventures to Lake Nyasa give way to the rivalry between Burton and Speke, who ventured north to Lakes Tanganyika, Victoria and Albert.H Details on the geopolitical consequences of finding the source of the Nilet are also presented. (History Today)

"Jeal's judicious account is a must-read for anyone hoping to understand the internal dynamics of modern statebuilding in central Africa." Booklist

Includes bibliographical references

Morrison, Dan

The **black** Nile; one man's amazing journey through peace and war on the world's longest river. Viking 2010 307p il map $26.95   **962**
    1. Canoes and canoeing 2. War and civilization
    ISBN 978-0-670-02198-7

LC 2010-4709

A foreign correspondent traces the four-thousand-mile plank-board boat journey he took with an inexperienced childhood friend along the Nile River from Lake Victoria to the Mediterranean Sea.

"Morrison's account transcends the travel genre to provide authentic and timely information on a complicated part of the world." Libr J

Strathern, Paul

Napoleon in Egypt; Bantam hardcover ed; Bantam Books 2008 480p il map $30   **962**
    1. Civilization -- Egyptian influences 2. Emperors
    ISBN 978-0-553-80678-6; 0-553-80678-5

LC 2008-28135

"Strathern's skillful use of memoir and other primary sources brings to life one of the most fascinating campaigns in military history." Libr J

Includes bibliographical references (p. 429-460)

Thompson, Jason

★ A **history** of Egypt; from earliest times to the present. Anchor Books 2008 382p il map pa $17   **962**
    ISBN 978-0-307-47352-3

The author "has masterfully undertaken the daunting task of presenting the 5000-year history of Egypt to the general reader, with each period given its due attention. Thompson captures the surprising continuity in Egyptian civilization despite the great cultural currents that have impacted the people over the millennia. . . . Thompson's compact, comprehensive, and balanced history of all periods of Egyptian civilization will serve a wide range of readers seeking to understand this enduring nation and people." Libr J

Includes bibliographical references

962.05   Egypt since 1922

Khalil, Ashraf

Liberation Square; Ashraf Khalil. St. Martin's Press 2012 x, 324p.p   **962.05**
    1. Journalists 2. Mubarak, Muhammad Husni, 1928- 3. Nonfiction
    ISBN 9781250006691; 9781429962445

LC 2011038194

This book covers "the rise and fall of Hosni Mubarak's dictatorship. . . . The . . . combination of judicial corruption and police brutality began to awake significant opposition, and the tipping point was the brutal beating death of Khalid Saieed in Alexandria on June 6, 2010. . . . [Author Ashraf] Khalils discussion of the role of the Internet and social media . . . [shows] how large numbers of people were organized to achieve specific objectives--for example, converging on Cairo's squares and other public areas. The author . . . examines how the opposition to Egypt's paramilitary police gained strength, and how American diplomacy contributed to the cause. Khalil closes with the battle for Tahrir Square and the overthrow of the dictatorship." (Kirkus)

962.4   Sudan and South Sudan

Deng, Benson

They poured fire on us from the sky; the true story of three lost boys from Sudan. [by] Benson Deng, Alephonsion Deng, Benjamin Ajak; with Judy Bernstein. Public Affairs 2005 xxiii, 311p map hardcover o.p. pa $13.95   **962.4**
    1. Child refugees -- Sudan 2. Genocide -- Sudan 3.

Refugee children -- Sudan 4. Refugees
ISBN 1-58648-269-6; 1-58648-388-9 pa
LC 2005-42566

"This collection is moving in its depictions of unbeliev-able courage." Publ Wkly

963   Ethiopia and Eritrea

Shah, Tahir
In search of King Solomon's mines. Little, Brown 2003 240p il map $24.95; pa $13.95 **963**
ISBN 1-55970-641-4; 1-55970-724-0 pa

This is an account of the author's search for "the myste-rious mines of Ophir, where King Solomon, the Bible's wis-est king, was supposed to have buried a fortune in gold. . . . According to his reckoning, the mines should be in modern-day Ethiopia, so he set out on an adventure of a lifetime with a shifty bookseller named (no kidding) Ali Baba. Along the way, readers are treated to his accounts of everything from the California gold rush to a sadistic Sultan." Libr J

Includes bibliographical references

964   Morocco, Ceuta, Melilla, Western Sahara, Canary Islands

Shah, Tahir
The **Caliph's** house; Tahir Shah. Bantam Books 2006 349p il $22 **964**
1. Authors 2. Biography, Individual 3. Nonfiction writers
ISBN 0-553-80399-9
LC 2005-53656

"Shah's picture of Moroccan society, its deeply held Is-lamic faith, its primitive superstition, and its raucous econo-my makes for endlessly fascinating reading." Booklist

965   Algeria

Macey, David
Frantz Fanon; a biography. Picador 2001 640p maps $40; pa $20 **965**
1. Algeria -- Biography 2. Diplomats 3. Intellectuals -- Algeria -- Biography 4. Political and social philosophers 5. Psychiatrists 6. Psychiatrists -- Algeria -- Biography 7. Revolutionaries 8. Revolutionaries -- Algeria -- Biography 9. Writers on medicine
ISBN 0-312-27550-1; 0-312-30042-5 pa
LC 2001-21807

"Macey's writing and research is rich with historical context and personal information that both Fanon loyalists and general readers will appreciate." Libr J

Includes bibliographical references

Morgan, Ted
My battle of Algiers; by Ted Morgan. Collins/Smithsonian 2006 284p maps $24.95 **965**
1. Authors 2. Biographers 3. Journalists 4. Memoirists

5. Nonfiction writers 6. Torture
ISBN 0-06-085224-0
LC 2005-52160

The author "recalls his service as a young officer in France's bitter war in Algeria. . . . Anyone interested in the origins of modern terrorist tactics will benefit from his recol-lections." Publ Wkly

966.68   Côte d'Ivoire (Ivory Coast)

Erdman, Sarah
Nine hills to Nambonkaha; two years in the heart of an African village. Holt & Co. 2003 322p $23; pa $14 **966.68**
1. British -- Côte d'Ivoire -- Nambonkaha
ISBN 0-8050-7381-7; 0-312-42312-8 pa
LC 2003-44955

"This is an engrossing, well-told tale certain to appeal to armchair travelers and to anyone—especially women—con-sidering international volunteer work." Publ Wkly

966.905   -1960

Maier, Karl
This house has fallen; midnight in Nigeria. Pub-licAffairs 2000 xxxvii, 327p hardcover o.p. pa $18 **966.905**
ISBN 0-8133-4045-4 pa
LC 00-28199

The author "explores the promise and paradox of Ni-geria. {He} . . . recounts the history of this nation cobbled together from British colonial interests in its formative years and dominated by international oil interests in more recent years." Booklist

Includes bibliographical references

967.5   Democratic Republic of the Congo, Rwanda, Burundi

Hochschild, Adam
★ **King** Leopold's ghost; a story of greed, terror, and heroism in Colonial Africa. Houghton Mifflin 1998 366p il map hardcover o.p. pa $15 **967.5**
1. Atrocities 2. Congo (Republic) -- History 3. Forced labor -- Congo (Democratic Republic) -- History -- 19th century 4. Forced labor -- Congo (Democratic Republic) -- History -- 20th century 5. Indigenous peoples -- Congo (Democratic Republic) -- History -- 19th century 6. Indigenous peoples -- Congo (Democratic Republic) -- History -- 20th century
ISBN 0-395-75924-2; 0-618-00190-5 pa
LC 98-16813

"Hochschild's impressively researched history records the roles of the famous and obscure, missionaries, journal-ists, opportunists, politicians, and royalty in this long-forgot-ten drama." Booklist

Includes bibliographical references

967.51   Democratic Republic of the Congo

Stearns, Jason K.

Dancing in the glory of monsters; the collapse of the Congo and the great war of Africa. PublicAffairs 2011 380p $28.99   **967.51**
  1. Genocide 2. Historical literature 3. Kabila, Laurent-Desire, 1939-2001 4. Massacres 5. Massacres -- Congo (Democratic Republic) 6. Political violence -- Congo (Democratic Republic)
  ISBN 978-1-58648-929-8; 1-58648-929-1
                                    LC 2010-43075
This book does not tell the story of the Rwanda genocide in 1994, in which 800,000 people—almost all civilians—were massacred by their ethnic rivals in the space of a hundred days. That great atrocity is now relatively well known. Instead, this book tells of the war that broke out in the same region two years later, and that was in many ways its consequence. . . . As the Rwandan invaders penetrated into the eastern Congo, atrocities broke out. The Rwandans murdered the Hutus who had not fled. . . . Robert Mugabe of Zimbabwe and Eduardo Dos Santos of Angola pulled their troops out of the war, warning Kabila to negotiate for peace. . . . As well as 'big men' actors, [Jason K.] Stearns questioned many survivors of battle and massacre. (New York Review of Books)
  A "look at the war that began in Congo in 1996 and that eventually involved nine countries and 20 different rebel movements, resulting in the deaths of more than five million people. In sheer brutality, this mostly unremarked upon cataclysm ranks with the two world wars, the Great Leap Forward and the Cambodia genocide. . . . Mr. Stearns has spoken to everyone—villagers, child soldiers, Mobutu's commanders, Kabila's ministers, Rwandan intelligence officers. In these conversations he found gold, bringing clarity—and humanity—to a place that usually seems inexplicable and barbaric. 'Dancing in the Glory of Monsters' is riveting and certain to become essential reading for anyone looking to understand Central Africa." Wall Street J

967.571   Rwanda

Gourevitch, Philip

We wish to inform you that tomorrow we will be killed with our families; stories from Rwanda. Farrar, Straus & Giroux 1998 355p hardcover o.p. pa $15   **967.571**
  1. Genocide 2. Genocide -- Rwanda
  ISBN 0-374-28697-3; 0-312-24335-9 pa
                                    LC 98-22132
This work is "readable and moving, Gourevitch is an impassioned and thoughtful observer. But this is not a work that gives much pleasure or comfort. Nor are its arguments fool-proof, its evidence complete, or its documentation thorough. . . . Still Gourevitch does struggle to come close to a great mystery of evil, and he makes us attend to great crimes." Commonweal

Hatzfeld, Jean

Machete season; the killers in Rwanda speak: a report. translated from the French by Linda Coverdale; preface by Susan Sontag. Farrar, Straus and Giroux 2005 253p il maps hardcover o.p. pa $14   **967.571**
  1. Genocide 2. Hutu (African people) 3. Tutsi (African people) 4. Tutsi (African people) -- Crimes against
  ISBN 0-374-28082-7; 0-312-42503-1 pa
                                    LC 2004-61600
"Steering clear of politics, this important book succeeds in offering the reader some grasp of how such unspeakable acts unfolded." Publ Wkly

The **antelope's** strategy; living in Rwanda after the genocide. a report by Jean Hatzfeld; translated from the French by Linda Coverdale. Farrar, Straus and Giroux 2009 242p map $25   **967.571**
  1. Genocide 2. Genocide -- Rwanda 3. Hutu (African people) 4. Tutsi (African people)
  ISBN 978-0-374-27103-9; 0-374-27103-8
                                    LC 2008-52489
This "is a book that illustrates vividly the thorny realities that accompany survival and appeasement." Washington Post

967.6   Uganda and Kenya

Beard, Peter H.

The **end** of the game; the last word from paradise. [by] Peter Beard; [foreword by Paul Theroux] Taschen 2008 280p il $39.99   **967.6**
  1. Hunting
  ISBN 978-3-83650-530-7; 3-83650-530-4
"This landmark book, with a chilling (and acerbic) new introduction by travel writer and novelist Paul Theroux, contains photographs many of them shocking that reveal the sad situation of African wildlife, and most particularly the elephant. Beard mourns the end of a continent from a diverse and interdependent ecosystem to a land suffocated by cement, wire, walls and ditches (not to mention war)." Stuart News (Stuart, Florida)

Chretien, Jean-Pierre

★ The **great** lakes of Africa; two thousand years of history. translated by Scott Straus. Zone Books 2003 504p map $36   **967.6**
  ISBN 1-89095-134-X
                                    LC 2002-191001
"This is an impressive and important book surveying 2,000 years of history. . . . The preeminence accorded Rwanda and Burundi . . . leads to the book's most significant contribution: to demonstrate that the region's recent interrelated conflicts claiming over four million lives are not based on ancient, unchanging 'ethnic' cleavages, most notably between Tutsi and Hutu." Choice
  Includes bibliographical references

Rice, Andrew

The **teeth** may smile but the heart does not forget; murder and memory in Uganda. Metropolitan Books/ Henry Holt and Co. 2009 363p il map $26   **967.6**
  1. Atrocities 2. Atrocities -- Uganda 3. Children of prominent persons 4. Generals 5. Government officials

6. Murder victims 7. Murderers 8. Presidents
ISBN 978-0-8050-7965-4; 0-8050-7965-3

LC 2008-41984

"At the core of the book is an unsolved disappearance: Eliphaz Laki, a local leader with ties to the anti-Amin opposition, vanished in the early days of the Amin regime. When his son, Duncan, uncovered a clue to his father's disappearance 30 years later, the investigation eventually implicated Amin's second-in-command, Maj. Gen. Yusuf Gowon. With Amin living out his years safely in Saudi Arabia, the trial of Gowon forced Uganda to confront its brutal past. Treating the Lakis' story as a microcosm of Uganda's own, the author weaves together the family's search for truth and justice with Uganda's history." Publ Wkly

967.62   Kenya

Anderson, David M.

Histories of the hanged; the dirty war in Kenya and the end of the empire. [by] David Anderson. Norton 2005 406p il map $25.95; pa $15.95   **967.62**
ISBN 0-393-05986-3; 0-393-32754-X pa

LC 2004-24804

This "history of the last days of the British Empire in Kenya focuses on the colonial judicial system, which sent over 1,000 native Kenyans to the gallows between 1952 and 1959, during the state of emergency triggered by the Mau Mau insurrection. . . . This is vital reading for any student of British colonial and African history." Publ Wkly

Includes bibliographical references

Dinesen, Isak

★ **Out** of Africa and Shadows on the grass. Vintage Bks. 1989 462p pa $13.95   **967.62**
ISBN 0-679-72475-3

LC 89-40144

Out of Africa is a recording of the author's life on a Kenya coffee plantation. Shadows on the grass consists of four short essays which present the author's recollections of her servants in Africa.

967.730   -1960

Bowden, Mark

Black Hawk down; a story of modern war. Atlantic Monthly Press 1999 386p il maps $25; pa $13.95   **967.730**
1. Operation Restore Hope, 1992-1993
ISBN 0-87113-738-0; 0-14-028850-3 pa

LC 98-46688

The author describes "both sides of the October 1993 raid into the heart of Mogadishu, Somalia, a raid that quickly became the most intensive close combat Americans have engaged in since the Vietnam War. But Bowden's gripping narrative of the fighting is only a framework for an examination of the internal dynamics of America's elite forces and a critique of the philosophy of sending such high-tech units into combat with minimal support." Publ Wkly

968   Republic of South Africa and neighboring southern African countries

Thompson, Leonard Monteath

A **history** of South Africa; {by} Leonard Thompson. 3rd ed; Yale Univ. Press 2001 xxiv, 358p il maps hardcover o.p. pa $17.95   **968**
ISBN 0-300-08776-4 pa

LC 00-32101

This is an exploration of South Africa's "history, from the earliest known human inhabitation of the region to the present, focusing primarily on the experiences of its black inhabitants." Publisher's note

Includes bibliographical references

968.04   1814-1910

Meredith, Martin

Diamonds, gold, and war; the British, the Boers, and the making of South Africa. PublicAffairs 2007 570p il map $35   **968.04**
1. Colonial administrators 2. Diamond industry and trade -- South Africa 3. Diamond industry and trade -- South Africa -- History 4. Gold industry -- South Africa 5. Gold industry -- South Africa -- History -- 19th century 6. Government officials 7. Philanthropists 8. South African War, 1899-1902 9. South African War, 1899-1902 -- Causes 10. Statesmen
ISBN 978-1-58648-473-6; 1-58648-473-7

LC 2007-34540

A history of the tumultuous period leading up to the 1910 founding of the modern state of South Africa explores how the discovery of vast diamond and gold deposits led to a fierce struggle between the British and the Boers for control of the region.

"Meredith thoroughly involves us in this gripping history. Highly recommended for all libraries." Libr J

Includes bibliographical references (p. 540-550)

968.06   Period as Republic, 1961-

Carlin, John

Playing the enemy; Nelson Mandela and the game that made a nation. Penguin 2008 274p il $24.95   **968.06**
1. Human rights activists 2. Nobel laureates for peace 3. Political leaders 4. Political prisoners 5. Presidents 6. Rugby 7. Rugby football -- History 8. Sports -- Social aspects -- History
ISBN 978-1-59420-174-5; 1-59420-174-9

LC 2008-298721

"Deftly sketched characters make up both an audience for the big game and a gallery of South Africa, through which Carlin will recount the absorbing story of a country emerging from its cruelly absurd racist experiment." N Y Times Book Rev

Includes bibliographical references

Duke, Lynne

Mandela, Mobutu, and me; a newswoman's African journey. Doubleday 2003 294p $24 **968.06**
1. Generals 2. Human rights activists 3. Nobel laureates for peace 4. Political leaders 5. Political prisoners 6. Presidents
ISBN 0-385-50398-9

LC 2002-73365

The author covers "some of the bloodier postcolonial wars of southern Africa as well as one of the most constructive struggles: the shaping of a postapartheid government. Her interviews with Mandela and Mobutu 'bookend' . . . conversations with common folk: township women struggling for clean water, AIDS nurses battling superstitious villagers and even a quiet old Zulu man impressed to meet his 'first foreign black folk.' A consummate journalist, Duke gives readers concise but thorough background briefings on a country's relevant history before cutting to the chase: who's taken control now, why, and what that means for the balance of power. . . . She deftly combines solid information and personal perspective to produce a powerful, readable chronicle." Publ Wkly

Mandela, Nelson

★ **Mandela**; an illustrated autobiography. Little, Brown 1996 208p il map $29.95 **968.06**
1. Biography, Individual 2. Human rights activists 3. Nobel laureates for peace 4. Political leaders 5. Political prisoners 6. Presidents
ISBN 0-316-55038-8

LC 96-77497

"The photos, from a variety of archives and journalistic sources, ably illustrate Mandela and, even more so, the South Africa around him." Libr J

Tutu, Desmond

★ **No** future without forgiveness; [by] Desmond Mpilo Tutu. Doubleday 1999 287p hardcover o.p. pa $15.95 **968.06**
ISBN 0-385-49690-7 pa

LC 99-34451

The author reflects on his role "as chairman of the Truth and Reconciliation Commission. Tutu speaks frankly of . . . the struggle that preceded it and of the betrayals and jubilations of this unique commission. The TRC's work was unprecedented not only in its emphasis on restorative over retributive justice but in the spirituality that permeated its work, the bulk of which constituted hearings from the 'victims' and 'perpetrators' of apartheid." Publ Wkly
Includes bibliographical references

The **rainbow** people of God; the making of a peaceful revolution. edited by John Allen. Doubleday 1994 xxii, 281p il hardcover o.p. pa $15.95 **968.06**
1. Sermons
ISBN 0-385-48374-0 pa

LC 94-16011

This collection of Tutu's "speeches, letters, and sermons—from the time of the 1976 Soweto Uprising, through the long years of repression and defiance, up to the triumph of the democratic election—serves as an immediate contemporary history of South Africa. Tutu's media secretary,

John Allen, provides a general historical introduction and a connecting narrative that places the individuals pieces in dramatic context." Booklist
Includes bibliographical references

Waldmeir, Patti

Anatomy of a miracle; the end of apartheid and the birth of the new South Africa. Rutgers University Press 1998 289p pa $22.95 **968.06**
ISBN 0-8135-2582-9; 978-0-8135-2582-2

LC 98-15628

Waldmeir traces the political and personal struggles that ultimately contributed to the dismantling of apartheid in South Africa.

"Although Mandela attributes greatness to de Klerk for his courage, it is Mandela's own character that dominates this history. . . . Engrossing in its sweep, this account also describes the obstacles facing the regime." Publ Wkly
Includes bibliographical references

968.91 Zimbabwe

Lamb, Christina

House of stone; the true story of a family divided in war-torn Zimbabwe. Lawrence Hill Books 2007 290p il map **968.91**
1. Farmers 2. Land tenure -- Zimbabwe 3. Nannies 4. Whites -- Zimbabwe -- History
ISBN 978-1-55652-735-7; 1-55652-735-7

LC 2007-19814

"Through the parallel accounts of two people in Zimbabwe, one a poor black maid, one a rich white farmer, ... Lamb tells the compelling story of a country ravaged first by colonial settlers and now by brutal civil war. . . . The anguished personal detail, true to the changing viewpoints, makes for a gripping read." Booklist

Rogers, Douglas

The **last** resort; a memoir of Zimbabwe. Harmony Books 2009 309p map $24.99 **968.91**
1. Memoirists 2. Resorts 3. Travel writers
ISBN 978-0-307-40797-9; 0-307-40797-7

"A nuanced, funny, and heartbreaking story of one community's experience of survival in Mugabe's Zimbabwe." New Yorker

970 History of North America

Morgan, Ted

Wilderness at dawn; the settling of the North American continent. Simon & Schuster 1993 541p il maps hardcover o.p. pa $20 **970**
1. North America -- History
ISBN 0-671-88237-6 pa

LC 93-2628

Morgan "tells a good story, emphasizing the ordinary people who did the actual settlement. . . . A useful survey of the colonial frontier." Libr J
Includes bibliographical references

970.004   North American native peoples

Bragdon, Kathleen J.

The **Columbia** guide to American Indians of the Northeast. Columbia Univ. Press 2001 292p il maps $53.50; pa $25.50   **970.004**

1. Indians of North America -- Canada, Eastern -- History 2. Indians of North America -- Northeastern States -- History 3. Native Americans

ISBN 0-231-11452-4; 0-231-11453-2 pa

LC 2001-47341

This handbook "includes not only a broad overview of the history of Native Americans in the Northeast but also a partially annotated listing of materials for further research including published primary sources, oral traditions, films, and Internet sites." Libr J

Includes bibliographical references

Brown, Dee Alexander

★ **Bury** my heart at Wounded Knee; an Indian history of the American West. [by] Dee Brown. Thirtieth anniversary ed; Holt & Co. 2001 487p il hardcover o.p. pa $16   **970.004**

1. Civil engineers 2. Generals 3. Government officials 4. Indian chiefs 5. Indians of North America -- Wars -- West (U.S.) 6. Indians of North America -- West (U.S.) -- History 7. Native Americans -- Wars 8. Native Americans -- West (U.S.)

ISBN 0-8050-6634-9; 0-8050-6669-1 pa

LC 00-40958

This is an account of the experience of the American Indian during the white man's expansion westward.

Bruchac, Joseph

Our stories remember; American Indian history, culture, & values through storytelling. Fulcrum 2003 192p map pa $16.95   **970.004**

1. Indians of North America -- Folklore 2. Indians of North America -- History 3. Indians of North America -- Social life and customs 4. Native Americans -- History 5. Storytelling

ISBN 1-555-91129-3

LC 2002-151236

"This important volume includes a wealth of traditional stories and solid information." SLJ

Includes bibliographical references

Deloria, Vine

★ **Custer** died for your sins; an Indian manifesto. by Vine Deloria, Jr. University of Oklahoma Press 1988 278p pa $19.95   **970.004**

1. Native Americans

ISBN 0-8061-2129-7

LC 87-40561

The author examines how anthropologists, missionaries, and government agencies have mistreated American Indians.

Fenton, William Nelson

The **Great** Law and the Longhouse; a political history of the Iroquois Confederacy. {by} Willam N. Fenton. University of Okla. Press 1998 xxii, 786p il map $75   **970.004**

1. Iroquois Indians -- History 2. Iroquois Indians -- History -- Sources

ISBN 0-8061-3003-2

LC 97-19842

"If a library has only one book about the Iroquois . . . it should be this title." Libr J

Includes bibliographical references

Fowler, Loretta

The **Columbia** guide to American Indians of the Great Plains. Columbia Univ. Press 2003 283p il maps $53.50; pa $26.50   **970.004**

1. Indians of North America -- Great Plains 2. Native Americans -- Great Plains

ISBN 0-231-11700-0; 0-231-11701-9 pa

LC 2002-73708

"This work is divided into four parts: a general survey of the history and cultures of the native peoples of the region; alphabetically arranged entries focusing on individuals, places, and events; a chronology; and a listing of resources for further research that includes published primary sources, oral traditions, films, and Internet sites. . . . Highly recommended." Libr J

Includes bibliographical references

Harmon, Alexandra

Indians in the making; ethnic relations and Indian identities around Puget Sound. University of Calif. Press 1998 393p il maps hardcover o.p. pa $21.95   **970.004**

1. Frontier and pioneer life -- Washington (State) -- Puget Sound 2. Indians of North America -- Government relations -- Washington (State) -- Puget Sound 3. Indians of North America -- Washington (State) -- Puget Sound -- Ethnic identity 4. Indians of North America -- Washington (State) -- Puget Sound -- History 5. Native Americans -- Northwest Coast of North America 6. Washington (State) -- History

ISBN 0-520-22685-2 pa

LC 98-17665

The author "examines how both the federal government and the native peoples of western Washington were constantly redefining Indian identity to their advantage over a 150-year period. Harmon's examination of the native fishing rights controversy of the 1960s and 1970s is particularly useful." Libr J

Includes bibliographical references

Hendricks, Steve

The **unquiet** grave; the FBI and the struggle for the soul of Indian country. Thunder's Mouth Press 2006 490p il map $27.95   **970.004**

1. Dissenters 2. Educators 3. Indian leaders 4. Native Americans -- Government relations 5. Social activists

ISBN 1-56025-735-0; 978-1-56025-735-6

The author tells "the story of the American Indian Movement (AIM) to reclaim civil and treaty rights. . . . Bracketed by the 1976 murder of AIM activist Anna Mae Aquash and the 2004 trial related to it, Hendricks's swift narrative is riddled with judicial travesties, coverups, vigilantism,

COINTELPRO-style tactics, mounting paranoia and lawlessness on both sides, as activists and ordinary American Indians confront the devastating neglect and outright hostility of government authorities." Publ Wkly

Includes bibliographical references

Iverson, Peter

We are still here; American Indians in the twentieth century. Davidson, H. 1998 255p il pa $14.95 **970.004**
1. Indians of North America -- History -- 20th century 2. Native Americans
ISBN 0-88295-940-9

LC 97-38321

The author "begins at Wounded Knee and tells the stories of Indian communities throughout the United States, including not only political leaders and activists, but also professionals, artists, soldiers and athletes." Publisher's note

Includes bibliographical references

Johansen, Bruce E.

The **Native** peoples of North America; a history. Praeger 2005 2v il set $99.95 **970.004**
1. Indians of North America -- History 2. Native Americans -- History
ISBN 0-275-98159-2

LC 2004-28732

This is a history of "cultures indigenous to North America from their earliest origins to the present. . . . Encompassing not only traditional historical records but also oral histories and biographical sketches, these two volumes will undoubtedly become an integral part of Native American history, an increasingly popular field." Booklist

Includes bibliographical references

Johnson, Michael

Encyclopedia of native tribes of North America; color plates by Richard Hook. 3rd ed; Firefly Books 2007 320p il map $49.95 **970.004**
1. Native Americans -- Encyclopedias 2. Reference books
ISBN 978-1-55407-307-8; 1-55407-307-3

"The volume is organized into ten regionally based culture areas (Northwestern Woodlands, Southeastern Woodlands, Plains and Prairie, Plateau, Great Basin, California, Southwest, Northwest Coast, Subarctic, and Arctic); each area is introduced with general information on language, subsistence, religion, culture, and history. . . . The rich illustrations and supplemental sections make this volume worthwhile." Choice

Includes bibliographical references

Josephy, Alvin M.

The **Nez** Perce Indians and the opening of the Northwest; {by} Alvin M. Josephy, Jr. Houghton Mifflin 1997 xx, 705p il map pa $19 **970.004**
1. Nez Perce Indians 2. Nez Percé Indians
ISBN 0-395-85011-8

LC 96-54278

This history of the Nez Perce tribe traces its contact with white settlers from Lewis and Clark to Chief Joseph and war in 1877.

★ **Now** that the buffalo's gone; a study of today's American Indians. University of Okla. Press 1984 300p pa $24.95 **970.004**
1. Apache Indians 2. Dakota Indians 3. Iroquois Indians 4. Mohegan Indians 5. Muckleshoot Indians 6. Narraganset Indians 7. Native Americans 8. Nisqualli Indians 9. Paiute Indians 10. Pequot Indians 11. Pueblo Indians 12. Puyallup Indians 13. Seneca Indians 14. Timucua Indians
ISBN 0-8061-1915-2; 978-0-8061-1915-1

This look at American Indians focuses primarily on the Seminoles, the Pequots, the Senecas, and the Taos Pueblo Indians.

McLoughlin, William Gerald

After the Trail of Tears; the Cherokees' struggle for sovereignty, 1839-1880. {by} William G. McLoughlin. University of N.C. Press 1993 439p maps hardcover o.p. pa $21.95 **970.004**
1. Cherokee Indians 2. Cherokee Indians -- Government relations 3. Cherokee Indians -- History 4. Cherokee Indians -- Politics and government 5. Indian chiefs
ISBN 0-8078-4433-0 pa

LC 93-18532

The author "recounts the tragedy that continued to afflict the Cherokee Nation after their forced removal from their traditional home to Oklahoma during the 1820s and 1830s. In Oklahoma the Cherokee Nation set out to reconstruct their society, reestablishing their newspaper, which published in the Cherokee language, and governing themselves according to a constitution modeled on that of the United States. . . . McLoughlin vividly depicts the conflicts between 'full-bloods,' who sought to live by more traditional ways, and Cherokees of mixed ancestry who favored assimilation into the dominant culture." Publ Wkly

Includes bibliographical references

McReynolds, Edwin C.

The **Seminoles**. University of Okla. Press 1957 397p il maps hardcover o.p. pa $21.95 **970.004**
1. Seminole Indians
ISBN 0-8061-1255-7 pa

"This is almost strictly a military and political history, in great detail, spiced with a few incidents which reveal the courageous character of the Seminoles, and stressing their relations with the Creeks." Libr J

Includes bibliographical references

Milton, Giles

Big Chief Elizabeth; the adventures and fate of the First English Colonists in America. Farrar, Straus & Giroux 2000 358p il maps hardcover o.p. pa $14 **970.004**
1. Indians of North America -- First contact with Europeans 2. Indians of North America -- Government relations 3. Indians, Treatment of -- North America 4.

Native Americans 5. Queens
ISBN 0-312-42018-8 pa

LC 00-31522

"Nearly 500 years ago, a small group of white men landed on the shores of North America and named it Virginia (for the Virgin Queen [Elizabeth]). Their purpose was to capture some natives and bring them to England to learn their language and everything else they could about the country they wished to colonize. . . . [Milton] chronicles the century-long battle to establish a permanent settlement in Virginia." Christ Sci Monit

Includes bibliographical references

Osborn, William M.

The **wild** frontier; atrocities during the American-Indian War from Jamestown Colony to Wounded Knee. Random House 2000 363p hardcover o.p. pa $19　　　　　　　　　　　　　　　　　**970.004**

1. Atrocities -- United States -- History 2. Frontier and pioneer life 3. Frontier and pioneer life -- United States 4. Indians of North America -- Government relations 5. Indians of North America -- Wars -- United States 6. Native Americans -- Government relations 7. Native Americans -- Wars
ISBN 0-375-75856-9 pa

LC 00-27171

"Characterizing the years between 1622 and 1890 as the era of the American-Indian War, Osborn provides a balanced analysis of the vicious atrocities committed by white settlers and Native Americans during the prolonged period of westward expansion. . . . Laden with stark, unsparing descriptions . . . the detailed narrative retains an admirable objectivity." Booklist

Includes bibliographical references

Perdue, Theda

The **Columbia** guide to American Indians of the Southeast; [by] Theda Perdue and Michael D. Green. Columbia Univ. Press 2001 325p il maps $53.50; pa $27.50　　　　　　　　　　　　　　　　　**970.004**

1. Indians of North America -- Southern States -- History 2. Indians of North America -- Southern States -- Social life and customs 3. Native Americans -- Southern States
ISBN 0-231-11570-9; 0-231-11571-7 pa

LC 2001-35338

"The first half of the text focuses on the history and culture of the region's native groups. This includes not only the Mississippian Moundbuilder cultures that arose between 800 and 1000 C.E. but also well-known native groups such as the Cherokee and Creeks. . . . Immediately following the survey are alphabetically arranged entries focusing on individuals, places, and events. The final two sections are a chronology and a listing of resources for further research, which include published primary sources, oral traditions, films, and Internet sites. . . . An essential purchase for all libraries collecting books about Native Americans." Libr J

Includes bibliographical references

Philip, Neil

The **great** circle; a history of the First Nations. foreword by Dennis Hastings. Clarion Books 2006 153p il map $25　　　　　　　　　　　　　　　　　**970.004**

1. Indians of North America -- History -- Juvenile literature 2. Native Americans 3. Young adult literature -- Works
ISBN 978-0-618-15941-3; 0-618-15941-X

LC 2005032743

"Philip takes on a huge challenge here: to present a unified narrative that explains the complex and confrontational relationships between Native Americans and white settlers. . . . He pulls it off, however, thanks to solid research, an engaging writing style, and a talent for making individual stories serve the whole. . . . Top marks, too, for the volume's photographs and historical renderings, which so intensely illustrate the pages." Booklist

Includes bibliographical references

Pritzker, Barry

A **Native** American encyclopedia; history, culture, and peoples. [by] Barry M. Pritzker. Oxford Univ. Press 2000 591p il hardcover o.p. pa $29.95　　　　　　　　　　　　　　　　　**970.004**

1. Indians of North America -- Encyclopedias 2. Native Americans -- Encyclopedias 3. Reference books
ISBN 0-19-513897-X; 0-19-513877-5 pa

LC 99-53677

"Organized geographically, each section begins with an introduction to the area and its original inhabitants. Tribal entries follow, with some smaller related groups discussed together. Each article includes sections on location, population, language, history, religion, government, customs, dwellings, diet, key technology, trade, notable arts, transportation, dress, and war/weapons. A contemporary section follows, with information on government/reservations, economy, legal status, and daily life." Libr J [review of 1998 edition]

Includes bibliographical references

Rajtar, Steve

Indian war sites; a guidebook to battlefields, monuments, and memorials, state by state with Canada and Mexico. McFarland & Co. 1999 330p $39.95　　　　　　　　　　　　　　　　　**970.004**

1. Battlefields -- North America 2. Historic sites -- North America 3. Indians of North America -- History 4. Indians of North America -- Wars 5. Native Americans -- Wars 6. War memorials -- North America
ISBN 0-7864-0710-7

LC 99-25893

This is a "reference to hundreds of conflicts, both major and minor, between American Indians and Europeans. Divided alphabetically by state and then chronologically within each, entries include name and date, a nonspecific location (e.g., Spring River), a brief description, and bibliographic sources. If the battle was a part of a larger war Rajtar also gives the name of the war; and if there is a monument, he tells its location and briefly describes what's there." Libr J

Includes bibliographical references and indexes

Richter, Daniel K.

Facing east from Indian country; a Native history of early America. Harvard Univ. Press 2001 317p il maps $27.50; pa $15.95 **970.004**
1. Indians of North America -- First contact with Europeans 2. Indians of North America -- History -- Colonial period, ca. 1600-1775 3. Indians, Treatment of -- United States -- History 4. Native Americans
ISBN 0-674-00638-0; 0-674-01117-1 pa

LC 2001-24997

The author "recasts early American history from the Native American point of view and in doing so illuminates as much about the Europeans as about the original Americans. . . . Exploring the varying complexities of different native people's relationships with England, France and Spain, he argues that the Native Americans were safer during the colonial era than after the Revolution. . . . Gracefully written and argued, Richter's compelling research and provocative claims make this an important addition to the literature for general readers of both Native American and U.S. studies." Publ Wkly

Includes bibliographical references and index

Robbins, Catherine C.

All Indians do not live in teepees (or casinos) University of Nebraska Press 2011 385p il map $26.95 **970.004**
1. Native Americans -- Social life and customs
ISBN 978-0-8032-3973-9; 0-8032-3973-4

LC 2011011320

"A solid, insightful overview of the way American Indians live now." Kirkus

Includes bibliographical references

Roberts, David

Once they moved like the wind; Cochise, Geronimo, and the Apache wars. Simon & Schuster 1993 368p il hardcover o.p. pa $22 **970.004**
1. Apache Indians 2. Apache Indians -- History 3. Apache Indians -- Wars 4. Biography, Individual 5. Indian chiefs 6. Native Americans -- Wars
ISBN 0-671-70221-1; 0-671-88556-1 pa

LC 93-7112

"The book is history at its most engrossing." Publ Wkly
Includes bibliographical references

Waldman, Carl

Atlas of the North American Indian; 3rd ed; Facts on File 2009 450p il map $85; pa $24.95 **970.004**
1. Atlases 2. Indians of North America 3. Native Americans 4. Reference books
ISBN 978-0-8160-6858-6; 0-8160-6858-5; 978-0-8160-6859-3 pa; 0-8160-6859-3 pa

LC 2008-40736

"This is a very well-designed book, a bargain for any library." Voice Youth Advocates [review of 2000 edition]
Includes glossary and bibliographical references

Encyclopedia of Native American tribes; 3rd rev ed; Facts on File 2006 xxiv, 360p il map $75; pa $21.95 **970.004**
1. Indians of North America 2. Native Americans -- Encyclopedias 3. Reference books
ISBN 978-0-8160-6273-7; 0-8160-6273-0; 978-0-8160-6274-4 pa; 0-8160-6274-9 pa

LC 2006-12529

"This well-written and easily accessible encyclopedia of a good starting point for research on Native American tribes." Libr Media Connect
Includes bibliographical references

Weatherford, J. McIver

Native roots; how the Indians enriched America. [by] Jack Weatherford. Fawcett 1992 310p il map pa $13.95 **970.004**
1. Native Americans
ISBN 978-0-449-90713-9; 0-449-90713-9
"A valuable corrective to the sentimentality with which we regard the first U.S. settlers and developers." Booklist
Includes bibliographical references

Wilson, James

The **earth** shall weep; the history of Native Americans. Atlantic Monthly Press 1999 xxix, 466p maps hardcover o.p. pa $16 **970.004**
1. Indians of North America -- Government policy 2. Indians of North America -- History 3. Indians, Treatment of -- North America 4. Native Americans
ISBN 0-8021-3680-X pa

LC 99-13098

"Employing elegiac prose and steady narrative momentum, Wilson has written a richly informative history that places Native Americans 'at the center of the historical stage.'" Publ Wkly
Includes bibliographical references

Woodard, Colin

American nations; a history of the eleven rival regional cultures of North America. Viking 2011 371p map $30 **970.004**
1. Multiculturalism 2. Regionalism -- North America
ISBN 978-0-670-02296-0

LC 2011015196

The author's "take on American history identifies the original cultural settlements that became the United States, and proceeds with the thesis that these regional and cultural divisions are responsible for clashes stretching back to Revolutionary times. The 11 nations don't follow state or even country territory lines, but rather the paths taken by the earliest settlers of these areas; while later immigrants added to the mix, they didn't change the fundamental culture. . . . The book's compelling explanations and apt descriptions will fascinate anyone with an interest in politics, regional culture, or history." Publ Wkly
Includes bibliographical references

America in 1492; the world of the Indian peoples before the arrival of Columbus. edited and with an introduction by Alvin Josephy, Jr.; developed by Frederick E. Hoxie. Knopf 1992 477p il maps hardcover o.p. pa $20   **970.004**
1. Indians -- History 2. Native Americans -- Antiquities 3. Native Americans -- History
ISBN 0-394-56438-3; 0-679-74337-5 pa
LC 90-26222
These essays depict "the diverse lives of the approximately 75 million people living in the Americas around the turn of the fifteenth century. Geography guides the first section. . . . Another section focuses on languages, spiritual beliefs and customs, art, and 'systems of knowledge.'" Booklist
Includes bibliographical references

American Indians; consulting editor, Harvey Markowitz. Salem Press 1995 3v il maps set $331   **970.004**
1. Indians of Mexico -- Dictionaries 2. Indians of North America -- Dictionaries 3. Native Americans -- Encyclopedias 4. Native Americans -- Mexico -- Encyclopedias 5. Reference books
ISBN 0-89356-757-4
LC 94-47633
"This set contains 1,129 articles ranging in length from 200 to 3,000 words. The entries cover a wide range of persons, tribes, organizations, cultural and historical events, and contemporary issues of U.S., Canadian, and some Mesoamerican Indian groups. Individual entries appear for 275 North American tribes. Entries are arranged alphabetically and are illustrated with 250 black-and-white photographs, maps, charts, tables, and drawings." Booklist

Documents of American Indian diplomacy; treaties, agreements, and conventions, 1775-1979. {compiled by} Vine Deloria, Jr., and Raymond J. DeMallie; with a foreword by Daniel K. Inouye. University of Okla. Press 1999 2v set $125   **970.004**
1. Indians of North America -- Treaties 2. Native Americans -- Government relations 3. Treaties
ISBN 0-8061-3118-7
LC 98-45365
This is a collection of hundreds of treaties and agreements made by American Indian nations with the Continental Congress, England, Spain, and other foreign countries, the Confederacy, the Republic of Texas, railroad companies, other Indian nations, and the U.S. government, with chapter introductions which put them in historical and political context.
"A must for all libraries." Libr J
Includes bibliographical references (p. {1496}-1500) and index

Encyclopedia of Native American wars and warfare; general editors, William B. Kessel, Robert Wooster. Facts on File 2005 398p il map $75; pa $21.95   **970.004**
1. Indians of North America -- Warfare 2. Indians of North America -- Wars 3. Native Americans -- Wars -- Encyclopedias 4. Reference books
ISBN 0-8160-3337-4; 0-8160-6430-X pa
LC 00-56200
"This encyclopedia offers readers a wide range of information about Native American history in North America after 1492." Choice
Includes bibliographical references

Native America in the twentieth century; an encyclopedia. edited by Mary B. Davis; assistant editors, Joan Berman, Mary E. Graham, Lisa A. Mitten. Garland 1994 xxxvii, 787p il maps hardcover o.p. pa $50   **970.004**
1. Indians of North America 2. Native Americans -- Encyclopedias 3. Reference books
ISBN 0-8153-2583-5 pa
LC 94-768
This volume offers "tribal-specific information on the art, daily life, economic development, and religion of 20th-century American Indians and Alaskan Natives and the government policy that affects them." Libr J

★ Native American testimony; a chronicle of Indian-white relations from prophecy to the present, 1492-2000. edited by Peter Nabokov; with a foreword by Vine Deloria, Jr. Rev and updated ed; Penguin Bks. 1999 xxiii, 506p il maps pa $16.95   **970.004**
1. Native Americans -- Government relations 2. Native Americans -- History -- Sources
ISBN 0-14-028159-2
"A collection of primary-source material, grouped by key issues that arose during 500 years of Indian and white encounters in North America. Nabokov uses traditional narratives, old government transcripts, reservation newspapers, and firsthand interviews to highlight this chronological volume. Photographs appear throughout." SLJ {review of 1991 edition}
Includes bibliographical references

970.01   Historical periods

Adovasio, J. M.
    The **first** Americans; in pursuit of archaeology's greatest mystery. {by} J.M. Adovasio with Jake Page. Random House 2002 328p il maps hardcover o.p. pa $14.95   **970.01**
1. Indians -- Origin 2. Native Americans -- Origin 3. Paleo-Indians
ISBN 0-375-75704-X pa
LC 2002-69766
"Readers get a lively, close-up view of how archaeologists study America's original discoverers." Booklist
Includes bibliographical references

Dillehay, Tom D.

★ The **settlement** of the Americas; a new pre-history. {by} Thomas D. Dillehay. Basic Bks. 2000 xxi, 371p il hardcover o.p. pa $22   **970.01**
1. Prehistoric peoples -- America
ISBN 0-465-07669-6 pa

LC 00-27572

This "is a seminal work in the field that is accessible to lay readers." Libr J
Includes bibliographical references

Duncan, David Ewing

Hernando de Soto; a savage quest in the Americas. University of Okla. Press 1997 570p map il pa $29.95   **970.01**
1. Colonial administrators 2. Explorers
ISBN 0-8061-2977-8; 978-0-8061-2977-8

LC 97-10455

"Duncan's scholarship and documentation are impeccable, and his chronology unfolds like a superbly crafted novel." Booklist
Includes bibliographical references

Horwitz, Tony

★ A **voyage** long and strange; rediscovering the new world. Henry Holt and Co. 2008 445p il map $27.50   **970.01**
1. Explorers 2. Explorers -- America -- History 3. Explorers -- North America -- History
ISBN 978-0-8050-7603-5; 0-8050-7603-4

LC 2007-45883

"Realizing that his knowledge of American history between Columbus's discovery and Plymouth Rock over 100 years later was sketchy at best, . . . [the author] sets out to educate himself with his own explorations. He intertwines his experiences retracing the early conquistadors, adventurers, and entrepreneurs through such regions as Newfoundland, the Dominican Republic, and the American South, Southwest, and New England with thoroughly researched accounts of the territories themselves, the natives who were historically affected, and the motives of the explorers. . . . This readable and vastly entertaining history travelog is highly recommended for public libraries." Libr J
Includes bibliographical references

Mann, Charles C.

1491; new revelations of the Americas before Columbus. Knopf 2005 465p il maps   **970.01**
1. Indians -- Antiquities 2. Indians -- History 3. Indians -- Origin 4. Native Americans -- History
ISBN 1-4000-3205-9 pa; 1-4000-4006-X

LC 2005-42178

This is a portrait "of the Americas before the arrival of the Europeans in 1492." (Publisher's note) Index.

"Mann navigates adroitly through the controversies. He approaches each in the best scientific tradition, carefully sifting the evidence, never jumping to hasty conclusions, giving everyone a fair hearing—the experts and the amateurs; the accounts of the Indians and their conquerors. And rarely is he less than enthralling." N Y Times Book Rev
Includes bibliographical references

National Museum of Natural History (U.S.)

Vikings: the North Atlantic saga; edited by William W. Fitzhugh and Elisabeth I. Ward. Smithsonian Institution Press 2000 432p il maps hardcover o.p. pa $34.95   **970.01**
1. Northmen 2. Vikings 3. Vikings -- Material culture
ISBN 1-56098-970-X; 1-56098-995-5 pa

LC 99-57983

This book is "well designed, heavily illustrated and almost encyclopedic in scope and detail." Publ Wkly
Includes bibliographical references

Schneider, Paul

Brutal journey: the epic story of the first crossing of North America. Holt 2006 366p il maps $26   **970.01**
1. Colonial administrators 2. Explorers 3. Government officials 4. Historians 5. Indians of North America -- First contact with Europeans 6. Indians of North America -- Florida -- First contact with Europeans 7. Indians of North America -- History -- 16th century 8. Travel writers
ISBN 978-0-8050-6835-1; 0-8050-6835-X

LC 2005-50246

"Equally able in his dramatizations of the privations and brutalities suffusing this extraordinary tale, Schneider scores big with fans of historical (mis)adventure." Booklist
Includes bibliographical references

Schobinger, Juan

★ The **ancient** Americans; a reference guide to the art, culture, and history of pre-Columbian North and South America. translation, Carys Evans-Corrales; consultant, Susan Kart. Sharpe, M.E. 2000 2v il maps set $159   **970.01**
1. Indian art 2. Indians -- Antiquities 3. Native American art 4. Native Americans -- Antiquities 5. Petroglyphs -- America 6. Rock drawings, paintings, and engravings 7. Rock paintings -- America
ISBN 0-7656-8034-3

LC 00-56280

This reference "surveys the entire Western Hemisphere prior to the arrival of Europeans in the Americas. This copiously illustrated work is especially notable for its numerous full-color plates of Native American rock art." Libr J
Includes bibliographical references

Archaeology of prehistoric native America; an encyclopedia. editor, Guy Gibbon; associate editors, Kenneth M. Ames [et al.] Garland 1998 lxxvii, 941p il map $205   **970.01**
1. Archaeology -- North America 2. Indians of North America -- Antiquities -- Encyclopedias 3. Native Americans -- Antiquities -- Encyclopedias 4. North America -- Antiquities -- Encyclopedias 5. Reference books
ISBN 0-8153-0725-X

LC 98-11443

This encyclopedia includes alphabetically arranged entries covering North American prehistory and archaeology.

"This superb reference source . . . has no equal in its coverage of Native American cultures in North America prior to European contact." Libr J

Includes bibliographical references

971 Countries and localities

Gray, Charlotte

Gold diggers; striking it rich in the Klondike. Counterpoint 2010 413p il map $29.95 **971**
1. Biography, Collective 2. Frontier and pioneer life -- Klondike River valley (Yukon) 3. Frontier and pioneer life -- Yukon Territory -- Klondike River valley 4. Gold mines and mining
ISBN 978-1-58243-611-1

LC 2010-17805

This is "an enchanting recitation of lives—and deaths— in the Klondike during the gold rush over 100 years ago. Combining a keen eye for detail and firsthand histories of contemporary witnesses, Gray sets forth the lives of six 'stampeders,' including Jack London (who almost died in the wild before writing so wonderfully of those who did), Mountie Sam Steele, business wiz Belinda Mulrooney, highborn journalist Flora Shaw, devoted Jesuit priest William Judge, and, most of all, Bill Haskell, a simple soul who left America with a dream of exploration and riches." Libr J

Includes bibliographical references

MacDonald, Laura M.

Curse of the Narrows. Walker & Co. 2005 355p il maps $26 **971**
1. Explosions
ISBN 0-8027-1458-7

LC 2005-44255

This "book captures in vivid detail the history of this catastrophe." Booklist

Includes bibliographical references

Mowat, Farley

High latitudes; an Arctic journey. foreword by Margaret Atwood. Steerforth Press 2003 300p map pa $15.95 **971**
1. Natural history -- Canada
ISBN 1-58642-061-5

LC 2002-151151

"In 1966, Mowat's publisher, Jack McClelland, sent Mowat into northern Canada to research an illustrated volume on the region. This book is the tale of that journey. Hopscotching by creaky plane from one isolated settlement to another, Mowat witnesses the devastation being wrought on the native peoples by encroaching white men, lured by a mirage of the north's supposedly limitless minerals and the raw beauty of the land and its people. A cavalcade of vivid, fiction-worthy characters fills these pages. . . . Voiced with a passionate sense of justice, this work is stirring reading from the bard of the Canadian north." Publ Wkly

Riendeau, Roger E.

★ A brief history of Canada; [by] Roger Riendeau. 2nd ed; Facts on File 2007 444p il map $45 **971**
ISBN 978-0-8160-6335-2

LC 2006-47130

This is a history of Canada "beginning with the exploration of the Northern American frontier and continuing through the rise and fall of the French and British empires to the foundations of Canadian nationhood and the present day." Publisher's note

Includes bibliographical references

Weihs, Jean Riddle

Facts about Canada, its provinces and territories; {by} Jean Weihs; illustrations by Cameron Riddle. Wilson, H.W. 1995 246p il maps $60 **971**
ISBN 0-8242-0864-1

LC 94-23275

Coverage includes "geography and climate, parks and historic sites, demography, government and politics, financial and economic information, history, culture and education, motor vehicle use statistics, trivia about the 'first, biggest and best,' information sources and a selected bibliography. Weihs provides very current information and has clearly researched her topic extensively." Voice Youth Advocates

972 Mexico, Central America, West Indies, Bermuda

Coe, Michael D.

The Maya; Michael D. Coe. 7th ed fully rev and expanded; Thames and Hudson 2005 272p il map pa $22.50 **972**
1. Indians of Central America -- Antiquities 2. Indians of Mexico -- Antiquities 3. Mayas 4. Mayas -- Antiquities
ISBN 978-0-500-28505-3; 0-500-28505-5

An illustrated survey of the Maya civilization, focusing on the achievements of the Classic Period, A.D. 300-900.

Diaz del Castillo, Bernal

The discovery and conquest of Mexico, 1517-1521; translated by A.P. Maudslay. Da Capo Press 2003 478p il map pa $24 **972**
ISBN 0-306-81319-X; 978-0-306-81319-1

"The memoirs of an old man, who began to write of his experiences half a century after they occurred and completed his account at the age of 84, they are not free from minor inaccuracies, but they are the most reliable narrative that exists." Chicago Sunday Trib

Foster, Lynn V.

★ A brief history of Mexico; 4th ed; Facts On File 2009 324p il map $49.50; pa $19.95 **972**
ISBN 978-0-8160-7405-1; 978-0-8160-7406-8 pa

LC 2009-18298

An overview of Mexican history covering pre-Columbian civilizations and contemporary indigenous cultures. Language, art, religion, politics and economics are discussed. A chronology and bibliography are included.

Henderson, Timothy J.
The **Mexican** Wars for Independence. Hill and Wang 2009 xxiii, 246p il map $27.50 **972**
ISBN 978-0-8090-9509-4; 0-8090-9509-2
LC 2008-48141
"A solid overview of a decidedly difficult time and place, and a lucid introduction for those unfamiliar with Mexican history." Kirkus
Includes bibliographical references

Kirkwood, Burton
The **history** of Mexico; 2nd ed.; Greenwood Press/ABC-CLIO 2010 258p il map $49.95 **972**
ISBN 978-0-313-36601-7; 0-313-36601-2
LC 2009036964
A historical survey of Mexico and its people from the arrival of the first humans in the Western Hemisphere to the first decade of the 21st century. Topics range from Mexico's cultural past to more current issues such as the war on drugs and the North American Free Trade Agreement.

Meyer, Michael C.
★ The **course** of Mexican history; [by] Michael C. Meyer, William L. Sherman, Susan M. Deeds. 8th ed.; Oxford University Press 2007 688p il map hardcover o.p. pa $64.95 **972**
ISBN 0-19-517835-1; 978-0-19-517835-7; 0-19-517836-X pa; 978-0-19-517836-4 pa
LC 2006-51741
A chronologically arranged survey of the political, economic, social, and cultural history of Mexico, ranging from the pre-Columbian period to the present.

Prescott, William Hickling
History of the conquest of Mexico. Modern Lib. 1998 xxvi, 1005p hardcover o.p. pa $17.95 **972**
1. Aztecs 2. Colonial administrators 3. Explorers
ISBN 0-375-75803-8 pa
LC 98-10173
This is a history of the subjugation of the Aztec people by Hernan Cortez and his soldiers between 1519 and 1522.

Smith, Michael Ernest
The **Aztecs**; [by] Michael E. Smith. 2nd ed; Blackwell 2003 367p il maps hardcover o.p. pa $29.95 **972**
1. Aztecs 2. Aztecs -- Antiquities 3. Aztecs -- History 4. Aztecs -- Social life and customs
ISBN 0-631-23015-7; 0-631-23016-5 pa
LC 2001-6950
The author "summarizes the results of archaeological research conducted largely in the past 30 years into the everyday lives of ordinary people in the villages, hamlets, and farmsteads from many regions of central Mexico. His method permits a fresh view of such topics as agricultural methods, population size, market system, relations between city-states and the empire, and even human sacrifice. Smith carries his social account of these people through transfor-

mation under Spanish rule and their legacy in modern Mexico." Libr J [review of 1996 edition]
Includes bibliographical references

Townsend, Richard F.
The **Aztecs**; 3rd ed; Thames & Hudson 2009 256p il map pa $24.95 **972**
1. Aztecs
ISBN 978-0-500-28791-0
LC 2008-908216
"Examines the history of these accomplished people through a review of the monuments and artifacts they left behind; exploring how their water-control projects worked, the purposes of their ceremonial centers, and the way they built their incredible ancient structures that still stand today." Publisher's note
Includes bibliographical references

The **Oxford history** of Mexico; edited by Michael C. Meyer and William H. Beezley. Oxford Univ. Press 2000 709p il maps $45 **972**
ISBN 0-19-511228-8
LC 99-56044
The editors "have compiled 20 previously unpublished essays by experts who explore Mexico from precolonial times to the present. . . . Examining the country with new and different approaches, the contributors challenge traditional historical concepts on a variety of issues." Libr J
Includes bibliographical references

972.08   Mexico since 1867

Fuentes, Carlos
A **new** time for Mexico; translated from the Spanish by Marina Gutman Castañeda and the author. University of Calif. Press 1997 226p pa $16.95 **972.08**
ISBN 0-520-21183-9
LC 97-8427
In these essays "Fuentes calls on Mexican president Ernesto Zedillo to take definitive steps toward a full democracy—electoral reform; equal access of candidates to the media; independent, aggressive labor unions; and, above all, true separation between the ruling party and the government. . . . Offering lapidary, lyrical meditations on Mexico as a land of continual metamorphosis, Fuentes nostalgically reminisces about his home in Veracruz, whose port his father defended against a Yankee invasion in 1914." Publ Wkly

Katz, Friedrich
The **life** and times of Pancho Villa. Stanford Univ. Press 1998 985p hardcover o.p. pa $30.95 **972.08**
1. Outlaws 2. Revolutionaries 3. Revolutionaries -- Mexico -- Biography
ISBN 0-8047-3046-6 pa
LC 97-47271
The author "traces Pancho Villa's rise from relatively obscure outlaw to national leader of the Mexican Revolution (1910-20) and his subsequent decline to guerrilla leader. . .

.{This} is likely to be the definitive account of Villa for years to come." Libr J

Includes bibliographical references

Lewis, Oscar

★ The **children** of Sanchez; autobiography of a Mexican family. Random House 1961 xxxi, 499p hardcover o.p. pa $17   **972.08**

1. Family 2. Mexico City (Mexico) -- Social conditions 3. Poor -- Mexico City (Mexico)

ISBN 0-394-70280-8 pa

"Oscar Lewis has made something brilliant and of singular significance, a work of such unique concentration and sympathy." N Y Times Book Rev

Womack, John

Zapata and the Mexican Revolution. Knopf 1969 435p il hardcover o.p. pa $17   **972.08**

1. Revolutionaries

ISBN 0-394-70853-9 pa

The author reconstructs the "history of the agrarian revolution in southern Mexico from the late Diaz period to about 1920. The work is well written {and} carefully conceived." Choice

972.8   Other parts of Middle America

Perez-Brignoli, Hector

A **brief** history of Central America; translated by Ricardo B. Sawrey A. and Susana Stettri de Sawrey. University of Calif. Press 1989 223p maps hardcover o.p. pa $18.97   **972.8**

ISBN 0-520-06832-7 pa

LC 89-31889

This book presents the economic, political and cultural history of Guatemala, Honduras, El Salvador, Nicaragua and Costa Rica, the five national states of Central America.

"For interested laypersons, this is an excellent introduction with an accurate sense of the region." Libr J

Includes bibliographical references

972.81   Guatemala

Goldman, Francisco

The **art** of political murder; who killed the Bishop? Grove Press 2007 396p il map $25   **972.81**

1. Bishops 2. Human rights activists 3. Murder victims 4. Trials (Homicide) 5. Trials (Murder) -- Guatemala

ISBN 978-0-8021-1828-8; 0-8021-1828-3

This book "is a tour de force, not just for . . . [the author's] reportorial tenacity . . . but because his novelist's eye and his deep understanding of Guatemalan society take you places no other reporter could." Nation

Includes bibliographical references

972.87   Panama

McCullough, David G.

★ The **path** between the seas; the creation of the Panama Canal, 1870-1914. [by] David McCullough. Simon & Schuster 1977 698p il maps hardcover o.p. pa $18   **972.87**

1. Army officers 2. Diplomats 3. Governors 4. Nobel laureates for peace 5. Panama Canal 6. Physicians 7. Presidents 8. Public health officials 9. Vice-presidents

ISBN 0-671-24409-4

LC 76-57967

"Not only is this a well-told story of the building of the Panama Canal but it also supplies welcome background for the . . . debate on the canal's role in inter-American relations." Booklist

Includes bibliographical references

972.9   West Indies (Antilles) and Bermuda

Kincaid, Jamaica

A **small** place. Farrar, Straus & Giroux 1988 81p hardcover o.p. pa $11   **972.9**

ISBN 0-374-52707-5 pa

LC 88-376

Antiguan Kincaid addresses foreign visitors to her country. In this essay, she discusses the poverty and political corruption of the island, which she views as a legacy of British colonialism and also as a result of an economy controlled by tourism.

Von Tunzelmann, Alex

Red heat; conspiracy, murder, and the Cold War in the Caribbean. Henry Holt 2011 449p il $30; ebook $14.99   **972.9**

1. Communist leaders 2. Generals 3. Physicians 4. Political leaders 5. Presidents 6. Revolutionaries

ISBN 978-0-8050-9067-3; 978-1-4299-6673-3 ebook

LC 2010-37585

"Three dictators, circa 1960—Castro in Cuba, François Duvalier in Haiti, and Rafael Trujillo in the Dominican Republic—are the principals in von Tunzelmann's political history. Recounting alarms that trio set off in Washington, she ponders how well the Eisenhower and Kennedy administrations understood situations on the islands of Cuba and Hispaniola. Not very realistically, runs the tenor of von Tunzelmann's narrative. . . . Punctuated by accounts of such major incidents as the Bay of Pigs, the assassination of Trujillo, the Cuban missile crisis, and LBJ's 1965 intervention in the Dominican Republic, von Tunzelmann's diligent work will widen the eyes of cold war buffs." Booklist

Includes bibliographical references

972.91   Cuba

Guillermoprieto, Alma

Dancing with Cuba; a memoir of the revolution. translated from the Spanish by Esther Allen. Pantheon 2004 290p $25; pa $13   **972.91**
1. Authors 2. Biography, Individual 3. Journalists
ISBN 0-375-42093-2; 0-375-72581-4 pa
LC 2003-44200

"Guillermoprieto vividly and purposefully recounts her acute discomfort with the strained and ludicrous rhetoric of the revolution, her sorrow over Castro's catastrophic failures, her astonishment at the great valor of Cuba's people, and her gradual recognition of her true calling as a journalist." Booklist

Martinez-Fernandez, Luis

Encyclopedia of Cuba; people, history, culture. edited by Luis Martinez-Fernández [et al.] Greenwood Press 2003 2v il maps set $174.95   **972.91**
1. Reference books
ISBN 1-57356-334-X
LC 2002-70030

"The editors intend this work to be a non-politicized look at Cuban people, politics, history, and culture. Chapters cover topics such as history, government, and popular culture. Within each chapter, entries are in alphabetical order. An excellent introduction to a colorful and important nation." Booklist

Includes bibliographical references

Perez, Louis A.

Cuba; between reform and revolution. Oxford University Press 2006 442p il map $77.95; pa $34.95   **972.91**
ISBN 0-19-517911-0; 978-0-19-517911-8; 0-19-517912-9 pa; 978-0-19-517912-5 pa
LC 2004-65477

"A narrative history that emphasizes the antecedents of the Cuban revolution and concludes with an analysis of Fidel Castro's successes and failures." N Y Public Libr Book of How & Where to Look It Up [entry for 1988 edition]

Includes bibliographical references

Rasenberger, Jim

The **brilliant** disaster; JFK, Castro, and America's doomed invasion of Cuba's Bay of Pigs. Scribner 2011 460p il   **972.91**
1. Communist leaders 2. Members of Congress 3. Presidents 4. Senators
ISBN 978-1-4165-9650-9
LC 2011-4178

"On Apr., 17, 1961, a CIA-trained brigade of 1,400 Cuban exiles, mostly students and former soldiers, made an unsuccessful amphibious assault on the Bay of Pigs, in southern Cuba, hoping to spur a popular revolt and overthrow the Castro regime. Fifty years later, Rasenberger . . . succeeds admirably in offering a nuanced view of the entire botched operation, from its planning in two U.S. administrations to the Cuban armed forces' quick defeat of the exiles, whose attack lacked air cover and the element of surprise." Kirkus

Includes bibliographical references

Suchlicki, Jaime

Cuba; from Columbus to Castro and beyond. {by} Jaime Suchlicki. 5th ed; Brassey's 2002 285p pa $24.95   **972.91**
ISBN 1-57488-436-0
LC 2002-3953

A summary of Cuba's development, with emphasis on the twentieth century and the factors that led to the Cuban revolution.

Symmes, Patrick

The **boys** from Dolores; Fidel Castro's schoolmates from revolution to exile.   Pantheon Books 2007 352p $26.95   **972.91**
1. Communist leaders 2. Presidents
ISBN 978-0-375-42283-6; 0-375-42283-8
LC 2006-30323

"The author writes of Castro's schoolmates from Dolores, the private Jesuit academy in Santiago de Cuba on the island's eastern end, and he visits several of them. . . . Among the Dolores students were Castro's brothers Raul and Ramon and a future star in North American television, Desi Arnaz. But it is Cuban intellectuals like Lundy Aguilar to whom Symmes turns for insights into Cuba before and after Castro's revolution. The result is a remarkable account of the country and its people." Libr J

972.910   -1899

Gimbel, Wendy

Havana dreams; a story of Cuba. Knopf 1998 234p il hardcover o.p. pa $13   **972.910**
1. Children of prominent persons 2. Communist leaders 3. Defectors 4. Mistresses 5. Mistresses -- Cuba -- Biography 6. Presidents 7. Socialites
ISBN 0-679-75070-3 pa
LC 98-14571

Gimbel "succeeds in showing the complexity of family relationships resulting from the Cuban revolution, which extends into two countries." Libr J

Includes bibliographical references

Quirk, Robert E.

Fidel Castro. Norton 1993 898p il maps hardcover o.p. pa $19.95   **972.910**
1. Biography, Individual 2. Communist leaders 3. Presidents
ISBN 0-393-31327-1 pa
LC 92-39300

"Quirk's richly detailed, psychologically acute portrait reveals more about Castro's unique personality and character than do previous biographies." Publ Wkly

Includes bibliographical references

973 United States

American Association for State and Local History

Directory of historical organizations in the United States and Canada; 15th ed.; American Assn. for State & Local Hist. 2002 1358p pa $149.95 **973**
1. Reference books
ISBN 0-7591-0002-0
This publication "lists historical societies geographically, giving mailing address, number of members, museums, hours and size of library, publication program, etc." Ref Sources for Small & Medium-sized Libr. 5th edition

Anzovin, Steven

★ **Famous** first facts about American politics; [by] Steven Anzovin & Janet Podell. Wilson, H.W. 2001 756p $180 **973**
ISBN 0-8242-0971-0
LC 00-49960
This offers over 5,000 entries of firsts in national, state, and local U.S. politics from the founding of the nation through the 2000 election and includes five indexes: subject, name, year, day, and place.

Appleby, Joyce Oldham

Inheriting the revolution; the first generation of Americans. {by} Joyce Appleby. Belknap Press 2000 322p il hardcover o.p. pa $16 **973**
ISBN 0-674-00236-9; 0-674-00663-1 pa
LC 99-49787
"This book provides a splendid introduction to the period for students and general readers." Libr J
Includes bibliographical references

Boller, Paul F.

Presidential inaugurations; {by} Paul F. Boller, Jr. Harcourt 2001 298p $25; pa $14 **973**
1. Presidents -- United States -- History 2. Presidents -- United States -- Inauguration 3. Presidents -- United States -- Inauguration -- History
ISBN 0-15-100546-X; 0-15-600759-2 pa
LC 00-49893
The author "examines the events and controversies surrounding Presidential inaugurations. . . . Written with elegance and wit, this is a wonderful addition to the very thin literature available on Presidential inaugurations." Libr J
Includes bibliographical references

Boorstin, Daniel J.

The **Americans**: The democratic experience. Random House 1973 717p hardcover o.p. pa $19 **973**
1. Advertising 2. American art 3. Americanisms 4. Automobile industry 5. Cities and towns -- United States 6. Higher education
ISBN 0-394-71011-8 pa

This volume is concerned with the democratization of the national character over the past hundred years and the growth of technology.

The **Americans**: The national experience. Random House 1965 517p hardcover o.p. pa $16 **973**
1. African Americans -- Religion 2. American national characteristics 3. Americanisms 4. Colleges and universities -- United States 5. Constitutional history -- United States 6. Federal government 7. Heroes and heroines
ISBN 0-394-70358-8 pa
A cultural interpretation of American history, this book traces "the roots of contemporary American life to the years between the Revolution and the Civil War." Booklist
Includes bibliographical references

Hidden history; selected and edited by Daniel J Boorstin and Ruth F. Boorstin. Vintage Books 1989 332p pa $15 **973**
ISBN 978-0-679-72223-6; 0-679-72223-8
"A collection of essays and abridgments from [Boorstin's] books that investigates certain overlooked or disregarded corners of history. . . . History engagingly written, deeply felt, widely appealing." Booklist

Churchill, Winston

★ The **great** republic; a history of America. edited by Winston S. Churchill. Random House 1999 454p hardcover o.p. pa $15.95 **973**
1. Large print books
ISBN 0-375-50320-X; 978-0-375-75440-1 pa; 0-375-75440-7 pa
LC 99-28511
"The first half of the volume offers an old-fashioned narrative history of America's political development, from the age of exploration to the 1880s. The second half reprints articles that Churchill penned for English publications on such themes as Prohibition, the muckraking of Upton Sinclair and the death of Franklin Delano Roosevelt." Libr J
Includes bibliographical references

Commager, Henry Steele

The **American** mind; an interpretation of American thought and character since the 1880's. Yale Univ Press 1950 476p hardcover o.p. pa $14.95 **973**
1. Authors 2. Authors, American 3. College teachers 4. Economics 5. Economists 6. Journalism 7. Law -- United States 8. Law teachers 9. Lawyers 10. National characteristics, American 11. Nonfiction writers 12. Philosophers 13. Pragmatism 14. Psychologists 15. Social critics 16. Sociologists 17. Sociology 18. Supreme Court justices 19. Writers on science
ISBN 0-300-00046-4 pa

Cornelison, Pam

★ The **great** American history fact-finder; the who, what, where, when, and why of American history. [by] Pam Cornelison and Ted Yanak. 2nd ed, up

dated and expanded; Houghton Mifflin 2004 608p il, maps pa $14.95 **973**
1. Reference books
ISBN 0-618-43941-2

LC 2004-47480

This book provides "information about significant persons as well as political, legal, sporting, and cultural events in American history. Entries are alphabetically arranged, and related entries cross-referenced. . . . Besides an index, there are suggested readings and information on the states, presidents, vice presidents, population, Supreme Court, Articles of Confederation, Declaration of Independence, and US Constitution (with signers and nonsigners). This is a good quick reference." Choice

Feiler, Bruce S.

America's prophet; Moses and the American story. [by] Bruce Feiler. William Morrow 2009 352p il $26.99 **973**
1. Biblical characters 2. Prophets 3. Religion and politics -- United States
ISBN 978-0-06-057488-8

An exploration of how the story of Moses has influenced American history traces the biblical figure's role in inspiring change, from the Pilgrims' journey and the visions of the Founding Fathers to the ideologies of the civil rights movement.

The author's argument is "an eye-opening contention, beautifully argued. . . . Fascinating and thought-provoking." Booklist

Includes bibliographical references and index

Grande, Reyna

The **distance** between us; a memoir. Reyna Grande. Atria Books 2012 336 p. (hardcover) $25.00 **973**
1. Abused children -- United States -- Biography 2. Immigrants -- United States -- Biography 3. Memoirs 4. Mexican American women authors -- Biography 5. Mexican Americans -- Biography 6. Mexican Americans -- California -- Los Angeles -- Biography
ISBN 1451661770; 9781451661774; 9781451661781; 9781451661804

LC 2012001634

This book presents a memoir by "[a]ward-winning novelist . . . [Reyna] Grande. . . . [F]our-year-old Grande and her two siblings lived with their cruel grandmother after both parents departed for the U.S. in search of work. . . . Eight years later her father returned and reluctantly agreed to take his children to the States. . . . Surrounded by family turmoil, Grande discovered a love of writing . . . and went on to become the first person in her family to graduate from college." (Publishers Weekly)

Gregorian, Vartan

The **road** to home; my life and times. Simon & Schuster 2003 354p il hardcover o.p. pa $15 **973**
1. College presidents 2. Foundation officials 3. Library directors
ISBN 0-684-80834-X; 978-0-7432-5565-3; 0-7432-5565-8 pa

LC 2003-45566

In this "memoir, Gregorian explains how he went from a childhood in a poor section of Tabriz, Iran, to become president of the New York Public Library and, later, the president of Brown University." Publ Wkly

Hofstadter, Richard

The **American** political tradition, and the men who made it; with a foreword by Christopher Lasch. 25th anniversary ed; Knopf 1973 xxxiii, 378p hardcover o.p. pa $14 **973**
1. Abolitionists 2. Architects 3. Authors 4. College presidents 5. Essayists 6. Generals 7. Governors 8. Handicapped 9. Lawyers 10. Members of Congress 11. Nobel laureates for peace 12. Orators 13. Philanthropists 14. Philatelists 15. Political leaders 16. Presidential candidates 17. Presidents 18. Secretaries of commerce 19. Secretaries of state 20. Secretaries of war 21. State legislators 22. Statesmen 23. Vice-presidents
ISBN 0-679-72315-3 pa

This volume contains twelve essays, ten of which analyze the political careers of Lincoln, Jefferson, Jackson, Calhoun, Wendell Phillips, Bryan, Theodore Roosevelt, Wilson, Hoover and Franklin D. Roosevelt.

Kammen, Michael G.

In the past lane; historical perspectives on American culture. {by} Michael Kammen. Oxford Univ. Press 1997 277p il hardcover o.p. pa $25 **973**
1. Popular culture -- United States
ISBN 0-19-513091-X pa

LC 97-21613

These essays "range from the influence of the personal experiences of prominent historians on their work to the changing attitudes toward the 'unique' aspects of American history as reflected in the views of historians, past and present. For professional historians or serious students of history, Kammen's essays provide an excellent opportunity to gauge how those who chronicle our past both influence and are influenced by national and personal experiences." Booklist

Includes bibliographical references

Lepore, Jill

★ The **mansion** of happiness; a history of life and death. Jill Lepore. 1st ed. Alfred A. Knopf 2012 xxxiii, 282 p.p $27.95 **973**
1. Death -- Social aspects -- United States -- History 2. Happiness -- Social aspects -- United States -- History 3. Life (Biology) -- Social aspects -- United States -- History 4. Life -- Social aspects -- United States -- History 5. Life cycle, Human -- Social aspects -- United States -- History 6. Politics and culture -- United States -- History 7. Popular culture -- United States -- History
ISBN 0307592995; 9780307592996

LC 2011050566

In this book Jill Lepore examines "the history of American ideas about life and death. . . . Lepore starts . . . with the story of a seventeenth-century Englishman who had the idea that all life begins with an egg and ends it with an American who, in the 1970s, began freezing the dead. . . . Investigating the surprising origins of the stuff of everyday life--from board games to breast pumps--Lepore argues that the age of discovery, Darwin, and the Space Age turned ideas about life on earth topsy-turvy." (Publisher's note)

Loewen, James W.

Lies across America; what our historic sites get wrong. Simon & Schuster 2007 464p pa $16 **973**

1. Historic sites 2. Monuments

ISBN 978-0-7432-9629-8; 0-7432-9629-X

"The book consists of 95 brief commentaries on specific sites from Alaska to Florida to Maine, sandwiched between essays that offer advice on how to interpret what you read or are told at historic sites." N Y Times Book Rev [review of 1999 edition]

Marcus, Greil

The **shape** of things to come; prophecy and the American voice. Farrar, Straus & Giroux 2006 320p $25 **973**

1. American national characteristics 2. National characteristics, American 3. Nationalism -- United States

ISBN 978-0-374-10438-2; 0-374-10438-7

LC 2005-33139

Marcus "posits that the United States of America is a cultural construction, grounded in the Declaration of Independence and the Constitution. Without those bedrocks, Marcus believes, the nation would be 'little more than a collection of buildings and people who have no special reason to speak to each other, and nothing to say.' Marcus builds his own erudite vision upon John Winthrop's 1630 speech 'A Modell of Christian Charity,' Abraham Lincoln's second inaugural address in 1865, Martin Luther King Jr.'s 1963 exhortation from the steps of the Lincoln Memorial in Washington, the later novels of Philip Roth, the films of David Lynch and the music of David Thomas with his band Pere Ubu. More than most books, Marcus's latest tour de force is quite likely to divide readers into two camps: those who find it brilliant and those who find it baffling." Publ Wkly

Morison, Samuel Eliot

A **concise** history of the American Republic; {by} Samuel Eliot Morison, Henry Steele Commager, William E. Leuchtenburg. 2nd ed; Oxford Univ. Press 1983 765p il maps hardcover o.p. pa $58.95 **973**

ISBN 0-19-503180-6 pa

LC 82-3621

The **growth** of the American Republic; {by} Samuel Eliot Morison, Henry Steele Commager, and William E. Leuchtenburg. 7th ed; Oxford Univ. Press 1980 2v il maps ea $59.95 **973**

ISBN 0-19-502593-8 v1; 0-19-502594-6 v2

LC 79-52432

A history of the United States that deals with military, political, economic, social, literary and spiritual aspects of the nation's development.

"A good general history, well-written." Sheehy. Guide to Ref Books. 10th edition

New York Public Library

The **New** York Public Library American history desk reference; 2nd ed; Hyperion 2003 576p il maps pa $21.95 **973**

1. Reference books

ISBN 0-7868-6847-3

LC 2003-56655

"{This is a} well-designed, convenient-size volume filled with lists, charts, tables, and short articles. . . . {This} volume should be {a} useful ready-reference compilation for public and academic libraries." Booklist {review of 1997 edition}

Includes bibliographical references

Olson, James Stuart

Encyclopedia of the industrial revolution in America; {by} James S. Olson; technical editor: Robert L. Shadle. Greenwood Press 2002 xxv, 313p il $69.95 **973**

1. Industrial revolution -- Encyclopedias 2. Reference books

ISBN 0-313-30830-6

LC 00-52129

"A well-organized and comprehensive ready reference." Voice Youth Advocates

Includes bibliographical references

Remini, Robert Vincent

Short history of the United States; [by] Robert V. Remini. HarperCollins Publishers 2008 373p il map $27.95 **973**

ISBN 978-0-06-083144-8; 0-06-083144-8

LC 2007-34811

The author "deftly wraps his expertise and deep knowledge of his subject in stripped-down prose that provides everything a casual (or bewildered) reader needs to know about the United States from the first English colonists until the beginning of 2008." Publ Wkly

Includes bibliographical references

Reynolds, David, 1952-

America, empire of liberty; a new history of the United States. Basic Books 2009 563p map **973**

ISBN 9780465015009

LC 2009-17831

This is "a one-volume history of the United States, from the mound-builders of the 11th century to the challenges facing President Barack Obama. . . . Mr. Reynold's book provides an entertaining and fair-minded introduction to American history." Economist

Includes bibliographical references

Said, Edward W.

Out of place; a memoir. Knopf 1999 295p il $26.95; pa $14 **973**

1. Authors 2. Essayists 3. Intellectuals -- United States -- Biography 4. Literary critics 5. Palestinian Americans -- Biography 6. Social critics 7. Writers on politics

ISBN 0-394-58739-1; 0-679-73067-2 pa

LC 99-31106

In this memoir Said offers an "account of his intellectual and moral development. At the heart of Said's story is the sense of dislocation experienced by a boy whose father was a Palestinian-born American citizen, whose mother was Lebanese, and who was raised in Egypt under the colonial rule of the British. This is the moving tale of a man who is always an outsider." Publ Wkly

Schlesinger, Arthur M.

The **cycles** of American history; {by} Arthur M. Schlesinger, Jr. Houghton Mifflin 1986 498p hardcover o.p. pa $16   **973**
  ISBN 0-395-95793-1 pa

                                    LC 86-7706
"For this volume, Schlesinger has revised and updated papers, reviews, and essays that have appeared in various forms over the past quarter-century. . . . Each of the 14 essays that make up the book offers a fresh, demanding, and lively argument about important issues in American intellectual, political, or diplomatic history." Choice
  Includes bibliographical references

The **disuniting** of America; reflections on a multicultural society. rev & enl ed; Norton 1998 208p $21.95; pa $12.95   **973**
  1. Multicultural education 2. Multicultural education -- United States 3. Multiculturalism 4. Pluralism (Social sciences) -- United States
  ISBN 0-393-04580-3; 0-393-31854-0 pa

                                    LC 97-25124
The author argues against radical multiculturalism, bilingual education, and the influence of ethnic, political, and religious pressure groups on the teaching of history. Includes an epilogue that assesses the impact of radical multiculturalism and radical monoculturalism on the Bill of Rights and concludes with an annotated reading list of titles essential for understanding the American experience

Shenkman, Richard

Legends, lies & cherished myths of American history. HarperPerennial 1989 213p il pa $13 **973**
  1. Legends -- United States
  ISBN 978-0-06-097261-5; 0-06-097261-0
The author "debunks a host of popular myths associated with U.S. history. From the Founding Fathers to the Reagan presidency, heretofore undisputed facts are exposed as fiction. Misquotes, misinterpretations, and downright fabrications are all duly recorded in an amusing and illuminating fashion. An irresistible browsing item." Booklist
  Includes bibliographical references

Stark, Peter

The **last** empty places; a past and present journey through the blank spots on the American map. Ballantine Books 2010 325p il map $26   **973**
  1. Wilderness areas
  ISBN 978-0-345-49537-2; 0-345-49537-3

                                    LC 2010-09942
Stark writes "about exploring Maine's northern woods and the St. John River, the forests and glens of western Pennsylvania, the vast empty deserts of southeast Oregon and the High Desert of New Mexico, deep within the Gila

Wilderness. Often he takes his family with him, and we get to read about the trials and tribulations of tents, backpacks, river crossings, switchbacks, towering cliffs and shadowy canyons. At the same time he intersperses his journeys with historical tales and horrors. . . . Stark keeps his writing sharp and clear and, wonderfully, does not slip into celebration of some mystical state of oneness with nature." Providence J
  Includes bibliographical references

Steinbeck, John

Travels with Charley; in search of America. Viking 1962 246p hardcover o.p. pa $14   **973**
  ISBN 0-670-72508-0; 0-14-200070-1 pa
The Nobel laureate recounts his impressions and observations of America gathered during a trip through forty states in the company of his French poodle Charley.

Steltenkamp, Michael F.

Black Elk, holy man of the Oglala. University of Okla. Press 1993 xxiii, 211p il maps hardcover o.p. pa $17.95   **973**
  1. Biography, Individual 2. Indian leaders 3. Oglala Indians 4. Shamans
  ISBN 0-8061-2988-3 pa

                                    LC 93-22089
This "is the story of Black Elk's later years, when the holy man converted to Roman Catholicism and worked actively as a catechist, converting the Lakota to his new religion." Antioch Rev
  Includes bibliographical references

Virga, Vincent

Eyes of the nation; a visual history of the United States. by Vincent Virga and curators of the Library of Congress; historical commentary by Alan Brinkley. Knopf 1997 399p il $75   **973**
  1. United States -- History -- Pictorial works
  ISBN 0-679-44330-4

                                    LC 97-36603
This visual history "showcases more than 500 illustrations, manuscripts, engravings, prints, movie stills and other artifacts stretching back to the 15th century. The accompanying text by the historian Alan Brinkley rolls through the high and low points of the nation's history, but it is the captions that sparkle the brightest, adding context while offering surprising information." N Y Times Book Rev

Wetterau, Bruce

Congressional Quarterly's desk reference on the Presidency. CQ Press 2000 311p il $49.95   **973**
  1. Executive power -- United States -- Handbooks, manuals, etc 2. Presidents -- United States 3. Presidents -- United States -- Handbooks, manuals, etc
  ISBN 1-56802-589-0

                                    LC 00-63024
Over 500 questions and answers on the organization, procedures, and history of the office and on the presidents and their wives. Topics covered include scandals, elections, the White House, and the executive branch.

Wills, Garry

A **necessary** evil; a history of American distrust of government. Simon & Schuster 1999 365p hardcover o.p. pa $15   **973**

1. Dissenters -- United States -- History 2. Government, Resistance to -- United States -- History 3. Resistance to government

ISBN 0-684-87026-6 pa

LC 99-35879

This "analysis of the distorted mythology that has grown up around government in the U.S. takes on hot-button issues from the Second Amendment and term limits to the idea that the Founders sought to create an inefficient government. Provocative and enlightening." Booklist

Includes bibliographical references

Zimmermann, Warren

First great triumph; how five Americans made their country a world power. Farrar, Straus & Giroux 2002 562p il $30; pa $15   **973**

1. Admirals 2. Biographers 3. Diplomats 4. Governors 5. Historians 6. Lawyers 7. Nobel laureates for peace 8. Poets 9. Presidents 10. Secretaries of state 11. Secretaries of war 12. Senators 13. Spanish-American War, 1898 14. Statesmen 15. Vice-presidents

ISBN 0-374-17939-5; 0-374-52893-4 pa

LC 2002-25015

The author credits five men "for the vision, determination and political skill that first gave the United States its global ambition. His book is a history of the American rise to power and a collective biography of [his] five heroes: Theodore Roosevelt, the assistant secretary of the Navy and later president; Alfred T. Mahan, the naval strategist; Senator Henry Cabot Lodge of Massachusetts; Secretary of State John Hay; and the first American colonial administrator, Elihu Root." N Y Times (Late N Y Ed)

Includes bibliographical references

The American presidency; edited by Alan Brinkley and Davis Dyer. Houghton Mifflin Co 2004 572p il pa $19.95   **973**

1. Presidents -- United States

ISBN 0-618-38273-9

LC 2003-62513

This work assesses "how presidents shape and define culture and society and, at the same time, reflect them. . . . {This} can serve as a beginning point for research and should engage casual readers as well as students of the American presidency." Choice

Includes bibliographical references

Americans at war; society, culture, and the homefront. John P. Resch, Editor in Chief. Macmillan Reference USA 2005 4v il set $395   **973**

1. War and civilization

ISBN 0-02-865806-X

LC 2004-17314

This book "delivers well-written articles and would make an excellent addition to high-school, academic, and public libraries." Booklist

Includes bibliographical references

Daily life through American history in primary documents; Randall M. Miller, general editor. Greenwood 2012 1099 p.   **973**

1. Everyday life 2. Historical literature 3. Reference books 4. United States -- History 5. United States -- History -- Sources

ISBN 161069032X; 1610690338; 9781610690324; 9781610690331

LC 2011040023

In this history book, four volumes are organized chronologically and then thematically and present the many small things that made up Americans daily life. Volumes are The Colonial Period through the American Revolution, The American Revolution to the Civil War, The Civil War to World War I, and World War I to the Present. Each volume begins with a time line of selected events and a lengthy historical-overview essay describing significant themes, events, and concerns of the period. This is followed by about 100 primary documents that illustrate daily life. . . . These include speeches, court and legislative documents, book excerpts, newspaper articles, diaries, letters, and more. Each entry is prefaced by a brief introduction that gives context to the document. (Booklist)

Encyclopedia of American cultural and intellectual history; edited by Mary Kupiec Cayton and Peter W. Williams. Scribner 2000 3v il set $400 **973**

1. Reference books

ISBN 0-684-80561-8

LC 2001-20005

Art movements, education and academia, the counterculture, the sciences, domestic life, social classes, Hollywood, and post-structuralism are among the topics covered. Each article includes illustrations, boxed biographies, or documentary excerpts

★ Encyclopedia of American historical documents; edited by Susan Rosenfeld. Facts on File 2004 3v set $300   **973**

ISBN 0-8160-4995-5

LC 2003-51610

"Each section begins with an overview of the period and each document is introduced with commentary on when and why it was created and its significance, then and now. Entries include material 'with resonance for the 21st century' that represents turning points in U.S. history, and documents of a controversial nature. Students can read Supreme Court justices' opinions, presidential announcements and inaugural addresses, excerpts from noteworthy books that influenced American thought and action, and speeches of women and people of color. . . . Students and teachers will welcome this mammoth resource." SLJ

Includes bibliographical references

Encyclopedia of American history; Gary B. Nash, general editor. Rev. ed.; Facts on File 2010 11v il map set $1,150   **973**

1. Reference books

ISBN 978-0-8160-7136-4

LC 2008-35422

This encyclopedia provides a "presentation of the political, social, economic, and cultural events that have shaped the land and the nation." Publisher's note
Includes bibliographical references

The Encyclopedia of American political history; edited by Paul Finkelman, Peter Wallenstein. CQ Press 2001 xxxii, 494p il map $140   **973**
1. Political science -- United States -- History 2. Political science -- United States -- History -- Encyclopedias 3. Reference books
ISBN 1-56802-511-4

LC 00-66812
This reference tool covers "significant events, people {and} concepts in U.S. political history. Organized alphabetically, the 225 entries vary in length from a few paragraphs to several pages. The book opens with a descriptive time line of political events and ends with an appendix of acronyms and abbreviations used in U.S. history." Libr J
Includes bibliographical references

Encyclopedia of U.S. political history.   CQ Press 2009 7v il map set $1200   **973**
1. Political science -- Encyclopedias 2. Reference books
ISBN 978-0-87289-320-7

LC 2010-2253
"An impressive work remarkable for its breath and scope, this encyclopedia covers U.S. political history chronologically from the year 1500 to the present day. . . . Written in a vivid and accessible yet scholarly manner, this wonderful synthesis of history and political science will greatly benefit students, lovers of political history, and academics alike." Libr J
Includes bibliographical references

Encyclopedia of rural America; the land and people. Gary A. Goreham, editor. 2nd ed; Grey House Pub. 2008 2v il map set $250   **973**
1. Country life -- United States -- Encyclopedias 2. Reference books
ISBN 978-1-59237-115-0; 1-59237-115-9
"This encyclopedia covers a broad range of topics, such as agriculture, the arts, economics, the environment, health, humanities, and political and social science. The . . . alphabetically arranged entries, from addiction to worker's compensation, are listed in the front of each volume for handy reference." Booklist [review of 1997 edition]
Includes bibliographical references

Encyclopedia of the new American nation; the emergence of the United States, 1754-1829. Paul Finkelman, editor in chief. Thomson Gale 2005 3v il map set $395   **973**
1. Reference books
ISBN 0-684-31346-4

LC 2005-17783
The editor and contributors "have produced a wonderful reference source." Ref & User Services Quarterly
Includes bibliographical references

★ Eyewitness to America; 500 years of America in the words of those who saw it happen. edited by David Colbert. Pantheon Bks. 1997 xxx, 599p hardcover o.p. pa $16.95   **973**
ISBN 0-679-44224-3; 0-679-76724-X pa

LC 96-24150
This volume contains a "panorama of first-person accounts of moments in the country's story that stretch from an October 10, 1492, diary entry by one of Columbus's crewmen to a 1994 e-mail message from Bill Gates. The nearly 300 entries tend to be short, preceded by informative introductions. The result is a feeling for history that is both immediate and dramatic." Publ Wkly
Includes bibliographical references

Facts about the states; editors, Joseph Nathan Kane, Janet Podell, Steven Anzovin. 2nd ed; Wilson, H.W. 1994 624p il $115   **973**
1. State governments   2.   State governments -- Miscellanea
ISBN 0-8242-0849-8

LC 93-30328
Provides geographic, demographic, economic, political, and cultural facts about the fifty states, Puerto Rico, and the District of Columbia. Part I presents state entries in alphabetical order. Part II provides comparative tables that rank states in categories such as population, geography, education, and finance.

★   The Greenwood encyclopedia of American regional cultures;   William Ferris, consulting editor. Greenwood Press 2004 8v il map set $699.95   **973**
1. Reference books
ISBN 0-313-33266-5
This "set explores the history and culture of U.S. regions from the Atlantic to the Pacific. The essay-long articles examine at length each region's art, ethnicity, fashion, film, folklore, food, literature, religion, sports, and more." Libr J
Includes bibliographical references

The Greenwood library of American war reporting; David A. Copeland, general editor.   Greenwood Press 2005 8v il set $995   **973**
ISBN 0-313-33435-8

LC 2005-10122
"Beginning with 1753 and ending in April 2004 with photographs depicting the mistreatment of Iraqi prisoners at Abu Ghraib, these volumes offer primary documents, mainly newspaper and magazine articles and radio and television transcripts. Indispensable to the study of war reporting and the most definitive . . . reference work available on the subject." Booklist
Includes bibliographical references

The New encyclopedia of American scandal;   George Childs Kohn, editor. Facts on File 2001 455p il $71.50; pa $24.95   **973**
1. Scandals -- United States -- History -- Dictionaries
ISBN 0-8160-4225-X; 0-8160-4420-1 pa

LC 00-34099

This compendium includes "more than 450 people and incidents from the 1600s to the present, surveying episodes of graft, bribery, deception, and outrage by people in high places. Although the tragic, career-derailing impact of historic humiliations cannot be denied, this frank book entertains as well as informs." Choice

Includes bibliographical references

The Oxford companion to United States history; editor in chief, Paul S. Boyer; editors, Melvyn Dubofsky {et al.} Oxford Univ. Press 2001 xliv, 940p il maps $75   **973**
1. Reference books
ISBN 0-19-508209-5

LC 00-55801

This reference work contains 1,400 alphabetically arranged signed entries. See and see also references are provided. Coverage starts with the colonial period and examines notable men and women and major events in U.S. history.

State by state; a panoramic portrait of America. edited by Matt Weiland & Sean Wilsey. Ecco 2008 xxxi, 572p il map $29.95   **973**
ISBN 978-0-06-147090-5; 0-06-147090-2

LC 2008-300642

"Taking as their inspiration the state guides published by the Federal Writers' Project during and shortly after the Great Depression, Weiland and Wilsey assembled 50 of America's finest writers and asked them to contribute essays on the same general theme: why my state is special—or not. The result is a funny, moving, rousing collection, greater than the sum of its excellent parts, a convention of literary super-delegates, each one boisterously nominating his or her piece of the Republic." N Y Times Book Rev

973.2   Colonial period, 1607-1775

Anderson, Fred
The **crucible** of war; the Seven Years' War and the fate of empire in British North America, 1754-1766. with illustrations from the William L. Clements Library. Knopf 2000 862p il hardcover o.p. pa $21   **973.2**
1. Seven Years' War, 1756-1763
ISBN 0-375-70636-4 pa

LC 99-18512

The author "demonstrates that the conflict was more than just a peripheral squabble that anticipated the American Revolution. Not only did the war decisively alter relations among the French, the English and the Native American allies of the two powers, who for decades had played the English and French off one another to their own advantage, but just as critical, argues Anderson, the war also changed the character of British imperialism, with the mother country trying to reshape the terms of empire and the colonists' place in it." Publ Wkly

The **dominion** of war; empire and liberty in North America, 1500-2000. [by] Fred Anderson and Andrew Cayton. Viking 2005 520p il maps $27.95; pa $16   **973.2**
1. War and society -- United States -- History
ISBN 0-670-03370-7; 0-14-303651-3 pa

The authors provide an "account of the U.S. rise to global preeminence over five centuries. Central to their thesis is the assertion that military conflict has been essential in determining the cultural and political evolution of North America. . . . Anderson and Cayton have provided a well-written and important reinterpretation of our past." Booklist

Includes bibliographical references

Bailyn, Bernard
The **peopling** of British North America; an introduction. Knopf 1986 177p hardcover o.p. pa $12   **973.2**
ISBN 0-394-75779-3 pa

LC 85-82144

In this introductory volume of a projected multivolume work, the author "gives first airing to his overall argument on settling patterns in history. Though designed to introduce the subsequent volumes, this superbly articulate study is understandable on its own." Booklist

Includes bibliographical references

Boorstin, Daniel J.
The **Americans**: The colonial experience. Random House 1958 434p hardcover o.p. pa $15 **973.2**
1. American national characteristics 2. Americanisms 3. Colleges and universities -- United States 4. Law -- United States 5. Puritans 6. Society of Friends
ISBN 0-394-70513-0 pa

"This study of colonial America attempts to show that it was not merely an offshoot of the mother country, but a new civilization. . . . The author centers his highly informative work on colonial education, the special qualities of American speech, and the growth of a distinct culture." Booklist

Includes bibliographical references

Demos, John
The **unredeemed** captive; a family story from early America. Knopf 1994 315p maps hardcover o.p. pa $14   **973.2**
1. Clergy 2. Indian captives 3. Mohawk Indians
ISBN 0-679-75961-1 pa

LC 93-23907

This "is a lively introduction to an authentically multicultural colonial North America." N Y Times Book Rev

Fowler, William M.
Empires at war; the French & Indian War and the struggle for North America, 1754-1763. [by] William M. Fowler, Jr. Walker & Company 2005 xxv, 332p il maps $27; pa $15   **973.2**
ISBN 0-8027-1411-0; 0-8027-7737-6 pa

LC 2004-43064

In this history of the French and Indian War, the author "glances occasionally at the European and Caribbean theaters of this 'first world war,' but concentrates on the North American operations that determined Britain's victory over France in the struggle for imperial supremacy. . . . The result is a judicious, well-paced and engaging introduction to a turning point in American and world history." Publ Wkly

Includes bibliographical references

Goetzmann, William H.

Beyond the Revolution; a history of American thought from Paine to pragmatism. Basic Books 2009 456p $35 **973.2**

1. American philosophy 2. Philosophy, American 3. Political science -- United States -- History

ISBN 978-0-465-00495-9; 0-465-00495-4

LC 2008-25590

"It's conventional to spin American history as a story of unfolding freedom, a quest to perfect our founding ideals, but Beyond the Revolution introduces something of a countervailing narrative. The country was as free and limitless as it would ever want to be right after the founding, Mr. Goetzmann contends, and the task since then has been to find a workable frame to harness that freedom. . . . [This book argues that] the entire frenzy of American enterprise from the founding to the present can be understood as an effort to invent, peddle, connive or discern, a model for how to choose and what to value in country where anything is possible." N Y Observer

Includes bibliographical references (p. 403-436)

Hawke, David Freeman

Everyday life in early America. Harper & Row 1988 195p il hardcover o.p. pa $13 **973.2**

ISBN 0-06-091251-0 pa

LC 87-17667

The author "provides enlightening and colorful descriptions of early Colonial Americans and debunks many widely held assumptions about 17th century settlers." Publ Wkly

Includes bibliographical references

Lepore, Jill

The **name** of war; King Philip's War and the origins of American identity. Knopf 1998 xxviii, 337p il maps hardcover o.p. pa $15 **973.2**

1. Indians of North America -- Wars -- 1600-1750 2. King Philip's War, 1675-1676 3. Native Americans -- Wars

ISBN 0-375-70262-8 pa

LC 97-2820

"This is a powerful book that doesn't shy away from depicting the sheer horror of what must be termed a race war." Booklist

Includes bibliographical references

Philbrick, Nathaniel

★ **Mayflower**; a story of courage, community, and war. Viking 2006 461p il $29.95; pa $16 **973.2**

1. Indians of North America -- Wars -- 1600-1750 2. Pilgrims (New England colonists) 3. Pilgrims (New Plymouth Colony)

ISBN 0-670-03760-5; 978-0-670-03760-5; 978-0-14-311197-9 pa; 0-14-311197-3 pa

LC 2005-58470

The author "has written a judicious, fascinating work of revisionist history. 'Mayflower' is a surprise-filled account of what are supposed to be some of the best-known events in

this country's past but are instead an occasion for collective amnesia." N Y Times (Late N Y Ed)

Includes bibliographical references

Remini, Robert Vincent

★ The **Battle** of New Orleans; {by} Robert V. Remini. Viking 1999 226p il maps hardcover o.p. pa $14 **973.2**

1. New Orleans, Battle of, New Orleans, La., 1815

ISBN 0-14-100179-8 pa

LC 99-19837

This "book establishes the War of 1812 historically as our second War of Independence, and describes its climactic battle in the maze of cypress swamps and bayous along the winding Mississippi. Remini, . . . unforgettably portrays individuals on both sides, and provides good maps to help us follow the action." New Yorker

Includes bibliographical references

Schultz, Eric B.

King Philip's War; the history and legacy of America's forgotten conflict. {by} Eric B. Schultz, Michael J. Tougias. Countryman Press 1999 416p il maps hardcover o.p. pa $18.95 **973.2**

1. Indians of North America -- Government relations -- To 1789 2. Indians of North America -- New England -- History 3. King Philip's War, 1675-1676 4. Native Americans -- Government relations

ISBN 0-88150-483-1 pa

LC 99-23481

The first part of this volume provides a "chronological retelling of the war. The second part, organized geographically and the heart of the volume, takes readers through New England to various sites associated with the conflict. . . . The third part offers three contemporary narratives reflecting the significance of the war on the people of the era. Useful maps assist the reader throughout." Libr J

Includes bibliographical references

Woodward, Hobson

A **brave** vessel; the true tale of the castaways who rescued Jamestown and inspired Shakespeare's The tempest. Viking 2009 268p il map $25.95 **973.2**

1. Authors 2. Colonists 3. Dramatists 4. Poets 5. Seafaring life 6. Shipwrecks

ISBN 978-0-670-02096-6

LC 2008-51325

"A skillfully written history of the trials of some the earliest American colonists." Kirkus

Includes bibliographical references

973.3 Periods of Revolution and Confederation, 1775-1789

Archer, Richard

As if an enemy's country; the British occupation of Boston and the origins of revolution. Oxford University Press 2010 284p il map $24.95 **973.3**

ISBN 978-0-19-538247-1; 0-19-538247-1

LC 2009-39919

Archer "utilizes a wealth of primary sources, from diaries to depositions, to provide an edifying account of the 17-month British occupation of Boston from October 1768 to the winter of 1770. . . . The uniqueness of Archer's superbly crafted tale lies in his discussion of how the politics of nonimportation polarized the elite of Boston society on the eve of revolution. Combining engaging prose and a wealth of interesting characters, Archer has provided students and general enthusiasts alike with a concise, appealing work of first-rate scholarship." Libr J

Includes bibliographical references and index

Becker, Carl

The **Declaration** of Independence; a study in the history of political ideas. Knopf 1942 286p hardcover o.p. pa $11   **973.3**

1. Architects 2. Essayists 3. Presidents 4. Vice-presidents

ISBN 0-394-70060-0 pa

"A study of the Declaration, the philosophy that lay behind it, the history of its several drafts, an estimate of its literary quality." Wis Libr Bull

Includes bibliographical references

Blumrosen, Alfred W.

Slave nation; how slavery united the colonies & sparked the American Revolution. [by] Alfred W. Blumrosen and Ruth G. Blumrosen; introduction by Eleanor Holmes Norton. Sourcebooks 2005 336p il map $24.95   **973.3**

1. African Americans -- History 2. Blacks -- History 3. Slavery -- History 4. Slavery -- United States

ISBN 1-4022-0400-0

LC 2004-27271

The authors "use the Somerset case of 1772, which freed all slaves in Britain, to illustrate how the price of freedom from English rule ensured continued bondage for slaves in the American South. The Blumrosens argue that Southerners feared that the ruling might be extended to the entire empire and therefore joined the move to win independence from Britain. . . . This well-researched book is sure to be controversial." Libr J

Includes bibliographical references

Bobrick, Benson

Angel in the whirlwind; the triumph of the American Revolution. Penguin Bks. 1998 553p map pa $18   **973.3**

ISBN 0-14-027500-2; 978-0-14-027500-1

LC 97-11320

"Many of the stories are familiar—Paul Revere's ride, Arnold's descent into infamy—but the book's strength lies in its many lesser-known details on the battlefield and beyond. . . . Though the format demands only brief treatment of complicated issues, what emerges is a highly impressive show of exhaustive research and engaging storytelling." Publ Wkly

Includes bibliographical references

Breen, T. H.

American insurgents, American patriots; the revolution of the people. Hill and Wang 2010 337p $27   **973.3**

ISBN 978-0-8090-7588-1; 0-8090-7588-1

LC 2009-42496

Breen "uses correspondence, diaries, outtakes from clergy sermons and newspaper reports to build a mosaic representation of the popular mood, and the escalating willingness to take up arms. . . . [The] book shows an energetic and necessarily untidy process of invention on the part of a people, and captures well its improvisatory nature." Chicago Trib

Includes bibliographical references and index

Cohen, I. Bernard

Science and the founding fathers; science in the political thought of Jefferson, Franklin, Adams and Madison. Norton 1995 368p il hardcover o.p. pa $15.95   **973.3**

1. Architects 2. Authors 3. Diplomats 4. Essayists 5. Inventors 6. Members of Congress 7. Political science 8. Presidents 9. Science -- United States 10. Science -- United States -- History 11. Scientists 12. Secretaries of state 13. Senators 14. Statesmen 15. United States -- Politics and government -- 1775-1783, Revolution 16. Vice-presidents 17. Writers on science

ISBN 0-393-31510-X pa

LC 94-26731

The author "analyzes how Thomas Jefferson, Benjamin Franklin, John Adams, and James Madison incorporated their scientific beliefs and knowledge into their political lives. Cohen examines each man's scientific education and then searches for examples of how that knowledge was expressed in their published works. He looks closely at phrases from the Declaration of Independence and the Constitution and shows that they have a Newtonian basis." Libr J

Davis, William C.

Battle at Bull Run; a history of the first major campaign of the Civil War. Louisiana State University Press 1981 298p il map pa $19.95   **973.3**

1. Bull Run, 1st Battle of, 1861

ISBN 978-0-8071-0867-3; 0-8071-0867-7

In this account of the war's first major engagement Davis' "sketches of the commanders, which will particularly delight Civil War enthusiasts, delve into the officer's backgrounds and unusual characteristics and include critical appraisals of their leadership capabilities. In addition, Davis includes fascinating human interest stories about the troops." Libr J

Includes bibliographical references

Draper, Theodore

A **struggle** for power; the American Revolution. Times Bks. 1996 544p hardcover o.p. pa $13.56   **973.3**

ISBN 0-679-77642-7 pa

LC 95-11605

This is an "elegantly written, masterful study. . . . Drawing freely on period pamphlets, letters, petitions, travelogues and assembly minutes, [the author] vividly evokes the populist discontent, intellectual gymnastics and mob violence that led to revolution." Publ Wkly

Includes bibliographical references

Dunn, Susan

Sister revolutions; French lightning, American light. Faber & Faber 1999 258p il hardcover o.p. pa $14   **973.3**

ISBN 0-571-19989-5 pa

LC 99-18178

"The American Revolution, according to Dunn, was more peaceful and practical, in part because its leaders were both intellectuals and men of political experience. The French Revolution, on the other hand, veered into extravagant abstractions because its leaders were intellectuals with litttle or no previous political experience. This book is clearly written and should appeal particularly to undergraduate students and members of the general public." Choice

Includes bibliographical references

Egerton, Douglas R.

Death or liberty; African Americans and revolutionary America. Oxford University Press 2009 342p il map $29.95   **973.3**

1. African Americans -- History 2. African Americans -- History -- 18th century 3. Blacks -- History 4. Slavery -- History 5. Slavery -- United States 6. Slavery -- United States -- History -- 18th century

ISBN 978-0-19-530669-9; 0-19-530669-4

LC 2008-27862

The author "traverses the rise and the debatable inevitability of slavery in the United States between the end of the Seven Years' War (1763) and Jefferson's election (1800), arguing that the 'division of the Republic into free wage labor sections and proslavery regions did not have to happen that way.'" Publ Wkly

Includes bibliographical references and index

Ellis, Joseph J.

American creation; triumphs and tragedies at the founding of the republic. A. A. Knopf 2007 283p   **973.3**

1. Founding Fathers of the United States 2. National characteristics, American

ISBN 978-0-307-26369-8; 0-307-26369-X

LC 2007-5273

The author "selects 'certain propitious moments' from the American Revolution and early republic, dramatizes them, and analyzes their crucial ramifications for America's future. ... A history bound for phenomenal popularity." Booklist

Includes bibliographical references

Ferling, John E.

Setting the world ablaze; Washington, Adams, and Jefferson and the American Revolution. {by} John Ferling. Oxford Univ. Press 2000 xxiv, 392p il maps hardcover o.p. pa $19.95   **973.3**

1. Architects 2. Essayists 3. Generals 4. Presidents 5. Statesmen -- United States 6. Vice-presidents

ISBN 0-19-515084-8 pa

LC 99-89686

In this history Ferling profiles "the three men who were, in his view, the most important leaders of the American Revolution. Thomas Jefferson was the 'pen,' John Adams the 'tongue,' and George Washington the 'sword.' Ferling's command of the material is sure-footed, though not everyone will agree with his views." Libr J

Includes bibliographical references

Fischer, David Hackett

Paul Revere's ride. Oxford Univ. Press 1994 445p il maps $37.50; pa $19.95   **973.3**

1. Artisans 2. Concord (Mass.), Battle of, 1775 3. Concord, Battle of, 1775 4. Lexington (Mass.), Battle of, 1775 5. Lexington, Battle of, 1775 6. Metalworkers 7. Revolutionaries 8. United States -- History -- 1775-1783, Revolution

ISBN 0-19-508847-6; 0-19-509831-5 pa

LC 93-25739

"Fischer's solid study of Paul Revere and his infamous ride debunks the myths surrounding the event, reconstructing the circumstances leading to the Battle of Lexington and Concord. Fischer's extensive use of primary sources affords an intimate glimpse of the participants' thoughts and feelings." Booklist

Includes bibliographical references

Washington's crossing. Oxford University Press 2004 564p il maps $35; pa $16.95   **973.3**

1. Generals 2. Presidents

ISBN 0-19-517034-2; 0-19-518159-X pa

LC 2003-19858

The author describes how "Washington, his officers, and their men turn the early military defeats of Long Island and New York City into victory at Trenton and Princeton. The opening chapter is devoted to the painting Washington Crossing the Delaware. Then the author discusses the British, Hessian, and American military units that were involved in these campaigns and gives background on their officers. This is Fischer's strong suit: he tells stories and gives details that bring history alive. ... In the hands of such a thorough researcher and talented writer, this is powerful stuff." SLJ

Includes bibliographical references

Fleming, Thomas J.

Washington's secret war; the hidden history of Valley Forge. [by] Thomas Fleming. Smithsonian Books/Collins 2005 384p il map $27.95; pa $14.95   **973.3**

1. Generals 2. Presidents

ISBN 0-06-082962-1; 0-06-087293-4 pa

LC 2005-52157

"Fleming has provided an original and provocative reinterpretation of a critical period in the struggle for independence." Booklist

Includes bibliographical references

Foner, Eric

Tom Paine and Revolutionary America; Updated ed; Oxford University Press 2005 xxxvi, 326p $71.50; pa $34.95   **973.3**

1. Essayists 2. Pamphleteers 3. Political and social philosophers 4. Writers on politics 5. Writers on

religion

ISBN 0-19-517486-0; 0-19-517485-2 pa

LC 2004-54799

The author examines the roots of Paine's thought within the social, economic and political context of colonial America.

Fowler, William M.

American crisis; George Washington and the dangerous two years after Yorktown, 1781-1783. Walker & Co. 2011 340p il map $28 **973.3**

1. Generals 2. Presidents

ISBN 978-0-8027-1706-1; 0-8027-1706-3

The author "artfully records the dangerous situation in the United States during the time between Cornwallis's surrender at Yorktown in 1781 and the evacuation of British troops from New York two years later. Drawing from a wealth of letters, he describes General Washington's skill as a leader, his humble and respectful character, and his noble motives in fighting to keep the army organized and disciplined. . . . This well-documented and highly readable account will engage and enrich scholars and general readers alike." Libr J

Includes bibliographical references

Hibbert, Christopher

★ **Redcoats** and rebels; the American Revolution through British eyes. Norton 1990 xx, 375p il maps hardcover o.p. pa $18.95 **973.3**

ISBN 0-393-02895-X; 0-393-32293-9 pa

LC 90-31753

"Mr. Hibbert has an eye for the telling anecdote and the graphic quotation, and his bibliography indicates that he has consulted a wealth of manuscript material as well as research published during the last 30 years that illuminates what lay behind the British defeat." N Y Times Book Rev

Hogeland, William

Declaration; the nine tumultuous weeks when America became independent, May 1-July 4, 1776. Simon & Schuster 2010 273p il $26; ebook $12.99 **973.3**

ISBN 978-1-4165-8409-4; 1-4165-8409-9; 978-1-4165-8425-4 ebook

LC 2010-3239

The author "forges a compelling narrative from the dozens of intricate political imbroglios that culminated with the signing of the Declaration of Independence. By casting a light on the daily interests of colonial Americans, particularly those whose homes and businesses patterned the spaces of bustling 18th-century Philadelphia, the author animates the discontents of the soon-to-be independent citizenry. With charming detail, the narrative brings together the diverse political players working during the nine weeks prior to the signing of the Declaration. These included rural militias, landed aristocrats, city merchants and immigrants, all of whom found a voice in Philadelphia." Kirkus

Includes bibliographical references

Howard, Hugh

Houses of the founding fathers; original photography by Roger Straus III. Artisan 2007 354p il $50 **973.3**

1. Historic buildings -- United States 2. Politicians -- United States 3. Statesmen -- United States

ISBN 978-1-57965-275-3; 1-57965-275-1

LC 2006-48015

"A prolific and popular architecture writer specializing in Colonial and early American historic preservation, teams up with veteran architecture photographer . . . to offer a sumptuously illustrated American history primer-cum-historic house tour. . . . A pleasantly flowing text interweaves historic events, details of daily life, personal anecdotes, and architectural insights into descriptions of the homes built and occupied by the era's upper social stratum." Libr J

Includes bibliographical references

Jasanoff, Maya

Liberty's exiles; Maya Jasanoff. Alfred A. Knopf 2011 xvi, 460p.p col. ill., maps $30 **973.3**

1. American Loyalists 2. American loyalists 3. Refugees

ISBN 978-1-4000-4168-8; 1-4000-4168-6; 978-0-307-59530-0 e-book

LC 201023514

"At the end of the American Revolution, sixty thousand Americans loyal to the British cause fled the United States and became refugees throughout the British Empire. . . . [This book offers a] global history of the loyalist exodus to Canada, the Caribbean, Sierra Leone, India, and beyond. . . . [Loyalists discussed include] Elizabeth Johnston, a young mother from Georgia, who led her growing family to Britain, Jamaica, and Canada, questing for a home; black loyalists such as David George, who escaped from slavery in Virginia and went on to found Baptist congregations in Nova Scotia and Sierra Leone; and Mohawk Indian leader Joseph Brant, who tried to find autonomy for his people in Ontario." (Publisher's note) Bibliography. Index.

"Combining compelling narrative with insightful analysis, Jasanoff has produced a work that is both distinct in perspective and groundbreaking in its originality." Libr J

Includes bibliographical references and index.

Ketchum, Richard M.

Saratoga; turning point of America's Revolutionary War. Holt & Co. 1997 545p il maps hardcover o.p. pa $18 **973.3**

1. Saratoga Campaign, 1777

ISBN 0-8050-6123-1 pa

LC 97-2773

A "narrative account of the Saratoga campaign of 1777. . . . Ketchum provides the full political context within which the fighting took place while penning dozens of colorful portraits of the principal characters. The author also succeeds in his goal of telling the story from the perspective of the participants, illustrating what the American Revolution in upstate New York meant for soldiers and civilians alike." Libr J

Includes bibliographical references

Lockhart, Paul Douglas

The **whites** of their eyes; Bunker Hill, the first American Army, and the emergence of George Washington. Harper 2011 414p il map $27.99   **973.3**
1. Bunker Hill (Boston, Mass.), Battle of, 1775   2. Generals 3. Presidents
ISBN 978-0-06-195886-1; 0-06-195886-7
LC 2010-43033
"Lockhart's shrewd, well-judged interpretation corrects myths about the battle and the men who fought it while doing full justice to their achievement in creating an army—and a nation—out of chaos." Publ Wkly
Includes bibliographical references

Maier, Pauline

American scripture; making the Declaration of Independence. Knopf 1997 xxi, 304p hardcover o.p. pa $14   **973.3**
ISBN 0-679-77908-6 pa
LC 97-2769
"In the spring of 1776, with a British invasion fleet on its way, the Second Continental Congress appointed a committee to compose a statement explaining America's decision to seek independence. Thomas Jefferson was the principal drafter of the statement, but Maier makes it clear that his task was to express the sentiments of the Congress, not his personal views, and she shows that when the congressmen edited his draft they improved it greatly (rather than 'mangling' it, as Jefferson ever after maintained). The Declaration of Independence is, she argues, a profoundly collective document, both in its origins and in our still-evolving interpretation of its self-evident truths." New Yorker

McCullough, David G.

1776; [by] David McCullough. Simon & Schuster 2005 386p il map $32   **973.3**
ISBN 0-7432-2671-2
LC 2005-42505
"This is a narrative tour de force, exhibiting all the hallmarks the author is known for: fascinating subject matter, expert research and detailed, graceful prose." Publ Wkly
Includes bibliographical references

Middlekauff, Robert

★ The **glorious** cause; the American Revolution, 1763-1789. Rev. and expanded ed.; Oxford University Press 2004 736p il map $37.50   **973.3**
ISBN 0-19-516247-1
LC 2004-16295
"This is narrative history at its best, written in a conversational and engaging style." Libr J
Includes bibliographical references

Morgan, Edmund Sears

★ The **birth** of the Republic, 1763-89; 3rd ed; University of Chicago Press 1992 206p hardcover o.p. pa $13   **973.3**
ISBN 0-226-53756-0; 0-226-53757-9 pa
LC 92-8871
A brief study of the American revolutionary period from 1763 to 1789.

Nelson, James L.

With fire & sword; the battle of Bunker Hill and the beginning of the American Revolution. Thomas Dunne Books 2011 364p il map $27.99; ebook $14.99   **973.3**
1. Bunker Hill (Boston, Mass.), Battle of, 1775
ISBN 978-0-312-57644-8; 978-1-4299-6807-2 ebook
LC 2010-40653
"This rousing history rescues Bunker Hill from its folkloric shroud and presents it as one of the revolution's more significant and dramatic battles. . . . Nelson's gripping portrait of the battle caps a lively chronicle of the early days of the rebellion in Massachusetts and of the revolutionaries' scramble to establish a government and organize an army as they edged uneasily toward independence." Publ Wkly
Includes bibliographical references

Paul, Joel R.

Unlikely allies; how a merchant, a playwright, and a spy saved the American Revolution. [by] Joel Richard Paul. Riverhead Books 2009 405p il $25.95   **973.3**
1. Authors 2. Diplomats 3. Dramatists 4. Saratoga Campaign, 1777 5. Secret service -- United States 6. Spies 7. Transvestites
ISBN 978-1-59448-883-2; 1-59448-883-5
LC 2009-34986
"A rip-roaring account of the American Revolution, told from a fresh, and undeniably offbeat, perspective." Booklist
Includes bibliographical references (p. 384-396)

Rakove, Jack

Revolutionaries; a new history of the invention of America. [by] Jack Rakove. Houghton Mifflin Harcourt 2010 487p $30   **973.3**
1. Revolutionaries -- United States -- History -- 18th century 2. Statesmen -- United States
ISBN 978-0-618-26746-0
LC 2009-47557
The author "reflects on how a group of lawyers and planters came to wage the American Revolution. Instead of focusing on the battlefield, the author examines what might be called a revolution of the mind—that is, how the early Founding Fathers' ideas developed and took hold. . . . An ambitious, intelligent exploration into the intellectual underpinnings of the Revolution." Kirkus
Includes bibliographical references

Raphael, Ray

★ A **people's** history of the American Revolution; how common people shaped the fight for independence. 1st Perennial ed; Perennial 2002 506p pa $13.95   **973.3**
ISBN 0-06-000440-1
LC 2002-16992
"Moving from broad overviews to stories of small groups or individuals, Raphael's study is impressive in both its sweep and its attention to the particular." Publ Wkly
Includes bibliographical references

Thomas, Evan

★ **John** Paul Jones; sailor, hero, father of the American Navy. Simon & Schuster 2003 383p il hardcover o.p. pa $16   **973.3**

1. Admirals -- United States -- Biography 2. Naval officers

ISBN 0-7432-0583-9; 978-0-7432-5804-3; 0-7432-5804-5 pa

LC 2003-42411

"The complex portrait is rendered with nautical precision—the author knows his topsail from his topgallant—and a lively eye for such details as the Enlightenment virtues espoused by Freemasonry or the proper way to kiss a French lady in the eighteenth century." Publ Wkly

Includes bibliographical references

Tuchman, Barbara Wertheim

The **first** salute; [by] Barbara W. Tuchman. Knopf 1988 347p il maps hardcover o.p. pa $16.95   **973.3**

1. Large print books

ISBN 0-394-55333-0; 0-345-33667-4 pa

LC 88-45216

"The book is a tightly woven narrative, ingeniously structured. It is not a blow-by-blow account of the conflict; familiarity with issues and events is assumed. Instead, Tuchman takes a specific incident and through it elucidates the course and outcome of the war." Christ Sci Monit

Includes bibliographical references

Unger, Harlow Giles

American tempest; how the Boston Tea Party sparked a revolution. [by] Harlow Giles Unger. Da Capo Press 2011 288p il map $26   **973.3**

1. Boston Tea Party, 1773

ISBN 978-0-306-81962-9; 0-306-819627

LC 2010-47734

"As Unger makes clear, the true impact of the Boston Tea Party came from Britain's ill-advised overreaction to the symbolic act of vandalism. It was exactly the response [Sam] Adams had dreamed of, with an enraged British government closing the port of Boston, sending more troops, imposing martial law, and requiring permits for any large Boston meetings. These 'Coercive Acts,' along with Adams's constant drumbeat of anti-British propaganda, helped unify the colonies around the idea of independence. Unger ends the book with British soldiers marching out to Lexington and Concord hoping to arrest Adams and Hancock (who, tipped off by Paul Revere, had fled). The rest, as they say, is history, and Unger has brought it brilliantly to life." Boston Globe

Includes bibliographical references

Weintraub, Stanley

Iron tears; America's battle for freedom, Britain's quagmire, 1775-1783. Free Press 2005 375p il maps $28   **973.3**

1. Public opinion -- Great Britain -- History -- 18th century

ISBN 0-7432-2687-9

LC 2004-56363

The author "examines the possibility that the British lost the war because of protest and lack of support at home. . . . The British failure to win a war against ill-trained but determined guerrilla forces in often unpredictable circumstances and weather appears now as an eerie harbinger of modern conflicts such as the Vietnam War. Weintraub's fast-paced narrative and impeccable historical research provide a stimulating challenge to conventional histories of the Revolutionary War that focus exclusively on the heroism of American forces." Publ Wkly

Includes bibliographical references

Wood, Gordon S.

The **radicalism** of the American Revolution. Knopf 1992 447p hardcover o.p. pa $16   **973.3**

1. United States -- History -- 1775-1783, Revolution 2. United States -- Politics and government -- 1775-1783, Revolution

ISBN 0-679-73688-3 pa

LC 91-19719

"Under the broad categories of monarchy, republicanism, and democracy, Wood explains how the US was transformed from a society that took for granted a nonworking elite and a dependent servile underclass to one in which the free-standing individualist, who worked for a living, became the norm. . . . {A} readable book based on hundreds of primary and secondary sources." Choice

Includes bibliographical references

The American Revolution: writings from the War of Independence. Library of Am. 2001 878p $40   **973.3**

ISBN 1-88301-191-4

LC 00-45373

"This work will serve as a marvelous research tool for specialists, but general readers with an interest in American history will also find fascinating gems." Booklist

Includes bibliographical references

973.4   Constitutional period, 1789-1809

Brookhiser, Richard

America's first dynasty; the Adamses, 1735-1918. Free Press 2002 244p il $25; pa $14 **973.4**

1. Authors 2. Diplomats 3. Essayists 4. Historians 5. Historians -- United States -- Biography 6. Members of Congress 7. Novelists 8. Political leaders 9. Presidents 10. Presidents -- United States -- Biography 11. Secretaries of state 12. Senators 13. Statesmen -- United States -- Biography 14. Vice-presidents

ISBN 0-684-86881-4; 0-684-86864-4 pa

LC 2001-51276

An "account of the lives of John, John Quincy, Charles Francis and Henry, four generations of men often brilliant but often shortsighted as well: two presidents, one diplomat and, finally, a historian who felt he had failed the ancestors." N Y Times Book Rev

Includes bibliographical references

Burstein, Andrew

Madison and Jefferson; [by] Andrew Burstein and Nancy Isenberg. Random House 2010 809p il map $35; e-book $35 **973.4**
1. Architects 2. Biography, Individual 3. Bishops 4. College presidents 5. Essayists 6. Members of Congress 7. Presidents 8. Presidents -- United States 9. Secretaries of state 10. Vice-presidents
ISBN 978-1-4000-6728-2; 978-0-679-60410-5 e-book
LC 2010-5884

This "dual biography promotes Madison from junior partner to full-fledged colleague of the 'more magnetic' Jefferson. According to the authors, Madison's popular image peaked in 1789 as 'father of the Constitution.' But Burstein . . . and Isenberg . . . see him as a canny, effective politician for four decades, from the Continental Congress through his two terms as America's fourth president. . . . An important, thoughtful, and gracefully written political history from the viewpoint of the young nation's two most intellectual founding fathers." Publ Wkly

Includes bibliographical references and index

Cerami, Charles A.

Jefferson's great gamble; the remarkable story of Jefferson, Napoleon and the men behind the Louisiana Purchase. Sourcebooks 2003 309p il $22.95; pa $14.95 **973.4**
1. Architects 2. Emperors 3. Essayists 4. Louisiana Purchase 5. Presidents 6. Vice-presidents
ISBN 1-57071-945-4; 1-40220-240-7 pa
LC 2002-153440

"Anyone wanting to read the story of a momentous turning point in American history, a story of diplomatic maneuvering and international politics, will be hard-pressed to find a better version than this." Publ Wkly

Includes bibliographical references

Ellis, Joseph J.

American sphinx: the character of Thomas Jefferson. Knopf 1997 365p $29.95; pa $15 **973.4**
1. Architects 2. Essayists 3. Presidents 4. Vice-presidents
ISBN 0-679-44490-4; 0-679-76441-0 pa
LC 96-26171

"Penetrating Jefferson's placid, elegant facade, this extraordinary biography brings the sage of Monticello down to earth without either condemning or idolizing him." Publ Wkly

Founding brothers; the revolutionary generation. Knopf 2000 288p $26.95; pa $14 **973.4**
1. Architects 2. Authors 3. Diplomats 4. Essayists 5. Generals 6. Inventors 7. Members of Congress 8. Presidents 9. Presidents -- United States 10. Presidents -- United States -- Biography -- Anecdotes 11. Scientists 12. Secretaries of state 13. Secretaries of the treasury 14. Statesmen 15. Statesmen -- United States -- Biography -- Anecdotes 16. United States -- History -- 1783-1815 -- Anecdotes 17. United States -- Politics and government -- 1783-1809 -- Anecdotes 18.

Vice-presidents 19. Writers on science
ISBN 0-375-40544-5; 0-375-70524-4 pa
LC 99-59304

"Ellis' essays are angled, fascinating, and perfect for general-interest readers." Booklist

Includes bibliographical references

Gordon-Reed, Annette

Thomas Jefferson and Sally Hemings; an American controversy. University Press of Va. 1997 xx, 288p hardcover o.p. pa $14.95 **973.4**
1. Architects 2. Essayists 3. Mistresses 4. Presidents 5. Slaves 6. Vice-presidents
ISBN 0-8139-1833-2 pa
LC 96-34550

"Hemings, a slave who was one-quarter African, was also a half sister of Jefferson's deceased wife, and she lived at Monticello for many years. In this understated, brilliant study an African-American law professor examines the allegation that Jefferson was the father of Hemings' children." New Yorker

Includes bibliographical references

Hamilton, Alexander

Writings. Library of Am. 2001 1108p $40 **973.4**
1. Secretaries of the treasury 2. Statesmen
ISBN 1-931082-04-9
LC 2001-23043

"The text consists of more than 170 letters, speeches, essays, reports, and memoranda written between 1769 and 1804, including all of Hamilton's material presented in The Federalist. This additionally sports several conflicting eyewitness accounts of Hamilton's lethal duel with Aaron Burr." Libr J

Includes bibliographical references

Hogeland, William

★ The **Whiskey** Rebellion; George Washington, Alexander Hamilton, and the frontier rebels who challenged America's newfound sovereignty. Scribner 2006 302p map $26.95; pa $16 **973.4**
1. Whiskey Rebellion, Pa., 1794
ISBN 978-0-7432-5490-8; 0-7432-5490-2; 978-0-7432-5491-5 pa; 0-7432-5491-0 pa
LC 2005-56340

"Soon after Americans ousted inequitable British taxation, Secretary of Finance Alexander Hamilton, hatched a plan to put the new nation on steady financial footing by imposing the first American excise tax, on whiskey makers. The tax favored large distillers over small farmers with stills in the mountains of Pennsylvania, Maryland and Virginia, and the farmers fomented their own new revolution— a challenge to the sovereignty of the new government and the power of the wealthy eastern seaboard. In a fast-paced, blow-by-blow account of this 'primal national drama,' journalist Hogeland energetically chronicles the skirmishes that made the Whiskey Rebellion from 1791 to 1795 a symbol of the conflict between republican ideals and capitalist values." Publ Wkly

Includes bibliographical references

Kranish, Michael

Flight from Monticello; Thomas Jefferson at war. Michael Kranish. Oxford University Press 2010 xii, 388 p.p   **973.4**
1. Governors -- Virginia -- Biography 2. Presidents -- United States -- Biography
ISBN 0195374622; 9780195374629 (acid-free paper)
LC 2009018156
This is an account of Jefferson's life during the period when he served as governor of Virginia. He became governor "in 1779 and had to face repeated invasions of his state by British forces." (Newsweek) Index.

"Crisply written and well documented, this book is popular history at its best and will appeal to a wide readership. Highly recommended." Libr J
Includes bibliographical references (p. [371]-373)

Kukla, Jon

A **wilderness** so immense; the Louisiana Purchase and the destiny of America. Knopf 2003 430p il map $30; pa $16   **973.4**
1. Louisiana Purchase
ISBN 0-375-40812-6; 0-375-70761-1 pa
LC 2002-27395
"This judicious, aptly illustrated work will gratify all its readers. Rarely does a work of history combine grace of writing with such broad authority." Publ Wkly
Includes bibliographical references

McCullough, David G.

John Adams; {by} David McCullough. Simon & Schuster 2001 751p il maps $35; pa $18.95 **973.4**
1. Large print books 2. Presidents 3. Presidents -- United States 4. Vice-presidents
ISBN 0-684-81363-7; 0-7432-2313-6 pa
LC 2001-27010
"This is a wonderfully stirring biography; to read it is to feel as if you are witnessing the birth of a country firsthand." Booklist
Includes bibliographical references

Miller, John Chester

The **Federalist** era, 1789-1801; by John C. Miller. Waveland Press 1998 304p il pa $16.95 **973.4**
1. Architects 2. Essayists 3. Presidents 4. Secretaries of the treasury 5. Statesmen 6. Vice-presidents
ISBN 978-1-57766-031-6; 1-57766-031-5
A chronicle of the administrations of George Washington and John Adams, concentrating on the politics and diplomacy.

Purcell, Sarah J.

The **early** national period; [by] Sarah Purcell. Facts on File 2004 420p il map $75   **973.4**
ISBN 0-8160-4769-3
LC 2003-14969
"A serious history student will find this book invaluable." Libr Media Connect
Includes bibliographical references

Randall, Willard Sterne

George Washington; a life. Holt & Co. 1997 548p hardcover o.p. pa $18   **973.4**
1. Biography, Individual 2. Generals 3. Presidents 4. Presidents -- United States
ISBN 0-8050-5992-X pa
LC 97-19125
"Chronicling less the adaptive leader of the struggling rebellion or the persuasive conciliator of the infant republic, Randall . . . portrays instead the vain, restless, ambitious provincial who got 'tremendously lucky'. . . . Altogether human, Randall's demythologized Washington comes vividly to life." Publ Wkly
Includes bibliographical references

Staloff, Darren

Hamilton, Adams, Jefferson; the politics of enlightenment and the American founding. Hill & Wang 2005 419p $30   **973.4**
1. Architects 2. Enlightenment 3. Essayists 4. Presidents 5. Secretaries of the treasury 6. Statesmen 7. Vice-presidents
ISBN 0-8090-7784-1; 978-0-8090-7784-7
LC 2005-40433
"Staloff has created a work that is a must-read for any serious scholar of US history." Choice
Includes bibliographical references

Stewart, David O.

American emperor; Aaron Burr's challenge to Jefferson's America. Simon & Schuster 2011 xx, 410p il map $30; ebook $14.99   **973.4**
1. Architects 2. Essayists 3. Presidents 4. Presidents -- United States -- Election -- 1800 5. Vice-presidents
ISBN 978-1-4391-5718-3; 978-1-4391-6032-9 ebook
LC 2011002647
Traces the career of the third U.S. vice president and would-be secession leader, discussing his acrimonious relationship with Thomas Jefferson; his ambitious vision of expansion; and his historical, self-defended trial for treason.

"A persuasive, engaging examination of the post-political career of a shadowy and much-maligned figure from the era of the Founders." Kirkus
Includes bibliographical references

Vidal, Gore

Inventing a nation: Washington, Adams, Jefferson. Yale University Press 2003 224p $22; pa $14   **973.4**
1. Architects 2. Essayists 3. Generals 4. Presidents 5. Vice-presidents
ISBN 0-300-10171-6; 0-300-10592-4 pa
LC 2003-015612
Vidal offers "characteristically brilliant and acerbic reflections on power and personality. . . . This entertaining and enlightening reappraisal of the Founders is a must for buffs of American civilization and its discontents." Booklist

Washington, George

★ **George** Washington's diaries; an abridgment. Dorothy Twohig, editor. University Press of Va. 1999 xxxi, 453p il $65; pa $22.95 **973.4**
1. Generals 2. Presidents 3. Presidents -- United States 4. Presidents -- United States -- Diaries
ISBN 0-8139-1856-1; 0-8139-1857-X pa

LC 98-11681
"Culled from the six volumes of The Diaries of George Washington completed in 1979, this selection of entries . . . reveals the lifelong preoccupations of the public and private man." Publisher's note
Includes bibliographical references

★ **Writings**. Library of Am. 1997 xxiii, 1149p $40 **973.4**
ISBN 1-883011-23-X

LC 96-9665
This "selection of Washington's letters, speeches, diary entries, maxims and military orders reveals a writer of surprising versatility and a statesman consciously involved with the forging of our national character." Publ Wkly

Wiencek, Henry

★ An **imperfect** god; George Washington, his slaves, and the creation of America. Farrar, Straus and Giroux 2003 404p il map $26; pa $15 **973.4**
1. Generals 2. Presidents 3. Presidents -- United States
ISBN 0-374-17526-8; 0-374-52951-5 pa

LC 2003-6984
"This work of stylish scholarship and genealogical investigation makes Washington an even greater and more human figure than he has seemed before." Publ Wkly
Includes bibliographical references

Wills, Garry

Henry Adams and the making of America. Houghton Mifflin 2005 467p hardcover o.p. pa $15.95 **973.4**
1. Authors 2. Essayists 3. Historians 4. Novelists
ISBN 0-618-13430-1; 0-618-87266-3 pa

LC 2005-40305
"Those unfamiliar with Adams' historical writings will find Wills a helpful and accessible guide; those who know Adams already will enjoy revisiting his histories with this knowledgeable and learned companion." Foreign Affairs
Includes bibliographical references

Wood, Gordon S.

★ **Empire** of liberty; a history of the early Republic, 1789-1815. Oxford University Press 2009 778p il map $35 **973.4**
1. National characteristics, American
ISBN 978-0-19-503914-6

LC 2009-10762
"Skillfully traversing seminal topics such as slavery, westward expansion, social leveling, diplomacy, evangelicalism, the arts and sciences, and the transformation of the American legal system, Wood's authoritative and compelling narrative presents a picture of early Americans engaged in pursuit of cultural, social, and economic self-discovery. .

. . [This is] a brilliant, definitive, and thought-provoking historical synthesis; sure to become indispensable to any study of the era." Libr J
Includes bibliographical references

Zacks, Richard

The **pirate** coast; Thomas Jefferson, the first marines, and the secret mission of 1805. Hyperion 2005 432p il map $25.95; pa $15.95 **973.4**
1. Architects 2. Army officers 3. Diplomats 4. Essayists 5. Pirates -- North Africa -- History -- 19th century 6. Presidents 7. Vice-presidents
ISBN 1-401-30003-0; 1-401-30849-X pa

LC 2004-60635
"This is the book that Captain Eaton has long deserved." Publ Wkly
Includes bibliographical references

The Louisiana Purchase; a historical and geographical encyclopedia. Junius P. Rodriguez, editor. ABC-CLIO 2002 xxxv, 513p il maps $95 **973.4**
1. Louisiana Purchase 2. Louisiana Purchase -- Encyclopedias
ISBN 1-57607-188-X

LC 2002-3228
"The reasons for as well as the immediate and historical repercussions of the purchase are explored in nearly 300 articles written by 85 distinguished scholars. Coverage includes native peoples, noteworthy personalities, and geographical areas associated with a land acquisition that nearly doubled the size of our nation. An extensive bibliography, 49 pertinent documents, a chronology, and an index round out this excellent volume." Libr J
Includes bibliographical references

973.5 1809-1845

Allgor, Catherine

A **perfect** union; Dolley Madison and the creation of the American nation. Henry Holt & Co. 2006 493p il $30 **973.5**
1. Biography, Individual 2. Spouses of presidents
ISBN 0-8050-7327-2; 978-0-8050-7327-0

LC 2005-55127
"In this evocative study a remarkable woman, creator of the 'first lady' role, comes vividly to life. " N Y Times Book Rev
Includes bibliographical references

Collins, Gail

William Henry Harrison; Gail Collins. Times Books/Henry Holt and Co. 2012 xviii, 153 p.p The American presidents **973.5**
1. Governors -- Indiana -- Biography 2. Presidents -- United States -- Biography 3. Presidents -- United States -- Election -- 1840
ISBN 9780805091182

LC 2011018976
This book offers a biography of U.S. former president William Henry Harrison. "Despite the legendary 1840 campaign featuring a 'log cabin, hard cider' frontiersman with

humble origins, Harrison was born on a Virginia plantation, built himself a mansion as governor of the rough Indiana frontier territory, and avoided alcohol. His fame rested on two victories: the 1811 battle of Tippecanoe against the Shawnee Indians, and the 1813 Battle of the Thames during the War of 1812, in which the Indian leader Tecumseh was killed. For decades afterward, he struggled as a farmer and Ohio politician; he lost the 1836 presidential election but won four years later." (Publishers Weekly)

Daughan, George C.

1812: the Navy's war; George C. Daughan. Basic Books 2011 xxix, 491p il map $32.50   **973.5**
1. Historical literature 2. United States -- History -- War of 1812 3. United States -- History -- War of 1812 -- Naval operations 4. War of 1812
ISBN 978-0-465-02046-1; 978-0-465-02808-5 ebook
LC 2011020923

This book provides an account of the U.S. Navy's surprising performance in the war that finally reconciled the British to America's independence. . . . If the U.S. Navy . . . didn't win the War of 1812, it probably kept the nation from losing. The . . . exploits of outstanding officers like Isaac Hull, David Porter, Stephen Decatur and Oliver Hazard Perry earned new respect for America's fleet; victories by the Essex, the Hornet and the Constitution . . . set off national celebrations.

"Daughan supplies just enough of the big picture—the dismal struggles of both armies, Napoleon's offstage machinations that determined so much of the war's progress, the outcome of domestic political squabbles upon which the navy's survival depended—to place the navy's role in context, but he focuses on the personalities, ships and battles that prevented the British from suffocating the infant nation's maritime ambitions. . . . A smart salute to a defining moment in the history of the U.S. Navy." Kirkus
Includes bibliographical references

Groom, Winston

Patriotic fire; Andrew Jackson and Jean Laffite at the Battle of New Orleans. Alfred A. Knopf 2006 xxiv, 292p il map $26   **973.5**
1. Generals 2. Pirates 3. Presidents
ISBN 1-4000-4436-7; 978-1-4000-4436-8
LC 2005-51001

"This is a beautifully written and exciting work of popular history." Booklist
Includes bibliographical references

Howe, Daniel Walker

★ **What** hath God wrought; the transformation of America, 1815-1848. Oxford University Press 2007 904p il map $35   **973.5**
1. Social change -- United States
ISBN 978-0-19-507894-7; 0-19-507894-2
LC 2007-12370

The author "narrates a crucial period in U.S. history—a time of territorial growth, religious revival, booming industrialization, a recalibrating of American democracy and the rise of nationalist sentiment. . . . Supported by engaging prose, Howe's achievement will surely be seen as one of the most outstanding syntheses of U.S. history published this decade." Publ Wkly
Includes bibliographical references

Langguth, A. J.

Driven West; Andrew Jackson and the Trail of Tears to the Civil War. Simon & Schuster 2010 466p il map $30; ebook $14.99   **973.5**
1. Generals 2. Indians of North America -- Relocation 3. Presidents 4. Trail of Tears, 1838-1839
ISBN 978-1-4165-4859-1; 1-4165-4859-9; 978-1-4391-9327-3 ebook; 1-4391-9327-4 ebook
LC 2010-20455

Langguth argues "that the passage of the Indian Removal Act of 1830, Jackson's breaking of Indian treaties and his support of the Southern states, especially Georgia, in resisting a Supreme Court ruling in favor of the Cherokees were 'salvos . . . fired in the nation's first civil war'." (N Y Times Book Rev) Bibliography. Index.

"A disturbing reconsideration of a key period of history and a powerful indictment of its main actors." Kirkus
Includes bibliographical references

Lincoln, Abraham

★ **Speeches** and writings, 1832-1858; speeches, letters, and miscellaneous writings: the Lincoln Douglas debates. Library of Am. 1989 898p $35   **973.5**
1. Lincoln-Douglas debates, 1858
ISBN 0-940450-43-7
LC 88-82723

Based on the "eight volumes of 'The Collected Works of Abraham Lincoln,' edited by Roy P. Basler, Marion Dolores Pratt and Lloyd A. Dunlap, the present . . . [volume contains] all seven of the Lincoln-Douglas debates, as well as the . . . speeches, before and after the debates, that attacked the repeal of the Missouri Compromise of 1820 and 'squatter sovereignty' in the territories." N Y Times Book Rev
Includes bibliographical references

Miller, William Lee

Arguing about slavery; the great battle in the United States Congress. Knopf 1996 577p hardcover o.p. pa $17   **973.5**
1. Members of Congress 2. Presidents 3. Secretaries of state 4. Senators 5. Slavery 6. Slavery -- United States
ISBN 0-679-76844-0 pa
LC 95-35075

"Miller lays out the arcane workings of the proceedings with admirable detail, clarity, and verve." Christ Sci Monit
Includes bibliographical references

Oates, Stephen B.

The **approaching** fury; voices of the storm, 1820-1861. Buz Wyeth, editor. HarperCollins Pubs. 1997 495p hardcover o.p. pa $15   **973.5**
ISBN 0-06-092885-9 pa
LC 96-31965

"Taken on its own terms, this book powerfully re-creates some of the momentous events that produced the catastrophe of 1861. Mr. Oates succeeds in bringing his characters alive

and in creating highly dramatic scenes for them to act out."
N Y Times Book Rev

Includes bibliographical references

Remini, Robert Vincent

John Quincy Adams; [by] Robert V. Remini.
Times Bks. 2002 172p $20   **973.5**
1. Members of Congress 2. Presidents 3. Presidents --
United States 4. Presidents -- United States -- Biography
5. Secretaries of state 6. Senators
ISBN 0-8050-6939-9

LC 2002-24210

The author's "judicious, eloquent survey of the sixth
president's life and career intends not to proffer new and explosive ideas but to fashion recent scholarship into a highly
readable overview for the general reader." Booklist

Includes bibliographical references

Reynolds, David S.

Waking giant; America in the age of Jackson.
Harper 2008 466p il $29.95   **973.5**
1. Generals 2. Presidents
ISBN 978-0-06-082656-7

LC 2007-51751

This is "a terrific introduction of succinct length to . . . a
time when the foundations of much of modern America were
laid." N Y Times (Late N Y Ed)

Includes bibliographical references

Taylor, Alan

The **civil** war of 1812; American citizens, British subjects, Irish rebels, & Indian allies. Alfred A.
Knopf 2010 620p il map $35; e-book $35   **973.5**
1. War of 1812
ISBN 978-1-4000-4265-4; 1-4000-4265-8; 978-0-307-
59459-4 e-book

LC 2010-12783

In this book, Alan "Taylor examines themes pertinent to
the period and the war [of 1812], blending narrative with
analysis. He sees this upheaval, and the earlier American
Revolution, as part of a anglophone civil war that defined
America, Canada, and the British Empire in the nineteenth
century. It was a peculiar type of civil war, to be certain, as
it involved more than one state and more than one culture. .
. . Many Canadians were in fact displaced American loyalists who hoped to undo the revolution. . . . Taylor draws on
the conceptual frameworks created in the burgeoning field
of borderlands history to construct his study. He uses this
approach to situate the character of the war along the Amer-
ican-Canadian border, which he sees as central to the entire
conflict." (American Historical Review)

"Instead of a traditional narrative of the war from its beginnings in June 1812 to its end in early 1815, [this] book
is structured topically. . . . Such a neat and methodical organization helps Taylor bring the confused and chaotic events
of the war under control. It also allows him to present an
enormous amount of material—on persons, events, and stories—without overwhelming the reader. And the amount of
material is enormous." N Y Rev Books

Includes bibliographical references

Tocqueville, Alexis de

Democracy in America; with an introduction
by Alan Ryan. Knopf 1994 lxxii, 434, xi, 394p
$27   **973.5**
1. American national characteristics 2. Democracy
ISBN 978-0-679-43134-3; 0-679-43134-9

LC 94-1752

Based partly on the French author's observations of
American political and social conditions during a visit in
1831-1832. "It remains the best philosophical discussion
of Democracy illustrated by the experience of the United
States, up to the time when it was written, which can be
found in any language." Pratt Alcove

Includes bibliographical references

Wilentz, Sean

The **rise** of American democracy; Jefferson to
Lincoln. Norton 2005 xxiii, 1044p il $35   **973.5**
1. Democracy 2. Democracy -- United States
ISBN 0-393-05820-4

LC 2004-29466

The author traces the evolution of democratic principles
in the United States from the American Revolution to the
Civil War.

This "is a magnificent chronicle, the life of an idea that,
although it is mentioned nowhere in the Constitution, nevertheless slowly elbowed its way into the heart of American
life. . . . Wilentz shows what [the] fight has cost, and why it's
worth it." Newsweek

Includes bibliographical references

Wills, Garry

James Madison. Times Bks. 2002 xx, 184p
$20   **973.5**
1. Members of Congress 2. Presidents 3. Presidents --
United States 4. Presidents -- United States -- Biography
5. Secretaries of state
ISBN 0-8050-6905-4

LC 2002-19692

The author "maintains that Madison possessed qualities
that served him well early in his career but proved to be a
handicap during his Presidency. . . . Written with flair, this
clear and balanced account is based on a sure handling of the
material." Libr J

Includes bibliographical references

Encyclopedia of the United States in the nineteenth
century; Paul Finkelman, editor in chief. Scribner 2001 3v il maps set $400   **973.5**
1. Reference books
ISBN 0-684-80500-6

LC 00-45811

In this historical overview: "population, politics and
government, economy and work, society and culture, religion, social problems and reform, everyday life, and foreign
policy are explored in more than 600 A-to-Z articles. Complete with more than 400 illustrations and maps, this set includes . . . {a} year-by-year chronology, original documents
{and} tables." Publisher's note

973.6   1845-1861

Bordewich, Fergus M.

America's great debate; Henry Clay, Stephen A. Douglas, and the compromise that preserved the Union. Fergus M. Bordewich. Simon & Schuster 2012 x, 480 p.p   **973.6**
   1. Compromise of 1850 2. Slavery -- United States -- History -- 19th century
   ISBN 1439124604; 9781439124604; 9781439141687
                      LC 2011029547

In this book, Historian [Fergus M.] Bordewich . . . recounts the amazing story of the cliffhanging compromise hammered out in both houses of Congress in 1850 that pitted the rival pro- and antislavery factions against each other and saved the country, temporarily, from dissolution. . . . Bordewich portrays a colorful cast of characters--Democrats, Whigs, Free Soilers and abolitionists--whose passionate rhetoric attained lyrical heights and brought the debate about America's very identity to the forefront. Chief architect Henry Clay . . . warned his colleagues of the dire consequences of disunion. . . . Warring factions . . . threatened to defeat the omnibus bill, until the rhetorical arm-wringing by . . . Stephen A. Douglas squeezed a compromise and the necessary passage. (Kirkus)

Dusinberre, William

Slavemaster president; the double career of James Polk. Oxford Univ. Press 2003 258p il map $35   **973.6**
   1. Governors 2. Members of Congress 3. Plantation owners -- Mississippi 4. Plantation owners -- Tennessee 5. Presidents 6. Presidents -- United States 7. Slavery -- Mississippi -- History -- 19th century 8. Slavery -- Tennessee -- History -- 19th century 9. Slavery -- United States 10. Speakers of the House
   ISBN 0-19-515735-4
                      LC 2002-74852

This book focuses on "Polk's management of his slaves and his public positions on slavery and related issues. The author suggests that Polk's policies were critical to the development of the secessionist movement in the South and that these policies derived from his personal financial interests. . . . Dusinberre's research also expands our understanding of the management of plantations. Essential reading for anyone wanting greater insight into the factors that led to the Civil War, this work is highly recommended." Libr J
   Includes bibliographical references

Guelzo, Allen C.

Lincoln and Douglas; the debates that defined America. Simon & Schuster 2008 xxvii, 383p il map $26   **973.6**
   1. Lawyers 2. Lincoln-Douglas debates, 1858 3. Members of Congress 4. Political leaders 5. Presidential candidates 6. Presidents 7. Senators 8. State legislators
   ISBN 978-0-7432-7320-6; 0-7432-7320-6
                      LC 2007-44254

"This Lincoln-Douglas rendition will engage every interest in Civil War and black history." Booklist
   Includes bibliographical references

973.7   Administration of Abraham Lincoln, 1861-1865

Ash, Stephen V.

Firebrand of liberty; the story of two Black regiments that changed the course of the Civil War. W.W. Norton & Co. 2008 282p il map $25.95   **973.7**
   1. African American soldiers 2. African American soldiers -- History 3. African American soldiers -- History -- 19th century 4. Clergy 5. Memoirists 6. Social reformers
   ISBN 978-0-393-06586-2; 0-393-06586-3
                      LC 2008-2503

"The titular firebrand in this revealing history is not an individual but a curious and ambitious project: the establishment, in March 1863, of a permanent Union outpost in Florida to serve as a haven for fugitive slaves and to 'help ignite the destruction of Southern slavery from within.' In readable prose and relying exclusively on primary sources, historian Ash . . . tells the little-known but crucial story of how 900 newly freed slaves, under the leadership of white abolitionist officers, captured Jacksonville." Publ Wkly
   Includes bibliographical references (p. [256]-265) and index.

Blanton, DeAnne

They fought like demons; women soldiers in the American Civil War. {by} DeAnne Blanton and Lauren M. Cook. Louisiana State Univ. Press 2002 277p il $29.95   **973.7**
   1. Women soldiers 2. Women soldiers -- United States -- History -- 19th century
   ISBN 0-8071-2806-6
                      LC 2002-4441

"The authors reconstruct the reasons why women entered the armed forces: many were simply patriotic, while others followed their husbands or lovers and yet others yearned to break free from the constraints that Victorian society had laid on them as women. Blanton and Cook detail women soldiers in combat, on the march, in camp and in the hospital, where many were discovered after getting sick. Some even wound up in grim prisons kept by both sides, while a few hid pregnancies and were only discovered after giving birth. . . . Solid research by the authors, including a look at the careers of a few women soldiers after the war, makes this a compelling book that belongs in every Civil War library." Publ Wkly
   Includes bibliographical references (p. {215}-230) and index

Blight, David W.

American oracle. Belknap Press of Harvard University Press 2011 314p $27.95   **973.7**
   1. African Americans -- Civil rights -- History -- 20th century 2. Authors 3. Civil rights movements -- United States -- History -- 20th century 4. Dramatists 5. Essayists 6. Historians 7. Historical literature 8. Journalists 9. Literary critics 10. Magazine editors 11. Nonfiction 12. Novelists 13. Poets 14. Poets laureate 15. Screenwriters 16. Short story writers 17. United States -- History -- Civil War, 1861-1865 -- Centennial celebrations, etc. 18. Writers on politics 19. Young

adult authors
ISBN 978-0-674-04855-3

LC 2011006653

This book examines how we handled the centennial [of the U.S. Civil War,] which occurred at the infancy of the civil rights movement, and the persistent questioning about all the elements that were at the heart of the nation-rending civil conflict. "History and great literature blend together . . . as Blight conducts his examination of the works of four writers -- Robert Penn Warren, southern-born novelist; Bruce Catton, historian and journalist; Edmund Wilson, literary critic; and James Baldwin, northern-born essayist and race critic -- providing background and context for their works and their views of the centennial and all its commercialism and hypocrisy." (Booklist)

Includes bibliographical references

Blount, Roy

★ **Robert** E. Lee; a Penguin life. [by] Roy Blount, Jr. Lipper/Viking Bk. 2003 210p $19.95; pa $13 **973.7**
1. College presidents 2. Generals 3. Generals -- Confederate States of America -- Biography
ISBN 0-670-03220-4; 0-14-303866-4 pa

LC 2002-32423

This is a biography of "the famous Southern general admired for his military leadership but also scorned for defending the Confederacy. Blount's concise writing keeps his biography trim and succinct, and his admiration for the subject allows for enjoyable reading." Booklist

Includes bibliographical references

Boatner, Mark Mayo

The **Civil** War dictionary; by Mark Mayo Boatner III; maps and diagrams by Allen C. Northrop and Lowell I. Miller. 1st Vintage Civil War Library ed.; Vintage Civil War Library 1991 974p il map pa $24 **973.7**
1. Reference books
ISBN 0-679-73392-2; 978-0-679-73392-8

LC 91-50013

"With more than 4,000 entries . . . this dictionary remains the most comprehensive and consistently accurate reference tool on the American Civil War. In addition to the biographical sketches there are entries relating to campaigns and battles, naval engagements, weapons, issues and incidents, military terms and definitions, politics, literature, and statistics." Choice

Includes bibliographical references

Bordewich, Fergus M.

★ **Bound** for Canaan; the epic story of the underground railroad, America's first integrated civil rights movement. Fergus M. Bordewich. Amistad 2005 540p il map $27.95; pa $14.95 **973.7**
1. Slavery -- United States 2. Underground railroad
ISBN 0-06-052430-8; 0-06-052431-6 pa

LC 2004-52082

"The men and women of this remarkable account will remain with readers for a long time to come." Publ Wkly

Includes bibliographical references

Boritt, G. S.

The **Gettysburg** gospel; the Lincoln speech that nobody knows. Simon & Schuster 2006 415p il $28 **973.7**
1. Lawyers 2. Members of Congress 3. Presidents 4. State legislators
ISBN 978-0-7432-8820-0; 0-7432-8820-3

LC 2006-50578

"The author sets the speech in its contemporary context and, most interestingly, demonstrates that it was not only minimally noticed by Lincoln's peers and the press at the time but was virtually forgotten to history until the 20th century. He addresses many of the myths surrounding the address, such as that Lincoln wrote it in haste on the train to Gettysburg. In fact, it went through a number of careful revisions. He includes images of the known copies of the handwritten address, broadsides and programs relating to the dedication ceremony at Gettysburg, selections of photos from the era, and a line-byline analysis of the various drafts of the address. Boritt's narrative style will appeal to lay readers . . . , while his extensive research and insightful conclusions will appeal to scholars." Libr J

Catton, Bruce

A **stillness** at Appomattox. Doubleday 1953 438p maps hardcover o.p. pa $14.95 **973.7**
1. Appomattox Campaign, 1865
ISBN 0-385-04451-8 pa

The author's "approach is judicious, his interpretation unbiased and his coverage comprehensive." N Y Times Book Rev

Includes bibliographical references

Center for the National Archives Experience

Discovering the Civil War; by the National Archives Experience's "Discovering the Civil War" Exhibition Team with a message from David S. Ferriero, Archivist of the United States; foreword by Ken Burns. D. Giles Ltd. 2010 208p il map $44.95 **973.7**
ISBN 978-1-904832-91-1

LC 2010-27924

"Created to accompany the major National Archives Civil War exhibit that mined our national trove of photographs, manuscripts, maps, ephemera, realia, and more, this book is spectacular in its presentation of the wide array of seemingly mundane but surprisingly revealing sources from both the well known and the obscure. . . . The intelligent framing of issues (e.g., government controls, technological and scientific innovation) for each chapter will invite readers to consider many questions about war and society, war making, and the economy of war." Libr J

Includes bibliographical references

Clinton, Catherine

Harriet Tubman: the road to freedom. Little, Brown 2004 272p hardcover o.p. pa $14.95 **973.7**
1. Abolitionists 2. African American women 3. African American women -- Biography 4. Antislavery movements 5. Antislavery movements -- United States -- History -- 19th century 6. Slaves -- United States --

Biography 7. Underground railroad
ISBN 0-316-14492-4; 0-316-15594-2 pa

LC 2003-56185

"Clinton turns sobriquets into meaningful descriptors of a unique person. In her hands, a familiar legend acquires human dimension with no diminution of its majesty and power." Publ Wkly

Includes bibliographical references

Colaiaco, James A.

Frederick Douglass and the Fourth of July. Palgrave Macmillan 2006 247p hardcover o.p. pa $16.95   **973.7**
1. Abolitionists 2. African Americans -- Civil rights -- History 3. Antislavery movements 4. Antislavery movements -- United States 5. Authors 6. Civil rights -- Constitutional history 7. Constitutional history -- United States 8. Fourth of July orations 9. Memoirists 10. Political rhetoric 11. Slavery -- History 12. Slavery -- United States 13. Slaves
ISBN 1-4039-7033-5; 1-4039-8072-1 pa

LC 2005-51520

"Colaiaco's careful study recaptures Douglass' reputation as one of America's greatest orators." Booklist

Includes bibliographical references

Cooper, William J.

Jefferson Davis, American. Knopf 2000 757p il maps $35; pa $18   **973.7**
1. Political leaders 2. Presidents -- Confederate States of America -- Biography 3. Secretaries of war 4. Senators 5. Statesmen
ISBN 0-394-56916-4; 0-375-72542-3 pa

LC 00-62006

In this biography of the president of the Confederacy, the author traces Davis' political career and personal life, including his days at West Point, as Secretary of War in the Mexican War, and as U.S. senator from Mississippi.

"In the already cluttered field of Civil War history, Cooper's is the definitive biography; readers will be particularly pleased to discover the compelling power of his narrative." Publ Wkly

Includes bibliographical references

Craughwell, Thomas J.

Stealing Lincoln's body. Belknap Press of Harvard University Press 2007 250p il $24.95   **973.7**
1. Counterfeits and counterfeiting 2. Grave robbing 3. Lawyers 4. Members of Congress 5. Presidents 6. State legislators
ISBN 978-0-674-02458-8; 0-674-02458-3

LC 2006-50842

"Summoning the raw spirit of crime novels and horror stories, as well as the forensic detail of a coroner's inquest, Thomas J. Craughwell has turned the eerie final chapter of the Lincoln story into a guilty pleasure." Washington Post Book World

Includes bibliographical references

Daniel, Larry J.

Shiloh; the battle that changed the Civil War. Simon & Schuster 1997 430p il map hardcover o.p. pa $14   **973.7**
1. Shiloh (Tenn.), Battle of, 1862
ISBN 0-684-83857-5 pa

LC 96-51539

The author "has crafted a superbly researched volume that will appeal to both the beginning Civil War reader as well as those already familiar with the course of fighting in the wooded terrain bordering the Tennessee River." Publ Wkly

Includes bibliographical references

Davis, Burke

Sherman's march. Random House 1980 335p il maps hardcover o.p. pa $14   **973.7**
1. Bentonville (N.C.), Battle of, 1865 2. Generals 3. Memoirists 4. Secretaries of war
ISBN 0-394-75763-7 pa

LC 79-5550

The author "reconstructs Sherman's infamous, but vastly consequential march through Georgia and the Carolinas, which sent the Confederacy into its death throes. Basing his narrative on eyewitness accounts, Davis brings the event down to a personal level." Booklist

Includes bibliographical references

To Appomattox; nine April days, 1865. Burford Books 2002 433p map pa $18.95   **973.7**
1. Appomattox Campaign, 1865
ISBN 1-580-80097-1; 978-1-580-80097-6

LC 2001-56744

"The story of the last nine days of the Civil War from the march on Richmond to the surrender at Appomattox. Quotations from diaries, letters, newspapers and military reports create a sense of immediacy as the reader follows each day's events in the city, in the Confederate camp, and with the Union Army." Publ Wkly

Includes bibliographical references

Davis, William C.

An honorable defeat; the last days of the Confederate government. Harcourt 2001 496p il maps $30; pa $16   **973.7**
1. Generals 2. Political leaders 3. Presidential candidates 4. Secretaries of war 5. Senators 6. Statesmen 7. Vice-presidents
ISBN 0-15-100564-8; 0-15-600748-7 pa

LC 00-46143

Davis "knows his two principal players well, and a marvelous supporting cast of politicians and soldiers helps him to fashion a story rich in pathos and humor." N Y Times Book Rev

Includes bibliographical references

Detzer, David

Allegiance; Fort Sumter, Charleston, and the beginning of the Civil War. Harcourt 2001 367p $27 **973.7**
 1. Charleston (S.C.) -- History
 ISBN 0-15-100641-5
LC 00-50570

"The central figure in this drama is Maj. Robert Anderson, commander of the Union garrison in Charleston Harbor. . . . Detzer's writing style brings the reader into close contact with soldiers, civilians and politicians as they struggle to solve the fate of Anderson and his men." Publ Wkly
 Includes bibliographical references

Egerton, Douglas R.

Year of meteors; Stephen Douglas, Abraham Lincoln, and the election that brought on the Civil War. Bloomsbury Press 2010 399p il $29 **973.7**
 1. Presidents -- United States -- Election -- 1860
 ISBN 978-1-59691-619-7
LC 2010-4965

The author "examines the importance of race in the presidential election of 1860, when a relatively unknown candidate came from behind to be elected to the nation's highest office. Following the fortunes of Democrat Stephen Douglas, Republican Abraham Lincoln, and a host of others significant to the election, Egerton highlights the central role played by race in the dynamics of political party, sectionalism, and politics generally in the election after which the nation was plunged into Civil War. . . . Heavily documented, relying on substantial primary and manuscript sources, this book sheds new light on an often researched topic. All those with an interest in the importance of race in the nation's history will want to acquire this highly readable work." Libr J
 Includes bibliographical references and index.

Eicher, David J.

The longest night; a military history of the Civil War. foreword by James M. McPherson; maps by Lee Vande Visse. Simon & Schuster 2001 990p maps $40; pa $22 **973.7**
 ISBN 0-684-84944-5; 0-684-84945-3 pa
LC 2001-34153

An account of battles and military strategies in the Civil War.

"Civil War buffs and military history scholars will find Eicher's superb analyses and original insights into oft-neglected theaters of operations extremely valuable. An important work that will be an essential component of Civil War collections." Booklist
 Includes bibliographical references (p. {897}-938) and index

Faust, Drew Gilpin

Mothers of invention; women of the slaveholding South in the American Civil War. University of N.C. Press 1996 326p il $37.50; pa $19.95 **973.7**
 1. United States -- History -- 1861-1865, Civil War -- Women 2. White women 3. Women -- Southern States
 ISBN 0-8078-2255-8; 0-8078-5573-1 pa
LC 95-8896

Based on journals, letters and memoirs, this is an "analysis of the impact of secession, invasion and conquest on Southern white women. Antebellum images based on helplessness and dependence were challenged as women assumed an increasing range of social and economic responsibilities. . . . Faust's provocative analysis of a complex subject merits a place in all collections of U.S. history." Publ Wkly
 Includes bibliographical references

This republic of suffering; death and the American Civil War. Alfred A. Knopf 2008 346p il $27.95 **973.7**
 1. Burial -- History 2. Death 3. Death -- Social aspects -- United States
 ISBN 978-0-375-40404-7; 0-375-40404-X
LC 2007-14658

The author "surveys the many ways the Civil War generation coped with the trauma: the concept of the Good Death—conscious, composed and at peace with God; the rise of the embalming industry; the sad attempts of the bereaved to get confirmation of a soldier's death, sometimes years after war's end; the swelling national movement to recover soldiers' remains and give them decent burials; the intellectual quest to find meaning—or its absence—in the war's carnage. . . . The result is an insightful, often moving portrait of a people torn by grief." Publ Wkly
 Includes bibliographical references

Fellman, Michael

The making of Robert E. Lee. Johns Hopkins Univ. Press 2003 360p il pa $19.95 **973.7**
 1. College presidents 2. Generals
 ISBN 0-8018-7411-4
LC 2002-43290

"Struggling to subdue his ambitions and passions in a peacetime military career whose monotony was only momentarily breached by the Mexican American War and at Harpers Ferry, Lee found in the Civil War a chance to express himself fully. In a study rich with discussions of Lee's religious beliefs and political opinions, the author skewers previous efforts to detach Lee from slavery, racism, and the mentality of the Lost Cause. Sure to arouse debate, this book challenges and delights." Libr J
 Includes bibliographical references

Ferguson, Andrew

Land of Lincoln; adventures in Abe's America. Atlantic Monthly Press 2007 279p il $24 **973.7**
 1. Lawyers 2. Members of Congress 3. Presidents 4. Public opinion -- United States 5. State legislators
 ISBN 978-0-871-13967-2; 0-871-13967-7
LC 2006-52634

An "offbeat tour of Lincoln shrines, statues, cabins and museums. The 16th president comes in many forms, and every one, it seems, has a following, right down to Lincoln the chief executive officer, dispenser of corporate leadership tips. . . . Along with the silly statues, the bogus exhibits and Abe's get-rich-quick tips, Mr. Ferguson includes some genuinely touching, if strange, examples of Lincoln love. . . . The Land of Lincoln turns out to be a big place: bigger than Illinois, bigger even than the United States, stranger than anyone would have thought. Mr. Ferguson maps it expertly, with an understated Midwestern sense of humor that Lincoln, master of the funny story, would have been the first to appreciate." N Y Times (Late N Y Ed)

Foner, Eric

The **fiery** trial; Abraham Lincoln and American slavery. W.W. Norton 2010 426p il map $29.95   **973.7**

1. Biography, Individual 2. Lawyers 3. Members of Congress 4. Presidents 5. Slavery -- United States 6. Slaves -- Emancipation -- United States 7. State legislators

ISBN 978-0-393-06618-0; 0-393-06618-5

LC 2010-23425

The book presents "a sustained argument for [U.S. President Abraham] Lincoln's growth into greatness." (London Review of Books) It presents the "history of Lincoln and the end of slavery in America" with a particular focus on "his capacity for moral and political growth through real engagement with allies and critics alike . . . Although 'naturally anti-slavery' . . . Lincoln . . . holds to the position that the Constitution protects the institution in the original slave states. But the political landscape is transformed in 1854 when the Kansas-Nebraska Act makes the expansion of slavery a national issue. . . . Lincoln navigates the dynamic politics . . . taking measured steps, often along a path forged by abolitionists and radicals in his party . . . As president of a divided nation and commander in chief at war . . . Lincoln finally embraces what he calls the Civil War's 'fundamental and astounding' result: the immediate, uncompensated abolition of slavery and recognition of blacks as American citizens." (books.wwnorton.com)

The author "explores the evolution—from frontier lawyer to Great Emancipator—of Lincoln's thought about and response to slavery. The book . . . showcases Foner's engaging style and insight, while keeping a tight focus on Lincoln in his own historical context. [This work] explains how a man who was more skilled politician than reformer came to issue one of the most sweeping, consequential edicts in American history." Am Scholar

Includes bibliographical references

Foote, Shelby

The **Civil** War; a narrative. Random House 1958 3v maps set $165; pa $75   **973.7**

1. United States -- History -- 1861-1865, Civil War

ISBN 0-394-49517-9; 0-394

"In objectivity, in range, in mastery of detail, in beauty of language and feeling for the people involved, this work surpasses anything else on the subject." New Repub

Includes bibliographical references

Ford, Lacy K.

Deliver us from evil; the slavery question in the old South. Oxford University Press 2009 673p $34.95   **973.7**

1. Slavery -- United States 2. Slavery -- United States -- History

ISBN 978-0-19-511809-4; 0-19-511809-X

LC 2008-47533

This book provides "an intricate, textured argument about the intellectual, social, and political interests shaping

'the slavery question,' as well as a reminder that Southern white commitment to a hardened proslavery position was not preordained or one-dimensional. Essential for all students of this subject." Libr J

Includes bibliographical references

Foreman, Amanda

A **world** on fire; Britain's crucial role in the American Civil War. Random House 2011 958p il map $35   **973.7**

1. Great Britain -- Foreign relations -- United States 2. United States -- History -- 1861-1865, Civil War -- Foreign public opinion, British 3. United States -- History -- 1861-1865, Civil War 4. United States -- History -- 1861-1865, Civil War -- Participation, British

ISBN 978-0-375-50494-5; 0-375-50494-X

"Ranging from the drawing rooms of Washington and London to the battlefields of Gettysburg and Antietam, to the high seas, and to Confederate and Union home fronts, Foreman has written a diplomatic, military, and social kaleidoscope of the Civil War. She superbly conveys the horror, pathos, and chaos of battle, the political and moral ambiguities, and the devotion of those who fought. She has also restored an international dimension missing from many histories. The fall of Fort Sumter in April 1861 set off a furious diplomatic contest between North and South for the favors of Great Britain, then the world's superpower. Britain had a tangle of economic interests in the United States; it was bound to the South by cotton, which kept the British textile industry spinning, and British investors held millions in stocks and securities." Boston Globe

Fredrickson, George M.

Big enough to be inconsistent; Abraham Lincoln confronts slavery and race. Harvard University Press 2008 156p $19.95   **973.7**

1. African Americans -- Civil rights 2. African Americans -- Civil rights -- History 3. Federal government 4. Lawyers 5. Members of Congress 6. Presidents 7. Racism -- United States -- History 8. Slavery -- Constitutional history 9. Slavery -- United States 10. Slavery -- United States -- History 11. State legislators 12. States' rights -- History

ISBN 978-0-674-02774-9; 0-674-02774-4

LC 2007-34018

The author "wades into a controversial arena: was Lincoln a heroic emancipator or a racist who didn't care about slaves at all? Stating that in between 'pathological' racism and egalitarianism lies a spectrum of possibilities, Fredrickson says that Lincoln is not easily classified. . . . This brief book will be widely discussed by historians and will provide nonacademic readers a lucid introduction to some of the most heated debates about the 16th president." Publ Wkly

Includes bibliographical references

Fredriksen, John C.

Civil War almanac. Facts on File, Inc. 2007 858p il map $85   **973.7**

1. United States -- History -- 1861-1865, Civil War

ISBN 0-8160-6459-8; 978-0-8160-6459-5

LC 2006-29985

This book contains a "day-by-day chronology of the events and people of this monumental war, along with an A-to-Z dictionary offering biographical information on leading military and political figures involved in the conflict." Publisher's note

Includes bibliographical references

Freeman, Douglas Southall

Lee; an abridgment in one volume, by Richard Harwell, of the four-volume R. E. Lee. with a new foreword by James M. McPherson. Scribner 1991 xxiii, 601p il maps hardcover o.p. pa $18   **973.7**
1. College presidents 2. Generals
ISBN 0-684-82953-3 pa

LC 91-20088

"Students of history will continue to want and to use the original four-volume work but most general readers will find this abridgment more convenient and adequate to their interest. All footnotes and all of the appendix have been omitted as well as details of Civil War action that are not necessary to show the main course of Lee's life and action." Booklist

Furgurson, Ernest B.

Chancellorsville, 1863; the souls of the brave. Knopf 1992 405p il maps hardcover o.p. pa $16   **973.7**
1. Chancellorsville (Va.), Battle of, 1863
ISBN 0-679-72831-7 pa

LC 91-47059

"Mr. Furgurson has written what should become the standard account of the battle. He is especially good at discussing both larger tactical issues and the experiences of ordinary soldiers. He is also evenhanded." N Y Times Book Rev

Includes bibliographical references

Freedom rising; Washington in the Civil War. Knopf 2004 463p il hardcover o.p. pa $16 **973.7**
1. Lawyers 2. Members of Congress 3. Presidents 4. State legislators
ISBN 0-375-40454-6; 0-375-70409-4 pa

LC 2004-40820

"Furgurson paints a compelling portrait of a dynamic, rapidly evolving city on edge. . . . This is a well-written and informative account of a city and its citizens passing through a traumatic national ordeal." Booklist

Includes bibliographical references

Not war but murder; Cold Harbor, 1864. Knopf 2000 328p il maps hardcover o.p. pa $14 **973.7**
1. Cold Harbor (Va.), Battle of, 1864 2. Cold Harbor, Battle of, Va., 1864
ISBN 0-679-78139-0 pa

LC 99-37147

The author's "engagement with the people he writes about comes through in every line, making one of the most wrenching incidents of the war grimly immediate." Publ Wkly

Includes bibliographical references

Gallagher, Gary W.

★ The **Confederate** War. Harvard Univ. Press 1997 218p il hardcover o.p.   **973.7**
1. Confederate States of America 2. United States -- History -- 1861-1865, Civil War
978-0-674-16056-9

LC 97-2495

This book "is the best thing that has happened to Confederate historiography in many years. Gallagher has a more thorough command of the sources for Confederate history than any other historian I have read and he brings that mastery to bear in a concise, hard-hitting book." NY Rev Books

Includes bibliographical references

The **union** war. Harvard University Press 2011 215p il $27.95   **973.7**
1. Historical literature 2. Liberty 3. Lincoln, Abraham, 1809-1865 4. Popular culture -- United States -- History -- 19th century 5. United States -- History -- Civil War, 1861-1865 -- Causes 6. United States -- History -- Research
ISBN 978-0-674-04562-0; 0-674-04562-9

LC 2010-51977

In this book, Gary Gallagher argues . . . that Northerners, ranging from President Lincoln all the way down to the conscripts in the Army of the Potomac, didn't fight the Civil War to free the slaves or to topple white supremacy in the South. Instead, they fought for the Union, an admittedly diffuse concept, Gallagher admits, but nevertheless their central animating principle. This point, he claims, "has been almost completely effaced from popular understanding of the conflict." And because of a relentless 'focus on emancipation and race,' he fears that in collective memory and scholarship alike, the war now has scant meaning apart from these issues -- and especially that the Union victory has little or no value without emancipation." (TLS)

"Brimming with insights, eloquent in argument, and filled with new evidence from the men who fought for the Union, this revisionist history will cause readers to rethink many of the now-standard Civil War interpretations. An essential work." Libr J

Includes bibliographical references

Gienapp, William E.

Abraham Lincoln and Civil War America; a biography. Oxford Univ. Press 2001 239p il maps hardcover o.p. pa $24.95   **973.7**
1. Lawyers 2. Members of Congress 3. Presidents 4. Presidents -- United States 5. Presidents -- United States -- Biography 6. State legislators
ISBN 0-19-515099-6; 0-19-515100-3 pa

LC 2001-50056

This biography focuses on the American president's leadership during the Civil War.

"In spite of the book's size, its discriminating history of Lincoln's life is surprisingly rich, and the narrative of his presidency and the unfolding of the war is crisp and coherent." Bookmarks

Includes bibliographical references

Goldfield, David R.

★ **America** aflame; how the Civil War created a nation. [by] David Goldfield. Bloomsbury Press 2011 632p il $35   **973.7**

1. United States -- History -- 1861-1865, Civil War - Influence 2. United States -- History -- 1861-1865, Civil War - Causes 3. United States -- History -- 1861-1865, Civil War -- Social aspects 4. United States -- History -- 1861-1865, Civil War - Campaigns

ISBN 978-1-59691-702-6; 1-59691-702-4
LC 2010-25241

"A provocatively written, scrupulously researched, and well-framed consideration of evangelical religion's questionable role in the antebellum, Civil War, and Reconstruction periods of our history." Libr J

Includes bibliographical references

Goodheart, Adam

★ **1861**; the Civil War awakening. 1st ed.; Alfred A. Knopf 2011 481p il $28.95   **973.7**

1. United States -- Politics and government -- 1861-1865 2. United States -- History -- 1861-1865, Civil War - Causes 3. United States -- Intellectual life

ISBN 978-1-4000-4015-5; 1-4000-4015-9
LC 2010-51326

"Goodheart leads us on a journey through the frenzied, frightening months between Abraham Lincoln's election to the presidency in 1860 — followed with breakneck speed by the secession of the Confederate States and the outbreak of war — and July 4, 1861, when President Lincoln delivered his first message to Congress, laying out the case not only for the necessity of war, but for a more democratic vision of the United States. The election of Lincoln and the secession crisis is, of course, familiar terrain. But Goodheart's version is at once more panoramic and more intimate than most standard accounts, and more inspiring. This is fundamentally a history of hearts and minds, rather than of legislative bills and battles." N Y Times Book Rev

Gopnik, Adam

Angels and ages; a short book about Darwin, Lincoln, and modern life. Alfred A. Knopf 2009 211p $24.95   **973.7**

1. Civilization, Modern 2. Lawyers 3. Members of Congress 4. Modern civilization 5. Naturalists 6. Presidents 7. State legislators 8. Travel writers 9. Writers on science

ISBN 978-0-307-27078-8; 0-307-27078-5
LC 2008-36224

"The book is worth reading . . . for the author's unquestioned skill as a craftsman and the light he sheds on what has become, for many, settled history." Bookmarks

Groom, Winston

Shiloh, 1862; the first great and terrible battle of the civil war. Winston Groom. National Geographic Books 2012 446 p.   **973.7**

1. Shiloh, Battle of, Tenn., 1862

ISBN 9781426208744
LC 2012372339

This book presents Shiloh, fought on April 6-7 in western Tennessee, as a turning point in the [U.S. Civil War].

(Kirkus) [Winston] Groom . . . compels the reader to appreciate the enormous toll to both sides owing to advanced arms, outmoded battle tactics, and poor generalship. Although Groom lays responsibility on both sides, he especially blames General [Ulysses] Grant and General [William] Sherman . . . for failure to fortify positions, properly reconnoiter, read the signs of enemy advances, and have a battle plan in case of attack. . . . Groom sees Shiloh as a learning experience for Grant, who finally understood that no single battle, no matter how costly or geographically significant, could end the rebellion: the Union could be restored only through the total conquest of the South. (Libr J)

Vicksburg, 1863. Alfred A. Knopf 2009 482p il $30   **973.7**

1. Generals 2. Presidents

ISBN 978-0-307-26425-1
LC 2008-45984

"Rarely has the story of such a lengthy and complicated campaign been told with such clarity and grace." Washington Post

Includes bibliographical references

Harper, Judith E.

Women during the Civil War; an encyclopedia. Routledge 2003 472p il map $170; pa $59.95 **973.7**

1. Reference books

ISBN 0-415-93723-X; 0-415-95574-2 pa
LC 2003-7181

"The 128 entries range in length from 400 to 4000 words, and include biographies of women from all regions of the U.S. Well-known figures such as Harriet Tubman, Clara Barton, Louisa May Alcott, and Mary Todd Lincoln are represented but so too are African-American sculptor Edmonia Lewis, poet Lucy Larcom, and Emma LeConte. . . . As well as biographies, there are superb thematic entries on women living in the West, prostitutes, industrial workers, family life, and invasion and occupation. . . . This encyclopedia is a welcomed addition to reference collections." SLJ

Includes bibliographical references

Horwitz, Tony

Confederates in the attic; dispatches from the unfinished Civil War. Pantheon Bks. 1998 406p map hardcover o.p. pa $14.95   **973.7**

ISBN 0-679-75833-X pa
LC 97-26759

This "is the work of a skilled journalist looking at how— and why—the War Between the States continues to live in so many issues still with us." Libr J

Howard, David

Lost rights; the misadventures of a stolen American relic. Houghton Mifflin Harcourt 2009 344p $26   **973.7**

1. Manuscripts 2. Theft

ISBN 978-0-618-82607-0; 0-618-82607-6
LC 2009-18046

"The tale pulsates with dynamic personalities greatly affected by their connection to one of the rarest, most influential and valuable documents in American history. Howard has produced a marvelously compelling read." Publ Wkly

Includes bibliographical references

Hyslop, Stephen G.

Atlas of the Civil War; a comprehensive guide to the tactics and terrain of battle. edited by Neil Kagan; narrative by Stephen G. Hyslop; introduction by Harris J. Andrews. National Geographic Society 2009 255p il map $40 **973.7**

1. Historical atlases 2. Reference books
ISBN 978-1-4262-0347-3

LC 2008-35066

"Arranged chronologically, this atlas combines period photographs and illustrations, rare period maps and modern cartography, with just enough narrative to explain the two-page spread devoted to each subject (the majority being about particular battles or campaigns). . . . The text also features numerous sidebars throughout, offering micro-timelines, biographies, and images showing the human side of the war. All of these special features make this large-format atlas a superior choice for Civil War buffs as well as those new to the subject." Libr J

Keegan, John

The **American** Civil War; a military history. Alfred A. Knopf 2009 396p il map $35 **973.7**

1. Military geography -- United States
ISBN 978-0-307-26343-8; 0-307-26343-6

LC 2009-19469

The author "provides the single best one-volume assessment of the military character and conduct of America's ordeal by fire." Libr J

Includes bibliographical references

Klein, Maury

Days of defiance; Sumter, secession, and the coming of the Civil War. Knopf 1997 496p il hardcover o.p. pa $16 **973.7**

ISBN 0-679-76882-3 pa

LC 96-39156

"With a novelist's skill, Klein has crafted an engrossing portrait of the nation's descent into chaos and war." Publ Wkly

Includes bibliographical references

Leonard, Elizabeth D.

All the daring of the soldier; women of the Civil War armies. Norton 1999 368p il hardcover o.p. pa $22.95 **973.7**

1. Women soldiers 2. Women soldiers -- United States -- History -- 19th century 3. Women spies -- United States -- History -- 19th century
ISBN 978-0-393-04712-7; 0-393-04712-1; 978-0-393-33547-7 pa; 0-393-33547-X pa

LC 98-52304

The author presents "stories of dozens of women who served in both the Union and Confederacy during the Civil War. Some were spies, but many more adopted men's names, dressed in men's clothes and lived and fought and died alongside mostly unsuspecting men." Publ Wkly

Includes bibliographical references

Lincoln, Abraham

★ **Speeches** and writings, 1859-1865; speeches, letters, and miscellaneous writings, presidential messages and proclamations. Library of Am. 1989 xxxiii, 787p $35 **973.7**

1. United States -- Politics and government -- 1861-1865, Civil War
ISBN 0-940450-63-1

LC 89-45349

This volume is based upon The Collected Works of Abraham Lincoln. It includes public statements, business letters, "poems, personal letters, telegrams to generals in the field, and other [writings]." Libr J

Includes bibliographical references

Marten, James

Civil War America; voices from the home front. ABC-CLIO 2003 346p il $85 **973.7**

1. United States -- History -- 1861-1865, Civil War -- Personal narratives
ISBN 1-576-07237-1

LC 2002-154377

"Marten offers a view of the war through the eyes of diverse noncombatants. Four parts of this five-part work each deal with Southerners, Northerners, children, and African Americans . . . Part five, 'Aftermaths,' includes descriptions of the postwar lives of veterans, orphans, and ex-slaves, and concludes with a chapter on the Civil War stories by Ambrose Bierce. Readers will find Marten's overarching theme of change—both immediate and long-range—revelatory and instructional." SLJ

Includes bibliographical references

Masur, Louis P.

The **Civil** War: a concise history. Oxford University Press 2011 118p il $18.95 **973.7**

ISBN 978-0-19-974048-2

LC 2010-19460

The author provides "a concise but compelling narrative of the Civil War era, packing in the critical information to track the trajectory of secession, war, emancipation, and Reconstruction. He focuses on the political and the military, with Lincoln, Jefferson Davis, and the generals especially getting their due." Libr J

Includes bibliographical references

McPherson, James M.

Abraham Lincoln and the second American Revolution. Oxford Univ. Press 1991 173p hardcover o.p. pa $16.95 **973.7**

1. Lawyers 2. Members of Congress 3. Presidents 4. State legislators
ISBN 0-19-507606-0 pa

LC 90-6885

The author "examines Lincoln's role in the transformation wrought by the Civil War—the liberation of four million slaves, the overthrow of the social and political order of the South." Publ Wkly

Includes bibliographical references

Battle cry of freedom; the Civil War era. Oxford Univ. Press 1988 904p il maps $47.50; pa $18.95   **973.7**

ISBN 0-19-503863-0; 0-19-516895-X pa

LC 87-11045

A narrative history of events from the Mexican War through Appomattox. The author describes military campaigns, tactics and leaders. How the war changed the American political, social and economic landscape is explored.

This volume "is comprehensive yet succinct, scholarly without being pedantic, eloquent but unrhetorical. It is compellingly readable." N Y Times Book Rev

Includes bibliographical references

★ **Drawn** with the sword; reflections on the American Civil War. Oxford Univ. Press 1996 258p $45; pa $18.95   **973.7**

1. Abolitionists 2. Authors 3. Children's authors 4. Generals 5. Lawyers 6. Members of Congress 7. Nonfiction writers 8. Novelists 9. Orators 10. Presidents 11. Secretaries of state 12. Secretaries of war 13. Short story writers 14. State legislators 15. Statesmen 16. Vice-presidents

ISBN 0-19-509679-7; 0-19-511796-4 pa

LC 95-38107

"These pieces provide a lively reminder that the best scholarship is also often a pleasure to read." N Y Times Book Rev

For cause and comrades; why men fought in the Civil War. Oxford Univ. Press 1997 237p $25; pa $15.95   **973.7**

1. Soldiers -- United States

ISBN 0-19-509023-3; 0-19-512499-5 pa

LC 96-24760

"Volumes have been written on the causes of the Civil War, but less has been written on what caused soldiers to risk their lives on the battlefield. McPherson . . . fills the gap. After studying thousands of letters and diaries, he discusses what really led soldiers to enlist, what kept them in the army, and what led them to the front lines." Libr J

Includes bibliographical references

Hallowed ground; a walk at Gettysburg. Crown Publishers 2003 144p map $16   **973.7**

1. Gettysburg (Pa.), Battle of, 1863 2. Gettysburg, Battle of, Gettysburg, Pa., 1863 3. Walking -- Pennsylvania -- Gettysburg National Military Park -- Guidebooks

ISBN 0-609-61023-6

LC 2002-35154

"If it were only a pointer to the physical ground and commemorative markers, this guide would be ordinary, but McPherson so articulately injects reminders—as of a free black farmer who fled the approaching battle lest Confederates enslave him—of what the Civil War was about as to

display the crystalline style that has made him one of our finest Civil War historians." Booklist

★ **This** mighty scourge; perspectives on the Civil War. Oxford University Press 2007 260p $28 **973.7**

1. Lawyers 2. Members of Congress 3. Presidents 4. State legislators

ISBN 0-19-531366-6

LC 2006-35523

These essays "stand as a remarkably elegant and clarifying narrative exploration of the most basic questions concerning the Civil War, issues over which scholars and activists still contend. . . 'This Mighty Scourge,' in fact, is an exemplary exercise in the contribution a great historian and eloquent writer can make to a people's understanding of themselves." Los Angeles Times

Nolan, Alan T.

Lee considered; General Robert E. Lee and Civil War history. University of N.C. Press 1991 231p il $29.95; pa $16.95   **973.7**

1. College presidents 2. Generals 3. United States -- History -- 1861-1865, Civil War

ISBN 0-8078-1956-5; 0-8078-4587-6 pa

LC 90-48296

"Nolan uses sources cleverly to build his case and adroitly pits this new 'truth' against the words of Lee's historically staunchest promoters." Booklist

Includes bibliographical references

Paludan, Phillip S.

The **presidency** of Abraham Lincoln; {by} Phillip Shaw Paludan. University Press of Kan. 1994 xx, 384p $29.95; pa $15.95   **973.7**

1. Lawyers 2. Members of Congress 3. Presidents 4. State legislators 5. United States -- Politics and government -- 1861-1865, Civil War

ISBN 0-7006-0671-8; 0-7006-0745-5 pa

LC 93-46830

The author "traces the year-by-year chronology of a Presidency engaged with recruiting, placating, appeasing and coercing the various and competing factions of the war years, and sees in Lincoln 'a commitment to the political-constitutional system that would itself move the nation toward its highest ambitions.' . . . Equally interesting is Mr. Paludan's depiction of how the war transformed the national Government, not only establishing the foundations for the Gilded Age but more subtly strengthening and enriching the role of government." NY Times Book Rev

Includes bibliographical references

Perry, James M.

Touched with fire; five presidents and the Civil War battles that made them. PublicAffairs 2003 335p il map $26; pa $16   **973.7**

1. Generals 2. Governors 3. Members of Congress 4. Presidents 5. Presidents -- United States 6. Presidents -- United States -- Biography 7. Presidents -- United States -- History 8. Senators 9. Soldiers -- United States -- Biography

ISBN 1-586-48114-2; 1-586-48290-4 pa

LC 2003-46625

"All chief executives during the Gilded Age volunteered for the Union in the Civil War (excluding Grover Cleveland, who paid for a substitute). Perry here recounts their war records with an eye to the subsequent electoral advertising of their bravery and patriotism. . . . Perry, a wry storyteller, delivers the regimental-level detail that buffs crave while dusting events with the skepticism that presidential electoral campaigning invites." Booklist
Includes bibliographical references

Pitch, Anthony

They have killed Papa dead! the road to Ford's Theatre, Abraham Lincoln's murder, and the rage for vengeance. Steerforth Press 2008 493p il $29.95   **973.7**
1. Assassins -- United States -- History -- 19th century 2. Lawyers 3. Members of Congress 4. Political culture -- United States -- History -- 19th century 5. Presidents 6. Presidents -- United States -- Assassination 7. Revenge 8. State legislators
ISBN 978-1-5864-2158-8; 1-5864-2158-1
                LC 2008-43222
The author presents "new evidence that Lincoln was under genuine threat as early as the eve of his first inauguration, not just after his second one. The result is a fast-moving telling of the multiple plots on Lincoln's life, the implementation of the successful one, its complex aftermath and the way it threw the nation into deep mourning and despair. . . . A real page-turner about real history." Publ Wkly
Includes bibliographical references

Rable, George C.

God's almost chosen peoples; a religious history of the American Civil War. University of North Carolina Press 2010 586p il $35   **973.7**
1. Civil religion 2. Evangelicalism -- United States -- History 3. Historical literature 4. War -- Religious aspects -- Christianity
ISBN 978-0-8078-3426-8; 0-8078-3426-2
                LC 2010-23646
This book offers a history of the religious aspects of the U.S. Civil War, with archival research and . . . [a] reading that reaches beyond the waras marquee names to exhume the voices and jottings of ministers, diarists, and combatants, who never fail to remark the presence (or absence) of God in the proceedings. Indeed, the stated occasion for [George C.] Rable's study is the notion that most of the war's actors would judge the scant "'attention to religion' in the grand and sweeping narratives of the sectional crisis' to be a curious omission. . . . Rable responds to this curiosity with a religious narrative of the conflict . . . that showcases a war among and between rival interpretations of God s providential guidance." (Journal of Religion)
"Rable draws upon newspapers, sermons, diaries, letters, and journals to show that many people on both sides of the conflict turned to faith to help explain the war's causes, course, and consequences. Rable demonstrates that both Northerners and Southerners tried to make sense of the brutal war by thumbing through their Bibles, listening to their preachers, and interpreting battles as a fulfillment of a divine plan. . . . Because of its thorough research and its chronicle of the lives of ordinary people, Rable's engrossing study of

the role of religion in the Civil War will stand as the definitive religious history of America's most divisive conflict." Publ Wkly
Includes bibliographical references and index

Roper, Robert

Now the drum of war; Walt Whitman and his brothers in the Civil War. Walker & Co. 2008 421p il $28   **973.7**
1. Army officers 2. Authors 3. Biography, Individual 4. Essayists 5. Poets
ISBN 978-0-8027-1553-1; 0-8027-1553-2
This is a "history of the Civil War by means of a family portrait, presenting the war through the eyes and words of the Whitman family. . . . The book provides a simultaneous historical perspective on the war and on an exceptional family, giving general readers and students a vivid depiction of both and a deeper understanding of one of America's greatest poets." Libr J
Includes bibliographical references and index

Sears, Stephen W.

★ **Chancellorsville**. Houghton Mifflin 1996 593p hardcover o.p. pa $17   **973.7**
1. Chancellorsville (Va.), Battle of, 1863 2. Generals
ISBN 0-395-87744-X pa
                LC 96-31220
In this history of the campaign that ended in Chancellorsville, the author argues that "a chain of errors, assumptions, and communications failures combined with the genuine brilliance and good luck of the Confederates to lead to a stinging if indecisive Union defeat." Booklist
Includes bibliographical references

Gettysburg. Houghton Mifflin 2003 623p il map $30; pa $17   **973.7**
1. Gettysburg (Pa.), Battle of, 1863 2. Gettysburg, Battle of, Gettysburg, Pa., 1863
ISBN 0-395-86761-4; 0-618-48538-4 pa
             LC 2002-191259
This is an "assessment of the battle of Gettysburg and the events leading up to it. . . . Sears examines several turning points during the battle's buildup and three-day duration. The resulting insights add to the excellent and dramatic narrative flow. . . . For all Civil War collections and academic libraries." Libr J
Includes bibliographical references

Landscape turned red; the Battle of Antietam. Houghton Mifflin 2003 431p il pa $17   **973.7**
1. Antietam (Md.), Battle of, 1862
ISBN 978-0-618-34419-2; 0-618-34419-5
This "account of the Battle of Antietam, the bloodiest day of the Civil War, is wide-ranging, detailed, and copiously documented. Stephen Sears . . . describes the tension-filled days preceding September 17, 1862, especially the political

climate of Union pessimism and Confederate optimism. . . . The battle itself is then exhaustively recounted." Booklist

★ **To** the gates of Richmond; the peninsula campaign. Mariner 2001 468p il map pa $17   **973.7**
1. Peninsular Campaign, 1862
ISBN 978-0-618-12713-9; 0-618-12713-5
"The campaign on the peninsula between the James and York rivers in Virginia in the spring of 1862 was McClellan's major strategic effort and the first major Union offensive in the East. . . . Sears does an outstanding job in making intelligible an extremely complex campaign." Booklist
Includes bibliographical references

Slotkin, Richard
No quarter; the Battle of the Crater, 1864. Random House 2009 411p il map $28   **973.7**
1. African American soldiers -- History 2. Petersburg Crater, Battle of, Va., 1864
ISBN 978-1-4000-6675-9; 1-4000-6675-1
LC 2008-36260
"By 1864, the North and South had settled into a positional war around Richmond and Petersburg, VA, with trenches, cannon, disease, and delay. Gen. Grant decided to try a mine, digging under a portion of the fortifications and cramming the tunnel with explosives. It was the largest explosion ever seen at the time—and led to a crushing Union defeat, with 4500 dead. There have been lots of books about the Crater, but the eminent Slotkin does a respectable job. Civil War history enthusiasts will want this." Libr J
Includes bibliographical references

Slotkin, Richard, 1942-
Long Road to Antietam; how the Civil War became a revolution. Richard Slotkin. Liveright Publishing Corporation 2012 512 p. (hardcover) $32.95   **973.7**
1. Antietam, Battle of, Md., 1862
ISBN 0871404117; 9780871404114
LC 2012007795
This book looks at the germination of the U.S. Civil War which became a revolution in summer 1862, when Lincoln acknowledged that peaceful compromise was at that point impossible and thoroughly committed himself to war. First up in this new strategy: the Emancipation Proclamation. As Lincoln clashed with ambitious general George McClellan, the country started on the bloody road to Antietam. (Library Journal)

Snodgrass, Mary Ellen
★ The **Underground** Railroad; an encyclopedia of people, places, and operations. Sharpe Reference 2007 2v il map set $199   **973.7**
1. Reference books 2. Slavery -- United States -- Encyclopedias 3. Underground railroad -- Encyclopedias
ISBN 978-0-7656-8093-8
LC 2007-9199
The author "has compiled an important and extensively researched encyclopedia of the Underground Railroad. Beginning with a concise, informative general introduction, this ambitious two-volume set neatly identifies the key people, places, documents, organizations, and publications

of the Underground Railroad movement, along with significant actions, events, and ideas underlying it in the US and Canada. Offering photographs, bookplates, sketches, and handbills, the set is visually attractive." Choice
Includes bibliographical references

Stout, Harry S.
Upon the altar of the nation: a moral history of the American Civil War. Viking 2006 552p il $29.95   **973.7**
1. Just war doctrine 2. War -- Moral and ethical aspects
ISBN 0-670-03470-3
LC 2005-42420
"Impeccably sourced and highly engaging, the book will surely be controversial—the best histories often are." Booklist
Includes bibliographical references

Swanson, Mark
Atlas of the Civil War, month by month; major battles and troop movements. maps by Mark Swanson, with Jacqueline D. Langley. University of Georgia Press 2004 141p il map $39.95   **973.7**
1. Historical atlases 2. Reference books
ISBN 0-8203-2658-5
LC 2004-12264
This Civil War atlas depicts "multiple aspects of the war's action in a month-by-month sequence from April 1861 to June 1865. . . . An absolute must for Civil War studies." Univ Press Books for Public and Second Sch Libr, 2006
Includes bibliographical references

Thomas, Emory M.
Robert E. Lee; a biography. Norton 1995 472p il maps pa $17.95   **973.7**
1. Biography, Individual 2. College presidents 3. Generals
ISBN 0-393-31631-9 pa
LC 95-10522
"Civil War historian Thomas presents Lee as neither an icon nor a flawed figure, but rather as a man who made the best of his lot, whose comic vision of life ultimately shaped him into an individual who was both more and less than his legend." Publ Wkly
Includes bibliographical references

Tobin, Jacqueline
Hidden in plain view; the secret story of quilts and the underground railroad. [by] Jacqueline L. Tobin and Raymond G. Dobard. Doubleday 1999 208p il map hardcover o.p. pa $14   **973.7**
1. African American quilts -- Social aspects -- History -- 19th century 2. Ciphers 3. Ciphers -- History -- 19th century 4. Fugitive slaves -- United States -- Communication -- History -- 19th century 5. Quilts 6. Underground railroad
ISBN 0-385-49137-9; 0-385-49767-9 pa
LC 98-49804
This is "a needed and valuable contribution to the literature of African American culture." Libr J
Includes bibliographical references

Trudeau, Noah Andre

Like men of war; black troops in the Civil War, 1862-1865. Little, Brown 1998 xxii, 548p il maps hardcover o.p. pa $18   **973.7**

1. African American soldiers

ISBN 0-316-85325-9; 0-316-85344-5 pa

LC 97-15380

A "study of the battlefield experiences of black Union regiments. Some 60 maps help the reader make sense of famous engagements (Fort Wagner and the Crater) and notorious incidents (Fort Pillow) in which black soldiers fought, as well as scores of lesser-known clashes. Rich archival research is integrated into a lively narrative that places the raising and deployment of black regiments in broader contexts. This book will become a basic source of information on the subject." Libr J

Includes bibliographical references

Ward, Andrew

★ The **slaves'** war; the Civil War in the words of former slaves. Houghton Mifflin Co. 2008 386p il $28   **973.7**

1. Freedmen -- United States 2. Slavery -- United States 3. Slaves -- Southern States -- Biography

ISBN 978-0-618-63400-2; 0-618-63400-2

LC 2008-1532

The author "has provided a . . . narrative that gives voice to the experiences and attitudes of slaves who endured the conflict. Ward utilizes testimonials, diaries, and letters, and organizes them in chronological order from the months before the commencement of hostilities to the aftermath of the surrender at Appomattox. . . . This is a work that will interest both scholars and general readers." Booklist

Includes bibliographical references

Ward, Geoffrey C.

The **Civil** War; an illustrated history. {by} Geoffrey C. Ward with Ken Burns and Ric Burns. Knopf 1990 425p il maps $75; pa $29.95   **973.7**

1. United States -- History -- 1861-1865, Civil War

ISBN 0-394-56285-2; 0-679-74277-8 pa

LC 89-43475

"A companion to a nine-part Public Broadcasting System documentary, this superbly designed book easily stands on its own." N Y Times Book Rev

Includes bibliographical references

Wert, Jeffry D.

Mosby's Rangers. Simon & Schuster 1990 384p il hardcover o.p. pa $14   **973.7**

ISBN 0-671-74745-2 pa

LC 90-37917

"Well-researched, objectively written, this is a first-class history." Publ Wkly

Includes bibliographical references

White, Ronald C.

★ **Lincoln's** greatest speech; the second inaugural. {by} Ronald C. White Jr. Simon & Schuster 2002 254p il hardcover o.p. pa $14   **973.7**

1. Lawyers 2. Members of Congress 3. Presidents

4. Presidents -- United States -- Inaugural addresses 5. Speeches, addresses, etc., American -- History and criticism 6. State legislators

ISBN 0-7432-1299-1 pa

LC 2001-54234

"White breaks down the speech phrase by phrase, then integrates it according to its rhetorical framework of past, present, and future. He seeks sources for the speech's ideas in Lincoln's ambiguous stance toward organized religion, in the sermons of preachers he listened to, and in his Bible-reading habit. . . . Must-have Lincolnalia." Booklist

Includes bibliographical references

Wiley, Bell Irvin

The **life** of Billy Yank; the common soldier of the Union. with a foreword by James I. Robertson, Jr. Updated ed.; Louisiana State University Press 2008 454p il pa $21.95   **973.7**

ISBN 978-0-8071-3375-0; 0-8071-3375-2

LC 2008-24243

"The soldiers' own writings—their letters and diaries—are . . . used as chief source for a picture of the response of the Union men to the call to arms, their training, army life, reactions to Southerners they encountered, opinions of Negroes, and comments on their Reb counterparts." Booklist

Includes bibliographical references

The **life** of Johnny Reb; the common soldier of the Confederacy. Updated ed.; Louisiana State University Press 2008 444p il pa $21.95   **973.7**

ISBN 978-0-8071-3325-5

LC 2007-33859

"Composite biography of the ordinary soldier of the Confederacy—his behavior in camp and under fire, his food, clothing, weapons, religion, amusements, attitude toward women, and so on. Taken mostly from firsthand accounts in letters, diaries, and records." New Yorker

Includes bibliographical references

Williams, David

★ **Bitterly** divided; the South's inner Civil War. David Williams. New Press 2008 310p ill., ports. (hbk.) o.p.; (pbk.) $14; (hbk.) o.p.   **973.7**

1. Social classes -- Southern States -- History -- 19th century 2. Social conflict -- Southern States -- History -- 19th century

ISBN 1-59558-108-1; 978-1595584755; 9781595581082

LC 2007045285

In this book, author and historian David Williams lays bare the myth of a united confederacy, revealing that the South was in fact fighting two civil wars—an external one that we know so much about and an internal one about which there is scant literature and virtually no public awareness. . . . [The book] shows that from the Confederacy's very beginnings white Southerners were as likely to have opposed secession as supported it, and they undermined the Confederate war effort at nearly every turn. In just one of many telling examples in . . . narrative history, Williams shows that when planters grew too much cotton and tobacco and exempted themselves from the draft, plain folk called the conflict a "rich man's war" and rioted. Many formed armed anti-Confederate bands. Southern blacks, in what W.E.B. DuBois called "a general strike against the Confederacy," resisted in increasingly overt ways, escaped by the thousands, and forced a change in the war's direction that led to emancipation. (Publisher s note)

"Williams marshals abundant evidence to demonstrate that the Confederacy also lost an internal civil war during 1861-65. . . . This firm repudiation of the myth of the solid Confederate South is absolutely essential Civil War reading." Booklist

Includes bibliographical references (p. [275]-291) and index

Wills, Garry
Lincoln at Gettysburg;   the words that remade America. Simon & Schuster 1992 317p hardcover o.p. pa $14   **973.7**
1. Large print books 2. Lawyers 3. Members of Congress 4. Presidents 5. State legislators
ISBN 0-671-86742-3 pa
                                                    LC 92-3546
This is a "tour de force that will cause much discussion and argument." Libr J
Includes bibliographical references

Woodworth, Steven E.
Atlas of the Civil War; by Steven Woodworth and Kenneth J. Winkle; foreword by James M. McPherson. Oxford University Press 2004 400p il map $75   **973.7**
1. Historical atlases 2. Reference books
ISBN 0-19-522131-1
                                                LC 2004-53112
"Richly illustrated, this publication will be wanted by all types of libraries. . . . The text entries are useful, while the maps and illustrations are both informative and eye-catching." Choice

The Causes of the Civil War; edited by Kenneth M. Stampp. 3rd rev ed; Simon & Schuster 1991 255p pa $14   **973.7**
1. Nationalism 2. Slavery -- United States 3. State rights
ISBN 0-671-75155-7
                                                LC 91-36819
This book integrates the conclusions of various post-war historians with the thoughts of contemporary commentators like Jefferson Davis, Horace Greeley, and Lincoln. Political, cultural and economic aspects are emphasized.

★ The Civil War; the first year told by those who lived it. edited by Brooks D. Simpson, Stephen W. Sears, Aaron Sheehan-Dean. Library of America 2011 xxv, 814p map $37.50   **973.7**
1. United States -- History -- 1861-1865, Civil War -- Personal narratives 2. United States -- History -- 1861-1865, Civil War -- Sources
ISBN 978-1-59853-088-9; 1-59853-088-7
                                                LC 2010-931718
"Drawing on diaries, letters, speeches, newspaper reports and editorials, memoirs, songs, poems, and other sources, the editors bring together a rich variety of voices relating or

remembering the crisis of the Union from Lincoln's election in 1860 through the first year of war. . . . Readable and riveting, this 'you are there' collection makes real the sense of urgency that gripped Americans as the nation came apart and as the war began, 175 years ago. An excellent primer on why the Civil War mattered to those living it." Libr J

Includes bibliographical references

The Civil War: a visual history; [produced in association with the Smithsonian Institution] DK Publishing 2011 360p il map $40   **973.7**
1. United States -- History -- 1861-1865, Civil War -- Pictorial works
ISBN 978-0-7566-7185-3
"Drawing on Smithsonian Institution collections, this fact-filled and richly illustrated history brings the war fully to life, along with time lines, sidebars on particular issues, chapter introductions, lengthy captions, and detailed maps. The emphasis throughout is on the military. Multiple examples of weapons, supplies, uniforms, camp life necessities, transport, and battle scenes dominate and show the variety, complexity, and prolixity of making war. Espionage, the home front, and politics get a nod, but this book is for those wanting to smell the sulfur and hear the thunder of guns." Libr J

★ Encyclopedia of the American Civil War; a political, social, and military history. David S. Heidler and Jeanne T. Heidler, editors; foreword by James W. McPherson; David J. Coles, associate editor; Gary W. Gallagher, James M. McPherson, Mark E. Neely, Jr., editorial board. ABC-CLIO 2000 5v il maps set $425   **973.7**
1. Reference books
ISBN 1-57607-066-2
                                                LC 00-11195
"The editors have compiled a comprehensive source that provides a first-stop reference on broad areas or specific topics on the Civil War. The contemporary photographs and lithographs bring the human element into the encyclopedia, a type of reference known more for facts and figures than emotions. The primary-source-documents volume brings obscure resources together, which will further illumine the period for students." "Outstanding Reference Sources." American Libraries, May 2001

Hearts touched by fire; the best of battles and leaders of the Civil War. edited with an introduction by Harold Holzer; with contributions by James M. McPherson ... [et al.] Modern Library 2011 xxiii, 1230p il map $38   **973.7**
1. United States -- History -- 1861-1865, Civil War -- Personal narratives
ISBN 978-0-679-64364-7
An anthology of excerpts from the four-volume classic "Battles and Leaders of the Civil War" features firsthand recollections by the Civil War's commanders and subordinates on both sides, with commentary by such leading scholars as James McPherson and Joan Waugh.

Lincoln on war; edited and with an introduction by Harold Holzer. Algonquin Books of Chapel Hill 2011 xxvi, 304p il $24.95; ebook $24.95 **973.7**
1. United States -- History -- 1861-1865, Civil War -- Sources
ISBN 978-1-56512-378-6; 978-1-61620-060-2 ebook
LC 2010-44569
"A wisely chosen, expertly arranged collection." Kirkus

973.709 Biography

Stahr, Walter
Seward; Lincoln's indispensable man. by Walter Stahr. Simon & Schuster 2012 720 p. $32.50; (hardcover) $32.50 **973.709**
1. Biographies 2. Cabinet officers -- United States -- Biography 3. Statesmen -- United States -- Biography
ISBN 9781439127940; 1439121168; 9781439121160; 9781439121184
LC 2011052984
This book presents a biography of William Henry Seward, U.S. Secretary of State under President Abraham Lincoln. "Seward was New York governor and senator, then a rival for Lincoln's place on the 1860 presidential ticket, finally senior cabinet officer.... Among other things, he kept Britain out of the Civil War, then negotiated the acquisition of Alaska for the U.S." (Publishers Weekly)

Leaders of the American Civil War; a biographical and historiographical dictionary. edited by Charles F. Ritter and Jon L. Wakelyn. Greenwood Press 1998 xxxiv, 465p $85 **973.709**
1. Reference books
ISBN 0-313-29560-3
LC 98-12156
This dictionary "includes 47 articles on outstanding military and civilian Union and Confederate leaders as well as entries for other significant figures, including Frederick Douglass, Clara Barton, Dorothea Dix, and even Walt Whitman." Libr J
Includes bibliographical references

973.8 Reconstruction period, 1865-1901

Algeo, Matthew
The **president** is a sick man; wherein the supposedly virtuous Grover Cleveland survives a secret surgery at sea and vilifies the courageous newspaperman who dared expose the truth. Chicago Review Press 2011 255p il $24.95 **973.8**
1. District attorneys 2. Governors 3. Journalism 4. Journalists 5. Mayors 6. Presidents
ISBN 978-1-56976-350-6; 1-56976-350-X
LC 2010-44639
"Incredibly, shortly after his second term began in 1893, Cleveland boarded a friend's yacht and sailed into the Long Island Sound where surgeons, in a makeshift operating theater, cut away cancerous tissue in his mouth and part of his jawbone.... Cancer was virtually taboo in Cleveland's day.

He didn't want to lose public confidence or become a spectacle like former President Grant, who had died from cancer. Also, Cleveland was in a contentious political struggle over whether the U.S. should return to the gold standard to back its money (his position), or continue with a policy that also accepted silver, the view of his vice president, Adlai Stevenson. Cleveland feared that should he become incapacitated, Stevenson would assume power and sway the country's financial direction. The yacht's crew and surgeons kept mum, except for a dentist serving as anesthetist, who told a fellow doctor. Word found its way to Philadelphia Press reporter E.J. Edwards, who confirmed enough of the tale to print it. Cleveland's circle squatted on the scoop and undermined the reporter's reputation.... Only decades later would one of the surgeons tell all in an article, and make amends to Edwards for the harm done to him." Milwaukee J Sentinel
Includes bibliographical references

Connell, Evan S.
★ **Son** of the Morning Star. North Point Press 1984 441p il hardcover o.p. pa $18 **973.8**
1. Army officers 2. Generals 3. Little Bighorn, Battle of the, 1876
ISBN 0-86547-160-6; 0-86547-510-5 pa
LC 84-60681
This book is "impressive in its massive presentation of information, and in the conclusions it draws about the probable events that led to the fracas on the banks of the Little Bighorn. But its strength lies in the way the author has shaped his material." N Y Times Book Rev
Includes bibliographical references

Diner, Steven J.
A **very** different age; Americans of the progressive era. Hill & Wang 1997 320p hardcover o.p. pa $14 **973.8**
1. Progressivism (United States politics)
ISBN 0-8090-1611-7 pa
LC 97-3801
The author examines the "social, economic, political, and other changes experienced by Americans during the first two decades of the 20th century.... The writing is succinct and fluid.... This rewarding social history is an excellent book for both experienced historians and novices." Libr J
Includes bibliographical references

Donovan, Jim
A **terrible** glory; Custer and the Little Bighorn-- the last great battle of the American West. [by] James Donovan. Little, Brown and Co. 2008 528p il map $26.99; pa $16.99 **973.8**
1. Army officers 2. Generals 3. Indians of North America -- Government relations 4. Little Bighorn, Battle of the, 1876 5. Little Bighorn, Battle of the, Mont., 1876
ISBN 978-0-316-15578-6; 0-316-15578-0; 978-0-316-06747-8 pa; 0-316-06747-4 pa
LC 2007-26156
The author "collects the multiple threads that led to the 1876 massacre at Little Big Horn.... Exhaustive research, lively prose and fresh interpretation make for a valuable ad-

dition to literature on this otherwise well-trodden historical event." Publ Wkly

Includes bibliographical references (p. [487]-511) and index

Douglass, Frederick

★ **Autobiographies**. Library of Am. 1994 1126p $35; pa $13.95   **973.8**

1. Abolitionists 2. African Americans -- Biography 3. Authors 4. Biography, Individual 5. Memoirists 6. Slaves

ISBN 0-940450-79-8; 1-883011-30-2 pa

LC 93-24168

"This one volume containing Douglass's seminal works is highly recommended for black history collections." Libr J

Includes bibliographical references

My bondage and my freedom; edited with an introduction and notes by John David Smith. Penguin Bks. 2003 lx, 366p pa $12   **973.8**

1. Abolitionists 2. Abolitionists -- United States -- Biography 3. African American abolitionists -- Biography 4. African Americans -- Biography 5. Antislavery movements -- United States -- History -- 19th century 6. Authors 7. Fugitive slaves -- Maryland -- Biography 8. Memoirists 9. Plantation life -- Maryland -- History -- 19th century 10. Slaves 11. Slaves -- Maryland -- Social conditions -- 19th century

ISBN 0-14-043918-8

LC 2002-28992

In this autobiography Douglass tells of his life as a slave and his early years in the abolitionist movement.

Foner, Eric

Forever free; the story of emancipation and Reconstruction. illustrations edited and with commentary by Joshua Brown. Knopf 2005 xxx, 268p il $27.50; pa $15   **973.8**

1. Reconstruction (1865-1876) 2. Slavery -- United States

ISBN 0-375-40259-4; 978-0-375-40259-3; 0-375-70274-1 pa; 978-0-375-70274-7 pa

LC 2005-40706

This "is an invaluable and timely book about a subject central to U.S. history and still of obvious significance today—slavery, the Civil War, emancipation, Reconstruction, and both the immediate aftermath and longer-term consequences of those things." Rev Am Hist

Includes bibliographical references

★ **Reconstruction**; America's unfinished revolution, 1863-1877. HarperCollins Pubs. 1988 xxvii, 690p il maps hardcover o.p. pa $23.95   **973.8**

1. Reconstruction (1865-1876)

ISBN 0-06-093716-5 pa

LC 87-45615

"Incorporating much eyewitness material, this book emphasizes the centrality of the Black experience. The book also examines the themes of race and class, the remodeling of Southern society, and the national context. A complete,

modern, scholarly text." N Y Public Libr Book of How & Where to Look It Up

Includes bibliographical references

Franklin, John Hope

Reconstruction after the Civil War; 2nd ed; University of Chicago Press 1994 265p hardcover o.p. pa $16   **973.8**

1. Reconstruction (1865-1876)

ISBN 0-226-26079-8 pa

LC 94-27366

This is an "account of American life in a time of great challenge, unfamiliar problems, and uncertain leadership. Discusses the Radicals' effort to secure racial justice in the South, the fact that corruption existed not only in the South, and that some worthwhile measures emerged from 'carpetbag' legislatures." Guide to Read in Am Hist {review of 1961 edition}

Includes bibliographical references

Graff, Henry F.

Grover Cleveland. Times Bks. 2002 154p il $20   **973.8**

1. District attorneys 2. Governors 3. Mayors 4. Presidents 5. Presidents -- United States 6. Presidents -- United States -- Biography

ISBN 0-8050-6923-2

LC 2002-20315

A biography of the only American president to serve two nonconsecutive terms.

This "volume is a valuable addition to the literature on the Presidency and is a compelling argument for taking Cleveland seriously as a President." Libr J

Includes bibliographical references

Grant, Ulysses S.

★ **Memoirs** and selected letters; personal memoirs of U.S. Grant, selected letters, 1839-1865. Library of Am. 1990 2v in 1 il maps $35   **973.8**

1. Biography, Individual 2. Generals 3. Presidents

ISBN 0-940450-58-5

LC 90-60013

This volume includes Grant's personal memoirs, first published in 1885 and 175 letters written between 1839 and 1865.

Grumet, Bridget Hall

Reconstruction era: primary sources; Lawrence W. Baker, project editor. UXL 2004 xxv, 228p il $60   **973.8**

1. Reconstruction (1865-1876)

ISBN 0-7876-9219-0

LC 2004-17309

This book "contains 19 complete or partial documents, such as the Fourteenth Amendment of the U.S. Constitution and Rutherford B. Hayes' inaugural address. Each document is accompanied by an introduction, keys to reading the document, a discussion of subsequent events related to the document, and other material." Booklist

Includes bibliographical references

Howes, Kelly King

Reconstruction era: almanac; Lawrence W. Baker, project editor. UXL 2004 xxxvii, 228p il map $60 **973.8**

1. Reconstruction (1865-1876)
ISBN 0-7876-9217-4

LC 2004-17301

This book "covers the political and social aspects of Reconstruction, including carpetbaggers and scalawags, amnesty for white Southerners, 'Black Codes,' the impeachment of President Johnson, the rise of the Ku Klux Klan, attempts to restore the old order in the South and much more." Publisher's note

Includes bibliographical references

Lears, T. J. Jackson

Rebirth of a nation; the making of modern America, 1877-1920. [by] Jackson Lears. Harper-Collins 2009 418p il $27.99 **973.8**

ISBN 978-0-06-074749-7; 0-06-074749-8

"A fascinating cultural history. . . . [This] is a major work by a leading historian at the top of his game—at once engaging and tightly argued. Like the best histories, it is also a book that speaks to our own time." N Y Times Book Rev

Millard, Candice

The **destiny** of the republic; Candice Millard. Doubleday 2011 x, 319 p., [16] p. of platesp ill. **973.8**

1. Medical instruments and apparatus -- United States -- History -- 19th century 2. Medicine -- United States -- History -- 19th century 3. Political culture -- United States -- History -- 19th century 4. Power (Social sciences) -- United States -- History -- 19th century 5. Presidents -- Medical care -- United States -- History -- 19th century 6. Presidents -- United States -- Biography
ISBN 9780307939654; 0385535007; 9780385526265; 9780385535007

LC 2011001549

This book explores U.S. history during the presidency and assassination of U.S. president James Garfield. "As [the author] . . . builds to the presidents fatal encounter with his assassin, she details the intra-party struggle among Republicans that led to Garfield's surprise 1880 nomination. . . . During the nearly three excruciating months Garfield lay dying, Alexander Graham Bell . . . scrambled to perfect his induction balance (a metal detector) in time to locate the lead bullet lodged in the stricken president's back. Meanwhile, Garfield's medical team persistently failed to observe British surgeon Joseph Lister's methods of antisepsis—the American medical establishment rejected the idea of invisible germs as ridiculous—a neglect that almost surely killed the president." (Kirkus)

Miller, Scott

The **President** and the assassin; McKinley, terror, and empire at the dawn of the American century. Random House 2011 422p il **973.8**

1. Anarchism -- United States -- History 2. Anarchism and anarchists 3. Anarchists 4. Governors 5. Members of Congress 6. Murderers 7. Presidents
ISBN 1-4000-6752-9; 978-1-4000-6752-7

LC 2010-38857

"Miller examines the social, economic and political forces that underlay the transformation of the U.S. after the Civil War from a feeble newcomer in world affairs to the global power we know today in a way that keeps you learning and turning pages at the same time. Rewarding as it is to be able to grasp at last such late 19th-century mysteries as the monetary debates that have befuddled college students ever since, what makes the book compelling is neither the narrative nor the explanations but the sense of familiarity that pervades it all. Indeed, so many of the circumstances and events of the earlier time have parallels in our own that the experience of reading it is practically eerie." Oregonian

Includes bibliographical references (p. [385]-403) and index

Philbrick, Nathaniel

★ The **last** stand; Custer, Sitting Bull, and the Battle of the Little Bighorn. Viking 2010 466p il map $30 **973.8**

1. Army officers 2. Dakota Indians 3. Dakota Indians -- Wars, 1876 4. Generals 5. Indian chiefs 6. Little Bighorn, Battle of the, 1876 7. Little Bighorn, Battle of the, Mont., 1876
ISBN 978-0-670-02172-7

LC 2009-47209

The author "writes a lively narrative that brushes away the cobwebs of mythology to reveal the context and realities of Custer's unexpected 1876 defeat at the hands of his Indian enemies under Sitting Bull, and the character of each leader. Judicious in his assessments of events and intentions, Philbrick offers a rounded history of one of the worst defeats in American military history, a story enhanced by his minute examination of the battle's terrain and interviews with descendants in both camps." Publ Wkly

Includes bibliographical references

Rauchway, Eric

Murdering McKinley; the making of Theodore Roosevelt's America. Hill & Wang 2003 250p il $25; pa $14 **973.8**

1. Anarchists 2. Biography, Individual 3. Governors 4. Members of Congress 5. Murderers 6. Nobel laureates for peace 7. Presidents 8. Vice-presidents
ISBN 0-8090-7170-3; 0-8090-1638-9 pa

LC 2003-40666

The author "uses a search for the motive of President William McKinley's assassin as a means to comment on the Progressive Era and show how Theodore Roosevelt manipulated the emotions of rage and despair after the tragic event to give it meaning, thereby advancing his own political vision. . . . Novel in its conception and well written, the book is appropriate for public as well as academic libraries." Choice

Includes bibliographical references

Sandoz, Mari

★ The **Battle** of the Little Bighorn. Lippincott 1966 191p maps hardcover o.p. pa $12.95 **973.8**

1. Army officers 2. Generals 3. Little Bighorn, Battle

of the, 1876
ISBN 0-397-00410-9; 0-8032-9100-0 pa
"An account of the United States Army expedition against the Sioux Nation with emphasis on the political motives and ambitions of General Custer." Publ Wkly
Includes bibliographical references

Schlereth, Thomas J.

Victorian America; transformations in everyday life, 1876-1915. HarperCollins Pubs. 1991 363p hardcover o.p. pa $15   **973.8**
　　1. United States -- Social life and customs
　　ISBN 0-06-092160-9 pa

LC 89-46555

The author surveys the objects, events, experiences, products and tastes that comprised what he terms America's Victorian culture (1876-1915) and shows how its values shaped modern life.

"What a wonderful book. . . . Schlereth is no wry compiler of trivia. His analysis of social context reveals truly profound, intangible transformations in how and where Americans spent their time during four pivotal decades." Booklist
Includes bibliographical references

Smith, Jean Edward

Grant. Simon & Schuster 2001 781p il $35; pa $20   **973.8**
　　1. Generals 2. Generals -- United States -- Biography 3. Presidents 4. Presidents -- United States -- Biography
　　ISBN 0-684-84926-7; 0-684-84927-5 pa

LC 00-53794

This biography surveys the career and achievements of the 18th U.S. president, from his days at West Point to the Civil War campaigns and his subsequent elevation to the presidency.

"While he acknowledges Grant's failure to rein in his 'friends' and cabinet members as president, Smith convincingly illustrates how Grant's backbone and political skills were used to advance the cause of former slaves in the South. This is an outstanding and long overdue reevaluation of the life and career of a great American." Booklist
Includes bibliographical references

Thomas, Evan

The **war** lovers; Roosevelt, Lodge, Hearst, and the rush to empire, 1898. Little, Brown and Co. 2010 471p il $29.99   **973.8**
　　1. Biographers 2. Business and politics -- United States -- History -- 19th century 3. Governors 4. Members of Congress 5. Newspaper editors 6. Newspaper executives 7. Nobel laureates for peace 8. Political leaders 9. Presidents 10. Senators 11. Spanish-American War, 1898 12. Spanish-American War, 1898 -- Causes 13. Speakers of the House 14. Vice-presidents
　　ISBN 0-316-00409-X; 978-0-316-00409-1

LC 2009-43616

This book focuses on the "Spanish American War and [on the involvement of] Roosevelt, Lodge, Hearst, McKinley, William James, and Thomas Reed." (Publisher's note) Index.

The author's multifaceted portraits lend the book a sweeping, almost cinematic quality. A lively, well-rounded look at politics and personalities in late-19th-century America. Kirkus
Includes bibliographical references

Utley, Robert Marshall

Custer: cavalier in buckskin; {by} Robert M. Utley. rev ed; University of Okla. Press 2001 176p il map $29.95; pa $17.95   **973.8**
　　1. Army officers 2. Generals 3. Native Americans -- Wars
　　ISBN 0-8061-3347-3; 0-8061-3387-2 pa

LC 2001-27356

The author offers theories and facts regarding the mythology surrounding Custer, telling how he promoted himself as an American hero in an effort to increase his rank in the army.

This "is a fair and full-bodied account that cogently interprets the facts, provides the proper psychological analysis, and offers solid grounding for the development of the considerable myth." Booklist {review of 1988 edition}
Includes bibliographical references

Wall, Joseph Frazier

Andrew Carnegie. University of Pittsburgh Press 1989 1137p il hardcover o.p. pa $22.50   **973.8**
　　1. Carnegie libraries 2. Metal industry executives 3. Philanthropists
　　ISBN 0-8229-5904-6 pa

LC 88-38160

This biography follows Carnegie from his boyhood in Scotland through his emigration to America, his rise in the business world, and his early ventures in oil, railroads, telegraphy, and the iron and steel industries.

Welch, James

Killing Custer; the Battle of the Little Bighorn and the fate of the Plains Indians. by James Welch with Paul Stekler. Norton 1994 320p il hardcover o.p. pa $14.95   **973.8**
　　1. Little Big Horn, Battle of the, 1876 2. Little Bighorn, Battle of the, 1876 3. Native Americans -- Wars
　　ISBN 0-393-32939-9 pa

LC 94-5617

"Welch produced this history of the Indian wars of the northern plains as a by-product of his work scripting a television documentary on the Battle of the Little Bighorn. In addition to military history, it contains long sections describing the life of the Plains Indians, accounts of contemporary Indian radical groups, and Welch's reactions while visiting the various historic sites in the area." Libr J
Includes bibliographical references

Wert, Jeffry D.

Custer; the controversial life of George Armstrong Custer. Simon & Schuster 1996 462p il maps hardcover o.p. pa $20   **973.8**
　　1. Army officers 2. Biography, Individual 3. Generals
　　ISBN 0-684-81043-3; 0-684-83275-5 pa

LC 96-7290

"Focusing on Custer's Civil War actions, Wert methodically examines a man often considered an enigma in American history. Clear writing and excellent use of primary source materials demonstrate how history should be written." Booklist

West, Elliott
    The **last** Indian war; the Nez Perce story. Oxford University Press 2009 397p il map   **973.8**
    1. Big Hole, Battle of the, 1877 2. Indian chiefs 3. Nez Percé Indians -- History -- 19th century 4. Nez Percé Indians -- Wars, 1877 5. Nez Percé War, 1877
    ISBN 9780195136753
                                        LC 2008051382
    This is an account of the 1877 war between the Nez Perce Indians and the United States government. Chronology. Index.
    The author "uses the story of the Nez Percé War of 1877 and its origins and aftermath to illuminate the era of expansion and consolidation between 1845 and 1877 that forged the American identity, a period he calls the 'Greater Reconstruction.' . . . This well-written book is an excellent place to start in understanding the Nez Percé War and is highly recommended for all libraries." Libr J
    Includes bibliographical references (p. 325-328) and index.

★ American eras. Gale Res. 1997 8v il set $1235   **973.8**
    1. Reference books
    ISBN 0-7876-1477-7
    This reference set "provides information on U.S. history, including social history, prior to the twentieth century. Each era-specific volume includes an introductory essay describing the time period to provide context and an overview, 150 illustrations, an index of photographs, a bibliography, a subject index and a list of contributors." Publisher's note

Encyclopedia of the Gilded Age and Progressive Era; edited by John D. Buenker and Joseph Buenker. M.E. Sharpe 2005 3v il set $299   **973.8**
    1. Reference books
    ISBN 0-7656-8051-3
                                        LC 2003-24653
    This set focuses "on a period between 1870 and 1920, when the United States emerged as an urban and industrial world power. Some 900 A-Z entries cover key individuals, events, and organizations of the times, and 17 essays discuss broad themes like the economy, politics, religion, and pop culture." Libr J
    Includes bibliographical references

973.9 1901-

Caro, Robert A.
    The **path** to power. Knopf 1982 xxiii, 882p il $49.95; pa $19.95   **973.9**
    1. Biography, Individual 2. Members of Congress 3. Presidents 4. Presidents -- United States 5. Senators

6. Vice-presidents
    ISBN 0-394-49973-5; 0-679-72945-3 pa
                                        LC 90-201781
    This volume, the first volume of a projected four-volume biography of Lyndon B. Johnson, "follows him from the Hill Country to New Deal Washington, from his boyhood through the years of the Depression to his debut as Congressman, his . . . defeat in his first race for the Senate, and his attainment, nonetheless, at age 31, of the national power for which he hungered." Publisher's note
    Includes bibliographical references

Cooke, Alistair
    Letter from America, 1946-2004. Knopf 2004 xx, 503p il $35   **973.9**
    ISBN 1-4000-4402-2
                                        LC 2004-304550
    "Arranged into chapters by decades, these commentaries reveal not only Cooke's mastery of clear prose but also the range of American topics that caught his interest, from politics to culture. . . . A book for appreciators of American culture in the second half of the previous century as well as those who relish the essay in either oral or written form." Booklist

Galbraith, John Kenneth
    Name-dropping; from F.D.R. on. Houghton Mifflin 1999 194p $26; pa $14   **973.9**
    1. Advertising executives 2. Architects 3. Columnists 4. Diplomats 5. Editors 6. Government officials 7. Governors 8. Handicapped 9. Humanitarians 10. Lawyers 11. Members of Congress 12. Memoirists 13. Nazi leaders 14. Nonfiction writers 15. Philatelists 16. Politicians -- United States 17. Politicians -- United States -- Anecdotes 18. Presidential candidates 19. Presidents 20. Prime ministers 21. Senators 22. Social activists 23. Socialites 24. Spouses of presidents 25. Statesmen 26. United Nations officials 27. United States -- Politics and government -- 1945-1989 -- Anecdotes 28. United States -- Politics and government -- 1989- -- Anecdotes 29. Vice-presidents 30. War criminals
    ISBN 0-395-82288-2; 0-618-15453-1 pa
                                        LC 99-20070
    The author "reminisces about important figures with whom he has been involved in his long and distinguished life in the public arena. Among the brief portraits are those of Franklin and Eleanor Roosevelt, Harry Truman, JFK, LBJ, Nehru, and others. More than the self-effacing title indicates, this book offers important insights into the people and times on which its author reflects. Galbraith writes with a wit, style, and elegance few can match." Libr J

Gould, Lewis L.
    The **modern** American presidency; foreword by Richard Norton Smith. 2nd ed., rev. and updated.; University Press of Kansas 2009 318p il $34.95; pa $17.95   **973.9**
    1. Presidents -- United States
    ISBN 978-0-7006-1683-1; 0-7006-1683-7; 978-0-7006-1684-8 pa; 0-7006-1684-5 pa
                                        LC 2009-20161

"Gould traces the decline of the party system, the increasing importance of the media and its role in creating the president-as-celebrity, and the growth of the White House staff and executive bureaucracy. He also shows us a succession of chief executives who increasingly have known less and less about the business of governing the country, observing that most would have had a better historical reputation if they had contented themselves with a single term." Publisher's note

Includes bibliographical references

Grose, Peter

Gentleman spy; the life of Allen Dulles. University of Mass. Press 1996 641p il pa $19.95 **973.9**
1. Diplomats 2. Government officials 3. Intelligence service officials 4. Lawyers
ISBN 1-55849-044-2; 978-1-55849-044-4
LC 96-19010

This biography of the CIA director under Eisenhower and Kennedy "renders the interplay of person and public event and allows readers to enter the dark world of US-sponsored terror and covert paramilitary operations. . . . Grose sets forth in fascinating and often unfamiliar detail the spectacular CIA covert operations: in Iran, Guatemala, Indonesia; the U2 incident; the Bay of Pigs." Choice

Menand, Louis

The **Metaphysical** Club. Farrar, Straus & Giroux 2001 546p il $30; pa $15 **973.9**
1. Educators 2. Logicians 3. Metaphysics 4. Metaphysics -- History 5. National characteristics, American 6. Philosophers 7. Psychologists 8. Supreme Court justices 9. Writers on science
ISBN 0-374-19963-9; 0-374-52849-7 pa
LC 00-66279

"Menand brings rare common sense and graceful, witty prose to his richly nuanced reading of American intellectual history." N Y Times Book Rev

Includes bibliographical references

Morgan, Ted

Reds: McCarthyism in twentieth-century America. Random House 2003 685p $35; pa $16.95 **973.9**
1. Anticommunist movements 2. Communism -- United States 3. Senators
ISBN 0-679-44399-1; 0-812-97302-X pa
LC 2003-46509

"Senator Joseph McCarthy's demagogic career is just part of this sweeping account of anti-Communist purges and Communist espionage." N Y Times Book Rev

Includes bibliographical references

Slotkin, Richard

Gunfighter nation; the myth of the frontier in twentieth-century America. University of Oklahoma Press 1998 850p pa $32.95 **973.9**
1. Frontier and pioneer life -- West (U.S.) 2. Popular culture -- United States
ISBN 0-8061-3031-8; 978-0-8061-3031-6
LC 97-32043

"On the premise that myth is spread by mass media, Slotkin examines numerous elements of popular culture

ranging from James Fenimore Cooper's Hawkeye in The last of the Mohicans to John Wayne's Green Berets film to demonstrate how the myth affects American perceptions regarding foreign and domestic issues." Libr J

Includes bibliographical references

Tintori, Karen

Trapped: the 1909 Cherry Mine disaster. Simon & Schuster 2002 273p il $25; pa $14 **973.9**
1. Cherry Mine Disaster, Cherry, Ill., 1909 2. Coal mine accidents -- Illinois -- Cherry 3. Coal mines and mining -- Accidents 4. Mine accidents -- Illinois -- Cherry
ISBN 0-7434-2194-9; 0-7434-2195-7 pa
LC 2002-104596

"On November 13, 1909, a fire trapped 480 coal miners . . . 400 feet below ground in a mine at Cherry, Illinois. Only 221 escaped. . . . Tintori describes the life-and-death struggle of the miners below ground and the terror of the women and children gathered at the mine's entrance. . . . Tintori's graphic account of this tragedy is a sad but gripping story." Booklist

American decades. Gale Res. 1994 11v set $1495 **973.9**
1. United States - Civilization 2. United States -- History -- 20th century
ISBN 0-7876-5076-5

"A series of volumes covering the twentieth century by decades. . . . Fun to browse, each volume is divided into 13 sections covering topics such as the arts, government and politics, lifestyles and social trends, medicine and health, and sports. Each section opens with a chronology and overview and closes with short biographies, deaths, and a bibliography of important books published in the decade. Sidebars highlight events and prominent individuals." Am Libr

American decades primary sources; Cynthia Rose, project editor. Gale 2004 10v il map set $1495 **973.9**
1. United States -- Civilization 2. United States -- History -- 20th century - Sources
ISBN 0-7876-6587-8
LC 2002-8155

"A treasure trove of more than 2,000 primary sources on U.S. history and culture, ranging from speeches and literary works to graphs and architectural drawings. Although many of the sources might be found on the Internet, they lack the organization and context provided here." Booklist

St. James encyclopedia of popular culture; editors, Tom Pendergast and Sara Pendergast; with an introduction by Jim Cullen. St. James Press 1999 5v il set $695 **973.9**
1. Popular culture -- United States -- Encyclopedias 2. Reference books
ISBN 1-55862-400-7
LC 99-46540

This is an "overview of popular culture in twentieth-century America with a particular emphasis on the second half of the century. In more than 2,700 entries, the nearly 450 contributors attempt to cover the major personalities, productions, products, events, and developments from film, music, print culture, social life, sports, television and radio, art, and performances (which include theater, dance, stand-up comedy, and other live performances). . . . The entries seldom sink to trivialization. They are generally thoughtful and well written, providing information and insight. . . . The editors have done a masterful job of providing something for nearly everyone." Am Ref Books Annu, 2001

Includes bibliographical references

973.91   1901-1953

Allen, Frederick Lewis
Only yesterday; an informal history of the 1920's. Wiley 1997 285p $21.95   **973.91**
ISBN 0-471-18952-9

LC 97-19930
"An account of the years from the spring of 1919 to . . . {1931}. It is a kaleidoscopic picture of American politics, society, manners, morals, and economic conditions." Booklist

Includes bibliographical references

Beam, Alex
A **great** idea at the time; the rise, fall, and curious afterlife of the Great Books. PublicAffairs 2008 245p il $24.95   **973.91**
1. Books and reading 2. Books and reading -- Social aspects 3. Books and reading -- Social aspects -- United States 4. Canon (Literature) 5. Education, Humanistic -- United States -- History -- 20th century 6. Popular culture -- United States -- History 7. Popular culture -- United States -- History -- 20th century
ISBN 978-1-58648-487-3; 1-58648-487-7

LC 2008-33115
This is a "look at the marketing phenomenon and cultural-icon status of the Great Books of Western Civilization, a 54-volume collection compiled by university-affiliated academics. . . . Beam's book will have readers looking at volumes in the series from a whole new perspective owing to its witty handling of popular culture." Libr J

Includes bibliographical references (p. 223-228) and index

Brands, H. W.
★ **Woodrow** Wilson. Times Books 2003 169p il $20   **973.91**
1. College presidents 2. Governors 3. Nobel laureates for peace 4. Presidents 5. Presidents -- United States 6. Presidents -- United States -- Biography
ISBN 0-8050-6955-0

LC 2002-41393
The author "presents Wilson as a moralistic, idealistic intellectual who came to the presidency well versed in domestic policy but sadly lacking in knowledge and experience of international affairs, a leader who ultimately sacrificed his health and his presidential legacy in a doomed battle with Sen. Henry Cabot Lodge to have the League of Nations ratified. . . . Brands's brief, skillful life of the President is recommended for all public libraries." Libr J

Includes bibliographical references

Burns, James MacGregor
The **three** Roosevelts; patrician leaders who transformed America. by James MacGregor Burns & Susan Dunn. Atlantic Monthly Press 2001 678p il $37.50; pa $18   **973.91**
1. Columnists 2. Diplomats 3. Governors 4. Handicapped 5. Humanitarians 6. Nobel laureates for peace 7. Philatelists 8. Presidents 9. Presidents -- United States -- Biography 10. Presidents' spouses -- United States -- Biography 11. Social activists 12. Social reformers -- United States -- Biography 13. Spouses of presidents 14. United Nations officials 15. Upper class -- United States -- Biography 16. Vice-presidents
ISBN 0-87113-780-1; 0-8021-3872-1 pa

LC 00-60896
Burns and Dunn "succeed in approaching their subjects with grace, respect and insight. In the end, they do great justice to three remarkable lives." Publ Wkly

Includes bibliographical references

Davis, Deborah
Guest of honor; Booker T. Washington, Theodore Roosevelt, and the White House dinner that shocked a nation. by Deborah Davis. Atria Books 2012 x, 308 p.p   **973.91**
1. Presidents -- United States -- Biography
ISBN 1439169810; 9781439169810; 9781439169827; 9781439169834

LC 2012009045
This book is a portrayal of the . . . oppressive racial attitudes prevalent at the turn of the twentieth century. As [Deborah] Davis indicates, even many so-called Progressives adhered to pseudoscientific doctrines of social Darwinism and Anglo-Saxon racial superiority Given that context, the unprecedented dinner invitation extended by President Teddy Roosevelt to preeminent black educator Booker T. Washington assumed great importance. Davis first expends considerable effort in drawing parallels between the two men . . . showing both as intense strivers. . . . When she gets to the meeting itself and the reactions to it, she . . . provid[es a] . . . snapshot of the prejudices and schisms in American society a century ago. (Booklist)

Dickstein, Morris
Dancing in the dark; a cultural history of the Great Depression. W. W. Norton 2009 598p il $29.95   **973.91**
1. Arts and society -- United States -- History -- 20th century 2. Depressions -- 1929 -- United States 3. Great Depression, 1929-1939 4. Popular culture -- United States 5. Popular culture -- United States -- History -- 20th century
ISBN 978-0-393-07225-9

LC 2009-17389
A cultural history of the 1930s explores the anxiety, despair, and optimism of the period while evaluating such factors as the Dust Bowl migrations, "screwball comedy," and swing band music to evaluate how period culture provided a dynamic lift to the country's morale.

"Whether discussing Citizen Kane or Porgy and Bess, the poetry of Langston Hughes, William Carlos Williams or

Robert Frost, Faulkner's unique achievement and odd relation to the period, the films of Cary Grant or the elegance and energy of Art Deco, Dickstein always has something smart and lively to say. His scintillating commentary illuminates an important dimension of a decade too often considered only in political or economic terms. It's hard to imagine a more astute, more graceful guide to a remarkably creative period." Kirkus

Includes bibliographical references

Egan, Timothy

★ The **big** burn; Teddy Roosevelt and the fire that saved America. Houghton Mifflin Harcourt 2009 324p il map $27   **973.91**

1. Conservationists 2. Forest conservation 3. Forest conservation -- United States 4. Forest conservation -- United States -- History 5. Forest fires 6. Forest fires -- United States -- History 7. Foresters 8. Governors 9. National parks and reserves -- United States 10. National parks and reserves -- United States -- History 11. Nature conservation 12. Nature conservation -- United States -- History 13. Nobel laureates for peace 14. Presidents 15. Vice-presidents

ISBN 978-0-618-96841-1; 0-618-96841-5

LC 2009-21881

"This is history that is well researched, vividly set into the context of the early twentieth century, and written with such skill in character development and pacing that readers will be lost in a vivid reimagining of those surreal days in 1910 when an ecological event unfolded with the spectacle of a modern summer blockbuster." Orion

Includes bibliographical references (p. [287]-305) and index.

Hagedorn, Ann

Savage peace; hope and fear in America, 1919. Simon & Schuster 2007 543p il $30   **973.91**

1. World War, 1914-1918 -- Influence 2. World War, 1914-1918 -- Peace 3. World War, 1914-1918 -- Social aspects -- United States

ISBN 978-0-7432-4371-1; 0-7432-4371-4

LC 2006-51258

Hagedorn "weaves numerous threads of history together to provide a clear vision of American society at the dawn of the modern age. This is not the dull history of academia: Her writing is concise, colorful and compelling." PopMatters

Includes bibliographical references (p. [499]-510) and index.

Hofstadter, Richard

The **age** of reform from Bryan to F.D.R. Knopf 1955 328, xxp hardcover o.p. pa $12.95   **973.91**

1. United States -- Politics and government -- 20th century

ISBN 0-394-70095-3 pa

This analysis of the reform movements in American politics from 1890-1940 reviews: The agrarian uprising that found its expression in the Populist movement of the 1890's; The Progressive movement from about 1900-1914; The New Deal of the 1930's. Emphasis is placed upon the ideas of the leading political reformers.

Kennedy, David M.

★ **Freedom** from fear; the American people in depression and war, 1929-1945. Oxford Univ. Press 1999 936p il maps $39.95; pa $22.50   **973.91**

ISBN 0-19-503834-7; 0-19-514403-1 pa

LC 98-49580

This narrative history of the United States spans the period from the Great Depression to the end of the Second World War.

"Rarely does a work of historical synthesis combine such trenchant analysis and elegant writing. For its scope, its insight and its purring narrative engine, Kennedy's book will stand for years to come as the definitive account of the critical decades of the American century." Publ Wkly

Includes bibliographical references

Millard, Candice

The **river** of doubt; Theodore Roosevelt's darkest journey. Doubleday 2005 416p il map $26 **973.91**

1. Army officers 2. Children of presidents 3. Explorers 4. Governors 5. Marshals 6. Natural history -- Amazon River region 7. Natural history -- Amazon River valley 8. Nobel laureates for peace 9. Presidents 10. Rain forests -- Amazon River valley 11. Shipping executives 12. Vice-presidents

ISBN 0-385-50796-8

LC 2005-46541

This is an account of the Amazon expedition Theodore Roosevelt undertook in 1912, with his son Kermit and the Brazilian explorer Col. Candido Rondon.

The author "turns this incredible story into one that easily matches an Indiana Jones screen adventure." Libr J

Includes bibliographical references

Miller, Nathan

New world coming; the 1920s and the making of modern America. Da Capo Press 2004 433p pa $19.95   **973.91**

1. Authors 2. Novelists 3. Screenwriters 4. Short story writers

ISBN 978-0-306-81379-5; 0-306-81379-3

LC 2004-56140

The author "illuminates the United States as it existed under presidents Harding, Coolidge and Hoover, using the life of F. Scott Fitzgerald, with all its peaks and valleys during the 1920s, as the backbone of his narrative. . . . In addition to events in the arts and sciences, Miller details bitter labor struggles, the rise of the reconstituted Ku Klux Klan and Prohibition. . . . This volume comprises an excellent chronicle of that turbulent, troubled and tempestuous decade called 'the roaring '20s.'" Publ Wkly

Includes bibliographical references

Moore, Lucy

Anything goes; a biography of the roaring twenties. Overlook Press 2010 352p il $25.95 **973.91**

ISBN 978-1-59020-313-2

LC 2009-46437

"Rather than presenting her material as an extended survey of the period, Moore focuses on a single Jazz Age trope per chapter, resulting in easily digestible takes on prohibition and the high-spirited criminal culture it engendered; the explosion in popularity of jazz music; the evolution of the flapper; the emergence of Hollywood as creator of a national cultural consciousness; the financial scandals of the Harding presidency; the Sacco/Vanzetti and Scopes trials; the resurgence of the Ku Klux Klan; the Algonquin round table and the founding of the New Yorker; Charles Lindbergh's historic trans-Atlantic flight; the spectacular boxing career of Jack Dempsey; and the financial devastation of the Wall Street crash that ended the party and ushered in the Great Depression. . . . Snappy, vivid account of America's most glittering decade." Kirkus

Includes bibliographical references

Morris, Edmund

★ **Theodore** Rex. Random House 2001 772p il map $35; pa $16.95 **973.91**
    1. Governors 2. Nobel laureates for peace 3. Presidents 4. Presidents -- United States 5. Presidents -- United States -- Biography 6. Vice-presidents
    ISBN 0-394-55509-0; 0-8129-6600-7 pa
                      LC 2001-19366

"The second entry in Morris's . . . three-volume life of Theodore Roosevelt focuses on the presidential years 1901 through early 1909." Publ Wkly

Includes bibliographical references

Pietrusza, David

1920: the year of the six presidents. Carroll & Graf 2007 533p il $28.95 **973.91**
    1. Presidents -- United States -- Election 2. Presidents -- United States -- Election -- 1920
    ISBN 978-0-78671-622-7; 0-7867-1622-3

"Six men—a sitting president, former president, and four eventual presidents—competed in the 1920 presidential election. . . . [The author] contends that this election marked the birth of modern American politics. . . . The many issues and forces that swirled during that time, from the fear of Communists and Socialists and the terrorism they allegedly perpetrated to technological advances and Prohibition, make for a fascinating and compelling tale of an often-overlooked election in our history." Libr J

Includes bibliographical references

Schlesinger, Arthur M.

The **crisis** of the old order, 1919-1933; [by] Arthur M. Schlesinger, Jr. Houghton Mifflin 2003 557p pa $17 **973.91**
    1. Depressions -- 1929 -- United States 2. Governors 3. Handicapped 4. Philatelists 5. Presidents
    ISBN 0-618-34085-8
                      LC 2003-47884

This is the first of three volumes which interpret the political, economic, social, and intellectual life of the United States during the time when Franklin D. Roosevelt was in office. This volume covers the years preceding his first term.

A **life** in the twentieth century; innocent beginnings, 1917-1950. [by] Arthur M. Schlesinger, Jr. Houghton Mifflin 2000 557p il $28.95; pa $15 **973.91**
    1. Authors 2. Biographers 3. Government officials 4. Historians 5. Historians -- United States 6. Nonfiction writers
    ISBN 0-395-70752-8; 0-618-21925-0 pa
                      LC 00-61322

This first volume of Schlesinger's autobiography covers the author's life through the publication of The Age of Jackson and The Vital Center.

Schlesinger's "autobiography, skillfully interweaving the personal and the historical, is elegantly simple and marvellously clear. Complex thoughts are set forth with a lucidity that conceals the depth of the intellectual analysis. Wit, humour and the resources of a natural storyteller sweep the reader along." Economist

Shlaes, Amity

The **forgotten** man; a new history of the Great Depression. HarperCollins Publishers 2007 464p il $26.95 **973.91**
    1. Depressions -- 1929 -- United States 2. Economic stabilization -- United States -- History -- 20th century 3. Great Depression, 1929-1939 4. New Deal, 1933-1939 5. Presidents -- United States -- Policies
    ISBN 978-0-06-621170-1; 0-06-621170-0
                      LC 2006-49761

"Reminding readers that the reputedly do-nothing Hoover pulled hard on the fiscal levers (raising tariffs, increasing government spending), Shlaes nevertheless emphasizes that his enthusiasm for intervention paled against the ebullient FDR's glee in experimentation. She focuses closely on the influence of his fabled Brain Trust, her narrative shifting among Raymond Moley, Rexford Tugwell, and other prominent New Dealers. Businesses that litigated their resistance to New Deal regulations attract Shlaes' attention, as do individuals who coped with the despair of the 1930s through self-help, such as Alcoholics Anonymous cofounder Bill Wilson. The book culminates in the rise of Wendell Willkie, and Shlaes' accent on personalities is an appealing avenue into her skeptical critique of the New Deal." Booklist

Includes bibliographical references

Starobin, Paul

After America; narratives for the next global age. Viking 2009 358p $26.95 **973.91**
    1. International relations
    ISBN 978-0-670-02094-2
                      LC 2008-46685

This "is a narrative of extraordinary range and contemporary relevance." Publ Wkly

Includes bibliographical references

Terkel, Studs

★ **Hard** times; an oral history of the great depression. Norton 2000 462p pa $14.95 **973.91**
    1. Great Depression, 1929-1939
    ISBN 1-56584-656-7
                      LC 2003-389318

"Persons of all ages, occupations, and classes scattered across the U.S. remember what they experienced or were told about the economic crisis of the 1930's. The result is a social document of immense interest." Booklist

Watkins, T. H.

The **hungry** years; a narrative history of the Great Depression in America. Holt & Co. 1999 587p il hardcover o.p. pa $17   **973.91**

1. Depressions -- 1929 -- United States 2. Depressions -- 1929 -- United States -- Personal narratives 3. Great Depression, 1929-1939

ISBN 0-8050-6506-7 pa

           LC 99-10391

"The vignettes Watkins selects are gritty, visceral, and seamlessly sutured to the federal programs that rolled out in the course of the decade, making this a signal addition to the rich historiography of the Depression." Booklist

Includes bibliographical references

973.917   Administration of Franklin Delano Roosevelt, 1933-1945

Cook, Blanche Wiesen

Eleanor Roosevelt. v1 Penguin Bks. 1993 587p v1 il pa $18   **973.917**

1. Columnists 2. Diplomats 3. Humanitarians 4. Presidents' spouses -- United States 5. Social activists 6. Spouses of presidents 7. United Nations officials

ISBN 0-14-009460-1

           LC 87-40632

"A feminist biography that regards its subject not only as a mostly 19th-century woman who invented her own life with very little help, but also as a self-created political figure of considerable significance." N Y Times Book Rev

Includes bibliographical references

Davis, Kenneth Sydney

FDR, into the storm, 1937-1940; a history. {by} Kenneth S. Davis. Random House 1993 691p hardcover o.p. pa $29   **973.917**

1. Biography, Individual 2. Governors 3. Handicapped 4. Philatelists 5. Presidents 6. Presidents -- United States

ISBN 0-8129-8205-9 pa

           LC 92-21640

This is the fourth volume of a five-volume biography begun with FDR, the beckoning destiny, 1882-1928 (1972); FDR, the New York years, 1928-1933 (1985); FDR, the New Deal years, 1933-1937 (1986).

In this study "particular emphasis is laid on Roosevelt's attempt to 'pack' the Supreme Court, his response to the growing threat of fascism in Europe, and the unexpectedly strong challenge by Republican Wendell Wilkie in the 1940 presidential campaign." Publ Wkly

Includes bibliographical references

Jackson, Robert Houghwout

That man: an insider's portrait of Franklin D. Roosevelt; [by] Robert H. Jackson; edited and introduced by John Q. Barrett; with a foreword by William E. Leuchtenburg. Oxford University Press 2003 xx-viii, 290p il hardcover o.p. pa $17.95   **973.917**

1. Governors 2. Handicapped 3. Philatelists 4.

Presidents 5. Presidents -- United States

ISBN 0-19-516826-7; 0-19-517757-6 pa

           LC 2003-9275

This "is a lively, revealing and suddenly relevant book. Jackson's memoir sheds new light—not always flattering—on important events and on a president who too often appears only in silhouette." N Y Times Book Rev

Includes bibliographical references

Leuchtenburg, William Edward

Franklin D. Roosevelt and the New Deal, 1932-1940; {by} William E. Leuchtenburg. Harper & Row 1963 393p il hardcover o.p. pa $16 **973.917**

1. Governors 2. Handicapped 3. New Deal, 1933-1939 4. Philatelists 5. Presidents

ISBN 0-06-133025-6 pa

This treatment of Roosevelt's first two terms in office emphasizes the economic crisis and New Deal reforms. The author shows how social forces influenced government action: the San Francisco strike in 1934, the careers of Huey Long and Father Coughlin, the sharecroppers' revolt, and unemployment.

This book "is comprehensive, logically organized, and written with clarity and detachment." Am Hist Rev

Includes bibliographical references

Schlesinger, Arthur M.

The **coming** of the New Deal, 1933-1935; {by} Arthur M. Schlesinger, Jr. Houghton Mifflin 2003 669p pa $17   **973.917**

1. Depressions -- 1929 -- United States 2. Governors 3. Handicapped 4. New Deal, 1933-1939 5. Philatelists 6. Presidents

ISBN 0-618-34086-6

           LC 2003-47859

"This second volume of 'The Age of Roosevelt' continues the work begun with 'The Crisis of the Old Order, 1919-1933'. . . . The dramatic story of how representative democracy began the battle to conquer economic collapse is followed through the first two years of the New Deal." Libr J

Includes bibliographical references

The **politics** of upheaval, 1935-1936; {by} Arthur M. Schlesinger, Jr. Houghton Mifflin 2003 749p pa $17   **973.917**

1. Depressions -- 1929 -- United States 2. Governors 3. Handicapped 4. New Deal, 1933-1939 5. Philatelists 6. Presidents

ISBN 0-618-34087-4

           LC 2003-47889

This third volume of The age of Roosevelt "concentrates on the turbulent concluding years of Franklin D. Roosevelt's first term." Publisher's note

Includes bibliographical references

973.918 Administration of Harry S Truman, 1945-1953

McCullough, David G.

Truman; {by} David McCullough. Simon & Schuster 1992 1117p il $40; pa $22 **973.918**
1. Biography, Individual 2. Presidents 3. Senators 4. Vice-presidents
ISBN 0-671-45654-7; 0-671-86920-5 pa

LC 92-5245

This biography of the 33rd president "not only conveys in rich detail Truman's accomplishments as a politician and statesman, but also reveals the character and personality of this constantly-surprising man—as schoolboy, farmer, soldier, merchant, county judge, senator, vice president and chief executive. The book relates how Truman overcame the stigma of business failure and debt . . . and acquired a reputation for honesty, reliability and common sense." Publ Wkly
Includes bibliographical references

973.92 1953-2001

Bloom, Allan David

The **closing** of the American mind. Simon & Schuster 1987 392p hardcover o.p. pa $14 **973.92**
1. Higher education
ISBN 0-671-65715-1 pa

LC 86-24768

This is the author's assessment of liberal arts education today. "In essence, he argues that over the last 25 years the academy has all but abandoned the intellectual and moral principles that have traditionally informed and given substance to liberal education, becoming prey to the enthusiasms—increasingly politicized—of the moment." N Y Times Book Rev

Duffy, Michael

★ The **presidents** club; inside the world's most exclusive fraternity. Nancy Gibbs and Michael Duffy. Simon & Schuster 2012 vii, 641 p.p **973.92**
1. Bush, George W. (George Walker), 1946- 2. Bush, George, 1924- 3. Clinton, Bill, 1946- 4. Eisenhower, Dwight D. (Dwight David), 1890-1969 5. Ex-presidents -- United States -- History 6. Historical literature 7. Interpersonal relations 8. Presidents -- United States -- History 9. Truman, Harry S., 1884-1972
ISBN 1439127700; 9781439127704

LC 2011042047

This book "chart[s] the zigzag arc of relationships among the men who have occupied the White House since the mid 20th century. . . . [T]he authors present numerous instances of presidents warming to their predecessors. . . . Sometimes mutual admiration was already in place (Truman and Eisenhower--though it later disintegrated); sometimes, antipathy (Clinton and Bush II). But almost always the sitting presidents found in their predecessors some solace, willing ears and sound advice." (Kirkus)

Frank, Thomas

The **wrecking** crew; how conservatives rule. Metropolitan Books 2008 369p il $25 **973.92**
1. Conservatism 2. Conservatism -- United States
ISBN 978-0-8050-7988-3; 0-8050-7988-2

LC 2008-15802

The author offers his assessment of the conservative Republican approach to government.

This "is a useful introduction to a world of pricey lobbyists, crackpot theorists, bought legislators and hapless government. And, in part through these very caricatures, the book gets at some essential questions about politics and markets in a democratic society." Nation
Includes bibliographical references

Frum, David

How we got here; the 70's: the decade that brought you modern life (for better or worse) Basic Bks. 2000 xxiv, 418p il hardcover o.p. pa $18.95 **973.92**
1. Nineteen seventies
ISBN 0-465-01496-5 pa

The author "aims 'to describe—and to judge' the transformation of American values during the '70s. Surveying politics, legal cases and opinion polls as well as popular culture, he links what he sees as America's loss of faith in government, the rise of 'sourness and cynicism' and the culture of licentiousness and divorce, among other social changes, to events in that decade." Publ Wkly
Includes bibliographical references

Gregory, Ross

Cold War America, 1946 to 1990; Richard Balkin, general editor. Facts on File 2003 670p il map $105 **973.92**
1. Cold War -- Social aspects -- United States 2. Cold war
ISBN 0-8160-3868-6

LC 2001-51136

"This is a treasure trove of statistical information documenting the enormous changes in American life from 1945 to 1990. . . . Found herein are data on everything from the population by sex . . . region, and race, business formations and failures, bull and bear markets, and operations of the postal service to the federal debt, high school seniors and drugs, executions by gender and race, and recipients of National Book Awards and Pulitzer Prizes. . . . Enhancing the work's appeal are photographs throughout the text and an exhaustive index." Am Ref Books Annu, 2003
Includes bibliographical references

Halberstam, David

The **fifties**. Villard Bks. 1993 800p il hardcover o.p. pa $17.95 **973.92**
1. Popular culture -- United States
ISBN 0-449-90933-6 pa

LC 92-56815

This is a social history of the United States during the 1950s.

The author's "sources are secondary and derivative, but his instinct for the revealing anecdote, his ear for the memorable quote, and his awesome powers of organization add up to a variegated overview that moves seamlessly between the serious shenanigans of Chief Justice Earl Warren and the frivolous ones of . . . Grace Metalious." Natl Rev

Includes bibliographical references

Hayden, Tom

The **long** sixties; from 1960 to Barack Obama. Paradigm Publishers 2009 272p $26.95   **973.92**

1. Lawyers 2. Nobel laureates for peace 3. Presidents 4. Senators 5. Social change 6. Social movements 7. State legislators

ISBN 978-1-59451-739-6; 1-59451-739-8

"With elements of a new Rules for Radicals and knowing takes on such old New Left moments as The Port Huron Statement, Hayden's book could be a worthy foundational document." Kirkus

Includes bibliographical references

Hodgson, Godfrey

The **gentleman** from New York: Daniel Patrick Moynihan: a biography. Houghton Mifflin 2000 452p il $38   **973.92**

1. Ambassadors -- United States 2. Diplomats 3. Legislators -- United States 4. Nonfiction writers 5. Political scientists 6. Senators 7. United Nations officials

ISBN 0-395-86042-3

LC 00-38921

"A cold war liberal, more of a regular Democrat than a reformer, Moynihan will no doubt be remembered as one of the smarter, more thoughtful elected officials of the late twentieth century. Others will probably produce more critical biographies, but, for now, Hodgson has supplied a fairly balanced overview." Booklist

Includes bibliographical references

Huchthausen, Peter A.

America's splendid little wars; a short history of U.S. military engagements, 1975-2000. Viking 2003 254p il, maps $25.95; pa $15   **973.92**

1. Intervention (International law) 2. Intervention (International law) -- History -- 20th century 3. Presidents -- United States -- History -- 20th century

ISBN 0-670-03232-8; 0-14-200465-0 pa

LC 2002-38025

This is "a review of America's conflicts since the fall of Saigon in 1975. Each of the 15 chronologically arranged conflicts has its own chapter, and they are also grouped by presidential administration, with the author demonstrating how U.S. foreign policy changed during each administration. The author does an excellent job of describing the circumstances surrounding the different conflicts, including eyewitness testimony and solid research to tell each story. . . . This book should appeal to subject specialists and casual readers alike." Libr J

Includes bibliographical references and index

King, Martin Luther

The **trumpet** of conscience; [by] Martin Luther King, Jr. Beacon Press 2010 80p $22; pa $12   **973.92**

ISBN 978-0-8070-0071-7; 0-8070-0071-X; 978-0-

8070-0170-7 pa; 0-8070-0170-8 pa

LC 2010007881

"In November and December 1967, Dr. Martin Luther King, Jr., delivered five lectures for the renowned Massey Lecture Series of the Canadian Broadcasting Corporation. The collection was immediately released as a book under the title Conscience for Change, but after King's assassination in 1968, it was republished as The Trumpet of Conscience. The collection . . . is his final testament on racism, poverty, and war. Each oration in this volume encompasses a distinct theme, . . . addressing issues of equality, conscience and war, the mobilization of young people, and nonviolence." Publisher's note

Kirkpatrick, Rob

1969; the year everything changed. Skyhorse Pub. 2009 302p $24.95   **973.92**

ISBN 978-1-60239-366-0

LC 2008-43073

The author "asserts that 1969 was the birth of modern America and sets out to relate how this incredible year reflected deep underlying changes in American culture. The book is divided into four parts that roughly outline the year, including 'sexual revolutions of springtime' and 'the apocalyptic standoffs at year's end.' A riveting look at a pivotal year." Booklist

Includes bibliographical references

Klosterman, Chuck

Eating the dinosaur. Scribner 2009 245p $25   **973.92**

1. Consumption (Economics) 2. Popular culture -- United States 3. Sports

ISBN 978-1-4165-4420-3; 1-4165-4420-8

LC 2009-18719

"Klosterman delivers his findings like earth-shattering epiphanies, letting the layers of subtle humor and irony fill in any gaps in logic. The result is a collection as much about the author and his way of thinking as it is about his topics. In both cases, the author is unique. Funny, irreverent and fascinating—Klosterman at his best." Kirkus

Kort, Michael

★ The **Columbia** guide to the Cold War. Columbia Univ. Press 1998 366p $60; pa $19.50 **973.92**

1. Cold war

ISBN 0-231-10772-2; 0-231-10773-0 pa

LC 98-7154

The author begins "with a narrative survey of the Cold War which explains some of the historiographical debates that have occupied historians for more than 50 years. Following this section is a mini-encyclopedia consisting of one- or two-page essays on a wide range of Cold War topics. The book concludes with a concise chronology and a comprehensive bibliography of books, films, novels, journal articles, and archival sources. Finally . . . Kort points out some of the relevant current websites and CD-ROM products." Libr J

Kuralt, Charles

Charles Kuralt's America. Anchor Books 1996
279p il pa $14.95 **973.92**
1. United States -- Social life and customs 2. United
States -- Description and travel
ISBN 0-385-48510-7; 978-0-385-48510-4
LC 96-18992
"Kuralt is not in search of crises or epiphanies; he values nature and good food, neighborliness and craftsmanship,
quaintness and quirkiness. Though no literary match for
American chroniclers like Calvin Trillin, the effable Kuralt
does, in un-fancy style, convey his enthusiasm and his engagement." Publ Wkly

On the road with Charles Kuralt. Fawcett 1986
363p il pa $19 **973.92**
1. United States -- Social life and customs 2. United
States -- Description and travel
ISBN 0-449-00740-5; 978-0-449-00740-2
"As a CBS reporter specializing in 'soft' news, Kuralt
has been roaming around the U.S. since 1967 in search of
'just plain folks.' Some 100 of the television interviews that
resulted from that search have been transcribed for this collection. Loosely organized by themes emphasizing the individuality, altruism, and humor that characterize small town
and rural Americans, the interviews and anecdotes are consistently entertaining." Booklist

Lifton, Robert Jay, 1926-

Witness to an extreme century; a memoir. Free
Press 2011 xv, 428 p.p il **973.92**
1. Authors 2. Biography, Individual 3. College
teachers 4. Nonfiction writers 5. Psychiatrists
ISBN 9781416590767; 9781416597186 ebook; 978-
1-4165-9076-7; 978-1-4165-9718-6 ebook
LC 2010046148
This book presents "a memoir of [American psychiatrist
Robert J.] Lifton's life and career." It "is a work of intellectual autobiography. . . . At bottom, [it] is a book about
scholarship and activism, and the links between the two. . .
. [Lifton's] passions include disarmament and social justice,
and he possesses a firm belief in the virtues of the autonomous intellect. The enemy is what he calls "totalism," by
which he means systems of political or religious belief that
seek to stamp out the possibility for independent thought. .
. . Lifton has tried throughout his life to develop and apply
a morally and politically consistent standard for humane behavior to his own nation as well as to others. In doing so, he
became an outspoken critic of the Vietnam War, developing
a close relationship in the early 1970s with antiwar Vietnam
veterans, whom he served as both clinician and advocate.
(N Y Times)

Marling, Karal Ann

As seen on TV; the visual culture of everyday life
in the 1950s. Harvard Univ. Press 1994 328p il map
$27.50; pa $20.50 **973.92**
1. Popular culture -- United States 2. Television --
Social aspects 3. Television broadcasting
ISBN 0-674-04882-2; 0-674-04883-0 pa
LC 94-2814

"A nostalgic, informative and sometimes funny view of
1950's American culture." Publ Wkly
Includes bibliographical references

Morrow, Lance

Second drafts of history; essays. Lance Morrow.
Basic Books 2006 323p $26.95 **973.92**
1. United States -- Politics and government -- 1989- 2.
United States -- Social conditions
ISBN 0-4650-4750-5
LC 2005-17092
"Loosely arranged by subject, these essays cover the
gamut of human experience, seen through Morrow's practiced yet unjaundiced point of view. Whether offering a fact-
laden piece on the AIDS epidemic or a personal meditation
on the Jonesboro, Ark., school shootings, Morrow manages—without becoming sentimental—to evoke the spirit of a
collective America. . . . Since Morrow is a weekly columnist,
the news of the day is often the primary subject." Publ Wkly

Patterson, James T.

Grand expectations; the United States, 1945-
1974. James T. Patterson. Oxford Univ. Press 1996
xviii, 829p ill., maps The Oxford history of the United States (pbk.) $27.95; o.p. **973.92**
1. United States -- Politics and government -- 1945- 2.
United States -- History -- 1945- 3. United States --
Economic conditions
ISBN 9780195117974; 019507680X
LC 9513878
In this book, author "James T. Patterson[s] . . . work .
. . weaves [together] the major political, cultural, and economic events of . . . America from 1945 through Watergate.
. . . [The book explores events from] the bloody campaigns
in Korea and . . . McCarthyism to the assassinations of the
Kennedys and Martin Luther King, to the Vietnam War, Watergate, and Nixon's resignation. Patterson . . . portray[s] the
. . . [economic] growth after World War II . . . as well as
the resultant buoyancy of spirit reflected in everything from
streamlined toasters, to big, flashy cars, to the soaring, butterfly roof of TWA's airline terminal in New York. . . . [A]n
important thread running through the book is a . . . depiction
of the civil rights movement--from the electrifying Brown v.
Board of Education decision, to the violent confrontations in
Little Rock, Birmingham, and Selma, to the landmark civil
rights acts of 1964 and 1965." (Publisherss note)

Restless giant; the United States from Watergate
to Bush v. Gore. James T. Patterson. Oxford University Press 2005 xii, 448p ill., maps $45 **973.92**
1. United States -- Politics and government -- 1945- 2.
United States -- History -- 1945-
ISBN 019512216X; 9780195122169
LC 2005016711
This book provides an "assessment of the twenty-
seven years between the resignation of Richard Nixon and
the election of George W. Bush in a . . . narrative that . .
. weaves together social, cultural, political, economic, and
international developments. . . . [Author James T.] Patterson
describes how America began facing bewildering developments in places such as Panama, Somalia, Bosnia, and Iraq,
and discovered that it was far from easy to direct the out-

come of global events, and at times even harder for political parties to reach a consensus over what attempts should be made. At the same time, domestic issues such as the persistence of racial tensions, high divorce rates, alarm over crime, and urban decay led many in the media to portray the era as one of decline." (Publisher's note)

Pietrusza, David

1960: LBJ vs. JFK vs. Nixon; the epic campaign that forged three presidencies. Union Square Press 2008 xx, 523p il $24.95   **973.92**
1. Members of Congress 2. Nonfiction writers 3. Presidents 4. Presidents -- United States -- Election -- 1960 5. Senators 6. Vice-presidents
ISBN 978-1-402-76114-0

LC 2009-291219

"The 1960 presidential campaign season was dominated by the personalities of three men, each of whom became president. . . . Pietrusza chronicles their roles and character in a stirring, hard-edged political saga." Booklist
Includes bibliographical references

Rather, Dan

The **American** dream; stories from the heart of our nation. Morrow 2001 xxii, 266p hardcover o.p. pa $12.95   **973.92**
1. American national characteristics
ISBN 0-688-17892-8; 0-06-093770-X pa

LC 2001-30031

In this book Rather tells stories of individual Americans and their dreams. He "groups his material into chapters that focus on elements of our national aspirations: liberty, enterprise, pursuit of happiness, family, fame, education, innovation, and 'giving back.' The Americans that Rather describes are a diverse group but, he urges, their stories are an inspirational reminder of the power of the nation's fundamental ideas to motivate a wide range of people." Booklist

Schwartz, Richard Alan

Cold War culture; media and the arts, 1945-1990. [by] Richard A. Schwartz. Facts on File 1998 376p il $60.50; pa $24.95   **973.92**
1. Cold War 2. Popular culture -- United States 3. Popular culture -- United States -- History -- 20th century
ISBN 0-8160-3104-5; 0-8160-4264-0 pa

LC 96-29642

This work "covers the various influences on American culture during the years 1945 to 1990. Schwartz organizes Cold War culture alphabetically within the following broad categories: art, cartoons, consumer goods, dance, film, games and toys, television and theater. . . . This reference source is easy to read and hard to put down as a browsing item." SLJ
Includes bibliographical references

Shelley, Fred M.

★ **Atlas** of American politics, 1960-2000; [by] Fred M. Shelley [et al.] CQ Press 2002 242p maps $156.25   **973.92**
1. United States -- Politics and government -- Maps
ISBN 1-56802-665-X

LC 2001-18267

This work "examines U.S. government and politics at the congressional district, state, and national levels from a combined historical, geographical, and political perspective. More than 200 maps from a variety of government and private sources show the relationship between the nation's geography and its political life. . . . This book provides a unique look at U.S. politics during the last 40 years and will be useful to students and researchers from the high-school level up." Booklist
Includes bibliographical references

Sirota, David

Back to our future; how the 1980s explains the world we live in now--our culture, our politics, our everything. Ballantine Books 2011 276p $25; ebook $12.99   **973.92**
1. Nineteen eighties 2. Political culture -- United States 3. Popular culture -- United States
ISBN 978-0-345-51878-1; 0-345-51878-0; 978-0-345-51880-4 ebook

LC 2010-41627

"The scope of the author's period knowledge is indisputable, and he parlays his experience as a Democratic strategist into politically charged discussions about the anti-governmental preaching on The A-Team, Ronald Reagan's questionable approach to Vietnam veterans and the bulletproof vigor of movies like Rambo, Red Dawn and Top Gun. . . . A sharp, dizzying history lesson that packs a punch." Kirkus
Includes bibliographical references.

Wheen, Francis

Strange days indeed; the golden age of paranoia. Public Affairs 2010 344p $26.95   **973.92**
1. Cold War 2. Espionage -- History 3. Members of Congress 4. Members of Parliament 5. Nineteen seventies 6. Nonfiction writers 7. Paranoia 8. Presidents 9. Prime ministers 10. Senators 11. Vice-presidents 12. World politics -- 1945-1991 13. World politics -- 1965-1975 14. World politics -- 1975-1985
ISBN 978-1-58648-845-1; 1-58648-845-7

LC 2009-941854

"A hugely entertaining book that makes you laugh, think, and look over your shoulder—sometimes all at the same time." Booklist
Includes bibliographical references

Woodward, Bob

Shadow; five presidents and the legacy of Watergate. Simon & Schuster 1999 592p il hardcover o.p. pa $16   **973.92**
1. Actors 2. Diplomats 3. Governors 4. Members of Congress 5. Nobel laureates for peace 6. Nonfiction writers 7. Parents of presidents 8. Presidents 9. Presidents -- United States 10. Senators 11. United Nations officials 12. Vice-presidents 13. Watergate Affair, 1972-1974
ISBN 0-684-85263-2 pa

LC 99-37045

Woodward examines the long-term effect of the Watergate Affair on the presidencies of Gerald Ford, Jimmy Carter, Ronald Reagan, George Bush, and Bill Clinton.

The author is an "effective investigative journalist. These skills are on full display in Shadow. . . . {The book} is most interesting as a reconstruction of the many scandals that have troubled the Clinton Administration." Nation

Includes bibliographical references

American empire, 1945-2000; the rise of a global power, the democratic revolution at home. Joshua Freeman. Viking 2012 512 p. Penguin history of the United States **973.92**
1. United States -- Economic conditions -- 20th century 2. United States -- Foreign relations 3. United States -- Politics and government -- 1945- 4. United States -- History -- 1945-
ISBN 0670023787; 9780670023783
LC 2011049263
In this book, author Joshua B. Freeman examines a postwar dominant America . . . . Covering the glory years of 1945-2000, Freeman . . . turns his critical eye on America's turbulent internal affairs, delving into Truman's contested Fair Deal reforms, the McCarthy communist witch-hunts, Eisenhower's cautious civil rights record, LBJ's ambitious Great Society programs, Nixon's Watergate disgrace, the return of corporate capitalism and Reagan conservatism. Freeman deals with the Clinton administration's economic policies . . . followed by the Republican victory in 2000. Though at its peak, America's power exceeded that of the Roman and British empires in cultural, economic, military, and political terms, the nation's postwar dreams were never completely fulfilled, says Freeman. (Publishers Weekly)

Postwar America; an encyclopedia of social, political, cultural, and economic history. James Ciment, editor. M.E. Sharpe 2006 4v il set $399 **973.92**
1. Reference books
ISBN 0-7656-8067-X; 978-0-7656-8067-9
LC 2004-13120
"A-Z entries address specific persons, groups, concepts, events, geographical locations, organizations, and cultural and technological phenomena. Sidebars highlight primary source materials, items of special interest, statistical data, and other information; and Cultural Landmark entries chronologically detail the music, literature, arts, and cultural history of the era. Bibliographies covering literature from the postwar era and about the era are also included, as well as illustrations and specialized indexes." Publisher's note
Includes bibliographical references

973.921 Administration of Dwight David Eisenhower, 1953-1961

Branch, Taylor
★ **Parting** the waters: America in the King years, 1954-63. Simon & Schuster 1988 1064p il hardcover o.p. pa $22 **973.921**
1. African Americans -- Civil rights 2. Civil rights activists 3. Clergy 4. Nobel laureates for peace 5. Nonfiction writers
ISBN 0-671-46097-8; 0-671-68742-5 pa
LC 88-24033

This history of the American civil rights movement from 1954 to 1963 focuses on the life of Dr. Martin Luther King.
The author "has searched out the hidden reality and often tragic human drama of the King years. On his best pages, the past, miraculously, seems to spring back to life. King himself appears human, all too human. Yet when the reader is done, his remarkable virtues and ordinary vices seem of a piece, the component parts of a coherent, towering personality." Newsweek
Includes bibliographical references

Eisenhower, Susan
Mrs. Ike; memories and reflections on the life of Mamie Eisenhower. Capital Bks. 2002 398p il pa $16.95 **973.921**
1. Presidents' spouses -- United States 2. Spouses of presidents
ISBN 1-931868-04-2; 978-1-931868-04-4
LC 2002-31378
"Enhanced by unpublished letters . . . this work is a good attempt at exploring a woman of another time who lived in a different state of grace." Libr J
Includes bibliographical references

Johnson, Haynes Bonner
The **age** of anxiety; McCarthyism to terrorism. [by] Haynes Johnson. Harcourt 2005 609p il $26 **973.921**
1. Anti-communist movements -- United States 2. Anticommunist movements 3. Senators 4. Terrorism -- Government policy -- United States 5. United States -- Politics and government -- 2001- 6. War on terrorism
ISBN 0-15-101062-5; 978-0-15-101062-2
LC 2005-13117
The author "offers an engrossing account of the career of red-baiting demagogue Joseph McCarthy and a chilling description of his legacy for today." Publ Wkly
Includes bibliographical references

Smith, Jean Edward
Eisenhower; in war and peace. by Jean Edward Smith. Random House 2012 950 p. (hbk : alk. paper) $40.00 **973.921**
1. Biographies 2. College presidents 3. Generals 4. Presidents 5. Presidents -- United States
ISBN 9781400066933; 140006693X; 9780679644293
LC 2011008605
This book presents a biography of former U.S. President Dwight D. Eisenhower. "Drawing on . . . untapped primary sources, [Jean Edward] Smith provides . . . insight into Ikes . . . apprenticeship under Douglas MacArthur in Washington and the Philippines. Then the whole panorama of World War II unfolds, with Eisenhowers . . . generalship forging the Allied path to victory through multiple reversals of fortune in North Africa and Italy, culminating in the triumphant invasion of Normandy. Smith also gives us an . . . examination of Ikes finances, details his wartime affair with Kay Summersby, and reveals the inside story of the 1952 Republican convention that catapulted him to the White House. . . . Smith . . . portrays an Eisenhower who engineered an end to America's three-year no-win war in Korea, resisted calls for preventative wars against the Soviet Union and China,

and . . . deployed the Seventh Fleet to protect Formosa from invasion. This Eisenhower, Smith shows us, stared down Khrushchev over Berlin and forced the withdrawal of British, French, and Israeli forces from the Suez Canal. . . . Domestically, Eisenhower reduced defense spending, balanced the budget, constructed the interstate highway system, and provided social security coverage for millions who were self-employed." (Publisher's note)

Wicker, Tom

Dwight D. Eisenhower. Times Bks. 2002 158p $20   **973.921**
1. College presidents 2. Generals 3. Presidents 4. Presidents -- United States 5. Presidents -- United States -- Biography
ISBN 0-8050-6907-0
LC 2002-20397
This work "captures the key events of the Eisenhower presidency in a way that is highly accessible and intellectually compelling." Libr J
Includes bibliographical references

Shooting star: the brief arc of Joe McCarthy. Harcourt 2006 212p $22   **973.921**
1. Biography, Individual 2. Senators
ISBN 978-0-15-101082-0; 0-15-101082-X
LC 2005-20990
This is a biography of the Senator from Wisconsin who led the House Committee on Un-American Activities and was censured by the Senate in 1954.
"This perceptive, well-written book should have wide appeal." Choice
Includes bibliographical references

973.922 Administration of John Fitzgerald Kennedy, 1961-1963

Bugliosi, Vincent

Reclaiming history; the assassination of President John F. Kennedy. W.W. Norton & Co. 2007 xlv, 1612p il $49.95   **973.922**
1. Conspiracies 2. Members of Congress 3. Murderers 4. Presidents 5. Senators
ISBN 978-0-393-04525-3; 0-393-04525-0
LC 2007-01545
The author argues that Lee Harvey Oswald was the lone assassin of John F. Kennedy.
"Destined to be the most significant challenge (save the Warren Report) to conspiracy theories, Bugliosi's study will provoke controversy and debate." Booklist
Includes bibliographical references

Dallek, Robert

An **unfinished** life: John F. Kennedy, 1917-1963. Little, Brown 2003 838p il $30; pa $17.95 **973.922**
1. Members of Congress 2. Presidents 3. Presidents -- United States 4. Senators
ISBN 0-316-17238-3; 0-316-90792-8 pa
LC 2002-116388
This is a biography of the thirty-fifth president of the United States.

The author "has written the most accessible, balanced, and scholarly biography yet of JFK. . . . It is the Kennedy biography against which others will be measured." Libr J
Includes bibliographical references

Dobbs, Michael

★ **One** minute to midnight; Kennedy, Khrushchev, and Castro on the brink of nuclear war. Alfred A. Knopf 2008 426p $28.95   **973.922**
1. Communist leaders 2. Cuban Missile Crisis, 1962 3. Heads of state 4. Members of Congress 5. Political leaders 6. Presidents 7. Senators
ISBN 978-1-4000-4358-3; 1-4000-4358-1
LC 2007-52250
The author discusses the Cuban Missile Crisis of 1962.
This book "is filled with . . . insights that will change the views of experts and help inform a new generation of readers." N Y Times Book Rev
Includes bibliographical references

Freedman, Lawrence

Kennedy's wars; Berlin, Cuba, Laos, and Vietnam. Oxford Univ. Press 2000 xx, 528p il hardcover o.p. pa $18.95   **973.922**
1. Berlin Wall, Berlin, Germany, 1961-1989 2. Cuban Missile Crisis, 1962 3. Members of Congress 4. Military policy -- United States 5. Presidents 6. Senators 7. Vietnam War, 1961-1975 8. Vietnamese Conflict, 1961-1975
ISBN 0-19-513453-2; 0-19-515243-3 pa
LC 99-87898
"Lawrence's book is an excellent treatment of U.S. foreign policy during this dynamic era and an insightful portrait of John F. Kennedy as a leader." Libr J
Includes bibliographical references

Fursenko, A. V.

One hell of a gamble; Khrushchev, Castro, and Kennedy, 1958-1964. {by} Aleksandr Fursenko and Timothy Naftali. Norton 1997 420p il hardcover o.p. pa $15.95   **973.922**
1. Cuban Missile Crisis, 1962
ISBN 0-393-31790-0 pa
LC 97-1022
For this diplomatic history of the Cuban Missile Crisis, the authors were granted "permission to review Krushchev's papers; they were also able to draw on archival material from other official Soviet sources." N Y Times Book Rev
Includes bibliographical references

Gitlin, Todd

★ The **sixties**; years of hope, days of rage. Bantam Bks. 1987 513p hardcover o.p. pa $19.95   **973.922**
1. College students -- Political activity 2. Radicalism -- United States 3. Students -- Political activity
ISBN 0-553-37212-2 pa
LC 87-47575
"Though ex-SDS leader Gitlin occasionally falls prey to the self-indulgence that snares most sixties' commentators, his analysis of the decade's politics is thought-provoking and clearheaded. Rather than singing the familiar hymn of

praise to youthful idealism, Gitlin carefully dissects why the activist spirit developed when it did and what its legacy has been." Am Libr
Includes bibliographical references

Halberstam, David

The **best** and the brightest; foreword by John McCain. Modern Library ed; Modern Lib. 2001 xxviii, 780p $24.95; pa $16,95 **973.922**
1. Army officers 2. Authors 3. Bankers 4. College teachers 5. Diplomats 6. Educators 7. Foundation officials 8. Generals 9. Government officials 10. International organization officials 11. Members of Congress 12. Nobel laureates for peace 13. Nonfiction writers 14. Political scientists 15. Presidential advisers 16. Presidents 17. Secretaries of defense 18. Secretaries of state 19. Senators 20. Statesmen 21. Vice-presidents
ISBN 0-679-64099-1; 0-449-90870-4 pa
LC 2001-31261
"The author describes analytically rather than narratively, how the Kennedy-Johnson intellectual (McNamara, Bundy, Rusk, Ball, Taylor, et al.) men praised as 'the best and the brightest' men of this century, became the architects of the disastrous American policy of Indochina." Libr J
Includes bibliographical references

Hill, Clint

Mrs. Kennedy and me; Clint Hill; with Lisa McCubbin. Gallery Books 2012 viii, 343 p.p **973.922**
1. Presidents' spouses -- Protection -- United States
ISBN 1451648448; 9781451648447; 9781451648461
LC 2011051017
This book is a memoir of guarding First Lady Jacqueline Kennedy through the young and sparkling years of the Kennedy presidency and the dark days following the assassination. Secret Service Special Agent [Clint] Hill . . . first met a young and pregnant soon-to-be First Lady in November 1960. For the next four years Hill would seldom leave her side. Theirs would be an odd relationship of always-proper formality combined with deep intimacy crafted through close proximity and mutual trust and respect. . . .When the bullet ripped into the president's brain with Hill not five feet away, he remained with her, through the public and private mourning. . . . Soon after, both would go on with their lives, but Hill would . . . never stop feeling he could have done more to save the president. (Kirkus)

Kaiser, David E.

The **road** to Dallas; the assassination of John F. Kennedy. [by] David Kaiser. Belknap Press of Harvard University Press 2008 509p il map $35 **973.922**
1. Members of Congress 2. Presidents 3. Senators
ISBN 978-0-674-02766-4; 0-674-02766-3
LC 2007-27305
"This is a deeply disturbing look at a national tragedy, and Kaiser's sober tone and reasoned analysis may well convince some in the Oswald-was-a-lone-nut camp." Publ Wkly
Includes bibliographical references

Kennedy, Caroline, 1957-

Jacqueline Kennedy; foreword by Caroline Kennedy; introduction and annotations by Michael Beschloss. Hyperion 2011 xxxii, 368 p.p 8 sound discs **973.922**
1. Presidents -- United States -- Biography 2. Presidents spouses -- United States -- Interviews
ISBN 9781401324254; 1401324258
LC 2012372265
This book, accompanied by a set of 8 compact discs (CDs), presents "seven historic interviews" by U.S. First Lady Jacqueline Kennedy "about her life with John F. Kennedy" (JFK). Recorded in 1964, "shortly after President . . . Kennedy's assassination," the interviews discuss JFK's political career and his views on various subjects, "including his thoughts and feelings about his brothers Robert and Ted, and his take on world leaders past and present." (Publisher's note) Other topics include JFK's reading habits, U.S. relations with Cuba, and Kennedy's relationship with her husband.

Kennedy, Robert F.

Make gentle the life of this world; the vision of Robert F. Kennedy. edited and with an introduction by Maxwell Taylor Kennedy. Broadway Books 1999 188p il pa $15 **973.922**
1. Quotations
ISBN 0-7679-0371-4
LC 98-55988
This is a collection of quotations by Robert F. Kennedy and the authors who inspired him.
"Chapters are arranged by issues that were most important to Kennedy and remain timely today—the responsibilities of citizens to their government, the tragedy of poverty in the midst of plenty, the importance of dissent in a democratic society, and work as the solution for the welfare crises. The book's haunting photos convey Kennedy's spirit as successfully as the words." Libr J
Includes bibliographical references

Thirteen days; a memoir of the Cuban missile crisis. with introductions by Robert S. McNamara and Harold Macmillan. Norton 1969 224p il hardcover o.p. pa $12.95 **973.922**
1. Cuban Missile Crisis, 1962
ISBN 0-393-31834-6 pa
A behind-the-scenes account of the Cuban Missile Crisis of 1962. Includes reproductions of pertinent documents and speeches by both President Kennedy and Nikita Khrushchev.

Leaming, Barbara

Mrs. Kennedy; the missing history of the Kennedy years. Free Press 2001 406p il $25; pa $14 **973.922**
1. Editors 2. Large print books 3. Presidents' spouses -- United States -- Biography 4. Socialites 5. Spouses of presidents
ISBN 0-684-86209-3; 0-7432-2749-2 pa
LC 2001-40442
"Asserting that Jacqueline Kennedy's role in shaping her husband's presidency has been under-examined, Leam-

ing . . . offers a corrective in this intimate look at a very private woman. Initially inclined to keep herself as much in the background as possible, says Leaming, Jacqueline Kennedy became an increasingly visible and vocal first lady as she realized how effective she could be as an image maker. It's in this capacity that Leaming convincingly depicts her as being instrumental in shaping the course of her husband's administration." Publ Wkly

Includes bibliographical references

Matthews, Chris

Kennedy & Nixon; the rivalry that shaped postwar America. {by} Christopher Matthews. Simon & Schuster 1996 377p il hardcover o.p. pa $14   **973.922**
   1. Members of Congress 2. Nonfiction writers 3. Presidents 4. Senators 5. Vice-presidents
   ISBN 0-684-83246-1 pa

LC 96-15677

This exploration of the rift between Kennedy and Nixon "shows how these two anti-New Dealers, anti-Communists, and freshmen members of Congress in 1946 became enemies as their political careers advanced." Libr J

Includes bibliographical references

Posner, Gerald L.

Case closed; Lee Harvey Oswald and the assassination of JFK. [by] Gerald Posner. Anchor Books 2003 608p il pa $17.95   **973.922**
   1. Members of Congress 2. Murderers 3. Presidents 4. Senators
   ISBN 1-400-03462-0; 978-1-400-03462-8

LC 2003-283539

In this book Posner argues that Lee Harvey Oswald was solely responsible for the assassination of President Kennedy and that none of the theories alleging conspiracy is valid.

"One of the strongest and most important features of the book, indeed, is Posner's painstaking dissection of each and every one of the competing conspiracy theories. None of them stands up under scrutiny." Natl Rev

Includes bibliographical references

Reeves, Richard

President Kennedy; profile of power. Simon & Schuster 1993 798p il hardcover o.p. pa $22   **973.922**
   1. Biography, Individual 2. Members of Congress 3. Presidents 4. Presidents -- United States 5. Senators
   ISBN 0-671-89289-4 pa

LC 93-24805

"Reeves doesn't try to soft-pedal the distasteful, but his account of the Kennedy presidency is resolutely matter of fact and not an indictment." Time

Includes bibliographical references

Taraborrelli, J. Randy

After Camelot; an intimate history of the Kennedy family, 1968 to the present. J. Randy Taraborrelli. Grand Central Pub. 2012 602 p.   **973.922**
   ISBN 9780446553902

LC 2011029518

For this book, which document[s] America's royal family, . . . [J. Randy Taraborrelli] conducted interviews with [Kennedy] family members and their intimates, such people as Eunice Kennedy Shriver, Oleg Cassini, Robert McNamara, Pierre Salinger, Arthur Schlesinger Jr., and numerous confidential sources. He also relied heavily on the 40 years of personal correspondence between Jackie Kennedy and Lady Bird Johnson. . . . [The book offers] a . . . view of family dynamics in crises both public and private: financial negotiations before Jackies marriage to Onassis; family interference in Pat Kennedy and Peter Lawford's troubled marriage; Ted Kennedys bad behavior at Chappaquiddick and his support of Caroline's abortive Senate run to carry on the family dynasty. (Publishers Weekly)

Thomas, Evan

★ **Robert** Kennedy; his life. Simon & Schuster 2000 509p il hardcover o.p. pa $15   **973.922**
   1. Attorneys general 2. Legislators -- United States -- Biography 3. Presidential candidates 4. Senators 5 Siblings of presidents
   ISBN 0-7432-0329-1 pa

LC 00-41995

"A solid, judicious life of a politician whose tragic death inspired a generation of what-if history." Booklist

Includes bibliographical references

973.923   Administration of Lyndon Baines Johnson, 1963-1969

Branch, Taylor

★ **At** Canaan's edge; America in the King years 1965-68. Simon & Schuster 2006 1039p il hardcover o.p.   **973.923**
   1. African Americans -- Civil rights 2. African Americans -- Civil rights -- History -- 20th century 3 Civil rights activists 4. Civil rights movements 5. Civil rights movements -- United States -- History -- 20th century 6. Clergy 7. Nobel laureates for peace 8 Nonfiction writers
   ISBN 0-684-85712-X; 0-684-85713-8 pa

LC 2005-40177

This is "the third and final volume of Taylor Branch's . . history of the life and times of King." (N Y Times (Late N Y Ed)) Index.

In this history that follows the life of Martin Luther King "from the protest at Selma and the 1966 Meredith March through King's expanding political concern for the poor to his 1968 assassination in Memphis, Tenn., Branch gives us not only the civil rights leader's life but also the rapidly changing pulse of American culture and politics. . . . This magisterial book is a fitting tribute to a magisterial man." Publ Wkly

Includes bibliographical references

Busby, Horace W.

The thirty-first of March; an intimate portrait of Lyndon Johnson's final days in office. [by] Horace Busby; with a preface by Scott Busby and an intro-

duction by Hugh Sidey. Farrar, Straus and Giroux 2005 250p il $24; pa $14 **973.923**
1. Members of Congress 2. Presidents 3. Senators 4. Vice-presidents
ISBN 0-374-27574-2; 0-374-53021-1 pa
This book "covers the 20 years during which Busby served as a trusted advisor and speechwriter for Johnson. This previously unpublished manuscript was discovered by Busby's son after his father's death in 2000. . . . This is an engrossing and important contribution to our understanding of a compelling political personality." Booklist

Caro, Robert A.
★ The **passage** of power; Robert A. Caro. Alfred A. Knopf 2012 xix, 712 p.p The years of Lyndon Johnson **973.923**
1. Biography 2. Johnson, Lyndon B. (Lyndon Baines), 1908-1973 3. United States -- Politics and government -- 1945- 4. Presidents -- United States -- Biography
ISBN 0679405070; 9780679405078
LC 2012010752
This book is part four of the author Robert A. Caro's biography of U.S. President Lyndon B. Johnson. This part covers both the most frustrating and the most triumphant periods of his career1958 to 1964. It is a time that would see him trade the extraordinary power he had created for himself as Senate Majority Leader for what became the wretched powerlessness of a Vice President in an administration that disdained and distrusted him. Yet it was, as well, the time in which the presidency, the goal he had always pursued, would be thrust upon him in the moment it took an assassin's bullet to reach its mark. (Publisher's note)

Risen, Clay
A **nation** on fire; America in the wake of the King assassination. John Wiley & Sons 2009 292p il $25.95 **973.923**
1. African Americans -- Social conditions 2. Civil rights activists 3. Clergy 4. Nobel laureates for peace 5. Nonfiction writers 6. Riots
ISBN 978-0-470-17710-5
LC 2008-26789
The author "has crafted a crucial addition to civil rights history, sure to absorb anyone interested in the times, the movement or MLK Jr." Publ Wkly
Includes bibliographical references

Witcover, Jules
The **year** the dream died; revisiting 1968 in America. Warner Bks. 1997 544p $25; pa $16 **973.923**
1. Presidents -- United States -- Election -- 1968
ISBN 0-446-51849-2; 0-446-67471-0 pa
LC 96-42017
Political columnist Witcover reviews "the tumultuous year in which the nation came 'unglued.' Nixon and Agnew vie for the villain's role, although neither would have been significant, contends the author, had LBJ not eroded his Kennedy legacy by escalating American involvement in Vietnam. . . . This backward look is enriched by the 20/20 hindsight of surviving participants, some still prominent in public life." Publ Wkly

The Columbia guide to America in the 1960s; David Farber and Beth Bailey, editors. Columbia Univ. Press 2001 508p il map $60; pa $25 **973.923**
1. United States -- Social conditions 2. United States -- History -- 1961-1974
ISBN 0-231-11372-2; 0-231-11373-0 pa
LC 00-65577
This reference work includes "a dictionary, an extensive annotated bibliography, a chronology of the era, and statistical information [and] two extraordinary bonuses: a section 'Debating the Sixties,' which includes ten essays by prominent historians . . . and an excellent 77-page history of the 1960s. This book is a fine addition to any library's collection." Choice
Includes bibliographical references

Taking charge; the Johnson White House tapes, 1963-1964. edited and with commentary by Michael R. Beschloss. Simon & Schuster 1997 591p il hardcover o.p. pa $16 **973.923**
1. Members of Congress 2. Presidents 3. Senators 4. Vice-presidents
ISBN 0-684-84792-2 pa
LC 97-26749
This book is a "selection of conversations taped by Lyndon B. Johnson during the first nine months of his Presidency—beginning on the day of the Kennedy assassination and continuing through the close of the Democratic National Convention in 1964. . . . There are no stunning revelations and no recorded moments of epochal importance. But 'Taking Charge' is a riveting book nevertheless. This is partly because it has been superbly edited and annotated by the historian Michael R. Beschloss, who has made everything—even the most arcane references—accessible to ordinary readers." N Y Times Book Rev

The Times were a changin' the sixties reader. edited by Irwin Unger and Debi Unger. Three Rivers Press (NY) 1998 355p hardcover o.p. pa $16 **973.923**
ISBN 0-609-80337-9 pa
LC 97-39844
"The broad range of viewpoints and the easy access to such an array of primary sources make the book a powerful adjunct for study of the sixties, as well as an interesting book for browsing." Book Rep

973.924 Administration of Richard Milhous Nixon, 1969-1974

Bernstein, Carl
All the president's men; {by} Carl Bernstein, Bob Woodward. Simon & Schuster 1999 349p il hardcover o.p. pa $14 **973.924**
1. Watergate Affair, 1972-1974
ISBN 0-684-86355-3; 0-671-89441-2 pa
LC 98-54773
The two Washington Post reporters whose investigative journalism first revealed the Watergate scandal tell the way it happened from the first suspicions, through the trail of false

leads, lies, secrecy, and high-level pressure, to the final moments when they were able to put the pieces of the puzzle together and write the series that won the Post a Pulitzer Prize.

Emery, Fred

Watergate; the corruption of American politics and the fall of Richard Nixon. Touchstone 1994 xvi, 559p il pa $25.95   **973.924**

1. Members of Congress 2. Nonfiction writers 3. Presidents 4. Senators 5. Vice-presidents 6. Watergate Affair, 1972-1974

ISBN 0-684-81323-8

LC 95-12511

"In addition to an introductory section on the cast of characters involved, Emery provides a detailed examination of the Committee To Reelect the President (CRP) and its dirty tricks: wiretapping, money laundering campaigns, and the infamous burglary of Democratic National Committee headquarters. Unlike much of the psychopersonal material that has come out on Nixon, Emery's book focuses on the tough political problems, documenting the need for impeachment and ultimately endorsing it. Riveting reading that is based on an unprecedented combing of the primary sources." Libr J

Includes bibliographical references

Feldstein, Mark

Poisoning the press; Richard Nixon, Jack Anderson, and the rise of Washington's scandal culture. [by] Mark Feldstein. Farrar, Straus and Giroux 2010 461p il $30; ebook $14.99   **973.924**

1. Political culture -- United States -- History -- 20th century 2. Political culture -- Washington (D.C.) 3. Presidents -- United States -- Press relations 4. Press -- Government policy 5. Press and politics -- United States -- History -- 20th century

ISBN 978-0-374-23530-7; 978-1-4299-7897-2 ebook

LC 2010-10272

"This fast-moving narrative will fascinate readers of recent American political and journalism history." Libr J

Includes bibliographical references

Killen, Andreas

1973 nervous breakdown; Watergate, Warhol, and the birth of post-sixties America. Bloomsbury 2006 312p $24.95   **973.924**

1. Nineteen seventies 2. Watergate Affair, 1972-1974

ISBN 1-59691-059-3; 978-1-59691-059-1

LC 2005-23661

This "is a high-definition snapshot, both nostalgic and perceptive, of a transitional time." Libr J

Includes bibliographical references

Kissinger, Henry

Years of renewal. Simon & Schuster 1999 1151p il maps hardcover o.p. pa $24   **973.924**

1. Cabinet officers -- United States -- Biography 2. College teachers 3. International relations specialists 4. Nobel laureates for peace 5. Nonfiction writers 6. Presidential advisers 7. Secretaries of state 8. Writers on politics

ISBN 0-684-85572-0 pa

LC 98-41038

"Statecraft defies simple solutions, and one of the merits of Kissinger's memoir—especially this somber and reflective third volume—is that he so rarely provides them." N Y Times Book Rev

Includes bibliographical references

Olson, Keith W.

Watergate; the presidential scandal that shook America. University Press of Kansas 2003 220p il $35; pa $15.95   **973.924**

1. Watergate Affair, 1972-1974

ISBN 0-7006-1250-5; 0-7006-1251-3 pa

LC 2002-38058

The author describes "the White House-approved break-in at Democratic National Committee headquarters in Washington's Watergate complex and its aftermath—most importantly, the dramatic proceedings of the Senate Watergate Committee.... {This} book provides an excellent, compact narrative of a crucial moment in the history of the American presidency." Publ Wkly

Includes bibliographical references

Perlstein, Rick

★ **Nixonland**; the rise of a president and the fracturing of America. Scribner 2008 881p il **973.924**

1. Members of Congress 2. Nonfiction writers 3. Presidents 4. Presidents -- United States 5. Senators 6. Vice-presidents

ISBN 0743243021; 074324303X; 9780743243025; 9780743243032 pa

LC 20080273706

The author discusses America's political landscape during the 1960s and 1970s and Richard Nixon's rise to the presidency.

This "is an exceptionally broad and thorough social, cultural and political history of eight tumultuous years. . . . It sings with outstanding storytelling and insight." Washington Monthly

Includes bibliographical references

Reeves, Richard

President Nixon; alone in the White House. Simon & Schuster 2001 702p il $35; pa $16 **973.924**

1. Members of Congress 2. Nonfiction writers 3. Presidents 4. Presidents -- United States 5. Senators 6. Vice-presidents

ISBN 0-684-80231-7; 0-7432-2719-0 pa

LC 2001-34417

This narrative "is chronological, from Nixon's inauguration in January 1969 to April 1973, when he realized that he had lost control over the Watergate scandals. . . . In between are Vietnam and crime in the streets, affirmative action and the end of the gold standard, Chile and the antiballistic missile treaty, the opening to China and, of course, Watergate. A fascinating study of the brilliant, profoundly flawed man elected to lead the nation through a troubled time." Booklist

Includes bibliographical references

Reston, James

The **conviction** of Richard Nixon; the untold story of the Frost/Nixon interviews. Harmony Books 2007 207p $22   **973.924**
1. Members of Congress 2. Nonfiction writers 3. Presidents 4. Presidents -- United States 5. Senators 6. Talk show hosts 7. Television producers 8. Vice-presidents 9. Watergate Affair, 1972-1974
ISBN 978-0-307-39420-0; 0-307-39420-4
LC 2007-1238
"In 1977, three years after his resignation, Richard Nixon returned to the public eye in a series of interviews with British television journalist David Frost, for which Nixon received $1 million. Figuring his political and lawyerly skills were more than a match for Frost's interrogation, Nixon instead found himself doing exactly what his successor, Gerald Ford, had tried to prevent with a presidential pardon: publicly admitting that he had broken the law. Reston Jr. was one of the aides Frost hired to help him plan his line of attack; this book, written at the time of the interviews, is being published for the first time now. . . . Reston's passion for finding the chinks in Nixon's armor makes for fascinating reading." Publ Wkly

Woodward, Bob

★ The **final** days; {by} Bob Woodward, Carl Bernstein. Simon & Schuster 1976 476p il hardcover o.p. pa $16   **973.924**
1. Members of Congress 2. Nonfiction writers 3. Presidents 4. Senators 5. Vice-presidents 6. Watergate Affair, 1972-1974
ISBN 0-7432-7406-7 pa
The title refers to the final days of the Nixon Presidency. The authors have "constructed a two-part narrative, the first half covering the period from April 30, 1973—the day John Dean was fired as White House counsel—until late July 1974, and the second half covering the last two weeks in detail." N Y Times Book Rev

★ Abuse of power; the new Nixon tapes. edited with an introduction and commentary by Stanley I. Kutler. Free Press 1997 xxiii, 675p hardcover o.p. pa $30.95   **973.924**
1. Members of Congress 2. Nonfiction writers 3. Political corruption -- United States -- History -- 20th century 4. Presidents 5. Senators 6. Vice-presidents 7. Watergate Affair, 1972-1974
ISBN 0-684-85187-3 pa
LC 97-32096
"This is an edited collection of transcripts of President Nixon's Watergate-related conversations made available under a 1974 Congressional directive covering tapes related to 'abuse of governmental power.' More than 90 percent of the volume covers the year after the June 1972 break-in and focuses on Watergate." Choice

973.925 Administration of Gerald Rudolph Ford, 1974-1977

Schulman, Bruce J.

The **seventies**; the great shift in American culture, society, and politics. Da Capo 2002 334p pa $17.95   **973.925**
ISBN 0-306-81126-X; 978-0-306-81126-5
"This is an important contribution to modern American social history and the literature of popular culture." Publ Wkly
Includes bibliographical references

973.926 Administration of Jimmy (James Earl) Carter, 1977-1981

Carter, Jimmy

An **hour** before daylight; memories of my rural boyhood. Simon & Schuster 2001 284p il hardcover o.p. pa $15   **973.926**
1. Country life -- Georgia -- Plains -- History -- 20th century 2. Farmers -- Georgia -- Plains 3. Governors 4. Nobel laureates for peace 5. Plains (Ga.) 6. Plains (Ga.) -- Social life and customs -- 20th century 7. Plains Region (Ga.) -- Rural conditions 8. Presidents 9. Presidents -- United States
ISBN 0-7432-1193-6; 0-7432-1199-5 pa
LC 00-48248
In this memoir, the thirty-ninth president of the United States remembers his childhood in rural Georgia.
This "is social and agricultural history as plain and honest as one of the tables the author makes in his workshop—an American classic." New Yorker

Morris, Kenneth Earl

Jimmy Carter, American moralist; {by} Kenneth E. Morris. University of Ga. Press 1996 397p il $29.95; pa $19.95   **973.926**
1. Biography, Individual 2. Governors 3. Nobel laureates for peace 4. Presidents 5. Presidents -- United States
ISBN 0-8203-1862-0; 0-8203-1949-X pa
LC 96-6350
The author asserts that "the Carter family is not quite the downhome, folksy clan of campaign advertising; they were actually rural gentry perched atop their county's segregated social pyramid. Members of the family were internally estranged, according to Morris, and Jimmy was a loner—a persona confirmed at Annapolis, where he left no discernible impression besides good grades. Yet Carter surmounted these aspects of himself and his background to become a gregarious integrationist, an indefatigable campaigner, and after a 1966 electoral defeat, a born-again Christian." Booklist
Includes bibliographical references

973.927   Administration of Ronald Reagan, 1981-1989

Brokaw, Tom

The **time** of our lives; past, present, promise. Random House 2011 xxii, 291p il $26; ebook $12.99   **973.927**
1. American national characteristics 2. Social problems
ISBN 978-1-4000-6458-8; 978-0-679-64392-0 ebook
LC 2011022825

"At this troubled point in the nation's history, . . . Brokaw offers a perspective from his own life and career. Drawing on interviews and observations, he ponders how the U.S. has come to a point where the country is suffering from eroding confidence, a financial crisis, declining education, and fears about China's progress. . . . Through the prism of his family and career, Brokaw looks back on the Great Depression, the civil rights era, the Cold War, and more recent history and looks forward to the future for his grandchildren and the nation. With commonsense values, he appeals to Americans to recommit to family and community, increase civic engagement, and make sacrifices in an effort to ensure some security for generations to come. An engaging recollection of the achievements of the past, the realities of the present, and the promise of the future." Booklist

D'Souza, Dinesh

Ronald Reagan; how an ordinary man became an extraordinary leader. Free Press 1997 292p hardcover o.p. pa $13   **973.927**
1. Actors 2. Governors 3. Presidents 4. Presidents -- United States 5. United States -- Politics and government -- 1974-1989
ISBN 0-684-84823-6 pa
LC 97-31396

The author's "provocative argument for Reagan's greatness opens a necessary and complicated debate." Commentary
Includes bibliographical references

FitzGerald, Frances

Way out there in the blue; Reagan, Star Wars, and the end of the Cold War. Simon & Schuster 2000 592p hardcover o.p. pa $17   **973.927**
1. Actors 2. Cold War 3. Cold war 4. Governors 5. Nuclear arms control -- United States -- History 6. Presidents 7. Strategic Defense Initiative
ISBN 0-7432-0023-3 pa
LC 99-59913

Fitzgerald offers a history of U.S. missile-defense programs over the last two decades, focusing particular attention on the Strategic Defense Initiative (SDI) supported by President Reagan.

"Explaining the Star Wars saga, Fitzgerald delivers all the information that any nonexpert could absorb." Booklist
Includes bibliographical references

Glenn, John

John Glenn; a memoir. [by] John Glenn with Nick Taylor. Bantam Bks. 1999 422p il $27; pa $7.99   **973.927**
1. Astronauts 2. Astronauts -- United States -- Biography

3. Large print books 4. Legislators -- United States -- Biography 5. Senators
ISBN 0-553-11074-8; 0-553-58157-0 pa
LC 99-42672

This is Glenn's account of how a "small-town Ohio boy weathers the Depression nurtured by conservative patriotic values, marries his high school sweetheart, flies combat missions in two wars, is selected as one of the original Mercury astronauts, becomes an instant national hero as the first American to orbit the earth, is elected to the Senate, and, after serving for four terms . . . returns to space aboard the Shuttle at age 77." Libr J

Johnson, Haynes Bonner

Sleepwalking through history; America in the Reagan years. {by} Haynes Johnson. Norton 1991 524p il hardcover o.p. pa $15.95   **973.927**
1. Actors 2. Governors 3. Presidents 4. United States -- History -- 1974-1989 5. United States -- Politics and government -- 1974-1989
ISBN 0-393-32434-6 pa
LC 90-38623

This is a study of American politics, history, and culture during the 1980s.

The author "concentrates on major events like the Iran-contra affair and the Wall Street scene, and briefly touches on other domestic scandals. . . . Not the definitive history of the 1980s, but recommended as an important book by an important author." Libr J
Includes bibliographical references

Mann, James

The **rebellion** of Ronald Reagan; a history of the end of the Cold War. [by] James Mann. Viking 2009 396p il   **973.927**
1. Actors 2. Cabinet members 3. Cold War 4. Cold war 5. Communist leaders 6. Governors 7. Nobel laureates for peace 8. Political leadership -- United States -- History -- 20th century 9. Presidents
ISBN 0670020540; 9780670020546
LC 2008029029

Mann discusses what President Reagan did, and did not do, to help bring America's four-decade conflict with the Soviet Union to a close. . . . [He examines] secret messages between Reagan and Moscow; internal White House intrigues; and battles with leading figures such as Nixon and Kissinger, who repeatedly questioned Reagan's unfolding diplomacy with Mikhail Gorbachev. He details the background and fierce debate over Reagan's famous Berlin Wall speech and [seeks to] show how it fit into Reagan's policies. (Publisher's note) Index.

Ronald Reagan did not win the Cold War, nor was he just historically lucky, as two contrasting viewpoints would sometimes have it. Instead, . . . [the author writes,] after a career of hard line anticommunism Reagan proved more flexible and visionary than many other leaders of American foreign policy and more opportunistic and insightful into the motives of Mikhail Gorbachev when the Soviet leader signaled change in the USSR's own conventional hard-line position. . . . Mann bases his argument upon impressive original research, including interviews with principals who range from George Shultz, to Colin Powell, to Helmut Kohl, to Nancy Reagan. Libr J

Includes bibliographical references

Ratnesar, Romesh

Tear down this wall; a city, a president, and the speech that ended the Cold War. Simon & Schuster 2009 229p $27   **973.927**

1. Actors 2. American speeches 3. Cabinet members 4. Cold war 5. Communist leaders 6. Governors 7. Nobel laureates for peace 8. Presidents

ISBN 978-1-4165-5690-9

LC 2009-24213

Drawing on interviews with Reagan administration officials, journalists, historians, and eyewitnesses, the author focuses on Ronald Reagan's June 1987 speech at the Brandenburg Gate and his historic challenge to Mikhail Gorbachev to tear down the Berlin Wall.

"This book may be read with pleasure by many, from trained historians to curious general readers. Generally objective in its approach, it will yet lead readers to understand why Reagan is remembered fondly by many and why both he and Gorbachev were key figures in this significant element of 20th-century history." Libr J

Includes bibliographical references

Reagan, Ronald

Reagan, in his own hand; edited, with an introduction and commentary by Kiron K. Skinner, Annelise Anderson, Martin Anderson; with a foreword by George P. Schultz. Free Press 2001 xxvi, 549p il $30; pa $16   **973.927**

ISBN 0-7432-0123-X; 0-7432-1938-4 pa

LC 00-66304

"A collection of . . . manuscripts is presented here, just as Reagan wrote them, including his corrections and notes. With a few exceptions, they are very short radio commentaries delivered during the pre-presidential period (1975-1979), focusing mostly on foreign policy and the economy." Publ Wkly

Reeves, Richard

President Reagan: the triumph of imagination. Simon & Schuster 2005 571p il $30   **973.927**

1. Actors 2. Biography, Individual 3. Governors 4. Presidents

ISBN 0-7432-3022-1

LC 2005-54198

This is an examination of the Reagan presidency.

This book "is a compelling read, fast-paced and scrupulously fair. . . . Anybody who is interested in Reagan's extraordinary presidency needs to reckon with Reeves." N Y Times Book Rev

Includes bibliographical references

Wilber, Del Quentin

Rawhide down; the near assassination of Ronald Reagan. Henry Holt and Co. 2011 305p il **973.927**

1. Actors 2. Governors 3. Presidents 4. Presidents -- United States -- Assassination

ISBN 0-805-09346-X; 978-0-8050-9346-9

LC 2010-49808

"On March 30, 1981, President Reagan walked out of a hotel in Washington, D.C. and was shot by a would-be assassin. For years, few people knew the truth about how close the president came to dying. . . . [Now, drawing on] new interviews, Del Quentin Wilber tells the [story]." (Publisher's note)

"A welcome addition to the literature of the Reagan era—and, for that matter, of political violence." Kirkus

Includes bibliographical references

The Iran-Contra scandal; the declassified history. edited by Peter Kornbluh and Malcolm Byrne. New Press 1993 xxxiii, 412p hardcover o.p. pa $24.95   **973.927**

1. Iran-Contra Affair, 1985-1990

ISBN 1-56584-047-X pa

LC 92-53732

This volume contains "one hundred documents concerning the Iran-Contra Scandal, covering the period from Reagan's original presidential finding of Dec. 1, 1981 to Bush's grant of executive clemency of Dec. 24, 1992. With a helpful chronology of key events and a glossary of major participants, the volume sets forth with contextual introductions the documents, the paper trail of this major controversy in contemporary American politics." Libr J

Includes bibliographical references

973.928   Administration of George Bush, 1989-1993

Parmet, Herbert S.

George Bush; the life of a Lone Star Yankee. with a new introduction by the author. Transaction Pubs. 2001 576p il pa $29.95   **973.928**

1. Diplomats 2. Members of Congress 3. Parents of presidents 4. Presidents 5. Presidents -- United States 6. Presidents -- United States -- Biography 7. United Nations officials 8. Vice-presidents

ISBN 0-7658-0730-0; 978-0-7658-0730-4

LC 00-42597

This biography of the forty-first president of the United States details his "climb up the business and political ladder in Texas . . . [then focuses on his] first runs for office, in 1964, when he faced a problem that dogged him his entire career: convincing right-wing Republicans that he was a true-blue Goldwater conservative. But he wasn't, and Parmet astutely analyzes both the contributors to and the forces within the Republican Party with which the unideological Bush had to contend." Booklist

Includes bibliographical references

Schell, Jonathan

Writing in time; a political chronicle. Moyer Bell 1997 303p hardcover o.p. pa $14.95 **973.928**

ISBN 1-55921-295-0 pa

LC 96-8516

This volume "traces the 1992 Presidential campaign, the election and President Clinton's first term through Jonathan Schell's columns for Newsday. This chronicle is a distinctly partisan one: Schell's views of the White House and its wannabes are seen strictly from the left. But the author's eye for issues and motives is so sure that even those who detest his opinions will find 'Writing in Time' a lively refresher course on five years of American history." N Y Times Book Rev

Woodward, Bob

★ The **commanders**. Simon & Schuster 1991 398p il hardcover o.p. pa $16   **973.928**
1. Admirals 2. Air force officers 3. Diplomats 4. Energy industry executives 5. Generals 6. Government officials 7. Members of Congress 8. Parents of presidents 9. Persian Gulf War, 1991 10. Presidential advisers 11. Presidents 12. Secretaries of defense 13. Secretaries of state 14. United Nations officials 15. Vice-presidents
ISBN 0-671-41367-8; 0-7432-3475-8 pa
LC 91-13037
This book discusses "top-level White House [and] Pentagon decisionmaking, first in the attack on Panama, and then in the 5½ months of diplomatic and especially military maneuvering that preceded the [1991] war with Iraq." Christ Sci Monit

973.929   Administration of Bill Clinton, 1993-2001

Applebome, Peter

Dixie rising; how the South is shaping American values, politics, and culture. Harcourt Brace 1997 393p il pa $14   **973.929**
ISBN 0-15-600550-6; 978-0-15-600550-0
LC 97-27787
The author explores the "contradictions of the modern South. Not only does the South exercise disproportionate political power (Dixie now claims leadership of Congress as well as the White House); most of our serious conflicts over race and religion continue to play out dramatically in the old Confederacy. Applebome's unusual historical literacy helps him understand a region drenched in the tradition and legends of the Civil War, racist demagoguery and the battles over integration." Publ Wkly
Includes bibliographical references

Clinton, Hillary Rodham

Living history. Simon & Schuster 2003 562p il $28; pa $16   **973.929**
1. Lawyers 2. Legislators -- United States -- Biography 3. Presidential candidates 4. Presidents' spouses -- United States -- Biography 5. Secretaries of state 6. Senators 7. Spouses of presidents 8. Women legislators -- United States -- Biography
ISBN 0-7432-2224-5; 0-7432-2225-3 pa
LC 2003-276264
"This book is important not because of the history Senator Clinton records, but because of the history she doesn't record, and what that airbrushing tells us about the history she aspires to shape." N Y Times Book Rev

Gormley, Ken

The **death** of American virtue; Clinton vs. Starr. Crown Publishers 2010 789p il $35   **973.929**
1. Clothing industry executives 2. Government

officials 3. Governmental investigations -- United States 4. Governors 5. Interns 6. Judges 7. Law teachers 8. Lawyers 9. Misconduct in office 10. Misconduct in office -- United States 11. Political ethics 12. Presidential aides 13. Presidential candidates 14. Presidents 15. Secretaries of state 16. Senators 17. Special prosecutors -- United States 18. Spouses of presidents 19. Whitewater Inquiry, 1993-2000
ISBN 978-0-307-4094-4; 0-307-40944-9
For those wishing to understand exactly what happened during this confusing, dismal time, Gormley's informed reporting and evenhanded analysis is the place to start. The entire nightmare vividly recalled. Kirkus
Includes bibliographical references

McDougal, Susan

The **woman** who wouldn't talk; {by} Susan McDougal with Pat Harris; introduction by Helen Thomas. Carroll & Graf Pubs. 2003 384p il $25; pa $14   **973.929**
1. Governors 2. Intimidation -- United States -- Case studies 3. Presidents 4. Prisoners 5. Real estate developers 6. Spouses of prominent persons 7. Whitewater Inquiry, 1993-2000 8. Witnesses -- United States -- Biography
ISBN 0-7867-1128-0; 0-7867-1302-X pa
LC 2002-192705
"In the 1996 Whitewater investigation, McDougal was indicted for fraud over a $300,000 loan, claiming that only her ex-husband, Jim McDougal, knew the money's intended purpose. Kenneth Starr, head of the Office of the Independent Counsel investigating Whitewater, offered her leniency if she would implicate President Clinton and Hillary Clinton. McDougal refused to testify, she writes, because she didn't want her statements about the Clintons' innocence twisted into perjury by the Starr Commission. She spent the next 21 months in prison on a charge of civil contempt. McDougal has written an engaging, sometimes gossipy, insightful biography, notable for its accounts of her different trials and more so for the depiction of life in women's prisons." Libr J

Reich, Robert B.

Locked in the cabinet. Knopf 1997 338p hardcover o.p. pa $15   **973.929**
ISBN 0-375-70061-7 pa
LC 97-71921
The author writes about his tenure as Secretary of Labor in the first Clinton administration.
"Reich has an acid pen, and he is by turns witty, churlish, and plain vulgar. . . . The specificity of detail in this book adds up not only to an absorbing accounting of failed service in the Cabinet but also to a powerful indictment of the Clinton Presidency." New Leader

Stephanopoulos, George

All too human; a political education. Little, Brown 1999 456p $32; pa $14.95   **973.929**
1. Governors 2. Presidents 3. Presidents -- United States
ISBN 0-316-92919-0; 0-316-93016-4 pa
LC 99-13817

This is a political memoir by a former senior advisor to President Clinton.

"A fascinating if controversial insiders account of life inside the Clinton pressure cooker administration during its early years." Libr J

Includes bibliographical references

Toobin, Jeffrey R.

A **vast** conspiracy; the real story of the sex scandal that nearly brought down a president. 1st Touchstone ed.; Simon & Schuster 2000 422p pa $20   **973.929**
    1. Governors 2. Presidents
    ISBN 0-7432-0413-1; 978-0-7432-0413-2

LC 00-59524
"Even for those who disagree with [Toobin's] assessment, the book is still hugely entertaining. There are plenty of scandal pellets to be found scattered throughout the analysis." Christ Sci Monit

Includes bibliographical references

Will, George F.

The **woven** figure; conservatism and America's fabric, 1994-1997. Scribner 1997 384p hardcover o.p. pa $21.95   **973.929**
    1. Conservatism
    ISBN 0-684-84820-1 pa

LC 97-34731
This is a collection of previously published newspaper columns presenting the author's views on such topics as affirmative action, abortion, welfare reform, the Clinton administration, multiculturalism, and campaign finance reform

973.93   -2001

Schama, Simon

The **American** future; a history. Ecco 2009 400p il $29.99   **973.93**
    1. American national characteristics
    ISBN 978-0-06-053923-8; 0-06-053923-2

LC 2009-358875
Schama "has begun wandering through the literature of the American past to snap up unconsidered trifles. The result is a book of mixed genre-history, memoir and journalism-and none the worse for that. In four successive chapters, Schama considers the American relationship to war, religion, immigration and prosperity. Within each, he moves between historical narratives and vignettes from the contemporary scene, usually involving his own presence. So the book's architecture is crisp, even as its rationale is mysterious." Times Lit Suppl

Shorris, Earl

The **politics** of heaven; America in fearful times. Norton 2007 371p $25.95   **973.93**
    1. Christian fundamentalism 2. Christianity and politics 3. Christianity and politics -- United States 4. Conservatism 5. Political culture -- United States 6. United States -- Politics and government -- 2001-
    ISBN 978-0-393-05963-2; 0-393-05963-4

LC 2007-12726

The author "offers a historical perspective on religion in the U.S., from Calvinist doctrine marrying religion and capitalism to the conservative modern-day gospels as preached by Billy Graham and Jerry Falwell. Drawing on research and interviews with political figures and advisors, academics, and theologians, Shorris examines the confluence of history, philosophy, experiences, and 'elemental feelings' that have gained enough momentum to become a movement of the fearful . . . Shorris eloquently offers a penetrating and unsettling look at American fear birthed by the horrors of the atom bomb and nurtured by 9/11 that promises to have an enduring impact on global and domestic policy for generations to come.." Booklist

973.931   Administration of George W. Bush, 2001-2009

Bernstein, Richard

Out of the blue; the story of September 11, 2001, from Jihad to Ground Zero. {by} Richard Bernstein and the staff of the New York Times. Times Bks. 2002 287p il hardcover o.p. pa $15   **973.931**
    1. September 11 terrorist attacks, 2001 2. Terrorism 3. Terrorism -- United States 4. Victims of terrorism -- New York (State) -- New York
    ISBN 0-8050-7240-3; 0-8050-7410-4 pa

LC 2002-20396
This account of the September 11, 2001 terrorist attacks focuses "on the personal—the victims, the perpetrators and heroes whose lives became tangled in catastrophe. . . . It uses these stories as a jumping-off point for a comprehensive look at the terror attacks—the reactions of New Yorkers, the nation and the world; the criticism of U.S. government agencies; the lingering effects of the tragedy. While some of this information has been published elsewhere, it has not been gathered so comprehensively—nor has it been written so well." Publ Wkly

Brill, Steven

After: how America confronted the September 12 era. Simon & Schuster 2003 723p $29.95; pa $16   **973.931**
    1. Disaster relief -- United States -- Finance 2. September 11 terrorist attacks, 2001 3. Terrorism -- United States 4. Victims of terrorism -- Services for -- United States -- Finance 5. War on Terrorism, 2001-
    ISBN 0-7432-3709-9; 0-7432-3710-2 pa

LC 2003-42727
This "book gives a sophisticated demonstration of the strengths and weaknesses of 21-century commercial democracy under pressure." N Y Times Book Rev

Includes bibliographical references

Bruni, Frank

Ambling into history: the unlikely odyssey of George W. Bush. HarperCollins Pubs. 2002 278p hardcover o.p. pa $12.95   **973.931**
    1. Baseball executives 2. Children of presidents 3. Energy industry executives 4. Governors 5. Large print books 6. Presidents 7. Presidents -- United States 8.

Presidents -- United States -- Election -- 2000
ISBN 0-06-093782-3 pa

The author, who covered Bush's 2000 presidential campaign for the New York Times, focuses on Bush's personality and mannerisms as well as his basic interactions with family, friends, and the public.

"Given [Bruni's] familiarity with Bush, one would expect his book to contain revealing insights, and this superb, incisive, and surprising account does not disappoint." Booklist

Includes bibliographical references

Buchanan, Patrick

Where the right went wrong; how neoconservatives subverted the Reagan revolution and hijacked the Bush presidency. [by] Patrick J. Buchanan. Thomas Dunne Books 2004 264p $24.95; pa $14.95   **973.931**
1. Conservatism 2. Economic policy -- United States 3. War on terrorism
ISBN 0-312-34115-6; 0-312-34116-4 pa
LC 2004-558171

This is a critique of the present-day conservative movement in the United States.

"Whether or not one agrees with [his] conclusions, Buchanan's book is provocative and will certainly ruffle feathers on both sides of the party line." Publ Wkly

Clarke, Richard A.

Against all enemies; inside America's war on terror. Free Press 2004 304p $27; pa $14   **973.931**
1. Baseball executives 2. Children of presidents 3. Counterterrorism 4. Energy industry executives 5. Governors 6. Presidents 7. September 11 terrorist attacks, 2001 8. Terrorism -- Government policy -- United States 9. War on Terrorism, 2001- 10. War on terrorism
ISBN 0-7432-6024-4; 0-7432-6045-7 pa
LC 2004-273844

"Richard A. Clarke knows too much, and 'Against All Enemies' is too good to be ignored. . . . It is a rarity among Washington-insider memoirs—it's a thumping good read." N Y Times Book Rev

Corn, David

The **lies** of George W. Bush; mastering the politics of deception. Crown 2003 337p $24; pa $12.95   **973.931**
1. Baseball executives 2. Children of presidents 3. Energy industry executives 4. Governors 5. Presidents
ISBN 1-4000-5066-9; 1-400-05067-7 pa
LC 2003-18347

The author chronicles "the lies, falsehoods, and misrepresentations of President George W. Bush. . . . He also shows that Bush committed them for a reason, engaging in 'strategic lying' in an effort to cover up his past and pave his way to governance. . . . From lies about his arrest and National Guard records, to environmental and energy concerns, to the war against Iraq, Corn has painstakingly unearthed a bill of particulars against the President that is as damaging as it is thorough." Libr J

Dowd, Maureen

Bushworld; enter at your own risk. G.P. Putnam's Sons 2004 523p $25.95; pa $15   **973.931**
1. Baseball executives 2. Children of presidents 3. Energy industry executives 4. Governors 5. Presidents
ISBN 0-399-15258-X; 0-425-20276-3 pa
LC 2004-48798

The author "is scorching in her analysis of the Bushes, putting them 'on the couch,' as they have contemptuously labeled efforts to delve into their relationship. . . . Bush detractors will love Dowd's sharp analysis, but even his fans should acknowledge her wit." Booklist

Draper, Robert

★ **Dead** certain; the presidency of George W. Bush. Free Press 2007 463p il $28   **973.931**
1. Baseball executives 2. Children of presidents 3. Energy industry executives 4. Governors 5. Presidents 6. Presidents -- United States 7. United States -- Foreign relations -- 2001- 8. United States -- Politics and government -- 2001-
ISBN 978-0-7432-7728-0; 0-7432-7728-7
LC 2007-23471

This book gives "the reader an intimate sense of the president's personality and how it informs his decision making." N Y Times (Late N Y Ed)

Includes bibliographical references

Farmer, John J.

The **ground** truth; the untold story of America under attack on 9/11. [by] John Farmer. Riverhead Books 2009 388p $26.95   **973.931**
1. Baseball executives 2. Children of presidents 3. Energy industry executives 4. Governors 5. National security -- United States 6. Political leadership -- United States 7. Presidents 8. September 11 terrorist attacks, 2001 9. Terrorism 10. Terrorism -- United States
ISBN 978-1-59448-894-8; 1-59448-894-0
LC 2009-23297

The author "presents a dismaying catalogue of incompetence and dissembling before and after the attack on the World Trade Center and the Pentagon. The author makes excellent use of declassified primary-source documents from 9/11—including transcriptions of frantic last-minute phone calls of air-traffic controllers—to demonstrate how a massively funded national-security system, a relic of the Cold War, failed to counter a small band of terrorists. . . . An important systematic brief on how an elaborately constructed national-defense system was penetrated, and why lessons of that day for disaster response remain dimly understood." Kirkus

Includes bibliographical references

Franks, Tommy

American soldier; [by] Tommy Franks, with Malcolm McConnell. Regan Bks. 2004 590p il map $27.95; pa $16.95   **973.931**
1. Biography, Individual 2. Generals
ISBN 0-06-073158-3; 0-06-077954-3 pa
LC 2004-558617

"The real value of 'American Soldier' . . . is not what it says about the war on terror, but what it reveals about

Tommy Franks. . . . The chapter on Vietnam, where Franks spent a year in brutal combat as a field artillery officer, is a cleareyed, mordant memoir." N Y Times Book Rev

Friedman, Thomas L.

Longitudes and attitudes; exploring the world after September 11. Farrar, Straus & Giroux 2002 383p $23   **973.931**

  1. September 11 terrorist attacks, 2001 2. Terrorism 3. Terrorism -- Press coverage -- New York (State) -- New York 4. United States -- Foreign relations -- 2001- 5. United States -- Politics and government -- 2001-

  ISBN 0-374-19066-6

                  LC 2002-74321

"Unapologetically pro-American, Friedman's deliberation on what changed on September 11 outside of the U.S. ultimately centers on the strength of American society and our place in the world." Publ Wkly

  Includes bibliographical references

Hersh, Seymour M.

  ★ **Chain** of command; the road from 9/11 to Abu Ghraib. HarperCollins 2004 394p map $25.95; pa $14.95   **973.931**

  1. Baseball executives 2. Children of presidents 3. Energy industry executives 4. Governors 5. Iraq War, 2003 6. Iraq War, 2003- 7. Presidents 8. September 11 terrorist attacks, 2001 9. Terrorism -- Government policy -- United States 10. War on Terrorism, 2001- 11. War on terrorism

  ISBN 0-06-019591-6; 0-06-095537-6 pa

"This sobering book is the closest anyone without a security clearance will get to operatives in the inner sanctums of America's intelligence, military, political and diplomatic worlds." Publ Wkly

Kaplan, Robert D.

Imperial grunts; the American military on the ground. Random House 2005 421p maps $27.95   **973.931**

  1. Military policy -- United States 2. Soldiers -- United States 3. Soldiers -- United States -- History 4. Special forces (Military science) -- United States 5. War on Terrorism, 2001- 6. World politics -- 1995-2005

  ISBN 1-4000-6132-6

                  LC 2004-61466

Kaplan's "on-the-ground reportage makes for riveting reading." N Y Times (Late N Y Ed)

  Includes bibliographical references

Kessler, Ronald

The **CIA** at war; inside the secret campaign against terror. St. Martin's Press 2003 362p il $27.95; pa $15.95   **973.931**

  1. War on terrorism

  ISBN 0-312-31932-0; 0-312-31933-9 pa

                  LC 2003-58487

The author "takes us from the formation of the CIA as an outgrowth of World War II OSS intelligence activities, when most agents were East Coast Ivy League elites focused on cold war scrimmages, through the current war on terror, where the enemy is often unknown and the agency elite are

somewhat more diverse. Through numerous interviews with both agents and operatives, Kessler brings to life a world generally described only in fiction." Booklist

  Includes bibliographical references

Mayer, Jane

The **dark** side; the inside story of how the war on terror turned into a war on American ideals. Doubleday 2008 392p il $27.50   **973.931**

  1. Military interrogation 2. September 11 terrorist attacks, 2001 3. September 11 terrorist attacks, 2001 -- Influence 4. United States -- Politics and government -- 2001- 5. War and emergency powers 6. War and emergency powers -- United States 7. War on Terrorism, 2001- 8. War on terrorism

  ISBN 978-0-385-52639-5; 0-385-52639-3

                  LC 2008-299452

This is an account of how the Bush administration has fought the war on terror.

  This is a "brilliantly researched and deeply unsettling book." N Y Times Book Rev

  Includes bibliographical references (p. 361-369)

Miller, John

The **cell**: inside the 9/11 plot and why the FBI and CIA failed to stop it; {by} John Miller and Michael Stone, with Chris Mitchell. Hyperion 2002 336p $24.95; pa $13.95   **973.931**

  1. Intelligence service -- United States 2. Large print books 3. September 11 terrorist attacks, 2001 4. Terrorism 5. Terrorism -- Government policy -- United States 6. Terrorism -- United States -- Prevention

  ISBN 0-7868-6900-3; 0-7868-8782-6 pa

                  LC 2002-27322

The authors analyze the circumstances inside and outside the United States that culminated in the September 11 terrorist attack. Included is an account of Miller's face-to-face meeting with Osama bin Laden in Afghanistan in 1998.

  This is a "frightening and important book." Publ Wkly

National Commission on Terrorist Attacks Upon the United States

  ★ The **9/11** Commission report; final report of the National Commission on Terrorist Attacks Upon the United States. Norton 2004 567p il $19.95; pa $10   **973.931**

  1. National security -- United States 2. September 11 terrorist attacks, 2001 3. Terrorism 4. War on terrorism

  ISBN 0-393-06041-1; 0-393-32671-3 pa

                  LC 2004-57564

This work aims to describe how the terrorist attacks of September 11, 2001 occurred and to provide recommendations for the prevention of future attacks.

  This book "reads like a Shakespearean drama. . . . This multi-author document produces an absolutely compelling narrative intelligence, one with clarity, a sense of shared mission and an overriding desire to do something about the situation." Publ Wkly

  Includes bibliographical references

Noonan, Peggy

A **heart,** a cross & a flag; America today. Free Press 2003 270p hardcover o.p. pa $19.95 **973.931**
1. American national characteristics 2. National characteristics, American 3. September 11 terrorist attacks, 2001 4. War on terrorism
ISBN 0-7432-5005-2; 978-0-7432-5048-1; 0-7432-5048-6

LC 2003-48336

"Noonan's essays are thoughtful, introspective, and deeply patriotic. Although she is devastated by the horror of 9/11, her spirits are lifted by the heroism and kindness she sees in her fellow New Yorkers, from the firemen who bravely raced into the doomed towers to the people who turned out to cheer on the rescue workers and firemen who toiled in the wreckage." Booklist

Ramo, Joshua Cooper

The **age** of the unthinkable; why the new world disorder constantly surprises us and what we can do about it. Little, Brown and Company 2009 279p $25.99 **973.931**
1. Military policy -- United States 2. United States -- Foreign relations -- 2001- 3. World politics -- 1991- 4. World politics -- 21st century
ISBN 978-0-316-11808-8; 0-316-11808-7

LC 2009-00854

This is "a fascinating look at various aspects of today's complicated world and how interconnecting systems often come to bear in unexpected ways." Libr J

Includes bibliographical references

Soufan, Ali H.

★ The **black** banners; the inside story of 9/11 and the war against Al-Qaeda. [by] Ali H. Soufan; with Daniel Freedman. W.W. Norton & Co. 2011 xxvi, 572p il map $26.95 **973.931**
1. September 11 terrorist attacks, 2001 2. Terrorism 3. Terrorism -- United States -- Prevention 4. War on Terrorism, 2001- 5. War on terrorism
ISBN 978-0-393-07942-5; 0-393-07942-2

LC 2011026938

A former FBI special agent offers an insider's account of how the September 11th attacks could have been prevented, as well as his role in the war on terror.

"The best and most original book published in the West on al-Qaeda, this is highly recommended." Libr J

Includes bibliographical references

Suskind, Ron

The **one** percent doctrine; deep inside America's pursuit of its enemies since 9/11. Simon & Schuster 2006 367p $27 **973.931**
1. Terrorism 2. Terrorism -- United States -- Prevention 3. War on Terrorism, 2001- 4. War on terrorism
ISBN 0-7432-7109-2; 978-0-7432-7109-7

LC 2006-279373

"Relying on . . . access to former and current government officials, this book [seeks to] . . . reveal for the first time how the U.S. government—from President Bush on down—is frantically improvising to fight a new kind of war." Publisher's note

Woodward, Bob

State of denial. Simon & Schuster 2006 560p il hardcover o.p. pa $16 **973.931**
1. Baseball executives 2. Children of presidents 3. Energy industry executives 4. Governors 5. Iraq War, 2003 6. Iraq War, 2003- 7. Presidents 8. War on Terrorism, 2001- -- Political aspects
ISBN 0-7432-7223-4; 978-0-7432-7223-0; 0-7432-7224-2 pa; 978-0-7432-7224-7 pa

LC 2006-285190

This is a critique of the Bush administration's handling of the war in Iraq.

"If journalism is the first page of history, then Woodward's opus will be required reading for any would-be historians of the time." Publ Wkly

Includes bibliographical references

Wright, Lawrence

The **looming** tower; Al Qaeda and the road to 9/11. Knopf 2006 469p map $27.95 **973.931**
1. Intelligence service -- United States 2. September 11 terrorist attacks, 2001 3. Terrorism 4. Terrorism -- Government policy -- United States
ISBN 0-375-41486-X

LC 2006-41032

The author "goes back—way back—to 1948 to dissect the personal influences and political radicalization that would lead to al Qaeda's attack on America." Libr J

Includes bibliographical references

The torture papers; the road to Abu Ghraib. edited by Karen J. Greenberg, Joshua L. Dratel; introduction by Anthony Lewis. Cambridge University Press 2005 xxxiv, 1249p il $30 **973.931**
1. Iraq War, 2003 2. Iraq War, 2003 -- Atrocities 3. Iraq War, 2003- 4. Prisoners of war -- Iraq 5. Torture 6. Torture -- Iraq 7. War on Terrorism 8. War on terrorism
ISBN 0-521-85324-9

"A gripping and alarming read about the use of government power." Choice

Includes bibliographical references

973.932   Administration of Barack Obama, 2009-

Balz, Daniel J.

The **battle** for America, 2008; the story of an extraordinary election. [by] Dan Balz and Haynes Johnson. Viking Press 2009 415p $29.95 **973.932**
1. Lawyers 2. Members of Congress 3. Nobel laureates for peace 4. Political campaigns -- United States -- History 5. Presidential candidates 6. Presidents 7. Presidents -- United States -- Election -- 2008 8. Prisoners of war 9. Secretaries of state 10. Senators 11. Spouses of presidents 12. State legislators 13. United States -- Politics and government -- 2001-
ISBN 978-0-670-02111-6; 0-670-02111-3

LC 2009-17129

This is an account of the 2008 American presidential campaign and election.

"Although we all know how things turned out, the authors know how to work a cliffhanger, and, as they effectively demonstrate, things could have turned out differently at any number of turns. Essential for watchers of politics and a model for similar electoral analyses in the future." Kirkus

Includes bibliographical references

Berry, Mary Frances

Power in words; the stories behind Barack Obama's speeches, from the state house to the White House. [by] Mary Frances Berry, Josh Gottheimer; foreword by Ted Sorensen. Beacon Press 2010 xxxiii, 267p $24.95   **973.932**

1. American speeches 2. Presidents -- United States -- Election -- 2008
ISBN 978-0-8070-0104-2

LC 2010004085

Collection of 18 of Obama's most memorable speeches between 2002 and 2008, each introduced by Berry and Gottheimer with political analysis, historical context, and commentary from the speechwriters.

"A book to savor and return to for subsequent readings." Kirkus

Includes bibliographical references

Frank, Justin A.

Obama on the couch; inside the mind of a president. Justin A. Frank. 1st Free Press hardcover ed.; Free Press 2011 256p $26   **973.932**

1. Lawyers 2. Nobel laureates for peace 3. Presidents 4. Presidents -- United States 5. Senators 6. State legislators 7. United States -- Politics and government -- 2009-
ISBN 978-1-4516-2063-4; 978-1-4516-2065-8 ebook

LC 2011025377

Maraniss, David

★ **Barack** Obama; the story. David Maraniss. Simon & Schuster 2012 xxiii, 641 p.p $32.50 **973.932**

1. Biographies 2. Politicians -- United States -- Biography 3. Presidents -- United States -- Biography
ISBN 1439160406; 9781439160404; 9781439160411; 9781439167533

LC 2011052983

This book offers a biography of Barack Obama, "the 44th president [of the United States,] through the age of 27." Topics include the "confluence of Kenya and Kansas in Obama's veins," "the legacy of his father's keen intellect, his mother's self-possession, social conscience, and anthropologists neutrality, and Obamas cosmopolitan childhood spent bouncing between Hawaii and Indonesia." (Publishers Weekly)

Taibbi, Matt

Griftopia; bubble machines, vampire squids, and the long con that is breaking America. Spiegel & Grau 2010 252p $26   **973.932**

1. Deception -- Political aspects 2. Despotism 3. Global Financial Crisis, 2008-2009 4. Political corruption 5. Political corruption -- United States
ISBN 978-0-385-52995-2; 978-0-385-52997-6 ebook

LC 2010-15067

This is a study of the causes and consequences of the 2008 financial crisis.

"Taibbi's glib prose is punctuated with just enough irreverence and wit to allow him to appeal to more casual readers while providing sufficient detail to satisfy those looking for a serious discussion of the high-level manipulation of the economy. Recommended for anyone interested in understanding the economy and how it got that way." Libr J

974   Specific states of United States

Vowell, Sarah

The **wordy** shipmates. Riverhead Books 2008 254p map $25.95   **974**

1. Pilgrims (New England colonists) 2. Puritans 3. Puritans -- New England -- History -- 17th century
ISBN 978-1-59448-999-0; 1-59448-999-8

LC 2008-30491

"A book dense with detail, insight, and humor." Booklist

★ The Encyclopedia of New England; the culture and history of an American region. edited by Burt Feintuch and David H. Watters; foreword by Donald Hall. Yale University Press 2005 xxiii, 1564p il map $65   **974**

1. Reference books
ISBN 0-300-10027-2

LC 2005-10353

For a fuller review, see: Booklist, Nov. 15, 2005

This "work aims to serve as an authoritative resource of information about people, places, events, culture, and ideas of the region. . . . [This is] a valuable tool for students, researchers, and casual readers alike." Libr J

Includes bibliographical references

974.4   Massachusetts

Bradford, William

Of Plymouth Plantation, 1620-1647; the complete text, with notes and an introduction by Samuel Eliot Morison. Knopf 1952 xliii, 448p maps $25   **974.4**

1. Pilgrims (New England colonists)
ISBN 0-394-43895-7

"The opening book sketches the origin of the Separatist movement, the flight from England to Holland, the settlement at Leiden, the plans for the settlement in New England, and the Mayflower voyage. The second book, which includes the major part of the history, is in the form of annals from 1620 to 1646, and describes every aspect of the life of the Pilgrims. Besides being a primary historical source, the work has artistic value because of its dignified, sonorous style, deriving from the Geneva Bible." Oxford Companion to Am Lit. 5th edition

Bremer, Francis J.

John Winthrop; America's forgotten founding father. Oxford University Press 2003 478p il hardcover o.p. pa $21.95   **974.4**

1. Clergy 2. Colonial administrators 3. Government officials

ISBN 0-19-514913-0; 978-0-19-517981-1 pa; 0-19-517981-1 pa

LC 2002-38143

"Bremer's definitive biography gracefully portrays Winthrop as a man of his time, whose influence in the new colony grew out of his own struggles to establish his identity before he left England." Publ Wkly

Includes bibliographical references

Bunker, Nick

★ **Making** haste from Babylon; the Mayflower Pilgrims and their world: a new history. Alfred A. Knopf 2010 489p il map $30   **974.4**

1. Pilgrims (New England colonists) 2. Pilgrims (New Plymouth Colony)

ISBN 978-0-307-26682-8; 0-307-26682-6

LC 2009038520

This is an "account of the Mayflower project and the first decade of the Plymouth Colony." (Publisher's note)

"Never before has such a comprehensive and thoroughly researched study of the subject appeared. . . . [This book] scoops up every relevant character and links all to the basic tale of indomitable courage, religious faith, commercial ambition, international rivalry, and domestic politics. The results are stunning. Certain to be the dominating work on the Pilgrims for decades." Publ Wkly

Includes bibliographical references

Cliff, Nigel

The **Shakespeare** riots; revenge, drama, and death in nineteenth-century America. Random House 2007 312p il $26.95   **974.4**

1. Actors 2. Astor Place Riot, New York, 1849 3. Authors 4. Dramatists 5. Poets 6. Riots -- New York (N.Y.) 7. Theater -- New York (N.Y.) -- History -- 19th century

ISBN 9780345486943; 0-345-48694-3

LC 2006-49139

"Cliff argues persuasively that 'the Astor Place riot,' as it came to be known, marked a turning point in America's search for a national identity. . . . [This] is an intriguing, thought-provoking book." Washington Post Book World

Includes bibliographical references

Corbett, Christopher

Poker bride; the first Chinese in the Wild West. Atlantic Monthly Press 2010 218p il $24   **974.4**

1. Chinese -- California -- San Francisco 2. Chinese American women -- History 3. Chinese Americans -- History 4. Pioneers

ISBN 978-0-8021-1909-4; 0-8021-1909-3

This book mixes a "mystery-wrapped story with the larger picture of Chinese immigration into the American West. The central story concerns a young Chinese woman sold by her family in 1872 into indentured prostitution. She turns up as a concubine in Idaho, is said then to have been won

by another man in a poker game, and became Polly Bemis, the winner's legal, beloved wife in the remote wilderness of Idaho. Polly emerged into public view only in 1923, a tiny old woman on horseback, her identity and story known only to a few old-timers. Corbett wisely sets Bemis's life into the context of Chinese immigration, gold-country anti-Chinese prejudice, and life in the mining communities." Publ Wkly

Includes bibliographical references

East, Elyssa

Dogtown; death and enchantment in a New England ghost town. Free Press 2009 291p map $26   **974.4**

ISBN 978-1-4165-8704-0; 1-4165-8704-7

LC 2009-17197

"A true-crime story, an art appreciation course and an American history lesson stitched together, and it succeeds as all three. . . . Plaudits to East for exploring the relationship of the land to artists, as well as to the people who live upon it, in this case for generations." N Y Times Book Rev

Francis, Richard

Fruitlands; the Alcott family and their search for utopia. Yale University Press 2010 321p il $30   **974.4**

1. Authors 2. Biography, Collective 3. Communal living 4. Educators 5. Journalists 6. Nonfiction writers 7. Philosophers 8. Social reformers 9. Transcendentalism 10. Utopias

ISBN 978-0-300-14041-5; 0-300-14041-X

LC 2010-19705

The book "examin[es] . . . the complicated intellectual and emotional entanglements not just between Fruitlands' titular 'heads,' New Englander Amos Bronson Alcott and Englishman Charles Lane, but . . . the many people with whom they interacted before and during the community's brief seven-month existence, from June to December 1843. . . . Francis begins his examination of Fruitlands a few years earlier with the failure and collapse of Bronson Alcott's infamous Temple School in Boston, and the controversial educator's subsequent vilification. . . . Alcott's fall from grace as an innovative and progressive educator was accompanied by his nearly simultaneous apotheosis overseas among the English Transcendentalists. Francis devotes the first third of the book to this crucial period of cross-cultural germination . . . The second two-thirds of Francis's study examines the months immediately preceding the utopian experiment fourteen miles west of Concord, day-to-day life at Fruitlands itself, and its demise in December 1843." (American Historical Review)

"Though obviously sympathetic to the Fruitlands experiment, Mr. Francis gives us enough facts to let us draw our own conclusions. . . . Along the way he adumbrates the ways in which idealism can slide into megalomania." Wall Street J

Includes bibliographical references

Kidder, Tracy

Home town. Washington Square Press 2000 432p pa $14.95   **974.4**

1. City and town life

ISBN 978-0-671-78521-5; 0-671-78521-4

This "acutely observed, crisply written, and utterly absorbing documentary proves that there is nothing on this spinning earth more amazing and full of grace than everyday life." Booklist

Includes bibliographical references

Manegold, Catherine

Ten Hills Farm; the forgotten history of slavery in the North. [by] C.S. Manegold. Princeton University Press 2010 317p il map $29.95   **974.4**
1. Slave trade -- Massachusetts 2. Slavery -- Massachusetts 3. Slavery -- United States 4. Slaves -- Massachusetts
ISBN 978-0-691-13152-8; 0-691-13152-X
LC 2009030875
This book tells the story "of five generations of slave owners in colonial New England. Settled in 1630, . . . Ten Hills Farm, a six-hundred-acre estate just north of Boston, passed from the Winthrops to the Ushers, to the Royalls—all . . . dynasties tied to the Native American and Atlantic slave trades." (Publisher's note) Index.
"Full of rich historical detail, this is a story that needed to be told." Kirkus

Includes bibliographical references

Masur, Louis P.

The **soiling** of Old Glory; the story of a photograph that shocked America. Bloomsbury Press 2008 224p il $24.95   **974.4**
1. African Americans -- Massachusetts -- Boston 2. Busing (School integration) 3. Busing for school integration -- Massachusetts -- Boston -- History 4. Demonstrations 5. Flags -- Desecration 6. Photojournalism 7. Photojournalists
ISBN 978-1-59691-364-6; 1-59691-364-9
LC 2007-31215
"On April 5, 1976, an antibusing rally in Boston grew violent when African American lawyer Ted Landsmark was attacked by some of the protesters. News photographer Stanley Forman captured the ruckus on film; one photo gained international attention and is the subject of this . . . study by Masur. . . . Masur writes descriptively about the photo while creating an ethnographic history of 1970s Boston, with diversions into the political and cultural uses of the American flag and the history of photojournalism in the United States. He also describes the aftermath of the photo's front-page publication. . . . A compelling story; highly recommended for all high school, public, and academic libraries." Libr J

Includes bibliographical references

Nugent, Rory

Down at the docks. Pantheon Books 2009 290p $24.95   **974.4**
1. Commercial fishing
ISBN 978-0-375-42064-1; 0-375-42064-9
LC 2008-20104
The author "describes his sometime home of New Bedford, Massachusetts. Long famous for whaling—Melville set sail from there—the city remains a major fishing port and produces the most valuable annual catch of any in the country. But in the past two decades consolidation and legislation have shackled what Nugent eulogizes as the fleet's 'frontier

mentality.' This canny self-reliance took a variety of forms; Nugent documents two kinds of insurance fraud and a 'night menu' of drugs smuggled to supplement the legitimate catch. Nugent strings together his subjects' boasts, banter, and laments into an engagingly anecdotal social history, fleshed out by strokes of fine description." New Yorker

Schama, Simon

Dead certainties; unwarranted speculations. Knopf 1991 333p hardcover o.p. pa $16   **974.4**
1. Generals 2. Historians 3. Historiography 4. Horticulturists 5. Murder victims 6. Physicians
ISBN 0-679-73613-1 pa
LC 90-52902
This exploration of the nature of historical writing consists of two stories. The first one "is concerned with the battlefield death of James Wolfe, British commander in the North American campaign of the Seven Years' War; the second with the murder ninety years later of a Harvard Medical School professor, George Parkman." New Repub

974.5   Rhode Island

Barry, John M.

Roger Williams and the creation of the American soul; church, state, and the birth of liberty. John M. Barry. Viking 2012 464 p.   **974.5**
ISBN 0670023051; 9780670023059
LC 2011032995
This book by John M. Barry offers a look at how Roger Williams shaped the nature of religion, political power, and individual rights in America. . . . Americans have [always] wrestled with . . . two concepts that define the nature of the nation: the proper relation between church and state and between a free individual and the state. These debates began with the extraordinary thought and struggles of Roger Williams. . . . This is a story . . . set against Puritan America and the English Civil War. Williams's interactions with King James, Francis Bacon, Oliver Cromwell, and his mentor Edward Coke set his course, but his fundamental ideas came to fruition in America, as Williams, though a Puritan, collided with John Winthrop's vision of his City upon a Hill. (Publishers note)

974.7   New York

Anasi, Robert

The **last** bohemia; scenes from the life of Williamsburg, Brooklyn. Robert Anasi. Farrar, Straus and Giroux 2012 240 p. (alk. paper) $15.00 **974.7**
1. Bohemianism -- New York (State) -- New York 2. City and town life -- New York (State) -- New York 3. Social change -- New York (State) -- New York
ISBN 0374533318; 9780374533311
LC 2011051267
This memoir about Brooklyn, New York focuses on the "eternal clash between authenticity, art, and real estate development." Author "[Robert] Anasi witnessed Williamsburgs progress in the 1990s and 2000s from crime-ridden working-class neighborhood overshadowed by crumbling

factories . . . to edgy arts scene and hipster mecca to end-stage self-parody as an unaffordably upscale 'Bohemian theme park.'" (Publishers Weekly)

Bloom, Ken

Broadway; its history, people, and places: an encyclopedia. 2nd ed; Routledge 2003 679p il $95   **974.7**

1. Theater -- New York (N.Y.)

ISBN 0-415-93704-3

LC 2003-2692

"Following a brief historical overview, . . . {the author} presents 394 alphabetical entries with multiple cross references for easy browsing. The most substantial entries cover theaters, playwrights, composers, directors, performers, and producers, with a special emphasis on composers and lyricists. . . . Bloom adds a touch of atmosphere with entries on critics, restaurants, publicity stunts, nightclubs, and other periphery characters and incidents that are so much a part of the Great White Way. As much a storyteller as a chronicler, he uses anecdotes and a plethora of black-and-white photographs, many never before published, to produce an entertaining as well as an informative work. Highly recommended for all theater collections." Libr J

Includes bibliographical references

Burns, Cherie

The **great** hurricane--1938. Atlantic Monthly Press 2005 240p il $24   **974.7**

1. Hurricanes

ISBN 0-8711-3893-X

LC 2005-41211

The author discusses the hurricane of September 1938, which affected the northeastern United States from Long Island to Providence, Rhode Island.

The author "has dug up old newspaper accounts and local histories to reconstruct the terror and destruction that accompanied the 1938 hurricane. Those who suffered the most, of course, did not survive to tell their tales. Nearly 700 people died, and about 63,000 were left homeless. . . . Survivor's stories, however, give ample feeling for the power of the rain, tide, and wind." Nat Hist

Burrows, Edwin G.

Gotham; a history of New York City to 1898. {by} Edwin G. Burrows and Mike Wallace. Oxford Univ. Press 1998 xxiv, 1383p il maps hardcover o.p. pa $29.95   **974.7**

ISBN 0-19-514049-4 pa

LC 97-39308

This history "begins with the Indian settlements and the subsequent seizure of the city by the Dutch in 1626 and continues up to the consolidation of the five boroughs in 1898. The authors . . . cover an extraordinary range of topics, including religion, race, gender and class, architecture, society and the arts, noted personalities, sports and the special customs immigrants brought with them." America

Includes bibliographical references

Dwyer, Jim

102 minutes; the untold story of the fight to survive inside the Twin Towers. [by] Jim Dwyer and

Kevin Flynn. Times Books 2005 322p il $26; pa $15   **974.7**

1. September 11 terrorist attacks, 2001 2. World Trade Center terrorist attack, 2001

ISBN 0-8050-7682-4; 0-8050-8032-5 pa

LC 2004-55321

Dwyer and Flynn have "given us a fitting tribute to the people caught up in one of the great dramas of our time. And for people still haunted by the events of that day, reading '102 Minutes' provides a cathartic release." N Y Times Book Rev

Friend, David

Watching the world change; the stories behind the images of 9/11. Farrar, Straus and Giroux 2006 435p il $30   **974.7**

1. Documentary photography 2. September 11 terrorist attacks, 2001 3. September 11 terrorist attacks, 2001 -- Pictorial works

ISBN 978-0-374-29933-0; 0-374-29933-1

LC 2005-36158

In this "analysis of how images of 9/11 and the 'war on terror' have altered our understanding of power, world politics, religion and identity, . . . [the author] successfully merges reportage and analysis as he interprets the images of falling towers, panic in Manhattan streets and prisoners at Abu Ghraib that have been burned into our brains." Publ Wkly

Includes bibliographical references

Gage, Beverly

The **day** Wall Street exploded; a story of America in its first age of terror. Oxford University Press 2009 400p il   **974.7**

1. Bombings 2. Terrorism 3. Terrorism -- New York (N.Y.) 4. Terrorism -- United States -- History 5. Wall Street (New York, N.Y.)

ISBN 0-19-514824-X; 978-0-19-514824-4

LC 2008022074

This is an account of the "1920 terrorist attack on Wall Street—why it happened [and] how it shaped American politics." (Publisher's note) Index.

"Gage has performed a real service, both in presenting such a complicated case in such a fair and balanced way and in reminding readers how large a space terrorism once occupied on the political landscape." San Francisco Chron

Includes bibliographical references

Gill, Jonathan

Harlem; the four hundred year history from Dutch village to capital of black America. Grove Press 2011 520p il map $29.95   **974.7**

ISBN 978-0-8021-1910-0

"Comprehensive and compassionate—an essential text of American history and culture." Kirkus

Includes bibliographical references

Goodman, Matthew

The **Sun** and the moon; the remarkable true account of hoaxers, showmen, dueling journalists, and

lunar man-bats in nineteenth-century New York. Basic Books 2008 350p il $26; pa $15 **974.7**
1. Fraud 2. Journalism
ISBN 978-0-465-00257-3; 0-465-00257-9; 978-0-465-01900-7 pa; 0-465-01900-5 pa

LC 2008-23617

"These incredible events occurred during a great democratization of media, with affordable news for all and the seeds of pop culture beginning to take root. To read The Sun and the Moon is to enter a world of aeronauts, automaton chess players, and glorious lunar temples. It is the old New York of P.T. Barnum brought into incredible focus and Goodman's research couldn't be more comprehensive." PopMatters

Includes bibliographical references

Gopnik, Adam

Through the children's gate; a home in New York. Alfred A. Knopf 2006 318p $25 **974.7**
1. Art critics 2. Authors 3. Essayists 4. Journalists 5. Novelists 6. Young adult authors
ISBN 1-4000-4181-3; 978-1-4000-4181-7

LC 2006-45260

"You don't have to be a New Yorker or even necessarily an enthusiast of the city to be alternately amused, touched, and charmed by Gopnik's well-crafted pieces." Christ Sci Monit

Homberger, Eric

The **historical** atlas of New York City; a visual celebration of nearly 400 years of New York City's history. Alice Hudson, cartographic consultant. Holt & Co. 1994 192p il maps hardcover o.p. pa $22 **974.7**
1. Historical atlases
ISBN 0-8050-6004-9 pa

LC 94-18992

This is an "encyclopedic overview of the history of New York City. . . . Detailed color maps abound, accompanied by a running commentary of major historical and cultural eras. Many of the most detailed maps are rendered schematically for easier reading. Each period treated features historical photos and illustrations along with accompanying map(s). . . . A visual delight." Libr J

Khan, Yasmin Sabina

Enlightening the world; the creation of the Statue of Liberty. Cornell University Press 2010 231p il $24.95 **974.7**
1. Artists 2. National monuments 3. Sculptors
ISBN 978-0-8014-4851-5; 0-8014-4851-4

LC 2009035711

This is "a lucid account connecting France's widespread grief over Abraham Lincoln's 1865 assassination with that country's own struggles to establish a lasting democracy. Khan shows how Édouard-René Lefebvre de Laboulaye, a legal scholar and celebrant of French-American friendship, led others to design and construct what was officially called Liberty Enlightening the World. . . . An important book for general audiences." Publ Wkly

Includes bibliographical references

Langewiesche, William

American ground, unbuilding the World Trade Center. North Point Press 2002 205p $22; pa $13 **974.7**
1. September 11 terrorist attacks, 2001
ISBN 0-86547-582-2; 0-86547-675-6 pa

LC 2002-75153

"This is a genuinely monumental story, told without melodrama, an intimate depiction of ordinary Americans reacting to grand-scale tragedy at their best—and sometimes their worst." Publ Wkly

Lepore, Jill

New York burning; liberty, slavery, and conspiracy in an eighteenth-century Manhattan. Alfred A. Knopf 2005 323p il maps $26.95 **974.7**
1. African Americans -- New York (N.Y.) -- History -- 18th century 2. Slavery -- United States
ISBN 1-4000-4029-9

LC 2004-57625

"In this first-rate social history, Lepore not only adroitly examines the case's travesty, questioning whether such a conspiracy ever existed, but also draws a splendid portrait of the struggles, prejudices and triumphs of a very young New York City in which fully 'one in five inhabitants was enslaved.'" Publ Wkly

Includes bibliographical references

MacColl, Gail

To marry an English Lord; by Gail MacColl and Carol McD. Wallace. Workman Pub. 1989 x, 403 p.p ill. (pbk.) $15.95; o.p. **974.7**
ISBN 9780761171959; 0894809393

LC 85040529

This book traces how "[f]rom the Gilded Age until 1914, more than 100 American heiresses invaded Britannia and swapped dollars for titles--just like Cora Crawley, Countess of Grantham, the first of the Downton Abbey characters Julian Fellowes was inspired to create [for the television program] after reading 'To Marry An English Lord.' Filled with . . . personalities, . . . anecdotes, grand houses, and . . . period details--plus photographs, illustrations, quotes, and the finer points of Victorian and Edwardian etiquette--'To Marry An English Lord' is [a] social history." (Publisher's note)

McCourt, Malachy

Singing my him song. HarperCollins Pubs. 2000 242p hardcover o.p. pa $14 **974.7**
1. Actors 2. Irish Americans -- New York (State) -- New York -- Biography
ISBN 0-06-095548-1 pa

LC 00-59774

In this sequel to A monk swimming, "McCourt tells us the rest of his story; how he got from there to here, how he went from living the headlong and heedless life of a world-class drunk to becoming a sober, loving father and grandfather, still happily married after thirty-five years." Publisher's note

A monk swimming. Hyperion 1998 290p $23.95; pa $14 **974.7**
1. Actors 2. Irish Americans -- New York (State) --

New York -- Biography
ISBN 0-7868-6398-6; 0-7868-8414-2 pa

LC 97-46720

"The memoir, which covers ground through 1963, will have readers smiling and laughing constantly." Publ Wkly

New York Historical Society

The **encyclopedia** of New York City; edited by Kenneth T. Jackson. 2nd ed; New-York Historical Society 2010 1561p il map $65   **974.7**

1. Reference books
ISBN 978-0-300-11465-2; 0-300-11465-6

LC 2010-31294

This encyclopedia "amasses the collective knowledge on New York City into a volume small enough to pick up and hold and large enough to satisfy the scholars, students, and enthusiasts native to New York or just passing through. . . . [Entries] describe and contextualize the people, places, events, and phenomena that tell the story of New York City." Libr J

Schecter, Barnet

★ The **devil's** own work; the Civil War draft riots and the fight to reconstruct America. Barnet Schecter. Walker & Co. 2005 434p il $28   **974.7**

1. Riots
ISBN 0-8027-1439-0

LC 2005-18089

"Copiously researched and highlighted with a wealth of period commentary, his lucid narrative colorfully recreates a historical watershed and offers a rich exploration of the Civil War's unfinished business." Publ Wkly
Includes bibliographical references

Schneider, Paul

The **Adirondacks**; a history of America's first wilderness. Holt & Co. 1997 368p il maps hardcover o.p. pa $16   **974.7**

1. Adirondack Mountains (N.Y.) -- History
ISBN 0-8050-5990-3 pa

LC 96-39844

The author presents a "history of New York State's Adirondack region. He relates here the life and lore of these scenic mountains and lakes (Whiteface, Mt. Marcy, Fulton Chain Lakes) from the region's earliest inhabitants (Haudenosaunce/Iroquois) through the advent of Henry Hudson (1609), the Revolutionary War, abolitionists (John Brown), 19th-century homesteaders, Hudson River School artists, tuberculosis patients to Melville Dewey's Lake Placid Club, the Adirondack Mountain Club, and the present environmental conservation efforts." Libr J

Smith, Dennis

A **decade** of hope; stories of grief and endurance from 9/11 families and friends. [by] Dennis Smith with Deirdre Smith. Viking 2011 364p $26.95 **974.7**

1. September 11 terrorist attacks, 2001 -- Personal narratives
ISBN 978-0-670-02293-9

LC 2011023325

The author, "a former firefighter, collects 25 moving personal narratives in this significant addition to the literature of September 11. Featuring notable figures such as NYPD Commissioner Ray Kelly and Congressman Peter King alongside rescue workers and victims' family members and loved ones, Smith's interviewees offer their experiences of that tragic day, illustrating how the pain and losses are still acutely felt. . . . With restraint and pathos, Smith's book provides powerful tribute and testimony." Publ Wkly

Taylor, Alan

The **divided** ground; Indians, settlers and the northern borderland of the American Revolution. Alfred A. Knopf 2006 542p il maps $35; pa $16.95   **974.7**

1. Educators 2. Indian chiefs 3. Indians of North America -- Government relations 4. Indians of North America -- Land tenure 5. Iroquois Indians 6. Iroquois Indians -- Government relations 7. Iroquois Indians -- History 8. Iroquois Indians -- Land tenure 9. Missionaries
ISBN 0-679-45471-3; 1-4000-7707-9 pa

LC 2005-43582

"Taylor's exquisite writing and thorough research in both Canadian and US archives and manuscript collections make this a major work." Choice
Includes bibliographical references

Tribble, Scott

A **colossal** hoax; the giant from Cardiff that fooled America. Rowman & Littlefield Publishers, Inc. 2009 311p il   **974.7**

1. Cardiff giant 2. Impostors and imposture
ISBN 0-7425-6050-3; 978-0-7425-6050-5

LC 2008-25178

"Tribble tells the tale of the 1869 'discovery' of a tenfoot giant reputed to be either a petrified Biblical-era man or an ancient statue fashioned by pre-American Indian inhabitants of North America. The story focuses on huckster George Hull, who commissioned the fake fossil's carving out of gypsum and planted it for profit derived from paid viewings by a gullible public. . . . After exposure, the giant had an afterlife at fairs and museums; he is still on display as an example of American innocence and humbug. Engagingly written in a thorough treatment that this popular culture phenomenon has not usually received." Libr J
Includes bibliographical references

Von Drehle, Dave

★ **Triangle**: the fire that changed America. Atlantic Monthly Press 2003 340p il hardcover o.p. pa $14   **974.7**

1. Clothing industry 2. Factories 3. Fires 4. Large print books
ISBN 0-87113-874-3; 0-8021-4151-X pa

LC 2003-41835

"Von Drehle's engrossing account, which emphasizes the humanity of the victims and the theme of social justice, brings on of the pivotal and most shocking episodes of American labor history to life." Publ Wkly
Includes bibliographical references

Ward, Geoffrey C.

A **disposition** to be rich; how a small-town pastor's son ruined an American president, brought on a Wall Street crash, and made himself the best-hated man in the United States. by Geoffrey C. Ward. Alfred A. Knopf 2012 418 p. **974.7**
1. Capitalists and financiers -- United States -- Biography 2. Children of clergy -- New York (State) -- Biography 3. Financial crises -- United States -- History -- 19th century 4. Ponzi schemes -- New York (State) -- New York -- History -- 19th century 5. Swindlers and swindling -- United States -- Biography
ISBN 0679445307; 9780679445302
LC 2011035140

In this book, [a]mong the ranks of past American financial swindlers is the scoundrel Ferdinand Ward, here vividly profiled by his great-grandson. [Geoffrey C.] Ward . . . mines personal archives, letters, and diaries. . . . The secret of [Ferdinand Wards] success was the classic pyramid scheme, which entailed paying off earlier investors with proceeds from newer ones. . . . In 1884, it all came crashing down . . . ruining countless individuals . . . and arguably contributing to the Panic of 1884. Ward went to prison but never acknowledged responsibility. . . . This . . . biography of a notorious ancestor successfully balances the truth about Ferdinand Ward's personal life with his scandalous role in this all-too-familiar American rags-to-riches-to-criminality saga. (Libr J)

White, Shane

Stories of freedom in Black New York. Harvard Univ. Press 2002 260p il $27.95 **974.7**
1. African Americans -- New York (N.Y.) 2. Architects 3. Authors 4. Diplomats 5. Dramatists 6. Essayists 7. Journalists 8. Local government officials 9. Painters
ISBN 0-674-00893-6
LC 2002-68540

The author "makes a persuasive case for the company's cultural importance, particularly as a forerunner of the Harlem Renaissance that was still a century away." Publ Wkly
Includes bibliographical references

★ After the fall; edited by Mary Marshall Clark ... [et al.] New Press 2011 xxiii, 263 p.p $26.95 **974.7**
1. Columbia University. Oral History Research Office 2. Interviews 3. Oral history 4. September 11 Terrorist Attacks, 2001 5. September 11 Terrorist Attacks, 2001 -- Personal narratives 6. September 11 terrorist attacks, 2001 -- Personal narratives
ISBN 978-1-59558-647-6; 9781595586476
LC 2011012833

This book was produced by Columbia University's Oral History Research Office, headed by [the bookss editor,] Mary Marshall Clark, [who] went to work immediately after September 11, 2001, and has now issued a selection from its hundreds of interviews with those most directly involved— first responders, victims' families, residents of lower Manhattan. . . . The interviews make clear the distance between those who will go on distressfully reliving their experience forever and those of us who were merely bystanders. (Columbia Journalism Review)

"The Columbia Center for Oral History (CCOH) is committed to building 'repositories of living memory,' and after 9/11 began to gather narratives from a variety of New York survivors and witnesses, eventually collecting over 600 histories. The skilled interviewers . . . are trained in oral history methods and richly summon forth from interviewees the repercussions of the attack on individuals, families, and communities. Those interviewed reflect a variety of perspectives, including both professional and unskilled workers in the Twin Towers, neighbors, first responders, and many of New York's immigrant groups, including Muslims." Libr J

★ The encyclopedia of New York State; editor in chief, Peter Eisenstadt; managing editor, Laura-Eve Moss; foreword by Carole F. Huxley. 1st ed.; Syracuse University Press 2005 xxviii, 1921p il map $95 **974.7**
1. Reference books
ISBN 0-8156-0808-X
LC 2005-1032

"The alphabetically arranged entries include all cities, towns, and counties (more than 1,500), with an additional 3,000-plus entries for information on a wide range of topics. . . . This ambitious project is a definite success." Booklist
Includes bibliographical references

974.8 Pennsylvania

Pennsylvania: a history of the Commonwealth; edited by Randall M. Miller and William Pencak. Pennsylvania State Univ. Press 2002 xxxi, 654p il maps $49.95; pa $29.95 **974.8**
ISBN 0-271-02213-2; 0-271-02214-0 pa
LC 2002-5457

"More than half of this book is an unusual and inspired hybrid of history and nine other disciplines from geography to literature. . . . The editors profess to discover the sources of Pennsylvania's greatness and significance but also expose its faults and declining significance in the 20th century. They succeed at both." Choice

974.9 New Jersey

Wolff, Daniel

4th of July, Asbury Park; a history of the promised land. Bloomsbury 2005 277p hardcover o.p. pa $14.95 **974.9**
1. Rock musicians 2. Singers 3. Songwriters
ISBN 1-58234-509-0; 1-59691-114-X pa
LC 2004-26965

The author "creates popular history at its best. Springsteen fans will love it, and so will anyone interested in American social history." Booklist
Includes bibliographical references

975 Southeastern United States (South Atlantic states)

Blount, Roy
Long time leaving; dispatches from up South. [by] Roy Blount, Jr. Knopf 2007 383p $25 **975**
1. North and south
ISBN 978-0-307-26618-7; 0-307-26618-4
LC 2007-6799
"This delightful collection is not only fun and funny but insightful as well." Libr J

Bragg, Rick
Ava's man. Knopf 2001 259p $25; pa $13 **975**
1. Carpenters 2. Depressions -- 1929 -- Southern States 3. Factory workers 4. Working class whites -- Southern States -- Biography
ISBN 0-375-41062-7; 0-375-72444-3 pa
LC 2001-32677
In this account of his maternal grandfather's life as a roofer and bootlegger in Appalachia, the author "creates a soulful, poignant portrait of working-class Southern life." Publ Wkly

Cash, Wilbur Joseph
The mind of the South; with a new introduction by Bertram Wyatt-Brown. Vintage Bks. 1991 xliv, 444p pa $16 **975**
ISBN 0-679-73647-6
LC 91-50042
A psychological, cultural, and social history of the old South.

Dent, Tom
Southern journey; a return to the civil rights movement. University of Georgia Press 2001 400p pa $18.95 **975**
1. African Americans -- Civil rights
ISBN 0-8203-2291-1; 978-0-8203-2291-9
LC 00-61990
"Dent compellingly reveals that ordinary Southerners fundamentally changed the region and are poised to make more substantive changes." Libr J
Includes bibliographical references

Lemann, Nicholas
Redemption: the last battle of the Civil War. Farrar, Straus and Giroux 2006 257p $24 **975**
1. African Americans -- Civil rights 2. African Americans -- Civil rights -- Southern States 3. African Americans -- Segregation 4. Generals 5. Governors 6. Reconstruction (U.S. history, 1865-1877) 7. Senators 8. Violence -- Southern States 9. Violence -- Southern States -- History -- 19th century
ISBN 978-0-374-24855-0; 0-374-24855-9
LC 2006-91
This book "offers a vigorous, necessary reminder of how racist reaction bred an American terrorism that suppressed black political activity and crushed Reconstruction in the South." N Y Times Book Rev
Includes bibliographical references

975.3 District of Columbia (Washington)

Bordewich, Fergus M.
Washington: the making of the American capital. Amistad 2008 367p map $27.95; pa $15.99 **975.3**
1. City planning -- Washington (D.C.) -- History -- 18th century
ISBN 978-0-06-084238-3; 0-06-084238-5; 978-0-06-084239-0 pa; 0-06-084239-3 pa
LC 2007-52053
The author explains "how the city's site was chosen and how political scheming, personal conflicts, and greed almost doomed the project of designing and constructing a capital city from scratch. Two themes are woven throughout his narrative: the important but often overlooked role played by slaves and former freed slaves and the constant North-South debate at the root of the bitter dispute over the capital's locale. . . . Bordewich introduces readers to the key players: George Washington, Thomas Jefferson, African American surveyor Benjamin Banneker, intractable and ill-fated architect and city planner Maj. Pierre Charles L'Enfant, the city's triumvirate of commissioners, and a host of pernicious financial speculators." Libr J
Includes bibliographical references

Gugliotta, Guy
Freedom's cap; Guy Gugliotta. Hill and Wang 2012 viii, 486 p.p **975.3**
ISBN 9780809046812
LC 2011025750
This book takes place in "Washington [in the] 1850s. . . . [Author Guy Gugliotta provides an] account of the transformation of the U. S. Capitol from a[n] . . . inadequate . . . structure into todays massive marble symbol of democracy. . . . The author begins in the mid-1850s with the issue of Thomas Crawford's statue, 'Freedom,' now perched atop the Capitol dome. The . . . contest that Gugliotta outlines was between Army engineer Montgomery C. Meigs and architect Thomas Ustick Walter, both of whom would, at times, have control of the project. Both had ferocious work ethics, as well as enormous egos. . . . Gugliotta . . . includ[es] stories about marble quarries and ironworks; John Brown (whom he labels a terrorist); Presidents Fillmore, Pierce, Buchanan and Lincoln; and the many artisans and artists, principally Constantino Brumidi." (Kirkus)

Lusane, Clarence
The Black history of the White House. City Lights Books 2011 575p il **975.3**
1. African Americans -- Washington (D.C.) 2. Presidents -- United States -- Staff 3. Slavery -- United States
ISBN 978-0-8728-6532-7
LC 2010-36925
The author "offers a comprehensive and well-documented account of African Americans who have graced the White House as builders, slaves, servants, entertainers, policy professionals, and finally as the nation's First Family. . . . This is an important work of historical scholarship, bringing together chronicles of the African Americans who have played major roles in the annals of the presidential mansion." Libr J
Includes bibliographical references

Monkman, Betty C.

★ The **White** House; its historic furnishings and first families. principal photography by Bruce White. Abbeville Press 2000 320p il $65   **975.3**
1. House furnishings -- United States 2. Presidents -- Dwellings -- United States
ISBN 0-7892-0624-2

LC 00-27085

"Monkman, the White House curator, documents the furnishings and decorative objects as well as the metamorphoses of White House interiors. The impact of the presidents and first ladies is particularly intriguing." Libr J
Includes bibliographical references

White House Historical Association

The **White** House; actors and observers. edited by William Seale. Northeastern Univ. Press 2002 xxii, 214p il $40   **975.3**
1. Presidents -- United States 2. Presidents -- United States -- Congresses 3. Presidents -- United States -- Family -- Congresses 4. Presidents -- United States -- Pictorial works
ISBN 1-55553-547-X

LC 2002-9087

This is "a pictorial history of the presidential residence. Accompanied by a succession of essays presented at a symposium honoring the 200th anniversary of the White House, this stunning collection of paintings, drawings, and photographs chronicles two centuries of presidential life. . . . This irresistible gallery of pictures will appeal to scholars and browsers alike." Booklist
Includes bibliographical references

Katharine Graham's Washington; {compiled by} Katharine Graham. Knopf 2002 813p il $30; pa $16.95   **975.3**
ISBN 0-375-41471-1; 1-4000-3059-5 pa

LC 2002-111640

"The late newspaper publisher's posthumous legacy is a delightful and insightful anthology of writings on the city that formed so much of her personality and her professional life. She draws from her personal collection of writings by a range of writers, many of them personal friends." Booklist

975.5   Virginia

Fox, James

Five sisters; the Langhornes of Virginia. Simon & Schuster 2000 496p il $30; pa $16   **975.5**
1. Americans -- Great Britain -- Biography 2. Members of Parliament 3. Spouses of prominent persons
ISBN 0-684-80812-9; 0-7432-0042-X pa

LC 99-41815

"Irene Langhorne, the last great Southern belle, moved North in 1895, when she married Charles Dana Gibson, creator of the Gibson girl. In her wake, three younger sisters (her elder, Lizzie, was already married) burst onto the glittering society stage. Nancy, the most famous, married Waldorf Astor and threw herself into English political activism; Phyllis, the author's grandmother, was more introverted; Nora, with 'a heart like a hotel,' repeatedly led the family

to the brink of scandal. Fox brings intimacy to these semi-public personalities, elevating a century's gossip and legend into absorbing history." New Yorker
Includes bibliographical references

Furgurson, Ernest B.

Ashes of glory; Richmond at war. Knopf 1996 419p il maps hardcover o.p. pa $16   **975.5**
1. United States -- History -- 1861-1865, Civil War -- Campaigns
ISBN 0-679-74660-9 pa

LC 95-49591

The author "tells the story of a city that between 1861 and 1865 epitomized the experience of the Civil War as a revolutionary one. Capital of a state that had long opposed secession, Richmond now became the symbol of Southern independence. It also remained a center of clandestine Unionism that hosted a struggle between espionage networks matching anything seen in Cold War Berlin." Publ Wkly
Includes bibliographical references

Horn, James P. P.

A **land** as God made it; Jamestown and the birth of America. [by] James Horn. Basic Books 2005 337p il maps $26   **975.5**
ISBN 0-465-03094-7

LC 2005-13054

"Possessing Jamestown's inherent drama, this is a solid rendition of the saga." Booklist
Includes bibliographical references

Noel Hume, Ivor

The **Virginia** adventure; Roanoke to James Towne: an archaeological and historical odyssey. University Press of Va. 1997 xxviii, 491p il map pa $19.95   **975.5**
ISBN 0-8139-1758-1

LC 97-16651

The author discusses "the historical archaeology of the Roanoke and James Fort (later James Towne) settlements. Drawing extensively on firsthand accounts and other textual sources, he conjures up the feel of the Elizabethan experience that gave life to these settlements. . . . Hume also includes masterly and generous accounts of the history of the excavation of these sites and offers his well-informed views on where future work needs to be done. Written with wit, compassion, and tremendous attention to detail, this is historical archaeology at its best." Libr J

Price, David

★ **Love** and hate in Jamestown; John Smith, Pocahontas, and the heart of a new nation. {by} David A. Price. Knopf 2003 305p maps $25.95; pa $14.95   **975.5**
1. Colonists 2. Indian leaders 3. Indians of North America -- First contact with Europeans 4. Indians of North America -- First contact with Europeans -- Virginia -- Jamestown 5. Powhatan Indians 6. Princesses 7. Travel writers
ISBN 0-375-41541-6; 1-4000-3172-9 pa

LC 2002-43437

"For those general readers who wish to move beyond the myths and obtain a better understanding of them and the early years of the colony, this book will be an enjoyable and valuable tool." Booklist

Includes bibliographical references

975.6   North Carolina

Horn, James

A **kingdom** strange; the brief and tragic history of the lost colony of Roanoke. [by] James Horn. Basic Books 2010 296p il map $26   **975.6**

ISBN 978-0-465-00485-0

LC 2010-563

"The author creates an engaging, you-are-there feel to the narrative, with rich descriptions of European politics, colonists' daily struggles and the vagaries of relations between Native American tribes. . . . A satisfying recounting of some of the earliest American history." Kirkus

Includes bibliographical references

975.7   South Carolina

Ball, Edward

Slaves in the family. Ballantine Books 1999 505p il map pa $17.95   **975.7**

1. Plantation life 2. Plantation owners 3. Slaveholders 4. Slavery -- United States

ISBN 978-0-345-43105-9; 0-345-43105-7

"For nearly a hundred and seventy years before the Civil War, members of the Ball family owned a string of plantations worked by slaves along South Carolina's Cooper River. After the war, the author's ancestors lost or sold their land and scattered to make new lives, but he wondered what happened to the slaves. This book, a brilliant blend of archival research and oral history, tells what he found." New Yorker

Includes bibliographical references

975.8   Georgia

Berendt, John

Midnight in the garden of good and evil; a story of Savannah. Random House 1994 388p $25; pa $14   **975.8**

1. Large print books 2. Savannah (Ga.) -- Description 3. Savannah (Ga.) -- Social life and customs

ISBN 0-679-42922-0; 0-679-75152-1 pa

LC 93-3955

"Berendt has fashioned a Baedeker to Savannah that, while it flirts with condescension, is always contagiously affectionate. Few cities have been introduced more seductively." Newsweek

Jones, Jacqueline

Saving Savannah; the city and the Civil War. Alfred A. Knopf 2008 510p il map $30   **975.8**

1. African Americans -- Georgia -- Savannah

ISBN 978-1-4000-4293-7; 1-4000-4293-3

LC 2008-11508

"Synthesizing the perspectives of the mercantile elite, the aristocratic upper crust and the downtrodden, . . . [the author has] fashioned a compelling social and political history." Washington Post Book World

Includes bibliographical references

★ Foxfire 40th anniversary book; faith, family, and the land. edited by Angie Cheek, Lacy Hunter Nix, and Foxfire students. Anchor Books 2006 xxxix, 512p il pa $17.95   **975.8**

1. Country life -- Georgia 2. Handicraft

ISBN 0-307-27551-5; 978-0-307-27551-6

LC 2006-45311

"Drawing on the magazine's published talks by local high school students with elderly rural inhabitants, the books have explored the crafts, cooking, music, gardening and stories that have been passed down through the generations. The focus in this anniversary volume is on devotion to religion, family and the land. Collecting pieces from 40 years' worth of the magazine, the book inevitably covers topics covered in previous Foxfire collections, including snake handling, childhood toys and recipes. But the spoken words remain captivating, eloquent if plainspoken." Publ Wkly

975.9   Florida

Gaines, Steven S.

Fool's paradise; players, poseurs, and the culture of excess in South Beach. Crown Publishers 2009 274p il $25.95   **975.9**

ISBN 978-0-307-34627-8; 0-307-34627-7

LC 2008-36067

This is a "terrific social history buffet. . . . [Gaines is] a gifted storyteller. He fills the book with telling anecdotes and bons mots, but the narrative never gets off track. It would be easy to focus on the drug-and-sleaze aspect of South Beach. But Gaines lets a little bit go a long way. He could fill the book with stupid celebrity tricks. But again, less is more. This book succeeds not because of star power but because of story power. The centerpiece of the book is a war of dueling architects and builders fighting to build the iconic Fontainebleau hotel and then to destroy it out of spite." St. Petersburg Times

Includes bibliographical references

Grunwald, Michael

The **swamp**; the Everglades, Florida, and the politics of paradise. Simon & Schuster 2005 450p il map hardcover o.p. pa $15   **975.9**

ISBN 0-7432-5105-9; 978-0-7432-5105-1; 978-0-7432-5107-5 pa; 0-7432-5107-5 pa

LC 2005-56329

This is a "chronicle of the history of the Everglades. . . . [This] is a riveting tale of ambition versus ecological reality, politics versus science, and, on the upside, our gradual awakening to the true nature of nature." Booklist

Includes bibliographical references

Roberts, Diane

Dream state; eight generations of swamp lawyers, conquistadors, Confederate daughters, banana Republicans, and other Florida wildlife. Free Press 2004 355p il $25 **975.9**

ISBN 0-7432-5206-3

LC 2004-56276

"With hurricane-force prose, . . . Roberts hits the land of orange groves, theme parks and mobile homes with a torrential outpouring of love and hate, affection and disgust." Publ Wkly

Includes bibliographical references

976.1   Alabama

Agee, James

Let us now praise famous men; [by] James Agee, Walker Evans; with an introduction to the new edition by John Hersey. Houghton Mifflin il $30; pa $18 **976.1**

1. Farm tenancy

ISBN 978-0-395-95771-4; 0-395-95771-0; 978-0-618-12749-8 pa; 0-618-12749-6 pa

This work documents "the ways of life of three Alabama tenant-farming families. . . . It is a unique and complex book, deeply honest and compassionate, and remarkable for its extraordinary descriptive, lyric, and meditative prose." Benet's Reader's Ency of Am Lit

McWhorter, Diane

Carry me home; Birmingham, Alabama: the climactic battle of the civil rights revolution. Simon & Schuster 2001 701p il hardcover o.p. pa $17 **976.1**

1. African Americans -- Civil rights   2. African Americans -- Civil rights -- Alabama -- Birmingham -- History -- 20th century   3. Civil rights movements -- Alabama -- Birmingham -- History -- 20th century

ISBN 0-684-80747-5; 0-7432-1772-1 pa

LC 00-53827

McWhorter presents an account of the struggle for civil rights in Birmingham, Ala., both from a personal and societal perspective.

"A daughter of Birmingham's privileged elite, McWhorter weaves a personal narrative through this startling account of the history, events, and major players on both sides of the civil rights battle in that city." Booklist

Includes bibliographical references

976.2   Mississippi

Welty, Eudora

One time, one place; Mississippi in the Depression: a snapshot album. rev ed; University Press of Miss. 1996 115p il $35 **976.2**

1. Mississippi -- Pictorial works

ISBN 0-87805-866-4

LC 95-46057

This is a "collection of photographs of Mississippians that Welty took in the 1930s, when she worked for the Works Progress Administration (WPA). This Silver Anniversary Edition contains a great foreword by William Maxwell that absolutely nails the importance of the book for many readers." Booklist

976.3   Louisiana

Baum, Dan

Nine lives; death and life in New Orleans. Spiegel & Grau 2009 335p $26 **976.3**

1. Biography, Collective   2. Hurricane Katrina, 2005

ISBN 978-0-385-52319-6; 0-385-52319-X

LC 2008-31483

"Baum's in-depth reporting (he was on scene during Katrina, even turning himself in at the Convention Center to chronicle the out-of-sight outrages) is evident on every page." Booklist

Includes bibliographical references

Brinkley, Douglas

The **great** deluge; Hurricane Katrina, New Orleans, and the Mississippi Gulf Coast. Morrow 2006 716p il hardcover o.p. pa $17.95 **976.3**

1. Disaster relief   2. Hurricane Katrina, 2005

ISBN 0-06-112423-0; 0-06-114849-0 pa

LC 2006-43338

This is an account of Hurricane Katrina, which ravaged the Gulf Coast in late summer 2005.

The author "captures the human toll of Katrina as graphically as the most vivid newspaper and television accounts did, and by pulling together a huge, choral portrait of what happened during that first week of havoc and distress (from Saturday, Aug. 27, through Saturday, Sept. 3), he gives the reader a richly detailed timeline of disaster—a timeline in which the sheer cumulative power of details impresses upon us, again, just how abysmally inept relief efforts were on every level, from FEMA to the Red Cross to the New Orleans police department, from the federal government to state and local authorities." N Y Times (Late N Y Ed)

Clark, Joshua

Heart like water; surviving Katrina and life in its disaster zone. Free Press 2007 356p map $25 **976.3**

1. Authors   2. Editors   3. Hurricane Katrina, 2005   4. Publishing executives   5. Travel writers

ISBN 978-1-4165-3763-2; 1-4165-3763-5

LC 2007-5157

"Clark was among the few hearty or hapless souls who remained in New Orleans during Hurricane Katrina. . . . In this riveting first-person account, Clark recalls the static in the air as the hurricane approached; the unnerving silence afterwards without even the sound of birds; and 'shopping' for supplies at a local store where the owner had apparently given permission before fleeing. . . . This is a raw, revealing, and highly personal look at surviving Hurricane Katrina." Booklist

Dyson, Michael Eric

Come hell or high water; Hurricane Katrina and the color of disaster. Basic Civitas 2006 258p $23; pa $14.95 **976.3**
1. African Americans -- Social conditions 2. Democracy 3. Disaster relief 4. Hurricane Katrina, 2005
ISBN 978-0-465-01761-4; 0-465-01761-4; 978-0-465-01772-0 pa; 0-465-01772-X pa
LC 2007-310210
This book on Hurrican Katrina "not only chronicles what happened when, it also argues that the nation's failure to offer timely aid to Katrina's victims indicates deeper problems in race and class relations. . . . [The author's] contention that Katrina exposed a dominant culture pervaded not only by 'active malice' toward poor blacks but also by a long history of 'passive indifference' to their problems is both powerful and unsettling." Publ Wkly
Includes bibliographical references

Horne, Jed

★ **Breach** of faith; Hurricane Katrina and the near death of a great American city. Random House 2006 412p map hardcover o.p. pa $16 **976.3**
1. Disaster relief 2. Hurricane Katrina, 2005
ISBN 978-1-4000-6552-3; 1-4000-6552-6; 978-0-8129-7650-2 pa; 0-8129-7650-9 pa
LC 2006-46468
This book does "an admirable job of detailing the design flaws that left New Orleans underwater." New Repub
Includes bibliographical references

Lane, Charles

The **day** freedom died; the Colfax massacre, the Supreme Court, and the betrayal of Reconstruction. Henry Holt and Co. 2008 326p il map $27 **976.3**
1. African Americans -- Crimes against -- History 2. African Americans -- History 3. Massacres 4. Massacres -- Louisiana -- Colfax 5. Racism -- Louisiana -- Colfax 6. Reconstruction (1865-1876) 7. Reconstruction (U.S. history, 1865-1877) -- Louisiana -- Colfax 8. Trials (Homicide)
ISBN 978-0-8050-8342-2; 0-8050-8342-1
LC 2007-37514
"The Colfax Massacre . . . took place on an Easter Sunday afternoon in 1873. Within four hours, at least eighty black American men had been brutally murdered by white vigilantes in Colfax, La. Journalist Lane's groundbreaking and persuasive work illustrates this 'pivotal event in the political and constitutional history of post-Civil War America' and its social, political and judicial aftermath. . . . Students of American and African-American history will find it particularly valuable; fans of American history will find it a moving and instructive drama." Publ Wkly
Includes bibliographical references

Rasmussen, Daniel

American uprising; the untold story of America's largest slave revolt. Harper 2011 276p map **976.3**
1. African Americans -- Louisiana 2. African Americans -- Louisiana -- New Orleans 3. Slave insurrections -- Louisiana -- New Orleans 4. Slavery -- Louisiana -- New Orleans 5. Slavery -- United States
ISBN 0061995215; 0062084356; 9780061995217; 9780062084354
LC 2010017855
This is a history of the 1811 slave rebellion in New Orleans. Bibliography. Index.
This is an "account of a large-scale, three-day slave revolt on the sugar plantations near New Orleans during the 1811 Carnival (Mardi Gras) season. The author argues that the slave-rebels, who had learned warfare tactics in their native Africa, were inspired by the successful Haitian revolution. . . . This is a welcome addition to popular history and an engaging read for anyone interested in this important chapter in the tragic story of American slavery." Libr J
Includes bibliographical references

Van Heerden, Ivor Ll.

The **storm**; what went wrong and why during Hurricane Katrina. [by] Ivor van Heerden and Mike Bryan. Viking 2006 308p il map hardcover o.p. pa $15 **976.3**
1. Disaster relief 2. Hurricane Katrina, 2005
ISBN 0-670-03781-8; 0-14-311213-9 pa
LC 2006-44727
This book focuses on public mismanagement relating to Hurricane Katrina.
"This serious, scientific explanation of what exactly happened in the hours—and years—leading up to Hurricane Katrina's devestation of New Orleans brings a fresh perspective to a tragedy that has generated remarkably similar news accounts over the past eight months." Publ Wkly
Includes bibliographical references

★ **Voices** rising; stories from the Katrina Narrative Project. edited by Rebeca Antoine; [afterword by Fredrick Barton] UNO Press 2008 244p pa $12.95 **976.3**
1. Hurricane Katrina, 2005 -- Personal narratives
ISBN 978-0-9728143-6-2; 0-9728143-6-1
In this "collection of personal narratives, readers come face-to-face with the stark reality wrought by Hurricane Katrina and the failure of the federal levees. . . . Every aspect of the post-Katrina New Orleans experience is present here, from areas as divergent as the I10 overpass, the French Quarter, and shelters across the South. The rescuers and rescued have equal voices and share memories poignant and startling. . . . Miles away from academic analysis, this is American social history from the ground up and staggering in its significance." Booklist

976.4 Texas

Davis, William C.

★ **Three** roads to the Alamo; the lives and fortunes of David Crockett, James Bowie and William

Barret Travis. HarperCollins Pubs. 1998 791p il hardcover o.p. pa $20   **976.4**
    1. Army officers 2. Lawyers 3. Members of Congress 4. Pioneers 5. Soldiers
    ISBN 0-06-093094-2 pa

                  LC 97-43815
    This "is a readable, stimulating, and exceptionally well-researched narrative history." Libr J
    Includes bibliographical references

Valby, Karen

    Welcome to Utopia; notes from a small town. Spiegel & Grau 2010 238p il $25   **976.4**
    1. City and town life
    ISBN 978-0-385-52286-1; 0-385-52286-X

                  LC 2009-37970
    "Entertainment Weekly magazine sent intrepid reporter Karen Valby into the great flyover zone in 2006 in search of a 'small town somewhere in America without popular culture.' She found Utopia, a town of a few hundred souls 90 miles west of the nation's seventh-largest city, San Antonio. Utopia is not exactly off the grid, and one suspects that its name appealed to Valby more than its isolation. Her book . . . is a pleasant moment-in-time postcard of a typical U.S. town." Minneapolis Star Tribune
    Includes bibliographical references

976.6   Oklahoma

Hirsch, James S.

    Riot and remembrance; the Tulsa race war and its legacy. Houghton Mifflin 2002 358p il $25; pa $14   **976.6**
    1. African Americans -- Oklahoma -- History 2. African Americans -- Oklahoma -- Tulsa -- History -- 20th century 3. African Americans -- Tulsa (Okla.) 4. Racism -- Oklahoma -- History 5. Riots 6. Riots -- Oklahoma -- History 7. Violence -- Oklahoma -- History
    ISBN 0-618-10813-0; 0-618-34076-9 pa
                  LC 2001-51615
    "Hirsch unearths an important episode in U.S. history with verve, intelligence and compassion." Publ Wkly
    Includes bibliographical references

977   North central United States

Barry, John M.

    Rising tide; the great Mississippi flood of 1927 and how it changed America. Simon & Schuster 1997 524p il maps hardcover o.p. pa $16   **977**
    1. Bridge engineers 2. Floods -- Mississippi River 3. Generals 4. Military engineers
    ISBN 0-684-84002-2 pa

                  LC 96-40077
    This is the "story of human defeat by a savage, unpredictable river. . . . The flood of 1927, three times greater than the flood of 1993, was an unprecedented disaster that spurred a political innovation. Congress's agreement to

rebuild the Mississippi's shattered flood-control system marked the federal government's first assumption of full financial responsibility for a regional calamity. Much of the book recounts how the greed of New Orleans bankers and Delta planters increased the sufferings of the rural poor. . . . Barry's book is a virtuoso piece of exposition." New Yorker
    Includes bibliographical references

Dennis, Jerry

    The **living** Great Lakes; searching for the heart of the inland seas. Thomas Dunne Bks. 2003 296p il maps hardcover o.p. pa $14.95   **977**
    ISBN 0-312-25193-9; 0-312-33103-7 pa
                  LC 2002-32500
    The author offers a "description of being a crew member on the schooner Malabar on a six-week trip through the waters of Lakes Huron, Ontario, Michigan, Erie and Superior. . . . Dennis weaves anecdotes from his childhood, such as a family-fishing trip on Lake Michigan, together with informed commentary on the natural history of the lakes and the people who live there." Publ Wkly
    Includes bibliographical references

Eckert, Allan W.

    A **sorrow** in our heart: the life of Tecumseh. Bantam Bks. 1992 862p maps hardcover o.p. pa $7.99   **977**
    1. Biography, Individual 2. Indian chiefs 3. Shawnee Indians
    ISBN 0-553-56174-X pa
                  LC 91-31858
    This is a "narrative biography of Tecumseh, the remarkable Shawnee warrior and statesman who succeeded in organizing a group of disparate tribes into a cohesive confederacy of nations. . . . Eckert places his subject firmly within his proper social and historical context by providing a tremendous amount of meticulously researched and authenticated background information, including illuminating details of tribal life and Shawnee culture." Booklist
    Includes bibliographical references

Laskin, David

    The **children's** blizzard. HarperCollins 2004 307p map $24.95; pa $13.95   **977**
    1. Blizzards
    ISBN 0-06-052075-2; 0-06-052076-0 pa
                  LC 2005-295018
    "An adroit, sensitive drama and a skillful addition to a popular genre." Booklist
    Includes bibliographical references

977.1   Ohio

Frazier, Ian

    Family. Farrar, Straus & Giroux 1994 386p il maps hardcover o.p. pa $16   **977.1**
    1. Biography, Individual 2. City and town life 3. City life 4. Ohio -- Social life and customs
    ISBN 0-312-42059-5 pa
                  LC 94-14730

"An extraordinary history of an ordinary family, in which the author plays the roles of gossip, pedant and loyal member, yielding a reunion strangers are welcome—and fortunate—to attend." N Y Times Book Rev

Gup, Ted

A **secret** gift; how one man's kindness--and a trove of letters--revealed the hidden history of the Great Depression. Penguin Press 2010 365p il $25.95   **977.1**

1. Businesspeople 2. Charity 3. Great Depression, 1929-1939 4. Philanthropists
ISBN 978-1-59420-270-4; 1-59420-270-2
                                        LC 2010-17302

"As Gup interweaves the sagas of recipient families with the life of their anonymous benefactor, 'A Secret Gift' never fails to entertain, inform and sometimes astound." Cleveland Plain Dealer

Ryan, Terry

The **prize** winner of Defiance, Ohio; how my mother raised 10 kids on 25 words or less. foreword by Suze Orman. Simon & Schuster 2001 351p il $24; pa $13   **977.1**

1. Defiance (Ohio) -- Biography 2. Homemakers 3. Prize contests in advertising 4. Prizewinners
ISBN 0-7432-1122-7; 0-7432-1123-5 pa
                                        LC 2001-18379

The author recounts the life of her mother, "a small-town Ohio housewife in the nineteen-fifties who lived on the brink of dire poverty, thanks to a brood of ten kids and an ineffectual drunk of a husband. Since Evelyn couldn't work outside her home, she worked inside it, penning hundreds of product jingles and entering them in the national contests that drove the advertising industry of the day." New Yorker

977.3   Illinois

Abbott, Karen

Sin in the Second City; madams, ministers, playboys, and the battle for America's soul. Random House 2007 xxiv, 356p il $25.95   **977.3**

1. Madams 2. Prostitution 3. Prostitution -- Illinois -- Chicago
ISBN 978-1-4000-6530-1; 1-4000-6530-5
                                        LC 2006-51878

"Lavish in her details, nicely detached in her point of view, [and with] scrupulous concern for historical accuracy, Ms. Abbott has written an immensely readable book. Sin in the Second City offers much in the way of reflection for those interested in the unending puzzle that goes by the name of human nature." Wall Street Journal
Includes bibliographical references

Cohen, Adam

American pharaoh: Mayor Richard J. Daley: his battle for Chicago and the nation; {by} Adam Cohen and Elizabeth Taylor. Little, Brown 2000 614p map hardcover o.p. pa $16.95   **977.3**

1. Mayors 2. Mayors -- Illinois -- Chicago -- Biography

3. Political party leaders
ISBN 0-316-83489-0 pa
                                        LC 99-42157

"Penetrating, nonsensationalistic and exhaustive, this is an impressive and important biography." Publ Wkly
Includes bibliographical references

Miller, Donald L.

City of the century; the epic of Chicago and the making of America. {by} Donald Miller. Simon & Schuster 1996 704p il maps hardcover o.p. pa $18   **977.3**

ISBN 0-684-83138-4 pa
                                        LC 96-4018

In this account of Chicago's history in the nineteenth century "Miller tells of Chicago's historical and literary figures, reform leaders, architects, industrialists, and entrepreneurs." Libr J

Newberry Library

The **Encyclopedia** of Chicago; edited by James R. Grossman, Ann Durkin Keating, Janice L. Reiff; cartographic editor, Michael P. Conzen. University of Chicago Press 2004 xxix, 1117p il map $65 **977.3**

1. Reference books
ISBN 0-226-31015-9
                                        LC 2004-3487

"The main alphabetical section of the Encyclopedia, comprising more than 1,400 entries, covers . . . Chicago's neighborhoods, suburbs, and ethnic groups, as well as the city's cultural institutions, technology and science, architecture, religions, immigration, transportation, business history, labor, music, health and medicine, and hundreds of other topics." Publisher's note

Pacyga, Dominic A.

Chicago; a biography. University of Chicago Press 2009 462p il map $35   **977.3**

ISBN 9780226644318; 0-226-64431-6
                                        LC 2009-1192

The author "has written an urban biography that captures the spirit of Chicago. . . . Pacyga portrays Chicago with time-lapse velocity as it morphs from a swampy portage to a city of skyscrapers. Concentrating on Chicago's ever-changing cultural diversity, notorious politics, and the crucial role technology played in the city's rapid rise, Pacyga seeds the big picture with cameos of fascinating individuals. . . . A vivid, streamlined, and superbly well-illustrated portrait of an essential American city." Booklist
Includes bibliographical references

Preib, Martin

The **wagon** and other stories from the city. University of Chicago Press 2010 167p $20   **977.3**

1. Police -- Chicago (Ill.)
ISBN 978-0-226-67980-8; 0-226-67980-2
                                        LC 2009-36010

"The book is anchored by 'The Wagon.' . . . In it, Preib details his work on the vehicle the CPD uses to pick up dead bodies. It seems incongruous to describe such a gut-wrenching story as gorgeous, but gorgeous it is; Preib's musings on the recently, often ignominiously departed are particularly affecting, with flashes of morbid humor for relief. Other trenchant essays touch on the trials of police work, his years as a doorman and a union organizer, his hitchhiking escapades as a young man, and his observations of Chicago. One thing's for sure: Preib isn't a cop moonlighting as a writer. He's a writer who happens to work as a cop." Chicago Reader

977.4   Michigan

Martelle, Scott

Detroit; a biography. Scott Martelle. Chicago Review Press 2012 xvi, 288 p.p   **977.4**
   1. African Americans -- Michigan -- Detroit -- History
ISBN 156976526X; 9781569765265
                                               LC 2011041173
   This book on Detroit, Michigan recounts the rise and downfall of a once-great city, from its origins as a French military outpost to protect fur traders and tame local Indian tribes, to the industrial giant, known colloquially as Motown, and now when its economy seized up like an engine run dry. Founded by a French naval officer named Cadillac, the city became a vibrant river town with the Erie Canal's opening, exporting both to the east and westward to Chicago. The 1855 opening of Lake Superior later expanded its postbellum shipping capacity and brought heavy industry. . . . But a series of downturns ravaged the city: the 1973 OPEC oil embargo helped destroy the city's auto-industry dominance, and drug-dealing gangs caused a murder rate that far out-stripped New York's. (Publishers Wkly)

978   Western United States

Brown, Dee Alexander

   The **American** West; photos edited by Martin F. Schmitt. Scribner 1994 461p il maps hardcover o.p. pa $17   **978**
   1. Apache Indians 2. Cheyenne Indians 3. Cowhands 4. Dakota Indians 5. Frontier and pioneer life -- West (U.S.) 6. Indian chiefs 7. Kiowa Indians 8. Little Bighorn, Battle of the, 1876 9. Nez Perce Indians 10. Nez Percé Indians 11. Outlaws 12. Rodeos 13. West (U.S.) -- History
ISBN 0-684-80441-7 pa
                                               LC 94-37444
   "This narrative history of westward expansion paints a vivid portrait of the settlers, pioneers, entrepreneurs, and Native Americans of the old West. Useful as collateral research material and for recreational reading." Booklist
   Includes bibliographical references

Calloway, Colin G.

   One vast winter count; the Native American West before Lewis and Clark. University of Nebraska Press 2003 631p il $39.95   **978**
   1. Indians of North America -- History 2. Indians of North America -- Western States 3. Native Americans -- West (U.S.)
ISBN 0-8032-1530-4
                                             LC 2003-44757

   "Calloway concentrates on the Indian experience from the Appalachians to the Pacific, in a time frame from prehistory to the 18th century. The scope is staggering, but Calloway masters it, demonstrating a remarkable command of a broad spectrum of historical, ethnographic and archeological sources including printed material and oral traditions." Publ Wkly
   Includes bibliographical references

Carter, Robert A.

   Buffalo Bill Cody; the man behind the legend. Wiley 2000 496p il hardcover o.p. pa $18.95 **978**
   1. Circus executives 2. Circus performers 3. Entertainers 4. Entertainers -- United States 5. Frontier and pioneer life -- West (U.S.) 6. Hunters 7. Pioneers -- West (U.S.) 8. Scouts 9. Scouts and scouting -- West (U.S.) 10. West (U.S.)
ISBN 0-471-31996-1; 0-471-07780-1 pa
                                             LC 00-20368
   This is "a stolid sifting of facts from fiction." Booklist
   Includes bibliographical references

Dary, David

   ★ The **Oregon** Trail; an American saga. Knopf 2004 414p il map $35   **978**
   1. Frontier and pioneer life -- West (U.S.) 2. Frontier and pioneer life -- Western States 3. Oregon Trail 4. Oregon Trail -- History
ISBN 0-375-41399-5
                                             LC 2004-46512
   The author "looks at the men and women who trekked the trouble-strewn paths to the nation's northwest coast. . . . Dary opens with 18th-century maritime explorers and carries us into the late 19th century, when the trail west from Independence, Mo., had ceded its importance to the railroads. . . . His closing chapter on the Oregon Trail's rebirth as a tourist draw in the 20th century is a real contribution to modern western lore. It's hard to imagine a more informative introduction to the westering itch along the Oregon Trail and to those who responded to it." Publ Wkly
   Includes bibliographical references

Egan, Timothy

   The **worst** hard time; the untold story of those who survived the great American dust bowl. Timothy Egan. Houghton Mifflin Co. 2006 340p ill., map $28; $28   **978**
   1. Depressions -- 1929 -- Great Plains 2. Droughts -- Great Plains -- History -- 20th century 3. Dust Bowl Era, 1931-1939 4. Dust storms 5. Dust storms -- Great Plains -- History -- 20th century
ISBN 061834697X; 9780618346974
                                             LC 2005-08057
   This book presents an account of how America's . . . plains turned to dust, and how the ferocious plains winds stirred up an endless series of "black blizzards" . . . in what became known as the Dust Bowl. But the plague was man-made, as Egan shows: the plains weren't suited to farming, and plowing up the grass to plant wheat, along with a confluence of economic disaster—the Depression—and natural disaster—eight years of drought—resulted in an ecological and human catastrophe. . . . [The author] grounds his tale in

portraits of the people who settled the plains: hardy Americans and immigrants desperate for a piece of land to call their own and lured by the lies of promoters who said the ground was arable. (Publishers Weekly)

"With characters who seem to have sprung from a novel by Sinclair Lewis or Steinbeck, and Egan's powerful writing, this account will long remain in readers' minds." Publ Wkly

Includes bibliographical references (p. 315-327) and index

Luchetti, Cathy

★ **Children** of the West; family life on the frontier. Norton 2001 253p il $39.95   **978**
1. Children -- West (U.S.) 2. Family -- West (U.S.) -- History -- 19th century 3. Family -- West (U.S.) -- History -- 19th century -- Pictorial works 4. Frontier and pioneer life -- West (U.S.) 5. Frontier and pioneer life -- West (U.S.) -- Pictorial works 6. Pioneer children -- West (U.S.) -- Pictorial works 7. Pioneer children -- West (U.S.) -- Social conditions 8. Pioneer children -- West (U.S.) -- Social life and customs
ISBN 0-393-04913-2

                         LC 00-53287

"In the nineteenth and early twentieth centuries, the children who resided in the sparsely populated plains and prairies of the western U.S. were subject to a unique variety of hardships and joys. . . . Utilizing more than 100 vintage photographs and excerpts from letters, diaries, and journals, Luchetti examines aspects of childbearing, child rearing, childhood, and adolescence on the American frontier." Booklist

Includes bibliographical references

McLynn, Frank

Wagons west; the epic story of America's overland trails. Grove Press 2002 509p il maps $32.50; pa $16.50   **978**
1. Frontier and pioneer life -- West (U.S.) 2. Overland journeys to the Pacific
ISBN 0-8021-1731-7; 0-8021-4063-7 pa

                       LC 2002-33859

This "account of the westward migration covers the years 1840-49, spanning the time between the eclipse of the mountain men and the beginning of the gold rush. . . . Relying on original diaries and memoirs, McLynn eloquently illustrates how diverse groups of people, including midwestern farmers, Native Americans, Mormons, and missionaries, played their parts in transforming the West while being transformed by it. This work will be a valuable addition to western history collections." Booklist

Includes bibliographical references

Morgan, Ted

A **shovel** of stars; the making of the American West, 1800 to the present. Simon & Schuster 1995 559p il maps hardcover o.p. pa $25   **978**
1. Frontier and pioneer life -- West (U.S.) 2. West (U.S.) -- History
ISBN 0-684-81492-7 pa

                       LC 94-43838

"This grandly inspired work—a completely satisfying read—embraces the texture and the drama of the West in all its heartbreak and heroism." Booklist

Includes bibliographical references

Parkman, Francis

The **Oregon** trail; The conspiracy of Pontiac. Literary Classics of the United States, Distributed to the trade in the U.S. and Canada by the Viking Press 1991 951p il $40   **978**
1. Frontier and pioneer life -- West (U.S.) 2. Native Americans 3. Oregon Trail 4. Pontiac's Conspiracy, 1763-1765
ISBN 0-940450-54-2

                       LC 90-62264

In The Conspiracy of Pontiac (1851), the author describes Native American resistance to white expansion in the Northeast after the French's loss of the Seven Years' War. The Oregon Trail is "an account of a trip made in 1846 by the author and his cousin Quincy Adams Shaw. They traveled together from St. Louis to Fort Laramie; there they separated, Parkman going to live for some weeks with a tribe of Sioux Indians. The Oregon Trail provides valuable descriptions of the prairies at the most fascinating period of their history and a remarkable ethnological study of the Indians." Benet's Reader's Ency of Am Lit

Includes bibliographical references

Raban, Jonathan

Bad land; an American romance. Pantheon Bks. 1996 324p hardcover o.p.   **978**
1. Frontier and pioneer life -- West (U.S.) 2. West (U.S.) -- Description 3. West (U.S.) -- History
ISBN 0-679-75906-9 pa

                       LC 96-13432

This "book about Montana examines the present remains and historical origins of the last great wave of American western settlement, the migration of homesteaders to eastern Montana in the first decade of this century." (London Rev Books)

Raban "turns Montana into a profound symbol for America's sense of displacement; for its tragic romance with rootlessness, its search for identity under that big blue sky." New Statesman (1913)

Schlissel, Lillian

Far from home; families of the westward journey. [by] Lillian Schlissel, Byrd Gibbens, Elizabeth Hampsten; foreword by Robert Coles. University of Nebraska Press 2002 264p il pa $14.95   **978**
1. Frontier and pioneer life -- West (U.S.)
ISBN 0-8032-9295-3

"An immensely readable book that peers closely into the lives of ordinary American frontier families." Booklist

Includes bibliographical references

Schmidt, Thomas

The **Lewis** & Clark Trail; foreword by Stephen E. Ambrose. Bicentennial ed completely rev;

National Geographic Soc. 2002 192p il maps pa
$16 **978**
    ISBN 0-7922-6471-1

                    LC 2001-7003
    Color photographs and maps provide a guide to the Lewis and Clark National Historic Trail.

Sides, Hampton

    Blood and thunder; an epic of the American West. Doubleday 2006 460p il $26.95 **978**
    1. Frontier and pioneer life -- West (U.S.) 2. Navajo Indians 3. Navajo Indians -- History 4. Pioneers 5. Scouts
    ISBN 978-0-385-50777-6; 0-385-50777-1

                    LC 2006-16579
    This book "will surely capture readers, and it ought to. It's a riveting account of a vast swath of history with which few Americans are familiar." New Yorker
    Includes bibliographical references

Slatta, Richard W.

    The **cowboy** encyclopedia. Norton 1996 474p il pa $17 **978**
    1. Cowhands -- Encyclopedias 2. Reference books
    ISBN 0-393-31473-1

                    LC 94-19824
    "Focusing on the cowboy experience in North and South America, The Cowboy Encyclopedia provides history, definitions, and commentary in an A-to-Z arrangement with major topics such as saddles and cowboy films receiving longer topical entries. Excellent cross-references and an extensive index provide easy access to all aspects of a topic. Appendixes cover cowboy films and videotape sources, museums, periodicals, and western cultural happenings." Am Libr

Slaughter, Thomas P.

    Exploring Lewis and Clark; reflections on men and wilderness. Knopf 2003 231p il maps $24; pa $14 **978**
    1. Explorers 2. Guides (Persons) 3. Interpreters 4. Slaves 5. Territorial governors
    ISBN 0-375-40078-8; 0-375-70071-4 pa

                    LC 2002-69376
    "It may be easy to dismiss as a nitpicking revisionist potshot at our beloved heroes, but as the expedition's bicentennial approaches, this book's perspective will help keep our understanding well nuanced and grounded in fact." Booklist
    Includes bibliographical references

Ward, Geoffrey C.

    The **West**; an illustrated history. narrative by Geoffrey C. Ward; based on a documentary film script by Geoffrey C. Ward and Dayton Duncan; with a preface by Stephen Ives and Ken Burns; and contributions by Dayton Duncan {et al.} Little, Brown 1996 445p il hardcover o.p. pa $24.95 **978**
    1. West (U.S.) -- History
    ISBN 0-316-73589-2 pa

                    LC 96-4323
    "The book's eight chapters, each written by a different historian, are arranged according to the corresponding PBS series. Beginning with Western America in the 1500s, the work presents all aspects of Western culture from the reality to the myth, moving chronologically from the Spanish exploration of the West, Native Americans, Hispanic Westerners, women in the West, and the Gold Rush, and ending with Buffalo Bill's Wild West Show. If one is looking for an in-depth, comprehensive history of the westward movement, this is not it, but as an introduction, this work is an enjoyable and interesting place to start." Libr J

Encyclopedia of the Great Plains; David J. Wishart, editor. University of Nebraska Press 2004 919p il map $75 **978**
    1. Reference books
    ISBN 0-8032-4787-7

                    LC 2003-21037
    "Here is a unique reference book that cuts a broad swath through parts of the U.S. and Canada, the region known as the heartland. The book's topical arrangement perfectly suits the cross-boundary approach." Booklist

The New encyclopedia of the American West; edited by Howard R. Lamar. Yale Univ. Press 1998 1324p il maps $60 **978**
    1. Frontier and pioneer life -- West (U.S.) -- Encyclopedias 2. Reference books
    ISBN 0-300-07088-8

                    LC 98-6231
    This reference work covers "the history, geography, culture, literature, art, and natural history of both the real and the imaginary West. . . . {Coverage spans} prehistory to the present, and . . . {includes} events in the history of the trans-Mississippi West . . . {as well as} the frontier or 'western' stage of all 50 American states. Entries range from important events in the expansion of the U.S. . . . to the first European and American discoverers, among them Coronado, LaSalle, and Lewis and Clark." Publisher's note
    Includes bibliographical references

978.1   Kansas

Frank, Thomas

    What's the matter with Kansas? how conservatives won the heart of America. Metropolitan Books 2004 306p map $24; pa $14 **978.1**
    1. Conservatism
    ISBN 0-8050-7339-6; 0-8050-7774-X pa

                    LC 2004-44824
    This is "a brilliant book, one of the best so far this decade on American politics." Nation
    Includes bibliographical references

Stratton, Joanna L.

    Pioneer women; voices from the Kansas frontier. introduction by Arthur M. Schlesinger, Jr. Simon & Schuster 1981 319p il hardcover o.p. $15 **978.1**
    1. Frontier and pioneer life -- Kansas 2. Women -- Kansas
    ISBN 0-671-44748-3 pa

                    LC 80-15960

"A unique book based on the memoirs of nearly 800 pio-neer women who lived in Kansas between 1854 and 1890. . . . The book presents personal and detailed accounts of life inside homes, the schools, and the social organizations of early Kansas." Choice

Includes bibliographical references

978.7   Wyoming

Black, George

Empire of shadows; the epic story of Yellow-stone. George Black. St. Martin's Press 2012 548 p   **978.7**
1.   Yellowstone National Park -- Discovery and exploration 2. Yellowstone National Park -- History
ISBN 9780312383190; 9781429989749
LC 2011041351

This book is an account of the discovery and imagina-tive creation of Yellowstone National Park is told through the lives of the park's colorful and often tragically egotis-tic explorers and promoters. . . . Waging an irreverent battle against now traditional fakelore, [George] Black particu-larly emphasizes Native American presence in the region of geysers, hot springs, and the headwaters of the Yellowstone River and the role of Lt. Gustavus Doane's military explo-ration, which opened the wonderland to international atten-tion. (Libr J) Divided into five sections and beginning with the familiar expedition of Lewis and Clark, the book spans nearly the entire 19th century. . . . As the book continues, the government enters with paleontologists, entomologists, botanists, and mineralogists, among others. (Kirkus)

Meyer, Judith L.

The **spirit** of Yellowstone; the cultural evolution of a national park. photographs by Vance Howard. Roberts Rinehart 2003 145p il pa $19.95   **978.7**
1.   Human beings -- Effect of environment on -- Yellowstone National Park 2. Human influence on nature
ISBN 1-570-98395-X
LC 2002-156320

The author "pays tribute to the park and all its glories, covering the park's history, its prime landmarks, and its prominence in art. The photographs are truly striking and not the typical landscape fare. Howard plays with light and texture to capture images that will amaze even those already familiar with the park's unprecedented beauty." Libr J

Includes bibliographical references

978.9   New Mexico

Childs, Craig Leland

House of rain; tracking a vanished civiliza-tion across the American Southwest. [by] Craig Childs. Little, Brown and Co. 2006 496p il map $24.99   **978.9**
1.   Pueblo Indians 2. Southwestern States -- Antiquities
ISBN 978-0-316-60817-6; 0-316-60817-3
LC 2006-19112

"Beginning at the monumental cultural center of Chaco Canyon, where the Anasazi flourished, Childs's quest to un-derstand their apparent disappearance leads him to the nu-merous great houses of New Mexico, such as Pueblo Bonito, to the Four Corners area of northeastern Arizona, southern Colorado and Utah, and beyond to northern Mexico. In these places, he identifies features that had not appeared prior to the apparent abandonment of Chaco (thus implying that the Anasazi migrated to these areas). Childs vividly weaves his personal narrative, imbued with a deep respect for the ge-ography and cultural landscape, with scientific research and numerous interactions with foremost scholars." Libr J

979   Great Basin and Pacific Slope region of United States

Durham, Michael S.

Desert between the mountains; Mormons, min-ers, padres, mountain men, and the opening of the Great Basin, 1772-1869. University of Oklahoma Press 1999 336p il map pa $19.95   **979**
1.   Frontier and pioneer life -- Great Basin 2. Frontier and pioneer life -- West (U.S.) 3. Mormon pioneers -- Great Basin -- History 4. Mormons 5. Pioneers -- Great Basin -- History
ISBN 0-8061-3186-1; 978-0-8061-3186-3
LC 99-23572

This is a history of the settlement of the Great Basin area in what is now Utah and Nevada.

"This is well-written history at its most easygoing." Publ Wkly

Includes bibliographical references

Groom, Winston

Kearny's march; the epic journey that created the American southwest, 1846-1847. Alfred A. Knopf 2011 310p il map $27.95; ebook $13.99   **979**
1.   Generals
ISBN 978-0-307-27096-2; 978-0-307-70141-1 ebook
LC 2011013889

"Groom brings to life the events of 1846–47 that trans-formed northern Mexico into the American Southwest dur-ing the Mexican War. He highlights General Stephen Ke-arny's Army of the West and the taking of New Mexico and California, Captain John Charles Fremont's expedition to California and his administrative battle with Kearny, the Mormon Battalion attached to Kearny's army, Colonel Al-exander Doniphan's capture of Chihuahua, and the civilian emigration horror of the Reed-Donner overland wagon train disaster. Groom's narrative of national political scheming and the constant threat of British involvement in the Mexi-can War creates an intriguing international drama." Libr J

Includes bibliographical references

979.1   Arizona

Dolnick, Edward

Down the great unknown; John Wesley Powell's 1869 journey of discovery and tragedy through the

Grand Canyon. HarperCollins Pubs. 2001 367p il maps $27.50; pa $13.95 **979.1**

1. Explorers 2. Explorers -- United States -- Biography 3. Geologists 4. Large print books

ISBN 0-06-019619-X; 0-06-095586-4 pa

LC 2001-24819

"Dolnick, a science journalist who has rafted down the Grand, turns in a most estimable rendition of that storied expedition. It skillfully integrates the notes and journals of expedition members with technical insight about the perils of roiling whitewater." Booklist

Includes bibliographical references

Nasdijj

The **blood** runs like a river through my dreams; a memoir. Houghton Mifflin 2000 216p $23; pa $13 **979.1**

1. Authors 2. Indians of North America -- Mixed descent 3. Memoirists 4. Navajo Indian Reservation -- Social conditions 5. Navajo Indians -- Biography 6. Navajo Indians -- Social conditions 7. Navajo Indians -- Social life and customs

ISBN 0-618-04892-8; 0-618-15448-5 pa

LC 00-38916

"Born on the Navajo reservation in 1950 to migrant workers (a Navajo storytelling mother and a white cowboy father) . . . Nasdijj writes about the life and death of his son, Tommy Nothing Fancy, their fishing trips, his travails as a committed but unpublished writer, life on the reservation, homelessness, ethnic cleansing in America, love, survival, hope. Illuminating both the comic and the tragic, his writing is a striking blend of 'tell it like it is' truths that hit right between the eyes and sensuous, expressive, poetic passages that urgently bid the reader to reread, linger, share, and appreciate. The stories and their implications are heartbreaking; but more importantly, they are heart expanding." Booklist

Pasternak, Judy

Yellow dirt; an American story of a poisoned land and a people betrayed. Free Press 2010 317p il map $26; ebook $12.99 **979.1**

1. Navajo Indians 2. Uranium mines and mining

ISBN 1416594825; 1439100462; 9781416594826; 9781439100462

LC 2010-5546

"In the 1940s, when the U.S. government was embarking on developing atomic weapons, it discovered huge uranium deposits in Navajo territory covering parts of Utah, New Mexico, and Arizona. . . . The Navajo themselves saw little of the huge profits from uranium but as workers and land dwellers would suffer radiation exposure four times that of the Japanese targeted by the A-bomb. . . . Pasternak follows four generations of Navajo families, from the patriarch who warned against violating the land to those tempted by the prospects of jobs and money. . . . A stunning look at a shameful chapter in American history with long-lasting implications for all Americans concerned with environmental justice." Booklist

Includes bibliographical references

979.2   Utah

Walker, Ronald W.

★ **Massacre** at Mountain Meadows; an American tragedy. by Ronald W. Walker, Richard E. Turley, Jr., [and] Glen M. Leonard. Oxford University Press 2008 430p il map $29.95 **979.2**

1. Mormons -- History 2. Mountain Meadows Massacre, 1857

ISBN 978-0-19-516034-5

LC 2008-14451

The authors tell the story of "the titular 1857 tragedy in which 157 emigrants traveling to California were killed by local Mormons. With its understated prose, an essential purchase." Libr J

Includes bibliographical references

979.3   Nevada

D'Agata, John

About a mountain. W. W. Norton 2010 236p $23.95 **979.3**

1. Radioactive waste disposal -- Nevada -- Yucca Mountain

ISBN 978-0-393-06818-4; 0-393-06818-8

LC 2009-39295

D'Agata "uses the federal government's highly controversial (and recently rejected) proposal to entomb the U.S.'s nuclear waste located in Yucca Mountain, near Las Vegas, as his way into a spiraling and subtle examination of the modern city, suicide, linguistics, Edvard Munch's The Scream, ecological and psychic degradation, and the gulf between information and knowledge. Acting as a counterpoint to Yucca is the story of a teenager named Levi who leapt to his death off Las Vegas' Stratosphere Motel. . . . A sublime reading experience, aesthetically rewarding and marked by moral courage and humility." Publ Wkly

Denton, Sally

The **money** and the power; the making of Las Vegas and its hold on America, 1947-2000. by Sally Denton and Roger Morris. Knopf 2001 479p hardcover o.p. pa $15 **979.3**

1. Celebrities -- Nevada -- Las Vegas -- History -- 20th century 2. Gambling 3. Organized crime 4. Organized crime -- Nevada -- Las Vegas -- History -- 20th century 5. Political corruption 6. Political corruption -- United States -- History -- 20th century 7. Politicians -- Nevada -- Las Vegas -- History -- 20th century

ISBN 0-375-70126-5 pa

LC 00-62011

"The idea of Las Vegas as the epitome of crass American pop culture has become at least a surface truism in most circles. But Denton and Morris . . . go much deeper than the surface in this sobering account of the famous Nevada resort town." Booklist

Includes bibliographical references

979.4   California

Cannon, Lou

Official negligence; how Rodney King and the riots changed Los Angeles and the LAPD. Westview Press 1999 706p il pa $27   **979.4**

1. Construction workers 2. Riots 3. Victims of crimes
ISBN 978-0-8133-3725-8; 0-8133-3725-9

This work represents "the best kind of reportage—meticulous, unbiased and complete." Publ Wkly

Didion, Joan

Where I was from. Knopf 2003 226p $23; pa $13.95   **979.4**

1. American national characteristics
ISBN 0-679-43332-5; 0-679-75286-2 pa
                                        LC 2002-43325

This "is a complex and challenging memoir, difficult to enter into but just as difficult to put down. . . . Those who have long admired the clarity and precision of her prose will not be disappointed with this partly autobiographical, partly historical, but fully engrossing account." Libr J

Lee, Helie

In the absence of sun; a Korean American woman's promise to reunite three lost generations of her family. Harmony Bks. 2002 342p il maps hardcover o.p. pa $18.95   **979.4**

1. Korean Americans
ISBN 0-449-91171-3 pa
                                        LC 2002-1680

"Lee's Still Life with Rice (1996) was a novelized account of her grandmother's life and escape from what would become North Korea. As she now recounts her and her father's struggles to get other people out of the North, she continues to wrestle with her own Korean heritage—in particular, the paternalistic and patronizing attitudes toward women." Booklist

Muir, John

The **Yosemite**; the original John Muir text. illustrated with photographs by Galen Rowell; each photograph accompanied by an excerpt from the works of John Muir and an annotation by Galen Rowell; introduction by the photographer. Sierra Club Bks. 1989 218p il hardcover o.p. pa $14.95   **979.4**

ISBN 0-87156-782-2 pa
                                        LC 88-34919

New photographs complement Muir's classic 1912 natural history of the national park.

Winchester, Simon

★ A **crack** in the edge of the world; America and the great California earthquake of 1906. HarperCollins 2005 462p il maps $27.95   **979.4**

1. Earthquakes -- California 2. Earthquakes -- California -- San Francisco -- History -- 20th century
ISBN 0-06-057199-3
                                        LC 2005-46009

"In this brawny page-turner, . . . [the author] has crafted a magnificent testament to the power of planet Earth and the efforts of humankind to understand her." Publ Wkly

Includes bibliographical references

979.7   Washington

Kluger, Richard

The **bitter** waters of Medicine Creek; a tragic clash between white and native America. Alfred A. Knopf 2011 330p il map $28.95   **979.7**

1. Generals 2. Indian chiefs 3. Native Americans -- Washington (State) 4. Nisqualli Indians -- Government relations 5. Nisqualli Indians -- History 6. Territorial governors 7. Territorial legislators
ISBN 978-0-307-26889-1; 0-307-26889-6
                                        LC 2010-34249

"When Isaac Stevens, territorial governor of Washington, implemented plans to move the Nisquallies from their ancestral lands to reservations in 1853, Chief Leschi turned from 'good Indian' to incendiary. Implacably opposed to removal to a place 'where the sting of an insect killed like the stroke of a spear, and the streams were foul and muddy,' he organized armed resistance to the whites in Washington. Gov. Stevens' resolve to punish him became an obsession. . . . [Kluger] recounts the confrontation between the two men. Meticulously researched, elegantly written and sophisticated, the book uses this all but forgotten episode in American history to give a human face to the injustices visited on Indians in treaty-making, on the battlefield and, surprisingly, in the courtroom." Minneapolis Star Tribune

Krist, Gary

The **white** cascade; the Great Northern Railway disaster and America's deadliest avalanche. Henry Holt and Company 2007 315p il map $26   **979.7**

1. Avalanches 2. Railroad accidents
ISBN 978-0-8050-7705-6; 0-8050-7705-7
                                        LC 2006-49047

"This is a tale in which snow falls, a mountain looms, and most of the protagonists simply sit. The outcome is predetermined. Mr. Krist does wonders with this unpromising material, however. Adopting a restrained, documentary tone, he slowly builds a picture of massing natural forces and helpless humanity, brought closer and closer to catastrophe with each tick of the clock. The pacing is expertly judged, and the potentially confusing narrative threads, involving multiple actors in scattered locations, are tied together neatly." N Y Times (Late N Y Ed)

Includes bibliographical references

979.8   Alaska

Borneman, Walter R.

★ **Alaska**: saga of a bold land. HarperCollins Pubs. 2003 608p il maps $34.95; pa $16.95 **979.8**

ISBN 0-06-050306-8; 0-06-050307-6 pa
                                        LC 2002-27271

"Separated into nine chronologically based chapters, the text explores a recurring theme in Alaska's development:

conflict among disparate groups over how the land would be used for personal enrichment, . . . Engaging chapters detail the important events and those who helped shape Alaska's history. . . . This expansive, comprehensive history is recommended for all libraries." Libr J

Includes bibliographical references

Jenkins, Peter

Looking for Alaska. St. Martin's Press 2002 434p il $25.95; pa $14.95 **979.8**
1. Alaska -- Social life and customs
ISBN 0-312-26178-0; 0-312-30289-4 pa
LC 2001-48871
This book "sparkles with adventure, quirky characters, unbelievable hardships, and indescribable beauty." Libr J

McPhee, John A.

Coming into the country; {by} John McPhee. Farrar, Straus & Giroux 1977 438p maps hardcover o.p. pa $15 **979.8**
ISBN 0-374-52287-1 pa
LC 77-12249
This book "is actually three lengthy bulletins about Alaska. . . . The first describes a canoe trip that McPhee and four companions took. . . . Second, McPhee tells of a helicopter ride with a committee looking for a site on which to build a new state capital. The last and longest section covers some wintry months spent in Eagle, a tiny settlement on the Yukon River." Time

Raban, Jonathan

Passage to Juneau; a sea and its meanings. Pantheon Bks. 1999 435p $26.50; pa $15 **979.8**
1. Indians of North America -- Northwest, Pacific -- Art 2. Indians of North America -- Northwest, Pacific -- Folklore 3. Northwest Coast of North America -- Description 4. Northwest, Pacific -- Description and travel 5. Romanticism -- History -- 18th century
ISBN 0-679-44262-6; 0-679-77614-1 pa
LC 99-28777
"Long fascinated by the Inside Passage (the protected waterway that runs from Washington State up to Alaska), Raban casts off in his 35' ketch from his home port in Seattle to follow in the wake of generations of salmon fishermen. He draws a rather dark portrait of the region as he fills out its history, through the cranky journals of Captain Vancouver and others, and meditates on the beautiful but threatening and lonesome landscape, with its struggling communities, submerged mountains, tricky waters, and names like Deception Pass and Desolation Sound." Libr J

980   History of South America

Casey, Michael

Che's afterlife; the legacy of an image. Vintage Books 2009 388p il pa $15.95 **980**
1. Imagery (Psychology) 2. Marketing 3. Photographers 4. Photography -- Social aspects 5. Physicians 6. Portrait photography 7. Revolutionaries
ISBN 978-0-307-27930-9; 0-307-27930-8
LC 2008-32186

Casey "has written a book that is not only a cultural history of an image, but also a sociopolitical study of the mechanisms of fame. It is a book about how ideas travel and mutate in this age of globalization, how concepts of political ideology have increasingly come to be trumped by notions of commerce and cool and chic, and how the historical Che Guevara gave way, postmortem, to a host of other Ches." N Y Times (Late N Y Ed)

Includes bibliographical references.

Chasteen, John Charles

Born in blood and fire; a concise history of Latin America. 2nd ed; W.W. Norton 2006 372p il map pa $43.25 **980**
ISBN 978-0-393-92769-6; 0-393-92769-5
LC 2005-48248
"Chasteen focuses on major political, social and economic topics and trends that helped shape Latin America, including liberalism, the caste system, the mixing of races, nationalism and the Western notion of 'Progress'; he also examines the role that Europe and the United States played in the development of these phenomena. Also refreshing is Chasteen's examination of the periods he covers from the perspective of women." Publ Wkly [review of 2000 edition]

Includes bibliographical references

Thomas, Hugh

Rivers of gold; the rise of the Spanish Empire, from Columbus to Magellan. Random House 2003 xxi, 696p il map $35 **980**
ISBN 0-375-50204-1
LC 2003-69316
"Engagingly presented, this book clearly shows the author's passion for his subject." Booklist

Includes bibliographical references

Williamson, Edwin

The **Penguin** history of Latin America. Penguin Books 1992 631p map pa $18 **980**
ISBN 0-14-012559-0
LC 2005-412242
"The book is organized topically, rather than by country, and the author wisely selected regional examples of his major themes, rather than attempting a detailed analysis of each country. The work ends with an unusual exploration of literature and culture in relation to identity and modernization, followed by a helpful bibliographic essay." Libr J

Includes bibliographical references

The **Cambridge** history of Latin America; edited by Leslie Bethell. Cambridge Univ. Press 1984 10v in 11 v1 $205; v2 $236; v3 $225; v4 $205; v5 $236; v6 pt. 1 $162; v6 pt. 2 $162; v7 $205; v8 $205; v10 $162; v11 $178 **980**
ISBN 0-521-23223-6 v1; 0-521-24516-8 v2; 0-521-23224-4 v3; 0-521-23225-2 v4; 0-521-24517-6 v5; 0-521-23226-0 v6 pt. 1; 0-521-46556-7 v6 pt. 2; 0-521-24518-4 v7; 0-521-26652-1 v8; 0-521-49594-6 v10; 0-521-39525-9 v11
LC 83-19036
"History of the areas south of the United States from just prior to the European invasions to the present. . . . Covers

general themes in Latin American history with chronological accounts of the individual countries. Bibliographical essays are appended to each chapter." NY Public Libr Book of How & Where to Look It Up

★ Encyclopedia of Latin American history and culture; Jay Kinsbruner, editor in chief; Erick D. Langer, senior editor. 2nd ed.; Gale 2008 6v il map set $695   **980**
1. Reference books
ISBN 978-0-684-31270-5
LC 2008-3461

"This reference set covers the Western Hemisphere from Mexico to the tip of South America. . . . [This is] an outstanding encyclopedia that will serve a wide range of users from high school students to Latin American scholars." Libr J
Includes bibliographical references

981 Brazil

Meade, Teresa
A **brief** history of Brazil; [by] Teresa A. Meade. 2nd ed; Facts On File 2009 280p il $49.50; pa $19.95   **981**
ISBN 978-0-8160-7788-5; 0-8160-7788-6; 978-0-8160-7789-2 pa; 0-8160-7789-4 pa; 978-1-4381-2736-1 ebook
LC 2009-33853

An account of Brazil's political, economic, and cultural landscape.

Reel, Monte
The **last** of the tribe; the epic quest to save a lone man in the Amazon. Scribner 2010 273p il map $26   **981**
1. Native Americans -- Brazil
ISBN 978-1-4165-9474-1; 1-4165-9474-4
LC 2009-37974

"In the opening scene of Monte Reel's 'The Last of the Tribe,' Brazilian government workers approach the deep jungle hideout of an Amazonian Indian they suspect to be the last living member of his tribe. The Indian sits in his hut, cornered, an arrow drawn on his bow, and waits. After two hours, the standoff ends. The government workers leave; the Indian disappears into the jungle. Again. 'The Last of the Tribe' is the story of the 20-year pursuit of that solitary Indian by aid workers who want to contact and protect him, and by loggers and miners who want him dead or moved before he gives the government a reason to protect more land from resource extraction. . . . Reel's tale is expertly told: perfectly timed, thoroughly researched and descriptively written." San Francisco Chron
Includes bibliographical references

Skidmore, Thomas E.
Brazil; five centuries of change. Oxford Univ. Press 1999 254p maps hardcover o.p. pa $28.95 **981**
ISBN 0-19-505810-0 pa
LC 98-23122

Skidmore explores the country's "history, its political and economic development, and social and racial relationships. . . . This is a well-researched look at a fascinating country." Booklist
Includes bibliographical references

Whitaker, Robert
The **mapmaker's** wife; a true tale of love, murder, and survival in the Amazon. Basic Books 2004 352p il maps $25   **981**
1. Scientific expeditions 2. Scientific expeditions -- Ecuador -- History 3. Travelers
ISBN 0-7382-0808-6; 978-0-7382-0808-4
LC 2003-26902

"The harrowing journey of Isabel Godin across the Andes and down the Amazon to rejoin her husband after a 20-year separation is only a small part of the extended history of the Charles-Marie de la Condamine expedition, which in turn is set within its context of the history of Enlightenment science, 18th-century mapping methods, the debate over the shape of the earth, and the sorry history of the Spanish and Portuguese conquest of South America." Sci Books Films
Includes bibliographical references

982 Argentina

Brown, Jonathan C.
A **brief** history of Argentina; 2nd ed; Facts On File 2010 354p il map $49.50; pa $19.95   **982**
ISBN 978-0-8160-7796-0; 978-0-8160-8361-9 pa; 978-1-4381-3111-5 ebook
LC 2010004887

This book covers "Argentina's diverse geography and its varied natural resources; the origins of the deep-seated practices of discrimination, which continue today; the effects of neoliberalism on Argentina's large working class and urban poor, culminating in the caserola movement, the piqueteros movement, and the birth of the cartoneros; the impact a changing global economy has had within Argentina's borders; [and] the rich culture of Argentina, which has created five Nobel laureates, vibrant cities that draw millions of tourists annually, and sports teams that have won multiple world championships." Publisher's note
Includes bibliographical references

Parrado, Nando
★ **Miracle** in the Andes; 72 days on the mountain and my long trek home. [by] Nando Parrado with Vince Rause. Crown Publishers 2006 291p il map hardcover o.p. pa $13.95   **982**
1. Businesspeople 2. Memoirists 3. Rugby players 4. Survival after airplane accidents, shipwrecks, etc. 5. Television producers
ISBN 1-4000-9767-3; 978-1-4000-9767-8; 1-4000-9769-X pa; 978-1-4000-9769-2 pa
LC 2005-21629

"In October 1972, a plane carrying an Uruguayan rugby team crashed in the Andes. Not immediately rescued, the survivors turned to cannibalism to survive and after 72 days were saved. Rugby team member Parrado has written a beautiful story of friendship, tragedy and perseverance." Publ Wkly

985   Peru

Adams, Mark

Turn right at Machu Picchu. Dutton 2011 333p il map $26.95   985
1. Explorers 2. Governors 3. Historians 4. Senators
ISBN 978-0-525-95224-4; 0-525-95224-1
LC 2011-10211

Traces the author's recreation of Hiram Bingham III's discovery of the ancient citadel, Machu Picchu, in the Andes Mountains of Peru, describing his struggles with rudimentary survival tools and his experiences at the sides of local guides.

"While some readers may prefer a more straightforward version of Bingham's exploits . . . , those favoring a quirkier retelling will relish Mr. Adams's wry, revealing romp through the Andes." Wall Street J

Bingham, Hiram

★ Lost city of the Incas; the story of Machu Picchu and its builders. with an introduction by Hugh Thomson; photographs by Hugh Thomson. Sterling 2002 274p il hardcover o.p. pa $12.95   985
1. Archaeological expeditions -- Peru -- Machu Picchu Site 2. Incas 3. Incas -- Peru -- Antiquities
ISBN 0-2976-0759-6; 1-84212-585-0 pa
LC 2002-483039

"In 1911 Bingham, an American explorer, found the Inca city of Machu Picchu, which had been lost for 300 years. In this volume he tells of its origin, how it came to be lost and how it was finally discovered." Libr J
Includes bibliographical references

Hunefeldt, Christine

A brief history of Peru; 2nd ed; Facts On File 2010 xx, 332p il map $49.50   985
ISBN 978-0-8160-8144-8; 978-1-4381-0828-5 ebook
LC 2010-20748

This is a history of Peru ranging "from its ancient peoples and the Inca Empire through . . . recent political, social, and economic developments." Publisher's note
Includes bibliographical references

MacQuarrie, Kim

The last days of the Incas. Simon & Schuster 2007 522p il map $30; pa $16.95   985
1. Incas
ISBN 978-0-7432-6049-7; 0-7432-6049-X; 978-0-7432-6050-3 pa; 0-7432-6050-3 pa
LC 2007-61700

This "is a first-rate reference work of ambitious scope that will most likely stand as the definitive account of these people." Booklist
Includes bibliographical references

Moseley, Michael Edward

★ The Incas and their ancestors; the archaeology of Peru. rev ed; Thames & Hudson 2001 288p il maps $27.50   985
1. Incas
ISBN 0-500-28277-3
LC 00-108866

This account of Andean prehistory and archaeology takes us from the first settlement of 10,000 years ago to the Spanish conquest.

"Clearly presented, with a generous ration of maps and illustrations, {the volume} is thoughtful and welcome." Times Lit Suppl {review of 1992 edition}
Includes bibliographical references

Thomson, Hugh

The white rock; an exploration of the Inca heartland. Overlook Press 2003 316p il map $27.95; pa $16.95   985
1. Inca architecture -- Peru -- Cuzco (Province) 2. Incas 3. Incas -- Peru -- Cuzco (Province) -- Antiquities 4. Incas -- Peru -- Cuzco (Province) -- History 5. Motion picture directors 6. Television directors
ISBN 1-585-67355-2; 1-585-67503-2 pa
LC 2002-34606

"So entertaining and appealing is Thomson's story of his exploration of the Inca empire that readers will wish they could take off and follow in his footsteps. . . . Thomson's wit, eye for detail and reverence for humanity set him apart from the average travel-adventure writer—he is as good a companion as a traveler could hope for." Publ Wkly
Includes bibliographical references

986.6   Ecuador

Kane, Joe

★ Savages. Knopf 1995 273p il map hardcover o.p. pa $14   986.6
1. Human ecology 2. Waorani Indians
ISBN 0-679-74019-8 pa
LC 95-4258

"In the Ecuadorian Amazon the author befriends Moi, a Huaorani warrior who is learning new strategies in his fight to keep American oil companies from destroying his homeland. Moi not only smuggles Kane past Ecuadorian military check-points into Huaorani territory but also returns with him to confront the savages in the conference halls of Washington." New Yorker
Includes bibliographical references

990   History of Australasia, Pacific Ocean islands, Atlantic Ocean islands, Arctic islands, Antarctica, extraterrestrial worlds

Michener, James A.

Return to paradise. Random House 1951 437p hardcover o.p. pa $7.99   990
ISBN 0-449-20650-5 pa

"Alternate chapters describe each island followed by a short story set against the region described." Ont Libr Rev

994 Australia

Clarke, F. G.

The **history** of Australia. Greenwood Press 2002 236p $45   994

ISBN 0-313-31498-5

LC 2001-54704

This volume "begins with a timeline of historical events. The first chapter is a very short overview of Australia (geography, climate, culture, and so on). The rest of the text is a chronological study in short, concise chapters beginning 60,000 years ago with Aboriginal Australia and ending with 2001 and beyond. Each chapter is broken down into smaller sections, with headings, covering such essential topics as colonization, war, government, and politics. The work ends with smaller sections for notable people, notes, a bibliographic essay, and an index." Recomm Ref Books for Small & Medium-sized Libr & Media Cent, 2003

Includes bibliographical references (p. {225}-227) and index

Clendinnen, Inga

Dancing with strangers; Europeans and Australians at first contact. Inga Clendinnen. Cambridge University Press 2005 324p il map $60; pa $21.99   994

1. Aboriginal Australians 2. Australian aborigines 3. British -- Cultural assimilation -- Australia 4. Europeans -- Cultural assimilation -- Australia 5. National characteristics, Australian

ISBN 0-5218-5137-8; 0-5216-1681-6 pa

LC 2005-11523

"In January 1788, the First Fleet arrived in New South Wales, Australia and a thousand British men and women encountered the people who would be their new neighbors. . . . [This book] tells the story of what happened between the first British settlers of Australia and these Aborigines." Publisher's note

Includes bibliographical references

Hughes, Robert

★ The **fatal** shore. Knopf 1987 688p il maps hardcover o.p. pa $18   994

1. Penal colonies

ISBN 0-394-75366-6 pa

LC 86-45272

"This epic account chronicles the history of Australia during the 80 years (1788-1868) of England's convict transportation system, when some 160,000 convicts reached 'the fatal shore.' Interweaving his own lucid narrative with untapped original sources—including the diaries and letters of the prisoners themselves—Hughes shows the evolution of the system and of the fledgling nation that emerged from the brutal penal colony." Libr J

Includes bibliographical references

Keneally, Thomas

A **commonwealth** of thieves; the improbable birth of Australia. Nan A. Talese/Doubleday 2006 385p map hardcover o.p. pa $15.95   994

1. Admirals 2. Colonial administrators 3. Frontier and pioneer life -- Australia 4. Penal colonies

ISBN 0-385-51459-X; 978-0-385-51459-0; 1-4000-7956-X pa; 978-1-4000-7956-8 pa

LC 2006-44470

This "book offers an engaging treatment of a subject which over the years has provoked a long and sometimes heated debate." Times Lit Suppl

Includes bibliographical references

The **Australian** people; an encyclopedia of the nation, its people and their origins. edited by James Jupp. Cambridge Univ. Press 2001 xx, 940p il maps $150   994

1. Australia -- Encyclopedias 2. Australian aborigines -- Social conditions 3. Immigrants -- Australia -- Social conditions 4. Minorities -- Australia -- History 5. Reference books

ISBN 0-521-80789-1

LC 2001-37896

This "documents the dramatic history of Australian settlement and describes the rich ethnic and cultural inheritance of the nation through the contributions of its people." Publisher's note

Includes bibliographical references (p. 868-930) and index

995.3 Papua New Guinea

Flannery, Tim F.

Throwim way leg; tree-kangaroos, possums, and penis gourds--on the track of unknown mammals in wildest New Guinea. [by] Tim Flannery. Atlantic Monthly Press 1998 326p il map hardcover o.p. pa $14   995.3

1. Ethnology -- New Guinea 2. Indigenous peoples -- New Guinea

ISBN 0-8021-3665-6 pa

LC 98-38435

This "is more than an account of [the author's] fieldwork. It is an enthralling introduction to the mountain people of New Guinea." N Y Times Book Rev

996 Polynesia and other Pacific Ocean islands

Alexander, Caroline

The **Bounty**: the true story of the mutiny on the Bounty. Viking 2003 491p il hardcover o.p. pa $17   996

1. Admirals 2. Bounty Mutiny, 1789 3. Colonial administrators 4. Explorers 5. Government officials 6. Mutineers 7. Naval officers

ISBN 978-0-670-03133-7; 0-670-03133-X; 978-0-14-200469-2 pa; 0-14-200469-3 pa

LC 2003-50158

"A rollicking sea adventure told with enormous confidence and style." Booklist

Includes bibliographical references

Severin, Timothy

In search of Robinson Crusoe. Basic Bks. 2002 333p il hardcover o.p. pa $16.95 **996**
1. Authors 2. Essayists 3. Historians 4. Literature and history -- England -- History -- 17th century 5. Novelists 6. Pamphleteers 7. Sailors 8. Survival after airplane accidents, shipwrecks, etc. 9. Survival after airplane accidents, shipwrecks, etc., in literature 10. Writers on politics
ISBN 0-465-07699-8 pa

LC 2002-71661

The author examines "the fictional Crusoe alongside the historic realities of colonization and human ingenuity. . . . Readers learn about the history of marooning among plunderers, blockade navies and other piratical sailors, as well as the ethnography of the so-called 'Moskito Man' (aka Man Friday) and all the ways to provide for oneself on a deserted island. . . . The work is energetic and Severin is an ideal guide to the world behind the word. This will surely appeal to the lovers of maritime history." Publ Wkly

996.9 Hawaii and neighboring north central Pacific Ocean islands

Vowell, Sarah

Unfamiliar fishes. Riverhead Books 2011 238p il map $25.95 **996.9**
ISBN 978-1-59448-787-3

LC 2010-47943

"While Vowell's take on Hawaii's Americanization is abbreviated, it's never bereft of substance—her repartee manages to be filling, her insights astute and comprehensive." N Y Times Book Rev

Includes bibliographical references

998 Arctic islands and Antarctica

Alexander, Caroline

The Endurance; Shackleton's legendary Antarctic expedition. Knopf 1998 211p il $29.95 **998**
1. Explorers
ISBN 0-375-40403-1

In 1914, Sir Ernest Shackleton "sailed to Antarctica with 27 men in hopes of being the first human to transverse the continent. But his ship, the Endurance, was trapped, then crushed, by ice in the Weddell Sea, propelling the party into a nightmare of cold and near starvation. Alexander, relying extensively on journals by crew members, some never published, as well as on myriad other sources, delivers a spellbinding story of human courage. . . . What makes this book especially exciting, however, are the 170 previously unpublished photos by the expedition's photographer, Frank Hurley." Publ Wkly

Avery, Tom

To the end of the earth; our epic journey to the North Pole and the legend of Peary and Henson. St. Martin's Press 2009 321p il map $26.95 **998**
1. Admirals 2. Explorers
ISBN 978-0-312-55186-5; 0-312-55186-X

LC 2008-44069

"To vindicate a controversial claim in Arctic annals (whether or not Robert Peary attained the . . . [North Pole] in 1909), Avery and his companions brave the unforgiving ice cap, confront numerous deadly situations, and return to Britain in triumph—only to weather heavy criticism about the exact significance of their feat. . . . A highly enjoyable chronicle of contemporary exploration." Booklist

Ehrlich, Gretel

This cold heaven; seven seasons in Greenland. Pantheon Bks. 2001 377p il maps hardcover o.p. pa $14 **998**
1. Inuit
ISBN 0-679-44200-6; 0-679-75852-6 pa

LC 00-69277

"Ehrlich began traveling to Greenland during her recovery from a nearly fatal lightning strike, and her keen, often poetic responses to the beauty of the frigid landscape and the warmth of Inuit families, combined with a profound immersion in Greenland history, infuse her captivating account with both drama and reflection." Booklist

Includes bibliographical references

Emmerson, Charles

The future history of the Arctic. PublicAffairs 2010 405p il map **998**
1. Geopolitics
ISBN 978-1-58648-636-5

LC 2009-35094

"It's easy to romanticise the Arctic, and over the years plenty of authors have. Oddly though, given the region's increasing geopolitical significance, it's rare to find books that treat it as something other than a chilly adventure playground or an excuse for reams of purple prose. Thank goodness, then, for Charles Emmerson. In this book he looks at how the frozen north has played a key role in world affairs in the past and how it could prove more important in the years to come." Scotsman

Includes bibliographical references

Griffiths, Tom

Slicing the silence; voyaging to Antarctica. Harvard University Press 2007 399p map $29.95 **998**
ISBN 978-0-674-02633-9; 0-674-02633-0

LC 2007-06549

"Believing that to understand the experiences of explorers and the history of Antarctica one must experience its mighty winds, cold, danger, and silence, the author, in 2002, joined a ship delivering scientists and supplies to Casey Station. This book is part diary of that voyage and part history of that most southerly land. . . . This enjoyable and highly readable book would be an excellent addition to any natural history, polar history, or adventure travel collection." Libr J

Includes bibliographical references

Kavenna, Joanna

The ice museum; in search of the lost land of Thule. Viking 2006 294p il map $24.95; pa $15 **998**

1. Journalists

ISBN 0-670-03473-8; 0-14-303846-X pa

The author "chronicles her personal journey into the myth and reality of the legendary Arctic land of Thule. . . . [This book] transcends all genre description, and holds its own as a journey into a world that somehow vibrantly exists on paper and nowhere else." Booklist

McGonigal, David

Antarctica; secrets of the southern continent. chief consultant, David McGonigal. Firefly Books 2008 400p il map $59.95 **998**

ISBN 978-1-55407-398-6; 1-55407-398-7

This "book covers all aspects of the continent, including ecology, geography, wildlife, and exploration. . . . Sumptuously illustrated with photos, maps, and paintings, this will be the go-to reference on Antarctica for years to come. A truly superb production." Booklist

Riffenburgh, Beau

Shackleton's forgotten expedition; the voyage of the Nimrod. by Beau Riffenburgh. Bloomsbury, Distributed to the trade by Holtzbrinck Publishers 2004 xxiv, 358p il map $25.95; pa $15.95 **998**

1. Explorers

ISBN 1-58234-488-4; 1-58234-611-9 pa

LC 2004-11999

The author recounts Shackleton's "voyage to the Antarctic from 1907 to 1909, during which he led a small group of men to within 97 miles of the South Pole. . . . For those who thrilled to the Endurance saga, Riffenburgh offers an equally gripping adventure, which laid the foundations of Shackleton's capacity for brilliant leadership under pressure." Publ Wkly

Includes bibliographical references

Smith, Roff

Life on the ice; no one goes to Antarctica alone. National Geographic 2005 208p pa $16 **998**

ISBN 0-7922-9345-2

LC 2005-298454

"Smith is the most exceptional of travel writers: his portraits of people are deeply sympathetic, while his language is at once lyrical and knowledgeable. Not to be missed." Booklist

Streever, Bill

Cold; adventures in the world's frozen places. Little, Brown and Co. 2009 292p $24.99; pa $14.99 **998**

1. Biologists 2. Cold

ISBN 978-0-316-04291-8; 0-316-04291-9; 978-0-316-04292-5 pa; 0-316-04292-7 pa

LC 2008-45350

Strever "delivers a poetic, anecdotal narrative complete with polar expeditions, Ice Age mysteries, igloos, permafrost and hailstorms. . . . This is a wonderful collection of one man's first-rate observations and commentary about the history and importance of cold to the earth and its occupants." Publ Wkly

Includes bibliographical references

Encyclopedia of the Arctic; Mark Nuttall, editor. Routledge 2005 3v il map set $525 **998**

1. Reference books

ISBN 1-57958-436-5

LC 2004-16694

For a fuller review see: Booklist, Jan. 1 & 15, 2005

Nuttall "has put together a multidisciplinary work that covers indigenous peoples, explorers, scientists, history, environment, climate, plants and animals, geography, current research concerns, and more. The 1200 alphabetically arranged entries, all written by experts from 20 countries (a number of them native to the Arctic), range in length from 500 to 5000 words." Libr J

The ends of the earth; an anthology of the finest writing on the Arctic and the Antarctic. Bloomsbury 2007 2v in 1 map $29.95 **998**

ISBN 1-59691-443-2; 978-1-59691-443-8

The editors "present an anthology of writings about the Arctic and Antarctic, which is actually two books in one. Halfway through, readers can turn the book upside down for writings about the opposite end of the earth. . . . Included are primary-source accounts by early explorers such as Ernest Shackleton, John Franklin, and Kund Rasmussen, nature writings by Barry Lopez and Gretel Ehrlich, excerpts from novels by Jules Verne, Jack London, and H.P. Lovecraft, and essays by journalists and scientists. Each excerpt is just long enough to whet the reader's appetite. Great reading for the armchair adventurer." Libr J

AUTHOR, TITLE, AND SUBJECT INDEX

This index to the books in the Classified Collection includes author, title, and subject entries; added entries for publishers' series, illustrators, joint authors, and editors of works entered under title; and name and subject cross-references; all arranged in one alphabet.

The number or symbol in boldface type at the end of each entry refers to the Dewey Decimal Classification or to the Fiction (Fic) or Story Collection (S C), or Easy Books (E) section where the main entry for the book will be found. Works classed in 92 will be found under the headings for the biographies' subject.

Keene, D. Five modern Japanese novelists **895.6**

Abegg, Martin G.

The Dead Sea scrolls **296.1**

Abel, Jessica

Drawing words & writing pictures **741.5**

Abigail Adams. Holton, W. **92**

ABILITIES *See* Ability

ABILITY

Shenk, D. The genius in all of us **155.2**

Syed, M. Bounce **650.1**

ABILITY—TESTING

See also Educational tests and measurements;
Intelligence tests; Psychological tests

Gould, S. J. The mismeasure of man **153.9**

ABILITY GROUPING IN EDUCATION

See also Education; Educational psychology;
Grading and marking (Education)

Abingdon Press

The New Interpreter's dictionary of the Bible **220.3**

ABNORMAL CHILDREN *See* Exceptional children; Handicapped children

ABNORMAL PSYCHOLOGY

See also Mind and body; Nervous system

Hicks, J. W. Fifty signs of mental illness **616.89**

Ronson, J. The psychopath test **616.85**

Smoller, J. The other side of normal **591.5**

ABNORMALITIES, HUMAN

Wynbrandt, J. The encyclopedia of genetic disorders and birth defects **616**

ABOLITION OF CAPITAL PUNISHMENT *See* Capital punishment

ABOLITION OF SLAVERY *See* Abolitionists; Slavery; Slaves—Emancipation

ABOLITIONISTS

Abdul-Jabbar, K. Black profiles in courage **920**

Benfey, C. E. G. A summer of hummingbirds **920**

Berkin, C. Civil War wives **920**

Carretta, V. Equiano, the African **92**

Clinton, C. Fanny Kemble's civil wars **792**

Clinton, C. Harriet Tubman: the road to freedom **973.7**

Colaiaco, J. A. Frederick Douglass and the Fourth of July **973.7**

Douglass, F. Autobiographies **973.8**

Douglass, F. My bondage and my freedom **973.8**

Douglass, F. Narrative of the life of Frederick Douglass, an American slave **92**

Failure is impossible **92**

Hague, W. J. William Wilberforce **92**

Hedrick, J. D. Harriet Beecher Stowe **92**

Hofstadter, R. The American political tradition, and the men who made it **973**

Horwitz, T. Midnight rising **92**

Humez, J. M. Harriet Tubman **92**

Larson, K. C. Bound for the promised land **92**

McPherson, J. M. Drawn with the sword **973.7**

Painter, N. I. Sojourner Truth **305.5**

Reynolds, D. S. John Brown, abolitionist **92**

Reynolds, D. S. Mightier than the sword **813**

Slaughter, T. P. The beautiful soul of John Woolman, apostle of abolition **92**

Tobin, J. From Midnight to Dawn **322**

Wills, G. Certain trumpets **303.3**

Wilson, E. Patriotic gore **810**

Winch, J. A gentleman of color: the life of James Forten **326**

ABOLITIONISTS—GREAT BRITAIN—HISTORY—19TH CENTURY

Desmond, A. J. Darwin's sacred cause **92**

ABOLITIONISTS—UNITED STATES—BIOGRAPHY

Douglass, F. My bondage and my freedom **973.8**

ABORIGINAL AUSTRALIANS

Chatwin, B. The songlines **919**

Clendinnen, I. Dancing with strangers **994**

Hooper, C. Tall man **364.1**

ABORIGINAL AUSTRALIANS—CRIMES AGAINST

Hooper, C. Tall man **364.1**

ABORIGINAL AUSTRALIANS—CRIMINAL JUSTICE SYSTEM

Hooper, C. Tall man **364.1**

ABORIGINAL AUSTRALIANS—SOCIAL CONDITIONS

The Australian people **994**

Abortion. Rose, M. **363.46**

ABORTION

Abortion wars **363.46**

Moreno, J. D. The body politic **303.48**

Press, E. Absolute convictions **363.46**

Reagan, L. J. When abortion was a crime **363.46**

Rose, M. Abortion **363.46**

Solinger, R. Beggars and choosers **363.46**

Tribe, L. H. Abortion: the clash of absolutes **363.46**

Weddington, S. R. A question of choice **363.46**

ABORTION—ENCYCLOPEDIAS

Palmer, L. J. Encyclopedia of abortion in the United States **363.46**

ABORTION—ETHICAL ASPECTS

See also Ethics

ABORTION—LAW AND LEGISLATION

Hull, N. E. H. Roe v. Wade **344**

ABORTION—LAW AND LEGISLATION

See also Law; Legislation

ABORTION—SOCIAL ASPECTS—UNITED STATES

Solinger, R. Beggars and choosers **363.46**

ABORTION—UNITED STATES—HISTORY

Rose, M. Abortion **363.46**

ABORTION PROVIDERS

Press, E. Absolute convictions **363.46**

ABORTION RIGHTS MOVEMENT *See* Pro-

See also Painting

ACRYLIC PAINTING—TECHNIQUE

All about techniques in acrylics **751.4**

ACT ASSESSMENT

Ehrenhaft, G. Barron's ACT **378.1**

An **act** of state. Pepper, W. F. **364.1**

ACTING

2010: the best men's stage monologues and scenes **808.82**

2010: the best women's stage monologues and scenes **808.82**

Adler, S. Stella Adler: the art of acting **792**

The best stage scenes of 2007 **808.82**

Brestoff, R. The actor's wheel of connection **792**

Chekhov, M. To the actor **792**

Hagen, U. Respect for acting **792**

Mamet, D. True and false **792**

Marasco, R. Notes to an actor **792**

Moore, S. The Stanislavski system **792**

Stanislavsky, K. An actor's work **792**

Stanislavsky, K. Creating a role **792**

The Ultimate audition book **808.82**

ACTING

See also Drama; Public speaking

ACTING—PSYCHOLOGICAL ASPECTS

Stanislavsky, K. An actor's work **792**

ACTING—STUDY AND TEACHING

Stanislavsky, K. An actor's work **792**

ACTING—TECHNIQUE

Stanislavsky, K. An actor's work **792**

Active liberty. Breyer, S. G. **342**

Active living every day. Blair, S. N. **613.7**

ACTIVITY PROGRAMS IN EDUCATION

Rupp, R. The complete home learning sourcebook **371.04**

An **actor** and his time. Gielgud, J. **92**

The **actor's** wheel of connection. Brestoff, R. **792**

An **actor's** work. Stanislavsky, K. **792**

ACTORS

See also Entertainers

Abbott, K. American rose **92**

Alexander, P. Boulevard of broken dreams **92**

Andrews, J. Home **92**

Angelou, M. Letter to my daughter **92**

Angelou, M. I know why the caged bird sings **92**

Angelou, M. A song flung up to heaven **818**

Arkin, A. An improvised life **92**

Bacall, L. By myself and then some **92**

Bach, S. Leni: the life and work of Leni Riefenstahl **92**

Balbirer, N. Take your shirt off and cry **92**

Becker, C. It's the pictures that got small **791.45**

Belafonte, H. My song **92**

Berg, A. S. Kate remembered **92**

Bernhardt, S. My double life: the memoirs of Sarah Bernhardt **792**

Biskind, P. Star **92**

Black women writers (1950-1980) **810**

Bogle, D. Heat wave **92**

Bosworth, P. Marlon Brando **791.43**

Bozza, A. Whatever you say I am **92**

Brynner, R. Empire & odyssey **920**

Buckley, W. F. The Reagan I knew **92**

Buford, K. Burt Lancaster **92**

Carroll, D. The legs are the last to go **92**

Clarke, G. Get happy: the life of Judy Garland **782.421**

Cliff, N. The Shakespeare riots **974.4**

Clinton, C. Fanny Kemble's civil wars **792**

Croall, J. Gielgud **792**

Curtis, J. Spencer Tracy **92**

Denton, S. The pink lady **92**

Douglas, K. My stroke of luck **362.1**

D'Souza, D. Ronald Reagan **973.927**

Dukakis, O. Ask me again tomorrow **92**

Dyson, M. E. Holler if you hear me: searching for Tupac Shakur **782.421**

The essential Chaplin **92**

Fey, T. Bossypants **92**

Fine, M. Accidental genius **791**

Fisher, C. Wishful drinking **92**

FitzGerald, F. Way out there in the blue **973.927**

Flinn, C. Brass diva **92**

Foote, H. Beginnings **812**

Fox, M. J. Always looking up **92**

Fox, M. J. Lucky man **92**

Friedwald, W. Sinatra! the song is you **782.421**

Gates, H. L. Thirteen ways of looking at a black man **920.71**

Gavin, J. Stormy weather **92**

Gehring, W. D. James Dean: rebel with a cause **92**

George-Warren, H. Public cowboy no. 1 **92**

Giddins, G. Bing Crosby: a pocketful of dreams: the early years, 1903-1940 **92**

Gielgud, J. An actor and his time **92**

Gillespie, M. A. Maya Angelou **92**

Gillies, I. Happens every day **92**

Goudsouzian, A. Sidney Poitier **92**

Green, S. The world of musical comedy **920**

Guralnick, P. Careless love: the unmaking of Elvis Presley **92**

Guralnick, P. Last train to Memphis: the rise of Elvis Presley **782.421**

Hepburn, K. Me **92**

Holroyd, M. A strange eventful history **92**

Hoskyns, B. Lowside of the road **92**

Ice-T Ice **92**

Jackson, C. Hattie: the life of Hattie McDaniel **92**

Jaffrey, M. Climbing the mango trees **92**

Johnson, H. B. Sleepwalking through history **973.927**

Kanfer, S. Ball of fire **791.45**

Kaplan, J. Frank 92
Kashner, S. Furious love 92
Kaufman, D. Doris Day 92
Keaton, E. Buster Keaton remembered 791.43
Kissinger, H. Diplomacy 327.2
Lax, E. Conversations with Woody Allen 791.43
Leaming, B. Katharine Hepburn 92
Leaming, B. Marilyn Monroe 791.43
Leider, E. W. Myrna Loy 92
Leider, E. W. Becoming Mae West 791.43
Leider, E. W. Dark lover: the life and death of Rudolph Valentino 791.43
Levy, S. Paul Newman 92
Lewis, J. Dean & me 92
Lewis, R. The real life of Laurence Olivier 792
Life stories 920
Lynn, K. S. Charlie Chaplin and his times 791.43
Mann, J. The rebellion of Ronald Reagan 973.927
Mann, J. About face 327
Mann, W. J. Kate: the woman who was Hepburn 92
Martin, S. Born standing up 92
Mason, B. A. Elvis Presley 782.421
McCabe, J. Cagney 92
McCann, G. Cary Grant 791.43
McCourt, M. A monk swimming 974.7
McCourt, M. Singing my him song 974.7
Meade, M. Buster Keaton 92
Min, A. Red Azalea 92
Mooney, P. Black is the new white 92
Moore, M. T. Growing up again 92
Moore, S. The Stanislavski system 792
Palin, M. Halfway to Hollywood 92
Pierpont, C. R. Passionate minds 810
Playwrights at work 812
Plummer, C. In spite of myself 92
Poitier, S. The measure of a man 92
Quirk, L. J. Bob Hope: the road well-traveled 92
Ratnesar, R. Tear down this wall 973.927
Reagan, R. Reagan 92
Reagan, R. My father at 100 92
Reeve, C. Still me 92
Reeves, R. President Reagan: the triumph of imagination 973.927
Rhodes, R. Hedy's folly 92
Ripken, C. The only way I know 792
Robeson, P. Here I stand 92
Robeson, P. The undiscovered Paul Robeson 782
Robinson, R. American original: a life of Will Rogers 792.7
Santopietro, T. Sinatra in Hollywood 92
Schickel, R. Clint Eastwood 791.43
Scovell, J. Oona 791.43
Server, L. Ava Gardner 791
Shearer, S. M. Beautiful 92
Singer, M. Character studies 920
Spitz, M. Bowie 92

Spoto, D. Notorious 92
Sudhalter, R. Stardust melody: the life and music of Hoagy Carmichael 782
Swanson, J. L. Manhunt 364.152
Taraborrelli, J. R. The secret life of Marilyn Monroe 92
Thomson, D. Bette Davis 92
Thomson, D. Gary Cooper 92
Thomson, D. Humphrey Bogart 92
Thomson, D. Ingrid Bergman 92
Thomson, D. Rosebud: the story of Orson Welles 92
Thursby, J. S. Critical companion to Maya Angelou 818
Trimborn, J. Leni Riefenstahl 92
Victor, A. The Elvis encyclopedia 781.66
Walker, A. Audrey 92
Wallach, E. The good, the bad, and me 92
Ware, S. Letter to the world 920.72
Wasson, S. Fifth Avenue, 5 AM 791.43
Watts, J. Hattie McDaniel 92
Waxman, S. Rebels on the backlot 920
Whitfield, E. Pickford 92
Wilber, D. Q. Rawhide down 973.927
Woodward, B. Shadow 973.92
Wranovics, J. Chaplin and Agee 92
Yagoda, B. Will Rogers 792.7

ACTORS—DICTIONARIES
Monush, B. Screen world presents the encyclopedia of Hollywood film actors 920.003
Otfinoski, S. Latinos in the arts 920.003

ACTORS—FRANCE—BIOGRAPHY
Bernhardt, S. My double life: the memoirs of Sarah Bernhardt 792

ACTORS—GREAT BRITAIN—BIOGRAPHY
Clinton, C. Fanny Kemble's civil wars 792
Croall, J. Gielgud 792

ACTORS—UNITED STATES
    See also Actors
Robeson, P. The undiscovered Paul Robeson 782
Turan, K. Free for all 92

ACTORS—UNITED STATES—BIOGRAPHY
Spacek, S. My extraordinary ordinary life 791.43

ACTORS AND ACTRESSES *See* Actors

ACTRESSES
    See also Actors
Bosworth, P. Jane Fonda 791.43
Kaling, M.   Is everyone hanging out without me? (and other concerns) 818

Acts of faith. Patel, E. 92

ACUPRESSURE
    See also Alternative medicine; Massage

ACUPUNCTURE
    See also Alternative medicine

Aczel, Amir D.
The artist and the mathematician 500
Chance: a guide to gambling, love, the stock market

Aderkas, P. von

Turner, N. J. The North American guide to common poisonous plants and mushrooms **581.6**

ADIRONDACK MOUNTAINS (N.Y.)—HISTORY

Schneider, P. The Adirondacks **974.7**

The **Adirondacks.** Schneider, P. **974.7**

ADJUSTABLE RATE MORTGAGES

Andrews, E. L. Busted **332.7**

ADJUSTMENT (PSYCHOLOGY)

See also Psychology

Brehony, K. A. After the darkest hour **155.9**

Brizendine, J. Stunned by grief **248**

Gonzales, L. Surviving survival **155.9**

Kingma, D. R. The ten things to do when your life falls apart **155.9**

Seligman, M. E. P. Learned optimism **155.2**

Weiss, M. C. Living well beyond breast cancer **616.99**

Adkin, Mark

The Trafalgar companion **940.2**

Adkins, Lesley

Handbook to life in ancient Greece **938**

Adkins, Roy

Adkins, L. Handbook to life in ancient Greece **938**

Adland. Tungate, M. **659.1**

Adler, Dennis

The art of the sports car **629.222**

Adler, Margot

Drawing down the moon **133.4**

Adler, Mortimer J.

Aristotle for everybody **185**

How to think about the great ideas **080**

Adler, Moshe

Economics for the rest of us **330**

Adler, Robert E.

Medical firsts **610**

Science firsts: from the creation of science to the science of creation **509**

Adler, Stella

Stella Adler: the art of acting **792**

Adler, Stephen J.

(ed) Women's letters **305.4**

Adler, William M.

The man who never died **92**

ADMINISTRATION *See* Civil service; Management; Public administration

ADMINISTRATION—HANDBOOKS, MANUALS, ETC.

Larson, J. C. The public library policy writer **025.1**

Stanley, M. J. Managing library employees **023**

Tucker, D. C. Crash course in library supervision **023**

ADMINISTRATION OF CRIMINAL JUSTICE

Bogira, S. Courtroom 302 **345**

Burns, S. The Central Park Five **364.1**

Encyclopedia of crime & justice **364**

Encyclopedia of crime and punishment **346**

Famous American crimes and trials **364**

Feige, D. Indefensible **345**

Geoghegan, T. In America's court **345**

Oshinsky, D. M. Worse than slavery **365**

Stuntz, W. J. The collapse of American criminal justice **364.4**

ADMINISTRATION OF CRIMINAL JUSTICE

See also Administration of justice; Criminal law

ADMINISTRATION OF CRIMINAL JUSTICE—DICTIONARIES

Encyclopedia of American prisons **365**

ADMINISTRATION OF JUSTICE

Legal systems of the world **340**

ADMINISTRATIVE ABILITY *See* Executive ability

ADMINISTRATIVE AGENCIES

Kettl, D. F. The next government of the United States **351**

ADMINISTRATIVE AGENCIES—LAW AND LEGISLATION *See* Administrative agencies

Administrative assistant's and secretary's handbook. Stroman, J. **651.3**

Admiral of the ocean sea: a life of Christopher Columbus. Morison, S. E. **92**

ADMIRALS

See also Military personnel; Navies

Adkin, M. The Trafalgar companion **940.2**

Alexander, C. The Bounty: the true story of the mutiny on the Bounty **996**

Avery, T. To the end of the earth **998**

Beyer, K. W. Grace Hopper and the invention of the information age **92**

Connell, E. S. The Aztec treasure house **814**

Hibbert, C. Nelson **92**

Keneally, T. A commonwealth of thieves **994**

Pocock, T. The terror before Trafalgar **940.2**

Spencer, C. E. M. S. Prince Rupert **92**

Sugden, J. Nelson: a dream of glory, 1758-1797 **92**

Vincent, E. Nelson **940.2**

Woodward, B. The commanders **973.928**

Zimmermann, W. First great triumph **973**

ADMIRALS—BIOGRAPHY—DICTIONARIES

Ancell, R. M. The biographical dictionary of World War II generals and flag officers **920.003**

ADMIRALS—GREAT BRITAIN—BIOGRAPHY

Vincent, E. Nelson **940.2**

ADMIRALS—UNITED STATES—BIOGRAPHY

Thomas, E. John Paul Jones **973.3**

ADMISSIONS APPLICATIONS *See* College applications

Admissions confidential. Toor, R. **378.1**

cans in art

AFRO-AMERICANS IN LITERATURE *See* African Americans in literature

AFRO-AMERICANS IN TELEVISION BROAD-CASTING *See* African Americans in television broadcasting

AFRO-AMERICANS ON TELEVISION *See* African Americans on television

After. Hirshfield, J.   **811**

After 9/11: America's war on terror (2001-) Jacobson, S.   **741.5**

After all. Matthews, W.   **811**

After America. Starobin, P.   **973.91**

After Camelot. Taraborrelli, J. R.   **973.922**

After cancer treatment. Silver, J. K.   **616.99**

AFTER DINNER SPEECHES

    See also Speeches

After Dolly. Wilmut, I.   **176**

After Jihad. Feldman, N.   **321.8**

After photography. Ritchin, F.   **775**

After such knowledge. Hoffman, E.   **940.53**

After the ball. Beard, P.   **368.32**

After the darkest hour. Brehony, K. A.   **155.9**

After the diagnosis. Pikula, D. L.   **610.69**

After the fall.   **974.7**

After the Holocaust. Brenner, M.   **943.087**

After the prophet. Hazleton, L.   **297**

After the storm.   **305**

After the Trail of Tears. McLoughlin, W. G.   **970.004**

After the war zone. Slone, L. B.   **616.85**

After: how America confronted the September 12 era. Brill, S.   **973.931**

AFTERLIFE *See* Future life

Aftermath. Rosen, N.   **956.7**

AFTERNOON TEAS

    See also Cooking

Aftershock. Reich, R. B.   **330.9**

Against all enemies. Clarke, R. A.   **973.931**

Against depression. Kramer, P. D.   **616.85**

Against the tide. Dean, C.   **333.91**

Agassi, Andre

    Open   **92**

Agatston, Arthur

    The South Beach diet   **613.2**

AGE—PHYSIOLOGICAL EFFECT *See* Aging

AGE DISCRIMINATION

    See also Discrimination

The **age** of anxiety. Johnson, H. B.   **973.921**

The **age** of anxiety. Tone, A.   **615**

Age of delirium. Satter, D.   **947.085**

The **age** of empathy. De Waal, F.   **152.4**

The **age** of entanglement. Gilder, L.   **530.1**

Age of greed. Madrick, J. G.   **330.9**

The **age** of insight. Kandel, E. R.   **154.2**

The **age** of movies. Kael, P.   **791.43**

The **age** of reform from Bryan to F.D.R. Hofstadter, R.   **973.91**

The **age** of revolution 1789-1848. Hobsbawm, E. J.   **940.2**

Age of Roosevelt [series]

    Schlesinger, A. M. The coming of the New Deal, 1933-1935   **973.917**

    Schlesinger, A. M. The crisis of the old order, 1919-1933   **973.91**

    Schlesinger, A. M. The politics of upheaval, 1935-1936   **973.917**

The **age** of science. Piel, G.   **509**

The **age** of the unthinkable. Ramo, J. C.   **973.931**

The **age** of turbulence. Greenspan, A.   **92**

The **age** of wonder. Holmes, R.   **509**

AGED *See* Elderly

AGED—ATTITUDES

    Alford, H. How to live   **155.67**

AGED—CONDUCT OF LIFE

    Chittister, J. The gift of years   **200**

AGED—CRIMES AGAINST—UNITED STATES—PREVENTION

    Carnot, E. J. Is your parent in good hands?   **362.6**

AGED—ENCYCLOPEDIAS

    Encyclopedia of aging   **305.26**

AGED—HEALTH AND HYGIENE

    The Johns Hopkins medical guide to health after 50   **613**

AGED—HEALTH AND HYGIENE—ENCYCLOPEDIAS

    Kandel, J. The encyclopedia of senior health and well being   **613**

AGED—PSYCHOLOGY

    Chittister, J. The gift of years   **200**

AGED—UNITED STATES

    Jacoby, S. Never say die   **305.26**

AGED PARENTS *See* Aging parents

Agee, James

    Let us now praise famous men   **976.1**

AGEING *See* Aging

Ageless body, timeless mind. Chopra, D.   **612.6**

Ageless yoga. Reichmann, R.   **613.7**

Agent Garbo. Talty, S.   **940.5**

Agent Zigzag. Macintyre, B.   **92**

The **ages** of Gaia. Lovelock, J.   **570.1**

AGGREGATES *See* Set theory

AGGRESSIVE BEHAVIOR *See* Aggressiveness (Psychology)

AGGRESSIVENESS (PSYCHOLOGY)

    See also Human behavior; Psychology

    Simmons, R. Odd girl out   **305.23**

AGGRESSIVENESS IN CHILDREN

    Simmons, R. Odd girl out   **305.23**

The **agile** gene. Ridley, M.   **155.7**

AGING

    See also Age; Elderly; Gerontology; Longevity; Middle age; Old age

Aldred, Cyril
  Akhenaten: King of Egypt **932**
Aldrich, Nelson W.
  (ed) George, being George **92**
Aldridge, Alan
  The man with kaleidoscope eyes **741.6**
Aleixandre, Vicente
  A longing for the light **861**
The **Aleppo** Codex. Friedman, M. **221**
Aletti, Vince
  (ed) Thompson, M. Michael Thompson: Portraits **779**
Alexander Hamilton. Randall, W. S. **92**
Alexander Hamilton. Chernow, R. **92**
Alexander Hamilton, American. Brookhiser, R. **92**
Alexander, Caroline
  The Bounty: the true story of the mutiny on the Bounty **996**
  The Endurance **998**
  The war that killed Achilles **883**
Alexander, Charles K.
  (ed) Standard handbook of electronic engineering **621.381**
Alexander, David E.
  Why don't jumbo jets flap their wings? **629.13**
Alexander, Elizabeth
  Crave radiance **811**
  (ed) Brooks, G. The essential Gwendolyn Brooks **811**
Alexander, Ivy L.
  (ed) AIDS sourcebook **362.1**
Alexander, Kelly
  Hometown appetites **92**
Alexander, Larry
  Biggest brother **92**
Alexander, Paul
  Boulevard of broken dreams **92**
Alexander, William
  52 loaves **641.8**
Alexie, Sherman
  Face **811**
Alexis De Tocqueville. Epstein, J. **92**
Alford, Henry
  How to live **155.67**
Alford, Jeffrey
  Beyond the Great Wall **641.5**
Alfred E. Smith, the happy warrior. Finan, C. M. **92**
Alfred Kazin's journals. Cook, R. M. **92**
Alfred Stieglitz: the key set. Stieglitz, A. **770**
ALGAE
  Barker, R. And the waters turned to blood **615.9**
Algar, Ayla Esen
  Classical Turkish cooking **641.59**
ALGEBRA
  See also Mathematical analysis; Mathematics
Algeo, Matthew

  The president is a sick man **973.8**
ALGERIA—BIOGRAPHY
  Macey, D. Frantz Fanon **965**
The **Algeria** Hotel. Nossiter, A. **940.53**
ALGORITHMS
  Berlinski, D. The advent of the algorithm **511**
  Michael, T. S. How to guard an art gallery and other discrete mathematical adventures **511**
Ali, Khaliah
  Fighting weight **92**
Ali, Nujood
  I am Nujood, age 10 and divorced **92**
Alibis. Aciman, A. A. **814**
Alice. Cordery, S. A. **92**
Alice Neel. Hoban, P. **92**
Alice Walker. **813**
Alice Walker's The color purple. **813**
ALIEN LABOR
  See also Labor
  Bacon, D. Illegal people **331.6**
ALIEN LABOR—UNITED STATES
  Bacon, D. Illegal people **331.6**
ALIEN LABOR, MEXICAN—NEW YORK—NEW YORK—BIOGRAPHY
  Breslin, J. The short sweet dream of Eduardo Gutierrez **331.6**
ALIEN PLANTS—CONTROL
  Bright, C. Life out of bounds **578.6**
ALIENATION (SOCIAL PSYCHOLOGY)
  See also Social psychology
ALIENS
  See also Minorities
ALIENS—UNITED STATES
  Bray, I. M. How to get a green card **342**
ALIENS FROM OUTER SPACE *See* Extraterrestrial beings
ALIMONY
  See also Divorce
Alinder, Mary Street
  Adams, A. Ansel Adams, an autobiography **770**
  Ansel Adams **770**
Alison, Jane
  The sisters antipodes **92**
Alive. Read, P. P. **910.4**
Alix G. Mautner memorial lectures [series]
  Feynman, R. P. QED **539.7**
All about roasting. **641.7**
All about techniques [series]
  All about techniques in acrylics **751.4**
All about techniques in acrylics. **751.4**
All American. Crawford, B. **92**
All creatures great and small. Herriot, J. **92**
All for love. Dryden, J. **822**
All God's children. Butterfield, F. **364.1**
All governments lie. MacPherson, M. **92**
All hopped up and ready to go. Fletcher, T. **781.64**

All in the dances: a brief life of George Balanchine. Teachout, T. **92**

All Indians do not live in teepees (or casinos) Robbins, C. C. **970.004**

All is change. Sutin, L. **294.3**

All music guide to classical music. **016**

All my dogs. Henderson, B. **92**

All my patients have tales. Wells, J. **636**

All new square foot gardening. Bartholomew, M. **635**

All of it singing. Gregg, L. **811**

All of us. Carver, R. **811**

All over but the shoutin' Bragg, R. **070**

All over the map. Fraser, L. **92**

All rivers run to the sea. Wiesel, E. **813**

All the best, George Bush. Bush, G. **92**

All the daring of the soldier. Leonard, E. D. **973.7**

All the devils are here. McLean, B. **330.9**

All the laws but one. Rehnquist, W. H. **342**

All the poems of Muriel Spark. Poems **821**

All the president's men. Bernstein, C. **973.924**

All the Shah's men. Kinzer, S. **327**

All the stops. Whitney, C. R. **786.5**

All the way home. Giffels, D. **92**

All the way to Berlin. Megellas, J. **940.54**

All the whiskey in heaven. Bernstein, C. **811**

All things Austen. Olsen, K. **823**

All things Shakespeare. Olsen, K. **822.3**

All things shining. Dreyfus, H. L. **200**

All too human. Stephanopoulos, G. **973.929**

The **all-natural** diabetes cookbook. Newgent, J. **641.5**

All-new hints from Heloise. Heloise **640**

Allaby, Michael
The encyclopedia of Earth **910**
The Facts on File weather and climate handbook **551.6**

Allan Pinkerton. Mackay, J. A. **363.28**

Allan, Tony
Life, myth, and art in Ancient Rome **937**

Allawi, Ali A.
The occupation of Iraq **956.7**

ALLEGED CRIMINALS
Heard, A. The eyes of Willie McGee **364.66**

Allegiance. Detzer, D. **973.7**

ALLEGORIES
See also Fiction

ALLEGORY
See also Arts; Fiction

Allen, Arthur
Vaccine **614.4**

Allen, Frederick Lewis
Only yesterday **973.91**

Allen, John
Tutu, D. The rainbow people of God **968.06**

Allen, R.

(ed) Bulletproof feathers **570.1**

Allen, Stewart Lee
In the devil's garden **641**

Allen, William Francis
Ware, C. P. Slave songs of the United States **781.62**

Allen, Woody
Side effects **817**
Without feathers **817**

Allende, Isabel
My invented country **863**
Paula **92**
The sum of our days **92**

ALLERGIES *See* Allergy

ALLERGIES, FOOD *See* Food allergy

ALLERGY
Brody, J. E. Jane Brody's allergy fighter **616.2**
Pescatore, F. The allergy and asthma cure **616.97**
Walsh, W. E. Food allergies **616.97**

ALLERGY—ALTERNATIVE TREATMENT
Pescatore, F. The allergy and asthma cure **616.97**

ALLERGY—ENCYCLOPEDIAS
Lipkowitz, M. Encyclopedia of allergies **616.97**
The **allergy** and asthma cure. Pescatore, F. **616.97**

ALLERGY, FOOD *See* Food allergy

Allert, Tilman
The Hitler salute **395**

Alley, Richard B.
Earth **621**

Allgor, Catherine
A perfect union **973.5**

Allied Forces/Supreme Headquarters/Psychological Warfare Division/Intelligence Team
The Buchenwald report **940.53**

ALLIGATORS
See also Reptiles

Allin, Craig W.
(ed) Encyclopedia of environmental issues **363.7**
(ed) Encyclopedia of global resources **333.7**

Allison, Graham T.
Nuclear terrorism **363.32**

Allison, Jay
(ed) This I believe **170**
(ed) This I believe II **170**

Allison, Nancy
(ed) The Illustrated encyclopedia of body-mind disciplines **615.5**

Allitt, Patrick
The conservatives **320.5**

Allman, Gregg
My cross to bear **780**

ALLOCATION OF TIME *See* Time management

ALLOSAURUS
See also Dinosaurs

Allport, Alan
Demobbed **305.9**

ALLUSIONS

American Cancer Society's guide to complementary and alternative cancer methods. American Cancer Society **616.99**

American Canoe Association

Canoeing **797.1**

Kayaking **797.1**

The **American** century. Haskell, B. **709**

American century series

Hughes, L. I wonder as I wander **818**

AMERICAN CHARACTERISTICS *See* American national characteristics

American chica. Arana, M. **92**

An **American** childhood. Dillard, A. **92**

American Civil Liberties Union

The rights of women **346.01**

American Civil Liberties Union handbook [series]

American Civil Liberties Union The rights of women **346.01**

The **American** Civil War. Keegan, J. **973.7**

AMERICAN CIVIL WAR *See* United States—History—1861-1865, Civil War

American College of Physicians complete home medical guide. **616.02**

American College of Sports Medicine

Complete guide to fitness & health **613.7**

AMERICAN COLONIAL STYLE IN ARCHITECTURE

See also Architecture

AMERICAN COLONIES *See* United States—History—1600-1775, Colonial period

AMERICAN COOKING

See also Cooking

American Council of Learned Societies

American national biography **920.003**

American countercultures. Misiroglu, G. R. **306**

American creation. Ellis, J. J. **973.3**

American crescent. Qazwini, H. **92**

American crisis. Fowler, W. M. **973.3**

American crossroads [series]

Harmon, A. Indians in the making **970.004**

An **American** daughter. Wasserstein, W. **812**

American decades. **973.9**

American decades primary sources. **973.9**

American Diabetes Association

American Diabetes Association complete guide to diabetes **616.4**

What to expect when you have diabetes **616.4**

Walker, R. A. Diabetes: a practical guide to managing your health **616.4**

American Diabetes Association complete guide to diabetes. American Diabetes Association **616.4**

AMERICAN DIARIES

See also American literature; Diaries

AMERICAN DIARIES—WOMEN AUTHORS

Adamson, L. G. Notable women in American history **016**

American Dietetic Association complete food and nutrition guide. Duyff, R. L. **613.2**

AMERICAN DRAMA

See also American literature; Drama

Critical survey of drama **809**

AMERICAN DRAMA—20TH CENTURY

Gurney, A. R. Love letters and two other plays: The golden age and What I did last summer **812**

AMERICAN DRAMA—20TH CENTURY—HISTORY AND CRITICISM

Playwrights at work **812**

AMERICAN DRAMA—DICTIONARIES

Bordman, G. M. The Oxford companion to American theatre **792**

Critical survey of drama **809**

AMERICAN DRAMATISTS

See also American authors; Dramatists

The **American** dream. Rather, D. **973.92**

American earth. **333.72**

American Eden. Graham, W. **712**

American electricians' handbook. **621.3**

American emperor. Stewart, D. O. **973.4**

American empire project [series]

Dreyfuss, R. Devil's game **327**

The American empire project [series]

McCoy, A. W. A question of torture **323.4**

American empire, 1945-2000. **973.92**

American encounters/global interactions [series]

Levi, H. The world of lucha libre **796.8**

American eras. **973.8**

AMERICAN ESPIONAGE

See also Espionage

Laird, T. Into Tibet **327.12**

AMERICAN ESSAYS

See also American literature; Essays

As consciousness is harnessed to flesh **B**

Baker, N. The way the world works **814**

Bissell, T. Magic hours **153.35**

Dower, J. W. Ways of forgetting, ways of remembering **940.53**

Flanagan, C. Girl land **305.235**

Franzen, J. Farther away **814**

Kaling, M. Is everyone hanging out without me? (and other concerns) **818**

Robinson, M. When I was a child I read books **814**

American experience [series]

Reef, C. Poverty in America **362.5**

Reef, C. Working in America **305**

Schneider, D. Slavery in America **326**

AMERICAN FICTION

See also American literature; Fiction

The Facts on File companion to the American novel **813**

Helbig, A. Dictionary of American young adult fiction, 1997-2001 **028.5**

AMERICAN FICTION—20TH CENTURY

The Columbia companion to the twentieth-century American short story **813**

Society for the Study of the Short Story A Reader's companion to the short story in English **809**

AMERICAN FICTION—20TH CENTURY—BIO-BIBLIOGRAPHY—DICTIONARIES

Helbig, A. Dictionary of American children's fiction, 1995-1999 **028.5**

Helbig, A. Dictionary of American young adult fiction, 1997-2001 **028.5**

AMERICAN FICTION—20TH CENTURY—DICTIONARIES

Helbig, A. Dictionary of American children's fiction, 1995-1999 **028.5**

Helbig, A. Dictionary of American young adult fiction, 1997-2001 **028.5**

AMERICAN FICTION—20TH CENTURY—HISTORY AND CRITICISM

The Columbia companion to the twentieth-century American short story **813**

AMERICAN FICTION—BIO-BIBLIOGRAPHY

The Columbia companion to the twentieth-century American short story **813**

Contemporary Jewish-American novelists **813**

The Facts on File companion to the American novel **813**

AMERICAN FICTION—ENCYCLOPEDIAS

The Facts on File companion to the American novel **813**

AMERICAN FICTION—HISTORY AND CRITICISM

The Columbia companion to the twentieth-century American short story **813**

The Facts on File companion to the American novel **813**

AMERICAN FICTION—JEWISH AUTHORS

Contemporary Jewish-American novelists **813**

AMERICAN FOLK ART

See also American art; Folk art

Encyclopedia of American folk art **745**

American Folk Art Museum

Encyclopedia of American folk art **745**

AMERICAN FOLK DRAMA

See also American drama; Folk drama

American food writing. **641.5**

AMERICAN FOREIGN AID

See also Foreign aid

American foreign relations since 1600. **016**

AMERICAN FURNITURE

See also Furniture

The **American** future. Schama, S. **973.93**

American Gothic. Biel, S. **759.13**

AMERICAN GOVERNMENT *See* United States—Politics and government

American grace. Campbell, D. E. **201**

American ground, unbuilding the World Trade Cen-

ter. Langewiesche, W. **974.7**

American Heart Association

New American Heart Association cookbook The new American Heart Association cookbook **641.5**

The **American** Heritage dictionary of business terms. Scott, D. L. **650**

The **American** Heritage dictionary of idioms. Ammer, C. **423**

The **American** Heritage dictionary of the English language. **423**

The **American** Heritage guide to contemporary usage and style. Houghton Mifflin Co. **423**

The **American** Heritage science dictionary. **503**

American heroes. Morgan, E. S. **920**

American heroines. Hutchison, K. B. **920**

AMERICAN HISTORY *See* America—History; United States—History

The **American** history cookbook. Zanger, M. H. **641.59**

American history series

Iverson, P. We are still here **970.004**

American home front, 1941-1942. Cooke, A. **940.53**

American Horticultural Society

American Horticultural Society encyclopedia of plants and flowers **635.9**

The American Horticultural Society gardening manual **635**

Pruning & training **635.9**

New encyclopedia of gardening techniques **635**

The **American** Horticultural Society A-Z encyclopedia of garden plants. **635.9**

American Horticultural Society encyclopedia of plants and flowers. **635.9**

The **American** Horticultural Society gardening manual. American Horticultural Society **635**

American hymns old and new. **782.27**

American icon. Thompson, T. **796.357**

American impressionism. Gerdts, W. H. **759.13**

American Indian ethnic renewal. Nagel, J. **305.8**

American Indians. **970.004**

AMERICAN INDIANS *See* Native Americans

American Institute for Cancer Research

The new American plate cookbook **641.5**

American Institute of Parliamentarians/Revision Committee

Sturgis, A. The standard code of parliamentary procedure **060.4**

American insurgents, American patriots. Breen, T. H. **973.3**

American inventors, entrepreneurs & business visionaries. Carey, C. W. **920**

American Islam. Barrett, P. M. **297**

American Jewish Historical Society

American Jewish history **305.8**

American Jewish history. **305.8**

American Jewish year book 2007. **296**

Denmead, K. Geek dad **790**
Lithgow, J. A Lithgow palooza! **793**
Amusing ourselves to death. Postman, N. **302.23**
AMYOTROPHIC LATERAL SCLEROSIS
Albom, M. Tuesdays with Morrie **378.1**
AMYOTROPHIC LATERAL SCLEROSIS—PA-TIENTS
Weiner, J. His brother's keeper **616.8**
AMYOTROPHIC LATERAL SCLEROSIS—PA-TIENTS—UNITED STATES—BIOGRAPHY
Albom, M. Tuesdays with Morrie **378.1**
An Deming
Yang Lihui Handbook of Chinese mythology **299.5**
ANABOLIC STEROIDS *See* Steroids
ANACONDAS
Murphy, J. C. Tales of giant snakes **597.96**
ANAESTHETICS *See* Anesthetics
The **Analects**. Confucius **181**
ANALYSIS (MATHEMATICS) *See* Calculus; Functions; Mathematical analysis
ANALYSIS OF FOOD *See* Food—Analysis; Food adulteration and inspection
ANALYTIC GEOMETRY
See also Geometry
ANALYTICAL CHEMISTRY
See also Chemistry
Analyzing library collection use with Excel. Greiner, T. **025.2**
Anan, Ruth
Turkington, C. The encyclopedia of autism spectrum disorders **616.85**
Ananthaswamy, Anil
The edge of physics **530**
ANARCHISM—FRANCE—HISTORY
Merriman, J. M. The dynamite club **363.32**
ANARCHISM—HISTORY
Butterworth, A. The world that never was **335**
Watson, B. Sacco and Vanzetti **345**
ANARCHISM—UNITED STATES—HISTORY
Miller, S. The President and the assassin **973.8**
ANARCHISM AND ANARCHISTS
See also Freedom; Political crimes and offenses; Political science
Butterworth, A. The world that never was **335**
Merriman, J. M. The dynamite club **363.32**
Miller, S. The President and the assassin **973.8**
Tuchman, B. W. The proud tower **909.82**
ANARCHISM AND ANARCHISTS—GRAPHIC NOVELS
Rudahl, S. A dangerous woman **335**
ANARCHISTS
Merriman, J. M. The dynamite club **363.32**
Miller, S. The President and the assassin **973.8**
Rauchway, E. Murdering McKinley **973.8**
Rudahl, S. A dangerous woman **335**
Watson, B. Sacco and Vanzetti **345**

Anasi, Robert
The gloves **796.83**
The last bohemia **974.7**
Anastasia, Paula J.
Bristow, R. E. A guide to survivorship for women with ovarian cancer **616.99**
ANATOMY
See also Biology; Medicine
Richardson, R. The making of Mr. Gray's Anatomy **611**
Anatomy of a business plan. Pinson, L. **658.4**
Anatomy of a miracle. Waldmeir, P. **968.06**
Anatomy of an epidemic. Whitaker, R. **616.89**
The **anatomy** of fascism. Paxton, R. O. **321.9**
The **anatomy** of hope. Groopman, J. E. **616**
The **anatomy** of influence. Bloom, H. **801**
The **anatomy** of prejudices. Young-Bruehl, E. **303.3**
The **anatomy** of racial inequality. Loury, G. C. **305.896**
An **anatomy** of thought. Glynn, I. **612.8**
ANATOMY, ARTISTIC *See* Artistic anatomy
Ancell, R. Manning
The biographical dictionary of World War II generals and flag officers **920.003**
ANCESTOR WORSHIP
See also Religion
The **ancestor's** tale. Dawkins, R. **576.8**
ANCESTRY *See* Genealogy; Heredity
Anchor Bible reference library [series]
Brown, R. E. An introduction to the New Testament **225**
Meier, J. P. A marginal Jew **232.9**
The **ancient** Americans. Schobinger, J. **970.01**
ANCIENT ARCHITECTURE
See also Archeology; Architecture
ANCIENT ART
See also Art
Frankfort, H. The art and architecture of the ancient Orient **709.3**
The **ancient** Celts. Cunliffe, B. **936**
ANCIENT CIVILIZATION
See also Ancient history; Civilization
Cantor, N. F. Antiquity: the civilization of the ancient world **930**
Freeman, C. Egypt, Greece, and Rome **909**
Hancock, G. Underworld: the mysterious origins of civilization **551.7**
Hunt, P. Ten discoveries that rewrote history **930.1**
Kriwaczek, P. Babylon **935**
The Oxford history of the biblical world **220.9**
Teresi, D. Lost discoveries **509**
Wilson, C. The Atlantis blueprint **001.94**
ANCIENT CIVILIZATION—ENCYCLOPE-DIAS
Encyclopedia of the ancient world **930**
Ancient Europe 8000 B.C.-A.D. 1000. **936**

ERVATION—MORAL AND ETHICAL AS-
PECTS
Childs, C. L. Finders keepers   **930.1**
**ANTIQUITIES, PREHISTORIC—EASTER IS-
LAND**
Van Tilburg, J. Among stone giants   **930.1**
ANTIQUITY OF MAN *See* Human origins
Antiquity: the civilization of the ancient world.
Cantor, N. F.   **930**
Antisemitism.   **305.8**
ANTISEMITISM
    See also Prejudices
Arendt, H. Origins of totalitarianism   **321.9**
Baldwin, N. Henry Ford and the Jews   **305**
Bredin The affair   **944.081**
Chesler, P. The new anti-semitism   **305.8**
Craig, G. A. The Germans   **943**
Derfler, L. The Dreyfus affair   **944.081**
Glass, J. M. Life unworthy of life   **940.53**
Goldhagen, D. Hitler's willing executioners **940.53**
Goldhagen, D. A moral reckoning   **940.53**
Gross, J. T. Fear: anti-semitism in Poland after
  Auschwitz   **305.8**
Kamen, H. The Spanish Inquisition   **272**
Kertzer, D. I. The Popes against the Jews   **261.2**
Lipstadt, D. E. Denying the Holocaust   **940.53**
Read, P. P. The Dreyfus affair   **944.081**
Smith, H. W. The butcher's tale   **305.892**
Those who forget the past   **305.8**
Wasserstein, B. On the eve   **305.892**
Watts, S. The people's tycoon   **92**
The World reacts to the Holocaust   **940.53**
ANTISEMITISM—ENCYCLOPEDIAS
Antisemitism   **305.8**
**ANTISEMITISM—EUROPE—HISTORY—
20TH CENTURY**
Wasserstein, B. On the eve   **305.892**
**ANTISEMITISM—FRANCE—HISTORY—
19TH CENTURY**
Read, P. P. The Dreyfus affair   **944.081**
ANTISEMITISM—GERMANY—HISTORY
Gilbert, M. Kristallnacht   **940.53**
ANTISEMITISM—GERMANY—KÖNITZ
Smith, H. W. The butcher's tale   **305.892**
ANTISEMITISM—ITALY
Zuccotti, S. Under his very windows   **940.53**
ANTISEMITISM—UNITED STATES
Baldwin, N. Henry Ford and the Jews   **305**
ANTISLAVERY *See* Abolitionists; Slavery;
  Slaves—Emancipation
ANTISLAVERY MOVEMENTS
Clinton, C. Harriet Tubman: the road to free-
  dom   **973.7**
Colaiaco, J. A. Frederick Douglass and the Fourth
  of July   **973.7**
ANTISLAVERY MOVEMENTS—GREAT BRIT-

AIN—HISTORY—18TH CENTURY
Hochschild, A. Bury the chains   **326**
**ANTISLAVERY MOVEMENTS—GREAT BRIT-
AIN—HISTORY—19TH CENTURY**
Hochschild, A. Bury the chains   **326**
ANTISLAVERY MOVEMENTS—HISTORY
Hague, W. J. William Wilberforce   **92**
ANTISLAVERY MOVEMENTS—UNITED
STATES
Colaiaco, J. A. Frederick Douglass and the Fourth
  of July   **973.7**
ANTISLAVERY MOVEMENTS—UNITED
STATES—HISTORY—19TH CENTURY
Clinton, C. Harriet Tubman: the road to free-
  dom   **973.7**
Douglass, F. Frederick Douglass: selected speeches
  and writings   **326**
Douglass, F. My bondage and my freedom **973.8**
ANTITRUST LAW
    See also Commercial law
ANTIVIVISECTION MOVEMENT *See* Animal
  rights movement
Antoine, Rebeca
(ed) Voices rising   **976.3**
Anton Chekhov's life and thought. Chekhov, A.
P.   **92**
Antony and Cleopatra. Goldsworthy, A. K.   **92**
The **ants.** Holldobler, B.   **595.79**
ANTS
    See also Insects
Holldobler, B. The ants   **595.79**
Holldobler, B. Journey to the ants   **595.79**
Holldobler, B. The leafcutter ants   **595.7**
Keller, L. The lives of ants   **595.7**
Moffett, M. W. Adventures among ants   **595.7**
ANTS—BEHAVIOR
Moffett, M. W. Adventures among ants   **595.7**
ANTS—ECOLOGY
Moffett, M. W. Adventures among ants   **595.7**
Ants on the melon. Adair, V. H.   **811**
Antunes, Antonio Lobo
The fat man and infinity   **869**
ANXIETIES *See* Anxiety
ANXIETY
    See also Emotions; Neuroses; Stress (Psy-
  chology)
Alcabes, P. Dread   **614.4**
Amen, D. Change your brain, change your
  life   **616.89**
Clark, T. Nerve   **152.4**
Foa, E. B. If your adolescent has an anxiety disor-
  der   **618.92**
Hallowell, E. M. Worry   **616.85**
Root, B. A. Understanding panic and other anxiety
  disorders   **616.85**
Tillich, P. The courage to be   **179**

See also United States

APPARATUS, ELECTRONIC *See* Electronic apparatus and appliances

APPARITIONS

See also Parapsychology; Spirits

The **appearance** of impropriety. Morgan, P. W. **306**

APPEARANCE, PERSONAL *See* Personal appearance

Appelbaum, Judith

How to get happily published   **070.5**

APPERCEPTION

See also Educational psychology; Psychology

Appetite city. Grimes, W.   **394.1**

Appetite for America. Fried, S.   **92**

Appetite for life. Fitch, N. R.   **92**

An **appetite** for poetry. Kermode, F.   **801**

Appetite for self-destruction. Knopper, S.   **384**

APPETIZERS

See also Cooking

Andres, J. Tapas   **641.8**

Appiah, Anthony

(ed) Africana: the encyclopedia of the African and African American experience   **909**

APPLE *See* Apples

The **apple** trees at Olema. Hass, R.   **811**

Applebaum, Anne

Gulag   **365**

Applebaum, Wilbur

(ed) Encyclopedia of the scientific revolution   **509**

Applebome, Peter

Dixie rising   **973.929**

Appleby, Joyce

The relentless revolution   **330.1**

Appleby, Joyce Oldham

Inheriting the revolution   **973**

Appleby, J. The relentless revolution   **330.1**

Appleby, R. Scott

Almond, G. A. Strong religion   **200.9**

Applegate, Debby

The most famous man in America   **92**

APPLES

See also Fruit

Hubbell, S. Shrinking the cat   **660.6**

Means, H. B. Johnny Appleseed   **92**

Pollan, M. The botany of desire   **306.4**

Apples and oranges. Brenner, M.   **92**

Apples are from Kazakhstan. Robbins, C.   **958.4**

APPLIANCES, ELECTRONIC *See* Electronic apparatus and appliances

APPLICATIONS FOR COLLEGE *See* College applications

APPLICATIONS FOR POSITIONS

See also Job hunting; Personnel management

The Adams resume almanac   **331**

Beatty, R. H. 175 high-impact cover letters **650.14**

Beatty, R. H. The interview kit   **650.14**

Enelow, W. S. Cover letter magic   **650.14**

Jackson, T. The perfect resume   **650.14**

Resumes and cover letters that have worked   **331**

Yate, M. J. Knock 'em dead 2011   **650.14**

APPLIED MECHANICS

See also Mechanics

APPLIED PSYCHOLOGY

See also Psychology

Beattie, M. Beyond codependency   **616.86**

Bloomfield, H. H. Making peace with your past **158**

Carnegie, D. How to win friends and influence people   **158**

Csikszentmihalyi, M. Flow: the psychology of optimal experience   **155.2**

Jacobs, C. S. Management rewired   **658**

Kessel, B. It's not about the money   **332.024**

Klauser, H. A. Write it down, make it happen **158**

May, R. Freedom and destiny   **158**

Michels, B. The tools   **158**

Peale, N. V. The power of positive living   **248**

Peck, M. S. Further along the road less traveled **158**

Peck, M. S. The road less traveled   **158**

Peck, M. S. The road less traveled and beyond **158**

Robbins, T. Awaken the giant within   **158**

Robbins, T. Unlimited power   **158**

APPLIED SCIENCE *See* Technology

APPLIQUÉ

See also Needlework

APPOMATTOX CAMPAIGN, 1865

See also United States—History—1861-1865, Civil War—Campaigns

Catton, B. A stillness at Appomattox   **973.7**

Davis, B. To Appomattox   **973.7**

APPORTIONMENT (ELECTION LAW)

See also Representative government and representation

APPRAISAL OF BOOKS *See* Book reviewing; Books and reading; Criticism; Literature—History and criticism

APPRECIATION OF ART *See* Art appreciation

APPRECIATION OF MUSIC *See* Music appreciation

The **apprentice:** my life in the kitchen. Pepin, J.   **641.5**

APPRENTICES

See also Labor; Technical education

The **approaching** fury. Oates, S. B.   **973.5**

APPROXIMATE COMPUTATION

Mahajan, S. Street-fighting mathematics   **510**

APRIL FOOLS' DAY

See also Holidays

APTITUDE *See* Ability

AQUACULTURE

See also Agriculture; Marine resources

AQUARIAN AGE MOVEMENT *See* New Age movement

Aquarium fish. Mills, D.   **639.34**

Aquarium owner's manual. Sandford, G.   **639.34**

Aquariums. Maitre-Allain, T.   **639.34**

AQUARIUMS
> Maitre-Allain, T. Aquariums   **639.34**
> Mills, D. Aquarium fish   **639.34**
> Sandford, G. Aquarium owner's manual   **639.34**

AQUARIUMS
> *See also* Freshwater biology; Natural history

AQUATIC ANIMALS
> *See also* Animals

AQUATIC EXERCISES
> *See also* Exercise

AQUATIC GARDENS *See* Water gardens

AQUATIC PLANTS
> *See also* Freshwater plants; Marine plants

Speichert, C. G. Encyclopedia of water garden plants   **635**

AQUEDUCTS
> *See also* Civil engineering; Hydraulic structures; Water supply

Aquino, Lucia
> Leonardo Da Vinci   **92**

ARAB AMERICAN YOUTH
> Bayoumi, M. How does it feel to be a problem?   **305.8**

ARAB AMERICANS—ETHNIC IDENTITY
> Bayoumi, M. How does it feel to be a problem?   **305.8**

ARAB AMERICANS—SOCIAL CONDITIONS
> Bayoumi, M. How does it feel to be a problem?   **305.8**
> Eggers, D. Zeitoun   **92**
> Malek, A. A country called Amreeka   **305.8**

Arab and Jew. Shipler, D. K.   **956.94**

ARAB CIVILIZATION
> Hourani, A. H. A history of the Arab peoples **909**
> Rogan, E. The Arabs   **909**
> Theroux, P. Sandstorms: days and nights in Arabia   **953**

ARAB COUNTRIES
> *See also* Islamic countries; Middle East

ARAB COUNTRIES—DESCRIPTION
> Theroux, P. Sandstorms: days and nights in Arabia   **953**

ARAB COUNTRIES—POLITICS AND GOVERNMENT
> *See also* Politics

ARAB REFUGEES
> *See also* Refugees

ARAB-ISRAEL CONFLICTS *See* Israel-Arab conflicts

ARAB-ISRAEL WAR, 1948-1949 *See* Israel-Arab War, 1948-1949

ARAB-ISRAEL WAR, 1967 *See* Israel-Arab War, 1967

ARAB-ISRAELI CONFLICT
> Chesler, P. The new anti-semitism   **305.8**
> Goldberg, J. Prisoners   **92**
> La Guardia, A. War without end   **956.940**
> Lozowick, Y. Right to exist   **956.940**
> Morris, B. Righteous victims   **956**
> Shipler, D. K. Arab and Jew   **956.94**
> Shlaim, A. The iron wall   **956.04**
> Shlaim, A. Israel and Palestine   **956.04**
> Tolan, S. The lemon tree   **956.94**

ARAB-ISRAELI CONFLICT—1948-1967
> Sacco, J. Footnotes in Gaza   **956.04**

ARAB-ISRAELI CONFLICT—1973-1993
> Grossman, D. The yellow wind   **956.95**

ARAB-ISRAELI CONFLICT—1993——INFLUENCE
> La Guardia, A. War without end   **956.940**

ARAB-ISRAELI CONFLICT—1993——PEACE
> Morris, B. Righteous victims   **956**
> Said, E. W. The end of the peace process **956.05**

ARAB-ISRAELI CONFLICTS *See* Israel-Arab conflicts

The **Arab-Israeli** wars. Herzog, C.   **956**

ARAB-JEWISH RELATIONS *See* Jewish-Arab relations

Arabesque: a taste of Morocco, Turkey, and Lebanon. Roden, C.   **641.5**

ARABIC CIVILIZATION
> *See also* Civilization

ARABIC LANGUAGE
> *See also* Language and languages

ARABIC LITERATURE
> *See also* Literature

ARABIC LITERATURE—COLLECTIONS
> Anthology of modern Palestinian literature **892.7**
> Night and horses and the desert   **892.7**

ARABIC LITERATURE—HISTORY AND CRITICISM
> Night and horses and the desert   **892.7**

ARABIC POETRY—20TH CENTURY—HISTORY AND CRITICISM
> Hoffman, A. My happiness bears no relation to happiness   **92**

ARABIC POETRY—20TH CENTURY—TRANSLATIONS INTO ENGLISH
> The Poetry of Arab women   **892.7**

ARABIC POETRY—COLLECTIONS
> Music of a distant drum   **808.81**
> The Poetry of Arab women   **892.7**

ARABIC POETRY—WOMEN AUTHORS—TRANSLATIONS INTO ENGLISH
> The Poetry of Arab women   **892.7**

The **Arabs.** Rogan, E.   **909**

ARABS
> Braude, J. The honored dead   **364.152**
> Lawrence, T. E. Seven pillars of wisdom   **940.4**

film **791.43**
ARMY *See* Armies; Military art and science
An **army** at dawn. Atkinson, R. **940.54**
ARMY BASES *See* Military bases
ARMY LIFE *See* Soldiers
ARMY OFFICERS
  Alexander, L. Biggest brother **92**
  Bredin The affair **944.081**
  Brighton, T. Patton, Montgomery, Rommel **920**
  Cesarani, D. Major Farran's hat **956.94**
  Connell, E. S. Son of the Morning Star **973.8**
  Davis, W. C. Three roads to the Alamo **976.4**
  Derfler, L. The Dreyfus affair **944.081**
  D'Este, C. Patton **92**
  Donovan, J. A terrible glory **973.8**
  Falkner, D. Great time coming: the life of Jackie Robinson, from baseball to Birmingham **92**
  Halberstam, D. The best and the brightest **973.922**
  Hanson, V. D. The soul of battle **355**
  Hennessey, P. The Junior Officers' Reading Club **92**
  Hirshson, S. P. General Patton: a soldier's life **355**
  Jordan, J. W. Brothers, rivals, victors **940.54**
  Kaplan, A. Y. The interpreter **940.54**
  Kennedy, J. F. Profiles in courage **920**
  Mansoor, P. R. Baghdad at sunrise **956.7**
  McCullough, D. G. The path between the seas **972.87**
  Millard, C. The river of doubt **973.91**
  Moore, W. The other Wes Moore **92**
  Peters, C. J. Virus hunter **614.4**
  Philbrick, N. The last stand **973.8**
  Roper, R. Now the drum of war **973.7**
  Sandoz, M. The Battle of the Little Bighorn **973.8**
  Schama, C. Wild romance **92**
  Schwartz, R. A. Encyclopedia of the Persian Gulf War **956.704**
  Sheehan, N. A bright shining lie: John Paul Vann and America in Vietnam **959.704**
  Showalter, D. E. Patton and Rommel **92**
  Sielski, M. Fading echoes **92**
  Tuchman, B. W. The proud tower **909.82**
  Tygiel, J. Baseball's great experiment **796.357**
  Utley, R. M. Custer: cavalier in buckskin **973.8**
  Wert, J. D. Custer **973.8**
  Wilson, E. Patriotic gore **810**
  Zacks, R. The pirate coast **973.4**
ARMY POSTS *See* Military bases
Arnason, H. Harvard
  History of modern art **709.04**
Arnell, Charles
  Bennett, J. The complete snowboarder **796.9**
Arnold, James R.
  Jungle of snakes **355**
Arnot, Bob
  The breast health cookbook **616.99**
  Wear and tear **616.7**

Arnot, Michelle
  Four-letter words **793.73**
Aron, Wendy
  Hide & seek **92**
Aronowitz, Nona Willis
  Out of the vinyl deeps **781.66**
Aronson, Amy
  (ed) Men and masculinities **305.31**
Aronson, Ronald
  (ed) Sartre, J. P. Truth and existence **121**
Around America. Cronkite, W. **917**
Around my French table. Greenspan, D. **641.5**
Arousal, the secret logic of sexual fantasies. Bader, M. J. **306.7**
Arrested. Denham, W. **362.82**
Arrington, Leonard J.
  Japanese Americans, from relocation to redress **940.53**
Arrival city. Saunders, D. **307.24**
The **ARRL** handbook for radio communications 2011. **621.384**
Arrogant capital. Phillips, K. P. **351**
Arsenals of folly. Rhodes, R. **355**
Arsenault, Raymond
  Freedom riders **323**
ARSON
  Wambaugh, J. Fire lover **364.16**
ARSON—CALIFORNIA—CASE STUDIES
  Wambaugh, J. Fire lover **364.16**
ARSONISTS
  Wambaugh, J. Fire lover **364.16**
ART
  See also Arts
  Dutton, D. The art instinct **701**
The **art** & craft of making jewelry. Gollberg, J. **739.27**
The **art** & elegance of beadweaving. Wells, C. W. **745.58**
Art & ideas [series]
  Escritt, S. Art Nouveau **709.03**
  Lowden, J. Early Christian & Byzantine art **709.02**
ART—15TH AND 16TH CENTURIES
  Adams, L. Italian Renaissance art **709.02**
  Brewer, J. The American Leonardo **759**
ART—19TH CENTURY
  Craske, M. Art in Europe, 1700-1830 **709.03**
ART—20TH CENTURY
  Acocella, J. R. Twenty-eight artists and two saints **920**
  Barnitz, J. Twentieth-century art of Latin America **709**
  Fineberg, J. D. Art since 1940 **709.04**
  Lucie-Smith, E. Art today **709.04**
  Tomkins, C. Lives of the artists **920**
ART—20TH CENTURY—ENCYCLOPEDIAS
  Dempsey, A. Art in the modern era **709.04**

ART, RUSSIAN—20TH CENTURY
Wullschlager, J. Chagall   **92**
Art: a new history. Johnson, P.   **709**
Art: over 2,500 works from cave to contemporary.
   King, R.   **709**

ARTHRITIS
   See also Diseases
Arnot, B. Wear and tear   **616.7**
The encyclopedia of arthritis   **616.7**

ARTHRITIS—ENCYCLOPEDIAS
The encyclopedia of arthritis   **616.7**

ARTHROPODA—CONSERVATION
Fortey, R. Horseshoe crabs and velvet worms   **595**
Arthur Conan Doyle. Doyle, A. C.   **92**
Arthur Miller. Bigsby, C.   **92**
Arthur Miller. Gottfried, M.   **92**
Arthur, W. Brian
The nature of technology   **600**

ARTHURIAN ROMANCES
Gawain and the Grene Knight (Middle English
   poem) Sir Gawain and the Green Knight   **398.2**
The **artificial** ape. Taylor, T.   **599.93**

ARTIFICIAL FLIES
   See also Fishing—Equipment and supplies;
   Fly casting
Rosenbauer, T. The Orvis guide to the essential
   American flies   **799.1**
Schullery, P. The rise   **799.1**

ARTIFICIAL FLOWERS
   See also Decoration and ornament

ARTIFICIAL FOODS
   See also Food; Synthetic products

ARTIFICIAL HEART
   See also Artificial organs; Heart

ARTIFICIAL INTELLIGENCE
   See also Computer science
Baker, S. Final Jeopardy   **006.3**
Brooks, R. A. Flesh and machines   **629.8**
Christian, B. The most human human   **128**
Devlin, K. J. Goodbye, Descartes   **128**
Gutkind, L. Almost human   **629.8**
Menzel, P. Robo sapiens: evolution of a new spe-
   cies   **629.8**
Wood, G. Edison's Eve   **629.8**

ARTIFICIAL LANGUAGES
Okrent, A. In the land of invented languages   **499**

ARTIFICIAL ORGANS
   See also Surgery

ARTIFICIAL RESPIRATION
   See also First aid

ARTIFICIAL SATELLITES
   See also Astronautics
Brzezinski, M. Red moon rising   **629.4**
Dickson, P. Sputnik: the shock of the centu-
   ry   **629.46**
ARTIFICIAL SATELLITES IN TELECOMMU-

NICATION
   See also Telecommunication

ARTIFICIAL SATELLITES, RUSSIAN
Brzezinski, M. Red moon rising   **629.4**

**ARTIFICIAL SATELLITES, RUSSIAN—PO-
LITICAL ASPECTS**
Dickson, P. Sputnik: the shock of the centu-
   ry   **629.46**

ARTIFICIAL SELECTION *See* Breeding

ARTIFICIAL SWEETENERS *See* Sugar substitutes

ARTIFICIAL WEATHER CONTROL   *See*
Weather control

Artigas, Mariano
Shea, W. R. Galileo in Rome   **92**

ARTILLERY
   See also Military art and science

ARTISANS
Faber, T. Faberge's eggs   **739.2**
Fischer, D. H. Paul Revere's ride   **973.3**
Lepore, J. A is for American   **306.44**
The **artist** and the mathematician. Aczel, A. D. **500**
The **artist** as critic. Wilde, O.   **824**
The **artist** blacksmith. Parkinson, P.   **682**
An **artist** in treason. Linklater, A.   **92**
The **artist's** handbook. Smith, R.   **702.8**
The **artist,** the philosopher, and the warrior. Strath-
ern, P.   **920**

ARTISTIC ANATOMY
Hart, C. Human anatomy made amazingly
easy   **743.4**

ARTISTIC ANATOMY
   See also Anatomy; Art; Drawing; Nude in art

ARTISTIC PHOTOGRAPHY
   See also Art; Photography
Adams, R. Summer nights, walking   **779**
Barnes, R. Animal logic   **779**
Brandow, T. Edward Steichen   **779**
Burtynsky, E. Burtynsky: oil   **779**
Coles, R. When they were young   **779**
Eggleston, W. William Eggleston   **779**
Leibovitz, A. Annie Leibovitz at work   **779**
Maisel, D. Library of dust   **779**
Mermelstein, J. Twirl/run   **779**
Newhall, B. Beaumont's kitchen   **641.5**
Penn, I. Irving Penn: small trades   **779**
Photography past forward: Aperture at 50   **770.9**
Roden, S. . . . i listen to the wind that obliterates my
traces   **781.64**
Smith, J. Edward Steichen: the early years   **779**
Sommer, F. The art of Frederick Sommer   **779**
Steinmetz, M. Greater Atlanta   **779**
Thompson, M. Michael Thompson: Portraits   **779**
Veasey, N. X-ray   **779**
Wolf, M. The transparent city   **779**

ARTISTIC PHOTOGRAPHY—ENCYCLOPE-

Cracking the hidden job market **650.14**

Ashes of glory. Furgurson, E. B. **975.5**

Ashin, Deborah

Take charge of your child's eating disorder **618.92**

Ashley, Dwayne

Williams, J. I'll find a way or make one **378**

Ashton, Nigel John

King Hussein of Jordan **92**

ASIA—CIVILIZATION

See also Civilization; East and West

ASIA—CIVILIZATION—ENCYCLOPEDIAS

Higham, C. Encyclopedia of ancient Asian civilizations **950**

ASIA—ENCYCLOPEDIAS

Levinson, D. Encyclopedia of modern Asia **950**

ASIA—POLITICS AND GOVERNMENT

See also Politics

ASIAN AMERICANS

See also Ethnic groups

ASIAN AMERICANS—HISTORY

Avakian, M. Atlas of Asian-American history **305.8**

Takaki, R. T. Strangers from a different shore **305.8**

ASIAN AMERICANS—SOCIAL CONDITIONS

Takaki, R. T. Strangers from a different shore **305.8**

ASIAN ARCHITECTURE

See also Architecture

Ruan Xing New China architecture **720.9**

ASIAN ART

See also Art

ASIAN COOKING

Chang, D. Momofuku **641.5**

Hair, J. The steamy kitchen cookbook **641.5**

Jaffrey, M. At home with Madhur Jaffrey **641.5**

Trang, C. Essentials of Asian cuisine **641.5**

Tsai, M. Blue Ginger **641.5**

ASIAN MYTHOLOGY

Yang Lihui Handbook of Chinese mythology **299.5**

ASIAN MYTHOLOGY—DICTIONARIES

Leeming, D. A. A dictionary of Asian mythology **201**

ASIAN NATIONAL CHARACTERISTICS

Bernstein, R. The East, the West, and sex **306.7**

ASIAN PHILOSOPHY

A Companion to world philosophies **100**

ASIAN STUDIES SPECIALISTS

Grant, R. Crazy river **916**

Lovell, M. S. A rage to live: a biography of Richard and Isabel Burton **92**

Salzman, M. Lost in place **813**

Salzman, M. True notebooks **371.9**

Ask a lawyer [series]

Strauss, S. D. Landlord and tenant **346.04**

Strauss, S. D. Wills and trusts **346.05**

Ask me again tomorrow. Dukakis, O. **92**

Aslan, Reza

No god but God **297**

Asleep. Crosby, M. C. **362.1**

Asleson, Robyn

Albert Moore **759.2**

Asma, Stephen T.

On monsters **398.2**

Stuffed animals & pickled heads **508**

Asmal, Kader

(ed) In his own words **92**

ASPCA complete cat care manual. Edney, A. T. B. **636.8**

ASPCA complete dog care manual. Fogle, B. **636.7**

ASPCA complete guide to cats. Richards, J. R. **636.8**

ASPERGER SYNDROME

Ozonoff, S. A parent's guide to asperger syndrome and high-functioning autism **618.92**

ASPERGER'S SYNDROME

See also Autism

Attwood, T. The complete guide to Asperger's syndrome **616.85**

Bashe, P. R. The oasis guide to Asperger syndrome **618.92**

Hewetson, A. The stolen child **616.89**

Jackson, L. Freaks, geeks and asperger syndrome **618.92**

Osborne, L. American normal **616.89**

Robison, J. E. Look me in the eye **92**

Tammet, D. Born on a blue day **92**

ASPERGER'S SYNDROME—PATIENTS

Jackson, L. Freaks, geeks and asperger syndrome **618.92**

ASPERGER'S SYNDROME—PATIENTS—FAMILY RELATIONSHIPS

Jackson, L. Freaks, geeks and asperger syndrome **618.92**

ASPERGER'S SYNDROME—POPULAR WORKS

Ozonoff, S. A parent's guide to asperger syndrome and high-functioning autism **618.92**

ASSASSINATION

See also Crime; Homicide; Political crimes and offenses

Hakkakiyan, R. Assassins of the Turquoise Palace **364.152**

Sides, H. Hellhound on his trail **364.152**

Assassination vacation. Vowell, S. **920**

ASSASSINS—UNITED STATES—HISTORY—19TH CENTURY

Pitch, A. They have killed Papa dead! **973.7**

Vowell, S. Assassination vacation **920**

Assassins of the Turquoise Palace. Hakkakiyan, R. **364.152**

The **assassins'** gate. Packer, G. **956.7**

ASSAULT, CRIMINAL *See* Offenses against the person

ASSAULT, SEXUAL *See* Rape

ASSERTIVENESS (PSYCHOLOGY)

See also Aggressiveness (Psychology); Psychology

Assessing service quality. Hernon, P. **025.5**

The **assist.** Swidey, N. **796.323**

ASSISTANCE IN EMERGENCIES *See* Helping behavior

ASSISTANCE TO DEVELOPING AREAS *See* Foreign aid; Technical assistance

ASSISTED LIVING
See also Housing

ASSISTED REPRODUCTION *See* Reproductive technology

ASSISTED SUICIDE
Humphry, D. Final exit **179.7**
McKhann, C. F. A time to die **179.7**
Yount, L. Right to die and euthanasia **179.7**

ASSOCIATIONS, INTERNATIONAL *See* International agencies

ASSYRIOLOGY
Damrosch, D. The buried book **809**

Asteroids. Peebles, C. **523.44**

ASTEROIDS
See also Astronomy; Solar system
Burrows, W. E. The survival imperative **629.4**
Peebles, C. Asteroids **523.44**

ASTHMA
Adams, F. V. The asthma sourcebook **616.2**
Brazelton, T. B. To listen to a child **155.4**
Freedman, M. R. Living well with asthma **616.2**
Pescatore, F. The allergy and asthma cure **616.97**

ASTHMA
See also Allergy; Lungs—Diseases

ASTHMA—ALTERNATIVE TREATMENT
Pescatore, F. The allergy and asthma cure **616.97**

ASTHMA—DIET THERAPY
Pescatore, F. The allergy and asthma cure **616.97**

The **asthma** sourcebook. Adams, F. V. **616.2**

ASTOR PLACE RIOT, NEW YORK, 1849
Cliff, N. The Shakespeare riots **974.4**

ASTRAL PROJECTION
See also Parapsychology

ASTROBIOLOGY *See* Life on other planets; Space biology

ASTROGEOLOGY
See also Geology

ASTROLOGY
See also Astronomy; Divination; Occultism
Goodman, L. Linda Goodman's star signs **130**
Goodman, L. Linda Goodman's sun signs **133.5**
Lewis, J. R. The astrology book **133.5**
Miller, S. Planets and possibilities **133.5**
Snodgrass, M. E. Signs of the zodiac **133.5**

ASTROLOGY—ENCYCLOPEDIAS
Lewis, J. R. The astrology book **133.5**

The **astrology** book. Lewis, J. R. **133.5**

ASTRONAUTICS

See also Aeronautics
Burrows, W. E. The survival imperative **629.4**
Burrows, W. E. This new ocean **629.4**
Dickson, P. Sputnik: the shock of the century **629.46**
Dyson, G. Project Orion **629.47**
National Geographic encyclopedia of space **629.4**
Schefter, J. L. The race **629.45**
Williamson, M. The Cambridge dictionary of space technology **629.4**
Zimmerman, R. The chronological encyclopedia of discoveries in space **500.5**

ASTRONAUTICS—COMMUNICATION SYSTEMS
See also Interstellar communication; Telecommunication

ASTRONAUTICS—DICTIONARIES
Angelo, J. A. The Facts on File dictionary of space technology **629.4**
Williamson, M. The Cambridge dictionary of space technology **629.4**

ASTRONAUTICS—INTERNATIONAL COOPERATION
Launius, R. D. Frontiers of space exploration **629.45**

ASTRONAUTICS—SOVIET UNION
Brzezinski, M. Red moon rising **629.4**
Cadbury, D. Space race **629.4**
French, F. In the shadow of the moon **629.45**
Hardesty, V. Epic rivalry **629.4**

ASTRONAUTICS—UNITED STATES
Barbree, J. Live from Cape Canaveral **629.45**
Brzezinski, M. Red moon rising **629.4**
Cadbury, D. Space race **629.4**
French, F. In the shadow of the moon **629.45**
Hardesty, V. Epic rivalry **629.4**
Kranz, E. F. Failure is not an option **629.45**
Nelson, C. Rocket men **629.45**
Pyne, S. J. Voyager **919**
Space exploration **629**
Walsh, P. J. Echoes among the stars **629.4**
Wolfe, T. The right stuff **629.45**

ASTRONAUTICS—UNITED STATES—HISTORY
French, F. In the shadow of the moon **629.45**
Hardesty, V. Epic rivalry **629.4**
Nelson, C. Rocket men **629.45**
Pyne, S. J. Voyager **919**
Sheehan, N. A fiery peace in a cold war **92**
Walsh, P. J. Echoes among the stars **629.4**

ASTRONAUTICS AND CIVILIZATION
See also Aeronautics and civilization; Astronautics; Civilization

ASTRONAUTICS AND STATE—UNITED STATES—PUBLIC OPINION
Dickson, P. Sputnik: the shock of the centu-

Encyclopedia of modern worldwide extremists and
extremist groups **320.5**

Atkinson, Rick
An army at dawn **940.54**
Crusade **956.7**
The day of battle **940.54**
In the company of soldiers **956.7**
Atlantic. Winchester, S. **551.46**
Atlantic fever. Jackson, J. **629.130**
ATLANTIC OCEAN
See also Ocean
The **Atlantic** slave trade. Postma, J. **306.3**
ATLANTIC STATES
See also United States
ATLANTIS
Ellis, R. Imagining Atlantis **001.94**
Wilson, C. The Atlantis blueprint **001.94**
The **Atlantis** blueprint. Wilson, C. **001.94**
Atlas. Atlas, T. **92**
ATLAS (MISSILE)
See also Ballistic missiles; Intercontinental
ballistic missiles
Atlas of American politics, 1960-2000. Shelley, F.
M. **973.92**
Atlas of Asian-American history. Avakian, M. **305.8**
The **atlas** of bird migration. **598**
The **atlas** of birds. Unwin, M. **598**
The **atlas** of climate change. Dow, K. **551.6**
Atlas of exploration. **911**
The **atlas** of global conservation. Hoekstra, J.
M. **333.95**
Atlas of human anatomy. Netter, F. H. **611**
The **atlas** of new librarianship. Lankes, R. D. **020**
The **atlas** of the Arab world. Fargues, P. **909**
Atlas of the Civil War. **973.7**
Atlas of the Civil War. Woodworth, S. E. **973.7**
Atlas of the Civil War, month by month. Swanson,
M. **973.7**
Atlas of the great plains. Lavin, S. J. **912**
Atlas of the North American Indian. Waldman,
C. **970.004**
Atlas of the transatlantic slave trade. Eltis, D. **381**
Atlas of world art. **709**
Atlas, James
Bellow **813**
Atlas, Teddy
Atlas **92**
ATLASES
See also Geography; Maps
Atlas of world art **709**
Bambaradeniya, C. N. B. The illustrated atlas of
wildlife **591.9**
Dow, K. The atlas of climate change **551.6**
Eltis, D. Atlas of the transatlantic slave trade **381**
Gilbert, M. The Routledge atlas of the Holo-
caust **940.53**

Hammond world atlas **912**
Hayes, D. Historical atlas of the United States **911**
Hoekstra, J. M. The atlas of global conserva-
tion **333.95**
Lavin, S. J. Atlas of the great plains **912**
Magocsi, P. R. Historical atlas of Central Eu-
rope **911**
National Geographic atlas of the world **912**
National Geographic visual atlas of the world **912**
The new atlas of the Arab world **912**
Oxford atlas of the world **912**
Times comprehensive atlas of the world **912**
Unwin, M. The atlas of birds **598**
Waldman, C. Atlas of the North American Indi-
an **970.004**
World atlas of great apes and their conserva-
tion **599.8**
ATMOSPHERE
See also Air; Earth
Encyclopedia of atmospheric sciences **551.5**
Newton, D. E. Encyclopedia of air **551**
Roston, E. The carbon age **577**
Walker, G. An ocean of air **551.5**
ATMOSPHERE—ENCYCLOPEDIAS
Encyclopedia of atmospheric sciences **551.5**
Newton, D. E. Encyclopedia of air **551**
ATMOSPHERE—POLLUTION *See* Air pollu-
tion
ATMOSPHERE, UPPER *See* Upper atmosphere
ATMOSPHERIC GREENHOUSE EFFECT *See*
Global warming
The **atom** and the apple. Balibar, S. **530**
The **atomic** bazaar. Langewiesche, W. **355**
ATOMIC BOMB
See also Bombs; Nuclear weapons
Baggott, J. E. The first war of physics **355.8**
Conant, J. 109 East Palace **623.4**
Conant, J. Tuxedo Park **530**
Degroot, G. J. The bomb **623.4**
Feynman **741.5**
Hersey, J. Hiroshima **940.54**
Lifton, R. J. Hiroshima in America **940.54**
Preston, D. Before the fallout **355.8**
Rhodes, R. The making of the atomic bomb **623.4**
Takaki, R. T. Hiroshima **940.54**
Walker, M. Nazi science **509**
**ATOMIC BOMB—GERMANY—HISTORY—
20TH CENTURY**
Cassidy, D. C. Beyond uncertainty **92**
ATOMIC BOMB—HISTORY
Baggott, J. E. The first war of physics **355.8**
Preston, D. Before the fallout **355.8**
ATOMIC BOMB—PHYSIOLOGICAL EFFECT
Hersey, J. Hiroshima **940.54**
**ATOMIC BOMB—UNITED STATES—HISTO-
RY**

AUTISTIC CHILDREN—CARE AND TREAT-MENT

Wing, L. The autistic spectrum   **618.92**

AUTISTIC CHILDREN—EDUCATION

Siegel, B. Helping children with autism learn **371.9**

AUTISTIC CHILDREN—FAMILY RELATION-SHIPS

Harris, S. L. Siblings of children with autism **649**

AUTISTIC CHILDREN—POPULAR WORKS

Children with autism   **618.92**

AUTISTIC DISORDER

Ozonoff, S. A parent's guide to asperger syndrome and high-functioning autism   **618.92**

The autistic spectrum. Wing, L.   **618.92**

AUTISTIC SPECTRUM DISORDERS *See* Autism

AUTISTIC YOUTH

Jackson, L. Freaks, geeks and asperger syndrome   **618.92**

Auto da Fay. Weldon, F.   **823**

AUTOBIOGRAPHICAL GRAPHIC NOVELS

B., D. Epileptic   **616.8**

Bechdel, A. Are you my mother?   **741.5**

Bechdel, A. Fun home   **741.5**

Beland, T. True story swear to God archives, vol. 1   **741.5**

My friend Dahmer   **FIC**

Persepolis/English The complete Persepolis **741.5**

Santiago, W. 21   **741.5**

Satrapi, M. Persepolis   **741.5**

Satrapi, M. Persepolis 2   **741.5**

Small, D. Stitches   **741.5**

Spiegelman, A. MetaMaus   **741.5**

Torres, A. American widow   **741.5**

AUTOBIOGRAPHICAL GRAPHIC NOVELS

See also Graphic novels

AUTOBIOGRAPHICAL MEMORY

Bloomfield, H. H. Making peace with your past **158**

Autobiographies. Douglass, F.   **973.8**

AUTOBIOGRAPHIES

See also Biography

Auster, P. Winter journal   **818**

Baldwin, R. Paris, I love you but you're bringing me down   **944**

Castner, B. The long walk   **956.704**

Churchill, B. E. Notes on a century   **956**

Cody, J. [Sic]   **362.196**

Deford, F. Over time   **070.449**

Ebert, R. Life itself   **92**

Fey, T. Bossypants   **92**

Jacobs, A. J. The year of living biblically   **220**

James, E. Paris in love   **92**

Johnson, M. An unquenchable thirst   **271**

Lanzmann, C. The Patagonian hare   **791.43**

Lifton, R. J. Witness to an extreme century **973.92**

Marshall, R. No time to lose   **616.9**

McWilliam, C. What to look for in winter **823.914**

The moment   **818**

Rosenblatt, R. Kayak morning   **300**

Scott-Heron, G. The last holiday   **920**

Smith, C. B. The rules of inheritance   **616.99**

Unferth, D. O. Revolution   **920**

AUTOBIOGRAPHIES—UNITED STATES

The Norton book of American autobiography **920**

Autobiography. Mill, J. S.   **92**

AUTOBIOGRAPHY

See also Biography as a literary form

AUTOBIOGRAPHY

Baroni, B. Fat kid got fit   **362.196**

Conway, J. K. When memory speaks   **808**

Encyclopedia of women's autobiography **920.003**

The Norton book of American autobiography **920**

Yagoda, B. Memoir   **809**

AUTOBIOGRAPHY—HISTORY AND CRITI-CISM *See* Autobiography

AUTOBIOGRAPHY—TECHNIQUE *See* Autobiography

AUTOBIOGRAPHY—WOMEN AUTHORS

Adamson, L. G. Notable women in American history   **016**

Adamson, L. G. Notable women in world history   **016**

Conway, J. K. When memory speaks   **808**

AUTOBIOGRAPHY—WOMEN AUTHORS—BIBLIOGRAPHY

Adamson, L. G. Notable women in world history   **016**

AUTOBIOGRAPHY AS A LITERARY FORM

See Autobiography

Autobiography of a recovering skinhead. Meeink, F.   **92**

The **autobiography** of Alice B. Toklas. Stein, G. **92**

The **autobiography** of Benjamin Franklin. Franklin, B.   **92**

The **autobiography** of Lincoln Steffens. Steffens, L.   **92**

The **autobiography** of Malcolm X. Malcolm X **92**

The **autobiography** of Mark Twain. Twain, M. **92**

Autobiography of Mark Twain.   **92**

The **autobiography** of Martin Luther King, Jr. King, M. L.   **323**

The **autobiography** of Medgar Evers: a hero's life and legacy revealed through his writings, letters, and speeches. Evers, M. W.   **92**

Autobiography of red. Carson, A.   **811**

Autobiography, Poor Richard, and later writings. Franklin, B.   **818**

AUTOGRAPHED EDITIONS

See also Autographs; Editions

AUTOGRAPHS

See also Biography; Writing

Tingey, J. The Englishman who posted himself and

other curious objects **92**

The **autoimmune** connection. Baron-Faust, R. **616.97**

AUTOIMMUNE DISEASES

See also Diseases

Nakazawa, D. J. The autoimmune epidemic **616.97**

AUTOIMMUNE DISEASES—ENCYCLOPE-DIAS

Cassell, D. K. The encyclopedia of autoimmune diseases **616.97**

The **autoimmune** epidemic. Nakazawa, D. J. **616.97**

AUTOMATA *See* Robots

AUTOMATED CATALOGING

See also Cataloging

AUTOMATIC DATA PROCESSING *See* Data processing

AUTOMATIC DRAFTING *See* Computer graphics

AUTOMATIC DRAWING *See* Computer graphics

AUTOMATIC SPEECH RECOGNITION

See also Speech processing systems; Voice

AUTOMATION OF LIBRARY PROCESSES—HANDBOOKS, MANUALS, ETC.

Cohn, J. M. The complete library technology planner **025**

AUTOMATION OF LIBRARY PROCESSES—TEACHING

Core technology competencies for librarians and library staff **020**

AUTOMATONS *See* Robots

Automats, taxi dances, and vaudeville. Freeland, D.

AUTOMOBILE DRIVER EDUCATION

See also Education

AUTOMOBILE DRIVERS

Vanderbilt, T. Traffic **629.28**

AUTOMOBILE DRIVERS—PSYCHOLOGY

Vanderbilt, T. Traffic **629.28**

AUTOMOBILE DRIVING *See* Automobile drivers

AUTOMOBILE EXECUTIVES

Baldwin, N. Henry Ford and the Jews **305**

Brinkley, D. Wheels for the world **338.7**

Grandin, G. Fordlandia **307.7**

Lutz, B. Car guys vs. bean counters **338.7**

Watts, S. The people's tycoon **92**

AUTOMOBILE INDUSTRY

See also Industries

Baldwin, N. Henry Ford and the Jews **305**

Boorstin, D. J. The Americans: The democratic experience **973**

Brinkley, D. Wheels for the world **338.7**

Lutz, B. Car guys vs. bean counters **338.7**

Magee, D. How Toyota became #1 **658.4**

Sperling, D. Two billion cars **388.3**

Vlasic, B. Once upon a car **338.4**

AUTOMOBILE INDUSTRY AND TRADE—

UNITED STATES—FINANCE

Lutz, B. Car guys vs. bean counters **338.7**

AUTOMOBILE INDUSTRY AND TRADE—UNITED STATES—HISTORY

Baldwin, N. Henry Ford and the Jews **305**

Watts, S. The people's tycoon **92**

AUTOMOBILE INDUSTRY AND TRADE—UNITED STATES—HISTORY—20TH CENTURY

Brinkley, D. Wheels for the world **338.7**

AUTOMOBILE INSURANCE

See also Insurance

AUTOMOBILE PARTS

See also Automobiles

AUTOMOBILE RACING

Baime, A. J. Go like hell **796.72**

Bechtel, M. He crashed me so I crashed him back **796.72**

Donovan, B. Hard driving: the Wendell Scott story **92**

Hawley, S. J. Speed duel **796.72**

Menzer, J. The wildest ride **796.72**

Waltrip, M. In the blink of an eye **796.72**

Wright, J. D. Fixin' to git **796.72**

AUTOMOBILE RACING DRIVERS

Donovan, B. Hard driving: the Wendell Scott story **92**

Hawley, S. J. Speed duel **796.72**

Levy, S. Paul Newman **92**

Waltrip, M. In the blink of an eye **796.72**

AUTOMOBILE TRAVEL

See also Transportation; Travel; Voyages and travels

AUTOMOBILE TRAVEL—GUIDEBOOKS

See also Maps

AUTOMOBILES

See also Highway transportation; Motor vehicles; Vehicles

The Beaulieu encyclopedia of the automobile **629.222**

Ladd, B. Autophobia **303.4**

Sobey, E. A field guide to automotive technology **629.2**

AUTOMOBILES—DESIGN AND CONSTRUCTION

See also Industrial design

AUTOMOBILES—DRIVING *See* Automobile drivers

AUTOMOBILES—ENCYCLOPEDIAS

The Beaulieu encyclopedia of the automobile **629.222**

AUTOMOBILES—ENVIRONMENTAL ASPECTS

Sperling, D. Two billion cars **388.3**

AUTOMOBILES—FUEL CONSUMPTION

Sperling, D. Two billion cars **388.3**

AUTOMOBILES—LAW AND LEGISLATION
See also Law; Legislation

AUTOMOBILES—MAINTENANCE AND RE-PAIR
Christensen, L. Clueless about cars **629.28**
Kachur, B. Every woman's quick & easy car care **629.28**
Ramsey, D. Teach yourself visually car care & maintenance **629.28**

AUTOMOBILES—MAINTENANCE AND RE-PAIR—POPULAR WORKS
Kachur, B. Every woman's quick & easy car care **629.28**

AUTOMOBILES—POPULAR WORKS
Kachur, B. Every woman's quick & easy car care **629.28**

AUTOMOBILES—RACING *See* Automobile racing

AUTOMOBILES—SOCIAL ASPECTS
Ladd, B. Autophobia **303.4**

AUTOMOBILES—TECHNOLOGICAL INNOVATIONS
See also Technological innovations

AUTOMOBILES, FOREIGN *See* Foreign automobiles

AUTOMOTIVE INDUSTRY *See* Automobile industry

AUTONOMOUS ROBOTS
Gutkind, L. Almost human **629.8**

AUTONOMY (PSYCHOLOGY)
See also Psychology
Autophobia. Ladd, B. **303.4**

AUTUMN
See also Seasons
Autumn in the Heavenly Kingdom. Platt, S. R. **951**
AV market place 2008. **371.3**
Ava Gardner. Server, L. **791**
Ava's man. Bragg, R. **975**

AVAILABILITY OF HEALTH SERVICES *See* Access to health care

Avakian, Monique
Atlas of Asian-American history **305.8**

AVALANCHES
See also Snow
Fredston, J. A. Snowstruck **551.3**
Krist, G. The white cascade **979.7**

Avallone, Eugene A.
(ed) Marks' standard handbook for mechanical engineers **621**

AVANT-GARDE (AESTHETICS)
See also Aesthetics; Modernism (Aesthetics)
Indiana, G. Andy Warhol and the can that sold the world **759.13**
Weber, N. F. The Bauhaus group **920**

AVANT-GARDE (AESTHETICS)—GERMANY—HISTORY—20TH CENTURY

Weber, N. F. The Bauhaus group **920**

AVANT-GARDE (AESTHETICS)—UNITED STATES—HISTORY—20TH CENTURY
FitzGerald, M. C. Picasso and American art **709**

AVARICE
See also Sin
The **avengers.** Cohen, R. **940.53**

Aveni, Anthony F.
Empires of time **529**

AVERAGE
See also Arithmetic; Probabilities; Statistics
Averno. Gluck, L. **811**

AVERSION
Palca, J. Annoying **612.8**

AVERSIVE STIMULI
Palca, J. Annoying **612.8**

Avery, Kevin
Everything is an afterthought **92**

Avery, Tom
To the end of the earth **998**

AVIATION *See* Aeronautics

AVIATION ACCIDENTS *See* Aircraft accidents

AVIATION MEDICINE
See also Medicine

AVIATORS *See* Air pilots

Avise, John C.
Genetics in the wild **591.3**
Avoid boring people. Watson, J. D. **92**

Avorn, Jerry
Powerful medicines **338.4**
Awaken the giant within. Robbins, T. **158**
Awakening the mind. Wise, A. **615.8**

AWARDS
Awards, honors, & prizes **001.4**
Awards, honors, & prizes. **001.4**

Axelrod, Alan
The encyclopedia of the American armed forces **355**
Phillips, C. Encyclopedia of wars **355**
(ed) Van Nostrand's concise encyclopedia of science **503**

AXIOLOGY *See* Values

Ayala, Francisco J.
Darwin's gift to science and religion **576.8**
The **Ayatollah** begs to differ. Majd, H. **955**

Aycoberry, Pierre
The social history of the Third Reich **943.086**

Ayers, Edward L.
(ed) The Oxford book of the American South **810**

Aykroyd, Peter
A history of ghosts **133.1**
Ayn Rand and the world she made. Heller, A. C. **92**

Ayres, Alex
(ed) Twain, M. The wit and wisdom of Mark Twain **818**

Ayres, Chris

BACTERIAL WARFARE *See* Biological warfare
BACTERIOLOGY
  See also Microbiology
Friedman, M. Medicine's 10 greatest discoveries **610**
The **bad** & the beautiful. Kashner, S. **791.43**
BAD BEHAVIOR
  See also Human behavior
Bad dog. Kihn, M. **636.7**
Bad elements. Buruma, I. **951.05**
Bad girls go everywhere: the life of Helen Gurley Brown. Scanlon, J. **92**
The **bad** guys won. Pearlman, J. **796.357**
Bad land. Raban, J. **978**
Bad science. Goldacre, B. **500**
BAD SPORTSMANSHIP *See* Sportsmanship
Bade, Patrick
  Manca, J. 1000 sculptures of genius **730.9**
Bader, Christopher D.
  Paranormal America **133.8**
Bader, Michael J.
  Arousal, the secret logic of sexual fantasies **306.7**
Bader, Philip
  African-American writers **920.003**
Badger, David
  Snakes **597.96**
BADGERS
  See also Mammals
Baek, Hongyong, 1912-2002
  About
  Lee, H. In the absence of sun **979.4**
Báez, Fernando
  A universal history of the destruction of books **900**
Bagemihl, Bruce
  Biological exuberance **591.56**
Bagg, Mary
  (ed) Berkshire encyclopedia of China **951**
Baggett, Jennifer
  The lost girls **910.4**
Baggett, Jennifer (American marketing executive)
  About
  Baggett, J. The lost girls **910.4**
Baggott, J. E.
  The first war of physics **355.8**
  Baggott, J. The quantum story **530.1**
Baggott, Jim
  The quantum story **530.1**
Baghdad at sunrise. Mansoor, P. R. **956.7**
Baghdad without a map, and other misadventures in Arabia. Horwitz, T. **915**
BAHAI FAITH
  See also Religions
Bahn, Paul G.
  Lister, A. Mammoths **569**
Baiev, Khassan
  The Oath **947.5**

Baigrie, Brian S.
  (ed) History of modern science and mathematics **500**
Baile de Laperriere, Charles
  Who's who in art **920.003**
Bailey, Anthony
  Velazquez: surrendering at Breda **759**
Bailey, Beth L.
  (ed) The Columbia guide to America in the 1960s **973.923**
Bailey, Blake
  Cheever **92**
  A tragic honesty: the life and work of Richard Yates **813**
Bailey, Covert
  Smart exercise **613.7**
Bailey, Elisabeth Tova
  The sound of a wild snail eating **92**
Bailey, Frankie Y.
  (ed) Famous American crimes and trials **364**
Bailey, R. A.
  Rittner, D. Encyclopedia of chemistry **540**
Bailey, Rebecca Anne
  Easy to love, difficult to discipline **155**
Baillio, Joseph
  Claude Monet, 1840-1926 **759**
Bailyn, Bernard
  The peopling of British North America **973.2**
Baime, A. J.
  Go like hell **796.72**
Bain, David Haward
  Empire express **385**
Bainbridge, David
  Beyond the zonules of Zinn **611**
Bainton, Roland Herbert
  Here I stand: a life of Martin Luther **92**
Bair, Deirdre
  Simone de Beauvoir **848**
Bais, Sander
  In praise of science **500**
Bakalar, Nick
  Where the germs are **616**
Baker, David
  The 50 most extreme places in our solar system **523.2**
Baker, Deborah
  The convert **92**
Baker, Houston A.
  (ed) Douglass, F. Narrative of the life of Frederick Douglass, an American slave **92**
Baker, James A.
  The Iraq Study Group report **956.7**
Baker, James W.
  Thanksgiving **394.26**
Baker, Jean H.
  Margaret Sanger **92**

Beans, B. E. Eagle's plume   598

BALDNESS—TREATMENT

Greenwood-Robinson, M. Hair savers for women   616.5

Baldrige, Letitia

Letitia Baldrige's new manners for new times 395

Baldwin, James

Collected essays   814

Baldwin, Jan

Stow, J. The African kitchen   641.5

Baldwin, Lewis V.

(ed) Thou, dear God   242

Baldwin, Neil

Henry Ford and the Jews   305

Baldwin, Rosecrans

Paris, I love you but you're bringing me down 944

Balf, Todd

Major   92

Balibar, Sebastien

The atom and the apple   530

Balken, Debra Bricker

Abstract expressionism   709.04

BALL GAMES

See also Games

Chetwynd, J. The secret history of balls   796.3

Ball of fire. Kanfer, S.   791.45

Ball, Edward

Slaves in the family   975.7

The sweet hell inside   920

Ball, Philip

The devil's doctor   610

Nature's patterns   500.2

The **ballad** of Bob Dylan. Epstein, D. M.   92

The **ballad** of Dorothy Wordsworth. Wilson, F.   92

BALLADS

See also Literature; Poetry; Songs

American ballads and folk songs   781.62

Our singing country   781.62

Ballance, Laura Jane

Cook, J. Our noise   338

Ballard, Robert D.

The eternal darkness   551.46

Return to Midway   940.54

BALLERINAS—UNITED STATES—BIOGRAPHY.

Tallchief, M. Maria Tallchief   92

BALLET

See also Dance; Drama; Performing arts;
Theater

Craine, D. The Oxford dictionary of dance 792.8

Goldner, N. Balanchine variations   792.8

Gottlieb, R. A. George Balanchine: the ballet maker   92

Homans, J. Apollo's angels   792.8

Reynolds, N. No fixed points   792.8

Teachout, T. All in the dances: a brief life of George

Balanchine   92

Volynskii, A. L. Ballet's magic kingdom   792.8

BALLET—HISTORY

Goldner, N. Balanchine variations   792.8

Homans, J. Apollo's angels   792.8

BALLET—HISTORY—20TH CENTURY

Reynolds, N. No fixed points   792.8

BALLET—RUSSIA (FEDERATION)

Volynskii, A. L. Ballet's magic kingdom   792.8

BALLET DANCERS

See also Dancers

Diaghilev   92

Kavanagh, J. Nureyev   92

Life stories   920

Marshall, L. Every step you take   92

Tallchief, M. Maria Tallchief   92

Volynskii, A. L. Ballet's magic kingdom   792.8

Ballet's magic kingdom. Volynskii, A. L.   792.8

BALLETS *See* Ballet

BALLISTIC MISSILES

See also Guided missiles; Nuclear weapons;
Rockets (Aeronautics)

Sheehan, N. A fiery peace in a cold war   92

BALLOON ASCENSIONS—ARCTIC REGIONS

Wilkinson, A. The ice balloon   910.91

BALLOONS

See also Aeronautics

Wilkinson, A. The ice balloon   910.91

BALLOONS, DIRIGIBLE *See* Airships

BALLOT *See* Elections

BALLROOM DANCING

See also Dance

Ballyhoo! Reaves, W. W.   741.6

Ballyhoo, buckeroo, and spuds. Quinion, M.   422

Balmer, Randall Herbert

Religion in twentieth century America   200.9

Butler, J. Religion in American life   200.9

Balsamo, John

Balsamo, W. Young Al Capone   92

Balsamo, William

Young Al Capone   92

Balz, Daniel J.

The battle for America, 2008   973.932

Balzac. Robb, G.   92

Bambaradeniya, Channa N. B.

The illustrated atlas of wildlife   591.9

Bambi vs. Godzilla. Mamet, D.   791.43

Bamford, James

The shadow factory   327.12

Ban Breathnach, Sarah

A man's journey to simple abundance   158.1

BANANA TRADE—LOUISIANA—NEW ORLEANS—HISTORY

Cohen, R. The fish that ate the whale   338.7

BAND LEADERS

Armstrong, L. Louis Armstrong, in his own

Ferguson, N. High financier **92**

BANKS AND BANKING—ITALY—FLORENCE

Parks, T. Medici money **332.1**

BANKS AND BANKING—UNITED STATES

Grind, K. The lost bank **332.3**

BANKS AND BANKING—UNITED STATES— HISTORY

Rockefeller, D. Memoirs **332.1**

BANKS AND BANKING—WASHINGTON (STATE)—SEATTLE—HISTORY

Grind, K. The lost bank **332.3**

BANKS AND BANKING, INTERNATIONAL

Rhodes, W. R. Banker to the world **92**

Banks, Adam

Caplin, S. The complete guide to digital illustration **760**

Banks, Amy Elizabeth

(ed) The Complete guide to mental health for women **616.89**

Bankston, Carl L.

(ed) Great lives from history: Notorious lives **920.003**

Banned in the U.S.A. Foerstel, H. N. **025.2**

Banned plays. Sova, D. B. **792.09**

Banquet at Delmonico's. Werth, B. **303.4**

BANQUETS See Dining; Dinners

Banyas, Stephanie

Flay, B. Bobby Flay's grilling for life **641.5**

BAPTISTS

Ault, J. M. Spirit and flesh **306**

BAPTISTS—UNITED STATES—CLERGY—BIOGRAPHY

Dyson, M. E. I may not get there with you: the true Martin Luther King, Jr **323**

King, M. L. The autobiography of Martin Luther King, Jr **323**

Winters, M. S. God's right hand **322**

BAR See Lawyers

Barack Obama. Maraniss, D. **973.932**

Barajas, Louis

Small business, big life **658**

Baraka, Imamu Amiri

Dutchman, and The slave **812**

The LeRoi Jones/Amiri Baraka reader **818**

Baranczak, Stanislaw

Szymborska, W. Monologue of a dog **891.8**

Szymborska, W. Poems, new and collected, 1957-1997 **891.8**

Szymborska, W. View with a grain of sand **891.8**

Barash, David P.

The myth of monogamy **306.7**

Baratay, Eric

Zoo: a history of zoological gardens in the West **590.73**

Barbara Bush. Bush, B. **92**

Barbara Kraus' calories and carbohydrates. Kraus,

B. **613.2**

The **Barbary** plague. Chase, M. **362.1**

Barbash, Tom

Lutnick, H. On top of the world **332.6**

BARBECUE COOKERY See Barbecue cooking

BARBECUE COOKING

See also Outdoor cooking

Batali, M. Italian grill **641.5**

Flay, B. Bobby Flay's grilling for life **641.5**

Jamison, C. A. The big book of outdoor cooking and entertaining **641.5**

Lang, A. P. Serious barbecue **641.5**

Mallmann, F. Seven fires **641.5**

Neely, P. Down home with the Neelys **641.5**

Schlesinger, C. The thrill of the grill **641.7**

Barbed wire. Razac, O. **323.4**

BARBED WIRE

Razac, O. Barbed wire **323.4**

BARBED WIRE—POLITICAL ASPECTS

Razac, O. Barbed wire **323.4**

Barber, Marianne S.

The parent's guide to food allergies **618.92**

BARBERING See Hair

Barbero, Alessandro

The Battle **940.2**

Barbour, Ian G.

When science meets religion **261.5**

Barbour, Julian B.

The end of time **530.11**

Barbree, Jay

Live from Cape Canaveral **629.45**

The **bard.** Crawford, R. **92**

Bard, Elizabeth

Lunch in Paris **92**

Bare bones young adult services. Vaillancourt, R. J. **027.62**

Barefoot Contessa (East Hampton, N.Y.: Store)

Garten, I. Barefoot Contessa family style **641.5**

Barefoot Contessa family style. Garten, I. **641.5**

BARGAINING See Negotiation

Barken, Frederick M.

Out of practice **610.6**

Barker, Rodney

And the waters turned to blood **615.9**

Barker, Teresa

Deak, J. Girls will be girls **649**

Barkley, Charles

I may be wrong but I doubt it **796.323**

Barkley, Russell A.

Taking charge of ADHD **618.92**

Taking charge of adult ADHD **616.85**

Barlow, Ellen

Eisenstat, S. A. Every woman's guide to diabetes **616.4**

Barlow, John

Everything but the squeal **641**

and novelist)

About

Daugherty, T. Hiding man	92

Barthelme, Frederick

Double down	616.85

Barthelme, Steve

Barthelme, F. Double down	616.85

Bartholet, Elizabeth

Nobody's children	362.76

Bartholomew, Mel

All new square foot gardening	635

Bartiromo, Maria

The 10 laws of enduring success	650.1
The weekend that changed Wall Street	330.9

Bartle, Lisa R.

Burgess, M. Reference guide to science fiction, fantasy, and horror	016

Bartlett's familiar quotations. Bartlett, J.	808.88
Bartlett's Roget's thesaurus. Little, B. &. C. I.	423

Bartlett, Allison Hoover

The man who loved books too much	92

Bartlett, John

Bartlett's familiar quotations	808.88

Bartlett, Rosamund

Tolstoy	891.7

Bartok, Mira

The memory palace	92

Barton, John

(ed) Oxford Bible commentary	220.7

Bartusiak, Marcia

The day we found the universe	520

Barzun, Jacques

From dawn to decadence	940.2
Begin here	371.1

Basbanes, Nicholas A.

Every book its reader	028
Patience & fortitude	002

Bascomb, Neal

Hunting Eichmann	943.086
The new cool	629.8

BASEBALL

See also Ball games; Sports

Achorn, E. Fifty-nine in '84	796.357
Angell, R. Game time: a baseball companion	796.357
Angell, R. Once more around the park	796.357
Barra, A. Clearing the bases	796.357
Barra, A. Rickwood Field	796.357
Barry, D. Bottom of the 33rd	796.357
Baseball: a literary anthology	810
Boston, T. 1939, baseball's tipping point	796.357
Bryant, H. Shut out	796.357
Costas, B. Fair ball	796.357
Dickson, P. The hidden language of baseball	796.357
Frost, M. Game six	796.357

Geist, B. Little League confidential	796.357
Gentile, D. Splitters, squeezes, and steals	796.357
Giamatti, A. B. A great and glorious game	796.357
Goodwin, D. K. Wait till next year	796.357
Gould, S. J. Triumph and tragedy in Mudville	796.357
Hample, Z. Watching baseball smarter	796.357
Hogan, L. D. Shades of glory	796.357
Kahn, R. Beyond the boys of summer	796.357
Kahn, R. The head game	796.357
Kelly, J. Bushville	796.357
Kurlansky, M. The Eastern stars	796.357
Lewis, M. Moneyball	796.357
Madden, B. Pride of October	796.357
Murphy, C. Crazy '08	796.357
Pearlman, J. The bad guys won	796.357
Posnanski, J. The soul of baseball	796.357
Prager, J. The echoing green	796.357
Ripken, C. Play baseball the Ripken way	796.357
Ruck, R. Raceball	796.357
Shapiro, M. Bottom of the ninth	796.357
Shapiro, M. The last good season	796.357
Smith, R. Red Smith on baseball	796.357
Snyder, B. Beyond the shadow of the Senators	796.357
Thompson, T. American icon	796.357
Thorn, J. Baseball in the Garden of Eden	796.357
Tofel, R. J. A legend in the making	796.357
Turbow, J. The baseball codes	796.357
Tygiel, J. Baseball's great experiment	796.357
Vecsey, G. Baseball: a history of America's favorite game	796.357
Ward, G. C. Baseball: an illustrated history	796.357
Weber, B. As they see 'em	796.357
Weintraub, R. The house that Ruth built	796.357
Wendel, T. High heat	796.357
Whitaker, L. In the time of Bobby Cox	796.357
Will, G. F. Men at work	796.35

BASEBALL—BIOGRAPHY

Barra, A. Yogi Berra	92
Biddle, D. R. Tasting freedom	92
Breslin, J. Branch Rickey	92
Bryant, H. The last hero	92
Clavin, T. Roger Maris	92
Creamer, R. W. Babe	92
D'Antonio, M. Forever blue	92
Darling, R. The complete game	92
Dawidoff, N. The crowd sounds happy	92
Eig, J. Luckiest man	92
Feinstein, J. Living on the black	92
Fox, W. P. Satchel Paige's America	92
Halberstam, D. The teammates	796
Hirsch, J. S. Willie Mays	92
Honig, D. The fifth season	92
Kennedy, K. 56	92
Leavy, J. The last boy	92

Bastianich, Lidia
Lidia cooks from the heart of Italy   **641.5**
Lidia's family table   **641.5**
Lidia's Italian table   **641.59**
Lidia's Italian-American kitchen   **641.59**
Baszile, Jennifer
The Black girl next door   **92**
Batali, Mario
Italian grill   **641.5**
Bate, Jonathan
John Clare: a biography   **92**
Soul of the age   **822.3**
BATHING CUSTOMS—HISTORY
Ashenburg, K. The dirt on clean   **391**
BATHROOMS
See also Rooms
BATHS
See also Cleanliness; Hygiene; Physical
therapy
Bathsheba's breast. Olson, J. S.   **616.99**
Bathurst, Bella
The wreckers   **910.4**
BATIK
See also Dyes and dyeing
Batker, David K.
De Graaf, J. What's the economy for, any-
way?   **330.9**
BATMAN (FICTIONAL CHARACTER)
Batman unauthorized   **741.5**
Batman unauthorized.   **741.5**
BATS
See also Mammals
Batstone, David B.
Saving the corporate soul & (who knows?) maybe
your own   **658.4**
BATTERED WIVES *See* Abused women
BATTERED WOMEN *See* Abused women
The **batterer.** Dutton, D. G.   **362.82**
BATTERIES, ELECTRIC *See* Electric batteries;
Storage batteries
BATTERING OF WIVES *See* Wife abuse
The **battery.** Schlesinger, H. R.   **621.31**
BATTING (BASEBALL)
Kennedy, K. 56   **92**
The **Battle.** Barbero, A.   **940.2**
Battle at Bull Run. Davis, W. C.   **973.3**
Battle at sea. Grant, R. G.   **359**
BATTLE CASUALTIES—HISTORY
Stephenson, M. The last full measure   **305.9**
Battle cries and lullabies. De Pauw, L. G.   **355**
Battle cry of freedom. McPherson, J. M.   **973.7**
The **battle** for America, 2008. Balz, D. J.   **973.932**
The **battle** for God. Armstrong, K.   **200.9**
The **battle** for Rome. Katz, R.   **940.54**
The **battle** for Social Security. Altman, N. J.   **368.4**
Battle of Britain. Holland, J.   **940.54**

The **Battle** of New Orleans. Remini, R. V.   **973.2**
The **Battle** of the Little Bighorn. Sandoz, M.   **973.8**
BATTLE SHIPS *See* Warships
BATTLEFIELDS
See also Battles
BATTLEFIELDS—NORTH AMERICA
Rajtar, S. Indian war sites   **970.004**
BATTLES
See also Military art and science; Military his-
tory; War
Hanson, V. D. Carnage and culture   **904**
Keegan, J. Fields of battle   **355.009**
BATTLESHIPS *See* Warships
Batuman, Elif
The possessed   **891.7**
Baudelaire, Charles
Les fleurs du mal   **841**
Poems   **841**
Bauer, Jeni Britton
Jeni's splendid ice creams at home   **641.8**
Baughman, Judith
(ed) Fitzgerald, F. S. A life in letters   **813**
The **Bauhaus** group. Weber, N. F.   **920**
Baum, Dan
Nine lives   **976.3**
Baumann, Martin
(ed) Religions of the world   **200**
Baumeister, Theodore
(ed) Marks' standard handbook for mechanical en-
gineers   **621**
Baur, Gene
Farm Sanctuary   **179**
Bausch, Paul
Dornfest, R. Google hacks   **025.04**
Bausell, R. Barker
Snake oil science   **615.5**
Bawer, Bruce
Stealing Jesus   **277**
Surrender   **297**
Baxter, Angus
In search of your European roots   **929**
Baxter, John
The most beautiful walk in the world   **914**
Bayless, Deann Groen
Bayless, R. Fiesta at Rick's   **641.5**
Bayless, R. Rick Bayless's Mexican kitchen   **641.59**
Bayless, Rick
Fiesta at Rick's   **641.5**
Rick Bayless's Mexican kitchen   **641.59**
Bayley, John
Elegy for Iris   **823**
Bayley, John
About
Bayley, J. Elegy for Iris   **823**
Bayly, C. A.
Forgotten armies   **940.54**

Beatrix Farrand. Tankard, J. B.   92
Beatrix Potter. Lear, L. J.   92
BEATS *See* Beat generation
Beattie, Melody
  Beyond codependency   616.86
  Codependent no more   616.86
  Codependents' guide to the twelve steps   616.86
Beatty, Michael A.
  County name origins of the United States   917
Beatty, Richard H.
  175 high-impact cover letters   650.14
  The interview kit   650.14
Beatty, Scott
  The DC Comics encyclopedia   741.5
Beaty, H. Wayne
  (ed) Standard handbook for electrical engineers   621.3
The **Beaulieu** encyclopedia of the automobile.   629.222
Beaumarchais. Lever, M.   92
Beaumont's kitchen. Newhall, B.   641.5
BEAUTIFICATION OF LANDSCAPE *See* Landscape protection
Beautiful. Shearer, S. M.   92
Beautiful & pointless. Orr, D.   809.1
The **beautiful** and the damned. Deb, S.   954.05
Beautiful child. Hayden, T. L.   371.9
The **beautiful** cigar girl. Stashower, D.   364.152
Beautiful minds. Bearzi, M.   599.8
The **beautiful** soul of John Woolman, apostle of abolition. Slaughter, T. P.   92
The **beautiful** struggle. Coates   92
BEAUTY *See* Aesthetics
The **beauty** and the sorrow. Englund, P.   940.3
BEAUTY CONTEST WINNERS
  Schiller, L. Perfect murder, perfect town   364.15
BEAUTY CULTURE—UNITED STATES—HISTORY
  Peiss, K. L. Hope in a jar   391.6
The **beauty** myth. Wolf, N.   305.4
The **beauty** of the husband. Carson, A.   811
BEAUTY PARLORS *See* Beauty shops
BEAUTY SALONS *See* Beauty shops
BEAUTY SHOPS
  See also Business enterprises
  Rodriguez, D. Kabul Beauty School   305.4
BEAUTY, PERSONAL *See* Personal appearance; Personal grooming
Beauty: the new basics. Berg, R.   646.7
Beauvoir, Simone de
  The second sex   305.4
Beavan, Colin
  No impact man   333.72
BEAVERS
  See also Furbearing animals; Mammals
Because I said so.   306.8

Beccaloni, Jan
  Arachnids   595.4
Bechdel, Alison, 1960- (American cartoonist and graphic novelist)
  Are you my mother?   741.5
  Fun home   741.5
Bechdel, Alison, 1960- (American cartoonist and graphic novelist)
About
  Bechdel, A. Fun home   741.5
Bechtel, Mark
  He crashed me so I crashed him back   796.72
Beck, Astrid B.
  (ed) Eerdmans dictionary of the Bible   220.3
Beck, Simone
  Child, J. Mastering the art of French cooking   641.5
Beck, Warren A.
  Historical atlas of the American West   911
Becker, Annette
  Audoin-Rouzeau, S. 14-18, understanding the Great War   940.3
Becker, Carl
  The Declaration of Independence   973.3
Becker, Charlotte B.
  (ed) Encyclopedia of ethics   170
Becker, Christine
  It's the pictures that got small   791.45
Becker, Ethan
  Rombauer, I. v. S. Joy of cooking   641.5
Becker, Jasper
  The Chinese   951.05
Becker, Lawrence C.
  (ed) Encyclopedia of ethics   170
Becker, Marion Rombauer
  Rombauer, I. v. S. Joy of cooking   641.5
Becker, Norman
  The complete book of home inspection   643
Becker, Suzy
  I had brain surgery, what's your excuse?   92
Becker, Suzy
About
  Becker, S. I had brain surgery, what's your excuse?   92
Beckerman, Gal
  When they come for us we'll be gone   305.8
Beckett, Kenneth A.
  Gardening basics   635
Beckett, Samuel
  Collected poems in English and French   841
  Dramatic works   842
Beckett, Samuel, 1906-1989 (Irish playwright and novelist)
About
  Samuel Beckett's Waiting for Godot   842
Beckett, Wendy
  Sister Wendy's American collection   709

Behan, Brendan
  The complete plays   **822**
BEHAVIOR *See* Animal behavior; Human behavior

BEHAVIOR GENETICS
  See also Genetics; Psychology
  Avise, J. C. Genetics in the wild   **591.3**
  Clark, W. R. Are we hardwired?   **155.7**
  Hamer, D. H. Living with our genes   **155.2**
  Smoller, J. The other side of normal   **591.5**
  Weiner, J. Time, love, memory   **591.5**

BEHAVIOR MODIFICATION
  See also Applied psychology; Human behavior; Psychology of learning

BEHAVIOR OF CHILDREN *See* Child psychology; Children—Conduct of life; Etiquette for children and teenagers

BEHAVIOR OF TEENAGERS *See* Adolescent psychology; Etiquette for children and teenagers; Teenagers—Conduct of life

BEHAVIOR PROBLEMS (CHILDREN) *See* Emotionally disturbed children

BEHAVIOR, HELPING *See* Helping behavior

BEHAVIORAL OPTOMETRY
  Barry, S. Fixing my gaze   **617.7**

BEHAVIORAL PSYCHOLOGY *See* Psychophysiology

BEHAVIORISM
  See also Human behavior; Psychology; Psychophysiology
  Skinner, B. F. About behaviorism   **150.19**

BEHAVIORISTIC PSYCHOLOGY *See* Behaviorism

Behind closed doors. Vickery, A.   **306.8**
Behind my eyes. Lee   **811**
Behind the beautiful forevers. Boo, K.   **305.5**
Behind the Berkshire Hathaway curtain. Chan, R. W.   **658.4**
Behind the palace doors. Farquhar, M.   **941**
Behind the screen. Mann, W. J.   **791.43**
Behnke, Robert J.
  Trout and salmon of North America   **597**
The **beholder's** eye.   **814**
Behr, Edward
  Prohibition   **363.4**
Beier, Ulli
  (ed) The Penguin book of modern African poetry   **896**
Beilock, Sian L.
  Choke   **153.9**
Being America. Purdy, J.   **327**
Being and nothingness. Sartre, J. P.   **142**
Being and time. Heidegger, M.   **111**
Being Jewish. Goldman, A. L.   **296.4**
Being wrong. Schulz, K.   **153**
Beisner, Robert L.

  (ed) American foreign relations since 1600   **016**
Bekoff, Marc
  Minding animals   **591.5**
  Wild justice   **591.5**
  (ed) Encyclopedia of animal behavior   **591.5**
  (ed) Encyclopedia of animal rights and animal welfare   **179**
  Goodall, J. The ten trusts   **333.95**
Belafonte, Harry
  My song   **92**
Beland, Tom
  True story swear to God archives, vol. 1   **741.5**
Beland, Tom, 1962- (American cartoonist)
      About
  Beland, T. True story swear to God archives, vol. 1   **741.5**
Belcher, Judy
  Polymer clay creative traditions   **731.4**
Belfiore, Michael
  The department of mad scientists   **355**
BELIEF AND DOUBT
  See also Philosophy; Theory of knowledge
  Barrett, J. L. Born believers   **200.1**
  Hecht, J. M. Doubt: a history   **121**
  Shermer, M. The believing brain   **153.4**
  Shermer, M. Why people believe weird things **001.9**
  This I believe   **170**
  This I believe II   **170**
Belief beyond boundaries.   **209**
Beliefs and blasphemies. Adair, V. H.   **811**
Believer, beware.   **200.9**
The **believing** brain. Shermer, M.   **153.4**
Believing is seeing. Morris, E.   **770.9**
Bell, Anne Olivier
  (ed) Woolf, V. A moment's liberty: the shorter diary   **92**
Bell, Dana
  (comp) Smithsonian atlas of world aviation **629.13**
Bell, Eric Temple
  Men of mathematics   **920**
Bell, Laura
  Claiming ground   **92**
Bell, Madison Smartt
  Toussaint Louverture   **92**
Bell, Suzanne
  Encyclopedia of forensic science   **363.2**
Bellamy, Charles L.
  Evans, A. V. An inordinate fondness for beetles   **595.7**
Bellamy, David
  David Bellamy's complete guide to watercolour painting   **751.42**
Bellec, Francois
  Unknown lands   **910.4**
Bellenir, Karen
  (ed) Breast cancer sourcebook   **616.99**

BEQUESTS *See* Gifts; Inheritance and succession; Wills

Beranbaum, Rose Levy
The cake bible   **641.8**

Bercovitch, Sacvan
(ed) The Cambridge history of American literature   **810**

BEREAVEMENT
See also Emotions

Attig, T. The heart of grief   **155.9**
Berns, N. Closure   **155.9**
The Book of eulogies   **808.8**
Brizendine, J. Stunned by grief   **248**
Dresser, N. Saying goodbye to someone you love   **155.9**
Edelman, H. Motherless daughters   **155.9**
Edelman, H. Motherless mothers   **155.9**
Emswiler, M. A. Guiding your child through grief   **155.9**
Gilbert, S. M. Death's door   **155.9**
Groom, K. I wore the ocean in the shape of a girl   **92**
Hood, A. Comfort   **92**
Jamison, K. R. Nothing was the same   **92**
Kohn, I. A silent sorrow   **618.3**
Levy, A. The orphaned adult   **152.4**
Levy, N. To begin again   **296.7**
McCracken, E. An exact replica of a figment of my imagination   **92**
Oates, J. C. A widow's story   **92**
O'Rourke, M. The long goodbye   **92**
Remembrances and celebrations   **808.8**
Roiphe, A. R. Epilogue   **92**
Rosenblatt, R. Making toast   **92**
Sheeler, J. Final salute   **956.7**
Sife, W. The loss of a pet   **155.9**
Smith, C. B. The rules of inheritance   **616.99**
Strayed, C. Wild   **813**
Winner, L. F. Still   **283**

BEREAVEMENT—PSYCHOLOGICAL ASPECTS

Attig, T. The heart of grief   **155.9**
Kohn, I. A silent sorrow   **618.3**
Levy, A. The orphaned adult   **152.4**
Smith, C. B. The rules of inheritance   **616.99**

BEREAVEMENT—PSYCHOLOGICAL ASPECTS—CASE STUDIES
Attig, T. The heart of grief   **155.9**

BEREAVEMENT—RELIGIOUS ASPECTS—JUDAISM
Levy, N. To begin again   **296.7**

BEREAVEMENT IN CHILDREN
Emswiler, M. A. Guiding your child through grief   **155.9**

Berenbaum, Michael
The world must know   **940.53**
(ed) Encyclopaedia Judaica   **296**

(ed) The Holocaust and history   **940.53**

Berendt, Joachim Ernst
Grosse Jazzbuch./English The jazz book   **781.65**

Berendt, John
The city of falling angels   **945**
Midnight in the garden of good and evil   **975.8**

Berg, A. Scott
Kate remembered   **92**
Lindbergh   **629.13**

Berg, Barbara J.
Sexism in America   **305.4**

Berg, Rona
Beauty: the new basics   **646.7**

Bergen, Peter L.
Holy war, Inc.   **303.6**
The longest war   **909.83**

BERGEN-BELSEN (GERMANY: CONCENTRATION CAMP)
See also Concentration camps

Berger, David G.
Hinton, M. Playing the changes   **92**

Berger, James
(ed) Keller, H. The story of my life   **92**

Berger, Joel
The better to eat you with   **591.5**

Berger, John
Bento's sketchbook   **741.9**

BERGER, JOHN—THEMES, MOTIVES
Berger, J. Bento's sketchbook   **741.9**

Berger, Lisa
Goldman, B. Brain fitness   **153.1**

Berger, William
Puccini without excuses   **92**
Verdi with a vengeance   **782.1**
Wagner without fear   **782**

Bergner, Daniel
The other side of desire   **306.7**

Bergreen, Laurence
Capone   **364.1**
Marco Polo   **92**
Over the edge of the world   **910.4**

Berkin, Carol
A brilliant solution   **342**
Civil War wives   **920**

Berkow, Ira
The minority quarterback, and other lives in sports   **796**

Berkshire encyclopedia of China.   **951**
Berkshire encyclopedia of world history.   **903**

Berkson, Bill
Portrait and dream   **811**

Berley, Peter
The modern vegetarian kitchen   **641.5**

Berlin at war. Moorhouse, R.   **943**
Berlin journal, 1989-1990. Darnton, R.   **943.087**
BERLIN WALL, BERLIN, GERMANY, 1961-

A timbered choir   **811**

Berryman, John
Collected poems, 1937-1971   **811**
The dream songs   **811**

Bertholf, Robert J.
(ed) Duncan, R. E. Selected poems   **811**

Bertholle, Louisette
Child, J. Mastering the art of French cooking **641.5**

Berthon, Simon
Warlords   **940.53**

Beschloss, Michael R.
The conquerors: Roosevelt, Truman, and the destruction of Hitler's Germany, 1941-1945 **940.53**
Jacqueline Kennedy   **973.922**
(ed) Taking charge   **973.923**

Beschloss, Michael R., 1955-
(ed) Jacqueline Kennedy   **973.922**

Bessel, Richard
Germany 1945   **943.087**

The **best** alternative medicine. Pelletier, K. R. **615.5**
The **best** American crime reporting, 2010.   **364.1**
The **best** American essays 2010.   **814**
The **Best** American essays of the century.   **814**
The **best** American poetry 2011.   **811**
The **best** American recipes 2005-2006.   **641.5**
The **best** American science and nature writing 2010.   **500**

The Best American series
The best American essays 2010   **814**
The best American recipes 2005-2006   **641.5**
The best American science and nature writing 2010   **500**
The best American sports writing 2010   **796**
The best American short plays.   **812**
The best American sports writing 2010.   **796**
The best American sports writing of the century.   **796**

The **best** and the brightest. Halberstam, D. **973.922**

BEST BOOKS
See also Books
Alabaster, C. Developing an outstanding core collection   **025.2**
Basbanes, N. A. Every book its reader   **028**
Covert, J. The 100 best business books of all time   **016.6**
Dirda, M. Book by book   **028**
Ellington, E. A year of reading   **011**
Fiction core collection   **016**
Helbig, A. Dictionary of American children's fiction, 1995-1999   **028.5**
Helbig, A. Dictionary of American young adult fiction, 1997-2001   **028.5**
Horror: another 100 best books   **823**
Isabella, T. 1,000 comic books you must read **741.5**
Major, D. C. 100 one-night reads   **001**
Masterpieces of world literature   **809**

Moyer, J. E. The readers' advisory handbook **025.5**
Pearl, N. Book lust   **011**
Pearl, N. More book lust   **025**
Pearl, N. Now read this III   **016**
Recommended reference books for small and medium-sized libraries and media centers, Vol. 30 **011**
Required reading   **301**
Rosow, L. V. Accessing the classics   **011.6**
Saricks, J. G. The readers' advisory guide to genre fiction   **025.5**
Silvey, A. 100 best books for children   **011.6**
What do I read next? 2011   **016**

BEST BOOKS—UNITED STATES
Helbig, A. Dictionary of American children's fiction, 1995-1999   **028.5**
The **best** chicken recipes. Cook's illustrated (Periodical)   **641.6**
The **best** game ever. Bowden, M.   **796.332**
The **best** International recipe. Cook's illustrated (Periodical)   **641.5**
Best music writing 2008.   **781.64**
The **best** of Abbie Hoffman. Hoffman, A.   **303.4**
The **best** of all possible worlds. Nadler, S. M. **190**
The **best** of it. Ryan, K.   **811**
Best of the brain from Scientific American. Scientific American (Periodical)   **612.8**
The **best** one-dish suppers.   **641.8**
The **best** plays of 2006-2007.   **808.82**
Best plays theater yearbook [series]
The best plays of 2006-2007   **808.82**
The **Best** poems of the English language.   **821**
The **best** quick breads. Hensperger, B.   **641.8**
BEST SELLERS (BOOKS)
See also Books and reading
Best skillet recipes. Cook's illustrated (Periodical)   **641.7**
The **best** stage scenes of 2007.   **808.82**
The **best** year of their lives. Morrow, L.   **920**
Best, Joel
Stat-spotting   **301**
BEST-BOOK LISTS *See* Best books
BESTIARIES
See also Books
Bethell, Leslie
(ed) The Cambridge history of Latin America **980**
Betjeman. Wilson, A. N.   **92**
Betrayal of trust. Garrett, L.   **362.1**
The **betrayal** of work. Shulman, B.   **331.2**
Betrayed. Diebel, L.   **364.152**
BETROTHAL
See also Courtship; Marriage
Betsy Ross and the making of America. Miller, M. R.   **92**
Bette Davis. Thomson, D.   **92**
Bettelheim, Bruno
Freud and man's soul   **150.19**

BINDING OF BOOKS *See* Bookbinding

Bing Crosby: a pocketful of dreams: the early years, 1903-1940. Giddins, G.   **92**

BINGE EATING BEHAVIOR *See* Bulimia

BINGE-PURGE BEHAVIOR *See* Bulimia

Bingham, Hiram

Lost city of the Incas   **985**

Bingham, Hiram, 1875-1956

About

Adams, M. Turn right at Machu Picchu   **985**

Bingham, H. Lost city of the Incas   **985**

Heaney, C. Cradle of gold   **92**

Binns, Brigit Legere

Psilakis, M. How to roast a lamb   **641.5**

BINOCULARS

Scagell, R. Stargazing with binoculars   **523.8**

Binyon, T. J.

Pushkin: a biography   **92**

BIOCHEMISTRY

See also Biology; Chemistry; Medicine

Harold, F. M. The way of the cell   **571.6**

BIOCHEMISTRY—DICTIONARIES

The Facts on File dictionary of biochemistry   **572**

BIOCHEMISTRY—RESEARCH

Watson, J. D. The double helix   **572.8**

BIOCHEMISTS

Blum, A. Breaking trail   **796.522**

Flowers, C. Instability rules   **509**

Friedman, M. Medicine's 10 greatest discoveries   **610**

Gunn, J. E. Isaac Asimov   **813**

Horvitz, L. A. Eureka!: scientific breakthroughs that changed the world   **509**

Ridley, M. Francis Crick   **92**

Winchester, S. The man who loved China   **92**

BIODIVERSITY

See also Biology

BIODIVERSITY CONSERVATION

See also Conservation of natural resources

Bright, C. Life out of bounds   **578.6**

Fraser, C. Rewilding the world   **333.95**

BIOENGINEERING

Frenay, R. Pulse   **620**

BIOETHICS

See also Ethics

Clones and clones   **174**

The Double-edged helix   **599.93**

Encyclopedia of bioethics   **174**

Fox, M. W. Beyond evolution   **174**

United States/President's Council on Bioethics Human cloning and human dignity   **174**

BIOETHICS—ENCYCLOPEDIAS

Encyclopedia of bioethics   **174**

BIOFEEDBACK TRAINING

See also Feedback (Psychology); Mind and body; Psychology of learning; Psychotherapy

BIOGEOGRAPHY

See also Ecology; Geography

Bambaradeniya, C. N. B. The illustrated atlas of wildlife   **591.9**

World atlas of great apes and their conservation   **599.8**

BIOGRAPHERS

Bair, D. Simone de Beauvoir   **848**

Blackburn, J. The three of us   **92**

Bloom, H. The anatomy of influence   **801**

Brookhiser, R. Right time, right place   **92**

Existentialism from Dostoevsky to Sartre   **142**

Farrell, S. E. Critical companion to Kurt Vonnegut   **813**

Fraser, K. Ornament and silence   **809**

Goodwin, D. K. Wait till next year   **796.357**

Grimes, T. Mentor   **92**

Hollis, L. London rising   **942**

Jarrell, R. No other book   **809**

Kapuscinski, R. Travels with Herodotus   **930**

King, D. Patrick O'Brian   **823**

Maraniss, D. Into the story   **92**

Martin, P. A life of James Boswell   **828**

Morgan, T. My battle of Algiers   **965**

Morris, W. My dog Skip   **813**

Oates, J. C. A widow's story   **92**

Parini, J. The art of teaching   **371.1**

Reiss, T. The Orientalist   **92**

Richardson, J. The sorcerer's apprentice   **92**

Schlesinger, A. M. Journals: 1952-2000   **92**

Schlesinger, A. M. A life in the twentieth century   **973.91**

Shields, C. J. And so it goes: Kurt Vonnegut: a life   **92**

Simon, J. F. What kind of nation   **342**

Sisman, A. Boswell's presumptuous task   **828**

Smith, J. E. John Marshall   **347**

Spurling, H. Pearl Buck in China   **92**

Stannard, M. Muriel Spark   **92**

Starr, W. W. Whisky, kilts, and the Loch Ness Monster   **914**

Steffens, L. The autobiography of Lincoln Steffens   **92**

Sutherland, J. Stephen Spender   **92**

Thomas, E. The war lovers   **973.8**

Thomson, D. Try to tell the story   **92**

Thurman, J. Secrets of the flesh: a life of Colette   **92**

Ulrich, L. Well-behaved women seldom make history   **305.4**

Von Mehren, J. Minerva and the muse: a life of Margaret Fuller   **818**

White, E. City boy   **92**

White, E. The flaneur   **944.083**

White, E. My lives   **813**

Zimmermann, W. First great triumph   **973**

BIOGRAPHERS—GREAT BRITAIN—BIOG-

BISEXUALITY

See also Sex

BISEXUALS

Gambone, P. Travels in a gay nation   **306.76**

BISEXUALS—UNITED STATES—HISTORY—ENCYCLOPEDIAS

Encyclopedia of lesbian, gay, bisexual, and transgender history in America   **306.76**

The **bishop's** daughter. Moore, H.   **92**

Bishop, Bill

The big sort   **305.8**

Bishop, Elizabeth

The collected prose   **818**

Edgar Allan Poe & the juke-box   **811**

Poems, prose, and letters   **S**

BISHOPS

See also Clergy

Burstein, A. Madison and Jefferson   **973.4**

Goldman, F. The art of political murder   **972.81**

Kung, H. Great Christian thinkers   **230**

Moore, H. The bishop's daughter   **92**

Newman, R. S. Freedom's prophet   **92**

Russell, B. A history of Western philosophy   **109**

Wills, G. Saint Augustine   **270.2**

Biskind, Peter

Easy riders, raging bulls   **791.43**

Star   **92**

Biskupic, Joan

Sandra Day O'Connor   **92**

Bismarck. Steinberg, J.   **92**

BISON

See also Mammals

Rinella, S. American buffalo   **599.64**

Biss, Eula

Notes from no man's land   **305.8**

Bissell, Tom

Extra lives   **794.8**

The father of all things   **959.704**

Magic hours   **153.35**

Bissinger, H. G.

Friday night lights   **796.332**

Three nights in August   **796.357**

Bitchfest.   **305.4**

Bite the hand that feeds you. Fairlie, H.   **814**

The **bitter** sea. Li, C. N.   **92**

Bitter spring. Pugliese, S. G.   **92**

The **bitter** waters of Medicine Creek. Kluger, R.   **979.7**

Bitter winds. Wu, H.   **951.05**

The **bitter** withy. Revell, D.   **811**

Bitterly divided. Williams, D.   **973.7**

Bittman, Mark

The food matters cookbook   **641.3**

How to cook everything   **641.5**

How to cook everything vegetarian   **641.5**

Mark Bittman's Kitchen express   **641.5**

Bix, Herbert P.

Hirohito and the making of modern Japan   **92**

Bizony, Piers

The man who ran the moon   **629**

Bizot, Francois

The gate   **959.604**

Bjork, Daniel W.

B.F. Skinner   **92**

Bjornerud, Marcia

Reading the rocks   **551.7**

Blachford, Stacey

(ed) Drugs and controlled substances   **362.29**

Black. Pastoureau, M.   **155.9**

BLACK

Pastoureau, M. Black   **155.9**

Black & Decker Corp.

The complete guide to finishing basements   **643**

The complete guide to flooring   **690**

The complete guide to patios & walkways   **690**

The complete guide to plumbing   **696**

The complete guide to roofing, siding & trim   **695**

The complete guide to wiring   **621.31**

The complete photo guide to home improvement   **643**

The complete photo guide to home repair   **643**

Black & white pipeline. Dillard, T.   **778.3**

The **black** 100. Salley, C.   **920**

BLACK ACTORS

See also Actors

BLACK AMERICANS *See* African Americans

BLACK ART

See also Art

BLACK ART (MAGIC) *See* Magic; Witchcraft

BLACK ARTISTS

See also Artists

BLACK ATHLETES

See also Athletes

BLACK AUTHORS

See also Authors

The **black** banners. Soufan, A. H.   **973.931**

Black belt tae kwon do. Park, Y. H.   **796.8**

Black boy. Wright, R.   **92**

BLACK BUSINESSPEOPLE

See also Businesspeople

BLACK CHILDREN

See also Children

Black cinema treasures. Jones, G. W.   **791.43**

BLACK DEATH *See* Plague

The **black** death and the transformation of the west. Herlihy, D.   **940.1**

BLACK DIASPORA *See* African diaspora

Black earth. Meier, A.   **947.086**

Black Elk

Black Elk speaks   **92**

Black Elk speaks. Black Elk   **92**

Black Elk, holy man of the Oglala. Steltenkamp, M.

(comp) Index to poetry for children and young people 808.81

Blackburn, Julia
Old man Goya 92
The three of us 92
With Billie 92

Blackburn, Lorraine A.
(comp) Index to poetry for children and young people 808.81

Blackburn, Paul
The collected poems of Paul Blackburn 811

Blackburn, Simon
The Oxford dictionary of philosophy 103
Think: a compelling introduction to philosophy 100
Truth 121

BLACKFACE ENTERTAINERS—UNITED STATES
Tosches, N. Where dead voices gather 782

Blackmon, Douglas A.
Slavery by another name 305.8

BLACKS
Africana: the encyclopedia of the African and African American experience 909
Litwack, L. F. How free is free? 323.1

BLACKS—AMERICA—RELIGION
The Encyclopedia of African and African-American religions 299.6

BLACKS—BIOGRAPHY
See also Biography

BLACKS—CIVIL RIGHTS
See also Blacks—Political activity; Civil rights

BLACKS—ECONOMIC CONDITIONS
See also Economic conditions

BLACKS—EDUCATION
See also Education

BLACKS—ENCYCLOPEDIAS
Africana: the encyclopedia of the African and African American experience 909

BLACKS—FOLKLORE
See also Folklore

BLACKS—HISTORY
Blumrosen, A. W. Slave nation 973.3
Egerton, D. R. Death or liberty 973.3
Grant, G. M. At the elbows of my elders 920

BLACKS—HISTORY—MISCELLANEA
Black firsts: 4,000 ground-breaking and pioneering historical events 305.8

BLACKS—HOUSING
See also Housing

BLACKS—INTELLECTUAL LIFE
See also Intellectual life

BLACKS—RACE IDENTITY
Touré Who's afraid of post-blackness?

BLACKS—RACE IDENTITY
See also Race awareness

BLACKS—RELIGION
The Encyclopedia of African and African-American religions 299.6

BLACKS—RELIGION
See also Religion

BLACKS—SEGREGATION
See also Segregation

BLACKS—SOCIAL LIFE AND CUSTOMS
See also Manners and customs

BLACKS—SOUTH AFRICA—SOCIAL CONDITIONS
Gevisser, M. A legacy of liberation 92

BLACKS—UNITED STATES *See* African Americans

BLACKS IN LITERATURE
Black literature criticism 809

BLACKS IN MOTION PICTURES
See also Minorities in motion pictures; Motion pictures
Bogle, D. Bright boulevards, bold dreams 791.43

BLACKS IN THE MOTION PICTURE INDUSTRY
See also Minorities in the motion picture industry; Motion picture industry
Bogle, D. Bright boulevards, bold dreams 791.43
Jones, G. W. Black cinema treasures 791.43
The **blacks**: a clown show. Genet, J. 842

BLACKSMITHING
Parkinson, P. The artist blacksmith 682

Blackwell companions to philosophy [series]
A Companion to world philosophies 100

Blackwell critical biographies [series]
Brown, T. The life of W.B. Yeats 821

Blackwell guides to literature [series]
MacGowan, C. J. Twentieth-century American poetry 811

Blainey, Geoffrey
Sea of dangers 92

Blair, Clay
Hitler's U-boat war 940.54

Blair, Louise
Worrall-Thompson, A. The essential diabetes cookbook 641.5

Blair, Sheila
Bloom, J. The Grove encyclopedia of Islamic art and architecture 709.1

Blair, Steven N.
Active living every day 613.7

Blair, Tony
A journey 92

Blais, Madeleine
In these girls, hope is a muscle 796.323

Blake, William
The complete poetry and prose of William Blake 821

Blake-Krebs, Barbara

Bragdon, Kathleen J.
The Columbia guide to American Indians of the Northeast   **970.004**

Bragg, Melvyn
The adventure of English   **420**
The book of books   **220.5**

Bragg, Rick
All over but the shoutin'   **070**
Ava's man   **975**
The prince of Frogtown   **92**

BRAHMANISM
  See also Religions

BRAIDS (HAIRSTYLING)
  See also Hair

BRAILLE
  See also Writing

BRAILLE BOOKS
  See also Books

BRAIN
  See also Head; Nervous system
Aamodt, S. Welcome to your brain   **612.8**
Amen, D. Change your brain, change your life   **616.89**
Bainbridge, D. Beyond the zonules of Zinn   **611**
Buonomano, D. Brain bugs   **612.8**
Calvin, W. H. How brains think   **153.9**
Carter, R. The human brain book   **612.8**
Chorost, M. World wide mind   **612.8**
Damasio, A. R. The Scientific American book of the brain   **612.8**
Doidge, N. The brain that changes itself   **612.8**
Dowling, J. E. Creating mind   **612.8**
Eagleman, D. Incognito   **153**
Eliot, L. What's going on in there?   **612.8**
Gazzaniga, M. S. Human   **612.8**
Glynn, I. An anatomy of thought   **612.8**
Greenfield, S. The private life of the brain   **612.8**
Horstman, J. The Scientific American day in the life of your brain   **616.8**
Johnson, S. Mind wide open   **612.8**
Linden, D. J. The accidental mind   **612.8**
McDermott, T. 101 theory drive   **612.8**
Pinker, S. How the mind works   **153**
Ramachandran, V. S. The tell-tale brain   **616.8**
Ratey, J. J. A user's guide to the brain   **612.8**
Restak, R. M. Mozart's brain and the fighter pilot   **612.8**
Sagan, C. The dragons of Eden   **153**
Schacter, D. L. Searching for memory   **153.1**
Scientific American (Periodical) Best of the brain from Scientific American   **612.8**
Tammet, D. Embracing the wide sky   **612.8**
Turkington, C. The encyclopedia of the brain and brain disorders   **612.8**
Victoroff, J. I. Saving your brain   **612.8**
Wise, A. Awakening the mind   **615.8**

Wolf, M. Proust and the squid   **612.8**
Zimmer, C. Soul made flesh   **612.8**

BRAIN—AGING
Victoroff, J. I. Saving your brain   **612.8**

BRAIN—CANCER—PATIENTS
Servan-Schreiber, D. Anticancer   **616.99**

BRAIN—DISEASES
  See also Diseases
Damasio, A. R. The Scientific American book of the brain   **612.8**
Lemon, A. Happy   **92**
Turkington, C. The encyclopedia of the brain and brain disorders   **612.8**

BRAIN—ENCYCLOPEDIAS
Turkington, C. The encyclopedia of the brain and brain disorders   **612.8**

BRAIN—EVOLUTION
Linden, D. J. The accidental mind   **612.8**
Wolf, M. Proust and the squid   **612.8**

BRAIN—PATHOPHYSIOLOGY
Amen, D. Change your brain, change your life   **616.89**

BRAIN—PHYSIOLOGY
Gonzales, L. Surviving survival   **155.9**

BRAIN—POPULAR WORKS
Ratey, J. J. A user's guide to the brain   **612.8**
Restak, R. M. Mozart's brain and the fighter pilot   **612.8**

BRAIN—SEX DIFFERENCES
Eliot, L. Pink brain, blue brain   **612.6**

BRAIN—SURGERY
El-Hai, J. The lobotomist   **92**

BRAIN—SURGERY—PATIENTS—BIOGRAPHY
Becker, S. I had brain surgery, what's your excuse?   **92**

BRAIN—SURGERY—PATIENTS—CARICATURES AND CARTOONS
Becker, S. I had brain surgery, what's your excuse?   **92**

BRAIN—SURGERY—PATIENTS—HUMOR
Becker, S. I had brain surgery, what's your excuse?   **92**

BRAIN—TUMORS
Gunther, J. Death be not proud   **92**

BRAIN—WOUNDS AND INJURIES
Mason, M. P. Head cases   **617**

BRAIN—WOUNDS AND INJURIES—PATIENTS—REHABILITATION
Mason, M. P. Head cases   **617**
Brain bugs. Buonomano, D.   **612.8**

BRAIN DAMAGE—PATIENTS—CARE
Shulman, A. K. To love what is   **92**

BRAIN DAMAGED CHILDREN
  See also Exceptional children; Handicapped children

BREAK DANCING

See also Dance

Break on through: the life and death of Jim Morrison. Riordan, J. **782.421**

Break, blow, burn. Paglia, C. **809.1**

BREAKERS *See* Ocean waves

Breakfast at Sally's. LeMieux, R. **92**

BREAKFASTS

See also Cooking; Menus

Breaking clean. Blunt, J. **92**

Breaking free, starting over. Dalpiaz, C. M. **362.82**

Breaking night. Murray, L. **92**

Breaking the spell. Dennett, D. C. **200**

Breaking trail. Blum, A. **796.522**

BREAKTHROUGHS, SCIENTIFIC *See* Discoveries in science

The **breakup** 2.0. Gershon, I. **303.4**

BREAST

Love, S. M. Dr. Susan Love's breast book **618.1**

BREAST—CANCER

Gabriel, S. Eating pomegranates **92**

BREAST—CANCER *See* Breast cancer

BREAST—CANCER—ALTERNATIVE TREATMENT

Breast cancer **616.99**

Breast cancer. Hirshaut, Y. **616.99**

BREAST CANCER

See also Cancer; Women—Diseases

Arnot, B. The breast health cookbook **616.99**

Breast cancer **616.99**

Breast cancer sourcebook **616.99**

Corrigan, K. The middle place **92**

Gabriel, S. Eating pomegranates **92**

Hirshaut, Y. Breast cancer **616.99**

Lerner, B. H. The breast cancer wars **616.99**

Link, J. The breast cancer survival manual **616.99**

Olson, J. S. Bathsheba's breast **616.99**

Queller, J. Pretty is what changes **92**

Schultz, N. L. Mrs. Mattingly's miracle **362.1**

Silver, M. Breast cancer husband **616.99**

Weiss, M. C. Living well beyond breast cancer **616.99**

Wheelwright, J. The wandering gene and the Indian princess **616.99**

Breast cancer. **616.99**

BREAST CANCER—ENCYCLOPEDIAS

Turkington, C. The encyclopedia of breast cancer **616.99**

BREAST—CANCER—HISTORY

Olson, J. S. Bathsheba's breast **616.99**

BREAST—CANCER—PATIENTS

Romm, R. The mercy papers **92**

Schultz, N. L. Mrs. Mattingly's miracle **362.1**

BREAST—CANCER—PATIENTS—FAMILY RELATIONSHIPS

Silver, M. Breast cancer husband **616.99**

BREAST—CANCER—POPULAR WORKS

Breast cancer **616.99**

Silver, M. Breast cancer husband **616.99**

BREAST—CANCER—PSYCHOLOGICAL ASPECTS

Silver, M. Breast cancer husband **616.99**

BREAST—CANCER—UNITED STATES—HISTORY—20TH CENTURY

Lerner, B. H. The breast cancer wars **616.99**

Breast cancer husband. Silver, M. **616.99**

Breast cancer sourcebook. **616.99**

The **breast** cancer survival manual. Link, J. **616.99**

The **breast** cancer wars. Lerner, B. H. **616.99**

BREAST FEEDING

Huggins, K. The nursing mother's companion **649**

Neifert, M. R. Great expectations **649**

The Nursing mother's problem solver **649**

Pryor, G. Nursing mother, working mother **649**

The Womanly art of breastfeeding **649**

BREAST FEEDING—POPULAR WORKS

The Nursing mother's problem solver **649**

The **breast** health cookbook. Arnot, B. **616.99**

BREAST NEOPLASMS—GENETICS

Wheelwright, J. The wandering gene and the Indian princess **616.99**

Breath. Levine, P. **811**

Breathless homicidal slime mutants. Brower, S. **741.6**

Brecht and company. Fuegi, J. **92**

Bredin, Alice

The virtual office survival handbook **658**

Bredin, Jean-Denis

The affair **944.081**

BREEDING

Hubbell, S. Shrinking the cat **660.6**

Palumbi, S. R. The evolution explosion **576.8**

BREEDING BEHAVIOR *See* Sexual behavior in animals

Breen, Michael

The Koreans **951.9**

Breen, Nancy

(ed) 2009 poet's market **808.1**

Breen, T. H.

American insurgents, American patriots **973.3**

Bregman, Ahron

A history of Israel **956.94**

Brehony, Kathleen A.

After the darkest hour **155.9**

Breitman, Richard

The architect of genocide **92**

Official secrets **940.54**

Bremer, Francis J.

John Winthrop **974.4**

Brendon, Piers

The decline and fall of the British Empire, 1781-1997 **909**

Decoration and ornament; Metalwork; Sculpture

Brook, Peter
The empty space 792

Brookhiser, Richard
Alexander Hamilton, American 92
America's first dynasty 973.4
Founding father: rediscovering George Washington 92
Right time, right place 92
What would the Founders do? 320

BROOKLYN (NEW YORK, N.Y.)
Anasi, R. The last bohemia 974.7

BROOKLYN (NEW YORK, N.Y.)—SOCIAL CONDITIONS
Salamon, J. Facing the wind 364.15

Brookover, Sophie
Pop goes the library 021.2

Brooks, Christopher Antonio
(ed) The African American almanac 305.8

Brooks, David
The social animal 305.5

Brooks, F. Erik
Starks, G. L. How your government really works 320.4

Brooks, Geraldine
Nine parts of desire 305.48

Brooks, Gwendolyn
The essential Gwendolyn Brooks 811
In Montgomery, and other poems 811

Brooks, M.
13 things that don't make sense 500

Brooks, Robert B.
Raising resilient children 649

Brooks, Rodney Allen
Flesh and machines 629.8

Brooks, Tim
The complete directory to prime time network and cable TV shows, 1946-present 791.45

Brosens, Koenraad
European tapestries in the Art Institute of Chicago 746.3

The **brother** gardeners. Wulf, A. 635
Brother, I'm dying. Danticat, E. 92

BROTHERS
See also Men; Siblings
Gigante, D. The Keats brothers 920
Louvin, C. Satan is real 920

BROTHERS AND SISTERS *See* Siblings
Brothers, rivals, victors. Jordan, J. W. 940.54

Brothers, Thomas David
Armstrong, L. Louis Armstrong, in his own words 781.65

Brott, Armin A.
The expectant father 649
Brought to light. 779

Broven, John
Record makers and breakers 781.64

Brower, Sam
Prophet's prey 306.8

Brower, Steven
Breathless homicidal slime mutants 741.6

Brown, Alan
Haunted Georgia 133.1
Haunted Kentucky 133.1
Haunted South Carolina 133.1
Haunted Tennessee 133.1
Haunted Texas 133.1

Brown, Archie
The rise and fall of communism 320.5

Brown, Bobbi
Bobbi Brown beauty evolution 646.7

Brown, Brandon P.
(ed) Magill's medical guide 610

Brown, Carolyn
Chance and circumstance 92

Brown, Claude
Manchild in the promised land 92

Brown, Cynthia Stokes
A big history 909

Brown, Daniel
The indifferent stars above 92
Under a flaming sky 634.9

Brown, David Alan
Leonardo da Vinci 759

Brown, David E.
Inventing modern America 609

Brown, Dee Alexander
The American West 978
Bury my heart at Wounded Knee 970.004

Brown, Elaine
The condemnation of Little B 364.15

Brown, Ethan
Shake the devil off 364.152

Brown, Frederick
Flaubert 92
For the soul of France 944.081

Brown, Ian, 1954-
The boy in the moon 618.92

Brown, James
James Brown, the godfather of soul 92
The Los Angeles diaries 92

Brown, John Russell
(ed) The Oxford illustrated history of theatre 792.09

Brown, Jonathan C.
A brief history of Argentina 982

Brown, Judith M.
Nehru: a political life 92

Brown, Lesley
(ed) Shorter Oxford English dictionary on historical principles 423

Brown, Malcolm

M. **332.6**

Bull's-eye: unraveling the medical mystery of Lyme disease. Edlow, J. A. **616.9**

Bull, John L.
The National Audubon Society field guide to North American birds, Eastern region **598**

Bull, Lorena Novak
Ong, J. S. The everything guide to macrobiotics **641.5**

Bullard, Sara
Teaching tolerance **649**

Bullard, Thomas E.
The myth and mystery of UFOs **001.9**

Bulletproof feathers. **570.1**

BULLFIGHTERS
Lewine, E. Death and the sun **791.8**

BULLFIGHTS
See also Sports
Hemingway, E. The dangerous summer **791.8**
Hemingway, E. Death in the afternoon **791.8**
Lewine, E. Death and the sun **791.8**

BULLFIGHTS—SPAIN
Lewine, E. Death and the sun **791.8**

BULLIES
See also Aggressiveness (Psychology)

Bulliet, Richard W.
(ed) The Columbia history of the 20th century **909.82**

Bullock, Alan
Hitler and Stalin **92**

Bullock-Prado, Gesine
Confections of a closet master baker **92**

Bully for brontosaurus. Gould, S. J. **508**

Bumiller, Elisabeth
May you be the mother of a hundred sons **305.409**

Bungalow style. Crochet, T. **747**

BUNKER HILL (BOSTON, MASS.), BATTLE OF, 1775
See also Battles; United States—History—1775-1783, Revolution—Campaigns
Lockhart, P. D. The whites of their eyes **973.3**
Nelson, J. L. With fire & sword **973.3**

Bunker, Nick
Making haste from Babylon **974.4**

Bunson, Margaret R.
Encyclopedia of ancient Egypt **932**

Bunson, Matthew
Encyclopedia of the Roman Empire **937**
(ed) Catholic Almanac, 2008 **282**

Bunting, Basil
Complete poems **821**

Bunting, Josiah
Ulysses S. Grant **92**

Buonomano, Dean
Brain bugs **612.8**

Burana, Lily

I love a man in uniform **92**

Burch, Mary R.
Citizen canine **636.7**

Burchfield, R. W.
Fowler, H. W. Fowler's modern English usage **428**

Burck, Charles
Bossidy, L. A. Execution: the discipline of getting things done **658.4**

Burckhardt, Jacob
The Greeks and Greek civilization **938**
About
Burckhardt, J. The Greeks and Greek civilization **938**

Burd-Sharps, Sarah
The measure of America **306**

Burdick, Alan
Out of Eden **577**

The **bureau** and the mole. Vise, D. A. **327.12**

BUREAUCRACY
See also Political science; Public administration
Chandrasekaran, R. Little America **958.104**

Burfoot, Amby
(ed) Runner's world complete book of running **796.42**

Burg, David F.
Almanac of World War I **940.3**

Burger, Joanna
Birds: a visual guide **598**

Burgess, Colin
French, F. In the shadow of the moon **629.45**

Burgess, Michael
Reference guide to science fiction, fantasy, and horror **016**

Burgin, R. V.
Islands of the damned **940.54**

BURGLARS *See* Thieves

BURGLARY PROTECTION
See also Crime prevention

Burhans, Dirk E.
Crunch! **338.4**

BURIAL
See also Archeology; Public health
Kammen, M. G. Digging up the dead **393**

BURIAL—HISTORY
Faust, D. G. This republic of suffering **973.7**

BURIAL—UNITED STATES
Kammen, M. G. Digging up the dead **393**
The **burial** at Thebes. Heaney, S. **822**

BURIAL CUSTOMS *See* Burial

Burial for a King. Burns, R. **92**

BURIAL STATISTICS *See* Mortality; Registers of births, etc.; Vital statistics

The **buried** book. Damrosch, D. **809**

BURIED CITIES *See* Extinct cities

BURIED TREASURE

Moss, R. W. Strauss's handbook of business information **650**

BUSINESS INTELLIGENCE

Javers, E. Broker, trader, lawyer, spy **364.1**

BUSINESS LAW *See* Commercial law

BUSINESS LETTERS

Lindsell-Roberts, S. Strategic business letters and e-mail **651.7**

Phillips, E. H. Shocked, appalled, and dismayed! **651.7**

BUSINESS MANAGEMENT *See* Management

BUSINESS MANAGERS

McCourt, A. A long stone's throw **92**

BUSINESS MATHEMATICS

See also Mathematics

BUSINESS MORTALITY *See* Bankruptcy; Business failures

BUSINESS ORGANIZATIONS *See* Business enterprises

BUSINESS PEOPLE *See* Businesspeople

Business periodicals index. **650**

BUSINESS PLANNING

McKeever, M. P. How to write a business plan **658.1**

Pinson, L. Anatomy of a business plan **658.4**

The power of habit **158.1**

Business: the ultimate resource. **658**

BUSINESSES *See* Business enterprises

BUSINESSMEN

See also Businesspeople

Cohen, R. The fish that ate the whale **338.7**

Kurlansky, M. Birdseye **338.7**

Rathbone, J. P. The sugar king of Havana **92**

Renehan, E. J. Commodore **92**

Stiles, T. J. The first tycoon **92**

Walton, S. Sam Walton, made in America **92**

Wolff, M. The man who owns the news **92**

BUSINESSMEN—NEW YORK (N.Y.)—HISTORY—20TH CENTURY

Beard, P. After the ball **368.32**

BUSINESSMEN—UNITED STATES—BIOGRAPHY

Kurlansky, M. Birdseye **338.7**

Lewis, M. The new new thing **338.4**

BUSINESSPEOPLE

See also Business

Carey, C. W. American inventors, entrepreneurs & business visionaries **920**

Fenn, D. Alpha dogs **658**

Gup, T. A secret gift **977.1**

Keefe, P. R. The snakehead **364.1**

Parrado, N. Miracle in the Andes **982**

Strouse, J. Morgan **92**

BUSINESSPEOPLE—UNITED STATES—BIOGRAPHY

Isaacson, W. Steve Jobs **621.39**

BUSINESSWOMEN

See also Businesspeople; Women

Bacon, L. The boss of you **658**

Lemmon, G. T. The dressmaker of Khair Khana **92**

Levinson, D. J. The seasons of a woman's life **155.6**

BUSINESSWOMEN—ENCYCLOPEDIAS

Krismann, C. Encyclopedia of American women in business **920.003**

BUSING (SCHOOL INTEGRATION)

See also School children—Transportation; School integration

Lukas, J. A. Common ground **305.8**

Masur, L. P. The soiling of Old Glory **974.4**

BUSING FOR SCHOOL INTEGRATION—MASSACHUSETTS—BOSTON—HISTORY

Masur, L. P. The soiling of Old Glory **974.4**

Buskin, Richard

Diller, P. Like a lampshade in a whorehouse **92**

Buss, David M.

The murderer next door **364.152**

Buss, Katharina

Big book of knitting **746.43**

Bussagli, Marco

Angels **704.9**

Busted. Andrews, E. L. **332.7**

Buster Keaton. Meade, M. **92**

Buster Keaton remembered. Keaton, E. **791.43**

The **busy** family's guide to volunteering. Friedman, J. L. **302**

But dad! Gross, G. **306.874**

The **butcher's** tale. Smith, H. W. **305.892**

Butcher, Carmen Acevedo

Man of blessing **271**

Butcher, Tim

Chasing the Devil **916**

Butler's Lives of the saints. **920.003**

Butler, Alban

Butler's Lives of the saints **920.003**

Butler, Colin

The practical Shakespeare **822.3**

Butler, Jon

Religion in American life **200.9**

Butler, Rebecca P.

Copyright for teachers & librarians in the 21st century **346**

Butler, Robert Olen

From where you dream **808.3**

Butler, Rosa Johnson

Gillespie, M. A. Maya Angelou **92**

Butler, Susan

East to the dawn **629.13**

BUTTER

See also Dairy products

Butterfield, Fox

All God's children **364.1**

BUTTERFLIES

See also Insects

The **Cambridge** history of Italian literature.   **850**
The **Cambridge** history of Judaism.   **296**
The **Cambridge** history of Judaism.   **296.09**
The **Cambridge** history of Judaism.   **296**
The **Cambridge** history of Latin America.   **980**
The **Cambridge** history of Latin American literature. Gonzalez Echevarria, R.   **860**
The **Cambridge** history of Russian literature. **891.7**
The **Cambridge** history of Spanish literature.   **860**
The **Cambridge** illustrated dictionary of natural history. Lincoln, R. J.   **508**
Cambridge illustrated history [series]
 The Cambridge illustrated history of religions **200.9**
 The Cambridge illustrated history of the Islamic world   **909**
 The Cambridge illustrated history of the Roman world   **937**
The **Cambridge** illustrated history of medicine. **610**
The **Cambridge** illustrated history of religions. **200.9**
The **Cambridge** illustrated history of the British Empire.   **941.08**
The **Cambridge** illustrated history of the Islamic world.   **909**
The **Cambridge** illustrated history of the Roman world.   **937**
The **Cambridge** introduction to modern British fiction, 1950-2000. Head, D.   **823**
The **Cambridge** star atlas. Tirion, W.   **523.8**
Cambridge texts in the history of political thought [series]
 Plato The republic   **888**
The **Cambridge** thesaurus of American English. Lutz, W.   **423**
The **Cambridge** world history of food.   **641.3**
CAMELS
 See also Desert animals; Mammals
CAMERAS
 See also Photography; Photography—Equipment and supplies
Cameron, Angus
 The L.L. Bean game and fish cookbook   **641.6**
Camfield, Gregg
 (ed) The Oxford companion to Mark Twain   **818**
Camoes, Luis de
 Selected sonnets   **869**
CAMORRA—HISTORY
 Saviano, R. Gomorrah   **364.1**
CAMOUFLAGE (BIOLOGY)
 See also Animal defenses
 Forbes, P. Dazzled and deceived   **578.4**
CAMOUFLAGE (MILITARY SCIENCE)
 See also Military art and science; Naval art and science
CAMP COOKING *See* Outdoor cooking
Camp, Jim
 Start with no   **658.4**

Campaign and election reform. Henderson, H. **324.6**
CAMPAIGN FUNDS
 See also Elections; Politics
CAMPAIGN FUNDS—LAW AND LEGISLATION—UNITED STATES
 Henderson, H. Campaign and election reform **324.6**
CAMPAIGN FUNDS—UNITED STATES
 Drew, E. The corruption of American politics **364.1**
 Henderson, H. Campaign and election reform **324.6**
CAMPAIGN LITERATURE
 See also Literature; Politics
CAMPAIGNS, POLITICAL *See* Politics
Campbell, Amy
 Beaser, R. S. The Joslin guide to diabetes   **616.4**
Campbell, David E.
 American grace   **201**
Campbell, Don G.
 The Mozart effect   **615.8**
Campbell, Donovan
 Joker one   **956.7**
Campbell, Gordon
 John Milton   **92**
Campbell, Greg
 Selby, S. A. Flawless   **364.1**
Campbell, James T.
 Middle passages   **916**
Campbell, Jeremy
 The liar's tale   **177**
Campbell, Jonathan
 The venomous reptiles of the Western Hemisphere   **597.96**
Campbell, Joseph
 Creative mythology   **201**
 Occidental mythology   **201**
 Oriental mythology   **201**
 The power of myth   **201**
 Primitive mythology   **201**
Campbell, Julieann
 Setting the truth free   **941.6**
Campbell, Keith
 Wilmut, I. The second creation   **174**
Campbell, Susan
 Nelson, G. Beyond Earth Day   **333.72**
Campbell, W. Joseph
 Getting it wrong   **071**
Campbell-Kelly, Martin
 From airline reservations to Sonic the Hedgehog   **005**
CAMPING
 Callan, K. The happy camper   **796.54**
Campo, Juan Eduardo
 Encyclopedia of Islam   **297**
CAMPS
 See also Recreation
CAMPS—DIRECTORIES
 Guide to summer camps and summer schools

See also Biochemistry; Nutrition
Steward, H. L. The new sugar busters! **613.2**

CARBOLIC ACID
See also Acids; Chemicals

CARBON
See also Chemical elements
Berners-Lee, M. How bad are bananas? **363.7**
Roston, E. The carbon age **577**

CARBON 14 DATING *See* Radiocarbon dating
The **carbon** age. Roston, E. **577**

CARBON DIOXIDE GREENHOUSE EFFECT
See Global warming

CARCINOMA *See* Cancer

CARD GAMES
See also Games
Bellin, A. Poker nation **795.4**
Hoyle, E. Hoyle's rules of games **795.4**
Scarne, J. Scarne's encyclopedia of card games **795.4**

CARD TRICKS
See also Card games; Magic tricks; Tricks
Carde, Ring T.
Encyclopedia of insects **595.7**
Cardello, Hank
Stuffed **616.3**
Cardenal, Ernesto
Pluriverse **861**

CARDIAC DISEASES *See* Heart diseases

CARDIAC RESUSCITATION
See also Emergency medicine
Gupta, S. Cheating death **616.02**

CARDIFF GIANT
Tribble, S. A colossal hoax **974.7**

CARDIOVASCULAR SYSTEM
See also Anatomy; Physiology

CARDS, GREETING *See* Greeting cards
Carduff, Christopher
(ed) Higher gossip **818**

CARE GIVERS *See* Caregivers

CARE OF CHILDREN *See* Child care

CARE OF THE DYING *See* Terminal care

CAREER CHANGES
See also Age and employment; Vocational guidance
Martini, K. Thank you for firing me! **650.14**
Wendleton, K. Building a great resume **650.14**
Career comeback. Richardson, B. G. **650.14**
CAREER COUNSELING *See* Vocational guidance
CAREER DEVELOPMENT *See* Personnel management; Vocational guidance
Career development series
Brestoff, R. The actor's wheel of connection **792**
CAREER GUIDANCE *See* Vocational guidance
CAREERS *See* Occupations; Professions; Vocational guidance

CAREGIVERS
See also Volunteer work
Caregiving: a step-by-step resource for caring for the person with cancer at home **649.8**
Carnot, E. J. Is your parent in good hands? **362.6**
Carter, R. Helping yourself help others **649.8**
Coste, J. K. Learning to speak Alzheimer's **362.1**
Federico, M. Welcome to the departure lounge **92**
Gillies, A. Keeper **616.8**
James, V. E. The Alzheimer's advisor **344**
Kessler, L. Dancing with Rose **362.1**
Kuhn, D. Alzheimer's early stages **616.8**
McFarlane, R. The complete bedside companion **649.8**
Phillips, K. J. The moon in the water **306.8**
Silver, M. Breast cancer husband **616.99**
Twelve breaths a minute **616**

CAREGIVERS—LAW AND LEGISLATION—UNITED STATES
Carnot, E. J. Is your parent in good hands? **362.6**

CAREGIVERS—POPULAR WORKS
Coste, J. K. Learning to speak Alzheimer's **362.1**
Caregiving: a step-by-step resource for caring for the person with cancer at home. **649.8**
Careless love: the unmaking of Elvis Presley. Guralnick, P. **92**
Carey, Charles W.
American inventors, entrepreneurs & business visionaries **920**
Carey, Jacqui
Japanese braiding **746.2**
Carey, Sarah
Stewart, M. Martha Stewart's cooking school **641.5**
Cargas, Harry J.
Wiesenthal, S. The sunflower **179.7**
CARIBBEAN ART—ENCYCLOPEDIAS
Encyclopedia of Latin American & Caribbean art **709**
CARICATURES AND CARTOONS *See* Cartoons and caricatures
Caring for a child with autism. Ives, M. **618.92**
Caring for your parents. Delehanty, H. **362.6**
Caring for your school-age child. **649**
Carl Sagan. Davidson, K. **520**
Carl, Deborah Ann
Bentley, E. P. Directory of family associations **929**
Carleton Watkins: the complete mammoth photographs. Watkins, C. E. **778.9**
Carley, Michael Jabara
1939 **940.53**
Carlin, George
Napalm & silly putty **817**
Carlin, John
Playing the enemy **968.06**
(ed) Masters of American comics **741.5**
Carlin, Richard

Carroll, David L.
Zugibe, F. T. Dissecting death   614
Carroll, Diahann
The legs are the last to go   92
Carroll, James
Constantine's sword   261.2
House of war   355
Jerusalem, Jerusalem   956.94
Practicing Catholic   92
Toward a new Catholic Church   282
Carroll, Rebecca
(ed) Uncle Tom or new Negro   370
Carroll, Robert P.
Bible   The Bible: Authorized King James Version   220.5
Carroll, Sean B.
Endless forms most beautiful   571.8
The making of the fittest   572.8
Remarkable creatures   508
Carroll, Sean M.
From eternity to here   530.1
Carruth, Hayden
Toward the distant islands   811
Carruthers, Gerard
(ed) Burns, R. Burns   821
Carry me home. McWhorter, D.   976.1
CARS (AUTOMOBILES) *See* Automobiles
Carson McCullers. Savigneau, J.   813
Carson, Anne
Carson, A. Nox   811
Autobiography of red   811
The beauty of the husband   811
Decreation   818
Men in the off hours   811
(tr) Sappho If not, winter   884
Carson, Anne, 1950-
Nox   811
Carson, Clayborne
Malcolm X: the FBI file   92
(ed) The Eyes on the prize civil rights reader 323.1
(ed) King, M. L. The autobiography of Martin Luther King, Jr   323
Carson, Rachel, 1907-1964
Carson, R. Silent spring   363.7
The edge of the sea   577.7
Lost woods   570
The sea around us   551.46
Under the sea wind   578.7
Carson, Rob
Mount St. Helens: the eruption and recovery of a volcano   551.2
Carson, Susannah
(ed) A truth universally acknowledged   823
Carter, Alice A.
The Red Rose girls   759.13
Carter, David

(ed) Spontaneous mind   811
Carter, Graydon
Vanity Fair, the portraits   779
Carter, Gregg Lee
(ed) Guns in American society   363.33
Carter, Jimmy, 1924- (American president)
Carter, J. White House diary   92
Everything to gain   92
An hour before daylight   973.926
Keeping faith: memoirs of a president   92
Living faith   248.4
Our endangered values   306
Sharing good times   92
Sources of strength   248.4
The virtues of aging   305.26
Carter, Jimmy

About
Carter, J. An hour before daylight   973.926
Carter, J. Living faith   248.4
Morris, K. E.   Jimmy Carter, American moralist   973.926
Carter, Miranda
Anthony Blunt: his lives   92
George, Nicholas, and Wilhelm   940.3
Carter, Rita
Exploring consciousness   153
The human brain book   612.8
Carter, Robert A.
Buffalo Bill Cody   978
Carter, Rosalynn
Carter, J. Everything to gain   92
Helping someone with mental illness   616.89
Helping yourself help others   649.8
Carter, Stephen L.
Integrity   170
Carter, Susan B.
(ed) Historical statistics of the United States   317
Carter, Thomas L.
Evans, G. E. Introduction to library public services   025.5
Carter, William C.
Marcel Proust   843
CARTHAGE (EXTINCT CITY)
See also Extinct cities
Cartledge, Paul
Ancient Greece   938
CARTOGRAPHERS
Lester, T. The fourth part of the world   912
Cartographies of time. Grafton, A.   902
CARTOGRAPHY *See* Map drawing; Maps
CARTOGRAPHY—HISTORY
Lester, T. The fourth part of the world   912
Cartooning. Brunetti, I.   741.5
CARTOONING
See also Cartoons and caricatures; Wit and humor

Chadwick, Henry
   (ed) Augustine Confessions   242
Chadwick, Ruth F.
   (ed) Encyclopedia of applied ethics   170
Chafe, William Henry
   (ed) Remembering Jim Crow   305.896
Chagall. Wullschlager, J.   92
Chaikin, Andrew
   Air and space   629.13
   A man on the moon   629.45
Chain of command. Hersh, S. M.   973.931
CHAIN STORES
   See also Retail trade; Stores
   Mitchell, S. Big-box swindle   381
CHAIR CANING
   See also Handicraft
CHAIRS
   See also Furniture
CHAKRAS
   See also Yoga
CHALK TALKS
   See also Public speaking
Chalker, Sylvia
   The Oxford dictionary of English grammar   428
Chalker-Scott, Linda
   The informed gardener   635
Challenger, Melanie
   (ed) Stolen voices   920
Chalmers, David Mark
   Hooded Americanism: the history of the Ku Klux Klan   322.4
CHAMBER MUSIC
   See also Instrumental music; Music
CHAMBERS OF COMMERCE
   See also Commerce
Chambers, Diane P.
   Communicating in sign   419
Chambers, John Whiteclay
   (ed) The Oxford companion to American military history   355.009
Chambers, Whittaker
   Witness   92
The **chameleon** couch. Komunyakaa, Y.   811
Chametzky, Jules
   (ed) Jewish American literature   810
Champlain's dream. Fischer, D. H.   92
The **Chan's** great continent. Spence, J. D.   951
CHAN, CHARLIE (FICTIONAL CHARACTER)
   Yunte Huang Charlie Chan   92
CHAN, CHARLIE (FICTITIOUS CHARAC-TER)
   Yunte Huang Charlie Chan   92
Chan, Ronald W.
   Behind the Berkshire Hathaway curtain   658.4
Chan, Simon
   (ed) Zondervan dictionary of Christian spiritual-

ity   248
CHANCE
   Aczel, A. D. Chance: a guide to gambling, love, the stock market & just about everything else   519.2
   Dolnick, B. Luck   130
   Mlodinow, L. The Drunkard's walk   519.2
   Rosenthal, J. Struck by lightning   519.2
Chance and circumstance. Brown, C.   92
Chance: a guide to gambling, love, the stock market & just about everything else. Aczel, A. D.   519.2
Chancellorsville. Sears, S. W.   973.7
CHANCELLORSVILLE (VA.), BATTLE OF, 1863
   Furgurson, E. B. Chancellorsville, 1863   973.7
   Sears, S. W. Chancellorsville   973.7
Chancellorsville, 1863. Furgurson, E. B.   973.7
Chandler, Charlotte
   It's only a movie   92
Chandrasekaran, Rajiv
   Imperial life in the emerald city   956.704
   Little America   958.104
CHANEL NO. 5 PERFUME
   Mazzeo, T. J. The secret of Chanel No. 5   338.7
Chang, Andrew C.
   (comp) Cheng & Tsui English-Chinese lexicon of business terms with pinyin   495.1
Chang, David
   Momofuku   641.5
Chang, Iris
   The Chinese in America   305.8
   The rape of Nanking   951.04
Chang, Jeff
   Can't stop, won't stop   306
Chang, Jung
   Mao: the unknown story   92
   Wild swans   951.05
Chang, Leslie T.
   Factory girls   331.4
Chang, Tina
   (ed) Language for a new century   808.81
The **change.** Greer, G.   618.1
CHANGE
   See also Metaphysics
CHANGE (PSYCHOLOGY)
   See also Psychology
   Heath, C. Switch   303.4
   Lunden, J. Wake-up calls   155.2
   McGraw, P. C. Life strategies   158
   Michels, B. The tools   158
   The power of habit   158.1
   Weber, R. J. The created self   155.2
CHANGE OF LIFE IN WOMEN *See* Menopause
CHANGE OF SEX *See* Transsexualism
Change the culture, change the game. Connors, R.   658.4
Change your brain, change your life. Amen,

Garfield, S. Mauve **666**

Gordin, M. D. A well-ordered thing: Dmitrii Mendeleev and the shadow of the periodic table **92**

Guillen, M. Five equations that changed the world **530.1**

Hager, T. The alchemy of air **92**

Hamblyn, R. The invention of clouds **551.57**

Hirshfeld, A. The electric life of Michael Faraday **530**

Horvitz, L. A. Eureka!: scientific breakthroughs that changed the world **509**

Hunter, M. Boyle **92**

Johnson, S. The invention of air **92**

Levi, P. The periodic table **92**

Maddox, B. Rosalind Franklin: the dark lady of DNA **92**

Malone, J. W. It doesn't take a rocket scientist **920**

Oakes, E. H. A to Z of chemists **920.003**

Pauling, L. C. Linus Pauling in his own words **081**

Quinn, S. Marie Curie **540**

Stern, J. Denial **92**

CHEMISTS—ENGLAND—BIOGRAPHY

Garfield, S. Mauve **666**

CHEMISTS—FRANCE

Dry, S. Curie **92**

CHEMISTS—POLAND

Dry, S. Curie **92**

Chen, Da

Colors of the mountain **92**

Sounds of the river **951.05**

Chen, Pauline W.

Final exam **92**

Cheney, Annie

Body brokers **617.9**

Cheng & Tsui English-Chinese lexicon of business terms with pinyin. **495.1**

Cheng, Linsun

(ed) Berkshire encyclopedia of China **951**

Cheng, Nien

Life and death in Shanghai **92**

Chermak, Steven M.

(ed) Famous American crimes and trials **364**

Chernow, Ron

Alexander Hamilton **92**

Titan: the life of John D. Rockefeller, Sr. **92**

The Warburgs **920**

Washington **92**

CHEROKEE INDIANS

Mankiller, W. Mankiller: a chief and her people **92**

McLoughlin, W. G. After the Trail of Tears **970.004**

CHEROKEE INDIANS—GOVERNMENT RELATIONS

McLoughlin, W. G. After the Trail of Tears **970.004**

CHEROKEE INDIANS—HISTORY

McLoughlin, W. G. After the Trail of Tears **970.004**

CHEROKEE INDIANS—POLITICS AND GOVERNMENT

McLoughlin, W. G. After the Trail of Tears **970.004**

CHERRY MINE DISASTER, CHERRY, ILL., 1909

Tintori, K. Trapped: the 1909 Cherry Mine disaster **973.9**

Chesler, Phyllis

The new anti-semitism **305.8**

CHESS

See also Board games

Brady, F. Endgame **92**

Capablanca, J. R. Chess fundamentals **794.1**

Fischer, B. Bobby Fischer teaches chess **794.1**

Hallman, J. C. The chess artist **794.1**

United States Chess Federation U.S. Chess Federation's official rules of chess **794.1**

CHESS—RULES

United States Chess Federation U.S. Chess Federation's official rules of chess **794.1**

The **chess** artist. Hallman, J. C. **794.1**

Chess fundamentals. Capablanca, J. R. **794.1**

CHESS PLAYERS

Brady, F. Endgame **92**

Chester Himes. Sallis, J. **813**

Chesterman, Charles W.

The Audubon Society field guide to North American rocks and minerals **549**

CHESTS

See also Furniture

Chetham, Deirdre

Before the deluge **951**

Chetwynd, Josh

The secret history of balls **796.3**

Chevallier, Andrew

Encyclopedia of herbal medicine **615**

Chevannes, Barry

Rastafari: roots and ideology **299.6**

Chewy gooey crispy crunchy melt-in-your-mouth cookies. Medrich, A. **641.8**

CHEYENNE INDIANS

Brown, D. A. The American West **978**

Chic simple [series]

Gross, K. J. Woman's face **646.7**

Chic sweats. Webber, C. **746.9**

Chicago. Pacyga, D. A. **977.3**

CHICAGO (ILL.)—ANTIQUITIES

See also Antiquities

CHICAGO (ILL.)—BIOGRAPHY

See also Biography

CHICAGO (ILL.)—CLIMATE

See also Climate

CHICAGO (ILL.)—COMMERCE

See also Commerce

CHICAGO (ILL.)—DIRECTORIES

See also Directories

CHICAGO (ILL.)—ECONOMIC CONDITIONS

CHILD CUSTODY

See also Divorce mediation; Parent-child relationship

Woo, I. The great divorce   **92**

CHILD DEVELOPMENT

See also Children

Barnet, A. B. The youngest minds	**155.4**
Brazelton, T. B. The irreducible needs of chil-dren	**155.4**
Brazelton, T. B. To listen to a child	**155.4**
Brazelton, T. B. Touchpoints birth to 3	**649**
Brazelton, T. B. Touchpoints three to six	**305.231**
Bronson, P. Nurtureshock	**305.23**
Bruer, J. T. The myth of the first three years	**155.4**
Caring for your school-age child	**649**
Egan, A. Is it a big problem or a little problem?	**649**
Eliot, L. Pink brain, blue brain	**612.6**
Gopnik, A. The scientist in the crib	**155.4**
Karr-Morse, R. Scared sick	**155.9**
Konner, M. The evolution of childhood	**305.23**
Leach, P. Your baby & child	**649**
Levine, M. D. A mind at a time	**370.15**
Mayes, L. C. The Yale Child Study Center guide to understanding your child	**649**
Spock, B. Dr. Spock's the first two years	**649**
Spock, B. Dr. Spock's the school years	**649**

A **child** is born. Nilsson, L.   **612.6**

CHILD LABOR

See also Age and employment; Child welfare;
Labor; Social problems

Levine, M. J. Children for hire   **331.3**

CHILD LABOR—UNITED STATES

Levine, M. J. Children for hire   **331.3**

CHILD MARRIAGE

Ali, N. I am Nujood, age 10 and divorced   **92**

CHILD MOLESTING *See* Child sexual abuse

CHILD NEGLECT *See* Child abuse

CHILD PLACING *See* Adoption; Foster home care

CHILD PORNOGRAPHY

See also Pornography

CHILD PROSTITUTION *See* Juvenile prostitution

CHILD PSYCHIATRY

See also Psychiatry

Terr, L. Magical moments of change   **618.92**

CHILD PSYCHOLOGY

See also Psychology

Barnet, A. B. The youngest minds	**155.4**
Barrett, J. L. Born believers	**200.1**
Brazelton, T. B. The irreducible needs of chil-dren	**155.4**
Brazelton, T. B. To listen to a child	**155.4**
Brazelton, T. B. Touchpoints birth to 3	**649**
Brazelton, T. B. Touchpoints three to six	**305.231**
Bronson, P. Nurtureshock	**305.23**

Egan, A. Is it a big problem or a little problem?	**649**
Greenspan, S. I. The child with special needs	**362.1**
Karr-Morse, R. Scared sick	**155.9**
Kubler-Ross, E. On children and death	**155.9**
Louv, R. Last child in the woods	**155.4**
Papolos, D. F. The bipolar child	**618.92**
Piaget, J. The moral judgment of the child	**155.4**
Sears, W. Parenting the fussy baby and high-need child	**649**
Seligman, M. E. P. The optimistic child	**155.4**
Shapiro, L. E. How to raise a child with a high EQ	**649**
White, B. L. The new first three years of life	**155.4**
Young-Eisendrath, P. The self-esteem trap	**155.2**

CHILD PSYCHOLOGY—UNITED STATES

Greenspan, S. I. The child with special needs   **362.1**

CHILD RAISING *See* Child rearing

CHILD REARING

See also Child care; Child-adult relationship;
Parent-child relationship

Ames, L. B. Your eight-year-old	**649**
Ames, L. B. Your five-year-old	**649**
Ames, L. B. Your four-year-old	**649**
Ames, L. B. Your one-year-old	**649**
Ames, L. B. Your seven-year-old	**649**
Ames, L. B. Your six-year-old	**649**
Ames, L. B. Your two-year-old	**649**
Bailey, R. A. Easy to love, difficult to discipline	**155**
Barkley, R. A. Taking charge of ADHD	**618.92**
Barnet, A. B. The youngest minds	**155.4**
Brazelton, T. B. The irreducible needs of chil-dren	**155.4**
Brazelton, T. B. Touchpoints birth to 3	**649**
Brazelton, T. B. Touchpoints three to six	**305.231**
Bronson, P. Nurtureshock	**305.23**
Brooks, R. B. Raising resilient children	**649**
Caring for your school-age child	**649**
Deak, J. Girls will be girls	**649**
Deutsch, F. Halving it all	**649**
Edelman, M. W. The measure of our success	**170**
Elias, M. J. Emotionally intelligent parenting	**649**
Elman, N. M. The unwritten rules of friendship	**649**
Emswiler, M. A. Guiding your child through grief	**155.9**
Furedi, F. Paranoid parenting	**649**
Garbarino, J. Parents under siege	**649**
Garber, S. W. Monsters under the bed and other childhood fears	**649**
Hopgood How Eskimos keep their babies warm	**649**
Hulbert, A. Raising America	**649**
Ilg, F. L. Your three-year-old	**649**
Karp, H. The happiest baby on the block	**649**
Leach, P. The essential first year	**649**
Lederman, J. The ups and downs of raising a bipo-lar child	**618.92**
Mayes, L. C. The Yale Child Study Center guide to	

Jacobson, S. Anne Frank **92**

Jones, G. Killing monsters **302.23**

Konner, M. The evolution of childhood **305.23**

Kozol, J. Ordinary resurrections **305.23**

Kubler-Ross, E. On children and death **155.9**

Matthews, J. Bringing Adam home **364.1**

Ozick, C. Quarrel & quandary **814**

Prose, F. Anne Frank **839.3**

Schiller, L. Perfect murder, perfect town **364.15**

Summerscale, K. The suspicions of Mr. Whicher **364.152**

Toffler, A. Future shock **303.4**

CHILDREN—ABUSE See Child abuse

CHILDREN—ADOPTION See Adoption

CHILDREN—ANTHROPOMETRY

Konner, M. The evolution of childhood **305.23**

CHILDREN—BOOKS AND READING

See also Books and reading

Allyn, P. What to read when **028.5**

The Cambridge guide to children's books in English **028.5**

Marcus, L. S. Minders of make-believe **070.5**

CHILDREN—BOOKS AND READING—HISTORY

Marcus, L. S. Minders of make-believe **070.5**

CHILDREN—CARE See Child care

CHILDREN—CHARITIES, PROTECTION, ETC. See Child welfare

CHILDREN—CHINA

Xinran Message from an unknown Chinese mother **305.4**

CHILDREN—CIVIL RIGHTS

See also Civil rights

CHILDREN—CONDUCT OF LIFE

See also Conduct of life

CHILDREN—CRIMES AGAINST—COLORADO—BOULDER—CASE STUDIES

Schiller, L. Perfect murder, perfect town **364.15**

CHILDREN—CUSTODY See Child custody

CHILDREN—DEATH

See also Death

CHILDREN—DEVELOPMENT See Child development

CHILDREN—DISEASES

See also Diseases

Brown, I. The boy in the moon **618.92**

Cohen, S. Normal at any cost **618.92**

CHILDREN—DISEASES—ENCYCLOPEDIAS

The Gale encyclopedia of children's health **618.92**

CHILDREN—EDUCATION See Elementary education; Preschool education

CHILDREN—EMPLOYMENT See Child labor

CHILDREN—ENGLAND—HISTORY

Orme, N. Medieval children **305.23**

CHILDREN—EUROPE—HISTORY

Nicholas, L. H. Cruel world **940.53**

CHILDREN—EUROPE—HISTORY—20TH CENTURY

Nicholas, L. H. Cruel world **940.53**

CHILDREN—GROWTH

See also Child development

CHILDREN—HEALTH AND HYGIENE

See also Health; Hygiene

Brazelton, T. B. To listen to a child **155.4**

Diller, L. H. Running on Ritalin **618.92**

Ferber, R. Solve your child's sleep problems **618.92**

Martin, K. L. Does my child have a speech problem? **618.92**

Shabecoff, A. Poisoned profits **618.92**

CHILDREN—HEALTH AND HYGIENE—ENCYCLOPEDIAS

The Gale encyclopedia of children's health **618.92**

CHILDREN—HEALTH AND HYGIENE—UNITED STATES

Levine, M. J. Children for hire **331.3**

CHILDREN—HISTORY

Orme, N. Medieval children **305.23**

CHILDREN—INSTITUTIONAL CARE

See also Child welfare; Institutional care

Bartholet, E. Nobody's children **362.76**

CHILDREN—INSTITUTIONAL CARE—UNITED STATES

Bartholet, E. Nobody's children **362.76**

CHILDREN—INTELLIGENCE LEVELS

Barnet, A. B. The youngest minds **155.4**

CHILDREN—LANGUAGE

See also Language and languages

CHILDREN—MANAGEMENT See Child rearing

CHILDREN—MEDICAL CARE

Johnson, C. M. Your critically ill child **618.92**

CHILDREN—MENTAL HEALTH See Child psychiatry

CHILDREN—MOLESTING See Child sexual abuse

CHILDREN—NUTRITION

See also Children—Health and hygiene; Nutrition

Sears, W. The family nutrition book **613.2**

The Yale guide to children's nutrition **613.2**

CHILDREN—NUTRITION—POPULAR WORKS

Sears, W. The family nutrition book **613.2**

CHILDREN—PHYSICAL FITNESS

See also Children—Health and hygiene; Physical fitness

CHILDREN—PICTORIAL WORKS

Coles, R. When they were young **779**

CHILDREN—PLACING OUT See Adoption; Foster home care

CHILDREN—PSYCHOLOGY See Child psychology

Mumford, L. The culture of cities   **307.7**

CITY PLANNING—CITIZEN PARTICIPATION

    See also Political participation; Social action

CITY PLANNING—ROME

    McGregor, J. H. Rome from the ground up   **711**

CITY PLANNING—WASHINGTON (D.C.)— HISTORY—18TH CENTURY

    Bordewich, F. M. Washington: the making of the American capital   **975.3**

City room. Gelb, A.   **92**

CITY TRAFFIC

    Vanderbilt, T. Traffic   **629.28**

Ciuraru, Carmela

    (ed) Beat poets   **811**

    Nom de plume   **929.4**

CIVICS *See* Citizenship; Political science

CIVIL DEFENSE

    See also Military art and science

CIVIL DISOBEDIENCE

    See also Resistance to government

CIVIL DISORDERS *See* Riots

CIVIL ENGINEERING

    See also Engineering

    Petroski, H. Engineers of dreams   **624.2**

CIVIL ENGINEERING—HISTORY

    The Seventy wonders of the modern world   **720.9**

CIVIL ENGINEERS

    Brown, D. A. Bury my heart at Wounded Knee   **970.004**

    Hiltzik, M. A. Colossus   **627**

    Petroski, H. Engineers of dreams   **624.2**

    Winchester, S. The map that changed the world   **526**

CIVIL GOVERNMENT *See* Political science

CIVIL LIBERTY *See* Freedom

CIVIL PROCEDURE

    See also Courts

CIVIL RIGHTS

    See also Constitutional law; Human rights; Political science

Brands, H. W. The man who saved the union   **355.009**

Dershowitz, A. M. Preemption   **363.32**

Dershowitz, A. M. Rights from wrongs   **323**

Dickey, C. Securing the city   **363.32**

Ford, R. T. Rights gone wrong   **342**

Kenney, D. N. Asylum denied   **92**

Maddex, R. L. International encyclopedia of human rights   **323**

Marshall, T. Thurgood Marshall   **347**

Rehnquist, W. H. All the laws but one   **342**

Shipler, D. K. The rights of the people   **323**

CIVIL RIGHTS (INTERNATIONAL LAW) *See* Human rights

CIVIL RIGHTS—CONSTITUTIONAL HISTORY

Arsenault, R. Freedom riders   **323**

Colaiaco, J. A. Frederick Douglass and the Fourth

of July   **973.7**

CIVIL RIGHTS—ENCYCLOPEDIAS

Maddex, R. L. International encyclopedia of human rights   **323**

CIVIL RIGHTS—HISTORY

Grant, G. M. At the elbows of my elders   **920**

CIVIL RIGHTS—PUBLIC OPINION

Bawer, B. Surrender   **297**

CIVIL RIGHTS—UNITED STATES

Shipler, D. K. The rights of the people   **323**

CIVIL RIGHTS—UNITED STATES—HISTORY

Foner, E. The story of American freedom   **323.44**

CIVIL RIGHTS—UNITED STATES—HISTORY—19TH CENTURY

Rehnquist, W. H. All the laws but one   **342**

CIVIL RIGHTS—UNITED STATES—HISTORY—20TH CENTURY

Sullivan, P. Lift every voice   **323.1**

CIVIL RIGHTS ACTIVISTS

Abdul-Jabbar, K. Black profiles in courage   **920**

Baraka, I. A. The LeRoi Jones/Amiri Baraka reader   **818**

Branch, T. At Canaan's edge   **973.923**

Branch, T. Parting the waters: America in the King years, 1954-63   **973.921**

Branch, T. Pillar of fire   **323.1**

Brinkley, D. Rosa Parks   **323**

Burns, R. Burial for a King   **92**

Carson, C. Malcolm X: the FBI file   **92**

Cleaver, E. Target zero   **323**

Dyson, M. E. I may not get there with you: the true Martin Luther King, Jr   **323**

Ellison, R. The collected essays of Ralph Ellison   **814**

Evanzz, K. The messenger: the rise and fall of Elijah Muhammad   **297.8**

Evers, M. W. The autobiography of Medgar Evers: a hero's life and legacy revealed through his writings, letters, and speeches   **92**

Gardell, M. In the name of Elijah Muhammad   **297**

Gates, H. L. The future of the race   **305.896**

Giddings, P. Ida: a sword among lions   **92**

Halberstam, D. The children   **323.1**

Harlan, L. R. Booker T. Washington: the making of a black leader, 1856-1901   **92**

Harlan, L. R. Booker T. Washington: the wizard of Tuskegee, 1901-1915   **92**

Jackson, T. Becoming King   **92**

Joseph, P. E. Dark days, bright nights   **323.1**

Joseph, P. E. Waiting 'til the midnight hour   **323.1**

King, M. L. The autobiography of Martin Luther King, Jr   **323**

Kotz, N. Judgment days   **323**

Lewis, D. L. W.E.B. Du Bois   **92**

Malcolm X The autobiography of Malcolm X   **92**

Marable, M. Malcolm X   **92**

CLASSICAL LANGUAGES *See* Greek language; Latin language

CLASSICAL LITERATURE
    See also Literature

CLASSICAL LITERATURE—COLLECTIONS
The Norton book of classical literature   **880**
The Oxford book of classical verse in translation   **881**

CLASSICAL LITERATURE—DICTIONARIES
Grant, M. Greek and Latin authors, 800 B.C.-A.D. 1000   **920.003**
The Oxford companion to classical literature   **880**

CLASSICAL MUSIC *See* Music
Classical music 101. Plotkin, F.   **781.6**
Classical music in America. Horowitz, J.   **781.6**

CLASSICAL MUSICIANS
Eisler, B. Chopin's funeral   **92**
Ellison, R. The collected essays of Ralph Ellison   **814**
Lang, L. Journey of a thousand miles   **92**
Quasthoff, T. The voice   **92**
Schonberg, H. C. The great pianists   **920**
Wilson, E. Jacqueline du Pre   **787.4**

CLASSICAL MYTHOLOGY
    See also Mythology
Graves, R. The Greek myths   **292**
The Oxford dictionary of classical myth and religion   **292**

CLASSICAL MYTHOLOGY—CATALOGS
Reid, J. D. The Oxford guide to classical mythology in the arts, 1300-1990s   **700**

CLASSICAL MYTHOLOGY—DICTIONARIES
Impelluso, L. Gods and heroes in art   **700**
The Oxford dictionary of classical myth and religion   **292**

CLASSICAL POETRY—COLLECTIONS
The Oxford book of classical verse in translation   **881**
The **classical** style. Rosen, C.   **780.9**
Classical Turkish cooking. Algar, A. E.   **641.59**
The **classical** world. Lane Fox, R.   **938**

CLASSICISM
    See also Aesthetics; Literature

CLASSICISM IN ARCHITECTURE
    See also Architecture; Classicism

CLASSICISTS
Mendelsohn, D. The lost   **92**
Classics for pleasure. Dirda, M.   **814**
Classics of naval literature [series]
Morison, S. E. John Paul Jones   **92**

CLASSIFICATION OF SCIENCES
Tyson, N. D. G. The Pluto files   **523.4**

CLASSIFICATION, DEWEY DECIMAL *See* Dewey Decimal Classification

CLASSROOM MANAGEMENT
    See also School discipline; Teaching

Claude Monet, 1840-1926. Baillio, J.   **759**
Claude-Pierre, Peggy
The secret language of eating disorders   **616.85**
Clausen, Ruth Rogers
Dreamscaping   **712**
Clausen, Tammy Hennigh
Spratford, B. S. The horror readers' advisory **025.5**
Clauser, Henry R.
Brady, G. S. Materials handbook   **620.1**
Clausewitz, Carl von
On war   **355**
Clavin, Thomas
Roger Maris   **92**
Clawson, Calvin C.
Mathematical mysteries   **512.7**
Clawson, Dan
(ed) Required reading   **301**
CLAY
    See also Ceramics; Soils
Belcher, J. Polymer clay creative traditions **731.4**
Otterbein, K. Polymer clay 101   **738.1**
Pavelka, L. The complete book of polymer clay   **738.1**

CLAY MODELING *See* Modeling
Clay, Catrine
King, Kaiser, Tsar   **920**
Clayman, Charles B.
(ed) The Human body   **612**
CLEANING
    See also Sanitation
Consumer Reports how to clean and care for practically anything   **648**
Friedman, V. M. Field guide to stains   **648**
CLEANING COMPOUNDS
    See also Cleaning
CLEANLINESS
    See also Hygiene; Sanitation
A **clearing** in the distance: Frederick Law Olmsted and America in the nineteenth century. Rybczynski, W.   **712**
Clearing the bases. Barra, A.   **796.357**
Cleaver, Eldridge
Soul on ice   **305.8**
Target zero   **323**
Cleaver, Kathleen
(ed) Cleaver, E. Target zero   **323**
Clee, Nicholas
Eclipse   **798.4**
Cleland, Max
Heart of a patriot   **92**
CLEMENCY
    See also Administration of criminal justice; Executive power
Clemente. Maraniss, D.   **92**
Clendinnen, Inga
Dancing with strangers   **994**

Cohn, Lawrence

(ed) Nothing but the blues **781.643**

Cohn, Roy, 1927-1986 (American lawyer)

About

Kushner, T. Angels in America **812**

Cohn, Samuel K.

Herlihy, D. The black death and the transformation of the west **940.1**

Cohodas, Nadine

Princess Noire **92**

COIFFURE See Hair

Coile, D. Caroline

Encyclopedia of dog breeds **636.7**

COINAGE

See also Money

COINAGE OF WORDS See New words

COINS

See also Money

Cuhaj, G. S. 2012 standard catalog of world coins, 1901-2000 **737.4**

Yeoman, R. S. A guide book of United States coins **737.4**

Yeoman, R. S. Handbook of United States coins 2009 **737.4**

Cokinos, Christopher

The fallen sky **523.5**

Colaiaco, James A.

Frederick Douglass and the Fourth of July **973.7**

Colbert, David

(ed) Eyewitness to America **973**

Colby, Vineta

(ed) European authors, 1000-1900 **920.003**

(ed) World authors, 1975-1980 **920.003**

(ed) World authors, 1980-1985 **809**

(ed) World authors, 1985-1990 **809**

Cold. Streever, B. **998**

COLD

Streever, B. Cold **998**

COLD (DISEASE)

See also Communicable diseases; Diseases

Ackerman, J. Ah-choo! **616.2**

A cold case. Gourevitch, P. **364.1**

COLD HARBOR (VA.), BATTLE OF, 1864

Furgurson, E. B. Not war but murder **973.7**

COLD HARBOR, BATTLE OF, VA., 1864

Furgurson, E. B. Not war but murder **973.7**

The cold war. Ossip, K. **811**

The Cold War. Hillstrom, K. **909.82**

COLD WAR

Bizony, P. The man who ran the moon **629**

Brzezinski, M. Red moon rising **629.4**

Cadbury, D. Space race **629.4**

Carlson, P. K blows top **947.085**

Dallek, R. The lost peace **909.82**

FitzGerald, F. Way out there in the blue **973.927**

Foner, E. The story of American freedom **323.44**

Gaddis, J. L. George F. Kennan **327**

Gates, R. M. From the shadows **327**

Gregory, R. Cold War America, 1946 to 1990 **973.92**

Grose, P. Operation Rollback **327.12**

Hardesty, V. Epic rivalry **629.4**

Haynes, J. E. Spies **327.12**

Hillstrom, K. The Cold War **909.82**

Johnson, I. A mosque in Munich **297**

Kissinger, H. Diplomacy **327.2**

Kort, M. The Columbia guide to the Cold War **973.92**

Mann, J. The rebellion of Ronald Reagan **973.927**

Ratnesar, R. Tear down this wall **973.927**

Rhodes, R. Arsenals of folly **355**

Rhodes, R. Dark sun **623.4**

Schwartz, R. A. Cold War culture **973.92**

Sheehan, N. A fiery peace in a cold war **92**

Stafford, D. Spies beneath Berlin **327.12**

Taubman, P. Secret empire **327.12**

Theoharis, A. G. Abuse of power **363.325**

Thompson, N. The hawk and the dove **92**

Wheen, F. Strange days indeed **973.92**

COLD WAR—DIPLOMATIC HISTORY

Gaddis, J. L. George F. Kennan **327**

COLD WAR—ENCYCLOPEDIAS

Encyclopedia of the Cold War **909.82**

COLD WAR—SOCIAL ASPECTS—UNITED STATES

Gregory, R. Cold War America, 1946 to 1990 **973.92**

COLD WAR—SOURCES

Hillstrom, K. The Cold War **909.82**

Cold War America [series]

Schwartz, R. A. Cold War culture **973.92**

Cold War America, 1946 to 1990. Gregory, R. **973.92**

Cold War culture. Schwartz, R. A. **973.92**

The coldest March. Solomon, S. **919**

The coldest war. Brady, J. **951.9**

The coldest winter. Halberstam, D. **951.9**

Cole Porter. McBrien, W. **782.1**

Cole, Henri

Middle earth **811**

Cole, K. C.

First you build a cloud **530**

The hole in the universe **530.01**

Mind over matter **500**

Something incredibly wonderful happens **92**

Cole, Natalie

Angel on my shoulder **92**

Cole, Peter

Sacred trash **296.09**

Cole, Trevor

(ed) American Horticultural Society encyclopedia of plants and flowers **635.9**

Cole, Tyson

The **collected** poems of James Merrill. Merrill, J. **811**

The **collected** poems of Jean Toomer. Toomer, J. **811**

The **collected** poems of John Ciardi. Ciardi, J. **811**

The **collected** poems of Kathleen Raine. Raine, K. **821**

The **collected** poems of Kenneth Koch. Koch, K. **811**

The **collected** poems of Octavio Paz, 1957-1987. Paz, O. **861**

The **collected** poems of Odysseus Elytis. Elytes, O. **889**

The **collected** poems of Paul Blackburn. Blackburn, P. **811**

The **collected** poems of Philip Whalen. Whalen, P. **811**

The **collected** poems of Robert Creeley. Creeley, R. **811**

The **collected** poems of Robert Penn Warren. **811**

The **collected** poems of Ted Berrigan. Poems/Selections **811**

The **collected** poems of Tennessee Williams. Williams, T. **811**

The **collected** poems of Theodore Roethke. Roethke, T. **811**

The **collected** poems of W.B. Yeats. Yeats, W. B. **821**

The **collected** poems of William Carlos Williams. Williams, W. C. **811**

Collected poems, 1909-1962. Eliot, T. S. **811**

Collected poems, 1912-1944. **811**

Collected poems, 1917-1982. MacLeish, A. **811**

Collected poems, 1920-1954. Montale, E. **851**

Collected poems, 1937-1971. Berryman, J. **811**

Collected poems, 1943-2004. Wilbur, R. **811**

Collected poems, 1945-1990. Howes, B. **811**

Collected poems, 1947-1997. Ginsberg, A. **811**

Collected poems, 1948-1984. Walcott, D. **811**

Collected poems, 1953-1993. Updike, J. **811**

The **collected** poems, 1956-1998. Herbert, Z. **891.8**

Collected poems, 1957-1982. Berry, W. **811**

Collected poems, prose, & plays. Frost, R. **811**

Collected poetry and prose. Stevens, W. **811**

The **collected** poetry of Nikki Giovanni, 1968-1998. Giovanni, N. **811**

The **collected** poetry of Robinson Jeffers. Jeffers, R. **811**

The **collected** prose. Bishop, E. **818**

Collected works. Niedecker, L. **811**

The **collected** works. Gibran, K. **818**

Collected works [series]
  Wilson, L. The Talley trilogy **812**

COLLECTIBLE CARD GAMES
  See also Card games

COLLECTIBLES

See also Collectors and collecting

COLLECTIBLES—UNITED STATES
  Prisant, C. Antiques roadshow primer **745.1**

COLLECTING *See* Collectors and collecting

COLLECTING OF ACCOUNTS
  See also Commercial law; Credit; Debt; Debtor and creditor

COLLECTION DEVELOPMENT
  Kovacs, D. K. The Kovacs guide to electronic library collection development **025**
  Slote, S. J. Weeding library collections **025.2**

COLLECTIONS OF ART, PAINTING, ETC. *See* Art collections; Art museums

COLLECTIONS OF OBJECTS *See* Collectors and collecting

COLLECTIVE BARGAINING
  See also Industrial relations; Labor; Labor disputes; Negotiation

COLLECTIVE IDENTITY *See* Group identity

COLLECTIVE MEMORY—GERMANY
  Fritzsche, P. Life and death in the Third Reich **943.086**

COLLECTIVE MEMORY—JAPAN—HISTORY—20TH CENTURY
  Dower, J. W. Ways of forgetting, ways of remembering **940.53**

COLLECTIVE SECURITY *See* International security

COLLECTIVE SETTLEMENTS
  See also Communism; Cooperation; Socialism

COLLECTIVISM
  See also Economics; Political science

COLLECTORS
  Singer, M. Character studies **920**
  Tingey, J. The Englishman who posted himself and other curious objects **92**

COLLECTORS AND COLLECTING
  See also Antiques; Art; Hobbies
  Frost, R. O. Stuff **616.85**
  Jamieson, D. Mint condition **796.357**
  Jasanoff, M. Edge of empire **909.08**

COLLECTORS AND COLLECTING—HISTORY
  Jasanoff, M. Edge of empire **909.08**

COLLECTS *See* Prayers

COLLEGE ADMINISTRATORS
  Rice, C. Extraordinary, ordinary people **92**
  Roosevelt, C. Too close to the sun **92**

COLLEGE ADMISSIONS ESSAYS *See* College applications

COLLEGE AND SCHOOL DRAMA
  See also Amateur theater; Drama; Student activities

COLLEGE AND SCHOOL JOURNALISM
  See also Journalism; Student activities

See also Community life; Social work

Community quilts. Kavaya, K.   **746.46**

COMMUNITY SERVICES

    See also Social work

COMPACT CARS

    See also Automobiles

COMPACT DISC INDUSTRY

    Knopper, S. Appetite for self-destruction   **384**

COMPACT DISC READ-ONLY MEMORY *See* CD-ROMs

COMPACT DISCS

    See also Optical storage devices; Sound recordings

Compagno, Leonard J. V.

    Sharks of the world   **597**

COMPANIES *See* Business enterprises; Corporations; Partnership

Companies we keep. Abrams, J.   **338.7**

Companion to Asian studies [series]

    Keene, D. The pleasures of Japanese literature   **895.6**

Companion to Narnia. Ford, P. F.   **823**

The **Companion** to southern literature.   **810**

A **Companion** to world philosophies.   **100**

COMPANION-ANIMAL PARTNERSHIP *See* Pet therapy

The **company.** Micklethwait, J.   **338.7**

Company of moths. Palmer, M.   **811**

COMPANY SYMBOLS *See* Trademarks

The **company** town. Green, H.   **307.7**

COMPANY TOWNS—UNITED STATES—HISTORY

    Green, H. The company town   **307.7**

The **company** we keep. Chadwick, D. H.   **333.95**

COMPARATIVE ANATOMY

    See also Anatomy; Zoology

COMPARATIVE CIVILIZATION

    Morris, I. Why the West rules—for now   **909**

COMPARATIVE GOVERNMENT

    See also Political science

    Fukuyama, F. The origins of political order   **320**

COMPARATIVE LAW

    Legal systems of the world   **340**

COMPARATIVE LINGUISTICS *See* Linguistics

COMPARATIVE LITERATURE

    See also Literature

COMPARATIVE MORPHOLOGY *See* Morphology

COMPARATIVE PHILOLOGY *See* Linguistics

COMPARATIVE PHILOSOPHY

    See also Philosophy

COMPARATIVE PHYSIOLOGY

    See also Physiology

    Holmes, H. The well-dressed ape   **612**

    Hughes, H. C. Sensory exotica   **573.8**

    Widmaier, E. P. Why geese don't get obese (and we

do)   **571.1**

COMPARATIVE PSYCHOLOGY

    See also Zoology

    Bearzi, M. Beautiful minds   **599.8**

    Calvin, W. H. How brains think   **153.9**

    Masson, J. M. When elephants weep   **591.5**

    Waal, F. d. Our inner ape   **156**

COMPARATIVE RELIGION *See* Christianity and other religions; Religions

COMPARISON OF CULTURES *See* Cross-cultural studies

COMPASS

    See also Magnetism; Navigation

    Aczel, A. D. The riddle of the compass   **912**

COMPASS—HISTORY

    Aczel, A. D. The riddle of the compass   **912**

The **compass** of pleasure. Linden, D. J.   **612.8**

COMPASSION

    See also Emotions

    Armstrong, K. Twelve steps to a compassionate life   **177**

    Bstan-'dzin-rgya-mtsho, D. L. X. How to be compassionate   **294.3**

COMPENSATION *See* Pensions; Salaries, wages, etc.; Workers' compensation

COMPETENCE *See* Performance

Competing voices from the Russian Revolution.   **947.084**

COMPETITION

    See also Business; Business ethics; Commerce

COMPETITION (PSYCHOLOGY)

    See also Interpersonal relations; Motivation (Psychology); Psychology

COMPETITION—UNITED STATES—CASE STUDIES

    Brenner, J. G. The emperors of chocolate   **338.7**

COMPETITIONS *See* Awards; Contests

The **complete** bedside companion. McFarlane, R.   **649.8**

The **complete** Bible handbook. Bowker, J.   **220.6**

The **complete** book of cacti & succulents. Hewitt, T.   **635.9**

The **complete** book of hair loss answers. Panagotacos, P. J.   **616.5**

The **complete** book of hairstyling. Worthington, C.   **646.7**

The **complete** book of home crafts.   **745.5**

The **complete** book of home inspection. Becker, N.   **643**

The **complete** book of jewelry making. Codina, C.   **739.27**

The **Complete** book of pasta and noodles.   **641.8**

The **complete** book of pickling. Mackenzie, J.   **641.4**

The **complete** book of polymer clay. Pavelka, L.   **738.1**

Crais, Clifton C.
Sara Baartman and the Hottentot Venus   92

Cram, David L.
Answers to frequently asked questions in Parkinson's disease   616.8
Coping with psoriasis   616.5

Cramer, Alfred William
(ed) Musicians & composers of the 20th century   920.003

Cramer, Deborah
Smithsonian ocean   578.7

Cramer, James J.
Confessions of a street addict   332.6

Cramer, Richard Ben
Joe DiMaggio   796.357

Cran, William
Do you speak American? (Television program) Do you speak American?   427
McCrum, R. The story of English   420

Crane, George
Bones of the master   294.3

Crane, Hart
Complete poems and selected letters   811

Crane, Kathleen
Sea legs   92

Crane, Stephen
Prose and poetry   813

CRANES (BIRDS)
Nigge, K. Whooping crane   598

Cranioklepty. Dickey, C.   612.7

CRANIOLOGY—HISTORY
Fabian, A. The skull collectors   599.9

CRANKS *See* Eccentrics and eccentricities

Cranston, Maurice
Jean-Jacques: the early life and work of Jean-Jacques Rousseau, 1712-1754   92
The noble savage: Jean-Jacques Rousseau, 1754-1762   92
The solitary self: Jean-Jacques Rousseau in exile and adversity   92

Crapol, Edward P.
John Tyler   92

Crash course [series]
Ford, C. Crash course in reference   025.5

Crash course in library services to people with disabilities. Roberts, E. A.   027.6

Crash course in library supervision. Tucker, D. C.   023

Crash course in reference. Ford, C.   025.5

Crash course series
Roberts, E. A. Crash course in library services to people with disabilities   027.6
Tucker, D. C. Crash course in library supervision   023

Crash of the titans. Farrell, G.   332.1

Crash out. Goewey, D.   365

CRASHES (FINANCE) *See* Financial crises

Crashing through. Kurson, R.   92

Craske, Matthew
Art in Europe, 1700-1830   709.03

Craughwell, Thomas J.
Saints behaving badly   270
Stealing Lincoln's body   973.7

Crave radiance. Alexander, E.   811

Craven, Wayne
American art   709

Crawford, Bill
All American   92

Crawford, Dorothy H.
The invisible enemy   579.2

Crawford, Matthew B.
Shop class as soulcraft   331

Crawford, Richard
America's musical life   780.9

Crawford, Robert
The bard   92

Crazy '08. Murphy, C.   796.357

Crazy basketball. Rosen, C.   796.323

Crazy for the storm. Ollestad, N.   92

Crazy Horse. McMurtry, L.   92

Crazy quilting. Michler, J. M.   746.46

CRAZY QUILTS
Michler, J. M. The magic of crazy quilting   746.46

Crazy river. Grant, R.   916

CRC handbook of chemistry and physics.   540

CRC standard mathematical tables and formulae.   510

Creamer, Robert W.
Babe   92
Stengel   796.357

Crease, Robert P.
The great equations   509
The prism and the pendulum   509

Create dangerously. Danticat, E.   92

The **created** self. Weber, R. J.   155.2

Creating a role. Stanislavsky, K.   792

Creating characters. Swain, D. V.   808.3

Creating mind. Dowling, J. E.   612.8

Creating minds. Gardner, H.   153.3

Creating the not so big house. Susanka, S.   728

Creating their own image. Farrington, L. E.   709

Creating your best life. Miller, C. A.   158

Creating your library brand. Doucett, E.   659.1

CREATION (LITERARY, ARTISTIC, ETC.)
See also Genius; Imagination; Intellect; Inventions
Boorstin, D. J. The creators   909
Dillard, A. The writing life   818
Doctorow, E. L. Creationists: selected essays, 1993-2006   814
Peacock, M. The paper garden   92

CREATION—STUDY AND TEACHING *See*

Creationism; Evolution—Study and teaching

CREATIONISM

Ayala, F. J. Darwin's gift to science and religion **576.8**

Deloria, V. Evolution, creationism, and other modern myths **201**

Humes, E. Monkey girl **231.7**

Montgomery, D. R. The rocks don't lie **551.48**

Pennock, R. T. Tower of Babel **576.8**

Young, C. C. Evolution and creationism **576.8**

Creationists: selected essays, 1993-2006. Doctorow, E. L. **814**

Creations of fire. Cobb, C. **540**

CREATIVE ABILITY

See also Ability

Bissell, T. Magic hours **153.35**

Csikszentmihalyi, M. Creativity **153.3**

Edwards, B. The new drawing on the right side of the brain **741.2**

Gardner, H. Creating minds **153.3**

Guber, P. Tell to win **658.4**

Kotter, J. P. Buy-in **650.1**

May, R. The courage to create **153.3**

Nugent, B. American nerd **305.9**

Peters, T. J. The circle of innovation **658.4**

CREATIVE ABILITY—HISTORY—20TH CENTURY

Nugent, B. American nerd **305.9**

CREATIVE ABILITY IN OLD AGE

Peacock, M. The paper garden **92**

CREATIVE ABILITY IN SCIENCE

Shermer, M. Why people believe weird things **001.9**

CREATIVE ACTIVITIES

See also Amusements; Elementary education; Kindergarten

Creative country construction. Inwood, R. **690**

The **creative** destruction of medicine. Topol, E. **610.28**

Creative metal clay jewelry. Wire, C. **745.59**

Creative mythology. Campbell, J. **201**

Creative Publishing International

The complete photo guide to window treatments **646.2**

Creative Publishing International, Inc.

The complete photo guide to sewing **646.2**

CREATIVE THINKING

See also Creative ability

Csikszentmihalyi, M. Creativity **153.3**

Godin, S. Linchpin **650.1**

Sawyer, R. K. Group genius **658.4**

Creative visualization. Gawain, S. **153.3**

CREATIVE WRITING

See also Authorship; Creation (Literary, artistic, etc.); Language arts

Grimes, T. Mentor **92**

Prose, F. Anne Frank **839.3**

Prose, F. Reading like a writer **808**

Salzman, M. True notebooks **371.9**

Stein, S. How to grow a novel **808.3**

The Writer's digest guide to good writing **808**

CREATIVE WRITING—GRAPHIC NOVELS

Barry, L. What it is **741.5**

Creativity. Csikszentmihalyi, M. **153.3**

CREATIVITY *See* Creative ability

The **creators.** Boorstin, D. J. **909**

CREATURE FILMS *See* Horror films

Creatures of a day. Gibbons, R. **811**

CREDIBILITY *See* Truthfulness and falsehood

CREDIT

See also Finance; Money

Leonard, R. Solve your money troubles **346**

CREDIT—UNITED STATES

Scurlock, J. D. Maxed out **332.7**

CREDIT CARD FRAUD

See also Fraud; Swindlers and swindling

CREDIT CARDS

See also Consumer credit

Weisman, S. 50 ways to protect your identity and your credit **364.1**

CREDIT CARDS—UNITED STATES

Scurlock, J. D. Maxed out **332.7**

CREDIT DERIVATIVES

Tett, G. Fool's gold **332.6**

Credit repair. Leonard, R. **332.7**

CREDIT REPORTS

Weisman, S. 50 ways to protect your identity and your credit **364.1**

CREDITOR *See* Debtor and creditor

CREEDS

See also Doctrinal theology

Creeley, Robert

The collected poems of Robert Creeley **811**

CREMATION

See also Public health; Sanitation

Mitford, J. The American way of death revisited **338.4**

Crenshaw, Mary Ann

Dibra, B. Dogspeak **636.7**

CREOLES

See also Ethnic groups

Crescent and star. Kinzer, S. **956.1**

CREWELWORK

See also Embroidery

Crews, Kambri

Burn down the ground **306.874**

Crews, Kenneth D.

Copyright law for librarians and educators **346.04**

Crichton, Sarah

Pearl, M. A mighty heart **070.92**

Cricket radio. Himmelman, J. **595.7**

CRICKETS

See also Insects

CRITICAL THINKING

   See also Decision making; Logic; Problem solving; Reasoning; Thought and thinking

CRITICALLY ILL—HOME CARE

CRITICALLY ILL CHILDREN—CARE

CRITICALLY ILL CHILDREN—MENTAL HEALTH

CRITICISM

   See also Aesthetics; Literature; Rhetoric

CRITICISM—POLITICAL ASPECTS

CRITICISM—UNITED STATES—HISTORY

CRITICISM AND INTERPRETATION *See* Criticism

CRITICISM, FEMINIST *See* Feminist criticism

CRITICISM, INTERPRETATION, ETC. *See* Criticism

CRITICS—GREAT BRITAIN—BIOGRAPHY

The **crowded** universe. Boss, A. P.   523.2

CROWDS
  Surowiecki, J. The wisdom of crowds   303.3

Crowe, David
  Oskar Schindler   92

Crowe, Lauren Goldstein
  The towering world of Jimmy Choo   391

Crowe, Lynn
  The diabetes manifesto   616.4

Crowell, Rodney
  Chinaberry sidewalks   92

Crowfoot, Jane
  Ultimate crochet bible   746.43

Crowley, Roger
  Empires of the sea   359

Crown Journeys series
  McPherson, J. M. Hallowed ground   973.7

The **crucible** of war. Anderson, F.   973.2

CRUDE OIL *See* Petroleum

Crude world. Maass, P.   338.2

Cruden's Complete concordance. Cruden, A.   220.5

Cruden, Alexander
  Cruden's Complete concordance   220.5

Cruel world. Nicholas, L. H.   940.53

CRUELTY
  See also Ethics
  Nelson, M. The art of cruelty   700

CRUELTY IN ART
  Nelson, M. The art of cruelty   700

CRUELTY TO ANIMALS *See* Animal welfare

CRUELTY TO CHILDREN *See* Child abuse

Crumb, R.
  Bible/O.T./Genesis The book of Genesis   222
  R. Crumb: the complete record cover collection   741.6

Crump, R. W.
  (ed) Rossetti, C. G. Christina Rossetti   821

Crumpacker, Bunny
  How to slice an onion   641.5

Crunch! Burhans, D. E.   338.4

Crusade. Atkinson, R.   956.7

The **Crusades.**   909.07

CRUSADES
  Andrea, A. J. Encyclopedia of the crusades 909.07
  Asbridge, T. The crusades   909.07
  The Crusades   909.07
  The Oxford illustrated history of the Crusades   909.07
  Phillips, J. Holy warriors   909.07
  Tuchman, B. W. A distant mirror   944

The **crusades.** Asbridge, T.   909.07

CRUSADES—ENCYCLOPEDIAS
  Andrea, A. J. Encyclopedia of the crusades 909.07
  The Crusades   909.07

CRUSHES
  See also Friendship; Love

Cruz, Nilo
  Anna in the tropics   812

CRYING IN INFANTS
  Karp, H. The happiest baby on the block   649

CRYOBIOLOGY
  See also Biology; Cold; Low temperatures

CRYONICS
  See also Burial

CRYOSURGERY
  See also Cold—Therapeutic use; Surgery

CRYPTOGRAPHY
  See also Signs and symbols; Writing
  Lee, B. Marching orders   940.54
  Sebag-Montefiore, H. Enigma: the battle for the code   940.54

CRYPTOGRAPHY—UNITED STATES—HISTORY—SOURCES
  Haynes, J. E. Venona   327.12

CRYSTAL GAZING *See* Divination

CRYSTAL METH (DRUG)
  See also Designer drugs; Methamphetamine

Crystal, David
  The story of English in 100 words   422

Crystal, David
  By hook or by crook   427
  The Cambridge encyclopedia of language   400
  The Cambridge encyclopedia of the English language   420
  A dictionary of language   410
  English as a global language   420
  How language works   401
  Language and the internet   410
  The stories of English   427

CRYSTALLIZATION *See* Crystals

CRYSTALLOGRAPHY *See* Crystals

CRYSTALS
  Holden, A. Crystals and crystal growing   548
  Johnsen, O. Minerals of the world   549

Crystals and crystal growing. Holden, A.   548

Csikszentmihalyi, Mihaly
  Creativity   153.3
  Flow: the psychology of optimal experience   155.2

Cuba. Suchlicki, J.   972.91

Cuba. Perez, L. A.   972.91

Cuba: art and history, from 1868 to today.   709

CUBAN AMERICANS
  Eire, C. M. N. Learning to die in Miami   92

CUBAN AMERICANS—BIOGRAPHY
  Eire, C. M. N. Waiting for snow in Havana   92

CUBAN AMERICANS—DRAMA
  Cruz, N. Anna in the tropics   812

CUBAN ART
  Cuba: art and history, from 1868 to today   709

CUBAN MISSILE CRISIS, 1962
  Dobbs, M. One minute to midnight   973.922
  Freedman, L. Kennedy's wars   973.922

Fursenko, A. V. One hell of a gamble   **973.922**

Kennedy, R. F. Thirteen days   **973.922**

CUBAN REFUGEES

Eire, C. M. N. Learning to die in Miami   **92**

CUBISM

See also Art

Cuddon, J. A.

The Penguin dictionary of literary terms and literary theory   **803**

Cuhaj, George S.

2012 standard catalog of world coins, 1901-2000   **737.4**

Culinary Institute of America

Techniques of healthy cooking   **641.5**

Vegetables   **641.6**

Kolpan, S. Exploring wine   **641.2**

Culkin, Jennifer

A final arc of sky   **92**

Cullen, Dave

Columbine   **364.152**

Cullen, Heidi

The weather of the future   **551.63**

Cullin, Robert

Bolan, K. Technology made simple   **025**

Cullina, William

Understanding perennials   **635.9**

Cullinane, Jan

The new retirement   **646.7**

CULTIVATED PLANTS

See also Agriculture; Gardening; Plants

Cultivating delight. Ackerman, D.   **508**

CULTS

See also Religions

Atkins, S. E. Encyclopedia of modern American extremists and extremist groups   **320.53**

Atkins, S. E. Encyclopedia of modern worldwide extremists and extremist groups   **320.5**

Belief beyond boundaries   **209**

The encyclopedia of cults, sects, and new religions   **200**

CULTS—UNITED STATES

Atkins, S. E. Encyclopedia of modern American extremists and extremist groups   **320.53**

CULTS—UNITED STATES—ENCYCLOPEDIAS

The encyclopedia of cults, sects, and new religions   **200**

Cultural amnesia. James, C.   **920**

CULTURAL ANTHROPOLOGY *See* Ethnology

Cultural atlas of Russia and the former Soviet Union. Milner-Gulland, R. R.   **947**

CULTURAL CHANGE *See* Social change

CULTURAL CHARACTERISTICS

Gilman, S. L. Making the body beautiful   **617.9**

CULTURAL CRITIQUE

Bissell, T. Magic hours   **153.35**

Deb, S. The beautiful and the damned   **954.05**

Nelson, M. The art of cruelty   **700**

Yalom, M. How the French invented love   **944**

The **cultural** encyclopedia of baseball. Light, J. F.   **796.357**

CULTURAL HERITAGE *See* Cultural property

CULTURAL INDUSTRIES

Lessig, L. Remix   **346**

CULTURAL LIFE *See* Intellectual life

CULTURAL PATRIMONY *See* Cultural property

CULTURAL POLICY

See also Culture; Intellectual life

CULTURAL PROGRAMS

Librarians as community partners   **021.2**

CULTURAL PROPERTY

See also Property

Cole, P. Sacred trash   **296.09**

Felch, J. Chasing Aphrodite   **930**

CULTURAL PROPERTY—MORAL AND ETHICAL ASPECTS

Childs, C. L. Finders keepers   **930.1**

CULTURAL PROPERTY—PROTECTION

Amery, C. Vanishing histories   **363.6**

Atwood, R. Stealing history   **364.1**

CULTURAL PROPERTY—REPATRIATION—ITALY

Felch, J. Chasing Aphrodite   **930**

CULTURAL RELATIONS

See also Intellectual cooperation; International cooperation; International relations

CULTURALLY DEPRIVED CHILDREN *See* Socially handicapped children

CULTURALLY HANDICAPPED CHILDREN *See* Socially handicapped children

CULTURE

Bitchfest   **305.4**

Bloom, H. The Lucifer principle   **128**

Huxley, A. Brave new world revisited   **303.3**

Hyde, L. Common as air   **346.04**

Klein, R. G. The dawn of human culture   **599.93**

Pagel, M. Wired for culture   **303.4**

Sowell, T. Migrations and cultures   **304.8**

Culture & Politics of Health Care Work [series]

Barken, F. M. Out of practice   **610.6**

CULTURE—ORIGIN

Klein, R. G. The dawn of human culture   **599.93**

CULTURE—PSYCHOLOGICAL ASPECTS

Triandis, H. C. Fooling ourselves   **155.2**

CULTURE CONFLICT

See also Ethnic relations; Ethnopsychology; Race relations

Encyclopedia of modern ethnic conflicts   **305.8**

Fadiman, A. The spirit catches you and you fall down   **306.4**

CULTURE CONFLICT—CALIFORNIA—SAN FRANCISCO—HISTORY—20TH CENTU-

The **dance** of intimacy. Lerner, H. G.   155.6
The **dance** of molecules. Sargent, T.   620
DANCE TEACHERS
  Gardner, H. Creating minds   153.3
  Tallchief, M. Maria Tallchief   92
  Ware, S. Letter to the world   920.72
  Wills, G. Certain trumpets   303.3
Dance, Stanley
  The world of Count Basie   920
DANCERS
    See also Entertainers
  Brown, C. Chance and circumstance   92
  Gardner, H. Creating minds   153.3
  Gates, H. L. Thirteen ways of looking at a black man   920.71
  Goldner, N. Balanchine variations   792.8
  Gottlieb, R. A. George Balanchine: the ballet maker   92
  Kurth, P. Isadora   792.8
  Life stories   920
  Sontag, S. Where the stress falls   814
  Streb, E. Streb   92
  Teachout, T. All in the dances: a brief life of George Balanchine   92
  Vaill, A. Somewhere   92
  Volkov, S. St. Petersburg   947
  Ware, S. Letter to the world   920.72
  Wills, G. Certain trumpets   303.3
DANCERS—UNITED STATES—BIOGRAPHY
  Kurth, P. Isadora   792.8
DANCES *See* Dance
Danchin, Antoine
  The Delphic boat   572.8
DANCING *See* Dance
Dancing in the dark. Dickstein, M.   973.91
Dancing in the glory of monsters. Stearns, J. K.   967.51
Dancing to a black man's tune: a life of Scott Joplin. Curtis, S.   780
Dancing to the precipice: Lucie de la Tour du Pin and the French Revolution. Moorehead, C.   92
Dancing with Cuba. Guillermoprieto, A.   972.91
Dancing with Rose. Kessler, L.   362.1
Dancing with strangers. Clendinnen, I.   994
Dando, Marc
  Compagno, L. J. V. Sharks of the world   597
Danger on peaks. Snyder, G.   811
Danger to self. Linde, P. R.   616.89
DANGEROUS ANIMALS
    See also Animals
  Grice, G. Deadly kingdom   591.6
  Quammen, D. Monster of God   591.6
Dangerous doses. Eban, K.   363.1
Dangerous games. MacMillan, M.   901
Dangerous nation. Kagan, R.   327
The **dangerous** summer. Hemingway, E.   791.8

A **dangerous** woman. Rudahl, S.   335
The **dangerous** world of butterflies. Laufer, P. 595.7
Dangerously funny. Bianculli, D.   791.45
Daniel Boone. Faragher, J. M.   92
Daniel Johnston. Johnston, D.   741
Daniel Webster. Remini, R. V.   328
Daniel, Jessica Henderson
  (ed) The Complete guide to mental health for women   616.89
Daniel, Larry J.
  Shiloh   973.7
Daniel, Nancy Brenan
  The art of the handmade quilt   746.4
Daniell, David
  The Bible in English   220.4
Daniels, Cora
  Black Power Inc.   658.4
Daniels, Les
  Marvel   741.5
Daniels, Patricia
  The new solar system   523.2
Daniels, Roger
  Coming to America   325
  Prisoners without trial   940.53
  (ed) Japanese Americans, from relocation to redress   940.53
Danielsen, Anne
  Presence and pleasure   781.644
Daniloff, Nicholas
  Baiev, K. The Oath   947.5
Daniloff, Ruth
  Baiev, K. The Oath   947.5
DANISH LANGUAGE
    See also Language and languages; Norwegian language; Scandinavian languages
DANISH LITERATURE
    See also Literature; Scandinavian literature
Danner, Mark
  Torture and truth   956.7
Danson, Edwin
  Weighing the world   526
Dante Alighieri
  The divine comedy   851
  The Inferno   851
  Paradiso   851
  The portable Dante   851
  Purgatorio   851
Dante Alighieri, 1265-1321 (Italian poet)
     About
  Ruud, J. Critical companion to Dante   850
Danticat, Edwidge
  Brother, I'm dying   92
  Create dangerously   92
Dare to repair. Sussman, J.   643
Daring young men. Reeves, R.   943.087
Darion, Joe

The sisters who would be queen 920

De Madariaga, Isabel
Ivan the Terrible 92

De Marly, Diana
Dress in North America 391

De Pauw, Linda Grant
Battle cries and lullabies 355

De Pree, Christopher Gordon
(ed) Van Nostrand's concise encyclopedia of science 503

De Quincey, Thomas
The confessions of an English opium-eater and other writings 824

De Sola, Ralph
(ed) Abbreviations dictionary 421

De Vecchi, Pierluigi
Raphael 759

De Villiers, Marq
The end 363.34
Sahara: a natural history 508
Windswept 551.51

De Vito, Carlo
The encyclopedia of international organized crime 364.1

De Vito, Dominique
World atlas of dog breeds 636.7

De Voto, Avis
Child, J. As always, Julia 92

De Voto, Avis, 1904-1989 (American editor)
About
Child, J. As always, Julia 92

De Waal, Edmund
The hare with amber eyes 920

De Waal, Frans
The age of empathy 152.4

De Young, Karen
Soldier: the life of Colin Powell 92

The **de-voicing** of society. Locke, J. L. 302.3

DEAD

See also Burial; Cremation; Death; Funeral rites and ceremonies; Obituaries

Roach, M. Stiff 611
The **dead** beat. Johnson, M. 070.4
Dead by sunset. Rule, A. 364.1
Dead certain. Draper, R. 973.931
Dead certainties. Schama, S. 974.4
Dead men do tell tales. Maples, W. R. 614
Dead pool. Powell, J. L. 363.6
The **Dead** Sea scrolls. Abegg, M. G. 296.1

Dead Sea scrolls
Abegg, M. G. The Dead Sea scrolls 296.1

Deadly choices. Offit, P. A. 614.4
Deadly feasts. Rhodes, R. 614.5
Deadly kingdom. Grice, G. 591.6
Deadly monopolies. Washington, H. A. 338.4

DEAF

See also Hearing impaired; Physically handicapped

Crews, K. Burn down the ground 306.874
Gibson, W. The miracle worker 812
Greenstein, G. Portraits of discovery 920
Herrmann, D. Helen Keller 92
Keller, H. Helen Keller: selected writings 92
Keller, H. The story of my life 92
Sacks, O. W. Seeing voices 362.4
Uhlberg, M. Hands of my father 92

DEAF—EDUCATION
See also Education

DEAF—MEANS OF COMMUNICATION
See also Communication

DEAF—MEANS OF COMMUNICATION—UNITED STATES
Grayson, G. Talking with your hands, listening with your eyes 419

DEAF—SIGN LANGUAGE *See* Sign language

DEAF—UNITED STATES—SOCIAL CONDITIONS
Grayson, G. Talking with your hands, listening with your eyes 419

DEAF WOMEN—UNITED STATES—BIOGRAPHY
Keller, H. The story of my life 92

DEAFNESS
Myers, D. G. A quiet world 617.8

Deak, JoAnn
Girls will be girls 649

The **deal** from hell. O'Shea, J. 92

Dealing with difficult people in the library. Willis, M. R. 025.5

Dean & me. Lewis, J. 92

Dean, Cornelia
Against the tide 333.91

Dean, Eddie
Kagarise, L. Pure country 781.642
Stanley, R. Man of constant sorrow 92

Dear ghosts, Gallagher, T. 811
Dear Prudence. Trinidad, D. 811
Dear Sandy, hello. Berrigan, T. 92

Dearborn, Mary V.
Mailer 813

Deardorff, David C.
What's wrong with my plant (and how do I fix it?) 635

DEATH

See also Biology; Eschatology; Life

Attig, T. The heart of grief 155.9
Auster, P. Winter journal 818
Barnes, J. Nothing to be frightened of 92
Benecke, M. The dream of eternal life 612.6
Brody, J. E. Jane Brody's guide to the great beyond 616.02
Brown, S. M. In heaven as it is on earth 236

Delmolino, Lara

Incentives for change   649

Deloria, Vine

Custer died for your sins   970.004

Evolution, creationism, and other modern myths   201

(comp) Documents of American Indian diplomacy   970.004

The **Delphic** boat. Danchin, A.   572.8

Delta blues. Gioia, T.   781.643

DELUSIONS

Freeman, D. Paranoia   616.89

The **deluxe** food lover's companion. Herbst, S. T.   641

DeMallie, Raymond J.

(comp) Documents of American Indian diplomacy   970.004

DeMasco, Karen

The craft of baking   641.8

Dement, William C.

The promise of sleep   612.8

Demetz, Peter

The air show at Brescia, 1909   629.13

Prague in black and gold   943.71

(ed) Lessing, G. E. Nathan the Wise, Minna von Barnhelm, and other plays and writings   832

Demick, Barbara

Nothing to envy   951.93

Demobbed. Allport, A.   305.9

DEMOCRACY

See also Constitutional history; Constitutional law; Political science

Broder, D. S. Democracy derailed   328.2

Buruma, I. Taming the gods   322

Dyson, M. E. Come hell or high water   976.3

Ferris, T. The science of liberty   303.4

Fukuyama, F. The origins of political order   320

Kalman, M. And the pursuit of happiness   170

Lasch, C. The revolt of the elites   306

Morozov, E. The net delusion   303.48

Patel, R. The value of nothing   330.1

Schoen, D. E. The power of the vote   324

Seeley, T. D. Honeybee democracy   551.7

Tocqueville, A. d. Democracy in America   973.5

Toffler, A. Future shock   303.4

Wilentz, S. The rise of American democracy   973.5

DEMOCRACY—CAMBODIA

Brinkley, J. Cambodia's curse   959.6

DEMOCRACY—HISTORY

Fukuyama, F. The origins of political order   320

Szpiro, G. G. Numbers rule   510

DEMOCRACY—RELIGIOUS ASPECTS

Buruma, I. Taming the gods   322

DEMOCRACY—RELIGIOUS ASPECTS—ISLAM

Feldman, N. After Jihad   321.8

DEMOCRACY—UNITED STATES

Broder, D. S. Democracy derailed   328.2

Joseph, P. E. Dark days, bright nights   323.1

Schlesinger, A. M. War and the American presidency   327.1

Wilentz, S. The rise of American democracy   973.5

DEMOCRACY—UNITED STATES—HISTORY

Han, L. C. Handbook to American democracy   320.4

Democracy and education. Dewey, J.   370.1

Democracy derailed. Broder, D. S.   328.2

Democracy in America. Tocqueville, A. d.   973.5

DEMOCRACY IN LITERATURE

Pinsky, R. Democracy, culture, and the voice of poetry   811

Democracy, culture, and the voice of poetry. Pinsky, R.   811

DEMOCRATIC PARTY (U.S.)

See also Political parties

Demon fish. Eilperin, J.   597

The **demon** in the freezer. Preston, R.   616.9

The **demon** under the microscope. Hager, T.   615

DEMONIAC POSSESSION

See also Demonology

DEMONOLOGY

See also Occultism

Guiley, R. E. The encyclopedia of demons and demonology   133.4

Messadie, G. A history of the devil   200

DEMONOLOGY—ENCYCLOPEDIAS

Guiley, R. E. The encyclopedia of demons and demonology   133.4

DEMONSTRATIONS

See also Crowds; Public meetings

Anderson, T. H. The movement and the sixties   303.48

Masur, L. P. The soiling of Old Glory   974.4

DEMONSTRATIONS FOR CIVIL RIGHTS *See* Civil rights demonstrations

Demos, John

The unredeemed captive   973.2

Dempsey, Amy

Art in the modern era   709.04

DeNapoli, Dyan

The great penguin rescue   639.9

DENATURED ALCOHOL

See also Alcohol

DENAZIFICATION

Taylor, F. Exorcising Hitler   943.087

Denckla, Tanya

The organic gardener's home reference   635

Deng Xiaoping and the transformation of China. Vogel, E. F.   951.05

Deng, Alephonsion

Deng, B. They poured fire on us from the sky   962.4

Deng, Benson

STATES

Greenspan, S. I. The child with special needs **362.1**

DEVELOPMENTALLY DISABLED CHILDREN—UNITED STATES—LIFE SKILLS GUIDES

Greenspan, S. I. The child with special needs **362.1**

DEVELOPMENTALLY DISABLED CHILDREN—UNITED STATES—PSYCHOLOGY

Greenspan, S. I. The child with special needs **362.1**

DEVIANCY See Deviant behavior

DEVIANT BEHAVIOR

See also Human behavior

Kipnis, L. How to become a scandal **306.7**

Devices and desires. Tone, A. **363.9**

DEVIL

Messadie, G. A history of the devil **200**

Pagels, E. H. The origin of Satan **235**

Wray, T. J. The birth of Satan **235**

The **devil** and Mr. Casement. Goodman, J. **305.8**

The **devil** and Sherlock Holmes. Grann, D. **814**

Devil in the mountain. Lamb, S. **551**

The **devil** in the shape of a woman. Karlsen, C. F. **133.4**

The **devil** in the white city. Larson, E. **364.15**

A **devil's** chaplain. Dawkins, R. **500**

The **devil's** doctor. Ball, P. **610**

Devil's game. Dreyfuss, R. **327**

The **devil's** highway. Urrea, L. A. **304.8**

The **devil's** own work. Schecter, B. **974.7**

Devine, Carol

Human rights **323**

Devine, T. M.

The Scottish nation 1700-2000 **941.1**

Devlin, Keith J.

Goodbye, Descartes **128**

The math gene **510**

The unfinished game **519.2**

Devonshire, William Cavendish, Duke of, 1748-1811

About

Foreman, A. Georgiana, Duchess of Devonshire **941.07**

DEVOTION See Prayer; Worship

DEVOTIONAL CALENDARS

See also Calendars; Devotional literature

DEVOTIONAL EXERCISES

Hendey, L. M. A book of saints for Catholic moms **248.8**

DEVOTIONAL THEOLOGY See Devotional exercises; Prayer

Devotions. Smith, B. **811**

DEVOTIONS See Devotional exercises

DeVoto, Mark

(ed) Harmony **781.2**

DeWalt, G. Weston

Boukreev, A. The climb **796.522**

Dewdney, A. K.

200[percent] of nothing **510**

A mathematical mystery tour **510**

Dewey. Myron, V. **636.8**

DEWEY DECIMAL CLASSIFICATION

Dewey decimal classification and relative index **025.4**

Dewey decimal classification and relative index. **025.4**

Dewey, John

Democracy and education **370.1**

The philosophy of John Dewey **191**

The school and society, and The child and the curriculum **372**

Dewey, Melvil

Dewey decimal classification and relative index **025.4**

DeWolf, Thomas Norman

Inheriting the trade **326**

DeWoskin, Rachel

Foreign babes in Beijing **951**

Di Giovanni, Janine

Madness visible **949.7**

Di Giovanni, Janine (American journalist)

About

Di Giovanni, J. Madness visible **949.7**

Diabesity. Kaufman, F. R. **362.1**

DIABETES

See also Diseases

American Diabetes Association American Diabetes Association complete guide to diabetes **616.4**

American Diabetes Association What to expect when you have diabetes **616.4**

Beaser, R. S. The Joslin guide to diabetes **616.4**

Crowe, L. The diabetes manifesto **616.4**

Diabetes sourcebook **616.4**

Eisenstat, S. A. Every woman's guide to diabetes **616.4**

Hirsch, J. S. Cheating destiny **616.4**

Hurley, D. Diabetes rising **362.1**

Kaplan-Mayer, G. Insulin pump therapy demystified **616.4**

Kaufman, F. R. Diabesity **362.1**

Mayo Clinic (Rochester, M. Mayo Clinic: the essential diabetes book **616.4**

Moore, M. T. Growing up again **92**

Walker, R. A. Diabetes: a practical guide to managing your health **616.4**

DIABETES—DIET THERAPY

Bernstein, R. K. The diabetes diet **641.5**

Newgent, J. The all-natural diabetes cookbook **641.5**

Scalpi, G. The everything diabetes cookbook **641.5**

Warshaw, H. S. The diabetes food & nutrition bible **616.4**

Worrall-Thompson, A. The essential diabetes cookbook **641.5**

DIABETES—TREATMENT

Kaplan-Mayer, G. Insulin pump therapy demystified **616.4**

The **diabetes** diet. Bernstein, R. K. **641.5**

The **diabetes** food & nutrition bible. Warshaw, H. S. **616.4**

The **diabetes** manifesto. Crowe, L. **616.4**

Diabetes rising. Hurley, D. **362.1**

Diabetes sourcebook. **616.4**

Diabetes: a practical guide to managing your health. Walker, R. A. **616.4**

Diaghilev. **92**

DIAGNOSIS

See also Medicine

Groopman, J. E. How doctors think **610**

Groopman, J. E. Second opinions **610**

The Johns Hopkins consumer guide to medical tests **616.07**

Pagana, K. D. Mosby's diagnostic and laboratory test reference **616.07**

Sanders, L. Every patient tells a story **616.07**

Segen, J. C. The patient's guide to medical tests **616.07**

Diagnosis, cancer. Harpham, W. S. **616.99**

DIAGNOSTIC ERRORS

DeGrandpre, R. J. Ritalin nation **618.92**

DIAGNOSTIC IMAGING

See also Pathology

Diagram Group

Lambert, D. The field guide to geology **551**

DIALECTICAL MATERIALISM

See also Communism; Socialism

DIALECTICS *See* Logic

Diamandis, Peter H.

Abundance **303.48**

Diamant, Anita

Pitching my tent **296.7**

The **diamond** dog. Wakoski, D. **811**

DIAMOND INDUSTRY AND TRADE—SOUTH AFRICA

Meredith, M. Diamonds, gold, and war **968.04**

DIAMOND INDUSTRY AND TRADE—SOUTH AFRICA—HISTORY

Meredith, M. Diamonds, gold, and war **968.04**

Diamond, Jared M.

Collapse: how societies choose to fail or succeed **304.2**

Guns, germs, and steel **303.4**

The third chimpanzee **599.93**

Diamond: a journey to the heart of an obsession. Hart, M. **553.8**

DIAMONDS

See also Carbon; Precious stones

Hart, M. Diamond: a journey to the heart of an obsession **553.8**

Selby, S. A. Flawless **364.1**

Zoellner, T. The heartless stone **553.8**

Diamonds, gold, and war. Meredith, M. **968.04**

The **Diana** chronicles. Brown, T. **92**

Diane Fitzgerald's shaped beadwork. Fitzgerald, D. **745.58**

DIARIES

See also Literature

Diehn, G. Real life journals: designing & using handmade books **686.3**

DIARIES—WOMEN AUTHORS

Adamson, L. G. Notable women in world history **016**

DIARIES—WOMEN AUTHORS—BIBLIOGRAPHY

Adamson, L. G. Notable women in world history **016**

Diaries of a young poet. Rilke, R. M. **92**

The **diaries** of Kenneth Tynan. Tynan, K. **792**

DIARISTS

Berr, H. The journal of Helene Berr **92**

Blight, D. W. A slave no more **326**

The diary of Anne Frank: the critical edition **940.53**

Frank, A. The diary of a young girl: the definitive edition **940.53**

Hertog, S. Anne Morrow Lindbergh **92**

Hollis, L. London rising **942**

Jacobson, S. Anne Frank **92**

Klemperer, V. I will bear witness **943.086**

LaPlante, E. Salem witch judge **92**

Lee, H. Virginia Woolf's nose **820**

Lindbergh, R. Under a wing **92**

Long, J. The plot against Pepys **941.06**

Ozick, C. Quarrel & quandary **814**

Pepys, S. The diary of Samuel Pepys **941.06**

Pierpont, C. R. Passionate minds **810**

Prose, F. Anne Frank **839.3**

Slaughter, T. P. The beautiful soul of John Woolman, apostle of abolition **92**

Tomalin, C. Samuel Pepys **941.06**

Wilson, F. The ballad of Dorothy Wordsworth **92**

Winters, K. C. Anne Morrow Lindbergh **92**

DIARISTS—GREAT BRITAIN—BIOGRAPHY

Tomalin, C. Samuel Pepys **941.06**

The **diary** of a young girl: the definitive edition. Frank, A. **940.53**

The **diary** of Anne Frank. Goodrich, F. **812**

The **diary** of Anne Frank: the critical edition. **940.53**

The **diary** of Frida Kahlo. Kahlo, F. **92**

The **diary** of Samuel Pepys. Pepys, S. **941.06**

DIASPORA, AFRICAN *See* African diaspora

DIASPORA, JEWISH *See* Jewish diaspora

Diaspora: homelands in exile. Brenner, F. **909**

Diaz del Castillo, Bernal

The discovery and conquest of Mexico, 1517-1521 **972**

DIEN BIEN PHU, BATTLE OF, 1954
Morgan, T. Valley of death   **959.704**

Dierker, Larry
This ain't brain surgery   **796**

DIES (METALWORKING)
See also Metalwork

DIESEL AUTOMOBILES
See also Automobiles

DIET
See also Health; Hygiene
Diet and nutrition sourcebook   **613.2**
Guiliano, M. French women don't get fat **613.2**
Nesheim, M. Why calories count   **613.2**
Nestle, M. What to eat   **613.2**
Shintani, T. The good carbohydrate revolution   **613.2**
Vileisis, A. Kitchen literacy   **641.5**

DIET—THERAPEUTIC USE *See* Diet therapy
DIET—UNITED STATES—HISTORY
Vileisis, A. Kitchen literacy   **641.5**
Diet and nutrition sourcebook.   **613.2**
Diet for a hot planet. Lappé, A.   **641**

DIET IN DISEASE
Hagman, B. The gluten-free gourmet   **641.5**

DIET SUPPLEMENTS *See* Dietary supplements
DIET THERAPY
See also Cooking for the sick; Diet in disease; Therapeutics
Haynes, A. J. The food intolerance bible **616.97**
Marks, D. R. The headache prevention cookbook   **616.8**
Pascal, C. The whole foods allergy cookbook **641.5**
Pescatore, F. The allergy and asthma cure **616.97**

DIETARY SUPPLEMENTS
See also Nutrition; Vitamins
Graedon, J. The people's pharmacy guide to home and herbal remedies   **615**
Kuhn, C. Pumped   **617.1**
Murray, M. T. Encyclopedia of nutritional supplements   **613.2**
Talbott, S. A guide to understanding dietary supplements   **615**

DIETARY SUPPLEMENTS—ENCYCLOPEDIAS
The Encyclopedia of vitamins, minerals, and supplements   **613.2**
Murray, M. T. Encyclopedia of nutritional supplements   **613.2**

DIETETIC FOODS
See also Diet; Food

DIETETICS *See* Diet
DIETING *See* Weight loss
DIETS, REDUCING *See* Weight loss
Dietz, Maggie
(ed) Americans' favorite poems   **808.81**
(ed) Poems to read   **808.81**

Different hours. Dunn, S.   **811**

DIFFERENTIAL EQUATIONS
See also Calculus
Difficult conversations. Stone, D.   **158**

DIFFUSION OF INNOVATION
Topol, E. The creative destruction of medicine   **610.28**

DIGESTION
See also Physiology

DIGESTIVE ORGANS—DISEASES
Minocha, A. The encyclopedia of the digestive system and digestive disorders **616.3**

DIGESTIVE ORGANS—ENCYCLOPEDIAS
Minocha, A. The encyclopedia of the digestive system and digestive disorders **616.3**

DIGESTIVE SYSTEM
See also Anatomy
Digging for dirt. Lowe, J.   **92**
Digging through the Bible. Freund, R. A. **220.9**
Digging up the dead. Kammen, M. G.   **393**

DIGITAL ART
Ligon, S. Digital art revolution   **776**
Digital art revolution. Ligon, S.   **776**

DIGITAL CAMERAS
Ang, T. Digital photographer's handbook **775**
Johnson, D. How to do everything: digital camera   **775**

DIGITAL CIRCUITS *See* Digital electronics
DIGITAL ELECTRONICS
See also Electronics
Ritchin, F. After photography   **775**

DIGITAL LIBRARIES
See also Information systems; Libraries
Kovacs, D. K. The Kovacs guide to electronic library collection development   **025**
Mitchell, A. M. Cataloging and organizing digital resources   **025.3**
More technology for the rest of us   **025**
White, A. C. E-metrics for library and information professionals   **025.2**

DIGITAL LIBRARIES—COLLECTION DEVELOPMENT
Kovacs, D. K. The Kovacs guide to electronic library collection development   **025**

DIGITAL MEDIA
Gershon, I. The breakup 2.0   **303.4**
Handley, A. Content rules   **658.8**
Mainwaring, S. We first   **658.8**

DIGITAL MEDIA—SOCIAL ASPECTS
Lanier, J. You are not a gadget   **303.4**
Digital photographer's handbook. Ang, T. **775**

DIGITAL PHOTOGRAPHY
Ang, T. Digital photographer's handbook **775**
Ang, T. Digital photography masterclass **775**
Dillard, T. Black & white pipeline   **778.3**
Freeman, M. The photographer's mind **775**

Watman, M. Chasing the white dog   **363.4**

The **distinctive** home. Eck, J.   **728**

Distinguished African Americans in aviation and space science. Gubert, B. K.   **629.13**

Distinguished African Americans series

    Gubert, B. K. Distinguished African Americans in aviation and space science   **629.13**

DISTRIBUTION (ECONOMICS) *See* Commerce; Marketing

DISTRIBUTION OF ANIMALS AND PLANTS

    See Biogeography

DISTRIBUTION OF WEALTH *See* Economics; Wealth

DISTRIBUTION, COOPERATIVE *See* Cooperation

DISTRIBUTORS

    Lansky, A. Outwitting history   **002.07**

District and circle. Heaney, S.   **821**

DISTRICT ATTORNEYS

    Algeo, M. The president is a sick man   **973.8**

    Bogdanos, M. Thieves of Baghdad   **956.7**

    Giuliani, R. W. Leadership   **658.4**

    Graff, H. F. Grover Cleveland   **973.8**

    Hull, N. E. H. Roe v. Wade   **344**

    Karabell, Z. The last campaign   **324.9**

    Kirtzman, A. Rudy Giuliani   **92**

    Rule, A. —and never let her go   **364.1**

    Siegel, F. F. The prince of the city   **92**

Disturbing the solar system. Rubin, A. E.   **521**

The **disuniting** of America. Schlesinger, A. M. **973**

Ditkoff, Beth Ann

    The thyroid guide   **616.4**

Divan-i Shams-i Tabrizi./English./Selections

    Rumi: the big red book   **891**

DIVERS

    Cousteau, J. Y. The human, the orchid, and the octopus   **333.95**

    Finch, P. Diving into darkness   **627**

    Matsen, B. Jacques Cousteau   **92**

DIVERSITY IN THE WORKPLACE

    See also Multiculturalism; Personnel management

DIVERSITY IN THE WORKPLACE—UNITED STATES

    Lasch-Quinn, E. Race experts   **305.8**

DIVERSITY MOVEMENT *See* Multiculturalism

The **diversity** of life. Wilson, E. O.   **333.95**

The **divided** ground. Taylor, A.   **974.7**

DIVIDENDS *See* Securities; Stocks

DIVINATION

    See also Occultism

    I ching The classic of changes   **299.5**

The **divine** comedy. Dante Alighieri   **851**

DIVINE HEALING *See* Spiritual healing

The **divine** milieu. Teilhard de Chardin, P.   **230**

Divine wind. Emanuel, K. A.   **551.55**

DIVING

    See also Swimming; Water sports

    Finch, P. Diving into darkness   **627**

Diving into darkness. Finch, P.   **627**

Divino, Cynthia L.

    Freedman, M. R. Living well with asthma   **616.2**

DIVISION OF POWERS *See* Separation of powers

DIVORCE

    See also Family

    Moffett, K. Not your mother's divorce   **306.89**

    Wallerstein, J. S. Second chances   **306.89**

    Winner, L. F. Still   **283**

    Woo, I. The great divorce   **92**

Divorce & money. Woodhouse, V.   **346.01**

DIVORCE—LAW AND LEGISLATION

    Doskow, E. Nolo's essential guide to divorce **346.01**

    Green, J. Divorce after 50   **306.89**

    Sherman, C. E. Make any divorce better!   **346.01**

    Woodhouse, V. Divorce & money   **346.01**

DIVORCE—PSYCHOLOGICAL ASPECTS

    Moffett, K. Not your mother's divorce   **306.89**

Divorce after 50. Green, J.   **306.89**

DIVORCE MEDIATION

    See also Divorce

DIVORCED FATHERS

    See also Divorced parents; Divorced people; Fathers

DIVORCED MOTHERS

    See also Divorced parents; Divorced people; Mothers

DIVORCED PARENTS

    See also Divorced people; Parents

DIVORCED PEOPLE

    See also Single people

DIVORCED WOMEN

    See also Divorced people; Single women

Dixie rising. Applebome, P.   **973.929**

Dixie, Quinton Hosford

    Williams, J. This far by faith   **200**

Dixon, Anne

    The handweaver's pattern directory   **746.1**

Dixon, Wheeler W.

    A short history of film   **791.43**

Đ

ĐIỆN BIÊN PHU (VIETNAM), BATTLE OF, 1954

    Morgan, T. Valley of death   **959.704**

D

Django: the life and music of a Gypsy legend. Dregni, M.   **92**

Djupe, Paul A.

    Encyclopedia of American religion and politics **322**

DNA. Stephenson, F. H.   **616**

DOGS

See also Domestic animals; Mammals

Adams, M. B. Shaggy muses **920**

American Kennel Club The complete dog book **636.7**

Breslin, E. Drinking with Miss Dutchie **92**

Budiansky, S. The truth about dogs **636.7**

Coppinger, R. Dogs **636.7**

Coren, S. Why we love the dogs we do **636.7**

De Vito, D. World atlas of dog breeds **636.7**

Dibra, B. Dogspeak **636.7**

The Doctor's book of home remedies for dogs and cats **636.7**

Dodman, N. H. Dogs behaving badly **636.7**

Dogs: the ultimate care guide **636.7**

Doty, M. Dog years **92**

Fogle, B. ASPCA complete dog care manual **636.7**

Fogle, B. Dog owner's manual **636.7**

Fogle, B. Dog: the definitive guide for dog owners **636.7**

Franklin, J. The wolf in the parlor **636.7**

Geeson, E. Ultimate dog grooming **636.7**

Gorant, J. The lost dogs **636.08**

Halligan, K. Doc Halligan's What every pet owner should know **636**

Healy, T. I have heard you calling in the night **636.7**

Henderson, B. All my dogs **92**

Herriot, J. James Herriot's dog stories **636.7**

Hugo, L. Where the trail grows faint **615.8**

Katz, J. The new work of dogs **636.7**

Kerasote, T. Merle's door **636.7**

Kihn, M. Bad dog **636.7**

Kotler, S. A small furry prayer **636.7**

Lane, M. The Humane Society of the United States complete guide to dog care **636.7**

Lufkin, E. To the rescue **636.7**

McConnell, P. For the love of a dog **636.7**

McGinnis, T. The well dog book **636.7**

Morris, W. My dog Skip **813**

The original dog bible **636.7**

Palika, L. K.I.S.S. guide to raising a puppy **636.7**

Petspeak **636.089**

Schaffer, M. One nation under dog **636.7**

Thomas, E. M. The social lives of dogs **636.7**

Woestendiek, J. Dog, Inc. **636.7**

DOGS—BEHAVIOR

Budiansky, S. The truth about dogs **636.7**

Dibra, B. Dogspeak **636.7**

McConnell, P. For the love of a dog **636.7**

Petspeak **636.089**

DOGS—BEHAVIOR—NEW HAMPSHIRE—ANECDOTES

Thomas, E. M. The social lives of dogs **636.7**

DOGS—BEHAVIOR—NEW JERSEY—MONTCLAIR—ANECDOTES

Katz, J. The new work of dogs **636.7**

DOGS—BREEDING

See also Breeding

DOGS—DISEASES

Eldredge, D. Dog owner's home veterinary handbook **636.7**

McGinnis, T. The well dog book **636.7**

DOGS—ENCYCLOPEDIAS

Coile, D. C. Encyclopedia of dog breeds **636.7**

Fogle, B. The new encyclopedia of the dog **636.7**

DOGS—NEW JERSEY—MONTCLAIR—ANECDOTES

Katz, J. The new work of dogs **636.7**

DOGS—PSYCHOLOGY

See also Animal intelligence; Comparative psychology; Psychology

Budiansky, S. The truth about dogs **636.7**

McConnell, P. For the love of a dog **636.7**

DOGS—SOCIAL ASPECTS—NEW HAMPSHIRE—ANECDOTES

Thomas, E. M. The social lives of dogs **636.7**

DOGS—TRAINING

Arden, A. Dog-friendly dog training **636.7**

Burch, M. R. Citizen canine **636.7**

Dibra, B. Dogspeak **636.7**

Fogle, B. New dog **636.7**

Katz, J. Katz on dogs **636.7**

Monks of New Skete How to be your dog's best friend **636.7**

Pelar, C. Living with kids and dogs—without losing your mind **636.7**

Rutherford, C. How to raise a puppy you can live with **636.7**

Taylor, D. Old dog, new tricks **636.7**

Dogs behaving badly. Dodman, N. H. **636.7**

Dogs that know when their owners are coming home. Sheldrake, R. **133.8**

Dogs: the ultimate care guide. **636.7**

Dogspeak. Dibra, B. **636.7**

Dogtown. East, E. **974.4**

Doh, Jenny

Signature styles **646.4**

Doherty, Gerard M.

(ed) Current surgical diagnosis & treatment **617**

Dohrmann, George

Play their hearts out **796.323**

Doidge, Norman

The brain that changes itself **612.8**

Doing nothing. Lutz, T. **174**

Dojny, Brooke

The New England cookbook **641.5**

Dolin, Eric Jay

Fur, fortune, and empire **381**

Leviathan **639.2**

Dolnick, Barrie

Luck **130**

Dolnick, Edward

Dubofsky, Melvyn
Labor in America   **331.8**
(ed) The Oxford companion to United States history   **973**
Dubois, Laurent
Soccer empire   **796.334**
Dubus, Andre, 1959-
Townie   **92**
Duca, Michael
Turbow, J. The baseball codes   **796.357**
Duchamp. Tomkins, C.   **709**
DUCKS
    See also Birds; Poultry
Dudden, Faye E.
Fighting chance   **324.6**
Due considerations. Updike, J.   **814**
DUE PROCESS OF LAW
    See also Administration of justice; Civil rights
DUELING
    See also Manners and customs; Martial arts
Duffield, Mary Rose
Plants for dry climates   **635.9**
Duffy, Eamon
Saints & sinners   **282**
Duffy, Michael
The presidents club   **973.92**
Duflo, Esther
(jt. auth) Banerjee, A. Poor economics   **339.4**
Dufty, William
Holiday, B. Lady sings the blues   **92**
Dugan, Alan
Poems seven   **811**
Duguid, Naomi
Alford, J. Beyond the Great Wall   **641.5**
Duhamel, Denise
Ka-ching!   **811**
Duiker, William J.
Ho Chi Minh   **959.704**
Duino elegies. Rilke, R. M.   **831**
Dukakis, Olympia
Ask me again tomorrow   **92**
Duke University/Center for Documentary Studies
Hirsch, E. How to read a poem   **808.1**
Duke, Kacy
The show it love workout   **613.7**
Duke, Lynne
Mandela, Mobutu, and me   **968.06**
Duke, Patty
A brilliant madness   **616.89**
Dulles, Foster Rhea
Dubofsky, M. Labor in America   **331.8**
Dumanoski, Dianne
The end of the long summer   **551.6**
DUMPS, TOXIC *See* Hazardous waste sites
Dunaway, David King
How can I keep from singing?   **92**

Dunbar, R. I. M.
Grooming, gossip, and the evolution of language   **599.93**
Duncan, David Ewing
Hernando de Soto   **970.01**
Duncan, Dayton
Lewis & Clark   **917**
The national parks   **333.7**
Ward, G. C. The West   **978**
Duncan, Robert Edward
Selected poems   **811**
Dungy, Camille T.
(ed) Black nature   **808**
Dunham, William
The mathematical universe   **510**
Dunlop, Nic
The lost executioner   **959.6**
Dunn, Erica H.
Birds at your feeder   **598**
Dunn, Jon
Alderfer, J. National Geographic birding essentials   **598**
Dunn, Patricia A.
Grammar rants   **428**
Dunn, Rob
The wild life of our bodies   **579**
Dunn, Stephen
Different hours   **811**
Local visitations   **811**
Loosestrife   **811**
New & selected poems, 1974-1994   **811**
Dunn, Susan
Burns, J. M. The three Roosevelts   **973.91**
Sister revolutions   **973.3**
Dunne, Dominick
Justice   **345**
Dunne, John Gregory
Monster   **791.43**
Dunne, Pete
Bayshore summer   **508**
Pete Dunne on bird watching   **598**
Pete Dunne's essential field guide companion   **598**
Dunnigan, James F.
The Pacific War encyclopedia   **940.54**
Dunning, John
On the air   **791.44**
Dunning, John B.
(ed) Sibley, D. The Sibley guide to bird life & behavior   **598**
Duplacey, James
(comp) Official guide to the players of the Hockey Hall of Fame   **796.962**
DuPriest, Laura
Natural beauty   **646.7**
Dupuy, Jessica
Cole, T. Uchi: the cookbook   **641.6**

E

E. Bodanis, D.   **530.1**

E. B. White. Elledge, S.   **92**

E.E. Cummings. Sawyer-Laucanno, C.   **92**

E-habits. Charnock, E.   **302.23**

E-MAIL *See* Electronic mail systems

**E-MAIL REFERENCE SERVICES (LIBRAR-
IES)** *See* Electronic reference services (Libraries)

E-metrics for library and information professionals.
White, A. C.   **025.2**

Eaarth. McKibben, B.   **253**

Eady, Cornelius

    Brutal imagination   **811**

Eagan, Daniel

    America's film legacy   **791.43**

Eagle against the sun. Spector, R.   **940.54**

Eagle blue. D'Orso, M.   **796.323**

Eagle's plume. Beans, B. E.   **598**

Eagleman, David

    Incognito   **153**

EAGLES

    See also Birds; Birds of prey

Earle, Sylvia A.

    The world is blue   **551.46**

EARLY CHILDHOOD EDUCATION

    See also Education

Early Christian & Byzantine art. Lowden, J. **709.02**

EARLY CHRISTIAN LITERATURE

    See also Christian literature; Literature; Me-
dieval literature

The early national period. Purcell, S. J.   **973.4**

EARLY PRINTED BOOKS

    See also Books

EARLY PRINTED BOOKS—17TH CENTURY

    Collins, P. The book of William   **822.3**

**EARLY PRINTED BOOKS—GREAT BRIT-
AIN—17TH CENTURY**

    Collins, P. The book of William   **822.3**

Early spring. Seidl, A.   **363.7**

Earth. Alley, R. B.   **621**

EARTH

    See also Planets; Solar system

Earth.   **550**

Earth. Fortey, R. A.   **551.7**

EARTH—AGE

    Hazen, R. M. The story of Earth   **550**

EARTH—CRUST

    See also Earth—Internal structure

EARTH—GRAVITY *See* Gravity

EARTH—INTERNAL STRUCTURE

    Hazen, R. M. The story of Earth   **550**

EARTH DAY

    Nelson, G. Beyond Earth Day   **333.72**

Earth in the balance. Gore, A.   **304.2**

The earth moved. Stewart, A.   **592**

The **Earth** moves. Hofstadter, D.   **509**

Earth ponds A to Z. Matson, T.   **627**

EARTH SCIENCES

    See also Physical sciences; Science

    Flannery, T. Here on Earth   **551**

    Gates, A. E. A to Z of earth scientists   **920.003**

    Hazen, R. M. The story of Earth   **550**

    Morton, R. L. Music of the earth   **550**

EARTH SCIENCES—DICTIONARIES

    The Facts on File dictionary of earth science   **550**

EARTH SCIENCES—ENCYCLOPEDIAS

    Allaby, M. The encyclopedia of Earth   **910**

    Kusky, T. M. Encyclopedia of earth science   **550**

EARTH SCIENCES—HISTORY

    Flannery, T. Here on Earth   **551**

EARTH SCIENCES—MEASUREMENT

    Nicastro, N. Circumference   **526**

EARTH SCIENTISTS

    Gates, A. E. A to Z of earth scientists   **920.003**

The **earth** shall weep. Wilson, J.   **970.004**

EARTH SHELTERED HOUSES

    See also House construction; Houses; Under-
ground architecture

Earth under fire. Braasch, G.   **363.7**

The **earth's** biosphere. Smil, V.   **577**

EARTH, EFFECT OF MAN ON *See* Human influence on nature

Earth, the sequel. Krupp, F. D.   **621**

EARTH-FRIENDLY TECHNOLOGY *See* Green
technology

EARTHENWARE *See* Pottery

Earthly measures. Hirsch, E.   **811**

EARTHQUAKE SEA WAVES *See* Tsunamis

EARTHQUAKES

    See also Earth; Geology; Natural disasters;
Physical geography

    Gates, A. E. Encyclopedia of earthquakes and vol-
canoes   **551.2**

    Hough, S. E. Richter's scale   **92**

    Palmer, J. Heaven cracks, earth shakes   **951**

    Zeilinga de Boer, J. Earthquakes in human his-
tory   **363.34**

EARTHQUAKES—CALIFORNIA

    Winchester, S. A crack in the edge of the
world   **979.4**

**EARTHQUAKES—CALIFORNIA—SAN
FRANCISCO—HISTORY—20TH CENTU-
RY**

    Winchester, S. A crack in the edge of the
world   **979.4**

EARTHQUAKES—ENCYCLOPEDIAS

    Gates, A. E. Encyclopedia of earthquakes and vol-
canoes   **551.2**

EARTHQUAKES—HISTORY

    Zeilinga de Boer, J. Earthquakes in human his-
tory   **363.34**

EARTHQUAKES—MISSOURI—NEW MADRID REGION

Feldman, J. When the Mississippi ran backwards **551.2**

EARTHQUAKES—UNITED STATES

Feldman, J. When the Mississippi ran backwards **551.2**

Earthquakes in human history. Zeilinga de Boer, J. **363.34**

EARTHWORKS (ART)

See also Art

EARTHWORMS

Stewart, A. The earth moved **592**

Easson, Angus

(ed) Gaskell, E. C. The life of Charlotte Bronte **92**

EAST AFRICA

See also Africa

EAST AND WEST

See also International relations

Bernstein, R. The East, the West, and sex **306.7**

Ernst, C. W. Following Muhammad **297**

Fuller, G. E. A world without Islam **297**

Morris, I. Why the West rules—for now **909**

EAST INDIAN AMERICANS

Rao, C. In Hanuman's hands **92**

EAST INDIAN ART *See* Indian art

EAST INDIANS

Hajratwala, M. Leaving India **92**

EAST INDIANS—ENGLAND—LONDON

Seth, V. Two lives **92**

EAST INDIANS—TRINIDAD—SOCIAL LIFE AND CUSTOMS

Naipaul, V. S. Reading & writing **92**

East to the dawn. Butler, S. **629.13**

East, Elyssa

Dogtown **974.4**

The **East,** the West, and sex. Bernstein, R. **306.7**

EASTER

See also Christian holidays; Holy Week

Easter everywhere. Steinke, D. **92**

EASTERN CHURCHES

See also Christian sects; Christianity

Eastern Europe. **940**

Eastern religions. **200.9**

The **Eastern** stars. Kurlansky, M. **796.357**

Easy. Ponsot, M. **811**

EASY AND QUICK COOKING *See* Quick and easy cooking

An **easy** burden. Young, A. **92**

Easy information sources for ESL, adult learners, & new readers. Riechel, R. **016**

EASY READING MATERIALS

See also Children's literature; Reading materials

Easy riders, raging bulls. Biskind, P. **791.43**

Easy to love, difficult to discipline. Bailey, R. A. **155**

Eat, drink and be healthy. Willett, W. **613.2**

Eat, pray, love. Gilbert, E. **92**

Eat, sleep, poop. Cohen, S. W. **618.92**

EATING *See* Dining; Gastronomy

EATING (PHILOSOPHY)

Grescoe, T. Bottomfeeder **641.6**

Eating animals. Foer, J. S. **641.3**

EATING CUSTOMS

See also Diet; Human behavior; Nutrition

Allen, S. L. In the devil's garden **641**

Cardello, H. Stuffed **616.3**

Collingham, E. M. Curry **394.1**

Colquhoun, K. Taste: the story of Britain through its cooking **641.3**

Davidson, A. The Oxford companion to food **641**

The food of a younger land **394.1**

Grimes, W. Appetite city **394.1**

Hopp, S. L. Animal, vegetable, miracle **381**

Lappé, A. Diet for a hot planet **641**

Lee, J. 8. The fortune cookie chronicles **641.5**

Mayle, P. French lessons **394.1**

McWilliams, J. E. Just food **394.1**

Nesheim, M. Why calories count **613.2**

New Yorker (Periodical) Secret ingredients **641**

Perche agli Italiani piace/English Why Italians love to talk about food **641.5**

Pollan, M. In defense of food **613**

Pollan, M. The omnivore's dilemma **394.1**

Standage, T. An edible history of humanity **394.1**

Tye, D. Baking as biography **92**

Vileisis, A. Kitchen literacy **641.5**

Wrangham, R. W. Catching fire **641.3**

Wright, C. A. A Mediterranean feast **641**

EATING CUSTOMS—ECONOMIC ASPECTS

Cowen, T. An economist gets lunch **394.1**

EATING CUSTOMS—FRANCE

Guiliano, M. French women don't get fat **613.2**

EATING CUSTOMS—GREAT BRIATAIN—HISTORY

Spencer, C. British food **394.1**

EATING CUSTOMS—GREECE

Kochilas, D. The glorious foods of Greece **641.59**

EATING CUSTOMS—HISTORY

Allen, S. L. In the devil's garden **641**

Wrangham, R. W. Catching fire **641.3**

EATING CUSTOMS—INDIA—HISTORY

Collingham, E. M. Curry **394.1**

EATING CUSTOMS—ITALY—HISTORY

Perche agli Italiani piace/English Why Italians love to talk about food **641.5**

EATING CUSTOMS—ITALY—TUSCANY

Buford, B. Heat **641.5**

EATING CUSTOMS—NEW YORK (N.Y.)

Grimes, W. Appetite city **394.1**

EATING CUSTOMS—PSYCHOLOGICAL ASPECTS

Sandel, M. J. What money can't buy   **330.1**

ECONOMICS—PSYCHOLOGICAL ASPECTS

Dubner, S. J. Freakonomics   **330**

Fox, J. The myth of the rational market   **332.6**

Levitt, S. D. Superfreakonomics   **330**

ECONOMICS—SOCIOLOGICAL ASPECTS

Dubner, S. J. Freakonomics   **330**

Levitt, S. D. Superfreakonomics   **330**

ECONOMICS—TERMINOLOGY

Romans, C. How to speak money   **332.024**

ECONOMICS AND CHRISTIANITY *See* Christianity and economics

Economics for the rest of us. Adler, M.   **330**

An **economist** gets lunch. Cowen, T.   **394.1**

ECONOMISTS

Commager, H. S. The American mind   **973**

Ebenstein, A. O. Milton Friedman   **92**

Ellison, R. The collected essays of Ralph Ellison   **814**

Greenspan, A. The age of turbulence   **92**

Heilbroner, R. L. The worldly philosophers   **330.1**

Hollis, L. London rising   **942**

Johnson-Sirleaf, E. This child will be great   **92**

Martin, J. Greenspan   **92**

McPhee, J. A. The ransom of Russian art   **709**

Mill, J. S. Autobiography   **92**

Overtveldt, J. v. Bernanke's test   **332.1**

Snyder, L. J. The philosophical breakfast club   **509**

Wessel, D. In Fed we trust   **332.1**

Woodward, B. Maestro: Greenspan's Fed and the American boom   **331.1**

Ecosystem [series]

Day, T. Oceans   **551.46**

ECOSYSTEMS *See* Ecology

ECOTERRORISM

See also Environmental movement; Terrorism

Potter, W. Green is the new red   **320.5**

The **ecstasy** of influence. Lethem, J.   **814**

ECUMENICAL COUNCILS *See* Councils and synods

EDAPHOLOGY *See* Soil ecology

EDDAS

See also Old Norse literature; Poetry; Scandinavian literature

Eddy, Mary Baker

Science and health, with key to the Scriptures   **289.5**

Edelman, Hope

Motherless daughters   **155.9**

Motherless mothers   **155.9**

Edelman, Marian Wright

Lanterns   **92**

The measure of our success   **170**

Edelman, Shimon

The happiness of pursuit   **153**

Edelson, Mat

Katz, R. The cancer-fighting kitchen   **641.5**

Edelson, Mitchell

Turkington, C. The encyclopedia of women's reproductive cancer   **616.99**

Eden's outcasts. Matteson, J.   **92**

Edey, Maitland Armstrong

Johanson, D. C. Lucy: the beginnings of humankind   **599.93**

Edgar A. Poe. Silverman, K.   **92**

Edgar Allan Poe & the juke-box. Bishop, E.   **811**

Edgar Cayce. Kirkpatrick, S.   **92**

Edgar, Blake

Johanson, D. C. From Lucy to language   **599.93**

Klein, R. G. The dawn of human culture   **599.93**

Edge of empire. Jasanoff, M.   **909.08**

The **edge** of medicine. Hanson, W.   **610.28**

The **edge** of physics. Ananthaswamy, A.   **530**

The **edge** of the sea. Carson, R.   **577.7**

Edgerton, David

The shock of the old   **600**

An **edible** history of humanity. Standage, T.   **394.1**

EDIBLE PLANTS

See also Economic botany; Food; Plants

Angier, B. Field guide to edible wild plants   **581.6**

The Cambridge world history of food   **641.3**

Chilies to chocolate   **641.3**

Gibbons, E. Stalking the wild asparagus   **581.6**

Van Wyk Food plants of the world   **581.6**

EDIFICES *See* Buildings

Edison. Israel, P.   **92**

Edison's Eve. Wood, G.   **629.8**

Edith Wharton. Lee, H.   **92**

EDITING

See also Authorship; Publishers and publishing

EDITIONS

See also Bibliography

EDITORS

Alice Walker   **813**

Alice Walker's The color purple   **813**

Arana, M. American chica   **92**

Athill, D. Somewhere towards the end   **92**

Black women writers (1950-1980)   **810**

Bloom, H. The anatomy of influence   **801**

Bowles, H. Jacqueline Kennedy   **92**

Breslin, E. Drinking with Miss Dutchie   **92**

Burana, L. I love a man in uniform   **92**

Child, J. As always, Julia   **92**

Clark, J. Heart like water   **976.3**

Danticat, E. Brother, I'm dying   **92**

Danticat, E. Create dangerously   **92**

Davis, J. H. Jacqueline Bouvier   **92**

Ehrlich, G. A match to the heart   **617.1**

Galbraith, J. K. Name-dropping   **973.9**

Gardner, H. Creating minds   **153.3**

Gass, W. H. Finding a form: essays   **814**

Gates, H. L. The future of the race   **305.896**

A. **616.8**

Encyclopedia of American business. **338**

Encyclopedia of American cultural and intellectual history. **973**

Encyclopedia of American ethnic literature [series]

Encyclopedia of American Indian literature **810**

Encyclopedia of American folk art. **745**

Encyclopedia of American folklife. **398**

Encyclopedia of American foreign policy. Hastedt, G. P. **327**

Encyclopedia of American gospel music. **782.25**

Encyclopedia of American historical documents. **973**

Encyclopedia of American history. **973**

Encyclopedia of American Indian costume. Paterek, J. **391**

Encyclopedia of American Indian literature. **810**

Encyclopedia of American literature. Facts on File, I. **810**

Encyclopedia of American military history. **355**

Encyclopedia of American poetry, the twentieth century. **811**

The Encyclopedia of American political history. **973**

Encyclopedia of American prisons. **365**

Encyclopedia of American radio, 1920-1960. Sies, L. F. **791.44**

Encyclopedia of American religion and politics. Djupe, P. A. **322**

Encyclopedia of American religious history. Queen, E. L. **200.9**

Encyclopedia of American women in business. Krismann, C. **920.003**

Encyclopedia of ancient Asian civilizations. Higham, C. **950**

Encyclopedia of ancient Egypt. Bunson, M. R. **932**

Encyclopedia of animal behavior. **591.5**

Encyclopedia of animal rights and animal welfare. **179**

Encyclopedia of applied ethics. **170**

Encyclopedia of aquarium & pond fish. Alderton, D. **639.34**

The encyclopedia of arthritis. **616.7**

Encyclopedia of artists. **709**

Encyclopedia of associations. **061**

Encyclopedia of atmospheric sciences. **551.5**

The encyclopedia of autism spectrum disorders. Turkington, C. **616.85**

The encyclopedia of autoimmune diseases. Cassell, D. K. **616.97**

Encyclopedia of bioethics. **174**

The Encyclopedia of blindness and vision impairment. **362.4**

The encyclopedia of breast cancer. Turkington, C. **616.99**

Encyclopedia of business information sources. **650**

The encyclopedia of cancer. Turkington, C. **616.99**

Encyclopedia of careers and vocational guidance. J.G. Ferguson Publishing Company **331.7**

The encyclopedia of censorship. Green, J. **363.31**

Encyclopedia of chemistry. Rittner, D. **540**

The Encyclopedia of Chicago. **977.3**

Encyclopedia of Christmas and New Year's celebrations. Gulevich, T. **394.26**

Encyclopedia of classical philosophy. **180**

Encyclopedia of clothing and fashion. **391**

The encyclopedia of complementary and alternative medicine. Navarra, T. **615.5**

Encyclopedia of computer science and technology. Henderson, H. **004**

Encyclopedia of conflicts since World War II. **909.82**

Encyclopedia of constitutional amendments, proposed amendments, and amending issues, 1789-2010. Vile, J. R. **342**

Encyclopedia of contemporary Japanese culture. **952.04**

The encyclopedia of cosmetic and plastic surgery. Rinzler, C. A. **617.9**

The Encyclopedia of country music. **781.642**

Encyclopedia of crime & justice. **364**

Encyclopedia of crime and punishment. **346**

Encyclopedia of criminology. **364**

Encyclopedia of Cuba. Martinez-Fernandez, L. **972.91**

The encyclopedia of cults, sects, and new religions. **200**

Encyclopedia of death and dying. **306.9**

The encyclopedia of demons and demonology. Guiley, R. E. **133.4**

Encyclopedia of diet fads. Bijlefeld, M. **613.2**

Encyclopedia of dinosaurs. **567.9**

Encyclopedia of disability. **362.4**

Encyclopedia of dog breeds. Coile, D. C. **636.7**

Encyclopedia of domestic violence. **362.82**

Encyclopedia of early Christianity. **270.1**

The encyclopedia of Earth. Allaby, M. **910**

Encyclopedia of earth science. Kusky, T. M. **550**

Encyclopedia of earthquakes and volcanoes. Gates, A. E. **551.2**

Encyclopedia of education. **370**

The encyclopedia of endocrine diseases and disorders. Petit, W. **616.4**

Encyclopedia of environmental issues. **363.7**

Encyclopedia of environmental science. Mongillo, J. F. **363.7**

Encyclopedia of ethics. **170**

Encyclopedia of exploration. Waldman, C. **910.3**

Encyclopedia of forensic science. Bell, S. **363.2**

Encyclopedia of forensic science. Conklin, B. G. **363.25**

Encyclopedia of fundamentalism. **200.9**

Encyclopedia of gardens. **635**

The encyclopedia of genetic disorders and birth de-

See also Medicine

ENDOWMENTS

See also Finance

ENDOWMENTS—DIRECTORIES

The Foundation directory	061
Endpoint and other poems. Updike, J.	811
The **ends** of the earth.	998
The **Endurance.** Alexander, C.	998

ENDURANCE, PHYSICAL *See* Physical fitness

Enelow, Wendy S.

Cover letter magic	650.14
Enemies. Weiner, T.	363.25
Enemies of the people. Marton, K.	92
Enemy of the state. Newton, M. A.	345

ENERGY *See* Energy resources; Force and energy

ENERGY AND STATE *See* Energy policy

ENERGY CONSERVATION

See also Conservation of natural resources; Energy resources

Feynman, R. P. Six easy pieces	530
Krupp, F. D. Earth, the sequel	621

ENERGY CONSUMPTION

See also Energy resources

ENERGY DEVELOPMENT

See also Energy resources

Alley, R. B. Earth	621

ENERGY INDUSTRY EXECUTIVES

Bruni, F. Ambling into history: the unlikely odyssey of George W. Bush	973.931
Burrough, B. The big rich	338.2
Bush, G. W. (. W. Decision points	92
Chernow, R. Titan: the life of John D. Rockefeller, Sr.	92
Clarke, R. A. Against all enemies	973.931
Corn, D. The lies of George W. Bush	973.931
Dershowitz, A. M. Supreme injustice	324.9
Dowd, M. Bushworld	973.931
Draper, R. Dead certain	973.931
Epstein, E. J. Dossier	92
Farmer, J. J. The ground truth	973.931
Hersh, S. M. Chain of command	973.931
Miller, T. C. Blood money	956.7
Minutaglio, B. First son: George W. Bush and the Bush family dynasty	92
Schlesinger, A. M. (. M. War and the American presidency	327.1
Schwartz, R. A. Encyclopedia of the Persian Gulf War	956.704
Walsh, J. The J. Paul Getty Museum and its collections	708.1
Woodward, B. The commanders	973.928
Woodward, B. Plan of attack	956.7
Woodward, B. State of denial	973.931

ENERGY INTAKE—PHYSIOLOGY

Nesheim, M. Why calories count	613.2

ENERGY POLICY

McGraw, S. The end of country	333.79
Yergin, D. The quest	333.79

ENERGY POLICY

See also Energy resources; Industrial policy

ENERGY RESOURCES

Friedman, T. L. Hot, flat, and crowded	363.7
McGraw, S. The end of country	333.79
Yergin, D. The quest	333.79

ENERGY RESOURCES—GOVERNMENT POLICY *See* Energy policy

ENERGY RESOURCES DEVELOPMENT *See* Energy development

Engard, Nicole C.

(ed) Library mashups	020

Engel, Beverly

The nice girl syndrome	155.6

Engel, Jonathan

American therapy	616.89

Engel, Peter

10-fold origami	736

Engelberg, Stephen

Germs	358

Engelbreit, Mary

Mary Engelbreit's children's companion	645

Engels, Friedrich

Marx, K. The Communist manifesto	335.4

ENGINEERING

See also Industrial arts; Technology

Molotch, H. L. Where stuff comes from	620
Petroski, H. The essential engineer	620
Petroski, H. Invention by design	620
Petroski, H. Remaking the world	620
Petroski, H. Success through failure	620
Van Nostrand's concise encyclopedia of science	503

ENGINEERING—ENCYCLOPEDIAS

Van Nostrand's concise encyclopedia of science	503

ENGINEERING—HISTORY

American Society of Mechanical Engineers/History and Heritage Committee Landmarks in mechanical engineering	621
Berlow, L. H. The reference guide to famous engineering landmarks of the world	620
Tobin, J. Great projects	609

ENGINEERING—SOCIAL ASPECTS

Petroski, H. Invention by design	620
Tobin, J. Great projects	609

ENGINEERING—STUDY AND TEACHING

Poe, M. Learning to communicate in science and engineering	501

ENGINEERING DESIGN

Petroski, H. Success through failure	620

ENGINEERING GEOLOGY

Goodell, J. How to cool the planet	551.6

ENGINEERING, GENETIC *See* Genetic engineering

ENGINEERS

See also Environment; Natural disasters

Ladd, B. Autophobia	**303.4**
McKibben, B. Eaarth	**253**
Novacek, M. J. Terra	**576.8**
Safina, C. The view from Lazy Point	**508**
Wilcove, D. S. No way home	**591.56**
Wilson, E. O. The future of life	**333.95**

ENVIRONMENTAL DESTRUCTION *See* Environmental degradation

ENVIRONMENTAL DETERIORATION *See* Environmental degradation

ENVIRONMENTAL ECONOMICS

Berry, W. Citizenship papers **338.1**

ENVIRONMENTAL ENGINEERING

Goodell, J. How to cool the planet **551.6**

ENVIRONMENTAL ENGINEERING—UNITED STATES

Humes, E. Garbology **628.4**

ENVIRONMENTAL ETHICS

See also Ethics

ENVIRONMENTAL HEALTH

See also Environmental influence on humans; Public health

Boyd, D. R. Dodging the toxic bullet	**615.9**
Callahan, J. R. Biological hazards	**615.9**
Davis, D. The secret history of the war on cancer	**616.99**
Environmental health sourcebook	**616.9**
Gonzalez, J. Fallout	**363.7**
Johansen, B. E. The dirty dozen: toxic chemicals and the earth's future	**363.738**
Markowitz, G. E. Deceit and denial	**615.9**
May, J. C. Jeff May's healthy home tips	**613**
Shabecoff, A. Poisoned profits	**618.92**
Smith, R. Slow death by rubber duck	**615.9**
Sustaining life	**333.95**
Walters, M. J. Six modern plagues and how we are causing them	**614.4**

ENVIRONMENTAL HEALTH—POPULAR WORKS

Walters, M. J. Six modern plagues and how we are causing them **614.4**

ENVIRONMENTAL HEALTH—SOCIAL ASPECTS

Markowitz, G. E. Deceit and denial **615.9**

Environmental health sourcebook. **616.9**

ENVIRONMENTAL ILLNESS *See* Environmentally induced diseases

ENVIRONMENTAL INFLUENCE ON HUMANS

Ackerman, D. Dawn light	**508.2**
Diamond, J. M. Guns, germs, and steel	**303.4**
Hansen, J. E. Storms of my grandchildren	**363.7**
Louv, R. Last child in the woods	**155.4**
Louv, R. The nature principle	**128**
Lynas, M. Six degrees	**551.6**

ENVIRONMENTAL INFLUENCE ON HUMANS

See also Adaptation (Biology); Human ecology; Human geography

ENVIRONMENTAL LAW

See also Environmental policy; Environmental protection; Law

ENVIRONMENTAL LITERATURE

American earth **333.72**

ENVIRONMENTAL LOBBY *See* Environmental movement

ENVIRONMENTAL MOVEMENT

See also Environment; Social movements

American earth	**333.72**
Friedman, T. L. Hot, flat, and crowded	**363.7**
Gessner, D. My green manifesto	**304.2**
Kostigen, T. M. The green book	**333.72**
Lear, L. J. Rachel Carson	**570**
Lytle, M. H. The gentle subversive	**92**
Nelson, G. Beyond Earth Day	**333.72**
Potter, W. Green is the new red	**320.5**

ENVIRONMENTAL POLICY

Diamond, J. M. Collapse: how societies choose to fail or succeed	**304.2**
Gore, A. Earth in the balance	**304.2**
Gore, A. Our choice	**363.7**
Pooley, E. The climate war	**363.7**
Speth, J. G. The bridge at the end of the world	**333.7**

ENVIRONMENTAL POLICY—CHINA

Watts, J. When a billion Chinese jump **363.7**

ENVIRONMENTAL POLICY—ENCYCLOPEDIAS

Hosansky, D. The environment A-Z **363.7**

ENVIRONMENTAL POLICY—UNITED STATES

Blatt, H. America's environmental report card	**363.7**
Chadwick, D. H. The company we keep	**333.95**
Friedman, T. L. Hot, flat, and crowded	**363.7**
Gore, A. An inconvenient truth	**363.7**
Jones, V. The green-collar economy	**363.7**
Speth, J. G. Red sky at morning	**363.7**

ENVIRONMENTAL POLICY—WESTERN STATES

Powell, J. L. Dead pool **363.6**

ENVIRONMENTAL POLLUTION *See* Pollution

ENVIRONMENTAL PROTECTION

See also Ecology; Environment

American earth	**333.72**
Beavan, C. No impact man	**333.72**
Brinkley, D. The quiet world	**333.72**
Buchmann, S. The forgotten pollinators	**577**
Gessner, D. My green manifesto	**304.2**
Goleman, D. Ecological intelligence	**333.7**
Gore, A. Earth in the balance	**304.2**
Gore, A. An inconvenient truth	**363.7**
Gore, A. Our choice	**363.7**

The selected essays of Gore Vidal **814**
The **essence** of style. DeJean, J. E. **391**
Essence total makeover. **646.7**
ESSENCES AND ESSENTIAL OILS
    See also Distillation; Oils and fats
ESSENES
    See also Jews
The **essential** agrarian reader. **338.1**
The **essential** Chaplin. **92**
The **essential** credit repair handbook. McNaughton, D. **332.024**
The **essential** cuisines of Mexico. Kennedy, D. **641.59**
The **essential** diabetes cookbook. Worrall-Thompson, A. **641.5**
The **essential** engineer. Petroski, H. **620**
The **essential** feminist reader. **305.4**
The **essential** first year. Leach, P. **649**
The **essential** guide to psychiatric drugs. Gorman, J. M. **615**
The **essential** Gwendolyn Brooks. Brooks, G. **811**
Essential Judaism. Robinson, G. **296**
The **essential** Jung. **150.19**
Essential manager's manual. Heller, R. **658.4**
The **essential** Mediterranean. Jenkins, N. H. **641.5**
The **essential** Middle East. Hiro, D. **956**
The **essential** New York Times cook book. Hesser, A. **641.5**
Essential Pepin. Pepin, J. **641.5**
The **essential** Rumi. Selections/English **891**
The **essential** transcendentalists. **141**
The **essential** writings of James Weldon Johnson. Johnson, J. W. **818**
Essentials of Asian cuisine. Trang, C. **641.5**
Essentials of classic Italian cooking. Hazan, M. **641.59**
Essex, Myron E.
    Dow, U. Saturday is for funerals **614.5**
ESTABLISHMENT CLAUSE
    Greenawalt, K. Does God belong in public schools? **379**
ESTATE PLANNING
    See also Personal finance; Planning
    Clifford, D. Make your own living trust **346.05**
    Clifford, D. Plan your estate **346.05**
    Shotwell, B. Pass it on **346.05**
    Strauss, S. D. Wills and trusts **346.05**
ESTATE PLANNING—CARICATURES AND CARTOONS
    Shotwell, B. Pass it on **346.05**
ESTATE PLANNING—HUMOR
    Shotwell, B. Pass it on **346.05**
ESTATE PLANNING—UNITED STATES—POPULAR WORKS
    Shotwell, B. Pass it on **346.05**
Estes, Angie

Tryst **811**
ESTHETICS *See* Aesthetics
ESTIMATION (MATHEMATICS) *See* Approximate computation
Estonia: a ramble through the periphery. Theroux, A. **947.98**
Estrine, Darryl
    Harvest to heat **641.5**
ESTROGEN
    Seaman, B. The greatest experiment ever performed on women **615**
ESTROGEN—THERAPEUTIC USE
    Seaman, B. The greatest experiment ever performed on women **615**
ETCHERS
    See also Artists; Engravers
    Blackburn, J. Old man Goya **92**
    Hughes, R. Goya **760**
    Schama, S. Rembrandt's eyes **92**
ETCHING
    See also Art; Pictures
Etcoff, Nancy L.
    Survival of the prettiest **391.6**
Eteraz, Ali
    Children of dust **92**
The **eternal** city. Graber, K. **811**
The **eternal** darkness. Ballard, R. D. **551.46**
Eternal enemies. **891.8**
The **eternal** frontier. Flannery, T. F. **508**
Eternal life. Spong, J. S. **236**
ETERNAL LIFE *See* Eternity; Future life; Immortality
ETERNAL PUNISHMENT *See* Hell
ETERNITY
    Eire, C. M. N. A very brief history of eternity **236**
    Spong, J. S. Eternal life **236**
ETERNITY—HISTORY OF DOCTRINES
    Eire, C. M. N. A very brief history of eternity **236**
Etherington, Mark
    Revolt on the Tigris **956.7**
ETHICISTS
    Beckwith, J. R. Making genes, making waves **576.5**
Ethics. **170**
ETHICS
    See also Philosophy
    Aristotle Nicomachean ethics **170**
    Armstrong, K. Twelve steps to a compassionate life **177**
    Carter, S. L. Integrity **170**
    Cicero, M. T. On the good life **878**
    Coles, R. Lives of moral leadership **170**
    Comte-Sponville, A. A small treatise on the great virtues **170**
    Edelman, M. W. The measure of our success **170**
    Encyclopedia of ethics **170**
    Ethics **170**

EVOLUTION (BIOLOGY)—SOCIAL ASPECTS

Rose, M. R. Darwin's spectre   **576.8**

EVOLUTION—DICTIONARIES

Mai, L. L. The Cambridge Dictionary of human biology and evolution   **612**

EVOLUTION—ENCYCLOPEDIAS

The Cambridge encyclopedia of human evolution   **599.93**

EVOLUTION—GRAPHIC NOVELS

Keller, M. Charles Darwin's On the Origin of Species   **576.8**

EVOLUTION—HISTORY

Flannery, T. Here on Earth   **551**

EVOLUTION—STUDY AND TEACHING

Long, J. Darwin's devices   **629.8**

EVOLUTION—STUDY AND TEACHING—DRAMA

Lawrence, J. Inherit the wind   **812**

EVOLUTION AND CHRISTIANITY See Creationism

Evolution and creationism. Young, C. C.   **576.8**

The **evolution** explosion. Palumbi, S. R.   **576.8**

Evolution for everyone. Wilson, D. S.   **576.8**

The **evolution** of childhood. Konner, M.   **305.23**

The **evolution** of physics. Einstein, A.   **530**

The **evolution** of useful things. Petroski, H.   **609**

Evolution, creationism, and other modern myths. Deloria, V.   **201**

Evolution: the remarkable history of a scientific theory. Larson, E. J.   **576.8**

EVOLUTIONARY ECONOMICS

McMillan, J. Reinventing the bazaar   **330.12**

EVOLUTIONARY GENETICS

Avise, J. C. Genetics in the wild   **591.3**

Pagel, M. Wired for culture   **303.4**

EVOLUTIONARY PALEOBIOLOGY

Horner, J. R. How to build a dinosaur   **567.9**

Schopf, J. W. Cradle of life   **576.8**

EVOLUTIONARY ROBOTICS

Long, J. Darwin's devices   **629.8**

Evolving God. King, B. J.   **200**

Ewans, Martin

Afghanistan   **958.1**

Ewen, David

American songwriters   **784**

(ed) Musicians since 1900   **920.003**

Ewing, Heather P.

The lost world of James Smithson   **92**

Ewing, Rex A.

Got sun? go solar   **697**

Ewing, William A.

Brandow, T. Edward Steichen   **779**

EX-CONVICTS—DRAMA.

Wilson, A. King Hedley II   **812**

EX-NUNS

See also Nuns

EX-PRESIDENTS—UNITED STATES—HISTORY

Duffy, M. The presidents club   **973.92**

EX-PRIESTS

See also Catholic Church—Clergy; Priests

An **exact** replica of a figment of my imagination. McCracken, E.   **92**

EXAMINATIONS

See also Questions and answers; Teaching

Examined lives. Miller, J.   **190**

EXCAVATION

See also Civil engineering; Tunnels

EXCAVATIONS (ARCHAEOLOGY)

Hunt, P. Ten discoveries that rewrote history **930.1**

EXCAVATIONS (ARCHAEOLOGY)—EGYPT

Hawass, Z. A. Hidden treasures of ancient Egypt   **932**

EXCAVATIONS (ARCHAEOLOGY)—GREECE

Great moments in Greek archaeology   **938**

EXCAVATIONS (ARCHEOLOGY)

See also Archeology

EXCAVATIONS (ARCHEOLOGY)—EGYPT

Hawass, Z. A. Hidden treasures of ancient Egypt   **932**

Ryan, D. P. Beneath the sands of Egypt   **92**

EXCAVATIONS (ARCHEOLOGY)—GREECE

Great moments in Greek archaeology   **938**

EXCAVATIONS (ARCHEOLOGY)—ITALY

Pellegrino, C. R. Ghosts of Vesuvius   **937**

EXCEL (COMPUTER PROGRAM)

Greiner, T. Analyzing library collection use with Excel   **025.2**

EXCEPTIONAL CHILDREN

See also Children; Elementary education

EXCEPTIONAL CHILDREN—EDUCATION—DIRECTORIES

The directory for exceptional children   **371.9**

EXCHANGE

See also Commerce

EXCHANGE OF PRISONERS OF WAR See Prisoners of war

EXCHANGE RATES See Foreign exchange

The **excruciating** history of dentistry. Wynbrandt, J.   **617.6**

EXCUSES

See also Etiquette; Manners and customs

Execution: the discipline of getting things done. Bossidy, L. A.   **658.4**

EXECUTIONERS

Dunlop, N. The lost executioner   **959.6**

EXECUTIONS AND EXECUTIONERS

See also Criminal law; Criminal procedure

EXECUTIONS AND EXECUTIONERS—UNITED STATES

Solotaroff, I. The last face you'll ever see   **364.66**

EXECUTIVE ABILITY

Experiment central. **507.8**

Experimental drawing. Kaupelis, R. **741.2**

EXPERIMENTAL FILMS

See also Motion pictures

EXPERIMENTAL MUSIC

Moore, T. No wave **781.66**

EXPERIMENTAL THEATER

See also Theater

EXPERIMENTATION ON ANIMALS See Animal experimentation

EXPERIMENTATION ON HUMANS, MEDICAL See Human experimentation in medicine

EXPERT SYSTEMS (COMPUTER SCIENCE)

See also Artificial intelligence; Data processing; Information systems

EXPERTISE

Schulz, K. Being wrong **153**

Explaining Hitler. Rosenbaum, R. **943.086**

EXPLORATION

See also Adventure and adventurers; Geography; History

Macleod, A. Explorers **910.4**

National Geographic Society (U.S.) National Geographic eyewitness to the 20th century **909.82**

The Oxford companion to world exploration **910.3**

Waldman, C. Encyclopedia of exploration **910.3**

EXPLORATION—ATLASES

Atlas of exploration **911**

EXPLORATION—ENCYCLOPEDIAS

Waldman, C. Encyclopedia of exploration **910.3**

EXPLORATION—HISTORY

Bellec, F. Unknown lands **910.4**

Lester, T. The fourth part of the world **912**

EXPLORATIONS See Exploration

EXPLORER (ARTIFICIAL SATELLITE)

See also Artificial satellites

Explorers. Macleod, A. **910.4**

EXPLORERS

See also Adventure and adventurers; Heroes and heroines

EXPLORERS—AMERICA—HISTORY

Horwitz, T. A voyage long and strange **970.01**

EXPLORERS—BIOGRAPHY

World explorers and discoverers **920.003**

EXPLORERS—BIOGRAPHY—ENCYCLOPEDIAS

Waldman, C. Encyclopedia of exploration **910.3**

EXPLORERS—DICTIONARIES

World explorers and discoverers **920.003**

EXPLORERS—GREAT BRITAIN—BIOGRAPHY

Preston, D. A first rate tragedy **919**

EXPLORERS—HISTORY

Bellec, F. Unknown lands **910.4**

EXPLORERS—NORTH AMERICA—HISTORY

Horwitz, T. A voyage long and strange **970.01**

EXPLORERS—SWEDEN

Wilkinson, A. The ice balloon **910.91**

EXPLORERS—SWEDEN—BIOGRAPHY

Wilkinson, A. The ice balloon **910.91**

EXPLORERS—UNITED STATES—BIOGRAPHY

Dolnick, E. Down the great unknown **979.1**

Explorers of the Nile. Jeal, T. **962**

Exploring consciousness. Carter, R. **153**

Exploring Lewis and Clark. Slaughter, T. P. **978**

Exploring wine. Kolpan, S. **641.2**

EXPLOSIONS

See also Accidents

MacDonald, L. M. Curse of the Narrows **971**

EXPLOSIVES

See also Chemistry

EXPORTS

See also International trade

EXPRESS HIGHWAYS

See also Roads; Traffic engineering

EXPRESS SERVICE

See also Railroads; Transportation

EXPRESSIONISM (ART)

See also Art

EXPROPRIATION See Eminent domain

EXPULSION See Penal colonies

Exquisite little knits. Kimmelstiel, L. **746.43**

EXTENDED CARE FACILITIES See Long-term care facilities

EXTERIOR FORMS

Ball, P. Nature's patterns **500.2**

EXTERMINATION OF PESTS See Pest control

EXTINCT ANIMALS

See also Animals

Barrow, M. V. Nature's ghosts **333.95**

Lister, A. Mammoths **569**

Weidensaul, S. The ghost with trembling wings **591.68**

EXTINCT CITIES

See also Archeology; Cities and towns

Hunt, P. Ten discoveries that rewrote history **930.1**

Extinct humans. Tattersall, I. **599.93**

EXTINCTION (BIOLOGY)

Barrow, M. V. Nature's ghosts **333.95**

Powell, J. L. Night comes to the Cretaceous **576.8**

Extra lives. Bissell, T. **794.8**

Extra virginity. Mueller, T. **664.362**

EXTRAGALACTIC NEBULAE See Galaxies

EXTRAMARITAL RELATIONSHIPS See Adultery

Extraordinary, ordinary people. Rice, C. **92**

EXTRASENSORY PERCEPTION

See also Parapsychology

Sheldrake, R. Dogs that know when their owners are coming home **133.8**

Sheldrake, R. The sense of being stared at **133.8**

Waldman, C. Encyclopedia of exploration **910.3**

Facts on File library of world literature [series]

Baker, W. Critical companion to Jane Austen **823**

Boyce, C. Critical companion to William Shakespeare **822.3**

Davis, P. B. Critical companion to Charles Dickens **823**

DeGategno, P. J. Critical companion to Jonathan Swift **828**

The Facts on File companion to the British novel **823**

Fargnoli, A. N. Critical companion to James Joyce **823**

Manser, M. H. Critical companion to the Bible **220.6**

Maunder, A. The Facts on File companion to the British short story **823**

Quinn, E. Critical companion to George Orwell **828**

Rollyson, C. Critical companion to Herman Melville **813**

Ross, D. A. Critical companion to William Butler Yeats **821**

Ruud, J. Critical companion to Dante **850**

Sova, D. B. Banned plays **792.09**

Thorburn, J. E. The Facts on File companion to classical drama **880**

The **Facts** on File marine science handbook. McCutcheon, S. **551.46**

Facts on File of American literature [series]

Thursby, J. S. Critical companion to Maya Angelou **818**

The Facts on File science and math handbooks [series]

McCutcheon, S. The Facts on File marine science handbook **551.46**

Facts on File science library [series]

Allaby, M. The Facts on File weather and climate handbook **551.6**

Angelo, J. A. Encyclopedia of space exploration **629.4**

Bell, S. Encyclopedia of forensic science **363.2**

Blauvelt, R. P. Encyclopedia of pollution **363.7**

Gates, A. E. Encyclopedia of earthquakes and volcanoes **551.2**

Gorini, C. A. The Facts on File geometry handbook **516**

Henderson, H. Encyclopedia of computer science and technology **004**

Kusky, T. M. Encyclopedia of earth science **550**

Longshore, D. Encyclopedia of hurricanes, typhoons, and cyclones **551.55**

Rittner, D. Encyclopedia of chemistry **540**

Rosen, J. Encyclopedia of physics **530**

Tanton, J. S. Encyclopedia of mathematics **510**

Wyman, B. C. The Facts on File dictionary of environmental science **363.7**

The **Facts** on File weather and climate handbook. Allaby, M. **551.6**

Facts on File, Inc.

The Facts on File companion to the American novel **813**

The Facts on File dictionary of earth science **550**

Encyclopedia of American literature **810**

Maunder, A. The Facts on File companion to the British short story **823**

FACTS, MISCELLANEOUS *See* Books of lists; Curiosities and wonders

FACULTY (EDUCATION) *See* Colleges and universities—Faculty; Educators; Teachers

Faderman, Lillian

Gay L.A. **306.76**

Fadiman, Anne

The spirit catches you and you fall down **306.4**

Fadiman, Clifton

(ed) World poetry **808.81**

Fading echoes. Sielski, M. **92**

FADS

> *See also* Manners and customs; Popular culture

The **faerie** queene. Spenser, E. **821**

Faerm, Steven

Fashion: design course **746.9**

Fagan, Brian M.

Fish on Friday **639.2**

The long summer: how climate changed civilization **551.6**

(ed) The Oxford companion to archaeology **930.1**

Fagan, Deirdre

Critical companion to Robert Frost **811**

Fagen, Herb

The encyclopedia of westerns **791.43**

Fagin, Dan

Toxic deception **615.9**

Fahey, David M.

(ed) Alcohol and temperance in modern history **362.292**

Fahey, Thomas D.

Basic weight training for men and women **613.7**

FAIENCE *See* Pottery

Faigman, David L.

Laboratory of justice **347**

Failed crusade. Cohen, S. F. **327**

FAILURE (PSYCHOLOGY)

Beilock, S. L. Choke **153.9**

Hallinan, J. T. Why we make mistakes **153**

Riess, J. Flunking sainthood **248.4**

FAILURE IN BUSINESS *See* Bankruptcy; Business failures

Failure is impossible. **92**

Failure is not an option. Kranz, E. F. **629.45**

FAILURE OF BANKS *See* Bank failures

FAILURES, STRUCTURAL *See* Structural fail-

FAMILY

See also Interpersonal relations; Sociology

Friedman, J. L. The busy family's guide to volunteering **302**

Gore, A. Joined at the heart **306.85**

Hewlett, S. A. The war against parents **649**

Hite, S. The Hite report on the family **306.85**

Lewis, O. The children of Sanchez **972.08**

Nathans, S. To free a family **306.3**

Tannen, D. I only say this because I love you **306.87**

Toffler, A. Future shock **303.4**

Westheimer, R. The value of family **306.85**

Family & friends' guide to domestic violence. Weiss, E. **362.82**

FAMILY—ECONOMIC ASPECTS

Hochschild, A. R. The outsourced self **306.85**

FAMILY—ENGLAND—HISTORY—19TH CENTURY

Victorian house Inside the Victorian home **306**

FAMILY—NEW YORK (STATE)—NEW YORK—CASE STUDIES

LeBlanc, A. N. Random family **305.5**

FAMILY—RELIGIOUS LIFE

See also Religious life

FAMILY—TIME MANAGEMENT

Friedman, J. L. The busy family's guide to volunteering **302**

FAMILY—UNITED STATES

Friedman, J. L. The busy family's guide to volunteering **302**

Gore, A. Joined at the heart **306.85**

Westheimer, R. The value of family **306.85**

FAMILY—WEST (U.S.)—HISTORY—19TH CENTURY

Luchetti, C. Children of the West **978**

FAMILY—WEST (U.S.)—HISTORY—19TH CENTURY—PICTORIAL WORKS

Luchetti, C. Children of the West **978**

Family affair. **305.8**

Family Bible. Delbridge, M. J. **92**

Family Britain, 1951-1957. Kynaston, D. **941.085**

FAMILY CAREGIVERS *See* Caregivers

FAMILY DEVOTIONS *See* Devotional exercises; Family—Religious life

FAMILY FARMS

See also Farms

Berry, W. Bringing it to the table **630**

FAMILY FINANCE *See* Personal finance

Family Handyman

Refresh your home **643**

FAMILY HISTORIES *See* Genealogy

Family history 101. Melnyk, M. Y. **929**

The **family** intervention guide to mental illness. Morey, B. **616.89**

FAMILY LIFE

See also Family

FAMILY LIFE—GRAPHIC NOVELS

Small, D. Stitches **741.5**

FAMILY LIFE EDUCATION

See also Education

The **family** meal. Adrià, F. **641.5**

FAMILY MEDICINE

See also Medicine

The **family** nutrition book. Sears, W. **613.2**

FAMILY PLANNING *See* Birth control

FAMILY PLANNING ADVOCATES

Baker, J. H. Margaret Sanger **92**

Rudahl, S. A dangerous woman **335**

Family planning sourcebook. **363.9**

FAMILY POLICY—UNITED STATES

Hewlett, S. A. The war against parents **649**

FAMILY PRAYERS *See* Devotional exercises; Family—Religious life

Family properties. Satter, B. **363.5**

FAMILY RELATIONS *See* Domestic relations; Family life

FAMILY REUNIONS—MASSACHUSETTS—CAMBRIDGE—HISTORY—19TH CENTURY

Nathans, S. To free a family **306.3**

FAMILY SIZE

See also Family

The **family** that couldn't sleep. Max, D. T. **616.8**

FAMILY THERAPY

See also Counseling; Psychotherapy

FAMILY TRADITIONS

See also Family life; Manners and customs

FAMILY TREES *See* Genealogy

FAMILY VIOLENCE *See* Domestic violence

FAMILY VIOLENCE—NEW YORK (STATE)—NEW YORK

Salamon, J. Facing the wind **364.15**

FAMINES

See also Food supply; Starvation

FAMINES—CHINA

Dikötter, F. Mao's great famine **951.05**

Famous American crimes and trials. **364**

Famous first facts. Kane, J. N. **031.02**

Famous first facts about American politics. Anzovin, S. **973**

Famous first facts about sports. Franck, I. M. **796**

Famous first facts about the environment. **363.7**

Famous first facts, international edition. **031.02**

Famous lines. Andrews, R. **080**

FAMOUS PEOPLE *See* Celebrities

FAN FICTION

See also Fiction

FAN FILMS

Young, C. Homemade Hollywood **791.43**

FANATICISM

See also Emotions

Fang Lizhi

(ed) Encyclopedia of the new American nation **973**

(ed) Encyclopedia of the United States in the nineteenth century **973.5**

Landmark decisions of the United States Supreme Court **347**

Millard Fillmore **92**

Finn, Robert
Organ transplants **617.9**

Finneran, Richard J.
(ed) Yeats, W. B. The collected poems of W.B. Yeats **821**

Finney, Nikky
Head off & split **811**

FINNO-RUSSIAN WAR, 1939-1940 *See* Russo-Finnish War, 1939-1940

Fiore's summer library reading program handbook. Fiore, C. D. **027.62**

Fiore, Carole D.
Fiore's summer library reading program handbook **027.62**

Firdawsi
Shahnameh **891**

Fire. Junger, S. **909.82**

FIRE
See also Chemistry
Wrangham, R. W. Catching fire **641.3**

FIRE—HISTORY
Wrangham, R. W. Catching fire **641.3**

Fire and ashes. Maclean, J. N. **363.3**

Fire and rain. Browne, D. **781.66**

FIRE ECOLOGY
See also Ecology

FIRE ENGINES
See also Engines; Fire fighting

FIRE EXTINCTION—NEW YORK (STATE)— NEW YORK—HISTORY
Golway, T. So others might live **363.37**

FIRE FIGHTERS
Downey, T. The last men out **363.34**
Halberstam, D. Firehouse **363.34**
Maclean, J. N. The Thirtymile fire **634.9**
Smith, D. Report from ground zero **363.34**
Taylor, M. A. Jumping fire **634.9**

FIRE FIGHTERS—NEW YORK (STATE)— NEW YORK
Golway, T. So others might live **363.37**

FIRE FIGHTING
See also Fire prevention; Fires
Golway, T. So others might live **363.37**
Taylor, M. A. Jumping fire **634.9**

FIRE IN MYTHOLOGY
See also Mythology

Fire in the city. Martines, L. **92**

Fire in the lake. FitzGerald, F. **959.704**

FIRE INSURANCE
See also Insurance

FIRE LOOKOUT STATIONS
Connors, P. Fire season **634.9**

FIRE LOOKOUTS
Connors, P. Fire season **634.9**

Fire lover. Wambaugh, J. **364.16**

The **fire** of his genius: Robert Fulton and the American dream. Sale, K. **620**

FIRE PREVENTION
See also Fires
Fire protection handbook **628.9**
Fire protection handbook. **628.9**
Fire season. Connors, P. **634.9**
Fire to fire. Doty, M. **811**
The **fire** within the eye. Park, D. **535**

FIREARMS
See also Weapons
Chivers, C. J. The gun **623.4**
Gun digest 2009 **623.4**
Yenne, B. Tommy gun **623.4**

FIREARMS—CATALOGS
Shooter's bible **623.4**

FIREARMS—LAW AND LEGISLATION *See* Gun control

FIREARMS—LAW AND LEGISLATION— UNITED STATES
Utter, G. H. Encyclopedia of gun control and gun rights **363.33**

FIREARMS CONTROL *See* Gun control

FIREARMS INDUSTRY
See also Industries

FIREARMS OWNERSHIP—UNITED STATES
Guns in American society **363.33**

Firebrand of liberty. Ash, S. V. **973.7**

FIREFIGHTERS
Wambaugh, J. Fire lover **364.16**

Firefly atlas of the universe. **523**

Firefly encyclopedia of the vivarium. Alderton, D. **639.3**

Firefly guide to gems. Oldershaw, C. **553.8**

Firehouse. Halberstam, D. **363.34**

FIREMEN AND FIREWOMEN *See* Fire fighters

FIREPLACES
See also Architecture—Details; Buildings; Heating; Space heaters

FIREPROOFING
See also Fire insurance; Fire prevention

FIRES
Von Drehle, D. Triangle: the fire that changed America **974.7**

FIRES
See also Accidents; Disasters; Fire

The **fires** of Vesuvius. Beard, M. **937**

The **fireside** cook book. Beard, J. **641.5**

FIREWORKS
See also Amusements

The **Firm:** the troubled life of the House of Windsor.

Junor, P.   **941.085**

Firmage, George James

(ed) Cummings, E. E. Complete poems, 1904-1962   **811**

FIRMS *See* Business enterprises

The **first** 20 minutes. Reynolds, G.   **613.7**

FIRST AID

     See also Health self-care; Home accidents; Medicine; Nursing; Rescue work; Sick

The American Red Cross first aid and safety handbook   **616.02**

Ryder, C. S. Take your pediatrician with you **618.92**

The **first** American: the life and times of Benjamin Franklin. Brands, H. W.   **92**

The **first** Americans. Adovasio, J. M.   **970.01**

First as tragedy, then as farce. Zizek, S.   **337**

First contact. Kaufman, M.   **576.8**

First darling of the morning. Umrigar, T. N.   **92**

The **first** emancipator. Levy, A.   **92**

First families. Angelo, B.   **920**

The **first** family. Dash, M.   **364.1**

First fire, then birds. Hix, H. L.   **811**

FIRST GENERATION CHILDREN *See* Children of immigrants

First great triumph. Zimmermann, W.   **973**

The **first** heroes. Nelson, C.   **940.54**

The **first** idea. Greenspan, S. I.   **153.7**

First in. Schroen, G. C.   **958.1**

First in his class: a biography of Bill Clinton. Maraniss, D.   **92**

First ladies. Schneider, D.   **920.003**

First ladies. Caroli, B. B.   **920**

FIRST LADIES—UNITED STATES *See* Presidents' spouses—United States

FIRST LOVES—FRANCE—BIOGRAPHY

Maitland, L. Crossing the borders of time   **940.53**

The **first** Paul. Borg, M. J.   **227**

First person: an astonishingly frank self-portrait. **92**

A **first** rate tragedy. Preston, D.   **919**

The **first** salute. Tuchman, B. W.   **973.3**

First son: George W. Bush and the Bush family dynasty. Minutaglio, B.   **92**

First they killed my father. Ung, L.   **959.6**

First things first. Covey, S. R.   **158**

The **first** tycoon. Stiles, T. J.   **92**

The **first** war of physics. Baggott, J. E.   **355.8**

The **first** word. Kenneally, C.   **400**

The **First** World War. Gilbert, M.   **940.3**

FIRST WORLD WAR *See* World War, 1914-1918

The **First** World War. Strachan, H.   **940.3**

The **first** year—fibromyalgia. Marek, C.   **616.7**

First you build a cloud. Cole, K. C.   **530**

FISCAL POLICY

     See also Economic policy; Public finance

Reinhart, C. M. This time is different   **338.5**

Fischer, Bobby

Bobby Fischer teaches chess   **794.1**

Fischer, David Hackett

Champlain's dream   **92**

Liberty and freedom   **323.44**

Paul Revere's ride   **973.3**

Washington's crossing   **973.3**

Fischer, Klaus P.

Nazi Germany   **943.086**

Fischer, Victor

(ed) Autobiography of Mark Twain   **92**

FISH *See* Fish as food; Fishes

FISH AS FOOD

     See also Cooking; Fishes; Food

Fagan, B. M. Fish on Friday   **639.2**

A **fish** caught in time. Weinberg, S.   **597.3**

FISH CULTURE

Greenberg, P. Four fish   **333.95**

FISH FARMING *See* Fish culture

FISH HATCHERIES *See* Fish culture

Fish on Friday. Fagan, B. M.   **639.2**

FISH POPULATIONS—RESEARCH

Rigney, M. In pursuit of giants   **597**

The **fish** that ate the whale. Cohen, R.   **338.7**

Fish without a doubt. Moonen, R.   **641.6**

The **fish's** eye. Frazier, I.   **799.1**

Fisher investments series

Fisher, K. L. How to smell a rat   **364.1**

Fisher, Carrie

Wishful drinking   **92**

Fisher, David

Fisher, E. Been there, done that   **782.421**

Read, A. The fall of Berlin   **940.54**

Fisher, Eddie

Been there, done that   **782.421**

Fisher, Edwin B.

Goldfarb, T. L. American Lung Association 7 steps to a smoke-free life   **616.86**

Fisher, James Terence

On the Irish waterfront   **331.7**

Fisher, John H.

Chaucer, G. The complete poetry and prose of Geoffrey Chaucer   **821**

Fisher, Kathleen

Taylor's guide to shrubs   **635.9**

Fisher, Kenneth L.

How to smell a rat   **364.1**

Fisher, M. F. K.

A stew or a story   **641**

Fisher, Marc

Something in the air   **384.54**

Fisher, Marshall

A terrible splendor   **796.342**

Fisher, Mary

Sleep with the angels   **362.1**

Fisher, Roy

Selected poems   **821**

Cohen, R. Sweet and low   920
D'Antonio, M. Hershey   92
FOOD INSPECTION *See* Food adulteration and inspection
The **food** intolerance bible. Haynes, A. J.   616.97
The **food** matters cookbook. Bittman, M.   641.3
The **food** of a younger land.   394.1
FOOD OF ANIMAL ORIGIN
 See also Food
 Masson, J. M. The face on your plate   641.3
The **food** of Portugal. Anderson, J.   641.5
FOOD PLANTS *See* Edible plants
Food plants of the world. Van Wyk   581.6
FOOD POISONING
 See also Poisons and poisoning
FOOD PREFERENCES—ECONOMIC AS-PECTS
 Cowen, T. An economist gets lunch   394.1
FOOD PREPARATION *See* Cooking; Food industry
FOOD PREPARATION INDUSTRY *See* Food industry
FOOD PROCESSING *See* Food industry
FOOD PROCESSING INDUSTRY *See* Food industry
FOOD RELIEF
 See also Charities; Disaster relief; Public welfare; Unemployed
 Astyk, S. A nation of farmers   338.1
FOOD SERVICE
 See also Food industry; Service industries
FOOD STAMPS
 See also Food relief
FOOD SUPPLEMENTS *See* Dietary supplements
FOOD SUPPLY
 Astyk, S. A nation of farmers   338.1
 Bloom, J. American wasteland   363.7
 Diamond, J. M. Guns, germs, and steel   303.4
 Dikötter, F. Mao's great famine   951.05
 Hesterman, O. B. Fair food   338.1
 Hewitt, B. The town that food saved   338.1
 Lappé, A. Diet for a hot planet   641
FOOD SUPPLY—CHINA
 Dikötter, F. Mao's great famine   951.05
FOOD SUPPLY—UNITED STATES
 Pollan, M. The omnivore's dilemma   394.1
FOOD TRADE *See* Food industry
FOOD WRITING
 Jacob, D. Will write for food   808
FOOD, CANNED *See* Canning and preserving
FOOD, COST OF *See* Cost and standard of living
Food, inc. Pringle, P.   363.1
Food52
 The Food52 cookbook   641.5
The **Food52** cookbook. Food52   641.5
Foods that harm, foods that heal. Reader's Digest

Association, I.   613.2
Fool for love, and other plays. Shepard, S.   812
Fool me twice. Otto, S.   303.4
Fool's gold. Tett, G.   332.6
Fool's paradise. Gaines, S. S.   975.9
Fooling ourselves. Triandis, H. C.   155.2
FOOLS AND JESTERS
 See also Comedians; Courts and courtiers; Entertainers
FOOT
 See also Anatomy
Football. Rielly, E. J.   796.332
FOOTBALL
 See also Ball games; Sports
 Anderson, L. Carlisle vs. Army   796.332
 Barra, A. The last coach: a life of Paul Bear Bryant   92
 Billick, B. More than a game   796.332
 Bissinger, H. G. Friday night lights   796.332
 Bowden, M. The best game ever   796.332
 Cosell, G. The games that changed the game   796.332
 Curtis, B. Every week a season   796.332
 Dent, J. The Junction boys   796.332
 Dent, J. Resurrection   796.332
 Dent, J. The undefeated   796.332
 Feinstein, J. Next man up   796.332
 Green, T. The dark side of the game   796.332
 Lazarus, A. Super Bowl Monday   796.332
 Miller, J. J. The big scrum   796.332
 Piascik, A. Gridiron gauntlet   796.332
 St. John, W. Rammer jammer yellow hammer   796.332
FOOTBALL—BIOGRAPHY
 Fatsis, S. A few seconds of panic   92
 Harris, D. The genius   92
 Lewis, M. The blind side   92
 Maki, A. Football's greatest stars   920
 Peter, J. Hero of the underground   92
 Sielski, M. Fading echoes   92
FOOTBALL—COACHING
 Walsh, B. The score takes care of itself   658.4
FOOTBALL—COACHING—UNITED STATES
 Dent, J. The Junction boys   796.332
FOOTBALL—ENCYCLOPEDIAS
 Rielly, E. J. Football   796.332
FOOTBALL—SOCIAL ASPECTS—TEXAS—ODESSA
 Bissinger, H. G. Friday night lights   796.332
FOOTBALL—UNITED STATES—HISTORY
 Miller, J. J. The big scrum   796.332
FOOTBALL—UNITED STATES—HISTORY—20TH CENTURY
 Bowden, M. The best game ever   796.332
FOOTBALL COACHES
 Anderson, L. Carlisle vs. Army   796.332

See also Conservation of natural resources

Egan, T. The big burn   **973.91**

FOREST CONSERVATION—KENYA

Maathai, W. Unbowed   **92**

FOREST CONSERVATION—UNITED STATES

Egan, T. The big burn   **973.91**

FOREST   CONSERVATION—UNITED STATES—HISTORY

Egan, T. The big burn   **973.91**

FOREST ECOLOGY

See also Ecology

FOREST FIRES

See also Fires

Brown, D. Under a flaming sky   **634.9**

Connors, P. Fire season   **634.9**

Egan, T. The big burn   **973.91**

Taylor, M. A. Jumping fire   **634.9**

FOREST FIRES—UNITED STATES—HISTORY

Egan, T. The big burn   **973.91**

FOREST INFLUENCES

See also Climate; Water supply

FOREST PLANTS

Darke, R. The American woodland garden   **635.9**

FOREST PRESERVATION *See* Forest conservation

FOREST PRODUCTS

See also Commercial products; Economic botany; Raw materials

The **forest** unseen. Haskell, D. G.   **577.3**

FORESTERS

Egan, T. The big burn   **973.91**

Miller, C. Gifford Pinchot and the making of modern environmentalism   **333.7**

FORESTS AND FORESTRY

See also Agriculture; Natural resources

FORESTS AND FORESTRY—TENNESSEE

Haskell, D. G. The forest unseen   **577.3**

Forever blue. D'Antonio, M.   **92**

Forever free. Foner, E.   **973.8**

The **forever** war. Filkins, D.   **956.7**

The **forger's** spell. Dolnick, E.   **759**

FORGERS

Worrall, S. The poet and the murderer   **364.15**

FORGERY

See also Crime; Fraud; Impostors and imposture

Burleigh, N. Unholy business   **933**

Worrall, S. The poet and the murderer   **364.15**

FORGERY—UTAH—SALT LAKE CITY

Worrall, S. The poet and the murderer   **364.15**

FORGERY OF MANUSCRIPTS—UTAH—SALT LAKE CITY

Worrall, S. The poet and the murderer   **364.15**

FORGETFULNESS

See also Memory; Personality

The **forgetting:** Alzheimer's, portrait of an epidemic. Shenk, D.   **616.8**

FORGING

See also Manufacturing processes; Metalwork

FORGIVENESS

See also Virtue

Kraybill, D. B. Amish grace   **364.152**

Kushner, H. S. How good do we have to be? **296.7**

Wiesenthal, S. The sunflower   **179.7**

FORGIVENESS—RELIGIOUS   ASPECTS— CHRISTIANITY

Kraybill, D. B. Amish grace   **364.152**

Forgotten armies. Bayly, C. A.   **940.54**

Forgotten founder, drunken prophet. Kauffman, B.   **92**

The **forgotten** man. Shlaes, A.   **973.91**

The **forgotten** pollinators. Buchmann, S.   **577**

FORM IN BIOLOGY *See* Morphology

FORMAL GARDENS *See* Gardens

Formica, Ronald J.

(ed) Famous first facts about the environment **363.7**

Fornay, Alfred

The African American woman's guide to successful makeup and skincare   **646.7**

Forni, Pier Massimo

The civility solution   **395**

Fornino, Stephanie

De Vito, D. World atlas of dog breeds   **636.7**

Forrest, Emma

Your voice in my head   **362.196**

Forten, James, 1766-1842 (American sailmaker and abolitionist)

About

Winch, J. A gentleman of color: the life of James Forten   **326**

Fortey, Richard

Horseshoe crabs and velvet worms   **595**

Fortey, Richard A.

Earth   **551.7**

Fossils   **560**

Life   **576.8**

Trilobite!   **560**

Forthcoming books.   **015**

FORTIFICATION

See also Military art and science

Fortin, Francois

Sports: the complete visual reference   **796**

Fortunate sons. Leibovitz, L.   **951.05**

Fortunato, Alfred

Rabiner, S. Thinking like your editor   **808**

FORTUNE *See* Fate and fatalism; Probabilities; Success

The **fortune** cookie chronicles. Lee, J. 8.   **641.5**

FORTUNE TELLING

See also Amusements; Divination

FORTUNES *See* Income; Wealth

Fortunoff Video Archive for Holocaust Testimonies

Witness   940.53

FORUMS (DISCUSSIONS) *See* Discussion groups

Forward, Susan

Toxic parents: overcoming their hurtful legacy and reclaiming your life   362.82

Fossey, Dian

Gorillas in the mist   599.88

FOSSIL HOMINIDS

See also Archeology; Fossils

Johanson, D. C. From Lucy to language   599.93

Sarmiento, E. The last human   569.9

Swisher, C. C. Java Man   599.93

Switek, B. Written in stone   576.8

Tattersall, I. Extinct humans   599.93

Walker, A. The wisdom of the bones   599.93

FOSSIL MAMMALS

See also Fossils; Mammals

Johanson, D. C. Lucy: the beginnings of humankind   599.93

FOSSIL PLANTS

See also Fossils; Plants

FOSSIL REPTILES

See also Fossils; Reptiles

The **fossil** trail. Tattersall, I.   599.93

Fossils. Fortey, R. A.   560

FOSSILS

See also Biology; Natural history; Science; Stratigraphic geology

Coenraads, R. R. Rocks and fossils   552

Fortey, R. A. Fossils   560

Fortey, R. A. Trilobite!   560

Larson, P. L. Rex appeal   567.9

Nothdurft, W. E. The lost dinosaurs of Egypt 567.9

Poinar, G. O. The quest for life in amber   560

Rea, T. Bone wars   560

Sampson, S. D. Dinosaur odyssey   567.9

Schopf, J. W. Cradle of life   576.8

Switek, B. Written in stone   576.8

Tattersall, I. The fossil trail   599.93

Thompson, I. The Audubon Society field guide to North American fossils   560

Travels with the fossil hunters   560

Wallace, D. R. The bonehunters' revenge   560

FOSSILS—COLLECTION AND PRESERVATION

Travels with the fossil hunters   560

FOSSILS—COLLECTION AND PRESERVATION—WEST (U.S.)—HISTORY—19TH CENTURY

Wallace, D. R. The bonehunters' revenge   560

FOSSILS—ENCYCLOPEDIAS

Encyclopedia of paleontology   560

Fossils, finches, and Fuegians. Keynes, R. D.   508

FOSTER CHILDREN

See also Children

FOSTER CHILDREN—LEGAL STATUS, LAWS, ETC—NEW YORK (STATE)—NEW YORK

Bernstein, N. The lost children of Wilder   362.73

FOSTER CHILDREN—NEW YORK (STATE)—NEW YORK

Bernstein, N. The lost children of Wilder   362.73

FOSTER GRANDPARENTS

See also Grandparents; Volunteer work

FOSTER HOME CARE

See also Child welfare

Bartholet, E. Nobody's children   362.76

Bernstein, N. The lost children of Wilder   362.73

FOSTER HOME CARE—UNITED STATES

Bartholet, E. Nobody's children   362.76

Foster, David K.

Angier, B. Field guide to edible wild plants 581.6

Foster, Gwendolyn Audrey

Dixon, W. W. A short history of film   791.43

Foster, Lynn V.

A brief history of Mexico   972

Foster, Nelson

(ed) Chilies to chocolate   641.3

Foster, Rick

How we choose to be happy   158

Foster, Russell G.

Rhythms of life   571.7

Foster, Steven

National Geographic desk reference to nature's medicine   615

Foster, Stephen Collins

Stephen Foster & Co.   782.42

Fothergill, Alastair

Planet Earth   508

Foulds, Adam

The broken word   821

Foulkes, Christopher

(ed) Larousse encyclopedia of wine   641.2

The **Foundation** directory.   061

Foundation for the National Archives

Center for the National Archives Experience Discovering the Civil War   973.7

FOUNDATION OFFICIALS

Conant, J. Tuxedo Park   530

Gregorian, V. The road to home   973

Halberstam, D. The best and the brightest 973.922

Seidl, A. Early spring   363.7

FOUNDATIONS

See also Architecture—Details; Buildings; Structural engineering

FOUNDING

See also Manufacturing processes; Metalwork

Founding brothers. Ellis, J. J.   973.4

Founding faith. Waldman, S.   342

Founding father: rediscovering George Washington.

Freed, Curt
Healing the brain   **616.8**

FreeDarko presents the macrophenomenal pro basketball almanac.   **796.323**

Freedman, David Noel
(ed) Eerdmans dictionary of the Bible   **220.3**

Freedman, Estelle B.
(ed) The essential feminist reader   **305.4**
No turning back   **305.4**

Freedman, Lawrence
Kennedy's wars   **973.922**

Freedman, Michael R.
Living well with asthma   **616.2**

Freedman, Samuel G.
Jew vs. Jew   **296**

FREEDMEN
Blight, D. W. A slave no more   **326**

FREEDMEN—UNITED STATES
Ward, A. The slaves' war   **973.7**

FREEDOM
See also Democracy; Political science
Fischer, D. H. Liberty and freedom   **323.44**
Foner, E. The story of American freedom   **323.44**
Pipes, R. Property and freedom   **323.4**
Purdy, J. A tolerable anarchy   **320**

Freedom and destiny. May, R.   **158**
Freedom evolves. Dennett, D. C.   **153.8**
Freedom from fear. Kennedy, D. M.   **973.91**
Freedom from fear, and other writings. Aung San Suu Kyi   **959.1**
Freedom in exile. Dalai Lama   **92**
Freedom is not enough. Walters, R. W.   **324.6**

FREEDOM MARCHES FOR CIVIL RIGHTS
See Civil rights demonstrations

FREEDOM OF ASSEMBLY
See also Civil rights; Freedom

FREEDOM OF ASSOCIATION
See also Civil rights; Freedom

FREEDOM OF CHOICE *See* Free will and determinism

FREEDOM OF CHOICE MOVEMENT *See* Prochoice movement

FREEDOM OF CONSCIENCE
See also Conscience; Freedom; Toleration

FREEDOM OF INFORMATION
See also Civil rights; Intellectual freedom
Morozov, E. The net delusion   **303.48**

FREEDOM OF MOVEMENT
See also Civil rights; Freedom

FREEDOM OF RELIGION
See also Civil rights; Freedom; Toleration
Nussbaum, M. C. Liberty of conscience   **342**
Waldman, S. Founding faith   **342**
Wexler, J. Holy hullabaloos   **342**

FREEDOM OF RELIGION—UNITED STATES
Nussbaum, M. C. Liberty of conscience   **342**

Waldman, S. Founding faith   **342**

FREEDOM OF SPEECH
See also Censorship; Civil rights; Freedom; Intellectual freedom
Bawer, B. Surrender   **297**
Bezanson, R. P. How free can the press be?   **342**
Burn this book   **814**
Rabban, D. M. Free speech in its forgotten years   **342**
Stone, G. R. Perilous times   **323.44**

FREEDOM OF THE PRESS
See also Civil rights; Freedom; Intellectual freedom; Press

FREEDOM OF THE PRESS AND FAIR TRIAL
See also Fair trial; Freedom of the press; Press

FREEDOM OF THE WILL *See* Free will and determinism

FREEDOM OF WORSHIP *See* Freedom of religion

Freedom on my mind.   **305.8**
Freedom riders. Arsenault, R.   **323**
Freedom rising. Furgurson, E. B.   **973.7**
Freedom summer. Watson, B.   **323.1**
Freedom's battle. Bass, G. J.   **341.5**
Freedom's cap. Gugliotta, G.   **975.3**
Freedom's forge. Herman, A.   **940.53**
Freedom's prophet. Newman, R. S.   **92**
Freeing the natural voice. Linklater, K.   **808.5**

FREELANCERS *See* Self-employed

Freeland, David
Automats, taxi dances, and vaudeville

Freeman, Charles
The closing of the Western mind   **940.1**
Egypt, Greece, and Rome   **909**

Freeman, Daniel
Paranoia   **616.89**

Freeman, Douglas Southall
Lee   **973.7**

Freeman, Jason
Freeman, D. Paranoia   **616.89**

Freeman, Joanne B.
Affairs of honor   **306.2**

Freeman, Joshua Benjamin
Working-class New York   **305.5**

Freeman, Mark
Gardening in your greenhouse   **635.9**

Freeman, Michael
The photographer's mind   **775**

The **Freemasons.** Ridley, J. G.   **366**

Freethinkers: a history of American secularism. Jacoby, S.   **211**

FREEZING *See* Cryobiology; Frost; Ice; Refrigeration

FREIGHT
See also Maritime law; Materials handling;

Murphy, M. Pelvic health and childbirth **618.4**

GENITALIA *See* Reproductive system

Genius. Bloom, H. **153.9**

The **genius.** Harris, D. **92**

GENIUS

See also Psychology

Bloom, H. Genius **153.9**

Murray, C. A. Human accomplishment **908**

GENIUS—CASE STUDIES

Murray, C. A. Human accomplishment **908**

The **genius** in all of us. Shenk, D. **155.2**

Genius on the edge. Imber, G. **92**

Genius: the life and science of Richard Feynman. Gleick, J. **92**

Gennari, John

Blowin' hot and cool **306**

GENOCIDE

Akcam, T. A shameful act **956.6**

Balakian, P. The burning Tigris **956.6**

de Bellaigue, C. Rebel land **956**

Goldhagen, D. J. Worse than war **364.1**

Gourevitch, P. We wish to inform you that tomorrow we will be killed with our families **967.571**

Hatzfeld, J. The antelope's strategy **967.571**

Hatzfeld, J. Machete season **967.571**

Kidder, T. Strength in what remains **92**

Palakean, G. Armenian Golgotha **956**

Snyder, T. Bloodlands **940.54**

Stearns, J. K. Dancing in the glory of monsters **967.51**

Wiesenthal, S. The sunflower **179.7**

GENOCIDE—BURUNDI

Kidder, T. Strength in what remains **92**

GENOCIDE—ENCYCLOPEDIAS

Encyclopedia of genocide and crimes against humanity **304.6**

GENOCIDE—EUROPE

Snyder, T. Bloodlands **940.54**

GENOCIDE—GERMANY

Breitman, R. Official secrets **940.54**

GENOCIDE—PSYCHOLOGICAL ASPECTS

Goldhagen, D. J. Worse than war **364.1**

GENOCIDE—RWANDA

Gourevitch, P. We wish to inform you that tomorrow we will be killed with our families **967.571**

Hatzfeld, J. The antelope's strategy **967.571**

GENOCIDE—SUDAN

Deng, B. They poured fire on us from the sky **962.4**

GENOCIDE—TURKEY

Balakian, P. The burning Tigris **956.6**

Palakean, G. Armenian Golgotha **956**

Genome. Ridley, M. **599.93**

GENOME *See* Genomes

GENOME MAPPING *See* Gene mapping

GENOMES

See also Genetics

Danchin, A. The Delphic boat **572.8**

Gee, H. Jacob's ladder **599.93**

The Genomic revolution **599.93**

Ridley, M. Genome **599.93**

Rothman, B. K. Genetic maps and human imaginations **599.93**

The **Genomic** revolution. **599.93**

GENOMICS

McElheny, V. K. Drawing the map of life **611**

Roberts, D. Fatal invention **305.8**

GENOMICS—POPULAR WORKS

The Genomic revolution **599.93**

Genovese, Michael A.

Encyclopedia of the American presidency **920.003**

GENRE PAINTING

See also Painting

Genrefied classics. Frolund, T. **016**

Genreflecting advisory series

Frolund, T. Genrefied classics **016**

Herald, D. T. Fluent in fantasy **016**

Herald, D. T. Strictly science fiction **016**

Pawuk, M. G. Graphic novels **016**

Ramsdell, K. Romance fiction **016**

Gentile, Derek

Splitters, squeezes, and steals **796.357**

Gentile, Mary C.

Giving voice to values **174**

Gentile, Olivia

Life list **92**

The **gentle** subversive. Lytle, M. H. **92**

The **gentleman** from New York: Daniel Patrick Moynihan: a biography. Hodgson, G. **973.92**

A **gentleman** of color: the life of James Forten. Winch, J. **326**

Gentleman spy. Grose, P. **973.9**

Gentry, Ann

The Real Food Daily cookbook **641.5**

Gentry, April

Rollyson, C. Critical companion to Herman Melville **813**

Gentry, Curt

Bugliosi, V. Helter skelter **364.1**

J. Edgar Hoover **353**

GEOCHEMISTRY

See also Chemistry; Earth sciences; Petrology

GEOCHEMISTS

Maddox, B. Rosalind Franklin: the dark lady of DNA **92**

GEOCHRONOMETRY

Macdougall, J. D. Nature's clocks **551.7**

GEODESY

See also Earth; Measurement

Ferreiro, L. D. Measure of the Earth **526**

GEODESY—EUROPE—HISTORY

Ferreiro, L. D. Measure of the Earth **526**

George Balanchine: the ballet maker. Gottlieb, R. A. **92**

George Bush. Parmet, H. S. **973.928**

George Eliot. Hughes, K. **823**

George F. Kennan. Gaddis, J. L. **327**

George Gershwin. Hyland, W. G. **780**

George Gershwin. Pollack, H. **92**

George Mason, forgotten founder. Broadwater, J. **92**

George Sand. Harlan, E. **92**

George Sand. Jack, B. E. **843**

George Washington. Randall, W. S. **973.4**

George Washington and the new nation, 1783-1793. Flexner, J. T. **92**

George Washington Carver. Macceca, S. **630**

George Washington's diaries. Washington, G. **973.4**

George Washington: anguish and farewell 1793-1799. Flexner, J. T. **92**

George Washington: the forge of experience, 1732-1775. Flexner, J. T. **92**

George Washington: the Founding Father. Johnson, P. **92**

George, being George. **92**

George, Daniel
  Whitehouse, P. J. The myth of Alzheimer's **616.8**

George, John H.
  Boller, P. F. They never said it **808.88**

George, Nelson
  (ed) Best music writing 2008 **781.64**
  Hip hop America **782.421**

George, Nicholas, and Wilhelm. Carter, M. **940.3**

George, Rose
  The big necessity **363.7**

George-Warren, Holly
  Public cowboy no. 1 **92**
  Lang, M. The road to Woodstock **781.66**

Georgia O'Keeffe: a life. Robinson, R. **709**

The **Georgian** star. Lemonick, M. D. **92**

Georgiana, Duchess of Devonshire. Foreman, A. **941.07**

The **Georgics** of Virgil. Virgil **872**

GEOSCIENCE *See* Earth sciences; Geology

GEOTHERMAL RESOURCES
  See also Geochemistry; Ocean energy resources; Renewable energy resources

Geraghty, Tony
  Soldiers of fortune **355.3**

Gerald Durrell. Botting, D. **590**

Gerardi, Juan, 1922-1998 (Guatemalan bishop)
  About
  Goldman, F. The art of political murder **972.81**

Gerasimo, Luisa
  (comp) McGraw-Hill's big red book of resumes **650.14**

Gerber, Michael E.
  The most successful small business in the world **658**

Gerding, Stephanie K.
  Winning grants **025.1**

Gerdts, William H.
  American impressionism **759.13**

Gerges, Fawaz
  Obama and the Middle East **327**

Gerges, Fawaz A.
  (jt. auth) Gerges, F. Obama and the Middle East **327**
  Journey of the Jihadist **322.4**

Gerhards, Paul
  How to sell what you make **658.8**

GERIATRICS—ENCYCLOPEDIAS
  Kandel, J. The encyclopedia of senior health and well being **613**

GERM THEORY OF DISEASE
  See also Communicable diseases
  Bakalar, N. Where the germs are **616**
  Biddle, W. A field guide to germs **616**

GERM WARFARE *See* Biological warfare

GERMAN COOKING
  Anderson, J. The new German cookbook **641.59**

GERMAN ESPIONAGE
  Vaughan, H. Sleeping with the enemy **92**

The **German** genius. Watson, P. **943**

GERMAN LANGUAGE
  See also Language and languages

GERMAN LANGUAGE—DICTIONARIES
  Random House Webster's German-English, English-German dictionary **433**

German library [series]
  Lessing, G. E. Nathan the Wise, Minna von Barnhelm, and other plays and writings **832**

GERMAN LITERATURE
  See also Literature
  Encyclopedia of German literature **830**

GERMAN LITERATURE—20TH CENTURY—HISTORY AND CRITICISM
  Sebald, W. G. On the natural history of destruction **833**

GERMAN LITERATURE—BIO-BIBLIOGRAPHY
  Encyclopedia of German literature **830**
  Garland, H. B. The Oxford companion to German literature **830**

GERMAN LITERATURE—DICTIONARIES
  Garland, H. B. The Oxford companion to German literature **830**

GERMAN LITERATURE—ENCYCLOPEDIAS
  Encyclopedia of German literature **830**

GERMAN LITERATURE—HISTORY AND CRITICISM
  The Cambridge history of German literature **830**
  Sebald, W. G. On the natural history of destruction **833**

GERMAN OCCUPATION OF FRANCE, 1940-1945 *See* France—History—1940-1945, German

Boylan, J. F. I'm looking through you **92**
Brown, A. Haunted Georgia **133.1**
Brown, A. Haunted Kentucky **133.1**
Brown, A. Haunted South Carolina **133.1**
Brown, A. Haunted Tennessee **133.1**
Brown, A. Haunted Texas **133.1**
Farnsworth, C. Haunted Connecticut **133.1**
Farnsworth, C. Haunted Hudson Valley **133.1**
Farnsworth, C. Haunted Massachusetts **133.1**
Farnsworth, C. Haunted New York **133.1**
Farnsworth, C. Haunted New York City **133.1**
Godfrey, L. S. Haunted Wisconsin **133.1**
Guiley, R. E. The encyclopedia of ghosts and spir-
its **133.1**
Martinelli, P. A. Haunted Delaware **133.1**
Martinelli, P. A. Haunted New Jersey **133.1**
Nesbitt, M. Haunted Pennsylvania **133.1**
Norman, M. Haunted America **133.1**
Okonowicz, E. Haunted Maryland **133.1**
Ramsland, K. M. Ghost **133.1**
Stansfield, C. A. Haunted Arizona **133.1**
Stansfield, C. A. Haunted Jersey shore **133.1**
Stansfield, C. A. Haunted Maine **133.1**
Stansfield, C. A. Haunted northern California **133.1**
Stansfield, C. A. Haunted Ohio **133.1**
Stansfield, C. A. Haunted Southern Califor-
nia **133.1**
Stansfield, C. A. Haunted Vermont **133.1**
Taylor, L. B. Haunted Virginia **133.1**
Taylor, T. Haunted Illinois **133.1**
Thuma, C. Haunted Florida **133.1**
Wilson, P. A. Haunted North Carolina **133.1**
Wilson, P. A. Haunted West Virginia **133.1**

GHOSTS—ENCYCLOPEDIAS
Guiley, R. E. The encyclopedia of ghosts and spirits **133.1**

GHOSTS—UNITED STATES
Ramsland, K. M. Ghost **133.1**
The **ghosts** of Cannae. O'Connell, R. L. **937**
The **ghosts** of Manila. Kram, M. **796.83**
Ghosts of Spain. Tremlett, G. **946**
Ghosts of Vesuvius. Pellegrino, C. R. **937**

Giamatti, A. Bartlett
A great and glorious game **796.357**

Giangreco, D. M.
Hell to pay **940.54**
The **giant** of the French Revolution. Lawday, D. **92**

GIANT PANDA
Croke, V. The lady and the panda **599.78**
Nicholls, H. The way of the panda **599.7**

GIANTS
See also Folklore; Monsters

Gibbens, Byrd
Schlissel, L. Far from home **978**

Gibbon, Edward
The decline and fall of the Roman empire **937**

Gibbon, Guy E.
(ed) Archaeology of prehistoric native America **970.01**

Gibbon, Piers
Tribe **305.8**

Gibbons, Euell
Stalking the wild asparagus **581.6**

Gibbons, Reginald
Creatures of a day **811**
It's time: poems **811**

Gibbs, Nancy
(jt. auth) Duffy, M. The presidents club **973.92**

Gibilisco, Stan
(ed) The illustrated dictionary of electronics **621.381**

Gibler, John
To die in Mexico **363.45**

Gibran, Kahlil
The collected works **818**
The Prophet **811**

Gibson, Ian
Federico Garcia Lorca: a life **92**

Gibson, James
(ed) Poems Thomas Hardy **821**

Gibson, William
The miracle worker **812**

Giddings, Paula
Ida: a sword among lions **92**

Giddins, Gary
Bing Crosby: a pocketful of dreams: the early years,
1903-1940 **92**
Jazz **781.65**
Visions of jazz **781.65**
Warning shadows **791.45**
Weather bird **781.65**
Gideon's trumpet. Lewis, A. **345**
Gielgud. Croall, J. **792**

Gielgud, John
An actor and his time **92**

Gienapp, William E.
Abraham Lincoln and Civil War America **973.7**

Gierach, John
No shortage of good days **799.1**

Gies, David Thatcher
(ed) The Cambridge history of Spanish literature **860**

Gies, Frances
Life in a medieval village **940.1**
Gies, J. Life in a medieval castle **940.2**
Gies, J. Life in a medieval city **940.1**

Gies, Joseph
Gies, F. Life in a medieval village **940.1**
Life in a medieval castle **940.2**
Life in a medieval city **940.1**

Gies, Miep
Anne Frank remembered **940.53**

Saltzman, C. Portrait of Dr. Gachet   **759.9**
Silverman, D. Van Gogh and Gauguin   **759**
Thomson, B. Van Gogh paintings   **759.9**
Going home to glory. Eisenhower, D.   **92**
Going sane. Phillips, A.   **616.89**
Going solo. Klinenberg, E.   **306.81**
Going to the territory. Ellison, R.   **818**
Golant, Susan K.
    Carter, R. Helping someone with mental illness   **616.89**
    Carter, R. Helping yourself help others   **649.8**
    Dutton, D. G. The batterer   **362.82**
Golay, Michael
    Fargnoli, A. N. Critical companion to William Faulkner   **813**
Golb, Norman
    Who wrote the Dead Sea scrolls?   **296.1**
GOLD
    See also Chemical elements; Precious metals
    Bernstein, P. L. The power of gold   **398**
Gold diggers. Gray, C.   **971**
Gold in the water. Mullen, P. H.   **797.2**
GOLD INDUSTRY—SOUTH AFRICA
    Meredith, M. Diamonds, gold, and war   **968.04**
GOLD INDUSTRY—SOUTH AFRICA—HISTORY—19TH CENTURY
    Meredith, M. Diamonds, gold, and war   **968.04**
GOLD MINES AND MINING
    Gray, C. Gold diggers   **971**
GOLD RUSH *See* Gold mines and mining
GOLD RUSHES *See* Gold mines and mining
Gold, Alison Leslie
    Gies, M. Anne Frank remembered   **940.53**
Goldacre, Ben
    Bad science   **500**
Goldbarth, Albert
    The kitchen sink   **811**
Goldberg, Bessie, d. 1963 (American homemaker and murder victim)
    About
    Junger, S. A death in Belmont   **364.152**
Goldberg, Dave
    A user's guide to the universe   **530**
Goldberg, Jeffrey
    Prisoners   **92**
Goldberg, Paul
    (jt. auth) Brawley, O. W. How we do harm **362.109**
Goldberg, Philip
    Bloomfield, H. H. Making peace with your past **158**
    American Veda   **294.5**
The **golden** age of American gardens. Griswold, M. K.   **712**
Golden book [series]
    The golden book of desserts   **641.8**
The **golden** book of desserts.   **641.8**
The **golden** bough. Frazer, J. G.   **201**

GOLDEN GATE BRIDGE (SAN FRANCISCO, CALIF.)
    See also Bridges
GOLDEN GLOVES TOURNAMENT
    Anasi, R. The gloves   **796.83**
The **golden** ratio. Livio, M.   **516.2**
The **golden** road. Millner, C.   **92**
GOLDEN RULE
    See also Ethics
GOLDEN SECTION
    Livio, M. The golden ratio   **516.2**
Golden, Alisa
    Making handmade books   **686.3**
Goldensohn, Lorrie
    (ed) American war poetry   **811**
Goldfarb, Toni L.
    American Lung Association 7 steps to a smoke-free life   **616.86**
Goldfield, David R.
    America aflame   **973.7**
The **goldfinches** of Baghdad. Adamson, R.   **821**
GOLDFISH
    See also Fishes
Goldhagen, Daniel
    Goldhagen, D. J. Worse than war   **364.1**
    Hitler's willing executioners   **940.53**
    A moral reckoning   **940.53**
Goldhagen, Daniel Jonah
    Worse than war   **364.1**
Goldman, Aaron
    Everything I know about marketing I learned from Google   **658.8**
Goldman, Ari L.
    Being Jewish   **296.4**
Goldman, Bob
    Brain fitness   **153.1**
Goldman, Emma, 1869-1940 (American anarchist)
    About
    Rudahl, S. A dangerous woman   **335**
Goldman, Francisco
    The art of political murder   **972.81**
Goldman, Merle
    Fairbank, J. K. China   **951**
Goldmann, David R.
    (ed) American College of Physicians complete home medical guide   **616.02**
Goldner, Nancy
    Balanchine variations   **792.8**
Goldschmidt, Arthur
    A brief history of Egypt   **962**
Goldsmith, Barbara
    Other powers   **92**
Goldsmith, Donald
    Tyson, N. D. G. Origins: fourteen billion years of cosmic evolution   **523.1**
Goldsmith, Francisca

The **Good** Housekeeping cookbook. Good housekeeping (Periodical) **641.5**

Good housekeeping drop 5 lbs. Jones, H. K. **613.2**

Good Housekeeping great American classics cookbook. **641.5**

Good Housekeeping Institute (New York, N.Y.)
Jones, H. K. Good housekeeping drop 5 lbs **613.2**

The **Good** Housekeeping step-by-step cookbook. **641.4**

Good morning blues: the autobiography of Count Basie. Basie, C. **92**

The **good** neighbor cookbook. Quessenberry, S. **641.5**

Good poems. **811**

The **good** rat. Breslin, J. **364.1**

The **good** soldiers. Finkel, D. **956.7**

Good to great. Collins, J. C. **658**

A **good** walk spoiled. Feinstein, J. **796.352**

The **good** war. **940.54**

The **good,** the bad, and me. Wallach, E. **92**

Goodall, Jane
Beyond innocence **92**
In the shadow of man **599.8**
Reason for hope **92**
The ten trusts **333.95**
Through a window **599.8**

Goodall, Tiffany
The ultimate student cookbook **641.5**

Goodbody, Mary
Barrenechea, T. The Basque table **641.59**
Lobel, S. The meat bible **641.6**

Goodbye, darkness. Manchester, W. **940.54**

Goodbye, Descartes. Devlin, K. J. **128**

Goodchild, Peter
Edward Teller, the real Dr Strangelove **92**

Goode, J. J.
Lang, A. P. Serious barbecue **641.5**

Goodell, Jeff
How to cool the planet **551.6**

Goodheart, Adam
1861 **973.7**

Goodman, Ellen
I know just what you mean **158.2**

Goodman, Jordan
The devil and Mr. Casement **305.8**
(ed) Tobacco in history and culture **394.1**

Goodman, Jordan Elliot
Downes, J. Finance and investment handbook **332.6**

Goodman, Linda
Linda Goodman's star signs **130**
Linda Goodman's sun signs **133.5**

Goodman, Martin
Rome and Jerusalem **933**

Goodman, Matthew
The Sun and the moon **974.7**

Goodman, Robert L.

How electronic things work—and what to do when they don't **621.381**

Goodrich, Frances
The diary of Anne Frank **812**

Goodrich, Norma Lorre
King Arthur **942.01**

Goodstein, David L.
Feynman's lost lecture **521**
Out of gas **333.8**

Goodstein, Judith R.
Goodstein, D. L. Feynman's lost lecture **521**

Goodwin, Brian C.
How the leopard changed its spots **576.8**

Goodwin, Doris Kearns
Team of rivals **92**

Goodwin, Doris Kearns
No ordinary time **92**
Team of rivals **92**
Wait till next year **796.357**

Goodwin, Jan
Price of honor **305.4**

Goodwin, Jason
Lords of the horizons **956.1**

Goodwin, Nancy
Montrose **712**

Goodwin, Scott C.
What your doctor may not tell you about fibroids **616.99**

The **Goodyear** story. Korman, R. **678**

GOOGLE
See also Web search engines; Web sites

GOOGLE (WEB SITE)
Dornfest, R. Google hacks **025.04**
Goldman, A. Everything I know about marketing I learned from Google **658.8**
Levy, S. In the plex **338.7**
Stross, R. E. Planet Google **338.7**
Vaidhyanathan, S. The Googlization of everything **338.7**

Google hacks. Dornfest, R. **025.04**

The **google** resume. Laakmann McDowell, G. **650.14**

The **Google** story. Vise, D. A. **338.7**

Googled. Auletta, K. **338.7**

The **Googlization** of everything. Vaidhyanathan, S. **338.7**

Gopnik, Adam
Angels and ages **973.7**
Through the children's gate **974.7**

Gopnik, Alison
The scientist in the crib **155.4**

Gora, Susannah
You couldn't ignore me if you tried **791.43**

Gorant, Jim
The lost dogs **636.08**

Gorbachev, Mikhail

On my country and the world   **947.085**

Gordimer, Nadine
Conversations with Nadine Gordimer   823

Gordin, Michael D.
Red cloud at dawn   355
A well-ordered thing: Dmitrii Mendeleev and the
    shadow of the periodic table   92

Gordon, Andrew
The modern history of Japan   952.03

Gordon, Charlotte
Mistress Bradstreet   92

Gordon, Deborah
Sperling, D. Two billion cars   388.3

Gordon, Elisabeth
Keller, L. The lives of ants   595.7

Gordon, James Samuel
Comprehensive cancer care   616.99

Gordon, Joanne
Schultz, H. Onward   647.9

Gordon, John Steele
A thread across the ocean   384.1

Gordon, Linda
Dorothea Lange   92

Gordon, Lois G.
The world of Samuel Beckett, 1906-1946   848

Gordon, Lyndall
Charlotte Bronte   92
Lives like loaded guns   92
T.S. Eliot   92
Vindication   92
Virginia Woolf, a writer's life   92

Gordon, Maggi McCormick
The needlecraft book   746.4

Gordon, Mary
Circling my mother   92
Joan of Arc   944
Reading Jesus   232

Gordon, Matthew
Understanding Islam   297

Gordon, Michael R.
The generals' war   956.7

Gordon, Robert
Can't be satisfied: the life and times of Muddy Wa-
    ters   782.421

Gordon-Reed, Annette
Andrew Johnson   92
The Hemingses of Monticello   920
Thomas Jefferson and Sally Hemings   973.4

Gore, Al
Earth in the balance   304.2
An inconvenient truth   363.7
Joined at the heart   306.85
Our choice   363.7

Gore, Al, 1948- (American vice-president)
About
Dershowitz, A. M. Supreme injustice   324.9

Gore, Tipper
Gore, A. Joined at the heart   306.85

Gore: a political life. Zelnick, B.   92

Goreham, Gary
(ed) Encyclopedia of rural America   973

Gorenberg, Gershom
The accidental empire   956.94

GORGE-PURGE SYNDROME *See* Bulimia

GORILLAS
    See also Apes
Fossey, D. Gorillas in the mist   **599.88**
Mowat, F. Woman in the mists: the story of Dian
    Fossey and the mountain gorillas of Africa   599

Gorillas in the mist. Fossey, D.   **599.88**

Gorini, Catherine A.
The Facts on File geometry handbook   516

Gorman, Jack M.
The essential guide to psychiatric drugs   615

Gorman, James
Horner, J. R. How to build a dinosaur   567.9

Gorman, Robert F.
(ed) Great events from history: The 20th century,
    1901-1940   **909.82**
(ed) Great events from history: The 20th century,
    1941-1970   **909.82**
(ed) Great events from history: The 20th century,
    1971-2000   **909.82**
(ed) Great lives from history: the 20th century,
    1901-2000   **920.003**

Gormley, Ken
The death of American virtue   973.929

Gorn, Elliott J.
Dillinger's wild ride   92
Mother Jones   331.88

Gorn, Michael H.
Expanding the envelope   629.13

Gorokhova, Elena
A mountain of crumbs   92

Gorra, Michael Edward
The bells in their silence   943

Gorst, Martin
Measuring eternity   115

Gortemaker, Heike B.
Eva Braun   92

Gosling, Sam
Snoop   155.9

Gosnell, Mariana
Ice   551.3

GOSPEL MUSIC
    See also African American music; Church
    music; Popular music
Ward-Royster, W. How I got over   920

GOSPEL MUSIC—ENCYCLOPEDIAS
Encyclopedia of American gospel music   782.25

GOSSIP
    See also Journalism; Libel and slander

Dunbar, R. I. M. Grooming, gossip, and the evolution of language **599.93**

GOSSIP COLUMNISTS

Walls, J. The glass castle **92**

Got sun? go solar. Ewing, R. A. **697**

Gotham. Burrows, E. G. **974.7**

GOTHIC ARCHITECTURE

See also Medieval architecture

GOTHIC ART

See also Medieval art

GOTHIC REVIVAL (ARCHITECTURE)

See also Architecture

GOTHIC REVIVAL (ART)

See also Art

GOTHIC REVIVAL (LITERATURE)

See also Literature

GOTHS

See also Teutonic peoples

Gotsch, Gwen

(ed) The Womanly art of breastfeeding **649**

Gott, J. Richard

Time travel in Einstein's universe **530.11**

Gottesman, Ronald

(ed) Violence in America **303.6**

Gottfried, Martin

Arthur Miller **92**

Gottheimer, Josh

Berry, M. F. Power in words **973.932**

Gottlieb, Anthony

The dream of reason **180**

Gottlieb, Daniel

Learning from the heart **170**

Gottlieb, Robert Adams

George Balanchine: the ballet maker **92**

Lives and letters **814**

Goudsouzian, Aram

Sidney Poitier **92**

Gould, Elizabeth

Fitzgerald, P. Invisible history **958.1**

Gould, Jonathan

Can't buy me love **920**

Gould, K. Lance

Heal your heart **616.1**

Gould, Lewis L.

Grand Old Party **324.273**

The modern American presidency **973.9**

Gould, Stephen Jay

Bully for brontosaurus **508**

The flamingo's smile **500**

Hen's teeth and horse's toes **576.8**

Leonardo's mountain of clams and the Diet of Worms **508**

The lying stones of Marrakesh **508**

The mismeasure of man **153.9**

The panda's thumb **576.8**

The richness of life **508**

The structure of evolutionary theory **576.8**

Triumph and tragedy in Mudville **796.357**

An urchin in the storm **570**

Goulston, Mark

Just listen **650.1**

Gourevitch, Philip

A cold case **364.1**

Standard operating procedure **956.7**

We wish to inform you that tomorrow we will be killed with our families **967.571**

The **gourmet** cookbook. **641.5**

The **Gourmet** cookie book. **641.8**

Gourmet today. **641.5**

GOUT

See also Arthritis; Rheumatism

Gove, Philip Babcock

(ed) Webster's third new international dictionary of the English language, unabridged **423**

Govenar, Alan B.

Lightnin' Hopkins **92**

Texas blues **781.64**

GOVERNESSES

Landon, M. Anna and the King of Siam **92**

GOVERNMENT See Political science

GOVERNMENT AGENCIES See Administrative agencies

GOVERNMENT AID

See also Government aid; Public finance

GOVERNMENT AID TO LIBRARIES

See also Government aid; Libraries—Government policy; Library finance

GOVERNMENT AND BUSINESS See Economic policy

GOVERNMENT BUSINESS ENTERPRISES

See also Business enterprises

GOVERNMENT EMPLOYEES

Conant, J. 109 East Palace **623.4**

Higham, S. Finding Chandra **364.152**

GOVERNMENT INFORMATION—DIRECTORIES

The United States government internet directory **025.04**

GOVERNMENT LENDING

See also Domestic economic assistance; Economic policy; Loans; Public finance

GOVERNMENT LIABILITY—UNITED STATES—STATES

Noonan, J. T. Narrowing the nation's power: the Supreme Court sides with the states **342**

GOVERNMENT OFFICIALS

Alexander, C. The Bounty: the true story of the mutiny on the Bounty **996**

Ambrose, S. E. The wild blue **940.54**

Bernstein, J. Oppenheimer **530**

Beschloss, M. R. The conquerors: Roosevelt, Truman, and the destruction of Hitler's Germany,

GOVERNMENT OWNERSHIP

See also Economic policy; Industrial policy; Socialism

GOVERNMENT POLICY *See* Buy national policy; Commercial policy; Cultural policy; Economic policy; Energy policy; Environmental policy; Fiscal policy; Industrial policy; Labor policy; Medical policy; Military policy; Monetary policy; Social policy; Wage-price policy

GOVERNMENT PUBLICATIONS—UNITED STATES

GOVERNMENT PUBLICATIONS—UNITED STATES—HANDBOOKS, MANUALS, ETC

GOVERNMENT, COMPARATIVE *See* Comparative government

GOVERNMENT, RESISTANCE TO *See* Resistance to government

GOVERNMENT, RESISTANCE TO—UNITED STATES—HISTORY

GOVERNMENTAL INVESTIGATIONS

See also Administration of justice

GOVERNMENTAL INVESTIGATIONS—UNITED STATES

GOVERNORS

See also State governments

Clarke, R. A. Against all enemies **973.931**

Clinton, B. My life **92**

Cooper, J. M. The warrior and the priest: Woodrow Wilson and Theodore Roosevelt **92**

Cooper, J. M. Woodrow Wilson **92**

Cordery, S. A. Alice **92**

Corn, D. The lies of George W. Bush **973.931**

Crapol, E. P. John Tyler **92**

Davis, K. S. FDR, into the storm, 1937-1940 **973.917**

Dershowitz, A. M. Supreme injustice **324.9**

DiSilvestro, R. L. Theodore Roosevelt in the Badlands **92**

Dowd, M. Bushworld **973.931**

Draper, R. Dead certain **973.931**

D'Souza, D. Ronald Reagan **973.927**

Dusinberre, W. Slavemaster president **973.6**

Egan, T. The big burn **973.91**

Farmer, J. J. The ground truth **973.931**

Feldman, N. Scorpions **920**

Felsenthal, C. Clinton in exile **92**

Fenster, J. M. FDR's shadow **92**

Finan, C. M. Alfred E. Smith, the happy warrior **92**

FitzGerald, F. Way out there in the blue **973.927**

Fried, A. F.D.R. and his enemies **92**

Galbraith, J. K. Name-dropping **973.9**

Goodwin, D. K. No ordinary time **92**

Goodwin, D. K. Team of rivals **92**

Gordon-Reed, A. Andrew Johnson **92**

Gormley, K. The death of American virtue **973.929**

Graff, H. F. Grover Cleveland **973.8**

Greenberg, S. B. Dispatches from the war room **324.7**

Hair, W. I. The Kingfish and his realm: the life and times of Huey P. Long **92**

Halberstam, D. War in a time of peace **327**

Heaney, C. Cradle of gold **92**

Hersh, S. M. Chain of command **973.931**

Hofstadter, R. The American political tradition, and the men who made it **973**

Jackson, R. H. That man: an insider's portrait of Franklin D. Roosevelt **973.917**

Johnson, H. B. Sleepwalking through history **973.927**

Karabell, Z. The last campaign **324.9**

Kennedy, J. F. Profiles in courage **920**

Kissinger, H. Diplomacy **327.2**

Lemann, N. Redemption: the last battle of the Civil War **975**

Leuchtenburg, W. E. Franklin D. Roosevelt and the New Deal, 1932-1940 **973.917**

MacMillan, M. Paris 1919 **940.3**

Mann, J. The rebellion of Ronald Reagan **973.927**

Mann, J. About face **327**

Maraniss, D. First in his class: a biography of Bill Clinton **92**

May, G. John Tyler **92**

McCullough, D. G. Mornings on horseback **92**

McCullough, D. G. The path between the seas **972.87**

McDougal, S. The woman who wouldn't talk **973.929**

Merry, R. W. A country of vast designs **92**

Millard, C. The river of doubt **973.91**

Miller, C. Gifford Pinchot and the making of modern environmentalism **333.7**

Miller, J. J. The big scrum **796.332**

Miller, S. The President and the assassin **973.8**

Miller, T. C. Blood money **956.7**

Minutaglio, B. First son: George W. Bush and the Bush family dynasty **92**

Morris, E. The rise of Theodore Roosevelt **92**

Morris, E. Theodore Rex **973.91**

Morris, K. E. Jimmy Carter, American moralist **973.926**

Morris, R. Fraud of the century **324.9**

Olson, L. Citizens of London **940.54**

O'Toole, P. When trumpets call **92**

Perry, J. M. Touched with fire **973.7**

Persico, J. E. Franklin and Lucy **920**

Phillips, K. P. William McKinley **92**

Ratnesar, R. Tear down this wall **973.927**

Rauchway, E. Murdering McKinley **973.8**

Reagan, R. Reagan **92**

Reagan, R. My father at 100 **92**

Reeves, R. President Reagan: the triumph of imagination **973.927**

Roberts, A. Masters and commanders **940.54**

Roosevelt, C. Too close to the sun **92**

Schlesinger, A. M. War and the American presidency **327.1**

Schlesinger, A. M. The coming of the New Deal, 1933-1935 **973.917**

Schlesinger, A. M. The crisis of the old order, 1919-1933 **973.91**

Schlesinger, A. M. The politics of upheaval, 1935-1936 **973.917**

Sears, S. W. George B. McClellan **92**

Shesol, J. Supreme power **347**

Smith, J. E. FDR **92**

Stephanopoulos, G. All too human **973.929**

Stinnett, R. B. Day of deceit **940.54**

Talbott, S. The Russia hand **327**

Taylor, N. American-made **331.1**

Thomas, E. The war lovers **973.8**

Toobin, J. R. A vast conspiracy **973.929**

Traister, R. Big girls don't cry **324**

Tuchman, B. W. Practicing history **907**

Wilber, D. Q. Rawhide down **973.927**

Wills, G. Certain trumpets **303.3**

Wilson, E. Patriotic gore **810**

Woodward, B. Plan of attack **956.7**

See also Family

GRANDPARENTS AS PARENTS

See also Grandparents; Parenting

Rosenblatt, R. Making toast   92

Grange, Kevin

Beneath blossom rain   915

Granger, Edith

The Columbia Granger's index to poetry in anthologies   808.81

GRANITE

See also Rocks; Stone

Grann, David

The devil and Sherlock Holmes   814

The lost city of Z   918

Grant. Smith, J. E.   973.8

Grant and Sherman. Flood, C. B.   92

Grant moves south. Catton, B.   92

Grant takes command. Catton, B.   92

Grant Wood. Evans, R. T.   92

Grant writing 101. Johnson, V. M.   658.1

Grant's final victory. Flood, C. B.   92

Grant, Colin

The natural mystics   920

Grant, Edward

Science and religion, 400 B.C. to A.D. 1550   261.5

Grant, Gail Milissa

At the elbows of my elders   920

Grant, Gail Milissa (American art historian and diplomat)

About

Grant, G. M. At the elbows of my elders   920

Grant, James

John Adams   92

Grant, Michael

(tr) Cicero, M. T. On the good life   878

Collapse and recovery of the Roman Empire   937

Greek and Latin authors, 800 B.C.-A.D. 1000   920.003

A guide to the ancient world   913

Grant, R. G.

Battle at sea   359

Flight: 100 years of aviation   629.13

Grant, Richard

Crazy river   916

Grant, Ulysses S.

Memoirs and selected letters   973.8

Grant, Ulysses S., 1822-1885

About

Perry, J. M. Touched with fire   973.7

Grant, Ulysses S., 1822-1885 (American president)

About

Bunting, J. Ulysses S. Grant   92

GRANTS *See* Grants-in-aid; Subsidies

GRANTS-IN-AID

See also Public finance

Gerding, S. K. Winning grants   025.1

Johnson, V. M. Grant writing 101   **658.1**

GRAPES

See also Fruit

GRAPH THEORY

See also Algebra; Mathematical analysis; Topology

GRAPHIC ARTS

See also Art

Aldridge, A. The man with kaleidoscope eyes **741.6**

I heart design   **741.6**

GRAPHIC FICTION *See* Graphic novels

Graphic novels. Pawuk, M. G.   **016**

GRAPHIC NOVELS

See also Comic books, strips, etc.; Fiction

B., D. Epileptic   **616.8**

Batman unauthorized   **741.5**

Bechdel, A. Fun home   **741.5**

Beland, T. True story swear to God archives, vol. 1   **741.5**

Bible/O.T./Genesis The book of Genesis   **222**

Delisle, G. Pyongyang: a journey in North Korea   **741**

Geary, R. J. Edgar Hoover   **363.2**

Geary, R. The Lindbergh child   **364.1**

Glidden, S. How to understand Israel in 60 days or less   **741.5**

Goldsmith, F. The readers' advisory guide to graphic novels   **025.2**

Guibert, E. Alan's war   **741.5**

Guibert, E. The photographer   **741.5**

Hennessey, J. The United States Constitution   **342**

Jacobson, S. The 9/11 report   **741.5**

Jacobson, S. After 9/11: America's war on terror (2001-)   **741.5**

Jacobson, S. Anne Frank   **92**

Keller, M. Charles Darwin's On the Origin of Species   **576.8**

Kleist, R. Johnny Cash   **741.5**

Neufeld, J. A.D.   **741.5**

Pawuk, M. G. Graphic novels   **016**

Pekar, H. Students for a Democratic Society **378.1**

Pendergast, T. U-X-L graphic novelists   **920.003**

Persepolis/English The complete Persepolis **741.5**

Rosenkranz, P. Rebel visions: the underground comix revolution, 1963-1975   **741.5**

Rudahl, S. A dangerous woman   **335**

Sacco, J. Footnotes in Gaza   **956.04**

Santiago, W. 21   **741.5**

Satrapi, M. Embroideries   **741**

Satrapi, M. Persepolis   **741.5**

Satrapi, M. Persepolis 2   **741.5**

Small, D. Stitches   **741.5**

Spiegelman, A. In the shadow of no towers   **741**

Spiegelman, A. Maus   **940.53**

Spiegelman, A. MetaMaus   **741.5**

Studio space   **741.5**

GREAT BRITAIN—ARMED FORCES—RE-CRUITING AND ENLISTMENT—BIOGRA-PHY

Hollis, M. Now all roads lead to France   821

GREAT BRITAIN—COLONIES

  See also Colonies

GREAT BRITAIN—HISTORY

MacColl, G. To marry an English Lord   974.7

GREAT BRITAIN—HISTORY—1066-1154, NORMAN PERIOD

Thomas Becket   942.03

GREAT BRITAIN—HISTORY—1455-1485, WARS OF THE ROSES

Weir, A. The Wars of the Roses   942.04

GREAT BRITAIN—HISTORY—1485-1603, TU-DORS

De Lisle, L. The sisters who would be queen   920

Fraser, A. Mary Queen of Scots   92

Fraser, A. The wives of Henry VIII   920

Hibbert, C. The virgin queen: Elizabeth I, genius of the Golden Age   92

Honan, P. Christopher Marlowe   92

Meyer, G. J. The Tudors   942.05

Nicholl, C. The reckoning   92

Porter, L. Katherine the queen   92

Starkey, D. Six wives: the queens of Henry VIII   942.05

Strachey, L. Elizabeth and Essex   92

Weir, A. Henry VIII   942.05

Weir, A. The lady in the tower   92

Weir, A. The life of Elizabeth I   942.05

Weir, A. The six wives of Henry VIII   942.05

GREAT BRITAIN—HISTORY—1714-1837

Clee, N. Eclipse   798.4

GREAT BRITAIN—HISTORY—1853-1856, CRIMEAN WAR *See* Crimean War, 1853-1856

GREAT BRITAIN—HISTORY—HENRY II, 1154-1189—BIOGRAPHY

Thomas Becket   942.03

Weir, A. Eleanor of Aquitaine   942.03

GREAT BRITAIN—HISTORY—MEDIEVAL PERIOD, 1066-1485—HISTORIOGRAPHY

Norwich, J. J. Shakespeare's kings   822.3

GREAT BRITAIN—HISTORY—STUARTS, 1603-1714—BIOGRAPHY

Tomalin, C. Samuel Pepys   941.06

GREAT BRITAIN—KINGS AND RULERS

  See also Kings and rulers

GREAT BRITAIN—KINGS AND RULERS—FICTION.

Ackroyd, P. The death of King Arthur   398.2

Great Britain: a reference guide from the Renaissance to the present. Tompson, R. S.   941

Great Catherine. Erickson, C.   947

The **great** Chinese revolution: 1800-1985. Fairbank, J. K.   951

Great Christian thinkers. Kung, H.   230

The **great** circle. Philip, N.   970.004

The **great** crash, 1929. Galbraith, J. K.   338.5

The **great** deluge. Brinkley, D.   976.3

GREAT DEPRESSION, 1929-1939

  See also Depressions; Economic conditions

Dickstein, M. Dancing in the dark   973.91

Egan, T. The worst hard time   978

Galbraith, J. K. The great crash, 1929   338.5

Gup, T. A secret gift   977.1

Shlaes, A. The forgotten man   973.91

Terkel, S. Hard times   973.91

Watkins, T. H. The hungry years   973.91

Great discoveries [series]

Goldstein, R. Incompleteness   92

Johnson, G. Miss Leavitt's stars   92

Krauss, L. M. Quantum man   92

Leavitt, D. The man who knew too much   92

Lemonick, M. D. The Georgian star   92

Nuland, S. B. The doctors' plague   92

Quammen, D. The reluctant Mr. Darwin   92

Reeves, R. A force of nature   92

Vollmann, W. T. Uncentering the Earth   92

The **great** disruption. Gilding, P.   304.2

The **great** divergence.   339.2

The **great** divorce. Woo, I.   92

The **great** emergence. Tickle, P.   270

The **great** enigma.   839.7

The **great** equations. Crease, R. P.   509

The **great** escape. Marton, K.   920

Great events from history, The 17th century, 1601-1700.   909

Great events from history, The 18th century, 1701-1800.   909.7

Great events from history, The 19th century, 1801-1900.   909.81

Great events from history: The 20th century, 1901-1940.   909.82

Great events from history: The 20th century, 1941-1970.   909.82

Great events from history: The 20th century, 1971-2000.   909.82

Great events from history, The ancient world, prehistory-476 C.E.   930

Great events from history, The Middle Ages, 477-1453.   909.07

Great events from history, The Renaissance & early modern era, 1454-1600.   909

Great expectations. Neifert, M. R.   649

The **great** father. Prucha, F. P.   323.1

The **great** gamble. Feifer, G.   958.1

Great garden formulas.   635

Great generals series

Frank, R. B. MacArthur   92

Remini, R. V. Andrew Jackson   92

Woodworth, S. E. Sherman   92

Gregg, Linda
All of it singing 811
GREGORIAN CHANT See Chants (Plain, Gregorian, etc.)
Gregorian, Vartan
The road to home 973
Gregory, R. L.
(ed) The Oxford companion to the mind 128
Gregory, Ross
Cold War America, 1946 to 1990 973.92
Greiner, Tony
Analyzing library collection use with Excel 025.2
Grendler, Paul F.
(ed) Encyclopedia of the Renaissance 940.2
(ed) The Renaissance 940.2
Grene, David
(ed) Aeschylus Aeschylus 882
(ed) Euripides Euripides 882
(ed) Euripides Euripides [2] 882
(ed) Sophocles Sophocles 882
Grennan, Conor
Little princes 92
Grescoe, Taras
Bottomfeeder 641.6
Gresham, John
Clancy, T. Special forces 356
Gribbin, John R.
Almost everyone's guide to science 500
The birth of time 523.1
The fellowship 509
In search of Schrodinger's cat 530.1
The origins of the future 523.1
Q is for quantum 539.7
Schrodinger's kittens and the search for reality 530.1
The scientists 509
The search for superstrings, symmetry, and the theory of everything 539.7
Stardust 523
White, M. Stephen Hawking 530
Gribbin, Mary
Gribbin, J. R. Almost everyone's guide to science 500
(ed) Gribbin, J. R. Q is for quantum 539.7
Gribbin, J. R. Stardust 523
Gribbon, Deborah Ann
Walsh, J. The J. Paul Getty Museum and its collections 708.1
Grice, Gordon
Deadly kingdom 591.6
The grid book. Higgins, H. B. 701
Gridiron gauntlet. Piascik, A. 796.332
GRIDS (CRISSCROSS PATTERNS)
Higgins, H. B. The grid book 701
GRIEF
See also Emotions

Attig, T. The heart of grief 155.9
The Book of eulogies 808.8
Gilbert, S. M. Death's door 155.9
Rosenblatt, R. Kayak morning 300
Wieseltier, L. Kaddish 296.4
GRIEF—CASE STUDIES
Attig, T. The heart of grief 155.9
Grieve, Michael
(ed) MacDiarmid, H. Selected poetry 821
Grieve, Paul
A brief guide to Islam 297
Griffin, Benjamin
(ed) Autobiography of Mark Twain 92
Griffin, David Ray
(ed) Process and reality 113
Griffin, Donald Redfield
Animal minds 591.5
Griffin, Farah Jasmine
If you can't be free, be a mystery 92
Griffin, Jasper
(ed) The Oxford history of the Roman world 937
Griffin, John Howard
Black like me 305.8
Griffith, Victoria
Kurtzman, J. MBA in a box 658
Griffiths, Tom
Slicing the silence 998
Griftopia. Taibbi, M. 973.932
GRILL COOKING See Barbecue cooking
GRILLING See Barbecue cooking
Grimes, Tom
Mentor 92
Grimes, William
Appetite city 394.1
Grimshaw, John
(ed) Johnson, H. The world of trees 582.16
Grind, Kirsten
The lost bank 332.3
Grinker, Roy Richard
Unstrange minds 616.85
Grinspoon, David Harry
Venus revealed 523.4
Grippo, Robert M.
Macy's 381
Griswold, Eliza
The tenth parallel 297
Griswold, Mac K.
The golden age of American gardens 712
The grizzly almanac. Busch, R. 599.784
GRIZZLY BEAR
Busch, R. The grizzly almanac 599.784
Grmek, Mirko D.
History of AIDS 616.97
Grob's basic electronics. Schultz, M. E. 621.381
GROCERY SHOPPING
See also Home economics; Shopping

Grout, Donald Jay
A history of western music   **780.9**
A short history of opera   **792.5**
The **Grove** book of opera singers.   **920**
The **Grove** encyclopedia of American art.   **709**
The **Grove** encyclopedia of Islamic art and architecture. Bloom, J.   **709.1**
The **Grove** encyclopedia of materials and techniques in art.   **702.8**
Grove library of world art [series]
Encyclopedia of Latin American & Caribbean art   **709**
Grove Press poetry series
Ryan, K. The Niagara River   **811**
Grover Cleveland. Graff, H. F.   **973.8**
Grow your money! Pond, J. D.   **332.024**
Growing a garden city. Smith, J. N.   **635**
Growing up. Baker, R.   **92**
Growing up again. Moore, M. T.   **92**
Grown up all wrong. Christgau, R.   **781.66**
GROWN-UP ABUSED CHILDREN *See* Adult child abuse victims
GROWTH
See also Physiology
Hall, S. S. Size matters   **612.6**
GROWTH DISORDERS
See also Metabolism
GROWTH DISORDERS—HORMONE THERAPY
Cohen, S. Normal at any cost   **618.92**
The **growth** of the American Republic. Morison, S. E.   **973**
Gruber, Jonathan
Health care reform   **362.1**
Gruen, Bob
New York Dolls   **781.66**
Grumet, Bridget Hall
Reconstruction era: primary sources   **973.8**
Grummer, Arnold E.
Trash-to-treasure papermaking   **676**
Grun, Bernard
The timetables of history   **902**
Grundy, Valerie
(ed) Correard The Oxford-Hachette French dictionary   **443**
Grunstein, Michael
Clark, W. R. Are we hardwired?   **155.7**
Grunwald, Lisa
(ed) Women's letters   **305.4**
Grunwald, Michael
Douglas, M. S. The Everglades   **577.6**
The swamp   **975.9**
Gruver, Ed
Koufax   **796.357**
Guadalupi, Gianni
Manguel, A. The dictionary of imaginary plac-

es   **809**
GUAM—DESCRIPTION
Sacks, O. W. The island of the colorblind   **617.7**
GUARANTEED ANNUAL INCOME
See also Income
Guaranteed to fail. Acharya, V. V.   **332.7**
Guare, John
Six degrees of separation   **812**
Gubar, Susan
Memoir of a debulked woman   **616.99**
Judas   **92**
Guber, Peter
Tell to win   **658.4**
Gubert, Betty Kaplan
Distinguished African Americans in aviation and space science   **629.13**
Guelzo, Allen C.
Lincoln and Douglas   **973.6**
GUERILLAS *See* Guerrillas
Guernica: the biography of a twentieth-century icon. Hensbergen, G. v.   **759**
GUERRILLA WARFARE
See also Insurgency; Military art and science; Tactics; War
Kilcullen, D. The accidental guerrilla   **355.4**
GUERRILLAS
Roy, A. Walking with the comrades   **954**
Guest of honor. Davis, D.   **973.91**
Guest, Barbara
The collected poems of Barbara Guest   **811**
Guest, Barbara, 1920-2006 (American poet)
About
Guest, B. The collected poems of Barbara Guest   **811**
Guest, Hadley Haden
(ed) Guest, B. The collected poems of Barbara Guest   **811**
GUESTS *See* Entertaining
Gugliotta, Guy
Freedom's cap   **975.3**
Guha, Ramachandra
India after Gandhi   **954.04**
Guibert, Emmanuel
Alan's war   **741.5**
The photographer   **741.5**
GUIDANCE, VOCATIONAL *See* Vocational guidance
A **guide** book of United States coins. Yeoman, R. S.   **737.4**
GUIDE DOGS
See also Animals and the handicapped; Working dogs
A **guide** to amphibians and reptiles.   **597.9**
Guide to British cinema. Mayer, G.   **791.43**
Guide to Congress. Congressional Quarterly, I. **328**
The **guide** to good health for teens & adults with

Down syndrome. Chicoine, B.   **618.92**

Guide to machine quilting. Gaudynski, D.   **746.46**

Guide to reference books.   **011**

Guide to reference materials for school library media centers. Safford, B. R.   **011.6**

Guide to summer camps and summer schools 2008/2009.   **796.54**

A **guide** to survivorship for women with ovarian cancer. Bristow, R. E.   **616.99**

A **guide** to the ancient world. Grant, M.   **913**

Guide to the presidency.   **352.23**

Guide to U.S. elections. Congressional Quarterly, I.   **324.6**

A **guide** to understanding dietary supplements. Talbott, S.   **615**

GUIDED MISSILES
> *See also* Bombs; Projectiles; Rocketry; Rockets (Aeronautics)

GUIDES (PERSONS)
Clark, E. E. Sacagawea of the Lewis and Clark expedition   **92**
Hari, D. The translator   **92**
Slaughter, T. P. Exploring Lewis and Clark   **978**

Guiding your child through grief. Emswiler, M. A.   **155.9**

Guiley, Rosemary Ellen
The encyclopedia of demons and demonology **133.4**
The encyclopedia of ghosts and spirits   **133.1**
The encyclopedia of saints   **282**
The encyclopedia of vampires & werewolves **398**
The encyclopedia of witches, witchcraft, and Wicca   **133.4**

Guiliano, Mireille
French women don't get fat   **613.2**

GUILLAIN-BARRÉ SYNDROME
Manguso, S. The two kinds of decay   **362**

Guillemin, Jeanne
Biological weapons   **358**

Guillen, Michael
Five equations that changed the world   **530.1**

Guillermoprieto, Alma
Dancing with Cuba   **972.91**

GUILT
> *See also* Conscience; Emotions; Ethics; Good and evil; Sin

Kushner, H. S. How good do we have to be? **296.7**

Guinagh, Kevin
Dictionary of foreign phrases and abbreviations **422**

A **guinea** pig's history of biology. Endersby, J. **576.5**

Guinier, Lani
The miner's canary   **323.1**

Guinn, Jeff
Go down together   **364.1**

Guinness world records.   **032.02**

GUITAR *See* Guitars

Guitar all-in-one for dummies. Chappell, J. **787.87**

GUITAR MUSIC
> *See also* Instrumental music

GUITARISTS
The Beatles anthology   **782.421**
Brightman, C. Sweet chaos   **920**
Clapton, E. Clapton   **92**
Cross, C. R. Heavier than heaven: a biography of Kurt Cobain   **92**
Cross, C. R. Room full of mirrors   **92**
Dance, S. The world of Count Basie   **920**
Dregni, M. Django: the life and music of a Gypsy legend   **92**
Gordon, R. Can't be satisfied: the life and times of Muddy Waters   **782.421**
Govenar, A. B. Lightnin' Hopkins   **92**
Gray, M. Hand me my travelin' shoes   **92**
Jackson, B. Garcia   **92**
King, B. B. Blues all around me   **781.643**
Kruth, J. To live's to fly   **92**
McDermott, J. Ultimate Hendrix   **781.66**
McDonough, J. Shakey: Neil Young's biography   **782.421**
Murray, C. S. Crosstown traffic: Jimi Hendrix and the post-war rock'n'roll revolution   **787.87**
Richards, K. Life   **92**
Schumacher, M. Crossroads   **92**
Spitz, B. The Beatles: the biography   **920**
Wald, E. Escaping the delta   **92**
Wareham, D. Black postcards   **92**
Wolfe, C. K. The life and legend of Leadbelly   **92**
Zappa, F. The real Frank Zappa book   **92**

GUITARS
Chapman, R. The new complete guitarist   **787.87**
Chappell, J. Guitar all-in-one for dummies **787.87**

GUJARATI AMERICANS
Hajratwala, M. Leaving India   **92**

Gulag. Applebaum, A.   **365**

Gulag. Kizny, T.   **365**

The **Gulag** Archipelago, 1918-1956 v1. Solzhenitsyn, A.   **365**

The **Gulag** Archipelago, 1918-1956 v2. Solzhenitsyn, A.   **365**

The **Gulag** Archipelago, 1918-1956 v3. Solzhenitsyn, A.   **365**

Guldin, Bob
(ed) Choosing the president 2008   **324.**

Gulevich, Tanya
Encyclopedia of Christmas and New Year's celebrations   **394.2**

Gulf music. Pinsky, R.   **81**

GULF STATES (U.S.)
> *See also* United States

The **Gulf** Stream. Ulanski, S. L.   **551.4**

GULF STREAM
Ulanski, S. L. The Gulf Stream   **551.4**

GULF WAR, 1991 *See* Persian Gulf War, 1991

Gull, Imtiaz
The most dangerous place 954.91
GUMS AND RESINS
See also Forest products; Industrial chemistry; Plastics
The **gun.** Chivers, C. J. 623.4
Gun control. Henderson, H. 363.33
GUN CONTROL
See also Law; Legislation
Guns in American society 363.33
Henderson, H. Gun control 363.33
Sugarmann, J. Every handgun is aimed at you 363.33
Utter, G. H. Encyclopedia of gun control and gun rights 363.33
GUN CONTROL—UNITED STATES
Guns in American society 363.33
Sugarmann, J. Every handgun is aimed at you 363.33
Utter, G. H. Encyclopedia of gun control and gun rights 363.33
Gun digest 2009. 623.4
Gunfighter nation. Slotkin, R. 973.9
Gunn, James E.
Isaac Asimov 813
Gunn, Thom
Boss Cupid 821
Collected poems 821
(ed) Winters, Y. Selected poems 811
GUNPOWDER
See also Explosives; Firearms
GUNPOWDER PLOT, 1605
Fraser, A. Faith and treason 942.06
GUNS *See* Firearms; Ordnance; Rifles; Shotguns
GUNS—CONTROL *See* Gun control
Guns in American society. 363.33
The **guns** of August. Tuchman, B. W. 940.3
Guns, germs, and steel. Diamond, J. M. 303.4
Gunther, John
Death be not proud 92
Gunton, Mike
(jt. auth) Barrington, R. Life 578.4
Gup, Ted
Book of honor 327.12
A secret gift 977.1
Gupta, Sanjay
Cheating death 616.02
Gur, Janna
The book of New Israeli food 641.5
Guralnick, Peter
Careless love: the unmaking of Elvis Presley 92
Dream boogie 92
Last train to Memphis: the rise of Elvis Presley 782.421
Gurney, A. R.
Love letters and two other plays: The golden age

and What I did last summer 812
Gurock, Jeffrey S.
(ed) American Jewish history 305.8
Gurstelle, William
Adventures from the technology underground 621.8
Gussow, Mel
Edward Albee 92
Guth, Dorothy Lobrano
(ed) White, E. B. Letters of E.B. White 92
Guthrie, James W.
(ed) Encyclopedia of education 370
Guthrie, Woody
The Woody Guthrie songbook 782.42
Gutjahr, Paul C.
The Book of Mormon 289.3
Gutkind, Lee
Almost human 629.8
(ed) Twelve breaths a minute 616
Gutman, Robert W.
Mozart 780
Gutman, Roy
How we missed the story 327
Gutmann, Amy
(ed) The lives of animals 179
Guttenplan, D. D.
American radical 92
The Holocaust on trial 940.53
Guttmann, Allen
The Olympics, a history of the modern games 796.48
Women's sports 796
Guy, Richard K.
Conway, J. H. The book of numbers 512.7
GWICH'IN INDIANS
D'Orso, M. Eagle blue 796.323
Gwynne, S. C.
Empire of the summer moon 92
GYMNASTICS
See also Athletics; Exercise; Sports
GYNECOLOGISTS
Press, E. Absolute convictions 363.46
GYPSIES
Lewy, G. The Nazi persecution of the gypsies 940.53
GYPSIES—ENGLAND—BIOGRAPHY
Walsh, M. Gypsy boy 305.891
GYPSUM
See also Minerals
Gypsy boy. Walsh, M. 305.891

H

H. D.Collected poems, 1912-1944 811

Haab, Sherri
The art of metal clay 739.27
Haaga, John
(ed) The American people 304.6

Handal, Kathleen A.
  (ed) The American Red Cross first aid and safety handbook **616.02**
Handal, Nathalie
  (ed) Language for a new century **808.81**
  (ed) The Poetry of Arab women **892.7**
Handbook of Chinese mythology. Yang Lihui **299.5**
Handbook of death & dying. **306.9**
Handbook of denominations in the United States. Atwood, C. D. **280**
The **handbook** of knots. Pawson, D. **623.88**
Handbook of model rocketry. Stine, G. H. **629.47**
Handbook of United States coins 2009. Yeoman, R. S. **737.4**
Handbook to American democracy. Han, L. C. **320.4**
Handbook to life in ancient Egypt. David, A. R. **932**
Handbook to life in ancient Greece. Adkins, L. **938**
Handbooks of world mythology [series]
  Yang Lihui Handbook of Chinese mythology **299.5**
Handel. Hogwood, C. **92**
HANDGUN CONTROL *See* Gun control
HANDGUNS
  See also Firearms
HANDICAPPED
  Berthon, S. Warlords **940.53**
  Beschloss, M. R. The conquerors: Roosevelt, Truman, and the destruction of Hitler's Germany, 1941-1945 **940.53**
  Brands, H. W. Traitor to his class **92**
  Burns, J. M. The three Roosevelts **973.91**
  Connolly, K. M. Double take **92**
  Davis, K. S. FDR, into the storm, 1937-1940 **973.917**
  Feldman, N. Scorpions **920**
  Fenster, J. M. FDR's shadow **92**
  Fried, A. F.D.R. and his enemies **92**
  Galbraith, J. K. Name-dropping **973.9**
  Goodwin, D. K. No ordinary time **92**
  Hofstadter, R. The American political tradition, and the men who made it **973**
  Jackson, R. H. That man: an insider's portrait of Franklin D. Roosevelt **973.917**
  Kissinger, H. Diplomacy **327.2**
  Leuchtenburg, W. E. Franklin D. Roosevelt and the New Deal, 1932-1940 **973.917**
  Persico, J. E. Franklin and Lucy **920**
  Reeve, C. Still me **92**
  Roberts, A. Masters and commanders **940.54**
  Roosevelt, C. Too close to the sun **92**
  Schlesinger, A. M. The coming of the New Deal, 1933-1935 **973.917**
  Schlesinger, A. M. The crisis of the old order, 1919-1933 **973.91**
  Schlesinger, A. M. The politics of upheaval, 1935-1936 **973.917**
  Shesol, J. Supreme power **347**

  Smith, J. E. FDR **92**
  Stinnett, R. B. Day of deceit **940.54**
  Susskind, L. The black hole war **530.1**
  Taylor, N. American-made **331.1**
  White, M. Stephen Hawking **530**
  Wills, G. Certain trumpets **303.3**
HANDICAPPED—CLOTHING
  See also Clothing and dress
HANDICAPPED—ENCYCLOPEDIAS
  Encyclopedia of disability **362.4**
HANDICAPPED—NAZI PERSECUTION
  See also Persecution; World War, 1939-1945—Atrocities
HANDICAPPED—SALARIES, WAGES, ETC.
  See also Salaries, wages, etc.
HANDICAPPED—SERVICES FOR
  See also Human services; Social work
HANDICAPPED—TRAVEL
  See also Travel
HANDICAPPED AND ANIMALS *See* Animals and the handicapped
HANDICAPPED CHILDREN
  See also Children; Exceptional children; Handicapped
  Greenspan, S. I. The child with special needs **362.1**
  Siegel, L. M. The complete IEP guide **371.9**
HANDICAPPED STUDENTS
  Fertig, B. Why cant U teach me 2 read? **372.4**
  Mooney, J. The short bus **92**
HANDICRAFT
  See also Arts
  Bried, E. How to sew a button **640**
  The complete book of home crafts **745.5**
  Foxfire 40th anniversary book **975.8**
  Gerhards, P. How to sell what you make **658.8**
  Kilby, J. E. By hand **745.5**
  Marshall, M. H. Shell chic **745.55**
  Martha Stewart living Martha Stewart's encyclopedia of crafts **745.5**
  Mary Engelbreit's children's companion **645**
  Pickering Rothamel, S. Encyclopedia of greeting card tools and techniques **745.59**
  Searle, T. Felt jewelry **746**
  Tapper, J. Craft activism **745.5**
  Taylor, T. Altered art **745.5**
  Wasinger, S. Eco-craft **745.5**
  White, C. Uniquely felt **746**
HANDICRAFT—UNITED STATES
  Kilby, J. E. By hand **745.5**
Handing one another along. Coles, R. **820**
Handley, Ann
  Content rules **658.8**
Handlin, Oscar
  The uprooted **325**
Hands of my father. Uhlberg, M. **92**
Hands to work. Hancock, L. **361.6**

Food52   The Food52 cookbook   **641.5**
The essential New York Times cook book   **641.5**
Hessler, Peter
Country driving   **303.4**
Oracle bones   **951**
Hesson, James L.
Weight training for life   **613.7**
Hesterman, Oran B.
Fair food   **338.1**
Hewetson, Ann
The stolen child   **616.89**
Hewitt, Ben
The town that food saved   **338.1**
Hewitt, Don
Tell me a story   **791.45**
Hewitt, Terry
The complete book of cacti & succulents   **635.9**
Hewlett, Sylvia Ann
Off-ramps and on-ramps   **658.3**
The war against parents   **649**
Hexham, Irving
Understanding world religions   **200**
Heyerdahl, Thor
Kon-Tiki   **910.4**
Heylin, Clinton
So long as men can breathe   **822.3**
Heynen, Jennifer
Ceramic bead jewelry   **745.59**
Heywood, V. H.
Flowering plant families of the world   **582.13**
Heywood, W.
(ed) The little flowers of St. Francis of Assisi   **242**
Hibbert, Christopher
The Borgias and their enemies   **945**
The House of Medici   **920**
Nelson   **92**
Queen Victoria   **92**
Redcoats and rebels   **973.3**
The virgin queen: Elizabeth I, genius of the Golden Age   **92**
Wellington   **92**
HIBERNATION
   See also Animal behavior
Hickam, Homer H.
The Coalwood way   **813**
Rocket boys   **629.1**
Hickam, Homer H., 1943- (American aerospace engineer and memoirist)
   About
Hickam, H. H. The Coalwood way   **813**
Hickam, H. H. Rocket boys   **629.1**
Hickey, Michael
The Korean War   **951.904**
Hickey, Michael C.
(ed) Competing voices from the Russian Revolution   **947.084**

Hicks, George
The comfort women   **940.54**
Hicks, Greg
Foster, R. How we choose to be happy   **158**
Hicks, James Whitney
Fifty signs of mental illness   **616.89**
The **hidden** brain. Vedantam, S.   **154.2**
HIDDEN CHILDREN (HOLOCAUST)
   See also Jewish children in the Holocaust
Hidden harmonies. Kaplan, E.   **516.2**
Hidden history. Boorstin, D. J.   **973**
Hidden in plain view. Tobin, J.   **973.7**
The **hidden** language of baseball. Dickson, P.   **796.357**
The **hidden** life of Otto Frank. Lee, C. A.   **92**
Hidden minds. Tallis, F.   **154.2**
The **hidden** people of North Korea. Hassig, R.   **951.93**
Hidden power. Marton, K.   **920**
The **hidden** reality. Greene, B. (.   **530.1**
The **hidden** room. Page, P. K.   **811**
Hidden treasures of ancient Egypt. Hawass, Z. A.   **932**
Hidden value. O'Reilly, C. A.   **658**
The **hidden** Wordsworth. Johnston, K. R.   **821**
Hide & seek. Aron, W.   **92**
Hider, James
The spiders of Allah   **956.05**
Hiding man. Daugherty, T.   **92**
HIEROGLYPHICS
   See also Inscriptions; Writing
Ceram, C. W. Gods, graves, and scholars   **930.1**
Connell, E. S. The Aztec treasure house   **814**
Mertz, B. Temples, tombs, & hieroglyphs   **932**
Hieronymus Bosch. Bosch, H.   **759.9**
Higdon, Hal
Marathon: the ultimate training guide   **796.42**
Higginbotham, Evelyn Brooks
(ed) African American lives   **920**
(ed) The African American national biography   **920.003**
Franklin, J. H. From slavery to freedom   **305.8**
Higgins, Charlotte
It's all Greek to me   **938**
Higgins, Hannah B.
The grid book   **701**
Higgins, Kathleen Marie
Solomon, R. C. A passion for wisdom   **109**
Solomon, R. C. What Nietzsche really said   **193**
Higginson, William J.
The haiku handbook   **808.1**
High financier. Ferguson, N.   **92**
High heat. Wendel, T.   **796.357**
HIGH INTEREST-LOW VOCABULARY BOOKS
Riechel, R. Easy information sources for ESL,

Hill, Clint
Mrs. Kennedy and me   973.922
Hill, Fionna
Microgreens   635
Hill, Geoffrey
The orchards of Syon   821
Selected poems   821
The triumph of love   821
Without title   821
Hill, Lewis
Bulbs   635.9
Hill, Nancy
Hill, L. Bulbs   635.9
Hill, Napoleon
Think and grow rich   650.1
Hill, Rosemary
Stonehenge   936
Hill, Samuel S.
Atwood, C. D. Handbook of denominations in the
United States   280
Hill, Sonya D.
(ed) Small business sourcebook   658.1
Hill, Tony
The contemporary encyclopedia of herbs and spic-
es   641.3
HILLBILLY MUSIC *See* Country music
Hillenbrand, Laura
Seabiscuit   798.4
Unbroken   940.54
Hillerbrand, Hans J.
(ed) The encyclopedia of Protestantism   280
Hillerman, Tony
Seldom disappointed   813
The **Hillier** gardener's guide to trees & shrubs. 635.9
Hillier, Malcolm
Container gardening through the year   635.9
Flowers   745.92
Hillman, Brenda
Cascadia   811
Pieces of air in the epic   811
Hillman, Robert
Ghahramani, Z. My life as a traitor   92
Hillstrom, Kevin
(ed) Contemporary women artists   920.003
The Cold War   909.82
Hillstrom, Laurie
(ed) Contemporary women artists   920.003
The Thanksgiving book   394.26
Hilts, Philip J.
Protecting America's health   353.9
Hiltzik, Michael A.
Colossus   627
Him, Chanrithy
When broken glass floats   959.604
HIMALAYA MOUNTAINS—DESCRIPTION
Matthiessen, P. The snow leopard   915

Himelstein, Shmuel
(ed) The New encyclopedia of Judaism   296
Himmelfarb, Gertrude
The moral imagination   190
The roads to modernity   190
Himmelman, John
Cricket radio   595.7
Hinden, Stan
How to retire happy   646.7
HINDI LANGUAGE
See also Indian languages; Language and lan-
guages
Hindle, Tim
Heller, R. Essential manager's manual   658.4
Hinds, P. Mignon
(ed) Essence total makeover   646.7
HINDU PHILOSOPHY
See also Philosophy
HINDUISM
See also Religions
Eastern religions   200.9
Goldberg, P. American Veda   294.5
Hine, Darlene Clark
(ed) Black women in America   920.003
Hine, Thomas
The rise and fall of the American teenager 305.235
Hines, Emmett W.
Fitness swimming   613.7
Hiney, Tom
Raymond Chandler   813
The **hinge** of fate. Churchill, W.   940.53
Hinges of history [series]
Cahill, T. The gifts of the Jews   909
Cahill, T. Sailing the wine-dark sea   909
Hingley, Brian D.
Furniture repair & restoration   684.1
Hinton, Milt
Playing the changes   92
Hip hop America. George, N.   782.421
Hip hop matters. Watkins, S. C.   781.64
HIP-HOP
Chang, J. Can't stop, won't stop   306
Charnas, D. The big payback   306
Dyson, M. E. Holler if you hear me: searching for
Tupac Shakur   782.421
Grandmaster Flash The adventures of Grandmas-
ter Flash   92
Watkins, S. C. Hip hop matters   781.64
HIP-HOP—UNITED STATES
George, N. Hip hop America   782.421
HIP-HOP CULTURE
See also Popular culture—United States
HIPPIES
See also Bohemianism
MacLean, R. Magic bus   915
Hippocrates' shadow. Newman, D. H.   610.69

Anissimov, M. Primo Levi 92

Brenner, M. After the Holocaust 943.087

Chiger, K. The girl in the green sweater 92

Kirshenblatt, M. They called me Mayer July 92

Klemperer, V. I will bear witness 943.086

Kramer, C. Clara's war 92

Lee, C. A. The hidden life of Otto Frank 92

Levi, P. The periodic table 92

Nothing makes you free 808.8

Pick, H. Simon Wiesenthal 940.53

Segev, T. Simon Wiesenthal 92

Wiesel, E. All rivers run to the sea 813

Wiesel, E. And the sea is never full 813

HOLOCAUST SURVIVORS—BIOGRAPHY

Wiesel, E. And the sea is never full 813

HOLOCAUST SURVIVORS—GRAPHIC NOVELS

Spiegelman, A. MetaMaus 741.5

HOLOCAUST VICTIMS

Berr, H. The journal of Helene Berr 92

The diary of Anne Frank: the critical edition 940.53

Frank, A. The diary of a young girl: the definitive edition 940.53

Jacobson, S. Anne Frank 92

Ozick, C. Quarrel & quandary 814

Prose, F. Anne Frank 839.3

HOLOCAUST, 1933-1945

Ackerman, D. The zookeeper's wife 940.53

Berenbaum, M. The world must know 940.53

Breitman, R. Official secrets 940.54

The Chronicle of the Lodz ghetto, 1941-1944 943.8

Cohen, R. The avengers 940.53

Dawidowicz, L. S. The war against the Jews, 1933-1945 940.53

The diary of Anne Frank: the critical edition 940.53

Dwork, D. Holocaust: a history 940.53

Fleming, G. Hitler and the final solution 943.086

Frank, A. The diary of a young girl: the definitive edition 940.53

Friedlander, S. Nazi Germany and the Jews 940.53

Friedlander, S. The years of extermination 940.53

Fritzsche, P. Life and death in the Third Reich 943.086

Gies, M. Anne Frank remembered 940.53

Gilbert, M. Holocaust journey 940.53

Glass, J. M. Life unworthy of life 940.53

Goldhagen, D. Hitler's willing executioners 940.53

Goldhagen, D. A moral reckoning 940.53

Goldsmith, M. The inextinguishable symphony 940.53

Gross, J. T. Fear: anti-semitism in Poland after Auschwitz 305.8

Hoffman, E. After such knowledge 940.53

The Holocaust and history 940.53

Horwitz, G. J. Ghettostadt 940.53

Johnson, E. A. What we knew 943.086

Kershaw, I. Hitler, the Germans, and the final solution 940.53

Kruk, H. The last days of the Jerusalem of Lithuania 940.53

Langer, L. L. Admitting the Holocaust 940.53

Lee, C. A. The hidden life of Otto Frank 92

Lifton, R. J. The Nazi doctors 940.53

Linenthal, E. T. Preserving memory 940.5

Lipstadt, D. E. The Eichmann trial 345

Mendelsohn, D. The lost 92

Nicholas, L. H. Cruel world 940.53

Rees, L. Auschwitz: a new history 940.53

Silver, D. B. Refuge in hell 362.1

Snyder, T. Bloodlands 940.54

Wiesel, E. And the sea is never full 813

The World reacts to the Holocaust 940.53

Zuccotti, S. Under his very windows 940.53

HOLOCAUST, 1933-1945—COMIC BOOKS, STRIPS, ETC.

Spiegelman, A. Maus 940.53

HOLOCAUST, 1933-1945—DICTIONARIES

Epstein, E. J. Dictionary of the Holocaust 940.53

HOLOCAUST, 1933-1945—ENCYCLOPEDIAS

Encyclopedia of Jewish life before and during the Holocaust 940.53

Encyclopedia of the Holocaust 940.53

The Holocaust encyclopedia 940.53

HOLOCAUST, 1933-1945—ETHICAL ASPECTS

Langer, L. L. Admitting the Holocaust 940.53

HOLOCAUST, 1933-1945—GRAPHIC NOVELS

Jacobson, S. Anne Frank 92

Spiegelman, A. Maus 940.53

Spiegelman, A. MetaMaus 741.5

HOLOCAUST, 1933-1945—HISTORIOGRAPHY

Clendinnen, I. Reading the Holocaust 940.53

Evans, R. J. Lying about Hitler 940.53

Guttenplan, D. D. The Holocaust on trial 940.53

Langer, L. L. Admitting the Holocaust 940.53

Lipstadt, D. E. Denying the Holocaust 940.53

Lipstadt, D. E. History on trial 940.53

HOLOCAUST, 1933-1945—MAPS

Gilbert, M. The Routledge atlas of the Holocaust 940.53

HOLOCAUST, 1933-1945—PERSONAL NARRATIVES

Berr, H. The journal of Helene Berr 92

The Buchenwald report 940.53

Chiger, K. The girl in the green sweater 92

Frankl, V. E. Man's search for meaning 92

Kramer, C. Clara's war 92

Prose, F. Anne Frank 839.3

Rosenfeld, O. In the beginning was the ghetto 940.53

Smith, L. Remembering, voices of the holocaust 940.53

Holoman, D. Kern
Berlioz   **780**
Holroyd, Michael
A book of secrets   **306.874**
A strange eventful history   **92**
Holt, Saxon
Greenlee, J. The American meadow garden   **635.9**
Holton, James R.
(ed) Encyclopedia of atmospheric sciences   **551.5**
Holton, Wendy M.
Dalton, K. Depression after childbirth   **616.85**
Holton, Woody
Abigail Adams   **92**
HOLY GHOST *See* Holy Spirit
Holy hullabaloos. Wexler, J.   **342**
HOLY OFFICE *See* Inquisition
Holy people of the world.   **920.003**
Holy roller. Wilson, D.   **92**
HOLY ROMAN EMPIRE
Reston, J. Defenders of the faith   **940.2**
HOLY SEE *See* Papacy; Popes
HOLY SPIRIT
    See also God—Christianity; Trinity
Cox, H. G. The future of faith   **270**
Holy war. Cliff, N.   **909**
HOLY WAR (ISLAM) *See* Jihad
Holy war, Inc. Bergen, P. L.   **303.6**
Holy warriors. Phillips, J.   **909.07**
HOLY WEEK
Benedict XVI, P. Jesus of Nazareth. part two **232.9**
Holzer, Harold
Lincoln president-elect   **92**
(ed) Hearts touched by fire   **973.7**
(ed) The Lincoln anthology   **92**
(ed) Lincoln on war   **973.7**
Homans, Jennifer
Apollo's angels   **792.8**
Homberger, Eric
The historical atlas of New York City   **974.7**
Home. Andrews, J.   **92**
HOME
Halpern, J. Braving home   **363**
Hooks, B. Belonging   **92**
HOME ACCIDENTS
    See also Accidents
Warner, M. L. The complete guide to Alzheimer's-proofing your home   **362.1**
Home and exile. Achebe, C.   **823**
HOME AND SCHOOL
    See also Education
HOME BUSINESS *See* Home-based business
HOME CARE *See* Home care services
HOME CARE SERVICES
    See also Medical care
Carter, R. Helping yourself help others   **649.8**
Home comforts. Mendelson, C.   **640**

HOME CONSTRUCTION *See* House construction
Home cooking with Jean-Georges. Ko, G.   **641.5**
Home dairy with Ashley English. English, A.   **637**
HOME DECORATION *See* Interior design
Home Depot, Inc.
Home improvement 1-2-3   **643**
HOME ECONOMICS
Bried, E. How to sew a button   **640**
Coyne, K. Making it   **640.73**
Heloise All-new hints from Heloise   **640**
Mendelson, C. Home comforts   **640**
Nakone, L. Organizing for your brain type   **640**
Walsh, P. How to organize just about everything   **640**
HOME EDUCATION *See* Correspondence schools and courses; Home schooling; Self-instruction
HOME EQUITY LOANS
    See also Loans
Home ground.   **917**
HOME HEALTH CARE *See* Home care services
Home improvement 1-2-3. Home Depot, I.   **643**
HOME INSTRUCTION *See* Home schooling
HOME LABOR *See* Home-based business
HOME LIFE *See* Family life
HOME LOANS *See* Mortgages
HOME MEDICAL CARE *See* Home care services
HOME NURSING
    See also Home care services; Nursing
McFarlane, R. The complete bedside companion   **649.8**
HOME NURSING—METHODS
Caregiving: a step-by-step resource for caring for the person with cancer at home   **649.8**
Home outside. Messervy, J. M.   **712**
HOME SCHOOLING
    See also Education
Rupp, R. The complete home learning sourcebook   **371.04**
HOME SCHOOLING—UNITED STATES—HANDBOOKS, MANUALS, ETC
Rupp, R. The complete home learning sourcebook   **371.04**
HOME STORAGE *See* Storage in the home
HOME TEACHING BY PARENTS *See* Home schooling
Home town. Kidder, T.   **974.4**
HOME VIDEO SYSTEMS—MAINTENANCE AND REPAIR
Capelo, G. R. VCR troubleshooting & repair   **621.388**
HOME-BASED BUSINESS
    See also Business; Self-employed; Small business
Arden, L. The work-at-home sourcebook   **338.7**
Bredin, A. The virtual office survival handbook **658**

Hooper, Chloe
Tall man   **364.1**

Hooper, Dan
Dark cosmos   **523.1**

Hooper, Judith
Of moths and men   **576.8**

Hoopla. Prain, L.   **746.44**

Hoops. Jackson, M.   **811**

HOOVER DAM (ARIZ. AND NEV.)
Hiltzik, M. A. Colossus   **627**

Hoover, J. Edgar, 1895-1972 (American FBI director)
About
Geary, R. J. Edgar Hoover   **363.2**

HOPE
> *See also* Emotions; Spiritual life; Virtue

Groopman, J. E. The anatomy of hope   **616**
Wright, N. T. Surprised by hope   **236**

HOPE—RELIGIOUS ASPECTS—CHRISTIANITY
Norris, K. Acedia & me   **92**
Wright, N. T. Surprised by hope   **236**

Hope against hope. Mandelstam, N.   **891.71**

Hope in a jar. Peiss, K. L.   **391.6**

Hope in hell. Bortolotti, D.   **610**

Hopgood, Mei-Ling
How Eskimos keep their babies warm   **649**

Hopkins, Edward J.
Buckley, B. Weather: a visual guide   **551.5**

Hopkins, Gerard Manley
Poems and prose   **821**

Hopkins, Jerry
No one here gets out alive   **92**

Hopkins, Kate
99 drams of whiskey   **641.2**

Hopp, Steven L.
Animal, vegetable, miracle   **381**

Horace
The epistles of Horace   **871**
The odes of Horace   **874**

Horbury, William
(ed) The Cambridge history of Judaism   **296.09**

HORMONE THERAPY
Cohen, S. Normal at any cost   **618.92**

HORMONES
Love, S. M. Dr. Susan Love's menopause and hormone book   **618.1**

Horn, James
A kingdom strange   **975.6**

Horn, James P. P.
A land as God made it   **975.5**
Horn, J. A kingdom strange   **975.6**

Horn, Miriam
Krupp, F. D. Earth, the sequel   **621**

Hornbacher, Marya
Wasted: a memoir of anorexia and bulimia   **616.85**

Hornblower, Simon
(ed) The Oxford classical dictionary   **938**

Horne, Alistair
La belle France   **944**
Seven ages of Paris   **944**

Horne, Jed
Breach of faith   **976.3**

Horner, John R.
How to build a dinosaur   **567.9**

Hornet's sting. Ryan, M.   **92**

Hornfischer, James D.
Ship of ghosts   **940.54**

HOROLOGY *See* Clocks and watches; Sundials; Time

HOROSCOPES
> *See also* Astrology

Horovitz, David Phillip
A little too close to God   **956.940**
(ed) Shalom, friend: the life and legacy of Yitzhak Rabin   **92**

Horowitz, Joseph
Classical music in America   **781.6**

Horowitz, Sari
Higham, S. Finding Chandra   **364.152**

HORROR
> *See also* Emotions; Fear

HORROR COMIC BOOKS, STRIPS, ETC.
The Horror! The horror!   **741.5**

HORROR FICTION
> *See also* Fiction

HORROR FICTION—HISTORY AND CRITICISM
Horror: another 100 best books   **823**
Spratford, B. S. The horror readers' advisory   **025.5**

HORROR FILMS
> *See also* Motion pictures

Zinoman, J. Shock value   **791.43**

HORROR FILMS—HISTORY AND CRITICISM
Zinoman, J. Shock value   **791.43**

HORROR GRAPHIC NOVELS
> *See also* Graphic novels

HORROR MOVIES *See* Horror films

HORROR PLAYS
> *See also* Drama

HORROR RADIO PROGRAMS
> *See also* Radio programs

The **horror** readers' advisory. Spratford, B. S.   **025.5**

HORROR TALES
Spratford, B. S. The horror readers' advisory   **025.5**

HORROR TALES—BIBLIOGRAPHY
Spratford, B. S. The horror readers' advisory   **025.5**

HORROR TALES—HISTORY AND CRITICISM
Burgess, M. Reference guide to science fiction, fantasy, and horror   **016**

How to read the Bible. Kugel, J. L.   **221**

How to retire happy. Hinden, S.   **646.7**

How to roast a lamb. Psilakis, M.   **641.5**

How to sell what you make. Gerhards, P.   **658.8**

How to sew a button. Bried, E.   **640**

How to slice an onion. Crumpacker, B.   **641.5**

How to smell a rat. Fisher, K. L.   **364.1**

How to speak money. Romans, C.   **332.024**

HOW TO START A BUSINESS *See* New business enterprises

How to survive and prosper as an artist. Michels, C.   **702**

How to talk so kids will listen & listen so kids will talk. Faber, A.   **649**

How to talk to anyone, anytime, anywhere. King, L.   **302.3**

How to think about the great ideas. Adler, M. J. **080**

How to travel practically anywhere. Stellin, S. **910.2**

How to travel with a salmon & other essays. Eco, U.   **854**

How to understand Israel in 60 days or less. Glidden, S.   **741.5**

How to win friends and influence people. Carnegie, D.   **158**

How to work with an interior designer. Sheridan, J.   **747**

How to wreck a nice beach. Tompkins, D. **621.382**

How to write a business plan. McKeever, M. P. **658.1**

How to write a children's book and get it published. Seuling, B.   **808.06**

How to write and give a speech. Detz, J.   **808.5**

How to write killer fiction. Wheat, C.   **808.3**

How Toyota became #1. Magee, D.   **658.4**

How wars end. Rose, G.   **355**

How we choose to be happy. Foster, R.   **158**

How we decide. Lehrer, J.   **153.8**

How we die. Nuland, S. B.   **616.07**

How we do harm. Brawley, O. W.   **362.109**

How we got here. Frum, D.   **973.92**

How we invented the airplane. Wright, O.   **92**

How we missed the story. Gutman, R.   **327**

How we talk. Metcalf, A. A.   **427**

How your government really works. Starks, G. L.   **320.4**

How your house works. Wing, C.   **643**

How-to-do-it manual for librarians [series]

    John, L. Z. Running book discussion groups   **374**

How-to-do-it manuals for librarians [series]

    Gerding, S. K. Winning grants   **025.1**

    Halsted, D. D. Disaster planning   **025.8**

    Mitchell, A. M. Cataloging and organizing digital resources   **025.3**

    Ross, C. S. Conducting the reference interview   **025.5**

HOW-TO-STOP-SMOKING PROGRAMS *See* Smoking cessation programs

Howard Cosell. Ribowsky, M.   **92**

Howard, David

    Lost rights   **973.7**

Howard, Hugh

    Houses of the founding fathers   **973.3**

Howard, Jason

    (jt. auth) House, S. Something's rising   **338.2**

Howard, Jean

    Jean Howard's Hollywood   **791.43**

Howard, Johnette

    The rivals   **92**

Howard, Judith A.

    Zebrowski, E. Category 5   **363.34**

Howard, Michael Eliot

    (ed) The Oxford history of the twentieth century   **909.82**

Howard, Richard

    (tr) Baudelaire, C. Les fleurs du mal   **841**

    Inner voices   **811**

    The silent treatment   **811**

    Without saying   **811**

Howarth, Glennys

    (ed) Encyclopedia of death and dying   **306.9**

Howatson, M. C.

    (ed) The Oxford companion to classical literature   **880**

Howe, Ben Ryder

    My Korean deli   **92**

Howe, Daniel Walker

    What hath God wrought   **973.5**

Howe, Susan

    Souls of the Labadie tract   **811**

    That this   **811**

Howell, Georgina

    Gertrude Bell   **92**

Howell, Karen

    Painting on glass & ceramic   **748.5**

Howes, Barbara

    Collected poems, 1945-1990   **811**

Howes, Kelly King

    Reconstruction era: almanac   **973.8**

Howey, Noelle

    Dress codes of three girlhoods—my mother's, my father's, and mine   **306.8**

Howlett, Mike

    The weird world of Eerie Publications   **741.5**

Hoyle's rules of games. Hoyle, E.   **795.4**

Hoyle, Edmond

    Hoyle's rules of games   **795.4**

Hoyt, Mike

    (ed) Reporting Iraq   **070**

Hrabowski, Freeman A.

    Overcoming the odds   **305**

Hubbell, Sue

    A book of bees   **638**

    Shrinking the cat   **660.6**

I

Impey, Chris
  How it began   **523.1**
Impey, Chris
  How it ends   **523.1**
The **importance** of being earnest and other plays.
  Wilde, O.   **822**
The **importance** of music to girls. Greenlaw, L. **92**
IMPORTS
  See also International trade
IMPOSTORS
  Massie, R. K. The Romanovs   **947.08**
IMPOSTORS AND IMPOSTURE
  See also Crime; Criminals
  Miller, W. I. Faking it   **179**
  Salisbury, L. Provenance   **92**
  Tribble, S. A colossal hoax   **974.7**
IMPOTENCE
  See also Diseases
  Loe, M. The rise of Viagra   **616.6**
  Sheehy, G. Understanding men's passages **305.244**
Impresario. Maguire, J.   **92**
IMPRESSIONISM (ART)
  See also Art
  Baillio, J. Claude Monet, 1840-1926   **759**
  Gerdts, W. H. American impressionism   **759.13**
  Impressionism and post-impressionism in the Art
    Institute of Chicago   **759.05**
  Kelder, D. The great book of French impression-
    ism   **759**
  King, R. The judgment of Paris   **759**
  Roe, S. The private lives of the impressionists **759**
IMPRESSIONISM (ART)—FRANCE
  King, R. The judgment of Paris   **759**
  Roe, S. The private lives of the impressionists **759**
IMPRESSIONISM (ART)—UNITED STATES
  Gerdts, W. H. American impressionism   **759.13**
Impressionism and post-impressionism in the Art
  Institute of Chicago.   **759.05**
IMPRESSIONIST ARTISTS
  Roe, S. The private lives of the impressionists **759**
**IMPRESSIONIST ARTISTS—UNITED
  STATES—BIOGRAPHY**
  Mathews, N. M. Mary Cassatt   **759.13**
IMPRISONMENT *See* Prisons
IMPRISONMENT—SOVIET UNION
  Figes, O. Just send me word   **365**
An **improvised** life. Arkin, A.   **92**
In a cardboard belt! Epstein, J.   **814**
In a desert garden. Alcock, J.   **595.7**
In a sunburned country. Bryson, B.   **919**
In America's court. Geoghegan, T.   **345**
In cold blood. Capote, T.   **364.1**
In command of history. Reynolds, D.   **940.53**
In defense of food. Pollan, M.   **613**
In Europe. Mak, G.   **940.5**
In Fed we trust. Wessel, D.   **332.1**

In focus. National Geographic Society (U.S.) **779**
In Hanuman's hands. Rao, C.   **92**
In heaven as it is on earth. Brown, S. M.   **236**
In heaven everything is fine. Frank, J.   **92**
In his own words.   **92**
In Montgomery, and other poems. Brooks, G. **811**
In other worlds. Atwood, M.   **809**
In our image. Karnow, S.   **959.9**
In our own best interest. Schulz, W. F.   **323**
In our time. Brownmiller, S.   **305.42**
In Patagonia. Chatwin, B.   **918**
In praise of science. Bais, S.   **500**
In pursuit of giants. Rigney, M.   **597**
In pursuit of silence. Prochnik, G.   **155.9**
In pursuit of the unknown. Stewart, I.   **551.3**
In reckless hands. Nourse, V. F.   **344**
In retrospect. McNamara, R. S.   **959.704**
In rough country. Oates, J. C.   **814**
In search of King Solomon's mines. Shah, T. **963**
In search of memory. Kandel, E. R.   **153**
In search of nature. Wilson, E. O.   **113**
In search of Nella Larsen. Hutchinson, G.   **92**
In search of our roots. Gates, H. L.   **305.8**
In search of Robinson Crusoe. Severin, T.   **996**
In search of Schrodinger's cat. Gribbin, J. R. **530.1**
In search of small gods. Harrison, J.   **811**
In search of the blues. Minutaglio, B.   **305.8**
In search of the promised land. Franklin, J. H. **929**
In search of the Trojan War. Wood, M.   **939**
In search of Tiger. Callahan, T.   **92**
In search of time. Falk, D.   **529**
In search of your European roots. Baxter, A. **929**
In Siberia. Thubron, C.   **957**
In spite of myself. Plummer, C.   **92**
In the absence of sun. Lee, H.   **979.4**
In the American grain. Williams, W. C.   **814**
In the arms of others. Filene, P. G.   **179.7**
In the beginning. Armstrong, K.   **222**
In the beginning was the ghetto. Rosenfeld,
  O.   **940.53**
In the belly of the beast. Abbott, J. H.   **365**
In the blink of an eye. Waltrip, M.   **796.72**
In the company of soldiers. Atkinson, R.   **956.7**
In the crevice of time. Jacobsen, J.   **811**
In the dark. Stone, R.   **811**
In the dark before dawn. Merton, T.   **811**
In the devil's garden. Allen, S. L.   **641**
In the footsteps of Marco Polo. Belliveau, D. **915**
In the garden of beasts. Larson, E.   **92**
In the green kitchen. Waters, A.   **641.5**
In the land of invented languages. Okrent, A. **499**
In the name of Elijah Muhammad. Gardell, M. **297**
In the name of identity. Maalouf, A.   **302.4**
In the next galaxy. Stone, R.   **811**
In the past lane. Kammen, M. G.   **973**
In the pines. Notley, A.   **811**

INDIANS OF NORTH AMERICA—SOUTHERN STATES—SOCIAL LIFE AND CUSTOMS

Perdue, T. The Columbia guide to American Indians of the Southeast **970.004**

INDIANS OF NORTH AMERICA—TREATIES

Documents of American Indian diplomacy **970.004**

INDIANS OF NORTH AMERICA—WARFARE

Encyclopedia of Native American wars and warfare **970.004**

INDIANS OF NORTH AMERICA—WARS

Encyclopedia of Native American wars and warfare **970.004**

Rajtar, S. Indian war sites **970.004**

Remini, R. V. Andrew Jackson **92**

INDIANS OF NORTH AMERICA—WARS— 1600-1750

Lepore, J. The name of war **973.2**

Philbrick, N. Mayflower **973.2**

INDIANS OF NORTH AMERICA—WARS— UNITED STATES

Osborn, W. M. The wild frontier **970.004**

INDIANS OF NORTH AMERICA—WARS— WEST (U.S.)

Brown, D. A. Bury my heart at Wounded Knee **970.004**

INDIANS OF NORTH AMERICA—WASHINGTON (STATE)—PUGET SOUND—ETHNIC IDENTITY

Harmon, A. Indians in the making **970.004**

INDIANS OF NORTH AMERICA—WASHINGTON (STATE)—PUGET SOUND—HISTORY

Harmon, A. Indians in the making **970.004**

INDIANS OF NORTH AMERICA—WEST (U.S.)—HISTORY

Brown, D. A. Bury my heart at Wounded Knee **970.004**

INDIANS OF NORTH AMERICA—WESTERN STATES

Calloway, C. G. One vast winter count **978**

INDIANS OF NORTH AMERICA—WOMEN

See Native American women

INDIANS OF SOUTH AMERICA—AMAZON RIVER REGION

Everett, D. L. Don't sleep, there are snakes **305.8**

INDIANS OF SOUTH AMERICA—SOCIAL CONDITIONS

Goodman, J. The devil and Mr. Casement **305.8**

INDIANS, TREATMENT OF

Gallay, A. The Indian slave trade **326**

INDIANS, TREATMENT OF—NORTH AMERICA

Milton, G. Big Chief Elizabeth **970.004**

Wilson, J. The earth shall weep **970.004**

INDIANS, TREATMENT OF—SOUTHERN STATES—HISTORY—17TH CENTURY

Gallay, A. The Indian slave trade **326**

INDIANS, TREATMENT OF—UNITED STATES—HISTORY

Richter, D. K. Facing east from Indian country **970.004**

INDIC ART *See* Indian art

INDIC COOKING

Ramineni, S. Entice with spice **641.5**

The **indifferent** stars above. Brown, D. **92**

INDIGENOUS PEOPLES

See also Ethnology

INDIGENOUS PEOPLES—AMERICA *See* Native Americans

INDIGENOUS PEOPLES—CONGO (DEMOCRATIC REPUBLIC)—HISTORY—19TH CENTURY

Hochschild, A. King Leopold's ghost **967.5**

INDIGENOUS PEOPLES—CONGO (DEMOCRATIC REPUBLIC)—HISTORY—20TH CENTURY

Hochschild, A. King Leopold's ghost **967.5**

INDIGENOUS PEOPLES—NEW GUINEA

Flannery, T. F. Throwim way leg **995.3**

INDIVIDUAL DIFFERENCES

Harris, J. R. No two alike **155.2**

INDIVIDUAL DIFFERENCES IN CHILDREN

Levine, M. D. A mind at a time **370.15**

INDIVIDUAL RETIREMENT ACCOUNTS

See also Pensions; Retirement income

INDIVIDUALISM

See also Economics; Equality; Political science; Sociology

Fairlie, H. Bite the hand that feeds you **814**

INDIVIDUALITY

See also Consciousness; Psychology

Harris, J. R. No two alike **155.2**

INDIVIDUALIZED INSTRUCTION

Siegel, L. M. The complete IEP guide **371.9**

Indivisible by two. Segal, N. L. **155.4**

INDOCHINESE WAR, 1946-1954

Logevall, F. Embers of War **959.704**

Morgan, T. Valley of death **959.704**

INDOCTRINATION, FORCED *See* Brainwashing

INDOLENCE *See* Laziness

Indonesia: peoples and histories. Taylor, J. G. **959.8**

INDOOR AIR POLLUTION

See also Air pollution

INDOOR GAMES

See also Games

Botermans, J. The book of games **794**

INDOOR GARDENING

See also Gardening

Courtier, J. Indoor plants **635.9**

Smith, P. A. P. Allen Smith's bringing the garden indoors **747**

Indoor plants. Courtier, J. **635.9**

Clifford, D. Make your own living trust   **346.05**

INHERITANCE AND SUCCESSION
See also Wealth

INHERITANCE AND TRANSFER TAX
See also Estate planning; Inheritance and succession; Internal revenue; Taxation

The **inheritance** of Rome. Wickham, C.   **940.1**

Inheriting the Holy Land. Miller, J.   **956.94**

Inheriting the revolution. Appleby, J. O.   **973**

Inheriting the trade. DeWolf, T. N.   **326**

Inhumane society. Fox, M. W.   **179**

INIA GEOFFRENSIS—AMAZON RIVER REGION

Montgomery, S.   Journey of the pink dolphins   **599.53**

INITIALISMS *See* Acronyms

INITIATION RITES
See also Rites and ceremonies

INITIATIVE AND REFERENDUM *See* Referendum

INJUNCTIONS
See also Constitutional law; Labor unions

INJURIES *See* Accidents; First aid; Wounds and injuries

INJURIOUS INSECTS *See* Insect pests

INLAND NAVIGATION
See also Navigation; Shipping; Transportation

INNER CITIES
See also Cities and towns

Kozol, J. Amazing grace   **362.7**

INNER CITIES—NEW YORK (STATE)—CASE STUDIES

LeBlanc, A. N. Random family   **305.5**

INNER CITY GHETTOS *See* Inner cities

INNER CITY PROBLEMS *See* Inner cities

Inner voices. Howard, R.   **811**

INNOVATIONS, TECHNOLOGICAL *See* Technological innovations

INNS *See* Hotels and motels

INNUIT *See* Inuit

INOCULATION *See* Vaccination

An **inordinate** fondness for beetles. Evans, A. V.   **595.7**

INORGANIC CHEMISTRY
See also Chemistry

INQUISITION
See also Catholic Church

Hofstadter, D. The Earth moves   **509**

Kamen, H. The Spanish Inquisition   **272**

Perez, J. The Spanish Inquisition   **272**

INQUISITION—ITALY

Hofstadter, D. The Earth moves   **509**

INSANE *See* Mentally ill

INSANITY—JURISPRUDENCE—UNITED STATES

Lombardo, P. A.   Three generations, no imbeciles   **344**

INSANITY DEFENSE
See also Criminal law

The **insanity** offense. Torrey, E. F.   **362.1**

INSCRIPTIONS
See also Ancient history; Archeology

INSCRIPTIONS, CUNEIFORM *See* Cuneiform inscriptions

INSECT PESTS
See also Economic zoology; Insects; Pests

Stewart, A. Wicked bugs   **632**

Waldbauer, G. Insights from insects   **632**

INSECT SOCIETIES

Holldobler, B. The superorganism   **595.7**

INSECTICIDES
See also Agricultural chemicals; Pesticides

INSECTICIDES—TOXICOLOGY
See also Poisons and poisoning

Insectopedia. Raffles, H.   **595.7**

INSECTS
See also Animals

Alcock, J. In a desert garden   **595.7**

Alderton, D. Firefly encyclopedia of the vivarium   **639.3**

Eisner, T. For love of insects   **595.7**

Eisner, T. Secret weapons   **595.7**

Holldobler, B. The superorganism   **595.7**

Milne, L. J. The Audubon Society field guide to North American insects and spiders   **595.7**

Raffles, H. Insectopedia   **595.7**

Waldbauer, G. Insects through the seasons   **595.7**

Waldbauer, G. Insights from insects   **632**

Waldbauer, G. Millions of monarchs, bunches of beetles   **595.7**

Waldbauer, G. What good are bugs?   **595.7**

Zuk, M. Sex on six legs   **595.7**

INSECTS—BEHAVIOR

Waldbauer, G. Millions of monarchs, bunches of beetles   **595.7**

INSECTS—ECOLOGY

Waldbauer, G. What good are bugs?   **595.7**

INSECTS—ENCYCLOPEDIAS

Encyclopedia of insects   **595.7**

INSECTS—MIGRATION

Pyle, R. M. Mariposa road   **595.7**

INSECTS—WAR USE

Lockwood, J. A. Six-legged soldiers   **358**

INSECTS AS CARRIERS OF DISEASE
See also Insect pests

Lockwood, J. A. Six-legged soldiers   **358**

INSECTS AS CARRIERS OF PLANT DISEASE

Lockwood, J. A. Six-legged soldiers   **358**

Insects through the seasons. Waldbauer, G.   **595.7**

Inseminating the elephant. Perillo, L. M.   **811**

Inseparable. Donoghue, E.   **809**

See also Islam; Sects

ISLAMIC SERMONS
See also Islamic literature; Sermons

ISLAMIC WOMEN *See* Muslim women

ISLAND ECOLOGY
See also Ecology

The **island** of the colorblind. Sacks, O. W.   **617.7**

Islands of the damned. Burgin, R. V.   **940.54**

. . . **isms**: understanding art. Little, S.   **709**

ISOLATIONISM
See also International relations

ISOTOPES
See also Atoms

ISRAEL
See also Middle East

ISRAEL—SOCIAL CONDITIONS

Horovitz, D. P. A little too close to God   **956.940**

Shipler, D. K. Arab and Jew   **956.94**

Israel and Palestine. Shlaim, A.   **956.04**

Israel is real. Cohen, R.   **956.94**

Israel, Fred L.
(ed) My fellow citizens   **352.23**

Israel, Paul
Edison   **92**

ISRAEL-ARAB CONFLICTS

Al Jundi, S. The hour of sunlight   **92**

Chesler, P. The new anti-semitism   **305.8**

Farsoun, S. K. Palestine and the Palestinians **956.94**

Goldberg, J. Prisoners   **92**

How Israelis and Palestinians negotiate   **956.94**

La Guardia, A. War without end   **956.940**

LeBor, A. City of oranges   **956.94**

Lozowick, Y. Right to exist   **956.940**

Miller, A. D. The much too promised land **956.05**

Miller, J. Inheriting the Holy Land   **956.94**

Morris, B. Righteous victims   **956**

Nusseibeh, S. Once upon a country   **92**

Sadat, J. My hope for peace   **956.05**

Said, E. W. The end of the peace process   **956.05**

Shehadeh, R. Palestinian walks   **956.95**

Shipler, D. K. Arab and Jew   **956.94**

Shlaim, A. The iron wall   **956.04**

Shlaim, A. Israel and Palestine   **956.04**

Timmerman, K. R. Preachers of hate   **956.94**

Tolan, S. The lemon tree   **956.94**

Winslow, P. C. Victory for us is to see you suffer   **956.95**

ISRAEL-ARAB   CONFLICTS—GRAPHIC NOVELS

Glidden, S. How to understand Israel in 60 days or less   **741.5**

Sacco, J. Footnotes in Gaza   **956.04**

ISRAEL-ARAB WAR, 1948-1949
See also Israel-Arab conflicts

Collins, L. O Jerusalem!   **956.94**

ISRAEL-ARAB WAR, 1967

See also Israel-Arab conflicts

Oren, M. Six days of war   **956.04**

ISRAEL-ARAB WAR, 1973
See also Israel-Arab conflicts

ISRAELI COOKING

Gur, J. The book of New Israeli food   **641.5**

ISRAELI NATIONAL CHARACTERISTICS

Horovitz, D. P. A little too close to God   **956.940**

How Israelis and Palestinians negotiate   **956.94**

La Guardia, A. War without end   **956.940**

The **Israeli** secret services and the struggle against terrorism. Pedahzur, A.   **363.32**

ISRAELI-ARAB CONFLICTS *See* Israel-Arab conflicts

ISRAELIS
See also Jews

ISRAELITES *See* Jews

Issenberg, Sasha
The sushi economy   **641.6**

Isserman, Maurice
The other American: the life of Michael Harrington   **300**

Issues of our time [series]
Dershowitz, A. M. Preemption   **363.32**

Istanbul. Pamuk, O.   **949.6**

It doesn't take a hero: General H. Norman Schwarzkopf. Schwarzkopf, H. N.   **92**

It doesn't take a rocket scientist. Malone, J. W. **920**

It pays to talk. Schwab-Pomerantz, C.   **332.024**

It's about that time. Cook, R.   **92**

It's all Greek to me. Higgins, C.   **938**

It's go in horizontal. Scalapino, L.   **811**

It's not about the bike. Armstrong, L.   **92**

It's not about the money. Kessel, B.   **332.024**

It's not just who you know. Spaulding, T.   **650.1**

It's only a movie. Chandler, C.   **92**

It's our day. Jellison, K.   **392**

It's the pictures that got small. Becker, C.   **791.45**

It's time: poems. Gibbons, R.   **811**

ITALIAN ART

Adams, L. Italian Renaissance art   **709.02**

Levey, M. Florence   **945**

Wittkower, R. Art and architecture in Italy, 1600-1750   **709**

ITALIAN COOKING

Bastianich, L. Lidia cooks from the heart of Italy   **641.5**

Bastianich, L. Lidia's family table   **641.5**

Bastianich, L. Lidia's Italian table   **641.59**

Bastianich, L. Lidia's Italian-American kitchen   **641.59**

Batali, M. Italian grill   **641.5**

Buford, B. Heat   **641.5**

David, E. Italian food   **641.5**

Fant, M. B. Rome   **641.5**

Hazan, M. Amarcord, Marcella remembers   **92**

JEWELERS
Faber, T. Faberge's eggs   **739.2**
JEWELRY
See also Clothing and dress; Costume; Decorative arts
Codina, C. The complete book of jewelry making   **739.27**
DeCoster, M. Marcia DeCoster's beaded opulence   **739.27**
Deeb, M. The beader's color palette   **745.594**
Gollberg, J. The art & craft of making jewelry   **739.27**
Haab, S. The art of metal clay   **739.27**
Heynen, J. Ceramic bead jewelry   **745.59**
Michaels, C. F. Teach yourself visually jewelry making & beading   **745.59**
Miller, J. Miller's costume jewelry   **739.27**
Searle, T. Felt jewelry   **746**
Wells, C. W. The art & elegance of beadweaving   **745.58**
Wire, C. Creative metal clay jewelry   **745.59**
Young, A. The workbench guide to jewelry techniques   **739.27**
JEWELRY—DESIGN
Wells, C. W. The art & elegance of beadweaving   **745.58**
JEWELRY MAKING
Codina, C. The complete book of jewelry making   **739.27**
JEWELS *See* Gems; Jewelry; Precious stones
Jewish American literature.   **810**
JEWISH AUTHORS—BIOGRAPHY
Wiesel, E. And the sea is never full   **813**
JEWISH BANKERS
Weintraub, S. Charlotte and Lionel   **92**
JEWISH BANKERS—GREAT BRITAIN—BIOGRAPHY
Weintraub, S. Charlotte and Lionel   **92**
The **Jewish** Bible.   **221**
JEWISH BUSINESSPEOPLE—LOUISIANA—NEW ORLEANS—BIOGRAPHY
Cohen, R. The fish that ate the whale   **338.7**
JEWISH CHILDREN IN THE HOLOCAUST
Nicholas, L. H. Cruel world   **940.53**
JEWISH CIVILIZATION
See also Civilization
Cultures of the Jews   **909**
JEWISH COOKING
Marks, G. The world of Jewish cooking   **641.5**
Nathan, J. Jewish cooking in America   **641.5**
Nathan, J. Quiches, kugels, and couscous   **641.5**
The New York Times Jewish cookbook   **641.5**
The New York Times Passover cookbook   **641.5**
Jewish cooking in America. Nathan, J.   **641.5**
JEWISH DIASPORA
See also Human geography; Jews

Brenner, F. Diaspora: homelands in exile   **909**
Jewish encounters [series]
Century, D. Barney Ross   **92**
Lehman, D. A fine romance   **782.42**
Lipstadt, D. E. The Eichmann trial   **345**
Pinsky, R. The life of David   **92**
JEWISH ETHICS
See also Ethics
Telushkin, J. Biblical literacy   **221**
Telushkin, J. Jewish wisdom   **296.3**
JEWISH FAMILIES—CZECH REPUBLIC—PRAGUE—BIOGRAPHY
Albright, M. K. Prague winter   **943.71**
JEWISH FAMILIES—NEW YORK (STATE)—NEW YORK
Roiphe, A. R. 1185 Park Avenue   **813**
JEWISH FICTION
Nothing makes you free   **808.8**
JEWISH HOLIDAYS
See also Judaism; Religious holidays
Goldman, A. L. Being Jewish   **296.4**
JEWISH LANGUAGE   *See* Hebrew language; Yiddish language
JEWISH LEADERS
Pick, H. Simon Wiesenthal   **940.53**
Segev, T. Simon Wiesenthal   **92**
JEWISH LITERATURE
See also Literature; Religious literature
JEWISH MEN
See also Men
JEWISH MOURNING CUSTOMS
Wieseltier, L. Kaddish   **296.4**
JEWISH MUSICIANS—GERMANY
Goldsmith, M. The inextinguishable symphony   **940.53**
Jewish people in America [series]
Diner, H. R. A time for gathering   **305.8**
Faber, E. A time for planting   **305.8**
Feingold, H. L. A time for searching   **305.8**
Shapiro, E. S. A time for healing   **305.8**
Sorin, G. A time for building   **305.8**
JEWISH PHILOSOPHY
Buber, M. I and thou   **181**
Friedman, M. S. Encounter on the narrow ridge: a life of Martin Buber   **92**
JEWISH PHYSICIANS—SOVIET UNION
Brent, J. Stalin's last crime   **947.084**
Jewish Publication Society
Eisenberg, R. L. The JPS guide to Jewish traditions   **296.4**
JEWISH REFUGEES
Marton, K. The great escape   **920**
JEWISH REFUGEES—BIOGRAPHY
Maitland, L. Crossing the borders of time   **940.53**
JEWISH REFUGEES—UNITED STATES—BIOGRAPHY

finding your next job   650.14

JOB INTERVIEWS

   See also Applications for positions; Interviewing

JOB PLACEMENT GUIDANCE *See* Vocational guidance

JOB SATISFACTION

   See also Attitude (Psychology); Employee morale; Personnel management; Work

   Hallowell, E. M. Shine   **658.3**

JOB SEARCHING *See* Job hunting

JOB SECURITY

   See also Personnel management

JOB STRESS

   See also Stress (Physiology); Stress (Psychology)

JOBLESS PEOPLE *See* Unemployed

JOBLESSNESS *See* Unemployment

JOBS *See* Occupations; Professions

JOCKEYS

   Drape, J. Black maestro   **92**

Joe DiMaggio. Cramer, R. B.   **796.357**

Joe Louis. Roberts, R.   **92**

Joe Turner's come and gone. Wilson, A.   **812**

Joel, Lewin G.

   Every employee's guide to the law   **344**

JOGGING

   See also Running

Johann Sebastian Bach. Geck, M.   **92**

Johann Sebastian Bach. Wolff, C.   **780**

Johannes Brahms. Swafford, J.   **780**

Johansen, Bruce E.

   The dirty dozen: toxic chemicals and the earth's future   **363.738**

   The Native peoples of North America   **970.004**

Johanson, Donald C.

   From Lucy to language   **599.93**

   Lucy: the beginnings of humankind   **599.93**

   Lucy's legacy   **569.9**

John Adams. Grant, J.   **92**

John Adams. McCullough, D. G.   **973.4**

John and Robin Diskson series in Texas music [series]

   Govenar, A. B. Texas blues   **781.64**

John Brown, abolitionist. Reynolds, D. S.   **92**

John Clare: a biography. Bate, J.   **92**

John Dryden. Selections.   **821**

John Ford. Gallagher, T.   **791.43**

John Ford. Davis, R. L.   **791.43**

John Glenn. Glenn, J.   **973.927**

John Gutmann. Stein, S.   **779**

John Huston. Meyers, J.   **92**

John James Audubon. Rhodes, R.   **92**

John Lennon. Norman, P.   **92**

John Marshall. Smith, J. E.   **347**

John Milton. Hawkes, D.   **92**

John Milton. Campbell, G.   **92**

John Muir. Wilkins, T.   **333.7**

John Osborne. Heilpern, J.   **92**

John Paul

   Crossing the threshold of hope   **282**

John Paul II. Flynn, R.   **92**

John Paul Jones. Thomas, E.   **973.3**

John Paul Jones. Morison, S. E.   **92**

John Quincy Adams. Nagel, P. C.   **92**

John Quincy Adams. Remini, R. V.   **973.5**

John Steinbeck.   **813**

John Tyler. Crapol, E. P.   **92**

John Tyler. May, G.   **92**

John Wesley. Tomkins, S.   **287**

John Winthrop. Bremer, F. J.   **974.4**

John, Catherine Rachel

   Attwater, D. The Penguin dictionary of saints   **920.003**

John, Lauren Z.

   Running book discussion groups   **374**

Johnny Appleseed. Means, H. B.   **92**

Johnny Cash. Kleist, R.   **741.5**

Johnny Cash. Streissguth, M.   **92**

The **Johns** Hopkins consumer guide to medical tests.   **616.07**

The **Johns** Hopkins medical guide to health after 50.   **613**

Johns Hopkins Press health book [series]

   Bristow, R. E. A guide to survivorship for women with ovarian cancer   **616.99**

   Cassel, G. H. The eye book   **617.7**

   Mace, N. L. The 36-hour day   **618.97**

   Mondimore, F. M. Adolescent depression   **616.85**

   Palmer, S. Spinal cord injury   **617**

   Ryder, C. S. Take your pediatrician with you   **618.92**

   Silver, J. K. After cancer treatment   **616.99**

Johns Hopkins, poetry and fiction [series]

   Jacobsen, J. In the crevice of time   **811**

   Smith, W. J. The world below the window   **811**

Johns, Adrian

   Death of a pirate   **384.54**

Johnsen, Ole

   Minerals of the world   **549**

Johnson, Catherine

   Grandin, T. Animals in translation   **591.5**

   Grandin, T. Animals make us human   **636**

Johnson, Charles Richard

   Africans in America: America's journey through slavery   **326**

   Turning the wheel   **814**

Johnson, Charles Richard

        About

   Johnson, C. R. Turning the wheel   **814**

Johnson, Christopher M.

   Your critically ill child   **618.92**

Johnson, Clay

Giddings, P. Ida: a sword among lions	92
Gilbert, E. Eat, pray, love	92
Gillies, A. Keeper	616.8
Girardet, E. Killing the cranes	958.4
Giridharadas, A. India calling	954.05
Godwin, P. When a crocodile eats the sun	92
Goldberg, J. Prisoners	92
Gopnik, A. Through the children's gate	974.7
Graham, K. Personal history	070.5
Greenberg, M. Beg, borrow, steal	92
Grogan, J. The longest trip home	92
Guillermoprieto, A. Dancing with Cuba	972.91
Guttenplan, D. D. American radical	92
Hajratwala, M. Leaving India	92
Halpern, J. Braving home	363
Hardy, J. In the valley of mist	954
Heilbroner, R. L. The worldly philosophers	330.1
Heilbrun, C. G. The education of a woman	92
Heller, E. Yossarian slept here	92
Hendrickson, P. Hemingway's boat	92
Herman, A. Gandhi and Churchill	92
Hessler, P. Country driving	303.4
Hilburn, R. Cornflakes with John Lennon	92
Hillerman, T. Seldom disappointed	813
Hiss, T. The view from Alger's window	364.1
Hitchens, C. Hitch-22	92
Holmes, H. The well-dressed ape	612
Houze, D. Twilight people	92
Jacobs, A. J. The know-it-all	031
Jeal, T. Stanley	92
Johnson, T. Tragedy in crimson	294.3
Jones, M. Little boy blues	92
Joseph Roth	92
Junger, S. A death in Belmont	364.152
Kaplan, A. Y. The collaborator: the trial & execution of Robert Brasillach	848
Kapuscinski, R. Travels with Herodotus	930
Katz, J. Dog days	636
Kavenna, J. The ice museum	998
Kimball, K. The dirty life	92
Kurson, R. Crashing through	92
Latus, J. If I am missing or dead	92
Leake, J. Entering Hades	364.152
Lelyveld, J. Great soul	92
Levy, B. H. Who killed Daniel Pearl?	070.92
Life stories	920
Lobdell, W. Losing my religion	92
Lukas, C. Blue genes	92
Lynn, K. S. Hemingway	92
MacFarquhar, N. The media relations department of Hizbollah wishes you a happy birthday	956.04
Mackall, J. Plain secrets	289.7
MacPherson, M. All governments lie	92
Majd, H. The Ayatollah begs to differ	955
Maraniss, D. Into the story	92
Martin, G. Gabriel Garcia Marquez	92
Marton, K. Enemies of the people	92
Marton, K. The great escape	920
McBride, J. The color of water	92
McCall, N. Makes me wanna holler	305.38
McKeen, W. Outlaw journalist	92
McPhee, J. A. Silk parachute	814
Meier, A. Black earth	947.086
Mellow, J. R. Hemingway	813
Mendelsohn, D. The lost	92
Millner, C. The golden road	92
Moaveni, A. Honeymoon in Tehran	92
Moaveni, A. Lipstick jihad	92
Mohandas Gandhi	92
Montgomery, S. Birdology	598
Moore, H. G. We are soldiers still	959.704
Morgan, T. My battle of Algiers	965
Morris, J. M. Pulitzer	92
Morris, J. Contact!	910.4
Morris, R. Ambrose Bierce	92
Morris, W. My dog Skip	813
Moser, B. Why this world	92
Moyers, W. C. Broken: my story of addiction and redemption	92
Naipaul, V. S. Between father and son	823
Naipaul, V. S. Reading & writing	92
Navasky, V. S. A matter of opinion	92
Norris, M. The grace of silence	92
O'Meara, A. Chasing medical miracles	615.5
O'Reilly, B. A bold fresh piece of humanity	92
O'Shea, J. The deal from hell	92
Paul, A. Big in China	92
Pearl, M. A mighty heart	070.92
Politkovskaya, A. A Russian diary	947.086
Prochnau, W. W. Once upon a distant war	959.704
Proulx, A. Bird cloud	92
Remnick, D. Reporting	814
Reynolds, M. S. Hemingway: the 1930's	813
Reynolds, M. S. Hemingway: the homecoming	92
Reynolds, M. S. Hemingway: the Paris years	92
Reynolds, M. S. The young Hemingway	92
Rideau, W. In the place of justice	92
Rinella, S. American buffalo	599.64
Rivard, R. Trail of feathers: searching for Philip True	364.152
Rooney, A. A. My war	940.54
Rosenblatt, R. Making toast	92
Ross, L. Here but not here	070
Sabar, A. My father's paradise	305.8
Sabbag, R. Down around midnight	92
Scammell, M. Koestler	92
Scheeres, J. Jesus land	92
Schmidle, N. To live or to perish forever	954.91
Seierstad, A. The angel of Grozny	947.5
Seierstad, A. A hundred and one days	956.7
Shields, C. J. And so it goes: Kurt Vonnegut: a life	92

(ed) Family planning sourcebook 363.9

Khalil, Ashraf
Liberation Square 962.05

Khalili, Nasser D.
Islamic art and culture 709.1

Khan, Mahvish Rukhsana
My Guantanamo diary 909.83

Khan, Yasmin Sabina
Enlightening the world 974.7

Khlevniuk, Oleg V.
The history of the Gulag 365

Khrushchev. Taubman, W. 92

Kiberd, Declan
Ulysses and us 823

Kicked, bitten, and scratched. Sutherland, A. 636.088

Kidder, Tracy
Home town 974.4
House 690
Mountains beyond mountains 92
Strength in what remains 92

KIDNAP VICTIMS
Cesarani, D. Major Farran's hat 956.94
Geis, G. Crimes of the century 345
Heidenry, J. Zero at the bone 364.152
Matthews, J. Bringing Adam home 364.1

KIDNAPPERS
Geis, G. Crimes of the century 345
Heidenry, J. Zero at the bone 364.152

KIDNAPPING
> See also Criminal law; Offenses against the person

Heidenry, J. Zero at the bone 364.152
Levy, B. H. Who killed Daniel Pearl? 070.92
Matthews, J. Bringing Adam home 364.1

KIDNAPPING—GRAPHIC NOVELS
Geary, R. The Lindbergh child 364.1

KIDNAPPING—MISSOURI—SAINT LOUIS
Heidenry, J. Zero at the bone 364.152

KIDNAPPING, PARENTAL See Parental kidnapping

KIDNEYS
Rose, D. A. Larry's kidney 915

Kiernan, Ben
The Pol Pot regime 959.6

Kiernan, Denise
D'Agnese, J. The money book for freelancers, part-time, and the self-employed 332.024

Kiernan, Frances
Seeing Mary plain: a life of Mary McCarthy 818

Kiernan, Stephen P.
Last rights 179.7

Kihn, Martin
Bad dog 636.7

Kiki de Montparnasse. Bocquet 759.4

Kilby, Janice Eaton
By hand 745.5

Kilcullen, David
The accidental guerrilla 355.4

Killen, Andreas
1973 nervous breakdown 973.924

The **killer** of little shepherds. Starr, D. 364.152

Killer stuff and tons of money. Stanton, M. 381

Killian, Johnny H.
(ed) United States/Constitution The Constitution of the United States of America 342

Killian, Kevin
(ed) Spicer, J. My vocabulary did this to me 811

Killing Custer. Welch, J. 973.8

Killing monsters. Jones, G. 302.23

The **killing** of Crazy Horse. Powers, T. 92

Killing the cranes. Girardet, E. 958.4

Killing yourself to live. Klosterman, C. 781.66

Kim, Susan
Stein, E. Flow 612.6

Kimball, Chad T.
(ed) Vegetarian sourcebook 613.2

Kimball, Charles
When religion becomes lethal 201

Kimball, George
At the fights 796.8
Four kings 920

Kimball, Kristin
The dirty life 92

Kimball, Robert
(ed) Porter, C. Selected lyrics 782.42

Kimbrell, Andrew
(ed) Fatal harvest 630

Kimmel, Michael S.
(ed) Men and masculinities 305.31

Kimmelstiel, Laurie
Exquisite little knits 746.43

Kincaid, Jamaica
A small place 972.9

A **kind** of grace. Joyner-Kersee, J. 796.42

KINDERGARTEN
> See also Elementary education; Schools

KINDERGARTEN TEACHERS
Tolan, S. The lemon tree 956.94

The **kindness** of strangers: the life of Tennessee Williams. Spoto, D. 92

Kindred spirits. Schoen, A. M. 636.089

Kindred, Dave
Sound and fury 796

Kindsvatter, Peter S.
American soldiers 355

KINESIOLOGY
> See also Human locomotion; Physical fitness

KINETIC ART
> See also Art

KINETIC SCULPTURE
> See also Kinetic art; Sculpture

McAllester, M. Beyond the Mountains of the Damned **949.71**

KOSOVO (SERBIA)—HISTORY—CIVIL WAR, 1998-

Di Giovanni, J. Madness visible **949.7**

KOSOVO (SERBIA)—HISTORY—CIVIL WAR, 1998-1999—PERSONAL NARRATIVES, AMERICAN

Clark, W. K. Waging modern war **949.703**

Kostigen, Thomas M.

The green book **333.72**

Kostiukovich, Elena

Perche agli Italiani piace/English Why Italians love to talk about food **641.5**

Kot, Greg

DeRogatis, J. The Beatles vs. the Rolling Stones **781.66**

Ripped **780.2**

Kotkin, Stephen

Uncivil society **947**

Kotler, Steven

(jt. auth) Diamandis, P. H. Abundance **303.48**

Kotler, Steven

A small furry prayer **636.7**

Kotter, John P.

Buy-in **650.1**

Kotz, Nick

Judgment days **323**

Koufax. Gruver, E. **796.357**

Kouzes, James M.

The truth about leadership **658.4**

Kovach, Bill

Blur **070**

The **Kovacs** guide to electronic library collection development. Kovacs, D. K. **025**

Kovacs, Diane K.

Genealogical research on the Web **929**

The Kovacs guide to electronic library collection development **025**

Kovel, Ralph M.

Kovels' dictionary of marks: pottery and porcelain **738**

Kovels' new dictionary of marks **738**

Kovel, Terry H.

Kovel, R. M. Kovels' dictionary of marks: pottery and porcelain **738**

Kovel, R. M. Kovels' new dictionary of marks **738**

Kovels' dictionary of marks: pottery and porcelain. Kovel, R. M. **738**

Kovels' new dictionary of marks. Kovel, R. M. **738**

Kovsky, Matt

Perkins, J. Attack proof **613.6**

Kozol, Jonathan

Amazing grace **362.7**

Letters to a young teacher **371.1**

Ordinary resurrections **305.23**

Rachel and her children **362.5**

Savage inequalities **371.9**

The shame of the nation **379**

Krag, Karen J.

Turkington, C. The encyclopedia of breast cancer **616.99**

Kragh, Helge

Quantum generations **530**

Krakatoa: the day the world exploded, August 27, 1883. Winchester, S. **551.2**

Krakauer, Jon

Into thin air **796.522**

Under the banner of heaven **289.3**

Kram, Mark

The ghosts of Manila **796.83**

Kramer, Clara

Clara's war **92**

Kramer, Eddie

McDermott, J. Ultimate Hendrix **781.66**

Kramer, Peter D.

Against depression **616.85**

Listening to Prozac **616.85**

Krames, Jeffrey A.

The Rumsfeld way **658.4**

Krane, Jim

City of gold **953**

Kranish, Michael

Flight from Monticello **973.4**

Krantz, Les

Not till the fat lady sings **796**

Kranz, Eugene F.

Failure is not an option **629.45**

Kranz, Gene

About

Kranz, E. F. Failure is not an option **629.45**

Krapp, Kristine M.

(ed) Drugs and controlled substances **362.29**

(ed) The Gale encyclopedia of children's health **618.92**

(ed) Notable black American scientists **509**

Krass, Peter

Carnegie **338.7**

Kraus, Barbara

Barbara Kraus' calories and carbohydrates **613.2**

Krauss, Erich

Wave of destruction **959.3**

Krauss, Lawrence Maxwell

Fear of physics **530**

Quantum man **92**

Kravets, Marybeth

The K & W guide to colleges for students with learning disabilities or attention deficit hyperactivity disorder **378**

Kraybill, Donald B.

Amish grace **364.152**

Concise encyclopedia of Amish, Brethren, Hutter-

LANDSCAPE DESIGN *See* Landscape architecture

LANDSCAPE GARDENING

> *See also* Gardening; Horticulture

Adam, J. Landscape planning **635**

Buchanan, R. Taylor's master guide to landscaping **712**

Chalker-Scott, L. The informed gardener **635**

Dirr, M. Dirr's Hardy trees and shrubs **635.9**

Dirr, M. Dirr's trees and shrubs for warm climates **635.9**

DiSabato-Aust, T. The well-designed mixed garden **635**

Greenlee, J. The American meadow garden **635.9**

Hayward, G. Stone in the garden **712**

Joyce, D. Topiary and the art of training plants **635.9**

King, M. Gardening with grasses **635.9**

Miller, L. Parks, plants, and people **712**

Newbury, T. The ultimate garden designer **712**

The plant finder **635.9**

Reader's Digest Association Beginner's guide to gardening **635**

Speichert, C. G. Encyclopedia of water garden plants **635**

Taylor's master guide to gardening **635.9**

LANDSCAPE IN LITERATURE

Home ground **917**

LANDSCAPE PAINTING

> *See also* Painting

Wilton, A. American sublime **759.13**

LANDSCAPE PHOTOGRAPHY

Drager, K. Scenic photography 101 **770.2**

Landscape planning. Adam, J. **635**

LANDSCAPE PLANTS—SUNBELT STATES

Dirr, M. Dirr's trees and shrubs for warm climates **635.9**

LANDSCAPE PROTECTION

> *See also* Environmental protection; Nature conservation

House, S. Something's rising **338.2**

LANDSCAPE PROTECTION—APPALACHIAN REGION, SOUTHERN—CITIZEN PARTICIPATION

House, S. Something's rising **338.2**

Landscape turned red. Sears, S. W. **973.7**

LANDSLIDES

> *See also* Natural disasters

Lane Fox, Robin

The classical world **938**

Lane, Anthony

Nobody's perfect **791.43**

Lane, Charles

The day freedom died **976.3**

Lane, Marion

The Humane Society of the United States complete guide to dog care **636.7**

Lane, Nancy E.

The osteoporosis book **616.7**

Lang, Adam Perry

Serious barbecue **641.5**

Lang, Anthony E.

Parkinson's disease **616.8**

Lang, Kenneth R.

The Cambridge guide to the solar system **523.2**

Lang, Lang

Journey of a thousand miles **92**

Lang, Michael

The road to Woodstock **781.66**

Lang, Paul Henry

Music in Western civilization **780.9**

Lang, Susan S.

Patt, R. B. The complete guide to relieving cancer pain and suffering **616.99**

Langdon, Helen

Caravaggio **709**

Lange Current series

Current medical diagnosis and treatment 2008 **610**

Lange's handbook of chemistry. **540**

Lange, Norbert Adolph

(ed) Lange's handbook of chemistry **540**

Langer, Erick Detlef

(ed) Encyclopedia of Latin American history and culture **980**

Langer, Howard J.

(ed) World War II **940.53**

Langer, Lawrence L.

Admitting the Holocaust **940.53**

Langewiesche, William

American ground, unbuilding the World Trade Center **974.7**

The atomic bazaar **355**

Sahara unveiled **916**

Langguth, A. J.

Driven West **973.5**

Our Vietnam **959.704**

Langland, William

Piers Plowman **821**

Langley, Jacqueline D.

Swanson, M. Atlas of the Civil War, month by month **973.7**

Langmuir, Erika

Yale dictionary of art and artists **703**

Langone, John

The new how things work **600**

LANGUAGE *See* Language and languages

LANGUAGE ACQUISITION

Barnet, A. B. The youngest minds **155.4**

LANGUAGE AND CULTURE

> *See also* Culture; Language and languages

LANGUAGE AND LANGUAGES

> *See also* Anthropology; Communication; Ethnology

Pakistan   **954.91**

Lieven, D. C. B.

  Russia against Napoleon   **940.2**

Life. Richards, K.   **92**

Life. Barrington, R.   **578.4**

LIFE

  Auster, P. Winter journal   **818**

  Benecke, M. The dream of eternal life   **612.6**

  Davies, P. C. W. The fifth miracle   **576.8**

  Deutsch, D. The fabric of reality   **530**

  Lepore, J. The mansion of happiness   **973**

Life. Fortey, R. A.   **576.8**

Life & times [series]

  Dry, S. Curie   **92**

LIFE (BIOLOGY)

  See also Biology

  Capra, F. The web of life   **570.1**

  Gribbin, J. R. Stardust   **523**

  Harold, F. M. The way of the cell   **571.6**

  Keller, E. F. Making sense of life   **570.1**

  Lovelock, J. The ages of Gaia   **570.1**

  Margulis, L. What is life?   **570.1**

  Ward, P. D. Life as we do not know it   **576.8**

**LIFE (BIOLOGY)—SOCIAL ASPECTS—UNIT-
ED STATES—HISTORY**

  Lepore, J. The mansion of happiness   **973**

LIFE—ORIGIN

  See also Evolution

  Davies, P. C. W. The fifth miracle   **576.8**

  Fortey, R. A. Life   **576.8**

  Frank, A. About time   **523.1**

  Gribbin, J. R. The origins of the future   **523.1**

  Hawking, S. W. (. W. The grand design   **530.1**

  Koerner, D. Here be dragons   **576.8**

  Macdougall, J. D. A short history of planet earth   **551.7**

  Margulis, L. What is life?   **570.1**

  Sagan, C. Shadows of forgotten ancestors   **304**

  Sasselov, D. The life of super-Earths   **576.8**

  Schopf, J. W. Cradle of life   **576.8**

  Tyson, N. D. G. Origins: fourteen billion years of cosmic evolution   **523.1**

  Ward, P. D. Life as we do not know it   **576.8**

**LIFE—SOCIAL ASPECTS—UNITED
STATES—HISTORY**

  Lepore, J. The mansion of happiness   **973**

LIFE AFTER DEATH *See* Future life; Immortality

Life after life. Moody, R. A.   **133.9**

Life and death in Shanghai. Cheng, N.   **92**

Life and death in the Third Reich. Fritzsche, P.   **943.086**

The **life** and death of smallpox. Glynn, I.   **616.9**

The **life** and legacy of Annie Oakley. Riley, G. **796.3**

The **life** and legend of Leadbelly. Wolfe, C. K.   **92**

The **life** and many deaths of Harry Houdini. Bran-

don, R.   **793.8**

The **life** and times of Little Richard. White, C.   **782.421**

The **life** and times of Pancho Villa. Katz, F. **972.08**

The **life** and times of the thunderbolt kid. Bryson, B.   **92**

Life as we do not know it. Ward, P. D.   **576.8**

Life at the zoo: behind the scenes with the animal doctors. Robinson, P. T.   **590.73**

LIFE CHANGE EVENTS

  James, E. Paris in love   **92**

**LIFE CHANGE EVENTS—PSYCHOLOGICAL
ASPECTS**

  Brehony, K. A. After the darkest hour   **155.9**

**LIFE CYCLE, HUMAN—RELIGIOUS AS-
PECTS—JUDAISM**

  Goldman, A. L. Being Jewish   **296.4**

**LIFE CYCLE, HUMAN—SOCIAL ASPECTS—
UNITED STATES—HISTORY**

  Lepore, J. The mansion of happiness   **973**

LIFE CYCLES *See* Life cycles (Biology)

LIFE CYCLES (BIOLOGY)

  See also Biology; Cycles; Life (Biology)

  Heinrich, B. Life everlasting   **591.7**

Life disrupted. Edwards, L.   **618.92**

Life drawing class. Watson, L.   **743**

Life everlasting. Heinrich, B.   **591.7**

LIFE EXPECTANCY

  See also Age; Life; Vital statistics

LIFE HISTORIES *See* Biography

Life in a medieval castle. Gies, J.   **940.2**

Life in a medieval city. Gies, J.   **940.1**

Life in a medieval village. Gies, F.   **940.1**

Life in cold blood. Attenborough, D.   **597.9**

A **life** in letters. Fitzgerald, F. S.   **813**

Life in photographs. McCartney, L.   **779**

Life in rewind. Murphy, T. W.   **92**

A **life** in secrets. Helm, S.   **92**

Life in the treetops. Lowman, M.   **577.34**

A **life** in the twentieth century. Schlesinger, A. M.   **973.91**

Life in the undergrowth. Attenborough, D.   **592**

Life in year one. Korb, S.   **933**

LIFE INSURANCE

  See also Insurance

  Schultz, E. Retirement heist   **331.2**

Life itself. Rensberger, B.   **571.6**

Life itself. Ebert, R.   **92**

Life lessons. Kubler-Ross, E.   **170**

Life list. Gentile, O.   **92**

The **life** of Billy Yank. Wiley, B. I.   **973.7**

The **life** of birds. Attenborough, D.   **598**

The **life** of Charlotte Bronte. Gaskell, E. C.   **92**

The **life** of David. Pinsky, R.   **92**

The **life** of Elizabeth I. Weir, A.   **942.05**

The **life** of Graham Greene. Sherry, N.   **92**

ry   **909.82**

Louisa May Alcott. Reisen, H.   **92**

The **Louisiana** Purchase.   **973.4**

LOUISIANA PURCHASE

    Cerami, C. A. Jefferson's great gamble   **973.4**

    Kukla, J. A wilderness so immense   **973.4**

    The Louisiana Purchase   **973.4**

LOUISIANA PURCHASE—ENCYCLOPEDIAS

    The Louisiana Purchase   **973.4**

Lourie, Bruce

    Smith, R. Slow death by rubber duck   **615.9**

Lourie, Richard

    Sakharov   **323**

Loury, Glenn C.

    The anatomy of racial inequality   **305.896**

Louv, Richard

    Last child in the woods   **155.4**

    The nature principle   **128**

Louvin, Charlie, 1927-2011

    Satan is real   **920**

Louvish, Simon

    Monkey business   **920**

LOVE

    See also Emotions; Human behavior

    Ackerman, D. A natural history of love   **152.4**

    Fromm, E. The art of loving   **152.4**

    Gilligan, C. The birth of pleasure   **152.4**

    Hooks, B. Salvation   **306.7**

    Lewis, T. A general theory of love   **152.4**

    Peck, M. S. The road less traveled   **158**

    Richardson, B. L. What mama couldn't tell us about love   **158**

    Shulman, A. K. To love what is   **92**

Love & survival. Ornish, D.   **616.1**

LOVE—PHYSIOLOGICAL ASPECTS

    Lewis, T. A general theory of love   **152.4**

LOVE—RELIGIOUS ASPECTS

    Chapman, G. D. Love as a way of life   **241**

LOVE—UNITED STATES

    Hooks, B. Salvation   **306.7**

Love and capital. Gabriel, M.   **92**

Love and hate in Jamestown. Price, D.   **975.5**

Love and Louis XIV. Fraser, A.   **92**

Love as a way of life. Chapman, G. D.   **241**

LOVE CANAL CHEMICAL WASTE LANDFILL (NIAGARA FALLS, N.Y.)

    See also Hazardous waste sites; Landfills

Love goes to buildings on fire. Hermes, W.   **781.64**

Love had a compass.   **811**

LOVE IN LITERATURE

    Yalom, M. How the French invented love   **944**

Love in the driest season. Tucker, N.   **362.7**

Love letters and two other plays: The golden age and What I did last summer. Gurney, A. R.   **812**

LOVE POETRY

    See also Poetry

Amichai, Y. Poems of Jerusalem; and, Love poems   **892**

A Book of love poetry   **808.81**

Rekdal, P. Animal eye   **811**

Yeros, D. Shades of love   **778**

Love soup. Thomas, A.   **641.5**

LOVE STORIES

    See also Fiction

    Bouricius, A. The romance readers' advisory   **016**

    Figes, O. Just send me word   **365**

    Maitland, L. Crossing the borders of time   **940.53**

    Ramsdell, K. Romance fiction   **016**

LOVE STORIES—APPRECIATION

    Bouricius, A. The romance readers' advisory   **016**

LOVE STORIES—BIBLIOGRAPHY

    Bouricius, A. The romance readers' advisory   **016**

    Ramsdell, K. Romance fiction   **016**

LOVE STORIES—HISTORY AND CRITICISM

    Bouricius, A. The romance readers' advisory   **016**

    Ramsdell, K. Romance fiction   **016**

LOVE STORIES—STORIES, PLOTS, ETC

    Bouricius, A. The romance readers' advisory   **016**

LOVE STORIES—TECHNIQUE

    See also Authorship

LOVE STORIES, AMERICAN—BIBLIOGRAPHY—METHODOLOGY

    Bouricius, A. The romance readers' advisory   **016**

LOVE STORIES, ENGLISH—BIBLIOGRAPHY—METHODOLOGY

    Bouricius, A. The romance readers' advisory   **016**

Love thy neighbor. Maass, P.   **949.702**

Love, life, Goethe. Armstrong, J.   **92**

Love, Robert

    The Great Oom   **92**

Love, Susan M.

    Dr. Susan Love's breast book   **618.1**

    Dr. Susan Love's menopause and hormone book   **618.1**

    Live a little!   **613**

LOVE-LETTERS

    Kerouac, J. Door wide open   **813**

Lovell, Mary S.

    A rage to live: a biography of Richard and Isabel Burton   **92**

    The sound of wings: the life of Amelia Earhart   **629.13**

Lovelock, James

    The ages of Gaia   **570.1**

Lovesick blues. Hemphill, P.   **92**

Loving, Jerome

    Mark Twain   **92**

LOW FAT DIET

    Brody, J. E. Jane Brody's good seafood book **641.6**

    Wenner, P. F. Garden cuisine   **613.2**

LOW TEMPERATURE RESEARCH

    Shachtman, T. Absolute zero and the conquest of

nedy 92

Mai, Larry L.

The Cambridge Dictionary of human biology and evolution 612

MAIASAURA

See also Dinosaurs

Maida Heatter's book of great desserts. Heatter, M. 641.8

The **maids** [and] Deathwatch. Genet, J. 842

Maier, Karl

This house has fallen 966.905

Maier, Pauline

American scripture 973.3

Ratification 342

MAIL-ORDER BUSINESS

See also Business; Direct selling; Selling

Mailer. Dearborn, M. V. 813

Mailer, Norris Church

A ticket to the circus 92

Mailhot, Claire B.

Surgery: a patient's guide from diagnosis to recovery 617

The **Maine** woods. Thoreau, H. D. 917

Mainlines, blood feasts and bad taste. Bangs, L. 781.66

MAINSTREAMING IN EDUCATION

See also Education; Exceptional children; Handicapped children

MAINTENANCE AND REPAIR *See* Repairing

MAINTENANCE OF BIODIVERSITY *See* Biodiversity conservation

MAINTENANCE SERVICES EXECUTIVES

St. John, W. Outcasts united 796.334

MAINTENANCE WORKERS

Junger, S. A death in Belmont 364.152

Mainwaring, Simon

We first 658.8

Mair, Victor H.

(ed) The Columbia history of Chinese literature 895.1

(ed) The Shorter Columbia anthology of traditional Chinese literature 895.1

Maisel, David

Library of dust 779

Maitland, Leslie

Crossing the borders of time 940.53

Maitre-Allain, Thierry

Aquariums 639.34

MAIZE *See* Corn

Majd, Hooman

The Ayatollah begs to differ 955

Major. Balf, T. 92

Major acts of Congress. 348

Major Barbara. Shaw, B. 822

Major Farran's hat. Cesarani, D. 956.94

Major, David C.

100 one-night reads 001

Major, John S.

Major, D. C. 100 one-night reads 001

(ed) World poetry 808.81

Mak, Geert

In Europe 940.5

Make any divorce better! Sherman, C. E. 346.01

Make gentle the life of this world. Kennedy, R. F. 973.922

Make it in America. Liveris, A. 330.9

Make job loss work for you. Deems, R. S. 650.14

Make mine a mystery. Niebuhr, G. W. 809

Make your own living trust. Clifford, D. 346.05

Makes me wanna holler. McCall, N. 305.38

MAKEUP (COSMETICS) *See* Cosmetics

MAKEUP, THEATRICAL *See* Theatrical makeup

Maki, Allan

Football's greatest stars 920

Making a baby. Bruce, D. F. 618.2

Making a winning short. Levy, E. 070

Making an elephant. Swift, G. 828

Making certain it goes on. Hugo, R. F. 811

Making comics. McCloud, S. 741.5

Making genes, making waves. Beckwith, J. R. 576.5

Making handmade books. Golden, A. 686.3

Making haste from Babylon. Bunker, N. 974.4

Making history [series]

Gilbert, M. Kristallnacht 940.53

Roberts, A. Waterloo: June 18, 1815 940.2

Making it. Coyne, K. 640.73

Making movies. Lumet, S. 791.43

The **Making** of a poem. 821

The **making** of a writer. Godwin, G. 92

The **making** of African America. Berlin, I. 305.8

The **making** of modern Japan. Jansen, M. B. 952

The **making** of Mr. Gray's Anatomy. Richardson, R. 611

The **making** of Robert E. Lee. Fellman, M. 973.7

The **making** of the atomic bomb. Rhodes, R. 623.4

The **making** of the fittest. Carroll, S. B. 572.8

Making our democracy work. Breyer, S. G. 347

Making PCR. Rabinow, P. 572.8

Making peace with your past. Bloomfield, H. H. 158

Making saints. Woodward, K. L. 235

Making sense of life. Keller, E. F. 570.1

Making the body beautiful. Gilman, S. L. 617.9

Making the most of your money now. Quinn, J. B. 332.024

Making toast. Rosenblatt, R. 92

Making your own days. Koch, K. 809.1

MALADJUSTED CHILDREN *See* Emotionally disturbed children

MALADJUSTMENT (PSYCHOLOGY) *See* Adjustment (Psychology)

MALARIA

See also Diseases

MacColl, G. To marry an English Lord **974.7**
Roiphe, A. R. Married **306.81**
Roiphe, K. Uncommon arrangements **920**
Shulman, A. K. To love what is **92**
Waite, L. J. The case for marriage **306.81**
Yalom, M. A history of the wife **306.872**
MARRIAGE—HISTORY
Yalom, M. A history of the wife **306.872**
MARRIAGE—POETRY
Carson, A. The beauty of the husband **811**
MARRIAGE CONTRACTS
See also Contracts; Marriage
MARRIAGE COUNSELING
See also Counseling; Family life education; Marriage
MARRIAGE CUSTOMS AND RITES
See also Manners and customs; Marriage; Rites and ceremonies; Weddings
Bride's book of etiquette **395**
Jellison, K. It's our day **392**
Monger, G. Marriage customs of the world **392**
Post, P. Emily Post's wedding etiquette **395**
Marriage customs of the world. Monger, G. **392**
MARRIAGE REGISTERS *See* Registers of births, etc.
MARRIAGE, INTERRACIAL *See* Interracial marriage
MARRIE COUPLES—UNITED STATES—PSY-CHOLOGY
Waite, L. J. The case for marriage **306.81**
Married. Roiphe, A. R. **306.81**
MARRIED LIFE *See* Marriage
MARRIED MEN *See* Husbands
MARRIED PEOPLE
See also Family; Marriage
Waite, L. J. The case for marriage **306.81**
MARRIED PEOPLE—DRAMA
Albee, E. Who's afraid of Virginia Woolf? **812**
MARRIED PEOPLE—GREAT BRITAIN—BI-OGRAPHY
Bayley, J. Elegy for Iris **823**
MARRIED PEOPLE—POETRY
Carson, A. The beauty of the husband **811**
MARRIED PERSONS *See* Married people
MARRIED WOMEN—HISTORY
Yalom, M. A history of the wife **306.872**
MARRIED WOMEN—UNITED STATES—HIS-TORY
Berkin, C. Civil War wives **920**
Marriott, Edward
Plague: a story of science, rivalry, and the scourge that won't go away **614.5**
Marrs, Richard P.
Dr. Richard Marrs' fertility book **616.6**
Marrs, Suzanne
Eudora Welty: a biography **92**

(ed) What there is to say we have said **92**
Mars. Sheehan, W. **523.43**
MARS (PLANET)
See also Planets
MARS (PLANET)—PICTORIAL WORKS
See also Space photography
Marsalis, Wynton, 1961-
Moving to higher ground **781.65**
Marsden, George M.
Jonathan Edwards **92**
MARSH ECOLOGY
See also Ecology
Marsh, Earle
Brooks, T. The complete directory to prime time network and cable TV shows, 1946-present **791.45**
Marshall Cavendish Corporation
Encyclopedia of social issues **306**
Marshall Editions Ltd.
Courtier, J. Indoor plants **635.9**
Marshall McLuhan. Coupland, D. **92**
MARSHALL PLAN *See* Reconstruction (1939-1951)
Marshall, Carmia
Webber, C. Chic sweats **746.9**
Marshall, Gary
(ed) Studio space **741.5**
Marshall, I. N.
Who's afraid of Schrodinger's cat? **500**
Marshall, Jim
Trust **781.66**
Marshall, Leslie
Every step you take **92**
Marshall, Marlene Hurley
Shell chic **745.55**
Marshall, P. J.
(ed) The Cambridge illustrated history of the British Empire **941.08**
Marshall, Paule
Triangular road **92**
Marshall, Ruth
No time to lose **616.9**
Marshall, Thurgood
Thurgood Marshall **347**
MARSHALS
Brighton, T. Patton, Montgomery, Rommel **920**
Fraser, D. Knight's cross: a life of Field Marshal Erwin Rommel **92**
Millard, C. The river of doubt **973.91**
Roberts, A. Masters and commanders **940.54**
Showalter, D. E. Patton and Rommel **92**
Marshes. Burt, W. **578.7**
MARSHES
Burt, W. Marshes **578.7**
Marston, Daniel
(ed) The Pacific War **940.54**
MARSUPIALS

Martines, L. Fire in the city **92**

Martyrs' Day. Kelly, M. **956.7**

Martz, Louis Lohr
(ed) Collected poems, 1912-1944 **811**

Marvel. Daniels, L. **741.5**

Marvel, William
Burgin, R. V. Islands of the damned **940.54**

Marvell, Andrew
Poems **821**

Marx's general. Hunt, T. **92**

Marx, Karl
Capital: an abridged edition **330.1**
The Communist manifesto **335.4**

MARXIAN THEORY *See* Marxism

MARXISM
See also Economics; Philosophy; Political
science; Sociology
Gabriel, M. Love and capital **92**

MARXIST THEORY *See* Marxism

MARY (BLESSED VIRGIN, SAINT)
See also Saints

MARY (BLESSED VIRGIN, SAINT) — ART
See also Art; Christian art

**MARY (BLESSED VIRGIN, SAINT) —
PRAYERS**
See also Prayers

Mary Baker Eddy. Gill, G. **289.5**

Mary Cassatt. Mathews, N. M. **759.13**

Mary Engelbreit's children's companion. **645**

Mary Magdalene. Chilton, B. **226**

Mary Queen of Scots. Fraser, A. **92**

Mary Shelley. Seymour, M. **92**

Mary Shelley. Sunstein, E. W. **823**

Mary through the centuries. Pelikan, J. J. **232.91**

Mary Todd Lincoln. Baker, J. H. **92**

Mary, Queen of Scots, 1542-1587
About
Fraser, A. Mary Queen of Scots **92**
Schiller, F. Don Carlos and Mary Stuart **832**
Weir, A. Mary, Queen of Scots, and the murder of
Lord Darnley **92**

Mary, Queen of Scots, and the murder of Lord Darnley. Weir, A. **92**

Mary: a flesh-and-blood biography of the Virgin
Mother. Hazleton, L. **92**

Maryland paperback bookshelf [series]
Mencken, H. L. A second Mencken chrestomathy **818**

Marzollo, Jean
Fathers & babies **306**

MASCULINITY
Bordo, S. The male body **305.31**
Jones, S. Y: the descent of men **599.93**

MASCULINITY (PSYCHOLOGY) *See* Masculinity

MASCULINITY—UNITED STATES

Canada, G. Reaching up for manhood **305.23**
Sheehy, G. Understanding men's passages **305.244**

MASCULINITY IN POPULAR CULTURE
Bordo, S. The male body **305.31**

MASKS (PLAYS)
See also Drama; Pageants; Theater

MASKS (SCULPTURE)
See also Sculpture

The masks of God [series]
Campbell, J. Creative mythology **201**
Campbell, J. Occidental mythology **201**
Campbell, J. Oriental mythology **201**
Campbell, J. Primitive mythology **201**

Maslon, Laurence
Kantor, M. Broadway: the American musical **792.6**

Maslow, Abraham Harold
Toward a psychology of being **155.2**

Mason, Bobbie Ann
Elvis Presley **782.421**

Mason, David
(ed) Twentieth-century American poetry **811**

Mason, Julian D.
(ed) The poems of Phillis Wheatley **811**

Mason, Michael Paul
Head cases **617**

MASONRY
See also Building; Stone

The masque of Africa. Naipaul, V. S. **200.9**

Masquerade: the life and times of Deborah Sampson, Continental soldier. Young, A. F. **92**

MASS COMMUNICATION *See* Communication;
Mass media; Telecommunication

MASS CULTURE *See* Popular culture

Mass destruction. LeCain, T. J. **338.2**

MASS EXTINCTION OF SPECIES
Alvarez, W. T. rex and the Crater of Doom **551.7**
Powell, J. L. Night comes to the Cretaceous **576.8**

MASS MEDIA
See also Communication
Coupland, D. Marshall McLuhan **92**
Durham, M. G. The Lolita effect **302.23**
Gonzalez, J. News for all the people **302.23**
History of the mass media in the United
States **302.23**
The influencing machine **302.23**
Jones, G. Killing monsters **302.23**
McLuhan, M. The global village **302.23**
Postman, N. Amusing ourselves to death **302.23**
Wolff, M. The man who owns the news **92**

MASS MEDIA—AUSTRALIA
Wolff, M. The man who owns the news **92**

MASS MEDIA—HISTORY
Wu, T. The master switch **384**

MASS MEDIA—SOCIAL ASPECTS
Shirky, C. Cognitive surplus **303.4**

MASS MEDIA—UNITED STATES—HISTORY

See also Antiquities; Archeology; Monuments

MEGALITHIC MONUMENTS—ENGLAND
Hill, R. Stonehenge   **936**

MEGALITHIC MONUMENTS—GREAT BRITAIN
Hill, R. Stonehenge   **936**

Megellas, James
All the way to Berlin   **940.54**

Mehta, Suketu
Maximum city   **954**

Mehus-Roe, Kristin
(ed) The original dog bible   **636.7**

Meier, Andrew
Black earth   **947.086**

Meier, John J.
(ed) Dinosaurs   **567.9**

Meier, John P.
A marginal Jew   **232.9**

Meier, Matt S.
Notable Latino Americans   **305.868**

Meier, Richard
Building the Getty   **708**

Meiji, Emperor of Japan, 1852-1912
About
Keene, D. Emperor of Japan: Meiji and His world, 1852-1912   **952.03**
Seagrave, S. The Yamato dynasty   **952.03**

Mein Kampf. Hitler, A.   **92**

MELANCHOLIA *See* Depression (Psychology); Manic-depressive illness

MELANCHOLY
See also Emotions; Mood (Psychology)
Norris, K. Acedia & me   **92**

Melichson, Henya
The art of paper cutting   **745.54**

Mellon. Cannadine, D.   **92**

Mellor, Don
Trailside (Television program)   Rock climbing   **796.522**

Mellow, James R.
Hemingway   **813**

Melnyk, Marcia Yannizze
Family history 101   **929**

MELODRAMA
See also Drama

Melton's encyclopedia of American religions. Melton, J. G.   **200.9**

Melton, J. Gordon
Melton's encyclopedia of American religions   **200.9**
The vampire book   **398**
(ed) Religions of the world   **200**

Meltzer, Allan H.
A history of the Federal Reserve   **332.1**

Meltzer, Marisa
Girl power   **781.64**

Meltzoff, Andrew N.
Gopnik, A. The scientist in the crib   **155.4**

Melville. Robertson-Lorant, L.   **813**

Melville. Delbanco, A.   **92**

Melville, Herman, 1819-1891 (American novelist)
The poems of Herman Melville   **811**
About
Rollyson, C. Critical companion to Herman Melville   **813**
Said, E. W. Reflections on exile and other essays   **814**

The **member** of the wedding. McCullers, C.   **812**

MEMBERS OF CONGRESS
Abuse of power   **973.924**
Ambrose, S. E. The wild blue   **940.54**
Baker, N. The World on Sunday   **071**
Balz, D. J. The battle for America, 2008   **973.932**
Berman, L. No peace, no honor   **959.704**
Black, C. M. Richard M. Nixon   **92**
Boritt, G. S. The Gettysburg gospel   **973.7**
Borneman, W. R. Polk   **92**
Brackett, E. Pay to play   **92**
Brands, H. W. The first American: the life and times of Benjamin Franklin   **92**
Brookhiser, R. America's first dynasty   **973.4**
Bugliosi, V. Reclaiming history   **973.922**
Burlingame, M. Abraham Lincoln   **92**
Burstein, A. Madison and Jefferson   **973.4**
Busby, H. W. The thirty-first of March   **973.923**
Bush, B. Barbara Bush   **92**
Bush, G. All the best, George Bush   **92**
Caro, R. A. Master of the senate   **92**
Caro, R. A. Means of ascent   **92**
Caro, R. A. The path to power   **973.9**
Carwardine, R. Lincoln: a life of purpose and power   **92**
Clinton, C. Mrs. Lincoln   **92**
Cohen, I. B. Science and the founding fathers **973.3**
Crapol, E. P. John Tyler   **92**
Craughwell, T. J. Stealing Lincoln's body   **973.7**
Dallek, R. Let every nation know   **92**
Dallek, R. Nixon and Kissinger   **92**
Dallek, R. An unfinished life: John F. Kennedy, 1917-1963   **973.922**
Davis, W. C. Three roads to the Alamo   **976.4**
Denton, S. The pink lady   **92**
Dershowitz, A. M. Supreme injustice   **324.9**
Dobbs, M. One minute to midnight   **973.922**
Donald, D. H. Lincoln   **92**
Dusinberre, W. Slavemaster president   **973.6**
Ellis, J. J. Founding brothers   **973.4**
Emery, F. Watergate   **973.924**
Ferguson, A. Land of Lincoln   **973.7**
Finger, S. Doctor Franklin's medicine   **610**
Finkelman, P. Millard Fillmore   **92**
Foner, E. The fiery trial   **973.7**

Martial Epigrams 878

The **modern** library writer's workshop. Koch, S. 808.3

MODERN LITERATURE *See* Literature; Modernism in literature

Modern midges. Takahashi, R. 799.1

MODERN PHILOSOPHY
> *See also* Philosophy

Berlin, I. The sense of reality 190
Gay, P. The rise of modern paganism 190
Gay, P. The science of freedom 190
Himmelfarb, G. The moral imagination 190
Nadler, S. M. The best of all possible worlds 190
Robinson, M. Absence of mind 201
Sedgwick, P. Descartes to Derrida 190

Modern physics and ancient faith. Barr, S. M. 201

The **modern** vegetarian kitchen. Berley, P. 641.5

Modern war studies [series]
Inside the Pentagon papers 959.704
Kindsvatter, P. S. American soldiers 355
Skiba, K. M. Sister in the Band of Brothers 956.7

MODERNISM *See* Modernism (Aesthetics); Modernism (Theology)

MODERNISM (AESTHETICS)
> *See also* Aesthetics

Wilson, E. Literary essays and reviews of the 1920s & 30s 814
Wilson, E. Literary essays and reviews of the 1930s & 40s 814

MODERNISM (ART)—EUROPE
Fineberg, J. D. Art since 1940 709.04

MODERNISM (ART)—UNITED STATES
Fineberg, J. D. Art since 1940 709.04

MODERNISM (ARTS) *See* Modernism (Aesthetics)

MODERNISM (LITERATURE) *See* Modernism in literature

MODERNISM IN ARCHITECTURE
> *See also* Architecture; Modernism (Aesthetics)

MODERNISM IN ART
> *See also* Art; Modernism (Aesthetics)

MODERNISM IN LITERATURE
> *See also* Literature; Modernism (Aesthetics)

The collected poems of Eugenio Montale 1925-1977 851

MODERNISM IN SCULPTURE
> *See also* Modernism (Aesthetics); Sculpture

MODERNIST-FUNDAMENTALIST CONTROVERSY *See* Christian fundamentalism; Modernism (Theology)

MODERNIZATION (SOCIOLOGY)
> *See also* Social change

Modigliani. Secrest, M. 92

Moeller, Hans-Georg
The moral fool 171

Moffat, Wendy
A great unrecorded history 92

Moffett, Kay
Not your mother's divorce 306.89

Moffett, Mark W.
Adventures among ants 595.7

Moffitt, Perry-Lynn
Kohn, I. A silent sorrow 618.3

Moffitt, Sean
Wikibrands 658.8

MOGUL EMPIRE
McLeod, J. The history of India 954
Wolpert, S. A. A new history of India 954

Mohandas
Gandhi 92

MOHAWK INDIANS
Demos, J. The unredeemed captive 973.2

MOHEGAN INDIANS
Josephy, A. M. Now that the buffalo's gone **970.004**

Moker, Molly
(ed) The official guide to America's national parks 917

Mokyr, Joel
(ed) The Oxford encyclopedia of economic history 330

The **mold** in Dr. Florey's coat. Lax, E. 615

MOLDS (FUNGI)
> *See also* Fungi

MOLECULAR BIOCHEMISTRY *See* Molecular biology

MOLECULAR BIOLOGISTS
Flowers, C. Instability rules 509
Friedman, M. Medicine's 10 greatest discoveries 610
Horvitz, L. A. Eureka!: scientific breakthroughs that changed the world 509
Watson, J. D. Avoid boring people 92
Watson, J. D. Genes, girls, and Gamow 92

MOLECULAR BIOLOGISTS—BIOGRAPHY
Watson, J. D. The double helix 572.8

MOLECULAR BIOLOGISTS—UNITED STATES—BIOGRAPHY
Segrà, G. Ordinary geniuses 572.8
Watson, J. D. Genes, girls, and Gamow 92

MOLECULAR BIOLOGY
> *See also* Biochemistry; Biophysics

Lewontin, R. C. The triple helix 572.8
Morange, M. A history of molecular biology 572.8
Rensberger, B. Life itself 571.6

MOLECULAR BIOLOGY—ENGLISH
Genetics 576.5

MOLECULAR BIOLOGY—HISTORY
Morange, M. A history of molecular biology 572.8
Zimmer, C. Microcosm 579.3

MOLECULAR BIOLOGY—PHILOSOPHY
Lewontin, R. C. The triple helix 572.8

Morris, Patrick

(jt. auth) Barrington, R. Life   **578.4**

Morris, Robert D.

The blue death   **614.4**

Morris, Roger

Denton, S. The money and the power   **979.3**

Morris, Roy

Ambrose Bierce   **92**

Fraud of the century   **324.9**

Morris, Sylvia Jukes

Rage for fame: the ascent of Clare Boothe Luce   **92**

Morris, Vanessa Irvin

The readers' advisory guide to street literature   **016**

Morris, William

Morris dictionary of word and phrase origins   **422**

Morris, Willie

My dog Skip   **813**

Morris-Suzuki, Tessa

To the Diamond Mountains   **915**

Morrison, Dan

The black Nile   **962**

Morrison, Grant

Supergods   **741.5**

Morrison, Joanna

Charles, J. A. The mystery readers' advisory **025.2**

Morrison, Phylis

Holden, A. Crystals and crystal growing   **548**

Morrison, Terri

Kiss, bow, or shake hands   **395**

Morrison, Toni, 1931- (American novelist)

(ed) Burn this book   **814**

About

Gillespie, C. Critical companion to Toni Morrison   **813**

Morrow, Bradford

(ed) The Inevitable   **814**

Morrow, Lance

The best year of their lives   **920**

Second drafts of history   **973.92**

Morrow-Cribbs, Briony

Stewart, A. Wicked bugs   **632**

MORSE CODE *See* Cipher and telegraph codes

Mortal coil. Haycock, D. B.   **571.8**

Mortenson, Greg

Stones into schools   **371.82**

Three cups of tea   **371.82**

MORTGAGE LOANS *See* Mortgages

MORTGAGE-BACKED SECURITIES

McLean, B. All the devils are here   **330.9**

MORTGAGES

See also Loans; Securities

Acharya, V. V. Guaranteed to fail   **332.7**

Andrews, E. L. Busted   **332.7**

Hudson, M. The monster   **332.6**

McLean, B. All the devils are here   **330.9**

Morgenson, G. Reckless endangerment   **332.7**

Morthland, John

(ed) Bangs, L. Mainlines, blood feasts and bad taste   **781.66**

MORTICIANS *See* Undertakers and undertaking

Mortimer, Gavin

Chasing Icarus   **629.13**

The great swim   **920**

The longest night   **940.53**

Morton, Brian

Cook, R. The Penguin guide to jazz recordings   **781.65**

Morton, Oliver

Eating the sun   **572**

Mapping Mars   **523.43**

Morton, R. L.

Music of the earth   **550**

MORTUARY CUSTOMS *See* Cremation; Funeral rites and ceremonies

MOSAICS

See also Decoration and ornament; Decorative arts

Mosby's diagnostic and laboratory test reference. Pagana, K. D.   **616.07**

Mosby's medical dictionary.   **610**

Mosby's Rangers. Wert, J. D.   **973.7**

Mosby, Rebekah Presson

(ed) Poetry speaks expanded   **811**

Moseley, Michael Edward

The Incas and their ancestors   **985**

Mosenfelder, Donn

Fischer, B. Bobby Fischer teaches chess   **794.1**

Moser, Benjamin

Why this world   **92**

Moser, Charles A.

(ed) The Cambridge history of Russian literature   **891.7**

Moses (Hebrew prophet)

About

Feiler, B. S. America's prophet   **973**

Moses, Kate

(ed) Because I said so   **306.8**

Moses, Sam

At all costs   **940.54**

Mosier, John

The myth of the Great War   **940.4**

Moskowitz, Isa Chandra

Vegan pie in the sky   **641.5**

MOSLEMS *See* Muslims

Mosley, Anthony D.

The encyclopedia of Parkinson's disease   **616.8**

Mosley, Charlotte

(ed) The Mitfords   **920**

Mosley, Shelley

Tucker, D. C. Crash course in library supervision   **023**

A **mosque** in Munich. Johnson, I.   **297**

Mamet, D. On directing film **791.43**
Reilly, T. A. The big picture **791.43**
Waxman, S. Rebels on the backlot **920**
MOTION PICTURES—REVIEWS
Ebert, R. Roger Ebert's movie yearbook 2010 **791.43**
Farber, M. Farber on film **791.43**
Kael, P. The age of movies **791.43**
Lane, A. Nobody's perfect **791.43**
MOTION PICTURES—UNITED STATES
Fine, M. Accidental genius **791**
Jones, G. W. Black cinema treasures **791.43**
MOTION PICTURES—UNITED STATES—HISTORY
Sragow, M. Victor Fleming **92**
MOTION PICTURES—UNITED STATES—HISTORY—20TH CENTURY
Thomson, D. The moment of Psycho **791.43**
MOTION PICTURES AND CHILDREN
See also Children; Motion pictures
MOTION PICTURES IN EDUCATION
See also Audiovisual education; Motion pictures; Teaching—Aids and devices
MOTION STUDY
See also Factory management; Industrial efficiency; Job analysis; Personnel management; Production standards
Motion, Andrew
Keats **821**
MOTIVATION (PSYCHOLOGY)
See also Psychology
Delmolino, L. Incentives for change **649**
Godin, S. Linchpin **650.1**
Hallowell, E. M. Shine **658.3**
Kelly, M. The dream manager **658.3**
Maslow, A. H. Toward a psychology of being **155.2**
Myers, B. Take the lead **158**
Tracy, B. Full engagement! **658.3**
Vedantam, S. The hidden brain **154.2**
MOTIVATION IN ANIMALS
Bekoff, M. Wild justice **591.5**
MOTIVATIONAL SPEAKERS
Meeink, F. Autobiography of a recovering skinhead **92**
Mooney, J. The short bus **92**
Murray, L. Breaking night **92**
Motley, Isolde
Caughman, S. You can adopt **362.7**
MOTOR CARS *See* Automobiles
MOTOR CYCLES *See* Motorcycles
MOTOR TRUCKS *See* Trucks
MOTOR VEHICLE INDUSTRY *See* Automobile industry
MOTOR VEHICLES—FUEL CONSUMPTION
Sperling, D. Two billion cars **388.3**
MOTORBOATS

See also Boats and boating
MOTORCYCLE GANGS
Queen, W. Under and alone **364.1**
Motorcycle owner's manual. Wilson, H. **629.28**
MOTORCYCLES
See also Bicycles
Johnson, W. Live to ride **796.7**
MOTORCYCLES—MAINTENANCE AND REPAIR
Wilson, H. Motorcycle owner's manual **629.28**
MOTORCYCLING
See also Cycling
Mott-Smith, Geoffrey
(ed) Hoyle, E. Hoyle's rules of games **795.4**
MOUNDS AND MOUND BUILDERS
See also Archeology; Burial; Tombs
Mount St. Helens: the eruption and recovery of a volcano. Carson, R. **551.2**
MOUNTAIN ANIMALS
See also Animals
MOUNTAIN BIKES
See also All terrain vehicles; Bicycles
MOUNTAIN BIKING
See also Cycling
MOUNTAIN CLIMBING *See* Mountaineering
MOUNTAIN ECOLOGY
See also Ecology
Mountain home. **895.1**
MOUNTAIN LIFE—ILLINOIS
Biggers, J. Reckoning at Eagle Creek **333.73**
MOUNTAIN MEADOWS MASSACRE, 1857
Walker, R. W. Massacre at Mountain Meadows **979.2**
A **mountain** of crumbs. Gorokhova, E. **92**
MOUNTAIN PEOPLE
See also Ethnology
Mountain rescue doctor. Van Tilburg, C. **616**
MOUNTAINEERING
See also Outdoor life
Blum, A. Breaking trail **796.522**
Boukreev, A. The climb **796.522**
Coburn, B. Everest: mountain without mercy **796.522**
Grange, K. Beneath blossom rain **915**
Jamling Tenzing Norgay Touching my father's soul **796.522**
Krakauer, J. Into thin air **796.522**
Taylor, J. E. Pilgrims of the vertical **796.52**
Trailside (Television program) Rock climbing **796.522**
Van Tilburg, C. Mountain rescue doctor **616**
MOUNTAINEERING—PERSONAL NARRATIVES
Krakauer, J. Into thin air **796.522**
MOUNTAINEERING ACCIDENTS—EVEREST, MOUNT (CHINA AND NEPAL)

See also Art; Cities and towns

MUNICIPAL ENGINEERING
 See also Engineering; Public works

MUNICIPAL FINANCE
 See also Municipal government; Public finance

MUNICIPAL GOVERNMENT
 See also Local government; Political science

MUNICIPAL OWNERSHIP
 See also Corporations; Economic policy; Government ownership

MUNICIPAL PLANNING *See* City planning

MUNICIPALITIES *See* Cities and towns; Municipal government

MUNITIONS *See* Defense industry; Military weapons

Munro, Nell
 Ives, M. Caring for a child with autism **618.92**

Munson, Ronald
 Raising the dead **174**

Murakami, Haruki
 Underground **364.1**

MURAL PAINTING AND DECORATION
 See also Decoration and ornament; Interior design; Painting
 Felisbret, E. Graffiti New York **751.7**
 Ganz, N. Graffiti world **751**
 King, R. Michelangelo & the Pope's ceiling **759**

MURAL PAINTING AND DECORATION, AMERICAN—NEW YORK (STATE)—NEW YORK
 Felisbret, E. Graffiti New York **751.7**

MURAL PAINTING AND DECORATION, ITALIAN
 King, R. Michelangelo & the Pope's ceiling **759**

MURAL PAINTING AND DECORATION, ITALIAN—VATICAN CITY
 King, R. Michelangelo & the Pope's ceiling **759**

MURAL PAINTING AND DECORATION, RENAISSANCE
 King, R. Michelangelo & the Pope's ceiling **759**

MURAL PAINTING AND DECORATION, RENAISSANCE—VATICAN CITY
 King, R. Michelangelo & the Pope's ceiling **759**

MURDER *See* Homicide

MURDER—ENGLAND
 Summerscale, K. The suspicions of Mr. Whicher **364.152**

MURDER—GEORGIA—ATLANTA
 Brown, E. The condemnation of Little B **364.15**

MURDER—GERMANY—HISTORY
 Robisheaux, T. The last witch of Langenburg **133.4**

MURDER—INVESTIGATION—COLORADO—BOULDER—CASE STUDIES
 Schiller, L. Perfect murder, perfect town **364.15**

MURDER—INVESTIGATION—JAPAN—TO-KYO
 Parry, R. L. People who eat darkness **364.152**

MURDER—KANSAS—CASE STUDIES
 Capote, T. In cold blood **364.1**

MURDER—LOUISIANA—NEW ORLEANS
 Brown, E. Shake the devil off **364.152**

MURDER—MISSOURI—SAINT LOUIS
 Heidenry, J. Zero at the bone **364.152**

MURDER—NEW YORK (STATE)—NEW YORK
 Salamon, J. Facing the wind **364.15**

MURDER—TEXAS—JASPER
 King, J. Hate crime: the story of a dragging in Jasper, Texas **364.15**

MURDER—WASHINGTON (D.C.)
 Higham, S. Finding Chandra **364.152**
 Murder city. Bowden, C. **364.152**
 Murder in Amsterdam. Buruma, I. **364.152**

MURDER IN MASS MEDIA
 Brown, E. The condemnation of Little B **364.15**
A **murder** in Virginia. Lebsock, S. **364.1**

MURDER INVESTIGATION—NEW YORK (STATE)—NEW YORK—CASE STUDIES
 Gourevitch, P. A cold case **364.1**

MURDER MYSTERIES *See* Mystery and detective plays; Mystery fiction; Mystery films; Mystery radio programs; Mystery television programs
The **murder** of Nikolai Vavilov. Pringle, P. **92**
The **murder** of the century. Collins, P. **364.152**
The **murder** of Tutankhamen. Brier, B. **932**

MURDER TRIALS *See* Trials (Homicide)

MURDER VICTIMS
 Abdul-Jabbar, K. Black profiles in courage **920**
 Brown, E. Shake the devil off **364.152**
 Cesarani, D. Major Farran's hat **956.94**
 Diebel, L. Betrayed **364.152**
 Dornstein, K. The boy who fell out of the sky **92**
 Gage, N. Eleni **92**
 Geis, G. Crimes of the century **345**
 Goldman, F. The art of political murder **972.81**
 Heidenry, J. Zero at the bone **364.152**
 Herlihy, D. V. The lost cyclist **92**
 Higham, S. Finding Chandra **364.152**
 Junger, S. A death in Belmont **364.152**
 Kersten, J. Journal of the dead **364.15**
 King, J. Hate crime: the story of a dragging in Jasper, Texas **364.15**
 Latus, J. If I am missing or dead **92**
 Malcolm, J. Iphigenia in Forest Hills **345**
 Matthews, J. Bringing Adam home **364.1**
 May, G. The informant **364.152**
 Mowat, F. Woman in the mists: the story of Dian Fossey and the mountain gorillas of Africa **599**
 O'Brien, G. The fall of the house of Walworth **920**
 Rice, A. The teeth may smile but the heart does not forget **967.6**

My prison, my home. Esfandiari, H.　　92

My Russian grandmother and her American vacuum cleaner. Shalev, M.　　92

My sister, guard your veil; my brother guard, your eyes.　　305

My song. Belafonte, H.　　92

My start-up life. Casnocha, B.　　338.7

My stroke of luck. Douglas, K.　　362.1

My sweet Mexico. Gerson, F.　　641.5

My Tibet. Dalai Lama　　951

My Times in black and white. Boyd, G. M.　　92

My vocabulary did this to me. Spicer, J.　　811

My war. Rooney, A. A.　　940.54

My wars are laid away in books. Habegger, A.　　92

My year of flops. Rabin, N.　　791.43

MYCOLOGY See Fungi

Myer, Valerie Grosvenor
(ed) The Continuum encyclopedia of British literature　　810

Myers, Allen C.
(ed) Eerdmans dictionary of the Bible　　220.3

Myers, Ann
Koestler, A. J.　Understanding chronic pain　　616

Myers, Betsy
Take the lead　　158

Myers, David G.
A quiet world　　617.8

Myers, Isabel Briggs
Gifts differing　　155.2

Myers, Peter B.
Myers, I. B.　Gifts differing　　155.2

Myerson, Joel
(ed) Transcendentalism　　810

Myne. Presley, F.　　821

MYOFASCIAL PAIN SYNDROMES
Patarca, R.　The concise encyclopedia of fibromyalgia and myofascial pain　　616.7

Myrick, Leslie Diane
(ed) Autobiography of Mark Twain　　92

Myrna Loy. Leider, E. W.　　92

Myron, Vicki
Dewey　　636.8

Myself when I am real: the life and music of Charles Mingus. Santoro, G.　　781.65

Myself with others. Fuentes, C.　　864

MYSPACE (WEB SITE)
See also Social networking; Web sites
Angwin, J.　Stealing MySpace　　338.7

MYSTERIES See Mysteries and miracle plays; Mystery and detective plays; Mystery fiction; Mystery films; Mystery radio programs; Mystery television programs

MYSTERIES AND MIRACLE PLAYS
See also Bible plays; English drama; Pageants; Religious drama; Theater
Everyman, and medieval miracle plays　　822

MYSTERY AND DETECTIVE FICTION
Charles, J. A.　The mystery readers' advisory　025.2

MYSTERY AND DETECTIVE FICTION—BIBLIOGRAPHY
Trott, B.　Read on . . . crime fiction　　016

MYSTERY AND DETECTIVE FILMS See Mystery films

MYSTERY AND DETECTIVE PLAYS
See also Drama

The **mystery** and meaning of the Dead Sea scrolls. Shanks, H.　　296.1

Mystery and suspense writers.　　809

MYSTERY COMIC BOOKS, STRIPS, ETC.
See also Comic books, strips, etc.

MYSTERY FICTION
See also Fiction

MYSTERY FICTION—BIBLIOGRAPHY
Bleiler, R.　Reference and research guide to mystery and detective fiction　　016
Charles, J. A.　The mystery readers' advisory　025.2
Niebuhr, G. W.　Make mine a mystery　　809
Trott, B.　Read on . . . crime fiction　　016

MYSTERY FICTION—DICTIONARIES
Mystery and suspense writers　　809

MYSTERY FICTION—HISTORY AND CRITICISM
Critical survey of mystery and detective fiction　809
James, P. D.　Talking about detective fiction　　823
Niebuhr, G. W.　Make mine a mystery　　809
Symons, J.　Bloody murder　　809

MYSTERY FICTION—TECHNIQUE
Roberts, G.　You can write a mystery　　808.3
Wheat, C.　How to write killer fiction　　808.3

MYSTERY FILMS
See also Motion pictures
Decharne, M.　Hardboiled Hollywood　　791.43
Film noir　　791.43

MYSTERY GRAPHIC NOVELS
See also Graphic novels
Geary, R.　The Lindbergh child　　364.1

The **mystery** of capital. Soto, H. d.　　330.12

The **mystery** of the hidden driveway. Knox, J. L.　　811

MYSTERY PLAYS See Mysteries and miracle plays; Mystery and detective plays

MYSTERY RADIO PROGRAMS
See also Radio programs

The **mystery** readers' advisory. Charles, J. A. 025.2

MYSTERY TELEVISION PROGRAMS
See also Television programs

MYSTERY WRITERS
Barr, N.　Seeking enlightenment—hat by hat　　92
Dirda, M.　On Conan Doyle; or, The whole art of storytelling　　823
Doyle, A. C.　Arthur Conan Doyle　　92
Hillerman, T.　Seldom disappointed　　813

See also Drugs; Materia medica; Psychotropic drugs

NARCOTICS DEALERS
Schou, N. Orange sunshine   **363.45**

NARRAGANSET INDIANS
Josephy, A. M. Now that the buffalo's gone **970.004**

NARRATIONS *See* Monologues; Recitations

Narrative of the life of Frederick Douglass, an American slave. Douglass, F.   **92**

NARRATIVE POETRY
     See also Poetry

Narrowing the nation's power: the Supreme Court sides with the states. Noonan, J. T.   **342**

Narth, Angela
Aykroyd, P. A history of ghosts   **133.1**

NASA OFFICIALS
Biddle, W. Dark side of the moon   **92**
Bizony, P. The man who ran the moon   **629**
Neufeld, M. J. Von Braun   **92**

Nasaw, David
Andrew Carnegie   **92**
The chief: the life of William Randolph Hearst **070.5**

Nasdijj
The blood runs like a river through my dreams **979.1**

Nash, Gary B.
(ed) Encyclopedia of American history   **973**

Nash, George
Do-it-yourself housebuilding   **690**

Nash, Jay Robert
The great pictorial history of world crime   **364**

Naskrecki, Piotr
The smaller majority   **591.7**

Nasr, Seyyed Hossein
Islam: religion, history, and civilization   **297**

Nasr, Vali
The Shia revival   **297**

Nat King Cole. Epstein, D. M.   **92**

NATAL ASTROLOGY
Lewis, J. R. The astrology book   **133.5**

Nathan I. Huggins lectures [series]
Litwack, L. F. How free is free?   **323.1**

Nathan the Wise, Minna von Barnhelm, and other plays and writings. Lessing, G. E.   **832**

Nathan, Debbie
Sybil exposed   **92**

Nathan, Joan
Jewish cooking in America   **641.5**
Quiches, kugels, and couscous   **641.5**

Nathan, John
Japan unbound   **320**

Nathans, Sydney
To free a family   **306.3**

Nather, David
The new health care system   **344**

A nation of farmers. Astyk, S.   **338.1**

NATION OF ISLAM *See* Black Muslims

A nation on fire. Risen, C.   **973.923**

A nation under our feet. Hahn, S.   **305.8**

National Air and Space Museum (U.S.)
Chaikin, A. Air and space   **629.13**
Hardesty, V. Black wings   **920**

National anthem. Prufer, K.   **811**

NATIONAL ANTHEMS *See* National songs

National anthems of the world.   **782.42**

National Audubon Society
Bull, J. L. The National Audubon Society field guide to North American birds, Eastern region **598**
Chartrand, M. R. The Audubon Society field guide to the night sky   **523**
Chesterman, C. W. The Audubon Society field guide to North American rocks and minerals **549**
Folkens, P. A. National Audubon Society guide to marine mammals of the world   **599.5**
Little, E. L. The Audubon Society field guide to North American trees   **582.16**
Ludlum, D. M. The Audubon Society field guide to North American weather   **551.6**
McKnight, K. H. A field guide to mushrooms, North America   **579.6**
Milne, L. J. The Audubon Society field guide to North American insects and spiders   **595.7**
Bird   **598**
National Audubon Society guide to nature photography   **778.9**
Pyle, R. M. The Audubon Society field guide to North American butterflies   **595.7**
Sibley, D. The Sibley guide to bird life & behavior   **598**
Sibley, D. The Sibley guide to birds   **598**
Smith, C. L. National Audubon Society field guide to tropical marine fishes of the Caribbean, the Gulf of Mexico, Florida, the Bahamas, and Bermuda   **597**
Thompson, I. The Audubon Society field guide to North American fossils   **560**
Udvardy, M. D. F. National Audubon Society field guide to North American birds, Western region   **598**
Whitaker, J. O. National Audubon Society field guide to North American mammals   **599**

National Audubon Society field guide series
Thieret, J. W. National Audubon Society field guide to North American wildflowers: eastern region   **582.13**

National Audubon Society field guide to fishes, North America. Gilbert, C. R.   **597**

The National Audubon Society field guide to North American birds, Eastern region. Bull, J. L.   **598**

National Audubon Society field guide to North American birds, Western region. Udvardy, M. D. F.   **598**

National Audubon Society field guide to North

National Geographic guide to the state parks of the United States **917**

National Geographic visual history of the world **902.2**

Through the lens **779**

Schmidt, T. The Lewis & Clark Trail **978**

Wiencek, H. National Geographic guide to America's great houses **728.8**

National Geographic visual atlas of the world. **912**

National Geographic visual history of the world. National Geographic Society (U.S.) **902.2**

NATIONAL HEALTH INSURANCE
See also Health insurance

NATIONAL HERITAGE *See* Cultural property

NATIONAL HOLIDAYS *See* Holidays

NATIONAL HYMNS *See* National songs

NATIONAL INTEREST *See* Public interest

NATIONAL LANDMARKS *See* National monuments

NATIONAL LIBERATION MOVEMENTS
See also Nationalism; Revolutions

NATIONAL LIBRARIES—WASHINGTON (D.C.)—HISTORY—19TH CENTURY
Conaway, J. America's library **027.5**

NATIONAL LIBRARIES—WASHINGTON (D.C.)—HISTORY—20TH CENTURY
Conaway, J. America's library **027.5**

NATIONAL MONUMENTS
See also Monuments; National parks and reserves

Khan, Y. S. Enlightening the world **974.7**

National Museum of Natural History (U.S.)

Vikings: the North Atlantic saga **970.01**

National park ranger. Farabee, C. R. **363.6**

The **national** parks. Duncan, D. **333.7**

NATIONAL PARKS AND RESERVES
See also Parks; Public lands

NATIONAL PARKS AND RESERVES—UNITED STATES
Duncan, D. The national parks **333.7**

Egan, T. The big burn **973.91**

Farabee, C. R. National park ranger **363.6**

National Geographic Society (U.S.) National Geographic guide to the national parks of the United States **917**

The official guide to America's national parks **917**

NATIONAL PARKS AND RESERVES—UNITED STATES—HISTORY
Egan, T. The big burn **973.91**

National party conventions, 1831-2008. Congressional Quarterly, I. **324.5**

NATIONAL PATRIMONY *See* Cultural property

NATIONAL PLANNING *See* Economic policy; Social policy

NATIONAL PSYCHOLOGY *See* Ethnopsychology; National characteristics

National Public Radio (U.S.)

Hoffman, M. The NPR classical music companion **780**

NATIONAL RESOURCES *See* Economic conditions; Natural resources; United States—Economic conditions

NATIONAL SECURITY
Hart, G. The fourth power **327**

NATIONAL SECURITY—INDIAN OCEAN REGION
Kaplan, R. D. Monsoon **327**

NATIONAL SECURITY—UNITED STATES
Graff, G. M. The threat matrix **363.325**

Maddow, R. Drift **306.2**

Weiner, T. Enemies **363.25**

NATIONAL SECURITY—UNITED STATES—HISTORY—20TH CENTURY
Thompson, N. The hawk and the dove **92**

NATIONAL SELF-DETERMINATION
See also Nationalism

NATIONAL SERVICE
See also Public welfare

NATIONAL SOCIALISM
See also Fascism; World War, 1939-1945—Causes

Allert, T. The Hitler salute **395**

Aycoberry, P. The social history of the Third Reich **943.086**

Breitman, R. The architect of genocide **92**

Evans, R. J. The coming of the Third Reich **943.08**

Evans, R. J. The Third Reich in power, 1933-1939 **943.086**

Fest, J. C. Speer: the final verdict **92**

Fischer, K. P. Nazi Germany **943.086**

Fisher, M. A terrible splendor **796.342**

Fritzsche, P. Life and death in the Third Reich **943.086**

Fulbrook, M. A concise history of Germany **943**

Gay, P. My German question **943**

Goldhagen, D. Hitler's willing executioners **940.53**

Hitler, A. Mein Kampf **92**

Kershaw, I. Hitler, 1936-1945: nemesis **943.086**

Kershaw, I. Hitler, the Germans, and the final solution **940.53**

Larson, E. In the garden of beasts **92**

Lewy, G. The Nazi persecution of the gypsies **940.53**

Mazower, M. Hitler's empire **940.53**

Nelson, A. Red Orchestra **943.086**

Petropoulos, J. The Faustian bargain **709**

Rempel, G. Hitler's children **943.086**

Rosenbaum, R. Explaining Hitler **943.086**

Sereny, G. Albert Speer **92**

Toland, J. Adolf Hitler **92**

Tubach, F. C. German voices **943.086**

Turner, H. A. Hitler's thirty days to power **943.086**

Walker, M. Nazi science   509

NATIONAL SOCIALISM—AUSTRIA

Weyr, T. The setting of the pearl   940.53

NATIONAL SOCIALISM—GERMANY

Larson, E. In the garden of beasts   92

NATIONAL SOCIALISM—HISTORY

Evans, R. J. The coming of the Third Reich 943.08

Evans, R. J. The Third Reich in power, 1933-1939   943.086

NATIONAL SOCIALISM—SOCIAL ASPECTS—GERMANY

Allert, T. The Hitler salute   395

NATIONAL SOCIALISM AND ART

Petropoulos, J. The Faustian bargain   709

NATIONAL SOCIALISM AND YOUTH

Nicholas, L. H. Cruel world   940.53

NATIONAL SONGS

> *See also* Songs

National anthems of the world   782.42

NATIONAL SONGS—UNITED STATES

> *See also* American songs

NATIONAL STATE

Bobbitt, P. The shield of Achilles   327

National Story Project (U.S.)

I thought my father was God and other true tales from the National Story Project   810

National survey of state laws.   349

National trade and professional associations of the United States.   061

NATIONAL TREASURE *See* Cultural property

National Wildlife Federation

McKnight, K. H. A field guide to mushrooms, North America   579.6

NATIONALISM

> *See also* International relations; Political science

Berlin, I. The sense of reality   190

The Causes of the Civil War   973.7

Said, E. W. Reflections on exile and other essays   814

NATIONALISM—ARAB COUNTRIES—HISTORY

Rogan, E. The Arabs   909

NATIONALISM—EUROPE—HISTORY—20TH CENTURY

Ousby, I. The road to Verdun   940.4

NATIONALISM—FRANCE

Brown, F. For the soul of France   944.081

NATIONALISM—FRANCE—HISTORY—19TH CENTURY

Brown, F. For the soul of France   944.081

NATIONALISM—UNITED STATES

Marcus, G. The shape of things to come   973

Zeskind, L. Blood and politics   305.8

NATIONALISTS—INDIA

Wolpert, S. A. Gandhi's passion   954.03

NATIONALITY (CITIZENSHIP) *See* Citizenship

NATIONS

> *See also* Political science

Native America in the twentieth century.   970.004

NATIVE AMERICAN ARCHITECTURE

> *See also* Architecture

NATIVE AMERICAN ART

> *See also* Art

Berlo, J. C. Native North American art   709.01

Schobinger, J. The ancient Americans   970.01

NATIVE AMERICAN AUTHORS

> *See also* Authors

NATIVE AMERICAN CHILDREN

> *See also* Children

NATIVE AMERICAN COSTUME—ENCYCLOPEDIAS

Paterek, J. Encyclopedia of American Indian costume   391

A **Native** American encyclopedia. Pritzker, B.   970.004

NATIVE AMERICAN GAMES

> *See also* Games; Native Americans—Social life and customs

NATIVE AMERICAN LANGUAGES

> *See also* Language and languages

NATIVE AMERICAN LITERATURE

> *See also* Literature

NATIVE AMERICAN LITERATURE—ENCYCLOPEDIAS

Encyclopedia of American Indian literature   810

NATIVE AMERICAN LITERATURE—HISTORY AND CRITICISM

The Cambridge companion to Native American literature   897

NATIVE AMERICAN MEDICINE

> *See also* Medicine

NATIVE AMERICAN MUSIC

> *See also* Music

Native American mythology A to Z. Lynch, P. A.   398.2

NATIVE AMERICAN NAMES

> *See also* Names

NATIVE AMERICAN SIGN LANGUAGE

> *See also* Sign language

Native American son. Buford, K.   92

Native American testimony.   970.004

NATIVE AMERICAN WOMEN

> *See also* Women

Sifters: Native American women's lives   920

NATIVE AMERICANS

Bragdon, K. J. The Columbia guide to American Indians of the Northeast   970.004

Deloria, V. Custer died for your sins   970.004

Dorris, M. The broken cord   362.292

Hogan, L. The woman who watches over the world   818

Iverson, P. We are still here   **970.004**
Josephy, A. M. Now that the buffalo's gone **970.004**
Milton, G. Big Chief Elizabeth   **970.004**
Nagel, J. American Indian ethnic renewal   **305.8**
Parkman, F. The Oregon trail; The conspiracy of Pontiac   **978**
Philip, N. The great circle   **970.004**
Richter, D. K. Facing east from Indian country   **970.004**
Waldman, C. Atlas of the North American Indian   **970.004**
Weatherford, J. M. Native roots   **970.004**
Wilson, J. The earth shall weep   **970.004**

NATIVE AMERICANS—AGRICULTURE
See also Agriculture

NATIVE AMERICANS—ANTIQUITIES
See also Antiquities
America in 1492   **970.004**
Schobinger, J. The ancient Americans   **970.01**

NATIVE AMERICANS—ANTIQUITIES—EN-CYCLOPEDIAS
Archaeology of prehistoric native America **970.01**

NATIVE AMERICANS—BIOGRAPHY
Black Elk Black Elk speaks   **92**
Buford, K. Native American son   **92**
Crawford, B. All American   **92**
McMurtry, L. Crazy Horse   **92**

NATIVE AMERICANS—BRAZIL
Reel, M. The last of the tribe   **981**

NATIVE AMERICANS—CAPTIVITIES
See also Frontier and pioneer life

NATIVE AMERICANS—DICTIONARIES
Notable native Americans   **920.003**

NATIVE AMERICANS—ECONOMIC CONDI-TIONS
See also Economic conditions

NATIVE AMERICANS—EDUCATION
See also Education

NATIVE AMERICANS—ENCYCLOPEDIAS
American Indians   **970.004**
Johnson, M. Encyclopedia of native tribes of North America   **970.004**
Native America in the twentieth century   **970.004**
Pritzker, B. A Native American encyclopedia   **970.004**
Waldman, C. Encyclopedia of Native American tribes   **970.004**

NATIVE AMERICANS—ETHNOBOTANY
See also Ethnobotany

NATIVE AMERICANS—FOLKLORE
See also Folklore
Lynch, P. A. Native American mythology A to Z   **398.2**

NATIVE AMERICANS—GOVERNMENT RE-LATIONS
Documents of American Indian diplomacy **970.004**

Hendricks, S. The unquiet grave   **970.004**
Native American testimony   **970.004**
Osborn, W. M. The wild frontier   **970.004**
Prucha, F. P. The great father   **323.1**
Schultz, E. B. King Philip's War   **973.2**
Wallace, A. F. C. The long bitter trail   **323.1**

NATIVE AMERICANS—GREAT PLAINS
Fowler, L. The Columbia guide to American Indians of the Great Plains   **970.004**

NATIVE AMERICANS—HISTORY
America in 1492   **970.004**
Bruchac, J. Our stories remember   **970.004**
Johansen, B. E. The Native peoples of North America   **970.004**
Mann, C. C. 1491   **970.01**

NATIVE AMERICANS—HISTORY—SOURC-ES
Native American testimony   **970.004**

NATIVE AMERICANS—HOUSING
See also Housing

NATIVE AMERICANS—HUNTING
See also Hunting

NATIVE AMERICANS—INDUSTRIES
See also Industries

NATIVE AMERICANS—MEDICAL CARE
See also Medical care

NATIVE AMERICANS—MEXICO—ENCY-CLOPEDIAS
American Indians   **970.004**

NATIVE AMERICANS—NORTHWEST COAST OF NORTH AMERICA
Harmon, A. Indians in the making   **970.004**

NATIVE AMERICANS—ORIGIN
Adovasio, J. M. The first Americans   **970.01**

NATIVE AMERICANS—POLITICS AND GOV-ERNMENT
See also Politics

NATIVE AMERICANS—PSYCHOLOGY
See also Ethnopsychology

NATIVE AMERICANS—RELIGION
See also Religion
Nabokov, P. Where the lightning strikes   **299.7**
Popol vuh Popol vuh   **299.7**

NATIVE AMERICANS—RITES AND CERE-MONIES
See also Rites and ceremonies

NATIVE AMERICANS—SOCIAL LIFE AND CUSTOMS
See also Manners and customs
Robbins, C. C. All Indians do not live in teepees (or casinos)   **970.004**

NATIVE AMERICANS—SOUTH AMERICA
Goodman, J. The devil and Mr. Casement **305.8**

NATIVE AMERICANS—SOUTHERN STATES
Gallay, A. The Indian slave trade   **326**
Perdue, T. The Columbia guide to American Indi-

NAVAJO INDIANS—HISTORY

Sides, H. Blood and thunder **978**

NAVAJO INDIANS—SOCIAL CONDITIONS

Nasdijj The blood runs like a river through my dreams **979.1**

NAVAJO INDIANS—SOCIAL LIFE AND CUSTOMS

Nasdijj The blood runs like a river through my dreams **979.1**

NAVAJO WOMEN

See also Native American women; Navajo Indians

NAVAL ADMINISTRATION *See* Naval art and science

NAVAL AERONAUTICS *See* Military aeronautics

NAVAL AIRPLANES *See* Military airplanes

NAVAL ARCHITECTURE

See also Architecture

NAVAL ART AND SCIENCE

Grant, R. G. Battle at sea **359**

NAVAL ART AND SCIENCE—DICTIONARIES

Dictionary of military terms **355**

NAVAL ART AND SCIENCE—ENCYCLOPEDIAS

Naval warfare **359**

NAVAL BATTLES

See also Battles

Crowley, R. Empires of the sea **359**

NAVAL BIOGRAPHY—ENCYCLOPEDIAS

Naval warfare **359**

NAVAL EDUCATION

See also Education

NAVAL HISTORY

See also History

Grant, R. G. Battle at sea **359**

Mostert, N. The line upon a wind **940.2**

NAVAL HISTORY—DICTIONARIES

Dictionary of military terms **355**

NAVAL HISTORY—ENCYCLOPEDIAS

Bruce, A. An encyclopedia of naval history **359**

Naval warfare **359**

NAVAL PERSONNEL *See* Sailors

NAVAL SCIENCE *See* Naval art and science

NAVAL STRATEGY *See* Strategy

Naval warfare. **359**

NAVAL WARFARE *See* Naval art and science; Naval battles; Submarine warfare

Navarra, Tova

(comp) The Encyclopedia of vitamins, minerals, and supplements **613.2**

Lipkowitz, M. Encyclopedia of allergies **616.97**

The encyclopedia of complementary and alternative medicine **615.5**

Navasky, Victor S.

A matter of opinion **92**

NAVIES

Jane's fighting ships 2008-2009 **623.8**

NAVIGATION

Cutler, T. J. Dutton's nautical navigation **623.89**

NAVIGATION (AERONAUTICS)

See also Aeronautics

NAVIGATION (ASTRONAUTICS)

See also Astrodynamics; Astronautics

NAVIGATION—HISTORY

Bellec, F. Unknown lands **910.4**

NAVIGATORS *See* Explorers; Sailors

NAVY *See* Naval art and science; Navies; Sea power

NAVY YARDS AND NAVAL STATIONS

See also Naval art and science

NAZI

Segev, T. Simon Wiesenthal **92**

The **Nazi** doctors. Lifton, R. J. **940.53**

Nazi Germany. Fischer, K. P. **943.086**

Nazi Germany and the Jews. Friedlander, S. **940.53**

NAZI HUNTERS

Pick, H. Simon Wiesenthal **940.53**

Segev, T. Simon Wiesenthal **92**

NAZI LEADERS

Ahamed, L. Lords of finance **332.1**

Bascomb, N. Hunting Eichmann **943.086**

Berthon, S. Warlords **940.53**

Breitman, R. The architect of genocide **92**

Bullock, A. Hitler and Stalin **92**

Cornwell, J. Hitler's pope: the secret history of Pius XII **92**

Craig, G. A. The Germans **943**

Fest, J. C. Speer: the final verdict **92**

Fischer, K. P. Nazi Germany **943.086**

Fleming, G. Hitler and the final solution **943.086**

Fulbrook, M. A concise history of Germany **943**

Galbraith, J. K. Name-dropping **973.9**

Hitler, A. Mein Kampf **92**

Kershaw, I. Hitler **92**

Kershaw, I. Hitler, 1889-1936: hubris **92**

Kershaw, I. Hitler, 1936-1945: nemesis **943.086**

Kershaw, I. Hitler, the Germans, and the final solution **940.53**

Kissinger, H. Diplomacy **327.2**

Lifton, R. J. The Nazi doctors **940.53**

Lipstadt, D. E. The Eichmann trial **345**

Parssinen, T. M. The Oster conspiracy of 1938 **943.086**

Pool, J. Hitler and his secret partners **943.086**

Rosenbaum, R. Explaining Hitler **943.086**

Ryback, T. W. Hitler's private library **027**

Sereny, G. Albert Speer **92**

Shirer, W. L. The rise and fall of the Third Reich **943.086**

Snyder, T. Bloodlands **940.54**

Speer, A. Inside the Third Reich **943.086**

Taylor, F. Exorcising Hitler **943.087**

Nelson, Gaylord
  Beyond Earth Day   **333.72**
Nelson, Glenn C.
  Ceramics: a potter's handbook   **738.1**
Nelson, James Carl
  The remains of Company D   **920**
Nelson, James L.
  With fire & sword   **973.3**
Nelson, Maggie
  The art of cruelty   **700**
Nelson, Michael
  (ed) Guide to the presidency   **352.23**
  (ed) The presidency A to Z   **352.23**
Nelson, Miriam E.
  Strong women eat well   **613.2**
  Strong women, strong bones   **616.7**
Nelson: a dream of glory, 1758-1797. Sugden, J. **92**
Nemat, Marina
  Prisoner of Tehran   **92**
Neme, Laurel A.
  Animal investigators   **363.2**
Nemeroff, Charles B.
  (ed) The Corsini encyclopedia of psychology and
  behavioral science   **150**
Nemerov, Howard
  The selected poems of Howard Nemerov   **811**
Nemiroff, Robert
  Hansberry, L. To be young, gifted, and Black   **92**
NEO-FASCISM See Fascism; Neo-Nazis
NEO-IMPRESSIONISM (ART) See Impression-
  ism (Art)
NEO-NAZIS
  See also Fascism
The **neocon** reader.   **320.5**
NEOPAGANISM
  See also Religions
  Hutton, R. The triumph of the moon   **133.4**
NEOPLASMS—NURSING
  Caregiving: a step-by-step resource for caring for
  the person with cancer at home   **649.8**
NEPTUNE (PLANET)
  See also Planets
Neruda, Pablo, 1904-1973 (Chilean poet)
  The poetry of Pablo Neruda   **861**
  About
  Neruda, P. The poetry of Pablo Neruda   **861**
Nerve. Clark, T.   **152.4**
NERVES
  See also Nervous system
NERVOUS SYSTEM
  See also Anatomy; Physiology
  Bainbridge, D. Beyond the zonules of Zinn   **611**
  Chase, V. D. Shattered nerves   **616.8**
  Iacoboni, M. Mirroring people   **573.8**
  Kandel, E. R. In search of memory   **153**
  Ramachandran, V. S. The tell-tale brain   **616.8**

Sacks, O. The mind's eye   **616.85**
Scientific American (Periodical) Best of the brain
  from Scientific American   **612.8**
Turkington, C. The encyclopedia of the brain and
  brain disorders   **612.8**
NERVOUS SYSTEM—DISEASES
  See also Diseases
  Sacks, O. W. An anthropologist on Mars   **616.8**
  Sacks, O. W. The man who mistook his wife for a
  hat and other clinical tales   **616.8**
  Weiner, J. His brother's keeper   **616.8**
Nesbitt, Mark
  Haunted Pennsylvania   **133.1**
Nesheim, Malden
  Why calories count   **613.2**
Ness, Bryan D.
  (ed) Magill's encyclopedia of science   **580**
NEST BUILDING
  See also Animal behavior; Animals—Habita-
  tions
Nestle, Marion
  (jt. auth) Nesheim, M. Why calories count **613.2**
  Pet food politics   **363.1**
  Safe food   **363.19**
  What to eat   **613.2**
The **net** delusion. Morozov, E.   **303.48**
**Netherlands State Institute for War Documenta-
tion**
  The diary of Anne Frank: the critical edition **940.53**
Netter, Frank H.
  Atlas of human anatomy   **611**
Nettle, Daniel
  Happiness   **152.4**
NETWORK THEORY See System analysis
NETWORKS, COMPUTER See Computer net-
  works
NETWORKS, INFORMATION See Information
  networks
Netzley, Patricia D.
  The encyclopedia of movie special effects   **778.5**
  Encyclopedia of women's travel and explora-
  tion   **910.4**
Neubauer, Alexander
  (ed) Poetry in person   **809.1**
Neubauer, Linda
  (ed) The complete photo guide to window treat-
  ments   **646.2**
Neuburger, Emily K.
  Marcus, L. S. Minders of make-believe   **070.5**
Neufeld, Josh
  The influencing machine   **302.23**
  A.D.   **741.5**
Neufeld, Michael J.
  Von Braun   **92**
Neugeboren, Jay
  Transforming madness   **616.89**

NEW BUSINESS ENTERPRISES—UNITED STATES—MANAGEMENT

Casnocha, B. My start-up life   338.7

New California poetry [series]

Scalapino, L. It's go in horizontal   811

Waldrop, K. Transcendental studies   811

The **New** Cambridge medieval history.   940.1

New Catholic encyclopedia.   282

New China architecture. Ruan Xing   720.9

New collected poems. Oppen, G.   811

New collected poems. Boland, E.   821

New collected poems. Berry, W.   811

The **new** complete book of food. Rinzler, C. A.   641.3

New complete guide to sewing. Reader's Digest Association, I.   646.2

The **new** complete guitarist. Chapman, R.   787.87

The **new** cool. Bascomb, N.   629.8

NEW DEAL, 1933-1939

Brands, H. W. Traitor to his class   92

Downey, K. The woman behind the New Deal   92

Leuchtenburg, W. E. Franklin D. Roosevelt and the New Deal, 1932-1940   973.917

Schlesinger, A. M. The coming of the New Deal, 1933-1935   973.917

Schlesinger, A. M. The politics of upheaval, 1935-1936   973.917

Shlaes, A. The forgotten man   973.91

Taylor, N. American-made   331.1

Welky, D. The thousand-year flood   363.34

The **new** dictionary of cultural literacy. Kett, J. F.   031

New dictionary of scientific biography.   920.003

The **New** Directions anthology of classical chinese poetry.   895.1

New dog. Fogle, B.   636.7

The **new** drawing on the right side of the brain. Edwards, B.   741.2

A **new** earth. Tolle, E.   158

The **new** encyclopaedia Britannica.   031

New encyclopedia of Africa.   960

The **New** encyclopedia of American scandal.   973

New encyclopedia of gardening techniques.   635

The **New** encyclopedia of Judaism.   296

The **new** encyclopedia of science.   503

The **new** encyclopedia of snakes. Mattison, C.   597.96

The **New** encyclopedia of the American West.   978

The **new** encyclopedia of the dog. Fogle, B.   636.7

The **new** encyclopedia of the saltwater aquarium. Jennings, G.   639.34

NEW ENGLAND

See also United States

The **New** England cookbook. Dojny, B.   641.5

The **new** faces of Christianity. Jenkins, P.   270

The **new** first three years of life. White, B. L.   155.4

New fix-it-yourself manual. Reader's Digest Association, I.   643

The **new** German cookbook. Anderson, J.   641.59

The **New** Grove dictionary of jazz.   781.65

The **New** Grove dictionary of music and musicians.   780

The **New** Grove dictionary of opera.   782.1

The **new** Harvard guide to women's health. Carlson, K. J.   613

The **new** hate. Goldwag, A.   306.2

The **new** health care system. Nather, D.   344

The **new** historical dictionary of the American film industry. Slide, A.   384

New histories of science, technology, and medicine [series]

Weart, S. R. The discovery of global warming   551.6

A **new** history of India. Wolpert, S. A.   954

The **new** history of the world. Roberts, J. M.   909

The **new** how things work. Langone, J.   600

The **New** Interpreter's dictionary of the Bible.   220.3

The **new** Jerusalem Bible. Bible   220.5

The **new** joys of Yiddish. Rosten, L.   422

New kidspace idea book. Jordan, W. A.   747

A **new** literary history of America.   810

The **New** living heart diet. DeBakey, M. E.   616.1

The **new** Mediterranean diet cookbook. Jenkins, N. H.   641.5

NEW MEXICO

Connors, P. Fire season   634.9

New narratives in American history [series]

Franklin, J. H. In search of the promised land   929

NEW NEGRO MOVEMENT See Harlem Renaissance

The **New** new journalism.   071

The **new** new thing. Lewis, M.   338.4

The **new** normal. Wann, D.   306

NEW ORLEANS, BATTLE OF, NEW ORLEANS, LA., 1815

Remini, R. V. The Battle of New Orleans   973.2

New Orleans, mon amour. Codrescu, A.   814

New Oxford American dictionary.   423

The **New** Oxford book of Irish verse.   821

The **New** Oxford book of literary anecdotes.   828

The **New** Oxford book of Victorian verse.   821

The **New** Oxford companion to literature in French.   840

The **new** parrot handbook.   636.6

The **new** Partridge dictionary of slang and unconventional English.   427

New passages. Sheehy, G.   305.24

A **new** path to the waterfall. Carver, R.   811

New poems. Rilke, R. M.   831

The **new** Portuguese table. Leite, D.   641.5

The **New** Princeton encyclopedia of poetry and poetics.   808.1

NEW PRODUCTS

See also Commercial products; Industrial re-

Nolo's quick reference series
Stim, R. Contracts   **346**
Nolt, Steven M.
(jt. auth) Kraybill, D. B. Amish grace   **364.152**
Nom de plume. Ciuraru, C.   **929.4**
Nomad's hotel. Nootebooms hotel./English   **910.4**
NOMADS
See also Primitive societies
NON-FICTION
Drew, B. A. 100 most popular nonfiction authors   **920.003**
NON-PROLIFERATION OF NUCLEAR WEAPONS *See* Arms control
NONCONFORMITY *See* Conformity; Counter culture; Dissent
NONINDIGENOUS PESTS
Hamilton, G. Super species   **578.6**
NONINDIGENOUS PESTS—CONTROL
Bright, C. Life out of bounds   **578.6**
NONLINGUISTIC COMMUNICATION *See* Nonverbal communication
NONNUTRITIVE SWEETENERS *See* Sugar substitutes
Nonpareil book [series]
Davenport, G. The geography of the imagination   **814**
NONPRESCRIPTION DRUGS
See also Drugs
Physicians desk reference for nonprescription drugs, dietary supplements, and herbs 2008   **615**
Nonrequired reading. Szymborska, W.   **028.1**
NONSENSE LITERATURE, ENGLISH
Lear, E. The complete verse and other nonsense **821**
NONSENSE VERSES
See also Children's poetry; Humorous poetry; Wit and humor
Lear, E. The complete verse and other nonsense **821**
NONSENSE VERSES, ENGLISH
Lear, E. The complete verse and other nonsense **821**
Nontraditional careers for women and men. McKenna, A.   **331.702**
NONVERBAL COMMUNICATION
See also Communication
Dimitrius Reading people   **155.2**
Pease, A. The definitive book of body language   **153.6**
NONVIOLENCE
Gandhi, M. Gandhi on non-violence   **322.4**
A testament of hope   **323.1**
NONVIOLENT NONCOOPERATION *See* Passive resistance
Noonan, John Thomas
Narrowing the nation's power: the Supreme Court sides with the states   **342**
Noonan, Peggy
A heart, a cross & a flag   **973.931**

Noonan, Raymond J.
(ed) The Continuum complete international encyclopedia of sexuality   **306.7**
The **noonday** demon. Solomon, A.   **616.85**
Nooteboom, Cees
Nootebooms hotel./English Nomad's hotel   **910.4**
Nootebooms hotel./English
Nomad's hotel   **910.4**
Norcross, Beverly Gore
Corson, R. Stage makeup   **792**
Nordhaus, Hannah
The beekeeper's lament   **638**
NORDIC PEOPLES *See* Teutonic peoples
Norgaard, Mette
(jt. auth) Conant, D. R. Touchpoints   **658.4**
Norgren, Jill
Belva Lockwood   **92**
Norlin, Elaina
Usability testing for library websites   **025.04**
NORM (PHILOSOPHY)
Smoller, J. The other side of normal   **591.5**
Normal at any cost. Cohen, S.   **618.92**
Norman Rockwell. Hennessey, M. H.   **759.13**
Norman Rockwell. Claridge, L. P.   **759.13**
Norman, Elizabeth M.
Norman, M. Tears in the darkness   **940.54**
Norman, Jill
Herbs & spices   **641.3**
Norman, Marsha
Collected plays   **812**
Norman, Michael
Haunted America   **133.1**
Tears in the darkness   **940.54**
Norman, Philip
John Lennon   **92**
NORMANDY (FRANCE), ATTACK ON, 1944
Ambrose, S. E. D-Day, June 6, 1944   **940.54**
Beevor, A. D-day   **940.54**
Macintyre, B. Double cross   **940.54**
Talty, S. Agent Garbo   **940.5**
NORMANS
See also Great Britain—History—1066-1154, Norman period
Norrell, Robert J.
Up from history   **92**
Norris, Kathleen
Acedia & me   **92**
The cloister walk   **255**
Journey: new and selected poems, 1969-1999   **811**
Norris, Michele
The grace of silence   **92**
Norris, Robert S.
Racing for the bomb: General Leslie R. Groves, the Manhattan Project's indispensable man   **92**
NORSE LITERATURE *See* Old Norse literature; Scandinavian literature

Now read this III. Pearl, N.   **016**
Now that the buffalo's gone. Josephy, A. M. **970.004**
Now the drum of war. Roper, R.   **973.7**
Now write! screenwriting.   **808.2**
Now, build a great business! Thompson, M.   **658**
Nowak, M. A. (Martin A.)
   (jt. auth) Highfield, R. Supercooperators   **519.3**
Nowak, Ronald M.
   Walker's mammals of the world   **599**
Nowlan, Robert A.
   (ed) A Dictionary of quotations in mathematics **510**
   Born this day   **808.88**
Nox. Carson, A.   **811**
The **NPR** classical music companion. Hoffman, M.   **780**
NUCLEAR ARMS CONTROL—UNITED STATES—HISTORY
   FitzGerald, F. Way out there in the blue   **973.927**
NUCLEAR DISARMAMENT
   Rhodes, R. The twilight of the bombs   **327.1**
NUCLEAR ENERGY
   See also Nuclear physics
NUCLEAR ENGINEERING
   See also Engineering; Nuclear energy; Nuclear physics
   Hodge, N. A nuclear family vacation   **623.4**
A **nuclear** family vacation. Hodge, N.   **623.4**
NUCLEAR FUSION
   See also Nuclear physics
   Seife, C. Sun in a bottle   **539.7**
NUCLEAR INDUSTRY
   See also Industries
NUCLEAR MEDICINE
   See also Medicine
NUCLEAR NON-PROLIFERATION *See* Arms control
NUCLEAR NONPROLIFERATION
   Hodge, N. A nuclear family vacation   **623.4**
   Langewiesche, W. The atomic bazaar   **355**
   Rhodes, R. The twilight of the bombs   **327.1**
NUCLEAR PARTICLES *See* Particles (Nuclear physics)
NUCLEAR PHYSICS
   See also Physics
   Gribbin, J. R. The search for superstrings, symmetry, and the theory of everything   **539.7**
   Johnson, G. Strange beauty: Murray Gell-Mann and the revolution in twentieth-century physics   **530**
   Kane, G. The particle garden   **539.7**
   Magueijo, J. A brilliant darkness   **92**
NUCLEAR PHYSICS—HISTORY
   Magueijo, J. A brilliant darkness   **92**
NUCLEAR POWER PLANTS—ENVIRONMENTAL ASPECTS
   See also Environment; Environmental health

NUCLEAR POWER PLANTS—FIRES AND FIRE PREVENTION
   See also Fire prevention; Fires
NUCLEAR REACTORS
   See also Nuclear energy; Nuclear engineering; Nuclear physics
NUCLEAR ROCKETS
   Dyson, G. Project Orion   **629.47**
NUCLEAR SUBMARINES
   See also Nuclear propulsion; Submarines
   Brownfield, C. J. My nuclear family   **92**
Nuclear terrorism. Allison, G. T.   **363.32**
NUCLEAR TERRORISM—UNITED STATES—PREVENTION
   Allison, G. T. Nuclear terrorism   **363.32**
NUCLEAR TEST BAN *See* Arms control
NUCLEAR WARFARE
   See also War
   Allison, G. T. Nuclear terrorism   **363.32**
   Degroot, G. J. The bomb   **623.4**
   Rosenbaum, R. How the end begins   **355**
NUCLEAR WEAPONS
   See also Military weapons
   Degroot, G. J. The bomb   **623.4**
   Gordin, M. D. Red cloud at dawn   **355**
   Hodge, N. A nuclear family vacation   **623.4**
   Iversen, K. Full body burden   **363.17**
   Karpin, M. I. The bomb in the basement   **355**
   Langewiesche, W. The atomic bazaar   **355**
   Rhodes, R. Arsenals of folly   **355**
   Rhodes, R. The twilight of the bombs   **327.1**
   Rosenbaum, R. How the end begins   **355**
   Sheehan, N. A fiery peace in a cold war   **92**
   Weapons of mass destruction   **358**
NUCLEAR WEAPONS—HISTORY
   Degroot, G. J. The bomb   **623.4**
   Gordin, M. D. Red cloud at dawn   **355**
NUCLEAR WEAPONS—PICTORIAL WORKS
   Light, M. 100 suns, 1945-1962   **355.8**
NUCLEAR WEAPONS—RESEARCH
   Hargittai, I. The Martians of science   **920**
NUCLEAR WEAPONS—TESTING
   Light, M. 100 suns, 1945-1962   **355.8**
NUCLEAR WEAPONS—UNITED STATES
   Trulock, N. Code name Kindred Spirit   **327.12**
NUCLEAR WEAPONS—UNITED STATES—HISTORY
   Sheehan, N. A fiery peace in a cold war   **92**
NUCLEAR WEAPONS PLANTS—HEALTH ASPECTS—COLORADO
   Iversen, K. Full body burden   **363.17**
NUCLEIC ACIDS
   See also Biochemistry
NUCLEONS *See* Particles (Nuclear physics)
Nugent, Benjamin
   American nerd   **305.9**

OBSCENE MATERIALS *See* Obscenity (Law); Pornography

Obscene, indecent, immoral, and offensive. Tropiano, S.   **791.43**

OBSCENITY (LAW)
   See also Criminal law

OBSESSION (PSYCHOLOGY) *See* Obsessive-compulsive disorder

OBSESSIVE-COMPULSIVE DISORDER
   Frost, R. O. Stuff   **616.85**
   Murphy, T. W. Life in rewind   **92**

OBSESSIVE-COMPULSIVE DISORDER—POPULAR WORKS
   Osborn, I. Tormenting thoughts and secret rituals   **616.85**

Obsessive-compulsive disorders. Penzel, F. **616.85**

OBSESSIVE-COMPULSIVE NEUROSES *See* Obsessive-compulsive disorder

OBSESSIVE-COMPULSIVE NEUROSIS
   Osborn, I. Tormenting thoughts and secret rituals   **616.85**
   Penzel, F. Obsessive-compulsive disorders **616.85**

OBSTETRICS *See* Childbirth

Obstfeld, Raymond
   Abdul-Jabbar, K. On the shoulders of giants   **92**

Occhiogrosso, Peter
   Zappa, F. The real Frank Zappa book   **92**

OCCIDENTAL CIVILIZATION *See* Western civilization

Occidental mythology. Campbell, J.   **201**

OCCULT FICTION
   See also Fiction

OCCULT SCIENCES *See* Occultism

OCCULTISM
   See also Religions; Supernatural
   Goodman, L. Linda Goodman's star signs   **130**

OCCULTISTS
   Schmidt, L. E. Heaven's bride   **92**

The **occupation.** Cockburn, P.   **956.7**

The **occupation** of Iraq. Allawi, A. A.   **956.7**

OCCUPATION, MILITARY *See* Military occupation

OCCUPATIONAL ACCIDENTS *See* Industrial accidents

OCCUPATIONAL DISEASES
   See also Diseases

OCCUPATIONAL GUIDANCE *See* Vocational guidance

OCCUPATIONAL HEALTH AND SAFETY
   See also Environmental health; Management; Public health

OCCUPATIONAL HEALTH SERVICES
   See also Medical care

OCCUPATIONAL INJURIES *See* Industrial accidents

Occupational outlook handbook 2010-2011. United States/Bureau of Labor Statistics   **331.7**

OCCUPATIONAL RETRAINING
   See also Employees—Training; Labor supply; Occupational training; Technical education; Unemployed; Vocational education

OCCUPATIONAL THERAPY
   See also Mental health; Physical therapy; Physically handicapped—Rehabilitation; Therapeutics

OCCUPATIONS
   Farr, J. M. 100 fastest-growing careers   **331.7**
   Ferguson Publishing The top 100   **331.7**
   McKenna, A. Nontraditional careers for women and men   **331.702**
   United States/Bureau of Labor Statistics Occupational outlook handbook 2010-2011   **331.7**

OCCUPATIONS—ENCYCLOPEDIAS
   J.G. Ferguson Publishing Company Encyclopedia of careers and vocational guidance   **331.7**

OCCUPIED TERRITORY *See* Military occupation

OCEAN
   See also Earth; Physical geography; Water
   Carson, R. The sea around us   **551.46**
   Cramer, D. Smithsonian ocean   **578.7**
   Day, T. Oceans   **551.46**
   Kunzig, R. The restless sea   **551.46**
   Pilkey, O. H. The rising sea   **363.34**
   Prager, E. J. Chasing science at sea   **551.46**
   Roberts, C. The ocean of life   **551.46**
   Roberts, C. The unnatural history of the sea   **909**
   Stow, D. A. V. Oceans: an illustrated reference   **551.46**

OCEAN—ECONOMIC ASPECTS *See* Marine resources; Shipping

OCEAN—ENCYCLOPEDIAS
   Ellis, R. Encyclopedia of the sea   **551.46**

OCEAN—HISTORY
   Roberts, C. The ocean of life   **551.46**

OCEAN AND CIVILIZATION
   Roberts, C. The ocean of life   **551.46**
   Winchester, S. Atlantic   **551.46**

OCEAN BOTTOM
   See also Ocean; Submarine geology

OCEAN CABLES *See* Submarine cables

OCEAN CURRENTS
   See also Navigation; Ocean
   Ebbesmeyer, C. Flotsametrics and the floating world   **551.46**

OCEAN DRILLING PLATFORMS *See* Drilling platforms

OCEAN ENERGY RESOURCES
   See also Energy resources; Marine resources; Ocean engineering

OCEAN ENGINEERING
   See also Engineering; Marine resources;

OFFICE WORKERS
See also Employees
Conant, J. 109 East Palace   **623.4**
Karp, B. The girl's guide to homelessness   **92**
Kelley, R. E. How to be a star at work   **658**
OFFICE WORKERS—SALARIES, WAGES, ETC.
See also Salaries, wages, etc.
The **official** ABMS directory of board certified medical specialists, 2010.   **610.69**
The **Official** Catholic directory 2008.   **282**
Official Congressional directory, 2009-2010.   **328**
The **official** guide to America's national parks.   **917**
Official guide to the players of the Hockey Hall of Fame.   **796.962**
OFFICIAL MISCONDUCT *See* Misconduct in office
The **Official** museum directory.   **069**
Official negligence. Cannon, L.   **979.4**
Official red book series
Yeoman, R. S. A guide book of United States coins   **737.4**
The **Official** Scrabble players dictionary.   **793.73**
Official secrets. Breitman, R.   **940.54**
OFFICIAL SECRETS—UNITED STATES—HISTORY—20TH CENTURY
Moynihan, D. P. Secrecy   **352.3**
Offit, Paul A.
Deadly choices   **614.4**
Vaccinated   **92**
OFFSET PRINTING
See also Lithography; Printing
OFFSHORE OIL INDUSTRY
See also Petroleum industry
OFFSHORE OIL WELL DRILLING
Achenbach, J. A hole at the bottom of the sea **363.7**
Freudenburg, W. R. Blowout in the Gulf   **363.7**
OFFSHORE OIL WELL DRILLING—SAFETY MEASURES
Magner, M. Poisoned legacy   **338.7**
OFFSHORE WATER POLLUTION *See* Marine pollution
Ogden Nash. Parker, D. M.   **92**
OGLALA INDIANS
Black Elk Black Elk speaks   **92**
McMurtry, L. Crazy Horse   **92**
Powers, T. The killing of Crazy Horse   **92**
Steltenkamp, M. F. Black Elk, holy man of the Oglala   **973**
Ohanian, Hans C.
Einstein's mistakes   **530**
OHIO—ANTIQUITIES
See also Antiquities
OHIO—BIOGRAPHY
See also Biography
OHIO—CHURCH HISTORY

See also Church history
OHIO—CIVILIZATION
See also Civilization
OHIO—CLIMATE
See also Climate
OHIO—COMMERCE
See also Commerce
OHIO—DIRECTORIES
·*See also* Directories
OHIO—ECONOMIC CONDITIONS
See also Economic conditions
OHIO—GAZETTEERS
See also Gazetteers
OHIO—INTELLECTUAL LIFE
See also Intellectual life
OHIO—LOCAL HISTORY
See also Local history
OHIO—MAPS
See also Maps
OHIO—MORAL CONDITIONS
See also Moral conditions
OHIO—OFFICIALS AND EMPLOYEES—SALARIES, WAGES, ETC.
See also Salaries, wages, etc.
OHIO—RACE RELATIONS
See also Race relations
OHIO—RELIGION
See also Religion
OHIO—SOCIAL LIFE AND CUSTOMS
Frazier, I. Family   **977.1**
OHIO—SOCIAL LIFE AND CUSTOMS
See also Manners and customs
OHIO—STATISTICS
See also Statistics
Oil. Sanmiguel, D.   **751.45**
OIL *See* Oils and fats; Petroleum
OIL DRILLING PLATFORMS *See* Drilling platforms
OIL INDUSTRY *See* Petroleum industry
Oil on the brain. Margonelli, L.   **338.2**
OIL PAINTING
See also Painting
Oil painting for the absolute beginner. Willenbrink, M.   **751.45**
OIL SPILLS
Achenbach, J. A hole at the bottom of the sea **363.7**
DeNapoli, D. The great penguin rescue   **639.9**
Freudenburg, W. R. Blowout in the Gulf   **363.7**
OIL SPILLS—ENVIRONMENTAL ASPECTS
Magner, M. Poisoned legacy   **338.7**
OIL SPILLS AND WILDLIFE
DeNapoli, D. The great penguin rescue   **639.9**
OIL WELL DRILLING
See also Drilling and boring (Earth and rocks); Petroleum industry
OIL WELL DRILLING, OFFSHORE *See* Off-

shore oil well drilling

OIL WELL DRILLING, SUBMARINE *See* Offshore oil well drilling

OIL WELLS

See also Petroleum industry

OIL WELLS—BLOWOUTS

Magner, M. Poisoned legacy   **338.7**

Ojaide, Tanure

(ed) The New African poetry   **896**

OJIBWA INDIANS

Erdrich, L. Books and islands in Ojibwe country **92**

Okinawa. Leckie, R.   **940.54**

OKINAWA, BATTLE OF, 1945

Leckie, R. Okinawa   **940.54**

Oklahoma western biographies [series]

Davis, R. L. John Ford   **791.43**

Riley, G. The life and legacy of Annie Oakley **796.3**

Wilkins, T. John Muir   **333.7**

Okonowicz, Ed

Haunted Maryland   **133.1**

Okrent, Arika

In the land of invented languages   **499**

Okrent, Daniel

Last call   **363.4**

OLD AGE

Athill, D. Somewhere towards the end   **92**

Friedan, B. The fountain of age   **305.26**

Jacoby, S. Never say die   **305.26**

Lawrence-Lightfoot, S. The third chapter   **305.26**

Pillemer, K. A. 30 lessons for living   **305.26**

OLD AGE PENSIONS

See also Pensions; Retirement income

Old dog, new tricks. Taylor, D.   **636.7**

OLD GROWTH FOREST ECOLOGY—TEN-NESSEE

Haskell, D. G. The forest unseen   **577.3**

OLD GROWTH FORESTS—TENNESSEE

Haskell, D. G. The forest unseen   **577.3**

Old man Goya. Blackburn, J.   **92**

Old masters, new world. Saltzman, C.   **759.9**

OLD NORSE LANGUAGE

See also Language and languages; Scandinavian languages

OLD NORSE LITERATURE

See also Literature; Medieval literature

The Sagas of Icelanders   **839**

**OLD NORSE LITERATURE—TRANSLATIONS
INTO ENGLISH**

The Sagas of Icelanders   **839**

OLD NORTHWEST

See also United States

OLD ORDER MENNONITES

Kraybill, D. B. On the backroad to heaven **289.7**

The **old** Patagonian express. Theroux, P.   **918**

OLD SOUTHWEST

See also United States

Old time radios! Carr, J. J.   **621.384**

Old world, new world. Burk, K.   **327**

**OLDER PEOPLE—CIVIL RIGHTS—UNITED
STATES—POPULAR WORKS**

Sember, B. M. Seniors' rights   **346.01**

**OLDER PEOPLE—LEGAL STATUS, LAWS,
ETC—UNITED STATES—POPULAR
WORKS**

Sember, B. M. Seniors' rights   **346.01**

OLDER PERSONS *See* Elderly

Oldershaw, Cally

Firefly guide to gems   **553.8**

Oldroyd, D. R.

Thinking about the earth   **551.09**

Olds, Jacqueline

The lonely American   **302.5**

Olds, Sharon

Blood, tin, straw   **811**

The unswept room   **811**

The wellspring   **811**

OLIVE—FOLKLORE

Mueller, T. Extra virginity   **664.362**

OLIVE—HISTORY

Mueller, T. Extra virginity   **664.362**

OLIVE OIL

Mueller, T. Extra virginity   **664.362**

OLIVE OIL—HISTORY

Mueller, T. Extra virginity   **664.362**

**OLIVE OIL INDUSTRY—MORAL AND ETHI-
CAL ASPECTS**

Mueller, T. Extra virginity   **664.362**

Oliver, Charles M.

Critical companion to Ernest Hemingway   **813**

Critical companion to Walt Whitman   **811**

Oliver, Chris

Introducing RDA   **025.3**

Oliver, Evelyn Dorothy

Lewis, J. R. The dream encyclopedia   **154.6**

Oliver, Jamie

Cook with Jamie   **641.5**

Oliver, Mary

The leaf and the cloud   **811**

New and selected poems   **811**

A poetry handbook   **808.1**

The Truro bear and other adventures   **811**

West wind   **811**

Winter hours   **811**

Oliver, Vicky

301 smart answers to tough business etiquette questions   **395**

Ollestad, Norman

Crazy for the storm   **92**

Olmos, Edward James

Monterrey, M. Americanos   **305.8**

Olsen, Jack

I: the creation of a serial killer   **364.1**

Olsen, Kirstin
  All things Austen   **823**
  All things Shakespeare   **822.3**
Olshaker, Mark
  Douglas, J. E. The cases that haunt us   **364.1**
  Peters, C. J. Virus hunter   **614.4**
Olson, Carl
  Historical dictionary of Buddhism   **294.3**
Olson, Charles
  The collected poems of Charles Olson   **811**
  The Maximus poems   **811**
Olson, James Stuart
  Bathsheba's breast   **616.99**
  Encyclopedia of the industrial revolution in America   **973**
Olson, Keith W.
  Watergate   **973.924**
Olson, Laura R.
  Djupe, P. A. Encyclopedia of American religion and politics   **322**
Olson, Lynne
  Citizens of London   **940.54**
Olson, Randy
  Don't be such a scientist   **501**
Olson, Richard
  Science and religion, 1450-1900   **261.5**
Olson, Steve
  Mapping human history   **599.9**
Olstein, Lisa
  Lost alphabet   **811**
OLYMPIC ATHLETES
  Anderson, L. Carlisle vs. Army   **796.332**
  Armstrong, L. Every second counts   **796.6**
  Armstrong, L. It's not about the bike   **92**
  Coyle, D. Lance Armstrong's war   **92**
  Crawford, B. All American   **92**
  Halberstam, D. Playing for keeps: Michael Jordan and the world he made   **92**
  Hillenbrand, L. Unbroken   **940.54**
  Hoffer, R. Something in the air   **796.4**
  Joyner-Kersee, J. A kind of grace   **796.42**
  Kimball, G. Four kings   **920**
  Schaap, J. Triumph   **92**
  Strickland, B. Tour de Lance   **92**
  Ware, S. Letter to the world   **920.72**
OLYMPIC GAMES
  See also Athletics; Contests; Games; Sports
  Guttmann, A. The Olympics, a history of the modern games   **796.48**
  Miller, S. G. Ancient Greek athletics   **796**
  Spivey, N. J. The ancient Olympics   **796.48**
  Wallechinsky, D. The complete book of the Winter Olympics   **796.98**
OLYMPIC GAMES (19TH: 1968: MEXICO CITY, MEXICO)
  Hoffer, R. Something in the air   **796.4**

OLYMPIC GAMES (ANCIENT)
  Miller, S. G. Ancient Greek athletics   **796**
OLYMPIC GAMES, 1936 (BERLIN, GER.)
  Schaap, J. Triumph   **92**
OLYMPIC GAMES, 1968 (MEXICO CITY, MEX.)
  Hoffer, R. Something in the air   **796.4**
OLYMPIC GAMES, 1996 (ATLANTA, GA.)
  See also Olympic games
OLYMPIC GAMES, 2000 (SYDNEY, AUSTRALIA)
  Mullen, P. H. Gold in the water   **797.2**
Olympic guides [series]
  United States Olympic Committee A basic guide to ice hockey   **796.962**
OLYMPICS *See* Olympic games
OLYMPICS—HISTORY
  Guttmann, A. The Olympics, a history of the modern games   **796.48**
The **Olympics,** a history of the modern games. Guttmann, A.   **796.48**
Omaha blues. Lelyveld, J.   **92**
OMBUDSMAN
  See also Administrative law; Public interest
An **omelette** and a glass of wine. David, E.   **641**
Omeros. Walcott, D.   **811**
The **omnivore's** dilemma. Pollan, M.   **394.1**
On apology. Lazare, A.   **155.9**
On architecture. Huxtable, A. L.   **724**
On becoming a novelist. Gardner, J.   **808.3**
On becoming a person. Rogers, C. R.   **616.89**
On being human. Fromm, E.   **150.19**
On children and death. Kubler-Ross, E.   **155.9**
On Conan Doyle; or, The whole art of storytelling. Dirda, M.   **823**
On death and dying. Kubler-Ross, E.   **155.9**
On desire. Irvine, W. B.   **128**
On directing film. Mamet, D.   **791.43**
On grief and reason. Brodsky, J.   **814**
On history. Hobsbawm, E. J.   **901**
On love. Hirsch, E.   **811**
On monsters. Asma, S. T.   **398.2**
On moral fiction. Gardner, J.   **801**
On my country and the world. Gorbachev, M.   **947.085**
On second thought. Herbert, W.   **153.4**
On Sunset Boulevard: the life and times of Billy Wilder. Sikov, E.   **92**
On the air. Dunning, J.   **791.44**
On the backroad to heaven. Kraybill, D. B.   **289.7**
On the brink. Paulson, H. M.   **330.9**
On the bus with Rosa Parks. Dove, R.   **811**
On the courthouse lawn. Ifill, S. A.   **364.1**
On the edge. Koch, K.   **811**
On the eve. Wasserstein, B.   **305.892**
On the good life. Cicero, M. T.   **878**

See also Labor; Labor contract; Labor unions

Open closed open. Amichai, Y.   **892.4**

OPEN HOUSING *See* Discrimination in housing

Open media [series]

Gibler, J. To die in Mexico   **363.45**

Open Media series

Lusane, C. The Black history of the White House   **975.3**

The **open** road. Iyer, P.   **92**

Opened ground. Heaney, S.   **821**

The **opening** of the American mind. Levine, L. W.   **001.1**

Opening the Qur'an. Wagner, W. H.   **297.1**

OPERA

    See also Drama; Musical form; Performing arts; Vocal music

Berger, W. Puccini without excuses   **92**

Berger, W. Wagner without fear   **782**

Grout, D. J. A history of western music   **780.9**

Grout, D. J. A short history of opera   **792.5**

The Grove book of opera singers   **920**

Wills, G. Verdi's Shakespeare   **822.3**

OPERA—DICTIONARIES

The New Grove dictionary of opera   **782.1**

OPERA—NEW YORK (STATE)—NEW YORK—HISTORY AND CRITICISM

Fiedler, J. Molto agitato   **782.1**

OPERA—SOUND RECORDINGS

    See also Sound recordings

OPERA—STORIES, PLOTS, ETC.

Osborne, C. The complete operas of Mozart **792.5**

Osborne, C. The complete operas of Puccini **792.5**

Osborne, C. The complete operas of Richard Wagner   **792.5**

OPERA SINGERS

Gage, N. Greek fire   **782.1**

Keiler, A. Marian Anderson   **92**

Scott, M. Maria Meneghini Callas   **782.1**

Ware, S. Letter to the world   **920.72**

OPERAS *See* Opera

Operation Bite Back. Kuipers, D.   **92**

OPERATION DESERT STORM *See* Persian Gulf War, 1991

Operation homecoming.   **956.7**

Operation Mincemeat. Macintyre, B.   **940.54**

OPERATION RESTORE HOPE, 1992-1993

Bowden, M. Black Hawk down   **967.730**

Operation Rollback. Grose, P.   **327.12**

OPERATION STOPWATCH\GOLD, BERLIN, GERMANY, 1955-1956

Stafford, D. Spies beneath Berlin   **327.12**

OPERATIONS RESEARCH

    See also Research; System theory

OPERATIONS, SURGICAL *See* Surgery

OPERETTA

    See also Musical form; Opera; Vocal music

Opie, Iona Archibald

(ed) The Oxford dictionary of nursery rhymes **398.8**

Opie, Peter

(ed) The Oxford dictionary of nursery rhymes **398.8**

OPINION, PUBLIC *See* Public opinion

Opium. Booth, M.   **362**

Opium. Chouvy   **363.45**

OPIUM

Booth, M. Opium   **362**

Chouvy Opium   **363.45**

Oppen, George

New collected poems   **811**

Oppenheim, Thomas

(ed) The muses go to school   **700**

Oppenheim, Tom

(ed) The muses go to school   **700**

Oppenheimer. Bernstein, J.   **530**

Oppenheimer, Betty

Candlemaker's companion   **745.59**

Oppenheimer, Clive

Eruptions that shook the world   **551.2**

The **opposite** of fate. Tan, A.   **814**

OPPRESSION (PSYCHOLOGY)—UNITED STATES

Richardson, B. L. What mama couldn't tell us about love   **158**

OPTICAL DATA PROCESSING

    See also Data processing

OPTICAL ILLUSIONS

    See also Hallucinations and illusions; Psychophysiology; Vision

OPTICAL IMAGES

Frankel, F. On the surface of things   **530.4**

OPTICS

    See also Physics

Park, D. The fire within the eye   **535**

OPTIMISM

Ehrenreich, B. Bright-sided   **155.2**

Ridley, M. The rational optimist   **339.2**

The **optimistic** child. Seligman, M. E. P.   **155.4**

Or to begin again. Lauterbach, A.   **811**

Oracle bones. Hessler, P.   **951**

ORACLES

    See also Occultism

ORAL COMMUNICATION—HISTORY

White, S. The sounds of slavery   **326**

ORAL CONTRACEPTIVES

May, E. T. America and the pill   **363.9**

Seaman, B. The greatest experiment ever performed on women   **615**

ORAL CONTRACEPTIVES—SOCIAL ASPECTS

May, E. T. America and the pill   **363.9**

ORAL HISTORY

    See also History

ORAL INTERPRETATION OF POETRY

Pinsky, R. The sounds of poetry   **808.5**

Orange sunshine. Schou, N.   **363.45**

ORATIONS *See* Speeches

ORATORIO

    See also Church music; Musical form; Vocal music

ORATORS

    Everitt, A. Cicero   **92**

    Goldsworthy, A. K. Antony and Cleopatra   **92**

    Hofstadter, R. The American political tradition, and the men who made it   **973**

    Johnson, M. An unquenchable thirst   **271**

    McPherson, J. M. Drawn with the sword   **973.7**

ORATORS—ROME—BIOGRAPHY

    Everitt, A. Cicero   **92**

ORATORY *See* Public speaking

Orbach, Susie

    Bodies   **362.1**

Orbanes, Philip

    The game makers   **338.7**

Orbinski, James

    An imperfect offering   **610**

ORBITAL LABORATORIES *See* Space stations

ORBITAL RENDEZVOUS (SPACE FLIGHT)

    See also Space flight; Space stations; Space vehicles

ORBITING VEHICLES *See* Artificial satellites; Space stations

ORCHARDS *See* Fruit culture

The **orchards** of Syon. Hill, G.   **821**

ORCHESTRAL MUSIC

    See also Instrumental music; Music; Orchestra

Orchestration. Piston, W.   **784**

ORCHESTRATION *See* Instrumentation and orchestration

Orchid fever. Hansen, E.   **635.9**

ORCHID INDUSTRY

    Hansen, E. Orchid fever   **635.9**

ORCHIDS

    Hansen, E. Orchid fever   **635.9**

Ordaining women. Chaves, M.   **262**

ORDERS, MONASTIC *See* Monasticism and religious orders

Ordinary geniuses. Segrà, G.   **572.8**

Ordinary resurrections. Kozol, J.   **305.23**

ORDINATION

    See also Rites and ceremonies; Sacraments

ORDINATION OF WOMEN

    Chaves, M. Ordaining women   **262**

ORDNANCE

    See also Military art and science

    Stephenson, M. The last full measure   **305.9**

ORDNANCE DISPOSAL UNITS

    Castner, B. The long walk   **956.704**

ORDNANCE DISPOSAL UNITS—IRAQ

Castner, B. The long walk   **956.704**

ORDNANCE DISPOSAL UNITS—UNITED STATES

    Castner, B. The long walk   **956.704**

ORE DEPOSITS

    See also Geology

The **Oregon** Trail. Dary, D.   **978**

OREGON TRAIL

    See also Overland journeys to the Pacific; United States

    Dary, D. The Oregon Trail   **978**

    Parkman, F. The Oregon trail; The conspiracy of Pontiac   **978**

OREGON TRAIL—HISTORY

    Dary, D. The Oregon Trail   **978**

The **Oregon** trail; The conspiracy of Pontiac. Parkman, F.   **978**

Oren, Michael

    Six days of war   **956.04**

Orenstein, Catherine

    Little Red Riding Hood uncloaked   **398.2**

Orenstein, Peggy

    Cinderella ate my daughter   **305.23**

ORES

    See also Minerals

Oreskes, Naomi

    (jt. auth) Conway, E. M. Merchants of doubt   **174**

The **Oresteia.** Aeschylus   **882**

ORGAN *See* Organs (Musical instruments)

ORGAN (MUSICAL INSTRUMENT)—UNITED STATES—HISTORY

    Whitney, C. R. All the stops   **786.5**

ORGAN BUILDERS—UNITED STATES

    Whitney, C. R. All the stops   **786.5**

ORGAN MUSIC

    See also Church music; Instrumental music; Music

ORGAN PRESERVATION (ANATOMY) *See* Preservation of organs, tissues, etc.

ORGAN TRAFFICKING

    Carney, S. The red market   **364.1**

Organ transplants. Finn, R.   **617.9**

ORGAN TRANSPLANTS *See* Transplantation of organs, tissues, etc.

ORGANIC AGRICULTURE *See* Organic farming

ORGANIC CHEMISTRY

    See also Chemistry

ORGANIC COMPOUNDS

    See also Chemicals; Organic chemistry

ORGANIC FARMING

    See also Agriculture

    Adamchak, R. W. Tomorrow's table   **664**

    Coleman, E. Winter harvest handbook   **635**

    Fatal harvest   **630**

    Kimball, K. The dirty life   **92**

ORGANIC FARMING—UNITED STATES

PALESTINIAN ARABS

See also Arabs

Al Jundi, S. The hour of sunlight   **92**

Farsoun, S. K. Palestine and the Palestinians **956.94**

Grossman, D. The yellow wind   **956.95**

How Israelis and Palestinians negotiate   **956.94**

La Guardia, A. War without end   **956.940**

Nusseibeh, S. Once upon a country   **92**

Said, E. W. Reflections on exile and other essays   **814**

Shipler, D. K. Arab and Jew   **956.94**

Shlaim, A. Israel and Palestine   **956.04**

PALESTINIAN ARABS—ETHNIC IDENTITY

La Guardia, A. War without end   **956.940**

PALESTINIAN ARABS—ISRAEL—SOCIAL CONDITIONS

LeBor, A. City of oranges   **956.94**

Palestinian walks. Shehadeh, R.   **956.95**

PALESTINIANS *See* Palestinian Arabs

Palfrey, John

Born digital   **302.23**

Palgrave essential histories [series]

Bregman, A. A history of Israel   **956.94**

Palika, Liz

K.I.S.S. guide to raising a puppy   **636.7**

Palin, Michael (English actor and screenwriter)

Halfway to Hollywood   **92**

About

Palin, M. Halfway to Hollywood   **92**

Palisca, Claude V.

Grout, D. J. A history of western music   **780.9**

Palladio, Andrea, 1508-1580 (Italian architect)

The four books on architecture   **720**

About

Boucher, B. Andrea Palladio   **720.9**

Palmer, Arnold

A golfer's life   **92**

Palmer, Colin A.

(ed) Encyclopedia of African-American culture and history   **305.8**

Palmer, Craig T.

Thornhill, R. A natural history of rape   **364.15**

Palmer, James

Heaven cracks, earth shakes   **951**

The bloody white baron   **92**

Palmer, Jeffrey B.

Palmer, S. Spinal cord injury   **617**

Palmer, Louis J.

Encyclopedia of abortion in the United States **363.46**

Palmer, Melissa

Dr. Melissa Palmer's guide to hepatitis & liver disease   **616.3**

Palmer, Michael

Company of moths   **811**

Palmer, Robert

Blues & chaos   **781.64**

Palmer, Sara

Spinal cord injury   **617**

Palmer, Xueyan Z.

Palmer, L. J. Encyclopedia of abortion in the United States   **363.46**

Palmisano, Joseph M.

(ed) World of sociology   **301**

PALMISTRY

See also Divination; Fortune telling; Occultism

Reid, L. The art of hand reading   **133.6**

PALSY *See* Parkinson's disease

Paludan, Phillip S.

The presidency of Abraham Lincoln   **973.7**

Palumbi, Stephen R.

The evolution explosion   **576.8**

Pampel, Fred C.

Drugs and sports   **362.29**

PAMPHLETEERS

Collins, P. The trouble with Tom: the strange afterlife and times of Thomas Paine   **92**

DeGategno, P. J. Critical companion to Jonathan Swift   **828**

Foner, E. Tom Paine and Revolutionary America   **973.3**

Severin, T. In search of Robinson Crusoe   **996**

PAMPHLETS

See also Press

PAMPHLETS—DESIGN

See also Design

Pamuk, Orhan

Istanbul   **949.6**

Other colors   **894**

PAN AM FLIGHT 103 BOMBING INCIDENT, 1988

Dornstein, K. The boy who fell out of the sky   **92**

Pan, Philip P.

Out of Mao's shadow   **951.05**

Panagotacos, Peter J.

The complete book of hair loss answers   **616.5**

PANAMA—DESCRIPTION

Royte, E. The Tapir's morning bath   **577.34**

PANAMA CANAL

McCullough, D. G. The path between the seas   **972.87**

The **panda's** thumb. Gould, S. J.   **576.8**

Pandora's baby. Henig, R. M.   **618.1**

Panek, Richard

The 4 percent universe   **523.1**

PANEL DISCUSSIONS *See* Discussion groups

Panic.   **338.5**

PANIC DISORDERS

See also Abnormal psychology; Neuroses

Root, B. A. Understanding panic and other anxiety disorders   **616.85**

Panic in level 4. Preston, R.   **616.02**

The **Paris** review book of heartbreak, madness, sex, love, betrayal, outsiders, intoxication, war, whimsy, horrors, God, death, dinner, baseball, travels, the art of writing, and everything else in the world since 1953. **808.8**

Paris to the past. Caro, I. **914**

Paris was ours. **944**

Paris, I love you but you're bringing me down. Baldwin, R. **944**

Pariser, Eli
   The filter bubble **025.04**

PARISH REGISTERS *See* Registers of births, etc.

Parisi, Joseph
   (ed) 100 essential modern poems **821**
   (ed) The Poetry anthology, 1912-2002 **811**

Parisians. Robb, G. **944**

PARK RANGERS
   Barr, N. Seeking enlightenment—hat by hat **92**

PARK RANGERS—UNITED STATES—HISTORY
   Farabee, C. R. National park ranger **363.6**

Park, Clara Claiborne
   Exiting nirvana **616.89**

Park, David
   The fire within the eye **535**

Park, Robert L.
   Voodoo science **500**

Park, Yeon Hwan
   Black belt tae kwon do **796.8**

Parker's wine buyer's guide. Wine buyer's guide **641.2**

Parker, Barry R.
   Albert Einstein's vision **530.1**
   Quantum legacy **530.12**

Parker, Dorothy
   The portable Dorothy Parker **818**

Parker, Douglas M.
   Ogden Nash **92**

Parker, Robert M.
   Wine buyer's guide *See* Parker's wine buyer's guide **641.2**

Parker, Steve
   Morris, D. Planet ape **599.8**

Parker, Yana
   The damn good resume guide **650.14**

Parkes, Clara
   The knitter's book of socks **746.43**

Parkinson's disease. Duvoisin, R. C. **616.8**

PARKINSON'S DISEASE
   Cram, D. L. Answers to frequently asked questions in Parkinson's disease **616.8**
   Duvoisin, R. C. Parkinson's disease **616.8**
   Freed, C. Healing the brain **616.8**
   Hauser, R. A. Parkinson's disease: questions and answers **616.8**
   Lang, A. E. Parkinson's disease **616.8**

Lieberman, A. 100 questions & answers about Parkinson {sic} disease **616.8**

Lieberman, A. Shaking-up Parkinson disease **616.8**

Mosley, A. D. The encyclopedia of Parkinson's disease **616.8**

Sacks, O. W. The island of the colorblind **617.7**

When Parkinson's strikes early **616.8**

Parkinson's disease. Lang, A. E. **616.8**

PARKINSON'S DISEASE—ENCYCLOPEDIAS
   Mosley, A. D. The encyclopedia of Parkinson's disease **616.8**

PARKINSON'S DISEASE—PATIENTS—UNITED STATES—BIOGRAPHY
   Havemann, J. A life shaken **362.1**

PARKINSON'S DISEASE—PERSONAL NARRATIVES
   Fox, M. J. Always looking up **92**
   Fox, M. J. Lucky man **92**
   Havemann, J. A life shaken **362.1**

PARKINSON'S DISEASE—POPULAR WORKS
   Duvoisin, R. C. Parkinson's disease **616.8**
   When Parkinson's strikes early **616.8**

PARKINSON'S DISEASE—TREATMENT—POPULAR WORKS
   Freed, C. Healing the brain **616.8**

Parkinson's disease: questions and answers. Hauser, R. A. **616.8**

Parkinson, Peter
   The artist blacksmith **682**

Parkman, Francis
   The Oregon trail; The conspiracy of Pontiac **978**

PARKS
   See also Cities and towns; Landscape architecture
   Miller, L. Parks, plants, and people **712**

PARKS—UNITED STATES
   National Geographic Society (U.S.) National Geographic guide to the state parks of the United States **917**

Parks, plants, and people. Miller, L. **712**

Parks, Suzan-Lori
   Topdog/underdog **812**

Parks, Tim
   Medici money **332.1**
   Teach us to sit still **616**

Parkyn, Neil
   (ed) The Seventy wonders of the modern world **720.9**

PARLIAMENTARY GOVERNMENT *See* Representative government and representation

PARLIAMENTARY PRACTICE
   See also Debates and debating; Legislation; Legislative bodies; Public meetings
   Robert, H. M. Robert's Rules of order newly revised **060.4**
   Robert, H. M. Webster's New World Robert's rules

Past masters series
    Hare, R. M. Plato   **184**
PASTA PRODUCTS
    Pasta, a. d. p. t. Encyclopedia of pasta   **641.8**
PASTA PRODUCTS—ENCYCLOPEDIAS
    Pasta, a. d. p. t. Encyclopedia of pasta   **641.8**
Pasta, atlante dei prodotti tipici/English
    Encyclopedia of pasta   **641.8**
PASTEL DRAWING
    Price, M. Painting with pastels   **741.2**
Pasternak, Judy
    Yellow dirt   **979.1**
PASTIMES See Amusements; Games; Recreation
PASTORAL DRAMA
    See also Drama
PASTORAL FICTION
    See also Fiction
PASTORAL POETRY
    See also Poetry
PASTORAL POETRY, LATIN—TRANSLA-TIONS INTO ENGLISH
    Virgil The eclogues of Virgil   **871**
PASTORAL PSYCHIATRY See Pastoral psychology
PASTORAL PSYCHOLOGY
    See also Applied psychology; Church work; Psychology of religion
    Peale, N. V. The power of positive living   **248**
PASTORAL THEOLOGY
    See also Theology
Pastorelles. Taggart, J.   **811**
PASTORS See Clergy; Priests
Pastoureau, Michel
    Black   **155.9**
PASTRY
    See also Baking; Cooking
PASTURES
    See also Agriculture; Land use
The **Patagonian** hare. Lanzmann, C.   **791.43**
Patarca, Roberto
    The concise encyclopedia of fibromyalgia and myofascial pain   **616.7**
Patchett, Ann
    Truth & beauty   **92**
PATCHWORK
    See also Needlework
PATCHWORK—PATTERNS
    Michler, J. M. The magic of crazy quilting **746.46**
PATCHWORK QUILTS See Quilts
Patel, Eboo
    Acts of faith   **92**
Patel, Raj
    The value of nothing   **330.1**
Patell, Cyrus R. K.
    (ed) The Cambridge history of American literature   **810**

Patent it yourself. Pressman, D.   **346**
PATENT MEDICINES See Nonprescription drugs
Patent, copyright & trademark. Stim, R.   **346**
Patent, Greg
    Baking in America   **641.8**
Patently female. Vare, E. A.   **609.2**
PATENTS
    See also Manufactures
    Hyde, L. Common as air   **346.04**
    Petroski, H. The evolution of useful things   **609**
    Pressman, D. Patent it yourself   **346**
    Stim, R. Patent, copyright & trademark   **346**
    Wherry, T. L. Intellectual property   **346.04**
Paterek, Josephine
    Encyclopedia of American Indian costume   **391**
Paterson. Williams, W. C.   **811**
Paterson, Don
    Rain   **821**
The **path** between the seas. McCullough, D. G.   **972.87**
The **path** to power. Caro, R. A.   **973.9**
PATHOLOGICAL PSYCHOLOGY See Abnormal psychology
PATHOLOGISTS
    Friedman, M. Medicine's 10 greatest discoveries   **610**
PATHOLOGY
    See also Medicine
    Zuk, M. Riddled with life   **616.07**
PATIENCE
    See also Human behavior; Virtue
    Partnoy, F. Wait   **153.8**
Patience & fortitude. Basbanes, N. A.   **002**
The **patient's** guide to medical tests. Segen, J. C.   **616.07**
Patient-centered guides [series]
    Finn, R. Organ transplants   **617.9**
    Janes-Hodder, H. Childhood cancer   **618.92**
PATIENTS
    Groopman, J. E. The anatomy of hope   **616**
    Pikula, D. L. After the diagnosis   **610.69**
PATIOS
    See also Landscape architecture
    Black & Decker Corp. The complete guide to patios & walkways   **690**
Patoski, Joe Nick
    Willie Nelson   **92**
Patricia Wells' trattoria. Wells, P.   **641.5**
Patrick Moore's data book of astronomy.   **520**
Patrick O'Brian. King, D.   **823**
Patrick, Jane
    The weaver's idea book   **746.1**
Patrick, William
    Bogdanos, M. Thieves of Baghdad   **956.7**
Patrimony. Roth, P.   **813**
Patriotic fire. Groom, W.   **973.5**

Lowenstein, R. While America aged   **331.2**

Matthews, J. L. Social security, Medicare & government pensions   **344**

Schultz, E. Retirement heist   **331.2**

PENSIONS—UNITED STATES

Lowenstein, R. While America aged   **331.2**

The **Pentagon**. Vogel, S.   **355.6**

PENTAGON

Carroll, J. House of war   **355**

PENTAGON (VA.) TERRORIST ATTACK, 2001

See September 11 terrorist attacks, 2001

PENTATHLETES

Anderson, L. Carlisle vs. Army   **796.332**

Crawford, B. All American   **92**

PENTECOSTAL CHURCHES

See also Christian sects; Protestantism

PENTECOSTALISM

See also Christianity

Pentimento. Hellman, L.   **92**

Penzel, Fred

Obsessive-compulsive disorders   **616.85**

Penzler, Otto

(ed) The best American crime reporting, 2010 **364.1**

PEOPLE *See* Ethnic groups; Indigenous peoples; Persons

A **people** adrift. Steinfels, P.   **282**

PEOPLE IN SPACE *See* Space flight

People who eat darkness. Parry, R. L.   **364.152**

PEOPLE WITH DISABILITIES—EDUCATION—UNITED STATES

Keller, H. The story of my life   **92**

PEOPLE WITH VISUAL DISABILITIES—DICTIONARIES

The Encyclopedia of blindness and vision impairment   **362.4**

PEOPLE WITH VISUAL DISABILITIES—POETRY

Stone, R. In the dark   **811**

A **people's** history of the American Revolution. Raphael, R.   **973.3**

People's movements, people's press. Ostertag, B.   **071**

The **people's** pension. Frank, J.   **368.4**

The **people's** pharmacy guide to home and herbal remedies. Graedon, J.   **615**

A **people's** tragedy. Figes, O.   **947.084**

The **people's** tycoon. Watts, S.   **92**

Peoples and empires. Pagden, A.   **909**

Peoples of America [series]

Smith, M. E. The Aztecs   **972**

The **peopling** of British North America. Bailyn, B.   **973.2**

Pepin, Claudine

Pepin, J. Jacques Pepin celebrates   **641.5**

Pepin, Jacques

Child, J. Julia and Jacques cooking at home **641.59**

The apprentice: my life in the kitchen   **641.5**

Essential Pepin   **641.5**

Jacques Pepin celebrates   **641.5**

Pepper, William F.

An act of state   **364.1**

PEPPERED MOTH

Hooper, J. Of moths and men   **576.8**

Pepperell, Julian G.

Fishes of the open ocean   **597**

Pepys, Samuel

The diary of Samuel Pepys   **941.06**

PEQUOT INDIANS

Josephy, A. M. Now that the buffalo's gone **970.004**

PERCEPTION

See also Intellect; Psychology; Senses and sensation; Theory of knowledge; Thought and thinking

Abram, D. The spell of the sensuous   **128**

Chabris, C. The invisible gorilla   **153.7**

Edelman, S. The happiness of pursuit   **153**

Hoffman, D. D. Visual intelligence   **152.14**

Kandel, E. R. The age of insight   **154**

Klein, S. The secret pulse of time   **153.7**

Sacks, O. The mind's eye   **616.85**

Vedantam, S. The hidden brain   **154.2**

Perche agli Italiani piace/English

Why Italians love to talk about food   **641.5**

PERCUSSION INSTRUMENTS

See also Musical instruments

PERCUSSIONISTS

Grant, C. The natural mystics   **920**

Percy, Ann

(ed) Castle, J. James Castle   **709.04**

Percy, Walker, 1916-1990

Lost in the cosmos   **818**

Signposts in a strange land   **818**

About

Elie, P. The life you save may be your own   **810**

Percy, W. Signposts in a strange land   **818**

Perdue, Theda

The Columbia guide to American Indians of the Southeast   **970.004**

(ed) Sifters: Native American women's lives   **920**

The **perennial** philosophy. Huxley, A.   **210**

PERENNIALS

See also Cultivated plants; Flower gardening; Flowers

Cullina, W. Understanding perennials   **635.9**

DiSabato-Aust, T. The well-tended perennial garden   **635.9**

Ellis, B. W. Taylor's guide to perennials   **635.9**

Hodgson, L. Perennials for every purpose   **635.9**

McGowan, A. Bulbs in the basement, geraniums on the windowsill   **635.9**

PERENNIALS—ENCYCLOPEDIAS

Bryant, G. Annuals and perennials   **635.9**

Attack proof   **613.6**

Perlstein, Rick
Nixonland   **973.924**

Pernoud, Regine
Joan of Arc: her story   **92**

Perper, Timothy
(ed) Graphic novels beyond the basics   **025.2**

Perrins, Christopher M.
(ed) The Princeton encyclopedia of birds   **598**

Perry, Arthur W.
Straight talk about cosmetic surgery   **617.9**

Perry, Bruce
Malcolm   **92**

Perry, James M.
Touched with fire   **973.7**

Perry, Michael
Coop   **92**
Truck: a love story   **629.223**

PERSECUTION
See also Atrocities
Conroy, J. Unspeakable acts, ordinary people **323.4**
God is red   **275.1**

PERSECUTIONS *See* Persecution

PERSEPHONE (GREEK DEITY)
See also Gods and goddesses

Persepolis. Satrapi, M.   **741.5**

Persepolis 2. Satrapi, M.   **741.5**

Persepolis/English
The complete Persepolis   **741.5**

PERSEVERANCE
See also Ethics

PERSIAN GULF WAR, 1991
Atkinson, R. Crusade   **956.7**
Clancy, T. Into the storm   **956.704**
Gordon, M. R. The generals' war   **956.7**
Lazarus, A. Super Bowl Monday   **796.332**
Newell, C. R. Historical dictionary of the Persian Gulf War, 1990-1991   **956.704**
Schwartz, R. A. Encyclopedia of the Persian Gulf War   **956.704**
Schwarzkopf, H. N. It doesn't take a hero: General H. Norman Schwarzkopf   **92**
Woodward, B. The commanders   **973.928**

PERSIAN GULF WAR, 1991—CAUSES
Haass, R. War of necessity: war of choice   **956.7**

PERSIAN GULF WAR, 1991—ENCYCLOPE-DIAS
The encyclopedia of Middle East wars   **355**
Schwartz, R. A. Encyclopedia of the Persian Gulf War   **956.704**

PERSIAN GULF WAR, 1991—PERSONAL NARRATIVES
Kelly, M. Martyrs' Day   **956.7**
Swofford, A. Jarhead: a Marine's chronicle of the Gulf War and other battles   **956.704**

PERSIAN GULF WAR, 1991—PERSONAL

NARRATIVES, AMERICAN
Swofford, A. Jarhead: a Marine's chronicle of the Gulf War and other battles   **956.704**

PERSIAN GULF WAR, 1991—POLITICAL AS-PECTS
Haass, R. War of necessity: war of choice   **956.7**

PERSIAN POETRY—COLLECTIONS
Music of a distant drum   **808.81**
Persian poets   **891**

Persian poets.   **891**

Persico, Joseph E.
Franklin and Lucy   **920**
Powell, C. L. My American journey   **92**

Persistence.   **306.76**

PERSISTENCE
See also Personality

PERSISTENT PAIN *See* Chronic pain

PERSISTENT POLLUTANTS—ENVIRON-MENTAL ASPECTS
Johansen, B. E. The dirty dozen: toxic chemicals and the earth's future   **363.738**

PERSISTENT POLLUTANTS—HEALTH AS-PECTS
Johansen, B. E. The dirty dozen: toxic chemicals and the earth's future   **363.738**

PERSISTENT VEGETATIVE STATE
Teresi, D. The undead   **610**

PERSONAL APPEARANCE
Berg, R. Beauty: the new basics   **646.7**
Bordo, S. The male body   **305.31**
Brandon, R. Ugly beauty   **646.7**
Brown, B. Bobbi Brown beauty evolution   **646.7**
DuPriest, L. Natural beauty   **646.7**
Essence total makeover   **646.7**
Etcoff, N. L. Survival of the prettiest   **391.6**
Fornay, A. The African American woman's guide to successful makeup and skincare   **646.7**
Hall, S. S. Size matters   **612.6**
Kashuk, S. Real beauty   **646.7**
Peiss, K. L. Hope in a jar   **391.6**
Wolf, N. The beauty myth   **305.4**

PERSONAL APPEARANCE—SOCIAL AS-PECTS
Etcoff, N. L. Survival of the prettiest   **391.6**

PERSONAL BELONGINGS
Tracy, L. Objects of our affection   **745**

PERSONAL CLEANLINESS *See* Hygiene

PERSONAL COMPUTERS
See also Computers

PERSONAL CONDUCT *See* Conduct of life

PERSONAL DEVELOPMENT *See* Personality; Self-improvement; Success

PERSONAL FINANCE
See also Finance
Armstrong, F. The retirement challenge— will you sink or swim?   **332.024**

Boeckh, J. A. The great reflation **332.6**

Bradford, S. L. The Wall Street Journal: financial guidebook for new parents **332.024**

Click millionaires **658.8**

D'Agnese, J. The money book for freelancers, part-time, and the self-employed **332.024**

Downes, J. Finance and investment handbook **332.6**

Glink, I. R. 50 simple things you can do to improve your personal finances **332.024**

Hirshman, S. L. Does this make my assets look fat? **332.024**

Huff, D. The complete how to figure it **640**

Jason, J. The AARP Retirement Survival Guide **332.024**

Kessel, B. It's not about the money **332.024**

McNaughton, D. The essential credit repair handbook **332.024**

Orman, S. The money class **332.024**

Quinn, J. B. Making the most of your money now **332.024**

Romans, C. How to speak money **332.024**

Schwab-Pomerantz, C. It pays to talk **332.024**

Solin, D. R. The smartest retirement book you'll ever read **332.024**

Tobias, A. P. The only investment guide you'll ever need **332.024**

Walsh, P. Lighten up **332.024**

Weltman, B. J.K. Lasser's guide for tough times **332.024**

Yeager, J. The cheapskate next door **332.024**

Yeager, J. The ultimate cheapskate's road map to true riches **332.024**

PERSONAL FREEDOM *See* Freedom

PERSONAL GROOMING

See also Hygiene; Personal appearance

Ashenburg, K. The dirt on clean **391**

Gross, K. J. Woman's face **646.7**

Toselli, L. Pro nail care **646.7**

PERSONAL HEALTH *See* Health

PERSONAL HEALTH SERVICES *See* Medical care

Personal history. Graham, K. **070.5**

PERSONAL HYGIENE *See* Hygiene

PERSONAL INCOME TAX *See* Income tax

PERSONAL LIFE SKILLS *See* Life skills

PERSONAL LOANS

See also Consumer credit; Loans

The **personal** MBA. Kaufman, J. **650**

PERSONAL NAMES

See also Names

PERSONAL NAMES—DICTIONARIES

Latham, E. A dictionary of names, nicknames, and surnames of persons, places, and things **929.4**

PERSONAL NAMES—UNITED STATES

Dictionary of American family names **929.4**

Shankle, G. E. American nicknames **929.4**

Twentieth century American nicknames **929.4**

PERSONAL NARRATIVES *See* Autobiographies; Biography

PERSONAL PARAPHERNALIA

Gosling, S. Snoop **155.9**

PERSONAL SPACE

See also Interpersonal relations; Nonverbal communication; Space and time

PERSONAL TIME MANAGEMENT *See* Time management

PERSONALITY

See also Consciousness; Psychology

Dimitrius Reading people **155.2**

Hamer, D. H. Living with our genes **155.2**

Harris, J. R. No two alike **155.2**

LeDoux, J. E. Synaptic self **612.8**

Maslow, A. H. Toward a psychology of being **155.2**

Myers, I. B. Gifts differing **155.2**

Whybrow, P. C. A mood apart **616.89**

PERSONALITY—GENETIC ASPECTS

Hamer, D. H. Living with our genes **155.2**

PERSONALITY ASSESSMENT—MISCELLA-NEA

Dimitrius Reading people **155.2**

PERSONALITY DISORDERS

See also Abnormal psychology

Kramer, P. D. Listening to Prozac **616.85**

Whybrow, P. C. A mood apart **616.89**

PERSONALITY IN LITERATURE

Bloom, H. Shakespeare: the invention of the human **822.3**

PERSONALITY, MULTIPLE *See* Multiple personality

PERSONNEL—ADMINISTRATION

Stanley, M. J. Managing library employees **023**

PERSONNEL ADMINISTRATION *See* Personnel management

PERSONNEL MANAGEMENT

See also Industrial relations; Management

Giesecke, J. Fundamentals of library supervision **023**

Jacobs, C. S. Management rewired **658**

Kelly, M. The dream manager **658.3**

Lancaster, L. C. When generations collide **658.3**

Richardson, B. G. Career comeback **650.14**

Stanley, M. J. Managing library employees **023**

Sutton, R. I. Good boss, bad boss **658.4**

Tracy, B. Full engagement! **658.3**

PERSONS

See also Human beings

PERSPECTIVE

See also Descriptive geometry; Geometrical drawing; Optics; Painting

PERSUASION (PSYCHOLOGY)

See also Communication; Conformity

Cialdini, R. B. Influence: the psychology of persua-

PHYSICAL APPEARANCE *See* Personal appearance

PHYSICAL CHEMISTRY
See also Chemistry; Physics

PHYSICAL CONSTANTS—POPULAR WORKS
Barrow, J. D. The constants of nature **530.8**

PHYSICAL EDUCATION
See also Education

PHYSICAL EDUCATION AND TRAINING— PHYSIOLOGICAL ASPECTS
Reynolds, G. The first 20 minutes **613.7**

PHYSICAL FITNESS
See also Exercise; Health; Health self-care; Physical education
Adams, M. Mister America **92**
Arnot, B. Wear and tear **616.7**
Bailey, C. Smart exercise **613.7**
Baroni, B. Fat kid got fit **362.196**
Blair, S. N. Active living every day **613.7**
Burke, L. The complete guide to food for sports performance **613.2**
Callahan, L. The fitness factor **613.7**
Carmichael, C. The ultimate ride **796.6**
Complete guide to fitness & health **613.7**
Decker, J. The world's fittest you **613.7**
Duke, K. The show it love workout **613.7**
Fitness and exercise sourcebook **613.7**
Fitness over fifty **613**
Hines, E. W. Fitness swimming **613.7**
Kolata, G. Ultimate fitness **613.7**
Pagano, J. Strength training for women **613.7**
Reynolds, G. The first 20 minutes **613.7**
Sivananda Yoga Vedanta Center (London, E. Yoga **613.7**

PHYSICAL FITNESS—POPULAR WORKS
Reynolds, G. The first 20 minutes **613.7**

PHYSICAL FITNESS CENTERS
See also Physical fitness

PHYSICAL FITNESS FOR WOMEN
Callahan, L. The fitness factor **613.7**

PHYSICAL GEOGRAPHY
See also Geography; Geology

PHYSICAL SCIENCES
See also Science
Notable women in the physical sciences **500.2**

PHYSICAL STAMINA *See* Physical fitness

PHYSICALLY HANDICAPPED
See also Handicapped
Encyclopedia of disability **362.4**
Reeve, C. Still me **92**
Schlachter, G. A. Financial aid for the disabled and their families, 2010-2012 **378.3**

PHYSICALLY HANDICAPPED—HOUSING
See also Housing

PHYSICALLY HANDICAPPED ATHLETES
Connolly, K. M. Double take **92**

PHYSICALLY HANDICAPPED CHILDREN
See also Handicapped children; Physically handicapped
Physician's desk reference 2008. **615**

PHYSICIAN-PATIENT RELATIONSHIP
Groopman, J. E. The anatomy of hope **616**
Groopman, J. E. Your medical mind **610**
Lown, B. The lost art of healing **610**
Newman, D. H. Hippocrates' shadow **610.69**

PHYSICIANS
Anderson, J. L. Che Guevara **92**
Ball, P. The devil's doctor **610**
Boyle, K. Arc of justice **345**
Brock, P. Charlatan **92**
Callow, P. Chekhov, the hidden ground **891.7**
Carrell, J. L. The speckled monster **614.5**
Casey, M. Che's afterlife **980**
Chekhov, A. P. Anton Chekhov's life and thought **92**
Donaldson, R. I. The Lassa ward **92**
Friedman, D. M. The immortalists **610.28**
Friedman, M. Medicine's 10 greatest discoveries **610**
Gawande, A. Better **616**
Groopman, J. E. How doctors think **610**
Halberstam, D. The children **323.1**
Hollis, L. London rising **942**
Jarrell, R. No other book **809**
Johnson, S. The ghost map **614.5**
Kidder, T. Mountains beyond mountains **92**
Kluger, J. Splendid solution: Jonas Salk and the conquest of polio **92**
Lattin, D. The Harvard Psychedelic Club **920**
Leibowitz, H. A. Something urgent I have to say to you: the life and works of William Carlos Williams **92**
Lifton, R. J. The Nazi doctors **940.53**
Mah, A. Y. Falling leaves **305.48**
Malcolm, J. Reading Chekhov **891.7**
Marion, R. Genetic rounds **92**
McCullough, D. G. The path between the seas **972.87**
McGoogan, K. Race to the Polar Sea **92**
Nabokov, V. V. Lectures on Russian literature **891.7**
Nuland, S. B. The doctors' plague **92**
Orbinski, J. An imperfect offering **610**
Sacks, O. W. Uncle Tungsten **616.8**
Sagan, C. Broca's brain **500**
Saltzman, C. Portrait of Dr. Gachet **759.9**
Schama, S. Dead certainties **974.4**
Schweitzer, A. Out of my life and thought **610**
Starr, D. The killer of little shepherds **364.152**
Stewart, J. B. Blind eye **364.1**
Tucker, H. Blood work **615**
Von Tunzelmann, A. Red heat **972.9**
Webster, C. Paracelsus **92**

PHYSICIANS (GENERAL PRACTICE)—

cine   **615.5**

PLACEBO (MEDICINE)

Bausell, R. B. Snake oil science   **615.5**

Scott, R. A. Miracle cures   **231.7**

The **places** as preludes. Sobin, G.   **811**

PLAGIARISM

> See also Authorship; Offenses against property

McKillop, A. B. The spinster & the prophet **941.08**

PLAGIARISM—GREAT BRITAIN—HISTORY—20TH CENTURY

McKillop, A. B. The spinster & the prophet **941.08**

PLAGUE

> See also Communicable diseases; Epidemics

Cantor, N. F. In the wake of the plague   **614.5**

Chase, M. The Barbary plague   **362.1**

Frist, B. When every moment counts   **613.6**

Herlihy, D. The black death and the transformation of the west   **940.1**

Kelly, J. The great mortality   **614.5**

Marriott, E. Plague: a story of science, rivalry, and the scourge that won't go away   **614.5**

Oldstone, M. B. A. Viruses, plagues, and history   **614.4**

Tuchman, B. W. A distant mirror   **944**

PLAGUE—CALIFORNIA—SAN FRANCISCO—HISTORY—20TH CENTURY

Chase, M. The Barbary plague   **362.1**

A **plague** of frogs. Souder, W. E.   **597.8**

Plague: a story of science, rivalry, and the scourge that won't go away. Marriott, E.   **614.5**

PLAIN CHANT See Chants (Plain, Gregorian, etc.)

Plain secrets. Mackall, J.   **289.7**

Plain, honest men. Beeman, R.   **342**

PLAINS (GA.)

Carter, J. An hour before daylight   **973.926**

PLAINS (GA.)—SOCIAL LIFE AND CUSTOMS—20TH CENTURY

Carter, J. An hour before daylight   **973.926**

PLAINS REGION (GA.)—RURAL CONDITIONS

Carter, J. An hour before daylight   **973.926**

PLAINSONG See Chants (Plain, Gregorian, etc.)

Plait, Philip C.

Death from the skies!   **520**

Plan of attack. Woodward, B.   **956.7**

Plan your estate. Clifford, D.   **346.05**

PLANE CRASHES See Aircraft accidents

PLANE GEOMETRY

> See also Geometry

Planet ape. Morris, D.   **599.8**

Planet Earth. Fothergill, A.   **508**

Planet Google. Stross, R. E.   **338.7**

A **planet** of viruses. Zimmer, C.   **362.196**

PLANETARIUMS

> See also Astronomy

PLANETOIDS See Asteroids

The **planets.** Sobel, D.   **523.2**

PLANETS

> See also Astronomy; Solar system

Brown, M. How I killed Pluto and why it had it coming   **523.48**

Goodstein, D. L. Feynman's lost lecture   **521**

Ridpath, I. Stars and planets   **520**

Sobel, D. The planets   **523.2**

Weintraub, D. A. Is Pluto a planet?   **523.4**

PLANETS—EXPLORATION

Pyne, S. J. Voyager   **919**

Planets and possibilities. Miller, S.   **133.5**

Planisphere. Ashbery, J.   **811**

PLANNED COMMUNITIES

> See also City planning

PLANNED COMMUNITIES—BRAZIL

Grandin, G. Fordlandia   **307.7**

PLANNED PARENTHOOD See Birth control

PLANNING

> See also Creation (Literary, artistic, etc.); Executive ability; Management

Klauser, H. A. Write it down, make it happen **158**

Planning parenthood. Clark, R. A.   **618.1**

PLANNING, LIBRARY

Cohn, J. M. The complete library technology planner   **025**

Laughlin, S. The quality library   **025.1**

PLANS See Geometrical drawing; Map drawing; Maps; Mechanical drawing

PLANT BREEDING

> See also Agriculture; Breeding; Horticulture

Smith, J. S. The garden of invention   **92**

PLANT BREEDING—UNITED STATES—HISTORY

Smith, J. S. The garden of invention   **92**

PLANT COLLECTORS

Hansen, E. Orchid fever   **635.9**

PLANT CONSERVATION

> See also Conservation of natural resources; Economic botany; Endangered species; Nature conservation

Fortey, R. Horseshoe crabs and velvet worms **595**

PLANT DISEASES

> See also Agricultural pests; Diseases; Fungi

Deardorff, D. C. What's wrong with my plant (and how do I fix it?)   **635**

PLANT ECOLOGY

> See also Ecology

The **plant** finder.   **635.9**

PLANT GENETICISTS

Pringle, P. The murder of Nikolai Vavilov   **92**

PLANT INTRODUCTION

> See also Economic botany

Bright, C. Life out of bounds   **578.6**

PLANT PATHOLOGY See Plant diseases

Hemisphere **597.96**

O'Shea, M. Venomous snakes of the world **597.96**

POISONOUS SUBSTANCES *See* Poisons and poisoning

POISONS

Turkington, C. The encyclopedia of poisons and antidotes **615.9**

POISONS—HISTORY

Emsley, J. The elements of murder **615.9**

POISONS AND POISONING

See also Accidents; Hazardous substances; Homicide; Medical jurisprudence

Barker, R. And the waters turned to blood **615.9**

Blum, D. The poisoner's handbook **614**

Callahan, J. R. Biological hazards **615.9**

Emsley, J. The elements of murder **615.9**

POISONS AND POISONING—ENCYCLOPE-DIAS

Turkington, C. The encyclopedia of poisons and antidotes **615.9**

Poitier, Sidney

The measure of a man **92**

POKER

See also Card games

McManus, J. Cowboys full **795.4**

McManus, J. Positively Fifth Street **795.4**

POKER—HISTORY

McManus, J. Cowboys full **795.4**

Poker bride. Corbett, C. **974.4**

Poker nation. Bellin, A. **795.4**

The **Pol** Pot regime. Kiernan, B. **959.6**

Polanka, Sue

(ed) No shelf required **025.17**

POLAR BEAR

Ellis, R. On thin ice **599.78**

POLAR EXPEDITIONS *See* Antarctica—Exploration; Arctic regions—Exploration; Scientific expeditions

POLAR REGIONS—EXPLORATION

Wilkinson, A. The ice balloon **910.91**

POLICE

See also Administration of criminal justice; Law enforcement

Queen, W. Under and alone **364.1**

POLICE—AUSTRALIA

Hooper, C. Tall man **364.1**

POLICE—CHICAGO (ILL.)

Preib, M. The wagon and other stories from the city **977.3**

POLICE—COMPLAINTS AGAINST *See* Police brutality; Police corruption

POLICE—CORRUPT PRACTICES *See* Police corruption

POLICE—NEW YORK (N.Y.)

Conway, J. N. The big policeman **92**

Dickey, C. Securing the city **363.32**

Levitt, L. NYPD confidential **364.1**

POLICE BRUTALITY

See also Police

Conroy, J. Unspeakable acts, ordinary people **323.4**

Hendrickson, P. Sons of Mississippi **305.8**

Lehr, D. The fence **364.1**

POLICE CORRUPTION

See also Misconduct in office; Police

Lehr, D. The fence **364.1**

Levitt, L. NYPD confidential **364.1**

POLICE CRUELTY *See* Police brutality

POLICE OFFICERS *See* Police

POLICE OFFICIALS

Conway, J. N. The big policeman **92**

Dickey, C. Securing the city **363.32**

POLICE REPRESSION *See* Police brutality

POLICE VIOLENCE *See* Police brutality

POLICEMEN *See* Police

POLICEWOMEN

See also Police; Women

Polio. Oshinsky, D. M. **614.5**

POLIO *See* Poliomyelitis

The **polio** paradox. Bruno, R. L. **616.8**

POLIOMYELITIS

See also Diseases

Bruno, R. L. The polio paradox **616.8**

Kluger, J. Splendid solution: Jonas Salk and the conquest of polio **92**

Oldstone, M. B. A. Viruses, plagues, and history **614.4**

Wilson, D. J. Living with polio **616.8**

POLIOMYELITIS—HISTORY

Oshinsky, D. M. Polio **614.5**

POLIOMYELITIS VACCINE

See also Vaccination

Oshinsky, D. M. Polio **614.5**

POLISH LITERATURE

Milosz, C. Legends of modernity **891.8**

POLISH POETRY—TRANSLATIONS INTO ENGLISH

Herbert, Z. The collected poems, 1956-1998 **891.8**

POLITENESS *See* Courtesy; Etiquette

POLITICAL ACTIVISTS

Abad, H. Oblivion **868**

Biddle, D. R. Tasting freedom **92**

Duberman, M. B. A saving remnant **92**

Kreisler, H. Political awakenings **920**

Lewis, A. B. The shadows of youth **323.1**

Liu, X. June fourth elegies **811**

Potter, W. Green is the new red **320.5**

POLITICAL ACTIVISTS—COLOMBIA—BI-OGRAPHY

Abad, H. Oblivion **868**

POLITICAL ACTIVISTS—CRIMES AGAINST

Abad, H. Oblivion **868**

POLITICAL ACTIVISTS—UNITED STATES

Smith, R. Slow death by rubber duck   **615.9**

POLLUTION—ENCYCLOPEDIAS

Blauvelt, R. P. Encyclopedia of pollution   **363.7**

Encyclopedia of environmental issues   **363.7**

POLLUTION—HEALTH ASPECTS

Markowitz, G. E. Deceit and denial   **615.9**

POLLUTION—MATHEMATICAL MODELS

   See also Mathematical models

POLLUTION—UNITED STATES

Blatt, H. America's environmental report card **363.7**

POLLUTION—UNITED STATES—CASE STUDIES

Lerner, S. Sacrifice zones   **363.738**

POLLUTION CONTROL INDUSTRY

   See also Industries

POLLUTION OF AIR *See* Air pollution

Polo, Marco, 1254-1323? (Italian traveler)

About

Bergreen, L. Marco Polo   **92**

Polonsky, Rachel

Molotov's magic lantern   **947**

POLTERGEISTS *See* Ghosts

POLYGAMY

   See also Marriage

Brower, S. Prophet's prey   **306.8**

Solomon, D. A. Predators, prey, and other kinfolk   **92**

POLYGLOT DICTIONARIES

   See also Encyclopedias and dictionaries

Polymer clay 101. Otterbein, K.   **738.1**

POLYMER CLAY CRAFT

   See also Handicraft

Polymer clay creative traditions. Belcher, J. **731.4**

POLYMERIZATION *See* Polymers

POLYMERS

Rabinow, P. Making PCR   **572.8**

POLYRADICULONEURITIS

Manguso, S. The two kinds of decay   **362**

POLYTHEISM

   See also Religion; Theism

Pomes all sizes. Kerouac, J.   **811**

Pomfret, John

Chinese lessons   **951.05**

Pomper, Philip

Lenin's brother   **92**

POND ECOLOGY

   See also Ecology

Pond, Jonathan D.

Grow your money!   **332.024**

PONDS

   See also Water

Matson, T. Earth ponds A to Z   **627**

Pong, David

(ed) Encyclopedia of modern China   **951**

PONIES

   See also Horses

Ponsot, Marie

Easy   **811**

Springing   **811**

PONTIAC'S CONSPIRACY, 1763-1765

   See also Native Americans—Wars; United States—History—1600-1775, Colonial period

Parkman, F. The Oregon trail; The conspiracy of Pontiac   **978**

The **pontiff** in winter. Cornwell, J.   **92**

Pontius Pilate. Wroe, A.   **226**

PONZI SCHEMES—NEW YORK (STATE)—NEW YORK—HISTORY—19TH CENTURY

Ward, G. C. A disposition to be rich   **974.7**

Ponzi's scheme. Zuckoff, M.   **364**

POOL (GAME)

   See also Billiards

Byrne, R. Byrne's new standard book of pool and billiards   **794.7**

McCumber, D. Playing off the rail   **794.7**

POOL PLAYERS

McCumber, D. Playing off the rail   **794.7**

Pool, James

Hitler and his secret partners   **943.086**

Pool, Robert

Fat   **616.3**

Poole, Adrian

(ed) The Oxford book of classical verse in translation   **881**

Poole, Hilary

Devine, C. Human rights   **323**

Pooley, Eric

The climate war   **363.7**

POOR

   See also Poverty; Public welfare

Grande, R. The distance between us   **973**

Vollmann, W. T. Poor people   **362.5**

POOR—MEDICAL CARE

   See also Medical care

POOR—MEXICO CITY (MEXICO)

Lewis, O. The children of Sanchez   **972.08**

POOR—NEW YORK (N.Y.)

Hancock, L. Hands to work   **361.6**

Kozol, J. Amazing grace   **362.7**

LeBlanc, A. N. Random family   **305.5**

POOR—SOCIAL CONDITIONS

Tough, P. Whatever it takes   **362.7**

POOR—UNITED STATES

Reef, C. Poverty in America   **362.5**

Rivlin, G. Broke, USA   **339.4**

Zucchino, D. Myth of the welfare queen   **305.42**

POOR CHILDREN—UNITED STATES

Coles, R. Children of crisis   **305.23**

Poor economics. Banerjee, A.   **339.4**

Poor people. Vollmann, W. T.   **362.5**

POOR PEOPLE *See* Poor

POOR PERSONS *See* Poor

Post, Stephen Garrard
(ed) Encyclopedia of bioethics   **174**
The **post**-American world. Zakaria, F.   **303.49**
POST-COMMUNISM—RUSSIA (FEDERATION)
Meier, A. Black earth   **947.086**
POST-MODERNISM *See* Postmodernism
POST-TRAUMATIC STRESS DISORDER
   See also Anxiety; Neuroses; Stress (Psychology)
Castner, B. The long walk   **956.704**
Coleman, P. Flashback   **616.85**
England, D. The post traumatic stress disorder relationship   **616.85**
Matsakis, A. Vietnam wives   **616.85**
Slone, L. B. After the war zone   **616.85**
POST-ZIONISM
Hazony, Y. The Jewish state   **320.54**
POSTAL DELIVERY CODE *See* Zip code
POSTAL SERVICE
   See also Communication; Transportation
POSTAL SERVICE—EXAMINATIONS
Bobrow, J. Barron's comprehensive postal exam, 473/473-C   **383**
Damp, D. V. Post office jobs   **383**
POSTAL SERVICE—GREAT BRITAIN
Tingey, J. The Englishman who posted himself and other curious objects   **92**
POSTAL SERVICE—VOCATIONAL GUIDANCE
Damp, D. V. Post office jobs   **383**
Postcards from Tomorrow Square. Fallows, J. M.   **951.05**
POSTCOLONIALISM
   See also Political science
The **poster**.   **741.6**
POSTERS
Aldridge, A. The man with kaleidoscope eyes **741.6**
Donahue, D. Ultraviolet   **741.6**
Hayes, C. Gig posters volume 1   **741.6**
The poster   **741.6**
Reaves, W. W. Ballyhoo!   **741.6**
POSTERS
   See also Advertising; Commercial art
POSTIMPRESSIONISM (ART)
   See also Art
Postma, Johannes
The Atlantic slave trade   **306.3**
Postman, Neil
Amusing ourselves to death   **302.23**
The end of education   **370.9**
Technopoly   **303.48**
POSTMODERNISM
Ferry, L. A brief history of thought   **100**
POSTMODERNISM
   See also Aesthetics

POSTMODERNISM—EUROPE
Fineberg, J. D. Art since 1940   **709.04**
POSTMODERNISM—UNITED STATES
Fineberg, J. D. Art since 1940   **709.04**
POSTPARTUM DEPRESSION
Dalton, K. Depression after childbirth   **616.85**
POSTPARTUM DEPRESSION
   See also Depression (Psychology)
POSTPOLIOMYELITIS SYNDROME
Bruno, R. L. The polio paradox   **616.8**
POSTTRAUMATIC STRESS DISORDER *See* Post-traumatic stress disorder
POSTURE
   See also Physical fitness
Postwar. Judt, T.   **940.55**
Postwar America.   **973.92**
POSTWAR RECONSTRUCTION
Van Buren, P. We meant well   **956.7044**
POSTWAR RECONSTRUCTION—IRAQ
Chandrasekaran, R. Imperial life in the emerald city   **956.704**
POT (DRUG) *See* Marijuana
The **pot** of gold, and other plays. Plautus, T. M. **872**
POTASH
   See also Fertilizers
Potato. Reader, J.   **635**
POTATO CHIPS
Burhans, D. E. Crunch!   **338.4**
POTATOES
   See also Vegetables
Pollan, M. The botany of desire   **306.4**
Reader, J. Potato   **635**
A **potent** spell. Smith, J. M.   **306.8**
POTPOURRI
   See also Herbs; Nature craft; Perfumes
The **potter's** dictionary of materials and techniques. Hamer, F.   **738.1**
The **potter's** studio handbook. Muller, K.   **738.1**
Potter, Beatrix, 1866-1943 (English children's author and illustrator)
About
Lear, L. J. Beatrix Potter   **92**
Potter, Christopher
You are here   **523.1**
Potter, Deborah
Wenger, D. H. Advancing the story   **070.1**
POTTER, HARRY (FICTITIOUS CHARACTER)
Highfield, R. The science of Harry Potter   **500**
Potter, John
(ed) The Cambridge companion to singing   **782**
Potter, Will
Green is the new red   **320.5**
POTTERS
   See also Artists
POTTERY

The **power** of positive living. Peale, N. V. **248**
Power of the news media. Henderson, H. **070.1**
The **power** of the vote. Schoen, D. E. **324**
POWER POLITICS *See* Balance of power; Cold war
POWER RESOURCES *See* Energy resources
POWER RESOURCES—POLITICAL ASPECTS
  Yergin, D. The quest **333.79**
POWER RESOURCES—RESEARCH
  Krupp, F. D. Earth, the sequel **621**
POWER RESOURCES CONSERVATION *See* Energy conservation
POWER RESOURCES DEVELOPMENT *See* Energy development
Power rules. Gelb, L. H. **327**
Power sewing step-by-step. Betzina, S. **646.4**
POWER SUPPLY *See* Energy resources
Power tools. Nagyszalanczy, S. **621.9**
POWER TOOLS
  See also Tools
  Nagyszalanczy, S. Power tools **621.9**
  Warner, P. The router book **684**
POWER TRANSMISSION
  See also Mechanical engineering; Power (Mechanics)
Power, Samantha
  Chasing the flame **92**
Powerful medicines. Avorn, J. **338.4**
The **powers** of heaven and earth. Nims, J. F. **811**
Powers, Bruce R.
  McLuhan, M. The global village **302.23**
Powers, Michael D.
  (ed) Children with autism **618.92**
Powers, Ron
  Bradley, J. Flags of our fathers **940.54**
  Mark Twain **92**
POWERS, SEPARATION OF *See* Separation of powers
Powers, Thomas
  The killing of Crazy Horse **92**
Powershift. Toffler, A. **303.49**
POWHATAN INDIANS
  Price, D. Love and hate in Jamestown **975.5**
POWS *See* Prisoners of war
POWWOWS
  See also Festivals; Native Americans—Rites and ceremonies; Native Americans—Social life and customs
Pox Americana. Fenn, E. A. **614.5**
Pox: genius, madness, and the mysteries of syphilis. Hayden, D. **616.95**
Poynter, Dan
  The self-publishing manual **070.5**
PRACTICAL JOKES
  See also Jokes; Wit and humor
PRACTICAL NURSES

See also Nurses
PRACTICAL NURSING
  See also Nursing
PRACTICAL POLITICS *See* Politics
PRACTICAL PSYCHOLOGY *See* Applied psychology
PRACTICAL REASON
  Ridley, M. The rational optimist **339.2**
The **practical** Shakespeare. Butler, C. **822.3**
Practically radical. Taylor, W. **658.4**
PRACTICE OF LAW—UNITED STATES—ANECDOTES
  Geoghegan, T. In America's court **345**
Practicing Catholic. Carroll, J. **92**
Practicing history. Tuchman, B. W. **907**
Prados, John
  (ed) Inside the Pentagon papers **959.704**
  Presidents' secret wars **327.12**
Praeger perspectives [series]
  Famous American crimes and trials **364**
Prager, Dennis
  Happiness is a serious problem **158**
Prager, Ellen J.
  Chasing science at sea **551.46**
Prager, Emily
  Wuhu diary **951**
Prager, Emily
       About
  Prager, E. Wuhu diary **951**
Prager, Joshua
  The echoing green **796.357**
Prager, LuLu, 1994-
       About
  Prager, E. Wuhu diary **951**
PRAGMATISM
  See also Philosophy; Positivism; Realism; Theory of knowledge
  Commager, H. S. The American mind **973**
PRAGUE (CZECH REPUBLIC)—HISTORY
  Demetz, P. Prague in black and gold **943.71**
Prague in black and gold. Demetz, P. **943.71**
Prague winter. Albright, M. K. **943.71**
Prahlad, Anand
  The Greenwood encyclopedia of African American folklore **398**
Prain, Leanne
  Hoopla **746.44**
PRAIRIE ECOLOGY
  See also Ecology; Grassland ecology
  Apfelbaum, S. I. Nature's second chance **639.9**
Praise of folly. Erasmus, D. **877**
Prakash, Vikramaditya
  Ching, F. A global history of architecture **720.9**
Prange, Gordon William
  At dawn we slept **940.54**
Pratt, Doug

Fowler, B. Iceman **937**

Hancock, G. Underworld: the mysterious origins of civilization **551.7**

Leakey, R. E. The origin of humankind **599.93**

Leakey, R. E. Origins reconsidered **599.93**

Wrangham, R. W. Catching fire **641.3**

PREHISTORIC PEOPLES—AMERICA

Dillehay, T. D. The settlement of the Americas **970.01**

PREHISTORIC PEOPLES—FOOD

Wrangham, R. W. Catching fire **641.3**

PREHISTORY See Archeology; Fossil hominids; Prehistoric peoples

Preib, Martin

The wagon and other stories from the city **977.3**

Prejean, Helen

The death of innocents **364.66**

PREJUDICE See Prejudices

PREJUDICE-MOTIVATED CRIMES See Hate crimes

PREJUDICES

See also Attitude (Psychology); Emotions; Interpersonal relations

Bullard, S. Teaching tolerance **649**

Goldhagen, D. J. Worse than war **364.1**

Griffin, J. H. Black like me **305.8**

Young-Bruehl, E. The anatomy of prejudices **303.3**

PREJUDICES—UNITED STATES—DICTIONARIES

Herbst, P. Talking terrorism **303.6**

PREMATURE BURIAL

See also Burial

PREMATURE INFANTS

Linden, D. W. Preemies **618.92**

PREMENSTRUAL SYNDROME

See also Menstruation

PREMIERS See Prime ministers

Preminger, Alex

(ed) The New Princeton encyclopedia of poetry and poetics **808.1**

PRENATAL CARE

See also Pregnancy

Block, J. Pushed **618.4**

Curtis, G. B. Your pregnancy week by week **618.2**

Murkoff, H. E. What to expect before you're expecting **618.2**

Riley, L. You & your baby: pregnancy **618.2**

Van der Ziel, C. Big, beautiful & pregnant **618.2**

PRENATAL DIAGNOSIS

See also Diagnosis

Paul, A. M. Origins **618.3**

PREPARED CEREALS

See also Breakfasts; Food

PRESBYTERIAN CHURCH—SERMONS

See also Sermons

PRESCHOOL CHILDREN

Brazelton, T. B. Touchpoints three to six **305.231**

PRESCHOOL CHILDREN See Children

PRESCHOOL EDUCATION

See also Education

Prescott, William Hickling

History of the conquest of Mexico **972**

PRESCRIPTION PRICING

Avorn, J. Powerful medicines **338.4**

Prescriptions for living. Siegel, B. S. **158**

Presence and pleasure. Danielsen, A. **781.644**

Present at the creation. Aczel, A. D. **539.7**

Present at the future. Flatow, I. **500**

Present company. Merwin, W. S. **811**

PRESENTS See Gifts

PRESERVATION OF BIODIVERSITY See Biodiversity conservation

PRESERVATION OF FORESTS See Forest conservation

PRESERVATION OF LIBRARY MATERIALS—HANDBOOKS, MANUALS, ETC.

Schechter, A. A. Basic book repair methods **025.7**

PRESERVATION OF NATURAL RESOURCES See Conservation of natural resources

PRESERVATION OF NATURAL SCENERY See Landscape protection; Natural monuments; Nature conservation

PRESERVATION OF ORGANS, TISSUES, ETC.

Friedman, D. M. The immortalists **610.28**

PRESERVATION OF SPECIMENS See Taxidermy

PRESERVATION OF WILDLIFE See Wildlife conservation

PRESERVATIONISM (HISTORIC PRESERVATION) See Historic preservation

PRESERVING See Canning and preserving

Preserving memory. Linenthal, E. T. **940.5**

The **presidency** A to Z. **352.23**

The **presidency** of Abraham Lincoln. Paludan, P. S. **973.7**

The **President** and the assassin. Miller, S. **973.8**

The **president** is a sick man. Algeo, M. **973.8**

President Kennedy. Reeves, R. **973.922**

President Nixon. Reeves, R. **973.924**

President Reagan: the triumph of imagination. Reeves, R. **973.927**

PRESIDENTIAL ADVISERS

Berman, L. No peace, no honor **959.704**

Dallek, R. Nixon and Kissinger **92**

Feldman, N. Scorpions **920**

Fenster, J. M. FDR's shadow **92**

Greenspan, A. The age of turbulence **92**

Halberstam, D. The best and the brightest **973.922**

Kissinger, H. Years of renewal **973.924**

Mann, J. About face **327**

Martin, J. Greenspan **92**

Millman, C. The detonators **940.4**

dency   **327.1**

Schlesinger, A. M. The coming of the New Deal, 1933-1935   **973.917**

Schlesinger, A. M. The crisis of the old order, 1919-1933   **973.91**

Schlesinger, A. M. The politics of upheaval, 1935-1936   **973.917**

Schwartz, R. A. Encyclopedia of the Persian Gulf War   **956.704**

Shenk, J. W. Lincoln's melancholy   **92**

Shesol, J. Supreme power   **347**

Simon, J. F. What kind of nation   **342**

Smith, D. J. Young Mandela   **92**

Smith, J. E. FDR   **92**

Smith, J. E. Grant   **973.8**

Sorensen, T. C. Counselor   **92**

Staloff, D. Hamilton, Adams, Jefferson   **973.4**

Stephanopoulos, G. All too human   **973.929**

Stewart, D. O. American emperor   **973.4**

Stinnett, R. B. Day of deceit   **940.54**

Swanson, J. L. Manhunt   **364.152**

Symmes, P. The boys from Dolores   **972.91**

Symonds, C. L. Lincoln and his admirals   **92**

Szulc, T. Fidel   **92**

Taking charge   **973.923**

Talbott, S. The Russia hand   **327**

Taylor, J. The generalissimo   **92**

Taylor, N. American-made   **331.1**

Thomas, E. The war lovers   **973.8**

Tolstaia, T. Pushkin's children   **891.7**

Toobin, J. R. A vast conspiracy   **973.929**

Tuchman, B. W. Practicing history   **907**

Tuchman, B. W. Stilwell and the American experience in China, 1911-45   **327**

Unger, H. G. The last founding father   **92**

Vidal, G. Inventing a nation: Washington, Adams, Jefferson   **973.4**

Von Tunzelmann, A. Red heat   **972.9**

Walker, C. E. Mongrel nation   **305.8**

Wallace, A. F. C. The long bitter trail   **323.1**

Walsh, J. E. Moonlight   **345**

Washington, G. George Washington's diaries   **973.4**

Weintraub, S. 15 stars   **920**

Wheen, F. Strange days indeed   **973.92**

White, R. C. A. Lincoln   **92**

White, R. C. The eloquent president: a portrait of Lincoln through his words   **92**

White, R. C. Lincoln's greatest speech   **973.7**

Wicker, T. Dwight D. Eisenhower   **973.921**

Widmer, E. L. Martin Van Buren   **92**

Wiencek, H. An imperfect god   **973.4**

Wilber, D. Q. Rawhide down   **973.927**

Wilentz, S. Andrew Jackson   **92**

Williams, C. The last great Frenchman   **944**

Wills, G. Certain trumpets   **303.3**

Wills, G. James Madison   **973.5**

Wills, G. Lincoln at Gettysburg   **973.7**

Wills, G. "Negro president"   **326**

Wilson, E. Patriotic gore   **810**

Woods, R. B. LBJ   **92**

Woodward, B. The commanders   **973.928**

Woodward, B. The final days   **973.924**

Woodward, B. Plan of attack   **956.7**

Woodward, B. Shadow   **973.92**

Woodward, B. State of denial   **973.931**

Zacks, R. The pirate coast   **973.4**

Zelizer, J. E. Jimmy Carter   **92**

Zimmermann, W. First great triumph   **973**

PRESIDENTS—CHINA

Taylor, J. The generalissimo   **92**

PRESIDENTS—CONFEDERATE STATES OF AMERICA—BIOGRAPHY

Cooper, W. J. Jefferson Davis, American   **973.7**

PRESIDENTS—DWELLINGS—UNITED STATES

Monkman, B. C. The White House   **975.3**

PRESIDENTS—FRANCE—BIOGRAPHY

Williams, C. The last great Frenchman   **944**

PRESIDENTS—LIBERIA

Johnson-Sirleaf, E. This child will be great   **92**

PRESIDENTS—MEDICAL CARE—UNITED STATES—HISTORY—19TH CENTURY

Millard, C. The destiny of the republic   **973.8**

PRESIDENTS—POWERS *See* Executive power

PRESIDENTS—SOUTH AFRICA

Mandela, N. Conversations with myself   **92**

PRESIDENTS—TAIWAN

Taylor, J. The generalissimo   **92**

PRESIDENTS—UNITED STATES

Brands, H. W. The man who saved the union **355.009**

Duffy, M. The presidents club   **973.92**

Hatch, P. J. A rich spot of earth   **635**

Maraniss, D. Barack Obama   **973.932**

PRESIDENTS—UNITED STATES—ASSASSINATION

See also Assassination

Hill, C. Mrs. Kennedy and me   **973.922**

Millard, C. The destiny of the republic   **973.8**

PRESIDENTS—UNITED STATES—BIOGRAPHY

Caro, R. A. The passage of power   **973.923**

Collins, G. William Henry Harrison   **973.5**

Davis, D. Guest of honor   **973.91**

Raphael, R. Mr. president   **352.23**

Smith, J. E. Eisenhower   **973.921**

PRESIDENTS—UNITED STATES—BIOGRAPHY—ANECDOTES

Ellis, J. J. Founding brothers   **973.4**

PRESIDENTS—UNITED STATES—CONGRESSES

The White House   **975.3**

PRESIDENTS—UNITED STATES—CORRE-

Raine, Kathleen
The collected poems of Kathleen Raine   821
Raines, Ben
Cleland, M. Heart of a patriot   92
Rainforest Alliance
Jukofsky, D. Encyclopedia of rainforests   **578.73**
A **raisin** in the sun. Hansberry, L.   812
Raising a child with a neuromuscular disorder.
Thompson, C. E.   **618.92**
Raising a child with autism. Richman, S.   **618.92**
Raising a happy, unspoiled child. White, B. L. **649**
Raising America. Hulbert, A.   649
Raising baby green. Greene, A. R.   **618.2**
Raising resilient children. Brooks, R. B.   649
Raising the dead. Munson, R.   174
Rajan, Raghuram G.
Fault lines   **330.9**
Rajtar, Steve
Indian war sites   **970.004**
United States holidays and observances   **394.26**
Rakove, Jack N.
(ed) The annotated U.S. Constitution and Declaration of Independence   342
Rakove, J. Revolutionaries   **973.3**
RALLIES (PROTEST) *See* Demonstrations
Ralph Ellison. Rampersad, A.   92
Ralston, John
Port, D. The caveman's pregnancy companion   **618.2**
Ramachandran, V. S.
The tell-tale brain   **616.8**
Ramage, Ken
(ed) Gun digest 2009   **623.4**
The **Ramayana**. Narayan, R. K.   891
Ramazani, Jahan
(ed) The Norton anthology of modern and contemporary poetry   821
Ramineni, Shubhra
Entice with spice   **641.5**
Ramke, Bin
Aerial   811
Ramm, David
(ed) World authors, 2000-2005   **920.003**
Rammer jammer yellow hammer. St. John, W.   **796.332**
Ramo, Joshua Cooper
The age of the unthinkable   **973.931**
Ramonet, Ignacio
Castro, F. Fidel Castro: my life   92
Rampersad, Arnold
(ed) The Oxford anthology of African-American poetry   811
The life of Langston Hughes Volume I: 1902-1941   92
The life of Langston Hughes Volume II: 1941-1967   818

Ralph Ellison   92
Ramsdell, Kristin, 1940-
Romance fiction   016
Ramsey, Dan
Teach yourself visually car care & maintenance   **629.28**
Ramsey, Dave
Entreleadership   **658.4**
Ramsey, JonBenet
About
Schiller, L. Perfect murder, perfect town   **364.15**
Ramsey, Judy
Ramsey, D. Teach yourself visually car care & maintenance   **629.28**
Ramsland, Katherine M.
Ghost   **133.1**
RANCH LIFE
See also Farm life; Frontier and pioneer life
Bell, L. Claiming ground   92
DiSilvestro, R. L. Theodore Roosevelt in the Badlands   92
RANCH LIFE—MONTANA
Blunt, J. Breaking clean   92
RANCHERS
Blunt, J. Breaking clean   92
Milner, C. A. As big as the West   92
Rand, Ayn
Journals of Ayn Rand   92
Letters of Ayn Rand   813
The virtue of selfishness   171
The voice of reason; essays in objectivist thought   191
Randal, Jonathan C.
Osama: the making of a terrorist   92
Randall, David K.
Dreamland   **612.8**
Randall, Harry G.
Cassel, G. H. The eye book   **617.7**
Randall, John Herman
(ed) The Renaissance philosophy of man   189
Randall, Lisa
Knocking on heaven's door   500
Randall, Otelio Sye
The encyclopedia of the heart and heart disease   **612.1**
Randall, Willard Sterne
Alexander Hamilton   92
George Washington   **973.4**
Thomas Jefferson   92
Randel, Don Michael
(ed) The Harvard biographical dictionary of music   780
(ed) The Harvard concise dictionary of music and musicians   780
(ed) The Harvard dictionary of music   780
RANDOM ACCESS MEMORY

Rashid, Ahmed
Descent into chaos 954
Taliban 958.1
Rasmussen, Daniel
American uprising 976.3
Rasmussen, Eric
The Shakespeare thefts 822.3
Rasmussen, R. Kent
(ed) Cyclopedia of literary places 809
Critical companion to Mark Twain 818
RASTAFARI MOVEMENT
Chevannes, B. Rastafari: roots and ideology 299.6
Rastafari: roots and ideology. Chevannes, B. 299.6
Ratcliff, Todd
Baker, D. The 50 most extreme places in our solar
system 523.2
Ratey, John J.
Hallowell, E. M. Delivered from distraction 616.85
Hallowell, E. M. Driven to distraction 616.85
A user's guide to the brain 612.8
Rath, Sara
The complete pig 636.4
Rathbone, Belinda
Walker Evans 92
Rathbone, John Paul
The sugar king of Havana 92
Rather, Dan
The American dream 973.92
Ratification. Maier, P. 342
Ratio. Ruhlman, M. 641.5
RATIO AND PROPORTION
See also Arithmetic; Geometry
**RATIONAL EXPECTATIONS (ECONOMIC
THEORY)**
Fox, J. The myth of the rational market 332.6
The **rational** optimist. Ridley, M. 339.2
RATIONALISM
See also Philosophy; Religion; Secularism;
Theory of knowledge
Ratliff, Ben
Coltrane 92
The jazz ear 781.65
Jazz: a critic's guide to the 100 most important re-
cordings 781.65
Ratnesar, Romesh
Tear down this wall 973.927
Rattlesnake. Rubio, M. 597.96
RATTLESNAKES
See also Poisonous animals; Snakes
Rubio, M. Rattlesnake 597.96
Rauchway, Eric
Murdering McKinley 973.8
Rause, Vince
Parrado, N. Miracle in the Andes 982
Ravago, Miguel
Tausend, M. Cocina de la familia 641.5

RAVENS
Heinrich, B. Mind of the raven 598.8
RAVENS—ANECDOTES
Heinrich, B. Mind of the raven 598.8
Ravitch, Diane
The death and life of the great American school sys-
tem 379
Raw energy. Tourles, S. L. 641.5
RAW MATERIALS
See also Commercial products
Rawhide down. Wilber, D. Q. 973.927
Ray, Barbara E.
Not quite adults 306.8
Ray, C. Claiborne
The New York Times second book of science ques-
tions and answers 500
Raymo, Chet
An intimate look at the night sky 520
Walking zero 526
Raymond Carver. Sklenicka, C. 92
Raymond Carver. Halpert, S. 813
Raymond Chandler. Hiney, T. 813
Razac, Olivier
Barbed wire 323.4
RDZOGS CHEN
Thondup, T. Enlightened journey 294.3
Rea, Tom
Bone wars 560
Reach for the skies. Branson, R. 629.1
Reaching up for manhood. Canada, G. 305.23
REACTION (POLITICAL SCIENCE) *See* Con-
servatism
Reactions. Atkins, P. 541
REACTIONS, CHEMICAL *See* Chemical reac-
tions
Read on . . . crime fiction. Trott, B. 016
Read on . . . fantasy fiction. Hollands, N. 016
Read on series
Hollands, N. Read on . . . fantasy fiction 016
Saricks, J. G. Read on—audiobooks 011
Trott, B. Read on . . . crime fiction 016
Read on—audiobooks. Saricks, J. G. 011
Read, Anthony
The fall of Berlin 940.54
Read, J. Leighton
Reeves, B. Total engagement 303.4
Read, Piers Paul
Alive 910.4
Read, Piers Paul, 1941-
The Dreyfus affair 944.081
READER GUIDANCE
Bouricius, A. The romance readers' advisory 016
Buker, D. M. The science-fiction and fantasy read-
ers' advisory 025.5
Charles, J. A. The mystery readers' advisory 025.2
Hooper, B. The short story readers' advisory 028

REGGAE MUSICIANS
Grant, C. The natural mystics   **920**

REGIONAL DEVELOPMENT *See* Community development; Regional planning

REGIONAL HISTORY *See* Local history

REGIONAL LIBRARIES
See also Public libraries

REGIONAL PLANNING
Mumford, L. The culture of cities   **307.7**

REGIONAL PLANNING
See also Land use; Planning

REGIONALISM
See also Geography; Politics

REGIONALISM—NORTH AMERICA
Woodard, C. American nations   **970.004**

REGIONALISM—POLITICAL ASPECTS
Bishop, B. The big sort   **305.8**

REGIONALISM—UNITED STATES
Bishop, B. The big sort   **305.8**

REGISTERS *See* Registers of births, etc.

REGISTERS OF BIRTHS, ETC.
See also Genealogy

Kemp, T. J. International vital records handbook   **929**

REGULATORY AGENCIES *See* Administrative agencies

REGULATORY AGENCY OFFICIALS
Feldman, N. Scorpions   **920**
Greenspan, A. The age of turbulence   **92**
Leamer, L. The Kennedy men   **920**
Mahoney, R. D. Sons and brothers: the days of Jack and Bobby Kennedy   **92**
Martin, J. Greenspan   **92**
Overtveldt, J. v. Bernanke's test   **332.1**
Perino, M. A. The hellhound of Wall Street   **330.9**
Wessel, D. In Fed we trust   **332.1**
Woodward, B. Maestro: Greenspan's Fed and the American boom   **331.1**

Rehak, Melanie
Girl sleuth   **813**

Rehnquist, William H.
All the laws but one   **342**

Reich, Eugenie Samuel
Plastic fantastic   **92**

Reich, Robert B.
Aftershock   **330.9**
The future of success   **306.3**
Locked in the cabinet   **973.929**

Reich, Steven A.
(ed) Encyclopedia of the great Black migration   **307**

Reichl, Ruth
(ed) The gourmet cookbook   **641.5**
(ed) Gourmet today   **641.5**
Comfort me with apples   **92**
Garlic and sapphires   **92**

Reichmann, Rosie

Ageless yoga   **613.7**

Reid, Anna
Leningrad   **940.5421**

Reid, Constance
From zero to infinity   **512.7**

Reid, Jane Davidson
The Oxford guide to classical mythology in the arts, 1300-1990s   **700**

Reid, Lori
The art of hand reading   **133.6**

Reid, T. R.
The healing of America   **362.1**

Reiff, Janice L.
(ed) The Encyclopedia of Chicago   **977.3**

REIKI (HEALING SYSTEM)
Quest, P. Reiki for life   **615.8**
Reiki for life. Quest, P.   **615.8**

Reill, Peter Hanns
(ed) Wilson, E. J. Encyclopedia of the Enlightenment   **940.2**

Reilly, Thomas A.
The big picture   **791.43**
Reimagining equality. Hill, A.   **305.8**

Reiman, Donald H.
(ed) Shelley's poetry and prose   **821**

REINDEER
See also Deer; Domestic animals; Mammals

Reiner, Jon
The man who couldn't eat   **92**

REINFORCED CONCRETE
See also Building materials; Concrete

Reinhart, Carmen M.
Reinhart, C. M. This time is different   **338.5**

Reinhart, Carmen M., 1955-
This time is different   **338.5**

Reinisch, June
The Kinsey Institute new report on sex   **306.7**
Reinventing comics. McCloud, S.   **741.5**
Reinventing the bazaar. McMillan, J.   **330.12**

Reischauer, Edwin O.
Japan   **952**
The Japanese today   **952**

Reisen, Harriet
Louisa May Alcott   **92**

Reiss, Tom
The Orientalist   **92**

Reistad-Long, Sara
The big New York sandwich book   **641.8**

Reiter, Margaret E.
Leonard, R. Solve your money troubles   **346**

Reitman, Janet
Inside Scientology   **299**

REJECTION (PSYCHOLOGY)
See also Psychology
Gershon, I. The breakup 2.0   **303.4**

Rejwan, Nissim

Stebbins, R. C. A field guide to Western reptiles and amphibians **597.9**

REPTILES—CANADA—IDENTIFICATION
Conant, R. A field guide to reptiles & amphibians **597.9**

REPTILES—NORTH AMERICA—IDENTIFICATION
Stebbins, R. C. A field guide to Western reptiles and amphibians **597.9**

REPTILES—PHYSIOLOGY
See also Physiology

REPTILES—UNITED STATES—IDENTIFICATION
Conant, R. A field guide to reptiles & amphibians **597.9**

REPTILES—WEST (U.S.)—IDENTIFICATION
Stebbins, R. C. A field guide to Western reptiles and amphibians **597.9**

The **republic.** Plato **888**

The **republic;** and, The laws. Cicero, M. T. **320.1**

REPUBLICAN PARTY (U.S.)
See also Political parties

REPUBLICS
See also Constitutional history; Constitutional law; Political science

Required reading. **301**

Resch, John Phillips
(ed) Americans at war **973**

The **rescue** artist. Dolnick, E. **364.1**

RESCUE DOGS
See also Rescue work; Working dogs
Charleson, S. Scent of the missing **636.7**

RESCUE WORK
Tougias, M. Ten hours until dawn **363.34**
Van Tilburg, C. Mountain rescue doctor **616**

RESEARCH
Ronson, J. The psychopath test **616.85**

RESEARCH—MISCELLANEA
Maddox, J. R. What remains to be discovered **500**

RESEARCH—NEW YORK (STATE)—TUXEDO PARK—HISTORY—20TH CENTURY
Conant, J. Tuxedo Park **530**

RESEARCH—UNITED STATES—HISTORY—20TH CENTURY
Finkbeiner, A. K. The Jasons **920**

RESEARCH AND DEVELOPMENT *See* Research

RESEARCH PAPER WRITING *See* Report writing

Research-based readers' advisory. Moyer, J. E. **025.5**

The **researcher's** guide to American genealogy. Greenwood, V. D. **929**

Resh, Vincent H.
(ed) Encyclopedia of insects **595.7**

RESIDENCES *See* Domestic architecture; Houses

RESILIENCE (PERSONALITY TRAIT)
Gonzales, L. Surviving survival **155.9**

RESILIENCE (PERSONALITY TRAIT) IN CHILDREN
Brooks, R. B. Raising resilient children **649**

Resistance. Humbert, A. **92**

RESISTANCE TO DRUGS IN MICROORGANISMS *See* Drug resistance in microorganisms

RESISTANCE TO GOVERNMENT
See also Political ethics; Political science
Stern, K. S. A force upon the plain **306.2**
Wills, G. A necessary evil **973**

Resistance, rebellion, and death. Camus, A. **844**

Resnick, Lynda
Rubies in the orchard **658.8**

RESORTS
See also Recreation
Rogers, D. The last resort **968.91**

RESOURCE MANAGEMENT *See* Conservation of natural resources

RESOURCEFULNESS
Gonzales, L. Surviving survival **155.9**

RESOURCES, MARINE *See* Marine resources

Respect for acting. Hagen, U. **792**

RESPIRATION
See also Physiology

RESPIRATORY SYSTEM
See also Anatomy; Physiology

RESPIRATORY SYSTEM—DISEASES
Brody, J. E. Jane Brody's allergy fighter **616.2**

RESPITE CARE *See* Home care services

RESPONSIBILITY
See also Ethics
Connors, R. Change the culture, change the game **658.4**

REST
Benson, H. The relaxation response **155.9**

REST
See also Health; Hygiene

REST—RELIGIOUS ASPECTS
Shulevitz, J. The Sabbath world **296.4**

REST—RELIGIOUS ASPECTS—CHRISTIANITY
Shulevitz, J. The Sabbath world **296.4**

REST—RELIGIOUS ASPECTS—JUDAISM
Shulevitz, J. The Sabbath world **296.4**

Rest in peace. Laderman, G. **393**

The **rest** of love. Phillips, C. **811**

Restak, Richard M.
Mozart's brain and the fighter pilot **612.8**

RESTAURANTS
Cowen, T. An economist gets lunch **394.1**
Fellows, W. Gay bar **306.76**
Fried, S. Appetite for America **92**
Grimes, W. Appetite city **394.1**
Lee, J. 8. The fortune cookie chronicles **641.5**

Rubio, Manny
Rattlesnake   597.96

Ruchti, Ulrich
Walker, A. Stanley Kubrick, director   791.43

Ruck, Rob
Raceball   796.357

Rudacille, Deborah
Roots of steel   338.4
The scalpel and the butterfly   179

Rudahl, Sharon
A dangerous woman   335

Rudd, Mark
Underground   92

Ruden, Sarah
Paul among the people   225.9

Rudman, Peter Strom
The Babylonian theorem   510

Rudnick, Paul
I shudder   92

Rudof, Joanne Weiner
(ed) Witness   940.53

Rudolph, Joseph R.
(ed) Encyclopedia of modern ethnic conflicts 305.8
Rudy Giuliani. Kirtzman, A.   92
Rudyard Kipling. Ricketts, H.   92

Ruefle, Mary
Poems./Selections   Selected poems   811

RUGBY
Carlin, J. Playing the enemy   968.06

RUGBY FOOTBALL—HISTORY
Carlin, J. Playing the enemy   968.06

RUGBY PLAYERS
Parrado, N. Miracle in the Andes   982

Ruger, Axel
Liedtke, W. A. Vermeer and the Delft school **759.9**

Ruggero, Ed
Duty first   355

RUGS AND CARPETS
    See also Decorative arts; Interior design

Ruhlman, Michael
Ratio   641.5

RUINS *See* Antiquities; Excavations (Archeology);
    Extinct cities

Rukeyser, Muriel
Selected poems   811

RULE OF LAW—UNITED STATES
Shipler, D. K. The rights of the people   323

Rule, Ann
—and never let her go   364.1
Dead by sunset   364.1
The stranger beside me   92
Too late to say goodbye   364.152

RULERS *See* Emperors; Heads of state; Kings and
    rulers; Queens
Rules for renegades. Comaford, C.   650.1
The **rules** of inheritance. Smith, C. B.   616.99

RULES OF ORDER *See* Parliamentary practice
Rumi: the big red book. Divan-i Shams-i Tabrizi./
English./Selections   891

RUMMAGE SALES
    See also Secondhand trade; Selling
A **rumor** of war. Caputo, P.   959.704

Rump, Eric S.
(ed) Sheridan, R. B. The school for scandal and
other plays   822

Rumpf, Teri P.
The Sjogren's syndrome survival guide   616.97
The **Rumsfeld** way. Krames, J. A.   658.4
Rumspringa. Shachtman, T.   305.23

RUNAWAY ADULTS
    See also Desertion and nonsupport; Missing
    persons

RUNAWAY CHILDREN
    See also Children; Homeless persons; Miss-
    ing children

RUNAWAY SLAVES *See* Fugitive slaves

RUNAWAY TEENAGERS
    See also Homeless persons; Missing persons;
    Teenagers

Runciman, David
Political hypocrisy   320.1
Runner's world complete book of running.   796.42
Runner's world complete book of women's running.
Scott, D.   796.42

RUNNERS (ATHLETES)
Hillenbrand, L. Unbroken   940.54
Hoffer, R. Something in the air   796.4
Schaap, J. Triumph   92

RUNNERS (SPORTS)—BIOGRAPHY
Robbins, L. A race like no other   796.42

RUNNING
Runner's world complete book of running   796.42
Scott, D. Runner's world complete book of wom-
en's running   796.42
Running away to home. Wilson, J.   305.8
Running book discussion groups. John, L. Z.   374
Running on Ritalin. Diller, L. H.   618.92
Running with scissors. Burroughs, A.   813

Rupp, Rebecca
The complete home learning sourcebook   371.04

RURAL CHURCHES
    See also Church work

RURAL DEVELOPMENT
    See also Agriculture—Government policy;
    Community development; Economic develop-
    ment; Regional planning

RURAL ELECTRIFICATION—MALAWI
Kamkwamba, W. The boy who harnessed the
wind   92

RURAL LIFE *See* Country life; Farm life; Outdoor life

RURAL SCHOOLS

Ryan, Evelyn
About
Ryan, T. The prize winner of Defiance, Ohio **977.1**
Ryan, Evelyn, d. 1998 (American homemaker and prizewinner)
About
Ryan, T. The prize winner of Defiance, Ohio **977.1**
Ryan, Frank
Virus-X   **614.4**
Ryan, Kay
The best of it   **811**
Elephant rocks   **811**
The Niagara River   **811**
Say uncle   **811**
Ryan, Mark
Hornet's sting   **92**
Ryan, Michael
(ed) The encyclopedia of literary and cultural theory   **801**
Ryan, Terry
The prize winner of Defiance, Ohio   **977.1**
Ryan, William B. F.
Noah's flood   **930.1**
Ryback, Timothy W.
Hitler's private library   **027**
Rybczynski, Witold
A clearing in the distance: Frederick Law Olmsted and America in the nineteenth century   **712**
The look of architecture   **721**
The perfect house: a journey with the Renaissance architect Andrea Palladio   **720.9**
Ryder, Christopher S.
Take your pediatrician with you   **618.92**

S

S. Mark Taper Foundation imprint in Jewish studies [series]
Kirshenblatt, M. They called me Mayer July   **92**
Saba, Umberto
Songbook   **851**
Sabar, Ariel
My father's paradise   **305.8**
Sabbag, Robert
Down around midnight   **92**
Sabbagh, Karl
The Riemann hypothesis   **512.7**
SABBATH
See also Judaism
Shulevitz, J. The Sabbath world   **296.4**
The **Sabbath** world. Shulevitz, J.   **296.4**
SABIN VACCINE *See* Poliomyelitis vaccine
Sabor, Peter
(ed) Carlyle, T. Sartor resartus   **824**
SABOTAGE
See also Offenses against public safety; Strikes; Subversive activities; Terrorism

Millman, C. The detonators   **940.4**
SABOTAGE—UNITED STATES—HISTORY—20TH CENTURY
Millman, C. The detonators   **940.4**
Sacagawea of the Lewis and Clark expedition. Clark, E. E.   **92**
Sacco and Vanzetti. Watson, B.   **345**
Sacco, Joe
Footnotes in Gaza   **956.04**
Sacco, Nicola, 1891-1927 (Italian anarchist)
About
Watson, B. Sacco and Vanzetti   **345**
The **Sacco-Vanzetti** Affair. Temkin, M.   **345**
SACCO-VANZETTI CASE
Temkin, M. The Sacco-Vanzetti Affair   **345**
Watson, B. Sacco and Vanzetti   **345**
SACCO-VANZETTI TRIAL, DEDHAM, MASS., 1921
Temkin, M. The Sacco-Vanzetti Affair   **345**
Watson, B. Sacco and Vanzetti   **345**
Sachar, Howard Morley
Dreamland   **940**
A history of Israel   **956.94**
A history of the Jews in the modern world   **909**
Sachs, Dana
The house on Dream Street   **959.7**
Sachs, Harvey
The Ninth   **785**
Sachs, Jeffrey D.
The price of civilization   **330.9**
Sack, Steven Mitchell
The employee rights handbook   **344**
The **Sackett** companion. L'Amour, L.   **813**
Sacks, David
Encyclopedia of the ancient Greek world   **938**
Sacks, Oliver W.
An anthropologist on Mars   **616.8**
The island of the colorblind   **617.7**
The man who mistook his wife for a hat and other clinical tales   **616.8**
The mind's eye   **616.85**
Seeing voices   **362.4**
Uncle Tungsten   **616.8**
Sacks, O. The mind's eye   **616.85**
SACRAMENTS
See also Church; Grace (Theology); Rites and ceremonies
SACRED ART *See* Religious art
SACRED BOOKS
Gutjahr, P. C. The Book of Mormon   **289.3**
Sacred cows and golden geese. Greek, C. R.   **179**
SACRED MUSIC *See* Church music
SACRED SPACE
Nabokov, P. Where the lightning strikes   **299.7**
SACRED SPACE—UNITED STATES
Nabokov, P. Where the lightning strikes   **299.7**

Levy, M. Why buildings fall down   **690**

SALVAGE

Bloom, J. American wasteland   **363.7**

Wasinger, S. Eco-craft   **745.5**

SALVAGE—CHINA

Humes, E. Garbology   **628.4**

SALVAGE (WASTE, ETC.) *See* Salvage

Salvation. Hooks, B.   **306.7**

SALVATION

    See also Doctrinal theology

SALVATION—HISTORY OF DOCTRINES

    See also Doctrinal theology

Salvation: scenes from the life of St. Francis. Martin, V.   **92**

Salzberg, Sharon

Real happiness   **158**

Salzman, Jack

(ed) The Cambridge handbook of American literature   **810**

Salzman, Mark

Iron & silk   **951.05**

Lost in place   **813**

True notebooks   **371.9**

Sam Shepard; seven plays. Shepard, S.   **812**

Sam Walton, made in America. Walton, S.   **92**

Sambuchino, Chuck

(ed) 2009 guide to literary agents   **070.5**

The **same** river twice. Walker, A.   **813**

SAME-SEX MARRIAGE

    See also Marriage

Moats, D. R. Civil wars   **306.8**

SAME-SEX MARRIAGE—LAW AND LEGISLATION—UNITED STATES

Moats, D. R. Civil wars   **306.8**

SAME-SEX MARRIAGE—LAW AND LEGISLATION—VERMONT

Moats, D. R. Civil wars   **306.8**

SAME-SEX MARRIAGE—UNITED STATES

Moats, D. R. Civil wars   **306.8**

SAME-SEX MARRIAGE—VERMONT

Moats, D. R. Civil wars   **306.8**

Samet, Elizabeth D.

Soldier's heart   **810**

SAMI (EUROPEAN PEOPLE)

Beach, H. A year in Lapland   **948.97**

Samii, Ali

Mosley, A. D. The encyclopedia of Parkinson's disease   **616.8**

SAMOAN ISLANDS—SOCIAL LIFE AND CUSTOMS

Mead, M. Coming of age in Samoa   **306**

Sample, Ian

Massive   **539.7**

SAMPLERS

    See also Embroidery; Needlework

SAMPLING (STATISTICS)

    See also Probabilities; Statistics

Sampson, Anthony

Nelson Mandela   **92**

Sampson, Curt

Masters   **796.352**

Sampson, Scott D.

Dinosaur odyssey   **567.9**

Samuel Beckett's Waiting for Godot.   **842**

Samuel Beckett: the Grove centenary edition [series]

Beckett, S. Dramatic works   **842**

Samuel Johnson.   **828**

Samuel Johnson. Meyers, J.   **92**

Samuel Johnson. Martin, P.   **92**

Samuel Pepys. Tomalin, C.   **941.06**

Samuel, Rhian

(ed) The Norton/Grove dictionary of women composers   **780.92**

Samuelsson, Marcus

The soul of a new cuisine   **641.5**

SAN FRANCISCO (CALIF.)—HISTORY

Talbot, D. Season of the witch   **306**

San Francisco Museum of Modern Art.

Brought to light   **779**

SANATORIUMS

    See also Long-term care facilities

SANCTIONS (INTERNATIONAL LAW)

    See also Economic policy; International economic relations; International law

SANCTUARY MOVEMENT

    See also Asylum; Church and social problems; Social movements

Sand. Welland, M.   **553.6**

SAND

Welland, M. Sand   **553.6**

A **Sand** County almanac. Leopold, A.   **508**

SAND DUNES

    See also Seashore

SAND SCULPTURE

    See also Nature craft; Sculpture

Sandburg, Carl

Abraham Lincoln: The prairie years and The war years   **92**

The American songbag   **781.62**

The complete poems of Carl Sandburg   **811**

Sandel, Michael J.

Justice   **172**

What money can't buy   **330.1**

Sanders, Andrew

The short Oxford history of English literature   **820**

Sanders, Donald Theodore

Zeilinga de Boer, J. Earthquakes in human history   **363.34**

Sanders, Ed

Let's not keep fighting the Trojan War   **811**

Thirsting for peace in a raging century   **811**

The battery **621.31**

Schlesinger, Stephen C.
(ed) Schlesinger, A. M. Journals: 1952-2000 **92**

Schlissel, Lillian
Far from home **978**

Schlosberg, Suzanne
Quessenberry, S. The good neighbor cookbook **641.5**

Schlosser, Eric
Fast food nation **394.1**

Schmidle, Nicholas
To live or to perish forever **954.91**

Schmidt, Elizabeth
(ed) The poets laureate anthology **811**

Schmidt, Leigh Eric
Heaven's bride **92**

Schmidt, Michael
Lives of the poets **821**

Schmidt, Thomas
The Lewis & Clark Trail **978**

Schneider, Carl J.
Schneider, D. First ladies **920.003**
Schneider, D. Slavery in America **326**

Schneider, Dorothy
First ladies **920.003**
Slavery in America **326**

Schneider, Edward L.
What your doctor hasn't told you and the health store clerk doesn't know **615.5**

Schneider, Paul
The Adirondacks **974.7**
Brutal journey: the epic story of the first crossing of North America **970.01**

Schobinger, Juan
The ancient Americans **970.01**

Schoch, Richard W.
The secrets of happiness **170**

Schoen, Allen M.
Kindred spirits **636.089**

Schoen, Douglas E.
The power of the vote **324**

Schoenberger, Nancy
Kashner, S. Furious love **92**

Schoenherr, Matthew
House transformed **690**

Schoepflin, Rennie B.
Christian Science on trial **289.5**

Schoerke, Meg
(ed) Twentieth-century American poetry **811**

Schoeser, Mary
World textiles: a concise history **677**

SCHOLARSHIP *See* Learning and scholarship
SCHOLARSHIP FUNDS *See* Scholarships
SCHOLARSHIPS
See also Education; Endowments; Student aid

Peterson's how to get money for college **378.3**
Schlachter, G. A. Financial aid for the disabled and their families, 2010-2012 **378.3**

SCHOLARSHIPS, FELLOWSHIPS, ETC. *See* Scholarships
SCHOLASTIC APTITUDE TEST *See* Scholastic Assessment Test
SCHOLASTIC ASSESSMENT TEST
Green, S. Barron's SAT **378.1**
SCHOLASTICISM
Rubenstein, R. E. Aristotle's children **189**

Schom, Alan
Napoleon Bonaparte **92**
One hundred days **944.05**

Schonberg, Harold C.
The great pianists **920**
The lives of the great composers **780**

SCHOOL ADMINISTRATORS
Halberstam, D. The children **323.1**
Rodriguez, D. Kabul Beauty School **305.4**
The **school** among the ruins: poems, 2000-2004. Rich, A. **811**
The **school** and society, and The child and the curriculum. Dewey, J. **372**

SCHOOL ATHLETICS *See* School sports
SCHOOL BOOKS *See* Textbooks
SCHOOL BUILDINGS
See also Buildings; Schools
SCHOOL BUSING *See* Busing (School integration); School children—Transportation
SCHOOL CHILDREN
See also Children; Students
Caring for your school-age child **649**
SCHOOL CHILDREN—FOOD
See also Children—Nutrition; Diet; Food
SCHOOL CHILDREN—TRANSPORTATION
See also Transportation
SCHOOL CHOICE
See also Education
Ravitch, D. The death and life of the great American school system **379**
SCHOOL DESEGREGATION *See* School integration
SCHOOL DISCIPLINE
See also Schools—Administration; Teaching
SCHOOL FAILURE—UNITED STATES
Gross, M. L. The conspiracy of ignorance **371.01**
The **school** for scandal and other plays. Sheridan, R. B. **822**
SCHOOL HYGIENE
See also Children—Health and hygiene; Health education; Hygiene; Public health; Sanitation
SCHOOL IMPROVEMENT PROGRAMS—UNITED STATES
Brill, S. Class warfare

Kohn, A. The schools our children deserve **371.2**

SCHOOL INTEGRATION

See also Race relations

Lukas, J. A. Common ground **305.8**

Margolick, D. Elizabeth and Hazel **92**

SCHOOL INTEGRATION—ARKANSAS—LITTLE ROCK—HISTORY—20TH CENTURY

Margolick, D. Elizabeth and Hazel **92**

SCHOOL LIBRARIES

See also Instructional materials centers; Libraries

SCHOOL LIBRARIES—CATALOGS

Safford, B. R. Guide to reference materials for school library media centers **011.6**

SCHOOL LIFE *See* Students

SCHOOL MEDIA CENTERS *See* Instructional materials centers

SCHOOL MUSIC *See* Music—Study and teaching; School songbooks; Singing

SCHOOL NURSES

See also Nurses

SCHOOL PRAYER

Greenawalt, K. Does God belong in public schools? **379**

SCHOOL PSYCHOLOGISTS

See also Psychologists

SCHOOL REFORM

Hirsch, E. D. The schools we need and why we don't have them **370.9**

Postman, N. The end of education **370.9**

SCHOOL REPORTS

See also Report writing

SCHOOL SHOOTINGS

See also Crime; School violence

Cullen, D. Columbine **364.152**

SCHOOL SHOOTINGS—COLORADO

Cullen, D. Columbine **364.152**

SCHOOL SONGBOOKS

See also Songbooks; Songs

SCHOOL SPORTS

See also Sports; Student activities

D'Orso, M. Eagle blue **796.323**

Kreidler, M. Four days to glory **796.8**

Merlino, D. The hustle **796.323**

Sielski, M. Fading echoes **92**

Swidey, N. The assist **796.323**

SCHOOL STORIES

See also Fiction

SCHOOL SUPERVISION

See also Schools—Administration; Teaching

SCHOOL TEACHING *See* Teaching

SCHOOL VIOLENCE

See also Juvenile delinquency; Violence

SCHOOLS—AFGHANISTAN

Mortenson, G. Stones into schools **371.82**

Mortenson, G. Three cups of tea **371.82**

SCHOOLS—EQUIPMENT AND SUPPLIES

See also Furniture

SCHOOLS—PAKISTAN

Mortenson, G. Stones into schools **371.82**

Mortenson, G. Three cups of tea **371.82**

SCHOOLS—SELECTION *See* School choice

The **schools** our children deserve. Kohn, A. **371.2**

The **schools** we need and why we don't have them. Hirsch, E. D. **370.9**

Schopf, J. William

Cradle of life **576.8**

Schoppa, R. Keith

The Columbia guide to modern Chinese history **951.05**

Schor, Edward L.

(ed) Caring for your school-age child **649**

Schorr, Daniel

Staying tuned **070**

Schou, Nicholas

Orange sunshine **363.45**

Schoultz, Lars

That infernal little Cuban republic **327**

Schrag, Philip G.

Kenney, D. N. Asylum denied **92**

Schreiber, Cory

Rustic fruit desserts **641.8**

Schreiber, Flora Rheta

Sybil **616.85**

Schreier, Iris

Kimmelstiel, L. Exquisite little knits **746.43**

Schrodinger's kittens and the search for reality. Gribbin, J. R. **530.1**

Schroeder, Alayna

Bray, I. M. Nolo's essential guide to buying your first home **643**

(ed) Steingold, F. The employer's legal handbook **344**

Schroeder, Alice D.

The snowball: Warren Buffett and the business of life **92**

Schroen, Gary C.

First in **958.1**

Schroth, Raymond A.

Bob Drinan **92**

Schrott, Allen

(ed) All music guide to classical music **016**

Schulberg, Budd

Sparring with Hemingway and other legends of the fight game **796.8**

Schuler, Judith

Curtis, G. B. Your pregnancy week by week **618.2**

Schulian, John

(ed) At the fights **796.8**

Schulkind, Jeanne

(ed) Woolf, V. Moments of being **823**

Schullery, Paul

The rise 799.1

Schulman, Bruce J.
The seventies 973.925

Schulman, Grace
(ed) Moore, M. The poems of Marianne Moore 811
Days of wonder 811

Schulmann, Robert J.
(ed) Einstein, A. Einstein on politics 92

Schultz, David A.
(ed) Encyclopedia of the First Amendment 342
Encyclopedia of the United States Constitution 342

Schultz, Ellen
Retirement heist 331.2

Schultz, Eric B.
King Philip's War 973.2

Schultz, Howard
Onward 647.9

Schultz, Jeffrey D.
Critical companion to John Steinbeck 813

Schultz, Ken
Ken Schultz's field guide to saltwater fish 597

Schultz, Mitchel E.
Grob's basic electronics 621.381

Schultz, Nancy Lusignan
Mrs. Mattingly's miracle 362.1

Schultz, Philip
My dyslexia 92

Schulz and Peanuts. Michaelis, D. 92

Schulz, Kathryn
Being wrong 153

Schulz, William F.
In our own best interest 323

Schulze, Hagen
Germany 943

Schumacher, Michael
Crossroads 92
Will Eisner 92

Schuyler, James
Collected poems 811
Other flowers 811

Schwab, Charles
Schwab-Pomerantz, C. It pays to talk 332.024

Schwab-Pomerantz, Carrie
It pays to talk 332.024

Schwalbe, Will
Shipley, D. Send 658

Schwantes, Carlos A.
The West the railroads made 338

Schwartz, Anna
Cancer fitness 616.99

Schwartz, David Joseph
The magic of thinking big 158

Schwartz, Jeffrey H.
What the bones tell us 599.93
Tattersall, I. Extinct humans 599.93

Schwartz, Lloyd

(ed) Bishop, E. Poems, prose, and letters S

Schwartz, Maxime
How the cows turned mad 616.8

Schwartz, Peter
Rand, A. The voice of reason; essays in objectivist thought 191

Schwartz, Richard Alan
The 1990s 909.82
Cold War culture 973.92
Encyclopedia of the Persian Gulf War 956.704

Schwartz, Richard S.
(jt. auth) Olds, J. The lonely American 302.5

Schwartz, Sanford
Kael, P. The age of movies 791.43

Schwarzkopf, H. Norman
It doesn't take a hero: General H. Norman Schwarzkopf 92

Schweid, Richard
Consider the eel 597

Schweitzer, Albert
Out of my life and thought 610

Schweninger, Loren
Franklin, J. H. In search of the promised land 929

Science. Fara, P. 509

SCIENCE
Angier, N. The canon 500
Bais, S. In praise of science 500
The best American science and nature writing 2010 500
Bronowski, J. Science and human values 500
Brooks, M. 13 things that don't make sense 500
Bryson, B. A short history of nearly everything 500
Cole, K. C. Mind over matter 500
Dolnick, E. The clockwork universe 509
Dyson, F. J. The scientist as rebel 500
Eiseley, L. C. The unexpected universe 500
The Encyclopedia of science and technology 503
Feynman, R. P. The meaning of it all 500
Feynman, R. P. The pleasure of finding things out 500
Flatow, I. Present at the future 500
Gardner, M. Did Adam and Eve have navels? 500
Great thinkers of the Western world 190
Gribbin, J. R. Almost everyone's guide to science 500
The handy science answer book 500
Highfield, R. The science of Harry Potter 500
Kaku, M. Physics of the future 303.49
Kipfer, B. A. How it happens 500
Maddox, J. R. What remains to be discovered 500
Marshall, I. N. Who's afraid of Schrodinger's cat? 500
McGraw-Hill dictionary of scientific and technical terms 503
Moreno, J. D. The body politic 303.48
The new encyclopedia of science 503

SCRAPBOOKS

Helfand, J. Scrapbooks: an American history **745.54**

Ure, S. Scrapbooking your vacations **745.593**

Scrapbooks: an American history. Helfand, J. **745.54**

Scraptherapy cut the scraps! Ford, J. **746.46**

A **scream** goes through the house. Weinstein, A. **801**

Screen world presents the encyclopedia of Hollywood film actors. Monush, B. **920.003**

Screenplay. Field, S. **808.2**

SCREENPLAYS

See also Drama

SCREENWRITERS

Abbotson, S. C. W. Critical companion to Arthur Miller **812**

Bigsby, C. Arthur Miller **92**

Blight, D. W. American oracle **973.7**

Didion, J. The year of magical thinking **92**

Eller, J. R. Becoming Ray Bradbury **92**

Ellison, R. The collected essays of Ralph Ellison **814**

Fargnoli, A. N. Critical companion to William Faulkner **813**

Fey, T. Bossypants **92**

Fisher, J. T. On the Irish waterfront **331.7**

Fitzgerald, F. S. A life in letters **813**

Foote, H. Beginnings **812**

Forrest, E. Your voice in my head **362.196**

Fraser, A. Must you go? **92**

Gates, H. L. Thirteen ways of looking at a black man **920.71**

Gora, S. You couldn't ignore me if you tried **791.43**

Gottfried, M. Arthur Miller **92**

Green, S. The world of musical comedy **920**

Hiney, T. Raymond Chandler **813**

Jentz, T. Strange piece of paradise **364.1**

John Steinbeck **813**

Kazin, A. An American procession **810**

Lardner, R. I'd hate myself in the morning **813**

Lax, E. Conversations with Woody Allen **791.43**

Leider, E. W. Becoming Mae West **791.43**

Life stories **920**

Martin, S. Born standing up **92**

McGilligan, P. Oscar Micheaux **92**

Meade, M. Dorothy Parker **92**

Meade, M. Lonelyhearts **92**

Meyers, J. John Huston **92**

Miller, N. New world coming **973.91**

Mooney, P. Black is the new white **92**

Palin, M. Halfway to Hollywood **92**

Parini, J. One matchless time **92**

Pierpont, C. R. Passionate minds **810**

Playwrights at work **812**

Rapoport, R. Citizen Moore **92**

Rudnick, P. I shudder **92**

Salamon, J. Wendy and the lost boys **920**

Schultz, J. D. Critical companion to John Steinbeck **813**

Sikov, E. On Sunset Boulevard: the life and times of Billy Wilder **92**

Simon, N. The play goes on **812**

Simon, N. Rewrites **812**

Stone, R. Prime green **92**

Tate, M. J. Critical companion to F. Scott Fitzgerald **813**

Vidal, G. Point to point navigation **92**

Waters, J. Role models **92**

Waxman, S. Rebels on the backlot **920**

Weller, S. The Bradbury chronicles **92**

William Faulkner **813**

Wranovics, J. Chaplin and Agee **92**

SCREENWRITERS—UNITED STATES—BIOGRAPHY

Foote, H. Beginnings **812**

Lardner, R. I'd hate myself in the morning **813**

The **Screwtape** letters. Lewis, C. S. **248**

The **Scribner** encyclopedia of American lives. **920.003**

The **Scribner** encyclopedia of American lives, The 1960s. **920.003**

Scribner library of daily life [series]

Encyclopedia of clothing and fashion **391**

Scribner library of modern Europe [series]

Europe 1789 to 1914 **940.2**

Europe since 1914 **940.5**

Scribner turning points library [series]

Tobacco in history and culture **394.1**

Scribner writers series

Latino and Latina writers **810**

Supernatural fiction writers **809**

Script and scribble. Florey, K. B. **652**

Scroggins, Deborah

Wanted women **305.48**

Scroogenomics. Waldfogel, J. **339.4**

Scuba diving. Graver, D. **797.2**

SCUBA DIVING

Graver, D. Scuba diving **797.2**

Scull, Andrew T.

Madhouse **616.89**

Scull, Christina

Hammond, W. G. J.R.R. Tolkien, artist & illustrator **760.9**

Scully, Pamela

(jt. auth) Crais, C. C. Sara Baartman and the Hottentot Venus **92**

Sculpting basics. Hessenberg, K. **731.4**

SCULPTORS

See also Artists

Dippie, B. W. The Frederic Remington Art Museum collection **709**

Khan, Y. S. Enlightening the world **974.7**

Searching for memory. Schacter, D. L.   **153.1**
SEARCHING THE INTERNET *See* Internet searching
Searle, Teresa
  Felt jewelry   **746**
Sears list of subject headings.   **025.4**
Sears, Martha
  Sears, W. Parenting the fussy baby and high-need child   **649**
Sears, Robert
  The vaccine book   **614.4**
Sears, Stephen W.
  Chancellorsville   **973.7**
  (ed) The Civil War   **973.7**
  George B. McClellan   **92**
  Gettysburg   **973.7**
  Landscape turned red   **973.7**
  To the gates of Richmond   **973.7**
Sears, William
  The Baby book   **649**
  The family nutrition book   **613.2**
  Parenting the fussy baby and high-need child   **649**
SEAS
  See also Earth; Physical geography; Water
SEASHORE
  Carson, R. The edge of the sea   **577.7**
SEASHORE ECOLOGY
  See also Ecology
  Dean, C. Against the tide   **333.91**
Season of the witch. Talbot, D.   **306**
SEASONS
  See also Astronomy; Climate; Meteorology
  Ackerman, D. Dawn light   **508.2**
  Haskell, D. G. The forest unseen   **577.3**
  Waldbauer, G. Insects through the seasons   **595.7**
SEASONS—TENNESSEE
  Haskell, D. G. The forest unseen   **577.3**
The **seasons** of a man's life. Levinson, D. J.   **155.6**
The **seasons** of a woman's life. Levinson, D. J.   **155.6**
Seaver, Barton
  For cod and country   **641.6**
SEAWEEDS *See* Algae
Sebag-Montefiore, Hugh
  Enigma: the battle for the code   **940.54**
Sebald, Winfried Georg
  On the natural history of destruction   **833**
Sebald, Winfried Georg, 1944-2001
  Across the land and the water   **831**
Sebestyen, Victor
  Revolution 1989   **947**
Sebold, Alice
  Lucky   **362.883**
SECESSION—SOUTHERN STATES
  See also United States—History—1861-1865, Civil War
  Williams, D. Bitterly divided   **973.7**

SECLUSION *See* Solitude
SECOND ADVENT
  See also Eschatology
  Second chances. Wallerstein, J. S.   **306.89**
  The **Second** City unscripted. Thomas, M.   **792**
  The **second** creation. Wilmut, I.   **174**
  Second drafts of history. Morrow, L.   **973.92**
  The **second** family. Taffel, R.   **306.874**
  A **second** Mencken chrestomathy. Mencken, H. L.   **818**
  Second nature. Balcombe, J.   **591.5**
  A **second** opinion. Relman, A.   **362.1**
  Second opinions. Groopman, J. E.   **610**
  The **second** sex. Beauvoir, S. d.   **305.4**
  The **Second** World War. Keegan, J.   **940.53**
  The **Second** World War. Gilbert, M.   **940.53**
SECOND WORLD WAR *See* World War, 1939-1945
Second World War [series]
  Churchill, W. Closing the ring   **940.53**
  Churchill, W. The gathering storm   **940.53**
  Churchill, W. The grand alliance   **940.53**
  Churchill, W. The hinge of fate   **940.53**
  Churchill, W. Their finest hour   **940.53**
  Churchill, W. Triumph and tragedy   **940.53**
The **Second** World War. Beevor, A.   **940.54**
SECONDARY EDUCATION
  See also Education
SECONDHAND TRADE
  See also Selling
  Secrecy. Moynihan, D. P.   **352.3**
Secrest, Meryle
  Frank Lloyd Wright   **92**
  Modigliani   **92**
Secret agents. Drexler, M.   **614.4**
Secret empire. Taubman, P.   **327.12**
A **secret** gift. Gup, T.   **977.1**
Secret historian. Spring, J.   **92**
The **secret** history of balls. Chetwynd, J.   **796.3**
The **secret** history of the war on cancer. Davis, D.   **616.99**
Secret ingredients. New Yorker (Periodical)   **641**
The **secret** language of eating disorders. Claude-Pierre, P.   **616.85**
The **secret** life of Marilyn Monroe. Taraborrelli, J. R.   **92**
The **secret** life of words. Hitchings, H.   **422**
The **secret** lives of buildings. Hollis, E.   **720.9**
The **secret** lives of Somerset Maugham. Hastings, S.   **92**
The **secret** of Chanel No. 5. Mazzeo, T. J.   **338.7**
The **secret** of scent. Turin, L.   **668**
The **secret** pulse of time. Klein, S.   **153.7**
The **secret** room. Laughlin, J.   **811**
SECRET SERVICE
  See also Police

lishing

Serious barbecue. Lang, A. P.   641.5

Serious business. Kanfer, S.   741.5

A **serious** way of wondering. Price, R.   241

Seriously funny. Nachman, G.   792.7

SERMONS

    American sermons   252

    King, M. L. Strength to love   252

    Tutu, D. The rainbow people of God   968.06

Seroussi, Karyn

    Unraveling the mystery of autism and pervasive developmental disorder   618.92

SERPENTS *See* Snakes

Servadio, Gaia

    Rossini   92

Servan-Schreiber, David

    Anticancer   616.99

Server, Lee

    Ava Gardner   791

SERVICE (IN INDUSTRY) *See* Customer services

Service and style. Whitaker, J.   381

SERVICE DOGS

    See also Working dogs

SERVICE INDUSTRIES

    See also Industries

SERVICE STATIONS

    See also Automobile industry; Petroleum industry

SERVICE, CUSTOMER *See* Customer services

Service, Robert

    A history of twentieth-century Russia   947.084

    Lenin—a biography   947.084

    Stalin   92

    Trotsky   92

SERVICES, CUSTOMER *See* Customer services

SERVITUDE *See* Peonage; Slavery

Sestets. Wright, C.   811

SET DESIGNERS

    Brainard, J. The Nancy book   759

    Holroyd, M. A strange eventful history   92

    Ross, C. The world of Edward Gorey   700.92

SET THEORY

    Stillwell, J. Roads to infinity   511.3

    See also Mathematics

Seth, Vikram, 1952-

    Two lives   92

SETS (MATHEMATICS) *See* Set theory

Settersten, Richard

    (jt. auth) Ray, B. E. Not quite adults   306.8

The **setting** of the pearl. Weyr, T.   940.53

Setting the truth free. Campbell, J.   941.6

Setting the world ablaze. Ferling, J. E.   973.3

Settled in the wild. Shetterly, S. H.   508

The **settlement** of the Americas. Dillehay, T. D.   970.01

Seuling, Barbara

How to write a children's book and get it published   808.06

Seven ages of Paris. Horne, A.   944

The **seven** daughters of Eve. Sykes, B.   599.93

Seven days in the art world. Thornton, S. 709.05

Seven experiments that could change the world. Sheldrake, R.   507.8

Seven fires. Mallmann, F.   641.5

Seven guitars. Wilson, A.   812

Seven pillars of wisdom. Lawrence, T. E.   940.4

Seven pleasures. Spiegelman, W.   814

The **seven** sins of memory. Schacter, D. L. 153.1

The **seven** storey mountain. Merton, T.   92

SEVEN WONDERS OF THE WORLD

    See also Ancient architecture; Ancient art

SEVEN YEARS' WAR, 1756-1763

    Anderson, F. The crucible of war   973.2

    McLynn, F. 1759: the year Britain became master of the world   941.07

The **seventies.** Schulman, B. J.   973.925

The **Seventy** wonders of the modern world.   720.9

Severin, Timothy

    In search of Robinson Crusoe   996

Severson, Marilyn S.

    Masterpieces of French literature   843

SEWAGE

    George, R. The big necessity   363.7

SEWAGE DISPOSAL

    See also Public health; Refuse and refuse disposal

    George, R. The big necessity   363.7

Seward. Stahr, W.   973.709

Sewell, Darrel

    (ed) Thomas Eakins   759.13

SEWERAGE

    See also House drainage; Municipal engineering; Plumbing; Sanitary engineering

SEWING

    See also Home economics

    Bednar, N. The encyclopedia of sewing machine techniques   646.2

    Betzina, S. Power sewing step-by-step   646.4

    Betzina, S. Sandra Betzina sews for your home   646.2

    Cheetham, K. Singer perfect plus   646.2

    Colgrove, D. Teach yourself visually sewing 646.2

    Creative Publishing International, I. The complete photo guide to sewing   646.2

    Doh, J. Signature styles   646.4

    James, C. The complete serger handbook   646.2

    Lee, L. Sewing edges and corners   646.2

    The new sewing essentials   646.2

    Reader's Digest Association, I. New complete guide to sewing   646.2

    Wasinger, S. The feisty stitcher   746

Sewing edges and corners. Lee, L.   646.2

Yes means yes!   306.7

SEX ROLE—ENGLAND—HISTORY—18TH CENTURY

Vickery, A. Behind closed doors   306.8

SEX ROLE—HISTORY

Adovasio, J. M. The invisible sex   305.4

SEX THERAPY

See also Psychotherapy

Sex, time, and power. Shlain, L.   306.7

SEXISM

See also Attitude (Psychology); Prejudices

Berg, B. J. Sexism in America   305.4

Yes means yes!   306.7

Sexism in America. Berg, B. J.   305.4

Sexton, Anne

The complete poems   811

SEXUAL ABSTINENCE

See also Asceticism; Sex

SEXUAL ABUSE *See* Child sexual abuse; Sex crimes; Sexual harassment

SEXUAL ASSAULT *See* Rape

SEXUAL ATTRACTION

Etcoff, N. L. Survival of the prettiest   391.6

Shlain, L. Sex, time, and power   306.7

SEXUAL BEHAVIOR

Ackerman, D. A natural history of love   152.4

Bader, M. J. Arousal, the secret logic of sexual fantasies   306.7

Barash, D. P. The myth of monogamy   306.7

Bergner, D. The other side of desire   306.7

Block, J. D. Sex over 50   613.9

Comfort, A. The joy of sex   613.9

The Continuum complete international encyclopedia of sexuality   306.7

Etcoff, N. L. Survival of the prettiest   391.6

Heap, C. C. Slumming   305.8

Hite, S. The Hite report on the family   306.85

Knust, J. W. Unprotected texts   220.8

Levine, J. Harmful to minors   306.7

McConnachie, J. The book of love   306.7

Moalem, S. How sex works   612.6

Pagels, E. H. Adam, Eve, and the serpent   241

Pincott, J. Do gentlemen really prefer blondes?   155.3

Pisani, E. The wisdom of whores   614.5

Reinisch, J. The Kinsey Institute new report on sex   306.7

Sheehy, G. Understanding men's passages   305.244

Small, M. F. What's love got to do with it?   576.8

Sugar in my bowl   306.7

SEXUAL BEHAVIOR *See* Sex

SEXUAL BEHAVIOR IN ANIMALS

Barash, D. P. The myth of monogamy   306.7

Zuk, M. Sexual selections   591.56

Zuk, M. Sex on six legs   595.7

SEXUAL BEHAVIOR IN ANIMALS

See also Animal behavior; Sex—Physiological aspects

SEXUAL DEVIATION

See also Sex; Sexual disorders

SEXUAL DIVISION OF LABOR—HISTORY

Adovasio, J. M. The invisible sex   305.4

SEXUAL ETHICS

See also Ethics

SEXUAL HARASSMENT

See also Sex; Sexual ethics

Bordo, S. The male body   305.31

SEXUAL HYGIENE

See also Hygiene

SEXUAL IDENTITY *See* Sex role

SEXUAL MINORITIES

Riggle, E. D. B. A positive view of LGBTQ   155.3

SEXUAL PRACTICES *See* Sex

Sexual selections. Zuk, M.   591.56

SEXUALITY *See* Sex; Sex—Physiological aspects; Sex—Psychological aspects

SEXUALLY ABUSED CHILDREN *See* Child sexual abuse

Sexually transmitted diseases. Marr, L.   616.95

SEXUALLY TRANSMITTED DISEASES

See also Communicable diseases

Marr, L. Sexually transmitted diseases   616.95

Seymour, Corey

Wenner, J. S. Gonzo   92

Seymour, Marilyn Dallman

(ed) Conversations with Nadine Gordimer   823

Seymour, Miranda

Mary Shelley   92

Shabecoff, Alice

Poisoned profits   618.92

Shabecoff, Philip

(jt. auth) Shabecoff, A. Poisoned profits   618.92

Shabtai, Aharon

Poems./English./Selections War & love, love & war   892.4

Shachtman, Tom

Absolute zero and the conquest of cold   536

Airlift to America   378.1

Rumspringa   305.23

Shackleton's forgotten expedition. Riffenburgh, B.   998

SHAD

McPhee, J. A. The founding fish   597

SHAD FISHING—NORTH AMERICA—HISTORY

McPhee, J. A. The founding fish   597

Shades of glory. Hogan, L. D.   796.357

Shades of love. Yeros, D.   778

Shadid, Anthony

Night draws near   956.7

Shadow. Woodward, B.   973.92

The shadow factory. Bamford, J.   327.12

The **shadow** of a great rock. Bloom, H. 220.5
The **shadow** of Sirius. Merwin, W. S. 811
Shadow of the Silk Road. Thubron, C. 911
SHADOW PANTOMIMES AND PLAYS
    See also Amateur theater; Pantomimes; Puppets and puppet plays; Shadow pictures; Theater
SHADOW PICTURES
    See also Amusements
Shadow voyage. Huchthausen, P. A. 940.53
Shadowing the ground. Ignatow, D. 811
SHADOWPACT (FICTIONAL CHARACTERS)
    See also Fictional characters; Superheroes
Shadows of forgotten ancestors. Sagan, C. 304
The **shadows** of youth. Lewis, A. B. 323.1
Shaffer, Peter
    Equus 822
    Peter Shaffer's Amadeus 822
Shaggy muses. Adams, M. B. 920
Shah, Saira
    The storyteller's daughter 958.1
Shah, Sonia
    The body hunters 362.1
    The fever 614.5
Shah, Tahir
    The Caliph's house 964
    In search of King Solomon's mines 963
Shahnameh. Firdawsi 891
Shake the devil off. Brown, E. 364.152
The **Shaker** experience in America. Stein, S. J. 289
SHAKERS
    Stein, S. J. The Shaker experience in America 289
    Woo, I. The great divorce 92
SHAKERS—NEW YORK (STATE)
    Woo, I. The great divorce 92
Shakespeare. Bryson, B. 822.3
Shakespeare after all. Garber, M. 822.3
Shakespeare and modern culture. Garber, M. 822.3
The **Shakespeare** riots. Cliff, N. 974.4
Shakespeare the thinker. Nuttall, A. D. 822.3
The **Shakespeare** thefts. Rasmussen, E. 822.3
The **Shakespeare** wars. Rosenbaum, R. 822.3
Shakespeare's kings. Norwich, J. J. 822.3
Shakespeare's language. Kermode, F. 822.3
Shakespeare, Nicholas
    (ed) Chatwin, B. Under the sun 92
    Bruce Chatwin 823
Shakespeare, William
    The Columbia dictionary of quotations from Shakespeare 822.3
    The complete works 822.3
Shakespeare, William, 1564-1616 (English dramatist and poet)
About

    Bate, J. Soul of the age 822.3
    Bloom, H. Hamlet: poem unlimited 822.3

Bloom, H. Shakespeare: the invention of the human 822.3
Bloom, H. The Western canon 809
Boyce, C. Critical companion to William Shakespeare 822.3
Bryson, B. Shakespeare 822.3
Butler, C. The practical Shakespeare 822.3
Cliff, N. The Shakespeare riots 974.4
Collins, P. The book of William 822.3
Frye, N. Northrop Frye on Shakespeare 822.3
Garber, M. Shakespeare after all 822.3
Garber, M. Shakespeare and modern culture 822.3
Greenblatt, S. J. Will in the world 822.3
The Greenwood companion to Shakespeare 822.3
Heylin, C. So long as men can breathe 822.3
Kermode, F. Shakespeare's language 822.3
Lamb, C. Tales from Shakespeare 822.3
Norwich, J. J. Shakespeare's kings 822.3
Nuttall, A. D. Shakespeare the thinker 822.3
Olsen, K. All things Shakespeare 822.3
The Oxford companion to Shakespeare 822.3
Rasmussen, E. The Shakespeare thefts 822.3
Rosenbaum, R. The Shakespeare wars 822.3
Shakespeare, W. The Columbia dictionary of quotations from Shakespeare 822.3
Shakespeare, W. The complete works 822.3
Shapiro, J. Contested Will 822.3
Shapiro, J. A year in the life of William Shakespeare, 1599 822.3
Stoppard, T. Rosencrantz and Guildenstern are dead 822
Wells, S. W. Shakespeare: for all time 822.3
Wills, G. Verdi's Shakespeare 822.3
Woodward, H. A brave vessel 973.2
Yoshino, K. A thousand times more fair 822.3
SHAKESPEARE, WILLIAM, 1564-1616 — ALLUSIONS
    See also Allusions
SHAKESPEARE, WILLIAM, 1564-1616 — AUTHORSHIP
    See also Authorship
SHAKESPEARE, WILLIAM, 1564-1616 — BIBLIOGRAPHY
    See also Bibliography
SHAKESPEARE, WILLIAM, 1564-1616 — CRITICISM
    See also Criticism
SHAKESPEARE, WILLIAM, 1564-1616 — DICTIONARIES
    See also Encyclopedias and dictionaries
SHAKESPEARE, WILLIAM, 1564-1616 — ETHICS
    See also Ethics
SHAKESPEARE, WILLIAM, 1564-1616 — PSYCHOLOGY
    See also Psychology

D.   **582.1**

The **shrubberies.** Johnson, R.   **811**

SHRUBS

     See also Plants; Trees

Dirr, M. Dirr's Hardy trees and shrubs   **635.9**

Dirr, M. Dirr's trees and shrubs for warm climates   **635.9**

Fisher, K. Taylor's guide to shrubs   **635.9**

The Hillier gardener's guide to trees & shrubs **635.9**

O'Sullivan, P. The homeowner's complete tree & shrub handbook   **635.9**

Symonds, G. W. D. The shrub identification book   **582.1**

SHRUBS—DICTIONARIES

Dirr, M. Dirr's Hardy trees and shrubs   **635.9**

Shteir, Rachel

    The steal   **364.1**

Shubin, Neil

    Your inner fish   **611**

Shugaar, Antony

    Storia della mafia./English   History of the mafia   **364.1**

Shulevitz, Judith

    The Sabbath world   **296.4**

Shulevitz, Uri

    Writing with pictures   **808.06**

Shulman, Alix Kates

    To love what is   **92**

Shulman, Beth

    The betrayal of work   **331.2**

Shulman, Lisa M.

    Lang, A. E. Parkinson's disease   **616.8**

Shulman, Seth

    The telephone gambit   **621.3**

Shultz, Richard H.

    The secret war against Hanoi   **959.704**

Shut out. Bryant, H.   **796.357**

SHYNESS

     See also Emotions

The **Sibley** field guide to birds of Eastern North America. Sibley, D.   **598**

The **Sibley** field guide to birds of Western North America. Sibley, D.   **598**

The **Sibley** guide to bird life & behavior. Sibley, D.   **598**

The **Sibley** guide to birds. Sibley, D.   **598**

The **Sibley** guide to trees. Sibley, D.   **582.16**

Sibley's birding basics. Sibley, D.   **598**

Sibley, David

    The Sibley field guide to birds of Eastern North America   **598**

    The Sibley field guide to birds of Western North America   **598**

    The Sibley guide to bird life & behavior   **598**

    The Sibley guide to birds   **598**

    The Sibley guide to trees   **582.16**

Sibley's birding basics   **598**

Siblin, Eric

    The cello suites   **787.3**

SIBLING RIVALRY

     See also Child psychology; Siblings

SIBLINGS

     See also Family

Harris, S. L. Siblings of children with autism **649**

Scheeres, J. Jesus land   **92**

Siblings of children with autism. Harris, S. L. **649**

SIBLINGS OF PRESIDENTS

Clarke, T. The last campaign   **92**

English, B. Last lion   **92**

Kennedy, E. M. True compass   **92**

Mahoney, R. D. Sons and brothers: the days of Jack and Bobby Kennedy   **92**

Schlesinger, A. M. Robert Kennedy and his times   **92**

Thomas, E. Robert Kennedy   **973.922**

[Sic] Cody, J.   **362.196**

Sichel, Deborah

    Women's moods   **616.89**

Sicherer, Scott H.

    Understanding and managing your child's food allergies   **618.92**

Sicherman, Barbara

    (ed) Notable American women: the modern period   **920.003**

SICK

     See also Handicapped

Filene, P. G. In the arms of others   **179.7**

Gunther, J. Death be not proud   **92**

Lown, B. The lost art of healing   **610**

Reiner, J. The man who couldn't eat   **92**

Weiner, J. His brother's keeper   **616.8**

Whitehouse, B. The match   **92**

SICK—PRAYERS

     See also Prayers

SICKLE CELL ANEMIA

Bloom, M. Understanding sickle cell disease **616.1**

SICKNESS *See* Diseases

Side effects. Allen, W.   **817**

Sides, Hampton

    Blood and thunder   **978**

    Ghost soldiers   **940.54**

    Hellhound on his trail   **364.152**

SIDING (BUILDING MATERIALS)

Black & Decker Corp. The complete guide to roofing, siding & trim   **695**

Sidney Poitier. Goudsouzian, A.   **92**

Siegal, Allan

    The New York times manual of style and usage **808**

Siegel, Barbara

    Siegel, S. The encyclopedia of Hollywood **791.43**

Siegel, Bernie S.

    Prescriptions for living   **158**

See also Color printing; Stencil work

Silko, Leslie

Storyteller   818

The turquoise ledge   92

SILKWORMS

See also Beneficial insects; Insects; Moths

Silone, Ignazio, 1900-1978 (Italian novelist and essayist)

About

Pugliese, S. G. Bitter spring   92

SILVER

See also Chemical elements; Precious metals

The **silver** spoon.   641.5

Silver, Alain

(ed) Film noir   791.43

Silver, Brian L.

The ascent of science   303.48

Silver, Daniel B.

Refuge in hell   362.1

Silver, Julie K.

After cancer treatment   616.99

Silver, Marc

Breast cancer husband   616.99

Silverman, Debora

Van Gogh and Gauguin   759

Silverman, Kathy Kirtland

Marrs, R. P. Dr. Richard Marrs' fertility book   616.6

Silverman, Kenneth

Begin again   92

Edgar A. Poe   92

Lightning man   621.383

Silverman, Sharon Hernes

Basic crocheting   746.43

Silverton, Nancy

A twist of the wrist   641.5

SILVERWORK

See also Art metalwork; Metalwork; Silver

Silvey, Anita

100 best books for children   011.6

Simic, Charles

Master of disguises   811

Selected early poems   811

That little something   811

The voice at 3:00 a.m   811

Simmons, Bill

The book of basketball   796.323

Simmons, Rachel

Odd girl out   305.23

Simon Wiesenthal. Pick, H.   940.53

Simon Wiesenthal. Segev, T.   92

Simon, Daniel

(ed) Hoffman, A. The best of Abbie Hoffman   303.4

(ed) Vonnegut, K. A man without a country   814

Simon, James F.

What kind of nation   342

Simon, Neil

Brighton Beach memoirs   812

The collected plays of Neil Simon   812

Lost in Yonkers   812

The play goes on   812

Rewrites   812

Simone de Beauvoir. Bair, D.   848

Simone Weil. Gray, F. d. P.   194

Simons, Daniel

(jt. auth) Chabris, C. The invisible gorilla   153.7

Simons, Robin

Greenspan, S. I. The child with special needs   362.1

SIMPLE MACHINES

See also Machinery; Mechanical movements; Mechanics

The **simple** science of flight. Tennekes, H.   629.132

The **simple** truth. Levine, P.   811

SIMPLICITY

See also Conduct of life

Coyne, K. Making it   640.73

Simply Einstein. Wolfson, R.   530.1

Simpson, Brooks D.

(ed) The Civil War   973.7

Simpson, Colton

Inside the Crips   364

Simpson, J. A.

(ed) The Oxford English dictionary   423

Simpson, John W.

Dam!   363.6

Simpson, Louis Aston Marantz

The owner of the house   811

Simpson, William Kelly

Smith, W. S. The art and architecture of ancient Egypt   709.3

Sims, Marsha

Felton, S. Organizing your day   650.1

Sims, Michael

Apollo's fire   529

SIMULATION GAMES

See also Game theory

SIMULATION GAMES IN EDUCATION

See also Education; Educational games; Game theory

Sin. Anderson, G. A.   241

SIN

See also Ethics; Good and evil; Theology

Anderson, G. A. Sin   241

Jacobs, A. Original sin   233

SIN—BIBLICAL TEACHING

Anderson, G. A. Sin   241

SIN—CHRISTIANITY

Anderson, G. A. Sin   241

Sin in the Second City. Abbott, K.   977.3

SIN, ORIGINAL—HISTORY OF DOCTRINES

Jacobs, A. Original sin   233

SIN, ORIGINAL, IN LITERATURE

Jacobs, A. Original sin   233

SINGLE WOMEN
> *See also* Single people; Women

SINGLE-PARENT FAMILIES
Winik, M. The lunch-box chronicles   **306.85**

SINGLE-PARENT FAMILIES
> *See also* Family

The **singularity** is near. Kurzweil, R.   **153.9**

Sinister resonance. Toop, D.   **781.1**

SINO-JAPANESE CONFLICT, 1937-1945
Chang, I. The rape of Nanking   **951.04**
Hicks, G. The comfort women   **940.54**
Tuchman, B. W. Stilwell and the American experi-
ence in China, 1911-45   **327**

**SINO-JAPANESE CONFLICT, 1937-1945—
PERSONAL NARRATIVES**
Hicks, G. The comfort women   **940.54**

Sinton, Nan
Michener, D. Taylor's guide to ground covers **635.9**

Sir Banister Fletcher's A history of architecture.
Fletcher, B. F.   **720.9**

Sir Gawain and the Green Knight. Gawain and the
Grene Knight (Middle English poem)   **398.2**

SIRIUS
> *See also* Stars

Sirota, David
Back to our future   **973.92**

Sisman, Adam
Boswell's presumptuous task   **828**

Sisson, C. H.
Selected poems   **821**

Sister Aimee: the life of Aimee Semple McPherson.
Epstein, D. M.   **92**

Sister Bernadette's barking dog. Florey, K. B. **428**

Sister in the Band of Brothers. Skiba, K. M. **956.7**

Sister revolutions. Dunn, S.   **973.3**

Sister Wendy's American collection. Beckett,
W.   **709**

SISTERS
> *See also* Siblings; Women

SISTERS (RELIGIOUS) *See* Nuns

SISTERS AND BROTHERS *See* Siblings

The **sisters** antipodes. Alison, J.   **92**
The **sisters** of Sinai. Soskice, J. M.   **92**
The **sisters** Rosensweig. Wasserstein, W.   **812**
The **sisters** who would be queen. De Lisle, L. **920**

SIT-INS FOR CIVIL RIGHTS *See* Civil rights
demonstrations

Sitting Bull. Yenne, B.   **92**

Sitting Bull: the life and times of an American patriot. Utley, R. M.   **92**

Sivan, Emmanuel
Almond, G. A. Strong religion   **200.9**

**Sivananda Yoga Vedanta Center (London, Eng-
land)**
Yoga   **613.7**
Yoga mind & body   **294.5**

SIX DAY WAR, 1967 *See* Israel-Arab War, 1967

Six days of war. Oren, M.   **956.04**
Six degrees. Lynas, M.   **551.6**
Six degrees of separation. Guare, J.   **812**
Six easy pieces. Feynman, R. P.   **530**
Six frigates. Toll, I. W.   **359**
Six modern plagues and how we are causing them.
Walters, M. J.   **614.4**
The **six** wives of Henry VIII. Weir, A.   **942.05**
Six wives: the queens of Henry VIII. Starkey,
D.   **942.05**
Six-legged soldiers. Lockwood, J. A.   **358**
The **sixteen** satires. Juvenal   **877**

SIXTEENTH CENTURY
Great events from history, The Renaissance & early
modern era, 1454-1600   **909**
The **sixties**. Gitlin, T.   **973.922**
The **Sixties**. Diski, J.   **92**

SIZE
> *See also* Concepts; Perception

Cohen, S. Normal at any cost   **618.92**

SIZE AND SHAPE *See* Shape; Size
Size matters. Hall, S. S.   **612.6**
Sizwe's test. Steinberg, J.   **362.1**

SJOGREN'S SYNDROME
Rumpf, T. P. The Sjogren's syndrome survival
guide   **616.97**

SJOGREN'S SYNDROME—TREATMENT
Rumpf, T. P. The Sjogren's syndrome survival
guide   **616.97**
The **Sjogren's** syndrome survival guide. Rumpf, T.
P.   **616.97**

SKATEBOARDING
Connolly, K. M. Double take   **92**
Skating on stilts. Baker, S. A.   **363.32**

SKELETAL REMAINS *See* Anthropometry

Skemp, Vicki
Kavaya, K. Community quilts   **746.46**
The **skeptic:** the life of H.L. Mencken. Teachout,
T.   **92**

SKEPTICISM
> *See also* Free thought; Philosophy; Rational-
> ism

Keller, T. J. The reason for God   **239**

Skerrett, P. J.
Willett, W. Eat, drink and be healthy   **613.2**
Sketches from a life. Kennan, G. F.   **92**
The **sketches** of Louisa May Alcott. Alcott, L.
M.   **818**

Skiba, Katherine M.
Sister in the Band of Brothers   **956.7**

Skidmore, Thomas E.
Brazil   **981**

SKIERS
Connolly, K. M. Double take   **92**
Kurson, R. Crashing through   **92**

Slave songs of the United States. Ware, C. P. **781.62**

SLAVE TRADE

See also International law; Slavery

Berlin, I. The making of African America	**305.8**
DeWolf, T. N. Inheriting the trade	**326**
Gallay, A. The Indian slave trade	**326**
Hartman, S. V. Lose your mother	**323**
Johnson, W. Soul by soul	**326**
Postma, J. The Atlantic slave trade	**306.3**
Segal, R. Islam's Black slaves	**306.3**

SLAVE TRADE—AFRICA—HISTORY

Postma, J. The Atlantic slave trade	**306.3**

SLAVE TRADE—AMERICA—HISTORY

Postma, J. The Atlantic slave trade	**306.3**

SLAVE TRADE—CUBA—HISTORY

DeWolf, T. N. Inheriting the trade	**326**

SLAVE TRADE—EUROPE—HISTORY

Postma, J. The Atlantic slave trade	**306.3**

SLAVE TRADE—GHANA

Hartman, S. V. Lose your mother	**323**

SLAVE TRADE—GREAT BRITAIN—HISTO-RY—17TH CENTURY

Gallay, A. The Indian slave trade	**326**

SLAVE TRADE—MAPS

Eltis, D. Atlas of the transatlantic slave trade	**381**

SLAVE TRADE—MASSACHUSETTS

Manegold, C. Ten Hills Farm	**974.4**

SLAVE TRADE—NEW ENGLAND—HISTORY

DeWolf, T. N. Inheriting the trade	**326**

SLAVE TRADE—SOUTHERN STATES

Gallay, A. The Indian slave trade	**326**

SLAVE TRADE—SOUTHERN STATES—HIS-TORY—17TH CENTURY

Gallay, A. The Indian slave trade	**326**

SLAVE TRADE—UNITED STATES

Berlin, I. The making of African America	**305.8**

SLAVE TRADE—WEST AFRICA—HISTORY

DeWolf, T. N. Inheriting the trade	**326**

SLAVE TRADERS

DeWolf, T. N. Inheriting the trade	**326**

SLAVEHOLDERS

Ball, E. Slaves in the family	**975.7**

Slavemaster president. Dusinberre, W. **973.6**

SLAVERY

Baker, J. F. The Washingtons of Wessyngton Plantation	**920**
Desmond, A. J. Darwin's sacred cause	**92**
Hochschild, A. Bury the chains	**326**
Miller, W. L. Arguing about slavery	**973.5**
Segal, R. Islam's Black slaves	**306.3**
Stark, R. For the glory of God	**201**
Wise, S. M. Though the heavens may fall	**342**

SLAVERY—CONSTITUTIONAL HISTORY

Fredrickson, G. M. Big enough to be inconsistent	**973.7**

SLAVERY—HISTORY

Blumrosen, A. W. Slave nation	**973.3**
Colaiaco, J. A. Frederick Douglass and the Fourth of July	**973.7**
Egerton, D. R. Death or liberty	**973.3**
Encyclopedia of slave resistance and rebellion	**326**
Horton, J. O. Slavery and the making of America	**326**
Jordan, D. White cargo	**326**
White, S. The sounds of slavery	**326**

SLAVERY—ISLAMIC COUNTRIES—HISTORY

Segal, R. Islam's Black slaves	**306.3**

SLAVERY—LAW AND LEGISLATION

Schneider, D. Slavery in America	**326**
Wise, S. M. Though the heavens may fall	**342**

SLAVERY—LEGAL HISTORY—GREAT BRITAIN

Wise, S. M. Though the heavens may fall	**342**

SLAVERY—LOUISIANA—NEW ORLEANS

Rasmussen, D. American uprising	**976.3**

SLAVERY—LOUISIANA—NEW ORLEANS—HISTORY—19TH CENTURY

Johnson, W. Soul by soul	**326**

SLAVERY—MASSACHUSETTS

Manegold, C. Ten Hills Farm	**974.4**

SLAVERY—MISSISSIPPI—HISTORY—19TH CENTURY

Dusinberre, W. Slavemaster president	**973.6**

SLAVERY—POETRY

Young, K. Ardency	**811**

SLAVERY—SOCIAL ASPECTS

White, S. The sounds of slavery	**326**

SLAVERY—SOUTHERN STATES

Fox-Genovese, E. Within the plantation household	**305.4**

SLAVERY—TENNESSEE—HISTORY—19TH CENTURY

Dusinberre, W. Slavemaster president	**973.6**

SLAVERY—UNITED STATES

Ball, E. Slaves in the family	**975.7**
Berlin, I. Generations of captivity	**326**
Blackmon, D. A. Slavery by another name	**305.8**
Blight, D. W. A slave no more	**326**
Blumrosen, A. W. Slave nation	**973.3**
Bordewich, F. M. Bound for Canaan	**973.7**
Brackman, B. Facts & fabrications: unraveling the history of quilts and slavery	**746.46**
The Causes of the Civil War	**973.7**
Colaiaco, J. A. Frederick Douglass and the Fourth of July	**973.7**
DeWolf, T. N. Inheriting the trade	**326**
Dusinberre, W. Slavemaster president	**973.6**
Egerton, D. R. Death or liberty	**973.3**
Encyclopedia of slave resistance and rebellion	**326**
Foner, E. The fiery trial	**973.7**
Foner, E. Forever free	**973.8**

Moondust 920

Smith, Andrew F.

(ed) The Oxford encyclopedia of food and drink in America 641.3

Smith, Bonnie G.

(ed) The Oxford encyclopedia of women in world history 305.4

Smith, Brian H.

Kolpan, S. Exploring wine 641.2

Smith, Bruce

Devotions 811

Smith, C. Lavett

National Audubon Society field guide to tropical marine fishes of the Caribbean, the Gulf of Mexico, Florida, the Bahamas, and Bermuda 597

Smith, Charles Sprague

(comp) American hymns old and new 782.27

Smith, Charles W. G.

The beginner's guide to edible herbs 635

Smith, Chris

Russell, T. The Penguin guide to blues recordings 781.643

Smith, Claire Bidwell

The rules of inheritance 616.99

Smith, Darren L.

(ed) Counties USA 352.13

Smith, David James

Young Mandela 92

Smith, Deirdre

Smith, D. A decade of hope 974.7

Smith, Dennis

A decade of hope 974.7

Report from ground zero 363.34

Smith, Douglas W.

Decade of the wolf 599.77

Smith, Edward C.

The vegetable gardener's bible 635

The vegetable gardener's container bible 635

Smith, George E.

(ed) The Cambridge companion to Newton 530

Smith, Gordon T.

(ed) Zondervan dictionary of Christian spirituality 248

Smith, Gregory White

(jt. auth) Naifeh, S. Van Gogh 759.9

Smith, Harriet Elinor

(ed) Autobiography of Mark Twain 92

Smith, Hedrick

The power game 320

Smith, Helmut Walser

The butcher's tale 305.892

Smith, Jacqueline

(ed) The Facts on File dictionary of earth science 550

Smith, James D.

(ed) Zondervan dictionary of Christian spiritual-

ity 248

Smith, Jane Idleman

Islam in America 297.092

Smith, Jane S.

The garden of invention 92

Smith, Janna Malamud

My father is a book 92

A potent spell 306.8

Smith, Jean Edward

Eisenhower 973.921

FDR 92

Grant 973.8

John Marshall 347

Smith, Jennie Erin

Stolen world 364.1

Smith, Jeremy N.

Growing a garden city 635

Smith, Jessie Carney

(ed) Black firsts: 4,000 ground-breaking and pioneering historical events 305.8

(ed) Notable black American men, book II 920.003

(ed) Notable black American women, book I 920.003

(ed) Notable black American women, Book III 920.003

Smith, Joel

Edward Steichen: the early years 779

Smith, John David

(ed) Douglass, F. My bondage and my freedom 973.8

Smith, Joseph, 1805-1844 (American Mormon leader)

About

Bushman, R. L. Mormonism 289.3

Smith, Josh

Nothdurft, W. E. The lost dinosaurs of Egypt 567.9

Smith, Kerry L.

Encyclopedia of indie rock 781.66

Smith, Larry

(ed) Iwo Jima 940.54

(ed) The moment 818

Smith, Laurence C.

The world in 2050 304.2

Smith, Lyn

Remembering, voices of the holocaust 940.53

Smith, Merril D.

(ed) Encyclopedia of rape 362.883

Smith, Michael Ernest

The Aztecs 972

Smith, Michael G.

(ed) The Art of natural building 690

Smith, Norris

(ed) Homeland security 363.32

Smith, P. Allen

P. Allen Smith's bringing the garden indoors 747

Smith, P. D.

Vickery, A. Behind closed doors   **306.8**

SOCIAL CRITICS

Commager, H. S. The American mind   **973**

Devlin, K. J. Goodbye, Descartes   **128**

Heilbroner, R. L. The worldly philosophers   **330.1**

Hooks, B. Belonging   **92**

Hooks, B. Wounds of passion   **92**

Isserman, M. The other American: the life of Michael Harrington   **300**

Kozol, J. Letters to a young teacher   **371.1**

My life as author and editor   **818**

Queenan, J. Closing time   **92**

Rapoport, R. Citizen Moore   **92**

Rodgers, M. E. Mencken   **92**

Said, E. W. Out of place   **973**

Teachout, T. The skeptic: the life of H.L. Mencken   **92**

Wills, G. Outside looking in   **92**

SOCIAL CUSTOMS *See* Manners and customs

SOCIAL DARWINISM

Werth, B. Banquet at Delmonico's   **303.4**

SOCIAL DEMOCRACY *See* Socialism

SOCIAL DEVIANCE *See* Deviant behavior

SOCIAL DISTINCTIONS *See* Social classes

SOCIAL DRINKING *See* Drinking of alcoholic beverages

SOCIAL ECOLOGY *See* Human ecology

SOCIAL EQUALITY *See* Equality

SOCIAL ETHICS

    See also Ethics; Sociology

Callahan, D. The cheating culture   **174**

Corning, P. The fair society   **303.3**

Moeller The moral fool   **171**

SOCIAL EVOLUTION *See* Social change

SOCIAL EVOLUTION—PHILOSOPHY

Wilson, E. O. The social conquest of earth **599.93**

SOCIAL GROUP WORK

    See also Counseling; Social work

SOCIAL GROUPS

    See also Sociology

Robbins, A. The geeks shall inherit the Earth

Rosenberg, T. Join the club   **303.3**

SOCIAL HISTORY

Burns, E. The spirits of America   **394.1**

Ekirch, A. R. At day's close   **306.4**

Encyclopedia of plague and pestilence   **614.4**

SOCIAL HISTORY—MEDIEVAL, 500-1500

Orme, N. Medieval children   **305.23**

SOCIAL HISTORY—SOURCES

Daily life through world history in primary documents   **909**

The **social** history of the Third Reich. Aycoberry, P.   **943.086**

SOCIAL HYGIENE *See* Public health; Sexual hygiene

SOCIAL IDENTITY *See* Group identity

SOCIAL INSURANCE *See* Social security

Social intelligence. Goleman, D.   **158**

SOCIAL INTERACTION—MATHEMATICAL MODELS

Baker, S. The numerati   **303.4**

SOCIAL ISOLATION *See* Loneliness

SOCIAL ISOLATION—UNITED STATES

Olds, J. The lonely American   **302.5**

Social issues in America.   **361**

SOCIAL JUSTICE

    See also Equality; Justice

Corning, P. The fair society   **303.3**

Sowell, T. The quest for cosmic justice   **303.3**

SOCIAL JUSTICE—UNITED STATES

Shaw, R. Beyond the fields   **331.8**

SOCIAL JUSTICE—UNITED STATES—HISTORY

Duberman, M. B. A saving remnant   **92**

SOCIAL LEARNING *See* Socialization

SOCIAL LIFE AND CUSTOMS *See* Manners and customs

The **social** lives of dogs. Thomas, E. M.   **636.7**

SOCIAL MEDIA

Shirky, C. Cognitive surplus   **303.4**

SOCIAL MEDICINE

    See also Medicine; Public health; Public welfare; Sociology

Elliott, C. Better than well   **306.4**

Encyclopedia of plague and pestilence   **614.4**

Sommer, A. Getting what we deserve   **362.1**

SOCIAL MEDICINE—HISTORY

Porter, R. The greatest benefit to mankind   **610**

SOCIAL MEDICINE—UNITED STATES

Elliott, C. Better than well   **306.4**

Fadiman, A. The spirit catches you and you fall down   **306.4**

SOCIAL MOBILITY

Pickett, K. The spirit level   **305**

SOCIAL MOBILITY—UNITED STATES

Murray, C. Coming apart   **305.8**

SOCIAL MOVEMENTS

    See also Social conditions; Social psychology

Hayden, T. The long sixties   **973.92**

Nader, R. The good fight   **323**

Ostertag, B. People's movements, people's press   **071**

Tapper, J. Craft activism   **745.5**

SOCIAL MOVEMENTS—UNITED STATES

Nader, R. The good fight   **323**

SOCIAL NETWORKING

Charnock, E. E-habits   **302.23**

Fertik, M. Wild west 2.0   **659.2**

Kirkpatrick, D. The Facebook effect   **338.7**

Mainwaring, S. We first   **658.8**

Penenberg, A. L. Viral loop   **303.4**

Shirky, C. Cognitive surplus   **303.4**

Hernon, P. Assessing service quality **025.5**

SOCIAL SETTLEMENTS

See also Charities; Industrial welfare; Social work

SOCIAL SKILLS

See also Interpersonal relations; Life skills

SOCIAL SKILLS IN CHILDREN

Elman, N. M. The unwritten rules of friendship **649**

SOCIAL STANDING *See* Social status

SOCIAL STATUS

See also Social psychology

Brooks, D. The social animal **305.5**

SOCIAL STATUS—ENGLAND

Vickery, A. Behind closed doors **306.8**

SOCIAL STATUS—UNITED STATES

Epstein, J. Snobbery: the American version **305.5**

SOCIAL STRUCTURE—GREAT BRITAIN

Nicolson, J. The perfect summer **942**

SOCIAL STUDIES *See* Geography; History; Social sciences

SOCIAL SURVEYS

See also Social sciences; Surveys

SOCIAL SYSTEMS

See also Sociology; System theory

SOCIAL VALUES

See also Values

Bork, R. H. Slouching towards Gomorrah **306**

Carter, J. Our endangered values **306**

Global values 101 **170**

Haidt, J. The righteous mind **201**

Moeller The moral fool **171**

Wann, D. The new normal **306**

Westheimer, R. The value of family **306.85**

SOCIAL VALUES—UNITED STATES

Carter, J. Our endangered values **306**

Cose, E. The envy of the world **305.38**

Gladwell, M. What the dog saw and other adventures **814**

SOCIAL WELFARE *See* Charities; Public welfare; Social problems; Social work

SOCIAL WELFARE LEADERS

Edelman, M. W. Lanterns **92**

Elshtain, J. B. Jane Addams and the dream of American democracy **361.9**

Gibson, W. The miracle worker **812**

Herrmann, D. Helen Keller **92**

Keller, H. Helen Keller: selected writings **92**

Keller, H. The story of my life **92**

Knight, L. W. Jane Addams **92**

Oates, S. B. A woman of valor: Clara Barton and the Civil War **92**

Tough, P. Whatever it takes **362.7**

SOCIAL WORK

Ackerman, D. A slender thread **362.28**

Reef, C. Poverty in America **362.5**

SOCIAL WORK WITH THE ELDERLY

See also Elderly; Social work

SOCIALISM

See also Collectivism; Economics; Political science

Berlin, I. The sense of reality **190**

Sayrafiezadeh, S. When skateboards will be free **92**

Tuchman, B. W. The proud tower **909.82**

SOCIALISM—SOVIET UNION

Zubok, V. Zhivago's children **305.5**

SOCIALIST LEADERS

Duberman, M. B. A saving remnant **92**

SOCIALISTS—UNITED STATES—BIOGRAPHY

Isserman, M. The other American: the life of Michael Harrington **300**

SOCIALITES

Bowles, H. Jacqueline Kennedy **92**

Buckley, C. T. Losing Mum and Pup **92**

Cordery, S. A. Alice **92**

Davis, J. H. Jacqueline Bouvier **92**

Foreman, A. Georgiana, Duchess of Devonshire **941.07**

Galbraith, J. K. Name-dropping **973.9**

Gimbel, W. Havana dreams **972.910**

Leaming, B. Mrs. Kennedy **973.922**

SOCIALIZATION

See also Acculturation; Child rearing; Education; Sociology

Elman, N. M. The unwritten rules of friendship **649**

Sheehy, G. New passages **305.24**

SOCIALLY HANDICAPPED

See also Handicapped; Social adjustment

SOCIALLY HANDICAPPED CHILDREN

Coles, R. Children of crisis **305.23**

Kozol, J. Amazing grace **362.7**

Kozol, J. Savage inequalities **371.9**

SOCIALLY HANDICAPPED CHILDREN

See also Handicapped children; Socially handicapped

SOCIETIES—DIRECTORIES

Encyclopedia of associations **061**

The Europa world of learning **060**

SOCIETY—RELIGIOUS ASPECTS *See* Religion and sociology

SOCIETY AND ART *See* Art and society

SOCIETY AND LANGUAGE *See* Sociolinguistics

SOCIETY AND RELIGION *See* Religion and sociology

Society for the Study of the Short Story

A Reader's companion to the short story in English **809**

Society of Biblical Literature

The HarperCollins Bible commentary **220.7**

The HarperCollins Bible dictionary **220.3**

SOCIETY OF FRIENDS

Boorstin, D. J. The Americans: The colonial expe-

SPACE LABORATORIES *See* Space stations

SPACE LAW

  See also Astronautics and civilization; International law; Law

SPACE MEDICINE

  See also Medicine; Space biology; Space sciences

SPACE OPTICS

  See also Optics; Space sciences

SPACE PERCEPTION

  Ellard, C. You are here   153.7

SPACE PHOTOGRAPHY

  See also Photography; Photography—Scientific applications

  Benson, M. Far out   778.3

SPACE PLATFORMS *See* Space stations

Space race. Cadbury, D.   629.4

SPACE RACE

  Biddle, W. Dark side of the moon   92

  Brzezinski, M. Red moon rising   629.4

  French, F. In the shadow of the moon   629.45

  Hardesty, V. Epic rivalry   629.4

SPACE RESCUE OPERATIONS

  See also Rescue work

SPACE RESEARCH *See* Outer space—Exploration; Space sciences

Space sciences.   500.5

SPACE SCIENCES

  See also Science

  Cole, K. C. The hole in the universe   530.01

  Space sciences   500.5

SPACE SCIENCES—HISTORY

  Neufeld, M. J. Von Braun   92

SPACE STATIONS

  See also Artificial satellites; Astronautics; Space vehicles

  Space exploration   629

SPACE SURVEILLANCE—UNITED STATES— HISTORY—20TH CENTURY

  Taubman, P. Secret empire   327.12

SPACE TRAVEL *See* Interplanetary voyages; Space flight

SPACE VEHICLE ACCIDENTS

  See also Accidents

SPACE VEHICLES

  See also Rocketry

SPACE VEHICLES—DESIGN

  Biddle, W. Dark side of the moon   92

SPACE VEHICLES—PILOTING

  See also Astronauts; Navigation (Astronautics)

SPACE VEHICLES—THERMODYNAMICS

  See also Thermodynamics

SPACE WARFARE

  See also Outer space; War

SPACE WEAPONS

  See also Military weapons; Space warfare

Space, in chains. Kasischke, L.   811

Spacek, Sissy

  My extraordinary ordinary life   791.43

SPACEK, SISSY

  Spacek, S. My extraordinary ordinary life   791.43

Spaeth, Paul J.

  (ed) A thing that is   811

Spaethling, Robert

  (ed) Mozart, W. A. Mozart's letters, Mozart's life   780

SPAGHETTI WESTERNS

  Fagen, H. The encyclopedia of westerns   791.43

Spagna, Ana Maria

  Test ride on the Sunnyland bus   323.1

SPAIN—DESCRIPTION

  Hemingway, E. The dangerous summer   791.8

  Stewart, C. Driving over lemons   946.083

SPAIN—HISTORY—1898, WAR OF 1898 *See* Spanish-American War, 1898

Spain: a history.   946

SPANISH AMERICAN LITERATURE *See* American literature (Spanish); Latin American literature

SPANISH COOKING

  Andres, J. Tapas   641.8

  Ortega, S. 1080 recipes   641.5

The **Spanish** Inquisition. Perez, J.   272

The **Spanish** Inquisition. Kamen, H.   272

SPANISH LANGUAGE

  See also Language and languages; Romance languages

SPANISH LANGUAGE—DICTIONARIES

  Houghton Mifflin Co. The Concise American Heritage Spanish dictionary   463

SPANISH LANGUAGE—DICTIONARIES— ENGLISH

  Houghton Mifflin Co. The Concise American Heritage Spanish dictionary   463

SPANISH LITERATURE

  See also Literature; Romance literature

SPANISH LITERATURE—HISTORY AND CRITICISM

  The Cambridge history of Spanish literature   860

SPANISH POETRY—COLLECTIONS

  The Penguin book of Spanish verse   861

SPANISH-AMERICAN WAR, 1898

  See also Spain—History; United States— History—1865-1898; United States—History—1898-1919

  Thomas, E. The war lovers   973.8

  Zimmermann, W. First great triumph   973

SPANISH-AMERICAN WAR, 1898—CAUSES

  Thomas, E. The war lovers   973.8

Spark, Muriel

  Poems All the poems of Muriel Spark   821

SPORTS DRAMA (RADIO PROGRAMS)
See also Radio programs

SPORTS DRAMA (TELEVISION PROGRAMS)
See also Television programs

SPORTS FOR THE HANDICAPPED
See also Handicapped

SPORTS FOR WOMEN
See also Sports

Sports history and society [series]
Levine, P. Ellis Island to Ebbet's Field   **796**

SPORTS IN TELEVISION *See* Television broadcasting of sports

SPORTS JOURNALISM
Deford, F. Over time   **070.449**

SPORTS LITERATURE—UNITED STATES
The Best American sports writing of the century   **796**

SPORTS MEDICINE
See also Medical care; Medicine

SPORTS MEDICINE—ENCYCLOPEDIAS
Oakes, E. H. The encyclopedia of sports medicine   **617.1**

SPORTS RECORDS
See also Sports
Brenkus, J. The perfection point   **612**

SPORTS STORIES, AMERICAN
The Best American sports writing of the century   **796**

SPORTS TEAMS
See also Sports

SPORTS TOURNAMENTS
See also Contests; Sports

SPORTS TRAINERS
Atlas, T. Atlas   **92**
Remnick, D. Reporting   **814**
Sports: the complete visual reference. Fortin, F.   **796**

SPORTSCASTERS
Barkley, C. I may be wrong but I doubt it   **796.323**
Bloom, J. There you have it   **92**
Dent, J. Resurrection   **796.332**
Dierker, L. This ain't brain surgery   **796**
Dutton, D. G. The batterer   **362.82**
Gates, H. L. Thirteen ways of looking at a black man   **920.71**
Geis, G. Crimes of the century   **345**
Halberstam, D. The teammates   **796**
Kindred, D. Sound and fury   **796**
Life stories   **920**
Ribowsky, M. Howard Cosell   **92**
White, B. Uppity   **92**
Will, G. F. Men at work   **796.35**

SPORTSCASTERS—UNITED STATES—BIOGRAPHY
Dierker, L. This ain't brain surgery   **796**

SPORTSMANSHIP
See also Human behavior; Sports

Bradley, B. Values of the game   **796.323**

SPORTSWRITERS
Angell, R. Let me finish   **070**
Blount, R. Alphabet juice   **817**
Blount, R. Be sweet   **818**
Dawidoff, N. The crowd sounds happy   **92**
George, being George   **92**
Honig, D. The fifth season   **92**
Rosen, C. Crazy basketball   **796.323**
Watman, M. Chasing the white dog   **363.4**
Weber, B. As they see 'em   **796.357**
Wertheim, L. J. Blood in the cage   **92**

Spotila, James R.
Sea turtles   **597.92**

Spoto, Donald
The dark side of genius   **791.43**
The kindness of strangers: the life of Tennessee Williams   **92**
Notorious   **92**
Spellbound by beauty   **92**

SPOTTING (CLEANING)
Friedman, V. M. Field guide to stains   **648**

SPOUSES *See* Husbands; Wives

SPOUSES OF HEADS OF STATE—GERMANY—BIOGRAPHY
Gortemaker, H. B. Eva Braun   **92**

SPOUSES OF PROMINENT PERSONS
Berkin, C. Civil War wives   **920**
Buckley, C. T. Losing Mum and Pup   **92**
Conant, J. A covert affair   **940.54**
Flanders, J. A circle of sisters   **920**
Foreman, A. Georgiana, Duchess of Devonshire   **941.07**
Fox, J. Five sisters   **975.5**
Gabriel, M. Love and capital   **92**
Hazleton, L. After the prophet   **297**
Hertog, S. Anne Morrow Lindbergh   **92**
Life stories   **920**
Lindbergh, R. Under a wing   **92**
Mailer, N. C. A ticket to the circus   **92**
Mallon, T. Mrs. Paine's garage and the murder of John F. Kennedy   **364.1**
McDougal, S. The woman who wouldn't talk   **973.929**
Meade, M. Lonelyhearts   **92**
Mitchell, A. Talking back—to presidents, dictators, and assorted scoundrels   **92**
Oates, J. C. A widow's story   **92**
Persico, J. E. Franklin and Lucy   **920**
Rickford, R. J. Betty Shabazz: a remarkable story of survival and faith before and after Malcolm X   **92**
Scovell, J. Oona   **791.43**
Tate, M. J. Critical companion to F. Scott Fitzgerald   **813**
Urrutia, M. My life with Pablo Neruda   **92**

(ed) The Oxford book of war poetry | **808.81**

Staloff, Darren

Hamilton, Adams, Jefferson | **973.4**

STAMINA, PHYSICAL *See* Physical fitness

STAMMERING *See* Speech disorders

Stamolis, Tony

Frezno | **779**

STAMP COLLECTING

See also Collectors and collecting

Stampp, Kenneth M.

(ed) The Causes of the Civil War | **973.7**

Stan Lee's How to draw comics. Lee, S. | **741.5**

Stand up, fight back. Dionne, E. J. | **306**

STAND-UP COMEDY—UNITED STATES— HISTORY—20TH CENTURY

Nachman, G. Seriously funny | **792.7**

Standage, Tom

An edible history of humanity | **394.1**

A history of the world in 6 glasses | **394.1**

Standard and Poor's register of corporations, directors, and executives. | **338.7**

The **standard** code of parliamentary procedure. Sturgis, A. | **060.4**

Standard handbook for electrical engineers. | **621.3**

Standard handbook of electronic engineering. | **621.381**

STANDARD OF LIVING *See* Cost and standard of living

STANDARD OF VALUE *See* Money

Standard operating procedure. Gourevitch, P. | **956.7**

STANDARD TIME *See* Time

Standiford, Les

(jt. auth) Matthews, J. Bringing Adam home | **364.1**

Standing in the light. Russell, S. A. | **211**

Standring, Susan

(ed) Gray's anatomy | **611**

Stanford, Craig B.

Bearzi, M. Beautiful minds | **599.8**

Stanford, David

(ed) Kerouac, J. Jack Kerouac and Allen Ginsberg | **92**

The **Stanislavski** system. Moore, S. | **792**

Stanislavsky, Konstantin

An actor's work | **792**

Creating a role | **792**

Stanley. Jeal, T. | **92**

Stanley Kubrick. LoBrutto, V. | **92**

Stanley Kubrick, director. Walker, A. | **791.43**

Stanley, Mary J.

Managing library employees | **023**

Stanley, Ralph

Man of constant sorrow | **92**

Stannard, Martin

Muriel Spark | **92**

Stannard, Russell

The end of discovery | **501**

Stanovich, Keith E.

What intelligence tests miss | **153.9**

Stansfield, Charles A.

Martinelli, P. A. Haunted New Jersey | **133.1**

Haunted Arizona | **133.1**

Haunted Jersey shore | **133.1**

Haunted Maine | **133.1**

Haunted northern California | **133.1**

Haunted Ohio | **133.1**

Haunted Southern California | **133.1**

Haunted Vermont | **133.1**

Stanton, Elizabeth Cady, 1815-1902 (American suffragist)

About

Ulrich, L. Well-behaved women seldom make history | **305.4**

Stanton, Maureen

Killer stuff and tons of money | **381**

Stanton, Tom

Road to Cooperstown | **92**

Star. Biskind, P. | **92**

Star dust. Bidart, F. | **811**

The **star** guide. Kerrod, R. | **523.8**

The **star** thrower. Eiseley, L. C. | **818**

STAR WARS (BALLISTIC MISSILE DEFENSE SYSTEM) *See* Strategic Defense Initiative

STAR WARS FILMS

See also Motion pictures; Science fiction films

Starbucked. Clark, T. | **338**

The **Starbucks** experience. Michelli, J. A. | **658**

Stardust. Gribbin, J. R. | **523**

Stardust melody: the life and music of Hoagy Carmichael. Sudhalter, R. | **782**

Stargardt, Nicholas

Witnesses of war | **940.53**

Stargazing with binoculars. Scagell, R. | **523.8**

Stark, Peter

The last empty places | **973**

Stark, Rodney

For the glory of God | **201**

One true God | **201**

Stark, Steven D.

Meet the Beatles | **920**

Starkey, David

Six wives: the queens of Henry VIII | **942.05**

Starks, Glenn L.

How your government really works | **320.4**

Starlanyl, Devin

Fibromyalgia & chronic myofascial pain syndrome | **616.7**

Starobin, Paul

After America | **973.91**

Starr, Douglas

The killer of little shepherds | **364.152**

Starr, Paul

Remedy and reaction | **362.1**

STATUES *See* Monuments; Sculpture

STATURE

Cohen, S. Normal at any cost   **618.92**

STATURE, SHORT—PSYCHOLOGICAL AS-PECTS

Hall, S. S. Size matters   **612.6**

STATURE, SHORT—SOCIAL ASPECTS

Hall, S. S. Size matters   **612.6**

STATUS, SOCIAL *See* Social status

Stauffer, Andrew M.

(ed) Browning, R. Robert Browning's poetry   **821**

Stavans, Ilan

(ed) Neruda, P. The poetry of Pablo Neruda   **861**

(ed) The Norton anthology of Latino literature   **810**

Staying tuned. Schorr, D.   **070**

Stead, Christina, 1902-1983 (Australian novelist, short story writer and translator)

         About

Jarrell, R. No other book   **809**

Steak. Schatzker, M.   **641.6**

The **steal.** Shteir, R.   **364.1**

Steal away. Wright, C. D.   **811**

STEALING *See* Theft

Stealing history. Atwood, R.   **364.1**

Stealing Jesus. Bawer, B.   **277**

Stealing Lincoln's body. Craughwell, T. J.   **973.7**

Stealing MySpace. Angwin, J.   **338.7**

STEAM

    See also Heat; Power (Mechanics); Water

STEAM ENGINEERING

    See also Engineering

STEAM ENGINES

Jensen, J. Steam: an enduring legacy   **625.2**

STEAM LOCOMOTIVES

    See also Locomotives

STEAM NAVIGATION

    See also Navigation; Steam engineering; Transportation

STEAM TURBINES

    See also Steam engines; Steam navigation; Turbines

Steam: an enduring legacy. Jensen, J.   **625.2**

STEAMBOATS

    See also Boats and boating; Naval architecture; Ocean travel; Shipbuilding; Ships

STEAMBOATS—HISTORY

Sale, K. The fire of his genius: Robert Fulton and the American dream   **620**

Stiles, T. J. The first tycoon   **92**

The **steamy** kitchen cookbook. Hair, J.   **641.5**

Stearns, Jason K.

Dancing in the glory of monsters   **967.51**

Steavenson, Wendell

The weight of a mustard seed   **92**

Stebbins, Robert C.

A field guide to Western reptiles and amphib-

ians   **597.9**

Steegmuller, Francis

Hazzard, S. The ancient shore   **945**

STEEL

    See also Iron; Metalwork

STEEL CONSTRUCTION

    See also Building; Structural engineering

STEEL INDUSTRY

    See also Industries

Rudacille, D. Roots of steel   **338.4**

STEEL INDUSTRY—QUALITY CONTROL

    See also Quality control

STEEL INDUSTRY—TECHNOLOGICAL IN-NOVATIONS

    See also Technological innovations

STEEL INDUSTRY AND TRADE *See* Steel industry

STEEL INDUSTRY AND TRADE—HISTORY

Krass, P. Carnegie   **338.7**

STEEL INDUSTRY AND TRADE—UNITED STATES—HISTORY

Krass, P. Carnegie   **338.7**

Steel, Rodney

Sharks of the world   **597**

Steele, Timothy

(ed) Cunningham, J. V. The poems of J.V. Cunningham   **811**

Steele, Valerie

(ed) Encyclopedia of clothing and fashion   **391**

Steffens, Lincoln

The autobiography of Lincoln Steffens   **92**

STEGOSAURUS

    See also Dinosaurs

Stein on writing. Stein, S.   **808**

Stein, C. Michael

(ed) The encyclopedia of arthritis   **616.7**

Stein, David E.

(ed) Bible/O.T./Pentateuch The contemporary Torah   **222**

Stein, Elissa

Flow   **612.6**

Stein, Gertrude

The autobiography of Alice B. Toklas   **92**

Writings, 1903-1932   **818**

Writings, 1932-1946   **818**

Stein, Howard

(ed) The Best American short plays   **812**

Stein, Marc

(ed) Encyclopedia of lesbian, gay, bisexual, and transgender history in America   **306.76**

Stein, Sally

John Gutmann   **779**

Stein, Sol

How to grow a novel   **808.3**

Stein on writing   **808**

Stein, Stephen J.

The **story** of my father. Miller, S.   92

The **story** of my life. Keller, H.   92

The **story** of painting. Beckett, W.   759

The **story** of philosophy. Durant, W. J.   109

The **story** of philosophy. Magee, B.   190

The **story** of stuff. Leonard, A.   306.4

Storyteller. Silko, L.   818

Storyteller. Sturrock, D.   92

The **storyteller's** daughter. Shah, S.   958.1

STORYTELLING

     See also Children's literature

     Bruchac, J. Our stories remember   970.004

     Flaherty, F. The elements of story   808.5

     Guber, P. Tell to win   658.4

     Seeger, P. Pete Seeger's storytelling book   372.6

     World folklore for storytellers   398

Stott, Carole

     Kerrod, R. Hubble   522

Stott, Rebecca

     Darwin's ghosts   576.8

Stout, Glenn

     (ed) The best American sports writing 2010   796

     Fenway 1912   796.357

Stout, Harry S.

     Upon the altar of the nation : a moral history of the American Civil War   973.7

Stover, Kaite Mediatore

     (jt. auth) Moyer, J. E. The readers' advisory handbook   025.5

Stow, Dorrik A. V.

     Oceans: an illustrated reference   551.46

Stow, Josie

     The African kitchen   641.5

Stowe, Harriet Beecher, 1811-1896 (American novelist)

     About

     Benfey, C. E. G. A summer of hummingbirds   920

     McPherson, J. M. Drawn with the sword   973.7

STRABISMUS

     Barry, S. Fixing my gaze   617.7

Strachan, Hew

     The First World War   940.3

     (ed) World War I   940.3

Strachey, Lytton

     Elizabeth and Essex   92

Straight talk about cosmetic surgery. Perry, A. W.   617.9

Straight talk from Claudia Black. Black, C.   362.29

STRAIN (PSYCHOLOGY) *See* Stress (Psychology)

STRAINS AND STRESSES

     See also Mechanics; Statics; Structural analysis (Engineering)

Strand, Mark

     (ed) 100 great poems of the twentieth century   821

     Barnes, R. Animal logic   779

     (ed) The Making of a poem   821

     Blizzard of one   811

     Man and camel   811

Strange angel. Pendle, G.   92

Strange beauty: Murray Gell-Mann and the revolution in twentieth-century physics. Johnson, G.   530

The **strange** career of Jim Crow. Woodward, C. V.   305.8

Strange days indeed. Wheen, F.   973.92

A **strange** eventful history. Holroyd, M.   92

Strange new worlds. Jayawardhana, R.   523.2

Strange piece of paradise. Jentz, T.   364.1

A **strange** stirring. Coontz, S.   305.4

The **stranger** beside me. Rule, A.   92

The **stranger** from paradise: a biography of William Blake. Bentley, G. E.   821

Strangers from a different shore. Takaki, R. T.   305.8

Strangers: homosexual love in the nineteenth century. Robb, G.   306.76

The **strangest** man. Farmelo, G.   92

Strassler, Robert B.

     (ed) Herodotus, c. B. C. The landmark Herodotus   938

     (ed) The Landmark Xenophon's Hellenika   938

Strategic business letters and e-mail. Lindsell-Roberts, S.   651.7

STRATEGIC DEFENSE INITIATIVE

     See also Military policy—United States; Space warfare; United States—Defenses

     FitzGerald, F. Way out there in the blue   973.927

STRATEGIC MANAGEMENT *See* Strategic planning

STRATEGIC PLANNING

     See also Planning

     Collins, J. C. Good to great   658

     Matthews, J. R. Scorecards for results   027.4

     Welch, J. F. Winning   658.4

STRATEGY

     See also Military art and science; Naval art and science

     D'Este, C. Warlord   92

     Gaddis, J. L. Surprise, security, and the American experience   355

     Overy, R. J. Why the Allies won   940.53

STRATEGY—HISTORY—20TH CENTURY

     Roberts, A. Masters and commanders   940.54

Strathern, Paul

     The artist, the philosopher, and the warrior   920

     Napoleon in Egypt   962

STRATIGRAPHIC GEOLOGY

     See also Geology

     Fortey, R. A. Earth   551.7

     Hancock, G. Underworld: the mysterious origins of civilization   551.7

     Macdougall, J. D. A short history of planet earth   551.7

Winchester, S. The map that changed the world **526**

STRATOSPHERE

   See also Upper atmosphere

Stratton, Joanna L.

   Pioneer women **978.1**

Stratton, Stephen E.

   The encyclopedia of HIV and AIDS **616.97**

Straus, Roger

   Howard, H. Houses of the founding fathers **973.3**

Strauss's handbook of business information. Moss, R. W. **650**

Strauss, Neil

   Everyone loves you when you're dead **920**

Strauss, Steven D.

   Landlord and tenant **346.04**

   The small business bible **658**

   Wills and trusts **346.05**

Stravinsky inside out. Joseph, C. M. **780**

Stravinsky: a creative spring. Walsh, S. **92**

Stravinsky: the second exile. Walsh, S. **92**

Strayed, Cheryl

   Wild **813**

Strayer, Joseph Reese

   (ed) Dictionary of the Middle Ages **909.07**

STREAM ANIMALS

   See also Animals; Rivers

STREAM ECOLOGY

   See also Ecology; Freshwater ecology

STREAMLINING *See* Aerodynamics

Streatfeild, Dominic

   Cocaine **362.29**

Streb. Streb, E. **92**

Streb, Elizabeth

   Streb **92**

Strebeigh, Fred

   Equal **342**

STREET ART

   Beever, J. Pavement chalk artist **741**

   Felisbret, E. Graffiti New York **751.7**

   Ganz, N. Graffiti world **751**

STREET ART—NEW YORK (STATE)—NEW YORK

   Felisbret, E. Graffiti New York **751.7**

STREET CLEANING

   See also Cleaning; Municipal engineering; Public health; Roads; Sanitary engineering; Streets

STREET ENTERTAINERS

   Lopez, S. The soloist **92**

Street fighters. Kelly, K. **332.6**

Street gang. Davis, M. **791.45**

STREET GANGS *See* Gangs

STREET LIFE

   See also City and town life

STREET LIFE—FICTION—BIBLIOGRAPHY

   Morris, V. I. The readers' advisory guide to street

literature **016**

STREET PEOPLE *See* Homeless persons

STREET RAILROADS

   See also Local transit; Railroads

STREET TRAFFIC *See* City traffic; Traffic engineering

Street-fighting mathematics. Mahajan, S. **510**

A **streetcar** named desire. Williams, T. **812**

STREETS

   See also Cities and towns; Civil engineering; Transportation

STREETS—LIGHTING

   See also Lighting

Streever, Bill

   Cold **998**

Streiff, Fritz

   The art of simple food **641.5**

Streissguth, Michael

   Johnny Cash **92**

Strength in what remains. Kidder, T. **92**

STRENGTH OF MATERIALS

   See also Mechanics; Structural analysis (Engineering)

Strength to love. King, M. L. **252**

STRENGTH TRAINING *See* Weight lifting

Strength training for women. Pagano, J. **613.7**

STRESS (PHYSIOLOGY)

   See also Adaptation (Biology); Physiology

   Benson, H. The relaxation response **155.9**

   Goldman, B. Brain fitness **153.1**

   Kahn, A. P. The encyclopedia of stress and stress-related diseases **616.9**

STRESS (PHYSIOLOGY)—ENCYCLOPEDIAS

   Kahn, A. P. The encyclopedia of stress and stress-related diseases **616.9**

STRESS (PSYCHOLOGY)

   See also Mental health; Psychology

   Benson, H. The relaxation response **155.9**

   Kahn, A. P. The encyclopedia of stress and stress-related diseases **616.9**

   Taylor, S. E. The tending instinct **304.5**

STRESS (PSYCHOLOGY)—ENCYCLOPEDIAS

   Kahn, A. P. The encyclopedia of stress and stress-related diseases **616.9**

STRESS MANAGEMENT

   See also Health

   Goldman, B. Brain fitness **153.1**

STRETCHING EXERCISES

   See also Exercise

Strickland, Bill

   Tour de Lance **92**

Strickland, Bonnie R.

   (ed) The Gale encyclopedia of psychology **150**

Strictly science fiction. Herald, D. T. **016**

STRIKES

Summer of '49. Halberstam, D. 796.357
A **summer** of hummingbirds. Benfey, C. E. G. 920
SUMMER RESORTS
    See also Resorts
SUMMER SCHOOLS
    See also Public schools; Schools
SUMMER THEATER
    See also Theater
Summer world. Heinrich, B. 591.7
Summerscale, Kate
    The suspicions of Mr. Whicher 364.152
Summits. Reynolds, D. 909.82
Sumner, Judith
    The natural history of medicinal plants 581.6
SUN
    See also Astronomy; Solar system
The **Sun** and the moon. Goodman, M. 974.7
Sun in a bottle. Seife, C. 539.7
The **sun** kings. Clark, S. 523.7
Sun Shuyun
    The Long March 951.04
SUN WORSHIP
    See also Religion
The **sun's** heartbeat. Berman, B. 523.7
Sun-tzu
    Sunzi bing fa The illustrated art of war 355
SUNDAY SCHOOLS
    See also Church work; Religious education
SUNDIALS
    See also Clocks and watches; Garden ornaments and furniture; Time
Sundown towns. Loewen, J. W. 363.5
Sundquist, Eric J.
    (ed) The Oxford W. E. B. Du Bois reader 305.896
The **sunflower.** Wiesenthal, S. 179.7
Sunflowers. Pappalardo, J. 583
SUNFLOWERS
    Pappalardo, J. Sunflowers 583
SUNKEN CITIES *See* Extinct cities
SUNNIS
    Hazleton, L. After the prophet 297
SUNNITES
    Nasr, V. The Shia revival 297
SUNNITES *See* Sunnis
SUNSPOTS
    See also Meteorology; Solar radiation; Sun
Sunstein, Cass R.
    (ed) Clones and clones 174
Sunstein, Emily W.
    Mary Shelley 823
Sunzi bing fa
    The illustrated art of war 355
SUPER BOWL (GAME)
    See also Football; Sports tournaments
SUPER BOWL GAME (FOOTBALL)
    Lazarus, A. Super Bowl Monday 796.332

Super Bowl Monday. Lazarus, A. 796.332
Super species. Hamilton, G. 578.6
Superbug. McKenna, M. 616.9
Superclass. Rothkopf, D. J. 305.5
SUPERCOMPUTERS
    See also Computers
SUPERCONDUCTORS
    See also Electric conductors; Electronics
Supercooperators. Highfield, R. 519.3
Superfreakonomics. Levitt, S. D. 330
Supergods. Morrison, G. 741.5
SUPERHERO COMIC BOOKS, STRIPS, ETC.
    See also Comic books, strips, etc.
SUPERHERO FILMS—ENCYCLOPEDIAS
    Muir, J. K. The encyclopedia of superheroes on film and television 791.43
SUPERHERO GRAPHIC NOVELS
    See also Graphic novels
    Wednesday comics 741.5
SUPERHERO TELEVISION PROGRAMS—ENCYCLOPEDIAS
    Muir, J. K. The encyclopedia of superheroes on film and television 791.43
SUPERHEROES
    Morrison, G. Supergods 741.5
SUPERHEROES (FICTIONAL CHARACTERS)—PSYCHOLOGY
    The psychology of superheroes 741.5
SUPERMAN (FICTIONAL CHARACTER)
    See also Fictional characters; Superheroes
SUPERMAN (FICTITIOUS CHARACTER)
    De Haven, T. Our hero 741.5
SUPERMARKETS
    See also Grocery trade; Retail trade; Stores
SUPERNATURAL
    See also Religion
    Steinmeyer, J. Charles Fort 92
Supernatural fiction writers. 809
SUPERNATURAL GRAPHIC NOVELS
    See also Graphic novels
SUPERNATURAL IN LITERATURE
    Supernatural fiction writers 809
SUPERNOVAE
    Gribbin, J. R. Stardust 523
SUPERNOVAE *See* Supernovas
SUPERNOVAS
    See also Stars
    Dauber, P. M. The three big bangs 523.1
    Gribbin, J. R. Stardust 523
The **superorganism.** Holldobler, B. 595.7
SUPERSONIC AERODYNAMICS
    See also Aerodynamics; High speed aeronautics
SUPERSTITION
    See also Folklore
    Dolnick, B. Luck 130

Swain, Dwight V.
Creating characters   808.3
Techniques of the selling writer   808.3
The **swamp.** Grunwald, M.   975.9
SWAMP ANIMALS
    See also Animals
SWAMP ECOLOGY
    See also Ecology; Wetland ecology
Swan, Annalyn
De Kooning: an American master   92
Swanepoel, Stefan
Surviving your Serengeti   650.1
Swanson, James A.
Strong, J. The strongest Strong's exhaustive concordance of the Bible   220.5
Swanson, James L.
Manhunt   364.152
Swanson, Mark
Atlas of the Civil War, month by month   973.7
Swartzwelder, Scott
Kuhn, C. Buzzed   615
Kuhn, C. Pumped   617.1
SWEATERS
Kagan, S. Sasha Kagan's country inspiration   746.43
KnitLit: sweaters and their stories and other writing about knitting   746.43
SWEATSHIRTS
Webber, C. Chic sweats   746.9
SWEDISH LANGUAGE
    See also Language and languages; Scandinavian languages
SWEDISH LITERATURE
    See also Literature; Scandinavian literature
Sweet and low. Cohen, R.   920
Sweet chaos. Brightman, C.   920
The **sweet** hell inside. Ball, E.   920
Sweet land of liberty. Sugrue, T. J.   323
The **sweet** science and other writings. Liebling, A. J.   818
Sweet thunder. Haygood, W.   92
Sweetness & light. Ellis, H.   595.7
SWEETS *See* Candy; Confectionery
SWELL *See* Ocean waves
Swenson, May
Nature   811
The **swerve.** Greenblatt, S. J.   940.2
Swidey, Neil
The assist   796.323
Swift, Daniel
Bomber County   821
Swift, Graham
Making an elephant   828
Swift, Jonathan, 1667-1745 (Irish satirist, poet and pamphleteer)
A tale of a tub, and other work   823
About

DeGategno, P. J. Critical companion to Jonathan Swift   828
Swift, Sally
Splendid table (Radio program) The Splendid table's how to eat supper   641.5
SWIMMERS
Cox, L. Swimming to Antarctica   92
SWIMMERS—UNITED STATES—BIOGRAPHY
Mullen, P. H. Gold in the water   797.2
SWIMMING
Hines, E. W. Fitness swimming   613.7
Mullen, P. H. Gold in the water   797.2
SWIMMING—TRAINING—UNITED STATES
Mullen, P. H. Gold in the water   797.2
Swimming to Antarctica. Cox, L.   92
Swindells, Philip
The water garden encyclopedia   635.9
Swindled. Wilson, B.   363.1
SWINDLERS
Brock, P. Charlatan   92
Salisbury, L. Provenance   92
Zuckoff, M. Ponzi's scheme   364
SWINDLERS AND SWINDLING
    See also Crime; Criminals
Fisher, K. L. How to smell a rat   364.1
Partnoy, F. The match king   92
SWINDLERS AND SWINDLING—UNITED STATES—BIOGRAPHY
Ward, G. C. A disposition to be rich   974.7
SWINDLERS AND SWINDLING—UNITED STATES—HISTORY
Ward, G. C. A disposition to be rich   974.7
SWINE *See* Pigs
SWINE BREEDS
Rath, S. The complete pig   636.4
Swisher, Carl C.
Java Man   599.93
Switch. Heath, C.   303.4
SWITCHBOARD HOTLINES *See* Hotlines (Telephone counseling)
Switek, Brian
Written in stone   576.8
Switzer, Janet
Canfield, J. The success principles   158
Swofford, Anthony
Jarhead: a Marine's chronicle of the Gulf War and other battles   956.704
Sword of the spirit, shield of faith. Preston, A.   322
SWORDS
    See also Weapons
Sybil. Schreiber, F. R.   616.85
Sybil exposed. Nathan, D.   92
Syed, Mathew
Bounce   650.1
Sykes, Bryan

Adam's curse **599.93**
DNA USA **559.9**
The seven daughters of Eve **599.93**
Sylvia Plath. Wagner-Martin, L. **92**
SYMBIOGENESIS
Margulis, L. Symbiotic planet **576.8**
SYMBIOSIS
See also Biology; Ecology
Margulis, L. Symbiotic planet **576.8**
Symbiotic planet. Margulis, L. **576.8**
SYMBOLIC LOGIC
See also Logic; Mathematics
Dyson, G. Turing's cathedral **004**
Livio, M. Is God a mathematician? **510**
Stillwell, J. Roads to infinity **511.3**
SYMBOLISM
See also Art; Mythology
Jung, C. G. Man and his symbols **150.19**
SYMBOLISM IN LITERATURE
See also Literature; Symbolism
SYMBOLISM OF NUMBERS
See also Symbolism
SYMBOLS *See* Signs and symbols
Symmes, Patrick
The boys from Dolores **972.91**
SYMMETRY
Livio, M. The equation that couldn't be solved **512**
Stewart, I. Why beauty is truth **539.7**
SYMMETRY (PHYSICS)
Stewart, I. Why beauty is truth **539.7**
Symonds, Craig L.
Lincoln and his admirals **92**
Symonds, George W. D.
The shrub identification book **582.1**
Symons, Julian
Bloody murder **809**
SYMPATHY
See also Conduct of life; Emotions
Armstrong, K. Twelve steps to a compassionate life **177**
SYMPHONIES *See* Symphony
The **symphony.** Steinberg, M. **784.2**
SYMPHONY
Steinberg, M. The symphony **784.2**
SYMPTOMS *See* Diagnosis
SYNAGOGUES
See also Buildings; Religious institutions; Temples
Synaptic self. LeDoux, J. E. **612.8**
SYNCHRONIZED SWIMMING
See also Swimming
Synge, J. M.
The complete plays **822**
SYNODS *See* Councils and synods
SYNTHESIZER MUSIC *See* Electronic music
SYNTHETIC BIOLOGY

Sasselov, D. The life of super-Earths **576.8**
SYNTHETIC FABRICS
See also Fabrics; Synthetic products
SYNTHETIC RUBBER
See also Plastics; Synthetic products
Sypeck, Jeff
Becoming Charlemagne **92**
SYPHILIS
See also Sexually transmitted diseases
Hayden, D. Pox: genius, madness, and the mysteries of syphilis **616.95**
SYRIA
Friedman, M. The Aleppo Codex **221**
SYRUPS
See also Sugar
SYSTEM ANALYSIS
See also Cybernetics; Mathematical models; System theory
Buchanan, M. Nexus: small worlds and the groundbreaking science of networks **530**
SYSTEM DESIGN
See also System analysis
SYSTEM FAILURES (ENGINEERING)
Petroski, H. Success through failure **620**
SYSTEM THEORY
See also Science
Capra, F. The web of life **570.1**
Goodwin, B. C. How the leopard changed its spots **576.8**
SYSTEMATIC THEOLOGY *See* Doctrinal theology
SYSTEMIC LUPUS ERYTHEMATOSUS
Lahita, R. G. Lupus Q&A **616.7**
SYSTEMS ANALYSIS *See* System analysis
SYSTEMS ENGINEERING
See also Automation; Cybernetics; Engineering; Industrial design; System analysis; System theory
SYSTEMS, DATABASE MANAGEMENT *See* Database management
SYSTEMS, THEORY OF *See* System theory
Szabo, Lynn
(ed) Merton, T. In the dark before dawn **811**
Szarmach, Paul E.
(ed) Medieval England **942**
Szpiro, George G.
Numbers rule **510**
Poincare's prize **510**
Szulc, Tad
Fidel **92**
Szwed, John F.
Alan Lomax **92**
Szymanski, Stefan
Kuper, S. Soccernomics **796.334**
Szymborska, Wislawa
Monologue of a dog **891.8**

Seeger, P. Pete Seeger's storytelling book   372.6

Tales from Ovid. Ovid   873

Tales from Shakespeare. Lamb, C.   822.3

Tales from the morgue. Wecht, C. H.   614

Tales from the underground. Wolfe, D. W.   578.7

Tales of a new Jerusalem [series]

Kynaston, D. Austerity Britain   941.085

Tales of giant snakes. Murphy, J. C.   597.96

Taliban. Rashid, A.   958.1

TALIBAN

Chandrasekaran, R. Little America   958.104

TALK SHOW HOSTS

Ali, K. Fighting weight   92

Baraka, I. A. The LeRoi Jones/Amiri Baraka reader   818

Life stories   920

O'Reilly, B. A bold fresh piece of humanity   92

Reston, J. The conviction of Richard Nixon 973.924

Terkel, S. Touch and go   92

Walters, B. Audition   92

TALK SHOWS

See also Interviewing; Radio programs; Television programs

Talk to the hand. Truss, L.   395

TALKING *See* Conversation

Talking about detective fiction. James, P. D.   823

Talking about movies with Jesus. Kirby, D.   811

Talking back—to presidents, dictators, and assorted scoundrels. Mitchell, A.   92

Talking dirty to the gods. Komunyakaa, Y.   811

Talking terrorism. Herbst, P.   303.6

Talking with your hands, listening with your eyes. Grayson, G.   419

Tall man. Hooper, C.   364.1

TALL TALES

See also Folklore; Legends; Wit and humor

Tallchief, Maria

Maria Tallchief   92

Taller when prone. Murray, L.   821

The **Talley** trilogy. Wilson, L.   812

Tallis, Frank

Hidden minds   154.2

TALMUD

See also Hebrew literature; Jewish literature; Judaism

Talty, Stephan

Agent Garbo   940.5

Escape from the land of snows   92

The illustrious dead   940.2

Tamborlane, William V.

(ed) The Yale guide to children's nutrition   613.2

Taming the beloved beast. Callahan, D.   338.4

Taming the gods. Buruma, I.   322

Tammet, Daniel

Born on a blue day   92

Embracing the wide sky   612.8

Tammy Wynette. McDonough, J.   92

Tan, Amy

The opposite of fate   814

Tanacredi, John T.

(ed) Experiment central   507.8

Tanakh. Bible/O.T.   221

Tang, Jean

Reistad-Long, S. The big New York sandwich book   641.8

Tanis, David

Heart of the artichoke and other kitchen journeys   641.5

A platter of figs and other recipes   641.5

Tanizaki, Jun'ichirō, 1886-1965 (Japanese novelist)

About

Keene, D. Five modern Japanese novelists   895.6

TANK WARFARE

See also War

Tankard, Judith B.

Beatrix Farrand   92

Tannen, Deborah

I only say this because I love you   306.87

You just don't understand   302.2

Tanning, Dorothea

Coming to that   811

Tanton, James S.

Encyclopedia of mathematics   510

Tanzi, Rudolph E.

Decoding darkness   616.8

TAO

See also Philosophy

The **tao** of travel. Theroux, P.   910.4

Tao te ching. Lao-tzu   299.5

TAOISM

See also Religions

Eastern religions   200.9

TAP DANCING

See also Dance

Tapas. Andres, J.   641.8

TAPE RECORDINGS, AUDIO *See* Sound recordings

TAPE RECORDINGS, VIDEO *See* Videotapes

Tape, Ken D.

The changing arctic landscape   551.69

TAPESTRY

See also Decoration and ornament; Decorative arts; Interior design; Needlework

Brosens, K. European tapestries in the Art Institute of Chicago   746.3

TAPESTRY—EUROPE

Brosens, K. European tapestries in the Art Institute of Chicago   746.3

The **Tapir's** morning bath. Royte, E.   577.34

Tapper, Joan

Craft activism   745.5

Tapply, William G.
Every day was special   **799.1**

Tapscott, Don, 1947-
Macrowikinomics   **303.4**

Tapscott, Stephen
(ed) Twentieth century Latin American poetry **861**

Taraborrelli, J. Randy
After Camelot   **973.922**
The secret life of Marilyn Monroe   **92**

TARAHUMARA INDIANS
McDougall, C. Born to run   **796.42**

Target zero. Cleaver, E.   **323**

TARIFF
    See also Commercial policy; Economic policy; Public finance

Tarn, Nathaniel
Selected poems   **811**

TAROT
    See also Card games; Fortune telling; Playing cards

Tarr-Whelan, Linda
Women lead the way   **658.4**

Tartine bread. Robertson, C.   **641.8**

Tartuffe and other plays. Moliere   **842**

TASTE
    See also Senses and sensation

TASTE (AESTHETICS) *See* Aesthetics
The **taste** of country cooking. Lewis, E.   **641.5**
The **taste** of wine. Peynaud, E.   **641.2**
Taste: the story of Britain through its cooking.
Colquhoun, K.   **641.3**

Tasting freedom. Biddle, D. R.   **92**

Tate, James
The ghost soldiers   **811**
Selected poems   **811**
Shroud of the gnome   **811**
Worshipful Company of Fletchers   **811**

Tate, Mary Jo
Critical companion to F. Scott Fitzgerald   **813**

Tattersall, Ian
Masters of the planet   **599.93**

Tattersall, Ian
Extinct humans   **599.93**
The fossil trail   **599.93**
Masters of the planet   **599.93**
The monkey in the mirror   **599.93**

TATTLING
    See also Gossip

TATTOO ARTISTS
Spring, J. Secret historian   **92**

TATTOOING
    See also Manners and customs; Personal appearance

Tattoos on the heart. Boyle, G. J.   **277**

Tatum, Beverly Daniel
Why are all the Black kids sitting together in the caf-

eteria? and other conversations about race   **305.8**

Tatum, Doug
No man's land   **658.4**

Tatzkow, Monika
Verlorene Bilder, V. L. Lost lives, lost art   **709**

Taub, Michael
(ed) Contemporary Jewish-American novelists **813**

The Tauber Institute for the Study of European Jewry [series]
Breitman, R. The architect of genocide   **92**

Taubes, Gary
Why we get fat and what to do about it   **613.7**

Taubman, Philip
Secret empire   **327.12**

Taubman, William
Khrushchev   **92**

Taunton's build like a pro [series]
German, R. Remodeling a basement   **643**

Taunton's complete illustrated guide to woodworking. Bird, L.   **684**

Tausend, Marilyn
Cocina de la familia   **641.5**

Tavormina, M. Teresa
(ed) Medieval England   **942**

Tavris, Carol
Anger   **152.4**

TAX ASSESSMENT
    See also Taxation; Valuation

TAX CREDITS
    See also Income tax

TAX EVASION
    See also Criminal law; White collar crimes

TAX PLANNING
    See also Personal finance; Planning; Taxation

TAXATION
    See also Political science; Public finance
Weltman, B. J.K. Lasser's guide for tough times   **332.024**

TAXES *See* Taxation

TAXIDERMISTS
Milgrom, M. Still life   **590.75**

TAXIDERMY
Milgrom, M. Still life   **590.75**

Tayler, Jeffrey
Angry wind   **916**

Taylor's encyclopedia of garden plants.   **635.9**

Taylor's guide to annuals. Ellis, B. W.   **635.9**

Taylor's guide to gardening [series]
Ellis, B. W. Taylor's guide to perennials   **635.9**

Taylor's guide to ground covers. Michener, D.   **635.9**

Taylor's guide to perennials. Ellis, B. W.   **635.9**

Taylor's guide to roses. Ondra, N. J.   **635.9**

Taylor's guide to shrubs. Fisher, K.   **635.9**

Taylor's guides to gardening [series]
Ellis, B. W. Taylor's guide to annuals   **635.9**
Fisher, K. Taylor's guide to shrubs   **635.9**

Michener, D. Taylor's guide to ground covers **635.9**

Ondra, N. J. Taylor's guide to roses **635.9**

Taylor's encyclopedia of garden plants **635.9**

Taylor's master guide to gardening. **635.9**

Taylor's master guide to landscaping. Buchanan, R. **712**

Taylor, A. J. P.
English history, 1914-1945 **942**

Taylor, Alan
The civil war of 1812 **973.5**

Taylor, Alan
The civil war of 1812 **973.5**
The divided ground **974.7**

Taylor, Barbara Brown
An altar in the world **92**

Taylor, Benjamin
(ed) Bellow, S. Saul Bellow **92**
Naples declared **945**

Taylor, C. James
(ed) Adams, J. My dearest friend **92**

Taylor, D. J.
Bright young people **305.24**

Taylor, David
Old dog, new tricks **636.7**

Taylor, David J.
Orwell: the life **92**

Taylor, Elizabeth
Cohen, A. American pharaoh: Mayor Richard J. Daley: his battle for Chicago and the nation **977.3**

Taylor, Fred
Exorcising Hitler **943.087**

Taylor, Gary
(ed) Shakespeare, W. The complete works **822.3**

Taylor, Guy
(ed) The encyclopedia of arthritis **616.7**

Taylor, Jay
The generalissimo **92**

Taylor, Jean Gelman
Indonesia: peoples and histories **959.8**

Taylor, Joseph E.
Pilgrims of the vertical **796.52**

Taylor, L. B.
Haunted Virginia **133.1**

Taylor, Larissa
(ed) Great events from history, The 17th century, 1601-1700 **909**
(ed) Great lives from history, The 17th century, 1601-1700 **920.003**

Taylor, Leslie
The healing power of rainforest herbs **615**

Taylor, Murry A.
Jumping fire **634.9**

Taylor, Nick
Glenn, J. John Glenn **973.927**
American-made **331.1**

Taylor, Sandra C.

(ed) Japanese Americans, from relocation to redress **940.53**

Taylor, Shelley E.
The tending instinct **304.5**

Taylor, Sybil
Walker, A. Stanley Kubrick, director **791.43**

Taylor, Terry
Altered art **745.5**

Taylor, Timothy
The artificial ape **599.93**
The instant economist **330**

Taylor, Todd W.
The Companion to southern literature **810**
Walker, J. R. The Columbia guide to online style **808**

Taylor, Troy
Haunted Illinois **133.1**

Taylor, William
Practically radical **658.4**

Taylor, Yuval
(ed) Douglass, F. Frederick Douglass: selected speeches and writings **326**

Tayman, John
The Colony **614.5**

TEA
See also Beverages
Rose, S. For all the tea in China **382**

TEA—HISTORY
Standage, T. A history of the world in 6 glasses **394.1**

Teach us to sit still. Parks, T. **616**

Teach yourself visually car care & maintenance. Ramsey, D. **629.28**

Teach yourself visually crochet. Keim, C. **746.43**

Teach yourself visually jewelry making & beading. Michaels, C. F. **745.59**

Teach yourself visually knitting. Turner, S. **746.43**

Teach yourself visually sewing. Colgrove, D. **646.2**

Teacher man. McCourt, F. **92**

TEACHER-STUDENT RELATIONSHIP
See also Child-adult relationship; Interpersonal relations; Teaching

TEACHER-STUDENT RELATIONSHIPS—DRAMA
Bennett, A. The history boys **822**

TEACHER-STUDENT RELATIONSHIPS—UNITED STATES—CASE STUDIES
Albom, M. Tuesdays with Morrie **378.1**

TEACHERS
See also Educators
Bush, L. Spoken from the heart **92**
Johnson, M. An unquenchable thirst **271**
Parini, J. The art of teaching **371.1**
Rudd, M. Underground **92**
Solomon, D. A. Predators, prey, and other kinfolk **92**

Walker-Hill, H. From spirituals to symphonies **780**

Teachers & Writers Collaborative

The Art of the personal essay **808.84**

TEACHERS—TRAINING

See also Education—Study and teaching; Teaching

TEACHERS—UNITED STATES

Kozol, J. Letters to a young teacher **371.1**

TEACHERS—UNITED STATES—HANDBOOKS, MANUALS, ETC

Crews, K. D. Copyright law for librarians and educators **346.04**

TEACHERS AND STUDENTS—COLLEGES AND UNIVERSITIES

Albom, M. Tuesdays with Morrie **378.1**

TEACHERS OF THE BLIND

Gibson, W. The miracle worker **812**

TEACHERS OF THE DEAF

Gibson, W. The miracle worker **812**

Gray, C. Reluctant genius **92**

Lepore, J. A is for American **306.44**

Shulman, S. The telephone gambit **621.3**

TEACHING

See also Education

Begin here **371.1**

Kozol, J. Letters to a young teacher **371.1**

Parini, J. The art of teaching **371.1**

Teaching a stone to talk. Dillard, A. **818**

TEACHING TEAMS

See also Teaching

Teaching tolerance. Bullard, S. **649**

The **teachings** of Don Juan. Castaneda, C. **299.7**

Teachout, Terry

(ed) Mencken, H. L. A second Mencken chrestomathy **818**

All in the dances: a brief life of George Balanchine **92**

Pops **92**

The skeptic: the life of H.L. Mencken **92**

Team of rivals. Goodwin, D. K. **92**

TEAM PROBLEM SOLVING *See* Group problem solving

TEAM WORK IN THE WORKPLACE *See* Teams in the workplace

The **teammates.** Halberstam, D. **796**

TEAMS IN THE WORKPLACE

See also Social groups; Work environment

Kelley, R. E. How to be a star at work **658**

TEAMWORK IN THE WORKPLACE *See* Teams in the workplace

Tear down this wall. Ratnesar, R. **973.927**

Tearing down the wall of sound. Brown, M. **92**

TEAROOMS

See also Restaurants; Tea industry

Tears in the darkness. Norman, M. **940.54**

TEASING

See also Aggressiveness (Psychology); Interpersonal relations

The **tech** writer's survival guide. Van Wicklen, J. **808**

TECHNICAL ASSISTANCE

See also Foreign aid; International economic relations

TECHNICAL EDUCATION

See also Education; Higher education; Technology

TECHNICAL SERVICE *See* Customer services

TECHNICAL WRITING

See also Authorship; Technology—Language

Van Wicklen, J. The tech writer's survival guide **808**

Techniques of healthy cooking. Culinary Institute of America **641.5**

Techniques of the selling writer. Swain, D. V. **808.3**

TECHNOLOGICAL CHANGE *See* Technological innovations

TECHNOLOGICAL FORECASTING

Diamandis, P. H. Abundance **303.48**

Long, J. Darwin's devices **629.8**

TECHNOLOGICAL INNOVATIONS

See also Inventions; Technology

Burke, J. J. Neal-Schuman library technology companion **025**

Carr, N. The big switch **303.4**

Core technology competencies for librarians and library staff **020**

Gershon, I. The breakup 2.0 **303.4**

Hanson, W. The edge of medicine **610.28**

Lanier, J. You are not a gadget **303.4**

Petroski, H. The essential engineer **620**

Popular mechanics magazine. The wonderful future that never was **609**

Stewart, I. In pursuit of the unknown **551.3**

Tapscott, D. Macrowikinomics **303.4**

Tenner, E. Our own devices **303.48**

Topol, E. The creative destruction of medicine **610.28**

TECHNOLOGICAL INNOVATIONS—ECONOMIC ASPECTS

Friedman, T. L. The Lexus and the olive tree **337**

TECHNOLOGICAL INNOVATIONS—FORECASTING

Diamandis, P. H. Abundance **303.48**

Long, J. Darwin's devices **629.8**

TECHNOLOGICAL INNOVATIONS—MANAGEMENT

Collins, J. C. Good to great **658**

TECHNOLOGICAL INNOVATIONS—SOCIAL ASPECTS

Friedman, T. L. The Lexus and the olive tree **337**

Lanier, J. You are not a gadget **303.4**

Palfrey, J. Born digital **302.23**

TELEVISION—PRODUCTION AND DIREC-TION

See also Television broadcasting

TELEVISION—REPAIRING

Davidson, H. L. TV repair for beginners **621.388**

TELEVISION—SOCIAL ASPECTS

Marling, K. A. As seen on TV **973.92**

TELEVISION—STAGE LIGHTING *See* Stage lighting

TELEVISION ACTORS *See* Actors

TELEVISION ADAPTATIONS

See also Television plays; Television programs; Television scripts

TELEVISION ADVERTISING

See also Advertising; Television broadcasting

TELEVISION AND CHILDREN

See also Children; Television

TELEVISION AND POLITICS

See also Politics; Television

TELEVISION AUTHORSHIP

See also Authorship

Gervich, C. Small screen, big picture **791.45**

TELEVISION BROADCASTING

See also Broadcasting; Mass media; Television

Marling, K. A. As seen on TV **973.92**

Postman, N. Amusing ourselves to death **302.23**

TELEVISION BROADCASTING—VOCATION-AL GUIDANCE

See also Vocational guidance

TELEVISION BROADCASTING OF NEWS

See also Broadcast journalism; Television broadcasting

Ghiglione, L. CBS's Don Hollenbeck **92**

TELEVISION BROADCASTING OF SPORTS

See also Broadcast journalism; Television broadcasting

Bloom, J. There you have it **92**

Miller, J. A. Those guys have all the fun **791.45**

TELEVISION COVERAGE OF NEWS *See* Television broadcasting of news

TELEVISION CRITICS

Barnes, J. Nothing to be frightened of **92**

Coupland, D. Marshall McLuhan **92**

TELEVISION DIRECTORS

Lukas, C. Blue genes **92**

Thomson, H. The white rock **985**

Zuckoff, M. Robert Altman **92**

TELEVISION GAMES *See* Video games

TELEVISION INDUSTRY *See* Television broadcasting; Television supplies industry

TELEVISION JOURNALISM *See* Broadcast journalism; Television broadcasting of news

TELEVISION JOURNALISTS—UNITED STATES—BIOGRAPHY

Brokaw, T. A long way from home **070**

TELEVISION JOURNALISTS—UNITED STATES—DIARIES

Koppel, T. Off camera **070.92**

TELEVISION MODERATORS

Koppel, T. Off camera **070.92**

O'Reilly, B. A bold fresh piece of humanity **92**

Terkel, S. Touch and go **92**

TELEVISION MOVIES

See also Motion pictures; Television programs

TELEVISION NEWS *See* Television broadcasting of news

TELEVISION NEWS ANCHORS

Brokaw, T. A long way from home **070**

Cronkite, W. A reporter's life **070**

Edwards, B. Edward R. Murrow and the birth of broadcast journalism **92**

Koppel, T. Off camera **070.92**

Olson, L. Citizens of London **940.54**

Sperber, A. M. Murrow, his life and times **92**

Walters, B. Audition **92**

TELEVISION NEWS ANCHORS—UNITED STATES—BIOGRAPHY

Brokaw, T. A long way from home **070**

TELEVISION PERSONALITIES

Baraka, I. A. The LeRoi Jones/Amiri Baraka reader **818**

Bianculli, D. Dangerously funny **791.45**

Bloom, J. There you have it **92**

Bourdain, A. Kitchen confidential **92**

Bourdain, A. Medium raw **92**

Buford, B. Heat **641.5**

Child, J. As always, Julia **92**

Child, J. My life in France **92**

Conant, J. A covert affair **940.54**

Deen, P. H. Paula Deen **92**

Fitch, N. R. Appetite for life **92**

Frank, J. In heaven everything is fine **92**

Gabler, N. Winchell **070**

Kanfer, S. Groucho: the life and times of Julius Henry Marx **92**

Kindred, D. Sound and fury **796**

Lewis, J. Dean & me **92**

Life stories **920**

Maguire, J. Impresario **92**

Pepin, J. The apprentice: my life in the kitchen **641.5**

Ribowsky, M. Howard Cosell **92**

Rodriguez, R. Hunger of memory **92**

TELEVISION PERSONALITIES

See also Celebrities

TELEVISION PLAYS

See also Drama; Television programs

TELEVISION PLAYS—TECHNIQUE

See also Drama—Technique; Television authorship

TELEVISION PRODUCERS

Tenenbaum, Frances
  (ed) Taylor's encyclopedia of garden plants **635.9**
  (ed) Taylor's master guide to gardening **635.9**
Tenet, Stephanie
  Sussman, J. Dare to repair **643**
Tennant, Richard A.
  The American Sign Language handshape diction-
  ary **419**
Tennekes, H.
  The simple science of flight **629.132**
Tenner, Edward
  Our own devices **303.48**
**TENNESSEE—HISTORY—1861-1865, CIVIL
  WAR**
  Groom, W. Shiloh, 1862 **973.7**
Tenney, Merrill C.
  (ed) Zondervan illustrated Bible dictionary **220.3**
TENNIS
      See also Sports
  Agassi, A. Open **92**
  Fisher, M. A terrible splendor **796.342**
  Wertheim, L. J. Strokes of genius **796.342**
TENNIS—BIOGRAPHY
  Agassi, A. Open **92**
  Howard, J. The rivals **92**
TENNIS—TOURNAMENTS
  Fisher, M. A terrible splendor **796.342**
TENNIS PLAYERS
  Agassi, A. Open **92**
  Fisher, M. A terrible splendor **796.342**
  Howard, J. The rivals **92**
  McEnroe, J. You cannot be serious **796.342**
  Wertheim, L. J. Strokes of genius **796.342**
Tennyson, Alfred Tennyson
  Poems **821**
TENSION (PHYSIOLOGY) *See* Stress (Physiol-
  ogy)
TENSION (PSYCHOLOGY) *See* Stress (Psychol-
  ogy)
The **tenth** muse. Jones, J. **92**
The **tenth** parallel. Griswold, E. **297**
TENTS
      See also Camping
Terence
  Terence, the comedies **872**
  Terence, the comedies. Terence **872**
  Teresa of Avila. Medwick, C. **282**
Teresi, Dick
  The undead **610**
Teresi, Dick
  Lederman, L. M. The God particle **539.7**
  Lost discoveries **509**
**TEREZIN (CZECHOSLOVAKIA: CONCEN-
  TRATION CAMP)**
      See also Concentration camps
Terkel, Studs

  (ed) The good war **940.54**
  And they all sang **780.9**
  Hard times **973.91**
  My American century **920**
  The spectator **791**
  Touch and go **92**
  Will the circle be unbroken? **128**
  Working **331.2**
TERM PAPER WRITING *See* Report writing
TERMINAL CARE
      See also Medical care
  Brody, J. E. Jane Brody's guide to the great be-
  yond **616.02**
  Kaufman, S. R. —And a time to die **362.1**
  Kiernan, S. P. Last rights **179.7**
  Kubler-Ross, E. On death and dying **155.9**
  McFarlane, R. The complete bedside compan-
  ion **649.8**
  Twelve breaths a minute **616**
TERMINAL CARE—ETHICAL ASPECTS
  Chen, P. W. Final exam **92**
  Kaufman, S. R. —And a time to die **362.1**
  Wanzer, S. H. To die well **179.7**
TERMINALLY ILL
      See also Sick
  Brody, J. E. Jane Brody's guide to the great be-
  yond **616.02**
  Romm, R. The mercy papers **92**
  Twelve breaths a minute **616**
TERMINALLY ILL CHILDREN
      See also Terminally ill
  Hilden, J. M. Shelter from the storm **618.92**
  Johnson, C. M. Your critically ill child **618.92**
  Kubler-Ross, E. On children and death **155.9**
TERMINATION OF PREGNANCY *See* Abortion
TERMS AND PHRASES
      See also Names
TERNS
      See also Birds; Water birds
Terr, Lenore
  Magical moments of change **618.92**
  Terra. Novacek, M. J. **576.8**
TERRA COTTA
      See also Building materials; Decoration and
  ornament; Pottery
Terrace, Vincent
  Television sitcom factbook **791.45**
TERRAIN SENSING, REMOTE *See* Remote
  sensing
TERRAPINS *See* Turtles
TERRARIUMS
      See also Indoor gardening
  Alderton, D. Firefly encyclopedia of the vivari-
  um **639.3**
  Martin, T. The new terrarium **635.9**
Terras, Victor

Wilson, E. O. Consilience   **121**

THEORY OF NUMBERS *See* Number theory

THEORY OF SYSTEMS *See* System theory

The **theory** of the leisure class. Veblen, T.   **305.5**

THEOSOPHY

> *See also* Mysticism; Religions

THERAPEUTIC SYSTEMS *See* Alternative medicine

THERAPEUTICS

> *See also* Medicine; Pathology

THERAPEUTICS, PHYSIOLOGICAL

Null, G. AIDS: a second opinion   **616.97**

THERAPY, PSYCHOLOGICAL *See* Psychotherapy

There are words. Turnbull, G.   **821**

There goes my everything. Sokol, J.   **305.8**

There is no freedom without bread! Pleshakov, K.   **947**

There is no me without you. Greene, M. F.   **92**

There is power in a union. Dray, P.   **331.8**

There you have it. Bloom, J.   **92**

Thermageddon: countdown to 2030. Hunter, R.   **363.7**

THERMODYNAMICS

> *See also* Dynamics; Physical chemistry; Physics

Shachtman, T. Absolute zero and the conquest of cold   **536**

Von Baeyer, H. C. Maxwell's demon   **536**

Theroux, Alexander

Estonia: a ramble through the periphery   **947.98**

Theroux, Paul

Dark star safari   **916**

The great railway bazaar   **915**

The happy isles of Oceania   **919**

The old Patagonian express   **918**

Riding the iron rooster   **915**

The tao of travel   **910.4**

Theroux, Peter

Sandstorms: days and nights in Arabia   **953**

Theroux, Phyllis

(ed) The Book of eulogies   **808.8**

THESAURI *See* Subject headings

These are my rivers. Ferlinghetti, L.   **811**

THESES *See* Dissertations

They all laughed at Christopher Columbus. Weil, E.   **621.43**

They called me Mayer July. Kirshenblatt, M.   **92**

They fought like demons. Blanton, D.   **973.7**

They have killed Papa dead! Pitch, A.   **973.7**

They lift their wings to cry. Haxton, B.   **811**

They made America. Evans, H.   **920**

They marched into sunlight. Maraniss, D.   **956.704**

They never said it. Boller, P. F.   **808.88**

They poured fire on us from the sky. Deng, B.   **962.4**

A **thief** of strings. Revell, D.   **811**

Thieret, John W.

National Audubon Society field guide to North American wildflowers: eastern region   **582.13**

THIEVES

> *See also* Criminals

Bartlett, A. H. The man who loved books too much   **92**

Macintyre, B. Agent Zigzag   **92**

Nourse, V. F. In reckless hands   **344**

Rideau, W. In the place of justice   **92**

Scotti, R. A. Vanished smile   **759**

Stiles, T. J. Jesse James   **364.15**

Thieves of Baghdad. Bogdanos, M.   **956.7**

Thieves of paradise. Komunyakaa, Y.   **811**

Thin ice. Bowen, M.   **551.51**

A **thing** that is.   **811**

Things I didn't know. Hughes, R.   **92**

Things I've been silent about. Nafisi, A.   **92**

Think and grow rich. Hill, N.   **650.1**

THINK TANKS *See* Group problem solving

Think: a compelling introduction to philosophy. Blackburn, S.   **100**

THINKING *See* Thought and thinking

Thinking about the earth. Oldroyd, D. R.   **551.09**

Thinking like your editor. Rabiner, S.   **808**

Thinking the twentieth century. Judt, T.   **320.092**

Thinking, fast and slow. Kahneman, D.   **153.4**

The **third** chapter. Lawrence-Lightfoot, S.   **305.26**

The **third** chimpanzee. Diamond, J. M.   **599.93**

THIRD PARTIES (UNITED STATES POLITICS)

> *See also* Political parties; United States—Politics and government

The **Third** Reich. Burleigh, M.   **943.086**

The **Third** Reich at war. Evans, R. J.   **940.53**

The **Third** Reich in power, 1933-1939. Evans, R. J.   **943.086**

Third World America. Huffington, A.   **330.9**

THIRD WORLD WAR *See* World War III

Thirsting for peace in a raging century. Sanders, E.   **811**

Thirteen days. Kennedy, R. F.   **973.922**

Thirteen ways of looking at a black man. Gates, H. L.   **920.71**

Thirteen ways of looking at the novel. Smiley, J.   **813**

The **Thirty** Years War. Wilson, P. H.   **940.2**

THIRTY YEARS' WAR, 1618-1648

Wilson, P. H. The Thirty Years War   **940.2**

The **thirty-first** of March. Busby, H. W.   **973.923**

The **Thirtymile** fire. Maclean, J. N.   **634.9**

This ain't brain surgery. Dierker, L.   **796**

This ain't the summer of love. Waksman, S.   **781.66**

This book is overdue! Johnson, M.   **020**

This boy's life: a memoir. Wolff, T.   **92**

This child will be great. Johnson-Sirleaf, E.   **92**

This cold heaven. Ehrlich, G.   **998**

This craft of verse. Borges, J. L.   809.1

This far by faith. Williams, J.   200

This house has fallen. Maier, K.   **966.905**

This I believe.   170

This I believe II.   170

This is biology. Mayr, E.   570

This is my God: the Jewish way of life. Wouk, H.   296

This is reggae music. Bradley, L.   781.646

This life is in your hands. Coleman, M.   92

This mighty scourge. McPherson, J. M.   973.7

This new ocean. Burrows, W. E.   629.4

This republic of suffering. Faust, D. G.   973.7

This time. Stern, G.   811

This time is different. Reinhart, C. M.   338.5

This will change everything.   501

Thomas

  Imitation of Christ   The imitation of Christ   242

  Selected writings   189

Thomas Becket.   942.03

Thomas Eakins.   759.13

Thomas Hardy. Tomalin, C.   92

Thomas Hardy. Poems   821

Thomas Jefferson. Bernstein, R. B.   92

Thomas Jefferson. Randall, W. S.   92

Thomas Jefferson and Sally Hemings. Gordon-Reed, A.   973.4

Thomas Jefferson: author of America. Hitchens, C.   92

The **Thomas** Kinkade story. Kinkade, T.   92

Thomas Mann. Kurzke, H.   92

Thomas, Abigail

  A three dog life   92

Thomas, Anna

  Love soup   641.5

Thomas, Aquinas, Saint, 1225?-1274

About

  Davies, B. The thought of Thomas Aquinas   189

  Kung, H. Great Christian thinkers   230

  Russell, B. A history of Western philosophy   109

  Thomas   Selected writings   189

Thomas, Dylan

  A child's Christmas in Wales   828

  The poems of Dylan Thomas   821

  Under milk wood   822

Thomas, Elizabeth Marshall

  The social lives of dogs   636.7

  The tribe of tiger   599.74

Thomas, Emory M.

  Robert E. Lee   973.7

Thomas, Evan

  John Paul Jones   973.3

  Robert Kennedy   973.922

  Sea of thunder   940.54

  The war lovers   973.8

Thomas, Hugh

  Rivers of gold   980

Thomas, Kenneth R.

  (ed) United States/Constitution   The Constitution of the United States of America   342

Thomas, Lewis

  The lives of a cell   570.1

Thomas, Mike

  The Second City unscripted   792

Thomas, Nicholas

  Cook   910

Thomas, Robert McG.

  52 McGs   920

THOMPSON SUBMACHINE GUN

  Yenne, B. Tommy gun   623.4

Thompson, Andrea

  Nachman, P. A. You and your only child   649

Thompson, Charlotte E.

  Raising a child with a neuromuscular disorder   618.92

Thompson, Cliff

  (ed) Current biography yearbook, 2010   920.003

  (ed) World authors, 1990-1995   809

  (ed) World authors, 1995-2000   809

  (ed) World musicians   920.003

Thompson, Dave

  I hate new music   781.66

  London's burning   781.66

Thompson, David

  Fertik, M. Wild west 2.0   659.2

  Thai food   641.5

Thompson, Dick

  Volcano cowboys   551.21

Thompson, Gary Richard

  (ed) Poe, E. A. Essays and reviews   809

Thompson, Gordon

  Please please me   781.64

Thompson, Hunter S., 1937-2005

  Fear and loathing at Rolling Stone   070.17

  Fear and loathing in America   070

  The great shark hunt   818

  The kingdom of fear   070.92

  (jt. auth) Thompson, H. S. Fear and loathing at Rolling Stone

Thompson, Ida

  The Audubon Society field guide to North American fossils   560

Thompson, Jason

  A history of Egypt   962

  Manga: the complete guide   016

Thompson, Leonard Monteath

  A history of South Africa   968

Thompson, Mark

  Now, build a great business!   658

  The white war   940.4

Thompson, Michael

  Michael Thompson: Portraits   779

THREE STOOGES FILMS

See also Comedy films; Motion pictures

Three strides before the wire. Mitchell, E. **798.4**

Three ways to capsize a boat. Stewart, C. **797.1**

THRIFTINESS

Yeager, J. The cheapskate next door **332.024**

The **thrill** of the grill. Schlesinger, C. **641.7**

Thriving with heart disease. Sotile, W. M. **362.1**

THROAT

See also Anatomy

The **throne** of Psyche. Youmans, M. **811**

Through a window. Goodall, J. **599.8**

Through the children's gate. Gopnik, A. **974.7**

Through the eyes of the Vikings. Haas, R. B. **779**

Through the language glass. Deutscher, G. **410**

Through the lens. National Geographic Society (U.S.) **779**

Throwim way leg. Flannery, T. F. **995.3**

Thubron, Colin

In Siberia **957**

Shadow of the Silk Road **911**

To a mountain in Tibet **915**

Thubron, Colin

About

Thubron, C. In Siberia **957**

Thucydides. Kagan, D. **938**

Thucydides

The history of the Peloponnesian War **938**

The landmark Thucydides **938**

Thuma, Cynthia

Haunted Florida **133.1**

THUNDERSTORMS

See also Meteorology; Storms

Thunderstruck. Larson, E. **364.152**

Thurgood Marshall. Williams, J. **347**

Thurgood Marshall. Marshall, T. **347**

Thurman, Judith

Isak Dinesen **92**

Secrets of the flesh: a life of Colette **92**

Thurman, Robert A. F.

Why the Dalai Lama matters **294.3**

Thursby, Jacqueline S.

Critical companion to Maya Angelou **818**

Thurschwell, Pamela

Sigmund Freud **150.19**

Thurston, Herbert

(ed) Butler's Lives of the saints **920.003**

Thus spoke Zarathustra. Nietzsche, F. W. **193**

THYROID GLAND—DISEASES

Ditkoff, B. A. The thyroid guide **616.4**

THYROID GLAND—DISEASES—POPULAR WORKS

Ditkoff, B. A. The thyroid guide **616.4**

The **thyroid** guide. Ditkoff, B. A. **616.4**

TIANANMEN SQUARE INCIDENT, BEIJING (CHINA), 1989—POETRY

Liu, X. June fourth elegies **811**

TIBET (CHINA)—FOREIGN PUBLIC OPINION

Schell, O. Virtual Tibet **951**

TIBET (CHINA)—IN MOTION PICTURES

Schell, O. Virtual Tibet **951**

TIBET (CHINA)—PICTORIAL WORKS

Dalai Lama My Tibet **951**

The **Tibetan** book of living and dying. Sogyal **294.3**

A **ticket** to the circus. Mailer, N. C. **92**

Tickle, Phyllis

The great emergence **270**

TICKS

Beccaloni, J. Arachnids **595.4**

Stewart, A. Wicked bugs **632**

Vanderhoof-Forschner, K. Everything you need to know about Lyme disease and other tick-borne disorders **616.9**

TIDAL WAVES *See* Tsunamis

TIDE POOL ECOLOGY

See also Ecology

TIDES

See also Ocean

TIE DYEING

See also Dyes and dyeing

Tierney, Lawrence M.

(ed) Current medical diagnosis and treatment 2008 **610**

The **tiger.** Vaillant, J. **599.75**

Tiger Force. Sallah, M. **959.704**

TIGER HUNTING

Vaillant, J. The tiger **599.75**

Tiger trap. Wise, D. **327**

A **tiger's** heart. Shen, A. J. **92**

Tiger, tiger. Fragoso, M. **92**

TIGERS

Matthiessen, P. Tigers in the snow **599.756**

Thomas, E. M. The tribe of tiger **599.74**

Vaillant, J. The tiger **599.75**

Tigers & ice. Hoagland, E. **814**

TIGERS—BEHAVIOR

Vaillant, J. The tiger **599.75**

TIGERS—RUSSIA (FEDERATION)—RUSSIAN FAR EAST

Matthiessen, P. Tigers in the snow **599.756**

Tigers in the snow. Matthiessen, P. **599.756**

Tigges, Julie A.

(ed) Women's legal guide **346.01**

TIGRIS RIVER

Kriwaczek, P. Babylon **935**

TILES

See also Building materials; Ceramics

Garskof, J. Tiling **698**

Tiling. Garskof, J. **698**

Till I end my song. **808.81**

Tillich, Paul

The Cambridge star atlas   **523.8**

Tirnady, Frank
   Lee, H. C. Blood evidence   **363.25**

Tirone Smith, Mary-Ann
   Girls of tender age   **92**

'**Tis.** McCourt, F.   **92**

Tischler, Nancy M.
   Men and women of the Bible   **220.9**

TISSUE AND ORGAN HARVESTING
   Teresi, D. The undead   **610**

TISSUES—TRANSPLANTATION *See* Transplantation of organs, tissues, etc.

Titan unveiled. Lorenz, R.   **523.2**

Titan: the life of John D. Rockefeller, Sr. Chernow,
   R.   **92**

TITHES
   See also Church finance; Ecclesiastical law;
   Taxation

Titian. Hudson, M.   **92**

Tito. West, R.   **949.7**

To a mountain in Tibet. Thubron, C.   **915**

To Appomattox. Davis, B.   **973.7**

To be young, gifted, and Black. Hansberry, L.   **92**

To begin again. Levy, N.   **296.7**

To begin where I am. Milosz, C.   **891.8**

To conquer the air. Tobin, J.   **629.13**

To die in Mexico. Gibler, J.   **363.45**

To die well. Wanzer, S. H.   **179.7**

To end all wars. Hochschild, A.   **940.3**

To free a family. Nathans, S.   **306.3**

To hell on a fast horse. Gardner, M. L.   **92**

To life! Kushner, H. S.   **296**

To listen to a child. Brazelton, T. B.   **155.4**

To live or to perish forever. Schmidle, N.   **954.91**

To live's to fly. Kruth, J.   **92**

To love what is. Shulman, A. K.   **92**

To marry an English Lord. MacColl, G.   **974.7**

To see the earth before the end of the world. Roberson, E.   **811**

To the actor. Chekhov, M.   **792**

To the castle and back. Havel, V.   **92**

To the Diamond Mountains. Morris-Suzuki, T.   **915**

To the end of the earth. Avery, T.   **998**

To the flag. Ellis, R.   **323.6**

To the gates of Richmond. Sears, S. W.   **973.7**

To the rescue. Lufkin, E.   **636.7**

TOADS
   Beltz, E. Frogs: inside their remarkable world **597.8**

TOADSTOOLS *See* Mushrooms

Toasts.   **808.88**

TOASTS
   See also Epigrams; Speeches
   Toasts   **808.88**

Tobacco. Gately, I.   **394.1**

TOBACCO
   Gately, I. Tobacco   **394.1**

TOBACCO—ENCYCLOPEDIAS
   Tobacco in history and culture   **394.1**

TOBACCO—HISTORY
   Gately, I. Tobacco   **394.1**
   Tobacco in history and culture   **394.1**

TOBACCO—SOCIAL ASPECTS—HISTORY
   Gately, I. Tobacco   **394.1**

TOBACCO HABIT
   See also Habit; Smoking
   Goldfarb, T. L. American Lung Association 7 steps
   to a smoke-free life   **616.86**
   Tobacco in history and culture.   **394.1**

TOBACCO INDUSTRY
   See also Industries

Tobias, Andrew P.
   The only investment guide you'll ever need **332.024**

Tobias, Sheila
   Overcoming math anxiety   **510**

Tobias, Steven E.
   Elias, M. J. Emotionally intelligent parenting   **649**

Tobin, Daniel R.
   Hilden, J. M. Shelter from the storm   **618.92**

Tobin, Jacqueline
   From Midnight to Dawn   **322**
   Hidden in plain view   **973.7**

Tobin, James
   Reporting America at war   **070.4**
   Ernie Pyle's war   **070.4**
   Great projects   **609**
   To conquer the air   **629.13**

Tocqueville, Alexis de
   Democracy in America   **973.5**

Todd, Kim
   Tinkering with Eden   **591.6**

Todd, Olivier
   Albert Camus   **848**

TODDLERS
   Murkoff, H. E. What to expect the second year **649**

Toerge, John E.
   (ed) Managing stroke   **616.8**

Tofel, Richard J.
   A legend in the making   **796.357**
   Restless genius   **92**

Toffler, Alvin
   Future shock   **303.4**
   Powershift   **303.49**

TOILET TRAINING
   See also Child rearing

TOILETRIES
   See also Personal grooming

Tolan, Sandy
   The lemon tree   **956.94**

Toland, John
   Adolf Hitler   **92**

A **tolerable** anarchy. Purdy, J.   **320**

TOLERANCE *See* Toleration

PSYCHOLOGICAL ASPECTS
Hemingway, L. A world turned over   363.34
Toropov, Brandon
Woodger, E. Encyclopedia of the Lewis and Clark Expedition   917
TORPEDOES
   See also Explosives; Naval art and science; Submarine warfare
Torre, Joe
The Yankee years   92
Torre, Monica de la
Reversible monuments   861
Torres, Alissa
American widow   741.5
Torres, Gerald
Guinier, L. The miner's canary   323.1
Torres, Joseph
(jt. auth) Gonzalez, J. News for all the people   302.23
Torrey, E. Fuller (Edwin Fuller), 1937-
The insanity offense   362.1
Surviving prostate cancer   616.99
TORTOISES *See* Turtles
Tortoises and turtles. Ferri, V.   597.92
Tortora, Phyllis G.
Calasibetta, C. M. The Fairchild dictionary of fashion   391
(ed) Fairchild's dictionary of textiles   677
Tortorella, Neil
Starting your career as a freelance web designer   006.7
TORTURE
   See also Criminal procedure; Cruelty; Punishment
Conroy, J. Unspeakable acts, ordinary people   323.4
Danner, M. Torture and truth   956.7
McCoy, A. W. A question of torture   323.4
Morgan, T. My battle of Algiers   965
The torture papers   973.931
TORTURE—IRAQ
The torture papers   973.931
Torture and truth. Danner, M.   956.7
The **torture** papers.   973.931
Tosches, Nick
Where dead voices gather   782
Toselli, Leigh
Pro nail care   646.7
TOTAL ABSTINENCE *See* Temperance
Total engagement. Reeves, B.   303.4
TOTAL QUALITY MANAGEMENT
Laughlin, S. The quality library   025.1
TOTALITARIANISM
   See also Political science
Arendt, H. Origins of totalitarianism   321.9
Huxley, A. Brave new world revisited   303.3
TOTEMS AND TOTEMISM

   See also Ethnology; Mythology
Totten, Herman L.
Larson, J. C. The public library policy writer **025.1**
Touborg, Sarah
Moffett, K. Not your mother's divorce   306.89
TOUCH
   See also Senses and sensation
Bruce, D. F. Miracle touch   615.5
TOUCH—THERAPEUTIC USE
Bruce, D. F. Miracle touch   615.5
Touch and go. Terkel, S.   92
Touched with fire. Perry, J. M.   973.7
Touching my father's soul. Jamling Tenzing Norgay   796.522
Touchpoints. Conant, D. R.   658.4
Touchpoints birth to 3. Brazelton, T. B.   649
Touchpoints three to six. Brazelton, T. B.   305.231
The **touchstone** of life. Loewenstein, W. R.   571.6
Tough, Paul
Whatever it takes   362.7
The **toughest** show on earth. Volpe, J.   92
Tougias, Mike
Schultz, E. B. King Philip's War   973.2
Ten hours until dawn   363.34
Toulouse-Lautrec. Frey, J.   92
Tour de Lance. Strickland, B.   92
Touré, 1971-
Who's afraid of post-blackness?
TOURETTE SYNDROME
Kushner, H. I. A cursing brain?   **616.8**
TOURETTE SYNDROME—HISTORY
Kushner, H. I. A cursing brain?   **616.8**
TOURING, BICYCLE *See* Bicycle touring
TOURISM *See* Tourist trade; Travel
TOURIST ACCOMMODATIONS *See* Hotels and motels; Youth hostels
TOURIST TRADE
   See also Commerce
TOURISTS *See* Tourist trade; Travelers
Tourles, Stephanie L.
Raw energy   641.5
Tourville, Jacqueline
Van der Ziel, C. Big, beautiful & pregnant   618.2
Toussaint Louverture. Bell, M. S.   92
Toward a new Catholic Church. Carroll, J.   282
Toward a psychology of being. Maslow, A. H. 155.2
Toward the distant islands. Carruth, H.   811
Towell, Larry
The world from my front porch   779
Tower of Babel. Pennock, R. T.   576.8
The **towering** world of Jimmy Choo. Crowe, L. G.   391
TOWN LIFE *See* City and town life
TOWN PLANNING *See* City planning
The **town** that food saved. Hewitt, B.   338.1
Townie. Dubus, A.   92

TRAIL RIDING
See also Horsemanship

TRAILS
See also Roads

Trailside (Television program)
Rock climbing   **796.522**

Trailside series guide [series]
Trailside (Television program)   Rock climbing   **796.522**

A **train** in winter. Moorehead, C.

TRAIN WRECKS *See* Railroad accidents

TRAINING OF CHILDREN *See* Child rearing

Trainor, Bernard E.
Gordon, M. R. The generals' war   **956.7**

TRAINS *See* Railroads

Traister, Rebecca
Big girls don't cry   **324**

Traitor to his class. Brands, H. W.   **92**

Traitors among us. Herrington, S. A.   **327.12**

TRAMPS
See also Homeless persons; Poor
Wyman, M. Hoboes   **305.5**

Tran, G. B.
Vietnamerica   **741.5**

Trang, Corinne
Essentials of Asian cuisine   **641.5**

TRANQUILIZING DRUGS
Tone, A. The age of anxiety   **615**

TRANSACTIONAL ANALYSIS
See also Psychotherapy

TRANSATLANTIC FLIGHTS
Lindbergh, C. The spirit of St. Louis   **629.13**

TRANSATLANTIC FLIGHTS—HISTORY—20TH CENTURY
Jackson, J. Atlantic fever   **629.130**

Transatlantic relations series
Britain and the Americas   **303**

TRANSCENDENTAL MEDITATION
See also Meditation

Transcendental studies. Waldrop, K.   **811**

Transcendentalism.   **810**

TRANSCENDENTALISM
See also Philosophy
The essential transcendentalists   **141**
Francis, R. Fruitlands   **974.4**

TRANSCENDENTALISM—COLLECTIONS
Transcendentalism   **810**

Transcircularities. Troupe, Q.   **811**

TRANSCONTINENTAL JOURNEYS (AMERICAN CONTINENT) *See* Overland journeys to the Pacific

TRANSCULTURAL MEDICAL CARE—CALIFORNIA—CASE STUDIES
Fadiman, A. The spirit catches you and you fall down   **306.4**

TRANSCULTURAL STUDIES *See* Cross-cultural studies

TRANSFER PAYMENTS
See also Domestic economic assistance; Economic policy; Subsidies

Transfigurations. Wright, J.   **811**

The **transformation** of American religion. Wolfe, A.   **200.9**

The **transformation** of Ireland. Ferriter, D.   **941.5**

Transforming madness. Neugeboren, J.   **616.89**

TRANSGENDER PEOPLE
Vollmann, W. T. Kissing the mask   **792.7**

TRANSGENDERED PEOPLE
Gambone, P. Travels in a gay nation   **306.76**
Vollmann, W. T. Kissing the mask   **792.7**

TRANSGENICS *See* Genetic engineering

TRANSISTORS
See also Electronics; Semiconductors

The **transits** of Venus. Sheehan, W.   **523.9**

TRANSLATING AND INTERPRETING
See also Language and languages
Grossman, E. Why translation matters   **418**
The Oxford guide to literature in English translation   **820**
Remnick, D. Reporting   **814**

Translations from the Asian classics [series]
Haiku before haiku   **895.6**
I ching The classic of changes   **299.5**
The Shorter Columbia anthology of traditional Chinese literature   **895.1**

Translations from the Oriental classics [series]
The Columbia book of Chinese poetry   **895.1**

The **translator.** Hari, D.   **92**

TRANSLATORS
Athill, D. Somewhere towards the end   **92**
Bloom, H. The Western canon   **809**
Boyd, B. Stalking Nabokov   **813**
Boyd, B. Vladimir Nabokov: the American years   **813**
Boyd, B. Vladimir Nabokov: the Russian years **813**
Draitser, E. Stalin's Romeo spy   **92**
Friedman, M. S. Encounter on the narrow ridge: a life of Martin Buber   **92**
Gioia, D. Can poetry matter?   **809.1**
Heaney, S. Finders keepers   **821**
Jarrell, R. No other book   **809**
Majd, H. The Ayatollah begs to differ   **955**
Mandelstam, N. Hope against hope   **891.71**
Manguel, A. A reader on reading   **818**
Milosz, C. To begin where I am   **891.8**
Nabokov, V. V. Speak, memory   **813**
O'Driscoll, D. Stepping stones   **821**
Seth, V. Two lives   **92**
Williamson, E. Borges, a life   **92**
Zubok, V. Zhivago's children   **305.5**

TRANSMUTATION (CHEMISTRY)
See also Atoms; Nuclear physics; Radioac-

See also Multiple birth; Siblings

Tripp, Charles

A history of Iraq   956.7

Tris Speaker. Gay, T. M.   92

Triumph. Schaap, J.   92

Triumph and tragedy. Churchill, W.   940.53

Triumph and tragedy in Mudville. Gould, S. J.   796.357

The **triumph** of love. Hill, G.   821

The **triumph** of music. Blanning, T. C. W.   306.4

The **triumph** of numbers. Cohen, I. B.   519.5

The **triumph** of the moon. Hutton, R.   133.4

TRIVIA *See* Curiosities and wonders; Questions and answers

TROJAN WAR

See also Greek mythology; Troy (Extinct city)

Alexander, C. The war that killed Achilles   883

Homer The Iliad   883

Tuchman, B. W. The march of folly   909.08

Wood, M. In search of the Trojan War   939

TROJAN WAR—LITERATURE AND THE WAR

Alexander, C. The war that killed Achilles   883

Manguel, A. Homer's The Iliad and The Odyssey   883

Trombetta, Jim

(ed) The Horror! The horror!   741.5

TROMBONISTS

Dance, S. The world of Count Basie   920

TROODON

See also Dinosaurs

Tropiano, Stephen

Obscene, indecent, immoral, and offensive   791.43

TROPICAL FISH

See also Fishes

Smith, C. L. National Audubon Society field guide to tropical marine fishes of the Caribbean, the Gulf of Mexico, Florida, the Bahamas, and Bermuda   597

TROPICAL FRUIT

Gollner, A. The fruit hunters   641.3

TROPICAL MEDICINE

See also Medicine

TROPICAL PLANTS

Taylor, L. The healing power of rainforest herbs   615

Trotsky. Service, R.   92

Trott, Barry

Read on . . . crime fiction   016

TROUBADOURS

See also French poetry; Minstrels; Poets

The **trouble** with physics. Smolin, L.   530.1

The **trouble** with poetry and other poems. Collins, B.   811

The **trouble** with Tom: the strange afterlife and times of Thomas Paine. Collins, P.   92

Troublemaker. Wu, H.   951.05

The **troubles.** Coogan, T. P.   941.6

Troupe, Quincy

Davis, M. Miles, the autobiography   92

Gardner, C. The pursuit of happyness   92

Miles and me: biography of Miles Davis   780.92

Transcircularities   811

TROUT

Trout and salmon of North America   597

TROUT—NORTH AMERICA

Trout and salmon of North America   597

Trout and salmon of North America.   597

TROUT FISHING

See also Fishing

Harrop, R. Learning from the water   799.1

Schullery, P. The rise   799.1

Troutt, David Dante

(ed) After the storm   305

Troyat, Henri

Catherine the Great   92

TRUCK FARMING

See also Agriculture; Gardening; Horticulture

Truck: a love story. Perry, M.   629.223

TRUCKING

See also Freight; Transportation

TRUCKING EXECUTIVES

Russell, T. Out of the jungle   92

TRUCKS

See also Automobiles; Highway transportation; Motor vehicles

Perry, M. Truck: a love story   629.223

Trudeau, Noah Andre

Like men of war   973.7

True and false. Mamet, D.   792

True compass. Kennedy, E. M.   92

True green @ work. McKay, K.   363.7

True north. Conway, J. K.   92

True notebooks. Salzman, M.   371.9

True story swear to God archives, vol. 1. Beland, T.   741.5

Trulock, Notra

Code name Kindred Spirit   327.12

Truman. McCullough, D. G.   973.918

Truman Capote. Plimpton, G.   813

Truman Capote, enfant terrible. Long, R. E.   92

Trumble, Angus

The finger   306.4

TRUMPET

Gabbard, K. Hotter than that   788

TRUMPET—HISTORY

Gabbard, K. Hotter than that   788

TRUMPET—METHODS (JAZZ)

Gabbard, K. Hotter than that   788

The **trumpet** of conscience. King, M. L.   973.92

TRUMPET PLAYERS

Armstrong, L. Louis Armstrong, in his own words   781.65

Collier, J. L. Louis Armstrong, an American ge-

gration

URBANIZATION

See also Cities and towns; Rural sociology; Social change; Social conditions; Urban sociology

DeStefano, S. Coyote at the kitchen door **578.7**

Duany, A. Suburban nation **307.76**

Saunders, D. Arrival city **307.24**

URBANIZATION—ENVIRONMENTAL ASPECTS

DeStefano, S. Coyote at the kitchen door **578.7**

URBANIZATION—UNITED STATES

Duany, A. Suburban nation **307.76**

An **urchin** in the storm. Gould, S. J. **570**

Urdang, Laurence

(ed) The timetables of American history **902**

(ed) Twentieth century American nicknames **929.4**

Ure, Susan

Scrapbooking your vacations **745.593**

URINARY INCONTINENCE

Genadry, R. A woman's guide to urinary incontinence **616.6**

URINARY INCONTINENCE—ETIOLOGY

Murphy, M. Pelvic health and childbirth **618.4**

Urofsky, Melvin I.

Finkelman, P. Landmark decisions of the United States Supreme Court **347**

(ed) The Supreme Court justices: a biographical dictionary **920.003**

Louis D. Brandeis **92**

UROGYNECOLOGY

Murphy, M. Pelvic health and childbirth **618.4**

Urquhart, Rachel

Gross, K. J. Woman's face **646.7**

Urrea, Luis Alberto

The devil's highway **304.8**

Urrutia, Matilde

My life with Pablo Neruda **92**

Ury, William

Getting past no **158**

US *See* United States

USA *See* United States

Usability testing for library websites. Norlin, E. **025.04**

The **use** and abuse of literature. Garber, M. **801**

USE STUDIES

Greiner, T. Analyzing library collection use with Excel **025.2**

Use your head to get your foot in the door. Mackay, H. **650.14**

USER INTERFACES (COMPUTER SYSTEMS)—TESTING

Norlin, E. Usability testing for library websites **025.04**

A **user's** guide to the brain. Ratey, J. J. **612.8**

A **user's** guide to the universe. Goldberg, D. **530**

USSR *See* Russia—History—1917-1991, Soviet Union

USURY

Mayer, R. Quick cash **332**

UTERINE FIBROIDS

Goodwin, S. C. What your doctor may not tell you about fibroids **616.99**

UTILITARIANISM

See also Ethics

UTILIZATION OF WASTE *See* Salvage

Utley, Robert Marshall

Billy the Kid **364.1**

Custer: cavalier in buckskin **973.8**

Sitting Bull: the life and times of an American patriot **92**

UTOPIAN FICTION

See also Fantasy fiction; Science fiction

UTOPIAN LITERATURE *See* Utopian fiction; Utopias

Utopianism and communitarianism [series]

Chevannes, B. Rastafari: roots and ideology **299.6**

UTOPIAS

See also Political science; Socialism

Francis, R. Fruitlands **974.4**

Heilbroner, R. L. The worldly philosophers **330.1**

Plato The republic **888**

Utter, Glenn H.

Encyclopedia of gun control and gun rights **363.33**

UXORICIDE—NEW YORK (STATE)—NEW YORK

Salamon, J. Facing the wind **364.15**

V

V.S. Pritchett: a working life. Treglown, J. **92**

VACATION HOMES

See also Houses

VACATIONS

See also Recreation

Vaccari, John A.

Brady, G. S. Materials handbook **620.1**

Vaccinated. Offit, P. A. **92**

VACCINATION

See also Immunization; Preventive medicine; Public health

Allen, A. Vaccine **614.4**

Friedman, M. Medicine's 10 greatest discoveries **610**

Kirby, D. Evidence of harm **614.4**

Offit, P. A. Deadly choices **614.4**

Offit, P. A. Vaccinated **92**

Sears, R. The vaccine book **614.4**

VACCINATION—HISTORY

Allen, A. Vaccine **614.4**

VACCINATION OF CHILDREN

Offit, P. A. Deadly choices **614.4**

VACCINATION OF CHILDREN—COMPLICA-

Food plants of the world   **581.6**

Vance, Ellie
Gordon, M. M. The needlecraft book   **746.4**

Vance, Jeffrey
Keaton, E. Buster Keaton remembered   **791.43**

Vancouver, George
About
Raban, J. Passage to Juneau   **979.8**

VanDeMark, Brian
McNamara, R. S. In retrospect   **959.704**

Vanderbilt, Tom
Traffic   **629.28**

Vanderhoof-Forschner, Karen
Everything you need to know about Lyme disease and other tick-borne disorders   **616.9**

VanderKam, James C.
(ed) The Encyclopedia of the Dead Sea scrolls **296.1**

VanderVelde, Lea
Mrs. Dred Scott   **92**

VanDyne, Stacia N.
(ed) Encyclopedia of American business   **338**

Vanished smile. Scotti, R. A.   **759**

A **vanished** world. Lowney, C.   **946**

Vanishing histories. Amery, C.   **363.6**

The **vanishing** hitchhiker. Brunvand, J. H.   **398.2**

VANISHING SPECIES *See* Endangered species

Vanity Fair, the portraits. Carter, G.   **779**

Vannucci, Lynn
Buckley, J. A. Healing our autistic children   **618**

Vanzetti, Bartolomeo, 1888-1927 (Italian anarchist)
About
Watson, B. Sacco and Vanzetti   **345**

Vardaman, Lisa
(ed) Our new public, a changing clientele   **025.1**

Vare, Ethlie Ann
Patently female   **609.2**

Vargas Llosa, Mario
The language of passion   **864**

VARIATION (BIOLOGY)
See also Biology; Genetics; Heredity

The **varieties** of religious experience. James, W. **210**

VARIETY SHOWS (RADIO PROGRAMS)
See also Radio programs

VARIETY SHOWS (TELEVISION PROGRAMS)
See also Television programs

Varmus, Harold
The art and politics of science   **92**

VARSITY SPORTS *See* College sports

VASECTOMY
See also Sterilization (Birth control)

Vassallo, Jody
Vegetable basics   **641.6**

VASSALS *See* Feudalism

Vassiliev, Alexander
Haynes, J. E. Spies   **327.12**

Weinstein, A. The haunted wood   **327.12**

A **vast** conspiracy. Toobin, J. R.   **973.929**

VATICAN COUNCIL (2ND: 1962-1965)
See also Councils and synods

VAUDEVILLE
See also Amusements; Theater
Trav S. D. No applause, just throw money; or, The book that made vaudeville famous   **792.7**

VAUDEVILLE—UNITED STATES
Trav S. D. No applause, just throw money; or, The book that made vaudeville famous   **792.7**

Vaughan, Christopher
Dement, W. C. The promise of sleep   **612.8**

Vaughan, Hal
Sleeping with the enemy   **92**

Vaughan, William
(ed) Encyclopedia of artists   **709**

VCR troubleshooting & repair. Capelo, G. R.   **621.388**

VD *See* Sexually transmitted diseases

Veasey, Nick
X-ray   **779**

Veblen, Thorstein
The theory of the leisure class   **305.5**

Vecsey, George
Baseball: a history of America's favorite game   **796.357**
Wu, H. Troublemaker   **951.05**

VEDANTA
See also Hinduism; Theosophy
Goldberg, P. American Veda   **294.5**

Vedantam, Shankar
The hidden brain   **154.2**

VEDAS
See also Hinduism; Sacred books

Vega, Lope de
Three major plays   **862**

VEGAN COOKERY
Robertson, R. Vegan planet   **641.5**

Vegan pie in the sky. Moskowitz, I. C.   **641.5**

Vegan planet. Robertson, R.   **641.5**

Vegetable basics. Vassallo, J.   **641.6**

The **vegetable** gardener's bible. Smith, E. C.   **635**

The **vegetable** gardener's container bible. Smith, E. C.   **635**

VEGETABLE GARDENING
See also Gardening; Horticulture
The backyard homestead   **641**
Bartholomew, M. All new square foot gardening   **635**
Coleman, E. Winter harvest handbook   **635**
Homegrown harvest   **635**
Pleasant, B. Starter vegetable gardens   **635**
Smith, E. C. The vegetable gardener's bible   **635**
Smith, E. C. The vegetable gardener's container bible   **635**

Verner, Miroslav
  The pyramids   **932**
The **Verneys.** Tinniswood, A.   **920**
VERSE SATIRE, ENGLISH.
  Poems./Selections Selected poetry   **821**
Versed. Armantrout, R.   **811**
VERSIFICATION
  See also Authorship; Poetics; Rhythm
VERTEBRATES
  See also Animals
The **vertical** farm. Despommier, D. D.   **630**
Vertigo. Auiler, D.   **791.43**
The **vertigo** years. Blom, P.   **940.2**
A **very** brief history of eternity. Eire, C. M. N.   **236**
A **very** different age. Diner, S. J.   **973.8**
Very short introductions [series]
  Bushman, R. L. Mormonism   **289.3**
  Close, F. E. Nothing   **530**
VESTA (ROMAN DEITY)
  See also Gods and goddesses
Vesuvius: a biography. Scarth, A.   **551.2**
VETERANS
  See also Military art and science; Veterans
  Alexander, L. Biggest brother   **92**
  Allport, A. Demobbed   **305.9**
  Bissell, T. The father of all things   **959.704**
  Burgin, R. V. Islands of the damned   **940.54**
  Cadillac Man Land of the lost souls   **92**
  Cleland, M. Heart of a patriot   **92**
  Coleman, P. Flashback   **616.85**
  Dyer, G. The missing of the Somme   **940.4**
  Guibert, E. Alan's war   **741.5**
  Heard, A. The eyes of Willie McGee   **364.66**
  Hillenbrand, L. Unbroken   **940.54**
  Kaplan, A. Y. The interpreter   **940.54**
  Matsakis, A. Vietnam wives   **616.85**
  Nelson, J. C. The remains of Company D   **920**
  Slone, L. B. After the war zone   **616.85**
  Voices of war   **355**
VETERANS—EDUCATION
  See also Education
VETERANS—UNITED STATES
  Cleland, M. Heart of a patriot   **92**
VETERANS—UNITED STATES—BIOGRA-PHY
  Voices of war   **355**
VETERANS DAY
  See also Holidays
VETERINARIANS
  Herriot, J. All creatures great and small   **92**
  Herriot, J. James Herriot's dog stories   **636.7**
VETERINARY ACUPUNCTURE
  Schoen, A. M. Kindred spirits   **636.089**
VETERINARY MEDICINE
  See also Medicine
  Goldstein, M. The nature of animal healing **636.089**

Herriot, J. All creatures great and small   **92**
Pinney, C. C. The complete home veterinary guide   **636.089**
Schoen, A. M. Kindred spirits   **636.089**
Wells, J. All my patients have tales   **636**
VETERINARY MEDICINE—DICTIONARIES
  Black's veterinary dictionary   **636.089**
VETERINARY MEDICINE—HANDBOOKS, MANUALS, ETC.
  The Merck veterinary manual   **636.089**
  The Merck/Merial manual for pet health   **636.089**
Vetri, Marc
  Il viaggio di Vetri   **641.5**
VIADUCTS *See* Bridges
VIBRATION
  See also Mechanics; Sound
VICE
  See also Conduct of life; Ethics; Human behavior
The **vice** presidents. Waldrup, C. C.   **920.003**
VICE-PRESIDENTS
  See also Presidents
  Abuse of power   **973.924**
  Adams, J. My dearest friend   **92**
  Becker, C. The Declaration of Independence **973.3**
  Berman, L. No peace, no honor   **959.704**
  Bernstein, R. B. Thomas Jefferson   **92**
  Beschloss, M. R. The conquerors: Roosevelt, Truman, and the destruction of Hitler's Germany, 1941-1945   **940.53**
  Black, C. M. Richard M. Nixon   **92**
  Brookhiser, R. America's first dynasty   **973.4**
  Burns, J. M. The three Roosevelts   **973.91**
  Burstein, A. Madison and Jefferson   **973.4**
  Busby, H. W. The thirty-first of March   **973.923**
  Bush, B. Barbara Bush   **92**
  Bush, G. All the best, George Bush   **92**
  Caro, R. A. Master of the senate   **92**
  Caro, R. A. Means of ascent   **92**
  Caro, R. A. The path to power   **973.9**
  Cerami, C. A. Jefferson's great gamble   **973.4**
  Cohen, I. B. Science and the founding fathers **973.3**
  Cooper, J. M. The warrior and the priest: Woodrow Wilson and Theodore Roosevelt   **92**
  Cordery, S. A. Alice   **92**
  Crapol, E. P. John Tyler   **92**
  Dallek, R. Harry S. Truman   **92**
  Dallek, R. Nixon and Kissinger   **92**
  Davis, W. C. An honorable defeat   **973.7**
  Dershowitz, A. M. Supreme injustice   **324.9**
  DiSilvestro, R. L. Theodore Roosevelt in the Badlands   **92**
  Egan, T. The big burn   **973.91**
  Ellis, J. J. American sphinx: the character of Thomas Jefferson   **973.4**
  Ellis, J. J. Founding brothers   **973.4**

Ferguson Publishing The top 100 **331.7**

Hawley, C. F. 10 make-or-break career moments **650.1**

Jerrard, J. Crisis in employment **025.5**

Martini, K. Thank you for firing me! **650.14**

McKenna, A. Nontraditional careers for women and men **331.702**

Parini, J. The art of teaching **371.1**

Richardson, B. G. Career comeback **650.14**

Tortorella, N. Starting your career as a freelance web designer **006.7**

United States/Bureau of Labor Statistics Occupational outlook handbook 2010-2011 **331.7**

VOCATIONAL GUIDANCE—ENCYCLOPEDIAS

J.G. Ferguson Publishing Company Encyclopedia of careers and vocational guidance **331.7**

VOCATIONAL GUIDANCE—INFORMATION SERVICES

Jerrard, J. Crisis in employment **025.5**

VOCATIONAL GUIDANCE—UNITED STATES

Gardella, R. The Harvard Business School guide to finding your next job **650.14**

VOCATIONAL GUIDANCE—UNITED STATES—JUVENILE LITERATURE

McKenna, A. Nontraditional careers for women and men **331.702**

VOCATIONAL GUIDANCE FOR THE HANDICAPPED

See also Handicapped; Vocational guidance

VOCATIONAL GUIDANCE IN LIBRARIES

Jerrard, J. Crisis in employment **025.5**

VOCATIONS *See* Occupations; Professions

VOCODER

Tompkins, D. How to wreck a nice beach **621.382**

VODUN *See* Voodooism

Vogel, Ezra F.

Deng Xiaoping and the transformation of China **951.05**

Vogel, Steve

The Pentagon **355.6**

Vogel, Steven

Cats' paws and catapults **571.4**

Vogler, Amy

Lang, A. P. Serious barbecue **641.5**

Vogue knitting stitchionary: cables. **746.43**

The **voice.** Quasthoff, T. **92**

VOICE

See also Language and languages; Throat

Karpf, A. The human voice **153**

Linklater, K. Freeing the natural voice **808.5**

VOICE—POETRY

Fay-LeBlanc, G. Death of a ventriloquist **811**

The **voice** at 3:00 a.m. Simic, C. **811**

VOICE CULTURE

See also Public speaking; Singing; Speech

Voice of America. Heil, A. L. **384.54**

The **voice** of reason; essays in objectivist thought. Rand, A. **191**

Voices in our blood. **323.1**

Voices of war. **355**

Voices rising. **976.3**

VOLCANISM—ITALY

Scarth, A. Vesuvius: a biography **551.2**

The **volcano** adventure guide. Lopes, R. M. C. **910.2**

Volcano cowboys. Thompson, D. **551.21**

VOLCANOES

See also Geology; Mountains; Physical geography

Calderazzo, J. Rising fire: volcanoes and our inner lives **551.2**

Gates, A. E. Encyclopedia of earthquakes and volcanoes **551.2**

Lopes, R. M. C. The volcano adventure guide **910.2**

Oppenheimer, C. Eruptions that shook the world **551.2**

Scarth, A. Vesuvius: a biography **551.2**

Thompson, D. Volcano cowboys **551.21**

Winchester, S. Krakatoa: the day the world exploded, August 27, 1883 **551.2**

VOLCANOES—ENCYCLOPEDIAS

Gates, A. E. Encyclopedia of earthquakes and volcanoes **551.2**

VOLCANOES—UNITED STATES

Carson, R. Mount St. Helens: the eruption and recovery of a volcano **551.2**

VOLCANOLOGICAL RESEARCH—HISTORY—20TH CENTURY

Thompson, D. Volcano cowboys **551.21**

Volkogonov, Dmitrii Antonovich

Lenin **947.084**

Volkov, Solomon

Romanov riches **891.7**

St. Petersburg **947**

Vollers, Maryanne

(jt. auth) Spacek, S. My extraordinary ordinary life **791.43**

VOLLEYBALL

See also Ball games; Sports

Vollmann, William T.

Kissing the mask **792.7**

Poor people **362.5**

Uncentering the Earth **92**

Vollstedt, Maryana

The big book of soups & stews **641.8**

Volpe, Joseph

The toughest show on earth **92**

Volpone and other plays. Jonson, B. **822**

Voltaire

The portable Voltaire **848**

Voltaire almighty. Pearson, R. **92**

VOLUME (CUBIC CONTENT)

Wall Street journal book [series]

Noonan, P. A heart, a cross & a flag   **973.931**

A Wall Street Journal book [series]

Rabinowitz, D. No crueler tyrannies   **345**

The **Wall** Street Journal complete home owner's guidebook. Crook, D.   **643**

The **Wall** Street Journal essential guide to management. Wall Street journal   **658**

The **Wall** Street Journal: financial guidebook for new parents. Bradford, S. L.   **332.024**

Wall, Cheryl A.

(ed) Folklore, memoirs, and other writings   **398**

Women of the Harlem Renaissance   **810**

Wall, Joseph Frazier

Andrew Carnegie   **973.8**

Wallace, Anthony F. C.

The long bitter trail   **323.1**

Wallace, Benjamin

The billionaire's vinegar   **641.2**

Wallace, Carol McD

(jt. auth) MacColl, G. To marry an English Lord   **974.7**

Wallace, Daniel

Beatty, S. The DC Comics encyclopedia   **741.5**

Wallace, Daniel J.

Fibromyalgia: an essential guide for patients and their families   **616.7**

Wallace, Danny

Friends like these   **92**

Wallace, David Foster

Consider the lobster   **814**

Wallace, David Rains

The bonehunters' revenge   **560**

Wallace, Janice Brock

Wallace, D. J. Fibromyalgia: an essential guide for patients and their families   **616.7**

Wallace, Joseph

A gathering of wonders   **508**

Wallace, Michael

Burrows, E. G. Gotham   **974.7**

Wallace, Tim

McKay, K. True green @ work   **363.7**

Wallach, Edward E.

Hysterectomy: exploring your options   **618.1**

Wallach, Eli

The good, the bad, and me   **92**

Wallach, Janet

Desert queen   **956**

Wallechinsky, David

The complete book of the Winter Olympics   **796.98**

Wallenstein, Peter

(ed) The Encyclopedia of American political history   **973**

Waller, Maureen

Sovereign ladies   **920**

Wallerstein, Judith S.

Second chances   **306.89**

Wallis, Michael

Mankiller, W. Mankiller: a chief and her people **92**

Billy the Kid   **92**

Route 66: the mother road   **917**

WALLPAPER

See also Interior design

WALLS

See also Buildings; Civil engineering

The **walls** came tumbling down. Stokes, G. **947.085**

Walls, Jeannette

The glass castle   **92**

Walsh, Bill

The score takes care of itself   **658.4**

Walsh, Craig

Walsh, B. The score takes care of itself   **658.4**

Walsh, Jim

The Replacements: all over but the shouting   **920**

Walsh, John

The J. Paul Getty Museum and its collections **708.1**

Public enemies   **364.1**

Walsh, John Evangelist

Midnight dreary   **818**

Moonlight   **345**

Walsh, Judith E.

A brief history of India   **954**

Walsh, Kenneth T.

Air Force One   **387.7**

Walsh, Keri

(ed) The letters of Sylvia Beach   **92**

Walsh, Michael

Jordan, D. White cargo   **326**

The dirt riddles   **811**

Walsh, Mikey

Gypsy boy   **305.891**

Walsh, Patrick J.

Echoes among the stars   **629.4**

Walsh, Peter

How to organize just about everything   **640**

Lighten up   **332.024**

Walsh, Stephen

Stravinsky: a creative spring   **92**

Stravinsky: the second exile   **92**

Walsh, William E.

Food allergies   **616.97**

Walter Benjamin at the Dairy Queen. McMurtry, L.   **818**

Walter, Carole

Great pies & tarts   **641.8**

Walters, Barbara

Audition   **92**

Walters, Mark Jerome

Six modern plagues and how we are causing them   **614.4**

Walters, Ronald W.

Freedom is not enough   **324.6**

Hip hop matters	781.64
Watkins, T. H.	
The hungry years	973.91
Watman, Max	
Chasing the white dog	363.4
WATSON (COMPUTER)	
Baker, S. Final Jeopardy	006.3
Watson, Bruce	
Freedom summer	323.1
Sacco and Vanzetti	345
Watson, Burton	
(ed) The Columbia book of Chinese poetry	895.1
Watson, James D., 1928-	
Avoid boring people	92
The double helix	572.8
Genes, girls, and Gamow	92
Watson, Lucy	
Life drawing class	743
Watson, Lyall	
Dark nature	111
Jacobson's organ and the remarkable nature of smell	612.8
Watson, Peter	
The German genius	943
Watson, Richard A.	
Cogito ergo sum: the life of Rene Descartes	92
Watson, Victor	
(ed) The Cambridge guide to children's books in English	028.5
Watstein, Sarah Barbara	
(jt. auth) Stratton, S. E. The encyclopedia of HIV and AIDS	616.97
Watters, David H.	
(ed) The Encyclopedia of New England	974
Watters, James	
Howard, J. Jean Howard's Hollywood	791.43
Watterson, Bill	
The complete Calvin and Hobbes	741.5
Watts, Alan	
The way of Zen	294.3
Watts, Duncan J.	
Everything is obvious	153.4
Watts, Jill	
Hattie McDaniel	92
Watts, Jonathan	
When a billion Chinese jump	363.7
Watts, Steven	
Mr. Playboy	92
The people's tycoon	92
Waugh, Alexander	
Fathers and sons	920
The House of Wittgenstein	920
Wauson, Jennifer	
Stroman, J. Administrative assistant's and secretary's handbook	651.3
The **wave**. Casey, S.	551.46

WAVE MECHANICS
> *See also* Mechanics; Quantum theory; Waves

Wave of destruction. Krauss, E.	959.3
Wax, Imy F.	
Kravets, M. The K & W guide to colleges for students with learning disabilities or attention deficit hyperactivity disorder	378
Waxman, Sharon	
Rebels on the backlot	920
The **way** it is. Stafford, W. E.	811
Way more West. Dorn, E.	811
A **way** of being. Rogers, C. R.	150.19
The **way** of the cell. Harold, F. M.	571.6
The **way** of the panda. Nicholls, H.	599.7
The **way** of Zen. Watts, A.	294.3
Way out there in the blue. FitzGerald, F.	973.927
The **way** the world works. Baker, N.	814
The **way** to cook. Child, J.	641.5
The **way** to write for children. Aiken, J.	808.06
Way, Lawrence W.	
(ed) Current surgical diagnosis & treatment	617
Wayne, Tiffany K.	
Critical companion to Ralph Waldo Emerson	818
Ways of forgetting, ways of remembering. Dower, J. W.	940.53
We are Americans. Perez, W.	371.82
We are our mothers' daughters. Roberts, C.	305.4
We are soldiers still. Moore, H. G.	959.704
We are still here. Iverson, P.	970.004
We care guides [series]	
Green volunteers	333.72
World volunteers	361.7
We first. Mainwaring, S.	658.8
We have met the enemy. Akst, D.	153.8
We meant well. Van Buren, P.	956.7044
We shall overcome. Boyd, H.	323.1
We tell ourselves stories in order to live. Didion, J.	814
We were soldiers once—and young. Moore, H. G.	959.704
We wish to inform you that tomorrow we will be killed with our families. Gourevitch, P.	967.571
WEALTH	
See also Economics; Finance	
Atwood, M. Payback	332.7
Bernstein, W. The birth of plenty	339.2
The great divergence	339.2
Madrick, J. G. Age of greed	330.9
Milanovic, B. The haves and the have-nots	339.2
Orman, S. The money class	332.024
Phillips, K. P. Wealth and democracy	305.5
Ridley, M. The rational optimist	339.2
WEALTH—HISTORY	
Milanovic, B. The haves and the have-nots	339.2
WEALTH—MORAL AND ETHICAL ASPECTS	
Madrick, J. G. Age of greed	330.9

Webb, Robyn
Warshaw, H. S. The diabetes food & nutrition bible | **616.4**

Webber, Carmen
Chic sweats | **746.9**

Weber, Bruce
As they see 'em | **796.357**

Weber, Eugen
Apocalypses | **200**

Weber, Mark Christopher
Brushwork essentials | **751.4**

Weber, Nancy S.
Smith, A. H. The mushroom hunter's field guide | **579.6**

Weber, Nicholas Fox, 1947-
The Bauhaus group | **920**

Weber, R. David
Schlachter, G. A. Financial aid for the disabled and their families, 2010-2012 | **378.3**

Weber, Robert J.
The created self | **155.2**

Weber, Thomas
Hitler's first war | **940.4**

WEBLOGS
See also Diaries; Online journalism
Wasik, B. And then there's this | **303.4**

WEBSITES *See* Web sites

Webster's New World Robert's rules of order. Robert, H. M. | **060.4**

Webster's third new international dictionary of the English language, unabridged. | **423**

Webster, Charles
Paracelsus | **92**

Webster, Raymond B.
African American firsts in science and technology | **508**

Wecht, Cyril H.
Tales from the morgue | **614**

The **wedding** book. Weiss, M. | **395**
A **wedding** in Haiti. Alvarez, J. | **FIC**
Wedding of the waters. Bernstein, P. L. | **386**

WEDDINGS
See also Marriage
Alvarez, J. A wedding in Haiti | **FIC**
Bride's book of etiquette | **395**
Into the garden | **808.8**
Mead, R. One perfect day | **392**
Outcalt, T. Your beautiful wedding on any budget | **395**
Post, P. Emily Post's wedding etiquette | **395**
Vivaldo, D. Do it for le$$! weddings | **395**
Warner, D. How to have a big wedding on a small budget | **395**
Weiss, M. The wedding book | **395**

WEDDINGS—SOCIAL ASPECTS
Mead, R. One perfect day | **392**

Weddington, Sarah Ragle
A question of choice | **363.46**

Wednesday comics. | **741.5**

A **weed** by any other name. Gift, N. | **635.9**

Weeding library collections. Slote, S. J. | **025.2**

Weeds. Mabey, R. | **632**

WEEDS
See also Agricultural pests; Economic botany; Gardening; Plants
Gift, N. A weed by any other name | **635.9**
Mabey, R. Weeds | **632**

WEEK
See also Calendars; Chronology
A **week** on the Concord and Merrimack rivers; Walden, or, Life in the woods; The Maine woods; Cape Cod. Thoreau, H. D. | **818**

The **weekend** that changed Wall Street. Bartiromo, M. | **330.9**

The **weekend** woodworker's project collection. Popular woodworking | **684**

Weems, David B.
Designing, building, and testing your own speaker system with projects | **621.382**

The **weeping** goldsmith. Kress, W. J. | **508**

Weidensaul, Scott
The ghost with trembling wings | **591.68**
Living on the wind | **598**
Of a feather | **598**
Return to wild America | **578**

Weigel, George
Witness to hope: the biography of Pope John Paul II | **92**

Weighing the world. Danson, E. | **526**

WEIGHT
See also Physics

WEIGHT CONTROL *See* Weight loss

WEIGHT LIFTING
See also Athletics; Exercise
Fahey, T. D. Basic weight training for men and women | **613.7**
Hesson, J. L. Weight training for life | **613.7**
Pagano, J. Strength training for women | **613.7**

WEIGHT LOSS
Agatston, A. The South Beach diet | **613.2**
Ali, K. Fighting weight | **92**
Atkins, R. C. Dr. Atkins' new diet revolution | **613.2**
Baroni, B. Fat kid got fit | **362.196**
Bijlefeld, M. Encyclopedia of diet fads | **613.2**
Jones, H. K. Good housekeeping drop 5 lbs | **613.2**
Kolata, G. Rethinking thin | **613.2**
The Mayo Clinic diet | **613.2**
Nesheim, M. Why calories count | **613.2**
Nichter, M. Fat talk | **613.2**
Steward, H. L. The new sugar busters! | **613.2**
Taubes, G. Why we get fat and what to do about it | **613.7**

Weiss, Michael A.
Kolpan, S. Exploring wine   **641.2**

Weiss, Mindy
The wedding book   **395**

Weiss, Mitch
Sallah, M. Tiger Force   **959.704**

Weisskopf, Michael
Blood brothers   **92**

Weiswasser, Janet Z.
(ed) The Yale guide to children's nutrition   **613.2**

Welch, Craig
Shell games   **364.1**

Welch, James
Killing Custer   **973.8**

Welch, John F.
Winning   **658.4**

Welch, Robert
(ed) The Oxford companion to Irish literature   **820**

Welch, Suzy
Welch, J. F. Winning   **658.4**

Welcome to the departure lounge. Federico, M.   **92**

Welcome to Utopia. Valby, K.   **976.4**

Welcome to your brain. Aamodt, S.   **612.8**

WELDING
    See also Blacksmithing; Forging; Ironwork; Manufacturing processes; Metalwork

Weldon, Fay
Auto da Fay   **823**

WELFARE RECIPIENTS—EMPLOYMENT—NEW YORK (STATE)—NEW YORK—CASE STUDIES
Hancock, L. Hands to work   **361.6**

WELFARE RECIPIENTS—NEW YORK (STATE)—NEW YORK—CASE STUDIES
Hancock, L. Hands to work   **361.6**

WELFARE REFORM *See* Public welfare

WELFARE STATE
    See also Economic policy; Public welfare; Social policy; State, The

WELFARE WORK *See* Charities; Social work

WELFARE, PUBLIC *See* Public welfare

Welky, David
The thousand-year flood   **363.34**

The **well** cat book. McGinnis, T.   **636.8**

The **well** dog book. McGinnis, T.   **636.7**

Well-behaved women seldom make history. Ulrich, L.   **305.4**

The **well-designed** mixed garden. DiSabato-Aust, T.   **635**

The **well-dressed** ape. Holmes, H.   **612**

A **well-ordered** thing: Dmitrii Mendeleev and the shadow of the periodic table. Gordin, M. D.   **92**

The **well-tended** perennial garden. DiSabato-Aust, T.   **635.9**

Welland, Michael
Sand   **553.6**

Weller's war. Weller, G.   **940.53**

Weller, Anthony
(ed) Weller, G. Weller's war   **940.53**

Weller, Eleanor
Griswold, M. K. The golden age of American gardens   **712**

Weller, George
Weller's war   **940.53**

Weller, Sam
The Bradbury chronicles   **92**

Weller, Sheila
Girls like us   **920**

Wellington. Hibbert, C.   **92**

WELLS
    See also Hydraulic engineering

Wells, C. M.
Sailing from Byzantium   **940.2**

Wells, Carol Wilcox
The art & elegance of beadweaving   **745.58**

Wells, Diana
100 flowers and how they got their names   **582.13**
Lives of the trees   **582.16**

Wells, H. G., 1866-1946 (English science fiction novelist)

        About
McKillop, A. B. The spinster & the prophet **941.08**

Wells, Jeff
All my patients have tales   **636**

Wells, Patricia
Patricia Wells' trattoria   **641.5**
The Provence cookbook   **641.5**
Vegetable harvest   **641.6**

Wells, Stanley W.
(ed) The Oxford companion to Shakespeare   **822.3**
(ed) Shakespeare, W. The complete works   **822.3**
Shakespeare: for all time   **822.3**

The **wellspring.** Olds, S.   **811**

Welsh, James Michael
(ed) Siegel, S. The encyclopedia of Hollywood   **791.43**

Weltman, Barbara
J.K. Lasser's guide for tough times   **332.024**

Welty, Eudora
One time, one place   **976.2**
One writer's beginnings   **92**
What there is to say we have said   **92**

Wenborn, Neil
(ed) The Columbia companion to British history   **941**

Wendel, Tim
High heat   **796.357**

Wendleton, Kate
Building a great resume   **650.14**

Wendy and the lost boys. Salamon, J.   **920**

Wenger, Debora Halpern
Advancing the story   **070.1**

Wenger, J. Michael

Goldstein, D. M. The Vietnam War: the story and photographs **959.704**

Wenner, Jann S.

(ed) Thompson, H. S. Fear and loathing at Rolling Stone **070.17**

Gonzo **92**

Wenner, Paul F.

Garden cuisine **613.2**

Werblowsky, R. J. Zwi

(ed) The Oxford dictionary of the Jewish religion **296**

WEREWOLVES

See also Folklore

Guiley, R. E. The encyclopedia of vampires & werewolves **398**

WEREWOLVES—ENCYCLOPEDIAS

Guiley, R. E. The encyclopedia of vampires & werewolves **398**

Werker, Kim P.

Keim, C. Teach yourself visually crochet **746.43**

Werlin, Laura

Laura Werlin's cheese essentials **641.6**

Werlock, Abby H. P.

(ed) The Facts on File companion to the American novel **813**

Wernick, Sarah

Henschke, C. I. Lung cancer **616.99**

Nelson, M. E. Strong women, strong bones **616.7**

Wert, Jeffry D.

Cavalryman of the lost cause **92**

Custer **973.8**

Mosby's Rangers **973.7**

Werth, Barry

Banquet at Delmonico's **303.4**

Wertheim, L. Jon

Blood in the cage **92**

Strokes of genius **796.342**

Wertheim, Margaret

Physics on the fringe **530.1**

Wertkin, Gerard C.

(ed) Encyclopedia of American folk art **745**

Wescott, Glenway, 1901-1987 (American novelist and poet)

About

Sontag, S. Where the stress falls **814**

Weski, Thomas

(ed) Eggleston, W. William Eggleston **779**

Wesleyan film [series]

Becker, C. It's the pictures that got small **791.45**

Wesleyan poetry [series]

Armantrout, R. Versed **811**

Brathwaite, E. K. Elegguas **811**

Guest, B. The collected poems of Barbara Guest **811**

Hillman, B. Cascadia **811**

Ignatow, D. I have a name **811**

Ignatow, D. Shadowing the ground **811**

Komunyakaa, Y. Thieves of paradise **811**

Roberson, E. To see the earth before the end of the world **811**

Shockley, E. The new black **811**

Tarn, N. Selected poems **811**

Valentine, J. Door in the mountain **811**

Wessel, David

In Fed we trust **332.1**

The **West**. Ward, G. C. **978**

WEST (U.S.)

See also United States

Carter, R. A. Buffalo Bill Cody **978**

WEST (U.S.)—DESCRIPTION

Frazier, I. Great Plains **917**

Raban, J. Bad land **978**

WEST (U.S.)—EXPLORATION

Black, G. Empire of shadows **978.7**

WEST (U.S.)—HISTORY

See also United States—History

Ambrose, S. E. Nothing like it in the world **385**

Bain, D. H. Empire express **385**

Beck, W. A. Historical atlas of the American West **911**

Brown, D. A. The American West **978**

Brown, D. A. Bury my heart at Wounded Knee **970.004**

Calloway, C. G. One vast winter count **978**

Fried, S. Appetite for America **92**

Groom, W. Kearny's march **979**

Gwynne, S. C. Empire of the summer moon **92**

Lockwood, J. A. Locust **632**

Morgan, R. Lions of the West **920**

Morgan, T. A shovel of stars **978**

Raban, J. Bad land **978**

Schwantes, C. A. The West the railroads made **338**

Sides, H. Blood and thunder **978**

Utley, R. M. Custer: cavalier in buckskin **973.8**

Ward, G. C. The West **978**

Wyman, M. Hoboes **305.5**

WEST (U.S.)—IN ART

Dippie, B. W. The Frederic Remington Art Museum collection **709**

WEST (U.S.)—SOCIAL LIFE AND CUSTOMS

Frazier, I. Great Plains **917**

Luchetti, C. Children of the West **978**

Schlissel, L. Far from home **978**

WEST (U.S.) IN ART

Dippie, B. W. The Frederic Remington Art Museum collection **709**

WEST AFRICA

See also Africa

WEST INDIAN LITERATURE (FRENCH)

See also Literature

West of Kabul, East of New York. Ansary, M.

Wheels for the world. Brinkley, D.   338.7

Wheelwright, Jeff
The wandering gene and the Indian princess **616.99**

Wheen, Francis
Karl Marx   335.4
Strange days indeed   973.92

When a billion Chinese jump. Watts, J.   363.7

When a crocodile eats the sun. Godwin, P.   92

When abortion was a crime. Reagan, L. J.   363.46

When affirmative action was white. Katznelson, I.   323.1

When bad things happen to good people. Kushner, H. S.   296.3

When Baghdad ruled the Muslim world. Kennedy, H.   956.7

When broken glass floats. Him, C.   959.604

When China rules the world. Jacques, M.   327

When do fish sleep? and other imponderables of everyday life. Feldman, D.   031.02

When elephants weep. Masson, J. M.   591.5

When every moment counts. Frist, B.   613.6

When everything changed. Collins, G.   305.4

When gadgets betray us. Vamosi, R.   004

When generations collide. Lancaster, L. C.   658.3

When God talks back. Luhrmann, T. M.   277

When Hollywood had a king. Bruck, C.   338.7

When I am playing with my cat, how do I know she is not playing with me? Frampton, S.   844

When I was a child I read books. Robinson, M.   814

When London was capital of America. Flavell, J.   305.8

When March went mad. Davis, S.   796.323

When memory speaks. Conway, J. K.   808

When Parkinson's strikes early.   616.8

When pride still mattered: a life of Vince Lombardi. Maraniss, D.   92

When religion becomes lethal. Kimball, C.   201

When science meets religion. Barbour, I. G.   261.5

When skateboards will be free. Sayrafiezadeh, S.   92

When that rough god goes riding. Marcus, G.   782.42

When the Garden was Eden. Araton, H.   796.323

When the Mississippi ran backwards. Feldman, J.   551.2

When they come for us we'll be gone. Beckerman, G.   305.8

When they were young. Coles, R.   779

When trumpets call. O'Toole, P.   92

When walking fails. Iezzoni, L.   362.4

When you are engulfed in flames. Sedaris, D.   814

Where China meets India. Thant Myint-U   959.1

Where dead voices gather. Tosches, N.   782

Where did you sleep last night? Senna, D.   92

Where do we go from here. King, M. L.   323.1

Where hell freezes over. Kearns, D. A.   613

Where I was from. Didion, J.   979.4

Where shall I wander. Ashbery, J.   811

Where stuff comes from. Molotch, H. L.   620

Where the dark and the light folks meet. Sandke, R.   781.65

Where the germs are. Bakalar, N.   616

Where the lightning strikes. Nabokov, P.   299.7

Where the right went wrong. Buchanan, P.   973.931

Where the stress falls. Sontag, S.   814

Where the trail grows faint. Hugo, L.   615.8

Where the wild things were. Stolzenberg, W.   577

Wherry, Timothy Lee
Intellectual property   346.04

While America aged. Lowenstein, R.   331.2

While America sleeps. Feingold, R.   327

WHISKEY
Hopkins, K. 99 drams of whiskey   641.2
The **Whiskey** Rebellion. Hogeland, W.   973.4

WHISKEY REBELLION, PA., 1794
Hogeland, W. The Whiskey Rebellion   973.4

Whisky, kilts, and the Loch Ness Monster. Starr, W. W.   914

The **whisperers.** Figes, O.   947.084

WHISTLE BLOWING
     See also Political corruption; Public interest
Bolkovac, K. The whistleblower   92
The **whistleblower.** Bolkovac, K.   92

WHISTLEBLOWING *See* Whistle blowing

Whitaker, Jan
Service and style   381

Whitaker, John O.
National Audubon Society field guide to North American mammals   599

Whitaker, Lang
In the time of Bobby Cox   796.357

Whitaker, Richard
Buckley, B. Weather: a visual guide   551.5

Whitaker, Robert
Anatomy of an epidemic   616.89
Mad in America   616.89
The mapmaker's wife   981

White apples and the taste of stone. Hall, D.   811

White cargo. Jordan, D.   326

The **white** cascade. Krist, G.   979.7

White coat, black hat. Elliott, C.   174.2

WHITE COLLAR CRIMES
     See also Crime

White egrets. Walcott, D.   811

White heat. Wineapple, B.   92

The **White** House. Monkman, B. C.   975.3

The **White** House.   975.3

White House diary. Carter, J.   92

White House Historical Association
The White House   975.3

White Mughals. Dalrymple, W.   954

The **white** rock. Thomson, H.   985

WHITE SUPREMACIST MOVEMENTS *See* White supremacy movements

birds

The **wild** frontier. Osborn, W. M.	**970.004**
Wild justice. Bekoff, M.	**591.5**
The **wild** life of our bodies. Dunn, R.	**579**
The **wild** places. Macfarlane, R.	**914**
Wild romance. Schama, C.	**92**
Wild swans. Chang, J.	**951.05**
The **wild** trees. Preston, R.	**577.3**
Wild west 2.0. Fertik, M.	**659.2**

WILD WEST SHOWS
Warren, L. S. Buffalo Bill's America · **92**

WILDCATS *See* Wild cats

Wilde, Oscar
The artist as critic · **824**
The importance of being earnest and other plays **822**

Wilde, Ralph
Devine, C. Human rights · **323**

The **Wilder** life. McClure, W. · **813**

Wilder, Laura Ingalls, 1867-1957 (American children's and young adult author)

About
McClure, W. The Wilder life · **813**

Wilder, Thornton
Collected plays & writings on theater · **812**
Our town · **812**

WILDERNESS AREAS
Hart, J. Walking softly in the wilderness · **796.51**
Macfarlane, R. The wild places · **914**
Stark, P. The last empty places · **973**

WILDERNESS AREAS—UNITED STATES
Brinkley, D. The wilderness warrior · **92**

Wilderness at dawn. Morgan, T. · **970**

A **wilderness** so immense. Kukla, J. · **973.4**

WILDERNESS SURVIVAL
See also Camping; Outdoor life; Survival skills
Stilwell, A. The encyclopedia of survival techniques · **613.6**
Survival wisdom & know-how · **613.6**
Wiseman, J. SAS survival handbook · **613.6**

The **wilderness** warrior. Brinkley, D. · **92**

The **wildest** ride. Menzer, J. · **796.72**

WILDFIRES
See also Fires
Maclean, J. N. Fire and ashes · **363.3**
Maclean, J. N. The Thirtymile fire · **634.9**

Wildflower. Seal, M. · **92**

WILDFLOWERS *See* Wild flowers

WILDLIFE
See also Animals
Shetterly, S. H. Settled in the wild · **508**

WILDLIFE AND PESTICIDES *See* Pesticides and wildlife

WILDLIFE ATTRACTING
See also Animals

WILDLIFE CONSERVATION
See also Conservation of natural resources; Economic zoology; Endangered species; Environmental protection; Nature conservation
Anthony, L. Babylon's ark · **590.73**
Barrow, M. V. Nature's ghosts · **333.95**
Carson, R. Lost woods · **570**
Chadwick, D. H. The company we keep · **333.95**
DeStefano, S. Coyote at the kitchen door · **578.7**
Fraser, C. Rewilding the world · **333.95**
Goodall, J. The ten trusts · **333.95**
Lebbin, D. J. The American Bird Conservancy guide to bird conservation · **333.95**
The monarch butterfly · **595.7**
Neme, L. A. Animal investigators · **363.2**
Nicholls, H. The way of the panda · **599.7**
Owens, D. The eye of the elephant · **333.95**
Owens, M. Secrets of the savanna · **599**
Schappert, P. The last Monarch butterfly · **595.7**
World atlas of great apes and their conservation · **599.8**

WILDLIFE CONSERVATION—UNITED STATES—HISTORY
Barrow, M. V. Nature's ghosts · **333.95**

WILDLIFE CONSERVATIONISTS—GREAT BRITAIN—BIOGRAPHY
Botting, D. Gerald Durrell · **590**

WILDLIFE CRIMES
Neme, L. A. Animal investigators · **363.2**

WILDLIFE PHOTOGRAPHY
See also Nature photography; Photography

WILDLIFE REFUGES
See also Wildlife conservation
Anthony, L. The elephant whisperer · **599.67**
Westoll, A. The chimps of Fauna Sanctuary · **636.9**

WILDLIFE REHABILITATION
Zickefoose, J. The bluebird effect · **598**

WILDLIFE REHABILITATION—SOUTH AFRICA—CAPE TOWN REGION
DeNapoli, D. The great penguin rescue · **639.9**

WILDLIFE REHABILITATION—UNITED STATES—ANECDOTES
Zickefoose, J. The bluebird effect · **598**

WILDLIFE REHABILITATORS—UNITED STATES—ANECDOTES
Zickefoose, J. The bluebird effect · **598**

WILDLIFE RESCUE—SOUTH AFRICA—CAPE TOWN REGION
DeNapoli, D. The great penguin rescue · **639.9**

WILDLIFE SANCTUARIES *See* Wildlife refuges

WILDLIFE SMUGGLING
Smith, J. E. Stolen world · **364.1**

Wilentz, Sean
Andrew Jackson · **92**
Bob Dylan in America · **92**
The rise of American democracy · **973.5**

Wiley electrical and electronics engineering diction-

Wireless nation. Murray, J. B.   **384.5**

WIRETAPPING

>*See also* Criminal investigation; Right of privacy

Theoharis, A. G. Abuse of power   **363.325**

WIRING, ELECTRIC *See* Electric wiring

Wirtz, James J.

>(ed) Weapons of mass destruction   **358**

Wirzba, Norman

>(ed) The essential agrarian reader   **338.1**

Wischnitzer, Edith

>Wischnitzer, S. Barron's guide to medical & dental schools   **610.69**

Wischnitzer, Saul

>Barron's guide to medical & dental schools   **610.69**

Wisconsin Milk Marketing Board

>The great big cheese cookbook   **641.6**

Wisconsin studies in autobiography [series]

>Humez, J. M. Harriet Tubman   **92**

Wisconsin studies in film [series]

>Neupert, R. A history of the French new wave cinema   **791.43**

Wisdom. Hall, S. S.   **179**

WISDOM

>Alford, H. How to live   **155.67**

Wisdom for a livable planet. McDaniel, C. N. **333.72**

The **wisdom** of crowds. Surowiecki, J.   **303.3**

The **wisdom** of the bones. Walker, A.   **599.93**

The **wisdom** of whores. Pisani, E.   **614.5**

Wise, Anna

>Awakening the mind   **615.8**

Wise, David

>Cassidy's run   **327.12**

>Spy: the inside story of how the FBI's Robert Hanssen betrayed America   **327.12**

>Tiger trap   **327**

Wise, Michael Owen

>Abegg, M. G. The Dead Sea scrolls   **296.1**

Wise, Nicole

>Rosenfeld, A. A. The over-scheduled child   **649**

Wise, Steven M.

>Drawing the line   **179**

>Though the heavens may fall   **342**

Wiseman, Carter

>Shaping a nation   **720.9**

Wiseman, John

>SAS survival handbook   **613.6**

Wish I could be there. Shawn, A.   **92**

Wishart, David J.

>(ed) Encyclopedia of the Great Plains   **978**

WISHES

>*See also* Motivation (Psychology)

Wishful drinking. Fisher, C.   **92**

Wisnia, Saul

>Alpert, M. J. Spinal cord injury and the family **617**

Wit. Edson, M.   **812**

WIT AND HUMOR

>*See also* Literature

Carlin, G. Napalm & silly putty   **817**

Nachman, G. Seriously funny   **792.7**

Oxford dictionary of humorous quotations   **808.88**

Toasts   **808.88**

The **wit** and wisdom of Mark Twain. Twain, M. **818**

WITCHCRAFT

>*See also* Folklore; Occultism

Adler, M. Drawing down the moon   **133.4**

Carlson, L. M. A fever in Salem   **133.4**

Guiley, R. E. The encyclopedia of demons and demonology   **133.4**

Hoffer, P. C. The Salem witchcraft trials   **345**

Hutton, R. The triumph of the moon   **133.4**

Karlsen, C. F. The devil in the shape of a woman   **133.4**

Robisheaux, T. The last witch of Langenburg **133.4**

Stark, R. For the glory of God   **201**

WITCHCRAFT—ENCYCLOPEDIAS

>Guiley, R. E. The encyclopedia of witches, witchcraft, and Wicca   **133.4**

WITCHCRAFT—GERMANY—HISTORY

>Robisheaux, T. The last witch of Langenburg **133.4**

WITCHCRAFT—HISTORY

>Guiley, R. E. The encyclopedia of witches, witchcraft, and Wicca   **133.4**

WITCHCRAFT—MASSACHUSETTS—SALEM—HISTORY—17TH CENTURY

>Carlson, L. M. A fever in Salem   **133.4**

WITCHES

>*See also* Witchcraft

Guiley, R. E. The encyclopedia of witches, witchcraft, and Wicca   **133.4**

Ward, M. C. Voodoo queen   **92**

Witcover, Jules

>The year the dream died   **973.923**

With Billie. Blackburn, J.   **92**

With fire & sword. Nelson, J. L.   **973.3**

With God on our side. Martin, W. C.   **261.8**

With speed and violence. Pearce, F.   **551.6**

With wings like eagles. Korda, M.   **940.54**

Within the plantation household. Fox-Genovese, E.   **305.4**

Without a map. Hall, M.   **92**

Without end. Zagajewski, A.   **891.8**

Without feathers. Allen, W.   **817**

Without saying. Howard, R.   **811**

Without title. Hill, G.   **821**

Witness. Chambers, W.   **92**

Witness.   **940.53**

Witness to an extreme century. Lifton, R. J. **973.92**

Witness to hope: the biography of Pope John Paul II. Weigel, G.   **92**

WITNESSES

>*See also* Litigation; Trials

WORKING CLASS—HISTORY

Murolo, P. From the folks who brought you the weekend **331**

WORKING CLASS—NEW YORK (STATE)—NEW YORK—HISTORY—20TH CENTURY

Freeman, J. B. Working-class New York **305.5**

WORKING CLASS—UNITED STATES—HISTORY

Murolo, P. From the folks who brought you the weekend **331**

WORKING CLASS WHITES—SOUTHERN STATES—BIOGRAPHY

Bragg, R. Ava's man **975**

WORKING CLASS WOMEN—UNITED STATES—BIOGRAPHY

Gorn, E. J. Mother Jones **331.88**

WORKING CLASS WOMEN—UNITED STATES—HISTORY

Kessler-Harris, A. Out to work **331.4**

WORKING CLASSES *See* Working class

WORKING COUPLES *See* Dual-career families

WORKING DOGS

Orlean, S. Rin Tin Tin **636.7**
See also Dogs; Working animals

Working for yourself. Fishman, S. **343**

Working in America. Reef, C. **305**

Working solo. Lonier, T. **658**

Working-class New York. Freeman, J. B. **305.5**

Works and days; and Theogony. Hesiod **881**

The **world** almanac and book of facts, 2011. **031.02**

World artists, 1950-1980. **920.003**

World artists, 1980-1990. **920.003**

A **world** at arms. Weinberg, G. L. **940.53**

World atlas of dog breeds. De Vito, D. **636.7**

World atlas of great apes and their conservation. **599.8**

World authors, 1950-1970. **920.003**

World authors, 1970-1975. **920.003**

World authors, 1975-1980. **920.003**

World authors, 1980-1985. **809**

World authors, 1985-1990. **809**

World authors, 1990-1995. **809**

World authors, 1995-2000. **809**

World authors, 2000-2005. **920.003**

The **world** below the window. Smith, W. J. **811**

The **World** Book encyclopedia. **031**

World cheese book. **641.3**

WORLD CUP (SOCCER)

Dubois, L. Soccer empire **796.334**

Hirshey, D. The ESPN World Cup companion **796.334**

WORLD ECONOMICS *See* Commercial geography; Commercial policy; Economic conditions; International competition

World explorers and discoverers. **920.003**

World folklore for storytellers. **398**

The **world** from my front porch. Towell, L. **779**

WORLD HEALTH

Garrett, L. Betrayal of trust **362.1**

World heritage sites. Unesco **910.2**

WORLD HISTORY

See also History

Brown, C. S. A big history **909**

McKillop, A. B. The spinster & the prophet **941.08**

National Geographic concise history of world religions **200**

National Geographic Society (U.S.) National Geographic visual history of the world **902.2**

The Oxford history of the twentieth century **909.82**

Pagden, A. Peoples and empires **909**

Roberts, J. M. The new history of the world **909**

Solomon, S. Water **553.7**

Standage, T. A history of the world in 6 glasses **394.1**

WORLD HISTORY—12TH CENTURY

See also Middle Ages

WORLD HISTORY—13TH CENTURY

See also Middle Ages

WORLD HISTORY—14TH CENTURY

See also Middle Ages

Tuchman, B. W. A distant mirror **944**

WORLD HISTORY—15TH CENTURY

Cliff, N. Holy war **909**

WORLD HISTORY—15TH CENTURY

Great events from history, The Renaissance & early modern era, 1454-1600 **909**
See also Middle Ages

WORLD HISTORY—16TH CENTURY

Great events from history, The Renaissance & early modern era, 1454-1600 **909**

WORLD HISTORY—17TH CENTURY

Great events from history, The 17th century, 1601-1700 **909**

Great lives from history, The 17th century, 1601-1700 **920.003**

WORLD HISTORY—18TH CENTURY

Craske, M. Art in Europe, 1700-1830 **709.03**

Great events from history, The 18th century, 1701-1800 **909.7**

Great lives from history Great lives from history, The 18th century, 1701-1800 **920.003**

WORLD HISTORY—1945-

Kreisler, H. Political awakenings **920**

Kurlansky, M. 1968 **909.82**

Reynolds, D. One world divisible **909.82**

WORLD HISTORY—19TH CENTURY

Great events from history, The 19th century, 1801-1900 **909.81**

Great lives from history, The 19th century, 1801-1900 **920.003**

Tuchman, B. W. The proud tower **909.82**

WORLD HISTORY—20TH CENTURY

Ramo, J. C. The age of the unthinkable   **973.931**
WORLD POLITICS—FORECASTING
Zakaria, F. The post-American world   **303.49**
**WORLD POLITICS—HANDBOOKS, MANU-
ALS, ETC.**
United States/Central Intelligence Agency   The
CIA world factbook 2011   **910**
WORLD POLITICS, 1945-1989
Dallek, R. The lost peace   **909.82**
WORLD POLITICS, 1945-1989—SOURCES
Hillstrom, K. The Cold War   **909.82**
WORLD POLITICS, 1985-1995—SOURCES
Hillstrom, K. The Cold War   **909.82**
The **World** reacts to the Holocaust.   **940.53**
WORLD RECORDS
See also Curiosities and wonders
**WORLD RECORDS—UNITED STATES—MIS-
CELLANEA**
Black firsts: 4,000 ground-breaking and pioneering
historical events   **305.8**
World religions. Bowker, J.   **200**
WORLD SERIES (BASEBALL)
Frost, M. Game six   **796.357**
World textiles: a concise history. Schoeser, M.   **677**
The **world** that never was. Butterworth, A.   **335**
WORLD TRADE CENTER (NEW YORK, N.Y.)
Dwyer, J. 102 minutes   **974.7**
Friend, D. Watching the world change   **974.7**
Langewiesche, W. American ground, unbuilding
the World Trade Center   **974.7**
Lutnick, H. On top of the world   **332.6**
Smith, D. Report from ground zero   **363.34**
**WORLD TRADE CENTER (NEW YORK, N.Y.)
TERRORIST ATTACK, 2001** *See* September
11 terrorist attacks, 2001
**WORLD TRADE CENTER TERRORIST AT-
TACK, 2001**
Downey, T. The last men out   **363.34**
Dwyer, J. 102 minutes   **974.7**
Gonzalez, J. Fallout   **363.7**
Halberstam, D. Firehouse   **363.34**
Magnum Photos, I. New York September 11   **770**
Smith, D. Report from ground zero   **363.34**
A **world** turned over. Hemingway, L.   **363.34**
World volunteers.   **361.7**
World War I.   **940.3**
WORLD WAR I *See* World War, 1914-1918
World War I almanac. Woodward, D. R.   **940.3**
World War I: the African Front. Paice, E.   **940.4**
World War II.   **940.53**
WORLD WAR II *See* World War, 1939-1945
World War II.   **940.53**
World War II writings. Liebling, A. J.   **940.54**
WORLD WAR III
See also War; World politics
Rosenbaum, R. How the end begins   **355**

World War One. Stone, N.   **940.3**
WORLD WAR, 1914-1918
See also Europe—History—1871-1918;
World history—20th century; World politics
Audoin-Rouzeau, S. 14-18, understanding the
Great War   **940.3**
Barr, J. A line in the sand   **956**
Burg, D. F. Almanac of World War I   **940.3**
Clay, C. King, Kaiser, Tsar   **920**
Competing voices from the Russian Revolu-
tion   **947.084**
Dyer, G. The missing of the Somme   **940.4**
Gilbert, M. The First World War   **940.3**
Kissinger, H. Diplomacy   **327.2**
Liddell Hart, B. H. The real war, 1914-1918 **940.4**
McMeekin, S. The Berlin-Baghdad express   **940.3**
Neiberg, M. Fighting the Great War   **940.4**
Rehnquist, W. H. All the laws but one   **342**
Stone, N. World War One   **940.3**
Strachan, H. The First World War   **940.3**
Tuchman, B. W. The guns of August   **940.3**
The United States in the First World War   **940.3**
Weber, T. Hitler's first war   **940.4**
Woodward, D. R. World War I almanac   **940.3**
World War I   **940.3**
WORLD WAR, 1914-1918—ARMISTICES
Dallas, G. 1918: war and peace   **940.4**
WORLD WAR, 1914-1918—BIOGRAPHY
Hollis, M. Now all roads lead to France   **821**
WORLD WAR, 1914-1918—CAMPAIGNS
D'Este, C. Warlord   **92**
Eisenhower, J. S. D. Yanks: the epic story of the
American Army in World War I   **940.4**
Mosier, J. The myth of the Great War   **940.4**
Ousby, I. The road to Verdun   **940.4**
Weber, T. Hitler's first war   **940.4**
**WORLD WAR, 1914-1918—CAMPAIGNS—
EAST AFRICA**
Paice, E. World War I: the African Front   **940.4**
**WORLD WAR, 1914-1918—CAMPAIGNS—
FRANCE**
Bloody victory   Three armies on the Somme **940.4**
Hart, P. The Somme   **940.4**
Herwig, H. H. The Marne, 1914   **940.4**
Nelson, J. C. The remains of Company D   **920**
Ousby, I. The road to Verdun   **940.4**
**WORLD WAR, 1914-1918—CAMPAIGNS—IT-
ALY**
Thompson, M. The white war   **940.4**
**WORLD WAR, 1914-1918—CAMPAIGNS—
MIDDLE EAST**
Korda, M. Hero   **92**
**WORLD WAR, 1914-1918—CAMPAIGNS—
TURKEY**
Korda, M. Hero   **92**
WORLD WAR, 1914-1918—CAMPAIGNS—

Ambrose, S. E. The wild blue **940.54**
Frank, R. B. Downfall **940.54**
Grayling, A. C. Among the dead cities **940.54**
Hillenbrand, L. Unbroken **940.54**
Korda, M. With wings like eagles **940.54**
Mortimer, G. The longest night **940.53**
Nelson, C. The first heroes **940.54**
Sheftall, M. G. Blossoms in the wind **940.54**
**WORLD WAR, 1939-1945—AERIAL OPERA-
TIONS, AMERICAN**
Ambrose, S. E. The wild blue **940.54**
Grayling, A. C. Among the dead cities **940.54**
Nelson, C. The first heroes **940.54**
Zuckoff, M. Lost in Shangri-la **940.54**
**WORLD WAR, 1939-1945—AERIAL OPERA-
TIONS, BRITISH**
Grayling, A. C. Among the dead cities **940.54**
Korda, M. With wings like eagles **940.54**
**WORLD WAR, 1939-1945—AERIAL OPERA-
TIONS, GERMAN**
Korda, M. With wings like eagles **940.54**
**WORLD WAR, 1939-1945—AFRICAN AMERI-
CANS**
See also African Americans
Kaplan, A. Y. The interpreter **940.54**
**WORLD WAR, 1939-1945—AMPHIBIOUS OP-
ERATIONS**
See also World War, 1939-1945—Naval op-
erations
WORLD WAR, 1939-1945—ART AND THE WAR
See also Art
Dolnick, E. The forger's spell **759**
Scott-Clark, C. The Amber Room **940.54**
WORLD WAR, 1939-1945—ASIA
Bayly, C. A. Forgotten armies **940.54**
Thompson, R. S. Empires on the Pacific **362.7**
WORLD WAR, 1939-1945—ATLANTIC OCEAN
Blair, C. Hitler's U-boat war **940.54**
WORLD WAR, 1939-1945—ATROCITIES
See also Atrocities
Breitman, R. Official secrets **940.54**
Hicks, G. The comfort women **940.54**
Lewy, G. The Nazi persecution of the gyp-
sies **940.53**
Lifton, R. J. The Nazi doctors **940.53**
Norman, M. Tears in the darkness **940.54**
Snyder, T. Bloodlands **940.54**
A woman in Berlin **940.53**
WORLD WAR, 1939-1945—AUSTRIA
Weyr, T. The setting of the pearl **940.53**
**WORLD WAR, 1939-1945—AUSTRIA—VIEN-
NA**
Weyr, T. The setting of the pearl **940.53**
**WORLD WAR, 1939-1945—BATTLES, SIEGES,
ETC.** *See* World War, 1939-1945—Aerial op-
erations; World War, 1939-1945—Campaigns;

World War, 1939-1945—Naval operations
WORLD WAR, 1939-1945—BIOGRAPHY
See also Biography
Ancell, R. M. The biographical dictionary of World
War II generals and flag officers **920.003**
Brighton, T. Patton, Montgomery, Rommel **920**
**WORLD WAR, 1939-1945—BIOGRAPHY—
DICTIONARIES**
Ancell, R. M. The biographical dictionary of World
War II generals and flag officers **920.003**
WORLD WAR, 1939-1945—CAMPAIGNS
Ambrose, S. E. The victors **940.54**
D'Este, C. Warlord **92**
Liebling, A. J. World War II writings **940.54**
Megellas, J. All the way to Berlin **940.54**
Patton, G. S. War as I knew it **940.54**
Roberts, A. Masters and commanders **940.54**
Weintraub, S. 15 stars **920**
Weller, G. Weller's war **940.53**
**WORLD WAR, 1939-1945—CAMPAIGNS—AF-
RICA, NORTH**
Atkinson, R. An army at dawn **940.54**
**WORLD WAR, 1939-1945—CAMPAIGNS—AT-
LANTIC OCEAN**
Blair, C. Hitler's U-boat war **940.54**
**WORLD WAR, 1939-1945—CAMPAIGNS—
EASTERN FRONT**
Merridale, C. Ivan's war **940.54**
Murphy, D. E. What Stalin knew **940.54**
Pleshakov, K. Stalin's folly **940.54**
**WORLD WAR, 1939-1945—CAMPAIGNS—EU-
ROPE**
Ambrose, S. E. Citizen soldiers **940.54**
Ambrose, S. E. The victors **940.54**
Jordan, J. W. Brothers, rivals, victors **940.54**
**WORLD WAR, 1939-1945—CAMPAIGNS—
FRANCE**
Ambrose, S. E. Citizen soldiers **940.54**
Ambrose, S. E. D-Day, June 6, 1944 **940.54**
**WORLD WAR, 1939-1945—CAMPAIGNS—IT-
ALY**
Atkinson, R. The day of battle **940.54**
**WORLD WAR, 1939-1945—CAMPAIGNS—ITA-
LY—SICILY**
Atkinson, R. The day of battle **940.54**
**WORLD WAR, 1939-1945—CAMPAIGNS—JA-
PAN**
Giangreco, D. M. Hell to pay **940.54**
**WORLD WAR, 1939-1945—CAMPAIGNS—
NORMANDY**
Beevor, A. D-day **940.54**
**WORLD WAR, 1939-1945—CAMPAIGNS—
NORTH AFRICA**
Atkinson, R. An army at dawn **940.54**
**WORLD WAR, 1939-1945—CAMPAIGNS—
OKINAWA ISLAND**

Fussell, P. Wartime: understanding and behavior in
 the Second World War   940.54
Goodwin, D. K. No ordinary time   92
Spector, R. Eagle against the sun   940.54
Takaki, R. T. Double victory   940.53
Takaki, R. T. Hiroshima   940.54
WORLD WAR, 1939-1945—VETERANS
    See also Veterans
Allport, A. Demobbed   305.9
WORLD WAR, 1939-1945—WOMEN
    See also Women
Hicks, G. The comfort women   940.54
A woman in Berlin   940.53
Yellin, E. Our mothers' war   940.53
**WORLD WAR, 1939-1945—WOMEN—UNITED
STATES**
Yellin, E. Our mothers' war   940.53
**WORLD WAR, 1939-1945—UNDERGROUND
MOVEMENTS—FRANCE**
Moorehead, C. A train in winter
**WORLD WAR, 1939-1945—WOMEN—
FRANCE—BIOGRAPHY**
Moorehead, C. A train in winter
World wide mind. Chorost, M.   612.8
WORLD WIDE WEB
    See also Internet
Kemp, T. J. Virtual roots 2.0   929
Pariser, E. The filter bubble   025.04
**WORLD WIDE WEB (INFORMATION RE-
TRIEVAL SYSTEM)** *See* World Wide Web
WORLD WIDE WEB PAGES *See* Web sites
WORLD WIDE WEB SEARCHING *See* Internet
searching; Web search engines
WORLD WIDE WEB SITES *See* Web sites
A **world** without ice. Pollack, H. N.   551.3
A **world** without Islam. Fuller, G. E.   297
The World's classics [series]
Carlyle, T. Sartor resartus   824
Swift, J. A tale of a tub, and other work   823
The **world's** fittest you. Decker, J.   613.7
The **World's** great speeches.   808.85
A **worldly** country. Ashbery, J.   811
The **worldly** philosophers. Heilbroner, R. L.   330.1
Worldmark encyclopedia of cultures and daily
life.   306
Worldwatch environmental alert series
Bright, C. Life out of bounds   578.6
WORMS
    See also Animals
Stewart, A. The earth moved   592
Worrall, Simon
The poet and the murderer   364.15
Worrall-Thompson, Antony
The essential diabetes cookbook   641.5
Worry. Hallowell, E. M.   616.85
WORRY

    See also Emotions
Hallowell, E. M. Worry   616.85
Worse than slavery. Oshinsky, D. M.   365
Worse than war. Goldhagen, D. J.   364.1
WORSHIP
    See also Religion; Theology
Worshipful Company of Fletchers. Tate, J.   811
The **worst** hard time. Egan, T.   978
Worster, Donald
A passion for nature   92
WORTH *See* Values
Worthen, John
D.H. Lawrence   92
D.H. Lawrence, the early years, 1885-1912   92
Worthington, Charles
The complete book of hairstyling   646.7
Wouk, Herman
This is my God: the Jewish way of life   296
Wouldn't take nothing for my journey now. Ange-
lou, M.   814
WOUNDED, FIRST AID TO *See* First aid
WOUNDS AND INJURIES
    See also Accidents
Wounds of passion. Hooks, B.   92
The **woven** figure. Will, G. F.   973.929
Wozniak, Paul R.
Nelson, G. Beyond Earth Day   333.72
Wrangham, Richard W.
Catching fire   641.3
Wranovics, John
Chaplin and Agee   92
Wrapped in rainbows. Boyd, V.   92
WRATH *See* Anger
Wray, T. J.
The birth of Satan   235
What the Bible really tells us   220.6
The **wreckers.** Bathurst, B.   910.4
WRECKERS (OF SHIPS)
Bathurst, B. The wreckers   910.4
The **wrecking** crew. Frank, T.   973.92
WRECKS *See* Accidents
WRESTLERS
Kreidler, M. Four days to glory   796.8
WRESTLING
    See also Athletics
Kreidler, M. Four days to glory   796.8
Levi, H. The world of lucha libre   796.8
WRESTLING—MEXICO
Levi, H. The world of lucha libre   796.8
The **Wright** style. Lind, C.   728
Wright, C. D.
One with others   811
Steal away   811
Wright, Charles
Appalachia   811
Negative blue   811

lem? 305.8

YOUNG MEN—UNITED STATES

Bayoumi, M. How does it feel to be a problem? 305.8

Young Owl, Marcus

Mai, L. L. The Cambridge Dictionary of human biology and evolution 612

YOUNG PEOPLE *See* Teenagers; Youth

YOUNG PERSONS *See* Teenagers; Youth

Young Stalin. Montefiore, S. 92

YOUNG WOMEN

See also Women; Youth

Kirsch, M. The girl's guide to absolutely everything 646.7

YOUNG WOMEN—CONDUCT OF LIFE

Moffett, K. Not your mother's divorce 306.89

YOUNG WOMEN—CRIMES AGAINST—JAPAN—TOKYO

Parry, R. L. People who eat darkness 364.152

YOUNG WOMEN—EMPLOYMENT—CHINA

Chang, L. T. Factory girls 331.4

YOUNG WOMEN—LIFE SKILLS GUIDES

Moffett, K. Not your mother's divorce 306.89

YOUNG WOMEN—PSYCHOLOGY

Moffett, K. Not your mother's divorce 306.89

Young, Alfred Fabian

Masquerade: the life and times of Deborah Sampson, Continental soldier 92

Young, Anastasia

The workbench guide to jewelry techniques 739.27

Young, Andrew

An easy burden 92

Young, Bruce

Miscarriage, medicine & miracles 618.3

Young, Christian C.

Evolution and creationism 576.8

Young, Clive

Homemade Hollywood 791.43

Young, Glenn

(ed) The Best American short plays 812

Young, Jon

What the robin knows 598.8

Young, Kevin

(ed) The best American poetry 2011 811

(ed) Blues poems 811

(ed) Jazz poems 811

Ardency 811

Young, Rob

(jt. auth) Pilkey, O. H. The rising sea 363.34

Electric Eden 781.62

Young, Robyn V.

(ed) Notable mathematicians 920.003

Young, Stephen

(ed) The Poetry anthology, 1912-2002 811

Young-Bruehl, Elisabeth

The anatomy of prejudices 303.3

Young-Eisendrath, Polly

The self-esteem trap 155.2

Youngerman, Barry

Wahab, S. A brief history of Afghanistan 958.1

The **youngest** minds. Barnet, A. B. 155.4

Yount, Lisa

Right to die and euthanasia 179.7

A to Z of biologists 920.003

Your adolescent. 155.5

Your baby & child. Leach, P. 649

Your beautiful wedding on any budget. Outcalt, T. 395

Your call is (not that) important to us. Yellin, E. 658.8

Your critically ill child. Johnson, C. M. 618.92

Your developing baby, conception to birth. Doublet, P. M. 612.6

Your eight-year-old. Ames, L. B. 649

Your first resume. Fry, R. W. 650.14

Your five-year-old. Ames, L. B. 649

Your flying car awaits. Milo, P. 909.82

Your four-year-old. Ames, L. B. 649

Your inner fish. Shubin, N. 611

Your medical mind. Groopman, J. E. 610

Your one-year-old. Ames, L. B. 649

Your pregnancy week by week. Curtis, G. B. 618.2

Your seven-year-old. Ames, L. B. 649

Your six-year-old. Ames, L. B. 649

Your three-year-old. Ilg, F. L. 649

Your time to bake. Blakeslee, R. L. 641.8

Your two-year-old. Ames, L. B. 649

Your voice in my head. Forrest, E. 362.196

Yours ever. Mallon, T. 808.86

YOUTH—BOOKS AND READING

Helbig, A. Dictionary of American young adult fiction, 1997-2001 028.5

YOUTH—DRUG USE

Cermak, T. L. Marijuana: what's a parent to believe? 362.29

YOUTH—DRUG USE—NEW YORK (STATE)—NEW YORK

LeBlanc, A. N. Random family 305.5

YOUTH—EDUCATION

Ray, B. E. Not quite adults 306.8

YOUTH—EMPLOYMENT

Ray, B. E. Not quite adults 306.8

YOUTH—EMPLOYMENT—UNITED STATES

Levine, M. J. Children for hire 331.3

YOUTH—HEALTH AND HYGIENE

Columbia University/Health Service The Go ask Alice book of answers 613

YOUTH—HEALTH AND HYGIENE—UNITED STATES

Levine, M. J. Children for hire 331.3

YOUTH—NEW YORK (N.Y.)

LeBlanc, A. N. Random family 305.5